VideoHound's® GOLDEN MOVIE RETRIEVER®

VideoHound's® GOLDEN MOVIE RETRIEVER®

Michael J. Tyrkus, Editor

GALE
A Cengage Company

GALE
A Cengage Company

VideoHound's Golden Movie Retriever® 2021

Project Editor: Michael J. Tyrkus

Editorial Support Services: Natasha Mikheyeva

Manufacturing: Rita Wimberley

Composition and Prepress: Charlie Montney

For product information and technology assistance, contact us at
Gale Customer Support, 1-800-877-4253.
For permission to use material from this text or product,
submit all requests online at **www.cengage.com/permissions.**
Further permissions questions can be emailed to
permissionrequest@cengage.com

Gale, A Cengage Company
27500 Drake Rd.
Farmington Hills, MI, 48331-3535

ISBN-13: ISBN 978-0-02-867698-2

ISSN 1095-371X

This title is also available as an e-book
ISBN-13: 978-0-02-867751-4
Contact your Gale, A Cengage Company sales representative for ordering information.

Printed in the United States of America
1 2 3 4 5 6 7 24 23 22 21 20

Credits:
or Who Does What

Project Editor
Michael J. Tyrkus

Editorial Coordinator
Dawn Redmond

Editorial Support Services
Natasha Mikheyeva

Product Design
Kristine Julien

Manufacturing
Rita Wimberley

Animal Control Officer
Shirelle Phelps

Review Crew
Tom Burns
James A. Cook
Martin Craddock
Lisa DeShantz-Cook
Deborah Draper
Scott Estes
Beth A. Fhaner
Jeff Hermann
Lynne Konstantin
Keith Lindsay
Peter Tigger Lunney
Stuart Mammel
Robyn Parton
Annette Petrusso
Joel Potrykus
Dawn Redmond
Chris Scanlon
Amanda Scheid
Brian Tallerico
Chris Tomassini
Michael J. Tyrkus
Hilary White

Special Assignment Research
Keith Lindsay

Typesetter Extraordinaire
Charlie Montney

Contents

Introduction

Since the mid-1970s, the summer movie release schedule has served as the barometer as to what would be the "blockbuster" films of that year. However, the year 2020, to put it mildly, was an absolute terror for the domestic (and worldwide) box office. Amidst the coronavirus shuttering movie theaters throughout the country, the summer blockbuster season was effectively eliminated, as were the bulk of yearly revenues typically earned by most films (and studios).

In past volumes, this space has been used to recap the highest grossing films of the previous year. That practice seems particularly irrelevant this year when the highest grossing film of the year, *Bad Boys for Life* grossed only $204.4 million domestically and $424.6 million worldwide. Compare that to the domestic box-office leader the previous year, *Avengers: Endgame*, which took in $858 million domestically and $2.8 billion worldwide, and it is easy to see that the numbers make very little sense (as do most other matters) in these strange and unusual times.

That being said, several viable platforms emerged during this time to provide hope that the art of cinema is not completely dead (only on hiatus) as streaming video and Premium VOD (PVOD) services saw a considerable boost as moviegoers enjoyed the remaining theatrical releases of the year from the confines of their own homes. In fact, many not-yet-released films have already altered their future schedules to debut on PVOD and bypass a theatrical release altogether. Streaming video, too, also played a large role in shaping the future of theatrical releases as films such as the oft-delayed *Artemis Fowl*, which was finally released on Disney's new streaming service Disney Plus in June rather than holding out for a post-pandemic theatrical release.

As of this writing, theaters were tentatively planning their reopening strategies and many first-run films were being scheduled for release in early Fall. However, as the aftermath of the pandemic continues to play itself out, it is impossible to forecast exactly how audiences will respond to the return of films to theaters (or theaters for that matter). Rest assured though, as films are eventually released on video, *VideoHound's Golden Movie Retriever* will be ever present, keeping a watchful eye over everything for you.

So, dear devotees of the Hound, we will once again look forward to next year with hope that the movies will surprise and delight us yet again (assuming that everything gets back to some semblance of normal of course). Hopefully, you feel the same way and continue to choose to bring us along with you as you explore the ever-expanding galaxy of movies available for your home entertainment purposes.

We here at VideoHound realize that every movie is potentially someone's favorite. That is precisely why we have created and maintained so many ways to help you find new and different movies within these pages. A film you love may lead you to one you love even more, either through an engaging screenplay, a thrilling visual style, a favorite actor, or previously undiscovered virtuoso director. There are as many ways to discover a movie using your handy copy of *VideoHound Golden Movie Retriever 2021* as there are possible movies to discover. As always, we want to be the ones you look to for help with those discoveries.

To that end, we hope you will let us continue to serve as your go-to-guide when looking for information and helpful reviews about the latest movies available in a variety of home entertainment formats. As always, we have added a few more Category and Kibbles subjects and subsequently removed some existing categories that were either redundant, confusing, or simply too big or too small to be useful anymore, to make room for more movie entries—over 500 new ones, give or take. Again, we strive to be as complete as possible for theatrical and higher-profile direct-to-video titles. While we still cover niche, foreign, and documentary movies, we have had to be more selective in their inclusion to make sure we can still bind this puppy into a somewhat manageable size. We have also continued to expand the Gale eBook version of *VideoHound* so that it now includes all the content we simply could not physically fit into the current print edition. If you are interested in perusing the electronic version, your local library should have access to it. That is yet another in a long list of great reasons to visit the library! You can also contact a Gale sales representative directly (via gale.com) to find out how to order your very own personal electronic copy of the book.

Finally, the VideoHound staff would like to extend a deep and heartfelt thank you to you, the reader, for your continued support and assistance throughout the many years we have been tolling away at this labor of love. It would not have been possible, or worthwhile, without those of you who truly love the Hound and share and abide in his love of movies.

As always, we want to know what you think about the films you love, hate, or whatever, as well as your thoughts on the book in general. What should we keep? What should we cut? What other changes would you like to see? Should we continue? So, keep calling, writing, emailing, etc. But, please bear in mind, that you need to provide us with a valid mailing address (and payment, especially if you are looking to order a copy of the book; unfortunately, we cannot deliver them to post office boxes). So, just in case you have forgotten, or have never written to us before, here is how to reach us directly:

VideoHound's Golden Movie Retriever
Editor, Michael J. Tyrkus
Gale, A Cengage Company
27500 Drake Road
Farmington Hills, MI 48331-3535
or, via email at: mike.tyrkus@cengage.com
or, via an old-fashioned phone call at: 248-699-8552

Using VideoHound

Alphabetization

Titles are arranged on a word-by-word basis, including articles and prepositions. Leading articles (such as A, An, and The) are ignored in English-language titles. The equivalent foreign articles are not ignored, however. Therefore, *The Abyss* appears under "A" while *Les Miserables* appears under "L." **Other points to keep in mind:**

- Acronyms appear alphabetically as if they are regular words. For example, *C.H.U.D.* is alphabetized as "Chud" and *M*A*S*H* as "Mash."
- Common abbreviations in titles file as if they were spelled out, so *St. Elmo's Fire* will be found under "Saint Elmo's Fire" and *Mr. Hollandís Opus* will be alphabetized as "Mister Holland's Opus."
- Proper names in titles are alphabetized beginning with the individual's first name; for instance, *Monty Python's The Meaning of Life* can be found under "M" and *Eddie Murphy: Raw* is under "E."
- Titles with numbers (*2001: A Space Odyssey*) are alphabetized as if the number were spelled out under the appropriate letter, in this case "Two Thousand One." When numeric titles gather in close proximity to each other (*2000 Year Old Man*, *2001*, or *2010: The Year We Make Contact*), the titles will be arranged in a low (*2000*) to high (*2010*) numeric sequence.

Indexes

Alternate Title Index. A number of films, particularly older, foreign, or B-type releases, may have variant titles. These alternate titles are listed alphabetically and refer the reader to the title under which the entry is listed. The alternate titles are also noted within the review.

Category Index. Subject categories ranging from the orthodox to the slightly eccentric permit you to video sleuth from broad type to significant themes to signature scenes. The mix, arranged alphabetically by category, includes hundreds of traditional film genres and sub-genres as well as a feast of *VideoHound* exclusives. Integrated into this index are cross references, while preceding the index is a list of definitions. Release year will help differentiate between titles of the same name. **A tipped triangle (▸) indicates a movie rated three bones or above.**

Kibbles and Series Index. Not your everyday categories, Kibbles span the literary side of movie-making (i.e. Adapted from a Play, Books to Film: Ernest Hemingway, etc.) and point out key producers and special effects masters. Yearly box-office winners (that are now available for home viewing) since 1939 are listed, along with classic movies, four-bone delights, trash films, modern interpretations of Shakespeare, Disney fare, significant on-screen and director/actor pairings. The Series portion of this index provides listings of major movie series, ranging from James Bond to National Lampoon to Indiana Jones. Recurring cinematic collaborations and partnerships of note are also listed, including Hope & Crosby, Abbott & Costello, De Niro & Scorsese, Rafelson & Nicholson, and even a 1973 Oldsmobile Delta 88 & Sam Raimi. A complete list of the categories precedes the index. Release year will help differentiate between titles of the same name. **As in the Category Index, tipped triangles (▸) indicate quality views.**

Awards Index. The Awards Index lists over 7,000 films honored by national and international award bodies, representing some 90 categories of competition. This information is also contained in the review following the credits. Nominations are also included in this index. A star (★) denotes the winner. **Only features available on home video and reviewed in the main section are listed in this index; movies not yet released for home viewing are NOT covered.** As award-winning and nominated films find their way to the home market, they will be added to the review section and covered in this index. Awards listed include the American Academy Awards; British Academy of Film and Television Arts; Golden Globes; Directors Guild of America; Independent Spirit; Writers' Guild of America; Screen Actors Guild; National Film Registry; and the Golden Raspberries.

The **Cast Index** provides full videographies for all actors and actresses listed in *VideoHound* with **two or more movies on their resume.** A (V) designation after a film title indicates that the actor lent only vocal talents to that movie, as in animation features. An (N) depicts narration duties. Birth and death dates (year only) follow the person's name in the citations. While they are not yet complete, they will continue to be updated, with more added to every edition. **Cross-references for actors and actresses who have appeared under more than one name assist in finding complete videographies.**

The **Director Index** also lists the works of any director who has made at least two films. Although listed in a first name, last name sequence, the names are alphabetized by last name. Film titles, complete with initial year of release, are arranged in chronological order, starting with their earliest appearance.

Writer Index. Screenwriters and script doctors with at least two credits are listed with their vital works. Names are arranged alphabetically by last name. Works are arranged chronologically.

Cinematographer Index. Directors of Photography with more than two credits are listed alphabetically by last name, along with their work, which is arranged chronologically.*

Composer Index. Videographies of movie music composers, arrangers, lyricists, and so on with more than two credits listed. Arranged alphabetically by last name.*

Video Sources Guide. Lists many mail order and independent video dealers where videos of all formats (VHS, DVD, Blu-ray, etc.) and streaming content can be obtained.

Web Site Guide. Lists Internet web sites for studios; general entertainment information; film festivals; and filmmaker resources; as well as sites for gossip, upcoming releases, video ordering outlets, and trivia.

* This index is still available via the Gale eBook electronic version of *VideoHound.*

Sample Review

Each *VideoHound* review contains up to 19 items, ranging from title, to the review, to cast listings, to awards received. The information in these reviews is designed to help you choose something you'll like, increase your enjoyment of a movie as you watch (especially by answering that nagging question of "What else have I seen that guy in?"), and increase your knowledge of movie trivia.

1 Tainted 2 🦴🦴 **3** *Angry Young Vampires* **4 1998 5 (R) 6** Ever wonder what would happen if the guys from "Clerks" fell in with a bunch of vampires? Well, lucky you. Now you can find out. Video clerks Ryan and J.T. hitch a ride to the midnight movie with their new co-worker Alex, who just happens to be a vampire whose ex is shacking up with the new vamp in town, who wants to taint the city's blood supply with undead blood. Script has many laughs, lots of attitude, and plenty of pop-culture knowledge, but gets a bit windy at times. Sometimes the actors seem to be trying a little too hard, but it doesn't detract from the story. Filmed in Detroit with lots of excellent local product placement. **7** ♫Bottoms Up; Rats!; One More for the Road.

8&9 64m/C 10 VHS, DVD. 11 ***GB*** **12** Brian Evans, Sean Farley, Dusan "Dean" Cechvala, Greg James, Jason Brouwer, Tina Kapousis; **13** ***D:*** Brian Evans; **14** ***W:*** Sean Farley; **15** ***C:*** Brian Evans; **16** ***M:*** Jessie McClear. **17** ***Nar:*** Bela Lugosi. **18** Academy Awards '98: Best Adapted Screenplay; Independent Spirit Awards '99: Best First Feature; Writers Guild of America '98: Best Original Screenplay. **19 VIDEO**

1. Title
2. One- to four-bone rating (or *Woof!*)
3. Alternate Title (we made this up)
4. Year released
5. MPAA rating
6. Description/review
7. Songs (made these up, too)
8. Length (in minutes)
9. Black & White (B) or Color (C)
10. Format (VHS, DVD, CD-I, Blu-ray, HD DVD, UMD, Streaming, On-demand, Widescreen, closed captioned, or 8mm)
11. Country of origin (made up)
12. Cast (*V:* indicates voiceovers; also includes cameos)
13. Director
14. Writer(s)
15. Cinematographer(s)
16. Composer(s)/Lyricist(s)
17. Narrator (made up)
18. Awards (yet again, made up)
19. Made-for-Television/Cable/Video identification

The movie used in this sample is a real movie, it was filmed in Detroit and released by Troma.

Alternate Titles Index

The Alternate Titles Index provides variant and foreign titles for movies with more than one name. Titles are listed in alphabetical order, followed by a cross-reference to the appropriate entry in the main video review section. If you don't find a movie you're looking for in the main section, this is the best place to look next.

Al Di La Della Legge *See* Beyond the Law (1968)
Al-Jenna-An *See* Paradise Now (2005)
Al-Massir *See* Destiny (1997)
Al midan *See* The Square (2013)
Al-Ris-Alah *See* The Message (1977)
Al 33 di Via Orologio fa Sempre Freddo *See* Shock (1979)
Alan Partridge: Alpha Papa *See* Alan Partridge (2013)
Alceste a Bicyclette *See* Bicycling With Moliere (2013)
Aleksandra *See* Alexandra (2007)
Alfie Darling *See* Oh, Alfie (1975)
Alhos Azuis *See* Blue Eyes (2009)
The Alibi *See* Lies & Alibis (2006)
Alicja *See* Alice (1986)
Alien 2 *See* Aliens (1986)
Alien 2: Sulla Terra *See* Alien 2 on Earth (1980)
Alien Thunder *See* Dan Candy's Law (1973)
Alien *vs.* Alien *See* Showdown at Area 51 (2007)
Alien Within *See* Evil Spawn (1987)
The Alien Within *See* Unknown Origin (1995)
Alien Women *See* Zeta One (1969)
Alien Zone *See* House of the Dead (1978)
Alistair MacLean's Death Train *See* Detonator (1993)
Alistair MacLean's Night Watch *See* Detonator 2: Night Watch (1995)
Alive by Night *See* Evil Spawn (1987)
All for Love *See* St. Ives (1998)
All for One *See* Return to Paradise (1998)
All Forgotten *See* Lover's Prayer (1999)
All Good Citizens *See* All My Good Countrymen (1968)
All in Place *See* All Screwed Up (1974)
All Monsters Attack *See* Destroy All Monsters (1968)
All That Money Can Buy *See* The Devil & Daniel Webster (1941)
All the Mornings of the World *See* Tous les Matins du Monde (1992)
All the Rage *See* It's the Rage (1999)
All the Way *See* The Night We Called It a Day (2003)
All Weekend Lovers *See* The Killing Game (1967)
Alle Anderen *See* Everyone Else (2009)
Aller-Simple Pour Manhattan *See* Petty Crimes (2002)
Alles Auf Zucker! *See* Go for Zucker (2005)
The Alley of Miracles *See* Midaq Alley (1995)
Alley of Nightmares *See* She-Freak (1967)
Alligators *See* The Great Alligator (1981)
Almok a hazrol *See* 25 Fireman's Street (1973)
Almost Human *See* Shock Waves (1977)
Alone *See* Horton Foote's Alone (1997)
Alone *See* Phobia (2013)
Alone Together *See* Crisscross (1992)
Alphaville, a Strange Case of Lemmy Caution *See* Alphaville (1965)
Alphaville, Une Etrange Aventure de Lemmy Caution *See* Alphaville (1965)
Altamira *See* Finding Altamira (2016)
The Alternate *See* Agent of Death (1999)
Alvin and the Chipmunks the Road Chip *See* Alvin and the Chipmunks: Road Chip (2015)
The Alzheimer Affair *See* The Memory of a Killer (2003)
Am zhan 2 *See* Running Out of Time 2 (2006)
Am zin 2 *See* Running Out of Time 2 (2006)
L'Amante di Paride *See* Loves of Three Queens (1954)
Amanti d'Oltretomba *See* Nightmare Castle (1965)
Amarelo Manga *See* Mango Yellow (2002)
Amateur Hour *See* I Was a Teenage TV Terrorist (1987)
The Amateurs *See* The Moguls (2005)
Amator *See* Camera Buff (1979)
The Amazing Panda Rescue *See* The Amazing Panda Adventure (1995)
Amazing Racer *See* Shannon's Rainbow (2009)
Amazon: Savage Adventure *See* Cut and Run (1985)
Amazon Women *See* Gold of the Amazon Women (1979)
Amazonia: The Catherine Miles Story *See* White Slave (1986)
Ambush in Waco *See* In the Line of Duty: Ambush in Waco (1993)
Amelia and the King of Plants *See* Bed of Roses (1995)
Amelie from Montmartre *See* Amelie (2001)
American Battleship *See* American Warships (2001)
American Beauty Hostages *See* She Devils in Chains (1976)
An American Daughter *See* Trial by Media (2000)
American Fork *See* Humble Pie (2007)
American Nightmares *See* Combat Shock (1984)
American Pie 3 *See* American Wedding (2003)
American Pie 5: The Naked Mile *See* American Pie Presents: The Naked Mile (2006)
American Raspberry *See* Prime Time (1977)
American Streetifighters *See* Miami Connection (1987)
American Warrior *See* American Ninja (1985)
The American Way *See* Riders of the Storm (1988)
Amerikaner Shadkhn *See* American Matchmaker (1940)
L'Ami de Mon Ami *See* Boyfriends & Girlfriends (1988)
Amigo/Amado *See* Beloved/Friend (1999)
Amityville 3-D *See* Amityville 3: The Demon (1983)
The Amityville Horror: The Evil Escapes, Part 4 *See* Amityville 4: The Evil Escapes (1989)
Amok *See* Schizo (1977)
Amor Perjudica Seriamente la Salud *See* Love Can Seriously Damage Your Health (1996)
Amores Possiveis *See* Possible Loves (2000)
The Amorous General *See* Waltz of the Toreadors (1962)
L'Amour a Mort *See* Love Unto Death (1984)
Amour de Poche *See* Girl in His Pocket (1957)
Amour et Turbulences *See* Love is in the Air (2013)
L'Amour l'Apres-midi *See* Chloe in the Afternoon (1972)
AmStarDam *See* Stoner Express (2016)
Amy Fisher: My Story *See* Lethal Lolita-Amy Fisher: My Story (1992)
Amy Foster *See* Swept from the Sea (1997)
Amy's Orgasm *See* Amy's O (2002)
Anacardium *See* Deranged (2001)
Anatomie *See* Anatomy (2000)
Anatomie 2 *See* Anatomy 2 (2003)
Anatomie de L'Enfer *See* Anatomy of Hell (2004)
And Comes the Dawn...But Colored Red *See* Web of the Spider (1970)
And Life Goes On . . . *See* Life and Nothing More . . . (1992)
And Once Upon a Love *See* Fantasies (1973)
And Then There Were None *See* Ten Little Indians (1975)
...And They Lived Happily Ever After *See* Happily Ever After (2004)
And Woman. . .Was Created *See* And God Created Woman (1957)
And Your Mother Too *See* Y Tu Mama Tambien (2001)
Anderson Falls *See* Darkness Falls (2020)
Anderson's Angels *See* Chesty Anderson USN (1976)
Andoromedia *See* Andromedia (2000)
Andrews' Raiders *See* The Great Locomotive Chase (1956)
Andron *See* Andron: The Black Labyrinth (2016)
Andy Colby's Incredibly Awesome Adventure *See* Andy and the Airwave Rangers (1989)
Andy Warhol's Flesh *See* Flesh (1968)
Andy Warhol's Heat *See* Heat (1972)
Andy Warhol's Young Dracula *See* Andy Warhol's Dracula (1974)
Angel *See* Danny Boy (1982)
Angel of Vengeance *See* Ms. 45 (1981)
Angel Street *See* Gaslight (1940)
Angelique et le Roy *See* Angelique and the King (1966)
Angelique et le Sultan *See* Angelique and the Sultan (1968)
Angelique, Marquise des Anges *See* Angelique (1964)
Angelique, Marquise of Angels *See* Angelique (1964)
L'Angelo Bianco *See* The White Angel (1955)
Angels & Airwaves Love *See* Love (2011)
Angels for Kicks *See* Wild Riders (1971)
Angels in the Attic *See* The Robin Hood Gang (1998)
Angie *See* Open Road (2013)
Angie X *See* MDMA (2018)
Angry Birds *See* The Angry Birds Movie (2016)
Angst Essen Selle auf *See* Ali: Fear Eats the Soul (1974)
Angst vor der Angst *See* Fear of Fear (1975)
Animal House *See* National Lampoon's Animal House (1978)
Ann Rule's And Never Let Her Go *See* And Never Let Her Go (2001)
Anne and Muriel *See* Two English Girls (1972)
Anne Frank *See* Anne Frank: The Whole Story (2001)
Anne of Green Gables: The Sequel *See* Anne of Avonlea (1987)
The Anniversary *See* Run Hide Die (2015)
Anno Domini *See* A.D. (1985)
Anno Zero - Guerra Nello Spazio *See* War in Space (1977)
Ano natsu, ichiban shizukana umi *See* A Scene at Sea (1992)
Anoche Sone Contigo *See* Dreaming About You (1992)
Anokoku Shinwa *See* The Dark Myth (1990)
Ansikte mot Ansikte *See* Face to Face (1976)
Ant-Man 2 *See* Ant-Man and the Wasp (2018)
Anthropophagus *See* Anthropophagus: The Grim Reaper (1980)
Antikorper *See* Antibodies (2005)
Antinea, l'Amante Della Citta Sepolta *See* Journey Beneath the Desert (1961)
Antisocial Behaviour *See* Antisocial Behavior (2007)
Antropophagus *See* Anthropophagus: The Grim Reaper (1980)
The Anxious Years *See* Dark Journey (1937)
Any Special Way *See* Business is Business (1971)
Anyone for Venice? *See* The Honey Pot (1967)
Anything for Love *See* 11 Harrowhouse (1974)
Aoi haru *See* Blue Spring (2001)
Aoki Okami: Chi Hate Umi Tsukiru Made *See* Genghis Khan: To the Ends of the Earth and Sea (2007)
Apa *See* Father (1967)
Apache Vengeance *See* The Desperados (1970)
The Apartment on the 13 Floor *See* Cannibal Man (1971)
Apocalipsis Canibal *See* Hell of the Living Dead (1983)
Appuntamento col Disonore *See* Night of the Assassin (1970)
Apres l'Amour *See* Love After Love (1994)
Après mai *See* Something in the Air (2013)
Apres-Ski *See* Snowballin' (1971)
Apu Sansat *See* The World of Apu (1959)
Apur Sansar *See* The World of Apu (1959)
The Aqua Sex *See* The Mermaids of Tiburon (1962)
Arctic Heat *See* Born American (1986)
Arctic Justice *See* Arctic Dogs (2019)
Are We Officially Dating? *See* That Awkward Moment (2014)
Are You Dying Young Man? *See* Beast in the Cellar (1970)
L'Argent de Poche *See* Small Change (1976)
Arlen Faber *See* The Answer Man (2009)
L'Armee des Ombres *See* Army of Shadows (1969)
L'Armee du Crime *See* The Army of Crime (2010)
Armored Attack *See* The North Star (1943)
Armour of God *See* Operation Condor 2: The Armour of the Gods (1986)
Arms and the Woman *See* Mr. Winkle Goes to War (1944)
Army in the Shadows *See* Army of Shadows (1969)
Army Mystery *See* Criminals Within (1941)
L'Arnacoeur *See* Heartbreaker (2010)
The Arrangement *See* Blood Money (1998)
Arritmia *See* Guantanamero (2007)
Arrivano Django e Sartana...è la fine *See* Django and Sartana; It's the End (1970)
Artaud *See* My Life and Times with Antonin Artaud (1993)
Artefacts *See* Artifacts (2008)
Arthur et les Minimoys *See* Arthur and the Invisibles (2006)
Artie Lange's Beer League *See* Beer League (2006)
Arven *See* The Inheritance (1976)
As Man to Man *See* Death Rides a Horse (1969)
As Tres Marias *See* The 3 Marias (2003)
Ascenseur pour L'Echafaud *See* Frantic (1958)
Ascent to Heaven *See* Mexican Bus Ride (1951)
Ashanti *See* Ashanti, Land of No Mercy (1979)
Ashura-jo no hitomi *See* Ashura (2005)
Asian Stories: Book 3 *See* Asian Stories (2006)

Bewitching Scatterbrain *See* Ravishing Idiot (1964)

Beyond Bedlam *See* Nightscare (1993)

Beyond Christmas *See* Beyond Tomorrow (1940)

Beyond Control *See* The Amy Fisher Story (1993)

Beyond Justice *See* Guardian Angel (1994)

Beyond Loch Ness *See* Loch Ness Terror (2007)

Beyond Obsession *See* Beyond the Door (1975)

Beyond the Call of Duty *See* Beyond the Call to Duty (2016)

Beyond the City Limits *See* Rip It Off (2002)

Beyond the Door 2 *See* Shock (1979)

Beyond the Fog *See* Tower of Evil (1972)

Beyond the Gates *See* Shooting Dogs (2005)

Beyond the Living *See* Hospital of Terror (1978)

Beyond the Living Dead *See* The Hanging Woman (1972)

Beyond the Rising Moon *See* Outerworld (1987)

Bez Konca *See* No End (1984)

Bian cheng san xia *See* The Magnificent Trio (1966)

Bice Skoro Propast Sveta *See* It Rains In My Village (1968)

The Big Bang Theory *See* Bang (1995)

The Big Bankroll *See* The King of the Roaring '20s: The Story of Arnold Rothstein (1961)

The Big Boss *See* Fists of Fury (1973)

The Big Boss *See* Rulers of the City (1976)

Big Boss *See* Rulers of the City (1977)

The Big Brawl *See* Battle Creek Brawl (1980)

The Big Carnival *See* Ace in the Hole (1951)

The Big Dance *See* DC 9/11: Time of Crisis (2004)

Big Deal at Dodge City *See* A Big Hand for the Little Lady (1966)

Big Duel in the North *See* Godzilla *vs.* the Sea Monster (1966)

Big Enough and Old Enough *See* Savages from Hell (1968)

The Big Escape *See* Eagles Attack at Dawn (1970)

The Big Grab *See* Any Number Can Win (1963)

The Big Heart *See* Miracle on 34th Street (1947)

The Big Lobby *See* Rosebud Beach Hotel (1985)

Big Monster on Campus *See* Boltneck (1998)

The Big One: The Great Los Angeles Earthquake *See* The Great Los Angeles Earthquake (1991)

The Big Risk *See* Classe Tous Risque (1960)

The Big Search *See* East of Kilimanjaro (1957)

Big Time Operators *See* The Smallest Show on Earth (1957)

The Biggest Fight on Earth *See* Ghidrah the Three Headed Monster (1965)

Biggles: Adventures in Time *See* Biggles (1985)

Bijita Q *See* Visitor Q (2001)

Bijo to Ekitainigen *See* H-Man (1959)

Bikini Bloodbath Car Wash *See* Bikini Bloodbath Carwash (2008)

Bikur Ha-Tizmoret *See* The Band's Visit (2007)

Bill *See* Meet Bill (2007)

Bio Creature Rasing *See* The Absence of Light (2006)

Bir zamanlar Anadolu'da *See* Once Upon a Time in Anatolia (2012)

The Bird with the Glass Feathers *See* The Bird with the Crystal Plumage (1970)

The Birder *See* The Bird Men (2013)

The Birdmen *See* Colditz: Escape of the Birdmen (1971)

Birds of a Feather *See* The Birdcage (1995)

Birds of a Feather *See* La Cage aux Folles (1978)

Birds of Prey *See* Beaks: The Movie (1987)

Birthmark *See* The Omen (1976)

Birumano Tategoto *See* The Burmese Harp (1956)

Bis ans Ende der Welt *See* Until the End of the World (1991)

The Bitter End *See* Love Walked In (1997)

Bitter Harvest *See* How Harry Became a Tree (2001)

Bittere Ernte *See* Angry Harvest (1985)

Black Angel *See* Angel Negro (2000)

Black Arrow Strikes *See* Black Arrow (1948)

The Black Book *See* Reign of Terror (1949)

The Black Bounty Hunter *See* Boss (1974)

The Black Bounty Killer *See* Boss (1974)

The Black Buccaneer *See* The Black Pirate (1926)

Black Cat *See* Kuroneko (1968)

Black Cat's Revenge *See* Blind Woman's Curse (1970)

Black Christmas *See* Black Sabbath (1964)

Black Dragon *See* Miracles (1989)

Black Eliminator *See* Kill Factor (1978)

Black Emmanuelle *See* Emmanuelle, the Queen (1979)

Black Evil *See* Ganja and Hess (1973)

Black Fist *See* Fist (1976)

Black Fist *See* Homeboy (1975)

Black Forest *See* Hyper Space (1989)

Black Frankenstein *See* Blackenstein (1973)

Black Gold *See* Day of the Falcon (2011)

Black Kingpin *See* The Italian Connection (1973)

Black Out *See* Midnight Heat (1995)

Black Out: The Moment of Terror *See* Ganja and Hess (1973)

Black Rider *See* Joshua (1976)

Black River *See* Dean Koontz's Black River (2001)

Black Scorpion 2: Aftershock *See* Black Scorpion 2: Ground Zero (1996)

The Black Streetfighter *See* Fist (1976)

Black Tigress *See* Lola Colt (1967)

The Black Torrent *See* Estate of Insanity (1964)

Black Vampire *See* Ganja and Hess (1973)

The Black Velvet Gown *See* Catherine Cookson's The Black Velvet Gown (1992)

Black Vengeance *See* Poor Pretty Eddie (1973)

Black Werewolf *See* The Beast Must Die (1975)

Black, White and Blues *See* Redemption Road (2010)

The Blackbird *See* The Black Bird (1926)

Blackboard Massacre *See* Massacre at Central High (1976)

Blackout *See* Contraband (1940)

Blackout in Rome *See* Era Notte a Roma (1960)

Blade of Steel *See* The Far Pavilions (1984)

Blair Witch 2 *See* Book of Shadows: Blair Witch 2 (2000)

Blake Edwards' Son of the Pink Panther *See* Son of the Pink Panther (1993)

Blast-Off *See* Those Fantastic Flying Fools (1967)

Blazing Arrows *See* Fighting Caravans (1931)

Bleach the Movie: Hell Verse *See* Bleach the Movie 4: Hell Verse (2010)

Blikende Lygter *See* Flickering Lights (2001)

Blind Alley *See* Perfect Strangers (1984)

Blind Fairies *See* His Secret Life (2001)

The Blind Swordsman: Zatoichi *See* Zatoichi (2003)

Blind Terror *See* See No Evil (1971)

Bl,.m *See* Bloom (2003)

Blonde Bombshell *See* Bombshell (1933)

The Blonde From Peking *See* The Peking Blond (1968)

A Blonde in Love *See* Loves of a Blonde (1965)

Blondie Has Servant Trouble *See* Blondie Has Trouble (1940)

Blood and Bullets *See* Rulers of the City (1976)

Blood and Concrete *See* Blood & Concrete: A Love Story (1991)

The Blood Baron *See* Torture Chamber of Baron Blood (1972)

Blood Bath *See* Track of the Vampire (1966)

Blood Beast from Outer Space *See* Night Caller from Outer Space (1966)

Blood Brides *See* Hatchet for the Honeymoon (1970)

The Blood Brothers *See* Heroes Two (1973)

Blood Castle *See* The Blood Spattered Bride (1972)

Blood Couple *See* Ganja and Hess (1973)

Blood Creature *See* Terror Is a Man (1959)

The Blood Crowd *See* The McMasters (1970)

The Blood Cult of Shangri-La *See* The Thirsty Dead (1974)

Blood Demon *See* The Torture Chamber of Dr. Sadism (1969)

Blood Doctor *See* Mad Doctor of Blood Island (1968)

Blood Evil *See* Demons of the Mind (1972)

Blood Feast *See* Night of a Thousand Cats (1972)

Blood Fiend *See* Theatre of Death (1967)

Blood for Dracula *See* Andy Warhol's Dracula (1974)

Blood Freaks *See* Blood Freak (1972)

Blood Gets in your Eyes *See* Ashura (2005)

Blood Hunger *See* Vampyres (1974)

Blood Hunt *See* The Thirsty Dead (1974)

Blood in the Streets *See* Revolver (1975)

Blood Is My Heritage *See* Blood of Dracula (1957)

Blood Lake: Attack of the Killer Lampreys *See* Blood Lake (2014)

Blood Mad *See* The Glove (1978)

Blood Money *See* Full Clip (2006)

Blood Money *See* The Killer's Edge (1990)

Blood Money *See* Red Serpent (2002)

Blood Money *See* Requiem for a Heavyweight (1962)

Blood Money *See* Under Oath (1997)

Blood Moon *See* The Werewolf *vs.* the Vampire Woman (1970)

Blood Oath *See* Prisoners of the Sun (1991)

Blood of Frankenstein *See* Dracula *vs.* Frankenstein (1971)

Blood of Fu Manchu *See* Kiss and Kill (1968)

Blood of the Demon *See* Blood of Dracula (1957)

Blood of the Man Devil *See* House of the Black Death (1965)

Blood of the Undead *See* Schizo (1977)

Blood on His Lips *See* Hideous Sun Demon (1959)

Blood Orgy *See* The Gore-Gore Girls (1972)

Blood Rust *See* Space Master X-7 (1958)

The Blood Seekers *See* Cain's Cutthroats (1971)

Blood Snow *See* Lady Snowblood (1973)

The Blood Suckers *See* Alien Massacre (1967)

Blood: The Ultimate Death *See* Blood (2009)

Blood Thirst *See* Salem's Lot (1979)

Blood Waters of Dr. Z *See* Attack of the Swamp Creature (1975)

Blood Will Have Blood *See* Demons of the Mind (1972)

Bloodline *See* Hush (1998)

Bloodsilver *See* Beyond the Law (1968)

Bloodsucking Bosses *See* Bloodsucking Bastards (2015)

Bloodsucking Nazi Zombies *See* Oasis of the Zombies (1982)

The Bloody Bushido Blade *See* The Bushido Blade (1980)

Bloody Fiance *See* The Blood Spattered Bride (1972)

Bloody Fists *See* Heroes Two (1973)

Bloody Pom Poms *See* Cheerleader Camp (1988)

The Bloody Scream of Dracula *See* Dracula, Prince of Darkness (1966)

Bloody Weekend *See* Loaded (1994)

Blow Back *See* TKO (2006)

The Blow-Out *See* La Grande Bouffe (1973)

Blue *See* Trois Couleurs: Bleu (1993)

Blue Eyes *See* Retribution Road (2007)

Blue Heat *See* The Last of the Finest (1990)

Blue Jean Cop *See* Shakedown (1988)

Blue Manhattan *See* Hi, Mom! (1970)

Blue Sierra *See* Courage of Lassie (1946)

Blue Vision *See* In Dreams (1998)

Blue Wolf: To the Ends of the Earth and Sea *See* Genghis Khan: To the Ends of the Earth and Sea (2007)

Blues for Lovers *See* Ballad in Blue (1966)

Bluff Storia di Truffe e di Imbroglioni *See* The Switch (1976)

Blumhouse's Truth or Dare *See* Truth or Dare (2018)

Blut an den Lippen *See* Daughters of Darkness (1971)

Bo biu *See* Have Sword, Will Travel (1969)

The Boat *See* Das Boot (1981)

The Boat That Rocked *See* Pirate Radio (2009)

Bob Dylan: Don't Look Back *See* Don't Look Back (1967)

Bob, Son of Battle *See* Thunder In the Valley (1947)

Bob the Gambler *See* Bob le Flambeur (1955)

Boca a Boca *See* Mouth to Mouth (1995)

Bodas de Sangre *See* Blood Wedding (1981)

Bodres Bear Traces of Carnal Violence *See* Torso (1973)

Body and Sword *See* Intimate Confessions of a Chinese Courtesan (1972)

Body Parts *See* Harold Robbins' Body Parts (1999)

Body Work *See* Bodywork (1999)

The Bodyguard *See* Have Sword, Will Travel (1969)

The Bodyguards *See* La Scorta (1994)

Bog Bodies *See* Legend of the Bog (2008)

Bogus Bandits *See* The Devil's Brother (1933)

Bokkou *See* Battle of the Warriors (2006)

Boksuneun naui geot *See* Sympathy for Mr. Vengeance (2002)

A Bold Affair *See* Interlocked (1998)

The Bold Cavalier *See* The Bold Caballero (1936)

Bolero: An Adventure in Ecstasy *See* Bolero (1984)

Bolgen *See* The Wave (2015)

Bolt *See* Rebel Run (1994)

Bom Yeorum Gaeul Gyeoul Geurigo. . .Bom *See* Spring, Summer, Fall, Winter. . . and Spring (2003)

Bombsight Stolen *See* Cottage to Let (1941)

Bone *See* Housewife (1972)

Bonjour Anne *See* Paris Can Wait (2017)

Boogievision *See* Boogie Vision (1977)

Book chon bang hyang *See* The Day He Arrives (2011)

Book of Beasts *See* Merlin and the Book of Beasts (2009)

Book of Blood *See* Clive Barker's Book of Blood (2008)

Book of Love *See* American Pie Presents: Book of Love (2009)

Bookworm *See* The Edge (1997)

Bor Lei Jun *See* Gorgeous (1999)

Bordello of Blood *See* Tales from the Crypt Presents Bordello of Blood (1996)

Border Heat *See* Deadly Stranger (1988)

Borg McEnroe *See* Borg *vs.* McEnroe (2017)

Born 2 Race: Face Track *See* Born to Race: Fast Track (2014)

Born to Be a Star *See* Bucky Larson: Born to Be a Star (2011)

Born to Be Sold *See* Baby Broker (1981)

Born to Kill *See* Cockfighter (1974)

Bosambo *See* Sanders of the River (1935)

Bosque de Sombras *See* The Backwoods (2006)

Boss Nigger *See* Boss (1974)

Boudu Sauve des Eaux *See* Boudu Saved from Drowning (1932)

The Bounceback *See* Love & Air Sex (2014)

Bound by Honor *See* Blood In . . . Blood Out: Bound by Honor (1993)

A Bout Pourtant *See* Point Blank (2010)

Boven is het stil *See* It's All So Quiet (2013)

Bowfinger's Big Thing *See* Bowfinger (1999)

The Box Collector *See* Love at First Kill (2008)

The Boxer *See* Blade Boxer (1997)

The Boxer *See* Counter Punch (1971)

The Boy Who Had Everything *See* Winner Takes All (1984)

The Boyfriend School *See* Don't Tell Her It's Me (1990)

Boyichi and the Supermonster *See* Gamera *vs.* Gaos (1967)

The Boynton Beach Bereavement Club *See* The Boynton Beach Club (2005)

The Boys are Back in Town *See* The Boys Are Back (2009)

The Boys from Brooklyn *See* Bela Lugosi Meets a Brooklyn Gorilla (1952)

The Boys From County Clare *See* The Boys and Girl From County Clare (2003)

Boze Cialo *See* Corpus Christi (2019)

Brain Candy *See* Kids in the Hall: Brain Candy (1996)

Brain Damage *See* Brain of Blood (1971)

The Brain Machine *See* Mind Warp (1972)

The Brain of Frankenstein *See* Abbott and Costello Meet Frankenstein (1948)

Braindead *See* Dead Alive (1993)

Bram Stoker's Burial of the Rats *See* Burial of the Rats (1995)

Bram Stoker's Count Dracula *See* Count Dracula (1971)

Bram Stoker's Dracula *See* Dracula (1973)

Bran Nue Dae *See* Brand New Day (2010)

Brand New Day *See* Love Happens (2009)

Brand New-U *See* Identicals (2016)

Brandy Ashore *See* Green Grow the Rushes (1951)

Brat *See* Brother (1997)

Brave Archer 4 *See* The Brave Archer and His Mate (1982)

The Brave Young Men of Weinberg *See* Up the Academy (1980)

Breach of Faith: A Family of Cops 2 *See* Family of Cops 2: Breach of Faith (1997)

A Bread Factory, Part One: For the Sake of Gold *See* A Bread Factory, Part One (2018)

A Bread Factory, Part Two: Walk with Me a While *See* A Bread Factory, Part Two (2018)

Break In *See* Loophole (1983)

Breakdance *See* Breakin' (1984)

Breakdance 2: Electric Boogaloo *See* Breakin' 2: Electric Boogaloo (1984)

The Breakup *See* La Rupture (1970)

Brendan and the Secret of Kells *See* The Secret of Kells (2009)

Brenn, Hexe, Brenn *See* Mark of the Devil (1969)

Briar Patch *See* Plain Dirty (2004)

Bride of Fengriffen *See* And Now the Screaming Starts (1973)

Bride of the Atom *See* Bride of the Monster (1955)

Brides of Blood *See* Brides of the Beast (1968)

Brigands, chapitre VII *See* Brigands: Chapter VII (1997)

Brijes 3D *See* Guardians of the Lost Code (2010)

Brilliantlove *See* The Orgasm Diaries (2010)

Britannia Mews *See* The Forbidden Street (1949)

Brodre *See* Brothers (2004)

Broken April *See* Behind the Sun (2001)

Broken Lizard's Club Dread *See* Club Dread (2004)

Broken Lizard's Super Troopers *See* Super Troopers (2001)

Broken Lizard's Super Troopers 2 *See* Super Troopers 2 (2018)

Bronenosets Potemkin *See* The Battleship Potemkin (1925)

Bronx Warriors *See* 1990: The Bronx Warriors (1983)

Brooklyn Love Story *See* Who Shot Pat? (1992)

Brotherhood of the Yakuza *See* The Yakuza (1975)

Brothers Five *See* Sword Masters: Brothers Five (1970)

Bruce Brown's The Endless Summer 2 *See* The Endless Summer 2 (1994)

Bruce Brown's The Endless Summer Revisited *See* The Endless Summer 2 (1994)

Bruce Lee's Game of Death *See* Game of Death (1979)

Bruno *See* The Dress Code (1999)

Bruoguminn *See* White Night Wedding (2008)

The Brute *See* El Bruto (1952)

Bu san *See* Goodbye, Dragon Inn (2003)

Buck Rogers *See* Destination Saturn (1939)

Buckaroo Banzai *See* The Adventures of Buckaroo Banzai Across the Eighth Dimension (1984)

Bud Abbott and Lou Costello In Hollywood *See* Abbott and Costello in Hollywood (1945)

The Buddy Factor *See* Swimming with Sharks (1994)

Buenos Aires, 1977 *See* Chronicle of an Escape (2006)

Bui bun si mun *See* The Master (1980)

Build a Fort Set It on Fire *See* Basquiat (1996)

Build My Gallows High *See* Out of the Past (1947)

A Bullet from God *See* God's Gun (1975)

Bullets, Blood & a Fistful of Cash *See* Ca$h (2006)

The Bully Project *See* Bully (2011)

Bump in the Night *See* The Final Terror (1983)

Bundy: An American Icon *See* Bundy: A Legacy of Evil (2008)

Bunhongsin *See* The Red Shoes (2005)

The Bunny Caper *See* Games Girls Play (1975)

Buon Funerale, Amigos! *See* Gunslinger (1970)

Buraddo *See* Blood (2009)

Bure Baruta *See* Cabaret Balkan (1998)

Burial Ground: Night of Terrors *See* Burial Ground (1985)

Buried on Sunday *See* Northern Extremes (1993)

Burn, Hollywood, Burn *See* An Alan Smithee Film: Burn, Hollywood, Burn (1997)

Burn, Witch, Burn *See* Mark of the Devil (1969)

Burning Cross *See* The Klansman (1974)

Burning Hearts *See* Kolberg (1945)

The Burning Man *See* Dangerous Summer (1982)

The Burning Question *See* Reefer Madness (1938)

Bushdio zankoku monogatari *See* Bushido: The Cruel Code of the Samurai (1963)

Bushido, Samurai Saga *See* Bushido: The Cruel Code of the Samurai (1963)

Bushwhacked *See* French Twist (1995)

Bustin' Bonaparte: The Story of an African Farm *See* The Story of an African Farm (2004)

Busu *See* The Booth (2006)

The Butcher *See* Le Boucher (1969)

The Butchers *See* Murderer's Keep (1970)

The Butler *See* Lee Daniels' The Butler (2013)

Butterfly: A Grimm Love Story *See* Grimm Love (2006)

Butterfly Lovers *See* The Assassin's Blade (2008)

Butterfly on a Wheel *See* Shattered (2007)

Butterfly's Tongue *See* Butterfly (1998)

Buying Aleksandr *See* Aleksandr's Price (2013)

By Hook or By Crook *See* I Dood It (1943)

By Rocket to the Moon *See* Woman in the Moon (1929)

Ca commence aujourd'hui *See* It All Starts Today (1999)

Cabiria *See* Nights of Cabiria (1957)

Caccia alla Volpe *See* After the Fox (1966)

Caceria *See* Manhunt (2001)

Cache *See* Hidden (2005)

Cactus Jack *See* The Villain (1979)

A Cada Lado *See* On Each Side (2007)

Cafe of the Seven Sinners *See* Seven Sinners (1940)

The Cage *See* My Sister, My Love (1978)

Caged Females *See* Caged Heat (1974)

Cain's Way *See* Cain's Cutthroats (1971)

California addio *See* California (1977)

California Axe Massacre *See* Axe (1974)

The California Dolls *See* . . .All the Marbles (1981)

California Holiday *See* Spinout (1966)

California Hot Wax *See* The Bikini Car Wash Company (1990)

California Man *See* Encino Man (1992)

Call Harry Crown *See* 99 & 44/100 Dead (1974)

Call It Love *See* She's So Lovely (1997)

Call It Murder *See* Midnight (1934)

The Call of the Savage *See* Savage Fury (1935)

The Call of the Wild: Dog of the Yukon *See* Jack London's The Call of the Wild (1997)

Calling Northside 777 *See* Call Northside 777 (1948)

Cama Adentro *See* Live-In Maid (2004)

Cammina Cammina *See* Keep Walking (1982)

Camp Hope *See* Camp Hell (2010)

Campanadas a Medianoche *See* Chimes at Midnight (1967)

Campsite Massacre *See* The Final Terror (1983)

Can a Song Save Your Life? *See* Begin Again (2013)

A Candle for the Devil *See* It Happened at Nightmare Inn (1970)

Cani Arrabbiati *See* Kidnapped (1974)

Canicule *See* Dog Day (1983)

Cannibal Ferox 3: Land of Death *See* Land of Death (2003)

Cannibal Holocaust 3: Cannibal *vs.* **Commando** *See* Land of Death (2003)

Cannibal Orgy, or the Maddest Story Ever Told *See* Spider Baby (1964)

The Cannibal's Daughter *See* Lucia, Lucia (2003)

Cannibals in the City *See* Cannibal Apocalypse (1980)

Cannibals in the Streets *See* Cannibal Apocalypse (1980)

Can't Be Heaven *See* Forever Together (2000)

Caos Calmo *See* Quiet Chaos (2008)

Capers *See* The Brooklyn Heist (2008)

Capharnaüm *See* Capernaum (2018)

Captain America *See* Captain America: The First Avenger (2011)

Captain Conan *See* Capitaine Conan (1996)

Captain Hurricane *See* Captain Calamity (1936)

Captive *See* Sex and the Other Man (1995)

The Captive Female *See* Amputee with an Axe (1973)

Captive Women *See* 1,000 Years From Now (1952)

Captive Women 3: Sweet Sugar *See* Sweet Sugar (1972)

Captured *See* Agent Red (2000)

The Car *See* El Carro (2004)

Caravan *See* Himalaya (1999)

The Card *See* The Promoter (1952)

Cardigan's Last Case *See* State's Attorney (1931)

Care of the Spitfire Grill *See* The Spitfire Grill (1995)

A Caribbean Mystery *See* Agatha Christie's A Caribbean Mystery (1983)

Caricies *See* Caresses (1997)

Carlo Collodi's Pinocchio *See* The Adventures of Pinocchio (1996)

Carmen of the Streets *See* As Tears Go By (1988)

Dr. Black and Mr. White *See* Dr. Black, Mr. Hyde (1976)

Doctor Blood Bath *See* Horror Hospital (1973)

Dr. Cadman's Secret *See* The Black Sleep (1956)

The Doctor from Seven Dials *See* Corridors of Blood (1958)

Doctor Gore *See* The Body Shop (1972)

Dr. Jekyll *vs.* **the Werewolf** *See* Dr. Jekyll and the Wolfman (1971)

Dr. Jekyll y el Hombre Lobo *See* Dr. Jekyll and the Wolfman (1971)

Dr. Jekyll's Dungeon of Darkness *See* Dr. Tarr's Torture Dungeon (1975)

Dr. Mabuse, Parts 1 & 2 *See* Dr. Mabuse, The Gambler (1922)

Doctor Maniac *See* House of the Living Dead (1973)

Dr. Orloff's Invisible Monster *See* Orloff and the Invisible Man (1970)

Dr. Phibes *See* The Abominable Dr. Phibes (1971)

Dr. Seuss' The Grinch *See* The Grinch (2018)

Dr. Sleep *See* Close Your Eyes (2002)

Dr. Terror's Gallery of Horrors *See* Alien Massacre (1967)

Dr. Terror's Gallery of Horrors *See* Gallery of Horrors (1967)

Doctors Wear Scarlet *See* The Bloodsuckers (1970)

The Does *See* Les Biches (1968)

Dog Soldiers *See* Who'll Stop the Rain? (1978)

Dog Years *See* The Last Movie Star (2017)

Dogboys *See* Tracked (1998)

Dogpound Shuffle *See* Dog Pound Shuffle (1975)

A Dog's Life *See* Mondo Cane (1963)

Dogwater *See* Since You've Been Gone (1997)

Doin' It *See* The First Time (1969)

Doing Life *See* Truth or Die (1986)

Doing Time *See* Porridge (1991)

Dokhtari ba kafsh-haye-katani *See* The Girl in the Sneakers (1999)

Doktor Mabuse der Spieler *See* Dr. Mabuse, The Gambler (1922)

The Dolls *See* Bambole (1965)

Dolor y gloria *See* Pain and Glory (2019)

Dolphins *See* Octane (2007)

Dom Durakov *See* House of Fools (2002)

Dom Over Dod Man *See* The Last Sentence (2012)

Dom Za Vesanje *See* Time of the Gypsies (1990)

Domestic Import *See* Nanny Insanity (2006)

Domicile Conjugal *See* Bed and Board (1970)

Dominick Dunne Presents Murder in Greenwich *See* Murder in Greenwich (2002)

Dominique is Dead *See* Dominique (1979)

The Domino Killings *See* The Domino Principle (1977)

Don Jon's Addiction *See* Don Jon (2013)

Don Juan *See* Private Life of Don Juan (1934)

Don Juan 73 *See* Don Juan (Or If Don Juan Were a Woman) (1973)

Don Kikhot *See* Don Quixote (1957)

Doña Clara *See* Aquarius (2016)

Dona Flor e Seus Dois Maridos *See* Dona Flor and Her Two Husbands (1978)

Dona Herlinda y Su Hijo *See* Dona Herlinda & Her Son (1986)

Dong *See* The Hole (1998)

Dong Fang San Xia *See* The Heroic Trio (1993)

Dong Mau Anh Hung *See* The Rebel (2008)

Donggong, Xigong *See* East Palace, West Palace (1996)

Donne facili *See* Les Bonnes Femmes (1960)

Donny's Boy *See* That's My Boy (2012)

The Don's Analyst *See* National Lampoon's The Don's Analyst (1997)

Don't Go Near the Park *See* Nightstalker (1981)

Don't Look Now, We've Been Shot At *See* La Grande Vadrouille (1966)

Don't Tempt Me! *See* No News from God (2001)

Don't Touch the Axe *See* The Duchess of Langeais (2007)

Donzoko *See* The Lower Depths (1957)

Doomed *See* Ikiru (1952)

The Doomsday Machine *See* Escape from Planet Earth (1967)

The Door *See* Shadow People (2013)

The Door with Seven Locks *See* Chamber of Horrors (1940)

Doorway to Heaven *See* Heaven's Door (2012)

Dope Addict *See* Reefer Madness (1938)

Doped Youth *See* Reefer Madness (1938)

Doppelganger *See* Journey to the Far Side of the Sun (1969)

Doppleganger *See* Doppelganger: The Evil Within (1990)

Dorothy and the Witches of Oz *See* The Witches of Oz (2011)

Dos hombres van a morir *See* Ringo, the Lone Rider (1968)

Dos Tipos Duros *See* Two Tough Guys (2003)

Dos Veces Judas *See* Twice a Judas (1969)

Dou fo sin *See* Flash Point (2007)

The Double *See* Kagemusha (1980)

The Double Con *See* Trick Baby (1972)

Double Down *See* Stacy's Knights (1983)

Double Hit *See* The Arab Conspiracy (1976)

Double Possession *See* Ganja and Hess (1973)

Double Trouble *See* No Deposit, No Return (1976)

Double Your Pleasure *See* The Reluctant Agent (1989)

Doubles vies *See* Non-Fiction (2018)

Doubting Thomas *See* Spy School (2008)

Douce Violence *See* Sweet Ecstasy (1962)

Doulos-The Finger Man *See* Le Doulos (1961)

Down *See* The Shaft (2001)

Down Among the Z Men *See* Goon Movie (1952)

Down Among the Z-Men *See* Goon Movie (1952)

Down the Hill *See* Footnote (2011)

Down Went McGinty *See* The Great McGinty (1940)

Dracula *See* Bram Stoker's Dracula (1992)

Dracula *See* The Horror of Dracula (1958)

Dracula 3D *See* Argento's Dracula 3D (2013)

Dracula and the Seven Golden Vampires *See* The Legend of the 7 Golden Vampires (1973)

Dracula Cerca Sangue di Vergine e...Mori de Sete *See* Andy Warhol's Dracula (1974)

Dracula Contra Frankenstein *See* Dracula *vs.* Frankenstein (1971)

Dracula in Pakistan *See* The Living Corpse (2003)

Dracula in the Castle of Blood *See* Web of the Spider (1970)

Dracula Is Dead and Well and Living in London *See* The Satanic Rites of Dracula (1973)

Dracula 71 *See* Count Dracula (1971)

Dracula: The Love Story *See* To Die For (1989)

Dracula, the Terror of the Living Dead *See* The Hanging Woman (1972)

Dracula Today *See* Dracula A.D. 1972 (1972)

Dracula *vs.* **Frankenstein** *See* The Screaming Dead (1972)

Dracula Vuole Vivere: Cerca Sangue de Vergina *See* Andy Warhol's Dracula (1974)

Dracula's Castle *See* Blood of Dracula's Castle (1969)

Dracula's Dog *See* Zoltan. . . Hound of Dracula (1978)

Dracula's Virgin Lovers *See* Dracula's Great Love (1972)

The Dragon and the Cobra *See* Fist of Fear, Touch of Death (1980)

Dragon Forever *See* Dragons Forever (1988)

Dragon Lady *See* G.I. Executioner (1971)

Dragon Wars: D-War *See* Dragon Wars (2007)

Drawing Blood *See* Sergio Lapel's Drawing Blood (1999)

The Dreaded Persuasion *See* The Narcotics Story (1958)

A Dream of Murder *See* A Nightmare Come True (1997)

Dream Slayer *See* Blood Song (1982)

The Dreamcatcher *See* The Dream Catcher (1999)

Dreaming of Julia *See* Cuban Blood (2003)

Dreams *See* Akira Kurosawa's Dreams (1990)

Drei Sterne *See* Mostly Martha (2001)

Dripping Deep Red *See* Deep Red: Hatchet Murders (1975)

Driven to Kill *See* Ruslan (2009)

Drivers to Hell *See* Wild Ones on Wheels (1962)

Drole de Drama *See* Bizarre Bizarre (1939)

Dronningen *See* Queen of Hearts (2019)

Drops of Blood *See* Mill of the Stone Women (1960)

The Drug *See* Kids in the Hall: Brain Candy (1996)

The Drum *See* Drums (1938)

Drunk Shaolin Challenges Ninja *See* Heroes of the East (2008)

Drunken Master 2 *See* The Legend of Drunken Master (1994)

Du bi quan wang da po xue di zi *See* Master of the Flying Guillotine (1975)

Du Rififi Chez les Hommes *See* Rififi (1954)

Du Zhan *See* Drug War (2013)

Dubei dao *See* The One-Armed Swordsman (1967)

Duck, You Sucker *See* A Fistful of Dynamite (1972)

The Duckweed Story *See* Drifting Weeds (1959)

Due Er Ikke Alene *See* You Are Not Alone (1978)

Due Notti Con Cleopatra *See* Two Nights with Cleopatra (1954)

Due Occhi Diabolici *See* Two Evil Eyes (1990)

Due Volte Guida *See* Twice a Judas (1969)

The Duel *See* Anton Chekhov's The Duel (2009)

Duel of the Gargantuas *See* War of the Gargantuas (1970)

Duel of the Space Monsters *See* Frankenstein Meets the Space Monster (1965)

Duello Nel Texas *See* Gunfight at Red Sands (1963)

Duelyant *See* The Duelist (2016)

Duet wan ling *See* The Bells of Death (1968)

Duk bei kuen wong daai poh huet dik ji *See* Master of the Flying Guillotine (1975)

Dumb Dicks *See* Detective School Dropouts (1985)

Dumbo Drop *See* Operation Dumbo Drop (1995)

D'Une Femme a L'Autre *See* A Business Affair (1993)

Dung che sai duk *See* Ashes of Time (1994)

Dungeons and Dragons *See* Mazes and Monsters (1982)

Dunwich *See* Hollow (2011)

Duo hun ling *See* The Bells of Death (1968)

Duoluo Tianshi *See* Fallen Angels (1995)

Dusting Cliff Seven *See* The Last Assassins (1996)

Duvar *See* The Wall (1983)

The Dwelling Place *See* Catherine Cookson's The Dwelling Place (1994)

The Dyatlov Pass Incident *See* Devil's Pass (2013)

Dylda *See* Beanpole (2020)

Dynamite Women *See* The Great Texas Dynamite Chase (1976)

E Dio Disse a Caino *See* And God Said to Cain (1969)

E Tu Vivrai Nel Terrore-L'aldila *See* The Beyond (1982)

E venne il giorno dei limoni neri *See* Black Lemons (1970)

Eamanuel and the Truth About Fishes *See* The Truth About Emanuel (2013)

Earth *See* Tierra (1995)

Earth Defense Forces *See* The Mysterians (1958)

The Earth Will Tremble *See* La Terra Trema (1948)

East Broadway *See* Falling for Grace (2006)

East Great Falls High *See* American Pie (1999)

East of Shanghai *See* Rich and Strange (1932)

East of the Rising Sun *See* Malaya (1949)

Easy Go *See* Free and Easy (1930)

Eat Your Heart Out *See* Skinned Alive (2008)

Eaten Alive *See* Emerald Jungle (1980)

Eaten Alive by Cannibals *See* Emerald Jungle (1980)

Eaters of the Dead *See* The 13th Warrior (1999)

Ebirah, Terror of the Deep *See* Godzilla *vs.* the Sea Monster (1966)

Eboli *See* Christ Stopped at Eboli (1979)

Ebony, Ivory, and Jade *See* She Devils in Chains (1976)

Echo Effect *See* Chain of Command (2015)

Echte Kerle *See* Regular Guys (1996)

Ecks *vs.* **Sever** *See* Ballistic: Ecks *vs.* Sever (2002)

Ecorches *See* Twisted Souls (2005)

Ecstasy *See* Extasis (1996)

L'Ecume des Jours *See* Mood Indigo (2013)

Eddie the Eagle: Alles ist Möglich *See* Eddie the Eagle (2016)

Edgar Allan Poe's Conqueror Worm *See* The Conqueror Worm (1968)

Edgar Allan Poe's the Pit and the Pendulum *See* The Pit and the Pendulum (2009)

Edgar Allan Poe's The Oblong Box *See* The Oblong Box (1969)

The Edge of Hell *See* Rock 'n' Roll Nightmare (1985)

Exploring the Kinsey Report *See* One Plus One (1961)

Expose *See* Footsteps (1998)

Exquisite Tenderness *See* The Surgeon (1994)

Extase *See* Ecstasy (1933)

Extreme Close-Up *See* Sex Through a Window (1972)

The Eye 10 *See* The Eye 3 (2005)

Eye of the Black Cat *See* Your Vice is a Closed Room and Only I Have the Key (1972)

Eyes of Dr. Chaney *See* Mansion of the Doomed (1976)

Eyes of Hell *See* The Mask (1961)

Eyes without a Face *See* The Horror Chamber of Dr. Faustus (1959)

The Fabulous Destiny of Amelie Poulain *See* Amelie (2001)

Faccia d'angelo *See* Long Days of Revenge (1967)

Face of a Stranger *See* The Promise (1979)

Face of Fear *See* Peeping Tom (1960)

Face the Music *See* Black Glove (1954)

Face to Face with El Diablo *See* Lola Colt (1967)

The Faceless Monsters *See* Nightmare Castle (1965)

Fag Hag *See* Okoge (1993)

Fair Trade *See* Skeleton Coast (1989)

Fairytale *See* The Haunting of Helena (2012)

Fairytales *See* Fairy Tales (1976)

Faites Vous Jeux, Mesdames *See* Make Your Bets Ladies (1965)

Faith, Fraud and Minimum Wage *See* Hoax for the Holidays (2010)

Fake Identity *See* Double Identity (2010)

The Fakers *See* Hell's Bloody Devils (1970)

Fallen *See* Falling (2006)

Fallen Knight *See* The Minion (1998)

Falltime *See* Fall Time (1994)

False Faces *See* Let 'Em Have It (1935)

False Witness *See* The Diplomat (2008)

Falstaff *See* Chimes at Midnight (1967)

Familia Rodante *See* Rolling Family (2004)

The Familiar Stranger *See* My Husband's Double Life (2001)

Family Resemblances *See* Un Air de Famille (1996)

Family Wedding *See* Our Family Wedding (2010)

A Family's Decision *See* Too Young to Be a Dad (2002)

Fanatic *See* Die! Die! My Darling! (1965)

Fanfan the Tulip *See* Fanfan la Tulipe (1951)

Fang Shiyu yu Hong Xiguan *See* Heroes Two (1973)

Fangelse *See* Devil's Wanton (1949)

Fangoria Presents: Inhuman Resources *See* Inhuman Resources (2012)

Fanny by Gaslight *See* Man of Evil (1948)

Fanny Hawthorne *See* Hindle Wakes (1927)

Fanny Och Alexander *See* Fanny and Alexander (1983)

Fan's Video *See* Otaku No Video (1991)

The Fantastic Disappearing Man *See* Return of Dracula (1958)

The Far Country *See* Nevil Shute's The Far Country (1985)

Farewell Bender *See* Wasted (2006)

Farewell, Friend *See* Honor Among Thieves (1968)

Farewell, My Love *See* Murder, My Sweet (1944)

Farinelli Il Castrato *See* Farinelli (1994)

Farinelli the Castrato *See* Farinelli (1994)

The Farm *See* The Curse (1987)

Farm Girl *See* The Farmer's Other Daughter (1965)

The Farmhouse *See* Eye of the Storm (1998)

Fashion House of Death *See* Blood and Black Lace (1964)

Fashions *See* Fashions of 1934 (1934)

Fast & Furious 7 *See* Furious 7 (2015)

Fast Fortune *See* 11 Harrowhouse (1974)

Fast Track *See* The Ex (2007)

Fatal Affair *See* Stalker (1998)

Fatal Assassin *See* African Rage (1978)

Fate Ignoranti *See* His Secret Life (2001)

Father & Son: Dangerous Relations *See* Dangerous Relations (1993)

Father Goose *See* Fly Away Home (1996)

The Father Kino Story *See* Mission to Glory (1980)

Father Master *See* Padre Padrone (1977)

Father, Son and the Mistress *See* For Richer, for Poorer (1992)

Faubourg 36 *See* Paris 36 (2008)

Faust-Eine deutsche Volkssage *See* Faust (1926)

Faustrecht der Freiheit *See* Fox and His Friends (1975)

Fauteuils d'Orchestre *See* Avenue Montaigne (2006)

The FBI Murders *See* In the Line of Duty: The FBI Murders (1988)

The Fear *See* Gates of Hell (1980)

Fear *See* Night Creature (1979)

Fear 2 *See* The Fear: Halloween Night (1999)

fear dot com *See* Feardotcom (2002)

Fear Eats the Soul *See* Ali: Fear Eats the Soul (1974)

Fear in the City of the Living Dead *See* Gates of Hell (1980)

Fear in the Night *See* Dynasty of Fear (1972)

Fear: Resurrection *See* The Fear: Halloween Night (1999)

Fearless *See* Jet Li's Fearless (2006)

Fearless Little Soldier *See* Fanfan la Tulipe (1951)

The Feast of All Saints *See* Anne Rice's The Feast of All Saints (2001)

Feast of Flesh *See* Blood Feast (1963)

February *See* The Blackcoat's Daughter (2017)

Federico Fellini: Sono un gran bugiardo *See* Fellini: I'm a Born Liar (2003)

Federico Fellini's 8 1/2 *See* 8 1/2 (1963)

Federico Fellini's Intervista *See* Intervista (1987)

Feel the Heat *See* Catch the Heat (1987)

A Fei jing juen *See* Days of Being Wild (1991)

Fei Ying *See* Silver Hawk (2004)

A Fei zheng zhuan *See* Days of Being Wild (1991)

Fellini: Je suis un grand menteur *See* Fellini: I'm a Born Liar (2003)

Fellini: Sono un gran bugiardo *See* Fellini: I'm a Born Liar (2003)

Felons *See* First Degree (1998)

Female Fiend *See* Theatre of Death (1967)

Femmine Infernali *See* Escape from Hell (1979)

Feng Yue *See* Temptress Moon (1996)

Fengriffen *See* And Now the Screaming Starts (1973)

Ferpect Crime *See* El Crimen Perfecto (2004)

Festen *See* The Celebration (1998)

Feuchtgebiete *See* Wetlands (2013)

Feux rouges *See* Red Lights (2004)

A Few Days in the Life of I.I. Oblomov *See* Oblomov (1981)

Fidelio: Alice's Journey *See* Fidelio: Alice's Odyssey (2014)

Fidelio, l'odyssee d'Alice *See* Fidelio: Alice's Odyssey (2014)

The Fiend with the Atomic Brain *See* Blood of Ghastly Horror (1972)

The Fiend with the Electronic Brain *See* Blood of Ghastly Horror (1972)

Fiendish Ghouls *See* The Flesh and the Fiends (1960)

Fierce *See* Fighting Mad (1977)

The Fifteen Streets *See* Catherine Cookson's The Fifteen Streets (1990)

The Fifth Chair *See* It's in the Bag! (1945)

The 51st State *See* Formula 51 (2001)

Fifty-Nothing *See* About Fifty (2011)

50 Violins *See* Music of the Heart (1999)

50 Ways to Leave Your Lover *See* How to Lose Your Lover (2004)

51 *See* Area 51 (2011)

52 Miles to Terror *See* Hot Rods to Hell (1967)

The Fighting Seventh *See* Little Big Horn (1951)

Figli de Annibale *See* Children of Hannibal (1998)

A Film about Love *See* Love Film (1970)

Film d'Amore et d'Anarchia *See* Love and Anarchy (1973)

Filofax *See* Taking Care of Business (1990)

Fin Aout Debut Septembre *See* Late August, Early September (1998)

Final Call *See* One Missed Call 3: Final (2006)

Final Conflict...Django Against Sartana *See* Django and Sartana; It's the End (1970)

The Final Crash *See* Steelyard Blues (1973)

Final Cut *See* Death Games (1980)

Final Destination 4 *See* The Final Destination (2009)

Final Destination: Death Trip 3D *See* The Final Destination (2009)

Final Recourse *See* Taken for Ransom (2013)

Final Target *See* The Vanquisher (2010)

Finally, Sunday *See* Confidentially Yours (1983)

Finding Kelly *See* Mystery Kids (1999)

Fine and Dandy *See* The West Point Story (1950)

Fine Mrtve Djevojke *See* Fine Dead Girls (2002)

Fine Things *See* Danielle Steel's Fine Things (1990)

Fink! *See* Pros and Ex-cons (2005)

Fir Crazy *See* Oh Christmas Tree! (2013)

Fire in Eden *See* Tusks (1989)

Fire Maidens of Outer Space *See* Fire Maidens from Outer Space (1956)

The Firebird *See* Phoenix (1978)

The First and the Last *See* 21 Days (1940)

The First Great Train Robbery *See* The Great Train Robbery (1979)

First Light *See* At First Light (2018)

The First of the Few *See* Spitfire (1942)

The First Rebel *See* Allegheny Uprising (1939)

First Strike *See* Jackie Chan's First Strike (1996)

The First Time *See* The Fighter (1952)

Fish Out of Water *See* The Witness (1999)

Fist of Fear *See* Fist of Fear, Touch of Death (1980)

Fist of Fury *See* Chinese Connection (1973)

Fist Right of Freedom *See* Fox and His Friends (1975)

Fistful of the Dragon *See* Chinese Connection 2 (1977)

Fists of Fury 2 *See* Chinese Connection 2 (1977)

5 bambole per la luna d'agosto *See* Five Dolls for an August Moon (1970)

Five Bloody Days to Tombstone *See* Gun Riders (1969)

Five Bloody Graves *See* Gun Riders (1969)

Five Days *See* Paid to Kill (1954)

Five Days Without Nora *See* Nora's Will (2009)

5 Dolls for an August Moon *See* Five Dolls for an August Moon (1970)

5 Fingers of Death *See* King Boxer (1972)

Five Minutes to Live *See* Door to Door Maniac (1961)

Five Savage Men *See* The Desperados (1970)

Five the Hard Way *See* The Sidehackers (1969)

Five Times Two *See* 5x2 (2004)

5 Up 2 Down *See* Getting High (2006)

Five Venoms *See* Five Deadly Venoms (1978)

Five Women *See* Gonin 2 (1996)

Five Women Around Utamaro *See* Utamaro and His Five Women (1946)

Fixing the Shadow *See* Beyond the Law (1992)

Flame Over India *See* North West Frontier (1959)

Flanagan *See* Walls of Glass (1985)

The Flanagan Boy *See* Bad Blonde (1953)

Flanders' Dog *See* Barking Dogs Never Bite (2000)

Flandersui gae *See* Barking Dogs Never Bite (2000)

Flash Gordon: Rocketship *See* Rocketship (1936)

Flash Gordon's Trip to Mars *See* Flash Gordon: Mars Attacks the World (1939)

Flashpoint *See* Flash Point (2007)

The Flesh Creatures *See* Horror of the Blood Monsters (1970)

Flesh Creatures of the Red Planet *See* Horror of the Blood Monsters (1970)

Flesh for Frankenstein *See* Andy Warhol's Frankenstein (1974)

Fleur Bleue *See* The Apprentice (1971)

Flickan Som Lekte Med Elden *See* The Girl Who Played With Fire (2010)

The Flight Commander *See* The Dawn Patrol (1930)

Flight of the Dove *See* The Spy Within (1994)

The Flight of the White Stallions *See* The Miracle of the White Stallions (1963)

Flip Out *See* Get Crazy (1983)

Flipper and the Pirates *See* Flipper's New Adventure (1964)

Floating Weeds *See* Drifting Weeds (1959)

Flood *See* Hard Rain (1997)

Flores Rares *See* Reaching for the Moon (2013)

Flower of the Arabian Nights *See* Arabian Nights (1974)

Flowers and Snakes *See* Flower & Snake '74 (1974)

Flu Bird Horror *See* Flu Birds (2008)

Flugel und Fesseln *See* The Future of Emily (1985)

Flukt *See* Escape (2012)

Flying Aces *See* The Flying Deuces (1939)

The Flying Dutchman *See* Frozen in Fear (2000)

Flying Wild *See* Fly Away Home (1996)

Focus *See* Shot (2001)

Fog *See* A Study in Terror (1966)

Folies Bourgeoises *See* The Twist (1976)

The Folks at Red Wolf Inn *See* Terror at Red Wolf Inn (1972)

Follow That Bird *See* Sesame Street Presents: Follow That Bird (1985)

Follow the Hunter *See* Fangs of the Wild (1954)

Fontane Effi Briest *See* Effi Briest (1974)

Foo gwai lit che *See* Shanghai Express (1986)

Footprints *See* Primal Impulse (1974)

For a Few Bullets More *See* Any Gun Can Play (1967)

For a Few Extra Dollars *See* Fort Yuma Gold (1966)

For Men Only *See* Tall Lie (1953)

For the Cause *See* Final Encounter (2000)

Forbidden Alliance *See* The Barretts of Wimpole Street (1934)

Forbidden Love *See* Freaks (1932)

Forbidden Paradise *See* Hurricane (1979)

Forbidden Son *See* Bulldance (1988)

The Forbin Project *See* Colossus: The Forbin Project (1970)

Forbrydelsens Element *See* The Element of Crime (1984)

Forces Spéciales *See* Special Forces (2011)

Ford Fairlane *See* The Adventures of Ford Fairlane (1990)

A Foreign Affair *See* 2 Brothers & a Bride (2003)

The Forest Primeval *See* The Final Terror (1983)

The Forgotten *See* Don't Look in the Basement (1973)

The Forsyte Saga *See* That Forsyte Woman (1950)

Fortune Hunters *See* The Million Dollar Kid (1999)

The Fortunes and Misfortunes of Moll Flanders *See* Moll Flanders (1996)

47 Samurai *See* 47 Ronin, Part 1 (1942)

Forushande *See* The Salesman (2016)

Forward March *See* Doughboys (1930)

Foster *See* Angel in the House (2011)

The Fotographer of Panic *See* Peeping Tom (1960)

The Four 3 *See* Kingdom of Blood: The Final Battle (2016)

Four Against Fate *See* Derby Day (1952)

Four Dark Hours *See* The Green Cockatoo (1937)

Four Dollars for Vengeance *See* Four Dollars of Revenge (1966)

Four Just Men *See* The Secret Four (1939)

4 Luni, 3 Saptamani si 2 Zile *See* 4 Months, 3 Weeks and 2 Days (2007)

4...3...2...1...Morte *See* Mission Stardust (1968)

Foxforce *See* She Devils in Chains (1976)

F.P. 1 Antwortet Nicht *See* F.P. 1 Doesn't Answer (1933)

F.P. 1 Doesn't Answer *See* F.P. 1 (1933)

Fra Diavolo *See* The Devil's Brother (1933)

Francesco, giullare di Dio *See* The Flowers of St. Francis (1950)

Francis *See* Francis the Talking Mule (1949)

Francis Ford Coppola Presents: The Legend of Suriyothai *See* The Legend of Suriyothai (2002)

Francis, God's Jester *See* The Flowers of St. Francis (1950)

Frank Herbert's Dune *See* Dune (2000)

Frank Miller's Sin City *See* Sin City (2005)

Frank Miller's Sin City: A Dame to Kill For *See* Sin City: A Dame to Kill For (2014)

Frankenstein *See* Andy Warhol's Frankenstein (1974)

Frankenstein *See* Mary Shelley's Frankenstein (1994)

The Frankenstein Experiment *See* Andy Warhol's Frankenstein (1974)

Frankenstein Made Woman *See* Frankenstein Created Woman (1966)

Frankenstein Meets the Giant Devil Fish *See* Frankenstein Conquers the World (1964)

Frankenstein Meets the Spacemen *See* Frankenstein Meets the Space Monster (1965)

Frankenstein Monsters: Sanda *vs.* **Gairath** *See* War of the Gargantuas (1970)

Frankenstein *vs.* **Baragon** *See* Frankenstein Conquers the World (1964)

Frankenstein *vs.* **the Giant Devil Fish** *See* Frankenstein Conquers the World (1964)

Frankenstein *vs.* **the Subterranean Monster** *See* Frankenstein Conquers the World (1964)

Frankie Go Boom *See* 3, 2, 1...Frankie Go Boom (2012)

Frasier the Lovable Lion *See* Frasier the Sensuous Lion (1973)

Fraternally Yours *See* Sons of the Desert (1933)

The Freak from Suckweasel Mountain *See* Geek Maggot Bingo (1983)

Freak Talks About Sex *See* Blowin' Smoke (1999)

Free to Live *See* Holiday (1938)

Freedom for Us *See* A Nous la Liberte (1931)

The Freedom Seekers *See* The Bloodsuckers (1970)

Freefall *See* Firefall (1994)

The Freeze Bomb *See* Kill Factor (1978)

Freier Fall *See* Free Fall (2013)

The French Woman *See* Madame Claude (1977)

Frenzy *See* Torment (1944)

Fresa y Chocolate *See* Strawberry and Chocolate (1993)

Fresh Bait *See* L'Appat (1994)

A Friday Night Date *See* Road Rage (2001)

Friday the 13th: The Orphan *See* The Orphan (1979)

Friday's Child *See* Age Out (2019)

Friends For Life *See* A Killer Among Friends (1992)

The Fright *See* Visiting Hours (1982)

Frightened City *See* The Killer That Stalked New York (1947)

The Frightened Lady *See* The Case of the Frightened Lady (1939)

Frightmare 2 *See* Frightmare (1974)

Frissons *See* They Came from Within (1975)

Fritt vilt II *See* Cold Prey II (2008)

Friz Freleng's Looney Looney Looney Bugs Bunny Movie *See* Looney Looney Looney Bugs Bunny Movie (1981)

Frogmen Operation Stormbringer *See* U.S. SEALs: Dead or Alive (2002)

Froken Julie *See* Miss Julie (1950)

From a Whisper to a Scream *See* The Offspring (1987)

From Hell to Victory *See* Eagles Attack at Dawn (1970)

From the Mixed-Up Files of Mrs. Basil E. Frankweiler *See* The Hideaways (1973)

The Front *See* Patricia Cornwell's The Front (2010)

Frost *See* The Last International Playboy (2008)

Frozen Terror *See* Macabre (1980)

Fruhlingssinfonie *See* Spring Symphony (1986)

F.T.W. *See* The Last Ride (1994)

Fu Gui Lie Che *See* The Millionaire's Express (1986)

Fu gui lie che *See* Shanghai Express (1986)

Fuera de Carta *See* Chef's Special (2008)

Fugitive Lovers *See* Runaways (1975)

Fukkatsu no Hi *See* Virus (1982)

Fukusho Suruwa Ware Ni Ari *See* Vengeance Is Mine (1979)

Full Moon of the Virgins *See* Devil's Wedding Night (1973)

Fulltime Killer *See* Full Time Killer (2001)

The Fun House *See* Last House on Dead End Street (1977)

Fun Loving *See* Quackser Fortune Has a Cousin in the Bronx (1970)

The Funeral Curtain *See* Acts of Death (2007)

Funeral Home *See* Mortuary (1981)

Funeral Rites *See* The Funeral (1984)

Fungus of Terror *See* Matango (1963)

Funny Little Dirty War *See* Funny, Dirty Little War (1983)

Fuoco Fatuo *See* The Fire Within (1964)

Fuocoammare *See* Fire at Sea (2016)

Fuori dal Mondo *See* Not of This World (1999)

Furankenshutain No Kaiju: Sanda tai Gailah *See* War of the Gargantuas (1970)

Furankenshutain tai chitai kaiju Baragon *See* Frankenstein Conquers the World (1964)

Furankensuten to Baragon *See* Frankenstein Conquers the World (1964)

Furin Kazan *See* Samurai Banners (1969)

The Further Adventures of Ma and Pa Kettle *See* Ma and Pa Kettle (1949)

Fury Is a Woman *See* Siberian Lady Macbeth (1961)

Fury of Samson *See* The Fury of Hercules (1961)

Fury of the Succubus *See* Demon Rage (1982)

Fury of the Vikings *See* The Invaders (1963)

The Future *See* Il Futuro (2013)

Future Cop *See* Trancers (1984)

Fyra Ar Till *See* Four More Years (2010)

Gadjo Dilo *See* The Crazy Stranger (1998)

A Gai Waak *See* Project A (1983)

Gainsbourg: Vie Heroique *See* Gainsbourg: A Heroic Life (2010)

Gake no Ue no Ponyo *See* Ponyo (2008)

The Gallery Murders *See* The Bird with the Crystal Plumage (1970)

Gallery of Horror *See* Alien Massacre (1967)

Gambara *vs.* **Barugon** *See* Gamera *vs.* Barugon (1966)

Gamblin' Man *See* Cockfighter (1974)

The Gambling Man *See* Catherine Cookson's The Gambling Man (1998)

Game *See* Gamer (2009)

The Game of Death *See* Robert Louis Stevenson's The Game of Death (1999)

Gamera *See* Gamera, the Invincible (1966)

Gamera: Chiisaki yusha-tachi *See* Gamera the Brave (2006)

Gamera: Little Braves *See* Gamera the Brave (2006)

Gamera Tai Barugon *See* Gamera *vs.* Barugon (1966)

Gamera Tai Gaos *See* Gamera *vs.* Gaos (1967)

Gamera Tai Guiron *See* Gamera *vs.* Guiron (1969)

Gamera Tai Shinkai Kaiju Jigara *See* Gamera *vs.* Zigra (1971)

Gamera Tai Uchukaiju Bairasu *See* Destroy All Planets (1968)

Gamera Tai Viras *See* Destroy All Planets (1968)

Gamera *vs.* **Gyaos** *See* Gamera *vs.* Gaos (1967)

Gamera *vs.* **Outer Space Monster Viras** *See* Destroy All Planets (1968)

Gamera *vs.* **the Deep Sea Monster Zigra** *See* Gamera *vs.* Zigra (1971)

Gamera *vs.* **Viras** *See* Destroy All Planets (1968)

Gamma Sango Uchu Daisakusen *See* The Green Slime (1968)

Gamma 693 *See* The Chilling (1989)

Gamma 693 *See* Night of the Zombies (1981)

Gammera *See* Gamera, the Invincible (1966)

Gang War *See* Odd Man Out (1947)

Gangland *See* Mean Machine (1973)

Gangland Boss *See* A Better Tomorrow, Part 1 (1986)

Gangs, Inc. *See* Paper Bullets (1941)

Gangster *See* Hoodlum (1996)

The Garden of Eden *See* Hemingway's Garden of Eden (2008)

Garden of Evil *See* Seeds of Destruction (2011)

The Gardener *See* Seeds of Evil (1976)

The Gargon Terror *See* Teenagers from Outer Space (1959)

Gas-Oil *See* Hijack Highway (1955)

Gas-s-s-s. . . or, It May Become Necessary to Destroy the World in Order to Save It *See* Gas-s-s-s! (1970)

A Gathering of Old Men *See* Murder on the Bayou (1991)

Gaugua Cochina *See* Nasty Baby (2015)

The Gay Divorce *See* The Gay Divorcee (1934)

The Gay Mrs. Trexel *See* Susan and God (1940)

The Gaze of Ulysses *See* Ulysses' Gaze (1995)

Gazon Maudit *See* French Twist (1995)

Geezer *See* Ordinary World (2016)

Gegen die Wand *See* Head On (2004)

Geheimecode Wildganse *See* Code Name: Wild Geese (1984)

Geheimecode Wildganse *See* Codename: Wildgeese (1984)

Gei Ba Ba de Xin *See* Jet Li's The Enforcer (1995)

Gekijouban Poketto monsuta: Minna no Monogatari *See* Pokemon the Movie: The Power of Us (2018)

Gekko no sasayaki *See* Moonlight Whispers (1999)

The Gemini Twins *See* Twins of Evil (1971)

Genealogies d'un Crime *See* Genealogies of a Crime (1997)

Genova *See* A Summer in Genoa (2008)

The Gentleman Tramp *See* La Collectionneuse (1967)

Gently Before She Dies *See* Your Vice is a Closed Room and Only I Have the Key (1972)

Geomeun jip *See* Black House (2007)

George A. Romero's Diary of the Dead *See* Diary of the Dead (2007)

George A. Romero's Survival of the Dead *See* Survival of the Dead (2009)

The George McKenna Story *See* Hard Lessons (1986)

Georgia's Friends *See* Four Friends (1981)

Germania Anno Zero *See* Germany Year Zero (1948)

Gernika *See* Guernica (2016)

Gestapo *See* Night Train to Munich (1940)

Get Down *See* Treed Murray (2001)

Get Rita *See* Lady of the Evening (1975)

Get Well Soon *See* Visiting Hours (1982)

Getting Even *See* Fight for Your Life (1977)

Getting Married in Buffalo Jump *See* Buffalo Jump (1990)

Incident at Victoria Falls *See* Sherlock Holmes and the Incident at Victoria Falls (1991)

L'inconnu du lac *See* Stranger by the Lake (2013)

Inconvenienced *See* Held Up (2000)

The Incredible Praying Mantis *See* The Deadly Mantis (1957)

The Incredible Torture Show *See* Bloodsucking Freaks (1975)

The Incredibly Strange Creatures *See* Incredibly Strange Creatures Who Stopped Living and Became Mixed-Up Zombies (1963)

L'Incroyable Mme. Ritchie *See* The Incredible Mrs. Ritchie (2003)

Incubo Sulla Citta Contaminata *See* City of the Walking Dead (1980)

Independence *See* Best Men (1998)

Indian Love Call *See* Rose Marie (1936)

Indian Summer *See* Alive and Kicking (1996)

Indiana Jones and the Raiders of the Lost Ark *See* Raiders of the Lost Ark (1981)

Indigenes *See* Days of Glory (2006)

Indiscretion *See* Christmas in Connecticut (1945)

Indiscretion *See* Dangerous Beauty (1998)

Indomptable Angelique *See* Untamable Angelique (1967)

Infection *See* Invasion (2007)

L'Infermiera di Campagna *See* Emmanuelle in the Country (1978)

Infernal Affairs: End Inferno 3 *See* Infernal Affairs 3 (2003)

Infernal Affairs II *See* Infernal Affairs 2 (2003)

Infernal Affairs III *See* Infernal Affairs 3 (2003)

The Infernal Idol *See* Craze (1974)

Inferno *See* Desert Heat (1999)

Inferno in Diretta *See* Cut and Run (1985)

Infested *See* Ticks (1993)

The Infra Superman *See* Infra-Man (1976)

Inglorious Bastards *See* Deadly Mission (1978)

Inn of the Frightened People *See* Revenge (1971)

Innocence is Bliss *See* Miss Grant Takes Richmond (1949)

L'Innocente *See* The Innocent (1976)

Insane World *See* Mondo Cane 2 (1964)

Insanely Happy *See* Happy, Happy (2010)

The Insect *See* The Insect Woman (1963)

Inside I'm Dancing *See* Rory O'Shea Was Here (2004)

Inside Ring *See* Ultimate Heist (2009)

The Inspector *See* Lisa (1962)

L'Instinct de Mort *See* Mesrine: Part 1-Killer Instinct (2008)

L'insulte *See* The Insult (2017)

An Intelligent Muscle Man *See* Running on Karma (2003)

Intensity *See* Dean Koontz's Intensity (1997)

Interlude *See* Intermezzo (1936)

Intermezzo: A Love Story *See* Intermezzo (1939)

Intern Academy *See* White Coats (2004)

Intersections *See* Collision (2013)

Intervention *See* The Art of War 3: Retribution (2008)

L'intervention *See* 15 Minutes of War (2019)

Intramuros *See* The Walls of Hell (1964)

Intruder *See* Intruso (1993)

The Intruder *See* Shame (1961)

L'Intrus *See* The Intruder (2004)

The Invaders *See* The Forty-Ninth Parallel (1941)

Invasion *See* Robin Cook's Invasion (1997)

Invasion Earth 2150 A.D. *See* Daleks-Invasion Earth 2150 A.D. (1966)

Invasion Force *See* Hangar 18 (1980)

Invasion from Inner Earth *See* They (1977)

Invasion of Mars *See* The Angry Red Planet (1959)

Invasion of Planet X *See* Godzilla *vs.* Monster Zero (1968)

Invasion of the Astro-Monsters *See* Godzilla *vs.* Monster Zero (1968)

Invasion of the Astros *See* Godzilla *vs.* Monster Zero (1968)

Invasion of the Flesh Hunters *See* Cannibal Apocalypse (1980)

Invasion of the Flying Saucers *See* Earth *vs.* the Flying Saucers (1956)

Invasion of the Zombies *See* Horror of Party Beach (1964)

Investigating Sex *See* Intimate Affairs (2001)

An Investigation of Murder *See* The Laughing Policeman (1974)

Invincible Pole Fighter *See* 8 Diagram Pole Fighter (1984)

The Invisible Dead *See* Orloff and the Invisible Man (1970)

The Invisible Horror *See* The Invisible Dr. Mabuse (1962)

An Invited Guest *See* Uninvited Guest (1999)

Io e lei *See* Me, Myself and Her (2016)

Io e Te *See* Me and You (2012)

Io Non Ho Paura *See* I'm Not Scared (2003)

Io Speriamo Che Me La Cavo *See* Ciao, Professore! (1994)

Io sto con gli ippopotami *See* I'm for the Hippopotamus (1979)

Ip Man 2: Legend of the Grandmaster *See* Ip Man 2 (2010)

¿Quien diablos es Juliette? *See* Who the Hell is Juliette? (1998)

L'ira di Achille *See* Fury of Achilles (1962)

The Iron Hand *See* Chinese Connection (1973)

Iron Invader *See* Metal Shifters (2011)

The Iron Kiss *See* Naked Kiss (1964)

The Iron Ladies 2: Before and After *See* The Iron Ladies 2 (2003)

The Iron Ladies II: The Early Years *See* The Iron Ladies 2 (2003)

Iron Monkey: The Young Wong Fei-hung *See* Iron Monkey (1993)

The Ironman *See* Tetsuo: The Iron Man (1992)

Irving Berlin's Alexander's Ragtime Band *See* Alexander's Ragtime Band (1938)

Iskanderija, Kaman oue Kaman *See* Alexandria Again and Forever (1990)

Island of Monte Cristo *See* Sword of Venus (1953)

Island of Shame *See* The Young One (1961)

Island of Terror *See* Five Dolls for an August Moon (1970)

Island of the Alive *See* It's Alive 3: Island of the Alive (1987)

Island of the Burning Damned *See* Island of the Burning Doomed (1967)

Island of the Fishmen *See* Screamers (1980)

The Island of the Last Zombies *See* Doctor Butcher M.D. (1980)

Island of the Living Dead *See* Zombie (1980)

Island of the Living Horror *See* Brides of the Beast (1968)

Island Rescue *See* Appointment With Venus (1951)

Isle of Lost Women *See* 99 Women (1969)

Isle of the Living Dead *See* The Snake People (1968)

Isle of the Snake People *See* The Snake People (1968)

Ismach Hatani *See* The Women's Balcony (2016)

It Ain't No Sin *See* Belle of the Nineties (1934)

It Came From Beyond Space *See* Alien Trespass (2009)

It Comes Up Murder *See* The Honey Pot (1967)

It Fell from the Sky *See* Alien Dead (1979)

It Happened at Lakewood Manor *See* Ants (1977)

It Happened in Paris *See* The Lady in Question (1940)

It Happened One Summer *See* State Fair (1945)

It Hurts Only When I Laugh *See* Only When I Laugh (1981)

It Lives Again *See* It's Alive 2: It Lives Again (1978)

It Lives By Night *See* The Bat People (1974)

It Only Take Five Minutes *See* Five Minutes to Love (1963)

It Runs in the Family *See* My Summer Story (1994)

It Stalked the Ocean Floor *See* Monster from the Ocean Floor (1954)

It! The Vampire from Beyond Space *See* It! The Terror from Beyond Space (1958)

The Italian Connection *See* Hired to Kill (1973)

The Italian Connection *See* Manhunt (1973)

Italianetz *See* The Italian (2005)

Italiensk for Begyndere *See* Italian for Beginners (2001)

It's My Life *See* My Life to Live (1962)

It's Only Money *See* Double Dynamite (1951)

It's Trad, Dad *See* Ring-a-Ding Rhythm (1962)

Ivan Groznyi *See* Ivan the Terrible, Part 1 (1944)

Ivan Groznyi 2 *See* Ivan the Terrible, Part 2 (1946)

Ivan the Terrible, Part 2: The Boyars' Plot *See* Ivan the Terrible, Part 2 (1946)

Ivan's Childhood *See* My Name Is Ivan (1962)

L'Ivresse du Pouvoir *See* Comedy of Power (2006)

Ja Cuba *See* I Am Cuba (1964)

Jack London's Call of the Wild *See* Call of the Wild (2004)

Jack London's Klondike Fever *See* Klondike Fever (1979)

Jackals *See* American Justice (1986)

Jacked *See* Jacked Up (2001)

Jackie Chan Is the Prisoner *See* The Prisoner (1990)

Jackie Chan's Police Force *See* Police Story (1985)

Jackie Chan's Police Story *See* Police Story (1985)

Jackie Chan's Project A *See* Project A (1983)

Jackie Chan's Project A2 *See* Project A: Part 2 (1987)

Jackie Collins' Hollywood Wives: The New Generation *See* Hollywood Wives: The New Generation (2003)

Jackie, Ethel, Joan: Women of Camelot *See* Jackie, Ethel, Joan: The Kennedy Women (2001)

Jack's Wife *See* Season of the Witch (1973)

Jacqueline Susann's Once is Not Enough *See* Once Is Not Enough (1975)

Jadesoturi *See* Jade Warrior (2006)

Jag ar nyfiken-en film i gult *See* I Am Curious (Yellow) (1967)

Jag ar nyfiken-gul *See* I Am Curious (Yellow) (1967)

Jag, en Kvinna *See* I, a Woman (1966)

Jagten *See* The Hunt (2013)

J'ai Pas Sommeil *See* I Can't Sleep (1993)

J'ai perdu mon corps *See* I Lost My Body (2019)

J'ai Tue Ma Mere *See* I Killed My Mother (2009)

Jail Birds *See* Pardon Us (1931)

J'Aimerais pas Crever un Dimache *See* Don't Let Me Die on a Sunday (1998)

Jakob der Lugner *See* Jacob the Liar (1974)

James A. Michener's Texas *See* Texas (1994)

James Cameron's Sanctum *See* Sanctum (2011)

James Clavell's Shogun *See* Shogun (1980)

James Dean: Race with Destiny *See* James Dean: Live Fast, Die Young (1997)

Jane Austen's Emma *See* Emma (1997)

Jane Austen's Mafia! *See* Mafia! (1998)

Jangsa-ri 9.15 *See* Battle of Jangsari (2019)

The Janitor *See* Eyewitness (1981)

Janu Nakts *See* Midsummer Madness (2007)

Jatszani Kell *See* Lily in Love (1985)

Jaws 3-D *See* Jaws 3 (1983)

Jayne Mansfield: A Symbol of the '50s *See* The Jayne Mansfield Story (1980)

Je Rentre a la Maison *See* I'm Going Home (2000)

Je Suis Heureux que Ma Mere Soit Vivante *See* I'm Glad My Mother Is Alive (2009)

Je Veux Rentrer a la Maison *See* I Want to Go Home (1989)

Je Vous Salue, Mafia *See* Hail Mafia (1965)

Je Vous Salue Marie *See* Hail Mary (1985)

Jealousy *See* L'Enfer (1993)

Jean de Florette 2 *See* Manon of the Spring (1987)

Jeanne et le Garcon Formidable *See* Jeanne and the Perfect Guy (1998)

Jeanne la Pucelle: Les Batailles *See* Jeanne la Pucelle (1994)

Jeanne la Purcelle: Les Prisons *See* Jeanne la Pucelle (1994)

Jeder fur Sich und Gott gegen Alle *See* Every Man for Himself & God Against All (1975)

Jekyll's Inferno *See* The Two Faces of Dr. Jekyll (1960)

J'embrasse Pas *See* I Don't Kiss (1991)

Jennie *See* Portrait of Jennie (1948)

Jennifer's Shadow *See* Chronicle of the Raven (2004)

Jenseits der Stille *See* Beyond Silence (1996)

Jerome Bixby's Man from Earth *See* The Man from Earth (2007)

Jerry Springer's Ringmaster *See* Ringmaster (1998)

A Jersey Tale *See* Bought and Sold (2003)

Jesus de Montreal *See* Jesus of Montreal (1989)

The Jesus Video *See* Ancient Relic (2002)

Jette un Sort *See* Rough Magic (1995)

Jeu de Massacre *See* The Killing Game (1967)

Jeune et Jolie *See* Young & Beautiful (2013)

Jeunes filles impudiques *See* Schoolgirl Hitchhikers (1973)

Kirschbluesten-Hanami *See* Cherry Blossoms (2008)

Kiru *See* Kill! (1968)

Kiseki *See* I Wish (2011)

A Kiss from Eddie *See* The Arousers (1970)

Kiss Me, Kill Me *See* Baba Yaga (1973)

Kiss My Butterfly *See* I Love You, Alice B. Toklas! (1968)

Kiss of Evil *See* Kiss of the Vampire (1962)

Kjaerlighetens Kjotere *See* Zero Degrees Kelvin (1995)

KKK *See* The Klansman (1974)

Klip *See* Clip (2013)

Klovn: The Movie *See* Klown (2012)

The Knack. . .and How to Get It *See* The Knack (1965)

Knafayim Shvurot *See* Broken Wings (2002)

Koara Kacho *See* Executive Koala (2006)

Kohi jikou *See* Cafe Lumiere (2005)

Komissar *See* Commissar (1968)

Kommissar X-Drei gelbe Katzen *See* Death is Nimble, Death is Quick (1967)

Kommissar X-Jagd auf Unbekant *See* Kiss Kiss Kill Kill (1966)

Koneko Monogatari *See* The Adventures of Milo & Otis (1989)

Kong saan mei yan *See* An Empress and the Warriors (2008)

Kongen av Bastoy *See* King of Devil's Island (2010)

Konig der Diebe *See* King of Thieves (2004)

Konketsuji Rika *See* Rica (1972)

Konketsuji Rika: Hitoriyuku sasuraitabi *See* Rica 2: Lonely Wanderer (1973)

Konna Yume Wo Mita *See* Akira Kurosawa's Dreams (1990)

Kootenai Brown *See* Showdown at Williams Creek (1991)

Korkarlen *See* The Phantom Carriage (1921)

Koroshi no Rakuin *See* Branded to Kill (1967)

Koroshiya Ichi *See* Ichi the Killer (2001)

Koukaku Kidoutai *See* Ghost in the Shell (1995)

Kozure Okami: Shinikazeni mukau ubaguruma *See* Shogun Assassin 2: Lightning Swords of Death (1973)

Kraftidioten *See* In Order of Disappearance (2014)

Krai *See* The Edge (2010)

Krajobraz Po Bitwie *See* Landscape After Battle (1970)

Krampack *See* Nico and Dani (2000)

Krasnaya Palatka *See* Red Tent (1969)

Krigen *See* A War (2015)

Kriget ar Slut *See* La Guerre Est Finie (1966)

Kronos *See* Captain Kronos: Vampire Hunter (1974)

Kronprinz Rudolf *See* The Crown Prince (2006)

Krug and Company *See* Last House on the Left (1972)

Kuai Huo Lin *See* The Delightful Forest (1972)

Kuga no ori: Nami dai-42 zakkyobo *See* Chain Gang Girls (2008)

Kuhle Wampe, Oder Wen Gehort die Welt? *See* Kuhle Wampe, Or Who Owns the World? (1932)

Kumonosujo, Kumonosu-djo *See* Throne of Blood (1957)

Kung Fu Invaders *See* Heroes Two (1973)

Kung Fu Kingdom *See* Kung Fu Killer (2008)

Kung Fu Warlords *See* The Brave Archer (1977)

Kurîpî: Itsuwari no rinjin *See* Creepy (2016)

Kuroi Ame *See* Black Rain (1988)

Kuroi Ie *See* The Black House (2000)

Kuronezumi *See* Black Rat (2010)

Kurozu Zero *See* Crows Zero (2007)

Kushka *See* The Cuckoo (2002)

KVC: Komodo *vs.* **Cobra** *See* Komodo *vs.* Cobra (2005)

Kvinnors Vantan *See* Secrets of Women (1952)

Kvish L'Lo Motzah *See* Dead End Street (1983)

Kynodontas *See* Dogtooth (2009)

Kyoko *See* Because of You (1995)

Kyoryuu: Kaicho no densetsu *See* Legend of the Dinosaurs and Monster Birds (1977)

Kyua *See* Cure (1997)

L Change the World *See* Death Note 3: L Change the World (2008)

La Banda J.&S. Cronaca Criminale del Far West *See* Sonny and Jed (1973)

La Barriera della Legge *See* Barrier of the Law (1954)

La Bataille d'Alger *See* The Battle of Algiers (1966)

La Bataille du Rail *See* Battle of the Rails (1946)

La Battaglia di Algeri *See* The Battle of Algiers (1966)

La Battaglia d'Inghilterra *See* Eagles Over London (1969)

La Belle Endormie *See* The Sleeping Beauty (2010)

La belle et la bête *See* Beauty and the Beast (1946)

La Belle Personne *See* The Beautiful Person (2008)

La Belle Saison *See* Summertime (2016)

La Belva Col Mitra *See* Mad Dog Killer (1977)

La Bestia nel Cuore *See* Don't Tell (2005)

La Bestia nello spazio *See* The Beast in Space (1980)

La Bestia Uccide a Sangue Freddo *See* Slaughter Hotel (1971)

La Bete *See* The Beast (1975)

La Bionda *See* The Blonde (1992)

La Bonne Annee *See* Happy New Year (1973)

La Bride sur le Cou *See* Please Not Now! (1961)

La Camara del Terror *See* The Fear Chamber (1968)

La camarista *See* The Chambermaid (2019)

La Casa 4 *See* Witchery (1988)

La Casa con la Scala Nel Buio *See* A Blade in the Dark (1983)

La Casa Dell'Exorcismo *See* Lisa and the Devil (1975)

La Caza *See* The Hunt (1965)

La Chambre Ardente *See* The Burning Court (1962)

La Chambre Verte *See* The Green Room (1978)

La Chiesa *See* The Church (1998)

La chute de l'empire americain *See* The Fall of the American Empire (2019)

La Ciel Sur la Tete *See* Times Have Been Better (2006)

La Ciociara *See* Two Women (1961)

La Cite des Enfants Perdus *See* The City of Lost Children (1995)

La Citte delle Donne *See* City of Women (1981)

La Coda dello Scorpione *See* The Case of the Scorpion's Tail (1971)

La Code a Change *See* Change of Plans (2009)

La Commare Secca *See* The Grim Reaper (1962)

La Comtesse Perverse *See* The Perverse Countess (1973)

La Confusion des Genres *See* Confusion of Genders (2000)

La Curee *See* The Game Is Over (1966)

La dame dans l'auto avec des lunettes et un fusil *See* The Lady in the Car with Glasses and a Gun (2016)

La Danza de la Realidad *See* The Dance of Reality (2014)

La Decade Prodigieuse *See* Ten Days Wonder (1972)

La Decima Vittima *See* 10th Victim (1965)

La Delicatesse *See* Delicacy (2012)

La Demoiselle d'Honneur *See* The Bridesmaid (2004)

La Desenchantee *See* The Disenchanted (1990)

La Diagonale du Fou *See* Dangerous Moves (1984)

La Dixieme Victime *See* 10th Victim (1965)

La Donna E Donna *See* A Woman Is a Woman (1960)

La Doppia Ora *See* The Double Hour (2009)

La Double Vie de Veronique *See* The Double Life of Veronique (1991)

La Doublure *See* The Valet (2006)

La Dueda Interna *See* Veronico Cruz (1987)

La Face Cachee de la Lune *See* Far Side of the Moon (2003)

La Faute a Fidel *See* Blame It on Fidel (2006)

La Femme d'a Cote *See* The Woman Next Door (1981)

La Femme de Chambre du Titanic *See* The Chambermaid on the Titanic (1997)

La Femme de Gilles *See* Gilles' Wife (2004)

La Femme de L'Aviateur *See* The Aviator's Wife (1980)

La Femme Mariee *See* A Married Woman (1965)

La Figlia di Frankenstein *See* Lady Frankenstein (1972)

La Fille Coupee en Deux *See* A Girl Cut in Two (2007)

La Fille de D'Artagnan *See* Revenge of the Musketeers (1994)

La Fille de Monaco *See* The Girl From Monaco (2008)

La Fille Du Puisatier *See* Well-Digger's Daughter (1946)

La Fille du Puisatier *See* The Well-Digger's Daughter (2011)

La Fille du RER *See* The Girl on the Train (2009)

La fille inconnue *See* The Unknown Girl (2017)

La Fille Seule *See* A Single Girl (1996)

La Finestra di Fronte *See* Facing Windows (2003)

La Flor de My Secreto *See* The Flower of My Secret (1995)

A la Folie *See* Six Days, Six Nights (1994)

La folie Almayer *See* Almayer's Folly (2012)

A la Folie. . .Pas de Tout *See* He Loves Me . . . He Loves Me Not (2002)

La Folle des Grandeurs *See* Delusions of Grandeur (1976)

La Francaise et L'Amour *See* Love and the Frenchwoman (1960)

La French *See* The Connection (2015)

La Frontiere de L'aube *See* Frontier of Dawn (2008)

La Furia del Hombre Lobo *See* The Fury of the Wolfman (1970)

La Furia Di Ercole *See* The Fury of Hercules (1961)

La Gangster del Pupa *See* Lady of the Evening (1975)

La Gloire de Mon Pere *See* My Father's Glory (1991)

La grande bellezza *See* The Great Beauty (2013)

La Grande Illusion *See* Grand Illusion (1937)

La grande notte di Ringo *See* Ringo's Big Night (1966)

La Grande Seduction *See* Seducing Doctor Lewis (2003)

La Grande Speranza *See* Submarine Attack (1954)

La Grande Strada Azzurra *See* The Wide Blue Road (1957)

La Guerra dei Robot *See* Reactor (1978)

La Guerre est Declaree *See* Declaration of War (2011)

La Haine *See* Hate (1995)

La Hija del Canibal *See* Lucia, Lucia (2003)

La Historia Oficial *See* The Official Story (1985)

La Horriplante Bestia Humana *See* Night of the Bloody Apes (1968)

La Isla Del Tersoro *See* Treasure Island (1972)

La jalousie *See* Jealousy (2013)

La Joven *See* The Young One (1961)

La Legge *See* Where the Hot Wind Blows (1959)

La Leggenda del Pianista Sull'Oceano *See* The Legend of 1900 (1998)

La Lengua Asesina *See* Killer Tongue (1996)

La Lengua de las Mariposas *See* Butterfly (1998)

La Ley del Deseo *See* Law of Desire (1986)

La Linea *See* The Line (2008)

La Llorona *See* The Wailer (2006)

La Loi *See* Where the Hot Wind Blows (1959)

La Lune Dans le Caniveau *See* Moon in the Gutter (1983)

La Mala Educacion *See* Bad Education (2004)

La Mala Ordina *See* The Italian Connection (1973)

La Mala Ordina *See* Manhunt (1973)

La Maldición *See* The Stranger (2015)

La Mariee Etait en Noir *See* The Bride Wore Black (1968)

La Maschera del Demonio *See* Black Sunday (1960)

La Masseria delle Allodole *See* The Lark Farm (2007)

La Matriarca *See* The Libertine (1969)

La Meglio Gioventu *See* Best of Youth (2003)

La Meilleure Facon de Marcher *See* The Best Way (1976)

La Migliore Offerta *See* The Best Offer (2013)

La Misma Luna *See* Under the Same Moon (2007)

La Moglie del Prete *See* The Priest's Wife (1971)

La Moglie Giovane *See* Death Will Have Your Eyes (1974)

La Mome *See* La Vie en Rose (2007)

La montagna di luce *See* Sandok (1965)

La Mort en Ce Jardin *See* Death in the Garden (1956)

La Morte de Staline *See* The Death of Stalin (2017)

La Morte Vestita di Dollar *See* Dog Eat Dog (1964)

La Morte Viene Dalla Spazio *See* The Day the Sky Exploded (1957)

La Morte Vivante *See* The Living Dead Girl (1982)

La Motocyclette *See* The Girl on a Motorcycle (1968)

Les raisins de la mort *See* The Grapes of Death (1978)

Les reines du ring *See* Queens of the Ring (2013)

Les Repos du Guerrier *See* Love on a Pillow (1962)

Les Revenants *See* They Came Back (2004)

Les Rivieres Pourpres *See* The Crimson Rivers (2001)

Les Rivieres Pourpres II: Les Anges de L'apocalypse *See* Crimson Rivers 2: Angels of the Apocalypse (2005)

Les Roseaux Sauvages *See* Wild Reeds (1994)

Les Soeurs Bronte *See* The Bronte Sisters (1979)

Les Somnambules *See* Mon Oncle d'Amerique (1980)

Les Temoins *See* The Witnesses (2007)

Les Temps Qui Changent *See* Changing Times (2004)

Les Temps Qui Reste *See* Time to Leave (2005)

Les Tontons Flingueurs *See* Monsieur Gangster (1963)

Les Triplettes de Belleville *See* The Triplets of Belleville (2002)

Les Trois Visages de la Peur *See* Black Sabbath (1964)

Les Vacances de Monsieur Hulot *See* Mr. Hulot's Holiday (1953)

Les Vaincus *See* The Vanquished (1952)

Les Valseuses *See* Going Places (1974)

Les Visiteurs *See* The Visitors (1995)

Les Yeux sans Visage *See* The Horror Chamber of Dr. Faustus (1959)

Lesbian Twins *See* The Virgin Witch (1970)

Lesbian Vampire Killers *See* Vampire Killers (2009)

L'Ete Meurtrier *See* One Deadly Summer (1983)

Let's Kill Bobby Z *See* Bobby Z (2007)

Let's Make Friends *See* I Love You, Man (2009)

Letter to Daddy *See* Jet Li's The Enforcer (1995)

Letyat Zhuravit *See* The Cranes Are Flying (1957)

L'Evangile Selon Saint-Matthieu *See* The Gospel According to St. Matthew (1964)

Levres de Sang *See* Lips of Blood (1975)

Lewis Carroll's Alice in Wonderland *See* Alice in Wonderland (1933)

L'Histoire d'Adele H. *See* The Story of Adele H. (1975)

L-Homme a Femmes *See* Murder By Two (1960)

L'Homme du Train *See* The Man on the Train (2002)

L'Homme Qui Aimait les Femmes *See* The Man Who Loved Women (1977)

L'Homme Qui J'aime *See* The Man I Love (1997)

L'Humanite *See* Humanity (1999)

Liar *See* Deceiver (1997)

Libertador *See* The Liberator (2013)

Lie to Me *See* Fling (2008)

Liebe Ist Kalter Als Der Tod *See* Love Is Colder Than Death (1969)

The Life and Adventures of Nicholas Nickleby *See* Nicholas Nickleby (1946)

The Life and Death of Bobby Z *See* Bobby Z (2007)

The Life and Loves of Beethoven *See* Beethoven (1936)

Life/Drawing *See* Apartment 12 (2006)

Life During Wartime *See* The Alarmist (1998)

Life Is a Fairy Tale *See* Life Is a Bed of Roses (1983)

The Life of Adele *See* Blue is the Warmest Color (2013)

Life of Brian *See* Monty Python's Life of Brian (1979)

The Life of Jack London *See* Jack London (1944)

Lifebreath *See* Last Breath (1996)

Lifesavers *See* Mixed Nuts (1994)

The Light Fantastic *See* Love Is Better Than Ever (1952)

Lighthouse *See* Dead of Night (1999)

Lightning *See* Ed McBain's 87th Precinct: Lightning (1995)

Lightning Fists of Shaolin *See* Opium and Kung-Fu Master (1984)

Lights of Variety *See* Variety Lights (1951)

Like a Crow on a June Bug *See* Sixteen (1972)

Like Minds *See* Murderous Intent (2006)

Lila *See* Mantis in Lace (1968)

Lila Dit Ca *See* Lila Says (2004)

Lilacs in the Spring *See* Let's Make Up (1955)

The Limb Salesman *See* Re-Generation (2004)

The Limit *See* Gone Dark (2003)

Limited Partners *See* Like a Boss (2020)

Limonadovy Joe aneb Konska Opera *See* Lemonade Joe (1964)

L'Inafferrabile Invincible *See* Mr. Superinvisible (1973)

Lincoln *See* Gore Vidal's Lincoln (1988)

Linkeroever *See* Left Bank (2008)

The Lion *See* La Leon (2007)

A Lion in the Streets *See* A Lion Is in the Streets (1953)

The Liquid Sword *See* Legend of the Liquid Sword (1993)

Lisa e il Diavolo *See* Lisa and the Devil (1975)

Lisa, Lisa *See* Axe (1974)

Lisbon *See* Lisboa (1999)

L'Isola Degli Uomini Pesce *See* Screamers (1980)

Little Fellas *See* Petits Freres (2000)

Little Fish, Strange Pond *See* Frenemy (2009)

Little Jerusalem *See* La Petite Jerusalem (2005)

Little Lili *See* La Petite Lili (2003)

The Little Martyr *See* The Children Are Watching Us (1944)

Little Miss Millions *See* Home for Christmas (1993)

Little Monsters *See* 2 Little Monsters (2015)

Little Pal *See* Healer (1936)

Little Panda *See* The Amazing Panda Adventure (1995)

Little Tough Guy *See* Dead End Kids: Little Tough Guy (1938)

Liu lang di qiu *See* The Wandering Earth (2019)

Liu Xiao Feng Zhi Jue Zhan Quian Hou *See* The Duel of the Century (1981)

Live a Little, Steal a Lot *See* Murph the Surf (1975)

Live Bait *See* L'Appat (1994)

Live Die Repeat: Edge of Tomorrow *See* Edge of Tomorrow (2014)

Live to Love *See* The Devil's Hand (1961)

Live Virgin *See* American Virgin (1998)

The Liver Eaters *See* Spider Baby (1964)

Living *See* Ikiru (1952)

The Living Dead at Manchester Morgue *See* Let Sleeping Corpses Lie (1974)

The Living Dead Man *See* Feu Mathias Pascal (1926)

Living Hell *See* Organizm (2008)

Living Nightmare *See* Echoes (1983)

Living With the Dead *See* Talking to Heaven (2002)

Ljubarni Slucaj *See* The Love Affair, or The Case of the Missing Switchboard Operator (1967)

Lo chiamavano California *See* California (1977)

Lo Chiamavano King *See* His Name Was King (1971)

Lo Chiamavano Trinita *See* They Call Me Trinity (1972)

Lo Sbarco di Anzio *See* Anzio (1968)

Lo Sceicco Bianco *See* The White Sheik (1952)

Lo Sono L'Amore *See* I Am Love (2009)

Lo Spettro *See* The Ghost (1963)

Lo Spettro de Dr. Hitchcock *See* The Ghost (1963)

Lo Squartatore de New York *See* New York Ripper (1982)

Lo Strangolatore di Vienna *See* The Mad Butcher (1972)

Loaded Weapon 1 *See* National Lampoon's Loaded Weapon 1 (1993)

The Lodger: A Case of London Fog *See* The Lodger (1926)

L'Oeuvre au Noir *See* The Abyss (1989)

Lola *See* Beyond Erotica (1974)

Lola + Bilikid *See* Lola and Billy the Kid (1998)

Lola Colt: Faccia a faccia con El Diablo *See* Lola Colt (1967)

Lola gegen den Rest der Welt *See* Lola Versus (2012)

Lola Rennt *See* Run Lola Run (1998)

Lolita 2000 *See* Lolida 2000 (1997)

The Lolly-Madonna War *See* Lolly-Madonna XXX (1973)

Lone Wolf and Cub: Baby Cart in Peril *See* Lone Wolf and Cub 4 (1972)

Lone Wolf and Cub: Baby Cart to Hades *See* Shogun Assassin 2: Lightning Swords of Death (1973)

Lone Wolf and Cub: Sword of Vengeance *See* Lone Wolf and Cub (1972)

The Lonely Hearts Killers *See* Honeymoon Killers (1970)

The Lonely Maiden *See* The Maiden Heist (2008)

Lonely Man *See* Gun Riders (1969)

The Lonely Wife *See* Charulata (1964)

The Lonely Woman *See* Voyage in Italy (1953)

The Loner *See* Ruckus (1981)

Lonesome Dove: Streets of Laredo *See* Larry McMurtry's Streets of Laredo (1995)

The Long, Dark Night *See* The Pack (1977)

Long Days of Vengeance *See* Long Days of Revenge (1967)

Long hu men *See* Dragon Tiger Gate (2007)

Long John Silver Returns to Treasure Island *See* Long John Silver (1954)

The Long Shot *See* African Rage (1978)

Long Time, Nothing New *See* No Looking Back (1998)

Long Way Home *See* Raising Victor Vargas (2003)

Long Weekend *See* Nature's Grave (2008)

Longxiong Hudi *See* Operation Condor 2: The Armour of the Gods (1986)

The Look *See* Charlotte Rampling: The Look (2011)

The Look of Ulysses *See* Ulysses' Gaze (1995)

Lookin' Italian *See* Showdown (1994)

Loonies on Broadway *See* Zombies on Broadway (1944)

Looters *See* Trespass (1992)

L'Opera De Quat'Sous *See* The Threepenny Opera (1931)

The Lorax *See* Dr. Seuss' The Lorax (2012)

Lorca *See* The Disappearance of Garcia Lorca (1996)

Lord Mountbatten: The Last Viceroy *See* Mountbatten: The Last Viceroy (1986)

Lord of the Elves *See* Age of the Hobbits (2012)

Lords of Treason *See* Secret Honor (1985)

L'Oro Di Napoli *See* The Gold of Naples (1954)

L'Orribile Segreto del Dr. Hichcock *See* The Horrible Dr. Hichcock (1962)

Los Abrazos Rotos *See* Broken Embraces (2009)

Los Amantes del Circulo Polar *See* Lovers of the Arctic Circle (1998)

Los amantes pasajeros *See* I'm So Excited (2013)

Los Ambiciosos *See* Fever Mounts at El Pao (1959)

Los cuatro salvajes *See* Ringo's Mark of Vengeance (1967)

Los Despiadados *See* Hellbenders (1967)

Los Lunes al Sol *See* Mondays in the Sun (2002)

Los Ojos de Julia *See* Julia's Eyes (2010)

Los sin nombre *See* The Nameless (1999)

Loser Take All *See* Strike It Rich (1990)

The Lost Atlantis *See* The Mistress of Atlantis (1932)

The Lost Coast Tapes *See* Bigfoot: The Lost Coast Tapes (2012)

The Lost Glory of Troy *See* The Avenger (1962)

The Lost Illusion *See* The Fallen Idol (1949)

Lost in Time *See* Waxwork 2: Lost in Time (1991)

Lost Planet Airmen *See* King of the Rocketmen (1949)

Lost Women *See* Mesa of Lost Women (1952)

Lost Women of Zarpa *See* Mesa of Lost Women (1952)

The Loudest Whisper *See* The Children's Hour (1961)

Louis L'Amour's Conagher *See* Conagher (1991)

Louis L'Amour's 'The Shadow Riders' *See* The Shadow Riders (1982)

Love a la Carte *See* Adua and Her Friends (1960)

Love and Death in Saigon *See* A Better Tomorrow, Part 3 (1989)

The Love Cage *See* Joy House (1964)

The Love Factor *See* Zeta One (1969)

Love in Las Vegas *See* Viva Las Vegas (1963)

Love Is the Drug *See* Addicted to Her Love (2006)

Love Lessons *See* All Things Fair (1995)

Love Madness *See* Reefer Madness (1938)

The Love Maniac *See* Blood of Ghastly Horror (1972)

A Love Story *See* Song of Love (1947)

Love, the Magician *See* El Amor Brujo (1986)

The Lovelorn Minstrel *See* Ashik Kerib (1988)

Lover of the Great Bear *See* Smugglers (1975)

Lovers and Liars *See* Criminal Desire (1998)

Lovers from Beyond the Tomb *See* Nightmare Castle (1965)

Lovers Must Learn *See* Rome Adventure (1962)

Love's a Bitch *See* Amores Perros (2000)

Loves of a Scoundrel *See* Death of a Scoundrel (1956)

The Loves of Count Yorga, Vampire *See* Count Yorga, Vampire (1970)

The Loves of Irina *See* Female Vampire (1973)

Loving Moments *See* Bleak Moments (1971)

Low Altitude *See* Low Heights (2002)

Low Rent *See* Apartment 12 (2006)

The Loyal 47 Ronin *See* 47 Ronin, Part 1 (1942)

Luca il Contrabbandiere *See* Contraband (1980)

Luce Dei Miei Occhi *See* Light of My Eyes (2001)

L'Ucello dalle Plume di Cristallo *See* The Bird with the Crystal Plumage (1970)

Luci del Varieta *See* Variety Lights (1951)

Lucia y el Sexo *See* Sex and Lucia (2001)

The Lucifer Project *See* Barracuda (1978)

Lucky Break *See* Paperback Romance (1996)

Lucky Day *See* Mary Higgins Clark: Lucky Day (2002)

Lucky 13 *See* Running Hot (1983)

Luftslottet Som Sprangdes *See* The Girl Who Kicked the Hornet's Nest (2010)

Luk jong si *See* Six Strong Guys (2004)

The Lullaby *See* The Sin of Madelon Claudet (1931)

L'Ultimo Bacio *See* The Last Kiss (2001)

L'Ultimo Uomo Della Terra *See* The Last Man on Earth (1964)

Lulu *See* Pandora's Box (1928)

Lung Boonmee Raluek Chat *See* Uncle Boonmee Who Can Recall His Past Lives (2010)

Lung fu moon *See* Dragon Tiger Gate (2007)

L'Uomo Dalle Due Ombre *See* Cold Sweat (1971)

Lust for Evil *See* Purple Noon (1960)

Lust och Fagring Stor *See* All Things Fair (1995)

Lust of the Vampires *See* I, Vampiri (1956)

Lysets Hjerte *See* Heart of Light (1997)

Lyubovnitsky *See* Mistresses (2019)

M. Hire *See* Monsieur Hire (1989)

M:I 2 *See* Mission: Impossible 2 (2000)

M:I 6-Mission Impossible *See* Mission: Impossible-Fallout (2018)

M1187511 *See* In This World (2003)

Ma and Pa Kettle Go to Paris *See* Ma and Pa Kettle on Vacation (1953)

Ma Femme est une Actrice *See* My Wife is an Actress (2001)

Ma noot Ihek lai *See* Mercury Man (2006)

Ma Nuit Chez Maud *See* My Night at Maud's (1969)

Ma Part du Gateau *See* My Piece of the Pie (2011)

Ma-seu-teo *See* Master (2016)

Ma vie de Courgette *See* My Life as a Zucchini (2016)

Ma Vie Sexuelle...Comment Je Me Suis Dispute *See* My Sex Life. . . Or How I Got into an Argument (1996)

Ma Vraie Vie a Rouen *See* My Life on Ice (2002)

Maboroshi no Hikari *See* Maborosi (1995)

Macabra *See* Demonoid, Messenger of Death (1981)

Macabre Serenade *See* Dance of Death (1968)

Maccheroni *See* Macaroni (1985)

Macchie solari *See* Autopsy (1975)

Maciste Alla Corte Del Gran Khan *See* Samson and the 7 Miracles of the World (1962)

Maciste at the Court of the Great Khan *See* Samson and the 7 Miracles of the World (1962)

Maciste Contro I Mongoli *See* Hercules Against the Mongols (1963)

Maciste Contro i Mostri *See* Fire Monsters Against the Son of Hercules (1962)

Maciste, Il Gladiatore piu Forte del Monte *See* Colossus of the Arena (1962)

Maciste la Regina di Samar *See* Hercules against the Moon Men (1964)

Maciste, L'Eroe Piu Grande Del Mondo *See* Goliath and the Sins of Babylon (1964)

The Mad Butcher of Vienna *See* The Mad Butcher (1972)

Mad Dog *See* Mad Dog Morgan (1976)

Mad Dog Time *See* Trigger Happy (1996)

Mad Dogs and Englishmen *See* Shameless (1994)

The Mad Hatter *See* Breakfast in Hollywood (1946)

The Mad Killers *See* Death Merchants (1973)

Mad Magazine's Up the Academy *See* Up the Academy (1980)

Mad Max 2 *See* The Road Warrior (1982)

Mad Trapper of the Yukon *See* Challenge To Be Free (1976)

Mad Wednesday *See* The Sin of Harold Diddlebock (1947)

Madame *See* Madame Sans-Gene (1962)

Madame De... *See* The Earrings of Madame De. . . (1954)

Madame Frankenstein *See* Lady Frankenstein (1972)

A Madea Christmas *See* Tyler Perry's A Madea Christmas (2013)

Mademoiselle France *See* Reunion in France (1942)

Mademoiselle Strip-tease *See* The Nude Set (1957)

Mademoiselle Striptease *See* Plucking the Daisy (1956)

Madmen of Mandoras *See* They Saved Hitler's Brain (1964)

Madness of Love *See* Mad Love (2001)

Madonna Truth or Dare *See* Truth or Dare (1991)

Maend & hons *See* Men & Chicken (2015)

Mafia Docks *See* Desperate Crimes (1993)

Mafia Junction *See* Super Bitch (1973)

The Mafia Terminator *See* Crime Boss (1972)

The Mafu Cage *See* My Sister, My Love (1978)

The Magic Hour *See* Twilight (1998)

The Magic Roundabout *See* Doogal (2005)

The Magnificent One *See* Le Magnifique (1976)

Magnificent Pole Fighters *See* 8 Diagram Pole Fighter (1984)

The Magnificent Seven *See* Seven Samurai (1954)

The Magnificent Showman *See* Circus World (1964)

Major Movie Star *See* Private Valentine: Blonde & Dangerous (2008)

Making It *See* Going Places (1974)

Mako: The Jaws of Death *See* Jaws of Death (1976)

Malastrana *See* Short Night of Glass Dolls (1971)

Malenka, the Vampire *See* Fangs of the Living Dead (1968)

Malenkaya Vera *See* Little Vera (1988)

Malibu Hot Summer *See* Sizzle Beach U.S.A. (1974)

Malice in Wonderland *See* The Rumor Mill (1986)

Malli *See* The Terrorist (1998)

Mamba Snakes *See* Fair Game (1989)

Mam'zelle Pigalle *See* That Naughty Girl (1958)

Man Against the Mob: The Chinatown Murders *See* The Chinatown Murders: Man against the Mob (1989)

Man and His Mate *See* One Million B.C. (1940)

A Man Called Blade *See* Mannaja: A Man Called Blade (1977)

Man Cheng Jin Dai Huang Jin Jia *See* Curse of the Golden Flower (2006)

Man-Eater *See* Shark! (1968)

A Man Escaped, or the Wind Bloweth Where It Listeth *See* A Man Escaped (1957)

The Man from C.O.T.T.O.N. *See* Purlie Victorious (1963)

The Man From C.O.T.T.O.N., Purlie Victorious *See* Gone Are the Days (1963)

Man from Music Mountain *See* Texas Legionnaires (1943)

The Man From Nevada *See* The Nevadan (1950)

The Man From the Folies Bergere *See* Folies Bergere de Paris (1935)

The Man Hunter *See* Devil Hunter (2008)

Man in a Cocked Hat *See* Carlton Browne of the F.O. (1959)

A Man in Mommy's Bed *See* With Six You Get Eggroll (1968)

The Man in Possession *See* Personal Property (1937)

Man of Bronze *See* Jim Thorpe: All American (1951)

Man of the Hour *See* Colonel Effingham's Raid (1945)

Man Som Hatar Kvinnor *See* The Girl With the Dragon Tattoo (2009)

The Man Who Cried *See* Catherine Cookson's The Man Who Cried (1993)

The Man With 100 Faces *See* Crackerjack (1938)

The Man With Rain in His Shoe *See* Twice upon a Yesterday (1998)

The Man With The Deadly Lens *See* Wrong Is Right (1982)

The Man with the Green Carnation *See* The Trials of Oscar Wilde (1960)

The Man with the Synthetic Brain *See* Blood of Ghastly Horror (1972)

The Man with the X-Ray Eyes *See* X: The Man with X-Ray Eyes (1963)

The Man with Thirty Sons *See* The Magnificent Yankee (1950)

Manbiki kazoku *See* Shoplifters (2018)

Manchester Prep *See* Cruel Intentions 2 (1999)

Mandingo Manhunter *See* Devil Hunter (2008)

Mangiati Vivi dai Cannibali *See* Emerald Jungle (1980)

Manhattan Project: The Deadly Game *See* The Manhattan Project (1986)

Manhunt *See* The Italian Connection (1973)

Mania *See* The Flesh and the Fiends (1960)

Mania Days *See* Touched With Fire (2016)

The Maniacs Are Loose *See* The Thrill Killers (1965)

Mannequins for Rio *See* Party Girls for Sale (1954)

Manner wie wir *See* Guys and Balls (2004)

Manners of the Sky *See* Navy Blues (1937)

Manon 70 *See* Manon (1968)

Manon des Sources *See* Manon of the Spring (1987)

Mansion of Madness *See* Dr. Tarr's Torture Dungeon (1975)

Mansquito *See* Mosquito Man (2005)

The Manster-Half Man, Half Monster *See* The Manster (1959)

Manuela's Loves *See* Le Jupon Rouge (1987)

Mar Adentro *See* The Sea Inside (2004)

Marc Bolan and T-Rrex: Born to Boogie *See* Born to Boogie (1972)

Marc Mato, Agent S.077 *See* Espionage in Tangiers (1965)

Marcelino *See* The Miracle of Marcelino (1955)

Marcelino, Pan y Vino *See* The Miracle of Marcelino (1955)

Marching Along *See* Stars and Stripes Forever (1952)

Marco Polo Junior Versus the Red Dragon *See* Marco Polo, Jr. (1972)

The Marconi Bros. *See* The Wedding Bros. (2008)

Maria Larssons Eviga Ogonblick *See* Everlasting Moments (2008)

Maria, llena eres de gracia *See* Maria Full of Grace (2004)

Maria Marten *See* Murder in the Old Red Barn (1936)

Maria's B Movie Mayhem: Vampire at Midnight *See* Vampire at Midnight (1988)

Marie Walewska *See* Conquest (1937)

Marijuana the Devil's Weed *See* She Shoulda Said No (1949)

Mario Puzo's The Last Don *See* The Last Don (1997)

Mario Puzo's The Last Don 2 *See* The Last Don 2 (1998)

Marius et Jeannette: Un Conte de L'Estaque *See* Marius and Jeannette (1997)

Mark of Terror *See* Drums of Jeopardy (1931)

The Mark: Redemption *See* The Mark 2: Redemption (2013)

Mark Twain *See* The Adventures of Mark Twain (1985)

Marquis de Sade's Justine *See* Justine (1969)

A Married Woman *See* Une Femme Mariee (1964)

Mars Invades Puerto Rico *See* Frankenstein Meets the Space Monster (1965)

The Marseille Contract *See* The Destructors (1974)

The Marsupials: Howling 3 *See* Howling 3: The Marsupials (1987)

Martha, Meet Frank, Daniel and Laurence *See* The Very Thought of You (1998)

Martin Lawrence You So Crazy *See* You So Crazy (1994)

Marusa No Onna *See* A Taxing Woman (1987)

Marvel's The Avengers *See* The Avengers (2012)

The Marx Brothers at the Circus *See* At the Circus (1939)

Marx Brothers Go West *See* Go West (1940)

Mary Bryant *See* The Incredible Journey of Mary Bryant (2005)

Mary Jane's Last Dance *See* New Best Friend (2002)

Maryland *See* Disorder (2016)

Macskajatek *See* Cat's Play (1974)

Masculin Feminin *See* Masculine Feminine (1966)

Mask of Dust *See* Race for Life (1955)

Mask of Satan *See* Black Sunday (1960)

The Masked Pirate *See* The Pirates of Capri (1949)

Maskerade *See* Mask Maker (2010)

Massacre at Fort Holman *See* A Reason to Live, a Reason to Die (1973)

Massage Parlor Hookers *See* Massage Parlor Murders (1973)

Massa'ot James Be'eretz Hakodesh *See* James' Journey to Jerusalem (2003)

The Master Killer *See* The 36th Chamber of Shaolin (1978)

The Master Mystery *See* The Houdini Serial (1920)

Master of Dragonard Hill *See* Dragonard (1988)

Moscow Distrusts Tears *See* Moscow Does Not Believe in Tears (1980)
Moscow Nights *See* I Stand Condemned (1936)
Moskwa Sljesam Nje Jerit *See* Moscow Does Not Believe in Tears (1980)
Most Dangerous Man in the World *See* The Chairman (1969)
Mosura *See* Mothra (1962)
Mosura *See* Rebirth of Mothra (1996)
Mosura 2 *See* Rebirth of Mothra 2 (1997)
Mosura tai Gojira *See* Godzilla *vs.* Mothra (1964)
The Moth *See* Catherine Cookson's The Moth (1996)
Mother *See* Madeo (2009)
Mother Goose A Go-Go *See* The Unkissed Bride (1966)
Mother Riley Meets the Vampire *See* My Son, the Vampire (1952)
A Mother's Fight for Justice *See* Crash Course (2000)
Mothra *See* Rebirth of Mothra (1996)
Mothra 2 *See* Rebirth of Mothra 2 (1997)
Mothra *vs.* **Godzilla** *See* Godzilla *vs.* Mothra (1964)
Motor Rods and Rockers *See* Motor Psycho (1965)
Mou gaan dou II *See* Infernal Affairs 2 (2003)
Mou gaan dou III: Jung mik mou gaan *See* Infernal Affairs 3 (2003)
Mou lam sing foh gam *See* Holy Flame of the Martial World (1983)
The Moustache *See* La Moustache (2005)
The Moutie *See* The Way of the West (2011)
Movie Struck *See* Pick a Star (1937)
The Moving Target *See* Harper (1966)
Mowgli *See* Mowgli: Legend of the Jungle (2018)
Mowgli and Baloo: Jungle Book 2 *See* Rudyard Kipling's the Second Jungle Book: Mowgli and Baloo (1997)
MS One: Maximum Security *See* Lockout (2012)
Much Ado about Murder *See* Theatre of Blood (1973)
Mugen no junin *See* Blade of the Immortal (2017)
Muhomatsu no Issho *See* Rikisha-Man (1958)
Mui du du Xanh *See* The Scent of Green Papaya (1993)
Mujeres al Borde de un Ataque de Nervios *See* Women on the Verge of a Nervous Breakdown (1988)
Muk Gong *See* Battle of the Warriors (2006)
The Mule *See* Border Run (2012)
The Mummy *See* Bram Stoker's The Mummy (1997)
Mumsy, Nanny, Sonny, and Girly *See* Girly (1970)
Mundo Depravados *See* World of the Depraved (1967)
Mur *See* Wall (2004)
Murder at Midnight *See* Murder by Invitation (1941)
Murder by Proxy *See* Blackout (1954)
The Murder Gang *See* Black Heat (1976)
Murder in the Ring *See* Counter Punch (1971)
The Murder in Thorton Square *See* Gaslight (1944)
Murder, Inc. *See* The Enforcer (1951)
Murder is Easy *See* Agatha Christie's Murder is Easy (1982)
Murder on the Air *See* The Twenty Questions Murder Mystery (1950)
Murder One *See* Death Sentence (1974)
The Murder Room *See* P.D. James: The Murder Room (2004)
Murder Rooms: The Dark Origins of Sherlock Holmes *See* Dr. Bell and Mr. Doyle: The Dark Beginnings of Sherlock Holmes (2000)
Murder Will Out *See* The Voice of Merrill (1952)
Murder with Mirrors *See* Agatha Christie's Murder with Mirrors (1985)
The Murderer Dmitri Karamazov *See* The Brothers Karamazov (1958)
Muriel, Or the Time of Return *See* Muriel (1963)
Muriel, Ou le Temps d'Un Retour *See* Muriel (1963)
Murieta *See* Revenge of Sartana (1965)
Musa *See* Musa: The Warrior (2001)
Music in Darkness *See* Night Is My Future (1947)
The Music Room *See* Jalsaghar (1958)
Musime si Pomahat *See* Divided We Fall (2000)
Mussolini: The Decline and Fall of Il Duce *See* Mussolini & I (1985)
Mutant *See* Forbidden World (1982)
The Mutation *See* The Freakmaker (1973)
Mutations *See* The Freakmaker (1973)
The Mutilator *See* The Dark (1979)
Mutter Kusters Fahrt Zum Himmel *See* Mother Kusters Goes to Heaven (1976)
Mutter und Sohn *See* Mother and Son (1997)
Mutters Courage *See* My Mother's Courage (1995)
Muyeong geom *See* The Legend of the Shadowless Sword (2008)
MVP 3 *See* MXP: Most Xtreme Primate (2003)
My Angel *See* Christmas Angel (2011)
My Bollywood Bride *See* My Faraway Bride (2006)
My Brother, the Outlaw *See* My Outlaw Brother (1951)
My Brother's Keeper *See* Brother's Keeper (2002)
My Crazy Life *See* Mi Vida Loca (1994)
My Father Is a Hero *See* Jet Li's The Enforcer (1995)
My Father, My Master *See* Padre Padrone (1977)
My Favorite Season *See* Ma Saison Preferee (1993)
My Favourite Year *See* My Favorite Year (1982)
My Forgotten Man *See* Flynn (1996)
My Girlfriend's Boyfriend *See* Boyfriends & Girlfriends (1988)
My Heart Goes Crazy *See* London Town (1946)
My Hero *See* A Southern Yankee (1948)
My Idiot Brother *See* Our Idiot Brother (2011)
My Idol *See* Whatever You Say (2002)
My Life in Pink *See* Ma Vie en Rose (1997)
My Love Letters *See* Love Letters (1983)
My Name Is Zora *See* Zora Is My Name! (1990)
My Neighbor's Daughter *See* Angel Blue (1997)
My Night with Maud *See* My Night at Maud's (1969)
My Posse Don't Do Homework *See* Dangerous Minds (1995)
My Son Alone *See* American Empire (1942)
My Teenage Daughter *See* Teenage Bad Girl (1959)
My Uncle *See* Mon Oncle (1958)
My Uncle, Mr. Hulot *See* Mon Oncle (1958)
My Undercover Years With the KKK *See* Undercover With the KKK (1978)
My World Dies Screaming *See* Terror in the Haunted House (1958)
Mysterious Island *See* Jules Verne's Mysterious Island (2010)
The Mysterious Magician *See* Again, the Ringer (1964)
Mystery Monsters! *See* Goobers! (1997)
The Mystery of Kaspar Hauser *See* Every Man for Himself & God Against All (1975)
The Mystery of Spoon River *See* The Ghost of Spoon River (2000)
Mystery of the Black Jungle *See* The Black Devils of Kali (1955)
The Mystery of the Golden Eye *See* The Golden Eye (1948)
The Myth *See* Jackie Chan's The Myth (2005)
Nachts wenn Dracula Erwacht *See* Count Dracula (1971)
Nader and Simin, a Separation *See* A Separation (2011)
A Nagy Fuzet *See* The Notebook (2013)
The Naked Goddess *See* The Devil's Hand (1961)
Naked Massacre *See* Born for Hell (1976)
The Naked Night *See* Sawdust & Tinsel (1953)
Naked Space *See* Spaceship (1981)
Naked under Leather *See* The Girl on a Motorcycle (1968)
Naked Warriors *See* The Arena (1973)
Nam's Angels *See* The Losers (1970)
Namu, My Best Friend *See* Namu, the Killer Whale (1966)
Nan Fang Che Zhan De Ju Hui *See* The Wild Goose Lake (2020)
Nanguo Zaijian, Nanguo *See* Goodbye South, Goodbye (1996)
Nanjing! Nanjing! *See* City of Life and Death (2009)
Nankai No Daikaiju *See* Yog, Monster from Space (1971)
Nankai No Kai Ketto *See* Godzilla *vs.* the Sea Monster (1966)
Nannerl, la Soeur de Mozart *See* Mozart's Sister (2010)
Nannerl, Mozart's Sister *See* Mozart's Sister (2010)
Nanny McPhee and the Big Bang *See* Nanny McPhee Returns (2010)
NaPolA *See* Before the Fall (2004)
Napszállta *See* Sunset (2018)
Nara Livet *See* Brink of Life (1957)
Narayama-Bushi-Ko *See* The Ballad of Narayama (1983)
Narayama bushiko *See* The Ballad of Narayama (1958)
Nasty Hunter *See* Lady Terminator (1989)
Nathaniel Hawthorne's 'Twice Told Tales' *See* Twice-Told Tales (1963)
The Nation *See* Hot Type: 150 Years of The Nation (2015)
National Lampoon Presents Repli-Kate *See* Repli-Kate (2001)
National Lampoon's Cousin Eddie's Christmas Vacation Lost *See* National Lampoon's Christmas Vacation 2: Cousin Eddie's Big Island Adventure (2003)
Nattens Engel *See* Angel of the Night (1998)
Nattvardsgaesterna *See* The Winter Light (1962)
Nature's Mistakes *See* Freaks (1932)
Naughty Girl *See* That Naughty Girl (1958)
Navy Cross *See* G.I. Jane (1997)
Navy Diver *See* Men of Honor (2000)
Ne le Dis a Personne *See* Tell No One (2006)
Ne Touchez pas la Hache *See* The Duchess of Langeais (2007)
Ne Zha zhi mo tong jiang shi *See* Ne Zha (2019)
The Necessary Death of Charlie Countryman *See* Charlie Countryman (2013)
Neco Z Alenky *See* Alice (1988)
Necromancy *See* The Witching (1972)
Ned Blessing: The Story of My Life and Times *See* Lone Justice 2 (1993)
Ned Kelly, Outlaw *See* Ned Kelly (1970)
Negatibu happi chenso ejji *See* Negative Happy Chainsaw Edge (2008)
Neighborhood Watch *See* The Watch (2012)
Neighbouring Sounds *See* Neighboring Sounds (2012)
Neil Simon's Biloxi Blues *See* Biloxi Blues (1988)
Neil Simon's Brighton Beach Memoirs *See* Brighton Beach Memoirs (1986)
Neil Simon's Lost in Yonkers *See* Lost in Yonkers (1993)
Neil Simon's The Odd Couple 2 *See* The Odd Couple 2 (1998)
Neil Simon's The Slugger's Wife *See* The Slugger's Wife (1985)
Nella Cita L'Inferno *See* And the Wild, Wild Women (1959)
Nella Stretta M Orsa Del Ragno *See* Web of the Spider (1970)
Nella terra dei cannibali *See* Land of Death (2003)
Nelly and Mr. Arnaud *See* Nelly et Monsieur Arnaud (1995)
Nelyubov *See* Loveless (2018)
The Neptune Disaster *See* Neptune Factor (1973)
Nes en 68 *See* Born in 68 (2008)
Neskolko Dnel iz Zhizni I.I. Oblomov *See* Oblomov (1981)
The Nest *See* Sisters (2015)
Netforce *See* Tom Clancy's Netforce (1998)
Nettoyage a Sec *See* Dry Cleaning (1997)
Neurosis *See* Revenge in the House of Usher (1982)
Nevada Heat *See* Fake Out (1982)
Never Cry Devil *See* Night Visitor (1989)
The Never Dead *See* Phantasm (1979)
Never Ever *See* Circle of Passion (1997)
Never Give an Inch *See* Sometimes a Great Notion (1971)
Never Take Sweets From a Stranger *See* Never Take Candy From a Stranger (1960)
NeverWhere *See* Neil Gaiman's NeverWhere (1996)
The New Adventures of Don Juan *See* Adventures of Don Juan (1949)
New Adventures of Tarzan *See* Tarzan and the Green Goddess (1938)
The New Barbarians *See* Warriors of the Wasteland (1983)
New Mafia Boss *See* Crime Boss (1972)
New Moon *See* The Twilight Saga: New Moon (2009)
The New Ninja *See* Shinobi No Mono 3: Resurrection (2009)
New Tales of the Taira Clan *See* Shin Heike Monogatari (1955)
New Wine *See* Melody Master (1941)
The Newcomers *See* The Wild Country (1971)
The Next Man *See* The Arab Conspiracy (1976)
The Next Race *See* Dark Metropolis (2010)
Ng duk *See* Five Deadly Venoms (1978)
Ng fu tiu lung *See* Sword Masters: Brothers Five (1970)
Ng Leung bat gwa gwun *See* 8 Diagram Pole Fighter (1984)
Ngo Hai Sui *See* Jackie Chan's Who Am I (1998)
Ni le ciel ni la terre *See* Neither Heaven Nor Earth (2016)
Nicholas Nickleby *See* The Life and Adventures of Nicholas Nickleby (1981)

One for Sorrow, Two for Joy *See* Signs of Life (1989)
One for the Money, Two for the Show *See* On the Run (1973)
One Horse Town *See* Small Town Girl (1953)
One Hundred Percent Pure *See* The Girl from Missouri (1934)
120 battements par minute *See* BPM (Beats Per Minute) (2017)
One in a Million *See* Dangerous Appointment (1934)
One-Man Mutiny *See* The Court Martial of Billy Mitchell (1955)
One Missed Call Final *See* One Missed Call 3: Final (2006)
One Plus One *See* Sympathy for the Devil (1970)
One Point O *See* Paranoia 1.0 (2004)
One Shot *See* Jack Reacher (2012)
The One That Got Away *See* Gossip (2008)
Ong Bak: The Beginning *See* Ong Bak 2 (2008)
Only Blackness *See* The Bloodstained Shadow (1978)
Only for Love *See* Please Not Now! (1961)
Only the French Can! *See* French Can-Can (1955)
Onmyoji: The Yin Yang Master *See* Onmyoji (2001)
Onna Ga Kaidan O Agaru Toki *See* When a Woman Ascends the Stairs (1960)
Onna hisatsu ken: kiki ippatsu *See* Sister Street Fighter 2: Hanging by a Thread (1974)
Oopsie Poopsie *See* Get Rita (1975)
Oopsie Poopsie *See* Lady of the Evening (1975)
Oorlogswinter *See* Winter in Wartime (2010)
OpenCam *See* Open Cam (2005)
Operacione Paura *See* Kill, Baby, Kill (1966)
Operation Cicero *See* Five Fingers (1952)
Operation Espionage *See* Billion Dollar Brain (1967)
Operation M *See* Hell's Bloody Devils (1970)
Operation Monsterland *See* Destroy All Monsters (1968)
Operation Overthrow *See* Power Play (1978)
Operation Serpent *See* Fer-De-Lance (1974)
Operation Undercover *See* Report to the Commissioner (1975)
Operazione Goldman *See* Lightning Bolt (1967)
Operetta tanuki goten *See* Princess Raccoon (2005)
Opium Connection *See* The Poppy Is Also a Flower (1966)
The Opposite Sex *See* A Bet's a Bet (2014)
Oprah Winfrey Presents: Mitch Albom's For One More Day *See* For One More Day (2007)
L'Ora di Punta *See* The Trial Begins (2007)
L'ora di religione *See* My Mother's Smile (2002)
The Oracle *See* The Horse's Mouth (1958)
Orazi e Curiazi *See* Duel of Champions (1961)
Orca-Killer Whale *See* Orca (1977)
Orchestra Seats *See* Avenue Montaigne (2006)
Order of Death *See* Corrupt (1984)
Ore Ni Sawaru to Abunaize *See* Black Tight Killers (1966)
Orfeu Negro *See* Black Orpheus (1958)
Orgasmo *See* Paranoia (1969)
Orgy of the Dead *See* The Hanging Woman (1972)
Original Sins *See* Acts of Contrition (1995)
Orion's Key *See* Alien Chaser (1996)
Orkobefogadas *See* Adoption (1975)
Orlacs Hande *See* The Hands of Orlac (1925)
Orloff Against the Invisible Man *See* Dr. Orloff and the Invisible Man (1972)
Orloff Against the Invisible Man *See* Orloff and the Invisible Man (1970)
Oro per i Caesari *See* Gold for the Caesars (1963)
Oroi *See* Jitters (2010)
Orphee *See* Orpheus (1949)
Orson Welles' Don Quixote *See* Don Quixote (1992)
Orson Welles's Othello *See* Othello (1952)
Oru Kaiju Daishingeki *See* Godzilla's Revenge (1969)
Osombie: Axis of the Evil Dead *See* Osombie (2012)
Ososhiki *See* The Funeral (1984)
OSS 117: Le Caire Nid d'Espions *See* OSS 117: Cairo, Nest of Spies (2006)
OSS 117: Rio Ne Repond Plus *See* OSS 117: Lost in Rio (2009)
Ostre Sledovane Vlaky *See* Closely Watched Trains (1966)
Ostwind 2 *See* Whisper 2: L'Aventure Continue (2016)
Otac na Sluzbenom Putu *See* When Father Was Away on Business (1985)
Otets I Syn *See* Father and Son (2003)
The Other World *See* Black Heaven (2010)
Otto e mezzo *See* 8 1/2 (1963)
Our Daily Bread *See* City Girl (1930)
Our Girl Friday *See* The Adventures of Sadie (1955)
Our Man in Marrakesh *See* Bang! Bang! You're Dead! (1966)
Our Mothers, Our Fathers *See* Generation War (2013)
Our Music *See* Our Music (2004)
Our Story *See* Notre Histoire (1984)
L'Ours *See* The Bear (1989)
Out of Inferno *See* Out of the Inferno (2013)
Out of Omaha *See* California Dreaming (2007)
Out of Rosenheim *See* Bagdad Cafe (1988)
Out of Synch *See* Lip Service (2000)
Out of the Darkness *See* Night Creature (1979)
Out of the Darkness *See* Teenage Caveman (1958)
Out of the Night *See* Strange Illusion (1945)
Outback Vampires *See* The Wicked (1989)
The Outcast *See* Man in the Saddle (1951)
The Outcry *See* Il Grido (1957)
Outer Reach *See* Spaced Out (1980)
Outlaw Gun *See* A Minute to Pray, a Second to Die (1967)
The Outlawed Planet *See* Planet of the Vampires (1965)
Outomlionnye Solntsem *See* Burnt by the Sun (1994)
Outpost 3: Rise of the Spetsnaz *See* Outpost: Rise of the Spetsnaz (2013)
Outside Satan *See* Hors Satan (2011)
The Outsider *See* Fatal Error (1983)
Outsider in Amsterdam *See* Fatal Error (1983)
The Outsiders *See* Band of Outsiders (1964)
Over Her Dead Body *See* Enid Is Sleeping (1990)
Over the Edge *See* A Deadly Encounter (2004)
Ozombie *See* Osombie (2012)
The Pace That Kills *See* Cocaine Fiends (1936)
Painted Angels *See* The Wicked, Wicked West (1997)
Painted Skin 2 *See* Painted Skin: The Resurrection (2012)
The Painting *See* Soldiers of Change (2006)
Pajaros de Verano *See* Birds of Passage (2018)
The Palace Thief *See* The Emperor's Club (2002)
Palata No. 6 *See* Ward No. 6 (2009)
The Pale Horse *See* Agatha Christie's The Pale Horse (1996)
Palomino *See* Danielle Steel's Palomino (1991)
Pan deng zhe *See* The Climbers (2019)
Pan si dong *See* The Cave of the Silken Web (1967)
Panama Menace *See* South of Panama (1941)
Pane, Amore e Fantasia *See* Bread, Love and Dreams (1953)
Pane e Cioccolata *See* Bread and Chocolate (1973)
Pane e Tulipani *See* Bread and Tulips (2001)
Panic at Lakewood Manor *See* Ants (1977)
Panic in Detroit *See* Corrupted Minds (2006)
Panic in the Trans-Siberian Train *See* Horror Express (1972)
Panic on the Trans-Siberian Express *See* Horror Express (1972)
Panico en el Transiberiano *See* Horror Express (1972)
Panny z Wilka *See* Maids of Wilko (1979)
Panther Squadron *See* Men of the Fighting Lady (1954)
Panzer Chocolate *See* Panzer (2013)
Paoda Shuang Deng *See* Red Firecracker, Green Firecracker (1993)
Paper Bullets *See* Gangs, Inc. (1941)
Par-dela les Nuages *See* Beyond the Clouds (1995)
Paradies: Glaube *See* Paradise: Faith (2012)
Paradies: Hoffnung *See* Paradise: Hope (2013)
Paradise Lagoon *See* The Admirable Crichton (1957)
Paradise Lost *See* Escobar: Paradise Lost (2015)
Paralyzed *See* Short Night of Glass Dolls (1971)
The Parasite Murders *See* They Came from Within (1975)
Parde *See* Closed Curtain (2013)
Pardon Me, Your Teeth Are in My Neck *See* The Fearless Vampire Killers (1967)
Parfait Amour *See* Perfect Love (1996)
Paris Brule-t-il? *See* Is Paris Burning? (1966)
Paris Does Strange Things *See* Elena and Her Men (1956)
Paris, I Love You *See* Paris, je t'aime (2006)
Paris pieds nus *See* Lost in Paris (2017)
Paris vu Par *See* Six in Paris (1968)
Paris Willouby *See* Meet the Guilbys (2015)
Park Plaza *See* Norman Conquest (1953)
Parlez-Moi de la Pluie *See* Let It Rain (2008)
Paroles et Musique *See* Love Songs (1984)
Paroxismus *See* Venus in Furs (1970)
Parts: The Clonus Horror *See* The Clonus Horror (1979)
The Party *See* Can't Hardly Wait (1998)
The Party at Kitty and Stud's *See* The Italian Stallion (1973)
Pasqualino Settebellezze *See* Seven Beauties (1976)
Pasqualino: Seven Beauties *See* Seven Beauties (1976)
The Pass *See* Highway Hitcher (1998)
The Passion Flower Hotel *See* Boarding School (1983)
Passion Play *See* Love Letters (1983)
Passions *See* The Passing of Evil (1970)
Patterns of Power *See* Patterns (1956)
Patton: A Salute to a Rebel *See* Patton (1970)
Patton: Lust for Glory *See* Patton (1970)
Paul Bowles: Halbmond *See* Halfmoon (1995)
Pauline a la Plage *See* Pauline at the Beach (1983)
Paura in citta *See* Street War (1976)
Paura Nella Citta Dei Morti Viventi *See* Gates of Hell (1980)
Pay the Devil *See* Man in the Shadow (1957)
Pazzi borghesi *See* The Twist (1976)
P.D. James: A Mind to Murder *See* A Mind to Murder (1996)
P.D. James: Devices & Desires *See* Devices and Desires (1991)
Peace and Riot *See* Girl Meets Boy (2013)
The Peace Game *See* The Gladiators (1970)
Peace Virus *See* Terminal Error (2002)
Peacemaker *See* The Ambassador (1984)
Peau d'Ane *See* Donkey Skin (1970)
Peau d-Espion *See* To Commit a Murder (1967)
Peccato Che Sia una Canaglia *See* Too Bad She's Bad (1954)
Pellet *See* El Bola (2000)
Pelvis *See* Toga Party (1977)
Pembalasan ratu pantai selatan *See* Lady Terminator (1989)
Pensionat Oskar *See* Like It Never Was Before (1995)
People Toys *See* Devil Times Five (1974)
People's Enemy *See* Prison Train (1938)
Per Pochi Dollari Ancora *See* Fort Yuma Gold (1966)
Per Saldo Mord *See* Swiss Conspiracy (1977)
Perceval Le Gallois *See* Perceval (1978)
Perche Quelle Strane Gocce di Sangre sul Corpo di Jennifer? *See* The Case of the Bloody Iris (1972)
Perche si uccide un magistrato *See* How to Kill a Judge (1975)
Perdita Durango *See* Dance with the Devil (1997)
A perdre la raison *See* Our Children (2012)
Perfect Life *See* Perfect Victims (2008)
The Perfect Model *See* Sweet Perfection (1990)
Perfect Strangers *See* Almost Strangers (2001)
Perfect Strangers *See* Vacation from Marriage (1945)
A Perfect Vacation *See* Awaken (2015)
The Perfect You *See* Crazy Little Thing (2002)
The Perfumed Garden *See* Tales of the Kama Sutra: The Perfumed Garden (1998)
Perils from Planet Mongo *See* Flash Gordon: Rocketship (1940)
The Perils of Gwendoline in the Land of the Yik-Yak *See* The Perils of Gwendoline (1984)

Queen of Destiny *See* Sixty Glorious Years (1938)

Queen of the Cannibals *See* Doctor Butcher M.D. (1980)

Queen of the Gorillas *See* The Bride & the Beast (1958)

The Queen's Husband *See* The Royal Bed (1931)

Quei Temerari Sulle Loro Pazze, Scatenate, Scalcinate Carriole *See* Those Daring Young Men in Their Jaunty Jalopies (1969)

Quel Maldetto Treno Blindato *See* The Inglorious Bastards (1978)

Quel maledetto giorno d'inverno... Django e Sartana all'ultimo sangue *See* One Fine Day, When Django Met Sartana (1970)

Quella Villa Accanto Al Cimitero *See* The House by the Cemetery (1983)

Quelqu' Un Derriere la Porte *See* Someone Behind the Door (1971)

Quelques Jours en Septembre *See* A Few Days in September (2006)

Quemimada! *See* Burn! (1970)

Quentin Tarantino's Death Proof *See* Death Proof (2007)

The Quest *See* The Longest Drive (1976)

Qui a tu Bambi? *See* Who Killed Bambi? (2003)

Quien Sabe? *See* A Bullet for the General (1968)

A Quiet Place to Kill *See* Paranoia (1969)

Quoi De Neuf, Pussycat? *See* What's New Pussycat? (1965)

Rabid Dogs *See* Kidnapped (1974)

The Raccoon War *See* Pom Poko (1994)

Race for the Yankee Zephyr *See* Treasure of the Yankee Zephyr (1983)

Race Gang *See* The Green Cockatoo (1937)

Racket Girls *See* Pin Down Girls (1951)

The Radical *See* Katherine (1975)

Radio Ranch *See* The Phantom Empire (1935)

Radon *See* Rodan (1956)

Radon the Flying Monster *See* Rodan (1956)

The Rag Nymph *See* Catherine Cookson's The Rag Nymph (1996)

Rage *See* Rabid (1977)

Rage of the Buccaneers *See* The Black Pirate (1926)

Ragewar *See* Dungeonmaster (1983)

Ragged Angels *See* They Shall Have Music (1939)

Raging Waters *See* The Green Promise (1949)

Rags to Riches *See* Callie and Son (1981)

Raiders in the Sky *See* Appointment in London (1953)

The Rain *See* Dark Fields (2009)

Rainbow on the River *See* It Happened in New Orleans (1936)

The Rainmaker *See* John Grisham's The Rainmaker (1997)

The Raisins of Death *See* The Grapes of Death (1978)

Rak ti Khon Khaen *See* Cemetery of Splendor (2015)

Ralph Breaks the Internet: Wreck-It Ralph 2 *See* Ralph Breaks the Internet (2018)

Ramblin' Man *See* Concrete Cowboys (1979)

Rang-e Khoda *See* The Color of Paradise (1999)

The Ranger, The Cook and a Hole in the Sky *See* Hole in the Sky (1995)

Ransom *See* Maniac (1977)

Rape Me *See* Baise Moi (2000)

The Rape of Richard Beck *See* Broken Badge (1985)

Rapt au Deuxieme Bureau *See* Operation Abduction (1958)

Rapunzel *See* Tangled (2010)

Rare Flowers *See* Reaching for the Moon (2013)

Rasputin: The Mad Monk *See* Rasputin and the Empress (1933)

Rat Pfink and Boo Boo *See* Rat Pfink a Boo-Boo (1966)

Ratko: The Dictator's Son *See* National Lampoon's Ratko: The Dictator's Son (2009)

The Rats of Tobruk *See* The Fighting Rats of Tobruk (1944)

The Raven *See* Le Corbeau (1943)

Raye Makhfi *See* Secret Ballot (2001)

Re-Animator 2 *See* Bride of Re-Animator (1989)

RE: Lucky Luciano *See* Lucky Luciano (1974)

Real Men *See* Regular Guys (1996)

The Rebel *See* The Bushwackers (1952)

Rebel with a Cause *See* The Loneliness of the Long Distance Runner (1962)

Rebelle *See* War Witch (2012)

Rebellion *See* Samurai Rebellion (1967)

Recoil *See* Silent Venom (2008)

Record of a Living Being *See* I Live in Fear (1955)

Red *See* Trois Couleurs: Rouge (1994)

Red Blooded American Girl 2 *See* Hot Blooded (1998)

The Red Circle *See* Le Cercle Rouge (1970)

Red Dragon *See* Manhunter (1986)

The Red Hangman *See* The Bloody Pit of Horror (1965)

The Red Head *See* Poil de Carotte (1931)

The Red Headed Corpse *See* Sweet Spirits (1971)

Red Hot Wheels *See* To Please a Lady (1950)

Red-Light District *See* Street of Shame (1956)

The Red Lips *See* Daughters of Darkness (1971)

Red on Red *See* Scarred (1984)

The Red Phone: Manhunt *See* Anti-Terrorist Cell: Manhunt (2001)

The Red Sign of Madness *See* Hatchet for the Honeymoon (1970)

The Red Tide *See* Blood Tide (1982)

Redd Inc. *See* Inhuman Resources (2012)

The Redeemer *See* Class Reunion Massacre (1977)

Redneck County *See* Hootch Country Boys (1975)

Redneck County *See* Poor Pretty Eddie (1973)

The Refuge *See* Hideaway (2009)

The Refugee *See* Three Faces West (1940)

Regeneration *See* Behind the Lines (1997)

Regina Roma *See* Regina (1983)

Rehearsal for a Crime *See* The Criminal Life of Archibaldo de la Cruz (1955)

Rekopis Znaleziony W Saragossie *See* The Saragossa Manuscript (1965)

Relatos Salvajes *See* Wild Tales (2014)

Religious Racketeers *See* Mystic Circle Murder (1939)

The Reluctant Professor *See* The Rewrite (2015)

Remando al Viento *See* Rowing with the Wind (1988)

Remembrance of Love *See* Holocaust Survivors. . . Remembrance of Love (1983)

Remo: Unarmed and Dangerous *See* Remo Williams: The Adventure Begins (1985)

Remove Lum & Abner *See* So This Is Washington (1943)

Renacer *See* Reborn (1981)

Rendezvous with Dishonour *See* Night of the Assassin (1970)

Renegade Girls *See* Caged Heat (1974)

The Rescue *See* Let's Get Harry (1987)

The Rescue *See* Out of Reach (2004)

Rescue Force *See* Terminal Force (1988)

Resentment *See* Any Day (2015)

Resident Evil: Afterlife: An IMAX 3D Experience *See* Resident Evil: Afterlife (2010)

Respectable Families *See* Un Air de Famille (1996)

Respiro: Grazia's Island *See* Respiro (2002)

The Rest of the Warrior *See* Love on a Pillow (1962)

Rest Stop 2 *See* Rest Stop: Don't Look Back (2008)

Rest Stop: Dead Ahead *See* Rest Stop (2006)

Rester Vertical *See* Staying Vertical (2016)

The Resurrection Syndicate *See* Nothing But the Night (1972)

Retik, the Moon Menace *See* Radar Men from the Moon (1952)

Retornados *See* The Returned (2014)

Return from the Past *See* Alien Massacre (1967)

The Return of Captain America *See* Captain America (1944)

The Return of Captain Nemo *See* The Amazing Captain Nemo (1978)

The Return of Maxwell Smart *See* The Nude Bomb (1980)

The Return of Mr. H. *See* They Saved Hitler's Brain (1964)

The Return of She *See* The Vengeance of She (1968)

Return of the Blind Dead *See* Return of the Evil Dead (1975)

Return of the Boomerang *See* Adam's Woman (1970)

The Return of the Corsican Brothers *See* The Bandits of Corsica (1953)

The Return of the Duchess Dracula *See* Devil's Wedding Night (1973)

The Return of the Giant Monsters *See* Gamera *vs.* Gaos (1967)

Return of the Living Dead *See* Messiah of Evil (1974)

Return of the Seven *See* Return of the Magnificent Seven (1966)

Return of the Texas Chainsaw Massacre *See* The Texas Chainsaw Massacre 4: The Next Generation (1995)

Return of the Wolfman *See* The Craving (1980)

Return of the Zombies *See* The Hanging Woman (1972)

Return to Jelucia *See* Message from Space (1978)

Return to Sender *See* Convicted (2004)

Return to the Horrors of Blood Island *See* Beast of Blood (1971)

Reunion *See* Reunion in France (1942)

Revenant *See* Modern Vampires (1998)

Revenge *See* Blood Feud (1979)

Revenge *See* Fallen Angel (1999)

The Revenge *See* Zemsta (2002)

Revenge of a Kabuki Actor *See* An Actor's Revenge (1963)

The Revenge of Al Capone *See* Capone (1989)

Revenge of Dracula *See* Dracula, Prince of Darkness (1966)

The Revenge of Dracula *See* Dracula *vs.* Frankenstein (1971)

The Revenge of Milady *See* The Four Musketeers (1975)

The Revenge of the Blood Beast *See* The She-Beast (1965)

Revenge of the Colossal Man *See* War of the Colossal Beast (1958)

Revenge of the Dead *See* Night of the Ghouls (1959)

Revenge of the Dead *See* Zeder (1983)

Revenge of the Innocents *See* South Bronx Heroes (1985)

Revenge of the Living Dead *See* Children Shouldn't Play with Dead Things (1972)

Revenge of the Ninja Warrior *See* The Dagger of Kamui (1985)

Revenge of the Savage Bees *See* Terror Out of the Sky (1978)

Revenge of the Screaming Dead *See* Messiah of Evil (1974)

Revenge of the South Seas Queen *See* Lady Terminator (1989)

Revenge of the Sun Demon *See* What's Up, Hideous Sun Demon? (1983)

Revenge of the Vampire *See* Black Sunday (1960)

Revenge of the Zombie *See* Kiss Daddy Goodbye (1981)

Revenge! The Killing Fist *See* The Street Fighter's Last Revenge (1974)

The Revenger: An Unromantic Comedy *See* For Love or Money (2019)

The Revengers' Comedies *See* Sweet Revenge (1998)

Rex: Le cyber chien *See* Cybermutt (2002)

Rhen zhe wu di *See* Five Element Ninjas (1982)

Ricco *See* Mean Machine (1973)

Rice, Beans and Ketchup *See* Manhattan Merenque! (1995)

The Richest Man in the World: The Story of Aristotle Onassis *See* Onassis (1988)

Richie *See* The Death of Richie (1976)

Rickshaw Man *See* Rikisha-Man (1958)

Ride a Dark Horse *See* Man & Boy (1971)

Rien ne va plus *See* The Swindle (1997)

Riffraff *See* Riff Raff (1935)

Riget *See* The Kingdom (1995)

Riget II *See* The Kingdom 2 (1997)

Rika the Mixed Blood Girl *See* Rica (1972)

Ring of Fire *See* Cowboy Up (2000)

Ring of the Nibelungs *See* Dark Kingdom: The Dragon King (2004)

The Ringer *See* Again, the Ringer (1964)

Ringo: Face of Revenge *See* Ringo's Mark of Vengeance (1967)

Ringo, il cavaliere solitario *See* Ringo, the Lone Rider (1968)

Ringu 0: Basudei *See* Ringu 0 (2001)

Rio, Eu Te Amo *See* Rio, I Love You (2014)

Rio Vengeance *See* Motor Psycho (1965)

Riot *See* Riot in the Streets (1996)

Rip-Off *See* The Squeeze (1980)

Ripped Off *See* Counter Punch (1971)

The Ripper *See* New York Ripper (1982)

Riri Shushu no subete *See* All About Lily Chou-Chou (2001)

The Rise *See* Wasteland (2013)

The Rise of Catherine the Great *See* Catherine the Great (1934)

The Rise of Helga *See* Susan Lenox: Her Fall and Rise (1931)

Rise of the Apes *See* Rise of the Planet of the Apes (2011)

Rising to Fame *See* Susan Lenox: Her Fall and Rise (1931)

Riso Amaro *See* Bitter Rice (1949)

Riten *See* The Rite (1969)

Rites of Summer *See* White Water Summer (1987)

The Ritual *See* The Rite (1969)

Ritual *See* Tales from the Crypt Presents Ritual (2002)

Ritual Dos Sadicos *See* Awakenings of the Beast (1968)

Schwestern Oder die Balance des Glucks See Sisters, Or the Balance of Happiness (1979)

Scorched See Incendies (2010)

The Scotland Yard Mystery See The Living Dead (1933)

The Scoundrel's Wife See The Home Front (2002)

Scouts v. Zombies See Scout's Guide to the Zombie Apocalypse (2015)

Scream Again See Scream 2 (1997)

Scream Bloody Murder See Amputee with an Axe (1973)

Screamer See Scream and Scream Again (1970)

Screwface See Marked for Death (1990)

Scrooge See A Christmas Carol (1951)

The Scythian See The Last Warrior (2018)

Se, Jie See Lust, Caution (2007)

Sea Change See Jesse Stone: Sea Change (2007)

The Sea Witches See The Sea is Watching (2002)

The Sea Wolf See Sea Wolf: The Pirate's Curse (2005)

Sea Wyf and Biscuit See Sea Wife (1957)

Seagulls Over Sorrento See Crest of the Wave (1954)

Search for the Jewel of Polaris: Mysterious Museum See Mysterious Museum (1999)

Search for the Mother Lode See Mother Lode (1982)

Seated At His Right See Black Jesus (1968)

The Second Arrival See The Arrival 2 (1998)

Second Breath See Le Deuxieme Souffle (1966)

The Second Coming See Messiah of Evil (1974)

The Second Jungle Book: Mowgli and Baloo See Rudyard Kipling's the Second Jungle Book: Mowgli and Baloo (1997)

The Second Lieutenant See The Last Lieutenant (1994)

Secondloitnanten See The Last Lieutenant (1994)

Seconds to Live See Viva Knievel (1977)

The Secret See Catherine Cookson's The Secret (2000)

Secret File: Hollywood See Secret File of Hollywood (1962)

Secret Honor: A Political Myth See Secret Honor (1985)

Secret Honor: The Last Testament of Richard M. Nixon See Secret Honor (1985)

The Secret Lives of Pigs See Cold Case Hammarskjöld (2019)

The Secret of Dr. Mabuse See The Thousand Eyes of Dr. Mabuse (1960)

The Secret of Dorian Gray See Dorian Gray (1970)

The Secret Pact See The Pact (1999)

Secret Santa See Dear Santa (1998)

Secret Weapon See Sherlock Holmes and the Secret Weapon (1942)

Secrets of the Red Bedroom See Secret Weapons (1985)

The Sect See The Devil's Daughter (1991)

Secuestrados See Kidnapped (2010)

Seddok, l'Erede di Satana See Atom Age Vampire (1961)

Sedotta e Abbandonata See Seduced and Abandoned (1964)

The Seducers See Death Game (1977)

The Seductress See The Teacher (1974)

Seduta Alla Sua Destra See Black Jesus (1968)

Seed of Terror See Grave of the Vampire (1972)

Seeds of Wrath See Man in the Shadow (1957)

The Seekers See Land of Fury (1955)

Segunda Piel See Second Skin (1999)

Sei Donne per l'Assassino See Blood and Black Lace (1964)

The Sell-Out See The Sellout (1976)

Selvmords Turisten See Exit Plan (2020)

Semana Santa See Angel of Death (2002)

Sen to Chihiro'No Kamikakushi See Spirited Away (2001)

Senior Trip See National Lampoon's Senior Trip (1995)

Sensations See Sensations of 1945 (1944)

Sensuous Vampires See The Vampire Hookers (1978)

Sentimental Destinies See Les Destinees (2000)

The Sentinel See La Sentinelle (1992)

Seom See The Isle (2001)

Separate Beds See The Wheeler Dealers (1963)

Separate Rooms See Notre Histoire (1984)

Seppuku See Harakiri (1962)

Sept Fois Femme See Woman Times Seven (1967)

Serbuan maut See The Raid: Redemption (2011)

Serial Killing 4 Dummys See Serial Killing 101 (2004)

The Serpent See Night Flight from Moscow (1973)

Seryozha See A Summer to Remember (1961)

The Set-Up See The Sellout (1976)

Sette Orchide Macchiate di Rosso See Seven Blood-Stained Orchids (1972)

Sette Volte Donna See Woman Times Seven (1967)

Seul contre tous See I Stand Alone (1998)

Seunlau Ngaklau See Time and Tide (2000)

Se7en See Seven (1995)

Seven Bad Men See Rage at Dawn (1955)

The Seven Brothers Meet Dracula See The Legend of the 7 Golden Vampires (1973)

7 Cajas See 7 Boxes (2014)

Seven Days to Live See 7 Days to Live (2000)

Seven Different Ways See Quick, Let's Get Married (1971)

Seven Doors of Death See The Beyond (1982)

Seven Graves for Rogan See Time to Die (1983)

Seven Sisters See The House on Sorority Row (1983)

Seven Stages to Achieve Eternal Bliss by Passing Through the Gateway Chosen by the Holy Storsh See Seven Stages to Achieve Eternal Bliss (2020)

7-10 Split See Strike (2007)

Seven Thunders See The Beasts of Marseilles (1957)

7th Cavalry See Seventh Cavalry (1956)

78/52 See 78/52: Hitchcock's Shower Scene (2017)

7eventy 5ive See Dead Tone (2007)

75 Degrees in July See 75 Degrees (2000)

Sex Crime of the Century See Last House on the Left (1972)

Sex Play See Games Girls Play (1975)

Sex Quartet See The Queens (1966)

Sexo canibal See Devil Hunter (2008)

Sexton Blake and the Hooded Terror See The Hooded Terror (1938)

SF: Episode One See Samurai Fiction (1999)

Sha chu di yu mun See Heaven & Hell (1978)

Sha shou hao See Battle Creek Brawl (1980)

Shadow See Unsane (1982)

The Shadow Army See Army of Shadows (1969)

Shadow of the Werewolf See The Werewolf vs. the Vampire Woman (1970)

Shadow Play See Portraits Chinois (1996)

The Shadow Versus the Thousand Eyes of Dr. Mabuse See The Thousand Eyes of Dr. Mabuse (1960)

The Shadow Warrior See Kagemusha (1980)

Shadow Zone: My Teacher Ate My Homework See My Teacher Ate My Homework (1998)

Shadowbuilder See Bram Stoker's Shadowbuilder (1998)

Shadowless Sword See The Legend of the Shadowless Sword (2008)

Shadows of Our Ancestors See Shadows of Forgotten Ancestors (1964)

Shadows of Our Forgotten Ancestors See Shadows of Forgotten Ancestors (1964)

Shaft Returns See Shaft (2000)

Shaka Zulu: The Citadel See Shaka Zulu: The Last Great Warrior (2001)

Shakespeare's Sister See The Proposition (1997)

Shalimar See Deadly Thief (1978)

Shall We Dansu? See Shall We Dance? (1996)

Shame of the Sabine Women See The Rape of the Sabines (1961)

Shan he gu ren See Mountains May Depart (2016)

Shanghai Express See The Millionaire's Express (1986)

Shao Lin shan shi liu fang See The 36th Chamber of Shaolin (1978)

Shao Lin yu Wu Dang See Shaolin & Wu Tang (1981)

Shao Lin yu Wu Dang See Sword Masters: Two Champions of Shaolin (1980)

Shao Nian Huang Fei Hong Zhi Tie Ma Liu See Iron Monkey (1993)

Shaolin Avenger See King Boxer (1972)

Shaolin Hellgate See Heaven & Hell (1978)

Shaolin Master Killer See The 36th Chamber of Shaolin (1978)

The Shaolin Swallow See Golden Swallow (1968)

Shaolin Temple, Part II See Shaolin & Wu Tang (1981)

Shaolin Wu Tang See Shaolin & Wu Tang (1981)

Sharayet See Circumstance (2011)

Shark Week See Shark Island (2012)

Shatter See Call Him Mr. Shatter (1974)

Shattered Silence See Sexting in Suburbia (2012)

Shatterhand See Apache's Last Battle (1964)

She Devil See Drums O'Voodoo (1934)

She Diao Ying Xiang Chuan See The Brave Archer (1977)

She Gets What She Wants See Slap Her, She's French (2002)

She Got What She Asked For See Yesterday, Today and Tomorrow (1964)

She Knew No Other Way See Last Resort (1986)

She Monster of the Night See Frankenstein's Daughter (1958)

She-Wolf See The Legend of the Wolf Woman (1977)

She Wolves of the Wasteland See Phoenix the Warrior (1988)

Sheer Bliss See Winter Break (2002)

Shelf Life See Subhuman (2004)

Shelter See 6 Souls (2013)

Shen Diao Zia Liu See The Brave Archer and His Mate (1982)

Shen hua See Jackie Chan's The Myth (2005)

Shenanigans See Great Bank Hoax (1978)

The Shepherd See Cybercity (1999)

Sherlock Holmes See The Adventures of Sherlock Holmes (1939)

Sherlock Holmes and the Prince of Crime See Hands of a Murderer (1990)

Sherlock Holmes and the Scarlet Claw See Scarlet Claw (1944)

Sherlock Holmes and the Woman in Green See The Woman in Green (1949)

Sherlock Holmes Grosster Fall See A Study in Terror (1966)

Sherlock Holmes: The Silver Blaze See Murder at the Baskervilles (1937)

Sherlock Holmes und das Halsband des Todes See Sherlock Holmes and the Deadly Necklace (1962)

She's De Lovely See De-Lovely (2004)

She's De Lovely See She's So Lovely (1997)

Shi See Poetry (2010)

Shi ba ban wu yi See Legendary Weapons of China (1982)

Shi Fu See The Final Master (2016)

Shi gan See Time (2006)

Shi qi sui de tian kong See Formula 17 (2004)

Shi San Tai Bo See The Heroic Ones (1970)

Shi yao See Corpse Mania (1981)

Shichinin No Samurai See Seven Samurai (1954)

Shimian Maifu See House of Flying Daggers (2004)

Shimotsuma monogatari See Kamikaze Girls (2004)

Shin Gojira See Shin Godzilla (2016)

Shin Jingi No Hakaba See Graveyard of Honor (2002)

Shin Kanashiki Hittoman See Another Lonely Hitman (1995)

Shin shinobi no mono See Shinobi No Mono 3: Resurrection (2009)

Shinju Ten No Amijima See Double Suicide (1969)

Shinobi: Heart Under Blade See Shinobi (2005)

Ship of Fools See The Imposters (1998)

The Ship was Loaded See Carry On Admiral (1957)

Shiqisuide Danche See Beijing Bicycle (2001)

Shiryo No Wana 2: Hideki See Evil Dead Trap 2: Hideki (1991)

Shiryoha See Dead Waves (2006)

Shiver See Night Train to Terror (1984)

Shivers See They Came from Within (1975)

Shiza See Schizo (2004)

Shizuka Naru Ketto See A Quiet Duel (1949)

Shock See Le Choc (1982)

Shock See Shock (1979)

Shocked See Mesmerized (1984)

Shockwave See The Arrival (1996)

Shogun Island See Raw Force (1981)

Shomerei Ha'saf See The Gatekeepers (2012)

Shoot the Pianist See Shoot the Piano Player (1962)

The Shooter See Hidden Assassin (1994)

Shooting Star See Lady Terminator (1989)

Shootout See Shoot Out (1971)

The Shop on High Street See The Shop on Main Street (1965)

The Shrieking See Charms (1973)

Shu Dan Long Wei See Meltdown (1995)

Shu Shan *See* Zu: Warriors from the Magic Mountain (1983)

Shu shan zheng zhuan *See* Zu Warriors (2001)

Shuang Long Hui *See* Twin Dragons (1992)

Shuang Tong *See* Double Vision (2002)

Shuban *See* Scandal (1950)

Shuffleton's Barbershop *See* Norman Rockwell's Shuffleton's Barbershop (2013)

Shui Ngai Miu Si *See* Journey of the Doomed (1985)

The Shunning *See* Beverly Lewis' The Shunning (2011)

Shura-yuki-hime: Urami Renga *See* Lady Snowblood: Love Song of Vengeance (1974)

Shura Yukihime *See* The Princess Blade (2002)

Shurayukihime *See* Lady Snowblood (1973)

Shussho Iwai *See* The Wolves (1982)

Shut In *See* Intruders (2016)

Shut Up and Dance *See* Dance with Me (1998)

Shutter: They Are Around Us *See* Shutter (2005)

The Shuttered Room *See* Blood Island (1968)

Si da ming bu *See* The Four (2012)

Si da ming bu 3 *See* Kingdom of Blood: The Final Battle (2016)

Si Don Juan Etait une Femme *See* Don Juan (Or If Don Juan Were a Woman) (1973)

Si J'Etais Toi *See* The Secret (2007)

Si Te Dicen Que Cai *See* If They Tell You I Fell (1989)

Si yiu *See* Corpse Mania (1981)

Sibirska Ledi Magbet *See* Siberian Lady Macbeth (1961)

Sid & Nancy: Love Kills *See* Sid & Nancy (1986)

Sidney Hall *See* The Vanishing of Sidney Hall (2017)

Sidney Sheldon's If Tomorrow Comes *See* If Tomorrow Comes (1986)

Siegfried's Death *See* Siegfried (1924)

Siegfrieds Tod *See* Siegfried (1924)

Signal One *See* Bullet Down Under (1994)

Significant Other *See* When a Man Loves a Woman (1994)

The Silence After the Shot *See* The Legend of Rita (1999)

Silencio Roto *See* Broken Silence (2001)

The Silent Flute *See* Circle of Iron (1978)

Silent Night, Evil Night *See* Black Christmas (1975)

Silken Skin *See* The Soft Skin (1964)

Silver Blaze *See* Murder at the Baskervilles (1937)

The Silver Brumby *See* The Silver Stallion: King of the Wild Brumbies (1993)

Simba: Mark of Mau Mau *See* Simba (1955)

Simbad Contro I Sette Saraceni *See* Ali Baba and the Seven Saracens (1964)

Simon: An English Legionnaire *See* Deserter (2002)

Simon och ekarna *See* Simon and the Oaks (2012)

Simoom: A Passion in the Desert *See* Passion in the Desert (1997)

Simple Lies *See* Rx (2006)

Simple Moves *See* Aleksandr's Price (2013)

A Simple Noodle Story *See* A Woman, a Gun and a Noodle Shop (2010)

Sin Eater *See* The Order (2003)

Sin Noticias de Dios *See* No News from God (2001)

Sin of Esther Waters *See* Esther Waters (1948)

Sinbad Against the Seven Saracens *See* Ali Baba and the Seven Saracens (1964)

The Singing Musketeer *See* The Three Musketeers (1939)

The Single Moms' Club *See* Tyler Perry's The Single Moms' Club (2014)

Singularidades de uma Rapariga Loura *See* Eccentricities of a Blonde-Haired Girl (2010)

The Sinners *See* La Piscine (1969)

Sins of Love *See* Test Tube Babies (1948)

Sir Arthur Conan Doyle's Sherlock Holmes *See* Sherlock Holmes (2010)

Sir Arthur Conan Doyle's The Lost World *See* The Lost World (1960)

Siren's Kiss *See* Body Strokes (1995)

The Sister of Satan *See* The She-Beast (1965)

Sisters *See* Some Girls (1988)

Sitting Bull's History Lesson *See* Buffalo Bill & the Indians (1976)

Siu hap Cho Lau Heung *See* Legend of the Liquid Sword (1993)

Siu lam juk kau *See* Shaolin Soccer (2001)

Siulam Chukkau *See* Shaolin Soccer (2001)

Siunin Wong Fei-hung Tsi Titmalau *See* Iron Monkey (1993)

600 Millas *See* 600 Miles (2016)

Six Inches Tall *See* Attack of the Puppet People (1958)

Six Underground *See* 6 Underground (2019)

Six Women for the Murderer *See* Blood and Black Lace (1964)

The Sixth of June *See* D-Day, the Sixth of June (1956)

Ski Lift to Death *See* Snowblind (1978)

Skif *See* The Last Warrior (2018)

Skipper *See* The Todd Killings (1971)

Skjult *See* Hidden (2009)

Sky is Falling *See* Bloodbath (1976)

Sky Terror *See* Skyjacked (1972)

Skylark *See* Sarah, Plain and Tall: Skylark (1993)

The Slammer *See* Short Eyes (1979)

The Slasher *See* Cosh Boy (1952)

The Slasher *See* Tough Guy (1953)

Slasher in the House *See* Home Sweet Home (1980)

The Slaughterers *See* Cannibal Apocalypse (1980)

Slave Coast *See* Cobra Verde (1988)

Slave Girls *See* Prehistoric Women (1967)

Slave of the Cannibal God *See* Mountain of the Cannibal God (1979)

Slaves of the Invisible Monster *See* The Invisible Monster (1950)

Sleep No More *See* Invasion of the Body Snatchers (1956)

Sleepaway Camp 5: The Return *See* Return to Sleepaway Camp (2008)

Slip Slide Adventures *See* Water Babies (1979)

Slow Burn *See* Wilder (2000)

Slow Motion *See* Every Man for Himself (1979)

A Small Miracle *See* Simon Birch (1998)

Small Town Massacre *See* Strange Behavior (1981)

Smashing the Crime Syndicate *See* Hell's Bloody Devils (1970)

Smokey and the Bandit Ride Again *See* Smokey and the Bandit 2 (1980)

Smorgasbord *See* Cracking Up (1983)

Smultron-Stallet *See* Wild Strawberries (1957)

Snabba Cash *See* Easy Money (2010)

Snabba Cash II *See* Easy Money: Hard to Kill (2012)

Snake Eyes *See* Dangerous Game (1993)

Snake Fist Fighter *See* Master with Cracked Fingers (1971)

The Snake King *See* Snakeman (2005)

Snapshot *See* The Night After Halloween (1979)

Snitch *See* Monument Ave. (1998)

Snow Days *See* Let It Snow (1999)

Snow Shark: Ancient Snow Beast *See* Snow Shark (2011)

Snow White *See* Grimm's Snow White (2012)

Snow White *See* Mirror Mirror (2012)

Snow White and the Three Clowns *See* Snow White and the Three Stooges (1961)

Snow White in the Black Forest *See* Snow White: A Tale of Terror (1997)

Snuffy Smith *See* Snuffy Smith, Yard Bird (1942)

So Evil, My Sister *See* The Sibling (1972)

So Sad About Gloria *See* Visions of Evil (1975)

So Sweet, So Perverse *See* Kiss Me, Kill Me (1973)

So This Is Romance? *See* Romance and Rejection (1996)

Sobre las Olas *See* Over the Waves (1949)

Social Nightmare *See* Mother (2013)

Sodome et Gomorrhe *See* Sodom and Gomorrah (1962)

Soft Target *See* Crooked (2005)

Solamente Nero *See* The Bloodstained Shadow (1978)

Solar Strike *See* Solar Attack (2006)

Soldaat van Oranje *See* Soldier of Orange (1978)

The Soldiers *See* Les Carabiniers (1963)

Solntse *See* The Sun (2005)

Solo de Otono *See* Autumn Sun (1998)

Solomon Northrup's Odyssey *See* Half Slave, Half Free (1985)

Solyaris *See* Solaris (1972)

Some Girl *See* Men (1997)

Some Like It Cool *See* Sex on the Run (1978)

Someone is Killing the Great Chefs of Europe *See* Who Is Killing the Great Chefs of Europe? (1978)

Someone to Love *See* And Then There Was You (2013)

Someone's Killing the World's Greatest Models *See* She's Dressed to Kill (1979)

Something Is Out There *See* Day of the Animals (1977)

Something Like the Truth *See* The Offence (1973)

Something Waits in the Dark *See* Screamers (1980)

Something's Gotta Give *See* Move Over, Darling (1963)

Sometimes Always Never (Triple Word Score) *See* Sometimes Always Never (2019)

Sommaren Med Monika *See* Summer With Monica (1953)

Sommarlek *See* Summer Interlude (1950)

Sommarnattens Leende *See* Smiles of a Summer Night (1955)

Sommer '04 *See* Summer of '04 (2006)

Somos Lo Que Hay *See* We Are What We Are (2011)

The Son *See* The String (2009)

Son of Blob *See* Beware! The Blob (1972)

The Son of Hercules and Five Giants *See* Ursus in the Land of Fire (1963)

The Son of Hercules in the Land of Fire *See* Ursus in the Land of Fire (1963)

Son of Spartacus *See* The Slave (1962)

Sondagsengler *See* The Other Side of Sunday (1996)

Song for Marion *See* Unfinished Song (2012)

The Song of the Road *See* Pather Panchali (1954)

The Songs of My Homeland *See* Marooned in Iraq (2002)

Sono Otoko, Kyobo ni Tsuki *See* Violent Cop (1989)

Sons and Warriors *See* Some Mother's Son (1996)

Sons of Satan *See* The Cats (1968)

Sons of the Legion *See* Sons of the Desert (1933)

Sons of the Musketeers *See* At Sword's Point (1951)

Sons of the Wind *See* The Great Challenge (2004)

Sophie Scholl: Die Letzten Tage *See* Sophie Scholl: The Final Days (2005)

Sorgenfri *See* What We Become (2016)

The Sorrow *See* A Sierra Nevada Gunfight (2013)

Sorstalansag *See* Fateless (2005)

S.O.S. Eisberg *See* S.O.S. Iceberg (1933)

Soshite chichi ni naru *See* Like Father, Like Son (2013)

Sotto gli Occhi dell'Assassino *See* Unsane (1982)

Soul *See* Earth (1930)

Soul Man 2 *See* Far Out Man (1989)

Soulmates *See* Evil Lives (1992)

Souls for Sale *See* Confessions of an Opium Eater (1962)

Sound From a Million Years Ago *See* Sound of Horror (1964)

Soup to Nuts *See* Waitress (1981)

Sous le Sable *See* Under the Sand (2000)

Sous les Toits de Paris *See* Under the Roofs of Paris (1929)

South Pacific *See* Rodgers & Hammerstein's South Pacific (2001)

South Sea Woman *See* Pearl of the South Pacific (1955)

Southside *See* Cock & Bull Story (2003)

Southwest to Sonora *See* The Appaloosa (1966)

Soy Cuba *See* I Am Cuba (1964)

Space: 1999-Destination Moonbase Alpha *See* Destination Moonbase Alpha (1975)

The Space Amoeba *See* Yog, Monster from Space (1971)

The Space Devils *See* The Snow Devils (1967)

Space Invasion from Lapland *See* Invasion of the Animal People (1962)

Space Invasion of Lapland *See* Invasion of the Animal People (1962)

Space Men *See* Assignment Outer Space (1961)

Space Mission of the Lost Planet *See* Horror of the Blood Monsters (1970)

Space Monster Dagora *See* Dagora, the Space Monster (1965)

Space Mutants *See* Planet of the Vampires (1965)

Space Soldiers *See* Flash Gordon: Rocketship (1940)

Space Station *See* Black Horizon (2001)

Space Travellers *See* Marooned (1969)

Space Twister *See* Super Storm (2012)

The Space Vampires *See* The Astro-Zombies (1967)

Spaceship to the Unknown *See* Flash Gordon: Rocketship (1940)

The Spanish Apartment *See* L'Auberge Espagnole (2002)

Spanish Rose *See* Point of Impact (1993)

Spara Forte, Piu Forte...Non Capisco *See* Shoot Loud, Louder, I Don't Understand! (1966)

Sparkling Cyanide *See* Agatha Christie's Sparkling Cyanide (1983)

Spawn *See* Todd McFarlane's Spawn (1997)

The Spawning *See* Piranha 2: The Spawning (1982)

Special Unit AT 13 *See* Anti-Terrorist Cell: Manhunt (2001)

The Specter of Freedom *See* Phantom of Liberty (1974)

The Spectre *See* The Ghost (1963)

The Spell of Amy Nugent *See* Spellbound (1941)

Spell of the Hypnotist *See* Fright (1956)

The Spider *See* Earth *vs.* the Spider (1958)

The Spider *See* The Killer Must Kill Again (1975)

Spider Baby, or the Maddest Story Ever Told *See* Spider Baby (1964)

Spiders 3D *See* Spiders (2013)

Spies-A-Go-Go *See* Nasty Rabbit (1964)

Spinal Tap *See* This Is Spinal Tap (1984)

Spione *See* Spies (1928)

Spiral *See* Uzumaki (2000)

Spirit of the Dead *See* The Asphyx (1972)

Spirit of the People *See* Abe Lincoln in Illinois (1940)

The Spiritualist *See* The Amazing Mr. X (1948)

Spivs *See* I Vitelloni (1953)

The Split *See* The Manster (1959)

Spook Warfare *See* The Great Yokai War (2005)

Spooks: The Greater Good *See* MI-5 (2015)

The Spooky Movie Show *See* The Mask (1961)

Spoorloos *See* The Vanishing (1988)

Spotlight on Scandal *See* Spotlight Scandals (1943)

Spotlight Revue *See* Spotlight Scandals (1943)

Spotswood *See* The Efficiency Expert (1992)

Spring Break USA *See* Lauderdale (1989)

Spring Fever USA *See* Lauderdale (1989)

The Spy in White *See* Secret of Stamboul (1936)

The Spy Who Never Was *See* Death Merchants (1973)

Spyder *See* Blackbelt 2: Fatal Force (1993)

Squadron of Doom *See* Ace Drummond (1936)

The Squeeze *See* The Rip Off (1978)

Stadt Land Fluss *See* Harvest (2011)

Stadt ohne Mitleid *See* Town without Pity (1961)

The Stag *See* The Bachelor Weekend (2013)

Stairs *See* Black Ops (2020)

Stakeout 2 *See* Another Stakeout (1993)

The Stand *See* Stephen King's The Stand (1994)

Standard Time *See* Anything But Love (2002)

Star *See* Danielle Steel's Star (1993)

The Star Man *See* The Star Maker (1995)

Star Quest: Beyond the Rising Moon *See* Outerworld (1987)

Star Runner *See* The Kumite (2003)

Star Spangled Banners *See* Banner 4th of July (2013)

Star Trek: The Future Begins *See* Star Trek (2009)

Star Vehicle *See* Bleading Lady (2010)

Star Wars: Episode 4-A New Hope *See* Star Wars (1977)

Star Wars: Episode 5-The Empire Strikes Back *See* The Empire Strikes Back (1980)

Star Wars: Episode 6-Return of the Jedi *See* Return of the Jedi (1983)

Star Wars: Episode IX-The Rise of Skywalker *See* Star Wars: The Rise of Skywalker (2019)

Star Wars: Episode VIII-The Last Jedi *See* Star Wars: The Last Jedi (2017)

Star Wars: Episode VII-The Force Awakens *See* Star Wars: The Force Awakens (2015)

Stardust *See* Mad About Money (1937)

Starknight *See* Star Knight (1985)

Starlight Slaughter *See* Eaten Alive (1976)

A State of Shock *See* Power Play (1978)

The Statutory Affair *See* Lola (1969)

Stauffenberg *See* Operation Valkyrie (2004)

Stay *See* Sleeping Dogs Lie (2006)

Staying Alive *See* Fight for Your Life (1977)

The Steam Experiment *See* The Chaos Experiment (2009)

Steel Edge of Revenge *See* Goyokin (1969)

Steiner-Das Eiserne Kreuz *See* Cross of Iron (1976)

Stella Star *See* Star Crash (1978)

Step Up 4 *See* Step Up Revolution (2012)

Stepfather *See* Beau Pere (1981)

Stephen King's A Good Marriage *See* A Good Marriage (2014)

Stephen King's Bag of Bones *See* Bag of Bones (2011)

Stephen King's Cat's Eye *See* Cat's Eye (1985)

Stephen King's Graveyard Shift *See* Graveyard Shift (1990)

Stephen King's Silver Bullet *See* Silver Bullet (1985)

Stephen King's Sleepwalkers *See* Sleepwalkers (1992)

Steppin' Up: Save the Last Dance 2 *See* Save the Last Dance 2 (2006)

Stesti *See* Something Like Happiness (2005)

Steven Spielberg Presents: Taken *See* Taken (2002)

Still Smokin' *See* Cheech and Chong: Still Smokin' (1983)

Still Waters *See* Under Still Waters (2008)

Stolen Hearts *See* Two If by Sea (1995)

Stolen Lives *See* Stolen (2009)

Stone Bros. *See* Stoned Bros. (2009)

Stone Cold *See* Jesse Stone: Stone Cold (2005)

The Stone House *See* Red Sands (2009)

Storm *See* Storm Tracker (1999)

Storm of the Century *See* Stephen King's The Storm of the Century (1999)

Storm Riders *See* Wind and Cloud: The Storm Riders (2004)

Storm War *See* Weather Wars (2011)

Storm Watch *See* Code Hunter (2002)

Stormbreaker *See* Alex Rider: Operation Stormbreaker (2006)

Story of a Marriage *See* On Valentine's Day (1986)

The Story of Gosta Berling *See* The Atonement of Gosta Berling (1924)

The Story of Robin Hood *See* The Story of Robin Hood & His Merrie Men (1952)

Strafsache 4 Ks 2/63: Auschwitz Vor Dem Frankfurter Schwurgericht *See* Verdict on Auschwitz: The Frankfurt Auschwitz Trial 1963-1965 (1993)

Straight Edge *See* Boot Camp (2007)

Straight on Till Morning *See* Dressed for Death (1974)

Straight to Hell *See* Cut and Run (1985)

Straightheads *See* Closure (2007)

Stranded *See* Black Horizon (2001)

The Strange Adventure of David Gray *See* Vampyr (1931)

Strange Affection *See* The Scamp (1957)

The Strange Case of Dr. Jekyll and Mr. Hyde *See* Dr. Jekyll and Mr. Hyde (1968)

The Strange Case of Madeleine *See* Madeleine (1950)

Strange Hearts *See* Road to Riches (2001)

Strange Incident *See* The Ox-Bow Incident (1943)

Strange Interval *See* Strange Interlude (1932)

Strange Journey *See* Fantastic Voyage (1966)

The Strange Ones *See* Les Enfants Terrible (1950)

Strange Skirts *See* When Ladies Meet (1941)

Strange Tales of a Dragon Tattoo *See* Blind Woman's Curse (1970)

Strangeland *See* Dee Snider's Strangeland (1998)

The Stranger *See* Shame (1961)

The Stranger Beside Me *See* Ann Rule Presents: The Stranger Beside Me (2003)

A Stranger Came Home *See* Unholy Four (1954)

The Stranger In Between *See* Hunted (1952)

Stranger in Our House *See* Summer of Fear (1978)

Stranger in the House *See* Black Christmas (1975)

Stranger on the Campus *See* Monster on the Campus (1959)

Strangers *See* Voyage in Italy (1953)

Stranger's Face *See* Face of Another (1966)

Stranger's Gold *See* Gunslinger (1970)

Strangest Dreams: Invasion of the Space Preachers *See* Invasion of the Space Preachers (1990)

The Strangler of Vienna *See* The Mad Butcher (1972)

Strangler's Morgue *See* The Crimes of Stephen Hawke (1936)

Stray Dog: Kerberos Panzer Cops *See* Stray Dog (1991)

Stray Dogs *See* Stray Dog (1991)

Stray Dogs *See* U-Turn (1997)

Street Fighter Counterattacks *See* The Street Fighter's Last Revenge (1974)

Street Gang *See* Vigilante (1983)

Street Gun *See* Thugs (1996)

Street Legal *See* The Last of the Finest (1990)

Street Love *See* Scarred (1984)

Street of Shadows *See* The Shadow Man (1953)

Street of Sorrow *See* Joyless Street (1925)

Strictly Confidential *See* Broadway Bill (1934)

Strictly for Pleasure *See* The Perfect Furlough (1959)

Strike! *See* All I Wanna Do (1998)

Strike the Tent *See* The Last Confederate: The Story of Robert Adams (2005)

Striking Back *See* Search and Destroy (1981)

Striptease *See* Insanity (1976)

Striptease Lady *See* Lady of Burlesque (1943)

Stryker's War *See* Thou Shalt Not Kill. . .Except (1987)

Subarashiki Nichiyobi *See* One Wonderful Sunday (1947)

Subida Al Cielo *See* Mexican Bus Ride (1951)

Sublet *See* Codename: Jaguar (1998)

Subspecies 2 *See* Bloodstone: Subspecies 2 (1992)

Subspecies 3 *See* Bloodlust: Subspecies 3 (1993)

Subspecies 4 *See* Bloodstorm: Subspecies 4 (1998)

Subspecies 4: Bloodstorm-The Master's Revenge *See* Bloodstorm: Subspecies 4 (1998)

Succubus *See* The Devil's Nightmare (1971)

Sud pralad *See* Tropical Malady (2004)

Sudden Terror *See* Eye Witness (1970)

Suffering Man's Charity *See* Ghost Writer (2007)

The Suicide Club *See* Robert Louis Stevenson's The Game of Death (1999)

Suicide Run *See* Too Late the Hero (1970)

Suiryothai *See* The Legend of Suriyothai (2002)

A Suitable Case for Treatment *See* Morgan: A Suitable Case for Treatment (1966)

Sukai kurora *See* The Sky Crawlers (2008)

Sukkar Banat *See* Caramel (2007)

The Sullivans *See* The Fighting Sullivans (1942)

Sullivan's Marauders *See* Commandos (1973)

Sult *See* Hunger (1966)

Summer Fling *See* The Last of the High Kings (1996)

Summer Love *See* Dead Man's Bounty (2006)

Summer Madness *See* Summertime (1955)

Summer of Innocence *See* Big Wednesday (1978)

Summer with Monika *See* Monika (1952)

Summerplay *See* Summer Interlude (1950)

Summer's Blood *See* Summer's Moon (2009)

Summertime Killer *See* Ricco (1974)

Sumurun *See* One Arabian Night (1920)

The Sun Demon *See* Hideous Sun Demon (1959)

Suna No Onna *See* Woman in the Dunes (1964)

Sunburst *See* Slashed Dreams (1974)

Sundance Cassidy and Butch the Kid *See* Sundance and the Kid (1969)

Sunless *See* Sans Soleil (1982)

Sunrise-A Song of Two Humans *See* Sunrise (1927)

Sunset of a Clown *See* Sawdust & Tinsel (1953)

The Sunset Warrior *See* Heroes Shed No Tears (1986)

Sunshine Even by Night *See* Night Sun (1990)

Super Dragon *See* Secret Agent Super Dragon (1966)

Super Inframan *See* Infra-Man (1976)

The Super Inframan *See* Infra-Man (1976)

Super Ninjas *See* Five Element Ninjas (1982)

Superargo the Giant *See* Superargo (1967)

Superfighters *See* The Legend of the Shadowless Sword (2008)

Supersnooper *See* Super Fuzz (1981)

Superstition *See* The Gallows (2015)

SuperVixens Eruption *See* Supervixens (1975)

Sur Mes Levres *See* Read My Lips (2001)

Surf Warriors *See* Surf Ninjas (1993)

The Surrogate *See* The Sessions (2012)

Survival Run *See* Spree (1979)

Susan's Plan *See* Dying to Get Rich (1998)

Suspense *See* Shock (1979)

Svitati *See* Screw Loose (1999)

Swamp Diamonds *See* Swamp Women (1955)

Swamp Fever *See* Convict Women (1974)

Swamp Fever *See* Thunder County (1974)

Swamp Volcano *See* Miami Magma (2011)

Three Evil Masters *See* The Master (1980)

The Three Faces of Fear *See* Black Sabbath (1964)

The Three Faces of Terror *See* Black Sabbath (1964)

3 foi 20 ans *See* Late Bloomers (2011)

Three Heroes of Border Town *See* The Magnificent Trio (1966)

3 Holiday Tails *See* A Golden Christmas 2: The Second Tail (2011)

The Three Musketeers *See* Mickey, Donald, Goofy: The Three Musketeers (2004)

Three Ninjas: Showdown at Mega Mountain *See* 3 Ninjas: High Noon at Mega Mountain (1997)

Three On a Weekend *See* Bank Holiday (1938)

Three Rascals in the Hidden Fortress *See* The Hidden Fortress (1958)

Three Steps to the Gallows *See* White Fire (1953)

The Three Stooges Go Around the World in a Daze *See* Around the World in a Daze (1963)

Three Way Split *See* 3-Way (2004)

Through the Looking Glass *See* The Velvet Vampire (1971)

Throw of the Dice *See* A Throw of Dice (1929)

Throwing Stars *See* Who's Your Monkey (2007)

Thunder County *See* Convict Women (1974)

Thunder County *See* Women's Prison Escape (1974)

Thunder Mountain *See* Shadow of Chikara (1977)

Thy Neighbor's Wife *See* Poison (2001)

Tian jiang xiong shi *See* Dragon Blade (2015)

Tian long ba bu *See* Sword Masters: The Battle Wizard (1977)

Tian Tang Kou *See* Blood Brothers (2007)

Tian xia *See* Wind and Cloud: The Storm Riders (2004)

Tian xia di yi quan *See* King Boxer (1972)

Tian Yu *See* Xiu Xiu: The Sent Down Girl (1997)

Tian zhu ding *See* A Touch of Sin (2013)

Tic *See* Mob Rules (2010)

Ticket to Ride *See* Post Grad (2009)

Tidal Wave *See* Portrait of Jennie (1948)

The Tide of Life *See* Catherine Cookson's The Tide of Life (1996)

Tien ya ming yue dao *See* The Magic Blade (2008)

The Ties That Bind *See* The Unsaid (2001)

The Tiger *See* Tiger Warsaw (1987)

Tiger in the Sky *See* The McConnell Story (1955)

Tiger, Leopard, Dragon, Snake, Eagle *See* 7 Grand Masters (2004)

Tiger Mask *See* Lone Tiger (1994)

Tiger of Bengal *See* Journey to the Lost City (1958)

The Tiger of Eschanapur *See* The Indian Tomb (1921)

Tigers Don't Cry *See* African Rage (1978)

Tight Little Island *See* Whiskey Galore (1948)

Til Dawn Do Us Part *See* Dressed for Death (1974)

Till Death Us Do Part *See* The Blood Spattered Bride (1972)

Till Gladje *See* To Joy (1950)

Tilly Trotter *See* Catherine Cookson's Tilly Trotter (1999)

Tim Burton's The Nightmare Before Christmas *See* The Nightmare Before Christmas (1993)

Tim Sullivan's 2001 Maniacs: Field of Screams *See* 2001 Maniacs: Field of Screams (2010)

Timber Tramps *See* The Big Push (1975)

Time Bomb *See* Terror on a Train (1953)

Time Breaker *See* Jackie Chan's The Myth (2005)

Time Lost and Time Remembered *See* I Was Happy Here (1966)

The Time of Return *See* Muriel (1963)

Time of the Wolves *See* Carbon Copy (1969)

Time Warp Terror *See* Bloody New Year (1987)

Timecode *See* Time Code (2000)

The Timeshifters *See* Thrill Seekers (1999)

Timeslip *See* The Atomic Man (1956)

Timewarp *See* Day Time Ended (1980)

Tin lung bat bou *See* Sword Masters: The Battle Wizard (1977)

Tin ngai ming yuet do *See* The Magic Blade (2008)

Tini Zabutykh Predkiv *See* Shadows of Forgotten Ancestors (1964)

Tirez sur le Pianiste *See* Shoot the Piano Player (1962)

Titan Find *See* Creature (1985)

Titanium Rain *See* Jackie Chan's The Myth (2005)

Titas Ekti Nodir Naam *See* A River Called Titas (1973)

Tito and I *See* Tito and Me (1992)

Tito i Ja *See* Tito and Me (1992)

TMNT 2 *See* Teenage Mutant Ninja Turtles: Out of the Shadows (2016)

To Be a Man *See* Cry of Battle (1963)

To Catch a Spy *See* Catch Me a Spy (1971)

To Die For *See* Heaven's a Drag (1994)

To Have and to Hold *See* When a Man Loves a Woman (1994)

To Koritsi Me Ta Mavra *See* Girl in Black (1956)

To Live *See* Ikiru (1952)

To Love a Vampire *See* Lust for a Vampire (1971)

To Our Loves *See* A Nos Amours (1984)

To Return *See* Volver (2006)

To Telefteo Psemma *See* A Matter of Dignity (1957)

To Vlemma Tou Odyssea *See* Ulysses' Gaze (1995)

Toca Para Mi *See* Play for Me (2001)

Tod eines Fremden *See* Death Merchants (1973)

Todo Sobre Mi Madre *See* All About My Mother (1999)

Todos lo saben *See* Everybody Knows (2018)

Todos queremos a alguien *See* Everybody Loves Somebody (2017)

Toemarok *See* The Soul Guardians (1998)

A Toi de Faire, Mignonne *See* Your Turn Darling (1963)

Toi et Moi *See* You and Me (2006)

Toivon Tuolla Puolen *See* The Other Side of Hope (2017)

Tokaido obake dochu *See* Along with Ghosts (1969)

Tokarev *See* Rage (2014)

Tokyo Monogatari *See* Tokyo Story (1953)

Tokyo Raiders 2 *See* Seoul Raiders (2005)

Tomb of the Cat *See* Tomb of Ligeia (1964)

Tomb of the Living Dead *See* Mad Doctor of Blood Island (1968)

Tomb Raider *See* Lara Croft: Tomb Raider (2001)

The Tommyknockers *See* Stephen King's The Tommyknockers (1993)

Tong qiao tai *See* The Assassins (2012)

Tong que tai *See* The Assassins (2012)

Too Many Chefs *See* Who Is Killing the Great Chefs of Europe? (1978)

Too Much *See* Wish You Were Here (1987)

Top of the Food Chain *See* Invasion! (1999)

Topio Stin Omichli *See* Landscape in the Mist (1988)

Torment *See* L'Enfer (1993)

Tornado Warning *See* Alien Storm (2012)

Torpedo Zone *See* Submarine Attack (1954)

Torso: The Evelyn Dick Story *See* Torso (2002)

Torture Chamber *See* The Fear Chamber (1968)

Torture Zone *See* The Fear Chamber (1968)

Toto the Hero *See* Toto le Heros (1991)

Tou Ming Zhuang *See* Warlords (2008)

The Touch of Flesh *See* You've Ruined Me, Eddie (1958)

The Touch of Melissa *See* The Touch of Satan (1970)

Touchez pas au Grisbi *See* Grisbi (1953)

Tough Guy *See* Counter Punch (1971)

Tournee *See* On Tour (2010)

Tout Contre Leo *See* Close to Leo (2002)

A Toute Vitesse *See* Full Speed (1996)

A Town Called Bastard *See* A Town Called Hell (1972)

Town Creek *See* Blood Creek (2009)

The Town That Cried Terror *See* Maniac (1977)

T.R. Sloane *See* Death Ray 2000 (1981)

Trading Christmas *See* Debbie Macomber's Trading Christmas (2011)

The Tragedy of Othello: The Moor of Venice *See* Othello (1952)

Trailing the Killer *See* Call of the Wilderness (1932)

Train of Terror *See* Terror Train (1980)

Trainwreck: My Life as an Idiot *See* American Loser (2007)

Traitement de Choc *See* Shock Treatment (1981)

Trance *See* The External (1999)

Trancers 6 *See* Trancers 6: Life After Deth (2002)

Transformers 4 *See* Transformers: Age of Extinction (2014)

Transformers 5 *See* Transformers: The Last Knight (2017)

Transparency *See* Takedown (2010)

The Transvestite *See* Glen or Glenda? (1953)

Tras el Cristal *See* In a Glass Cage (1986)

Trauma *See* Dario Argento's Trauma (1993)

Trautmann *See* The Keeper (2018)

Traveling Birds *See* Winged Migration (2001)

Travels with Anita *See* Lovers and Liars (1981)

Tre Fratelli *See* Three Brothers (1980)

Tre Passi nel Delirio *See* Spirits of the Dead (1968)

The Treasure of Monte Cristo *See* The Secret of Monte Cristo (1961)

Treasure of the Living Dead *See* Oasis of the Zombies (1982)

Tree of Liberty *See* The Howards of Virginia (1940)

Trespassing *See* Evil Remains (2004)

Trial by Combat *See* Choice of Weapons (1976)

Trial by Fire *See* Smoke Jumpers (2008)

Trick of the Eye *See* Primal Secrets (1994)

Tricks of Love *See* Tricks of a Woman (2008)

A Trip with Anita *See* Lovers and Liars (1981)

Triple Trouble *See* Kentucky Kernels (1934)

Tristan and Isolde *See* Lovespell (1979)

Triumph des Willens *See* Triumph of the Will (1934)

Trmavomodry Svet *See* Dark Blue World (2001)

Troglodyte *See* Sea Beast (2008)

Trois Histoires Extraordinaires d'Edgar Poe *See* Spirits of the Dead (1968)

Trois Hommes et un Couffin *See* Three Men and a Cradle (1985)

Trois souvenirs de ma jeunesse *See* My Golden Days (2015)

The Trojan War *See* The Trojan Horse (1962)

The Trollenberg Terror *See* The Crawling Eye (1958)

Trollhunter *See* The Troll Hunter (2011)

Trolljegeren *See* The Troll Hunter (2011)

Trolosa *See* Faithless (2000)

Trop Belle pour Toi *See* Too Beautiful for You (1988)

Trouble Chaser *See* Li'l Abner (1940)

The Trout *See* La Truite (1983)

Trudno Byt Bogom *See* Hard to Be a God (2013)

True Crimes *See* Dark Crimes (2016)

The True Story of My Life in Rouen *See* My Life on Ice (2002)

Truman Capote's One Christmas *See* One Christmas (1995)

Truman Capote's The Glass House *See* The Glass House (1972)

The Truth *See* A Dark Truth (2012)

The Truth About Tully *See* Tully (2000)

Try and Find It *See* Hi Diddle Diddle (1943)

Try Seventeen *See* All I Want (2002)

Tsubaki Sanjuro *See* Sanjuro (1962)

Tsvet Granata *See* The Color of Pomegranates (1969)

Tudor Rose *See* Nine Days a Queen (1936)

Tulitkkutehtaan Tytto *See* The Match Factory Girl (1990)

The Tunnel *See* Transatlantic Tunnel (1935)

Tunnels *See* Criminal Act (1988)

Turist *See* Force Majeure (2014)

Turkey Shoot *See* Escape 2000 (1981)

Turnaround *See* The Big Turnaround (1988)

Tuzolto utca 25 *See* 25 Fireman's Street (1973)

The 12 Disasters of Christmas *See* 12 Disasters (2012)

Twelve Miles Out *See* The Second Woman (1951)

Twelve to the Moon *See* 12 to the Moon (1960)

12 Wishes of Christmas *See* 12 Christmas Wishes For My Dog (2011)

24 Hours *See* Trapped (2002)

2047: Sights of Death *See* Death Squad (2014)

24 Hours *See* SWAT: Unit 887 (2015)

24 jours *See* 24 Days (2014)

Twenty-One Days Together *See* 21 Days (1940)

Twenty Twelve *See* 2012 (2009)

2012: Supernova *See* Supernova (2009)

Twice Bitten *See* The Vampire Hookers (1978)

Twilight: New Moon *See* The Twilight Saga: New Moon (2009)

Twilight of the Dead *See* Gates of Hell (1980)

Twinkle, Twinkle, Killer Kane *See* The Ninth Configuration (1979)

Twinky *See* Lola (1969)
The Twins Effect *See* Vampire Effect (2003)
Twins of Dracula *See* Twins of Evil (1971)
Twist of Fate *See* Psychopath (1997)
Twisted *See* Medusa (1974)
The Twisted Road *See* They Live by Night (1949)
Two Brothers, One Death *See* Ringo, the Lone Rider (1968)
Two Champions of Death *See* Sword Masters: Two Champions of Shaolin (1980)
Two Champions of Shaolin *See* Sword Masters: Two Champions of Shaolin (1980)
2 Cries in the Night *See* Funeral Home (1982)
2 Guns: Zero Tolerance *See* Zero Tolerance (2015)
The Two-Headed Monster *See* The Manster (1959)
Two If By Sea *See* Stolen Hearts (1995)
Two Minds for Murder *See* Someone Behind the Door (1971)
Two Mothers *See* Adore (2013)
2 S.I.C.K. *See* Mr. Jingles (2006)
Two Weeks in September *See* A Coeur Joie (1967)
2BPerfectlyHonest *See* 2B Perfectly Honest (2004)
Tyler Perry's A Madea Family Funeral *See* A Madea Family Funeral (2019)
Tyler Perry's Acrimony *See* Acrimony (2018)
Tyler Perry's Boo 2! A Madea Halloween *See* Boo 2! A Madea Halloween (2017)
Tyler Perry's Boo! A Madea Halloween *See* Boo! A Madea Halloween (2016)
Tyler Perry's Daddy's Little Girls *See* Daddy's Little Girls (2007)
Tyler Perry's I Can Do Bad All By Myself *See* I Can Do Bad All By Myself (2009)
Tyler Perry's Madea Goes to Jail *See* Madea Goes to Jail (2009)
Tyler Perry's Madea's Big Happy Family *See* Madea's Big Happy Family (2011)
Tyler Perry's Madea's Witness Protection *See* Madea's Witness Protection (2012)
Tyler Perry's The Family That Preys *See* The Family That Preys (2008)
Tyrannosaurus Wrecks *See* The Eden Formula (2006)
The Tyrant of Syracuse *See* Damon and Pythias (1962)
Tystnaden *See* The Silence (1963)
Tyubeu *See* Tube (2003)
U-67 *See* The Sea Ghost (1931)
U-Boat *See* In Enemy Hands (2004)
U-Boat 29 *See* Spy in Black (1939)
U-238 and the Witch Doctor *See* Jungle Drums of Africa (1953)
Uccellacci e Uccellini *See* The Hawks & the Sparrows (1967)
Uccidero Un Uomo *See* This Man Must Die (1970)
Uccidi Django... uccidi per primo!!! *See* Kill Django (1971)
Uchu Daikaiiju Dogora *See* Dagora, the Space Monster (1965)
Uchu Kaisoku-sen *See* Invasion of the Neptune Men (1961)
Uchu kara no messeji *See* Message from Space (1978)
Uchudai Dogora *See* Dagora, the Space Monster (1965)
U.F.O. *See* Alien Uprising (2012)
Ugetsu Monogatari *See* Ugetsu (1953)
Ugly Dolls *See* UglyDolls (2019)
Ukigusa *See* Drifting Weeds (1959)
Ulisse *See* Ulysses (1955)
Ulisse contro Ercole *See* Ulysses Against the Son of Hercules (1961)
A Ultima Vez Que Vi Macau *See* The Last Time I Saw Macao (2013)
Ultimi Giorni di Pompeii *See* The Last Days of Pompeii (1960)
L'ultimo killer *See* Django: Last Killer (1967)
L'Ultimo Tango a Parigi *See* Last Tango in Paris (1973)
L'Ultimo Treno della Notte *See* Night Train Murders (1975)
Ultra Force *See* Royal Warriors (1986)
Ulysses Against Hercules *See* Ulysses Against the Son of Hercules (1961)
Umarete Wa Mita Keredo *See* I Was Born But. . . (1932)
The Umbrella Woman *See* The Good Wife (1986)
U.M.C. *See* Operation Heartbeat (1969)
Umi wa miteita *See* The Sea is Watching (2002)
Umi yori mo mada fukaku *See* After the Storm (2017)
Umimachi Diary *See* Our Little Sister (2016)
Un Amour De Swann *See* Swann in Love (1984)
Un Angelo per Satan *See* An Angel for Satan (1966)
Un Arma de Dos Filos *See* Shark! (1968)
Un Autre Homme, Une Autre Chance *See* Another Man, Another Chance (1977)
Un bacio *See* One Kiss (2016)
Un Baiser S'il Vous Plait? *See* Shall We Kiss? (2007)
Un beau soleil intérieur *See* Let the Sunshine In (2017)
Un Chapeau de Paille d'Italie *See* Italian Straw Hat (1927)
Un Condamne a Mort s'est Echappe, Ou le Vent Souffle ou il Vent *See* A Man Escaped (1957)
Un Conte de Noel *See* A Christmas Tale (2008)
Un, Deux, Trois, Quatre! *See* Black Tights (1960)
Un dia sin mexicanos *See* A Day Without a Mexican (2004)
Un Dimanche a la Campagne *See* A Sunday in the Country (1984)
Un Divan a New York *See* A Couch in New York (1995)
Un Esercito di 5 Uomini *See* The Five Man Army (1969)
Un Ete Brulant *See* A Burning Hot Summer (2011)
Un Fiume di Dollari *See* The Hills Run Red (1967)
Un Grand Amour de Beethoven *See* Beethoven (1936)
Un Homme Amoureux *See* A Man in Love (1987)
Un Homme et Un Femme *See* A Man and a Woman (1966)
Un Homme et Une Femme: Vingt Ans Deja *See* A Man and a Woman: 20 Years Later (1986)
Un long dimanche de fiancailles *See* A Very Long Engagement (2004)
Un Minuto Per Pregare, Un Istante Per Morire *See* A Minute to Pray, a Second to Die (1967)
Un monde presque paisible *See* Almost Peaceful (2002)
Un Monstre a Paris *See* A Monster in Paris (2011)
Un monstruo de mil cabezas *See* A Monster with a Thousand Heads (2015)
Un Nomme La Rocca *See* A Man Named Rocca (1961)
Un Partie de Plaisir *See* A Piece of Pleasure (1974)
Un Prophete *See* A Prophet (2009)
Un Tipo con Una Faccia Strana ti Cerca per Ucciderti *See* Mean Machine (1973)
Un Tranquillo Posto di Campagna *See* A Quiet Place in the Country (1969)
Un Uomo da Rispettare *See* Master Touch (1974)
Una Giornata Speciale *See* A Special Day (1977)
Una Hacha para la Luna de Miel *See* Hatchet for the Honeymoon (1970)
Una Lucertola con la Pelle di Donna *See* A Lizard in a Woman's Skin (1971)
Una Mujer Fantastica *See* A Fantastic Woman (2018)
Una pistola per cento bare *See* Gun for 100 Graves (1968)
Una Pura Formalita *See* A Pure Formality (1994)
Una Ragione Per Vivere e Una Per Morire *See* A Reason to Live, a Reason to Die (1973)
Una Sombra Ya Pronto Seras *See* A Shadow You Soon Will Be (1994)
Unagi *See* The Eel (1996)
Unakrsna Vatra *See* Operation Cross Eagles (1969)
Uncle Harry *See* The Strange Affair of Uncle Harry (1945)
Uncle Silas *See* Inheritance (1947)
Unconventional Linda *See* Holiday (1938)
Under California Skies *See* Under California Stars (1948)
Under Heaven *See* In the Shadows (1998)
Under Pressure *See* Escape under Pressure (2000)
Under sandet *See* Land of Mine (2015)
Under Solen *See* Under the Sun (1998)
Under the Banner of Samurai *See* Samurai Banners (1969)
Under the Clock *See* The Clock (1945)
Underground *See* The Lower Depths (1936)
An Underwater Odyssey *See* Neptune Factor (1973)
Underworld 4: Awakening *See* Underworld: Awakening (2012)
Underworld: New Dawn *See* Underworld: Awakening (2012)
Undue Influence *See* Steve Martini's Undue Influence (1996)
Une Affaire de Femmes *See* The Story of Women (1988)
Une Femme de Menage *See* The Housekeeper (2002)
Une Femme Est une Femme *See* A Woman Is a Woman (1960)
Une Femme Fidele *See* Game of Seduction (1976)
Une Hirondelle a Fait le Printemps *See* The Girl from Paris (2002)
Une Liaison d'Amour *See* An Affair of Love (1999)
Une Liaison Pornographique *See* An Affair of Love (1999)
Une Noire de. . . *See* Black Girl (1966)
Une nouvelle amie *See* The New Girlfriend (2014)
Une Pure Formalite *See* A Pure Formality (1994)
Unearthed *See* Mandrake (2010)
The Unearthing *See* Aswang (2003)
The Unfaithful Wife *See* La Femme Infidele (1969)
Ungarische Rhapsodie *See* Hungarian Rhapsody (1928)
The Ungodly *See* The Perfect Witness (2007)
U.S. Navy SEALS: Dead or Alive *See* U.S. SEALs: Dead or Alive (2002)
U.S. SEALs 3: Frogmen *See* U.S. SEALs: Dead or Alive (2002)
U.S. Vice *See* Black Heat (1976)
The Unknown *See* Clawed: The Legend of Sasquatch (2005)
The Unnamable Returns *See* The Unnamable 2: The Statement of Randolph Carter (1992)
Uno dopo l'altro *See* One After Another (1968)
Unseen Evil 2 *See* Alien 3000 (2004)
Unsere Mutter, Unsere Vater *See* Generation War (2013)
Untel Pere et Fils *See* Heart of a Nation (1943)
Unter dem Pflaster Ist der Strand *See* Under the Pavement Lies the Strand (1975)
The Untold *See* Sasquatch (2002)
The Unvanquished *See* Aparajito (1958)
Uomini Si Nasce Politziotti Si Muore *See* Live Like a Cop, Die Like a Man (1976)
Uomini Uomini Uomini *See* Men Men Men (1995)
Uomo Dalla Pelle Dura *See* Counter Punch (1971)
L'Uomo delle Stelle *See* The Star Maker (1995)
L'uomo, L'orgoglio, la vendetta *See* Man, Pride and Vengeance (1967)
Up Frankenstein *See* Andy Warhol's Frankenstein (1974)
Up in Smoke *See* Cheech and Chong's Up in Smoke (1979)
Upper World *See* Upperworld (1934)
The Upstate Murders *See* Savage Weekend (1980)
Urban Justice *See* Under Oath (1997)
Urban Killas: Blood Billz *See* Blood Billz (2003)
Urban Killaz: Thugz *See* Thugz (2004)
Ursus *See* The Mighty Ursus (1961)
Ursus *See* Ursus in the Valley of the Lions (1962)
Ursus nella terra di fuoco *See* Ursus in the Land of Fire (1963)
The Usual Unidentified Thieves *See* Big Deal on Madonna Street (1958)
Utamaro O Meguru Gonin No Onna *See* Utamaro and His Five Women (1946)
Vacation *See* National Lampoon's Vacation (1983)
The Valdez Horses *See* Chino (1975)
Valdez the Half Breed *See* Chino (1975)
Vale Abraao *See* Abraham's Valley (1993)
Valentine's Day *See* Protector (1997)
Valley of Abraham *See* Abraham's Valley (1993)
Valley of Fear *See* Sherlock Holmes and the Deadly Necklace (1962)
Valley of the Swords *See* The Castilian (1963)
Vals in Bashir *See* Waltz with Bashir (2008)
The Vampire *See* Vampyr (1931)
The Vampire and the Robot *See* My Son, the Vampire (1952)
The Vampire-Beast Craves Blood *See* Blood Beast Terror (1967)
Vampire Castle *See* Captain Kronos: Vampire Hunter (1974)
Vampire Men of the Lost Planet *See* Horror of the Blood Monsters (1970)
Vampire Orgy *See* Vampyres (1974)
Vampire Over London *See* My Son, the Vampire (1952)
Vampire Playgirls *See* Dracula's Great Love (1972)
Vampires *See* John Carpenter's Vampires (1997)
The Vampire's Assistant *See* Cirque du Freak: The Vampire's Assistant (2009)
Vampires: Los Muertos *See* John Carpenter Presents Vampires: Los Muertos (2002)
The Vampire's Niece *See* Fangs of the Living Dead (1968)
Vampire's Night Orgy *See* Orgy of the Vampires (1973)

Vampire's Thirst *See* The Body Beneath (1970)

Vampyr, Der Traum des David Gray *See* Vampyr (1931)

Vampyr, Ou l'Etrange Aventure de David Gray *See* Vampyr (1931)

Vampyres, Daughters of Dracula *See* Vampyres (1974)

Van Wilder *See* National Lampoon's Van Wilder (2002)

Van Wilder 2: The Rise of Taj *See* National Lampoon's Van Wilder 2: The Rise of Taj (2006)

Vanishing Body *See* The Black Cat (1934)

Vargtimmen *See* Hour of the Wolf (1968)

Variete *See* Variety (1925)

Vaudeville *See* Variety (1925)

Vaya con dios gringo *See* Go With God Gringo (1966)

V.C. Andrews' Rain *See* Rain (2006)

Vegas, Baby *See* Bachelor Party Vegas (2005)

The Veil *See* Haunts (1977)

Veiled Truth *See* What Comes Around (2006)

Veillees d'armes *See* The Troubles We've Seen (1994)

Velka voda *See* The Great Water (2004)

The Velocity of Gary (Not His Real Name) *See* The Velocity of Gary (1998)

Velvet House *See* Crucible of Horror (1969)

Vendetta *See* Long Days of Revenge (1967)

A Vendre *See* For Sale (1998)

Vendredi Soir *See* Friday Night (2002)

Venere Imperiale *See* Imperial Venus (1963)

Venganza de Barrio *See* Hood Vengeance (2009)

Vengeance *See* I Am Vengeance (2018)

Vengeance of a Soldier *See* Soldier's Revenge (1984)

Vengeance: The Demon *See* Pumpkinhead (1988)

The Vengeful Dead *See* Kiss Daddy Goodbye (1981)

Venice *See* Dangerous Beauty (1998)

Venkovsky Ucitel *See* The Country Teacher (2008)

Venus in Peltz *See* Venus in Furs (1970)

The Venusian *See* Stranger from Venus (1954)

Venuto al Mondo *See* Twice Born (2012)

Vercingetorix *See* Druids (2001)

The Veritas Project: Hangman's Curse *See* Hangman's Curse (2003)

Vers le Sud *See* Heading South (2005)

A Very Big Weekend *See* A Man, a Woman, and a Bank (1979)

A Very Cool Christmas *See* Too Cool for Christmas (2004)

Vessel of Wrath *See* Beachcomber (1938)

The Veteran *See* Deathdream (1972)

Viagem ao Principio do Mundo *See* Voyage to the Beginning of the World (1996)

The Vicious Circle *See* Woman in Brown (1948)

Victory *See* Vincere (2009)

The Vienna Strangler *See* The Mad Butcher (1972)

Vig *See* Money Kings (1998)

Viking Massacre *See* Knives of the Avenger (1965)

The Vintner's Luck *See* A Heavenly Vintage (2009)

Violated *See* Party Girls for Sale (1954)

Violence et Passion *See* Conversation Piece (1975)

Violent City *See* The Family (1970)

The Violent Hour *See* Dial 1119 (1950)

Violent Midnight *See* Psychomania (1963)

Violent Streets *See* Thief (1981)

Violeta se fue a los cielos *See* Violeta Went to Heaven (2013)

Violette Noziere *See* Violette (1978)

Viperes *See* Posers (2002)

Virgin Hunters *See* Test Tube Teens from the Year 2000 (1993)

The Virgin Vampires *See* Twins of Evil (1971)

Virtual Storm *See* Code Hunter (2002)

The Virtuous Tramps *See* The Devil's Brother (1933)

Virus *See* Cannibal Apocalypse (1980)

Virus Undead *See* Beast Within (2008)

Visages villages *See* Faces Places (2017)

Viskingar Och Rop *See* Cries and Whispers (1972)

Visszaesok *See* Forbidden Relations (1983)

Vital Parts *See* Harold Robbins' Body Parts (1999)

Vitelloni *See* I Vitelloni (1953)

Vitez se peharom *See* Knight of Cups (2015)

Viva Las Nowhere *See* Dead Simple (2001)

Vivement Dimanche! *See* Confidentially Yours (1983)

The Vivero Letter *See* Forgotten City (1998)

Vivi O, Prefeibilmente, Morti *See* Sundance and the Kid (1969)

Vivid *See* Luscious (1997)

Vivo per la Tua Morte *See* A Long Ride From Hell (1968)

Vivre Sa Vie *See* My Life to Live (1962)

The Vixen *See* The Women (1968)

Vixens *See* Supervixens (1975)

Voces inocentes *See* Innocent Voices (2004)

Voci dal Profondo *See* Voices from Beyond (1990)

Voleurs de Chevaux *See* In the Arms of My Enemy (2007)

Voodoo Blood Bath *See* I Eat Your Skin (1964)

Voodoo Girl *See* Sugar Hill (1974)

Voor een Verloren Soldaat *See* For a Lost Soldier (1993)

Vor *See* The Thief (1997)

Vortex *See* Day Time Ended (1980)

Voskhozhdeniye *See* The Ascent (1976)

Vous N'avez Encore Rien Vu *See* You Ain't Seen Nothin' Yet (2012)

Voyage to a Prehistoric Planet *See* Voyage to the Prehistoric Planet (1965)

Voyage to Italy *See* Voyage in Italy (1953)

Vraie Jeanne, fausse Jeanne *See* The Real Joan of Arc (2008)

Vredens Dag *See* Day of Wrath (1943)

Vs *See* All Superheroes Must Die (2011)

Vsichni Moji Blizci *See* All My Loved Ones (2000)

Vuelven *See* Tigers Are Not Afraid (2019)

The VVitch: A New-England Folktale *See* The Witch (2016)

Vzlomschik *See* Burglar (1987)

W Pustyni I W Puszczy *See* In Desert and Wilderness (2001)

Wages of Fear *See* Sorcerer (1977)

Waiting Women *See* Secrets of Women (1952)

Wajda: Czlowiek Z Zelaza *See* Man of Iron (1981)

Wake *See* Beneath the Dark (2010)

Wake in Fright *See* Outback (1971)

Wake Up *See* Awake (2019)

The Waking Hour *See* The Velvet Vampire (1971)

Wakolda *See* The German Doctor (2014)

Wakusei daikaiju Negadon *See* Negadon: The Monster from Mars (2005)

Waldo Warren: Private Dick Without a Brain *See* Maximum Thrust (1988)

Walking with the Dead *See* Walking Deceased (2015)

Wandafuru Raifu *See* After Life (1998)

Wang jiao ka men *See* As Tears Go By (1988)

The Wannabes *See* Criminal Ways (2003)

Wannseekonferenz *See* The Wannsee Conference (1984)

Want a Ride, Little Girl? *See* Impulse (1974)

Wanted *See* Crime Spree (2003)

The Wanton Contessa *See* Senso (1954)

War Between the Planets *See* Planet on the Prowl (1965)

War Games *See* Suppose They Gave a War and Nobody Came? (1970)

The War Is Over *See* La Guerre Est Finie (1966)

The War of the Monsters *See* Gamera *vs.* Barugon (1966)

War of the Monsters *See* Godzilla *vs.* Monster Zero (1968)

War of the Planets *See* Cosmos: War of the Planets (1980)

War of the Robots *See* Reactor (1978)

War of the Worlds *See* H.G. Wells' War of the Worlds (2005)

W.A.R., Women Against Rape *See* Lethal Victims (1987)

WarGames 2 *See* WarGames: The Dead Code (2008)

The Warm-Blooded Spy *See* Ravishing Idiot (1964)

Warnung Vor Einer Helligen Nutte *See* Beware of a Holy Whore (1970)

Warrior *See* Mexican Blow (2002)

The Warrior of Waverly Street *See* Star Kid (1997)

The Warrior Princess *See* Musa: The Warrior (2001)

The Warriors Gate *See* Enter the Warriors Gate (2017)

Warrior's Rest *See* Le Repos du Guerrier (1962)

Waru Yatsu Hodo Yoku Nemuru *See* The Bad Sleep Well (1960)

Warum Lauft Herr R Amok? *See* Why Does Herr R. Run Amok? (1969)

Was Tun, Wenn's Brennt? *See* What to Do in Case of Fire (2002)

Wasps' Nest *See* The Nest (2002)

Watch That Man *See* The Man Who Knew Too Little (1997)

Watchtower *See* Cruel and Unusual (2001)

Water Cyborgs *See* Terror Beneath the Sea (1966)

The Watts Monster *See* Dr. Black, Mr. Hyde (1976)

The Way Ahead *See* Immortal Battalion (1944)

The Way of Life *See* They Call It Sin (1932)

The Way We Are *See* Quiet Days in Hollywood (1997)

Ways of the Flesh *See* The Heart Specialist (2006)

WAZ *See* The Killing Gene (2007)

We Met on the Vineyard *See* The Big Day (1999)

Weapon *See* Cyborg Soldier (2008)

The Web of Death *See* Sword Masters: Web of Death (1976)

Wedding Bells *See* Royal Wedding (1951)

Wedding Breakfast *See* The Catered Affair (1956)

A Wedding for Bella *See* The Bread, My Sweet (2001)

The Wedding Wish *See* How I Married My High School Crush (2007)

Wee Geordie *See* Geordie (1955)

Week of the Killer *See* Cannibal Man (1971)

Weekend Babysitter *See* Weekend with the Babysitter (1970)

Wei Xian Guan Xi *See* Dangerous Liaisons (2012)

Welcome Home Brother Charles *See* Soul Vengeance (1975)

Welcome to Jericho *See* Last Man Standing (1996)

Welcome to Planet Earth *See* Alien Avengers (1996)

The Well-Made Marriage *See* Le Beau Mariage (1982)

Welt am Draht *See* World on a Wire (1973)

Wendy Cracked a Walnut *See* . . .Almost (1990)

We're in the Army Now *See* Pack Up Your Troubles (1932)

Werewolf Warrior *See* Kibakichi (2004)

Werewolf Woman *See* The Legend of the Wolf Woman (1977)

Werk ohne Autor *See* Never Look Away (2018)

Wes Craven Presents Carnival of Souls *See* Carnival of Souls (1998)

Wes Craven Presents: Don't Look Down *See* Don't Look Down (1998)

Wes Craven Presents Dracula 2: Ascension *See* Dracula 2: Ascension (2003)

Wes Craven Presents: Dracula 2000 *See* Dracula 2000 (2000)

Wes Craven Presents Wishmaster *See* Wishmaster (1997)

West Beyrouth *See* West Beirut (1998)

The Westing Game *See* Get a Clue! (1998)

Wet Bum *See* Surfacing (2014)

The Wettest County in the World *See* Lawless (2012)

We've Got Christmas Mail *See* Christmas Mail (2010)

What *See* The Whip and the Body (1963)

What a Man *See* Never Give a Sucker an Even Break (1941)

What Are Those Strange Drops of Blood on the Body of Jennifer? *See* The Case of the Bloody Iris (1972)

What Ever Happened to Baby Jane *See* What Ever Happened To. . . (1993)

What Happened to Tully *See* Tully (2000)

What Lola Wants *See* Damn Yankees (1958)

What the Swedish Butler Saw *See* A Man with a Maid (1973)

What We Did That Night *See* Murder at Devil's Glen (1999)

What Would Jesus Do? *See* WWJD: What Would Jesus Do? (2010)

What's Wrong With Virginia *See* Virginia (2010)

The Wheel *See* La Roue (1923)

The Wheelchair *See* El Cochecito (1960)

When Andrew Came Home *See* Taming Andrew (2000)

When I Fall in Love *See* Everybody's All American (1988)

When Knighthood Was in Flower *See* The Sword & the Rose (1953)

When Michael Calls *See* Shattered Silence (1971)

When Strangers Marry *See* Betrayed (1944)

When the Girls Meet the Boys *See* Girl Crazy (1943)

When Youth Conspires *See* Old Swimmin' Hole (1940)

Where is the Friend's Home? *See* Where Is My Friend's House? (1987)

Video A-Z

A. I.: Artificial Intelligence 2001 **(PG-13)** The uneasy melding of an homage directed by Spielberg of a long-cherished idea by late director Stanley Kubrick. Global warming submerges the world's coastal cities but advanced humanoid robots, or "mechas," keep things going. Professor Hobby (Hurt) made a child mecha, David (Osment), designed to be loving and extremely loyal—in this case to his human mother Monica (O'Connor) who eventually abandons him to the cruel world. Having heard the Pinocchio story, David searches for the Blue Fairy who can make David a "real" boy. En route, David meets mecha Gigolo Joe (Law), who advises David about human beings' perfidy. An acquired taste--it's long, dark, confusing, sometimes boring, and sometimes touching. Law's role is small but Osment carries the picture. Based on Brian Aldiss' 1969 short story "Supertoys Last All Summer Long." **145m/C; VHS, DVD.** Haley Joel Osment; Jude Law; Frances O'Connor; Sam Robards; Brendan Gleeson; William Hurt; Jake Thomas; Clara Bellar; Enrico Colantoni; Adrian Grenier; Emmanuelle Chriqui; ***V:*** Robin Williams; Chris Rock; Meryl Streep; Jack Angel; ***Nar:*** Ben Kingsley; ***D:*** Steven Spielberg; ***W:*** Steven Spielberg; ***C:*** Janusz Kaminski; ***M:*** John Williams.

A Lot Like Love 2005 **(PG-13)** More like "A Lot Like a Million Other Disposable Romantic Comedies." On a plane from New York to L.A., shy Oliver (Kutcher) meets aggressive Emily (Peet), who goads Oliver into joining the Mile High Club and unceremoniously dumps him once they land, claiming he's not her type. Apparently the universe and the writers disagree. Over the next seven years, their paths keep crossing, and they wonder if perhaps it's true love. Kutcher and Peet do their best to fake on-screen chemistry, but come off as the poor man's Tom Hanks and Meg Ryan. **95m/C; DVD.** Ashton Kutcher; Amanda Peet; Kathryn Hahn; Kal Penn; Taryn Manning; James Read; Molly Cheek; Gabriel Mann; Ty(rone) Giordano; Aimee Garcia; Ali Larter; Amy Aquino; Jeremy Sisto; Holmes Osborne; Lee Garlington; Linda Hunt; Melissa van der Schyff; ***D:*** Nigel Cole; ***W:*** Colin Patrick Lynch; ***C:*** John de Borman; ***M:*** Alex Wurman.

A Nos Amours *To Our Loves* **1984 (R)** Craving the attention she is denied at home, a young French girl searches for love and affection from numerous boyfriends in hopes of eradicating her unhappy home. Occasional lapses in quality and slow pacing hamper an otherwise excellent effort. The characterization of the girl Suzanne is especially memorable. In French with English subtitles. **99m/C; VHS, DVD,** ***FR*** Sandrine Bonnaire; Dominique Besnehard; Maurice Pialat; Evelyne Ker; ***D:*** Maurice Pialat; ***W:*** Maurice Pialat; Arlette Langmann; ***C:*** Jacques Loiseleux; ***M:*** Henry Purcell.

A Nous la Liberte *Freedom for Us* **1931** Two tramps encounter industrialization and automation, making one into a wealthy leader, the other into a nature-loving iconoclast. A poignant, fantastical masterpiece by Clair, made before he migrated to Hollywood. Though the view of automation may be dated, it influenced such films as Chaplin's "Modern Times." In French with English subtitles. **87m/B; VHS, DVD.** ***FR*** Henri Marchand; Raymond Cordy; Rolla France; Paul Olivier; Jacques Shelly; Andre Michaud; ***D:*** Rene Clair; ***W:*** Rene Clair; ***C:*** Georges Perinal; ***M:*** Georges Auric.

The A-Team **2010 (PG-13)** The 1983-87 TV series successfully takes to the big screen, and its four members are now Iraq War vets trying to clear their names after being framed for a heist of some American currency engraving plates. Perfectly cast, with just the right tone for summer blockbuster season, Carnahan delivers exactly what the show did: Mindless, loud, and fun entertainment. You don't necessarily have to be a fan of the show to enjoy it, but it might help. Stephen J. Cannell, who created and produced the TV show, is a producer of the film version. **117m/C; Blu-Ray.** Liam Neeson; Bradley Cooper; Sharlto Copley; Quinton 'Rampage' Jackson; Jessica Biel; Patrick Wilson; Brian Bloom; Gerald McRaney; Henry Czerny; Omari Hardwick; Jon Hamm; Yul Vazquez; Maury Sterling; ***Cameo(s):*** Dirk Benedict; Dwight Schultz; ***D:*** Joe Carnahan; ***W:*** Skip Woods; Michael Brandt; Derek Haas; ***C:*** Mauro Fiore; ***M:*** Alan Silvestri.

Aaliyah: The Princess of R&B 1/2 **2014** Unfortunately shallow Lifetime biopic of the young singer, who was killed in a plane crash in 2001. Aaliyah's family objected to her portrayal and they blocked the rights to using her hits, so there are few songs. The singer was no diva and there's also not a lot of drama, except for her controversial relationship with fellow singer R. Kelly. Shipp is pleasant and attractive in the title role. **90m/C; DVD.** Alexandra Shipp; Cle Bennett; Lyriq Bent; Rachael Crawford; Elise Neal; Izaak Smith; ***D:*** Bradley Walsh; ***W:*** Michael Elliot; ***C:*** Andre Pienarr. **CABLE**

Aardvark **2018 (PG-13)** Writer/director Shoaf manages to turn three interesting and talented actors downright boring. Slate plays Emily, a therapist who begins treating mentally ill Josh (Quinto), who's prone to hallucinations, typically involving his celebrity brother (Hamm). Committing a huge therapist no-no, Emily begins dating said brother; meanwhile Josh starts seeing a new woman...but can anyone else? Doesn't matter. This film makes no statement, and the only impression it leaves is one of pity over having squandered its cast. **89m/C; DVD, Blu-Ray.** Zachary Quinto; Jenny Slate; Sheila Vand; Jon Hamm; Tonya Pinkins; ***D:*** Brian Shoaf; ***W:*** Brian Shoaf; ***C:*** Eric Lin; ***M:*** Heather McIntosh.

Aaron Loves Angela **1975 (R)** Puerto Rican girl falls in love with a black teen amidst the harsh realities of the Harlem ghetto. "Romeo and Juliet" meets "West Side Story" in a cliched comedy drama. **99m/C; VHS, DVD.** Kevin Hooks; Irene Cara; Moses Gunn; Robert Hooks; ***Cameo(s):*** Jose Feliciano; ***D:*** Gordon Parks, Jr.; ***C:*** Richard Kratina; ***M:*** Jose Feliciano.

Abandon 1/2 **2002 (PG-13)** "Traffic" screenwriter Stephen Gaghan makes his directorial debut in this psychological thriller that centers on bookworm college student Katie (Holmes) and her mysteriously missing boyfriend Embry (Hunnam). When police detective Wade (Bratt) arrives to question Katie two years after the disappearance of the eccentric Embry, she begins to see glimpses of him all over campus. The "twist" ending is fairly predictable, but the cast, particularly Union, Mann and Deschanel as Katie's classmates, get the most out of the script. Based on the book "Adam's Fall" by Sean Desmond. **99m/C; VHS, DVD.** Katie Holmes; Benjamin Bratt; Charlie Hunnam; Zooey Deschanel; Gabrielle Union; Gabriel Mann; Mark Feuerstein; Melanie Lynskey; Will McCormack; Philip Bosco; Tony Goldwyn; Fred Ward; ***D:*** Stephen Gaghan; ***W:*** Stephen Gaghan; ***C:*** Matthew Libatique; ***M:*** Clint Mansell.

Abandoned 1/2 *Abandoned Woman* **1947** A young woman goes missing in Los Angeles, and her sister starts searching. Turns out the missing girl had a baby—but the baby is nowhere to be found. The police are disinterested until a local crime reporter gets involved and winds up finding a shady detective and black market baby ring. **78m/B; DVD.** Dennis O'Keefe; Gale Storm; Marjorie Rambeau; Raymond Burr; Will Kuluva; Jeff Chandler; Meg Randall; Jeannette Nolan; ***D:*** Joseph M. Newman; ***W:*** Irwin Gielgud; William Bowers.

Abandoned WOOF! 2010 (PG-13) Distressingly bad, low-budget medical thriller that was the last completed film feature for Murphy, who looks much worse than even her unstable character warrants. Mary takes new boyfriend Kevin to an L.A. hospital for some minor surgery but he vanishes and there's no record he was ever a patient. Because of her own mental issues, Mary is suspected of being a nutcase but, because she works as a bank manager, there's more involved that just delusions. **93m/C; DVD, Blu-Ray.** Brittany Murphy; Dean Cain; Peter Bogdanovich; Mimi Rogers; Jay Pickett; Tim Thomerson; ***D:*** Michael Feifer; ***W:*** Peter Sullivan; ***C:*** Denis Maloney; ***M:*** Andres Boulton. **VIDEO**

Abandoned and Deceived **1995** ABC TV movie based on a true story. Gerri's (Loughlin) ex-husband Doug (Kerwin) doesn't pay his child support and even though she works two jobs the bills pile up. Not getting any help from social services, Gerri and her two sons move in with her parents and she decides to place a newspaper ad asking for moms in similar situations to contact her, leading to the founding of the Association for Enforcement of Child Support. **90m/C; DVD.** Lori Loughlin; Brian Kerwin; Farrah Forke; Anthony Tyler Quinn; Eric Lloyd; Gordon Clapp; Bibi Besch; Linden Chiles; ***D:*** Joseph Dougherty; ***W:*** Joseph Dougherty; ***C:*** Thomas Del Ruth; ***M:*** Laura Karpman. **TV**

Abattoir **2017 (R)** Reporter Julia Talben's (Lowndes) sister is killer by a sociopath. She discovers that the room in which her loved one dies has been taken by a mysterious man (Callie) who is collecting places in which people were murdered to form an ultimate haunted house. Maybe. That could be it. A truly nonsensical and non-scary horror flick. Bousman officially runs out of the steam granted him by directing three "Saw" lesser sequels with this horror disaster that even makes those tolerable. **98m/C; DVD.** Jessica Lowndes; Joe Anderson; Dayton Callie; Lin Shaye; John McConnell; ***D:*** Darren Lynn Bousman; ***W:*** Christopher Monfette; ***C:*** Michael Fimognari; ***M:*** Mark Sayfritz.

Abbott and Costello Go to Mars 1/2 *On to Mars; Rocket and Roll* **1953** Poor parody of sci-fi films finds the frantic duo aboard a rocket ship and accidentally heading off into outer space. They don't land on Mars, but Venus, which is populated by lots of pretty women and no men. Even this duo looks good to the ladies. Cheapie production and uninspired buffoonery. **77m/B; VHS, DVD.** Bud Abbott; Lou Costello; Mari Blanchard; Robert Paige; Martha Hyer; Horace McMahon; Jack Kruschen; Anita Ekberg; Jean Willes; Joe (Joseph) Kirk; Jackie Loughery; James Flavin; ***D:*** Charles Lamont; ***W:*** John Grant; D.D. Beauchamp; ***C:*** Clifford Stine; ***M:*** Joseph Gershenson.

Abbott and Costello in Hollywood *Bud Abbott and Lou Costello In Hollywood* **1945** Bud and Lou appear as a barber and porter of a high-class tonsorial parlor in Hollywood. A rather sarcastic look at backstage Hollywood, Abbott & Costello style. Ball makes a guest appearance. **111m/B; VHS, DVD.** Bud Abbott; Lou Costello; Frances Rafferty; Warner Anderson; Jean Porter; Robert Stanton; Mike Mazurki; ***D:*** S. Sylvan Simon; ***M:*** George Bassman.

Abbott and Costello in the Foreign Legion 1/2 **1950** Fight promoters Jonesy and Max trail their runaway fighter to Algiers where they're tricked into joining the French Foreign Legion. They have to cope with a sadistic sergeant, a sexy spy, and still find their man. Most amusement comes from Lou's wild desert mirages. **80m/B; VHS, DVD.** Bud Abbott; Lou Costello; Walter Slezak; Patricia Medina; Douglass Dumbrille; Leon Belasco; Marc Lawrence; Tor Johnson; ***D:*** Charles Lamont; ***W:*** John Grant; Martin Ragaway; Leonard Stern; ***C:*** George Robinson.

Abbott and Costello Meet Captain Kidd **1952** With pirates led by Captain Kidd on their trail, Abbott and Costello follow a treasure map. Bland A&C swashbuckler spoof with a disinterested Laughton impersonating the Kidd. One of the duo's few color films. **70m/C; VHS, DVD.** Bud Abbott; Lou Costello; Charles Laughton; Hillary Brooke; Fran Warren; Bill (William) Shirley; Leif Erickson; ***D:*** Charles Lamont.

Abbott and Costello Meet Dr. Jekyll and Mr. Hyde **1952** Slim (Abbott) and Tubby (Costello) are a couple of cops sent to London, who become involved with crazy Dr. Jekyll (Karloff), who has transformed himself into Mr. Hyde via an experimental serum, and is terrorizing London. Naturally, he goes after the boys. A lame attempt at recapturing the success of "Abbott and Costello Meet Frankenstein" but Karloff is top-notch as always. **77m/B; VHS, DVD.** Bud Abbott; Lou Costello; Boris Karloff; Craig Stevens; Helen Westcott; Reginald Denny; John Dierkes; Marjorie Bennett; Lucille Lamarr; Patti McKay; ***D:*** Charles Lamont; ***W:*** John Grant; Leo Loeb; Howard Dimsdale; ***C:*** George Robinson.

Abbott and Costello Meet Frankenstein *Abbott and Costello Meet the Ghosts; Meet the Ghosts; The Brain of Frankenstein* **1948** Big-budget A&C classic is one of their best efforts and was rewarded handsomely at the boxoffice. Unsuspecting baggage clerks Chick (Abbott) and Wilbur (Costello) deliver a crate containing the last but not quite dead remains of Dracula (Lugosi) and Dr. Frankenstein's monster (Strange) to a wax museum. When Drac revives, he replaces the monster's brain with Wilbur's so he'll be easier to control. Chaney Jr. makes a special wolfish appearance to warn the boys that trouble looms. Last film to use the Universal creature pioneered by Karloff in 1931. **83m/B; VHS, DVD, Blu-Ray.** Bud Abbott; Lou Costello; Lon Chaney, Jr.; Bela Lugosi; Glenn Strange; Lenore Aubert; Jane Randolph; Frank Ferguson; Charles Bradstreet; Howard Negley; Clarence Straight; ***V:*** Vincent Price; ***D:*** Charles T. Barton; ***W:*** John Grant; Robert Lees; Frederic Rinaldo; ***C:*** Charles Van Enger; ***M:*** Frank Skinner. Natl. Film Reg. '01.

Abbott and Costello Meet the Invisible Man **1951** Abbott and Costello play newly graduated detectives who take on the murder case of a boxer (Franz) accused of killing his manager. Using a serum that makes people invisible, the boxer helps Costello in a prizefight that will frame the real killers, who killed the manager because the boxer refused to throw a fight. Great special effects and hilarious gags make this one of the best from the crazy duo. **82m/B; VHS, DVD, Blu-Ray.** Bud Abbott; Lou Costello; Nancy Guild; Adele Jergens; Sheldon Leonard; William Frawley; Gavin Muir; Arthur Franz; Syd Saylor; Bobby Barber; ***D:*** Charles Lamont; ***W:*** Frederic Rinaldo; John Grant; Robert Lees; ***C:*** George Robinson; ***M:*** Hans J. Salter.

Abbott and Costello Meet the Keystone Kops 1/2 **1954** It's 1912 and the boys are bilked into buying a fake movie studio by a clever con man. When they find out they've been tricked, the duo head to Hollywood to track him down and find out the crook is trying to cheat Sennett's film company. Sennett himself trained A&C and the new Keystone Kops in their recreations of his silent screen routines. Good final chase sequence but the earlier work is tired. **79m/B; VHS, DVD.** Bud Abbott; Lou Costello; Fred Clark; Lynn Bari; Mack Sennett; Maxie "Slapsie" Rosenbloom; Frank Wilcox; Harold Goodwin; ***D:*** Charles Lamont; ***W:*** John Grant; ***C:*** Reggie Lanning; ***M:*** Joseph Gershenson.

Abbott and Costello Meet the Killer, Boris Karloff *Abbott and Costello Meet the Killer* **1949** Unremarkable Abbott and Costello murder mystery. Karloff plays a psychic who tries to frame Lou for murder. Pleasant enough but not one of their best. **84m/B; VHS, DVD.** Bud Abbott; Lou Costello; Boris Karloff; Lenore Aubert; Gar Moore; Donna Martell; Alan Mowbray; James Flavin; Roland Winters; Nicholas Joy; Mikel Conrad; Morgan Farley; Victoria Horne; ***D:*** Charles T. Barton; ***W:*** John Grant; Hugh Wedlock, Jr.; Howard Snyder; ***C:*** Charles Van Enger; ***M:*** Milton Schwarzwald.

Abbott and Costello Meet the Mummy 1/2 **1955** Okay comedy from the duo has them stranded in Egypt with a valuable medallion which will lead to secret treasure and the mummy who guards the tomb. The last of the films the twosome made for Universal. **90m/B; VHS, DVD, Blu-Ray.** Bud Abbott; Lou Costello; Marie Windsor; Michael Ansara; Dan Seymour; Kurt Katch; Richard Deacon; Mel Welles; Edwin Parker; Richard Karlan; George Khoury; ***D:*** Charles Lamont; ***W:*** John Grant; ***C:*** George Robinson; ***M:*** Joseph Gershenson; Hans J. Salter.

ABCD 1/2 **1999** Touching story of an Asian Indian-American family living in New York. Siblings Raj and Nina have grown up in America, and have struggled with the competing pressures of their peers and their parent's old-world expectations. Their widowed mother wants them to settle down with suitable Indian spouse. Patel shows humor, and largely avoids stereotypes (although the mother ventures dangerously close), and the kids manage to be fully-realized characters. **102m/C; VHS, DVD.** Madhur Jaffrey; Faran Tahir; Sheetal Sheth; Aasif Mandvi; Adriane Forlana Erdos; Rex Young; ***D:*** Krutin Patel; ***W:*** Krutin Patel; James McManus; ***C:*** Milton Kam; ***M:*** Deirdre Broderick.

The ABCs of Death 1/2 **2012** Twenty-six vignettes offer death-by-alphabet. Some fun, some repulsive, and some head-scratchers, 26 directors are set loose in each of their segments, making for some fairly twisted storytelling. No filmmaker was limited in style, direction or subject; thus, there are multiple languages and formats, keeping things interesting. And, fortunately none are very long, as 26 letters are represented in the anthology's two-plus hours of runtime, so if D is for Dogfight is bringing you down, hang on because F is for Fart isn't far behind. **123m/C; DVD, Blu-Ray.** *RU* Ivan Gonzalez; Kyra Zagorsky; ***V:*** Ingrid Bolso Berdal; ***D:*** Kaare Andrews; Angela Bettis; Hélène Cattet; Ernesto Diaz Espinoza; Jason Eisener; Bruno Forzani; Andria Bogliano; Xavier Gens; Lee Hardcastle; Noboru Iguchi; Thomas Cappelen Maaling; Jorge Grau; Anders Morgenthaler; Yoshihiro Nishimura; Banjong Pisanthanakun; Marcel Samiento; Jon Schnepp; Timo Tjahjanto; Srdjan Spasojevic; Andrew Traucki; Nacho Vigalondo; Jake West; Ti West; Ben Wheatley; Adam Wingard; Yudai Yamaguchi; ***W:*** Kaare Andrews; Hélène Cattet; Bruno Forzani; Andria Bogliano; Lee Hardcastle; Noboru Iguchi; Yoshihiro Nishimura; Simon Rumley; Srdjan Spasojevic; Nacho Vigalondo; Ti West; Yudai Yamaguchi; Simon Barrett; Dimitrie Vojnov; ***C:*** Harris Charalambous; Manuel Dacosse; Magnus Flato; Ernesto Herrera; Karim Hussain; Nicolás Ibieta; Nemanja Jovanov; Antoine Marteau; Shu G. Momose; Yasutaka Nagano; Laurie Rose; ***M:*** Phillip Blackford; Simon Boswell; Yasuhiko Fukuda; Nobuhiko Morino; Kou Nakagawa; Julio Pillado; Johannes Ringen.

The ABCs of Death 2 1/2 **2014** Better than the first film but still bad, this anthology horror flick follows the same formula—26 short films, all based on a different letter of the alphabet. So, for example, "C is for Capital Punishment" and "H is for Head Games." The title of the short isn't given till the end of it, adding a bit of mystery to each segment. The batting average here is less than 50% but there are a few standout entries, and the idea that this series introduces horror fans to 26 different, mostly new, filmmakers is pretty fun. **125m/C; DVD, Blu-Ray.** ***D:*** Dennison Ramalho; Bruno Samper; Lancelot Imasuen; Larry Fessenden; Todd Rohal; Rodney Ascher; Marvin Kren; Vincenzo Natali; Jerome Sable; Steven Kostanski; Soichi Umezawa; Chris Nash; Evan Katz; Julian Barratt; Robert Morgan; Bill Plympton; Erik Matti; Robert Boocheck; Hajime Ohata; Juan Martinez Moreno; Jen Soska; Sylvia Soska; Julien Maury; Julian Gilbey; Alejandro Brugues; Aharon Keshales; Jim Hosking; ***W:*** Robert Boocheck; Hajime Ohata; Juan Martinez Moreno; Jen Soska; Sylvia Soska; Julien Maury; Julian Gilbey; Alejandro Brugues; Aharon Keshales; Jim Hosking.

The Abdication 1/2 **1974** Unconvincing historical bio of Sweden's Queen Christina (Ullmann) who relinquishes her 17th-century throne after converting to Catholicism. She heads to Rome but rather than finding herself dedicated to God, Christina becomes more interested in Cardinal Azzolino (Finch). Wolff adapted from her play. Garbo did it much better in 1933's "Queen Christina." **102m/C; DVD.** *GB* Peter Finch; Cyril Cusack; Graham Crowden; Michael Dunn; Liv Ullman; Kathleen Byron; ***D:*** Anthony Harvey; ***W:*** Ruth Wolff; ***C:*** Geoffrey Unsworth; ***M:*** Nino Rota.

Abducted: The Carlina White Story 1/2 **2012** True crime from the Lifetime Channel. In 1987, new mom Joy White has her infant daughter kidnapped from a Harlem hospital by a woman posing as a nurse. Some years later, pregnant teen Netty Pettway (Parker) needs her birth certificate and social security info, which her mom Ann (Ellis) doesn't have. A long investigation ensues but it's not entirely a happy ending. **90m/C; DVD.** Keke Palmer; Aunjanue Ellis; Sherri Shepherd; Roger R. Cross; ***D:*** Vondie Curtis-Hall; ***W:*** Elizabeth Hunter; ***C:*** Thomas M. (Tom) Harting; ***M:*** Terence Blanchard. **CABLE**

The Abduction 1/2 **1996** Fact-based melodrama about Kate Olavsky (Principal) and her abusive marriage to cop Paul (Hays). Afraid to press charges, she finally manages to leave him and get on with her life. But Paul refuses to let Kate go, constantly hounding her, until he takes Kate hostage at gunpoint. **91m/C; VHS, DVD.** Victoria Principal; Robert Hays; Christopher Lawford; William Greenblatt; ***D:*** Larry Peerce; ***W:*** Marshall Goldberg; ***C:*** Tony Imi; ***M:*** Fred Mollin. **CABLE**

Abduction **2007 (R)** Low budget crapfest about a New Jersey town that kidnaps tourists so they can sell women and babies to the wealthy and cut up everyone else to harvest their organs. **106m/C; DVD.** John Orrichio; Tony Rugnetta; Roberto Lombardi; ***D:*** John Orrichio; ***W:*** John Orrichio; ***C:*** John Orrichio; ***M:*** John Orrichio. **VIDEO**

Abduction **WOOF! 2011 (PG-13)** A young man (Lautner) discovers his secret past and must go on the run when his whereabouts are revealed to people seeking him for over a decade. Lautner is unbelievable as the strong leading man type and the film completely flies off the rails in a rushed and senseless final act. And what was the accomplished Weaver thinking when she signed on? Filled with plot holes more interesting to think about than the actual plot. **106m/C; DVD, Blu-Ray.** Taylor Lautner; Lily Collins; Alfred Molina; Jason Isaacs; Maria Bello; Michael Nyqvist; Sigourney Weaver; ***D:*** John Singleton; ***W:*** Shawn Christensen; ***C:*** Peter Menzies, Jr.; ***M:*** Edward Shearmur.

The Abductors **1972 (R)** Caffaro's super-agent takes on international white slavery, a worthy target for any exploitation effort. While the novelty is a tough and intelligent on-screen heroine, sufficient sleaze and violence bring it all down to the proper level of swampland video. Sequel to the never-to-be-forgotten "Ginger." **90m/C; VHS, DVD.** Cheri Caffaro; William Grannel; Richard Smedley; Patrick Wright; Laurie Rose; Jeramie Rain; ***D:*** Don Schain; ***W:*** Don Schain; ***C:*** R. Kent Evans; ***M:*** Robert G. Orpin.

Abdulla the Great *Abdullah's Harem* **1956** A dissolute Middle Eastern monarch falls for a model, who spurns him for an army officer. While distracted by these royal shenanigans, the king is blissfully unaware of his subjects' disaffection—until they revolt. Dares to lampoon Egypt's dead King Farouk, going against conventional Hollywood wisdom ("Farouk in film is boxoffice poison"). **89m/C; VHS, DVD.** *GB* Gregory Ratoff; Kay Kendall; Syd Chaplin; Alexander D'Arcy; ***D:*** Gregory Ratoff; ***C:*** Lee Garmes; ***M:*** Georges Auric.

Abe **2020** Tween Abe (Schnapp) is an aspiring chef who lives in Brooklyn with his half-Israeli and half-Palestinian family. Family dinner times are often scenes of culture clash between the sides, and Abe sometimes is forced to referee their arguments. At the same, he is learning to cook the foods of both cultures and shares his experiences on his video blog. Over time, enthusiastic Abe's culinary experiments blend the flavors of both sides together in unique fashion and bring his family together in unexpected ways. The charming coming of age comedy is well intentioned but rather dull except for Schnapp's zestful performance. **85m/C; DVD.** Noah Schnapp; Seu Jorge; Dagmara Dominczyk; Arian Moayed; Mark Margolis; ***D:*** Fernando Grostein Andrade; ***W:*** Lameece Issaq; Jacob Kader; ***C:*** Blasco Giurato; ***M:*** Gui Amabis.

Abe Lincoln in Illinois *Spirit of the People* **1940** Massey considered this not only his finest film but a part he was "born to play." Correct on both counts, this Hollywood biography follows Lincoln from his log cabin days to his departure for the White House. The Lincoln-Douglass debate scene and Massey's post-presidential election farewell to the citizens of Illinois are nothing short of brilliant. Written by Sherwood from his Pulitzer-Prize winning play. Contrasted with the well-known "Young Mr. Lincoln" (Henry Fonda), its relative anonymity is perplexing. **110m/B; VHS, DVD.** Raymond Massey; Gene Lockhart; Ruth Gordon; Mary Howard; Dorothy Tree; Harvey Stephens; Minor Watson; Alan Baxter; Howard da Silva; Maurice Murphy; Clem Bevans; Herbert Rudley; ***D:*** John Cromwell; ***W:*** Robert Sherwood; ***C:*** James Wong Howe; ***M:*** Roy Webb.

Abel's Field 1/2 **2012 (PG)** Solid, if predictable, faith-based drama. High school senior Seth McArdle (Davis) is caring for his younger sisters after his mother's death and his father's abandonment. Seth gets into trouble and is assigned to after-school work, supervised by groundskeeper Abel (Sorbo), who may be the only one to help Seth before he makes some seriously bad decisions. **104m/C; DVD; Closed Captioned.** Samuel

Davis; Kevin Sorbo; Richard Dillard; *D:* Gordie Haakstad; *W:* Aron Flasher; *C:* Ian Ellis; *M:* Jeff Toyne. **VIDEO**

Aberdeen **2000** Ambitious London attorney Kaisa (Headey) gets a call from her terminally ill mother Helen (Rampling), who lives in Aberdeen, Scotland. Helen wants Kaisa to travel to Oslo and retrieve Tomas (Skargard), her alcoholic and estranged father, so Helen and he can have a deathbed reconciliation. Assertive Kaisa tracks the drunk down and makes him come with her on a nightmare trip back. Lead performances are utterly unsentimental. **103m/C; VHS, DVD.** *NO GB* Stellan Skarsgard; Lena Headey; Ian Hart; Charlotte Rampling; *D:* Hans Petter Moland; *W:* Hans Petter Moland; Kristin Amundsen; *C:* Philip Ogaard; *M:* Zbigniew Preisner.

Aberration **1997 (R)** Amy (Gidley) has traveled to her parents remote cabin and notices a lizard infestation. So she heads to the store for some exterminating equipment and meets biologist Marshall (Bossell), who studies eco-abnormalities. Seems the lizards are vicious mutants who eat Amy's cat and are working their way up the food chain. Doesn't offer many scares. **93m/C; VHS, Streaming.** *AU GB* Pamela Gidley; Simon Bossell; Valery (Valeri Nikolayev) Nikolaev; *D:* Tim Boxell; *W:* Darrin Oura; Scott Lew; *C:* Allen Guilford. **VIDEO**

Abe's Tomb **2007** Micro budget indie film wherein the United States is being devastated by vampires. Small town locals get the idea to resurrect a powerful demon named Abe to stop the vampires despite the fact that they're ancestors were resonsible for putting Abe in the ground. Had the budget been bigger they may have been able to do more with the premise. **94m/C; DVD, Streaming.** Amanda Fire; Ray Basham; Lisa Adore; Manda Webster; Marisa Karoutsos; Stacey Sparks; Timothy Herron; Carl R. Merritt; Danielle Webster; Sherri Foxx; *D:* Amanda Fire; Nikky Irene; Carl R. Merritt; *C:* Amanda Fire; Nikky Irene; Ray Basham; Lisa Adore; Cody Einsfeld; James Merz; Carl R. Merritt; Sherri Foxx; *M:* Pitch Blak; Peter John Ross; Danielle Webster. **VIDEO**

Abigail's Party **1977** Steadman plays the hostess for a very ill-fated dinner party, especially when she realizes her husband has just died on her new carpet. **105m/C; VHS, DVD.** *GB* Alison Steadman; *D:* Mike Leigh. **TV**

Abilene Town **1946** In a post-Civil War Kansas town far from the freeway, Scott is the tough marshal trying to calm the conflict between cattlemen and homesteaders. He also finds time to participate in a romantic triangle with dance hall vixen Dvorak and heart-of-gold Fleming. Snappy pace keeps it interesting. Based on a novel by Ernest Haycox. **90m/B; VHS, DVD.** Randolph Scott; Ann Dvorak; Edgar Buchanan; Rhonda Fleming; Lloyd Bridges; *D:* Edwin L. Marin; *W:* Harold Shumate; *C:* Archie Stout.

Ablaze 1/2 **2000 (R)** Greedy developer Wendell Mays (Arnold) arranges for his industrial refinery to be torched and the ensuing fire and explosion taxes both the fire fighters and the hospital that has to deal with the casualties. Wynorski directs under the pseudonym Jay Andrews. **97m/C; VHS, DVD.** John Bradley; Tom Arnold; Michael Dudikoff; Ice-T; Amanda Pays; Cathy Lee Crosby; Pat Harrington, Jr.; Edward Albert; Mary Jo Catlett; Richard Biggs; *D:* Jim Wynorski; *W:* Steve Latshaw; *C:* Andrea V. Rossotto; *M:* Neal Acree. **VIDEO**

Abner the Invisible Dog **2013** When incompetent thieves swipe a top secret formula, they unintentionally create havoc in the lives of family and their dog. The thieves are able to steal two secret formulas developed by the government. One gives animals speech, while the other creates invisibility. The thieves hide their stash in a chemistry set they think is safe in toy store. However, a father buys the set for his son Chad's (Zykov) 13th birthday and the family dog, Abner, licks both vials. The thieves try to steal their stash back when the boy's parents are away, but Abner helps save the day! **90m/C; DVD, Blu-Ray, Streaming, Download.** David DeLuise; David Chokachi; Daniel Zykov; Molly Morgen Lamont; Robert (Bobby Ray) Shafer; *D:* Fred Olen Ray; *W:* Pat Moran; *C:* Theo Angell; *M:* Matthew Janszen.

Abolition 1/2 **2011** A handyman is taken in by a fallen priest before suffering from blackouts that result in him always waking up near someone in trouble. His compulsions to hlep them out only seem to cause suffering for someone else. **82m/C; DVD, Blu-Ray, Streaming.** *CA* Caroline Williams; Reggie Bannister; Emily Alatalo; Elissa Dowling; Andrew Roth; *D:* Mike Klassen; *W:* Mike Klassen; Chris Lawson; Chantelle Kadyschuk; *C:* Nick Remy Matthews; *M:* Colin Parrish. **VIDEO**

Abominable **2006 (R)** A man wheelchair bound after a mountain climbing incident watched Bigfoot devour a cabin of co-eds next door but no one believes him. **94m/C; DVD, Blu-Ray.** Matt McCoy; Jeffrey Combs; Michael Deak; Paul Gleason; Hayley Joel; Lance Henriksen; Tiffany Shepis; *D:* Ryan Schifrin; *W:* Ryan Schifrin; James Morrison; *C:* Neal Fredericks; *M:* Lalo Schifrin. **VIDEO**

Abominable 1/2 **2019 (PG)** After a playful yeti breaks free from confinement in a Chinese city, he makes his way to a rooftop where he encounters tough girl Yi (Bennett). After healing the yeti's wound and naming him Everest, she teams up with two neighbors, Peng (Tsai) and Jin (Norgay Trainor), to get him home and reunited with his family. As they travel across the country, the group is followed by Dr. Zara (Paulsen) and rare animal collector Burnish (Izzard), who want Everest for their own purposes. The animated feature is sweet and simple to the point of boring, despite an appealing story and moments of graceful imagery. **97m/C; DVD, Blu-Ray.** Chloe Bennet; Albert Tsai; Tenzing Norgay Trainor; Joseph Izzo; Eddie Izzard; *D:* Jill Culton; *W:* Jill Culton; *C:* Robert Edward Crawford; *M:* Rupert Gregson-Williams.

The Abominable Dr. Phibes *Dr. Phibes; The Curse of Dr. Phibes* **1971 (PG)** After being disfigured in a freak car accident that killed his wife, an evil genius decides that the members of a surgical team let his wife die and shall each perish by a different biblical plague. High camp with the veteran cast in top form. **90m/C; VHS, DVD, Blu-Ray.** *GB* Vincent Price; Joseph Cotten; Hugh Griffith; Terry-Thomas; Virginia North; Susan Travers; Alex Scott; Caroline Munro; Peter Jeffrey; Peter Gilmore; Edward Burnham; Sean Bury; David Hutcheson; Maurice Kaufmann; Charles Farrell; *D:* Robert Fuest; *W:* William Goldstein; James Whiton; *C:* Norman Warwick; *M:* Basil Kirchin; Jack Nathan.

The Abominable Snowman *The Abominable Snowman of the Himalayas* **1957** Corny Hammer horror about adventurer Tom Friend (Tucker), Dr. John Rollason (Cushing), and guide Ed Shelley (Brown) searching for the legandary Yeti. The harsh conditions cause the explorers to lose their grip and, after Shelley shoots a Yeti, Rollason begins to suspect that the creatures practice mind control. **91m/B; VHS, DVD, Blu-Ray.** *GB* Peter Cushing; Forrest Tucker; Robert Brown; Richard Wattis; Maureen Connell; *D:* Val Guest; *W:* Nigel Kneale; *C:* Arthur Grant; *M:* Humphrey Searle.

The Abomination **1988 (R)** After a 5,000-year-old creature possesses him during a nightmare, a boy goes on an eye-gouging frenzy. Only the audience gets hurt. **100m/C; VHS, DVD.** Van Connery; Victoria Chaney; Gaye Bottoms; Suzy Meyer; Jude Johnson; Blue Thompson; Scott Davis; *D:* Max Raven.

About a Boy **2002 (PG-13)** After "Bridget Jones's Diary," Grant continues the role of charming cad. This time, he's Will, a 38-year-old bachelor who doesn't work thanks to his father's legacy and eschews lasting emotional commitments. Will's latest dating scheme is that of a single parent who joins support groups to hit on the single mums. Here he meets Marcus (Hoult), the 12-year-old misfit son of seriously depressed Fiona (Collette). Will likes Marcus despite himself and becomes his confidante. He finds romance with single mum Rachel (Weitz) but that's almost beside the point. Adapted from Nick Hornby's novel. **100m/C; VHS, DVD, Blu-Ray.** *US GB* Hugh Grant; Rachel Weisz; Toni Collette; Nicholas Hoult; Isabel Brook; Victoria Smurfit; *D:* Chris Weitz; Paul Weitz; *W:* Chris Weitz; Paul Weitz; Peter Hedges; *C:* Remi Adefarasin; *M:* Badly Drawn Boy.

About Adam **2000 (R)** Adam (Townsend) is a duplicitous Dublin charmer who worms his way into the Owens family. Waitress Lucy (Hudson) falls in love with Adam and takes him to meet her family and before anyone realizes what's happening, Adam seduces both her sisters, telling each woman exactly what she needs to hear. And no one holds a grudge! **98m/C; VHS, DVD.** *IR GB* Stuart Townsend; Kate Hudson; Frances O'Connor; Charlotte Bradley; Rosaleen Linehan; Brendan F. Dempsey; Alan Maher; Tommy Tiernan; Cathleen Bradley; *D:* Gerard Stembridge; *W:* Gerard Stembridge; *C:* Bruno de Keyzer; *M:* Adrian Johnston.

About Alex **2014 (R)** Another riff on "The Big Chill" starts when Alex (Ritter) tries to kill himself, pushing college friends Ben (Parker), Siri (Grace), Josh (Greenfield), Isaac (Minghella) and Sarah (Plaza) into a cabin weekend with their old friend. Old insecurities and resentments sprout up, along with the requisite amount of healing. It's relatively predictable stuff filmed with all the flavor of a TV movie but the cast is remarkably likable, which wins half the battle. **96m/C; DVD, Blu-Ray, Streaming.** Aubrey Plaza; Maggie Grace; Max Minghella; Nate Parker; Max Greenfield; Jason Ritter; Jane Levy; *D:* Jesse Zwick; *W:* Jesse Zwick; *C:* Andre Lascaris; *M:* Joel P. West.

About Cherry 1/2 **2012 (R)** Traditional coming of age story about an abused young woman moving to the big city to procure fame in the adult entertainment industry and a powerful boyfriend with a massive drug addiction. **102m/C; DVD, Blu-Ray, Streaming.** Ashley Hinshaw; Lili Taylor; Dev Patel; Diane Farr; Johnny Weston; *D:* Stephen Elliott; *W:* Stephen Elliott; Lorelei Lee; *C:* Darren Genet; *M:* Jeff Russo.

About Fifty *Fifty-Nothing* **2011 (R)** Amusing midlife comedy. Miserable, heading towards divorce Adam is talked into a golf weekend in Palm Springs by his single pal Jon as they both unwillingly negotiate the facts of middle age. Jon still thinks he can bed half-his-age Alix, who's too smart to fall for his shtick, but she does introduce Adam to her divorced mom Kate. **80m/C; DVD.** Martin Grey; Drew Pillsbury; Wendie Malick; Michaela McManus; Anne-Marie Johnson; Jessalyn Gilsig; *D:* Thomas Johnston; *W:* Martin Grey; Drew Pillsbury; Thomas Johnston; *C:* Keith J. Duggan.

About Last Night. . . **1986 (R)** Semi-realistic comedy-drama which explores the ups and downs of one couple's (Lowe, Moore) relationship. Mostly quality performances, especially Perkins and Belushi as friends of the young lovers. Based on David Mamet's play "Sexual Perversity in Chicago," but considerably softened so that more people would buy tickets at the boxoffice, the film acts as a historical view of contemporary mating rituals before the onset of the AIDS crisis. **113m/C; VHS, DVD, Blu-Ray.** Rob Lowe; Demi Moore; Elizabeth Perkins; James Belushi; George DiCenzo; Robin Thomas; Michael Alldredge; *D:* Edward Zwick; *W:* Tim Kazurinsky; Denise DeClue; *C:* Andrew Dintenfass; *M:* Miles Goodman.

About Last Night 1/2 **2014 (R)** A modern take on a 1974 David Mamet play, previously brought to the big screen in 1986 with Rob Lowe and Demi Moore in the leads. This time around Kevin Hart cranks the raunch-factor to the max as Bernie, a hard-partying player who meets his match in Joan (Hall). The new couple fight over all things sexual, and one-up each other in every phase of life. On paper, it shouldn't have worked, but the razor sharp banter and dynamite chemistry between Hall and Hart overcome all mediocre in story, even as the credits roll. **100m/C; DVD, Blu-Ray.** Kevin Hart; Michael Ealy; Joy Bryant; Regina Hall; Christopher McDonald; Paula Patton; Adam Rodriguez; *D:* Steve Pink; *W:* Leslye Headland; *C:* Michael Barrett; *M:* Marcus Miller.

About Schmidt 1/2 **2002 (R)** Jack's back and playing against type as Warren Schmidt, a man left with virtually no identity once he retires from his ho-hum insurance job. Left only with time to reflect on a meaningless life, he questions everything he once took for granted, including Helen (Squibb), his wife of 42 years. The day after his retirement, the couple shares breakfast before Helen suddenly dies. With nothing left to lose, Schmidt hits the road in a Winnebago to visit his daughter and try to find some meaning in his poorly thought-out life. In Denver, he meets and immediately hates his daughter's cheesy salesman fiance Randall (Mulroney), while Randall's flowsy mother Roberta (Bates) tries to seduce the lonely introvert in a hot tub. Combines humor, pathos, and hope with a first rate performance by Nicholson, who quashes any of his characteristic animation. Davis, Mulroney, and especially Bates are also excellent. **124m/C; VHS, DVD, Blu-Ray.** Jack Nicholson; Hope Davis; Dermot Mulroney; Kathy Bates; Len Cariou; Howard Hesseman; June Squibb; *D:* Alexander Payne; *W:* Alexander Payne; Jim Taylor; *C:* James Glennon; *M:* Rolfe Kent. Golden Globes '03: Actor--Drama (Nicholson), Screenplay; L.A. Film Critics '02: Actor (Nicholson), Film, Screenplay; Natl. Bd. of Review '02: Support. Actress (Bates).

About Scout **2015** Indie drama centered on a young girl's quest to find her younger sister. A native of rural Texas, Scout (Ennenga) is a rebellious Goth who forms an instantaneous bond with Sam (Frecheville) when they first meet. Sam is a suicidal mental patient and a native of New York. After Scout's deadbeat father takes her younger sister Lulu (Aprile), she convinces Sam to take a road trip across West Texas in search of her beloved sibling. As they travel through small Texas towns, the pair botch a convenience store robbery which makes their road trip into a quest to evade law enforcement. **109m/C; DVD, Streaming, Download.** India Ennenga; James Frecheville; Onata Aprile; Jane Seymour; Nikki Reed; *D:* Laurie Weltz; *W:* Laurie Weltz; *C:* Austin F. Schmidt; *M:* John Dragonetti.

About Sunny **2012** Star Ambrose propels this recession-themed examination of a single mother trying to keep her head above water and hold on to her daughter as best she can. Writer/director Wizemann doesn't hold back from presenting his conflicted protagonist in a three-dimensional way that's heartbreaking. The fact is that Angela may not be able to give her daughter Sunny (Scott) what she needs and that the girl could conceivably be better off without her economically- and responsibility-deprived mother. Ambrose gives a fantastic performance by making a possibly clichéd character feel devastatingly real. **104m/C; Streaming.** Lauren Ambrose; Audrey P. Scott; Dylan Baker; David Conrad; Penelope Ann Miller; *D:* Bryan Wizemann; *W:* Bryan Wizemann; *C:* Mark Schwartzbard; *M:* Jeff Grace.

About Time 1/2 **2013 (R)** A rom com about a young man, Tim (Gleeson), who can time travel may sound like a recipe for drivel, but writer/director Curtis ends up with a wistful, sentimental gem. Though he time travels, he can't drastically alter history but he can fine-tune his life, starting with Mary (a luminous McAdams) with whom he has fallen in love. Tim has the glorious gift of being able to hit restart to come up with the perfect date, romantic proposal, etc. Curtis' comedy is gentle and sweet, anchored by characters you truly hope finally get it right. **123m/C; DVD, Blu-Ray.** Domhnall Gleeson; Rachel McAdams; Bill Nighy; Tom Hollander; Margot Robbie; *D:* Richard Curtis; *W:* Richard Curtis; *C:* John Guleserian; *M:* Nick Laird-Clowes.

Above and Beyond **1953** Good performance by Taylor as Col. Paul Tibbets, the man who piloted the Enola Gay, which dropped the atomic bomb on Hiroshima. Focuses on the secrecy of the mission and the strain this puts on Tibbets marriage. Exciting action sequences of the mission itself. **122m/B; VHS, DVD.** Robert Taylor; Eleanor Parker; James Whitmore; Larry Keating; Larry Gates; Robert Burton; Jim Backus; Marilyn Erskine; Steve (Stephen) Dunne; John Pickard; Hayden Rorke; Lawrence (Larry) Dobkin; Jack Raine; Jeff Richards; Barbara Ruick; Harlan Warde; John Close; Frank Gerstle; Dabbs Greer; Ewing Mitchell; Gregory Walcott; John Baer; Jonathon Cott; Dick Simmons; John McKee; G. Pat Collins; John Hedloe; Mack Williams; Dorothy Kennedy; *D:* Melvin Frank; Norman Panama; *W:* Melvin Frank; Norman Panama; Beirne Lay, Jr.; *C:* Ray June; *M:* Hugo Friedhofer.

Above and Beyond **2006** In 1940, German U-boats prevent American ships from transporting plane parts to England so the Atlantic Ferry Command is set up. The RAF will fly the planes from Gander, Newfoundland to England instead. Capt. Don Bennett is commissioned to start the operation at the airfield run by Nathan Burgess, who isn't happy about the increased military presence. Nathan also isn't happy when ex-girlfriend Shelagh returns as a liaison since she's now interested in pilot Bill Jacobson. Has a number of inaccuracies (particularly regarding the planes) that will bother those in the know but otherwise is a decent Canadian TV miniseries. **179m/C; DVD.** *CA* Richard E. Grant; Liane Balaban; Jonathan Scarfe; Allan Hawco; Kenneth Welsh; Jason Priestley; Joss Ackland; Peter MacNeill; Robert Wisden; ***D:*** Sturla Gunnarsson; ***W:*** John W. Doyle; Lisa Porter; ***C:*** Rene Ohashi; ***M:*** Jonathan Goldsmith. **TV**

Above Suspicion **1943** MacMurray and Crawford are American honeymooners (poor Fred!) asked to assist an international intelligence organization. They engage the Nazis in a tense battle of wits. Well-made and engaging. **91m/B; VHS, DVD.** Joan Crawford; Fred MacMurray; Conrad Veidt; Basil Rathbone; Reginald Owen; Richard Ainley; Cecil Cunningham; ***D:*** Richard Thorpe; ***W:*** Patricia Coleman; ***C:*** Robert Planck; ***M:*** Bronislau Kaper.

Above Suspicion **1995 (R)** Dempsey Cain (Reeve) seems to be the perfect cop, as well as a loving husband and father and a mentor to his younger brother. But when Cain is paralyzed by a drug dealer's bullet, he begins to notice just how close his wife (Cattrall) and brother (Kerr) are. There's adultery, there's murder, and there's the cop who just may be a cold-blooded killer. Unnervingly, Reeve plays a paraplegic in the last movie he made before his own paralyzing riding accident. **92m/C; VHS, DVD.** Christopher Reeve; Kim Cattrall; Joe Mantegna; Edward Kerr; ***D:*** Steven Schachter. **CABLE**

Above Suspicion **2000 (R)** James Stockton (Bakula) seems like the perfect family man but his wife Lisa (Sciorra) starts becoming suspicious of his past—fearing that he's a killer on the lam. **99m/C; VHS, DVD.** Scott Bakula; Annabella Sciorra; George Dzundza; Ed Asner; Jack Blessing; ***D:*** Steven La Rocque.

Above the Law **1988 (R)** In his debut, Seagal does his wooden best to portray a tough Chicago police detective planning an enormous drug bust of one of the biggest felons in the state. Unfortunately, the FBI has ordered him to back off and find another bust. The reasons are almost as complex as Seagal's character, and like most details of the flick, stupid. However, people don't watch these movies for the acting or the plot, but for the fight scenes, which are well-choreographed and violent. Watch it with someone you love. **99m/C; VHS, DVD, Blu-Ray.** Steven Seagal; Pam Grier; Henry Silva; Sharon Stone; Ron Dean; Daniel Faraldo; Chelcie Ross; Thalmus Rasulala; Michael Rooker; ***D:*** Andrew Davis; ***W:*** Andrew Davis; Steven Pressfield; ***C:*** Robert Steadman; ***M:*** David Michael Frank.

Above the Rim **½ 1994 (R)** Vulgar, violent hoopster drama about a fiercely competitive inner-city playground game. Kyle-Lee Watson (Martin), a self-involved high school star raised by a saintly single mom (Pinkins), is torn between the lure of the streets and his college recruiting chances. His odds aren't made any easier by homeboy hustler Birdie (Shakur), who wants to improve his chances of making money on the local games by making sure Watson plays for his team. Energetic b-ball sequences, strong performances lose impact amid formulaic melodrama and the usual obscenities. Debut for director Pollack. **97m/C; VHS, DVD.** Duane Martin; Tupac Shakur; Leon; Marlon Wayans; Tonya Pinkins; Bernie Mac; ***D:*** Jeff Pollack; ***W:*** Jeff Pollack; Barry Michael Cooper; ***M:*** Marcus Miller.

Above Us the Waves **1955** During WWII, the British navy immobilizes a huge German battleship off the coast of Norway. Effectively dramatizes the British naval preparations for what seemed a suicidal mission: using midget submarines to plant underwater explosives on the hull of the German vessel and detonating them before the Germans could detect the danger. **92m/C; VHS, DVD.** *GB* John Mills; John Gregson; Donald Sinden; James Robertson Justice; Michael Medwin; James Kenney; O.E. Hasse; Theodore Bikel; Thomas Heathcote; Lee Patterson; Lyndon Brook; Anthony Newley; ***D:*** Ralph Thomas.

Abraham **½ 1994** Biblical epic chronicling the Old Testament story of humble shepherd Abraham (Harris), who's commanded by God to lead his family into the promised land of Canaan. Among his family's many trials will be God's command that Abraham sacrifice his son Isaac as a test of faith and obedience. Filmed on location in Morocco with a commanding performance by Harris that somewhat redeems the film's dullness. **175m/C; VHS, DVD.** Richard Harris; Barbara Hershey; Maximilian Schell; Vittorio Gassman; Carolina Rosi; Gottfried John; Kevin McNally; ***D:*** Joseph Sargent; ***W:*** Robert McKee; ***C:*** Raffaele Mertes; ***M:*** Ennio Morricone; Marco Frisina. **CABLE**

Abraham Lincoln **½ 1930** Griffith's first talking movie takes Abraham Lincoln from his birth through his assassination. This restored version includes the original slavery sequences which were believed to be lost, but obviously were not. Musical score included. **97m/B; VHS, DVD, Blu-Ray.** Walter Huston; Una Merkel; Kay Hammond; E. Alyn (Fred) Warren; Hobart Bosworth; Henry B. Walthall; Russell Simpson; Ian Keith; Frank Campeau; ***D:*** D.W. Griffith; ***C:*** Karl Struss.

Abraham Lincoln: Vampire Hunter **½ 2012 (R)** Working from Seth Grahame-Smith's 2010 bestselling novel (who adapted the script), producer Tim Burton and director Bekmambetov drain the life out of this unique concept by presenting something remarkably lacking in personality. The basis of the 3D action extravaganza is simple enough--the legendary President is re-imagined as a killer of the undead after seeing his mom die at the fangs of a vampire as a child. But, save for two clever action scenes, the result is bloody (literally) boring. It doesn't help that the leading man has all the charisma of a robot at Disney's Hall of Presidents. **105m/C; DVD, Blu-Ray, Streaming.** Benjamin Walker; Dominic Cooper; Anthony Mackie; Mary Elizabeth Winstead; Rufus Sewell; ***D:*** Timur Bekmambetov; ***W:*** Seth Graham-Smith; ***C:*** Caleb Deschanel; ***M:*** Henry Jackman.

Abraham Lincoln vs. Zombies **WOOF! 2012 (R)** Another attempt by Asylum to cash in on making a film with a name similar to a much bigger studio release. President Lincoln has to rehearse the Gettysburg Address while sneaking into Georgia with the Secret Service to quell a zombie uprising. **90m/C; DVD, Blu-Ray, Streaming.** Bill Oberst, Jr.; Jason Vail; Don McGraw; Richard Schenkman; Baby Norman; ***D:*** Richard Schenkman; ***W:*** Richard Schenkman; Karl T. Hirsch; J. Lauren Proctor; ***C:*** Tim Gill; ***M:*** Chris Ridenhour. **VIDEO**

Abraham's Valley *Vale Abraao; Valley of Abraham* **1993** Beautiful Ema (Silveira) is forced into a wealthy marriage to a friend of her father's and they move to the vineyards of Abraham's Valley where the bride knows no one. Unhappy, Ema refuses to submit to her husband and decides to take a lover of her own. Based on the novel by Augustina Bessa-Luis. Portuguese with subtitles. **180m/C; VHS, DVD.** *PT* Leonor Silveira; Luis Miguel Cintra; Diogo Doria; Ruy de Carvalho; Luis Lima Barreto; ***D:*** Manoel de Oliveira; ***W:*** Manoel de Oliveira; ***C:*** Mario Barroso.

Abraxas: Guardian of the Universe **½** *Abraxas* **1990 (R)** Good space cop versus bad space cop with an ecological twist. Good-guy Abraxas (Ventura) has the task of stopping planets from destroying their environments and fighting senseless wars. His ex-partner Secundas (Ole-Thorsen) has his own mission, seeking an anti-life power which could destroy the universe. They decide to fight it out, using Earth as the battleground. Also available in an edited PG-13 version. **90m/C; VHS, DVD.** Jesse Ventura; Sven-Ole Thorsen; Damian Lee; Marjorie Bransfield; Ken Quinn; Marilyn Lightstone; Moses Znaimer; Layne Coleman; Sonja Belliveau; James Belushi; ***D:*** Damian Lee; ***W:*** Damian Lee; ***C:*** Curtis Petersen.

The Absence of Light *Bio Creature Rasing* **2006** Lame micro budget flick about a scientist discovering the secret of life who immediately becomes pursued by agents of the two mega corporations secretly controlling America. **77m/C; DVD.** Tom Savini; Caroline Munro; ***D:*** Patrick Desmond; ***W:*** Patrick Desmond; ***C:*** Patrick Desmond; ***M:*** Andy L. Halter; Todd Skeie. **VIDEO**

Absence of Malice **½ 1981 (PG)** High-minded story about the harm that the news media can inflict. Field is the earnest reporter who, after being fed some facts by an unscrupulous federal investigator, writes a story implicating Newman in a murder he didn't commit. Field hides behind journalistic confidentiality privilege to put off the outraged Newman, who loses a friend to suicide during the debacle. Interesting performances by Field and Newman. **116m/C; VHS, DVD.** Paul Newman; Sally Field; Bob Balaban; Melinda Dillon; Luther Adler; Barry Primus; Josef Sommer; John Harkins; Don Hood; Wilford Brimley; ***D:*** Sydney Pollack; ***W:*** Kurt Luedtke; ***C:*** Owen Roizman; ***M:*** Dave Grusin.

Absence of the Good **1999 (R)** Homicide detective Caleb Barnes (Baldwin) is mourning the accidental death of his only child while investigating a series of murders in Salt Lake City. He's under pressure to solve the case, even as his home life is disintegrating, and Caleb's investigation leads to a family's malignant history. **99m/C; VHS, DVD.** Stephen Baldwin; Tyne Daly; Allen Garfield; Robert Knepper; ***D:*** John Flynn; ***W:*** James Reid.

The Absent **2011** Twin brothers part ways when one of them poisons their parents after he finds out they plan to murder him for insurance money. Fast forward 25 years and he's released and free to interfere with his brother's life again. **80m/C; DVD, Streaming.** Jesse Gullion; Lucas Dick; Bryan Kirkwood; Denny Kirkwood; Matthew Josten; Sam Ball; Kelly B. Eviston; Jamielyn Kane; Moniqua Plante; Vanessa Zima; Yvonne Zima; Jennifer Blanc; ***D:*** Sage Bannick; ***W:*** Sage Bannick; Damon Abdallah; Ari Bernstein; ***C:*** Eric Curtis. **VIDEO**

The Absent-Minded Professor **½ 1961** Classic dumb Disney fantasy of the era. A professor accidentally invents an anti-gravity substance called flubber, causing inanimate objects and people to become airborne. Great sequence of the losing school basketball team taking advantage of flubber during a game. MacMurray is convincing as the absent-minded genius in this newly colored version. Followed by "Son of Flubber." **97m/C; VHS, DVD, Blu-Ray.** Fred MacMurray; Nancy Olson; Keenan Wynn; Tommy Kirk; Leon Ames; Ed Wynn; Edward Andrews; Wally Brown; Wendell Holmes; ***D:*** Robert Stevenson; ***W:*** Bill Walsh; ***C:*** Edward Colman; ***M:*** George Bruns.

Absentia **2011 (R)** Callie (Katie Parker) moves in with her sister, to help her get her life back together after her husband's disappearance. She quickly discovers many local disappearances all connected to a nearby tunnel. **91m/C; DVD, Streaming.** Katie Parker; Courtney Bell; Dave Levine; Morgan Peter Brown; Justin Gordon; ***D:*** Mike Flanagan; ***W:*** Mike Flanagan; ***C:*** Rustin Cerveny; ***M:*** Ryan David Leack. **VIDEO**

Absolute Beginners **1986 (PG)** Fervently stylish camp musical exploring the lives of British teenagers in the 1950s never quite gets untracked, although MTV video moments fill out a spare plotline. Based on a novel by Colin MacInnes. **107m/C; VHS, DVD, Blu-Ray.** *GB* David Bowie; Ray Davies; Mandy Rice-Davies; James Fox; Eddie O'Connell; Patsy Kensit; Anita Morris; Sade Adu; Sandie Shaw; ***D:*** Julien Temple; ***W:*** Richard Burridge; Don MacPherson; ***C:*** Oliver Stapleton.

Absolute Deception **½ 2013 (R)** Generic action-thriller. Magazine reporter Rebecca Scott (Vaugier) is informed by FBI agent John Nelson (Gooding Jr.) that her long-presumed dead husband Miles has, in fact, just been murdered. Miles was an informant and Rebecca and John travel to Australia's Gold Coast for amswers from people who want to stop their investigation in the same deadly manner. **92m/C; DVD.** Cuba Gooding, Jr.; Emmanuelle Vaugier; Evert McQueen; Ty Hungerford; ***D:*** Brian Trenchard-Smith; ***W:*** Kraig Wenman; ***C:*** Dan Macarthur; ***M:*** Michael Richard Plowman. **VIDEO**

Absolute Power **½ 1997 (R)** Eastwood is "In the Line of Fire," (against the very agents he previously glorified) as an expert thief being pursued by rogue Secret Service men in this fast-paced thriller. While looting a Washington official's place, Luther (Eastwood) inadvertently witnesses a murder committed by none other than U.S. President Richmond (Hackman) and his goons. Immediately, a cover-up is organized by his unbalanced chief-of-staff (Davis) and Luther becomes the prime suspect. Harris gives his usual solid performance as the homicide detective. Eastwood's simple directorial style keeps up the suspense and propels the film steadily forward, alongside a generally solid plot that gets a bit improbable near the end. Based on the novel by David Baldacci. **120m/C; VHS, DVD, Blu-Ray.** Clint Eastwood; Gene Hackman; Ed Harris; Laura Linney; Judy Davis; Scott Glenn; Dennis Haysbert; E.G. Marshall; Melora Hardin; ***D:*** Clint Eastwood; ***W:*** William Goldman; ***C:*** Jack N. Green; ***M:*** Lennie Niehaus.

Absolute Zero **2005** Climatologist David Koch (Fahey) warns that a shift in the earth's polarity (thanks to global warming) could quickly cause a second ice age. When his predictions start coming true, scientist have to find a way to prevent the temps from reaching absolute zero and destroying life as we know it. **86m/C; DVD.** Jeff Fahey; Erika Eleniak; Bill Dow; Jessica Amlee; Michael Ryan; Fred Ewanuick; Brittney Irvin; ***D:*** Robert Lee; ***W:*** Sarah Watson; ***C:*** Adam Sliwinski; ***M:*** Annette Ducharme; John Webster. **CABLE**

Absolutely Anything **½ 2017 (R)** A group of CGI aliens (voiced by Monty Python alums) grant a human (Pegg) infinite powers as a test: unless he uses them for good, they'll destroy the planet. Sure, he'll get around to that, but first the childish vignettes -- seeing the hot neighbor in her underwear, increasing the size of his manhood, giving his dog (Williams) speech. Pegg plays a likeable enough goof, but there's not enough originality here to elicit more than a few grins. **85m/C; DVD.** Simon Pegg; Kate Beckinsale; Sanjeev Bhaskar; Rob Riggle; ***V:*** Robin Williams; ***D:*** Terry Jones; ***W:*** Terry Jones; Gavin Scott; ***C:*** Peter Hannan; ***M:*** George Fenton.

Absolutely Fabulous: The Movie **2016 (R)** Edina (Saunders) and Patsy's (Lumley) boozy, self-centered life is brought to a halt when they accidentally knock model Kate Moss into the river Thames. Fleeing the resulting media firestorm, they wind up in France, scheming for a way to become wealthy enough to never work again. Longtime fans of the TV show will love, but it will be lost on other audiences. **91m/C; DVD, Blu-Ray, Streaming.** *UK US* Jennifer Saunders; Joanna Lumley; Julia Sawalha; Jane Horrocks; June Whitfield; ***D:*** Mandie Fletcher; ***W:*** Jennifer Saunders; ***C:*** Chris Goodger; ***M:*** Jake Monaco.

Absolution **1981 (R)** Two English boys trapped in a Catholic boarding school conspire to drive a tyrannical priest over the edge of sanity. As a result, bad things (including murder) occur. Burton is interesting in sadistic character study. Not released in the U.S. until 1988 following Burton's death, maybe due to something written in the will. **105m/C; VHS, DVD, Blu-Ray.** *GB* Richard Burton; Dominic Guard; Dai Bradley; Andrew Keir; Billy Connolly; Willoughby Gray; Preston Lockwood; James Ottaway; Brook Williams; Jon Plowman; Robin Soans; Trevor Martin; ***D:*** Anthony Page; ***W:*** Anthony Shaffer; ***C:*** John Coquillon; ***M:*** Stanley Myers.

Absolution **WOOF!** *The Journey: Absolution* **1997** Bad acting, bad dialogue, cretinous plot even by low-budget sci fi standards. A meteor causes severe planetary destruction and one set of survivors lives in an Arctic military colony. Ryan Murphy is sent to investigate the disappearance of a soldier and sees that the colony's tyrannical leader has the inhabitants involved in some weird outer space conspiracy. **100m/C; DVD.** Mario Lopez; Jaime Pressly; Richard Grieco; Greg Serano; Justin Walker; ***D:*** David DeCoteau; ***W:*** Chris Chaffin; ***C:*** Howard Wexler; ***M:*** Marco Marinangeli. **VIDEO**

Absolution **2003** An angel who wants to know what being human is like becomes involved in a deal to turn chemicals used in nuclear weapons into vhs tape shells and ships them overseas disguised as porn. **99m/B; DVD.** John Specht; Jonas Moses; Paul Wendell; Terry Hopper; Eric Whitman; Daniel Byington; Bryan Lane; Eric Peniston; Leah Schumacher; Emily Haack; Halley Moore; Anna Knobeloch; *D:* John Specht; *W:* John Specht; Jonas Moses; Stacy Key. **VIDEO**

Absolution **2005** New York journalist Bettina hasn't been back to her Ohio hometown in years but gets an assignment to investigate a man who's allegedly performing hands-on miracles. She's shocked to find out it's her high school boyfriend Paolo, who's now comatose but whose mother Maria lays his hands on the sick. Flashbacks show why Bettina had to get away from her own dysfunctional family. **90m/C; DVD.** Samantha Mathis; Stephen McHattie; Nicky Guadagni; Dan Petronijevic; Peter Mooney; Maria Ricossa; Stefano DiMatteo; *D:* Holly Dale; *W:* Bethany Rooney; *C:* Malcolm Cross; *M:* Zack Ryan. **CABLE**

The Abyss *L'Oeuvre au Noir* **1989 (PG-13)** Underwater sci-fi adventure about a team of oil-drilling divers pressed into service by the navy to locate and disarm an inoperative nuclear submarine. A high-tech thriller with fab footage underwater and pulsating score. **140m/C; VHS, DVD.** Ed Harris; Mary Elizabeth Mastrantonio; Todd Graff; Michael Biehn; John Bedford Lloyd; J.C. Quinn; Leo Burmester; Kidd Brewer, Jr.; Kimberly Scott; Adam Nelson; George Robert Kirk; Chris Elliott; Jimmie Ray Weeks; *D:* James Cameron; *W:* James Cameron; *C:* Mikael Salomon; *M:* Alan Silvestri. Oscars '89: Visual FX.

Acapulco Gold ½ **1978 (PG)** Mockumentary follows Gortner as he's framed for drug smuggling and becomes entangled in a Hawaiian drug deal. Not worth the time it'll take to track down a copy. **105m/C; DVD, Blu-Ray.** Marjoe Gortner; Robert Lansing; Ed Nelson; John Harkins; Lawrence Casey; Phil Hoover; *D:* Burt Brinckerhoff; *W:* Don Enright; *C:* Robert Steadman; *M:* Craig Safan.

Accatone! **1961** Accatone (Citti), a failure as a pimp, tries his luck as a thief. Hailed as a return to Italian neo-realism, this is a gritty, despairing, and dark look at the lives of the street people of Rome. Pasolini's first outing, adapted by the director from his novel, "A Violent Life." Pasolini served as mentor to Bernardo Bertolucci, listed in the credits as an assistant director. **116m/B; VHS, DVD.** *IT* Franco Citti; Franca Pasut; Roberto Scaringelli; Silvana Corsini; Paolo Guidi; Adriana Asti; *D:* Pier Paolo Pasolini; *W:* Pier Paolo Pasolini; *C:* Tonino Delli Colli.

Acceptable Risk **2001** Pharmaceutical scientist Edward Wells (Lowe) discovers a strange fungus in a walled-in part of his basement. He takes it into the lab, finds unusual healing properties in the substance, and immediately begins to test it on himself. At first, he feels superhuman, but monstrous side effects quickly surface. There is some suspense in this TV movie, but the inconsistent story and poor performances are hard to get past. **92m/C; DVD.** Chad Lowe; Kelly Rutherford; Sean Patrick Flanery; Patty McCormack; Danielle von Zerneck; *D:* William A. Graham; *W:* Michael J. Murray; *C:* Eyal Grodin. **TV**

Acceptance ½ **2009** Disjointed and sentimental Lifetime comedy about high school seniors and the stress-ridden process of college applications. Taylor's (Whitman) parents have separated, Maya's (Daryanani) immigrant parents expect her to pursue science studies while she prefers the arts, and Harry (Keltz) is only (and obsessively) interested in going to Harvard. There are some minor subplots featuring the adults but they don't add up to much. Adaptation of the Susan Coll novel. **90m/C; DVD.** Mae Whitman; Deepti Daryanani; Jonathan Keltz; Joan Cusack; Mark Moses; Kiersten Warren; Brigid Brannagh; Rob Mayes; *D:* Sanaa Hamri; *W:* Suzette Couture; *C:* Anthony B. Richmond; *M:* Richard (Rick) Marvin; Alan Derian. **CABLE**

Accepted ½ **2006 (PG-13)** Flunky campus farce about what to do after getting one too many thin envelopes from college admissions offices: create your own university. Bartleby (Long) and his buds pretend to matriculate at the fictitious South Harmon Institute of Technology. So-so jokes about beer and babes and that oh-so-hilarious acronym abound, until the tale attempts to take an unexpectedly touching turn. Ultimately lands on the failing side of the campus-movie bell curve (with "Animal House" and "Back to School" at the top of the class). **92m/C; DVD.** Justin Long; Blake Lively; Mark Derwin; Anthony Heald; Adam Herschman; Jonah Hill; Columbus Short; Maria Thayer; Lewis Black; Ann Cusack; Travis Van Winkle; Hannah Marks; Diora Baird; *D:* Steve Pink; *W:* Mark Perez; Adam Cooper; Bill Collage; *C:* Matthew F. Leonetti; *M:* David Schommer.

Accident ½ **1967** A tangled web of guilt, remorse, humor and thwarted sexuality is unravelled against the background of the English countryside in this complex story of an Oxford love triangle. An inside view of English repression at the university level adapted for the screen by Pinter from the novel by Nicholas Mosley. Long-winded but occasionally engrossing character study with interesting performances. **100m/C; VHS, DVD, Blu-Ray.** *GB* Dirk Bogarde; Michael York; Stanley Baker; Jacqueline Sassard; Delphine Seyrig; Alexander Knox; Vivien Merchant; Freddie Jones; Harold Pinter; *D:* Joseph Losey; *W:* Harold Pinter; *C:* Gerry Fisher; *M:* John Dankworth. Cannes '67: Grand Jury Prize.

The Accidental Husband ½ **2008 (PG-13)** In this feeble romcom, New York firefighter Patrick Sullivan (Morgan) is incensed when his fiancee dumps him, thanks to the advice of frigid radio therapist Emma Lloyd (Thurman). In an unlikely chain of events, Patrick forges a marriage license between himself and the doc that throws a wrench into Emma's plans with her own stuffy fiance Richard (Firth). Morgan is hunky but Thurman is boring. **91m/C; DVD.** Uma Thurman; Jeffrey Dean Morgan; Colin Firth; Justina Machado; Sam Shepard; Lindsay Sloane; Ajay Naidu; Keir Dullea; *D:* Griffin Dunne; *W:* Mimi Hare; Clare Naylor; Bonnie Sikowitz; *C:* William Rexer; *M:* Andrea Guerra. **VIDEO**

Accidental Love **2015 (PG-13)** Production on this stinker started in 2008 (as "Nailed") under the directorial hand of David O. Russell, who completely disowned the final product. Financial difficulties caused its ultimate demise, even after most of it was filmed, and so a quiet release under a new name and a director title (of the fake Stephen Greene) raised eyebrows. It's clear why this story of a small-town waitress (Biel) accidentally shot in the head by a nail gun and made hypersexual as a result was buried for years. Despite game work by Gyllenhaal and Biel--it's no accident that it's awful. **100m/C; DVD, Blu-Ray.** Jessica Biel; Raymond L. Brown, Jr.; Jenny Gulley; Beverly D'Angelo; Steve Boles; *D:* David O. Russell; *W:* Kristin Gore; Matthew Silverstein; Dave Jeser; *C:* Max Malkin; *M:* John Swihart.

The Accidental Spy ½ **2001 (R)** Salesman Bei (Chan) longs for some excitement in his life but gets more than anticipated when he foils the plans of two bank robbers. The resulting publicity leads Bei to discover that he's the long-lost son of a wealthy Korean businessman who also turns out to be a spy and Bei decides to join the family profession. **87m/C; VHS, DVD.** *CH* Jackie Chan; Eric Tsang; Vivian Hsu; Alfred Cheung; Min-jeong Kim; Hsing-kuo Wu; *D:* Teddy Chen; *W:* Ivy Ho; *C:* Wing-Hung Wong; *M:* Peter Kam.

The Accidental Tourist ½ **1988 (PG)** A bittersweet and subtle story, adapted faithfully from Anne Tyler's novel, of an introverted, grieving man who learns to love again after meeting an unconventional woman. After his son's death and subsequent separation from wife Turner, Macon Leary (Hurt) avoids emotional confrontation, burying himself in routines with the aid of his obsessive-compulsive siblings. Kooky dogtrainer Muriel Pritchett (an exuberant Davis) wins his attention, but not without struggle. Hurt effectively uses small gestures to describe Macon's emotional journey, while Davis grabs hearts with her open performance. Outstanding supporting cast. **121m/C; DVD, Blu-Ray.** William Hurt; Geena Davis; Kathleen Turner; Ed Begley, Jr.; David Ogden Stiers; Bill Pullman; Amy Wright; *D:* Lawrence Kasdan; *W:* Lawrence Kasdan; *C:* John Bailey; *M:* John Williams. Oscars '88: Support. Actress (Davis); N.Y. Film Critics '88: Film.

Accidents ½ **1989 (R)** A scientist discovers that his invention has been stolen and is going to be used to cause worldwide havoc. He becomes concerned and spends the remainder of the movie trying to relieve himself of anxiety. **90m/C; VHS, Streaming.** Edward Albert; Leigh Taylor-Young; Jon Cypher; *D:* Gideon Amir.

Accidents Happen ½ **2009 (R)** Meandering melodrama finds a tragedy pulling apart the dysfunctional Conway family. Since he can't connect with his bitter, grief-stricken mom (Davis), 15-year-old Billy (Gilbertson) copes by shunning responsibility and getting involved in pranks that usually backfire. **92m/C; DVD.** *AU* Geena Davis; Harrison Gilbertson; Harry Cook; Joel Tobeck; Anthony (Tony) Vorno; Sarah Woods; *D:* Andrew Lancaster; *W:* Brian Carbee; *C:* Ben Nott; *M:* Antony Partos.

The Accompanist ½ **2020** Recently divorced, Jason Holden (Keeve) works as an accompanist at a dance studio where his children once took lessons. Jason becomes the object of desire of troubled yet talented ballet dancer Brandon (Palomino). After inviting Jason to become his private accompanist, Jason begins to return his feelings. The growing romance faces roadblocks because Brandon is reluctant to leave his physically abusive relationship with his current boyfriend. Though the film tries to be moving in its melodramatic exploration of gay romance and features strong performances by Keeve, it is repetitive and full of tangents. **93m/C; DVD.** Juliet Doherty; Angelle Brooks; Frederick Keeve; Ricky Palomino; Jeanette Driver; *D:* Frederick Keeve; *W:* Frederick Keeve; *C:* David M. Parks; *M:* Frederick Keeve. **VIDEO**

According to Greta *Greta* **2008 (PG-13)** Duff acquits herself quite well as a suicidal teen who's fobbed off on her grandparents for the summer by her preoccupied mother. Greta gets a job as a waitress and starts an interracial romance with the unfortunately-named Julie (Ross), the cook. But her grandparents really freak when they find out the boy has a criminal past. **91m/C; DVD.** Hilary Duff; Evan Ross; Ellen Burstyn; Michael Murphy; Melissa Leo; *D:* Nancy Bardawil; *W:* Michael Gilvary; *C:* Michael Lohmann; *M:* Joseph E. Nordstrom.

The Accountant **2016 (R)** This action-thriller features a very solid performance from Affleck but comes undone by the time the credits roll. Christian Wolff (Affleck) is a high-functioning autistic man who serves as the accountant for numerous criminal enterprises, and ends up having a highly trained set of killer skills as well. He's kind of like Jason Bourne with more math skills and fewer social ones. It's decent, but gets too silly for its own good in a twist-filled climax. **128m/C; DVD, Blu-Ray.** Ben Affleck; Anna Kendrick; J.K. Simmons; Jon Bernthal; Jeffrey Tambor; *D:* Gavin O'Connor; *W:* Bill Dubuque; *C:* Seamus McGarvey; *M:* Mark Isham.

The Accursed ½ **1957** A 'dark old house' mystery. A group of former WWII resistance fighters meet each year at the home of Col. Charles Price (Wolfit) to commemorate the murder of their leader by the Nazis. Price gets a phone call saying they were betrayed and the traitor is now killing off the rest of the group, but the caller is killed before he reveals the name. Now, everyone is a suspect when they meet. **74m/B; DVD.** *UK* Donald Wolfit; Robert Bray; Jane Griffiths; Anton Diffring; Christopher Lee; Karel Stepanek; Carl Jaffe; *D:* Michael McCarthy; *W:* Michael McCarthy; *C:* Bert Mason; *M:* Jackie Brown.

Accused ½ **1936** Married dancers Fairbanks and Del Rio are working in a Parisian revue when the show's sultry leading lady (Desmond) makes a pass at Fairbanks. Though he's turned her down, through a series of misunderstandings Del Rio believes the worst and the two women get into a vicious argument. When the star is found dead guess who gets the blame? Del Rio is lovely, Desmond is spiteful, and Fairbanks serves as a fine object of two women's affections. **83m/B; VHS, DVD.** *GB* Douglas Fairbanks, Jr.; Dolores Del Rio; Florence Desmond; Basil Sydney; Athole Stewart; Esme Percy; Googie Withers; Cecil Humphreys; *D:* Thornton Freeland.

The Accused **1988 (R)** Provocative treatment of a true story involving a young woman gang raped in a bar while onlookers cheer. McGillis is the assistant district attorney who takes on the case and must contend with the victim's questionable past and a powerful lawyer hired by a wealthy defendant's parents. As the victim with a past, Foster gives an Oscar-winning performance that won raves for its strength and complexity. **110m/C; VHS, DVD.** Jodie Foster; Kelly McGillis; Bernie Coulson; Leo Rossi; Ann Hearn; Carmen Argenziano; Steve Antin; Tom O'Brien; Peter Van Norden; Woody Brown; *D:* Jonathan Kaplan; *W:* Tom Topor; *C:* Ralf Bode; *M:* Brad Fiedel. Oscars '88: Actress (Foster); Golden Globes '89: Actress--Drama (Foster); Natl. Bd. of Review '88: Actress (Foster).

Accused at 17 **2009** Lifetime drama. High schooler Bianca complains to her best friends Fallyn and Sarah that her boyfriend Chad has cheated with slut Dory. A revenge plot goes awry when Fallyn loses her temper and kills Dory. When the cops start investigating, she pins the blame on Bianca and tries bullying Sarah into keeping quiet while Bianca's mom Jacqui works to prove her daughter's innocence. **90m/C; DVD.** Nicole Gale Anderson; Janet Montgomery; Stella Maeve; Cynthia Gibb; Jason Brooks; Lindsay Taylor; Reiley McClendon; Linden Ashby; William R. Moses; Barbara Niven; *D:* Doug Campbell; *W:* Christine Conradt; *C:* Robert Ballo; *M:* Steve Gurevitch. **CABLE**

Ace Drummond *Squadron of Doom* **1936** The complete 13-chapter serial about a murder organization that tries to stop several countries from forming a worldwide clipper ship air service and government troubleshooter Ace Drummond who's out to stop them. **260m/B; VHS, DVD.** John "Dusty" King; Jean Rogers; Noah Beery, Jr.; *D:* Ford Beebe.

Ace High ½ **1968** Spaghetti western about a ruthless outlaw named Cat Stevens trying to save himself from the noose. Patterned after the famous Sergio Leone-Clint Eastwood westerns, with less of a budget and more camp tendencies. **120m/C; VHS, DVD.** *IT* Eli Wallach; Terence Hill; Bud Spencer; Brock Peters; Kevin McCarthy; *D:* Giuseppe Colizzi.

Ace in the Hole *The Big Carnival* **1951** Moralist Wilder brilliantly captures a cynical media circus. Alcoholic SOB reporter Chuck Tatum (Douglas) is bored crazy working a podunk paper in New Mexico when he gets a big scoop. Unhappy Lorraine (Sterling) tells Tatum her husband Leo (Benedict) was searching for Indian artifacts and is now trapped in a cave-in. Tatum teams up with corrupt local sheriff Gus Kretzer (Teal) to delay rescue operations to milk the story for maximum exposure while poor Leo suffers and the public come to gawk. Based on the Floyd Collins mining disaster of the 1920s. **111m/B; DVD, Blu-Ray.** Kirk Douglas; Richard Benedict; Ray Teal; Jan Sterling; Robert Arthur; Porter Hall; Frank Cady; Gene Evans; Lewis Martin; Harry Harvey; Richard Gaines; *D:* Billy Wilder; *W:* Billy Wilder; Lesser Samuels; Walter Newman; *C:* Charles B(ryant) Lang, Jr.; *M:* Hugo Friedhofer. Natl. Film Reg. '17.

Ace of Aces **1933** An American sculptor is reviled, particularly by his girlfriend, when he does not join fellows in enlisting in what becomes WWI. Out to prove he's not lacking testosterone, he becomes a pilot in France, but is embittered by his experiences. Dated but well-acted war melodrama. **77m/B; DVD.** Richard Dix; Elizabeth Allan; Theodore Newton; Ralph Bellamy; William Cagney; Frank Conroy; *D:* J. Walter Ruben; *W:* John Monk Saunders; *C:* Henry Cronjager; *M:* Max Steiner.

The Ace of Hearts **1921** Betray your ideals or your friends? Farallone (Chaney Sr.) and Forrest (Bowers) belong to a secret socialist society of vigilantes who target greedy, capitalist tycoons for death. The assassin is chosen by a random drawing of the ace of hearts but Forrest has fallen in love with Lilith (Joy) and can't kill. He's become the target after Farallone draws the deadly card. Silent drama is a subtle, sympathetic role for Chaney. **74m/B; Silent; DVD.** Lon Chaney, Sr.; John Bowers; Leatrice Joy; Hardee Kirkland; Raymond Hatton; *D:* Wallace Worsley, II; *W:* Ruth Wightman; *C:* Don Short.

Ace of Hearts ½ **2008 (PG)** Officer Daniel Harding (Cain) is a member of the K-9 unit with his German Shepherd police partner, Ace. When Ace is unjustly accused of mauling a suspect, an over-zealous DA wants the dog euthanized. But Dan and his family are determined to clear Ace's name and save his furry life. **99m/C; DVD.** Dean Cain; Mike Dopud; Anne Marie Deluise; Matthew Harrison; Britt Mckillip; David Patrick Green; ***D:*** David McKay; ***W:*** Frederick Ayeroff; ***C:*** Gordon Verheul; ***M:*** Michael Richard Plowman. **VIDEO**

Ace Ventura Jr.: Pet Detective **2008 (PG)** Eccentric 12-year-old Ace Jr. (Flitter) is following in his dad's footsteps when his mom (Cusack) is falsely accused of stealing a zoo's baby panda. He teams up with girl-next-door Laura (Lockhart) and gizmo-crazy pal A-Plus (Rogers) to clear the family name. Alrighty then! **93m/C; DVD.** Josh Flitter; Emma Lockhart; Austin Rogers; Ann Cusack; Ralph Waite; Brian Patrick Clarke; Art LaFleur; Reed Alexander; Cullen Douglas; ***D:*** David Mickey Evans; ***W:*** David Mickey Evans; Jeffrey Sank; Jason Heimberg; Justin Heimberg; ***C:*** Mark Irwin; ***M:*** Laura Karpman. **VIDEO**

Ace Ventura: Pet Detective **1993 (PG-13)** Shamelessly silly comedy casts human cartoon Carrey, he of the rubber limbs and spasmodic facial muscles, as Ace, the guy who'll find missing pets, big or small. When the Miami Dolphins' mascot Snowflake is kidnapped, he abandons his search for an albino pigeon to save the lost dolphin just in time for the Super Bowl. This is brain candy, running full throttle with juvenile humor, some charm, and the hyper-energetic Carrey, not to mention Young as the police chief with a secret. Critically trashed boxoffice smash catapulted Carrey into nearly instant stardom after seven seasons as the geeky white guy on "In Living Color." **87m/C; VHS, DVD, Blu-Ray.** Jim Carrey; Courteney Cox; Sean Young; Tone Loc; Noble Willingham; Troy Evans; Udo Kier; ***Cameo(s):*** Dan Marino; ***D:*** Tom Shadyac; ***W:*** Jim Carrey; Tom Shadyac; Jack Bernstein; ***C:*** Julio Macat; ***M:*** Ira Newborn. Blockbuster '95: Comedy Actor, V. (Carrey), Male Newcomer, V. (Carrey).

Ace Ventura: When Nature Calls *Ace Ventura Goes to Africa* **1995 (PG-13)** Ace is back on the case as the pet dick (Carrey) ventures to Africa to restore peace among rival tribes by finding an albino bat that's M.I.A. Plot is secondary, however, to multi-million dollar man Carrey's outrageous brand of physical comedy combined with his unique ability to deliver junior high level lines with pseudo-suave savoir-faire. Contains only a handful of outstanding gags, the best with Ace and a mechanical rhino. Mainly for Carrey aficionados (of which there are many) and original "Ace" fans—the low-brow humor runs a bit thin by the end. **94m/C; VHS, DVD, Blu-Ray.** Jim Carrey; Ian McNeice; Simon Callow; Maynard Eziashi; Bob Gunton; Sophie Okonedo; Tommy Davidson; ***D:*** Steve Oedekerk; ***W:*** Steve Oedekerk; ***C:*** Donald E. Thorin; ***M:*** Robert Folk. MTV Movie Awards '96: Comedic Perf. (Carrey), Male Perf. (Carrey); Blockbuster '96: Comedy Actor, T. (Carrey).

Aces: Iron Eagle 3 **1992 (R)** Colonel "Chappy" Sinclair returns once again in this air adventure. He's been keeping busy flying in air shows when he stumbles across the nefarious activities of a Peruvian drug baron working out of a remote village. Sinclair recruits a team of maverick air circus pilots and they "borrow" a fleet of WWII vintage aircraft to raid the village, coming up against a fellow Air Force officer who turns out to be another villain. Lots of action and a stalwart cast. **98m/C; VHS, DVD, Blu-Ray.** Louis Gossett, Jr.; Rachel McLish; Paul Freeman; Horst Buchholz; Christopher Cazenove; Sonny Chiba; Fred Dalton Thompson; Mitchell Ryan; Rob(ert) Estes; J.E. Freeman; ***D:*** John Glen.

Aces 'n Eights **2008** Luke Rivers (Van Dien) has retired as a gunslinger and is now working on an Arizona ranch owned by crusty Thurmond Prescott (Borgnine). The local land owners band together to fight ruthless railroad mogul Howard (Atherton), who uses intimidation and murder to seize their land. Looks like Rivers is going to have to strap on his six-guns and go up against some of his old saddle-mates in order to defend his new life. Title refers to poker's so-called "dead man's hand," held by Wild Bill Hickok when he was killed. **87m/C; DVD.** Casper Van Dien; Bruce Boxleitner; Ernest Borgnine; William Atherton; Jeff Kober; Jack Noseworthy; Jake Thomas; Rodney Scott; Deirdre Quinn; ***D:*** Craig R. Baxley; ***W:*** Ronald M. Cohen; Dennis Shryack; ***C:*** Yaron Levy. **TV**

The Acid House **1/2 1998** Trilogy of tales written by Irving Welsh, author of "Trainspotting," similarly centers on down-on-their-luck Scottish hooligans ravaged by drugs and drink. Its tone, however, makes its predecessor look like a light-hearted romp in the countryside. In "The Granton Star Cause," freeloading loser Boab (McCole) gets turned into a fly by God during a trip to the pub. He proceeds to exact some disgusting revenge on those he feels have wronged him. "A Soft Touch" depicts the twisted relationship between brow-beaten Johnny (McKidd) and kinky wife Catriona (Gomez), who is sleeping with psycho neighbor Larry (McCormack). In the last chapter, "The Acid House," tripped-out rave party boy Coco (Bremner) exchanges personalities with the newborn baby of suburban couple Rory (Clunes) and Jenny (Redgrave). First-time director McGuigan does a good job of translating the material to the screen, but sometimes goes over the top in showing these skanky Scots. Also, be warned that the Scottish accents are so thick that the movie ran with subtitles during its limited U.S. theatre run. If you liked "Trainspotting," however, you'll probably like this similar entry in the "if it's Scottish, it's crap!" genre. **118m/C; VHS, DVD.** Stephen McCole; Maurice Roeves; Garry Sweeney; Kevin McKidd; Ewen Bremner; Martin Clunes; Jemma Redgrave; Arlene Cockburn; Jenny McCrindle; Michelle Gomez; Tam Dean Burn; Gary McCormack; Jane Stabler; ***D:*** Paul McGuigan; ***W:*** Irvine Welsh; ***C:*** Alasdair Walker.

A.C.O.D. **2013 (R)** As it has so many times, divorce becomes the basis for comedy in this tale of a grown man named Carter (Scott) who discovers that his childhood of divorce was used as the basis of a hit book. Years later, when his brother is about to get married, Carter is forced to play peacekeeper again between his antagonistic parents (scene-stealing O'Hara & Jenkins). The ensemble cast is uniformly great but the film goes off on too many tangents (a brief affair with Alba, as another "child of divorce" is totally superfluous) and it kind of just ends. **88m/C; DVD, Blu-Ray.** Adam Scott; Richard Jenkins; Catherine O'Hara; Mary Elizabeth Winstead; Jessica Alba; ***D:*** Stuart Zicherman; ***W:*** Stuart Zicherman; Ben Karlin; ***C:*** John Bailey; ***M:*** Nick Urata.

Acolytes **2008** A couple of high school kids have a serious bully problem and decide to blackmail a local serial killer into fixing it when they find one of his victims. **91m/C; DVD.** *AU* Joel Edgerton; Michael Dorman; Sebastian Gregory; Joshua Payne; Hanna Mangan Lawrence; Belinda McClory; ***D:*** Jon Hewitt; ***W:*** Jon Hewitt; Shane Krause; Shayne Armstrong; ***C:*** Mark Pugh; ***M:*** David Franzke. **VIDEO**

Acrimony *Tyler Perry's Acrimony* **2018 (R)** A drama about a wrathful woman enraged by how a man ruined her life. Talking directly to the camera and in voiceover, Melinda (Henson) recounts how Robert (Bent) seduced her with lies, took her love and money, and mother's home, and betrayed her. Though Robert is working on an invention that he claims will make them rich, he is unlucky for many years, which strains their relationship. After things start going his way, the wronged Melinda becomes resentful and obsessive. Though Henson gives a strong performance, the film's message about her and her mental illness is muddled. **120m/C; DVD, Blu-Ray.** Taraji P. Henson; Lyriq Bent; Crystle Stewart; Jazmyn Simon; Ptosha Storey; ***D:*** Tyler Perry; ***W:*** Tyler Perry; ***C:*** Richard J. Vialet; ***M:*** Christopher Lennertz.

Across 110th Street **1972 (R)** Gritty, violent cop thriller in the blaxploitation genre. Both the Mafia and the cops hunt down three black hoods who, in a display of extremely bad judgment, knocked over a mob-controlled bank while disguised as police. Lots of bullets create buckets of blood. Filmed on location in Harlem. **102m/C; DVD, Blu-Ray.** Anthony Quinn; Yaphet Kotto; Anthony (Tony) Franciosa; Paul Benjamin; Ed Bernard; Antonio Fargas; Tim O'Connor; Lewis Gilbert; Richard Ward; ***D:*** Barry Shear; ***W:*** Luther Davis; ***C:*** Jack Priestley.

Across the Bridge **1/2 1957** A man on the run from Scotland Yard for stealing a fortune flees to Mexico, in the process killing a man and assuming his identity. An ironic twist and his love for a dog seal his final destiny. Steiger's psychological study as the fugitive is compelling. Based on a novel by Graham Greene. **103m/B; DVD.** *UK* Rod Steiger; David Knight; Marla Landi; Noel Willman; Bernard Lee; ***D:*** Ken Annakin; ***W:*** Guy Elmes; Denis Freeman; ***C:*** Reginald Wyer; ***M:*** James Bernard.

Across the Great Divide **1/2 1976 (G)** Two orphans must cross the rugged snow-covered Rocky Mountains in 1876 in order to claim their inheritance—a 400-acre plot of land in Salem, Oregon. Pleasant coming-of-age tale with majestic scenery. **102m/C; VHS, DVD.** Robert F. Logan; George "Buck" Flower; Heather Rattray; Mark Hall; ***D:*** Stewart Raffill; ***W:*** Stewart Raffill; ***M:*** Angelo Badalamenti.

Across the Hall **1/2 2009 (R)** Somewhat slow-paced and non-linear modern noir, with plot twists you may see coming. June (Murphy) has checked into a seedy hotel, followed by fiance Terry (Pino) who's sure she's meeting some other guy. Distraught, Terry rents a room and calls his best friend Julian (Vogel), threatening to use the gun he's waving around although he agrees to wait until Julian shows up. Based on Merkin's 2005 short film. **93m/C; DVD.** Danny Pino; Brittany Murphy; Mike Vogel; Brad Greenquist; Arie Verveen; Natalia Smyka; Guillermo Diaz; Dov Davidoff; ***D:*** Alex Merkin; ***W:*** Julian Schwab; Jesse Mittletadt; ***C:*** Andrew Carranza; ***M:*** Bobby Tahouri.

Across the Line **1/2 2000 (R)** Miranda (Erez) crosses the border from Mexico into the U.S. and immediately witnesses the murder of a tourist and her husband by corrupt Border Patrol officers. A sheriff (Johnson) tries to protect his witness even as he falls in love with her. **97m/C; VHS, DVD.** Brad Johnson; Sigal Erez; Brian Bloom; Marshall Teague; Adrienne Barbeau; ***D:*** Martin Spottl; ***W:*** Sigal Erez. **VIDEO**

Across the Line: The Exodus of Charlie Wright **2010** Las Vegas financier Charlie Wright ripped off his investors for two billion in a ponzi scheme and fled to Tijuana, Mexico. The head of a Mexican crime family, Russian mobsters, and the FBI all want Charlie—and more importantly—his money. **95m/C; DVD.** Aidan Quinn; Mario Van Peebles; Luke Goss; Andy Garcia; Danny Pino; Corbin Bernsen; Jordan Belfi; Bokeem Woodbine; Raymond J. Barry; Gina Gershon; Claudia Ferri; Gary Daniels; ***D:*** R. Ellis Frazier; ***W:*** R. Ellis Frazier; ***C:*** Anthony J. Rickert-Epstein; ***M:*** Kim Carroll.

Across the Moon **1994 (R)** A road trip to the desert takes Carmen and Kathy away from their incarcerated boyfriends but into troubles with cowboys and prospectors. **88m/C; VHS, DVD.** Elizabeth Pena; Christina Applegate; Tony Fields; Peter Berg; James Remar; Michael McKean; Burgess Meredith; Jack Nance; Jack Kehler; ***D:*** Lisa Gottlieb; ***W:*** Stephen Schneck; ***C:*** Andrzej Sekula; ***M:*** Christopher Tyng; Exene Cervenka.

Across the Pacific **1/2 1942** Classic Bogie/Huston vehicle made on the heels of "The Maltese Falcon." Bogie is an American Army officer booted out of the service on false charges of treason. When no other military will accept him, he sails to China (via the Panama Canal) to offer his services to Chiang Kai-Shek. On board, he meets a variety of seedy characters who plan to blow up the canal. Huston again capitalizes on the counterpoint between the rotundly acerbic Greenstreet, who plays a spy, and stiff-lipped Bogart, who's wooing Astor. Great Bogie moments and fine direction make this an adventure classic. When he departed for the service just prior to filming the final scenes, Huston turned over direction to Vincent Sherman. Also available colorized. **97m/B; VHS, DVD.** Humphrey Bogart; Mary Astor; Sydney Greenstreet; Charles Halton; Victor Sen Yung; Roland Got; Keye Luke; Richard Loo; Frank Wilcox; Paul Stanton; Lester Matthews; Tom Stevenson; Roland Drew; Monte Blue; Rudy Robles; Lee Tung Foo; Chester Gan; Kam Tong; Spencer Chan; Philip Ahn; Frank Faylen; Frank Mayo; ***D:*** John Huston; ***W:*** Richard Macaulay; ***C:*** Arthur Edeson; ***M:*** Adolph Deutsch.

Across the Tracks **1989 (PG-13)** Two brothers, Billy (Schroder), a juvie-home rebel, and Joe (Pitt), a straight-A jock, are at odds when the black sheep is pressured into selling drugs. In an attempt to save his brother from a life of crime, saintly Joe convinces Billy to join him on the school track team, and the brothers are forced to face off in a big meet. Fairly realistic good guy/bad guy who's really a good guy teen drama. **101m/C; VHS, DVD.** Rick Schroder; Brad Pitt; Carrie Snodgress; ***D:*** Sandy Tung; ***W:*** Sandy Tung; ***C:*** Michael Delahoussaye; ***M:*** Joel Goldsmith.

Across the Universe **2007 (PG-13)** Director Julie Taymor has certainly crafted a mystical tour, from middle America to bohemian Greenwich Village to Vietnam. Whether this portrayal of the Vietnam era, using gorgeous visuals, a stylized 60s aesthetic, a nice chunk of the Beatles songbook, and surprisingly little spoken dialogue, is also magical is debatable. Lucy Even (Wood) moves from a small town to New York City, where she and her brother Max (Anderson) meet and befriend a number of predictable characters including Jude (Sturgess), a Brit from—where else??Liverpool. The music has been tasked with propelling the plot along via a vision of this revolutionary time from hippie idealism through the duty of military service to the anti-war counter culture, which is where the message of the film finally lands. See it for the stunning visuals and the fresh interpretation of Beatles classics. **133m/C; DVD, Blu-Ray.** Evan Rachel Wood; Joe Anderson; Jim Sturgess; Dana Fuchs; Martin Luther McCoy; T.V. Carpio; ***Cameo(s):*** Bono; ***D:*** Julie Taymor; ***W:*** Dick Clement; Ian La Frenais; ***C:*** Bruno Delbonnel; ***M:*** Elliot Goldenthal.

Across the Wide Missouri **1/2 1951** Pioneer epic stars Gable as a rugged fur trapper who marries an Indian woman (Marques) so he can trap beaver pelts on her people's rich land. On the journey to the Indian territory however, the trapper truly falls in love with his bride. Superior historical drama is marred slightly by the use of narration (provided by Howard Keel). Look for lively performances from Menjou as a French tippler and Naish as the quirky Indian Chief. Beautiful scenery filmed in the spectacular Rocky Mountains. **78m/C; VHS, DVD, Streaming.** Clark Gable; Ricardo Montalban; John Hodiak; Adolphe Menjou; Maria Elena Marques; J. Carrol Naish; Jack Holt; Alan Napier; ***Nar:*** Howard Keel; ***D:*** William A. Wellman; ***C:*** William Mellor.

Across to Singapore **1928** Convoluted family/romantic drama based on the Ben Ames Williams novel "All the Brothers Were Valiant." Childhood friends Joel Shore (Novarro) and Priscilla Crowninshield (Crawford) have grown up in seafaring New England. When Joel's older brother Mark (Torrence) returns home from a long voyage, he's immediately smitten by Priscilla and both fathers agree to their marriage (without consulting Priscilla). Joel refuses to hear Priscilla's pleas that she loves only him and agrees to join his brothers on a voyage to Singapore where multiple tragedies strike. **85m/B; Silent; DVD.** Ramon Novarro; Joan Crawford; Ernest Torrence; Jim Mason; Frank Currier; Louis Wolheim; Duke Martin; Edward Connelly; Anna May Wong; ***D:*** William Nigh; ***W:*** Joe Farnham; ***C:*** John Seitz.

The Act of Killing **2013** A rare documentary that sheds light on a horrific period of history in a way that glorifies it into a surreal nightmare. Director Oppenheimer not only sits down with a pair of gangsters considered heroes in their native Indonesia for executing an untold number of so-called communists following the 1965 government overthrow, but the director somehow gets the killers to reenact their brutality in elaborately staged send ups and musical interpretations of the slaughters. **115m/C; DVD, Blu-Ray.** *DK NO UK* ***D:*** Christine Cynn; Joshua Oppenheimer; ***C:*** Lars Skree; Carlos Arango De Montis; ***M:*** Simon Thamdrup Jensen. British Acad. '13: Feature Doc.

Act of Valor **2012 (R)** Combination of combat footage featuring active duty Navy SEALs and a plot involving a kidnapped CIA operative that reveals a coordinated terrorist plot leading Bandito Platoon to the U.S.-Mexico border. **110m/C; DVD, Blu-Ray.** Alex Veadov; Roselyn Sanchez; Jason Cottle; Nestor Serrano; Emilio Rivera; Gonzalo Menendez; Ailsa Marshall; ***D:*** Scott Waugh; Mike McCoy; ***W:*** Kurt Johnstad; ***C:*** Shane Hurlbut; ***M:*** Nathan Furst.

Act of Violence 1/2 **1948** Postwar melodrama. Small-town businessman and war hero Frank Enley (Heflin) has a pretty wife (Leigh), a young son, and a good life that gets him recognition. But this brings Frank to the attention of embittered, crippled vet Joe Parkson (Ryan), who's got a beef. Seems both were POWs in a German camp and Enley informed on the men's escape plans, which got everyone but Parkson killed. As Parkson pursues Enley through the seedier sides of L.A., Astor enters the picture as a down-heels dame at a dive bar who offers Enley some assistance that results in a lot more trouble. **82m/B; DVD.** Van Heflin; Robert Ryan; Janet Leigh; Mary Astor; Phyllis Thaxter; Berry Kroeger; Taylor Holmes; ***D:*** Fred Zinnemann; ***W:*** Robert L. Richards; ***C:*** Robert L. Surtees; ***M:*** Bronislau Kaper.

Act of War **1996** Disgraced diplomat/spy Jack Gracey (Scalia) has to stop renegade communists who've taken over a remote nuclear missile site from pressing the button on a missile aimed directly at the White House. Lots of action should hold viewers' interest. **100m/C; VHS, DVD.** *CA CZ* Jack Scalia; Ingrid Torrance; Douglas Arthurs; ***D:*** Robert Lee; ***W:*** Michael Bafaro; ***C:*** David Pelletier; ***M:*** Peter Allen. **VIDEO**

Action Force: The Movie *G.I. Joe: The Movie; G.I. Joe: A Real American Hero-The Movie* **1987** Terrorist group COBRA awakens an ancient race of snake people after immobilizing most of G.I. Joe, forcing some new recruits to try saving the world. **93m/C; DVD, Blu-Ray.** ***V:*** Don Johnson; Burgess Meredith; Robert Remus; Richard Gautier; Chris Latta; ***D:*** Don Jurwich; ***W:*** Ron Friedman; ***M:*** Johnny Douglas; Robert J. Walsh. **TV**

Action in Arabia **1944** A newsman uncovers a Nazi plot to turn the Arabs against the Allies while investigating a colleague's murder in Damascus. The desert teems with spies, double agents, and sheiks as suave Sanders goes about his investigative business. Quintessential wartime B-movie. **75m/B; VHS, Streaming.** George Sanders; Virginia Bruce; Lenore Aubert; Gene Lockhart; Robert Armstrong; H.B. Warner; Alan Napier; Michael Ansara; ***D:*** Leonide Moguy.

Action in the North Atlantic **1943** Massey and Bogart are the captain and first mate of a Merchant Marine vessel running the lone supply route to the Soviet Union. Eventually they wind up locking horns with a Nazi U-boat. Plenty of action and strenuous flag waving in this propagandorama. Gordon fans won't want to miss her as Massey's wife. Also available colorized. **126m/B; VHS, DVD.** Humphrey Bogart; Raymond Massey; Alan Hale; Julie Bishop; Ruth Gordon; Sam Levene; Dane Clark; Peter Whitney; Minor Watson; J.M. Kerrigan; Dick Hogan; Kane Richmond; Chick Chandler; Donald "Don" Douglas; Creighton Hale; Iris Adrian; Elliott Sullivan; Glenn Strange; ***D:*** Lloyd Bacon; ***W:*** A(lbert) I(saac) Bezzerides; W.R. Burnett; John Howard Lawson; ***C:*** Ted D. McCord; ***M:*** Adolph Deutsch.

Action Jackson **1988 (R)** Power-hungry auto tycoon Nelson tries to frame rebellious black police sergeant Weathers for murder. Being a graduate of Harvard and a tough guy, the cop doesn't go for it. Nelson eats up the screen as the heavy with no redeeming qualities, while Weathers is tongue-in-cheek as the resourceful good guy who keeps running afoul of the law in spite of his best efforts. Lots of action, violence, and a few sexy women help cover the plot's lack of common sense. **96m/C; VHS, DVD, Blu-Ray.** Carl Weathers; Vanity; Craig T. Nelson; Sharon Stone; Thomas F. Wilson; Mary Ellen Trainor; ***D:*** Craig R. Baxley; ***W:*** Robert Reneau; ***C:*** Matthew F. Leonetti; ***M:*** Herbie Hancock; Michael Kamen.

Action Man *Le Soleil des Voyous; Leather and Nylon* **1967** Ferrand (Gabin) has reformed his criminal ways to run a restaurant but he's bored and ready to get involved in one last caper with crooked pal Beckley (Stack). The bank job goes fine but drug dealers kidnap Ferrand's wife and want the loot in exchange for her life. French with subtitles. **95m/C; DVD.** *FR IT* Jean Gabin; Robert Stack; Suzanne Flon; Georges Aminel; Walter Giller; Jean Topart; Margaret Lee; ***D:*** Jean Delannoy; ***W:*** Jean Delannoy; Alphonse Boudard; ***C:*** Walter Wottitz; ***M:*** Francis Lai.

Action Point **2018 (R)** Johnny Knoxville proves that a man can grow older but not necessarily up. The former Jackass star brings the same old slapstick stunts and gratuitous sex jokes to the story of an amusement park owner who finds a competitive edge by offering rides designed to inflict maximum "fun." Props to Knoxville, though, for performing his own stunts, many of which landed him in the emergency room during filming. Inspired by Action Park, a New Jersey amusement park that caused six fatalities before it was shuttered in 1996. **85m/C; DVD, Blu-Ray.** Johnny Knoxville; Eleanor Worthington-Cox; Brigette Lundy-Paine; Susan Yeagley; Johnny Pemberton; ***D:*** Tim Kirkby; ***W:*** John Altschuler; Dave Krinsky; ***C:*** Michael Snyman; ***M:*** Deke Dickerson; Andrew Feltenstein; John Nau.

Actium Maximus: War of the Alien Dinosaurs *Actium Maximus* **2005** A ship captain is ordered to find sock puppets (sorry we meant dinosaurs) to compete in a gladiatorial arena for the amusement of a dictator modeled on old Rome. Meant for the fans of films so indescribably bad they're beyond belief. **78m/C; DVD, Streaming.** Jonathan Daniel McCuin; Mark Hicks; Jennifer Hamil; David Matt Duncan; Selwyn Findley; ***D:*** Mark Hicks; ***W:*** Mark Hicks; ***C:*** Mark Hicks; ***M:*** Mark Hicks. **VIDEO**

Active Stealth **1999 (R)** The Army's most secret weapon, an undetectable fighter jet, is hijacked by terrorists during a training mission. Now, it's up to Jefferson Pike (Baldwin) to lead a team into the Central American jungles to retrieve the military's property. **99m/C; VHS, DVD.** Daniel Baldwin; Fred Williamson; Hannes Jaenicke; Chick Vennera; Lisa Vidal; ***D:*** Fred Olen Ray. **VIDEO**

Actors and Sin 1/2 **1952** Two-part film casting a critical eye toward actors and Hollywood. "Actor's Blood" is the melodramatic story of Shakespearean actor Robinson and his unhappy actress daughter. She commits suicide and he sets out to prove it was murder. Heavy going. Lighter and more entertaining is "Woman of Sin," which relates a Hollywood satire involving a theatrical agent and his newest client, a precocious nine-year-old. **82m/B; VHS, DVD.** Edward G. Robinson; Marsha Hunt; Eddie Albert; Alan Reed; Dan O'Herlihy; Tracey Roberts; Rudolph Anders; Paul Guilfoyle; Alice Key; Douglas Evans; Rick Roman; Jenny Hecht; Jody Gilbert; John Crawford; ***D:*** Lee Garmes; Ben Hecht; ***W:*** Ben Hecht; ***C:*** Lee Garmes; ***M:*** George Antheil.

An Actor's Revenge *Yukinojo Henge; Revenge of a Kabuki Actor* **1963** In the early 19th century, a female impersonator in a Kabuki troupe takes revenge on the three men who killed his parents. Fascinating study of opposites—male/female, stage/life, love/hate. In Japanese with English subtitles. **110m/C; VHS, DVD, Blu-Ray.** *JP* Kazuo Hasegawa; Fujiko Yamamoto; Ayako Wakao; Ganjiro Nakamura; ***D:*** Kon Ichikawa; ***W:*** Teinosuke Kinugasa; Daisuke Ito; Natto Wada; ***C:*** Setsuo Kobayashi; ***M:*** Yashushi Akutagawa.

The Actress 1/2 **1953** Solid performances from Tracy and Wright as the concerned parents although Simmons seems out of her depth (although it befits the character). Working-class Clinton Jones is dismayed that his daughter Ruth is stagestruck and tries to persuade her to a more conventional life. When she is rejected for theater roles in Boston, dad finally realizes how much being an actress means to his little girl and he gives Ruth his only valuable possession to sell so she can move to New York. Film debut of Perkins as the suitor. Based on Gordon's autobiographical play "Years Ago." **90m/B; DVD.** Spencer Tracy; Jean Simmons; Teresa Wright; Anthony Perkins; Ian Wolfe; Mary Wickes; ***D:*** George Cukor; ***W:*** Ruth Gordon; ***C:*** Harold Rosson.

Acts of Contrition 1/2 *Original Sins* **1995** Boston radio talk-show host Jonathan Franye (Harmon) has his listeners call in and confess their deepest secrets. Then one caller confesses to a murder and Jonathan decides to investigate and see if the claim is true. But bringing a murderer to justice could be hazardous to his own health. **89m/C; DVD.** Mark Harmon; Julianne Phillips; Sarah Trigger; Ron Perlman; David Clennon; Gustave Johnson; Betty Miller; ***D:*** Jan Egleson; ***W:*** John Pielmeier; ***C:*** Andrzej Sekula; ***M:*** Gary Chang. **TV**

Acts of Death *The Funeral Curtain* **2007 (R)** Re-imagining of 'I Know What You Did Last Summer' set in a locked college theater with various fraternity types paying for an accident they covered up from the day before. **103m/C; DVD.** Bill Vincent; Reggie Bannister; Jason Carter; Derek J. Dubuque; Nathaniel Nose; James Ohngren; Glenn Shadix; Finn Wrisely; Niki Huey; Monica Percich; Erin Scheiner; ***D:*** Jeff Burton; ***W:*** Bill Vincent; Jeff Burton; Erik F. Hill; ***C:*** Jeff Burton; ***M:*** John Roome. **VIDEO**

Acts of Vengeance 1/2 **2017 (R)** Taking a page from the playbooks of Liam Neeson and the casts of *The Expendables*, Banderas is the latest late-middle-ager to reemerge as an action hero. After his wife and daughter are murdered, Frank Valera punishes himself for failing to protect them by joining an underground fight club, then taking a vow of silence, and finally seeking revenge using the skills he gained from those first two pursuits: pugilistic prowess and, incredibly, enhanced hearing. A by-the-numbers action-drama that won't disappoint fans with low expectations of the genre. **87m/C; DVD, Blu-Ray.** Antonio Banderas; Karl Urban; Paz Vega; Cristina Serafini; Atanas Srebrev; ***D:*** Isaac Florentine; ***W:*** Matt Venne; ***C:*** Yaron Scharf; ***M:*** Frederick Wiedmann.

Acts of Violence 1/2 **2018 (R)** An action-drama that explores an incident of vigilantism and human trafficking. At the bachelorette party of bride-to-be Mia (Bolona), she argues with goons for local crime boss Max Livingston (Epps). As retaliation, they kidnap her and plan to use her to begin their human trafficking operation. Convinced the police will not act, Mia's fiance, Roman (Holmes), and his two military vet brothers work to track her down and kill anyone who stands in their way. Along the way, police detective James Avery (Willis) assists the group. Simplistic and exploitative, the film also suffers from poor pacing and uninspired performances. **86m/C; DVD, Blu-Ray.** Bruce Willis; Cole Hauser; Shawn Ashmore; Ashton Holmes; Melissa Bolona; ***D:*** Brett Donowho; ***W:*** Nicolas Aaron Mezzanatto; ***C:*** Edd Lukas; ***M:*** James T. Sale.

Acts of Worship 1/2 **2001 (R)** Kicked out by her boyfriend, junkie Alix finds a safe haven with Digna, a former addict. But her attempt to straighten Alix out leads Digna back to her old, bad habits. **94m/C; VHS, DVD.** Ana Reeder; Michael Hyatt; Nestor Rodriguez; Christopher Kadish; ***D:*** Rosemary Rodriguez; ***W:*** Rosemary Rodriguez; ***C:*** Luke Geissbuhler; ***M:*** Jim Coleman. **VIDEO**

A.D. 1/2 *Anno Domini* **1985** Set shortly after Jesus' death, this rather low-budget miniseries chronicles the life and adventures of Christ's disciples (especially Peter and Paul) and the growing conflicts between Jewish zealots, early Christians, and the power of the Roman empire. Based on the Acts of the Apostles. **540m/C; VHS, DVD.** Denis Quilley; Philip Sayer; Anthony Andrews; Colleen Dewhurst; Ava Gardner; Richard Kiley; James Mason; David Hedison; John Houseman; John McEnery; Ian McShane; Jennifer O'Neill; Fernando Rey; Richard Roundtree; Ben Vereen; Susan Sarandon; Diane Venora; Anthony Zerbe; Jack Warden; Amanda Pays; Millie Perkins; Michael Wilding, Jr.; ***D:*** Stuart Cooper; ***W:*** Anthony Burgess; ***C:*** Ennio Guarnieri; ***M:*** Lalo Schifrin. **TV**

Ad Astra **2019 (PG-13)** Set in the near future, astronaut Roy McBride (Pitt) is famous for being unshakeable. When thousands are killed on Earth by a power surge that originated near Neptune, space officials send Roy to Mars to contact his father, H. Clifford McBride (Jones), in hopes of saving the planet. The elder McBride was part of a famous space mission that went to the edge of the universe in search of intelligent life but was presumed dead. Besides all the obstacles of the mission, Roy also confronts his long-held angst toward Clifford for leaving him behind as a child. Reflective and visually stunning, Pitt's star shines brilliantly, countering the at-times lifeless storytelling. **123m/C; DVD, Blu-Ray.** Brad Pitt; Tommy Lee Jones; Ruth Negga; Donald Sutherland; Kimberly Elise; ***D:*** James Gray; ***W:*** James Gray; Ethan Gross; ***C:*** Hoyte Van Hoytema; ***M:*** Max Richter.

Ada 1/2 **1961** Southern-fried, Depression-era setting adds to the melodrama, which is based on Wirt Williams' novel, "Ada Dallas." Crooked party boss Sylvester Marin (Hyde-White) picks pliable country boy sheriff Bo Gillis (Martin) and pushes through his election to governor. Bo's ambitious wife Ada (Hayward) wants Bo to be his own man so Marin uses her ex-prostitute past to create a scandal and more dirty tactics to keep political power. **108m/C; DVD.** Susan Hayward; Dean Martin; Wilfrid Hyde-White; Ralph Meeker; Martin Balsam; Frank Maxwell; ***D:*** Daniel Mann; ***W:*** Arthur Sheekman; ***C:*** Joseph Ruttenberg; ***M:*** Bronislau Kaper.

Adam 1/2 **1983** Docu-drama based on a tragic, true story. John and Reve Williams (Travanti and Williams) desperately search for their six-year-old son abducted during an outing. During their long search and struggle, they lobby Congress for use of the FBI's crime computer. Eventually their efforts led to the creation of the Missing Children's Bureau. Sensitive, compelling performances by Travanti and Williams as the agonized, courageous parents. **100m/C; VHS, DVD.** Daniel J. Travanti; JoBeth Williams; Martha Scott; Richard Masur; Paul Regina; Mason Adams; ***D:*** Michael Tuchner. **TV**

Adam 1/2 **2009 (PG-13)** New York-set romantic drama with a twist. Having just moved into her apartment building, teacher Beth (Byrne) becomes intrigued by good-looking neighbor Adam (Dancy) although he's ill at ease socially. After gaining his trust, Adam explains to Rose that he has Asperger's syndrome (a form of autism) and doesn't understand empathy or what people are thinking. Still recovering from a painful breakup, Rose is uncertain if she wants to get involved or how much Adam can participate in a romantic relationship, especially when her parents' reservations and problems begin interfering. Dancy never overdoes his role and Byrne is sympathetic without being cloying. **97m/C; Blu-Ray, On Demand.** Hugh Dancy; Rose Byrne; Frankie Faison; Amy Irving; Peter Gallagher; Mark Linn-Baker; ***D:*** Max Mayer; ***W:*** Max Mayer; ***C:*** Seamus Tierney; ***M:*** Christopher Lennertz.

Adam & Steve **2005** Contrived but generally amusing gay romance begins in 1987 when shy goth boy Adam (writer/director Chester) meets glittery party boy Steve (Gets) and their trick turns into disaster. They meet cute 17 years later, don't recognize each other, and start a romance fraught with individual neuroses that stem from that fateful night. Each man also comes complete with the prerequisite straight best friend: for Adam, it's former-fatty turned skinny comic Rhonda (Posey) and for Steve it's caustic roommate Michael (Kattan). A couple of musical fantasy sequences provide some unexpected distraction. **99m/C; DVD.** Craig Chester; Malcolm Gets; Parker Posey; Chris Kattan; Sally Kirkland; Noah Segan; ***D:*** Craig Chester; ***W:*** Craig Chester; ***C:*** Carl F. Bartels; ***M:*** Roddy Bottum.

Adam at 6 a.m. **1970 (PG)** Douglas is a young college professor who decides to spend a summer laboring in Missouri, where life, he thinks, is simpler. Of course, he learns that life in the boonies has its own set of problems, but unfortunately it takes him the entire movie before he catches the drift. **100m/C; VHS, DVD; Open Captioned.** Michael Douglas; Lee Purcell; Joe Don Baker; Charles Aidman; Marge Redmond; Louise Latham; Grayson Hall; Dana Elcar; Meg Foster; Richard Derr; Anne Gwynne; ***D:*** Robert Scheerer.

Adam Had Four Sons 1/2 **1941** Satisfying character study involving the typical turn-of-the-century family nearly consumed by love, jealousy, and hatred. In the early part of the century, a goodly governess (Bergman in her second U.S. film) watches sympathetically over four sons of an American businessman after their mother dies. Economic necessity separates Bergman from the family for several years. Upon her return, she tangles with scheming bride-to-be Hayward, a bad girl intent on dividing and conquering the family before walking down the aisle with one of the sons. Based on a novel by Charles Bonner. **81m/B; VHS, DVD.** Ingrid Bergman; Warner Baxter; Susan Hayward; Fay Wray; Richard Denning; June Lockhart; Robert Shaw; Johnny Downs; ***D:*** Gregory Ratoff.

Adam Resurrected 🦴 1/2 **2008 (R)** An unsettling story, with a brilliant lead performance by Goldblum, but Schrader's tone veers uncertainly. Adam Stein (Goldblum) was a successful Jewish cabaret performer in Berlin until the Nazis came to power. Sent to a concentration camp, Adam survives because the camp's Commandant (Defoe) is an admirer. But he also treats Adam (literally) like a dog so it's no wonder that Adam eventually winds up in an Israeli mental hospital for Holocaust survivors. He's still using humor as a coping mechanism but circumstances and survivors' guilt undermine an already shaky foundation. Based on the novel by Yoram Kaniuk. **106m/C; Blu-Ray.** *GE IS* Jeff Goldblum; Willem Dafoe; Derek Jacobi; Ayelet Zurer; Moritz Bleibtreu; Hana Laszlo; Tudor Rapiteanu; ***D:*** Paul Schrader; ***W:*** Noah Stollman; ***C:*** Sebastian Edscmid; ***M:*** Gabriel Yared.

Adam Sandler's 8 Crazy Nights 🦴🦴 *8 Crazy Nights* **2002 (PG-13)** Parents should be warned that Adam Sandler's foray into animated holiday fare is more for the big kids than the tiny tots. When eyes are aglow, it's usually the bloodshot peepers of party animal Davey Stone (voiced by Sandler), who harbors a grudge against the holiday season. After he goes on a spree of booze-soaked vandalism, the judge is about to throw the book at Davey until Whitey, the ref of a youth basketball league, intercedes for him. Davey proceeds to torment Whitey and his sister Eleanor (both also voiced by Sandler) until the last act less-than-believably transforms him into a good guy. At turns offensive and interesting, this foul-mouthed cartoon does manage to set a record for animated product placement. **71m/C; VHS, DVD.** ***V:*** Adam Sandler; Kevin Nealon; Rob Schneider; Norm Crosby; Jackie Titone; Austin Stout; Jon Lovitz; ***D:*** Seth Kearsley; ***W:*** Adam Sandler; Allen Covert; Brooks Arthur; Brad Isaacs; ***M:*** Marc Ellis; Ray Ellis; Teddy Castellucci.

Adam's Apples 🦴🦴 *Adams Aebler* **2005 (R)** Danish black comedy about a Neo-Nazi forced to finish a prison sentence doing community service at a church. Adam (Thomsen) is EVIL and meets his opposite in the positive-to-a-fault priest Ivan (Mikkelsen). Adam promises Ivan that he'll make a pie from the apples that grow in the churchyard, but as crows and disease peck away at the apples, Adam decides to break Ivan down, mentally and physically. Alternately bleak and ludicrous, the movie is mostly style over substance and rarely digs deeper than the basic absurdity of its premise. **93m/C; DVD.** *CZ* Ulrich Thomsen; Mads Mikkelsen; Paprika Steen; Nikolaj Lie Kaas; Nicolas Bro; Ali Kazim; Ole Thestrup; ***D:*** Anders Thomas Jensen; ***W:*** Anders Thomas Jensen; ***C:*** Sebastian Blenkov; ***M:*** Jeppe Kaas.

Adam's Rib 🦴🦴🦴🦴 **1950** Classic war between the sexes cast Tracy and Hepburn as married attorneys on opposite sides of the courtroom in the trial of blonde bombshell Holliday, charged with attempted murder of the lover of her philandering husband. The battle in the courtroom soon takes its toll at home as the couple is increasingly unable to leave their work at the office. Sharp, snappy dialogue by Gordon and Kanin with superb direction by Cukor. Perhaps the best of the nine movies pairing Tracy and Hepburn. Also available colorized. **101m/B; VHS, DVD.** Spencer Tracy; Katharine Hepburn; Judy Holliday; Tom Ewell; David Wayne; Jean Hagen; Hope Emerson; Polly Moran; Marvin Kaplan; Paula Raymond; Tommy Noonan; ***D:*** George Cukor; ***W:*** Garson Kanin; Ruth Gordon; ***C:*** George J. Folsey; ***M:*** Miklos Rozsa. Natl. Film Reg. '92.

Adam's Woman 🦴🦴 1/2 *Return of the Boomerang* **1970** In the 1840s, American sailor Adam (Bridges) is falsely convicted of a crime while on shore leave in Liverpool and is transported to an outback Australian penal colony. He's recaptured after escaping with brutal inmate Dyson (Booth) and offered a chance by reform-minded governor Sir Philip (Mills) to marry fellow prisoner Bess (Merrow) and start a new settlement. However, Dyson and his band of marauders comes calling. **116m/C; DVD.** *GR* Beau Bridges; Jane Merrow; James Booth; John Mills; Andrew Keir; Peter O'Shaughnessy; Tracy Reed; ***D:*** Philip Leacock; ***W:*** Richard Fielder; ***C:*** Wilmer C. Butler; ***M:*** Bob Young.

Adaptation 🦴🦴🦴 1/2 **2002 (R)** Quirky but highly entertaining comedy about blocked L.A. screenwriter Charlie Kaufman (Cage), hired to adapt author Susan Orlean's (Streep) book "The Orchid Thief." The book recounts the story of John Laroche (Cooper), one of a breed of orchid-obsessed con men who schemes to steal the desirable plants from the Florida Everglades. At a loss as to how to treat the story, the neurotic Charlie becomes obsessed with Orlean, gazing at her picture while his lesser twin brother Donald (also Cage), breezily announces the sales of his own million dollar screenplay, which he wrote after one seminar. Meanwhile, Orlean travels to Florida to interview the gap-toothed Laroche and begins her own minor obsession. Plot twists keep you on your toes right down to the surprise ending. Cage is at his best as the twin writers, while Streep shows off her comic chops and Cooper turns in a career-making performance. Deftly directed by Jonze. **114m/C; VHS, DVD.** Nicolas Cage; Meryl Streep; Chris Cooper; Tilda Swinton; Cara Seymour; Brian Cox; Judy Greer; Maggie Gyllenhaal; Ron Livingston; Stephen Tobolowsky; Jay Tavare; Litefoot; Gary Farmer; Peter Jason; Curtis Hanson; ***D:*** Spike Jonze; ***W:*** Charlie Kaufman; ***C:*** Lance Acord; ***M:*** Carter Burwell. Oscars '02: Support. Actor (Cooper); British Acad. '02: Adapt. Screenplay; Golden Globes '03: Support. Actor (Cooper), Support. Actress (Streep); L.A. Film Critics '02: Support. Actor (Cooper); Natl. Bd. of Review '02: Screenplay, Support. Actor (Cooper); N.Y. Film Critics '02: Screenplay.

The Addams Family 🦴🦴 1/2 **1991 (PG-13)** Everybody's favorite family of ghouls hits the big screen, but something is lost in the translation. An imposter claiming to be long-lost Uncle Fester (Lloyd), who says he was in the Bermuda Triangle for 25 years, shows up at the Addams' home to complete a dastardly deed—raid the family's immense fortune. Although Fester's plan is foiled, a series of plot twists highlight the ghoulish family's eccentricities. Darkly humorous but eventually disappointing: Julia, Huston, and Ricci (as Gomez, Morticia, and Wednesday, respectively) are great in their roles and the sets look good, but the plot is thin. Much closer to the original comic strip by Charles Addams than the popular TV show ever was. **102m/C; VHS, DVD, Blu-Ray.** Anjelica Huston; Raul Julia; Christopher Lloyd; Dan Hedaya; Elizabeth Wilson; Judith Malina; Carel Struycken; Dana Ivey; Paul Benedict; Christina Ricci; Jimmy Workman; Christopher Hart; John Franklin; ***Cameo(s):*** Marc Shaiman; ***D:*** Barry Sonnenfeld; ***W:*** Caroline Thompson; Larry Thompson; ***C:*** Owen Roizman; ***M:*** Marc Shaiman. Golden Raspberries '91: Worst Song ("Addams Groove").

The Addams Family 🦴🦴 **2019 (PG)** To escape angry neighbors threatening Morticia (Theron) and Gomez (Isaac) on their wedding night, the couple moves to a former asylum in Assimilation, New Jersey. Thirteen years later, the family fears that son Pugsley (Wolfhard) will not be able to complete the required dance for the traditional coming-of-age ceremony. At the same time, Margaux Needler (Janney), the mother of daughter Wednesday's (Moretz) public school chum, wants to makeover the Addams to help her reality show and real estate business. A dull, uninspired animated take on the macabre Addams clan. **87m/C; DVD, Blu-Ray.** Oscar Isaac; Charlize Theron; Chloë Grace Moretz; Nick Kroll; ***D:*** Greg Tiernan; Conrad Vernon; ***W:*** Matt Lieberman; Pamela Pettler; ***C:*** Finn Wolfhard; ***M:*** Jeff Danna; Mychael Danna.

Addams Family Values 🦴🦴 1/2 **1993 (PG-13)** The creepy Addams' are back, but this time they leave the dark confines of the mansion to meet the "real" world. New baby Pubert causes homicidal jealousy in sibs Wednesday and Pugsley, causing Mom and Dad to hire a gold-digging, serial-killing nanny (Cusack) with designs on Uncle Fester to watch over the tot. A step above its predecessor, chock full of black humor, sub-plots, and one-liners. Cusack fits right in with an outrageously over the top performance and Ricci nearly steals the show again as the deadpan Wednesday. **93m/C; VHS, DVD.** Anjelica Huston; Raul Julia; Christopher Lloyd; Joan Cusack; Carol Kane; Christina Ricci; Jimmy Workman; Kaitlyn Hooper; Kristen Hooper; Carel Struycken; David Krumholtz; Christopher Hart; Dana Ivey; Peter MacNichol; Christine Baranski; Mercedes McNab; ***D:*** Barry Sonnenfeld; ***W:*** Paul Rudnick; ***M:*** Marc Shaiman. Golden Raspberries '93: Worst Song ("WHOOMP! There It Is").

The Adderall Diaries 🦴 1/2 **2016 (R)** An exploration of a murder case's effect on the life of an author, based on the best-selling memoir by Stephen Elliott. Told from the point of view of Elliott (Franco), the film explores his troubled state of mind. He struggles with writer's block, the pressures of past successes, and the trouble caused by the reappearance of his long-gone father (Harris). Neil Elliott now says that his son made up the stories of his troubled childhood which made him famous. Also dealing with substance abuse problems—including a fondness for Adderall—Elliott finds unexpected inspiration in the form of the 2007 trial of Hans Reiser (Slater) who is accused of murdering his wife and an unexpected new romance. **105m/C; DVD, Blu-Ray, Streaming, Download.** James Franco; Amber Heard; Christian Slater; Wilmer Valderrama; Ed Harris; ***D:*** Pamela Romanowsky; ***W:*** Pamela Romanowsky; ***C:*** Bruce Thierry Cheung; ***M:*** Michael Andrews.

Addicted 🦴 **2014 (R)** This sleazy film nonsense is based on sleazy book nonsense by Zane, the kind of pulpy sexy romance meant for an airplane or beach read, but never a movie. Zoe Reynard (Leal) is a successful businesswoman who seems to have it all, including a dream husband and two beautiful children. Of course, she's addicted to sex, and risks losing everything by entering into an illicit affair. It's cheaply made, never sexy, and the kind of soap opera that even fans of made-for-cable movies would call inferior. Avoid at all costs. **105m/C; DVD.** Sharon Leal; Boris Kodjoe; William Levy; Tyson Beckford; Tasha Smith; Kat Graham; Emayatzy Corinealdi; ***D:*** Bille Woodruff; ***W:*** Christina Welsh; Ernie Basbarash; ***C:*** Joseph White; ***M:*** Aaron Zigman.

Addicted to Fresno 🦴 **2015 (R)** Black comedy featuring gleefully malicious behavior that quickly turns sour. Director Babbitt's misanthropic misfire follows the strained relationship of sisters Shannon (Greer) and Martha (Lyonne), who work as hotel maids in Fresno. Shannon is a sex addict who hates that she's forced to work a blue-collar job with Martha and lets everyone know it. After unintentionally killing a guest, their cover-up leads to more-unbelievable-than-wacky hijinks. None of the nonsense unfortunately leads to a single likeable character. **85m/C; DVD, Blu-Ray.** Judy Greer; Natasha Lyonne; Aubrey Plaza; Fred Armisen; Molly Shannon; ***D:*** Jamie Babbit; ***W:*** Karey Dornetto; ***C:*** Jeffrey Waldron; ***M:*** Nathan Mathew David.

Addicted to Her Love 🦴 1/2 *Love Is the Drug* **2006 (R)** Boilerplate troubled-teen drama about a working class student obsessed with a rich girl at his private high school where everyone seems to drink, drug, and have casual sex. Jonah (Amedori) works at a pharmacy, which gets him an in with Sara (Caplan) and her spiteful crowd. He becomes a pill supplier but, not surprisingly, the partying gets out of control and there's a tragedy. **98m/C; DVD.** John Patrick Amedori; Lizzy Caplan; D.J. Cotrona; Jonathan Trent; Jenny Wade; Daryl Hannah; Bruce A. Young; ***D:*** Elliott Lester; ***W:*** Wesley Strick; Steve Allison; ***C:*** Florian Stadler.

Addicted to Love 🦴🦴 1/2 **1996 (R)** Warning: Do not rent this movie with your significant other if you're thinking about breaking up with them. After they're both dumped, mild-mannered Sam (Broderick) and wild woman Maggie (Ryan) discover they have a lot in common. First of all, their exes Linda (Preston) and Anton (Karyo) are dating each other. Secondly, they're both stalkers! Yep! A romantic comedy about stalking. Sam wants nothing more than to reclaim Linda as his own. Maggie wants nothing less than Anton's head on a plate. Interesting comedy wavers between dark and light moments, aided by the rather murky sets and lighting. Directorial debut for Dunne, who makes his father eat a bug in one scene. **100m/C; VHS, DVD.** Meg Ryan; Matthew Broderick; Kelly Preston; Tcheky Karyo; Maureen Stapleton; Remak Ramsay; Nesbitt Blaisdell; Dominick Dunne; ***D:*** Griffin Dunne; ***W:*** Robert Gordon; ***C:*** Andrew Dunn; ***M:*** Rachel Portman.

Addicted to Murder 🦴🦴 **1995** Joel Winter (McCleery) was abused as a child and now takes his anger out on women by killing them. Then he meets vampire Angie (Graham), who decides to transform him since he's already a predator. But Joel develops a conscience and tries to reform, which ticks Angie off and she frames him for a murder he didn't commit. Which ticks Joel off so he becomes a vampire (and a vampire hunter) to get even. **90m/C; VHS, DVD.** Michael (Mick) McCleery; Sasha Graham; Laura McLaughlin; ***D:*** Kevin J. Lindenmuth; ***W:*** Kevin J. Lindenmuth; ***C:*** Kevin J. Lindenmuth. **VIDEO**

Addicted to Murder 2: Tainted Blood 🦴 1/2 **1997** It's a case of diminishing returns as is usual with sequels in this plotwise mishmash. New York City is the happy hunting grounds for a rogue vamp who's turning others whom Angie (Graham) doesn't considered worthy of getting "The Gift." So she intends to put a stop to it. And just around for more laughs is Joel (McCleery)?the serial killer turned vampire turned vampire hunter. **80m/C; VHS, DVD.** Sasha Graham; Michael (Mick) McCleery; Sarah K. Lippmann; Robbi Firestone; Ted Grayson; Joe Moretti; Joel D. Wynkoop; Tom NonDorf; ***Cameo(s):*** Ted V. Mikels; ***D:*** Kevin J. Lindenmuth; ***W:*** Kevin J. Lindenmuth. **VIDEO**

Addicted to Murder 3: Bloodlust 🦴 1/2 **1999** Serial killer Joel Winter (McCleery) continues his quest to eliminate vampires in revenge for his own transformation. One master vamp thinks he has a secure haven but he's very wrong. **85m/C; VHS, DVD.** Michael (Mick) McCleery; Sarah K. Lippmann; Nick Kostopoulos; Cloud Michaels; Grant Cramer; Frank Lopez; Joe Zaso; Jon Sanborne; Reid Ostrowski; ***D:*** Kevin J. Lindenmuth; Tom Vollmann; ***W:*** Kevin J. Lindenmuth; Tom Vollmann. **VIDEO**

Address Unknown 🦴🦴 **1944** Martin Schulz (Lukas) and Max Eisenstein (Carnovsky) are German immigrants working as art dealers in San Francisco. Their long friendship tears apart when Martin returns to Germany and is swayed by Nazi propaganda, which causes a series of family tragedies. The title isn't explained until the end of the movie. **75m/B; DVD, Blu-Ray.** Paul Lukas; Morris Carnovsky; K.T. Stevens; Mady Christians; Peter Van Eyck; Carl Esmond; ***D:*** William Cameron Menzies; ***W:*** Herbert Dalmas; Kressman Taylor; ***C:*** Rudolph Mate; ***M:*** Ernst Toch.

Address Unknown 🦴🦴 1/2 **1996 (PG)** A ten-year-old letter and a priceless stamp provide a teenager with clues to dad's mysterious death. **92m/C; VHS, DVD.** Kyle Howard; Johna Stewart; Patrick Renna; Corbin Allred; Michael Flynn; ***D:*** Shawn Levy.

Adios Amigo 🦴🦴 **1975 (PG)** Offbeat western comedy has ad-libbing Pryor hustling as a perennially inept con man. Script and direction (both provided by Williamson) are not up to Pryor's level, although excessive violence and vulgarity are avoided in a boring attempt to provide good clean family fare. **87m/C; VHS, DVD.** Fred Williamson; Richard Pryor; Thalmus Rasulala; James Brown; Robert Phillips; Mike Henry; ***D:*** Fred Williamson; ***W:*** Fred Williamson.

Adios, Sabata 🦴 1/2 **1971 (PG-13)** Brynner took over the role for one sequel. In 1873, Sabata comes to the aid of a band of Mexican revolutionaries who want to steal a wagonload of gold from sadistic Austrian interloper, Colonel Von Skimmel. **102m/C; DVD, Blu-Ray.** *IT* Yul Brynner; Pedro Sanchez; Gerard Herter; Dean Reed; Sal Borgese; Franco Fantasia; ***D:*** Gianfranco Parolini; ***W:*** Gianfranco Parolini; Renato Izzo; ***C:*** Sandro Mancori; ***M:*** Bruno Nicolai.

The Adjuster 🦴🦴 1/2 **1991 (R)** Critics either loved or hated this strange film. Insurance adjuster Noah Render's clients look to him for all sorts of comfort, so much so that his own identity becomes a blurred reflection of their tragedies. Wife Hera is a film censor who secretly tapes the pornographic videos she watches at work. Their carefully organized lives are invaded by Bubba and Mimi, a wealthy couple who pass themselves off as filmmakers who want to use the Render house as a movie set. They are instead looking to involve the Renders in their latest and most elaborate erotic fantasy. Lots of symbolism, but little substance. **102m/C; VHS, DVD.** *CA* Elias Koteas; Arsinee Khanjian; Maury Chaykin; Gabrielle Rose; David Hemblen; Jennifer Dale; Don McKellar; Raoul Trujillo; ***D:*** Atom Egoyan; ***W:*** Atom Egoyan; ***C:*** Paul Sarossy; ***M:*** Mychael Danna. Toronto-City '91: Canadian Feature Film.

The Adjustment Bureau 🦴🦴 ½ **2011 (PG-13)** Big Brother IS watching. The movie, loosely based on a 1954 story by Philip K. Dick, who didn't include the love story that's really the heart of Nolfi's sci-fi/romance/thriller. David Norris (Damon) has just lost his senatorial bid when he meets ballet dancer Elise (Blunt) and they discover an instant rapport. Then fate, literally in the form of guys wearing suits and fedoras, strives to keep them apart so they won't alter the future. However, David believes he should control his own destiny and he and Elise refuse to give each other up despite increasing pressures (and multiple chase scenes). **106m/C; Blu-Ray, On Demand.** Matt Damon; Emily Blunt; Anthony Mackie; John Slattery; Anthony Michael Ruivivar; Michael Kelly; Terence Stamp; ***D:*** George Nolfi; ***W:*** George Nolfi; ***C:*** John Toll; ***M:*** Thomas Newman.

The Admirable Crichton 🦴🦴 ½ *Paradise Lagoon* **1957** Social satire about an aristocratic family and their butler who are marooned on a tropical island. Crichton (More), the butler, has a good deal more practical experience and sense than his employers so he's soon in charge of their survival. Filmed in Bermuda and based on the play by James M. Barrie. **93m/C; VHS, DVD, Blu-Ray.** *GB* Kenneth More; Cecil Parker; Sally Ann Howes; Diane Cilento; Martita Hunt; Jack Watling; Peter Graves; Gerald Harper; ***D:*** Lewis Gilbert; ***W:*** Vernon Harris; ***C:*** Wilkie Cooper; ***M:*** Douglas Gamley.

The Admiral Was a Lady 🦴🦴 **1950** Four ex-GIs try to get by in life without going to work. Hendrix walks into their lives as a winning ex-Wave gifted with a knack for repartee who is disgusted by their collective lack of ambition. Nevertheless, she is pursued by the zany quartet with predictable results. **87m/B; VHS, DVD.** Edmond O'Brien; Wanda Hendrix; Rudy Vallee; Steve Brodie; ***D:*** Albert Rogell.

Admission 🦴🦴 ½ **2013 (PG-13)** Portia Nathan (Fey) is an admissions officer at Princeton University and follows a structured routine. While on a recruiting visit to an alternative high school run by old friend John Pressman (Rudd), she's stunned to come face-to-face with a young man who may be the son she gave up years ago. Questioning the decisions she's made and facing new romance, Fey does her best with material that isn't nearly as smart as it should be. The apt and charming cast can't quite get this comedy applicant into the school of success. **107m/C; DVD, Blu-Ray.** Tina Fey; Paul Rudd; Nat Wolff; Michael Sheen; Wallace Shawn; Gloria Reuben; Lily Tomlin; Sarita Choudhury; ***D:*** Paul Weitz; ***W:*** Karen Croner; ***C:*** Declan Quinn; ***M:*** Stephen Trask.

Adolf Hitler: My Part in His Downfall 🦴 ½ **1974** Mild war comedy based on Spike Milligan's memoirs. Young jazz drummer Spike (Dale) is forced into duty when WWII begins and there are various absurd mishaps with Spike and his fellow recruits during basic training with the Royal Artillery. Milligan himself plays his father Leo. **103m/C; DVD.** *UK* Jim Dale; Arthur Lowe; Bill Maynard; Tony Selby; Spike Milligan; ***D:*** Norman Cohen; ***W:*** Norman Cohen; Johnny Byrne; ***C:*** Terry Maher; ***M:*** Wilfred Burns.

Adopt a Highway 🦴🦴 ½ **2019** Russ Millings, imprisoned for two decades for possession of an ounce of marijuana, is finally paroled. Depressed and afraid of the outside world, he is emotionally reawakened after finding a baby abandoned in a Dumpster. It's a well-acted and moving film, but a shade too corny to inspire awe. **78m/C; DVD, Blu-Ray.** Ethan Hawke; Elaine Hendrix; Chris Sullivan; Christopher Heyerdahl; Betty Gabriel; ***D:*** Logan Marshall-Green; ***W:*** Logan Marshall-Green; ***C:*** Pepe Avila del Pino; ***M:*** Jason Isbell.

Adopt a Sailor 🦴🦴 **2008** Character drama based on writer/director Evered's own experiences. A nameless, naive young Arkansas sailor (Peck) is visiting New York during Fleet Week and is spending the evening with Patricia (Neuwirth) and Richard (Coyote) who have agreed to look after him. Only wealthy passive-aggressive Patricia and her dilettante filmmaker hubby have a now-loveless marriage and more-than-embarrassing issues that are revealed during a very uncomfortable dinner. **85m/C; DVD.** Ethan Peck; Bebe Neuwirth; Peter Coyote; ***D:*** Charles Evered; ***W:*** Charles Evered; ***C:*** Ulf Soderqvist; ***M:*** Joshua Fardon.

Adopted WOOF! **2009 (R)** The movie is supposed to be intentionally stupid and offensive but Shore's flick just goes beyond that into unwatchable. Shore plays himself as a burned-out party guy who decides to go respectable by adopting an African orphan like some other better-known celebrities. But his American ignorance and arrogance makes the entire process trickier. It's a really looong 80 minutes and you really have to like Shore to endure even more than a few of those. **80m/C; DVD.** Pauly Shore; ***D:*** Pauly Shore; ***W:*** Pauly Shore; ***C:*** Bruce Cunningham; Grant Nelson; ***M:*** The Newton Brothers. **VIDEO**

Adoption 🦴🦴🦴 *Orkobefogadas* **1975** The third of Meszaros's trilogy, involving a middle-aged Hungarian woman who longs for a child and instead forms a deep friendship with a 19-year-old orphan. In Hungarian with English subtitles. **89m/B; VHS, DVD.** *HU* Kati Berek; Laszlo Szabo; Gyongyver Vigh; Dr. Arpad Perlaky; ***D:*** Marta Meszaros; ***W:*** Marta Meszaros; Gyula Hernadi; ***C:*** Lajos Koltai; ***M:*** Gyorgy Kovacs. Berlin Intl. Film Fest. '75: Golden Berlin Bear.

The Adorable Cheat 🦴🦴 **1928** A low-budget, late-silent melodrama about a young woman who tries to get involved in the family business, despite her father's refusal of her help. Once in the business, she finds love. **76m/B; Silent; DVD.** Lila Lee; Cornelius Keefe; Burr McIntosh; ***D:*** Burton King.

Adoration 🦴🦴 **2008 (R)** High-school French teacher Sabine (Khanjian) gives her class a translation exercise based on a news story about a terrorist and his pregnant girlfriend. Student Simon (Bostick) has a lot of unresolved feelings about his parents' death in a car crash, especially since his bigoted grandfather (Welsh) has led Simon to believe that his Lebanese father deliberately caused the accident. Simon uses the article to imagine himself as the terrorist's now-grown son but presents his work as fact not fiction when he uses a webcam to take the story to internet chat rooms, which has the deception spiraling out of control. English and French with subtitles. **101m/C; Blu-Ray, On Demand.** *CA FR* Arsinee Khanjian; Scott Speedman; Rachel Blanchard; Noam Jenkins; Kenneth Welsh; Devon Bostick; ***D:*** Atom Egoyan; ***W:*** Atom Egoyan; ***C:*** Paul Sarossy; ***M:*** Mychael Danna.

Adore 🦴 ½ *Two Mothers* **2013 (R)** Solemn yet sudsy melodrama of two blonde, 40-something lifelong best friends who each have a sexual relationship with the other's son. Widow Lil (Watts) and married Roz (Wright) live next door to each other along the Australian coast. Though they have jobs, the women seem to spend most of their time sunbathing and watching their sons, Tom (Frechville) and Ian (Samuel), also best friends, surf. After Tom witnesses an encounter between his mother Roz and Ian, he seduces Lil. There are some momentary pangs of conscience but that doesn't stop them from carrying on. Adapted from Doris Lessing's novel, "The Grandmothers." **100m/C; DVD, Blu-Ray.** *AU FR* Robin Wright; Naomi Watts; James Frecheville; Xavier Samuel; Ben Mendelsohn; Sophie Lowe; Jessica Tovey; Gary Sweet; ***D:*** Anne Fontaine; ***W:*** Christopher Hampton; ***C:*** Christophe Beaucarne; ***M:*** Christopher Gordon.

Adrenalin: Fear the Rush 🦴 **1996 (R)** Dull future thriller in the deadly virus category. In 2007, a plague in Eastern Europe causes those that survive to turn into cannabalistic killers. The U.S. has started quarantine camps, one of which is in Boston, and two cops (Henstridge and Lambert) must track down an infected killer who's escaped. Not worth your time. **77m/C; VHS, DVD.** Christopher Lambert; Natasha Henstridge; Norbert Weisser; Craig Davis, MD; Elizabeth Barondes; Xavier DeClie; ***D:*** Albert Pyun; ***W:*** Albert Pyun; ***C:*** George Mooradian; ***M:*** Tony Riparetti.

Adrenaline Drive 🦴🦴 *Adorenarin Doraibu* **1999** Sad sack Suzuki (Ando), who's working for a car rental company, accidentally plows a car into the Jaguar of yakuza big guy Kuroiwa (Matushige). Before punishment can be exacted, there's an explosion that lands them in the hospital. There shy nurse Shizuko (Ishida) latches on both to Suzuki and to a yakuza suitcase full of money and drags both on a road trip to freedom. Silly, good-natured comedy. Japanese with subtitles. **111m/C; VHS, DVD.** *JP* Hikari Ishida; Mansanobu Ando; Yataka Matushige; Kazue Tsunogae; ***D:*** Shinobu Yaguchi; ***W:*** Shinobu Yaguchi; ***C:*** Takashi Hamada; ***M:*** Seiichi Yamamoto.

Adrift 🦴🦴 ½ **2018 (PG-13)** Based on the true story of survival, a young couple's (Woodley and Claflin) encounter leads them first to love, and then on the adventure of a lifetime as they sail from Tahiti to San Diego. Things go horribly wrong as they fight to survive one of history's most devastating hurricanes. Woodley, who often carries the film solo, delivers a gritty yet emotional performance right up through the unforeseen conclusion. Based on the book *Red Sky in Mourning* by Tami Ashcraft. **96m/C; DVD, Blu-Ray.** Shailene Woodley; Sam Claflin; Grace Palmer; Jeffrey Thomas; Elizabeth Hawthorne; ***D:*** Baltasar Kormakur; ***W:*** Aaron Kandell; Jordan Kandell; David Branson Smith; ***C:*** Robert Richardson; ***M:*** Volker Bertelmann.

Adrift in Manhattan 🦴🦴 **2007 (R)** Chance encounters change the lives of three lonely New Yorkers. Simon (Rasuk) is a young man with a passion for photography. Snapping street pics, he finds his muse in depressed optometrist Rose (Graham), who's estranged from her husband (Baldwin) after their young child's death. Rose's patient Tommaso (Chianese), a painter, is going blind and she encourages him to find comfort with someone, deciding to take her own advice after Simon gets the courage to introduce himself. **91m/C; DVD, Blu-Ray.** Heather Graham; William Baldwin; Victor Rasuk; Dominic Chianese; Elizabeth Pena; Marta Colon; Erika Michels; ***D:*** Alfredo de Villa; ***W:*** Alfredo de Villa; Nat Moss; ***C:*** John Foster; ***M:*** Michael A. Levine.

Adua and Her Friends 🦴🦴 *Love a la Carte; Adua e le Compagne* **1960** When Rome's legalized brothels are shut down, four prostitutes use their savings to buy a rundown restaurant but they need a front man to get the property and licenses. Ercoli agrees for a hefty commission and only if they will continue to offer their services in the upstairs rooms. The restaurant is a success but the women become increasingly frustrated when they can't shake their pasts. Italian with subtitles. **98m/B; DVD, Blu-Ray.** *IT* Simone Signoret; Sandra Milo; Emmanuelle Riva; Gina Rovere; Claudio Gora; Marcello Mastroianni; Gianrico Tedeschi; ***D:*** Antonio Pietrangeli; ***W:*** Antonio Pietrangeli; Ruggero Maccari; Ettore Scola; ***C:*** Armando Nannuzzi; ***M:*** Piero Piccioni.

Adult World 🦴🦴 ½ **2013 (R)** When not stuck working in a dinky porn shop, hopeful writer Amy (Roberts) spends most of her time stalking her idol, the once-famous poet Rat Billings (Cusack). Yes, his name is Rat. Set in a wintry Syracuse, the back-and-forth resistance from the petulant has-been, pushing away his diehard fan, is loaded with biting dark humor. An original coming-of-age story that never dives into sentimentality or melodrama, with a sharp performance from Cusack at his most wry and witty. **97m/C; On Demand.** Emma Roberts; John Cusack; Evan Peters; John Cullum; Cloris Leachman; ***D:*** Scott Coffey; ***W:*** Andy Cochran; ***C:*** James Laxton; ***M:*** B.C. Smith.

Advance to the Rear 🦴🦴 ½ **1964** Light-hearted military comedy. A misfit band of Union Army soldiers are sent westward to do as little damage as possible while they frustrate their by-the-book captain, Jared Heath (Ford). Instead, they manage to get involved in protecting a gold shipment from southern sympathizer Zattig (Griffith) and get vamped by some beautiful Confederate spies, including Martha Lou (Stevens) who's very interested in Jared. **97m/B; DVD.** Glenn Ford; Stella Stevens; Melvyn Douglas; Joan Blondell; James J. Griffith; Jim Backus; Andrew Prine; Alan Hale, Jr.; Whit Bissell; Britt Ekland; ***D:*** George Marshall; ***W:*** Samuel A. Peeples; William Bowers; ***C:*** Milton Krasner; ***M:*** Randy Sparks.

Adventure in Baltimore 🦴🦴 **1949** Lightweight comedy set in 1905. Independent-minded Dinah is sent back in disgrace to her Baltimore hometown from her ladies' finishing school. She shocks the locals in several ways (she's a suffragette!) and exasperates her usually understanding minister father. However, Dinah's unconventional ways may derail his promotion to bishop and she also causes humiliation for her beau, Tom. **89m/B; DVD.** Shirley Temple; Robert Young; John Agar; Albert Sharpe; Josephine Hutchinson; Johnny Sands; ***D:*** Richard Wallace; ***W:*** Lionel Houser; ***C:*** Robert De Grasse; ***M:*** Frederick "Friedrich" Hollander.

Adventure in Manhattan 🦴🦴 ½ **1936** Smug crime reporter/criminologist George Melville (McCrea) is investigating a series of art thefts when he falls for Claire (Arthur), who's actually an actress hired to puncture his ego. Claire's starring in a WWI-set play (complete with loud explosions) that's a front for a jewel heist masterminded by the very man George has been pursuing. **73m/B; DVD.** Joel McCrea; Jean Arthur; Reginald Owen; Thomas Mitchell; Victor Kilian; ***D:*** Edward Ludwig; ***W:*** Sidney Buchman; Harry Sauber; Jack Kirkland; ***C:*** Henry Freulich; ***M:*** William Grant Still.

An Adventure in Space and Time 🦴🦴 ½ **2013** A behind-the-scenes look at how pioneering female producer Verity Lambert and the BBC got "Doctor Who," a science fiction TV series intended for children, on the air in 1963. When it becomes an unexpected hit, the show also revives the fading career of irascible character actor William Hartnell, who plays the time-traveling Doctor until ill health eventually forces him off the program. **90m/C; DVD, Blu-Ray.** *UK* David Bradley; Jessica Raine; Brian Cox; Sacha Dhawan; Lesley Manville; ***D:*** Terry McDonough; ***W:*** Mark Gatiss; ***C:*** John Pardue; ***M:*** Edmund Butt. **TV**

Adventure in Washington 🦴 **1941** Unbelievable political drama has DC gossip maven Jane Scott (Bruce), the girlfriend of Senator John Coleridge (Marshall), revealing that someone is selling government info. Coleridge discovers it's Senate page Marty Driscoll (Reynolds), a troubled youth Coleridge tried to help by getting him the job. How the plot plays out next is ridiculous. **82m/B; DVD.** Herbert Marshall; Virginia Bruce; Gene Reynolds; Samuel S. Hinds; Ralph Morgan; Vaughan Glaser; ***D:*** Alfred E. Green; ***W:*** Arthur Caesar; Lewis R. Foster; ***C:*** Henry Sharp; ***M:*** W. Franke Harling.

Adventureland 🦴🦴🦴 **2009 (R)** With his post-college dreams of a European trip squashed by his dad's financial problems, James (Eisenberg) instead must move back home to Pennsylvania in the summer of 1987 and with his limited degree can only find work at the "Adventureland," the ragged local amusement park. Still a virgin, James encounters Em (Stewart), a sexually-experienced though troubled young woman who can't stand her stepmother and is having an affair with the park's married handyman (Reynolds). The pair genuinely connect, in large part to the actors, particularly Stewart. Yes, it's a coming-of-age comedy and has the usual sophomoric jokes, vulgarity, and drug use but they are just background to a charming love story. Based in part on writer-director Mottola's own life, also features a great '80s soundtrack and a fun pairing of SNLers Wiig and Hader as the park's married owners. **107m/C; Blu-Ray.** Jesse Eisenberg; Kristen Stewart; Martin Starr; Bill Hader; Kristen Wiig; Ryan Reynolds; ***D:*** Greg Mottola; ***W:*** Greg Mottola; ***C:*** Terry Stacey.

The Adventurer: The Curse of the Midas Box 🦴🦴 ½ **2013 (PG)** When his parents go missing and his younger brother is kidnapped, 17-year-old Mariah Mundi follows clues that lead him to the mysterious Prince Regent Hotel. There he learns about an artifact with supernatural powers that can grant limitless wealth and that there are monsters who steal children. Brit fantasy based on the young adult novel by G.P. Taylor. **98m/C; DVD, Blu-Ray.** *UK* Aneurin Barnard; Michael Sheen; Sam Neill; Ioan Gruffudd; Keeley Hawes; Lena Headey; Tristan Gemmill; ***D:*** Jonathan Newman; ***W:*** Christian Taylor; Matthew Huffman; ***C:*** Unax Mendia; ***M:*** Fernando Velazquez.

The Adventurers WOOF! 1970 (R) Sleazy Harold Robbins novel retains its trashy aura on film. Unfortunately, this turkey is also long and boring. Set in South America, it tells the tale of a rich playboy who uses and destroys everyone who crosses his path. His vileness results from having seen his mother murdered by outlaws, but his obsession is to avenge his father's murder. Blood, gore, revolutions, and exploitive sex follow him everywhere. Watch and be amazed at the big-name stars who signed on for this one. **171m/C; DVD.** Candice Bergen; Olivia de Havilland; Bekim Fehmiu; Charles Aznavour; Alan Badel; Ernest Borgnine; Leigh Taylor-Young; Fernando Rey; Thommy Berggren; John Ireland; Sydney Tafler; Rossano Brazzi; Anna Moffo; Christian Roberts; Yorgo Voyagis; Angela Scoular; Yolande Donlan; Ferdinand "Ferdy" Mayne; Jaclyn Smith; Peter Graves; Roberta Haynes; ***D:*** Lewis Gilbert.

Adventures in Babysitting 🦴🦴 1/2 *A Night on the Town* **1987 (PG-13)** Pleasant comedy has its moments when a babysitter and her charges leave peaceful suburbia for downtown Chicago to rescue a friend in trouble. After a flat tire strands them on the freeway, trouble takes on a new meaning. Shue is charming as the hapless sitter, unexpectedly dateless, who finds herself doing a lot more than just watching the kids. Ludicrous at times, but still fun to watch. **102m/C; VHS, DVD, Blu-Ray.** Elisabeth Shue; Keith Coogan; Maia Brewton; Anthony Rapp; Calvin Levels; Vincent D'Onofrio; Penelope Ann Miller; George Newbern; John Ford Noonan; Lolita Davidovich; Albert Collins; ***D:*** Chris Columbus; ***W:*** David Simkins; ***C:*** Ric Waite; ***M:*** Michael Kamen.

Adventures in Zambezia 🦴 1/2 *Zambezia* **2012 (G)** A young falcon leaves for the big city to make his mark on the world. **83m/C; DVD, Blu-Ray.** *SA* Leonard Nimoy; Jeremy Suarez; Abigail Breslin; Jeff Goldblum; Samuel L. Jackson; ***D:*** Wayne Thornley; ***W:*** Wayne Thornley; Andrew Cook; Raffaella Delle Donne; Anthony Silverston; ***M:*** Bruce Retief. **VIDEO**

Adventures of a Teenage Dragonslayer 🦴🦴 1/2 2010 (PG) Fantasy adventure flick that hits its young target audience. Junior high dweeb Arthur is being bullied at school when he's rescued by Bart the troll, who tells Arthur he's the only one who can stop a dragon's destruction. After convincing his divorced mom Laura that what's happening is real, she, videogamer Shane, Bart, and Arthur team up to save the world. **88m/C; DVD.** Hunter Allan; Lea Thompson; Richard Sellers; Eric Lutes; Wendie Malick; Jordan Reynolds; Amy Pietz; ***D:*** Andrew Lauer; ***W:*** Jamie Nash; ***C:*** Luis M. Robinson; ***M:*** Mark Oates. **VIDEO**

The Adventures of Baron Munchausen 🦴🦴🦴 1/2 1989 (PG) From the director of "Time Bandits," "Brazil," and "The Fisher King" comes an ambitious, imaginative, chaotic, and under-appreciated marvel based on the tall (and often confused) tales of the Baron. Munchausen encounters the King of the Moon, Venus, and other odd and fascinating characters during what might be described as a circular narrative in which flashbacks dovetail into the present and place and time are never quite what they seem. Wonderful special effects and visually stunning sets occasionally dwarf the actors and prove what Gilliam can do with a big budget. **126m/C; VHS, DVD.** *GB GE* John Neville; Eric Idle; Sarah Polley; Valentina Cortese; Oliver Reed; Uma Thurman; Sting; Jonathan Pryce; Bill Paterson; Peter Jeffrey; Alison Steadman; Charles McKeown; Winston Dennis; Jack Purvis; Don Henderson; Andrew MacLachlan; ***Cameo(s):*** Robin Williams; ***D:*** Terry Gilliam; ***W:*** Terry Gilliam; Charles McKeown; ***C:*** Giuseppe Rotunno; ***M:*** Michael Kamen.

The Adventures of Buckaroo Banzai Across the Eighth Dimension 🦴🦴🦴 *Buckaroo Banzai* **1984 (PG)** A man of many talents, Buckaroo Banzai (Weller) travels through the eighth dimension in a jet-propelled Ford Fiesta to battle Planet 10 aliens led by the evil Lithgow. Buckaroo incorporates his vast knowledge of medicine, science, music, racing, and foreign relations to his advantage. Offbeat and often humorous cult sci-fi trip. **100m/C; VHS, DVD, Blu-Ray.** Peter Weller; Ellen Barkin; Jeff Goldblum; Christopher Lloyd; John Lithgow; Lewis Smith; Rosalind Cash; Robert Ito; Pepe Serna; Vincent Schiavelli; Dan Hedaya; Yakov Smirnoff; Jamie Lee Curtis; Ronald Lacey; Matt Clark; Clancy Brown; Carl Lumbly; Boyd 'Red' Morgan; Damon Hines; Billy Vera; Bill Henderson; Jonathan Banks; John Ashton; James Saito; ***D:*** W.D. Richter; ***W:*** Earl MacRauch; ***C:*** Fred W. Koenekamp; ***M:*** Michael Boddicker.

The Adventures of Bullwhip Griffin 🦴🦴 1/2 1966 A rowdy, family-oriented comedy-adventure set during the California Gold Rush. Light Disney farce catches Russell at the tail end of his teenage star days. Pleshette and McDowall embark upon an ocean trip from Boston to San Francisco to find her brother, Russell, who's out west digging for gold. Assorted comedic adventures take place. **110m/C; VHS, DVD.** Roddy McDowall; Suzanne Pleshette; Karl Malden; Harry Guardino; Bryan Russell; ***D:*** James Neilson; ***C:*** Edward Colman; ***M:*** George Bruns.

Adventures of Don Juan 🦴🦴🦴 1/2 *The New Adventures of Don Juan* **1949** Flynn's last spectacular epic features elegant costuming and loads of action. Don Juan saves Queen Margaret from her evil first minister. He then swashbuckles his way across Spain and England in an effort to win her heart. Grand, large-scale fun and adventure with Flynn at his self-mocking best. **111m/C; VHS, DVD.** Errol Flynn; Viveca Lindfors; Robert Douglas; Romney Brent; Alan Hale; Raymond Burr; Aubrey Mather; Ann Rutherford; ***D:*** Vincent Sherman; ***M:*** Max Steiner. Oscars '49: Costume Des. (C).

The Adventures of Ford Fairlane WOOF! *Ford Fairlane* **1990 (R)** The Diceman plays an unusual detective specializing in rock 'n' roll cases. When a heavy metal singer dies on stage, he takes the case in his own inimitable fashion, pursuing buxom gals, sleazy record executives, and even his ex-wife. Not surprisingly, many of his stand-up bits are worked into the movie. Clay, the ever-so-controversial comic in his first (and likely last) starring role haplessly sneers his way through this rock 'n' roll dud of a comedy thriller. A quick effort to cash in on Clay's fading star. Forget about it. **101m/C; VHS, DVD, Blu-Ray.** Andrew Silverstein; Wayne Newton; Priscilla Presley; Morris Day; Lauren Holly; Maddie Corman; Gilbert Gottfried; David Patrick Kelly; Brandon Call; Robert Englund; Ed O'Neill; Sheila E; Kari Wuhrer; Tone Loc; ***D:*** Renny Harlin; ***W:*** David Arnott; Daniel Waters; James Cappe. Golden Raspberries '90: Worst Actor (Silverstein), Worst Picture, Worst Screenplay.

The Adventures of Gallant Bess 🦴🦴 1948 The time-honored story of a rodeo man torn between his girl and his talented horse (the Bess of the title). **73m/C; VHS, DVD.** Cameron Mitchell; Audrey Long; Fuzzy Knight; James Millican; ***D:*** Lew Landers.

The Adventures of Huck Finn 🦴🦴🦴 1993 (PG) Decent Disney attempt at adapting an American favorite by Mark Twain. Mischievious Huck and runaway slave Jim travel down the muddy Mississippi, working on life and friendship and getting into all sorts of adventures in the pre-Civil War era. Fast-paced and amusing with good performances by Wood (in the title role) and Broadway trained Vance (as Jim). Racial epithets and minstrel show dialect have been eliminated in this version. Some material, including Jim's close call with a lynch mob and Huck's drunken, brutal father may be too strong for immature children. **108m/C; VHS, DVD.** Elijah Wood; Courtney B. Vance; Robbie Coltrane; Jason Robards, Jr.; Ron Perlman; Dana Ivey; Anne Heche; James Gammon; Paxton Whitehead; Tom Aldredge; Curtis Armstrong; Mary Louise Wilson; Frances Conroy; ***D:*** Stephen Sommers; ***W:*** Stephen Sommers; ***C:*** Janusz Kaminski; ***M:*** Bill Conti.

The Adventures of Huckleberry Finn 🦴🦴🦴 1939 Mark Twain's classic story about a boy who runs away and travels down the Mississippi on a raft, accompanied by a runaway slave, is done over in MGM-style. Rooney is understated as Huck (quite a feat), while the production occasionally floats aimlessly down the Mississippi. An entertaining follow-up to "The Adventures of Tom Sawyer." **89m/B; VHS, DVD, Streaming.** Mickey Rooney; Lynne Carver; Rex Ingram; William Frawley; Walter Connolly; ***D:*** Richard Thorpe.

The Adventures of Huckleberry Finn 🦴🦴 1/2 1960 A lively adaptation of the Twain saga in which Huck and runaway slave Jim raft down the Mississipi in search of freedom and adventure. Miscasting of Hodges as Huck hampers the proceedings, but Randall shines as the treacherous King. Strong supporting cast includes Keaton as a lion-tamer and boxing champ Moore as Jim. **107m/C; DVD.** Tony Randall; Eddie Hodges; Archie Moore; Patty McCormack; Neville Brand; Mickey Shaughnessy; Judy Canova; Andy Devine; Sherry Jackson; Buster Keaton; Finlay Currie; Josephine Hutchinson; Parley Baer; John Carradine; Royal Dano; Sterling Holloway; Harry Dean Stanton; ***D:*** Michael Curtiz.

The Adventures of Huckleberry Finn 🦴🦴 1/2 1985 An adaptation of the Mark Twain story about the adventures encountered by Huckleberry Finn and a runaway slave as they travel down the Mississippi River. Top-notch cast makes this an entertaining version. Originally made in a much longer version for PBS's "American Playhouse." **121m/C; VHS, DVD.** Sada Thompson; Lillian Gish; Richard Kiley; Jim Dale; Barnard Hughes; Patrick Day; Frederic Forrest; Geraldine Page; Butterfly McQueen; Samm-Art Williams; ***D:*** Peter H. Hunt. **TV**

The Adventures of Ichabod and Mr. Toad 🦴🦴🦴 1/2 1949 Disney's wonderfully animated versions of Kenneth Grahame's "The Wind in the Willows" and "The Legend of Sleepy Hollow" by Washington Irving. Rathbone narrates the story of Mr. Toad, who suffers from arrogance and eventually must defend himself in court after being charged with driving a stolen vehicle (Disney did take liberties with the story). Crosby provides all the voices for "Ichabod," which features one of the all-time great animated sequences—Ichabod riding in a frenzy through the forest while being pursued by the headless horseman. A treat for all ages. **68m/C; VHS, DVD, Blu-Ray.** ***V:*** Jack Kinney; Bing Crosby; Eric Blore; Pat O'Malley; ***Nar:*** Basil Rathbone; ***D:*** Clyde Geronimi; James Nelson Algar; ***W:*** Winston Hibler; Erdman Penner; Joe Rinaldi; Ted Sears; Homer Brightman; Harry Reeves; ***M:*** Oliver Wallace.

The Adventures of Marco Polo 🦴🦴 1/2 1938 Lavish Hollywood production based on the exploits of 13th-century Venetian explorer Marco Polo (Cooper). He becomes the first white man to record his visit to the Eastern court of Kublai Khan, where he falls for a beautiful princess also desired by the evil Rathbone. Lots of action, though its hard to picture the laconic Cooper in the title role. **100m/B; DVD.** Gary Cooper; Sigrid Gurie; Basil Rathbone; Ernest Truex; George Barbier; Binnie Barnes; Alan Hale; H.B. Warner; ***D:*** Archie Mayo; ***W:*** Robert Sherwood; ***M:*** Hugo Friedhofer.

The Adventures of Mark Twain 🦴🦴🦴 1944 March stars as Mark Twain, the nom de plume of Samuel Clemens, the beloved humorist and writer. His travels and adventures along the Mississippi and on to the California gold rush would later result in the books and stories which would make him so well-known. March attains a quiet nobility as he goes from young man to old sage, along with Smith, who plays Olivia, Twain's beloved wife. **130m/B; DVD.** Fredric March; Alexis Smith; Donald Crisp; Alan Hale; Sir C. Aubrey Smith; John Carradine; William Henry; Robert Barrat; Walter Hampden; Percy Kilbride; ***D:*** Irving Rapper; ***W:*** Alan LeMay; Harry Chandlee; ***M:*** Max Steiner.

The Adventures of Mark Twain 🦴🦴🦴 *Mark Twain* **1985 (G)** A clay-animated fantasy based on, and radically departing from, the life and work of Mark Twain. Story begins with Twain flying into outer space in a blimp with stowaways Huck Finn, Tom Sawyer and Becky Thatcher and takes off from there. Above average entertainment for kids and their folks. **86m/C; VHS, DVD, Blu-Ray.** ***V:*** James Whitmore; Chris Ritchie; Gary Krug; Michele Mariana; ***D:*** Will Vinton; ***W:*** Susan Shadburne.

The Adventures of Milo & Otis 🦴🦴🦴 *Koneko Monogatari; The Adventures of Chatran* **1989 (G)** Delightful Japanese children's film about a farm-dwelling dog and cat and their odyssey after the cat is accidentally swept away on a river. Notable since no humans appear in the film. A record-breaking success in its homeland. Well received by U.S. children. Narrated by Dudley Moore. **76m/C; VHS, DVD, Blu-Ray.** *JP* ***Nar:*** Dudley Moore; ***D:*** Masanori Hata; ***W:*** Mark Saltzman; ***C:*** Hideo Fujii; Shinji Tomita; ***M:*** Michael Boddicker.

The Adventures of Pinocchio 🦴🦴 1/2 *Pinocchio; Carlo Collodi's Pinocchio* **1996 (G)** Live-action version of Carlo Collodi's story about woodcarver Gepetto (Landau) who carves himself a puppet son (Thomas) who longs to be a real boy. Story differs from the Disney cartoon version in that it's a little darker and the cat, the fox, and the cricket have larger roles. Jim Henson's Creature Shop provided the animatronic magic to bring Pinocchio to life. His head alone was jammed with wiring and 18 tiny motors to give the "boy" a full range of facial expressions. It took as many as five puppeteers at a time to animate the character. So lifelike was the puppet that some of the crew actually spoke to it as they did the human actors. **88m/C; VHS, DVD.** Martin Landau; Jonathan Taylor Thomas; Rob Schneider; Bebe Neuwirth; Udo Kier; ***D:*** Steven Barron; ***W:*** Steven Barron; Tom Benedek; Sherry Mills; ***C:*** Juan Ruiz-Anchia; ***M:*** Rachel Portman.

The Adventures of Pluto Nash WOOF! 2002 (PG-13) Pluto Nash (Murphy) owns a nightclub on the moon in the year 2087, and some gangsters want it. Murphy should save us all a lot of time, trouble, and wasted effort and hand it over. On the shelf for two years (and some good reasons), this steaming pile of "action-comedy" has nothing going for it. The performances are "collecting-a-paycheck" quality, the script and direction are a mess, and it's howlingly unfunny. If you avoid seeing one movie this year, make it this one. **97m/C; VHS, DVD.** Eddie Murphy; Rosario Dawson; Randy Quaid; Joe Pantoliano; Jay Mohr; John Cleese; Pam Grier; Peter Boyle; Luis Guzman; James Rebhorn; Burt Young; Miguel A. Nunez, Jr.; Illeana Douglas; Victor Varnado; ***D:*** Ron Underwood; ***W:*** Neil Cuthbert; ***C:*** Oliver Wood; ***M:*** John Powell.

The Adventures of Priscilla, Queen of the Desert 🦴🦴🦴 1994 (R) Quirky down-under musical-comedy follows two drag queens and a transsexual across the Australian Outback on their way to a gig in a small resort town. They make the drive in a pink bus nicknamed Priscilla. Along the way they encounter, and perform for, the usual unusual assortment of local characters. Scenes depicting homophobic natives play out as expected. Finest moments occur on the bus or onstage (all hail ABBA). Strong performances, especially by usually macho Stamp as the widowed Bernadette, rise above the cliches in what is basically a bitchy, cross-dressing road movie, celebrating drag as art and the nonconformity of its heroes. Costumes (by Lizzy Gardner and Tim Chappel) are a lark, the photography's surreal, and the soundtrack fittingly campy. **102m/C; VHS, DVD.** *AU* Terence Stamp; Hugo Weaving; Guy Pearce; Bill Hunter; Sarah Chadwick; Mark Holmes; Julia Cortez; Rebel Russell; June Marie Bennett; Alan Dargin; Margaret Pomeranz; ***D:*** Stephan Elliott; ***W:*** Stephan Elliott; ***C:*** Brian J. Breheny; ***M:*** Guy Gross. Oscars '94: Costume Des.; Australian Film Inst. '94: Costume Des.

Adventures of Red Ryder 🦴🦴 1940 The thrills of the rugged West are presented in this 12-episode serial. Based on the then-famous comic strip character. **240m/B; VHS, DVD.** Donald (Don "Red") Barry; Noah Beery, Sr.; Tommy Cook; Harry Worth; Wally Wales; William Farnum; Carleton Young; ***D:*** William Witney; John English; ***W:***

Frank (Franklyn) Adreon; Norman S. Hall; Barney A. Sarecky; ***C:*** William Nobles; ***M:*** Cy Feuer.

The Adventures of Robin Hood **1938** Rollicking technicolor tale of the legendary outlaw, regarded as the swashbuckler standard-bearer. The justice-minded Saxon knight battles the Normans, outwits evil Prince John, and gallantly romances Maid Marian. Grand Castle sets and lush forest photography display ample evidence of the huge (for 1938) budget of $2 million plus. Just entering his prime, Flynn enthusiastically performed most of his own stunts, including intricate swordplay and advanced tree and wall climbing. His Robin brims with charm and bravura. THe rest of the cast likewise attacks with zest: de Haviland, a cold, but ultimately sympathetic Marian; Rains's dastardly Prince John; and Rathbone's convincing Sir Guy to Robin's band of very merry men. Based on the many Robin Hood legends, as well as Sir Walter Scott's "Ivanhoe" and the opera "Robin Hood" by De Koven-Smith. **102m/C; VHS, DVD, Blu-Ray, HD-DVD.** Errol Flynn; Olivia de Havilland; Claude Rains; Basil Rathbone; Alan Hale; Una O'Connor; Patric Knowles; Eugene Pallette; Herbert Mundin; Melville Cooper; Ian Hunter; Montagu Love; ***D:*** Michael Curtiz; ***W:*** Seton I. Miller; Norman Reilly Raine; ***C:*** Gaetano Antonio "Tony" Gaudio; Sol Polito; ***M:*** Erich Wolfgang Korngold. Oscars '38: Film Editing, Orig. Score; Natl. Film Reg. '95.

The Adventures of Rocky & Bullwinkle **1/2 2000 (PG)** Flying squirrel and his moose pal--living on residuals since their TV show was cancelled--discover their old enemies, Russian spies Boris Badenov (Alexander), Natasha Fatale (Russo), and their Fearless Leader (De Niro), have escaped from their two-dimensional existence. The troublemaking trio heads for Hollywood and plots to--what else?—take over the world. Someone seriously miscalculated in targeting the Pokemon set (the show was 35 years old, and the majority of the jokes were aimed at adults), but it's more effective on the small screen, providing a few good laughs. **88m/C; VHS, DVD, Blu-Ray.** Robert De Niro; Jason Alexander; Rene Russo; Janeane Garofalo; Randy Quaid; Piper Perabo; Carl Reiner; Jonathan Winters; John Goodman; Kenan Thompson; Kel Mitchell; James Rebhorn; David Alan Grier; Norman Lloyd; Jon Polito; Whoopi Goldberg; Billy Crystal; Don Novello; Harrison Young; Dian Bachar; Paget Brewster; ***V:*** June Foray; Keith Scott; ***D:*** Des McAnuff; ***W:*** Kenneth Lonergan; ***C:*** Thomas Ackerman; ***M:*** Mark Mothersbaugh.

The Adventures of Sadie **1/2** *Our Girl Friday* **1955** Collins is stranded on a desert island with three men, two of whom continuously chase her around. Naturally, she falls for the guy who ignores her. Obvious sex comedy which plays on Collins' scantily clad physical assets. Based on the novel "The Cautious Amorist" by Norman Lindsay. **87m/C; VHS, DVD.** *GB* Joan Collins; George Cole; Kenneth More; Robertson Hare; Hermione Gingold; Walter Fitzgerald; ***D:*** Noel Langley; ***W:*** Noel Langley.

The Adventures of Sebastian Cole **1/2 1999 (R)** Sebastian (Grenier) is a misfit highschooler in upstate New York in 1983. Not only does he have to deal with the usual trials of adolescence but there's his unusual family problems. His mother, Joan (Colin), returns to her native England upon learning that Sebastian's stepdad, Hank (Gregg), has decided to become a woman. Sebastian eventually winds up living with Hank, who is now known as Henrietta, and who's still the most stable adult in the teen's fractured world. **99m/C; DVD.** Adrian Grenier; Clark Gregg; Aleksa Palladino; Margaret Colin; John Shea; Joan Copeland; Marni Lustig; Tom Lacy; ***D:*** Tod Harrison Williams; ***W:*** Tod Harrison Williams; ***C:*** John Foster; ***M:*** Lynne Geller.

The Adventures of Sharkboy and Lavagirl in 3-D **1/2 2005 (PG)** Multi-hyphenate Rodriguez uses a story from son Racer as the basis for this kid-friendly adventure. Ten year-old misfit Max (Boyd) dreams up a couple of young superheroes and finds them coming to life. Sharkboy (Lautner) and Lavagirl (Dooley) need Max's help to save their home world, Planet Drool, from the evil Mr. Electric (Lopez). The cartoonish gee-wizardry will no doubt appeal to its target audience, but might struggle to hold the attention of older kids. **94m/C; DVD, Blu-Ray, UMD.** Kristin Davis; David Arquette; George Lopez; Taylor Lautner; Taylor Dooley; Cayden Boyd; Jacob Davich; Sasha Pieterse; Rico Torres; Rebel Rodriguez; Racer Rodriguez; Rocket Rodriguez; ***D:*** Robert Rodriguez; ***W:*** Robert Rodriguez; ***C:*** Robert Rodriguez; ***M:*** John Debney; Graeme Revell.

The Adventures of Sherlock Holmes **1/2** *Sherlock Holmes* **1939** The immortal Sherlock Holmes and his assistant Dr. Watson conflict with Scotland Yard as they both race to stop arch-criminal Professor Moriarty. The Yard is put to shame as Holmes, a mere amateur sleuth, uses his brilliant deductive reasoning to save the damsel in distress and to stop Moriarty from stealing the Crown Jewels. Second in the series. **83m/B; VHS, DVD.** Basil Rathbone; Nigel Bruce; Ida Lupino; George Zucco; E.E. Clive; Mary Gordon; ***D:*** Alfred Werker; ***W:*** Edwin Blum; ***C:*** Leon Shamroy.

The Adventures of Sherlock Holmes' Smarter Brother **1978 (PG)** The unknown brother of the famous Sherlock Holmes takes on some of his brother's more disposable excess cases and makes some hilarious moves. Moments of engaging farce borrowed from the Mel Brooks school of parody (and parts of the Brooks ensemble as well). **91m/C; VHS, DVD.** Gene Wilder; Madeline Kahn; Marty Feldman; Dom DeLuise; Leo McKern; Roy Kinnear; John Le Mesurier; Douglas Wilmer; Thorley Walters; ***D:*** Gene Wilder; ***W:*** Gene Wilder.

Adventures of Smilin' Jack **1943** WWII flying ace Smilin' Jack Martin comes to life in this action-packed serial. Character from the Zack Mosley comic strip about air force fighting over China. **90m/B; VHS, DVD.** Tom Brown; Sidney Toler; ***D:*** Ray Taylor.

The Adventures of Tartu **1/2** *Tartu* **1943** A British secret agent, sent to blow up a Nazi poison gas factory in Czechoslovakia, poses as a Romanian. One of Donat's lesser films, in the style of "The 39 Steps." **103m/C; VHS, DVD.** *GB* Robert Donat; Valerie Hobson; Glynis Johns; ***D:*** Harold Bucquet.

The Adventures of Tarzan **1921** The screen's first Tarzan in an exciting jungle thriller. Silent. **153m/B; Silent; VHS, DVD.** Elmo Lincoln; Louise Lorraine; Lilian Worth; Frank Whitson; Frank Merrill; ***D:*** Robert F. "Bob" Hill; ***W:*** Robert F. "Bob" Hill.

The Adventures of the Wilderness Family **1976 (G)** The story of a modern-day pioneer family who becomes bored with the troubles of city life and heads for life in the wilderness. There, they find trouble in paradise. Family-oriented adventure offering pleasant scenery. Followed by "The Wilderness Family, Part 2." **100m/C; VHS, DVD.** Robert F. Logan; Susan Damante-Shaw; ***D:*** Stewart Raffill; ***W:*** Stewart Raffill.

The Adventures of Tintin **1/2 2011 (PG)** Spielberg explores both motion-capture animation and the world of 3D with his adaptation of the hit Belgian comic book series by Herge. With mo-cap work by Bell, Serkis, and Craig, Spielberg works straight from one of the original stories, "The Secret of the Unicorn." In the tale, reporter Tintin (Bell) and his fox terrier Snowy team up with an alcoholic sea captain to get to the bottom of the mystery behind a secret scroll found in a model ship. Some of the 3D sequences—which could only be accomplished in the motion-capture form—are undeniably tasty eye candy, but the whole experience feels remarkably hollow. **107m/C; DVD, Blu-Ray.** ***V:*** Jamie Bell; Daniel Craig; Andy Serkis; Simon Pegg; Toby Jones; Sebastien Roche; Mackenzie Crook; Gad Elmaleh; ***D:*** Steven Spielberg; ***W:*** Edgar Wright; Steven Moffatt; Joe Cornish; ***M:*** John Williams. Golden Globes '12: Animated Film.

The Adventures of Tom Sawyer **1938** The vintage Hollywood adaptation of the Mark Twain classic, with art direction by William Cameron Menzies. Not a major effort from the Selznick studio, but quite detailed and the best Tom so far. **91m/C; VHS, DVD, Blu-Ray; Open Captioned.** Tommy Kelly; Walter Brennan; Victor Jory; May Robson; Victor Kilian; Jackie Moran; Donald Meek; Ann Gillis; Marcia Mae Jones; David Holt; Margaret Hamilton; ***D:*** Norman Taurog; ***C:*** James Wong Howe; ***M:*** Max Steiner.

Advise and Consent **1962** An interesting political melodrama with a fascinating cast, based upon Allen Drury's novel. The President chooses a candidate for the Secretary of State position which divides the Senate and causes the suicide of a senator. Controversial in its time, though somewhat turgid today. Laughton's last film. **139m/B; VHS, DVD.** Don Murray; Charles Laughton; Henry Fonda; Walter Pidgeon; Lew Ayres; Burgess Meredith; Gene Tierney; Franchot Tone; Paul Ford; George Grizzard; Betty White; Peter Lawford; Edward Andrews; ***D:*** Otto Preminger; ***W:*** Wendell Mayes; ***C:*** Sam Leavitt. Natl. Bd. of Review '62: Support. Actor (Meredith).

The Advocate *The Hour of the Pig* **1993 (R)** Bizarre black comedy about 15th-century Paris lawyer Richard Courtois (Firth) who decides to ply his trade in the country, only to find things stranger than he can imagine. His first case turns out to be defending a pig that's accused of murdering a child. And the pig is owned by beautiful gypsy Samira (Annabi), so the idealistic lawyer can fall in love (or lust). There's religion and superstition, there's power struggles, there's ignorance versus knowledge—things sound very modern indeed. **102m/C; VHS, DVD.** *GB* Colin Firth; Amina Annabi; Nicol Williamson; Ian Holm; Lysette Anthony; Donald Pleasence; Michael Gough; Harriet Walter; Jim Carter; Dave Atkins; ***D:*** Leslie Megahey; ***W:*** Leslie Megahey.

AE: Apocalypse Earth **2013** The film follows a small group of survivors shipwrecked on a foreign world full of monsters after aliens invade Earth. **87m/C; DVD, Blu-Ray.** Adrian Paul; Richard Grieco; Bali Rodriguez; Gray Hawks; ***D:*** Thunder Levin; ***W:*** Thunder Levin; ***C:*** Richard J. Vialet; ***M:*** Chris Ridenhour. **VIDEO**

Aelita: Queen of Mars *Aelita: The Revolt of the Robots* **1924** Though the title has blockbuster potential, "Aelita" is a little-known silent Soviet sci-fi flick destined to remain little known. After building a rocket to fly to Mars, a Russian engineer finds it's no Martian holiday on the fourth planet from the sun, with the Martians in the midst of a revolution. Silent, with a piano score. **113m/B; Silent; VHS, DVD.** *RU* Yulia Solntseva; Nikolai Batalov; Nikolai Tseretelli; Vera Orlova; Pavel Poi; Konstantin Eggert; Yuri Zavadski; Valentina Kuindzi; N. Tretyakova; ***D:*** Yakov Protazanov; ***W:*** Fedor Ozep; Aleksey Fajko; ***C:*** Yuri Zhelyabuzhsky; Emil Schunemann.

Aeon Flux **1/2 2005 (PG-13)** It's hard to fault a movie ostensibly about Charlize Theron in spandex shooting people. Based on the MTV cartoon, Kusama's sci fi/actioner is a goofy guilty pleasure that succeeds largely due to Theron's on-screen charisma. Set 400 years in the future, a plague wipes out most of humanity and survivors live in Bregna, a walled city ruled by Trevor Goodchild's (Csokas) fascist government. A resistance movement sends their top assassin, Aeon Flux (Theron), to dispatch Goodchild but Aeon realizes some disturbing truths might lie behind her brave new world. Things get cheesy, but Kusama has fun with her wonky futuristic designs. **95m/C; DVD, Blu-Ray, HD-DVD.** Charlize Theron; Marton Csokas; Jonny Lee Miller; Sophie Okonedo; Frances McDormand; Pete Postlethwaite; Amelia Warner; Nikolai Kinski; Caroline Chikezie; ***D:*** Karyn Kusama; ***W:*** Phil Hay; Matt Manfredi; ***C:*** Stuart Dryburgh; ***M:*** Graeme Revell.

The Aeronauts **1/2 2019 (PG-13)** In nineteenth century Britain, James (Redmayne) is a scientist with original theories about weather that he desperately wants to prove even as his colleagues express serious skepticism. When he meets hot air balloon pilot Amelia (Jones), he believes he has found a solution to his dilemma. However, Amelia lost her husband in a ballooning accident and is initially reluctant to take his offer to pilot a balloon for scientific research. Though she finally agrees, both of their lives are put in peril. The historical fantasy, based partly on real people and events, features impressive cinematography but is otherwise deflating. **101m/C; DVD.** Felicity Jones; Eddie Redmayne; Vincent Perez; Phoebe Fox; Himesh Patel; ***D:*** Tom Harper; ***W:*** Jack Thorne; ***C:*** George Steel; ***M:*** Steven Price.

The Affair **1973** Songwriter/polio victim Wood falls in love for the first time with attorney Wagner. Delicate situation handled well by a fine cast. **74m/C; VHS, DVD.** Natalie Wood; Robert Wagner; Bruce Davison; Kent Smith; Frances Reid; Pat Harrington, Jr.; ***D:*** Gilbert Cates. **TV**

The Affair **1/2 1995 (R)** It's 1944 in a small English town, where a troop of black American soldiers are billeted prior to the D-Day invasion. Travis (Vance) falls for the married Maggie (Fox)?whose husband, Edward (Hinds), is supposed to be away at sea—and they begin an affair. Unfortunately, Edward arrives home unexpectedly and accuses Travis of raping his wife. If Maggie denies the accusation, she'll lose her home and family but if she confirms it, Travis, according to Army law, will be condemned to death. **105m/C; VHS, DVD.** *GB* Courtney B. Vance; Kerry Fox; Ciaran Hinds; Beatie Edney; Leland Gantt; Bill Nunn; Ned Beatty; ***D:*** Paul Seed; ***W:*** Pablo F. Fenjves; Bryan Goluboff; ***C:*** Ivan Strasburg; ***M:*** Christopher Gunning. **CABLE**

Affair in Trinidad **1952** Fun in the tropics as nightclub singer Hayworth enlists the help of brother-in-law Ford to find her husband's murderer. The trail leads to international thieves and espionage in a romantic thriller that reunites the stars of "Gilda." Hayworth sings (with Jo Ann Greer's voice) "I've Been Kissed Before." **98m/B; DVD.** Rita Hayworth; Glenn Ford; Alexander Scourby; Torin Thatcher; Valerie Bettis; Steven Geray; ***D:*** Vincent Sherman.

An Affair of Love **1/2** *Une Liaison Pornographique; A Pornographic Liaison; Une Liaison d'Amour* **1999 (R)** French love story sounds like "Last Tango in Paris" but really owes more to "sex, lies and videotape." Elle (Baye) places an ad in a sex magazine and arranges to meet a respondent, Lui (Lopez), for afternoon sexual encounters in a hotel. Virtually all of the physical action takes place behind a closed door. The point is emotional and so, in after-the-fact monologues, they both discuss (separately) what's happened. French with subtitles. **80m/C; VHS, DVD.** *FR BE LU* Nathalie Baye; Sergi Lopez; Paul Pavel; ***D:*** Frederic Fonteyne; ***W:*** Philippe Blasband; ***C:*** Virginie Saint-Martin; ***M:*** Andre Dziezuk; Marc Mergen; Jeannot Sanavia.

The Affair of the Necklace **1/2 2001 (R)** Louis XVI-era history is given a tabloid treatment in this costume drama concerning the vengeful efforts of orphaned Jeanne de la Motte-Valois to restore nobility to her family name. She conspires with a court rogue to hatch a sophisticated scam involving the cardinal of France, Marie Antoinette, German Illuminati, and the fabulous necklace of the title, paving the way for the French Revolution. Excessive narration and flashbacks bog the plot; film offers little other than eye candy in the form of intricate set pieces and fancy dress. Intriguing story potential is mishandled, and Swank is terribly miscast but looks nice in a corset. The remaining actors are underused, except Walken in a scene-chewing role as a Svengali-like mesmerist. **120m/C; VHS, DVD.** Hilary Swank; Jonathan Pryce; Simon Baker; Adrien Brody; Brian Cox; Joely Richardson; Christopher Walken; Paul Brooke; Peter Eyre; Simon Kunz; Hayden Panettiere; ***D:*** Charles Shyer; ***W:*** John Sweet; ***C:*** Ashley Rowe; ***M:*** David Newman.

An Affair to Remember **1/2 1957** McCarey remakes his own "Love Affair," with less success. Nightclub singer Kerr and wealthy bachelor Grant discover love on an ocean liner and agree to meet six months later on top of the Empire State Building to see if their feelings are the same. Not as good as the original, but a winner of a fairy tale just the same. Notable for causing many viewers to sob uncontrollably. "Affair" was gathering dust on store shelves until "Sleepless in Seattle" used it as a plot device and rentals skyrocketed. In 1994 real life couple Warren Beatty and Annette Bening attempted a third "Love Affair" remake. **115m/C; VHS, DVD, Blu-Ray.** Cary Grant; Deborah Kerr; Richard Denning; Cathleen Nesbitt; Neva Patterson; Robert Q. Lewis; Fortunio Bonanova; Matt Moore; Nora Marlowe; Sarah Selby; *D:* Leo McCarey; *W:* Leo McCarey; Delmer Daves; Donald Ogden Stewart; *C:* Milton Krasner; *M:* Hugo Friedhofer.

Affairs of Anatol ⚲⚲ **1921** Philandering playboy Anatol Spencer (Reid) finds no luck with women. He's robbed by one (Ayres), two-timed by another (Hawley), and even madam Satan Synne (Daniels) isn't what she seems. Then Anatol decides to return to his wife, Vivian (Swanson), only to discover that she's being amusing herself with another. Based on a play by Arthur Schnitzler. **117m/B; Silent; VHS, DVD.** Wallace Reid; Gloria Swanson; Bebe Daniels; Wanda (Petit) Hawley; Agnes Ayres; Monte Blue; Theodore Roberts; Elliott Dexter; *D:* Cecil B. DeMille; *W:* Beulah Marie Dix; *C:* Karl Struss; Alvin Wyckoff.

The Affairs of Dobie Gillis ⚲⚲ 1/2 **1953** Light musical-comedy about a group of college kids and their carefree antics. Complete with big-band tunes, dance numbers, and plenty of collegiate shenanigans, this '50s classic inspired a hit TV series, "The Many Loves of Dobie Gillis." **72m/B; VHS, DVD.** Debbie Reynolds; Bobby Van; Barbara Ruick; Bob Fosse; Lurene Tuttle; Hans Conried; Charles Lane; *D:* Don Weis; *W:* Max Shulman; *C:* William Mellor.

Affinity ⚲⚲ **2008** In 1870s Victorian England, a woman of Margaret Prior's (Madeley) upper social class and age should be married. Instead, she lives with her mother and is suffering a deep depression after the recent death of her father and the marriage of her best friend (and secret lover) Helen (Young) to her brother. Encouraged to do good works, Margaret mentors the female inmates of Milbank prison and becomes curious about Selina Dawes (Tapper), a so-called spirit medium incarcerated for murder after a seance gone wrong. At first skeptical of Selina's alleged gifts, Margaret becomes fascinated by the allure of the unknown. Based on the novel by Sarah Waters. **94m/C; DVD.** *GB* Anna Madeley; Zoe Tapper; Domini Blythe; Anne Reid; Amanda Plummer; Anna Massey; Ferelith Young; Vincent Leclerc; *D:* Tim Fywell; *W:* Andrew Davies; *C:* Bernard Couture; *M:* Frederic Weber. **TV**

Afflicted ⚲⚲ 1/2 **2014 (R)** Found-footage horror movies might be the most overdone genre du jour, but directors Prowse and Lee breathe some life into shaky-cam cinema with this tense first-person account of a young man's transformation into something else. Resembling "American Werewolf in London" more than "Paranormal Activity," the story follows two friends, Clif and Derek (played by the writer-directors), documenting their trip around the world. But, after Derek gets bit by a strange woman in Paris, his body starts changing and he develops a taste for blood. Prowse and Lee do a fantastic job of making their characters feel like real people, which only makes Derek's transformation that much creepier. **85m/C; DVD, Blu-Ray.** *US CA* Clif Prowse; Derek Lee; Baya Rehaz; Benjamin Zeitoun; Edo Van Breemen; *D:* Clif Prowse; Derek Lee; *W:* Clif Prowse; Derek Lee; *C:* Norm Li; *M:* Edo Van Breemen.

Affliction ⚲⚲⚲ 1/2 **1997 (R)** Nolte, Schrader, and Coburn turn in the finest work of their careers in this bleak tale of one man's battle with the demons of his past and the failures of the present. Nolte is small-town, small-time sheriff Wade Whitehouse, who wants to do the right things, but never does. Damaged beyond repair by his abusive alcoholic father (Coburn), he alienates or scares away anyone who might care for him, including his daughter (Tierney) and his girlfriend (Spacek). When a local businessman dies under mysterious circumstances, Wade sees a chance at redemption, but the investigation turns out to be the catalyst for his final degradation. Schrader has studied the beaten-down male psyche before, but never with this much discipline or implicit knowledge. He adapted the screenplay from Russell Banks' 1989 novel. **113m/C; VHS, DVD.** Nick Nolte; James Coburn; Sissy Spacek; Willem Dafoe; Mary Beth Hurt; Jim True-Frost; Marian Seldes; Brigid Tierney; Sean McCann; Wayne Robson; Holmes Osborne; *D:* Paul Schrader; *W:* Paul Schrader; *C:* Paul Sarossy; *M:* Michael Brook. Oscars '98: Support. Actor (Coburn); N.Y. Film Critics '98: Actor (Nolte); Natl. Soc. Film Critics '98: Actor (Nolte).

Afghan Knights ⚲ 1/2 **2007 (R)** An ex-Navy SEAL recruits some former comrades to go back to Afghanistan as mercenaries in order to sneak a warlord out of the country. They meet some opposition and are forced to hide out in a cave where they find some weapons that contain the spirit of Genghis Khan and his Mongol warriors. Said ghostly hordes are looking for some new recruits. Surprisingly, not as ridiculous as it sounds. **90m/C; DVD.** Francesco Quinn; Steve Bacic; Gary Stretch; Michael Madsen; Chris Kramer; *D:* Allan Harmon; *W:* Christine Stringer; *C:* Randal Platt; *M:* Jon Lee; Stu Goldberg. **VIDEO**

Afghan Luke ⚲ 1/2 **2011 (R)** Journalist Luke Benning (Stahl) quits his job after his story about a Canadian sniper mutilating corpses in Afghanistan is rejected. He returns to the war, accompanied by pal Tom (Wright), to get more evidence but they get caught up in various surreal situations. Maybe the onscreen hash haze spilled over because the film is rambling and incoherent. **97m/C; DVD, Blu-Ray.** *CA* Nick Stahl; Nicholas Wright; Ali Liebert; Stephen Lobo; Pascale Hutton; *D:* Mike Clattenberg; *W:* Mike Clattenberg; *C:* Jeremy Benning; *M:* Blaine Morris.

Afraid of the Dark ⚲⚲ **1992 (R)** Convoluted psycho-thriller from a child's point of view. Young Lucas is fearful for his blind mother. It seems a vicious slasher has been attacking blind women and Lucas' father, a policeman, has yet to apprehend the criminal. But...Lucas it seems has a problem with reality. With his fantasies and realities mixed, all the people in his life also play entirely different roles. Characters are so detached and unreal that a viewer is prevented from a clear understanding of anything that may, or may not, be going on. Directorial debut of Peploe. **91m/C; VHS, DVD.** *FR GB* Ben Keyworth; James Fox; Fanny Ardant; Paul McGann; Clare Holman; Robert Stephens; *D:* Mark Peploe; *W:* Mark Peploe; *C:* Bruno de Keyzer.

Africa Screams ⚲⚲ 1/2 **1949** Abbott and Costello go on an African safari in possession of a secret map. Unheralded independent A&C film is actually quite good in the stupid vein, with lots of jungle slapstick, generally good production values, and a supporting cast of familiar comedy faces. **79m/B; VHS, DVD.** Lou Costello; Bud Abbott; Shemp Howard; Hillary Brooke; Joe Besser; Clyde Beatty; Max Baer, Sr.; *D:* Charles T. Barton; *W:* Earl Baldwin; *M:* Walter Schumann.

Africa Texas Style ⚲⚲ **1967** An East African rancher hires an American cowboy and his Navajo sidekick to help run his wild game ranch. Decent family adventure which served as the pilot for the short-lived TV series "Cowboy in Africa." Features lots of wildlife footage and a cameo appearance by Hayley Mills. **109m/C; VHS, Streaming.** Hugh O'Brian; John Mills; Nigel Green; Tom Nardini; Adrienne Corri; *Cameo(s):* Hayley Mills; *D:* Andrew Marton; *M:* Malcolm Arnold. **TV**

An African Election ⚲⚲ **2011** Rather generic documentary has the Merz brothers looking at the sub-Saharan country of Ghana, which is preparing for the 2008 presidential elections. Although the country achieved independence in 1957, it's been subjected to five military regimes as well as three republics since then. The two main presidential candidates may represent leftist and right-wing parties but don't differ much politically. The most dramatic part of the film is the millions of citizens who show up at the polls on election day determined to exercise their democratic rights. English and various Ghanaian languages with subtitles. **89m/C; DVD.** *US SI D:* Jarreth Merz; Kevin Merz; *W:* Erika Tasini; Shjun Yantara Marcacci; *C:* Kevin Merz; Topher Osborn; *M:* Patrick Kirst.

The African Queen ⚲⚲⚲⚲ **1951** After Bible-thumping spinster Hepburn's missionary brother is killed in WWI Africa, hard-drinking, dissolute steamer captain Bogart offers her safe passage. Not satisfied with sanctuary, she persuades him to destroy a German gunboat blocking the British advance. The two spend most of their time battling aquatic obstacles and each other, rather than the Germans. Time alone on a African river turns mistrust and aversion to love, a transition effectively counterpointed by the continuing suspense of their daring mission. Classic war of the sexes script adapted from C.S. Forester's novel makes wonderful use of natural dialogue and humor. Shot on location in Africa. **105m/C; VHS, DVD, Blu-Ray.** *GB* Humphrey Bogart; Katharine Hepburn; Robert Morley; Theodore Bikel; Peter Bull; Walter Gotell; Peter Swanwick; Richard Marner; *D:* John Huston; *W:* John Huston; James Agee; *C:* Jack Cardiff. Oscars '51: Actor (Bogart); AFI '98: Top 100; Natl. Film Reg. '94.

African Rage ⚲⚲ *Tigers Don't Cry; The Long Shot; Target of an Assassin; Fatal Assassin* **1978** Little known release about an aging male nurse (yes, Quinn) who discovers he's dying of an incurable disease. With nothing left to lose, he plans the kidnapping of an African leader, hoping that the ransom will support his family. Meanwhile, another man is plotting the same leader's death. Decent performances help move along the improbable plot. **90m/C; VHS, DVD.** *SA* Anthony Quinn; John Phillip Law; Simon Sabela; Ken Gampu; Marius Weyers; Sandra Prinsloo; *D:* Peter Collinson.

African Treasure ⚲ 1/2 **1952** Bomba is summoned by jungle drum telegraph when two geologists turn out to actually be diamond smugglers. They're forcing the local tribe to get the gems for them and Bomba must defeat the villains in the 7th film in the Monogram series. **70m/B; DVD.** John(ny) Sheffield; Laurette Luez; Lyle Talbot; Lane Bradford; Arthur Space; Leonard Mudie; *D:* Ford Beebe; *W:* Ford Beebe; *C:* Harry Neumann; *M:* Raoul Kraushaar.

After ⚲ **2019 (PG-13)** After naive suburban teen Tessa (Langford) begins college, she meets complex bad boy Hardin Scott (Fiennes Tiffin) and the pair bond over their shared love of works of fiction. Dumping her high school boyfriend Noah (Arnold), Tessa and Hardin grow closer and closer and have sex. Though Hardin repeatedly states he does not exist, they fall into a relationship that becomes increasingly complicated for both of them and affects Tessa's relationship with her judgmental mother Carol (Blair). Based on a first book in a novel series by Anna Todd, it comes off more like a teen soap opera. **106m/C; DVD, Blu-Ray.** Hero Fiennes Tiffin; Josephine Langford; Selma Blair; Jennifer Beals; Peter Gallagher; *D:* Jenny Gage; *W:* Susan McMartin; *C:* Tom Betterton; Adam Silver; *M:* Justin Caine Burnett.

After Dark, My Sweet ⚲⚲⚲ **1990 (R)** A troubled young man in search of a little truth ends up entangled in a kidnapping scheme. Muddled direction is overcome by above average performances and gritty realism. Based on the novel by Jim Thompson. **114m/C; VHS, DVD.** Jason Patric; Rachel Ward; Bruce Dern; George Dickerson; James Cotton; Corey Carrier; Rocky Giordani; *D:* James Foley; *W:* Robert Redlin; James Foley; *C:* Mark Plummer; *M:* Maurice Jarre.

After Earth ⚲ **2013 (PG-13)** In this sci-fi blockbuster, Kitai Raige (Jaden Smith) and his legendary Ranger father Cypher (Will Smith) crash-land on a futuristic Earth that has been unable to sustain human life for centuries. With both of his legs broken, the elder Raige can only monitor and advise his adolescent son as he treks across the inhospitable planet in search of the other half of their ship, the one with the homing beacon...and the deadly alien creature. With more silly motivational nuggets ("Fear is a choice") than a midnight infomercial, the script for the pic is depressingly slight and the performances are stunningly ineffective. **100m/C; DVD, Blu-Ray.** Jaden Smith; Will Smith; Sophie Okonedo; Zoë Kravitz; Glenn Morshower; David Denham; *D:* M. Night Shyamalan; *W:* M. Night Shyamalan; Gary Whitta; *C:* Peter Suschitzky; *M:* James Newton Howard. Golden Raspberries '13: Worst Actor (Smith), Worst Ensemble Cast, Worst Support. Actor (Smith).

After Fall, Winter **WOOF!** **2011** And after yawning, boredom. Schaeffer's broke, self-pitying writer Michael Shiver moves to Paris and meets younger beauty, Sophie (Brochere), who inexplicably gets involved with him. She works as both a hospice nurse and a dominatrix while keeping the latter info from Michael. Too bad, since he's a closet masochist. Eventually, this all results in a cringe-inducing ending (if you've made it that far). The second part of Schaefer's projected film quartet, following 1997's "Fall." English and French with subtitles. **131m/C; DVD.** Eric Schaeffer; Lizzie Brochere; *D:* Eric Schaeffer; *W:* Eric Schaeffer; *C:* Zoran Veljkovic; *M:* Matthew Puckett.

After Hours ⚲⚲⚲ 1/2 **1985 (R)** An absurd, edgy black comedy that's filled with novel twists and turns and often more disturbing than funny. An isolated uptown New York yuppie (Dunne) takes a late night stroll downtown and meets a sexy woman in an all-night coffee shop. From there he wanders through a series of threatening and surreal misadventures, leading to his pursuit by a vigilante mob stirred by ice cream dealer O'Hara. Something like "Blue Velvet" with more Catholicism and farce. Or similar to "Something Wild" without the high school reunion. Great cameos from the large supporting cast, including Cheech and Chong as burglars. A dark view of a small hell-hole in the Big Apple. **97m/C; VHS, DVD.** Griffin Dunne; Rosanna Arquette; John Heard; Teri Garr; Catherine O'Hara; Verna Bloom; Linda Fiorentino; Dick Miller; Bronson Pinchot; Will Patton; Rockets Redglare; Rocco Sisto; Larry Block; Victor Argo; *Cameo(s):* Richard "Cheech" Marin; Thomas Chong; Martin Scorsese; *D:* Martin Scorsese; *W:* Joe Minion; *C:* Michael Ballhaus; *M:* Howard Shore. Cannes '86: Director (Scorsese); Ind. Spirit '86: Director (Scorsese), Film.

After Innocence ⚲⚲⚲ **2005** Sanders exposes the cracks in the criminal justice system by examining the cases of seven men—four white and three black—who were convicted on murder and rape charges. Eventually, after spending many years in prison, each was exonerated because of DNA evidence. Also examined are the roadblocks thrown up by authorities who don't want to admit to mistakes, the question of compensation after wrongful imprisonment, and life after release. Documentary was made in collaboration with the nonprofit legal clinic, the Innocence Project, now expanded into the Innocence Network. Since its founding in 1992 more than 160 people have been exonerated through DNA testing. **95m/C; DVD.** *D:* Jessica Sanders; *W:* Jessica Sanders; Marc H. Simon; *C:* Buddy Squires; Shana Hagan; *M:* Charles Bernstein.

After Life ⚲⚲ *Wandafuru Raifu* **1998** A drab office building turns out to be a metaphysical doorway and those who pass through are the recently deceased. Each person is assigned a caseworker and told that they have three days to decide on one particular memory to take with them into the after life. If they cannot chose, they will be forced to remain in the limbo of the processing center until they can do so. Japanese with subtitles. **118m/C; VHS, DVD.** *JP* Taketoshi Naito; Susumu Terajima; Arata; Erika Oda; Takashi Naito; Hisako Hara; *D:* Hirokazu Kore-eda; *W:* Hirokazu Kore-eda; *C:* Yutaka Yamazaki; Masayoshi Sukita; *M:* Yasuhiro Kasamatsu.

After Midnight ⚲⚲ **1989 (R)** Suspended in a central story about an unorthodox professor who preys upon the deepest fears of his students, a trio of terror tales come to life. From the writers of "The Fly II" and "Nightmare on Elm Street 4." Some chills, few thrills. **90m/C; VHS, DVD, Blu-Ray.** Marg Helgenberger; Marc McClure; Alan Rosenberg; Pamela Segall; Nadine Van Der Velde; Ramy Zada; Jillian McWhirter; Billy Ray Sharkey; Judie Aronson; Tracy Wells; Ed Monaghan; Monique Salcido; Penelope Sudrow; *D:* Jim Wheat; Ken Wheat; *W:* Jim Wheat; Ken Wheat; *M:* Marc Donahue.

After Office Hours ⚲⚲ **1935** The title's provocative but this rom com is standard 30s fare enlivened by the beautiful Bennett. New York newspaper editor Jim (Gable) sneers at society gal Sharon (Bennett) until he realizes she has the in to stories on the rich and scandalous. They bicker their way to romance until they wind up on opposites sides of a murder involving a society wife. **72m/B; DVD.** Clark Gable; Constance Bennett; Stuart Erwin; Billie Burke; Harvey Stephens; Katherine Alexander; Hale Hamilton; *D:* Robert Z. Leonard; *W:* Herman J. Mankiewicz; *C:* Charles Rosher.

After Sex ⚲⚲ *Post Coitum, Animal Triste; Post Coitum* **1997** Passion and madness—French style. Confident, middleaged

Diane (Rouan) has a successful career and a complacent marriage. Then she meets twentysomething hunk Emilio (Terral) and all bets are off. The twosome have a delirious affair but Diane's passion teeters towards obsession, with reckless disregard for her family. Then the affair ends and Diane falls apart. French with subtitles. **97m/C; VHS, DVD.** *FR* Brigitte Rouan; Boris Terral; Patrick Chesnais; Nils (Niels) Tavernier; Jean-Louis Richard; Francoise Arnoul; *D:* Brigitte Rouan; *W:* Brigitte Rouan; Jean-Louis Richard; Santiago Amigorena; Guy Zilberstein; *C:* Pierre Dupouey; *M:* Michel Musseau; Umberto Tozzi.

After Sundown 🦴 **2006 (R)** A vampire from the Old West is searching for his daughter and creating a small army of zombies in his wake. **90m/C; DVD.** Christopher Abram; Reece Rios; Natalie Jones; Susanna Gibb; *D:* Christopher Abram; Michael W. Brown; *W:* Christopher Abram; *C:* David Pinkston; *M:* Steven Barnett; Timothy Edward Smith. **VIDEO**

After the Deluge 🦴🦴🦴 **2003** Dogged with their own problems, three brothers must deal with their distant father's decline from Alzheimer's while he is pained by flashbacks of his WWII tour of duty. **103m/C; VHS, DVD.** David Wenham; Hugo Weaving; Samuel Johnson; Aden Young; Catherine McClements; Ray Barrett; Rachel Griffiths; Essie Davis; Kate Beahan; Vince Colosimo; Marta Dusseldorp; Bob Franklin; Marco Chiappi; Simon Burke; *D:* Brendan Maher; *W:* Deb Cox; Andrew Knight; *C:* Geoff Burton; *M:* Cezary Skubiszewski. **TV**

After the Fall of New York WOOF! **1985 (R)** Dim-witted post-apocalyptic tale set in New York after the fall of the "Big Bomb." A man, driven to search for the last normal woman, has reason to believe she is frozen alive and kept in the heart of the city. His mission: locate her, thaw her, engage in extremely limited foreplay with her, and repopulate the planet. A poorly dubbed dating allegory. **95m/C; VHS, DVD.** *IT FR* Michael Sopkiw; Valentine Monnier; Anna Kanakis; Roman Geer; Edmund Purdom; George Eastman; *D:* Sergio Martino.

After the Fox 🦴🦴 *Caccia alla Volpe* **1966** Sellers is a con artist posing as a film director to carry out a bizarre plan to steal gold from Rome. Features occasional backhand slaps at Hollywood, with Mature turning in a memorable performance as the has-been actor starring in Sellers' movie. Though the screenplay was co-written by Neil Simon, the laughs are marginal. **103m/C; VHS, DVD, Blu-Ray.** *GB IT* Peter Sellers; Victor Mature; Martin Balsam; Britt Ekland; *D:* Vittorio De Sica; *W:* Neil Simon; Cesare Zavattini; *C:* Leonida Barboni; *M:* Burt Bacharach.

After the Rain 🦴🦴 **1999 (R)** Hard-hitting apartheid story that unfortunately descends into melodrama. In 1970s South Africa, Steph (Bettany) is a conflicted soldier in love with dancer Emma (Lombard). After his brigade is posted, lonely Emma befriends a black co-worker, Joseph (Bakare). Upon learning that he is living on the streets, Emma invites Joseph to stay with her. Of course that just happens to be when Steph, who's deserted, returns and assumes the worst. Writer/director Kettle adapted the film from his play "Soweto's Burning." **110m/C; DVD.** *SA* Paul Bettany; Louise Lombard; Ariyon Bakare; *D:* Ross Kettle; *W:* Ross Kettle; *C:* Koos Roets; *M:* Hummie Mann.

After the Storm 🦴🦴 ½ **2001 (R)** Beachcomber Arno (Bratt) discovers a sunken yacht but can't salvage the loot, even with the help of girlfriend Coquina (Avital). So he hooks up with Jean-Pierre (Assante) and his wife Janine (Girard), but greed gets the best of everyone. Based on a story by Ernest Hemingway; filmed in Belize. **103m/C; VHS, DVD.** Benjamin Bratt; Armand Assante; Mili Avital; Simone-Elise Girard; Stephen Lang; *D:* Guy Ferland; *W:* A.E. Hotchner; *C:* Gregory Middleton; *M:* Bill Wandel. **CABLE**

After the Storm 🦴🦴🦴 *Umi yori mo mada fukaku* **2017** The great Japanese director Hirokazu Kore-eda delivers another heartfelt, humane drama about a man who can't live in the present. He's either reliving past glories from the one hit book he wrote or worrying about a future in which he'll become his father. Struggling to pay child support, he works on the side as a private detective, but longs for a reunion with his ex-wife and young son that will clearly never come. While his mother and ex appear to be moving on, he's stuck in time, until a vicious storm traps everyone in an apartment, and hard truths are realized. **117m/C; DVD, Blu-Ray.** Hiroshi Abe; Yoko Maki; Kirin Kiki; Riri Furanki; Satomi Kobayashi; *D:* Hirokazu Kore-eda; *W:* Hirokazu Kore-eda; *C:* Yutaka Yamazaki.

After the Sunset 🦴🦴 **2004 (PG-13)** Lightweight crime caper is as memorable as a soap bubble, although the scenery (Hayek in a variety of skimpy attire and the sun-drenched island setting) is appealing. Max (Brosnan) is a suave thief who, with partner Lola (Hayek), has pulled off a successful diamond heist that ruins the career of FBI agent Stan (Harrelson). The thieves then retire to the Bahamas where Max is soon bored, bored, bored, and ready for some action when an ocean liner docks in port with a priceless jewel exhibit onboard. Stan, of course, shows up, determined to finally outwit Max. Hayek plays another firecracker while Brosnan slums charmingly; Cheadle is wasted in a throwaway role as a gangster. **93m/C; VHS, DVD, Blu-Ray.** Pierce Brosnan; Salma Hayek; Woody Harrelson; Don Cheadle; Naomie Harris; Christopher Penn; Mykelti Williamson; Obba Babatunde; Russell Hornsby; Rex Linn; Kate Walsh; Troy Garity; *D:* Brett Ratner; *W:* Craig Rosenberg; Paul Zbyszewski; *C:* Dante Spinotti; *M:* Lalo Schifrin.

After the Thin Man 🦴🦴🦴 **1936** Second in a series of six "Thin Man" films, this one finds Nick, Nora and Asta, the lovable terrier, seeking out a murderer from Nora's own blue-blooded relatives. Fast-paced mystery with a witty script and the popular Powell/Loy charm. Sequel to "The Thin Man," followed by "Another Thin Man." **113m/B; VHS, DVD.** William Powell; Myrna Loy; James Stewart; Elissa Landi; Joseph Calleia; Jessie Ralph; Alan Marshal; *D:* W.S. Van Dyke.

After the Wedding 🦴🦴🦴 *Efter Brylluppet* **2006 (R)** Jacob (Mikkelsen), director of a struggling Indian orphanage, is given the opportunity to solve all his problems via a rich benefactor back in Denmark. Once he returns home, however, he finds things much more complicated than he expected, and he must choose between the world he knows in India and the obligations towards an ex-girlfriend and illegitimate daughter in Denmark. Oscar-nominated, poignant film teeters on the fine line between melodrama and soap opera. **120m/C; DVD.** *CZ* Mads Mikkelsen; Rolf Lassgard; Sidse Babett Knudsen; Stine Fischer Christensen; Christian Tafdrup; *D:* Suzanne (Susanne) Bier; *W:* Anders Thomas Jensen; *C:* Morten Soborg; *M:* Johan Soderqvist.

After the Wedding 🦴🦴 **2019 (PG-13)** For years, Isabel (Williams) has run an orphanage in India. She is summoned to America by Theresa Young (Moore), who is ready to sell her business, cash out, and use the funds to become the biggest benefactor of Isabel's organization. That same weekend, Grace (Quinn), the daughter of Theresa and Oscar Carlson (Crudup), is getting married. As events unfold, Isabel learns the truth about Theresa's donation and the characters' interconnected lives are revealed. An art-house drama full of contrivances and too many twists, it focuses on the repressed lives and problems of the ultrarich in an underwhelming manner. **112m/C; DVD, Blu-Ray.** Michelle Williams; Julianne Moore; Billy Crudup; Abby Quinn; Will Chase; *D:* Bart Freundlich; *W:* Bart Freundlich; *C:* Julio Macat; *M:* Mychael Danna.

After Tiller 🦴🦴🦴 **2013 (PG-13)** George Tiller was assassinated in 2009, leaving only four working doctors who perform late-term abortions, terminations of pregnancies in the final trimester, most often because of horrendous illnesses that would leave the child with no quality of life were they to be taken to term. This incredibly important film takes these four people who have been turned into demons by those who believe them wrong and heroes by those who believe them right and makes them human again. It's an incredibly hard film to watch at times but it perfectly captures the complexity of an issue that has divided us for decades and will likely continue to do so. **85m/C; DVD.** *D:* Martha Shane; Lana Wilson; *W:* Martha Shane; Lana Wilson; Greg O'Toole; *C:* Hilary Spera; Emily Topper; *M:* Andy Cabic; Eric D. Johnson.

After Tomorrow 🦴🦴 **1932** In this Depression-era film, Peter (Farrell) and Sidney (Nixon) struggle to work and save their money to get married but are frequently separated by hardship. Fearing she's losing her beau, Sidney suggests they go away together (there's a sex talk) while Peter nobly insists they wait until marriage. **70m/B; DVD.** Charles Farrell; Marion (Marian) Nixon; Minna Gombell; Josephine Hull; William Collier, Sr.; William Pawley; *D:* Frank Borzage; *W:* Sonya Levien; *C:* James Wong Howe.

Afterburn 🦴🦴🦴 **1992 (R)** When Ted, her Air Force pilot husband, is killed in a crash of his F-16 fighter, Janet Harduvel learns the official explanation is pilot error. Convinced that something was wrong with his plane, Janet sets out to investigate, and eventually sue, military contractor General Dynamics. Dern turns in a great performance as the tough widow determined to clear her husband's name. Based on a true story. **103m/C; VHS, DVD.** Laura Dern; Robert Loggia; Vincent Spano; Michael Rooker; Andy Romano; *D:* Robert Markowitz; *W:* Elizabeth Chandler. **CABLE**

Afterglow 🦴🦴 **1997 (R)** Romantic quadrangle skates by on the performances of its two veterans. Lucky Mann (Nolte) is experiencing marital boredom with his longtime wife Phyllis (the ever-beautiful Christie), a former B-movie actress. Meanwhile twenty-something Marianne Byron (Boyle), who is desperate to have a baby, is sexually frustrated by her workaholic hubby, Jeffrey (Miller). Repairman Lucky happens to come along to work on the Bryon's apartment and Marianne decides to throw herself at him. Then Jeffrey meets the sophisticated Phyllis and soon both couples have uncoupled and re-formed. **113m/C; VHS, DVD.** Nick Nolte; Julie Christie; Lara Flynn Boyle; Jonny Lee Miller; Jay Underwood; Domini Blythe; *D:* Alan Rudolph; *W:* Alan Rudolph; *C:* Toyomichi Kurita; *M:* Mark Isham. Ind. Spirit '98: Actress (Christie); N.Y. Film Critics '97: Actress (Christie); Natl. Soc. Film Critics '97: Actress (Christie).

After.life 🦴 ½ **2010 (R)** After a car crash, Anna (Ricci) wakes up on the mortuary table of sorta creepy undertaker Eliot Deacon (Neeson). She is quite certain she is still alive; he is equally certain she is dead. He can see and speak to the recently deceased while they are trying to adjust to the fact that they are, indeed, dead. Anna thinks he is some kind of serial killer keeping her prisoner since Deacon locks the door anytime he leaves the room. She gets hysterical and tries to escape, he is calm. Though Ricci is unselfconscious about her frequent nudity and the picture looks stylish (nice use of red), it's also boring and doesn't actually make much sense. **97m/C; Blu-Ray, On Demand.** Christina Ricci; Liam Neeson; Justin Long; Chandler Canterbury; Celia Weston; Josh Charles; *D:* Agnieszka Wojtowicz-Vosloo; *W:* Agnieszka Wojtowicz-Vosloo; Paul Vosloo; Jakub Korolczuk; *C:* Anastas Michos; *M:* Paul Haslinger.

Aftermath 🦴 ½ **1985** Three astronauts return to Earth and are shocked to discover that the planet has been ravaged by a nuclear war. Quickly they make new plans. **96m/C; VHS, DVD, Blu-Ray.** Steve Barkett; Larry Latham; Lynne Margulies; Sid Haig; Forrest J Ackerman; *D:* Ted V. Mikels.

Aftermath 🦴🦴 **2012 (R)** An action-thriller about surviving after an apocalypse and the intense uncertainty the situation creates. After a nuclear apocalypse, nine strangers huddle in a farmhouse cellar. As radioactive fallout blankets the world, the survivors must deal with a lack of supplies, their own personal sorrows, and zombie-like humans trying to enter their safe hiding place. The nine soon must make a decision about if they should stay and perhaps die in the cellar or face the unknown outside. **92m/C; DVD, Blu-Ray, Streaming, Download.** C.J. Thomason; Monica Keena; Edward Furlong; Andre Royo; Christine Kelly; *D:* Peter Engert; *W:* Christian McDonald; *C:* Scott Winig; *M:* Austin Wintory.

Aftermath 🦴🦴 **2017 (R)** Schwarzenegger is surprisingly subtle, though not quite masterful, in this tale of grief and revenge based on a true story. Arnold plays Roman, a man who recently lost his family in a plane crash. His grief is intensified by an offer of a financial settlement and the revelation that an air-traffic controller (McNairy) may have been to blame. The film slowly and unevenly builds toward their eventual confrontation, in the process missing numerous chances to explore grief on more than just a superficial level. Schwarzenegger makes a bid for serious actor status, but is undercut by the script's shortcomings. **94m/C; DVD, Blu-Ray.** Arnold Schwarzenegger; Scoot McNairy; Maggie Grace; Judah Nelson; Larry Sullivan; *D:* Elliott Lester; *W:* Javier Gullon; *C:* Pieter Vermeer; *M:* Mark D. Todd.

The Aftermath 🦴 ½ **2019 (R)** Shortly after the Allies defeated Germany, British military officer Lewis Morgan (Clarke) is charged with helping to keep order and finding Nazi loyalists in Hamburg. With his wife Rachel (Knightley), he is given a home in a large mansion requisitioned from German widower Stefan (Skarsgard). Treating locals with kindness, Lewis allows Stefan and his daughter to remain in the house instead of moving to a refugee camp. Though Rachel is initially unsure of the arrangement, her marriage becomes threatened by her relationship with Stefan. Based loosely on the novel by Rhidian Brook, the melodramatic period piece is visually appealing but there's nothing new here. **108m/C; DVD.** *UK GE US* Keira Knightley; Jason Clarke; Alexander Skarsgård; Flora Thiemann; Anna Katharina Schimrigk; *D:* James Kent; *W:* Joe Shrapnel; Anna Waterhouse; Rhidian Brook; *C:* Franz Lustig; *M:* Martin Phipps.

Afternoon Delight 🦴 ½ **2013 (R)** Debuting feature director Soloway tries for a female raunch comedy but her characters are generally self-absorbed and unlikeable with the exception of Temple's confident young exotic dancer McKenna. Bored wife/mother Rachel (Hahn) wants to spice up her sex life with husband Jeff (Radnor) so they go to a strip club, which is where Rachel encounters McKenna. Intrigued, Rachel's soon offering her a temporary place to live although McKenna definitely isn't interested in being reformed. Drinking and fantasies (men's and women's) are prominently featured but it never adds up to anything sexy, fun, or believable. **99m/C; DVD, Blu-Ray.** Kathryn Hahn; Juno Temple; Josh Radnor; Jane Lynch; Michaela Watkins; Josh Stamberg; John Kapelos; Keegan Michael Key; *D:* Jill Soloway; *W:* Jill Soloway; *C:* Jim Frohna; *M:* Craig Wedren.

Afternoon of a Faun 🦴🦴🦴 **2013** A biographical documentary look at the tragic life of ballerina Tanaquil Le Clerq. A beautiful dancer with an elongated physique, she danced with the New York City Ballet. Le Clerq defined a new aesthetic in dancers for choreographers George Balachine and Jerome Robbins. Also married to Balachine, Robbins created ballets for her, including Afternoon of a Faun for Tanny. Her career was cut short when she contracted polio at the age of 27, was paralyzed, and was unable to dance again. Le Clerq lived to the age of 80. **91m/C; DVD, Download.** *D:* Nancy Buirski; *W:* Nancy Buirski; *C:* R.E. Rodgers.

Afterschool 🦴🦴 **2008** Feature film debut for writer/director Campos who was 24 at the time of filming. Socially awkward, self-absorbed teen Robert (Miller) is boarding at a New England prep school where he's generally ignored and his roommate deals drugs. Repressed, Robert finds his sexual outlet in violent Internet porn. During an afterschool student film project, Robert accidentally films the drug overdose deaths of twin sisters who die in his arms. The school tries to cover up the scandal and Robert is asked to supply a tasteful memorial film, which turns out to be truthful and wildly inappropriate—much like the movie. **121m/C; On Demand.** Ezra Miller; Jeremy White; Emory Cohen; Christopher McCann; Michael Stuhlbarg; Addison Timlin; Lee Wilkof; *D:* Antonio Campos; *W:* Antonio Campos; *C:* Jody Lee Lipes; *M:* Rakotondrabe Gael.

Aftershock 🦴 ½ **1988 (R)** A beautiful alien and a mysterious stranger battle the Earth's repressive, evil government. **90m/C; VHS, DVD.** Jay Roberts, Jr.; Elizabeth Kaitan; Chris Mitchum; Richard Lynch; John Saxon; Russ Tamblyn; Michael Berryman; Chris De Rose; Chuck Jeffreys; *D:* Frank Harris; *W:* Michael Standing; *M:* Kevin Klinger; Bob Mamet.

Aftershock 🦴 ½ **2012 (R)** Part ho-hum horror/part disaster flick, it's the English-language debut of Chilean director Lopez. A vacationing American nicknamed Gringo (horror helmer Roth) heads to an underground club in Valparaiso with some friends when they get caught in an earthquake. Eventually making their way out, they emerge into chaos, a lot of disturbing violence thanks to a prison collapse and a group of escaped cons, and a lot more gore. English and Spanish with subtitles. **90m/C; DVD, Blu-Ray, Streaming.** *US CL* Eli Roth; Ariel Levy; Nicolas Martinez; Lorenza Izzo; Andrea Osvart; Natasha Yarovenko; ***D:*** Nicolas Lopez; ***W:*** Eli Roth; Nicolas Lopez; Guillermo Amoedo; ***C:*** Antonio Quercia; ***M:*** Manuel Riveiro.

Aftershock: Earthquake in New York 1/2 **1999** Typical TV disaster movie based on the novel by Chuck Scarborough. You're introduced to a bunch of nice people (there's quite a good cast), disaster strikes, death and destruction are everywhere and all it brings out (rather than hysteria, looting, violence and assorted evilness) is good deeds and rescues. Nifty special effects though. **139m/C; VHS, DVD.** Tom Skerritt; Sharon Lawrence; Charles S. Dutton; Lisa Nicole Carson; Cicely Tyson; Jennifer Garner; Rachel Ticotin; Frederick Weller; Erika Eleniak; Michell Ryan; ***D:*** Mikael Salomon; ***W:*** David Stevens; Paul Eric Meyers; Loren Boothby; ***C:*** Jon Joffin; ***M:*** Irwin Fisch. **TV**

Afterwards 1/2 **2008** Sentimental and slow-paced (and a little creepy). Successful New York lawyer Nathan Del Amico (Duris) encounters mysterious hospice physician, Dr. Kay (Malkovich), who claims to have supernatural abilities to see a white aura around people who will soon die. Thinking he's next, Nathan decide to make peace with his past, including his ex-wife Claire (Lilly), while trying to thwart what he thinks is supposed to be his destiny. **107m/C; DVD.** *FR GE* Romain Duris; John Malkovich; Evangeline Lilly; Pascale Bussieres; Reece Thompson; Sara Waisglass; ***D:*** Gilles Bourdos; ***W:*** Gilles Bourdos; Michel Spinosa; ***C:*** Mark Ping Bin Lee; ***M:*** Alexandre Desplat.

Again, the Ringer *Der Hexer; The Ringer; The Mysterious Magician* **1964** Well-done German adaptation of the Edgar Wallace novel "The Ringer" (also known as "The Squeaker"). The sister of a famous criminal, who's a master of disguise, is murdered in London and her brother seeks revenge. Meanwhile, Scotland Yard detectives think they finally have a chance of catching him. German with subtitles. **85m/B; DVD.** *GE* Joachim Fuchsberger; Heinz Drache; Siegfried Lowitz; Margot Trooger; Rene Deltgen; Siegfried Schurenberg; Sophie Hardy; Carl Lange; ***D:*** Alfred Vohrer; ***W:*** Herbert Reinecker; ***C:*** Karl Lob; ***M:*** Peter Thomas.

Against a Crooked Sky **1975 (G)** A young boy sets out with an elderly trapper to find his sister, who was captured by the Indians. Similiar story to "The Searchers," but no masterpiece. **89m/C; VHS, DVD.** Richard Boone; Stewart Petersen; Jewel Blanch; Geoffrey Land; Henry Wilcoxon; ***D:*** Earl Bellamy.

Against All Flags **1952** An enjoyable Flynn swashbuckler about a British soldier slashing his way through the Spanish fleet at the turn of the 18th century. Though the story has been told before, tight direction and good performances win out. O'Hara is a tarty eyeful as a hot-tempered pirate moll. **81m/C; VHS, DVD.** Errol Flynn; Maureen O'Hara; Anthony Quinn; Mildred Natwick; ***D:*** George Sherman.

Against All Odds 1/2 **1984 (R)** An interesting love triangle evolves when recently cut quarterback Terry Brogan (Bridges) is asked by his nightclub owning/bookie buddy, Jack (Woods), to travel to Mexico and bring back Jack's sultry girlfriend, Jessie (Ward). Then Terry discovers that Jessie is the daughter of Mrs. Wyler, the football team owner. Contains complicated plot, numerous double crosses, sensual love scenes, and a chase scene along Sunset Boulevard. As the good friend sans conscience, Woods stars. A remake of 1947's "Out of the Past." **122m/C; VHS, DVD.** Jeff Bridges; Rachel Ward; James Woods; Alex Karras; Jane Greer; Richard Widmark; Dorian Harewood; Swoosie Kurtz; Bill McKinney; Saul Rubinek; ***D:*** Taylor Hackford; ***W:*** Eric Hughes; ***C:*** Donald E. Thorin; ***M:*** Michel Colombier; Larry Carlton.

Against the Current 1/2 **2009** Maudlin and slow-paced drama. Paul (Fiennes) persuades his friend Jeff (Kirk) that it's time to carry through with his long-held wish to swim the 150 miles down the Hudson River from Troy, New York to Manhattan. Jeff and acquaintance Liz (Reaser) will provide assistance but Jeff soon realizes that it's the fifth anniversary of the death of Paul's pregnant wife and he has another purpose beyond swimming in mind. **98m/C; DVD.** Joseph Fiennes; Justin Kirk; Elizabeth Reaser; Pell James; Mary Tyler Moore; Michelle Trachtenberg; Amy Hargreaves; ***D:*** Peter Callahan; ***W:*** Peter Callahan; ***C:*** Sean Kirby; ***M:*** Anton Sanko.

Against the Dark **2008 (R)** Seagal vs. the vampires. In a post-apocalyptic world the few human survivors are being sucked dry by vampires. Trapped in a hospital, Commander Tao and his group of ex-military vigilantes are about to make their last stand. **94m/C; DVD.** Skye Bennett; Emma Catherwood; Keith David; Jenna Harrison; Linden Ashby; Steven Seagal; Tanoai Reed; ***D:*** Richard Crudo; ***W:*** Matthew Klickstein; ***C:*** William Trautvetter; ***M:*** Philip White. **VIDEO**

Against the Law 1/2 **1998** Criminal Rex (Grieco) prides himself on his abilities with a gun—leaving a trail of dead cops in his wake. His wants notoriety and, after spotting detective John Shepard (Mancuso) on a news show, decides that TV is the perfect medium to get his 15 minutes of infamy. **85m/C; VHS, DVD.** Richard Grieco; Nick Mancuso; Nancy Allen; Steven Ford; ***D:*** Jim Wynorski; ***W:*** Steve Mitchell; Bob Sheridan; ***C:*** Andrea V. Rossotto; ***M:*** Kevin Kiner. **VIDEO**

Against the Ropes **2004 (PG-13)** "Erin Brockovich" meets "Rocky" in this biopic loosely based on the life of Detroit boxing manager Jackie Kallen (although for some reason, they set it in Cleveland). Jackie (Ryan) is a tough, harried secretary for the Cleveland Coliseum who's smarter than her skimpy outfits would indicate. She sees her chance to go somewhere in the boxing world when she buys crackhead/boxer Luther's (Epps) contract from mobbed-up manager Sam (Shalhoub) for a dollar. Ryan plays Jackie as a walking cliche spouting lousy dialogue. Shalhoub injects the movie with a bit of fun doing his best Snidley Whiplash. Dutton does better playing Luther's trainer, Felix, than he does directing fight scenes that don't show the action with much clarity. There's no clear winner here, but the audience is definitely the loser. Paramount shelved the movie for a year and a half. **111m/C; VHS, DVD.** Meg Ryan; Omar Epps; Tony Shalhoub; Timothy Daly; Charles S. Dutton; Kerry Washington; Joe Cortese; ***D:*** Charles S. Dutton; ***W:*** Cheryl Edwards; ***C:*** Jack N. Green; ***M:*** Michael Kamen.

Against the Sun 1/2 **2015 (PG)** A drama based on a harrowing incident which occurred during World War II. Flying a torpedo bomber in the South Pacific theater, three U.S. Navy airmen are forced to crash land. Though they fly into the water, the trio manages to gather on a tiny life raft in the middle of the ocean without food or water. Despite enduring storms, sharks, and starvation, the three sail for a month hoping to be rescued as they sail towards safety hundreds of miles away. **100m/C; DVD, Blu-Ray, Streaming, Download.** Garret Dillahunt; Tom Felton; Jake Abel; Nadia Parra; Quinton Flynn; ***D:*** Brian Falk; ***W:*** Brian Falk; Mark David Keegan; ***C:*** Petr Cikhart; ***M:*** Paul Mills.

Against the Wall **1994** Compelling and tense dramatization of the 1971 Attica, New York prison uprising in which 10 guards were held hostage and state troopers and the National Guard killed 29 prisoners before regaining control. Partially fictionalized version of the story told from the viewpoints of a young prison guard (MacLachlan) and a politicized prisoner (Jackson). Filmed at a prison in Clarksville, Tennessee. **115m/C; VHS, DVD.** Kyle MacLachlan; Samuel L. Jackson; Clarence Williams, III; Frederic Forrest; Harry Dean Stanton; Tom Bower; Philip Bosco; Anne Heche; David Ackroyd; ***D:*** John Frankenheimer; ***W:*** Ron Hutchinson; ***M:*** Gary Chang. **CABLE**

Against the Wall *Quality of Life* **2004 (R)** Mikey (Garrison) and Curtis (Burnam) make their claim to fame as graffiti artists in San Francisco's hard-luck Mission District. But when their illegal activity gets them arrested, Mikey starts thinking about the future and going legit while Curtis violates his probation and his self-destructive behavior shatters their friendship. Debut for Morgan. **84m/C; DVD.** MacKenzie Firgens; Luis Saguar; Lane Garrison; Brian Burnam; ***D:*** Benjamin Morgan; ***W:*** Benjamin Morgan; ***C:*** Kev Robertson.

Against the Wild **2014 (PG)** A family adventure centered on two kids, their dog, and their survival in the Alaskan wilderness. While taking a small plane to visit their father (Whittall) at his job at a remote mining operation in Alaska, siblings Zach (Green) and Hannah (Pitt) survive an emergency landing after their plane has troubles. Traveling with their dog, the duo must make their way through the Alaskan terrain to safety using their survival skills and instincts for several days. **90m/C; DVD, Download.** CJ Adams; Erin Pitt; Natasha Henstridge; Ted Whittall; ***D:*** Richard Boddington; ***W:*** Richard Boddington; ***C:*** Stephen Chandler Whitehead; ***M:*** Varhan Orchestrovich Bauer.

Against the Wild II: Survive the Seregenti *Against the Wild 2: Survive the Serengeti* **2016 (PG)** A family adventure drama centered on a quest for survival in Africa. To visit their father at the mine when he works, Emma Croft (Ballentine) and her brother Ryan (Ruttan) must travel by plane through the African wilderness. When rebel forces shoot at and bring down the plane, the kids and the miner's dog are the only survivors. The trio must stick together and deal with the challenges that arise as they make their way to safety. **91m/C; DVD, Streaming, Download.** Jeri Ryan; John Paul Ruttan; Ella Ballentine; Ashley Dowds; Hlomla Dandala; ***D:*** Richard Boddington; ***W:*** Richard Boddington; ***C:*** Stephen Chandler Whitehead; ***M:*** Philip Miller.

Against the Wind 1/2 **1948** A motley crew is trained for a mission into Nazi Germany to blow up records and rescue a prisoner. The first half of the film focuses on the group's training, but despite its intensity they win only a pyrrhic victory. A well-done production with solid performances from the cast. **96m/B; VHS, DVD.** Robert Beatty; Jack Warner; Simone Signoret; Gordon Jackson; Paul Dupuis; Peter Illing; ***D:*** Charles Crichton.

Against the Wind *Contra el Viento* **1990** Juan (Banderas) takes refuge in a remote area of Andalusia in an effort to get away from a mutally obsessive love. But his exile is in vain when his lover appears—his sister (Suarez). Spanish with subtitles. **117m/C; VHS, DVD.** *SP* Antonio Banderas; Emma Suarez; ***D:*** Paco Perinan.

Agatha 1/2 **1979 (PG)** A speculative period drama about Agatha Christie's still unexplained disappearance in 1926, and a fictional American reporter's efforts to find her. Beautiful but lackluster mystery. Unfortunately, Hoffman and Redgrave generate few sparks. **98m/C; VHS, DVD.** Dustin Hoffman; Vanessa Redgrave; Timothy Dalton; Helen Morse; Tony Britton; Timothy West; Celia Gregory; Pam(ela) Austin; ***D:*** Michael Apted.

Agatha Christie: A Life in Pictures 1/2 **2004** In 1926, famed mystery writer Agatha Christie (Williams) went missing for 11 days. She was found at a hotel and couldn't remember what had happened to her, although hypnosis revealed that Christie knew her husband Archie (Coulthard) was an unfaithful wastrel. But Christie also left clues in her writings and, in 1962, the aged Agatha (Massey) speaks of her disappearance to a journalist. **90m/C; DVD.** *GB* Olivia Williams; Anna Massey; Raymond Coulthard; Stephen Boxer; Anthony O'Donnell; ***D:*** Richard Curson Smith; ***W:*** Richard Curson Smith; ***C:*** Jeff Baynes; ***M:*** Andrew Phillips. **TV**

Agatha Christie's A Caribbean Mystery 1/2 *A Caribbean Mystery* **1983** Miss Marple's vacation turns into another sluething adventure when she must solve the murder of a retired British Army officer. Faithful adaptation updates the action form the 1950s to the '80s in fine fashion. **96m/C; VHS, DVD.** Helen Hayes; Barnard Hughes; Jameson Parker; Season Hubley; Swoosie Kurtz; Cassie Yates; Zakes Mokae; Stephen Macht; Maurice Evans; Lynne Moody; George Innes; Brock Peters; ***D:*** Robert Lewis; ***W:*** Sue Grafton; Steve Humphrey; ***C:*** Ted Voightlander; ***M:*** Lee Holdridge. **TV**

Agatha Christie's Murder is Easy *Murder is Easy* **1982** Luke Williams (Bixby), an American computer expert, is on a train to London when he meets an old woman (Hayes) who confides that she is going to Scotland Yard to report some mysterious deaths in her village. When she is killd by a hit-and-run driver after leaving the train, he decides to investigate. When he reaches the village, he is aided by a local girl who also suspects foul play. So-so mystery suffers from attempts to update the mystery with computer technology. Adapted from the Agatha Christie novel "Easy to Kill." **95m/C; VHS, DVD.** Bill Bixby; Lesley-Anne Down; Olivia de Havilland; Helen Hayes; Patrick Allen; Freddie Jones; Shane Briant; Leigh Lawson; Jonathan Pryce; Carol MacReady; ***D:*** Claude Whatham; ***W:*** Carmen Culver; ***C:*** Brian Tufano; ***M:*** Gerald Fried. **TV**

Agatha Christie's Murder with Mirrors *Murder with Mirrors* **1985** Lightweight TV mystery has Miss Marple (Hayes) once again sleuthing about to help an old friend (Davis) who thinks she's going to be killed for her estate. Hayes is once again delightful, but things begin to fade about half way through. Look for Tim Roth spicing things up in an early role. **96m/C; VHS, DVD.** Helen Hayes; Bette Davis; Leo McKern; John Mills; John Laughlin; Dorothy Tutin; Anton Rodgers; John Woodvine; James Coombes; Tim Roth; ***D:*** Dick Lowry; ***W:*** George Eckstein; ***C:*** Brian West; ***M:*** Richard Rodney Bennett. **TV**

Agatha Christie's Sparkling Cyanide *Sparkling Cyanide* **1983** Somebody spiked the champagne—with cyanide! This really brings down a socialite couple's anniversary party as they have to set aside the hor's douvres to solve the whodunit. Cheesy but enjoyable, the twist ending adds to the fun. **96m/C; VHS, DVD.** Anthony Andrews; Deborah Raffin; Pamela Bellwood; Nancy Marchand; Josef Sommer; David Huffman; Christine Belford; June Chadwick; Harry (Henry) Morgan; Michael Woods; ***D:*** Robert Lewis; ***W:*** Robert M. Young; Sue Grafton; Steve Humphrey; ***C:*** Ted Voightlander. **TV**

Agatha Christie's The Pale Horse 1/2 *The Pale Horse* **1996** When writer Mark Easterbrook is accused of murdering a priest, the only clue to clearing himself is a mysterious list of names. Now he has to figure out the connection between the names if he expects to clear himself. **100m/C; VHS, DVD.** *GB* Michael Byrne; Ruth Madoc; Leslie Phillips; Jean Marsh; ***D:*** Charles Beeson. **TV**

Agatha Christie's Thirteen at Dinner *Thirteen at Dinner* **1985** Hercule Poirot must solve the case when an actress's ex-husband dies shortly after granting her a divorce. Lack of character development hurt this otherwise solid outing. Fine cast is highlighted by Ustinov and Dunaway. **91m/C; VHS, DVD.** Peter Ustinov; Faye Dunaway; David Suchet; Jonathan Cecil; Bill Nighy; Lee Horsley; Diane Keen; Allan Cuthbertson; John Barron; Amanda Pays; Lesley Dunlop; ***Cameo(s):*** David Frost; ***D:*** Lou Antonio; ***W:*** Rod Browning; ***C:*** Curtis Clark; ***M:*** John Addison. **TV**

The Age of Adaline **2015 (PG-13)** Adaline (Lively) is in an accident near her birth at the turn of the 20th century and learns that she can never age. Drama naturally ensues when this ageless ingénue meets a man (Huisman) with whom she can quite literally NOT grow old together. The Lively-Huisman melodrama is not interesting in the slightest but Harrison Ford and Ellen Burstyn pop up to show the younger cast members what real acting looks like. **112m/C; DVD, Blu-Ray.** Blake Lively; Michiel Huisman; Harrison Ford; Ellen Burstyn; Kathy Baker; ***D:*** Lee Toland Krieger; ***W:*** J. Mills Goodloe; Salvador Paskowitz; ***C:*** David Lanzenberg; ***M:*** Rob Simonsen.

Age of Consent **1969** Disillusioned painter Bradley Morahan (Mason) leaves his successful career in New York to return to his Australian homeland. He rents a house on a sparsely populated Great Barrier

Reef island and promptly notices the fleshy beauty of teenager Cora (Mirren), who agrees to pose nude for him, which reinvigorates Morahan in more than one way. Morahan's paradise is invaded by a mooching old friend (MacGowran) who steals from him, and Cora's alcoholic granny (Carr-Glynn) makes trouble. **103m/C; DVD, Blu-Ray.** *AU* James Mason; Dame Helen Mirren; Jack MacGowran; Andonia Katsaros; Neva Carr-Glynn; Michael Bodde; ***D:*** Michael Powell; ***W:*** Peter Yeldham; ***C:*** Hannes Staudinger; ***M:*** Peter Sculthorpe.

Age of Dinosaurs **2013** Reminiscent of 'Jurassic Park,' a fireman must work to save his daughter after cloned dinosaurs escape from a museum exhibit. **89m/C; DVD, Blu-Ray, Streaming.** Treat Williams; Ronny Cox; Jillian Rose Reed; Joshua Michael Allen; Andray Johnson; ***D:*** Joseph J. Lawson; ***W:*** Hank Woon, Jr.; ***C:*** Richard J. Vialet; ***M:*** Chris Ridenhour. **VIDEO**

The Age of Innocence ½ **1934** Best seen for the radiant Dunne's performance since Boles isn't quite up to the task as her romantic partner. In 1875 New York, lawyer Newland Archer (Boles) has just become engaged to oh-so-proper May Welland (Haydon). May's cousin Ellen, the Countess Olenska (Dunne), returns to the city seeking a divorce and asks Archer's advice. They become deeply attracted to one another but a scandal would cause social ruin. Based on the Edith Wharton novel; remade in 1993. **71m/B; DVD.** Irene Dunne; John Boles; Julie Haydon; Lionel Atwill; Helen Westley; Laura Hope Crews; Herbert Yost; ***D:*** Philip Moeller; ***W:*** Victor Heerman; Sarah Y. Mason; ***C:*** James Van Trees.

The Age of Innocence **1993 (PG)** Magnificently lavish adaptation of Edith Wharton's novel of passion thwarted by convention is visually stunning, but don't expect action since these people kill with a word or gesture. In 1870s New York, proper lawyer Newland Archer (Day-Lewis) is engaged to the equally proper May Welland (Ryder). He discovers unexpected romance when May's cousin, the rather scandalous Ellen Olenska (Pfeiffer), returns to the city from Europe but his hesitancy costs them dearly. Woodward's narration of Wharton's observations helps sort out what goes on behind the facades. Although slow, see this one for the beautiful period authenticity, thanks to Scorsese, who obviously labored over the small details. He shows up as a photographer; his parents appear in a scene on a train. **138m/C; VHS, DVD, Blu-Ray.** Daniel Day-Lewis; Michelle Pfeiffer; Winona Ryder; Martin Scorsese; Richard E. Grant; Alec McCowen; Miriam Margolyes; Mary Beth Hurt; Geraldine Chaplin; Stuart Wilson; Michael Gough; Alexis Smith; Jonathan Pryce; Robert Sean Leonard; ***Nar:*** Joanne Woodward; ***D:*** Martin Scorsese; ***W:*** Martin Scorsese; Jay Cocks; ***C:*** Michael Ballhaus; ***M:*** Elmer Bernstein. Oscars '93: Costume Des.; British Acad. '93: Support. Actress (Margolyes); Golden Globes '94: Support. Actress (Ryder); Natl. Bd. of Review '93: Director (Scorsese), Support. Actress (Ryder).

The Age of Shadows ½ **2016** An espionage thriller set in 1920s Korea that explores the Korean resistance to Japanese occupation. Police captain Lee Jung-chool (Kang-Ho) works for the Japanese but has positive childhood links to the resistance. Though charged with stopping the resistance, Lee's feelings of sympathy for the cause and its fighters grows when he infiltrates a group traveling to China for an explosives deal. Balancing out Lee's perspective is the resistance's new leader, Kim Woo-jin (Yoo) and the bloodthirsty Japanese agent Hashimoto (Tae-go). Though the overly long film has muddled plotting, a well-executed train sequence justifies the time investment. Korean, Japanese, and Mandarin with subtitles. **140m/C; DVD.** Byung-hun Lee; Kang-ho Song; Yoo Gong; Richard Epcar; Kyle Hebert; ***D:*** Jee-woon Kim; ***W:*** Jee-woon Kim; Ji-min Lee; Jong-dae Park; Kathy Pilon; ***C:*** Ji-yong Kim; ***M:*** Mowg.

Age of the Dragons ½ **2011 (PG-13)** In this reworking of Herman Melville's "Moby Dick" into a medieval fantasy, Ahab (Glover) was scarred by the white dragon that killed his sister. He and his crew rumble through the land in a boat-shaped contraption in a search for dragon's vitriol, the liquid that allows the beasties to breathe fire and serves as a power source for the local villages. It's a goof but the CGI's not bad for a low-budget indie. **92m/C; DVD, Blu-Ray.** Danny Glover; Corey Sevier; Kepa Kruse; Vinnie Jones; Sofia Pernas; David Morgan; Larry Bagby; McKay Daines; ***D:*** Ryan Little; ***W:*** McKay Daines; ***C:*** Ryan Little; ***M:*** J Bateman. **VIDEO**

Age of the Hobbits *Clash of the Empires; Lord of the Elves* **2012** A tribe of little people in ancient Thailand appeal to their neighbors to help them rescue their peers from dragon riding cavemen cannibals. **87m/C; DVD, Blu-Ray, Streaming.** Bai Ling; Sun Korng; Srogn; Khom Lyly; Christopher Judge; ***D:*** Joseph J. Lawson; ***W:*** Eric Forsberg; ***C:*** Richard J. Vialet; ***M:*** Chris Ridenhour. **VIDEO**

Age Old Friends ½ **1989** Crusty octogenarian Cronyn must choose. His daughter (played by real-life offspring Tandy) wants him to move out of a retirement home and into her house. But he's struggling to keep neighbor and increasingly senile friend Gardenia from slipping into "zombieland." An emotional treat with two fine actors deploying dignity and wit in the battle against old age. Originally adapted for HBO from the Broadway play, "A Month of Sundays" by Bob Larbey. **89m/C; VHS, DVD.** Vincent Gardenia; Hume Cronyn; Tandy Cronyn; Esther Rolle; Michelle Scarabelli; ***D:*** Allen Kroeker.

Age Out *Friday's Child* **2019** Eighteen-year-old Richie (Sheridan) has aged out of the foster care system. A bit lost, he finds an inexpensive place to live and tries to support himself with odd jobs. When troublemaker Swim (Jones) tells Richie that his landlady (Butler) is a known cheat, Richie breaks into her office looking for cash. When she is found dead the next day, a detective (Wright) wants to talk to Richie. Though Richie plans to leave town, he meets traumatized Joan (Poots) and makes unexpected decisions. The second feature by Edwards, the beautiful drama is impressionistic in its storytelling and visuals, and features memorable performances by the leads. **91m/C; DVD, Blu-Ray.** Tye Sheridan; Imogen Poots; Caleb Landry Jones; Jeffrey Wright; Brett Butler; ***D:*** A.J. Edwards; ***W:*** A.J. Edwards; ***C:*** Jeff Bierman; ***M:*** Colin Stetson.

The Agency *Mind Games* **1981 (R)** An advertising agency attempts to manipulate public behavior and opinion through the use of subliminal advertising. A good premise is bogged down by a dull script and plodding performances by all concerned. Based on a Paul Gottlieb novel. **94m/C; VHS, DVD.** *CA* Robert Mitchum; Lee Majors; Valerie Perrine; Saul Rubinek; Alexandra Stewart; ***D:*** George Kaczender; ***M:*** Lewis Furey.

Agent Cody Banks ½ **2003 (PG)** Muniz is Cody Banks, a seemingly normal 15-year-old kid who lives a secret life as a CIA spy. After training for a few years at a "junior spy" summer camp, he's given his first mission: talk to a girl! He must befriend and protect classmate Natalie (Duff), the daughter of a scientist (Donovan) who's created a nanotechnology that could help villains McShane and Vosloo CONTROL THE WORLD!!! Much junior 007 action ensues, mixed with some quirky comedy and innocent teen romance. "Spy Kids" had more charm, but the target audience probably won't mind the difference. Harmon keeps things interesting for the older set with her vavoom-ish wardrobe and surprising knack for comedy. If the characters aren't exactly fleshed out, at least the actors playing them seem to be enjoying themselves. **95m/C; VHS, DVD, Blu-Ray.** Frankie Muniz; Hilary Duff; Angie Harmon; Keith David; Cynthia Stevenson; Arnold Vosloo; Martin Donovan; Daniel Roebuck; Ian McShane; Darrell Hammond; ***D:*** Harald Zwart; ***W:*** Scott M. Alexander; Ashley Edward Miller; Zack Stentz; Larry Karaszewski; ***C:*** Denis Crossan; ***M:*** John Powell.

Agent Cody Banks 2: Destination London **2004 (PG)** Banks is back to take on more evildoers who want to RULE THE WORLD!!! AGAIN!!! Now it's British industrialist Lord Kenworth (Faulkner) and Diaz (Allen), Banks's CIA camp commander turned traitor, who have a device that allows them to control what people do and say. Off to London for the big showdown. Cody goes undercover in a youth symphony where he meets his handler (the funny Anderson, who's not given much to work with) and Hilary Duff fill-in Spearritt as Emily, the prerequisite pretty girl (albeit a drab one here). While the first effort thrived on the normal-teenager-becomes-secret-agent concept the second surprisingly ignores the first part and focuses on the at-times hard-to-follow action scenes. Muniz puts in another fine performance and the kids will probably still find it a fun ride, but a trilogy is probably not needed. **99m/C; VHS, DVD, Blu-Ray.** Frankie Muniz; Anthony Anderson; Cynthia Stevenson; Daniel Roebuck; Hannah Spearritt; Anna Chancellor; Keith Allen; James Faulkner; David Kelly; Santiago Segura; Connor Widdows; Keith David; ***D:*** Kevin Allen; ***W:*** Don Rhymer; Harald Zwart; ***C:*** Denis Crossan; ***M:*** Mark Thomas.

Agent of Death *The Alternate* **1999 (R)** Philandering President Beck is not Mr. Popularity and there's an election coming up. So his PR head arranges for a fake kidnapping to garner sympathy. But the plans goes wrong and he winds up in the hands of a psycho Secret Service agent (Genesse). And the one man (Roberts) who might be able to rescue the Prez doesn't want the job. **105m/C; VHS, DVD.** Ice-T; Eric Roberts; Michael Madsen; Bryan Genesse; John Beck; ***D:*** Sam Firstenberg; ***W:*** Bryan Genesse. **VIDEO**

Agent Red ½ *Captured* **2000 (R)** Oh so typical story done in a less-than-enthralling manner. Naval Specials Ops Commander Matt Hendricks (Lundgren) is aboard a U.S. sub, escorting a deadly chemical weapon to a safe storage facility. Then the sub is boarded by Russian terrorists who want to unleash the virus on New York City. Naturally, Hendricks must prevent that. **95m/C; VHS, DVD.** Dolph Lundgren; Randolph Mantooth; Meilani Paul; Alexander Kuznitsov; Natalie Radford; Steve Eastin; Tony Becker; ***D:*** Damian Lee; ***W:*** Damian Lee; ***C:*** Ken Blakey; ***M:*** David Wurst; Eric Wurst. **VIDEO**

The Aggression Scale **2012 (R)** Humor and gore are successfully combined in this sicko thriller. Mobster Reg's (Wise) getaway money is missing, and he sends henchman Lloyd (Ashbook) and his crew after the likely suspects. They descend on the Rutledge family and kill off the parents. It turns out that young weirdo Owen (Hartwig) and his older stepsister Lauren (Therese) are more ruthless than the hit men can imagine. **85m/C; DVD, Blu-Ray.** Ryan Hartwig; Fabianne Therese; Dana Ashbrook; Ray Wise; Derek Mears; Jacob Reynolds; Joseph McKelheer; ***D:*** Steven C. Miller; ***W:*** Ben Powell; ***C:*** Jeff Dolen; ***M:*** Kevin Riepl. **VIDEO**

Agnes Browne ½ **1999 (R)** Sentimental, old-fashioned saga concerning recent widow Agnes Browne (Huston), who's trying to cope with her seven children under difficult circumstances in Dublin in 1967. Agnes, who works a market stall, has one personal dream—she wants to see Tom Jones in an upcoming concert. Guess what happens. Director Huston does try to keep the bathos under control. Based on the novel "The Mammy" of Brendan O'Carroll. **91m/C; VHS, DVD.** Anjelica Huston; Ray Winstone; Arno Chevrier; Marion O'Dwyer; Ciaran Owens; Tom Jones; ***D:*** Anjelica Huston; ***W:*** John Goldsmith; Brendan O'Carroll; ***C:*** Anthony B. Richmond; ***M:*** Paddy Moloney.

Agnes of God **1985 (PG-13)** Stage to screen translation of John Pielmeier's play loses something in the translation. Coarse chain-smoking psychiatrist Fonda is sent to a convent to investigate whether young nun Tilly is fit to stand trial. Seems that the nun may have given birth to and then strangled her baby, although she denies ever having sexual relations and knows nothing about an infant. Naive Tilly is frightened by probing Fonda, while worldly mother-superior Bancroft is distrusting. Melodramatic stew of Catholicism, religious fervor, and science features generally good performances, although Fonda often seems to be acting (maybe it's the cigarettes). **98m/C; VHS, DVD, Blu-Ray.** Jane Fonda; Anne Bancroft; Meg Tilly; Anne Pitoniak; Winston Rekert; Gratien Gelinas; ***D:*** Norman Jewison; ***W:*** John Pielmeier; ***C:*** Sven Nykvist; ***M:*** Georges Delerue. Golden Globes '86: Support. Actress (Tilly).

The Agony and the Ecstasy ½ **1965** Big-budget (for 1965 anyway at $12 million) adaptation of the Irving Stone book recounts the conflict between Michelangelo and Pope Julius II after His Holiness directs the artist to paint the Sistine Chapel. Follow the tortured artist through his unpredictable creative process and the hours (it seems literal due to movie length) of painting flat on his back. Heston exudes quiet strength in his sincere interpretation of the genius artist, while Harrison has a fling as the Pope. Slow script is not up to the generally good performances. Disappointing at the boxoffice, but worth a look on the small screen for the sets alone. **136m/C; VHS, DVD, Blu-Ray.** Charlton Heston; Rex Harrison; Harry Andrews; Diane Cilento; Alberto Lupo; Adolfo Celi; ***D:*** Carol Reed; ***W:*** Philip Dunne; ***C:*** Leon Shamroy; ***M:*** Jerry Goldsmith; Alex North. Natl. Bd. of Review '65: Support. Actor (Andrews).

Agony of Love **1966** An unhappy homemaker rents a nearby apartment to live out her wildest fantasies and bring some excitment into her otherwise dull life. **?m/CVHS, DVD.** Pat Barrington; William Rotsler; ***D:*** William Rotsler; ***W:*** William Rotsler.

Agora **2009** Despite being a woman living in 4th-century Alexandria, philosopher, mathematician, and astronomer Hypatia (Weisz, who gives a dominating performance) teaches and spends her time in the city's fabled library. But the ancient pagan world is giving way to a firebrand cult of Christians who begin to dominate their Roman rulers to the detriment of such knowledge. Could use some editing with too much exposition and too many monologues slowing down the too-timely story of religious fundamentalist intolerance vs. personal freedom and reason. **141m/C; Blu-Ray, On Demand.** *SP* Rachel Weisz; Max Minghella; Oscar Isaac; Ashraf Barhoum; Rupert Evans; Michael (Michel) Lonsdale; Sami Samir; ***D:*** Alejandro Amenabar; ***W:*** Alejandro Amenabar; Mateo Gil; ***C:*** Xavi Gimenez; ***M:*** Dario Marianelli.

Aguirre, the Wrath of God ½ *Aguirre, der Zorn Gottes* **1972** Herzog at his best, combining brilliant poetic images and an intense narrative dealing with power, irony, and death. Spanish conquistadors in 1590 search for the mythical city of gold in Peru. Instead, they descend into the hell of the jungle. Kinski is fabulous as Aquirre, succumbing to insanity while leading a continually diminishing crew in this compelling, extraordinary drama shot in the jungles of South America. Both English- and German-language versions available. **94m/C; VHS, DVD, Blu-Ray.** *GE* Klaus Kinski; Ruy Guerra; Del Negro; Helena Rojo; Cecilia Rivera; Peter Berling; Danny Ades; ***D:*** Werner Herzog; ***W:*** Werner Herzog; ***C:*** Thomas Mauch; ***M:*** Popul Vuh. Natl. Soc. Film Critics '77: Cinematog.

Ah, Wilderness! ½ **1935** Delightful tale of a teen boy coming of age in small town America. Watch for the hilarious high school graduation scene. Based on the play by Eugene O'Neill. Remade in 1948 as "Summer Holiday," a musical with Mickey Rooney in the lead. **101m/B; VHS, DVD.** Wallace Beery; Lionel Barrymore; Aline MacMahon; Eric Linden; Cecilia Parker; Spring Byington; Mickey Rooney; Charley Grapewin; Frank Albertson; ***D:*** Clarence Brown; ***C:*** Clyde De Vinna.

Ai Weiwei: Never Sorry **2012 (R)** The title of Alison Klayman's brassy documentary refers to its subject matter, a Chinese artist who has become internationally renowned not just for his creative abilities but his activism. The filmmaker was granted access to the acclaimed public figure from 2008 to 2010 and watched as Ai went through small moments with his family to international ones with the Chinese government. As with several great documentaries about artistic figures who transcend their art form to become something greater, "Never Sorry" paints a fully-rounded picture of both the personal and the political side of its subject matter. **91m/C; DVD, Blu-Ray.** *US CH* ***D:*** Alison Klayman; ***W:*** Alison Klayman; ***C:*** Alison Klayman; ***M:*** Ilan Isakov.

Aileen: Life and Death of a Serial Killer **2003** Documentary studies the life and crimes of serial killer Aileen Wournos. In-depth work recounts her horrible childhood and the psychoses that led to her murderous spree. Chilling. **89m/C; VHS, DVD.** *D:* Joan Churchill; Nick Broomfield; *C:* Joan Churchill; *M:* Robert (Rob) Lane.

Aimee & Jaguar **1998** In 1943 Berlin, Jewish Felice (Schrader) is hiding her identity and working for a Nazi newspaper where she can gather information to leak to the resistance. She leads a hedonistic night life with a group of lesbian friends and, one night, encounters Lilly (Koehler), the unfaithful wife of an SS soldier who's away at the Russian front. The odd couple begin a risky affair (the title refers to the nicknames the women gave each other) until the inevitable discovery. Based on a true story from the 1994 book by Erica Fischer. German with subtitles. **125m/C; VHS, DVD.** *GE* Maria Schrader; Juliane Kohler; Johanna Wokalek; Heike Makatsch; Elisabeth Degen; Detlev Buck; *D:* Max Farberbock; *W:* Rona Munro; Max Farberbock; *C:* Tony Imi; *M:* Jan A.P. Kaczmarek.

Ain't In It For My Health: A Film About Levon Helm **2010** Compelling rock documentary by Hatley was filmed over more than two years at the Woodstock, New York home of multiple-Grammy winning singer/musician Levon Helm. It details the recording of his first studio album in 25 years, 2007's "Dirt Farmer," while also covering Helm's battle with throat cancer, which would leave him with a ravaged voice, as well as his, sometimes bitter, memories of his time with The Band. Includes archival footage and interviews. **83m/C; DVD, Blu-Ray.** *D:* Jacob Hatley; *C:* Emily Topper.

Ain't No Way Back *The Ghost of Fletcher Ridge* **1989** Two hunters stumble upon a feudin' bunch of moonshiners and must leave their city ways behind if they plan to survive. **90m/C; VHS, DVD.** Campbell Scott; Virginia Lantry; Bernie (Bernard) White; John Durbin; Len Lesser; Joe Mays; *D:* Michael Borden.

Ain't Them Bodies Saints **2013 (R)** Affleck & Mara star as lovers split by crime as the former goes to prison just as the latter is about to give birth. Years later, he escapes and works his way back to his true love, just as a cop involved with putting him away (Foster) gets closer to his family. Sometimes too sluggish for its own good, the stunning cinematography (set in Texas) and score mesmerize enough to overcome any storytelling flaws. Young writer/director Lowery's Sundance hit borrows liberally from the filmmaking school of Terrence Malick, but he's assembled a cast and crew who pulled off copying one of film's masters. **96m/C; Blu-Ray, Streaming.** Rooney Mara; Casey Affleck; Ben Foster; Keith Carradine; Nate Parker; *D:* David Lowery; *W:* David Lowery; *C:* Bradford Young; *M:* Daniel Hart.

Air America **1990 (R)** It's the Vietnam War and the CIA is operating a secret drug smuggling operation in Southeast Asia to finance the effort. Flyboys Gibson and Downey drop opium and glib lines all over Laos. Big-budget Gibson vehicle with sufficient action but lacking much of a story, which was adapted from a book by Christopher Robbins. **113m/C; VHS, DVD, Blu-Ray.** Mel Gibson; Robert Downey, Jr.; Marshall Bell; Nancy Travis; David Marshall Grant; Tim Thomerson; Lane Smith; *D:* Roger Spottiswoode; *W:* Richard Rush; *C:* Roger Deakins; *M:* Charles Gross.

Air Bud ½ **1997 (PG)** Buddy's a basketball-playing golden retriever (no relation) who befriends lonely misfit Josh (Zegers) and teaches him the nuances of the layup, fade-away J, and pick-and-roll. It's good to see dog athletes getting to stretch beyond the usual frisbee and stick-fetching roles. Teaming animals (especially canines) with kids usually adds up to success. This one's no exception, especially for the grade school crowd. **92m/C; VHS, DVD, Blu-Ray.** Kevin Zegers; Michael Jeter; Bill Cobbs; Wendy Makkena; Eric Christmas; Brendan Fletcher; Jay Brazeau; Stephen E. Miller; Nicola Cavendish; *D:* Charles Martin Smith; *W:* Paul Tamasy; Aaron Mendelsohn; *C:* Mike Southon; *M:* Brahm Wenger.

Air Bud 2: Golden Receiver **1998 (G)** Buddy, the canine Michael Jordan of last year's "Air Bud," is back for more organized team sports with small children. His owner, Josh (Zegers) is still mourning the death of his father and isn't ready to deal with his mother's budding romance with the new veterinarian in town (Harrison). Meanwhile, Josh joins the school's football team and finds himself thrust into the spotlight as the team's quarterback when the starter is injured (big surprise!), only to be bailed out by his multi-sport pooch. Actually, Buddy is played by four different Golden Retrievers, as the original died shortly after completing the original. This rehash tries to take itself seriously, with lessons about overcoming tragedy and adjusting to change, but isn't much more than sappy melodrama and cute dog tricks. **90m/C; VHS, DVD.** Kevin Zegers; Cynthia Stevenson; Gregory Harrison; Nora Dunn; Robert Costanzo; Tim Conway; Dick Martin; Perry Anzilotti; Suzanne Ristic; Jay Brazeau; *D:* Richard Martin; *W:* Paul Tamasy; Aaron Mendelsohn; *C:* Mike Southon; *M:* Brahm Wenger.

Air Bud 3: World Pup ½ **2000 (G)** Buddy went from basketball to football and now to soccer in this third installment. This time he teams up with the U.S. Women's Soccer Team and also becomes a dad. And wouldn't you know—just before the championship game, dad Buddy must rescue one of his pups from a gang of dog-nappers. **83m/C; VHS, DVD.** Kevin Zegers; Dale Midkiff; Caitlin Wachs; Martin Ferrero; Duncan Regehr; Brittany Paige Bouck; Briana Scurry; Brandi Chastain; Tisha Venturini; *D:* Bill Bannerman. **VIDEO**

Air Bud 4: Seventh Inning Fetch ½ **2002 (G)** Since Josh is off at college, it's his little sis Andrea who needs Buddy's help on her baseball team. But Buddy's got other problems—Rocky the Raccoon has kidnapped Buddy's puppies! **93m/C; VHS, DVD.** Richard Karn; Cynthia Stevenson; Kevin Zegers; Caitlin Wachs; *D:* Robert Vince. **VIDEO**

Air Bud 5: Buddy Spikes Back **2003 (G)** After her best friend moves to California, Andrea (Wachs) takes up volleyball so she can win a chance to visit. Naturally, all-around sports dog Buddy can do a little spiking of his own. **87m/C; VHS, DVD.** *CA* Caitlin Wachs; Katija Pevec; Jake D. Smith; Tyler Boissonnault; Edie McClurg; Patrick Cranshaw; Cynthia Stevenson; Rob Tinkler; *D:* Mike Southon; *C:* Adam Sliwinski. **VIDEO**

Air Bud 6: Air Buddies **2006 (PG)** When doggie parents Buddy and Molly are abducted, their five talking puppies—B-Dawg, RoseBud, Bud-dha, Mudbud, and Budderball—must come to the rescue. Yeah, it's cute—you expected more? **80m/C; DVD.** Slade Pearce; Trevor Wright; *V:* Abigail Breslin; Spencer Breslin; Josh Flitter; Spencer Fox; Michael Clarke Duncan; Don Knotts; Mike Southon; *D:* Robert Vince; *W:* Robert Vince; Anna McRoberts; *M:* Brahm Wenger. **VIDEO**

Air Eagles ½ **1931** Former WWI flying ace Bill Ramsey and his German counterpart Otto Schuman have teamed up for an aerial carnival act. Otto's engaged to circus star Eve but she discovers he plans to shoot down a mining company's plane to steal the payroll. Bill's kid brother Eddie is the pilot and Bill loads his Sopwith Camel's machine guns with live rounds and prepares for a final dogfight. **72m/B; DVD.** Lloyd Hughes; Norman Kerry; Shirley Grey; Matty Kemp; Berton Churchill; *D:* Philip H. (Phil, P.H.) Whitman; *W:* Hampton Del Ruth; *C:* James S. Brown, Jr.

Air Force ½ **1943** One of the finest of the WWII movies, Hawks' exciting classic has worn well through the years, in spite of the Japanese propaganda. It follows the hazardous exploits of a Boeing B-17 bomber crew who fight over Pearl Harbor, Manila, and the Coral Sea. Extremely realistic dogfight sequences and powerful, introspective real guy interfacing by the ensemble cast are masterfully combined by Hawks. **124m/B; DVD.** John Garfield; John Ridgely; Gig Young; Arthur Kennedy; Charles Drake; Harry Carey, Sr.; George Tobias; Ray Montgomery; James Brown; Stanley Ridges; Willard Robertson; Moroni Olsen; Edward Brophy; Richard Lane; Faye Emerson; Addison Richards; James Flavin; Ann Doran; Dorothy Peterson; William Forrest; Ward Wood; *D:* Howard Hawks; *W:* Dudley Nichols; William Faulkner; *C:* James Wong Howe; Elmer Dyer; Charles A. Marshall; *M:* Franz Waxman. Oscars '43: Film Editing.

Air Force One *AFO* **1997 (R)** Ford stars as U.S. President James Marshall, who is not only tough on crime but tough, period. His policy is to not negotiate with terrorists. Then Air Force One, with him, the First Lady and their daughter aboard is hijacked by Russian nationalists, led by ice cold Ivan (Oldman). Close is first woman Veep, Kathryn Bennett, stuck in D.C. coping with the situation. Ford is in fine form as the President who's forced to kick some Commie butt to save the day. Director Petersen ("In The Line of Fire") is becoming a master of building tension in confined places and puts his strong cast to good use. Nail-biting suspense and breath-taking action sequences cap off tour-de-force adventure. **124m/C; VHS, DVD, Blu-Ray, UMD.** Harrison Ford; Gary Oldman; Glenn Close; Dean Stockwell; William H. Macy; Wendy Crewson; Xander Berkeley; Paul Guilfoyle; Liesl Matthews; Bill Smitrovich; Elya Baskin; David Vadim; Tom Everett; Philip Baker Hall; Spencer Garrett; Donna Bullock; *Cameo(s):* Jurgen Prochnow; *D:* Wolfgang Petersen; *W:* Andrew Marlowe; *C:* Michael Ballhaus; *M:* Jerry Goldsmith.

Air Guitar Nation **2006 (R)** Suit up, grab your guitars...wait, you don't need them. First time director (and reality TV vet) Lipsitz follows rivals David "C. Diddy" Jung and Dan "Bjorn Turoque" Crane as they air guitar-battle their way from American competitions to the World Championships in Finland. Lipsitz doesn't push many boundaries with her direction or narrative, but still manages to create a film that's often hilarious without making its subjects the butt of the joke. **81m/C; DVD.** *D:* Alexandra Lipsitz; *C:* Anthony Sacco; *M:* Dan Crane.

Air Hawks **1935** Barry Eldon (Bellamy) owns a small air courier company and is after a big government contract. He refuses to be bought out by a larger firm that's also after the contract, they use a ray machine developed by one of their scientists that can cause a plane's engines to shut down and cause a crash. Famed aviator Wiley Post briefly appears as himself. **70m/B; DVD.** Ralph Bellamy; Robert "Tex" Allen; Douglass Dumbrille; Edward Van Sloan; Tala Birell; Billie Seward; *D:* Albert Rogell; *W:* Griffin Jay; *C:* Henry Freulich.

The Air I Breathe **2007 (R)** Four interlocking stories are delivered in the form of an allegorical gangster movie that ends up an overwrought mess. Characters Happiness (Whitaker), Pleasure (Fraser), Sorrow (Gellar), and Love (Bacon), named for the key emotions of a Chinese proverb, muddle through individual challenges while the menacing gangster Fingers (Garcia) casts a shadow over all their lives. Standout cast fails to overcome the challenges presented by such a poorly executed, pretentious movie. **97m/C; DVD, Blu-Ray.** Forest Whitaker; Brendan Fraser; Sarah Michelle Gellar; Kevin Bacon; Andy Garcia; Emile Hirsch; Julie Delpy; *D:* Jieho Lee; *W:* Jieho Lee; Bob DeRosa; *C:* Walt Lloyd; *M:* Marcelo Zarvos.

Air Rage **2001 (R)** General Prescott (Cord) screwed over five Marines, setting them up and sending them to prison in order to advance his career. Now they're out and have just hijacked a 747 with the general on board—they not only want revenge but $100 million as well. Captain Marshall (Ice-T) and his team are sent on a rescue mission but things go wrong and Marshall is left to tackle the bad guys on his own. Familiar but fast-paced. **99m/C; VHS, DVD.** Ice-T; Cyril O'Reilly; Steve Hytner; Gil Gerard; Alex Cord; Kim Oja; *D:* Fred Olen Ray; *W:* Sean O'Bannon; *C:* Mac Ahlberg. **VIDEO**

Air Raid Wardens ½ **1943** Laurel & Hardy play a couple of small-town failures who become the local air raid wardens during WWII. They even manage to make a mess of this but redeem themselves when they overhear a spy plot and save the town's munitions factory from a German spy ring. A so-so effort from the comic duo. **67m/B; VHS, DVD.** Stan Laurel; Oliver Hardy; Edgar Kennedy; Jacqueline White; Stephen McNally; Russell Hicks; Howard Freeman; Donald Meek; Henry O'Neill; *D:* Edward Sedgwick.

The Air Up There **1994 (PG)** Assistant basketball coach Jimmy Dolan (Bacon) heads to the African village of Winabi to recruit talented (and tall) Saleh (Maina) to play b-ball in the U.S. But Saleh is next in line to be the tribe's king and doesn't want to leave. Stupid American in foreign country learning from the natives story is lighthearted, but relies heavily on formula—and borders on the stereotypical, though climatic game is a lot of fun. **108m/C; VHS, DVD.** Kevin Bacon; Charles Gitona Maina; Sean McCann; Dennis Patrick; *D:* Paul Michael Glaser; *W:* Max Apple; *C:* Elliot Davis; *M:* David Newman.

Airborne ½ **1993 (PG)** Cool California rollerblade dude gets transplanted to Cincinnati for a school year, and has to prove himself when those good ol' midwestern boys come after him. Nothing short of a skate vehicle appealing largely, if not solely, to the high school contingent. **91m/C; VHS, DVD.** Shane McDermott; Seth Green; Brittney Powell; Edie McClurg; Jack Black; Chris Conrad; Alanna Ubach; Jacob Vargas; *D:* Rob Bowman; *W:* Bill Apablasa; *M:* Stewart Copeland.

Airborne **1998 (R)** Members of a covert Special Forces team are targeted for assassination after recovering a biochemical weapon from terrorists. But their leader (Guttenberg) decides to use the virus as bait to find out who wants them dead. Guttenberg tries but can't convince as a tough guy but there's lots of action to make up for this casting quirk. **94m/C; VHS, DVD.** Steve Guttenberg; Sean Bean; Colm Feore; *D:* Julian Grant. **VIDEO**

Airboss ½ **1997 (R)** A special forces team of FBI agents and the military must track down a hijacked shipment of plutonium before it falls into terrorist hands. When a team member is killed, fighter pilot Frank White (Zagarino) is called in. Lots of machinery, guns, and explosions make up for the lack of believable story. **90m/C; VHS, DVD.** Frank Zagarino; John Christian; Kayle Watson; Caroline Strong; Jerry Kokich; *D:* J. Christian Ingvordsen. **VIDEO**

Airheads ½ **1994 (PG-13)** "Wayne's World" meets "Dog Day Afternoon." Silly farce has three metal heads (Buscemi, Fraser, Sandler) holding a radio station hostage in order to get their demo tape played. Events snowball and they receive instant fame. Cast and crew rich with subversive comedic talents, including Sandler and Farley from "Saturday Night Live." Soundtrack authenticity supplied by White Zombie and The Galatic Cowboys. **81m/C; VHS, DVD, Blu-Ray.** Brendan Fraser; Steve Buscemi; Adam Sandler; Chris Farley; Michael McKean; Judd Nelson; Joe Mantegna; Michael Richards; Ernie Hudson; Amy Locane; Nina Siemaszko; John Melendez; Harold Ramis; Marshall Bell; David Arquette; Reg E. Cathey; Allen Covert; Sam Whipple; China Kantner; *D:* Michael Lehmann; *W:* Rich Wilkes; *C:* John Schwartzman; *M:* Carter Burwell.

Airline Disaster **2010** It's a disaster alright. President Franklin (Baxter) learns that her brother Joseph (Valentine) is flying a super-techno new passenger jet that has been hijacked by neo-Nazi terrorists. Now she must decide between saving the plane's crew and passengers or protecting the safety of those below. This time it's the Washington Monument that takes one for the team. **90m/C; DVD.** Meredith Baxter; Scott Valentine; Lindsey McKeon; Geoff Meed; Jude Gerard Prest; Matt Lagan; *D:* John Willis, III; *W:* Paul Shor; Victoria Dadi; *C:* Alexander Yellen; *M:* Chris Ridenhour. **VIDEO**

Airplane! ½ **1980 (PG)** Classic lampoon of disaster flicks is stupid but funny and launched a bevy of wanna-be spoofs. Former pilot Ted Striker (Hays), who's lost both his stewardess girlfriend Elaine (Hagerty) and his nerve, takes over the controls of a jet when the crew is hit with food poisoning. The passengers become increasingly crazed and ground support more surreal as our hero struggles to land the plane. Clever, fast-paced, and very funny parody mangles every Hollywood cliche within reach. The gags are so furiously paced that when one bombs it's hardly noticeable. Launched Nielsen's second career as a comic actor. And it ain't over till it's over: don't miss the amusing final credits. Followed by "Airplane 2: The Sequel." **88m/C; VHS, DVD, Blu-Ray.** Robert Hays; Julie Hagerty; Lloyd Bridges; Peter Graves; Robert Stack; Kareem Abdul-Jabbar; Leslie Nielsen; Stephen Stucker;

Ethel Merman; Jerry Zucker; Barbara Billingsley; Jim Abrahams; Lorna Patterson; Joyce Bulifant; David Zucker; James Hong; Maureen McGovern; Jimmie Walker; Rossie (Ross) Harris; *D:* Jerry Zucker; Jim Abrahams; David Zucker; *W:* Jerry Zucker; Jim Abrahams; David Zucker; *C:* Joseph Biroc; *M:* Elmer Bernstein. Natl. Film Reg. '10; Writers Guild '80: Adapt. Screenplay.

Airplane 2: The Sequel 1982 **(PG)** Not a Zucker, Abrahams and Zucker effort, and sorely missing their slapstick and script finesse. The first passenger space shuttle has taken off for the moon and there's a mad bomber on board. Given the number of stars mugging, it's more of a loveboat in space than a fitting sequel to "Airplane." Nonetheless, some funny laughs and gags. **84m/C; VHS, DVD, Blu-Ray.** Robert Hays; Julie Hagerty; Lloyd Bridges; Raymond Burr; Peter Graves; William Shatner; Sonny Bono; Chuck Connors; Chad Everett; Stephen Stucker; Rip Torn; Kent McCord; Sandahl Bergman; Jack Jones; John Dehner; Richard Jaeckel; ***Cameo(s):*** Ken Finkleman; *D:* Ken Finkleman; *W:* Ken Finkleman; *C:* Joseph Biroc; *M:* Elmer Bernstein.

Airplane vs. Volcano 2014 Pure cheese with tremendous overacting by everyone trying to sell this foolishness for all they're worth. An airliner is getting close to landing in Hawaii when it's suddenly trapped in a ring of active volcanoes. With the instruments not working and the plane stuck on autopilot, Rick Pierce (Cain) is flying through ash and debris while the first class passengers panic and volcano expert Lisa Whitmore (Givens) tries to come up with a solution on the ground. **90m/C; DVD, Blu-Ray.** Dean Cain; Robin Givens; Mike Jerome Putman; Lawrence-Hilton Jacobs; Matt Mercer; Tamara Goodwin; Morgan West; *D:* James Kondelik; Jon Kondelik; *W:* James Kondelik; Jon Kondelik; *C:* Alexander Yellen; *M:* Chris Ridenhour. **VIDEO**

Airport 1970 **(G)** Old-fashioned disaster thriller built around an all-star cast, fairly moronic script, and an unavoidable accident during the flight of a passenger airliner. A boxoffice hit that paved the way for many lesser disaster flicks (including its many sequels) detailing the reactions of the passengers and crew as they cope with impending doom. Considered to be the best of the "Airport" series; adapted from the Arthur Hailey novel. **137m/C; VHS, DVD, Blu-Ray.** Dean Martin; Burt Lancaster; Jean Seberg; Jacqueline Bisset; George Kennedy; Helen Hayes; Van Heflin; Maureen Stapleton; Barry Nelson; Lloyd Nolan; Dana Wynter; Barbara Hale; Gary Collins; Jessie Royce Landis; *D:* George Seaton; *W:* George Seaton; *C:* Ernest Laszlo; *M:* Alfred Newman. Oscars '70: Support. Actress (Hayes); Golden Globes '71: Support. Actress (Stapleton).

Airport '75 1975 **(PG)** After a mid-air collision, a jumbo 747 is left pilotless. Airline attendant Black must fly da plane. She does her cross-eyed best in this absurd sequel to "Airport" built around a lesser "all-star cast." Safe on the ground, Heston tries to talk the airline hostess/pilot into landing, while the impatient Kennedy continues to grouse as leader of the foam-ready ground crew. A slick, insincere attempt to find box office magic again (which unfortunately worked, leading to two more sequels). **107m/C; VHS, DVD, Blu-Ray.** Charlton Heston; Karen Black; George Kennedy; Gloria Swanson; Helen Reddy; Sid Caesar; Efrem Zimbalist, Jr.; Susan Clark; Dana Andrews; Linda Blair; Nancy Olson; Roy Thinnes; Myrna Loy; Ed Nelson; Larry Storch; *D:* Jack Smight; *W:* Don Ingalls; *C:* Philip H. Lathrop; *M:* John Cacavas.

Airport '77 1977 **(PG)** Billionaire Stewart fills his converted passenger jet with priceless art and sets off to Palm Beach for a museum opening, joined by an uninvited gang of hijackers. Twist to this in-flight disaster is that the bad time in the air occurs underwater, a novel (and some might say, desperate) twist to the old panic in the plane we're all gonna die formula. With a cast of familiar faces, some of them stars and some of them just familiar faces, this is yet another sequel to "Airport" and another boxoffice success, leading to the last of the tired series in 1979. **114m/C; VHS, DVD, Blu-Ray.** Jack Lemmon; James Stewart; Lee Grant; Brenda Vaccaro; Joseph Cotten; Olivia de Havilland; Darren McGavin; Christopher Lee; George Kennedy; Kathleen Quinlan; Monte Markham; *D:* Jack Smight.

Ajami 1/2 2009 A non-professional cast, many from Jaffa's multi-ethnic Ajami neighborhood, are featured in Copti and Shani's intense story of culture clash in Israel. A revenge killing has many repercussions that involve Palestinians and Israelis, Christians, Muslims, and Jews—all of whom are hostile to the differing communities. Moving, powerful portrait of a society where violence permeates even the most insignificant aspects of daily life. Arabic and Hebrew with subtitles. **120m/C; Blu-Ray, On Demand.** *IS* Shahir Kabaha; Fouad Habash; Ibrahim Frege; Youseff Sahwani; Ramin Karim; Eran Naim; Scandar Copti; *D:* Scandar Copti; Yaron Shani; *W:* Scandar Copti; Yaron Shani; *C:* Boaz Yehonatan Yaacov; *M:* Rabiah Buchari.

AKA 2002 **(R)** Unhappy with his family life, young man Dean leeches off of rich socialite Lady Gryffoyn until her son, Alex, smells a rat and Dean scampers away to Paris. Unable to forgo his taste for the good life, he opts to pass himself off as Alex—causing him to face his sexuality. British writer-director Roy uses offbeat three-screen device to tell his own real-life tale. **107m/C; VHS, DVD.** *GB* Diana Quick; Blake Ritson; Bill Nighy; Geoff Bell; Matthew Leitch; George Asprey; Lindsey Coulson; *D:* Duncan Roy; *W:* Duncan Roy. **VIDEO**

AKA Doc Pomus 2012 A revealing documentary look at the life, work, and influence of Jerome Felder, better known as Doc Pomus. Born in Brooklyn and paralyzed after suffering from polio as a child, Felder was first a blues singer before becoming better known as one of the greatest songwriters of rock and roll songs in the 1950s and early 1960s. Responsible for such songs as "This Magic Moment" and "Viva Las Vegas," he also mentored other songwriters over the next few decades. The film also explores the impact of his disability on his career, which only ended with his death at the age of 65. **98m/C; DVD, Streaming, Download.** *D:* William Hechter; Peter Miller; *C:* Antonio Rossi.

Akeelah and the Bee 1/2 2006 **(PG)** Inspirational story focuses on 11-year-old Akeelah (Palmer), a vocabulary whiz (thanks to her late father's Scrabble prowess) who doesn't want to be humiliated as a brainiac at her tough South Central L.A. school. But after a couple of spelling bee wins, and the coaching of no-nonsense UCLA English professor Larabee (Fishburne), Akeelah is encouraged to dream big and head for the National Spelling Bee. Bassett plays her overworked widow mom, who has too many other worries to help her daughter (at least at first). Palmer's character is both sweet and determined although the film may seem overly familiar. **107m/C; DVD, Blu-Ray.** Laurence Fishburne; Angela Bassett; Keke Palmer; Curtis Armstrong; Tzi Ma; Lee Thompson Young; Sahara Garey; J.R. Villarreal; Sean Michael Afable; *D:* Doug Atchison; *W:* Doug Atchison; *C:* M. David Mullen; *M:* Aaron Zigman.

Akira Kurosawa's Dreams 1/2 *Dreams; Yume; I Saw a Dream Like This; Konna Yume Wo Mita* **1990 (PG)** An anthological lesson regarding the simultaneous loss of humanity and nature that threatens us all from the renowned Japanese director. Although the startling and memorable imagery is still present, Kurosawa's lessons are strangely trite and consequently lack the power that is normally associated with his work. Watch for Scorsese as Van Gogh. With English subtitles. **120m/C; VHS, DVD, Blu-Ray.** *JP* Akira Terao; Mitsuko Baisho; Meiko Harada; Chishu Ryu; Hisashi Igawa; Mitsunori Isaki; Toshihiko Nakano; Yoshitaka Zushi; Toshie Negishi; Martin Scorsese; *D:* Akira Kurosawa; *W:* Akira Kurosawa; *C:* Kazutami Hara; Takao Saito; Masaharu Ueda; *M:* Shinichiro Ikebe.

Al Capone 1959 Film noir character study of one of the most colorful gangsters of the Roaring '20s. Sort of an underworld "How to Succeed in Business." Steiger chews scenes and bullets as they fly by, providing the performance of his career. Plenty of gangland violence and mayhem and splendid cinematography keep the fast-paced period piece sailing. **104m/C; VHS, DVD.** Rod Steiger; Fay Spain; Murvyn Vye; Nehemiah Persoff; Martin Balsam; Al Ruscio; Joe De Santis; *D:* Richard Wilson.

Aladdin 1/2 **1992 (G)** Boy meets princess, loses her, finds her, wins her from evil vizier and nasty parrot, while being aided by big blue genie. Superb animation triumphs over average songs and storyline by capitalizing on Williams' talent for ad-lib with lightning speed genie changes, lots of celebrity spoofs, and even a few pokes at Disney itself. Adults will enjoy the 1,001 impersonations while kids will get a kick out of the big blue genie and the songs, three of which are the late Ashman's legacy. Kane and Salonga are responsible for the singing voices of Aladdin and Jasmine; Gottfried is a riot as the obnoxious parrot sidekick. Be forewarned: small children may be frightened by some of the scarier sequences. **90m/C; VHS, DVD, Blu-Ray.** *V:* Robin Williams; Scott Weinger; Linda Larkin; Jonathan Freeman; Frank Welker; Gilbert Gottfried; Douglas Seale; Brad Caleb Kane; Lea Salonga; *D:* Ron Clements; John Musker; *W:* Ron Clements; John Musker; Ted Elliott; Terry Rossio; *M:* Alan Menken; *M:* Howard Ashman; Tim Rice. Oscars '92: Orig. Score, Song ("A Whole New World"); Golden Globes '93: Score, Song ("A Whole New World"); MTV Movie Awards '93: Comedic Perf. (Williams).

Aladdin 1/2 **2019 (PG)** Aladdin (Massoud) is an impoverished street urchin who gains possession of a magic lamp and magic carpet. Rubbing the lamp, he learns that he is able to summon a big blue genie (Smith). Using his new magical items, he sets out to win the heart of a princess, Jasmine (Scott), and prevent the treacherous official Jafar (Kenzari) from stealing Jasmine's father's kingdom away from him. Closely following the plot of the 1992 animated feature for the most part, this live action retelling of the classic fairytale still has an inspiring story and humorous moments but lacks the magic of the original. **128m/C; DVD, Blu-Ray.** Will Smith; Mena Massoud; Naomi Scott; Marwan Kenzari; Navid Negahban; *D:* Guy Ritchie; *W:* Guy Ritchie; John August; *C:* Alan Stewart; *M:* Alan Menken.

Aladdin and the King of Thieves 1996 Second-direct-to-video saga (following "The Return of Jafar") once again features Williams as the voice of the genie (after settling a dispute with Disney). On the eve of Aladdin's marriage to Jasmine, theives try to steal a magic talisman, sending Aladdin on a mission to find the thieves—and his father. Disney had such terrific success with "Return" that it was inevitable they would try again. **82m/C; VHS, DVD, Blu-Ray.** *V:* Robin Williams; Scott Weinger; Jerry Orbach; John Rhys-Davies; Gilbert Gottfried; Linda Larkin; CCH Pounder; Frank Welker; *D:* Ted Stones; *W:* Mark McCorkle; Robert Schooley; *M:* Mark Watters.

Alambrista! *The Illegal* **1977** Spare, affecting, unsentimental drama marks the directorial debut of Young. Mexican Roberto (Ambiz) becomes an illegal immigrant in California, doing backbreaking farm work to send money back to his destitute family. English and Spanish with subtitles. **110m/C; DVD, Blu-Ray.** Domingo Ambiz; Trinidad Silva; Linda Gillin; Paul Berrones; *D:* Robert M. Young; *W:* Robert M. Young; *C:* Robert M. Young; Tom Hurwitz; *M:* Michael Martin Murphey.

The Alamo 1960 Old-fashioned patriotic battle epic recounts the real events of the 1836 fight for independence in Texas. The usual band of diverse and contentious personalities, including Wayne as a coonskin-capped Davy Crockett, defend a small fort against a very big Mexican raiding party outside of San Antonio. Before meeting mythic death, they fight with each other, learn the meaning of life, and ultimately come to respect each other. Just to make it more entertaining, Avalon sings. Big-budget production features an impeccable musical score by Tiomkin and an impressive 7,000 extras for the Mexican army alone. Wayne reportedly received directorial assistance from John Ford, particularly during the big massacre finale. **161m/C; VHS, DVD.** John Wayne; Richard Widmark; Laurence Harvey; Frankie Avalon; Richard Boone; Carlos Arruza; Chill Wills; Veda Ann Borg; Linda Cristal; Patrick Wayne; Joan O'Brien; Joseph Calleia; Ken Curtis; Jester Hairston; Denver Pyle; John Dierkes; Guinn "Big Boy" Williams; Olive Carey; William Henry; Hank Worden; Ruben Padilla; Jack Pennick; *D:* John Wayne; *W:* James Edward Grant; *C:* William Clothier; *M:* Dimitri Tiomkin; Paul Francis Webster. Oscars '60: Sound; Golden Globes '61: Score.

The Alamo 1/2 **2004 (PG-13)** Dry as a tumbleweed epic is the latest and not so greatest in a dozen odd big-screen tries of dubious success at depicting the historic Texas battle. Thornton stars as Davy Crockett along with Wilson, Patric, and Quaid as William Travis, Jim Bowie, and Sam Houston who, along with 189 others, form the "Texican" holdouts who, after nearly two weeks of anxious waiting, battle the Mexican army of nearly 2,500 and their General, Santa Anna (Echevarria). Mostly tedious waiting, while the actual battle is surprisingly sterile. Thornton (if not his character) emerges unscathed with an excellent performance, especially in the winning rooftop fiddle serenade scene. Supporting work is more uneven. Big-budgeter looks great and is exacting in historical accuracy but ultimately lacks dramatic punch and a cohesive plot. **137m/C; DVD.** Dennis Quaid; Billy Bob Thornton; Jason Patric; Patrick Wilson; Emilio Echeverria; Jordi Molla; Leon Rippy; Marc Blucas; Tom Davidson; Robert Prentiss; Ken Page; Joe Stevens; Steven Prince; Tom Everett; Brandon Smith; Rance Howard; Stephen Bruton; Emily Deschanel; Laura Clifton; Edward "Blue" Deckert; *D:* John Lee Hancock; *W:* John Lee Hancock; Leslie Bohem; Stephen Gaghan; *C:* Dean Semler; John O'Connor; *M:* Carter Burwell.

Alamo Bay 1/2 **1985** A slow-moving but sincere tale of contemporary racism. An angry Vietnam veteran and his red-neck buddies feel threatened by Vietnamese refugees who want to go into the fishing business. Set in Texas, filled with Texas-sized characters, and based on a true Texas story, as interpreted by the French Malle. **99m/C; VHS, Blu-Ray, Streaming.** Ed Harris; Ho Nguyen; Amy Madigan; Donald Moffat; Cynthia Carle; Truyen V. Tran; Rudy Young; *D:* Louis Malle; *W:* Alice Arlen; *M:* Ry Cooder.

The Alamo: Thirteen Days to Glory 1987 The legendary Davy Crockett (Keith), Colonel William Travis (Baldwin), and Jim Bowie (Arness) overcome personal differences to unite against the Mexican Army, vowing to hold down the fort or die. It takes a true Texan to fully appreciate the merits of this rather pedestrian retelling of a familiar story, but the battle scenes are pretty heady (although they lose some of their froth on the small screen). If nothing else, the ever-versatile Julia is worth seeing as Santa Anna in this made-for-TV rendering of J. Lon Tinkle's "Thirteen Days to Glory." You may not want to remember the Alamo this way. **180m/C; VHS, Streaming.** James Arness; Lorne Greene; Alec Baldwin; Brian Keith; Raul Julia; Laura Elena Harring; *D:* Peter Werner; *M:* Peter Bernstein.

Alamut Ambush 1986 A federal agent is stalked by assassins, and decides to hunt them in return. Sequel to "Cold War Killer." **94m/C; VHS, DVD.** *GB* Terence Stamp; Michael Culver; *D:* Ken Grieve.

Alan Partridge *Alan Partridge: Alpha Papa* **2013 (R)** If you know who comedian Steve Coogan is, you've got Alan Partridge to thank for it. Partridge, Coogan's self-obsessed talk-show-host character--Britain's Ron Burgundy--made the comedian a UK fixture in the 1990s, inspiring various radio series, TV shows, and an autobiography. But this is Partridge's first movie and it succeeds largely thanks to an incredibly clever script by Coogan and Iannucci. Partridge is now a local DJ swept up in the media circus when disgruntled ex-co-worker Pat (Meaney) takes his radio station hostage. It's all very droll, very witty, and very, very English. (Titled "Alan Partridge: Alpha Papa" in the UK.) **90m/C; Blu-Ray, On Demand.** *UK* Steve Coogan; Colm Meaney; Felicity Montagu; Nigel Lindsay; Simon Greenall; Monica Dolan; *D:* Declan Lowney; *W:* Steve Coogan; Neil Gibbons; Armando Iannucci; *C:* Ben Smithard; *M:* Ilan Eshkeri.

An Alan Smithee Film: Burn, Hollywood, Burn 1/2 *Burn, Hollywood, Burn* **1997 (R)** Follows a British director (Idle), whose given name is Alan Smithee, as he kidnaps the reels of his own picture when he realizes he hates the movie but can't remove his name from it since the Directors Guild of America's official pseudonym for disputed films is "Alan Smithee."

O'Neal stars as the boorish producer who drives Smithee to the desperate act. This extended in-joke ran into its own problem when director Arthur Hiller, in what seemed like a publicity stunt, repudiated the version producer/writer Eszterhas recut and had his own name removed from the film, thus making "An Alan Smithee Film" one of the more than 30 Alan Smithee films in as many years. The tedious mockumentary style is relentless in narrating the story to the audience, who is never allowed to just watch what happens. Only interest is the parade of star cameos, including Stallone, Goldberg, and Chan (as themselves), along with writer Eszterhas in a scene with the director who declined credit for the film, Hiller. **86m/C; VHS, DVD.** Eric Idle; Ryan O'Neal; Coolio; Richard Jeni; Sandra Bernhard; Cherie Lunghi; Harvey Weinstein; M.C. Lyte; Stephen Tobolowsky; Chuck D; Leslie Stefanson; Gavin Polone; Marcello Thedford; Nicole Nagel; Dina Spybey; ***Cameo(s):*** Joe Eszterhas; Sylvester Stallone; Whoopi Goldberg; Jackie Chan; Larry King; Billy Bob Thornton; Dominick Dunne; Robert Evans; Shane Black; ***D:*** Arthur Hiller; ***W:*** Joe Eszterhas; ***C:*** Reynaldo Villalobos; ***M:*** Gary G-Wiz. Golden Raspberries '98: Worst New Star (Eszterhas), Worst Picture, Worst Screenplay, Worst Song ("I Wanna Be Mike Ovitz!"), Worst Support. Actor (Eszterhas).

Alarm ½ **2008** Irish psycho-thriller. Molly leaves Dublin a year after her father's death, the result of their being terrorized during a home invasion. She hopes for some peace and quiet in her country estate house but only experiences isolation. When her home is repeatedly broken into, Molly begins to have paranoid suspicions about everyone from her old friends to a new lover. **104m/C; DVD.** *IR* Alan Howley; Tom Hickey; Ruth Bradley; Aidan Turner; Anita Reeves; Owen Roe; ***D:*** Gerard Stembridge; ***W:*** Gerard Stembridge; ***C:*** Bruno de Keyzer.

The Alarmist *Life During Wartime* **1998** Tommy Hudler (Arquette) is the eager beaver new employee at the L.A. home-security company owned by slick super-salesman Heinrich Grigoris (Tucci). But Tommy's soon shocked to learn that Heinrich makes certain clients continue to need his services by breaking into their homes. Tommy makes his first sale to fortysomething widow Gale (Capshaw), who enjoys seducing the boyish innocent, and the two embark on a torrid affair. Then Gale and her teenaged son are murdered after a home break-in and Tommy suspects Heinrich went a little too far. Arquette's amusingly geeky but Tucci steals the film as his sleazy boss. **93m/C; VHS, DVD.** Stanley Tucci; David Arquette; Kate Capshaw; Ryan Reynolds; Mary McCormack; Tricia Vessey; ***D:*** Evan Dunsky; ***W:*** Evan Dunsky; ***C:*** Alex Nepomniaschy; ***M:*** Christophe Beck.

Alaska ½ **1996 (PG)** Fourteen-year-old Vincent Barnes (Kartheiser) and his 12-year-old sister Jessie (Birch) try to rescue their bush pilot father Jake (Benedict) whose plane has crashed in the wilderness. They also rescue an orphaned polar bear cub from an evil poacher (Heston) that manages to help them out along the way. See this flick if only to enjoy the lush backdrop of Alaska and British Columbia and, of course, the absolutely adorable polar cub. Director Fraser C. Heston directs dad Charlton, appropriate payback for landing him the role as the infant Moses in "The Ten Commandments." **109m/C; VHS, DVD.** Thora Birch; Vincent Kartheiser; Dirk Benedict; Charlton Heston; ***D:*** Fraser Heston; ***W:*** Andy Burg; Carol Fuchs; ***C:*** Tony Westman.

Albatross ½ **2011** Cliff House is a family-run hotel on England's south coast that is also the title of the one successful novel by owner Jonathan Fischer (Koch). His frustrated wife Joa (Ormond) isn't happy with the disruptive influence of new teenage maid Emelia (Findlay), who has writing aspirations and is supposedly being mentored by Jonathan, or her friendship with their serious daughter Beth (Jones). Nor should she be, since Emelia is doing more than sharpening her literary skills with Jonathan. **90m/C; DVD.** *UK* Jessica Brown-Findlay; Sebastian Koch; Julia Ormond; Felicity Jones; Harry Treadaway; Thomas Brodie-Sangster; ***D:*** Niall MacCormick; ***W:*** Tamzin Rafn; ***C:*** Jan Jonaeus; ***M:*** Jack C. Arnold.

Albert Nobbs ½ **2011 (R)** A passion project by Close results in one of the best film performances of her career as a 19th-century Irish woman who has to disguise herself as the title character to work as a hotel butler. When she meets a man (McTeer) who turns out to also be a woman in disguise, Albert is thrown out of her routine by the concept that she could have more happiness than her predictable life has provided, maybe even love with a co-worker (Wasikowska). Close and McTeer are subtle and often spectacular but the overall piece is relatively slight. **113m/C; DVD, Blu-Ray.** *IR* Glenn Close; Mia Wasikowska; Aaron Taylor-Johnson; Janet McTeer; Pauline Collins; Brenda Fricker; Jonathan Rhys Meyers; Brendan Gleeson; Mark Williams; Bronagh Gallagher; ***D:*** Rodrigo Garcia; ***W:*** Glenn Close; John Banville; Gabriella Prekop; ***C:*** Michael McDonough; ***M:*** Brian Byrne.

Albert's Memorial ½ **2009** In London, aged Harry and Frank agree to honor their dying friend Albert's last wish to be buried on the German hill where they fought together during WWII. The duo (and Albert's dead body) set off in Harry's cab but get lost in France and then rely on German hitchhiker Vicki to help them. She also uncovers a 55-year-old secret (revealed in flashbacks) that still haunts the men. **68m/C; DVD.** *GB* David Jason; David Warner; Judith Hoersch; Michael Jayston; Nick Bennett; Scott Harrison; Adam Flynn; ***D:*** David Richards; ***W:*** Thomas Ellice; ***C:*** Tony Coldwell; ***M:*** Hal Lindes. **TV**

Albino Alligator **1996 (R)** Three small-time crooks bungle a robbery and inadvertently run down a federal officer in Academy Award-winning actor Spacey's directorial debut. The trio, consisting of leader Dova (Dillon), brains Milo (Sinise) and brawn Law (Fichtner) hole up in a seedy bar and grab the occupants as hostages. The police soon surround the dive, and the crooks begin arguing among themselves and with brash barmaid Janet (Dunaway) about their chances and means for escape. All, however, is not as it seems. The claustrophobic setting seems more suitable for the stage than the screen, and the plot twists don't bend very far from predictable. Screenwriter Forte is the son of '60s teen idol Fabian. **94m/C; VHS, DVD, Blu-Ray.** Matt Dillon; Gary Sinise; Faye Dunaway; William Fichtner; Joe Mantegna; Viggo Mortensen; John Spencer; Skeet Ulrich; M. Emmet Walsh; ***D:*** Kevin Spacey; ***W:*** Christian Forte; ***C:*** Mark Plummer; ***M:*** Michael Brook.

Albino Farm ½ **2009 (R)** College kids travel to the Ozarks to research an urban legend and run afoul of inbred mutant rednecks. **90m/C; DVD.** Chris Jericho; Richard Christy; Duane Whitaker; Sunkrish Bala; Nick Richey; Kevin Blair Spirtas; Tammin Sursok; ***D:*** Joe Sanderson; ***W:*** Joe Sanderson; Sean McEwen; ***C:*** Rene Jung; ***M:*** Scott Rockenfield. **VIDEO**

The Alchemist **WOOF! 1981 (R)** See humans transformed into murderous zombies! A bewitched man seeks revenge upon the evil magician who placed a curse on him, causing him to live like an animal. Painfully routine, with a few chills along the way. Amonte is an alias for Charles Band. Filmed in 1981 and released four years later. **86m/C; VHS, DVD.** Robert Ginty; Lucinda Dooling; John Sanderford; Viola Kate Stimpson; Bob Glaudini; ***D:*** Charles Band; ***W:*** Alan J. Adler; ***M:*** Richard Band.

The Alchemists ½ **1999 (PG-13)** The world's leading pharmaceutical company is covering up the fact that their fertility drug has some serious side effects. Employees Show and Gemmell try to expose the corporate conspiracy. Based on the novel by Peter James. **150m/C; VHS, DVD.** Grant Show; Ruth Gemmell; Edward Hardwicke; ***D:*** Peter Smith; ***C:*** Peter Middleton; ***M:*** Rick Wentworth.

Alchemy ½ **2005 (PG-13)** Slight romantic comedy that gets a little extra oomph from its appealing leads. Professor Mal Downey (Cavanaugh) uses his new computer software to woo struggling actress Samantha Rose (Chalke) based on the responses the program generates. **85m/C; DVD.** Sarah Chalke; Nadia Dajani; Illeana Douglas; Celeste Holm; Tom Cavanaugh; James Barbour; Anna Belknap; Erik Palladino; ***D:*** Evan Oppenheimer; ***W:*** Evan Oppenheimer; ***C:*** Luke Geissbuhler; ***M:*** Peter Lurye.

Aleksandr's Price ½ *Simple Moves; Buying Aleksandr* **2013** Illegal Russian emigre Aleksandr doesn't know where to turn after his mother's death so he gets work dancing in gay clubs for the money and the feeling of being desired. Soon, he's working asa prostitute and becoming increasingly troubled as his desperate search for love turns into just another sexual encounter. Low-budget indie wth a familar story. **110m/C; DVD.** Pau Maso; Josh Berresford; ***D:*** Pau Maso; ***W:*** Pau Maso; ***C:*** David Damen; ***M:*** Dave Klotz.

Alex & Emma ½ **2003 (PG-13)** The original unwieldy title was "Loosely Based on a True Love Story" because it's loosely based on writer Fyodor Dostoyevsky's story "The Gambler," which was based on a true incident in his life. Or at least that's what the original hype for the movie maintained. Writer Alex (Wilson) has big gambling debts so he takes an advance from his publisher (Reiner) in exchange for churning out a book in 30 days. He hires stenographer Emma (Hudson) to take dictation of his very bad novel, which is set in 1924 and comes to life as Alex spins a story that Emma heartily criticizes. Lame romantic comedy wastes its leads, who have been much more charming in other films (and who have no chemistry together). Lovely blond Hudson is forced into a drab brunette persona that's as unappealing as her wardrobe. **96m/C; VHS, DVD.** Luke Wilson; Kate Hudson; Sophie Marceau; David Paymer; Francois Giroday; Rob Reiner; Cloris Leachman; Rip Taylor; ***D:*** Rob Reiner; ***W:*** Jeremy Leven; ***C:*** Gavin Finney; ***M:*** Marc Shaiman.

Alex Cross **WOOF! 2012 (PG-13)** A future MST3K entry from reel one, Perry's attempt to step into the shoes of the character made popular by Morgan Freeman in the first two films adapted from James Patterson's novels is laughable. The half-asleep Perry plays Cross as he tries to track down a maniacal assassin played with bug-eyed intensity by Fox in what is easily one of the most ridiculous performances of the young decade. At least Fox seems to be concerned with keeping the action moving, which is more than can be said for everyone else involved, especially the lackluster direction by Cohen. **101m/C; DVD, Blu-Ray; Closed Captioned.** Tyler Perry; Matthew Fox; Edward Burns; Rachel Nichols; Jean Reno; Cicely Tyson; Carmen Ejogo; ***D:*** Rob Cohen; ***W:*** Kerry Williamson; Marc Moss; ***C:*** Ricardo Della Rosa; ***M:*** John Debney.

Alex in Wonderland ½ **1970 (R)** A semi-autobiographical and satirical look at Hollywood from the standpoint of a young director who's trying to follow up his recent hit (in real life, "Bob & Carol & Ted & Alice") with a picture of some integrity that will keep the mass audience away. The confused plot provides obvious parallels to Fellini (who appears in a cameo) and some sharp, often bitter insights into the Hollywood of the early '60s. Strong performances by Sutherland and Burstyn compensate somewhat for the patience-trying self-indulgent arty whining of the script. **109m/C; VHS, DVD.** Donald Sutherland; Ellen Burstyn; Paul Mazursky; ***Cameo(s):*** Jeanne Moreau; Federico Fellini; ***D:*** Paul Mazursky; ***W:*** Larry Tucker; Paul Mazursky.

Alex Rider: Operation Stormbreaker *Stormbreaker* **2006 (PG)** Horowitz adapted the story from the first book in his own young adult series about 14-year-old Alex Rider (newcomer Pettyfer), who's basically a junior James Bond. Alex is orphaned and living with his spy uncle Ian (McGregor), who's quickly killed off, thus leaving Alex himself to be recruited by MI-6 boss Blunt (Nighy). Good thing the teen's already had all that special ops training. The villain is the ever-creepy Rourke, here playing some evil tycoon with a grudge, and Silverstone is Alex's helpful housekeeper, Jack. There's gadgets and action galore for the undemanding youngster while the adults can stick with Ian Fleming. **93m/C; DVD.** *GE* Ewan McGregor; Mickey Rourke; Bill Nighy; Sophie Okonedo; Alex Pettyfer; Alicia Silverstone; Missi Pyle; Sarah Bolger; Damian Lewis; Andy Serkis; Robbie Coltrane; Stephe Fry; ***D:*** Geoffrey Sax; ***W:*** Anthony Horowitz; ***C:*** Chris Seager; ***M:*** Alan Parker.

Alexander **2004 (R)** Looooong and somewhat farcical bio of Macedonian conqueror Alexander the Great. In Stone's depiction, Alexander (Farrell) is the pawn in a marital war between his swaggering, drunken father Philip (Kilmer) and his snake-worshipping mother Olympias (a sultry Jolie), who implies that her boy is really the progeny of the god Zeus. Tutored by Aristotle (Plummer), Alexander believes it's his destiny to subjugate as much of the known world as is possible. Lots of big battles ensue as Alexander forcibly unites the squabbling Greek city-states before challenging the might of the Persian empire. He does take some time out to marry hot-blooded Eastern princess, Roxanne (Dawson), while the ruler's relationship with constant companion Hephaistion (Leto) is reduced to meaningful glances. Farrell cannot overcome the fact that he isn't forceful enough to portray an epic figure. **175m/C; VHS, DVD, Blu-Ray.** Colin Farrell; Angelina Jolie; Val Kilmer; Christopher Plummer; Jared Leto; Rosario Dawson; Anthony Hopkins; Brian Blessed; Jonathan Rhys Meyers; Tim Pigott-Smith; Gary Stretch; John Kavanagh; Ian Beattie; Feodor Atkine; Connor Paolo; Nick Dunning; Marie Meyer; Elliot Cowan; Joseph Morgan; Denis Conway; Neil Jackson; Rory McCann; Raz Degan; Annelise Hesme; ***D:*** Oliver Stone; ***W:*** Oliver Stone; Laeta Kalogridis; Christopher Kyle; ***C:*** Rodrigo Prieto; ***M:*** Vangelis.

Alexander and the Terrible, Horrible, No Good, Very Bad Day ½ **2014 (PG)** Disney adaptation of Judith Viorst's 32-page children's book gets turned into a live action feature. The terrible day in question starts in the head of nice kid Alexander (Oxenbould) upon hearing that the most popular kid in school is throwing a major party the same night as his proposed 12th birthday party. This means no one will be there, not his busybody mom (Garner) or even his stay-at-home dad (Carell) who have more pressing matters. This straight-laced family comedy means well, but lacks the courage and bite of the original text, coming off as gooey and forgettable. **81m/C; DVD, Blu-Ray.** Ed Oxenbould; Steve Carell; Jennifer Garner; Dylan Minnette; Kerris Dorsey; Megan Mullally; Jennifer Coolidge; ***D:*** Miguel Arteta; ***W:*** Rob Lieber; ***C:*** Terry Stacey; ***M:*** Christophe Beck.

Alexander Nevsky ½ **1938** A story of the invasion of Russia in 1241 by the Teutonic Knights of Germany and the defense of the region by good old Prince Nevsky. Eisenstein's first completed project in nearly ten years, it was widely regarded as an artistic disappointment upon release and as pro-war propaganda for the looming conflict with the Nazis. Fabulous Prokofiev score illuminates the classic battle scenes, which used thousands of Russian army regulars. Russian with subtitles. **110m/B; VHS, DVD.** *RU* Nikolai Cherkassov; Nikolai P. Okhlopkov; Andrei Abrikosov; Alexandra Danilova; Dmitri Orlov; Vera Ivasheva; Sergei Blinnikov; Lev Fenin; Vladimir Yershov; Nikolai Arsky; Naum Rogozhin; Varvara O. Massalitinova; Vasili Novikov; Ivan Lagutin; ***D:*** Sergei Eisenstein; ***W:*** Sergei Eisenstein; Pyotr Pavlenko; ***C:*** Eduard Tisse; ***M:*** Sergei Prokofiev.

Alexander the Great ½ **1955** A lavish epic about the legendary Greek conqueror of the fourth century B.C., which provides Burton a rare chance at an adventure role. Here we find Alexander is the product of a dysfunctional royal family who hopes to create an idealized world modeled after Greek culture to make up for the love he lacks from daddy. This he does by conquering everything before dying at the age of 33. The great cast helps to overcome the sluggish pacing of the spectacle, while numerous battle scenes featuring loads of spears and arrows are staged effectively. **135m/C; VHS, DVD, Blu-Ray.** Richard Burton; Fredric March; Claire Bloom; Harry Andrews; Peter Cushing; Danielle Darrieux; Helmut Dantine; ***D:*** Robert Rossen; ***C:*** Robert Krasker.

Alexander the Last ½ **2009** Brief mumblecore drama from Swanberg with a lot of improvised dialogue by the actors that may be more realistic but isn't very interesting. Married actress Alex is rehearsing a very-Off Broadway play with costar Jamie in which the director needs them to simulate a sex scene and make it seem hot. With her husband out of town, Alex starts getting increasingly uncomfortable about her attraction to the other man. **72m/C; DVD.** Jess Weixler; Barlow Jacobs; Justin M. Rice; Jane Adams; Josh Hamilton; Amy Seimetz; Jo Schornikow; *D:* Joe Swanberg; *W:* Joe Swanberg; *C:* Joe Swanberg; *M:* Justin M. Rice; Jo Schornikow. **VIDEO**

Alexander: The Other Side of Dawn ♂♂ **1977** Tired sequel to the television movie "Dawn: Portrait of a Teenage Runaway." A young man turns to prostitution to support himself on the street of Los Angeles. **100m/C; VHS, DVD.** Leigh McCloskey; Eve Plumb; Earl Holliman; Juliet Mills; Jean Hagen; Lonny (Lonnie) Chapman; *D:* John Erman. **TV**

Alexander's Ragtime Band ♂♂♂ *Irving Berlin's Alexander's Ragtime Band* **1938** Energetic musical that spans 1915 to 1938 and has Power and Ameche battling for Faye's affections. Power is a society nabob who takes up ragtime. He puts together a band, naming the group after a piece of music (hence the title), and finds a singer (Faye). Ameche is a struggling composer who brings a Broadway producer to listen to their performance. Faye gets an offer to star in a show and becomes an overnight success. Over the years the trio win and lose success, marry and divorce, and finally end up happy. Corny but charming. **105m/B; VHS, DVD.** Tyrone Power; Alice Faye; Don Ameche; Ethel Merman; Jack Haley; Jean Hersholt; Helen Westley; John Carradine; Paul Hurst; Joe King; Ruth Terry; *D:* Henry King; *W:* Kathryn Scola; Lamar Trotti; *M:* Irving Berlin. Oscars '38: Score.

Alexandra ♂♂♂ *Aleksandra* **2007** A moving, dramatic war film that looks at the mechanisms of a military camp through the eyes of an outsider. Taking the train, an elderly woman, Aleksandra Nikolaevna (Vishnevskaya), travels to an isolated military outpost in Chechnya to visit her favorite grandson. Denis (Shevtsov) is an officer stationed there. Initially focused on exploring the barracks inside the compound, Aleksandra sees firsthand the complexities of the military life there. She also experiences the unexpected nature of war when she takes a trip to the nearby countryside where the enemy awaits. Russian and Chechen with subtitles. **95m/C; DVD.** Galina Vishnevskaya; Vasily Shevtsov; Raisa Gichaeva; Serge Makarov; Evgeniy Tkachuk; *D:* Aleksandr Sokurov; *W:* Aleksandr Sokurov; *C:* Aleksandr Burov; *M:* Andrey Sigle.

Alexandria Again and Forever ♂♂ *Iskanderija, Kaman oue Kaman* **1990** Yehia (Chahine) remembers his win as best director at the Berlin Film Festival a decade before for his political film "Alexandria...Why?" and thinks about that film's leading man with whom he fell in love. But when he meets and falls for Nadia, Yehia decides he will launch her career as the star of his new film. The final part of Chahine's Alexandria trilogy, following "Alexandria...Why?" and "An Egyptian Story." Arabic with subtitles. **105m/C; VHS, DVD.** *EG* Youssef Chahine; Zaki Abdel Wahab; Menha Batraoui; Teheya Cariocca; Amr Abdel Guelil; Yousra; *D:* Youssef Chahine; *W:* Youssef Chahine; *C:* Ingy Assolh; *M:* Mohammed Nouh.

Alexandria. . . Why? ♂♂ **1978** Schoolboy (director Chahine uses his adolescent recollections) tries to ignore the war in Alexandria in 1942 by escaping into the movies and his dreams of becoming a star. He also witnesses two love affairs—one between a Muslim man and a Jewish woman and the second betweeen an Arab nationalist and an English soldier. Part 1 of Chahine's Alexandria trilogy, followed by "An Egyptian Story" and "Alexandria Again and Forever." Arabic with subtitles. **133m/C; VHS, DVD.** *EG* Gerry Sundquist; Naglaa Fathi; Farid Shawqi; Mohsen Mohiedine; *D:* Youssef Chahine; *W:* Youssef Chahine; *C:* Mohsen Nasr; *M:* Foad El Zaheri.

Alfie ♂♂♂ **1966 (PG)** What's it all about, Alfie? Caine, in his first starring role, plays the British playboy out of control in mod London. Alfie is a despicable, unscrupulous and vile sort of guy who uses woman after woman to fulfill his basic needs and then casts them aside until...tragedy strikes. Though this box office hit was seen as a sophisticated take on current sexual mores upon release, it now seems a dated but engaging comedy, notable chiefly for its performances. From the play by Bill Naughton. The title song "Alfie," sung by Dionne Warwick, was a top ten hit. **114m/C; VHS, DVD.** *GB* Michael Caine; Shelley Winters; Millicent Martin; Vivien Merchant; Julia Foster; Jane Asher; Shirley Anne Field; Eleanor Bron; Denholm Elliott; Alfie Bass; Graham Stark; Murray Melvin; Sydney Tafler; *D:* Lewis Gilbert; *W:* Bill Naughton; *C:* Otto Heller; *M:* Burt Bacharach; Sonny Rollins. Cannes '67: Grand Jury Prize; Golden Globes '67: Foreign Film; Natl. Bd. of Review '66: Support. Actress (Merchant); Natl. Soc. Film Critics '66: Actor (Caine).

Alfie ♂♂ ½ **2004 (R)** Law plays a kinder, gentler lothario in this contemporary update of the 1966 film (which helped make Michael Caine a star), although Alfie still engages in a somewhat self-conscious running commentary directed to the camera. The charming, handsome Alfie is now a limo driver in New York who indulges himself with as many beautiful birds as will put up with him. These include the lonely, married Dorie (Krakowski); single mom Julie (Tomei), who kicks him out after realizing Alfie is a horn-dog; sexy, self-destructive party girl Nikki (Miller); and foxy Lonette (Long), the ex-girlfriend of his best friend Marlon (Epps). But even Alfie must pay for his dalliances when he suffers a bout of impotence and then meets his sexual match in worldly mature beauty Liz (Sarandon). While Alfie remains a narcissist (though ever-so-appealing as played by Law) at least the women characters are no longer complaisant or compliant. **106m/C; VHS, DVD.** Jude Law; Marisa Tomei; Omar Epps; Nia Long; Jane Krakowski; Sienna Miller; Susan Sarandon; Renee Taylor; Dick Latessa; Jefferson Mays; Gedde Watanabe; *D:* Charles Shyer; *W:* Charles Shyer; Elaine Pope; *C:* Ashley Rowe; *M:* Mick Jagger; David A. Stewart; John Powell. Golden Globes '05: Song ("Old Habits Die Hard").

Alfredo, Alfredo ♂♂ **1972 (R)** Hoffman plays a mild-mannered bank clerk who regrets marrying a sexy woman. Lightweight domestic comedy. In Italian with English subtitles (Hoffman's voice was dubbed). **97m/C; VHS, DVD.** *IT* Dustin Hoffman; Stefania Sandrelli; Carla Gravina; Clara Colosimo; Daniela Patella; Dulio Del Prete; *D:* Pietro Germi; *W:* Pietro Germi; Leonardo Benvenuti; *C:* Aiace Parolini; *M:* Carlo Rustichelli.

Algiers ♂♂♂ **1938** Nearly a scene-for-scene Americanized remake of the 1937 French "Pepe Le Moko" about a beautiful rich girl (Lamarr) who meets and falls in love with a notorious thief (Boyer, then a leading sex symbol). Pursued by French police and hiding in the underworld-controlled Casbah, Boyer meets up with Lamarr in a tragically fated romance done in the best tradition of Hollywood. Boyer provides a measured performance as Le Moko, while Lamarr is appropriately sultry in her American film debut (which made her a star). Later remade as the semi-musical "Casbah." **96m/B; DVD.** Charles Boyer; Hedy Lamarr; Sigrid Gurie; Gene Lockhart; Joseph Calleia; Alan Hale; *D:* John Cromwell; *C:* James Wong Howe.

Ali ♂♂ ½ **2001 (R)** Mann, a notorious obsessive, couldn't have picked a more ambitious topic. The herculean task proves too much, yielding a film that lacks focus or insight into its subject. Ali is depicted during a contentious decade (1964-1974), in which he converted to Islam, befriended civil rights icons, refused the draft, was stripped of his title, married three times, and blurred lines between sport, ethics and society. Perhaps it's no coincidence that screenwriter Roth, who previously penned "Forrest Gump," was chosen to chronicle Ali amid such historic happenings. Mann's visual skills are apparent, and Smith gives an inspired performance in and out of the ring. Other noteworthies include Foxx as cornerman "Bundini" Brown, and Voight as verbose sportscaster Cosell. Despite the charisma of its subject (and its lead), film feels distant and subdued. Lands a few clean blows, but certainly not a knockout. **158m/C; VHS, DVD, Blu-Ray.** Will Smith; Jamie Foxx; Jon Voight; Mario Van Peebles; Ron Silver; Jeffrey Wright; Mykelti Williamson; Jada Pinkett Smith; Michael Michele; Joe Morton; Paul Rodriguez; Nona Gaye; Bruce McGill; Barry (Shabaka) Henley; Giancarlo Esposito; Laurence Mason; LeVar Burton; Albert Hall; David Cubitt; Ted Levine; David Elliott; Michael Bentt; James N. Toney; Charles Shufford; Malick Bowens; Shari Watson; Victoria Dillard; Kim Robillard; Gailard Sartain; Rufus Dorsey; Robert Sale; Damien "Bolo" Wills; Michael Dorn; *D:* Michael Mann; *W:* Michael Mann; Stephen J. Rivele; Christopher Wilkinson; Eric Roth; *C:* Emmanuel Lubezki; *M:* Lisa Gerrard; Pieter Bourke.

Ali Baba and the Forty Thieves ♂♂ ½ **1943** Ali Baba and his gang of thieves do battle against Hulagu Khan, leader of the Mongols, to save Baghdad and its citizens from ruin and death. **87m/C; VHS, DVD.** Jon Hall; Turhan Bey; Maria Montez; Andy Devine; Kurt Katch; Frank Puglia; Fortunio Bonanova; Moroni Olsen; Scotty Beckett; *D:* Arthur Lubin; *W:* Edmund L. Hartmann; *C:* William Howard Greene.

Ali Baba and the Seven Saracens ♂ *Sinbad Against the Seven Saracens; Simbad Contro I Sette Saraceni; Hawk of Bagdad* **1964** The hero is either Sinbad or Ali Baba but it's never really clear (maybe it's the atrocious dubbing)?not that it matters anyway. The leaders of eight tribes must battle to the death until a winner is left to be the new ruler to the Golden Throne of the Majii. And whoever our hero is, he's a prime candidate. Dubbed. **92m/C; DVD.** *IT* Gordon Mitchell; Bella Cortez; Bruno Piergentili; Carla Calo; Tony Di Mitri; *D:* Emmimo Salvi.

Ali: Fear Eats the Soul ♂♂♂ *Fear Eats the Soul; Angst Essen Selle auf* **1974** A widow cleaning woman in her 60s has a love affair with a Moroccan man 30 years her junior. To no one's surprise, both encounter racism and moral hypocrisy in West Germany. Serious melodrama from Fassbinder, who wrote it and appears as the squirmy son-in-law. In German with English subtitles. **68m/C; VHS, DVD, Blu-Ray.** *GE* Brigitte Mira; El Hedi Ben Salem; Irm Hermann; *D:* Rainer Werner Fassbinder; *W:* Rainer Werner Fassbinder; *C:* Jurgen Jurges.

Alias Betty ♂♂ *Betty Fisher and Other Stories; Betty Fisher et Autres Histoires* **2001** Writer Betty (Kiberlain) has recently returned to Paris after separating from her lover. She is uneasily waiting for the arrival of her mother Margot (Garcia), a disturbed woman who abused Betty as a child. Betty's own young son Joseph (Setbon) suddenly dies in an accidental fall and she suffers a breakdown. Jose (Chatrian) is the abused young son of single mother Carole (Seigner). When Margot notices Jose alone in the streets, she takes him back to Betty as a replacement child and Betty debates whether to go along or go to the cops. Based on the book "The Tree of Hands" by Ruth Rendell. French with subtitles. **101m/C; VHS, DVD.** *FR CA* Sandrine Kiberlain; Nicole Garcia; Mathilde Seigner; Alexis Chatrian; Edouard Baer; Arthur Setbon; Luck Mervil; Stephane Freiss; *D:* Claude Miller; *W:* Claude Miller; *C:* Christophe Pollock.

Alias French Gertie ♂ ½ **1930** The leads are good, this early talkie not so much. Jewel thief Gertie poses as a French maid to rob dowagers of their gems. Her latest heist is interrupted by safecracker Jimmy Hartigan but the crime is thwarted by the arrival of Detective Kelcey. Jimmy takes the rap and Gertie is waiting for him when he gets out of prison, but now she wants to go straight and Jimmy isn't so sure. **67m/B; DVD.** Bebe Daniels; Ben Lyon; Robert Emmett O'Connor; John Ince; Daisy Belmore; *D:* George Archainbaud; *W:* Wallace Smith; *C:* J. Roy Hunt.

Alias Jesse James ♂♂ **1959 (PG)** Insurance agent Milford Farnsworth (Hope) is an eastern tenderfoot who holds a policy on Jesse James (Corey). So he heads west to make certain the outlaw doesn't get killed. Only Jesse sets Milford up as himself, hoping to collect on his own policy. Fleming's the local beauty. A number of western stars have cameos, coming to Hope's rescue. **92m/C; VHS, DVD.** Bob Hope; Rhonda Fleming; Wendell Corey; Jim Davis; Gloria Talbott; Will Wright; Mary (Marsden) Young; Joseph (Joe) Vitale; *Cameo(s):* Hugh O'Brian; Ward Bond; James Arness; Roy Rogers; Fess Parker; Gail Davis; James Garner; Gene Autry; Jay Silverheels; Bing Crosby; Gary Cooper; *D:* Norman Z. McLeod; *W:* William Bowers; D.D. Beauchamp; *C:* Lionel Lindon.

Alias John Preston ♂ ½ **1956** Yet another one of those pseudo-psychological to sleep perchance to dream movies. Lee plays a man haunted by dreams in which he's a murderer, and soon starts to question whether his dreams might not imitate life. It's been done before, it's been done since, and it's been done better. **66m/B; VHS, DVD.** *GB* Betta St. John; Alexander Knox; Christopher Lee; Sandra Dorne; Patrick Holt; Betty Ann Davies; John Longden; Bill Fraser; John Stuart; *D:* David MacDonald.

Alias the Doctor ♂ ½ **1932** Karl Brenner is the adopted son of Martha Brenner and both he and his drunken brother Stephan are studying medicine. He takes the blame for student Stephan's botched operation and goes to prison but Martha urges him to return to medicine upon his release. Since Stephan is dead, Karl passes himself off as his doctor brother and finds success in Vienna until his past is exposed. **69m/B; DVD.** Richard Barthelmess; Norman Foster; Lucille La-Verne; Marian Marsh; Adrienne Dore; Oscar Apfel; John St. Polis; George Rosener; Claire Dodd; *D:* Michael Curtiz; *W:* Houston Branch; Charles Kenyon; *C:* Barney McGill.

Alibi ♂♂ **1929** Low-budget crime drama from independent producer/director West. Gangster Chick Williams (Morris) reclaims his mob role after being released from prison. But when a cop is killed during a robbery, Williams is suspected of the crime and the detective squad will employ any method to bring him to justice. Noted for its experimental use of sound, its dazzling Art Deco sets, and its eccentric composition. **84m/B; VHS, DVD.** Chester Morris; Mae Busch; Regis Toomey; Harry Stubbs; *D:* Roland West; *W:* Roland West; C. Gardner Sullivan; *C:* Ray June; *M:* Hugo Riesenfeld.

Alibi Ike ♂♂ ½ **1935** Baseball comedy about rookie Cubs pitcher Frank Farrell (rubbery-faced comedian Brown), who is known as "Alibi Ike" because he's always making excuses, driving his manager Cap (Frawley) and his teammates crazy. He can't even be straight with his gal, Dolly (de Havilland). Next, Frank gets into trouble with gamblers who want him to throw games but he comes through in the end. Adapted from a story by Ring Lardner. **73m/B; VHS, DVD.** Joe E. Brown; Olivia de Havilland; William Frawley; Ruth Donnelly; Roscoe Karns; Joseph King; Paul Harvey; Selmer Jackson; *D:* Ray Enright; *W:* William Wister Haines; *C:* Arthur L. Todd.

Alice ♂♂ *Alicja* **1986** A twist on the "Alice in Wonderland" tale. Alice witnesses an attempted murder, faints, and awakens in a weird, yet strangely familiar environment. Adapted from the stage production. **80m/C; VHS, DVD.** Sophie Barjac; Susannah York; Jean-Pierre Cassel; Paul Nicholas; *D:* Jacek Bromski; Jerzy Gruza.

Alice ♂♂♂ ½ *Neco Z Alenky* **1988** An acclaimed surreal version of Lewis Carroll's already surreal "Alice in Wonderland," with the emphasis on Carroll's obsessiveness. Utilizing animated puppets and a live actor for Alice, Czech director Svankmajer injects grotesque images and black comedy into Wonderland. Not for the kids. **84m/C; VHS, DVD, Blu-Ray.** *CZ SI GB GE* Kristina Kohoutova; *D:* Jan Svankmajer; *W:* Jan Svankmajer; *C:* Svatopluk Maly.

Alice ♂♂♂ **1990 (PG-13)** Farrow is "Alice," a woman plagued with doubts about her lifestyle, her religion, and her happiness. Her perfect children, husband, and apartment don't prevent her backaches, and she turns to an Oriental "herbalist" for aid. She finds his methods unusual and the results of the treatments surprising. Lightweight fairytale of Yuppiedom gone awry. Fine performances, but superficial and pointed story that may leave the viewer looking for more. (Perhaps that's Allen's point.) Farewell performance from charactor actor Luke, unbilled cameo from Judith Ivey, and first time out for Dylan O'Sullivan Farrow, adopted daughter of Allen and Farrow, as Kate. **106m/C; VHS, DVD, Blu-Ray.** Mia Farrow; William Hurt; Joe Mantegna; Keye Luke; Alec Baldwin; Cybill Shepherd; Blythe Danner; Gwen Verdon; Bernadette Peters; Judy Davis; Patrick O'Neal; Julie Kavner; Caroline Aaron; Holland Taylor; Robin Bartlett; David Spielberg; Bob Balaban; Dylan O'Sullivan Farrow; Elle Macpherson; *D:* Woody Allen; *W:* Woody Allen; *C:* Carlo Di Palma. Natl. Bd. of Review '90: Actress (Farrow).

The Alice ♂ ½ **2004** A disparate group of characters come from all corners of Australia to the outback town of Alice Springs in order to witness a total eclipse of the sun in hopes that it will changes their lives. Apparently intended as an Australian TV pilot although it never went any farther. **98m/C; DVD.** *AU* Erik Thomson; Jessica Napier; Brett Stiller; Simon Burke; Caitlin McDougall; Luke Carroll; Kyaș Sherriff; ***D:*** Kate Dennis; ***W:*** Justin Mongo; ***C:*** Louis Irving. **TV**

Alice 2009 Syfy pic derived from "Alice in Wonderland" goes psychedelic with uneven results. This time Alice (Scorsone) is not only an adult but a martial arts instructor who tumbles through a mirror with the help of a ring given to her by beau Jack (Winchester). Wonderland is under the totalitarian control of the Queen of Hearts (Bates) and Alice teams up with such rebels as the Hatter (Potts) and the White Knight (Frewer) to battle the regime, which tends to turn unwelcome guests into zombies. **180m/C; DVD.** Caterina Scorsone; Kathy Bates; Philip Winchester; Andrew Lee Potts; Matt Frewer; Colm Meaney; Tim Curry; Allan Gray; Eugene Lipinski; Harry Dean Stanton; ***D:*** Nick Willing; ***W:*** Nick Willing; ***C:*** Jon Joffin; ***M:*** Ben Mink. **CABLE**

Alice Adams 1/2 **1935** Based on the classic Booth Tarkington novel about a poor girl from a small Midwestern town who falls in love with a man from the upper level of society. She tries desperately to fit in and nearly alienates her family and friends. The sets may be dated, but the insight on human behavior is timeless. **99m/B; VHS, DVD.** Katharine Hepburn; Fred MacMurray; Evelyn Venable; Fred Stone; Frank Albertson; Ann Shoemaker; Charley Grapewin; Grady Sutton; Hedda Hopper; Hattie McDaniel; ***D:*** George Stevens; ***M:*** Max Steiner.

Alice Doesn't Live Here Anymore 1/2 **1974 (PG)** Scorsese marries road opera with pseudo-feminist semi-realistic melodrama and produces uneven but interesting results. When Alice's husband dies suddenly, leaving her with their 11-year-old son, she leaves for California, but finds herself stranded in Phoenix, down to her last few bucks. There she lands a job as a waitress in a diner where she meets kindly rancher Kristofferson. Notable for its female point of view, it was also the basis for the once-popular TV show "Alice." Burstyn and Ladd lend key performances, while Kristofferson is typically wooden. **105m/C; VHS, DVD.** Ellen Burstyn; Kris Kristofferson; Diane Ladd; Jodie Foster; Harvey Keitel; Vic Tayback; Billy Green Bush; Laura Dern; ***D:*** Martin Scorsese; ***W:*** Robert Getchell; ***C:*** Kent Wakeford; ***M:*** Richard LaSalle. Oscars '74: Actress (Burstyn); British Acad. '75: Actress (Burstyn), Film, Screenplay, Support. Actress (Ladd).

Alice in Wonderland 1/2 *Lewis Carroll's Alice in Wonderland* **1933** Early black-and-white version of Lewis Carroll's classic with what was an all-star cast at the time. It's somewhat pressed for time as it includes both of Carroll's works, and is presented as more of a series of episodes then a standard plot. **77m/B; DVD, Blu-Ray, Streaming.** Richard Arlen; Gary Cooper; Cary Grant; Charlotte Henry; ***D:*** Norman Z. McLeod; ***W:*** Joseph L. Mankiewicz; William Cameron Menzies; ***C:*** Bert Glennon; Henry Sharp; ***M:*** Dimitri Tomkin.

Alice in Wonderland 1/2 **1950** Another version of the Lewis Carroll classic which combines the usage of Lou Bunin's puppets and live action to tell the story. Released independently to cash in on the success of the Disney version. Takes a more adult approach to the story and is worth viewing on its own merits. **83m/C; VHS, DVD, Blu-Ray.** *FR* Carol Marsh; Stephen Murray; Pamela Brown; Felix Aylmer; Ernest Milton; ***D:*** Dallas Bower.

Alice in Wonderland **1951 (G)** Classic Disney dream version of Lewis Carroll's famous children's story about a girl who falls down a rabbit hole into a magical world populated by strange creatures. Beautifully animated with some startling images, but served with a strange dispassion warmed by a fine batch of songs. Wynn's Mad Hatter and Holloway's Cheshire Cat are among the treats in store. **75m/C; VHS, DVD.** ***V:*** Kathryn Beaumont; Ed Wynn; Sterling Holloway; Jerry Colonna; ***D:*** Hamilton Luske; Wilfred Jackson; Clyde Geronimi.

Alice in Wonderland **1966** Minimalist re-telling of the classic story set in old mansions with the main characters in Victorian period costumes. The BBC decided for a darker more surrealistic tone for the film as opposed to what had been done before. **72m/B; DVD.** *UK* Anne-Marie Mallik; Michael Redgrave; Peter Cook; Michael Gough; Peter Sellers; ***D:*** Jonathan Miller; ***W:*** Jonathan Miller; ***C:*** Dick Bush; ***M:*** Ravi Shankar. **TV**

Alice in Wonderland 1/2 **1985** All-star updated adaptation of the Lewis Carroll classic. This time instead of Alice falling down a rabbit hole she falls through her television set. But her adventures still include the White Rabbit, Mad Hatter, March Hare, Cheshire Cat, and the King and Queen of Hearts. Followed by "Alice Through the Looking Glass." **90m/C; VHS, DVD.** Natalie Gregory; Anthony Newley; Ringo Starr; Telly Savalas; Robert Morley; Sammy Davis, Jr.; Steve Allen; Steve Lawrence; Eydie Gorme; Red Buttons; Ann Jillian; Scott Baio; Sid Caesar; Ernest Borgnine; Beau Bridges; Lloyd Bridges; Tom McLoughlin; Harvey Korman; Patrick Duffy; Donald O'Connor; Arte Johnson; Carol Channing; Sherman Hemsley; Roddy McDowall; Donna Mills; Imogene Coca; Karl Malden; Noriyuki "Pat" Morita; Sally Struthers; Martha Raye; Merv Griffin; Jack Warden; Louis Nye; Shelley Winters; John Stamos; Jonathan Winters; George Savalas; ***D:*** Harry Harris; ***W:*** Paul Zindel; ***C:*** Fred W. Koenekamp; ***M:*** Morton Stevens. **TV**

Alice in Wonderland 1/2 **1999** Visually elaborate but somewhat tedious version of the popular Lewis Carroll tale filled with scenery chewing by the real actors and the welcome presence of animatronic wonders from the Jim Henson Creature Shop. This time Alice is the poised Majorino, who seems more annoyed by the denizens of Wonderland than amazed at her adventures. **129m/C; VHS, DVD.** Tina Majorino; Martin Short; Miranda Richardson; Whoopi Goldberg; Ben Kingsley; Gene Wilder; Christopher Lloyd; Pete Postlethwaite; Peter Ustinov; George Wendt; Robbie Coltrane; ***D:*** Nick Willing; ***W:*** Peter Barnes; ***C:*** Giles Nuttgens; ***M:*** Richard Hartley. **TV**

Alice in Wonderland 1/2 **2010 (PG)** Burton's visually stunning flick combines Lewis Carroll's novels of Wonderland with his poem "The Jabberwocky" to tell the tale of an older Alice (Wasikowska). Now 19 years old and resisting an arranged marriage to an upper-class twit, Alice flees her engagement party and once again falls down the rabbit hole. She's reunited with her old friends the Mad Hatter (Depp) and the White Queen (Hathaway), as well as her old enemy the Red Queen (Bonham-Carter). The climactic battle scene seems forced and cribbed from other recent fantasy epics, but the characters retain their demented quirkiness. The movie was not actually shot in 3-D, which makes its release in this format (with sub-par results) seem curiouser and curiouser. **108m/C; Blu-Ray.** Mia Wasikowska; Johnny Depp; Anne Hathaway; Helena Bonham Carter; Crispin Glover; Michael Sheen; Alan Rickman; Christopher Lee; Stephen Fry; Matt Lucas; Marton Csokas; Lindsay Duncan; ***D:*** Tim Burton; ***W:*** Linda Woolverton; ***C:*** Dariusz Wolski; ***M:*** Danny Elfman. Oscars '10: Art Dir./Set Dec., Costume Des.; British Acad. '10: Costume Des., Makeup.

Alice Sweet Alice 1/2 *Holy Terror; Communion* **1976 (R)** Mediocre, gory who-killed-her, best remembered as the debut of Shields (in a small role). **112m/C; VHS, DVD, Blu-Ray.** Linda Miller; Paula Sheppard; Mildred Clinton; Niles McMaster; Jane Lowry; Rudolph Willrich; Brooke Shields; Alphonso de Noble; Gary Allen; Tom Signorelli; Lillian Roth; ***D:*** Alfred Sole; ***W:*** Alfred Sole; Rosemary Ritvo; ***C:*** John Friberg; Chuck Hall; ***M:*** Stephen Lawrence.

Alice Through the Looking Glass 1/2 **1966** Based on Lewis Carroll's classic adventure. Follows the further adventures of young Alice. After a chess piece comes to life, it convinces Alice that excitement and adventure lie through the looking glass. **72m/C; VHS, DVD.** Judi Rolin; Ricardo Montalban; Nanette Fabray; Robert Coote; Agnes Moorehead; Jack Palance; Jimmy Durante; Tom Smothers; Roy Castle; Richard Denning; ***D:*** Alan Handley.

Alice Through the Looking Glass **2016 (PG)** Loosely based on Lewis Carroll's Through the Looking Glass and following up on Tim Burton's 2010 hit, this disaster will forever be Evidence Exhibit A in the case that Hollywood doesn't understand what audiences want from a franchise. Burton's film was flawed but the follow-up enhances all of those flaws, coming off as a loud, CGI-heavy, completely hollow exercise in torture. Alice (Wasikowska) returns to Underland and finds the Mad Hatter (Depp) acting crazier than ever. All of it is merely an excuse for bad special effects and worse writing. Unlikely to appeal to even fans of the original. **113m/C; DVD, Blu-Ray.** Johnny Depp; Mia Wasikowska; Helena Bonham Carter; Anne Hathaway; Sacha Baron Cohen; ***D:*** James Bobin; ***W:*** Linda Woolverton; ***C:*** Stuart Dryburgh; ***M:*** Danny Elfman.

Alice Upside Down 1/2 **2007** Preteen Alice McKinley (Stoner) and her older brother Lester (Grabeel) struggle when their widowed dad Ben (Perry) decides to make a fresh start in St. Louis. Alice has a tough time adjusting to her new school and gets into trouble with her stern homeroom teacher Mrs. Plotkin (Marshall). But Alice learns two important lessons as adolescence hits: don't be judgmental and don't jump to conclusions. Adapted from Phyllis Reynolds Naylor's "Alice" novels. **90m/C; DVD.** Alyson Stoner; Luke Perry; Lucas Grabeel; Penny Marshall; Ann Dowd; Dylan McLaughlin; Parker McKenna Posey; ***D:*** Stanley Tung; ***W:*** Stanley Tung; Meghan Heritage; ***C:*** Mark Mervis.

Alice's Restaurant 1/2 **1969 (PG)** Based on the popular and funny 20-minute Arlo Guthrie song "Alice's Restaurant Massacre" about a Flower Child during the Last Big War who gets hassled for littering, man. Step back in time and study the issues of the hippie era, including avoiding the draft, dropping out of college, and dealing with the local pigs. Sort of a modern movie in the cinematic ambling genre, in that nothing really happens. **111m/C; VHS, DVD.** Arlo Guthrie; James Broderick; Pat Quinn; Geoff Outlaw; Pete Seeger; Lee Hays; Michael McClanathan; Tina Chen; Kathleen Dabney; William Obanhein; Graham Jarvis; M. Emmet Walsh; ***D:*** Arthur Penn; ***W:*** Arthur Penn; Venabel Herndon; ***C:*** Michael Nebbia; ***M:*** Arlo Guthrie; Garry Sherman.

Alien 1/2 **1979 (R)** Terse direction, stunning sets and special effects, and a well-seasoned cast save this from being another "Slimy monster from Outerspace" story. Instead it's a grisly rollercoaster of suspense and fear (and a huge boxoffice hit). Intergalactic freighter's crew is invaded by an unstoppable carnivorous alien intent on picking off the crew one by one. While the cast mostly bitches and banters while awaiting the horror of their imminent departure, Weaver is exceptional as Ripley, a self-reliant survivor who goes toe to toe with the Big Ugly. Futuristic, in the belly of the beast visual design creates a vivid sense of claustrophobic doom enhanced further by the ominous score. Oscar-winning special effects include the classic baby alien busting out of the crew guy's chest routine, a rib-splitting ten on the gore meter. Successfully followed by "Aliens" and "Alien 3." **116m/C; VHS, DVD, Blu-Ray.** *GB* Tom Skerritt; Sigourney Weaver; Veronica Cartwright; Yaphet Kotto; Harry Dean Stanton; Ian Holm; John Hurt; Bolaji Badejo; ***V:*** Helen Horton; ***D:*** Ridley Scott; ***W:*** Dan O'Bannon; ***C:*** Derek Vanlint; ***M:*** Jerry Goldsmith. Oscars '79: Visual FX; Natl. Film Reg. '02.

Alien 3 **1992 (R)** Picks up where "Aliens" left off as Ripley crash lands on Fiorina 161, a planet that serves as a penal colony for 25 celibate but horny men who smell bad. Ripley is forced to shave her head because of the planet's lice problem, and she sets out to survive on the cold, unfriendly planet until a rescue ship can come for her. Fending off sexual advances from the men, Ripley soon discovers she wasn't the only survivor of the crash—the alien survived too and has somehow implanted her with an alien of her own. Dark and disturbing, filled with religious allegories, and a universe removed from the two earlier Aliens. Intended as the final installment of the series. **135m/C; VHS, DVD, Blu-Ray.** Sigourney Weaver; Charles S. Dutton; Charles Dance; Paul McGann; Brian Glover; Ralph Brown; Danny (Daniel) Webb; Christopher John Fields; Holt McCallany; Lance Henriksen; ***D:*** David Fincher; ***C:*** Alex Thomson; ***M:*** Elliot Goldenthal.

Alien Abduction 1/2 **2014** Based on the real Brown Mountain Lights sightings in North Carolina, this thriller considers what happens when a family on a camping vacation comes into contact with hostile aliens. Among the family members is Riley (Polanski), an autistic child who uses a handheld camera to help him understand the bigger world. During the trip, he records the night sky and the growing alien threat against his family. **85m/C; DVD, Streaming.** Katherine Sigismund; Corey Eid; Riley Polanski; Jillian Clare; Jeff Bowser; ***D:*** Matty Beckerman; ***W:*** Robert Lewis; ***C:*** Luke Geissbuhler; ***M:*** Ben Weinman. **VIDEO**

Alien Agent 1/2 **2007 (R)** Agent Rykker (Dacascos) is sent to stop a renegade military unit that is building a portal between its dying homeworld and Earth. Seem Saylon (Zane), Isis (Cooke), and their band have decided they will exterminate the humans and move in. Good fights (director Johnson got his start as a stunt coordinator) but not much true sci-fi despite the plot. **95m/C; DVD.** Mark Dacascos; Billy Zane; Kim Coates; Amelia Cooke; Emma Lahana; ***D:*** Jesse Johnson; ***W:*** Vlady Pildysh; ***C:*** C. Kim Miles; ***M:*** Michael Richard Plowman. **VIDEO**

Alien Apocalypse **2005** A group of astronauts return to Earth after 40 years in suspended animation to discover that humanity is enslaved by giant termite aliens. Unsurprisingly, despite being outnumbered, outgunned, and just out everything'd, they lead a slave revolt to free humanity. **88m/C; DVD.** Bruce Campbell; Renee O'Connor; Remington Franklin; Michael Cory Davis; Peter Jason; ***D:*** Josh Becker; ***W:*** Josh Becker; Joseph LoDuca; ***C:*** David Worth. **CABLE**

Alien Avengers 1/2 *Roger Corman Presents: Alien Avengers; Welcome to Planet Earth* **1996 (R)** Naive, poor Joseph Collins (Brown) inherits a rundown roominghouse and before he knows it, he has his first tenants—Charlie (Wendt), Rhonda (Reed), and their teenaged daughter Daphne (Sakelaris). What Joseph doesn't know is the friendly trio are aliens (on vacation), who are fond of killing lowlifes and bringing home human parts for snacks. Goofy and gory cable movie. **120m/C; VHS, DVD.** George Wendt; Shanna Reed; Christopher Brown; Anastasia Sakelaris; ***D:*** Lev L. Spiro; ***W:*** Michael James McDonald; ***C:*** Christopher Baffa; ***M:*** Tyler Bates.

Alien Chaser *Orion's Key* **1996 (R)** Alien android Zagarino, who crashed in the African desert 5000 years ago, returns to life thanks to the unwitting aid of archeologists Jensen and MacDonald. They literally hold the key to stopping his destruction of mankind. **95m/C; VHS, DVD.** Frank Zagarino; Todd Jensen; Jennifer MacDonald; Brian O'Shaughnessy; ***D:*** Mark Roper; ***W:*** B.J. Nelson; ***C:*** Rod Stewart; ***M:*** Robert O. Ragland.

Alien Contamination **WOOF!** *Contamination* **1981 (R)** Tale of two astronauts who return to Earth from an expedition on Mars carrying some deadly bacterial eggs. Controlled by a Martian intent on conquering the world, the eggs squirt a gloppy juice that makes people explode on contact (a special effect). A cheap and sloppy attempt to cash in on the success of "Alien." Dubbed. **90m/C; VHS, DVD, Blu-Ray.** *IT* Ian McCulloch; Louise Monroe; Martin Mase; Siegfried Rauch; Lisa Hahn; Louise Marleau; ***D:*** Luigi Cozzi; ***W:*** Luigi Cozzi.

Alien: Covenant 1/2 **2017 (R)** Scott returns to the Alien franchise, and returns it to its roots in sci-fi horror, replacing the navel-gazing of "Prometheus" with the claustrophobic jump scares and gore of the original 1979 classic. In doing so, he also keeps it simple and familiar, luring another crew with another mysterious signal that they just HAVE to investigate. With the exception of Fassbender (playing a dual role of androids David and Walter), said crew is basically interchangeable alien chow, more notable for their method of demise than any unique characterization. Your enjoyment level will depend a lot on your franchise fatigue level. **122m/C; DVD, Blu-Ray.** Michael Fassbender; Katherine Waterston; Billy Crudup; Danny McBride; Demian Bichir; ***D:*** Ridley Scott; ***W:*** John Logan; Dante Harper; ***C:*** Dariusz Wolski; ***M:*** Jed Kurzel.

Alien Dead *It Fell from the Sky* **1979 (R)** The teenage victims of a bizarre meteor crash reincarnate as flesh-eating ghouls anxious for a new supply of human food in this extremely low-budget sleep inducer. **75m/C; VHS, DVD, Blu-Ray.** Buster Crabbe; Linda Lewis; Ray Roberts; Mike Bonavia; Dennis Underwood; ***D:*** Fred Olen Ray; ***W:*** Fred Olen Ray; Martin Allen Nicholas; ***C:*** Fred Olen Ray.

The Alien Factor 🦴 1/2 **1978 (PG)** Another low-budget crazed critter from outer-space dispatch, this one featuring multiple aliens, one of whom is good, who have the misfortune of crash landing near Baltimore. The grotesque extraterrestrials jolt a small town out of its sleepy state by wreaking havoc (except for the good one, of course). Decent special effects. **82m/C; VHS, DVD, Blu-Ray.** Don Leifert; Tom Griffith; Mary Mertens; Richard Dyszel; Richard Geiwitz; Eleanor Herman; Anne Frith; Christopher Gummer; George Stover; John Walker; Donald M. Dohler; ***D:*** Donald M. Dohler; ***W:*** Donald M. Dohler; ***M:*** Ken Walker.

Alien Factor 2: The Alien Rampage 🦴 1/2 **2001** An alien traps a town inside a force field and runs about shooting the inhabitants at will. **75m/C; DVD.** Patrick Bussink; Jonas Grey; Steven King; Bill Ulrich; George Stover; Joe Ripple; Richard Ruxton; Donna Sherman; Jaime Kulman; LauraLee O'Shell; Anne Frith; ***D:*** Don Dohler; ***W:*** Don Dohler. **VIDEO**

Alien 51 🦴 **2004 (R)** A monster escapes from Area 51 and is adopted by a traveling freak show. **90m/C; DVD.** Layton Matthews; Heidi Fleiss; Mia Riverton; ***D:*** Brennon Jones; Paul Wynne; ***W:*** Brennon Jones; ***C:*** Roderick E. Stevens; ***M:*** Collin Simon. **VIDEO**

Alien from L.A. **WOOF!** **1987 (PG)** Awesomely inept comedy about a California girl who unwittingly stumbles onto the famed continent of Atlantis and can't find a yogurt stand. Weakly plotted and acted and filmed. Like, really. **88m/C; VHS, DVD.** Kathy Ireland; Thom Mathews; Don Michael Paul; Linda Kerridge; William R. Moses; Richard Haines; Janie du Plessis; Russel Savadier; Simon Poland; Locher de Kock; Deep Roy; ***D:*** Albert Pyun; ***W:*** Albert Pyun; Debra Ricci; Regina Davis; ***C:*** Tom Fraser; ***M:*** James Saad.

Alien Hunter 🦴 1/2 **2003 (R)** Cobbled together compilation of a dozen sci fi movies. A cryptozoologist is called to the Antarctic to translate messages from an alien artifact in a plot that in no way owes a massive homage to "The Thing." Okay, actually it owes it in every way. **92m/C; DVD, Streaming.** *BL US* James Spader; Janine Eser; John Lynch; Nikolai Biney; Leslie Stefanson; ***D:*** Ron Krauss; ***W:*** Boaz Davidson; J.S. Cardone; ***C:*** Darko Suvac; ***M:*** Tim Wynne-Jones. **VIDEO**

Alien Intruder 🦴🦴 **1993 (R)** What happens when an evil demon appears before the soldiers of the future in the guise of a beautiful woman? Futuristic trash B-movie emerges from the depths. **90m/C; VHS, DVD, On Demand.** Billy Dee Williams; Tracy Scoggins; Maxwell Caulfield; ***D:*** Ricardo Jacques Gale.

Alien Invasion Arizona 🦴 *The Salena Incident* **2007 (R)** A group of death row inmates manage an escape from their prison bus, only to end up in a deserted town. Deserted, that is, except for the military covering up their experiments with alien life forms. A bad idea since they get freaked out and eat whatever's in reach. **87m/C; DVD.** Dan Southworth; Avery Clyde; Sam McConkey; James Luca McBride; Larry Jones; ***D:*** Dustin Rikert; ***W:*** Dustin Rikert; Soon Hee Newbold; ***C:*** Brian Lataille; ***M:*** Carl Rydlund. **VIDEO**

Alien Lockdown 🦴 *PredatorMan* **2004 (R)** Special Forces are required to infiltrate a genetics lab when it's super soldier experiment gets loose and goes on a killing spree. **92m/C; DVD, Streaming.** James Marshall; John Savage; Martin Kove; Michelle Goh; ***D:*** Tim Cox; ***W:*** Kenneth M. Badish; Boaz Davidson; Ross Helford; T. M. Van Ostrand; ***C:*** John S. Bartley; ***M:*** John Dickson. **VIDEO**

Alien Massacre **WOOF!** *Dr. Terror's Gallery of Horrors; Return from the Past; The Blood Suckers; Gallery of Horror* **1967** One of the worst films of all time—five short horror stories about zombies and vampires. Goes by many names—stinks in all of them. **90m/C; VHS, DVD.** Lon Chaney, Jr.; John Carradine; Rochelle Hudson; Roger Gentry; Mitch Evans; Joey Benson; Vic McGee; ***D:*** David L. Hewitt; ***W:*** Gary Heacock; David Prentiss; ***C:*** Austin McKinney.

Alien Nation 🦴🦴 1/2 **1988 (R)** A few hundred thousand alien workers land accidentally on Earth and slowly become part of its society, although widely discriminated against. One of the "newcomers" teams with a surly and bigoted human cop to solve a racially motivated murder. An inconsistent and occasionally transparent script looks at race conflicts and includes some humorous parallels with contemporary American life. Basis for the TV series. Producer Hurd was also the force behind "The Terminator" and "Aliens." **89m/C; VHS, DVD.** James Caan; Mandy Patinkin; Terence Stamp; Kevyn Major Howard; Peter Jason; Jeff Kober; Leslie Bevis; ***D:*** Graham Baker; ***W:*** Rockne S. O'Bannon; ***C:*** Adam Greenberg; ***M:*** Curt Sobel.

Alien Nation: Body and Soul 🦴🦴 1/2 **1995** The second TV movie sequel to the series finds detectives Francisco (Pierpoint) and Sykes (Graham) on a murder investigation that leads to a Newcomer scientist whose secret research deals with interspecies breeding. Meanwhile, Sykes' romance with Cathy (Treas) is heating up and he's becoming painfully aware of the sexual differences between humans and Newcomers. **87m/C; VHS, DVD.** Gary (Rand) Graham; Eric Pierpoint; Terri Treas; Michelle Scarabelli; Sean Six; Lauren Woodland; Kristin Davis; Tiny Ron; ***D:*** Kenneth Johnson; ***C:*** Shelly Johnson; ***M:*** David Kurtz.

Alien Nation: Dark Horizon 🦴🦴 1/2 **1994 (PG)** The alien Newcomers have successfully adapted to life on Earth but face continuing dangers when a human-supremacy group develops a virus to wipe them out and an alien infiltrator is plotting to return them to slavery on Tencton. Naturally, it's up to detectives Sykes and Francisco to save the day. Based on the TV series. Part of the 'Alien Nation: Ultimate Movie Collection'. **90m/C; VHS, DVD.** Gary (Rand) Graham; Eric Pierpoint; Scott Patterson; Terri Treas; Michelle Scarabelli; Lee Bryant; Sean Six; Lauren Woodland; Ron Fassler; Jeff Marcus; ***D:*** Kenneth Johnson; ***W:*** Diane Frolov; Andrew Schneider; ***M:*** David Kurtz.

Alien Nation: Millennium 🦴🦴 1/2 **1996** In this third TV sequel Matt (Graham) and George's (Pierpoint) latest police investigation hits very close to the Francisco home. Rebellious teenager Buck (Six) gets involved with a suspicious cult, lead by Newcomer Jennifer (Keane), that offers spiritual enlightenment at a very heavy price. **120m/C; VHS, DVD.** Eric Pierpoint; Gary (Rand) Graham; Sean Six; Kerrie Keane; Michelle Scarabelli; Terri Treas; Lauren Woodland; Jeff Marcus; Jenny Gago; David Faustino; ***D:*** Kenneth Johnson; ***W:*** Kenneth Johnson; ***C:*** Shelly Johnson; ***M:*** David Kurtz.

Alien Nation: The Enemy Within 🦴🦴 1/2 **1996** George (Pierpont) must deal with his own bigotry when he and Matt (Graham) investigate the death of an Eenos Newcomer. The underground-dwelling Eenos are shunned as an ignorant and savage subclass by other Newcomers but the detectives gradually discover some sinister goings-on involving a fierce Eenos/Newcomer mutant. Meanwhile, George's wife Susan (Scarabelli) is feeling neglected and Cathy (Treas) and Matt find living together causes a strain on their relationship. The fourth TV movie from the series. **120m/C; VHS, DVD.** Eric Pierpoint; Gary (Rand) Graham; Michelle Scarabelli; Terri Treas; Sean Six; Lauren Woodland; Joe Lando; Kerrie Keane; Tiny Ron; Ron Fassler; ***D:*** Kenneth Johnson.

Alien Outlaw 🦴 **1985** Disappointing hybrid of sci fi and westerns that's not the corny entertainment it should be given the plot. Sharpshooter Jesse Jamison (Anderson) has fallen on hard times when a trio of aliens lands their spaceship in a remote desert area with the intention of hunting and killing humans. And co-star Lash LaRue doesn't even have his bullwhip! **90m/C; DVD.** Kari Anderson; Lash LaRue; Sunset Carson; ***D:*** Phil Smoot; ***W:*** Phil Smoot; ***C:*** Paul Hughen; ***M:*** Marcus Kearns.

Alien Prey 🦴 1/2 *Prey* **1978 (R)** Two lesbians are making love when they are unexpectedly devoured by a hungry and indiscreet alien. No safe sex there. Graphic sex, violence, and cannibalism abound. Interesting twist to the old eat 'em and leave 'em genre. **85m/C; VHS, DVD, Blu-Ray.** *GB* Barry Stokes; Sally Faulkner; Glory Annen; Sandy Chinney; ***D:*** Norman J. Warren; ***W:*** Max Cuff; ***C:*** Derek V. Browne; ***M:*** Ivor Slaney.

Alien Raiders 🦴🦴 **2008 (R)** A family-owned supermarket in a small Arizona town is getting ready to close when it is taken over by armed men. They aren't robbers but scientists who have tracked an alien infestation to that store. Now the scientists have to discover who among the employees and customers were infected. Fast-paced and reasonably clever with a few twists. **85m/C; DVD.** Matthew St. Patrick; Rockmond Dunbar; Jeff(rey) Licon; Bonita Friedericy; Carlos Bernard; Courtney Ford; Derek Basco; Bryan Krasner; ***D:*** Ben Rock; ***W:*** David Simkins; Julia Fair; ***C:*** Walt Lloyd; ***M:*** Kays Alatrakchi. **VIDEO**

Alien: Resurrection 🦴🦴🦴 **1997 (R)** Despite her fiery end in the last film, Ripley is brought back, through cloning, by a team of scientist anxious to get their hands on the alien embryo that invaded her. A more buffed and equally strange Ripley (Weaver) results as some of her DNA gets mixed with her alien friend. Injecting new life into the franchise, director Jeunet creates a freaky and macabre journey as the aliens get loose on board the mysterious space craft Auriga and create messy havoc for new alien appetizers including Call (Ryder), who has a personal agenda of her own with Ripley. Ryder may be somewhat out of place, but the humor and energy from the supporting cast, along with the film's dank look raises this one from the bowels of formulaic action/horror. Includes some decent scares with a tense underwater sequence. **108m/C; VHS, DVD, Blu-Ray.** Sigourney Weaver; Winona Ryder; Ron Perlman; Dominique Pinon; Michael Wincott; Kim Flowers; Leland Orser; Brad Dourif; Dan Hedaya; J.E. Freeman; Raymond Cruz; ***D:*** Jean-Pierre Jeunet; ***W:*** Joss Whedon; ***C:*** Darius Khondji; ***M:*** John (Gianni) Frizzell.

Alien Seed 🦴 **1989** Aliens kidnap a woman and impregnate her. Estrada is the government scientist hot on her trail. (How far could a woman carrying alien offspring wander?) **88m/C; VHS, DVD.** Erik Estrada; Heidi Paine; Steven Blade; ***D:*** Bob James.

Alien Siege 🦴 1/2 **2005 (R)** Aliens descend upon Earth seeking human blood, which is the only cure for a virus killing their race. They destroy some cities to show they mean business. Since they need 8 million bodies, a lottery system is devised and the unlucky get to become alien vaccine. Scientist Steven Chase (Johnson) decides no fair when his only child, Heather (Ross), is chosen. Naturally, there's a resistance group that feels earthlings should be fighting the alien fiends and Steve joins. A Sci-Fi Channel original. **90m/C; DVD.** Brad Johnson; Carl Weathers; Nathan Anderson; Erin Ross; Lilas Lane; ***D:*** Robert Stadd; ***W:*** Robert Stadd; ***C:*** Lorenzo Senatore; ***M:*** Matthias Weber; Chris Walden. **CABLE**

Alien Storm 🦴 *Tornado Warning* **2012** Purely stupid effort from the SyFy Channel that doesn't even have the decency to fall into the so-bad-it's-good category. Only gets any credit because of pro dramatics from Fahey and Wuhrer. Storm chaser Gail wants to know why the bureaucrats are ignoring her warnings about destructive green-colored tornadoes--the same phenomena that destroyed Illinois farmer Judd's crops. It's evil aliens, of course, which the government doesn't want anyone to panic about. **87m/C; DVD.** Jeff Fahey; Kari Wuhrer; Stacey Asaro; Willard Pugh; Terry Kiser; David Jensen; ***D:*** Jeff Burr; ***W:*** Paul A. Birkett; ***C:*** Andrew Strahorn; ***M:*** Andrew Morgan Smith. **CABLE**

Alien Terminator 🦴 **1995 (R)** Scientists experimenting with DNA find themselves creating an organism capable of instant regeneration that also likes to nosh on living flesh. To make matters worse, the scientists are trapped in their lab complex, which happens to be located five miles below Los Alamos. **95m/C; VHS, DVD.** Maria Ford; Kevin Alber; Rodger Halston; Cassandra Leigh; Emile Levisetti; ***D:*** Dave Payne.

Alien 3000 **WOOF!** *Unseen Evil 2* **2004 (R)** This woofer is dull as well as stupid. A commando unit is sent into the forest to search for an invisible alien creature that is supposed to be guarding an unknown treasure in a cave no one can find. Ummm, maybe that's because it's really hard to tell what's going on and not worth the effort anyway. **81m/C; DVD.** Lorenzo Lamas; Priscilla Barnes; Corbin Timbrook; Scott Schwartz; ***D:*** Jeff Leroy; ***W:*** Garrett Clancy; ***C:*** Rachel Wyn Dunn; ***M:*** Collin Simon. **VIDEO**

Alien Trespass 🦴🦴 1/2 *It Came From Beyond Space* **2009 (PG)** In 1957, a spaceship crash-lands in the Mohave desert, witnessed only by a waitress and an astronomer. The occupants are a vicious omnivorous alien, Ghota, and its captor, Urp. In order to save mankind, Urp (McCormack) must take over the astronomer's body and capture the beast, with the waitress's help. Earnest tribute to 1950s drive-in movie monster flicks. **90m/C; Blu-Ray, On Demand.** Eric McCormack; Robert Patrick; Dan Lauria; Jenni Baird; Jody Thompson; Aaron Brooks; Sarah Smyth; Andrew Dunbar; ***D:*** R.W. Goodwin; ***W:*** Steve(n) Fisher; ***C:*** David Moxness; ***M:*** Louis Febre.

Alien 2 on Earth **WOOF!** *Alien 2: Sulla Terra* **1980** In this obscure, cheap Italian sci fi rip-off, telepathic speleologist Thelma Joyce discovers a space capsule that crashed to Earth has littered the coast with rocks that are actually alien life forms. After taking time out to go bowling (!), Thelma and her team get trapped in an underground cavern teaming with these alien/rock forms, which like to burrow inside humans. **84m/C; DVD.** *IT* Belinda Mayne; Michele (Michael) Soavi; Judy Perrin; Roberto Barrese; Benedetta Fantoli; ***D:*** Ciro Ippolito; ***W:*** Ciro Ippolito; ***C:*** Silvio Fraschetti; ***M:*** Guido de Angelis; Maurizio de Angelis.

Alien Uprising **WOOF!** *U.F.O.* **2012 (R)** Slow-moving, low-budget Brit sci fi. Friends have a drunken night out and wake the next day to discover the city has no power and no communications. Yes, aliens have invaded. They decide to find recluse survivalist George to help them out. Van Damme apparently took this small role because daughter Bianca Bree is one of the leads. Nice daddy gesture but it didn't help--the pic is still dumb and dreadful. **101m/C; DVD.** *UK* Sean Brosnan; Bianca Bree; Jazz Lintott; Simon Phillips; Maya Grant; Jean-Claude Van Damme; Sean Pertwee; ***D:*** Dominic Burns; ***W:*** Dominic Burns; ***C:*** Luke Bryant; ***M:*** Si Begg.

Alien vs. Predator 🦴 *AvP* **2004 (PG-13)** How to classify "AvP?" Is it an "Alien" or "Predator" movie? It doesn't really matter since it's the worst offering that either franchise has produced to date. Predictable, effects-laden prequel to the four-part "Alien" saga and a sequel to the two "Predator" films has a bunch of humans finding an arctic training base for adolescent Predators that uses Aliens as their prey. Of course, the silly humans get caught between them and bad things happen. Monster fest fails to enhance either franchise. **110m/C; VHS, DVD, Blu-Ray, UMD.** Sanaa Lathan; Raoul Bova; Lance Henriksen; Ewen Bremner; Colin Salmon; Tommy Flanagan; Joseph Rye; Agathe de la Boulaye; Carsten Norgaard; Sam Troughton; Ian Whyte; ***D:*** Paul W.S. Anderson; ***W:*** Paul W.S. Anderson; Dan O'Bannon; ***C:*** David C(lark) Johnson; ***M:*** Harald Kloser.

Alien Visitor 🦴🦴 *Epsilon* **1995 (PG-13)** Beautiful alien woman lands on Earth in the Australian outback where she meets a guy and is disappointed in her destination since Earth is considered so backwards. But he manages to show her some things that make Earth life worth living. **92m/C; VHS, DVD.** *AU* Syd Brisbane; Alethea McGrath; Chloe Ferguson; Phoebe Ferguson; Ulli Birve; ***D:*** Rolf de Heer; ***W:*** Rolf de Heer; ***C:*** Tony Clark; ***M:*** Graham Tardif.

Alienator 🦴 **1989 (R)** In the improbable future, an unstoppable android killer is sent after an intergalactic villain. An intentional "Terminator" rip-off. **93m/C; VHS, DVD, Blu-Ray.** Jan-Michael Vincent; John Phillip Law; Ross Hagen; Dyana Ortelli; Dawn Wildsmith; P.J. Soles; Teagan Clive; Robert Clarke; Leo Gordon; Robert Quarry; Fox Harris; Hoke Howell; Jay Richardson; ***D:*** Fred Olen Ray.

Aliens 🦴🦴🦴 1/2 *Alien 2* **1986 (R)** The bitch is back, some 50 years later. Popular sequel to "Alien" amounts to non-stop, ravaging combat in space. Contact with a colony on another planet has mysteriously stopped. Fresh from deep space sleep, Ripley and a slew of pulsar-equipped Marines return to confront the mother alien at her nest, which is also inhabited by a whole bunch of the nasty critters spewing for a fight. Something's gotta give, and the Oscar-winning special effects are especially inventive (and messy) in the alien demise department. Dimension (acting biz talk) is given to our hero Ripley, as she discovers maternal instincts lurking within her space suit while looking after a young girl, the lone survivor of the colony. Tension-filled gore blaster. Followed by "Aliens 3." **138m/C; VHS, DVD, Blu-Ray.** Sigourney Weaver; Michael Biehn; Lance Henriksen; Bill Paxton; Paul Reiser; Carrie Henn; Jenette Goldstein; William Hope; Al Matthews; Mark Rolston; Ricco Ross; Colette Hiller; ***D:*** James Cameron; ***W:*** James Cameron; Walter Hill; ***C:*** Adrian Biddle; ***M:*** James Horner. Oscars '86: Sound FX Editing, Visual FX.

Aliens from Spaceship Earth 🦴½ **1977** Are strange, celestial forces invading our universe? If they are, is man prepared to defend his planet against threatening aliens of unknown strength? Lame docudrama featuring the Hurdy Gurdy man himself, Donovan. **107m/C; VHS, DVD.** Donovan; Lynda Day George; ***D:*** Don Como.

Aliens in the Attic 🦴½ *They Came From Upstairs* **2009 (PG)** Youngsters will probably be at least mildly entertained by this live-action/(mediocre) CGI concoction. The extended Pearson family is staying at their vacation home in Michigan although the teens are less than thrilled about being there. Then brainiac Tom (Jenkins) discovers four pint-sized aliens have taken over the attic. The nasty aliens have a device (resembling a videogame joystick) that can control the minds and actions of the adults so it's up to the kids to improvise and save the planet. Silly and generally harmless, although Roberts as a martial arts-kicking granny is somewhat unnerving. **86m/C; Blu-Ray.** Carter Jenkins; Ashley Tisdale; Austin Butler; Ashley Boettcher; Doris Roberts; Robert Hoffman, III; Kevin Nealon; Andy Richter; Tim Meadows; Henri Young; Regan Young; Malese Jow; Maggie VandenBerghe; Megan Parker; ***V:*** Thomas Haden Church; Josh Peck; Ashley Peldon; Kari Wahlgren; J.K. Simmons; ***D:*** John Schultz; ***W:*** Mark Burton; Adam F. Goldberg; ***C:*** Don Burgess; ***M:*** John Debney.

Aliens vs. Predator: Requiem 🦴½ **2007 (R)** In this sequel to the 2004 flick, the extraterrestrial beasties are cool and the humans are interchangeable incubators and fodder. A mutant alien-predator crash-lands near a small Colorado town and begins using convenient humans for procreation vessels and a super-Predator shows up to dispatch the new critters. The locals are collateral damage. Everything moves along at a snappy pace and there's some action pieces that are watchable, which means if you're a fan you probably won't be disappointed. **86m/C; Blu-Ray.** Reiko Aylesworth; Johnny Lewis; Ariel Gade; Steven Pasquale; Sam Trammell; John Ortiz; Robert Joy; ***D:*** Colin Strause; Greg Strause; ***W:*** Shane Salerno; ***C:*** Daniel Pearl; ***M:*** Brian Tyler.

Alimony Madness 🦴½ **1933** Architect John Thurman is desperate to divorce his greedy wife Eloise, so he agrees to her excessive alimony demands. When the depression causes his business to collapse, he gets into legal trouble for non-payment. His frantic second wife Joan finally confronts Eloise--and winds up on trial for her murder. **66m/B; DVD.** Helen Chandler; Leon Ames; Charlotte Merriam; Edward Earle; ***D:*** B. Reeves Eason; ***W:*** John Thomas "Jack" Neville; ***C:*** Ernest Miller.

Alita: Battle Angel 🦴🦴½ **2019 (PG-13)** In a futuristic world, Alita (Salazar) is a teen cyborg found in a scrap heap by Dr. Ido (Waltz) and brought back to life. Made of superior technology and with a powerful heart, she is centuries old and the last of her kind. As Alita makes discoveries about herself and her abilities in the downtrodden Iron City, she manages a crush on human boy Hugo (Johnson) and becomes a warrior on behalf of humanity in the face of threats both human and cyborg. At times cumbersome, this adaptation of a popular manga is filled with exciting action and interesting characters. **125m/C; DVD, Blu-Ray.** Rosa Salazar; Christoph Waltz; Jennifer Connelly; Mahershala Ali; Ed Skrein; ***D:*** Robert Rodriguez; ***W:*** James Cameron; Laeta Kalogridis; ***C:*** Bill Pope; ***M:*** Junkie XL.

Alive 🦴🦴½ **1993 (R)** Recounts the true-life survival story of a group of Uruguayan rugby players in 1972. After their plane crashes in the remote, snowy Andes (in a spectacular sequence) they're forced to turn to cannibalism during a 10-week struggle to stay alive. Marshall doesn't focus on the gruesome idea, choosing instead to focus on all aspects of their desperate quest for survival. The special effects are stunning, but other parts of the film are never fully realized, including the final scene. Based on the nonfiction book by Piers Paul Read. **127m/C; VHS, DVD.** Ethan Hawke; Vincent Spano; Josh Hamilton; Bruce Ramsay; John Haymes Newton; David Kriegel; Kevin Breznahan; Sam Behrens; Illeana Douglas; Jack Noseworthy; Christian Meoli; Jake Carpenter; ***Nar:*** John Malkovich; ***D:*** Frank Marshall; ***W:*** John Patrick Shanley; ***C:*** Peter James; ***M:*** James Newton Howard.

Alive 🦴½ **2002** Tenshu Yashiro (Sakaki) has been sent to the chair for murdering the gang who raped and killed his girlfriend. Surviving his initial shock in the electric chair, he is given the choice of being jolted again or sharing a cell with another inmate who has also survived the chair. He'll be given anything he wants (within reason), as long as he stays in the cell. At first this doesn't seem like too bad a deal until he learns his cellmate is a violent serial rapist. **119m/C; DVD.** *JP* Shun Sugata; Hideo Sakaki; Erika Oda; Ryo; Koyuki; ***D:*** Ryuhei Kitamura; ***W:*** Ryuhei Kitamura; Yudai Yamaguchi; Isao Kiriyama; Daisuke Yano; ***C:*** Takumi Furuya; ***M:*** Nobuhiko Morino.

Alive and Kicking 🦴🦴½ *Indian Summer* **1996 (R)** Tonio (Flemyng) is a handsome, vain ballet dancer with AIDS, who hides his emotions beneath a witty facade and his work. At a club he meets the older, equally driven Jack (Sher), an AIDS counselor, who pursues him. Though they become lovers, Tonio's obsession with his latest (and last) dance role causes a rift between them. Subplot between Tonio and lesbian dancer Millie (Parish) is self-conscious and Tonio's theatrics can become annoying but both Flemyng and Sher do their best in somewhat one-note roles. **100m/C; VHS, DVD.** *GB* Jason Flemyng; Anthony Sher; Dorothy Tutin; Anthony (Corlan) Higgins; Diane Parish; Bill Nighy; ***D:*** Nancy Meckler; ***W:*** Martin Sherman; ***C:*** Chris Seager; ***M:*** Peter Salem.

Alive Inside 🦴🦴🦴 **2014** This moving documentary explores the power of music and how it can be used to address memory loss issues. Especially focusing on the work of Dan Cohen, a social worker and the founder of the nonprofit Music & Memory, the very act of listening to personalized music is shown to have a profound impact on combating memory loss and improving the sense of self of those suffering from such conditions and diseases as Alzheimer's and dementia. The documentary features interviews with neurologists, related scientists and experts, musicians, and family members who have seen how music has positively affected their loved ones. **78m/C; DVD, Blu-Ray, Streaming, Download.** ***D:*** Michael Rossato-Bennett; ***W:*** Michael Rossato-Bennett; ***C:*** Shachar Langlev; ***M:*** Itaal Shur.

Alive or Dead 🦴 **2008 (R)** After wrecking her car in a sordid and unique manner, a woman comes across the bloody aftermath of a crime scene on a deserted bus before being kidnapped by a mutant freak. **83m/C; DVD, Streaming.** Ann Henson; Angelica May; ***D:*** Stephen Goetsch; ***W:*** Stephen Goetsch; ***C:*** Stephen Goetsch; ***M:*** William Anderson. **VIDEO**

All About Eve 🦴🦴🦴🦴 **1950** One of the wittiest (and most cynical) flicks of all time follows aspiring young actress Eve Harrington (Baxter) as she ingratiates herself with a prominent group of theatre people so she can become a Broadway star without the usual years of work. The not-so-innocent babe becomes secretary to aging star Margo Channing (Davis) and ruthlessly uses everyone in her climb to the top, much to Davis' initial disbelief and eventual displeasure. Satirical, darkly funny view of the theatre world features exceptional work by Davis, Sanders, and Ritter. Based on "The Wisdom of Eve" by Mary Orr. Later staged as the musical "Applause." **138m/B; VHS, DVD, Blu-Ray.** Bette Davis; Anne Baxter; George Sanders; Celeste Holm; Gary Merrill; Thelma Ritter; Marilyn Monroe; Hugh Marlowe; Gregory Ratoff; Eddie Fisher; ***D:*** Joseph L. Mankiewicz; ***W:*** Joseph L. Mankiewicz; ***C:*** Milton Krasner; ***M:*** Alfred Newman. Oscars '50: Costume Des. (B&W), Director (Mankiewicz), Film, Screenplay, Sound, Support. Actor (Sanders); AFI '98: Top 100; British Acad. '50: Film; Cannes '51: Actress (Davis), Grand Jury Prize; Directors Guild '50: Director (Mankiewicz); Golden Globes '51: Screenplay; Natl. Film Reg. '90; N.Y. Film Critics '50: Actress (Davis), Director (Mankiewicz), Film.

All About Lily Chou-Chou 🦴🦴🦴 *Riri Shushu no subete* **2001** Yuichi's (Hayato Ichihara) mother has remarried, and he doesn't exactly like it. At school he is bullied horrifically, and he has to resort to crime to pay off the demands of his assailants, one of whom pimps out the other school boys to older men. His only respite is the website he runs about his favorite singer Lily Chou-Chou. Pic boasts some of the most beautiful cinematography to come out of Japan, but its subject matter is brutal and unforgiving, and the nonlinear story will cause some confusion. **146m/C; DVD, Blu-Ray.** *JP* Hayato Ichihara; Yu Aoi; Shugo Oshinari; Ayumi Ito; Takao Osawa; Miwako Ichikawa; Izumi Inamori; Kazusa Matsuda; Ryo Katsuji; ***D:*** Shunji Iwai; ***W:*** Shunji Iwai; ***C:*** Noboru Shinoda; ***M:*** Takeshi Kobayashi.

All About My Mother 🦴🦴🦴 *Todo Sobre Mi Madre* **1999 (R)** Manuela (Roth) is a single mom, emotionally dependent on her 17-year-old son, Esteban (Azorin). After seeing him killed in a car accident, the grief-stricken mom seeks to find Esteban's father—now a transvestite named Lola (Canto)?and meets an old friend, tranvestite prostitute Agrado (San Juan), who offers comfort. Adding to the female roundelay are Huma Rojo (Paredes), Esteban's favorite actress, and Sister Rosa (Cruz), a pregnant nun who runs a shelter. As Manuela encounters each of them, they help give her a renewed sense of hope and the strength to carry on. Spanish with subtitles. **102m/C; VHS, DVD, Blu-Ray.** *SP* Cecilia (Celia) Roth; Penelope Cruz; Marisa Paredes; Eloy Azorin; Toni Canto; Antonia San Juan; Candela Pena; ***D:*** Pedro Almodóvar; ***W:*** Pedro Almodóvar; ***C:*** Affonso Beato; ***M:*** Alberto Iglesias. Oscars '99: Foreign Film; British Acad. '99: Director (Almodóvar), Foreign Film; Cannes '99: Director (Almodóvar); Cesar '00: Foreign Film; Golden Globes '00: Foreign Film; L.A. Film Critics '99: Foreign Film; N.Y. Film Critics '99: Foreign Film; Broadcast Film Critics '99: Foreign Film.

All About Nina 🦴🦴½ **2018 (R)** A somewhat successful stand-up comedian Nina (Winstead) leads a trainwreck of a life. The New York City-based cynical comic drinks too much, has a violent married lover, and experiences self-destructive sexual encounters. Her life and career unexpectedly change when she auditions for a sketch comedy TV show in Los Angeles. While competing against other female comedians for a slot on the program, she finds an unlikely yet meaningful romantic connection in Rafe (Common). Though the film is cliched at times, it deftly explores one woman's righteous anger and the difficult world of women in comedy, and allows Winstead to give a deep, uncompromising performance. **97m/C; DVD.** Mary Elizabeth Winstead; Common; Chace Crawford; Camryn Manheim; Jay Mohr; ***D:*** Eva Vives; ***W:*** Eva Vives; ***C:*** Thomas Scott Stanton; ***M:*** John Dragonetti.

All About Steve 🦴 **2009 (PG-13)** Mary Magdalene Horowitz is a boring, clingy, delusional, cruciverbalist (crossword-puzzle designer) who after one blind date with cable news cameraman Steve (Cooper) misinterprets an innocent comment that leads her to relentlessly follow him across the country, egged on by a self-serving reporter, Hartman Hughes (Church). Amid the trek she befriends a variety of socially inept characters like herself that bring nothing but more uncomfortable irritation. Feature debut from director Traill falls seriously short of anything remotely funny, even with his notable cast, while writer Barker vies for the "most annoying character ever created" award. Even Bullock's charm and Cooper's hunky-ness can't spare this from being, in a five-letter word--"awful." **98m/C; Blu-Ray, On Demand.** Sandra Bullock; Bradley Cooper; Thomas Haden Church; Ken Jeong; DJ Qualls; Katy Mixon; ***D:*** Phil Traill; ***W:*** Kim Barker; ***C:*** Tim Suhrstedt; ***M:*** Christophe Beck. Golden Raspberries '09: Worst Actress (Bullock).

All About the Benjamins 🦴🦴 **2002 (R)** Cube and Epps re-team (2000's "Next Friday") as bounty hunter Bucum (Ice Cube) and two-bit con Reggie (Epps) who meet mobsters and mayhem in Miami in this hip-hop buddy flick. Bucum, who dreams of opening his own private-eye agency, is sent to track down Reggie, who seeks a lost lottery tickets which gets the mismatched duo mixed up in a diamond heist. As usual, Cube, straight man to Epps's clown, have the usual chemistry and deliver some amusing moments in this light caper comedy, but the director's penchant for gory violence interrupts the otherwise slapstick mood. The two leads would shine if not for being stuck in this nod to "Miami Vice" and Elmore Leonard without the character development and plot. Cube co-wrote with Levy. **98m/C; VHS, DVD.** Ice Cube; Mike Epps; Tommy Flanagan; Eva Mendes; Carmen Chaplin; Roger Guenveur Smith; Anthony Michael Hall; Valarie Rae Miller; Bow Wow; ***D:*** Kevin Bray; ***W:*** Ice Cube; Ronald Lang; ***C:*** Glen MacPherson; ***M:*** John Murphy.

All About You 🦴½ **2001 (PG)** Tired tale takes Nicole from lost love Robbie in L.A. to blossoming romance with Brian in San Fran. Naturally the new guy is the old guy's alienated brother. **100m/C; VHS, DVD.** Terron Brooks; Debbie Allen; LisaRaye; Renee Goldsberry; Lou Myers; Vanessa Bell Calloway; Bobby Hosea; Chris Spencer; Tico Wells; Adam Lazarre-White; Emily Liu; ***D:*** Christine Swanson; ***W:*** Christine Swanson; ***C:*** Wolf Baschung; David Scardina; ***M:*** John Bickerton. **VIDEO**

The All-American Boy 🦴 **1973** Voight plays one of the most unpleasant characters seen on screen in this sports drama that was shot in 1969. Manipulative, self-centered, petulant amateur boxer Vic Bealer has dreams of going to the Olympics but he doesn't have the talent or the heart. Instead he's just a user, especially with the women in his life. **118m/C; DVD.** Jon Voight; Anne Archer; Carol Androsky; Gene Borkan; Jeanne Cooper; Rosalind Cash; Ron Burns; ***D:*** Charles Eastman; ***W:*** Charles Eastman; ***C:*** Philip H. Lathrop.

All-American Murder 🦴🦴 **1991 (R)** A rebellious young man is enrolled in a typical, all-American college for one last shot at mainstream life. Things start out okay, as he meets an attractive young coed. Hours later, he finds himself accused of her grisly murder. The youth is then given 24 hours to prove his innocence by a canny homicide detective. Average performances highlight this film, which isn't able to rise above the mediocre. **94m/C; VHS, DVD.** Christopher Walken; Charlie Schlatter; Josie Bissett; Joanna Cassidy; Richard Kind; Woody Watson; J.C. Quinn; Amy Davis; ***D:*** Anson Williams; ***W:*** Barry Sandler.

All Ashore 🦴½ **1953** Generally mediocre Columbia Pictures musical comedy about three sailors on shore leave. They head to Catalina Island for some girl chasing fun but Rooney's gullible sailor is constantly being taken advantage of by his two supposed pals (Haynes, McDonald) and that's not a lot of laughs. **80m/C; DVD.** Mickey Rooney; Dick Haymes; Ray McDonald; Barbara Bates; Jody Lawrance; Peggy Ryan; ***D:*** Richard Quine; ***W:*** Richard Quine; Blake Edwards; ***C:*** Charles Lawton, Jr.

All at Sea 🦴½ *Barnacle Bill* **1957** The last comedy from Ealing Studios is fitfully amusing, buoyed by Guinness' performance. Capt. Ambrose's constant seasickness keeps him on shore, where he buys a run-down amusement pier in a resort town and turns it into a hotel and arcade catering to sailors. He makes it into a success but the devious Mayor wants the property to further his own plans and Ambrose fights back by declaring his pier a cruise ship and not subjected to land laws! **82m/B; DVD, Blu-Ray.** *UK* Alec Guinness; Maurice Denham; Irene Browne; George Rose; Victor Maddern; ***D:*** Charles Frend; ***W:*** T.E.B. Clarke; ***C:*** Douglas Slocombe; ***M:*** John Addison.

All Creatures Great and Small 🦴🦴🦴 **1974** Taken from James Herriot's bestselling novels, this is a delightful, quiet drama of a veterinarian's apprentice in rural England. Fine performance by Hopkins. Followed by "All Things Bright and Beautiful" and a popular British TV series. **92m/C; VHS, DVD.** *GB* Simon Ward; Anthony Hopkins; Lisa Harrow; Brian Stirner; Freddie Jones; T.P. McKenna; ***D:*** Claude Whatham; ***W:*** Hugh Whitemore; ***C:*** Peter Suschitzky; ***M:*** Wilfred Josephs.

All Dogs Go to Heaven 🦴🦴 **1989 (G)** Somewhat heavy-handed animated musical (Reynolds sings) about a gangster dog who is killed by his partner in business. On the way to Heaven, he discovers how to get back to Earth to seek his revenge. When he returns to Earth, he is taken in by a little girl and learns about something he missed in life the first time around: Love. Expertly animated, but the plot may not keep the grown-ups engrossed, and the kids may notice its lack of charm. **85m/C; VHS, DVD, Blu-Ray.** ***V:*** Burt Reynolds; Judith Barsi; Dom DeLuise; Vic Tayback; Charles Nelson Reilly; Melba Moore; Candy Devine; Loni Anderson; ***D:*** Don Bluth; ***W:*** Don Bluth; David N. Weiss; ***M:*** Ralph Burns.

All Dogs Go to Heaven 2 🦴🦴 **1/2 1995 (G)** Animated musical finds lovable scamp Charlie (Sheen) the dog discovering that the afterlife is not all it's cracked up to be and pining for dysfunction aplenty back on earth. He gets his chance when Gabriel's Horn is stolen and Charlie is assigned to retrieve it. Charlie teams up again with old buddy Itchy (Deluise) as the two come down from Dog Heaven to stop the villainous Carface (Borgnine) and demonic cat Red (Hearn). Along the way, Charlie falls in love with sexy Irish Setter Sasha (Easton), and finds a chance for redemption by helping a little boy in trouble. Animation not outstanding, but should keep the attention of small children. **82m/C; VHS, DVD, Blu-Ray.** ***V:*** Charlie Sheen; Sheena Easton; Ernest Borgnine; Dom DeLuise; George Hearn; Bebe Neuwirth; Hamilton Camp; Wallace Shawn; Bobby DiCicco; Adam Wylie; ***D:*** Paul Sabella; Larry Leker; ***W:*** Arne Olsen; Kelly Ward; Mark Young; ***M:*** Mark Watters; Barry Mann; Cynthia Weil.

All Eyez on Me 🦴 **1/2 2017 (R)** Factual yet superficial biopic of rapper/activist Tupac Shakur. Shipp's uncanny resemblance to the legendary performer is the best aspect of the film, which is otherwise dragged down by leaden dialogue and bullet points (no pun intended) of Shakur's story rather than any meaningful insight into it. **139m/C; DVD, Blu-Ray.** Demetrius Shipp, Jr.; Danai Gurira; Kat Graham; Hill Harper; Annie Ilonzeh; ***D:*** Benny Boom; ***W:*** Jeremy Haft; Eddie Gonzalez; Steven Bagatourian; ***C:*** Peter Menzies, Jr.; ***M:*** John Paesano.

All Fall Down 🦴🦴 **1/2 1962** A young man (de Wilde) idolizes his callous older brother (Beatty) until a tragedy forces him to grow up. Saint plays the older woman taken in by the brothers' family, who is seduced and abandoned. When she finds herself pregnant and alone, she commits suicide causing the younger brother, who loved her from afar, to vow to kill his older sibling. A well-acted melodrama. Also available colorized. **111m/B; VHS, DVD.** Eva Marie Saint; Brandon de Wilde; Warren Beatty; Karl Malden; Angela Lansbury; Constance Ford; Barbara Baxley; ***D:*** John Frankenheimer; ***W:*** William Inge; ***C:*** Lionel Lindon; ***M:*** Alex North.

All Good Things 🦴 **1/2 2010 (R)** Fictional account of the true crime story involving Robert A. Durst and the (unsolved) disappearance of his wife Kathie in 1982. David Marks (Gosling) doesn't want to follow his wealthy father Sanford (Langella) into the family's New York real estate business. He tries rebelling, including through his marriage to Katie (Dunst), but finally succumbs to parental pressure. As David gets increasingly angry, his marriage falls apart. Then Katie goes missing. Dunst is appealing but Gosling is stuck playing a repellent cipher. **101m/C; DVD.** Ryan Gosling; Kirsten Dunst; Frank Langella; Lily Rabe; Kristen Wiig; Diane Venora; Philip Baker Hall; Michael Esper; Nick Offerman; John Cullum; ***D:*** Andrew Jarecki; ***W:*** Marcus Hinchey; Marc Smerling; ***C:*** Michael Seresin; ***M:*** Rob Simonsen.

All Hallow's Eve 🦴🦴 **2013** The first entry in a horror series centered on a maniacal clown that terrorizes its human prey. Working as a babysitter for two children on Halloween, a bored young woman finds a VHS tape in one of her charge's trick or treat bag. She watches the video, which includes three tales of terror featuring a clown who kills. During the night, weird things begin to happen in the house. The babysitter soon finds that the clown is becoming part of her reality with mayhem on his mind. **83m/C; DVD, Blu-Ray, Streaming, Download.** Katie Maguire; Catherine Callahan; Marie Maser; Kayla Lian; Mike Giannelli; ***D:*** Damien Leone; ***W:*** Damien Leone; ***C:*** Christopher Cafaro; Christopher Eadicicco; George Steuber; Marvin Suarez; ***M:*** Noir Deco. **VIDEO**

All Hallow's Eve 2 🦴 **1/2 2015** The sequel to All Hallow's Eve, this horror flick centers on a pumpkin-faced killer who torments his young victim. On Halloween night, a young woman spending the evening alone finds a mysterious VHS tape outside her door. She watches the tape, which includes several horrific, realistic tales of horror. The woman soon discovers the pumpkin-faced killer featured therein is using the tape to come into her reality with the goal of spilling blood. **91m/C; DVD, Blu-Ray, Streaming, Download.** Andrea Monier; Damien Monier; Jonathan Nation; April Adamson; Drew Davis; ***D:*** Jesse Baget; Elias Benavidez; Andres Borghi; Jay Holben; Mike Kochansky; James Kondelik; Jon Kondelik; Bryan Norton; Antonio Padovan; Ryan M. Patch; Marc Roussel; ***W:*** Jesse Baget; Elias Benavidez; Andres Borghi; Jay Holben; Mike Kochansky; James Kondelik; Jon Kondelik; Bryan Norton; Antonio Padovan; Ryan M. Patch; Marc Roussel; ***C:*** Julian Batistuta; Graham Bremner; Michael Jari Davidson; Andrew Ellis; Aaron Moorhead; Christopher Probst; Kyle Stryker; Gordon Yu; ***M:*** Hamdiga Ajanovic; Pablo Borghi; Mark Byers; Sam Estes; Christopher Guglick; Michael John Mollo; Buck Sanders; Marco Werba. **VIDEO**

All Hands on Deck 🦴 **1/2 1961** Silly Naval comedy has young Lt. Victor Donald (Boone) assigned to keep crazy sailor Shrieking Eagle Garfield (Hackett)--and his pet turkey--out of trouble. Meanwhile, reporter Sally Hobson (Eden) wants a story, sneaks aboard, and falls for the crooning officer. **98m/C; DVD.** Pat Boone; Buddy Hackett; Dennis O'Keefe; Warren Berlinger; Gale Gordon; ***D:*** Norman Taurog; ***W:*** Jay Sommers; ***C:*** Barbara Eden; Leo Tover; ***M:*** Cyril Mockridge.

All Hat 🦴 **1/2 2007 (R)** And no particular brains or heart. Hot-head Ray Doakes (Kirby) just got out of prison. He returns to his Ontario hometown to find that lowdown land developer Sonny Stanton (Jenkins), who helped put Ray away, is still up to no good. When an expensive thoroughbred from Stanton's racing stables goes missing, the scumball uses it as an excuse to squeeze the local farmers into selling their property for his golf resort. Only Ray comes up with a plan to stop him. **91m/C; DVD.** *CA* Rachael Leigh Cook; Luke Kirby; Noam Jenkins; Keith Carradine; Ernie Hudson; David Alpay; Graham Greene; Gary Farmer; Lisa Ray; Stephen McHattie; Michelle Nolden; ***D:*** Leonard Farlinger; ***W:*** Brad Smith; ***C:*** Paul Sarossy; ***M:*** Bill Frisell. **VIDEO**

All Hell Broke Loose 🦴 **1/2 2009 (PG-13)** Worth a bone just to see Carradine in a western. Ian McHenry was a sharpshooter during the Civil War and becomes a hired gun after the fighting ends. Only he eventually decides to redeem himself by hunting the outlaws he once rode with. **90m/C; DVD.** David Carradine; Jim Hilton; Jerry Chesser; Alex Daniel; Michael Hilton; Scotty Sparks; ***D:*** Christopher Forbes; ***W:*** Jim Hilton; Christopher Forbes; ***C:*** Christopher Forbes; ***M:*** Christopher Forbes. **VIDEO**

All I Desire 🦴🦴 **1/2 1953** Estranged wife and mother (Stanwyck) returns to her hometown after fleeing years ago to pursue a stage career. She desires a new beginning with her family, but finds things have changed in her absence. The story examines the will of a strong woman and small town values. Director Sirk disagreed with the happy ending demanded by producers, but the drama is still noteworthy. **80m/B; VHS, DVD.** Barbara Stanwyck; Richard Carlson; Lyle Bettger; Maureen O'Sullivan; ***D:*** Douglas Sirk; ***W:*** James Gunn; Robert Blees; Carl Guthrie; Gina Kaus; ***M:*** Joseph Gershenson.

All I See Is You 🦴 **1/2 2017 (R)** A failed drama with what could have been an interesting premise in better hands. To outsiders, Gina (Lively) and James (Clarke) have an ideal marriage. The couple lives in Bangkok, Thailand, and though Gina is blind, James takes care of her and ensures she can interact with the world. After Gina undergoes surgery to restore her eyesight, the dynamic in the marriage shifts as her needs and desires change. The truths Gina finds through her regained sight are further compromised when her sight begins to fade again. Lacking exposition, character development, and balanced direction, the film is simply a visual curiosity. **110m/C; DVD, Blu-Ray.** Blake Lively; Jason Clarke; Ahna O'Reilly; Yvonne Strahovski; Wes Chatham; ***D:*** Marc Forster; ***W:*** Marc Forster; Sean Conway; ***C:*** Matthias Koenigwieser; ***M:*** Marc Streitenfeld.

All I Wanna Do 🦴🦴 **1/2** *The Hairy Bird; Strike!* **1998 (PG-13)** The students of an exclusive, and financially troubled, East Coast girls' school, circa 1963, are vigorously opposed to the merger of their school with a boys' academy. So they decide to stage a protest strike. Rather typical coming of age tale with a notable cast of up-and-comers. Film was briefly released in 1998 at 110 minutes under the title "Strike" and then re-edited and re-released under its current title in 2000. **94m/C; VHS, DVD.** Kirsten Dunst; Gaby Hoffman; Heather Matarazzo; Rachael Leigh Cook; Monica Keena; Merritt Wever; Lynn Redgrave; Vincent Kartheiser; Tom Guiry; Matthew Lawrence; Robert Bockstael; ***D:*** Sarah Kernochan; ***W:*** Sarah Kernochan; ***C:*** Anthony C. "Tony" Jannelli; ***M:*** Graeme Revell.

All I Want 🦴🦴 *Try Seventeen* **2002 (R)** Jones Dillon (Wood) is a 17-year-old wide-eyed Kansas university freshman who soon decides that dorm life is not for him. So he moves into the boarding house of Ma Mabley (Harry) and is soon pining after a couple of his neighbors—sweet would-be actress Lisa (Moore) and experienced photographer Jane (Potente). Coming of ager hasn't anything new to say but the three leads do well with their limited material. **96m/C; VHS, DVD.** Elijah Wood; Franka Potente; Mandy Moore; Deborah Harry; Aaron Pearl; Elizabeth Perkins; ***D:*** Jeffrey Porter; ***W:*** Charles Kephart; ***C:*** Blake T. Evans; ***M:*** Andrew Gross.

All I Want for Christmas 🦴🦴 **1991 (G)** Low-budget, sappy holiday tale of a young girl (Birch) who wants to reunite her divorced parents. Determined to fulfill her Christmas wish, Hallie seeks out the Santa Claus at Macy's department store to tell him the one thing she truly wants for Christmas. Birch is charming as are Bacall as her grandmother and Nielsen as Santa but the story is too squishy and bland to be believable. **92m/C; VHS, DVD.** Thora Birch; Leslie Nielsen; Lauren Bacall; Jamey Sheridan; Harley Jane Kozak; Ethan (Randall) Embry; Kevin Nealon; Andrea Martin; ***D:*** Ron Lieberman; ***W:*** Richard Kramer; Thom Eberhardt; Neal Israel; Gail Parent; ***C:*** Robbie Greenberg; ***M:*** Bruce Broughton.

All I Want for Christmas 🦴🦴 **1/2 2007** Wanting to help out his overworked, widowed mom Sarah (O'Grady), young Jesse (Pinchak) enters a national contest sponsored by a toy company with an essay about wanting a new husband to take care of his mom. When Jesse wins, it thrusts them into a national spotlight and Sarah just may wind up with the wrong guy. A Hallmark Channel original. **89m/C; DVD.** Gail O'Grady; Robert Mailhouse; Greg Germann; Amanda Foreman; Jimmy Pinchak; Bess Meyer; Robert Pine; ***D:*** Harvey Frost; ***W:*** Marc Rey; ***C:*** Dane Peterson; ***M:*** Stephen Graziano. **CABLE**

All In 2006 Alice "Ace" Anderson (Swain) has been raised by her poker-playing father (Madsen) in the world of backstreet gambling. With mounting debts from med school, Ace decides to recruit some fellow students to take on the best players and win at the World Series of Poker. Lame effort with some confusing and unnecessary subplots. **?m/CDVD.** Dominique Swain; Michael Madsen; James Russo; Louis Gossett, Jr.; Kristen Miller; Colleen Porch; Scott Whyte; Michelle Lombardo; Chris Backus; Johann Urb; Hayley DuMond; ***D:*** Nick Vallelonga; ***W:*** Loren Comitor; ***C:*** Jeff Baustert; ***M:*** Harry Manfredini.

All in a Night's Work 🦴🦴 **1/2 1961** The founder of a one-man publishing empire is found dead with a smile on his face. His nephew inherits the business and finds himself caught in a series of big and small business misunderstandings. He's also falling in love with the woman he suspects was responsible for his uncle's grin. Nicely paced sex and business comedy with warm performances. **94m/C; DVD.** Dean Martin; Shirley MacLaine; Cliff Robertson; Charlie Ruggles; ***D:*** Joseph Anthony; ***W:*** Sidney Sheldon; ***C:*** Joseph LaShelle; ***M:*** Andre Previn.

All is Lost 🦴🦴🦴 **2013 (PG-13)** Devastating in its brutal lack of Hollywoodization, writer/director Chandor's drama captures what it must really be like to be trapped alone with a seemingly inevitable death coming soon. A nameless man (played perfectly by Redford) is forced to deal with water, sun, and sharks when his boat is struck by a drifting cargo container in a sailing trip far from shore. With only about 45 seconds of dialogue, Chandor and Redford have crafted a film that desperately displays a portrait of human struggle against its most notable enemy, Mother Nature. Redford proves he still has the acting chops in a performance that feels completely real. **106m/C; DVD, Blu-Ray.** Robert Redford; ***D:*** J.C. Chandor; ***W:*** J.C. Chandor; ***C:*** Frank DeMarco; Peter Zuccarini; ***M:*** Alex Ebert. Golden Globes '14: Orig. Score.

All Is True 🦴🦴 **1/2 2018 (PG-13)** When London's Globe Theater burns to the ground in June 1613, playwright William Shakespeare (Branaugh) experiences a serious case of writer's block and decides to never write again. He returns to his home in Stratford-upon-Avon, and his wife Anne Hathaway (Dench) and two daughters, Susannah (Wilson) and Judith (Wilder). As William tries to work through his writing and personal issues, he is haunted by his dead son Hamnet and has a strained relationship with Judith, Hamnet's twin. An imagining of the last years of the life of Shakespeare, of which little is known, Branaugh has created a complex, entertaining story. **101m/C; DVD, Blu-Ray.** Kenneth Branagh; Dame Judi Dench; Kathryn Wilder; Lydia Wilson; Ian McKellen; ***D:*** Kenneth Branagh; ***W:*** Ben Elton; ***C:*** Zac Nicholson; ***M:*** Patrick Doyle.

All Mine to Give 🦴🦴 **1/2** *The Day They Gave the Babies Away* **1956** Sad saga of a Scottish family of eight who braved frontier hardships, epidemics, and death in the Wisconsin wilderness more than a century ago. Midway through, mom and dad die, leaving the oldest child struggling to keep the family together. A strange, though often effective, combination of pioneer adventures and tear-jerking moments that avoids becoming hopelessly soapy due to fine performances. Unless you're pretty weathered, you'll need some hankies. Based on the reminiscences of Dale and Katherine Eunson as detailed in a "Cosmopolitan" magazine article. **102m/C; VHS, DVD.** Glynis Johns; Cameron Mitchell; Rex Thompson; Patty McCormack; Ernest Truex; Hope Emerson; Alan Hale, Jr.; Royal Dano; Reta Shaw; Rita Johnson; Ellen Corby; Jon(athan) Provost; ***D:*** Allen Reisner; ***M:*** Max Steiner.

All My Good Countrymen 🦴🦴 **1/2** *All Good Citizens* **1968** A lyrical, funny film about the eccentric denizens of a small Moravian village soon after the socialization of Czechoslovakia in 1948. Completed during the Soviet invasion of 1968 and immediately banned. In Czech with English subtitles. **115m/C; VHS, DVD.** *CZ* Vladimir Mensik; Radoslav Brozobohaty; Pavel Pavlovsky; ***D:*** Vojtech Jasny. Cannes '69: Director (Jasny).

All My Loved Ones 🦴🦴 *Vsichni Moji Blizci* **2000** Moving fictionalized account by director Minac of his mother's recollections of being one of nearly 700 Czech Jewish children saved in the Kindertransport trains. Briton Nicholas Winton (Graves) is on holiday in Prague in 1938; recognizing the worsening situation for the Jews in Czechoslovakia, he discovers that both Sweden and Britain are willing to take in child refugees if he can transport them out of the country. One of these potential transportees is 10-year-old David (Holicek), a member of a weathy family who fail to recognize the seriousness of their situation. Czech with subtitles. **91m/C; VHS, DVD.** *CZ* Rupert Graves; Libuse Safrankova; Josef Abrham; Jiri Bartoska; Brano Holicek; Jiri Menzel; ***D:*** Matej Minac; ***W:*** Jiri Hubac; ***C:*** Dodo Simoncic; ***M:*** Janusz Stoklosa.

All Neat in Black Stockings 🦴 **1969** Dour Brit sex comedy that's equally insulting to men and women, even allowing for its late swinging 60s time period. Window washer Ginger and his pal Dwyer are incessant in their pursuit of pretty birds. Ginger meets Jill, admires her black fishnet stockings, and thinks maybe she's the one to settle down with, but Dwyer gets to her first. Jill tells Ginger she's pregnant and they get married, but it's not happily-ever-after. **98m/C; DVD.** *UK* Victor Henry; Jack Shepherd; Susan George; Anna Cropper; Harry Towb; ***D:*** Christopher Morahan; ***W:*** Jane Gaskell; ***C:*** Larry Pizer; ***M:*** Robert Cornford.

All New Adventures of Laurel and Hardy: For Love or Mummy ✓✓ 1/2 **1998 (PG)** Stan Laurel (Pinchot) and Oliver Hardy (Sartain) are the equally bumbling nephews of the original comedic duo. The would-be movers are hired to transport an Egyptian mummy to an American museum, where archeologist Leslie (Danford) is the unwitting object of an ancient curse that fortells her marrying the reanimated corpse. **84m/C; VHS, DVD.** Bronson Pinchot; Gailard Sartain; F. Murray Abraham; Susan Danford; ***D:*** John R. Cherry, III; Larry Harmon.

All Night Long ✓✓ **1962** Brit jazz version of Shakespeare's "Othello." Black pianist/band leader Aurelius Rex (Harris) is married to white, now-retired singer Delia (Stevens). They are celebrating their anniversary in a London club where ambitious drummer Johnny (McGoohan) is determined to cause trouble. If he can break them up and get Delia back singing, he can secure a contract for his own group and so the lies begin. **91m/B; DVD.** Patrick McGoohan; Paul Harris; Marti Stevens; Keith Michell; Richard Attenborough; Betsy Blair; Bernard Braden; ***D:*** Basil Dearden; ***W:*** Paul Jarrico; Nel King; ***C:*** Edward (Ted) Scaife; ***M:*** Philip Green.

All Night Long ✓✓✓ **1981 (R)** Offbeat middle-age crisis comedy about a burned-out and recently demoted drugstore executive in L.A. who leaves his wife, takes up with his fourth cousin by marriage, and begins a humorous rebellion, becoming an extremely freelance inventor while joining the drifters, weirdos and thieves of the night. An obscure, sometimes uneven little gem with Hackman in top form and an appealing supporting performance by Streisand. Highlighted by delightful malapropisms and satiric inversion of the usual cliches. **100m/C; VHS, DVD, Blu-Ray.** Gene Hackman; Barbra Streisand; Diane Ladd; Dennis Quaid; Kevin Dobson; William Daniels; ***D:*** Jean-Claude Tramont; ***W:*** W.D. Richter; ***M:*** Ira Newborn.

All Nighter ✓✓ **2017 (R)** A buddy comedy centered on an unexpected duo forced to work together to find a missing woman. About three months after Ginnie (Tipton) breaks up with Martin (Hirsch) and moves out of their shared home, her no-nonsense father Mr. Gallo (Simmons) shows up worried about his daughter. Mr. Gallo has not been able to reach Ginnie for several days. Martin reluctantly agrees to help Mr. Gallo retrace Ginnie's steps over the past three months. As they meet randomly quirky characters, the pair slowly bond and Mr. Gallo reveals his own issues. Both the script and direction are uninspired, wasting Simmons' solid performance. **86m/C; DVD.** Analeigh Tipton; Emile Hirsch; J.K. Simmons; Meta Golding; Jon Daly; ***D:*** Gavin Wiesen; ***W:*** Seth W. Owen; ***C:*** Seamus Tierney; ***M:*** Alec Puro.

All of Me ✓✓ 1/2 **1984 (PG)** A wealthy woman (Tomlin) dies and her guru accidentally transfers her soul to the right side of her lawyer's body, a modern version of existential hell. Lawyer Martin indulges in some funny slapstick as he discovers that his late client is waging an internal war for control of his body. Flat and cliched at times, but redeemed by the inspired clowning of Martin and witty Martin/Tomlin repartee. Based on the novel "Me Too" by Ed Davis. **93m/C; VHS, DVD.** Steve Martin; Lily Tomlin; Victoria Tennant; Madolyn Smith; Richard Libertini; Dana Elcar; Selma Diamond; Jason Bernard; Eric Christmas; Peggy (Margaret) Feury; ***D:*** Carl Reiner; ***W:*** Phil Alden Robinson; ***C:*** Richard H. Kline; ***M:*** Patrick Williams. N.Y. Film Critics '84: Actor (Martin); Natl. Soc. Film Critics '84: Actor (Martin).

All or Nothing ✓✓ **2002 (R)** A depressing tale about depressed and desperate people set in a grotty housing project in South London. Hangdog minicab driver Phil (Spall) can't even earn a decent wage to support his family, cashier common-law wife Penny (Manville), and their layabout son Rory (Corden) and misfit daughter Rachel (Garland). Their neighbors aren't any better off—stuck with abusive boyfriends, unplanned pregnancy, alcoholism, and the general dreariness of their daily lives. Leigh is known for his slice-of-life dramas but this just stays one-dimensional. **128m/C; VHS, DVD.** *GB FR* Timothy Spall; Lesley Manville; Alison Garland; James Corden; Paul Jesson; Ruth Sheen; Marion Bailey; Sally Hawkins; Ben Crompton; Helen Coker; Daniel Mays; ***D:*** Mike Leigh; ***W:*** Mike Leigh; ***C:*** Dick Pope; ***M:*** Andrew Dickson.

All or Nothing at All ✓✓ **1993** Leo Hopkins (Laurie) is a charming con man with a successful career and a wife and kids. He's also a gambling addict who can't help living life on the edge, until he finds himself about to fall off. **150m/C; DVD.** *GB* Hugh Laurie; Bob Monkhouse; Pippa Guard; Caroline Quentin; Jessica Turner; Steve Steen; Phyllida Law; ***D:*** Andrew Grieve; ***W:*** Guy Andrews. **TV**

All Out Dysfunktion! ✓ 1/2 **2016** Purporting to be a satire of common personality types found in L.A., Dysfunktion is just a retread story of young people trying to thwart the olds and have a big house party. In this case a bevy of narcissistic renters versus their evil party pooper landlady. It doesn't even really deliver the raunchy shenanigans it promises, letting down it's one intended audience. **85m/C; DVD, Blu-Ray, Streaming.** Bridgette B.; Rene Rosado; Angelica Chitwood; Vincent De Paul; Gerry Bednob; ***D:*** Ryan LeMasters; ***W:*** David Bianchi; ***C:*** Jeff Siljenberg; ***M:*** Paul Cristo. **VIDEO**

All Over Me ✓✓✓ **1996 (R)** Teen angst/coming of age set in New York's Hell's Kitchen. Ungainly wanna-be guitarist, 15-year-old Claudia-AKA-Claude (Folland), is best friends with flirty blonde Ellen (Subkoff). But their relationship changes when Ellen begins dating the macho older Mark (Hauser) and is soon into sex and drugs, while Claude's sexual quandries lead her to a lesbian bar and an interest in singer Lucy (Hailey). Good performances but a moody and somewhat awkward first feature from Sichel, whose sister wrote the screenplay. **90m/C; VHS, DVD.** Alison Folland; Tara Subkoff; Cole Hauser; Wilson Cruz; Leisha Hailey; Pat Briggs; Ann Dowd; ***D:*** Alex Sichel; ***W:*** Sylvia Sichel; ***C:*** Joe DeSalvo; ***M:*** Miki Navazio.

All Over the Guy ✓✓ 1/2 **2001 (R)** Writer/director Roos served as executive producer on this film, which re-unites some of the personnel from his hit "The Opposite of Sex." Unfortunately, the quality of that film isn't reproduced here. Eli (writer Bucatinsky adapted from his play) and Tom (Ruccolo) are two gay men who are set up on a blind date by Brett (Goldberg) and Jackie (Alexander). They don't really get along, but they find themselves very attracted to one another. The film then explores the ups and downs of their courtship, as each tries to deal with the baggage from the past which keeps them from succeeding in the present. The problem is it's incredibly unoriginal. There doesn't seem to be any real chemistry between the couple, so whether or not they stay together may become a moot point to some viewers. Some of the performances are good (Goldberg has some good lines), but Ruccolo looks very uncomfortable at times. **95m/C; VHS, DVD.** Dan Bucatinsky; Richard Ruccolo; Adam Goldberg; Sasha Alexander; Doris Roberts; Andrea Martin; Tony Abatemarco; Joanna Kerns; Nicolas Surovy; Christina Ricci; Lisa Kudrow; ***D:*** Julie Davis; ***W:*** Dan Bucatinsky; ***C:*** Goran Paviceric; ***M:*** Peter Stuart; Andrew Williams.

All Passion Spent ✓✓ 1/2 **1986** BBC TV production based on Vita Sackville-West's 1931 novel. After the death of her politically prominent husband, 85-year-old Lady Slane no longer wishes to be part of London society. Ignoring her children's expectations, she moves to a cottage in the country and intends to do as she pleases and keep company with only those people she likes (which doesn't include most of her family). **158m/C; DVD.** *UK* Wendy Hiller; Harry Andrews; Maurice Denham; Jane Snowden; Eileen Way; David Waller; ***D:*** Martyn Friend; ***W:*** Peter Buckman; ***C:*** Trevor Wimlett; ***M:*** Nigel Hess. **TV**

All Quiet on the Western Front ✓✓✓✓ **1930** Extraordinary and realistic anti-war epic based on the novel by Erich Maria Remarque. Seven patriotic German youths go together from school to the battlefields of WWI. They experience the horrors of war first-hand, stuck in the trenches and facing gradual extermination. Centers on experiences of one of the young men, Paul Baumer, who changes from enthusiastic war endorser to battle-weary veteran in an emotionally exact performance by Ayres. Boasts a gigantic budget (for the time) of $1.25 million, and features more than 2000 extras swarming about battlefields set up on ranchland in California. Relentless anti-war message is emotionally draining and startling with both graphic shots and haunting visual poetry. Extremely controversial in the U.S. and Germany upon release, the original version was 140 minutes long (some versions are available with restored footage) and featured ZaSu Pitts as Ayres mother (later reshot with Mercer replacing her). Remarque, who had fought and been wounded on the Western Front, was eventually forced to leave Germany for the U.S. due to the film's ongoing controversy. **103m/B; VHS, DVD, Blu-Ray.** Lew Ayres; Louis Wolheim; John Wray; Slim Summerville; Russell Gleason; Raymond Griffith; Ben Alexander; Beryl Mercer; Arnold Lucy; William "Billy" Bakewell; Scott Kolk; Owen Davis, Jr.; Walter Rodgers; Richard Alexander; Harold Goodwin; G. Pat Collins; Edmund Breese; ***D:*** Lewis Milestone; ***W:*** Maxwell Anderson; George Abbott; Del Andrews; ***C:*** Arthur Edeson; Karl Freund; ***M:*** David Broekman. Oscars '30: Director (Milestone), Film; AFI '98: Top 100; Natl. Film Reg. '90.

All Quiet on the Western Front ✓✓ 1/2 **1979** A big-budget TV remake of the 1930 masterpiece starring John Boy. Sensitive German youth Thomas plunges excitedly into WWI and discovers its terror and degradation. Nowhere near the original's quality. **150m/C; VHS, DVD, Blu-Ray.** Richard Thomas; Ernest Borgnine; Donald Pleasence; Patricia Neal; ***D:*** Delbert Mann; ***W:*** Paul Monash; ***C:*** John Coquillon; ***M:*** Allyn Ferguson. **TV**

All Roads Lead Home ✓✓ 1/2 **2008 (PG)** Twelve-year-old Belle (Cardone) begins acting out after her mother's death in a car accident. She thinks her father Cody (London), who must euthanize unwanted pets as part of his animal control job, is in some way responsible. Cody decides to send Belle to her maternal grandfather Hock's (Coyote) farm but Hock is having trouble dealing with his own grief and it has turned him indifferent to the plight of the animals on the property. Of course as Belle helps care for the various critters, she and her family begin to reach out to one another. Boyle's last film role. **112m/C; DVD.** Vivien Cardone; Peter Coyote; Jason London; Evan Dexter Parke; Peter Boyle; Patton Oswalt; Vanessa Branch; Shannon Knopke; ***D:*** Dennis Fallon; ***W:*** Douglas Delaney; ***C:*** Fred Paddock; ***M:*** Korey Ireland.

All Roads Lead to Rome ✓ 1/2 **2015 (PG-13)** A light, Italy-set romantic comedy. Maggie (Parker) struggles with being a tightly wound, single mother to a troubled teen, Summer (Day). To reconnect with Summer, Maggie takes her to the village in Tuscany she used to visit regularly as a youth. There, Maggie runs into a former lover, Luca (Bova), and his mother, Carmen (Cardinale). One day, Summer and Carmen make an off-the-cuff choice to steal Luca's car and go to Rome. Though Carmen his hoping for love for her son, Summer merely wants to return to New York. Maggie and Luca make their own connection as they road trip across Italy in pursuit of their loved ones. **90m/C; DVD, Streaming, Download.** Sarah Jessica Parker; Rosie Day; Raoul Bova; Claudia Cardinale; Paz Vega; ***D:*** Ella Lemhagen; ***W:*** Josh Appignanesi; Cindy Myers; ***C:*** Gergely Poharnok; ***M:*** Alfonso Gonzalez Aguilar.

All Saints ✓✓ 1/2 **2017 (PG)** The true story of a salesman-turned-pastor (Corbett), who, with the help of a group of Burmese refugees, attempts to revive a small church in rural Tennessee by supporting it with funds from their fledgling farm. Authentic acting, a likeable cast, and hopefulness drawn more from a sense of community than faith elevate this film from heavy-handed preachiness to touching inspiration. **108m/C; DVD, Blu-Ray.** John Corbett; Cara Buono; Barry Corbin; Chonda Pierce; Nelson Lee; ***D:*** Steve Gomer; ***W:*** Steve Armour; ***C:*** Eduardo Enrique Mayen.

All Saint's Day ✓✓ **1998** Tired of his going-nowhere life, Marco (Blatt) recruits four of his screw-up friends to help him rob the Brooklyn fish market where he works. Of course, since they're all losers this doesn't work out as planned. **82m/C; VHS, DVD.** Mickey Blatt; Thomas J. La Sorsa; James Patrick McArdle; Mark Love; Christopher Lynn; Anthony Mangano; Ray Garvey; Howard Simon; ***D:*** Thomas J. La Sorsa; ***W:*** Thomas J. La Sorsa; Christopher Lynn; ***C:*** Daniel Marracino.

All Screwed Up ✓✓✓ *All in Place; Nothing in Order* **1974** A group of young immigrants come to Milan and try to adjust to city life; they soon find that everything is in its place, but nothing is in order. Wertmuller in a lighter vein than usual. Part of 'Kino Classics Lina Wertmuller' collection. **104m/C; VHS, DVD, Blu-Ray.** *IT* Luigi Diberti; Lina Polito; ***D:*** Lina Wertmuller; ***W:*** Lina Wertmuller.

All Souls Day ✓ 1/2 *Dia de los Muertos* **2005** Vargas Diaz's 1892 brutal rampage in a small Mexican town on the symbolic "Day of the Dead" causes his murderous soul to haunt the locals for years, leading them to perform certain acts to keep the zombies at bay. First up to be terrorized is a 1950's family with a sick boy and a hot teenaged girl who takes the standard "something-bad-is-about-to-happen" steamy bath. Then, in the present, Joss (Wester) and Alicia (Ramirez) seem doomed when they unknowingly interrupt the long-standing rite and must flee the same creepy hotel. Sci-Fi Channel original should have let the walking dead lie. **90m/C; DVD.** Travis Wester; Nichole Hiltz; Laz Alonso; Laura Elena Harring; Marisa Ramirez; David Keith; Jeffrey Combs; Ellie Cornell; Julia Vera; Daniel Burgio; Mircea Monroe; Danny Trejo; Noah Luke; ***D:*** Jeremy Kasten; ***W:*** Mark Altman; ***C:*** Christopher Duddy; ***M:*** Joseph Gutowski. **CABLE**

All Superheroes Must Die ✓ *Vs* **2011** Four superheroes are abducted by a man who steals their powers and makes them take part in horrific challenges to save a whole town of people he's kidnapped. **78m/C; DVD, Blu-Ray.** Jason Trost; Lucas Till; James Remar; Sophie Merkley; Lee Valmassy; ***D:*** Jason Trost; ***W:*** Jason Trost; ***C:*** Amanda Treyz; ***M:*** George Holdcroft. **VIDEO**

All That Heaven Allows ✓✓✓ **1955** Attractive, wealthy middleaged widow Cary Scott (Wyman) falls for her 15-years-younger gardener, Ron Kirby (Hudson), and becomes the target of small-minded gossips and her disapproving family. Ron's no gigolo or fortune-hunter but societal pressure still gets to Cary and she breaks things off. But loneliness makes her realize what she's missing and she decides to make things up with Ron and forget her critics. Hopeful Sirk romance that still takes some jabs at conformity. **89m/B; VHS, DVD, Blu-Ray.** Jane Wyman; Rock Hudson; Conrad Nagel; Agnes Moorehead; Virginia Grey; Gloria Talbott; William Reynolds; ***D:*** Douglas Sirk; ***W:*** Peggy Fenwick; ***C:*** Russell Metty; ***M:*** Frank Skinner; Joseph Gershenson. Natl. Film Reg. '95.

All That Jazz ✓✓✓ 1/2 **1979 (R)** Fosse's autobiographical portrait with Scheider fully occupying his best role as the obsessed, pill-popping, chain-smoking choreographer/director dancing simultaneously with love and death. But even while dying, he creates some great dancing. Vivid and imaginative with exact editing, and an eerie footnote to Fosse's similar death almost ten years later. Egocentric and self-indulgent for sure, but that's entertainment. **120m/C; VHS, DVD, Blu-Ray.** Roy Scheider; Jessica Lange; Ann Reinking; Leland Palmer; Cliff Gorman; Ben Vereen; Erzebet Foldi; John Lithgow; Max Wright; Deborah Geffner; Michael (Lawrence) Tolan; Keith Gordon; David Margulies; Nicole Fosse; Anthony Holland; ***D:*** Bob Fosse; ***W:*** Bob Fosse; Robert Alan Aurthur; ***C:*** Giuseppe Rotunno; ***M:*** Ralph Burns. Oscars '79: Art Dir./Set Dec., Costume Des., Film Editing, Orig. Song Score and/or Adapt.; Cannes '80: Film; Natl. Film Reg. '01.

All the Boys Love Mandy Lane ✓ 1/2 **2006 (R)** Throwback indie slasher flick shelved for seven years until the studios dusted it off for reasons unknown, and unimportant. Titular character Mandy Lane (Heard) walks in slow motion through her Texas high school hallways, oozing untouchable sexuality and mystery. During a weekend blowout at a remote cattle ranch, her dimwitted classmates are picked off one-by-one as she's left to take the killer on alone. A juicy twist ending can't undo its otherwise formulaic blah. Nothing worth the seven-year wait. **90m/C; DVD, Blu-Ray.** Amber Heard; Anson Mount; Aaron Himelstein; Luke Grimes; Whitney Able; Melissa Price; Edwin Hodge; Michael Welch; ***D:*** Jonathan Levine; ***W:*** Jacob Forman; ***C:*** Darren Genet; ***M:*** Mark Schulz.

All the Brothers Were Valiant 1/2 **1953** Brothers Taylor and Granger are New England whaling captains but Granger decides to treasure hunt instead. He finds a priceless cache of black pearls on an island but angers the locals who regard the gems as sacred. When Taylor rescues him, Granger promptly turns his brother's crew into mutineers in order to return to the island and retrieve his prize. Lots of brawling and there's an incidental love story with Blyth desired by both men (she's married Taylor and just happens to be aboard). Last role for Stone. Based on the novel by Ben Ames Williams. **101m/C; VHS, DVD.** Robert Taylor; Stewart Granger; Ann Blyth; Betta St. John; Keenan Wynn; James Whitmore; Kurt Kasznar; Lewis Stone; Robert Burton; Peter Whitney; John Lupton; Billie Dove; ***D:*** Richard Thorpe; ***W:*** Harry Brown; ***C:*** George J. Folsey; ***M:*** Miklos Rozsa.

All the Good Ones Are Married 1/2 **2007** Alex (Hannah) is going through an amicable divorce from Ben (McGowan) until his mistress (Douglas) shows up at her door. Having been dumped herself, she thinks the two women scorned should team up, but Alex is naturally wary. Lifetime drama. **89m/C; DVD.** Daryl Hannah; Deborah Odell; Matthew Knight; Nick Baillie; James McGowan; Joanna Douglas; Matthew Broderick; Brittany Snow; Maura Tierney; Peter Facinelli; ***D:*** Terry Ingram; ***C:*** Marcus Elliott. **CABLE**

All the Kind Strangers *Evil in the Swamp* **1974** Traveling photographer Keach picks up a young hitchhiker and takes him to the boy's home. He discovers six other children there who want him as a father, his alternative being death. He and "Mother" Eggar plot their escape from the dangerous orphans. Thriller short on suspense. **72m/C; VHS, DVD.** Stacy Keach; Robby Benson; John Savage; Samantha Eggar; ***D:*** Burt Kennedy. **TV**

All the King's Men **1949** Grim and graphic classic set in the Depression follows the rise of a Louisiana farm-boy from angry and honest political hopeful to powerful but corrupt governor. Loosely based on the life (and death) of Huey Long and told by a newsman who's followed his career (Ireland). Willy Stark (Crawford, in his breakthrough role) is the politician who, while appearing to improve the state, rules dictatorially, betraying friends and constituents and proving once again that power corrupts. In her first major role, McCambridge delivers a powerful performance as the cunning political aide. Potent morality play based on the Robert Penn Warren book. **109m/B; VHS, DVD, Blu-Ray.** Broderick Crawford; Mercedes McCambridge; John Ireland; Joanne Dru; John Derek; Anne Seymour; Shepperd Strudwick; ***D:*** Robert Rossen; ***W:*** Robert Rossen; ***C:*** Burnett Guffey; ***M:*** Louis Gruenberg. Oscars '49: Actor (Crawford), Film, Support. Actress (McCambridge); Golden Globes '50: Actor--Drama (Crawford), Director (Rossen), Film--Drama, Support. Actress (McCambridge); Natl. Film Reg. '01; N.Y. Film Critics '49: Actor (Crawford), Film.

All the King's Men 1/2 **1999** In 1915, Frank Beck (Jason), the manager of the royal estate of Sandringham, trains a company of servants to be volunteer soldiers. Unfortunately, the raw recruits are posted to the disaster of Gallipoli and a battle against the Turks. The true fate of the company was unknown for many years and their disappearance became the stuff of myth (recent discoveries proved much grimmer) but the storyline is muddled and it's not easy to distinguish one youthful character from another (although the veterans do a notable job). Based on the novel by Nigel McCrery. **110m/C; VHS, DVD.** *GB* David Jason; Maggie Smith; Stuart Bunce; William Ash; James Murray; Sonya Walger; Eamon Boland; David Troughton; Emma Cunniffe; Adam Kotz; Patrick Malahide; Ed Waters; Tom Burke; Ben Crompton; Jo Stone-Fewings; James Hillier; Ian McDiarmid; Phyllis Logan; ***D:*** Julian Jarrold; ***W:*** Alma Cullen; ***C:*** David Odd; ***M:*** Adrian Johnston. **TV**

All the King's Men 1/2 **2006 (PG-13)** Based on Robert Penn Warren's 1946 novel, this bungled remake of the 1949 film focuses on the rise and fall of a Huey P. Long-like politician, with Penn all bug-eyed sputterings as southern demagogue Willie Stark. Besides the out-of-place Penn, there's a bunch of miscast Brits, including narrator Law as boozy journalist Jack Burden, Winslet as Stark's unrequited love Anne, and Hopkins as a judge that Willie wants dirt on. Louisiana native Clarkson and former child actor Haley are about the only two actors who probably won't make you squirm. **128m/C; DVD, Blu-Ray.** Sean Penn; Jude Law; Kate Winslet; James Gandolfini; Mark Ruffalo; Patricia Clarkson; Kathy Baker; Jackie Earle Haley; Anthony Hopkins; Kevin Dunn; Frederic Forrest; Talia Balsam; Glenn Morshower; ***D:*** Steven Zaillian; ***W:*** Steven Zaillian; ***C:*** Pawel Edelman; ***M:*** James Horner.

All the Light in the Sky **2013** Ultra-low-budget filmmaker Swanberg includes even less dramatic thrust than normal in this practically short film about aging actress Marie (Adams, a character-driven performer doing very personal work here) who spends a few days with her visiting niece Faye (Takal) in her apartment. They don't do much. The movie doesn't say much. And yet Swanberg and his cast develop a nice, gentle charm with their dialogue, particularly in scenes that suggest the woman realizes she's entering the twilight period of her life. It's a small film that's slow but immensely likable. **79m/C; DVD.** Jane Adams; Sophia Takal; Kent Osborne; Larry Fessenden; ***D:*** Joe Swanberg; ***W:*** Jane Adams; Joe Swanberg; ***C:*** Joe Swanberg; ***M:*** Orange Mighty Trio.

All the Little Animals 1/2 **1998 (R)** Twenty-four-year old Bobby (Bale) is brain damaged from a childhood accident. After his mother's death, he's left in the less-than-tender care of his malevolent stepfather, De Winter (Benzali), who's only interested in Bobby's inheritance. So Bobby runs away and is taken in by hermit, Mr. Summers (Hurt), who is devoted to burying the remains of animals killed in road accidents. But Bobby's idyll cannot last when his stepfather finds him—and Mr. Summers is also not quite what he seems. Based on the novel by Walker Hamilton. **104m/C; VHS, DVD.** *GB* John Hurt; Christian Bale; Daniel Benzali; James Faulkner; Amy Robbins; ***D:*** Jeremy Thomas; ***W:*** Eski Thomas; ***C:*** Mike Molloy; ***M:*** Richard Hartley.

. . .All the Marbles *The California Dolls* **1981 (R)** A manager of two beautiful lady wrestlers has dreams of going to the top. Aldrich's last film, and an atypical one, with awkward pacing and a thin veil of sex exploitation. Falk provides needed grace and humor as the seedy manager, with Young contributing his usual competent bit as a hustling promoter dabbling in criminal activity. One of the few tag-team women wrestling pictures, it builds to a rousing finale match in the "Rocky" tradition, although the shift in tone and mounting cliches effectively body slam the intent. **113m/C; VHS, DVD.** Peter Falk; Burt Young; Richard Jaeckel; Vicki Frederick; Claudette Nevins; Lenny Montana; ***D:*** Robert Aldrich; ***C:*** Joseph Biroc.

All the Money in the World 1/2 **2017 (R)** A kidnap thriller based on the true story of John Paul Getty III (Charlie Plummer). In the early 1970s, the teenaged Getty was kidnapped and held for $17 million in ransom. The scheme targets his grandfather, John Paul Getty (Christopher Plummer), the richest man in the world. Instead of paying the ransom, he haggles with the kidnappers as his grandson suffers. Young Getty's middle-class mother, Gail Harris (Williams), cannot afford to pay herself but grows angry and frustrated as the elder Getty demonstrates a lack of empathy. Strong performances, especially by last-minute replacement Christopher Plummer, make up for subpar script. **132m/C; DVD, Blu-Ray.** Michelle Williams; Christopher Plummer; Mark Wahlberg; Romain Duris; Charlie Plummer; ***D:*** Ridley Scott; ***W:*** David Scarpa; ***C:*** Dariusz Wolski; ***M:*** Daniel Pemberton.

All the President's Men 1/2 **1976 (PG)** True story of the Watergate break-in that led to the political scandal of the decade, based on the best-selling book by Washington Post reporters Bob Woodward and Carl Bernstein. Intriguing, terse thriller is a nail-biter even though the ending is no secret. Expertly paced by Pakula with standout performances by Hoffman and Redford as the reporters who slowly uncover and connect the seemingly isolated facts that ultimately lead to criminal indictments of the Nixon Administration. Deep Throat Holbrook and Robards as executive editor Ben Bradlee lend authenticity to the endeavor, a realistic portrayal of the stop and go of journalistic investigations. **135m/C; VHS, DVD, Blu-Ray.** Robert Redford; Dustin Hoffman; Jason Robards, Jr.; Martin Balsam; Jane Alexander; Hal Holbrook; F. Murray Abraham; Stephen Collins; Lindsay Crouse; Meredith Baxter; Ned Beatty; Penny Fuller; Dominic Chianese; David Arkin; Polly Holliday; James Karen; ***D:*** Alan J. Pakula; ***W:*** William Goldman; ***C:*** Gordon Willis; ***M:*** David Shire. Oscars '76: Adapt. Screenplay, Art Dir./Set Dec., Sound, Support. Actor (Robards); Natl. Bd. of Review '76: Director (Pakula), Support. Actor (Robards); Natl. Film Reg. '10; N.Y. Film Critics '76: Director (Pakula), Film, Support. Actor (Robards); Natl. Soc. Film Critics '76: Film, Support. Actor (Robards); Writers Guild '76: Adapt. Screenplay.

All the Pretty Horses **2000 (PG-13)** John Grady Cole (Damon) is a dispossessed Texas cowboy in the late 1940s who, along with his buddy Lacey Rawlins (Thomas) and teen misfit Blevins (Black), crosses the border for, he hopes, a better life in Mexico. What he finds is an ill-fated romance with the beautiful daughter (Cruz) of a possessive rancher (Blades). It's pretty, all right. But thanks to Thornton's uneven pacing and inability to settle on a visual style, the story, and splendor, of the book is lost somewhere along the way. Of the young (and also pretty) cast, Damon and especially Black fare the best. Based on the first book of Cormac McCarthy's Border Trilogy. **117m/C; VHS, DVD, Blu-Ray.** Matt Damon; Penelope Cruz; Ruben Blades; Lucas Black; Henry Thomas; Robert Patrick; Julio Oscar Mechoso; Miriam Colon; Bruce Dern; Sam Shepard; ***D:*** Billy Bob Thornton; ***W:*** Ted Tally; ***C:*** Barry Markowitz; ***M:*** Marty Stuart. Natl. Bd. of Review '00: Screenplay.

All the Queen's Men **2002** After his mission to steal a German Enigma encoding machine is torpedoed by an arrogant British officer, American OSS agent O'Rourke (LeBlanc) is assigned to multinational commando team to try again. Only this time they'll be infiltrating a Nazi factory—as female workers. Cross-dressing comic Izzard, as team member Tony, is invaluable here, as he's the only one who looks comfortable in a dress or supplies any comic flair. Jumbled plot and bumbled comedic opportunities combine to thwart a good premise and excellent cast. **99m/C; VHS, DVD.** Matt LeBlanc; Eddie Izzard; James Cosmo; Udo Kier; Edward Fox; Nicolette Krebitz; David Birkin; Oliver Korittke; Karl Markovics; ***D:*** Stefan Ruzowitzky; ***W:*** David Schneider; ***C:*** Wedigo von Schultzendorff; ***M:*** Joern-ewe Fahrenkrog-Petersen.

All the Real Girls 1/2 **2003 (R)** Sophomore effort of writer-director Green is a sincere and poignant look at youthful love. Paul (Schneider), a twentysomething Romeo who's broken more than a few hearts in town, finds the real thing in Noel (played wonderfully by Deschanel), the 18-year-old sister of his best friend, fresh out of boarding school. Fully captures the real and often awkward moments of young love and the pain and confusion that can come with it. Schneider also helped conceive and write the story. **108m/C; VHS, DVD.** Paul Schneider; Zooey Deschanel; Patricia Clarkson; Maurice Compte; Benjamin Mouton; Shea Whigham; Danny McBride; ***D:*** David Gordon Green; ***W:*** Paul Schneider; David Gordon Green; ***C:*** Tim Orr; ***M:*** David Wingo; Michael Linnen.

All the Right Moves 1/2 **1983 (R)** Cruise is the high school football hero hoping for a scholarship so he can vacate pronto the dying Pennsylvania mill town where he grew up. At least he thinks that's what he wants to do. Further mixing up his own mixed feelings are his pushy, ambitious coach (Nelson, doing what he does best), his understanding dad (Cioffi) and supportive girlfriend (Thompson, in a notable early role). Strong performances push the relatively cliched melodrama into field goal range. Cinematographer Chapman's directorial debut. **90m/C; VHS, DVD.** Tom Cruise; Lea Thompson; Craig T. Nelson; Christopher Penn; Charles Cioffi; Paul Carafotes; Dick Miller; ***D:*** Michael Chapman; ***W:*** Michael Kane; ***C:*** Jan De Bont; ***M:*** David (Richard) Campbell.

All the Vermeers in New York 1/2 **1991** A stressed-out Wall Street broker flees to the soothing recesses of the Metropolitan Museum's Vermeer Room. There he meets a beautiful, manipulative French actress dreaming of success in Manhattan. Amidst the opulent art world of New York, the two pursue their relationship to an ultimately tragic end. Jost offers an inside look at the collision of commerce and art and the corrupt underside of New York in this elegant contemporary film. **87m/C; VHS, DVD.** Emmanuelle Chaulet; Stephen Lack; Grace Phillips; Katherine Bean; Laurel Lee Kiefer; Gracie Mansion; Gordon Joseph Weiss; Roger Ruffin; ***D:*** Jon Jost; ***W:*** Jon Jost.

All the Way, Boys 1/2 **1973 (PG)** Two inept adventurers crash-land a plane in the Andes in the hope of discovering slapstick, but find none. "Trinity" cast up to no good. **105m/C; VHS, DVD, Streaming.** *IT* Terence Hill; Bud Spencer; Cyril Cusack; Michel Antoine; ***D:*** Giuseppe Colizzi.

All the Wilderness **2014** First-time writer/director Michael Johnson's coming-of-age drama looks beautiful, is acted pitch-perfectly, but nonetheless, goes nowhere. After his father's death, wayward teen James (Smit-McPhee), living in a remote cabin with his mother (Madsen), yearns for some kind of social connection or purpose in his life. As much as Johnson tries to shelter his characters from falling into cliches, there's still too much wishy-washy existential fluff. It's borderline silly when James meets a girl (Fuhrman) in his shrink's waiting room. What should be short and sweet at only 80 minutes, feel long and sour by the end. **80m/C; DVD, Blu-Ray.**

All the Wrong Places 1/2 **2000** Twenty-somethings Marisa (Hillis) and Paul (Klavens), the children of successful parents, are struggling to find their own identities and careers. Marisa is trying to make it as a filmmaker, while spending much of her time on her therapist's couch, while Paul is working on his first novel. They've got a lot in common but most of it is little above slacker whining. **95m/C; DVD.** Ali Hillis; Alyce LaTourelle; Brian Patrick Sullivan; Jeremy Klavens; Judy Del Guidice; ***D:*** Martin Edwards; ***W:*** Martin Edwards; ***C:*** Bing Rao; ***M:*** Jody Elff.

All Things Fair 1/2 *Lust och Fagring Stor; Love Lessons; Laererinden* **1995** Coming of age story set in neutral Sweden in 1943. Fifteen-year-old Stig (Widerberg, the director's son) has just arrived in Malmo to begin classes at his all-male school—a situation filled with sexual curiosity and repression. Stig is attracted to his beautiful teacher Viola (Lagercrantz), whose marriage to alcoholic traveling salesman Frank (von Bromssen) is less than ideal, and the duo begin an affair. Frank not only seems not to care but befriends his wife's youthful lover, although the situation is ripe for tragedy. Excellent performances, sensual air, though somewhat lacking in logical narrative. Swedish with subtitles. **128m/C; VHS, DVD.** *DK SW* Johan Widerberg; Marika Lagercrantz; Tomas von Bromssen; Bjorn Kjellman; Charles A. Palmer; ***D:*** Bo Widerberg; ***W:*** Bo Widerberg; ***C:*** Morten Bruus.

All Things to All Men **2013** Brit crime drama with an ordinary story and a good cast. In London, crooked cop Parker, his partner Sands, and rookie detective Dixon nab a drug dealer who turns out to be the son of crime boss Joseph Corso. So they leverage the son's arrest to have Corso set up safecracker/jewel thief Riley, who's about to pull another job. Of course nothing goes according to plan, but that's because the plan isn't so clear. **84m/C; DVD.** *UK* Rufus Sewell;

Toby Stephens; Gabriel Byrne; Terence Maynard; Leo Gregory; Julian Sands; ***D:*** George Isaac; ***W:*** George Isaac; ***C:*** Howard Atherton; ***M:*** Thomas Wanker. **VIDEO**

All This and Heaven Too **1940** When a governess arrives at a Parisian aristocrat's home in the 1840s, she causes jealous tension between the husband and his wife. The wife is soon found murdered. Based on Rachel Field's best-seller. **141m/B; VHS, DVD.** Charles Boyer; Bette Davis; Barbara O'Neil; Virginia Weidler; Jeffrey Lynn; Helen Westley; Henry Daniell; Harry Davenport; June Lockhart; Montagu Love; Anne Howard; ***D:*** Anatole Litvak; ***M:*** Max Steiner.

All Through the House 1/2 *A Nightmare Christmas* **2015** A glorious homage to 80's style slasher films, All Through the House takes everything from it's premise to it's killer straight from old school horror films (which may or may not be a good thing depending on your feelings about 80's horror movies). Once again a murderous Santa is cutting his way though a quiet neighborhood on Christmas Eve, and the usual final girl has to figure out how to stop him. **88m/C; DVD, Blu-Ray, Streaming.** Ashley Marie Nunes; Jessica Cameron; Melynda Kiring; Lito Velasco; Jennifer Wenger; ***D:*** Todd Nunes; ***W:*** Todd Nunes; ***C:*** Ryan J. Anderson; ***M:*** Irving Victoria. **VIDEO**

All Through the Night **1942** A very funny spy spoof as well as a thrilling crime story with Bogart playing a gambler who takes on a Nazi spy ring. Features memorable double-talk and a great auction scene that inspired the one with Cary Grant in "North by Northwest." Suspense builds throughout the film as Lorre appears in a sinister role as Pepi and Veidt gives a fine performance as the spymaster. **107m/B; VHS, DVD.** Humphrey Bogart; Conrad Veidt; Karen Verne; Jane Darwell; Frank McHugh; Peter Lorre; Judith Anderson; William Demarest; Jackie Gleason; Phil Silvers; Barton MacLane; Martin Kosleck; Wallace Ford; ***D:*** Vincent Sherman; ***C:*** Sidney Hickox; ***M:*** Adolph Deutsch.

All Tied Up 1/2 **1992 (R)** Ladies man Brian (Galligan) thinks he's found true love with Linda (Hatcher) but that doesn't mean he's stopped seeing other women. And when Linda finds out, she breaks it off. So Brian goes over to her house to work things out and gets tied up—literally—by Linda and her girlfriends. Talk about teaching a guy a lesson. **90m/C; VHS, DVD.** Zach Galligan; Teri Hatcher; Tracy Griffith; Lara Harris; ***D:*** John Mark Robinson; ***W:*** Robert Madero; I. Markie Lane; ***M:*** Bernardo Bonezzi.

All We Had **2016** The directorial debut of actress Katie Holmes is an obvious adaptation of the Annie Weatherwax novel. Rita (Holmes) is the irresponsible, reckless single mom of 14-year-old Ruthie (Owen). The pair gets stuck in a small town on their way to build their dream life in Boston. Getting jobs in the local diner, Rita and Ruthie form a family with diner's owner (Kind) and transgender waitress (Lindley). As Rita deals with her addiction issues, Ruthie works to fit in at her new school while she waits for her mother to make another poor choice. Strong casting and performances abound in this predictably plotted film. **105m/C; DVD.** Katie Holmes; Stefania LaVie Owen; Luke Wilson; Eve Lindley; Richard Kind; ***D:*** Katie Holmes; ***W:*** Josh Boone; Jill Killington; ***C:*** Brett Pawlak; ***M:*** Michael Brook.

All You Need Is Cash *The Rutles* **1978** "The Rutles" star in this parody of The Beatles' legend, from the early days of the "Pre-Fab Four" in Liverpool to their worldwide success. A marvelous pseudo-documentary, originally shown on NBC-TV and with various SNL alumni, which captures the development of the Beatles and '60s rock with devastating effect. Served as the inspiration for "This Is Spinal Tap." **70m/C; VHS, DVD, Blu-Ray.** *GB* Eric Idle; Neil Innes; Ricky Fataar; Dan Aykroyd; Gilda Radner; John Belushi; George Harrison; Paul Simon; Mick Jagger; John Halsey; Michael Palin; Bianca Jagger; Bill Murray; Gwen Taylor; Ron Wood; Jeannette Charles; Al Franken; Lorne Michaels; Tom Davis; ***D:*** Eric Idle; Gary Weis; ***W:*** Eric Idle; ***C:*** Gary Weis; ***M:*** Neil Innes. **TV**

Allan Quartermain and the Temple of Skulls 1/2 **2008 (R)** Passably enjoyable adventure (filmed in South Africa) is a retelling of H. Rider Haggard's "King Solomon Mines." Desperately in need of money, washed-up adventurer Allan Quartermain (Michael) is trying to sell his half of a treasure map to baddie Hartford (Adamson). Along comes Lady Anna (Stone) and her silly brother Sir Henry (Bonjour) with the other half of the map and the trio reluctantly agree to team up, which doesn't make Hartford too happy. **90m/C; DVD.** Sean Cameron Michael; Chris(topher) Adamson; Natalie Stone; Daniel Boujour; Wittly Jourdan; Nick Everhart; ***D:*** Mark Atkins; ***W:*** David Michael Latt; ***C:*** Mark Atkins; ***M:*** Kays Al-Atrakchi. **VIDEO**

Allan Quatermain and the Lost City of Gold 1/2 **1986 (PG)** While trying to find his brother, Quatermain discovers a lost African civilization, in this weak adaptation of an H. Rider Haggard adventure. An ostensible sequel to the equally shallow "King Solomon's Mines." **100m/C; VHS, DVD, Blu-Ray.** Richard Chamberlain; Sharon Stone; James Earl Jones; ***D:*** Gary Nelson; ***W:*** Gene Quintano; Lee Reynolds; ***C:*** Frederick Elmes.

Alleged 1/2 **2010** Simplistic drama with an emphasis on the movie's religious intentions. In 1925, ambitious Dayton, Tennessee newspaper reporter Charles Anderson becomes part of the media circus surrounding the so-called Scopes 'Monkey' Trial. Cynical columnist H.L. Mencken becomes Charles' mentor, much to the dismay of his fiance and fellow reporter Rose, who feels Charles isn't thinking for himself. **91m/C; DVD.** Nathan West; Colm Meaney; Ashley Johnson; Fred Dalton Thompson; Brian Dennehy; Jamie Kolacki; ***D:*** Tom Hines; ***W:*** Brian Godawa; ***C:*** John Samaras; ***M:*** John R. Graham. **VIDEO**

Allegheny Uprising 1/2 *The First Rebel* **1939** Set in 1759, the story of a frontiersman who clashes with a British military commander in order to stop the sale of firearms to Indians. The stars of "Stagecoach" are back on board in this lesser effort. Also available colorized. **81m/B; VHS, DVD.** John Wayne; Claire Trevor; George Sanders; Brian Donlevy; Chill Wills; Moroni Olsen; ***D:*** William A. Seiter.

Allegiance 1/2 **2012 (R)** One-dimensional drama set over a single day in 2004. White National Guard Lt. Danny Sefton (Gabel) gets homefront duty while his unit is being deployed to Iraq, thanks to his politican dad's intervention. Feeling guilty, he tries to help black medic Chris Reyes (Bow Wow), who can't get a transfer even though his young son is dying. **91m/C; DVD, Blu-Ray.** Seth Gabel; Bow Wow; Aidan Quinn; Pablo Schreiber; Malik Yoba; ***D:*** Michael Connors; ***W:*** Michael Connors; ***C:*** Daniel Vecchione.

Allegiant *The Divergent Series: Allegiant* **2016 (PG-13)** The YA dystopian trend has once again split a book in half, taking the third book in the Divergent series and cutting into two films. Tris (Woodley) continues to realize her importance in this futuristic world when she's taken in by the people who created the factions that define society. It was all a grand experiment, and Tris's abilities prove it worked. But she's not done rebelling. It's just flat, boring, clichéd young adult filmmaking lacking a spark of passion. **120m/C; Blu-Ray, Streaming.** Shailene Woodley; Theo James; Miles Teller; Jeff Daniels; Octavia Spencer; Naomi Watts; ***D:*** Robert Schwentke; ***W:*** Noah Oppenheim; Adam Cooper; Bill Collage; ***C:*** Florian Ballhaus; ***M:*** Joseph Trapanese.

Allegro Non Troppo **1976 (PG)** An energetic and bold collection of animated skits set to classical music in this Italian version of Disney's "Fantasia." Watch for the evolution of life set to Ravel's Bolero, or better yet, watch the whole darn movie. Features Nichetti (often referred to as the Italian Woody Allen, particularly by people in Italy) in the non-animated segments, who went on to write, direct, and star (he may have sold concessions in the lobby as well) in "The Icicle Thief." **75m/C; VHS, DVD.** *IT* Maurizio Nichetti; Nestor Garay; Maria Giovannini; ***D:*** Bruno Bozzetto; ***W:*** Maurizio Nichetti; Bruno Bozzetto; Guido Manuli; ***C:*** Mario Masini.

Alley Cat **1984 (R)** Woman uses martial arts to fight back against a street gang that attacked her. **82m/C; VHS, DVD.** Karin Mani; Robert Torti; Brit Helfer; Michael Wayne; Jon Greene; ***D:*** Edward Victor.

Allie & Me **1997** Gullible beautician Allie (Baron) wants to make some changes in her life but doesn't quite expect what happens when she teams up with wronged wife Michelle (Benson). They decide to take out their frustrations by committing a burglary but find the Beverly Hills abode occupied by stud Rodney (Wilder), whom they take as a hostage, and then Allie decides to fall in love with him. Lots of recognizable faces but the comedy doesn't quite come together. **86m/C; VHS, DVD.** Joanne Baron; Lyndie Benson; James Wilder; Steven Prince; Ed Lauter; Lainie Kazan; Dyan Cannon; Harry Hamlin; Julianne Phillips; ***D:*** Michael Rymer; ***W:*** Michael Rymer; ***C:*** Rex Nicholson.

Allied 1/2 **2016 (R)** Zemeckis displays his love for Casablanca in this WWII film of spies and lovers. Wing Commander Max Vatan (Pitt) is a member of the Canadian Air Force who drops into Morocco just outside Casablanca. There, he meets Marianne Beausejour (Cotillard), a member of the French Resistance, and the two team up for a mission to assassinate the German Ambassador. Things get dicey once it's revealed that one may in fact be a spy. Pitt and Cotillard bring blinding star power to this high-budget thriller. It's more hollow than it should be, but still a lot of fun. **124m/C; DVD, Blu-Ray.** Brad Pitt; Marion Cotillard; Lizzy Caplan; Jared Harris; Matthew Goode; ***D:*** Robert Zemeckis; ***W:*** Steven Knight; ***C:*** Don Burgess; ***M:*** Alan Silvestri.

Alligator **1980 (R)** Dumped down a toilet 12 long years ago, lonely alligator Ramon resides in the city sewers, quietly eating and sleeping. In addition to feasting on the occasional stray human, Ramon devours the animal remains of a chemical plant's experiment involving growth hormones and eventually begins to swell at an enormous rate. Nothing seems to satisfy Ramon's ever-widening appetite: not all the people or all the buildings in the whole town, but he keeps trying, much to the regret of the guilt-ridden cop and lovely scientist who get to know each other while trying to nab the gator. Mediocre special effects are only a distraction in this witty eco-monster take. **94m/C; VHS, DVD.** Robert Forster; Robin Riker; Jack Carter; Henry Silva; Dean Jagger; Michael V. Gazzo; Perry Lang; Bart Braverman; Angel Tompkins; Sue Lyon; Sydney Lassick; James Ingersoll; John Lisbon Wood; Robert Doyle; Patti Jerome; ***D:*** Lewis Teague; ***W:*** John Sayles; Frank Ray Perilli; ***C:*** Joseph Mangine; ***M:*** Craig Hundley.

Alligator 2: The Mutation **1990 (PG-13)** Not a sequel to 1980's surprisingly good "Alligator," but a bland rehash with a decent cast. Once again a toxic alligator grows to enormous size and menaces a community. A Donald-Trump-like villain and pro wrestlers (!) bring this up to date, but it's all on the level of a TV disaster movie; even the PG-13 rating is a bit too harsh. **92m/C; VHS, DVD.** Steve Railsback; Dee Wallace; Joseph Bologna; Woody Brown; Bill Daily; Brock Peters; Richard Lynch; Holly Gagnier; ***D:*** Jon Hess; ***W:*** Curt Allen; ***C:*** Joseph Mangine.

Alligator Alley **1972** When two young divers witness a major drug deal, they become entangled in a web of danger they never expected. **92m/C; VHS, DVD.** Steve Alaimo; John Davis Chandler; Willie Pastrano; Jeremy Slate; Cece Stone; ***D:*** William Grefe.

Alligator Eyes 1/2 **1990 (R)** Stranger wearing trouble like a cheap perfume enters the midst of a vacationing trio of New Yorkers. Their vulnerabilities are exposed by a young hitchhiker sporting a slinky polka dot ensemble and way cool sunglasses who insinuates herself into their vacation plans (not to mention their private lives), before the three realize she's blind and full of manipulative and vindictive tricks, thanks to the usual brutal childhood. Psycho-sexo-logical thriller has some fine performances and a promising beginning, before fizzling into celluloid cotton candy. **101m/C; VHS, DVD.** Annabelle Larsen; Roger Kabler; Mary McLain; Allen McCullough; John MacKay; ***D:*** John Feldman; ***W:*** John Feldman; ***M:*** Sheila Silver.

An Alligator Named Daisy 1/2 **1955** And what a troublesome reptile she turns out to be! Peter (Sinden) is set to marry wealthy Vanessa (Dors) when he suddenly acquires a baby alligator from another ferry boat passenger. He tries to dispose of Daisy in various ways but she's like a boomerang and keeps returning, as does zoo worker Moira (Carson) who urges Peter just to keep Daisy. But Vanessa gives him an ultimatum. **85m/C; DVD.** *GB* Donald Sinden; Diana Dors; Jeannie Carson; James Robertson Justice; Roland Culver; Avice Landone; Margaret Rutherford; Stanley Holloway; ***D:*** J. Lee Thompson; ***W:*** Jack Davies; ***C:*** Reg Wyer; ***M:*** Stanley Black.

The Allnighter **1987 (PG-13)** A college coed searches through the hypersexed beach-party milieu of her senior year for Mr. Right. Bangle Hoffs is directed by her mom, to no avail. **95m/C; VHS, DVD.** Susanna Hoffs; John Terlesky; Joan Cusack; Michael Ontkean; ***D:*** Tamar Simon Hoffs; ***W:*** Tamar Simon Hoffs; ***C:*** Joseph D. Urbanczyk; ***M:*** Charles Bernstein.

All's Faire in Love 1/2 **2009** Wannabe actress Kate (Ricci) takes a summer job at a Renaissance Faire where college quarterback Will (Benjamin) has been assigned to work by his irate professor as a punishment for blowing off class. There's a social hierarchy, headed by a Queen (Ann-Margret) who instills competition among her somewhat crazy subjects even as Kate and Will find romance. **108m/C; DVD, Blu-Ray.** Christina Ricci; Owen Benjamin; Ann-Margret; Cedric the Entertainer; Matthew Lillard; Bill Engvall; ***D:*** Scott Marshall; ***W:*** Scott Marshall; ***C:*** Mark Irwin; ***M:*** Jeff Cardoni; Julian Jackson.

Almayer's Folly 1/2 *La folie Almayer* **2012** An adaptation of Joseph Conrad's debut novel, centering on a Dutch trader living in Malaysia and exploring such issues as colonialism, cultural conflict, and despair. Set in the 1950s, Almayer (Merhar) is the trader who married the adopted Malay daughter of Captain Lingard (Barbe) to gain a promised inheritance. This inheritance has never materialized, and the greedy Almayer has been relegated to an isolated trading post. Almayer is bitter and unhappy, but focuses on his love on his daughter Nina (Marion). As much as emotionally invests in her, Nina loathes her father and all he represents. Yet Nina is the only reason Almayer keeps going and his pipe dream of success alive. **127m/C; DVD, Streaming, Download.** Stanislas Merhar; Marc Barbe; Aurora Marion; Zac Andrianasolo; Sakhna Oum; ***D:*** Chantal Akerman; ***W:*** Chantal Akerman; ***M:*** Raymond Fromont.

Almighty Thor **WOOF!** **2011** Almighty mess. The Asylum's boring rip-off of "Thor" debuted on the Syfy Channel. Evil Loki wants the Hammer of Invincibility so he can destroy Earth. Odin refuses, so Loki destroys Asgard and then heads to Earth anyway (specifically L.A.). A constantly whining Thor gets some extra training to battle his brother from Valkyrie Jarnsaxa, who eventually just gives the big lug an Uzi to cap anyone who gets in his way. **90m/C; DVD, Blu-Ray.** Richard Grieco; Patricia Velasquez; Kevin Nash; Cody Deal; Jess Allen; ***D:*** Christopher Ray; ***W:*** Erik Estenberg; ***C:*** Alexander Yellen; ***M:*** Chris Ridenhour. **CABLE**

. . .Almost *Wendy Cracked a Walnut* **1990 (PG)** Arquette plays a curiously giddy bookworm with a vivid imagination. When her husband disappears on their anniversary, the man of her dreams shows up to sweep her off her feet. Is he real or is he simply another daydream? Almost a good time. **87m/C; VHS, DVD.** *AU* Rosanna Arquette; Bruce Spence; ***D:*** Michael Pattinson.

Almost an Angel 1/2 **1990 (PG)** Another in a recent spate of angels and ghosts assigned back to earth by the head office. A life-long criminal (Hogan) commits a heroic act and finds himself a probationary angel returned to earth to gain permanent angel status. He befriends a wheelchair-bound man, falls in love with the guy's sister, and helps her out at a center for potential juvenile delinquents. Melodramatic and hokey in places, relying too much on Hogan's crocodilian charisma. **98m/C; VHS, DVD, Blu-Ray.** Paul Hogan; Linda Kozlowski; Elias Koteas; Doreen Lang; Charlton Heston; David Alan Grier; Larry Miller; Douglas Seale; Parley Baer; Hank Worden; ***D:*** John Cornell; ***W:*** Paul Hogan; ***C:*** Russell Boyd; ***M:*** Maurice Jarre.

Almost Angels **1962** Two boys romp in Austria as members of the Vienna Boys Choir. Lesser sentimental Disney effort that stars the actual members of the Choir; not much of a draw for today's Nintendo-jaded young viewers. **85m/C; VHS, DVD.** Vincent Winter; Peter Weck; Hans Holt; ***D:*** Steve Previn.

Almost Blue 1/2 **1993 (R)** A gigantic, slow-moving, movie cliche. Madsen is a sulky, hard-living sax player going off the deep end because of his wife's death. Walden is the good woman who comes along to save him from himself. Tenor saxman Ernie Watts doubles for Madsen. Do yourself a favor—skip the movie and listen to some good jazz instead. **98m/C; VHS, Streaming.** Michael Madsen; Lynette Walden; Garrett Morris; Gale Mayron; Yaphet Kotto; ***D:*** Keoni Waxman.

Almost Christmas 1/2 **2016 (PG-13)** Retired widower Walter (Glover) invites his four grown children (Gabrielle Union, Romany Malco, Jessie Usher, and Kimberly Elise) home for the holidays to rekindle a sense of family that he's now lost. Of course, each of the four kids comes with their own baggage, and some come with significant others. Writer/director Talbert's comedy is warm-hearted, funny, and kind. It is incredibly familiar, and breaks no new ground in its genre, but it's not designed to do so. It's just a sweet movie for the holidays, elevated by a truly excellent cast. **111m/C; DVD, Blu-Ray.** Kimberly Elise; Omar Epps; Danny Glover; John Michael Higgins; Romany Malco; ***D:*** David E. Talbert; ***W:*** David E. Talbert; ***C:*** Larry Blanford; ***M:*** John Paesano.

Almost Dead 1/2 **1994** Psychiatrist Katherine Roshak's (Doherty) mother committed suicide four years ago and suddenly her corpse is appearing to Katherine. When she visits Mom's grave, Katherine finds an empty coffin. So she teams up with a skeptical cop (Mandylor) to figure out what's going on. Lots of loose ends. Based on the novel "Resurrection" by William Valtos. **92m/C; VHS, Streaming.** Shannen Doherty; Costas Mandylor; John Diehl; William R. Moses; ***D:*** Ruben Preuss; ***W:*** Miguel Tejada-Flores; ***C:*** Zoran Hochstatter.

Almost Famous **2000 (R)** Fifteen-year-old budding rock critic William Miller's (Fugit) dream comes true after he bluffs his way into a Rolling Stone writing assignment covering a rising '70s rock band on tour. This ode to the music and youth culture of that decade may lack grit, but its sympathetic treatment of young Miller's coming-of-age amid groupies, drugs, rock and roll, and a worried, undupable mother (McDormand) achieves director Crowe's ends. The film's adoration of the music's energy and emotion appear to be the headliner here, but it never outperforms its devotion to character and relationship. Delicate performances by first-timer Fugit, and by Hudson as the more-than-a-groupie groupie, plus a memorable portrayal of the wise and slightly surly critic Lester Bangs by Hoffman. Based on Crowe's own experiences. **202m/C; VHS, DVD, Blu-Ray.** Patrick Fugit; Philip Seymour Hoffman; Frances McDormand; Jason Lee; Billy Crudup; Kate Hudson; John Fedevich; Mark Kozelek; Fairuza Balk; Bijou Phillips; Anna Paquin; Noah Taylor; Jimmy Fallon; Zooey Deschanel; Liz Stauber; Eion Bailey; Mark Pellington; Terry Chen; Peter Frampton; Zack (Zach) Ward; ***Cameo(s):*** Jann Wenner; ***D:*** Cameron Crowe; ***W:*** Cameron Crowe; ***C:*** John Toll; ***M:*** Nancy Wilson. Oscars '00: Orig. Screenplay; Golden Globes '01: Film--Mus./Comedy, Support. Actress (Hudson); L.A. Film Critics '00: Support. Actress (McDormand); Broadcast Film Critics '00: Orig. Screenplay, Support. Actress (McDormand).

Almost Friends 1/2 **2017** A gentle yet meandering coming-of-age comedy-drama. Twentysomething Charlie (Hightower) was on track to be a talented chef, but a traumatic event emotionally derailed him. Living at home with his mother (Helgenberger) and second husband (Moore), he works at a revival movie theater. Charlie begins to find meaning in life when he meets barista Amber (Rush), though she is still involved with self-absorbed track star Brad (Smith). The reappearance of Charlie's long-gone charismatic gambler father Howard (Meloni) further shakes him up. Lots of potential, but lackluster direction and uninspired performances drag it down. **101m/C; DVD, Blu-Ray.** Freddie Highmore; Odeya Rush; Christopher Meloni; Haley Joel Osment; Jake Abel; ***D:*** Jake Goldberger; ***W:*** Jake Goldberger; ***C:*** Jeremy Mackie; ***M:*** Eric V. Hachikian.

Almost Heaven **2006** Alcoholic Canadian director Mark Brady (Logue) is hired for a low-rated fishing program in Scotland that's hosted by his bitter ex-wife Taya (Collins). The village is filled with the usual quirky characters and Mark finds romance with independent fishing guide Nicki (Mitchell) but is she enough to help keep him sober? **102m/C; DVD.** *CA* Donal Logue; Tom Conti; Kirsty Mitchell; Joely Collins; Erin Karpluk; ***D:*** Shel Piercy; ***W:*** Shel Piercy; Richard Beattie; ***C:*** Oliver Cheesman; ***M:*** Richard G. Mitchell.

Almost Heroes 1/2 *Edwards & Hunt: The First American Road Trip* **1997 (PG-13)** Farley's last screen appearance teams him with Perry as explorers Edwards and Hunt, who are racing Lewis and Clark to the Pacific Ocean in 1804. Edwards (Perry) is a glory-seeking fop who's totally out of his league, Hunt (Farley) is a slovenly, clumsy tracker with a soft spot for toilet (or would that be outhouse?) humor. Along with a team of misfits and losers, the duo wreaks havok on the American frontier. Perry and Farley show some flashes of comic chemistry, but their left to fend for themselves by a script that's lost in the wilderness, sadly relying too much on Farley's patented self-destructive schtick. **87m/C; VHS, DVD.** Chris Farley; Matthew Perry; Eugene Levy; Bokeem Woodbine; Lisa Barbuscia; Kevin Dunn; Hamilton Camp; Lewis Arquette; ***V:*** Harry Shearer; ***D:*** Christopher Guest; ***W:*** Tom Wolfe; Mark Nutter; Boyd Hale; ***C:*** Adam Kimmel; Kenneth Macmillan; ***M:*** C.J. Vanston.

Almost Holy 1/2 *Crocodile Gennadiy* **2016 (R)** A documentary biography of Gennadiy Mohknenko, a Ukrainian pastor and civic leader. In the post-Soviet era, Ukraine suffered from social and political unrest. In this world Gennadiy worked to address issues related to street children. The founder of the children's rehab center/home for former street kids called Pilgrim's Republic, Gennadiy was controversial for his abductions of drug-addicted street kids as means of helping them get clean. Though Gennadiy's efforts have resulted in few homeless children in his city, another wave of upheaval in Ukraine has created more unrest in the city he has worked so hard to save. **96m/C; DVD, Streaming, Download.** ***D:*** Steve Hoover; ***W:*** Steve Hoover; ***C:*** John Pope; ***M:*** Bobby Krlic; Atticus Ross; Leopold Ross.

Almost Peaceful *Un monde presque paisible* **2002** In 1946, a Jewish tailor is restarting his business and attempting to regain a life of normalcy. Deville quietly follows the Jewish employees—some who have survived the camps, some who have escaped the horrors but have fought their own war—as they stitch, sew, and try to restore themselves. Intertwined stories flow marvelously, providing poignant observation of the Holocaust aftermath. **90m/C; DVD.** *FR* Simon Abkarian; Zabou Breitman; Denis Podalydes; Vincent Elbaz; Lubna Azabal; Stanislas Merhar; Clotilde Courau; Julie Gaynet; Malik Zidi; ***D:*** Michel DeVille; ***C:*** Andre Diot.

Almost Perfect **2011** Vanessa is a 34-year-old New Yorker who heads the philanthropic foundation at her family's company. She has no life of her own because she caters to everyone else's whims until she runs into old friend Dwayne, who admits he's always had a crush on her. Just as the romantic sparks are igniting, Vanessa's self-absorbed family comes to her with various crises and she has to decide whether to focus on their lives or her own. **106m/C; DVD.** Kelly Hu; Ivan Shaw; Christina Chang; Edson Chen; Tina Chen; Roger Rees; ***D:*** Bertha Bay-Sa Pan; ***W:*** Bertha Bay-Sa Pan; ***C:*** Sam Chase; ***M:*** Jeff Martin. **VIDEO**

An Almost Perfect Affair **1979 (PG)** Taxing romantic comedy about an ambitious independent American filmmaker who, after finishing a movie about an executed murderer, travels to the Cannes festival and proceeds to fall in love or lust with the wife of an Italian producer. Numerous inside jokes and capable performances nearly overcome script lethargy. **92m/C; VHS, DVD.** Keith Carradine; Monica Vitti; Raf Vallone; Christian de Sica; Dick Anthony Williams; ***D:*** Michael Ritchie; ***W:*** Walter Bernstein; ***M:*** Georges Delerue.

Almost Strangers *Perfect Strangers* **2001** Compelling thriller about family ties. Ernest Symon (Howell) arranges a complicated three-day family reunion at a London hotel, which is reluctantly attended by black sheep Raymond (Gambon) and his curious son Daniel (Macfadyen). Both see family photos of events neither of them can remember and then Daniel meets his up-to-no-good cousins Rebecca (Skinner) and Charles (Stephens). Are those family skeletons we hear rattling? **237m/C; DVD.** *GB* Michael Gambon; Matthew Macfadyen; Claire Skinner; Toby Stephens; Lindsay Duncan; Peter Howell; Anton Lesser; ***D:*** Stephen Poliakoff; ***W:*** Stephen Poliakoff; ***C:*** Cinders Forshaw; ***M:*** Adrian Johnston. **TV**

Almost You **1985 (R)** Normal marital conflicts and uncertainties grow exponentially when a wealthy New York City 30-something couple hires a lovely young nurse to help care for the wife after a car accident. An unsentimental marital comedy with a good cast that still misses. **91m/C; VHS, DVD.** Brooke Adams; Griffin Dunne; Karen Young; Marty Watt; Christine Estabrook; Josh Mostel; Laura Dean; Dana Delany; Miguel Pinero; Joe Silver; Suzzy Roche; Spalding Gray; ***D:*** Adam Brooks; ***M:*** Jonathan Elias.

Aloha 1/2 **2015 (PG-13)** Brian Gilcrest (Cooper) is a celebrated military contractor brought to Hawaii to, well, do something undefined with a gate. The something doesn't really matter as much as Gilcrest running into his old love (McAdams) and a potential new one (Stone). Of course, the girl helps the boy get over this bump in his life. It is a Cameron Crowe movie, after all, even if it's a faded carbon copy. Unfortunate that Cooper followed up his "American Sniper" role with this mess along with A-listers McAdams and Stone. **105m/C; DVD, Blu-Ray.** Bradley Cooper; Emma Stone; Rachel McAdams; Bill Murray; John Krasinski; ***D:*** Cameron Crowe; ***W:*** Cameron Crowe; ***C:*** Eric Gautier; ***M:*** Jon Thor Birgisson; Alex Somers.

Aloha, Bobby and Rose 1/2 **1974 (PG)** A mechanic and his girlfriend in L.A. become accidentally involved in an attempted robbery and murder and go on the run for Mexico, of course. Semi-satisfying drama in the surf, with fine location photography. **90m/C; VHS, DVD, Blu-Ray.** Paul LeMat; Dianne Hull; Robert Carradine; Tim McIntire; Noble Willingham; Leigh French; ***D:*** Floyd Mutrux; ***W:*** Floyd Mutrux; ***C:*** William A. Fraker.

Alone in the Dark **1982 (R)** Slash and dash horror attempt featuring four escaped patients from a mental hospital who decide that they must kill their doctor because they don't like him. Conveniently, a city-wide blackout provides the opportunity, as the good doctor defends home and family against the aging stars intent on chewing up as much scenery as possible. **92m/C; VHS, DVD.** Jack Palance; Donald Pleasence; Martin Landau; Dwight Schultz; ***D:*** Jack Sholder; ***W:*** Jack Sholder.

Alone in the Dark **WOOF!** **2005 (R)** If there's any justice, Tim Burton's grandson will one day film a lovingly campy biopic about director Uwe Boll. Heir apparent to Ed Wood, Boll follows up 2003's "House of the Dead" with yet another incoherent video game adaptation. Paranormal detective Edward Carnby (Slater) represses memories of an orphanage trauma as he travels the globe collecting mystical chotchkies and fighting poorly-lit bad guys. When his fellow orphans start disappearing, Carnby and his scientist girlfriend (Reid) team up to battle bargain-basement CGI terror dogs. The monsters are somehow tied to an extinct Indian tribe, but you'll be too busy groaning at Reid's phonetically sounded-out science talk or the ridiculously inane opening crawl to care. **96m/C; DVD.** *US CA GE* Christian Slater; Tara Reid; Stephen Dorff; Matthew (Matt) Walker; Will Sanderson; Darren Shahlavi; Karin Konoval; Ed Anders; Frank C. Turner; Mark Acheson; Craig Bruhnanski; Kwesi Ameyaw; Catherine Lough Haggquist; ***D:*** Uwe Boll; ***W:*** Elan Mastai; Michael Roesch; Peter Scheerer; ***C:*** Mathias Neumann; ***M:*** Bernd Wendlandt.

Alone in the Dark 2 **WOOF!** **2008 (PG-13)** Private eye Edward Carnby (Yune) gets caught in a feud between a group of witch hunters and witch Elizabeth Dexter (Lange) over a stolen (and cursed) dagger. Lead character Carnby has the same name as the character in the videogame (and the 2005 movie) but that's all and the plot actually makes little to no sense whatsoever. Infamously bad director Uwe Boll only produced this time around but it didn't seem to make any difference. **90m/C; DVD.** Rick Yune; Allison Lange; Rachel Specter; Bill Moseley; Ralph (Ralf) Moeller; Michael Paré; Jason Connery; P.J. Soles; Danny Trejo; Lance Henriksen; Natassia Malthe; Zack (Zach) Ward; ***D:*** Michael Roesch; Peter Scheerer; ***W:*** Michael Roesch; Peter Scheerer; ***C:*** Zoran Popovic; ***M:*** Jessica de Rooij. **VIDEO**

Alone in the Neon Jungle **1987** A glamorous big-city police captain is assigned to clean up the most corrupt precinct in town. Pleshette is untypically cast but still manages to make her role believable in a serviceable TV cop drama with more dialogue than action. **90m/C; VHS, DVD.** Suzanne Pleshette; Danny Aiello; Georg Stanford Brown; Frank Converse; Joe Morton; ***D:*** Georg Stanford Brown.

Alone in the Woods **1995 (PG)** Ten-year-old Justin mistakenly gets into the wrong van while on his way to his family's annual mountain vacation. Turns out the duo in the van are would-be kidnappers after Chelsea Stuart, the daughter of a toy magnate and now Justin must escape and rescue Chelsea. **81m/C; VHS, DVD.** Brady Bluhm; Chick Vennera; Matthias Hues; Laraine Newman; Daniel McVicar; Krystee Clark; ***D:*** John Putch; ***W:*** J. Riley Lagesen; ***C:*** Frank Johnson; ***M:*** David Lawrence. **VIDEO**

Alone with a Stranger **1999 (R)** Long lost Evil Twin (Moses) learns that he has a rich brother. Evil Twin and girlfriend (Peeples) plan to kidnap Good Twin, sell his company, and scoot with the loot. But what about Good Twin's wife (Niven) and family? **90m/C; DVD.** William R. Moses; Barbara Niven; Priscilla Barnes; Nia Peeples; Mindy Cohn; ***D:*** Peter Paul Liapis; ***W:*** Peter Paul Liapis; Richard Dana Smith; ***C:*** M. David Mullen; ***M:*** Alan Howarth.

Alone With Her 1/2 **2007** Clumsy thriller with camera as voyeur. Doug (Hanks) is obsessed with Amy (Talancon) and sets up surveillance on her with hidden cameras after breaking into her apartment. He orchestrates nasty little surprises and then turns up as Amy's concerned friend but the tension never particularly increases, even when Doug goes to what should have been more creepy extremes. **78m/C; DVD.** Ana Claudia Talancon; Colin Hanks; Jordana Spiro; Jonathan Trent; ***D:*** Eric Nicholas; ***W:*** Eric Nicholas; ***C:*** Nathaniel Wilson; ***M:*** David E. Russo.

Alone Yet Not Alone **2013 (PG-13)** Dreadful faith-based indie with historical inaccuracies and amateur ability in front of and behind the camera. In 1755 in the Ohio valley, frontier farms are under attack by hostile local tribes. During a raid, two sisters are taken but find comfort in their captivity through the titular hymn. After Barbara and her sister get separated, she decides to escape with other captives, but they must cross miles of wilderness to safety while being pursued. Based on the Tracey Leininger Craven "Alone Yet Not Alone: Their Faith Became Their Freedom." **103m/C; DVD.** Kelly Greyson; Natalie Racoosin; Jenn Gotzon; Clay Walker; Ozzie Torres; ***D:*** Ray Bengston; George D. Escobar; ***W:*** George D. Escobar; James Richards; ***C:*** James Suttles; ***M:*** William Ross.

Along Came a Spider **2001 (R)** Sequel to 1997's "Kiss the Girls" is actually a prequel storywise but Freeman does reprise his character of Detective Alex Cross. This time he must save a U.S. Senator's daughter who's been kidnapped by a serial killer. Freeman is easily the best thing in this convoluted, plot-deficient, murky mess. He makes every "yeah, right" moment (and there are many) palatable. Based on the novel by James Patterson. **103m/C; VHS, DVD, Blu-Ray.** Morgan Freeman; Monica Potter; Michael Wincott; Penelope Ann Miller; Michael Moriarty; Dylan Baker; Billy Burke; Jay O. Sanders; Kim Hawthorne; Mika Boorem; Anton Yelchin; ***D:*** Lee Tamahori; ***W:*** Marc Moss; ***C:*** Matthew F. Leonetti; ***M:*** Jerry Goldsmith.

Along Came Jones **1945** Cowboy Cooper, who can't handle a gun and is saddled with grumpy sidekick Demarest, is the victim of mistaken identity as both the good guys and the bad guys pursue him thinking he is a vicious killer. Young is the woman who rides to his defense. Offbeat and charming western parody based on a novel by Alan le May. **93m/B; VHS, DVD, Blu-Ray.** Gary Cooper; Loretta Young; Dan Duryea; William Demarest; ***D:*** Stuart Heisler; ***W:*** Nunnally Johnson; ***C:*** Milton Krasner; ***M:*** Arthur Lange.

Along Came Polly **2004 (PG-13)** There's something about Polly. Neurotic risk analyst (Stiller) meets wild child Polly (Aniston) and learns to let loose. Has the requisite number of sight gags involving bodily fluids and embarrassing situations (Stiller is a master at squeezing the humor out of both), but breaks no new ground and quickly become formulaic. Generic romantic comedy with a few laughs is otherwise forgettable. **91m/C; VHS, DVD, Blu-Ray.** Ben Stiller; Jennifer Aniston; Philip Seymour Hoffman; Debra Messing; Alec Baldwin; Hank Azaria; Bryan Brown; Michele Lee; Jsu Garcia; Bob (Robert) Dishy; Missi Pyle; Judah Friedlander; Kym E. Whitley; Kevin Hart; ***D:*** John Hamburg; ***W:*** John Hamburg; ***C:*** Seamus McGarvey; ***M:*** Theodore Shapiro.

Along Came the Devil **1/2** *Tell Me Your Name* **2018** Because of an absent mother and abusive father, high school student Ashley (Sweeney) and her sister Jordan (Deaver) are raised by their aunt, Tanya (Barth). When Jordan goes off to college, Ashley and Tanya move together to Ashley's hometown. As Ashley reunites with old friends, including best friend Hannah (Lintz), she also connects to the dark, demon-like force that may have played a role in her mother's suspicious disappearance. The low budget horror film is a copycat of other genre films, including The Exorcist, but with much lower standards. **89m/C; DVD.** Jessica Barth; Matt Dallas; Bruce Davison; Sydney Sweeney; Madison Lintz; ***D:*** Jason DeVan; ***W:*** Jason DeVan; Heather DeVan; ***C:*** Justin Duval.

Along Came the Devil 2 **1/2 2019** The sequel shifts focus to college student Jordan (Wiggins) from her demon-possessed sister of the first movie. Coming home from school, Jordan tries to figure out what happened to her missing sister. She reluctantly stays with her once emotionally abusive father Mark (Ashworth), who is now a recovering alcoholic, his new wife Karen (Fallon), and their odd son Xander (DeVan). Before long, Jordan learns that darker forces are still threatening her family. More coherent than its predecessor, the film is more about family issues than supernatural evil but is plagued by over-the-top dialogue and bland performances. **88m/C; DVD, Blu-Ray.** Laura Wiggins; Bruce Davison; Tiffany Fallon; Mark Ashworth; Bill Barrett; ***D:*** Jason DeVan; ***W:*** Jason DeVan; ***C:*** Jay Ruggieri; ***M:*** Kevin Coughlin; Chad Lanier.

Along for the Ride **1/2 2000 (R)** Seriously disturbed Lulu (Griffith) checks herself out of the mental hospital and informs old boyfriend Ben (Swayze) that when she was a teen, she gave birth to their son and put him up for adoption. Somehow she manages to persuade him on a cross-country journey to Wisconsin to meet the now-teenaged kid. Naturally, this idea doesn't sit that well with Ben's wife Claire (Miller) who decides to put a stop to the nonsense. Goopy sentiment. **99m/C; VHS, DVD.** Melanie Griffith; Patrick Swayze; Penelope Ann Miller; Joseph Gordon-Levitt; Richard Schiff; Annie Corley; Lee Garlington; Michael J. Pollard; Steven Bauer; ***D:*** John Kaye; ***W:*** John Kaye; ***C:*** Dion Beebe; ***M:*** Serge Colbert.

Along the Great Divide **1951** A U.S. marshal and his deputy battle pursuing vigilantes and the untamed frontier to bring a falsely accused murderer to trial (and of course, find the real bad guy). Douglas' first western has the usual horse opera cliches supported by excellent cinematography. **88m/B; VHS, DVD.** Kirk Douglas; John Agar; Walter Brennan; Virginia Mayo; ***D:*** Raoul Walsh.

Along the Rio Grande **1/2 1941** Ranch hands Jeff, Smokey, and Whopper's boss Pop Edwards is murdered and they are falsely accused of bank robbery and jailed. Rustler Doc Randall breaks one of his henchmen out of jail and they persuade him to let them join his gang with the intention of proving Randall's the real criminal. **65m/B; DVD.** Tim Holt; Ray Whitley; Emmett Lynn; Robert (Fisk) Fiske; Betty Jane Rhodes; Carl Stockdale; Slim Whitaker; Monte Montague; Harry Humphrey; Hal Taliaferro; Ruth Clifford; ***D:*** Edward Killy; ***W:*** Arthur V. Jones; Morton Grant; ***C:*** Frank Redman.

Along with Ghosts *Tokaido obake dochu; Yokai Monsters 3: Along with Ghosts; Journey With Ghost Along Yokaido Road* **1969** A young girl discovers proof of corruption in her town, and her grandfather is murdered because of it. She flees in search of her father. Because her grandfather was murdered on holy ground, the Yokai agree to protect her and take revenge on her behalf. This is the third film in the Yokai trilogy. The monsters are finally a little less cutesy looking for this sequel, which is fitting considering the mythological reputation of the Yokai. **90m/C; DVD.** *JP* Kojiro Hongo; Bokuzen Hidari; Pepe Hozumi; Masami Burukido; Mutsuhiro; Yoshito Yamaji; ***D:*** Yoshiyuki Kuroda; Kimiyoshi Yasuda; ***W:*** Tetsuro Yoshida; ***C:*** Hiroshi Imai; ***M:*** Michiaki Watanabe.

Alpha **1/2 2018 (PG-13)** A story of survival set 20,000 years ago, during the last Ice Age. A boy who's lost from his tribe encounters an injured wolf, and the pair tentatively form a bond that ushers in the concept of "man's best friend." Beautifully shot, dog lovers will howl with delight, though the perilous scenes may be too much for young pups. **96m/C; DVD, Blu-Ray.** Kodi Smit-McPhee; Jóhannes Haukur Jóhannesson; Leonor Varela; Natassia Malthe; Jens Hultén; ***D:*** Albert Hughes; ***W:*** Daniele Sebastian Wiedenhaupt; ***C:*** Martin Gschlacht; ***M:*** Joseph S. DeBeasi; Michael Stearns.

Alpha Alert *Event 15* **2013 (R)** Three vets, all suffering from PTSD, are trapped in an elevator after a terrorist attack on DC. Tensions increase as the situation brings up experiences from their wartime service, especially when it seems unlikely they'll be rescued. But are things as they seem? **84m/C; DVD.** Jennifer (Jenny) Morrison; Josh Stewart; Stephen Rider; James Frain; Kimberly Elise; Jude Ciccolella; ***D:*** Matthew Thompson; ***W:*** Matthew Thompson; Scott Bolger; ***C:*** Eduardo Enrique Mayen; ***M:*** Mark Russell. **VIDEO**

Alpha and Omega **1/2 2010 (PG)** Unambitious but not unappealing 3D animated kiddie comedy finds disciplined Alpha wolf Kate and fun-loving Omega wolf Humphrey transported from their Canadian national park home to Idaho as part of a wolf-relocation project. They want to get home but it's a thousand mile journey of bears, a helpful golfing duck, squabbles, and predictable adventures. Little ones will be generally amused, though it's mostly forgettable. Grown-ups beware that some rather obvious sexual references might prompt questions. **88m/C; Blu-Ray, On Demand.** ***V:*** Hayden Panettiere; Justin Long; Dennis Hopper; Danny Glover; Chris Carmack; Christina Ricci; Larry Miller; Eric Price; Vicki Lewis; ***D:*** Anthony Bell; Ben Gluck; ***W:*** Chris Denk; Steve Moore; ***M:*** Chris P. Bacon.

Alpha Dog **2006 (R)** True crime saga resulting from sheer stupidity. Wannabe white gangsta drug dealer Johnny Truelove (Hirsch) feels dissed when customer Jake (Foster) refuses to pay his tab. So Johnny and his equally wasted posse take advantage of a run-in with Jake's naive 15-year-old half brother Zack (Yelchin) and decide to hold him as collateral. Cohort Frankie (a convincing Timberlake) becomes Zack's de-facto babysitter and introduces him to their indulgent SoCal life—that is until someone finally realizes that kidnapping is a serious crime. A "River's Edge" for 21st-century teens. **117m/C; DVD, Blu-Ray, HD-DVD.** Emile Hirsch; Justin Timberlake; Ben Foster; Anton Yelchin; Shawn Hatosy; Bruce Willis; Sharon Stone; David Thornton; Fernando Vargas; Amanda Seyfried; Dominique Swain; Olivia Wilde; Lukas Haas; Vincent Kartheiser; Harry Dean Stanton; Alex Kingston; Heather Wahlquist; ***D:*** Nick Cassavetes; ***W:*** Nick Cassavetes; ***C:*** Robert Fraisse; ***M:*** Aaron Zigman.

The Alpha Incident **1/2 1976 (PG)** Time-worn doomsday drama about an alien organism with the potential to destroy all living things. Government works hard to cover up. **86m/C; VHS, DVD.** Ralph Meeker; Stafford Morgan; John Goff; Carol Irene Newell; John Alderman; ***D:*** Bill Rebane.

Alpha Male **1/2 2006** The time switch between the present and 10 years in the past can be confusing but this is an otherwise decent family drama. Wealthy Jim (Huston) has made a good life for wife Alice (Ehle) and their two children, despite his temper and domineering attitude. After Jim dies from cancer, officious son Jack (Wells) takes it badly when Alice decides to remarry, especially since widower Clive (Baladi) is his father's polar opposite. The situation comes to a boil when Alice throws Jack a lavish 21st birthday party. **100m/C; DVD.** *GB* Danny Huston; Jennifer Ehle; Amelia Warner; Christopher Egan; Mark Wells; Patrick Baladi; Trudie Styler; ***D:*** Dan Wilde; ***W:*** Dan Wilde; ***C:*** Shane Daly; ***M:*** Stephen Warbeck.

Alphabet City **1984 (R)** A drug kingpin who runs New York's Lower East Side has decided to turn over a new leaf, but first he must survive his last night as a criminal while figuring out a way to pay off his large debts. Very stylish and moody, but light on content and plot. **85m/C; VHS, DVD.** Vincent Spano; Michael Winslow; Kate Vernon; Jami Gertz; Zohra Lampert; Raymond Serra; Ken Marino; Daniel Jordano; Miguel Pinero; ***D:*** Amos Poe; ***W:*** Amos Poe.

The Alphabet Killer **2008 (R)** Loosely-based on the true story of a 1970s serial killer in Rochester, New York. Police detective Megan Paige (Dushku) becomes obsessed with a child killer case and has a breakdown after suffering hallucinations. Diagnosed as schizophrenic, Megan eventually returns to the force just as the killer, who chooses victims whose first and last names begin with the same letter, gets active again. Can she hold it together long enough to catch the killer this time? **100m/C; DVD, Blu-Ray.** Eliza Dushku; Cary Elwes; Timothy Hutton; Tom Malloy; Michael Ironside; Martin Donovan; Melissa Leo; Bill Moseley; Carl Lumbly; Tom Noonan; ***D:*** Rob Schmidt; ***W:*** Tom Malloy; ***C:*** Joe DeSalvo; ***M:*** Eric Perlmutter.

The Alphabet Murders *ABC Murders* **1965** Picture this: Randall playing Agatha Christie's famous Belgian sleuth, Hercule Poirot, and Rutherford—in a cameo'as Miss Marple. As if that wouldn't be enough to make Dame Agatha roll over in her grave, there's plenty of cloying wisecracking and slapsticking throughout. An adaptation of "The ABC Murders" in which Poirot stalks a literate killer who snuffs out his victims in alphabetical order. Hardly a must-see, unless you're hellbent on viewing the entire Randall opus. **90m/B; DVD.** Tony Randall; Anita Ekberg; Robert Morley; Maurice Denham; Guy Rolfe; Sheila Allen; Margaret Rutherford; Julian Glover; ***D:*** Frank Tashlin; ***W:*** David Pursall; Jack Seddon; ***C:*** Desmond Dickinson; ***M:*** Ronald Goodwin.

Alphaville *Alphaville, a Strange Case of Lemmy Caution; Alphaville, Une Etrange Aventure de Lemmy Caution* **1965** Engaging and inimitable Godard attempt at science fiction mystery. P.I. Lemmy Caution searches for a scientist in a city (Paris as you've never seen it before) run by robots and overseen by a dictator. The futuristic techno-conformist society must be upended so that Caution may save the scientist as well as nonconformists everywhere. In French with subtitles. **100m/B; VHS, DVD, Blu-Ray.** *FR* Eddie Constantine; Anna Karina; Akim Tamiroff; Howard Vernon; Laszlo Szabo; Michel Delahaye; Jean-Pierre Leaud; ***D:*** Jean-Luc Godard; ***W:*** Jean-Luc Godard; ***C:*** Raoul Coutard; ***M:*** Paul Misraki. Berlin Intl. Film Fest. '65: Golden Berlin Bear.

Already Dead **1/2 2007 (R)** Thomas Archer (Eldard) has a great job and a beautiful wife and son. Then the Archer home is robbed, his wife is brutalized, and his son is killed. The police can't find the criminals so Archer turns to a shadow group that promises to deliver those responsible and then give Archer the opportunity to deal with them as he sees fit. **93m/C; DVD.** Ron Eldard; Til Schweiger; Christopher Plummer; Patrick Kilpatrick; Marisa Coughlan; ***D:*** Joe Otting; ***W:*** Joe Chappelle; ***C:*** Eric Trageser; ***M:*** Nathan Furst. **VIDEO**

Altered **2006 (R)** Four men who were violated by aliens in the woods return 15 years later to get some revenge. **88m/C; DVD, Streaming.** Adam Kaufman; Brad William Henke; Michael C. Williams; Paul McCarthy-Boyington; James Gammon; Catherine Mangan; ***D:*** Eduardo Sanchez; ***W:*** Eduardo Sanchez; Jamie Nash; ***C:*** Steve Yedlin; ***M:*** Tony Cora; Exiquio Talavera. **VIDEO**

Altered Minds **1/2 2013** A psychological thriller centered one family's deepest secrets. Tommy Shellner (O'Nan) is under a lot of stress. Not only is his father Nathaniel Shellner (Hirsch) dying, he is experiencing terrifying visions that cause him much torment. In order to learn the truth about his family, he takes over a family reunion to try to get his father, a Nobel Prize-winning former CIA psychiatrist, to confess truths about the family. The situation only becomes more tense when Tommy reveals that his father allegedly adopted multiple children, including himself, as part of a psychological experiment. **106m/C; DVD, Streaming, Download.** Judd Hirsch; Ryan O'Nan; C.S. Lee; Jaime Ray Newman; Caroline Lagerfelt; ***D:*** Michael Z. Wechsler; ***W:*** Michael Z. Wechsler; ***C:*** Adrian Correia; ***M:*** Edmund Choi.

Altered States **1980 (R)** Obsessed with the task of discovering the inner man, Hurt's ambitious researcher ignores his family while consuming hallucinogenic drugs and floating in an immersion tank. He gets too deep inside, slipping way back through the evolutionary order and becoming a menace in the process. Confusing script based upon Chayefsky's (alias Sidney Aaron) confusing novel is supported by great special effects and the usual self-indulgent and provocative Russell direction. Chayefsky eventually washed his hands of the project after artistic differences with the producers. Others who departed from the film include initial director William Penn and special effects genius John Dykstra (relieved ably by Bran Ferren). Hurt's a solemn hoot in his first starring role. **103m/C; VHS, DVD, Blu-Ray.** William Hurt; Blair Brown; Bob Balaban; Charles Haid; Dori Brenner; Drew Barrymore; Miguel Godreau; Thaao Penghlis; Peter Brandon; Charles White Eagle; Meghan Jeffers; Jack Murdock; John Larroquette; ***D:*** Ken Russell; ***W:*** Paddy Chayefsky; Sidney Aaron; ***C:*** Jordan Cronenweth; ***M:*** John Corigliano.

Altitude **2010 (R)** Terror in the air. New pilot Sara persuades boyfriend Bruce and three friends that she can fly them to a concert. This is before the plane's instruments malfunction, they are forced into an uncontrolled climb, and they start seeing something horrible in the strange storm clouds that surround them. **90m/C; DVD.** *CA* Jessica Lowndes; Landon Liboiron; Julianna Guill; Jake Weary; Ryan Donowho; Mike Dopud; ***D:*** Kaare Andrews; ***W:*** Paul A. Birkett; ***C:*** Norm Li; ***M:*** Jeff Tymoschuk. **VIDEO**

Altitude **1/2 2017 (R)** A B-movie action romp set on a plane. After ignoring a direct order and being demoted, FBI agent Gretchen (Richards) is flying to her new assignment in Washington, D.C. On the plane ride, she strikes up a conversation with a well-dressed Brit Terry (Barker). Terry's demeanor changes when he sees Sharpe (Lundgren), Rawbones (Liddell), and Sadie (Grammer) board. Terry betrayed them all during a jewelry heist and the trio wants the gems and revenge. To save himself, Terry offers Gretchen $50 million to get him off the plane alive. The obviously low budget film makes the most of its cast and script. **88m/C; DVD.** Denise Richards; Dolph Lundgren; Jonathan Lipnicki; Kirk Barker; Greer Grammer; ***D:*** Alex Merkin; ***W:*** Jesse Mittelstadt; ***C:*** Dane Lawing; ***M:*** Bobby Tahouri.

Alucard **2008** A modern day remake of "Dracula." **156m/C; DVD, Streaming.** Jay Barber; Liam Smith; David Harscheid; Karthik Srinivasan; John VanPatten; Hal Handerson; John Johnson; Rebecca Taylor; Mariah Smith; Vicki Taylor; ***D:*** John Johnson; ***W:*** Spenser Tomson; ***C:*** John Johnson; Sergio Lescari; ***M:*** Lisa Hammer. **VIDEO**

Alvarez Kelly **1/2 1966** Offbeat western with Holden as the Mexican-Irish Kelly who has just sold a herd of cattle to the North during the Civil War. Confederate officer Widmark kidnaps Holden in an effort to have the cattle redirected to the South. Aided by the traditional women in the midst of men intent on double-crossing each other, a fierce hatred develops between the two, erupting into violence. Sleepy performance by Holden is countered by an intensive Widmark. Based on a true Civil War incident, the script occasionally wanders far afield with the cattle, who cleverly heighten the excitement by stampeding. **109m/C; VHS, DVD.** William Holden; Richard Widmark; Janice Rule; Patrick O'Neal; Harry Carey, Jr.; Victoria Shaw; Roger C. Carmel; Indus Arthur; ***D:*** Edward Dmytryk; ***W:*** Elliott Arnold; Franklin Coen; ***C:*** Joe MacDonald; ***M:*** Johnny Green.

Alvin and the Chipmunks ♂♂ 1/2 **2007 (PG)** Alvin, Simon, and Theodore (now digitally rendered) bring their chipmunk schtick into the twenty-first century, and mostly pull it off. Dave Seville (Lee) finds the trio in a muffin basket, quickly discovering their ability not only to speak, but to sing. Soon enough, a hustling promoter (Cross) takes their act on the road, where, sadly, the chipmunks fall victim to burn-out and must lip-sync the rest of their shows. (It ain't the '50s.) Lots of fun for nostalgic baby-boomers and kiddies alike; featuring techno and hip-hop remixes of the Chipmunks' classics. **92m/C; Blu-Ray, On Demand.** Jason Lee; David Cross; Cameron Richardson; Jane Lynch; ***V:*** Justin Long; Matthew Gray Gubler; Jesse McCartney; ***D:*** Tim Hill; ***W:*** Jon Vitti; Will McRobb; Chris Viscardi; ***C:*** Peter Lyons Collister; ***M:*** Christopher Lennertz.

Alvin and the Chipmunks: Chipwrecked ♂ 1/2 **2011 (G)** This third Chipmunks adventure is more of the silly same and modestly acceptable kiddy fare. The Chipmunks and Chipettes plus human minder Dave and nemesis Ian are onboard a cruise ship until they become 'chipwrecked' on an island thanks to Alvin's misbehavior. It's not as deserted as they thought since they find long-stranded treasure hunter Zoe (who's gone a little crazy). They practice some survival skills and then a volcano starts rumbling. **87m/C; DVD, Blu-Ray.** Jason Lee; Alyssa Milano; David Cross; Andy Buckley; ***V:*** Justin Long; Matthew Gray Gubler; Jesse McCartney; Amy Poehler; Anna Faris; Christina Applegate; ***D:*** Mike Mitchell; ***W:*** Jonathan Aibel; Glenn Berger; ***C:*** Thomas Ackerman.

Alvin and the Chipmunks: Road Chip ♂ *Alvin and the Chipmunks the Road Chip* **2015 (G)** The fourth film in this wretched franchise is also arguably its worst, revealing that the series is so completely bereft of idea that it's resorted to stealing them poorly from better films. The concept here isn't horrible: mimicking great road movies of the past, all the way back to the Crosby-Hope films, but this one has no rhythm or even a sense of humor. Alvin, Simon and Theodore take a road trip to Miami after they mistakenly think that Dave is going to propose to his girlfriend and leave them behind. The Hound recommends taking a detour. **86m/C; DVD, Blu-Ray.** Jason Lee; Justin Long; Matthew Gray Gubler; Jesse McCartney; Bella Thorne; Kimberly Williams; Tony Hale; Jennifer Coolidge; ***V:*** Christina Applegate; Kaley Cuoco; Anna Faris; ***D:*** Walt Becker; ***W:*** Randi Mayem Singer; Adam Sztykiel; ***C:*** Peter Lyons Collister; ***M:*** Mark Mothersbaugh.

Alvin and the Chipmunks: The Squeakuel ♂ 1/2 **2009 (PG)** The unruly rodent trio of Alvin, Simon, and Theodore are back! This time around, Dave Seville (Lee) is laid up in a French hospital (thanks to Alvin) and the boys are inevitably left in the care of Dave's lazy video-game playing cousin Toby (Levi). Former promoter Ian (Cross) is angry that the Chipmunks aren't his to manage anymore but soon comes across the female Chipettes—Eleanor, Jeanette, and Brittany—who he pits against the boys. Mayhem ensues with plenty of pop music mixes to entertain the kiddies though its weak and predictable plot makes it a far squeak from the original. **88m/C; Blu-Ray.** Jason Lee; Zachary Levi; David Cross; Bridgit Mendler; Wendie Malick; ***V:*** Justin Long; Matthew Gray Gubler; Jesse McCartney; Anna Faris; Christina Applegate; Amy Poehler; ***D:*** Betty Thomas; ***W:*** Jonathan Aibel; Glenn Berger; Ross Bagdasarian; Jon Vitti; ***C:*** Anthony B. Richmond; ***M:*** David Newman.

Always ♂♂♂ **1985 (R)** Jaglom fictionally documents his own divorce and reconciliation with Patrice Townsend: set in the director's home and starring his friends and family, the film provides comic insight into the dynamics of married/about-to-be-married/and used-to-be-married relationships. Set at a Fourth of July barbecue, this bittersweet romantic comedy is a veritable feast for Jaglom fans, but not everyone will find the director's free-form narrative to their taste. **105m/C; VHS, DVD.** Henry Jaglom; Patrice Townsend; Bob Rafelson; Melissa Leo; Andre Gregory; Michael Emil; Joanna Frank; Alan Rachins; Jonathan Kaufer; ***D:*** Henry Jaglom; ***W:*** Henry Jaglom; ***C:*** Hanania Baer.

Always ♂♂ 1/2 **1989 (PG)** A hotshot pilot (Dreyfuss) meets a fiery end and finds that his spirit is destined to become a guardian angel to the greenhorn fire-fighting flyboy (Johnson) who steals his girl's heart. Warm remake of "A Guy Named Joe," one of Spielberg's favorite movies. Sparks between Dreyfuss and Hunter eventually ignite, but Goodman delivers the most heat. Hepburn makes an appearance as the angel who guides Dreyfuss. An old-fashioned tree-burner romance that includes actual footage of the 1988 Yellowstone fire. **123m/C; VHS, DVD, Blu-Ray.** Holly Hunter; Richard Dreyfuss; John Goodman; Audrey Hepburn; Brad Johnson; Marg Helgenberger; Keith David; Roberts Blossom; Dale Dye; ***D:*** Steven Spielberg; ***W:*** Jerry Belson; ***C:*** Mikael Salomon; ***M:*** John Williams.

Always Be My Maybe ♂♂ 1/2 **2019 (PG-13)** Growing up in San Francisco, Sasha (Wong) and Marcus (Kim) were neighbors and friends. As teens, they lost their virginity to each other before a falling out. As adults, Sasha is a famous celebrity chef and engaged to restaurateur Brandon (Kim). When her wedding is delayed, she returns to San Francisco to open a new restaurant. After her fiance postpones their nuptials and asks to open their relationship, Marcus, still living at home and working in the family business, comes back into her life. Follows the expected rom-com formula but the lively cast more than makes up for that. And Keanu Reeves has a memorable appearance as himself. **101m/C; DVD.** Ali Wong; Randall Park; James Saito; Michelle Buteau; Keanu Reeves; ***D:*** Nahnatchka Khan; ***W:*** Ali Wong; Randall Park; Michael Golamco; ***C:*** Tim Suhrstedt.

Always Goodbye ♂♂ **1938** Typical '30s melodrama. Unmarried tough cookie Margot Weston (Stanwyck) gives up her baby for adoption to Phil Marshall (Hunter) and his wife. After becoming a successful businesswoman, Margot accidentally meets her son and learns his mother has died and his dad is getting remarried. Margot pushes her way into their lives, doesn't like Phil's fiance (Bari), and aims to break them up. **75m/B; DVD.** Barbara Stanwyck; Ian Hunter; Lynn Bari; Herbert Marshall; Cesar Romero; Binnie Barnes; ***D:*** Sidney Lanfield; ***W:*** Kathryn Scola; ***C:*** Robert Planck; ***M:*** Cyril Mockridge.

Always Outnumbered Always Outgunned ♂♂♂ **1998 (R)** Character study follows ex-con Socrates Fortlow (Fishburne in a dynamic performance). A convicted murderer, he's now trying to lead a non-violent life on the violent streets of L.A.'s Watts, maintain his dignity, and find a job. But none of this is easy. Adapted from the book by Mosley, who wrote the teleplay. **110m/C; VHS, DVD.** Laurence Fishburne; Bill Cobbs; Natalie Cole; Daniel Williams; Laurie Metcalf; Bill Nunn; Cicely Tyson; Isaiah Washington, IV; ***D:*** Michael Apted; ***W:*** Walter Mosley; ***C:*** John Bailey; ***M:*** Michael Franti. **CABLE**

Always Shine ♂♂♂ **2016** Mackenzie Davis and Caitlin FitzGerald give fantastic performances in this thriller/drama about identity, fame, jealousy, and the life of an actress. Beth (FitzGerald) is a performer just starting to get some success in indie films. Her good friend and fellow actress Anna (Davis) is joining her on a weekend getaway to Big Sur, but Anna is struggling, both in her career and possibly her sanity. Director Takal's film works best the less you know about it, but nothing is quite what it seems in this unique, challenging film. **85m/C; DVD, Blu-Ray.** Mackenzie Davis; Caitlin FitzGerald; Lawrence Michael Levine; Khan Baykal; Alexander Koch; ***D:*** Sophia Takal; ***W:*** Lawrence Michael Levine; ***C:*** Mark Schwartzbard; ***M:*** Michael Montes.

Always Will ♂♂ 1/2 **2006 (PG)** High-school senior Will discovers his elementary school's time capsule and it allows him to revisit his past and change decisions he now regrets. But his changes impact his present in unexpected ways and Will wonders if selfishness is the true problem and if he needs to accept his past and move on. **95m/C; DVD.** Andrew Baglini; John Schmidt; Mark Schroeder; Noelle Meixell; Bart Mallard; Jody Seymour; ***D:*** Michael Sammaciccia; ***W:*** Michael Sammaciccia; ***C:*** Michael Sammaciccia; ***M:*** Michael Aharon. **VIDEO**

Always Woodstock ♂♂ *There's Always Woodstock* **2015** A romantic comedy about finding yourself after seemingly losing it all. Though Catherine Brown (Miller) wanted to be a singer, she lives in New York City and works at a major label as a talent wrangler for a difficult singing star, Jody (Snow). Unexpectedly fired, Catherine goes home to find her finance Garret (Ritter) in a compromising situation with another woman. Making a major life change, she sells her engagement ring and moves back into her family home in Woodstock, New York. There, she throws herself into writing music and begins to find herself as a writer with local singing star Lee Ann (Sagal). Catherine also finds unexpected love with the town doctor, Noah (Wolk). **97m/C; DVD, Streaming, Download.** Allison Miller; James Wolk; Jason Ritter; Brittany Snow; Katey Sagal; ***D:*** Rita Merson; ***W:*** Rita Merson; ***C:*** Matthew Irving; ***M:*** Chris(topher) Westlake.

Amadeus ♂♂♂ 1/2 **1984 (PG)** Entertaining adaptation by Shaffer of his play about the intense rivalry between 18th century composers Antonio Salieri and Wolfgang Amadeus Mozart. Abraham's Salieri is a man who desires greatness but is tortured by envy and sorrow. His worst attacks of angst occur when he comes into contact with Hulce's Mozart, an immature, boorish genius who, despite his gifts, remains unaffected and delighted by the beauty he creates while irking the hell out of everyone around him. Terrific period piece filmed on location in Prague; excellent musical score, beautiful sets, nifty billowy costumes, and realistic American accents for the 18th century Europeans. **158m/C; VHS, DVD, Blu-Ray.** F. Murray Abraham; Tom Hulce; Elizabeth Berridge; Simon Callow; Roy Dotrice; Christine Ebersole; Jeffrey Jones; Kenny Baker; Cynthia Nixon; Vincent Schiavelli; ***D:*** Milos Forman; ***W:*** Peter Shaffer; ***C:*** Miroslav Ondricek; ***M:*** John Strauss. Oscars '84: Actor (Abraham), Adapt. Screenplay, Art Dir./Set Dec., Costume Des., Director (Forman), Film, Makeup, Sound; AFI '98: Top 100; Cesar '85: Foreign Film; Directors Guild '84: Director (Forman); Golden Globes '85: Actor--Drama (Abraham), Director (Forman), Film--Drama, Screenplay; L.A. Film Critics '84: Director (Forman), Film, Screenplay; Natl. Film Reg. '19.

Amanda Knox: Murder on Trail in Italy ♂ **2011** Lifetime usually does a better job with its true crime efforts, but this one is apparently pasted together from tabloid headlines. In 2007, Seattle exchange student Amanda Knox is accused by Italian authorities of murdering her British roommate Meredith Kercher, aided by her boyfriend and another male friend. The evidence is likely tainted and Prosecutor Mignini has been accused of misconduct but the trial goes on anyway. **92m/C; DVD.** Hayden Panettiere; Marcia Gay Harden; Vincent Riotta; Paolo Romio; Djirbi Kebe; Amanda Fernando Stevens; Clive Walton; ***D:*** Robert Dornhelm; ***W:*** Wendy Battles; ***M:*** Zack Ryan. **CABLE**

Amarcord ♂♂♂ 1/2 *I Remember* **1974 (R)** Semi-autobiographical Fellini fantasy which takes place in the village of Rimini, his birthplace. Focusing on the young Zanin's impressions of his town's colorful slices of life, Fellini takes aim at fascism, family life, and religion in 1930s Italy. Visually ripe, delivering a generous, occasionally uneven mix of satire, burlesque, drama, and tragicomedic lyricism. Considered by people in the know as one of Fellini's best films and the topic of meaningful discussions among art film students everywhere. **124m/C; VHS, DVD.** *IT* Magali Noel; Bruno Zanin; Pupella Maggio; Armando Brancia; ***D:*** Federico Fellini; ***W:*** Federico Fellini; Tonino Guerra; ***C:*** Giuseppe Rotunno; ***M:*** Nino Rota. Oscars '74: Foreign Film; N.Y. Film Critics '74: Director (Fellini), Film.

Amarilly of Clothesline Alley ♂♂ 1/2 **1918** Amarilly (Pickford) gets a job as a New York dance hall cigarette girl and is around to help wealthy slumming playboy Gordon Phillips (Kerry) after he gets into a fight. Phillips becomes convinced he loves Amarilly, despite her social inferiority, but Amarilly comes to realize she should stick with those that know her best, including neighborhood beau, Terry (Scott). **77m/B; Silent; VHS, DVD.** Mary Pickford; William Scott; Norman Kerry; Ida Waterman; Kate Price; Margaret Landis; ***D:*** Marshall Neilan; ***W:*** Frances Marion; ***C:*** Walter Stradling.

The Amateur ♂ 1/2 **1982 (R)** Computer technologist for the CIA dives into a plot of international intrigue behind the Iron Curtain when he investigates the death of his girlfriend, murdered by terrorists. Confused and ultimately disappointing spy drama cursed with a wooden script written by Littell, based on his novel. **112m/C; VHS, DVD.** John Savage; Christopher Plummer; Marthe Keller; Arthur Hill; Ed Lauter; ***D:*** Charles Jarrott; ***W:*** Robert Littell.

Amateur ♂♂♂ **1994 (R)** Former nun Huppert, trying to make a living writing pornography, hooks up with an amnesiac (Donovan) who turns out to have a criminal past and a porno actress wife (Lowensohn) who wants him dead. Blackmail plot has oddball characters racing through dark and evocative settings while unfolding a tale loaded with offbeat oppositions and an irresistibly bizarre romantic triangle. Lively and playful without becoming pretentious, Hartley's self-described "action thriller... with one flat tire" evokes his typical deadpan subtle style. **105m/C; VHS, DVD.** Isabelle Huppert; Martin Donovan; Elina Lowensohn; Damian Young; Chuck Montgomery; David Simonds; Pamela Stewart; Terry Alexander; ***D:*** Hal Hartley; ***W:*** Hal Hartley; ***C:*** Michael Spiller; ***M:*** Hal Hartley; Jeff Taylor.

Amateur Night ♂♂ **2016** A comedy about one man's indirect route to discovering he can handle fatherhood. Though Guy Carter (Biggs) was an award-winning graduate student of architecture, he has been out of school for a year. Guy has two things going for him: he is married to a beautiful woman, Anne (Mollen), and has a baby on the way. Out of desperation, Anne finds him a job as a driver on Craig's List. When Guy goes to the interview, he thinks it will be for food delivery but it actually is for driving around a group of female sex workers. During one wild night with these ladies, Guy proves to them and himself that he has the ability to be a responsible father and protector. **89m/C; DVD, Blu-Ray, Streaming.** Jason Biggs; Jenny Mollen; Janet Montgomery; Ashley Tisdale; Bria L. Murphy; ***D:*** Lisa Addario; Joe Syracuse; ***W:*** Lisa Addario; Joe Syracuse; ***C:*** Nicole Hirsch Whitaker; ***M:*** The Newton Brothers.

The Amazing Captain Nemo ♂ 1/2 *The Return of Captain Nemo* **1978** Captain Nemo (Ferrer) is awakened after a 100-year cryogenic freeze with the help of scientist Waldo Cunningham (Meredith) after Navy divers discover the Nautilus and take it to DC. Since Waldo is nuts, he decides to use Nemo and the Nautilus, threatening to destroy the capitol unless he gets a billion in gold. Originally broadcast as a three-part TV pilot from producer Irwin Allen and then recut for an international film release. **98m/C; DVD.** Jose Ferrer; Burgess Meredith; Mel Ferrer; Burr DeBenning; Horst Buchholz; Tom Hallick; Lynda Day George; ***D:*** Alex March; ***W:*** Robert Bloch; Robert C. Dennis; Norman Katkov; ***C:*** Lamar Boren; ***M:*** Richard LaSalle. **TV**

Amazing Dr. Clitterhouse ♂♂♂ **1938** Satirical gangster saga has criminologist Dr. Clitterhouse (Robinson) so fascinated by crime that he commits a few jewel robberies just to test out that bad guy rush. He contacts a fence, luscious Jo Keller (Trevor), who gets Clitterhouse an in with gangster Rocks Valentine (Bogart). Clitterhouse successfully masterminds some heists for Valentine—who becomes jealous of Clitterhouse's brain power and things just get more wacky from there (including a farcical trial). This is definitely Robinson's show. **87m/B; VHS, DVD.** Edward G. Robinson; Claire Trevor; Humphrey Bogart; Gale Page; Donald Crisp; Maxie "Slapsie" Rosenbloom; Thurston Hall; Allen Jenkins; John Litel; Henry O'Neill; Ward Bond; Curt Bois; ***D:*** Anatole Litvak; ***W:*** John Huston; John Wexley; ***C:*** Gaetano Antonio "Tony" Gaudio; ***M:*** Max Steiner.

Amazing Grace **1974** Some righteous mothers led by Moms Mabley go up against corrupt city politics in this extremely dated comedy that was cast with a sense of the absurd. **99m/C; VHS, DVD, Blu-Ray.** Moms (Jackie) Mabley; Slappy (Melvin) White; Moses Gunn; Rosalind Cash; Dolph Sweet; Butterfly McQueen; Stepin Fetchit; ***D:*** Stan Lathan; ***W:*** Matt Robinson; ***C:*** Edward R. Brown; Sol Negrin.

Amazing Grace **2006 (PG)** Sincere and forceful bio of evangelical Christian William Wilberforce (Gruffudd), a member of the House of Commons, who spent his years in the British Parliament introducing antislavery legislation. Tells the crusader's story with flashbacks, introducing both foes and friends, including former slave trader John Newton (Finney), who wrote the title hymn (rousingly sung by Gruffudd), as part of his atonement. Senegalese singer N'Dour makes his film debut as freed slave and author Oloudah Equiano. **111m/C; DVD.** *GB* Ioan Gruffudd; Romola Garai; Albert Finney; Michael Gambon; Rufus Sewell; Ciaran Hinds; Toby Jones; Nicholas Farrell; Sylvestria Le Touzel; Stephan Campbell Moore; Benedict Cumberbatch; Youssou N'Dour; ***D:*** Michael Apted; ***W:*** Steven Knight; ***C:*** Remi Adefarasin; ***M:*** David Arnold.

Amazing Grace **2019 (G)** Shot over two days in January 1972 in a Los Angeles Baptist church, this deeply moving concert film documents the recording of soul singer Aretha Franklin's best-selling, Grammy-winning gospel album Amazing Grace. The film captures Franklin at the height of her vocal powers and focuses on her other wordly singing and its effect on the audience. Also documenting the black Baptist church experience, Reverend James Cleveland acts as a master of ceremonies for the recording while the church choir, led by Alexander Hamilton, adds to the emotion that Franklin brings to each song. **87m/C; DVD.** Aretha Franklin; Rev. James Cleveland; ***D:*** Sydney Pollack; Alan Elliott.

Amazing Grace & Chuck **1987 (PG)** Perhaps the only anti-war/sports fantasy ever made. After a visit to a Minuteman missile site in Montana, 12-year-old Little Leaguer Chuck learns of the dangers of nuclear arms. He begins a protest by refusing to play until the nations come to a peace agreement. In a sudden surge of social conscience, athletes worldwide put down their equipment and join in droves, starting with pro-basketball star Amazing Grace Smith (Denver Nugget English). Capra-like fantasy has good intentions but ultimately lacks two key elements: coherency and plausibility. **115m/C; VHS, DVD.** Jamie Lee Curtis; Gregory Peck; William L. Petersen; Joshua Zuehlke; Alex English; ***D:*** Mike Newell; ***C:*** Robert Elswit; ***M:*** Elmer Bernstein.

The Amazing Howard Hughes ½ **1977** Reveals the full story of the legendary millionaire's life and career, from daring test pilot to inventor to Hollywood film producer to isolated wealthy paranoiac with a germ phobia. Lingers on the rich guy with big problems theme. Big-budget TV drama with a nice performance by Jones. **119m/C; VHS, DVD.** Tommy Lee Jones; Ed Flanders; James Hampton; Tovah Feldshuh; Lee Purcell; ***D:*** William A. Graham. **TV**

The Amazing Mrs. Holiday ½ **1943** Pleasant Durbin outing finds the star playing the daughter of missionaries working in China. Ruth accompanies a group of Chinese orphans aboard a ship bound for San Francisco, aided by steward Timothy (Fitzgerald). She wants the children to stay together, so Timothy passes Ruth off as the wife of a shipping magnate, who's been lost at sea. Ruth admits her deception to the man's grandson Tom (O'Brien) and convinces him that it's okay that she and the children stay in the family mansion. **98m/B; DVD.** Deanna Durbin; Edmond O'Brien; Barry Fitzgerald; Arthur Treacher; Harry Davenport; Grant Mitchell; Frieda Inescort; Elisabeth Risdon; ***D:*** Bruce Manning; ***W:*** Frank Ryan; John Jacoby; ***C:*** Elwood "Woody" Bredell; ***M:*** Frank Skinner; Hans J. Salter.

Amazing Mr. Blunden ½ **1972 (G)** Solid kidvid about two youngsters aided by a ghost who travel back in time to save the lives of two murdered children. Adapted by Jeffries from Antonia Barber's novel, "The Ghosts." **100m/C; VHS, DVD.** Laurence Naismith; Lynne Frederick; Garry Miller; Marc Granger; Rosalyn London; Diana Dors; ***D:*** Lionel Jeffries; ***M:*** Elmer Bernstein.

The Amazing Mr. X ½ *The Spiritualist* **1948** When a woman's husband dies, she tries to contact him via a spiritualist. Things are not as they seem however, and the medium may just be part of an intricate scheme to defraud the woman. **79m/B; VHS, DVD.** Turhan Bey; Lynn Bari; Cathy O'Donnell; Richard Carlson; Donald Curtis; Virginia Gregg; ***D:*** Bernard Vorhaus; ***W:*** Ian McLellan Hunter; Muriel Roy Boulton; ***C:*** John Alton.

The Amazing Panda Adventure ½ *Little Panda; The Amazing Panda Rescue* **1995 (PG)** Ryan (Slater) is off to China during his spring break to visit dad Michael (Lang), who's working on a project to rescue the dwindling panda population. But there's poacher trouble and Ryan and young translator Ling (Ding) decide to rescue the preserve's panda cub, which has been animal-napped (where's Ace Ventura when you need him). Family fare, with a mixture of totally adorable real and animatronic pandas; filmed in the Sichuan province of China, home to the Wolong Nature Reserve which is famous for its successful breeding of the endangered giant pandas. Slater, in his first starring role, is the younger brother of Christian. **84m/C; DVD.** Ryan Slater; Stephen Lang; Yi Ding; Wang Fei; ***D:*** Christopher Cain; ***W:*** Laurice Elehwany; Jeff Rothberg; ***C:*** Jack N. Green; ***M:*** William Ross.

The Amazing Spider-Man **2012 (PG-13)** The Marvel Comics franchise gets a fine (if a little long) 3D film reboot as awkward science nerd Peter Parker (Garfield) goes back to his high school outcast teen years, his crush on Gwen Stacy (Stone), and his family issues. Peter gets bitten by a spider at genetics research company Oscorp--where his dad's ex-partner, Dr. Curt Connors (Ifans) works. (Connors has a second identity as the villainous Lizard.) Spidey is perceived as a weirdo vigilante by Gwen's police captain dad (Leary). There's the usual big action sequences, including a rescue, and battling the destructive baddie. The end-credits give a peek at the inevitable sequel's villain. **136m/C; DVD, Blu-Ray.** Andrew Garfield; Rhys Ifans; Emma Stone; Martin Sheen; Sally Field; Denis Leary; Irrfan Khan; Chris Zylka; Campbell Scott; Embeth Davidtz; ***D:*** Marc Webb; ***W:*** James Vanderbilt; Alvin Sargent; Steve Kloves; ***C:*** John Schwartzman; ***M:*** James Horner.

The Amazing Spider-Man 2 **2014 (PG-13)** Peter Parker/Spider-man (Garfield) is back along with his girlfriend Gwen Stacy (Stone) and troubled friend Harry Osborn (DeHaan). Beleaguered Max Dillon (Foxx) suffers an accident at work that has electrifying consequences as he takes on his own alter ego, Electro. Besides this new threat, Spidey has to confront even more enemies--The Green Goblin, Rhino, and his own emotional drama. Some of the rapport between Garfield and Stone works (and Field steals the movie as Aunt May) but it's mostly too cluttered down with subplots and villains that it can't take flight. **142m/C; DVD, Blu-Ray.** Andrew Garfield; Emma Stone; Jamie Foxx; Dane DeHaan; Paul Giamatti; Colm Feore; Sally Field; Felicity Jones; ***D:*** Marc Webb; ***W:*** Alex Kurtzman; Roberto Orci; Jeff Pinkner; ***C:*** Dan(iel) Mindel; ***M:*** Hans Zimmer.

The Amazing Transplant **WOOF!** **1970** A sleaze-bag psycho has a "love enhancing" transplant, much to the pleasure of his sexual partners. Much to their and our dismay, however, he then kills them and bores us. **90m/C; VHS, DVD.** Juan Fernandez; Linda Southern; Larry Hunter; Kim Pope; ***D:*** Doris Wishman; ***W:*** Doris Wishman; ***C:*** C. Davis Smith.

Amazon Jail **1985** Scantily clad women go over the wall and promptly get caught by devil worshiping men in the jungle. They should have known better. Redeemed only by lingerie selection. **94m/C; VHS, DVD.** Elisabeth Hartmann; Mauricio Do Valle; Sondra Graffi; ***D:*** Oswald De Oliveira.

Amazon Women on the Moon *Cheeseburger Film Sandwich* **1987 (R)** A plotless, irreverent media spoof, depicting the programming of a slipshod TV station as it crams weird commercials and shorts around a comical '50s science fiction film. Inconsistent, occasionally funny anthology hangs together very loosely. Produced by Landis, with the usual amount of in-joke cameos and allusions to his other works of art. **85m/C; VHS, DVD.** Rosanna Arquette; Steve Guttenberg; Steve Allen; B.B. King; Michelle Pfeiffer; Arsenio Hall; Andrew Silverstein; Howard Hesseman; Lou Jacobi; Carrie Fisher; Griffin Dunne; Sybil Danning; Henny Youngman; Monique Gabrielle; Paul Bartel; Kelly Preston; Ralph Bellamy; Russ Meyer; Steve Forrest; Joey Travolta; Ed Begley, Jr.; Forrest J Ackerman; Archie Hahn; Phil Hartman; Peter Horton; Charlie Callas; T.K. Carter; Dick Miller; Roxie Roker; ***D:*** John Landis; Joe Dante; Carl Gottlieb; Robert Weiss; Peter Horton; ***W:*** Michael Barrie; Jim Mulholland; ***C:*** Daniel Pearl; ***M:*** Ira Newborn.

Amazons **1986 (R)** Tall, strong women who occasionally wander around nude search for a magical talisman that will overthrow an evil magician. **76m/C; VHS, DVD.** Mindi Miller; Penelope Reed; Joseph Whipp; Willie Nelson; Danitza Kingsley; ***D:*** Alex Sessa.

Amazons and Gladiators **2001 (R)** The title just says it all, doesn't it? Beautiful slave girl joins up with an Amazon queen and her band of warriors to fight an evil Roman governor. **89m/C; VHS, DVD.** *US GE* Jennifer Rubin; Patrick Bergin; Nichole Hiltz; Wendi Winburn; Melanie Gutteridge; Richard Norton; ***D:*** Zachary Weintraub; ***W:*** Zachary Weintraub; ***C:*** Thomas Hencz; ***M:*** Timothy S. (Tim) Jones. **VIDEO**

The Ambassador ½ *Peacemaker* **1984** An American ambassador (Mitchum) is sent to the Middle East to try to solve the area's deep political problems. He quickly becomes the target of terrorist attacks, and is blamed for the nation's unrest. To make matters worse, his wife is having an affair with a PLO leader. The President ignores him, forcing the ambassador to fend for himself. Talk about your bad days. Hudson's last feature. Based on Elmore Leonard's "52 Pickup," and remade a year later under its own title. **97m/C; VHS, DVD, Blu-Ray.** Robert Mitchum; Ellen Burstyn; Rock Hudson; Fabio Testi; Donald Pleasence; ***D:*** J. Lee Thompson.

The Ambassador ½ **2011** A dark comedy/documentary that uses humor as it exposes the business of selling diplomatic titles and the corruption found in third world countries. Mads Brugger, a filmmaker, journalist, and risk taker, assumes the persona of wealthy businessman who buys the title of Liberian ambassador to the Central African Republic. The film follows his exploits in the country, following him as he becomes involved in dangerous yet humorous situations.Through it all, Brugger reveals much about the blood diamond trade in Africa. **97m/C; DVD, Blu-Ray, Streaming, Download.** Mads Brügger; ***D:*** Mads Brügger; ***W:*** Mads Brügger; ***C:*** Johan Stahl Winthereik; ***M:*** Niklas Schak; Tin Soheili.

Ambassador Bill **1931** An Oklahoma rancher is appointed ambassador to a country in revolt. Rogers, of course, saves the day with his rustic witticisms. Based on the story "Ambassador from the United States" by Vincent Sheean. **68m/B; VHS, DVD.** Will Rogers; Marguerite Churchill; Greta Nissen; Ray Milland; Tad Alexander; Gustav von Seyffertitz; ***D:*** Sam Taylor.

The Ambassador's Daughter **1956** The Parisian adventures of an American ambassador's daughter De Havilland and soldier Forsythe, who, unaware of her position, falls in love with her. Faltering comedy is supported by an expert cast (although nearly 40, De Havilland is charming as the young woman) with especially good performances from Menjou and Loy. **102m/C; VHS, DVD.** Olivia de Havilland; John Forsythe; Myrna Loy; Adolphe Menjou; Edward Arnold; Francis Lederer; Tommy Noonan; Minor Watson; ***D:*** Norman Krasna; ***W:*** Norman Krasna.

The Ambulance ½ **1990 (R)** A New York cartoonist witnesses a mysterious ambulance at work and decides to investigate. His probings uncover a plot to sell the bodies of dying diabetics. A surprisingly good no-money feature from low-budget king Cohen. Includes an appearance by Marvel Comics' Stan Lee as himself. **95m/C; VHS, DVD, Blu-Ray.** Eric Roberts; James Earl Jones; Megan Gallagher; Richard Bright; Janine Turner; Eric Braeden; Red Buttons; Laurene Landon; Jill Gatsby; Nick (Nicholas) Chinlund; James Dixon; Stan Lee; ***D:*** Larry Cohen; ***W:*** Larry Cohen; ***C:*** Jacques Haitkin; ***M:*** Jay Chattaway.

Ambush **1950** Director Sam Wood's last film is a tough, lean western. Civilian scout Ward Kinsman is asked by Major Breverty to find Mary Carlyle, who was taken in an Apache raid. Ward refuses until Mary's beautiful sister Ann pleads and then insists on coming along. Ward learns where Mary is being held and reports her whereabouts to Capt. Lorrison who prepares to attack. First he and Ward have to settle their jealousy issues since both have fallen for Ann. **89m/B; DVD.** Robert Taylor; Arlene Dahl; John Hodiak; Leon Ames; Charles Stevens; Don Taylor; Jean Hagen; Bruce Cowling; Chief Thundercloud; John McIntire; Marta Mitrovich; ***D:*** Sam Wood; ***W:*** Marguerite Roberts; ***C:*** Harold Lipstein; ***M:*** Rudolph Kopp.

Ambush *Rukajarven Tie* **1999** Young lieutenant Eero is serving in the Finnish Army in 1941 pursuing Russian troops along the border. During his mission, Eero is able to briefly spend some time with his lovely fiancee Irina but must soon leave to go on a recon. He receives word that Irina has been killed by Russian soldiers and seeks revenge on any Russians he finds—turning from innocent soldier to dehumanized killer. Co-writer Tuuri adapted from his novel. Finnish with subtitles. **117m/C; VHS, DVD.** *FI* Peter Franzen; Irina Bjorklund; Kari Vaananen; Kari Heiskanen; Taisto Reimalvoto; ***D:*** Olli Saarela; ***W:*** Olli Saarela; Antti Tuuri; ***C:*** Kjell Lagerros; ***M:*** Tuomas Kantelinen.

Ambush at Tomahawk Gap **1953** Three released prisoners go in search of hidden loot and tempers rise when the goods don't turn up. Then the Apaches show up. **73m/C; DVD.** John Hodiak; John Derek; David Brian; Maria Elena Marques; Ray Teal; ***D:*** Fred F. Sears.

The Ambush Murders ½ **1982** True story of a stalwart white attorney defending a black activist accused of killing two cops. Not the compelling TV drama it could be, but still enjoyable. From Ben Bradlee Jr.'s novel. **100m/C; VHS, Streaming.** James Brolin; Dorian Harewood; Alfre Woodard; Louis Giambalvo; John McLiam; Teddy Wilson; Antonio Fargas; Amy Madigan; ***D:*** Steven Hilliard Stern. **TV**

Ambushed ½ *Rush* **2013 (R)** A couple of low-level L.A. coke dealers get in big trouble with their mobster boss and their antics bring in the DEA, including an undercover agent, as well as a crooked LAPD officer. The big action names (Lundgren, Jones, Couture) actually have supporting roles and leads Capaldi and Bonjour aren't nearly as interesting amidst the clichés. **96m/C; DVD, Blu-Ray.** Gianni Capaldi; Daniel Bonjour; Dolph Lundgren; Vinnie Jones; Randy Couture; Carly Pope; Cinthya Carmona; ***D:*** Giorgio Serafini; ***W:*** Augustin; ***C:*** Marco Cappetta. **VIDEO**

The Ambushers **WOOF!** **1967** Martin's third Matt Helm farce finds him handling a puzzling case involving the first United States spacecraft. When the craft is hijacked with Rule on board, it's Matt to the rescue, regaining control before unfriendly forces can take it back to Earth. Tired formula seems to have worn Martin out while the remainder of the cast goes to camp. Followed by "The Wrecking Crew." **102m/C; VHS, DVD.** Dean Martin; Janice Rule; James Gregory; Albert Salmi; Senta Berger; Kurt Kasznar; Beverly Adams; ***D:*** Henry Levin; ***W:*** Herbert Baker; ***C:*** Burnett Guffey; Edward Colman; ***M:*** Hugo Montenegro.

Amelia ½ **2009 (PG)** Good-looking, if old-fashioned, biography of famed celebrity aviatrix Amelia Earhart based on Susan Butler's "East to the Dawn" and Elgin Long's "Amelia Earhart: The Mystery Solved." Director Nair highlights the wonder (and danger) of flying in the 1920s and 30s through Swank's sparkling lead performance and how the adventuresome Amelia dealt with worldwide fame as well as her unconventional marriage to New York publisher George Putnam (Gere). **111m/C; DVD, Blu-Ray, On Demand.** Hilary Swank; Richard Gere; Ewan

McGregor; Christopher Eccleston; Mia Wasikowska; *D:* Mira Nair; *W:* Ronald Bass; Anna Hamilton Phelan; *C:* Stuart Dryburgh; *M:* Gabriel Yared.

Amelia Earhart: The Final Flight 1/2 **1994** Investigates the mysterious disappearance of pioneering aviatrix Amelia Earhart's 1937 flight to become the first pilot to circumnavigate the globe. Earhart (Keaton) and her navigator Fred Noonan (Hauer) disappeared over the Pacific Ocean and their fate has never been determined. Dern plays Earhart's husband, publisher George B. Putnam, who served as Amelia's manager and publicist. Based on the biography by Doris L. Rich. **95m/C; DVD.** Diane Keaton; Rutger Hauer; Bruce Dern; Paul Guilfoyle; Denis Arndt; David Carpenter; Diana Bellamy; *D:* Yves Simoneau; *W:* Anna Sandor; *C:* Lauro Escorel; *M:* George S. Clinton. **TV**

Amelie 1/2 *Amelie from Montmartre; The Fabulous Destiny of Amelie Poulain; Le Fabuleux Destin d'Amelie Poulain* **2001 (R)** Paris waitress Amelie (Tautou) has led a solitary, but not wholly unpleasant, existence. When she finds a box of childhood treasures behind a wall in her apartment, she sets out to return them to their original owner. Accomplishing this, she begins to secretly intervene in the lives of neighbors and coworkers, helping some find romance, others retribution for past wrongs. When her "missions" bring her into contact with a quirky local (Kassovitz), she begins a roundabout courtship involving a treasure hunt instead of approaching him directly. Director Jeunet leaves intact his stunning, and very stylized visual talents, but marshals them in service of a fresh, lighthearted comedy, in contrast to his previous, downcast work. Tautout has no problem carrying the movie and has the look of a budding major star. **120m/C; VHS, DVD, Blu-Ray.** *FR GE* Audrey Tautou; Mathieu Kassovitz; Rufus; Yolande Moreau; Dominique Pinon; Maurice Benichou; Artus de Penguern; Urbain Cancellier; Isabelle Nanty; Claire Maurier; Claude Perron; Clothilde Mollet; Serge Merlin; Jamel Debbouze; Flora Guiet; *Nar:* Andre Dussollier; *D:* Jean-Pierre Jeunet; *W:* Jean-Pierre Jeunet; Guillaume Laurant; *C:* Bruno Delbonnel; *M:* Yann Tiersen. British Acad. '01: Orig. Screenplay; Cesar '01: Art Dir./Set Dec., Director (Jeunet), Film, Score; Broadcast Film Critics '01: Foreign Film.

Amen **2002 (R)** Costa-Gavras dramatizes a Holocaust story with a somewhat heavy hand. SS. Lt. Kurt Gerstein (Tukur) is a chemist who uses prussic acid Zyklon B for fumigating camp barracks. Sent to a Polish concentration camp, he witnesses the deaths of Jewish prisoners by the gas. Appalled, Gerstein rishes reprisals by informing various church leaders, although no one is willing to speak out until he reaches the young Italian priest, Father Riccardo Fontana (Kassovitz), who has family ties to Pope Pius XII (Ιures). As head of the the Hygiene Institute, the SS expects Gerstein to continue to eliminate vermin of all kinds while Father Fontana heads to the Vatican in the hopes of getting the Pope to expose the genocide. An adaptation of Rolf Hochhuth's 1963 play, "The Deputy." **130m/C; DVD, Blu-Ray.** *FR* Ulrich Tukur; Mathieu Kassovitz; Marcel Iures; Ulrich Muhe; Michel Duchaussoy; Ion Caramitru; *D:* Constantin Costa-Gavras; *W:* Constantin Costa-Gavras; Jean-Claude Grumberg; *C:* Patrick Blossier; *M:* Armand Amar.

America 1/2 **1924** Young patriot Nathan Holden (Hamilton) is torn between his political beliefs and his love for the daughter of a Virignia Tory (Dempster). Meanwhile, evil redcoat Captain Butler (Barrymore) and his band of murderous Mohawks ruthlessly attack the colonists. **141m/B; Silent; VHS, DVD.** Neil Hamilton; Carol Dempster; Lionel Barrymore; Erville Alderson; Charles Bennett; Arthur Donaldson; Charles Emmet Mack; Frank McGlynn; Henry O'Neill; Ed Roseman; Harry Semels; Louis Wolheim; Hugh Baird; Lee Beggs; Downing Clarke; Sydney Deane; Arthur Dewey; Michael Donavan; Paul Doucet; John Dunton; Riley Hatch; Emil Hoch; Edwin Holland; W.W. Jones; William S. Rising; Frank Walsh; *D:* D.W. Griffith; *W:* Robert W. Chambers; *C:* Marcel Le Picard; Hendrik Sartov; Billy (G.W.) Bitzer.

America 1/2 **2009** Outstanding performance by newcomer Philip Johnson in the title role highlights this message movie that's based on the novel by E.R. Frank. Therapist Dr. Marie Brennan (O'Donnell) tries to help sullen 17-year-old America (Johnson), who's caught up in the overburdened foster care system. Flashbacks detail some of the abuse he's suffered while in the present America struggles to adjust to a group home. **90m/C; DVD.** Rosie O'Donnell; Phil Johnson; Raquel Castro; Timothy Edward Rhoze; Jade Yorker; Ruby Dee; *D:* Yves Simoneau; *W:* Joyce Eliason; *C:* John Aronson; *M:* Normand Corbeil. **TV**

America America 1/2 **1963** Overlong and slow-moving, but very personal, immigrant drama that Kazan adapted from his own book and based on his uncle's life. In 1896, young Stavros is sent by his family from Anatolia, Turkey--where the Greeks are an oppressed minority--to Constantinople. After various tribulations, Stavros decides to realize his own dream and emigrate to America but his idealism soon gives way to a frequently harsh reality. **177m/B; DVD.** Stathis Giallelis; Harry Davis; Elena Karam; Frank Wolff; Estelle Hemsley; Lou Antonio; John Marley; *D:* Elia Kazan; *W:* Elia Kazan; *C:* Haskell Wexler; *M:* Manos Hadjidakis. Oscars '63: Art Dir./Set Dec., B&W.

America: Imagine the World Without Her **2014 (PG-13)** Director/writer D'Souza continues his efforts to proclaim Barack Obama the "Worst President in U.S. History." The film purports to set up a vision of a "what if" world in which George Washington was killed and America never came into existence, but quickly becomes a political screed against the man that D'Souza believes is threatening the existence of the country in 2014, with a few shots at 2016's likely nominee, Hillary Clinton, for good measure. Ignoring the fear-mongering and lack of fact-checking, D'Souza's film is just poorly made on every level. **105m/C; DVD, Blu-Ray.** *Nar:* Dinesh D'Souza; *D:* Dinesh D'Souza; John Sullivan; *W:* Dinesh D'Souza; John Sullivan; Bruce Schooley; *C:* Benjamin Huddleston; *M:* Bryan Miller.

America So Beautiful 1/2 **2001** Set in Los Angeles in 1979 as the Iranian hostage crisis is taking place, it centers on Iranian immigrants attempting to make their own way in the United States and achieve their version of the American dream. Houshang (Manour) wants to become a partner in a disco to reach this goal, but lacks the funds. Trying to convince his family to invest, he takes them to disco for an evening in which the revelations occur and lives are transformed. Issues like identy, culture, and forbidden love are explored in unexpected ways. **91m/C; DVD, Download.** Shohreh Aghdashloo; Mansour; David Diaan; Diane Gaidry; Houshang Touzie; *D:* Babak Shokrian; *W:* Babak Shokrian; Brian Horiuchi; *C:* Tom Ryan; *M:* Ramin Torkian. **VIDEO**

The American **2001** Heavy-handed adaptation of Henry James's 1877 novel. Christopher Newman (Modine) makes a fortune in California and heads to Paris in the 1870s where he hopes to acquire both culture and a wife. He meets mysterious widow Claire de Cintre (Sullivan) but his proposal is rejected by her snobby aristocratic family, which is headed by Claire's imperious mother, Madame de Bellegarde (Rigg). Then Newman learns a family secret that could win him Claire's hand. **90m/C; VHS, DVD.** Matthew Modine; Aisling O'Sullivan; Diana Rigg; Brenda Fricker; Andrew Scott; Eva Birthistle; *D:* Paul Unwin; *W:* Michael Hastings. **TV**

The American **2010 (R)** A cold-blooded weapons-making assassin goes soft in this adaptation of the Martin Booth novel "A Very Private Gentleman." Knowing he's being hunted, Jack (Clooney) hides out in the Italian countryside. His lone wolf instincts are changed when he indulges the interest of Father Benedetto (Bonacelli) and moves from a client relationship with hooker Clara (Placido) to something more emotional. Neither situation is very believable but Clooney can certainly sell the cool. **105m/C; Blu-Ray.** *US GB* George Clooney; Paolo Bonacelli; Bruce Altman; Violante Placido; Thekla Reuten; Johan Leysen; *D:* Anton Corbijn; *W:* Rowan Joffe; *C:* Martin Ruhe; *M:* Herbert Gronemeyer.

American Adobo 1/2 **2002 (R)** An adobo is the Philippines' national dish, a savory concoction that must marinate to bring its flavors together. As it does five Filipino-American long-time friends around a dinner table in Queens. They are all doing well professionally but their personal lives could definitely use work. **99m/C; VHS, DVD.** Dina Bonnevie; Randy Becker; Cherry Pie Picache; Sol Ocoa; Christopher De Leon; Susan Valdez-LeGoff; Ricky Davao; Wayne Maugans; Paolo Montalban; Gloria Romero; *D:* Laurice Guillen; *W:* Vincent R. Nebrida; *C:* Lee Meily.

An American Affair 1/2 **1999** Washington, D.C., District Attorney Sam Brady (Bernsen) marries Genevieve (D'Abo) even though he's having an affair with her best friend, Barbara (Heitmeyer). But after Genevieve is murdered, her ghost begins to haunt him. And to make things more complicated, a senator seems to have it in for Sam. The two plotlines take too long to intersect, so the story never makes much sense. **90m/C; VHS, DVD.** *CA* Corbin Bernsen; Maryam D'Abo; Jayne Heitmeyer; Robert Vaughn; *D:* Sebastian Shah. **VIDEO**

An American Affair 1/2 **2009 (R)** In 1963, 13-year-old Adam (Bright), suffering from raging teen hormones, takes to peeping on his beautiful new Washington, DC neighbor Catherine (Mol), even working odd jobs in order to be near her. She's got lots of problems, including over-indulging in drugs and alcohol. Catherine, a divorced socialite artist, is also having an affair with the President and is a pawn for the CIA. Mol gives off that Marilyn Monroe vibe but the story is probably drawn from a tryst JFK had with a Washington socialite who was later murdered. **93m/C; DVD.** Gretchen Mol; Cameron Bright; Perrey Reeves; Noah Wyle; James Rebhorn; Mark Pellegrino; Kris Arnold; *D:* William Sten Olsson; *W:* Alex Metcalf; *C:* David Insley; *M:* Dustin O'Halloran.

American Animals **2018 (R)** The true story of four bored college freshmen who attempt a heist of their school's rare book collection. By the time they realize that they're dangerously out of their depth, their plan's taken a dramatic life of its own. Writer-director Layton delivers a caper thriller so smart and mesmerizing that it has an almost documentary feel. **76m/C; DVD, Blu-Ray.** Evan Peters; Barry Keoghan; Blake Jenner; Jared Abrahamson; Ann Dowd; *D:* Bart Layton; *W:* Bart Layton; *C:* Ole Bratt Birkeland; *M:* Anne Nikitin.

American Anthem **1986 (PG-13)** A young gymnast must choose between family responsibilities or the parallel bars. Olympic gymnast Gaylord makes his movie debut but doesn't get the gold. Good fare for young tumblers, but that's about it. Followed by two of the films' music videos and tape-ads featuring Max Headroom. **100m/C; VHS, DVD.** Mitch Gaylord; Janet Jones; Michelle Phillips; Michael Pataki; *D:* Albert Magnoli; *W:* Evan P. Archerd; Jeff Benjamin; *M:* Alan Silvestri.

American Assassin **2017 (R)** A flick that's as generic as its title. After terrorists kill his girlfriend, a revenge-bound Mitch Rapp (O'Brien) is recruited by the CIA, and teams up with his mentor Stan Hurley (Keaton) to bring down the mysterious bad guy behind seemingly random attacks around the world. Requisite car chases, shoot outs, and hand-to-hand bouts are there, but if this film (based on the Mitch Rapp series of novels by Vince Flynn) is aiming to launch the next Bourne, it misses the mark. **112m/C; DVD, Blu-Ray.** Dylan O'Brien; Michael Keaton; Sanaa Lathan; Taylor Kitsch; Shiva Negar; *D:* Michael Cuesta; *W:* Stephen Schiff; Michael Finch; Edward Zwick; Marshall Herskovitz; *C:* Enrique Chediak; *M:* Steven Price.

American Bandits: Frank and Jesse James 1/2 **2010 (PG)** Falls into the category of poorly acted, unexciting westerns. After Jesse (Stults) is shot, brother Frank (Abell) splits up the gang, planning to meet up again in four days. However, U.S. Marshal Kane (Fonda) is in pursuit and someone in the gang isn't loyal so a showdown is looming. **86m/C; DVD.** George Stults; Tim Abell; Peter Fonda; Jeffrey Combs; Anthony Tyler Quinn; Michael Gaglio; *D:* Fred Olen Ray; *W:* Fred Olen Ray; *C:* Theo Angell; *M:* Jason Solowsky. **VIDEO**

American Beauty 1/2 **1999 (R)** Lester Burnham (Spacey) is dead. This isn't any shock—Lester tells you this himself in his opening narration. It's the time leading up to his death Lester wants to remember. Lester is a middle-aged drone with a brittle, status-conscious wife, Carolyn (Bening), and a sullen teenaged daughter, Jane (Birch). Lester's world is rocked when he meets Jane's Lolita-like friend, Angela (Suvari), and his fantasies find him quitting his job, pumping iron, and smoking dope with Ricky (Bentley), the voyeuristic kid next door who has a thing for videotaping Jane. It's a suburban nightmare writ large with an excellent cast and some unexpected twists. **118m/C; VHS, DVD, Blu-Ray.** Kevin Spacey; Annette Bening; Mena Suvari; Thora Birch; Wes Bentley; Peter Gallagher; Chris Cooper; Allison Janney; Scott Bakula; Sam Robards; *D:* Sam Mendes; *W:* Alan Ball; *C:* Conrad L. Hall; *M:* Thomas Newman. Oscars '99: Actor (Spacey), Cinematog., Director (Mendes), Film, Orig. Screenplay; British Acad. '99: Actor (Spacey), Actress (Bening), Cinematog., Film, Film Editing, Score; Directors Guild '99: Director (Mendes); Golden Globes '00: Director (Mendes), Film--Drama, Screenplay; L.A. Film Critics '99: Director (Mendes); Natl. Bd. of Review '99: Film; Screen Actors Guild '99: Actor (Spacey), Actress (Bening), Cast; Writers Guild '99: Orig. Screenplay; Broadcast Film Critics '99: Director (Mendes), Film, Orig. Screenplay.

American Born 1/2 **1989** Murder Inc. returns to the dismay of one idealist who embarks on a battle he doesn't intend to lose. The mob had better look out. **90m/C; VHS, DVD, Streaming.** Joey Travolta; Andrew Zeller; *D:* Raymond Martino; *W:* Raymond Martino.

American Buffalo 1/2 **1995 (R)** Somewhat lackluster but decent screen adaptation of a classic American drama. Franz's junk shop owner Donny plans to steal back a rare Buffalo-head nickel that he feels he was swindled out of, with the help of his protege Bobby (Nelson). Hoffman's ferret-like Teach, one of Donny's card-playing buddies and an arrogant opportunist, tries to weasel in on the plan that never comes to fruition. Set in Corrente's hometown of Pawtucket, the director's reverence for the material is obvious and he plays it too safe. Top-notch performances raise the level. Mamet adapts his play for the screen. **88m/C; VHS, DVD, Blu-Ray.** Dustin Hoffman; Dennis Franz; Sean Nelson; *D:* Michael Corrente; *W:* David Mamet; *C:* Richard Crudo; *M:* Thomas Newman.

An American Carol WOOF! **2008 (PG-13)** An anti-American filmmaker named Michael Malone (Farley)--a shameless parody of real-life documentarian Michael Moore, down to the ubiquitous baseball cap—is out to abolish the 4th of July holiday when he is visited by three ghostly historic figures who try to get him to appreciate his country ala "A Christmas Carol." An overtly biased skewering of supposedly "liberal" politics and ideologies is ultimately a smear campaign masquerading as entertainment—and it's not even funny. Kevin Farley is the brother of the late Chris Farley. **84m/C; Blu-Ray, On Demand.** Kevin Farley; Kelsey Grammer; Jon Voight; Robert Davi; Chriss Anglin; Leslie Nielsen; Gail O'Grady; Trace Adkins; *D:* David Zucker; *W:* David Zucker; Lewis Freidman; Myrna Sokoloff; *C:* Brian Baugh; *M:* James L. Venable.

American Chai **2001 (R)** Indian-American college student Sureel is caught between pleasing his traditional parents, who think he's studying pre-med, and his own desires to be a professional musician. He meets another first generation student, the beautiful Maya, who's equally determined to pursue her career as a dancer. Now Sureel has to find the correct fusion in his personal life that he strives for in his music--a harmonious blending of East and West. **92m/C; DVD.** Aalok Mehta; Paresh Rawal; Sheetal Sheth; Josh Ackerman; Ajay Naidu; Aasif Mandvi; Bharati Desai; Jamie Hurley; Anand Chulani; Reena Shah; *D:* Anurag Mehta; *W:* Anurag Mehta; *C:* John Matkowsky; *M:* Aalok Mehta; Jack Bowden Faulkner.

American Chinatown 1/2 **1996** Orphaned tough guy is taken in by a powerful Chinatown mob family but gets into trouble when he falls for the head man's sister. He has a chance to redeem himself when he learns about a plot to overthrow the triad clan but will he take it? **90m/C; VHS, DVD.** Henry Lee; Robert Z'Dar; Liat Goodson; *D:* Richard W. Park.

An American Christmas Carol **1979** Charles Dickens' classic story is retold with limited charm in a TV effort. This time a greedy American financier (Winkler) learns about the true meaning of Christmas. **98m/C; VHS, DVD, Blu-Ray.** Henry Winkler; David Wayne; Dorian Harewood; ***D:*** Eric Till; ***M:*** Hagood Hardy. **TV**

American Commandos *Hitman* **1984 (R)** An ex-Green Beret slaughters the junkies who killed his son and raped his wife, and then joins his old buddies for a secret, Rambo-esque mission in Vietnam providing a tired rehash of Vietnam movie cliches. **96m/C; VHS, DVD.** Chris Mitchum; John Phillip Law; Franco Guerrero; ***D:*** Bobby Suarez.

American Cousins 1/2 **2002** New Jersey gangsters Gino and Settimo Bazaglia get into trouble with the Ukrainian mob while in Europe and are instructed to lay low in Glasgow with their distant cousin Roberto. Roberto is a mild-mannered, stamp-collecting fish & chips shop proprietor, who is clueless about his American cousins' true business. But they decide to repay his hospitality by helping Roberto out with some local thugs who are trying to muscle in on his business. Light-hearted culture clash comedy. **89m/C; DVD.** *GB* Danny Nucci; Dan Hedaya; Shirley Henderson; Vincent Pastore; Gerald Lepkowski; Russell Hunter; Stevan Rimkus; ***D:*** Donald Coutts; ***W:*** Sergio Casci; ***C:*** Jerry Kelly; ***M:*** Don Shaw.

American Cowslip 1/2 **2009 (R)** Overly quirky indie. Agoraphobic heroin addict Ethan lives in a remote California desert town. He's obsessed with his garden and is determined to win first prize in a gardening contest by growing a rare American cowslip. **107m/C; DVD.** Diane Ladd; Cloris Leachman; Lin Shaye; Rip Torn; Hanna Hall; Bruce Dern; Val Kilmer; Peter Falk; Priscilla Barnes; Ronnie Gene Blevins; ***D:*** Mark David; ***W:*** Mark David; Ronnie Gene Blevins; ***C:*** Mark David; ***M:*** Joseph Blaustein.

American Crime 1/2 **2004 (R)** A reporter disappears while researching a serial killer who films his victims, and her colleagues waste no time running to her aid in the tradition of amateur would-be cops everywhere. **92m/C; DVD.** Cary Elwes; Kip Pardue; Annabella Sciorra; Rachael Leigh Cook; ***D:*** Dan Mintz; ***W:*** Jeff Ritchie; ***C:*** Dan Mintz; ***M:*** Kurt Oldman. **VIDEO**

An American Crime **2007 (R)** A cringing, sordid true crime story set in 1965 in Indianapolis. Sylvia (Page) and her younger sister Jennie (McFarland) are left by their carny parents in the paid care of single mother Gertrude (Keener), who already has seven kids. Gert needs the money but she's soon over the edge (although booze and drugs help). Soon, the crazy sadist accuses Sylvia of all sorts of crimes and locks her in the basement. Then the real abuse starts until things end tragically with a trial. **92m/C; DVD.** Catherine Keener; Ellen Page; James Franco; Bradley Whitford; Ari Gaynor; Nick Searcy; Michael O'Keefe; Romy Rosemont; Hayley McFarland; ***D:*** Tommy O'Haver; ***W:*** Tommy O'Haver; Irene Turner; ***C:*** Byron Shah; ***M:*** Alan Ari Lazar. **CABLE**

American Crude **2007 (R)** That would be crude as in unfunny sex comedy and not as in oil production. Johnny (Livingston) is married to Jane (Watros) and they are both throwing separate engagement parties for their friends Bill (Schneider) and Olivia (Detmer) on the same night. There's also a bunch of other characters, including an amateur porn maker, a ho, and a runaway teen, and of course their stories will converge but you won't care in the slightest. **98m/C; DVD.** Ron Livingston; Cynthia Watros; Rob Schneider; Amanda Detmer; Jennifer Esposito; Michael Clarke Duncan; Missi Pyle; Raymond J. Barry; Sarah Foret; Nancy Marlow; ***D:*** Craig Sheffer; ***W:*** Craig Sheffer; ***C:*** James Mathers; ***M:*** Dennis Hamlin.

American Cyborg: Steel Warrior 1/2 **1994 (R)** Basic evil-machine-bent-on-mankind's-destruction movie—with a hero bent on rescuing the world. **95m/C; VHS, Streaming.** Joe Lara; John P. Ryan; ***D:*** Boaz Davidson; ***W:*** Bill Crounse.

American Dharma 1/2 **2018 (R)** A documentary look at Steve Bannon, a filmmaker and right-wing ideologue who briefly served as President Donald Trump's chief strategist. In the film, Bannon explains the history of his political evolution and current state of his political philosophy. After finding a foreign-made uniform at West Point, he developed a hard-line ideology that emphasizes strength and seeks a radical overhaul of the American system. Bannon then created documentaries and worked with Breitbart News before joining the White House. Though other documentaries about controversial figures by Morris involve informative scrutinization, the documentary about Bannon is less challenging and a more superficial, fan-like portrayal. **95m/C; DVD.** Steve Bannon; ***D:*** Errol Morris; ***C:*** Igor Martinovic; ***M:*** Paul Leonard-Morgan.

An American Dream 1/2 **1966** Stephen Rojack (Whitman) says his wife Deborah (Parker) committed suicide but the cops think it's murder and he's the prime suspect. Because the ruthless TV talk show host has been targeting police corruption, they may be prejudiced so Stephen turns to ex-flame Cherry (Leigh) for help. But you know what they say about a woman scorned. Adapted from the Norman Mailer bestseller. **103m/C; DVD.** Stuart Whitman; Janet Leigh; Eleanor Parker; Barry Sullivan; Lloyd Nolan; Murray Hamilton; J.D. Cannon; George Takei; ***D:*** Robert Gist; ***W:*** Mann Rubin; ***C:*** Sam Leavitt; ***M:*** Johnny Mandel.

American Dream **1990** Kopple's account of the Hormel labor strike, which devastated the small company town of Austin, Minnesota in the 1980s, makes a compelling documentary of big business versus worker demands. A mixture of interviews with major participants and location footage of the strikers and their families focuses also on the dispute between the local meatpackers and their parent union's lack of support and on the ultimately futile efforts of the union organizers. **100m/C; VHS, DVD.** ***D:*** Barbara Kopple; ***C:*** Phil Parmet. Oscars '90: Feature Doc.; Natl. Soc. Film Critics '92: Feature Doc.; Sundance '91: Aud. Award, Grand Jury Prize.

American Dreamer **1984 (PG)** A housewife wins a trip to Paris as a prize from a mystery writing contest. Silly from a blow on the head, she begins living the fictional life of her favorite literary adventure. Sporadic comedy with a good cast wandering about courtesy of a clumsy screenplay. **105m/C; VHS, DVD, Blu-Ray.** JoBeth Williams; Tom Conti; Giancarlo Giannini; Coral Browne; James Staley; ***D:*** Rick Rosenthal; ***M:*** Lewis Furey.

American Dreamz **2006 (PG-13)** Weitz's obvious satire has self-loathing, smarmy Brit Martin Tweed (Grant) hosting the universally popular reality show of the title. This latest version will be highlighted by the appearance of dim-witted, affable American President Staton (Quaid) as a guest judge. He has the time because the country is actually being run by his power-hungry chief of staff (Dafoe). Vying for celebrity status are small-town blonde Sally Kendoo (Moore), who hides her unholy ambitions behind a girl-next-door smile, and Omer (Golzari), a showtune-loving Iraqi who has been chosen as a suicide bomber. Grant and Moore fare best as conniving players who recognize and respect the dark streak in each other. **107m/C; DVD, Blu-Ray.** Hugh Grant; Dennis Quaid; Mandy Moore; Willem Dafoe; Chris Klein; Jennifer Coolidge; Marcia Gay Harden; John Cho; Sam Golzari; Seth Meyers; Judy Greer; Shohreh Aghdashloo; Bernie (Bernard) White; Tony Yalda; Marley Shelton; Lawrence Pressman; Noureen DeWulf; ***D:*** Paul Weitz; ***W:*** Paul Weitz; ***C:*** Robert Elswit; ***M:*** Stephen Trask.

American Eagle 1/2 **1990 (R)** A veteran goes crazy and seeks sadistic, bloody revenge on his war buddies. Now his war buddies are the only ones who can stop him. **92m/C; VHS, DVD.** Asher Brauner; Robert F. Lyons; Vernon Wells; Kai Baker; ***D:*** Robert J. Smawley.

American East **2007 (R)** Arab-American Moustafa is having a very bad day. He has problems with his children and sister and the customers at his rundown L.A. diner insist on arguing about politics. Then when he goes to pick up his cousin at the airport, Moustafa is detained and questioned by an FBI agent. His one dream is to open a classy Middle Eastern restaurant with his Jewish pal Sam (Shalhoub), but no one believes he can do that either. **110m/C; DVD.** Sayed Badreya; Tony Shalhoub; Anthony Azizi; Kais Nashef; Amanda Detmer; Erik Avari; Ray Wise; Tay Blessey; Sarah Shahi; ***D:*** Hesham Issawi; ***W:*** Sayed Badreya; Hesham Issawi; ***C:*** Michael G. Wojciechowski; ***M:*** Tony Humecke.

American Empire 1/2 *My Son Alone* **1942** Two Civil War heroes struggle to build a cattle empire in Texas and are hampered by rustlers, one of whom was their partner. A fine, veteran cast and a tight script keep things moving, including the cattle. **82m/B; VHS, DVD.** Preston Foster; Richard Dix; Frances Gifford; Leo Carrillo; ***D:*** William McGann.

American Fable 1/2 **2017** Peyton Kennedy gives a breakthrough performance as Gitty, an 11-year-old girl in the Midwest in the 1980s, in this throwback to adventure movies of that era. Gitty is stunned to discover the developer who has been buying up farmland in the area held prisoner in an abandoned grain silo on her family's farm. This discovery is just the beginning as fairy tale elements start to enter her humdrum life, including magical individuals. Delicate and visually striking film about those days in which magic still seemed possible but real-life concerns also created just as many nightmares. **96m/C; DVD.** Kip Pardue; Peyton Kennedy; Gavin MacIntosh; Rusty Schwimmer; Marci Miller; ***D:*** Anne Hamilton; ***W:*** Anne Hamilton; ***C:*** Wyatt Garfield; ***M:*** Gingger Shankar.

American Factory **2019** When a General Motors automotive plant in Dayton, Ohio, closed in 2008, the manufacturing jobs were feared to be permanently lost. Six years later, the factory was bought by Chinese billionaire Cao Dewang, who reopened it as an automotive glass company. Cao's plans included hiring 2,000 American workers, bringing 200 workers from China to help train the Americans, and bridging the cultural gap between them. The differences, including attitudes towards work, regulations, and unionization, soon lead to clashes. The first film produced by Barack and Michelle Obama's production company, it is a revealing documentary exploring the state of American labor in an engaging and entertaining fashion. **115m/C; DVD.** ***D:*** Steven Bognar; Julia Reichert; ***C:*** Steven Bognar; Julia Reichert; Aubrey Keith; Jeff Reichert; Erick Stoll; ***M:*** Chad Cannon. Oscars '19: Feature Doc.; Directors Guild '19: Documentary Director (Bognar), Documentary Director (Reichert); Ind. Spirit '20: Feature Doc.

American Flyers 1/2 **1985 (PG-13)** Two competitive brothers train for a grueling three-day bicycle race in Colorado while tangling with personal drama, including the spectre that one of them may have inherited dad's tendency for cerebral aneurisms and is sure to drop dead during a bike race soon. Written by bike movie specialist Tesich ("Breaking Away") with a lot of the usual cliches (the last bike ride, battling bros, eventual understanding), which are gracefully overridden by fine bike-racing photography. Interesting performances, especially Chong as a patient girlfriend and Amos as the trainer. **113m/C; VHS, DVD.** Kevin Costner; David Marshall Grant; Rae Dawn Chong; Alexandra Paul; John Amos; Janice Rule; Robert Townsend; Jennifer Grey; Luca Bercovici; ***D:*** John Badham; ***W:*** Steve Tesich; ***M:*** Lee Ritenour; Greg Mathieson.

The American Friend 1/2 *Der Amerikanische Freund* **1977** Tribute to the American gangster film helped introduce Wenders to American moviegoers. Young Hamburg picture framer thinks he has a terminal disease and is set up by American expatriate Hopper to become a hired assassin in West Germany. The lure is a promise of quick money that the supposedly dying man can then leave his wife and child. After the first assasination, the two bond. Hopper is the typical Wenders protagonist, a strange man in a strange land looking for a connection. Great, creepy thriller adapted from Patricia Highsmith's novel "Ripley's Game." Fuller and Ray (better known as directors) appear briefly as gangsters. **127m/C; VHS, DVD, Blu-Ray.** *FR GE* Bruno Ganz; Dennis Hopper; Elisabeth (Lisa) Kreuzer; Gerard Blain; Jean Eustache; Samuel Fuller; Nicholas Ray; Daniel Schmid; Lou Castel; Rudolf Schuendler; Sandy Whitelaw; ***Cameo(s):*** Wim Wenders; ***D:*** Wim Wenders; ***W:*** Wim Wenders; ***C:*** Robby Muller; ***M:*** Jurgen Knieper.

American Friends **1991 (PG)** Genteel story masquerades as high comedy. Palin is a fussy middle-aged Oxford classics tutor. On a holiday he meets American Hartley (Booth) and her adopted daughter, Elinor (Alvarado). Both women are immensely attracted to the don (for reasons that are unclear) and follow him back to Oxford, where he's engaged in a battle of succession with his rival Molina. Dismal screenplay lacks logic and urgency, making it difficult to care about the story or the characters. Script is said to have been inspired by an incident in the life of Palin's great-grandfather. If this sounds like your cup of tea, save your time and watch a Merchant Ivory film instead. **95m/C; VHS, Streaming.** *GB* Michael Palin; Connie Booth; Trini Alvarado; Alfred Molina; ***D:*** Tristam Powell; ***W:*** Michael Palin; Tristam Powell; ***M:*** Georges Delerue.

American Fusion 1/2 **2005 (PG-13)** Charming romance in a culture clash comedy. Middle-aged, divorced Yvonne (Chang) is the frustrated daughter in a crazy Chinese-American family. She falls in love with Hispanic dentist Jose (Morales) but her family disapproves and his family isn't too happy with the cultural diversity either. **107m/C; DVD.** Sylvia Chang; Esai Morales; Collin Chou; James Hong; Lan Yeung; Noriyuki "Pat" Morita; Randall Park; ***D:*** Frank Lin; ***W:*** Randall Park; Frank Lin; ***C:*** Jason Inouye; ***M:*** Dave Iwataki.

American Gangster **2007 (R)** Director Ridley Scott's shot at the gangster genre hits the mark, transcending the tough-guy norm in its purposeful juxtaposition of the two main characters: Frank Lucas (Washington), the near-perfect, respectable, yet cold-blooded criminal genius who is pursued by the unkempt, womanizing, but razor-straight cop, Ritchie Roberts (Crowe). Washington and Crowe are mesmerizing in this powerful story of the brutality and excess of the '70s era Harlem drug trade that would be over-the-top if it weren't true, and that revolutionized both the drug trade and the law enforcement of the period. **157m/C; DVD, Blu-Ray.** John Ortiz; Denzel Washington; Russell Crowe; Chiwetel Ejiofor; Cuba Gooding, Jr.; Josh Brolin; Ted Levine; Armand Assante; Clarence Williams, III; Lymari Nadal; RZA; Ruby Dee; Idris Elba; Carla Gugino; Common; Joe Morton; Jon Polito; Kevin Corrigan; Ruben Santiago-Hudson; Roger Bart; KaDee Strickland; ***D:*** Ridley Scott; ***W:*** Steven Zaillian; ***C:*** Harris Savides; ***M:*** Marc Streitenfeld. Screen Actors Guild '07: Support. Actress (Dee).

American Gigolo **1979 (R)** A Los Angeles loner who sexually services the rich women of Beverly Hills becomes involved with the wife of a California state senator and is then framed for a murder he did not commit. A highly stylized but empty view of seamy low lives marred by a contrived plot, with decent romp in the hay readiness displayed by Gere. **117m/C; VHS, DVD, Blu-Ray.** Richard Gere; Lauren Hutton; Hector Elizondo; Nina Van Pallandt; Bill Duke; K. Callan; ***Cameo(s):*** Paul Schrader; ***D:*** Paul Schrader; ***W:*** Paul Schrader; ***C:*** John Bailey; ***M:*** Giorgio Moroder.

American Girl: Chrissa Stands Strong 1/2 *Chrissa Stands Strong* **2009** When fourth-grader Chrissa's family moves in to help out her recently-widowed grandma, she's most afraid that she won't make friends at her new school. Chrissa's fears seem well-founded when Tara, queen of the mean girl clique, starts tormenting Chrissa and turns out to be her main rival on the swim team. Chrissa must figure out the best way to stand up to Tara's bullying. **90m/C; DVD.** Michael Learned; Annabeth Gish; Timothy Bottoms; Jennifer Tilly; Don Franklin; Sammi Hanratty; Adair Tishler; Austin Thomas; ***D:*** Martha Coolidge; ***W:*** Christine Coyle Johnson; Julie Prendiville Roux; ***C:*** Johnny E. Jensen; ***M:*** Jennie Muskett. **VIDEO**

American Gothic **WOOF!** *Hide and Shriek* **1988 (R)** Three couples headed for a vacation are instead stranded on an island and captured by a demented family headed by Steiger and De Carlo, a scary enough proposition in itself. Even worse, Ma and Pa have three middle-aged moronic offspring who still dress as children and are intent on killing the thwarted vacationers (who are none too bright themselves) one by bloody one. A stultifying career low for all involved. **89m/C; VHS, DVD, Blu-Ray.** *CA GB* Rod Steiger; Yvonne De Carlo; Michael J. Pollard; Sarah Torgov; Fiona Hutchinson; William Hootkins; Terry Kelly; Mark Ericksen; Caroline Barclay; Mark Lindsay Chapman; ***D:*** John Hough; ***W:*** Michael Vines; Bert Wetanson; ***C:*** Harvey Harrison; ***M:*** Alan Parker.

American Graffiti 🦴🦴🦴 ½ **1973 (PG)** Atmospheric, episodic look at growing up in the innocence of America before the Kennedy assassination and the Vietnam War. It all takes place on one hectic but typical night in the life of a group of recent California high school grads unsure of what the next big step in life is. So they spend their time cruising, listening to Wolfman Jack, and meeting at the drive-in. Slice of '60s life boasts a prudent script, great set design, authentic soundtrack, and consistently fine performances by the young cast. Catapulted Dreyfuss, Ford, and Somers to stardom, branded Lucas a hot directorial commodity with enough leverage to launch "Star Wars," and steered Howard and Williams towards continued age-of-innocence nirvana on "Happy Days." **112m/C; VHS, DVD, Blu-Ray.** Richard Dreyfuss; Ron Howard; Cindy Williams; MacKenzie Phillips; Paul LeMat; Charles Martin Smith; Suzanne Somers; Candy Clark; Harrison Ford; Bo Hopkins; Joe Spano; Kathleen Quinlan; Wolfman Jack; ***D:*** George Lucas; ***W:*** George Lucas; Gloria Katz; Willard Huyck; ***C:*** Jan D'Alquen; Ron Eversage. AFI '98: Top 100; Golden Globes '74: Film--Mus./Comedy; Natl. Film Reg. '95; N.Y. Film Critics '73: Screenplay; Natl. Soc. Film Critics '73: Screenplay.

American Grindhouse 🦴🦴 ½ **2010** This insightful documentary offers an in-depth look at the history of the exploitation film, from the 1950s to the present. Noting that they began as movies meant to appeal to rebellious teenagers, the documentary explores the evolution of the genre in the 1960s and 1970s as it moved into drug movies and Blaxploitation flicks. Including more than 200 clips and interviews with filmmakers, actors, and critics, the documentary shows how the genre changed with and reflected the eras in which the films were created. **80m/C; DVD, Streaming, Download.** Robert Forster; ***W:*** Elijah Drenner; Calum Waddell; ***C:*** Dan Greene; ***M:*** Jason Brandt.

American Guerrilla in the Philippines 🦴 ½ **1950** Listless war drama whose title says it all. After his boat is sunk, Ensign Chuck Palmer (Power) is among those stranded in the Philippines after the islands surrender to the Japanese invasion in 1942. Plamer joins the guerilla movement as they wait for Gen. Douglas MacArthur's promised return. **105m/C; DVD.** Tyrone Power; Micheline Presle; Tom Ewell; Tommy Cook; Juan Torena; Robert Barrat; ***D:*** Fritz Lang; ***W:*** Lamar Trotti; ***C:*** Harry Jackson; ***M:*** Cyril Mockridge.

American Gun 🦴🦴🦴 **2002 (R)** Coburn, in his last performance, is Martin Tillman, an anguished father whose daughter has recently been killed during a violent crime. He decides to trace the history of the gun that was used, and along the way deals with an incident from his service in the Korean War that still haunts him. Coburn's performance is magnificent, even if the material itself is a little uneven. **89m/C; VHS, DVD.** James Coburn; Barbara Bain; Virginia Madsen; Alexandra Holden; ***D:*** Alan Jacobs; ***W:*** Alan Jacobs; ***C:*** Phil Parmet; ***M:*** Anthony Marinelli.

American Gun 🦴 ½ **2005 (R)** Three generally uninvolving stories about guns from debuting director Avelino. In Oregon, Janet (Harden) and her teen son David (Marquete) are guilt-wracked community outcasts three years after her older son participated in a high school shooting rampage. At a gang-ridden Chicago school, Principal Carter (Whitaker) expels student Jay (Escarpeta) for having a handgun, and the pic follows the teen to his convenience store job where he tries to use the (fake) weapon as intimidation against would-be thieves. In Virginia, co-ed Mary Ann (Cardellini) sets aside her dislike of firearms and learns to shoot after a friend is date-raped. **94m/C; DVD.** Donald Sutherland; Forest Whitaker; Marcia Gay Harden; Linda Cardellini; Tony Goldwyn; Christopher Marquette; Nikki Reed; Garcelle Beauvais; Amanda Seyfried; Melissa Leo; Arlen Escarpeta; ***D:*** Aric Avelino; ***W:*** Aric Avelino; Steven Bagatourian; ***C:*** Nancy Schreiber; ***M:*** Peter Golub.

An American Haunting 🦴 ½ **2005 (PG-13)** Fictionalized account of Tennessee's "Bell Witch," adapted from Brent Monahan's novel. In 1818, a neighbor curses the prosperous Bell family for their greed and soon they are haunted by a poltergeist that eventually takes possession of pretty teen daughter Betsy (Hurd-Ward). Parents John (Sutherland) and Lucy (Spacek) try to fight the evil spirit. Lots of hokum, not many frights. **82m/C; DVD.** Donald Sutherland; Sissy Spacek; Rachel Hurd-Wood; James D'Arcy; Matthew Marsh; Thom Fell; Gaye Brown; ***D:*** Courtney Solomon; ***W:*** Courtney Solomon; ***C:*** Adrian Biddle; ***M:*** Caine Davidson.

American Heart 🦴🦴🦴 ½ **1992 (R)** Jack (Bridges) is a suspicious ex-con, newly released from prison, with few prospects and little hope. He also has a teenage son, Nick (Furlong), he barely remembers but who desperately wants to have his father back in his life. Jack is reluctantly persuaded to let Nick stay with him in his cheap hotel where Nick befriends fellow resident, Molly (Kaprisky), a teenage hooker, and other castoff street kids. Superb performances by both male leads—Furlong, both yearning and frustrated as he pursues his dream of having a family, and Bridges as the tough parolee, unwilling to open his heart. Hardboiled, poignant, and powerful. **114m/C; VHS, DVD.** Jeff Bridges; Edward Furlong; Lucinda Jenney; Tracey Kapisky; Don Harvey; Margaret Welsh; ***D:*** Martin Bell; ***W:*** Peter Silverman; ***C:*** James R. Bagdonas; ***M:*** James Newton Howard. Ind. Spirit '94: Actor (Bridges).

American Heist 🦴🦴 **2015 (R)** A crime drama about the the divergent paths taken by two brothers and what happens when they re-connect again. After brothers Frankie (Brody) and James (Christensen) commit a crime together, Frankie takes the blame while James goes free. As Frankie serves a decade in prison, James becomes a productive member of society with a special job as a mechanic and a stable relationship with girlfriend Emily (Brewster). But when Frankie is released, he has nothing and looks to Sugar (Akon), a friend from prison, for an illegal gig. Frankie and his friends also convince James to help with one last job robbing a bank to set them both up for life. **94m/C; DVD, Blu-Ray, Streaming, Download.** Hayden Christensen; Adrien Brody; Jordana Brewster; Akon; Tory Kittles; ***D:*** Sarik Andreasyan; ***W:*** Raul Inglis; ***C:*** Antonio Calvache; ***M:*** Akon.

American History X 🦴🦴 ½ **1998 (R)** Former skinhead Derek (Norton) is released from prison after a three-year stint for killing two black teens. He returns home having renounced his neo-Nazi ideology and lifestyle, only to find his younger brother Danny (Furlong) involved in a skinhead gang. Controversial not only due to its touchy subject matter and startling violence, but also because director Kaye waged a public war with New Line to remove his name from the film, believing his vision had been compromised by the studio. Ultimately, the fuss is much ado about not much, as the film falls short of expectations. The story is predictable and rather simplistic, the script uneven and sometimes preachy, and most of the characters are wafer-thin. Only Norton's mesmerizing, forceful performance and a commendable job by Furlong as the impressionable younger brother lend credibility. **118m/C; VHS, DVD, Blu-Ray.** Edward Norton; Edward Furlong; Fairuza Balk; Beverly D'Angelo; Avery Brooks; Stacy Keach; Jennifer Lien; Elliott Gould; William Russ; Joe Cortese; Ethan Suplee; Guy Torry; Giuseppe Andrews; Jordan Marder; Anne Lambton; Paul LeMat; ***D:*** Tony Kaye; ***W:*** David McKenna; ***C:*** Tony Kaye; ***M:*** Anne Dudley.

American Honey 🦴🦴 ½ **2016 (R)** European Andrea Arnold brings an outsider's viewpoint to the heartland of America in this invigorating story of youthful energy. Newcomer Sasha Lane fronts the film as Star, a young lady with a depressing home life who stumbles upon a group of teenagers and twentysomethings who travel the country selling magazines door to door. Arnold's film tries to capture America's limitless potential as seen through the eyes of characters who do little more than dream. It's a film that some will see as too long, but that matches its remarkable ambition. **163m/C; DVD, Blu-Ray.** Sasha Lane; Shia LaBeouf; Riley Keough; McCaul Lombardi; Arielle Holmes; ***D:*** Andrea Arnold; ***W:*** Andrea Arnold; ***C:*** Robbie Ryan.

American Hustle 🦴🦴🦴 ½ **2013 (R)** Director Russell brilliantly turns the '70s Abscam scandal into a story about the American ability to lie to survive. Irving Rosenfeld (Bale) and his lover Sydney Prosser (Adams) run cons in the art world when FBI agent Richie DiMaso (Cooper) catches them, making them employees of the federal government in his narcissistic quest to "get a big fish." The trio sets their sights on entrapping Atlantic City Mayor Carmine Polito (Renner) in a bribery scam that involves the mob as well as Irving's emotionally turbulent wife Rosalyn (a feisty Lawrence). And we get to see this truly dazzling ensemble don gaudy clothes of the era, and the boys' stunningly bad 'dos. **138m/C; DVD, Blu-Ray.** Christian Bale; Bradley Cooper; Amy Adams; Jennifer Lawrence; Jeremy Renner; Louis CK; Jack Huston; Michael Peña; Shea Wigham; Alessandro Nivola; Elisabeth Rohm; ***D:*** David O. Russell; ***W:*** David O. Russell; Eric Singer; ***C:*** Linus Sandgren; ***M:*** Danny Elfman. British Acad. '13: Actress--Supporting (Lawrence), Makeup, Orig. Screenplay; Golden Globes '14: Actress--Mus./Comedy (Adams), Actress--Supporting (Lawrence), Film--Mus./Comedy; Screen Actors Guild '13: Cast.

An American in Paris 🦴🦴🦴🦴 **1951** Lavish, imaginative musical features a sweeping score, and knockout choreography by Kelly. Ex-G.I. Kelly stays on in Paris after the war to study painting, supported in his efforts by rich American Foch, who hopes to acquire a little extra attention. But Kelly loves the lovely Caron, unfortunately engaged to an older gent. Highlight is an astonishing 17-minute ballet which holds the record for longest movie dance number—and one of the most expensive, pegged at over half a million for a month of filming. For his efforts, the dance king won a special Oscar citation. While it sure looks like Paris, most of it was filmed in MGM studios. **113m/C; VHS, DVD.** Gene Kelly; Leslie Caron; Oscar Levant; Nina Foch; Georges Guetary; ***D:*** Vincente Minnelli; ***W:*** Alan Jay Lerner; ***C:*** John Alton; ***M:*** Ira Gershwin. Oscars '51: Art Dir./Set Dec., Color, Color Cinematog., Costume Des. (C), Film, Scoring/Musical, Story & Screenplay; AFI '98: Top 100; Golden Globes '52: Film--Mus./Comedy; Natl. Film Reg. '93.

American Justice 🦴🦴 *Jackals* **1986 (R)** Two cops, one of whom looks suspiciously like a Simon of "Simon and Simon," fight political corruption and white slavery near the Mexican border. The chief white slaver bears a full resemblance to the other Simon. Sufficient action but less than original. **96m/C; VHS, DVD.** Jameson Parker; Gerald McRaney; Wilford Brimley; Jack Lucarelli; ***D:*** Gary Grillo.

American Kickboxer 1 🦴 ½ **1991 (R)** Barrett stars as B.J. Quinn, a down on his luck kickboxing champion who spends much of his time onscreen aimlessly wandering (apparently searching for the meaning of his life). Lackluster script and performances will make this one trying—even for kickboxing fans. Barrett is Chuck Norris' former workout partner, but there isn't enough action often enough for him to show off his formidable skills. **93m/C; VHS, DVD.** John Barrett; Keith Vitali; Brad Morris; Terry Norton; Ted Leplat; ***D:*** Frans Nel; ***W:*** Emil Kolbe; ***M:*** Frank Becker.

American Kickboxer 2: To the Death 🦴 ½ **1993 (R)** Lillian must find a way to get her cop ex-husband and her kickboxer ex-lover to work together to save her kidnapped daughter's life. **91m/C; VHS, DVD.** Dale "Apollo" Cook; Evan Lurie; Kathy Shower; Ted Markland; ***D:*** Jeno Hodi.

American Loser 🦴🦴 *Trainwreck: My Life as an Idiot* **2007 (R)** Adapted from comic Jeff Nichols' memoir "The Little Yellow Bus." New Yorker Jeff (Scott) is dyslexic, suffers from attention-deficit disorder and a mild case of Tourette's, and is a recovering alcoholic. He has little idea what a normal life is but Jeff likes to talk, so he attends multiple 12-step programs for a chance to share (truthfully or not). He meets down-on-her luck Lynn (Mol) at one meeting and she actually befriends him and tries to cope with his foibles while helping Jeff manage his life. **94m/C; DVD.** Seann William Scott; Gretchen Mol; Jeff Garlin; Deirdre O'Connell; Denis O'Hare; Kevin Conway; Ian Buchanan; ***D:*** Tod Harrison Williams; ***W:*** Tod Harrison Williams; ***C:*** Michael Simmonds; ***M:*** Marcelo Zarvos.

American Made 🦴🦴 ½ **2017 (R)** Based on the true story of Barry Seal and the Iran-Contra Affair, this appealing, if shallow, action-filled film runs on Tom Cruise's charisma. Hired by the CIA, Barry (Cruise) flies spy planes over South American countries taking photographs of suspected communist groups. After Barry is kidnapped by drug lord Pablo Escobar (Mejia), he begins to smuggle cocaine, as well as other drugs, money, and guns, while acting as a CIA operative. The film also explores the effect of Barry's activities on his family, including his wife Lucy (Wright). Imbued with a dark sense of humor, it's watchable though morally lacking. **115m/C; DVD, Blu-Ray.** Tom Cruise; Domhnall Gleeson; Sarah Wright; Jesse Plemons; Caleb Landry Jones; ***D:*** Doug Liman; ***W:*** Gary Spinelli; ***C:*** Cesar Charlone; ***M:*** Christophe Beck.

American Madness 🦴🦴 ½ **1932** Benevolent banker Dickson (Huston) has been making loans without sufficient collateral. The bank's board of directors give him a warning and then a robbery causes a run on the bank. The directors are ready to oust Dickson when the small businessmen he's helped rally to his defense. Tedious romantic subplot has Dickson's unhappy wife (Johnson) accusing him of neglect and dallying with unscrupulous bank clerk Cluett (Gordon). **75m/B; VHS, DVD, Blu-Ray.** Walter Huston; Pat O'Brien; Kay Johnson; Gavin Gordon; Constance Cummings; Robert Ellis; Walter Walker; Arthur Hoyt; ***D:*** Frank Capra; ***W:*** Robert Riskin; ***C:*** Joseph Walker.

The American Mall 🦴🦴 ½ **2008** An MTV-produced teen musical that finds songwriter Ally (Dobrev) working at her mother's failing mall music store. She falls for janitor/musician Joey (Mayes) and they would make beautiful music together if not for rich witch Madison (Reeser), whose daddy owns the property. A would-be fashion designer, Madison wants Joey to be her model and she wants to kick out Ally's mom so she can have the space to expand her own store. Satisfyingly chipper—if predictable—with cute leads and bright songs. **100m/C; DVD.** Nina Dobrev; Autumn Reeser; Al Sapienza; Rob Mayes; Yassmin Alers; Wade Allain-Marcus; Neil Haskell; Brooke Lyons; ***D:*** Shawn Ku; ***W:*** Margaret Grieco Oberman; ***C:*** Matthew Williams. **CABLE**

American Matchmaker 🦴🦴 ½ *Amerikaner Shadkhn* **1940** Nat Silver decides to go into the matchmaking business, after his own marriages fail miserably, hoping to experience happiness vicariously. However, he soon begins to realize that one of his clients is a better match for him than the man he chose for her. In Yiddish with English subtitles. **87m/B; VHS, DVD.** Leo Fuchs; Judith Abarbanel; Rosetta Bialis; Yudel Dubinsky; Abe Lax; ***D:*** Edgar G. Ulmer; ***W:*** S. (Shirley Ulmer) Castle; ***C:*** Edgar G. Ulmer.

American Me 🦴🦴🦴 **1992 (R)** Violent and brutal depiction of more than 30 years of gang wars and drugs in East Los Angeles. Santana founded a street gang as a teenager, but has spent the last 18 years in prison, where he's the boss of the so-called Mexican Mafia, which oversees the drugs, scams, murders, and violence that are an everyday fact of prison life. Released from Folsom, Santana goes back to his old neighborhood and attempts to distance himself from his old life but finds his gang ties are stronger than any other alliance. Unsparing and desolate directorial debut from Olmos. **119m/C; VHS, DVD, Blu-Ray, HD-DVD.** Edward James Olmos; William Forsythe; Pepe Serna; Danny De La Paz; Evelina Fernandez; Daniel Villarreal; Cary-Hiroyuki Tagawa; Sal Lopez; Tony Giorgio; ***D:*** Edward James Olmos; ***W:*** Floyd Mutrux; Desmond Nakano; ***C:*** Reynaldo Villalobos; ***M:*** Dennis Lambert.

American Meltdown 🦴🦴 *Meltdown* **2004** In this tense thriller six terrorists take over the San Juan nuclear power plant and the government tries to figure out how to respond to the threat without it leading to a meltdown. However, the terrorists aren't exactly who they seem. **90m/C; DVD.** Bruce Greenwood; Leslie Hope; Arnold Vosloo; James Remar; Susan Merson; Will Lyman; ***D:*** Jeremiah S. Chechik; ***W:*** Larry Barber; Paul Barber; ***C:*** Douglas Koch; ***M:*** tomandandy. **CABLE**

American Movie 🦴🦴🦴½ **1999 (R)** Would-be filmmaker Mark Borchardt's American Dream is to make his own independent film in his home of Menomonee Falls, Wisconsin. He doesn't have the money (or a particularly workable idea) but he does have lots of self-confidence and enthusiasm, as well as his mom, his 82-year-old Uncle Bill, and a cast of eccentrics. Smith's unlimited access shows Borchardt's almost limitless failures and obstacles, making the whole affair seem like a "Spinal Tap"-esque spoof, even though the people are sometimes painfully, sometimes hilariously real. **104m/C; VHS, DVD.** Mike Schank; Mark Borchardt; ***D:*** Chris Smith; ***C:*** Chris Smith; ***M:*** Mike Schank.

American Mystic 🦴🦴 **2010** This debut documentary by Alex Mar focuses on an insightful exploration of alternative religions in the United States. Focusing on rural regions, the documentary follows three young Americans who have chosen to forego comforts for their faith. They include a Lakota Sioux sundancer, a pagan priestess, and a Spiritualist medium, each of whom leaves behind a mainstream life to live a very different way of life. **81m/C; DVD, Streaming, Download. VIDEO**

American Nightmare 🦴½ **2000 (R)** To commemorate the killings of four college students on Halloween the year before, pirate radio show "American Nightmare" is broadcasting all night. The program's host, Caligari (Ryan), has listeners calling in with their worst fears and seven friends take turns calling. Too bad, the killer is also listening and decides to make their nightmares come true. **91m/C; VHS, DVD.** Debbie Rochon; Brandy Little; Johnny Sneed; Christopher Ryan; Brinke Stevens; ***D:*** Jon Keeyes; ***W:*** Jon Keeyes; ***C:*** Brad Walker; ***M:*** Peter Gannan; David Rosenblad.

American Ninja 🦴🦴 *American Warrior* **1985 (R)** American Dudikoff is G.I. Joe, a martial-arts expert stationed in the Philippines who alienates most everyone around him (he's a rebel). Deadly black-belt war begins with Joe confronting the army which is selling stolen weapons to the South American black market. Aided by one faithful pal, Joe uses his head-kicking martial arts skills to stop hundreds of ninja combatants working for the corrupt arms dealer. In his spare time he romances the base chief's daughter. Efficient rib-crunching chop-socky action wrapped in no-brainer plot and performed by nonactors. Cannon epic mercilessly followed by at least three sequels. **96m/C; VHS, DVD, Blu-Ray.** Michael Dudikoff; Guich Koock; Judie Aronson; Steve James; ***D:*** Sam Firstenberg; ***W:*** Gideon Amir; ***C:*** Hanania Baer; ***M:*** Michael Linn.

American Ninja 2: The Confrontation 🦴🦴 **1987 (R)** Soldiers Dudikoff and James are back again using their martial arts skills (in lieu of any acting) to take on a Caribbean drug-lord. Apparently he has been kidnapping Marines and taking them to his island, where he genetically alters them to become fanatical ninja assassins eager to do his dirty work. The script hardly gets in the way of the rib-crunching action, but is an improvement upon Ninja Number One. **90m/C; VHS, DVD, Blu-Ray.** Michael Dudikoff; Steve James; Larry Poindexter; Gary Conway; ***D:*** Sam Firstenberg; ***W:*** Gary Conway; James Booth.

American Ninja 3: Blood Hunt **WOOF! 1989 (R)** Second sequel in the American Ninja series. Bradley replaces Dudikoff as the martial arts good guy fighting the martial arts bad guys on a Caribbean island. He's pursued by ex-evangelist Marjoe, who wants to inject him with a nasty virus before unloading the germs to bad buys worldwide. Less ninjitsu; more uninspired martial arts. **90m/C; VHS, DVD, Blu-Ray.** David Bradley; Steve James; Marjoe Gortner; Michele Chan; Calvin Jung; ***D:*** Cedric Sundstrom; ***W:*** Paul DeMielche; Gary Conway; ***M:*** George S. Clinton.

American Ninja 4: The Annihilation **WOOF! 1991 (R)** Dudikoff returns after noticeable absence in last sequel. He should have stayed away from #4—it's a rehash of tired ideas that never gets off the ground. Forget this and see "American Ninja 2: The Confrontation," the best of this series. **99m/C; VHS, DVD, Blu-Ray.** Michael Dudikoff; David Bradley; James Booth; Dwayne Alexandre; Robin Stille; Ken Gampu; ***D:*** Cedric Sundstrom; ***W:*** David Geeves; ***M:*** Nicolas Tenbroek.

American Outlaws 🦴 **2001 (PG-13)** Look kids, it's N'Sync as the James Gang! Remember "Young Guns" (1988)? By the end of this, you'll be begging for Emilio Estevez's constant mugging and Kiefer Sutherland's ridiculous brooding. Jesse (Farrell) and Frank James (Macht), along with cousins Cole (Caan), Bob (McCormack) and Jim Younger (Smith) return from the Civil War to find Ma (Bates) and the family farm threatened by the railroad. So they commence to robbin' banks to help out the poor folk who been done wrong. Along the way Jesse courts purty young filly Zee (Larter). People have been writing the obituary of the Western for a few years now, but "Outlaws" may be the bullet in the genre's back. **95m/C; VHS, DVD, Blu-Ray.** Colin Farrell; Gabriel Macht; Scott Caan; Gregory Edward Smith; Will McCormack; Timothy Dalton; Kathy Bates; Nathaniel Arcand; Ali Larter; Ronny Cox; Harris Yulin; Terry O'Quinn; Ty O'Neal; Joe Stevens; ***D:*** Les Mayfield; ***W:*** John Rogers; Roderick Taylor; ***C:*** Russell Boyd; ***M:*** Trevor Rabin.

American Pastoral 🦴½ **2016 (R)** Philip Roth's award-winning novel was deemed unfilmable for about two decades, and it turns out those people were right. McGregor's directorial debut is a stunningly flat and boring film, a complete misreading of many of Roth's most interesting themes. McGregor plays "The Swede," the most popular guy in Middle America, who watches his life unravel when his daughter (Fanning) is drawn to the counterculture movement and accused of murder. Telling a story that takes place across multiple decades requires a tight directorial hand and this one gets away from McGregor. He never figured out what story to tell and the film just comes apart. **108m/C; DVD, Blu-Ray.** Ewan McGregor; Jennifer Connelly; Dakota Fanning; Peter Riegert; Rupert Evans; ***D:*** Ewan McGregor; ***W:*** John Romano; ***C:*** Martin Ruhe; ***M:*** Alexandre Desplat.

American Pie 🦴🦴🦴 *East Great Falls High* **1999 (R)** And you thought you loved dessert! Four high school seniors led by pastry molesting Jim (Biggs) vow to lose their virginity before the Prom. Unfortunately for them, the girls that they're chasing aren't your usual teenage sex comedy tarts. These smart little cookies make sure that the boys' quest is chock full of humiliation. The sensitivity to the female point-of-view is balanced by a heapin' helpin' of crude and disgusting humor for the guys. An absolute must-see for baked goods and the men who love them. **95m/C; VHS, DVD, Blu-Ray, UMD.** Jason Biggs; Thomas Ian Nicholas; Chris Owen; Chris Klein; Natasha Lyonne; Tara Reid; Mena Suvari; Alyson Hannigan; Shannon Elizabeth; Eugene Levy; Seann William Scott; Jennifer Coolidge; Eddie Kaye Thomas; Lawrence Pressman; Eric Lively; Molly Cheek; Clyde Kusatsu; John Cho; Eli Marienthal; Casey Affleck; Tara Subkoff; Christina Milian; ***D:*** Chris Weitz; Paul Weitz; ***W:*** Adam Herz; ***C:*** Richard Crudo; ***M:*** David Lawrence.

American Pie 2 🦴🦴½ **2001 (R)** No pie is abused in this movie, although everyone (including exec producers Chris and Paul Weitz) is back for a second helping. The story picks up a year later while everyone is on summer vacation from college and sharing a beach house. Jim (Biggs) is nervously anticipating a visit from Nadia, while getting sex tips from band camp geek Michelle (Hannigan). Entertaining sequel shares the original's appealing and effective combination of gross-out situations and sweet silliness, and while it's not quite as good, it doesn't miss by much. **105m/C; VHS, DVD, Blu-Ray, UMD.** Jason Biggs; Shannon Elizabeth; Alyson Hannigan; Chris Klein; Natasha Lyonne; Thomas Ian Nicholas; Tara Reid; Chris Owen; Seann William Scott; Mena Suvari; Eddie Kaye Thomas; Eugene Levy; Jennifer Coolidge; Christopher Penn; Eli Marienthal; Casey Affleck; Denise Faye; Molly Cheek; ***D:*** James B. Rogers; ***W:*** Adam Herz; ***C:*** Mark Irwin; ***M:*** David Lawrence.

American Pie Presents Band Camp 🦴 *Band Camp* **2005** Stiffler's equally obnoxious and horny younger brother Matt (Hilgenbrink) is sent to summer band camp as punishment for a prank gone wrong. He decides to liven up his stay by shooting "girls gone wild"-type videos of the band chicks, only to have a change of heart when he hooks up with old friend Elyse (Kebbel). Levy's is the only original cast member to sheepishly show up in this drivel. **94m/C; DVD, Blu-Ray.** Tad Hilgenbrink; Arielle Kebbel; Crystle Lightning; Eugene Levy; Jason Earles; ***D:*** Steve Rash; ***W:*** Brad Riddell; ***C:*** Victor Kemper; ***M:*** Robert Folk. **VIDEO**

American Pie Presents: Beta House 🦴 *Beta House* **2007 (R)** And the franchise just gets lamer and grosser. Dwight Stifler is the head of the infamous Beta frat, just pledged by his cousin Erik and his buds. But their house superiority is challenged by newcomer Geek House and power-hungry nerd Edgar. **89m/C; DVD.** Jake Siegel; John White; Steven Talley; Meghan Heffern; Nic Nac; Tyrone Savage; Sarah Power; Eugene Levy; Christopher McDonald; ***D:*** Andrew Waller; ***W:*** Erik Lindsay; ***M:*** Jeff Cardoni. **VIDEO**

American Pie Presents: Book of Love 🦴 *Book of Love* **2009 (R)** The seventh entry in the impossibly lame series finds high-school virgins Rob, Nathan, and Lube discovering the legendary love manual hidden in the school's library. So they vow to test its wisdom on various babes. None of the characters are appealing and this is merely a crude wannabe comedy. **94m/C; DVD.** Bug Hall; Brandon Hardesty; Kevin M. Horton; John Patrick Jordan; Eugene Levy; Cindy Busby; Jennifer Holland; Beth Behrs; Rosanna Arquette; ***D:*** John Putch; ***W:*** David H. Steinberg; ***C:*** Ross Berryman. **VIDEO**

American Pie Presents: The Naked Mile 🦴🦴 *American Pie 5: The Naked Mile* **2006 (R)** Raunchy and surprisingly funny sex comedy. Erik Stifler (White) is a high school virgin since sweet girlfriend Tracy (Schram) won't put out. Erik and his buddies are visiting his cousin Dwight (Talley) at college for the weekend in order to run in the annual naked mile. Feeling guilty, Tracy gives him a free pass to do whatever he wants—and then worries that what Erik wants is sex with some other girl. Humiliation and a wide variety of bodily fluids follow. Also available unrated. **97m/C; DVD, Blu-Ray.** John White; Steven Talley; Ross Thomas; Christopher McDonald; Jessy Schram; Jake Siegel; Eugene Levy; Candace Kroslak; ***D:*** Joe Nussbaum; ***W:*** Erik Lindsay; ***C:*** Eric Haase; ***M:*** Jeff Cardoni. **VIDEO**

American Pluck 🦴🦴 **1925** Before he can inherit anything, a playboy millionaire's son must go out into the world and prove he can make his own way. He meets a beautiful princess, who is pursued by a villainous count. Walsh, as the dashing hero, was the younger brother of director Raoul. Silent with original organ music. **91m/B; Silent; VHS, DVD.** George Walsh; Wanda (Petit) Hawley; Frank Leigh; Sidney De Grey; ***D:*** Richard Stanton.

American Pop 🦴🦴 **1981 (R)** Animated story of four generations of men told in music. Immigrant Zalmie starts off in vaudeville and winds up involved in the mob, his pianist son Benny gets killed in WWII, Benny's son Tony winds up in the early psychedelic rock scene in Haight-Asbury, and Tony's son Little Pete becomes a rock idol. **95m/C; VHS, DVD.** ***V:*** Ron Thompson; Marya Small; Lisa Jane Persky; Roz Kelly; Richard Singer; Jeffrey Lippa; ***D:*** Ralph Bakshi; ***W:*** Ronni Kern; ***M:*** Lee Holdridge.

The American President 🦴🦴🦴 **1995 (PG-13)** Widower president Andrew Shepherd (Douglas) decides it's time to get back into the dating game. But just what woman wants to find her romance in the public eye? Well, it turns out to be feisty environmental lobbyist Sydney Wade (the ever-charming Bening). But the Prez also has to put up with nasty opponent Bob Rumson (Dreyfuss), who's using their courtship as political fodder, approval ratings, and a nosy press. Glossy fairytale material expertly handled by both cast and director. **114m/C; VHS, DVD, Blu-Ray.** Michael Douglas; Annette Bening; Martin Sheen; Michael J. Fox; David Paymer; Samantha Mathis; John Mahoney; Anna Deavere Smith; Nina Siemaszko; Wendie Malick; Shawna Waldron; Richard Dreyfuss; Gabe Jarret; Anne Haney; Gail Strickland; Joshua Malina; Ron Canada; Jennifer Crystal Foley; Taylor Nichols; ***D:*** Rob Reiner; ***W:*** Aaron Sorkin; ***C:*** John Seale; ***M:*** Marc Shaiman.

American Psycho 🦴🦴 **1999 (R)** Trimmed-down and (slightly) cleaned-up version of Bret Easton Ellis's widely hated 1991 novel has Bale as '80s hotshot Wall Street exec and apparent serial-killer Patrick Bateman. Bateman is the poster child for Reaganera excess and preference for style over substance, a theme with which the film, while shooting for satire, beats you over the head. Like the decade it portrays, "Psycho" is far from subtle, and the characters barely register as two-dimensional, let alone three. They got the look right, but then, that's the point, isn't it? The production drew protests in Toronto, where some scenes were shot, and Leo DiCaprio was rumored to be in line to play the lead for a time. **103m/C; VHS, DVD, Blu-Ray, UMD.** Christian Bale; Willem Dafoe; Jared Leto; Reese Witherspoon; Samantha Mathis; Chloë Sevigny; Justin Theroux; Josh(ua) Lucas; Guinevere Turner; Matt Ross; William Sage; Cara Seymour; ***D:*** Mary Harron; ***W:*** Guinevere Turner; Mary Harron; ***C:*** Andrzej Sekula; ***M:*** John Cale.

American Psycho 2: All American Girl 🦴🦴 **2002 (R)** Rachelle Newman (Kunis) is the only victim who managed to escape from serial killer Patrick Bateman. But her ordeal left her obsessed with such killers and when she learns that college prof Robert Strickland (Shatner) was an FBI profiler specializing in the subject, Rachelle is determined to become his teaching assistant. Even if it means killing the competition. **88m/C; VHS, DVD, Blu-Ray.** Mila Kunis; William Shatner; Geraint Wyn Davies; Lindy Booth; Robin Dunne; ***D:*** Morgan J. Freeman; ***W:*** Karen Craig; Alex Sanger; ***C:*** Vanja Cernjul; ***M:*** Norman Orenstein. **VIDEO**

American Reunion 🦴🦴 **2012 (R)** The fourth film to feature the characters from 1999's "American Pie" also features the stalest comedy in the franchise. Jim (Biggs), Oz (Klein), Kevin (Nicholas), Finch (Thomas), and Stifler (Scott) are all back for some raunchy action (and are ably assisted by many of the supporting characters like Levy and Coolidge) but they forgot to write an interesting story for them. In typical fashion, the quintet of guys show up for their reunion in Michigan and sexually-charged hijinks ensue. Except for the occasional jolt of comic energy from Scott or Levy, the entire affair is like an actual reunion with people you never wanted to see again. **113m/C; DVD, Blu-Ray, Streaming.** Jason Biggs; Alyson Hannigan; Chris Klein; Thomas Ian Nicholas; Tara Reid; Seann William Scott; Mena Suvari; Eddie Kaye Thomas; Jennifer Coolidge; Eugene Levy; Natasha Lyonne; Shannon Elizabeth; Chris Owen; ***D:*** Jon Hurwitz; Hayden Schlossberg; ***W:*** Jon Hurwitz; Hayden Schlossberg; ***C:*** Daryn Okada; ***M:*** Lyle Workman; JoJo Villanueva.

An American Rhapsody 🦴🦴🦴 **2001 (PG-13)** A mother/daughter conflict steeped in history and based on the experiences of writer/director Gardos. Margit (Kinski) and her family flee Hungary during the communist takeover of the 1950s but she is forced to leave her infant daughter behind. While the family settles in L.A., Suzanne is being raised in the country by adoptive parents and knows nothing of her origins. She gets a rude awakening at the age of 6 when her grandmother Helen (Banfalvy) makes arrangements to reunite Suzy with her unknown "real" family. The child grows into a sullen teenager (Johansson) who longs to return to Budapest. Her father finally agrees to a solo trip and Suzanne learns just what her family suffered and where she truly belongs. **106m/C; VHS, DVD.** *US HU* Nastassja Kinski; Scarlett Johansson; Tony Goldwyn; Kelly Endresz-Banlaki; Agnes Banfalvy; Zsuzsi Czinkoczi; Balazs Galko; Zoltan Seress; Mae Whitman; Lisa Jane Persky; Emmy Rossum; ***D:*** Eva Gardos; ***W:*** Eva Gardos; ***C:*** Elemer Ragalyi; ***M:*** Cliff Eidelman.

An American Romance 🦴🦴 **1944** That would be a romance with the country and not your typical love match. Czech immigrant Steve Dangos (Donlevy) believes in the American Dream and strives to better himself. He eventually starts his own auto manufacturing company in Chicago, marries Ann (Richards), and raises a family. But the industrialist has a problem when his workers want to unionize and Steve's son Teddy (McNally) takes their side. Vidor's expensive propaganda piece was cut by the studio by some 30 minutes and Vidor himself eventually dismissed the movie. **121m/C; DVD.** Brian Donlevy; Ann Richards; Stephen McNally; John Qualen; Walter Abel; Mary McLeod; Bob Lowell; ***D:*** King Vidor; ***W:*** Herbert Dalmas; William Ludwig; ***C:*** Harold Rosson; ***M:*** Louis Gruenberg.

American Samurai 🦴 1/2 **1992 (R)** Drew is the adopted son of a Japanese samurai, who gives him the family's sacred sword. This gesture angers his stepbrother who gets involved with Japanese gangsters and illegal live-blade fighting, and who also vows revenge on this American upstart. Lots of sword play to go with the chop-socky action. **89m/C; VHS, DVD.** David Bradley; Mark Dacascos; John Fujioka; Valarie Trapp; ***D:*** Sam Firstenberg; ***W:*** John Corcoran.

The American Side 🦴🦴 1/2 **2016** An indie noir thriller-mystery with technology proposed by genius inventor Nikola Tesla at its center. Charlie Paczynski (Stuhr) is drawn into a case after his partner becomes caught up in a blackmail scheme gone sideways. When an unexplained suicide takes place at Niagara Falls as part of this situation, Charlie begins to further investigate the matter. What he finds is a conspiracy that focuses on finding and constructing a secret, long-lost invention designed by Tesla. **104m/C; DVD, Streaming, Download.** Greg Stuhr; Alicja Bachleda-Curus; Camilla Belle; Matthew Broderick; Robert Forster; ***D:*** Jenna Ricker; ***W:*** Greg Stuhr; Jenna Ricker; ***C:*** Frank Barrera; ***M:*** David Shire.

American Sniper 🦴🦴 1/2 **2014 (R)** Eastwood admirably but cold-heartedly adapts the true story of Chris Kyle, the most proficient U.S. sniper in military history. Played with striking realism by a beefed-up Cooper, Kyle's story of the role he felt ordained to play as the protector of his fellow soldiers is certainly one worth telling, but it's hard to know what to take away from the film. There's no actual statement made, and in not doing so, it feels incomplete as drama. Eastwood is technically proficient but the film is surprisingly thin for its thick subject matter. It's a gripping story nonetheless that has its moments of pulling at any patriot's heartstrings. **132m/C; DVD, Blu-Ray.** Bradley Cooper; Sienna Miller; Luke Grimes; Kyle Gallner; Jake McDorman; Cory Hardrict; ***D:*** Clint Eastwood; ***W:*** Jason Dean Hall; ***C:*** Tom Stern; ***M:*** Joseph S. DeBeasi; Clint Eastwood. Oscars '14: Sound FX Editing.

The American Soldier 🦴🦴 1/2 *Der Amerikanische Soldat* **1970** Fassbinder's homage to the American gangster film tells the story of Ricky, a charismatic hit man. Ricky always wears a gun in a shoulder holster, sports a fedora and a white double-breasted suit, and drinks Scotch straight from the bottle. He also carries out his assigned murders with complete efficiency and no emotion. In German with English subtitles. **80m/C; VHS, DVD.** *GE* Rainer Werner Fassbinder; Karl Scheydt; Elga Sorbas; Jan George; Ingrid Caven; Ulli Lommel; Kurt Raab; ***D:*** Rainer Werner Fassbinder; ***W:*** Rainer Werner Fassbinder; ***C:*** Dietrich Lohmann; ***M:*** Peer Raben.

American Soldiers WOOF! **2005 (R)** Incompetent mess mangles a serious subject and is only worth a groan for its ineptitude. In April 2004, an army platoon is ambushed by insurgents in Iraq and the surviving soldiers must make their way back to base through enemy territory. Filmed in Hamilton, Ontario, which cannot in any way pass for Iraq. **103m/C; DVD.** *CA* Curtis Morgan; Zan Calabretta; Jordan Brown; Eddie Della Siepe; ***D:*** Sidney J. Furie; ***W:*** Greg Mellott. **VIDEO**

American Son 🦴🦴 1/2 **2008 (R)** Well-done drama focuses on the personal rather than the military aspects of the Iraq War. Marine Pvt. Mike Holland (Cannon) gets a four-day Thanksgiving leave before shipping out to Iraq. While taking the bus from Camp Pendleton to Bakersfield, Mike is instantly smitten by fellow passenger Cristina (Diaz), a Mexican-American college student. Mike keeps postponing the moment he has to tell his troubled family he's leaving while dealing with his volatile friend, drug dealer Jake (O'Leary), who's upset that Mike has changed. Meanwhile, Mike tries to persuade Cristina to be his girlfriend despite his upcoming departure. **86m/C; DVD.** Nick Cannon; Melonie Diaz; Matt O'Leary; Jay Hernandez; Chi McBride; Tom Sizemore; April Grace; ***D:*** Neil Abramson; ***W:*** Eric Schmid; ***C:*** Kris Kachikis; ***M:*** Tim Bolland; Sam Retzer. **VIDEO**

American Son 🦴🦴 **2019** On a rainy Miami night, Kendra (Washington) anxiously waits in a police station because her teenage son Jamal is missing. The African-American mother's quest for answers is not helped by a young white police officer, Larkin (Jordan), who gives her evasive explanations as they await the arrival of another officer with more information. Kendra's estranged husband, white FBI agent Scott (Pasquale), shows up before the other officer, Stokes (Lee), and argues with his wife until they learn Jamal's fate. A Broadway play adaptation, the feature feels like a filmed play with overstated performances as it explores issues of race and privilege in obvious fashion. **90m/C; DVD.** Kerry Washington; Steven Pasquale; Jeremy Jordan; Eugene Lee; ***D:*** Kenny Leon; Melissa Kent; ***W:*** Christopher Demos-Brown; ***C:*** Kramer Morgenthau; ***M:*** Lisbeth Scott. **VIDEO**

American Splendor 🦴🦴🦴 1/2 **2003 (R)** Giamatti is brilliant as Harvey Pekar, a life-long file clerk in Cleveland who authored the R. Crumb-illustrated autobiographical graphic novels of the film's title. The unlikely courtship of misfits Pekar and his third wife Joyce Brabner (Davis) is comically portrayed as the two kindred souls mysteriously come together. Their unlikely romance mirrors the unlikelihood that a comic filled with the pessimism, cynicism, and wry comic observations of Pekar's admitted hum-drum life would somehow translate just as well onto the big screen. But it does. Documentarian directors Berman and Pulcini weave fiction with fact as the real Pekar narrates and cameos. They also make use of illustrated comic segments and footage from Pekar's frequent appearances on David Letterman's show. **101m/C; VHS, DVD.** Paul Giamatti; Hope Davis; Harvey Pekar; Joyce Brabner; Earl Billings; James Urbaniak; Judah Friedlander; Donal Logue; Molly Shannon; James McCaffrey; Shari Springer Berman; Robert Pulcini; ***D:*** Shari Springer Berman; Robert Pulcini; ***W:*** Shari Springer Berman; Robert Pulcini; ***C:*** Terry Stacey; ***M:*** Mark Suozzo. L.A. Film Critics '03: Film, Screenplay; N.Y. Film Critics '03: Actress (Davis); Natl. Soc. Film Critics '03: Film, Screenplay; Writers Guild '03: Adapt. Screenplay.

American Strays 🦴 1/2 **1996 (R)** Episodic black comedy about various oddballs (most of them violent) who cross paths (usually in Kane's roadside diner) in an isolated desert town. There's a masochist who wants help committing suicide, an unemployed family man on the verge of a breakdown, a serial killer, and more—mostly strange. **97m/C; VHS, DVD.** Carol Kane; Jennifer Tilly; Eric Roberts; John Savage; Luke Perry; Joe (Johnny) Viterelli; James Russo; Vonte Sweet; Sam Jones; Brion James; Toni Kalem; Melora Walters; Jack Kehler; ***D:*** Michael Covert; ***W:*** Michael Covert; ***C:*** Sead Muhtarevic; ***M:*** John Graham.

American Streetfighter 🦴🦴 **1996** Martial arts expert Jake Tanner gets involved with an illegal streetfighting ring to rescue his brother, Randy, who's the target of a drug courier. But what happens when his next opponent is his sibling? **80m/C; VHS, DVD.** Gary Daniels; Ian Jacklin; Tracy Dali; ***D:*** Steven Austin.

American Streetfighter 2: The Full Impact 🦴 1/2 **1997** Ex-cop becomes a bounty hunter tracking a serial killer who likes to kill his victims with his bare hands. **90m/C; VHS, DVD.** Gary Daniels; Graciela Casillas; ***D:*** Marc Messenger. **VIDEO**

An American Summer 🦴🦴 **1990** A Chicago kid spends a summer with his aunt in beach-rich Los Angeles in this coming-of-age tale filled with '90s teen idols. **100m/C; VHS, DVD.** Brian Austin Green; Joanna Kerns; Michael Landes; Tony Crane; Brian Krause; Wayne Pere; Amber Susa; ***D:*** James Slocum; ***W:*** James Slocum; ***C:*** Bruce Dorfman; ***M:*** Roger Neill.

American Swing 🦴🦴 **2008** The revealing documentary offers a profile of Plato's Retreat, a well-known sex club in New York City opened in 1977 as the sexual revolution was reaching its end. The film explores nightlife in the city in this period, and how the club came to be. The filmmakers note that its founder, Larry Levenson, was a swinger who was inspired to establish Plato's by the open sexuality found in New York's gay club. The documentary looks at the whole history of Plato's, until it closed on New Year's Eve in 1985 as the AIDS crisis took hold. Included in the documentary are interviews with Ed Koch, the former mayor of New York City, celebrities, journalists, and former employees. **81m/C; DVD, Streaming, Download.** ***D:*** Jon Hart; Mathew Kaufman; ***W:*** Jon Hart; ***C:*** Christian Hoagland; ***M:*** Jim Coleman.

An American Tail 🦴🦴 1/2 **1986 (G)** While emigrating to New York in the 1880s, a young Russian mouse (Fievel) is separated from his family. He matures as he learns to live on the Big Apple's dirty boulevards. The bad guys are of course cats. Excellent animation and a high-minded (though sentimental and stereotypical) plot keep it interesting for adults. Produced by Spielberg and the first big hit for the Bluth factory, a collection of expatriate Disney artists. Knowing better than to let a money-making mouse tale languish, Bluth followed with "An American Tale: Fievel Goes West." **81m/C; VHS, DVD, Blu-Ray.** ***V:*** Dom DeLuise; Madeline Kahn; Phillip Glasser; Christopher Plummer; Nehemiah Persoff; Will Ryan; John Finnegan; Cathianne Blore; ***D:*** Don Bluth; ***M:*** James Horner.

An American Tail: Fievel Goes West 🦴🦴 **1991 (G)** Fievel and the Mousekewitz family continue their pursuit of the American dream by heading West, where the intrepid mouse seeks to become a famous lawman while his sister looks to make it big as a dance hall singer. The score is performed by the London Symphony Orchestra. Unfortunately released at the same time as "Beauty and the Beast," "Fievel Goes West" suffers from comparison. Worthwhile viewing for the whole family, but it won't ever reach the heights of "B&B." The laser edition is letterboxed and features chapter stops. **75m/C; VHS, DVD, Blu-Ray.** ***V:*** John Cleese; Dom DeLuise; Phillip Glasser; Amy Irving; Jon Lovitz; Catherine Cavadini; Nehemiah Persoff; Erica Yohn; James Stewart; ***D:*** Phil Nibbelink; Simon Wells; ***W:*** Flint Dille; ***M:*** James Horner.

American Teen 🦴🦴 1/2 **2008 (PG-13)** Slick documentary following four teens through their senior year of high school in Warsaw, Indiana. Director Burstein shot 1000 hours of footage over 10 months, piecing together her version of "The Breakfast Club" for MTV. The popular girl, the basketball star, the band geek, and the art chick all suspiciously play exactly to stereotype, making it seem more like reality TV than a documentary. Nothing too thought provoking or unusual (zits, prom jitters, the big game, Internet drama) but it still touches a nerve and may bring back a few memories, good or bad. **95m/C; On Demand.** ***D:*** Nanette Burstein; ***C:*** Laela Kilbourn; Wolfgang Held; Robert Hanna; ***M:*** Michael Penn.

An American Tragedy 🦴🦴 **1931** Straightforward retelling of the Theodore Dreiser novel (although Dreiser sued Paramount because he didn't approve of the script). Ambitious factory boss Clyde Griffiths (Holmes) takes advantage of his distant connection to some wealthy relatives to hang around the fringes of high society. He romances moneyed beauty Sondra (Dee) but his plans are thrown into disarray when working-class Roberta (Sidney) tells Clyde she's pregnant. After a boating trip, Clyde becomes a criminal suspect leading to a long trial sequence. Remade as 1951's "A Place in the Sun." **96m/B; DVD.** Phillips Holmes; Sylvia Sidney; Frances Dee; Irving Pichel; Lucille LaVerne; Frederick Burton; Charles Middleton; Emmett Corrigan; ***D:*** Irving Pichel; Josef von Sternberg; ***W:*** Samuel Hoffenstein; ***C:*** Lee Garmes.

American Tragedy 🦴🦴 1/2 **2000 (PG-13)** Remember the O.J. Simpson trial? Well, if you don't, this cable drama is here to remind you as it explores the egos and infighting of Simpson's four defense lawyers: Johnny Cochran (Rhames), Bob Shapiro (Silver), F. Lee Bailey (Plummer), and Barry Scheck (Kirby). Based on the book by Schiller, who also directed. **170m/C; VHS, DVD.** Ving Rhames; Ron Silver; Christopher Plummer; Bruno Kirby; Nicholas Pryor; Robert LuPone; Ruben Santiago-Hudson; Richard Cox; Clyde Kusatsu; Jeff Kober; ***D:*** Lawrence Schiller; ***W:*** Norman Mailer; ***C:*** Bruce Surtees; ***M:*** Bill Conti. **CABLE**

American Ultra 🦴 1/2 **2015 (R)** Eisenberg and Stewart are slumming in this ineffective action-comedy that plays like a stoner variation on Jason Bourne. Mike (Eisenberg) is a small-town loser who has no idea that he was trained by the CIA to be a killing machine until he's "called" back into action after he's unexpectedly activated with a phrase. Why is Mike back in action? It turns out there's a good reason as he and his girlfriend (Stewart) are quickly targeted by mercenaries. Jesse and Kristen are fun, but you won't care if they live or die, and the movie is surprisingly vicious. **99m/C; DVD, Blu-Ray.** Jesse Eisenberg; Kristen Stewart; Topher Grace; Connie Britton; Walton Goggins; ***D:*** Nima Nourizadeh; ***W:*** Max Landis; ***C:*** Michael Bonvillain; ***M:*** Marcelo Zarvos.

American Vampire 🦴🦴 1/2 **1997 (R)** Teenager Frankie (Lussauer) has been left alone while his parents are on vacation. One night on the beach, he and his friend Bogie (Hitt) meet Moondoggie (Venokur), who promises to help them party the summer away. He soon reappears with two babes (Electra and Xavier) who appear to be undead. Frankie must turn to The Big Kahuna (West) to stop the vampires. Yes, the plot strictly follows the formula, but the effects are not bad for a low-budget production; the photography is better than it needs to be; and the humor is intentional. **99m/C; VHS, DVD.** Trevor Lissauer; Danny Hitt; Johnny Venokur; Carmen Electra; Debora Xavier; Adam West; Sydney Lassick; ***D:*** Luis Esteban; ***W:*** Rollin Jarrett; ***C:*** Jurgen Baum; Goran Paviceric. **VIDEO**

American Venus 🦴 1/2 **2007** Celia Lane (De Mornay) is the ultimate in crazy, controlling mothers. When her ice skating daughter Jenna (McGregor) chokes during a national-level competition, Jenna decides she's had enough and quits for good—much to coach/mom Celia's fury. So Jenna sneaks out of Spokane to live the college life in Vancouver, British Columbia—until Celia tracks her down. Celia's also the ultimate in ugly Americans in a foreign country and the viewer is never quite sure if Sweeney is aiming for satire or not. **80m/C; DVD.** *CA* Rebecca De Mornay; Jane McGregor; Matt Craven; Nicholas Lea; Agam Darshi; Anna Amoroso; ***D:*** Bruce Sweeney; ***W:*** Bruce Sweeney; ***C:*** David Pelletier; ***M:*** James Jandrisch. **VIDEO**

American Violence WOOF! **2017** Richards plays Amanda Tyler, a world-renowned psychologist (stop laughing) who interviews death row inmate Jackson Shea (Lyman-Mersereau) in the final days of his sentence to get to the root of American evil and the country's propensity for violence. The film consists primarily of flashbacks of Shea's story from petty criminal to death row inmate, making excuses for his behavior and providing viewers with just over an hour of horrendous dialogue and two-dimensional characters. This isn't just your standard bad movie. **107m/C; DVD, Blu-Ray.** Bruce Dern; Denise Richards; Kaiwi Lyman-Mersereau; Columbus Short; Johnny Messner; ***D:*** Timothy Woodward, Jr.; ***W:*** Al Lamanda; ***C:*** Pablo Diez; ***M:*** Andrew Joslyn.

American Violet 🦴🦴 1/2 **2009 (PG-13)** Docudrama of Dee Roberts (Beharie), a 24 year-old African-American single mother of four young girls living in a small Texas town barely able to make ends meet. While police drag Dee from work in handcuffs on trumped-up charges, dumping her in the women's county prison, the powerful local district attorney (O'Keefe) leads an extensive drug bust, sweeping her housing project and ultimately charging Dee as a drug dealer. With few choices, Dee and her ACLU attorney decide to sue the DA for unjust practices. Predictable outcome but does well in its portrayal of the plight of poor minorities caught up, legitimately or not, in a racially tainted justice system. Newcomer Beharie shines alongside veterans Woodard, Dutton, and Blake Nelson. Based on a true story that's set during the 2000 presidential campaign. **103m/C; Blu-Ray, On Demand.** Michael O'Keefe; Tim Blake Nelson; Will Patton; Alfre Woodard; Nicole Beharie; Xzibit; Scott A. Martin; ***D:*** Tim Disney; ***W:*** Bill Haney; ***C:*** Steve Yedlin.

American Virgin 🦴 *Live Virgin* **1998 (R)** Ronny Bartoloti (Loggia) is a successful Hollywood adult film director who has upset his virginal 18-year-old daughter, Katrina (Suvari), with his double-standard attitudes. So she decides to get even by sharing her first sexual experience with millions—by going live on camera on closed-circuit—with the help of Ronny's rival Joey Quinn (Hoskins). But can daddy get his determined little darling to change her mind? Exploitative would-be satire falls flat. **87m/C; VHS, DVD, On Demand.** Mena Suvari; Robert Loggia; Bob Hoskins; Gabriel Mann; Sally Kellerman; Bobbie Phillips; Lamont Johnson; Rick Peters; O-lan Jones; Alexandra Wentworth; ***D:*** Jean Pierre Marois; ***W:*** Jean Pierre Marois; Ira Israel; ***C:*** Eagle Egilsson.

American Virgin 🦴 **2009 (R)** Yeah, it's a stupid, low-budget, direct-to-DVD college sex comedy (and the female leads keep their clothes on) but said female leads try hard and even Schneider isn't completely offensive. Chaste college freshman Priscilla (Dewan) is horrified that her roommate Natalie (Davis) is the biggest slut on campus. Then Priscilla gets drunk (thanks to Natalie) at a frat party and displays her ta-tas for a "Girls Gone Crazy" video. Humiliated, she scrambles to get the footage back from sleazy producer Ed (Schneider), who's now down in New Orleans filming more unseemly behavior at Mardi Gras. **88m/C; DVD.** Jenna Dewan; Brianne Davis; Rob Schneider; Ebon Moss-Bachrach; Chase Ryan Jeffery; Ben Marten; Ashley Schneider; Bo Burnham; ***D:*** Clare Kilner; ***W:*** Lucas Jarach; Jason Price; Jeff Seeman; ***C:*** Oliver Curtis; ***M:*** John Hunter. **VIDEO**

American Warship 🦴 ½ **2012** The Asylum changed the title from American Battleship when it ran into some legal trouble but this low-budget copycat military adventure is surprisingly watchable. The USS Iowa, a WWII-era destroyer, is on its final voyage when Capt. Winston (Van Peebles) and his crew run into trouble. Naval vessels have been disappearing in the South Pacific and the enemy turn out to be aliens. **90m/C; DVD, Blu-Ray.** Mario Van Peebles; Carl Weathers; Brandon Clark; Johanna Watts; Nikki McCauley; Elijah Chester; ***D:*** Thunder Levin; ***W:*** Thunder Levin; ***C:*** Stuart Brereton; ***M:*** Chris Ridenhour. **VIDEO**

American Warships 🦴 *American Battleship* **2001** The U.S. Navy takes on aliens in the Asylum's mockbuster salute to "Battleship." **90m/C; DVD, Blu-Ray.** Mario Van Peebles; Carl Weathers; Johanna Watts; Nikki McCauley; Elijah Chester; ***D:*** Thunder Levin; ***W:*** Thunder Levin; ***C:*** Stuart Brereton; ***M:*** Chris Ridenhour. **CABLE**

American Wedding 🦴🦴 ½ *American Pie 3* **2003 (R)** In the finale of the epic trilogy Annakin and Amidala, no, wait. Frodo and Gollum...no, Neo and Trinity...that's not it either. Jim and Michelle are getting married, with the dubious help of most of the gang. Kevin and Finch are still around, but it's Stifler who has the biggest impact, throwing the bachelor party, battling Finch for the affections of Michelle's sister Cadence (Jones), and almost putting the kibosh on the whole wedding. Like the other two, it's pretty gross in parts, uproarious in others, but still has its sweet, charming moments. Levy and Willard make the most of their scenes as the father of the groom and bride, respectively. **96m/C; VHS, DVD, Blu-Ray, UMD.** Jason Biggs; Alyson Hannigan; Seann William Scott; Eddie Kaye Thomas; January Jones; Eugene Levy; Thomas Ian Nicholas; Fred Willard; Molly Cheek; Eric Allen Kramer; Deborah Rush; Jennifer Coolidge; Angela Paton; Lawrence Pressman; Amanda Swisten; Nikki Schieler Ziering; ***D:*** Jesse Dylan; ***W:*** Adam Herz; ***C:*** Lloyd Ahern, II; ***M:*** Christophe Beck.

An American Werewolf in London 🦴🦴🦴 **1981 (R)** Strange, darkly humorous version of the classic man-into-wolf horror tale became a cult hit, but never clicked with most American critics. Two American college students, David (Naughton) and Jack (Dunne), are backpacking through England when thy're viciously attacked by a werewolf one foggy night. Jack is killed, but keeps appearing (in progressively decomposed form) before the seriously wounded David, warning him of impending werewolfdom when the moon is full; Jack advises suicide. Seat-jumping horror and gore, highlighted by intensive metamorphosis sequences orchestrated by Rick Baker, are offset by wry humor, though the shifts in tone don't always work. Great moon songs permeate the soundtrack, including CCR's "Bad Moon Rising" and Van Morrison's "Moondance." Followed by "An American Werewolf in Paris" (1997). **97m/C; VHS, DVD, Blu-Ray, HD-DVD.** *GB* David Naughton; Griffin Dunne; Jenny Agutter; Frank Oz; Brian Glover; Lila Kaye; David Schofield; John Woodvine; Don McKillop; Paul Kember; Colin Fernandes; Rik Mayall; Paddy Ryan; ***D:*** John Landis; ***W:*** John Landis; ***C:*** Robert Paynter; ***M:*** Elmer Bernstein. Oscars '81: Makeup.

An American Werewolf in Paris 🦴🦴 **1997 (R)** More of a remake than a sequel, horror-comedy fails to live up to the wit and quirkiness of the original. Andy (Scott) is on a daredevil tour of Europe along with buddies Brad (Vieluf) and Chris (Buckman). As he attempts to bungee jump off of the Eiffel Tower, he spots a French femme attempting to plungee jump nearby. He saves her and immediately falls in love with her. The girl, Serafine (Delpy) warns him to stay away, but he keeps sniffing around. They tail her to a creepy house she shares with a guy named Claude (Cosso), where Andy secures a date and his friends are invited to a dinner party. Claude, however, is top dog in a pack of racist werewolves, and Andy's pals end up as the main course. Bitten himself, Andy learns that he's now a werewolf. Brad and the other victims pop up now and again to remind Andy that they're doomed to walk the earth until the werewolves that killed them are destroyed. Special effects have advanced a long way since the original and it shows, although the computer generated wolves are difficult to tell apart. **100m/C; VHS, DVD.** Julie Delpy; Tom Everett Scott; Julie Bowen; Anthony Waller; Pierre Cosso; Thierry Lhermitte; Vince Vieluf; Phil Buckman; Tom Novembre; Isabelle Constantini; ***D:*** Anthony Waller; ***W:*** Anthony Waller; Tim Burns; Tom Stern; ***C:*** Egon Werdin; ***M:*** Wilbert Hirsch.

American Woman 🦴🦴 ½ **2019 (R)** In a small Pennsylvania town, single mom Debra (Miller) lives in a chaotic home she shares with the daughter she had at 16, Bridget (Ferriera), and Jesse, the child of teenager Bridget. Debra is close to her sister Katherine (Hendricks), who lives with her husband (Sasso) and two children across the street. Debra relies on their support, and her need for it greatly increases when Bridget goes missing and Debra must raise Jesse as she navigates her own romantic life. Miller's complex performance is powerful and makes the story all the more potent. **111m/C; DVD, Blu-Ray.** Sienna Miller; Christina Hendricks; Aaron Paul; Sky Ferreira; Amy Madigan; ***D:*** Jake Scott; ***W:*** Brad Ingelsby; ***C:*** John Mathieson; ***M:*** Adam Wiltzie.

American Women 🦴🦴 *The Closer You Get* **2000 (PG-13)** Poor schlub County Donegal lads, weary of their lack of female companionship, send an ad to the Miami Herald, looking for young, nubile American women to come over and "see what happens." Hoping to see the American lasses in time for the social event of the season, the St. Martha's Day dance, they're disappointed when the day arrives but the girls don't. To make matters worse, the local ladies have brought in some Spanish fishermen to play music at the dance. Old fashioned ethnic comedy tries to cash in on the successes of "The Full Monty" and "Waking Ned Devine," but contains a wee bit too many Irish cliches, and the charm is squeezed out by the patronizing view of what is supposed to be modern-day Ireland. **90m/C; VHS, DVD.** *IR GB* Ian Hart; Sean McGinley; Niamh Cusack; Ruth McCabe; Ewan Stewart; Maureen O'Brien; Pat Laffan; Britta Smith; Pat Shortt; Cathleen Bradley; Sean McDonagh; Risteard Cooper; ***D:*** Aileen Ritchie; ***W:*** William Ivory; ***C:*** Robert Alazraki; ***M:*** Rachel Portman.

American Yakuza 🦴🦴 **1994 (R)** FBI agent Nick Davis (Mortensen) is sent to L.A. to infiltrate the American arm of the Yakuza, Japan's dangerous criminal underworld. He rises through the ranks and is adopted into the powerful Tendo family. Now Davis finds himself caught between the FBI, the Yakuza, and the vengeful American mafia. **95m/C; VHS, DVD.** Viggo Mortensen; Michael Nouri; Ryo Ishibashi; Franklin Ajaye; ***D:*** Frank Cappello; ***W:*** Max Strom; John Allen Nelson; ***C:*** Richard Clabaugh; ***M:*** David Williams.

American Zombie 🦴🦴 **2007** Mockumentary covering a small community of the living dead in Los Angeles and their attempts to fit in despite obvious discrimination, shortly before the usual social uprising. **91m/C; DVD, Streaming.** *SK US* Austin Basis; Al Vicente; John Solomon; Andrew Amondson; Kevin Michael Walsh; Paul Eiding; Jose Solomon; Philip Newby; Grace Lee; Jane Edith Wilson; Suzy Nakamura; Amy Higgins; ***D:*** Grace Lee; ***W:*** Grace Lee; Rebecca Sonnenshine; ***C:*** Matthias Grunsky; ***M:*** Woody Pak. **VIDEO**

Americana 🦴🦴 ½ **1981 (PG)** A troubled Vietnam vet tries to restore himself by rebuilding a merry-go-round in a small midwestern town, while dealing with opposition from the local residents. Offbeat, often effective post-Nam editorial that was produced and directed in 1973 by Carradine and then shelved. Hershey and Carradine were a couple back then. **90m/C; VHS, DVD.** David Carradine; Barbara Hershey; Michael Greene; John Drew (Blythe) Barrymore, Jr.; ***D:*** David Carradine; ***W:*** Richard Carr.

The Americanization of Emily 🦴🦴🦴 **1964** A happy-go-lucky American naval officer (Garner) with no appetite for war discovers to his horror that he may be slated to become the first casualty of the Normandy invasion as part of a military PR effort in this black comedy-romance. Meanwhile, he spreads the charisma in an effort to woo and uplift Emily (Andrews), a depressed English woman who has suffered the loss of her husband, father, and brother during the war. A cynical, often funny look at military maneuvers and cultural drift that was adapted by Paddy Chayefsky from William Bradford Huie's novel. Also available colorized. **117m/B; VHS, DVD, Blu-Ray.** James Garner; Julie Andrews; Melvyn Douglas; James Coburn; Joyce Grenfell; Keenan Wynn; Edward Binns; Liz Fraser; William Windom; ***D:*** Arthur Hiller; ***W:*** Paddy Chayefsky.

Americano 🦴🦴 **1955** A cowboy travelling to Brazil with a shipment of Brahma bulls discovers the rancher he's delivering them to has been murdered. An odd amalgam of western cliches and a South American setting. **85m/C; DVD, Blu-Ray.** Glenn Ford; Frank Lovejoy; Abbe Lane; Cesar Romero; ***D:*** William Castle.

Americano 🦴🦴 **2005 (R)** Recent college grad Chris (Jackson) and his friends Ryan (Sharp) and Michelle (Ruthanna Hopper) have been backpacking through Europe and wind up at the end of their trip in Pamplona, Spain, for the annual running of the bulls. Chris meets beautiful Adela (Varela), who takes pity on him and lets Chris stay at her house after his backpack is stolen. His feelings quickly turn romantic. Dennis Hopper plays an ex-pat bar owner proffering advice when Chris wonders if he's really ready to return home. **95m/C; DVD.** Joshua Jackson; Leonor Varela; Dennis Hopper; Timm Sharp; Ruthanna Hopper; ***D:*** Kevin Noland; ***W:*** Kevin Noland; ***C:*** Robert Christopher Webb; ***M:*** Peter Golub.

Americano 🦴🦴 **2011** Demy makes his feature directorial debut and also stars in this melancholy drama that features clips from his mother Agnes Varda's 1981 film "Documenteur" that show him as a child and are used as flashbacks. Martin, who has lived in France for years, returns to Los Angeles to sort out his estranged mom's estate. He knows little of her life but a letter and a photo has Martin searching in Tijuana for Lola (Hayek), who's working in a strip club called the Americano. English, French, and Spanish with subtitles. **106m/C; DVD, Blu-Ray.** *FR* Mathieu Demy; Salma Hayek; Geraldine Chaplin; Chiara Mastroianni; Carlos Bardem; ***D:*** Mathieu Demy; ***W:*** Mathieu Demy; ***C:*** Georges Lechaptois; ***M:*** Gregoire Hetzel.

America's Dream 🦴🦴🦴 **1995 (PG-13)** Trilogy of short stories covering black life from 1938 to 1958. In "Long Black Song," based on a short story by Richard Wright, Alabama farmer Silas (Glover) lives with lonely wife Sarah (Lifford), who succumbs to the charms of white travelling salesman, David (Donovan). "The Boy Who Painted Christ Black" is young Aaron (Golden), who gives the drawing to his teacher, Miss Williams (Calloway). But the portrait causes a great deal of controversy in Aaron's 1948 Georgia school, especially for ambitious principal George Du Vaul (Snipes). Based on a story by John Henrich Clarke. The last story is Maya Angelou's "The Reunion," about Chicago jazz pianist Philomena (Toussaint), who encounters her childhood nemesis, Beth Ann (Thompson), the daughter of the white family who employed her parents as servants. **87m/C; VHS, DVD.** Danny Glover; Tina Lifford; Tate Donovan; Dan Kamin; Wesley Snipes; Jasmine Guy; Vanessa Bell Calloway; Norman D. Golden, II; Timothy Carhart; Yolanda King; Rae'ven (Alyia Larrymore) Kelly; Lorraine Toussaint; Susanna Thompson; Carl Lumbly; Phyllis Cicero; ***D:*** Bill Duke; Kevin Rodney Sullivan; Paris Barclay; ***W:*** Ron Stacker Thompson; Ashley Tyler; ***C:*** Karl Herrmann; ***M:*** Patrice Rushen.

America's Heart and Soul 🦴🦴 **2004 (PG)** Series of vignettes seeks to capture the diversity and indomitable spirit of America, as a saccharine and ineffective answer to "Fahrenheit 9/11." Viewers literally fly over the U.S. and swoop down to meet a cowboy in Colorado, a rug weaver in Appalachia, a dairy farmer in Vermont, a trombone prodigy in Louisiana, a Methodist pastor in San Francisco, an Olympic boxer in Chicago and so on. Although the scenery is gorgeous and the people compelling, you're never with them for very long or reach any sort of depth. **84m/C; DVD.** ***D:*** Louis Schwartzberg; ***C:*** Louis Schwartzberg; ***M:*** Joel McNeely.

America's Sweethearts 🦴🦴 **2001 (PG-13)** This just in: Hollywood is shallow and fake, Julia Roberts is pretty, and entertainment reporters are freeloading numbskulls. These are the themes covered in this disappointing romantic comedy in which America's favorite on- and off-screen couple Eddie (Cusack) and Gwen (Zeta-Jones) pretend to reconcile during a disaster-filled press junket cooked up by desparate publicist Lee (Crystal). Complicating matters are the developing relationship between Gwen's sister and assistant Kiki (Roberts) and Eddie. Roth hasn't directed a film in over 10 years, and it shows here. But beneath the rust, there are some funny moments, mostly including Walken as the crazy director who has taken his own film hostage. **103m/C; VHS, DVD.** Julia Roberts; Catherine Zeta-Jones; John Cusack; Billy Crystal; Hank Azaria; Christopher Walken; Seth Green; Stanley Tucci; ***Cameo(s):*** Larry King; ***D:*** Joe Roth; ***W:*** Billy Crystal; Peter Tolan; ***C:*** Phedon Papamichael; ***M:*** James Newton Howard.

Americathon WOOF! **1979 (PG)** It is the year 1998 and the United States is almost bankrupt, so President Chet Roosevelt decides to stage a telethon to keep the country from going broke. Interesting satiric premise with a diverse cast, but a poor script and slack pacing spoil all the fun. The soundtrack features music by The Beach Boys and Elvis Costello while the narration is by George Carlin. **85m/C; VHS, DVD.** Peter Riegert; John Ritter; Nancy Morgan; Harvey Korman; Fred Willard; Meat Loaf Aday; Elvis Costello; Chief Dan George; Howard Hesseman; Jay Leno; Terence McGovern; Allan Arbus; David Opatoshu; John Lone; Cybill Shepherd; Dorothy Stratten; ***Cameo(s):*** Tommy Lasorda; Peter Marshall; ***Nar:*** George Carlin; ***D:*** Neal Israel; ***W:*** Monica Johnson; Neal Israel; ***M:*** Earl Brown, Jr.

Amerigeddon 🦴 ½ **2016 (PG-13)** An action flick that offers a potential scenario of the future in which the United States is in jeopardy. When the United Nations and a global terrorist group form an alliance, they work together to disable the power grid in the United States and institute martial law. Americans with survival skills band together to save the country and make it free again. **90m/C; DVD, Blu-Ray, Streaming, Download.** Aliya Astaphan; Rich Bentz; Giovannie Cruz; Jonny Cruz; Mike Daniel; ***D:*** Mike Norris; ***W:*** Gary Heavin; ***C:*** Akis Konstantakopoulos; ***M:*** Denis Kashoid.

Amexico 🦴 ½ **2016** A drama about migrants as they make their way in the United States and experience love, success, sorrow, and survival. Told from the point of view of Evelia Dominguez (Pena), a migrant who becomes a short-term housemaid to the Muehlhaus family. After the family is murdered in front of her, Evelia struggles to continue moving forward because of the trauma. Her migrant brother, Alejandro (Enrique), faces his own difficulties living in the United States and experiencing his own tragedies on the street. **86m/C; DVD.** Olivia Pena; Roberto Enrique; Richard Gleason; Maricela Ochoa; Bashar Rahal; ***D:*** Glenn Robert Smith; ***W:*** Glenn Robert Smith; ***C:*** Jim Orr; ***M:*** Emilio Kauderer. **VIDEO**

Amigo Undead 1/2 **2015** Kevin (played by an oft underestimated Randall Park) is invited by his estranged, dying brother to go camping with his buddies. They freak out when one of his brother's friends dies unexpectedly and bury him in an ancient Indian burial ground (sounds familiar doesn't it?). Kevin and company are being pursued by an indestructible dead man who sounds like a diesel engine with serious maintenance issues. Recommended for diehard fans of zombies or the aforementioned Mr. Park only. **92m/C; DVD, Blu-Ray, Streaming.** Randall Park; Steve Agee; Dave Sheridan; David Clennon; Jeff Bryan Davis; ***D:*** Ryan Nagata; ***W:*** Ryan Nagata; George Edelman; ***C:*** Ben Pluimer; ***M:*** Matt Bowen. **VIDEO**

Amira & Sam **2015** The first feature film by writer-director Sean Mullin focuses on an unexpected romance between an army veteran and a young Iraqi woman living in New York City. After returning from an overseas deployment, Sam (Starr) moves to New York. There, Sam meets up with his unit's Iraqi translator and his niece Amira (Shihabi). Though Amira initially has no interest in Sam because he is a solider, they become close friends after Sam hides Amira in his apartment to avoid immigration issues. Sam and Amira soon fall in love, but find their growing relationship threatened by circumstances outside of their control. **88m/C; DVD, Streaming, Download.** Martin Starr; Dina Shihabi; Paul Wesley; Laith Nakli; David Rasche; ***D:*** Sean Mullin; ***W:*** Sean Mullin; ***C:*** Daniel Vecchione; ***M:*** Heather McIntosh.

Amish Grace 1/2 **2010** Fact-based Lifetime movie taken from a book on the 2006 shootings of Amish schoolgirls in Pennsylvania. Ida Graber (Paisley-Williams), whose daughter was killed, grapples with the demands of her Old Order Amish faith that she forgive the sinner. Amy Roberts (Blanchard), a mother herself, must deal with the inexplicable and horrible aftermath that her husband was the killer. **90m/C; DVD.** Kimberly Williams; Tammy Blanchard; Matt Letscher; Fay Masterson; John Churchill; Madison Mason; Gary (Rand) Graham; ***D:*** Gregg Champion; ***W:*** Sylvie White; Teena Booth; ***C:*** Ross Berryman; ***M:*** Joseph Conlan. **CABLE**

Amistad **1997 (R)** Spielberg again creates an epic from another historic example of man's inhumanity, although not quite as effectively this time around. In 1839, African captives aboard the slaveship Amistad, led by a Mende tribesman named Cinque (Hounsou), free themselves and take over the ship in a bloody mutiny. Property attorney Robert Baldwin (McConaughey) must prove in lengthy court battles that the Africans were rightfully freed individuals in the eyes of the law. John Quincy Adams (Hopkins) presents the Africans' defense to the Supreme Court. Sequences depicting the horrors of slavery are bogged down with heavy handed musical orchestrations that elicit emotion, but at the price of storytelling. McConaughey seems a bit too Californian to be colonial and Morgan Freeman is reduced to periodic cameos as an abolitionist. Fortunately, thanks to an eye for rich detail and superb acting by dynamic newcomer Hounsou, the film nearly escapes the clutches of melodrama to emerge educational and moving. Film's release was marred by a French author accusing Spielberg and his Dreamworks studio of plagiarism. **152m/C; VHS, DVD, Blu-Ray.** Djimon Hounsou; Anthony Hopkins; Matthew McConaughey; Morgan Freeman; Nigel Hawthorne; David Paymer; Pete Postlethwaite; Stellan Skarsgard; Anna Paquin; Austin Pendleton; Tomas Milian; Paul Guilfoyle; ***D:*** Steven Spielberg; ***W:*** David Franzoni; ***C:*** Janusz Kaminski; ***M:*** John Williams. Broadcast Film Critics '97: Support. Actor (Hopkins).

The Amityville Horror **1979 (R)** Sometimes a house is not a home. Ineffective chiller that became a boxoffice biggie, based on a supposedly real-life occurrence in Amityville, Long Island. The Lutz family moves into the house of their dreams only to find it full of nightmares. Once the scene of a grisly mass murder, the house takes on a devilish attitude, plunging the family into supernatural terror. Pipes and walls ooze icky stuff, flies manifest in the strangest places, and doors mysteriously slam while exorcist Steiger staggers from room to room in scene-chewing prayer. Based on the Jay Anson book and followed by a number of sequels. **117m/C; VHS, DVD, Blu-Ray.** James Brolin; Margot Kidder; Rod Steiger; Don Stroud; Murray Hamilton; Helen Shaver; Amy Wright; Val Avery; Natasha Ryan; John Larch; K.C. Martel; Meeno Peluce; ***D:*** Stuart Rosenberg; ***W:*** Sandor Stern; ***C:*** Fred W. Koenekamp; ***M:*** Lalo Schifrin.

Amityville 2: The Possession
WOOF! 1982 (R) More of a prequel than a sequel to "The Amityville Horror" (1979). Relates the story of the house's early years as a haven for demonic forces intent on driving a father to beat the kids, a mother to prayer, and a brother to lust after his sister (before he murders them all). Young etc. portray an obnoxious family that you're actually glad to see wasted by the possessed son. A stupid, clumsy attempt to cash in on the success of the first film, which was also stupid and clumsy but could at least claim novelty in the bad housing development genre. Followed by "Amityville 3: The Demon" in 1983. **110m/C; VHS, DVD, Blu-Ray.** James Olson; Burt Young; Andrew Prine; Moses Gunn; Rutanya Alda; Jack Magner; Diane Franklin; ***D:*** Damiano Damiani; ***W:*** Tommy Lee Wallace; ***C:*** Franco Di Giacomo; ***M:*** Howard Blake; Lalo Schifrin.

Amityville 3: The Demon 1/2 *Amityville 3-D* **1983 (R)** America's worst real-estate value dupes another funky buyer. The infamous Amityville house is once again restless with terror and gore, though supported with even less plot than the usual smidgin. Cynical reporter Roberts moves in while trying to get to the bottom of the story by way of the basement. Courtesy of 3-D technology, monsters sprang at theatre patrons but the video version is strictly two-dimensional, forcing the viewer to press his or her face directly onto the TV screen in order to derive similar effect. **98m/C; VHS, DVD, Blu-Ray.** Tony Roberts; Tess Harper; Robert Joy; Candy Clark; John Beal; Leora Dana; John Harkins; Lori Loughlin; Meg Ryan; Rikke Borge; Jack Cardiff; ***D:*** Richard Fleischer; ***W:*** William Wales; David Ambrose; ***C:*** Fred Schuler; ***M:*** Howard Blake.

Amityville 4: The Evil Escapes 1/2 *The Amityville Horror: The Evil Escapes, Part 4* **1989 (R)** It's an unusual case of house-to-house transference as the horror from Amityville continues, now lodged in a Californian residence. The usual good-house-gone-bad story has the place creating a lot of unusual creaks and rattles before deciding to use its inherited powers to attack and possess a little girl. Special effects from Richard Stutsman ("The Lost Boys" and "Jaws"). **95m/C; VHS, DVD.** Patty Duke; Jane Wyatt; Norman Lloyd; Frederic Lehne; Brandy Gold; ***D:*** Sandor Stern; ***W:*** Sandor Stern; ***M:*** Rick Conrad. **TV**

Amityville: A New Generation 1/2 **1993 (R)** And the bad sequels just go on and on and on. Terry is a young photographer who's given an old mirror by a crazy homeless man (tell me why he took it). He shares a loft with three friends and all begin experiencing vivid and terrifying dreams of murder. Seems the mirror is tied to Amityville and its evil legacy and Terry is the designated inheritor. **92m/C; VHS, DVD, Blu-Ray.** Ross Partridge; Julia Nickson-Soul; David Naughton; Richard Roundtree; Terry O'Quinn; ***D:*** John Murlowski; ***W:*** Christopher DeFaria; Antonio Toro.

Amityville Dollhouse 1/2 **1996 (R)** Family moves into their Victorian dream home in Amityville, which comes complete with a replica dollhouse that charms the daughter. But the Amityville curse inhabits the plaything and soon the poltergeists make their nasty appearance. **97m/C; VHS, DVD, Blu-Ray.** Robin Thomas; Starr Andreeff; Allen (Culter) Cutler; Rachel Duncan; Jarrett Lennon; Clayton Murray; Frank Ross; Lenora Kasdorf; Lisa Robin Kelly; ***D:*** Steve White; ***W:*** Joshua Michael Stern; ***C:*** Thomas Callaway.

The Amityville Horror 1/2 **2005 (R)** Revamp of the Amityville tale swaps the understated chills of the original 1979 film with faster editing, more gore, and lots of goth imagery. George and Kathy Lutz (Reynolds and George) learn the meaning of "buyer beware" when they move their family into a lakeside colonial home, a real bargain thanks to the house's history of bone-chilling mass murders. After a series of strange incidents and ghostly visitations, Kathy begins catching on, just in time to watch her husband start channeling Jack Nicholson in "The Shining." The scares are familiar, but Douglas does an admirable job of creating a pervasively creepy, claustrophobic atmosphere throughout. **89m/C; DVD, Blu-Ray, UMD.** Ryan Reynolds; Melissa George; Jesse James; Jimmy Bennett; Rachel Nichols; Philip Baker Hall; Rich Komenich; Scott Kosar; Brendan Donaldson; Annabel Armour; Chloë Grace Moretz; Isabel Conner; Jose Taitano; David Gee; Danny McCarthy; Nancy Lollar; ***D:*** Andrew Douglas; ***C:*** Peter Lyons Collister; ***M:*** Steve Jablonsky.

Amityville 1992: It's About Time **1992 (R)** Time is of the essence in the sixth installment of the Amityville flicks. A vintage clock (from Amityville, of course), causes creepy goings-on in a family's house. Actually a halfway decent horror film with high-grade special effects, and much, much better than previous Amityville sequels, which isn't saying much. **95m/C; VHS, DVD, Blu-Ray.** Stephen Macht; Shawn Weatherly; Megan Ward; Damon Martin; Nita Talbot; Dick Miller; ***D:*** Tony Randel; ***W:*** Christopher DeFaria; Antonio Toro.

Amityville: The Awakening 1/2 **2017 (R)** This long-delayed entry in the Amityville franchise is awash in horror cliches and poor creative choices. Widowed mother Joan (Leigh) moves her three children into the home where the Amityville Horror took place years earlier as a cost-saving measure. Daughter Belle (Thorne) learns of the house's history when she is teased at school, and the whole family soon experiences the unexpected there. Among the strange things is the complete recovery of Belle's twin brother, James (Monaghan), who has long been in a coma. Though Belle uncovers the truth in interesting fashion, the film as a whole feels anything but awake. **85m/C; DVD, Blu-Ray.** Jennifer Jason Leigh; Bella Thorne; McKenna Grace; Cameron Monaghan; Thomas Mann; ***D:*** Franck Khalfoun; ***W:*** Franck Khalfoun; ***C:*** Steven Poster; ***M:*** Robin Coudert.

Amnesia **1996 (R)** Minister Paul Keller (Walker) is having an affair with his son's teacher, Veronica Dow (Tomanovich). Paul decides to fake his death, leaving wife Martha (Sheedy) with the insurance money, and allowing him to start a new life with Veronica. Only he has an accident that causes amnesia and runs into more trouble than he can imagine. Has more humor than you might imagine, thanks to its wacky characters, but as usual Kirkland is way over the top as a love-starved motel owner. **92m/C; VHS, DVD.** Nicholas Walker; Ally Sheedy; Sally Kirkland; John Savage; Dara Tomanovich; Vincent Berry; ***D:*** Kurt Voss.

Amnesiac **2015** Director Polish loses almost all of the indie cred he once had with this forgettable thriller. Bentley and Bosworth star as characters only credited as 'Man' and 'Woman'. They're in a car accident in the opening scene, with a girl in the backseat of the vehicle. When they wake up, the Man is in a bed in an old house, and cannot remember the identity of the Woman, who claims to be his wife. The girl goes unmentioned at all. Clearly, something odd is going on, and Bosworth has some fun with it, but you won't. **90m/C; DVD, Blu-Ray.** Kate (Catherine) Bosworth; Wes Bentley; Olivia Rose Keegan; Shashawnee Hall; Richard Riehle; ***D:*** Michael Polish; ***W:*** Amy Kolquist; Mike Le; ***C:*** Jayson Crothers; ***M:*** Aleks de Carvalho.

Among Brothers **2005** A "what if" based on a true crime from 1994. South Carolina frat boy Ethan doesn't take it well when co-ed Jennifer just wants to be friends, and she winds up dead in her apartment. Ethan whines to frat brothers Miles and Billy that it was an accident, so they torch the place to cover things up. Only the cops figure out Jennifer was murdered, so the boys try to shift the blame elsewhere. The real crime remains unsolved. **85m/C; DVD.** Matt Mercer; Lauren Schneider; Corey Cicci; Daniel J. Watts; Lindsay Ayliffe; ***D:*** John Schwert; ***W:*** John Schwert; ***C:*** Brad Hoover.

Among Giants **1998 (R)** Postlethwaite is Ray, the foreman of a crew of painters assigned to slap a new coat on the electrical towers that line the Yorkshire countryside. When a female Australian rock climber (Griffiths) wanders into town, joins the crew, and starts sleeping with Ray, she causes static between him and his best friend (Thornton). Understated to the point of being comatose, nothing much happens with the romance or the dangerous occupation angle. Postlethwaite does a fine job as the unlikely romantic lead, though. **93m/C; VHS, Streaming.** *GB* Pete Postlethwaite; Rachel Griffiths; James Thornton; Lennie James; Andy Serkis; Rob Jarvis; ***D:*** Sam Miller; ***W:*** Simon Beaufoy; ***C:*** Witold Stok; ***M:*** Tim Atack.

Among the Believers **2015** A feature-length documentary look at Muslim cleric Abdul Aziz Ghazi and his jihad against the Pakistani government. A supporter of ISIS and an ally of the Taliban, Aziz desires to impose Shariah law in Pakistan. To support his vision for Pakistan, Aziz is creating a network of Islamic seminaries for children. In addition to examining Aziz and his work, the documentary also follows teen students at his seminaries and their role in his ideological quest. Urdu and English with subtitles. **84m/C; DVD.** ***D:*** Mohammed Naqvi; Hemal Trivedi; ***W:*** Jonathan Goodman Levitt; ***C:*** Haider Ali; Habib Ur-Rehman; ***M:*** Milind Date.

Amongst Friends **1993 (R)** Three boyhood buddies, Trevor (McGaw), Billy (Lindsey), and Andy (Parlavecchio), from a nice Long Island neighborhood turn to crime out of boredom. Trevor gets busted and goes to prison for two years. Upon getting out, he finds his old cronies still share the taste for crime and general aimlessness but also still want that one big score. Trevor finally agrees to join Andy and Billy in a drug deal but the jealous Billy, who wants Trevor's old girlfriend Laura (Sorvino), plans a double-cross that will affect them all. Filled with cutting attacks on the society that spawns aimless youth. Debut of then 26-year-old writer/director Weiss. **88m/C; VHS, DVD.** Patrick McGaw; Steve Parlavecchio; Joseph Lindsey; Mira Sorvino; David Stepkin; Michael Artura; Louis Lombardi; ***D:*** Rob Weiss; ***W:*** Rob Weiss; ***C:*** Michael Bonvillain; ***M:*** Mick Jones.

Amongst Women **1998** Embittered ex-IRA soldier Michael Moran (Doyle) is desperate to keep his family together, but the widower's brutality only succeeds in driving his children to strong measures to make their own lives. Set in 1950s rural Ireland; based on the novel by John McGahern. **219m/C; DVD.** *IR* Tony Doyle; Susan Lynch; Ger Ryan; Geraldine O'Rawe; Anne-Marie Duff; Brian F. O'Byrne; ***D:*** Tom Cairns; ***W:*** Adrian Hodges; ***C:*** Sue Gibson; ***M:*** Niall Byrne. **TV**

Amores Perros *Love's a Bitch* **2000 (R)** A Mexico City car accident and the fortunes of a dog bring together three stories of love, loss, and redemption in director/producer Gonzalez Inarritu's impressive feature debut. Octavio's love for his brother's wife leads him to enter his dog, Cofi, in a dogfight for elopement money. When Cofi is wounded, it leads to a car chase, and the central accident. A woman, Valeria, is injured and permanently scarred in the accident. This affects her beau, who has just left his family to be with her. A homeless man, a former revolutionary turned hitman, witnesses the crash and rescues the dog, who becomes a part of his search for his estranged daughter. The plot structure invites comparisons to Tarantino, but these characters inhabit a more consequences-and-morality-oriented world than Q's characters ever did. Film came under fire from animal rights activists for the dogfight scenes, although it was made clear from the start that no animals were actually harmed. **153m/C; VHS, DVD, Blu-Ray.** *MX* Vanessa Bauche; Emilio Echeverria; Gael Garcia Bernal; Goya Toledo; Alvaro Guerrero; Jorge Salinas; Marco Perez; Rodrigo Murray; Humberto Busto; Gerardo Campbell; Rosa Maria Bianchi; Dunia Saldivar; Adriana Barraza; ***D:*** Alejandro Gonzalez Inarritu; ***W:*** Guillermo Arriaga; ***C:*** Rodrigo Prieto; ***M:***

Gustavo Santaolalla. British Acad. '01: Foreign Film; Natl. Bd. of Review '01: Foreign Film.

The Amorous Adventures of Moll Flanders 🦴🦴 **1965** An amusing romp set in 18th century England focusing on a poor orphan girl who seeks wealth. Moll plots to get ahead through an advantageous series of romances and marriages. Her plan is ruined when she falls in love and he turns out to be a wanted highwayman, landing her in prison. Not surprisingly, love (and money) conquers all. Based on the novel by Daniel Defoe. Novak tries in this female derivative of "Tom Jones," but this period piece isn't her style. **126m/C; VHS, Streaming.** Kim Novak; Richard Johnson; Angela Lansbury; Vittorio De Sica; Leo McKern; George Sanders; Lilli Palmer; ***D:*** Terence Young; ***C:*** Ted Moore; ***M:*** John Addison.

Amos and Andrew 🦴 ½ **1993 (PG-13)** Embarrassing attempt at comedy stops short of endorsing the stereotypes it tries to parody. Prizewinning African-American author Andrew Sterling (Jackson) is seen moving into a house on an island previously reserved for the uptight white, and the neighbors call the cops, assuming he's a thief. Chief of police (Coleman) eagerly gets into the act, then exploits drifter Amos (Cage) in a cover-up attempt when he realizes his mistake. Talented cast can't overcome lame jokes and transparent plot that serves as an opportunity to bring black and white together for a "see how much we have in common" bonding session. **96m/C; VHS, DVD, Blu-Ray.** Nicolas Cage; Samuel L. Jackson; Michael Lerner; Margaret Colin; Giancarlo Esposito; Dabney Coleman; Bob Balaban; Aimee Graham; Brad Dourif; Chelcie Ross; Jodi Long; ***D:*** E. Max Frye; ***W:*** E. Max Frye; ***M:*** Richard Gibbs.

Amour 🦴🦴🦴 **2012 (PG-13)** Writer/director Haneke's clinical approach to filmmaking takes on his most emotional subject matter in this tale of the inevitable common bond of life--the cruelty of death. Georges (Trintignant) and Anne (Riva) are a happy couple in their 80s until Anne has a stroke and goes unresponsive for long periods of time. The film merely chronicles, often like a fly on the wall, the final days of a decades-old relationship. Riva and Trintignant are stunningly real, adding to the feeling that this is so truthful, so private, and so emotionally raw that we shouldn't even be watching. **125m/C; DVD, Blu-Ray.** *FR AT* Jean-Louis Trintignant; Emmanuelle Riva; Isabelle Huppert; Alexandre Tharaud; William Shimell; ***D:*** Michael Haneke; ***W:*** Michael Haneke; ***C:*** Darius Khondji; ***M:*** Cecile Lenoir. Oscars '12: Foreign Film; British Acad. '12: Actress (Riva), Foreign Film; Golden Globes '13: Foreign Film; Ind. Spirit '13: Foreign Film.

The Amphibian Man 🦴🦴 **1961** What does a scientist do once he's created a young man with gills? Plunge him in the real world of aqua pura to experience life and love, albeit underwater. Trouble is, the protagonist, who's come to be known as the Sea Devil, takes a dive for a young pretty he's snatched from the jaws of death. A '60s Soviet sci-fi romance originally seen on American TV. **93m/C; VHS, DVD.** *RU* K. Korieniev; M. Virzinskaya; Mikhail Kozakov; Vladlen Davydov; ***D:*** Y. Kasancki; ***W:*** Aleksei Kapler.

Amputee with an Axe 🦴 ½ *Scream Bloody Murder; Claw of Terror; Matthew; The Captive Female* **1973 (R)** A young boy murders his father with a tractor for no apparent reason, and amputates his own arm in the process. After a long stay in the wacky bin, he relapses upon being released. Upon finding out his mother has remarried, he decides to replace her with a succession easily kidnapped women. **90m/C; DVD, Streaming.** Fred Holbert; Robert Knox; Angus Scrimm; Leigh Mitchell; Suzette Hamilton; ***D:*** Marc B. Ray; ***W:*** Marc B. Ray; Larry Alexander; ***C:*** Stephen Burum. **VIDEO**

Amreeka 🦴🦴🦴 **2009 (PG-13)** Palestinian divorced mom Muna (Faour), who lives on the West Bank, decides she and her 16-year-old son Fadi (Muallem) will have a better life joining her married sister Raghda (Abbass) in suburban Chicago. However, the U.S. has just invaded Iraq so all Arabs are under suspicion and Muna and her family face a number of indignities. Despite her professional background, the only job Muna can find is working at White Castle (a fact she keeps from her family) while Fadi tries to make his way through the hazards of high school. The cast is excellent with Faour expressing a particularly warm, bright, and strong presence. English and Arabic with subtitles. **96m/C; DVD.** *US CA* Nisreen Faour; Melkar Muallem; Hiam Abbass; Yussef Abu-Warda; Alia Shawkat; Joseph Ziegler; ***D:*** Cherien Dabis; ***W:*** Cherien Dabis; ***C:*** Tobias Datum; ***M:*** Kareem Roustom.

The Amsterdam Connection 🦴 **1978** Film company acts as a cover for prostitution and drug smuggling, with the girls acting as international couriers. **90m/C; VHS, DVD.** *CH* Chen Shing; Kid Sherrif; Yeung Sze; Jason Pai Piu; Fang Mui San; ***D:*** Fang Mui San; Lo Ke.

Amuck! 🦴🦴 ½ **1971** Vintage early '70s Euro-sleaze makes a belated debut on home video. Greta (Bouchet) is hired to be a secretary to world-famous author Richard Stuart (Granger). But Stuart's wife Eleanora (Neri) has designs on the young woman, and Greta has secrets of her own. Nostalgic treat for fans of the era. **98m/C; DVD.** *IT* Farley Granger; Barbara Bouchet; Rosalba Neri; Umberto Raho; Patrizia Viotti; Dino Mele; Petar Martinovic; Nino Segurini; ***D:*** Silvio Amandio; ***W:*** Silvio Amandio; ***C:*** Aldo Giordani; ***M:*** Teo Usuelli.

Amusement 🦴 **2008 (R)** There's nothing amusing about it. Longtime friends Tabitha, Shelby, and Lisa are held hostage in a maze of cells and traps as someone wants revenge for a long-past incident from their school days. **85m/C; DVD, Blu-Ray.** Katheryn Winnick; Laura Breckenridge; Jessica Lucas; Tad Hilgenbrink; Reid Scott; ***D:*** John Simpson; ***W:*** Jake Wade Hall; ***C:*** Mark Garret; ***M:*** Marco Beltrami. **VIDEO**

Amy 🦴🦴 ½ **1981 (G)** Set in the early 1900s, the story follows the experiences of a woman after she leaves her well-to-do husband to teach at a school for the deaf and blind. Eventually she organizes a football game between the handicapped kids and the other children in the neighborhood. Good Disney family fare. **100m/C; VHS, DVD, Streaming.** Jenny Agutter; Barry Newman; Kathleen Nolan; Margaret O'Brien; Nanette Fabray; Chris Robinson; Louis Fant; ***D:*** Vincent McEveety; ***M:*** Robert F. Brunner.

Amy 🦴🦴🦴 **2015 (R)** Amy Winehouse was an undeniable musical talent, whose life was cut short by the inevitable end of addiction at the age of 27. Director Asif Kapadia avoids most of the traps of the music bio-doc by focusing so intently on archival footage of the award-winning singer instead of merely taking heads pontificating about her importance. In fact, part of his point is how Winehouse could never avoid being recorded, and he very clearly implicates celebrity culture and the paparazzi in her death. The result is a commentary not just on music but how we steal the privacy of those we find talented. **128m/C; DVD, Blu-Ray, Streaming.** *US UK* ***D:*** Asif Kapadia; ***C:*** Ernesto Harrmann; ***M:*** Antonio Pinto. Oscars '15: Feature Doc.; British Acad. '15: Feature Doc.

The Amy Fisher Story 🦴🦴 *Beyond Control* **1993** Amy Fisher wishes she looked this good. Perhaps if she did, she could be acting in TV movies like Barrymore instead of providing fodder for them. The ABC account draws from a variety of sources to dramatize the relationship between Amy and her married, ahem, friend, and Amy's subsequent attack on his wife. Although it tries not to take sides, it does include some pretty hot sex scenes which could be why this docudrama garnered the highest ratings of the three network productions released on TV. See also: "Casualties of Love: The 'Long Island Lolita' Story" and "Lethal Lolita—Amy Fisher: My Story." **93m/C; VHS, DVD.** Drew Barrymore; Anthony John (Tony) Denison; Harley Jane Kozak; Tom Mason; Laurie Paton; Ken Pogue; Linda Darlow; Garry Davey; Dwight McFee; Gabe Khouth; Philip Granger; Stephen Cooper; ***D:*** Andy Tennant; ***W:*** Janet Brownell; ***C:*** Glen MacPherson; ***M:*** Michael Hoenig. **TV**

Amy's O 🦴🦴 *Amy's Orgasm* **2002** Amy (Davis) is a twentysomething L.A. single who has penned a self-help book about why women don't need men to feel complete. She's successful but doesn't believe her own work and is lonely and looking. She meets radio shock jock Matthew Starr (Chinlund), who turns out to be a pretty decent guy, although he's got some personal quirks Amy comes to resent. And Matthew finds some things about Amy he could live without. Of course, they're meant to be together if they could just get past their own egos. **87m/C; VHS, DVD.** Julie Davis; Nick (Nicholas) Chinlund; Caroline Aaron; Mitchell Whitfield; Mary Ellen Trainor; Charles Cioffi; Tina Lifford; Jennifer Bransford; ***D:*** Julie Davis; ***W:*** Julie Davis; ***C:*** Mark Mervis; Goran Paviceric.

Anaconda 🦴🦴 ½ **1996 (PG-13)** Snakes—lots and lots of snakes. Teeny baby snakes, little snakes, medium-sized snakes, large snakes, and one gigantic 40-foot long snake that likes to swallow people and then vomit them up again (the better to have room to swallow somebody else). Oh yeah, the minimal plot concerns a documentary film crew traveling the Amazon River looking for a legendary Indian tribe. They not only have to contend with the snakes but with crazy, snake-obsessed guide Paul Sarone (Voight). The actors react appropriately to becoming snake food. **90m/C; VHS, DVD, Blu-Ray.** Jon Voight; Jennifer Lopez; Ice Cube; Eric Stoltz; Owen Wilson; Kari Wuhrer; Jonathan Hyde; Vincent Castellanos; Danny Trejo; ***D:*** Luis Llosa; ***W:*** Jim Cash; Jack Epps, Jr.; Hans Bauer; ***C:*** Bill Butler; ***M:*** Randy Edelman.

Anaconda 3: The Offspring 🦴 **2008 (R)** It was filmed in Romania, has bad CGI, and a nonsensical plot—yep, it's another Sci-Fi Channel treasure. Scientist Amanda (Allen) has been working with Murdoch (Rhys-Davies), who has done some genetic tinkering that resulted in a mutated 60-foot long anaconda with a machete growing out of its tail (good for the gore factor but really silly looking). Of course the beastie gets loose and must be eradicated, which is where Hammett (Hasselhoff) and his mercenaries come in. **91m/C; DVD.** John Rhys-Davies; David Hasselhoff; Anthony Green; Crystal Allen; Patrick Regis; ***D:*** Don E. Fauntleroy; ***W:*** Nicholas Davidoff; David C. Olson; ***C:*** Don E. Fauntleroy; ***M:*** Peter Meisner. **CABLE**

Anacondas: The Hunt for the Blood Orchid 🦴🦴 **2004 (PG-13)** An enjoyably trashy quasi-sequel to the 1997 flick finds even more (and bigger) snakes to swallow the generally no-name cast. A pharmaceutical company sponsors a scientific expedition along a Borneo river to hunt for the rare title flower, which may extend life and youth. There's the usual mix of characters: fearless riverboat captain (Messner), arrogant scientist (Marsden), computer geek (Bryd), babe (Strickland), etc., and the standard situations: ramshackle boat, dense jungle, hungry snakes, and a really clever monkey for a little variety. The director and cast handle their parts efficiently and they know enough not to take it too seriously. Neither should you. **93m/C; VHS, DVD, UMD.** Johnny Messner; KaDee Strickland; Matthew Marsden; Eugene Byrd; Denis Arndt; Morris Chestnut; Salli Richardson-Whitfield; Nicholas Gonzalez; ***D:*** Dwight Little; ***W:*** Michael Miner; John Claflin; Daniel Zelman; Edward Neumeier; ***C:*** Stephen F. Windon; ***M:*** Nerida Tyson-Chew.

Anacondas: Trail of Blood 🦴 **2009 (R)** Yep, SciFi Channel does it again with cheap CGI that can't even get the snakes right (there's a couple of decent deaths which is why this isn't a woofer). In this fourth entry, scientist Amanda (Allen) has turned into a good girl and is trying to foil a corporate plot to get the super-snake's priceless venom. **88m/C; DVD.** John Rhys-Davies; Linden Ashby; Crystal Allen; Calin Stanciu; Danny Midwinter; Ana Ularu; ***D:*** Don E. Fauntleroy; ***W:*** David C. Olson; ***C:*** Don E. Fauntleroy; ***M:*** Peter Meisner. **CABLE**

Analyze That 🦴 ½ **2002 (R)** Woefully inferior sequel finds shrink Dr. Sobel (Crystal, becoming more irritating with every film), who's trying to deal with his father's death, also helping out mobster Vitti (De Niro), whose life is being threatened by mob factions with boundary issues. After Vitti fakes a breakdown to escape jailhouse hitmen, Sobel is forced by the FBI to house and rehabilitate him, incurring the wrath of his loving but running-out-of patience wife Laura (the sadly underused Kudrow). There are a few laughs to be had, mostly compliments of De Niro, but not enough to keep the inevitable "Analyze the Other Thing" off the Least Wanted list. **95m/C; VHS, DVD.** Billy Crystal; Robert De Niro; Lisa Kudrow; Joe (Johnny) Viterelli; Reg Rogers; Cathy Moriarty; John Finn; Kyle Sabihy; Callie (Calliope) Thorne; Pat Cooper; Frank Gio; Donnamarie Recco; ***D:*** Harold Ramis; ***W:*** Harold Ramis; Peter Steinfeld; Peter Tolan; ***C:*** Ellen Kuras; ***M:*** David Holmes.

Analyze This 🦴🦴🦴 **1998 (R)** Robert De Niro stars as anxiety-stricken mob boss Paul Vitti. He begins to see suburban shrink Ben (Crystal), and is so pleased with the results that he strong-arms the doc into seeing him whenever he wants. Unfortunately for Ben and fiance Laura (Kudrow), that usually happens to be when they're trying to get married. Palminteri is a rival gangster with whom Vitti "seeks closure." De Niro expertly winks at the mob genre (which he helped create) without losing the air of menace that surrounds the good fella character. His performance carries the movie despite the somewhat hokey ending. It's De Niro's underworld, Billy's just living in it. **110m/C; VHS, DVD.** Robert De Niro; Billy Crystal; Lisa Kudrow; Chazz Palminteri; Joe (Johnny) Viterelli; Bill Macy; Leo Rossi; Rebecca Schull; Molly Shannon; Max Casella; Pat Cooper; Richard C. Castellano; Jimmie Ray Weeks; Elizabeth Bracco; Tony Darrow; Kyle Sabihy; Donnamarie Recco; ***D:*** Harold Ramis; ***W:*** Harold Ramis; Peter Tolan; Kenneth Lonergan; ***C:*** Stuart Dryburgh; ***M:*** Howard Shore.

Anamorph 🦴 ½ **2007 (R)** Psycho-thriller gets too arty for its own good. Stan Aubray (Dafoe) is an OCD NYC police detective assigned to the case of a serial killer who arranges his victims using an artistic technique called anamorphosis (manipulating perspective). The killings may be related to a closed case where Aubray killed the prime suspect. Are the new murders being done by a copycat or did Aubray kill the wrong person? **107m/C; DVD.** Willem Dafoe; Scott Speedman; Clea DuVall; James Rebhorn; Peter Stormare; Amy Carlson; ***D:*** H.S. Miller; ***W:*** H.S. Miller; Tom Phelan; ***C:*** Fred Murphy; ***M:*** Reinhold Heil; Johnny Klimek.

Anastasia 🦴🦴🦴 ½ **1956** Bergman won her second Oscar, and deservedly so, for her classic portrayal of the amnesia victim chosen by Russian expatriate Brynner to impersonate Anastasia, the last surviving member of the Romanoff dynasty. As such, she becomes part of a scam to collect millions of rubles deposited in a foreign bank by her supposed father, the now-dead Czar. But is she just impersonating the princess? Brynner as the scheming White General and Hayes as the Grand Duchess who needs to be convinced turn in fine performances as well. Based on Marcelle Maurette's play. **105m/C; VHS, DVD, Blu-Ray.** Ingrid Bergman; Yul Brynner; Helen Hayes; Akim Tamiroff; Martita Hunt; Felix Aylmer; Ivan Desny; Sacha (Sascha) Pitoeff; ***D:*** Anatole Litvak; ***W:*** Arthur Laurents; ***C:*** Jack Hildyard. Oscars '56: Actress (Bergman); Golden Globes '57: Actress--Drama (Bergman); N.Y. Film Critics '56: Actress (Bergman).

Anastasia 🦴🦴 ½ **1997 (G)** Let's face it, this is a pretty weird story to turn into a cartoon fairy tale. Fox's first entry into the Disney-dominated full-length animated musical fray is the story of Princess Anastasia and the fall of the Romanov empire. She has been missing ever since the evil Rasputin put a curse on the Romanov family and started the Russian Revolution (Lenin must have flunked the screen test. Not "toon" enough). Ten years later, con artist Dimitri and ex-aristocrat Vladimir try to convince orphaned 18-year-old Anya that she's the ex-royal so they can claim a reward from the princess' grandmother. Little do they know that she actually is the lost princess, but they must battle Rasputin and his albino bat henchman to put things right. Among the big names lending their voices are Meg Ryan, John Cusack (Cossack?), and Christopher Lloyd. Now let me tell you how the Katzenjammer Kids started WWII. . . **90m/C; VHS, DVD, Blu-Ray.** ***V:*** Meg Ryan; John Cusack; Kelsey Grammer; Angela Lansbury; Christopher Lloyd; Hank Azaria; Bernadette Peters; Kirsten Dunst; ***D:*** Don Bluth; Gary Goldman; ***W:*** Bruce Graham; Susan Gauthier; Bob Tzudiker; Noni White; ***M:*** David Newman.

Anastasia: The Mystery of Anna 🦴🦴 ½ **1986** Irving stars as Anna Anderson, a woman who claimed to be the Grand Duchess Anastasia, the sole surviving daughter of Russian Czar Nicholas II. A powerful epic reliving her experience of royalty, flight from execution, and struggle to retain her heritage. The story of Anastasia remains as one of the greatest dramatic mysteries of the 20th century. Adapted from the book "Anastasia: The Riddle of Anna Anderson" by Peter Kurth. **190m/C; VHS, DVD.** Amy Irving; Olivia de Havilland; Jan Niklas; Nicolas Surovy; Susan Lucci; Elke Sommer; Edward Fox; Claire Bloom; Omar Sharif; Rex Harrison; ***D:*** Marvin J. Chomsky; ***W:*** James Goldman. **CABLE**

Anatomy 🦴🦴🦴 *Anatomie* **2000 (R)** Medical student Paula Henning (Potente) is accepted into a prestigious Heidelberg anatomy class. She's carrying on the family tradition of her grandfather, who's dying in the hospital he built, and her father, with whom she disagrees on almost everything. But when she gets to the new university, she finds that very creepy stuff is going on. Medical horror/thriller is right up there with "Coma." It's inventive, grotesque, and the special effects work very well. Franka Potente shows that the impression she made in "Run, Lola, Run" was no fluke. **100m/C; VHS, DVD, Blu-Ray.** *GE* Franka Potente; Benno Furmann; Anna Loos; Holger Spechhahn; Sebastian Blomberg; ***D:*** Stefan Ruzowitzky; ***W:*** Stefan Ruzowitzky; ***C:*** Peter von Haller; ***M:*** Marius Ruhland.

Anatomy 2 🦴 ½ *Anatomie 2* **2003 (R)** A cabal of mad scientists are implanting synthetic muscles into willing interns, only to learn the drugs needed to prevent their bodies from rejecting the foreign tissues drive them to insanity and murder. **101m/C; DVD, Blu-Ray.** *GE* Ariane Schnug; August Diehl; Herbert Knaup; Birgit von Ronn; Barnaby Metschurat; ***D:*** Stefan Ruzowitzky; ***W:*** Stefan Ruzowitzky; ***C:*** Andreas Berger; ***M:*** Marius Ruhland. **VIDEO**

Anatomy of a Murder 🦴🦴🦴🦴 **1959** Considered by many to be the best courtroom drama ever made. Small-town lawyer in northern Michigan faces an explosive case as he defends an army officer who has killed a man he suspects was his philandering wife's rapist. Realistic, cynical portrayal of the court system isn't especially concerned with guilt or innocence, focusing instead on the interplay between the various courtroom characters. Classic performance by Stewart as the down home but brilliant defense lawyer who matches wits with Scott, the sophisticated prosecutor; terse and clever direction by Preminger. Though tame by today's standards, the language used in the courtroom was controversial. Filmed in upper Michigan; based on the bestseller by judge Robert Traver. **161m/B; VHS, DVD, Blu-Ray.** James Stewart; George C. Scott; Arthur O'Connell; Ben Gazzara; Lee Remick; Orson Bean; Eve Arden; Duke Ellington; Kathryn Grant; Murray Hamilton; Joseph Welch; ***D:*** Otto Preminger; ***W:*** Wendell Mayes; ***C:*** Sam Leavitt; ***M:*** Duke Ellington. Natl. Film Reg. '12; N.Y. Film Critics '59: Actor (Stewart), Screenplay.

Anatomy of a Psycho 🦴 **1961** A man plans to avenge his gas chambered brother by committing mass murder. Very cheaply and poorly produced. **75m/B; VHS, DVD.** Ronnie Burns; Pamela Lincoln; Darrell Howe; Russ Bender; ***D:*** Boris L. Petroff.

Anatomy of a Seduction 🦴🦴 **1979** TV formula melodrama of a middle-aged divorcee's affair with her son's best friend. Age knows no boundaries when it comes to television lust. **100m/C; VHS, Streaming.** Susan Flannery; Jameson Parker; Rita Moreno; Ed Nelson; Michael LeClair; ***D:*** Steven Hilliard Stern; ***M:*** Hagood Hardy. **TV**

Anatomy of Hell WOOF! *Anatomie de L'Enfer* **2004** French pretentiousness at its most full-blown. An unnamed straight woman (Casar)--bored, stupid, mentally unbalanced or all three—slits her wrists in a gay disco and is attended to by a nameless gay man (Italian porn stud Siffredi) whom she then propositions. She'll pay him to accompany her to her creepy isolated house and look at her naked. This will help her confront her problems with intimacy or sexuality or something. Unless you're as masochistic as the characters, you won't care. Oh, and Casar has a body double for the more, ummm, close-up views but that's all Siffredi all the time. Adapted from Breillat's novel "Pornocratie"; French with subtitles. **87m/C; DVD.** *FR* Amira Casar; Rocco Siffredi; Catherine Breillat; ***D:*** Catherine Breillat; ***W:*** Catherine Breillat; ***C:*** Yorgos Arvanitis; Guillaume Schiffman; Miguel Malherios; Pedro da Santos; ***M:*** D'juiz.

Anchorman: The Legend of Ron Burgundy 🦴🦴 ½ **2004 (PG-13)** Back in the '80s, Chevy Chase specialized in clueless all-American goofs who thought they were smarter than they were. The crown has now been passed to Ferrell. Here, he plays Ron Burgundy, the top-rated anchorman in '70s-era San Diego. Ron is the booze swilling, cigarette smoking, female ogling, narcissistic leader of an all-male news team whose world is rocked by the arrival of a new female reporter—beautiful, talented, and ambitious Veronica Corningstone (Applegate). Ron falls for the babe even as he tries to retain his chauvinistic place at the top of the news chain. It's amusing shtick and a fair send-up of a time when men were pigs and women decided to bring home the bacon themselves. Besides Applegate, Ferrell is well supported by Koechner, Carell, and Rudd as his equally macho-wannabe news boys. **91m/C; DVD, Blu-Ray, HD-DVD.** Will Ferrell; Christina Applegate; David Koechner; Steve Carell; Paul Rudd; Fred Willard; Vince Vaughn; Chad Everett; Tara Subkoff; Stephen (Steve) Root; Danny Trejo; Jack Black; Ben Stiller; Missi Pyle; Chris Parnell; Tim Robbins; Luke Wilson; Laura Kightlinger; Kevin Corrigan; Fred Armisen; ***D:*** Adam McKay; ***W:*** Will Ferrell; Adam McKay; ***C:*** Thomas Ackerman; ***M:*** Alex Wurman.

Anchorman 2: The Legend Continues 🦴🦴 ½ **2013 (PG-13)** Less inspired than the original, McKay's follow-up to his cult hit still connects with the funny bone. Ron Burgundy (Ferrell) is back, pushed out of the New York news scene just as a company is about to create 24-hour news in the early '80s. Burgundy is called back in, reuniting with partners Brian (Rudd), Champ (Koechner), and Brick (Carell) in an effort to rise to the top again. Not every joke works but they come fast enough that the laughs outnumber the duds. **119m/C; DVD, Blu-Ray.** Will Ferrell; Steve Carell; Paul Rudd; David Koechner; Christina Applegate; Meagan Good; ***D:*** Adam McKay; ***W:*** Will Ferrell; Adam McKay; ***C:*** Oliver Wood; ***M:*** Andrew Feltenstein; John Nau.

Anchors Aweigh 🦴🦴🦴 **1945** Snappy big-budget (for then) musical about two horny sailors, one a girl-happy dancer and the other a shy singer. While on leave in Hollywood they return a lost urchin to his sister. The four of them try to infiltrate a movie studio to win an audition for the girl from maestro Iturbi. Kelly's famous dance with Jerry the cartoon Mouse (of "Tom and Jerry" fame) is the second instance of combining live action and animation. The young and handsome Sinatra's easy crooning and Grayson's near operatic soprano are blessed with music and lyrics by Styne and Cahn. Lots of fun, with conductor-pianist Iturbi contributing and Hollywood-style Little Mexico also in the brew. **139m/C; VHS, DVD, Blu-Ray.** Frank Sinatra; Gene Kelly; Kathryn Grayson; Jose Iturbi; Dean Stockwell; Carlos Ramirez; Pamela Britton; Sharon McManus; Leon Ames; ***D:*** George Sidney; ***M:*** Jule Styne; ***M:*** Sammy Cahn. Oscars '45: Scoring/Musical.

Ancient Evil: Scream of the Mummy 🦴 ½ **2000 (R)** Six archeology students discover accidentally revive an Aztec mummy and unleash a deadly curse that could destroy mankind. **86m/C; VHS, DVD.** Ariauna Albright; Jeff Peterson; Russell Richardson; Christopher Cullen; ***D:*** David DeCoteau. **VIDEO**

Ancient Relic 🦴 ½ *The Jesus Video* **2002 (R)** Confusing German miniseries focuses on a startling archeological discovery. Steffen Vogt is helping out at a dig site in Israel when he finds a 2,000-year-old skeleton holding instructions for a video camera. He leaps to the conclusion that the skeleton belongs to a time traveler who got actual footage of Jesus. His crackpot idea is given credence by expert Kaun, who's convinced the camera is hidden somewhere in Jerusalem's Wailing Wall. Then Steffen is abducted by your basic secret Vatican society who doesn't want the status quo upset. German with subtitles. **182m/C; DVD.** *GE* Naike Rivelli; Hans Diehl; Matthias Koeberlin; Heinrich Giskes; ***D:*** Sebastian Niemann; ***W:*** Martin Ritzenhoff; ***C:*** Gerhard Schirlo; ***M:*** Egon Riedel. **TV**

And Baby Makes Six 🦴🦴 ½ **1979** An unexpected pregnancy creates new challenges for a couple with grown children. Dewhurst is excellent as usual. Followed by "Baby Comes Home." **100m/C; VHS, DVD.** Colleen Dewhurst; Warren Oates; Maggie Cooper; Mildred Dunnock; Timothy Hutton; Allyn Ann McLerie; ***D:*** Waris Hussein; ***W:*** Shelley List. **TV**

And Everything Is Going Fine 🦴🦴 ½ **2010** Created by acclaimed filmmaker Steven Soderbergh, this feature-length documentary considers the whole of the life and career of Spalding Gray. This American actor and monologist had a long, rich career until his suicide in 2004. The documentary includes interviews with and excerpts from Gray's well-received one-man shows, resulting in a revealing portrait of the artist in his own words. **89m/C; DVD, Blu-Ray, Streaming, Download.** Spalding Gray; ***D:*** Steven Soderbergh; ***M:*** Forrest Gray.

And God Created Woman 🦴🦴 ½ *And Woman. . .Was Created; Et Dieu Crea la Femme* **1957 (PG)** Launching pad for Bardot's career as a sex siren, as she flits across the screen in a succession of scanty outfits and hangs out at the St. Tropez beach in what is euphemistically known as a swimsuit while turning up the heat for the males always in attendance. The plot concerns an 18-year-old nymphomaniac who is given a home by a local family with three handsome young sons. A cutting-edge sex film in its time that was boffo at the boxoffice. In French with English subtitles. **93m/C; VHS, DVD.** *FR* Brigitte Bardot; Curt Jurgens; Jean-Louis Trintignant; Christian Marquand; ***D:*** Roger Vadim; ***W:*** Roger Vadim; Raoul Levy; ***C:*** Armand Thirard; ***M:*** Paul Misraki.

And God Created Woman 🦴 ½ **1988 (R)** Loose, dull remake by Vadim of his own 1957 softcore favorite about a free-spirited woman dodging men and the law while yearning for rock and roll stardom. DeMornay is a prisoner who hopes to marry one of the local hunks (Spano) so she can be paroled. They marry, she strips, he frets, while political hopeful Langella smacks his lips in anticipation. Available in an unrated 100-minute version. **98m/C; VHS, DVD.** Rebecca De Mornay; Vincent Spano; Frank Langella; Donovan Leitch; Judith Chapman; Thelma Houston; ***D:*** Roger Vadim; ***M:*** Tom Chase; Steve Rucker.

And God Said to Cain 🦴 *E Dio Disse a Caino* **1969** Another Biblically titled western from the prolific Kinski, about a put-upon gunman who must fight for his life. **95m/C; VHS, DVD.** *IT* Klaus Kinski; Antonio Cantafora; Peter Carsten; Marcella Michelangeli; Alan Collins; Giuliano Raffaelli; ***D:*** Anthony M. Dawson; ***W:*** Anthony M. Dawson; Giovanni Addessi; ***C:*** Riccardo (Pallton) Pallottini; Luciano Trasatti; ***M:*** Carlo Savina.

. . .And God Spoke 🦴🦴 **1994 (R)** Low budget spoof takes on both religion and moviemaking with two schlockmeisters filming a biblical epic. Since the duo have no budget and are basic hacks with pretensions, they have to settle...so Sales plays Moses, "The Incredible Hulk" Ferrigno gets cast as Cain, while Plumb ("Jan" on "The Brady Bunch") does Mrs. Noah. Has some lulls but also covers very recognizable territory. Directorial debut of Borman. **82m/C; VHS, DVD.** Michael Riley; Stephen Rappaport; Soupy Sales; Lou Ferrigno; Eve Plumb; Andy Dick; R(ichard) C(arlos) Bates; Fred Kaz; Daniel Tisman; ***D:*** Arthur Borman; ***W:*** Gregory S. Malins; Michael Curtis; ***C:*** Lee Daniel.

And Justice for All 🦴🦴 ½ **1979 (R)** Earnest attorney Pacino questions the law and battles for justice in and out of the courtroom. He's hired to defend a detested judge from a rape charge, while dealing with a lost-soul caseload of eccentric and tragedy-prone clients. Overly melodramatic, an odd mix of satire, cynicism, and seemingly sincere drama that hits with a club when a stick will do. Jewison aims for black surrealism, permitting both Pacino and Warden (as a judge losing his sanity) to veer into histrionics, to the detriment of what is essentially a gripping behind-the-scenes story. Excellent cast creates sparks, including Lahti in her film debut. And Baltimore never looked lovelier. **120m/C; VHS, DVD.** Al Pacino; Jack Warden; Christine Lahti; Thomas G. Waites; Craig T. Nelson; John Forsythe; Lee Strasberg; Jeffrey Tambor; Dominic Chianese; ***D:*** Norman Jewison; ***W:*** Barry Levinson; Valerie Curtin; ***C:*** Victor Kemper; ***M:*** Dave Grusin.

And Never Let Her Go 🦴🦴 ½ *Ann Rule's And Never Let Her Go* **2001** CBS true crime miniseries based on the book by Ann Rule. Powerful Delaware lawyer Thomas Capano (Harmon) has an affair with vulnerable secretary Anne Marie Fahey (Morris) as well as keeping his longtime mistress, Christine (Ward). She breaks things off, but the obsessed, manipulative Capano won't let her go. Then Anne Marie disappears. The investigation is hindered because there's no body and by the sensational release of her diaries, but the detectives refuse to give up. **170m/C; DVD.** Mark Harmon; Kathryn Morris; Rachel Ward; Steven Eckholdt; Paul Michael Glaser; Rick Roberts; Olympia Dukakis; ***D:*** Peter Levin; ***W:*** Adam Greenman; ***C:*** Bruce Surtees; ***M:*** Harald Kloser. **TV**

And Now a Word From Our Sponsor 🦴 ½ **2013** Satire on the ad world is badly in need of new ideas. Chicago exec Adan Kundle (Greenwood) has a breakdown, lands in the hospital, and responds only by spouting commercial slogans. Widowed hospital volunteer Karen (Posey), who once attended a Kundle seminar, believes he's misunderstood and decides to take him in thus upsetting her teen daughter Meghan (MacDonald) and ruthless agency prez Lucas Foster (Blue) who wants Kundle declared incompetent. Debut director Bernbam doesn't seem to know how to make the cliches fresh. **87m/C; DVD, Streaming.** Bruce Greenwood; Parker Posey; Callum Blue; Allie MacDonald; ***D:*** Zack Bernbaum; ***W:*** Michael Hamilton-Wright; ***C:*** Stephen Whitehead; ***M:*** Erica Procunier.

And Now for Something Completely Different 🦴🦴🦴 **1972 (PG)** A compilation of skits from BBC-TV's "Monty Python's Flying Circus" featuring Monty Python's own weird, hilarious brand of humor. Sketches include "The Upper Class Twit of the Year Race," "Hell's Grannies," and "The Townswomen's Guild Reconstruction of Pearl Harbour." A great intro to Python for the uninitiated, or a chance for the converted to see their favorite sketches again. **89m/C; VHS, DVD.** *GB* John Cleese; Michael Palin; Eric Idle; Graham Chapman; Terry Gilliam; Terry Jones; Carol Cleveland; Connie Booth; ***D:*** Terry Gilliam; Ian McNaughton; ***W:*** John Cleese; Michael Palin; Eric Idle; Graham Chapman; Terry Gilliam; Terry Jones; ***C:*** David Muir; ***M:*** Douglas Gamley.

And Now Ladies and Gentlemen 🦴🦴 **2002 (PG-13)** Englishman Valentin (Irons) is a jewel thief who likes disguises and is suffering from mysterious blackouts. In Paris, jazz singer Jane Lester (Kaas) is also suffering from blackouts. They both wind up in Morocco, staying at the same hotel and seeing the same doctor (both turn out to have brain tumors). They flirt, there's a robbery at the hotel, a cop investigates...and the film continues to meander on and on. It all looks lovely but doesn't amount to much. English and French with subtitles. **126m/C; VHS, DVD.** *FR GB* Jeremy Irons; Patricia Kaas; Alessandra Martines; Thierry Lhermitte; Ticky Holgado; Yvan Attal; Claudia Cardinale; Amidou; Jean-Marie Bigard; ***D:*** Claude Lelouch; ***W:*** Claude Lelouch; Pierre Uytterhoeven; Pierre Leroux; ***C:*** Pierre William Glenn; ***M:*** Michel Legrand.

And Now My Love 🦴🦴 ½ **1974 (PG)** A French couple endeavor to maintain their romance despite interfering socio-economic factors—she's a millionaire and he's an excon filmmaker. Keller plays three roles spanning three generations, as Lelouch invests autobiographical details to invent a highly stylized, openly sentimental view of French folks in love with love. Along the way he comments on social mores and changing attitudes through the years. Dubbed in English. **121m/C; VHS, DVD.** *FR* Marthe Keller; Andre Dussollier; Carla Gravina; ***D:*** Claude Lelouch; ***W:*** Claude Lelouch. L.A. Film Critics '75: Foreign Film.

And Now the Screaming Starts 1/2 *Bride of Fengriffen; Fengriffen; I Have No Mouth But I Must Scream* **1973 (R)** The young bride-to-be of the lord of a British manor house is greeted by bloody faces at the window, a severed hand, and five corpses. Then Cushing shows up to investigate. Good-looking, sleek production with genuine chills. **91m/C; VHS, DVD, Blu-Ray.** *GB* Peter Cushing; Herbert Lom; Patrick Magee; Ian Ogilvy; Stephanie Beacham; Rosalie Crutchley; Guy Rolfe; Janet Key; Gillian Lind; ***D:*** Roy Ward Baker; ***W:*** Roger Marshall; ***C:*** Denys Coop; ***M:*** Douglas Gamley.

And So It Goes **2014 (PG-13)** Oren (Douglas) is a grumpy old coot who yells at everyone who crosses his path but in that supposedly lovable way that makes directors long past their prime think is sweet. Leah (Keaton) is the neighbor stuck in his path in this romantic dramedy that isn't romantic, dramatic, or comedic. So far out of touch with the way real people flirt, heal, and deal with life, Reiner's film is one of his worst and Douglas and Keaton are going through the motions with such little flair that one can almost see them getting bored. **94m/C; DVD, Blu-Ray.** Michael Douglas; Diane Keaton; Sterling Jerins; Scott Shepherd; Annie Parisse; Frances Sternhagen; ***D:*** Rob Reiner; ***W:*** Mark Andrus; ***C:*** Reed Morano; ***M:*** Marc Shaiman.

And So They Were Married 1/2 **1936** Amusing rom com with winning performances by the leads. Widower Stephen Blake (Douglas) and divorcee Edith Farnham (Astor) are temporarily stuck at a winter resort lodge at Christmas because of the weather. They begin an unexpected romance but their respective children have taken an instant dislike to each other and are determined to break them up. After succeeding, the kids have a change of heart and then scheme to get the adults back together. **74m/B; DVD.** Melvyn Douglas; Mary Astor; Edith Fellows; Jackie Moran; Donald Meek; ***D:*** Elliott Nugent; ***W:*** Doris Anderson; Joseph Anthony; ***C:*** Henry Freulich; ***M:*** Howard Jackson.

And Soon the Darkness **1970 (PG)** One of two vacationing young nurses disappears in France where a teenager was once murdered and the search is on. Predictable, ineffective suspenser. **94m/C; VHS, DVD, Blu-Ray.** *GB* Pamela Franklin; Michele Dotrice; Sandor Eles; John Nettleton; Claire Kelly; Hanna-Marie Pravda; ***D:*** Robert Fuest; ***W:*** Brian Clemens; Terry Nation; ***C:*** Ian Wilson; ***M:*** Laurie Johnson.

And Soon the Darkness **2010 (R)** Too many horror cliches make for boring viewing in this remake of the 1970 British film. Stephanie and Ellie go to rural Argentina on vacation but Ellie goes missing and the police seem to be indifferent. Stephanie turns to ex-pat American Michael, who's staying at the same hotel, but he may not be so trustworthy. **91m/C; DVD, Blu-Ray.** Amber Heard; Odette Annable; Karl Urban; Ceasar Vianco; ***D:*** Marcos Efron; ***W:*** Marcos Efron; Jennifer Derwingson; ***C:*** Gabriel Beristain; ***M:*** tomandandy.

And Starring Pancho Villa as Himself **2003** It's 1914, and Mexican revolutionary Pancho Villa finds himself in dire need of funding for his campaign against the military-run government. He strikes a deal with American filmmakers D.W. Griffith (Feore) and Harry Aiken (Broadbent) that provides them with full access to his war. Based upon actual events, their efforts resulted in the first feature length film. Splendid portrayal by the charismatic and superbly-cast Banderas in the title role of the complex and compelling Villa. **115m/C; VHS, DVD.** Antonio Banderas; Eion Bailey; Alan Arkin; Jim Broadbent; Matt(hew) Day; Colm Feore; Michael McKean; Alexa Davalos; Anthony Head; Kyle Chandler; Saul Rubinek; Damian Alcazar; Pedro Armendariz, Jr.; ***D:*** Bruce Beresford; ***W:*** Larry Gelbart; ***C:*** Andre Fleuren; Peter James; ***M:*** Joseph Vitarelli. **CABLE**

And the Band Played On **1993 (PG-13)** Randy Shilts's monumental, and controversial, 1987 book on the AIDS epidemic comes to TV in an equally controversial cable movie. Details the intricate medical research undertaken by doctors in France and the U.S. who fought to isolate and identify the mystery virus despite governmental neglect, red tape, clashing egos, and lack of funding. Various aspects of gay life are shown objectively, without sensationalizing. Celebrity cameos are somewhat distracting though most acquit themselves well. The script went through numerous rewrites; director Spottiswoode reportedly objected to HBO interference at the editing stage. **140m/C; VHS, DVD.** Matthew Modine; Alan Alda; Ian McKellen; Lily Tomlin; Glenne Headly; Richard Masur; Saul Rubinek; Charles Martin Smith; Patrick Bauchau; Nathalie Baye; Christian Clemenson; ***Cameo(s):*** Richard Gere; David Clennon; Phil Collins; Alex Courtney; David Dukes; David Marshall Grant; Ronald Guttman; Anjelica Huston; Ken Jenkins; Richard Jenkins; Tcheky Karyo; Swoosie Kurtz; Jack Laufer; Steve Martin; Dakin Matthews; Peter McRobbie; Lawrence Monoson; B.D. Wong; Donal Logue; Jeffrey Nordling; Stephen Spinella; ***D:*** Roger Spottiswoode; ***W:*** Arnold Schulman; ***C:*** Paul Elliott; ***M:*** Carter Burwell. **CABLE**

. . .And the Earth Did Not Swallow Him 1/2 *. . .Y No Se Lo Trago La Tierra* **1994** Family trials of migrant farm workers from the perspective of 12-year-old Marcos, who travels with his parents on their annual (it's 1952) move from Texas throughout the midwest during harvest season. Balances their struggles with the strong family bonds that allow them to endure. Based on the semi-autobiographical novel by Tomas Rivera. **99m/C; VHS, DVD.** Jose Alcala; Rose Portillo; Marco Rodriguez; ***D:*** Severo Perez; ***W:*** Severo Perez; ***C:*** Virgil Harper; ***M:*** Marcos Loya.

And the Ship Sails On *El la Nave Va* **1983 (PG)** On the eve of WWI, a group of devoted opera lovers take a luxury cruise to pay their respects to a recently deceased opera diva. Also on board is a group of fleeing Serbo-Croation freedom fighters. A charming and absurd autumnal homage-to-life by Fellini shot entirely in the studio. **130m/C; VHS, DVD.** *IT* Freddie Jones; Barbara Jefford; Janet Suzman; Peter Cellier; Philip Locke; Victor Poletti; Norma West; ***D:*** Federico Fellini; ***W:*** Federico Fellini; Tonino Guerra; ***C:*** Giuseppe Rotunno; ***M:*** Gianfranco Plenizio.

And the Wild, Wild Women *Hell in the City; Nella Cita L'Inferno* **1959** Italian women-behind-bars potboiler. Young Lina (Masina) is falsely convicted of robbery and sent to the slammer in Rome, where seasoned cellmate Egle (Magnani) decides to look after her. Lina is finally exonerated but, to Egle's regret, that doesn't mean Lina's life gets any better. Dubbed. **85m/B; DVD.** *IT FR* Anna Magnani; Giulietta Masina; Renato Salvatori; Alberto Sordi; Myriam Bru; Cristina Gaioni; ***D:*** Renato Castellani; ***W:*** Renato Castellani; ***C:*** Leonida Barboni; ***M:*** Roman Vlad.

And Then Came Lola **2009** Lesbian rom com inspired by the 1998 German film "Run, Lola, Run." This Lola is a talented but unreliable San Francisco photographer who is asked by her girlfriend to deliver some important photos to a meeting. Lola has three chances but gets waylaid by a no-nonsense meter maid, crazy dog owners, and beautiful babes, which could ruin both her personal and professional lives if she screws up. **70m/C; DVD.** Ashleigh Sumner; Jill Bennett; Cathy DeBuono; Jessica Graham; Candy Tolentino; Linda Ignazi; Angelyna Martinez; Jenoa Harlow; ***D:*** Ellen Seidler; Megan Siler; ***W:*** Ellen Seidler; Megan Siler; ***C:*** Jennifer Derbin.

And Then Came Love **2007** When Julie (Williams) decides to search for the anonymous sperm donor father of her six-year-old son, her idyllic world is suddenly turned upside-down. This color-blind romantic comedy provides unadulterated insight into complex relationships without being overly sappy or contrary. **98m/C; DVD.** Vanessa L(ynne) Williams; Kevin Daniels; Ben Vereen; Michael Boatman; Eartha Kitt; Tommy Nelson; Stephen Spinella; ***D:*** Richard Schenkman; ***W:*** Caytha Jentis; ***C:*** Timothy Naylor; ***M:*** Rebecca Lloyd.

And Then There Was You *Someone to Love* **2013** The process of mending a broken heart and broken trust are at the center of this romantic drama. Though Natalie (Beauvais) and Joshua (Robinson) seem to have the perfect marriage, it all falls apart when she learns he has a secret life which includes another family. Though her world has fallen apart, Natalie focuses on healing. In the process, she meets a new love interest, Darrell (White) with his own secrets, but must learn to fully trust before she can truly love again. **100m/C; DVD, Streaming, Download.** Garcelle Beauvais; Leon Robinson; Brian White; Lynn Whitfield; Scarlett Estevez; ***D:*** Leila Djansi; ***W:*** Leila Djansi; ***C:*** Aaron Wong; ***M:*** Thomas VanOosting. **VIDEO**

And Then There Were None 1/2 **1945** An all-star cast makes up the ten colorful guests invited to a secluded estate in England by a mysterious host. What the invitations do not say, however, is the reason they have been specifically chosen to visit—to be murdered, one by one. Cat and mouse classic based on Agatha Christie's book with an entertaining mix of suspense and black comedy. Remade in 1966 and again in 1975 as "Ten Little Indians," but lacking the force and gloss of the original. **97m/B; VHS, DVD, Blu-Ray.** Louis Hayward; Barry Fitzgerald; Walter Huston; Roland Young; Sir C. Aubrey Smith; Judith Anderson; Mischa Auer; June Duprez; ***D:*** Rene Clair; ***W:*** Rene Clair; Dudley Nichols; ***C:*** Lucien N. Andriot; ***M:*** Mario Castelnuovo-Tedesco.

And Then We Danced **2020** A gifted member of a respected folkdance troupe, Merab (Gelbakhiani) spends his days rehearsing and perfecting his every motion in a sexless environment. From an underachieving family of professional dancers, he works tirelessly at his craft to surpass them. Merab's life, perspective, and priorities are shifted when the more freewheeling Irakli (Bvalishvili) joins the troupe. The pair have instant chemistry, and their friendship turns into something more. The heartfelt drama offers empathetic insights into Georgian society and its strict dance culture, especially through Gelbakhiani's subtle performance, though it sometimes relies on cliches often found in coming of age films. Georgian with subtitles. **113m/C; DVD.** Levan Gelbakhiani; Bachi Valishvili; Ana Javakishvili; Kakha Gogidze; Ana Makharadze; ***D:*** Levan Akin; ***W:*** Levan Akin; ***C:*** Lisabi Fridell.

And They're Off 1/2 **2011 (PG-13)** What's really off here is the so-called comedy. Dusty Sanders (Astin) is a losing horse trainer with no horses, a volatile jockey girlfriend (Oteri), and a documentary crew following him around. A meeting with his former English teacher and her husband may change his luck because they're about to buy a horse and give Dusty the opportunity to train it. **90m/C; DVD.** Sean Astin; Cheri Oteri; Mark Moses; Gigi Rice; Martin Mull; Peter Jacobson; Mo Collins; Kevin Nealon; ***D:*** Rob Schiller; ***W:*** Alan Grossbard; ***C:*** Ulf Soderqvist; ***M:*** Lawrence Brown. **VIDEO**

And While We Were Here **2013 (R)** Young American writer Jane (Bosworth) and her violinist husband Leonard (Goldberg) travel to the island of Ischia, off the Amalfi Coast, as he prepares for a concert. Reading her grandmother's memoir about her WWII experiences (narrated by Bloom), Jane questions the mundane nature of her marriage contrasted against the passion in what she reads and what she feels far away from home. A romantic affair with younger man Caleb (Blackley) seems inevitable. Too slight and forgettable but the location-shooting captures the ability of beautiful places to crack people out of their well-worn patterns. **83m/C; DVD, Blu-Ray.** Kate (Catherine) Bosworth; Iddo Goldberg; Jamie Blackley; ***V:*** Claire Bloom; ***D:*** Kat Coiro; ***W:*** Kat Coiro; ***C:*** Doug Chamberlain; ***M:*** Mateo Messina.

And You Thought Your Parents Were Weird! 1/2 **1991 (PG)** A pair of introverted, whiz kid brothers invent a lovable robot to provide fatherly guidance as well as companionship for their widowed mother. Surprisingly charming, sentimental film is only slightly hampered by low-budget special effects. **92m/C; VHS, Streaming.** Marcia Strassman; Joshua John Miller; Edan Gross; John Quade; Sam Behrens; Susan Gibney; Gustav Vintas; Eric Walker; ***V:*** Alan Thicke; Richard Libertini; ***D:*** Tony Cookson; ***W:*** Tony Cookson; ***C:*** Paul Elliott; ***M:*** Randy Miller.

The Anderson Tapes **1971 (PG)** Newly released from prison, an ex-con assembles his professional pals and plans the million-dollar robbery of an entire luxury apartment house on NYC's upper east side. Of course, he's unaware that a hoard of law men from federal, state, and local agencies are recording their activities for a wide variety of reasons, though none of the surveillance is coordinated and it has nothing to do with the planned robbery. Based on the novel by Lawrence Sanders, the intricate caper is effectively shaped by Lumet, who skillfully integrates broad satire with suspense. Shot on location in New York City. Walken is The Kid, his first major role. **100m/C; VHS, DVD, Blu-Ray.** Sean Connery; Dyan Cannon; Martin Balsam; Christopher Walken; Alan King; Ralph Meeker; Garrett Morris; Margaret Hamilton; Val Avery; Dick Anthony Williams; Richard B. Shull; Conrad Bain; Paul Benjamin; ***D:*** Sidney Lumet; ***W:*** Frank Pierson; ***M:*** Quincy Jones.

Andersonville **1995** Andersonville was an infamous Confederate prison camp in Georgia that by August, 1864 contained more than 32,000 Union POWs—and was planned to hold 8,000 men. One in four soldiers died in the camp. The story is told through the eyes of Massachusetts Corporal Josiah Day (Emick), who is captured in 1864 and struggles to survive the hellish conditions. The commander of the Andersonville was a deranged German-Swiss captain named Wirz (Triska)?who became the only Civil War soldier to be hanged for war crimes (depicted in "The Andersonville Trial"). The TV miniseries was filmed some 150 miles from the original site. **168m/C; VHS, DVD.** Jarrod Emick; Frederic Forrest; Ted Marcoux; Jan Triska; Cliff DeYoung; Tom Aldredge; Frederick Coffin; Justin Henry; Kris Kamm; William H. Macy; Gabriel Olds; William Sanderson; Bud Davis; Carmen Argenziano; Peter Murnik; Thomas F. Wilson; ***D:*** John Frankenheimer; ***W:*** David W. Rintels; ***C:*** Ric Waite; ***M:*** Gary Chang. **TV**

The Andersonville Trial 1/2 **1970** Details the atrocities experienced by captured Union soldiers who were held in the Confederacy's notorious Andersonville prison during the American Civil War. Provides an interesting account of the war-crimes trial of the Georgia camp's officials, under whom more than 14,000 prisoners died. Moving, remarkable TV drama based on the book by Pulitzer prize-winner MacKinlay Kantor. **150m/C; VHS, DVD.** Martin Sheen; William Shatner; Buddy Ebsen; Jack Cassidy; Richard Basehart; Cameron Mitchell; ***D:*** George C. Scott. **TV**

Andre 1/2 **1994 (PG)** More human-animal interaction from the director of "The Man from Snowy River," telling the true story of an orphaned seal that was adopted by the local Maine harbormaster (Carradine) and his family. As they raise their houseguest, the question arises whether Andre should be returned to the wild. It'll remind you of "Free Willy" with an appealing smaller sea mammal and the equally appealing Majorino, as the youngster who befriends Andre. For those who are sticklers for accuracy, Andre is actually portrayed by a sea lion and not a seal. **94m/C; VHS, DVD.** Keith Carradine; Tina Majorino; Chelsea Field; Keith Szarabajka; Shane Meier; Joshua Jackson; ***D:*** George Miller; ***W:*** Dana Baratta; ***C:*** Thomas Burstyn; ***M:*** Bruce Rowland.

Andrei Rublev **1966** A 15th-century Russian icon painter must decide whether to record history or participate in it as Tartar invaders make life miserable. During the black and white portion, he becomes involved in a peasant uprising, killing a man in the process. After a bout of pessimism and a vow of silence, he goes forth to create artistic beauty as the screen correspondingly blazes with color. A brilliant historical drama censored by Soviet authorities until 1971. In Russian with English subtitles. **185m/C; VHS, DVD, Blu-Ray.** *RU* Anatoli (Otto) Solonitzin; Ivan Lapikov; Nikolai Grinko; Nikolai Sergeyev; ***D:*** Andrei Tarkovsky; ***W:*** Andrei Tarkovsky; Andrei Konchalovsky; ***C:*** Vadim Yusov; ***M:*** Vyacheslav Ovchinnikov.

Androcles and the Lion 1/2 **1952** Stage-bound Hollywood version of the George Bernard Shaw story about a tailor in Imperial Rome who saves Christians from a hungry lion he had previously befriended. Sharp dialogue and a plot that's relatively (within the bounds of Hollywood) faithful help a great play become a semi-satisfying cinematic morsel. Harpo Marx was originally cast as Androcles, but was fired by producer Howard Hughes five weeks into the shooting.

105m/B; VHS, DVD. Jean Simmons; Alan Young; Victor Mature; Robert Newton; Maurice Evans; Elsa Lanchester; ***D:*** Chester Erskine; ***C:*** Harry Stradling, Sr.

Android 1/2 **1982 (PG)** When an android who has been assisting a quirky scientist in space learns that he is about to be permanently retired, he starts to take matters into his own synthetic hands. Combines science fiction, suspense and cloned romance. A must for Kinski fans. **80m/C; VHS, DVD.** Klaus Kinski; Don Opper; Brie Howard; Norbert Weisser; Crofton Hardester; Kendra Kirchner; ***D:*** Aaron Lipstadt; ***W:*** Don Opper; James Reigle; ***C:*** Tim Suhrstedt; ***M:*** Don Preston.

The Android Affair 1/2 **1995 (PG-13)** Karen Garrett (Kozak) is studying at the Institute for Surgical Research where doctors practice experimental techniques on lifelike androids. Her next patient is William (Dunne), a handsome and charming android with a heart defect, who doesn't want to "die" during Karen's risky surgical procedure. What's worse is Karen finds this 'droid all too humanly appealing and decides to help him escape the Institute. From a story by Isaac Asimov and screenwriter Kletter. **90m/C; VHS, DVD.** Harley Jane Kozak; Griffin Dunne; Ossie Davis; Saul Rubinek; Peter Outerbridge; Natalie Radford; ***D:*** Richard Kletter; ***W:*** Richard Kletter; ***C:*** Berhard Salzmann; ***M:*** Simon Boswell.

Android Cop 1/2 **2014** In 2045, LA cop Hammond gets a new android partner. They are tasked with tracking down an android copy of the mayor's daughter and discover dirty cops and a conspiracy. An actually competent sci-fi actioner from The Asylum. **90m/C; DVD, Blu-Ray.** Michael Jai White; Randy Wayne; Kadeem Hardison; Larissa Vereza; Charles S. Dutton; ***D:*** Mark Atkins; ***W:*** Mark Atkins; ***C:*** Mark Atkins; ***M:*** Chris(topher) Cano. **VIDEO**

The Andromeda Strain 1/2 **1971 (G)** A satellite falls back to earth carrying a deadly bacteria that must be identified in time to save the population from extermination. The tension inherent in the bestselling Michael Crichton novel is talked down by a boring cast. Also available in letterbox format. **131m/C; VHS, DVD, Blu-Ray.** Arthur Hill; David Wayne; James Olson; Kate Reid; Paula Kelly; Ramon Bieri; George Mitchell; ***D:*** Robert Wise; ***W:*** Nelson Gidding; ***C:*** Richard H. Kline; ***M:*** Gil Melle.

The Andromeda Strain **2008** Creepy, updated, but over-extended adaptation of Michael Crichton's 1969 novel that was previously filmed for the big screen in 1971. An alien pathogen—code-named Andromeda—hitches a ride aboard a satellite that crashes near a small desert town in Utah. It either quickly kills the inhabitants or turns them into homicidal zombies. Dr. Jeremy Stone (Bratt) and his team are responsible for finding a cure but their efforts are hindered by government conspiracies as well as environmental activism and potential bioterrorism. Then a military snafu leads to an outbreak within the scientists' underground lab. **177m/C; DVD.** Benjamin Bratt; Christa Miller; Rick Schroder; Andre Braugher; Eric McCormack; Viola Davis; Justin Louis; Daniel Dae Kim; ***D:*** Mikael Salomon; ***W:*** Robert Schenkkan; ***C:*** Jim Joffin; ***M:*** Joel J. Richard. **CABLE**

Andromedia 1/2 *Andoromedia* **2000** Horribly sappy teen romance drama from director Takashi Miike featuring two Japanese pop bands as actors. A father resurrects his dead teen daughter as a computer program only to be murdered by a mega-corporation hell-bent on world domination. How they intend to achieve said domination with the archived memories of a dead teenager is anyone's guess. **109m/C; DVD.** *JP* Hiroko Shimabukoro; Eriko Imai; Takako Uehara; Hitoe Arakaki; Kenji Harada; Ryo Karato; Christopher Doyle; Tomorowo Taguchi; Issa Hentona; Shinobu Miyara; Yukinari Tamaki; Ken Okumoto; ***D:*** Takashi Miike; ***W:*** Itaru Era; Masa Nakamura; Kozy Watanabe; ***C:*** Christopher Doyle; Hideo Yamamoto.

Andron: The Black Labyrinth 1/2 *Andron* **2016 (R)** A sci-fi thriller about a futuristic society in which former slaves must fight for their freedom. It is the year 2154, and entertainment comes in the form of watching a group of people being thrown into a maze called the Black Labyrinth of Andron and betting on the outcome. When the group of men and women—all strangers to each other—are dropped in the tight space, they do not know how they got there or who they really are. They must work together to understand the codes and signals put before them as well as past tests—all to ensure their survival. **100m/C; DVD, Streaming, Download.** Alec Baldwin; Danny Glover; Michelle Ryan; Leo Howard; Gale Harold; ***D:*** Francesco Cinquemani; ***W:*** Francesco Cinquemani; ***C:*** Gherardo Gossi; ***M:*** Riccardo Eberspacher.

Andy and the Airwave Rangers *Andy Colby's Incredibly Awesome Adventure* **1989** Andy is whisked into the TV!! He finds adventure and excitement—car chases, intergalactic battles, and cartoons. **75m/C; VHS, DVD.** Dianne Kay; Vince Edwards; Bo Svenson; Richard Thomas; Erik Estrada; Randy Josselyn; Jessica Puscas; Chuck Kovacic; ***D:*** Deborah Brock.

Andy Hardy Comes Home 1/2 **1958** After a 12-year hiatus, Rooney and MGM tried to restart the Andy Hardy franchise to no effect. Andy's now married to bland Jane, has two trouble-prone young sons, and is a lawyer for an aviation factory in California. He and his family come back to Carvel to explore building a new plant. There's a crooked businessman who causes trouble but, since Judge Hardy has died, Andy must now make the moral choices. **80m/B; DVD.** Mickey Rooney; Patricia Breslin; Fay Holden; Cecilia Parker; Sara Haden; Frank Ferguson; Vaughn Taylor; ***D:*** Howard W. Koch; ***W:*** Edward Everett Hutshing; Robert Morris Donley; ***C:*** William W. Spencer; ***M:*** Van Alexander.

Andy Hardy Gets Spring Fever **1939** Andy falls for a beautiful acting teacher, and then goes into a funk when he finds she's engaged. Judge Hardy and the gang help heal the big wound in his heart. A lesser entry (and the seventh) from the popular series. **88m/B; DVD, Streaming.** Mickey Rooney; Lewis Stone; Ann Rutherford; Fay Holden; Cecilia Parker; Sara Haden; Helen Gilbert; ***D:*** W.S. Van Dyke; ***W:*** Kay Van Riper; ***C:*** Lester White; ***M:*** David Snell; Edward Ward.

Andy Hardy Meets Debutante 1/2 **1940** Seems like there should be an article in that title. Garland's second entry in series, wherein Andy meets and falls foolishly for glamorous debutante Lewis with Betsy's help while family is on visit to New York. Judy/Betsy sings "I'm Nobody's Baby" and "Singing in Rain." **86m/B; DVD, Streaming.** Mickey Rooney; Judy Garland; Lewis Stone; Ann Rutherford; Fay Holden; Sara Haden; Cecilia Parker; Diana Lewis; Tom Neal; ***D:*** George B. Seitz; ***W:*** Tom Seller; Annalee Whitmore; ***C:*** Charles Lawton, Jr.; Sidney Wagner; ***M:*** David Snell.

Andy Hardy's Blonde Trouble **1944** Andy's antics are sillier than usual in this 15th entry in the series as he deals with being a freshman at Wainwright College, his dad's alma mater that's just gone co-ed. Andy befriends Kay, who's more interested in faculty advisor, Mr. Standish, and is bewildered by a pert blonde who flirts with him one minute and ignores him the next. Andy's slow to discover these are the trouble-making Walker twins who cause hm to believe he should give up and go home until Judge Hardy comes to visit. **107m/B; DVD.** Mickey Rooney; Bonita Granville; Lee Wilde; Lyn Wilde; Herbert Marshall; Lewis Stone; ***D:*** George B. Seitz; ***W:*** Agnes Christine Johnston; William Ludwig; Harry Ruskin; ***C:*** Lester White; ***M:*** David Snell.

Andy Hardy's Double Life 1/2 **1942** In this entertaining installment from the Andy Hardy series, Andy proposes marriage to two girls at the same time and gets in quite a pickle when they both accept. Williams makes an early screen splash. **91m/B; DVD, Streaming.** Mickey Rooney; Lewis Stone; Ann Rutherford; Fay Holden; Sara Haden; Cecilia Parker; Esther Williams; William Lundigan; Susan Peters; Robert (Bobby) Blake; ***D:*** George B. Seitz; ***W:*** Agnes Christine Johnston; ***C:*** John Mescall; George J. Folsey; ***M:*** Daniele Amfitheatrof.

Andy Hardy's Private Secretary **1941** After Andy fails his high school finals he gets help from a sympathetic faculty member. As the secretary, Grayson makes a good first impression in one of her early screen appearances. The Hardy series was often used as a training ground for new MGM talent. **101m/B; DVD, Streaming.** Mickey Rooney; Kathryn Grayson; Lewis Stone; Fay Holden; Ian Hunter; Gene Reynolds; Ann Rutherford; ***D:*** George B. Seitz; ***W:*** Jane Murfin; Harry Ruskin; ***C:*** Lester White.

Andy Warhol's Bad **1977 (R)** In the John Waters' school of "crime is beauty," a Queens housewife struggles to make appointments for both her home electrolysis clinic and her all-female murder-for-hire operation, which specializes in children and pets (who are thrown out of windows and knived, respectively). Her life is further complicated by a boarder (King) who's awaiting the go-ahead for his own assignment, an autistic child unwanted by his mother. One of Warhol's more professional-appearing films, and very funny if your tastes run to the tasteless. **100m/C; VHS, DVD.** Perry King; Carroll Baker; Susan Tyrrell; Stefania Casini; Cyrinda Foxe; Lawrence Tierney; Tito Goya; ***D:*** Jed Johnson; ***C:*** Alan Metzger; ***M:*** Michael Bloomfield.

Andy Warhol's Dracula *Blood for Dracula; Young Dracula; Dracula Cerca Sangue di Vergine e...Mori de Sete; Dracula Vuole Vivere: Cerca Sangue de Vergina; Andy Warhol's Young Dracula* **1974 (R)** Sex and camp humor, as well as a large dose of blood, highlight Warhol's treatment of the tale. As Dracula can only subsist on the blood of pure, untouched maidens ("were-gins"), gardener Dallesandro rises to the occasion in order to make as many women as he can ineligible for Drac's purposes. Very reminiscent of Warhol's "Frankenstein," but with a bit more spoofery. Look for Roman Polanski in a cameo peek as a pub patron. Available in R and unrated versions. **106m/C; VHS, DVD.** *IT FR* Udo Kier; Arno Juerging; Maxine McKendry; Joe Dallesandro; Vittorio De Sica; Milena Vukotic; Dominique Darel; Stefania Casini; Silvia Dionisio; ***Cameo(s):*** Roman Polanski; ***D:*** Paul Morrissey; Anthony M. Dawson; ***W:*** Paul Morrissey; ***C:*** Luigi Kuveiller; ***M:*** Claudio Gizzi.

Andy Warhol's Frankenstein 1/2 *Flesh for Frankenstein; The Frankenstein Experiment; Up Frankenstein; The Devil and Dr. Frankenstein; Carne per Frankenstein; Frankenstein; Il Mostro e in Tavola...Barone Frankenstein* **1974 (X)** A most outrageous parody of Frankenstein, featuring plenty of gore, sex, and bad taste in general. Baron von Frankenstein (Kier) derives sexual satisfaction from his corpses (he delivers a particularly thought-provoking philosphy on life as he lustfully fondles a gall bladder); his wife seeks her pleasure from the monster himself (Dallesandro). Originally made in 3-D, this is one of Warhol's campiest outings. Also available on video in an R-rated version. **95m/C; VHS, DVD.** *GE FR IT* Udo Kier; Monique Van Vooren; Joe Dallesandro; Dalia di Lazzaro; Arno Juerging; Srdjan Zelenovic; Nicoletta Elmi; Marco Liofredi; Cristina Gajoni; Carla Mancini; Liu Bozizio; ***D:*** Paul Morrissey; ***W:*** Paul Morrissey; ***C:*** Luigi Kuveiller; ***M:*** Claudio Gizzi.

Angel 1/2 **1937** Melodrama finds Maria Barker (Dietrich) the bored wife of British diplomat Sir Frederick (Marshall). So she heads off to Paris to visit a friend and meets the dashing Anthony Halton (Douglas), with whom she has a fling. Too bad Halton's next stop is jolly old England where he runs into an old military chum (Sir Fred, of course). High gloss but no heart. **91m/B; DVD, Blu-Ray.** Marlene Dietrich; Herbert Marshall; Melvyn Douglas; Edward Everett Horton; Laura Hope Crews; ***D:*** Ernst Lubitsch; ***W:*** Guy Bolton; Samson Raphaelson; Russell Medcraft; ***C:*** Charles B(ryant) Lang, Jr.; ***M:*** Frederick "Friedrich" Hollander.

Angel 1/2 **1984 (R)** Low-budget leerer about a 15-year-old honor student who attends an expensive Los Angeles private school during the day and by night becomes Angel, a streetwise prostitute making a living amid the slime and sleaze of Hollywood Boulevard. But wait, all is not perfect. A psycho is following her, looking for an opportunity. **94m/C; VHS, DVD, Blu-Ray.** Donna Wilkes; Cliff Gorman; Susan Tyrrell; Dick Shawn; Rory Calhoun; John Diehl; Elaine Giftos; Ross Hagen; ***D:*** Robert Vincent O'Neil; ***W:*** Joseph M. Cala.

Angel 1/2 **2007** Over-ripe costumed melodrama set in Edwardian Britain and based on the 1957 novel by Elizabeth Taylor. Angel, the daughter of a provincial grocer, wants more from life and, through her writing of purple prose bestselling novels, she becomes wealthy. After buying a country mansion and hiring adoring secretary Lucy, Angel marries Lucy's brother Esme (a tortured artist, naturally) but World War I intrudes. Angel is remarkably unlikeable and almost every other character (with the exception of those of Neill and Rampling) is a cliché. **134m/C; DVD.** *GB* Romola Garai; Sam Neill; Michael Fassbender; Lucy Russell; Charlotte Rampling; Jacqueline Tong; Janine Duvitsky; Christopher Benjamin; Tom Georgeson; ***D:*** Francois Ozon; ***W:*** Francois Ozon; Martin Crimp; ***C:*** Denis Lenoir; ***M:*** Philippe Rombi.

Angel 3: The Final Chapter WOOF! 1988 (R) Former hooker Angel hits the streets to save her newly discovered sister from a life of prostitution. Trashy sequel with a better cast to tepid "Avenging Angel," which was the inept 1985 follow-up to 1984's tasteless "Angel." **100m/C; VHS, DVD, Blu-Ray.** Maud Adams; Mitzi Kapture; Richard Roundtree; Mark Blankfield; Kin Shriner; Tawny (Ellis) Fere; Toni Basil; ***D:*** Tom De Simone; ***M:*** Eric Allaman.

Angel-A **2005 (R)** Andre (Debbouze), a small-time crook, owes thugs all over Paris and he's at the end of the line. Contemplating a leap from a bridge to end his woes, a gorgeous blonde in a miniskirt beats him to it and leaps first. Of course he saves her. Of course she's his angel (a la "It's a Wonderful Life") and it's really her mission to save him. The spectacular Angela (Rasmussen) and Andre then traipse around town fixing Andre's mistakes, as well as Andre himself. Shot in black and white, with stunning images of Paris; the film's plot and actors, alas, do not fare as well. **91m/B; DVD.** *FR* Jamel Debbouze; Rie Rasmussen; Gilbert Melki; Serge Riaboukine; ***D:*** Luc Besson; ***W:*** Luc Besson; ***C:*** Thierry Arbogast.

Angel and the Badman **1947** When notorious gunslinger Wayne is wounded during a shoot-out, a pacifist family takes him in and nurses him back to health. While he's recuperating, the daughter in the family (Russell) falls for him. She begs him not to return to his previous life. But Wayne, though smitten, thinks that a Duke's gotta do what a Duke's gotta do. And that means finding the dirty outlaw (Cabot) who killed his pa. Predictable but nicely done, with a good cast and script. Wayne provides one of his better performances (and also produced). **100m/B; VHS, DVD, Blu-Ray.** John Wayne; Gail Russell; Irene Rich; Harry Carey, Sr.; Bruce Cabot; ***D:*** James Edward Grant; ***W:*** James Edward Grant; ***C:*** Archie Stout; ***M:*** Richard Hageman.

Angel and the Badman 1/2 **2009 (PG-13)** Wounded gunslinger Quirt Evans (Phillips) takes refuge with a family of Quakers and immediately starts romancing eldest daughter Temperance (Unger). But if he really expects to win her heart, he has to lay down his gun and not take revenge against bad guy Loredo (Perry). Dull remake of the 1947 western, which starred John Wayne, features Wayne's grandson Brendan in a small role. **92m/C; DVD.** Lou Diamond Phillips; Deborah Kara Unger; Luke Perry; Brendan Wayne; ***D:*** Terry Ingram; ***W:*** Jack Nasser; ***C:*** Anthony C. Metchie; ***M:*** Stu Goldberg. **CABLE**

An Angel at My Table **1989 (R)** New Zealand TV miniseries chronicling the life of Janet Frame, New Zealand's premiere writer/poet. At once whimsical and tragic, the film tells of how a mischievious, free-spirited young girl was wrongly placed in a mental institution for eight years, yet was ultimately able to cultivate her incredible storytelling gifts, achieving success, fame and happiness. Adapted from three of Frame's novels: "To the Is-land," "An Angel at My Table," and "The Envoy From Mirror City." Highly acclaimed the world over, winner of over 20 major international awards. **157m/C; VHS, DVD, Blu-Ray.** *NZ* Kerry Fox; Alexia Keogh; Karen Fergusson; Iris Churn; K.J. Wilson; Martyn Sanderson; ***D:*** Jane Campion; ***W:*** Laura Jones; ***C:*** Stuart Dryburgh. Ind. Spirit '92: Foreign Film. **TV**

Angel Baby 1/2 **1961** A mute girl struggles to re-define her faith when she is cured by preacher, but then sees him fail with others. Fine performances all around, notably Reynolds in his screen debut. Adapted from "Jenny Angel" by Elsie Oaks Barber. **97m/B; VHS, DVD.** George Hamilton; Salome Jens; Mercedes McCambridge; Joan Blondell; Henry Jones; Burt Reynolds; *D:* Paul Wendkos; Hubert Cornfield; *C:* Haskell Wexler.

Angel Blue ♪ 1/2 *My Neighbor's Daughter* **1997** All-around married nice guy Dennis Cromwell (Bottoms) lives with his wife, Jill (Eichhorn) and newborn child in his California hometown. He befriends newcomer Enrique (Rodriguez) and soon Enrique's daughter Angela (Behrens) is babysitting for the infant Cornwell. David should really know better when his friendship with the teen turns sexual and their secret gets out. **91m/C; VHS, DVD.** Sam Bottoms; Yeniffer Behrens; Lisa Eichhorn; Marco Rodriguez; Karen Black; Sandor Tecsy; *D:* Steven Kovacs; *W:* Steven Kovacs; *C:* Mickey Freeman; *M:* Joel Lindheimer. **CABLE**

Angel Dusted ♪ 1/2 **1981** This made-for-TV flick about the dangers of drug use looks sorta hysterical and dated but check out the performances by Stapleton and real-life son Putch as unsuspecting housewife/mom Betty Eaton and college boy Owen who winds up in restraints after smoking some PCP-laced reefer. He's had a major violent freakout and is committed to a psych hospital but his complete recovery is uncertain. Based on the book by Ursula Etons. **97m/C; DVD.** John Putch; Maureen Stapleton; Arthur Hill; Percy Rodriguez; Darlene Craviotto; Patrick Cassidy; Helen Hunt; *D:* Dick Lowry; *W:* Darlene Craviotto; *M:* James Horner. **TV**

Angel Eyes ♪♪ 1/2 **2001 (R)** Although the film's marketing campaign implied some supernatural elements, there's nothing unworldly about this romantic drama. And despite some capable performances by the leads, the film is utterly predictable as well. Tough Chicago police officer Sharon Pogue (Lopez) is still dealing with the effects of an abusive childhood when she meets another lost soul, Catch (Caviezel), who's grappling with the death of his wife and child. He saves her life, they fall for each other, but things are hardly that simple. They both have emotional issues and a past connection that's all too easy to determine. **104m/C; DVD.** Jennifer Lopez; James (Jim) Caviezel; Sonia Braga; Terrence Howard; Jeremy Sisto; Monet Mazur; Victor Argo; Shirley Knight; Jeremy Ratchford; Peter MacNeill; Stephen Kay; *D:* Luis Mandoki; *W:* Gerald Di Pego; *C:* Piotr Sobocinski; *M:* Marco Beltrami.

Angel Face ♪♪♪ **1952** An angel's face with a devil's heart is psycho rich girl Diane (Simmons), who wants to get rid of her hated stepmommy (O'Neil) so she can have daddy (Marshall) all to herself. Diane is infatuated with new chauffeur Frank (Mitchum) and he becomes an unwitting accomplice in her deadly scheme. Both are brought up on murder charges but Frank doesn't realize how far this crazy chick will go to keep what—and who'she wants. Wild noir melodrama from Preminger that gave good girl Simmons a chance to unleash her inner bad femme. Mitchum is his usual cool self. **92m/B; DVD.** Jean Simmons; Robert Mitchum; Herbert Marshall; Mona Freeman; Leon Ames; Barbara O'Neil; Kenneth Tobey; *D:* Otto Preminger; *W:* Frank Nugent; Oscar Millard; *C:* Harry Stradling, Sr.; *M:* Dimitri Tiomkin.

An Angel for Satan ♪ 1/2 *Un Angelo per Satan* **1966** Steele plays a dual role in her last major, Italian horror film. She gives a strong performance as a woman possessed by the spirit of a statue. In Italian with no subtitles. **90m/B; VHS, DVD.** *IT* Barbara Steele; Anthony Steffen; Aldo Berti; Mario Brega; Ursula Davis; Claudio Gora; *D:* Camillo Mastrocinque; *W:* Camillo Mastrocinque; *M:* Francesco De Masi.

Angel Has Fallen ♪♪ **2019 (R)** Secret Service agent Mike Banning (Butler) is the most loyal and trusted agent of U.S. President Allan Trumball (Freeman) and continues to guard him despite chronic pain and migraines caused by concussions. When the president is attacked by drones with smart bombs while enjoying a fishing trip, Banning is set up to take the fall for the attack when all the other Secret Service agents are killed and Trumball ends up in a coma. A rather bland and routine second sequel to Olympus Has Fallen though Butler and Nick Nolte (playing his father) provide some energy. **121m/C; DVD, Blu-Ray.** Gerard Butler; Frederick Schmidt; Danny Huston; Rocci Williams; Piper Perabo; *D:* Ric Roman Waugh; *W:* Ric Roman Waugh; Robert Mark Kamen; Matt Cook; *C:* Jules O'Loughlin; *M:* David Buckley.

Angel Heart ♪♪ 1/2 **1987 (R)** Exotic, controversial look at murder, voodoo cults, and sex in 1955 New Orleans. Bonet defiantly sheds her image as a young innocent (no more Cosby Show for you, young lady). Rourke is slimy as marginal NYC private eye Angel, hired by the devilish De Niro to track a missing big band singer who violated a "contract." His investigation leads him to the bizarre world of the occult in New Orleans, where the blood drips to a different beat. Visually stimulating, with a provocative sex scene between Bonet and Rourke, captured in both R-rated and unrated versions. Adapted by Parker from "Falling Angel" by William Hjortsberg. **112m/C; VHS, DVD, Blu-Ray.** Mickey Rourke; Robert De Niro; Lisa Bonet; Charlotte Rampling; Michael Higgins; Charles Gordone; Kathleen Wilhoite; Stocker Fountelieu; Brownie McGhee; Elizabeth Whitcraft; Eliott Keener; Dann Florek; *D:* Alan Parker; *W:* Alan Parker; *C:* Michael Seresin; *M:* Trevor Jones.

Angel in the House ♪♪ 1/2 *Foster* **2011 (PG)** The Morrison's marriage is rocky after the death of their child and their problems conceiving another. They decide to become foster parents instead and seven-year-old Eli suddenly appears on their doorstep, saying the agency sent him. Eli seems wise beyond his years and is not only a good listener but offers sound advice to put the Morrson's marriage back together. It's reliably charming and suitable for family viewing. **90m/C; DVD.** *UK* Toni Collette; Ioan Gruffudd; Maurice Cole; Hayley Mills; Richard E. Grant; Anne Reid; *D:* Jonathan Newman; *W:* Jonathan Newman; *C:* Dirk Nel; *M:* Mark Thomas.

The Angel Levine ♪♪ 1/2 **1970 (PG)** Morris (Mostel) is an old Jewish man who has lost his faith in God after a series of personal and professional losses. Alexander Levine (Belafonte) is a black angel who can earn his wings if he can convince Morris that his life does have meaning. As sentimental as it sounds but the leads are pros. Based on a story by Bernard Malamud. **104m/C; VHS, DVD.** Zero Mostel; Harry Belafonte; Ida Kaminska; Milo O'Shea; Gloria Foster; Eli Wallach; Anne Jackson; *D:* Jan Kadar; *W:* Bill Gunn; Ronald Ribman; *C:* Richard Kratina; *M:* William Eaton.

Angel Negro ♪♪ *Black Angel* **2000** Hyped as Chile's first horror film, it starts with the usual group of high school students celebrating in a manner that ends in one's inevitable death. Just as inevitably the survivors start getting murdered one by one years later by someone they assume is the dead girl. **85m/C; DVD.** *CL* Alvaro Morales; Andrea Freund; Blanca Lewin; *D:* Jorge Olguin; *W:* Jorge Olguin; *C:* Arnaldo Rodriquez; *M:* Juan Francisco Cueto. **VIDEO**

Angel of Death **WOOF!** **1986 (R)** A small mercenary band of Nazi hunters attempt to track down Josef Mengele in South America. Stupid entry in the minor "let's find the darn Nazi before he really causes trouble" genre. Director Franco is also known as A. Frank Drew White. **92m/C; VHS, DVD.** Chris Mitchum; Fernando Rey; Susan Andrews; *D:* Jess (Jesus) Franco.

Angel of Death ♪ *Semana Santa; Holy Week* **2002** Detective Maria Delgado (Sorvino) comes to Seville during Holly Week to investigate a series of ritual killings. With cops Quemada (Martinez) and Torillo (Atkine) assisting, Maria discovers a mysterious religious order, The Brotherhood of Christ, and an old woman (Valli) keeping a secret since the Spanish Civil War. Lackluster, miscast thriller adapted from the novel by David Hewson. **94m/C; DVD.** *GE SP GB FR IT DK* Mira Sorvino; Olivier Martinez; Feodor Atkine; Alida Valli; Luis Tosar; *D:* Pepe Danquart; *W:* Roy Mitchell; *C:* Ciro Cappellari; *M:* Andrea Guerra.

Angel of Death ♪ 1/2 **2009 (R)** Originally a 10-episode web series starring Bell as remorseless assassin Eve. After suffering severe head trauma, the hitwoman begins to hallucinate and is haunted by her victims. So Eve decides to seek revenge on her mob employers, who ordered the hits. **90m/C; DVD.** Zoe Bell; Lucy Lawless; Doug Jones; Vail Bloom; Theodore (Ted) Raimi; Brian Poth; Justin Huen; Jake Abel; *D:* Paul Etheredge-Ouzts; *W:* Ed Brubaker; *C:* Carl Herse.

Angel of Destruction ♪ 1/2 **1994 (R)** Undercover cop is assigned to protect controversial rock star from psycho fan. Cop gets killed and cop's sister decides to go after the killer. **80m/C; VHS, DVD.** Maria Ford; Charlie Spradling; *D:* Charles Philip Moore.

Angel of H.E.A.T. **WOOF!** *The Protectors, Book One* **1982 (R)** Porn-star Chambers is Angel, a female super-agent on a mission to save the world from total destruction. Sex and spies abound with trashy nonchalance. **90m/C; VHS, DVD.** Marilyn Chambers; Mary Woronov; Steve Johnson; *D:* Helen Sanford; Myrl A. Schreibman.

Angel of the Night ♪♪ *Nattens Engel* **1998 (R)** Rebecca inherits her grandmother's creepy mansion and invites her best friend and her boyfriend for a visit. While exploring, Rebecca discovers that great-grandpa Rico was a vampire and she inadvertently releases him from his tomb. Dubbed from Danish. **98m/C; VHS, DVD.** *DK* Ulrich Thomsen; Maria Karlsen; Erik Holmey; *D:* Shakey Gonzaless; *W:* Shakey Gonzaless; *C:* Jacob Kusk; *M:* Soren Hyldgaard.

Angel on My Shoulder ♪♪♪ **1946** A murdered convict makes a deal with the Devil (Rains) and returns to earth for revenge as a respected judge who's been thinning Hell's waiting list. Occupying the good judge, the murderous Muni has significant problems adjusting. Amusing fantasy with Muni in a rare and successful comic role. Co-written by Segall, who scripted "Here Comes Mr. Jordan," in which Rains played an angel. Remade in 1980. **101m/B; VHS, DVD.** Paul Muni; Claude Rains; Anne Baxter; Onslow Stevens; *D:* Archie Mayo; *W:* Harry Segall; *C:* James Van Trees; *M:* Dimitri Tiomkin.

Angel Rodriguez ♪♪ 1/2 **2005** Unsentimental story about the problems facing the trouble-prone title character. Angel (Everett) is a smart Brooklyn high schooler whose temper often gets the best of him. After getting into a fight with his dad's girlfriend, he's thrown out of the house and taken in for the night by his pregnant guidance counselor Nicole (Griffiths). But good intentions have a way of going wrong. **87m/C; DVD.** Rachel Griffiths; Denis O'Hare; David Zayas; Jonan Everett; Wallace Little; Jon Norman Schneider; Denise Burse; *D:* Jim McKay; *W:* Jim McKay; Hannah Weyer; *C:* Chad Davidson. **CABLE**

Angel Town ♪ **1989 (R)** A foreign exchange student, who happens to be a champion kick-boxer, is forced into combat with LA street gangs. **90m/C; VHS, DVD, Blu-Ray.** Olivier Gruner; Theresa Saldana; Frank Aragon; Tony Valentino; Peter Kwong; Mike Moroff; *D:* Eric Karson.

Angel Unchained ♪ 1/2 **1970** Typical biker exploitation flick has bikers and hippies joining together to fend off small-town redneck hostility. **92m/C; VHS, DVD, Blu-Ray.** Don Stroud; Tyne Daly; Luke Askew; Larry Bishop; Aldo Ray; Bill McKinney; *D:* Lee Madden; *W:* Jeffrey Alladin Fiskin.

Angel with the Trumpet ♪♪ **1950** Depressing character study of a woman who marries to please her family, rather than herself. When the Gestapo finds out about her Jewish ancestry, she must make the most important decision of her life. Currently only available as part of a collection 'The Nifty Fifties'. **98m/B; VHS, DVD.** *GB* Eileen Herlie; Basil Sydney; Norman Wooland; Maria Schell; Olga Edwards; Oskar Werner; Anthony Bushell; Wilfrid Hyde-White; *D:* Anthony Bushell.

Angela ♪♪ **1994** Exceedingly mystical film focuses on religiously obsessed 10-year-old Angela (Rhyne), who tells her six-year-old sister Ellie (Blythe) that unless they are very good the Devil will come to take them away. Meanwhile, she tries to cope with volatile family relationships, including their unstable mother. Good performances in a sometimes sluggish and abstract drama. **105m/C; VHS, DVD.** Miranda Stuart Rhyne; Charlotte Blythe; Anna Thomson; John Ventimiglia; Vincent Gallo; *D:* Rebecca Miller; *W:* Rebecca Miller; *C:* Ellen Kuras; *M:* Michael Rohatyn. Sundance '95: Cinematog., Filmmakers Trophy.

Angela ♪♪ **2002 (R)** Angela (Finochiarro) is married to the older Saro (Pupella), who runs the mob in Palermo. Angela helps out by using her shoe store as a front for his drug deals, but she's frustrated by being shut out of all the business decisions. Then hunky hood Masino (di Stefano) is hired and the two are soon hitting the sheets. A bad idea, not only because of what Saro will do but because it gives the cops, who have the mobsters under surveillance, the leverage they need to take Saro down. Italian with subtitles. **100m/C; DVD.** *IT* Andrea Di Stefano; Donatella Finochiarro; Mario Pupella; Toni Gambino; *D:* Roberta Torre; *W:* Roberta Torre; Massimo D'Anolfi; *C:* Daniele Cipri; *M:* Andrea Guerra.

Angela's Ashes ♪♪ 1/2 **1999 (R)** Frank McCourt's devastating memoir covers growing up poverty-stricken in Limerick during the 1930s, with an alcoholic father (Carlyle) and a mother (Watson) struggling to hold the family together while dealing with her own deep depression. The book had the saving graces of lyricism and wit. Unfortunately, the film misses all that and is merely bleak despite the talented cast (including the three actors who play Frank through the years). **145m/C; DVD, Blu-Ray.** *IR* Emily Watson; Robert Carlyle; Joe Breen; Ciaran Owens; Michael Legge; Ronnie Masterson; Pauline McLynn; *Nar:* Andrew Bennett; *D:* Alan Parker; *W:* Robert Carlyle; Laura Jones; *C:* Michael Seresin; *M:* John Williams.

Angelique ♪♪ 1/2 *Angelique, Marquise des Anges; Angelique, Marquise of Angels* **1964** The first of a five-picture series of mildly racy, bodice-ripping costumed pulp. Beautiful Angelique (Mercier) is forced to leave her lover Nicolas (Gemma) to marry wealthy (but disfigured) Count Joffrey de Peyrac (Hossein). A marriage of convenience turns into true love but Joffrey has powerful enemies, including a jealous Louis XIV (Toja), who accuses Joffrey of sorcery. Loosely based on the novels by Anne and Serge Colon; French with subtitles. **117m/C; DVD.** *FR* Michele Mercier; Robert Hossein; Jean Rochefort; Claude Giraud; Giuliano Gemma; Charles Regnier; Jacques Toja; *D:* Bernard Borderie; *W:* Claude Brule; Francis Cosne; *C:* Henri Persin; *M:* Michel Magne.

Angelique and the King ♪♪ 1/2 *Angelique et le Roy* **1966** The third in the series following "Angelique: The Road to Versailles." The Persian ambassador (Frey) falls in love with Angelique and holds her captive, hoping that she'll return his affections. When she finally returns to the court of King Louis (Toja) it's to rumors that she's his new mistress. Followed by "Untamable Angelique." French with subtitles. **104m/C; DVD.** *FR* Michele Mercier; Robert Hossein; Sami Frey; Jean Rochefort; Estella Blain; Jacques Toja; *D:* Bernard Borderie; *W:* Bernard Borderie; Francis Cosne; Alain Decaux; *C:* Henri Persin; *M:* Michel Magne.

Angelique and the Sultan ♪♪ 1/2 *Angelique et le Sultan* **1968** The fifth and last in the series, following "Untamable Angelique." Angelique continues to be threatened by d'Escrainville, who holds her aboard his ship. A battle ensues between the kidnapper and Joffrey but Angelique has already been sold to the Sultan of Morocco, so Joffrey must go rescue his wife. French with subtitles. **97m/C; DVD.** *FR* Michele Mercier; Robert Hossein; Roger Pigaut; Ettore Manni; Helmuth Schneider; Jean-Claude Pascal; Jacques Santi; Aly Ben-Ayed; *D:* Bernard Borderie; *W:* Bernard Borderie; Francis Cosne; *C:* Henri Persin; *M:* Michel Magne.

Angelique: The Road to Versailles ♪♪ 1/2 *Merveilleuse Angelique* **1965** The second in the series, following "Angelique." Believing her husband Joffrey is dead, Angelique hides out in Paris with her old love Nicolas but discovers he's changed from a sweet youth to a ruthless criminal. Still, Nicolas offers her protection and when Angelique is reunited with her children, she decides to try respectability by becoming a shop owner under an assumed name. Followed by "Angelique and the King." French with subtitles. **105m/C; DVD.** *FR* Michele Mercier; Robert Hossein; Giuliano

Gemma; Claude Giraud; Jean Rochefort; Charles Regnier; Claire Maurier; Jacques Toja; Jean-Louis Trintignant; ***D:*** Bernard Borderie; ***W:*** Claude Brule; Francis Cosne; ***C:*** Henri Persin; ***M:*** Michael Magne.

Angels & Demons 🦴🦴 **2009 (PG-13)** Sequel/prequel to Dan Brown's "The Da Vinci Code," is just as ridiculously plotted as the original, but is thankfully faster-paced and less exposition-intensive. Harvard symbologist Robert Langdon (Hanks) is in Rome trying to prevent the secret society, the Illuminati, from destroying the Vatican. It all adds up to a semi-entertaining mess that can be enjoyed if you don't think about it too much. **138m/C; DVD, Blu-Ray.** Tom Hanks; Ayelet Zurer; Ewan McGregor; Stellan Skarsgard; Armin Mueller-Stahl; ***D:*** Ron Howard; ***W:*** Akiva Goldsman; David Koepp; ***C:*** Salvatore Totino; ***M:*** Hans Zimmer.

Angels and Insects 🦴🦴🦴 **1995 (R)** Very strange Victorian-era romantic drama is definitely an acquired taste. The mysteries of nature are nothing compared to the mysteries of human life as naturalist William Adamson (Rylance) comes to discover when he takes up a position at the home of amateur insect collector, Sir Harald Alabaster (Kemp). He falls in love and quickly marries blondly beautiful Eugenia (Kensit), whose outward propriety hides a sensual nature and some decadent family secrets. Based on A.S. Byatt's novella "Morpho Eugenia." Take particular note of the costumes by Paul Brown, which mimic the exoticness of insects. **116m/C; VHS, DVD.** *GB* Mark Rylance; Patsy Kensit; Kristin Scott Thomas; Jeremy Kemp; Douglas Henshall; Chris Larkin; Annette Badland; Anna Massey; Saskia Wickham; ***D:*** Philip Haas; ***W:*** Belinda Haas; Philip Haas; ***C:*** Bernard Zitzermann; ***M:*** Alexander Balanescu.

Angels Crest 🦴 ½ **2011 (R)** Based on Leslie Schwartz's novel, this drama centers on the loss of a child, often a foundation for manipulative histrionics. Set in the titular Rocky Mountain town, Dellal's film is another tale of working class, already-troubled people dealing with intense, unimaginable tragedy. Young father Ethan (Dekker) is trying to take care of his son instead of the boy's alcoholic mother (Collins) but this snow-covered film quickly turns to melodrama. The cast seems up for the soap operatic challenge but the piece never develops the realism for the grave subject matter to have any weight. **92m/C; DVD, Blu-Ray.** Tom Decker; Jeremy Piven; Lynn Collins; Mira Sorvino; Elizabeth McGovern; Joseph Morgan; Kate Walsh; Barbara Williams; Julian Domingues; Ameko Eks Mass Carroll; ***D:*** Gaby Dellal; ***W:*** Catherine Triescmann; ***C:*** David Johnson; ***M:*** Stephen Warbeck.

Angel's Dance 🦴🦴 ½ **1999 (R)** Tony (Chandler) works for mobster Uncle Vinnie (Polito) and wants to be a hit man. So, Vinnie sends him to L.A. for training with Stevie Rossellini (Belushi) who, despite appearances, is an expert. Part of Tony's education is to choose and kill a victim at random and he selects Angel (Lee). This is Tony's big mistake, since this Angel is turns out to be the avenging kind. Gets a little too goofy but does provide some action. **102m/C; VHS, DVD.** James Belushi; Sheryl Lee; Kyle Chandler; Jon Polito; Ned Bellamy; Mac Davis; Frank John Hughes; Mark Carlton; ***D:*** David Corley; ***W:*** David Corley; ***C:*** Michael G. Wojciechowski; ***M:*** Tim Truman.

Angels Die Hard 🦴🦴 **1970 (R)** Novel biker story with the cyclists as the good guys intent on helping a town during a mining disaster. Grizzly Adams makes an early film appearance. **86m/C; VHS, DVD.** Tom Baker; R.G. Armstrong; Dan Haggerty; William (Bill) Smith; ***D:*** Richard Compton; ***W:*** Richard Compton; ***M:*** Bill Cone.

Angels Don't Sleep Here 🦴🦴 **2000** Forensic pathologist Michael Daniels returns to his hometown when his twin brother disappears. He gets involved with district attorney Kate, who was his brother's childhood girlfriend, and whose father is the town's mayor. Michael thinks his brother is stalking him and when the mayor is killed, he believes his brother is the culprit. But local detective Russell Stark thinks Michael is the real criminal. **97m/C; VHS, DVD.** Dana Ashbrook; Robert Patrick; Roy Scheider; Susan Allison; Gary Farmer; Kelly Rutherford; Christina Pickles; ***D:*** Paul Cade. **VIDEO**

Angels Fall 🦴🦴 ½ **2007** Reece Gilmore (Locklear) was the sole survivor of a mass killing at the Boston restaurant where she worked. Desperate for a fresh start, Reece hits the road until her car breaks down in a Wyoming town and she takes a diner job to get some cash. Settling in, Reece becomes interested in writer Brody (Schaech), who is the only one to help her when Reece claims she witnessed a murder, although the cops don't find any evidence of a crime. A Lifetime original movie based on the novel by Nora Roberts. **95m/C; DVD.** Heather Locklear; Johnathon Schaech; Gary Hudson; Derek Hamilton; Linda Darlow; ***D:*** Ralph Hamecker; ***W:*** Janet Brownell; ***C:*** Joel Ransom; ***M:*** Chris P. Bacon; Stuart M. Thomas. **CABLE**

Angels from Hell 🦴 **1968** Early application in the nutso 'Nam returnee genre. Disillusioned Vietnam veteran forms a massive biker gang for the sole purpose of wreaking havoc upon the Man, the Establishment and anyone else responsible for sending him off to war. The big gang invades a town, with predictably bloody results. Sort of a follow-up to "Hell's Angels on Wheels." **86m/C; VHS, Streaming.** Tom Stern; Arlene Martel; Ted Markland; Stephen Oliver; Paul Bertoya; James Murphy; Jack Starrett; Pepper Martin; Luana Talltree; ***D:*** Bruce Kessler.

Angels Hard As They Come 🦴🦴 **1971 (R)** Opposing Hell's Angels leaders clash in a hippie-populated ghost town. A semi-satiric spoof of the biker genre's cliches features an early Glenn appearance and Busey's film debut. **86m/C; VHS, DVD.** Gary Busey; Scott Glenn; James Iglehart; Gary Littlejohn; Charles Dierkop; Larry Tucker; Gilda Texter; Janet Wood; Brendan Kelly; ***D:*** Joe Viola; ***W:*** Jonathan Demme; Joe Viola; ***M:*** Richard Hieronymous.

Angels in America 🦴🦴🦴 **2003** Kushner exquisitely adapts his two-part award-winning play into this six-part miniseries that vividly intertwines the lives and sufferings of several New Yorkers as they grapple with such issues as AIDS, drug addiction, homosexuality, and abandonment during the mid-80s. Masterfully directed by Nichols, it presents a spiritual perspective featuring Thompson as an angel of mercy to a man dying of AIDS while Streep appears as an apparition to another. **360m/C; DVD.** Meryl Streep; Emma Thompson; Justin Kirk; Ben Shenkman; Mary-Louise Parker; Jeffrey Wright; Patrick Wilson; James Cromwell; Michael Gambon; Simon Callow; Brian Markinson; ***D:*** Mike Nichols; ***W:*** Al Pacino; Tony Kushner; ***C:*** Stephen Goldblatt; ***M:*** Thomas Newman. **CABLE**

Angels in Stardust 🦴🦴 **2014 (PG-13)** A teen girl struggles to find herself in this coming-of-age comedy-drama. Vallie Sue (Michalka) lives with her irresponsible mother Tammy (Silverstone) and younger brother at mystical yet dangerous impoverished community constructed on the lot of a deserted drive-in theater near the Texas-Oklahoma border. Full of imagination, Vallie Sue knows she has potential and longs for escape, using a fictional cowboy character (Burke) as a role model. When her mother breaks up the family, Vallie Sue must do all she can to move forward in the world. **101m/C; DVD, Streaming, Download.** AJ Michalka; Alicia Silverstone; Amelia Rose Blaire; Billy Burke; Sydney Sweeney; ***D:*** William Robert Carey; ***W:*** William Robert Carey; ***C:*** Alexandre Lehmann; ***M:*** John Hunter.

Angels in the Endzone 🦴🦴 ½ **1998** TV follow-up to Disney's 1994 "Angels in the Outfield" finds the heavenly troops trying to aid a failing high school football squad, especially the leading players (Gallagher and Lawrence) who are also trying to also handle the death of their father. **85m/C; VHS, DVD.** Matthew Lawrence; David Gallagher; Paul Dooley; Christopher Lloyd; ***D:*** Gary Nadeau. **TV**

Angels in the Infield 🦴🦴 ½ **2000** Third in the Disney series finds former baseball player Bob "The Bungler" Bugler (Grier) trying to earn his Guardian Angels wings by looking out for pitcher Eddie Everett (Warburton) who's lost his self-confidence. But with daughter Laurel (Irvin) praying for some heavenly intervention, things are certainly looking up. **93m/C; VHS, DVD.** David Alan Grier; Patrick Warburton; Kurt Fuller; Rebecca Jenkins; Colin Fox; Peter Keleghan; Duane Davis; Brittney Irvin; ***D:*** Robert King. **TV**

Angels in the Outfield 🦴🦴🦴 **1951** Enjoyable comedy fantasy about the lowly Pittsburgh Pirates who get a little celestial help in their race for the pennant. Naturally, it takes the prayers of young Bridget (Corcoran) to get the angel Gabriel to assist. Oh yeah, only the kid can actually see the angels (no special effects in this movie). Great performances all around, especially Douglas as gruff losing manager Guffy McGovern, with Janet Leigh as the reporter he makes a play for. Based on a story by Richard Conlin. **102m/B; DVD.** Paul Douglas; Janet Leigh; Keenan Wynn; Donna Corcoran; Lewis Stone; Spring Byington; Bruce Bennett; Marvin Kaplan; Ellen Corby; Jeff Richards; ***D:*** Clarence Brown; ***W:*** Dorothy Kingsley; George Wells; ***C:*** Paul Vogel.

Angels in the Outfield 🦴🦴 ½ **1994 (PG)** Remake of the 1951 fantasy about a lowly baseball team who, along with some heavenly animated help find themselves on a winning streak. The new lineup includes Glover as manager of the hapless California Angels, Danza as a washed-up pitcher, and Lloyd as captain of the celestial spirits. Gordon-Levitt plays the foster child who believes he'll get his family back together if the Angels win the pennant. Familar ground still yields good, heartfelt family fare. Oakland A's third baseman Carney Lansford served as technical advisor, molding actors into fair semblance of baseball team. **105m/C; DVD.** Danny Glover; Tony Danza; Christopher Lloyd; Brenda Fricker; Ben Johnson; Joseph Gordon-Levitt; Jay O. Sanders; Dermot Mulroney; ***D:*** William Dear; ***W:*** Holly Goldberg Sloan; ***C:*** Matthew F. Leonetti; ***M:*** Randy Edelman.

Angels of the City 🦴🦴 **1989** What's a girl got to do to join a sorority? A house prank turns vicious when two coeds take a walk on the wild side and accidentally observe a murder, making them the next targets. Credible exploitation effort, if that's not an oxymoron. **90m/C; VHS, DVD.** Lawrence-Hilton Jacobs; Cynthia Cheston; Kelly Galindo; Sandy Gershman; ***D:*** Lawrence-Hilton Jacobs; ***W:*** Lawrence-Hilton Jacobs; Raymond Martino; Joseph Merhi.

Angels One Five 🦴🦴 **1954** A worm's-eye view of British air power in WWII. What little "excitement" there is, is generated by flashing lights, plotting maps, and status boards. Hawkins and Denison are the only bright spots. **97m/B; VHS, DVD.** *GB* Jack Hawkins; Michael Denison; Dulcie Gray; John Gregson; Cyril Raymond; Veronica Hurst; Geoffrey Keen; Vida Hope; Andrew Osborn; ***D:*** George More O'Ferrall; ***W:*** Derek Twist; ***C:*** Christopher Challis; Stanley Grant; ***M:*** John Wooldridge.

Angels Over Broadway 🦴🦴🦴 **1940** Slick, fast-paced black comedy about con man Fairbanks, who plans to hustle suicidal thief Qualen during a poker game, but has a change of heart. With the help of call-girl Hayworth and drunken playwright Mitchell, he helps Qualen turn his life around. Ahead of its time with an offbeat morality, but a delight in the '90s. **80m/B; VHS, DVD.** Douglas Fairbanks, Jr.; Rita Hayworth; Thomas Mitchell; John Qualen; George Watts; ***D:*** Ben Hecht; Lee Garmes; ***W:*** Ben Hecht; ***C:*** Lee Garmes.

Angels Sing 🦴🦴 ½ **2013 (PG)** Austin, Texas set Christmas tale. Because of a holiday tragedy in his childhood, Michael Walker (Connick, Jr.) is a decidedly bah-humbug guy. The struggling family gets a great deal on a house from an elderly man named Nick (Nelson) but the catch is it's located in a neighborhood known for its elaborate Christmas displays. The neighbors besiege the Walkers to participate, meaning Michael finally has to make peace with his past. Cheerfully sentimental without the sappiness. **86m/C; DVD, Blu-Ray.** Harry Connick, Jr.; Connie Britton; Chandler Canterbury; Lyle Lovett; Fionnula Flanagan; Kris Kristofferson; Willie Nelson; Dana Wheeler-Nicholson; ***D:*** Tim McCanlies; ***W:*** Lou Berney; ***C:*** Kamal Derkaoui; ***M:*** Carl Thiel; Scott Warren.

Angels Wash Their Faces 🦴 ½ **1939** Warner Bros. tried to cash in on the 1938 James Cagney classic "Angels With Dirty Faces," which also featured the Dead End Kids, to little success. Newcomer Gabe (Thomas) is framed for arson by some local mobsters and the gang plan to clear his name with the help of Assistant District Attorney Patrick Remson (Reagan) who happens to love Gabe's sister Joy (Sheridan). **86m/B; DVD.** Billy Halop; Leo Gorcey; Bobby Jordan; Huntz Hall; Gabriel Dell; Bonita Granville; Frankie Thomas, Jr.; Ann Sheridan; Ronald Reagan; Bernard Punsley; Eduardo Ciannelli; Bernard Nedell; Margaret Hamilton; Marjorie Main; ***D:*** Ray Enright; ***W:*** Michael Fessier; Robert Buckner; Niven Busch; ***C:*** Arthur L. Todd; ***M:*** Adolph Deutsch.

Angels' Wild Women **WOOF! 1972** From the man who brought you "Dracula vs. Frankenstein" comes an amalgamation of hippies, motorcycle dudes, evil desert gurus and precious little plot. **85m/C; VHS, DVD.** Kent Taylor; Regina Carrol; Ross Hagen; Maggie Bemby; Vicki Volante; ***D:*** Al Adamson.

Angels with Dirty Faces 🦴🦴🦴🦴 **1938** Rousing classic with memorable Cagney twitches and the famous long walk from the cell to the chair. Two young hoods grow up on NYC's lower East Side with diverse results—one enters the priesthood and the other opts for crime and prison. Upon release from the pen, famed gangster Cagney sets up shop in the old neighborhood, where Father O'Brien tries to keep a group of young toughs (the Dead End Kids) from following in his footsteps. Bogart's his unscrupulous lawyer and Bancroft a crime boss intent on double-crossing Cagney. Reportedly they were blasting real bullets during the big shootout, no doubt helping Cagney's intensity. Adapted from a story by Rowland Brown. **97m/B; VHS, DVD.** James Cagney; Pat O'Brien; Humphrey Bogart; Ann Sheridan; George Bancroft; Billy Halop; Leo Gorcey; Huntz Hall; Bobby Jordan; Bernard Punsley; Gabriel Dell; Adrian Morris; ***D:*** Michael Curtiz; ***W:*** John Wexley; Warren Duff; Rowland Brown; ***C:*** Sol Polito; ***M:*** Max Steiner. N.Y. Film Critics '38: Actor (Cagney).

Anger Management 🦴🦴 **2003 (PG-13)** Disappointing comedy has mild-mannered, confrontation-averse Dave (Sandler) forced to attend anger management therapy after a misunderstanding on an airplane. Crazed anger therapist Dr. Buddy Rydell (Nicholson) is of the opinion that Dave isn't angry enough on the outside, so he proceeds, in increasingly ridiculous ways, to make him...angry, disrupting Dave's life and his relationship with girlfriend Linda (Tomei). While attempting to play off the two leads' screen and public personas, it succeds only rarely, due mainly to a weak script that takes the easy way out whenever it's offered, and by-the-numbers direction. Nicholson's obvious glee at not having to be restrained makes some scenes work on a pure comic level, while Sandler seems right at home, back in his element, after the smart comedy of "Punch-Drunk Love." **101m/C; VHS, DVD, Blu-Ray, UMD.** Adam Sandler; Jack Nicholson; Marisa Tomei; Luis Guzman; Allen Covert; Lynne Thigpen; Kurt Fuller; Jonathan Loughran; Krista Allen; January Jones; Woody Harrelson; John Turturro; Heather Graham; John C. Reilly; Kevin Nealon; Harry Dean Stanton; ***Cameo(s):*** Bobby Knight; John McEnroe; ***D:*** Peter Segal; ***W:*** David Dorfman; ***C:*** Donald McAlpine; ***M:*** Teddy Castellucci.

Angie 🦴🦴 **1994 (R)** Brassy Angie finds herself pregnant and unmarried. Tired of the advice and criticism she receives from her close knit neighborhood she strikes out of Brooklyn to find a new life for herself. Average "woman's movie" wrought with messages of pregnancy, childbirth, friendship, love, and family has far too much going on and relies too heavily on formula soap. Davis, in what could have been a juicy (read "Oscar") role is strong, but her performance is drowned by all the melodrama. Madonna was originally cast as Angie, but was bounced when the filming of "Snake Eyes" conflicted. Adapted from the book "Angie, I Says" by Avra Wing. **108m/C; VHS, DVD, Blu-Ray.** Geena Davis; Aida Turturro; Stephen Rea; Philip Bosco; James Gandolfini; Jenny O'Hara; ***D:*** Martha Coolidge; ***W:*** Todd Graff.

AngKor: Cambodia Express 🦴 **1981** An American journalist travels back to Vietnam to search for his long lost love. **96m/C; VHS, DVD.** Robert Walker, Jr.; Christopher George; ***D:*** Lek Kitiparaporn.

Anglo-Saxon Attitudes 1/2 **1992** Dreary TV adaptation of the 1956 Angus Wilson novel. At age 60, retired historian Gerald Middleton is estranged from his family and looks back over the mess he's made of his life. In 1912, Gerald is one of a group excavating a bishop's grave that also contains a pagan fertility idol, a find that is kept secret. The young Gerald also has an affair with Dollie, his friend Gilbert's fiance, and she will continue to be his mistress for years though he marries another woman. Everyone is miserable and not very interesting to watch. **229m/C; DVD.** *UK* Richard Johnson; Dorothy Tutin; Elizabeth Spriggs; Douglas Hodge; Tara Fitzgerald; Briony Glassco; Daniel Craig; ***D:*** Diarmuid Lawrence; ***W:*** Andrew Davies; ***C:*** Clive Tickner; ***M:*** Colin Towns. **TV**

The Angriest Man in Brooklyn **2014 (R)** This remake of a 1997 Israeli film follows agitated New Yorker Henry Altman (Williams) through his existential melt-down after a doctor tells him he has only 90 minutes to live. As he attempts to repair broken family ties and clear his head, his rage continues to get the best of him. And as simple as it may sound, the filmmakers seem just as confused as Henry, as they throw in odd flashbacks, clunky comedy, and force eye-rolling melodrama into the mix. A great ensemble cast is left out to dry, each of them searching for the same thing as Henry - the point of all this. **83m/C; DVD, Blu-Ray.** Robin Williams; Mila Kunis; Peter Dinklage; Hamish Linklater; Melissa Leo; James Earl Jones; ***D:*** Phil Alden Robinson; ***W:*** Daniel Taplitz; ***C:*** John Bailey; ***M:*** Mateo Messina.

The Angry Birds Movie *Angry Birds* **2016 (PG)** This annoying, hyperactive commercial for a series of video games never justifies its existence. It's a Happy Meal tie-in toy disguised as a film. Sudeikis voices Red, the angriest, loneliest resident of Bird Island (yes, that's about as smart as the writing gets). While Red is going through anger management training, a group of pigs (led by Hader) lands on Bird Island, and tries to steal the eggs of the residents there. Red leads the resistance. Ignoring the odd immigration analogy, this is just a loud movie that essentially ends in a final act that's not unlike watching someone else play the game. **97m/C; DVD, Blu-Ray.** Jason Sudeikis; Josh Gad; Danny McBride; Maya Rudolph; Bill Hader; ***D:*** Clay Kaytis; Fergal Reilly; ***W:*** Jon Vitti; ***M:*** Heitor Pereira.

The Angry Birds Movie 2 1/2 **2019 (PG)** After saving Bird Island from an invasion of green pigs, bird Red (Sudeikis) is a hero and no longer angry. He, the other birds, and the pigs face new challenges when bird Zeta (Jones) appears. The lanky leader of a third, ice-covered island begins a war with the birds and pigs, who must put aside their differences to take on this new enemy. A sequel also based on the mobile app game, it's the expected kid-oriented slapstick humor but also has social satire and themes that are more for adults, including sexual humor. The mix does not always come together. **100m/C; DVD, Blu-Ray.** Jason Sudeikis; Josh Gad; Leslie Jones; Bill Hader; Rachel Bloom; ***D:*** Thurop Van Orman; ***W:*** Peter Ackerman; Eyal Podell; Jonathon E. Stewart; ***C:*** Simon Dunsdon; ***M:*** Heitor Pereira.

Angry Harvest *Bittere Ernte* **1985** During the WWII German occupation of Poland, a gentile farmer shelters a young Jewish woman on the run, and a serious, ultimately interdependent relationship forms. Acclaimed; Holland's first film since her native Poland's martial law imposition made her an exile to Sweden. In German with English subtitles. Contains nudity and violence. **102m/C; VHS, DVD.** *GE* Armin Mueller-Stahl; Elisabeth Trissenaar; Wojciech Pszoniak; Margit Carstensen; Kurt Raab; Kathe Jaenicke; Hans Beerhenke; Isa Haller; ***D:*** Agnieszka Holland; ***W:*** Agnieszka Holland. Montreal World Film Fest. '85: Actor (Mueller-Stahl).

Angry Joe Bass **1976** Contemporary Native American Joe Bass faces government officials who continually usurp his fishing rights. Something like "Billy Jack" without the intelligence. **82m/C; VHS, DVD.** Henry Bal; Molly Mershon; ***D:*** Thomas G. Reeves.

The Angry Red Planet *Invasion of Mars; Journey to Planet Four* **1959** An unintentionally amusing sci-fi adventure about astronauts on Mars fighting off aliens and giant, ship-swallowing amoebas. Filmed using bizarre "Cinemagic" process, which turns almost everything pink. Wild effects have earned the film cult status. **83m/C; VHS, DVD, Blu-Ray.** Gerald Mohr; Les Tremayne; Jack Kruschen; Nora Hayden; Paul Hahn; J. Edward McKinley; Tom Daly; Don Lamond; ***D:*** Ib Melchior; ***W:*** Ib Melchior; Sidney W. Pink; ***C:*** Stanley Cortez; ***M:*** Paul Dunlap.

Anguish 1/2 **1988 (R)** Well-done horror thriller about a lunatic who, inspired to duplicate the actions of an eyeball-obsessed killer in a popular film, murders a movie audience as they watch the movie. Violence and gore abound. **89m/C; VHS, DVD.** *SP* Zelda Rubinstein; Michael Lerner; Talia Paul; Clara Pastor; ***D:*** Bigas Luna; ***W:*** Bigas Luna; ***C:*** Josep Civit; ***M:*** J(ose) M(anuel) Pagan.

Angus **1995 (PG-13)** Dull teen comedy about self-esteem revolves around the overweight Angus (Talbert), a friendly kid tormented by the usual school bullies. His best bud is twerp Troy (Owen), who tries to help Angus out with his crush on cute blonde Melissa (Ariana). There's even a schmaltzy prom scene. The profanity, though mild, and the boys sexual interests make this questionable for the pre-teen audience that could actually enjoy it. **87m/C; VHS, DVD.** Charlie Talbert; Kathy Bates; George C. Scott; Chris Owen; Ariana Richards; Lawrence Pressman; Rita Moreno; James Van Der Beek; Anna Thomson; ***D:*** Patrick Read Johnson; ***W:*** Jill Gordon; ***C:*** Alexander Grusynski; ***M:*** David E. Russo.

Angus, Thongs and Perfect Snogging 1/2 **2008 (PG-13)** Angus is a feral cat and 'snogging' is kissing in Brit-speak in this cheerful adaptation of the first two books in Louise Rennison's teen girl series. Plain 14-year-old Georgia (Groome) is obsessed with both her looks and inexperience with boys, which she writes about in her diary. Things look up in the boy department when two handsome brothers move into the neighborhood and she and Robbie (Johnson) bond over their fondness for cats. Too bad that he's already been claimed by her school rival Lindsay (Nixon). **100m/C; DVD.** *GB* Aaron Taylor-Johnson; Kimberly Nixon; Eleanor Tomlinson; Sean Bourke; Liam Hess; Alan J. Dachman; Karen Taylor; Manjeevan Grewal; Georgia Henshaw; Eva Drew; ***D:*** Gurinder Chadha; ***W:*** Gurinder Chadha; Paul Mayeda Berges; Will McRobb; Chris Viscardi; ***C:*** Richard Pope; ***M:*** Joby Talbot.

Anima **1998** Sam and Iris have long left their pasts in Nazi Germany behind them for a secluded life in a New England farmhouse. At least until young journalist Bill discovers them while researching an article on taxidermy and mummification and sees their bizarre private world. **88m/C; VHS, DVD.** Bray Poor; George Bartenieff; Jacqueline Bertrand; ***D:*** Craig Richardson; ***W:*** Craig Richardson; ***C:*** Randy Drummond; ***M:*** Joel Diamond; Adam Hurst.

The Animal 1/2 **2001 (PG-13)** Meek clerk Schneider is injured in a serious car accident and is rescued by a mad scientist who surgically replaces his damaged organs with animal parts. These animalistic traits tend to surface at the worst possible time for Schneider, just as he's realizing his dream of becoming a supercop. Haskell (from TV's first "Survivor") is pleasant in her big screen debut as the animal-rights advocate girlfriend, but Schneider is the one who makes this surprisingly enjoyable comedy work with his affable loser persona and willingness to go with the joke. **83m/C; VHS, DVD.** Rob Schneider; Guy Torry; John C. McGinley; Colleen Haskell; Michael Caton; Louis Lombardi; Ed Asner; Michael (Mike) Papajohn; ***D:*** Luke Greenfield; ***W:*** Rob Schneider; Tom Brady; ***C:*** Peter Lyons Collister; ***M:*** Teddy Castellucci.

Animal 1/2 **2005 (R)** James "Animal" Allen is a violent gangsta sent to prison, leaving behind young son Darius (Howard), who grows up following in pop's footsteps. When Animal emerges from prison reformed, he attempts to get Darius out of the life. Thoughtful and intelligent, with excellent performances by leads Howard and Rhames. **93m/C; DVD.** Ving Rhames; Terrence Howard; Jim Brown; Chazz Palminteri; Paula Jai Parker; Faizon Love; Wes Studi; Beverly Todd; ***D:*** David J. Burke; ***W:*** David C(lark) Johnson. **VIDEO**

Animal 2 **2007** Lifer James "Animal" Allen's (Rhames) prison transfer finds him doing time with younger son James Jr. (Collins), who was framed for murder by Animal's old foe Kasada (Dunn), who wants Animal to get back into the prison fight game. On the outside, elder son Darius (Shannon) is trying to find the evidence to clear his bro. **93m/C; DVD.** Ving Rhames; Vicellous Shannon; Conrad Dunn; K.C. Collins; ***D:*** Ryan Combs; ***W:*** Jacob L. Adams; ***M:*** Craig McConnell. **VIDEO**

Animal Crackers 1/2 **1930 (G)** The second and possibly the funniest of the 13 Marx Brothers films, "Animal Crackers" is a screen classic. Groucho is a guest at the house of wealthy matron Margaret Dumont and he, along with Zeppo, Chico, and Harpo, destroy the tranquility of the estate. Complete with the Harry Ruby music score—including Groucho's "Hooray for Captain Spaulding" with more quotable lines than any other Marx Brothers film: "One morning I shot an elephant in my pajamas. How he got into my pajamas, I'll never know." Based on a play by George S. Kaufman. **98m/B; VHS, DVD, Blu-Ray.** Groucho Marx; Chico Marx; Harpo Marx; Zeppo Marx; Lillian Roth; Margaret Dumont; Louis Sorin; Hal Thompson; Robert Greig; Margaret Irving; Edward Metcalf; Kathryn Reece; ***D:*** Victor Heerman; ***W:*** Morrie Ryskind; ***C:*** George J. Folsey; ***M:*** Bert Kalmar; Harry Ruby.

Animal Crackers **2017** After circus performers Buffalo Bob (Taylor) and acrobat Talia (Strong) marry, her gypsy mother gives them a magic box of animal cookies that allows them to become the animal of whatever cookie they eat. This gift permits the couple to found their own popular circus. After years of jealousy, Bob's brother Horatio (McKellan) sabotages the circus to learn the secret of Bob's magic animals. However, the animal cracker box falls into the hands of Owen (Krasinski), allowing him to live out his own circus dreams. An inventive story and a stellar cast brings the delightful characters to life, overcoming the cut-rate animation. **94m/C; DVD.** James Arnold Taylor; Tara Strong; Emily Blunt; John Krasinski; Ian McKellen; ***D:*** Tony Bancroft; Scott Christian Sava; ***W:*** Scott Christian Sava; Dean Lorey; ***M:*** Bear McCreary.

Animal Factory 1/2 **2000 (R)** When first-time felon Ron Decker (Furlong) is sentenced to two years in a decaying prison, he is introduced to a world where violence is a way of life. After witnessing a riot, Ron is taken under the wing of Earl Copen (Dafoe), the main-man on the cellblock, but the younger man soon discovers that life in prison is not about rehabilitation, it's about survival. Bunker wrote the screenplay based on his novel of the same name. **94m/C; VHS, DVD, Blu-Ray.** Willem Dafoe; Edward Furlong; Danny Trejo; John Heard; Mickey Rourke; Tom Arnold; Mark Boone, Jr.; Steve Buscemi; Seymour Cassel; Edward (Eddie) Bunker; ***D:*** Steve Buscemi; ***W:*** Edward (Eddie) Bunker; John Steppling; ***C:*** Phil Parmet; ***M:*** John Lurie.

Animal Farm **1955** An animated version of George Orwell's classic political satire about a barnyard full of animals who parallel the growth of totalitarian dictatorships. Not entirely successful, but probably best translation of Orwell to film. **73m/C; VHS, DVD.** ***V:*** Maurice Denham; Gordon Heath; ***D:*** John Halas; Joy Batchelor.

Animal Farm 1/2 **1999** Orwell's political satire is given the "Babe" treatment in this live-action version. Drunken farmer Mr. Jones (Postlethwaite) has his power overthrown by his barnyard animals, who in turn are ruled by the farm's pig population. Only porker Napoleon (Stewart) turns out to be as big a tyrant as his human counterpart. Far beyond the scope of children, this retelling is clunky and its propaganda value has certainly come and gone. (Orwell was originally satirizing Stalinist Russia.) **91m/C; DVD.** Pete Postlethwaite; ***V:*** Patrick Stewart; Kelsey Grammer; Ian Holm; Julia Ormond; Julia Louis-Dreyfus; Paul Scofield; Peter Ustinov; ***D:*** John Stephenson; ***W:*** Martyn Burke; Alan Janes; ***C:*** Mike Brewster; ***M:*** Richard Harvey. **CABLE**

Animal Instincts **1992 (R)** A woman takes a prescription drug that makes her a nymphomaniac, and her police officer husband discovers that he's turned on by videotaping her in bed with other men and women. One of the many in her constant stream of lovers is a politician whose campaign is based on shutting down all the town's sex clubs. Another in the string of sexual thrillers riding on the coattails of "Basic Instinct." **94m/C; VHS, DVD.** Maxwell Caulfield; Jan-Michael Vincent; Mitch Gaylord; Shannon Whirry; Delia Sheppard; John Saxon; David Carradine; ***D:*** Alexander Gregory (Gregory Dark) Hippolyte; ***W:*** Jon Robert Samsel; Georges des Esseintes; ***C:*** Paul Desatoff; ***M:*** Joseph Smith.

Animal Instincts 2 **1994 (R)** Joanna leaves her overbearing husband and moves into a supposedly quiet community. Neighbor Steve is a security expert—and a voyeur. He's hidden a camera in Joanna's bedroom but she knows he's watching. **92m/C; VHS, DVD.** Shannon Whirry; Woody Brown; Elizabeth Sandifer; Al Sapienza; ***D:*** Alexander Gregory (Gregory Dark) Hippolyte.

Animal Instincts 3: The Seductress **1995 (R)** Joanna (Schumacher) finds a new kind of sexual excitement when she gets involved with rock music promoter Alex (Matthew), whose kicks include feining blindness. The unrated version contains 12 more minutes of footage. **96m/C; VHS, DVD.** Wendy Schumacher; James Matthew; Marcus Graham; John Bates; Anthony Lesa; ***D:*** Alexander Gregory (Gregory Dark) Hippolyte; ***W:*** Selwyn Harris; ***C:*** Ernest Paul Roebuck.

The Animal Kingdom *The Woman in His House* **1932** A romantic triangle develops when Howard, married to Loy, has an affair with Harding. The problem is Harding acts more like a wife and Loy a mistress. Intelligently written and directed, with a marvelous performance from veteran character actor Gargan. **95m/B; VHS, DVD.** Ann Harding; Leslie Howard; Myrna Loy; Neil Hamilton; William Gargan; Henry Stephenson; Ilka Chase; ***D:*** Edward H. Griffith; ***W:*** Horace Jackson; ***C:*** George J. Folsey.

Animal Kingdom **2009 (R)** Feature debut from writer/director Michod is a contemporary noir following the disintegration of the Codys, a Melbourne family of criminals, ruled by monstrous mom Smurf whose specialty is the armed robberies she plans with her three psycho sons. When his mother ODs, teenaged grandson Joshua is brought into the fold but his allegiance might not lay where everyone thinks it should. Increasing violence and some cops getting killed brings too much scrutiny and trouble increases amidst the brutality and tension that Michod and his cast play with assurance. **112m/C; Blu-Ray, On Demand.** *AU* Jacki Weaver; Guy Pearce; Ben Mendelsohn; Joel Edgerton; James Frecheville; Luke Ford; Sullivan Stapleton; Daniel Wyllie; Anthony Hayes; Justin Rosniak; Susan Prior; Anne Lise Phillips; Laura Wheelwright; Mirrah Foulkes; Clayton Jacobson; ***D:*** David Michod; ***W:*** David Michod; ***C:*** Adam Arkapaw; ***M:*** Antony Partos.

Animal Room **1995** When high school student Arnold Mosk (Harris) is caught using drugs, he's place in the school's controversial isolation program that's nicknamed "The Animal Room." There are no rules and Arnold's life is threatened by delinquent thug, Doug (Lillard). But if Arnold expects to survive, he's going to have to learn how to fight. **98m/C; VHS, DVD.** Neil Patrick Harris; Matthew Lillard; Gabriel Olds; Catherine Hicks; Brian Vincent; ***D:*** Craig Singer.

Animals **2008** Lots of gratuitous nudity and sex scenes to make up for the stupid plot and lack of actual acting skills. Syd (Blucas) gets picked up by Nora (Aycox) in a small town Nevada bar. After a night of rough sex he wakes up infected by lycanthropy (that Nora was a biter). They keep hooking up but Nora's jealous and vicious lycan sire Vic (Andrews) wants her back. **93m/C; DVD.** Marc Blucas; Nicki Aycox; Naveen Andrews; Eva Amurri; Andy Comeau; Bart Johnson; Ron Rogge; ***D:*** Douglas Aarniokoski; ***W:*** Craig Spector; ***C:*** Matthew Williams; ***M:*** Alan Brewer.

Animals **2015** Director Schiffli's Chicago-set junkie drama earned deserved comparisons to Gus Van Sant's breakthrough in "Drugstore Cowboy." Like that film, it's a harrowing tale of co-dependency at its most damaging. Junkies Jude (Dastmalchian) and Bobbie (Shaw) are a homeless couple forced to escalating extremes to get their next fixes. As Jude's theft becomes more brazen and Bobbie sells her body to get drugs, the two realize that perhaps the only way they can get clean is to part ways. Both actors are excellent and Schiffli shows real skill with unforced drama. **90m/C; DVD, Blu-Ray.** David Dastmalchian; Kim Shaw; John Heard; John Hoogenakker; John Lister; ***D:*** Collin Schiffli; ***W:*** David Dastmalchian; ***C:*** Larkin Donley; ***M:*** Ian Hultquist.

The Ann Jillian Story 🦴 1/2 **1988** Jillian stars as herself in this melodrama recounting her battle with breast cancer. Several musical numbers are included. **96m/C; VHS, Streaming.** Ann Jillian; Tony LoBianco; Viveca Lindfors; Leighton Bewley; ***D:*** Corey Allen. **TV**

Ann Rule Presents: The Stranger Beside Me 🦴🦴 *The Stranger Beside Me* **2003** Crime writer Ann Rule (Hershey) is working at a Seattle crisis center in 1971 alongside charming volunteer Ted Bundy (Campbell). When Bundy comes under suspicion as a serial killer, Rule has trouble believing the accusations—until the truth comes out. Based on Rule's 1983 nonfiction bestseller about Bundy. **88m/C; DVD, Blu-Ray.** Barbara Hershey; Billy Campbell; Kevin Dunn; Jay Brazeau; Benjamin Ratner; Matthew Bennett; Suki Kaiser; ***D:*** Paul Shapiro; ***W:*** Matthew McDuffie; Matthew Tabak; ***C:*** Ronald Orieux; ***M:*** Joseph Conlan. **CABLE**

Anna 🦴🦴🦴 **1987 (PG-13)** Age, envy, and the theatrical world receive their due in an uneven but engrossing drama about aging Czech film star Anna, making a sad living in New York doing commercials and trying for off-Broadway roles. She takes in Krystyna, a young Czech peasant girl who eventually rockets to model stardom. Modern, strongly acted "All About Eve" with a story partially based on a real Polish actress. Kirkland drew quite a bit of flak for shamelessly self-promoting for the Oscar. She still lost. **101m/C; VHS, DVD.** Sally Kirkland; Paulina Porizkova; Robert Fields; Stefan Schnabel; Larry Pine; Ruth Maleczech; ***D:*** Yurek Bogayevicz; ***W:*** Yurek Bogayevicz; Agnieszka Holland; ***C:*** Bobby Bukowski; ***M:*** Greg Hawkes. Golden Globes '88: Actress--Drama (Kirkland); Ind. Spirit '88: Actress (Kirkland); L.A. Film Critics '87: Actress (Kirkland).

Anna 🦴🦴 **2019 (R)** After being recruited by the KGB to be an undercover agent, beautiful Anna (Luss) agrees to serve for five years so she can escape difficult circumstances. Three years later, while working in a market in Moscow, she is discovered by a French modeling agency scout and begins working in Paris. She then becomes the love interest of a wealthy Russian, who makes his money illegally and assassinates him. As Anna continues to use her modeling career as a cover, she finds herself entangled with the CIA. Tries to be a stylish European action-thriller, but lacks charisma. **118m/C; DVD, Blu-Ray.** *FR US* Sasha Luss; Dame Helen Mirren; Luke Evans; Cillian Murphy; Lera Abova; ***D:*** Luc Besson; ***W:*** Luc Besson; ***C:*** Thierry Arbogast; ***M:*** Éric Serra.

Anna and the King 🦴🦴 1/2 **1999 (PG-13)** Based on the story of English widow and schoolteacher Anna Leonowens (Foster) who, in 1862, is hired by the King Mongkut of Siam (Yun-Fat) to introduce his 58 children to the ideas of the West. The film looks stunning (it was filmed in Malaysia) and Yun-Fat is regal and charismatic but Foster is too stiff upper-lipped and remote and there's respect rather than any hint of romance. Previously filmed as 1946's "Anna and the King of Siam" and the 1956 musical "The King and I." **147m/C; VHS, DVD.** Jodie Foster; Chow Yun-Fat; Bai Ling; Tom Felton; Syed Alwi; ***D:*** Andy Tennant; ***W:*** Steve Meerson; Peter Krikes; ***C:*** Caleb Deschanel; ***M:*** George Fenton.

Anna and the King of Siam 🦴🦴🦴 1/2 **1946** Splendid adaptation, from the book by Margaret Landon, about the true life adventures of 33-year-old English widow Anna Leonowens. In 1862 Anna and her son travelled to the exotic kingdom of Siam to educate the harem and children of the king. Dunne is splendid as the strong-willed governess as is Harrison (in his first American film) as the authoritarian eastern ruler. Remade as the musical "The King and I." **128m/B; VHS, DVD.** Irene Dunne; Rex Harrison; Linda Darnell; Lee J. Cobb; Gale Sondergaard; Mikhail Rasumny; Dennis Hoey; Richard Lyon; John Abbott; ***D:*** John Cromwell; ***W:*** Sally Benson; Talbot Jennings; ***C:*** Arthur C. Miller; ***M:*** Bernard Herrmann. Oscars '46: Art Dir./Set Dec., B&W, B&W Cinematog.

Anna Christie 🦴🦴🦴 1/2 **1923** Silent production of Eugene O'Neill's play that even he liked. A young girl is sent away by her father, a seaman, and finds her way to Chicago, where she becomes a prostitute. Later she visits her father's barge and falls for a sailor. She shares her past life story, hoping they will understand. This film was acclaimed when it was released, and still remains a touching work of art. Remade in 1930. **75m/B; Silent; VHS, DVD.** Blanche Sweet; George F. Marion, Sr.; William Russell; Eugenie Besserer; Chester Conklin; George Siegmann; Victor Potel; Fred Kohler, Sr.; ***D:*** John Griffith Wray.

Anna Christie 🦴🦴 1/2 **1930** Garbo is the ex-prostitute who finds love with sailor Bickford. Bickford is unaware of his lover's tarnished past and she does her best to keep it that way. Garbo's first sound effort was advertised with the slogan "Garbo Talks." Adapted from the classic Eugene O'Neill play, the film is a slow but rewarding romantic drama. **90m/B; VHS, DVD.** Greta Garbo; Marie Dressler; Charles Bickford; George F. Marion, Sr.; ***D:*** Clarence Brown; ***C:*** William H. Daniels.

Anna Karenina 🦴🦴🦴 1/2 **1935** Cinematic Tolstoy with Garbo as sad, moody, married Anna willing to give up everything to be near Vronsky (March), the cavalry officer she's obsessed with. And since it's Russian, expect tragedy. A classic Garbo vehicle with March and Rathbone (as the cuckhold husband) providing excellent support. Interestingly, a remake of the Garbo and John Gilbert silent, "Love." **85m/B; VHS, DVD.** Greta Garbo; Fredric March; Freddie Bartholomew; Maureen O'Sullivan; May Robson; Basil Rathbone; Reginald Owen; Reginald Denny; ***D:*** Clarence Brown; ***W:*** S.N. Behrman; Clemence Dane; Salka Viertel; ***C:*** William H. Daniels; ***M:*** Herbert Stothart. N.Y. Film Critics '35: Actress (Garbo).

Anna Karenina 🦴🦴 1/2 **1948** Stiff version of Tolstoy's passionate story of illicit love between a married woman and a military officer. In spite of exquisite costumes, and Leigh and Richardson as leads, still tedious. **123m/C; VHS, DVD.** *GB* Vivien Leigh; Ralph Richardson; Kieron Moore; Sally Ann Howes; Niall MacGinnis; Martita Hunt; Michael Gough; ***D:*** Julien Duvivier; ***W:*** Julien Duvivier; ***C:*** Henri Alekan; ***M:*** Constant Lambert.

Anna Karenina 🦴🦴 1/2 *Leo Tolstoy's Anna Karenina* **1996 (PG-13)** The third film version of Tolstoy's tempestuous, tragic romance certainly looks good, even if the performances don't engender the passion the story demands. Beautiful Anna (Marceau) leaves stuffy husband Karenin (Fox) to travel to 1880 Moscow and mend the marriage of her philandering brother Stiva (Huston). She meets dashing soldier, Count Alexei Vronsky (Bean), who pursues the beauty, and the two begin an all-encompassing affair, leading to tragedy. This version also includes the secondary, contrasting romance between young Kitty (Kirshner) and Tolstoy's alter ego, aristo Levin (Molina). Filmed on location in St. Petersburg, Russia. **120m/C; VHS, DVD.** Sophie Marceau; Sean Bean; Alfred Molina; Mia Kirshner; James Fox; Danny Huston; Fiona Shaw; Phyllida Law; David Schofield; Saskia Wickham; ***D:*** Bernard Rose; ***W:*** Bernard Rose; ***C:*** Daryn Okada.

Anna Karenina 🦴🦴 1/2 **2000** Well-done British adaptation of the familiar Tolstoy drama although, frankly, Anna (McCrory) is a pill. Less tragic than headstrong, this willful Russian beauty runs from her passionless marriage to Karenin (Dillane) straight into the arms of dashing seducer Vronsky (McKidd). Of course, once they turn each other's lives to misery, what else is left but a tragic end. This version also includes the secondary love affair of Kitty (Baeza) and Levin (Henshall). **240m/C; VHS, DVD.** Helen McCrory; Kevin McKidd; Stephen (Dillon) Dillane; Douglas Henshall; Paloma Baeza; Amanda Root; Mark Strong; ***D:*** David Blair; ***W:*** Allan Cubitt; ***C:*** Ryszard Lenczewski; ***M:*** John Keane. **TV**

Anna Karenina 🦴 1/2 **2012 (R)** Director Wright found such creative success with his costume-heavy literary adaptations of "Pride & Prejudice" and "Atonement" that it makes sense that he would try to go for three hits with leading lady Knightley. Sadly, the umpteenth version of Tolstoy's 1877 drama is easily his worst film as his decision to present the entire piece as an elaborate stage play (complete with sets that fly in and visible light rigs) makes an already-cold story even more frigid. Knightley makes it out unscathed but Wright can't save a lot of the supporting cast, including a remarkably bad performance from Taylor-Johnson as Anna's paramour Vronsky. **130m/C; DVD, Blu-Ray.** *UK* Keira Knightley; Jude Law; Aaron Taylor-Johnson; Kelly Macdonald; Matthew Macfadyen; Emily Watson; Olivia Williams; Domhnall Gleeson; Alicia Vikander; ***D:*** Joe Wright; ***W:*** Tom Stoppard; ***C:*** Seamus McGarvey; ***M:*** Dario Marianelli. Oscars '12: Costume Des.; British Acad. '12: Costume Des.

Anna Nicole 🦴 1/2 **2013** The rags-to-riches tragedy of Anna Nicole Smith (Bruckner) gets a tacky biopic treatment from Lifetime. The small town Texas single mom becomes a buxom blonde with Marilyn Monroe as her idol and dreams of fame that lead to modeling, men, and a prescription drug habit. While working at a strip club, Anna Nicole meets elderly oil tycoon J. Howard Marshall (Landau), who's some 60 years her senior, but a willing sugar daddy to the young woman, whom he marries. His death leads to an ugly court battle with Marshall's family over his money and Anna Nicole's continuing decline. **89m/C; DVD.** Agnes Bruckner; Martin Landau; Cary Elwes; Adam Goldberg; Virginia Madsen; ***D:*** Mary Harron; ***W:*** Joe Batteer; John Rice; ***C:*** Michael Simmonds; ***M:*** Zack Ryan. **CABLE**

Anna to the Infinite Power 🦴🦴 1/2 **1984** Sci fi based on the book of the same name follows a young girl with telepathic powers. When the girl discovers that she has sisters as the result of a strange scientific experiment, she sets out to find them, drawing on her own inner strength. **101m/C; VHS, DVD.** Dina Merrill; Martha Byrne; Mark Patton; ***D:*** Robert Wiemer.

Annabelle 🦴🦴 **2014 (R)** After a brutal attack by Satanic cult members, newlyweds John (Horton) and Mia (Wallis) fall victim to a nasty evil spirit turning their world to Hell. Turns out Mia's new doll, Annabelle, is host to a demon, out for the soul of their newborn daughter. The tension is built effectively, but most of the thrill comes from cheap jump scares and bad decisions by every single character entering the cursed home. Director Leonetti does the best he can with a script that makes too many bonehead moves. **99m/C; DVD, Blu-Ray.** Annabelle Wallis; Ward Horton; Alfre Woodard; Tony Amendola; ***D:*** John R. Leonetti; ***W:*** Gary Dauberman; ***C:*** James Kniest; ***M:*** Joseph Bishara.

Annabelle Comes Home 🦴🦴 **2019 (R)** Religious paranormal researchers Ed (Wilson) and Lorraine (Farmiga) Warren know the Annabelle doll is possessed by a sinister presence and keep it contained in a blessed glass case hidden from their young daughter Judy (Grace). A gifted clairvoyant, Judy connects with teen babysitter Ellen (Iseman) who watches her while her parents are away. However, Ellen's friend Daniela (Sarife) sneaks into the forbidden room with artifacts including Annabelle to communicate with her deceased father and awakens the spirit in Annabelle. The sequential sequel to The Conjuring, the film has creepy moments, excellent costumes, and moments of humor but its story does not make sense. **106m/C; DVD.** Vera Farmiga; Patrick Wilson; McKenna Grace; Madison Iseman; Katie Sarife; ***D:*** Gary Dauberman; ***W:*** Gary Dauberman; ***C:*** Michael Burgess; ***M:*** Joseph Bishara.

Annabelle: Creation 🦴🦴 1/2 **2017 (R)** Skillfully directed by Sandburg, this horror-thriller prequel to The Conjuring (2013) and Annabelle (2014) offers the backstory of the possessed titular doll to great effect. Set in the mid-1950s, the paranormal comes into play when dollmaker Samuel Mullens (LaPaglia) and his wife Esther (Otto) offer space in their large farmhouse to a nun and six girls after an orphanage closes. The couple had lived in seclusion for 12 years after the tragic death of their young daughter Bee (Lee). Everyone is terrorized by the doll Annabelle, who was made by Samuel and is possessed by the couple's young daughter. An effective creepy explanation of the doll's origins. **109m/C; DVD, Blu-Ray.** Anthony LaPaglia; Samara Lee; Miranda Otto; Brad Greenquist; Lulu Wilson; ***D:*** David F. Sandberg; ***W:*** Gary Dauberman; ***C:*** Maxime Alexandre; ***M:*** Benjamin Wallfisch.

Annapolis 🦴 1/2 **2006 (PG-13)** Predictable military/boxing flick finds hot-headed, working-class Jake Huard (Franco) set on entering the U.S. Naval Academy at Annapolis. He's finally accepted and finds himself subjected to the berating of disciplinarian Lt. Cole (Gibson), who is certain Jake doesn't have what it takes. However, Jake is a really good boxer and starts training for the Academy's Brigades competition, hoping for a shot at the reigning champ—Cole. The fetching Brewster serves as Jake's superior officer, questionable trainer, and romantic object. **108m/C; DVD, Blu-Ray.** James Franco; Tyrese Gibson; Jordana Brewster; Donnie Wahlberg; Vicellous Shannon; Roger Fan; Chi McBride; Brian Goodman; Charles Napier; Zachery Ty Bryan; ***D:*** Justin Lin; ***W:*** Dave Collard; ***C:*** Phil Abraham; ***M:*** Brian Tyler.

Anna's Storm 🦴 **2007** Silly disaster flick finds Mayor Anna's (Wilson) small town being hit by meteor storms (with low-budget CGI) that are destroying everything in sight. This doesn't stop her from fretting more over her bothersome marriage. **90m/C; DVD.** Sheree J. Wilson; Peter Lacroix; Scott Hylands; Aaron Pearl; Desiree Loewen; Graham Wardle; Sarah Jane Redmond; ***D:*** Kristoffer Tabori; ***W:*** Steven B. Frank; Julie Ferber Frank; ***M:*** Michael Neilsen. **CABLE**

Anne Frank: The Whole Story 🦴🦴🦴 *Anne Frank* **2001** Solid made-for-TV entry into the pantheon of Anne Frank pathos, legend, or tragedy—take your pick. Romanian-born director Robert Dornhelm does his best work to date by taking a more intimate look at the day-to-day life of the young Anne Frank (played with great precision by Hannah Taylor-Gordon) during the years she and her family spent in hiding from the German invaders. Anne, as a human being, is fleshed out and painted with more detail than in other bio-pics covering the same ground (story is based on Melissa Muller's biography, and not on the famous diary). This has the effect of making her ultimate fate at Auschwitz all the more painful. **189m/C; DVD.** Ben Kingsley; Brenda Blethyn; Hannah Taylor Gordon; Joachim Krol; Lili Taylor; Tatjana Blacher; ***D:*** Richard Dornhelm; ***W:*** Kirk Ellis; ***C:*** Elemer Ragalyi; ***M:*** Graeme Revell. **TV**

Anne of Avonlea 🦴🦴🦴 1/2 *Anne of Green Gables: The Sequel* **1987** Equally excellent miniseries sequel to "Anne of Green Gables" in which the romantic heroine grows up and discovers romance. The same cast returns and Sullivan continues his tradition of lavish filming on Prince Edward Island and beautiful costumes. Based on the characters from L.M. Montgomery's classic novels "Anne of Avonlea," "Anne of the Island," and "Anne of Windy Poplars." CBC, PBS, and Disney worked together on this WonderWorks production. **224m/C; VHS, DVD.** *CA* Megan Follows; Colleen Dewhurst; Wendy Hiller; Frank Converse; Patricia Hamilton; Schuyler Grant; Jonathan Crombie; Rosemary Dunsmore; ***D:*** Kevin Sullivan; ***W:*** Kevin Sullivan; ***M:*** Hagood Hardy. **TV**

Anne of Green Gables 🦴🦴🦴 **1934** A lonely Canadian couple adopts an orphan who keeps them on their toes with her animated imagination, and wins a permanent place in their hearts. Warm (but loose) adaptation of Lucy Maud Montgomery's popular novel is entertaining although 1985 remake is far superior. Followed by "Anne of Windy Poplars." **79m/B; VHS, DVD.** Anne Shirley; Tom Brown; O.P. Heggie; Helen Westley; Sara Haden; Charley Grapewin; ***D:*** George Nicholls, Jr.; ***M:*** Max Steiner.

Anne of Green Gables 🦴🦴🦴 1/2 **1985** Splendid production of the famous Lucy Maud Montgomery classic about a young orphan girl growing to young adulthood with the help of a crusty brother and sister duo. The characters come to life under Sullivan's direction, and the movie is enhanced by the beautiful Prince Edward Island scenery and wonderful costumes. One of the few instances where an adaptation lives up to (if not exceeds) the quality of the original novel. A WonderWorks presentation that was made with the cooperation of the Disney channel, CBC, and PBS. Followed by "Anne of Avonlea." On two tapes. **197m/C; VHS, DVD, Blu-Ray.** *CA* Megan Follows; Colleen Dewhurst; Richard Farnsworth; Patricia Hamilton; Schuyler Grant; Jonathan Crombie; Marilyn Lightstone; Charmion King; Rosemary Radcliffe; Jackie Burroughs; Robert E. Collins; Joachim Hansen; Cedric Smith; Paul Bown; Miranda de Pencier; Jennifer Inch; Wendy Lyon; Christiane Kruger; Trish Nettleton; Morgan Chapman; ***D:*** Kevin Sullivan; ***W:*** Kevin Sullivan; Joe Wiesenfeld; ***C:*** Rene Ohashi; ***M:*** Hagood Hardy. **TV**

Anne of Green Gables: The Continuing Story 1/2 **1999** Anne (Follows) learns that fiance Gilbert (Blythe) has accepted a job in a New York hospital. She takes a job in a publishing house where she meets fast-living journalist Jack Garrison (Daddo). Gilbert and Anne return to Avonlea to marry just before WWI and Gilbert joins the army as a doctor and is sent to France. When he's declared MIA, Anne heads overseas with the Red Cross to search for him and runs into Jack again, who leads Anne into numerous intrigues. This far-fetched story is not based on one of Lucy Maud Montgomery's books but Anne at least retains her spunkiness and determination. **185m/C; VHS, DVD.** *CA* Megan Follows; Jonathan Crombie; Cameron Daddo; Schuyler Grant; Patricia Hamilton; Rosemary Radcliffe; Miranda de Pencier; Barry Morse; Martha Henry; Janet-Laine Green; Nigel Bennett; Shannon Lawson; ***D:*** Stefan Scaini; ***W:*** Kevin Sullivan; Laurie Pearson; ***C:*** Robert Saad; ***M:*** Peter Breiner. **TV**

Anne of the Thousand Days 1/2 **1969 (PG)** Lavish retelling of the life and loves of Henry the VIII. In 1526, Henry tosses aside his current wife for the young and devastatingly beautiful Anne Boleyn (Bujold). But after the birth of Princess Elizabeth, Henry tires of Anne and wishes to marry another. So he decides to rid himself of her presence—permanently. Burton's performance of the amoral king garnered him an Oscar nomination. Based on the 1948 play by Maxwell Anderson. Watch for Elizabeth Taylor as a masked courtesan at the costume ball. **145m/C; VHS, DVD, Blu-Ray.** Richard Burton; Genevieve Bujold; Irene Papas; Anthony Quayle; John Colicos; Michael Hordern; Michael Johnson; ***D:*** Charles Jarrott; ***W:*** Bridget Boland; John Hale; ***M:*** Georges Delerue. Oscars '69: Costume Des.; Directors Guild '70: Director (Jarrott); Golden Globes '70: Actress--Drama (Bujold), Director (Jarrott), Film--Drama, Screenplay.

Anne Rice's The Feast of All Saints 1/2 *The Feast of All Saints* **2001** It's not about vampires. Rice's novel is set in pre-Civil War New Orleans among free people of color. They enjoy certain privileges of middleclass society while still dealing with class, race, and sex. Cecil St. Marie (Ruben) is the mistress of white plantation owner Philippe Ferronnaire (Gallagher). He makes certain promises to his children by Cecil—Marcel (Ri'chard) and Marie (Lyn)?which he fails to keep, thus causing family dissension. As the children grow into adults they face romantic and societal dilemmas of their own. Excellent cast does well by the sometimes melodramatic story. Title refers to the day for remembering the dead. **212m/C; VHS, DVD.** Robert Ri'chard; Peter Gallagher; Gloria Reuben; Nicole Lyn; Jennifer Beals; Ossie Davis; Ruby Dee; Pam Grier; Jasmine Guy; Victoria Rowell; James Earl Jones; Eartha Kitt; Ben Vereen; Forest Whitaker; Bianca Lawson; Daniel Sunjata; ***D:*** Peter Medak; ***W:*** John Wilder; ***C:*** Edward Pei; ***M:*** Patrick Seymour. **CABLE**

Annie **1982 (PG)** Stagy big-budget adaption of the Broadway musical, which was an adaptation of the comic strip. A major financial disaster upon release, still it's an entertaining enterprise curiously directed by Huston and engagingly acted by Finney and Quinn. **128m/C; VHS, DVD, Blu-Ray.** Aileen Quinn; Carol Burnett; Albert Finney; Bernadette Peters; Ann Reinking; Tim Curry; ***D:*** John Huston; ***W:*** Thomas Meehan; ***C:*** Richard Moore; ***M:*** Ralph Burns. Golden Raspberries '82: Worst Support. Actress (Quinn).

Annie **1999** Lively and amusing adaptation of the smash Broadway musical that will make you forget that dud 1982 movie version. Scrappy urchin Annie (newcomer Morton) is incarcerated in a Depression-era orphange run by despotic Miss Hannigan (Bates) when she's offered the chance to spend the holidays with chilly moneybags Oliver Warbucks (Garber). Naturally, Annie thaws his frosty demeanor. Able support is provided by Warbucks' faithful assistant Grace (McDonald) and Miss Hannigan's wastrel brother Rooster (Cumming) and his floozy Lily (Chenoweth). **120m/C; VHS, DVD.** Alicia Morton; Victor Garber; Kathy Bates; Alan Cumming; Audra McDonald; Kristin Chenoweth; ***Cameo(s):*** Andrea McArdle; ***D:*** Rob Marshall; ***W:*** Irene Mecchi; ***C:*** Ralf Bode; ***M:*** Charles Strouse; ***M:*** Martin Charnin. **TV**

Annie **2014 (PG)** The remake of the classic musical for a new generation updates the rags-to-riches tale of the orphan who found love among the wealthy largely through its alteration of the racial backgrounds of its characters. Foxx steps into the Daddy Warbucks role while "Beasts of the Southern Wild" star Wallis charms in the title role. As with so many remakes/reboots of beloved family films, the modern Annie isn't necessarily wrong on its own terms but never justifies its existence. Except for young viewers unwilling to watch "old movies," it's hard to believe anyone would prefer it to the original. **118m/C; DVD, Blu-Ray.** Quvenzhane Wallis; Jamie Foxx; Cameron Diaz; Bobby Cannavale; Rose Byrne; David Zayas; ***D:*** Will Gluck; ***W:*** Will Gluck; Aline Brosh McKenna; ***C:*** Michael Grady; ***M:*** Greg Kurstin. Golden Raspberries '14: Worst Remake/Sequel.

Annie: A Royal Adventure 1/2 **1995** TV sequel to "Annie" finds the red-haired heroine (Johnson) traveling to England with her Daddy Warbucks (Hearn), who's about to be knighted in London. But the evil Lady Edwina Hogbottom (played to a high-camp hilt by Collins) has a plan to blow up Buckingham Palace and take over as queen. Naturally, it's up to Annie to defeat her and have a happy ending. **92m/C; VHS, DVD.** Ashley Johnson; George Hearn; Joan Collins; Emily Ann Lloyd; Camilla Belle; Ian McDiarmid; ***D:*** Ian Toynton; ***W:*** Trish Soodik; ***C:*** Alan Hume; ***M:*** David Michael Frank.

Annie Claus is Coming to Town 1/2 **2011** In this Hallmark Channel holiday movie, Santa's (Jason) naive daughter Annie (Thayer) leaves the North Pole for the first time to experience the real world by heading to L.A. where she is befrended by single mom Lucy (Fox) and her daughter Mia (Kirby). Annie goes to work for struggling toy shop owner Ted (Page), who is not feeling the Christmas spirit, and she needs to bring it back. **87m/C; DVD.** Maria Thayer; Sam Page; Vivica A. Fox; Nay Nay Kirby; Peter Jason; Vicki Lawrence; ***D:*** Kevin Connor; ***W:*** Nina Weinman; ***C:*** Maximo Munzi; ***M:*** Nathan Wang. **CABLE**

Annie Get Your Gun **1950** A lavish production of Irving Berlin's Broadway hit musical. Sharpshooting Annie Oakley (Hutton) is the queen of Buffalo Bill's Wild West show though her talents leave her loveless. Seems fellow marksman Frank Butler's (Keel) ego can't handle the fact that Annie keeps beating him. Lots of singing, with an enthusiastic lead performance by Hutton. **107m/C; VHS, DVD.** Betty Hutton; Howard Keel; Keenan Wynn; Louis Calhern; J. Carrol Naish; Edward Arnold; Clinton Sundberg; ***D:*** George Sidney; ***W:*** Sidney Sheldon; ***C:*** Charles Rosher; ***M:*** Irving Berlin. Oscars '50: Scoring/Musical.

Annie Hall **1977 (PG)** Acclaimed coming-of-cinematic-age film for Allen is based in part on his own life. His love affair with Hall/Keaton is chronicled as an episodic, wistful comedy commenting on family, love, loneliness, communicating, maturity, driving, city life, careers, and various other topics. Abounds with classic scenes, including future star Goldblum and his mantra at a cocktail party; Allen and the lobster pot; and Allen, Keaton, a bathroom, a tennis racket, and a spider. The film operates on many levels, as does Keaton's wardrobe, which started a major fashion trend. Don't blink or you'll miss several future stars in bit parts. Expertly shot by Gordon Willis. **94m/C; VHS, DVD.** Woody Allen; Diane Keaton; Tony Roberts; Carol Kane; Paul Simon; Colleen Dewhurst; Janet Margolin; Shelley Duvall; Christopher Walken; Marshall McLuhan; Dick Cavett; John Glover; Jeff Goldblum; Beverly D'Angelo; ***D:*** Woody Allen; ***W:*** Woody Allen; Marshall Brickman; ***C:*** Gordon Willis. Oscars '77: Actress (Keaton), Director (Allen), Film, Orig. Screenplay; AFI '98: Top 100; British Acad. '77: Actress (Keaton), Director (Allen), Film, Screenplay; Directors Guild '77: Director (Allen); Golden Globes '78: Actress--Mus./Comedy (Keaton); L.A. Film Critics '77: Screenplay; Natl. Bd. of Review '77: Support. Actress (Keaton); Natl. Film Reg. '92; N.Y. Film Critics '77: Actress (Keaton), Director (Allen), Film, Screenplay; Natl. Soc. Film Critics '77: Actress (Keaton), Film, Screenplay; Writers Guild '77: Orig. Screenplay.

Annie Oakley **1935** Energetic biographical drama based on the life and legend of sharpshooter Annie Oakley and her on-off relationship with Wild Bill Hickok. Stanwyck makes a great Oakley. Later musicalized as "Annie Get Your Gun." **90m/B; VHS, DVD.** Barbara Stanwyck; Preston Foster; Brad Johnson; Melvyn Douglas; Pert Kelton; Andy Clyde; Moroni Olsen; Chief Thundercloud; ***D:*** George Stevens.

Annie's Point 1/2 **2005 (G)** Recent widow Annie intends to fulfill her husband's final request: to have his ashes scattered on a bluff in California they called Annie's Point. Resentful son Richard doesn't approve, so Annie takes off on a cross-country road trip from Chicago with Richard's free-spirited daughter Ella instead. A Hallmark Channel family drama. **87m/C; DVD.** Betty White; Richard Thomas; Amy Davidson; Ellen A. Dow; Robert F. Lyons; John Dybdahl; James Keane; Rebecca Switzer; ***D:*** Michael Switzer; ***W:*** Mike Leonardo; ***C:*** Amit Bhattacharya; ***M:*** Steve Dorff. **CABLE**

Annihilation 1/2 **2018 (R)** A thought-provoking, category-defying science fiction film. When Kane (Isaac) returns after going missing during a mission, his scientist wife Lena (Portman) realizes he is not the same. She learns he was part of an exploratory mission into The Shimmer, which emerged after what looked like a meteor struck a lighthouse three years earlier. To uncover what happened to him, Lena joins an all-women team to reach the lighthouse. Once inside, it becomes clear that the invaders have impacted nature in unexpected ways--and cause a profound effect on Lena and her team. Ambitious, visionary, and unsettling. **115m/C; DVD, Blu-Ray.** Natalie Portman; Benedict Wong; Oscar Isaac; Jennifer Jason Leigh; Gina Rodriguez; ***D:*** Alex Garland; ***W:*** Alex Garland; ***C:*** Rob Hardy; ***M:*** Geoff Barrow; Ben Salisbury.

The Anniversary **1968** One-eyed monster mom Mrs. Taggart (Bette at her baddest) gives new meaning to the word "possessive." Thoroughly cowing her three grown sons, she manages to get them to come home each year on the wedding anniversary to the husband she despised. Only this time, the trio tell her they're going to live their own lives. Hah—not if mom has anything to do with it. Based on the play by Bill MacIlwraith. **93m/C; VHS, DVD.** *GB* Bette Davis; Jack Hedley; James Cossins; Christian Roberts; Sheila Hancock; Elaine Taylor; ***D:*** Roy Ward Baker; ***W:*** Jimmy Sangster; ***C:*** Henry Waxman; ***M:*** Philip Martell.

The Anniversary Party **2001 (R)** Leigh and Cumming co-write, co-direct, and star as the central couple in this impressive ensemble comedy-drama about a group of Hollywood friends celebrating said couple's sixth anniversary. Amid much career and personal angst, drug use, and sometimes nasty air-clearing, most of the characters are fleshed out nicely and the dialogue remains sharp throughout. The air is thick with genuine personal dread and interpersonal tension. Among the uniformly excellent performances, two especially stand out: Leigh as the aging actress on the cusp of career oblivion, and Cates as a former actress who's given up her career to focus on being a wife (to just-beyond-leading-man-status hubby Kline) and mother. Filmed in digital video in 19 days under the Dogme 95 guidelines. **117m/C; VHS, DVD.** Jennifer Jason Leigh; Alan Cumming; Gwyneth Paltrow; Kevin Kline; Phoebe Cates; John C. Reilly; Jane Adams; John Benjamin Hickey; Parker Posey; Denis O'Hare; Jennifer Beals; Mina Badie; Michael Panes; ***D:*** Jennifer Jason Leigh; Alan Cumming; ***W:*** Jennifer Jason Leigh; Alan Cumming; ***C:*** John Bailey; ***M:*** Michael Penn.

Anomalisa **2016 (R)** Kaufman and Johnson adapt their radio play into one of the most unique stop-motion animation pictures ever made. A man (voiced by Thewlis) ends up at a depressing Midwest hotel, where he meets a woman who stands out of the crowd. The "trick" of Kaufman's film is that everyone but Thewlis has been voiced by the same person (Noonan), symbolizing the way crowds blend into each other and how we can feel alone even among many. Then he meets Lisa, voiced by Jennifer Jason Leigh. It's a beautiful, moving film that explores loneliness and our need for connection. **90m/C; DVD, Blu-Ray.** David Thewlis; Jennifer Jason Leigh; Tom Noonan; ***D:*** Duke Johnson; Charlie Kaufman; ***W:*** Charlie Kaufman; ***C:*** Joe Passarelli; ***M:*** Carter Burwell.

The Anomaly **2015** An action-science fiction thriller about a man with less than 10 minutes to figure out why his life is in jeopardy. In a time in the not-to-distant future, Ryan Reeve (Clarke) is a former soldier who suffers from PTSD and has a very distinctive type of blackout amnesia. When he regains consciousness—be it days or weeks apart—it is only for nine minutes and 47 seconds. During these periods of reboot, he learns that he is now a deadly operative for a mysterious organization known as Anomaly. When he tries to put together his past in these periods, he also learns that Anomaly wants him dead. As the tries to avoid an Anomaly employee (Somerhalder) intent on his demise, Reeve tries to stay alive and destroy a global conspiracy in the process. **97m/C; DVD, Blu-Ray, Download.** Noel Clarke; Ian Somerhalder; Brian Cox; Alexis Knapp; Luke Hemsworth; ***D:*** Noel Clarke; Simon Lewis; ***C:*** David Katznelson; ***M:*** Tom Linden.

Anonymous 1/2 **2011 (PG-13)** Weaves a political thriller around the conspiracy theory that William Shakespeare didn't write his own works. Rather it was actually Edward De Vere, Earl of Oxford (played exceptionally by Ifans), who was forced to keep his gift secret by a political structure that devalued art. Director Emmerich changes gears after his string of CGI-driven end-of-the-world blockbusters, though this melodramatic piece is just as absurd. A wasted effort for Redgrave as Queen Elizabeth I. **130m/C; DVD, Blu-Ray.** Rhys Ifans; Vanessa Redgrave; Joely Richardson; David Thewlis; Jamie Campbell Bower; Rafe Spall; Xavier Samuel; Sebastian Armesto; Ed Hogg; Sam Reid; ***D:*** Roland Emmerich; ***W:*** John Orloff; ***C:*** Anna Foerster; ***M:*** Harald Kloser.

Anonymous Rex **2004** So dinosaurs didn't actually die off, they adapted and live side-by-side with humans. They wear holographic suits as disguises. Dino-detectives Vince Rubio and Ernie Watson are out to stop a mutant sect that wants to wipe out mankind. Based on the comic mysteries by Eric Garcia. **89m/C; DVD.** Sam Trammell; Daniel Baldwin; Faye Dunaway; Isaac Hayes; Tamara Gorski; Stephanie Lemelin; ***D:*** Julian Jarrold; ***W:*** Joe Menosky; ***C:*** Albert J. Dunk; Kit Whitmore; ***M:*** David Bergeaud. **CABLE**

Another Cinderella Story 1/2 **2008 (PG)** Same basic plot as 2004's "A Cinderella Story" with different characters. Our Cinderella is Mary (Gomez), whose mean stepsisters are trying to stop her from putting on her dancing shoes and going to a costume ball. But Mary makes it and dances with Joey (Seeley), the most popular guy around, who recognizes that this is his dream girl even behind a mask. When Mary has to make a quick exit to meet her curfew, Joey's only clue is the phone she left behind. **90m/C; DVD, Blu-Ray.** Jane Lynch; Katharine Isabelle; Emily Perkins; Marcus T. Paulk; Selena Gomez; Andrew Seeley; Jessica Parker Kennedy; ***D:*** Damon Santostefano; ***W:*** Masahiro Asakawa; Jessica Scott; ***C:*** Jon Joffin; ***M:*** John Paesano. **VIDEO**

Another Country 1/2 **1984** Mitchell's adaptation of his play based on the life of Guy Burgess, who became a spy for the Soviet Union. Guy Bennett (Everett) is an English boarding school upperclassman whose affected mannerisms and barely disguised homosexuality cause dissension among his schoolmates, while his one friend, Tommy Judd (Firth), is a fervant Marxist.

Rather fancifully depicted and loving recreation of 1930s English life. Although the film is inferior to the award-winning play, director Kanievska manages to transform a piece into a solid film, and Everett's performance as Bennett/Burgess is outstanding. **90m/C; VHS, DVD.** *GB* Rupert Everett; Colin Firth; Michael Jenn; Robert Addie; Anna Massey; Betsy Brantley; Rupert Wainwright; Cary Elwes; Arthur Howard; Tristan Oliver; Frederick Alexander; Adrian Ross-Magenty; Geoffrey Bateman; Philip Dupuy; Jeffrey Wickham; Gideon Boulting; Ivor Howard; Charles Spencer; ***D:*** Marek Kanievska; ***W:*** Julian Mitchell; ***C:*** Peter Biziou; ***M:*** Michael Storey.

Another Dawn **1937** Romantic melodrama finds Julia Ashton (Francis) broken-hearted after her fly boy fiancé is killed. Instead, she marries nice guy Col. John Wister (Hunter) and accompanies him to his base in the post-WWI Saharan desert. There, Julia meets Wister's dashing adjunct, Capt. Denny Roark (Flynn), and realizes she's with the wrong man. **73m/B; DVD.** Kay Francis; Errol Flynn; Ian Hunter; Frieda Inescort; ***D:*** William Dieterle; ***W:*** Laird Doyle; ***C:*** Tony Gaudio; ***M:*** Erich Wolfgang Korngold.

Another Day in Paradise **1998 (R)** Tulsa teen junkies Bobbie (Kartheiser) and Rosie (Wagner) team up with older junkie couple Mel (Woods) and Sidney (Griffith) and go from bad to worse. Mel's also a dealer and thief and is glad to add two would-be partners in crime to his and Sidney's traveling road to hell. Woods is all sly confidence while Griffith shows some seductive tough-chick grit and the younger twosome manage to hold their own nicely. Not a pic for the faint of heart or queasy of stomach. Based on the book by Eddie Little. **101m/C; VHS, DVD.** James Woods; Melanie Griffith; Vincent Kartheiser; Natasha Gregson Wagner; Paul Hipp; Brent Briscoe; Lou Diamond Phillips; ***D:*** Larry Clark; ***W:*** Christopher Landon; Stephen Chin; ***C:*** Eric Alan Edwards.

Another Earth **2011 (PG-13)** Cahill's expressionistic low-budget flick is melodramatic and compelling at the same time. A 10th planet—a duplicate Earth—is discovered and young MIT student Rhoda (co-writer Marling) is so busy looking at Earth 2 that she plows her SUV into another car and kills all but one of the occupants. After serving a prison term, a penitent Rhoda tries making amends by secretly befriending the lone survivor, isolated and grief-stricken composer John (Mapother), while still being obsessed with the possibility of an alternate reality on the alternate planet. **92m/C; DVD, Blu-Ray, On Demand.** Brit Marling; William Mapother; Jordan Baker; Flint Beverage; Kumar Pallana; ***D:*** Mike Cahill; ***W:*** Brit Marling; Mike Cahill; ***C:*** Mike Cahill; ***M:*** Fall on Your Sword.

Another 48 Hrs. **1/2 1990 (R)** Continuing chemistry between Nolte and Murphy is one of the few worthwhile items in this stodgy rehash. Any innovation by Murphy seems lost, the story is redundant of any other cop thriller, and violence and car chases abound. Pointlessly energetic and occasionally fun for only the true devotee. **98m/C; VHS, DVD.** Eddie Murphy; Nick Nolte; Brion James; Kevin Tighe; Bernie Casey; David Anthony Marshall; Ed O'Ross; Tisha Campbell; ***D:*** Walter Hill; ***W:*** Jeb Stuart; ***C:*** Matthew F. Leonetti; ***M:*** James Horner.

Another Happy Day **2011 (R)** An angry dysfunctional family portrait that unfortunately mistakes drama for comedy. Neurotic mother Lynn (Barkin) hits the road with her two youngest sons to Annapolis for the marriage of her oldest son Dylan (Nardelli) to Heather (Coover). Inflated ego trips lead to the inevitable, and cliched, clash with the in-laws, setting the stage for excellent, if a bit over-the-top performances from a great cast. Moore is especially in overdrive as a goofy, sexed up second wife of Lynn's abusive ex-husband Paul (Church). A feast for the performers, but doesn't give the audience much to digest. **119m/C; DVD, Blu-Ray.** Ellen Barkin; Kate (Catherine) Bosworth; Michael Nardelli; Daniel Yelsky; Ezra Miller; George Kennedy; Ellen Burstyn; Thomas Haden Church; Demi Moore; Laura Coover; Jeffrey DeMunn; ***D:*** Sam Levinson; ***W:*** Sam Levinson; ***C:*** Ivan Strasburg; ***M:*** Olafur Arnalds.

Another Life **1/2 2001** Based on the 1920s Thompson-Bywaters criminal case. Fanciful Edith (Little) makes a grave mistake by marrying staid Percy Thompson (Moran), whom she soon feels is dull, resentful, and cold. When Edith re-connects with exciting family friend Frederick Bywaters (Gruffudd), she strays, eventually confessing to Freddy that she wishes Percy were dead. He soon is and the adulterers stand trial for his murder. **101m/C; DVD.** *GB* Natasha Little; Nick Moran; Ioan Gruffudd; Imelda Staunton; Rachael Stirling; Tom Wilkinson; Liz McKechnie; ***D:*** Philip Goodhew; ***W:*** Philip Goodhew; ***C:*** Simon Archer; ***M:*** James McConnel.

Another Lonely Hitman *Shin Kanashiki Hittoman* **1995** Character study rather than a typical gangster flick. Old-school yakuza and former junkie Tachibana (Ishibashi) finds his ways badly out-of-date after he's released from a 10-year prison stretch. He tries to do the right thing by helping young druggie/hooker Yuki (Sawada) clean up (and the withdrawal scenes aren't pretty) and teach the younger hoods some manners. Based on the book by Yamanouchi, who did the screenplay; Japanese with subtitles. **105m/C; DVD.** *JP* Ryo Ishibashi; Asami Sawada; Kazuhiko Kanayama; Tatsuo Yamada; ***D:*** Rokuro Mochizuki; ***W:*** Yukio Yamanouchi; ***C:*** Naoki Imaizumi; ***M:*** Kazutoki Umezu.

Another Man, Another Chance *Un Autre Homme, Une Autre Chance* **1977 (PG)** Remake of Lelouch's "A Man and a Woman," set in the turn-of-the-century American West, pales by comparison to the original. Slow-moving tale casts widow Bujold and widower Caan as lovers. **132m/C; VHS, DVD.** *FR* James Caan; Genevieve Bujold; Francis Huster; Jennifer Warren; Susan Tyrrell; ***D:*** Claude Lelouch; ***W:*** Claude Lelouch.

Another Man's Poison **1/2 1952** Melodramatic crime drama with a showy, if stereotypical role, for Davis. She's mystery writer Janet Frobisher and lives on a secluded Yorkshire farm. Too bad her escaped con husband suddenly shows up (and gets killed by Janet). Her troubles aren't over. Hubby's partner, George Bates (Merrill), comes a-lookin' and agrees to dispose of the body if Janet will let him hide out. She tries to kill Bates as well but her scheming comes to an unexpected conclusion. Adapted from the play "Deadlock" by Leslie Sands. **90m/B; VHS, DVD, Blu-Ray.** *GB* Bette Davis; Gary Merrill; Emlyn Williams; Anthony Steel; Barbara Murray; Reginald Beckwith; Edna Morris; ***D:*** Irving Rapper; ***W:*** Val Guest; ***C:*** Robert Krasker; ***M:*** Paul Sawtell.

Another 9 1/2 Weeks WOOF! **1996 (R)** Uninteresting sequel finds suicidal John (Rourke) overwhelmed by his kinky memories of Elizabeth, so he flies to Paris determined to find her. Instead, he meets fashion designer Lea (Everhart), who claims to be Elizabeth's friend and who puts the sexual tease on the S/M devotee. Monotony sets in early and there's no real heat generated between the duo. **104m/C; VHS, DVD.** Mickey Rourke; Angie Everhart; Steven Berkoff; Agathe de la Fontaine; Dougray Scott; ***D:*** Anne Goursaud; ***W:*** Mick Davis; ***C:*** Robert Alazraki; ***M:*** Stephen Parsons; Francis Haines.

Another Pair of Aces: Three of a Kind **1991** Nelson and Kristofferson team up to clear the name of Torn, a Texas Ranger accused of murder. Video contains some scenes deemed too racy for TV. Sequel to "A Pair of Aces." **93m/C; VHS, DVD.** Willie Nelson; Kris Kristofferson; Joan Severance; Rip Torn; Dan Kamin; Ken Farmer; Richard Jones; ***D:*** Bill Bixby. **TV**

Another Public Enemy *Gonggongui Jeog 2* **2005 (R)** Prosecutor Kang investigates corrupt businessman Han, who is laundering his ill-gotten real estate gains in the U.S. Only his superiors suspect Kang's motives since the two were bitter high school rivals. Really, really, really long, which dilutes any action and suspense. Korean with subtitles. **148m/C; DVD.** *NK* Kyung-gu Sol; Jun-ho Jeong; Shin-il Kang; ***D:*** Woo-suk Kang; ***W:*** Woo-suk Kang; ***M:*** Jawe-kwon Han.

Another Stakeout **1/2** *Stakeout 2* **1993 (PG-13)** Sequel six years after the original finds Dreyfuss and Estevez partnered again for another stakeout, this time to keep an eye on Moriarty, a reluctant witness against the Mob. The two spying detectives find themselves in an upscale neighborhood where blending in is a hard thing to do. O'Donnell is a breath of fresh air as a wisecracking assistant district attorney. Stowe briefly reprises her role as Dreyfuss' girlfriend. Writer Kouf reportedly had difficulty penning the script, surprising since there isn't much new here. **109m/C; VHS, DVD, Blu-Ray.** Richard Dreyfuss; Emilio Estevez; Rosie O'Donnell; Cathy Moriarty; Madeleine Stowe; John Rubinstein; Marcia Strassman; Dennis Farina; Miguel Ferrer; ***D:*** John Badham; ***W:*** Jim Kouf; ***C:*** Roy Wagner.

Another Thin Man **1/2 1939** Powell and Loy team up for the third in the delightful "Thin Man" series. Slightly weaker series entry takes its time, but has both Powell and Loy providing stylish performances. Nick Jr. is also introduced as the newest member of the sleuthing team. Sequel to "After the Thin Man"; followed by "Shadow of the Thin Man." **105m/B; VHS, DVD.** William Powell; Myrna Loy; Virginia Grey; Otto Kruger; Sir C. Aubrey Smith; Ruth Hussey; ***D:*** W.S. Van Dyke.

Another Time, Another Place **1958** Sappy melodrama about an American journalist who suffers an emotional meltdown when her married British lover is killed during WWII. So she heads for Cornwall to console the widow and family. **98m/B; VHS, DVD.** *GB* Lana Turner; Barry Sullivan; Glynis Johns; Sean Connery; Terence Longdon; ***D:*** Lewis Allen; ***C:*** Jack Hildyard.

Another Way *Olelkezo Tekintetek* **1982** The director of 1971's much-lauded "Love" sets this politically charged love story in Hungary in 1958. Opening with a view of a female corpse, the story flashes backward to look at the woman's journalistic career and her relationship with a women colleague. Candid love scenes between women in Hungary of 1958, considered a cinematic novelty in many places outside Hungary. In Hungarian with English subtitles. **100m/C; VHS, DVD.** *HU* Jadwiga Jankowska Cieslak; Grazyna Szapolowska; Josef Kroner; Hernadi Judit; Andorai Peter; ***D:*** Karoly Makk. Cannes '82: Actress (Cieslak).

Another Woman **1988 (PG)** The study of an intellectual woman whose life is changed when she begins to eavesdrop. What she hears provokes her to examine every relationship in her life, finding things quite different than she had believed. Heavy going, with Rowlands effective as a woman coping with an entirely new vision of herself. Farrow plays the catalyst. Although Allen's comedies are more popular than his dramas, this one deserves a look. **81m/C; VHS, DVD, Blu-Ray.** Gena Rowlands; Gene Hackman; Mia Farrow; Ian Holm; Betty Buckley; Martha Plimpton; Blythe Danner; Harris Yulin; Sandy Dennis; David Ogden Stiers; John Houseman; Philip Bosco; Frances Conroy; Kenneth Welsh; Michael Kirby; ***D:*** Woody Allen; ***W:*** Woody Allen; ***C:*** Sven Nykvist.

Another Woman **1/2 1994** Lisa Temple (Bateman) was attacked and left for dead in an alley. She wakes up in the hospital with amnesia but her bitter husband Paul (Outerbridge) still wants a divorce. Lisa learns things about herself she doesn't like and vows to change but as her memories start to return she realizes just what put her in that alley in the first place. From the Harlequin Romance Series; adapted from the Margot Dalton novel. **91m/C; DVD.** *CA* Justine Bateman; Peter Outerbridge; Amy Stewart; Kenneth Welsh; James Purcell; Jackie Richardson; Michael Copeman; Elizabeth Lennie; ***D:*** Alan Smythe; ***W:*** Jim Henshaw; Lee Langley; Lyle Slack; ***C:*** Michael Storey; ***M:*** David Blamires. **TV**

Another Woman's Husband **1/2 2000** Traumatized as a child by the drowning death of her brother, Laurel (Rinna) finally decides to get over her fear of water by taking swimming lessons. Susan (O'Grady) is her swimming instructor and they become best friends. Until the women realize they also share the same man (Midkiff), who happens to be Susan's husband. Based on the novel "Swimming Lessons" by Anna Villegas and Lynne Hugo. **91m/C; VHS, DVD.** Lisa Rinna; Gail O'Grady; Dale Midkiff; Sally Kirkland; Charlotte Rae; ***D:*** Noel Nosseck; ***W:*** Susan Arnout Smith; ***C:*** Alan Caso; ***M:*** Mark Snow. **CABLE**

Another Year **2010 (PG-13)** Despite the PG13 rating, Leigh's film is all about adults—some who are and some who should be. This slice of life drama, set in North London, features a year (corresponding to the seasons) in an interconnected group of family and friends that longtime-marrieds Tom (Broadbent) and Gerri (Sheen) regularly see. Among them is increasingly desperate, self-pitying Mary (Manville, in a shockingly vulnerable performance) who drinks too much and embarrasses herself with inappropriate flirtations. **129m/C; Blu-Ray, On Demand.** *GB* Jim Broadbent; Ruth Sheen; Lesley Manville; Oliver Maltman; Peter Wight; David Bradley; Martin Savage; Philip Davis; Imelda Staunton; Karina Fernandez; Michele Austin; ***D:*** Mike Leigh; ***W:*** Mike Leigh; ***C:*** Dick Pope; ***M:*** Gary Yershon.

Another You **1991 (R)** Con man Wilder takes pathological liar Pryor under his care and decides to use his talents to his fullest advantage. Posing as successful businessmen, the duo initiate a scam so complicated that they may end up being double-crossed or worse yet, dead! Can the pair see their plan through without losing their lives? Sad to see how far these two gifted comedians have fallen. Their collaboration is tired and the movie generally dreadful. **98m/C; VHS, DVD.** Richard Pryor; Gene Wilder; Mercedes Ruehl; Vanessa L(ynne) Williams; Stephen Lang; Kevin Pollak; ***D:*** Maurice Phillips.

The Answer Man *Arlen Faber* **2009 (R)** Arlen Faber (Daniels) has suffered for 20 years as the author of a spiritual self-help guide that became a mass-media sensation. Unable to handle the fame, Arlen is a misanthropic recluse with back trouble that drives him into the arms of single mom/chiropractor Elizabeth (Graham) who thinks maybe Arlen could also be the new dad figure in her young son's life. Also having father issues is bookstore owner Kris (Pucci), just out of alcohol rehab, who turns to the reluctant Arlen for guidance. Pic skates on the emotional surface of some big issues but does have some nice turns by the leads. **96m/C; Blu-Ray, On Demand.** Jeff Daniels; Lauren Graham; Lou Taylor Pucci; Olivia Thirlby; Kat Dennings; Nora Dunn; Tony Hale; ***D:*** John Hindman; ***W:*** John Hindman; ***C:*** Oliver Bokelberg; ***M:*** Teddy Castellucci.

Answer This **1/2 2010 (PG-13)** Nerd comedy. Trivia whiz Paul Tarson (Gorham) doesn't know what he's going to do after grad school. He postpones his long-overdue dissertation yet again so he and some buddies can tackle the First Annual Ann Arbor Pub Trivia Tournament. **105m/C; DVD.** Christopher Gorham; Nelson Franklin; Evan Jones; Arielle Kebbel; Kip Pardue; Chris Parnell; Ralph Williams; ***D:*** Christopher Farah; ***W:*** Christopher Farah; ***C:*** Christian Sprenger; ***M:*** John Paesano. **VIDEO**

Answers to Nothing **1/2 2011 (R)** Competent but undistinguished drama. Stories about five days in the lives of some Los Angelenos suffering various crises converge around the highly publicized search for a kidnapped young girl, including the female detective assigned to the case and several suspects. There's a therapist with his family issues plus the problems of a couple of his patients and a recovering alcoholic who's the caregiver for her disabled brother. **124m/C; DVD.** Dane Cook; Elizabeth Mitchell; Julie Benz; Barbara Hershey; Zach Gilford; Erik Palladino; Mark Kelly; Kali Hawk; Aja Volkman; ***D:*** Matthew Leutwyler; ***W:*** Matthew Leutwyler; Gillian Vigman; ***C:*** David Robert Jones; ***M:*** Craig Richey.

The Ant Bully **1/2 2006 (PG)** Warner Bros. entry in the CGI-created insect category comes eight years after Pixar and DreamWorks set the standard with "A Bug's Life" and "Antz," respectively, and delivers nothing new. New kid on the block and neighborhood punching-bag Lucas, vents his frustration by picking on something smaller than him—an ant colony in his yard—only to be magically shrunken and transported into the ant's world to face his victims. Predictable life lessons about acceptance and teamwork, along with uninspired voice work from the star-studded cast drag down this visually impressive but all too familiar story. Based on the book by John Nickle. **88m/C; DVD, Blu-Ray.** ***V:*** Zach Tyler; Jake T. Austin; Nicolas Cage; Bruce Campbell; Meryl Streep; Julia Roberts; Paul Giamatti; Myles Jeffrey; Regina King; Cheri

Oteri; Lily Tomlin; Rob Paulsen; Allison Mack; Ricardo Montalban; Larry Miller; Austin Majors; Mark DeCarlo; Frank Welker; Nicole Sullivan; Vernee Watson-Johnson; ***D:*** John A. Davis; ***W:*** John A. Davis; ***M:*** John Debney.

Ant-Man 🦴🦴🦴 **2015 (PG-13)** More fun and clever than it had any right to be, Peyton Reed's first entry in the Marvel Cinematic Universe may not have the stature of an Iron Man or the scope of a Guardians of the Galaxy but it works on its own (small) terms. Douglas plays Hank Pym, a S.H.I.E.L.D. scientist who basically passes down his knowledge of the way to shrink down to ant size to become the titular hero to Scott Lang (played with a knowing wink by Rudd). **117m/C; DVD, Blu-Ray, Streaming.** Paul Rudd; Michael Douglas; Bobby Cannavale; Hayley Atwell; John Slattery; Evangeline Lilly; Corey Stoll; ***D:*** Peyton Reed; ***W:*** Paul Rudd; Edgar Wright; Joe Cornish; Adam McKay; ***C:*** Russell Carpenter; ***M:*** Christophe Beck.

Ant-Man and the Wasp 🦴🦴🦴 *Ant-Man 2* **2018 (PG-13)** If Paul Rudd isn't Hollywood's most charming actor, he's gotta be in the top five. Luckily for audiences, he brings that charisma to reprising his roles both on-screen as the titular character and off-screen as writer. In this sequel, Ant-Man partners with another bite-sized superhero, the Wasp (Lilly), to defeat The Ghost. It's a funny, easy-breezy respite from the emotionally heavy fare otherwise offered by the Marvel Cinematic Universe. **118m/C; DVD, Blu-Ray.** Paul Rudd; Evangeline Lilly; Michael Peña; Walton Goggins; Bobby Canavale; ***D:*** Peyton Reed; ***W:*** Paul Rudd; Chris McKenna; Erik Sommers; Andrew Barrer; Gabriel Ferrari; ***C:*** Dante Spinotti; ***M:*** Christophe Beck.

Antarctica 🦴 **1/2 2008 (R)** Various Tel Aviv residents look for love or merely a one-night stand in Hochner's interconnecting stories. Librarian Omer and dancer Danny are looking for commitment, journalist Ronen and choreographer Boaz prefer to play the field, and Shirley keeps trying to leave her girlfriend Michal. Hebrew with subtitles. **112m/C; DVD.** *IS* Ofer Regirer; Guy Zoaretz; Tomer Ilan; Yiftach Mizrahi; Lucy Dubinchik; Liat Ekta; ***D:*** Yair Hochner; ***W:*** Yair Hochner; ***C:*** Ziv Berkovich; ***M:*** Eli Soorani.

Antboy 🦴 **1/2 2014 (PG)** This is a weird one. This low-budget Danish kids' movie has been dubbed into English, but regional idioms aren't the only things lost in translation. A twelve-year-old kid named Pelle (Dietz) is bitten by a genetically-altered ant and gains the powers of... yeah, it's a cheap Danish Disney Channel-version of the "Spider-Man" story. Only Pelle's Antboy is decidedly wackier, with powers fueled by sugar and (kid you not) acid pee. (We are fortunately spared a scene where he uses that power on anyone living.) It's an odd, earnest superhero tale for the kiddies. **77 minutesm/C; DVD.** Oscar Dietz; Nicolas Bro; Samuel Ting Graf; Amalie Kruse Jensen; ***D:*** Ask Hasselbalch; ***W:*** Anders Olholm; ***C:*** Niels Johansen; ***M:*** Peter Peter.

Anthony Adverse 🦴🦴 **1/2 1936** March is a young man in the 19th century who searches for manhood across America and Mexico. He grows slowly as he battles foes, struggles against adversity and returns home to find his lover in this romantic swashbuckler. A star-studded cast, lush costuming, and an energetic musical score. Highly acclaimed in its time, but now seems dated. Based on the novel by Hervey Allen. **141m/B; DVD.** Fredric March; Olivia de Havilland; Anita Louise; Gale Sondergaard; Claude Rains; Edmund Gwenn; Louis Hayward; ***D:*** Mervyn LeRoy; ***W:*** Sheridan Gibney; ***C:*** Gaetano Antonio "Tony" Gaudio; ***M:*** Erich Wolfgang Korngold. Oscars '36: Cinematog., Film Editing, Score, Support. Actress (Sondergaard).

Anthropoid 🦴🦴 **1/2 2016 (R)** In their German-occupied country in December of 1941, two Czech soldiers (Dornan and Murphy) are a part of a resistance that plots to assassinate Reinhard Heydrich, the third-in-command of the Nazi Reich and one of the key architects of the Final Solution. Sean Ellis' historical action flick is often a bit too dry for its own good. There's a lot of discussion of action instead of action, but this rarely told chapter in the history of World War II offers proof of how many stories from that world-changing event remain to be told. **120m/C; DVD, Blu-Ray.** Cillian Murphy; Jamie Dornan; Anna Geislerova; Toby Jones; Charlotte Le Bon; ***D:*** Sean Ellis; ***W:*** Sean Ellis; Anthony Frewin; ***C:*** Sean Ellis; ***M:*** Robin Foster.

Anthropophagus: The Grim Reaper 🦴🦴 *The Grim Reaper; Anthropophagus; The Zombie's Rage; Antropophagus* **1980** Disturbing cult film about American tourists vacationing in Greece who stumble upon an island village that appears to be missing all its inhabitants. Infamously gory, and rarely available in its uncut form due to its graphic nature. **90m/C; DVD, Blu-Ray.** *IT* George Eastman; Saverio Vallone; Mark Bodin; Bob Larson; Tisa Farrow; Serena Grandi; Margaret Mazzantini; Rubina Rey; Zora Kerova; ***D:*** Joe D'Amato; ***W:*** George Eastman; Joe D'Amato; ***C:*** Enrico Biribicchi; ***M:*** Marcello Giombini. **VIDEO**

Anti-Terrorist Cell: Manhunt 🦴 *The Red Phone: Manhunt; Special Unit AT 13* **2001** The ATC is an international covert organization that hunts terrorists who escape government, military, and police agencies although this case involves a group of greedy mercenaries. Made as a TV pilot for the European market, it failed to sell—probably because it's cheap and boring. **92m/C; DVD.** *GE* Joe Penny; Michael Wincott; Arnold Vosloo; Michael Ironside; Ben Cross; Colin Salmon; ***D:*** Jerry Jameson; ***W:*** Terry Thompson; Steven Whitney; ***C:*** Fernando Arguelles; ***M:*** Martin Locker.

Antibodies 🦴🦴 *Antikorper* **2005** Captured serial killer Gabriel Engel (Hennicke) admits to the murders of 13 boys and is suspected in the death of a young girl in a rural community. Naive local cop Michael Martens (Mohring) travels to the city to question the now wheelchair-bound Engel and close his case. But Engel tries to convince him that someone else killed the girl and Michael learns more about the killer and himself that he could have imagined. German with subtitles. **128m/C; DVD.** *GE* Andre Hennicke; Wotan Wilke Mohring; Heinz Hoenig; Ulrike Krumbiegel; Jurgen Schornagel; ***D:*** Christian Alvart; ***W:*** Christian Alvart; ***C:*** Hagen Bogdanski; ***M:*** Michi Britsch.

Antibody 🦴🦴 **2002 (R)** Terrorist Moran (Vergov) has a nuclear bomb and the detonator chip is inside his body. He's shot and if he dies, the chip will go off. So it's up to security expert Richard Gaynes (Henriksen) and a team of scientists to send an experimental tracking craft inside Moran's bloodstream to find and extract the chip in time. **90m/C; VHS, DVD.** Lance Henriksen; Robin Givens; William Zabka; Julian Vergov; ***D:*** Christian McIntire; ***W:*** Micheal Baldwin; ***C:*** Adolfo Bartoli; ***M:*** Scott Clausen. **VIDEO**

Antichrist 🦴 **2009** Challenging in all the wrong ways, Von Tier's self-conscious, symbolic, misogynistic, psychosexual arthouse horror is divided into four chapters and begins with the accidental death of a toddler. The nameless traumatized mother (Gainsbourg) and her domineering husband (Dafoe), a professional therapist, go to their isolated home in the country in an effort to deal with their grief. Soon, her sanity is in question and Von Tier eventually tips over the edge in a graphically-depicted mutilation scene. In black and white and color. **105m/C; Blu-Ray, On Demand.** *DK GE FR SW IT PL* Charlotte Gainsbourg; Willem Dafoe; ***D:*** Lars von Trier; ***W:*** Lars von Trier; ***C:*** Anthony Dod Mantle.

Antisocial Behavior 🦴 *Antisocial Behaviour* **2007** A man known for his mental instability because he committed murder as a young boy is tomented by a gang of teens. The cops prove worthless to help him, and he falls back on old habits. **90m/C; DVD.** *UK* Simon Brewer; Aidan Cross; Okezie Morro; David Watkins; Posey Brewer; ***D:*** Vinson Pike; ***W:*** Vinson Pike; Kevin Ault; ***C:*** John Wilson; ***M:*** Steven Wilson. **VIDEO**

Antitrust 🦴 **1/2 2000 (PG-13)** Supernerd code writer Milo (Phillippe) leaves the garage for a Pacific Northwest software giant only to discover the company's mega-monied leader, Winston (Robbins), may not be on the up and up—in fact, the things he's doing to maintain industry supremacy could be downright evil. Robbins's bespectacled techie villain is spot-on Bill Gates, but the film borrows heavily from its paranoid predecessors and offers little of its own to the field. A mediocre thriller among other mediocre thrillers. **120m/C; VHS, DVD.** Ryan Phillippe; Tim Robbins; Rachael Leigh Cook; Claire Forlani; Douglas McFerran; Richard Roundtree; Yee Jee Tso; Tygh Runyan; ***D:*** Peter Howitt; ***W:*** Howard Franklin; ***C:*** John Bailey; ***M:*** Don Davis.

Antiviral 🦴🦴 **2012** Brandon Cronenberg (son of director David) debuts with some creepy ick of his own. In a star-obsessed, slightly near-future culture, the latest craze has Syd and the employees at Lucas Clinic injecting rabid fans with non-contagious viruses bought from the famous. Syd also runs a black-market sideline in live viruses, which backfires when he injects himself with some exotica taken from starlet Hannah. He quickly realizes something's gone wrong after Hannah dies and Syd himself becomes terminal. Not for those with weak stomachs as needles and bodily fluids are rampant. **109m/C; DVD, Blu-Ray.** *CA* Caleb Landry Jones; Sarah Gadon; Malcolm McDowell; Nicholas (Nick) Campbell; Sheila McCarthy; Joe Pingue; Wendy Crewson; ***D:*** Brandon Cronenberg; ***W:*** Brandon Cronenberg; ***C:*** Karim Hussain; ***M:*** E.C. Woodley.

Anton Chekhov's The Duel 🦴 **1/2** *The Duel* **2009** Adaptation of Chekov's 1891 novella. Self-absorbed aristocrat Laevsky has come to a seaside town with his married mistress Nadya. But now that they are together all the time, Laevsky grows bored and the flirtatious Nadya looks for other romantic prospects. Another visitor, zoologist Van Koren, becomes increasingly enraged by Laevsky's neurotic behavior and maneuvers him into a duel in a seeming reaction to the notion of survival of the fittest. **95m/C; DVD.** Andrew Scott; Tobias Menzies; Niall Buggy; Fiona Glascott; Michelle Fairley; Nicholas (Nick) Rowe; Jeremy Swift; ***D:*** Dover Kosashvili; ***W:*** Mary Bing; ***C:*** Paul Sarossy; ***M:*** Angelo Milli.

Antonia's Line 🦴🦴 **1/2 1995 (R)** 90-year-old Antonia (Van Ammelrooy) has decided that she is going to die today and so begins a 50-year-long flashback of her nonconformist life in a Dutch village. Her lesbian daughter Danielle (Dottermans) wants a child without bothering about a husband and Antonia obliging arranges a brief interlude that produces child prodigy Therese (Van Overloop), who eventually has her own daughter, Sarah (Ravesteijn). Lots of female bonding (the male characters are mostly on the periphery of the action) and a certain magic realism abound. Dutch with subtitles. **102m/C; VHS, DVD, Blu-Ray.** *NL* Willeke Van Ammelrooy; Els Dottermans; Veerle Van Overloop; Thyrza Ravesteijn; Jan Decleir; Mil Seghers; Jan Steen; Marina De Graaf; ***D:*** Marleen Gorris; ***W:*** Marleen Gorris; ***C:*** Willy Stassen; ***M:*** Ilona Sekacz. Oscars '95: Foreign Film.

Antonio 🦴🦴 **1973** A Texas millionaire on the run from his wife and her divorce lawyer alights in a small Chilean village and turns it upside down. **89m/C; VHS, DVD.** Larry Hagman; Trini Lopez; Noemi Guerrero; Pedro Becker; ***D:*** Claudio Guzman.

Antony and Cleopatra 🦴🦴 **1973 (PG)** Heston wrote, directed, and starred in this long, dry adaptation of the Shakespeare play that centers on the torrid romance between Mark Antony and Cleopatra. **150m/C; VHS, DVD, Blu-Ray.** Charlton Heston; Hildegard(e) Neil; Fernando Rey; Eric Porter; John Castle; Freddie Jones; Warren Clarke; Julian Glover; ***D:*** Charlton Heston.

Ants 🦴 **1/2** *Panic at Lakewood Manor; It Happened at Lakewood Manor* **1977** A mad bug parable for our planet-obsessed society. Insecticide-infected ants turn militant and check into a local hotel to vent their chemically induced foul mood on the unsuspecting clientele. The guest register includes a gaggle of celebrities who probably wish they'd signed on the Love Boat instead. Made for TV (an ant farm would probably be just too horrible on the big screen). **100m/C; VHS, DVD.** Suzanne Somers; Robert Foxworth; Myrna Loy; Lynda Day George; Gerald Gordon; Bernie Casey; Barry Van Dyke; Karen Lamm; Anita Gillette; Moosie Drier; Steve Franken; Brian Dennehy; Bruce French; Stacy Keach, Sr.; Rene Enriquez; James Storm; ***D:*** Robert Scheerer; ***W:*** Guerdon (Gordon) Trueblood; ***C:*** Bernie Abramson; ***M:*** Ken Richmond. **TV**

Antwone Fisher 🦴🦴🦴 **2002 (PG-13)** Washington's directorial debut is a drama based on the true story of Antwone Fisher, who also wrote the screenplay. Washington also stars as Jerome Davenport, the naval psychiatrist who helps the angry young Fisher (Luke) get past the demons of his foster childhood. The two knock heads and are both forced to change their own ideas, slowly coming to understand and trust one another. Davenport learns that Fisher was born in prison, his father murdered and his mother a convict. Davenport urges Fisher to confront his past, and some of the best scenes are with Fisher's aunt (Johnson), uncle (Billings) and mother (Davis), which resonate. Subplot with Davenport and wife Berta (Richardson) shows they have their own issues to work out, as well. A tearjerker in the best sense, the simply told tale is a triumph for Luke, who is impressive in his debut role. **113m/C; VHS, DVD, Blu-Ray.** Derek Luke; Denzel Washington; Joy Bryant; Salli Richardson-Whitfield; Earl Billings; Kevin Connolly; Viola Davis; Rainoldo Gooding; Novella Nelson; Vernee Watson-Johnson; Kente Scott; Yolonda Ross; Stephen Snedden; Malcolm David Kelly; ***D:*** Denzel Washington; ***W:*** Antwone Fisher; ***C:*** Philippe Rousselot; ***M:*** Mychael Danna. Ind. Spirit '03: Actor (Luke).

Antz 🦴🦴🦴 **1998 (PG)** Malcontent worker ant, Z (Allen), moans to his therapist about his insignificance and the depressing anonymity of "being born in the middle of five million." But after meeting the colony's princess, Bala (Stone), who is facing her own bleak future thanks to an arranged marriage with the colony's power-hungry General Mandible (Hackman), Z and Princess Bala embark on a dangerous mission to the surface in search of the mythical "Insectopia." Only the second film ever created entirely through computer animation ("Toy Story" being the first), pic is visually amazing. The fact that the ant characters do not resemble their performers' appearances makes the relationship between Z and the princess plausible, and actually adds depth to the characters' personalities. An interesting, rather elaborate storyline, along with excellent voice performances (even Stallone!) make this one fun for all ages. **83m/C; VHS, DVD, Blu-Ray.** ***V:*** Woody Allen; Sharon Stone; Sylvester Stallone; Anne Bancroft; Danny Glover; Christopher Walken; Jane Curtin; Jennifer Lopez; John Mahoney; Dan Aykroyd; Paul Mazursky; Gene Hackman; ***D:*** Eric Darnell; Tim Johnson; ***W:*** Chris Weitz; Paul Weitz; Todd Alcott; ***M:*** Harry Gregson-Williams; John Powell.

Anvil! The Story of Anvil 🦴🦴 **2009** Rockumentary about the aging, working-class Canadian metal band that seemed on the brink of stardom in the mid-1980s and instead faded into obscurity. Lead vocalist Steve 'Lips' Kudlow and drummer Robb Reiner have been playing together since the age of 14 and their early LPs influenced more successful speed-metal bands. But with only modest hits and a mismanaged European tour, they were dropped by their label. Still playing clubs (with two additional rotating members), they have day jobs to support their families while working on a comeback album. You have to admire their persistence and optimism if nothing else. **90m/C; DVD.** Steve "Lips" Kudlow; Robb Reiner; ***D:*** Sacha Gervasi; ***C:*** Christopher Soos. Ind. Spirit '10: Feature Doc.

Any Day 🦴 *Resentment* **2015** Ex-fighter Vian (Bean) is released from a stint in prison after a drunken fight ended very badly. Crashing on his sister Bethley's (Walsh) couch, he plays father figure to nephew Jimmy (Gross, giving one of the most cartoonish child performances ever) and gets a job at a local pizza joint run by Roland (Arnold). Vian even gets a love interest in Jolene (Longoria), who he fails to tell about his ex-con status because, well, it's a movie. And then Jimmy gets into an accident and the film gets truly manipulative. It's horrendous. **100m/C; DVD.** Sean Bean; Kate Walsh; Eva Longoria; Tom Arnold; Shane Black; ***D:*** Rustam Branaman; ***W:*** Rustam Branaman; ***C:*** Harlan Bosmajian; ***M:*** Elia Cmiral.

Any Day Now 🦴🦴🦴 **2012 (R)** Rudy (Cumming) and Paul (Dillahunt) are a loving gay couple who take in teenager Marco (Leyva) with Down syndrome and give him the acceptance and family that he's never found. When authorities try to take Marco away from them, a court battle ensues. Dillahunt and Cumming are two great actors who are allowed a timely showcase in this true story of gay parenthood in the '70s, and how the issues then remain ones today. **97m/C; DVD, Blu-Ray.** Alan Cumming; Garret Dillahunt; Isaac Leyva; Frances Fisher; Gregg Henry; Jamie Anne Allman; Kelli Williams; Chris Mulkey; Alan Rachins; ***D:*** Travis Fine; ***W:*** Travis Fine; George Arthur Bloom; ***C:*** Rachel Morrison; ***M:*** Joey Newman.

Any Given Sunday **1999 (R)** Stone sets aside his conspiracy theories on war and politics and effectively shines a spotlight on a different kind of battlefield to come up with the most commerical and entertaining film of his career. Pacino heads an all-star cast as the battered, yet wise and resilient coach of a struggling Miami football team who locks horns with not only young quarterback Foxx, but ruthless, ballbuster team owner Diaz. Epic-like runtime (which sprints along thanks to Stone's potent mix of raw camera work and hip-hop soundtrack) allows much of the cast plenty of room, with comedian Foxx holding his own with the big boys in a star-making performance as the hotdog player with a bad case of ego. With an intelligent script and a perfect cast, Stone creates the most realistic look at pro football since 1979's "North Dallas Forty." **170m/B; VHS, DVD, Blu-Ray.** Al Pacino; Dennis Quaid; Cameron Diaz; Jamie Foxx; Charlton Heston; James Woods; Matthew Modine; Ann-Margret; Lauren Holly; Lela Rochon; LL Cool J; Aaron Eckhart; Jim Brown; Bill Bellamy; Elizabeth Berkley; John C. McGinley; ***D:*** Oliver Stone; ***W:*** Oliver Stone; John Logan; ***C:*** Salvatore Totino; ***M:*** Robbie Robertson.

Any Gun Can Play *For a Few Bullets More* **1967** Typical spaghetti western. Three men (banker, thief, and bounty hunter) compete for a treasure of gold while wandering about the Spanish countryside. **103m/C; VHS, DVD.** *IT SP* Edd Byrnes; Gilbert Roland; George Hilton; Kareen O'Hara; Pedro Sanchez; Gerard Herter; ***D:*** Enzo G. Castellari.

Any Human Heart **2011** Boyd adapts his own novel, which follows three stages (and three actors) in the life of minor British writer Logan Mountstuart from his 1920s youth (Claflin) through WWII (Macfadyen) and his old age (Broadbent) in the 1970s. Various historical personages flit through (Hemingway, Ian Fleming, the Duke and Duchess of Windsor) while Logan endures a series of romantic encounters that are recounted through his journals. Melancholy and too long, though not as dismal as may be imagined. **240m/C; DVD.** *GB* Sam Claflin; Matthew Macfadyen; Jim Broadbent; James Musgrave; Ed Stoppard; Freddie Fox; Samuel West; Hayley Atwell; Holliday Grainger; Kim Cattrall; Charity Wakefield; Emerald Fennell; Tom Hollander; Gillian Anderson; Tobias Menzies; Julian Ovenden; ***D:*** Michael Samuels; ***W:*** William Boyd; ***C:*** Wojciech Szepel; ***M:*** Dan (Daniel) Jones. **TV**

Any Man's Death **1990 (R)** Savage is a globe-trotting reporter on the trail of a worldwide conspiracy who accidentally uncovers a Nazi war criminal in Africa. Well-meaning but confused tale. **105m/C; VHS, DVD.** John Savage; William Hickey; Mia Sara; Ernest Borgnine; Michael Lerner; ***D:*** Tom Clegg.

Any Number Can Play ½ **1949** Fast-moving drama about an ailing gambler who faces a series of crises. Gable gives a commanding performance as the noble dice-roller. Based on the novel by Edward Harris Heath. **102m/B; VHS, DVD.** Clark Gable; Alexis Smith; Wendell Corey; Audrey Totter; Frank Morgan; Mary Astor; Lewis Stone; Barry Sullivan; ***D:*** Mervyn LeRoy; ***W:*** Richard Brooks.

Any Number Can Win *Melodie en Sous-Sol; The Big Grab* **1963** Two ex-convicts, aging Charles (Gabin) and his former cellmate Francis (Delon), risk their lives and freedom for one last major heist: a gambling casino on the French Riviera. French with English subtitles. **118m/B; VHS, DVD.** *FR* Jean Gabin; Alain Delon; Viviane Romance; Maurice Biraud; Carla Marlier; Jose-Luis De Villalonga; Jean Carmet; Claude Cerval; ***D:*** Henri Verneuil; ***W:*** Henri Verneuil; Michel Audiard; Albert Simonin; ***C:*** Louis Page; ***M:*** Michel Magne.

Any Wednesday ½ *Bachelor Girl Apartment* **1966** Okay sex farce about powerful industrialist Robards' use of his mistress's apartment as a tax write-off. When a young company executive learns of the "company" apartment, he meets Robards' nonchalant wife for a tryst of their own. Based on Muriel Resnik's Broadway play; similar to the 1960 "The Apartment." **110m/C; VHS, DVD.** Jane Fonda; Jason Robards, Jr.; Dean Jones; Rosemary Murphy; ***D:*** Robert Ellis Miller; ***W:*** Julius J. Epstein; ***M:*** George Duning.

Any Which Way You Can **1980 (PG)** Bad brawler Philo Beddoe and his buddy Clyde, the orangutan, are back again in the sequel to "Every Which Way But Loose." This time Philo is tempted to take part in a big bout for a large cash prize. Clyde steals scenes, brightening up the no-brainer story. **116m/C; VHS, DVD.** Clint Eastwood; Sondra Locke; Ruth Gordon; Harry Guardino; William (Bill) Smith; Geoffrey Lewis; Barry Corbin; ***D:*** Buddy Van Horn; ***W:*** Stanford Sherman; ***C:*** David Worth.

Anything But Love ½ *Standard Time* **2002 (PG-13)** Predictable Hollywood love story. Writer/actor Isabel Rose plays Billie Golden, a not-so-young wanna-be torch singer wrestling with the choice of whether to marry her old high school crush (Bancroft) for security, or stay with her anguished true love (McCarthy), who better understands her. Meager budget is best spent on the elaborate dream sequences. Eartha Kitt appears as herself, providing crucial advice and a shining example of a true star. **99m/C; VHS, DVD.** Isabel Rose; Andrew McCarthy; Cameron Bancroft; Alix Korey; Victor Argo; Ilana Levine; Sean Arbuckle; Eartha Kitt; ***D:*** Robert Cary; ***W:*** Isabel Rose; Robert Cary; ***C:*** Horacio Marquinez; ***M:*** Andrew Hollander; Steven Lutvak.

Anything Else ½ **2003 (R)** With his last few outings, Allen has shown that he's a shadow of his former creative self, so he's logically picked Biggs to play a shadow of his former self. Biggs doesn't seem comfortable in his role as a neurotic psychoanalyst-dependent joke-writer trying to break up with the quirky, torturing girlfriend (Ricci) he's smitten with. The Woodman shows up as his alter-ego's paranoid, mean-spirited mentor and confidant. Flick is so short on new ideas that the young couple can only agree on their love of Bogie and old jazz records. Ricci spends most of the film walking around her apartment in her underwear, which isn't bad if you can keep the image of Allen leering just off-camera out of your head. If you insist on a Woody Allen movie, make it almost anything else but this mess. **108m/C; VHS, DVD.** Jason Biggs; Christina Ricci; Woody Allen; Stockard Channing; Danny DeVito; Jimmy Fallon; Erica Leerhsen; David Conrad; KaDee Strickland; Adrian Grenier; ***D:*** Woody Allen; ***W:*** Woody Allen; ***C:*** Darius Khondji.

Anything for Love ½ *Just One of the Girls* **1993** Teen musician is the object of a school bully's rage so he decides to dress up as a girl to escape the guy's fists. **90m/C; VHS, DVD.** *CA* Corey Haim; Nicole Eggert; Cameron Bancroft; Kevin McNulty; Wendy Van Riesen; Lochlyn Munro; Rachel Hayward; Molly Parker; ***D:*** Michael Keusch; ***M:*** Amin Bhatia.

Anything Goes **1956** Listless Paramount musical occasionally highlighted by the Cole Porter songs. Veteran Broadway star Bill Benson (Crosby) teams up with TV entertainer Ted Adams (O'Connor) for a new musical but they need a leading lady. Thanks to plot contrivances, each separately finds the perfect dame in Europe and the quartet meet up on the ocean liner heading home. However, their show is only designed for one female star. **106m/C; DVD.** Bing Crosby; Donald O'Connor; Mitzi Gaynor; Zizi Jeanmaire; Phil Harris; Kurt Kasznar; ***D:*** Robert Lewis; ***W:*** Sidney Sheldon; ***C:*** John F. Warren.

Anywhere But Here ½ **1999 (PG-13)** Just who's the Mom here? It certainly doesn't seem to be flaky Adele (Sarandon), who suddenly uproots teen daughter Ann (Portman) from provincial Wisconsin to relocate in sunny L.A., where Adele wants Ann to become an actress. Ann's definitely the practical one of the duo and she tries to rein in Adele's loopier flights of fantasy. Of course, Ann does have some plans (and dreams) of her own. The leads are both pros and there are enough tear-jerking moments to satisfy in this somewhat stereotypical drama. Based on the 1986 novel by Mona Simpson. **114m/C; VHS, DVD.** Susan Sarandon; Natalie Portman; Shawn Hatosy; Hart Bochner; Bonnie Bedelia; Eileen Ryan; Ray Baker; John Diehl; Caroline Aaron; Paul Guilfoyle; Mary Ellen Trainor; Ashley Johnson; ***D:*** Wayne Wang; ***W:*** Alvin Sargent; ***C:*** Roger Deakins; ***M:*** Danny Elfman.

Anzio *The Battle for Anzio; Lo Sbarco di Anzio* **1968** The historic Allied invasion of Italy during WWII as seen through the eyes of American war correspondent Mitchum. Fine cast waits endlessly to leave the beach, though big battle scenes are effectively rendered. Based on the book by Wynford Vaughan Thomas. **117m/C; VHS, DVD.** Robert Mitchum; Peter Falk; Arthur Kennedy; Robert Ryan; Earl Holliman; Mark Damon; Reni Santoni; Patrick Magee; Giancarlo Giannini; ***D:*** Edward Dmytryk; ***W:*** H.A.L. Craig; Frank De Felitta; ***C:*** Giuseppe Rotunno; ***M:*** Riz Ortolani.

Apache ½ **1954** Lancaster is the only Indian in Geronimo's outfit who refuses to surrender in this chronicle of a bitter battle between the Indians and the U.S. cavalry in the struggle for the West. First western for Aldrich is a thoughtful piece for its time that had the original tragic ending reshot (against Aldrich's wishes) to make it more happy. Adapted from "Bronco Apache" by Paul I. Wellman. **91m/C; VHS, DVD.** Burt Lancaster; John McIntire; Jean Peters; Charles Bronson; John Dehner; Paul Guilfoyle; ***D:*** Robert Aldrich; ***C:*** Ernest Laszlo.

Apache Blood ½ *Pursuit* **1975 (R)** An Indian Brave, the lone survivor of an Indian massacre by the U.S. Army, squares off with a cavalry scout in the forbidding desert. **92m/C; VHS, DVD.** Ray Danton; DeWitt Lee; Troy Neighbors; Diane Taylor; Eva Kovacs; Jason Clark; ***D:*** Thomas Quillen.

Apache Rifles **1964** Army Captain Jeff Stanton delivers a message to renegade Apache chief Victorio that if his tribe go back to the reservation, miners won't be allowed on their land. When gold is discovered, the miners break the treaty. Jeff has fallen in love with half-white, half-Comanche missionary Dawn and wants to restore the peace to prove himself to her. **92m/C; DVD.** Audie Murphy; Linda Lawson; Michael Dante; L.Q. Jones; Joseph (Joe) Vitale; ***D:*** William Witney; ***W:*** Charles B. Smith; ***C:*** Arch R. Dalzell; ***M:*** Richard LaSalle.

Apache Rose **1947** Gambling boat owner plots to gain control of oil found on Vegas Ranch. Roy and Dale oppose the idea. First of the series in color; the original, unedited version of the film. **75m/B; VHS, DVD.** Roy Rogers; Dale Evans; Olin Howlin; George Meeker; ***D:*** William Witney.

Apache Territory ½ **1958** Drifter Logan Cates (Calhoun) takes refuge with a group of settlers at Papago Wells who are fending off an Apache attack. But as the food and water run out, the settlers turn on each other while Cates decides to use the cover of a dust storm to strike back. Based on the Louis L'Amour novel "Last Stand at Papago Wells." **71m/C; DVD.** Rory Calhoun; Barbara Bates; John Dehner; Carolyn Craig; Tom Pitman; Leo Gordon; Myron Healey; ***D:*** Ray Nazarro; ***W:*** George W. George; Charles Marion; ***C:*** Irving Lippman.

Apache's Last Battle *Old Shatterhand; Shatterhand* **1964** A boundary scout discovers the ward of an Apache chief has been framed for murder by a cavalry officer who wants to start an Indian war in this exciting Euro western. **122m/C; VHS, DVD.** *GE YU FR IT* Lex Barker; Pierre Brice; Daliah Lavi; Guy Madison; Ralf Wolter; Gustavo Rojo; Rick (Rik) Battaglia; Bill Ramsey; ***D:*** Hugo Fregonese; ***W:*** Ladislas Fodor; Robert A. Stemmle; ***C:*** Siegfried Hold; ***M:*** Riz Ortolani.

Aparajito ½ *The Unvanquished* **1958** The second of the Apu trilogy, about a boy growing up in India, after "Pather Panchali," and before "The World of Apu." Apu is brought to Benares and his education seriously begins. The work of a master; in Bengali with English subtitles. **108m/B; VHS, DVD, Blu-Ray.** *IN* Pinaki Sen Gupta; Karuna Bannerjee; Kanu Bannerjee; Ramani Sen Gupta; ***D:*** Satyajit Ray; ***W:*** Satyajit Ray; ***C:*** Subrata Mitra; ***M:*** Ravi Shankar. Venice Film Fest. '57: Film.

Apart from Hugh **1994** Collin and Hugh have been living together for a year and to celebrate the occasion, Hugh decides to plan an anniversary party. Unfortunately, Collin hasn't told Hugh he's having second thoughts about their relationship. Directorial debut of FitzGerald. **87m/B; VHS, DVD.** Steve Arnold; David Merwin; Jennifer Reed; ***D:*** Jon FitzGerald; ***W:*** Jon FitzGerald; ***C:*** Randy Allred; ***M:*** James Clarke.

The Apartment ½ **1960** Lowly insurance clerk C.C. Baxter (Lemmon) tries to climb the corporate ladder by "loaning" his apartment out to executives having affairs. Problems arise, however, when he unwittingly falls for sweet elevator operator Fran Kubelik (MacLaine), the most recent girlfriend of his unfeeling boss J.D. Sheldrake (MacMurray). Highly acclaimed social satire. **125m/B; VHS, DVD, Blu-Ray.** Jack Lemmon; Shirley MacLaine; Fred MacMurray; Ray Walston; Jack Kruschen; Joan Shawlee; Edie Adams; Hope Holiday; David Lewis; ***D:*** Billy Wilder; ***W:*** I.A.L. Diamond; Billy Wilder; ***C:*** Joseph LaShelle; ***M:*** Adolph Deutsch. Oscars '60: Art Dir./Set Dec., B&W, Director (Wilder), Film, Film Editing, Story & Screenplay; AFI '98: Top 100; British Acad. '60: Actor (Lemmon), Actress (MacLaine), Film; Directors Guild '60: Director (Wilder); Golden Globes '61: Actor--Mus./Comedy (Lemmon), Actress--Mus./Comedy (MacLaine), Film--Mus./Comedy; Natl. Film Reg. '94; N.Y. Film Critics '60: Director (Wilder), Film, Screenplay.

Apartment for Peggy ½ **1948** Touching postwar drama. WWII vet Jason Taylor (Holden) is going to college on the GI Bill while he and his pregnant wife Peggy (Crain) struggle to find affordable housing in the postwar boom. Peggy charms elderly, depressed Henry Barnes (Gwenn) and he allows them to renovate his attic into an apartment. Their optimism about the future also gives the old man a new lease on life. **96m/C; DVD.** Jeanne Crain; William Holden; Edmund Gwenn; Gene Lockhart; ***D:*** George Seaton; ***W:*** George Seaton; ***C:*** Harry Jackson; ***M:*** David Raskin.

Apartment 1303 **2007** Sayaka throws an apartment-warming party, during which she freaks out and throws herself from the balcony after sucking down some dog food for no apparent reason, leaving her friends to wonder what the heck they just witnessed as the little kid from the hall says, "There goes another one". Sayaka's curious sister learns suicides happen pretty regularly among the tenants in that building, and of course there are ghosts involved. **94m/C; DVD.** *JP* Eriko Hatsune; Yuka Itaya; Naoko Otani; ***D:*** Byeong-ki Ahn; ***W:*** Byeong-ki Ahn; Brian O'Hara; ***C:*** Seok-hyeon Lee; ***M:*** Tae-beon Lee.

Apartment Troubles ½ **2015** A comedy-drama about two friends trying to make it in L.A. Conceptual artists and co-dependent roommates Olivia (Prediger) and Nicole (Weixler) believe they will be successful and famous. After getting evicted from their tiny apartment in New York City, they make a bold move to Los Angeles to visit Nicole's wealthy aunt Kimberley (Mullally). After a tarot card reading and some cajoling by Kimberley, the pair decide to use their background in performance art by auditioning for a reality television show produced by Kimberley. However, their friendship is challenged by these experiences as Olivia begins to see she may not need Nicole as much as she once thought. **95m/C; DVD, Streaming, Download.** Jess Weixler; Jennifer Prediger; Megan Mullally; Will Forte; Jeffrey Tambor; ***D:*** Jess Weixler; Jennifer Prediger; ***W:*** Jess Weixler; Jennifer Prediger; ***C:*** Daniel Sharnoff. **VIDEO**

Apartment 12 ½ *Low Rent; Life/Drawing* **2006 (R)** Artisan Alex (Ruffalo) is stunned when a gallery curator trashes his work and pulls his show, causing his shallow bombshell of a girlfriend to lose interest. Dejected and homeless, he takes a pizza shop job and moves into more affordable digs where he meets several interesting characters, including goofy and loveable Lori (Ulrich). They start dating but Alex's cold feet mess things up, though the neighbors can't avoid one another. Solid work by leads Ruffalo and Ulrich keep this average romantic tale from getting evicted. **90m/C; DVD.** Mark Ruffalo; Alan Gelfant; Manuel Cabral; Beth Ulrich; Mary Coleston; ***D:*** Dan Bootzin; ***W:*** Dan Bootzin; Elizabeth Rivera Bootzin. **VIDEO**

Apartment Zero ½ **1988 (R)** A decidedly weird, deranged psychological drama about the parasite/host-type relationship between two roommates in downtown Buenos Aires: one, an obsessive British movie nut, the other, a sexually mesmerizing stud who turns out to be a cold-blooded psycho. **124m/C; VHS, DVD.** *GB* Hart Bochner; Colin Firth; Fabrizio Bentivoglio; Liz Smith; Dora Bryan; James Telfer; Mirella D'Angelo; Juan Vitale; Francesca D'Aloja; Miguel Ligero; Elvia Andreoli; Marikeva Monti; ***D:*** Martin Donovan; ***W:*** Martin Donovan; David Koepp; ***C:*** Miguel Rodriguez; ***M:*** Elia Cmiral.

A*P*E* WOOF! *Attack of the Giant Horny Gorilla* **1976 (PG)** A*P*E* is 36 feet tall and ten tons of animal fury who destroys anything that comes between him and the actress he loves. Cheap rip-off of Kong. **87m/C; VHS, DVD, Blu-Ray.** *NK* Rod Arrants; Joanna Kerns; Alex Nicol; Francis Lee; ***D:*** Paul Leder; ***W:*** Paul Leder; Reuben Leder.

The Ape **2005** In search of solitude as he struggles to write his first great novel, Harry (Franco, also debuting as writer and director) leaves his wife and child for a studio apartment in NYC, where he is shocked to find that an ape already lives there—one that talks and wears a gaudy Hawaiian t-shirt. He somehow serves as Harry's inspiration despite stooping to lowbrow jokes and gags such as throwing poop. **93m/C; DVD.** James Franco; Brian Lally; Allison Bibicoff; Stacey Miller; Vince Jolivette; ***D:*** James Franco; ***W:*** James Franco; Merriwether Williams. **VIDEO**

The Apocalypse **1996 (R)** Space pilot J.T. Wayne (Bernhard) teams up with salvage operator Suarez (McCoy) and his crew to retrieve a cargo ship lost in space for 25 years. But crewman Vendler (Zagarino) hijacks the cargo for himself, with only Wayne and Lennon (Dye) as survivors. But it turn's out the ship is one big booby-trap rigged to crash into earth. Now Wayne and Lennon must not only save themselves but the planet as well. Low-budget, with a confusing plot. **96m/C; VHS, DVD.** Sandra Bernhard; Laura San Giacomo; Cameron Dye; Frank Zagarino; Matt McCoy; ***D:*** Hubert de la Bouillerie; ***C:*** Greg Gardiner.

The Apocalypse WOOF! 2007 There's some kind of end of days nonsense attached to this dreck but not even anyone interested in apocalyptic prophecies will be able to watch. Multiple asteroids trigger a series of disasters so Ashley and Jason decide they must travel to L.A. to spend their last four days with daughter Lindsey before an even bigger asteroid wipes out the planet. **90m/C; DVD.** Rhett Giles; Jill Stapley; Kristen Quintrall; Tom Nagel; Kim Little; Sarah Lieving; Shaley Scott; Amol Shah; Erica Roby; Michael Tower; ***D:*** Justin Jones; ***W:*** David Michael Latt; ***C:*** Adam Silver. **VIDEO**

Apocalypse Now **1979 (R)** Coppola's $40 million epic vision of the Vietnam War was inspired by Joseph Conrad's novella "Heart of Darkness," and continues to be the subject of debate. Disillusioned Army captain Sheen travels upriver into Cambodia to assassinate renegade colonel Brando. His trip is punctuated by surrealistic battles and a terrifying descent into a land where human rationality seems to have slipped away. Considered by some to be the definitive picture of war in its overall depiction of chaos and primal bloodletting; by others, over-wrought and unrealistic. May not translate as well to the small screen, yet worth seeing, if only for Duvall's ten minutes of scenery chewing as a battle-obsessed major. Stunning photography by Vittorio Storaro, awe-inspiring battle scenes, and effective soundtrack montage. Both Sheen and Coppola suffered emotional breakdowns during the prolonged filming, and that's a very young Fishburne in his major film debut. In 1991 a documentary detailing the making of the film, "Hearts of Darkness: A Filmmaker's Apocalypse," was released. **153m/C; VHS, DVD, Blu-Ray.** Marlon Brando; Martin Sheen; Robert Duvall; Frederic Forrest; Sam Bottoms; Scott Glenn; Albert Hall; Laurence Fishburne; Harrison Ford; G.D. Spradlin; Dennis Hopper; Cynthia Wood; Colleen Camp; Francis Ford Coppola; Linda Carpenter; Tom Mason; James Keane; Damien Leake; Jack Thibeau; R. Lee Ermey; Vittorio Storaro; ***D:*** Francis Ford Coppola; ***W:*** Francis Ford Coppola; John Milius; Michael Herr; ***C:*** Vittorio Storaro; ***M:*** Carmine Coppola. Oscars '79: Cinematog., Sound; AFI '98: Top 100; British Acad. '79: Director (Coppola), Support. Actor (Duvall); Cannes '79: Film; Golden Globes '80: Director (Coppola), Score, Support. Actor (Duvall); Natl. Film Reg. '00; Natl. Soc. Film Critics '79: Support. Actor (Forrest).

Apocalypse Pompeii **1/2 2014** Mt. Vesuvius blows its top again just when the wife and daughter of a Special Ops commando are playing tourist. So Jeff calls his former teammates to rescue his trapped family. Cheese all the way but consistent for a release from The Asylum. **87m/C; DVD, Blu-Ray.** Adrian Paul; Georgina Beedle; John Rhys-Davies; Jhey Castles; Dylan Vox; ***D:*** Ben Demaree; ***W:*** Jacob Cooney; Bill Hanstock; ***C:*** Ben Demaree; ***M:*** Joseph Metcalfe. **VIDEO**

The Apocalypse Watch *Robert Ludlum's the Apocalypse Watch* **1997** CIA analyst Drew (Bergin) takes over his field agent brother's assignment when the latter is killed. Drew hooks up with his bro's girlfriend/partner (Madsen) and their spying leads to a neo-Nazi organization. Based on the novel by Ludlum. **176m/C; VHS, DVD.** Patrick Bergin; Virginia Madsen; John Shea; Benedick Blythe; Christopher Neame; Malcolm Tierney; ***D:*** Kevin Connor; ***W:*** John Goldsmith; Christopher Canaan; ***C:*** Dennis C. Lewiston; ***M:*** Ken Thorne. **TV**

Apocalypto **2006 (R)** Set during ancient times against a lavish, peaceful backdrop in the Yucatan Peninsula. Producer/director/co-writer Gibson unleashes a savage nightmare that somehow surpasses the bloodbaths of his other works, "Passion of the Christ" and "Braveheart." Jaguar Paw (Youngblood, part of the all-native cast) and his forest tribe are viciously rounded up by Mayan attackers as their rulers desperately attempt to save their decaying civilization by sacrificing Paw's people to the gods. As the graphic slaughter begins, Paw slips away and triggers an intense 45-minute jungle chase as he tries to outrun his captors and return to his pregnant wife and young son who he'd hidden in a village well. Gibson's talent at creating no-holds-barred action is on full display. In the Mayan language of the Yucatec, with English subtitles. **137m/C; DVD, Blu-Ray.** Rudy Youngblood; Dalia Hernandez; Jonathan Brewer; Morris Birdyellowhead; Carlos Emilio Baez; Raoul Trujillo; Rodolfo Palacios; ***D:*** Mel Gibson; ***W:*** Mel Gibson; Farhad Safinia; ***C:*** Dean Semler; ***M:*** James Horner.

Apollo 13 **1/2 1995 (PG)** Realistic big-budget reenactment of the 1970 Apollo lunar mission that ran into a "problem" 205, 000 miles from home reunites Hanks and Sinese from "F. Gump" and Howard and Hanks from "Splash." And an enjoyable reunion it is. Explosion in one of two oxygen tanks helping power the spacecraft leaves the three astronauts (led by Hanks) tumbling through space. With the electrical system kaput and oxygen running low, the men seek refuge in the Lunar Excursion Module. Since it's based on the real event and the outcome is known, director Howard concentrates on the personalities and the details of the seven-day adventure at Mission Control and in space, in the process delivering the dramatic payload. Weightless shots are the real deal as crew filmed for ten days and made 600 parabolic loops in a KC-135 jet, NASA's "Vomit Comet," the long plunge creating 25 seconds of weightlessness. Special effects (by James Cameron's Digital Domain) and set design do the rest; no NASA footage is used, though original TV footage is used to dramatic effect. Script, with an uncredited rewrite by John Sayles, is based on the 1994 book, "Lost Moon," written by 13's Jim Lovell (who has a cameo as the Navy captain welcoming the astronauts aboard the recovery ship), while Apollo 15 commander David Scott served as a consultant. **140m/C; VHS, DVD, Blu-Ray, HD-DVD.** Tom Hanks; Kevin Bacon; Bill Paxton; Gary Sinise; Ed Harris; Kathleen Quinlan; Brett Cullen; Emily Ann Lloyd; Miko Hughes; Max Elliott Slade; Jean Speegle Howard; Tracy Reiner; Michelle Little; David Andrews; Mary Kate Schellhardt; Gabe Jarret; Chris Ellis; Joe Spano; Xander Berkeley; Marc McClure; Clint Howard; Loren Dean; Todd Louiso; ***D:*** Ron Howard; ***W:*** William Broyles, Jr.; Al Reinert; ***C:*** Dean Cundey; ***M:*** James Horner. Oscars '95: Film Editing, Sound; Directors Guild '95: Director (Howard); Screen Actors Guild '95: Cast, Support. Actor (Harris); Blockbuster '96: Drama Actor, T. (Hanks).

Apollo 18 **2011 (PG-13)** Shot in quasi-documentary style, this gimmicky, tedious sci fi wannabe thriller shows found classified film of a secret moon mission in 1974 that NASA later denied. American astronauts (two on the ground and one piloting the space module) find disturbing evidence of very unfriendly alien life forms on the dark side of the moon along with a Soviet spacecraft and a dead cosmonaut. Much of the plot isn't coherent and we're not just talking about the grainy footage beamed back to Earth. **90m/C; DVD, Blu-Ray.** Warren Christie; Ryan Robbins; ***D:*** Lloyd Owen; Gonzalo Lopez-Gallego; ***W:*** Brian Miller; ***C:*** Jose David Montero.

Apollo 11 **2019 (G)** Using previously unseen and unheard archival footage and audio recordings, this documentary offers a unique perspective on the first mission to the moon. Telling the story of the landing in present tense and with the wider context of the astronauts' feat, the documentary creates a feeling of immediacy to the events as they happen. Further enhancing the experience, exciting moments such as the liftoff from Earth and landing on the moon are depicted from a fixed point of view in mostly unbroken images. Playfully and effectively edited, the documentary's power and retro feel is only improved by a period-appropriate electronic score. **93m/C; DVD, Blu-Ray.** Edwin E. Aldrin, Jr.; Neil Armstrong; Walter Cronkite; Lyndon Baines Johnson; Richard M. Nixon; ***D:*** Todd Douglas Miller; ***C:*** Adam Holender; ***M:*** Matt Morton.

The Apostate *Michael Angel* **1998 (R)** A young Jesuit priest, whose gay prostitute brother has been murdered by a serial killer, heads home to Puerto Rico and offers his assistance to his police inspector uncle in catching the killer, who seems driven by religious torment. But the priest himself is torn by spiritual doubts about his calling and is plunged into a world of temptation and vengeance. **94m/C; VHS, DVD.** Richard Grieco; Dennis Hopper; Kristin Minter; Frank Medrano; Michael Cole; Efrain Figueroa; Bridget Ann White; ***D:*** Bill Gove; ***W:*** Bill Gove; ***C:*** Reinhart Pesche; ***M:*** Thomas Morse. **VIDEO**

The Apostle **1997 (PG-13)** No-holds-barred look at one man's search for religious redemption. Eulis Dewey (Duvall) is a devout, middle-aged, Pentecostal preacher in Texas, with a true gift for inspiring his congregation. Unfortunately, he's not so inspiring to his wife Jessie (Fawcett), who's cheating on him with younger minister, Horace (Allen). When Eulis discovers the infidelity, he strikes Horace with a bat, sending the man into a coma. Eulis escapes and winds up in the predominantly black town of Bayou Boutte, Louisiana, having shed his old identity for that of E.F., "The Apostle" of God. He zealously starts up a new church, seeking salvation, but his past comes back to haunt him. **134m/C; VHS, DVD.** Robert Duvall; Miranda Richardson; Farrah Fawcett; John Beasley; Todd Allen; June Carter Cash; Billy Bob Thornton; Rick Dial; Walton Goggins; Billy Joe Shaver; ***D:*** Robert Duvall; ***W:*** Robert Duvall; ***C:*** Barry Markowitz; ***M:*** David Mansfield. Ind. Spirit '98: Actor (Duvall), Director (Duvall), Film; L.A. Film Critics '97: Actor (Duvall); Natl. Soc. Film Critics '97: Actor (Duvall).

Apostle **1/2 2018** A gothic horror flick capitalizing on slow-burning dread to inflict maximum terror. In 1905, Thomas (Stevens) ventures to a remote island to free his sister from the religious cult that kidnapped her. Sneaking around the island, trying to remain hidden from the cult members, Thomas gradually bears witness to grisly rituals and a supernatural presence that suggest that this isn't going to be an easy search and recovery mission. Although it might have benefited from a 15-minute trim in the running time, this horror film won't disappoint. **130m/C; Streaming.** Dan Stevens; Richard Elfyn; Paul Higgins; Bill Milner; Catrin Aaron; ***D:*** Gareth Evans; ***W:*** Gareth Evans; ***C:*** Matt Flannery; ***M:*** Aria Prayogi; Fajar Yuskemal.

The Appaloosa **1/2** *Southwest to Sonora* **1966** A lamenting loner who decides to begin anew by breeding Appaloosas is ripped off by a desperate woman who steals his horse in order to get away from her abusive amour. Brando falls in love with the girl and the two amazingly survive a wealth of obstacles in their battle against Mexican bandits. **99m/C; VHS, DVD, Blu-Ray.** Marlon Brando; Anjanette Comer; John Saxon; ***D:*** Sidney J. Furie; ***W:*** James Bridges; ***C:*** Russell Metty.

Appaloosa **2008 (R)** Director, co-writer, co-producer, and star Harris brings the 2005 Robert B. Parker novel to the big screen with grit and grandeur. In 1880s New Mexico, two friends, Virgil Cole (Harris) and Everett Hitch (Mortensen), are hired to uphold the law in a small town overtaken by a tyrannical rancher (Irons). Their duty, as well as their friendship, is put to the test as a fetching young widow (Zellweger) strolls into town, stirring the hearts of both men. Beautifully shot and perfectly acted, with a smart and funny screenplay that keeps it above the genre cliches. **114m/C; Blu-Ray.** Ed Harris; Viggo Mortensen; Renée Zellweger; Jeremy Irons; Rex Linn; Tom Bower; Timothy Spall; James Gammon; Lance Henriksen; Ariadna Gil; ***D:*** Ed Harris; ***W:*** Ed Harris; Robert Knott; ***C:*** Dean Semler; ***M:*** Jeff Beal.

The Apparition WOOF! 2012 (PG-13) The scariest thing about this turgid mess is the thought of having to sit through it again. The creators of this absolute disaster did the bare minimum of work to produce an Asian horror rip-off years after most people thought that trend had mercifully ended. A boring couple is haunted by a boring ghost in a boring retread of better movies. Without a single memorable line of dialogue, scary moment, or actual twist, it's almost a non-horror movie, only terrifying when one considers that any effort was put into making it. **82m/C; DVD, Blu-Ray.** Ashley Greene; Sebastian Stan; Tom Felton; Julianna Guill; Luke Pasqualino; Rick Gomez; ***D:*** Todd Lincoln; ***W:*** Todd Lincoln; ***C:*** Daniel Pearl; ***M:*** tomandandy.

Appetite **1998 (R)** Try to stick with this slow-moving suspenser because it's got a wicked ending. A group of strangers, staying at the same hotel, play a game of cards where the loser must sleep in the reputedly haunted Room 207. **99m/C; VHS, DVD.** Ute Lemper; Trevor Eve; Christien Anholt; Edward Hardwicke; ***D:*** George Milton; ***W:*** Dominik Scherrer; ***C:*** Peter Thwaites.

Appetites **2015** A dark horror exploration of one cannibal-loving woman's bloodlust and what happens when she meets her match. On the surface, Daisy (Parkinson) seems like an ideal woman, except for her penchant for murder. She has spent much of her life living in the desert with her mentally challenged brother Bubba (Barrows). There, she hunts young men for sport and food. Yet Daisy's life is empty without love and she believes her romantic fortunes have changed after meeting John Doe (Roberts). Though the couple falls in love, Daisy soon learns that he has his own killer hobbies. She could be next on his hit list or, perhaps, his partner in crime. **106m/C; DVD, Streaming, Download.** Lauren Parkinson; Scott Barrows; Bret Roberts; James Duval; Travis Eberhard; ***D:*** Cameron Casey; ***W:*** Darren Bevill; ***C:*** Christopher Gosch; ***M:*** Tristan Clopet.

Applause **1929** Morgan plays a down-and-out burlesque star trying to protect her fresh from the convent daughter. Definitely dated, but a marvelous performance by Morgan. Film buffs will appreciate this early talkie. **78m/B; VHS, DVD.** Helen Morgan; Joan Peers; Fuller Mellish, Jr.; Henry Wadsworth; Dorothy (Dorothy G. Cummings) Cumming; ***D:*** Rouben Mamoulian; ***C:*** George J. Folsey. Natl. Film Reg. '06.

The Apple **1/2 1980 (PG)** Futuristic musical filmed in Berlin that features a young, innocent, folk-singing couple who nearly become victims of the evil, glitzy record producer who tries to recruit the couple into a life of sex and drugs. **90m/C; VHS, DVD, Blu-Ray.** Catherine Mary Stewart; Alan Love; Grace Kennedy; Joss Ackland; ***D:*** Menahem Golan; ***W:*** Menahem Golan.

The Apple Dumpling Gang **1975 (G)** Three frisky kids strike it rich and trigger the wildest bank robbery in the gold-mad West. Unmistakably Disney, a familial subplot and a wacky duo are provided. Mediocre yet superior to its sequel, "The Apple Dumpling Gang Rides Again." **100m/C; VHS, DVD, Blu-Ray.** Bill Bixby; Susan Clark; Don Knotts; Tim Conway; David Wayne; Slim Pickens; Harry (Henry) Morgan; ***D:*** Norman Tokar; ***M:*** Buddy (Norman Dale) Baker.

The Apple Dumpling Gang Rides Again **1979 (G)** Two lovable hombres terrorize the West in their bungling attempt to go straight. Fans of Conway or Knotts may appreciate this sequel to Disney's "The Apple Dumpling Gang." **88m/C; VHS, DVD.** Tim Conway; Don Knotts; Tim Matheson; Kenneth Mars; Harry (Henry) Morgan; Jack Elam; ***D:*** Vincent McEveety; ***M:*** Buddy (Norman Dale) Baker.

Appointment in Honduras
1953 An adventurer goes on a dangerous trek through the Central American jungles to deliver funds to the Honduran President. **79m/C; VHS, DVD.** Glenn Ford; Ann Sheridan; Zachary Scott; ***D:*** Jacques Tourneur.

Appointment in London 1/2
Raiders in the Sky **1953** In 1943, Wing Commander Tim Mason is trying to complete 90 German bombing missions before being consigned to desk duty. Under increasing strain, his superior officers ground him after his 89th mission but when another bomber pilot is injured, Mason defies orders and takes his place. **96m/C; DVD.** *GB* Dirk Bogarde; Ian Hunter; Bill Kerr; Bryan Forbes; William Sylvester; Dinah Sheridan; Walter Fitzgerald; ***D:*** Philip Leacock; ***W:*** Robert Westerby; John Wooldridge; ***C:*** Stephen Dade; ***M:*** John Wooldridge.

Appointment with Crime 1/2
1945 After serving a prison sentence, an ex-con sets out to avenge himself against the colleagues who double crossed him. Well done, highlighted by superior characterizations. Based on the story by Michael Leighton. **91m/B; VHS, Blu-Ray, Streaming.** *GB* William Hartnell; Raymond Lovell; Robert Beatty; Herbert Lom; Joyce Howard; Alan Wheatley; Cyril Smith; ***D:*** John Harlow; ***W:*** John Harlow.

Appointment With Danger
1951 Postal Inspection Service detective Al Goddard (Ladd) goes undercover to get the gang who murdered his partner after persuading the only witness, Sister Augustine (Calvert), to identity the killer. But psychotic gang member Joe (Webb) decides to take care of any loose ends that will prevent them from going after a million dollar mail heist. **89m/B; DVD, Blu-Ray.** Alan Ladd; Phyllis Calvert; Jack Webb; Harry (Henry) Morgan; Paul Stewart; Jan Sterling; ***D:*** Lewis Allen; ***W:*** Richard L. Breen; Warren Duff; ***C:*** John Seitz; ***M:*** Victor Young.

Appointment With Death 1/2
2010 Vacationing in Syria, Hercule Poirot (Suchet) joins in visiting the archeological expedition of Lord Greville Boynton (Curry), which is financed by his loathed second wife, domineering, wealthy American Lady Boynton (Campbell). It's no wonder she becomes a murder victim and the Belgian detective has numerous suspects, but his final act denouncement by gathering them all together proves somewhat long and tedious. Based on the Agatha Christie mystery. **90m/C; DVD.** *GB* David Suchet; Tim Curry; Cheryl Campbell; Tom Riley; Zoe Boyle; Emma Cunniffe; John Hannah; Elizabeth McGovern; Angela Pleasence; Paul Freeman; Beth Goddard; Mark Gatiss; Christian McKay; Christina Cole; ***D:*** Ashley Pearce; ***W:*** Guy Andrews; ***C:*** Peter Greenhalgh; ***M:*** Stephen McKeon. **TV**

Appointment With Venus *Island Rescue* **1951** In this silly WWII comedy, the Germans occupy the Channel Island of Armorel. The British Ministry of Agriculture and the War Office plan an operation to smuggle out a valuable, pedigreed Gurnsey milk cow named Venus via the Royal Navy. German commander Weiss wants Venus shipped to the Fatherland. **89m/B; DVD.** *UK* David Niven; Glynis Johns; George Coulouris; Kenneth More; Noel Purcell; Bernard Lee; ***D:*** Ralph Thomas; ***W:*** Nicholas Phipps; ***C:*** Ernest Steward; ***M:*** Benjamin Frankel.

The Apprentice 1/2 *Fleur Bleue* **1971** A directionless young French-Canadian man, growing up in Montreal, is involved with both his fanatical French separatist girlfriend and a free-spirited English-Canadian model. It's a love triangle that doesn't end well. An early role for Sarandon and a time capsule of the '70s separatist movement in Quebec. English and French with subtitles. **81m/C; DVD.** *CA* Susan Sarandon; Carole Laure; Gerard Parkes; Steve Fiset; Celine Bernier; Jean-Pierre Cartier; ***D:*** Larry Kent; ***W:*** Edward Steward; ***C:*** Jean-Claude Labrecque.

The Apprenticeship of Duddy Kravitz 1/2 **1974 (PG)** Young Jewish man in Montreal circa 1948 is driven by an insatiable need to be the "somebody" everyone has always told him he will be. A series of get-rich-quick schemes backfire in different ways, and he becomes most successful at driving people away. Young Dreyfuss is at his best. Made in Canada with thoughtful detail, and great cameo performances. Script by Richler, from his novel. **121m/C; VHS, DVD.** *CA* Richard Dreyfuss; Randy Quaid; Denholm Elliott; Jack Warden; Micheline Lanctot; Joe Silver; ***D:*** Ted Kotcheff; ***W:*** Mordecai Richler; Lionel Chetwynd. Berlin Intl. Film Fest. '74: Golden Berlin Bear; Writers Guild '74: Adapt. Screenplay.

Approaching the Unknown
2016 (R) A science fiction drama about a trip to Mars gone wrong. Ahead of colonization efforts on Mars, Captain William Stanaforth (Strong) is taking a one-way solo mission to establish a base there. The trip is fraught with peril, and he must overcome the unexpected to survive the journey to his new home. **90m/C; DVD, Streaming, Download.** Mark Strong; Luke Wilson; Sanaa Lathan; Anders Danielsen Lie; Charles Baker; ***D:*** Mark Elijah Rosenberg; ***W:*** Mark Elijah Rosenberg; ***C:*** Adam Newport; ***M:*** Paul Damian Hogan.

Appropriate Adult **2011** Chilling Brit true crime story finds unassuming social worker Janet Leach (West) brought in to monitor the police interrogations of serial killer Fred West (West) in 1994. Pleased to be so needed, Janet is out of her depth with the manipulative sociopath, caught between his evasions and the frustrations of the police in the highly publicized case. **135m/C; DVD.** *UK* Emily Watson; Dominic West; Robert Glenister; Sylvestria Le Touzel; Monica Dolan; ***D:*** Julian Jarrold; ***W:*** Neil McKay; ***C:*** Tony Slater-Ling; ***M:*** Dan Jones, PhD. **TV**

Appropriate Behavior 1/2 **2014** Writer/director/star Akhavan makes a confident debut with this story of a bisexual Persian dealing with life half-in and half-out of the closet in New York City. Shirin's (Akhavan) old-fashioned, Iranian parents would never accept their daughter's sexuality were she to come out to them, but the act of hiding herself has created a lack of self-confidence, which pushes her into an unhealthy relationship with lesbian Maxine. The film takes place on the day of their break-up, flashing back to the highlights of it and then pushing forward to her getting past it. Solid, if not a little too familiar. **82m/C; DVD.** *US UK* Desiree Akhavan; Rebecca Henderson; Halley Feiffer; Scott Adsit; ***D:*** Desiree Akhavan; ***W:*** Desiree Akhavan; ***C:*** Chris Teague; ***M:*** Josephine Wiggs.

Apres Lui *After Him* **2007** Divorcee Camille (Deneuve) is devastated when her 20-year-old son Mathieu (Jolivet) is killed in a car accident. She turns to her son's grief-stricken best friend Franck (Dumerchez), who was the driver of the car, and starts helping the less-privileged young man out with college, also giving him a job in her bookstore. Franck's bewildered by her concern, which becomes obsessive, especially when Camille follows him on vacation. French with subtitles. **89m/C; DVD.** *FR* Catherine Deneuve; Guy Marchand; Elodie Bouchez; Adrien Jolivet; Thomas Dumerchez; ***D:*** Gael Morel; ***W:*** Gael Morel; Christophe Honore; ***C:*** Jean-Max Bernard; ***M:*** Louis Sclavis.

Apres-Vous *After You* **2003 (R)** Sometimes you should just mind your own business. Parisian maitre d' Antoine (Auteuil) saves depressive loser Louis (Garcia) from hanging himself in a park and then feels responsible for making the man happy. He gets Louis a wine steward job, though he has no abilities whatsoever, and seeks to reconcile the sad sack with ex-lover Blanche (Kiberlain), except that Antoine falls for her himself. Auteuil is so good he can make any character believable (even this overzealous nice guy), but this familiar farce doesn't do much to stretch his talents. French with subtitles. **110m/C; DVD.** *FR* Daniel Auteuil; Jose Garcia; Sandrine Kiberlain; Marilyne Canto; Michele Moretti; Garance Clavel; Fabio Zenoni; Ange Ruze; ***D:*** Pierre Salvadori; ***W:*** Pierre Salvadori; Benoit Graffin; David Colombo Leotard; ***C:*** Gilles Henry; ***M:*** Camille Bazbaz.

April Fools **1969 (PG)** A bored stockbroker falls in love with a beautiful woman who turns out to be married to his boss. **95m/C; DVD.** Jack Lemmon; Catherine Deneuve; Sally Kellerman; Peter Lawford; Harvey Korman; Melinda Dillon; Kenneth Mars; ***D:*** Stuart Rosenberg; ***M:*** Marvin Hamlisch.

April Fools **2007** A teen is killed by a prank gone wrong, causing yet another killing spree to occur later when the group responsible begin to wonder who saw what they did. **72m/C; DVD.** Darrin Dewitt Henson; Aaliyah Franks; Dava Vaidya; ***D:*** Nancy Norman; ***W:*** Nancy Norman; ***C:*** Jeff Brown; ***M:*** Donald Hayes; Kenneth Hampton. **VIDEO**

April Fool's Day 1/2 **1986 (R)** Rich girl Muffy (Foreman) invites eight college friends to spend the April Fool's weekend with her at her family's isolated island mansion. Everyone is subjected to an endless series of practical jokes when things apparently turn deadly and several of the kids begin disappearing. Twist ending. Lame spoof of "Friday the 13th" and other teenagers-in-peril slasher films. **90m/C; VHS, DVD, Blu-Ray.** Deborah Foreman; Jay Baker; Pat Barlow; Lloyd Berry; Deborah Goodrich; Ken Olandt; Griffin O'Neal; Tom Heaton; Mike Nomad; Leah K. Pinsent; Clayton Rohner; Amy Steel; Thomas F. Wilson; ***D:*** Fred Walton; ***W:*** Danilo Bach; ***C:*** Charles Minsky; ***M:*** Charles Bernstein.

April Fool's Day WOOF! **2008 (R)** You'll be the fool if you're conned into watching this dreck done by the duo appropriately calling themselves the Butcher Brothers. Rich bitch Desiree (Cole) plays a prank on rival Milan (Aldridge) at a party, only things go way too far and Milan dies. A year later, the partygoers receive invitations to Milan's gravesite and are then warned that they too will die unless someone accepts responsibility for Milan's death. Shares nothing but the title with the 1986 slasher flick. **91m/C; DVD.** Sabrina Aldridge; Josh Henderson; Scout Taylor-Compton; Joe Egender; Samuel Child; Jennifer Siebel (Newsom); Joseph McKelheer; ***D:*** Phil Flores; Mitchell Altieri; ***W:*** Phil Flores; Mitchell Altieri; ***C:*** Michael Maley; ***M:*** James Stemple. **VIDEO**

April in Paris **1952** Dynamite Jackson (Day), a chorus girl accidentally sent by the State Department to perform in Paris, meets S. Winthrop Putnam (Bolger), a timid fellow trapped in an unpleasant marriage. They eventually sing and dance their way to warm feelings as they begin a lifelong romance and live happily ever after. **100m/C; VHS, DVD.** Doris Day; Ray Bolger; Claude Dauphin; Eve Miller; George Givot; Paul Harvey; ***D:*** David Butler; ***W:*** Jack Rose; Melville Shavelson.

April Love 1/2 **1957** Simple, pleasant romance/musical with Boone as the nicest juvenile delinquent you'll ever meet. After he's placed on probation for car theft in Chicago, Nick (Boone) is sent to stay at his Aunt Henrietta's (Nolan) and Uncle Jed's (O'Connell) Kentucky horse farm. The city boy is out of his element as he prefers horsepower to horses but he learns to train a horse and drive a racing sulky as well as romance pretty neighbor Liz (Jones)?once he gets over his crush on her sister Fran (Michaels). Filmed on location in Lexington, Kentucky. **97m/C; DVD, Blu-Ray.** Pat Boone; Shirley Jones; Jeannette Nolan; Arthur O'Connell; Dolores Michaels; Matt Crowley; Brandon T. Jackson; ***D:*** Henry Levin; ***W:*** Winston Miller; ***C:*** Wilfred M. Cline; ***M:*** Sammy Fain; Alfred Newman.

April Morning 1/2 **1988** A Hallmark Hall of Fame presentation based on the Howard Fast novel. April 19, 1775 marked the beginning of the American Revolution as British troops clashed with American militia. Moses Cooper (Jones) and his teenage son Adam (Lowe) are part of the Lexington Minutemen who oppose Major John Pitcairn (Colvey) and his redcoats in this well-done family/historical drama. **99m/C; DVD.** Tommy Lee Jones; Chad Lowe; Robert Urich; Peter Colvey; Rip Torn; Susan Blakely; Meredith Salenger; Vlasta Vrana; ***D:*** Delbert Mann; ***W:*** James Lee Barrett; ***C:*** Frank Tidy; ***M:*** Allyn Ferguson. **TV**

April's Shower 1/2 **2003 (R)** April's about to get married, but what few know is that April's been a lesbian most of her life. Her ex-lover, and now bridesmaid, has even kept it a secret. Up until now. A slew of one-dimensional stereotypes parade across the screen, almost like they're at a John Waters audition, to ruin the emotional core. Tries too hard to be comedic and outrageous and oh, so culturally hip, assuming it can elude criticism by playing the indie card. Nope. Even the gay and lesbian crowds will find little amusement. **98m/C; DVD.** Maria Cina; Zack (Zach) Ward; Lara Harris; Molly Cheek; Trish Doolan; Frank Grillo; Randall Batinkoff; Arly Jover; ***D:*** Trish Doolan; ***W:*** Trish Doolan; ***C:*** Kristian Bernier; Rory King; ***M:*** Jeff Cardoni.

Apt Pupil **1997 (R)** In 1984, high school senior Todd Bowden (Renfro) becomes fascinated by the Holocaust during a school project and is able to discern from an old photo that neighbor Kurt Dussander (McKellen) was a Nazi concentration camp commander and is a war criminal. Todd agrees to keep quiet if the old man will tell exactly what he did during the war. But Dussander hasn't stayed quiet all these years to have his secrets revealed by a nosy teen, so Todd gets an up close and personal lesson about the nature of evil. Very creepy adaptation of the Stephen King novella with a standout performance by McKellen. **111m/C; VHS, DVD.** Ian McKellen; Brad Renfro; Jan Triska; Bruce Davison; Joe Morton; Elias Koteas; David Schwimmer; Michael Byrne; Heather McComb; Ann Dowd; Joshua Jackson; Michael Artura; ***D:*** Bryan Singer; ***W:*** Brandon Boyce; ***C:*** Newton Thomas (Tom) Sigel; ***M:*** John Ottman.

Aqua Teen Hunger Force Colon Movie Film for Theaters 1/2 **2007 (R)** As intentionally nonsensical as its title. This component of the Cartoon Network's "Adult Swim" feature has New Jersey roomies (and fast-food items) Frylock, Master Shake, and Meatwad going full-length and big screen, battling the Insane-O-Flex home exercise machine that's actually an alien (the outer space kind). Familiar characters like Carl, Dr. Weird, Err, and others make their appearances. Only for those who already know "Aqua Teen" or just can't stand to be out of the pop culture loop. **86m/C; DVD.** ***V:*** Bruce Campbell; Matt Maiellaro; Dave Willis; Dana Snyder; Carey Means; Mike Schatz; Andy Merrill; C. Martin Croker; ***D:*** Matt Maiellaro; Dave Willis; ***W:*** Matt Maiellaro; Dave Willis.

Aquaman 1/2 **2018 (PG-13)** The laughing stock of the DC Universe gets his own flick, and -- surprise! -- it's not as bad as you might have guessed. Momoa plays Arthur Curry, heir to the underwater kingdom of Atlantis, who rises up to prevent a war with the land-dwellers. Momoa's Aquaman isn't some wimpy fish-talker; he's brawny, sarcastic, and as cool as a (sea) cucumber. The problem is that he's drowned out by overdone effects and plotlines that fishtail out of control. Although it's perfectly adequate, recent superhero movies have raised the bar so high that this one won't blow you out of the water. **143m/C; Blu-Ray.** *AU* Jason Momoa; Amber Heard; Willem Dafoe; Patrick Wilson; Nicole Kidman; ***D:*** James Wan; ***W:*** James Wan; Will Beall; Geoff Johns; David Leslie Johnson-McGoldrick; ***C:*** Don Burgess; ***M:*** Rupert Gregson-Williams.

Aquamarine 1/2 **2006 (PG)** Sweet tweener flick about best friends and a girl with a tail. Mermaid Aquamarine (Paxton) washes into a Florida beach club pool after a storm. She's discovered by 13-year-olds Claire (Roberts) and Hailey (Levesque) and the trio make a pact: Aqua needs to prove to her stern father that true love exists within three days or she will be forced to marry, and the girls want her to grant their wish to stop Hailey from moving away. Fortunately, Aqua is a blonde babe (her tail can conveniently vanish during daylight) who falls for cute lifeguard, Raymond (McDorman)?a romance the younger girls eagerly encourage. Generally comic calamities ensue. Based on the book by Alice Hoffman. **109m/C; DVD.** Sara Paxton; Emma Roberts; Arielle Kebbel; Claudia Karvan; Joanna "JoJo" Levesque; Jake McDorman; Bruce Spence; Roy Billing; Tammin Sursok; Julia Blake; Shaun Micallef; ***D:*** Elizabeth Allen; ***W:*** Jessica Bendinger; John Quaintance; ***C:*** Brian J. Breheny; ***M:*** David Hirschfelder.

Aquarius 1/2 *Doña Clara* **2016** Clara (the timeless Braga) lives in the titular apartment building in Recife, Brazil in the 1940s. All of her neighbors and friends are moving out after accepting offers of buy-outs from developers who are going to tear the unique building down and put up something predictable and bland. While the thought of a three-hour drama about real estate drama sounds like it might be a bit torturous, writer/director Kleber Mendonca Filho makes us care about what happens to Clara. The political messages are also striking, especially for a country currently in deep turmoil in that department. **142m/C; DVD.** Sonia Braga; Maeve Jinkings; Irandhir Santos; Humberto Carrão; Zoraide Coleto; ***D:*** Kleber Mendonca Filho; ***W:*** Kleber Mendonca Filho; ***C:*** Pedro Sotero; Fabricio Tadeu.

The Arab Conspiracy 🦴🦴 *The Next Man; Double Hit* **1976 (R)** Sharpe plays a hit-woman conspiring with assassins from all over the world to kill Arab leaders. One problem—she falls in love with Saudi Arabian ambassador Connery as he tries to gain peace with Palestine. **108m/C; VHS, DVD.** Sean Connery; Cornelia Sharpe; Albert Paulsen; Adolfo Celi; Charles Cioffi; ***D:*** Richard Sarafian; ***W:*** Alan R. Trustman; ***C:*** Michael Chapman; ***M:*** Michael Kamen.

Arabesque 🦴🦴 **1/2 1966** A college professor is drawn into international espionage by a beautiful woman and a plot to assassinate an Arab prince. Stylish and fast moving. From the novel "The Cipher" by Gordon Cotler. **105m/C; VHS, DVD, Blu-Ray.** Gregory Peck; Sophia Loren; George Coulouris; Alan Badel; Kieron Moore; ***D:*** Stanley Donen; ***M:*** Henry Mancini.

Arabian Adventure 🦴🦴 **1979 (G)** Pleasant enough fantasy adventure for the family. A prince enlists the aid of a peasant in order to prevent an evil wizard from obtaining a magical rose and taking over the kingdom. **98m/C; DVD, Blu-Ray.** *UK* Christopher Frank Carandini Lee; Milo O'Shea; Oliver Tobias; Emma Samms; Peter Cushing; ***D:*** Kevin Connor; ***W:*** Brian Hayles; ***C:*** Alan Hume; ***M:*** Ken Thorne.

Arabian Nights 🦴🦴 **1942** Two brothers fight for the throne of Turkey and the affection of the sultry dancing girl Scheherazade. Enchanting costumes and lavish sets augment the fantasy atmosphere. **87m/C; VHS, DVD.** Jon Hall; Maria Montez; Sabu; Leif Erickson; Edgar Barrier; Richard Lane; Turhan Bey; ***D:*** John Rawlins; ***W:*** Michael Hogan; ***C:*** Milton Krasner.

Arabian Nights 🦴🦴🦴 *Il Fiore delle Mille e Una Notte; Flower of the Arabian Nights; A Thousand and One Nights* **1974** The third of Pasolini's epic, explicit adaptations of classic portmanteau, featuring ten of the old Scheherazade favorites adorned by beautiful photography, explicit sex scenes and homoeroticism. In Italian with English subtitles; available dubbed. **130m/C; VHS, DVD, Blu-Ray.** *IT* Ninetto Davoli; Franco Merli; Ines Pellegrini; Luigina Rocchi; Franco Citti; ***D:*** Pier Paolo Pasolini; ***W:*** Pier Paolo Pasolini; ***C:*** Giuseppe Ruzzolini; ***M:*** Ennio Morricone.

Arabian Nights 🦴🦴 **1/2 2000** Lavish spectacle and good casting overcomes the somewhat sluggish storytelling that combines a number of familiar tales. Sultan Schahriar's (Scott) grip on reality is slim ever since his greedy brother (Frain) and his first (and now late) wife plotted to assassinate him. Although he agrees to marry lovely Scheherezade (Avital), he also plans to kill her the morning after. But the lady is bright and desperate, she sooths her savage sultan with a number of stories involving genies, flying carpets, 40 thieves, and magic in order to stay alive until his sanity returns. Filmed on location in Turkey and Morocco. **175m/C; VHS, DVD.** Mili Avital; Dougray Scott; James Frain; John Leguizamo; Rufus Sewell; Jason Scott Lee; Alan Bates; Tcheky Karyo; ***D:*** Steven Barron; ***W:*** Peter Barnes; ***C:*** Remi Adefarasin; ***M:*** Richard Harvey. **TV**

Arachnia 🦴 **1/2 2003 (R)** Giant stop motion spider puppets invade a farm as all that stands between them and the rest of Arizona are a paleontologist and his bumbling assistants. **82m/C; DVD.** David Bunce; ***D:*** Brett Piper; ***W:*** Brett Piper; ***M:*** David Giancola; Cheryl Friberg; Chuck Harding. **VIDEO**

Arachnid 🦴 **1/2 2001 (R)** Plane carrying a rescue crew on a mission to find a downed pilot crashes on a tropical island that contains a gigantic, carnivorous alien spider. Nothing that hasn't been seen before. **95m/C; VHS, DVD.** Chris Potter; Neus Asensi; Jose Sancho; Alex Reid; ***D:*** Jack Sholder; ***W:*** Mark Sevi; ***C:*** Carlos Gonzalez; ***M:*** Francesc Gener.

Arachnophobia 🦴🦴 **1/2 1990 (PG-13)** Big-budget big-bug horror story has a few funny moments as lots and lots of spiders wreak havoc in a white picket fence community somewhere off the beaten track. Lethal South American spider makes a trek to sunny California, meets up with local spiders, and rapidly multiplies. Utterly arachnophobic (read: totally scared of spiders) town doctor Daniels pairs with gung-ho exterminator Goodman to try and track down the culprits. The script's a bit yawn-inspiring but the cast and effects will keep you from dozing off. Directorial debut for Marshall, a longtime friend and producer for Spielberg. **109m/C; VHS, DVD, Blu-Ray.** Jeff Daniels; John Goodman; Harley Jane Kozak; Julian Sands; Roy Brocksmith; Stuart Pankin; Brian McNamara; Mark L. Taylor; Henry Jones; Peter Jason; James Handy; ***D:*** Frank Marshall; ***W:*** Wesley Strick; Don Jakoby; ***C:*** Mikael Salomon; ***M:*** Trevor Jones.

Ararat 🦴🦴🦴 **2002 (R)** The slaughter of more than one million Armenians by the Turks in 1915 is the difficult subject matter of Canadian/Armenian director Egoyan's historically-themed drama. Excellent ensemble cast portrays characters in modern-day Toronto who deal with pasts that have been affected by the event in different ways. A director (Aznavour) revisits his roots by making a movie about the Armenian genocide. An expert (Egoyan's wife Khanjian) on Armenian painter Gorky deals with her son (Alpay), whose father was killed after attempting to assassinate a Turkish diplomat, and stepdaughter (Croze), who's father committed suicide. Frequent Egoyan collaborator Greenwood turns up as an actor portraying a real-life U.S. doctor in Turkey during that era who published a book about the events. Stylistically intricate, which may leave some confused, but the heartfelt message is not lost in the crowd. **116m/C; VHS, DVD.** *CA* Charles Aznavour; Eric Bogosian; Brent Carver; David Alpay; Marie Josee Croze; Arsinee Khanjian; Bruce Greenwood; Elias Koteas; Christopher Plummer; Simon Abkarian; ***D:*** Atom Egoyan; ***W:*** Atom Egoyan; ***C:*** Paul Sarossy; ***M:*** Mychael Danna. Genie '02: Actress (Khanjian), Costume Des., Film, Score, Support. Actor (Koteas).

Araya 🦴🦴 **1959** Ethnographic documentary with separate narrations done in Spanish and French with subtitles. In 1957, writer/director Margo Benacerraf discovers the Araya peninsula, an isolated region in Northern Venezuela. The entire community is based on salt mining from the marshes next to the ocean and the exporting of the product. Trucks bring in the only fresh water and the inhabitants either fish or work in the communal salt production. Even as Benacerraf was making her only film, mechanization was being introduced, which would change a centuries-old way of life. **82m/B; DVD.** *VZ FR* ***Nar:*** Laurent Terzieff; Jose Ignacio Cabrujas; ***D:*** Margot Benacerraf; ***W:*** Margot Benacerraf; Pierre Seghers; ***C:*** Giuseppe Nisoli; ***M:*** Guy Bernard.

Arbitrage 🦴🦴🦴 **2012 (R)** Investment guru Robert Miller (Gere) comes off as an untouchable tycoon, with a beautiful wife (Sarandon), amped to sell his trading empire for a fortune. However, he's secretly millions in debt, trying to hush his spitfire mistress (Casta), and elude a detective (Roth) breathing down his neck. Soon enough, his world begins to collapse, leaving him running on empty. First-time feature director Jarecki pulls off a modern-day Hitchcockian miracle, making financial struggles chilling and exciting in this dense thriller. Leading the topnotch cast is Gere, whose portrayal of a desperate man is powerful. **107m/C; DVD, Blu-Ray.** Richard Gere; Susan Sarandon; Tim Roth; Brit Marling; Laetitia Casta; Nate Parker; ***D:*** Nicholas Jarecki; ***W:*** Nicholas Jarecki; ***C:*** Yorick Le Saux; ***M:*** Cliff Martinez.

Arc 🦴 **2006** Former L.A. cop Paris Pritchert (Facinelli) is now a junkie and drug dealer. In a last ditch effort at redemption, he tries to find a missing child, which leads to deceit, betrayal, and his own past. First-time director Gunnerson drags out the story and gets overly self-important for what should be a tight crime drama. **113m/C; DVD.** Peter Facinelli; Jonah Blechman; Ann Cusack; Logan Grove; Mel Harris; Ken Howard; Simone Moore; ***D:*** Robert Ethan Gunnerson; ***W:*** Robert Ethan Gunnerson; ***C:*** David J. Frederick; ***M:*** Monte Montgomery.

Arcade 🦴 **1/2 1993 (R)** All the kids in town are desperate to play the new virtual reality game Arcade, only the game is just a little too real. Seems it can transport you into another world with its stunning graphics and sound effects but you really put your life on the line. Only Alex (Ward) worries when kids start to disappear and she decides to battle the game for their lives. **85m/C; VHS, DVD.** Megan Ward; Peter Billingsley; John de Lancie; Sharon Farrell; Seth Green; Humberto Ortiz; Jonathan Fuller; Norbert Weisser; ***D:*** Albert Pyun; ***W:*** David S. Goyer; ***M:*** Alan Howarth.

Arch of Triumph 🦴🦴🦴 **1948** In Paris, an Austrian refugee doctor falls in love just before the Nazis enter the city. Big-budget boxoffice loser featuring fine cast but sluggish pace. Based on the Erich Maria Remarque novel. **120m/B; VHS, DVD, Blu-Ray.** Ingrid Bergman; Charles Boyer; Charles Laughton; Louis Calhern; Ruth Warrick; ***D:*** Lewis Milestone; ***W:*** Lewis Milestone; Harry Brown; ***C:*** Russell Metty.

Arch of Triumph 🦴🦴 **1/2 1985** A refugee doctor falls in love with a mystery woman as the Nazis enter Paris. TV remake of the 1948 film. **95m/C; VHS, DVD.** Anthony Hopkins; Lesley-Anne Down; Donald Pleasence; Frank Finlay; ***D:*** Waris Hussein; ***W:*** Charles Israel; ***M:*** Georges Delerue. **TV**

Archangel 🦴🦴 **1/2 2005 (R)** Based on the novel by Robert Harris, this thriller follows British historian Kelso (Craig), an expert on the Stalin-era USSR, to a Moscow conference. He's approached by an elderly man (Chernvak) claiming to know the whereabouts of Stalin's lost diary and he's plausible enough to have Kelso haring off to the port city of Archangel, accompanied by the man's daughter Zinaida (Rednikova) and reporter O'Brian (Macht). Only their search leads them to a dangerous underground movement to restore Stalinism to modern Russia. Originally broadcast as a BBC miniseries. **120m/C; DVD.** Daniel Craig; Yekaterina Rednikova; Gabriel Macht; Valery Chernvak; ***D:*** Jon Jones; ***W:*** Dick Clement; Ian La Frenais; ***C:*** Chris Seager; ***M:*** Robert (Rob) Lane. **TV**

Archer's Adventure 🦴 **1/2 1985** An Australian family film based on a true story. A horsetrainer's young apprentice delivers a prize racehorse to Melbourne, through 600 miles of tough frontier, devious bush rangers, and disaster. **120m/C; VHS, DVD.** *AU* Brett Climo; Nicole Kidman; ***D:*** Denny Lawrence.

The Architect 🦴🦴 **2006 (R)** Rickety construction undermines the cast. Affluent white architect Leo Waters (LaPaglia) lives with his dysfunctional family on Chicago's North Shore. Black activist Tonya Neely (Davis) is an occupant of a South Side housing tower that Leo designed, which in now gang-controlled and falling apart. Tonya, who has her own family issues, wants the towers torn down for new housing and thinks Leo's signature on her petition will help her efforts, but he's reluctant to participate. Based on a play by David Grieg. **82m/C; DVD.** Anthony LaPaglia; Viola Davis; Isabella Rossellini; Hayden Panettiere; Sebastian Stan; Paul James; Serena Reeder; Walton Goggins; ***D:*** Matt Tauber; ***W:*** Matt Tauber; ***C:*** John Bailey; ***M:*** Marcelo Zarvos.

Arctic 🦴🦴 **1/2 2018 (PG-13)** After his plane crashes in the middle of nowhere in the Arctic, Overgard (Mikkelsen) is alone but survives. He has a radio system, a systems for catching fish, and a watch alarm to organize his time. When the rescue helicopter crashes, he gains gear like a sled and some food but also a woman who survived the crash and is now in a coma. Mikkelsen gives a thoughtful performance that carries the somber, somewhat spiritless film. **98m/C; DVD, Blu-Ray.** *IC* Mads Mikkelsen; Maria Thelma Smaradottir; ***D:*** Joe Penna; ***W:*** Joe Penna; ***C:*** Tomas Orn Tomasson; ***M:*** Joseph Trapanese.

Arctic Blue 🦴 **1/2 1993 (R)** Alaskan biologist Walsh gets stuck being the local lawman when he's the only one willing to escort Hauer, a homicidal trapper, to a Fairbanks jail. But nothing's that easy—their plane crashes atop a glacier and the duo must battle each other and the elements to survive, while Hauer's brutal partners hunt Walsh. **95m/C; VHS, DVD.** Dylan Walsh; Rutger Hauer; Richard Bradford; ***D:*** Peter Masterson; ***W:*** Ross LaManna; ***C:*** Thomas Burstyn; ***M:*** Peter Melnick.

Arctic Dogs 🦴 **1/2** *Arctic Justice* **2019 (PG)** Swifty (Renner), an arctic fox, aspires to join the big dogs on the sledding team of the Arctic Blast Delivery Service. To prove he's up to the job, he makes a covert delivery to a mysterious location, and inadvertently unearths a plot by Otto Von Walrus (Cleese) to rule the world by melting the Arctic. Bland and joyless, with uninspired animation and a moral that's over the head of the intended audience. **92m/C; DVD, Blu-Ray.** *UK SK CA US* ***V:*** Jeremy Renner; Heidi Klum; James Franco; John Cleese; Omar Sy; ***D:*** Aaron Woodley; ***W:*** Aaron Woodley; Bob Barlen; Callan Brunker; ***M:*** David Buckley.

Arctic Tale 🦴🦴 **1/2 2007 (G)** We love pretending animals are just like us, don't we? Just add some disco music ("We Are Family") and a narrator (Queen Latifah) we all recognize and watch those wacky things animals do in the wild (like fart). Flick follows a polar bear and a walrus over six years, starting with their birth. The message is clear beyond our compulsion to humanize them, however; climate change, possibly caused by us, is dramatically affecting their habitat. Lush (if not chilly) backdrops and the directors' passion make this a fine family film. **96m/C; DVD, Blu-Ray, HD-DVD.** ***Nar:*** Queen Latifah; ***D:*** Adam Ravetch; Sarah Robertson; ***W:*** Linda Woverton; Moses Richards; Kristin Gore; ***C:*** Adam Ravetch; ***M:*** Joby Talbot.

The Ardennes 🦴 **1/2** *D'Ardennen* **2017** Dave (Perceval) and Kenneth (Janssens) are brothers and house robbers who split up when a job goes tragically wrong and Kenneth ends up in jail. Four years later, he's allowed out having never ratted out his brother, only to find his sibling with his girlfriend Sylvie (Baetens). The criminal trio reforms, but, of course, things aren't exactly stable. It's a decent crime thriller eventually but it takes forever to get going. Still, genre fans could do a lot worse than this Cain and Abel tale. **93m/C; DVD, Streaming.** *BE* Kevin Janssens; Jeroen Perceval; Veerle Baetens; Viviane de Muynck; Jan Bijvoet; ***D:*** Robin Pront; ***W:*** Jeroen Perceval; Robin Pront; ***C:*** Robrecht Heyvaert; ***M:*** Hendrik Willemyns.

Are We Done Yet? 🦴 **1/2 2007 (PG)** Apparently this sequel to "Are We There Yet?" is based on the 1948 Cary Grant comedy "Mr. Blandings Builds His Dream House" but don't count on it. Nick's (Ice Cube) married to divorcee-with-kids Suzanne (Long) and she announces she's preggers. Nick decides the family needs larger digs and leaves city life for a deceptively beautiful country house sold to them by slick/crazy contractor/building inspector/real estate salesman Chuck (scene-stealer McGinley). Of course their new abode is actually a homeowner's worst nightmare. If you liked the first Ice Cube family flick, this is more of the same. **92m/C; DVD, Blu-Ray.** Ice Cube; Nia Long; John C. McGinley; Aleisha Allen; Philip Daniel Bolden; ***D:*** Steve Carr; ***W:*** Hank Nelken; ***C:*** Jack N. Green; ***M:*** Teddy Castellucci.

Are We There Yet? 🦴 **2005 (PG)** Ice Cube is Nick Persons, an easygoing, charming ladies' man with a self-professed hatred of kids, when in walks his dream woman in the form of Suzanne (Long), an event planner. Suzanne, unfortunately for Nick, is a divorcee with two children, 11-year-old Lindsey (Allen) and 8-year-old Kevin (Bolden). Nick reconsiders his anti-kid rule, and decides to court Suzanne anyway. However, the two kids, who stubbornly believe that their parents will get back together, have decided to thwart any of their mother's would-be boyfriends. As luck would have it, their mother is needed in Vancouver to plan a New Year's Eve party and needs Nick to bring the kids to her. While Ice Cube is certainly enjoyable to watch, the kids are so obnoxious that the obvious question is, "is this movie done yet?" **91m/C; DVD, Blu-Ray, UMD.** Ice Cube; Nia Long; Jay Mohr; M.C. Gainey; Aleisha Allen; Philip Daniel Bolden; Tracy Morgan; Nichelle Nichols; ***D:*** Brian Levant; ***W:*** Steven Banks; Claudio Grazioso; J. David Stem; David N. Weiss; ***C:*** Thomas Ackerman; ***M:*** David Newman.

Are You Here 🦴 1/2 **2013 (R)** Weatherman Steve Dallas is a selfish, womanizing heel whose one friend is bipolar, semi-recluse Ben Baker. When Ben's estranged father dies, Ben persuades Steve to accompany him to Pennsylvania's Amish country for the reading of the will. Ben's control freak sister Terry thinks she'll have to battle their 20-something stepmom Angela over their inheritance, but it's bewildered Ben who's the major beneficiary of the family fortune. Writer/director Weiner's messy comedy generally doesn't work and the characters are annoying without being interesting. **113m/C; DVD, Blu-Ray.** Owen Wilson; Zach Galifianakis; Amy Poehler; Laura Ramsey; Alana de la Garza; Edward Herrmann; Peter Bogdanovich; ***D:*** Matthew Weiner; ***W:*** Matthew Weiner; ***C:*** Christopher Manley; ***M:*** David Carbonara.

Are You Listening? 🦴 1/2 **1932** Haines' last film on his MGM contract turns out to be a more somber affair as wise-cracking radio writer Bill is tricked into confessing to the accidental death of his greedy wife Alice (Morley) on a phone-in program. **73m/B; DVD.** William Haines; Karen Morley; Madge Evans; Anita Page; John Miljan; Neil Hamilton; Joan Marsh; Wallace Ford; Jean Hersholt; ***D:*** Harry Beaumont; ***W:*** Dwight Taylor; ***C:*** Harold Rosson.

Are You Scared 2 🦴 **2009 (R)** A group of young people competing in an online reality show involving treasure hunting are pursued by psychopaths sent by someone wishing to take advantage of their fame by murdering them all. **93m/C; DVD, Streaming.** Adam Busch; Tony Todd; Andrea Monier; Kathy Gardiner; ***D:*** John Lands; Russell Appling; ***W:*** John Lands; Russell Appling; ***C:*** John Lands; ***M:*** Kevin Gradnigo. **VIDEO**

Are You Scared? WOOF! 2006 Scared only by this movie—a dire rip-off/combination of "Saw" and TV's "Fear Factor." Six young people wake up in an abandoned factory and learn they are contestants on the reality TV show of the title. They all have to face their worst fear—or die trying. **79m/C; DVD.** Aletha Kutscher; Erin Consolvi; Carlee Avers; Soren Bowie; Kariem Marbury; Brad Ashten; Caia Coley; Brent Fidler; ***D:*** Andy Hurst; ***W:*** Andy Hurst; ***C:*** Jeffrey Smith. **VIDEO**

Area 51 🦴 1/2 *51* **2011 (R)** Syfy Channel feature that keeps all its sci-fi cliches briskly moving along. Public and political pressure finally forces the Air Force to allow selected journalists limited access to their Area 51 base. Of course, this proves to be a disaster when one alien captive uses the visit to free itself and some other aliens and they go on a killing spree. **90m/C; DVD.** Bruce Boxleitner; John Shea; Vanessa Branch; Lena Clark; Rachel Miner; Jason London; Damon Lipari; Billy Slaughter; ***D:*** Jason Connery; ***W:*** Lucy Mukerjee; ***C:*** Yaron Levy; ***M:*** Ian Honeyman.

Area 51 🦴 **2015 (R)** Three guys are obsessed with breaking into the titular location, the epicenter of all alien conspiracy theories for over a half-century. Much of the film consists of night-vision footage as the guys explore the warehouse that allegedly houses alien life. Of course, they find something scary. Director/writer Peli's follow-up to "Paranormal Activity" sat on the shelf for years before finally finishing re-shoots and heavy editing. It's easy to see why this boring mess barely got released but the real question is why anyone convinced themselves that there was a way to save it. **91m/C; DVD.** Glenn Campbell; Sandra Staggs; Jelena Nik; Suze Lanier-Bramlett; Roy Abramsohn; ***D:*** Oren Peli; ***W:*** Oren Peli; Christopher Denham; ***C:*** Todd Grossman.

The Arena 🦴🦴 *Naked Warriors* **1973 (R)** Ancient Romans capture beautiful women from around the world and force them to compete in gladiatorial games. New World exploitation gem featuring mostly Italian cast, including Bay, who starred in the previous year's "Lady Frankenstein." **75m/C; VHS, DVD.** Margaret Markov; Pam Grier; Lucretia Love; Paul Muller; Daniel Vargas; Marie Louise; Mary Count; Rosalba Neri; Vic Karis; Sid Lawrence; Peter Cester; Anna Melita; ***D:*** Steve Carver; ***W:*** John W. Corrington; Joyce H. Corrington; ***C:*** Joe D'Amato; ***M:*** Francesco De Masi.

Arena 🦴 1/2 **2011 (R)** What is Jackson doing in this violent, uninspired foolishness? A sadistic businessman (Jackson) runs an underground gladiatorial arena that kidnaps would-be fighters and forces them into death matches for online bettors. David's (Lutz) the latest combatant but winning becomes more than just a matter of survival for him. **94m/C; DVD.** Kellan Lutz; Samuel L. Jackson; Nina Dobrev; Daniel Dae Kim; Johnny Messner; James Remar; ***D:*** Jonah Loop; ***W:*** Robert Martinez; Martin Hultqvist; ***C:*** Nelson Cragg; ***M:*** Jeff Danna. **VIDEO**

Argento's Dracula 3D 🦴 *Dracula 3D* **2013** Schlocky kitsch horror filled with sex, gore, and cheap effects (just wait until Dracula turns into a giant praying mantis). Argento sticks to the basics of the Bram Stoker novel with Jonathan Harker coming to work for the bloodsucker who soon has designs on Harker's sweet wife, Mina. Meanwhile, Mina's sexy friend, Lucy, becomes a victim and Dracula is hunted by vampire slayer Van Helsing. **106m/C; Blu-Ray, On Demand.** *IT* Thomas Kretschmann; Marta Gastini; Asia Argento; Unax Ugalde; Rutger Hauer; Miriam Giovanelli; Giovanni Franzoni; ***D:*** Dario Argento; ***W:*** Dario Argento; Enrique Cerezo; ***C:*** Luciano Tovoli; ***M:*** Claudio Simonetti.

Argo 🦴🦴🦴🦴 **2012 (R)** Affleck's skillful retelling of a recently declassified aspect of the Iranian hostage crisis offers impressive attention to detail, but never loses sight of the emotional journey of the characters involved. The film details the invention of a faux Hollywood production in order to "exfiltrate" six Americans from Iran during the crisis. Affleck stars as the man with the daring plan, giving a remarkably strong if reserved performance that allows supporting players like Cranston, Arkin, and Goodman to shine. Producing tension in a story for which most viewers know the ending, Affleck proves his first two directorial efforts to be no mere flukes. **120m/C; DVD, Blu-Ray.** Ben Affleck; Alan Arkin; Bryan Cranston; John Goodman; Kyle Chandler; Rory Cochrane; Tate Donovan; Titus Welliver; Richard Kind; Victor Garber; Clea DuVall; Taylor Schilling; ***D:*** Ben Affleck; ***W:*** Chris Terrio; ***C:*** Rodrigo Prieto; ***M:*** Alexandre Desplat. Oscars '12: Adapt. Screenplay, Film, Film Editing; British Acad. '12: Director (Affleck), Film, Film Editing; Directors Guild '12: Director (Affleck); Golden Globes '13: Director (Affleck), Film--Drama; Screen Actors Guild '12: Cast; Writers Guild '12: Adapt. Screenplay.

Aria 🦴🦴 **1988 (R)** Ten directors were given carte blanche to interpret ten arias from well-known operas. Henry and D'Angelo star in Julian Temple's rendition of Verdi's "Rigoletto." In Fonda's film debut, she and her lover travel to Las Vegas and eventually kill themselves in the bathtub, just like "Romeo & Juliet." Jarman's piece (a highlight) shows an aged operatic star at her last performance remembering an early love affair. "I Pagliacci" is the one aria in which the director took his interpretation in a straightforward manner. **90m/C; VHS, DVD, Blu-Ray.** *GB* Theresa Russell; Anita Morris; Bridget Fonda; Beverly D'Angelo; Buck Henry; John Hurt; ***D:*** Ken Russell; Charles Sturridge; Robert Altman; Bill Bryden; Jean-Luc Godard; Bruce Beresford; Nicolas Roeg; Franc Roddam; Derek Jarman; Julien Temple; ***W:*** Ken Russell; Charles Sturridge; Robert Altman; Bill Bryden; Jean-Luc Godard; Bruce Beresford; Nicolas Roeg; Franc Roddam; Derek Jarman; Julien Temple; ***C:*** Caroline Champetier; Oliver Stapleton; Gale Tattersall.

Ariel 🦴🦴🦴 **1989** Refreshing, offbeat Finnish comedy by highly praised newcomer Kaurismaki. Hoping to find work in Southern Finland, an out-of-work miner from Northern Finland (Pajala) jets off in his white Cadillac convertible given to him in a cafe by a friend, who promptly shoots himself. There's no linear progression toward a happy ending, although antiheroic subject does find employment and romances a meter maid. Mostly, though, he's one of those it's hell being me guys who wouldn't have any luck if it weren't for bad luck. Strange slice-of-life sporting film noir tendencies, although essentially antistylistic. **74m/C; VHS, DVD.** *FI* Susanna Haavisto; Turo Pajala; Matti Pellonpaa; ***D:*** Aki Kaurismaki; ***W:*** Aki Kaurismaki; ***C:*** Timo Salminen. Natl. Soc. Film Critics '90: Foreign Film.

The Aristocats 🦴🦴🦴 **1970** Typically entertaining Disney animated story about pampered pussy Duchess (Gabor) and her three kittens, who are left a fortune in their mistress' will. The fortune goes to the butler if the cats don't survive, so he dumps them in the country hoping they won't find their way home. The cats are aided by tough alley denizen O'Malley (Harris)?it's kind of the feline version of "Lady and the Tramp." Maurice Chevalier sings the title tune. **78m/C; VHS, DVD, Blu-Ray.** ***V:*** Eva Gabor; Phil Harris; Sterling Holloway; Roddy Maude-Roxby; Bill Thompson; Hermione Baddeley; Carol(e) Shelley; Pat Buttram; Nancy Kulp; Paul Winchell; ***D:*** Wolfgang Reitherman; ***M:*** George Bruns.

Aristocrats 🦴🦴 1/2 **1999** Lavish BBC historical drama based on Stella Tillyard's biography about aristocratic life in 18th-century Britain and Ireland as seen through the eyes of the Lennox sisters. Daughters of the Duke of Richmond and great-granddaughters of Charles II (via an illegitimate son), the sisters find marriage, politics, and family ties intertwining. **293m/C; DVD.** *UK* Serena Gordon; Geraldine Somerville; Anne-Marie Duff; Jodhi May; Alun Armstrong; Ben Daniels; Julian Fellowes; Toby Jones; ***Nar:*** Sian Phillips; ***D:*** David Caffrey; ***W:*** Harriet O'Carroll; ***C:*** James Welland; ***M:*** Mark Thomas. **TV**

The Aristocrats 🦴🦴 1/2 **1999** True story of the scandalous 18th-century aristocratic Lennox family, including the four beautiful sisters whose elopements, liaisons, and intrigues provided ample English gossip. Based on the novel by Stella Tillyard. Three cassettes. **255m/C; VHS, DVD.** *GB* Jodhi May; Geraldine Somerville; Serena Gordon; Anne-Marie Duff; Alun Armstrong; Julian Fellowes; Ben Daniels; Diane Fletcher; Clive Swift; Sian Phillips; Richard Dempsey; ***D:*** David Caffrey; ***W:*** Harriet O'Carroll. **TV**

The Aristocrats 🦴🦴🦴 **2005** "A family walks into a talent agency..." and so begins the raunchiest joke in cinematic history. It might seem odd to dedicate an entire documentary to one joke, but co-directors Provenza and Jillette excel at demonstrating how different comedians bring their own unique interpretations to the same material. The all-star interviewees (George Carlin, Chris Rock, and Robin Williams, among many others) speak elegantly about the joys of working "blue," although the true tour-de-force performances come from Bob Saget, Gilbert Gottfried, and Sarah Silverman, who all give blisteringly filthy renditions of the titular joke that you'll be talking about for weeks to come. **87m/C; DVD.** ***D:*** Paul Provenza; ***M:*** Gary Stockdale.

Arizona 🦴🦴 *Men Are Like That* **1931** Wayne's inexperience shows in this romantic drama. West Point cadet Bob Gunton (Wayne) refuses to commit to girlfriend Evelyn (La Plante) and she marries his mentor Frank Bonham (Stanley). The Bonhams move to an Arizona Army post where Bob is also posted. Instead of being upset, Bob starts wooing Evelyn's younger sister Bonnie (Clyde), which definitely angers Evelyn. **70m/B; DVD.** Laura La Plante; John Wayne; Forrest Stanley; June Clyde; ***D:*** George B. Seitz; ***W:*** Robert Riskin; ***C:*** Ted Tetzlaff.

Arizona 🦴🦴 1/2 **1940** Arthur is a hellion in wild 1860 Tucson who falls for the wandering Holden. He's headed for California and she can't keep him in town so Arthur throws herself into business by establishing a freight line. Only warring Apaches try to burn her out and Holden rides in to save the day (with the cavalry and a stampeding cattle herd). Holden's first western is lively but long. **121m/B; VHS, DVD.** Jean Arthur; William Holden; Warren William; Porter Hall; Paul Harvey; George Chandler; Regis Toomey; Edgar Buchanan; ***D:*** Wesley Ruggles; ***W:*** Claude Binyon; ***M:*** Victor Young.

Arizona 🦴🦴 **2018** Real estate agent Cassie (DeWitt) is struggling. She quickly bought an overpriced house to get away from her former husband Scott (Wilson). In debt, she is regularly harassed by bill collectors. She also must deal with a slimy, greedy boss (Rogen). After one of his angry clients, Sonny (McBride), accidentally kills him, he kidnaps Cassie. Sonny tries to make Cassie see him as a good guy, but she tries to get away as he commits more crimes. A broad satire with a touch of horror, the film fails to live up to its potential as a social commentary about the subprime mortgage crisis. **85m/C; DVD.** Danny McBride; Rosemarie DeWitt; Lolli Sorenson; Luke Wilson; Elizabeth Gillies; ***D:*** Jonathan Watson; ***W:*** Luke Del Tredici; ***C:*** Drew Daniels; ***M:*** Joseph Stephens.

Arizona Bushwackers 🦴 1/2 **1967** Routine western that has Confederate spy Keel taking job as sheriff in small Arizona town. Once there, he has to straighten out a few bad guys who have been selling weapons to the Apaches. Notable for presence of old western-movie veterans Ireland, Donlevy, Brady, and MacLane. Based on a story by Steve Fisher. **87m/C; VHS, Streaming.** Howard Keel; Yvonne De Carlo; John Ireland; Marilyn Maxwell; Scott Brady; Brian Donlevy; Barton MacLane; ***D:*** Lesley Selander.

Arizona Dream 🦴🦴 **1994 (R)** Alex (Depp) is a New York drifter who gets stuck working for his uncle's (Lewis) car dealership in a small Arizona town. He meets an eccentric older woman (Dunaway) with a homemade plane and some dreams of her own. Tends toward the surreal and confusing. **119m/C; VHS, DVD.** Johnny Depp; Faye Dunaway; Jerry Lewis; Lili Taylor; Paulina Porizkova; Tricia Leigh Fisher; Vincent Gallo; ***D:*** Emir Kusturica; ***W:*** Emir Kusturica; David Atkins; ***C:*** Vilko Filac.

Arizona Raiders 🦴🦴 **1965** Arizona rangers hunt down killers who have been terrorizing the territory. **88m/C; VHS, DVD, Streaming.** Audie Murphy; Buster Crabbe; Gloria Talbott; ***D:*** William Witney.

Arizona Sky 🦴🦴 **2008** Kyle and Jake were teenaged best friends who could never follow through with their feelings for each other because of hometown prejudice. A stressed-out Jake returns to their desert community after 20 years and discovers Kyle hasn't been happy with his choices either. So the men decide to see if those old emotions are worth pursuing. **91m/C; DVD.** Patricia Place; Eric Dean; Jayme McCabe; Bernadette Murray; ***D:*** Jeff London; ***W:*** Jeff London; ***C:*** Matthew Skala. **VIDEO**

Arizona Summer 🦴🦴 1/2 **2003 (PG)** Brent (Barnett) makes friends and gets some life lessons at a summer camp run by Travers (Majors). Simple family entertainment. **90m/C; DVD.** Lee Majors; Greg Evigan; Morgan Fairchild; Bug Hall; Gemini Barnett; David Henrie; Lorenzo Henrie; Scott Clifton; ***D:*** Joey Travolta; ***W:*** Bill Blair.

Ark of the Sun God 🦴 **1982** Another adventurer battles the Nazis and nutsies for a 2000-year-old ark buried in the Sahara. **95m/C; VHS, DVD.** David Warbeck; John Steiner; Susie Sudlow; Alan Collins; Riccardo Palacio; ***D:*** Anthony M. Dawson.

Arlington Road 🦴🦴 1/2 **1999 (R)** The tranquility of surburban life is shattered for college professor Faraday (Bridges) when he suspects the picket fence and overly friendliness of new neighbor Lang (Robbins) is a cover for his right-wing terrorism. As Faraday slowly uncovers Lang's true identity, it becomes harder for him to convince friends to believe the conspiracy. Impressive nail-biter with an interesting twist has a solid performance from Bridges as the paranoid professor, and an eerie one from the otherwise affable Robbins. Director Pellington, with the aide of Badalamenti's haunting score maintains the film's objective of showing how evil can come from the most unlikely place. **119m/C; VHS, DVD, Blu-Ray.** Jeff Bridges; Tim Robbins; Joan Cusack; Hope Davis; Mason Gamble; Stanley Anderson; Robert Gossett; Spencer Treat Clark; ***D:*** Mark Pellington; ***W:*** Ehren Kruger; ***C:*** Bobby Bukowski; ***M:*** Angelo Badalamenti; tomandandy.

Arlo the Burping Pig 🦴🦴 1/2 **2016 (G)** A kid- and family-friendly flick about a girl who bonds with a tea-cup pig. When seven-year-old Talia (Blanchard) moves with her family to a new town, she finds it hard to fit in at her new school. She is also friendless until she finds Arlo (Bell), a small pig who has run away from the circus. Though she tries to keep him a secret, Arlo burps loudly! Though Arlo does not remain a secret, he helps save Talia's family. **80m/C; DVD, Streaming, Download.** Drake Bell; Joseph Lawrence; Jennifer Taylor; Lindsey Blanchard; Jonathan Lipnicki; ***D:*** Tom DeNucci; ***W:*** Eric Weinstock; ***C:*** Sam Eilersten; ***M:*** David Bateman. **VIDEO**

Armadillo 🦴🦴 1/2 **2011** An insightful, intimate documentary about the impact of war on soldiers, especially focusing on how combat affects different personalities. Created by Danish filmmaker Janus Metz Pedersen, he was imbedded with Danish soldiers at Camp Armadillo fighting the Taliban in southern Afghanistan. Metz centered on two soldiers in particular, Mads and Daniel, and shows the daily grind of warfare, the dangers faced by troops daily, and the murky ethical choices that are made. Danish with subtitles. **105m/C; DVD, Blu-Ray, Streaming, Download.** ***D:*** Janus Metz Pedersen.

Armageddon 🦴🦴 ½ **1998 (PG-13)** A Texas-sized asteroid is hurtling towards earth, NASA gets nervous, and it's up to oil driller Harry Stamper (Willis) and his misfit crew to turn astronaut, blast off into space, land on that rock, and blow the sucker to kingdom come. Ya get a little romance as hotshot A.J. Frost (Affleck) smooches with babe Grace (Tyler), who's Harry's nubile daughter. Lots of action (naturally), some humor, and some sappy, heart-tugging moments for perfect put-your-brain-on-hold entertainment. The second "space rock hits earth" movie, following the somber "Deep Impact." **150m/C; VHS, DVD, Blu-Ray.** Bruce Willis; Ben Affleck; Billy Bob Thornton; Steve Buscemi; Liv Tyler; Will Patton; Peter Stormare; Keith David; Owen Wilson; William Fichtner; Jessica Steen; Grayson McCouch; Jason Isaacs; Michael Clarke Duncan; Erik Per Sullivan; ***D:*** Michael Bay; ***W:*** Jonathan Hensleigh; J.J. (Jeffrey) Abrams; ***C:*** John Schwartzman; ***M:*** Trevor Rabin. MTV Movie Awards '99: Action Seq., Song ("I Don't Want to Miss a Thing"); Golden Raspberries '98: Worst Actor (Willis).

Armed and Dangerous 🦴🦴 **1986 (PG-13)** Candy and Levy are incompetent security guards assigned to a do-nothing job. Things get spiced up when a mobster tries to run a crime ring under their nose. Candy catches on and winds up in a full-fledged chase. Not as funny as it sounds, though occasionally has moments of genuine comedy. **88m/C; VHS, DVD.** John Candy; Eugene Levy; Kenneth McMillan; Brion James; Robert Loggia; Meg Ryan; Don Stroud; Jonathan Banks; Steve Railsback; Bruce Kirby; Tony Burton; Larry Hankin; Judy Landers; David Wohl; ***D:*** Mark L. Lester; ***W:*** Harold Ramis; Peter Torokvei; James Keach; Brian Grazer.

Armed Response 🦴🦴 **1986 (R)** Carradine leads a group of mercenaries in a battle against Chinatown mobsters. They race to locate a priceless jade statue before it can fall into the wrong hands. **86m/C; VHS, DVD.** David Carradine; Lee Van Cleef; Mako; Lois Hamilton; Ross Hagen; Brent Huff; ***D:*** Fred Olen Ray; ***C:*** Paul Elliott.

Armed Response 🦴 ½ *In Security* **2013 (R)** Likeable enough crime comedy. The buddy owners of a failing home security business take to robbing local houses to sell their products. They rob a mobster's house and get into major trouble, especially with the cops investigating the burglaries as well. **94m/C; DVD.** Ethan (Randall) Embry; Michael Gladis; Cary Elwes; Clea DuVall; Ving Rhames; Adam Arkin; Vinnie Jones; Alan Arkin; ***D:*** Adam Beamer; Evan Beamer; ***W:*** Adam Beamer; Evan Beamer; Craig Hildebrand; ***C:*** Akis Konstantakopoulos; ***M:*** Ben Zaral. **VIDEO**

Armistead Maupin's More Tales of the City 🦴🦴 ½ *More Tales of the City* **1997** More risque and odd adventures for the inhabitants of Barbary Lane. Sequel picks up some six weeks after the first adventures. In 1977 San Francisco, Mary Ann (Linney) and Mouse (Hopkins) hunt for romance on a Mexican cruise. Mary Ann falls for handsome amnesiac Burke (Ferguson) and tries to help him regain his memory, while Mouse reunites with ex-lover, Dr. Jon (Campbell). Meanwhile, Mona (Siemszko) searches for her roots, which leads to revelations from Mrs. Madrigal (Dukakis). Brian (Hubley) becomes a voyeur and DeDe (Garrick) awaits the birth of twins—whose father is not her supercilious husband Beauchamp (Gibson). **330m/C; VHS, DVD.** Laura Linney; Olympia Dukakis; Colin Ferguson; Billy Campbell; Paul Hopkins; Whip Hubley; Thomas Gibson; Barbara Garrick; Nina Siemaszko; Jackie Burroughs; Swoosie Kurtz; Francoise Robertson; Dan E. Butler; ***Cameo(s):*** Parker Posey; Ed Asner; Paul Bartel; Brian Bedford; Sheila McCarthy; Scott Thompson; ***D:*** Pierre Gang; ***W:*** Nicholas Wright; ***C:*** Serge Ladouceur; ***M:*** Richard Gregoire.

Armistead Maupin's Tales of the City 🦴🦴 ½ *Tales of the City* **1993** Carefree '70s San Francisco is the setting for the interconnected stories of the inhabitants of 28 Barbary Lane. There's mysterious landlady Mrs. Madrigal (Dukakis); free-spirit Mona Ramsey (Webb); her gay roomie, Michael "Mouse" Tolliver (D'Amico); hetero lawyer-turned-waiter Brian (Gross); nerdy, secretive Norman (DeSantis); and the naively sweet Mary Ann Singleton (Linney). Definite time-warp factor in this pre-AIDS depiction of sex and drugs, but also the timeless search for love and happiness. Maupin first wrote the stories as an ongoing serial for the "San Francisco Chronicle" and they were later turned into six novels. Made for British TV. **360m/C; VHS, DVD.** *GB* Olympia Dukakis; Donald Moffat; Chloe Webb; Laura Linney; Marcus D'Amico; Billy Campbell; Thomas Gibson; Paul Gross; Barbara Garrick; Nina Foch; Edie Adams; Meagen Fay; Lou Liberatore; Country Joe McDonald; Mary Kay Place; Parker Posey; Kevin Sessums; McLean Stevenson; Stanley DeSantis; Cynda Williams; Karen Black; Michael Jeter; Paul Bartel; Lance Loud; Ian McKellen; Bob Mackie; Marissa Ribisi; Mother Love; Don Novello; Rod Steiger; Janeane Garofalo; Armistead Maupin; ***D:*** Alastair Reid; ***W:*** Richard Kramer; ***M:*** John Keane. **TV**

Armored 🦴🦴 ½ **2009 (PG-13)** Unpretentious but generic heist movie. A six-man crew at an L.A. armored transport security firm are in on a robbery against their company with a $42 million dollar payoff. If only planner Cochrane (Dillon) can persuade Iraqi war vet Hackett (Short) to go along by reassuring him that nobody will get hurt. Of course, that turns out to be wrong and a conflicted Hackett then tries to do the right thing. **88m/C; Blu-Ray, On Demand.** Columbus Short; Jean Reno; Laurence Fishburne; Skeet Ulrich; Amaury Nolasco; Fred Ward; Matt Dillon; Milo Ventimiglia; Andre Jamal Kinney; ***D:*** Nimrod Antal; ***W:*** James V. Simpson; ***C:*** Andrzej Sekula; ***M:*** John Murphy.

Armored Car Robbery 🦴🦴 **1950** Talman and his buddies plot to rob an armored car but are foiled by McGraw and his crime-fighters. Surprisingly good B-crime drama. **68m/B; VHS, DVD.** Charles McGraw; Adele Jergens; William Talman; Steve Brodie; Douglas Fowley; Don McGuire; James Flavin; Gene Evans; ***D:*** Richard Fleischer; ***W:*** Gerald Drayson Adams; Earl Felton; ***C:*** Guy Roe; ***M:*** Paul Sawtell.

Armstrong 🦴🦴 ½ **2019** Narrated by Harrison Ford, this solid documentary tracks the life of Neil Armstrong, from his childhood in Ohio, through his early days as a fighter pilot, and to global stardom as the first man to walk on the moon. Interviews and archival footage grant an intimate look at the humble, remarkable man inside the spacesuit. Released on July 12, 2019, the 50th anniversary of his moon landing. **100m/C; DVD.** Neil Alden Armstrong; Janet Armstrong; Mark Armstrong; Rick Armstrong; ***Nar:*** Harrison Ford; ***D:*** David Fairhead; ***C:*** Tim Cragg; ***M:*** Chris Roe.

The Armstrong Lie 🦴🦴🦴 **2013 (R)** Expert documentarian Gibney just happened to be shooting a documentary on the life of infamous cyclist Lance Armstrong when his life and public persona collapsed, thereby changing the focus of the film that would be released. As Armstrong continuously tried to defend the now-revealed fact that he used performance enhancing drugs to become an international champion, Gibney holds him over the flame via interview segments, ultimately painting a portrait of a deeply troubled man who not only cheated but tried to ruin the lives of those who knew about it. It's too long for its own good but fascinating at times. **124m/C; DVD, Blu-Ray.** Lance Armstrong; ***Nar:*** Alex Gibney; ***D:*** Alex Gibney; ***W:*** Alex Gibney; ***C:*** Maryse Alberti; ***M:*** David Kahne.

The Army of Crime 🦴🦴 *L'Armee du Crime* **2010** Semi-fictional historical drama about French communists, the Resistance movement, and the Nazis. Armenian-born poet and militant Communist Missak Manouchian becomes the leader of a group of anti-fascist partisans. The Nazis begin a crackdown and Manouchian's group is eventually rounded up to be executed. French and German with subtitles. **139m/C; DVD.** *FR* Simon Abkarian; Virginie Ledoyen; Robinson Stevenin; Gregoire Leprince-Ringuet; Lola Naymark; Yann Tregouet; Ariane Ascaride; Jean-Pierre Darroussin; ***D:*** Robert Guediguian; ***W:*** Robert Guediguian; Serge Le Peron; Gilles Taurand; ***C:*** Pierre Milon; ***M:*** Alexandre Desplat.

Army of Darkness 🦴🦴🦴 *Evil Dead 3; The Medieval Dead* **1992 (R)** Campbell returns for a third "Evil Dead" round as the square-jawed, none too bright hero, Ash in this comic book extravaganza. He finds himself hurled back to the 14th-century through the powers of an evil book. There he romances a babe, fights an army of skeletons, and generally causes all those Dark Age knights a lot of grief, as he tries to get back to his own time. Raimi's technical exuberance is apparent and, as usual, the horror is graphic but still tongue-in-cheek. **77m/C; VHS, DVD, Blu-Ray, HD-DVD.** Bruce Campbell; Embeth Davidtz; Marcus Gilbert; Ian Abercrombie; Richard Grove; Michael Earl Reid; Tim Quill; Bridget Fonda; Patricia Tallman; Theodore (Ted) Raimi; Ivan Raimi; Donald Campbell; William Lustig; Josh Becker; ***D:*** Sam Raimi; ***W:*** Sam Raimi; Ivan Raimi; ***C:*** Bill Pope; ***M:*** Joseph LoDuca; Danny Elfman.

Army of One 🦴 ½ **1994 (R)** Santee (Lundgren) and his pal are hauling stolen cars across the desert when a cop pulls them over. Soon there's two dead bodies and Santee's in big trouble. An unrated version is also available. **102m/C; VHS, DVD, Blu-Ray.** Dolph Lundgren; George Segal; Kristian Alfonso; Geoffrey Lewis; Michelle Phillips; ***D:*** Vic Armstrong; ***W:*** Steven Pressfield; Joel Goldsmith.

Army of One 🦴🦴 ½ **2016 (R)** A comedy centered on one American civilian's efforts to find terrorist mastermind Osama Bin Laden, partially based on actual events. Unemployed ex-con handyman Gary Faulkner (Cage) receives a vision from God (Brand) telling him to capture Bin Laden. Using a sword purchased from a home-shopping network, Gary goes to Pakistan to complete his mission. During his mission, he sees old friends, makes new friends, and angers new enemies. **92m/C; DVD, Blu-Ray, Streaming, Download.** Nicolas Cage; Russell Brand; Wendi McLendon-Covey; Amer Chadha-Patel; Paul Scheer; ***D:*** Larry Charles; ***W:*** Rajiv Joseph; Scott Rothman; ***C:*** Anthony Hardwick; ***M:*** David Newman.

Army of Shadows 🦴🦴🦴 ½ *L'Armee des Ombres; Army in the Shadows; The Shadow Army* **1969** Melville's stunning adaptation of the 1943 Joseph Kessel novel focuses on members of the French Resistance in 1942. They lead shadow lives under false identities, struggling to survive while living in fear of betrayal. The head of this cell is Luc Jardie (Meurisse) but the most necessary of its members is field commander Philippe Gerbier (Ventura,) who metes out punishment for such betrayals. It's grim and dangerous and morally ambivalent and no one has time to be heroic (though they are) because there's too much at stake. You can't look away even if you want to. Melville himself was a member of the Resistance. French with subtitles. **140m/C; DVD, Blu-Ray.** *FR IT* Lino Ventura; Simone Signoret; Paul Meurisse; Jean-Pierre Cassel; Claude Mann; Paul Crauchet; Christian Barbier; Alain Libolt; Jean-Marie Robain; ***D:*** Jean-Pierre Melville; ***W:*** Jean-Pierre Melville; ***C:*** Pierre Lhomme; ***M:*** Eric Demarsen.

Army of the Dead 🦴 **2008 (R)** Some college students awaken a small army of dead spanish guys who are guarding a buried treasure. **89m/C; DVD.** Mike Hatfield; Malcolm Madera; Ross Kelly; Miguel Martinez; Audrey Anderson; Stefani Marchesi; ***D:*** Joseph Conti; ***W:*** Tom Woosley; Michael Ciccolini; ***C:*** John Grace; ***M:*** William T. Stromberg. **VIDEO**

Arn: The Knight Templar 🦴🦴 **2007 (R)** Historical epic that doesn't have as much action as the plot implies. In the 12th century, young Swedish nobleman Arn is being trained as a warrior when he impregnates love Cecilia. As penance for this scandal, Arn is sent to Jerusalem to join the Crusades, where his fighting ability will eventually be used to unify rival clans back home. **139m/C; DVD.** *SW* Joakim Natterqvist; Sofia Helin; Stellan Skarsgard; Michael Nyqvist; Bibi Andersson; Simon Callow; Vincent Perez; Sven-Bertil Taube; Milind Soman; Lina Englund; ***D:*** Peter Flinth; ***W:*** Hans Gunnarsson; ***C:*** Eric Kress; ***M:*** Tuomas Kantelinen.

Around a Small Mountain 🦴🦴 *36 Vues du Pic Saint-Loop* **2009** Melancholy, talky Rivette pic follows Kate as she returns to her late father's small traveling circus after a 15-year absence. When Vittorio helps her with her stalled car, Kate invites him to a village performance and he ingratiates himself with the troupe. His (non-romantic) interest in Kate makes Vittorio want to learn about the trouble that made her leave her family and life behind and why she came back. French with subtitles. **85m/C; DVD.** *FR* Jane Birkin; Sergio Castellitto; Andre Marcon; Jacques Bonnaffe; Julie-Marie Parmentier; Helene De Vallombreuse; Valintino Orsini; Vimala Pons; ***D:*** Jacques Rivette; ***W:*** Sergio Castellitto; Jacques Rivette; ***C:*** Irina Lubtchansky; ***M:*** Pierre Allio.

Around June 🦴🦴 **2008** Ever since June's (Armstrong) mother died when she was a girl, her grief-stricken father Murry (Gries) has dominated her life. But things change when June meets illegal immigrant Juan (Guerrero), who offers her a chance at happiness. **93m/C; DVD.** Samaire Armstrong; Oscar H. Guerrero; Jon(athan) Gries; Brad William Henke; Michael Goorjian; ***D:*** James Savoca; ***W:*** James Savoca; ***C:*** Peter Hawkins; ***M:*** Didier Rachou.

Around the Bend 🦴🦴 **2004 (R)** Dying patriarch Henry Lair (Caine) is being cared for by his grandson Jason (Lucas), who is also looking after his own young son, Zach (Bobo). Jason's black sheep father, Turner (Walken), abandoned him to Henry's care when he was a child. But Turner suddenly shows up, just in time to fulfill Henry's last request—he wants to be buried in a bizarre ritual that will mean a generational road trip from L.A. to Albuquerque. So does some male bonding occur? Boy, howdy, you betcha, but with Walken around the trip is never completely mundane. Feature debut of director/writer Roberts. **83m/C; DVD.** Christopher Walken; Josh(ua) Lucas; Michael Caine; Glenne Headly; Jonah Bobo; ***D:*** Jordan Roberts; ***W:*** Jordan Roberts; ***C:*** Michael Grady; ***M:*** David Bâerwald.

Around the Block 🦴 ½ **2013** Dedicated teacher helps at-risk student in this clichéd drama. Engaged to an Aussie, American Dino Chalmers (Ricci) moves to Sydney and gets a job as an English teacher in an underfunded school. She convinces the burned-out principal to let her stage "Hamlet" and it's Aboriginal 16-year-old Liam Wood (Page-Lochard) who surprises everyone, including himself, by winning the lead role. But Liam's troubled home life, which includes a father in prison and a brother who wants Liam to help him get revenge, might derail his chance at a different life. **104m/C; DVD.** *AU* Christina Ricci; Hunter Page-Lochard; Mark Coles Smith; Jack Thompson; Matthew Nable; Ursula Yovich; ***D:*** Sarah Spillane; ***W:*** Sarah Spillane; ***C:*** Martin McGrath; ***M:*** Nick Wales.

Around the Fire 🦴🦴 **1998 (R)** At boarding school, Simon (Sawa) tries to escape his emotional troubles by getting in with the school druggies, including Andrew (Mabius). He also begins a foray into the neo-hippie world of the Grateful Dead, where he falls for the free-spirited Jennifer (Reid). Simon does wind up in rehab, looking back on his life. **107m/C; VHS, DVD.** Devon Sawa; Eric Mabius; Bill Smitrovich; Tara Reid; Charlaine Woodard; Michael McKeever; ***D:*** John Jacobsen; ***W:*** John Comerford; Tommy Rosen; ***M:*** B.C. Smith. **VIDEO**

Around the World in 80 Days 🦴🦴🦴 **1956 (G)** Niven is the unflappable Victorian Englishman who wagers that he can circumnavigate the earth in four-score days. With his faithful manservant Cantinflas they set off on a spectacular journey. A perpetual favorite providing ample entertainment. Star-gazers will particularly enjoy the more than 40 cameo appearances by many of Hollywood's biggest names. Adapted from the novel by Jules Verne. **178m/C; VHS, DVD.** David Niven; Shirley MacLaine; Cantinflas; Robert Newton; Charles Boyer; Joe E. Brown; Martine Carol; John Carradine; Charles Coburn; Ronald Colman; ***Cameo(s):*** Melville Cooper; Noel Coward; Andy Devine; Reginald Denny; Fernandel; Marlene Dietrich; Hermione Gingold; Cedric Hardwicke; Trevor Howard; Glynis Johns; Buster Keaton; Evelyn Keyes; Peter Lorre; John Gielgud; Victor McLaglen; John Mills; Robert Morley; Jack Oakie; George Raft; Cesar Romero; Gilbert Roland; Red Skelton; Frank Sinatra; Beatrice Lillie; Ava Gardner; ***D:*** Michael Anderson, Sr.; ***W:*** James Poe; John Farrow; S.J. Perelman; ***C:*** Lionel Lindon; ***M:*** Victor Young. Oscars '56: Adapt. Screenplay, Color Cinematog., Film,

Film Editing, Orig. Dramatic Score; Golden Globes '57: Actor--Mus./Comedy (Cantinflas), Film--Drama; N.Y. Film Critics '56: Film, Screenplay.

Around the World in 80 Days 1/2 **1989** TV adaptation of the Jules Verne adventure novel that finds Victorian gentleman Phineas Fogg (Brosnan) wagering that he can circle the globe in 80 days. He's pursued by private detective Fix (Ustinov), who suspects him of a daring bank robbery, and faces many trials and much excitement along the way. On two cassettes. **270m/C; VHS, DVD.** Pierce Brosnan; Peter Ustinov; Eric Idle; Arielle Dombasle; Henry Gibson; John Hillerman; Jack Klugman; Christopher Lee; Patrick Macnee; Roddy McDowall; Darren McGavin; John Mills; Robert Morley; Lee Remick; Pernell Roberts; James B. Sikking; Jill St. John; Robert Wagner; Julia Nickson-Soul; ***D:*** Buzz Kulik.

Around the World in 80 Days **2004 (PG)** Phileas Fogg (Coogan) bets the London science community that he can circumnavigate the earth in 80 days, aided by assistant Passpartout (Chan). Surprising no one, a few people don't want him to make it. This time around Passpartout steals the show as a martial arts expert trying to return a stolen sacred heirloom to his village in China. In fact, Fogg's unworldly inventor seems at times like the sidekick. While departing wildly from the source material, it's lightweight fun better suited to the lowered expectations of a rental. As in the previous version, entertaining cameos add to the humor. Schwarzenegger is especially silly as an over-the-top lusty Turkish prince. **125m/C; DVD.** *GB IR GE* Steve Coogan; Jackie Chan; Cecile de France; Jim Broadbent; Kathy Bates; Arnold Schwarzenegger; John Cleese; Ian McNeice; Luke Wilson; Owen Wilson; Ewen Bremner; Rob Schneider; Mark Addy; Sammo Hung; Roger Hammond; David Ryall; Macy Gray; Daniel Wu; Will Forte; Robert Fyfe; Karen Joy Morris; Richard Branson; ***D:*** Frank Coraci; ***W:*** David Benullo; David Titcher; David Goldstein; ***C:*** Phil Meheux; ***M:*** Trevor Jones.

Around the World in a Daze 1/2 *The Three Stooges Go Around the World in a Daze* **1963** The Stooges are servants for Phileas Fogg's great-grandson, who has decided to repeat his ancestor's famous feat. Mayhem ensues when the three help out in their usual efficient, competent way. **93m/B; VHS, DVD.** Moe Howard; Larry Fine; Joe DeRita; Jay Sheffield; ***D:*** Norman Maurer.

Around the World Under the Sea **1965** Bunch of men and one woman scientist plunge under the ocean in an experiment to predict earthquakes. They plant earthquake detectors along the ocean floor and discover the causes of tidal waves. They have men-women battles. They see big sea critters. **111m/C; VHS, DVD, Streaming.** David McCallum; Shirley Eaton; Gary Merrill; Keenan Wynn; Brian Kelly; Lloyd Bridges; ***D:*** Andrew Marton.

Aroused **1966** Hollister is an apparently dedicated policeman who commits a number of blunders in the pursuit of a serial killer, including leaving his wife with the sociopath while he cavorts with the prostitute assigned to his protection. Director Holden's psychothriller was gorily ahead of its time. Includes heart-stopping castration sequence. **78m/B; VHS, DVD.** Janine Lenon; Steve Hollister; Fleurette Carter; Joanna Mills; Tony Palladino; Ted Gelanza; ***D:*** Anton Holden.

The Arousers WOOF! *Sweet Kill; A Kiss from Eddie* **1970** Hunk Hunter stars as a handsome, repressed California psycho in this cult item. Eddie travels the coast searching for a woman he is able to make love to; those who fail to arouse him come to tragic, climactic ends. Dreary, cheap exploitation with Roger Corman as executive producer for New World Pictures. **85m/C; DVD.** Tab Hunter; Cherie Latimer; Nadyne Turney; Isabel Jewell; ***D:*** Curtis Hanson; ***W:*** Curtis Hanson; ***C:*** Daniel Lacambre; ***M:*** Charles Bernstein.

The Arrangement 1/2 **1969 (R)** Veteran advertising executive Douglas attempts suicide and then sets out to search for the meaning of life. Along the way he attempts to patch up his "arrangements" with his wife, his mistress and his father. Forced, slow, and self-conscious, though well acted. Adapted by Kazan from the director's own novel. **126m/C; VHS, DVD.** Kirk Douglas; Faye Dunaway; Deborah Kerr; Richard Boone; Hume Cronyn; ***D:*** Elia Kazan; ***W:*** Elia Kazan; ***C:*** Robert L. Surtees; ***M:*** David Amram.

The Arrangement **1999 (R)** Jake (Keskhemnu) lives in Los Angeles. Luhann (James) is in New York. They're engaged until he admits to a one-night stand and invites her to experiment herself before the wedding. When she accepts, he is not pleased. Low-budget independent production is a bit obvious and slow moving in some respects, much more sophisticated in others. The details of everyday life are well observed and ring true. Editing is zippy and the characters are treated seriously. **90m/C; DVD.** Billie James; Keskhemnu; ***D:*** H.H. Cooper; ***W:*** H.H. Cooper; ***C:*** Douglas W. Shannon; ***M:*** Michael Bearden.

The Arrival 1/2 *Shockwave* **1996 (PG-13)** Radio astronomer Zane (Sheen) picks up a message from deep space and discovers a planned alien invasion. When he brings evidence of such to his boss Gordian (Silver) he finds himself on the run from both government operatives and morphing aliens. Starts off slow, but an intelligent script and premise makes this a grade above cheesy. The aliens, with their kooky flaps of skin and back bending knees, are fun to watch. Directorial debut for Twohy. **109m/C; VHS, DVD.** Charlie Sheen; Ron Silver; Lindsay Crouse; Teri Polo; ***D:*** David N. Twohy; ***W:*** David N. Twohy; ***C:*** Hiro Narita; ***M:*** Arthur Kempel.

Arrival **2016 (PG-13)** Director Villeneuve's sci-fi drama is remarkably ambitious, carried by one of the best performances of Adams' career. Adams plays a linguist, a surprisingly important person when an alien race lands on Earth with no obvious means of communication. What do they want? How can we convey our intentions? Villeneuve's film is a thought-provoking sci-fi movie that's more concerned with deeply human issues like how we get along with one another and how much pain we're willing to endure for brief happiness. **116m/C; DVD, Blu-Ray.** Amy Adams; Jeremy Renner; Forest Whitaker; Michael Stuhlbarg; Mark O'Brien; ***D:*** Denis Villeneuve; ***W:*** Eric Heisserer; ***C:*** Bradford Young; ***M:*** Johann Johannsson. Oscars '16: Sound FX Editing; British Acad. '16: Sound; Writers Guild '16: Adapt. Screenplay.

The Arrival 2 *The Second Arrival* **1998 (R)** Computer programmer Muldoon receives information describing an extraterrestrial conspiracy against earth. Dull story, dull cast. **101m/C; VHS, DVD.** Patrick Muldoon; Michael Sarrazin; Jane Sibbett; ***D:*** Kevin S. Tenney; ***W:*** Mark David Perry; ***C:*** Bruno Philip; ***M:*** Ned Bouhalassa. **VIDEO**

Arrowhead 1/2 **1953** A long-running argument between a tough Cavalry scout and an Apache chief pits the cowboys against the Indians in this western fantasy. The personal battles that become all-out wars turn back to fist-fights before the matter is finally settled. **105m/C; VHS, DVD.** Charlton Heston; Jack Palance; Katy Jurado; Brian Keith; Milburn Stone; ***D:*** Charles Marquis Warren; ***C:*** Ray Rennahan.

Arrowsmith 1/2 **1931** A small-town medical researcher battles his conscience as he juggles his selfish and unselfish motivations for the work he does. He travels to the West Indies to confront the issues of his life and come to terms with himself once and for all. A talented cast takes their time. Based on the classic Sinclair Lewis novel. Two edited versions available (99 and 89 minutes), both of which delete much of Loy. **95m/B; DVD.** Ronald Colman; Helen Hayes; Myrna Loy; ***D:*** John Ford; ***W:*** Sidney Howard; ***C:*** Ray June; ***M:*** Alfred Newman.

Arsenal **1929** Classic Russian propagandist drama about strikes affecting the Russian home front during WWI, marking Dovzhenko's first great achievement in the realm of Eisenstein and Pudovkin. Silent. **75m/B; Silent; VHS, DVD.** *RU* Semyon Svashenko; Luciano Albertini; ***D:*** Alexander Dovzhenko; ***W:*** Alexander Dovzhenko; ***C:*** Daniil Demutsky.

Arsenal 1/2 **2017 (R)** An uninspired crime drama centering on a small business owner trying to save his deadbeat brother from a violent crime boss. When Mikey (Schaech) is kidnapped by mobster Eddie King (Cage), JP (Grenier), a straight arrow with his own business, must figure out who has his brother and raise $35,000 for his ransom. JP feels he owes Mikey because of a childhood incident in which Mikey steered his younger brother away from harm. Many acts of bloody violence are interspersed with JP's work investigating his brother's disappearance. An unbalanced, muddled plot that limits Cage is but one of the film's many problems. **97m/C; DVD.** Nicolas Cage; John Cusack; Adrian Grenier; Johnathon Schaech; Lydia Hull; ***D:*** Steven C. Miller; ***W:*** Jason Mosberg; ***C:*** Brandon Cox; ***M:*** Ryan Franks; Scott Nickoley.

The Arsenal Stadium Mystery 1/2 **1939** Inspector Banks of Scotland Yard tracks down the killer of a football star in this clever but unassuming murder mystery. **85m/B; DVD.** *UK* Leslie Banks; Greta Gynt; Ian MacLean; Liane Linden; Anthony Bushell; Esmond Knight; ***D:*** Thorold Dickinson.

Arsene Lupin Returns 1/2 **1938** Having faked his death, the former jewel thief is living the life of a gentleman farmer. Despite his protests that he's retired, insurance detective Steve Emerson (William) is certain Lupin (Douglas) is behind the theft of a necklace owned by beautiful Lorraine De Grissac (Bruce). Played with more comic/mystery elements than 1932's "Arsene Lupin," which starred the Barrymore brothers. **81m/B; DVD.** Melvyn Douglas; Warren William; Virginia Bruce; John Halliday; Monty Woolley; Nat Pendleton; ***D:*** George Fitzmaurice; ***W:*** James Kevin McGuinness; George Harmon Coxe; Howard Emmett Rogers; ***C:*** George J. Folsey; ***M:*** Franz Waxman.

Arsenic and Old Lace 1/2 **1944** Set-bound but energetic adaptation of the classic Joseph Kesselring play. Easy-going drama critic Mortimer Brewster (Grant) is caught in a sticky situation when he learns of his aunts' favorite pastime. Apparently the kind, sweet, lonely spinsters lure gentlemen to the house and serve them elderberry wine with a touch of arsenic, then they bury the bodies in the cellar—a cellar which also serves as the Panama Canal for Mortimer's cousin (who thinks he's Theodore Roosevelt). Massey, as Brewster cousin Jonathan, and Lorre, as his plastic surgeon, excel in their sinister roles. One of the best madcap comedies of all time—a must-see. Shot in 1941 and released a wee bit later. **118m/B; VHS, DVD.** Cary Grant; Josephine Hull; Jean Adair; Raymond Massey; Jack Carson; Priscilla Lane; John Alexander; Edward Everett Horton; Peter Lorre; James Gleason; John Ridgely; ***D:*** Frank Capra; ***W:*** Julius J. Epstein; Philip G. Epstein; ***C:*** Sol Polito; ***M:*** Max Steiner.

Art Heist 1/2 **2005 (R)** The theft of a precious painting from a Barcelona art gallery causes art expert Sandra (Pompeo) to leave New York to work with Daniel (Folk), an old love interest, to investigate the crime. This doesn't sit well with her tough-guy ex-husband Bruce (Baldwin), an NYPD cop, who tracks Sandra down, only to find her in over her head with the menacing Russian mafia. **98m/C; VHS, DVD.** *SP* Ellen Pompeo; William Baldwin; Abel Folk; Simon Andreu; Ed Lauter; ***W:*** Diane Fine; Evan Spiliotopolos; ***C:*** Jacques Haitkin. **VIDEO**

Art House 1/2 **1998 (R)** Ray (O'Donahue) and his irritating pal Weston (irritating Hardwick) aspire to be filmmakers, but the road to success is blocked by rocky relationships, money problems, and lack of talent. The comic elements are fitfully funny but the image is so rough that only the most dedicated fans of low-budget ($200,000 according to the director) independent productions will be willing to stick with it. Those hoping to see a lot of Internet babe Weber will be disappointed. **89m/C; DVD.** Dan O'Donahue; Chris Hardwick; Luigi Amodeo; Rebecca McFarland; Adam Carolla; Cheryl Pollak; Amy Weber; ***D:*** Leigh Slawner; ***W:*** Dan O'Donahue; Leigh Slawner; ***C:*** Billy Beaird; ***M:*** Christopher Lennertz.

Art House **2016** A feature-length documentary look at the homes of 11 American artists. Exploring the handmade homes created by the artists themselves, the documentary considers how their aesthetic and use of building techniques from art practice impacted their building choices and expresses their spirt. Also examined is the nature of their individual expression and how living in the homes affected their art. **88m/C; DVD.** ***D:*** Don Freeman; ***C:*** Don Freeman; ***M:*** Jamie Rudolph. **VIDEO**

Art Machine **2012** Declan has had great success as a teenaged art prodigy but now he's old news. He's struggling to find something new to present, but seems stuck until he meets up with an art collective that includes Cassandra. Declan's inspired but the same can't be said for the movie, which is an uneasy satire that feels unfinished. **89m/C; DVD.** Joseph Cross; Jessica Szohr; Joey Lauren Adams; Damian Young; ***D:*** Doug Karr; ***W:*** Doug Karr; Nuno Viera Faustino; ***C:*** Adriana Correia; ***M:*** Mark Stephan Kondracki.

The Art of Dying **1990** A loony videophile decides to start staging productions of his all-time favorite scenes. Trouble is, his idea of a fabulous film moment calls for lots of blood and bile as he lures teenage runaways to his casting couch. Director Hauser stars as the cop who's none too impressed with the cinematic remakes, while cult favorite Pollard is his partner. If you like a little atmosphere and psychological depth in your slashers, you'll find this to be the stuff that populates film noir nightmares. **90m/C; VHS, DVD.** Wings Hauser; Michael J. Pollard; Sarah Douglas; Kathleen Kinmont; Sydney Lassick; Mitch Hara; Gary Werntz; ***D:*** Wings Hauser.

The Art of Getting By 1/2 *Homework* **2011 (PG-13)** Upper Manhattan prep school senior George (Highmore) is another rebel without a cause: privileged on paper, lonely in life. His life changes forever when he becomes friends with the like-minded Sally (Roberts), a beautiful yet troubled popular girl. This indie, coming of age story reads more as a self-important drama without any real, original substance. Inconsistent and shallow writing aside, Highmore and Roberts just don't have the magnetic presences that are vital to sell this. Teen angst flicks are a dime a dozen, and this one doesn't stand out. Debut of writer/director Wisesen. **84m/C; Blu-Ray.** Freddie Highmore; Emma Roberts; Michael Angarano; Elizabeth Reaser; Blair Underwood; Alicia Silverstone; Sam Robards; Rita Wilson; ***D:*** Gavin Wiesen; ***W:*** Gavin Wiesen; ***C:*** Ben Kutchins; ***M:*** Alec Puro.

The Art of Murder **1999 (R)** Married Elizabeth (Pacula) has a wealthy hubby (Moriarty) and a younger lover (Kesnter) to keep her motor running. But then sleazy Willie (Onorati) threatens to show her husband dirty pictures of the affair and blackmail is just the beginning. **97m/C; VHS, DVD.** Joanna Pacula; Michael Moriarty; Boyd Kestner; Peter Onorati; ***D:*** Ruben Preuss; ***W:*** Anthony Stark; ***C:*** John Tarver. **VIDEO**

The Art of Racing in the Rain 1/2 **2019 (PG)** Denny (Ventimiglia) is an aspiring race car driver who adopts Enzo (voiced by Costner) as a puppy. As Denny marries Eve (Seyfried) and becomes a father to Zoe (Armstrong), Enzo becomes a beloved member of the family and tries to help when there is stress and conflict. At the same time, Enzo enjoys watching racing with Denny and trips to the track where he races. Based on the best-selling book by race car driver Garth Stein, it's a nice insight into how a devoted dog views its owner but is too overly sentimental and the dog narration too grandiose. **109m/C; DVD.** Kevin Costner; Milo Ventimiglia; Amanda Seyfried; Ryan Kiera Armstrong; Ian Lake; ***D:*** Simon Curtis; ***W:*** Mark Bomback; ***C:*** Ross Emery; ***M:*** Volker Bertelmann; Dustin O'Halloran.

The Art of Self-Defense **2019 (R)** Accountant Casey Davies (Eisenberg) is timid and bland, and is most comfortable at home with his sweet dachshund. One night, he goes out to buy dog food and is robbed by a gang of helmeted motorcyclists. Though Casey willingly gives up his wallet, he is badly beaten. As he recovers, he decides to take karate lessons to protect himself. When Casey walks into dojo owned by Sensei (Nivola), he discovers acceptance and a new sense of self—at an unexpected price. The dark satirical comedy is an effective exploration of toxic masculinity and features inspired performances by the cast, especially Eisnberg and Nivola. **104m/C; DVD, Blu-Ray.** Jesse Eisenberg; Alessandro Nivola; Imogen Poots; Steve Terada; Phillip Andre Botello; *D:* Riley Stearns; *W:* Riley Stearns; *C:* Michael Ragen; *M:* Heather McIntosh.

The Art of the Steal **2013 (R)** A fitfully amusing, overly complicated crime comedy held together by Russell's enjoyable performance as semi-reformed art thief Crunch Calhoun. The ex-con is working as a low-rent motorcycle daredevil when he reluctantly agrees to a heist with his untrustworthy brother, Nicky (Dillon). The plan is to steal a rare book from a Niagara Falls border customs station but eager Interpol agent Bick's (Jones) out to stop them with Stamp delightfully disdainful as the thief coerced into helping him. **90m/C; DVD, Blu-Ray.** *CA* Kurt Russell; Matt Dillon; Jay Baruchel; Kenneth Welsh; Terence Stamp; Jason Jones; Katheryn Winnick; Chris Diamantopoulos; *D:* Jonathan Sobol; *W:* Jonathan Sobol; *C:* Adam Swica; *M:* Grayson Matthews.

The Art of Travel **2008 (R)** When Conner Layne (Masterson) finds his fiancee cheating, he dumps her at the altar and takes off for a solo Central American honeymoon. First he gets robbed, but then he's befriended by adventure junkies Darlene (Burns) and Christopher (Messner), who are planning to cross Darien Gap, 100 miles of roadless jungle separating Panama and Columbia. They invite Conner along and he's soon hooked on the travel and decides not to stop. **101m/C; DVD, On Demand.** Christopher K. Masterson; Brooke Burns; Johnny Messner; James Duval; Angelika Baran; Jake Muxworthy; Maria Conchita Alonso; Shalim Ortiz; *D:* Thomas Whelan; *W:* Thomas Whelan; Brian LaBelle; *C:* Lawson Deming; *M:* Steve Bartek.

The Art of War **1/2 2000 (R)** Disappointingly formulaic thriller has Snipes starring as top-secret U.N. operative Neil Shaw, who is framed for the assassination of a Chinese ambassador (Hong). Also involved is his boss, Eleanor Hooks (Archer), Chinese power broker David Chan (Tagawa), and interpreter Julia (Matiko), whom Shaw kidnaps to help him prove his innocence. Plot is both convoluted and obvious (you can pretty much guess what's coming) and you learn so little about the players that you won't be very interested in what happens to them. **117m/C; VHS, DVD, Blu-Ray.** Wesley Snipes; Marie Matiko; Cary-Hiroyuki Tagawa; Anne Archer; Maury Chaykin; Michael Biehn; Donald Sutherland; Liliana Komorowska; James Hong; *D:* Christian Duguay; *W:* Wayne Beach; Simon Davis Barry; *C:* Pierre Gill; *M:* Normand Corbeil.

Art of War 2: The Betrayal **2008 (R)** Dull plot isn't even redeemed by any good action and everyone looks bored. Neil Shaw (Snipes) is called out of retirement by his friend Garret (Munro), a senatorial candidate. Seems senators with oversight on defense spending are either being blackmailed or killed and Garret doesn't want to wind up a statistic. **103m/C; DVD.** Wesley Snipes; Lochlyn Munro; Athena Karkanis; Winston Rekert; Clifford W. Stewart; Ryan McDonald; *D:* Josef Rusnak; *W:* Jason Bourque; Keith Shaw; *C:* Neil Cerrin; *M:* Peter Allen. **VIDEO**

The Art of War 3: Retribution **1/2** *Intervention* **2008 (R)** Agent Shaw is on a mission to prevent North Korean terrorists from obtaining a nuclear bomb. Framed for murder and hunted on the streets, Shaw has to stop the terrorists before they can detonate the bomb at a U.N. peace conference. **88m/C; DVD.** Treach; Sung Hi Lee; Warren DeRosa; *D:* Gerry Lively; *W:* Joe Halpin; *C:* Suki Medencevic; *M:* James Bairian; Louis Castle. **VIDEO**

Art School Confidential **2006 (R)** Underdeveloped and frequently flat satire about the art world. Idealistic Jerome (Minghella) wants to be the next Picasso when he enters art school. He soon learns it's not about art, it's about hype and commerce. Generic character types include pretentious professor Sandiford (Malkovich), no-talent filmmaker Vince (Suplee), shallow-but-beautiful artists' model Audrey (Myles), drunken failed artist Jimmy (Broadbent), and Jerome's own cynical guide Bardo (Moore). Jerome becomes disillusioned and desperate, and not just because a serial killer is working the neighborhood. Clowes adapted from his comic strip. Buscemi is uncredited as trendy restaurant owner Broadway Bob. **102m/C; DVD, Blu-Ray.** Max Minghella; Sophia Myles; John Malkovich; Jim Broadbent; Matt Keeslar; Ethan Suplee; Anjelica Huston; Joel David Moore; Nick Swardson; Steve Buscemi; *D:* Terry Zwigoff; *W:* Daniel Clowes; *C:* Jamie Anderson; *M:* David Kitay.

Artemisia **1997 (R)** Artemisia (Cervi) is the teenaged daughter of well-known artist Orazio Gentileschi (Serrault), who encourages her artistic pursuits. He bullies the local art academy to admit Artemisia, a no-no in 17th-century Rome, and she even tries the forbidden territory of the male nude. Soon her artistic passion is matched by a sexual passion for fellow artist Agostino Tassi (Manojlovic), but this time her father isn't so understanding and Artemisia becomes the center of a rape trial. The real Artemisia is considered to be the first known female artist. French with subtitles. **95m/C; VHS, DVD.** *FR* Valentina Cervi; Michel Serrault; Miki (Predrag) Manojlovic; Luca Zingaretti; Brigitte Catillon; Frederic Pierrot; Maurice Garrel; Yann Tregouet; Jacques Nolot; *D:* Agnes Merlet; *W:* Agnes Merlet; *C:* Benoit Delhomme; *M:* Krishna Levy.

Arthur **1981 (PG)** Spoiled, alcoholic billionaire Moore stands to lose everything he owns when he falls in love with a waitress. He must choose between wealth and a planned marriage, or poverty and love. Surprisingly funny, with an Oscar for Gielgud as Moore's valet, and great performance from Minnelli. Arguably the best role Moore's ever had, and he makes the most of it, taking the one-joke premise to a Oscar nomination. **97m/C; VHS, DVD.** Dudley Moore; Liza Minnelli; John Gielgud; Geraldine Fitzgerald; Stephen Elliott; Jill Eikenberry; Lou Jacobi; Ted Ross; Barney Martin; *D:* Steve Gordon; *W:* Steve Gordon; *C:* Fred Schuler; *M:* Burt Bacharach; Peter Allen; *M:* Peter Allen. Oscars '81: Song ("Arthur's Theme"), Support. Actor (Gielgud); Golden Globes '82: Actor--Mus./Comedy (Moore), Film--Mus./Comedy, Song ("Arthur's Theme"), Support. Actor (Gielgud); L.A. Film Critics '81: Support. Actor (Gielgud); N.Y. Film Critics '81: Support. Actor (Gielgud); Writers Guild '81: Orig. Screenplay.

Arthur **2011 (PG-13)** Controversial funnyman Brand takes over the title role that Dudley Moore made famous in 1981. Arthur Bach is the punch-drunk zillionaire content with partying and always picking up the check. However, his controlling mother informs him that he'll be marrying rich young woman Susan (Garner) and finding a job to maintain the inheritance. All this just as he meets working girl Naomi (Gerwig), a woman with soul. Mirren puts more muscle into the part of the playboy's caretaker, previously filled by Arthur's aloof brother. A fairly faithful adaptation, with Brand never going over-the-top or doing a Moore impression. **110m/C; Blu-Ray, On Demand.** Russell Brand; Greta Gerwig; Jennifer Garner; Dame Helen Mirren; Nick Nolte; Geraldine James; Leslie Hendrix; Luis Guzman; *D:* Jason Winer; *W:* Peter Baynham; *C:* Uta Briesewitz; *M:* Theodore Shapiro.

Arthur 2: On the Rocks **1/2 1988 (PG)** When Arthur finally marries his sweetheart, it may not be "happily ever after" because the father of the girl he didn't marry is out for revenge. When Arthur discovers that he is suddenly penniless, a bit of laughter is the cure for the blues and also serves well when the liquor runs out. A disappointing sequel with few laughs. **113m/C; VHS, DVD.** Dudley Moore; Liza Minnelli; John Gielgud; Geraldine Fitzgerald; Stephen Elliott; Ted Ross; Barney Martin; Jack Gilford; *D:* Bud Yorkin; *W:* Andy Breckman; *C:* Stephen Burum; *M:* Burt Bacharach. Golden Raspberries '87: Worst Actress (Minnelli).

Arthur and the Invisibles *Arthur et les Minimoys* **2006 (PG)** Maybe it makes sense to the French. Besson tackles kiddie fantasy in this mishmash combo of CGI and live-action. Arthur (Highmore) lives with his grandma (Farrow), who is about to lose their debt-ridden home. Arthur needs to follow clues left by grandpa to some rubies hidden in the land of the Minimoys, who look like fairies and happen to live in the backyard. A little hocus-pocus, and Arthur becomes mini, gets some help from the inhabitants, and goes after the gems, which are held by evil Maltazard (Bowie). Film's voices are frequently out of sync (it was dubbed from French) and since it's remarkably talky, this is a notable distraction (at least to adult eyes). **102m/C; DVD.** *FR* Freddie Highmore; Mia Farrow; Adam LeFevre; Douglas Rand; Penny Balfour; *V:* David Bowie; Madonna; Jimmy Fallon; Robert De Niro; Anthony Anderson; Chazz Palminteri; Snoop Dogg; Jason Bateman; Harvey Keitel; Emilio Estevez; *D:* Luc Besson; *W:* Luc Besson; Celine Garcia; *C:* Thierry Arbogast; *M:* Éric Serra.

Arthur Christmas **1/2 2011 (PG)** Charming 3D animated Christmas fare from Aardman studios. Santa's youngest son, klutzy and kind Arthur, just loves the holiday and is in charge of the Letters to Santa department. However, Santa is now a figurehead as his impatient elder son Steve has turned the North Pole into a high-tech operation and is dismissive when one present gets left behind. Arthur is horrified and decides to personally deliver Gwen's bicycle (she wrote a letter, after all) aboard their old-fashioned wooden sleigh, accompanied by his opinionated Grandsanta and elf Bronwyn. **97m/C; DVD, Blu-Ray.** *US UK V:* James McAvoy; Hugh Laurie; Jim Broadbent; Bill Nighy; Imelda Staunton; Ashley Jensen; *D:* Sarah Smith; *W:* Sarah Smith; Peter Baynham.

Arthur Hailey's The Moneychangers *The Moneychangers* **1976** Corporate potboiler from Hailey shown as an NBC miniseries. A bank president steps down and leaves the board to choose his successor. Smooth-talking Alex Vandervoort (Douglas) has a rabble-rousing lawyer lover, Margot (Flannery), who wants to change bank policies. His rival, conservative Roscoe Heyward (Plummer), gets involved in a shady business deal and with high-end escort, Avril (Collins). There's also a number of subplots involving embezzlement and other questionable practices. **320m/C; DVD.** Kirk Douglas; Christopher Plummer; Anne Bancroft; Ralph Bellamy; Timothy Bottoms; Joan Collins; Susan Flannery; Robert Loggia; Jean Peters; *D:* Boris Sagal; *W:* Dean Riesner; Stanford Whitmore; *C:* Joseph Biroc; *M:* Henry Mancini. **TV**

Arthur's Quest **1/2 1999 (PG)** In this switcheroo on Mark Twain's "A Connecticut Yankee in King Arthur's Court" a five-year-old Arthur is transported by Merlin from his medieval home to the modern age because the wizard fears for the boy's safety. Merlin doesn't reappear for 10 years, so Arthur has become a typical American teen. Now, how do you convince a 15-year-old that he's really a medieval monarch who must return to save Camelot? **91m/C; VHS, DVD, On Demand.** Kevin Elston; Zach Galligan; Arye Gross; Clint Howard; Brion James; Katie Johnston; Neil Mandt; *D:* Neil Mandt. **VIDEO**

Article 99 **1992 (R)** Doctors in a Kansas City Veteran's Administration hospital try to heal patients while putting up with bureaucratic red tape and a stingy administrator. When rogue physician Sturgess (Liotta) is dismissed, the patients hold a siege. Sort of son of "M.A.S.H." (Big Daddy Sutherland did Hawkeye) that gets its title from a fictional rule that says veterans can be treated only for conditions related to military service. Erstwhile cast labors to combine comedic and dramatic intentions of script. **100m/C; VHS, DVD.** Ray Liotta; Kiefer Sutherland; Forest Whitaker; Lea Thompson; John C. McGinley; John Mahoney; Keith David; Kathy Baker; Eli Wallach; Noble Willingham; Julie Bovasso; Troy Evans; Lynne Thigpen; Jeffrey Tambor; Rutanya Alda; *D:* Howard Deutch; *W:* Ron Cutler; *C:* Rick Bota; *M:* Danny Elfman.

Artifacts *Artefacts* **2008 (R)** A young blonde has just broken up with her boyfriend to devote herself to her work. Then all her friends get murdered by their own look-alikes, and the boyfriend suddenly doesn't look so bad. Oh, and they both have the same weird chest implant that all their dead friends have. Is it the aliens? Is it the government? Will the boyfriend get wise and ditch her when he realizes he's being used as a meat shield? **75m/C; DVD.** Mary Stockley; Cecile Boland; Max Digby; Jason Morell; Felix Scott; Martin Swabey; Veronique Van de Ven; *D:* Giles Daoust; Emmanuel Jespers; *W:* Giles Daoust; Emmanuel Jespers; *C:* Bernard Vervoort; *M:* Ernst Meinrath. **VIDEO**

The Artist **2011 (PG-13)** A brilliant hybrid of homage to the golden age of Hollywood while also being a film that could, with only few alterations, have been released in the silent film era as well. George Valentin (Dujardin) refuses to give in to the next wave of cinema as talkies threaten to make the silent film star irrelevant. As his star falls, that of the stunning newcomer (Bejo) he discovered rises. The risky artistic decision to make a '20s silent film in 2011 pays off for director Hazanavicius, as the result is a delightful, alluring comedy that works on multiple levels. **100m/B; Silent; DVD, Blu-Ray.** *FR* Jean Dujardin; Berenice Bejo; John Goodman; James Cromwell; Penelope Ann Miller; Missi Pyle; Malcolm McDowell; Beth Grant; Ed Lauter; Ken Davitian; *D:* Michel Hazanavicius; *W:* Michel Hazanavicius; *C:* Guillaume Schiffman; *M:* Ludovic Bource. Oscars '11: Actor (Dujardin), Costume Des., Director (Hazanavicius), Film, Orig. Score; British Acad. '11: Actor (Dujardin), Cinematog., Costume Des., Director (Hazanavicius), Film, Orig. Score, Orig. Screenplay, Sound; Directors Guild '11: Director (Hazanavicius); Golden Globes '12: Actor--Mus./Comedy (Dujardin), Film--Mus./Comedy, Orig. Score; Ind. Spirit '12: Actor (Dujardin), Cinematog., Director (Hazanavicius), Film; Screen Actors Guild '11: Actor (Dujardin).

Artists and Models **1937** Mac Brewster's (Benny) struggling advertising agency lands a big ad campaign for Townsend Silver, and Mac promises his client that their spokesmodel will be queen of the Artists and Models Ball. But Alan Townsend (Arlen) rejects Mac's model girlfriend Paula (Lupino) because he wants someone from the social register. An angry Paula pretends to be a debutante while numerous variety acts perform at the event. Followed by "Artists and Models Abroad." **97m/B; DVD.** Jack Benny; Ida Lupino; Richard Arlen; Gail Patrick; Ben Blue; *D:* Raoul Walsh; *W:* Francis Martin; Walter DeLeon; *C:* Victor Milner; *M:* Victor Young.

Artists and Models **1/2 1955** Martin is a struggling comic book artist and Lewis his idiot roommate. The pair become mixed up in both romance and intrigue when Lewis begins talking in his sleep about spys and such. One of the duo's more pleasant cinematic outings. **109m/C; DVD.** Dean Martin; Jerry Lewis; Shirley MacLaine; Dorothy Malone; Eddie Mayehoff; Eva Gabor; Anita Ekberg; George Winslow; Jack Elam; Herbert Rudley; Nick Castle; *D:* Frank Tashlin; *W:* Frank Tashlin; Hal Kanter; Herbert Baker; *C:* Daniel F. Fapp.

Artists and Models Abroad **1/2 1938** Tedious in-name-only sequel to 1937's "Artists and Models." Buck Boswell (Benny) and his all-girl troupe of entertainers are stranded in Paris. Buck gets them jobs as fashion models, including newcomer Patricia Harper (Bennett), who's just pretending to be penniless as is her wealthy father James (Grapewin). The truth comes out when Buck's financial problems multiply. May be of some interest for the fashions on display from then-current French designers. **90m/B; DVD.** Jack Benny; Joan Bennett; Charley Grapewin; Mary Boland; Joyce Compton; Fritz Feld; Monty Woolley; *D:* Mitchell Leisen; *W:* Ken Englund; Howard Lindsay; *C:* Ted Tetzlaff.

As Above, So Below **1/2 2014 (R)** There are miles and miles of catacombs underneath one of the most beautiful cities in the world, Paris. Upon all that life, death sits below. A group of explorers goes to explore these darkened chambers and uncover a dark secret about them and the city. While the Parisian catacombs may seem like the perfect setting for a psychological horror flick, director Dowdle can't pull it off, opting for cheap scares and shaky camera tricks. There are some decent scenes and performances, but not enough for more than hardcore horror nuts. **93m/C; DVD, Blu-Ray.** Perdita Weeks; Ben Feldman; Edwin Hodge; Francois Civil; Marion Lambert; Ali Marhyar; *D:* John Erick Dowdle; *W:* John Erick Dowdle; Drew Dowdle; *C:* Leo Hinstin; *M:* Keefus Ciancia.

As Cool As I Am **2013 (R)** Clunky, melodramatic coming-of-age drama. Teen Lucy (Bolger) is realizing her parents, who had her when they were teenagers, have yet to become grown-ups. Lainee (Danes) suffers the effects of a long-distance marriage to lumberjack husband Chuck (Marsden) and the tension is affecting Lucy, who starts acting out. She and best friend Kenny (Mann) start experimenting sexually, which shocks their parents and causes more problems, especially for Lucy. **93m/C; DVD, Blu-Ray, Streaming.** Sarah Bolger; Claire Danes; James Marsden; Thomas Mann; Jeremy Sisto; Jon Tenney; Peter Fonda; Anika Noni Rose; ***D:*** Max Mayer; ***W:*** Virginia Korus Spragg; ***C:*** Tim Suhrstedt; ***M:*** Christopher Lennertz.

As Goes Janesville 🦴🦴 1/2 **2012** This insightful, feature-length documentary provides a look at the impact of the Great Recession on individuals in Janesville, Wisconsin, the home of the 2008 vice presidential candidate Paul Ryan. Following them from 2008 to 2011, the subjects of the documentary have been directly impacted by major events in their community, state, and country. That year, bankrupt General Motors shut down their plant in Janesville after a century and local business leaders vowed to bring companies by partnering with the union-busting governor Scott Walker. In all, the film offers a cautionary perspective for the rest of the country on these issues and those affected by them. **88m/C; DVD, Streaming, Download.** ***D:*** Brad Lichtenstein; ***W:*** Leslie Simmer; ***C:*** Brad Lichtenstein; ***M:*** Vernon Reid. **VIDEO**

As Good As Dead 🦴 1/2 **2010 (R)** Grisly and confusing revenge thriller. New York journalist Ethan is held captive in his apartment and tortured by Southern Christian extremists who somehow believe he's responsible for the murder of their leader 10 years earlier. They try to force Ethan to confess but they may just have the wrong man. **92m/C; DVD.** Cary Elwes; Andie MacDowell; Frank Whaley; Matt Dallas; Jess Weixler; Brian Cox; Nicole Ansari; ***D:*** Jonathan Mossek; ***W:*** Eve Pomerance; Erez Mossek; ***C:*** Frank Barrera; ***M:*** Greg Arnold. **VIDEO**

As Good As It Gets 🦴🦴🦴 *Old Friends* **1997 (PG-13)** Entertaining and enjoyable outing from Brooks racked up an impressive list of Oscar noms (including Best Picture). Obsessive-compulsive romance novelist Melvin Udall (Nicholson) is also the meanest guy in New York, liked by nobody and hating all. The only exception is single-mother/waitress Carol (Hunt), who puts up with his annoying habits at the local restaurant where he dines. Forced to look after gay neighbor Kinnear's fussy-but-cute dog, Udall falls into an improbable quest for love, friendship, and a life as "normal as it gets" in this sort of extended-sitcom universe. Snappy dialogue by Brooks and co-writer Andrus, and an easy-going non-stereotypical performance by Kinnear are highlights, almost overshadowing both Hunt's Jodie Foster-like portrayal, and Nicholson's typical but delightful role (both of which won Oscars). **130m/C; VHS, DVD, Blu-Ray.** Jack Nicholson; Helen Hunt; Greg Kinnear; Cuba Gooding, Jr.; Skeet Ulrich; Shirley Knight; Yeardley Smith; Lupe Ontiveros; Bibi Osterwald; Brian Doyle-Murray; Randall Batinkoff; Missi Pyle; Shane Black; Tara Subkoff; Danielle Brisebois; Harold Ramis; Jimmy Workman; ***Cameo(s):*** Lawrence Kasdan; Todd Solondz; Tom McGowan; ***D:*** James L. Brooks; ***W:*** Mark Andrus; James L. Brooks; ***C:*** John Bailey; ***M:*** Hans Zimmer. Oscars '97: Actor (Nicholson), Actress (Hunt); Golden Globes '98: Actor--Mus./Comedy (Nicholson), Actress--Mus./Comedy (Hunt), Film--Mus./Comedy; Natl. Bd. of Review '97: Actor (Nicholson), Support. Actor (Kinnear); Screen Actors Guild '97: Actor (Nicholson), Actress (Hunt); Writers Guild '97: Orig. Screenplay; Broadcast Film Critics '97: Actor (Nicholson).

As It Is In Heaven 🦴🦴 **2004** Well-known conductor Daniel Dareas returns to his northern Swedish village after a breakdown and is asked to give advice to the church choir. He's soon assuming the task of choirmaster and the group improves so much they are chosen for a prestigious competition. However, Daniel's role stirs up past jealousies and the problems of the isolated community as well as religious belief and romance. Swedish with subtitles. **132m/C; DVD.** *SW* Michael Nyqvist; Frida Hallgren; Ingela Olsson; Niklas Falk; Lennart Jahkel; Helen Sjoholm; ***D:*** Kay Pollak; ***W:*** Kay Pollak; ***C:*** Harald Gunnar Paalgard; ***M:*** Stefan Nilsson.

As Tears Go By 🦴🦴🦴 *Wong gok ka moon; Carmen of the Streets; Wang jiao ka men* **1988** A young gangster is visited by his pretty young cousin from the country because she needs medical treatment for her lung problems. He begins to fall for her but this is complicated by his unstable friend who has a habit of angering mob bosses. Soon he finds himself roped into a scheme to assassinate a witness before he can testify, in order to apologize for his friends' mistakes. **102m/C; DVD.** *CH* Andy Lau; Maggie Cheung; Jacky Cheung; ***D:*** Kar-Wai Wong; ***W:*** Kar-Wai Wong; ***C:*** Wai Keung (Andrew) Lau; ***M:*** Teddy Robin Kwan; Ting Yat Chung.

As You Like It 🦴🦴 1/2 **1936** A Duke's banished daughter poses as a man to win the attentions of one of her father's attendants in this highly stylized Shakespearean comedy adapted by J.M. Barrie and Robert Cullen. Early Shakespearean Olivier. **96m/B; VHS, DVD.** *GB* Elisabeth Bergner; Laurence Olivier; Henry Ainley; Felix Aylmer; ***D:*** Paul Czinner; ***W:*** J.M. Barrie; Robert Cullen; ***C:*** Jack Cardiff; Harold Rosson; ***M:*** William Walton.

As You Like It 🦴🦴 1/2 **2006 (PG)** Branagh sets this version of Shakespeare's romantic fantasy in 18th-century Japan with a group of Europeans who live in a trade colony. Because of a family conflict, Rosalind (Howard) and her entourage are forced to flee into the enchanted forest of Arden. Disguising herself (fetchingly unconvincingly) as a boy, Rosalind then proceeds to confuse the heck out of would-be love interest Orlando (Oyelowo). Kline is along as the melancholy Jacques with the "all the world's a stage" speech. **135m/C; DVD.** Bryce Dallas Howard; David Oyelowo; Kevin Kline; Alfred Molina; Adrian Lester; Brian Blessed; Janet McTeer; Romola Garia; Jade Jefferies; ***D:*** Kenneth Branagh; ***W:*** Kenneth Branagh; ***C:*** Roger Lanser; ***M:*** Patrick Doyle. **CABLE**

As Young As You Feel 🦴🦴🦴 **1951** A 65-year-old man is forced to retire from his job. He poses as the head of the conglomerate and convinces them to repeal their retirement policy. He then gains national publicity when he makes a speech about the dignity of man. Watch for Monroe as the boss's secretary. Fine comic performances enhance the script; based on a story by Chayefsky. **77m/C; VHS, DVD.** Monty Woolley; Thelma Ritter; David Wayne; Jean Peters; Constance Bennett; Marilyn Monroe; Allyn Joslyn; Albert Dekker; Clinton Sundberg; Minor Watson; ***D:*** Harmon Jones; ***W:*** Paddy Chayefsky.

The Ascent 🦴🦴🦴 *Voskhozhdeniye* **1976** During WWII, two Soviet partisans leave their comrades in order to obtain supplies from a nearby farm. Only the Germans have gotten there first, forcing the Soviets deeper into occupied territory, which leads to their eventual capture and interrogation. Russian with subtitles. **105m/B; VHS, DVD.** *RU* Boris Plotnikov; Vladimir Gostyukhin; ***D:*** Larisa Shepitko; ***W:*** Larisa Shepitko; Yuri Klepikov; ***C:*** Pavel Lebeshev; Vladimir Chukhnov; ***M:*** Alfred Schnittke.

Ash Is Purest White 🦴🦴🦴 *Jiang hu er nü* **2018** At the turn of the twentieth century, Qiao (Zhao) saves a local gangster Bin (Liao) from a brutal beating by youths as part of a larger turf war. For her efforts, she is sent to prison for five years. When Qiao leaves prison, it is 2006 and she takes a boat to find Bin. Along the way, she is robbed and deceived by those nearby. Qiao mourns the loss of a way of life, which greatly impacts her actions in 2018. The time-hopping drama successfully explores the changes in China through the lives of these somewhat tragic characters. Mandarin with subtitles. **136m/C; DVD, Blu-Ray.** Tao Zhao; Fan Liao; Yi'nan Diao; Xuan Li; Casper Liang; ***D:*** Zhangke Jia; ***W:*** Zhangke Jia; ***C:*** Eric Gautier; ***M:*** Giong Lim.

Ash Wednesday 🦴 **1973 (R)** Taylor endures the pain of cosmetic surgery in an effort to rescue her floundering union with Fonda. Another undistinguished performance by Liz. Fonda is especially slimy as the philandering husband, but only appears in the latter stages of the film. **99m/C; VHS, DVD, Streaming.** Elizabeth Taylor; Henry Fonda; Helmut Berger; Keith Baxter; Margaret Blye; Maurice Teynac; Monique Van Vooren; ***D:*** Larry Peerce; ***M:*** Maurice Jarre.

Ash Wednesday 🦴🦴 **2002 (R)** On Ash Wednesday, 1983, ex-Hell's Kitchen tough Francis Sullivan (Burns) is working in his bar when his younger brother Sean (Wood) suddenly turns up. Three years ago to the day, Sean killed some thugs after his bro and went into exile, allowing everyone to think he was dead, including his wife Grace (Dawson). In the intervening time, Grace and Francis have become more than just in-laws. Oh, and gangster Moran (Platt) still wants revenge on Sean for killing his goons. The penance references are all too obvious and Wood's an odd casting choice since he looks too young and innocent for his role. **98m/C; VHS, DVD.** Edward Burns; Elijah Wood; Rosario Dawson; Oliver Platt; Pat McNamara; James Handy; Michael Mulheren; Malachy McCourt; ***D:*** Edward Burns; ***W:*** Edward Burns; ***C:*** Russell Fine; ***M:*** David Shire.

Ashanti, Land of No Mercy 🦴🦴 *Ashanti* **1979** Caine of the week movie with Michael portraying a doctor acting as a missionary in South Africa who finds himself alone in a battle to rescue his wife from a band of slave traders. The chase spans many Middle Eastern countries and begins to look bleak for our man. Talented cast and promising plot are undone by slow pace. Based on the novel "Ebano" by Alberto Vasquez-Figueroa. **117m/C; VHS, DVD, Blu-Ray.** Michael Caine; Omar Sharif; Peter Ustinov; Rex Harrison; William Holden; Beverly Johnson; ***D:*** Richard Fleischer.

Ashes and Diamonds 🦴🦴🦴 1/2 *Popiol i Diament* **1958** In the closing days of WWII, young Polish resistance fighter Maciek (Cybulski) is sent to a small town to assassinate a Communist Party official. Waiting around in a hotel, Maciek romances the beautiful barmaid, Krystyna (Krzysewska), and questions the meaning of struggle. A seminal Eastern European masterpiece that defined a generation of pre-solidarity Poles. The last installment of the trilogy that includes "A Generation" and "Kanal" and based on a novel by Jerzy Andrzewski. Polish with subtitles. **105m/B; VHS, DVD.** *PL* Zbigniew Cybulski; Eva Krzyzewska; Adam Pawlikowski; Bogumil Kobiela; Waclaw Zastrzezynski; ***D:*** Andrzej Wajda; ***W:*** Andrzej Wajda; Jerzy Andrzejewski; ***C:*** Jerzy Wojcik; ***M:*** Jan Krenz; Filip Nowak.

Ashes and Embers 🦴🦴 **1982** A black Vietnam vet in Los Angeles has trouble fitting into society, eventually running afoul of the police. Ethiopian-born director Gerima endows vital subject matter with a properly alienated mood. **120m/C; VHS, DVD.** John Anderson; Evelyn Blackwell; ***D:*** Haile Gerima.

Ashes of Time 🦴🦴🦴 *Dung che sai duk* **1994** Mystical, brooding, and sumptiously lensed martial arts epic was filmed in mainland China, with respect paid to Sergio Leone. A swordsman, played by Tony Leung, is going blind and wants to see his wife one last time before the lights go out completely. Another, played by the other Tony Leung, possesses a magic wine that allows him to forget his haunted past. The two swordsmen are hired to kill and protect, respectively, the same person. The plot simmers and occasionally explodes into chaotic action peppered with sparkling geysers and such. **95m/C; DVD.** *CH* Tony Leung Chiu-Wai; Tony Leung Ka-Fai; Brigitte Lin; Jacky Cheung; Leslie Cheung; Maggie Cheung; Carina Lau; ***D:*** Wong Kar-Wai; ***W:*** Wong Kar-Wai; ***C:*** Christopher Doyle; ***M:*** Frankie Chan.

Ashes of Time Redux 🦴🦴 **2008 (R)** Hong Kong director Wong was never satisfied with his 1994 wuxia epic, feeling he didn't do his vision justice (though it originally took two years to film). Over the years the movie was subjected to various bootleg versions and the original negative was disintegrating, so Wong spent five years reassembling, restoring, color-correcting, and rescoring before releasing his updated cut. Not that the dense narrative is any easier to follow (though the subtitles are good). Set over five seasons, Ouyang (Cheung), disappointed that his true love married his brother, moves to the desert and becomes a middleman for those who want to hire a swordsman to settle a wrong. Chinese with subtitles. **93m/C; Blu-Ray, On Demand.** *CH* Leslie Cheung; Maggie Cheung; Brigitte Lin; Carina Lau; Tony Leung Ka-Fai; Jacky Cheung; Tony Leung Chiu-Wai; ***D:*** Wong Kar-Wai; ***W:*** Wong Kar-Wai; ***C:*** Christopher Doyle; ***M:*** Wu Tong.

Ashik Kerib 🦴🦴🦴 *The Lovelorn Minstrel; The Hoary Legends of the Caucasus* **1988** Ashik Kerib is a wandering minstrel who is rejected by a rich merchant as his daughter's suitor. He then journeys for 1,000 days trying to earn enough money to marry his beloved. Along the way he's imprisoned by an evil sultan and rides a flying horse, among other adventures. Wonderful use of exotic makeup and costumes highlight this Arabian Nights tale. Adapted from a story by Mikhail Lermontov. Paradjanov's last film. In Russian with English subtitles. **75m/C; VHS, DVD.** *RU* Yiur Mgoyan; Veronkia Metonidze; Levan Natroshvili; Sofiko Chiaureli; ***D:*** Dodo Abashidze; Sergei Paradjanov; ***W:*** Giya Badridze; ***M:*** Djavashir Kuliev.

Ashura 🦴🦴 1/2 *Ashura-jo no hitomi; Blood Gets in your Eyes* **2005** Set in what appears to be 19th century Japan, this Kabuki play turned film is centered on the life of Izumo (Somegoro Ichikawa), a Demon Slayer who has retired to become an actor after accidentally killing a child. A former comrade has gone over to the dark side in his absence however, and he has become the lover of a demon looking to resurrect her Queen Ashura who is now in human form. They believe an amnesiac thief that Izumo has fallen in love with may be the one they are looking for, and the inevitable sword battles ensue. **119m/C; DVD.** *JP* Somegoro Ichikawa; Rie Miyazawa; Kanako Higuchi; Atsuro Watabe; Fumiyo Kohinata; Takashi Naito; ***D:*** Yojiro Takita; ***W:*** Sei Kawaguchi; Kazuki Nakashima; Masashi Todayama; ***C:*** Katsumi Yanagijima; ***M:*** Yoko Kanno.

Asian Connection 🦴 1/2 **2016 (R)** An action crime thriller centering on a couple seeking revenge on a drug lord. While robbing banks in Southeast Asia, Jack (Lee) and Sam (Gibson), the pair of Americans living abroad unknowingly swipe money from a drug lord, Gan (Seagal). Targeted by the drug lord, Sam is killed by them. Teaming up a romantic interest, Jack seeks revenge on those who murdered his partner in crime. **90m/C; DVD, Streaming, Download.** John Edward Lee; Byron Gibson; Steven Seagal; Michael Jai White; Pim Bubear; ***D:*** Daniel Zirilli; ***W:*** D. Glase Lomond; ***C:*** Orlando Herrera; ***M:*** Ali Helnwein.

Asian Stories 🦴 1/2 *Asian Stories: Book 3* **2006** Not particularly interesting story about a man who thinks he wants to die. Chinese-American Jim (Lee) has been dumped by his fiancee two weeks before their Valentine's Day wedding. Depressed and in debt, Jim asks his hitman best friend Alex (Kishita) to kill him and they decide to head off to a mountain cabin for some quiet contemplation under the condition that the deed must be done before the dreaded lovers' holiday. Think Jim will change his mind? **98m/C; DVD.** James Kyson Lee; Kirt Kishita; Kathy Uyen; ***D:*** Ron Oda; Kris Chin; ***W:*** Ron Oda; ***C:*** Jonathan Hall; ***M:*** Thomas' Apartment.

Ask a Policeman 🦴 1/2 **1938** The village of Turnbottom Round has been crime-free for so long that bumbling Sgt. Dudfoot (Hay) and his constables Brown (Moffatt) and Harbottle (Marriott) may soon be unemployed. The trio decides to stage some bogus crimes, only to uncover a real smuggling operation. **83m/B; DVD.** *GB* Will Hay; Graham Moffatt; Moore Marriott; Glennis Lorimer; Peter Gawthorne; Charles Oliver; ***D:*** Marcel Varnel; ***W:*** Val Guest; Marriott Edgar; ***C:*** Derick Williams.

Ask the Dust 🦴🦴 **2006 (R)** Chasing an aspiring novelist's dream in 1930s Los Angeles, Arturo Bandini (Farrell)--the son of Italian immigrants but desperate to leave his heritage behind—collides into a turbulent love/hate affair with Camilla (Hayek), a Latina waitress with her own agenda to quickly ascend the social ladder. When Arturo comes into money to write his book, their relationship oddly cools off, while later he struggles with what success has cost him. Taken from John Fantes' 1939 novel of the same name and highlighted by brilliant desert scenery shot in South Africa. **117m/C; DVD.** Colin Farrell; Salma Hayek; Donald Sutherland; Eileen Atkins; Idina Menzel; Justin Kirk; Jeremy Crutchley; Richard Schickel; ***D:*** Robert Towne; ***W:*** Robert Towne; ***C:*** Caleb Deschanel; ***M:*** Ramin Djawadi; Hector Pereira.

Aspen Extreme 🦴 **1993 (PG-13)** Former Aspen ski instructor writes and directs a movie on (what else?) ski instructors in (where?) Aspen! Long on ski shots and short on plot, this movie never leaves the bunny hill. Two Detroiters leave Motown for Snowtown to pursue a life on the slopes. T.J

(Gross) soon has his hands full with two beautiful women (Polo and Hughes) who encourage his dream of becoming a writer. His friend Dexter (Berg), however, acquires a few bad habits, and the whole movie just goes downhill from there. **128m/C; VHS, DVD, Blu-Ray.** Paul Gross; Peter Berg; Finola Hughes; Teri Polo; Martin Kemp; Nicolette Scorsese; William Russ; Will MacMillan; ***D:*** Patrick Hasburgh; ***W:*** Patrick Hasburgh; ***C:*** Steven Fierberg; ***M:*** Michael Convertino.

The Asphalt Jungle 1950 An aging criminal emerges from his forced retirement (prison) and assembles a gang for one final heist. Then things start to go awry. A very realistic story line and a superb cast make this one of the best crime films ever made. Highly acclaimed. **112m/B; VHS, DVD, Blu-Ray.** Sterling Hayden; Louis Calhern; Jean Hagen; James Whitmore; Sam Jaffe; John McIntire; Marc Lawrence; Barry Kelley; Anthony Caruso; Teresa Celli; Marilyn Monroe; Brad Dexter; Strother Martin; Dorothy Tree; ***D:*** John Huston; ***W:*** Ben Maddow; W.R. Burnett; ***M:*** Miklos Rozsa. Natl. Bd. of Review '50: Director (Huston); Natl. Film Reg. '08; Venice Film Fest. '50: Actor (Hayden).

The Asphyx *Spirit of the Dead* **1972 (PG)** Nineteenth century doctor Stephens is studying death when he discovers The Asphyx, an aura that surrounds a person just before they die. Stephens delves deeper into his research and finds the keys to immortality. However, his irresponsibility in unleashing the obscure supernatural power on the world brings a swarm of unforeseen and irreversible troubles. High-class sci fi. **98m/C; VHS, DVD, Blu-Ray.** *GB* Robert Stephens; Robert Powell; Jane Lapotaire; Alex Scott; Ralph Arliss; Fiona Walker; John Lawrence; Paul Bacon; Terry Scully; ***D:*** Peter Newbrook; ***W:*** Brian Comfort; ***C:*** Frederick A. (Freddie) Young; ***M:*** Bill McGuffie.

Ass Backwards 2013 An unfunny comedy about stupid people. Delusional Kate and Chloe are best friends who are about to be evicted from their New York apartment. Just then, they get an invitation to attend the 50th anniversary celebration of their hometown's children's beauty pageant where they were dual last-place finishers. The road trip consists of one calamity after another, before they arrive to get involved in even more ridiculousness. **86m/C; Streaming.** June Diane Raphael; Casey Wilson; Jon Cryer; Vincent D'Onofrio; Brian Geraghty; Alicia Silverstone; ***D:*** Chris Nelson; ***W:*** June Diane Raphael; Casey Wilson; ***C:*** Andre Lascaris; ***M:*** Erica Weis.

Assassin 1986 (PG-13) Made for TV drama about a mad scientist who creates a bionic killer for a bizarre plot to take over the world. He programs the cyborg to assassinate the President and other key people to help carry out his plan. A retired CIA operative emerges to stop the scientist by trying to destroy the robot. **94m/C; VHS, DVD.** Robert Conrad; Karen Austin; Richard Young; Jonathan Banks; Robert Webber; ***D:*** Sandor Stern; ***W:*** Sandor Stern; ***C:*** Chuck (Charles G.) Arnold; ***M:*** Anthony Guefen. **TV**

The Assassin *Nie yin niang* **2015** Hou Hsaio-Hsien's visually sumptuous martial arts epic may not be as narratively riveting as fans of the genre would hope, but it's so mesmerizing to look at that most of them won't care. Set during the Tang Dynasty in 8th century China, the film tells the story of Nie Yinniang (Shu Qi), a female assassin who has been ordered by her master to slay corrupt government officials. She travels to a distant province to kill its governor, who happens to be her cousin to whom she was once betrothed. Hou understand how to use silence and stillness as a filmmaker in effective ways, making a film that's more poetry than prose. **105m/C; DVD, Blu-Ray.** *CH FR TW* Qi Shu; Chen "Chang Chen" Chang; Satoshi Tsumabuki; ***D:*** Hou Hsiao-hsien; ***W:*** Hou Hsiao-hsien; Cheng Ah; Tien-wen Chu; Hai-Meng Hsieh; Ping Bin Lee; ***C:*** Ping Bin Lee; ***M:*** Giong Lim.

Assassin in Love 1/2 *The Baker* **2007 (PG-13)** London hitman Milo decides he needs a career change after screwing up a job and making his boss angry. So he moves to a Welsh village and finds work as a baker. However, when the locals learn Milo's previous occupation they want him to settle their own petty problems. **86m/C; DVD.** *GB* Damian Lewis; Kate Ashfield; Nikolaj Coster-Waldau; Dyfan Dwyfor; Michael Gambon; Anthony O'Donnell; Steve Speirs; ***D:*** Gareth Lewis; ***W:*** Gareth Lewis; ***C:*** Sean Bobbitt; ***M:*** Alex Wurman.

Assassin of Youth 1/2 1935 Girl is introduced to marijuana and soon becomes involved in "the thrills of wild parties," and the horrors of the "killer weed." Camp diversion. **70m/B; VHS, DVD.** Luana Walters; Arthur Gardner; Earl Dwire; Fern Emmett; Dorothy Short; ***D:*** Elmer Clifton.

Assassin X *The Chemist* 2016 An action drama-thriller about an assassin in a difficult situation. Ronus Steele (Gruner) is an aging but skilled assassin who is given what he considers an untenable assignment: assassinating a woman he just met. Going on the run after being double crossed, he becomes the target of an assassin himself. He also finds himself having romantic feelings for the target he could not kill. When Steele learns a deep secret, his already skewed perspective on the situation changes completely. **102m/C; DVD, Streaming, Download.** Olivier Gruner; Patrick Kilpatrick; Martin Kove; Stephanie Gerard; Steven Dell; ***D:*** Art Camacho; ***W:*** James Dean Simington; ***C:*** Carmen Cabana; ***M:*** Ernesto Ueman; Rob Wasilauski. **VIDEO**

Assassination 1987 (R) A serious threat has been made to First Lady Ireland and no one is taking it lightly. Secret Service agent Bronson has been called as Ireland's personal bodyguard and suddenly they are both the target of terrorist attacks. Strangely though, the attacks seem to be directed from inside the White House. Bronson as you've seen him many times before. **93m/C; VHS, DVD, Blu-Ray.** Charles Bronson; Jill Ireland; Stephen Elliott; Michael Ansara; ***D:*** Peter Hunt; ***W:*** Richard Sale; ***C:*** Hanania Baer.

The Assassination Bureau **1969** Set in Victorian-era London, this amusing farce concerns a society of international assassins led by the charming Reed. Rigg is an intrepid reporter who pays Reed to have his own organization try to kill him. Reed in turn will try to get them first. A cross-European chase ends in a battle aboard a Zeppelin. Tongue-in-cheek whimsey with a fine cast. Based on a short story by Jack London. **106m/C; DVD.** *UK* Oliver Reed; Diana Rigg; Telly Savalas; Curt Jurgens; Philippe Noiret; Warren Mitchell; Beryl Reid; Clive Revill; Kenneth Griffith; Vernon Dobtcheff; Annabella Incontrera; ***D:*** Basil Dearden; ***C:*** Geoffrey Unsworth.

Assassination in Rome *Il Segreto del Vestito Rosso* **1965** American Shelley North (Charisse) and her husband are vacationing in Rome when he suddenly disappears. When she goes to the American embassy for help, Shelley is reunited with ex-lover, reporter Dick Sherman (O'Brian), who decides to help her out. A dead body in the Trevi fountain isn't the missing Mr. North but Dick thinks there's a connection and he and Shelley take their investigation to Venice. Available as a Drive-In Double Feature with "Espionage in Tangiers." **104m/C; DVD.** *IT SP* Cyd Charisse; Hugh O'Brian; Mario Feliciani; Juliette Mayniel; Alberto Closas; ***D:*** Silvio Amadio; ***W:*** Giovanni Simonelli; Silvio Amadio; ***C:*** Mario Pacheco; ***M:*** Armando Trovajoli.

Assassination of a High School President 2008 (R) Mainstream high school black comedy finds ambitious sophomore Bobby Funke (Thompson) assigned to write about seemingly perfect star jock and class president Paul Moore (Taylor). Bobby writes a school paper expose that puts Paul in a bad light and turns out to be riddled with errors. The wannabe journalist finally figures out that the high school's problems go far beyond what he first imagined. **99m/C; DVD.** Reece Thompson; Mischa Barton; Bruce Willis; Patrick Taylor; Melonie Diaz; Luke Grimes; Josh Pais; Kathryn Morris; Michael Rapaport; ***D:*** Brett Simon; ***W:*** Tim Calpin; Kevin Jakubowski; ***C:*** M. David Mullen.

The Assassination of Jesse James by the Coward Robert Ford 2007 (R) Calling this film a western is like calling a transcontinental railroad journey a trip to the coast. Tightly wound epic, brooding and dark yet visually spectacular, unfolds at a deliberate pace as a case study of James (Pitt) and his clinging young sycophant admirer, Robert Ford (Affleck), who would become the man who finally takes James' life. Ford's hero worship turns into jealousy and then disdain in the shadow of James' tabloid celebrity. A true film lover's film, director Dominik brings a style and texture that transcends the genre. See it if you worship the craft or Pitt, or both. **152m/C; DVD.** Brad Pitt; Casey Affleck; Sam Shepard; Mary-Louise Parker; Sam Rockwell; Paul Schneider; Jeremy Renner; Garret Dillahunt; Zooey Deschanel; Michael Parks; Ted Levine; Alison Elliott; James Carville; Tom Aldredge; ***Nar:*** Hugh Ross; ***D:*** Andrew Dominik; ***W:*** Andrew Dominik; ***C:*** Roger Deakins; ***M:*** Nick Cave; Warren Ellis.

The Assassination of Richard Nixon 1/2 2005 (R) Sam Bicke (Penn), a hopeless loser who shoots himself in the foot at every turn, ends up blaming Nixon for his downfall and decides to hijack a jet and fly it into the White House. Based on the true story of a failed plot, film focuses on showing Bicke's gradual but certain descent, played by Penn with gutwrenching nakedness. Incredibly dismal but revealing look at the making of a potential terrorist. **95m/C; DVD.** Sean Penn; Don Cheadle; Naomi Watts; Jack Thompson; Michael Wincott; Mykelti Williamson; Nick Searcy; Brad William Henke; Lily Knight; Tracy Middendorf; April Grace; Eileen Ryan; Jared Dorrance; ***D:*** Niels Mueller; ***W:*** Niels Mueller; Kevin Kennedy; ***C:*** Emmanuel Lubezki; ***M:*** Steven Stern.

Assassination of Trotsky **1972** Middling attempt to dramatize the last days of the Russian Revolutionary leader in Mexico before he's done in with an ice pick. **113m/C; VHS, DVD.** *FR GB IT* Richard Burton; Alain Delon; Romy Schneider; Valentina Cortese; Jean Desailly; ***D:*** Joseph Losey; ***C:*** Pasqualino De Santis.

Assassination Tango 2003 (R) Aging Brooklyn hit man John J. (Duvall), who dotes on girlfriend Maggie (Baker), and her daughter Jenny (Miller), and likes to hang out at the local dance hall, is sent to Argentina to kill a general. When the hit is delayed, he meets and is enchanted by Tango instructor Manuela, as well as the dance she teaches to him. Deep character study, beautifully shown in Duvall's performance, redeems film's slow, at times maddening pace. Duvall's direction, while not perfect, makes the proceedings interesting to watch, but requires patience. **114m/C; VHS, DVD.** Robert Duvall; Ruben Blades; Kathy Baker; Luciana Pedraza; Julio Oscar Mechoso; James Keane; Frank Gio; Katherine Micheaux Miller; ***D:*** Robert Duvall; ***W:*** Robert Duvall; ***C:*** Felix Monti; ***M:*** Luis Bacalov.

Assassins 1/2 1995 (R) Stallone gets to play elder statesman in the very deadly rivalry between two contract killers. Robert Rath (Stallone) is the man—number one with a bullet—whose reputation has caught up with him. Hot-headed Miguel Bain (the ever-smoldering Banderas) wants to off Rath and assume the position of top hitman. Caught in the middle of this macho posturing is surveillance expert—and potential murderee—Electra (Moore). It's Stallone to the rescue but his character pays more attention to Pearl, Electra's pampered Persian cat than to the lovely lady herself. But then romance isn't what this film is about—and director Donner does know his action. **132m/C; VHS, DVD, Blu-Ray.** Sylvester Stallone; Antonio Banderas; Julianne Moore; Anatoly Davydov; ***D:*** Richard Donner; ***W:*** Brian Helgeland; Lilly Wachowski; Lana Wachowski; ***C:*** Vilmos Zsigmond; ***M:*** Mark Mancina.

The Assassins *Tong que tai; Tong qiao tai* **2012** Set in China's Three Kingdoms Period, this follows the personal life of oft-used villain Cao Cao (Chow Yun-Fat) as opposed to the usual stories presenting him as a military tactician and villain. Cao Cao has grown in power so much that he dwarfs even the Emperor, and various factions are competing to see him dead. **103m/C; DVD, Blu-Ray, Streaming.** *CH* Chow Yun-Fat; Yifei Liu; Hiroshi Tamaki; Alec Su; ***D:*** Linshan Zhao; ***W:*** Bin Wang; ***C:*** Xiaoding Zhao; ***M:*** Shigeru Umebayashi. **VIDEO**

The Assassin's Blade 1/2 *Mo hup leung juk; Butterfly Lovers* **2008** A young woman disguises herself to enter an all male martial arts academy to learn the skills needed to defend her family. **102m/C; DVD, Blu-Ray.** *CH* Charlene (Cheuk-Yin) Choi; Chun Wu; Ge Hu; ***D:*** Jingle Ma; ***W:*** Jingle Ma; Po Chun Chan; Ka Keung Ng; Sin Ling Yeung; ***C:*** Jingle Ma; Chi Ying Chan; ***M:*** Tsang-Hei Chiu. **VIDEO**

Assassin's Bullet 2012 (R) Everyone tries hard not to look bored in this nondescript thriller. Former FBI agent Robert (Slater), retired after a personal tragedy, is a cultural attache in Sofia, Bulgaria. American Ambassador Ashdown (Sutherland) gets Robert to go back to his former profession to find a woman (Portnoy) who's assassinating Muslim jihadists. **91m/C; DVD, Blu-Ray.** Christian Slater; Elika Portnoy; Donald Sutherland; Timothy Spall; ***D:*** Isaac Florentine; ***W:*** Hans Feuersinger; ***C:*** Ross W. Clarkson; ***M:*** Simon Stevens.

Assassin's Creed 2016 (PG-13) In this adaptation of a video game, Callum Lynch (Fassbender) taps into the memories and fighting skills of a distant ancestor who was a member of a secret society of Assassins, charged with protecting an artifact known as the Apple of Eden. With its ridiculously talented cast – including leads Fassbender and Cotillard and supporting actors Irons, Gleeson, and Charlotte Rampling – there was reason to hope this would break the rule that video game adaptations are dreadful. Unfortunately talented people can still make pieces of nonsense. **115m/C; DVD, Blu-Ray.** Michael Fassbender; Marion Cotillard; Jeremy Irons; Brendan Gleeson; Charlotte Rampling; ***D:*** Justin Kurzel; ***W:*** Michael Lesslie; Adam Cooper; Bill Collage; ***C:*** Adam Arkapaw; ***M:*** Jed Kurzel.

Assault of the Killer Bimbos 1/2 **1988 (R)** A show girl gets framed for the murder of her boss and takes off for the border with a couple of girlfriends. On the way they get pursued by the expected dumb cops and meet up with horny, clean-cut hunks. In Mexico they encounter the villain and extract comic vengeance. Watchable mainly due to the likable female leads and pleasant, lightly camp execution, although it might prove too tame for most of its target audience. **85m/C; VHS, DVD.** Patti Astor; Christina Whitaker; Elizabeth Kaitan; Griffin O'Neal; Nick Cassavetes; Clayton Landey; Eddie Deezen; Arell Blanton; David Marsh; Tammara Souza; Jamie Bozian; Mike Muscat; Jeffrey Orman; John Quern; Jay O. Sanders; ***D:*** Anita Rosenberg; ***W:*** Ted Nicolaou; ***C:*** Thomas Callaway; ***M:*** Fred Lapides; Marc Ellis.

Assault of the Party Nerds 1989 **(R)** Nerds throw a wild party to try and attract new members to their fraternity, while a jock frat plots against them. Sound familiar? Little more than a ripoff of "Revenge of the Nerds" made especially for video. **82m/C; VHS, DVD.** Linnea Quigley; Troy Donahue; Richard Gabai; C. Paul Demsey; Marc Silverberg; Robert Mann; Richard Rifkin; Deborah Roush; Michelle (McClellan) Bauer; ***D:*** Richard Gabai. **VIDEO**

Assault of the Party Nerds 2: Heavy Petting Detective 1995 Detective tries to save a beauty from her scheming husband. **87m/C; VHS, DVD.** Linnea Quigley; Richard Gabai; Michelle (McClellan) Bauer; Arte Johnson; Burt Ward; ***D:*** Richard Gabai; ***W:*** Richard Gabai.

Assault of the Rebel Girls 1/2 *Cuban Rebel Girls; Attack of the Rebel Girls* **1959** A reporter gets involved with smuggling in Castro's Cuba. Flynn's last film, saving the worst for last. **66m/B; VHS, DVD.** Errol Flynn; Beverly Aadland; John MacKay; Jackie Jackler; Marie Edmund; ***D:*** Barry Mahon; ***W:*** Errol Flynn.

Assault of the Sasquatch *Sasquatch Assault* **2009** Police arrest a bear poacher and impound his truck which contains an unconscious Sasquatch. Unfortunately they don't bother to notice Bigfoot, and when he wakes up with a hangover from being shot multiple times he attacks the city. Despite his ability to rip off people's arms and use uprooted street signs as weapons, the local cops shrug off calling for help because "we got this." **85m/C; DVD, Streaming.** Kevin Shea; Greg Nutcher; Jason Criscoulo; Cristina Santiago; Andrea Saenz; ***D:*** Andrew Gernhard; ***W:*** John Doolan; ***C:*** Colin Theys; Matthew Wauhkonen; ***M:*** Shannon Gould; Matthew Llewellyn. **VIDEO**

Assault on a Queen 🦴 **1966** Stupid Sinatra vehicle about a group of con men who plot together to rob the Queen Mary on one of her trips. Their attack vessel is a renovated WWII German U-boat. The producers tried to capitalize on the popularity of "Ocean's Eleven," but they didn't even come close. Based on a novel by Jack Finney. **106m/C; VHS, DVD, Blu-Ray.** Frank Sinatra; Virna Lisi; Anthony (Tony) Franciosa; Richard Conte; Reginald Denny; ***D:*** Jack Donohue; ***W:*** Rod Serling; ***C:*** William H. Daniels.

Assault on Precinct 13 🦴🦴🦴 **1976** Urban horror invades LA. Lt. Bishop (Stoker) is assigned to oversee the final shutdown of Precinct 13. Nearly abandoned, except for a couple of secretaries and a few officers, the phones and electricity have already been shut off. First problem: a busload of criminals and officers are forced to make a stop to look after a sick prisoner. Second problem: a father, who just witnessed his daughter's murder by a brutal street gang, stumbles in. Then said street gang surrounds the precinct to get the witness. Paranoia abounds as the police are attacked from all sides and can see no way out. Carpenter's musical score adds to the excitement of this low-budget police exploitation story. Semi-acclaimed cult feature and very gripping. **91m/C; VHS, DVD, Blu-Ray.** Austin Stoker; Darwin Joston; Martin West; Tony Burton; Nancy Loomis; Kim Richards; Henry (Kleinbach) Brandon; Laurie Zimmer; Charles Cyphers; Peter Bruni; ***D:*** John Carpenter; ***W:*** John Carpenter; ***C:*** Douglas Knapp; ***M:*** John Carpenter.

Assault on Precinct 13 🦴🦴 **1/2 2005 (R)** Richet's remake of the Carpenter cult classic has the cons and cops, led by burned-out Sgt. Roenick (Hawke) and criminal kingpin Bishop (Fishburne) holed up in a soon-to-be-closed Precinct 13 on a snowy New Year's Eve against a squad of corrupt cops intent on eliminating Bishop, their not-quite-silent-enough partner. Generally solid, if standard, updating loses much credibility by plopping a forest in the middle of a heavily industrial part of Detroit, where this one is set. Hawke and Fishburne are appropriately conflicted and heroic as it's called for, but it's the supporting cast that gives this rendition its zest. Stick around for the helpful plot-summarizing rap song that plays over the closing credits. **109m/C; VHS, DVD, Blu-Ray, UMD, HD-DVD.** Ethan Hawke; Laurence Fishburne; Brian Dennehy; Drea De Matteo; Maria Bello; Gabriel Byrne; Ja Rule; Matt Craven; John Leguizamo; Fulvio Cecere; Currie Graham; Dorian Harewood; Kim Coates; Hugh Dillon; Titus Welliver; Aisha Hinds; ***D:*** Jean-Francois Richet; ***W:*** James DeMonaco; ***C:*** Robert Gantz; ***M:*** Graeme Revell.

The Assignment 🦴🦴 **1/2 1997 (R)** Workmanlike thriller is a case of deadly impersonation. Infamous terrorist Carlos the Jackal (Quinn) is shown plying his trade in Europe under the nose of CIA counterterrorism expert Jack Shaw (Sutherland). Later, in Israel, Mossad agent Amos (Kinglsey) captures a man whom he thinks is Carlos, only it's his double—U.S. Navy officer Annibal Ramirez (Quinn again). So Shaw and Amos decide to turn the seaman into the terrorist, in an elaborate plot to have Carlos' Russian handlers think the terrorist has betrayed them. There's a very long setup for a somewhat lame payoff. **115m/C; VHS, DVD.** *CA* Aidan Quinn; Donald Sutherland; Ben Kingsley; Liliana Komorowska; Claudia Ferri; Celine Bonnier; Vlasta Vrana; Von Flores; Al Waxman; ***D:*** Christian Duguay; ***W:*** Don Gordon; Sabi H. Shabtai; ***C:*** David Franco; ***M:*** Normand Corbeil.

The Assignment 🦴 **1/2 2017 (R)** A genre crime thriller with an unusual twist. Notorious San Francisco hitman Frank Kitchen (Rodriguez) crosses Dr. Rachel Kay (Weaver) by killing her brother, so the brilliant yet demented doctor decides to use Frank for an experiment. Enlisting crime boss Honest John Hartunian (LaPaglia), who brings Frank to her lab, the deranged doctor performs nonconsensual gender reassignment surgery on Frank to see if it will remove his desire to kill. After the surgery, Frank learns that the procedure cannot be reversed and vows to take revenge on everyone involved. Controversial because of its premise, the film's flaws do not overwhelm its intriguing aspects. **95m/C; DVD.** Michelle Rodriguez; Tony Shalhoub; Anthony LaPaglia; Caitlin Gerard; Ken Kirzinger; ***D:*** Walter Hill; ***W:*** Walter Hill; Denis Hamill; ***C:*** James Liston; ***M:*** Giorgio Moroder; Raney Shockne.

Assignment K 🦴 **1/2 1968** Uninspired spy thriller. While in Munich, British spy Philip Scott's (Boyd) cover as a toy manufacturer is blown and he's under surveillance by German intelligence. His girlfriend Toni (Sparv) is kidnapped to learn the names of his contacts. A lot of the so-called action takes place at a ski resort. **97m/C; DVD.** *UK* Stephen Boyd; Camilla Sparv; Leo McKern; Michael Redgrave; Jeremy Kemp; Robert Hoffmann; ***D:*** Val Guest; ***W:*** Val Guest; Maurice Foster; William Harold Strutton; ***C:*** Ken Hodges; ***M:*** Basil Kirchin.

Assignment Outer Space 🦴 *Space Men* **1961** A giant spaceship with bytes for brains is on a collision course with Earth. A team of astronauts is sent to save the world from certain peril. Seems they take the task lightly, though, and their mission (and hence the plot) revolves more around saving sexy sultress Farinon from certain celibacy. If you're into stultifying Italian space operas with a gratuitous sex sub-plot then look up this assignment, but don't say we didn't warn you. Director Margheriti is also known as Anthony Dawson, not to be confused with the actor of the same name. **79m/B; VHS, DVD.** *IT* Rik van Nutter; Gabriella Farinon; Archie Savage; Dave Montresor; Alan Dijon; ***Nar:*** Jack Wallace; ***D:*** Anthony M. Dawson.

Assignment: Paris 🦴🦴 **1/2 1952** Spy thriller finds reporter Jimmy Race (Andrews) sent from Paris to Budapest where his editor, Nick Strang (Sanders), assigns him to work with local Jeanne (Toren) on a potential political bombshell. Seems democratic elements within the Hungarian government are talking with Yugoslav president Tito about overthrowing the country's communist dictatorship. An incriminating photo is involved. **84m/B; DVD, Blu-Ray.** Dana Andrews; Marta Toren; George Sanders; Audrey Totter; Herbert Berghof; Sandro Giglio; Donald Ranolph; ***D:*** Robert Parrish; ***W:*** William Bowers; ***C:*** Burnett Guffey; Ray Cory; ***M:*** George Duning.

Assignment to Kill 🦴 **1969** Tedious thriller with only some pretty scenery (courtesy of Switzerland) to make it almost watchable. Insurance investigator Richard Cutting (O'Neal) is hired to find out why so many of shipping tycoon Curt Valayan's (Gielgud) vessels are sinking. It turns out to be sabotage. **98m/C; DVD.** Patrick O'Neal; John Gielgud; Herbert Lom; Joan Hackett; Oscar Homolka; Peter Van Eyck; Kent Smith; Fifi d'Orsay; Eric Portman; ***D:*** Sheldon Reynolds; ***W:*** Sheldon Reynolds; ***C:*** Enzo Barboni; Harold Lipstein; ***M:*** William Lava.

The Assisi Underground 🦴🦴 **1984** True but boringly told story of how the Catholic Church helped to save several hundred Italian Jews from being executed by the Nazis during the 1943 German occupation of Italy. Edited from 178 minutes, a good-will gesture from the producers. **115m/C; VHS, DVD.** James Mason; Ben Cross; Maximilian Schell; Irene Papas; Angelo Infanti; ***D:*** Alexander Ramati; ***M:*** Pino Donaggio.

The Assistants 🦴 **1/2 2009** Jack and his film school grad friends find it difficult to get their big break as they work on the showbiz fringes. As a joke they fake a coverage report for a nonexistent script but Jack's producer boss Gary sees it and wants to buy the property. Now they have to make the fake real, which in Hollywood should be a breeze (with certain complications of course). **100m/C; DVD.** Joe Mantegna; Stacy Keach; Aaron Himelstein; Chris Conner; Jane Seymour; Peter Douglas; Tate Hanyok; Kathleen Early; Jonathan Bennett; Reiko Aylesworth; Michael Grant Terry; ***D:*** Steve Morris; ***W:*** Steve Morris; ***C:*** Aaron Torres; ***M:*** Aaron R. Kaplan. **VIDEO**

The Associate 🦴🦴 *L'Associe* **1979 (R)** French farce about penniless financial consultant Julien Pardot (Serrault) who invents a fictitious partner, Mr. Davis, in order to get his business rolling. When his clients, his wife, and even his mistress are all more intrigued by the partner than Julien, he becomes so jealous he decides to "murder" his creation. Based on the novel "My Partner, Mr. Davis" by Jenaro Prieto. French with subtitles; remade in 1996 with Whoopi Goldberg. **93m/C; VHS, DVD.** *FR* Michel Serrault; Claudine Auger; Catherine Alric; Matthieu Carriere; ***D:*** Rene Gainville; ***W:*** Jean-Claude Carriere.

The Associate 🦴🦴 **1996 (PG-13)** Whoopi drags a 20-minute premise over almost two hours when she invents an elderly, white, male business partner to give her fledgling financial consulting business some prestige. After having all her moneymaking ideas appropriated by male colleagues, Laurel Ayres (Goldberg) starts her own business, only to find that no one wants to hire her. She creates the genius and the money comes rolling in. Everyone clamors to meet the mystery man, so she goes undercover as the elusive Robert S. Cutty. The sight of Goldberg in old white guy garb and makeup is jarring, and the payoff doesn't merit the overlong build up. Based on the French film "L'Associate" and the Jenaro Prieto novel "El Socio." **113m/C; VHS, DVD, Blu-Ray.** Whoopi Goldberg; Timothy Daly; Bebe Neuwirth; Dianne Wiest; Eli Wallach; ***D:*** Donald Petrie; ***W:*** Nick Thiel; ***C:*** Alex Nepomniaschy; ***M:*** Christopher Tyng.

Asteroid 🦴🦴 **1997** Re-edited version of the NBC TV miniseries emphasizes the special effects and action, which should help this routine disaster flick. Astronomer Lily McKee (Sciorra) discovers that several giant asteroids are on a collision course with Kansas City. She contacts FEMA and gets hotshot director Jack Wallach (Biehn) anxious to help out (and not just with the rock problem). Naturally, the citizens freak and one asteroid hits but there's an even bigger one on the way. **120m/C; VHS, DVD.** Michael Biehn; Annabella Sciorra; Don Franklin; Anne-Marie Johnson; Anthony Zerbe; Carlos Gomez; Jensen (Jennifer) Daggett; Michael Weatherly; Frank McRae; Denis Arndt; ***D:*** Bradford May; ***W:*** Robbyn Burger; Scott Sturgeon; ***C:*** David Hennings; Thomas Del Ruth; ***M:*** Shirley Walker. **TV**

Asteroid vs. Earth 🦴 **2014** Cheesy sci-fi disaster from The Asylum. An asteroid is on a collision course with Earth in this end of the world cheapie and the solution is to set off a series of nukes in the Pacific Ocean in the hope of wobbling the planet off its axis enough for the asteroid to pass harmlessly by. Yep, no consequences there. **91m/C; DVD, Blu-Ray.** Jason Brooks; Tia Carrere; Robert Davi; Charles Byun; Tim Russ; ***D:*** Christopher Ray; ***W:*** Adam Lipsius; ***C:*** Laura Beth Love; ***M:*** Chris Ridenhour. **VIDEO**

Astoria 🦴🦴 **2000 (R)** The Astoria section of Queens is heavily Greek-American with all its ethnic traditions. Alex (Stear) is 28 and wants to escape his stagnant life by joining an archeological expedition to find the lost tomb of Alexander the Great. His father Demo (Setrakian) expects Alex to help with the family business. Alex isn't happy until Greek art restorer Elena (Turco) pays a visit and suddenly things look a lot brighter. **103m/C; DVD.** Rick Stear; Ed Setrakian; Paige Turco; Joseph (Joe) D'Onofrio; ***D:*** Nick Efteriades; ***W:*** Nick Efteriades; ***C:*** Elia Lyssey; ***M:*** Nikos Papazoglou.

Astro Boy 🦴🦴 **1/2 2009 (PG)** Energetic—if somewhat violent—adaptation of the Japanese manga books and the 1963 anime TV series. Set in Metro City, an orbiting world above a polluted Earth, robot Astro Boy (Highmore) is created by grieving scientist Dr. Tenma (Cage) as a replacement for his deceased son. When he can't fulfill his "father's" expectations, the rejected Astro Boy finds a home amidst Earth's scavengers but must return to Metro City when he learns everyone is in danger from polluting red energy (Astro Boy is powered by clean blue energy) and save the day. **94m/C; Blu-Ray, On Demand.** *US CH* ***V:*** Freddie Highmore; Nicolas Cage; Donald Sutherland; Kristen Bell; Bill Nighy; Nathan Lane; Eugene Levy; Matt Lucas; Samuel L. Jackson; ***Nar:*** Charlize Theron; ***D:*** David Bowers; ***W:*** Timothy Harris; ***C:*** Pepe Valencia; ***M:*** John Ottman.

The Astro-Zombies **WOOF!** *The Space Vampires* **1967** A contender as one of the worst movies of all time. Carradine plays a mad scientist creating zombies who eat people's guts. Cult favorite Satana stars. Co-written and co-produced by Rogers of "M*A*S*H" fame. **83m/C; VHS, DVD, Blu-Ray.** Tura Satana; Wendell Corey; John Carradine; Tom Pace; Joan Patrick; Rafael Campos; William Bagdad; Joseph Hoover; Victor Izay; Vincent Barbi; Rod Wilmoth; ***D:*** Ted V. Mikels; ***W:*** Ted V. Mikels; Wayne Rogers; ***C:*** Robert Maxwell; ***M:*** Nico (Nicholas Carras) Karaski.

Astro-Zombies M3: Cloned 🦴 **2010** Eight years after the preceeding film, the government resurrects the Astro-Zombies to use in war not thinking that this is a B-movie and that bringing back monsters will bite them on the heinie. Had it not been shot on digital video cam it might have been much more fun. **104m/C; DVD.** Fletcher Sharp; Sean Morelli; Francine York; ***D:*** Ted V. Mikels; ***W:*** Ted V. Mikels; Cory Udler; ***C:*** Ted V. Mikels. **VIDEO**

Astro-Zombies M4: Invaders from Cyberspace 🦴 **2012** The Astro-Zombies are pretty upset over the last film in the series. Armed with their own planet, some nifty UFOs, and the ability to kill people over the Internet, they invade once again. **120m/C; DVD.** Sean Morelli; Jaime Preston Lynch; ***D:*** Ted V. Mikels; ***W:*** Ted V. Mikels; Cory Udler; ***C:*** Ted V. Mikels. **VIDEO**

The Astronaut Farmer 🦴🦴 **1/2 2007 (PG)** NASA engineer Charlie Farmer (Thornton) left the space program for his family's failing Texas ranch but never gave up his dream of being an astronaut. He's got his very own shiny silver space suit and is building an actual rocket in his barn. His family and friends see Charlie as a larger-than-life eccentric but when he tries to buy rocket fuel the feds think Charlie's some kind of homegrown terrorist. Film treats Charlie and his dreams matter-of-factly as does Thornton, with Madsen luminous as his devoted wife and Simmons blustering as his fed nemesis. **104m/C; DVD.** Billy Bob Thornton; Virginia Madsen; Bruce Dern; J.K. Simmons; Tim Blake Nelson; Max Thieriot; Jon(athan) Gries; Mark Polish; Jasper Polish; Logan Polish; ***Cameo(s):*** Bruce Willis; ***D:*** Michael Polish; ***W:*** Mark Polish; Michael Polish; ***C:*** M. David Mullen; ***M:*** Stuart Matthewman.

The Astronaut's Wife 🦴 **1/2 1999 (R)** Astronaut Spencer Armacost (Depp) just isn't the same guy after he returns from a nearly fatal space shuttle mission. He and his wife, Jillian (Theron), suddenly move to New York and she definitely notices some behavioral changes (he likes to listen to the test pattern on the TV screen). Oh, and then the little woman discovers she's pregnant and things get very "Rosemary's Baby." Theron's role is also very much like her beleagured wife in "The Devil's Advocate," since everyone seems to think Jillian's nuts. Disappointingly formulaic; Depp's more believable in quirky roles in quirky movies. **109m/C; VHS, DVD, Blu-Ray.** Johnny Depp; Charlize Theron; Joe Morton; Tom Noonan; Blair Brown; Nick Cassavetes; Clea DuVall; Donna Murphy; Samantha Eggar; ***D:*** Rand Ravich; ***W:*** Rand Ravich; ***C:*** Allen Daviau; ***M:*** George S. Clinton.

Asunder 🦴🦴 **1/2 1999** Slick thriller with a familiar storyline. Michael (Beach) and wife Lauren (Morgan) are at the fairground with best friends Chance (Underwood) and his pregnant wife Roberta (Hicks). Roberta is tragically killed in a fall while riding the Ferris wheel. Michael and Lauren invite Chance to stay with them and the viewer learns that Lauren and Chance once had an extramarital affair. Then Chance decides to wreck her marriage and get Lauren back. **102m/C; VHS, DVD.** Blair Underwood; Debbi (Deborah) Morgan; Michael Beach; Marva Hicks; ***D:*** Tim Reid; ***W:*** Eric Lee Bowers; ***C:*** Johnny (John W.) Simmons; ***M:*** Lionel Cole.

Aswang 🦴🦴 *The Unearthing* **2003** The Aswang are shapeshifting Filipino vampires with long tongues, who sit on the roofs of houses and drink blood from sleeping victims by inserting their tongues down the house into the sleeping occupants. Some are particularly fond of unborn children. Kat (Tina Ona Paukstelis) is unwed and pregnant, and would prefer to give her child up for adoption instead of having an abortion. A family of creepy rich eccentrics accepts her offer. You can pretty much see where this is going. **82m/C; DVD.** Norman Moses; Tina Ona Paukstelis; John Kishline; Flora Coker; Mildred Nierras; Jamie Jacobs Anderson; Daniel Demarco; Rosalie Seifert; ***D:*** Wyre Martin; Barry Poltermann; ***W:*** Wyre Martin; Barry Poltermann; Frank L. Anderson; ***C:*** Jim Zabilla; ***M:*** Ken Brahmstedt.

Asylum 🦴🦴 **1/2** *House of Crazies* **1972 (PG)** Four strange and chilling stories weave together in this film. A murderer's victim seeks retribution. A tailor seems to be collecting his bills. A man who makes voodoo dolls...only to become one later on. A woman plagued by a double. A doctor visiting the asylum tells each tale. Horrifying and grotesque, not as humorless as American horror films. **100m/C; VHS, DVD, Blu-Ray.** *GB* Peter Cushing; Herbert Lom; Britt Ekland; Barbara Parkins; Patrick Magee; Barry Morse; Robert Powell; Richard Todd; Charlotte Rampling; Ann(e) Firbank; Sylvia Syms; James Villiers; Geoffrey Bayldon; Megs Jenkins; ***D:*** Roy Ward Baker; ***W:*** Robert Bloch; ***C:*** Denys Coop.

Asylum **2005 (R)** Sex in the loony bin. In 1959, frustrated Stella Raphael (Richardson) accompanies her hubby Max (Bonneville) to the titular Victorian heap where he is the new superintendent. Stella meets hottie patient Edgar (Csokas), who helps out around the grounds, and the two are soon helping themselves to each other. Despite the fact that Edgar's locked up because he beat his wife to death in a jealous rage. Add to the mix Edgar's manipulative doctor, Peter Cleave (McKellen), and you've got a melodrama at high boil, just waiting to bubble over. As over-the-top as it sounds; adapted from the novel by Patrick McGrath. **90m/C; DVD.** *IR GB* Natasha Richardson; Ian McKellen; Marton Csokas; Hugh Bonneville; Judy Parfitt; Sean Harris; Gus Lewis; Wanda Ventham; Joss Ackland; ***D:*** David Mackenzie; ***W:*** Patrick Marber; Chrys Balis; ***C:*** Giles Nuttgens; ***M:*** Mark Mancina.

Asylum of Satan **1972** A beautiful concert pianist is savagely tortured by a madman in the Asylum of Satan. Filmed on location in Louisville, Kentucky. **87m/C; VHS, DVD.** Charles Kissinger; Carla Borelli; Nick Jolly; Sherry Steiner; ***D:*** William Girdler; ***W:*** William Girdler.

Asylum of the Damned *Hellborn* **2003 (R)** Naive psychologist believes he can tackle the worst offenders at the criminally insane asylum but isn't ready to deal with the hideous truth behind the high volume of vanishing inmates. **85m/C; VHS, DVD, Blu-Ray.** Bruce Payne; Tracy Scoggins; Tommy (Tiny) Lister; Gregory Wagrowski; Bill McKinney; Randall England; Kyle T. Heffner; Michael Earl Reid; David Thomas; Matt Stasi; Julia Lee; Joe Sabatino; Deborah Flora; Stefan Marchand; ***D:*** Philip Jones; ***W:*** Matthew McCombs; ***C:*** Mark Melville; ***M:*** Valentine Leone; Steve Bauman. **VIDEO**

At Close Range **1986 (R)** Based on the true story of Bruce Johnston Sr. and Jr. in Brandywine River Valley, Pennsylvania. Father, Walken, tempts his teenaged son, Penn, into pursuing criminal activities with talk of excitement and high living. Penn soon learns that his father is extremely dangerous and a bit unstable, but he's still fascinated by his wealth and power. Sometimes overbearing and depressing, but good acting and fancy camera work. A young cast of stars includes Masterson as the girl Penn tries to impress. Features Madonna's "Live to Tell." **115m/C; VHS, DVD.** Sean Penn; Christopher Walken; Christopher Penn; Mary Stuart Masterson; Crispin Glover; Kiefer Sutherland; Candy Clark; Tracey Walter; Millie Perkins; Alan Autry; David Strathairn; Eileen Ryan; ***D:*** James Foley; ***W:*** Nicholas Kazan; ***C:*** Juan Ruiz-Anchia; ***M:*** Patrick Leonard.

At Eternity's Gate **2018 (PG-13)** A look into Vincent van Gogh's final days in the south of France, as envisioned by writer/director Julian Schnabel, a painter himself. The pace is deliberate and the soundtrack mournful, and Willem Dafoe skillfully expresses the anguish that the now-revered the artist faced from both public ridicule and mental illness. **110m/C; DVD, Blu-Ray.** Willem Dafoe; Rupert Friend; Oscar Isaac; Mads Mikkelsen; Mathieu Amalric; ***D:*** Julian Schnabel; ***W:*** Julian Schnabel; Jean-Claude Carriere; Louise Kugelberg; ***C:*** Benoit Delhomme; ***M:*** Tatiana Lisovkaia.

At First Light *First Light* **2018** In a small town in California, high school student Sean (Pellerin) has an estranged relationship with long-time childhood friend and crush Alex (Scott) because she is dating big-mouth jock Tom (Wotherspoon). After Alex has an encounter with an alien life form, she calls Sean. The experience has affected her memory and given her a strange energy. As Sean tries to help her, he is accused of kidnapping Alex but discovers that others have already had deadly encounters with these visitors. An interesting combinationof first contact and coming of age. **89m/C; DVD, Blu-Ray.** Stefanie Scott; Theodore Pellerin; Kristin Booth; Josh Cruddas; Said Taghmaoui; ***D:*** Jason Stone; ***W:*** Jason Stone; ***C:*** David Robert Jones.

At First Sight 1/2 **1998 (PG-13)** Slow-paced romantic drama stars Kilmer as a blind masseuse who falls for high-strung architect Sorvino. She persuades him to have an operation that restores his sight, and he's forced to adapt to a world he has never seen. Excellent supporting performances by McGillis as Kilmer's sister and Lane as the doctor that eases his transition. Kilmer does an outstanding job in making his character neither pitiful nor over-sentimental, which is rare in movies that center on disabilities. Based loosely on a case study by Dr. Oliver Sacks, whose work was also the basis for "Awakenings." **128m/C; VHS, DVD, Blu-Ray.** Val Kilmer; Mira Sorvino; Kelly McGillis; Steven Weber; Bruce Davison; Nathan Lane; Ken Howard; ***D:*** Irwin Winkler; ***W:*** Steve Levitt; ***C:*** John Seale; ***M:*** Mark Isham.

At Middleton 1/2 **2013 (R)** In this love story, uptight George (Garcia) and free-spirit Edith (Vera Farmiga) meet at the title college--as parents visiting with their teenage children. Once the mismatched pair gets separated from the campus tour, they must get over their differences and realize they might have more in common than they think. Meanwhile George's preppy son Conrad (Lofranco) and Edith's ambitious, perfectionist daughter Audrey (Farmiga's younger sister Taissa) explore their own struggles with leaving home and entering adulthood. Story is predictable and chock-full of cliches, but as George and Edith, Garcia and Farmiga put up strong, chemistry-filled performances. **100m/C; DVD, Blu-Ray.** Andy Garcia; Vera Farmiga; Taissa Farmiga; Spencer Lofranco; Peter Riegert; Tom Skerritt; ***D:*** Adam Rodgers; ***W:*** Adam Rodgers; Glenn German; ***C:*** Emmanuel (Manu) Kadosh; ***M:*** Arturo Sandoval.

At Midnight, I'll Take Your Soul *A Meia-Noite Levarei Sua Alma* **1963** Brazilian import about sadistic gravedigger Coffin Joe (alter ego of director Jose Mojica Marins), who wanders the streets of his hometown in order to meet a desirable woman. His mission is to sire a son to continue his legacy and wiggle his lips at screaming women. A study in psycho-sexual horror, this makes "Apocalypse Now" look like a beach party. Coffin Joe, or "Ze do Caixao," is a kind of South American Freddy or Jason; Mojica Marin's movies—which are graphically sadistic—were banned by the Brazilian government. In Portugese with English subtitles. Followed by "Tonight I'll Be Incarnated in Your Corpse." **92m/B; VHS, DVD.** *BR* Jose Mojica Marins; Magda Mei; Nivaldo de Lima; ***D:*** Jose Mojica Marins; ***W:*** Jose Mojica Marins; ***C:*** Giorgio Attili.

At Sword's Point *Sons of the Musketeers* **1951** Adventure tale based on characters from Alexandre Dumas's "The Three Musketeers," although the story is original. The French Queen (Cooper) is disturbed by sinister Duke Lavalle (Douglas) who wishes to marry Princess Henriette (Gates) and gain power to the throne. But the children of the four original musketeers come to her rescue, including swordswoman Claire (O'Hara). **81m/C; VHS, DVD.** Cornel Wilde; Maureen O'Hara; Robert Douglas; Dan O'Herlihy; Alan Hale, Jr.; Blanche Yurka; Gladys Cooper; June Clayworth; Nancy Gates; ***D:*** Lewis Allen; ***W:*** Walter Ferris; Joseph Hoffman; ***C:*** Ray Rennahan; ***M:*** Roy Webb.

At the Circus 1/2 *The Marx Brothers at the Circus* **1939** Marx Brothers invade the circus to save it from bankruptcy and cause their usual comic insanity, though they've done it better before. Beginning of the end for the Marxes, a step down in quality from their classic work, though frequently darn funny. **87m/B; VHS, DVD.** Groucho Marx; Chico Marx; Harpo Marx; Margaret Dumont; Kenny L. Baker; Florence Rice; Eve Arden; Nat Pendleton; Fritz Feld; James Burke; Barnett Parker; ***D:*** Edward Buzzell; ***W:*** Irving Brecher; ***C:*** Leonard Smith; ***M:*** Harold Arlen.

At the Death House Door **2008** Acclaimed documentarians Steve James and Peter Gilbert explore complex issues related to the death penalty in the United States through the stories of a death house chaplain and a death row conflict widely believed to be innocent. Focusing on the "Walls" prison unit in Huntsville, Texas, the film describes the career of Carroll Pickett, who spent at least 15 years as the unit's death house chaplain and was involved in 95 executions. Pickett is one of many who believed that convict Carlos De Luna, though he was ultimately executed for his crimes. The documentary presents related evidence, including the information found by two Chicago Tribune reporters that suggest another man committed the crimes for which De Luna was convicted. **98m/C; DVD, Download.** ***D:*** Peter Gilbert; Steve James; ***C:*** Peter Gilbert.

At the Earth's Core **1976 (PG)** A Victorian scientist invents a giant burrowing machine, which he and his crew use to dig deeply into the Earth. To their surprise, they discover a lost world of subhuman creatures and prehistoric monsters. Based on Edgar Rice Burrough's novels. **90m/C; VHS, DVD, Blu-Ray.** *GB* Doug McClure; Peter Cushing; Caroline Munro; Cy Grant; Godfrey James; Keith Barron; ***D:*** Kevin Connor; ***W:*** Milton Subotsky; ***C:*** Alan Hume; ***M:*** Michael Vickers.

At the Midnight Hour 1/2 **1995** Elizabeth Guinness (Kensit) is hired as the new nanny to care for the troubled young son of widowed scientist Richard Keaton (MacCorkindale). She finds herself falling in love but then uncovers a secret about the death of Keaton's wife. From the Harlequin Romance series; adapted from the novel by Alicia Scott. **95m/C; DVD.** *CA* Patsy Kensit; Simon MacCorkindale; Keegan Macintosh; Lindsay Merrithew; Cynthia Dale; Kay Hawtrey; ***D:*** Charles Jarrott; ***W:*** Joe Wiesenfeld; ***C:*** Robert Fresco; ***M:*** Charles T. Cozens. **TV**

At War with the Army **1950** Serviceable comedy from Martin and Lewis in their first starring appearance, as the recruits get mixed up in all kinds of wild situations at their army base. Based on the play by James Allardice. **93m/B; DVD, Blu-Ray.** Dean Martin; Jerry Lewis; Polly Bergen; Mike Kellin; ***D:*** Hal Walker; ***W:*** Fred Finklehoffe; ***C:*** Stuart Thompson; ***M:*** Jerry Livingston.

Athena 1/2 **1954** Two sisters (Powell and Reynolds) from an eccentric, health-faddist family fall in love with their opposites. Purdom is the stuffy Boston lawyer who goes off with Powell and Reynolds entices a TV crooner (Damone). Routine romance with routine songs. Reeves, who would become a star as a movie muscleman, appears in a brief role. **96m/C; DVD.** Jane Powell; Debbie Reynolds; Edmund Purdom; Vic Damone; Louis Calhern; Evelyn Varden; Linda Christian; Virginia Gibson; Nancy Kilgas; Dolores Starr; Jane Fischer; Cecile Rogers; Steve Reeves; ***D:*** Richard Thorpe; ***W:*** William Ludwig; Leonard Spigelgass; ***M:*** Hugh Martin; Ralph Blane.

ATL **2006 (PG-13)** A pack of roller-skating Atlanta outsiders battle the streets and get their groove on to a bumpin' soundtrack (certain to be the perfect corporate tie-in). High-octane dazzle should satisfy most looking for a safe urban-teen flick not loaded with the normally obligatory f-bomb. But the poor-boy-meets-rich-girl romance is too fluffy, and an evil drug-dealer conflict still doesn't add the bite it needs. Music-video director Chris Robinson makes his wildly disobedient big-screen debut with bling and hoopla, but a lack of grit and coherence is all too apparent. **105m/C; DVD, Blu-Ray, UMD, HD-DVD.** Lonette McKee; Mykelti Williamson; Keith David; Jason Weaver; Tip "T.I." Harris; Lauren London; Evan Ross; Antwan Andre Patton; Jackie Long; Albert Daniels; Malika Khadijah; Tyree Simmons; ***D:*** Chris Robinson; ***W:*** Tina Gordon Chism; Antwone Fisher; ***M:*** Aaron Zigman.

Atlantic City **1944** Bradford Taylor (Brown) learns a hard lesson in humility when he decides to build a boardwalk amusement pier in 1915's Atlantic City and transform the sleepy town into a vacation destination. While his ventures are successful, he alienates himself from his family and friends. Probably more interesting for the popular featured performers, including Louis Armstrong, Paul Whiteman, Dorothy Dandridge, Buck and Bubbles, and Gallagher and Sheen among others. **86m/B; DVD.** Stanley Brown; Constance Moore; Charley Grapewin; Jerry Colonna; Robert Castaine; ***D:*** Ray McCarey; ***W:*** Gilbert Doris; Frank Gill, Jr.; George Carleton Brown; ***C:*** John Alton.

Atlantic City 1/2 *Atlantic City U.S.A.* **1981 (R)** A small-time, aging Mafia hood falls in love with a young clam bar waitress, and they share the spoils of a big score against the backdrop of Atlantic City. Wonderful character study that becomes something more, a piercing declaration about a city's transformation and the effect on the people who live there. Lancaster, in a sterling performance, personifies the city, both of them fading with time. **104m/C; VHS, DVD, Blu-Ray.** *FR CA* Burt Lancaster; Susan Sarandon; Kate Reid; Michel Piccoli; Hollis McLaren; Robert Joy; Al Waxman; ***D:*** Louis Malle; ***W:*** John Guare; ***C:*** Richard Ciupka; ***M:*** Michel Legrand. British Acad. '81: Actor (Lancaster), Director (Malle); Genie '81: Support. Actress (Reid); L.A. Film Critics '81: Actor (Lancaster), Film, Screenplay; Natl. Film Reg. '03; N.Y. Film Critics '81: Actor (Lancaster), Screenplay; Natl. Soc. Film Critics '81: Actor (Lancaster), Director (Malle), Film, Screenplay.

Atlantics *Atlantique* **2019** Unpaid construction workers building a giant tower In Dakar, Senegal, flee by sea in protest. One of the men, Souleiman (Traore), leaves behind his love Ada (Sane), who cannot shake her feelings for him despite her impending arranged marriage to the wealthy Omar (Sylla). On the wedding day, strange events occur including Omar's bed going up in flames, leading many to suspect Souleiman, even though no one has heard from the group of workers. The investigation seems to spark a series of strange events. A stunning debut for director Diop that uniquely melds drama and romance with the supernatural, highlighted by Sane's performance. **106m/C; DVD.** Mame Bineta Sane; Amadou Mbow; Ibrahima Traore; Nicole Sougou; Aminata Kane; ***D:*** Mati Diop; Ael Dallier Vega; ***W:*** Mati Diop; Olivier Demangel; ***C:*** Claire Mathon; ***M:*** Fatima Al Qadiri.

Atlantis, the Lost Continent **1961** If anything could sink the fabled lost continent of Atlantis it's this cheap fantasy flick. A greek sailor saves a princess and takes her back to her Atlantis home where he's promptly enslaved by the island's evil ruler. But this hero won't put up with any nonsense so he leads his fellow slaves in a revolt and gains his freedom before sinking both evil ruler and island (using atomic power no less!). **90m/C; VHS, DVD.** Anthony Hall; Joyce Taylor; John Dall; William (Bill) Smith; Edward Platt; Frank De Kova; ***Nar:*** Paul Frees; ***D:*** George Pal; ***W:*** Daniel Mainwaring; ***C:*** Harold E. Wellman; ***M:*** Russell Garcia.

Atlantis: The Lost Empire 1/2 **2001 (PG)** Fast-paced and action-packed animated Disney adventure about inexperienced explorer Milo Thatch (Fox) who uses his grandfather's secret journals to discover the whereabouts of the submerged city of Atlantis. Submarine Captain Rourke (Garner) leads the expedition, but the eccentric and multi-ethnic crew are not entirely who or what they seem to be. Once found, the city holds a love interest (Summer) for Milo, and treasures to tempt the less benevolent members of the crew. The animation is old-fashioned and the plotting is reminiscent of adventure movies such as "Raiders of the Lost Ark" and "20,000 Leagues Under the Sea," but these should be considered merits instead of liabilities, especially if you're under 13 years old. **95m/C; VHS, DVD, Blu-Ray.** ***V:*** Michael J. Fox; James Garner; Claudia Christian; Cree Summer; John Mahoney; Leonard Nimoy; David Ogden Stiers; Jim Varney; Phil Morris; Don Novello; Florence Stanley; Corey Burton; Jacqueline Obradors; ***D:*** Gary Trousdale; Kirk Wise; ***W:*** Tab Murphy; ***M:*** James Newton Howard.

Atlas **1960** The mighty Atlas takes on massive armies, one of which includes director Corman, in a bid to win the hand of a princess. About as cheap as they come, although it is one of the few Sword & Sandal epics that isn't dubbed. **84m/C; VHS, DVD.** Michael Forest; Frank Wolff; Barboura Morris; Walter Maslow; Christos Exarchos; Miranda Kounelaki; Theodore Dimitriou; Charles B. Griffith; Roger Corman; Dick Miller; ***D:*** Roger Corman; ***W:*** Charles B. Griffith; ***C:*** Basil Maros; ***M:*** Ronald Stein.

Atlas Shrugged: Part 1 **2011 (PG-13)** Low-budget, simplistic, and rushed adaptation of the 1957 Ayn Rand novel, the first in a supposed trilogy of films, tackles only the first third of the book and sets it in 2016.

Tough railroad heiress Dagny (Schilling) is merely a pretty-but-bland blonde businesswoman who gets involved with visionary manufacturer Hank Reardon (Bowler), whose formula for a new steel is expected to transform the nation's current economic crisis through free enterprise and rebuilding big business. **97m/C; Blu-Ray.** Taylor Schilling; Grant Bowler; Matthew Marsden; Edi Gathegi; Graham Beckel; Jsu Garcia; Jon Polito; Michael Lerner; Neill Barry; Rebecca Wisocky; Paul Johansson; ***D:*** Paul Johansson; ***W:*** Brian Patrick O'Toole; John Aglialoro; ***C:*** Ross Berryman; ***M:*** Elia Cmiral.

Atlas Shrugged 2: The Strike **WOOF! 2012 (PG-13)** The second part of the Ayn Rand novel is a cinematic nightmare with a different cast and director. Business moguls Dagny Taggart (Mathis) and Henry Rearden (Beghe) fiercely object to the government takeover of their industries just because the world's economy has gone to hell. Sadly, the movie that is clearly designed to invoke conversation about modern politics and ideals is just so deadly dull that it's more likely to start conversation about the failure of its creators. A bizarre piece of work that even its director can't seem to keep track of the storyline. **111m/C; DVD, Blu-Ray.** Samantha Mathis; Jason Beghe; Esai Morales; Patrick Fabian; Kim Rhodes; Diedrich Bader; Richard T. Jones; D.B. Sweeney; John Rubinstein; Robert Picardo; ***D:*** John Putch; ***W:*** Brian Patrick O'Toole; Duke Sandefur; Duncan Scott; ***C:*** Ross Berryman; ***M:*** Chris Bacon.

Atlas Shrugged 3: Who Is John Galt? **WOOF! 2014 (PG-13)** Someone not already enamored of Ayn Rand's screed is unlikely to care about John Galt or anyone else in this tedious, cheap-looking--and thankfully last--pic. The nation's economy is in a tailspin, the government is turning dictatorial, and only everyman Galt and his ideas and inventions can save the day. A third set of actors have been cast in the roles. **99m/C; DVD, Blu-Ray.** Kristoffer Polaha; Laura Regan; Peter Mackenzie; Rob Morrow; Joaquim de Almeida; Greg Germann; ***D:*** James Manera; ***W:*** James Manera; Harmon Kaslow; John Aglialoro; ***C:*** Gale Tattersall; ***M:*** Elia Cmiral.

ATM 🦴 1/2 **2012 (R)** In the tradition of thrillers such as "Speed" and "Phone Booth," director Brooks takes one common location and attempts to turn it into a nail-biting nightmare. This time it's a late-night ATM in a deserted parking lot. Three young urban professionals (Geraghty, Eve, Peck) enter the barely lit chamber after parking ridiculously far away only to turn around and see a hulking shadow in a parka. What does he want? And did he really just kill that guy who was walking his dog? As a series of unbelievable events pile up, the gimmick is out of order. **90m/C; DVD, Blu-Ray.** *CA US* Brian Geraghty; Alice Eve; Josh Peck; Mike O'Brian; ***D:*** David Brooks; ***W:*** Chris Sparling; ***C:*** Bengt Jonsson; ***M:*** David Buckley.

Atom Age Vampire **WOOF!** *Seddok, l'Erede di Satana* **1961** Mad scientist doing research on Japanese nuclear bomb victims falls in love with a woman disfigured in an auto crash. To remove her scars, he treats her with a formula derived from the glands of freshly killed women. English dubbed. Not among the best of its kind (a low-rent district if ever there was one), but entertaining in a mischievous, boy-is-this-a-stupid-film sort of way. **71m/B; VHS, DVD.** *IT* Alberto Lupo; Susanne Loret; Sergio Fantoni; Franca Parisi Strahl; Ivo Garrani; Andrea Scotti; Rina Franchetti; ***D:*** Anton Giulio Majano; ***W:*** Anton Giulio Majano; Alberto Bevilacqua; Gino De Santis; ***C:*** Aldo Giordani.

Atom Man vs. Superman 🦴🦴 **1950** Superman saves Metropolis from the machinations of his deadly foe, Atom Man, in this long-unseen second theatrical serial. Contains all 15 episodes on two tapes. **251m/B; VHS, DVD.** Kirk Alyn; Lyle Talbot; Noel Neill; Tommy "Butch" Bond; Pierre Watkin; ***D:*** Spencer Gordon Bennet.

Atom Nine Adventures 🦴 1/2 **2007** An astrophysicist and his homemade robot are pestered by terrorists after finding a meteorite with an alien organism in it. Fairly average sci fi thriller. **78m/C; DVD.** Christopher Farley; Paul Meade; Jennifer Ferguson; Colin Armstrong; ***D:*** Christopher Farley; ***W:*** Christopher Farley; ***C:*** Dave Arnold; Laura Beth Love; ***M:*** Robert Gulya. **VIDEO**

Atomic Blonde 🦴🦴 1/2 **2017 (R)** Charlize Theron doesn't just star in this stylish action-thriller; it was her production company that optioned the comic book it's based on, "The Coldest City." Set in Berlin before the wall came down, Theron's Lorraine is sent undercover to root out a double-agent using her smarts, sensuality, and killer moves, all while wearing stilettos. Plot weaknesses are easily forgiven by the fast-paced, colorful nod to 80s excess. **115m/C; DVD, Blu-Ray.** Charlize Theron; James McAvoy; Eddie Marsan; John Goodman; Toby Jones; ***D:*** David Leitch; ***W:*** Kurt Johnstad; ***C:*** Jonathan Sela; ***M:*** Tyler Bates.

The Atomic Brain **WOOF!** *Monstrosity* **1964** An old woman hires a doctor to transplant her brain into the body of a beautiful young girl. Of the three girls who are abducted, two become homicidal zombies and the third starts to act catty when she is given a feline brain. A must-see for bad-brain movie fans. **72m/B; VHS, DVD.** Frank Gerstle; Erika Peters; Judy Bamber; Marjorie Eaton; Frank Fowler; Margie Fisco; ***D:*** Joseph Mascelli; ***W:*** Jack Pollexfen; Vivian Russell; Dean Dillman, Jr; Sue Bradford.

The Atomic Cafe 🦴🦴🦴 **1982** A chillingly humorous compilation of newsreels and government films of the 1940s and '50s that show America's preoccupation with the A-Bomb. Some sequences are in black and white. Includes the infamous training film "Duck and Cover," which tells us what to do in the event of an actual bombing. **92m/C; VHS, DVD, Blu-Ray.** ***D:*** Kevin Rafferty; Jayne Loader; Pierce Rafferty; ***M:*** Miklos Rozsa. Natl. Film Reg. '16.

The Atomic City 🦴🦴 1/2 **1952** Barry plays a nuclear physicist at Los Alamos whose son is kidnapped by terrorists who want his bomb-making formulas. The bad guys hide out in the nearby mountains which at least makes for some pleasant scenery in this average thriller. **84m/B; VHS, DVD, Blu-Ray.** Gene Barry; Lee Aaker; Michael D. Moore; Lydia Clarke; Nancy Gates; Milburn Stone; ***D:*** Jerry Hopper.

The Atomic Kid 🦴 1/2 **1954** A man survives an atomic blast because of a peanut butter sandwich he was eating. As a result, he himself becomes radioactive and discovers that he has acquired some strange new powers which get him into what pass for hilarious predicaments. **86m/B; DVD, Blu-Ray.** Mickey Rooney; Robert Strauss; Elaine Davis; Bill Goodwin; Whit Bissell; ***D:*** Leslie Martinson; ***W:*** Blake Edwards; ***C:*** John L. "Jack" Russell; ***M:*** Van Alexander.

The Atomic Man 🦴 1/2 *Timeslip* **1956** Owing to radioactive experimentation, a scientist exists for a short time in the future. Once there, both good and evil forces want to use him for their own purposes. **78m/B; VHS, DVD.** *GB* Gene Nelson; Faith Domergue; Joseph Tomelty; Peter Arne; ***D:*** Ken Hughes.

Atomic Rulers of the World 🦴 1/2 *Atomic Rulers; Attack of the Flying Saucers* **1965** An alien council of robots concerned that possible nuclear war on Earth will contaminate the universe sends one of their own to oversee the planet in the form of superhero Starman. In this particular installment he fights criminals from a foreign land who intend to use A-bombs to rule the world. Campy sci fi fun. **83m/B; DVD.** *JP* Ken Utsui; ***D:*** Koreyoshi Akasaka; Teruo Ishii; Akira Mitsuwa; ***W:*** Ichiro Miyagawa; ***C:*** Takashi Watanabe; ***M:*** Michiaki Watanabe.

Atomic Submarine 🦴🦴 **1959** Futuristic sci fi plots government agents against alien invaders. The battle, however, takes place in the ocean beneath the Arctic and is headed by an atomic-powered submarine clashing with a special alien underwater saucer. We all live on the atomic submarine: fun for devotees. **80m/C; VHS, DVD.** Arthur Franz; Dick Foran; Bob Steele; Brett Halsey; Joi Lansing; Tom Conway; Paul Dubov; ***D:*** Spencer Gordon Bennet; ***W:*** Orville H. Hampton; ***C:*** Gilbert Warrenton; ***M:*** Alexander Laszlo.

Atomic Train 🦴 1/2 **1999 (PG-13)** Silly two-part TV mini about a runaway train that's packed with toxic waste and a nuclear bomb, which is headed straight for Denver. Lowe (who makes a surprisingly good action hero) is National Transportation Safety Board investigator John Seger, who must derail the disaster. Meanwhile, the relentless media coverage has brought on widespread panic (those fiends!). **168m/C; VHS, DVD.** Rob Lowe; Kristin Davis; Esai Morales; John Finn; Mena Suvari; Sean Smith; Edward Herrmann; Erik King; Blu Mankuma; ***D:*** Dick Lowry; David S. Jackson; ***C:*** Steven Fierberg; ***M:*** Lee Holdridge. **TV**

Atonement 🦴🦴🦴 **2007 (R)** In 1935 England, 13-year-old Briony (Ronan) sees her sister Cecilia (Knightley) and their cook's son Robbie (McAvoy) together (literally) and, out of jealousy, accuses Robbie of a crime he didn't commit. The once beloved Robbie is sent to jail and the family, who had been paying for him to attend college, rejects him. Only Cecilia believes he is innocent, and cannot forgive her sister. Five years later, the now grown Briony (Garai) and Cecilia are nurses in London and Robbie has been released from prison to fight in the war. Desperate for forgiveness for ruining Robbie's life, Briony tries to find a way to fix her mistake, but it may be too late. Knightley and McAvoy shine as the long-lost lovers, and Ronan's Briony is stellar. Beautifully shot period film is faithful to McEwan's novel, and to the tone and style of 1930s and '40s-era melodramas. **122m/C; Blu-Ray, On Demand.** *US GB* James McAvoy; Keira Knightley; Saoirse Ronan; Romola Garai; Vanessa Redgrave; Brenda Blethyn; Juno Temple; Patrick Kennedy; Benedict Cumberbatch; Harriet Walter; Gina McKee; ***D:*** Joe Wright; ***W:*** Christopher Hampton; ***C:*** Seamus McGarvey; ***M:*** Dario Marianelli. Oscars '07: Orig. Score; British Acad. '07: Film; Golden Globes '08: Film--Drama, Orig. Score.

The Atonement of Gosta Berling 🦴🦴🦴 *Gosta Berling's Saga; The Legend of Gosta Berling; The Story of Gosta Berling; The Saga of Gosta Berling* **1924** A priest, forced to leave the priesthood because of his drinking, falls in love with a young married woman. Garbo shines in the first role which brought her critical acclaim; Hanson's performance also makes this a memorable drama. Adapted from the novel by Selma Lagerlof. **91m/B; Silent; VHS, DVD.** *SW* Lars Hanson; Greta Garbo; Ellen Cederstrom; Mona Martenson; Jenny Hasselqvist; Gerda Lundequist; ***D:*** Mauritz Stiller.

Ator the Fighting Eagle **WOOF! 1983 (PG)** Styled after "Conan The Barbarian" this mythical action fantasy stars O'Keeffe as Ator, son of Thorn. Ator must put an end to the tragic Dynasty of the Spiders, thereby fulfilling the legend of his family at the expense of the viewer. Goofy low-budget sword and sandal stuff. D'Amato used the pseudonym David Hills. Followed by "The Blade Master." **98m/C; VHS, DVD, Blu-Ray.** *IT* Miles O'Keeffe; Sabrina Siani; Ritza Brown; Edmund Purdom; Laura Gemser; ***D:*** Joe D'Amato.

Atragon 🦴🦴 1/2 *Katei gunkan* **1963** The lost continent of Mu invades the surface world in order to reclaim its colonies. An embittered WWII veteran is asked to return to service in Japan's navy to construct the super-weapon intended to reverse Japan's fortunes before they surrendered to the Allies. **96m/C; DVD.** *JP* Tadao Takashima; Yoko Fujiyama; Yu Fujiki; Ken Uehara; Jun Tazaki; ***D:*** Ishiro Honda; ***W:*** Shinichi Sekizawa; ***C:*** Hajime Koizumi; ***M:*** Akira Ifukube.

Attack! 🦴🦴🦴 **1956** Cowardly Captain Cooney (Albert) is order to move one of his platoons into a forward position in 1944 Belgium. They are slowly surrounded by the enemy as platoon leader, Lt. Costa (Palance), calls headquarters for reinforcements. But Cooney won't commit his reserves even as the platoon is decimated. Expert portrayals of men under pressure. **107m/B; VHS, DVD.** Eddie Albert; Jack Palance; Lee Marvin; Robert Strauss; Richard Jaeckel; Buddy Ebsen; William (Bill) Smithers; Strother Martin; ***D:*** Robert Aldrich; ***W:*** James Poe; ***C:*** Joseph Biroc; ***M:*** Frank DeVol.

The Attack 🦴🦴🦴 *El atentado* **2013 (R)** A provocative drama, this Israeli film tells the story of a man caught between family, ethnicity, and origin in a powerful parable to the way history can collide with present day in the Middle East, leading to tragedy. An Arab doctor named Amin Jaafari (Suliman) has his world shattered when a suicide bombing in Tel Aviv is traced back to his wife Siham (Amsalem). Is it possible that the woman he shared his life with is a terrorist? An incredibly grounded performance from Suliman carries writer/director Ziad Doueiri's adaptation of the novel by Yasmina Khadra. **102m/C; DVD, Blu-Ray.** Ali Suliman; Reymond Amsalem; Uri Gavriel; ***D:*** Ziad Doueiri; ***W:*** Ziad Doueiri; Joelle Touma; ***C:*** Tommaso Fiorilli; ***M:*** Eric Neveux.

Attack Force **WOOF! 2006 (R)** Even judging by the low standards set by Seagal movies, this dreck isn't worth the effort to figure out what might be going on. After Special Agent Marshall Lawson's strike team is wiped out by a super-strong, drugged-out prostie, he's determined to figure out how it happened. This leads to a military/political conspiracy to infect the water supply with a drug that turns its users ultra-violent. Even the dialogue over-dubbing is ludicrous, with someone else obviously substituting for Seagal in various scenes. **95m/C; DVD.** Steven Seagal; David Kennedy; Danny (Daniel) Webb; Andrew Bicknell; Lisa Lovbrand; Matthew Chambers; ***D:*** Michael Keusch; ***W:*** Steven Seagal; Joe Halpin; ***C:*** Sonja Rom; ***M:*** Barry Taylor. **VIDEO**

Attack Force Z 🦴🦴 **1984** An elite corps of Australian military is Force Z. Volunteers are chosen for a dangerous mission: find the plane that crashed somewhere in the South Pacific and rescue the defecting Japanese government official on board, all before the end of WWII and the feature. Talented cast is effectively directed in low-key adventure featuring young Gibson. **84m/C; VHS, DVD, Blu-Ray.** *AU* Sam Neill; Chris Haywood; Mel Gibson; John Phillip Law; John Waters; ***D:*** Tim Burstall.

Attack from Mars 🦴🦴 1/2 *Midnight Movie Massacre* **1988** Retro splatterama has really gross vampire alien land outside a Burbank movie theatre in 1956, and the really weird movie patrons try to terminate it. **86m/C; VHS, DVD.** Robert Clarke; Ann (Robin) Robinson; ***D:*** Mark Stock; ***W:*** Mark Stock; David Houston.

Attack of the 50 Foot Cheerleader 🦴 1/2 **2012 (R)** A Roger Corman-inspired comedy about how a young women's desire to improve herself goes very, very wrong. More than anything, Cassie Stratford (Sims) wants to be a college cheerleader. Wiling to do anything to make the squad, she takes an experimental drug called Renew. At first, Renew seems to work as she gains beauty and the athletic ability to achieve her goal. She soon learns that the drug has an unexpected side effect—growth that turns her into a 50 foot giant. **83m/C; DVD, Streaming, Download.** Jena Sims; Sean Young; Treat Williams; Sasha Jackson; Olivia Alexander; ***D:*** Kevin ONeill; ***W:*** Mike MacLean; ***M:*** Andrew Johnson. **VIDEO**

Attack of the 50 Foot Woman 🦴🦴 1/2 **1958** A beautiful, abused housewife has a frightening encounter with a giant alien, causing her to grow to an enormous height. Then she goes looking for hubby. Perhaps the all-time classic '50s sci fi, a truly fun movie highlighted by the sexy, 50-foot Hayes in a giant bikini. Has intriguing psychological depth and social commentary done in a suitably cheezy manner. **72m/B; VHS, DVD.** Allison Hayes; William (Bill) Hudson; Roy Gordon; Yvette Vickers; George Douglas; Ken Terrell; Michael Ross; Frank Chase; Eileen Stevens; Otto Waldis; ***D:*** Nathan "Jerry" Juran; ***W:*** Mark Hanna; ***C:*** Jacques "Jack" Marquette; ***M:*** Ronald Stein.

Attack of the 50 Ft. Woman 🦴🦴 1/2 **1993** Campy remake of the 1958 sci-fi cult classic features the statuesque Hannah in the title role. Nancy's a put-upon hausfrau with zero self-esteem thanks to her domineering father (Windom) and loutish hubby (Baldwin). They should have been sweet to her because after an encounter with a flying saucer Nancy starts to grow...and grow...and grow. And then she decides to get some revenge. **90m/C; VHS, DVD.** Daryl Hannah; Daniel Baldwin; William Windom; Frances Fisher; Cristi Conaway; Paul Benedict; Lewis Arquette; Xander Berkeley; Hamilton Camp; Richard Edson; Victoria Haas; O'Neal Compton; ***D:*** Christopher Guest; ***W:*** Joseph Dougherty; ***M:*** Nicholas Pike. **TV**

Attack of the Gryphon 🦴 *Gryphon* **2007 (PG-13)** Royals from two rival kingdoms must band together to fight a wizard attempting to wipe them out with a giant monster in order to satisfy his evil wives. The low-budget special effects are evil in and of themselves. **89m/C; DVD, Streaming.** Jonathan LaPaglia; Larry Drake; Amber Benson; Andrew Pleavin; Douglas Roberts; ***D:*** Andrew Prowse; ***W:*** Sean Keller; Boaz Davidson; Tim Cox; Kenneth M. Badish; ***C:*** Viorel Sergovici, Jr.; ***M:*** John Dickson. **CABLE**

Attack of the Herbals 🦴 **2011** A pair of slackers try to save their small village from being bulldozed, and discover a way when a mysterious crate washes ashore. They have no idea what the contents are but decide to make tea out of them and it turns out surprisingly addictive. Only when they run out of the stuff do they notice the swastika on the bottom of the crate, and predictably all hell breaks loose. **86m/C; DVD.** *UK* Calum Booth; Steve Worsley; Richard Currie; Liam Matheson; Lee Hutcheon; ***D:*** David Ryan Keith; ***W:*** Liam Matheson; David Ryan Keith; Alisdair Cook; ***C:*** David Ryan Keith; ***M:*** Leah Kardos. **VIDEO**

Attack of the Jurassic Shark 🦴 *Jurassic Shark* **2012** An oil company unleashes a prehistoric shark which quickly traps a group of college girls on an island along with a gang of art thieves. **79m/C; DVD.** *CA* Emanuelle Carriere; Christine Emes; Celine Filion; Angela Parent; Duncan Milloy; ***D:*** Brett Kelly; ***W:*** David Lloyd; Trevor Payer; ***C:*** Amber Peters; ***M:*** Christopher Nickel. **VIDEO**

Attack of the Killer Tomatoes WOOF! 1977 (PG) Candidate for worst film ever made, deliberate category. Horror spoof that defined "low budget" stars several thousand ordinary tomatoes that suddenly turn savage and begin attacking people. No sci-fi cliche remains untouched in this dumb parody. A few musical numbers are performed in lieu of an actual plot. Followed by "Return of the Killer Tomatoes." Originally released at 87 minutes. **87m/C; VHS, DVD, Blu-Ray.** George Wilson; Jack Riley; Rock Peace; Eric Christmas; David Miller; Sharon Taylor; Jerry Anderson; Nigel Barber; John DeBello; ***D:*** John DeBello; ***W:*** Costa Dillon; John DeBello; ***C:*** John K. Culley.

Attack of the Moon Zombies 🦴 ½ **2011** Another Mihm homage to 50s drive-in monster movies. Scientists on the moon discover plant life. This is considered a good thing until the plants' spores turn humans into evil plant zombies. **99m/B; DVD, Blu-Ray, Streaming.** Michael Cook; Shannon McDonough; Michael G. Kaiser; Sid Korpi; Douglas Sidney; ***D:*** Christopher R. Mihm; ***W:*** Christopher R. Mihm. **VIDEO**

Attack of the Puppet People 🦴🦴 *Six Inches Tall* **1958** This alternative classic from the prolific Bert I. Gordon, a rival to Ed Wood Jr. in the schlock hall of fame, will not make anyone forget "The Incredible Shrinking Man." The insane dollmaker Dr. Franz (Hoyt) shrinks six people (including our heroes Agar and Kenny) to the size of Ken and Barbie. Can they escape the mad scientist? The dog? The rat? The effects are nostalgically charming. **79m/B; DVD, Blu-Ray.** John Agar; John Hoyt; June Kenney; Sally Reynolds; Susan Gordon; ***D:*** Bert I. Gordon; ***W:*** George Worthing Yates; ***C:*** Ernest Laszlo; ***M:*** Albert Glasser.

Attack of the Robots 🦴 ½ *Cartes sur Table* **1966** Silly spy spoof about powerful government officials who are being killed off by a mad scientist's robots. Interpol agent Lemmy Caution comes to the rescue. **88m/B; VHS, DVD, Blu-Ray.** *FR SP* Eddie Constantine; Fernando Rey; ***D:*** Jess (Jesus) Franco; ***W:*** Jean-Claude Carriere.

Attack of the Sabretooth 🦴 ½ **2005 (R)** Think cheap "Jurassic Park." Niles (Bell) invests his moolah in a combo tropical paradise resort and wildlife refuge that contains cloned sabretooth tigers. Naturally they escape and maul and munch any human in reach. **88m/C; DVD.** *AU* Robert Carradine; Nicholas Bell; Billy Aaron Brown; Brian Wimmer; Stacy Haiduk; Natalie Avital; Amanda Stephens; ***D:*** George Miller; ***W:*** Tom Woosley; ***C:*** Mark Melville; ***M:*** Timothy S. (Tim) Jones. **CABLE**

Attack of the 60-Foot Centerfold 🦴 ½ **1995 (R)** Angel Grace wants to be Centerfold of the Year so badly that she gets a doctor to enhance her endowments even more through a mystery formula. Only there's a little complication. Cheesy, with pretty women and no discernable acting (and a spoof of that '58 gem "Attack of the 50 Ft. Woman"). **83m/C; VHS, DVD.** J.J. North; Tammy Parks; John Lazar; Russ Tamblyn; Tommy Kirk; Stanley Livingston; Michelle (McClellan) Bauer; George Stover; Forrest J Ackerman; Ted Monte; Jim Wynorski; Raelyn Saalman; Tim Abell; Jay Richardson; Nikki Fritz; ***D:*** Fred Olen Ray; ***W:*** Steve Armogida; ***C:*** Gary Graver; Howard Wexler; ***M:*** Jeff Walton.

Attack of the Swamp Creature WOOF! *Blood Waters of Dr. Z; Zaat; The Legend of the Zaat Monster; Hydra* **1975** A deranged scientist transforms himself into a swamp critter and terrorizes a small town. **96m/C; VHS, DVD, Blu-Ray.** Marshall Grauer; Nancy Lien; Paul Galloway; Wade Popwell; Frank Crowell; David Robertson; Doug Thomas; ***D:*** Don Barton; Arnold Stevens; ***W:*** Lee Larew; Ron Kivett.

Attack on Darfur WOOF! *Darfur* **2009** Western journalists staying in a Sudanese village are gathering footage and interviews on atrocities. When they learn that the brutal Janjaweed militia is heading towards the village, the journalists don't know whether to leave or stay and help. Boll goes for importance and gets pretentious drama instead. **104m/C; DVD.** Billy Zane; Kristanna Loken; Edward Furlong; David O'Hara; Hakeem Kae-Kazim; Matt Frewer; ***D:*** Uwe Boll; ***W:*** Uwe Boll; Chris Roland; ***C:*** Mathias Neumann; ***M:*** Jessica de Rooij. **VIDEO**

Attack on Leningrad 🦴 ½ **2009 (PG-13)** Clunky exposition and some questionable acting doom this true story drama. In the winter of 1941, German troops cut the food and fuel supplies in an attempt to starve the people of Leningrad into submission. British journalist Kate Davis gets left behind during an evacuation and is hidden from Russian military authorities by officer Nina Tsvetkova as the siege continues and everyone struggles to survive amidst increasingly dire circumstances. **110m/C; DVD, Blu-Ray.** *GB RU* Mira Sorvino; Olga Sutulova; Gabriel Byrne; Armin Mueller-Stahl; Alexander Abdulov; Vladimir Ilin; ***D:*** Aleksandr (Sasha) Buravsky; ***W:*** Aleksandr (Sasha) Buravsky; ***C:*** Vladimir Klimov; ***M:*** Yurily Poteenko.

Attack the Block 🦴🦴 **2011 (R)** Debut feature from Cornish is fast and funny (although the slang may puzzle Americans). South London teen hoodlums mug nurse Sam before killing an alien (the outer-space kind) who had the bad luck to crash-land in their hood. The two incidents come together when their impetuous actions result in a full-on invasion that the authorities know nothing about since they're preoccupied with the fireworks on Guy Fawkes night. **88m/C; Blu-Ray, On Demand.** *GB* John Boyega; Jodie Whitaker; Alex Esmail; Franz Drameh; Leeon Jones; Simon Howard; Nick Frost; Luke Treadway; Jumayh Hunter; ***D:*** Joe Cornish; ***W:*** Joe Cornish; ***C:*** Tom Townsend; ***M:*** Steven Price; Felix Buxton; Simon Radcliffe.

Attack the Gas Station 🦴🦴 ½ *Juyuso seubgyuksageun* **1999 (R)** Four young slackers who have been successful at robbing gas stations take one over and pose as the attendants while keeping the real workers in back as hostages. They then indulge in other brilliant behavior by beating up the local gangsters, robbing the guys who deliver their takeout food, and cheesing off anyone they encounter. Eventually this ends in a comic slugfest between them, the cops, the mob, and several local Chinese restaurants. The police and organized crime are survivable but they're pretty brave taking on Chinese delivery boys. **109m/C; DVD.** *NK* Ji-tae Yu; Jun Jeong; Yu-won Lee; Sung-jae Lee; Oh-seong Yu; Seong-jin Kang; Yeong-gyu Park; ***D:*** Sang-jin Kim; ***W:*** Jeong-woo Park; ***C:*** Jeong-won Choi; ***M:*** Mu-hyeon Son.

Attention Shoppers 🦴🦴 **1999 (R)** Latin sitcom heartthrob Carbonell angers his wife and threatens his hunk status during a K-Mart publicity appearance in Houston that's taken over by his rival, soap star Perry. **87m/C; VHS, DVD.** Nestor Carbonell; Luke Perry; Martin Mull; Kathy Najimy; Michael Lerner; Cara Buono; Lin Shaye; Casey Affleck; ***D:*** Philip Charles MacKenzie; ***W:*** Nestor Carbonell. **VIDEO**

The Attic 🦴🦴 ½ **1980 (R)** Psycho-drama about an overbearing invalid father and his insecure and unmarried daughter. The girl learns to escape her unhappy life by hiding in the attic. Not horrifying, but a clear analytical look into the game of control. **92m/C; VHS, DVD.** Carrie Snodgress; Ray Milland; Rosemary Murphy; Ruth Cox; Frances Bay; Marjorie Eaton; ***D:*** George Edwards.

The Attic 🦴 **2006 (R)** Not very scary horror flick that also suffers in the script and acting departments. Emma Callan (Moss) and her family move into what seems to be a perfect Victorian home. Only Emma begins to have visions of her twin, who's supposedly dead, evil, and hiding in the attic. **85m/C; DVD, Blu-Ray.** Elisabeth Moss; Jason Lewis; John Savage; Catherine Mary Stewart; Tom Malloy; ***D:*** Mary Lambert; ***W:*** Tom Malloy; ***C:*** James Callanan; ***M:*** Mario Grigorov. **VIDEO**

The Attic Expeditions 🦴 ½ *Horror in the Attic* **2001 (R)** Very non-linear story about a man committed to an asylum for the murder of a girlfriend he doesn't remember. He begins to suspect the psychiatrists are implanting delusions in his mind (not that a lot of mental patients wouldn't say that). **100m/C; DVD, Streaming.** Andras Jones; Seth Green; Jeffrey Combs; Theodore (Ted) Raimi; Wendy Robie; ***D:*** Jeremy Kasten; ***W:*** Rogan Russell Marshall; ***C:*** Greg Littlewood; Michael Negrin; ***M:*** David Reynolds. **VIDEO**

The Attic: The Hiding of Anne Frank 🦴🦴 ½ **1988** Steenburgen is wonderful in the true story of Miep Gies, the Dutch woman who hid Otto Frank, her employer, and his family from the Nazis. Unusual because it is told from Gies's perspective, rather than from the more familiar Anne Frank story. Based on Gies's book, "Anne Frank Remembered." **95m/C; DVD.** Mary Steenburgen; Paul Scofield; Huub Stapel; Eleanor Bron; Miriam Karlin; Lisa Jacobs; Ronald Pickup; ***D:*** John Erman; ***W:*** William Hanley; ***M:*** Richard Rodney Bennett. **TV**

Attila 🦴 ½ **1954** Silly historical costumer. Attila (Quinn) and his brother Bleda (Manni) battle for control over the Huns. Attila wants to conquer Rome next but Bleda wants to make the Romans their allies. The weakling Roman emperor (Laydu) is willing to make peace and his ambitious sister Honoria (Loren) offers to wed Attila, but their powerful mother (Regis) refuses and tells Roman general Aetius (Vidal) to prepare the legions for battle. Italian with subtitles. **87m/C; DVD.** *IT* Anthony Quinn; Sophia Loren; Henri Vidal; Ettore Manni; Irene Papas; Christian Marquand; Claude Laydu; Colette Regis; ***D:*** Christian Marquand; Pietro Francisci; ***W:*** Primo Zeglio; Ennio De Concini; ***C:*** Aldo Tonti; ***M:*** Enzo Masetti.

Attila 🦴🦴 ½ **2001** Epic miniseries takes on the life of Attila the Hun. Early years of Attila are swiftly dealt with as his family is slaughtered and the boy is raised by his uncle—with his cousin as his rival for leadership. The adult Attila (Butler) is tough, charismatic, and bloodthirsty enough to unite the Hun tribes and challenge the domination of the Roman empire, which leads to the politically savvy Roman general Flavius Aetius (Boothe) being dispatched to get Attila on Rome's side. Lots of big battles as this part of history is treacherous indeed. **177m/C; VHS, DVD.** Gerard Butler; Powers Boothe; Alice Krige; Simmone MacKinnon; Tim Curry; Reg Rogers; Steven Berkoff; Tommy Flanagan; Pauline Lynch; Liam Cunningham; Jolyon Baker; Sian Phillips; Jonathan Hyde; ***D:*** Dick Lowry; ***W:*** Robert Cochran; ***C:*** Steven Fierberg; ***M:*** Nick Glennie-Smith. **CABLE**

Au Hasard Balthazar 🦴🦴 *Balthazar* **1966** Allegorical story from Bresson about donkey Balthazar and poor village girl Marie. Balthazar is taken from the children who love him and he's sold to a cruel master. Marie is also abused by the village men, including her jealous lover Gerard. It's supposed to be all about purity and cruelty in the world but instead it's just grim and drab. French with subtitles. **95m/B; DVD, Blu-Ray.** *FR* Anna Wiazemsky; Francois Lafarge; Walter Green; Philippe Asselin; ***D:*** Robert Bresson; ***W:*** Robert Bresson; ***C:*** Ghislan Cloquet; ***M:*** Jean Wiener.

Au Pair 🦴🦴 ½ **1999** MBA grad Jenny Morgan learns the job she's been hired for by widowed, wealthy business exec Oliver Caldwell is that of nanny to his two bratty kids, Kate and Alex. When the kids bond with Jenny, they decide she'd make a much-better stepmom than their dad's witchy fiancee, Vivian (Sibbert), and play matchmaker when they all travel to Paris. Originally shown on the Fox Family Channel. **90m/C; DVD.** Heidi Lenhart Seban; Gregory Harrison; Katie Volding; Jake Dinwiddie; John Rhys-Davies; Jane Sibbett; Michael Woolson; Richard Riehle; ***D:*** Mark Griffiths; ***W:*** Jeffrey C. Sherman; Cheryl Seban; ***C:*** Blake T. Evans; ***M:*** Inon Zur. **CABLE**

Au Pair 2: The Fairy Tale Continues 🦴🦴 ½ **2001** Nanny Jenny and her boss Oliver are keeping their romance a secret for fear of upsetting imperious Nell, his late wife's mother, who's willing to believe the worst about Jenny. But the bigger obstacle is the would-be merger of Oliver's firm with that of Karl Sennhauser, whose greedy grown children plan to use Jenny to ruin Oliver so they can take over instead. However, Oliver's smarter, younger kids have different ideas. Originally shown on the Fox Family Channel. **93m/C; DVD.** Gregory Harrison; Heidi Lenhart Seban; June Lockhart; Katie Volding; Jake Dinwiddie; Rachel York; Robin Dunne; Rory Johnston; Celine Massuger; Cliff Bemis; ***D:*** Mark Griffiths; ***W:*** Jeffrey C. Sherman; Cheryl Seban; ***C:*** Thomas Callaway; ***M:*** Inon Zur. **CABLE**

Au Pair 3: Adventure in Paradise 🦴🦴 **2009** Oliver and Jenny are married with a baby and they and his children Kate and Alex go on vacation to Puerto Rico. But it's not all fun in the sun as Jake refuses to be groomed to take over the family business and both Jake and Kate would rather go off on their own than hang out with the 'rents. An eight-year gap between sequels wasn't exactly kind to the cable family comedy and the brother/sister duo were more appealing characters when they were younger. Originally shown on ABC Family. **99m/C; DVD.** Heidi Lenhart Seban; Gregory Harrison; Jake Dinwiddie; Katie Volding; ***D:*** Mark Griffiths; ***W:*** Jeffrey C. Sherman. **CABLE**

Au Pair Girls 🦴🦴 ½ **1972** Four sexy young ladies leave their various homelands to embark on careers as au pair girls, making friends and love along the way. **86m/C; VHS, DVD, Blu-Ray.** *GB* Gabrielle Drake; Astrid Frank; Nancie Wait; Me Me Lai; Richard O'Sullivan; Johnny Briggs; Ferdinand "Ferdy" Mayne; ***D:*** Val Guest; ***W:*** Val Guest; David Adnopoz; ***C:*** John Wilcox; ***M:*** Roger Webb.

Au Revoir les Enfants 🦴🦴🦴🦴 *Goodbye, Children* **1987 (PG)** During the Nazi occupation of France in the 1940s, the headmaster of a Catholic boarding school hides three Jewish boys among the other students by altering their names and identities. Two of the students, Julien (Manesse) and Jean (Fejto), form a friendship that ends tragically when Jean and the other boys are discovered and taken away by the Gestapo. Compelling and emotionally wrenching coming of age tale based on an incident from director Malle's childhood is considered to be his best film to date and quite possibly the best he will ever make. In French with English subtitles. Other 1987 movies with similar themes are "Hope and Glory" and "Empire of the Sun." **104m/C; VHS, DVD, Blu-Ray.** *FR GE* Gaspard Manesse; Raphael Fejto; Francine Racette; Stanislas Carre de Malberg; Philippe Morier-Genoud; Francois Berleand; Peter Fitz; Francois Negret; Irene Jacob; Pascal Rivet; Benoit Henriet; Richard Leboeuf; Xavier Legrand; Arnaud Henriet; Jean-Sebastien Chauvin; Luc Etienne; ***D:*** Louis Malle; ***W:*** Louis Malle; ***C:*** Renato Berta. British Acad. '88: Director (Malle); Cesar '88: Art Dir./Set Dec., Cinematog., Director (Malle), Film, Sound, Writing; L.A. Film Critics '87: Foreign Film; Venice Film Fest. '87: Film.

Audition 🦴🦴 ½ *Odishon* **1999** Director Miike successfully illustrates a middle-aged widower's worst nightmares about remarrying a younger woman. The benign first half of the film, in which businessman Aoyama (Ishibashi) is persuaded by a producer friend to stage a fake movie audition in order to find a new bride, belies the gruesome turn of events revealed later. Seven years single, Aoyama wants a traditional, submissive young girl, which he finds in one of the actresses, Asami (Shiina). Aoyama's smitten, but buddy Yoshikawa (Kunimura) is decidedly less so, sensing something a tad askew in the graceful beauty. Something definitely is amiss, as numerous flashbacks showing the girl's sadistic bent attest. Soon enough, Aoyama is on the business end of Asami's macabre doings. Based on a story by Ryu Murakami. In Japanese with subtitles. **115m/C; VHS, DVD, Blu-Ray.** *JP* Ryo Ishibashi; Eihi Shiina; Tetsu Sawaki; Jun Kunimura; Miyuki Matsuda; ***D:*** Takashi Miike; ***W:*** Daisuke Tengan; ***C:*** Hideo Yamamoto; ***M:*** Koji Endo.

The Audrey Hepburn Story **2000 (PG)** When you play a movie icon, expect the critical brickbats to fly. Sweet Hewitt does her best in the title role (Hepburn's her longtime idol) but it's all surface gloss. Bio covers 1935 to 1960 as Hepburn deals with family crises (dad's a two-timing Nazi sympathizer who abandons his family), war years in Nazi-occupied Holland, Hepburn's beginnings as a dancer in England and her first small roles. Then it's onto New York and the world of theatre and films. Along the way there's a little romance, a marriage to actor Mel Ferrer (McCormack), and various re-creations of some Hepburn movie roles. **133m/C; VHS, DVD.** Jennifer Love Hewitt; Eric McCormack; Frances Fisher; Peter Giles; Keir Dullea; Gabriel Macht; Marcel Jeannin; Swede Svensson; Michael J. Burg; Ryan Hollyman; ***D:*** Steve Robman; ***W:*** Marsha Norman; ***C:*** Pierre Letarte; ***M:*** Lawrence Shragge. **TV**

Audrey Rose **1977 (PG)** Parents of a young girl are terrified when their darling daughter is having dreadful dreams. Mysterious friend Hopkins cements their fears when he declares that his dead daughter has been reincarnated in their child. The nightmares continue suggesting that none other than Lucifer could be at work. Good cast is hampered by slow-moving take-off on "The Exorcist" with a weak staged ending. Adapted by DeFelitta from his novel. **113m/C; VHS, DVD, Blu-Ray.** Marsha Mason; Anthony Hopkins; John Beck; John Hillerman; Susan Swift; Norman Lloyd; ***D:*** Robert Wise; ***W:*** Frank De Felitta; ***C:*** Victor Kemper.

Audrey's Rain **2003** Audrey (Smart) is already caring for her younger, mentally challenged sister Marguerite (Wilhoite) when she must take in her orphaned niece and nephew after another sister commits suicide. No wonder Audrey is grateful for the attentions of old boyfriend Terry Lloyd (Smart's husband Gilliland). But can they overcome their troubles to take a second chance on love? Packs too much story into a too-short run time but Smart is always a pleasure to watch. **88m/C; DVD.** Jean Smart; Richard Gilliland; Kathleen Wilhoite; Angus T. Jones; Carol Kane; ***D:*** Sam Pillsbury; ***W:*** Jennifer Schwalbach Smith; Kate Smith; ***C:*** James W. Wrenn; ***M:*** Stephen (Steve) Edwards. **CABLE**

August 1/2 **1995 (PG)** Yet another version of Chekov's "Uncle Vanya," this time transported to 1890s Wales. Hopkins (who makes his directorial debut and composed the score) stars as Ieuan Davies, a bitter drinker who manages the estate of brother-in-law Alexander Blathwaite (Phillips). Blathwaite arrives for his annual summer stay with unhappy, young second wife Helen (Burton), who's the object of desire for both Ieuan and the local doctor, Michael Lloyd (Grainger). It's a perfectedly adequate rendition but offers little that's new except a change of scenery. **93m/C; VHS, DVD.** *GB* Anthony Hopkins; Kate Burton; Leslie Phillips; Gawn Grainger; Rhian Morgan; Hugh Lloyd; Rhoda Lewis; Menna Tussler; ***D:*** Anthony Hopkins; ***W:*** Julian Mitchell; ***C:*** Robin Vidgeon; ***M:*** Anthony Hopkins.

August 1/2 **2008 (R)** In 2001, Tom Sterling (Hartnett) is riding the dot-com bubble as CEO of Landshark, a New York internet startup company whose services are actually created by his married brother Josh (Scott). The cracks begin to show, precipitating a cash-flow crisis Tom prefers to ignore. There's no particular urgency or surprise to the story and Tom is a hollow, unlikeable character blankly played by Hartnett. **88m/C; DVD.** Josh Hartnett; Adam Scott; Robin Tunney; Emmanuelle Chriqui; Andre Royo; Naomie Harris; Rip Torn; Caroline Lagerfelt; David Bowie; ***D:*** Austin Chick; ***W:*** Howard A. Rodman; ***C:*** Andrij Parekh; ***M:*** Nathan Larson.

August **2011** Gay romantic triangle set during a sweltering L.A. summer. Hunky Raoul (Gonzalez) has made a green card marriage so he can stay in the U.S. with his boyfriend Jonathan (Dugan). Despite Raoul's devotion, there's a snake in their paradise when Jonathan's ex Troy (Bartlett) shows up, trying to worm his way back into his heart and bed. Jonathan can't resist but isn't sure he can depend on Troy, and Raoul isn't giving up on his lover. **99m/C; DVD; Closed Captioned.** Daniel Dugan; Murray Bartlett; Adrian Gonzalez; Hillary Banks; ***D:*** Eldar Rapaport; ***W:*** Eldar Rapaport; ***C:*** James Adolphus.

August: Osage County 1/2 **2013 (R)** An all-star cast of undeniably talented actors fight over Oscar buzz in this blatant awards bait, a melodramatic dud that guts Tracy Letts' Pulitzer Prize-winning play of its core, leaving only the "major moments" and monologues. After years of dealing with his crazy wife (Streep), Beverly Weston (Shepard) has gone missing, leading to a family reunion from all branches of this deeply damaged tree. The cast is uniformly strong, particularly Nicholson and Martindale, but the dialogue feels forced and the plot farfetched as the characters are little more than a series of crises and revelations. **121m/C; DVD, Blu-Ray.** Meryl Streep; Julia Roberts; Chris Cooper; Ewan McGregor; Margo Martindale; Sam Shepard; Misty Upham; Julianne Nicholson; Juliette Lewis; Benedict Cumberbatch; ***D:*** John Wells; ***W:*** Tracy Letts; ***C:*** Adriano Goldman; ***M:*** Gustavo Santaolalla.

August Rush **2007 (PG)** Lyla (Russell) is a classical cellist who falls for club-band musician Louis (Rhys Myers) and soon finds herself pregnant with his child. Her overbearing stage father tells her the baby has died and ships him off to an orphanage. Fast-forward 11 years and little orphan Evan (adorable Highmore) hears music in everything. He thinks if he learns how to play an instrument, his parents—who he knows are musicians—will find him. Through sheer force, a few side players, a healthy dose of appropriately sappy music, and a whole lotta far-fetched coincidences, the family is reunited. Utterly and unapologetically predictable, but it won't matter a bit if your idea of a good film is one in which you need an entire box of tissues. **113m/C; Blu-Ray, On Demand.** Freddie Highmore; Keri Russell; Jonathan Rhys Meyers; Terrence Howard; Robin Williams; William Sadler; Leon G. Thomas, III; Jamia Simone Nash; ***D:*** Kristen Sheridan; ***W:*** Nick Castle; James V. Hart; ***C:*** John Mathieson; ***M:*** Mark Mancina; Hans Zimmer.

Augustine **2012** A 19-year-old kitchen maid named Augustine (Soko) has a seizure that gets her shipped off to a psychiatric hospital in this smart French drama that examines how women and their sexuality were treated by the 19th-century medical community. Augustine is left partially paralyzed by her seizure, but her symptoms manifest in ways that lead neurologist Charcot (Lindon) to become convinced that it's more hysteria than physical malady. And then things get really interesting when Charcot begins to experiment in the sexual arena. French with subtitles. **102m/C; DVD, Blu-Ray.** *FR* Soko; Vincent Lindon; Chiara Mastroianni; Olivier Rabourdin; ***D:*** Alice Winocour; ***W:*** Alice Winocour; ***C:*** Georges Lechaptois; ***M:*** Jocelyn Pook.

Auntie Mame **1958** A young boy is brought up by his only surviving relative—flamboyant and eccentric Auntie Mame. Mame is positive that "life is a banquet and most poor suckers are starving to death." Based on the Patrick Dennis novel about his life with "Auntie Mame." Part of the "A Night at the Movies" series, this tape simulates a 1958 movie evening, with a Road Runner cartoon, "Hook, Line and Stinker," a newsreel and coming attractions for "No Time for Sergeants" and "Chase a Crooked Shadow." **161m/C; VHS, DVD, Blu-Ray.** Rosalind Russell; Patric Knowles; Roger Smith; Peggy Cass; Forrest Tucker; Coral Browne; ***D:*** Morton DaCosta; ***W:*** Betty Comden; Adolph Green; ***C:*** Harry Stradling, Sr. Golden Globes '59: Actress--Mus./Comedy (Russell).

The Aura **2005** To escape his bleak life in Buenos Aires, Esteban (Darin)--a quiet, reserved taxidermist—has fantasies of carrying out the perfect crime using his photographic memory even though he's plagued by epileptic seizures that at first give him great clarity (the "aura") but then cause blackouts. Despite this, Esteban seizes a chance to make his crime dream come true when he figures out that Dietrich (Rodal), who he mistakenly kills while on a hunting trip, was plotting a real heist. He's able to convince Dietrich's wife and gang members that he's also in on the gig but much like his seizures the events that follow get out of control. Tense thriller was only the second movie directed by Bielinsky, who died of a heart attack after its completion. In Spanish with subtitles. **138m/C; DVD.** *AR FR SP* Ricardo Darin; Dolores Fonzi; Alejandro Awada; Pablo Cedron; Jorge d'Elia; Nahuel Perez; Walter Reyno; Manuel Rodal; Rafael Castejon; ***D:*** Fabian Bielinsky; ***W:*** Fabian Bielinsky; ***C:*** Checco Varese; ***M:*** Lucio Godoy.

Aurora 1/2 **2010** An intense murder mystery that centers on the motive, not the perpetrator. Viorel (Puiu) is a 42-year-old divorced man with two daughters. First, he is seen quietly talking about the inconsistencies in the story of Little Red Riding Hood with a woman so as to not awake a child in the next room. Next, he is seen amongst abandoned trailers on the outskirts of Bucharest waiting for an arrival. Finally, he is at a metallurgical factory to pick up two hand-made firing pins. The why links these varied scenes together as Viorel drives towards an unknown fate. Romanian with subtitles. **181m/C; DVD.** Cristi Puiu; Clara Voda; Catrinel Dumitrescu; Luminita Gheorghiu; Valentin Popescu; ***D:*** Cristi Puiu; ***W:*** Cristi Puiu; ***C:*** Viorel Sergovici, Jr.

Aurora Borealis 1/2 **2006 (R)** Sutherland happily chews scenery as aged Ronald, whose increasingly ill health is proving too much for his wife Ruth (Fletcher) to handle. Fortunately, their slacker grandson Duncan (Jackson) gets a handyman's job at their apartment building to help out. Ruth also hires free-spirited home healthcare worker Kate (Lewis), whom Duncan immediately fancies. But Kate doesn't like to stay in one place for too long so Duncan may have to make a tough decision about where his future lies. Title refers to Ronald's belief that he can see the northern lights from his window. **110m/C; DVD.** Joshua Jackson; Donald Sutherland; Juliette Lewis; Louise Fletcher; ***D:*** James C.E. Burke; ***W:*** Brent Boyd; ***C:*** Alar Kivilo; ***M:*** Mychael Danna.

The Aurora Encounter **1985 (PG)** Aliens surreptitiously infiltrate a small town in 1897, and spread benevolence everywhere. Family fare. **90m/C; VHS, DVD.** Jack Elam; Peter Brown; Carol Bagdasarian; Dottie West; George "Spanky" McFarland; ***D:*** Jim McCullough, Sr.; ***W:*** Jim McCullough, Jr.

Aussie and Ted's Great Adventure 1/2 **2009 (G)** Michael Brooks returns from Australia with a dog that immediately bonds with his young daughter Laney. However, Michael later buys Laney a very special teddy bear from a friend in Chinatown. Aussie gets jealous and manages to 'lose' Ted on the streets of their San Francisco hometown. Then doggie guilt sets in and Aussie hunts to find Ted, only to have the Brooks' move out to their aunt's farm in the meantime. **89m/C; DVD.** Dean Cain; Alyssa Shafer; Leo Howard; Kristin Eggers; Beverly D'Angelo; Emily Kuroda; Vanessa Bell Calloway; Timothy Starks; ***V:*** James Ryan; Nick Shafer; ***D:*** Shuki Levy; ***W:*** Shuki Levy; Tori Avey; ***C:*** James Mathers; ***M:*** Shuki Levy; Gil Feldman. **VIDEO**

Austenland **2013 (PG-13)** Jane Hayes (Russell) is a woman obsessed with Jane Austen's "Pride and Prejudice" to the degree that she travels to a British resort built around the author's work. The idea that grown adults can act like children at Disney World but with themes from Austen's work has comedic potential but the laughless script is stunningly bad as it tries to tell an odd story of the haves and have-nots at Austenland. Made years after the Austen buzz seems to have died down, director Hess based this upon co-screenwriter Shannon Hale's 2007 book. **97m/C; DVD, Blu-Ray.** *US UK* Keri Russell; Jennifer Coolidge; Bret McKenzie; J.J. Feild; James Callis; Georgia King; Ricky Whittle; Jane Seymour; Rupert Vansittart; ***D:*** Jerusha Hess; ***W:*** Jerusha Hess; Shannon Hale; ***C:*** Larry Smith; ***M:*** Ilan Eshkeri.

Austin Powers: International Man of Mystery **1997 (PG-13)** Hilarious spoof of '60s spy and babe movies. Groovy '60s spy Austin Powers (Myers) discovers that his arch-enemy, Dr. Evil (Myers again) has frozen himself in order to elude capture, so the swingin' dentally challenged Brit decides to do the same. They awaken 30 years later in the same state: woefully out of touch. Dr. Evil is attempting to blackmail the British government and deal with his Gen-X son, Scott Evil (Green). Austin, on the other hand, is trying to "shag" every "groovy bird" he sees. Teamed with Vanessa (Hurley), the daughter of his former partner, they try to stop the evil machinations of...well.Evil. Myers revels in playing the fool, and he may step over the line every once in a while, but he gets plenty of mileage out of the one-joke premise. **88m/C; VHS, DVD, Blu-Ray, UMD.** Mike Myers; Elizabeth Hurley; Michael York; Seth Green; Mimi Rogers; Robert Wagner; Fabiana Udenio; Paul Dillon; Charles Napier; Will Ferrell; Mindy Sterling; ***Cameo(s):*** Tom Arnold; Carrie Fisher; ***D:*** Jay Roach; ***W:*** Mike Myers; ***C:*** Peter Deming; ***M:*** George S. Clinton. MTV Movie Awards '98: Dance Seq. (Mike Myers/Londoners), Villain (Myers).

Austin Powers 2: The Spy Who Shagged Me **1999 (PG-13)** Old snaggle-tooth (Myers) returns and time travels back to 1969 in order to foil his look-alike nemesis, Dr. Evil, who steals Powers' mojo. Myers wisely highlights the not-so-good Dr., along with some hilarious new characters, instead of the periodically wearisome Powers. Again plot takes a back seat to the great dialogue, characters (including Rob Lowe doing a dead-on Robert Wagner and a third Myers incarnation, Fat Bastard), and kitchy eye candy. It all still works because of Myers' winking good nature. **95m/C; VHS, DVD, Blu-Ray.** Mike Myers; Heather Graham; Elizabeth Hurley; Seth Green; Robert Wagner; Rob Lowe; Verne Troyer; Kristen Johnston; Mindy Sterling; Gia Carides; Clint Howard; Michael York; Will Ferrell; Muse Watson; Charles Napier; Tim Robbins; Fred Willard; Jack Kehler; ***Cameo(s):*** Burt Bacharach; Elvis Costello; Rebecca Romijn; Woody Harrelson; Willie Nelson; Jerry Springer; ***D:*** Jay Roach; ***W:*** Mike Myers; Michael McCullers; ***C:*** Ueli Steiger; ***M:*** George S. Clinton. MTV Movie Awards '00: On-Screen Duo (Mike Myers/Verne Troyer), Villain (Myers).

Austin Powers In Goldmember 1/2 **2002 (PG-13)** Shag-happy superspy Austin Powers is back for the third installment of the spy-spoof franchise. Austin travels back to the 70's to find his secret agent dad Nigel (Caine), hook up with new love interest and fellow spy Foxxy Cleopatra (Knowles), and rescue the world. Myers again takes on numerous roles, this time adding new villain Goldmember, a disco-clad Dutchman with a gilded prosthetic and a penchant for world domination. Dr. Evil is in good form but soft newcomer Goldmember comes up short, and Myers is running out of funny ideas. Bond studio MGM raised a stink about the title (too close to "Goldfinger") but finally saw the light and allowed the parody to continue. **94m/C; VHS, DVD, Blu-Ray.** Mike Myers; Michael Caine; Seth Green; Beyonce Knowles; Verne Troyer; Michael York; Robert Wagner; Mindy Sterling; Fred Savage; Tommy (Tiny) Lister; Clint Howard; Nathan Lane; ***Cameo(s):*** Steven Spielberg; Gwyneth Paltrow; Tom Cruise; Kevin Spacey; Danny DeVito; John Travolta; Quincy Jones; Burt Bacharach; Britney Spears; Ozzy Osbourne; Donna D'Errico; Susanna Hoffs; ***D:*** Jay Roach; ***W:*** Mike Myers; Michael McCullers; ***C:*** Peter Deming; ***M:*** George S. Clinton.

Australia 1/2 **2008 (PG-13)** Luhrmann's near-three-hour epic, set in northern Australia shortly before WWII, finds English aristocrat Lady Sarah Ashley inheriting a sprawling cattle station, eyed by local barons looking to take over. So Lady Sarah joins forces with a stockman known only as The Drover to drive 2,000 head of cattle to market, only to then face the bombing of Darwin by the Japanese. Long and melodramatic all-things-Down-Under story is beautiful to watch, with astonishing photography, sweeping vistas, and easy-on-the-eyes leads in Kidman and Jackman, but is ultimately overwhelmed by its own grandiose ambitions (note the similarities between posters for "Australia" and "Gone With the Wind"). **165m/C; Blu-Ray, On Demand.** *AU US GB* Nicole Kidman; Hugh Jackman; David Wenham; Bryan Brown; Jack Thompson; Ben Mendelsohn; David Gulpilil; David Ngoombujarra; Yuen Wah; Barry Otto; Bruce Spence; Brandon Walters; Lillian Crombie; ***D:*** Baz Luhrmann; ***W:*** Baz Luhrmann; Stuart Beattie; Ronald Harwood; Richard Flanagan; ***C:*** Mandy Walker; ***M:*** David Hirschfelder.

The Australian Story 🦴🦴 *Kangaroo* **1952** After a botched robbery, Connor (Lawford) and Gamble (Boone) stumble across the McGuire ranch and convince drunken Michael McGuire (Currie) that Connor is the old man's long-lost son. This becomes a problem when Connor falls in love with his 'sister' Dell (O'Hara) as they help out on a cattle drive. **84m/C; DVD.** Maureen O'Hara; Finlay Currie; Peter Lawford; Richard Boone; Chips Rafferty; ***D:*** Lewis Milestone; ***W:*** Harry Kleiner; ***C:*** Charles G. Clarke; ***M:*** Sol Kaplan.

Author! Author! 🦴🦴 1/2 **1982 (PG)** Sweet, likable comedy about playwright Pacino who is about to taste success with his first big hit. Suddenly his wife walks out, leaving him to care for her four children and his own son. His views shift as he begins to worry about, among other things, who will watch the obnoxious kids on opening night. **100m/C; VHS, DVD.** Al Pacino; Tuesday Weld; Dyan Cannon; Alan King; Andre Gregory; ***D:*** Arthur Hiller; ***W:*** Israel Horovitz; ***M:*** Dave Grusin.

Author: The JT LeRoy Story 🦴🦴 1/2 **2016 (R)** There was a time when JT Leroy was literally the most popular author in the world. His stories of drug abuse, prostitution, and teenage sexuality were adapted into feature films and he became a staple in the New York bar scene. Celebrities wanted to meet him and tons of young authors wanted to be him. The twist was that he didn't exist. JT Leroy was really a creation of Laura Albert, who hired a friend to pretend to be her pseudonym in public. Feuerzeig's documentary skips a few of the more damning facts about how Albert used people but is still fascinating. **110m/C; DVD.** Laura Albert; Bruce Benderson; Dennis Cooper; Panio Gianopoulos; Winona Ryder; ***D:*** Jeff Feuerzeig; ***W:*** Jeff Feuerzeig; ***C:*** Richard Henkels; ***M:*** Walter Werzowa.

Authors Anonymous 🦴🦴 **2014 (PG-13)** A group of eccentric, unpublished writers welcome Hannah Rinaldi (Cuoco) into their crowd until she becomes a sudden success. Then jealousy and rivalries set in as they each try to find their own way to fame and fortune, but it ain't pretty. **92m/C; DVD, Blu-Ray.** Kaley Cuoco; Chris Klein; Dennis Farina; Teri Polo; Dylan Walsh; Jonathan Bennett; Tricia Helfer; Jonathan Banks; ***D:*** Ellie Kanner; ***W:*** David Congalton; ***C:*** Tobias Datum; ***M:*** Jeff Cardoni. **VIDEO**

Auto Focus 🦴🦴🦴 **2002 (R)** Paul Schrader examines the sordid life and death of "Hogan's Heroes" star Bob Crane (Kinnear). Kinnear's portrayal of Crane from the seemingly normal father and husband to the sexaholic who was found bludgeoned to death amongst his amateur pornography is startling. The trouble starts when he meets creepy pal (and possible murderer) Carpenter (Dafoe), who gets him drumming gigs in strip clubs. This easy access to women, along with his affable manner and Carpenter's array of video equipment lead to a torrent of carnal acts that the two obsessively commit to tape. Crane loses two wives (Wilson, Bello) and his wholesome image while remaining oblivious to the descent that his sex addiction is causing in his personal and professional life. The cast does a great job with difficult material, especially Kinnear and Ron Leibman as Crane's weary agent. **104m/C; VHS, DVD, Blu-Ray.** Greg Kinnear; Willem Dafoe; Rita Wilson; Maria Bello; Ron Leibman; Kurt Fuller; Ed Begley, Jr.; Michael E. Rodgers; Michael McKean; Bruce Solomon; Christopher Neiman; Lyle Kanouse; ***D:*** Paul Schrader; ***W:*** Michael Gerbosi; ***C:*** Fred Murphy; ***M:*** Angelo Badalamenti.

Auto Recovery 🦴🦴 **2008** Some films can still be pretty good even with a low budget, or even if the plot is cliched and overdone. This is not one of them. A repo man with a checkered past has to nab a pastor's car or do 20 years in prison. Steal a car or go to jail. How does that work exactly? Isn't it usually the other way around? That's kind of like saying "People who obey the speed limit will have their drivers license taken." **113m/C; DVD.** *IN* Pierre August; Larry Barry; Tim Bell; Shelli Boone; Tyrone Burton; Anthony Coleman; Corey Miguel Curties; Aaron A. Frazier; Leonard George, III; David Alan Graf; Brian Keith Hall; Sir Majesty; Jolin Miranda; Steven Slates; ***D:*** Ernest Johnson; ***W:*** Ernest Johnson; ***C:*** Dave Bouza; Crystal Burdette; ***M:*** Dwayne Madison; Dwight Madison.

The Autobiography of Miss Jane Pittman 🦴🦴🦴 1/2 **1974** The history of blacks in the South is seen through the eyes of a 110-year-old former slave. From the Civil War through the Civil Rights movement, Miss Pittman relates every piece of black history, allowing the viewer to experience the injustices. Tyson is spectacular in moving, highly acclaimed drama. Received nine Emmy awards; adapted by Tracy Keenan Wynn from the novel by Ernest J. Gaines. **110m/C; VHS, DVD.** Cicely Tyson; Odetta; Joseph Tremice; Richard Dysart; Michael Murphy; Katherine Helmond; ***D:*** John Korty; ***W:*** Tracy Keenan Wynn; ***C:*** James A. Crabe; ***M:*** Fred Karlin. **TV**

Automaton Transfusion WOOF! **2006 (R)** Dumb title, worse movie. It's cheap, gory zombie horror that has the advantage of at least having a short run-time. Teens in some backwater Florida burg find their town is being overrun by bloodthirsty zombies that are result of a misbegotten military experiment. **75m/C; DVD.** Garrett Jones; Juliet Reeves; Kendra Farner; Joel Hebner; Rowan Bousaid; William Howard Bowman; ***D:*** Steven C. Miller; ***W:*** Steven C. Miller; ***C:*** Jeff Dolan; ***M:*** Jamey Scott. **VIDEO**

Automatons 🦴 **2006** Micro-budget homage to old sci-fi movies. Humans take on robots in the aftermath of yet another pointless World War. **83m/B; DVD.** Christine Spencer; Angus Scrimm; Brenda Cooney; ***D:*** James Felix McKenney; ***W:*** James Felix McKenney; ***C:*** David W. Hale; ***M:*** Noah De Filippis. **VIDEO**

L'Automobile 🦴 1/2 *The Automobile* **1971** Longtime Roman prostitute Anna is tired of her usual routine. She buys an automobile to make herself feel normal and to give her a sense of freedom. A trip to the beach in her new car doesn't work out as Anna thought it would. Originally filmed for Italian TV as part of the "Tre Donne" miniseries. Italian with subtitles. **98m/C; DVD.** *IT* Anna Magnani; Vittorio Caprioli; Christian Hay; ***D:*** Alfredo Giannetti; ***W:*** Alfredo Giannetti; ***C:*** Pasqualino De Santis; ***M:*** Ennio Morricone. **TV**

Autopsy 🦴 *Tarot* **1973** A young gold-digger and a millionaire marry, and then cheat on each other, provoking blackmail and murder. **90m/C; VHS, DVD.** *FR SP* Fernando Rey; Gloria Grahame; Christian Hay; Sue Lyon; ***D:*** Jose Maria Forque; ***W:*** Rafael Azcona; ***C:*** Alejandro Ulloa; ***M:*** Michel Colombier.

Autopsy 🦴 1/2 *Macchie solari* **1975 (R)** Forensic pathologist Farmer is working at a morgue compiling statistics concerning suicides and murders staged to look like suicides. Farmer begins to go nuts when it seems a stalker is killing people around her using the fake suicide method. Then there's the fact that the pathological pathologist is also sexually repressed and everything and everyone starts to scream sex to her and things get really kinky (and gory). **100m/C; VHS, DVD.** *IT FR SP* Mimsy Farmer; Barry Primus; Angela Goodwin; Ray Lovelock; ***D:*** Armando Crispino; ***W:*** Armando Crispino; Lucio Battistrada; ***C:*** Carlo Carlini; ***M:*** Ennio Morricone.

Autopsy 🦴🦴 **2008 (R)** The usual band of young adults has a car accident on a lonely road and gets taken to a mostly abandoned country hospital full of evil doctors. **89m/C; DVD, Streaming.** Michael Bowen; Robert Patrick; Ross Kohn; Robert LaSardo; Jessica Lowndes; Ashley Schneider; Jenette Goldstein; Janine Venable; ***D:*** Adam Gierasch; ***W:*** Adam Gierasch; Jace Anderson; E. L. Katz; ***C:*** Anthony B. Richmond; ***M:*** Joseph Bishara. **VIDEO**

Autopsy: A Love Story 🦴🦴 1/2 **2002** Life is a cold, lonely place for morgue-worker Charlie, whose pushy boss has him knee-deep in the bootlegged organs business. Meanwhile, his cross, crippled girlfriend torments him. The arrival of a hot new amour at the office livens things up—even though she's dead—but the pitiful lad is thrown when her (living) twin sister shows up. **90m/C; VHS, DVD.** Joe Estevez; Paul DeGruccio; Dina Osmussen; Ginny Harman; Wendy Crawford; Robert McClure; Jill Seitz; Greg Hanson; Mike Watkis; Keith Arbo; Ashley Smith; John Scott Mills; ***D:*** Guy Crawford; ***W:*** Guy Crawford; Tamarie Hargrove. **VIDEO**

The Autopsy of Jane Doe 🦴🦴 1/2 **2016 (R)** Cox and Hirsch star as father and son, respectively, who happen to also be coroners. They're working late one night when a body comes in that the police cannot explain. A naked woman was found half-buried in the basement at a brutal crime scene, but her body appears unharmed. As the gentlemen perform the autopsy, the story of Jane Doe gets even stranger as her insides look as though she was brutally tortured. And then supernatural things start happening in the funeral home. This is a smart, tense haunted house story where the haunted house happens to be a morgue. **86m/C; DVD, Blu-Ray.** Emile Hirsch; Brian Cox; Ophelia Lovibond; Michael McElhatton; Olwen Catherine Kelly; ***D:*** André Ovredal; ***W:*** Ian Goldberg; Richard Naing; ***C:*** Roman Osin; ***M:*** Danny Bensi; Saunder Jurriaans.

An Autumn Afternoon 🦴🦴🦴 1/2 *Sanma No Aji* **1962** Ozu's final film is a beautiful expression of his talent. In postwar Tokyo, an aging widower loses his only daughter to marriage and begins a life of loneliness. A heart-wrenching tale of relationships and loss. In Japanese with English subtitles. **112m/C; VHS, DVD, Blu-Ray.** *JP* Chishu Ryu; Shima Iwashita; Shin-Ichiro Mikami; Mariko Okada; Keiji Sada; ***D:*** Yasujiro Ozu; ***W:*** Yasujiro Ozu; ***C:*** Yuuharu Atsuta; ***M:*** Kojun Saito.

Autumn Blood 🦴🦴 **2014 (R)** A dramatic thriller about two children doing all they can to survive in difficult circumstances. In remote mountain region, a widow (Le Saunier) with two children runs a small farm to keep her family going. When the mother suddenly dies, the children are alone and believe they will be split up if anyone learns they are orphans. Instead, they keep the death a secret, live off the land, and rely on each other. The 16-year-old girl (Lowe) is naive and in touch with nature, while her 10-year-old brother (Harnisch) is mute after witnessing his father's death. Soon, their world is further shattered when hunters, including the son of the nearby town's mayor, sexually assault her and destroy her innocence. Though a social worker arrives in the community to help them, the siblings learn who they can rely on for survival. **100m/C; DVD, Streaming, Download.** Sophie Lowe; Maximilian Harnisch; Jacqueline Le Saunier; Annica McCrudden; Peter Stormare; ***D:*** Markus Blunder; ***W:*** Markus Blunder; Stephen T. Barton; ***C:*** Reed Morano; ***M:*** Robert Miller.

Autumn Hearts: A New Beginning 🦴🦴 *Emotional Arithmetic* **2007** A notable cast in a story that's sentimental and somewhat familiar. In 1945, Jewish dissident Jakob protected youngsters Melanie and Christopher when they were all interred at a detention camp outside Paris. After 35 years, the trio is unexpectedly reunited at Melanie's (Sarandon) rural home in Quebec, where she lives unhappily with husband David (Plummer). Christopher (Byrne) has never gotten over his first love for Melanie and the strong emotional bonds of the past prove to be equally potent in the present. **100m/C; DVD.** *CA* Susan Sarandon; Christopher Plummer; Gabriel Byrne; Max von Sydow; Roy Dupuis; Kris Holden-Ried; Dakota Goya; Regan Jewitt; Alexandre Nachi; ***D:*** Paolo Barzman; ***W:*** Jefferson Lewis; ***C:*** Luc Montpellier; ***M:*** Normand Corbeil.

Autumn in New York 🦴 1/2 **2000 (PG-13)** Start with one clunky love story with no chemistry, then mix in cheesy melodrama and a dash of creepy Freudian undertones and what do you get? This recipe for disaster about a doomed May-December romance. Middle-aged Will Keane (Gere) leads a playboy's life as the owner of one of New York's most fashionable restaurants. He falls for much younger sensitive gal Charlotte (Ryder) after finding out that he dated her mother. Unfortunately, Charlotte is afflicted with a life-threatening disease whose symptoms include saying "Wow!" a lot and fainting at overly dramatic moments. Will's life is changed, and he rushes around trying to find some medical miracle or plot device which might be able to save her. Rent "Love Story" instead. Because love means never having to say you're sorry you wasted two hours of your life on this movie. **104m/C; VHS, DVD, Blu-Ray.** Richard Gere; Winona Ryder; Anthony LaPaglia; Elaine Stritch; Vera Farmiga; Sherry Stringfield; Jill(ian) Hennessey; ***D:*** Joan Chen; ***W:*** Allison Burnett; ***C:*** Changwei Gu; ***M:*** Gabriel Yared.

Autumn Moon 🦴🦴 *Qiuyue* **1992** Young Japanese tourist (Nagase) travels to Hong Kong to enjoy some sexual fun but instead he befriends a 15-year-old girl (Wai), who's afraid of her family's impending emigration to Canada. Not much happens but the Hong Kong setting is eye-catching. English and Cantonese with subtitles. **108m/C; VHS, DVD.** *CH* Masatoshi Nagase; Li Pui Wai; ***D:*** Clara Law; ***C:*** Tony Leung Siu Hung.

Autumn Sonata 🦴🦴🦴 *Hostsonaten* **1978** Nordic family strife as famed concert pianist Bergman is reunited with a daughter she has not seen in years. Bergman's other daughter suffers from a degenerative nerve disease and had been institutionalized until her sister brought her home. Now the three women settle old scores, and balance the needs of their family. Excellent performance by Bergman in her last feature film. **97m/C; VHS, DVD, Blu-Ray.** *SW* Ingrid Bergman; Liv Ullmann; Halvar Bjork; Lena Nyman; Gunnar Bjornstrand; Erland Josephson; ***D:*** Ingmar Bergman; ***W:*** Ingmar Bergman; ***C:*** Sven Nykvist. Golden Globes '79: Foreign Film; Natl. Bd. of Review '78: Actress (Bergman), Director (Bergman); N.Y. Film Critics '78: Actress (Bergman); Natl. Soc. Film Critics '78: Actress (Bergman).

Autumn Sun 🦴🦴🦴 *Solo de Otono* **1998** This is a love story for appreciative adults. Clara (Aleandro) is a middleaged Buenos Aires accountant whose personal ad for a Jewish gentleman caller is answered by older widower (and non-Jew) Raul Ferraro (Luppi). Still, they're attracted to each other, and since Clara needs a man to pose as her admirer for a visit from her long-absent brother, Raul agrees to the ruse and undergoes a crash course in Jewish customs. This isn't actually played for laughs but as a reflection on expanding one's horizons and taking chances. Spanish with subtitles. **103m/C; VHS, DVD.** *AR* Norma Aleandro; Federico Luppi; Jorge Luz; Cecilia Rossetto; ***D:*** Eduardo Mignogna; ***W:*** Eduardo Mignogna; Santiago Carlos Oves; ***C:*** Marcelo Camorino; ***M:*** Edgardo Rudnitzky.

Ava & Lala 🦴🦴 1/2 **2014 (PG)** A family animated feature about a spirited girl who makes animal friends and has an unexpected adventure. Imaginative Ava's world is changed forever when she meets Lala (Flanagan), an animal full of curiosity. Teaming up, they meet other animals as have new exploits. Ultimately, Ava, Lala, and their friends must work together to fight evil General Tiger (Simmons) to gain control of Cloud Land. **80m/C; DVD, Streaming, Download.** Maile Flanagan; Abraham Benrubi; J.K. Simmons; George Takei; Mira Sorvino; ***W:*** Michael Shear; ***M:*** Sebastien Pan. **VIDEO**

Avalanche 🦴 1/2 **1978 (PG)** Disasterama as vacationers at a new winter ski resort find themselves at the mercy of a monster avalanche leaving a so-called path of terror and destruction in its wake. Talented cast is buried by weak material, producing a snowbound adventure yawn. **91m/C; VHS, DVD, Blu-Ray.** Rock Hudson; Mia Farrow; Robert Forster; Rick Moses; ***D:*** Corey Allen; ***W:*** Corey Allen; ***C:*** Pierre William Glenn; ***M:*** William Kraft.

Avalanche 🦴 1/2 **1999 (PG-13)** Prototypical cheesy disaster flic. Alaskan chopper pilot Neil (Griffith) helps out Lia (Feeney), the widow of an old pal, who works for the EPA. She believes the establishment of an oil company's overland pipeline through the mountains will trigger an avalanche that could destroy the city of Juneau. Naturally, no one believes her until there's an avalanche. (Considering the movie's title, you could have guessed this.) **105m/C; VHS, DVD.** Thomas Ian Griffith; Caroleen Feeney; R. Lee Ermey; C. Thomas Howell; John Ashton; Hilary

Shepard; *D:* Steve Kroschel; *W:* Steve Kroschel; *C:* Steve Kroschel; Richard Pepin; *M:* K. Alexander (Alex) Wilkinson.

Avalanche Express **1979 (PG)** Marvin is a CIA agent who uses a defector (Shaw) to lure a scientist (Schell), specializing in biological warfare, aboard a European train. Marvin wants to eliminate Schell but all plans go awry when the snow begins to fall. Ineffective thriller. Director Robson's and actor Shaw's last film—much of Shaw's dialogue was dubbed due to his death before the film's soundtrack was completed. Based on a novel by Colin Forbes. **89m/C; VHS, DVD.** Lee Marvin; Robert Shaw; Maximilian Schell; Linda Evans; Mike Connors; Joe Namath; Horst Buchholz; David A(lexander) Hess; *D:* Mark Robson; *W:* Abraham Polonsky; *C:* Jack Cardiff.

Avalon **1990 (PG)** Powerful but quiet portrait of the break-up of the family unit as seen from the perspective of a Russian family settled in Baltimore at the close of WWII. Initally, the family is unified in their goals, ideologies, and social lives. Gradually, all of this disintegrates; members move to the suburbs and TV replaces conversation at holiday gatherings. Levinson based his film on experiences within his own family of Russian Jewish immigrants. **126m/C; VHS, DVD.** Armin Mueller-Stahl; Aidan Quinn; Elizabeth Perkins; Joan Plowright; Lou Jacobi; Leo Fuchs; Eve Gordon; Kevin Pollak; Israel Rubinek; Elijah Wood; Grant Gelt; Bernard Hiller; *D:* Barry Levinson; *W:* Barry Levinson; *C:* Allen Daviau; *M:* Randy Newman. Writers Guild '90: Orig. Screenplay.

Avanti! **½ 1972 (R)** Stuffy businessman Wendell Armbruster (Lemmon) heads to Italy to claim his father's body when the old man dies while on vacation. Then he discovers dad has been visiting his mistress lo these many years. While trying to get through mountains of red tape, Wendell finds himself romancing the woman's daughter (Mills). Too long but still amusing. **144m/C; VHS, DVD, Blu-Ray.** Jack Lemmon; Juliet Mills; Clive Revill; Edward Andrews; Gianfranco Barra; Franco Angrisano; *D:* Billy Wilder; *W:* I.A.L. Diamond; Billy Wilder.

Ava's Magical Adventure **½ 1994 (PG)** Ten-year-old Eddie decides to take Ava on a little adventure. Too bad she's a 2-ton elephant he's stolen from the circus. Based on the Mark Twain story "The Stolen White Elephant." **97m/C; VHS, DVD.** Timothy Bottoms; Georg Stanford Brown; Patrick Dempsey; Priscilla Barnes; David Lander; Kaye Ballard; Remi Ryan; *D:* Patrick Dempsey; Rocky Parker; *W:* Susan D. Nimm; *M:* Mark Holden.

Avatar **2009 (PG-13)** Cameron's first directorial effort since "Titanic" is an elaborate 3-D sci-fi adventure with dazzling technique and a behind-the-scenes story more interesting than what appears onscreen. Cameron created (in collaboration) advanced motion-capture at an alleged cost of more than $200 million and four years of actual production. The plot itself is fairly standard, set in 2154 when Earth has suffered some disaster. Paraplegic ex-Marine Jake Sully (Worthington) is taken to the human outpost on Pandora where a shady corporation is trying to mine a rare mineral. Because the atmosphere is toxic, humans are mind-linked to a remote-controlled biological body called an avatar. Jake's avatar allows him to walk again and he's supposed to infiltrate the indigenous Na'vi. Too bad Jake becomes completely intrigued with their civilization and warrior Neytiri (Saldana) and is torn between duty and the exotic alien world. **163m/C; Blu-Ray.** Sam Worthington; Zoe Saldana; Michelle Rodriguez; Sigourney Weaver; Giovanni Ribisi; Laz Alonso; Wes Studi; Stephen Lang; CCH Pounder; Joel David Moore; *D:* James Cameron; *W:* James Cameron; *C:* Mauro Fiore; *M:* James Horner. Oscars '09: Art Dir./Set Dec., Cinematog., Visual FX; British Acad. '09: Visual FX; Golden Globes '10: Director (Cameron), Film--Drama.

Avengement **½ 2019** Hardened prison convict Cain (Adkins) is given a furlough to see his dying mother. Arriving after her death with a large security detail, Cain escapes from their custody and goes to a secret pub in London. Unrecognized by the criminal gang there because of his facial scars, Cain holds the men hostage as he tells them the story of how he became so disfigured over the past seven years and had to fight for his life. The latest action film by director Johnson starring Adkins, the film features the expected brutal fight scenes as well as a engaging performance by the lead actor. **90m/C; DVD.** Scott Adkins; Craig Fairbrass; Thomas Turgoose; Nick Moran; Kierston Wareing; *D:* Jesse V. Johnson; *W:* Jesse V. Johnson; Stu Small; *C:* Jonathan Hall; *M:* Sean Murray.

The Avenger **½ 1960** The story of a criminal who cuts off the heads of people and mails them off makes for a shocker. Graphic violence will appeal to those who like a good mail-order gorefest and are not employed by the post office. **102m/B; VHS, DVD.** *GE* Ingrid van Bergen; Heinz Drache; Ina Duscha; Mario Litto; Klaus Kinski; *D:* Karl Anton.

The Avenger *The Lost Glory of Troy* **1962** This time muscleman Reeves plays Aeneas and leads the Trojans in battle against the Greeks. It's supposedly an adaptation of "The Aeneid" by Virgil. **108m/C; VHS, DVD.** *FR IT* Steve Reeves; Giacomo "Jack" Rossi-Stuart; Carla Marlier; Gianni "John" Garko; Liana Orfei; *D:* Giorgio Rivalta.

The Avengers **1998 (PG-13)** Based on the cutly '60s Brit TV series, this unfortunate big screen adaptation fails by choosing style over campy charm. Set in a surreal 1999 London, scientist (and leather-girl) Mrs. Emma Peel (Thurman) teams up with dapper secret agent John Steed (Fiennes) to defeat maximum baddie, Sir August de Wynter (Connery). Seems de Wynter has a machine that can manipulate the world's weather—and he's not intending to do good deeds. It's dull, the leads have no chemistry together (although they have their separate charms), and the creators have chosen to include some lesser aspects of the series, such as the boring character of Mother (Broadbent). Unforgiveably, Laurie Johnson's memorable TV theme is not used for the film's opening—replaced instead by generic music by McNeely. (Johnson's theme is heard later.) Original Steed, Patrick MacNee, does have an amusing cameo. **90m/C; VHS, DVD, Blu-Ray.** Ralph Fiennes; Uma Thurman; Sean Connery; Jim Broadbent; Fiona Shaw; Eileen Atkins; John Wood; Eddie Izzard; Carmen Ejogo; Keeley Hawes; ***Cameo(s):*** Patrick Macnee; *D:* Jeremiah S. Chechik; *W:* Don MacPherson; *C:* Roger Pratt; *M:* Joel McNeely. Golden Raspberries '98: Worst Remake/Sequel.

The Avengers **½** *Marvel's The Avengers* **2012 (PG-13)** Nick Fury, the director of international peacekeeping agency SHIELD, needs a superhero team to defeat Norse god Loki and his army. He recruits Iron Man, Captain America, Thor, the Incredible Hulk, Hawkeye, and Black Widow. Perfect blend of action and humor, helped along by superhero banter and the feeling that everyone involved is having a good time. **143m/C; DVD, Blu-Ray.** Samuel L. Jackson; Robert Downey, Jr.; Chris Evans; Mark Ruffalo; Chris Hemsworth; Scarlett Johansson; Jeremy Renner; Stellan Skarsgard; Tom Hiddleston; Clark Gregg; Cobie Smulders; Gwyneth Paltrow; Harry Dean Stanton; *V:* Paul Bettany; *D:* Joss Whedon; *W:* Zak Penn; Joss Whedon; *C:* Seamus McGarvey; *M:* Alan Silvestri.

Avengers: Age of Ultron **½ 2015 (PG-13)** Whedon disappoints slightly with his follow-up to one of the biggest films of all time, ending Marvel Universe 2.0 on a bit of a down note. Most of the ingredients are there—the big action set-pieces, the A-list cast, the witty dialogue—but the film suffers from the unbelievably common problem of the superhero sequel by overdoing the storylines and mistaking chaos for entertainment. Bruce Banner and Tony Stark kick-start an old peacekeeping program called Ultron and things go horribly wrong, forcing the Avengers to reunite to save the world...again. **141m/C; DVD, Blu-Ray.** Robert Downey, Jr.; Chris Hemsworth; Mark Ruffalo; Chris Evans; Scarlett Johansson; *D:* Joss Whedon; *W:* Joss Whedon; *C:* Ben Davis; *M:* Danny Elfman; Brian Tyler.

Avengers: Endgame **2019 (PG-13)** The Russo brothers conclude the epic "Infinity Saga" chapter of the Marvel Cinematic Universe with this appropriately titled and wickedly entertaining film. In this installment, heroes from over twenty previous Marvel films join forces to do battle with the tyrannical Thanos (Brolin) as he gathers the remaining Infinity Stones to bring his own version of "order" to the universe. In addition to stalwarts like the Avengers and the Guardians of the Galaxy, newcomers such as Captain Marvel (Larson) and Spider-Man (Holland) are given their time to shine. Despite the film's over three-hour run time, the story moves briskly and effortlessly thanks to a myriad of wonderful performances and epic action sequences. **181m/C; DVD, Blu-Ray.** Robert Downey, Jr.; Chris Evans; Mark Ruffalo; Chris Hemsworth; Scarlett Johansson; *D:* Anthony Russo; Joe Russo; *W:* Christopher Markus; Stephen McFeely; *C:* Trent Opaloch; *M:* Alan Silvestri.

Avengers: Infinity War **2018 (PG-13)** An epic superhero film that successfully brings together a decade of build-up of a series of Marvel films. Traveling through various star systems, fanatical bully Thanos (Brolin) and his minions torture and kill to gather the six Infinity Stones so Thanos can carry out his extermination agenda. Challenging Thanos are the dedicated members of the Avengers and Marvel characters from such films as Black Panther and Guardians of the Galaxy, but their desperate resistance seems futile. A whole lot of story, characters, action, and humor are packed into a 160-minute run time. **156m/C; DVD.** Robert Downey, Jr.; Chris Hemsworth; Mark Ruffalo; Chris Evans; Scarlett Johansson; *D:* Anthony Russo; Joe Russo; *W:* Christopher Markus; Stephen McFeely; *C:* Trent Opaloch; *M:* Alan Silvestri.

Avenging Angel **WOOF! 1985 (R)** Law student Molly "Angel" Stewart is back on the streets to retaliate against the men who killed the policeman who saved her from a life of prostitution. Worthless sequel to 1984's "Angel," exploiting the original's exploitative intent. Followed listlessly by "Angel III: The Final Chapter." **94m/C; VHS, DVD, Blu-Ray.** Betsy Russell; Rory Calhoun; Susan Tyrrell; Ossie Davis; Barry Pearl; Ross Hagen; Karin Mani; Robert Tessier; *D:* Robert Vincent O'Neil; *W:* Joseph M. Cala; *C:* Peter Lyons Collister; *M:* Paul Antonelli.

The Avenging Angel **½ 1995** Unusual take on religion and western justice. Brigham Young (Heston) and his Mormon sect have established themselves in Utah—with the aid of some sharpshooting vigilantes, including Miles Utley (Berenger). When an assassination attempt is made on Young's life, Utley finds he's stumbled into an ever-widening church conspiracy that threatens to consume him. Based on the novel by Gary Stewart. **100m/C; DVD.** Tom Berenger; Charlton Heston; James Coburn; Kevin Tighe; Jeffrey Jones; Tom Bower; Joanna Miles; *D:* Craig R. Baxley; *W:* Dennis Nemec; *C:* Mark Irwin; *M:* Gary Chang. **TV**

Avenging Angel **½ 2007** Cliches abound in this oater about a nameless preacher (Sorbo) who suffered a personal tragedy at the hands of greedy land baron Col. Cusack (Hauser) and his evil minions. The preacher turns bounty hunter before rethinking his path thanks to outcast single mother Maggie (Watros). But when Cusack turns to violence again to get rid of some pesky settlers, the preacher straps on his trusty six-shooter. **81m/C; DVD.** Kevin Sorbo; Cynthia Watros; Wings Hauser; Nick (Nicholas) Chinlund; Richard Lee Jackson; Jim Haynie; *D:* David S. Cass, Sr.; *W:* William Sims Myers; *C:* Maximo Munzi; *M:* Joe Kraemer. **CABLE**

Avenging Angelo **2002 (R)** The Hound thinks this flick is supposed to be a mobster comedy with some romance and, well, it's such a mess who knows what was intended, except it's not gonna revive Stallone's career. He's bodyguard Frankie Delano. He works for mob boss Angelo Allighieri (Quinn), who gets whacked. Frankie then decides Angelo's daughter Jennifer (Stowe) is in danger, so he goes to protect her. Only Jennifer was adopted and doesn't know she's a mobster's daughter and thinks Frankie is nuts—until she nearly gets whacked. Then she believes him and wants revenge. **96m/C; VHS, DVD.** Sylvester Stallone; Madeleine Stowe; Harry Van Gorkum; Raoul Bova; Anthony Quinn; *D:* Martyn Burke; *W:* Will Aldis; Steve Mackall; *C:* Ousama Rawi; *M:* Bill Conti.

Avenging Conscience *Thou Shall Not Kill* **1914** An early eerie horror film, based on tales of Edgar Allan Poe. D.W. Griffith's first large-scale feature. Silent. **78m/B; Silent; VHS, DVD.** Henry B. Walthall; Blanche Sweet; *D:* D.W. Griffith.

Avenging Disco Godfather **½** *Avenging Godfather; Disco Godfather* **1976 (R)** Moore parodies the "Godfather" and martial arts movies. **99m/C; VHS, DVD, Blu-Ray.** Rudy Ray Moore; Carol Speed; Jimmy Lynch; Jeny Jones; Lady Reeds; James H. Hawthorne; Frank Finn; Julius J. Carry, III; *D:* J. Robert Wagoner; *W:* J. Robert Wagoner; Cliff Roquemore; *C:* Arledge Armenaki; *M:* Ernie Fields, Jr.

Avenue Montaigne **½** *Fauteuils d'Orchestre; Orchestra Seats* **2006 (PG-13)** Sweet provincial gamine Jessica (De France) comes to Paris and gets a job at a cafe along the titular street. The cafe is particularly busy because three major events will be happening nearby: classical pianist Jean-Francois (Dupontel) is giving a concert; popular TV actress Catherine (Lemercier) is starring onstage; and aging businessman Jacques (Brasseur) is going to auction off his extensive art collection. Each are having personal difficulties, which come to a boil over a three-day period, with Jessica providing her common-sense reactions. French with subtitles. **100m/C; DVD.** *FR* Cecile de France; Valerie Lemercier; Albert Dupontel; Claude Brasseur; Dani; Laura Morante; Sydney Pollack; Annelise Hesme; Suzanne Flon; *D:* Daniele Thompson; *W:* Daniele Thompson; *C:* Jean-Marc Fabre; *M:* Nicola Piovani.

AVH: Alien vs. Hunter **WOOF! 2007** All-around rip-off woofer. Reporter Lee (Katt) goes to a small town to investigate what turns out to be the crash landing of two spaceships. One contains a vicious alien spider thingy and the other the alien hunter that is trying to kill it. But those pesky human residents are in the way! **85m/C; DVD, Blu-Ray.** William Katt; Dedee Pfeiffer; Randy Mulkey; Jennifer Couch; Jason S. Gray; *D:* Scott Harper; *W:* David Michael Latt; *C:* Mark Atkins. **VIDEO**

Avia: Vampire Hunter **2005** A mentally disturbed young woman discovers vampires are real and spends her life running about whacking them with a Samurai sword. Little known fact: apparently American vampires are allergic to Japanese steel. **90m/C; DVD.** Rodney Jackson; Allison Valentino; *D:* Leon Hunter; *W:* Leon Hunter; *C:* Leon Hunter. **VIDEO**

The Aviator **1985 (PG)** Pilot Reeve, haunted by the memory of a fatal crash, tries to find a new line of work. Large sums of money persuade him to transport spoiled Arquette to Washington. When the biplane crashes in the mountain wilderness, the two fall in love between scavenging for food and fighting wild animals. From the director of "Man From Snowy River." **98m/C; VHS, DVD, Blu-Ray.** Christopher Reeve; Rosanna Arquette; Jack Warden; Tyne Daly; Marcia Strassman; Sam Wanamaker; Scott Wilson; *D:* George Miller; *W:* Marc Norman; *C:* David Connell; *M:* Dominic Frontiere.

The Aviator **½ 2004 (PG-13)** Scorsese's sweeping, rich biopic of eccentric movie producer/aviation pioneer Howard Hughes soars on many levels. The film follows Hughes from maverick producer taking Hollywood by storm in the '20s through his successes in aviation and the founding of TWA, and finally battling Pan Am and Congress in the '40s. Di Caprio, in full-on movie idol mode, captures the drive and intensity of Hughes, letting the audience see glimpses of the coming breakdown, but mostly keeping it bubbling below the surface (until a slightly over-the-top sequence about 90 minutes in). Blanchett also shines in a dazzling portrayal of Katharine Hepburn. Scorsese's eye for detail and love of Old Hollywood serve the proceedings well, providing fascinating peeks into the workings of the old studio system, the testing and building of experimental aircraft, and the wheeling and dealing of high-stakes politics. **166m/C; VHS, DVD, Blu-Ray, HD-DVD.** Leonardo DiCaprio; Cate Blanchett; Kate Beckinsale; John C. Reilly; Alec Baldwin; Alan Alda; Ian Holm; Danny Huston; Jude Law; Adam Scott; Matt Ross; Kelli Garner; Frances Conroy; Brent Spiner; Stanley DeSantis;

Edward Herrmann; Willem Dafoe; J.C. MacKenzie; Kenneth Welsh; Amy Sloan; Kevin O'Rourke; Lisa Bronwyn Moore; Gwen Stefani; Vincent Laresca; Josie Maran; ***D:*** Martin Scorsese; ***W:*** John Logan; ***C:*** Robert Richardson; ***M:*** Howard Shore. Oscars '04: Art Dir./Set Dec., Cinematog., Costume Des., Film Editing, Support. Actress (Blanchett); British Acad. '04: Film, Makeup, Support. Actress (Blanchett); Golden Globes '05: Actor--Drama (DiCaprio), Film--Drama, Orig. Score; Screen Actors Guild '04: Support. Actress (Blanchett).

The Aviator's Wife 🦴🦴🦴 *La Femme de L'Aviateur* **1980** The first in Rohmer's Comedies and Proverbs series is a comedy of errors involving a post-office worker (Marlaud) who believes that his older girlfriend (Riviere) is seeing another man, a pilot (Carriere). He enlists the aid of a young girl (Meury) to help him spy on his romantic obsession. French with subtitles. **104m/C; VHS, DVD.** *FR* Philippe Marlaud; Marie Riviere; Anne-Laure Meury; Matthieu Carriere; ***D:*** Eric Rohmer; ***W:*** Eric Rohmer; ***C:*** Bernard Lutic; ***M:*** Jean-Louis Valero.

Awake 🦴 1/2 **2007 (R)** Wealthy Clayton Beresford (Christensen), stricken with a heart defect, must undergo a transplant to save his life. Unfortunately, something goes wrong, and he experiences "anesthesia awareness," which means that he appears asleep but is actually awake and fully aware of everything going on during his operation. Rather than build suspense and tension from such an intense premise, the story's twists and surprises (including an absurd-even-by-horror-movie-standards plot for poor Clay to die on the operating table) pile on ad nauseum, and Christensen is expected to carry much of the movie while flat on his back. **78m/C; Blu-Ray, On Demand.** Hayden Christensen; Jessica Alba; Terrence Howard; Lena Olin; Arliss Howard; Christopher McDonald; Fisher Stevens; Sam Robards; Georgina Chapman; ***D:*** Joby Harold; ***W:*** Joby Harold; ***C:*** Russell Carpenter; ***M:*** Graeme Revell.

Awake 🦴 1/2 *Wake Up* **2019** When he wakes up in the hospital, John Doe (Rhys Meyers) has no idea who he is. He learns that he is the prime suspect in the murder of five women and the police have evidence that links him to the crimes. Sympathetic nurse Diana (Eastwood) shares his doubts about his guilt and goes on the run with him as he tries to remember who he is and prove he is not a murderer. A mess of a mystery-thriller that starts off strong only to end up sleepwalking. **92m/C; DVD.** Jonathan Rhys Myers; Francesca Ruth Eastwood; Malik Yoba; James Austin Kerr; Erin Elizabeth Cook; ***D:*** Aleksandr Chernyaev; ***W:*** Elana Zeltser; ***C:*** Fedor Lyass; ***M:*** Alex Kharlamov. **VIDEO**

Awaken 🦴 1/2 *A Perfect Vacation* **2015 (R)** A action-horror-mystery hybrid centering on lost people stranded on an island and the sinister plot behind their disappearance. Awakening on the shore of the island, a group of people does not know one another nor why they are there. They soon discover that they are being hunted and that they had been kidnapped by organ harvesters who only want their body parts. The captives try their best to avoid this fate. **89m/C; DVD, Streaming, Download.** Daryl Hannah; Edward Furlong; Vinnie Jones; Jason London; David Keith; ***D:*** Mark Atkins; ***W:*** Mark Atkins; Ryan Priest; ***M:*** Kays Al-Atrakchi; Brian Ralston. **VIDEO**

The Awakening 🦴 1/2 **1980 (R)** An archeologist discovers the tomb of a murderous queen, but upon opening the coffin, the mummy's spirit is transferred to his baby daughter, born at that instant. They call that bad luck. **101m/C; VHS, Streaming.** *GB* Charlton Heston; Susannah York; Stephanie Zimbalist; Patrick Drury; Ian McDiarmid; Bruce Myers; Nadim Sawalha; Jill Townsend; ***D:*** Mike Newell; ***W:*** Allan Scott; Chris Bryant; Clive Exton; ***C:*** Jack Cardiff; ***M:*** Claude Bolling.

The Awakening 🦴 1/2 **1995** Smalltown Sara (Geary) has had to turn the family home into a boardinghouse in order to meet expenses. Bounty hunter Flynn (Beecroft) moves in while pursuing an antiques smuggler and he and Sara join forces to find romance as well as adventure. From the Harlequin Romance Series; adapted from the Patricia Coughlin novel. **95m/C; DVD.** *CA* Cynthia Geary; David Beecroft; Sheila McCarthy; Maurice Godin; ***D:*** George Bloomfield; ***W:*** Maria Nation; ***C:*** Manfred Guthe; ***M:*** Amin Bhatia. **TV**

The Awakening 🦴🦴 **2011 (R)** Florence Cathcart (Hall) spends her time debunking false reports of hauntings but finds herself challenged when she investigates an orphanage that reportedly has a ghostly child roaming its halls. Set in 1921 England, director Murphy's film starts with some promising themes regarding loneliness, survivor's guilt, and depression but becomes a rather generic affair as its supernatural angles work toward a twist ending that doesn't have nearly the power that its filmmakers believe it does. Hall delivers the dramatic goods and there's an interesting sense of setting but the overall production ends up more monotonous than terrifying. **107m/C; DVD, Blu-Ray.** *UK* Rebecca Hall; Dominic West; Imelda Staunton; Isaac Hempstead-Wright; Shaun Dooley; Joseph Mawle; ***D:*** Nick Murphy; ***W:*** Nick Murphy; Stephen Volk; ***C:*** Eduard Grau.

The Awakening Land 🦴🦴 1/2 **1978** Well-acted miniseries based on Conrad Richter's trilogy follows the fortunes of the pioneering Luckett family in the Ohio Territory from 1790 through 1817. Illiterate homesteader Sayward Luckett (Montgomery) falls in love and marries frontier lawyer Portius Wheeler (Holbrook), who's rightly known as "The Solitary." It's up to Sayward to raise their children and make a go of their lives amidst various hardships and many changes. **333m/C; DVD.** Elizabeth Montgomery; Hal Holbrook; Jane Seymour; Louise Latham; Steven Keats; Jeannette Nolan; Tony Mockus, Jr.; William H. Macy; ***D:*** Boris Sagal; ***W:*** James Lee Barrett; Liam O'Brien; ***C:*** Michel Hugo; ***M:*** Fred Karlin. **TV**

Awakening the Zodiac 🦴🦴 **2017 (R)** A modern-day trio, with their eyes on the prize reward of $100,000, try to uncover the identity of the Zodiac killer, who thoughtfully filmed his 1968 murders and abandoned the reels in a storage unit. Shadowy figures and mysterious callers factor in to this cat-and-mouse yarn, and devotees of true crime might enjoy a new spin on an unsolved case, but an implausible ending undoes the fun. **100m/C; DVD.** Shane West; Leslie Bibb; Matt Craven; Stephen McHattie; Nicholas (Nick) Campbell; ***D:*** Jonathan Wright; ***W:*** Jonathan Wright; Jennifer Archer; Mike Horrigan; ***C:*** Boris Mojsovski; ***M:*** Mark Korven.

Awakenings 🦴🦴🦴 1/2 **1990 (PG-13)** Marshall's first dramatic effort is based on the true story of Dr. Oliver Sacks, from his book of the same title. It details his experimentation with the drug L-dopa which inspired the "awakening" of a number of catatonic patients, some of whom had been "sleeping" for as long as 30 years. Occasionally oversentimental, but still providing a poignant look at both the patients—who find themselves confronted with lost opportunities and faded youth—and at Sacks, who must watch their exquisite suffering as they slip away. De Niro's performance as the youngest of the group is heart-rending, while Williams offers a subdued, moving performance as the doctor. **120m/C; VHS, DVD.** Robin Williams; Robert De Niro; John Heard; Julie Kavner; Penelope Ann Miller; Max von Sydow; Anne Meara; Dexter Gordon; Alice Drummond; Richard Libertini; Judith Malina; Barton Heyman; Bradley Whitford; Peter Stormare; Laura Esterman; Vincent Pastore; Vin Diesel; ***D:*** Penny Marshall; ***W:*** Steven Zaillian; ***M:*** Randy Newman. Natl. Bd. of Review '90: Actor (De Niro), Actor (Williams); Natl. Soc. Film Critics '90: Actor (De Niro).

Awakenings of the Beast 🦴 *Ritual Dos Sadicos; Ritual of the Maniacs* **1968** Documents the protracted sufferings of an LSD drug user who is beset with hallucinatory visions and is prone to fits of frenzied violence. Director Jose Mojica Marins (AKA Coffin Joe) steps out of his Ze do Ciaxia character in this disjointed mix of drugs and sex intercut with Mojica Marins himself on trial for his offensive movies, followed by a case study on drugs and sexual behavior. By the end of the movie, there is a point—that drugs aren't the cause of evil behavior—but it's very painful getting there. In Portugese with English subtitles. **93m/B; VHS, DVD.** *BR* Jose Mojica Marins; Sergio Hingst; Andrea Bryan; Mario Lima; ***D:*** Jose Mojica Marins; ***W:*** Jose Mojica Marins; Rubens Francisco Lucchetti; ***C:*** Giorgio Attili.

Away All Boats 🦴🦴 1/2 **1956** The true story of one Captain Hawks, who led a crew of misfits to victory in WWII Pacific aboard transport USS Belinda. Battle scenes are well done; look for early (and brief) appearance by young Clint Eastwood. **114m/B; VHS, DVD.** Jeff Chandler; George Nader; Richard Boone; Julie Adams; Keith Andes; Lex Barker; Clint Eastwood; ***D:*** Joseph Pevney; ***W:*** Ted Sherdeman; ***C:*** William H. Daniels; ***M:*** Frank Skinner.

Away From Her 🦴🦴🦴 **2006** Polley makes her directorial debut with this adaptation of the Alice Munro story "The Bear Who Came Over the Mountain." Grant (Pinsent) and Fiona (Christie) have been married more than 40 years when she is diagnosed with Alzheimer's. As her mental acuity deteriorates, Fiona insists on entering a nursing home, where she befriends another married patient (Murphy), while Grant struggles to cope with the changes. Gracefully aging '60s British icon Christie is well-matched by Canadian actor Pinsent in a tender story about love and loss that shouldn't be seen by cynics. **110m/C; DVD.** *CA* Julie Christie; Gordon Pinsent; Olympia Dukakis; Michael Murphy; Wendy Crewson; Alberta Watson; Kristen Thomson; ***D:*** Sarah Polley; ***W:*** Sarah Polley; ***C:*** Luc Montpellier; ***M:*** Jonathan Goldsmith. Golden Globes '08: Actress--Drama (Christie); Screen Actors Guild '07: Actress (Christie).

Away We Go 🦴🦴 **2009 (R)** Thirty-somethings Burt (Krasinski) and Verona (Rudolph) are a longtime unmarried couple who are expecting their first child. Uncommitted to their life in Colorado, they decide to travel around the U.S., visiting various cities to see if any appeal as the perfect place to start their family. Along the way, they have misadventures and find fresh connections with an assortment of relatives and old friends who just might help them discover "home" for the first time. The leads are appealing but the writers seem determined to showcase various domestic hells and condescending caricatures with their secondary characters. **97m/C; Blu-Ray, On Demand.** John Krasinski; Jeff Daniels; Maggie Gyllenhaal; Melanie Lynskey; Maya Rudolph; Allison Janney; Catherine O'Hara; Jim Gaffigan; Carmen Ejogo; Josh Hamilton; Chris Messina; Paul Schneider; ***D:*** Sam Mendes; ***W:*** Dave Eggers; Vendela Vida; ***C:*** Ellen Kuras; ***M:*** Alex Murdoch.

Awesome! I F*in' Shot That!** 🦴🦴🦴 **2006 (R)** Combination of professional and fans' footage of The Beastie Boys' October 9, 2004 show at Madison Square Garden. The band encouraged fans to film the concert and send them the results. Works as both a document of the show and as an experiment in cooperation and collaboration between the artists and their fans. **90m/C; DVD.** ***D:*** Adam "MCA" Yauch; ***C:*** Alexis Boling; ***M:*** Adam "MCA" Yauch; Adam Horovitz; Mike D.

The Awful Dr. Orloff 🦴 *Gritos en la Noche; The Demon Doctor* **1962** Set in a bygone era, Dr. Orloff (Vernon) is a retired prison physician who needs unblemished skin to remedy the horrible disfigurement of his daughter Melissa (Lorys), ravaged by fire. He abducts promising young women candidates with the help of his blind zombie henchman Morpho (Valle), who simply cannot be trusted with a scalpel. After several surgical mishaps, they kidnap the perfect specimen, a woman who bears an uncanny resemblance to Melissa. Unfortunately, she is engaged to suspicious police Inspector Tanner (San Martin). French version with English subtitles that includes more explicit gore is also available. **86m/B; DVD, Blu-Ray.** *SP FR* Howard Vernon; Diana Lorys; Frank Wolff; Riccardo Valle; Conrado San Martin; Perla Cristal; Maria Silva; Mara Laso; ***D:*** Jess (Jesus) Franco; ***W:*** Jess (Jesus) Franco; ***C:*** Godofredo Pacheco; ***M:*** Jose Pagan; Antonio Ramirez Angel.

Awful Nice 🦴 **2014 (R)** Deliberately obnoxious behavior highlights this indie comedy. Belligerently estranged brothers Jim and Dave start up their sibling rivalry once again by fighting at their dad's funeral. Then they learn they've equally inherited the family lakeside cottage in Branson, resulting in a road trip. Only the house is a disaster that they'll have to fix up in order to sell, which leads to a number of mishaps. **88m/C; DVD, Blu-Ray.** Alex Rennie; James Pumphrey; Christopher Meloni; Brett Gelman; Keeley Hazell; ***D:*** Todd A. Sklar; ***W:*** Alex Rennie; Todd A. Sklar; ***C:*** Adam Ginsberg; ***M:*** Mark Harrison.

The Awful Truth 🦴🦴🦴🦴 **1937** Lucy (Dunne) and Jerry (Grant) Warriner are a young couple who discard their marriage made in heaven and go their separate ways in search of happiness. Meticulously sabotaging each others' new relationships, they discover they really were made for each other. Grant is at his most charming with dead-on comic timing while Dunne is brilliant as his needling ex. The scene where Dunne poses as Grant's prodigal fan-dancing sister who pays a surprise cocktail-hour visit to the family of his stuffy, upper-class girlfriend (Lamont) is among the most memorable screwball vignettes of all time. And don't miss the custody battle they have over the family dog (Asta of "The Thin Man" fame). Based on Arthur Richman's 1922 play. Preceded by 1925 and 1929 versions; remade in 1953 as "Let's Do it Again." **92m/B; VHS, DVD, Blu-Ray.** Irene Dunne; Cary Grant; Ralph Bellamy; Alexander D'Arcy; Cecil Cunningham; Molly Lamont; Esther Dale; Joyce Compton; Robert "Tex" Allen; Robert Warwick; Mary Forbes; ***D:*** Leo McCarey; ***W:*** Vina Delmar. Oscars '37: Director (McCarey); Natl. Film Reg. '96.

An Awfully Big Adventure 🦴🦴 **1994 (R)** Coming-of-age saga set in postwar Liverpool around a provincial reperatory company. Stage-struck 16-year-old Stella (Cates) gets work as a company apprentice, immediately getting a crush on arch, callous theatre manager Meredith Potter (a deliciously nasty Grant), who enjoys degrading everyone around him. The company's chance for success rests on a production of "Peter Pan," with visiting actor P.L. O'Hara (dashing Rickman), who immediately seduces Stella and has more than a few secrets of his own. Theatrically exaggerated; based on the novel by Beryl Bainbridge. **113m/C; VHS, DVD.** *GB* Georgina Cates; Hugh Grant; Alan Rickman; Peter Firth; Alun Armstrong; Prunella Scales; Rita Tushingham; Alan Cox; Edward Petherbridge; Nicola Pagett; Carol Drinkwater; Clive Merrison; Gerard McSorley; ***D:*** Mike Newell; ***W:*** Charles Wood; ***C:*** Dick Pope; ***M:*** Richard Hartley.

Axe 🦴 1/2 *Lisa, Lisa; California Axe Massacre* **1974 (R)** After a group of thugs kill a man (on an embarrassingly shoddy set), they flee to the country, where they take over a farmhouse. The only residents of this farmhouse are a young girl, Lisa (Lee), and her invalid grandfather. The criminals force Lisa to cook a chicken dinner (NO!) and then generally terrorize the girl and her grandfather. Eventually, Lisa (who is actively hallucinating throughout this episode) gets the titular axe and seeks her revenge. The film is slow and boring, and the sub-amateur acting doesn't help. The only positive aspect is the suspense that mounts over the course of the movie. Having seen films like this before, and given the fact that nothing else is happening, the audience knows that Lisa is going to strike back at some time. **68m/C; DVD, Blu-Ray.** Leslie Lee; Jack Canon; Frederick Friedel; Frank Jones; ***D:*** Frederick Friedel; ***W:*** Frederick Friedel; ***C:*** Austin McKinney.

Axe **WOOF!** *Greed* **2006** Underwear acting. Babes Raven and Ashley (who spend a lot of time in their scanties) hit a desert bar after a rock-climbing expedition. After being harassed by a biker gang, they steal one of the bikes and wind up at a lonely motel with a satchel of cash. Oh, and there's an escaped con, Ivan the Axeman, on the loose as well. London has limited screen time as the bar owner in this incredibly stupid mishmash of genres. **92m/C; DVD.** Tim Sitarz; Jason London; Joe Goodrich; Andrea Bogart; Darlena Tejeiro; ***D:*** Ron Wolotzky; ***W:*** Eyal Sher; Dred Ross; ***C:*** Moshe Levin; Scott Carrithers; ***M:*** Erik Godal; Mark Fontana. **VIDEO**

A-X-L 🦴 1/2 **2018 (PG)** After corporate arms mogul Andric Crane (Rains) creates a finely tuned war machine mechanical canine named AXL (attack, exploration, logistics), the dog escapes and hides in the desert. There, AXL is found by Miles (Neustaedter), a teenage bike racer who does not see a bright future for himself despite his racing talent. After Miles repairs AXL, the pair bond and Miles, with the help of love interest Sara (G), tries to protect him from Crane's goons. A thin plot and poor presentation of AXL -- shifting between a visual effect and an obvious puppet -- undercuts everything else. **98m/C; DVD.** Alex Neustaedter; Becky G; Thomas Jane; Ted McGinley; Dominic Rains; ***D:*** Oliver Daly; ***W:*** Oliver Daly; ***C:*** Tim Orr; ***M:*** Ian Hultquist.

Azumi 🦴🦴🦴 **2003 (R)** In 19th century Japan, Azumi, a young orphan girl is raised, along with other orphans, to become an assassin. Azumi (Ueto) soon becomes the best of them. When they come of age, they are cruelly tested, and the survivors are given a mission to eliminate warlords who are tearing the country apart. The action is top-notch, as expected, and the script manages to show both the beauty and brutality of the end of the Samurai era in Japan. Not all Western audience will appreciate the humor, fatalism, or meandering storytelling, but patience and attention is definitely rewarded. **128m/C; DVD.** Shun Oguri; Yoshio Harada; Masato Ibu; Joe Odagiri; Naoto Takenaka; Aya Ueto; Hiroki Narimiya; Kenji Kohashi; Takatoshi Kaneko; Yuma Ishigaki; Yasuomi Sano; Shinji Suzuki; Eita Nagayama; Shogo Yamaguchi; Kazuki Kitamura; Kenichi Endo; Kazuya Shimizu; Ryo; Michael P. Greco; Shoichiro Masumoto; Minoru Matsumoto; Aya Okamoto; Tak Sakaguchi; Hideo Sakaki; ***D:*** Ryuhei Kitamura; ***W:*** Yu Koyama; Rikiya Mizushima; Isao Kiriyama; ***C:*** Takumi Furuya; ***M:*** Taro Iwashiro.

Azumi 2 🦴🦴 1/2 *Azumi 2: Death or Love; Azumi 2: Love or Duty...An Assassin Must Choose* **2005** Beginning directly where the first film leaves off, Azumi (Ueto) and Nagara (Ishigaki) continue their pursuit of their assigned target Masayuki Sanada (Nagasawa). He hires the Koga Ninja clan, a band of specialized assassins to take them out before they can reach him. The first film is required viewing for this one as there are no flashbacks or explanations given. Fans of "Kill Bill" should look for Chiaki Kuriyama (she played Go Go) as one of the ninja super assassins. **108m/C; DVD.** *JP* Aya Ueto; Yuma Ishigaki; Chiaki Kuriyama; Shun Oguri; Kenichi Endo; Kai Shishido; Tak Sakaguchi; Shoichiro Masumoto; Eugene Nomura; Aki Maeda; Toshie Negishi; Toshiya Nagasawa; Kenji Takechi; Shigeru Koyama; Mikijiro Hira; Kazuki Kitamura; Reiko Takashima; ***D:*** Shusuke (Shu) Kaneko; ***W:*** Yu Koyama; Yoshiaki Kawajiri; Mataichiro Yamamoto; ***C:*** Yoshitaka Sakamoto.

B. Monkey 🦴🦴 **1997 (R)** B—AKA Beatrice (Argento)--hopes she can escape her world of drugs and crime (she's a thief) with the romantic aid of schoolteacher Alan (Harris). But her past catches up with her when ex-partners Paul (Everett) and Bruno (Rhys Meyers) convince her to do one last job (she misses the rush). Based on the novel by Andrew Davies, this one is mainly cool Brit style over substance. **91m/C; VHS, DVD, Blu-Ray.** *GB* Asia Argento; Jared Harris; Rupert Everett; Jonathan Rhys Meyers; Tim Woodward; Ian Hart; ***D:*** Michael Radford; ***W:*** Michael Thomas; Chloe King; ***C:*** Ashley Rowe; ***M:*** Jennie Muskett.

The B-Side: Elsa Dorfman's Portrait Photography 🦴🦴 **2017 (R)** An enchanting documentary look at the life and work of photographer Elsa Dorfman. Between 1980 and 2015, the captivating Dorfman took revealing portraits with her large-format Polaroid Land 20x24 camera of the famous and the not so famous who stopped at her studio in Cambridge, Massachusetts. As she neared retirement, filmmaker Errol Morris explores her artistic style and vision, technology, and materials though the pictures she took as well as the place of her work in her personal and professional life. Though full of well-explained technical details, the film is driven by Dorfman's engaging personality and Morris's exploration of Dorfman as an artist. **66m/C; DVD.** Elsa Dorfman; ***D:*** Errol Morris; ***C:*** Nathan Swingle; Nathan Allen Swingle; ***M:*** Paul-Leonard Morgan.

Baadasssss! 🦴🦴🦴 1/2 *How to Get the Man's Foot Outta Your Asss!* **2003 (R)** Mario Van Peebles' fictionalized biopic of his father Melvin's efforts to get his influential indie film "Sweet Sweetback's Baadasssss Song" (the forerunner of the blaxploitation genre) made. Melvin (Mario, who also directed, co-wrote, and produced) is plagued with money and health problems, union troubles and lack of studio interest. Well-made and highly entertaining film was adapted from Melvin's "making of" book. Mario honors his father's work without over-romanticizing the often-imperfect man behind it. **108m/C; DVD.** Mario Van Peebles; Nia Long; David Alan Grier; Ossie Davis; Terry Crews; Rainn Wilson; Joy Bryant; Saul Rubinek; T.K. Carter; Paul Rodriguez; Vincent Schiavelli; Khleo Thomas; Len Lesser; Sally Struthers; Adam West; Glenn Plummer; Khalil Kain; Pamela Gordon; Joseph Culp; Karimah Westbrook; Ralph Martin; Robert Peters; Wesley Jonathan; John Singleton; ***D:*** Mario Van Peebles; ***W:*** Mario Van Peebles; Dennis Haggerty; ***C:*** Robert Primes; ***M:*** Tyler Bates.

The Baader Meinhof Complex 🦴🦴 **2008 (R)** Overstuffed drama crams ten years worth of history on the notorious 1960-70s West German terrorist group, the Red Army Faction (RAF), reducing it to re-enactments (albeit with some ferocious acting) with not much explanation for those not already familiar with the history. Left-wing journalist Ulricke Meinhof (Gedeck) uses the German government's heavy-handed reaction to student demonstrations to leave behind her life as a prosaic middle-class wife and mother. Instead, she becomes involved in the political activities of Andreas Baader (Bleibtrue) and Gudrun Ensslin (Wokalek) that were transformed from idealism to nihilism and violence, including bombings, hijackings, kidnappings, jailbreaks, and assassinations. Adapted from the book by Stefan Aust. English, German, French, and Arabic with subtitles. **150m/C; Blu-Ray, On Demand.** *GE* Martina Gedeck; Moritz Bleibtreu; Johanna Wokalek; Bruno Ganz; Nadja Uhl; Jan Josef Liefers; Stipe Erceg; Niels Bruno Schmidt; Vinzenz Kiefer; Simon Licht; ***D:*** Uli Edel; ***W:*** Uli Edel; Bernd Eichinger; ***C:*** Rainer Klausmann; ***M:*** Peter Hindertuer; Florian Tesslof.

Ba'al: The Storm God **WOOF!** **2008 (PG-13)** An archaeologist gathers four ancient amulets, designed to reawaken the storm god Ba'al, hoping their mystical properties will cure his terminal cancer. Cheapo Sci-Fi Channel movie with a lousy script and equally bad acting. **90m/C; DVD.** Jeremy London; Lexa Doig; Michael Kopsa; ***D:*** Paul Ziller; ***W:*** Paul Ziller; Andrew Black; ***C:*** Mahlon Todd Williams; ***M:*** Pinar Toprak. **CABLE**

Baaria 🦴🦴 **2009** Old-fashioned and over-extended multi-decade saga from writer/director Tornatore that focuses on the Sicilian Torrenuova clan, who survive through Fascism, WWII, and the political chaos of postwar Italy. In the 1930s, shepherd Ciccio works for corrupt landowner Giacinto, and his trials turn his son Peppino into an ambitious Communist activist. Peppino's son Pietro will become a photographer, recording the changes around him. The title is local dialect for the Sicilian town of Bagheria where Tornatore was born. Italian with subtitles. **150m/C; DVD, Blu-Ray.** *IT* Angela Molina; Enrico Lo Verso; Lina Sastri; Francesco Scianna; Margareth Made; Lollo Franco; Giovanni Gambino; Davide Viviani; Marco Iermano; Gaetano Aronica; ***D:*** Giuseppe Tornatore; ***W:*** Giuseppe Tornatore; ***C:*** Enrico Lucidi; ***M:*** Ennio Morricone.

Baba Yaga 🦴 *Kiss Me, Kill Me; The Devil Witch* **1973** Euro-horror loosely based on the erotic comic books of Guido Crepax. Talented young Milan photog Valentina accepts a late-night ride from the oddly-named Baba Yaga and then can't get the older woman out of her life. Valentina starts having kinky nightmares and her camera seems to be cursed. She discovers that Baba Yaga is literally a witch (and an S&M-loving lesbian). Dubbed. **83m/C; DVD, Blu-Ray.** *FR IT* Carroll Baker; Isabelle DeFunes; George Eastman; Ely Galleani; ***D:*** Corrado Farina; ***W:*** Corrado Farina; ***C:*** Aiace Parolini; ***M:*** Piero Umiliani.

The Babadook 🦴🦴🦴 **2014** Samuel (Wiseman) was born the day his father died, as he tried to get his mother Amelia (Davis) to the hospital to deliver. Naturally, this blend of grief and joy around Samuel's birthday leads to emotional turmoil, which results in a haunting of sorts in this excellent Australian boogeyman tale. Amelia and Samuel find a book they didn't know they had that tells the story of the deadly Babadook and how it's coming to get them. And then it does. Davis is fantastic in a tale that feels reminiscent of "The Shining" and "The Orphanage." **95m/C; DVD, Blu-Ray.** *AU* Essie Davis; Noah Wiseman; Daniel Henshall; ***D:*** Jennifer Kent; ***W:*** Jennifer Kent; ***C:*** Radek Kotatko; ***M:*** Jed Kurzel.

Babar: The Movie 🦴🦴 1/2 **1988 (G)** The lovable Babar, king of the elephants, must devise a plan to outwit an angry hoard of attacking rhinos. Based on the characters of Jean and Laurent de Brunhoff. **75m/C; VHS, DVD.** *CA FR* ***V:*** Gavin Magrath; Gordon Pinsent; Sarah Polley; Chris Wiggins; Elizabeth Hanna; ***D:*** Alan Bunce; ***W:*** Alan Bunce; John deKlein.

Babe! 🦴🦴🦴 1/2 **1975** A fine TV movie about the life of one of America's most famous woman athletes, Babe Didrickson. Adapted by Joanna Lee from Didrickson's autobiography "The Life I've Led." The movie was nominated for Outstanding Special of 1975-76 and Clark won an Emmy for her work. **120m/C; VHS, DVD.** Susan Clark; Alex Karras; Slim Pickens; Jeannette Nolan; Ellen Geer; Ford Rainey; ***D:*** Buzz Kulik; ***M:*** Jerry Goldsmith. **TV**

The Babe 🦴🦴 1/2 **1992 (PG)** Follows the life of legendary baseball player Babe Ruth, portrayed as a sloppy drunkard whose appetites for food, drink, and sex were as large as he was. Alvarado and McGillis do well as the Babe's first and second wives, but this is Goodman's show from start to finish. He's excellent as Ruth, and looks the part, but his fine performance can't make up for a lackluster script filled with holes. **115m/C; VHS, DVD, Blu-Ray.** John Goodman; Kelly McGillis; Trini Alvarado; Bruce Boxleitner; Peter Donat; J.C. Quinn; Richard Tyson; James Cromwell; Joe Ragno; Bernard Kates; Michael McGrady; Stephen Caffrey; Michael (Mike) Papajohn; ***D:*** Arthur Hiller; ***W:*** John Fusco; ***C:*** Haskell Wexler; ***M:*** Elmer Bernstein.

Babe 🦴🦴🦴 1/2 *Babe, the Gallant Pig* **1995 (G)** Totally charming fable has intelligent piglet Babe being raised by matriarch sheepdog Fly, and learning the art of sheep herding along with his new canine brothers. Farmer Hoggett (Cromwell), Babe's owner by virtue of a winning raffle ticket, sees that he's more than just a ham, and enters them in the world sheepdog herding championship. Whimsy that never crosses the line into treacle. Four different special effects houses were used to make the barnyard animals talk and walk. Filmed on location in Australia; based on Dick King-Smith's book "The Sheep-Pig." **91m/C; VHS, DVD, Blu-Ray.** *AU* James Cromwell; Magda Szubanski; ***V:*** Christine Cavanaugh; Miriam Margolyes; Danny Mann; Hugo Weaving; ***Nar:*** Roscoe Lee Browne; ***D:*** Chris Noonan; ***W:*** Chris Noonan; George Miller; ***C:*** Andrew Lesnie; ***M:*** Nigel Westlake. Oscars '95: Visual FX; Golden Globes '96: Film--Mus./Comedy; Natl. Soc. Film Critics '95: Film.

Babe: Pig in the City 🦴🦴 1/2 **1998 (PG)** Miller takes over the director's chair for this trip. And he brings along more money, more effects, more animals, and more unsettling images, including Mickey Rooney in a creepy clown suit, than anyone who saw the original would expect. Babe returns home to a hero's welcome, but the joy doesn't last long. Farmer Hoggett (Cromwell) is injured, and with foreclosure imminent, Babe and Mrs. Hoggett (Szubanski) head out to turn Babe's fame into a little cash. Along the way, they miss their connecting flight in "the city" and are forced to stay at a hotel that caters to animals. There, they meet the aforementioned Rooney and his three chimp partners, along with various dogs and cats. Technically well-done, and sporting an imaginative story, but may be a little dark for the younger kiddies. **96m/C; VHS, DVD, Blu-Ray.** James Cromwell; Magda Szubanski; Mickey Rooney; Mary Stein; Julie Godfrey; ***V:*** Elizabeth Daily; Danny Mann; Glenne Headly; Steven Wright; James Cosmo; Stanley Ralph Ross; Russi Taylor; Adam Goldberg; Nathan Kress; Myles Jeffrey; ***Nar:*** Roscoe Lee Browne; ***D:*** George Miller; ***W:*** Judy Morris; Mark Lamprell; ***C:*** Andrew Lesnie; ***M:*** Nigel Westlake.

Babe Ruth Story 🦴🦴 **1948** An overly sentimental biography about the famed baseball slugger. Bendix is miscast as the Bambino, but the actual film clips of the Babe are of interest. A movie to be watched during those infrequent bouts of sloppy baseball mysticism. **107m/B; VHS, DVD.** William Bendix; Claire Trevor; Charles Bickford; William Frawley; Sam Levene; Gertrude Niesen; ***D:*** Roy Del Ruth.

Babel 🦴🦴🦴 1/2 **2006 (R)** A father in a Moroccan village allows his two young sons to shoot his hunting rifle and an international incident is sparked. The boys innocently aim at a tourist bus, never believing the bullets could actually hit someone. They do, of course, and this one foolish act leads to complications that will encompass a Mexican nanny and her Anglo charges back in California and an angry deaf-mute teenaged girl in Tokyo. Somehow director Gonzalez Inarritu manages to tie the stories together (with a certain amount of unbelievability). Pitt and Blanchett join an impressive international cast who live up to this gritty, realistic dramatic puzzle. **142m/C; DVD, Blu-Ray, HD-DVD.** Brad Pitt; Cate Blanchett; Gael Garcia Bernal; Adriana Barraza; Elle Fanning; Koji Yakusho; Nathan Gamble; Rinko Kikuchi; Said Tarchani; Boubker Ait El Caid; Mustapha Rachidi; Abdelkader Bara; ***D:*** Alejandro Gonzalez Inarritu; ***W:*** Guillermo Arriaga; ***C:*** Rodrigo Prieto; ***M:*** Gustavo Santaolalla. Oscars '06: Orig. Score; British Acad. '06: Orig. Score; Golden Globes '07: Film--Drama.

Baberellas 🦴 1/2 **2003 (R)** In this parody of old scifi nudies like "Barbarella" or "Flesh Gordon" an evil alien queen hopes to steal all of the Earth's 'sexy energy' to promote her tv show (and incidentally killing off all life in the process). Standing in her way is an all girl rock band. **80m/C; DVD.** Shauna O'Brien; Julie K. Smith; Regina Russell; Julie Strain; ***D:*** Chuck Cirino; ***W:*** Chuck Cirino; Tip McPartland; Dave Nichols; Mark Wilde; ***C:*** David Winters; ***M:*** John Beal. **VIDEO**

Babes in Arms 🦴 1/2 **1939** The children of several vaudeville performers team up to put on a show to raise money for their financially impoverished parents. Loosely adapted from the Rodgers and Hart Broadway musical of the same name; features some of their songs as well as new additions. **91m/B; VHS, DVD.** Judy Garland; Mickey Rooney; Charles Winninger; Guy Kibbee; June Preisser; ***D:*** Busby Berkeley; ***M:*** George Bassman; Richard Rodgers; ***M:*** Lorenz Hart.

Babes in Toyland 🦴🦴 **1961** A lavish Disney production of Victor Herbert's timeless operetta, with Toyland being menaced by the evil Barnaby and his Bogeymen. Yes, Annette had a life after Mickey Mouse and before the peanut butter commercials. Somewhat charming, although the roles of the lovers seem a stretch for both Funicello and Kirk. But the flick does sport an amusing turn by Wynn. **105m/C; VHS, DVD, Blu-Ray.** Annette Funicello; Ray Bolger; Tommy Sands; Ed Wynn; Tommy Kirk; ***D:*** Jack Donohue; ***C:*** Edward Colman; ***M:*** George Bruns.

Babes on Broadway 🦴🦴 1/2 **1941** Mickey and Judy put on a show to raise money for a settlement house. Nearly the best of the Garland-Rooney series, with imaginative numbers staged by Berkeley. **118m/B; VHS, DVD.** Mickey Rooney; Judy Garland; Fay Bainter; Richard Quine; Virginia Weidler; Ray Macdonald; Busby Berkeley; ***D:*** Busby Berkeley; ***M:*** George Bassman.

Babette's Feast 🦴🦴🦴 1/2 *Babettes Gaestebud* **1987** A simple, moving pageant-of-life fable. Philippa (Kjer) and Martina (Federspiel) took over their late father's ministry in a small Danish coastal town. Widowed Frenchwoman Babette (Audran) has spent 14 years in their service and, after winning a lottery prize, decides she will prepare a lavish banquiet in honor of their father's 100th birthday. The religiously conservative villagers don't know what to make of such bounty—or the pleasure it brings to their senses. Adapted from a tale by Isak Dinesen. French and Danish with subtitles. **102m/C; VHS, DVD, Blu-Ray.** *DK FR* Stephane Audran; Bibi Andersson; Bodil Kjer; Birgitte Federspiel; Jean-Philippe LaFont; Ebbe Rode; Jarl Kulle; ***Nar:*** Ghita Norby; ***D:*** Gabriel Axel; ***W:*** Gabriel Axel; ***C:*** Henning Kristiansen; ***M:*** Per Norgard. Oscars '87: Foreign Film; British Acad. '88: Foreign Film.

Babies 🦴🦴🦴 *Bebes* **2010 (PG)** Gets extra bones for the awww factor. Director Balmes chronicles the first year of life for four babies (one boy, three girls) born in Mongolia, Namibia, San Francisco, and Tokyo. There's crying and various bodily functions to deal with; crawling, walking and exploring; and interacting with family and caregivers. There's no narration or subtitles to bother about. **79m/C; Blu-Ray, On Demand.** *FR* ***D:*** Thomas Balmes; ***C:*** Jerome Almeras; Steeven Petitteville; ***M:*** Bruno Coulais.

The Baby 1972 (PG) Bizarre story of a social worker who resorts to swinging an ax to cut the apron strings of "baby," a retarded man-child, from his over-protective and insane (bad combination) mother and sisters. Low-budget production looks and feels like a low-budget production, but any movie featuring a grown man wandering about in diapers can't be all bad. **85m/C; VHS, DVD, Blu-Ray.** Anjanette Comer; Ruth Roman; Marianna Hill; Suzanne Zenor; David Manzy; Michael Pataki; Erin O'Reilly; Virginia Vincent; ***D:*** Ted Post; ***W:*** Abe Polsky; ***C:*** Michael D. Margulies; ***M:*** Gerald Fried.

Baby 2000 John (Carradine) and Lily (Fawcett) Malone are unsuccessful in coping with their grief over the death of their infant son and in helping their 12-year-old daughter, Larkin (Pill), to deal with her own pain. Then a baby girl is abandoned on the Malone doorstep and Lily immediately wants to keep the child—much to the others' dismay. Formulaic weepie based on the novel by Patricia MacLachlan. **93m/C; DVD.** Farrah Fawcett; Keith Carradine; Jean Stapleton; Alison Pill; Vincent Berry; Ann Dowd; ***Nar:*** Glenn Close; ***D:*** Robert Allan Ackerman; ***W:*** Kerry Kennedy; Patricia MacLachlan; David Manson; ***C:*** Ron Garcia; ***M:*** Jeff Danna. **CABLE**

Baby Boom 1/2 1987 (PG) J.C. Wiatt (Keaton) is a hard-charging exec who becomes the reluctant mother to an orphaned baby girl (a gift from a long-lost relative). She adjusts with great difficulty to motherhood and life outside the rat race and New York City when J.C. decides she must make some radical changes to her routine. A fairly harmless collection of cliches bolstered by Keaton's usual nervous performance as a power-suited yuppie ad queen saddled with a noncareer-enhancing baby, who moves from manic career woman to jelly-packing Vermont store-owner/mom. Shepherd serves as her new, down-home, doctor beau. To best appreciate flick, see it with a bevy of five- and six-year-olds (a good age for applauding the havoc that a baby creates). **103m/C; VHS, DVD, Blu-Ray.** Diane Keaton; Sam Shepard; Harold Ramis; Sam Wanamaker; James Spader; Pat Hingle; Mary Gross; Victoria Jackson; Paxton Whitehead; Annie Golden; Dori Brenner; Robin Bartlett; Chris Noth; Britt Leach; ***D:*** Charles Shyer; ***W:*** Charles Shyer; Nancy Meyers; ***C:*** William A. Fraker; ***M:*** Bill Conti.

Baby Boy 1/2 2001 (R) Singleton's candid look at a culture that fosters and tolerates lack of emotional maturity in young African-American males. Jody (Gibson) is a 20-year-old manchild who still lives with his mother (Johnson), has two children with two different women, no job, and cheats on his current girl, Yvette. Jody's life changes when his mother's boyfriend moves in. Melvin (Rhames), an ex-con who's been down the road Jody is heading, shows no tolerance for his attitude. Real trouble starts when Rodney (Snoop Dogg), a street thug and Yvette's ex, is released from prison and refuses to leave her house. Singleton toys with two endings, but finishes the story with the message that the means to fix the problems he's described are within reach. **129m/C; VHS, DVD, UMD.** Tyrese Gibson; Omar Gooding; Taraji P. Henson; Adrienne-Joi (AJ) Johnson; Snoop Dogg; Tamara La Seon Bass; Ving Rhames; Angell Conwell; ***D:*** John Singleton; ***W:*** John Singleton; ***C:*** Charles Mills; ***M:*** David Arnold.

Baby Broker 1/2 *Born to Be Sold* 1981 Dated TV melodrama finds social worker Kate Carlin (Carter) learning that a 14-year-old client has agreed to a private adoption. When the teen tries to change her mind, a greedy lawyer who's arranging the black market baby sales hands the tyke over to paying-but-unfit parents anyway. Naturally Kate's in jeopardy when she starts investigating. **94m/C; DVD.** Lynda Carter; Harold Gould; Dean Stockwell; Sharon Farrell; Philip Sterling; Lloyd Haynes; Ed Nelson; Donna Wilkes; ***D:*** Burt Brinckerhoff; ***W:*** Karen Harris; ***C:*** William Cronjager; ***M:*** Johnny Harris. **TV**

The Baby Dance 1998 Well-off, middleaged Hollywood marrieds Rachel (Channing) and Richard (Reigert) Luckman have unsuccessfully tried to have a baby for years. Finally they place an adoption ad and receive a response from poor Louisiana trailer park inhabitants Wanda (Dern) and Art (Lineback) LeFauvre, who have an unwanted fifth child on the way. A meeting between the couples soon points out monetary, religious, and cultural differences that may derail their bargain. The two leading ladies carry the picture, which is based on director Anderson's Off-Broadway play. **95m/C; VHS, DVD.** Stockard Channing; Laura Dern; Peter Riegert; Richard Lineback; ***D:*** Jane Anderson; ***W:*** Jane Anderson; ***C:*** Jan Kiesser; ***M:*** Terry Allen. **CABLE**

Baby Doll 1956 Suggestive sex at its best, revolving around the love of cotton in Mississippi. Nubile Baker is married to slow-witted Malden, who runs a cotton gin. His torching of Wallach's cotton gin begins a cycle of sexual innuendo and tension, brought to exhilarating life on screen, without a single filmed kiss. Performers and sets ooze during the steamy exhibition, which was considered highly erotic when released. Excellent performances from entire cast, with expert pacing by director Kazan. Screenplay is based on Tennessee Williams' "27 Wagons Full of Cotton." **115m/B; VHS, DVD.** Eli Wallach; Carroll Baker; Karl Malden; Mildred Dunnock; Rip Torn; ***D:*** Elia Kazan; ***W:*** Tennessee Williams; ***C:*** Boris Kaufman. Golden Globes '57: Director (Kazan).

Baby Driver 2017 (R) Baby (Elgort) is an exceptional getaway driver because of his hearing disability -- he blares adrenaline pumping music to drown out his tinnitus and intensify his focus. He wants a fresh start with his new girlfriend, but he's forced to make one last run, a job that's doomed and will likely incur the wrath of his crime boss (Spacey). The soundtrack is thumping and the chase scenes are works of art. Sit back and enjoy the ride. **112m/C; DVD, Blu-Ray.** Ansel Elgort; Kevin Spacey; Lily James; Eiza González; Jon Hamm; Jamie Foxx; ***D:*** Edgar Wright; ***W:*** Edgar Wright; ***C:*** Bill Pope; ***M:*** Steven Price. British Acad. '17: Film Editing.

Baby Face 1933 A small town girl moves to the city when her father dies. There she gets a job at a bank and sleeps her way to the top of the business world, discarding used men left and right. The Hays Office was extremely upset with the then risque material and forced Warner to trim the first cut. **70m/B; VHS, DVD.** Barbara Stanwyck; George Brent; Donald Cook; John Wayne; Henry Kolker; Margaret Lindsay; Douglass Dumbrille; James Murray; ***D:*** Alfred E. Green; ***W:*** Gene Markey; Kathryn Scola; ***C:*** James Van Trees; ***M:*** Leo F. Forbstein. Natl. Film Reg. '05.

The Baby Formula 1/2 2008 Sentimental mockumentary with too many caricatures. Thanks to an experimental scientific procedure, married Toronto lesbians Athena (Vint) and Lilith (Fahlenbock) are able to have a baby using the DNA of both women. Now they're both pregnant and have to explain everything to their respective (and dysfunctional) families. Both actresses were actually pregnant during filming, which at least makes the awkward (and sometimes gross) situations very real (and the musical end credits very funny). **82m/C; DVD.** *CA* Megan Fahlenbock; Rosemary Dunsmore; Roger Dunn; Angela Vint; Hal Eisen; Jessica Booker; Michael Hanrahan; ***D:*** Allison Reid; Brian Harper; ***W:*** Richard Beattie; ***M:*** Robert Carli. **VIDEO**

Baby Geniuses 1/2 1998 (PG) Steals the most irritating parts of "Look Who's Talking," "Home Alone" and that creepy dancing baby and pastes them onto a lame good kids vs. evil adults plot. Turner and Lloyd are evil scientists attempting to crack the secret language of babies, which they believe holds the secrets of the universe (such as how to enjoy drooling and making in your pants). Standing in their way are nursery school operators Cattrall and MacNichol and an array of babies that spout inane dialogue thanks to an abuse of computer morphing. The effect is more disturbing than cute, and an excellent supporting cast is wasted. More interesting things can be found inside a diaper. **94m/C; VHS, DVD.** Kathleen Turner; Christopher Lloyd; Kim Cattrall; Peter MacNichol; Dom DeLuise; Ruby Dee; Kyle Howard; Leo Fitzgerald; Myles Fitzgerald; Gerry Fitzgerald; ***D:*** Bob (Benjamin) Clark; ***W:*** Bob (Benjamin) Clark; Steven Paul; Francisca Matos; Robert Grasmere; Greg Michael; ***C:*** Stephen M. Katz; ***M:*** Paul Zaza.

Baby Girl Scott 1/2 1987 Hurt and Lithgow play the parents of an extremely premature infant who is being kept alive by technology. They make a heartrending decision and then must battle doctors and the system to let their daughter die with dignity. **97m/C; VHS, Streaming.** John Lithgow; Mary Beth Hurt; Linda Kelsey; ***D:*** John Korty. **TV**

Baby It's You 1982 (R) In New Jersey in the '60s, the relationship between a smart, attractive Jewish girl who yearns to be an actress and a street-smart Catholic Italian boy puzzles their family and friends. It all works due to Arquette's strong acting and Sayles' script, which explores adolescent dreams, the transition to adulthood, class differences, and the late 1960s with insight and humor. Interesting period soundtrack (Woolly Bully and, for some reason, Bruce Springsteen) helps propel the film, a commercial job which helped finance Sayles' more independent ventures. **105m/C; VHS, DVD, Blu-Ray.** Rosanna Arquette; Vincent Spano; Jack Davidson; Joanna Merlin; Nick Ferrari; Leora Dana; Robert Downey, Jr.; Tracy Pollan; Matthew Modine; ***D:*** John Sayles; ***W:*** John Sayles; ***C:*** Michael Ballhaus.

The Baby Maker 1970 (R) A couple who cannot have children because the wife is sterile decides to hire a woman to have a child for them. However, the relationship between the husband and the surrogate progresses beyond what either of them wanted. Hershey stars as the free-love surrogate mama (just before she underwent the supreme 60s transformation into Barbara Seagull) and Bridges makes his directorial debut. Flick is interesting as a combo critique/exploitation of those wild and groovy 1960s. **109m/C; VHS, DVD.** Barbara Hershey; Collin Wilcox-Paxton; Sam Groom; Scott Glenn; Jeannie Berlin; ***D:*** James Bridges; ***W:*** James Bridges.

Baby Mama 1/2 2008 (PG-13) Predictable mom com starring Fey and Poehler, who got comfortable doing skits together on SNL. Single, 37-year-old workaholic Kate Holbrook (Fey) determines she now has the time and resources to have a baby, but dang if her biological clock hasn't stopped ticking. So Kate goes the surrogacy route and chooses an unlikely candidate—South Philly good-time gal Angie (Poehler), who's unwilling to follow Kate's precise pregnancy plans when the duo wind up as roommates. Naturally, over the course of nine months and lots of preggo jokes, they bond. The leads sell the weak material and are backed up by such pros as Weaver, Kinnear, and Martin. **99m/C; DVD, Blu-Ray.** Tina Fey; Amy Poehler; Greg Kinnear; Dax Shepard; Romany Malco; Holland Taylor; Sigourney Weaver; Maura Tierney; Steve Martin; Siobhan Fallon Hogan; ***D:*** Michael McCullers; ***W:*** Michael McCullers; ***C:*** Daryn Okada; ***M:*** Jeff Richmond.

Baby of the Bride 1/2 1991 Follow-up to "Children of the Bride," has McClanahan settling into wedded bliss with younger husband Shackleford when she discovers she's pregnant. Not only is she unsure about wanting to be a mom again at her age but then grown—and single—daughter McNichol announces she is also pregnant. The sheer silliness of this TV fare makes it fun to watch. **93m/C; VHS, DVD.** Rue McClanahan; Ted Shackleford; Kristy McNichol; John Wesley Shipp; Anne Bobby; Conor O'Farrell; ***D:*** Bill Bixby; ***W:*** Bart Baker. **TV**

Baby on Board 2008 (R) Witless pregnancy comedy. Chicago ad exec Angela (Graham), half of a power couple along with dopey husband Curtis (O'Donnell), is confounded by her unexpected pregnancy, which she feels will derail her career. Angela goes all hormonal and you won't really care what happens over the next nine months. **94m/C; DVD.** Heather Graham; Jerry O'Connell; Lara Flynn Boyle; John Corbett; Kate Finneran; Anthony Starke; ***D:*** Brian Herzlinger; ***W:*** Russell Sealise; ***C:*** Denis Maloney; ***M:*** Teddy Castellucci. **VIDEO**

Baby. . . Secret of the Lost Legend 1985 (PG) A sportswriter and his paleontologist wife risk their lives to reunite a hatching brontosaurus with its mother in the African jungle. Although this Disney film is not lewd in any sense, beware of several scenes displaying frontal nudity and some violence. **95m/C; VHS, DVD, Blu-Ray.** William Katt; Sean Young; Patrick McGoohan; Julian Fellowes; ***D:*** Bill W.L. Norton.

The Baby-Sitters' Club 1/2 1995 (PG) Centering on the summer vacation of seven enterprising Connecticut 13-year-olds and their teen trials with parents, boys, and babysitting, this film is sure to hit home with a crowd that is rarely featured, pre-teen girls. Director Mayron claims, "It's the 'Mystic Pizza' of their age." Young girls and girls young at heart should enjoy this touching look at the fragile years of our youth, leaving baby dolls behind and heading towards dating. Based on the best-selling book series by Ann Martin. Fisk, who plays club leader Kristy, is the daughter of actress Sissy Spacek and director Jack Fisk. **92m/C; VHS, DVD.** Schuyler Fisk; Bre Blair; Rachael Leigh Cook; Larisa Oleynik; Tricia Joe; Stacey Linn Ramsower; Zelda Harris; Brooke Adams; Peter Horton; Bruce Davison; Ellen Burstyn; Austin O'Brien; Aaron Michael Metchik; ***D:*** Melanie Mayron; ***W:*** Dalene Young; ***C:*** Willy Kurant; ***M:*** David Michael Frank.

Baby, Take a Bow 1934 (PG) Temple's first starring role. As a cheerful Pollyanna-type she helps her father, falsely accused of theft, by finding the true thief. **76m/B; VHS, DVD.** Shirley Temple; James Dunn; Claire Trevor; Alan Dinehart; ***D:*** Harry Lachman.

Baby, the Rain Must Fall 1964 A rockabilly singer, paroled from prison after serving time for a knifing, returns home to his wife and daughter, but his outbursts of violence make the reunion difficult. Unsentimental with realistic performances, but script is weak (although written by Foote, based on his play, "The Traveling Lady"). Theme song was a Top 40 hit. **100m/B; VHS, DVD, Blu-Ray.** Steve McQueen; Lee Remick; Don Murray; ***D:*** Robert Mulligan; ***W:*** Horton Foote; ***C:*** Ernest Laszlo; ***M:*** Elmer Bernstein.

Babycakes 1/2 1989 A marshmellow romance between an overweight mortuary attendant who decides to follow her heart when she falls for a hunky ice skater. Can she make him appreciate her inner beauty instead of just her not-the-normal-beauty-standard outward appearance? (Happy ending guaranteed.) TV remake of the darker German film "Sugarbaby." **94m/C; VHS, DVD.** Ricki Lake; Craig Sheffer; Paul Benedict; Betty Buckley; John Karlen; Nada Despotovich; ***D:*** Paul Schneider; ***W:*** Joyce Eliason; ***C:*** Tony Imi; ***M:*** William Olvis. **TV**

Babyfever 1/2 1994 (R) Women gather at a baby shower and tell stories about motherhood and related topics. May be viewed as a babblefest with video accompaniment or as an overdue cinematic exploration of a fairly important aspect of life (where would we be without mom?). That said, pace of the comedy drama is less than feverish, although director Jaglom captures the essence of the stories without disturbing their flow. Foyt, Jaglom's wife and co-screenwriter, makes her acting debut. **110m/C; VHS, DVD.** Matt Salinger; Eric Roberts; Frances Fisher; Victoria Foyt; Zack Norman; Dinah Lenney; Elaine Kagan; ***D:*** Henry Jaglom; ***W:*** Victoria Foyt; Henry Jaglom; ***C:*** Hanania Baer.

Babylon A.D. 2008 (PG-13) See if this sounds familiar: War-torn, post-apocalyptic, bleak future finds mercenary loner who is forced into a seemingly impossible transglobal mission where he is accosted by bad guys every step of the way. Thought so. In this version, Diesel plays Toorop , the brooding ex-pat who must transport Aurora (Thierry), a young woman with a potentially lethal secret, from Russia to New York by whatever means necessary, including a snowmobile! Someone forgot to tell French co-writer/director Kassovitz that Diesel cannot carry a movie, even with a decent French cast and a few visually interesting sets. Kassovitz disowned it in the end, calling it "stupid." Who are we to disagree? **90m/C; Blu-Ray.** *FR* Vin Diesel; Mélanie Thierry; Gerard Depardieu; Charlotte Rampling; Mark Strong; Lambert Wilson; Michelle Yeoh; Jerome Le Banner; ***D:*** Mathieu Kassovitz; ***W:*** Mathieu Kassovitz; Eric Besnard; ***C:*** Thierry Arbogast; ***M:*** Atli Orvarsson.

The Babymakers 2012 (R) Difficulty with getting his wife (Munn) pregnant forces Tommy (Schneider) to try and break into a sperm bank where the man believes his deposit from years ago may still contain a few good swimmers. A heist film set in a sperm bank is a recipe for bodily fluid disaster and leads Schneider and Munn are miscast in this misguided affair. But you can't really blame them. There are a few laughs here and there but the script's focus on gross-out humor is mostly shooting blanks. **93m/C; DVD, Blu-Ray.** Paul Schneider; Olivia Munn; Kevin Heffernan; Wood Harris; Nat Faxon; Aisha Tyler; Collette Wolfe; Hayes Macarthur; Jay Chandrasekhar; ***D:*** Jay Chandrasekhar; ***W:*** Peter Gaulke; Gerry Swallow; ***C:*** Frank DeMarco; ***M:*** Ed Shearmur.

Baby's Day Out 🦴🦴 1/2 **1994 (PG)** Poor man's "Home Alone" refits tired Hughes formula using little tiny baby for original spin. Adorable Baby Bink crawls his way onto the city streets, much to his frantic mother's dismay, and unwittingly outsmarts his would-be kidnappers. As in "HA I and II," the bad guys fall victim to all sorts of cataclysmic Looney Tunes violence. Small kids will get a kick out of this one. Particular problem for the moviemakers was that the nine-month old Worton twins were past the year mark by the end of the shoot, a world of difference in infantdom. Blue screens and out-of-sequence shooting were used to overcome the developmental gap. **99m/C; VHS, DVD.** Adam Worton; Jacob Worton; Joe Mantegna; Lara Flynn Boyle; Joe Pantoliano; Fred Dalton Thompson; John Neville; Brian Haley; Matthew Glave; ***D:*** Patrick Read Johnson; ***W:*** John Hughes; ***C:*** Thomas Ackerman; ***M:*** Bruce Broughton.

The Babysitter 🦴🦴 1/2 **1995 (R)** All-American teen Jennifer (Silverstone) becomes the unexpected object of desire for family man Harry (Walsh), whose wife Dolly (Garlington) is fantasizing about having an affair with a neighbor (Segal). But then Jennifer's boyfriend (London) gets caught up in a malicious prank that turns bad for everyone involved. Based on a short story by Robert Coover. **90m/C; VHS, DVD, Blu-Ray.** Alicia Silverstone; Jeremy London; J.T. Walsh; Lee Garlington; Nicky Katt; Lois Chiles; George Segal; ***D:*** Guy Ferland; ***W:*** Guy Ferland; ***M:*** Loek Dikker.

The Babysitter 🦴🦴 1/2 **2017** A stylish teen horror film. Though 12-year old Cole (Lewis) is almost too old for a babysitter, he is in love with his beautiful, understanding teenage sitter Bee (Weaving). When Cole's parents go on a weekend trip, he is happy Bee will be staying with him. That is, until Cole witnesses Bee and other teens take part in a Satanic cult ritual that involves human sacrifice in order to get everything they want. When the group wants to make Cole their next sacrifice, he must fight to survive the night. The balance between violence, humor, and cleverness make this film entertaining. **85m/C; DVD.** Judah Lewis; Samara Weaving; Robbie Amell; Hana Mae Lee; Bella Thorne; ***D:*** McG; ***W:*** Brian Duffield; ***C:*** Shane Hurlbut; ***M:*** Douglas Pipes.

Babysitter Wanted 🦴 1/2 **2008 (R)** A young college girl travels to a lonely farm for a babysitting job and quickly discovers why the other co-eds became strippers or waitresses instead of babysitters: because farmers with children are evil, evil people. **90m/C; DVD, Blu-Ray.** Matt Dallas; Tina Houtz; Sarah Thompson; Nana Visitor; Jillian Schmitz; ***D:*** Jonas Barnes; Michael Manasseri; ***W:*** Jonas Barnes; ***C:*** Alex Vendler; ***M:*** Kurt Oldman. **VIDEO**

The Babysitters 🦴 1/2 **2007 (R)** Married men in midlife crises turn to teen girls for sex. Babysitter Shirley (Waterston) is having an affair with married dad Mike (Leguizamo), who tips her very generously. Mike tells pal Jerry (Comeau) while Shirley tells friend Melissa (Birkell), who's willing to oblige Jerry with special services. Soon Shirley is recruiting a couple of other gals into her little sex ring and things start to get dicey before director Ross completely loses control of his sexcapade. **90m/C; DVD.** John Leguizamo; Andy Comeau; Denis O'Hare; Cynthia Nixon; Ethan Phillips; Katherine Waterston; Lauren Birkell; Louisa Krause; Halley Wegryn; Jason Dubin; ***D:*** David Ross; ***W:*** David Ross; ***C:*** Michael McDonough; ***M:*** Chad Fischer.

Babysitters Beware 🦴🦴 1/2 *The No-Sit List* **2008 (PG)** Seven-year-old Danny Parker is tired of being left with even the nicest babysitter while his parents go out to their endless business dinners. His friend Marco tells him if he's terrible enough, Danny will get on the 'no-sit list' and his folks will have to stay home. Then the Parkers hire former prison guard Clyde and the battle of wills is on. **70m/C; DVD.** Trenton Rogers; Danny Trejo; Rico Rodriguez; Kate Orsini; Chris Cleveland; Brittany Renee Finamore; Luis Anthony; Dee Wallace; Taylor Negron; ***D:*** Douglas Horn; ***W:*** Douglas Horn; ***C:*** Milton Santiago; ***M:*** Nathan Lanier. **VIDEO**

Babyteeth 🦴🦴🦴 **2020 117m/C; DVD.** Eliza Scanlen; Michelle Lotters; Toby Wallace; Sora Wakaki; Renee Billing; ***D:*** Shannon Murphy; ***W:*** Rita Kalnejais; ***C:*** Andrew Commis; ***M:*** Amanda Brown.

The Bachelor 🦴🦴 **1999 (PG-13)** Exec producer/star Chris O'Donnell's remake of Buster Keaton's 1925 silent comedy "Seven Chances" falls short of bringing the story to a modern audience. Well, an audience that's aware of the discovery of talkies, feminism and plot holes anyway. O'Donnell plays Jimmy, who stands to inherit a fortune from his grandfather (Ustinov) if he marries before the age of 30. Unfortunately, he receives this news immediately after his odious proposal to girlfriend Anne (Zellweger) is rejected...and of course his 30th birthday happens to be 27 hours away. Madcap antics allegedly ensue as Jimmy trolls for a wife from the pool of his ex-girlfriends and flees the husband-hunting horde who respond to a front-page ad placed by his pal Marco (Lange). **101m/C; VHS, DVD.** Chris O'Donnell; Renée Zellweger; Hal Holbrook; James Cromwell; Artie Lange; Ed Asner; Marley Shelton; Stacy Edwards; Rebecca Cross; Jennifer Esposito; Peter Ustinov; Mariah Carey; Brooke Shields; ***D:*** Gary Sinyor; ***W:*** Steve Cohen; ***C:*** Simon Archer; ***M:*** David A. Hughes; John Murphy.

The Bachelor and the Bobby-Soxer 🦴🦴🦴 *Bachelor Knight* **1947** Playboy Grant is brought before Judge Loy for disturbing the peace and sentenced to court her teenage sister Temple. Cruel and unusual punishment? Maybe, but the wise Judge hopes that the dates will help Temple over her crush on handsome Grant. Instead, Loy and Grant fall for each other. **95m/B; VHS, DVD.** Cary Grant; Myrna Loy; Shirley Temple; Rudy Vallee; Harry Davenport; Ray Collins; Veda Ann Borg; ***D:*** Irving Reis; ***W:*** Sidney Sheldon. Oscars '47: Orig. Screenplay.

The Bachelor Father 🦴🦴 **1931** Aging British peer Sir Basil (Smith) wants to get to know his three grown children (by three different mothers) and invites them to his country estate. He bonds the most with adventurous American Antoinette (Davies), who decides to meddle in his life as well. **84m/B; DVD.** Sir C. Aubrey Smith; Marion Davies; Ray Milland; Nina Quartero; Ralph Forbes; Guinn "Big Boy" Williams; David Torrence; Doris Lloyd; Halliwell Hobbes; ***D:*** Robert Z. Leonard; ***W:*** Laurence E. Johnson; ***C:*** Oliver Marsh.

Bachelor Flat 🦴 1/2 **1962** A broad, somewhat tiresome comedy. Professor Bruce Patterson (Terry-Thomas) is the unlikely lust object for numerous ladies, so he's happy to use fiancée Helen's (Holm) home when she goes out of town. Only Helen has neglected to mention her first marriage and her 17-year-old daughter, Libby (Weld), who shows up unaware of her mother's engagement and then pretends to be some juvenile delinquent after Patterson. **91m/C; DVD.** Terry-Thomas; Tuesday Weld; Richard Beymer; Celeste Holm; ***D:*** Frank Tashlin; ***W:*** Frank Tashlin; Budd Grossman; ***C:*** Daniel F. Fapp; ***M:*** John Williams.

Bachelor Games 🦴🦴 *Rules of the Game* **2016** Henry (Jack Gordon) is getting married, so for his stag weekend his friends take him hiking in the wilderness of Argentina. As the drunken weekend progresses, the group's camaraderie frays, particularly when they are stalked by what may be a local supernatural legend they were clearly warned about. Clearly Henry needs new friends. **88m/C; DVD, Blu-Ray, Streaming.** *AR UK* Charlie Bewley; Jack Gordon; Jack Doolan; Mike Noble; Obi Abali; ***D:*** Edward McGown; ***W:*** Chris Hill; Sam Mitchell; ***C:*** Lucio Bonelli; ***M:*** David Julyan. **VIDEO**

Bachelor in Paradise 🦴🦴 1/2 **1961** Silly tale starring Hope as a writer of books to the lovelorn who decides to do firsthand research on the sexual goings-on of a suburban California community. All the married ladies find him charming (much to their husbands' disgust) and the lone single woman, Turner, isn't single by the end of the movie. **109m/C; VHS, DVD.** Bob Hope; Lana Turner; Janis Paige; Jim Hutton; Paula Prentiss; Don Porter; Virginia Grey; Agnes Moorehead; John McGiver; ***D:*** Jack Arnold; ***W:*** Hal Kanter; Valentine Davies; ***M:*** Henry Mancini.

Bachelor Mother 🦴🦴🦴 **1939** A single salesgirl causes a scandal when she finds an abandoned baby and is convinced by her boss to adopt the child. Smart, witty comedy with nice performance by Rogers. **82m/B; VHS, DVD.** Ginger Rogers; David Niven; Charles Coburn; ***D:*** Garson Kanin.

Bachelor Party 🦴🦴 **1984 (R)** Rick (Hank) is silly, cute, and poor. Debbie (Kitaen) is intelligent, beautiful, and rich. It must be a marriage made in heaven, because no one in their right mind would put these two together. All is basically well, except that her parents hate him and his friends dislike her. Things are calm until right before the big event, when the bride-to-be objects to Rick's traditional pre-nuptial partying and with good reason. Light and semi-entertaining with scattered laughs. **105m/C; VHS, DVD, Blu-Ray.** Tom Hanks; Tawny Kitaen; Adrian Zmed; George Grizzard; Robert Prescott; William Tepper; Wendie Jo Sperber; Barry Diamond; Michael Dudikoff; Deborah Harmon; John Bloom; Toni Alessandra; Monique Gabrielle; Angela Aames; Rosanne Katon; Bradford Bancroft; ***D:*** Neal Israel; ***W:*** Pat Proft; ***C:*** Hal Trussel; ***M:*** Robert Folk.

Bachelor Party 2: The Last Temptation 🦴 **2008** Has, of course, nothing to do with the 1984 Tom Hanks comedy. Ron (Cooke) gets engaged to wealthy Melinda (Foster). Her scheming brother Todd (Christie) is convinced that the affable Ron will be anointed heir to the family business so he takes Ron and his buds to South Beach hoping some compromising situations will lead to the wedding being called off. An excuse for a lot of topless women to be on parade and men-behaving-badly stupidity. **103m/C; DVD.** Sara Foster; Danny A. Jacobs; Harland Williams; Emmanuelle Vaugier; Audrey Landers; Josh Cooke; Warren Christie; Greg Pitts; Maj. Mike Russell; ***D:*** James Ryan; ***W:*** Jay Longino; ***C:*** Roy Wagner; ***M:*** James Dooley. **VIDEO**

Bachelor Party in the Bungalow of the Damned 🦴 1/2 **2008** A wild bachelor party at a house in the Hamptons (complete with a creepy caretaker) goes awry amid the jiggle and debauchery when the gates of hell open up mid-bash, leaving some to wonder, can I get my shower present back? **90m/C; DVD.** Trina Analee; Monique Dupree; Gregg Aaron Greenburg; Kaitlyn Gutkes; Zoe Hunter; Sean Parker; Joseph Parker; Gelu Dan Rusu; Joe Testa; ***D:*** Brian Thomson; ***W:*** Brian Thomson; ***C:*** Demian Barba; ***M:*** Brian Thomson. **VIDEO**

Bachelor Party Vegas WOOF! *Vegas, Baby* **2005 (R)** Things go wrong for five friends when they head to Vegas and discover their bachelor party planner is a casino thief, which leads to all sorts of misunderstandings. Unbelievably crass and unfunny comedy that should have stayed in Vegas, preferably so the master print could have been shredded by one of Siegfried & Roy's white tigers. **90m/C; DVD.** Kal Penn; Jonathan Bennett; Donald Adeosun Faison; Charlie Talbert; Vincent Pastore; Jaime Pressly; Aaron Himelstein; Diora Baird; Lin Shaye; Graham Beckel; Daniel Stern; Steve Hytner; Kathy Griffin; ***D:*** Eric Bernt; ***W:*** Eric Bernt; ***C:*** Robert Primes.

The Bachelor Weekend 🦴🦴 *The Stag* **2013** A genial but forgettable comedy about a group of guys who head out on a "stag," the Irish tradition of reconnecting with friends and nature on a hike/camping trip before getting married. The uptight groom Fionnan (O'Conor) is nicely balanced out by best bud Davin (Scott) but the entire affair is threatened by the arrival of the soon-to-be brother-in-law known as The Machine (McDonald), an oafish jerk of a man. Of course, The Machine hides a good heart under all that bluster, secrets are revealed, and everyone comes home a better man. It has moments but you've seen a lot of them before. **94m/C; DVD.** *IR* Hugh O'Conor; Andrew Scott; Peter McDonald; Brian Gleeson; Michael Legge; Andrew Bennett; Amy Huberman; ***D:*** John Butler; ***W:*** Peter McDonald; John Butler; ***C:*** Peter Robertson; ***M:*** Stephen Rennicks.

Bachelorette 🦴 **2012 (R)** Foul-mouthed chick flicks that follow the success of "Bridesmaids" are fair game for comparisons--this falls far short. Regan (Dunst) spends the weekend organizing her friend's NYC wedding, and trying to look after the wilder, cocaine-laced members of the wedding party, Gena (Caplan) and Katie (Fisher). One misstep after another leads to an unsurprisingly chaotic wedding day. Drug abuse and casual sex are pushed to such an absurd limit that the romp loses all credibility in characters and circumstances. A mean-spirited, soulless, and dull debut for director Headland. **93m/C; DVD, Blu-Ray, Download.** Kirsten Dunst; Isla Fisher; Lizzy Caplan; Rebel Wilson; James Marsden; Adam Scott; Kyle Bornheimer; Hayes Macarthur; ***D:*** Leslye Headland; ***W:*** Leslye Headland; ***C:*** Doug Emmett; ***M:*** Andrew Feltenstein; John Nau.

BachelorMan 🦴🦴 **2003 (R)** Easygoing Ted Davis (DeLuise) considers himself an authority on bachelorhood. But when hot brunette Heather (Pyle) becomes his next-door neighbor, all Ted's tricks to woo her fail. Even worse, Ted realizes he's actually fallen in love. Based on the sketch comedy act of Rodney Lee Conover, who plays Ted's outspoken buddy Gordie. **90m/C; DVD.** David DeLuise; Missi Pyle; Karen Bailey; Rodney Lee Conover; ***D:*** John Putch; ***W:*** Jeffrey Hause; David Hines; ***C:*** Keith J. Duggan; ***M:*** Steve Bauman; J. Lynn Duckett. **VIDEO**

Back Against the Wall 🦴🦴 **2000** Shot in 16mm and black and white, this original art film by acclaimed underground director James Fotopoulos explores the darkness surrounding a lingerie model. The layers of the models life and the men, often corrupt, that she must service are exposed in this three-part feature. As the film progresses, her life grows more depressing and she experiences a serious downfall. Two men in her life—a jealous middle-aged man and his odd friend with no neck—also re-appear regularly. **94m/B; DVD.** Debbie Mulcahy; Martin Shannon; Ernie E. Frantz; Michael Wexler; Gary Sugarman; ***D:*** James Fotopoulos; ***W:*** James Fotopoulos; ***C:*** Dennis Best; John Wagner; ***M:*** Bob Davies; Alexander Horn; Tom Nicholl.

Back Door to Heaven 🦴🦴🦴 1/2 **1939** Traces the path of a young boy who is born into a poor family and the reasons for his turning to a life of crime. A grim and powerful drama with many convincing performances. **85m/B; VHS, DVD.** Wallace Ford; Aline MacMahon; Stuart Erwin; Patricia Ellis; Kent Smith; Van Heflin; Jimmy Lydon; ***D:*** William K. Howard.

Back Home 🦴🦴 1/2 **1990** A family reunion movie with pure Disney sentiment. A 12-year-old English girl, who has been living in America during WWII, is reunited with her family in postwar England. **103m/C; VHS, DVD.** Hayley Carr; Hayley Mills; Jean Anderson; Rupert Frazer; Brenda Bruce; Adam Stevenson; George Clark; ***D:*** Piers Haggard. **CABLE**

Back in Action 🦴 1/2 **1994 (R)** Veteran LA detective Rossi (Piper) is out to bust the ruthless drug gang who gunned down his partner. But he's got company—martial-arts expert Billy (Blanks) whose young sister has fallen prey to the same gang. So the two action junkies reluctantly team up to cause some major damage. **93m/C; VHS, DVD.** Roddy Piper; Billy Blanks; Bobbie Phillips; Matt Birman; Nigel Bennett; Damon D'Oliveira; Kai Soremekun; ***D:*** Paul Ziller; Steve DiMarco; ***W:*** Karl Schiffman.

Back in Business 🦴🦴 **1996 (R)** Joe Elkhart's (Bosworth) life is down the drain. After failing to expose a fellow police officer as corrupt, he's kicked off the force, abandoned by his friends, and divorced by his wife. Now working as a mechanic, Joe gets pulled back into the action when his ex-partner, Tony (Torry), goes undercover to bring down a major drug dealer and Joe discovers the corrupt cops that framed him are also behind the current heroin deal. **93m/C; VHS, Streaming.** Brian Bosworth; Joe Torry; Dara Tomanovich; Alan Scarfe; Brion James; Ron Glass; ***D:*** Philippe Mora; ***W:*** Ed Decatur; Ash Staley; ***C:*** Walter Bal.

Back in Business 🦴 **2006** Lame Brit crime caper. Con man Will Spencer (Kemp) and his various allies plot to steal a technologically advanced space exploration device developed by Britain and sought after by a number of foreign investors. But is ex-detective Jarvis (Waterman) planning to double-cross the crew or make the scam his own? **82m/C; DVD.** *GB* Martin Kemp; Dennis Waterman; Chris Barrie; Brian Blessed; Stefan Booth; Joanna Taylor; ***D:*** Chris Munro; ***W:*** Chris Munro; ***C:*** Martin Kenzie; ***M:*** Mark Thomas.

Back in the Day 🦴🦴 1/2 **2005 (R)** Reggie Cooper (Ja Rule) is living with his successful, divorced father (Esposito) in an effort to stay away from the 'hood that nearly cost him his life. But when Reggie reconnects with gangster mentor J-Bone (Rhames) it can only mean trouble because J-Bone has some scores to settle. Reggie gets involved in the murder of a local preacher (Morton), but tries to keep his part a secret after he falls for the man's daughter (Ali). Now he must choose between old loyalties and new love. Decent effort with a familiar cast doing professional work. **103m/C; DVD.** Ja Rule; Ving Rhames; Tatyana Ali; Giancarlo Esposito; Pam Grier; Joe Morton; Tia Carrere; Frank Langella; Debbi (Deborah) Morgan; Al Sapienza; Lahmard Tate; ***D:*** James Hunter; ***W:*** James Hunter; Michael Raffanello; ***C:*** Donald M. Morgan; ***M:*** Robert Folk. **VIDEO**

Back in the Day WOOF! 2014 (R) Dreary raunch that's a complete comic misfire. Jim Owens goes home to Indiana for his high school reunion, wanting to relive his past with some drunken partying while trying to get the girl that had the good sense to get away back then. **94m/C; DVD.** Michael Rosenbaum; Morena Baccarin; Nick Swardson; Harland Williams; Emma Caulfield; ***D:*** Michael Rosenbaum; ***W:*** Michael Rosenbaum; ***C:*** Bradley Stonesifer; ***M:*** Rob Danson. **VIDEO**

Back of Beyond 🦴🦴 **1995 (R)** Spectacular setting in the Australian outback can't make up for unfocused plot and characters with little impact. Tom (Mercutio) ran a remote desert gas station with his sister, Susan (Elmalogulou), before she was killed on his motorbike. When Connor's (Friels) car breaks down by the derelict station, he, girlfriend Charlie (Smart), and sidekick Nick (Polson) must wait while Tom tries to fix it. Only Connor is a diamond thief and patience isn't one of his virutes, especially when he notices the unhappy Charlie making friends with Tom. Mystical/supernatural elements involving ghosts and Aboriginal sites only add to the confusion. **85m/C; Streaming.** *AU* Paul Mercurio; Colin Friels; Dee Smart; John Polson; Rebekah Elmaloglou; Bob Maza; Terry Serio; ***D:*** Michael Robertson; ***W:*** Paul Leadon; A.M. Brooksbank; Richard I. Sawyer; ***C:*** Stephen Dobson; ***M:*** Mark Moffatt; Wayne Goodwin.

Back Road Diner 🦴 **1999** A couple of old friends go on a road trip leaving Harlem for the backwoods. It goes well until they meet the local redneck deputies who've been told they're drug dealers because unlike all the locals they happen to be African-American. Predictably their vacation quickly goes downhill. **89m/C; DVD.** Andre M. Carrington; Winston I. Dunlop, II; ***D:*** Winston I. Dunlop, II; ***C:*** Joseph Matina; ***M:*** William Brown. **VIDEO**

Back Roads 🦴🦴 **1981 (R)** Southern hooker meets a down-on-his-luck boxer and both head out for a better life in California, finding love along the way. Ritt road trip lacks any comedic rhythm and survives on Field and Jones working to entertain. **94m/C; VHS, DVD, Blu-Ray.** Sally Field; Tommy Lee Jones; David Keith; ***D:*** Martin Ritt; ***W:*** Gary De Vore; ***C:*** John A. Alonzo; ***M:*** Henry Mancini.

Back Street 🦴🦴 1/2 **1941** Pretty Rae Stevens (Sullavan) falls in love with Walter Saxel (Boyer) but, thanks to a misunderstanding, they part company. They meet again five years later and, although Walter is married and has children, begin an affair. Over the years, Rae is to learn that the life of a mistress is a lonely one. Based on the novel by Fannie Hurst; also filmed in 1932 and 1961. **89m/B; DVD.** Margaret Sullavan; Charles Boyer; Richard Carlson; Frank McHugh; Tim Holt; Frank Jenks; Esther Dale; Samuel S. Hinds; ***D:*** Robert Stevenson; ***W:*** Bruce Manning; Felix Jackson; ***C:*** William H. Daniels; ***M:*** Frank Skinner.

Back Street 🦴🦴 **1961** The forbidden affair between a married man and a beautiful fashion designer carries on through many anxious years to a tragic end. The lavish third film version of the Fannie Hurst novel. **107m/C; DVD.** Susan Hayward; John Gavin; Vera Miles; Charles Drake; Virginia Grey; Reginald Gardiner; ***D:*** David Miller; ***W:*** Eleanore Griffin; William Ludwig; ***C:*** Stanley Cortez; ***M:*** Frank Skinner.

Back to Back 🦴🦴 1/2 **1996 (R)** Ex-cop Malone (Rooker) must team up with hitman Koji (Ishibashi), who's holding Malone's daughter hostage, to double-cross a corrupt cop and stay alive while being hunted by the Mafia. **95m/C; VHS, DVD.** Michael Rooker; Ryo Ishibashi; John Laughlin; Danielle Harris; Bobcat Goldthwait; Vincent Schiavelli; ***D:*** Roger Nygard; ***W:*** Lloyd Keith; ***C:*** Mark W. Gray; ***M:*** Walter Werzowa.

Back to Bataan 🦴🦴 1/2 **1945** Colonel forms guerrilla army to raid Japanese in the Philippines and to help Americans landing on Leyte. Also available in a colorized version. **95m/B; VHS, DVD.** John Wayne; Anthony Quinn; Beulah Bondi; Fely Franquelli; Richard Loo; Philip Ahn; Lawrence Tierney; ***D:*** Edward Dmytryk.

Back to God's Country 🦴 1/2 **1953** Minor adventure based on the James Oliver Curwood novel. Former ship's captain Peter Keith is up in Alaska with his wife, Dolores, and a valuable load of furs. Both of which are coveted by bad guy Paul Blake. **78m/C; DVD.** Rock Hudson; Marcia Henderson; Steve Cochran; Hugh O'Brien; Chubby Johnson; ***D:*** Joseph Pevney; ***W:*** Tom Reed; ***C:*** Maury Gertsman; ***M:*** Frank Skinner.

Back to Hannibal: The Return of Tom Sawyer and Huckleberry Finn 🦴🦴 1/2 **1990** Mark Twain's characters Tom Sawyer and Huckleberry Finn are reunited as adults to solve a murder mystery. Tom is a lawyer, Finn a newspaper man, and it's Becky Thatcher's husband who's been murdered. Did a freed slave really commit the crime? **92m/C; VHS, DVD.** Raphael Sbarge; Mitchell Anderson; Megan Follows; William Windom; Ned Beatty; Paul Winfield; ***D:*** Paul Krasny; ***M:*** Lee Holdridge. **TV**

Back to 1942 🦴🦴 1/2 **2012** In Henan Province one of China's worst famines in history struck just as war with Japan was looming. Three million people starved to death on the trek west, hoping to avoid the Japanese army and somehow find food. Their quest amounts to little as the politicians of the time prefer to ignore the masses in preference for dining with the elite, a somewhat revisionist history as those same politicians were not on good terms with the Communist Party at the time. Based more on the novel "Remembering 1942" than actual events in particular, it still portrays a decent account of the death and degradation of the time's events. **145m/C; DVD, Blu-Ray.** *CH* Guoli Zhang; Adrien Brody; Mo Zhang; Ziwen Wang; Tim Robbins; ***D:*** Xiaogang Feng; ***W:*** Zhenyun Liu; ***C:*** Yue Lu; ***M:*** Jiping Zhao. **VIDEO**

Back to School 🦴🦴 1/2 **1986 (PG-13)** Dangerfield plays an obnoxious millionaire who enrolls in college to help his wimpy son, Gordon, achieve campus stardom. His motto seems to be "if you can't buy it, it can't be had." At first, his antics embarrass his shy son, but soon everyone is clamoring to be seen with the pair as Gordon develops his own self confidence. **96m/C; VHS, DVD, Blu-Ray.** Rodney Dangerfield; Keith Gordon; Robert Downey, Jr.; Sally Kellerman; Burt Young; Paxton Whitehead; Adrienne Barbeau; M. Emmet Walsh; Severn Darden; Ned Beatty; Sam Kinison; Kurt Vonnegut, Jr.; Robert Picardo; Terry Farrell; Edie McClurg; Jason Hervey; William Zabka; ***D:*** Alan Metter; ***W:*** Will Aldis; Steven Kampmann; Harold Ramis; Peter Torokvei; ***C:*** Thomas Ackerman; ***M:*** Danny Elfman.

Back to the Beach 🦴 1/2 **1987 (PG)** Frankie and Annette return to the beach as self-parodying, middle-aged parents with rebellious kids, and the usual run of sunbleached, lover's tiff comedy ensues. Plenty of songs and guest appearances from television past. Tries to bring back that surf, sun, and sand feel of the orignal "Beach Party" movies, but fails. **92m/C; DVD.** Frankie Avalon; Annette Funicello; Connie Stevens; Lori Loughlin; Tommy Hinkley; Demian Slade; John Calvin; Joe Holland; David Bowe; Paul (Pee-wee Herman) Reubens; Don Adams; Bob Denver; Alan Hale, Jr.; Tony Dow; Jerry Mathers; Dick Dale; Stevie Ray Vaughan; Edd Byrnes; Barbara Billingsley; ***D:*** Lyndall Hobbs; ***W:*** James Komack; Bill W.L. Norton; ***C:*** Bruce Surtees; ***M:*** Steve Dorff.

Back to the Future 🦴🦴🦴 **1985 (PG)** When neighborhood mad scientist Doc Brown (Lloyd) constructs a time machine from a DeLorean, his youthful companion Marty (Fox) accidentally transports himself to 1955. There, Marty must do everything he can to bring his high-school age parents together (so he can be born), elude the local bully, and get back...to the future. Solid fast-paced entertainment is even better due to Lloyd's inspired performance as the loony Doc while Fox is perfect as the boy completely out of his element. Soundtrack features Huey Lewis and the News. Followed by two sequels. **116m/C; VHS, DVD, Blu-Ray.** Michael J. Fox; Christopher Lloyd; Lea Thompson; Crispin Glover; Wendie Jo Sperber; Marc McClure; Thomas F. Wilson; James Tolkan; Casey Siemaszko; Billy Zane; George DiCenzo; Courtney Gains; Claudia Wells; Jason Hervey; Harry Waters, Jr.; Maia Brewton; J.J. (Jeffrey Jay) Cohen; ***Cameo(s):*** Huey Lewis; ***D:*** Robert Zemeckis; ***W:*** Robert Zemeckis; Bob Gale; ***C:*** Dean Cundey; ***M:*** Alan Silvestri. Natl. Film Reg. '07.

Back to the Future, Part 2 🦴🦴 1/2 **1989 (PG)** Taking up exactly where Part 1 left off, Doc Brown and Marty time-hop into the future (2015 to be exact) to save Marty's kids, then find themselves returning to 1955 to retrieve a sports almanac that causes havoc for the McFly family. Clever editing allows for Marty Part 2 to see Marty Part 1 at the school dance. Most of the cast returns, although Glover appears only in cuts from the original and Shue steps in as girlfriend Jennifer. Not up to the original, but still satisfying. Cliffhanger ending sets up Part 3, which was shot simultaneously with this. **107m/C; VHS, DVD, Blu-Ray.** Michael J. Fox; Christopher Lloyd; Lea Thompson; Thomas F. Wilson; Harry Waters, Jr.; Charles Fleischer; Joe Flaherty; Elisabeth Shue; James Tolkan; Casey Siemaszko; Jeffrey Weissman; Flea; Billy Zane; J.J. (Jeffrey Jay) Cohen; Darlene Vogel; Jason Scott Lee; Crispin Glover; Ricky Dean Logan; Elijah Wood; ***D:*** Robert Zemeckis; ***W:*** Robert Zemeckis; Bob Gale; ***C:*** Dean Cundey; ***M:*** Alan Silvestri.

Back to the Future, Part 3 🦴🦴🦴 **1990 (PG)** Picks up where Part 2 climaxed a la cliffhanger. Stuck in 1955, time-traveling hero Marty frantically searches for Doc Part 1 so he can return to 1985. Instead, he finds himself in the Wild West circa 1885, trying to save Doc's life. Plot is related to earlier BTTFs, so first time viewers might be confused. For those who've seen previous incarnations, the clever interconnections are really nifty. Nearly matches the original for excitement and offers some snazzy special effects. The complete trilogy is available as a boxed set. **118m/C; VHS, DVD, Blu-Ray.** Michael J. Fox; Christopher Lloyd; Mary Steenburgen; Thomas F. Wilson; Lea Thompson; Elisabeth Shue; Matt Clark; Richard Dysart; Pat Buttram; Harry Carey, Jr.; Dub Taylor; James Tolkan; Marc McClure; Wendie Jo Sperber; J.J. (Jeffrey Jay) Cohen; Ricky Dean Logan; Jeffrey Weissman; ***D:*** Robert Zemeckis; ***W:*** Robert Zemeckis; Bob Gale; ***C:*** Dean Cundey; ***M:*** Alan Silvestri.

Back to the Secret Garden 🦴🦴 1/2 **2001** Well-meaning but dull sequel based on characters from the novel by Frances Hodgson Burnett. It's now the 1940s and sullen Mary has grown into the elegant Lady Mary (Lunghi), the wife of the ambassador to the U.S. Mistlethwaite has turned into a sunny English orphanage that is run by Martha (Plowright). Lady Mary arranges for Brooklyn-born orphan Lizzie (Buelle) to join their little band, and the young girl just happens to be a gardening whiz. Which is a good thing, since Mary's special garden been badly neglected once again. **100m/C; VHS, DVD.** Camilla Belle; Cherie Lunghi; Joan Plowright; David Warner; Leigh Lawson; Florence Hoath; ***D:*** Michael Tuchner; ***W:*** Joe Wiesenfeld; ***C:*** Ian Wilson. **CABLE**

Back to You and Me 🦴🦴 1/2 **2005** Hallmark Channel family drama. Big city doctor Sydney Ludwick has been estranged from her widowed mom Helen ever since her dad's funeral. Needing a break, Syd decides to return home for her high school reunion and notices that her one-time boyfriend Gus is still a hunk and now a widower. His son Jake, who happens to need Syd's medical help, thinks she would also be a good choice for a stepmom. However, first Syd has to deal with her own mom issues. **85m/C; DVD.** Rue McClanahan; Lisa Hartman Black; Dale Midkiff; Blake Woodruff; Don Harvey; Lisa Long; Barbara Niven; Larry Manetti; ***D:*** David S. Cass, Sr.; ***W:*** Tom Amundsen; ***C:*** James W. Wrenn; ***M:*** Kevin Kliesch. **CABLE**

The Back Trail 1924 Unusual silent western that deals with post-war problems. Due to shell shock, WWI veteran Jeff Prouty has amnesia. The cowboy is manipulated by bad guy Gentleman Harry King into believing he's a criminal and then into breaking his father's will so King can gain access to Jeff's inheritance. **?m/B; Silent; DVD.** Jack Hoxie; Eugenia Gilbert; William Berke; Claude Payton; William (Bill, Billy) McCall; Al Hoxie; ***D:*** Cliff(ord) Smith; ***W:*** Isadore Bernstein; ***C:*** Harry Neumann.

The Back-Up Plan 🦴🦴 1/2 **2010 (PG-13)** Tepid romantic comedy (that packs on the schmaltz as well) with Lopez game for various outrageous and humiliating situations (she has a funny lament about what pregnancy has done to her curves, especially her butt). Pet shop-owner Zoe (Lopez) is tired of waiting for the right man to father her child so she goes the sperm donor route. Of course just when she gets pregnant, Zoe meets frequently shirtless, cheese-making goat farmer Stan (O'Loughlin) who may be a keeper since he's willing to stick around and help her with the pregnancy. But then the realization of upcoming parenthood sinks in, causing both of them to question the suddenness of their relationship. **106m/C; Blu-Ray, On Demand.** Jennifer Lopez; Eric Christian Olsen; Danneel Harris; Melissa McCarthy; Alex O'Loughlin; Anthony Anderson; Michaela Watkins; ***D:*** Alan Poul; ***W:*** Kate Angelo; ***C:*** Xavier Perez Grobet; ***M:*** Stephen Trask.

Backbeat 🦴🦴🦴 **1994 (R)** Backed by the beat of early Beatle tunes as rendered by some of today's top alternative musicians, the debut for director Softley explores the Fab Four's beginnings in Hamburg's underground music scene. Storyline is driven by the complications of a romantic triangle between John Lennon, Astrid Kirchherr (the photographer who came up with the band's signature look) and Stu Sutcliffe, Lennon's best friend and the original bass player for the Beatles. Hart's dead-on as Lennon, playing him a second time (check out "The Hours and Times"). Energetic and enjoyable, particularly when the Was-produced music takes center stage. **100m/C; VHS, DVD, Blu-Ray.** *GB* Stephen Dorff; Sheryl Lee; Ian Hart; Gary Bakewell; Chris O'Neill; Scot Williams; Kai Wiesinger; Jennifer Ehle; ***D:*** Iain Softley; ***W:*** Michael Thomas; Stephen Ward; Iain Softley; ***C:*** Ian Wilson; ***M:*** Don Was.

Backdraft 🦴🦴 1/2 **1991 (R)** High action story of Chicago firemen has some of the most stupendous incendiary special effects ever filmed. But then there's that plot, B-movie hokum about a mystery arsonist torching strategic parts of the community with the finesse of an expert and a brother-against-brother conflict. Straight-forward performances from most of the cast in spite of the weak storyline. Writer Widen wrote from experience—he used to be a fireman; real-life Chicago firefighters were reportedly very happy with the realistic and intense fire scenes. Forget the plot and just watch the fires. Also available in a letterboxed version. **135m/C; VHS, DVD, Blu-Ray, HD-DVD.** Kurt Russell; William Baldwin; Robert De Niro; Donald Sutherland; Jennifer Jason Leigh; Scott Glenn; Rebecca De Mornay; Jason Gedrick; J.T. Walsh; Tony Mockus, Sr.; Clint Howard; David Crosby; ***D:*** Ron Howard; ***W:*** Gregory Widen; ***C:*** Mikael Salomon; ***M:*** Hans Zimmer.

Backfield in Motion 🦴🦴 1/2 **1991** Silly but harmless comedy about a widowed mom who tries to get closer to her high-schooler son by organizing a mother-son football game. But it's the boys' football coach who really wants to get close—to mom. TV movie debut of both Arnolds (past and present). **95m/C; VHS, DVD.** Roseanne; Tom Arnold; Colleen Camp; Conchata Ferrell; Johnny Galecki; Kevin Scannell; ***D:*** Richard Michaels. **TV**

Backfire 🦴🦴 1/2 **1950** Bob Corey (MacRae) has spent months in an LA veterans hospital where he and Army nurse Julie

Benson (Mayo) fall in love. Bob's worried when he loses contact with buddy Steve Connolly (O'Brien) and, after his release, the cops tell him that Steve is on the lam for murdering a gambler. Bob doesn't believe them and he and Julie start investigating, which leads to a series of flashbacks narrated by different characters who don't all tell the truth. MacRae successfully moved on from his musical past to this postwar crime thriller. **91m/B; DVD.** Gordon MacRae; Virginia Mayo; Edmond O'Brien; Dane Clark; Viveca Lindfors; Ed Begley, Sr.; Monte Blue; Richard Rober; ***D:*** Vincent Sherman; ***W:*** Ben Roberts; Lawrence B. Marcus; Ivan Goff; ***C:*** Carl Guthrie; ***M:*** Daniele Amfitheatrof.

Backfire **1988 (R)** A mysterious stranger enters the lives of a disturbed 'Nam vet and his discontented wife, setting a pattern of murder and double-cross in motion. **90m/C; VHS, DVD.** Karen Allen; Keith Carradine; Jeff Fahey; Bernie Casey; Dinah Manoff; Dean Paul (Dino Martin Jr.) Martin; ***D:*** Gilbert Cates; ***W:*** Larry Brand; ***M:*** David Shire.

Backflash **2001 (R)** Ray (Patrick) runs a videostore and needs a little excitement in his life. He picks up pretty hitchhiker Harley (Esposito), who's just out of jail, and gets more than he's bargained for since Harley needs Ray to pretend to be her husband so she can get into a safety deposit box. But just who's conning who? **90m/C; VHS, DVD.** Robert Patrick; Jennifer Esposito; Melissa Joan Hart; ***D:*** Philip Jones; ***W:*** Philip Jones; Jennifer Farrell; Lillian Jackson; ***C:*** Maximo Munzi; ***M:*** Valentine Leone; Carl Wurtz.

Background to Danger **1943** A suspenseful WWII actioner about American agent Raft who travels to Turkey to receive secret documents from the soon-to-be-murdered Massen. Greenstreet is the Nazi master spy who also wants the documents as do Russian spies, Lorre and Marshall. Somewhat confusing plot but fast-paced. Based on the thriller "Uncommon Danger" by Eric Ambler. This film was Warner Bros.' follow-up to "Casablanca" with Raft in the Bogie role he had turned down in that cinema classic. **80m/B; VHS, DVD.** George Raft; Sydney Greenstreet; Peter Lorre; Brenda Marshall; Osa Massen; Turhan Bey; Kurt Katch; ***D:*** Raoul Walsh; ***W:*** W.R. Burnett.

Backlash **1/2** **1956** Jim Slater (Widmark) and Karyl Orton (Reed) are both searching for the surivors of an Apache attack. Karyl's husband is dead but one man got away with a fortune in gold and Jim is determined to find him. **84m/C; DVD.** Richard Widmark; Donna Reed; John McIntire; William Campbell; Barton MacLane; ***D:*** John Sturges; ***W:*** Borden Chase; ***C:*** Irving Glassberg; ***M:*** Herman Stein.

Backlash *Justice* **1999 (R)** Federal prosecutor Gina Gallagher (Needham) has gotten on the wrong side of the Colombian drug cartel. After her partner is killed, Gina works with veteran homicide detective Moe Ryan (Durning) and uncovers a government conspiracy—so maybe trusting a convict (Belushi) to protect her isn't such a bad idea. **103m/C; VHS, DVD, UMD.** Tracey Needham; Charles Durning; James Belushi; JoBeth Williams; Patrick Ersgard; Tony Plana; Henry Silva; Warren Berlinger; ***D:*** Joakim (Jack) Ersgard; ***W:*** Patrick Ersgard. **VIDEO**

Backlash: Oblivion 2 **1/2** *Oblivion 2* **1995 (PG-13)** Galactic supervillainess Lash stakes her claim to a rare derconium mine on the remote space outpost of Oblivion. Will cave monsters thwart her evil plan before space cowboys come to the town's rescue? **82m/C; VHS, DVD.** Andrew Divoff; Meg Foster; Isaac Hayes; Julie Newmar; Carel Struycken; George Takei; Musetta Vander; Jimmie F. Skaggs; Irwin Keyes; Maxwell Caulfield; ***D:*** Sam Irvin; ***W:*** Peter David; ***M:*** Pino Donaggio.

Backslash **1/2** *Back Slash; Backslash: The Ultimate Internet Predator* **2005** Members of a group of would-be moviemakers are being killed off one by one, when they notice all the victims are fit college girls who appeared on a local website. Which is not exactly a new theme for a slasher movie. **88m/C; DVD.** Steven J. Burge; Laura Bruner; ***D:*** Kevin Campbell; ***W:*** Kevin Campbell; ***C:*** Victor Zorba. **VIDEO**

Backstabbing for Beginners **2018 (R)** A political thriller based on the memoirs of American diplomat Michael Soussan. In 2002, the idealistic Soussan (James), then a former lobbyist, takes a job as a coordinator for the United Nations' Oil-for-Food program. This program provided much-needed humanitarian aid to Iraq in exchange for profits from selling Iraqi oil. Mentored by program undersecretary Pasha (Kingsley), Soussan regularly travels to Baghdad, and soon learns that the truths are being manipulated and shadowy agendas are ever-present. Though visually interesting, it suffers from the overuse of voiceovers to tell the story and James' lackluster acting. **108m/C; DVD, Blu-Ray, Streaming.** Theo James; Jacqueline Bisset; Belcim Bilgin; Rossif Sutherland; Rachel Wilson; ***D:*** Per Fly; ***W:*** Per Fly; Daniel Pyne; ***M:*** Todor Kobakov.

Backstairs at the White House **1/2** **1979** Drawn from Lillian Rogers Parks' 1961 novel "My Thirty Years Backstairs at the White House" and originally aired on NBC, recounts the head maid's real life as she works for eight presidents—from Taft through Eisenhower—and narrates a wide array of historical events during her 52 years of service. **540m/C; DVD.** Olivia Cole; Leslie Uggams; Louis Gossett, Jr.; Robert Hooks; Leslie Nielsen; Cloris Leachman; Hari Rhodes; Paul Winfield; Julie Harris; Victor Buono; David Downing; Helen Carroll; Robert Vaughn; Kim Hunter; James A. Watson, Jr.; Claire Bloom; Celeste Holm; George Kennedy; Ed Flanders; Lee Grant; Larry Gates; Eileen Heckart; John Anderson; Harry (Henry) Morgan; Estelle Parsons; Jan Sterling; Barbara Barrie; Andrew Duggan; Heather Angel; Matthew "Stymie" Beard; Bibi Besch; Gerry Black; Marilyn Chris; Tom Clancy; Ann Doran; BeBe Drake; Kevin Hooks; Nancy Morgan; Harrison Page; Woodrow Parfrey; Bill Quinn; Ford Rainey; John Randolph; Noble Willingham; Dana Wynter; Ian Abercrombie; Louise Latham; ***D:*** Michael O'Herlihy; ***W:*** Paul Dubov; ***C:*** Robert L. Morrison; ***M:*** Morton Stevens. **TV**

Backstreet Dreams **1990 (R)** The young parents of an autistic child find themselves torn apart due to their feelings of guilt. The father has an affair with a specialist hired to help the boy, causing further strife. Interesting story possibilities never get far. **104m/C; VHS, Streaming.** Brooke Shields; Jason O'Malley; Sherilyn Fenn; Tony Fields; Burt Young; Anthony (Tony) Franciosa; Nick Cassavetes; Ray "Boom Boom" Mancini; ***D:*** Rupert Hitzig; ***M:*** Bill Conti.

Backtrack *Catchfire* **1989 (R)** Foster co-stars in this thriller about an artist who accidentally witnesses a mob hit. The mob puts a hitman (Hopper) on her trail, and after studying her background and listening to audio tapes she recorded, he finds himself falling in love. Originally intended for a theatrical release, it hit the European screens in a different cut as "Catchfire"; Hopper restored his original version and it was released on cable TV in the U.S. **102m/C; VHS, DVD.** Dennis Hopper; Jodie Foster; Dean Stockwell; Vincent Price; John Turturro; Fred Ward; G. Anthony "Tony" Sirico; Julie Adams; Frank Gio; Sy Richardson; Helena Kallianiotes; Bob Dylan; ***Cameo(s):*** Charlie Sheen; Joe Pesci; ***D:*** Dennis Hopper; ***W:*** Ann Louise Bardach; ***M:*** Michel Colombier.

Backtrack **1/2** **2016 (R)** A suspenseful Michael Petroni mystery-thriller centered on one man who must face a secret from his past. Blaming himself for his daughter's death, psychologist Peter Bower (Brody) takes a job in Sydney, Australia, but soon realizes that all of his new patients are ghosts. Questioning his own mental health, Peter must look to his own past to understand his present position. He soon learns that his past holds a secret that he must correct to be free. **90m/C; DVD, Blu-Ray, Streaming, Download.** Adrien Brody; Sam Neill; Robin McLeavy; Bruce Spence; Jenni Baird; ***D:*** Michael Petroni; ***W:*** Michael Petroni; ***C:*** Stefan Duscio; ***M:*** Dale Cornelius.

Backwards **2012 (PG)** Standard sports drama. After 30-year-old Abi Brooks is again only chosen as an alternate for the Olympic rowing team, she decides to reevaluate her life and takes a coaching job at her Philadelphia alma mater. This also gives her the chance to renew a romance with ex-beau Geoff. Abi struggles until she discovers a couple of girls with real potential just as she gets a call from her former coach about her own Olympic chances. **89m/C; DVD.** Sarah Megan Thomas; James Van Der Beek; Glenn Morshower; Margaret Colin; Alexandra Metz; Meredith Apfelbaum; ***D:*** Ben Hickernell; ***W:*** Sarah Megan Thomas; ***C:*** Harlan Bosmajian; ***M:*** David Torn. **VIDEO**

Backwoods **1987 (R)** Two campers wish they had never encountered a mountain man when he begins to stalk them with murder in mind. **90m/C; VHS, DVD.** Jack O'Hara; Dick Kreusser; Brad Armacot; ***D:*** Dean Crow.

The Backwoods **1/2** *Bosque de Sombras* **2006 (R)** Weak, schlocky psycho-thriller. In 1978, Norman (Considine) and his unhappy wife Lucy (Ledoyen) visit Spain's Basque Country to stay at the isolated house that's being renovated by their friends Paul (Oldman) and Isabel (Sanchez-Gijon). When the guys go out hunting, they find a hut where a disfigured, feral young girl (Esteve) is chained. After freeing her, they bring her back to the house but for some reason this makes the locals very upset. English and Spanish with subtitles. **97m/C; DVD.** *GB FR SP* Gary Oldman; Paddy Considine; Virginie Ledoyen; Aitana Sanchez-Gijon; Lluis Homar; Yaiza Esteve; Andres Gertudix; Jon Arino; ***D:*** Koldo Serra; ***W:*** Koldo Serra; Jon Sagala; ***C:*** Unax Mendia; ***M:*** Fernando Verazquez.

Backwoods **2008 (R)** Despite the rating and subject matter, this is a remarkably tame horror show about computer programmers on a corporate wilderness retreat in Northern California. They are preyed on by religious fanatics/survivalists who are interested in the women for breeding purposes. The men are expendable. **84m/C; DVD.** Haylie Duff; Ryan Merriman; Danny Nucci; Mark Rolston; Troy Winbush; Deborah Van Valkenburgh; ***D:*** Marty Weiss; ***W:*** Anthony Jaswinski; ***C:*** James W. Wrenn; ***M:*** Paul D'Amour. **VIDEO**

Bacurau **1/2** *Nighthawk* **2020** If Quentin Tarantino made a sociopolitical American Western set in a small Brazilian village and invited Close Encounters of the Third Kind to do a fly-over, this film would be the result. Teresa (Colen) returns home for a funeral, only to discover that her poor village, which is literally wiped off the map, is vulnerable to attack by outsiders. While this genre-bending film isn't for everyone, it won several awards for best film at international film festivals. **131m/C; DVD.** Barbara Colen; Thomas Aquino; Silvero Pereira; Thardelly Lima; Rubens Santos; ***D:*** Juliano Dornelles; Kleber Mendonca Filho; ***W:*** Juliano Dornelles; Kleber Mendonca Filho; ***C:*** Pedro Sotero; ***M:*** Mateus Alves; Tomaz Alves Souza.

Bad Actress **2011** Has-been TV actress Alyssa is now doing commercials for hubby Bernie's appliance store chain. Their daughter dies in a bizarre accident and the media attention rejuvenates Alyssa but Bernie deals with the tragedy by turning spiritual and wanting to give all their money away. Alyssa refuses to be poor so Bernie has to go and the body count starts to rise. **85m/C; DVD.** Beth Broderick; Chris Mulkey; Whitney Able; Vincent Ventresca; Ryan Hansen; Keri Lynn Pratt; ***D:*** Robert Lee King; ***W:*** David M. Barrett; ***C:*** Andrew Huebscher; ***M:*** Frederik Wiedmann. **VIDEO**

The Bad and the Beautiful **1/2** **1952** The rise and fall of a Hollywood producer. Douglas stars as the ruthless, arrogant Jonathan Shields, who alienates actress Georgia (Turner), writer James Lee Bartlow (Powell), and director Fred Amiel (Sullivan) as he pursues his career. Much speculation at the time as to who the real-life models for the insider story actually were. Winner of five Oscars, a splendid drama. **118m/B; VHS, DVD, Blu-Ray.** Kirk Douglas; Lana Turner; Dick Powell; Gloria Grahame; Barry Sullivan; Walter Pidgeon; Gilbert Roland; Leo G. Carroll; Elaine Stewart; ***D:*** Vincente Minnelli; ***W:*** Charles Schnee; ***C:*** Robert L. Surtees; ***M:*** David Raksin. Oscars '52: Art Dir./Set Dec., B&W, B&W Cinematog., Costume Des. (B&W), Screenplay, Support. Actress (Grahame); Natl. Film Reg. '02.

Bad Ass **1/2** **2009** Corrado works as a hitman for Frankie who wants him to deal with elderly mob boss Vittorio. The hit goes bad when Corrado is surprised by the mobster's live-in nurse Julia. She gets blamed for the death by Vittorio's crazy son Paolo and Corrado decides to save Julia and himself by going on the lam. **84m/C; DVD.** Johnny Messner; Tom Sizemore; Ken Kercheval; Candace Elaine; Joseph Gannascoli; ***D:*** Adamo P. Cultraro; ***W:*** Adamo P. Cultraro; ***C:*** David Fox; ***M:*** Ryan Franks. **VIDEO**

Bad Attitude **1993 (R)** Leon is a narcotics officer on a mission to restore his badge after his careless pistol work gets him booted off the force. The quick-tempered cop relentlessly pursues druglord Finque with the help of an open-minded preacher (De Veaux) and his sexy, streetwise assistant (Lim). **87m/C; VHS, DVD.** Leon; Gina Lim; Nathaniel DeVeaux; Susan Finque; ***D:*** Bill Cummings.

The Bad Batch **2017 (R)** Despite having some big names attached, a spotty narrative and heavy reliance on atmospheric shots make this flick more gory art-house than gory mainstream. Arlen (Waterhouse) is one of thousands exiled to a desert wasteland, where she is partially eaten by roving cannibals. She skateboards on her back to a safe haven ruled by The Dream (Reeves), semi-adopts the orphan Honey, and gets the hots for ultra-muscled yet cannibalistic Miami Man. Jim Carrey's first non-speaking role. **118m/C; DVD, Blu-Ray.** Suki Waterhouse; Jason Momoa; Keanu Reeves; Yolonda Ross; Giovanni Ribisi; Jim Carrey; ***D:*** Ana Lily Amirpour; ***W:*** Ana Lily Amirpour; ***C:*** Lyle Vincent.

Bad Behavior **1/2** **1992 (R)** Unscripted character-driven drama. Gerry and Ellie McAllister are an Irish couple living in North London. He's tired of working for the local planning commission, she's bored being just a mum at home, and both are still a little uneasy living in England. When they decide to remodel the family bath, the unexpected problems lead to an emotional shakeup. Don't expect a lot of drama, the film works only if you accept the decency of the characters and the small moments of recognizable daily life. Director Blair wrote a basic script outline and had the actors improvise their dialogue, in character, over a long rehearsal period to develop their roles. **103m/C; VHS, DVD.** *GB* Stephen Rea; Sinead Cusack; Philip Jackson; Clare Higgins; Phil Daniels; Saira Todd; ***D:*** Les Blair; ***M:*** John Altman.

Bad Blonde **1/2** *The Flanagan Boy* **1953** Minor Brit crime melodrama would have benefited from some better acting. Giuseppe Vecchi (Valk) is the promoter of young prizefighter Johnny Flanagan (Wright), who makes the mistake of fooling around with Vecchi's hotsie, scheming wife Lorna (Payton). Lorna tells Johnny she's expecting and insists they get rid of her hubby so the lovers can be together. But Johnny can't take the guilt after doing the deed. **80m/B; DVD.** *GB* Barbara Payton; Tony Wright; Frederick Valk; John Slater; Sidney James; Marie Burke; ***D:*** Reginald LeBorg; ***W:*** Richard H. Landau; Guy Elmes; ***C:*** Walter J. (Jimmy W.) Harvey; ***M:*** Ivor Slaney.

Bad Blood **1981** The true story of Stan Graham, who went on a killing spree in the New Zealand bush when his farm was foreclosed and his life ruined. **104m/C; VHS, DVD.** *NZ* Jack Thompson; Carol Burns; Dennis (Denis) Lill; ***D:*** Mike Newell; ***W:*** Andrew Brown; ***C:*** Gary Hansen; ***M:*** Richard Hartley.

Bad Boy Bubby **1993** Bizarre black comedy about the extremely maladjusted Bubby (Hope), who becomes a pop culture phenomena. The 35-year-old childlike Bubby has been kept a virtual prisoner by his monstrous mom, who has told him the world outside is filled with poisonous gas. Wondering how his cat survived, Bubby wraps it in plastic wrap and is puzzled when it dies. Still, this gives Bubby an idea—he wraps mom in plastic and escapes outside, where he's soon adopted by a struggling rock band that writes a cult song hit about his experiences. It's even stranger than it sounds. **114m/C; VHS, DVD.** *IT AU* Nicholas Hope; Claire Benito; Carmel Johnson; Ralph Cotterill; Norman Kaye; Paul Philpot; Graham Duckett; Bridget Walters; ***D:*** Rolf de Heer; ***W:*** Rolf de Heer; ***M:*** Graham Tardif. Australian Film Inst. '94: Actor (Hope), Director (de Heer), Film Editing, Orig. Screenplay.

Bad Boys **1983 (R)** When a gang member's little brother is killed in a rumble, the teen responsible (Penn, who else?) goes to a reformatory, where he quickly (though somewhat reluctantly) takes charge. Meanwhile, on the outside, his rival attacks Penn's girlfriend (Sheedy, in her feature film debut) in retaliation, is incarcerated, and ends up vying with Penn for control of the cell block. Backed into a corner by their mutual hatred and escalating peer pressure, the two are pushed over the brink into a final and shattering confrontation. Not as violent as it could be, to its credit; attempts to communicate a message. **104m/C; VHS, DVD.** Sean Penn; Esai Morales; Reni Santoni; Jim Moody; Eric Gurry; Ally Sheedy; Clancy Brown; *D:* Rick Rosenthal; *W:* Richard Dilello; *C:* Donald E. Thorin; *M:* Bill Conti.

Bad Boys 1/2 **1995 (R)** And you thought the old buddy-cop formula was played out. Well, Hollywood sticks with what works, and pairing the two TV personalities definitely works at the minimalist level required. Mike (Smith) and Marcus (Lawrence) are Miami cops who must track down $100 million worth of heroin stolen from their evidence room before internal affairs shuts down the precinct. The case leads them to a vicious thief and a beautiful female witness to his murderous handiwork. Plot lacks depth, but high energy and dazzling action sequences keep things moving. Loud adventure is made louder still by cranking soundtrack. Satisfying addition to the odd-couple cops genre with potential to spawn a "Lethal Weapon"-type franchise. Feature film debut for director Bay. **118m/C; VHS, DVD, Blu-Ray.** Martin Lawrence; Will Smith; Tcheky Karyo; Tea Leoni; Theresa Randle; Marg Helgenberger; Joe Pantoliano; John Salley; Nestor Serrano; Michael Imperioli; Julio Oscar Mechoso; *D:* Michael Bay; *W:* Michael Barrie; Jim Mulholland; *C:* Howard Atherton; *M:* Mark Mancina. Blockbuster '96: Male Newcomer, T. (Smith).

Bad Boys 2 **2003 (R)** Bombastic sequel finds Miami narcs Mike Lowrey (Smith) and Marcus Burnett (Lawrence) going after a violent network of Ecstasy dealers. The duo also has personal problems when Mike falls for Marcus' sister, Syd (Union), an undercover cop. Meanwhile, Marcus ponders whether he wants to remain partners with Mike, and whether, in classic Det. Murtaugh style, he's getting too old for this...stuff. Typical action-flick paper-thin plot doesn't stop Smith and Lawrence from clicking as a comedy-action team. Since this flick is basically the original, amped up to a ridiculous degree, your enjoyment will hinge on your opinion of that one, and your tolerance for the Bruckheimer-Bay "make-go-boom!" style. **146m/C; VHS, DVD, Blu-Ray, UMD.** Will Smith; Martin Lawrence; Gabrielle Union; Joe Pantoliano; Theresa Randle; Jordi Molla; Peter Stormare; Michael Shannon; Jon Seda; Yul Vazquez; Henry Rollins; Jason Manuel Olazabel; Otto Sanchez; *D:* Michael Bay; *W:* Ron Shelton; Jerry Stahl; *C:* Amir M. Mokri.

Bad Boys for Life 1/2 **2020 (R)** After the birth of his first grandchild, Miami police detective Marcus Burnett (Lawrence) reconsiders his law enforcement career because he wants to spend more time with his family. His long-time partner, hotheaded Mike Lowery (Smith), tries to change his mind. As the duo works out their issues, they must reckon with Isabel Aretas (del Castillo), who has been broken out of Mexican prison by her son Armando (Scipio). Under his mother's orders, he is to exact revenge for his drug dealer father's death by killing targets, including Lowery. The entertaining third entry in the series has unexpected depth in its story and characterizations. **124m/C; DVD.** Will Smith; Martin Lawrence; Vanessa Anne Hudgens; Alexander Ludwig; Charles Melton; *D:* Adil El Arbi; Bilall Fallah; *W:* Chris Bremner; Peter Craig; Joe Carnahan; *C:* Robrecht Heyvaert; *M:* Lorne Balfe.

Bad Bunch **1976** A white liberal living in Watts tries to befriend a ruthless black street gang, but is unsuccessful. **82m/C; VHS, DVD.** Greydon Clark; Tom Johnigam; Pamela Corbett; Jacqulin Cole; Aldo Ray; Jock Mahoney; *D:* Greydon Clark.

Bad Bush **2009** Based on a true story, this thriller is centered on a woman fighting for the survival of herself and her baby. The mother of a newborn, Ophelia (Bianca) needs a safe haven and visits her sister in a remote farmhouse in the Australian Bush country. Her sister is deeply disturbed and leaves Ophelia alone with her drug-obsessed boyfriend who makes his living growing marijuana for outlaw bikers. For 24 hours, he torments Ophelia who does all she can to protect herself and her baby from his psychosis. **85m/C; DVD.** Viva Bianca; Chris Sadrinna; Jeremy Lindsay Taylor; Malcolm Kennard; Michael Labram; *D:* Samuel Genocchio; *W:* Samuel Genocchio; *C:* Paul Howard; *M:* Veren Grigorov. **VIDEO**

Bad Channels **1992 (R)** Radio goes awry when female listeners of station KDUL are shrunk and put into speciman jars by a way-out disc jockey and a visiting alien, who plans to take the women back to his planet. Mildly amusing comedy features ex-MTV VJ Quinn and score by Blue Oyster Cult. Also available with Spanish subtitles. **88m/C; VHS, DVD.** Paul Hipp; Martha Quinn; Aaron Lustig; Ian Patrick Williams; Charlie Spradling; Tim Thomerson; Sonny Carl Davis; Robert Factor; Michael Huddleston; *D:* Ted Nicolaou; *W:* Jackson Barr; *C:* Adolfo Bartoli.

Bad City *Dirty Work* **2006 (R)** Yes, gnomish Pendleton is playing a depraved Chicago crime lord named Julian Healy and he's scarily effective. Derek Manning (Reddick) is a tough detective with a gambling problem who is in debt to Healy, which makes investigating the murder of hooker Bridgette (McDonough) difficult. Then there's too-slick politico Frank Sullivan (McGlone) whose troublesome wife (Anglin) is also killed. **97m/C; DVD.** Lance Reddick; Mike McGlone; Austin Pendleton; Nutsa Kukhianidze; Tim Decker; Meghan Maureen McDonough; Karin Anglin; *D:* Bruce Terris; *W:* Bruce Terris; Rick Rose; *C:* David Blood; *M:* Mark Messing.

Bad Company 1/2 **1972 (PG)** Thoughtful study of two very different Civil War draft dodgers roaming the Western frontier and eventually turning to a fruitless life of crime. Both the cast and script are wonderful in an entertaining film that hasn't been given the attention it's due. **94m/C; DVD.** Jeff Bridges; Barry Brown; Jim Davis; John Savage; *D:* Robert Benton; *W:* Robert Benton; David Newman; *C:* Gordon Willis; *M:* Harvey Schmidt.

Bad Company **1994 (R)** Cynical thriller pits the bad against the worst. Vic Grimes (Langella) and Margaret Wells (Barkin) run a company of former secret agents who specialize in corporate dirty work. Nelson Crowe (Fishburne) is an ex-CIA agent who's their latest recruit. But maybe he's not so ex and maybe Margaret doesn't like sharing power and maybe the cold-blooded duo will get together to make some changes. Everything is stylish, including the leads, but there's a definite chill in the air. **118m/C; VHS, DVD.** Ellen Barkin; Laurence Fishburne; Frank Langella; Michael Beach; Gia Carides; David Ogden Stiers; Spalding Gray; James Hong; Daniel Hugh-Kelly; *D:* Damian Harris; *W:* Ross Thomas; *C:* Jack N. Green; *M:* Carter Burwell.

Bad Company 1/2 *Mauvaises Frequentations* **1999** Delphine (Forget) is a typically dissatisfied middle-class teen susceptible to her more-worldly peers, which include the attitudinal, punked-out Olivia (Doillon). Olivia takes Delphine clubbing and she meets requisite smoldering bad boy, Laurent (Stevenin). Delphine's hormones are soon out of control and she agrees to some very questionable suggestions to prove her "love." Frank and unsettling. French with subtitles. **98m/C; VHS, DVD.** *FR* Maud Forget; Lou Doillon; Robinson Stevenin; Maxime Mansion; Delphine Rich; Rene Berleand; Micheline Presle; Cyril Cagnat; *D:* Jean-Pierre Ameris; *W:* Alain Layrac; *C:* Yves Vanderemeeren; *M:* Lene Marlin; Giya Kanchell.

Bad Company **2002 (PG-13)** Hustler Rock discovers his twin brother was a CIA operative who has just been murdered. He gets recruited by agency honcho Hopkins to take over his bro's assignment, which involves terrorists, bombs, and New York City. Considering these elements, it's no wonder this one got delayed. Rock deserves a better movie, but he almost salvages this one, anyway...almost. He's up against a standard-issue plot that merely serves to get to the next action set piece which, this being a Bruckheimer production, are done well, but done too often. Schumacher manages to (mostly) subdue his worst instincts (see "Batman & Robin" to watch him surrender to them completely), but it doesn't really help. **111m/C; VHS, DVD.** Chris Rock; Anthony Hopkins; Matthew Marsh; Garcelle Beauvais; Kerry Washington; Gabriel Macht; Peter Stormare; John Slattery; Adoni Maropis; Brooke Smith; *D:* Joel Schumacher; *W:* Michael Browning; Jason Richman; *C:* Dariusz Wolski; *M:* Trevor Rabin.

Bad Country 1/2 **2014 (R)** This throwback action flick is set in the 1980s, which is appropriate because it's the kind of lazy crime story that would feel right at home on a not-often visited shelf of a VHS rental store. Detective Lt. Bud Carter (Dafoe, sporting an awesome mustache) pressures a notorious contract killer (Dillon) into becoming a police informant, a move that makes them both the targets of the even more notorious crime lord Lutin Adams (Berenger). Lots of angst, shooting, and terrible Cajun accents do nothing to improve director Brinker's tepid thriller. (Brinker, unfortunately, died during post-production.) **95m/C; DVD, Blu-Ray.** Willem Dafoe; Matt Dillon; Tom Berenger; Neal McDonough; Amy Smart; Christopher Marquette; *D:* Chris Brinker; *W:* Jonathan Hirschbein; *C:* Zoran Popovic; *M:* Jeff Danna; John Fee. **VIDEO**

Bad Day at Black Rock 1/2 **1954** Story of a one-armed man uncovering a secret in a Western town. Wonderful performances from all concerned, especially Borgnine. Fine photography, shot using the new Cinemascope technique. Based on the novel by Howard Breslin. **81m/C; VHS, DVD, Blu-Ray.** Spencer Tracy; Robert Ryan; Anne Francis; Dean Jagger; Walter Brennan; John Ericson; Ernest Borgnine; Lee Marvin; *D:* John Sturges; *C:* William Mellor; *M:* Andre Previn. Cannes '55: Actor (Tracy); Natl. Film Reg. '18.

Bad Day for the Cut 1/2 **2017** A compelling revenge drama set in Northern Ireland. Donal (O'Neill) lives a simple life with his aging mother (McCusker) on their small family farm. His life changes forever when he finds his mother murdered in what seems like a home invasion. After her funeral, two masked men try to stage Donal's suicide, but he kills one and imprisons the other. He learns that his prisoner, Bartosz (Pawloski), had been blackmailed to protect his sister (Prochniak), the captive of human traffickers. Together, the pair head to Belfast to rescue her and get payback. Well-crafted performances, colorful characters, and dark humor add to the film's appeal. **99m/C; DVD, Blu-Ray.** Nigel O'Neill; Susan Lynch; Jozef Pawlowski; Stuart Graham; David Pearse; *D:* Chris Baugh; *W:* Chris Baugh; Brendan Mullin; *C:* Ryan Kernaghan; *M:* James Everett.

Bad Dreams 1/2 **1988 (R)** The only surviving member of a suicidal religious cult from the '60s awakens in 1988 from a coma. She is pursued by the living-dead cult leader, who seeks to ensure that she lives up (so to speak) to the cult's pact. Blood begins flowing as her fellow therapy group members begin dying, but the only bad dreams you'd get from this flick would be over the money lost on the video rental. **84m/C; VHS, DVD, Blu-Ray.** Bruce Abbott; Jennifer Rubin; Richard Lynch; Harris Yulin; Dean Cameron; Elizabeth Daily; Susan Ruttan; Charles Fleischer; Sy Richardson; *D:* Andrew Fleming; *W:* Andrew Fleming; Steven E. de Souza; *C:* Alexander Grusynski; *M:* Jay Ferguson.

Bad Education *La Mala Educacion* **2004** Complicated film noir begins in 1980 Madrid where young movie director Enrique (Martinez) is seeking inspiration. It comes to him, literally, when old school friend Ignacio (Garcia Bernal) turns up and hands Enrique a story he's written about the sexual abuse he suffered at the hands of the principal of their Catholic boys' school. But something is wrong—and it's not just the fact that the wannabe actor returns demanding to play the part of transsexual prostitute Zahara (Garcia Bernal again—making quite a pretty woman) in the film, which plays out in Enrique's mind so you're watching two films at once. And if that's not confusing enough, the film has flashbacks to the boys' schooldays and a subsequent meeting in 1977. Somehow Almodovar makes it work. Spanish with subtitles. **104m/C; DVD.** Fele Martinez; Gael Garcia Bernal; Lluis Homar; Javier Camara; Petra Martinez; Nacho Perez; Raul Garcia Forneiro; Juan Fernandez; Daniel Gimenez Cacho; Alberto Ferreiro; Francisco Boira; *D:* Pedro Almodóvar; *W:* Pedro Almodóvar; *C:* Jose Luis Alcaine; *M:* Alberto Iglesias.

Bad for Each Other **1953** Predictable melodrama with a stiff Heston starring as a former-Korean War Army medico who is torn between helping the poor in his coal-mining hometown and becoming a society doc so he can romance an ice-cold socialite beauty (Scott). The beauty wins out for awhile until miners get trapped in a cave-in and the doc's conscience kicks in. **83m/B; DVD.** Charlton Heston; Lizabeth Scott; Dianne Foster; Mildred Dunnock; Arthur Franz; Ray Collins; *D:* Irving Rapper; *W:* Horace McCoy; Irving Wallace; *C:* Franz Planer; *M:* Mischa Bakaleinikoff.

Bad Girl **1931** Apparently sassy model Dorothy (Eilers) is a bad girl because she has sex with Eddie (Dunn) before marriage and gets herself into trouble. Eddie does the right thing and they get married, although he doesn't really want to be a father and isn't happy to give up his dreams to support his unexpected family. So they have to struggle to make things work amidst hard times. **90m/B; DVD, Blu-Ray.** James Dunn; Sally Eilers; Minna Gombell; William Pawley; Frank Darien; *D:* Frank Borzage; *W:* Edwin J. Burke; *C:* Chester Lyons.

Bad Girls 1/2 **1994 (R)** Latest in the current western craze turns the tables as women take their turns being the gunslingers. Four hooker chums hastily flee town after one kills a nasty customer—only to find the bank where their cash was stashed was robbed by baddies Loggia and Russo. Wearing stylish duds and with each hair perfectly in place the beauties manage to recover their loot. Unexciting script leaves a lot to be desired, but a strong performance from Stowe makes this nearly worthwhile. Lots of off-set drama with original director Tamra Davis fired, and the actresses reportedly having a less-than-bonding experience. **99m/C; VHS, DVD.** Andie MacDowell; Madeleine Stowe; Mary Stuart Masterson; Drew Barrymore; James Russo; Dermot Mulroney; Robert Loggia; James LeGros; Nick (Nicholas) Chinlund; Will MacMillan; Jim Beaver; *D:* Jonathan Kaplan; *W:* Ken Friedman; Yolande Finch; *M:* Jerry Goldsmith.

Bad Girls Dormitory **1984 (R)** At the New York Female Juvenile Reformatory, suicide seems a painless and welcome escape. Utilizes standard genre identifiers, including rape, drugs, soapy showers, bad docs, and desperate young women trapped in a web of frustration and desire. Cheap and mindless titillation. **95m/C; VHS, DVD.** Carey Zuris; Teresa Farley; *D:* Tim Kincaid.

Bad Girls from Mars **WOOF!** **1990 (R)** "B" movie sleaze-o-rama in which everyone is murdered, either before, after, or during sex, just like in real life. When the director of the film within this film hires an actress who is, shall we say, popular, to be the heroine of his latest sci-fier, the fun, slim as it is, begins. **86m/C; VHS, DVD.** Edy Williams; Brinke Stevens; Jay Richardson; Oliver Darrow; Dana Bentley; Jeffrey Culver; Jasae; *D:* Fred Olen Ray; *W:* Mark Thomas McGee; Fred Olen Ray; *C:* Gary Graver; *M:* Chuck Cirino.

Bad Girls Go to Hell **WOOF!** **1965** From the sultana of sleaze, Wishman, comes this winning entry into Joe Bob Briggs' "Sleaziest Movies in the History of the World" series. A ditsy-but-sexy housewife accidentally commits murder and what follows is a plethora of perversion involving hirsute men and gender-bending women who are hell-bent on showing her how hot it is where bad girls go. **98m/B; VHS, DVD.** Gigi Darlene; George La Rocque; Sam Stewart; Sandee Norman; Alan Yorke; Bernard L. Sankett; Darlene Bennett; Marlene Starr; Harold Key; *D:* Doris Wishman; *W:* Doris Wishman; Dawn Whitman; *C:* C. Davis Smith.

Bad Guys 1/2 **2008** A too-much-talk and too-little-action crime drama. Disbarred criminal attorney Zena hooks up with three former clients to make a fortune with a new designer drug. Unfortunately, the plan goes bad when Eddie gets inexplicably trigger-happy while meeting their drug connection, who works for the yakuza. **86m/C; DVD.** Kate del Castillo; Sherman Augustus; Danny Strong; Art LaFleur; Quinton 'Rampage' Jackson; Antonio Fargas; *D:* Rick Jacobsen; *W:* Timothy Cogshell; *C:* Brian Agnew; *M:* Dan Radlauer. **VIDEO**

Bad Influence 1/2 **1990 (R)** A lackluster effort in the evil-doppelganger school of psychological mystery, where a befuddled young executive (Spader) is led into the seamier side of life by a mysterious stranger (Lowe). **99m/C; VHS, DVD, Blu-Ray; Open Captioned.** Rob Lowe; James Spader; Lisa Zane; Christian Clemenson; Kathleen Wilhoite; *D:* Curtis Hanson; *C:* Robert Elswit; *M:* Trevor Jones.

Bad Jim 1/2 **1989 (PG)** A cowpoke buys Billy the Kid's horse and, upon riding it, becomes an incorrigible outlaw himself. First feature film for Hollywood legend Clark Gable's son. **110m/C; DVD.** James Brolin; Richard Roundtree; John Clark Gable; Harry Carey, Jr.; Ty Hardin; Pepe Serna; Rory Calhoun; *D:* Clyde Ware.

Bad Lieutenant **1992 (NC-17)** Social chaos and degeneration characterize story as well as nameless loner lieutenant Keitel, who is as corrupt as they come. Assigned to a case involving a raped nun, he's confronted by his own lagging Catholic beliefs and the need for saving grace. From cult filmmaker Ferrara ("Ms. 45") and filled with violence, drugs, and grotesque sexual situations. Tense, over-the-top, urban drama is not intended for seekers of the subtle. Rent it with "Reservoir Dogs" and prepare yourself for a long tense evening of top-rated Keitel and screen-splitting violence. "R" rated version is also available at 91 minutes. **98m/C; VHS, DVD.** Harvey Keitel; Brian McElroy; Frankie Acciario; Peggy Gormley; Stella Keitel; Victor Argo; Paul Calderon; Leonard Thomas; Frankie Thorn; Zoe Tamerlis; *D:* Abel Ferrara; *W:* Zoe Tamerlis; Abel Ferrara; *C:* Ken Kelsch; *M:* Joe Delia. Ind. Spirit '93: Actor (Keitel).

Bad Lieutenant: Port of Call New Orleans **2009 (R)** Loopy director Herzog does his 'reimaging' of Abel Ferrara's 1992 guilt-ridden cult flick "Bad Lieutenant" that starred an over-the-top Harvey Keitel. This time it's Cage as New Orleans homicide detective Terence McDonaugh, who's a gambling and drug addict who hallucinates evil iguanas. He also has a beautiful drug-addicted hooker girlfriend (Mendes) and a gangland slaying (that's drug related) to investigate. It's all just secondary to watching Cage act bizarrely, which (for a change) is actually in keeping with his erratic character. **121m/C; DVD, Blu-Ray.** Nicolas Cage; Val Kilmer; Eva Mendes; Fairuza Balk; Jennifer Coolidge; Brad Dourif; Michael Shannon; Shawn Hatosy; Denzel Whitaker; Shea Whigham; Xzibit; Tom Bower; Irma P. Hall; Vondie Curtis-Hall; *D:* Werner Herzog; *W:* William M. Finkelstein; *C:* Peter Zeitlinger; *M:* Mark Isham.

Bad Love 1/2 **1995 (R)** Unlucky Eloise (Gidley) stays true to nature when she falls for loser Lenny (Sizemore), who decides the big score lies with robbing the fading movie star (O'Neill) Eloise works for. Naturally, things go badly. Slick production for anyone who likes fringe romances. **93m/C; VHS, DVD.** Tom Sizemore; Pamela Gidley; Debi Mazar; Jennifer O'Neill; Margaux Hemingway; Richard Edson; Seymour Cassel; Joe Dallesandro; *D:* Jill Goldman; *C:* Gary Tieche; *M:* Rick Cox.

The Bad Man **1941** With a particularly ripe Mexican accent, Beery stars in a convoluted comedic western as bandit Pancho Lopez. Henry Jones (Barrymore) and his nephew Gil (Reagan) own a ranch in Mexico that's being unjustly foreclosed on by men who both think there's oil on the property. When not rustling the Jones? cattle and holding people for ransom, Pancho decides to save the ranch because Gil once saved his life. It's hard to tell who chews more scenery—Beery or Barrymore. **70m/B; DVD.** Wallace Beery; Lionel Barrymore; Ronald Reagan; Laraine Day; Tom Conway; Henry Travers; Nydia Westman; Chill Wills; *D:* Richard Thorpe; *W:* Wells Root; *C:* Clyde De Vinna; *M:* Franz Waxman.

The Bad Man of Brimstone 1/2 **1938** Rascally but violent outlaw Trigger Bill (Beery) discovers his estranged son Jeffrey (O'Keefe) is a prizefighter. Trigger wants his son to go to law school and promises to reform so they—ll both be legit but Bill is tested in one final showdown by villain Blackjack McCreedy (Cabot). **89m/B; DVD.** Wallace Beery; Dennis O'Keefe; Bruce Cabot; Virginia Bruce; Lewis Stone; Guy Kibbee; Cliff Edwards; Guinn "Big Boy" Williams; Noah Beery, Sr.; Joseph Calleia; *D:* J. Walter Ruben; *W:* Richard Maibaum; Cyril Hume; *C:* Clyde De Vinna; *M:* William Axt.

Bad Manners **1998 (R)** Pompous musicologist Matt (Rubinek) returns to Boston with his razor-tongued girlfriend Kim (Feeney) to give a lecture and check in on his old girlfriend, brittle unhappy Nancy (Bedelia), and her prissy academic husband Wes (Strathairn). It's a weekend in hell for houseguests and hosts as they play not-so-adult games of truth-or-dare. Based on Gilman's play "Ghost in the Machine." **88m/C; VHS, DVD.** David Strathairn; Bonnie Bedelia; Saul Rubinek; Caroleen Feeney; Julie Harris; *D:* Jonathan Kaufer; *W:* David Gilman; *C:* Denis Maloney; *M:* Ira Newborn.

Bad Man's River **1972** A Mexican revolutionary leader hires a gang of outlaws to blow up an arsenal used by the Mexican Army. **92m/C; VHS, DVD, Blu-Ray.** *IT SP* Lee Van Cleef; James Mason; Gina Lollobrigida; *D:* Eugenio (Gene) Martin; *W:* Philip Yordan; *C:* Alejandro Ulloa; *M:* Waldo de los Rios.

Bad Meat **2011** Unruly teens arriving at a boot camp intended to put them back on the path to more responsible behavior have more than the usual bad camp experience when a disease causes their sadistic counselors to put on leather outfits and run around eating people. **96m/C; DVD, Streaming.** *CA* Dave Franco; Elisabeth Harnois; Mark Pellegrino; Jessica Parker Kennedy; Monique Ganderton; *D:* Lulu Jarmen; *W:* Paul Gerstenberger. **VIDEO**

Bad Medicine **WOOF! 1985 (PG-13)** A youth who doesn't want to be a doctor is accepted by a highly questionable Latin American school of medicine. Remember that it was for medical students like these that the U.S. liberated Grenada. **97m/C; VHS, Streaming.** Steve Guttenberg; Alan Arkin; Julie Hagerty; Bill Macy; Curtis Armstrong; Julie Kavner; Joe Grifasi; Robert Romanus; Taylor Negron; Gilbert Gottfried; *D:* Harvey Miller; *W:* Harvey Miller.

Bad Men of Tombstone **1949** Gunslinger Tom Horn lands in a cell with outlaw William Morgan. His men break them out, and Morgan asks Horn to join them in stealing a fortune in gold. They hide out in lawless Tombstone where Horn's bride Julie wants to take their share and head out of town, but neither desperado is willing to split their ill-gotten gains. **74m/B; DVD.** Barry Sullivan; Broderick Crawford; Marjorie Reynolds; Guinn "Big Boy" Williams; Fortunio Bonanova; John Kellogg; *D:* Kurt Neumann; *W:* Philip Yordan; Arthur Strawn; *C:* Russell Harlan; *M:* Roy Webb.

Bad Moms 1/2 **2016 (R)** Amy (Kunis) is a working, married mom with two children, exhausted by the pressure to keep everything in place on a daily basis. Carla (Hahn) is a sexually-active single mom who has given up more of the societal standards of motherly love. Kiki (Bell) is stay-at-home mom with four kids, and almost no support from her husband in raising them. The unlikely trio become friends and decide to break out and have some fun in this sleeper hit comedy that has just enough laughs to merit a look but also feels like something of a wasted opportunity to be an instant classic. **100m/C; DVD, Blu-Ray.** Mila Kunis; Kathryn Hahn; Kristen Bell; Christina Applegate; Jada Pinkett Smith; *D:* Jon Lucas; Scott Moore; *W:* Jon Lucas; Scott Moore; *C:* Jim Denault; *M:* Christopher Lennertz.

A Bad Moms Christmas 1/2 **2017 (R)** A slapdash sequel to the unexpected comedy hit Bad Moms that explores similar themes with added bonus of another generation of moms and the pressures of the holidays. Moms Amy (Kunis), Kiki (Bell), and Carla (Hahn) must contend with visits from their problematic mothers over Christmas. Each mother-daughter relationship has its own emotional baggage which pushes the moms over the edge. Lacking the substance about the truths of motherhood, meaningful interactions among the three original moms, and a balance between raunchy and sweetness that gave the original its power, there are moments of hilarity but ultimately comes up short. **104m/C; DVD, Blu-Ray.** Mila Kunis; Kristen Bell; Kathryn Hahn; Christine Baranski; Susan Sarandon; *D:* Jon Lucas; Scott Moore; *W:* Jon Lucas; Scott Moore; *C:* Mitchell Amundsen; *M:* Christopher Lennertz.

Bad Moon 1/2 **1996 (R)** Let's put it this way, the werewolf in this movie is not the only thing that bites. Shortest (mercifully) studio release in recent history is a horror (in more ways than one) film with Pare leading the pack as Ted, a photojournalist who comes back from the Amazon a different, more nocturnally hirsute man. Fleeing from the site of his nightly gore, Ted takes refuge with his loving sister Janet (Hemingway) and her son Brett (Gamble). The real hero (and best actor) is a German shepherd named Thor (Primo) who discovers that Ted's a werewolf. Dog steals the show paws down (naturally). Decent special FX. Adapted from Wayne Smith's novel "Thor." **79m/C; DVD, Blu-Ray.** Mariel Hemingway; Michael Paré; Mason Gamble; Ken Pogue; *D:* Eric Red; *W:* Eric Red; *C:* Jan Kiesser; *M:* Daniel Licht.

The Bad Mother's Handbook 1/2 **2007 (PG-13)** Self-absorbed single mom Karen (Tate) thinks she can bend anyone to her will but learns differently in this BBC family drama. She expects her teenage daughter Charlotte (Grainger) to go to college but when Charlotte becomes pregnant, Karen refuses to help. Instead, the girl turns to geeky friend Daniel (Pattinson) and her grandmother Nancy (Reid) for comfort and Karen learns some hard lessons in parenting. Adaptation of the Kate Long novel. **90m/C; DVD.** *GB* Catherine Tate; Holliday Grainger; Anne Reid; Robert Pattinson; Steve John Shepherd; Steve Pemberton; *D:* Robin Shepperd; *W:* Kate Long; Kate O'Riordan; *M:* Mark Russell. **TV**

The Bad News Bears **1976 (PG)** Family comedy about a misfit Little League team that gets whipped into shape by a cranky, sloppy, beer-drinking coach who recruits a female pitcher. O'Neal and Matthau are top-notch. Spawned two sequels and a TV series. **102m/C; VHS, DVD.** Walter Matthau; Tatum O'Neal; Vic Morrow; Joyce Van Patten; Jackie Earle Haley; Chris Barnes; Erin Blunt; Gary Cavagnaro; Alfred Lutter; David Stambaugh; Brandon Cruz; Jaime Escobedo; Scott Firestone; George Gonzales; Brett Marx; David Pollock; Quinn Smith; *D:* Michael Ritchie; *W:* Bill Lancaster; *C:* John A. Alonzo; *M:* Jerry Fielding. Writers Guild '76: Orig. Screenplay.

The Bad News Bears **2005 (PG-13)** Here's some bad news: Indie darling Linklater hit a home run with his kid-friendly "School of Rock," but he couldn't squeeze any life of out this watered-down remake of the 1976 Walter Matthau classic. It's disturbing that the updated "Bears" is a million times less subversive, vulgar, and (let's face it) funny than the original, a film that was released almost thirty years ago. Isn't society supposed to be declining? Shouldn't Linklater's movie be raunchier than a film released during the Carter administration? Casting Thornton in the lead was an inspired choice, but the toothless script just forces him to do the PG version of his "Bad Santa" routine. Do yourself a favor and rent the original. **111m/C; DVD, UMD.** Billy Bob Thornton; Greg Kinnear; Marcia Gay Harden; Tyler Patrick Jones; Sammi Kraft; Timmy Deters; Ridge Canipe; Brandon Craggs; Jeff Davies; Carter Jenkins; Jeffrey Tedmori; Troy Gentile; Carlos Estrada; Emmanuel Estrada; Kenneth "K.C." Harris; Aman Johal; *D:* Richard Linklater; *W:* Glenn Ficarra; John Requa; Bill Lancaster; *C:* Rogier Stoffers; *M:* Ed Shearmur; Randall Poster.

The Bad News Bears Go to Japan **1978 (PG)** The second sequel, in which the famed Little League team goes to the Little League World Series in Tokyo. Comic adventure features Curtis as a talent agent out to exploit the team's fame. **92m/C; VHS, DVD.** Tony Curtis; Jackie Earle Haley; Tomisaburo Wakayama; George Wyner; Erin Blunt; George Gonzales; Brett Marx; David Pollock; David Stambaugh; Regis Philbin; *D:* John Berry; *W:* Bill Lancaster; *C:* Gene Polito; *M:* Paul Chihara.

The Bad News Bears in Breaking Training 1/2 **1977 (PG)** With a chance to take on the Houston Toros for a shot at the little league baseball Japanese champs, the Bears devise a way to get to Texas to play at the famed Astrodome. Disappointing sequel to "The Bad News Bears"; followed by "The Bad News Bears Go to Japan" (1978). **99m/C; VHS, DVD.** William Devane; Clifton James; Jackie Earle Haley; Jimmy Baio; Chris Barnes; Erin Blunt; George Gonzales; Jaime Escobedo; Alfred Lutter; Brett Marx; David Pollock; Quinn Smith; David Stambaugh; Dolph Sweet; *D:* Michael Pressman; *W:* Paul Brickman; *C:* Fred W. Koenekamp; *M:* Craig Safan.

The Bad Pack 1/2 **1998 (R)** Soldier of fortune puts together a team when he's hired to defend a town beseiged by a sadistic militia. **93m/C; VHS, DVD.** Robert Davi; Ralph (Ralf) Moeller; Roddy Piper; Brent Huff; Larry B. Scott; Patrick Dollaghan; Marshall Teague; *D:* Brent Huff. **VIDEO**

Bad Parents 1/2 **2012** Satire may get knowing nods from parents who cart their kids around to organized sports leagues. New Jersey housewife Kathy signs her younger daughter up for soccer not realizing the craziness that will ensue. The parents are obsessed with which team their girls are assigned to and how much playing time they get and they and Coach Nick are obsessed with winning, especially as the A team heads towards the state semi-finals. These adults couldn't even spell 'sportsmanship.' **100m/C; DVD.** Janeane Garofalo; Christopher Titus; Cheri Oteri; Kristen Johnston; Michael Boatman; Rebecca Budig; Reiko Aylesworth; Bill Sage; *D:* Caytha Jentis; *W:* Caytha Jentis; *C:* Anthony Savini; *M:* James Harrell. **VIDEO**

Bad Reputation **2005 (R)** Chillingly disturbing portrayal of victim's revenge. Michelle, though poor, attends an affluent school on scholarship. She chooses to keep buried in a book rather than mix with the shallow class populous. One night at a party, she is drugged and gang-raped. A metamorphosis follows, as the shy, smart, attractive girl becomes an avenging assassin, swiftly wiping out all who humiliated her. Excellent character development, smart script, and bright directing make for a very satisfying retaliation tale. **90m/C; DVD.** Angelique Hennessy; Jerad Anderson; Danielle Noble; Mark Kunzman; Kristina Conzen; *D:* Jim Hemphill; *W:* Jim Hemphill; *C:* Forrest Allison; *M:* John LeBec; Eric Choronzy. **VIDEO**

Bad Reputation 1/2 **2018 (R)** A documentary about the career of rocker Joan Jett, with significant input from the singer herself. Essentially narrated by Jett, the film follows the trajectory of her career from The Runaways to her solo years to her most recent musical activities. In addition to archival performances, it also has interview nuggets with fellow musicians and Kristen Stewart,who played Jett in a feature film about The Runaways. Focusing primarily on her music, it's superficial and dismisses major issues, such as Jett's drinking. However, it does show her dedication to her craft and the extent of her influence despite an uneven career. **95m/C; DVD.** *D:* Kevin Kerslake; *W:* Joel Marcus; *C:* Kevin Kerslake; Peter Alton; Greg Olliver; *M:* Jacques Brautbar.

Bad Ronald **1974** No, not a political biography of Ronald Reagan... Fascinating thriller about a disturbed teenager who kills a friend after being harassed repeatedly. The plot thickens after the boy's mother dies, and he is forced to hide out in a secret room when an unsuspecting family with three daughters moves into his house. The story is accurately recreated from the novel by John Holbrook Vance. **78m/C; VHS, DVD, Blu-Ray.** Scott Jacoby; Pippa Scott; John Larch; Dabney Coleman; Kim Hunter; John Fiedler; *D:* Buzz Kulik. **TV**

Bad Samaritan **2018 (R)** A serial killer horror-thriller that is simultaneously inane, charming, and unexpectedly entertaining. When petty thief/artiste Sean Falco (Sheehan) breaks into the luxurious Portland home of trust fund-rich Cale Erendreich (Tennant), he unexpectedly finds a scared woman, Helen (Brenner), tied to a chair. Sean soon learns that perverse Cale is a murderer with a special torture room in his garage. He feels Cale's wrath as he embarks upon systematically ruin Sean's life in unexpected ways. If not too much is read into basically nonsensical character motivations, it can be a highly amusing, if not enjoyable. **110m/C; DVD, Blu-Ray.** David Tennant; Robert Sheehan; Kerry Condon; Jacqueline Byers; ***Cameo(s):*** Carlito Olivero; *D:* Dean Devlin; *W:*

Brandon Boyce; *C:* David Connell; *M:* Joseph LoDuca.

Bad Santa 1/2 **2003 (R)** This is not your grandparents' Christmas movie. Or your kids' for that matter. Thornton is Willie Stokes, an alcoholic, vulgarian, self-loathing department store Santa who uses the gig to rob the store safe on Christmas Eve. His partner is sidekick/elf Marcus, the brains of the duo, who berates Willie for letting his liquor-soaked ways interfere with the job. When they set up shop in Phoenix, things get complicated when a doughy outcast kid leeches onto Willie. Sentimentality is crushed beneath the boot of bitter misanthropy as the movie swerves from tasteless to merely outrageous and back. Luckily, the commitment of the cast to their unsavory roles makes most of the comedy work. Zwigoff and the script let in a little light at the end, but not so much that it betrays what came before. Ritter is excellent in his final role, as the meek store manager. **91m/C; VHS, DVD, Blu-Ray.** Billy Bob Thornton; Tony Cox; Lauren Graham; Brett Kelly; John Ritter; Bernie Mac; Lauren Tom; Cloris Leachman; *D:* Terry Zwigoff; *W:* Glenn Ficarra; John Requa; *C:* Jamie Anderson; *M:* David Kitay.

Bad Santa 2 **2016 (R)** There's nothing less funny than a joke for which you know the punchline. Consider that when you think of watching this lame follow-up to a movie that really could never possibly justify a sequel, especially this long after the original. Willie (Thornton) and Marcus (Cox) team up again to rob a Chicago charity on Christmas Eve. Brett Kelly returns as a much-bigger version of Thurman Merman, the kid from the original, and Christina Hendricks and Kathy Bates try to replace lost stars Bernie Mac and John Ritter. Nothing here works as well as the first film. **92m/C; DVD, Blu-Ray.** Billy Bob Thornton; Kathy Bates; Tony Cox; Christina Hendricks; Brett Kelly; *D:* Mark Waters; *W:* Johnny Rosenthal; Shauna Cross; *C:* Theo van de Sande; *M:* Lyle Workman.

The Bad Seed 1/2 **1956** A mother makes the tortuous discovery that her cherubic eight-year-old daughter harbors an innate desire to kill. Based on Maxwell Anderson's powerful Broadway stage play. **129m/B; VHS, DVD, Blu-Ray.** Patty McCormack; Nancy Kelly; Eileen Heckart; Henry Jones; Evelyn Varden; Paul Fix; Jesse White; Gage Clark; Joan Croyden; Frank Cady; William Hopper; *D:* Mervyn LeRoy; *W:* John Lee Mahin; *C:* Harold Rosson; *M:* Alex North. Golden Globes '57: Support. Actress (Heckart).

The Bad Seed **1985** TV remake of the movie with the same name. Story about a sadistic little child who kills for her own evil purposes. Acting is not up to par with previous version. **100m/C; VHS, DVD.** Blair Brown; Lynn Redgrave; David Carradine; Richard Kiley; David Ogden Stiers; Carrie Wells; Chad Allen; Christa Denton; Anne Haney; Eve Smith; *D:* Paul Wendkos; *M:* Paul Chihara. **TV**

Bad Seed *Preston Tylk* **2000 (R)** Mild-mannered Preston (Wilson) storms out of the house when he discovers wife Emily (Avital) is having an affair. He returns home to find her murdered—maybe by her boyfriend Jonathan (Reedus) whom Preston then tries to track down. There's another murder, both men go on the lam, and Preston turns to a hard-luck PI, Dick (Farina), for help. Too bad the film doesn't hang together better since it had the makings of a fine little thriller. **92m/C; VHS, DVD.** Luke Wilson; Norman Reedus; Dennis Farina; Mili Avital; Vincent Kartheiser; *D:* Jon Bokenkamp; *W:* Jon Bokenkamp; *C:* Joey Forsyte; *M:* Kurt Kuenne.

The Bad Sleep Well 1/2 *The Worse You Are, the Better You Sleep; Waru Yatsu Hodo Yoku Nemuru* **1960** Japanese variation of the 1940 Warner Bros. crime dramas. A tale about corruption in the corporate world as seen through the eyes of a rising executive. **135m/B; VHS, DVD.** *JP* Toshiro Mifune; Masayuki Kato; Masayuki Mori; Takashi Shimura; Akira Nishimura; *D:* Akira Kurosawa; *W:* Akira Kurosawa; Shinobu Hashimoto; Ryuzo Kikushima; Hideo Oguni; *C:* Yuzuru Aizawa; *M:* Masaru Sato.

The Bad Son 1/2 **2007** A Seattle serial killer targets the women who come into his life, except for his mom who protects him because she actually works for the cops and has access to confidential documents. Whenever the police get too close, Frances cries harassment but two at-odds detectives are determined to bring him to justice. **90m/C; DVD.** Catherine Dent; Tom McBeath; Ben Cotton; Marilyn Norry; Paul Jarrett; Tegan Moss; Kimberly Warnat; *D:* Neill Fearnley; *W:* Richard Leder; *C:* Eric Goldstein; *M:* Jerry Lambert; Harry Manfredini. **CABLE**

Bad Taste **1988** A definite pleaser for the person who enjoys watching starving aliens devour the average, everyday human being. Alien fast-food manufacturers come to earth in hopes of harvesting all of mankind. The earth's fate lies in the hands of the government who must stop these rampaging creatures before the whole human race is gobbled up. Terrific make-up jobs on the aliens add the final touch to this gory, yet humorous cult horror flick. **90m/C; VHS, DVD.** *NZ* Peter Jackson; Pete O'Herne; Mike Minett; Terry Potter; Craig Smith; Doug Wren; Dean Lawrie; Peter Vere-Jones; Ken Hammon; Michael Gooch; *D:* Peter Jackson; *W:* Peter Jackson; Ken Hammon; Tony Hiles; *C:* Peter Jackson; *M:* Michelle Scullion.

Bad Teacher **2011 (R)** Wild-living and completely inappropriate 7th-grade teacher Elizabeth (Diaz) wants to dump her job for a wealthy match and sets her sights on a rich, handsome substitute teacher (Timberlake). However, she has competition from perfectly-behaved colleague Amy (Punch). Diaz and Segel are game, but the plot tries too hard to be raunchy and funny enough to join the "hard R comedy" revival, and comes up a bit short. **92m/C; DVD, Blu-Ray.** Cameron Diaz; Justin Timberlake; Lucy Punch; John Michael Higgins; Thomas Lennon; Jason Segel; *D:* Jake Kasdan; *W:* Gene Stupnitsky; Lee Eisenberg; *C:* Alar Kivilo; *M:* Michael Andrews.

Bad Times at the El Royale 1/2 **2018 (R)** In the early 1970s, a formerly upscale motel that straddles the California-Nevada border attracts a diverse group of guests, a decade after a crime was committed in one of the rooms and evidence was left behind. Father Daniel Flynn (Bridges) seems connected to this crime, while singer Darlene Sweet (Erivo) seeks a place to practice her craft. Salesman Laramie (Hamm) is not what he seems, while Emily Summerspring (Johnson) only wants to save her sister Ruth (Spaeny) from cult leader Billy Lee (Hemsworth). As the fates of the characters violently come together, the horror-thriller becomes a plot-heavy exercise in survival. **140m/C; DVD, Blu-Ray.** Jeff Bridges; Cynthia Erivo; Dakota Johnson; Jon Hamm; Chris Hemsworth; *D:* Drew Goddard; *W:* Drew Goddard; *C:* Seamus McGarvey; *M:* Michael Giacchino.

Bad Timing: A Sensual Obsession **1980** Perverse sex drama from Brit director Roeg. Milena (Russell) is admitted to a Vienna hospital nearly dead from an overdose, making the staff suspicious and Inspector Netusil (Keitel) is called in. It seems her ex-lover, psychologist Alex (Garfunkel), can't quite account for the time they spent together before he called for help. Flashbacks depict Milena's increasingly crazy behavior and Alex's unhealthy obsession with her. **123m/C; DVD.** *GB* Art Garfunkel; Theresa Russell; Harvey Keitel; Denholm Elliott; *D:* Nicolas Roeg; *W:* Yale Udoff; *C:* Anthony B. Richmond; *M:* Richard Hartley.

Bad Turn Worse 1/2 **2014** Debut directors Simon and Zeke Hawkins name drop Jim Thompson in the opening scene of this heat-drenched Texan noir and then go on to earn that comparison. B.J. (Huffman) is frustrated that his best friend Bobby (White) and girlfriend Sue (Davis) are heading off to college without him. He steals a large wad of cash from his boss's safe to have one last night of partying. He forgets that his boss is insane and his boss's boss is even crazier. Violence and betrayal ensues. It's smart, tense and remarkably clever; well-cast from top to bottom. **91m/C; Streaming.** Logan Huffman; Jeremy Allen White; Mackenzie Davis; Mark Pellegrino; William Devane; Jon(athan) Gries; *D:* Zeke Hawkins; Simon Hawkins; *W:* Dutch Southern; *C:* Jeff Bierman; *M:* Jonathan Keevil.

Bad 25 **2012** Documentary centering on the 25th anniversary of Michael Jackson's seventh studio album "Bad," released in 1987. Plays clips from the recording of the album, as well as many behind-the-scenes views of Jackson's life during the time "Bad" was recorded, and his first solo artist worldwide tour. Also features many people that were involved in his life at the time as well as interviews with those who worked with him. Fans will appreciate the inside look at a pivotal point the King of Pop's career. **123m/C; DVD, Blu-Ray.** *D:* Spike Lee; *C:* Kerwin Devonish.

Bad Words **2013 (R)** Bateman stars and makes his directorial debut as a foul-mouthed sore loser. Disgruntled 40-year-old Guy Trilby exploits a technicality in the spelling bee regulations that allows him to compete against the 8th-grade participants. Going on to the national spelling bee in L.A., he forms an unexpected bond with charming youngster Chaitanya Chopra (Chand)--they're both dealing with daddy issues--despite Guy's worst behavior. Joyfully irresponsible and uncensored. **88m/C; DVD, Blu-Ray.** Jason Bateman; Rohan Chand; Kathryn Hahn; Allison Janney; Philip Baker Hall; Ben Falcone; Anjul Nigam; *D:* Jason Bateman; *W:* Andrew Dodge; *C:* Ken Seng; *M:* Rolfe Kent.

The Badge **2002 (R)** Small-town sheriff Darl (Thornton) must set aside his personal distate to investigate the murder of a local transsexual, who was once married to stripper Scarlett (Arquette). But the deeper Darl digs, the more the powers that be want the incident covered up. Mediocre mystery despite the name cast. **103m/C; VHS, DVD.** Billy Bob Thornton; Patricia Arquette; Sela Ward; William Devane; Jena Malone; Tom Bower; Ray McKinnon; Julie Hagerty; Hill Harper; *D:* Robby Henson; *W:* Robby Henson; *C:* Irek Hartowicz; *M:* David Bergeaud.

Badge of Faith **2015** A dramatic story of recovery, based on a true story. For officer Bryan Lawrence (Lauer), his life is centered on his family and his faith. After an encounter with fugitives on the job, Bryan is paralyzed and doctors say he will never walk again. He grows despondent and wants his wife to divorce him so that he is not a burden to her. Bryan is especially upset that he cannot live up to his promise that he will walk his future daughter-in-law down the aisle when she marries his son. Because of this promise, Bryan does all he can to fulfill this promise. **98m/C; DVD.** Andrew Lauer; Rebecca Rogers, MD; Chase Pitts; Danny Vinson; Brandon Seth Chinault; *D:* Donald Leow; *W:* Rick Garside; *C:* James Burgess; *M:* John Doryk. **VIDEO**

Badge 373 1/2 **1973 (R)** In the vein of "The French Connection," a New York cop is suspended and decides to battle crime his own way. **116m/C; VHS, DVD, Blu-Ray, Streaming.** Robert Duvall; Verna Bloom; Eddie Egan; *D:* Howard W. Koch.

Badla 1/2 **2019** Naina (Pannu) is accused of murdering Arjun (Luke), a man she was allegedly having an affair with. Though only compelling circumstantial evidence links her to the crime, she is arrested and interrogated by police. Her lawyer Jimmy (Kaul) hires a more experienced investigative attorney Badal Gupta (Bachchan) to help defend her. As Badal interviews Naina about what happened, truths about related events and both characters slowly emerge. A whodunit murder mystery, the flashback-heavy film largely succeeds as an Indian remake of the Spanish film "The Invisible Guest." Both Pannu and Bachchan are compelling in their dialogue-heavy roles. Hindi with subtitles. **118m/C; DVD.** Amitabh Bachchan; Taapsee Pannu; Amrita Singh; Antonio Aakeel; Tony Luke; *D:* Sujoy Ghosh; *W:* Sujoy Ghosh; *C:* Avik Mukhopadhyay; *M:* Clinton Cerejo; Amal Mallik; Anupam Roy.

Badland 1/2 **2007 (R)** Overly-solemn and way too long. Marine reservist Jerry wound up with a dishonorable discharge and PTSD after a stint in Iraq. Now he's got a nothing job in a nowhere Wyoming town when his boss falsely accuses him of theft. When shrewish wife Nora nags once too often—well, Jerry takes young daughter Celia and hits the road. **165m/C; DVD.** Jamie Draven; Vinessa Shaw; Joe Morton; Chandra West; Grace Fulton; Patrick Richards; *D:* Francesco Lucente; *W:* Francesco Lucente; *C:* Carlo Varini; *M:* Ludek Drizhal.

The Badlanders **1958** A western remake of the 1950 crime drama "The Asphalt Jungle." In 1898, Peter 'The Dutchman' Van Hoek (Ladd) and John McBain (Borgnine) are released from Yuma state prison. Both wind up in Prescott, Arizona where the Dutchman is unwelcome since the mining engineer was framed and sent to the pen by gold mine owner Cyril Lounsberry (Smith). McBain wants to go straight but is drawn into the Dutchman's revenge scheme. **83m/C; DVD.** Alan Ladd; Ernest Borgnine; Kent Smith; Claire Kelly; Katy Jurado; Nehemiah Persoff; *D:* Delmer Daves; *W:* Richard Collins; *C:* John Seitz.

Badlands 1/2 **1974 (PG)** Based loosely on the Charlie Starkweather murders of the 1950s, this impressive debut by director Malick recounts a slow-thinking, unhinged misfit's killing spree across the midwestern plains, accompanied by a starry-eyed 15-year-old schoolgirl. Sheen and Spacek are a disturbingly numb, apathetic, and icy duo. **94m/C; VHS, DVD, Blu-Ray.** Martin Sheen; Sissy Spacek; Warren Oates; Ramon Bieri; Alan Vint; Gary Littlejohn; Charles Fitzpatrick; Howard Ragsdale; John Womack, Jr.; Dona Baldwin; ***Cameo(s):*** Terrence Malick; *D:* Terrence Malick; *W:* Terrence Malick; *C:* Tak Fujimoto; Stevan Larner; Brian Probyn; *M:* Carl Orff. Natl. Film Reg. '93.

Badman's Territory **1946** A straight-shooting marshal has to deal with such notorious outlaws as the James and Dalton boys in a territory outside of government control. **79m/B; VHS, DVD.** Randolph Scott; Ann Richards; George "Gabby" Hayes; Steve Brodie; *D:* Tim Whelan.

Baffled 1/2 **1972** Nimoy is a race car driver who has visions of people in danger. He must convince an ESP expert (Hampshire) of the credibility of his vision, and then try to save the lives of the people seen with his sixth sense. A failed NBC TV pilot movie. **90m/C; DVD, Streaming.** Leonard Nimoy; Susan Hampshire; Vera Miles; Rachel Roberts; Jewel Blanch; Christopher Benjamin; *D:* Philip Leacock; *W:* Theodore Apstein; *C:* Ken Hodges; *M:* Richard Hill. **TV**

The Bag Man **2014 (R)** Cusack continues his remarkable descent into less than B-movie nonsense with this insipid piece masquerading as a crime drama but actually little more than a paycheck movie for its lazy stars. The king of the paycheck movies in the current century, De Niro co-stars as a legendary crime boss (of course) who hires a bag man named Jack (Cusack) to wait at a seedy motel for his arrival. While Jack wonders what the crime boss has in store for him, he meets a stunner named Rivka (Da Costa). A waste of time on every level—ridiculous, repugnant, and just plain stupid. **109m/C; DVD, Blu-Ray.** John Cusack; Rebecca Da Costa; Robert De Niro; Dominic Purcell; Crispin Glover; Kirk "Sticky Fingaz" Jones; *D:* David Grovic; *W:* David Grovic; Paul Conway; *C:* Steve Mason; *M:* Tony Morales; Edward Rogers.

Bag of Bones *Stephen King's Bag of Bones* **2011** Underwhelming A&E miniseries finds bestselling novelist Mike Noonan (Brosnan) retreating to a New England lake house to grieve the sudden death of his wife Jo (Gish). Mike starts suffering from nightmares and it becomes clear that Jo is contacting him over long-ago secrets involving the disappearance of 1930s blues singer Sara Tidwell (Rose) and a town curse. Also involved are single mom Mattie (George), who's being harassed in a custody battle over her daughter by her evil, elderly father-in-law Max (Schallert) that also has ties to the past. Based on Stephen King's 1998 novel. **170m/C; DVD.** Pierce Brosnan; Melissa George; Annabeth Gish; Anika Noni Rose; William Schallert; Deborah Grover; Caitlin Carmichael; Matt Frewer; Jason Priestley; *D:* Mick Garris; *W:* Matt Venne; *C:* Barry Donlevy; *M:* Nicholas Pike. **CABLE**

A Bag of Hammers **2011** Offbeat indie comedy (with some maudlin moments) finds L.A. slacker buds Ben (Ritter) and Alan (Sandvig) living lives of irresponsibility and scams until they befriend neglected 12-year-old Kelsey (Canterbury), who's unstable single mom Lynette (Preston) abandons him to the guys' unlikely care. Can they actually assume adult responsibilities? **85m/C; DVD, Blu-Ray.** Jason Ritter; Jake Sandvig; Chandler Canterbury; Rebecca Hall; Carrie Preston; Todd Louiso; Gabriel Macht; Amanda Seyfried; *D:*

Brian Crano; **W:** Jake Sandvig; Brian Crano; **C:** Byron Shah; Quyen Tran; **M:** Johnny Flynn.

Bagdad Cafe ♪♪♪ *Out of Rosenheim* **1988 (PG)** A large German woman, played by Sagebrecht, finds herself stranded in the Mojave desert after her husband dumps her on the side of the highway. She encounters a rundown cafe where she becomes involved with the off-beat residents. A hilarious story in which the strange people and the absurdity of their situations are treated kindly and not made to seem ridiculous. Spawned a short-lived TV series with Whoopi Goldberg. **91m/C; VHS, DVD.** *GE* Marianne Saegebrecht; CCH Pounder; Jack Palance; Christine Kaufmann; Monica Calhoun; Darron Flagg; **D:** Percy Adlon; **W:** Percy Adlon; Eleonore Adlon; **C:** Bernd Heinl; **M:** Bob Telson. Cesar '89: Foreign Film.

Baggage Claim ♪ **2013 (PG-13)** Another offensive romantic comedy that posits that all women over 30 are desperate enough to get married that they'll act stupidly in their pursuit to do so. The ridiculously named Montana Moore (Patton) is a flight attendant who decides that her biological clock is ticking to the point that she goes back through her ex-boyfriends to find the one that got away. Montana goes on a 30-day, 30,000-mile expedition to find the right beau before her younger sister's wedding. It's one of those comedies that's not just unfunny but deeply misogynistic when it's not just deadly dull. **96m/C; DVD, Blu-Ray.** Paula Patton; Derek Luke; Taye Diggs; Boris Kodjoe; Jill Scott; **D:** David E. Talbert; **W:** David E. Talbert; **C:** Anastas Michos; **M:** Aaron Zigman.

Baghead ♪ **2008 (R)** Four wannabe actor/writers take a weekend retreat to a woodsy cabin so they can come up with a screenplay they can star in. The two sorta couples are having relationship issues and then some peeper, wearing a bag on his head, starts peering in the windows. But no one's sure if it's just a prank or something more sinister. A mumblecore indie mash-up of genres best appreciated by those who enjoy watching the self-absorbed yammer. **84m/C; DVD.** Ross Partridge; Greta Gerwig; Elise Muller; Steve Zissis; **D:** Mark Duplass; Jay Duplass; **W:** Mark Duplass; Jay Duplass; **C:** Jay Duplass; **M:** J. Scott Howard.

The Bagman ♪ **2002** A disfigured young man is murdered 'accidentally' while being hazed by his peers, and years later they start dying. The survivors begin to wonder if he's really dead in this hilariously awful re-imagining of every bad remake of "I Know What You Did Last Summer." **88m/C; DVD.** Mikul Robins; Ron Ford; Stephanie Beaton; **D:** Beverly Beaton; **W:** Beverly Beaton; **C:** Eric Lasher; **M:** Jay Woelfel. **VIDEO**

Bail Out ♪ **1990 (R)** Three bounty hunters, armed to the teeth, run a car-trashing police gauntlet so they may capture a valuable crook. **88m/C; VHS, DVD.** David Hasselhoff; Linda Blair; John Vernon; Tom Rosales; Charlie Brill; **D:** Max Kleven.

Bailey's Billion$ ♪♪ ½ **2005 (G)** Bailey (voiced by Lovitz) is a golden retriever who has been left a fortune by his late owner. Naturally, the woman's greedy nephew Caspar (Curry) and his scheming wife Dolores (Tilly) plot to get the money by kidnapping the dog. However, Bailey's guardian Theodore (Cain), a geeky animal behaviorist who can speak dog, and animal-rights activist Marge (Holden) team up to do right by him. **93m/C; DVD.** *CA* Dean Cain; Laurie Holden; Tim Curry; Jennifer Tilly; Angela Vallee; Max Baker; Sheila McCarthy; Kenneth Welsh; **V:** Jon Lovitz; **D:** David Devine; **W:** Heather Conkie; Mary Walsh; **C:** Gavin Finney; **M:** Lou Pomanti.

Baise Moi **WOOF!** *Rape Me* **2000** French porn dressed up for the arthouse crowd had critics spinning like tops to justify not calling the film what it is—exploitative trash, even if it is done by women. After Manu (Anderson) gets gang raped, she kills her boyfriend, steals his money, and hooks up with prostitute Nadine (Bach) to go on a sex and murder spree. Very, very graphic sex and violence and the literal translation of the French title is not "rape" but another four-letter word beginning with "f." Based on the novel by co-writer/director Despentes; French with subtitles. **77m/C; VHS, DVD.** *FR* Raffaela Anderson; Karen Bach; **D:** Virginie Despentes; Coralie Trinh Thi; **W:** Virginie Despentes; Coralie Trinh Thi; **C:** Benoit Chamaillard; **M:** Varou Jan.

Bait ♪ ½ **1954** Low-budget melodrama has longtime prospector Marko (Haas) finally striking it rich. Only he doesn't want to share the wealth with young partner, Ray (Agar). Marko decides to use his comely young wife Peggy (Moore) to lure Ray into an affair so he has an excuse to kill him, but neither Peggy nor Ray cooperate as expected. **79m/B; DVD, Blu-Ray.** Cleo Moore; John Agar; Hugo Haas; **D:** Hugo Haas; **W:** Samuel W. Taylor; **C:** Eddie (Edward) Fitzgerald; **M:** Vaclav Divina.

Bait ♪♪ **2000 (R)** Bait is what you use to catch bigger fish, and hopefully star Foxx can use his performance in this otherwise by-the-book action-comedy to snag bigger and better roles. Petty thief Alvin (Foxx) winds up in the clink after a botched seafood robbery. His cellmate Jaster (Pastorelli) is the double-crossing partner of prancing archvillain Bristol (Hutchinson), who has stolen $40 million in gold. Unfortunately for Alvin, Jaster winds up in the Big House in the sky before he can tell anyone where the hidden loot is stashed. Head Fed Clenteen (Morse), thinking that Alvin knows where the gold is hidden, has him unwittingly equipped with surveillance devices and springs him from the pokey. Alvin, now followed by Bristol and the feds, tries to find the stashed loot by piecing together the cryptic clues that Jaster has left him. Lots of action on a minimal (for these types of movies) budget. **119m/C; VHS, DVD.** Jamie Foxx; Doug Hutchison; David Morse; Jamie Kennedy; Robert Pastorelli; Kimberly Elise; David Paymer; Tia Texada; Mike Epps; Nestor Serrano; Megan Dodds; Jeffrey Donovan; Kirk Acevedo; **D:** Antoine Fuqua; **W:** Tom Gilroy; Jeff Nathanson; Adam Scheinman; Andrew Scheinman; **C:** Tobias Schliessler; **M:** Mark Mancina.

Bait ♪♪ ½ **2002** Jack Blake does a good deed on a cold, rainy night, taking in Pam and her daughter Stephanie when their car breaks down. Their gratitude is short-lived as Jack, still anguished over his daughter's unsolved murder years before, realizes that Stephanie looks like her and holds them captive so he can use her to catch the killer. **98m/C; VHS, DVD.** John Hurt; Sheila Hancock; Rachael Stirling; Angeline Ball; Jonathan Firth; Nicholas Farrell; Matthew Scurfield; **D:** Nicholas Renton; **W:** Daniel Boyle; **C:** Oliver Curtis; **M:** John Keane. **TV**

Bait Shop ♪ ½ **2008 (PG)** Good ole boy bait shop owner Bill (Engvall) is going to lose his business to the bank unless he can come up 15,000 smackers. His one chance is to win the annual Bass Tournament, which he's lost every previous year to smug rival Hot Rod Johnson (Cyrus). **85m/C; DVD.** Bill Engvall; Billy Ray Cyrus; Vincent Martella; Harve Presnell; Billy Joe Shaver; **D:** C.B. Harding; **W:** Bear Aderhold; Tomas D. Sullivan; **C:** Jamie Barber; **M:** Steven R. Phillips. **VIDEO**

Baja ♪♪ **1995 (R)** Bebe (Ringwald) hides out in Baja with her beau Alex (Logue) after a drug deal goes bad. They hold up in a sleazy motel while Bebe waits for dad, John (Bernsen), to bail her out. But instead, John persuades estranged hubby Michael (Nickles) to track down the runaways and Michael finds out that hitman Tom (Henriksen) is hunting for Alex. Must be the desert heat causing all the ensuing commotion. **92m/C; VHS, DVD.** Molly Ringwald; Lance Henriksen; Michael A. (M.A.) Nickles; Donal Logue; Corbin Bernsen; **D:** Kurt Voss; **W:** Kurt Voss; **C:** Denis Maloney; **M:** Reg Powell.

Baked in Brooklyn ♪♪ **2016** A comedy-drama about an inexperienced drug dealer who finds himself over his head. A recent college grad living in New York City, David (Brener) works hard, does not give up, and is creative, but cannot keep his job. He needs to make money quickly to cover rent and keep his long-suffering girlfriend happy. His solution is to sell marijuana over the Internet. At first, David is quite successful and spends all his time working to deliver his wares to his clients all over the city. Once he develops his own drug habit and demand begins to exceed supply, he realizes that he could be arrested, or even killed. David must decide how to re-take control of his life. **86m/C; DVD, Blu-Ray, Streaming, Download.** Josh Brener; Todd Bartels; Evangelo Bousis; Alexandra Daddario; Tyrone Brown; **D:** Rory Rooney; **W:** David Shapiro; **C:** Trevor Forrest; **M:** Kenny Woods. **VIDEO**

Baker's Hawk ♪♪ **1976** A young boy befriends a red-tailed hawk and learns the meaning of family and caring. **98m/C; VHS, DVD.** Clint Walker; Diane Baker; Burl Ives; Lee Montgomery; Alan Young; Danny Bonaduce; **D:** Lyman Dayton; **W:** Dan Greer; Hal Harrison, Jr.; **C:** Bernie Abramson; **M:** Lex de Azevedo.

Balalaika ♪♪ **1939** Rather dull operetta about the Russian revolution with Eddy playing a Russian prince. Eddy masquerades as a member of the proletariat in order to romance Massey, who was expected to become the next Garbo. Didn't happen, though. Eddy's rendition of "Stille Nacht" ("Silent Night") is highlight of film. Based on the operetta by Eric Maschwitz, George Ponford, and Bernard Gruen. **102m/B; VHS, Streaming.** Nelson Eddy; Ilona Massey; Charlie Ruggles; Frank Morgan; Lionel Atwill; Sir C. Aubrey Smith; Joyce Compton; **D:** Reinhold Schunzel; **W:** Leon Gordon; Charles Bennett; Jacques Deval; **C:** Karl Freund.

Balboa **WOOF!** **1982** Set on sun-baked Balboa Island, this is a melodramatic tale of high-class power, jealousy, and intrigue. Never-aired pilot for a TV miniseries, in the night-time soap tradition (even features Steve Kanaly from TV's "Dallas"). Special appearance by Cassandra Peterson, also known as horror hostess Elvira; and if that interests you, look for Sonny Bono, as well. **92m/C; VHS, DVD.** Tony Curtis; Carol Lynley; Chuck Connors; Sonny Bono; Steve Kanaly; Jennifer Chase; Lupita Ferrer; Martine Beswick; Henry Jones; Cassandra Peterson; **D:** James Polakof. **TV**

The Balcony ♪♪♪ **1963** A film version of the great Jean Genet play about a surreal brothel, located in an unnamed, revolution-torn city, where its powerful patrons act out their fantasies. Scathing and rude. **87m/B; VHS, DVD.** Peter Falk; Shelley Winters; Lee Grant; Kent Smith; Peter Brocco; Ruby Dee; Jeff Corey; Leonard Nimoy; Joyce Jameson; **D:** Joseph Strick; **W:** Ben Maddow; **C:** George J. Folsey.

Ball & Chain ♪♪ ½ **2004 (PG-13)** Although raised in America, Ameet (Malhotra) and Saima (Ray) can't escape the customs of India when their respective parents arrange their marriage. They want to break their engagement, so Ameet decides that if he behaves outrageously enough, his prospective in-laws will be so dismayed that they will call things off. Only the more time Ameet and Saima spend together, the more they realize that the arrangement could actually work. **90m/C; DVD.** Lisa Ray; Kal Penn; Purva Bedi; Suni Malhotra; Ismail Bashey; **D:** Shriaz Jafri; **W:** Thomas Mortimer; **C:** Peter Simonite; **M:** Deane Ogden.

Ball of Fire ♪♪♪ **1941** A gang moll hides out with a group of mundane professors, trying to avoid her loathsome boyfriend. The professors are busy compiling an encyclopedia and Stanwyck helps them with their section on slang in the English language. Cooper has his hands full when he falls for this damsel in distress and must fight the gangsters to keep her. Stanwyck takes a personal liking to naive Cooper and resolves to teach him more than just slang. **111m/B; VHS, DVD.** Gary Cooper; Barbara Stanwyck; Dana Andrews; Gene Krupa; Oscar Homolka; Dan Duryea; S.Z. Sakall; Henry Travers; **D:** Howard Hawks; **W:** Billy Wilder; Charles Brackett; **C:** Gregg Toland; **M:** Alfred Newman. Natl. Film Reg. '16.

Ball of Wax ♪ ½ **2003** Superstar baseball player Bret Packard (Mench) is a domination freak who plots the downfall of his teammates basically because he's a wealthy, arrogant sociopath and he can. Then manager Ingels (Morris) brings in motivational speaker Bob Tower (Tobias) to get the team back on track and Packard flips to find he's losing control of the situation. **90m/C; DVD.** Larry Tobias; Mark Mench; Justin Smith; Traci Dinwiddie; Cullen Moss; Daniel Morris; Kevin Scanlon; Stephanie Wallace; **D:** Daniel Kraus; **W:** Daniel Kraus; **C:** Michael Caporale; **M:** Eric Bachman.

Ballad in Blue ♪♪ *Blues for Lovers* **1966** Real life story of Ray Charles and a blind child. Tearjerker also includes some of Charles' hit songs. **89m/B; VHS, DVD.** *GB* Ray Charles; Tom Bell; Mary Peach; Dawn Addams; Piers Bishop; Betty McDowall; **D:** Paul Henreid.

Ballad of a Soldier ♪♪♪ ½ *Ballada o Soldate* **1960** As a reward for demolishing two German tanks, a 19-year-old Russian soldier receives a six-day pass so he can see his mother; however, he meets another woman. Well directed and photographed, while avoiding propaganda. Russian with subtitles. **88m/B; VHS, DVD.** *RU* Vladimir Ivashov; Shanna Prokhorenko; Antonina Maximova; Nikolai Kryuchkov; **D:** Grigori Chukhraj; **W:** Grigori Chukhraj; Valentin Yezhov; **C:** Sergei Mukhin; **M:** Mikhail Ziv. British Acad. '61: Film.

The Ballad of Andy Crocker ♪♪ ½ **1969** Early TV movie take on vets returning home from Vietnam. Andy (Majors) comes home to find his girlfriend has married someone else, his small business is in ruins, and his friends and family haven't a clue as to what has happened or what to expected from the disillusioned ex-soldier. **80m/C; VHS, DVD.** Lee Majors; Joey Heatherton; Jimmy Dean; Marvin Gaye; Agnes Moorehead; Pat Hingle; Jill Haworth; Peter Haskell; Bobby Hatfield; **D:** George McCowan; **W:** Stuart Margolin; **C:** Henry Cronjager, Jr.; **M:** Billy May. **TV**

The Ballad of Buster Scruggs ♪♪♪ **2018 (R)** An anthology of six stories, written by the Coen brothers over the course of 25 years, that explore different perspectives on the Old West, all relating to the singing, misanthropic gunslinger Buster Scruggs (Nelson) and all united in the theme of death. Some chapters work better than others, but they are beautifully shot and capture the dark humor, violence, and occasional silliness that the Coens are known and beloved for. **132m/C; Streaming.** Tim Blake Nelson; James Franco; Brendan Gleeson; Zoe Kazan; Liam Neeson; Tom Waits; **D:** Ethan Coen; Joel Coen; **W:** Ethan Coen; Joel Coen; **C:** Bruno Delbonnel; **M:** Carter Burwell.

Ballad of Cable Hogue ♪♪♪ **1970 (R)** A prospector, who had been left to die in the desert by his double-crossing partners, finds a waterhole. A surprise awaits his former friends when they visit the remote well. Not the usual violent Peckinpah horse drama, but a tongue-in-cheek comedy romance mixed with tragedy. Obviously offbeat and worth a peek. **122m/C; VHS, DVD, Blu-Ray.** Jason Robards, Jr.; Stella Stevens; David Warner; L.Q. Jones; Strother Martin; Slim Pickens; **D:** Sam Peckinpah; **C:** Lucien Ballard; **M:** Jerry Goldsmith.

The Ballad of Jack and Rose ♪♪♪ **2005 (R)** Absorbing story about an idealistic father and daughter living on their own like the last two hippies on earth in an abandoned commune. Rose (Belle) loves her father, Jack (Day-Lewis). A lot. Actually, she's probably in love with him. This is a touchy subject (not literally, don't worry) for Jack. Jack knows his daughter is too attached, is going to lose him one day, and may not make it on her own. After venturing into the real world for six months Jack begins dating a woman, mother to two boys, and asks her and the boys to move into the commune. Rose reacts with jealousy, trying to anger her father by seducing the sons. Writer/director Rebecca Miller, daughter of playwright Arthur Miller, sidesteps any cliches but piles on a few too many tricks at the end. **138m/C; DVD.** Daniel Day-Lewis; Catherine Keener; Camilla Belle; Beau Bridges; Jason Lee; Jena Malone; Paul Dano; Susanna Thompson; Ryan McDonald; **D:** Rebecca Miller; **W:** Rebecca Miller; **C:** Ellen Kuras; **M:** Michael Rohatyn. L.A. Film Critics '05: Actress (Keener).

The Ballad of Josie ♪ ½ **1967** Studio backlot western comedy. After managing to accidentally kill her drunken lout of a husband, perky frontier widow Josie (Day) needs a way to support herself and her son. She takes up sheep ranching--in cattle country--which makes her very unpopular with most everyone except good guy Jason Meredith (Graves). **103m/C; DVD.** Doris Day; Peter Graves; George Kennedy; Andy Devine; William Talman; David Hartman; **D:** Andrew V. McLaglen; **W:** Harold Swanton; **C:** Milton Krasner; **M:** Frank DeVol.

The Ballad of Lefty Brown 1/2 **2017** A western influenced by classic films in the genre while putting the sidekick at center. In 1889 Montana, rancher Edward (Fonda) heads east to take office as a newly elected senator accompanied by his longtime hand Lefty (Pullman). Edward is murdered during his journey and his widow Laura (Baker) accuses Lefty of failing him. The grieving Lefty decides to find Edward's killer. Meeting idealistic traveler Jeremiah (Josef) early on, the pair try to solve the mystery but face trouble themselves. With picturesque visuals and Pullman's grounded performance, the film is a both a love letter and a reaction to classic western themes and characters. **111m/C; DVD, Blu-Ray.** Bill Pullman; Peter Fonda; Joseph Lee Anderson; Michael Spears; Kathy Baker; ***D:*** Jared Moshe; ***W:*** Jared Moshe; ***C:*** David McFarland; ***M:*** H. Scott Salinas.

The Ballad of Little Jo 1/2 **1993 (R)** Inspired by a true story set during the 1866 gold rush. Easterner Josephine Monaghan is cast out of her wealthy family after she has a baby out of wedlock. Heading west, she passes herself off as a man—Little Jo'in an attempt to forestall harrassment. Solemn and overly earnest attempt by Greenwald to demystify the old west and bring a feminist viewpoint to a familiar saga. **110m/C; VHS, DVD.** Suzy Amis; Bo Hopkins; Ian McKellen; Carrie Snodgress; David Chung; Rene Auberjonois; Heather Graham; Anthony Heald; Sam Robards; Ruth Maleczech; ***D:*** Maggie Greenwald; ***W:*** Maggie Greenwald; ***C:*** Declan Quinn; ***M:*** David Mansfield.

The Ballad of Narayama *Narayama bushiko* **1958** Filmed in a style similar to traditional Kabuki plays, this is the story of a remote village near Narayama Mountain. Famine is so bad, that it has become policy that anyone reaching the age of 70 is to be carried off into the mountains by their family and left to die. **98m/C; DVD, Blu-Ray, Streaming.** *JP* Kinuyo Tanaka; Teiji Takahashi; Yuko Mochizuki; Danko Ichikawa; Keiko Ogasawara; ***D:*** Keisuke Kinoshita; ***W:*** Keisuke Kinoshita; ***C:*** Hiroshi Kusuda; ***M:*** Chuji Kinoshita; Matsunosuke Nozawa. **VIDEO**

The Ballad of Narayama *Narayama-Bushi-Ko* **1983** Director Imamura's subtle and vastly moving story takes place a vague century ago. In compliance with village law designed to control population among the poverty-stricken peasants, a healthy 70-year-old woman must submit to solitary starvation atop a nearby mountain. We follow her as she sets into motion the final influence she will have in the lives of her children and grandchildren, a situation described with detachment and without imposing a tragic perspective. In Japanese with English subtitles. **129m/C; VHS, DVD.** *JP* Ken Ogata; Sumiko Sakamoto; Takejo Aki; Tonpei Hidari; Shoichi Ozawa; ***D:*** Shohei Imamura; ***W:*** Shohei Imamura; ***C:*** Masao Tochizawa; ***M:*** Shinichiro Ikebe. Cannes '83: Film.

The Ballad of the Sad Cafe 1/2 **1991 (PG-13)** Unusual love story set in a small Southern town during the Depression. The everday lives of its townspeople are suddenly transformed when a distant relation of the town's outcast (Redgrave) unexpectedly shows up. A moving story that tries to portray both sides of love and its power to enhance and destroy simultaneously. Emotion never seems to come to life in a movie that's nice to watch, but is ultimately disappointing. Adapted from the play by Edward Albee, which was based on the critically acclaimed novella by Carson McCullers. A British/U.S. co-production. **100m/C; VHS, DVD.** *GB* Vanessa Redgrave; Keith Carradine; Cork Hubbert; Rod Steiger; Austin Pendleton; Beth Dixon; Lanny Flaherty; Mert Hatfield; Earl Hindman; Anne Pitoniak; ***D:*** Simon Callow; ***W:*** Michael Hirst; ***C:*** Walter Lassally; ***M:*** Richard Robbins.

Ballast **2008** Hammer's debut follows the misfortunes of a poor Mississippi Delta family and the little bit of hope that sustains them. Lawrence (Smith, Sr.) shot himself after his twin brother Darius OD'd. He's slowly recovering at home where he's confronted by Darius' reckless 12-year-old son James (Ross), who believes he and his ex-druggie mother Marlee (Riggs) are owed money from the small business the brothers ran. They need the cash since Marlee has just lost her job but there's a lot of bitterness on both sides to overcome. **96m/C; Blu-Ray, On Demand.** Tarra Riggs; JimMyron Ross; Michael J. Smith, Sr.; Johnny McPhail; ***D:*** Lance Hammer; ***W:*** Lance Hammer; ***C:*** Lol Crawley.

Ballet Shoes 1/2 **2007** Orphans Pauline (Watson), Petrova (Paige), and Posy (Boynton) are adopted by eccentric paleontologist Great Uncle Matthew (Griffiths), who leaves their raising to his niece Sylvia (Fox) while he's off exploring. Each girl has an ambition: Pauline wants to act, Posy wants to be a ballet dancer, and Petrova wants to be an aviatrix. Times are tough in 1930s London and Sylvia is forced to take boarders. Luckily dance teacher Theo (Cohu) is able to help out with the girls' desire to raise some money. Sweet adaptation of the novel by Noel Streatfeild. **84m/C; DVD.** *GB* Emma Watson; Yasmin Paige; Emilia Fox; Richard Griffiths; Victoria Wood; Lucy Cohu; Marc Warren; Eileen Atkins; Gemma Jones; Harriet Walter; Lucy Boynton; ***D:*** Sandra Goldbacher; ***W:*** Heidi Thomas; ***C:*** Peter Greenhalgh; ***M:*** Kevin Sargent. **TV**

Ballets Russes **2005** This feature-length documentary offers a broad examination of the history and influence of Ballet Russes. In its initial incarnation, the troupe, based in western Europe, featured only Russian exiles who fled their country during the Russian Revolution in the early twentieth century. The company is widely credited with setting the tone for modern ballet. The insightful documentary includes information on the Ballet Russes stars, their productions, and behind-the-scenes conflicts. **118m/C; DVD, Streaming, Download.** Marian Seldes; ***D:*** Dan Geller; Daniel Geller; Dayna Goldfine; ***W:*** Dan Geller; Daniel Geller; Dayna Goldfine; Celeste Schaefer Snyder; Gary Weimberg; ***C:*** Dan Geller; ***M:*** Todd Boekelheide; David Conte.

Ballistic: Ecks vs. Sever 1/2 *Ecks vs. Sever* **2002 (R)** Awkwardly titled actioner stars Banderes as Ecks, a disillusioned former FBI manhunter mourning his dead wife. Liu is code-name Sever, a former government-trained assassin. Ecks has been rehired to track Sever for kidnapping the son of her former boss Gant (Henry), chief of the Defense Intelligence Agency. Both agents are also on the lookout for a supposedly dangerous and supremely ridiculous techno virus. Once the operatives find they have a lot in common, including a common enemy, they join forces to gun down and blow up everything in sight. Superb, if overdone stunts take top billing, while dim lighting matches equally dim plot. Neophyte director Kaos (short for Kaosayananda) cops all the moves of "The Matrix." Based on the far more entertaining video game. **95m/C; VHS, DVD.** Antonio Banderas; Lucy Liu; Gregg Henry; Ray Park; Talisa Soto; Miguel (Michael) Sandoval; Terry Chen; Sandrine Holt; Roger R. Cross; Steve Bacic; Aidan Drummond; ***D:*** Kaos; ***W:*** Alan B. McElroy; ***C:*** Julio Macat; ***M:*** Don Davis.

Ballistica **2010** Stoic, action-oriented lead; eye candy in ridiculous role; solid, familiar faces as good guy backup and terrorists; fast pace (dumb plot). What more do you need for mindless entertainment? CIA field operative Sloan teams up with scientist Amanda who unwittingly developed a bomb for Russian terrorist Dragomir, who plans to set it off in L.A. **90m/C; DVD.** Paul Logan; Martin Kove; Robert Davi; Andrew Divoff; C.B. Spencer; ***D:*** Gary Jones; ***W:*** Sean Rourke; ***C:*** Mark Morris; ***M:*** Shie Rozow. **VIDEO**

Balloon Farm 1/2 **1997** Harvey Potter (Torn), using some magic, raises a crop of balloons on cornstalks. His drought-stricken fellow farmers see the miraculous crop as symbols of hope but grumpy farmer Wheezle (Blossom) is suspicious. And his suspcions begin to infect the rest of the community, except for spunky young Willow (Wilson). Based on Jerdine Nolen's children's book "Harvey Potter's Balloon Farm." **89m/C; VHS, DVD.** Rip Torn; Mara Wilson; Roberts Blossom; Laurie Metcalf; Neal McDonough; Frederic Lehne; Adam Wylie; ***D:*** William Dear; ***W:*** Steven M. Karczynski. **TV**

Balls of Fury 1/2 **2007 (PG-13)** Former child prodigy ping-pong star Randy Daytona (Fogler) finds himself fat and washed up at the ripe old age of 32. He's approached by the feds (Lopez as FBI agent) to take on a dangerous mission—infiltrate an underground ping-pong tournament run by shifty Chinese crime boss Feng (Walken), who also happens to be responsible for Randy's fathers' (Patrick) death. But Randy finds his mission has a dual purpose: avenge his father's murder, and attempt a high-stakes comeback. Of course every would-be hero needs a little help, and Randy's crackpot team includes blind restaurateur and ping-pong sage Master Wong (Hong) and his totally hot niece Maggie (Maggie Q). Some funny moments intertwine with a backdrop of Def Leppard in this ode to '80s nostalgia and martial arts, but it never fully takes off. **90m/C; DVD, HD-DVD.** Dan Fogler; Christopher Walken; George Lopez; James Hong; Terry Crews; Robert Patrick; Diedrich Bader; Aisha Tyler; Maggie Q; Thomas Lennon; Patton Oswalt; David Koechner; Jason Scott Lee; Masi Oka; David Proval; Jenny Robertson; Toby Huss; ***D:*** Robert Ben Garant; ***W:*** Thomas Lennon; Robert Ben Garant; ***C:*** Thomas Ackerman; ***M:*** Randy Edelman.

Balls Out: Gary the Tennis Coach 1/2 **2009 (R)** Raunchy, dumb sports comedy about a loser with dreams of greatness. High school janitor Gary Houseman (Scott) decides to coach the long-neglected, losing tennis team. Soon, despite his crude behavior, his unorthodox methods actually get the team to the state championships. **93m/C; DVD, Blu-Ray.** Seann William Scott; Randy Quaid; Leonor Varela; Deke Anderson; Justin Chon; Brent Anderson; ***D:*** Danny Leiner; ***W:*** Andy Stock; Rick Stempson; ***C:*** Rogier Stoffers; ***M:*** John Swihart. **VIDEO**

Baltic Deputy 1/2 **1937** An early forerunner of Soviet historic realism, where an aging intellectual deals with post-revolution Soviet life. In Russian with subtitles. **95m/B; VHS, DVD.** *RU* Nikolai Cherkassov; Boris Livanov; Marta Domasheva; Oleg Zhakov; ***D:*** Yosif Heifitz; Iosif Kheifits; Alexander Zarkhi; ***W:*** Iosif Kheifits; Alexander Zarkhi; ***C:*** Edgar Shtyrtskober; ***M:*** Nikolai Timofeyev.

Balto 1/2 **1995 (G)** Animated adventure, based on a true story, of a half-husky, half-wolf sled dog, Balto, who faces overwhelming odds to bring life-saving medicine to Nome, Alsaka. It's 1925, there's a diptheria epidemic, and Balto is the lead team dog on the final leg of the race to get the serum to Nome in time. Balto and the rest of the team dogs became instant heroes and even journeyed to Hollywood to star in their own silent film "Balto's Race to Nome." **78m/C; VHS, DVD, Blu-Ray.** ***V:*** Kevin Bacon; Bob Hoskins; Bridget Fonda; Jim (Jonah) Cummings; Phil Collins; Juliette Brewer; Danny Mann; Miriam Margolyes; ***D:*** Simon Wells; ***W:*** Cliff Ruby; Elana Lesser; David Steven Cohen; Roger S.H. Schulman; ***M:*** James Horner.

Balzac: A Life of Passion **1999** Bio of French writer Honore de Balzac (1799-1850)?a larger-then-life figure played by the larger-than-life Depardieu. He has mom problems (she never loved him) and turns to women who encourage him as his writing consumes him. There are balls and duels and all sorts of high and low society life during the Napoleonic era to enjoy. French with subtitles. **210m/C; VHS, DVD.** *FR* Gerard Depardieu; Jeanne Moreau; Fanny Ardant; Virna Lisi; Katja Riemann; Claude Rich; ***D:*** Josee Dayan; ***W:*** Didier Decoin; ***C:*** Willy Stassen; ***M:*** Bruno Coulais. **TV**

Balzac and the Little Chinese Seamstress *Balzac et la petite tailleuse Chinois; Xiao cai feng* **2002** Sijie dreamily adapts his own autobiographical novel depicting life in a remote Chinese mountain village in 1971. City boys Luo (Chen) and Ma (Liu) are sent to be re-educated under Mao's Cultural Revolution. The young men perform manual labor under the watchful eyes of the village chief (Wang) and both become attracted to the nameless young woman (Zhou) of the title, reading to her from a secreted cache of Western books (including Balzac, Flaubert, and Dumas) and teaching her to read and write. There is eventual separation and loss and an abrupt epilogue that shows the men 20 years later wondering whatever happened to the girl they once knew. Mandarin and French with subtitles. **111m/C; DVD.** *CH FR* Liu Ye; Hongwei Wang; Ziiou Xun; Chen Kun; Wang Shuangbao; Chung Zhijun; ***D:*** Dai Sijie; ***W:*** Dai Sijie; Nadine Perront; ***C:*** Jean-Marie Dreujou; ***M:*** Wang Pujian.

Bam Bam & Celeste **2005** Margaret Cho's screenplay features herself as Celeste, a social outcast on a quest to win a makeover on "Trading Faces," a popular show filmed in New York. On the road trip from Illinois to the Big Apple with her gay hairdresser, boyfriend/buddy Bam Bam (Daniels), the pair encounter offbeat characters and situations and a showdown with their high school rivals, while discovering beauty is more than skin deep. Cheeky, loose, cry-while-you're-laughing entertainment. **85m/C; DVD.** Margaret Cho; Bruce Daniels; Alan Cumming; Elaine Hendrix; Jane Lynch; John Cho; Wilson Cruz; Kathy Najimy; Butch Klein; ***D:*** Lorene Machado; ***W:*** Margaret Cho; ***C:*** Matthew Clark; ***M:*** Pat Irwin.

Bambi **1942 (G)** A true Disney classic, detailing the often harsh education of a newborn deer and his friends in the forest. Proves that Disney animation was—and still is—the best to be found. Thumper still steals the show and the music is delightful, including "Let's Sing a Gay Little Spring Song," "Love is a Song," "Little April Shower," "The Thumper Song," and "Twitterpated." Stands as one of the greatest children's films of all time; a genuine perennial from generation to generation. Based very loosely on the book by Felix Salten. **69m/C; VHS, DVD, Blu-Ray.** ***V:*** Bobby Stewart; Peter Behn; Stan Alexander; Cammie King; Donnie Dunagan; Hardie Albright; John Sutherland; Tim Davis; Sam Edwards; Sterling Holloway; Ann Gillis; Perce Pearce; ***D:*** David Hand; ***W:*** Larry Morey; ***M:*** Frank Churchill; Edward Plumb. Natl. Film Reg. '11.

Bambi II 1/2 **2006 (G)** The sequel might not be up to the standards of the original but it will keep the tykes occupied. Bambi's dad, the Great Prince, takes over the raising of his fawn when mom gets killed but he's having a tough time. Still, Bambi tries his best to learn despite clumsiness and teasing with some help from his pals Thumper and Flower. **72m/C; DVD, Blu-Ray.** ***V:*** Patrick Stewart; Alexander Gould; Brendon Baerg; Nicky Jones; ***D:*** Brian Pimental; ***W:*** Alicia Kirk; ***M:*** Bruce Broughton. **VIDEO**

Bambole 1/2 *The Dolls* **1965** Silly Italian sex farce with four sixties beauties in four separate, not very interesting stories from four different directors. Italian with subtitles. **109m/B; DVD.** *IT* Virna Lisi; Monica Vitti; Elke Sommer; Gina Lollobrigida; Nino Manfredi; Jean Sorel; Akim Tamiroff; ***D:*** Mauro Bolognini; Luigi Comencini; Dino Risi; Franco Rossi; ***W:*** Rodolfo Sonego; ***C:*** Leonida Barboni; Ennio Guarnieri; ***M:*** Armando Trovajoli.

The Bamboo Blonde 1/2 **1946** Wartime romance in which nightclub singer Louise (Langford) meets cute with B-29 pilot Patrick (Wade). She gives him her photograph and when he heads to Saipan, his bomber crew decides to paint Louise's picture on the nose of their plane for good luck. When the crew starts sinking Japanese ships and shooting down Zeros, the "Bamboo Blonde" becomes famous and Eddie (Edwards), the huckster club owner who employs Louise, gets rich by exploiting that fact. Told in flashbacks. **67m/B; DVD.** Frances Langford; Ralph Edwards; Russell Wade; Iris Adrian; Jane Greer; Richard Martin; Paul Harvey; ***D:*** Anthony Mann.

The Bamboo Saucer 1/2 *Collision Course* **1968** Russian and American scientists race to find a U.F.O. in Red China. **103m/C; DVD, Blu-Ray.** Dan Duryea; John Ericson; Lois Nettleton; Nan Leslie; ***D:*** Frank Telford; ***W:*** Frank Telford; John P. Fulton; ***C:*** Hal Mohr; ***M:*** Nicholas Carras; Edward Paul.

Bamboozled 1/2 **2000 (R)** Spike Lee aims for controversy once again as he criticizes Hollywood's portrayal of African-Americans as well as pointing the finger at the black community's complicity in the process. Fed-up black writer Pierre Delacroix (Wayans) comes up with a series idea for a fledgling TV network as a form of protest—a modern day minstrel show complete with performers in burnt cork blackface. Fully expecting the show to fail, he hires struggling street performers Manray (Glover) and Womack (Davidson), changing their names to Mantan and Sleep 'N Eat (a reference to '30s and '40s black actors Mantan Moreland and

Stepin Fetchit). The show becomes a surprise hit but also riles a militant black group, resulting in chaos in the lives of Delacroix and his assistant Sloan (Pinkett). The feel of the movie sways toward melodrama halfway through, but the wry observations of the artistic treatment of AfricanAmericans ring eerily true. Don't say it couldn't happen these days. **135m/C; VHS, DVD, Blu-Ray.** Damon Wayans; Jada Pinkett Smith; Savion Glover; Tommy Davidson; Michael Rapaport; Thomas Jefferson Byrd; Paul Mooney; Susan Batson; Mos Def; Sarah Jones; Gillian Iliana Waters; ***D:*** Spike Lee; ***W:*** Spike Lee; ***C:*** Ellen Kuras; ***M:*** Terence Blanchard.

Bananas 🦴🦴🦴 **1971 (PG-13)** Intermittently hilarious pre-"Annie Hall" Allen fare is full of the director's signature angst-ridden philosophical comedy. A frustrated product tester from New York runs off to South America, where he volunteers his support to the revolutionary force of a shaky Latin-American dictatorship and winds up the leader. Don't miss an early appearance by Stallone. Witty score contributes much. **82m/C; VHS, DVD, Blu-Ray.** Woody Allen; Louise Lasser; Carlos Montalban; Howard Cosell; Charlotte Rae; Conrad Bain; Allen Garfield; Sylvester Stallone; ***D:*** Woody Allen; ***W:*** Woody Allen; Mickey Rose; ***C:*** Andrew M. Costikyan; ***M:*** Marvin Hamlisch.

Band Aid 🦴🦴 **1/2 2017 (R)** With their marriage on the rocks, Anna (Lister-Jones) and Ben (Pally) turn their fights into songs, rocking out their issues as a garage band with their neighbor (Armisen). The dialog is sarcastic, prickly, funny, and ultimately real, and the chemistry between Lister-Jones and Pally carries the film through a flailing and somewhat melodramatic final quarter. A feature debut by writer/director Lister-Jones, who employed a nearly all-female production crew, that strikes the right chords. **91m/C; DVD.** Zoe Lister-Jones; Adam Pally; Fred Armisen; Susie Essman; Hannah Simone; ***D:*** Zoe Lister-Jones; ***W:*** Zoe Lister-Jones; ***C:*** Hillary Spera; ***M:*** Lucius.

A Band Called Death 🦴🦴🦴 **2013** In much the same vein as the Oscar-winning "Searching for Sugar Man," this punk roc doc offers hope that creativity and staying true to one's personal vision will someday lead to success. In the early '70s, before The Ramones and The Sex Pistols, three brothers from Detroit were revolutionizing rock in a punk style. With the name Death, fame eluded them (and their leader refused to change it) until their demos were found decades later and a new generation gave them the artistic credit they always deserved. Fun, poignant, and inspirational, pic captures the timeless power of passionate creativity. **96m/C; DVD, Blu-Ray.** ***D:*** Mark Christopher Covino; Jeff Howlett; ***C:*** Mark Christopher Covino; ***M:*** Tim Boland; Sam Retzer.

Band of Angels 🦴🦴 **1/2 1957** Orphaned Amantha (De Carlo) learns she has African-American blood and since it's the pre-Civil War era she promptly winds up on the auction block. She becomes both the property and the mistress of mysterious New Orleans landowner Hamish Bond (Gable). Then the Civil War comes along bringing threats and revelations. De Carlo looks properly sultry but this is a weak attempt at costume drama. Based on the novel by Robert Penn Warren. **127m/C; VHS, DVD.** Clark Gable; Yvonne De Carlo; Sidney Poitier; Efrem Zimbalist, Jr.; Rex Reason; Patric Knowles; Torin Thatcher; Andrea King; Ray Teal; ***D:*** Raoul Walsh; ***W:*** John Twist; Ivan Goff; ***M:*** Max Steiner.

Band of Brothers 🦴🦴🦴 **1/2 2001** Steven Spielberg and Tom Hanks executive produced this excellent adaptation of Stephen Ambrose's epic tale of the 101 Airborne's Easy Company as they made their way from D-Day through the capture of Hitler's "Eagle's Nest" compound. Although uniformly showing the influence of "Saving Private Ryan," each episode focuses on a separate sub-theme or character while not losing sight of the big-picture depth. Some characters are given short shrift, and sometimes it's hard to tell which characters lived or died during a battle, but that's a minor quibble with such a large and, in most cases, unknown, cast. Although they're young and mostly anonymous, they do give excellent, and in some cases, breakout performances. The battle scenes are bracing, harrowing, and well-constructed, and the quiet moments serve to underscore the bond that develops between the men as they become battle tested. **600m/C; VHS, DVD, Blu-Ray.** Eion Bailey; Jamie Bamber; Michael Cudlitz; Dale Dye; Scott Grimes; Frank John Hughes; Ron Livingston; James Madio; Neal McDonough; Rene L. Moreno; David Schwimmer; Donnie Wahlberg; Colin Hanks; Marc Warren; Damian Lewis; Kirk Acevedo; Rick Gomez; Richard Speight, Jr.; Jimmy Fallon; Ian Virgo; Tom (Thomas) Hardy; ***D:*** David Frankel; Tom Hanks; Richard Loncraine; Phil Alden Robinson; Mikael Salomon; David Nutter; David Leland; Tony To; ***W:*** Tom Hanks; E. Max Frye; Erik Jendresen; Bruce McKenna; Graham Yost; Stephen E. Ambrose; Erik Bork; John Orloff; ***C:*** Remi Adefarasin; ***M:*** Michael Kamen. **CABLE**

Band of Gold 🦴🦴🦴 **1995** Unflinching British miniseries follows the lives of Yorkshire prostitutes Rosie (James), Carol (Tyson), and Gina (Gemmell). They try to survive the streets of Bradford while a serial killer is targeting the local hookers. On six cassettes. **312m/C; VHS, DVD.** *GB* Geraldine James; Cathy Tyson; Ruth Gemmell; Barbara Dickson; David Schofield; Richard Moore; Rachel Davies; Samantha Morton; ***D:*** Richard Standeven; Richard Laxton; ***W:*** Kay Mellor; ***C:*** Peter Jessop; ***M:*** Hal Lindes.

Band of Outsiders 🦴🦴 **1/2** *Bande a Part; The Outsiders* **1964** A woman hires a pair of petty criminals to rip off her aunt; Godard vehicle for expousing self-reflexive comments on modern film culture. In French with English subtitles. **97m/B; VHS, DVD, Blu-Ray.** *FR* Sami Frey; Anna Karina; Claude Brasseur; Louisa Colpeyn; ***D:*** Jean-Luc Godard; ***W:*** Jean-Luc Godard; ***C:*** Raoul Coutard; ***M:*** Michel Legrand.

Band of the Hand 🦴 **1986 (R)** A "Miami Vice" type melodrama about five convicts who are trained to become an unstoppable police unit. The first feature film by Glaser, last seen as Starsky in "Starsky & Hutch." **109m/C; VHS, DVD, Blu-Ray.** Stephen Lang; Michael Carmine; Lauren Holly; Leon Robinson; ***D:*** Paul Michael Glaser; ***W:*** Jack Baran; Leo Garen.

The Band Wagon 🦴🦴🦴 **1953** A Hollywood song-and-dance man finds trouble when he is persuaded to star in a Broadway musical. Charisse has been called Astaire's most perfect partner, perhaps by those who haven't seen Rogers. **112m/C; VHS, DVD, Blu-Ray.** Fred Astaire; Cyd Charisse; Oscar Levant; Nanette Fabray; Jack Buchanan; Bobby Watson; ***D:*** Vincente Minnelli; ***W:*** Betty Comden; ***M:*** Arthur Schwartz; Howard Dietz. Natl. Film Reg. '95.

Bandidas 🦴🦴 **1/2 2006 (PG-13)** A New York bank wants to build a railroad line to Mexico, and decide the best way will be to buy up small banks in Mexico and evict anyone that owes the banks money. Opposing them is the daughter of one of the owners of the small banks, and a peasant woman who decide to become modern day Robin Hoods. Getting in their way of course is the fact that they've never robbed banks before. Considering that the guy sent from New York to take out the banks killed their father, they have some inspiration. **92m/C; DVD.** *MX FR* Penelope Cruz; Salma Hayek; Steve Zahn; Dwight Yoakam; Denis Arndt; Audra Blaser; Sam Shepard; Ismael Carlo; Gary Cervantes; Jose Maria Negri; Lenny Zundel; ***D:*** Joachim Ronning; Espen Sandberg; ***W:*** Luc Besson; Robert Mark Kamen; ***C:*** Thierry Arbogast; ***M:*** Eric Serra.

The Bandit of Sherwood Forest 🦴🦴 **1/2 1946** Technicolor swashbuckler with Wilde properly athletic and dashing as the true lead in this Robin Hood story. An aged Robin Hood (Hicks), now the respectable Robert of Huntington, and his namesake son Robert (Wilde) join again with the merry men to prevent usurper William of Pembroke (Daniell) from seizing the throne of England after he imprisons the young king and revokes the Magna Carta. **86m/C; DVD.** Cornel Wilde; Henry Daniell; Anita Louise; Russell Hicks; Jill Esmond; Edgar Buchanan; George Macready; John Abbott; Lloyd Corrigan; Ray Teal; Leslie Denison; ***D:*** George Sherman; Henry Levin; ***W:*** Melvin Levy; Wilfred Pettitt; ***C:*** Gaetano Antonio "Tony" Gaudio; George Meehan; William E. Snyder; ***M:*** Hugo Friedhofer.

Bandit Queen 🦴🦴 **1994** Phoolan Devi (Biswas) is a female Robin Hood in modern-day India. A lower-caste woman, Devi is sold into marriage at 11, brutalized by her husband (and many others throughout the film), and eventually winds up with an equally brutal group of hill bandits. Only this time around, Devi takes action by aiding the group in robbing, kidnapping (and murdering) the rich and higher castes. Devi surrendered to authorities in 1983 and spent 11 years in jail. Based on screenwriter Sen's biography "India's Bandit Queen: The True Story of Phoolan Devi" and Devi's diaries. In Hindi with subtitles. **119m/C; VHS, DVD, Blu-Ray.** *GB IN* Seema Biswas; Nirmal Pandey; Manoj Bajpai; Raghuvir Yadav; Rajesh Vivek; Govind Namdeo; ***D:*** Shekhar Kapur; ***W:*** Mala Sen; ***C:*** Ashok Mehta; ***M:*** Nusrat Fateh Ali Khan; Roger White.

Bandits 🦴🦴 **1999 (R)** Talk about your band on the run! Four young women form a prison rock-and-roll band called the Bandits. Their first gig on the outside is the policeman's ball, where they escape. They become folk heroes as they elude the police and a clandestine recording they sent to a music exec zooms up the charts. German with subtitles. **109m/C; VHS, DVD.** *GE* Katja Riemann; Jutta Hoffmann; Jasmin Tabatabai; Nicolette Krebitz; Hannes Jaenicke; Werner Schreyer; ***D:*** Katja von Garnier; ***W:*** Katja von Garnier; Uwe Wilhelm; ***C:*** Torsten Breuer.

Bandits 🦴🦴 **1/2 2001 (PG-13)** Willis and Thornton are Joe and Terry, quirky bank robbers known as the "sleepover bandits" for their unusual but non-violent heists. With Willis as the smirky brawn and Thornton as the neurotic brain, the two play the Butch-and-Sundance act until fate puts bored housewife Kate (Blanchett) in their path. She talks her way into their little gang, but can't decide which of the two she should fall for most. The plot then slams on the brakes, although Levinson adds enough padding to cushion the blow. Blanchett is excellent as the sultry, vulnerable Kate, but Thornton steals the show (and chomps on considerable scenery) as the omniphobic hypochondriac Terry (his fear of antique furniture is actually one of Thornton's well-documented quirks as well). **123m/C; VHS, DVD, Blu-Ray.** Bruce Willis; Billy Bob Thornton; Cate Blanchett; Troy Garity; Bobby Slayton; Brian F. O'Byrne; Azura Skye; Stacey Travis; William Converse-Roberts; Richard Riehle; Micole Mercurio; January Jones; ***D:*** Barry Levinson; ***W:*** Harley Peyton; ***C:*** Dante Spinotti; ***M:*** Christopher Young. Natl. Bd. of Review '01: Actor (Thornton).

The Bandits of Corsica 🦴 **1/2** *The Return of the Corsican Brothers* **1953** Swashbuckler has Greene playing identical twins who, though separated at birth, maintain a psychic connection. Mario Franchi wants to overthrow ruling despot Jonatto and bring freedom to the people of Corsica. He's hoping his gypsy brother Carlos will help him, but there's a complication when Carlos falls in love with Mario's wife Christina. Burr and Van Cleef make good in their bad guy roles. **82m/B; DVD.** Richard Greene; Raymond Burr; Lee Van Cleef; Paula Raymond; Dona Drake; Raymond Greenleaf; Frank Puglia; ***D:*** Ray Nazarro; ***W:*** Richard Schayer; ***C:*** George E. Diskant; ***M:*** Irving Gertz.

Bandolero! 🦴🦴 **1/2 1968 (PG)** In Texas, Stewart and Martin are two fugitive brothers who foil a hanging, escape to Mexico, and run into trouble with their Mexican counterparts. Enjoyable all-star Western boasts beautiful cinematography and solid performances all around. **106m/C; VHS, DVD, Blu-Ray.** James Stewart; Raquel Welch; Dean Martin; George Kennedy; Will Geer; Harry Carey, Jr.; Andrew Prine; Denver Pyle; ***D:*** Andrew V. McLaglen; ***C:*** William Clothier; ***M:*** Jerry Goldsmith.

The Band's Visit 🦴🦴🦴 *Bikur Ha-Tizmoret* **2007 (PG-13)** Eight members of an Egyptian police orchestra are accidentally stranded in the Israeli desert, far away from their intended destination. They end up in an Israeli town where they are anything but welcome. Through the culture clash, connections are made, and an unlikely attraction develops between band members and the beautiful restaurant owner who gives them a place to stay. Director Kolirin draws comedy out of the isolated, sad characters and their awkward situation without exploiting them. **89m/C; Blu-Ray, On Demand.** *FR IS US* Sasson Gabai; Ronit Elkabetz; Saleh Bakri; Shlomi Avraham; Khalifa Natour; Rubi Muscovich; ***D:*** Eran Kolirin; ***W:*** Eran Kolirin; ***C:*** Shai Goldman; ***M:*** Habib Shehadeh Hanna.

Bandslam 🦴🦴 **1/2 2009 (PG)** Awkward but pleasant teen musical. Geek introvert Will (Connell) is the new kid at New Jersey's Van Buren High School. He bonds over shared musical tastes with sullen Sam (Hudgens) and cheerleader-turned-singer Charlotte (Michalka) who want Will to manage her garage band. After a few changes and a lot of practice, Will figures they have a shot at the tri-state battle-of-the-bands competition. Music isn't terribly memorable but everyone is just so darn cute. **111m/C; On Demand.** Alyson Michalka; Scott Porter; Vanessa Anne Hudgens; Lisa Kudrow; Ryan Donowho; Gaelen Connell; Charlie Saxton; ***Cameo(s):*** David Bowie; ***D:*** Todd Graff; ***W:*** Todd Graff; Josh A. Cagan; ***C:*** Eric Steelberg; ***M:*** Junkie XL.

Bandwagon 🦴🦴 **1995** Four unlikely twentysomething guys decide to form a band in Raleigh, NC. Tony Ridge (Holmes) is the lead singer-songwriter who's so shy he practices in a closet; chatty drummer Charlie Flagg (Hennessey) has the rehearsal space; Wynn Knapp (Corrigan) is the band's perpetually stoned guitarist; and bass player Eric Ellwood's (Parlavecchio) hot temper has him in big trouble with a local loan shark. They finally come up with a name (Circus Monkey), get a gig (a raucous frat party), and are on their way when they acquire Zen-like road manager Linus Tate (MacMillan) and a battered van. Of course, life on the road proves to be a challenge. **99m/C; VHS, Streaming.** Kevin Corrigan; Steve Parlavecchio; Lee Holmes; Matthew Hennessey; Doug MacMillan; Lisa Keller; ***D:*** John Schultz; ***W:*** John Schultz; ***C:*** Shawn Maurer; ***M:*** Greg Kendall.

Bang 🦴🦴 *The Big Bang Theory* **1995** This $20,000 indie concerns a nameless, powerless Asian-American would-be actress (Narita) in L.A. She gets kicked out of her apartment, accosted by a homeless crazy (Greene), and sexually propositioned by a sleazy producer (Graff). Finally, she's accused of causing a public disturbance by a cop (Newland), who'll let her off in exchange for sexual favors. Instead, she grabs his gun, forces him to strip, ties him to a tree, puts on the cop's uniform, and steals his motorcycle. In uniform, she's suddenly viewed with authority and decides to take some time to see what that's like. **98m/C; VHS, DVD.** Darling Narita; Peter Greene; Michael Newland; David Alan Graf; Eric Schrody; Michael Arturo; James Sharpe; Luis Guizar; Art Cruz; Stanley Herman; ***D:*** Ash; ***W:*** Ash; ***C:*** Dave Gasperik.

The Bang Bang Club 🦴 **1/2 2010** Superficial true story of four photojournalists covering the last days of apartheid in South Africa before the country's first free elections in 1994. Unfortunately the story becomes repetitive as the four men compete for some dangerous assignment/shot, spend their downtime drinking and fooling around with some very willing women, and then go out and shoot some more pictures. **106m/C; DVD, Blu-Ray.** *CA SA* Ryan Phillippe; Taylor Kitsch; Frank Rautenbach; Neels Van Jaarsveld; Malin Akerman; ***D:*** Steven Silver; ***W:*** Steven Silver; ***C:*** Miroslaw Baszak; ***M:*** Philippe Miller.

Bang Bang Kid 🦴🦴 *Bang Bang* **1967 (G)** A western spoof about a klutzy gunfighter defending a town from outlaws. **78m/C; VHS, DVD.** Tom Bosley; Guy Madison; Sandra Milo; ***D:*** Stanley Prager.

Bang! Bang! You're Dead! 🦴 **1/2** *Our Man in Marrakesh* **1966** Generally silly, occasionally dull, spy comedy. American tourist Andrew Jessel (Randall) gets caught up with spies in Marrakesh when he's given the wrong hotel room and finds it already occupied by a dead body. It's a set-up for CIA agent Kyra Stanovy (Berger), involving crime boss Mr. Casimir (Lom) and some secret documents. It leads to Andrew and Kyra going on the lam, sought by Casimir's henchmen, including Jonquil (Kinski). **92m/C; DVD, Blu-Ray.** *UK* Tony Randall; Senta Berger; Herbert Lom; Klaus Kinski; Wilfrid Hyde-White; Terry-Thomas; John Le Mesurier; ***D:*** Don Sharp; ***W:*** Peter Yeldham; ***C:*** Michael Reed; ***M:*** Malcolm Lockyer.

Bang Rajan ½ **2000** Kind of a Thai version of the Alamo. The small village of Bang Rajan, circa 1765, finds itself geographically in the path of a very angry Burmese army on their way to the warring city of Ayudhay. With no outside help, the community must band together in hopes of protecting their land. One of the country's most legendary battles, told with Hollywood-like epic production helped the film become Thailand's biggest box office hit ever. One-upping "Braveheart," the film arguably contains the most violent images of warfare to date. Fan Oliver Stone helped secure U.S. release. **119m/C; DVD.** *TH* Winai Kraibutr; Bin Bunluerit; Chumphorn Thepphithak; Jaran Ngamdee; Suntharee Maila-or; ***D:*** Thanit Jitnukul; ***W:*** Thanit Jitnukul; Kongkiat Khomsiri; Bunthin Thuaykaew; Patikarn Phejmunee; Suttipong Muttanavee; ***C:*** Wichian Ruangwijchayakul; ***M:*** Chartachai Phongpraphaphan.

Bang the Drum Slowly **1973 (PG)** The touching story of a major league catcher who discovers that he is dying of Hodgkins disease and wants to play just one more season. De Niro is the weakening baseball player and Moriarty is the friend who helps him see it through. Based on a novel by Mark Harris. **97m/C; VHS, DVD.** Robert De Niro; Michael Moriarty; Vincent Gardenia; Phil Foster; Ann Wedgeworth; Heather MacRae; Selma Diamond; Danny Aiello; ***D:*** John Hancock. N.Y. Film Critics '73: Support. Actor (De Niro).

The Banger Sisters **2002 (R)** Fast forward "Almost Famous" thirty years and you'll find Kate Hudson has turned into her real-life mother, Hawn, who plays Suzette, a middle-aged former '60s/'70s "band-aid" turned, well, not turned at all, still living the wild, free-spirit life. Her partner in rock n' roll groupie-dom, Vinnie (Sarandon), however, has grown up and uptight; now she's suburban mom Lavinia living in the 'burbs. When Suzette loses her job, she drifts back into Vinnie's life and helps her get back to her sleazy, but more honest, roots. Sanitized-for-your-protection version of groupie life rings false throughout. Characters are essentially modeled on groupie legends the Plaster Casters. Material isn't worthy of these A-listers and nostalgia appeal runs thin. Amurri is Sarandon's real-life daughter. **97m/C; VHS, DVD.** Goldie Hawn; Susan Sarandon; Geoffrey Rush; Erika Christensen; Robin Thomas; Eva Amurri; Matthew Carey; ***D:*** Bob Dolman; ***W:*** Bob Dolman; ***C:*** Karl Walter Lindenlaub; ***M:*** Trevor Rabin.

Bangkok Dangerous **2000 (R)** A moderately interesting action film that inspired a horrible Hollywood remake that was somehow done by the same team of directors (you'd think they'd get it better the second time around). A deaf mute assassin who doesn't know sign language (good thing he can read) becomes a one-man army after deciding to leave the business for his girlfriend. **105m/C; DVD, Blu-Ray.** *TH* Pawalit Mongkolpisit; Premsinee Ratanasopha; Patharawarin Timkul; Pisek Intrakanchit; ***D:*** Oxide Pang Chun; Danny Pang; ***W:*** Oxide Pang Chun; Danny Pang; ***C:*** Decha Srimantra; ***M:*** Orange Music.

Bangkok Dangerous ½ **2008 (R)** The Pang Brothers come to Hollywood for the remake of their 1999 Hong Kong cult classic. Hitman Joe (Cage), not deaf like the original hitman, is sent to Thailand to complete four last jobs before he can retire. Struggling with culture shock, he hires street rat Kong (Yamnarm) as an interpreter/assistant. Each kill brings him closer to ending his career, but the progressive difficulties bring him closer to ending his life. Shelved for almost two years after production, with execs hoping Cage's career would pick up enough to guarantee box-office success. Instead, Cage's tendency towards wildly inconsistent performances continues, and he's utterly awful and joyless, not to mention silly-looking in his leather jacket and lousy haircut. Awkward title likely comes from studio heads assuming a semicolon would turn off American audiences. **100m/C; Blu-Ray, On Demand.** Nicolas Cage; Charlie Yeung; Shahkrit Yamnarm; Panward Hemmanee; James With; Dom Hetrakul; Philip Waley; Shaun Delaney; ***D:*** Danny Pang; Oxide Pang; ***W:*** Jason Richman; ***C:*** Decha Srimantra; ***M:*** Brian Tyler.

Banjo Hackett ½ *Banjo Hackett: Roamin' Free* **1976** Banjo (Meredith) and his orphaned nephew (Eisenmann) travel the West in search of a rare Arabian horse that was stolen from the boy's mother before she died. Also in pursuit are a millionaire and a devious bounty hunter who will stop at nothing to capture the missing steed. Although the storyline is as rambling as the West, it's heartfelt all the same. **100m/C; DVD.** Don Meredith; Ike Eisenmann; Carol Connors; Gloria De Haven; Jeff Corey; L.Q. Jones; Jan Murray; Dan O'Herlihy; Jennifer Warren; David Young; Richard Young; Anne Francis; Slim Pickens; ***D:*** Andrew V. McLaglen; ***W:*** Ken Trevey; ***C:*** Al Francis; ***M:*** Morton Stevens.

The Bank ½ **2001** Geeky mathematician/computer whiz Jim Doyle (Wenham) is offered a job by unscrupulous Centrabank CEO Simon O'Reilly (LaPaglia) to set up a computer program that will predict stock market fluctuations and increase the bank's profits. Victims of Centrabank's drive for profits are Wayne (Rodgers) and Diane (McElhinney) Davis, who are suing the bank as a cause of a family tragedy. The two stories come to overlap when O'Reilly pressures Doyle into questionable practices to resolve the various situations. **103m/C; VHS, DVD.** *AU* David Wenham; Anthony LaPaglia; Steve Rodgers; Mandy McElhinney; Mitchell Butel; Sibylla Budd; ***D:*** Robert Connolly; ***W:*** Robert Connolly; ***C:*** Tristan Milani; ***M:*** Alan John.

The Bank Dick *The Bank Detective* **1940** Fields wrote the screenplay (using an alias) and stars in this zany comedy about a man who accidentally trips a bank robber and winds up as a guard. Fields' last major role is a classic, a worthy end to his great career. **73m/B; VHS, DVD.** W.C. Fields; Cora Witherspoon; Una Merkel; Evelyn Del Rio; Jack Norton; Jessie Ralph; Franklin Pangborn; Shemp Howard; Grady Sutton; Russell Hicks; Richard Purcell; Reed Hadley; ***D:*** Edward F. (Eddie) Cline; ***W:*** W.C. Fields; ***C:*** Milton Krasner. Natl. Film Reg. '92.

Bank Holiday ½ *Three On a Weekend* **1938** Contrived weepie with some comic relief provided by the subplots. Nursing Catherine Lawrence is spending an illicit weekend with her boyfriend at a seaside resort but she can't stop thinking about her last case. Ann Howard died in childbirth and Catherine is worried about how new father and widower Stephen is coping. Meanwhile, Doreen and her friend Milly are interested in the local beauty pageant and Cockney Arthur is trying to find some peace away from his rambunctious family. **86m/B; DVD.** *UK* Margaret Lockwood; John Lodge; Hugh Williams; Wally Patch; Kathleen Harrison; Rene Ray; Merle Tottenham; ***D:*** Carol Reed; ***W:*** Rodney Ackland; Roger Burford; ***C:*** Arthur Crabtree.

The Bank Job ½ **2007** When inmate Kenny (Brad Jurjens, who is also the writer and director) gets out of prison he immediately hooks up with an old friend who intends to rob a bank. Things go bad, and to escape Kenny steals a car that incidentally has a dead body hidden in the trunk. God must really hate ex-cons. Watching this film you may think he's not very fond of the fans of action films either. **76m/C; DVD.** Johann Urb; Brad Jurjen; Perry Caravello; Rene Escapite; Alfred Soyyar; Renee Darmiento; Nano Cabello; ***D:*** Brad Jurjen; ***W:*** Brad Jurjen; ***C:*** "Mad" Marty Rockatansky; ***M:*** Brad Jurjen.

The Bank Job **2008 (R)** Terry (Statham) thinks his ex-lover Martine (Burrows) has recruited him to assemble a crew including his number two guy, porn king Kevin (Campbell Moore), for a straightforward cash heist. They end up involved in one of the greatest bank robberies in British history: the 1971 tunneled break in at the Baker Street branch of Lloyd's. The real-life investigation produced no arrests and recovered no loot, thus allowing writers Clement and La Frenais to construct an elaborate albeit fictionalized account that ties the crime to a conspiracy to retrieve sexually-compromising photos of a British royal from the safe deposit box of a black power operative (De Jersey). A near-perfect period heist-caper film that extracts terrific effect from the fashion and technology of the 70's. Particularly humorous are the giant walkie-talkies alleged to have played a role in the crime. **111m/C; DVD, Blu-Ray.** *GB US* Jason Statham; Saffron Burrows; Daniel Mays; David Suchet; Richard Lintern; James Faulkner; ***D:*** Roger Donaldson; ***W:*** Dick Clement; Ian La Frenais; ***C:*** Michael Coulter; ***M:*** J. Peter Robinson.

Bank Shot **1974** Hilarious comedy about a criminal who plans to rob a bank by stealing the entire building. Based on the novel by Donald Westlake, and the sequel to "The Hot Rock." **83m/C; VHS, DVD, Blu-Ray.** George C. Scott; Joanna Cassidy; Sorrell Booke; G(eorge) Wood; Clifton James; Bob Balaban; Bibi Osterwald; ***D:*** Gower Champion; ***W:*** Wendell Mayes; ***C:*** Harry Stradling, Jr.

The Banker ½ **2020 (PG-13)** The true story of Bernard Garrett (Mackie), an ambitious, business-savvy black man hampered only by his race in 1950s Los Angeles. He partners with entrepreneur Joe Morris (Jackson) to build a real estate and banking empire, and the two mold a working-class white man (Hoult) to be the face of the business while they pose as a janitor and a chauffeur. Inevitably, the FBI catches wind of the scheme. An important and interesting story, unfortunately delivered as a safe, rather bland biopic. **120m/C; DVD.** Anthony Mackie; Samuel L. Jackson; Nicholas Hoult; Nia Long; James DuMont; ***D:*** George Nolfi; ***W:*** George Nolfi; Niceole R. Levy; David Lewis Smith; Stan Younger; ***C:*** Charlotte Bruus Christensen; ***M:*** H. Scott Salinas.

The Bannen Way **2010** Slick, fast-paced, edited to feature film version of the web series. Con man Neil Bannen (co-creator Gantt) has a mobster uncle, a cop dad, and enough audacious charm to think he can maneuver out of any trouble he finds himself in. **94m/C; DVD.** Mark Gantt; Robert Forster; Autumn Reeser; Vanessa Marcil; Michael Ironside; Michael Lerner; Brynn Thayer; ***D:*** Jesse Warren; ***W:*** Mark Gantt; Jesse Warren; ***C:*** Roger Chingirian; ***M:*** Joseph Trapanese. **VIDEO**

Banner 4th of July ½ *Star Spangled Banners* **2013** Desiree Banner now owns a record company, but she used to be part of a music trio with her brothers Mitchell and Johnny. Desiree and Mitchell have been estranged for years until their mother's heart attack brings the siblings back to their hometown in time for the 4th of July celebration. Only it may be the community's last because the town faces bankruptcy unless they can make a land payment. From the Hallmark Channel. **85m/C; DVD.** Brooke White; Christian Campbell; Michael Barbuto; Mercedes Ruehl; ***D:*** Don McBrearty; ***W:*** Michael Vickerman; ***C:*** Peter Benison; ***M:*** Steve London. **CABLE**

Banshee ½ **2006 (R)** Kind of a woman-in-peril/action/psycho-thriller. Pro car thief Sage (Manning), nicknamed Banshee, is always in competition with boyfriend Tony (Kelly) for the hottest cars to boost. She steals a 1966 Dodge Charger, knowing it will bring top dollar, but not knowing the ride belongs to serial killer/DJ Larch (Campbell). Larch has this little kink about recording the screams of his victims and then mixing them in with his techno sounds. Larch not only wants his car back but he wants to teach Sage a very unpleasant lesson. **95m/C; DVD.** Taryn Manning; Christian Campbell; Morgan Kelly; Tony Calabretta; Mike Lombardi; ***D:*** Keri Skogland; ***W:*** Kirsten Elms; ***C:*** David Franco; ***M:*** Ned Bouhalassa. **CABLE**

Banshee!!! **2008** Some college kids on spring break meet up with a monster that uses sound to cause them to hallucinate. Odd that the film is called 'Banshee' considering that the monster bears little resemblance to the creature from Irish myth, nor are the victims in Ireland. **86m/C; DVD, Streaming.** Kevin Shea; Troy Walcott; Ashley Bates; Kerry McGann; Iris McQuillan-Grace; ***D:*** Colin Theys; ***W:*** John Doolan; Christian Pindar; Gregory Parker; ***C:*** Matthew Wauhkonen; Andrew Gernhard; ***M:*** Matthew Llewellyn. **VIDEO**

Banzai Runner **1986** A cop whose brother was killed in an exclusive desert-highway race decides to avenge by joining the race himself. **88m/C; VHS, DVD.** Dean Stockwell; John Shepherd; Charles Dierkop; ***D:*** John G. Thomas; ***W:*** Phil Harnage; ***C:*** Howard Wexler; ***M:*** Joel Goldsmith. **VIDEO**

B.A.P.'s ½ **1997 (PG-13)** Ghetto to riches story about Georgia waitresses Nisi (Berry) and Mickey (Desselle) who dream about opening their own business—a combo restaurant and hair salon. An L.A. audition offering $10,000 gets them to the sunny coast and eventually into the Beverly Hills mansion of Mr. Blakemore (Landau), where Nisi's persuaded to pose as the granddaughter of his lost love by Blakemore's money-grubbing nephew, Isaac (Fried). Everybody bonds and butler Manley (Richardson) instructs the women in taste and etiquette. Good cast is wasted and the comedy's lame when not offensive. **91m/C; VHS, DVD.** Halle Berry; Natalie Desselle; Martin Landau; Ian Richardson; Troy Beyer; Luigi Amodeo; Jonathan Fried; A.J. (Anthony) Johnson; ***D:*** Robert Townsend; ***W:*** Troy Beyer; ***C:*** Bill Dill; ***M:*** Stanley Clarke.

Bar-B-Q WOOF! 2000 A pro-ball player turned actor needs a break and heads home to have a Bar-B-Q with his girl and old homies. When word gets out the entire neighborhood shows up for the party. A lot of music and a lot of crude jokes and infantile humor make this poorly made, horribly acted film practically unwatchable. The 102-minute running time includes nearly 15 minutes of credits and what the cast and crew apparently considered humorous outtakes. **102m/C; DVD.** Layzie Bone; John West; Chanda Watts; Lea Griggs; ***D:*** Amanda Moss; John West; ***W:*** John West.

Bar Girls **1995 (R)** Mating rituals, set in L.A. wateringhole "The Girl Bar," finds usually tough cookie Loretta (Wolfe) spotting new face Rachael (D'Agostino) and deciding she likes what she sees. There's various mind games as they chart a rocky course to true love—with jealousy, possessiveness, and past romance all playing their parts. Hoffman adapted from her play and the staginess remains; film debut for director Giovanni. **95m/C; VHS, DVD.** Nancy Allison Wolfe; Liza D'Agostino; Justine Slater; Paula Sorge; Camila Griggs; Pam Raines; ***D:*** Marita Giovanni; ***W:*** Lauran Hoffman; ***C:*** Michael Ferris; ***M:*** Lenny Meyers.

Bar Hopping **2000** Disjointed series of vignettes about the singles scene in L.A. centered around a bar with Arnold as the bartender, narrating the action (or lack thereof). Lame. **88m/C; VHS, DVD.** Tom Arnold; Nicole Sullivan; Scott Baio; John Henson; Sally Kellerman; Kevin Nealon; Kelly Preston; Roy Thinnes; Linda Favila; Anson Downes; ***D:*** Steve Cohen; ***W:*** Linda Favila; Anson Downes; ***C:*** Joe Montgomery; ***M:*** Nick Loren. **CABLE**

Barabbas ½ **1962** Barabbas, a thief and murderer, is freed by Pontius Pilate in place of Jesus. He is haunted by this event for the rest of his life. Excellent acting, little melodrama, lavish production make for fine viewing. Based on the novel by Lagerkvist. **144m/C; VHS, DVD.** Anthony Quinn; Silvana Mangano; Arthur Kennedy; Jack Palance; Ernest Borgnine; Katy Jurado; Vittorio Gassman; ***D:*** Richard Fleischer; ***W:*** Diego Fabbri; Christopher Fry; Ivo Perilli; Nigel Balchin; ***C:*** Aldo Tonti; ***M:*** Mario Nascimbene.

Baraka **1993** Time-lapse photography transforms a fascinating array of scenic panoramas into a thought-provoking experience. No dialogue, but the captivating visuals, shot in 24 countries, are a feast for the eyes. Points of interest include Iguacu Falls in Argentina, Ayers Rock in Australia, the temples of Angkor Wat in Cambodia, and the Grand Canyon. Also tours Auschwitz and the streets of Calcutta, in an effort to warn the viewer of the planet's fragility. Filmed in 70mm. **96m/C; VHS, DVD, Blu-Ray.** ***D:*** Ron Fricke; ***W:*** Ron Fricke; Mark Magidson; Bob Green; ***C:*** Ron Fricke; ***M:*** Michael Stearns.

Barb Wire ½ **1996 (R)** "Don't call me babe!" That'll be difficult when the figure in question is Anderson Lee's big-screen take on Dark Horse comic book heroine Barb Wire. Barb runs the sleazy Hammerhead Bar & Grille in Steel Harbor, the only neutral city in an America torn by a second civil war, and reluctantly agrees to aid hunky resistance leader Axel (Morrison) on a dangerous peace mission. Pambo gives Stallone a fight for the action title—fetching in high heels and black leather—with lots of fire power and a take-no-prisoners attitude. Plot's secondary to pulchritude but, unfortunately, the movie's just not a lotta fun. **98m/C; DVD, Blu-Ray.** Pamela Anderson; Temuera Morrison; Jack Noseworthy; Victoria Rowell; Xander Berkeley; Udo Kier; Steve Railsback; Clint Howard; Tony Bill; ***D:*** David Glenn Hogan; ***W:*** Chuck Pfarrer; Ilene Chaiken; ***C:*** Rick Bota; ***M:*** Michel Colombier. Golden Raspberries '96: Worst New Star (Anderson).

Barbara Frietchie ✓✓ 1/2 **1924** Southern belle Barbara (Vidor) and Yankee captain William Trumbell (Lowe) are introduced by her brother Arthur (Delaney) and begin a romance. The war starts and his troops occupy the hometown of the Frietchies—Trumbell is wounded and Barbara thinks he's dying so she decides to defy the Confederacy to publicly declare her love. Adapted from Clyde Fitch's 1899 play. **103m/B; Silent; DVD.** Florence Vidor; Edmund Lowe; Joseph Bennett; Charles Delaney; Mattie Peters; Emmett King; Louis Fitzroy; Gertrude Short; George A. Billings; ***D:*** Lambert Hillyer; ***W:*** Lambert Hillyer; Agnes Christine Johnson; ***C:*** Henry Sharp.

Barbarella ✓✓ 1/2 *Barbarella, Queen of the Galaxy* **1968 (PG)** Based on the popular French sci-fi comic strip drawn by Jean-Claude Forest, this cult classic details the bizarre adventures of a space nymphette (Fonda) encountering fantastic creatures and super beings. You'll see sides of Fonda you never saw before (not even in the workout videos). Notorious in its day; rather silly, dated camp now. Don't miss the elbow-sex scene. Terry Southern contributed to the script. **98m/C; VHS, DVD, Blu-Ray.** *FR IT* Jane Fonda; John Phillip Law; David Hemmings; Marcel Marceau; Anita Pallenberg; Milo O'Shea; Ugo Tognazzi; Veronique Vendell; Giancarlo Cobelli; Serge Marquand; ***D:*** Roger Vadim; ***W:*** Roger Vadim; Terry Southern; Vittorio Bonicelli; Claude Brule; Tudor Gates; Clement Biddle Wood; Brian Degas; Jean-Claude Forest; ***C:*** Claude Renoir; ***M:*** Charles Fox.

The Barbarian ✓✓ **1933** Diana (Loy) travels to Cairo with her Uncle Cecil (Smith) and sharp-tongued companion Powers (Hale) to meet stuffy fiance Gerald (Denny). Arab guide Jamil (Navarro) is immediately attracted to the beauty, eventually kidnapping her and taking Diana on a desert trek to further his romantic plans after revealing to her that he's actually a prince. Pre-Code MGM production has a risque bathing scene by Loy and a questionable seduction scene common to the milieu. Based on Edgar Selwyn's racy play "The Arab." **84m/B; DVD.** Myrna Loy; Reginald Denny; Louise Closser Hale; Sir C. Aubrey Smith; Edward Arnold; Ramon Novarro; ***D:*** Sam Wood; ***W:*** Anita Loos; Elmer Harris; ***C:*** Harold Rosson; ***M:*** Herbert Stothart.

Barbarian and the Geisha ✓✓ **1958** The first US diplomat in Japan undergoes culture shock as well as a passionate love affair with a geisha, circa 1856. **104m/C; VHS, Blu-Ray, Streaming.** John Wayne; Eiko Ando; Sam Jaffe; So Yamamura; ***D:*** John Huston; ***M:*** Hugo Friedhofer.

The Barbarian Invasions ✓✓✓ *Les Invasions Barbares* **2003 (R)** Writer/director Arcand reunites characters from his 1986 film "The Decline of the American Empire" to capture the last days of lecherous, lustful divorced academic Remy (Girard), hospitalized with terminal cancer in his fifties. Through some pleading by his ex-wife (Berryman), estranged son Sebastian (Rousseau) reconnects with his father and deftly orchestrates his twilight days. He upgrades his medical care, persuades ex lovers and colleagues to come and see him off, and sneaks him heroin to ease the physical pain. Takes a few jabs at the Canadian health care system while showing how life and death can be celebrated. Sparkling performances by all, with clever writing that avoids being overly sentimental or maudlin, well deserving of its win in Cannes. **110m/C; VHS, DVD.** *CA FR* Remy Girard; Stephane Rousseau; Marie Josee Croze; Marina Hands; Dorothee Berryman; Johanne-Marie Tremblay; Dominique Michel; Louise Portal; Yves Jacques; Pierre Curzi; ***D:*** Denys Arcand; ***W:*** Denys Arcand; ***C:*** Guy Dufaux; ***M:*** Pierre Aviat. Oscars '03: Foreign Film; British Acad. '03: Orig. Screenplay; Cannes '03: Actress (Croze), Screenplay; Natl. Bd. of Review '03: Foreign Film.

Barbarian Queen ✓ **1985 (R)** Female warriors led by beauteous babe seek revenge for the capture of their men in this sword-and-sorcery epic. Low-budget rip-off "Conan the Barbarian" is laughable. Also available in an unrated version. Followed by "Barbarian Queen 2: The Empress Strikes Back." **71m/C; VHS, DVD.** *IT* Lana Clarkson; Frank Zagarino; Katt Shea; Dawn Dunlap; Susana Traverso; ***D:*** Hector Olivera; ***W:*** Howard R. Cohen; ***C:*** Rudy Donovan; ***M:*** Christopher Young.

Barbarian Queen 2: The Empress Strikes Back ✓ **1989 (R)** Apparently one movie wasn't enough to tell the beautiful Princess Athalia's story. This time she fights her evil brother Ankaris. He throws her in prison, she escapes, joins a band of female rebels, and leads them into battle. No better than the first attempt. **87m/C; VHS, DVD.** *IT* Lana Clarkson; Greg Wrangler; Rebecca Wood; Elizabeth Jaegen; Roger Cundy; ***D:*** Joe Finley; ***W:*** Howard R. Cohen; ***C:*** Francisco Bojorquez; ***M:*** Christopher Young.

Barbarians at the Gate ✓✓✓ 1/2 **1993 (R)** In the "greed is good" financial climate of the '80s, this movie chronicles the $25 billion battle in 1988 for RJR Nabisco, which at the time was working on developing a "smokeless cigarette." Garner is CEO F. Ross Johnson, who is confident that their "smokeless cigarette" will boost the stock's value—until he gets the test-marketing results. Unwilling to risk the product's failure, Johnson decides to buy the company and is challenged by master dealer Kravis (Pryce). Fascinating social commentary on the nastiest mega-deal in history. Based on the book by Bryan Burrough and John Helyar. **107m/C; VHS, DVD.** James Garner; Jonathan Pryce; Peter Riegert; Joanna Cassidy; Fred Dalton Thompson; Leilani Sarelle Ferrer; Matt Clark; Jeffrey DeMunn; ***D:*** Glenn Jordan; ***W:*** Larry Gelbart; ***C:*** Thomas Del Ruth; Nicholas D. Knowland; ***M:*** Richard Gibbs. **CABLE**

Barbarosa ✓✓✓ **1982 (PG)** Offbeat western about an aging, legendary outlaw constantly on the lam who reluctantly befriends a naive farmboy and teaches him survival skills. Nelson and Busey are a great team, solidly directed. Lovely Rio Grande scenery. **90m/C; VHS, DVD, Blu-Ray.** Willie Nelson; Gilbert Roland; Gary Busey; Isela Vega; ***D:*** Fred Schepisi; ***W:*** William D. Wittliff; ***C:*** Ian Baker; ***M:*** Bruce Smeaton.

Barbary Coast ✓✓✓ **1935** A ruthless club owner tries to win the love of a young girl by building her into a star attraction during San Francisco's gold rush days. **90m/B; VHS, DVD.** Edward G. Robinson; Walter Brennan; Brian Donlevy; Joel McCrea; Donald Meek; David Niven; Miriam Hopkins; ***D:*** Howard Hawks.

Barbershop ✓✓✓ **2002 (PG-13)** Ensemble comedy looks at the unique culture found in barbershops in the black male community. Cube plays Calvin, discontented owner of a barbershop he inherited from his father. In debt, Calvin sells the shop to a loan shark, which sends all the shop's regulars reeling, as their haven will be turned into a strip club. During the shop's final day, when the film takes place, Calvin must come to grips with his mistake and recognize the value of his father's legacy. Though two lesser subplots detract from the engrossing barbershop talk, a host of interesting characters mesh with an original and entertaining story. **102m/C; VHS, DVD, Blu-Ray, UMD.** Ice Cube; Anthony Anderson; Cedric the Entertainer; Eve; Sean Patrick Thomas; Troy Garity; Michael Ealy; Leonard Earl Howze; Keith David; Lahmard Tate; Tom Wright; Jazsmin Lewis; ***D:*** Tim Story; ***W:*** Mark Brown; Don D. Scott; Marshall Todd; ***C:*** Tom Priestley; ***M:*** Terence Blanchard.

Barbershop 2: Back in Business ✓✓✓ **2004 (PG-13)** Calvin and the rest of the crew are back. This time around, the shop faces a community crisis in the form of franchise cutters Nappy Cutz moving in across the street, threatening to put Calvin's shop out business. Lacks the fresh charm of the first one, but the strong cast and crisp writing save the day. **106m/C; VHS, DVD, Blu-Ray.** Ice Cube; Cedric the Entertainer; Sean Patrick Thomas; Eve; Troy Garity; Michael Ealy; Leonard Earl Howze; Harry J. Lennix; Robert Wisdom; Jazsmin Lewis; Carl Wright; Kenan Thompson; Queen Latifah; Garcelle Beauvais; ***D:*** Kevin Rodney Sullivan; ***W:*** Don D. Scott; ***C:*** Tom Priestley; ***M:*** Richard Gibbs.

Barbershop: The Next Cut ✓✓ 1/2 **2016 (PG-13)** It's rare that a three-quel, especially one this late in the game (the last movie in the franchise was 12 years ago) actually works, but Malcolm D. Lee's dramedy puts its focus on character first, and has something truthful and painful to say about urban city neighborhoods overrun by violence. The set-up is simple enough in that most of the story centers around the barbershop run by Calvin (Ice Cube), at which the unforgettable Eddie (Cedric the Entertainer) still works. A lot of things have changed in the last decade, including the fact that the shop is now co-ed. **111m/C; DVD, Blu-Ray.** Ice Cube; Cedric the Entertainer; Regina Hall; Sean Patrick Thomas; Eve; ***D:*** Malcolm Lee; ***W:*** Kenya Barris; Tracy Oliver; ***C:*** Greg Gardiner; ***M:*** Stanley Clarke.

Barcelona ✓✓✓ **1994 (PG-13)** Old-fashioned talkfest about two neurotic Americans experiencing sibling rivalry in Spain. Serious Ted (Nichols) is an American sales rep, posted to Barcelona, who can't quite get into the city's pleasure-loving rhythm. This is not a problem for Ted's cousin Fred (Eigeman), an obnoxious naval officer, with whom Ted has had a rivalry dating back to their boyhood. Set in the 1980s, the two must also deal with anti-Americanism, which leads both to violence and romantic developments. Tart dialogue, thoughtful performances, and exotic locales prove enticing in low-budget sleeper that effectively mixes drama and dry comedy. Watch for Eigeman in Tom Cruise's uniform from "A Few Good Men." **102m/C; VHS, DVD, Blu-Ray.** Taylor Nichols; Christopher Eigeman; Tushka Bergen; Mira Sorvino; Pep Munne; Francis Creighton; Thomas Gibson; Jack Gilpin; Nuria Badia; Hellena Schmied; ***D:*** Whit Stillman; ***W:*** Whit Stillman; ***C:*** John Thomas; ***M:*** Tom Judson; Mark Suozzo. Ind. Spirit '95: Cinematog.

Bardelys the Magnificent ✓✓ **1926** Boastful, womanizing swashbuckler the Marquis de Bardelys (Gilbert) sets out to woo Roxalanne (Boardman) who has already rejected the advances of sinister Chatellerault (D'Arcy). Bardelys assumes the disguise of a rebel leader, gets into trouble, and winds up on the gallows thanks to his rival. A gap in the surviving print is bridged with stills and footage from the original trailer. Based on the novel by Rafael Sabatini. **90m/B; Silent; DVD.** John Gilbert; Eleanor Boardman; Roy D'Arcy; Arthur Lubin; Lionel Belmore; Emily Fitzroy; ***D:*** King Vidor; ***W:*** Dorothy Farnum; ***C:*** William H. Daniels.

Bare Knuckles ✓ **1977 (R)** The adventures of a low-rent bounty hunter. **90m/C; VHS, DVD.** Robert Viharo; Sherry Jackson; Michael Heit; Gloria Hendry; John Daniels; ***D:*** Don Edmonds; ***C:*** Dean Cundey.

Bare Knuckles ✓ 1/2 **2010 (PG-13)** Inspired by a true story, single mother Samantha Rogers (Roxborough) struggles making a living as a cocktail waitress to support her young daughter. After meeting promoter Sonny Cool (Kove), she enters an underground bare knuckles boxing tournament for a chance to improve their lives. A good story but not well told. **90m/C; DVD.** Jeanette Roxborough; Martin Kove; Louis Mandylor; Bridgett "Baby Doll" Riley; Joanne Baron; ***D:*** Eric Etebari; ***W:*** Robert Redlin; ***C:*** George Reasner; ***M:*** Evan Frankfort. **VIDEO**

Barefoot ✓ **2014 (PG-13)** Misbegotten remake of a 2005 German comedy. Needing to convince his wealthy family he's changed, n'er-do-well Jay (Speedman) has innocent Daisy (Wood) pose as his girlfriend at his brother's New Orleans wedding. And where did they meet? In the mental ward of an L.A. hospital (he was a janitor, she was a patient). When Jay's plan doesn't work as intended, they steal his dad's vintage RV and road-trip back to Cali. Daisy's inappropriate behavior is meant to be charming but pic comes off as exploitative and rather icky. **90m/C; DVD, Blu-Ray.** Scott Speedman; Evan Rachel Wood; J.K. Simmons; Treat Williams; Kate Burton; ***D:*** Andrew Fleming; ***W:*** Stephen Zotnowski; ***C:*** Alexander Gruszynski; ***M:*** Michael Penn.

Barefoot Boy ✓ 1/2 **1938** An ex-con sends his snob of a son to the farm of an old friend to learn a few life lessons, which materialize in the form of a gang of crooks and a haunted house. **63m/B; DVD.** Jackie Moran; Marcia Mae Jones; Bradley Metcalfe; Johnnie Morris; Marilyn Knowlden; ***D:*** Karl Brown; ***W:*** John Thomas "Jack" Neville; ***C:*** Gilbert Warrenton. **VIDEO**

The Barefoot Contessa ✓✓✓ **1954** The story, told in flashback, of a Spanish dancer's rise to Hollywood stardom, as witnessed by a cynical director. Shallow Hollywood self-examination. **128m/C; VHS, DVD, Blu-Ray.** Ava Gardner; Humphrey Bogart; Edmond O'Brien; Valentina Cortese; Rossano Brazzi; Warren Stevens; Marius Goring; ***D:*** Joseph L. Mankiewicz; ***W:*** Joseph L. Mankiewicz; ***C:*** Jack Cardiff. Oscars '54: Support. Actor (O'Brien); Golden Globes '55: Support. Actor (O'Brien).

The Barefoot Executive ✓✓ **1971** A mailroom boy who works for a national TV network finds a chimpanzee that can pick hit shows in this Disney family comedy. **92m/C; VHS, DVD.** Kurt Russell; John Ritter; Harry (Henry) Morgan; Wally Cox; Heather North; Joe Flynn; ***D:*** Robert Butler; ***M:*** Robert F. Brunner.

Barefoot in the Park ✓✓✓ **1967** Neil Simon's Broadway hit translates well to screen. A newly wedded bride (Fonda) tries to get her husband (Redford, reprising his Broadway role) to loosen up and be as free-spirited as she is. **106m/C; VHS, DVD.** Robert Redford; Jane Fonda; Charles Boyer; Mildred Natwick; Herb Edelman; Mabel Albertson; ***D:*** Gene Saks; ***W:*** Neil Simon; ***C:*** Joseph LaShelle; ***M:*** Neal Hefti.

Barely Lethal ✓✓ **2015 (PG-13)** An action-adventure comedy about a teen special-ops agent gone rogue. Teen Megan (Steinfeld) is tired of the demands of her life as a special-ops agent and acts to have a normal life. After faking her own death, she hides in the suburbs and attends a local high school. She soon learns fitting in and being a normal teen comes with its own set of complications. Megan's plan goes further awry when her handler Victoria (Alba) sends another teen agent, Heather (Turner) to the school undercover with the goal of making Megan to service. **100m/C; DVD, Blu-Ray, Streaming, Download.** Hailee Steinfeld; Jessica Alba; Sophie Turner; Jaime King; Samuel L. Jackson; John D'Arco; ***D:*** Kyle Newman; ***C:*** Peter Lyons Collister; ***M:*** Mateo Messina.

Barfly ✓✓✓ **1987 (R)** Bukowski's semi-autobiographical screenplay is the story of a talented writer who chooses to spend his time as a lonely barfly, hiding his literary abilities behind glasses of liquor. Dunaway's character is right on target as the fellow alcoholic. **100m/C; VHS, DVD.** Mickey Rourke; Faye Dunaway; Alice Krige; Frank Stallone; J.C. Quinn; Jack Nance; Charles Bukowski; Pruitt Taylor Vince; Fritz Feld; Sandy Martin; Damon Hines; ***D:*** Barbet Schroeder; ***W:*** Charles Bukowski; ***C:*** Robby Muller; ***M:*** Jack Baran.

Bark! ✓ 1/2 **2002 (R)** L.A. dog walker Lucy (Morgan) begins to overly-identify with her clients when she stops speaking and begins barking and displaying other canine behavior. Her baffled husband Peter (Tergesen) consults Lucy's equally odd parents as well as a vet (Kudrow) and a shrink (D'Onofrio) and decides to have his wife committed. But when Lucy becomes catatonic in the hospital, Peter decides to take her home and learn to adapt. He's a lot more understanding than the viewer will be. **100m/C; VHS, DVD, On Demand.** Lee Tergesen; Lisa Kudrow; Vincent D'Onofrio; Heather Morgan; Hank Azaria; Mary Jo Deschanel; Scott Wilson; Aimee Graham; Wade Andrew Williams; ***D:*** Kasia Adamik; ***W:*** Heather Morgan; ***C:*** Irek Hartowicz; ***M:*** Eric Colvin.

Barking Dogs Never Bite ✓✓✓ *Flandersui gae; A Higher Animal; Flanders' Dog* **2000** Black comedy involving a janitor and a stressed academic, one of which could be a serial killer specializing in small dogs. May be distressing for lovers of cute fluffy animals. Scratch that, it will be traumatizing for fluffy animal lovers. **108m/C; DVD.** *NK* Sung-jae Lee; Doona Bae; ***D:*** Joon-ho Bong; ***W:*** Joon-ho Bong; Ji-ho Song; Derek Son Tae-woong; ***C:*** Yong-kyou Cho; Yeong-gyu Jo; ***M:*** Sung-woo Jo.

The Barkleys of Broadway ✓✓✓ **1949** The famous dancing team's last film together; they play a quarreling husband/wife showbiz team. **109m/C; VHS, DVD.** Fred Astaire; Ginger Rogers; Gale Robbins; Oscar Levant; Jacques Francois; Billie Burke; ***D:*** Charles Walters; ***W:*** Adolph Green; Betty Comden; ***C:*** Harry Stradling, Sr.; ***M:*** Ira Gershwin; Harry Warren.

Barn of the Naked Dead **WOOF!** *Nightmare Circus; Terror Circus* **1973** Prine plays a sicko who tortures women while his radioactive monster dad terrorizes the Nevada desert. Rudolph's first film, directed under the pseudonym Gerald Comier. **86m/C; VHS, DVD, Blu-Ray.** Andrew Prine; Manuella Thiess; Sherry Alberoni; Gylian Roland; Al Cormier; Jennifer Ashley; *D:* Alan Rudolph; *W:* Alan Rudolph; Roman Valenti.

Barney's Great Adventure 🦴🦴 **1998 (G)** First the bad news: that big purple dweebosaur made a movie and your three-year-old is going to make you buy the video. Now the good news: since it's on video you can cue it up for the young-uns and run screaming from the room. You see, they don't care what you think about Barney, who looks a little like a big lug in a purple felt suit, actually. In this extravaganza of not so special effects, Barney and two little girls chase a magical egg around town and encounter a parade, a circus and other allegedly wonderful things, all while trying to convince the older Kyle that Barney is "cool." In a surprise move, the egg hatches to reveal....that new stuffed animal you're going to have to buy! **75m/C; VHS, DVD.** George Hearn; Shirley Douglas; Kyla Pratt; Trevor Morgan; Diana Rice; Renee Madeleine Le Guerrier; *V:* Bob West; Julie Johnson; *D:* Steve Gomer; *W:* Stephen White; *C:* Sandi Sissel.

Barney's Version 🦴🦴 **2010 (R)** Necessarily compacted adaptation of Mordecai Richler's dense 1997 satire/memoir. It follows 40 years in the life of curmudgeonly, triple-married and divorced Montreal Jew Barney Panofsky (Giamatti) and his various excesses, which could include murder. Not a sympathetic character, Barney is self-involved and obsessive, particularly with near-saintly third wife Miriam (Pike). Also watch the close relationship between Barney and his sly cop father, Izzy (well-played by Hoffmann). **132m/C; Blu-Ray.** *CA IT* Paul Giamatti; Dustin Hoffman; Rosamund Pike; Minnie Driver; Rachelle Lefevre; Scott Speedman; Bruce Greenwood; Mark Addy; Saul Rubinek; *D:* Richard J. Lewis; *W:* Michael Konyves; *C:* Guy Dufaux; *M:* Pasquale Catalano. Golden Globes '11: Actor--Mus./Comedy (Giamatti).

Barnum 🦴🦴 ½ **1986** P.T. Barnum's life is focused upon in this biography about the man who helped to form "The Greatest Show On Earth." **100m/C; VHS, DVD.** Burt Lancaster; Hanna Schygulla; Jenny Lind; John Roney; *D:* Lee Philips.

Barnyard 🦴🦴 **2006 (PG)** Young Otis the cow (James) is unconcerned about keeping the secret that animals can not only talk, but like to dance, sing, party, and play pranks. But when the farmer's away, Otis is given the unexpected responsibility of looking after things. Cute, but probably more enjoyable for younger kids. Some jokes click for older kids and adults, but not quite enough. **89m/C; DVD.** *V:* Kevin James; Courteney Cox; Sam Elliott; Danny Glover; Andie MacDowell; Wanda Sykes; David Koechner; Steve Oedekerk; Rob Paulsen; Dom Irrera; Maria Bamford; Laraine Newman; Maurice LaMarche; Jeff Garcia; *D:* Steve Oedekerk; *W:* Steve Oedekerk; *M:* John Debney.

Barocco 🦴🦴 **1976** Crook kills his lookalike and takes his place and his girlfriend. Together the duo try blackmail to get the money they need to start a new life. Self-conscious would-be film noir. French with subtitles. **102m/C; VHS, DVD.** *FR* Gerard Depardieu; Isabelle Adjani; Marie-France Pisier; Jean-Claude Brialy; *D:* Andre Techine; *W:* Andre Techine; Marilyn Goldin; *C:* Bruno Nuytten; *M:* Philippe Sarde.

The Baron 🦴 ½ **1988** Vengeance is the name of the game when an underworld boss gets stiffed on a deal. Fast-paced no-brainer street drama. **88m/C; VHS, DVD.** Calvin Lockhart; Charles McGregor; Joan Blondell; Richard Lynch; Marlene Clark; *D:* Philip Fently.

The Baron and the Kid 🦴 **1984** A pool shark finds out that his opponent at a charity exhibition game is his long-lost son. Based on Johnny Cash's song. Made for TV. **100m/C; VHS, DVD.** Johnny Cash; Darren McGavin; June Carter Cash; Richard Roundtree; *D:* Gary Nelson; *M:* Brad Fiedel. **TV**

Baron Munchausen 🦴🦴🦴 **1943** The German film studio UFA celebrated its 25th anniversary with this lavish version of the Baron Munchausen legend, starring a cast of top-name German performers at the height of the Third Reich. Filmed in Agfacolor; available in English subtitled or dubbed versions. **120m/C; VHS, DVD.** *GE* Hans Albers; Kathe Haack; Hermann Speelmanns; Leo Slezak; *D:* Josef von Baky.

Baron of Arizona 🦴🦴🦴 **1951** Land office clerk almost succeeds in convincing the U.S. that he owned the state of Arizona. **99m/B; VHS, DVD.** Vincent Price; Ellen Drew; Beulah Bondi; Reed Hadley; Vladimir Sokoloff; *D:* Samuel Fuller; *W:* Samuel Fuller; *C:* James Wong Howe.

The Baroness and the Butler 🦴🦴 **1938** Johann (Powell) is butler to Baron Georg (Schildkraut) and his wife Katrina (Annabella), who is the daughter of the Hungarian Prime Minister. Politically active Johann becomes the opposition party leader and is elected to parliament--much to his employers' shock. Baron Georg happens to be a philanderer and it's no surprise when the Baroness and the butler find romance. Annabella's first American film. **80m/B; DVD.** William Powell; Annabella; Joseph Schildkraut; Henry Stephenson; Nigel Bruce; J. Edward Bromberg; *D:* Walter Lang; *W:* Sam Hellman; Lamar Trotti; Kathryn Scola; *C:* Arthur C. Miller.

Barracuda WOOF! *The Lucifer Project* **1978 (R)** Lots of innocent swimmers are being eaten by crazed killer barracudas. Currently only available as part of a collection. **90m/C; VHS, DVD, Streaming.** Wayne Crawford; Jason Evers; Roberta Leighton; *D:* Harry Kerwin.

Barracuda 🦴🦴 **2017** A thriller centered on half-sisters meeting for the first time. After hitchhiking across America, the mysterious Sinaloa (Reid) shows up at the Austin home of her half-sister Merle (Tolman) and Merle's fiance Raul (Bordonada). Merle was unaware of Sinaloa's existence, but their father was a famous country singer and had been in contact with her. At Raul's insistence, Merle invites Sinaloa to stay with them, but Sinaloa soon shows herself to be dominating and competitive in uexpected ways. As Sinaloa destabilizes Merle's orderly life, it is never clear what she wants. The character of Sinaloa is terrifyingly compelling, infusing dark energy into the film. **100m/C; DVD.** Allison Tolman; Sophie Reid; JoBeth Williams; Luis Bordonada; Larry Jack Dotson; *D:* Jason Cortlund; Julia Halperin; *W:* Jason Cortlund; *C:* Jonathan Nastasi; *M:* Chris Brokaw.

The Barrens 🦴🦴 **2012 (R)** Standard psycho/creep fare. A family travels to the Pine Barrens to scatter their grandfather's ashes only to encounter trouble as the other campers go missing. Instead of thinking they may have gotten lost they remember the urban legends about the Jersey Devil, and Dad immediately assumes the Devil is killing people. **97m/C; DVD, Blu-Ray, Streaming.** *CA US* Shawn Ashmore; Stephen Moyer; Peter DaCunha; Erik Knudsen; Mia Kirshner; Allie MacDonald; *D:* Darren Lynn Bousman; *W:* Darren Lynn Bousman; *C:* Joseph White; *M:* Bobby Johnston. **VIDEO**

The Barretts of Wimpole Street 🦴🦴🦴 *Forbidden Alliance* **1934** The moving, almost disturbing, account of poetess Elizabeth Barrett, an invalid confined to her bed, with only her poetry and her dog to keep her company. She is wooed by poet Robert Browning, in whose arms she finds true happiness and a miraculous recovery. Multi-faceted drama expertly played by all. **110m/B; DVD.** Fredric March; Norma Shearer; Charles Laughton; Maureen O'Sullivan; Katherine Alexander; Una O'Connor; Ian Wolfe; *D:* Sidney Franklin; *C:* William H. Daniels.

Barricade 🦴🦴 **1949** Massey practically twirls a mustache of evil in this odd western that's an alleged adaptation of Jack London's "The Sea Wolf." Gold mine owner Boss Kruger uses fugitives on the lam to dig for his ore, including new arrivals Bob (Clark) and Judith (Roman). They befriend lawyer Milburn (Douglas) who wants revenge on Kruger for murdering his brother, the mine's original owner. **75m/C; DVD.** Raymond Massey; Dane Clark; Ruth Roman; Robert Douglas; Morgan Farley; *D:* Peter Godfrey; *W:* William Sackheim; *C:* Carl Guthrie.

Barricade 🦴 ½ **2012 (PG-13)** A horror-thriller centered on a family trying to find peace amidst a tragedy but instead experiencing dark terror. After the unexpected death of his wife, psychiatrist Terrance Shade (McCormack) decides to take his two children to a secluded cabin in the mountains. There, he hopes, the family can heal after this major loss. Though the three have some fun, they soon find themselves cut off from civilization by a freak winter storm. Trapped, the Shade family finds themselves being terrorized by something unknown. As these horrific events occur, Terrance does all he can to make sure he and his children survive. **82m/C; DVD, Blu-Ray, Streaming, Download.** Eric McCormack; Jody Thompson; Conner Dwelly; Ryan Grantham; Donnelly Rhodes; *D:* Andrew Currie; *W:* Michaelbrent Collings; *C:* Robert Aschmann; *M:* Trevor Morris.

Barrier of the Law 🦴 ½ *La Barriera della Legge* **1954** In this Italian crime drama, cop Mario Grandi (Brazzi) goes undercover to infiltrate a gang of smugglers operating between the French and Italian Riviera. His cover may be blown when young Anna (Padovani) falls in love with him. Italian with subtitles. **81m/B; DVD.** *IT* Rossano Brazzi; Lea Padovani; Jacques Sernas; Cesare Fantoni; *D:* Piero Costa; *W:* Piero Costa; Guido Malatesta; *C:* Augusto Tiezzi; *M:* Franco D'Achiardi.

Barrio Wars 🦴 ½ **2002 (R)** Hip hop Latino Romeo and Juliet staged on the mean streets of L.A. Plato and Angelina are the star-crossed lovers from rival gangs sparking violence and turmoil all over the city. Nice try, but the standard no-budget acting style and a rather jarring soft-core sex scene defeats any intended purpose. But really, what's the point? Leonardo DiCaprio and Claire Danes have already done modern-day Shakespeare much better. **90m/C; VHS, DVD.** Sevier Crespo; Luchana Gatica; Anthony Martins; Beny Mena; Chino XL; *D:* Paul Wynne; *W:* Paul Wynne. **VIDEO**

Barry Lyndon 🦴🦴🦴 ½ **1975 (PG)** Ravishing adaptation of the classic Thackeray novel about the adventures of an Irish gambler moving from innocence to self-destructive arrogance in the aristocracy of 18th Century England. Visually opulent. Kubrick received excellent performances from all his actors, and a stunning display of history, but the end result still overwhelms. O'Neal has seldom been better. **185m/C; VHS, DVD, Blu-Ray.** Ryan O'Neal; Marisa Berenson; Patrick Magee; Hardy Kruger; Guy Hamilton; *D:* Stanley Kubrick; *W:* Stanley Kubrick; *C:* John Alcott. Oscars '75: Art Dir./Set Dec., Cinematog., Costume Des., Orig. Song Score and/or Adapt.; British Acad. '75: Director (Kubrick); L.A. Film Critics '75: Cinematog.; Natl. Bd. of Review '75: Director (Kubrick); Natl. Soc. Film Critics '75: Cinematog.

Barry McKenzie Holds His Own 🦴🦴 **1974** In this sequel to "The Adventures of Barry McKenzie," we find that after a young man's aunt is mistaken for the Queen of England, two emissaries of Count Plasma of Transylvania kidnap her to use as a Plasma tourist attraction. Based on the 'Private Eye' comic strip, this crude Australian film is as disappointing as the first of the Barry McKenzie stories. **93m/C; VHS, DVD.** *AU* Barry Humphries; Barry Crocker; Donald Pleasence; *D:* Bruce Beresford; *W:* Barry Humphries; Bruce Beresford.

Barry Munday 🦴 ½ **2010 (R)** Self-absorbed 30-something Barry (Wilson) crudely propositions every potentially available woman he sees. At least until his private parts are permanently injured by an irate father. At this neutered moment, Barry is told by one-night stand Ginger, whom he doesn't remember, that she is pregnant. Predictably, he has his doubts about fatherhood. **99m/C; DVD.** Patrick Wilson; Judy Greer; Chloë Sevigny; Jean Smart; Cybill Shepherd; Malcolm McDowell; Billy Dee Williams; Colin Hanks; Shea Whigham; Missi Pyle; Emily Procter; Christopher McDonald; *D:* Chris D'Arienzo; *W:* Chris D'Arienzo; *C:* Morgan Susser; *M:* Jude Christodal. **VIDEO**

Barrymore 🦴🦴 ½ **2011** Dramatic film based on a one man play about the life of actor John Barrymore. Old and in bad health, and no longer a leading actor, Barrymore (Christopher Plummer) has rented an old theater to rehearse for a backer's audtion of a revival of the play that made him famous. **84m/C; DVD, Blu-Ray, Streaming.** *CA* Christopher Plummer; *D:* Erik Canuel; *W:* Erik Canuel; *C:* Bernard Couture; *M:* Michael Corriveau. **VIDEO**

Barstool Cowboy 🦴 **2008** Boring and predictable low-budget indie. Unemployed, 30-something, self-pitying Mick is spending time on a barstool after a bad breakup when 19-year-old art student Arcy comes along. Despite the fact that she's too young to legally drink, she becomes a bar regular and she and Mick decide to spend some time together for no other reason than they're both alone. **90m/C; DVD.** Tim Woodward; Rachel Lien; *D:* Mark Thimijan; *W:* Mark Thimijan; *C:* Doug McMains; *M:* Natalie Ileana.

Bart Got a Room 🦴 ½ **2008 (PG-13)** All-too familiar plot overdoes the fact that Hollywood, Florida high school nerd Danny (Kaplan) lives in a geriatric haven. Danny spends a fortune renting a room for the prom (after he learns ever dweebier Bart has apparently scored) with the expectation of losing his virginity. But first he has to get a date and he keeps overlooking his best friend Camille (Shawkat). Maybe he can't think of her 'that way.' Funniest thing in the movie is Macy's (Danny's divorced, dating dad) Jewish 'fro. **80m/C; DVD.** Alia Shawkat; William H. Macy; Cheryl Hines; Ashley Benson; Jennifer Tilly; Steve Kaplan; Brandon Hardesty; Chad Jamian Williams; *D:* Brian Hecker; *W:* Brian Hecker; *C:* Hallvard Braein; *M:* Jamie Lawrence.

Bartleby 🦴🦴 ½ **1970** A new version of the classic Herman Melville short story. McEnery is Bartleby the clerk, who refuses to leave his job even after he's fired; Scofield is his frustrated boss. **79m/C; VHS, DVD.** Paul Scofield; John McEnery; Colin Jeavons; Thorley Walters; *D:* Anthony Friedman; *W:* Rodney Carr-Smith.

Bartleby 🦴🦴 **2001 (PG-13)** Contempo version of Herman Melville's 1856 novella "Bartleby the Scrivener." Eccentric Bartleby (Glover) is the model of efficiency when first hired to do clerical work in a nondescript records office. But gradually Bartleby begins to refuse tasks, then to do anything at all—even firing him has no effect to the consternation of his boss (Paymer) and the bewilderment of his co-workers. **83m/C; VHS, DVD.** Crispin Glover; David Paymer; Glenne Headly; Joe Piscopo; Maury Chaykin; Seymour Cassel; Carrie Snodgress; Dick Martin; *D:* Jonathan Parker; *W:* Jonathan Parker; Catherine Di Napoli; *C:* Wah Ho Chan; *M:* Jonathan Parker; Seth Asarnow.

Barton Fink 🦴🦴🦴 **1991 (R)** This eerie comic nightmare comes laden with awards (including the Palme D'Or from Cannes) but only really works if you care about the time and place. Fink is a trendy New York playwright staying in a seedy Hollywood hotel in the 1940s, straining to write a simple B-movie script. Macabre events, both real and imagined, compound his writer's block. Superb set design from Dennis Gassner complements an unforgettable cast of grotesques. **116m/C; VHS, DVD, Blu-Ray.** John Turturro; John Goodman; Judy Davis; Michael Lerner; John Mahoney; Tony Shalhoub; Jon Polito; Steve Buscemi; David Warrilow; Richard Portnow; Christopher Murney; *D:* Joel Coen; *W:* Joel Coen; Ethan Coen; *C:* Roger Deakins; *M:* Carter Burwell. Cannes '91: Actor (Turturro), Director (Coen), Film; L.A. Film Critics '91: Cinematog., Support. Actor (Lerner); N.Y. Film Critics '91: Cinematog., Support. Actress (Davis); Natl. Soc. Film Critics '91: Cinematog.

The Base 🦴🦴 ½ **1999 (R)** Army Intelligency officer Major John Murphy (Dacascos) is sent undercover to Fort Tilman to investigate the murder of an army operations officer. Murphy is assigned to a border patrol unit and discovers his fellow soldiers are muscling in on the Mexican/American drug trade. When he discovers who's behind the operation, Murphy's cover is blown and he's in for the fight of his life. **101m/C; VHS, DVD.** Mark Dacascos; Tim Abell; Paula Trickey; Noah Blake; Frederick Coffin; *D:* Mark L. Lester; *W:* Jeff Albert; William C. Martell; *C:* Jacques Haitkin; *M:* Paul Zaza. **VIDEO**

The Base 2: Guilty as Charged 🦴 ½ *Guilty as Charged* **2000 (R)** The U.S. Army sends an undercover investigator to look into mysterious deaths on one of their bases. Turns out a

Colonel and his unit have gone rogue and are executing enlisted men they believe were wrongly acquitted of crimes. Might be enjoyable to diehard action fans, presuming they haven't actually joined the military and gained any knowledge of how it works. **97m/C; DVD.** Antonio Sabato, Jr.; James Remar; Duane Davis; Yuji Okumoto; Melissa Lewis; Elijah Mahar; Emilio Rivera; Johnny Urbon; William Jones; Daron McBee; Randy Mulkey; Gary Cervantes; Robert Crow; Bob Rudd; ***D:*** Mark L. Lester; ***W:*** Jeff Albert; C. Courtney Joyner; ***C:*** George Mooradian; ***M:*** Andrew Kereztes.

BASEketball 1/2 **1998 (R)** Dude! Three slacker buddies ("South Park"'s Parker and Stone plus Bachar) invent a new game in their driveway—a combo of basketball with baseball rules—and see it turn into big business. Parkere gets to romance Jenna Reed (Bleeth), a social worker who helps "health-challenged" kids. Stone and Parker's penchant for gross-out humor and having their characters say whatever's on their minds (no matter how offensive) mixes well with Zucker's talent for sight gags and physical humor to create an enjoyably guilty pleasure. Based on a game that Zucker invented with friends. **103m/C; VHS, DVD, Blu-Ray.** Trey Parker; Matt Stone; Yasmine Bleeth; Jenny McCarthy; Ernest Borgnine; Dian Bachar; Robert Vaughn; Bob Costas; Al Michaels; Reggie Jackson; Robert Stack; Steve Garvey; Kareem Abdul-Jabbar; ***D:*** David Zucker; ***W:*** David Zucker; Robert Locash; Jeffrey Wright; Lewis Friedman; ***C:*** Steve Mason; ***M:*** Ira Newborn.

Baseline Killer **2008 (R)** Yet another film based (very) loosely on the exploits of a serial killer by obsessed director Ulli Lommel. This time, the subject is Mark Goudeau, also known as the Baseline Killer, who was convicted of nine murders along with a host of sexual assaults and robberies. **90m/C; DVD, Streaming.** Victoria Ullmann; Pia Pownall; ***D:*** Ulli Lommel; ***W:*** Ulli Lommel; ***C:*** Ulli Lommel; ***M:*** Ulli Lommel. **VIDEO**

The Basement 1/2 **1989** Cult horror anthology from the 80s that was thought lost. It opens with four people wandering a basement and encountering a towering figure who asks them to confess the sins they will commit in the future. Apparently their sins involve a demon, a psychopathic teacher, zombies, and a really angry snake in a pool. **79m/C; DVD.** Dennis Driscoll; Kathleen Heidinger; David Webber; Scott Corizzi; Traci Mann; ***D:*** Timothy O'Rawe; ***W:*** Timothy O'Rawe; ***C:*** Michael Raso. **VIDEO**

Basement Jack **2009 (R)** A serial killer who surprised his victims by hiding in their basements is released, and immediately travels home to pick up where he left off. Apparently the maximum sentence for wiping out several families is 10 years if you're a minor and no one thought to notify the public. **93m/C; DVD.** Eric Peter-Kaiser; Sam Skoryna; Michele Morrow; Lynn Lowry; ***D:*** Michael Shelton; ***W:*** Brian Patrick O'Toole; ***C:*** Matthew Rudenberg; ***M:*** Alan Howarth. **VIDEO**

The Bashful Bachelor **1942** Yokel joker Abner trades his delivery car for a race horse, hoping to win a big race. **78m/B; VHS, DVD.** Chester Lauck; Norris Goff; Zasu Pitts; Grady Sutton; Louise Currie; Irving Bacon; Earle Hodgins; Benny Rubin; ***D:*** Malcolm St. Clair.

Basic **2003 (R)** Travolta, swallowing scenery and his fellow actors in one gulp, is DEA agent and ex-Army Ranger Tom Hardy, brought in to investigate how a training mission ended in all but two soldiers being killed. Over the objections of the base's top cop, Capt. Julia Osborne (Nielsen, sporting an inconsistent Southern accent), he interrogates both survivors and gets two completely differing accounts, "Rashomon" style. In flashback, it's learned that the platoon's commander, Sgt. West, was universally hated, and the men were killed by each other, and some kind of drug smuggling ring may have been involved. Convoluted and confusing are two words you could use for this script, but both are woefully inadequate to describe how it messes with your head, and not in that good, "Wow, that was clever" way. It seems that the actors are as confused as the audience, and decide to cover that with epidemic over-acting. **95m/C; VHS, DVD.** John Travolta; Samuel L. Jackson; Connie Nielsen; Giovanni Ribisi; Brian Van Holt; Taye Diggs; Christian de la Fuente; Dash Mihok; Timothy Daly; Roselyn Sanchez; Harry Connick, Jr.; ***D:*** John McTiernan; ***W:*** James Vanderbilt; ***C:*** Steve Mason; ***M:*** Klaus Badelt.

Basic Instinct 1/2 **1992 (R)** Controversial thriller had tongues wagging months before its theatrical release. Burnt-out detective Douglas falls for beautiful, manipulative murder suspect Stone, perfectly cast as a bisexual ice queen who may or may not have done the deed. Noted for highly erotic sex scenes and an expensive (3 million bucks) script; ultimately the predictable plot is disappointing. Gay activists tried to interrupt filming because they objected to the depiction of Stone's character but only succeeded in generating more free publicity. The American release was edited to avoid an "NC-17" rating, but an uncut, unrated video version is also available. **123m/C; VHS, DVD, Blu-Ray.** Michael Douglas; Sharon Stone; George Dzundza; Jeanne Tripplehorn; Denis Arndt; Leilani Sarelle Ferrer; Bruce A. Young; Chelcie Ross; Dorothy Malone; Wayne Knight; Stephen Tobolowsky; ***D:*** Paul Verhoeven; ***W:*** Joe Eszterhas; ***C:*** Jan De Bont; ***M:*** Jerry Goldsmith. MTV Movie Awards '93: Female Perf. (Stone), Most Desirable Female (Stone).

Basic Instinct 2 **2006 (R)** It took 14 years for a sequel and this glossy, laughably overwrought mess is what we get? Stone tries too hard reprising her role as cold-blooded vamp Catherine Tramell, who's now living in London. After a fatal car crash, suspicious Scotland Yard detective Washburn (Thewlis) asks criminologist Michael Glass (Morrissey) to evaluate Catherine for possible criminal charges. His diagnosis is "risk addiction." Gee, doc, no kidding. Soon Michael is drawn into Catherine's possibly deadly web. Maybe this effort will become a midnight movie, just waiting to be mocked. **114m/C; DVD, Blu-Ray.** Sharon Stone; David Morrissey; David Thewlis; Charlotte Rampling; Hugh Dancy; Flora Montgomery; Iain Robertson; Indira Varma; Anne Caillon; Stan Collymore; Heathcote Williams; ***D:*** Michael Caton-Jones; ***W:*** Leora Barish; Henry Bean; ***C:*** Gyula Pados; ***M:*** John Murphy. Golden Raspberries '06: Worst Actress (Stone), Worst Picture, Worst Screenplay, Worst Sequel/Prequel.

Basic Training **WOOF! 1986 (R)** Three sexy ladies wiggle into the Pentagon in their efforts to clean up the government. **85m/C; VHS, DVD.** Ann Dusenberry; Rhonda Shear; Angela Aames; Walter Gotell; ***D:*** Andrew Sugarman.

Basil 1/2 **1998 (R)** Turn of the century English aristocrat Basil (Leto) strives for the approval of his overbearing father (Jacobi) while also trying to please the selfish woman he loves (Forlani). Based on the novel by Wilkie Collins. **113m/C; VHS, DVD.** Jared Leto; Claire Forlani; Christian Slater; Derek Jacobi; ***D:*** Radha Bharadwaj.

The Basket 1/2 **1999 (PG)** There's a lot going on in a small Washington community, circa 1918. Martin Conlon (Coyote) is the new teacher (he's from Boston) at the one-room schoolhouse who introduces opera and basketball into the curriculum. Then German orphans Helmut (Burke) and Brigitta (Willenborg) come to live with the local doctor and are persecuted for their nationality because of WWI. Mr. Emery (MacDonald) is especially hostile since his son was wounded in the war but Mrs. Emery (Allen) is willing to give the newcomers a chance. Helmut turns out to be a hoops natural and the team has a chance to compete in a national championship—if they can set their differences aside. **104m/C; VHS, DVD.** Karen Allen; Peter Coyote; Robert Karl Burke; Amber Willenborg; Jock MacDonald; Eric Dane; Casey Cowan; Brian Skala; Tony Lincoln; Patrick Treadway; Ellen Travolta; ***D:*** Rich Cowan; ***W:*** Rich Cowan; Frank Swoboda; Tessa Swoboda; ***C:*** Dan Heigh; ***M:*** Don Caron.

Basket Case **1982** A gory horror film about a pair of Siamese twins—one normal, the other gruesomely deformed. The pair is surgically separated at birth, and the evil disfigured twin is tossed in the garbage. Fraternal ties being what they are, the normal brother retrieves his twin—essentially a head atop shoulders—and totes him around in a basket (he ain't heavy). Together they begin twisted and deadly revenge, with the brother-in-a-basket in charge. Very entertaining, if you like this sort of thing. Followed by two sequels, if you just can't get enough. **89m/C; VHS, DVD, Blu-Ray.** Kevin Van Hentenryck; Terri Susan Smith; Beverly Bonner; Robert Vogel; Diana Browne; Lloyd Pace; Bill Freeman; Joe Clarke; Ruth Neuman; Richard Pierce; Dorothy Strongin; ***D:*** Frank Henenlotter; ***W:*** Frank Henenlotter; ***C:*** Bruce Torbet; ***M:*** Gus Russo.

Basket Case 2 1/2 **1990 (R)** Surgically separated teenage mutant brothers Duane and Belial are back! This time they've found happiness in a "special" family—until they're plagued by the paparazzi. Higher production values make this sequel slicker than its low-budget predecessor, but it somehow lacks the same charm. **90m/C; VHS, DVD, Blu-Ray.** Kevin Van Hentenryck; Annie Ross; Kathryn Meisle; Heather Rattray; Jason Evers; Ted (Theodore) Sorel; Matt Mitler; Ron Fazio; Leonard Jackson; Beverly Bonner; ***D:*** Frank Henenlotter; ***W:*** Frank Henenlotter; ***C:*** Robert M. "Bob" Baldwin, Jr.; ***M:*** Joe Renzetti.

Basket Case 3: The Progeny 1/2 **1992 (R)** In this sequel to the cult horror hits "Basket Case" and "Basket Case 2," Belial is back and this time he's about to discover the perils of parenthood as the mutant Mrs. Belial delivers a litter of bouncing mini-monsters. Everything is fine until the police kidnap the little creatures and chaos breaks out as Belial goes on a shocking rampage in his newly created mechanical body. Weird special effects make this a cult favorite for fans of the truly outrageous. **90m/C; VHS, DVD, Blu-Ray.** Annie Ross; Kevin Van Hentenryck; Gil Roper; Tina Louise Hilbert; Dan Biggers; Jim O'Doherty; Jackson Faw; Jim Grimshaw; ***D:*** Frank Henenlotter; ***W:*** Frank Henenlotter; Robert Martin; ***C:*** Bob Paone; ***M:*** Joe Renzetti.

The Basketball Diaries **1995 (R)** Disappointing adaptation of undeground writer/musician Jim Carroll's 1978 cult memoirs, with DiCaprio starring as the teen athlete whose life spirals into drug addiction and hustling on the New York streets. Carroll and friends Mickey (Wahlberg), Neutron (McGaw), and Pedro (Madio), form the heart of St. Vitus' hot hoopster team. But the defiant quartet really get their kicks from drugs, dares, and petty crime—leading to an ever-downward turn. The book takes place in the '60s but the film can't make up its mind what the decade is, although DiCaprio (and Wahlberg) are particularly effective in a self-conscious first effort from Kalvert. **102m/C; VHS, DVD.** Leonardo DiCaprio; Mark Wahlberg; Patrick McGaw; James Madio; Bruno Kirby; Ernie Hudson; Lorraine Bracco; Juliette Lewis; Josh Mostel; Michael Rapaport; Michael Imperioli; James Dennis (Jim) Carroll; ***D:*** Scott Kalvert; ***W:*** Bryan Goluboff; ***C:*** David Phillips; ***M:*** Graeme Revell.

Basketweave **2006** Her parents murdered by a serial killer, a young girl spends 10 years locked in a brutal mental institution being fed experimental drugs. She escapes after a series of difficult-to-believe subplots come to fruition, and meets her parents' murderer who has been happily waiting in the hospital all this time. **76m/C; DVD.** Vance Strickland; Anna Harden; ***D:*** Christopher Forbes; ***W:*** Christopher Forbes; Ken Forbes; Kevin Forbes; ***C:*** Richard Kelly; Michael G. Hennessy; ***M:*** Christopher Forbes; Ken Forbes. **VIDEO**

Basquiat *Build a Fort Set It on Fire* **1996 (R)** First-time writer/director and re-knowned '80s pop artist Schnabel paints a celluloid portrait of African-American artist Jean Michel Basquiat, who went from grafitti artist to overnight sensation in the mid-1980s before dying of a drug overdose at 27. Schnabel's first-hand knowledge provides details of the painters, the dealers, and the patrons of the whirlwind New York art scene of the time, using an all-star cast (no mean feat on a $3 million budget). Making the move from stage to screen, Wright is an aptly deep and elusive Basquiat and Bowie stands out in a marvelously concevied portrayal of Basquiat's pseudo-mentor, the equally sensational Warhol. Features authentic works of the artists portrayed and some very convincing Basquiat reproductions done by Schnabel. **108m/C; VHS, DVD.** Jeffrey Wright; David Bowie; Dennis Hopper; Gary Oldman; Christopher Walken; Michael Wincott; Benicio Del Toro; Parker Posey; Elina Lowensohn; Courtney Love; Claire Forlani; Willem Dafoe; Paul Bartel; Tatum O'Neal; Chuck Pfeiffer; ***D:*** Julian Schnabel; ***W:*** Julian Schnabel; ***C:*** Ron Fortunato; ***M:*** John Cale. Ind. Spirit '97: Support. Actor (Del Toro).

The Bastard 1/2 *The Kent Chronicles* **1978** Dashing (but alas, illegitimate) nobleman roams Europe on futile, "Roots"-like search, then settles for America during the Revolutionary War in this long-winded TV adaptation of John Jakes's equally cumbersome bestseller (part of his popular Bicentennial series). Stevens stars, along with many supporting performers merely keeping active. Followed by "The Rebels" and "The Seekers." **189m/C; DVD.** Andrew Stevens; Tom Bosley; Kim Cattrall; Buddy Ebsen; Lorne Greene; Olivia Hussey; Cameron Mitchell; Harry (Henry) Morgan; Patricia Neal; Eleanor Parker; Donald Pleasence; William Shatner; Barry Sullivan; Noah Beery, Jr.; William Daniels; Keenan Wynn; Peter Bonerz; James Gregory; Mark Neely; Ike Eisenmann; Charles Haid; Russell Johnson; James Whitmore, Jr.; Alan Napier; Stephen Furst; Philip Baker Hall; ***Nar:*** Raymond Burr; ***D:*** Lee H. Katzin; ***W:*** Guerdon (Gordon) Trueblood; ***C:*** Michel Hugo; ***M:*** John Addison. **TV**

Bastard out of Carolina **1996 (R)** Huston's steeped-in-controversy directorial debut tells the story of young mom Anney (Leigh), who lives a hardscrabble life in Greenville, South Carolina, with an illegitimate daughter nicknamed Bone (Malone). Working as a waitress, Anney's eager to find love and succumbs to the charms of laborer Glen (Eldard), despite his nasty temper. Eleven-year-old Bone and Glen are immediately at odds and he begins to beat her, with Anney unwilling to face the truth, until a final horrific event. Based on the 1992 semiautiobiographical novel by Dorothy Allison, the film was originally made for Ted Turner's TNT network but was rejected as unsuitable because of its graphic depiction of child abuse. **97m/C; VHS, DVD.** Jennifer Jason Leigh; Jena Malone; Ron Eldard; Glenne Headly; Lyle Lovett; Dermot Mulroney; Christina Ricci; Michael Rooker; Diana Scarwid; Susan Traylor; Grace Zabriskie; Sonny Shroyer; ***D:*** Anjelica Huston; ***W:*** Anne Meredith; ***C:*** Anthony B. Richmond; ***M:*** Van Dyke Parks. **TV**

The Bat **1926** A bat-obsessed killer stalks the halls of a spooky mansion in this early film version of the Mary Roberts Rinehart novel. **81m/B; Silent; VHS, DVD, Blu-Ray.** Andre de Beranger; Charles Herzinger; Emily Fitzroy; Louise Fazenda; Arthur Houseman; Robert McKim; Jack Pickford; Jewel Carmen; ***D:*** Roland West; ***W:*** Roland West.

The Bat **1959** A great plot centering around a murderer called the Bat, who kills hapless victims by ripping out their throats when he isn't busy searching for $1 million worth of securities stashed in the old house he is living in. Adapted from the novel by Mary Roberts Rinehart. **80m/B; VHS, DVD, Blu-Ray.** Vincent Price; Agnes Moorehead; Gavin Gordon; John Sutton; Lenita Lane; Darla Hood; ***D:*** Crane Wilbur; ***W:*** Crane Wilbur; ***C:*** Joseph Biroc; ***M:*** Louis Forbes.

The Bat People *It Lives By Night* **1974 (R)** Less-than-gripping horror flick in which Dr. John Bech is bitten by a bat while on his honeymoon. He then becomes a sadistic bat creature, compelled to kill anyone who stumbles across his path. The gory special effects make for a great movie if you've ever been bitten by that sort of thing. **95m/C; VHS, DVD, Blu-Ray.** Stewart Moss; Marianne McAndrew; Michael Pataki; Paul Carr; ***D:*** Jerry Jameson; ***C:*** Matthew F. Leonetti; ***M:*** Artie Kane.

Bat 21 **1988 (R)** Hackman, an American officer, is stranded in the wilds of Vietnam alone after his plane is shot down. He must rely on himself and Glover, with whom he has radio contact, to get him out. Glover and Hackman give solid performances in this otherwise average film. **112m/C; VHS, DVD, Blu-Ray.** Gene Hackman; Danny Glover; Jerry Reed; David Marshall Grant; Clayton Rohner; Erich Anderson; Joe Dorsey; ***D:*** Peter Markle; ***W:*** Marc Norman; William C. Anderson; ***C:*** Mark Irwin; ***M:*** Christopher Young.

The Bat Whispers 1/2 **1930** A masked madman is stalking the halls of a creepy mansion; eerie tale that culminates in an appeal to the audience to keep the plot under wraps. Unusually crafted film for its early era. Comic mystery based on the novel and play by Mary Roberts Rinehart and Avery Hopwood. **82m/B; VHS, DVD.** Chester Morris; Chance Ward; Richard Tucker; Wilson Benge; DeWitt Jennings; Una Merkel; Spencer Charters; *D:* Roland West; *W:* Roland West; *C:* Ray June; Robert Planck.

Bat Without Wings ♪♪ *Wu yi bian fu* **1980** The Shaw Brothers occasionally dabbled in horror films about black magic and the supernatural, which usually weren't quite as successful. There's a reason for that. They weren't as good. A villain known as The Bat (who is supposed to be long dead) returns, and kidnaps and murders a young woman. A local swordsman volunteers to track him down and bring him to justice. And so the really bad special effects begin. **92m/C; DVD.** *CH* Shen Chan; Feng Ku; Wah Yuen; *D:* Yuen Chor.

Bataan ♪♪ 1/2 **1943** A rugged war-time combat drama following the true story of a small platoon in the Philippines endeavoring to blow up a pivotal Japanese bridge. Also available in a colorized version. **115m/B; VHS, DVD.** Robert Taylor; George Murphy; Thomas Mitchell; Desi Arnaz, Sr.; Lee Bowman; Lloyd Nolan; Robert Walker; Barry Nelson; Phillip Terry; Tom Dugan; Roque Espiritu; Kenneth Spencer; Alex Havier; Donald Curtis; Lynne Carver; Bud Geary; Dorothy Morris; *D:* Tay Garnett; *W:* Robert D. (Robert Hardy) Andrews; *C:* Sidney Wagner; *M:* Bronislau Kaper; Eric Zeisl.

Bathing Beauty ♪♪ 1/2 **1944** This musical stars Skelton as a pop music composer with the hots for college swim teacher Williams. Rathbone is a music executive who sees the romance as a threat to Skelton's career and to his own profit margin. Full of aquatic ballet, Skelton's shtick, and wonderful original melodies. The first film in which Williams received star billing. **101m/C; VHS, DVD.** Red Skelton; Esther Williams; Basil Rathbone; Bill Goodwin; Jean Porter; Carlos Ramirez; Donald Meek; Ethel Smith; Helen Forrest; *D:* George Sidney; *C:* Harry Stradling, Sr.; *M:* Xavier Cugat.

Bathtubs Over Broadway ♪♪♪ **2018 (PG-13)** A comedy documentary exploration of the mid-twentieth industrial musicals created for a company for one-time use at a national or major regional sales meetings. These costly productions were never meant for commercial use and generally unknown to the general public yet were often written by future stars, including award-winning choreographer Bob Fosse and Tony Award-winning songwriter Sheldon Harnick, for everything from dog food and plastic wrap to Chevys and American Standard plumbing. The feature debut of documentarian Whisenant, the film takes a perspective of affection for the musicals while showing the work involved and the positive and negative effects on the creatives involved. **87m/C; DVD.** *D:* Dava Whisenant; *W:* Dava Whisenant; Ozzy Inguanzo; *C:* Nick Higgins; Natalie Kingston; *M:* Anthony DiLorenzo. Writers Guild '18: Documentary Screenplay.

Batkid Begins ♪♪ 1/2 **2015 (PG)** The story of Dana Nachman's heartwarming documentary is undeniably moving and fascinating, even if the filmmaking never quite justifies pushing it past TV special length to a feature running time. In November of 2013, an amazing percentage of the world stopped to see what was happening for one 5-year-old kid in San Francisco who dared to have a big dream for his Make-a-Wish choice. He wanted to be Batkid. And instead of doing it simply, the whole city shut down, sending Batkid on a journey through San Francisco that caught the world's attention, even the President. It's a heartwarming story about how we can come together to make a boy's wish come true. **87m/C; DVD, Streaming.** *D:* Dana Nachman; *W:* Dana Nachman; Kurt Kuenne; *C:* Don Hardy, Jr.

Batman ♪♪ 1/2 **1966** Holy television camp, Batman! Will the caped crusader win the Bat-tle against the combined forces of the Joker, the Riddler, the Penguin, and Catwoman? Will Batman and Robin save the United World Security Council from dehydration? Will the Bat genius ever figure out that Russian journalist Miss Kitka and Catwoman are one and the same? Biff! Thwack! Socko! Not to be confused with the Michael Keaton version of the Dark Knight, this is the potbellied Adam West Batman, teeming with Bat satire and made especially for the big screen. **104m/C; VHS, DVD, Blu-Ray.** Burt Ward; Adam West; Burgess Meredith; Cesar Romero; Frank Gorshin; Lee Meriwether; Alan Napier; Neil Hamilton; Stafford Repp; Madge Blake; Reginald Denny; Milton Frome; *D:* Leslie Martinson; *W:* Lorenzo Semple, Jr.; *C:* Howard Schwartz; *M:* Nelson Riddle.

Batman ♪♪♪ 1/2 **1989 (PG-13)** The blockbuster fantasy epic that renewed Hollywood's faith in media blitzing. The Caped Crusader (Keaton) is back in Gotham City, where even the criminals are afraid to walk the streets alone. There's a new breed of criminal in Gotham, led by the infamous Joker (Nicholson). Their random attacks via acid-based make-up are just the beginning. Keaton is surprisingly good as the dual personality hero though Nicholson steals the show with his campy performance. Basinger is blonde and feisty as photog Vicki Vale, who falls for mysterious millionaire Bruce Wayne (and the bat). Marvelously designed and shot. Followed by three sequels. **126m/C; VHS, DVD, Blu-Ray, UMD.** Michael Keaton; Jack Nicholson; Kim Basinger; Robert Wuhl; Tracey Walter; Billy Dee Williams; Pat Hingle; Michael Gough; Jack Palance; Jerry Hall; *D:* Tim Burton; *W:* Sam Hamm; Warren Skaaren; *C:* Roger Pratt; *M:* Danny Elfman; Prince. Oscars '89: Art Dir./Set Dec.

Batman and Robin ♪ 1/2 **1997 (PG-13)** Includes lots of flash but, as usual, not much substance in this fourth adventure, which features a less angst-ridden caped crusader in the charming persona of Clooney. O'Donnell, who apparently knows a good gig when he's got one, returns as Robin. They must battle evil industrialist, Mr. Freeze (an impressively costumed Schwarzenegger), and his partner-with-the-deady-kiss (but what a way to go!), Poison Ivy (Thurman), who have plans to freeze Gotham City. Our heroes have some additional help in the person of Batgirl (Silverstone), who's now butler Alfred's (Gough) niece (she was Commissioner Gordon's daughter in the comics). Story's simplified but the secondary characters still get lost in the crowd. Director Schumacher's already agreed to helm a fifth film, but don't hold your breath since he succeeded in doing the impossible: killing the franchise. **125m/C; VHS, DVD.** George Clooney; Chris O'Donnell; Arnold Schwarzenegger; Uma Thurman; Alicia Silverstone; Michael Gough; Pat Hingle; John Glover; Elle Macpherson; Vivica A. Fox; Vendela Thommessen; Jeep Swenson; *D:* Joel Schumacher; *W:* Joel Schumacher; Akiva Goldsman; *C:* Stephen Goldblatt; *M:* Elliot Goldenthal. Golden Raspberries '97: Worst Support. Actress (Silverstone).

Batman Begins ♪♪♪ **2005 (PG-13)** They got rid of the Bat-nipples? Joel Schumacher will be so disappointed. Fortunately for everyone else, Nolan rejects the other Bat-sequels' lame campiness and returns Batman to his gritty roots, showing us how a young Bruce Wayne (Bale) first became the Caped Crusader. After training abroad with the mysterious Ducard (Neeson) and Ra's Al Ghul (Watanabe), Wayne begins his one-man war on crime with the help of his butler Alfred (Caine), good cop Jim Gordon (Oldman), and tech-savvy Lucius Fox (Freeman). The cast is beyond stellar, and Nolan does an amazing job of making Batman's world seem almost plausible. There's a bit too much angsty pondering about the nature of fear, but you'll forget all that once you see the Lamborghini-inspired Batmobile. **141m/C; DVD, Blu-Ray, UMD, HD-DVD.** Christian Bale; Michael Caine; Ken(saku) Watanabe; Cillian Murphy; Tom Wilkinson; Morgan Freeman; Katie Holmes; Gary Oldman; Liam Neeson; Rutger Hauer; Mark Boone, Jr.; Linus Roache; Gus Lewis; *D:* Christopher Nolan; *W:* Christopher Nolan; David S. Goyer; *C:* Wally Pfister; *M:* Hans Zimmer; James Newton Howard.

Batman Forever ♪♪♪ **1995 (PG-13)** Holy franchise, Batman! Third-time actioner considerably lightens up Tim Burton's dark vision for a more family-oriented Caped Crusader (now played by Kilmer). The Boy Wonder also makes a first-time appearance in the bulked-up form of O'Donnell, a street-smart Robin with revenge on his mind. Naturally, the villains still steal the show in the personas of maniacal Carrey (the Riddler) and the sartorially splendid Jones as Harvey "Two-Face" Dent. Rounding out this charismatic cast is Kidman's slinky psychologist Chase Meridian, who's eager to find the man inside the bat. Lots of splashy toys for the boys and awe-inspiring sets to show you where the money went. **121m/C; VHS, DVD.** Val Kilmer; Tommy Lee Jones; Jim Carrey; Chris O'Donnell; Nicole Kidman; Drew Barrymore; Debi Mazar; Michael Gough; Pat Hingle; Jon Favreau; George Wallace; Don "The Dragon" Wilson; Ed Begley, Jr.; Rene Auberjonois; Joe Grifasi; Jessica Tuck; Kimberly Scott; *D:* Joel Schumacher; *W:* Janet Scott Batchler; Akiva Goldsman; Lee Batchler; *C:* Stephen Goldblatt; *M:* Elliot Goldenthal. Blockbuster '96: Action Actress, T. (Kidman).

Batman: Mask of the Phantasm ♪♪ 1/2 *Batman: The Animated Movie* **1993 (PG)** Based on the Fox TV series with the animated Batman fending off old enemy the Joker, new enemy the Phantasm, and dreaming of his lost first love. Cartoon film noir set in the 1940s but filled with '90s sarcasm. Complicated storyline with a stylish dark look may be lost on the kiddies but adults will stay awake. **77m/C; VHS, DVD.** *V:* Kevin Conroy; Dana Delany; Mark Hamill; Stacy Keach; Hart Bochner; Abe Vigoda; Efrem Zimbalist, Jr.; Dick Miller; *D:* Eric Radomski; Bruce W. Timm; *W:* Michael Reaves; Alan Burnett; Paul Dini; Martin Pako; *M:* Shirley Walker.

Batman Returns ♪♪ 1/2 **1992 (PG-13)** More of the same from director Burton, with Batman more of a supporting role overshadowed by provocative villains. DeVito is the cruely misshapen Penguin who seeks to rule over Gotham City; Pfeiffer is the exotic and dangerous Catwoman—who has more than a passing purr-sonal interest in Batman; Walken is the maniacal tycoon Max Shreck. Pfeiffer fares best in her wickedly sexy role and second-skin costume (complete with bullwhip). Plot is secondary to special effects and nightmarish settings. Despite a big budget, this grandiose sequel is of the love it or leave it variety. **126m/C; VHS, DVD, Blu-Ray.** Michael Keaton; Danny DeVito; Michelle Pfeiffer; Christopher Walken; Michael Gough; Michael Murphy; Cristi Conaway; Pat Hingle; Vincent Schiavelli; Jan Hooks; Paul (Pee-wee Herman) Reubens; Andrew Bryniarski; *D:* Tim Burton; *W:* Daniel Waters; *C:* Stefan Czapsky; *M:* Danny Elfman.

Batman v Superman: Dawn of Justice ♪♪ **2016 (PG-13)** Crash! Bang! Boom! The DC/Zack Snyder model of superhero storytelling continues to prove that it is primarily about being bigger/louder/faster more than anything else. The result is a sequel that almost punishes people into enjoying it. You WILL like this! Or else! Superman (Cavill) has been getting a little loose with his superpowers, and people are wondering if the collateral damage he causes makes him more enemy than hero. In steps Batman (Affleck) to stop the alien invader. Amy Adams returns as Lois while Gal Gadot steals the film as Wonder Woman. The less said about Eisenberg's Lex Luthor, the better. **151m/C; DVD, Blu-Ray, Streaming.** Ben Affleck; Henry Cavill; Amy Adams; Jesse Eisenberg; Diane Lane; Gal Gadot; *D:* Zack Snyder; *W:* Chris Terrio; David S. Goyer; *C:* Larry Fong; *M:* Junkie XL; Hans Zimmer. Golden Raspberries '16: Worst Director (Snyder), Worst Screenplay, Worst Sequel/Prequel, Worst Support. Actor (Eisenberg). **VIDEO**

Bats ♪ 1/2 **1999 (PG-13)** B-grade comedy/thriller proves that people with a warped vision can create something that'll suck the life right out of you. Unfortunately, they use dialogue and plot, and not the winged critters in the title. A mad scientist (Gunton) working for the military genetically engineers some extra-nasty super-intelligent bats. Mad scientists being notoriously bad at cage maintenance, they escape. They then rile up a bunch of normally docile bats, turning them into vicious killers through some type of rodent peer pressure. After several attacks on his small Texas town, Sheriff Kimsey (Phillips) summons the nearest beautiful female bat expert (Meyer) and comic relief sidekick (Leon) so the bats have someone to chase around until the finale. They decide to freeze the bats in their cave, at the risk of trudging through a lot of guano to reach the end. You'll know how they feel. **91m/C; VHS, DVD.** Lou Diamond Phillips; Dina Meyer; Bob Gunton; Leon; Carlos Jacott; Oscar Rowland; David Shawn McConnell; Marcia Dangerfield; *D:* Louis Morneau; *W:* John Logan; *C:* George Mooradian; *M:* Graeme Revell.

Bats: Human Harvest WOOF! **2007 (R)** Basically an in-name-only sequel to 1999's "Bats" (well, except for the genetically mutated flying rodents). A special ops squad is sent to Chechnya to retrieve a renegade doctor (Arana). Seems the doc has turned bats into flesh-eating monsters that are now infesting the local woods. Just terrible in every possible way, including its bad CGI. **84m/C; DVD.** Tomas Arana; Michael Jace; David Chokachi; Melissa De Sousa; *D:* Jamie Dixon; *W:* Chris Denk; *C:* Ivo Peitchev; *M:* James Bairian; Louis Castle. **CABLE**

***batteries not included** ♪♪ 1/2 **1987 (PG)** As a real estate developer fights to demolish a New York tenement, the five remaining residents are aided by tiny metal visitors from outer space in their struggle to save their home. Each resident gains a renewed sense of life in this sentimental, wholesome family film produced by Spielberg. Cronyn and Tandy keep the schmaltz from getting out of hand. Neat little space critters. **107m/C; VHS, DVD, Blu-Ray.** Hume Cronyn; Jessica Tandy; Frank McRae; Michael Carmine; Elizabeth Pena; Dennis Boutsikaris; James LeGros; *D:* Matthew Robbins; *W:* Matthew Robbins; Brad Bird; Brent Maddock; S.S. Wilson; *C:* John McPherson; *M:* James Horner.

Battle at Bloody Beach ♪ **1961** Craig Benson (Murphy) was separated from his bride, Ruth (Michaels), when the Japanese invaded Manila. Two years later, he's still searching for her and teams up with Army Sgt. Sackler (Crosby), who's working with Filipino insurgents. Ruth, thinking Craig died, is involved with guerilla leader Julio (Rey), when Craig finds her. Catalina Island made for a cheap location for this poorly-scripted, no-budget drama. **79m/B; DVD.** Audie Murphy; Dolores Michaels; Gary Crosby; Alejandro Rey; *D:* Herbert Coleman; *W:* Richard Maibaum; Willard Willingham; *C:* Kenneth Peach, Sr.; *M:* Henry Vars.

Battle Beneath the Earth ♪♪ **1968** The commies try to undermine democracy once again when American scientists discover a Chinese plot to invade the U.S. via a series of underground tunnels. Perhaps a tad jingoistic. **112m/C; VHS, DVD.** *GB* Kerwin Mathews; Peter Arne; Viviane Ventura; Robert Ayres; *D:* Montgomery Tully.

Battle Beyond the Stars ♪♪ 1/2 **1980 (PG)** The planet Akir must be defended against alien rapscallions in this intergalactic Corman creation. Sayles authored the screenplay and co-authored the story on which it was based. **105m/C; VHS, DVD.** Richard Thomas; Robert Vaughn; George Peppard; Sybil Danning; Sam Jaffe; John Saxon; Darlanne Fluegel; Jeff Corey; Morgan Woodward; Marta Kristen; Ron Ross; Eric Morris; *D:* Jimmy T. Murakami; *W:* John Sayles; *C:* Daniel Lacambre; *M:* James Horner.

Battle Beyond the Sun ♪♪ **1963** Former Russian movie "Nebo Zowet" is Americanized. Everyone is trying to send a mission to Mars. Roger Corman was the producer, director Coppola used the pseudonym Thomas Colchart. **75m/C; VHS, DVD.** Edd Perry; Arla Powell; Bruce Hunter; Andy Stewart; *D:* Francis Ford Coppola; *W:* Nicholas Colbert; Edwin Palmer; *M:* Les Baxter.

Battle Circus ♪ 1/2 **1953** Sappy drama casts Bogart as a surgeon at a M*A*S*H unit during the Korean War. Allyson is a combat nurse who finds love amongst the harsh reality of a war zone. Bogart was badly miscast and his performance proves it. Weak script and uninspired performances don't help this depressing story. **90m/B; DVD.** Humphrey Bogart; June Allyson; Keenan Wynn; Robert Keith; William Campbell; Perry Sheehan; Patricia Tiernan; Adele Longmire; Jonathon Cott; Ann Morrison; Helen Winston; Sarah Selby; Danny Chang; Philip Ahn; Steve Forrest; Jeff Richards; Dick Simmons; *D:* Richard Brooks; *W:* Richard Brooks; *C:* John Alton; *M:* Lennie Hayton.

Battle Creek Brawl ♪♪ *Battle Creek; The Big Brawl; Sha shou hao* **1980** Jerry Kwan (Jackie Chan) is forced to fight in a brutal martial arts competition to save the family business from a mobster. Ironically, Chan had fled the Triads (Chinese mobsters) who were sent after him by an angry ex director who wanted to make him the next Bruce Lee, only to make this film under another director who wanted to make him Bruce Lee. The irony of the real-life situation is probably the most interesting thing about the movie. **95m/C; DVD, Blu-Ray.** *CH* Jackie Chan; Jose Ferrer; Kristine DeBell; Mako; Ron Max; David S. Sheiner; Rosalind Chao; Lenny Montana; Pat E. Johnson; H.B. Haggerty; Chao-Li Chi; Joycelyne Lew; ***D:*** Robert Clouse; ***W:*** Robert Clouse; Fred Weintraub; ***C:*** Robert C. Jessup; ***M:*** Lalo Schifrin.

Battle Cry 🦴🦴🦴 **1955** A group of U.S. Marines train, romance, and enter battle in WWII. But it takes 'em a while to do it. Walsh's film focuses on the psychology of training men to fight, and to wait for the chance. Uris's script (from his own novel) also spends an inordinate amount of time on the love lives of the soldiers. **169m/C; VHS, DVD, Blu-Ray.** Van Heflin; Aldo Ray; Mona Freeman; Tab Hunter; Dorothy Malone; Anne Francis; James Whitmore; Raymond Massey; William Campbell; John Lupton; L.Q. Jones; Perry Lopez; Fess Parker; Jonas Applegarth; Tommy Cook; Felix Noriego; Nancy Olson; Susan Morrow; Carleton Young; Rhys Williams; Gregory Walcott; Frank Ferguson; Sarah Selby; Willis Bouchey; ***D:*** Raoul Walsh; ***W:*** Leon Uris; ***C:*** Sidney Hickox; ***M:*** Max Steiner.

Battle for Skyark 🦴 $^1/_2$ **2015 (PG-13)** A post-apocalyptic examination of one man's quest to save humanity. Far in the future, Earth is desolate and has been taken over by a mysterious race of aliens. To survive, humanity takes refuge in a city orbiting Earth called SkyArk. All is not well, there, however, and a rebellion breaks out against corrupt leaders. When the rebellion fails, the children of the rebels are condemned to live on Earth. Led by Rags (Mortenson), the son of the rebel leader, they fight the monsters to try to return to SkyArk and ensure the survival of the human race. **88m/C; DVD, Blu-Ray, Streaming, Download.** Caon Mortenson; Garrett Coffey; Charlene Tung; Taylor Coliee; Riley Jane; ***D:*** Simon Hung; ***W:*** Simon Hung; Guy Malim; ***C:*** Hiroyuki Haga; ***M:*** Josh Cruddas.

Battle for Terra 🦴🦴🦴 *Terra* **2009 (PG)** A sci-fi story with a moral and some great 3-D animation. Having ruined Earth, human survivors are seeking another planet to colonize. This leads them to peaceful Terra, where the Terrans have set aside weapons and war long ago. Rebellious teen Mala (Wood) saves the life of human pilot Jim (Wilson) and, in return, asks for his help in rescuing her father who is a prisoner. The Terrans themselves are in danger since General Hammer (Cox) wants to get rid of the pesky natives and make the planet Earthlings-only. Don't worry, it's still fun as well. **85m/C; Blu-Ray.** ***V:*** Evan Rachel Wood; Luke Wilson; Brian Cox; James Garner; Chris Evans; Dennis Quaid; David Cross; Danny Glover; Amanda Peet; ***D:*** Aristomenis Tsirbas; ***W:*** Evan Spiliotopolos; ***M:*** Abel Korzeniowski.

Battle for the Planet of the Apes 🦴🦴 *Battle of the Planet of the Apes* **1973 (G)** A tribe of human atomic bomb mutations are out to make life miserable for the peaceful ape tribe. The story is told primarily in flashback with the opening and closing sequences taking place in the year A.D. 2670. Final chapter in the five-movie simian saga. **96m/C; VHS, DVD, Blu-Ray.** Roddy McDowall; Lew Ayres; John Huston; Paul Williams; Claude Akins; Severn Darden; Natalie Trundy; Austin Stoker; Noah Keen; Michael Stearns; John Landis; ***D:*** J. Lee Thompson; ***W:*** John W. Corrington; Joyce H. Corrington; ***C:*** Richard H. Kline; ***M:*** Leonard Rosenman.

Battle Hymn 🦴🦴 $^1/_2$ **1957** After accidentally bombing an orphanage as a WWII fighter pilot, Dean Hess (Hudson) becomes a minister. He returns to the Air Force in 1950 to train Korean pilots in Seoul and winds up building a home for the local orphans. True story on which the real Hess served as technical advisor. **109m/C; VHS, DVD.** Rock Hudson; Dan Duryea; Martha Hyer; Anna Kashfi; Don DeFore; Jock Mahoney; Carl Benton Reid; Alan Hale, Jr.; Richard Loo; Philip Ahn; ***D:*** Douglas Sirk; ***W:*** Charles Grayson; Vincent B. Evans; ***C:*** Russell Metty; ***M:*** Frank Skinner.

Battle in Seattle 🦴🦴 **2007 (R)** Dramatic (and heavily biased) reenactment of five days in 1999 when the World Trade Organization convened in Seattle and was met with tens of thousands of activists upset with the corporate entity's globalization policies and damage to the environment. Soon, however, the protests turned violent, with the police donning riot gear and the National Guard swooping in to clean up the mess. All the players get their turn: good-guy cop Dale (Harrelson) and his pregnant wife Ella (Theron), protest leader Jay (Henderson) and his angry girlfriend Lou (Rodriguez), over-zealous newswoman Jean (Nielsen), and finally, non-fictionalized Mayor Tobin (Liotta) to ineffectively calm both groups' fears. Despite writer-director Townsend's attempt for grit and realism, silly monologues and overt melodrama reek of pure Hollywood. **100m/C; Blu-Ray, On Demand.** Andre Benjamin; Jennifer Carpenter; Michelle Rodriguez; Martin Henderson; Ray Liotta; Woody Harrelson; Charlize Theron; Connie Nielsen; Channing Tatum; Isaach de Bankole; Joshua Jackson; Rade Serbedzija; ***D:*** Stuart Townsend; ***W:*** Stuart Townsend; ***C:*** Barry Ackroyd; ***M:*** One Point Six.

Battle: Los Angeles 🦴🦴 **2011 (PG-13)** Sci-fi action for those who just want to be entertained by the loud, undemanding, and familiar. Stoic Marine Staff Sgt. Nantz (Eckhart) and his platoon are the last line of defense, first on the Santa Monica streets, and then L.A. when Earth is attacked by outer space invaders who want to colonize our planet. There's no wink-wink to the audience as the script and the actors take their mission seriously as good soldiers should amidst all the pyrotechnics. **116m/C; Blu-Ray.** Aaron Eckhart; Michelle Rodriguez; Bridget Moynahan; Ramon Rodriguez; Cory Hardrict; Michael Peña; Lucas Till; Bryce Cass; Ne-Yo; ***D:*** Jonathan Liebesman; ***W:*** Christopher Bertolini; ***C:*** Lukas Ettlin; ***M:*** Brian Tyler.

The Battle of Algiers 🦴🦴🦴 $^1/_2$ *La Bataille d'Alger; La Battaglia di Algeri* **1966** Famous, powerful, award-winning film depicting the uprisings against French Colonial rule in 1954 Algiers. A seminal documentary-style film which makes most political films seem ineffectual by comparison in its use of non-professional actors, gritty photography, realistic violence, and a boldly propagandistic sense of social outrage. **123m/B; VHS, DVD, Blu-Ray.** *AL IT* Yacef Saadi; Jean Martin; Brahim Haggiag; Tommaso Neri; Samia Kerbash; Fawzia el Kader; Michele Kerbash; Mohamed Ben Kassen; ***D:*** Gillo Pontecorvo; ***W:*** Gillo Pontecorvo; Franco Solinas; ***C:*** Marcello Gatti; ***M:*** Gillo Pontecorvo; Ennio Morricone. Venice Film Fest. '66: Film.

Battle of Britain 🦴🦴 $^1/_2$ **1969 (G)** A powerful retelling of the most dramatic aerial combat battle of WWII, showing how the understaffed Royal Air Force held off the might of the German Luftwaffe. **132m/C; VHS, DVD, Blu-Ray.** Harry Andrews; Michael Caine; Laurence Olivier; Trevor Howard; Kenneth More; Christopher Plummer; Robert Shaw; Susannah York; Ralph Richardson; Curt Jurgens; Michael Redgrave; Nigel Patrick; Edward Fox; Ian McShane; Patrick Wymark; ***D:*** Guy Hamilton; ***W:*** James Kennaway; Wilfred Greatorex; ***C:*** Frederick A. (Freddie) Young; ***M:*** Malcolm Arnold; Ronald Goodwin; William Walton.

The Battle of El Alamein 🦴🦴 **1968** Action filled movie about the alliance of Italy and Germany in a war against the British, set in a North African desert in the year 1942. Ferroni used the pseudonym Calvin Jackson Padget. **105m/C; VHS, DVD.** *IT FR* Frederick Stafford; Ettore Manni; Robert Hossein; Michael Rennie; George Hilton; Ira Furstenberg; ***D:*** Giorgio Ferroni.

Battle of Jangsari 🦴🦴 *Jangsa-ri 9.15* **2019** During the Korean War, many secondary school students in South Korea serve in the army, including a troop under Captain Lee Myung-joon (Myung-min). The soldiers are headed to the front to engage in combat at Jangsari beach. As they near the beach, adult team members are killed by machine gun fire from the shore as they try to help younger soldiers move from the ship to the shore. Many young soldiers suffer the same fate, though the rest must fight for their survival. Based on a true story, much of what's interesting is lost in the predictable presentation. Korean with subtitles. **104m/C; DVD, Blu-Ray.** Megan Fox; George Eads; David Lee McInnis; Minho Choi; Myung-Min Kim; ***D:*** Kyung-taek Kwak; ***W:*** Brian Chung; Cory Gustke; Man-Hee Lee; ***M:*** Komeil S. Hosseini.

Battle of Neretva 🦴🦴 **1969** During WWII, Yugoslav partisans are facing German and Italian troops and local Chetniks as they battle for freedom. Big budget war film lost continuity with U.S. cut. **106m/C; VHS, DVD, Streaming.** *YU* Yul Brynner; Curt Jurgens; Orson Welles; Hardy Kruger; Franco Nero; Sergei Bondarchuk; ***D:*** Veljko Bulajic.

Battle of Rogue River 🦴 $^1/_2$ **1954** Cavalry officer Frank Archer is told to obtain a truce with the local warring tribes so Oregon can gain statehood. There's the usual group of bad guys who prefer the fighting to continue so they can control the area's mineral wealth. **71m/C; DVD.** Richard Denning; George Montgomery; Charles Evans; Martha Hyer; Emory Parnell; John Crawford; Michael Granger; ***D:*** William Castle; ***W:*** Douglas Heyes; ***C:*** Henry Freulich.

The Battle of Shaker Heights 🦴 $^1/_2$ *Project Greenlight's The Battle of Shaker Heights* **2003 (PG-13)** Disappointing sophomore effort from the HBO series "Project Greenlight," backed once again by producers Ben Affleck and Matt Damon. Kelly Ernswiler (LaBeouf) is bright, middle-class Midwestern teen whose hobby is military re-enactment. He becomes best friends with Bart (Henson) after "saving his life" in a mock battle. He soon develops a crush on Bart's older sister Tabby, an engaged Yale grad student, much to the dismay of his supermarket co-worker Sarah (Appleby). This only adds to Kelly's mounting problems, which include myriad family problems with ex-addict dad (Sadler) and "art" entrepreneur mom (Quinlan). LaBeouf is appealing, rising above the disjointed, uninspired mess. If there is another "Project," they should look for a director who will provide satisfying drama on the big screen as well as on the show. **85m/C; VHS, DVD.** Shia LaBeouf; Elden (Ratliff) Henson; Amy Smart; Billy Kay; Shiri Appleby; Kathleen Quinlan; William Sadler; Ray Wise; Anson Mount; Philipp Karner; ***D:*** Kyle Rankin; Efram Potelle; ***W:*** Erica Beeney; ***C:*** Thomas Ackerman; ***M:*** Richard (Rick) Marvin.

Battle of the Bulbs 🦴 $^1/_2$ **2010** In this goofy Hallmark Channel flick, Bob has been the king of Christmas decorations in the neighborhhod until Stu and his family move in across the street. They turn out to be ex-friends, still holding a 25-year-old grudge, who now pit themselves against each other to win the prize for the best holiday display. There's a couple of sappy subplots than ruin the slapstick. **88m/C; Streaming.** Daniel Stern; Matt Frewer; Allison Hossack; Teryl Rothery; Emily Tennant; William Hutchinson; ***D:*** Harvey Frost; ***W:*** W. Paul Thompson; ***C:*** Paul Mitchnick; ***M:*** Hal Beckett. **CABLE**

Battle of the Bulge 🦴🦴 **1965** A re-creation of the famous offensive by Nazi Panzer troops on the Belgian front during 1944-45, an assault that could have changed the course of WWII. **141m/C; VHS, DVD, Blu-Ray, HD-DVD.** Henry Fonda; Robert Shaw; Robert Ryan; Dana Andrews; Telly Savalas; Ty Hardin; Pier Angeli; George Montgomery; Charles Bronson; Barbara Werle; Hans-Christian Blech; James MacArthur; Karl Otto Alberty; ***D:*** Ken Annakin; ***W:*** Philip Yordan; John Melson; ***C:*** Jack Hildyard; ***M:*** Benjamin Frankel.

Battle of the Coral Sea 🦴 $^1/_2$ **1959** Strictly a war B-movie all the way. The crew of a submarine is captured by the Japanese while on a recon mission in the Pacific and sent to a POW camp. Three officers escape in time to provide the needed intel before the titular 1942 battle, which is not shown. **86m/B; DVD.** Cliff Robertson; Gia Scala; Teru Shimada; L.Q. Jones; Gene Blakely; Rian Garrick; ***D:*** Paul Wendkos; ***W:*** Stephen Kandel; Daniel Ullman; ***C:*** Wilfred M. Cline; ***M:*** Ernest Gold.

Battle of the Damned 🦴 **2014 (R)** Killer Asian robots, a zombie-like plague, and even Dolph Lundgren can't make for much entertainment. A city is quarantined with a military blockade when a deadly virus is accidentally released. Former commando Max Gatling is hired to rescue a wealthy man's daughter from the chaos, but when he finds Jude, she refuses to abandon a group of survivors who are using robots to battle the zombie-like plague victims. **89m/C; DVD, Blu-Ray.** Dolph Lundgren; Melanie Zanetti; Matt Doran; David Field; ***D:*** Christopher Hatton; ***W:*** Christopher Hatton; ***C:*** Roger Chingirian; ***M:*** Joe Ng. **VIDEO**

Battle of the Eagles 🦴 $^1/_2$ **1979** Follows the true adventures of the "Partisan Squadron," the courageous airmen known as the "Knights of the Sky" during WWII in Yugoslavia. **102m/C; VHS, DVD.** Bekim Fehmiu; George Taylor; Gloria Samara; ***D:*** Tom Raymonth.

Battle of the Rails 🦴🦴🦴 *La Bataille du Rail* **1946** Docudrama based on actual events of French Resistance fighters who worked on the railways and, at great peril, stymied the Nazis efforts throughout World War II and aided the Allies during the D-Day invasion. Powerful debut feature film for French director Clement, who included real railroad workers in recreating events. In French with subtitles. **85m/B; DVD.** Marcel Barnault; Jean Clarieux; Jean Daurand; Jacques Desagneaux; Francois Joux; ***D:*** Rene Clement; ***W:*** Rene Clement. **VIDEO**

Battle of the Sexes 🦴🦴 **1928** Real estate tycoon Judson (Hersholt) abandons his wife (Bennett) and home for money-hungry flapper Marie (Haver). Based on the novel "The Single Standard" by Daniel Carson Goodman. Griffith's remake of his own 1913 film. **88m/B; Silent; VHS, DVD.** Jean Hersholt; Phyllis Haver; Belle Bennett; Don Alvarado; William "Billy" Bakewell; Sally O'Neil; ***D:*** D.W. Griffith; ***W:*** Gerrit J. Lloyd; ***C:*** Billy (G.W.) Bitzer; Karl Struss.

Battle of the Sexes 🦴🦴 $^1/_2$ **2017 (PG-13)** The true tale of the famous 1973 tennis match between reigning female star Billie Jean King (Stone) and hustler/former champ Bobby Riggs (Carell). While Riggs' motivation was likely a combination of ego and showmanship along with genuine sexism, King carried the weight of an entire gender's quest for respect and equality. In spite of such high stakes, Stone and Carell bring humor, thoughtfulness, and humanity to their roles. Might not be an ace of a flick, but it still scores. **121m/C; DVD, Blu-Ray.** Emma Stone; Steve Carell; Andrea Riseborough; Natalie Morales; Sarah Silverman; ***D:*** Jonathan Dayton; Valerie Faris; ***W:*** Simon Beaufoy; ***C:*** Linus Sandgren; ***M:*** Nicholas Britell.

Battle of the Warriors 🦴🦴 $^1/_2$ *A Battle of Wits; Mo Gong; Bokkou; Muk Gong* **2006 (R)** More commonly known as 'A Battle of Wits,' this story is set in 370 B.C. in China's warring states period. The kingdom of Zhao invades the smaller (and fictional) city-state of Liang with an army 25 times their size. Enter Ge Li (Andy Lau), a Mohist philosopher who wishes to warn the citizens and find a way to stop the invaders from killing them all. The King of Liang is threatened by Ge Li's popularity however, and Li must deal with his machinations while trying to slow down or turn aside the oncoming army. **131m/C; DVD, Blu-Ray.** *JP CH HK SK* Andy Lau; Sung-kee Ahn; Zhiwen Wang; Si Won Choi; Bingbing Fan; ***D:*** Chi Leung Cheung; ***W:*** Chi Leung Cheung; ***C:*** Yoshitaka Sakamoto; ***M:*** Kenji Kawai.

Battle of the Worlds 🦴 *Il Pianeta Degli Uomini Spenti; Planet of the Lifeless Men* **1961** Typical low-budget science fiction. A scientist tries to stop an alien planet from destroying the Earth. Even an aging Rains can't help this one. Poorly dubbed in English. **84m/C; VHS, DVD.** *IT* Claude Rains; Maya Brent; Bill Carter; Marina Orsini; Jacqueline Derval; ***D:*** Anthony M. Dawson.

Battle of the Year 🦴 $^1/_2$ **2013 (PG-13)** After losing his wife and son, washed-up, boozing dance coach Jason (Holloway) assembles a rag-tag team of street dancers to battle their way to the world championships. Little more than a fictional re-telling of director Benson's outstanding 2007 competitive breakdancing documentary, "Planet B-Boy," mixed with the usual "Rocky"-like underdog clichés. A flashy, fun, and ultimately dumb guilty pleasure that never takes itself too seriously. "Step Up" fans, step up. **110m/C; DVD, Blu-Ray.** Josh Holloway; Laz Alonso; Josh Peck; Caity Lotz; Chris Brown; ***D:*** Benson Lee; ***W:*** Brin Hill; Chris Parker; ***C:*** Michael Barrett; ***M:*** Christopher Lennertz.

Battle Planet 🦴 $^1/_2$ **2008** A special forces officer is sent to a desolate planet on a secret mission to capture an alien terrorist. All too quickly he learns the experimental battlesuit he was given has trapped him inside, and there's more to his mission than he has been told. **86m/C; DVD, Streaming.** Zack (Zach) Ward; Monica May; Kevin Thompson; John Duerler; ***V:*** Colleen Smith; ***D:*** Greg

Aronowitz; *W:* Greg Aronowitz; *C:* Dallas Sterling; *M:* Mel Lewis. **VIDEO**

Battle Queen 2020 **1999 (R)** In a frozen post-apocalyptic future (eternal winter after asteroid crash), Gayle (Strain) leads the downtrodden masses in a revolution against the Elites who live above ground. She's a courtesan by day, freedom fighter by night...or is the other way around? This one is at least as good as "Battlefield Earth." It's certainly shorter and was made by people who were under no illusions about what they were doing. **80m/C; DVD.** *CA* Julie Strain; Jeff Wincott; *D:* Daniel D'or; *W:* Michael B. Druxman; William Hulkower; William D. Bostjancic; Caron Nightengale; *C:* Billy Brao; *M:* Robert Duncan. **VIDEO**

Battle Royale 1/2 *Batoru Rowaiaru* **2000** Insightful condemnation of modern Japanese society and politics masquerading as a thriller. In the near future, Japan has more graduates than jobs. Each year a class of random middle school children is kidnapped and forced to murder each other one by one lest they all die. The winner gets a job, assuming they remain sane enough for it. **122m/C; DVD, Blu-Ray, Streaming.** *JP* Tatsuya Fujiwara; Aki Maeda; Taro Yamamoto; Takeshi "Beat" Kitano; Chiaki Kuriyama; *D:* Kinji Fukasaku; *W:* Kenta Fukasaku; *C:* Katsumi Yanagijima; *M:* Masamichi Amano.

Battle Zone 1/2 **1952** WWII vet Danny Young (Hodiak) re-enlists to fight in Korea, and he and combat photographer Mitch Turner (McNally) volunteer to gather intel from behind enemy lines. This means putting aside their romantic rivalry since Mitch is engaged to Red Cross nurse Jeanne (Christian), whom Danny was once involved with. **81m/B; DVD.** John Hodiak; Stephen McNally; Linda Christian; Martin Milner; Jack Larson; *D:* Lesley Selander; *W:* Steve Fisher; *C:* Ernest Miller; *M:* Marlin Skiles.

Battlefield America **2012 (PG-13)** From the creators of You Got Served, a group of kids prepare for a dance battle. Businessman Sean Lewis (Houston) is young, charismatic, and successful, but must finish community service hours after facing legal troubles. Working with a group of misfit kids known as Bad Boys in Long Beach, California, Sean helps them prep for a major underground dance competition. Realizing that the kids have little dance talent, Sean gets a professional dance instructor to help the kids and boost their confidence ahead of the big battle. **106m/C; DVD, Blu-Ray.** Marques Houston; Mekia Cox; Lynn Whitfield; Tristen M. Carter; Chandler Kinney; *D:* Chris Stokes; *W:* Marques Houston; Chris Stokes; *C:* Miko Dannels; *M:* Michael J. Leslie.

Battlefield Earth **WOOF! 2000 (PG-13)** In the year 3000, the Earth has been decimated by 10-foot tall aliens known as Psychlos who are stripping the planet of its natural resources. Only a few humans survive, including Pepper who becomes the leader of a rebellion. Travolta plays the leader of the bad aliens and is extremely evil-lookng but in a strangely campy way. Based on a 1982 novel by Scientology founder L. Ron Hubbard. Film generated controversy for that reason and supposedly "subliminal" church messages but you'll simply be stunned into submission by how badly it blows. **117m/C; VHS, DVD.** John Travolta; Barry Pepper; Forest Whitaker; Kelly Preston; Kim Coates; Richard Tyson; Sabine Karsenti; Michael Byrne; Sean Hewitt; Michel Perron; Shaun Austin-Olsen; Marie Josee Croze; *D:* Roger Christian; *W:* J. David Shapiro; Cory Mandell; *C:* Giles Nuttgens; *M:* Elia Cmiral. Golden Raspberries '00: Worst Actor (Travolta), Worst Director (Christian), Worst Picture, Worst Screenplay, Worst Support. Actor (Pepper), Worst Support. Actress (Preston).

Battleforce *The Battle of the Mareth Line; The Greatest Battle* **1978** Exciting battle scenes lose their power in the confusion of this mixed-up WWII film about Rommel's last days. Dubbed sequences, news-reel vignettes and surprise performances by big name stars are incomprehensibly glued together. **97m/C; VHS, DVD.** *GE YU* Henry Fonda; Stacy Keach; Helmut Berger; Samantha Eggar; Giuliano Gemma; John Huston; *Nar:* Orson Welles; *D:* Umberto Lenzi.

Battleground **1949** A tightly conceived post-WWII character drama, following a platoon of American soldiers through the Battle of the Bulge. Available in a Colorized version. **118m/B; VHS, DVD, Blu-Ray.** Van Johnson; John Hodiak; James Whitmore; George Murphy; Ricardo Montalban; Marshall Thompson; Jerome Courtland; Don Taylor; Bruce Cowling; Leon Ames; Douglas Fowley; Richard Jaeckel; Scotty Beckett; Herbert Anderson; Thomas E. Breen; Denise Darcel; James Arness; Brett King; *D:* William A. Wellman; *W:* Robert Pirosh; *C:* Paul Vogel; *M:* Lennie Hayton. Oscars '49: B&W Cinematog., Story & Screenplay; Golden Globes '50: Screenplay, Support. Actor (Whitmore).

Battles of Chief Pontiac **1952** Set in America before the Revolutionary war, a Colonial officer is attempting to broker a peace deal between Indian chief Pontiac (Lon Cheney Jr.) and the settlers. Complicating this is a Hessian mercenary company waging a campaign of extermination against the Indians. The film is unusual in that it is one of the few films of its age that portrays the Native Americans as the good guys, and white men as the evil bad guys. **72m/B; DVD.** Lex Barker; Helen Westcott; Lon Chaney, Jr.; Berry Kroeger; Roy Roberts; Larry Chance; Katherine Warren; Ramsay Hill; *D:* Felix Feist; *W:* Jack DeWitt; *C:* Charles Van Enger; *M:* Elmer Bernstein.

Battleship **2012 (PG-13)** Yep, it's based on Hasbro's combat game. Naval officer Alex Hopper (Kitsch) and his fellow crewman aboard the USS John Paul Jones are trapped by an unknown force that's destroying the planet. They fight back. As bloated as one would expect from a summer blockbuster that attempts to turn a straightforward child's game into a Transformers-esque CGI orgy, director Berg's film is popcorn entertainment at its most formulaic. Movies like this one are not unlike watching someone else play a video game--it may look good but there's no real involvement on your part. **131m/C; DVD, Blu-Ray, Streaming.** Taylor Kitsch; Alexander Skarsgård; Rhianna; Brooklyn Decker; Tadanobu Asano; Liam Neeson; Peter MacNichol; *D:* Peter Berg; *W:* Erich Hoeber; Jon Hoeber; *C:* Tobias Schliessler; *M:* Steve Jablonsky. Golden Raspberries '12: Worst Support. Actress (Rhianna).

The Battleship Potemkin *Potemkin; Bronenosets Potemkin* **1925** Eisenstein's best work documents mutiny aboard the Russian battleship Potemkin in 1905 which led to a civilian uprising against the Czar in Odessa, and the resulting crackdown by troops loyal to the Czar. Beautiful cinematography, especially the use of montage sequences, changed filmmaking. In particular, a horrifying sequence depicting the slaughter of civilians on an Odessa beach by soldiers coming down the stairs leading to it is exceptional; many movies pay homage to this scene including "The Untouchables" and "Love and Death." Viewers should overlook obvious Marxist overtones and see this film for what it is: a masterpiece. **71m/B; Silent; VHS, DVD, Blu-Ray.** *RU* Alexander Antonov; Vladimir Barsky; Grigori Alexandrov; Mikhail Gomorov; Sergei Eisenstein; I. Brobov; Beatrice Vitoldi; N. Poltavseva; Alexandr Levshin; Repnikova; Korobei; Levchenko; *D:* Grigori Alexandrov; Sergei Eisenstein; *W:* Sergei Eisenstein; Nina Agadzhanova Shutko; *C:* Eduard Tisse.

Battlestar Galactica 1/2 **1978 (PG)** Plot episode of the sci-fi TV series which was later released in the theatres. The crew of the spaceship Galactica must battle their robot enemies in an attempt to reach Earth. Contains special effects designed by John "Star Wars" Dykstra. Individual episodes are also available. **125m/C; VHS, DVD, Blu-Ray.** Lorne Greene; Dirk Benedict; Maren Jensen; Jane Seymour; Patrick Macnee; Terry Carter; John Colicos; Richard A. Colla; Laurette Spang; Richard Hatch; *D:* Richard A. Colla; *W:* Richard A. Colla; Glen Larson; *C:* Ben Colman; *M:* Stu Phillips. **TV**

Battlestar Galactica: The Plan **2009** The human-Cylon war, as seen through the eyes of the machines, opens with their destruction of Caprica. It then wanders off to show backstory on too many of the series's pivotal events in order to try and tie up some loose ends. A fans-only watch. **112m/C; DVD, Blu-Ray.** Edward James Olmos; Tricia Helfer; Dean Stockwell; Grace Park; Michael Hogan; Michael Trucco; Callum Keith Rennie; Kate Vernon; *D:* Edward James Olmos; *W:* Jane Espenson; *C:* Stephen McNutt; *M:* Bear McCreary. **VIDEO**

Battling Butler 1/2 **1926** Rich young Keaton tries to impress a young lady by impersonating a boxer. All goes well until he has to fight the real thing. Mostly charming if uneven; one of Keaton's more unusual efforts, thought to be somewhat autobiographical. Silent. **70m/B; Silent; VHS, DVD, Blu-Ray.** Buster Keaton; Sally O'Neil; Snitz Edwards; Francis McDonald; Mary O'Brien; Tom Wilson; Walter James; *D:* Buster Keaton; *W:* Al Boasberg; Lex Neal; Charles Henry Smith; Paul Girard Smith; *C:* Bert Haines; Devereaux Jennings.

Battling for Baby **1992** It's the war of the Grandmas. New mother Katherine decides to return to work and both her mother and mother-in-law want to look after the little tyke. Silly made-for-TV fluff. **93m/C; VHS, DVD.** Courteney Cox; Suzanne Pleshette; Debbie Reynolds; John Terlesky; Doug McClure; Leigh Lawson; Mary Jo Catlett; *D:* Art Wolff; *W:* Walter Lockwood; Nancy Silvers.

Battling with Buffalo Bill **1931** Twelve episodes of the vintage serial concerning the exploits of the legendary Indian fighter. **180m/B; VHS, DVD.** Tom Tyler; Rex Bell; Franklyn Farnum; Lucille Browne; Francis Ford; William Desmond; Jim Thorpe; Yakima Canutt; Chief Thunderbird; Bud Osborne; *D:* Ray Taylor; *W:* Ella O'Neill; George Plympton.

Baxter 1/2 **1989** A bull terrier lives his life with three different sets of masters. He examines all of humankind's worst faults and the viewer quickly realizes that Baxter's life depends on his refusal to obey like a good dog should. Based on the novel by Ken Greenhall. Funny, sometimes erotic, quirky comedy. In French with English subtitles. **82m/C; VHS, DVD.** *FR* Lisa (Lise) Delamare; Jean Mercure; Jacques Spiesser; Catherine Ferran; Jean-Paul Roussillon; Sabrina Leurquin; *D:* Jerome Boivin; *W:* Jerome Boivin; Jacques Audiard; *C:* Yves Angelo; *M:* Marc Hillman; Patrick Roffe.

The Baxter **2005 (PG-13)** Elliot Sherman (Showalter) is so CPA mega-nerd even his sweet grandmother knows he's "the Baxter," the also-ran, the nice, safe, dull guy who never gets the girl. In the opening scene he's dumped at the altar by his beautiful fiancee Caroline (Banks) when her high school flame Bradley (Theroux) reappears. You might want to feel something for Elliot, but he's so unlikable that sympathy will be hard to find. Soon it becomes apparent that Elliot's office temp Cecil (Williams), who has been right there under his nose, is the perfect woman for him. **91m/C; DVD.** Michael Showalter; Elizabeth Banks; Michelle Williams; Justin Theroux; Zak Orth; Michael Ian Black; Catherine Lloyd Burns; Peter Dinklage; Paul Rudd; *D:* Michael Showalter; *W:* Michael Showalter; *M:* Theodore Shapiro; Craig Wedren.

The Bay 1/2 **2012 (R)** A la "Blair Witch Project" and "Cloverfield's" found-footage style, this horror/mockumentary pits a sleepy, fictional town in Maryland's Chesapeake Bay against some bacterial enemy that's infected the water. Over the course of 24 hours, townspeople flock to the local ER with rashes, boils, and other gross symptoms. People are dying from a flesh-eating bacteria, and the living are panicking. The town is shut down, but the government is covering something up. The story unfolds through pieced-together clips from budding journalist, Donna (Donohue)--only it's three years later that the truth of this eco-disaster is unveiled. **84m/C; DVD.** Kristen Connolly; Kether Donohue; Christopher Denham; Stephen Kunken; Frank Deal; Nansi Aluka; *D:* Barry Levinson; *W:* Michael Wallach; *C:* Josh Nussbaum; *M:* Marcelo Zarvos.

The Baytown Outlaws **2012 (R)** Violent, cartoonish action filled with stereotypes. The dumber-than-dirt, redneck Alabama Oodie brothers are hired by Celeste to retrieve her wheelchair-bound godson Rob, who's been kidnapped by her sleazy criminal ex-husband Carlos, who wants the teen's trust fund. Getting Rob out of Carlos' Texas compound means going up against a series of violent (and weird) killers. **98m/C; DVD, Blu-Ray.** Clayne Crawford; Daniel Cudmore; Travis Fimmel; Andre Braugher; Eva Longoria; Billy Bob Thornton; Thomas Brodie-Sangster; Paul Wesley; *D:* Barry Battles; *W:* Barry Battles; Griffin Hood; *C:* Dave McFarland; *M:* Kostas Christides; Christopher Young. **VIDEO**

Baywatch 1/2 **2017 (R)** Comedy reboots of earnest, if silly, old TV shows, are all the rage. This one mostly follows that plan. It has the self-aware, "hey, we know this is ridiculous" wink of many of the recent offerings in the genre (21 Jump Street, CHiPs), and it amps up the original's jiggle and suggestive dialogue to R-rated lengths. Johnson and Efron seem to be having a blast as lifeguards who stumble upon a drug and murder plot that, unfortunately, sucks a lot of the fun out of the last act. It shoots for an outsized version of the original's escapism and campy fun, and mostly succeeds in that. For best results, turn off your brain, and wait an hour after eating. **116m/C; DVD, Blu-Ray.** Dwayne "The Rock" Johnson; Zac Efron; Priyanka Chopra; Alexandra Daddario; Kelly Rohrbach; *D:* Seth Gordon; *W:* Damian Shannon; Mark Swift; *C:* Eric Steelberg; *M:* Christopher Lennertz.

Be Cool **2005 (PG-13)** Paging Dr. Tarantino STAT! This turgid sequel to "Get Shorty" proves that Travolta is in need of another new-career-ectomy. Jettisoning anything even mildly cool about the witty original, director Gray instead focuses on bombast and pointless cameos in the continuing adventures of Hollywood shylock Chili Palmer (Travolta). This time, Chili tries to break into the music business with the help of a widowed record producer (Thurman) and a young ingenue (Milian). Standing in their way are Russian mobsters, gangsta rap kingpins, and Vince Vaughn doing the tired white-guy-who-thinks-he's-black routine. Even The Rock as a flamboyantly gay bodyguard can't inject any life into such a flat, unfunny mess. **112m/C; VHS, DVD, Blu-Ray, UMD.** John Travolta; Uma Thurman; Vince Vaughn; Cedric the Entertainer; Andre Benjamin; Robert Pastorelli; Christina Milian; Paul Adelstein; Debi Mazar; Gregory Alan Williams; Harvey Keitel; Dwayne "The Rock" Johnson; Danny DeVito; James Woods; *D:* F. Gary Gray; *W:* Peter Steinfeld; *C:* Jeffrey L. Kimball; *M:* John Powell.

Be Kind Rewind 1/2 **2008 (PG-13)** Simple guy Jerry (Black) lives in a trailer, works at a junkyard, and likes to hang out at Mr. Fletcher's (Glover) titular video rental store, where his buddy Mike (Def) works. After a mishap at a local power plant magnetizes Jerry, accidentally erases all of the videotapes (the store is VHS only), so Jerry and Mike enlist the talents of the very cute Alma (Diaz) from the nearby dry cleaner to help them re-enact and re-record all of the movies for rental as usual. The oddball store regulars get wise to their shenanigans and everyone wants to play a part, which makes Jerry, Mike and the video store unlikely celebrities. Black is Black and the whole thing is often silly and obvious, but entertaining nonetheless. **100m/C; DVD, Blu-Ray.** Jack Black; Mos Def; Danny Glover; Mia Farrow; Melonie Diaz; Arjay Smith; Sigourney Weaver; Chandler Parker; Irv Gooch; *D:* Michel Gondry; *W:* Michel Gondry; *C:* Ellen Kuras; *M:* Jean-Michel Bernard.

Be My Valentine **2013** A typical Hallmark Channel rom com. Young Tyler Farrell looks for advice from his widowed dad, Dan, when he gets his first crush on a girl at school. But it's been a long time since romance was part of the firefighter's life--at least until he and his crew respond to a call at Kate's flower shop. Dan falls for the florist and he and Kate seem to share some mutual feelings until her ex-boyfriend comes back into town. **90m/C; DVD.** William Baldwin; Natalie Brown; Christian Martyn; James Thomas; *D:* Graeme Campbell; *W:* David Titcher; *C:* Peter Benison; *M:* Trevor Yuile. **CABLE**

Be Yourself 1/2 **1930** Thin plot contrived for Ziegfeld Follies star Brice, who stars as nightclub entertainer Fanny Field. Fanny falls for a down-and-out-boxer (Armstrong) trying to make a comeback. Brice, who was married to impresario Billy Rose at the time, sings several songs co-written by Rose, including "Cookin' Breakfast for the One I Love." **65m/B; VHS, DVD.** Fanny Brice; Robert Armstrong; Harry Green; Gertrude Astor; G. Pat Collins; Marjorie "Babe" Kane; *D:* Thornton Freeland; *W:* Thornton Freeland; *C:* Karl Struss; Robert Planck.

The Beach **2000 (R)** DiCaprio's follow-up to the blockbuster "Titantic" is an uneven adaptation of the novel by Alex Garland concerning a group of hedonists trying to find paradise and destroying their ideal in the process. Cynical young journalist Richard (DiCaprio) meets the manic Daffy (Carlyle) in a Bangkok dive and is given a map to a supposedly unspoiled island off the Thai coast. Impulsively, Richard asks French acquaintances Francoise (Ledoyen) and Etienne (Canet) to accompany him and they discover an odd settlement of Euro-trash, headed by Sal (Swinton), amidst a marijuana plantation guarded by gun-wielding thugs. Paradise turns out to be less than paradisical. **120m/C; VHS, DVD.** Leonardo DiCaprio; Tilda Swinton; Virginie Ledoyen; Guillaume Canet; Robert Carlyle; Paterson Joseph; Peter Youngblood Hills; Jerry Swindall; ***D:*** Danny Boyle; ***W:*** John Hodge; ***C:*** Darius Khondji; ***M:*** Angelo Badalamenti.

Beach Babes 2: Cave Girl Island **1995** The babes crash land on a prehistoric planet populated by horny cavemen. **78m/C; VHS, DVD.** Sara Bellomo; Stephanie Hudson; Rodrigo Botero; ***D:*** David DeCoteau. **VIDEO**

Beach Blanket Bingo **1965** Fifth entry in the "Beach Party" series (after "Pajama Party") is by far the best and has achieved near-cult status. Both Funicello and Avalon are back, but this time a very young Evans catches Avalon's eye. Throw in a mermaid, some moon-doggies, skydiving, sizzling beach parties, and plenty of nostalgic golly-gee-whiz fun and you have the classic '60s beach movie. Totally implausible, but that's half the fun when the sun-worshipping teens become involved in a kidnapping and occasionally break into song. Followed by "How to Stuff a Wild Bikini." **96m/C; VHS, DVD, Blu-Ray.** Frankie Avalon; Annette Funicello; Linda Evans; Don Rickles; Buster Keaton; Paul Lynde; Harvey Lembeck; Deborah Walley; John Ashley; Jody McCrea; Marta Kristen; Timothy Carey; Earl Wilson; Bobbi Shaw; Brian Wilson; ***D:*** William Asher; ***W:*** William Asher; Sher Townsend; Leo Townsend; ***C:*** Floyd Crosby; ***M:*** Les Baxter.

The Beach Bum **2019 (R)** Moondog (McConaghey) is a somewhat famous poet and local colorful personality in Key West. Often high, he doesn't seem to care much about anything but does show love for those in his life. He is married to wealthy Minnie (Fisher), who is also involved with rapper Lingerie (Snoop Dogg). When Moondog and Minnie's daughter Heather (LaVie Owen) gets married, Moondog begins a life journey that forces him to confront hard truths about himself and those around him. Visually appealing with a strong soundtrack that pairs nicely with the flick, McConaghey successfully brings balance to the often abrasive Moondog. **95m/C; DVD, Blu-Ray.** Matthew McConaughey; Snoop Dogg; Isla Fisher; Stefania LaVie Owen; Zac Efron; ***D:*** Harmony Korine; ***W:*** Harmony Korine; ***C:*** Benoit Debie; ***M:*** John Debney.

Beach Girls **1982 (R)** Three voluptuous coeds intend to re-educate a bookish young man and the owner of a beach house. **91m/C; VHS, DVD, Blu-Ray.** Debra Blee; Val Kline; Jeana Tomasina; Adam Roarke; Paul Richards; ***D:*** Patrice Townsend; ***C:*** Michael D. Murphy.

The Beach Girls and the Monster *Monster in the Surf; Monster from the Surf* **1965** Here's one on the cutting edge of genre bending: while it meticulously maintains the philosophical depth and production values of '60s beach bimbo fare, it manages to graft successfuly with the heinous critter from the sea genre to produce a hybrid horror with acres o' flesh. **70m/B; VHS, DVD.** Jon Hall; Sue Casey; Walker Edmiston; Arnold Lessing; Elaine DuPont; Dale Davis; ***D:*** Jon Hall; ***W:*** Joan Gardner; ***C:*** Dale Davis; ***M:*** Frank Sinatra, Jr.

Beach Kings 1/2 *Green Flash* **2008 (PG-13)** Thirty-year-old Cameron Day (Charvet) is a former college basketball star who couldn't stand the pressure of trying to make a pro career. A chance meeting with Mia (DeVitto) has Cam returning to sports as a pro beach volleyball player but as the pressures build again so do his own insecurities. **95m/C; DVD.** David Charvet; Torrey DeVitto; Brody Hutzler; Kristin Cavallari; Court Young; Jaleel White; Bret Roberts; ***D:*** Paul Nihipali; ***W:*** Paul Nihipali; ***C:*** David Waldman; ***M:*** Craig Eastman. **VIDEO**

Beach Party **1963** Started the "Beach Party" series with the classic Funicello/Avalon combo. Scientist Cummings studying the mating habits of teenagers intrudes on a group of surfers, beach bums, and bikers, to his lasting regret. Typical beach party bingo, with sand, swimsuits, singing, dancing, and bare minimum in way of a plot. Followed by "Muscle Beach Party." **101m/C; VHS, DVD.** Frankie Avalon; Annette Funicello; Harvey Lembeck; Robert Cummings; Dorothy Malone; Morey Amsterdam; Jody McCrea; John Ashley; Candy Johnson; Dolores Wells; Yvette Vickers; Eva Six; Brian Wilson; Vincent Price; Peter Falk; Dick Dale; ***D:*** William Asher; ***W:*** Lou Rusoff; ***C:*** Kay Norton; ***M:*** Les Baxter.

Beach Patrol **1979** Lightweight ABC TV movie has pretty cop Jan Plummer transferring from the narcotics division to an L.A. police team that patrols the beaches in dune buggies. All because a drug lord has a hit out on her. Naturally, it's at her new job that Jan spots the fugitive bad guy. **75m/C; DVD.** Christine De Lisle; Jonathan Frakes; Paul Burke; Rick Hill; Michael Gregory; ***D:*** Bob Kelljan; ***W:*** Rick Edelstein; ***C:*** Archie Dalzell; ***M:*** Barry DeVorzon. **TV**

Beach Rats 1/2 **2017 (R)** A dark, character study of a Brooklyn teenager grappling with his sexuality while maintaining a façade of coolness with his gang of delinquent, macho pals. By day, Frankie (Dickinson) plays handball, gets high, and dates a young lady; by night, he cruises (weirdly outdated) gay websites for older men. Dickinson is star material, and not just for his killer bod -- his sensitive yet steely portrayal of an adolescent in the throes of self-discovery is spot-on. **98m/C; DVD, Blu-Ray.** Harris Dickinson; Madeline Weinstein; Kate Hodge; Neal Huff; Nicole Flyus; ***D:*** Eliza Hittman; ***W:*** Eliza Hittman; ***C:*** Helene Louvart; ***M:*** Nicholas Leone.

Beach Red **1967** American Marines storm an unnamed Pacific island held by the Japanese in WWII in this anti-war film. Unlike many war films from the '60s, it is somewhat gory (in other words they tried to be realistic with the combat scenes). It is also unusual in that it tells the story of each of the characters in flashback, including the Japanese soldiers, preventing them from being demonized. To increase the realism, all the actors wore full 40 pound gear during all scenes, and the director enlisted the help of the U.S. armed forces to create the film. **114m/C; DVD.** Cornel Wilde; Rip Torn; Burr DeBenning; Patrick Wolfe; Jean Wallace; Jaime Sanchez; Dale Ishimoto; Genki Koyama; Gene Blakely; Michael Parsons; Norman Pak; Dewey Stringer; Fred Galang; Hiroshi Kiyama; ***D:*** Cornel Wilde; ***W:*** Cornel Wilde; Peter Bowman; Clint Johnston; Don Peters; ***C:*** Cecil R. Cooney; ***M:*** Ismail Darbar.

Beachcomber *Vessel of Wrath* **1938** Comedy set in the Dutch East Indies about a shiftless beachcomber (Laughton) who falls in love with a missionary's prim sister (Lanchester), as she attempts to reform him. The real-life couple of Laughton and Lanchester are their usual pleasure to watch. Remade in 1954. Story by W. Somerset Maugham. **88m/B; VHS, DVD.** *GB* Charles Laughton; Elsa Lanchester; Robert Newton; Tyrone Guthrie; ***D:*** Erich Pommer.

Beaches 1/2 **1988 (PG-13)** Based on the novel by Iris Rainer Dart about two girls whose friendship survived the test of time. The friendship is renewed once more when one of the now middle-aged women learns that she is dying slowly of a fatal disease. **123m/C; VHS, DVD, Blu-Ray; Open Captioned.** Bette Midler; Barbara Hershey; John Heard; Spalding Gray; Lainie Kazan; James Read; Mayim Bialik; ***D:*** Garry Marshall; ***W:*** Mary Agnes Donoghue; ***C:*** Dante Spinotti; ***M:*** Georges Delerue.

The Beaches of Agnes 1/2 *Les plages d'Agnes* **2008** A documentary self-portrait by acclaimed French director Agnes Varda, who created such films as "The Gleaners and I" and "Cleo from 5 to 7." The filmmaker offers her reflections on her life, art, movies, and memories, as well as broader cultural forces like the feminist movement, the Black Panthers, and French New Wave Cinema. Additionally, Varda offers insights into the films of her husband, Jacques Demy, who directed "The Umbrellas of Cherbourg." French with subtitles. **110m/C; DVD.** Agnes Varda; ***D:*** Agnes Varda; ***W:*** Agnes Varda; ***C:*** Agnes Varda; Julia Fabry; Helene Louvart; Arlene Nelson; Alain Sakot; ***M:*** Joanna Bruzdowicz; Stephane Vilar.

Beaks: The Movie WOOF! *Birds of Prey* **1987 (R)** Two TV reporters try to figure out why birds of prey are suddenly attacking humans. Owes nothing to Hitchcock's "The Birds." **86m/C; VHS, DVD.** Christopher Atkins; Michelle Johnson; ***D:*** Rene Cardona, Jr.

Bean **1997 (PG-13)** Big screen adaptation of rubber-faced Atkinson's Mr. Bean character finds disaster-magnet hero working as a guard in London's National Gallery. When a famous painting is purchased by a museum in L.A., the Gallery's curators jump at the chance to send Bean along with the painting as an "expert," although he is nearly mute and definitely not qualified. David (MacNicol), the American curator, invites him to stay at his house, much to the dismay of his wife and children. Bean, of course, wrecks the painting, ruins David's marriage and career, and generally makes an ass out of himself. He then resourcefully (and sometimes accidentally) puts things right. Atkinson proves himself a master of the almost lost art of slapstick comedy. **92m/C; VHS, DVD, Blu-Ray.** *GB* Rowan Atkinson; Peter MacNichol; Pamela Reed; Harris Yulin; Burt Reynolds; Larry Drake; Johnny Galecki; Richard Gant; Tom McGowan; Dakin Matthews; Peter Capaldi; Sandra Oh; Tricia Vessey; Peter Egan; ***D:*** Mel Smith; ***W:*** Richard Curtis; Robin Driscoll; ***C:*** Francis Kenny; ***M:*** Howard Goodall.

Beanpole *Dylda* **2020** In post-World War II Leningrad, Masha (Perelygina) longs to find personal happiness while working as a hospital nurse. During the war, she served in the Russian army and suffers from post-traumatic stress disorder. Her friend and fellow veteran/nurse Iya (Miroshnickenko) also struggles with post-concussion syndrome and related paralysis. Masha's need for a child compels her to blackmail Iya to have sex with doctor Nikolay (Bykov) and give birth to son Pashka (Glazkov). Inspired by the stories of real Soviet war veterans, filmmaker Balagov's colorful debut film is a moving character study that touchingly portrays the depths of Masha and Iya's damaged psyches. **130m/C; DVD.** Viktoria Miroshnichenko; Vasilisa Perelygina; Andrey Bykov; Igor Shirokov; Konstantin Balakirev; ***D:*** Kantemir Balagov; ***W:*** Kantemir Balagov; Aleksandr Terekhov; ***C:*** Kseniya Sereda; ***M:*** Evgueni Galperine.

The Bear *L'Ours* **1989 (PG)** Breathtaking, effortlessly entertaining family film (from France) about an orphaned bear cub tagging after a grown Kodiak male and dealing with hunters. The narrative is essentially from the cub's point of view, with very little dialogue. A huge money-maker in Europe; shot on location in the Dolomites and the Candian Arctic. Based on the 1917 novel "The Grizzly King" by James Oliver Curwood. **92m/C; VHS, DVD.** *FR* Jack Wallace; Tcheky Karyo; Andre Lacombe; ***D:*** Jean-Jacques Annaud; ***W:*** Gerard Brach; Michael Kane; ***C:*** Philippe Rousselot; ***M:*** Bill Conti.

BearCity 1/2 **2010** Rom-com featuring a group of large, hairy, gay men supporting a younger friend who comes out about his love for older, hairy men who don't fit the usual ultra-toned and fit stereotype. **99m/C; DVD, Blu-Ray, Streaming.** Joe Conti; Brian Keane; Gerald McCullouch; Stephen Guarino; ***D:*** Douglas Langway; ***W:*** Douglas Langway; Lawrence Ferber; ***C:*** Michael Hauer; ***M:*** Kerry Muzzey.

Bears 1/2 **2014 (G)** Disney's Disneynature documentaries are experts at making wild animals humanlike, while making the kids inside all of us believe that ocean creatures and African cats all have cute names, funny quirks, and convenient three-act journeys. Co-directors Fothergill and Scholey turn their, admittedly, gorgeously cinematic gaze towards a family of bears this time, affectionately named Sky, Scout, and Amber. Their footage of the bears' trek across Alaska is jaw-droppingly beautiful and Reilly is a fine, friendly narrator, but the documentary could've benefitted from more actual wildlife information and less manufactured family drama. **78m/C; DVD, Blu-Ray.** ***Nar:*** John C. Reilly; ***D:*** Alastair Fothergill; Keith Scholey; ***M:*** George Fenton.

The Bears & I **1974 (G)** A young Vietnam vet helps Indians regain their land rights while raising three bear cubs. Beautiful photography in this Disney production. **89m/C; VHS, DVD.** Patrick Wayne; Chief Dan George; Andrew Duggan; Michael Ansara; ***D:*** Bernard McEveety; ***W:*** Jack Speirs; John Whedon; ***C:*** Ted D. Landon; ***M:*** Buddy (Norman Dale) Baker.

The Beast 1/2 *La Bete* **1975** Long considered taboo due to its erotic subject matter, this 1975 French film from director Borowczyk arrives in its uncensored form for the first time in 2000. Young heiress Lucy Broadhurst (Hummel) arrives at the de l'Esperance chateau, where she is to marry the young Mathurn de l'Esperance (Benedetti). After retiring to her room, Lucy finds herself dreaming of the 18th-century lady of the chateau, Romilda de l'Esperance (Lane), who according to legend, encountered a wild, sexual monster in the forest near the manor. Was this an isolated incident or does the Beast still roam the grounds? The once shocking sex scenes will be considered quite tame by today's audience, and some of them come across as quite silly. **94m/C; DVD.** Sirpa Lane; Lisbeth Hummel; Elizabeth Kaza; Pierre Benedetti; Guy Trejan; ***D:*** Walerian Borowczyk; ***W:*** Walerian Borowczyk; ***C:*** Bernard Daillencourt; Marcel Grignon.

The Beast 1/2 *The Beast of War* **1988 (R)** Violent and cliche-driven war drama notable for its novel twist: wild Russian tank officer becomes lost in the Afghanistan wilderness while being tracked by Afghan rebels with revenge in mind. Filmed in the Israel desert and adapted by William Mastrosimone from his play. **93m/C; VHS, DVD.** George Dzundza; Jason Patric; Steven Bauer; Stephen Baldwin; Don Harvey; Kabir Bedi; Erik Avari; Haim Gerafi; ***D:*** Kevin Reynolds; ***W:*** William Mastrosimone; ***C:*** Doug Milsome; ***M:*** Mark Isham.

The Beast *Peter Benchley's The Beast* **1996 (PG-13)** Benchley once again terrorizes a small coastal community with a giant sea creature that preys on sailors and divers. When a poacher's attempts to capture the creature result in further disaster, a fishing boat captain, a Coast Guard officer, and a marine biologist set sail to to kill the critter. **116m/C; VHS, DVD, Blu-Ray.** William L. Petersen; Karen Sillas; Charles Martin Smith; Ronald Guttman; Missy (Melissa) Crider; Sterling Macer; Denis Arndt; Larry Drake; ***D:*** Jeff Bleckner; ***W:*** J.B. White; ***C:*** Geoff Burton; ***M:*** Don Davis. **TV**

Beast **2017 (R)** Living with her parents on the island of Jersey, Moll (Buckley) is a young woman whose sadness and difficult family is on display at her birthday party. She helps care for her father as he descends into dementia, and her controlling mother limits her life. After Moll's sister announces she is pregnant at the party, Moll runs away to a bar, dances the night away, and is saved from a predatory man by charismatic Pascal (Flynn). Pascal gives Moll a new lease on life, though he challenges social norms. An interesting first feature from director Pearce, it features a break-out debut from Buckley. **107m/C; DVD, Blu-Ray.** Jessie Buckley; Johnny Flynn; Geraldine James; Hattie Gotobed; Charley Palmer Rothwell; ***D:*** Michael Pearce; ***W:*** Michael Pearce; ***C:*** Benjamin Kracun; ***M:*** Jim Williams.

Beast Cops *Yeshou Xingjing* **1998** Until the last quarter of the film, director Chan's "Beast Cops" is more of a buddy/buddy cop click than a shoot 'em up. But don't worry, once it passes that point, the cops live up to their titular name and deliver a brutal slaughter worthy of the finest and/or vilest of Hong Kong action films. The near-romantic build up makes the climax seem even all the more violent. Wong is excellent as the cop who loves the whoring and gambling that he uses to stay in touch with his mob contacts. **108m/C; DVD.** *CH* Anthony Wong; Michael Wong; Roy Cheung; ***D:*** Gordon Chan; ***W:*** Gordon Chan; Chan Hing-Kai.

The Beast from 20,000 Fathoms 1/2 **1953** Atomic testing defrosts a giant dinosaur in the Arctic; the hungry monster proceeds onwards to its former breeding grounds, now New York City. Oft-imitated saurian-on-the-loose formula is still fun, brought to life by Ray Harryhausen special effects. Based loosely on the Ray Bradbury story "The Foghorn." **80m/B; VHS, DVD, Blu-Ray.** Paul (Christian) Hubschmid; Paula Raymond; Cecil Kellaway; Kenneth Tobey; Donald Woods; Lee Van Cleef; Steve Brodie; Mary Hill; Jack Pennick; Ross Elliot; ***D:*** Eugene Lourie; ***W:*** Eugene Lourie; Fred Freiberger; Louis Morheim; Robert Smith; ***C:*** John L. "Jack" Russell; ***M:*** David Buttolph.

The Beast in Space *La Bestia nello spazio* **1980** Pointless reimagining of Walerian Borowyczyk's film "La Bete" set in space. The crew of a ship looking for rare elements is seduced by the computer of a faraway world. It convinces them all to get naked and party, not noticing the homicidal robot running around killing the natives. **92m/C; DVD.** *IT* Sirpa Lane; Vassili Karis; Umberto Ceriani; Maria D'Alessandro; Marina Hedman; ***D:*** Alfonso Brescia; ***W:*** Alfonso Brescia; Aldo Crudo; ***C:*** Silvio Fraschetti; ***M:*** Marcello Giombini. **VIDEO**

Beast in the Cellar 1/2 *Are You Dying Young Man?* **1970 (R)** Every family has something to hide, and in the case of two spinster sisters, it's their murderous inhuman brother, whom they keep chained in the cellar. Like all brothers, however, the "beast" rebels against his sisters' bossiness and escapes to terrorize their peaceful English countryside. The sisters' (Reid and Robson) performances aren't bad, but rest of effort is fairly disappointing. **85m/C; VHS, DVD, Blu-Ray.** *GB* Beryl Reid; Flora Robson; T.P. McKenna; ***D:*** James Kelly.

The Beast Must Die *Black Werewolf* **1975 (PG)** A millionaire sportsman invites a group of men and women connected with bizarre deaths or the eating of human flesh to spend the cycle of a full moon at his isolated lodge. **93m/C; VHS, DVD, Blu-Ray.** *GB* Peter Cushing; Calvin Lockhart; Charles Gray; Anton Diffring; Marlene Clark; Ciaran Madden; Tom Chadbon; Michael Gambon; ***D:*** Paul Annett; ***W:*** Michael Winder; ***C:*** Jack Hildyard; ***M:*** Douglas Gamley.

The Beast of Babylon Against the Son of Hercules *Goliath, King of the Slaves; Hero of Babylon; L'Eroe di Babilonia* **1963** Nippur (Gordon) probably doesn't have any filial bond to Hercules but it's a convenient hook for this dubbed Italian flick. Tyrant Balthazar (Lulli) rules Assyria, sacrificing virgins to the goddess Istar. Nippur, the rightful heir to the throne, leads a slave revolt to overthrow the bloodthirsty ruler. **98m/C; DVD.** *IT* Gordon Scott; Genevieve Grad; Pierro Lulli; Andrea Scotti; Moira Orfei; Mario Petri; ***D:*** Siro Marcellini; ***W:*** Siro Marcellini; Gian Paolo Callegari; Albert Valentin; ***C:*** Pier Ludovico Pavoni; ***M:*** Carlo Franci.

Beast of Blood 1/2 *Beast of the Dead; Horrors of Blood Island; Return to the Horrors of Blood Island* **1971** In this sequel to "Mad Doctor of Blood Island," an insane scientist finally captures the chlorophyll zombie, beheads him, and keeps the head alive to insult it daily. As opposed to the not-insane people who burn monsters so they can't somehow gain revenge (hint, hint). **90m/C; DVD.** *PH US* John Ashley; Eddie Garcia; Alfonso Carvajal; Bruno Punzalan; Celeste Yarnall; Liza Belmonte; Justo Paulino; ***D:*** Eddie Romero; ***W:*** Eddie Romero; Beverly Miller; ***M:*** Tito Arevalo. **VIDEO**

Beast of Morocco *Hand of Night* **1966** Interesting vampire film about a Moroccan vampire princess who sets her sights on seducing a noted archaeologist. Of course his girlfriend ends up being abducted by the vampire's servant. **88m/C; VHS, DVD.** *GB* William Sylvester; Alizia Gur; Terence de Marney; Diane Clare; Edward Underdown; William Dexter; Sylvia Marriott; ***D:*** Frederick Goode; ***W:*** Bruce Stewart; ***C:*** William Jordan; ***M:*** John Shakespeare.

The Beast of the City **1932** Crime melodrama that ends in a violent machine-gun rubout, making you wonder just who the good guys are. Chicago police captain Jim Fitzpatrick (Huston) is obsessed with cleaning up the city but crime boss Belmonte (Hersholt) gets off because he has city and police officials on his payroll. When Jim becomes a hero foiling a bank robbery, public opinion demands he be appointed the new police commissioner and his first order is to get Belmonte by any means necessary. Harlow plays gun moll Daisy. **85m/B; DVD.** Walter Huston; Jean Harlow; Jean Hersholt; Wallace Ford; Dorothy Peterson; Tully Marshall; Emmett Corrigan; ***D:*** Charles Brabin; ***W:*** John Lee Mahin; ***C:*** Norbert Brodine.

Beast of the Yellow Night WOOF! **1970 (R)** A dying soldier sells his soul to Satan at the close of WWII. Years later, existing without aging, he periodically turns into a cannibal monster. Although the first half is tedious, the monster turns things around when he finally shows up. Decent gore effects. **87m/C; VHS, DVD, Blu-Ray.** *PH* John Ashley; Mary Wilcox; Eddie Garcia; Vic Diaz; ***D:*** Eddie Romero.

The Beast With a Million Eyes **1956** Silly and very cheap Roger Corman-produced sci fi. The desert-dwelling Kelly family finds a spaceship has landed with an alien that plans to dominate earthlings with mind control. **78m/B; DVD.** Paul Birch; Lorna Thayer; Dona Cole; Chester Conklin; Dick Sargent; Leonard Tarver; ***D:*** David Kramarsky; ***W:*** Tom Filer; ***C:*** Everett Baker; ***M:*** John Bickford.

The Beast with Five Fingers 1/2 **1946** After a pianist mysteriously dies and leaves his fortune to his private nurse, the occupants of his villa are terrorized by a creature that turns out to be the pianist's hand which was severed by his personal secretary (Lorre). Lorre is also terrorized by hallucinations of the hand, and no matter what he does to stop it (nail it to a desk, throw it in the fire, etc.), nothing can keep the hand from carrying out its mission. A creepy thriller with inventive shots of the severed hand. **88m/B; DVD, Streaming.** Robert Alda; Andrea King; Peter Lorre; Victor Francen; J. Carrol Naish; Charles Dingle; ***D:*** Robert Florey; ***W:*** Curt Siodmak; ***C:*** Wesley Anderson; ***M:*** Max Steiner.

The Beast Within **1982 (R)** Young woman has the misfortune of being raped by an unseen creature in a Mississippi swamp. Seventeen years later, her son conceived from that hellish union begins to act quite strange, developing a penchant for shedding his skin before turning into an insect-like critter with a cannibalistic appetite. First film to use the air "bladder" type of prosthetic make-up popularized in later, and generally better, horror films. Contains some choice cuts in photo editing: the juxtaposition of hamburger and human "dead meat" is witty. Based on Edward Levy's 1981 novel. **98m/C; VHS, DVD, Blu-Ray.** Ronny Cox; Bibi Besch; L.Q. Jones; Paul Clemens; Don Gordon; Katherine Moffat; John Dennis Johnston; R.G. Armstrong; Logan Ramsey; Ron Soble; Meshach Taylor; ***D:*** Philippe Mora; ***W:*** Tom Holland; ***C:*** Jack L. Richards; ***M:*** Les Baxter.

Beast Within *Virus Undead* **2008 (R)** Yet another zombie flick with a too-predictable plot (this time from Germany). Medical student Robert and his friends are whooping it up in his grandfather's country mansion when zombies (infected by diseased birds) come a-callin'. **93m/C; DVD.** *GE* Philipp Danne; Anna Breuer; Marvin Gronen; Birthe Wolter; Alex Attimoneilli; ***D:*** Wolf Wolff; ***W:*** Wolf Janke; ***C:*** Heiko Rahnenfuhrer.

Beastly 1/2 **2011 (PG-13)** Modern retelling of the "Beauty and the Beast" story based on the novel by Alex Finn and intended for tween girls (and maybe some older sisters). Wealthy, handsome Kyle (Pettyfer) has a mean streak, but he humiliates the wrong classmate when witchy Kendra (Olsen) uses a spell to transform Kyle into a (somewhat) repulsive character with weird tribal tattoos, scars, and piercings. Banished to Brooklyn seclusion, his curse can only be lifted if Kyle can find someone to love him as he is. So he makes a deal with wrong side of the tracks Linda Taylor (Hudgens) who moves in and becomes his companion. **86m/C; Blu-Ray, On Demand.** Alex Pettyfer; Vanessa Anne Hudgens; Mary-Kate Olsen; Peter Krause; Neil Patrick Harris; Dakota Johnson; ***D:*** Daniel Barnz; ***W:*** Daniel Barnz; ***C:*** Mandy Walker; ***M:*** Marcelo Zarvos.

Beastly Boyz *Beastly Boyz: A Twisted Tale of Revenge; David DeCouteau's Beastly Boyz* **2006 (R)** A young man worms his way into an all-gay male sports camp to avenge the death of his twin sister because her ghost just can't let it go. **75m/C; DVD, Streaming.** *CA US* Sebastian Gacki; Emrey Wright; Charlie Marsh; Andrew Butler; Dean Hrycan; Tyler Burrows; ***D:*** David DeCoteau; ***W:*** David DeCoteau; David Grove; ***C:*** Todd Turner; ***M:*** Joe Silva. **TV**

Beastmaster **1982 (PG)** Adventure set in a wild and primitive world. The Beastmaster is involved in a life-and-death struggle with overwhelming forces of evil. Campy neanderthal flesh flick. **119m/C; VHS, DVD.** Marc Singer; Tanya Roberts; Rip Torn; John Amos; Josh Milrad; Billy Jacoby; Ben Hammer; ***D:*** Don A. Coscarelli; ***W:*** Don A. Coscarelli; Paul Pepperman; ***C:*** John Alcott; ***M:*** Lee Holdridge.

The Beasts Are On the Streets 1/2 **1978** A Hanna-Barbera live-action NBC TV disaster pic that has the animals from a safari tourist park escaping after a careening truck tears off the fencing. Park rangers and cops try to recapture the beasts while some of the public decide to go big game hunting and vet Dr. McCauley tries to stop the man vs. beast panic. **98m/C; DVD.** Carol Lynley; Dale Robinette; Billy Green Bush; Philip Michael Thomas; Casey Biggs; ***D:*** Peter R. Hunt; ***W:*** Laurence Heath; ***C:*** Chuck Arnold; ***M:*** Gerald Fried. **TV**

The Beasts of Marseilles *Seven Thunders* **1957** In 1943, two Brits escape from a POW camp and hide out among the refugees in the French port city of Marseilles. They're bored waiting to find a ship to take them back to England and get into trouble, including finding Dr. Martout, a friendly local who turns out to be a serial killer. (His character is based on the mass murderer Dr. Marcel Petiot.) **100m/B; DVD.** *UK* Stephen Boyd; Tony Wright; James Robertson Justice; Anna Gaylor; Kathleen Harrison; Anton Diffring; ***D:*** Hugo Fregonese; ***W:*** John Baines; ***C:*** Wilkie Cooper; ***M:*** Antony Hopkins.

Beasts of No Nation 1/2 **2015** Cary Joji Fukunaga adapts Uzodinma Iweala's stunning novel about a young boy in an unnamed African country dealing with the unimaginable horror of war. Abraham Attah plays Agu, a young boy who watches his family and village get killed, as he flees to the nearby bush. After avoiding the rebels who destroyed his village, he comes upon the Native Defense Force, and is recruited into being a child soldier by the charismatic Commandant (Idris Elba). Attah and Elba are phenomenal, and Fukunaga's vision is uncompromising and more horrific than any horror film, because it's based on truth. **137m/C; DVD.** Idris Elba; Abraham Attah; Emmanuel Affadzi; Ama K. Abebrese; Kobina Amissah-Sam; ***D:*** Cary Fukunaga; ***W:*** Cary Fukunaga; ***C:*** Cary Fukunaga; ***M:*** Daniel Romer. Ind. Spirit '16: Actor (Attah), Actor--Supporting (Elba); Screen Actors Guild '15: Actor--Supporting (Elba).

Beasts of the Southern Wild **2012 (PG-13)** This multi-award winner at the 2012 Sundance Film Festival is a daring post-Katrina tale of people living off the grid in the deep south. Six-year-old Hushpuppy (Wallis) narrates and most of the film's dream-like nature comes from the fact that it's clearly a story seen through the eyes of a child. As her father's health struggles and their house and lives are in peril, she manages to stay hopeful. Director Zeitlin's debut is stunning as it blends youth-like wonder with the true horrors of the real world into something that feels poetic, original, and mesmerizing. **93m/C; DVD, Blu-Ray.** Quvenzhane Wallis; Dwight Henry; Jean Battiste; Lowell Landes; ***D:*** Benh Zeitlin; ***W:*** Benh Zeitlin; Lucy Alibar; ***C:*** Ben Richardson; ***M:*** Benh Zeitlin; Daniel Romer. Ind. Spirit '13: Cinematog.

Beat **2000** Disappointing look at the events leading up to William S. Burroughs's shooting of his wife in Mexico in 1951. Tangled hetero- and homosexual relationships and unrequited longings between future literarati Burroughs (Sutherland), his wife (Love), Allen Ginsberg (Livingston), Lucien Carr (Reedus), and Jack Kerouac (Martinez) should've provided more spark, but the indifferent direction and poor script give the actors little to work with. **89m/C; VHS, DVD.** Courtney Love; Kiefer Sutherland; Ron Livingston; Kyle Secor; Daniel Martinez; Sam Trammell; ***D:*** Gary Walkow; ***W:*** Gary Walkow; ***C:*** Ciro Cabello; ***M:*** Ernest Troost.

Beat Girl *Wild for Kicks* **1960** Pouty rebellious teen Jennifer (Hill) spends her days in art school and her nights at a London beat hangout. She's jealous when daddy (Farrar) marries sexy French Nichole (Adam) and plots to break them up. When Jennifer discovers Nichole's sordid past she winds up in a burlesque club, attracting the unsavory attentions of owner Kenny (Lee). Then Kenny winds up dead. Singer Adam Faith performs and Reed has a bit as a youthful tough. **85m/B; VHS, DVD.** *GB* Gillian Hills; David Farrar; Noelle Adam; Christopher Lee; Shirley Anne Field; Oliver Reed; Nada Beall; Adam Faith; Nigel Green; Claire Gordon; ***D:*** Edmond T. Greville; ***W:*** Dail Ambler; ***C:*** Walter Lassally; ***M:*** John Barry.

The Beat My Heart Skipped *De batter mon coeur s'est arrete* **2005** In adapting James Toback's 1978 "Fingers," French director Audiard changed the place (from New York to Paris), the pace (more somber and less high-strung), and the names—but the heart of the story stayed the same. Here Thomas Seyr (Duris, in Harvey Keitel's "Johnny Fingers" role) does his dad's dirty collections work in crooked real estate schemes though it repulses him. But when his long-discarded dreams of becoming a concert pianist re-emerge, the pull between his two lives proves more than he can bear. **107m/C; DVD.** *FR* Romain Duris; Niels Arestrup; Linh Dan Pham; Emmanuelle Devos; Jonathan Zaccai; Gilles Cohen; Anton Yakovlev; Melanie Laurent; ***D:*** Jacques Audiard; ***W:*** Jacques Audiard; Tonino Benaquista; ***C:*** Stephane Fontaine. British Acad. '05: Foreign Film.

Beat Street 1/2 **1984 (PG)** Intended as a quick cash-in on the break dancing trend, this essentially plotless musical features kids trying to break into local show biz with their rapping and dancing skills. Features the music of Afrika Bambaata and the Soul Sonic Force, Grand Master Melle Mel and the Furious Five, and others. **106m/C; VHS, DVD, Blu-Ray.** Rae Dawn Chong; Leon Grant; Saundra Santiago; Guy Davis; Jon Chardiet; Duane Jones; Kadeem Hardison; ***D:*** Stan Lathan; ***W:*** Andrew Davis.

Beat the Devil **1953** Each person on a slow boat to Africa has a scheme to beat the other passengers to the uranium-rich land that they all hope to claim. An unusual black comedy which didn't fare well when released, but over the years has come to be the epitome of spy-spoofs. **89m/C; VHS, DVD, Blu-Ray.** Humphrey Bogart; Gina Lollobrigida; Peter Lorre; Robert Morley; Jennifer Jones; Edward Underdown; Ivor Barnard; Bernard Lee; Marco Tulli; ***D:*** John Huston; ***W:*** John Huston; Truman Capote; ***C:*** Oswald Morris; ***M:*** Franco Mannino.

Beatdown **2010 (R)** An MMA fighter flees the city after his brother is murdered for not paying off a debt to a gangster. He becomes involved in illegal cage-fighting while trying to figure a way out of the mess. **90m/C; DVD, Blu-Ray.** Rudy Youngblood; Michael Bisping; Bobby Lashley; Kyle Woods; Mike Swick; Susie Abromeit; ***D:*** Mike Gunther; ***W:*** Mike Gunther; Bobby Mort; Sean Patrick O'Reilly; ***C:*** Joe Passarelli; ***M:*** Alan Derian. **VIDEO**

The Beatnicks **2000** Weird, frustrating drama. Would-be L.A. beat poet Nick Beat (Reedus) and his bandmate Nick Nero (Boone Jr.) find a mysterious electronic box washed up on the beach that sparks their music. While trying to get gigs, Beat falls for Nica (Bouchez), the wife of mobster/club owner Mack (Roberts), and Nero just kinda hangs out in a daze. **96m/C; DVD.** Norman Reedus; Patrick Bauchau; Mark Boone, Jr.; Elodie Bouchez; Eric Roberts; Lisa Marie; Jon(athan) Gries; ***D:*** Nicholson Williams; ***W:*** Nicholson Williams; ***C:*** Joseph Montgomery; ***M:*** Zander Schloss. **VIDEO**

The Beatniks **1960** Story about the dark secrets of the beat generation in which a man is promised fame and fortune by an agent, but his dreams are dashed when his friend commits murder. A big waste of time.

78m/B; VHS, DVD. Tony Travis; Peter Breck; Karen Kadler; Joyce Terry; Sam Edwards; Bob Wells; *D:* Paul Frees; *W:* Paul Frees; *C:* Murray Deatley; *M:* Stanley Wilson.

Beatrice Cenci 🦴 1/2 **1969** Italian historical horror, based on a true story, set in the 16th-century. Teenaged Beatrice is locked in the Cenci castle dungeon by her crazy nobleman father Francesco who also abuses her. Beatrice, her stepmother Lucrezia, obsessed servant Olimpo, and local bandit Catalano come up with a plan to kill him. However, the Vatican gets involved because they want the Cenci fortune. Italian with subtitles. **99m/C; DVD.** *IT* Adrienne Larussa; Tomas Milian; Georges Wilson; Mavie; Pedro Sanchez; Raymond Pellegrin; *D:* Lucio Fulci; *W:* Lucio Fulci; Roberto Gianviti; *C:* Erico Menczer; *M:* Angelo Francesco Lavagnino.

Beatriz at Dinner 🦴🦴 1/2 **2017 (R)** Beatriz (Hayek), a natural healer who immigrated from a poor town in Mexico, is a reluctant guest at her wealthy L.A. client's dinner party, where she butts heads with an arrogant, big-game-hunting industrialist (Lithgow). At times, the main characters are two-dimensional and the sanctimony is heavy-handed, but outstanding performances and a surprise ending provide enough meat to sink your teeth into. **82m/C; DVD, Blu-Ray.** Salma Hayek; John Lithgow; Connie Britton; Jay Duplass; Amy Landecker; Chloë Sevigny; *D:* Miguel Arteta; *W:* Mike White; *C:* Wyatt Garfield; *M:* Mark Mothersbaugh.

Beats, Rhymes and Life: The Travels of a Tribe Called Quest 🦴🦴🦴 **2011 (R)** Actor and A Tribe Called Quest mega-fan Rapaport's feature directorial debut joins the 2008 reunion tour of the troubled hip-hop legends who try to recapture the magic of the 1980s and '90s. Rapaport doesn't shy away from the drama that led up to their 1998 breakup primarily due to squabbling between leads Q-Tip and Phife Dawg. Credible and engaging for non-fans as well, includes interviews with the group and industry folks. **95m/C; Blu-Ray, On Demand.** Q-Tip; Ali Shaheed Muhammad; Adam "MCA" Yauch; Phife Dawg; Jarobi White; Mike D; *D:* Michael Rapaport; *C:* Robert Benavides.

Beau Brummel 🦴🦴 1/2 **1924** The famous silent adaptation of the Clyde Fitch play about an ambitious English dandy's rise and fall. **80m/B; Silent; VHS, DVD.** John Barrymore; Mary Astor; Willard Louis; Irene Rich; Carmel Myers; Alec B. Francis; William Humphreys; *D:* Harry Beaumont.

Beau Brummell 🦴🦴🦴 **1954** Lavish production casts Granger in the role of the rags-to-riches dandy and chief adviser to the Prince of Wales. Born into a life of poverty, George Bryan Brummel uses wit and intelligence to meet the vain Prince and ingratiate himself to the future king (George IV). He also manages to catch the eye of Taylor, who falls in love with him. Outstanding period piece cinematography, sets, and costumes. Shot on location in England's beautiful countryside, many of the interior shots are from a 15th-century mansion, Ockwell Manor, located near Windsor Castle. Remake of the 1924 silent film starring John Barrymore. Based on the play by Clyde Fitch. **113m/C; VHS, Blu-Ray, Streaming.** Stewart Granger; Elizabeth Taylor; Peter Ustinov; Robert Morley; James Donald; James Hayter; Rosemary Harris; Paul Rogers; Noel Willman; Peter Dyneley; Charles Carson; *D:* Curtis Bernhardt; *W:* Karl Tunberg; *C:* Oswald Morris.

Beau Brummell: This Charming Man 🦴🦴 1/2 **2006** Brummell (Purefoy) is a Regency dandy who changes the powders, perfumes, and foppery of male dress to one of elegance and expensive simplicity. He does a makeover on the Prince of Wales (Bonneville) and uses his royal connection to further his extravagant lifestyle. Then Beau meets the much more fascinating Lord Byron (Rhys), falls out of royal favor, and winds up in greatly-reduced circumstances. Based on Ian Kelly's biography. **79m/C; DVD.** *GB* James Purefoy; Hugh Bonneville; Matthew Rhys; Anthony Calf; Nicholas (Nick) Rowe; Philip Davis; Zoe Telford; *D:* Philippa Lowthorpe; *W:* Simon Bent; *C:* Graham Smith; *M:* Peter Salem. **TV**

Beau Geste 🦴🦴🦴 1/2 **1939** The classic Hollywood adventure film based on the Percival Christopher Wren novel. To protect aging Lady Patricia (Thatcher), who raised the orphaned brothers, Beau Geste (Cooper) takes the blame for a jewel theft and decides to enlist in the Foreign Legion. He's followed by his brothers John (Milland) and Digby (Preston), and all face desert wars and despicable officers, including the psychotic Sgt. Markoff (Donlevy). A rousing, much-copied epic. **114m/B; VHS, DVD, Blu-Ray.** Gary Cooper; Ray Milland; Robert Preston; Brian Donlevy; Donald O'Connor; J. Carrol Naish; Susan Hayward; James Stephenson; Albert Dekker; Broderick Crawford; Charles T. Barton; Heather Thatcher; James Burke; G.P. (Tim) Huntley, Jr.; Harold Huber; Harvey Stephens; Stanley Andrews; Harry Woods; Arthur Aylesworth; Henry (Kleinbach) Brandon; Nestor Paiva; George Chandler; George Regas; *D:* William A. Wellman; *W:* Robert Carson; *C:* Theodor Sparkuhl; Louis Clyde Stouman; Archie Stout; *M:* Alfred Newman.

Beau Ideal 🦴 1/2 **1931** A young American man joins the French Foreign Legion in hopes of finding his captured childhood friend and rescuing him. The third film in a trilogy (along with "Beau Geste" and "Beau Sabreur"), it was such a massive financial failure at the box office that a planned remake of "Beau Geste" in 1939 almost didn't happen because it was considered too risky. It's one of the first movies with sound, which is also a nice way of saying the acting would be considered stiff and awkward even by standards in the 1950s. **82m/B; DVD.** Ralph Forbes; Loretta Young; Irene Rich; Lester Vail; Frank McCormick; Otto Matieson; Don Alvarado; Bernard Siegel; Myrtle Stedman; Leni Stengel; *D:* Herbert Brenon; *W:* Percival Christopher Wren; Paul Schofield; Elizabeth Meehan; *C:* J. Roy Hunt; *M:* Max Steiner.

Beau Pere 🦴🦴🦴 *Stepfather* **1981** Bittersweet satiric romp from Blier about the war zone of modern romance, wherein 14-year-old Besse pursues her 30-year-old irresponsible, widowed stepfather (Dewaere). Sharp-edged and daring. In French with subtitles. **125m/C; VHS, DVD.** *FR* Patrick Dewaere; Nathalie Baye; Ariel Besse; Maurice Ronet; Genevieve Mnich; Maurice Risch; Macha Meril; Rose Thiery; *D:* Bertrand Blier; *W:* Bertrand Blier; *C:* Sacha Vierny; *M:* Philippe Sarde.

Beau Travail 🦴🦴 1/2 **1998** Very loose adaptation of Melville's "Billy Budd" is set in the French Foreign Legion at an outpost near Djibouti in Africa. Second-in-command Galoup (Lavant) tries to break popular new soldier Sentain (Colin) before he can become the Commandant's favorite. Visual style and attention to the male form take precedence over the story itself, which is mostly provided in Galoup's flashback narration. French with subtitles. **89m/C; VHS, DVD.** *FR* Denis Lavant; Michel Subor; Gregoire Colin; *D:* Claire Denis; *W:* Claire Denis; Jean-Pol Fargeau; *C:* Agnes Godard.

Beaufort 🦴🦴🦴 1/2 **2007** A fascinating, intense look at the strife in the Middle East through the eyes of soldiers who have lived their entire lives under the shadow of conflict. As the 18-year Israeli occupation of the medieval Lebanese castle Beaufort comes to an end, the soldiers pray to survive random Hezbollah bombing attacks while waiting out the days until withdrawal. As the bombings increase, commander Liberti (Cohen) and his troops must hold on to hope while trying to manage the tedium of holding a castle for largely symbolic purposes. Film avoids political commentary and instead explores the minds of soldiers on the ground, to excellent effect. **125m/C; DVD.** *IS* Oshri Cohen; Ohad Knoller; Eli Eltonyo; Gal Friedman; Nevo Kimchi; Daniel Brook; *D:* Joseph Cedar; *W:* Joseph Cedar; *C:* Ofer Inov; *M:* Ishai Adar.

Beaumarchais the Scoundrel 🦴🦴 1/2 *Beaumarchais L'Insolent* **1996** Adapted from an unpublished play by Sacha Guitry. Beautifully filmed romp of the social-climbing and political-spying gadfly Pierre Augustin Caron de Beaumarchais. Molinaro has simplified the fantastic life of the 18th-century dramatist, courtier, and watchmaker to Louis XV (and author of the comic masterpieces "The Barber of Seville" and "The Marriage of Figaro") but the result is still dizzying. French with subtitles. **100m/C; VHS, DVD.** *FR* Fabrice Luchini; Jacques Weber; Michel Piccoli; Claire Nebout; Jean-Francois Balmer; Florence Thomassin; Michel Serrault; Dominique Besnehard; Jean-Claude Brialy; Murray Head; Jeff Nuttal; Jean Yanne; Manuel Blanc; Sandrine Kiberlain; Axelle Laffont; *D:* Edouard Molinaro; *W:* Edouard Molinaro; Jean-Claude Brisville; *C:* Michael Epp; *M:* Jean-Claude Petit.

The Beautician and the Beast 🦴🦴 **1997 (PG)** Evita meets Lucille Ball when TV's "Nanny" enters Eastern Europe whining to conquer fictional "Slovetzia" royalty. Camp comedy casts Drescher as Joy, a beautician who becomes a local hero after a fire in her beauty class and is subsequently hired by a visiting emissary to tutor the children of despotic dictator Pochenko (Dalton). Overridingly well-known caricatures, loosely based on the fairy tale "Beauty and the Beast," as well as a host of old-time, culture clash movies ("The King and I," "Sound of Music"), where the humble nanny attempts to bring joy (get it?) into the life of a man who carries the weight of the world on his shoulders. Lensed in Prague inside a Gothic, 17th-century castle. Pleasant enough, if not original, time-killer. **105m/C; DVD.** Fran Drescher; Timothy Dalton; Ian McNeice; Patrick Malahide; Lisa Jakub; Michael Lerner; Phyllis Newman; *D:* Ken Kwapis; *W:* Todd Graff; *C:* Peter Lyons Collister; *M:* Cliff Eidelman.

Beauties of the Night 🦴🦴 *Night Beauties; Les Belles de Nuit* **1952** Dreamy fantasy finds a shy music teacher (Philipe) escaping from his boring life into romantic adventures with beautiful women. But his dreams slowly turn nightmarish and he's forced to deal with reality—and real love. French with subtitles. **89m/B; VHS, DVD, Streaming.** *FR* Gerard Philipe; Gina Lollobrigida; Martine Carol; Magali Vendeuil; Paolo Stoppa; Raymond Bussieres; Raymond Cordy; *D:* Rene Clair; *W:* Rene Clair; *C:* Armand Thirard; *M:* Georges Van Parys.

Beautiful 🦴 **2000 (PG-13)** Field's directorial debut is a cloying beauty pageant satire that wants you to like it. REALLY wants you to like it. Unfortunately, the jokes and characters are U-G-L-Y and they ain't got no alibi. Minnie Driver is Mona, a bright girl from an abusive home who escapes her grim reality by trying to win beauty pageants. She's shown as a little ugly duckling who uses any means necessary to win her way up the escalating ladder of swimsuitability. Finally, she qualifies for the Holy Grail of beauty pageants, the Miss American Miss competition. Along the way, however, she has become a single mother, which automatically disqualifies her as a contestant. She comes up with a plan where her daughter Vanessa (Pepsi prodigy and demon-child Hallie Kate Eisenberg) is passed off as the child of her patient best friend Ruby (Adams). Mona then screeches complaints about the kid's behavior being a distraction to her goal (which is no way to treat your child, even if she is Satan's hand-puppet) while an ambitious reporter (Stefanson) tries to reveal her secret. Overly padded, and it doesn't even have a nice personality. **112m/C; VHS, DVD.** Minnie Driver; Hallie Kate Eisenberg; Joey Lauren Adams; Kathleen Turner; Leslie Stefanson; Bridgette Wilson-Sampras; Kathleen Robertson; Michael McKean; Gary Collins; Brent Briscoe; *D:* Sally Field; *W:* Jon Bernstein; *C:* Robert Yeoman; *M:* John (Gianni) Frizzell.

Beautiful 🦴🦴 **2009 (R)** Shy 14-year-old photographer Daniel is persuaded by his beautiful, manipulative, 17-year-old neighbor Suzy to help her investigate the disappearance of three teenage girls in their middle-class Australian suburb of Sunshine Hills. Suzy is convinced that the reclusive widow who lives in Number 46 is involved but getting too close to the crimes could prove dangerous. **103m/C; DVD, Blu-Ray.** *AU* Anthony (Tony) Vorno; Tahyna Tozzi; Peta Wilson; Deborra-Lee Furness; Erick Thomson; Aaron Jeffery; Socratis Otto; Asher Keddie; *D:* Dean O'Flaherty; *W:* Dean O'Flaherty; *C:* Kent Smith; *M:* Paul Mac.

Beautiful Beast 🦴🦴 *XX: Utukushiki Gakuen; XX Beautiful Beast* **1995** Mysterious Chinese warrior woman known as Black Orchid arrives in Japan and rubs out mob boss Ishizuka. Fleeing the scene, she hides out with bartender Yoichi Fujinami, who becomes torn between helping his old pal Yaguchi and the mystery girl that he's falling in love with. Foregoes a lot of empty soft-core sex in favor of providing more action. Director Toshiharu Ikeda is no John Woo, but at least Black Orchid's trunk full of high-powered weaponry provides a little fun. **87m/C; DVD.** *JP* Kaori Shimamura; Takanori Kikuchi; Hakuryu; Minako Ogawa; *D:* Toshiharu Ikeda; *W:* Tamiya Takehashi; Hiroshi Takehashi; *C:* Seizo Sengen.

The Beautiful Blonde from Bashful Bend 🦴🦴 1/2 **1949** Charming comedy-western gets better with age. Grable is the pistol packing mama mistaken for the new school teacher. Fun performances by all, especially Herbert. **77m/C; DVD, Blu-Ray, Streaming.** Betty Grable; Cesar Romero; Rudy Vallee; Olga San Juan; Hugh Herbert; Porter Hall; Sterling Holloway; El Brendel; *D:* Preston Sturges.

Beautiful Boy 🦴🦴 1/2 **2010 (R)** On the verge of separation, troubled married couple, Bill (Sheen) and Kate (Bello), are horrified by the news that their 18-year-old son Sam (Gallner) killed himself after committing a mass shooting at his college. As the media dogs them, the couple is forced to turn to each other as they attempt to cope with the consequences of the killer they brought into the world. Can they ever find happiness together again? Sheen and Bello are genuine and the concept is engaging, but it's distant and formulaic at times. **100m/C; DVD, Blu-Ray.** Michael Sheen; Maria Bello; Kyle Gallner; Moon Bloodgood; Austin Nichols; *D:* Shawn Ku; *W:* Shawn Ku; Michael Armbruster; *C:* Michael Fimognari; *M:* Trevor Morris.

Beautiful Boy 🦴 1/2 **2018 (R)** Based on the memoir "Beautiful Boy" by David Sheff and "Tweak" by his son, Nic Sheff, it chronicles the heartbreaking and inspiring experience of survival and recovery in a family coping with addiction over many years. **120m/C.** Steve Carell; Timothée Chalamet; Maura Tierney; Amy Ryan; Christian Convery; *D:* Felix van Groeningen; *W:* Felix van Groeningen; Luke Davies; *C:* Ruben Impens; *M:* Christoffer Franzén.

The Beautiful Country 🦴🦴 1/2 **2004 (R)** In 1990, 20-year-old Binh (Nguyen) lives with poverty and discrimination in Vietnam because of his mixed ancestry: his father was an American solider. Binh's dying mother sends him on an illegal journey to the U.S. in hopes of tracking down his dad in Houston. There's an extended sequence involving a Malaysian refugee camp (with Ling as a friendly prostitute) and a trip on a freighter (captained by Roth) before the young man makes it to the States and finally meets his dad (Nolte). Earnest, gentle, and sometimes harrowing (and rather too long). **137m/C; DVD.** *NO US* Nick Nolte; Tim Roth; Bai Ling; Temuera Morrison; Damien Nguyen; Nguyen Thi Huong Dung; Chau Thi Kim Xuan; Anh Thu; Khong Duc Thuan; Chapman To; Vu Tang; Nguyen Than Kien; Bui Ti Hong; John Hussey; *D:* Hans Petter Moland; *W:* Larry Gross; Sabina Murray; *C:* Stuart Dryburgh; *M:* Zbigniew Preisner.

Beautiful Creatures 🦴🦴 **2000 (R)** Fitful comedy/thriller follows the adventures of Petulia (Weisz) and Dorothy (Lynch), two Glasgow lasses with abusive boyfriends. Dorothy escapes a beating from her druggie boyfriend Tony (Glen), only to wind up aiding Petulia, who is being attacked in the street by drunken Brian (Mannion). Unfortunately, Brian dies and the women decides to make it look like he's been kidnapped and ask a ransom from his equally violent brother Ronnie (Roeves) so they can get out of town. Then a crooked detective (Norton) enters the scene and the women's plans turn a little complicated. **88m/C; VHS, DVD.** *GB* Rachel Weisz; Susan Lynch; Alex Norton; Iain Glen; Maurice Roeves; Tom Mannion; *D:* Bill Eagles; *W:* Simon Donald; *C:* James Welland; *M:* Murray Gold.

Beautiful Creatures 🦴🦴 **2013 (PG-13)** Yet another Hollywood attempt to cultivate that "Twilight" magic in this adaptation of the young adult novel by Kami Garcia and Margaret Stohl. Wanting to flee his suffocating small Southern town, Ethan (Ehrenreich) meets the lovely Lena (Englert), who carries dark secrets into this supernatural Romeo and Juliet. She is a caster, a creature not unlike a witch, who will be drawn to the light or dark side on her impending 16th birthday. Writer/director LaGravenese elicits charming performances from his leads and talented ensemble but even he seems bored by the generic source material. **124m/C; DVD, Blu-Ray.** Alden Ehrenreich; Alice Englert; Jeremy Irons; Emma Thompson; Emmy Rossum; Viola Davis; Thomas Mann; Kyle Gallner; Eileen Atkins; Margo Martindale; Pruitt Taylor Vince; ***D:*** Richard LaGravenese; ***W:*** Richard LaGravenese; ***C:*** Philippe Rousselot; ***M:*** Mary Ramos.

A Beautiful Day in the Neighborhood **2019 (PG)** Cynical journalist Lloyd Vogel (Rhys) is assigned an article on popular children's television show host Fred Rogers (Hanks). Though Lloyd is reluctant to write the article, his meeting with Rogers proves transformative as he encourages Lloyd to talk about himself, his new role as a father, and the long-term effects of his own estrangement from his father Jerry (Cooper). Rogers' connection with and compassion for Lloyd, and others, results in emotional breakthroughs. Based on a true story, the drama captures the power and influence of Mr. Rogers on people while also giving space for Rhys's character to undergo a life-changing journey. **108m/C; DVD, Blu-Ray.** Tom Hanks; Matthew Rhys; Chris Cooper; Susan Kelechi Watson; Maryann Plunkett; ***D:*** Marielle Heller; ***W:*** Micah Fitzerman-Blue; Noah Harpster; ***C:*** Jody Lee Lipes; ***M:*** Nate Heller.

Beautiful Dreamers 1/2 **1992 (PG-13)** Maurice Bucke is a young Canadian physician who runs the London Insane Asylum. After a chance meeting with poet Walt Whitman, both men discover their mutual outrage for current treatment of the mentally ill. Bucke persuades Whitman to visit his asylum in order to try Whitman's theory of human compassion on the asylum's inmates. However, Bucke runs into opposition from the local townspeople, scandalized by Whitman's radical reputation. Fairly humdrum with a larger-than-life performance by Torn as Whitman. Based on Whitman's visit to Canada in 1880. **108m/C; VHS.** *CA* Rip Torn; Colm Feore; Wendel Meldrum; Sheila McCarthy; Colin Fox; ***D:*** John Kent Harrison; ***W:*** John Kent Harrison.

This Beautiful Fantastic 1/2 **2017 (PG)** Librarian Bella Brown (Brown Findlay) was a foundling raised by nuns. As an adult, she receives support from and inspires men like her personal cook Vernon (Scott) and inventor Billy (Irvine). Though Bella has quirks about organizing her home life, she also is regularly late to work and has let the garden behind her home fall into disrepair. After menacing neighbor Alfie (Wilkinson) calls the authorities, Bella is given a month to fix the garden or be forced out of her rental home. Though the story has charm, questionable plotting mars it. **100m/C; DVD.** Jessica Brown Findlay; Andrew Scott; Tom Wilkinson; Jeremy Irvine; Anna Chancellor; ***D:*** Simon Aboud; ***W:*** Simon Aboud; ***C:*** Mike Eley; ***M:*** Anne Nikitin.

Beautiful Girls **1996 (R)** Slow but easy-going film highlights the differences between men, women, and relationships. A 10-year high school reunion brings together buddies Tommy (Dillon), Kev (Perlich), Paul (Rapaport), Mo (Emmerich), and Willie (Hutton). They ice-fish, drink, and talk about women (about whom they haven't a clue). All are smitten by Andera (Thurman), the gorgeous visiting cousin of another friend, and Willie becomes intrigued by Marty (Portman), his precociously tantalizing 13-year-old neighbor. The guys' whining gets annoying and the women are strictly secondary characters, but O'Donnell's tirade about fake femininity is just one of many amusing examples of smart dialogue. The Afghan Whigs are featured as the bar band. **110m/C; VHS, DVD.** Matt Dillon; Timothy Hutton; Michael Rapaport; Max Perlich; Noah Emmerich; Lauren Holly; Uma Thurman; Natalie Portman; Mira Sorvino; Martha Plimpton; Rosie O'Donnell; Annabeth Gish; Pruitt Taylor Vince; Sam Robards; David Arquette; Anne Bobby; Richard Bright; ***D:*** Ted (Edward) Demme; ***W:*** Scott Rosenberg; ***C:*** Adam Kimmel; ***M:*** David A. Stewart.

Beautiful Joe **2000 (R)** Joe (Connolly) decides to hit the road for adventure and discovers it in Louisville, Kentucky when he meets Hush (Stone), an ex-stripper turned con artist. Then Joe gets in trouble when he tries to help Hush with her debt to crime boss George the Geek (Holm) and the twosome take off to Vegas with Geek's henchman (Bellows) on their trail. **98m/C; VHS, DVD.** Billy Connolly; Sharon Stone; Gil Bellows; Ian Holm; Dann Florek; Barbara Tyson; ***D:*** Stephen Metcalfe; ***W:*** Stephen Metcalfe; ***C:*** Thomas Ackerman.

Beautiful Kate **2009 (R)** Writer/director feature debut of actress Ward is a haunting family drama. Forty-year-old author Ned reluctantly returns to the isolated farm where he grew up to see his belligerent, terminally ill father Bruce. They've been estranged for 20 years and their rancor goes back to the death of Ned's twin sister Kate and the subsequent suicide of Ned's elder brother Cliff. However, neither has ever wanted to face why the tragedies occurred. Adapted from Newton Thornburg's novel. **90m/C; DVD.** *AU* Ben Mendelsohn; Bryan Brown; Rachel Griffiths; Sophie Lowe; Scott O'Donnell; Josh McFarlane; Maeve Dermody; ***D:*** Rachel Ward; ***W:*** Rachel Ward; ***C:*** Andrew Commis; ***M:*** Tex Perkins; Murray Paterson.

A Beautiful Life **2008** Cliched, predictable drama with a very annoying lead character. Abused teenaged runaway Maggie comes to L.A. and is befriended by illegal immigrant David, who works as a janitor in a strip club. They also get romantically involved, though whiny Maggie is a thorough nuisance. The two are befriended by stripper Esther and librarian Susan who try to help after David loses his job and while Maggie searches for her mother. Adaptation of Wendy Hammond's play "Jersey City." **81m/C; DVD.** Angela Sarafyan; Jesse Garcia; Bai Ling; Debi Mazar; Dana Delaney; Jonathan LaPaglia; Rena Owen; ***D:*** Alejandro Chomski; ***W:*** Deborah Calla; Wendy Hammond; ***C:*** Nancy Schreiber; ***M:*** Ruy Folguera.

Beautiful Losers 1/2 **2008** This revealing feature-length documentary looks at the unexpected influence of a group of artistic friends who began challenging the artistic establishment in the early 1990s. Borne out of the New York gallery Alleged, this artistic community ultimately changed popular culture. With origins in the do-it-yourself subcultures such as skateboarding, graffiti, and hip hop, the group included skateboarder Ed Templeton, filmmaker Harmony Korine, and artist/filmmaker Mike Mills. A look at the cultures that spawned the art and interviews with the artists are included as well. **90m/C; DVD, Streaming, Download.** ***D:*** Aaron Rose; Joshua Leonard; ***W:*** Arty Nelson; ***C:*** Tobin Yelland; ***M:*** Money Mark.

A Beautiful Mind 1/2 **2001 (PG-13)** Loose adaptation of Sylvia Nasar's 1998 bio of Nobel Prize winning mathematician John Forbes Nash Jr. An anti-social genius at Princeton University, Nash wrote his thesis on game theory at 21 and worked for the government in the 1950s before succumbing to paranoid schizophrenia, necessitating his confinement to a mental institution. (The treatment scenes are not for the faint-hearted.) His apparent recovery, after some 30 years, led to sharing a Nobel award in economics in 1994. Director Howard manages to keep the inherent sentimentality and sensationalism generally under control thanks to some powerful performances from Crowe (as Nash), Connelly (as wife Alicia), and Harris (as a sinister government official). The usual controversies swirled about the accuracy of the biopic and what was left out. Ignore the petty carping. **129m/C; VHS, DVD, Blu-Ray.** Russell Crowe; Jennifer Connelly; Ed Harris; Paul Bettany; Christopher Plummer; Judd Hirsch; Adam Goldberg; Josh(ua) Lucas; Anthony Rapp; Austin Pendleton; Vivien Cardone; ***D:*** Ron Howard; ***W:*** Akiva Goldsman; ***C:*** Roger Deakins; ***M:*** James Horner. Oscars '01: Adapt. Screenplay, Director (Howard), Film, Support. Actress (Connelly); British Acad. '01: Actor (Crowe), Support. Actress (Connelly); Directors Guild '01: Director (Howard); Golden Globes '02: Actor--Drama (Crowe), Film--Drama, Screenplay, Support. Actress (Connelly); Screen Actors Guild '01: Actor (Crowe); Writers Guild '01: Adapt. Screenplay; Broadcast Film Critics '01: Actor (Crowe), Director (Howard), Film, Support. Actress (Connelly).

Beautiful Ohio **2006** Coming-of-age age story about sibling rivalry, set in the 1970s. Clive Messerman (Call) is a teen math prodigy who's grown distant from his once-idolized older brother William (Davern). William is not only jealous of his parents' hopes for Clive but covets his troubled girlfriend Sandra (Trachtenberg), which leads to an unexpected revelation. Directorial debut of Lowe. **90m/C; DVD.** Rita Wilson; William Hurt; Michelle Trachtenberg; Julianna Margulies; Thomas (Tom) McCarthy; David Call; Brett Davern; Hale Appleman; ***D:*** Chad Lowe; ***W:*** Ethan Canin; ***C:*** Stephen Kazmierski; ***M:*** Craig Wedren.

Beautiful People **1999 (R)** The war in Bosnia (circa 1993) comes to London when former neighbors-turned-enemies, one a Serbian and the other a Croatian, accidentally meet on a bus and try to kill each other. This chaos leads to a variety of intersecting situations: Portia (Coleman), a doctor and daughter of a snobby Tory MP, falls for a refugee; another doctor (Farrell) counsels a pregnant refugee who wants to abort her baby, who is the product of a rape; a druggy skinhead (Nussbaum) winds up experiencing battle firsthand, and on and on and on. **107m/C; VHS, DVD.** *GB* Charlotte Coleman; Nicholas Farrell; Danny Nussbaum; Edin Dzandzanovic; Charles Kay; Rosalind Ayres; Heather Tobias; Siobhan Redmond; Gilbert Martin; Linda Bassett; Steve Sweeney; ***D:*** Jasmin Dizdar; ***W:*** Jasmin Dizdar; ***C:*** Barry Ackroyd; ***M:*** Gary Bell.

The Beautiful Person *La Belle Personne* **2008** After the death of her mother, 16-year-old Junie starts over at a high school in Paris. The pouty beauty is pursued by a number of boys and chooses the reticent Otto to discourage the rest. Junie is really only interested in her foreign language teacher Mr. Nemours whose love life is already very complicated. French with subtitles. **97m/C; DVD.** *FR* Lea Seydoux; Louis Garrel; Gregoire Leprince-Ringuet; Esteban Carvajal-Alegria; Simon Truxillo; Agathe Benitzer; Anais Demoustier; ***D:*** Christophe Honore; ***W:*** Christophe Honore; Gilles Taurand; ***C:*** Laurent Brunet; ***M:*** Alexandre Beaupain.

Beautiful Something **2016** A look at the romantic trials and tribulations of four gay men who seek connection and unexpectedly find it with each other. Before this fateful meeting, Brian (Sheppard) has been unable to find love, while Jim (Ryan) usually is the heartbreaker. However, Zack is love with sculptor Drew (Domingo), who seems more interested in his work than much younger Zack. Bob (Lescault), a sixtysomething agent, tires to compensate for a lost love. One night in Philadelphia, they cross paths and their lives change forever. **97m/C; DVD, Streaming, Download.** Brian Sheppard; Zack Ryan; Colman Domingo; John Lescault; David Melissaratos; ***D:*** Joseph Graham; ***W:*** Joseph Graham; ***C:*** Matthew Boyd; ***M:*** Inu; Luke O'Malley; Windows to Sky.

The Beautiful, the Bloody and the Bare **1964** Sordid screamer in the Herschell Gordon Lewis tradition. Set in New York City in the '60s, a depraved artist kills the nude models who pose for him. **?m/C VHS, DVD.** Adela Rogers St. John; Marlene Denes; Debra Page; Jack Lowe; ***D:*** Sande N. Johnsen; ***W:*** Sande N. Johnsen; ***C:*** Jerry Denby; ***M:*** Steve Karmen.

Beautiful Thing **1995 (R)** Sweet, fairytalish, gay coming-of-age story set in a working-class southeast London housing estate. Shy teenager Jamie (Berry) lives with his barmaid mum, Sandra (Henry), and her lover, Tony (Daniels). Next-door is his best mate, the stoic Ste (Neal), who's regularly abused by his father and brother. But when things get too bad, he sleeps over with Jamie. And one night, nature hesitantly takes its course. Their tart-tongued, Mama Cass fanatic, friend Leah (Empson) starts rumors about the twosome that lead to some uneasy (but ultimately conciliatory) confrontations. Fine performances; Harvey adapted from his play. **89m/C; VHS, DVD.** *GB* Glen Berry; Scott Neal; Linda Henry; Tameka Empson; Ben Daniels; ***D:*** Hettie Macdonald; ***W:*** Jonathan Harvey; ***C:*** Chris Seager.

Beautiful Wave 1/2 **2011 (PG-13)** Cliched, coming-of-age surfer flick. Teenager Nicole (Teegarden) is having trouble dealing with her dad's death, and her mom sends her to California to stay with her grandma. Nicole befriends some surfers and aims to learn how to ride the waves herself. She also discovers that her surfer grandpa had a favorite spot in Mexico, leading Nicole and her new buddies to take a road trip in search of it. **96m/C; DVD, Blu-Ray.** Aimee Teegarden; Patricia Richardson; Lance Henriksen; Alicia Ziegler; Ben Milliken; Helen Slater; ***D:*** David Mueller; ***W:*** David Mueller; Lynn Salt; ***C:*** Kev Robertson; ***M:*** Edward White. **VIDEO**

Beauty and the Beast *La Belle et la Bete* **1946** The classic medieval fairy tale is brought to life on the big screen for the first time. Beauty takes the place of her father after he is sentenced to die by the horrible Beast and falls in love with him. Cocteau uses the story's themes and famous set-pieces to create a cohesive and captivating surreal hymn to romantic love that is still the definitive version of B&B. In French with subtitles. **90m/B; VHS, DVD, Blu-Ray.** *FR* Jean Marais; Josette Day; Marcel Andre; Mila Parely; Nane Germon; Michel Auclair; ***D:*** Jean Cocteau; ***W:*** Jean Cocteau; ***C:*** Henri Alekan; ***M:*** Georges Auric.

Beauty and the Beast **1991 (G)** Wonderful Disney musical combines superb animation, splendid characters, and lively songs about a beautiful girl, Belle, and the fearsome and disagreeable Beast. Supporting cast includes the castle servants (a delightful bunch of household objects). Notable as the first animated feature to be nominated for the Best Picture Oscar. Destined to become a classic. The deluxe video version features a work-in-progress rough film cut, a compact disc of the soundtrack, a lithograph depicting a scene from the film, and an illustrated book. **84m/C; VHS, DVD, Blu-Ray.** ***V:*** Paige O'Hara; Robby Benson; Rex Everhart; Richard White; Jesse Corti; Angela Lansbury; Jerry Orbach; David Ogden Stiers; Bradley Michael Pierce; Jo Anne Worley; Kimmy Robertson; ***D:*** Kirk Wise; Gary Trousdale; ***W:*** Linda Woolverton; ***M:*** Alan Menken; ***M:*** Howard Ashman. Oscars '91: Orig. Score, Song ("Beauty and the Beast"); Golden Globes '92: Film--Mus./Comedy; Natl. Film Reg. '02.

Beauty and the Beast 1/2 *La belle et la bête* **2014 (PG-13)** French director Christophe Gans brings his trademark visual flourish to the oft-told tale of the beautiful girl and the beast with whom she falls in love. The gorgeous Lea Seydoux plays the former and the always-fascinating Vincent Cassel plays the latter. This is one of those films that is so full of visual beauty that it can be overwhelming, almost suffocating the story in costume and production design. However, if one can appreciate the fact that Gans is purposefully going for as artistic an approach to this fairy tale as possible, it's a beautiful film. **112m/C; DVD.** Vincent Cassel; Lea Seydoux; Andre Dussollier; Eduardo Noriega; Myriam Charleins; ***D:*** Christophe Gans; ***W:*** Christophe Gans; Sandra Vo-Anh; ***C:*** Christophe Beaucarne; ***M:*** Pierre Adenot.

Beauty and the Beast 1/2 **2017 (PG)** The tale as old as time gets a high-priced retelling over a quarter-century after the Best Picture-nominated Disney classic. This time, Watson and Stevens play the title characters, a pair who realizes it's what's on the inside that counts. Watson is a charming lead as Belle, the bookworm who essentially becomes the Beast's prisoner, eventually falling in love with the cursed man. This is a lavish, expensive affair with gorgeous special effects and production values. It's not as magical as the animated classic, but it's a good time nonetheless. **?m/C; DVD, Blu-Ray.** Emma Watson; Dan Stevens; Luke Evans; Ewan McGregor; Kevin Kline; Josh Gad; ***D:*** Bill Condon; ***W:*** Evan Spiliotopoulos; Stephen Chbosky; ***C:*** Tobias A. Schliessler; ***M:*** Alan Menken.

Beauty and the Beast: A Dark Tale **2010 (R)** The Syfy Channel goes silly, gory, and cheap for this re-imagining of the classic fairytale. Mini-skirted peasant Belle is saved from a wolf by the Beast, who's being accused of numerous bloody crimes plaguing the local village. There's an evil Count, a witch, and a CGI troll involved. **90m/C; DVD.** Estella Warren; Victor Parascos; Rhett Giles; Vanessa Gray; Tony Bellette; Tony Thurbon; ***D:*** David Lister; ***W:*** Gavin Scott; ***C:*** Nino Martinetti; ***M:*** Garry MacDonald. **CABLE**

Beauty and the Boss 1/2 **1933** Playboy Viennese bank exec Josef von Ullrich (William) is too attracted to his pretty stenographer Olive (Doran) so he fires her and hires plain-but-efficient Susie (Marsh) instead. He thinks she won't be a distraction but when Susie gets romance on her mind, she also gets a makeover (thanks to Olive) that draws Josef's attention after all. Remade as 1934's "The Church Mouse." **66m/B; DVD.** Marian Marsh; Warren William; Mary Doran; Charles Butterworth; Frederick Kerr; David Manners; Robert Greig; ***D:*** Roy Del Ruth; ***W:*** Joseph Jackson; ***C:*** Barney McGill.

Beauty & the Briefcase 🦴🦴 ½ **2010** ABC Family cable rom com. Journalist Lane Daniels (Duff) gets a chance at a Cosmo cover story after pitching a "finding love in the workplace" story to editor Kate White (Pressly). Lane gets a job as a corporate assistant at a finance company and proceeds to date as many of her male coworkers as possible. She only falls for Liam (Carmack), who doesn't work in her office, and Lane may blow her chance when Kate doesn't go for her changes. **83m/C; DVD.** Hilary Duff; Chris Carmack; Matt Dallas; Michael McMillen; Jaime Pressly; Jennifer Coolidge; ***D:*** Gil Junger; Michael Horowitz; ***C:*** Greg Gardiner; ***M:*** Danny Lux. **CABLE**

Beauty Queen Butcher! 🦴 ½ **1991** A group of mean girls convince a fat girl to enter a beauty pageant to humiliate her. Of course she goes crazy and starts killing everyone in sight. Kind of insulting to all concerned as it implies all "hot" women are inherently evil and cruel, and all "non-hot" women are a cruel joke away from becoming psychopathic death machines. **118m/C; DVD.** Jim Boggess; Rhona Brody; Kathryn A. Mensik; Tammy Pescatelli; Kimberly Ann Kurtenbach; Laura Schutter; ***D:*** Jill Rae Zurborg; ***W:*** Jill Rae Zurborg; Shane Partlow; ***C:*** Jeff Carney; ***M:*** Dana P. Rowe. **VIDEO**

Beauty Shop 🦴🦴🦴 **2005 (PG-13)** Spinning off from the "Barbershop" series, familiar tale of female empowerment succeeds, thanks to Queen Latifah's classy, charismatic lead performance. Beautician Gina moves to Atlanta, landing a job working for pretentious upscale salon owner Jorge (Bacon). Frustrated with Jorge's lack of respect, Gina opens her own beauty shop in a working-class black neighborhood, gathering a group of good-natured, eccentric stylists like outspoken Ms. Josephine (Woodard) and clueless white girl Lynn (Silverstone). All of the community pride themes from the "Barbershop" movies are touched on here, but "Beauty" distinguishes itself with genuine characters. Bacon and Suvari are exceptions, choosing instead to go ridiculously broad. **105m/C; DVD, Blu-Ray, UMD.** Queen Latifah; Alicia Silverstone; Andie MacDowell; Alfre Woodard; Mena Suvari; Della Reese; Golden Brooks; Paige Hurd; LisaRaye; Keisha Knight Pulliam; Bryce Wilson; Kevin Bacon; Djimon Hounsou; Adele Givens; Miss Laura Hayes; Little JJ; Sherri Shepherd; Kimora Lee Simmons; Sheryl Underwood; ***D:*** Bille Woodruff; ***W:*** Kate Lanier; Norman Vance, Jr.; ***C:*** Theo van de Sande; ***M:*** Christopher Young.

The Beaver 🦴🦴 ½ **2011 (PG-13)** Formerly successful toy executive Walter Black's (Gibson) life is spiraling out of control as severe depression tears apart his marriage and his family. Nothing seems to help—except, of all things, a beaver hand puppet that he uses to communicate as "therapy." The title, premise, and the involvement of the controversial-at-the-time lead actor would all seem to contribute to a cinematic train wreck. Instead, director Foster (who also stars as Black's wife) has created a lovely, unexpected surprise. With a strong script that gives dignity to an emotional and psychological family drama, Gibson is charming, brave, and sincere. **91m/C; DVD, Blu-Ray, On Demand.** Mel Gibson; Jodie Foster; Anton Yelchin; Jennifer Lawrence; Riley Thomas Stewart; Zachary Booth; ***D:*** Jodie Foster; ***W:*** Kyle Killen; ***C:*** Hagen Bogdanski; ***M:*** Marcelo Zarvos.

Beavis and Butt-Head Do America 🦴🦴 ½ **1996 (PG-13)** Moronic MTV metalheads go on the road in search of their stolen TV and are somehow mistaken for criminal masterminds. Okay, enough about plot. If you're thinking of renting this one, you don't care about that stuff anyway. Director/writer/voice of B&B Judge is smart enough not to change our "heroes" just because they're on a bigger screen. They're still stupid, obsessed with chicks, (Yeah! Chicks are cool!) and blissfully unaware of what's happening around them. The opening sequence, a parody of 70s cop shows, is hilarious (and cool). For those who like the show, and for people who just don't admit that they do, the boys' movie debut (he said "but") doesn't suck. **82m/C; VHS, DVD.** ***V:*** Mike Judge; Robert Stack; Cloris Leachman; Demi Moore; Eric Bogosian; Richard Linklater; Pamela Blair; Tim Guinee; David Letterman; David Spade; Bruce Willis; Toby Huss; ***D:*** Mike Judge; ***W:*** Mike Judge; Joe Stillman; ***M:*** John (Gianni) Frizzell.

Bebe's Kids 🦴🦴 ½ **1992 (PG-13)** When ladies' man Robin falls for the lovely Jamika, he gets some unexpected surprises when he takes her out on a first date to an amusement park—and she brings along four kids. Animated comedy takes some funny pot-shots at both black and white culture and Disneyland. The children are amusing, especially baby PeeWee, a tot with chronically dirty diapers and Tone Loc's gravelly voice. Based on characters created by the late comedian Robin Harris. The video includes the seven-minute animated short "Itsy Bitsy Spider." **74m/C; VHS, DVD.** ***V:*** Faizon Love; Vanessa Bell Calloway; Wayne Collins; Jonell Green; Marques Houston; Tone Loc; Nell Carter; Myra J.; ***D:*** Bruce Smith; ***W:*** Reginald (Reggie) Hudlin; ***M:*** John Barnes.

Because I Said So 🦴🦴 **2007 (PG-13)** Keaton stars as Daphne, a well-intentioned but overprotective and meddling mom to three beautiful daughters. Maggie (Graham) and Mae (Perabo) are safely married and successful, but youngest chick Milly (Moore) has terrible taste in men, so Daphne places a personal ad and screens the replies. Daphne approves of architect Jason (Scott) but Milly is drawn to musician and single dad Johnny (Macht), whose own dad, Joe (Collins), strikes unexpected sparks with Daphne. Much over-the-top shtick follows but everything (and everyone) looks gorgeous. **102m/C; DVD.** Diane Keaton; Mandy Moore; Lauren Graham; Piper Perabo; Gabriel Macht; Tom Everett Scott; Stephen Collins; Ty Panitz; Colin Ferguson; Tony Hale; Matt Champagne; ***D:*** Michael Lehmann; ***W:*** Karen Leigh Hopkins; Jessie Nelson; ***C:*** Julio Macat; ***M:*** David Kitay.

Because of Him 🦴🦴 ½ **1945** Actress Kim Walker (Durbin) fakes a letter of introduction from famous thespian John Sheridan (Laughton) in order to impress Broadway producer Charles Gilbert (Ridges). It works and she's given the lead, much to the dismay of the playwright, Paul Taylor (Tone). Naturally, Kim turns out to be an opening night success and Paul comes around and realizes what a swell gal she is. Laughton is at his best as the hammy veteran performer. **88m/B; VHS, DVD.** Deanna Durbin; Franchot Tone; Charles Laughton; Stanley Ridges; Helen Broderick; Donald Meek; ***D:*** Richard Wallace; ***W:*** Edmund Beloin; ***C:*** Hal Mohr; ***M:*** Miklos Rozsa.

Because of Winn-Dixie 🦴🦴 ½ **2005 (PG)** Based on the popular children's book by Kate DiCamillo of the same name about a lonely young girl who adopts a stray dog. India Opal Buloni (played by Robb) is a lonely 10 year-old who's just moved to Florida with her preacher father (Daniels). Without friends, and missing her mother, who left her when she was three, Opal encounters a stray dog at the local grocery store. She adopts the dog as her own, naming him Winn-Dixie after the store. Slowly, the dog helps Opal ease her loneliness and she discovers some rare friendships in unusual places. While not perfect, the movie has more hits than misses and is helped along with a strong supporting cast, including Dave Matthews as a singing pet store clerk. **105m/C; DVD.** Jeff Daniels; Cicely Tyson; Eva Marie Saint; Courtney Jines; Elle Fanning; AnnaSophia Robb; Dave Matthews; Nick Price; Luke Benward; ***D:*** Wayne Wang; ***W:*** Joan Singleton; ***C:*** Karl Walter Lindenlaub; ***M:*** Rachel Portman.

Because of You 🦴🦴 *Kyoko* **1995 (R)** Jose (Osorio), a Cuban-American serviceman stationed in Japan, taught the young Kyoko how to do latin dancing. When she's 21, Kyoko (Takaoka) travels to New York to see Jose again. When she does find him, she discovers Jose has AIDS and no longer remembers much of his past, including Kyoko. Terminally ill, his one wish is to be reunited with his family in Miami. Kyoko decides to drive Jose home, hoping somehow he'll come to remember her. **85m/C; VHS, DVD.** Saki Takaoka; Carlos Osorio; Scott Whitehurst; Mauricio Bustamante; Oscar Colon; Bradford West; Angel Stephens; ***D:*** Ryu Murakami; ***W:*** Ryu Murakami; ***C:*** Sarah Cawley.

Because They're Young 🦴🦴 ½ **1960** Routine teen drama. Big city high school history teacher Neil Hendry (Dick Clark in his film debut) becomes a role model for some of his juvenile delinquent kids and still finds the time to romance school secretary Joan. Naturally, Principal Dolan is opposed to Neil befriending his students. **98m/B; DVD.** Dick Clark; Victoria Shaw; Warren Berlinger; Michael Callan; Tuesday Weld; Doug McClure; Wendell Holmes; Roberta Shore; Chris Robinson; Rudy Bond; ***D:*** Paul Wendkos; ***W:*** James Gunn; ***C:*** Wilfred M. Cline; ***M:*** John Williams.

Because Why? 🦴🦴 **1993** After travelling abroad for five years, Alex (Riley) returns to Montreal with a back pack, a skateboard, and an old girlfriend's address. The address only leads to a demolished building, so Alex finds himself a new home and—longing to belong somewhere—a potentially new family and friends. **104m/C; VHS, DVD.** *CA* Michael Riley; Martine Rochon; Doru Bandol; Heather Mathieson; ***D:*** Arto Paragamian; ***W:*** Arto Paragamian; ***C:*** Andre Turpin; ***M:*** Nana Vasconcelos.

Because You're Mine 🦴🦴 **1952** Lanza plays an opera star who is drafted and falls in love with Morrow, his top sergeant's sister. Plenty of singing—maybe too much at times, but Lanza's fans will enjoy it nonetheless. **103m/C; VHS, DVD.** Mario Lanza; James Whitmore; Doretta Morrow; Dean Miller; Rita (Paula) Corday; Jeff Donnell; Spring Byington; ***D:*** Alexander Hall.

Becket 🦴🦴🦴 **1964** Adaptation of Jean Anouilh's play about the tumultuous friendship between Henry II of England and the Archbishop of Canterbury Thomas Becket. Becket views his position in the church of little relation to the sexual and emotional needs of a man, until he becomes archbishop. His growing concern for religion and his shrinking need of Henry as friend and confidant eventually cause the demise of the friendship and the resulting tragedy. Flawless acting from every cast member, and finely detailed artistic direction make up for the occasional slow moment. **148m/C; VHS, DVD, Blu-Ray.** Richard Burton; Peter O'Toole; John Gielgud; Donald Wolfit; ***D:*** Peter Glenville; ***W:*** Edward Anhalt; ***C:*** Geoffrey Unsworth. Oscars '64: Adapt. Screenplay; Golden Globes '65: Actor--Drama (O'Toole), Film--Drama.

Becky Sharp 🦴🦴 ½ **1935** This premiere Technicolor film tells the story of Becky Sharp, a wicked woman who finally performs one good deed. **83m/C; VHS, DVD, Blu-Ray.** Miriam Hopkins; Frances Dee; Cedric Hardwicke; Billie Burke; Nigel Bruce; Pat Nixon; ***D:*** Rouben Mamoulian; ***C:*** Ray Rennahan. Natl. Film Reg. '19.

Becoming Jane 🦴🦴 ½ **2007 (PG)** Jane Austen's writing has withstood the test of time, but films about the writer and her writings are still fledgling. This one's a love story—supposedly her own—and takes place before Jane (Hathaway) is, well, Jane Austen as we know her. Penniless mom and dad (Walters and Cromwell) don't take the whole writing thing seriously and expect 20-year-old Jane to choose a wealthy suitor from among those that come calling. Then Thomas Lefroy (McAvoy) shows up, dashing and pushy, and Jane—after initial annoyance—entertains the thought of shelving her writing, at least temporarily. Alas, relatives from both sides disapprove of the match. No matter, she becomes a fantastic writer whom we still read, speak of, and make films about nearly 200 years later. Pretty costumes, but with a been-there-done-that (think "Pride and Prejudice" remake) feel. Still worthwhile for Austen fans and non-fans alike. **120m/C; DVD, Blu-Ray.** *US GB* Anne Hathaway; James McAvoy; Julie Walters; James Cromwell; Laurence Fox; Maggie Smith; Ian Richardson; Anna Maxwell Martin; Joe Anderson; Helen McCrory; Leo Bill; ***D:*** Julian Jarrold; ***W:*** Kevin Hood; Sarah Williams; ***C:*** Eigil Bryld; ***M:*** Adrian Johnston.

Becoming Mike Nichols 🦴🦴 ½ **2016** A documentary look at influential filmmaker Mike Nichols. This feature-length documentary features a series of discussions between theater director Jack O'Brien and Nichols about his life and work. Topics of focus include Nichols' early comedy collaborations with Elaine May, his stage directing work including 1963's "Barefoot in the Park" and 1965's "The Odd Couple," and his hit films "The Graduate" and "Who's Afraid of Virginia Woolf?" **72m/C; DVD, Download.** Mike Nichols; Jack O'Brien; ***D:*** Douglas McGrath; ***C:*** Tim Orr; ***M:*** David Lawrence.

Bed and Board 🦴🦴🦴 *Domicile Conjugal* **1970** The fourth film in the Antoine Doinel (Leaud) cycle finds him marrying Christine (Jade) and becoming a father. The responsibilities of adulthood upset him so much that Antoine leaves his new family and begins an affair. French with subtitles. **100m/C; VHS, DVD.** *FR* Jean-Pierre Leaud; Claude Jade; Barbara Laage; Hiroko Berghauer; Daniel Boulanger; Pierre Maguelon; Jacques Jouanneau; Jacques Rispal; Jacques Robiolles; Pierre Fabre; Billy Kearns; Daniel Ceccaldi; Daniele Girard; Claire Duhamel; Sylvana Blasi; Claude Vega; Christian de Tiliere; Annick Asty; Marianne Piketi; Guy Pierauld; Marie Dedieu; Marie Irakane; Yvon Lec; Ernest Menzer; Christophe Vesque; ***D:*** Francois Truffaut; ***W:*** Francois Truffaut; Bernard Revon; Claude de Givray; ***C:*** Nestor Almendros; ***M:*** Antoine Duhamel.

Bed & Breakfast 🦴🦴 **2010** Formulaic rom com. His wife leaves him and Jake Sullivan (Cain) gladly escapes to the bed and breakfast he's inherited in California's wine country. Unfortunately, Brazilian Ana (Paes) shows up with a deed to the same property, left to her by her father. Let the predictable romance ensue. **89m/C; DVD.** Dean Cain; Juliana Paes; Julian Stone; Bill Engvall; Eric Roberts; John Savage; Julia Duffy; ***D:*** Marcio Garcia; ***W:*** Leland Douglas; ***C:*** Craig Kief; ***M:*** John Hunter. **VIDEO**

Bed and Sofa 🦴🦴🦴 ½ **1927** Adultery, abortion, and women's rights are brought about by a housing shortage which forces a man to move in with a married friend. Famous, ground-breaking Russian silent. **73m/B; Silent; VHS, DVD.** *RU* Nikolai Batalov; Vladimar Fogel; ***D:*** Abram Room.

Bed of Roses 🦴🦴 ½ *Amelia and the King of Plants* **1995 (PG)** Wistful romance finds workaholic investment banker Lisa Walker (Masterson) receiving lavish floral tributes from an unknown admirer. When Lisa tracks her giver down, it turns out to be lovestruck widowed florist Lewis Farrell (Slater), who noticed Lisa crying through her apartment window and sent the flowers to cheer her up. Best friend Kim (Seagall) urges Lisa to go for Lewis but a problematic past has Lisa distrusting her emotions and their romantic path has a few bumps (easily overcome). Appealing leads, lots of cliches. Goldenberg's debut. **88m/C; VHS, DVD.** Christian Slater; Mary Stuart Masterson; Pamela Segall; Josh Brolin; Ally Walker; Debra Monk; ***D:*** Michael Goldenberg; ***W:*** Michael Goldenberg; ***C:*** Adam Kimmel; ***M:*** Michael Convertino.

The Bed Sitting Room 🦴 **1969** Too weird for words, episodic Brit black comedy. After the nuclear bombing of Britain, survivors living in the ruins of London try to establish some semblance of normal behavior. Despite the fact some of them seem to be mutating into objects like a chest of drawers and a bed sitting room. **90m/C; DVD.** *UK* Rita Tushingham; Ralph Richardson; Peter Cook; Dudley Moore; Spike Milligan; Michael Hordern; ***D:*** Richard Lester; ***W:*** John Antrobus; ***C:*** David Watkin; ***M:*** Ken Thorne.

The Bed You Sleep In 🦴🦴 **1993** Ray (Blair) is a struggling lumber mill owner, living with his wife Jean (McLaughlin) in a small Oregon town. The couple are torn apart when they receive a letter from their daughter, who's away at college, accusing her father of sexual abuse. The secrets and lies of the family soon echo throughout their community. **117m/C; VHS, DVD.** Tom Blair; Ellen McLaughlin; Kathryn Sannella; ***D:*** Jon Jost; ***W:*** Jon Jost; ***C:*** Jon Jost.

Bedazzled 🦴🦴🦴 **1968 (PG)** Short-order cook Stanley Moon (Moore) is saved from suicide by the devil, here known as George Spiggot (Cook), who makes Stanley an offer: seven wishes in exchange for his soul. What Stanley wants is waitress Margaret (Bron) but each of Stanley's wishes is granted with surprising consequences. Cult comedy is a sometimes uneven, but thoroughly entertaining and funny retelling of the Faustian story.

107m/C; VHS, DVD, Blu-Ray. *GB* Dudley Moore; Peter Cook; Eleanor Bron; Michael Bates; Raquel Welch; Bernard Spear; Parnell McGarry; Howard Goorney; Daniele Noel; Barry Humphries; Lockwood West; Robert Russell; Michael Trubshawe; Robin Hawdon; Evelyn Moore; Charles Lloyd-Pack; *D:* Stanley Donen; *W:* Dudley Moore; Peter Cook; *C:* Austin Dempster; *M:* Dudley Moore.

Bedazzled ½ **2000 (PG-13)** Mortals have been falling for this scam for centuries: seven wishes in exchange for your eternal soul. Once again the Devil finds a taker. Fraser plays Elliot, a nice but hopeless geek who will do anything to improve his lowly stature in life and nab the girl of his dreams (O'Connor). The Devil's (Hurley) misinterpretations of his requests result in Elliot becoming, among other things, a drug lord, an NBA star, and a much too sensitive bore. Will Elliot find a way out of his hellish obligation? Is there a lesson to be learned from his experiences? You probably know the answers. Ramis occasionally misfires, but the hits outnumber the misses. An updated remake of the Dudley Moore/Peter Cook film. **105m/C; VHS, DVD, Blu-Ray.** Brendan Fraser; Elizabeth Hurley; Frances O'Connor; Rudolf Martin; Orlando Jones; Gabriel Casseus; Miriam Shor; Brian Doyle-Murray; *D:* Harold Ramis; *W:* Harold Ramis; Larry Gelbart; Peter Tolan; *C:* Bill Pope.

Bedevilled ½ **1955** Dull MGM crime drama that doesn't make a lot of sense. What it does have going for it are the Paris locations and the CinemaScope cinematography by Freddie Young. Seminarian Gregory Fitzgerald (Forrest) stops in Paris before heading to Rome to receive his ordination as a priest. He gets mixed up with cynical cabaret singer Monica (Baxter), who's killed her married lover. She's hunted by the cops and the dead man's gangster brother. Greg offers to help her out. **85m/C; DVD.** Steve Forrest; Anne Baxter; Maurice Teynac; Simone Renant; Victor Francen; Joseph Tomelty; *D:* Mitchell Leisen; *W:* Jo Eisinger; *C:* Frederick A. (Freddie) Young; *M:* William Alwyn.

Bedford Incident ½ **1965** The U.S.S. Bedford discovers an unidentified submarine in North Atlantic waters. The Bedford's commander drives his crew to the point of exhaustion as they find themselves the center of a fateful controversy. **102m/B; VHS, DVD.** Richard Widmark; Sidney Poitier; James MacArthur; Martin Balsam; Wally Cox; Donald Sutherland; Eric Portman; *D:* James B. Harris.

Bedknobs and Broomsticks ½ **1971 (G)** A novice witch and three cockney waifs ride a magic bedstead and stop the Nazis from invading England during WWII. Celebrated for its animated art. **117m/C; VHS, DVD, Blu-Ray.** Angela Lansbury; Roddy McDowall; David Tomlinson; Bruce Forsyth; Sam Jaffe; *D:* Robert Stevenson; *W:* Don DaGradi; Bill Walsh; *C:* Frank V. Phillips; *M:* Richard M. Sherman; Robert B. Sherman. Oscars '71: Visual FX.

Bedlam **1945** Creeper set in the famed asylum in 18th-century London. A woman, wrongfully committed, tries to stop the evil doings of the chief (Karloff) of Bedlam, and endangers herself. Fine horror film co-written by producer Lewton. **79m/B; VHS, DVD.** Jason Robards, Sr.; Ian Wolfe; Glenn Vernon; Boris Karloff; Anna Lee; Billy House; Richard Fraser; Elizabeth Russell; Skelton Knaggs; Robert Clarke; Ellen Corby; Leyland Hodgson; Joan Newton; *D:* Mark Robson; *W:* Mark Robson; Val Lewton; *C:* Nicholas Musuraca; *M:* Roy Webb.

Bedroom Eyes **1986 (R)** A successful businessman becomes a voyeur by returning nightly to a beautiful woman's window, until she is killed and he is the prime suspect. Part comic, part disappointing thriller. **90m/C; VHS, DVD.** Kenneth Gilman; Dayle Haddon; Christine Cattall; *D:* William Fruet.

The Bedroom Window ½ **1987 (R)** Guttenberg is having an illicit affair with his boss' wife (Huppert), who witnesses an assault on another woman (McGovern) from the bedroom window. To keep the affair secret Guttenberg reports the crime, but since it is secondhand, the account is flawed and he becomes a suspect. Semi-tight thriller reminiscent of Hitchcock mysteries isn't always believable, but is otherwise interesting. **113m/C; VHS, DVD, Blu-Ray.** Steve Guttenberg; Elizabeth McGovern; Isabelle Huppert; Wallace Shawn; Paul Shenar; Carl Lumbly; Frederick Coffin; Brad Greenquist; *D:* Curtis Hanson; *W:* Curtis Hanson; *C:* Gilbert Taylor; *M:* Patrick Gleeson; Michael Shrieve; Felix Mendelessohn.

Bedrooms and Hallways ½ **1998** Single gay Leo (McKidd) is urged to join a new agey men's therapy group where, during one of their meetings, he expresses his interest in Brendan (Purefoy), who's breaking up with longtime lover, Sally (Ehle). After Leo and Brendan get together, Leo realizes that Sally is his old high school girlfriend and there's still a certain spark between them. And things just get more complicated. Zippy if glib humor, although the film tends to lose steam at the end. **96m/C; VHS, DVD.** *GB* Kevin McKidd; James Purefoy; Jennifer Ehle; Tom Hollander; Hugo Weaving; Simon Callow; Harriet Walter; Christopher Fulford; Julie Graham; *D:* Rose Troche; *W:* Robert Farrar; *C:* Ashley Rowe; *M:* Alfredo Troche.

Bedtime for Bonzo ½ **1951** A professor adopts a chimp to prove that environment, not heredity, determines a child's future. Fun, lighthearted comedy that stars a future president. Followed by "Bonzo Goes to College." **83m/B; VHS, DVD.** Ronald Reagan; Diana Lynn; Walter Slezak; Jesse White; Bonzo the Chimp; Lucille Barkley; Herbert (Hayes) Heyes; Herb Vigran; Harry Tyler; Edward Clark; *D:* Fred de Cordova; *W:* Lou Breslow; Val Burton; *C:* Carl Guthrie; *M:* Frank Skinner.

Bedtime Stories ½ **2008 (PG)** Skeeter (Sandler) is a lowly maintenance guy at the hotel now standing on the site of the motel he and his sister (Cox) grew up in. Skeeter's lifelong dream of running it as his father (Pryce) once did seems unlikely as he toils under the loathsome hotel manager, Kendall (Pearce), a pompous dream-crusher who's double-timing his girlfriend Violet (Palmer)?the hotel owner's daughter who Skeeter has a colossal crush on. Skeeter's luck begins to change when he realizes, while caring for his sister's kids, that his wild bedtime stories of heroic daring can show up in real life. Thus he concocts tales giving him the upper hand with his boss and catching the eye of his girl. Uneven story but the outrageous special effects deliver a wholesome family comedy. **99m/C; Blu-Ray.** Adam Sandler; Keri Russell; Guy Pearce; Courteney Cox; Teresa Palmer; Russell Brand; Lucy Lawless; Richard Griffiths; Jonathan Pryce; Aisha Tyler; Laura Ann Kesling; Madisen Beaty; *D:* Adam Shankman; *W:* Tim Herlihy; Matt Lopez; *C:* Michael Barrett; *M:* Rupert Gregson-Williams.

Bedtime Story **1963** Two con artists attempt to fleece an apparently wealthy woman and each other on the French Riviera. Re-made in 1988 as "Dirty Rotten Scoundrels." One of Brando's thankfully few forays into comedy. **99m/C; VHS, DVD.** Marlon Brando; David Niven; Shirley Jones; Dody Goodman; Marie Windsor; *D:* Ralph Levy.

Bee Movie **2007 (PG)** A bee named Barry B. Benson (Seinfeld) finds himself on a mission when he learns that humans have been profiting off bees forever. Wanting more out of life than his job at a honey-production company can offer, Barry goes out in search of adventure and meets florist Vanessa (Zellweger), a former lawyer wannabe. A budding legal eagle himself, Barry ends up taking on the honey industry with Vanessa's help, and by recruiting all sorts of folks to further his cause (Sting and Larry King, among others). The environmental tones are sound, but the big names behind this film (Seinfeld also co-wrote and co-produced) are the only real buzz. There are bursts of cuteness and the kids will enjoy it, but the frenetic pace and endless string of one-liners tend to come off as just too much busyness. **90m/C; DVD, Blu-Ray.** *V:* Jerry Seinfeld; Renée Zellweger; Matthew Broderick; John Goodman; Patrick Warburton; Chris Rock; Kathy Bates; Barry Levinson; Oprah Winfrey; Larry Miller; Megan Mullally; Rip Torn; Michael Richards; Larry King; Ray Liotta; Sting; *D:* Simon J. Smith; Steve Hickner; *W:* Jerry Seinfeld; Spike Feresten; Barry Marder; Andy Robin; *M:* Rupert Gregson-Williams.

Bee Season **2005 (PG-13)** Based on the bestselling novel by Myla Goldberg. Eleven-year-old Eliza (Cross), an average kid who lacks attention from her bright but aptly troubled parents, finds she's got a gift for spelling. Dad Saul (Gere), a religious studies professor and follower of Kabbalah mysticism, is at a loss as scientist wife Miriam (Binoche) teeters on the edge of instability. Meanwhile Eliza has fantastical visions of the words she is to spell as she wins local spelling bees and heads toward the national competition in Washington, D.C. Dad becomes obsessed with Eliza's gift, ignoring Miriam and their other child, Aaron (Minghella). Viewers who didn't read the book may be set adrift in this somewhat pretentious, but earnest film. **104m/C; DVD.** Richard Gere; Juliette Binoche; Flora Cross; Max Minghella; Kate (Catherine) Bosworth; *D:* Scott McGehee; David Siegel; *W:* Naomi Foner; *C:* Giles Nuttgens.

Beefcake **1999** Campy docudrama set in 1950s L.A. covers the muscle (or men's physique) magazine culture. Doting mama's boy Bob Mizer (MacIvor) found his talents as a still photographer and filmmaker, who also published Physique Pictorial, all of which featured chiseled studs. While Mizer insisted that his models were just clean-cut, all-American boys, he still fell afoul of pornography charges and operating a prostitution ring. The mock style turns harder-edged with Mizer's tribulations. To further confuse things, the film also includes present-day interviews with some of Mizer's one-time models and others familiar with the culture. **93m/C; VHS, DVD.** Daniel MacIvor; Josh Peace; Carroll Godsman; *D:* Thom Fitzgerald; *W:* Thom Fitzgerald; *C:* Thomas M. (Tom) Harting; *M:* John Roby.

Beer **1985 (R)** A female advertising executive devises a dangerous sexist campaign for a cheap beer, and both the beer and its nickname become nationwide obsessions. Not especially amusing. **83m/C; VHS, DVD, Streaming.** Loretta Swit; Rip Torn; Dick Shawn; David Alan Grier; William Russ; Kenneth Mars; Peter Michael Goetz; *D:* Patrick Kelly; *C:* Bill Butler; *M:* Bill Conti.

Beer for My Horses **2008 (PG-13)** Country singer Toby Keith writes and stars in this dim comedy adaptation of one of his songs. Rack and Lonnie are deputies in a usually quiet small southern town. Then Rack's girlfriend is kidnapped by a drug lord whose brother has been arrested, and the duo, joined by fellow lawman Skunk, go on a rescue mission. Stick to the music career, Toby. **86m/C; DVD.** Ted Nugent; Tom Skerritt; Claire Forlani; Greg Serano; Toby Keith; Rodney Carrington; Carlos Sanz; Barry Corbin; Willie Nelson; Gina Gershon; *D:* Mikael Salomon; *W:* Toby Keith; Rodney Carrington; *C:* Paul Elliott; *M:* Toby Keith; Jeff Cardoni. **VIDEO**

Beer League *Artie Lange's Beer League* **2006 (R)** Howard Stern sidekick Lange sticks to his booze, smokes, and broads persona as Artie DeVanzo, the head of a lousy New Jersey softball team at war with their perennial winning cross-town rivals. The deadbeat team of losers can't win a game, but that's okay, they've got beer and brawls. Except that the local law is fed up and demands the team either win or be forced to disband. Oh, the horror. If you actually know who Lange is, you know what to expect, and criticism is beside the point. Sit back and have another beer. **86m/C; DVD, Blu-Ray.** Artie Lange; Ralph Macchio; Anthony De Sando; Seymour Cassel; Cara Buona; Jimmy Palumbo; Joe Lo Truglio; Laurie Metcalf; *D:* Frank Sebastiano; *W:* Frank Sebastiano; *C:* David Phillips; *M:* B.C. Smith.

Beerfest **2006 (R)** It's from those Broken Lizard boys, so don't go looking for sophistication. American brothers Todd and Jan Wolfhouse travel to Germany's Oktoberfest and stumble across a secret, long-standing beer competition. They also meet the arrogant German branch of the family who humiliate the brothers when they attempt to enter the contest and stand up for American males' ability to drink themselves stupid. "Strange Brew" meets "Fight Club" as this raucous comedy will probably become an instructional video to aspiring frat boys everywhere. **111m/C; DVD, Blu-Ray.** Jay Chandrasekhar; Kevin Heffernan; Steve Lemme; Paul Soter; Erik Stolhanske; Eric Christian Olsen; Cloris Leachman; Donald Sutherland; Mo'Nique; Jurgen Prochnow; M.C. Gainey; Will Forte; Blanchard Ryan; Ralph (Ralf) Moeller; *D:* Jay Chandrasekhar; *W:* Jay Chandrasekhar; Kevin Heffernan; Steve Lemme; Paul Soter; Erik Stolhanske; *C:* Frank DeMarco; *M:* Nathan Barr.

Bees in Paradise **1944** Typical wartime comedy from Askey. Four airmen are forced to parachute out of their plane and they land on a tropical isle populated entirely by women. They think this is wonderful until they realize why there are no other men around. The women practice a marriage ceremony that requires the new hubby to commit suicide after the honeymoon. Arthur and his fellows try to convince the ladies that part of the ritual really isn't necessary. **72m/B; DVD.** *GB* Arthur Askey; Peter Graves; Jean Kent; Max Bacon; Ronald Shiner; Antoinette Cellier; Joy Shelton; Beatrice Varley; Anne Shelton; *D:* Val Guest; *W:* Val Guest; Marriott Edgar; *C:* Phil Grindrod.

Beeswax **2009** A charming comedy-drama about the lives and loves of two very different identical twin sisters living in Austin, Texas. Jeannie (Hatcher) has been a paraplegic since childhood, and is the co-owner of a vintage clothing store. Lauren (Hatcher) is more of a drifter and wants to move outside of the United States, but in the meantime, is looking for a steady job and personal understanding after breaking up with her boyfriend. Jeannie co-owns the store with Amanda (Dodge), a former friend who is threatening to sue Jeannie to end their partnership. Jeannie seeks help from her former boyfriend Merrill (Karpovsky), a law student. Ignoring his own issues, Merrill helps both sisters deal with their individual problems. **100m/C; DVD.** Tilly Hatcher; Maggie Hatcher; Alex Karpovsky; Anne Dodge; David Zellner; *D:* Andrew Bujalski; *W:* Andrew Bujalski; *C:* Matthias Grunsky.

Beethoven *Beethoven's Great Love; The Life and Loves of Beethoven; Un Grand Amour de Beethoven* **1936** Startling biography of the musical genius, filled with opulent, impressionistic visuals. French with subtitles. **116m/B; VHS, DVD.** *FR* Harry Baur; Jean-Louis Barrault; Marcel Dalio; *D:* Abel Gance; *W:* Abel Gance; *C:* Marc Fossard; Robert Lefebvre.

Beethoven ½ **1992 (PG)** Adorable St. Bernard puppy escapes from dognappers and wanders into the home of the Newtons, who, over dad's objections, adopt him. Beethoven grows into a huge, slobbering dog who sorely tries dad's patience. To make matters worse, two sets of villains also wreak havoc on the Newton's lives. Evil veterinarian Dr. Varnick plots to steal Beethoven for lab experiments, and yuppie couple Brad and Brie plot to take over the family business. Enjoyable cast, particularly Grodin as dad and Chris as Beethoven enable this movie to please more than the milk and cookies set. Followed by "Beethoven's 2nd." **89m/C; VHS, DVD, Blu-Ray.** Charles Grodin; Bonnie Hunt; Dean Jones; Oliver Platt; Stanley Tucci; Nicholle Tom; Christopher Castile; Sarah Rose Karr; David Duchovny; Patricia Heaton; Laurel Cronin; *D:* Brian Levant; *W:* John Hughes; Amy Holden Jones; *C:* Victor Kemper; *M:* Randy Edelman.

Beethoven's 2nd ½ **1993 (PG)** Sequel has awwww factor going for it as new daddy Beethoven slobbers over four adorable and appealing St. Bernard pups and his new love Missy. Same basic evil subplot as the first, with wicked kidnappers replacing evil vet. During the upheaval, the Newtons take care of the little yapping troublemakers, providing the backdrop for endless puppy mischief and exasperation on Grodin's part. Silly subplots and too many human moments tend to drag, but the kids will find the laughs (albeit stupid ones). **87m/C; VHS, DVD.** Charles Grodin; Bonnie Hunt; Nicholle Tom; Christopher Castile; Sarah Rose Karr; Debi Mazar; Christopher Penn; Ashley Hamilton; *D:* Rod Daniel; *W:* Len Blum; *C:* Bill Butler; *M:* Randy Edelman.

Beethoven's 3rd ½ **2000 (PG)** Dad Richard Newton (Reinhold) wants to take the family on vacation and, naturally, huge St. Bernard Beethoven is coming along. Suddenly, that rented luxury RV doesn't seem very big and dad's idea of fun is lame to the kids. Of course, it's not a typical vacation anyway, seems thieves Tommy (Ciccolini) and Bill (Marsh) need to retrieve a videotape that Richard has rented. Beethoven tries to protect his family while being blamed for every little mishap. A dog's life, indeed! **99m/C; VHS, DVD.** Judge Reinhold; Julia Sweeney; Joe Pichler; Michaela Gallo; Jamie Marsh; Michael Ciccolini; Frank Gorshin; Danielle Wiener; ***D:*** David Mickey Evans; ***W:*** Jeff Schechter; ***C:*** John Aronson; ***M:*** Philip Giffin. **VIDEO**

Beethoven's 4th 🦴 1/2 **2001** Unruly Beethoven is sent to obedience school where he's accidentally switched with a well-behaved St. Bernard. Imagine the family's confusion. **94m/C; VHS, DVD.** Judge Reinhold; Julia Sweeney; Joe Pichler; Michaela Gallo; Matt McCoy; Veanne Cox; Mark Lindsay Chapman; Art LaFleur; Kaleigh Krish; Natalie Marston; ***D:*** David Mickey Evans; ***W:*** John Loy; ***C:*** John Aronson. **VIDEO**

Beethoven's 5th 🦴🦴 1/2 **2003** Twelve-year-old Sara (Chase) and Beethoven spend the summer with eccentric Uncle Freddy (Thomas) in the old mining town of Quicksilver. Beethoven manages to dig up an old $10 bill that apparently comes from some loot buried by a couple of crooks in the 1920s and soon everyone in town is looking for the rest of the cash. **90m/C; VHS, DVD.** Daveigh Chase; Dave Thomas; Faith Ford; John Larroquette; Kathy Griffin; Tom Poston; Katherine Helmond; Clint Howard; ***D:*** Mark Griffiths; ***W:*** Elana Lesser; Cliff Ruby; ***C:*** Christopher Baffa; ***M:*** Adam Berry. **VIDEO**

Beethoven's Big Break 🦴🦴 1/2 **2008 (PG)** Struggling animal trainer Eddie gets his big break as the wrangler for a movie star St. Bernard. But the dog's fame means some criminal-types have come up with a kidnapping and ransom scheme. **101m/C; DVD.** Jonathan Silverman; Moises Arias; Rhea Perlman; Stephen Tobolowsky; Eddie Griffin; Osmar Nunez; Joey Fatone; Jennifer Finnigan; ***D:*** Mike Elliott; ***W:*** Derek Rydall; ***C:*** Stephen Campbell; ***M:*** Robert Folk. **VIDEO**

Beethoven's Christmas Adventure 🦴🦴 1/2 **2011 (PG)** Henry the elf accidentally takes off in Santa's toy-filled sleigh and crash lands in Beethoven's neighborhood. Santa's magic toy bag gets stolen and it's up to the St. Bernard (who now talks) and his human pal Mason to rescue Henry, retrieve the toy bag, and make sure that Christmas isn't ruined. **90m/C; DVD.** Kyle Massey; Munro Chambers; Kim Rhodes; Robert Picardo; John O'Hurley; Curtis Armstrong; ***V:*** Tom Arnold; ***Nar:*** John Cleese; ***D:*** John Putch; ***W:*** Daniel Altiere; Steven Altiere; ***C:*** Ross Berryman; ***M:*** Chris Bacon. **VIDEO**

Beetlejuice 🦴🦴🦴 1/2 **1988 (PG)** The after-life is confusing for a pair of ultra-nice novice ghosts Adam Maitland (Baldwin) and his wife Barbara (Davis), who are faced with chasing an obnoxious family of post-modern art lovers who move into their house. Then they hear of a poltergeist who promises to rid the house of all trespassers for a price. Things go from bad to impossible when the maniacal Keaton (as the demonic "Betelgeuse") works his magic. The calypso scene is priceless. A cheesy, funny, surreal farce of life after death with inventive set designs popping continual surprises. Ryder is striking as the misunderstood teen with a death complex, while O'Hara is hilarious as the yuppie art poseur. **92m/C; VHS, DVD, Blu-Ray.** Michael Keaton; Geena Davis; Alec Baldwin; Sylvia Sidney; Catherine O'Hara; Winona Ryder; Jeffrey Jones; Dick Cavett; Glenn Shadix; Robert Goulet; ***D:*** Tim Burton; ***W:*** Michael McDowell; Warren Skaaren; ***C:*** Thomas Ackerman; ***M:*** Danny Elfman. Oscars '88: Makeup; Natl. Soc. Film Critics '88: Actor (Keaton).

Before and After 🦴 1/2 **1995 (PG-13)** Disjointed drama depicts well-off suburban couple, Carolyn (Streep) and Ben (Neeson), who are thrown into chaos when their teenaged son Jacob (Furlong) is accused of murdering his girlfriend. Upon notification by the police that his son is the prime suspect and on the lam, Ben finds what seems to be bloody evidence in the family's car, which he destroys. The story loses steam from there. Based on the novel by Rosellen Brown, the focus is on the effect the death has on this picture book Massachusetts family. Neeson and Streep fall short of usually deliverable goods and director Schroeder takes the middle-of-the-road sentimental approach. **107m/C; VHS, DVD, Blu-Ray.** Meryl Streep; Liam Neeson; Edward Furlong; Alfred Molina; John Heard; Julia Weldon; Daniel von Bargen; Ann Magnuson; Alison Folland; Kaiulani Lee; ***D:*** Barbet Schroeder; ***W:*** Ted Tally; ***C:*** Luciano Tovoli; ***M:*** Howard Shore.

Before I Fall 🦴🦴 **2017 (PG-13)** If *Groundhog Day* and *Mean Girls* had humorectomies and then hooked up, this would be the result. Teenaged Samantha has a perfect family, boyfriend, and group of gal pals, but she dies in a car crash and is forced to repeat that day until she learns to be a nicer person. Zoey Deutch captivates as the lead, as does Halston Sage as her BFF, and the ending is surprisingly satisfying, but the bulk of the movie is too tedious and angsty to appeal to anyone outside the YA set. Based on a novel by Lauren Oliver. **98m/C; DVD, Blu-Ray.** Zoey Deutch; Halston Sage; Logan Miller; Kian Lawley; Elena Kampouris; ***D:*** Ry Russo-Young; ***W:*** Maria Maggenti; ***C:*** Michael Fimognari; ***M:*** Adam Taylor.

Before I Forget 🦴🦴 *Avant que J'oubile* **2007** When his wealthy benefactor dies after 30 years of support and he doesn't get an expected inheritance, former gigolo Pierre (Nolot) struggles insouciantly to cope with age, poverty, and the increasing complications of his HIV status. He pursues sex with rent boys though he doesn't seem to take any pleasure in it, except for gossiping with his friend Georges (Pommier) about the cost, and takes an unsentimental look back on his life while writing his memoirs. French with subtitles. **108m/C; DVD.** *FR* Jacques Nolot; Jean Pommier; Bastien d'Asnieres; Marc Rioufol; Jean-Pol Dubois; ***C:*** Josee Desaies.

Before I Go to Sleep 🦴 1/2 **2014 (R)** This one might actually help you deal with any problems with insomnia. Christine (Kidman) wakes up every morning with no memory of the last 15 years. She thinks she's 26 instead of 40 and doesn't recognize her husband Ben (Firth). Every morning, he has to explain that she was in an accident that gave her a rare form of amnesia that reboots her after every night's sleep. Christine distrusts Ben and works with Dr. Nasch (Strong) to discern why he's not being entirely truthful. It doesn't make any sense and features thin characters despite solid work by Kidman. Take a snooze instead. **92m/C; DVD, Blu-Ray.** *UK US* Nicole Kidman; Colin Firth; Mark Strong; Anne-Marie Duff; ***D:*** Rowan Joffe; ***W:*** Rowan Joffe; ***C:*** Ben Davis; ***M:*** Ed Shearmur.

Before I Say Goodbye 🦴 1/2 **2003** Political hopeful Nell's (Young) hubby faces accusations of crooked business deeds when he and his boat are blown to bits. But her desperate search for the truth might make her the next victim. A Mary Higgins Clark adaptation. **95m/C; VHS, DVD.** Sean Young; Lloyd Bochner; Peter DeLuise; Ursula Karven; ***D:*** Michael Storey; ***W:*** John Benjamin Martin; Jon Cooksey; Ali Matheson; ***C:*** David Pelletier. **TV**

Before I Wake 🦴 **2015 (PG-13)** After Jessie (Bosworth) and Mark (Jane) adopt a young boy (Tremblay), they learn of his intense fear of sleep, how his dreams and nightmares become reality, and take big risks to discover why. Normally successful in the horror/mystery genre, director Flanagan doesn't quite pull this one off. Unfortunately when a scary story isn't so much scary, then someone's nodded off somewhere. **?m/C; DVD.** Annabeth Gish; Kate (Catherine) Bosworth; Thomas Jane; Scottie Thompson; Dash Mihok; ***D:*** Mike Flanagan; ***W:*** Mike Flanagan; Jeff Howard.

Before Midnight 🦴🦴🦴 **2013 (R)** Linklater, Delpy, and Hawke continue the story of Jesse and Celine that began in "Before Sunrise" and continued through "Before Sunset" in the best film of the now-trilogy. The now-married couple walks to a hotel room for a night away from their twin girls at the tail end of a Grecian vacation and the conversation swirls around their romantic past and complicated future. Linklater and his co-writer/stars not only know these characters so completely but understand how people in long-term relationships fight and love each other even in the same heated moment. It's a mesmerizing character study of romance, resentment, and hope. **108m/C; DVD, Blu-Ray.** Julie Delpy; Ethan Hawke; ***D:*** Richard Linklater; ***W:*** Julie Delpy; Ethan Hawke; Richard Linklater; ***C:*** Christos Voudouris; ***M:*** Graham Reynolds.

Before Night Falls 🦴🦴🦴 **2000 (R)** Director Schnabel takes a quantum leap in skill in his second film (after "Basquiat"). This time his tortured artist is the literally tortured late Cuban poet Reinaldo Arenas (Bardem), who falls victim to Castro's repression against both his writings and his sexuality (he's gay). Arenas gets thrown into prison, eventually gets released after confessing his "crimes," and makes his escape as part of the 1980 Mariel boatlift. Ironically, freedom offers little solace to Arenas either in Miami or his last home in New York. Spanish actor Bardem is outstanding as the poet who only seeks to be true to himself and pays a tragic price. Based on the writer's autobiography. **134m/C; VHS, DVD.** Javier Bardem; Olivier Martinez; Andrea Di Stefano; Johnny Depp; Michael Wincott; Sean Penn; Hector Babenco; Najwa Nimri; ***D:*** Julian Schnabel; ***W:*** Julian Schnabel; Lazaro Gomez Carilles; Cunningham O'Keefe; ***C:*** Xavier Perez Grobet; Guillermo Rosas; ***M:*** Carter Burwell. Ind. Spirit '01: Actor (Bardem); Natl. Bd. of Review '00: Actor (Bardem); Natl. Soc. Film Critics '00: Actor (Bardem).

Before Sunrise 🦴🦴 1/2 **1994 (R)** Light, "getting-to-know-you," romance unfolds as two 20-somethings share an unlikely 14-hour date. Gen-Xer Jesse (Hawke) and French beauty (Delpy) meet on the Eurail and he convinces her to join him in exploring Vienna and their mutual attraction before he heads back to the States in the morning. The two exchange life experiences and philosophies in the typical Linklater conversational fashion, but the film strays from the comical accounts of earlier works "Slacker" and "Dazed and Confused." Cinematographer Daniel captures the Old World with finesse, especially in the inevitable "first kiss" atop the Ferris wheel made famous in Orson Welles' "The Third Man." **101m/C; VHS, DVD, Blu-Ray.** Ethan Hawke; Julie Delpy; ***D:*** Richard Linklater; ***W:*** Richard Linklater; Kim Krizan; ***C:*** Lee Daniel. Berlin Intl. Film Fest. '94: Director (Linklater).

Before Sunset 🦴🦴🦴 1/2 **2004 (R)** Sequel to Linklater's "Before Sunrise" reunites Jesse (Hawke) and Celine (Delpy), nine years after their Viennese fling, on the sidewalks of Paris. He's a writer promoting his book about their brief affair. She, a Parisian, shows up at his book signing. The two have only a few hours to catch up before Jesse has to fly back to America. In real time, they walk through Paris together, just talking. But what talking! They begin awkwardly polite and impersonal, but as the minutes slip away their questions and responses take on more urgency. Hawke and Delpy co-wrote the screenplay (with Hawke using his real-life divorce as inspiration) and there's real chemistry between them. Movie veers cleverly back and forth between them and ends ambiguously. Great date film (Sorry, guys). **80m/C; VHS, DVD, Blu-Ray.** Ethan Hawke; Julie Delpy; Rodolphe Pauly; ***D:*** Richard Linklater; ***W:*** Ethan Hawke; Julie Delpy; Richard Linklater; ***C:*** Lee Daniel; ***M:*** Julie Delpy; Glover Gill.

Before the Devil Knows You're Dead 🦴🦴🦴 **2007 (R)** At 83, director Lumet shows he still has crime chops in this grubby tragedy about a botched heist. Calculating, fleshy Andy (Hoffman) has a drug problem and a trophy wife, Gina (Tomei), while his sad-sack, skinny baby bro Hank (Hawke), who happens to be hitting the sheets with Gina, needs cash for his shrewish ex (Ryan). Andy plans a heist on their family's jewelry store but Hank manages to screw it up and things just get more complicated. Good performances by all concerned. **117m/C; DVD, Blu-Ray.** Philip Seymour Hoffman; Ethan Hawke; Marisa Tomei; Albert Finney; Rosemary Harris; Brian F. O'Byrne; Amy Ryan; Michael Shannon; Aleksa Palladino; ***D:*** Sidney Lumet; ***W:*** Kelly Masterson; ***C:*** Ron Fortunato; ***M:*** Carter Burwell.

Before the Fall 🦴🦴 *NaPolA* **2004** In 1942, teenager Friedrich Weimer (Riemelt) goes against his father's wishes to enter an exclusive Berlin school designed to educate future Nazi leaders. Friedrich distinguishes himself with his boxing prowess but eventually begins to question his indoctrination. German with subtitles. **110m/C; DVD.** *GE* Tom Schilling; Max Riemelt; Michael Schenk; Jonas Jagermeyr; Leon A. Kersten; Thomas Dreschel; ***D:*** Dennis Gansel; ***W:*** Dennis Gansel; Maggie Peren; ***C:*** Torsten Brewer; ***M:*** Angelo Badalamenti; Normand Corbeil.

Before the Flood 🦴🦴 1/2 **2016 (PG)** A cause-driven documentary exploration of climate change and global warming. Narrated by actor DiCaprio, the film features perspectives of scientists, officials, and others who have experience with or knowledge of climate change effects. The film outlines key ideas on such topics as the polar ice caps melting and the United States' electricity use for wide understanding and offers viewers easy ways to help, such as recycling or turning off lights. Though the documentary discusses the major issues about climate change, it only offers an emotional perspective on the topic and limits itself to defining related, obvious heroes and villains. **96m/C; DVD.** Leonardo DiCaprio; ***D:*** Fisher Stevens; ***W:*** Mark Monroe; ***C:*** Antonio Rossi; ***M:*** Mogwai; Trent Reznor; Atticus Ross; Gustavo Santaolalla.

Before the Rain 🦴🦴🦴 *Po Dezju; Pred dozhdot* **1994** War-torn Macedonia is the backdrop for Manchevski's first film (and first made in the newly declared republic of Macedonia). Powerful circular narrative joins three stories about the freedom of love and the pervasiveness of violence. "Words" finds young Macedonian monk Kiril (Colin) distracted from his spiritual duties by young Albanian Muslim Zamira (Mitevska), who takes refuge in his monastery. In "Faces," pregnant picture editor Anne (Cartlidge) is torn between her estranged husband and her lover, Aleksander (Serbedzija), a London-based war photographer who left his native Macedonia years before. "Pictures" finds Aleksandar returning to his old village—now torn by ethnic strife. In Macedonian, Albanian, and English, with subtitles. **120m/C; VHS, DVD.** *GB FR MA* Rade Serbedzija; Katrin Cartlidge; Gregoire Colin; Labina Mitevska; Phyllida Law; ***D:*** Milcho Manchevski; ***W:*** Milcho Manchevski; ***C:*** Manuel Teran; ***M:*** Anastasia. Ind. Spirit '96: Foreign Film; Venice Film Fest. '94: Golden Lion.

Before the Rains 🦴🦴 **2007 (PG-13)** Lavishly photographed period piece about Brits behaving badly in India. In 1937, spice baron Henry Moores (Roache) plans to build a road that will help expand his business but it needs to be completed before monsoon season. His right-man man T.K. (Bose) smooths the way but Moores is having an affair with married housemaid Sajani (Das), whose suspicious husband (Paul) beats her. When Sajani comes to Moores for help, he coldly turns her over to the loyal T.K. to deal with, causing more turmoil and eventual tragedy. **98m/C; DVD.** Linus Roache; Rahul Bose; Nandita Das; Jennifer Ehle; Lal Paul; John Standing; Leopold Benedict; ***D:*** Santosh Sivan; ***W:*** Cathy Rabin; ***C:*** Santosh Sivan; ***M:*** Mark Kilian.

Before We Go 🦴🦴 **2014 (PG-13)** Captain America himself, Chris Evans, makes his directorial debut with a romantic dramedy that feels inspired by Richard Linklater's "Before" trilogy but lacks the spark. Brooke Dalton (Eve) misses the last train home, and a street musician named Nick (Evans) helps her try to get back there before her husband does. Evans brings the his same affable charm to his direction, but the script here is thin and his filmmaking can't quite support it. He also has too little chemistry with Eve to make the romance work. **96m/C; DVD, Blu-Ray, Streaming.** Chris Evans; Alice Eve; Emma Fitzpatrick; Daniel Spink; Mark Kassen; John Cullum; ***D:*** Chris Evans; ***W:*** Ronald Bass; Jennifer Smolka; Chris Shafer; Paul Vicknair; ***C:*** John Guleserian; ***M:*** Chris(topher) Westlake.

Before Winter Comes 🦴 1/2 **1969** Starts off as a bland military comedy before it gets a little serious. In 1945, British Major Giles Burnside is assigned to oversee a displaced persons camp in Austria where there's friction between British and Russian troops and wrangling over zoning areas. Burnside's wheeler-dealer interpreter Janovic is found to be a Russian deserter and the Soviets want him back. **103m/C; DVD.** *UK* David Niven; Topol; John Hurt; Anna Karina; Anthony Quayle; Ori Levy; ***D:*** J. Lee Thompson; ***W:*** Andrew Sinclair; ***C:*** Gilbert Taylor; ***M:*** Ron Grainer.

Before You Say 'I Do' 🦴🦴 1/2 **2009** Undemanding rom com (with adorable leads) from the Hallmark Channel. George (Sutcliffe) proposes to Jane (Westfeldt) but she refuses because of her lousy first marriage to Doug (Roop)?who cheated on their wedding day. A car crash leads to George going back in time 10 years so he can stop Jane's wedding and get her to fall in love with him instead. **120m/C; DVD.** David Sutcliffe; Jennifer Westfeldt; Lauren Holly; Jeff Roop; Brad Borbridge; Brandon Firla; John Boylan; Roger Dunn; ***D:*** Paul Fox; ***W:*** Elena Krupp; ***C:*** David Makin; ***M:*** Lawrence Shragge. **CABLE**

Beg! 1/2 **1994** The wealthy owners of a mental institution announce possible cuts to an already-thin budget, and the staff immediately sets out to stab one another in the back. Quite literally in some cases. **108m/C; DVD, Streaming.** *UK* Philip Pelew; Julian Bleach; Olegar Fedoro; Jeremy Wilkin; Peta Lily; ***D:*** Robert Golden; ***W:*** Peta Lily; Robert Golden; David Glass; ***C:*** Chris Middleton; ***M:*** David Pearl; Stephen Parsons. **VIDEO**

Beggars in Ermine **1934** A handicapped, impoverished man organizes all the beggars in the world into a successful corporation. Unusual performance from Atwill. **70m/B; VHS, DVD.** Lionel Atwill; Henry B. Walthall; Betty Furness; Jameson Thomas; James Bush; Astrid Allwyn; George "Gabby" Hayes; ***D:*** Phil Rosen.

Beggars of Life **1928** In a panic, Nancy (Brooks) kills her abusive stepfather. She disguises herself as a boy and, with fellow runaway Jim (Arlen) serving as her protector, decides to hop a train to Canada. They wind up spending the night in a hobo camp, looked after by Oklahoma Red (Beery) who aids in their escape at great cost to himself. **100m/B; Silent; VHS, DVD, Blu-Ray.** Louise Brooks; Richard Arlen; Wallace Beery; Robert Perry; Roscoe Karns; Edgar "Blue" Washington; ***D:*** William A. Wellman; ***W:*** Benjamin Glazer; Jim Tully; ***C:*** Henry W. Gerrard; ***M:*** Karl Hajos.

Beggar's Opera **1954** Brooks' directorial debut was this adaptation of John Gay's 18th-century comic opera. Highwayman MacHeath (Olivier), a prisoner in Newgate who's condemned to hang, regales a beggar (Griffith) with his life story and the beggar decides to write an opera about him. Olivier did his own singing (badly) while most of the other performers were dubbed. **93m/C; DVD.** *GB* Laurence Olivier; Hugh Griffith; Stanley Holloway; Dorothy Tutin; George Devine; Mary Clare; Athene Seyler; Daphne Anderson; ***D:*** Peter Brooks; ***W:*** Christopher Fry; Denis Cannan; ***C:*** Guy Green; ***M:*** Arthur Bliss.

Begin Again 1/2 *Can a Song Save Your Life?* **2013 (R)** Director/writer Carney's long-awaited follow-up to "Once" strikes a few similar chords in the way it intertwines music and romance, but the song isn't quite as catchy. Knightley stars as Gretta, a songwriter abandoned by long-time boyfriend Dave (Levine). Of course, Gretta meets Dan (Ruffalo) just in time for both love and her chosen career. Dan is a record-label exec who falls for both Gretta's looks and her skills with a guitar. With more whimsy than the two characters in "Once," the two inspire and fall for one another. **104m/C; DVD, Blu-Ray.** Keira Knightley; Mark Ruffalo; Catherine Keener; Adam Levine; Hailee Steinfeld; James Corden; ***D:*** John Carney; ***W:*** John Carney; ***C:*** Yaron Orbach; ***M:*** Gregg Alexander.

Beginners **2010** Oliver (McGregor) is completely shocked when his elderly father, Hal (Plummer), declares that he is gay and dating a young man named Andy (Visnjic). As if that weren't enough, he also learns that his father has terminal lung cancer. As Oliver reflects on his father's unconventional and inspirational life, he strives to take a chance with new love Anna (Laurent) despite a long string of unsuccessful relationships. Profoundly funny and tragic as it explores life's bittersweet lessons—including how well we know even those closest to us. Autobiographical story from writer/director Mills. **105m/C; DVD, Blu-Ray.** Ewan McGregor; Christopher Plummer; Melanie Laurent; Goran Visnjic; Kai Lennox; Mary Page Keller; Keegan Boos; ***D:*** Mike Mills; ***W:*** Mike Mills; ***C:*** Kasper Tuxen; ***M:*** Roger Neill; David Palmer; Brian Reitzell. Oscars '11: Support. Actor (Plummer); British Acad. '11: Support. Actor (Plummer); Golden Globes '12: Support. Actor (Plummer); Ind. Spirit '12: Support. Actor (Plummer); Screen Actors Guild '11: Support. Actor (Plummer).

A Beginner's Guide to Endings 1/2 **2010 (R)** In this quirky black comedy, three brothers discover at the reading of their father's will that the quick cash drug trials he forced them into have severely shortened their own life spans. They decide to fulfill their individual bucket lists. Not everything works, but there's enough that does to make it entertaining. **92m/C; DVD.** Scott Caan; Jason Jones; Paulo Costanzo; J.K. Simmons; Tricia Helfer; Harvey Keitel; Wendy Crewson; ***D:*** Jonathan Sobol; ***W:*** Jonathan Sobol; ***C:*** Samy Inayeh. **VIDEO**

Beginning of the End 1/2 **1957** Produced the same year as "The Deadly Mantis," Gordon's effort adds to 1957's harvest of bugs on a rampage "B"-graders. Giant, radiation-spawned grasshoppers attack Chicago causing Graves to come to the rescue. Easily the best giant grasshopper movie ever made. **73m/B; VHS, DVD.** Peggy Castle; Peter Graves; Morris Ankrum; Richard Benedict; James Seay; Thomas B(rowne). Henry; Larry J. Blake; John Close; Frank Wilcox; ***D:*** Bert I. Gordon; ***W:*** Lester Gorn; Fred Freiberger; ***C:*** Jack Marta; ***M:*** Albert Glasser.

The Beguiled **1970 (R)** During the Civil War a wounded Union soldier is taken in by the women at a girl's school in the South. He manages to seduce both a student and a teacher, and jealousy and revenge ensue. Decidedly weird psychological melodrama from action vets Siegel and Eastwood. **109m/C; VHS, DVD, Blu-Ray.** Clint Eastwood; Geraldine Page; Elizabeth Hartman; Jo Ann Harris; ***D:*** Donald Siegel; ***W:*** Albert (John B. Sherry) Maltz; Irene (Grimes Grice) Kamp; ***C:*** Bruce Surtees; ***M:*** Lalo Schifrin.

The Beguiled 1/2 **2017 (R)** Writer/director Sofia Coppola's intriguing remake of the 1971 film. Like a fox in a hen house, Farrell's appearance at an all-girls' boarding school unleashes tension, but since this is the South during the Civil War, it's of the hospitable, courteous-while-I-eviscerate-you variety. Kidman's, Dunst's, and Fanning's characters subtlety and deftly portray their simmering jealousy and rivalry. Based on the 1966 novel by Thomas Cullinan. **93m/C; DVD, Blu-Ray.** Colin Farrell; Nicole Kidman; Kirsten Dunst; Elle Fanning; Oona Laurence; ***D:*** Sofia Coppola; ***W:*** Sofia Coppola; ***C:*** Philippe Le Sourd; ***M:*** Phoenix.

Behave Yourself! 1/2 **1952** A married couple adopts a dog who may be the key for a million-dollar hijacking setup by a gang of hoodlums. **81m/B; VHS, DVD.** Shelley Winters; Farley Granger; William Demarest; Lon Chaney, Jr.; Hans Conried; Elisha Cook, Jr.; Francis L. Sullivan; ***D:*** George Beck.

Behaving Badly 1/2 **1989** When Bridget's husband of 20 years left her for a younger woman, she didn't put up a fuss. But after five years of keeping a stiff upper lip, Bridget hasn't really moved on with her life and she decides to start over by changing her attitude and not being so accomodating. Some of the characters are little more than charicatures, which doesn't help the slow-moving story. **203m/C; DVD.** *UK* Dame Judi Dench; Ronald Pickup; Frances Barber; Joely Richardson; Douglas Hodge; ***D:*** David Tucker; ***W:*** Catherine Heath; Moira Williams; ***C:*** Andy Watt; ***M:*** Stephen Oliver. **TV**

Behemoth **2011** Part of the Syfy Channel's "Maneater" series. An earthquake reactivates a long-dormant volcano on Mount Lincoln and as scientists investigate, they find a subterranean creature has been released to cause havoc. The special effects are mostly shaky cams, steam, and monster parts since there's no budget for anything more. **90m/C; DVD.** Ed Quinn; Pascale Hutton; William B. Davis; Ty Olsson; Cindy Busby; James Kirk; Jessica Parker Kennedy; Garry Chalk; ***D:*** David (W.D.) Hogan; ***W:*** Rachelle S. Howie; ***C:*** Anthony C. Metchie; ***M:*** Michael Neilson. **CABLE**

Behind Enemy Lines 1/2 **1985 (R)** Special Forces soldier goes on a special mission to eliminate a possible Nazi spy. **83m/C; VHS, Blu-Ray, UMD.** Hal Holbrook; Ray Sharkey; David McCallum; Tom Isbell; Anne Twomey; Robert Patrick; ***D:*** Sheldon Larry. **TV**

Behind Enemy Lines **1996 (R)** Ex-Marine Mike Weston (Griffith) believes he was responsible for the death of his friend Jones (Mulkey) during assignment in Vietnam. When Weston discovers Jones is actually being hostage, he decides on a rescue mission. **89m/C; VHS, DVD, Blu-Ray.** Thomas Ian Griffith; Chris Mulkey; Courtney Gains; ***D:*** Mark Griffiths; ***W:*** Andrew Osborne; Dennis Cooley; ***C:*** Blake T. Evans; ***M:*** Arthur Kempel.

Behind Enemy Lines **2001 (PG-13)** Balkan civil war is mere scenery, and soldiers only caricatures, in this cartoonish cat-and-mouse chase movie. Ace Navy navigator Lt. Burnett (Wilson), tired of flying peace missions, yearns for some real action. When a routine reconnaissance operation goes awry—his plane shot down over Serbian territory and his pilot ruthlessly executed—Burnett gets his wish. Crusty Admiral Reigart (Hackman) wants to rescue his flyboy, but a pesky international peace agreement gets in the way. First-time director Moore, best known for Sega promos, takes a video game approach to war. Utterly unconvincing suspense, but action sequences do their duty. Despite a clear connection to the ordeal of real-life Air Force captain Scott O'Grady, this is no true story. **106m/C; VHS, DVD, Blu-Ray.** Owen Wilson; Gene Hackman; Joaquim de Almeida; David Keith; Gabriel Macht; Charles Malik Whitfield; Olek Krupa; Vladimir Mashkov; Marko Ogonda; ***D:*** John Moore; ***W:*** David Veloz; Zak Penn; ***C:*** Brendan Galvin; ***M:*** Don Davis.

Behind Enemy Lines 2: Axis of Evil 1/2 **2006 (R)** Navy SEALs are on a covert op to North Korea to take out a nuclear missile site. The mission is aborted when they are already on the ground so the soldiers decide to get it done anyway despite the bad guys hunting for them. Dumb but generally fast-paced escapist fare. **96m/C; DVD, Blu-Ray.** Nicholas Gonzalez; Keith David; Denis Arndt; Ben Cross; Bruce McGill; Peter Coyote; Glenn Morshower; Matt Bushell; Dennis James Lee; ***D:*** James Dodson; ***W:*** James Dodson; ***C:*** Lorenzo Senatore; ***M:*** Pinar Toprak. **VIDEO**

Behind Enemy Lines 3: Colombia 1/2 **2008 (R)** An in-name-only sequel that finds a team of Navy SEALS, on assignment in Colombia, falsely accused of assassinating the leaders of two opposing factions. With the U.S. government disavowing their mission, the commandoes are left to sort out the mess on their own. **94m/C; DVD.** Joe Manganiello; Kenneth Anderson; Keith David; Channon Roe; Yancey Arias; Steven Bauer; Tim Matheson; ***D:*** Tim Matheson; ***W:*** Tobias Iaconis; ***C:*** Claudio Chea; ***M:*** Joseph Conlan. **VIDEO**

Behind Office Doors **1931** Astor stars as the secretarial "power behind the throne" in this look at who really wields power in an office. Her boss takes her for granted until things go wrong. **82m/B; VHS, DVD.** Mary Astor; Robert Ames; Ricardo Cortez; Charles Sellon; ***D:*** Melville Brown; ***W:*** Carey Wilson.

Behind That Curtain 1/2 **1929** Charlie Chan (Park) makes a brief appearance as a Scotland Yard detective in this melodrama. Wealthy Eve Mannering (Moran) marries rotter Eric Durand (Strange) and they go off to India. Soon unhappy, Eve is eager to leave Eric behind when old friend John Beetham (Baxter) assures her of his love. They travel to San Francisco with a murderous Eric in pursuit. Boris Karloff makes an appearance in his first sound picture as a nameless servant. **91m/B; DVD.** Warner Baxter; Lois Moran; Philip Strange; Charles King; Gilbert Emery; E.L. Park; ***D:*** Irving Cummings; ***W:*** Sonya Levien; Clarke Silvernail; ***C:*** Conrad Wells.

Behind the Candelabra **2013** Soderbergh wraps Douglas and Damon in over-the-top (even for Vegas) glitz and secrecy in looking at the last decade of entertainer Liberace's life. In 1977, 18-year-old Scott Thorsen meets the 58-year-old 'Lee" and soon becomes his companion, even appearing onstage with him. There's something both kind and unnerving about Liberace, especially after he persuades Scott to undergo plastic surgery to look more like him with the help of supremely creepy Dr. Jack Startz (Lowe). But drugs enter their lavish lifestyle, Scott becomes an addict, and eventually realizes he's going to be replaced, leading to a palimony suit. Based on Thorson's book. **120m/C; DVD, Blu-Ray.** Michael Douglas; Matt Damon; Rob Lowe; Scott Bakula; Dan Aykroyd; Debbie Reynolds; Cheyenne Jackson; Mike O'Malley; ***D:*** Steven Soderbergh; ***W:*** Richard LaGravenese; ***C:*** Steven Soderbergh; ***M:*** Marvin Hamlisch. **CABLE**

Behind the Green Lights 1/2 **1935** Mary, who works for ruthless criminal lawyer Raymond Cortell, switches loyalties when her policeman father is shot by one of Cortell's acquitted clients. She then takes up with detective Dave Britten to help prove Cortell is dirty and put him behind bars. **68m/B; DVD.** Sidney Blackmer; Judith Allen; Norman Foster; Purnell Pratt; Theodore von Eltz; ***D:*** Christy Cabanne; ***W:*** James Gruen; ***C:*** Ernest Miller; Jack Marta.

Behind the Lines *Regeneration* **1997 (R)** Focuses on the friendship between WWI soldier/poets Siegfried Sassoon (Wilby) and Wilfred Owen (Bunce), who receive a brief reprieve from the war when they're treated for shell shock at Edinburgh's Craiglockhart Hospital in 1917. Another patient is working-class soldier Billy Prior (Miller), made mute from the horrors he's witnessed. But their compassionate doctor, William Rivers (Pryce), is himself becoming increasingly unstable over the ethical concerns his work engenders. If he cures his patients, they go back to the front to fight again. The first book in Pat Barker's war trilogy. **96m/C; VHS, DVD.** *GB CA* Jonathan Pryce; James Wilby; Jonny Lee Miller; Stuart Bunce; Tanya Allen; John Neville; Dougray Scott; David Hayman; David Robb; Julian Fellowes; Kevin McKidd; Jeremy Child; ***D:*** Gilles Mackinnon; ***W:*** Allan Scott; ***C:*** Glen MacPherson; ***M:*** Mychael Danna.

Behind the Mask 1/2 **1999** Mentally challenged janitor James Jones (Fox) is employed at a center run by workaholic doctor Bob Shushan (Sutherland). When the doc suffers a heart attack, it's James who saves him. Shushan takes this as a wake-up call and decides to help James find the father who abandoned him while reconnecting with his own neglected adult son, Brian (Whitford). Based on a true story. **90m/C; DVD.** Donald Sutherland; Matthew Fox; Bradley Whitford; Mary McDonnell; Sheila Larken; Currie Graham; Lorena Gale; Ron Sauve; ***D:*** Tom McLoughlin; ***W:*** Gregory Goodell; ***C:*** Arthur Albert. **TV**

Behind the Mask: The Rise of Leslie Vernon **2006 (R)** Hilarious satire of slasher films set in a world where killers apparently have enough fans to warrant documentary crews chasing them about to interview them. Crews composed of people who should, in theory, be smart enough to realize at some point that they might end up becoming victims because slashers are, you know, crazy. **92m/C; DVD, Blu-Ray, Streaming.** Nathan Baesel; Robert Englund; Scott Wilson; Ben Pace; Britain Spellings; Angela Goethals; Zelda Rubenstein; Bridgett Newton; Kate Johnson; ***D:*** Scott Glosserman; ***W:*** Scott Glosserman; David J. Stieve; ***C:*** Jaron Presant; ***M:*** Gordy Haab. **VIDEO**

Behind the Red Door **2002 (R)** Natalie (Sedgwick) hasn't spoken to her arrogant older brother Roy (Sutherland) for 10 years. A New York photographer, Natalie is tricked by her friend and agent Julia (Channing) into accepting an assignment in Boston that turns out to be for her brother's company. Roy then bullies Natalie into staying for his birthday party—later revealing to her that he's dying of AIDS. He wants to reconcile but a shaken Natalie (who blames Roy for some childhood traumas) insists she must return home. Good cast, but Sutherland's character is so secretive and obnoxious it's hard to dredge up any sympathy for him. **105m/C; VHS, DVD.** Kyra Sedgwick; Kiefer Sutherland; Stockard Channing; Jason Carter; Philip Craig; ***D:*** Matia Karrell; ***W:*** Matia Karrell; C.W. Cressler; ***C:*** Robert Elswit; ***M:*** David Fleury. **CABLE**

Behind the Sun *Abril Despedacado; Broken April* **2001 (PG-13)** A blood feud between two families nearly destroys them both in Salles' adaptation of Ismail Kadare's novel, which the director relocated to Brazil in 1910. The Ferreiras and the

Breveses are both sugarcane planters determined to protect their honor if nothing else. Tonho Breves (Santoro) is expected to avenge the death of his older brother at the hands of the Ferreiras. Tonho's young brother (Lacerda) can't understand why the pointless violence continues and when Tonho falls in love with traveling circus performer Clara (Antonio), the boy becomes determined to see his brother safe and happy. Portuguese with subtitles. **91m/C; VHS, DVD.** *BR FR SI* Jose Dumont; Rita Assemany; Rodrigo Santoro; Ravi Ramos Lacerda; Luiz Carlos Vasconcelos; Othon Bastos; Flavia Marco Antonio; *D:* Walter Salles; *W:* Walter Salles; Karim Ainouz; Sergio Machado; *C:* Walter Carvalho; *M:* Antonio Pinto. British Acad. '01: Foreign Film.

Behind the Wall 1/2 **2008 (R)** A small community in Maine has decided to renovate a local lighthouse that's reputed to be haunted because of a 20-year-old murder case, despite the objections of an elderly priest. The pace picks up in the latter half of this low-budget horrorfest. **94m/C; DVD.** Souleymane Sy Savane; Diana Franco-Galindo; Jody Richardson; Lindy Booth; Lawrence Dane; James Thomas; Andy Jones; *D:* Paul Schneider; *W:* Anna Singer; Michael Bafaro; *C:* Larry Lynn. **VIDEO**

Behind Your Eyes 1/2 **2011** A mystery-horror film full of twists and turns, centered on a young couple and hidden truths. When Steve (Sandoval) and Erika (Farrell) go on a weekend trip to meet his parents, they expect to have fun. Instead, they are kidnapped, held hostage, and tortured by an enigmatic abductor (Fanaberia). Through this experience, secrets come to light and perspectives shift. Though Erika manages to break away and escape, the situation grows more dire for her and Steven. **85m/C; DVD, Blu-Ray.** Frida Farrell; Tom Sandoval; Daniel Fanaberia; Arthur Roberts; Remy O'Neill; *D:* Clint Lien; *W:* Daniel Fanaberia; *C:* Akis Konstantakopoulos; *M:* Corey Wallace. **VIDEO**

Behold a Pale Horse 1/2 **1964** A Spanish police captain attempts to dupe Peck into believing that his mother is dying and he must visit her on her deathbed. Loyalist Spaniard Peck becomes privy to the plot against him, but goes to Spain anyway in this post Spanish Civil War film. **118m/B; VHS, DVD, Blu-Ray.** Gregory Peck; Anthony Quinn; Omar Sharif; Mildred Dunnock; *D:* Fred Zinnemann; *W:* J(ames) P(inckney) Miller; *M:* Maurice Jarre.

Beijing Bicycle *Shiqisuide Danche* **2001 (PG-13)** Guei (Lin) leaves his provincial home and gets a job as a bike messenger in Beijing where most of his meager wages go to purchase his mountain bike. His bike is stolen and Guei loses his job. He finally discovers that petulant high schooler Jian (Bin), whose father wouldn't buy him a bike of his own, has purchased Geui's from a flea market and, because he can now join his friends riding after school, he refuses to let it go. Their confrontation turns violent as more and more people become involved. Chinese with subtitles. **113m/C; VHS, DVD.** *TW FR* Cui Lin; Bin Li; Zhou Xun; Gao Yuanyuahn; Li Shuang; Zhao Yiwei; Pang Yan; *D:* Xiaoshuai Wang; *W:* Xiaoshuai Wang; Danian Tang; Peggy Chiao; Hsiang-Ming Hsu; *C:* Jie Liu; *M:* Wang Hsiao Feng.

The Being **1983 (R)** People in Idaho are terrorized by a freak who became abnormal after radiation was disposed in the local dump. Another dull monster-created-by-nuclear-waste non-event. Of limited interest is Buzzi. However, you'd be more entertained (read: amused) by Troma's "The Toxic Avenger," which takes itself much (much!) less seriously. **82m/C; VHS, DVD, Blu-Ray.** Ruth Buzzi; Martin Landau; Jose Ferrer; *D:* Jackie Kong.

Being Canadian **2015** This humorous documentary explores what it really means to be Canadian, beyond common stereotypes. Canadian filmmaker Cohen moved to Los Angeles to become a comedy writer. There, he found that most people knew nothing about the nation to the north of the United States. This chronicles his personal quest to show the truth about the whole of Canada through his extensive travels in his native country and interviews with many famous Canadians, including actor Mike Myers and seminal band Rush. **90m/C; DVD, Streaming, Download.** *D:* Robert Cohen; *W:* Robert Cohen; *C:* Megan Raney; *M:* Craig Northey.

Being Charlie **2016 (R)** Charlie (Robinson) is a troubled teenager who breaks out of a drug treatment clinic. He makes his way home to Los Angeles, but his parents force him to go to an adult rehab center instead, where he meets a girl named Eva (Saylor), and finally grows up. Some of the issues of addiction are dealt with superficially here but it's a humane, well-made film that takes a different approach to coming-of-age arcs than many of its peers. Director Reiner's son Nick co-wrote the script. **97m/C; DVD, Blu-Ray.** Nick Robinson; Common; Cary Elwes; Devon Bostick; Morgan Saylor; *D:* Rob Reiner; *W:* Matt Elisofon; Nick Reiner; *C:* Barry Markowitz; *M:* Chris Bacon.

Being Elmo: A Puppeteer's Journey 1/2 **2011 (PG)** Entertaining, but not particularly enlightening, documentary on African-American puppeteer Kevin Clash, who provides the movement and voice for furry, red, childlike Elmo. Clash always knew he wanted to be a puppeteer, made his own puppets, and started his career on a local Baltimore-area children's TV program. His talent eventually led to his meeting Jim Henson in the mid-1980s, joining "Sesame Street," and his work as Elmo. **80m/C; DVD.** Kevin Clash; *Nar:* Whoopi Goldberg; *D:* Philip Shane; Constance Marks; *W:* Philip Shane; Justin Weinstein; *C:* James Miller; *M:* Joel Goodman.

Being Flynn 1/2 **2012 (R)** Struggling writer Nick Flynn (Dano) takes a job at a homeless shelter as he searches to find meaning in his life. His mother committed suicide and his father Jonathan, a con man (De Niro), hasn't been around for 18 years. When Jonathan shows up at the shelter, the pair begin to forge a tenuous relationship. Jonathan is eccentric, unhinged, but also a writer; Nick's mother (Moore) shows up in flashbacks; and Nick is drawn to Denise (Thirlby), another lost soul looking for answers by working at the shelter. Based on Flynn's 2004 memoir, "Another Bullshit Night in Suck City." **102m/C; DVD.** Robert De Niro; Paul Dano; Julianne Moore; Olivia Thirlby; Eddie Rouse; Steve Cirbus; Lili Taylor; Victor Rasuk; *D:* Paul Weitz; *W:* Paul Weitz; *C:* Declan Quinn; *M:* Damon Gough.

Being Frank *You Can Choose Your Family* **2019 (R)** In 1992, business owner Frank (Gaffigan) has a tense relationship with his teenage son Philip (Miller). Frank's job takes him away for weeks at a time, and he is often difficult to be around at home. One day, Philip learns that his father has another family, including a wife and two teenagers, in a nearby town. As Philip infiltrates Frank's other family, Frank takes action to win over Philip. At the same time, Philip is pained to learn that his father treats his other family much better. Though the comedy/drama has a generally strong script, it's a tough topic to play up for laughs. **109m/C; DVD.** Jim Gaffigan; Logan Miller; Danielle Campbell; Gage Banister; Isabelle Phillips; *D:* Miranda Bailey; *W:* Glen Lakin; *C:* Yaron Scharf; *M:* Craig Richey.

Being Human 1/2 **1994 (PG-13)** Ambitious comedy drama promises more than it delivers, and shackles Williams in the process. Hector (Williams) is a regular guy continuously reincarnated throughout the milennia. He plays a caveman, a Roman slave, a Middle Ages nomad, a crew member on a 17th century new world voyage, and a modern New Yorker in separate vignettes that echo and/or extend the main themes of family, identity, and random fate. But he manages to emerge from each sketch as an unassuming everyman who never learns his lesson. One of Williams' periodic chancy ventures away from his comedic roots occasionally strikes gold, but often seems overly restrained. **122m/C; VHS, DVD.** Robin Williams; John Turturro; Anna Galiena; Vincent D'Onofrio; Hector Elizondo; Lorraine Bracco; Lindsay Crouse; Kelly Hunter; William H. Macy; Grace Mahlaba; Theresa Russell; Helen Miller; Robert Carlyle; Tony Curran; Bill Nighy; David Morrissey; Ewan McGregor; David Proval; *D:* Bill Forsyth; *W:* Bill Forsyth; *C:* Michael Coulter; *M:* Michael Gibbs.

Being John Malkovich **1999 (R)** Very weird comedy is the debut feature for Jonze. High-strung street puppeteer Craig Schwartz (Cusack) is married to frumpy pet-store worker Lotte (an unrecognizable Diaz). Forced to take a job as an office clerk in a building on floor seven-and-a-half, Craig falls for office vixen, Maxine (Keener), but his big discovery is a sealed door that reveals a tunnel leading directly into actor John Malkovich's mind. Craig views the world through the actor's eyes for 15 minutes at a time and decides to profit on his findings. Things just get more surreal when both Lotte and Maxine get involved. **112m/C; VHS, DVD, Blu-Ray, HD-DVD.** John Cusack; Cameron Diaz; Catherine Keener; John Malkovich; Orson Bean; Mary Kay Place; Charlie Sheen; *D:* Spike Jonze; *W:* Charlie Kaufman; *C:* Lance Acord; *M:* Carter Burwell. British Acad. '99: Orig. Screenplay; Ind. Spirit '00: First Feature, First Screenplay; L.A. Film Critics '99: Screenplay; MTV Movie Awards '00: New Filmmaker (Jonze); N.Y. Film Critics '99: Support. Actor (Malkovich), Support. Actress (Keener); Natl. Soc. Film Critics '99: Film, Screenplay.

Being Julia **2004 (R)** Bening triumphs in the title role as a larger-than-life stage actress suffering a midlife dip. But this delightful diva still has the deviousness to show a couple of whippersnappers what it means to be a star. Swanning about in 1938 London, Julia has a strong support system, led by her unfaithful but loving manager/husband Michael (Irons). However, she's bored and ready for a little fling with Tom (Evans), a fawning young fan with an agenda of his own, involving his ambitious actress girlfriend (Punch). When Julia discovers she's been used, she takes the opportunity not only to get revenge but as a step in revitalizing her life. Based on the novel "Theatre" by W. Somerset Maugham. **105m/C; DVD.** *HU CA GB* Annette Bening; Jeremy Irons; Bruce Greenwood; Miriam Margolyes; Juliet Stevenson; Shaun Evans; Lucy Punch; Maury Chaykin; Sheila McCarthy; Michael Gambon; Leigh Lawson; Rosemary Harris; Rita Tushingham; Thomas Sturridge; *D:* Istvan Szabo; *W:* Ronald Harwood; *C:* Lajos Koltai; *M:* Mychael Danna. Golden Globes '05: Actress--Mus./Comedy (Bening).

Being There 1/2 **1979 (PG)** A feeble-minded gardener, whose entire knowledge of life comes from watching TV, is sent out into the real world when his employer dies. Equipped with his prize possession, his remote control unit, the gardener unwittingly enters the world of politics and is welcomed as a mysterious sage. Sellers is wonderful in this satiric treat adapted by Jerzy Kosinski from his novel. **130m/C; VHS, DVD, Blu-Ray.** Peter Sellers; Shirley MacLaine; Melvyn Douglas; Jack Warden; Richard Dysart; Richard Basehart; *D:* Hal Ashby; *W:* Jerzy Kosinski; *C:* Caleb Deschanel; *M:* Johnny Mandel. Oscars '79: Support. Actor (Douglas); Golden Globes '80: Actor--Mus./Comedy (Sellers), Support. Actor (Douglas); L.A. Film Critics '79: Support. Actor (Douglas); Natl. Bd. of Review '79: Actor (Sellers); Natl. Film Reg. '15; N.Y. Film Critics '79: Support. Actor (Douglas); Natl. Soc. Film Critics '79: Cinematog.; Writers Guild '79: Adapt. Screenplay.

Beirut 1/2 **2018 (R)** A dramatic political thriller written by Bourne author Tony Gilroy. In 1972, Mason (Hamm) is an engaging American diplomat in Lebanon. After colleague Cal (Pellegrino) informs Mason that his 13-year-old ward Karim (Rosenberg) is the younger brother of a terrorist involved in Munich Olympics attack, Mason tries to peacefully negotiate Karim's extraction. The situation goes badly. A decade later, Mason is called back to Beirut, a city in crisis, when Cal has been kidnapped, allegedly by a grown-up Karim (Chender). A strong performance by Hamm and the supporting cast carries the film. **109m/C; DVD, Blu-Ray.** Rosamund Pike; Jon Hamm; Mark Pellegrino; Dean Norris; Shea Whigham; *D:* Brad Anderson; *W:* Tony Gilroy; *C:* Bjorn Charpentier; *M:* John Debney.

Bel Ami 1/2 **2012 (R)** Although Pattinson is attractive in his 19th-century finery, he doesn't display the necessary charisma to put over the scheming, charm, and ruthlessness of social climbing Georges Duroy in this adaptation of Guy de Maupassants's 1885 novel. Penniless in Paris, Georges takes advantage of a meeting with a former mentor to get a newspaper job and the first of several amours who'll pave his way to money and power. **102m/C; DVD, Streaming.** *UK IT* Robert Pattinson; Uma Thurman; Kristin Scott Thomas; Christina Ricci; Colm Meaney; Philip Glenister; Holliday Grainger; *D:* Declan Donnellan; Nick Ormerod; *W:* Rachel Bennette; *C:* Stefano Falivene; *M:* Rachel Portman; Lakshman Joseph De Saram.

Bel Canto 1/2 **2018** At a mansion located in an unstable country, wealthy partygoers attend a performance featuring famed American soprano Roxanne Coss (Moore). The party is interrupted by a group of rebels, led by Benjamin (Huerta), who holds the group of attendees hostage. The rebels demand the release of all political prisoners in exchange for releasing the hostages. As the situation grows more dire, bonds form between the hostages. A compelling adaptation of the highly regarded Ann Patchett novel based on a real hostage crisis that took place in Lima, Peru, during the mid-1990s. **102m/C; DVD.** Julianne Moore; Ken(saku) Watanabe; Sebastian Koch; Ryo Kase; Tenoch Huerta; *D:* Paul Weitz; *W:* Paul Weitz; *C:* Tobias Datum; *M:* David Majzlin.

Bela Lugosi Meets a Brooklyn Gorilla **WOOF!** *The Boys from Brooklyn; The Monster Meets the Gorilla* **1952** Two men who look like Dean Martin and Jerry Lewis (but aren't) get lost in the jungle, where they meet mad scientist Lugosi. Worse than it sounds. Real Jerry sued for unflattering imitation. **74m/B; VHS, DVD.** Bela Lugosi; Duke Mitchell; Sammy Petrillo; Charlita; Martin Garralaga; Al Kikume; Muriel Landers; Milton Newberger; *D:* William Beaudine; *W:* Tim Ryan; *C:* Charles Van Enger; *M:* Richard Hazard.

Believe 1/2 **1999 (PG-13)** Teen prankster Ben Stiles (Mabe) loves to scare people. In fact, his behavior gets him kicked out of prep school and sent to live with his no-nonsense grandfather (Rubes). But the fright's on him when Ben and his friend Katherine (Cuthbert) decide to turn the abandoned Wickwire House into a haunted mansion and a ghostly figure suddenly starts making appearances. **97m/C; VHS, DVD.** Ricky Mabe; Elisha Cuthbert; Jan Rubes; Ben Gazzara; Andrea Martin; Jayne Heitmeyer; *D:* Robert Tinnell. **VIDEO**

Believe 1/2 **2007 (PG)** After Adam Pendon loses his steel mill job he's recruited by salesman Mark Fuller to join Believe Industries, a multi-level marketing company promising wealth through direct sales opportunities that seems just too good to be true. Adam becomes a success pushing products and signing up new salespeople but there's trouble brewing from some ex-Believers. **80m/C; DVD.** Larry Bagby; Lincoln Hoppe; Jeff Olson; Craig Clyde; Vanessa DeHart; Brian Clark; Britani Bateman; Steve Anderson; Ann Bosler; K. Danor Gerald; *D:* Loki Mulholland; *W:* Loki Mulholland; *C:* Ryan Little; *M:* Aaron Merrill. **VIDEO**

Believe **2016 (PG)** A faith-based drama about a businessman who regains his faith by helping others. Matthew Peyton (O'Quinn) owns the last major business in his economically depressed community. Because his company is on the verge of bankruptcy, other financial setbacks, and a workers strike, he cannot fund the local Christmas pageant. After being attacked and beaten, Matthew is cared for by single mom Sharon (Nicolet) and her young son Clarence (Brown). He experiences redemption after using the factory as a shelter for the poor during a freeze and later hires them as replacement workers. Poor pacing and heavy-handed storytelling limit the effectiveness of good performances. **119m/C; DVD.** Ryan O'Quinn; Shawnee Smith; Danielle Nicolet; Kevin Sizemore; David DeLuise; *D:* Billy Dickson; *W:* Billy Dickson; *C:* Billy Dickson; *M:* Michael Reola.

Believe in Me **2006 (PG)** Formulaic, standard "inspiring story" sports film plays like a distaff "Hoosiers" but occasionally conjures up an interesting twist. Clay Driscoll (Donovan) moves to small-town America to discover that his new job coaching a high school boy's team has been taken from him and he's been given the girl's team instead. At first offended, he takes the young women from zeros (giggling losers) to heroes (state finals) through hard work, dedication, inspiring locker room speeches, and other well-mined sports cliches. Based on a true story (of course). **108m/C; DVD, Blu-Ray.** Jeffrey Donovan; Samantha Mathis; Bruce Dern; Bob Gunton; Heather Matarazzo; Alicia Lagano; ***D:*** Robert Collector; ***W:*** Robert Collector; ***C:*** James L. Carter; ***M:*** David Torn.

The Believer 🦴🦴 **2001** Inspired by the true story of neo-Nazi Daniel Burros and the New York Times expose that revealed he was Jewish. In Bean's version, Danny Balint (Gosling) is a ferociously intelligent former yeshiva student whose personal identity crisis has led him to a fascist movement led by Curtis Zampf (Zane) and to virulent anti-Semitism. But even while leading his own band of skinheads, Danny discovers he can't easily leave his Jewish heritage behind. **98m/C; VHS, DVD.** Ryan Gosling; Summer Phoenix; Billy Zane; Theresa Russell; Glenn Fitzgerald; ***D:*** Henry Bean; ***W:*** Henry Bean; ***C:*** Jim Denault; ***M:*** Joel Diamond.

The Believers 🦴🦴 **1/2 1987 (R)** Tense horror mystery set in New York city about a series of gruesome, unexplained murders. A widowed police psychologist investigating the deaths unwittingly discovers a powerful Santeria cult that believes in the sacrifice of children. Without warning he is drawn into the circle of the "Believers" and must free himself before his own son is the next sacrifice. Gripping (and grim), unrelenting horror. **114m/C; VHS, DVD, Blu-Ray.** Martin Sheen; Helen Shaver; Malick Bowens; Harris Yulin; Robert Loggia; Jimmy Smits; Richard Masur; Harley Cross; Elizabeth Wilson; Lee Richardson; Carla Pinza; ***D:*** John Schlesinger; ***W:*** Mark Frost; ***C:*** Robby Muller; ***M:*** J. Peter Robinson.

Believers 🦴 **1/2 2007 (R)** Two paramedics (Messner, Huertas) are kidnapped by a doomsday cult that believes the end is at hand so they're going to commit mass suicide. Not quite sure why a suicidal cult wants paramedics in its midst, but it's a creepy story. **101m/C; DVD.** Johnny Messner; Elizabeth Bogush; Daniel Benzali; Jon Huertas; John Farley; Deanna Russo; ***D:*** Daniel Myrick; ***W:*** Daniel Myrick; ***C:*** Andrew Huebscher; ***M:*** Kays Al-Atrakchi. **VIDEO**

Belizaire the Cajun 🦴🦴 **1/2 1986 (PG)** 19th-century Louisiana love story. White prejudice against the Cajuns is rampant and violent, but that doesn't stop sexy faith healer Assante from falling in love with the inaccessible Cajun wife (Youngs) of a rich local. Made with care on a tight budget. Worthwhile, though uneven. **103m/C; VHS, DVD.** Armand Assante; Gail Youngs; Will Patton; Stephen McHattie; Michael Schoeffling; Robert Duvall; Nancy Barrett; ***D:*** Glen Pitre; ***W:*** Glen Pitre; ***C:*** Richard Bowen; ***M:*** Michael Doucet; Howard Shore.

The Belko Experiment 🦴🦴 **2017 (R)** Visualize your worst day on the job and then multiply it by a hundred in Greg McLean's vicious horror flick and social satire. An American company in Colombia is turned into the scene of a massacre when the 80 employees are basically told that they have to kill their co-workers to survive. The lengths people go to in such an experiment should make for a fascinating genre exercise but McLean's is more along the lines of mildly entertaining. Bluntly, the director isn't ambitious enough to make the social satire work here, but genre fans should still be satisfied. **89m/C; DVD, Blu-Ray.** John Gallagher, Jr.; Tony Goldwyn; Adria Arjona; John C. McGinley; Melonie Diaz; ***D:*** Greg McLean; ***W:*** James Gunn; ***C:*** Luis David Sansans; ***M:*** Tyler Bates.

Bell, Book and Candle 🦴🦴 **1/2 1958** Gillian Holroyd (Novak) is a beautiful modern-day witch (from a family of witches) who has made up her mind to refrain from using her powers. That is until Sheperd Henderson (Stewart) moves into her building and she decides to enchant him with a love spell. But spells have a way of backfiring on those who cast them. Lanchester is romantic Aunt Queenie and Lemmon is a standout as Gillian's jazz-loving, bongo-playing brother, Nicky. **106m/C; VHS, DVD, Blu-Ray.** James Stewart; Kim Novak; Jack Lemmon; Elsa Lanchester; Ernie Kovacs; Hermione Gingold; Janice Rule; ***D:*** Richard Quine; ***W:*** Daniel Taradash; ***C:*** James Wong Howe; ***M:*** George Duning.

Bell from Hell 🦴🦴 **1974** A tale of insanity and revenge, wherein a young man, institutionalized since his mother's death, plots to kill his aunt and three cousins. **80m/C; VHS, DVD.** Viveca Lindfors; Renaud Verley; Alfredo Mayo; ***D:*** Claudio Guerin Hill.

The Bell Jar 🦴 **1/2 1979 (R)** Based on poet Sylvia Plath's acclaimed semi-autobiographical novel, this is the story of a young woman who becomes the victim of mental illness. Not for the easily depressed and a disjointed and disappointing adaptation of Plath's work. **113m/C; VHS, DVD.** Marilyn Hassett; Julie Harris; Barbara Barrie; Anne Bancroft; Robert Klein; Anne Jackson; ***D:*** Larry Peerce.

Bella 🦴🦴 **2006 (PG-13)** Saccharine storytelling, appealing leads. Jose (Verastegui) is the head chef at his brother Manny's (Perez) upscale Mexican restaurant in Manhattan. Intolerant of unprofessional behavior, Manny fires waitress Nina (Blanchard) when she's late for work. Jose discovers the reason is because the unmarried young woman has just learned she's pregnant, so he leaves as well. Jose then spends the day with Nina, trying to convince her to have the baby, with his motives slowly revealed through flashbacks. **91m/C; DVD.** Eduardo Verastegui; Tammy Blanchard; Manny Perez; Angelica Aragon; Jamie Tirelli; Ali Landry; Ramon Rodriguez; ***D:*** Alejandro Monteverde; ***W:*** Patrick Million; ***C:*** Andrew Cadelago; ***M:*** Stephen Altman.

Belladonna 🦴 **1/2 2008** Luke is in the midst of wedding plans with his high-strung, longtime girlfriend Katherine when he becomes attracted to Amelia. As his wedding draws closer, Luke is increasingly plagued by nightmares and finally goes into therapy. Under hypnosis, his nightmares reveal a medieval town, devil worship, and a romantic triangle that turns into a reincarnation story. **93m/C; DVD.** *AU* Katherine Kendall; Katie Jean Harding; Todd MacDonald; Indiana Avent; John Jacobs; Anne Cordiner; Katia Mazurek; Daryl Pellizzer; ***D:*** Annika Glac; ***W:*** Annika Glac; ***C:*** Marcus Struzina; ***M:*** Volmer Haas I.

The Bellboy 🦴🦴 **1/2 1960** Lewis makes his directorial debut in this plotless but clever outing. He also stars as the eponymous character, a bellboy at Miami's Fountainbleau Hotel. Cameos from Berle and Winchell are highlights. **72m/B; VHS, DVD.** Jerry Lewis; Alex Gerry; Bob Clayton; Sonny Sands; Bill Richmond; Larry Best; Maxie "Slapsie" Rosenbloom; ***Cameo(s):*** Milton Berle; Walter Winchell; ***D:*** Jerry Lewis; ***W:*** Jerry Lewis; ***C:*** Haskell Boggs; ***M:*** Walter Scharf.

Belle 🦴🦴 **1/2 2013 (PG)** A well-intentioned and well-staged drama that nonetheless feels flat. This period piece is based on the true story of Dido Elizabeth Belle (Mbatha-Raw), the illegitimate mixed-race daughter of a Royal Navy Admiral. Belle is raised by her great uncle Lord Mansfield (Wilkinson) and his wife (Watson) but occupies a unique place in history given the privilege allowed by her family's place in society balanced against the way she's treated for the color of her skin. With the help of those sympathetic to her cause and a little bit of love, Belle's story actually helped end slavery in England. **105m/C; DVD, Blu-Ray.** *UK* Gugu Mbatha-Raw; Tom Wilkinson; Emily Watson; Sarah Gadon; Sam Reid; James Norton; Tom Felton; Miranda Richardson; Penelope Wilton; ***D:*** Amma Asante; ***W:*** Misan Sagay; ***C:*** Ben Smithard; ***M:*** Rachel Portman.

Belle de Jour 🦴🦴🦴 **1/2 1967 (R)** Based on Joseph Kessel's novel, one of director Bunuel's best movies has all his characteristic nuances: the hypocrisy of our society; eroticism; anti-religion. Deneuve plays Severine, a chic, frigid Parisian newlywed, who decides to become a daytime prostitute, unbeknownst to her husband. Bunuel blends reality with fantasy, and the viewer is never sure which is which in this finely crafted movie. French with subtitles. **100m/C; VHS, DVD, Blu-Ray.** *FR* Catherine Deneuve; Jean Sorel; Genevieve Page; Michel Piccoli; Francisco Rabal; Pierre Clementi; Georges Marchal; Francoise Fabian; ***D:*** Luis Bunuel; ***W:*** Luis Bunuel; Jean-Claude Carriere; ***C:*** Sacha Vierny.

Belle Epoque 🦴🦴🦴 *The Age of Beauty* **1992 (R)** Young army deserter Fernando (Sanz) embarks on a personal voyage of discovery when he meets Manolo (Gomez), an eccentric old man, and father to four beautiful daughters. Fernando can't believe his luck—and the sisters share his interest, resulting in an amusing round of musical beds. Bittersweet tale set amidst the anarchy and war of 1930s Spain with a terrific screenplay that tastefully handles the material without stooping to the obvious leering possibilities. In addition to Oscar, won nine Spanish Goyas, including best picture, director, actress (Gil), and screenplay. Title ironically refers to the era at the end of the 19th century before the wars of the 20th century tore Europe apart. Spanish with English subtitles or dubbed. **108m/C; VHS, DVD, Blu-Ray.** *SP* Jorge Sanz; Fernando Fernan-Gomez; Ariadna Gil; Maribel Verdu; Penelope Cruz; Miriam Diaz-Aroca; Mary Carmen Ramirez; Michel Galabru; Gabino Diego; ***D:*** Fernando Trueba; ***W:*** Rafael Azcona; ***C:*** Jose Luis Alcaine; ***M:*** Antoine Duhamel. Oscars '93: Foreign Film.

A Belle for Christmas 🦴🦴 **2014 (PG)** A family Christmas movie about the importance of family, friendship, and dogs. After the death of his wife, Glenn Barrows (Cain) is raising his daughter Phoebe (Murphy) and son Elliot (Jurgensmeyer) alone. During the holidays, the family adopts a puppy named Belle that makes everyone happy. However, Glenn's girlfriend Dani (Swanson) hates dogs and wants Glenn's money, and makes Belle disappear. By Christmas Eve, Phoebe and Elliot must work together to try find their puppy and bring him home for the holidays. **91m/C; DVD, Streaming, Download.** Dean Cain; Kristy Swanson; Jet Jurgensmeyer; Meyrick Murphy; Haylie Duff; ***D:*** Jason Dallas; ***W:*** Jake Helgren; ***M:*** Sherief Abraham.

The Belle of New York 🦴🦴 **1952** A turn-of-the-century bachelor falls in love with a Salvation Army missionary in this standard musical. **82m/C; VHS, DVD.** Fred Astaire; Vera-Ellen; Marjorie Main; Keenan Wynn; Alice Pearce; Gale Robbins; Clinton Sundberg; ***D:*** Charles Walters.

Belle of the Nineties 🦴🦴 **1/2** *It Ain't No Sin* **1934** West struts as a 1890s singer who gets involved with a boxer. Her trademark sexual innuendos were already being censored but such lines as "It's better to be looked over than overlooked," done in West style, get the point across. **73m/B; DVD.** Mae West; Roger Pryor; Johnny Mack Brown; John Miljan; Katherine DeMille; Harry Woods; Edward (Ed) Gargan; ***D:*** Leo McCarey; ***W:*** Mae West; ***C:*** Karl Struss; ***M:*** Arthur Johnston.

Belle Starr 🦴 **1/2 1979** The career of Wild West outlaw Belle Starr is chronicled in this strange western pastiche about lawlessness and sexual agression. Wertmuller directed under the pseudonym Nathan Wich. Dubbed in English. **90m/C; VHS, DVD.** *IT* Elsa Martinelli; George Eastman; Dan Harrison; ***D:*** Lina Wertmuller.

Belle Toujours 🦴🦴🦴 **2006** Thirty-nine years after "Belle de Jour" comes this sequel—or perhaps more of an homage—from Manoel de Oliveira. A chance meeting after so many years places Henri Husson (Piccoli) and Severine (Ogier) at a candlelit dinner table where they discuss the past, the intervening years, and thoughts of the future. Severine, now a widow worn down by years of carrying secrets and lies, seems to care little about reliving their sexually complicated past and in fact is prepared to retire to a convent. Henri, still feeling the dart of her rejection, wants to recount the sordid history they share. In the earlier film the young Severine supported herself and her disabled husband as a daytime prostitute, a secret she meticulously kept from her husband; Henri wanted a relationship with her that never happened. Paris sparkles in this beautifully crafted work. **68m/C; DVD.** *FR PT* Michel Piccoli; Bulle Ogier; Ricardo Trepa; Leonor Baldaque; Julia Buisel; ***D:*** Manoel de Oliveira; ***W:*** Manoel de Oliveira; ***C:*** Sabine Lancelin.

The Belles of St. Trinian's 🦴🦴🦴 **1953** Sim is priceless in a dual role as the eccentric headmistress of a chaotic, bankrupt girls' school and her bookie twin brother who scheme the school into financial security. The first in a series of movies based on a popular British cartoon by Ronald Searles about a girls' school and its mischievous students. Followed by "Blue Murder at St. Trinian's," "The Pure Hell of St. Trinian's," and "The Great St. Trinian's Train Robbery." **86m/B; VHS, Blu-Ray, Streaming.** *GB* Alastair Sim; Joyce Grenfell; Hermione Baddeley; George Cole; Eric Pohlmann; Renee Houston; Beryl Reid; Balbina; Jill Braidwood; Annabelle Covey; Betty Ann Davies; Diana Day; Jack Doyle; Irene Handl; Arthur Howard; Sidney James; Lloyd Lamble; Jean Langston; Belinda Lee; Vivian Martin; Andree Melly; Mary Merrall; Guy Middleton; Joan Sims; Jerry Verno; Richard Wattis; ***D:*** Frank Launder; ***W:*** Frank Launder; Sidney Gilliat; Val Valentine; ***C:*** Stanley Pavey; ***M:*** Malcolm Arnold.

Belles on Their Toes 🦴🦴 **1952** Somewhat less charming sequel to 1950's "Cheaper by the Dozen" is big on nostalgia. Now widowed, Lillian Gilbreth (Loy) is struggling to support her large family, having to overcome women in the workplace prejudice. Using her industrial engineering degree, Lillian finally gets a job training young engineers, but this means eldest daughter Ann (Crain) must pick up the domestic slack. Which puts a crimp in Ann's budding romance with young Dr. Bob (Hunter). Based on the memoir by Gilbreth children Frank and Ernestine. **89m/C; DVD.** Myrna Loy; Jeanne Crain; Debra Paget; Jeffrey Hunter; Edward Arnold; Hoagy Carmichael; Barbara Bates; Robert Arthur; Martin Milner; Verna Felton; Carole Nugent; Tommy "T.V." Ivo; Jimmy Hunt; Robert Easton; Cecil Weston; ***D:*** Henry Levin; ***W:*** Henry Ephron; Phoebe Ephron; ***C:*** Arthur E. Arling; ***M:*** Cyril Mockridge.

Bellflower 🦴🦴 **2011 (R)** A queasy, hot mess of a male fantasy with on-the-edge Woodrow (played by debut writer/director Glodell) and his equally grungy friend Aiden (Dawson) drinking too much and obsessing over sex, muscle cars, and a post-apocalyptic "Mad Max" world as well as setting things on fire with their homemade flamethrower. Woodrow falls for tough blond Milly (Wiseman) and seems to be making a play towards adulthood until she cheats on him and the situation gets violent instead. **104m/C; DVD.** Evan Glodell; Tyler Dawson; Jessie Wiseman; Vincent Grashaw; Rebekah Brandes; ***D:*** Evan Glodell; ***W:*** Evan Glodell; ***C:*** Joel Hodge; ***M:*** Jonathan Keevil.

Bellissima 🦴🦴🦴 **1951** A woman living in an Italian tenement has unrealistic goals for her plain but endearing daughter when a famous director begins casting a role designed for a child. The mother's maternal fury and collision with reality highlight a poignant film. Italian with subtitles. **130m/B; VHS, DVD.** *IT* Anna Magnani; Walter Chiari; Alessandro Blasetti; Tina Apicella; Gastone Renzelli; ***D:*** Luchino Visconti; ***W:*** Luchino Visconti; Cesare Zavattini; Francesco Rosi; Suso Cecchi D'Amico; ***C:*** Piero Portalupi; Paul Ronald.

Bellman and True 🦴🦴 **1/2 1988 (R)** Rewarding, but sometimes tedious character study of a mild mannered computer whiz who teams with a gang of bank robbers. Fine performances, especially subtle dangerous gang characters. **112m/C; VHS, Streaming.** *GB* Bernard Hill; Kieran O'Brien; Richard Hope; Frances Tomelty; Derek Newark; John Kavanagh; Ken Bones; ***D:*** Richard Loncraine; ***W:*** Desmond Lowden; ***C:*** Ken Westbury; ***M:*** Colin Towns.

The Bells 🦴🦴🦴 **1926** The mayor of an Alsatian village kills a wealthy merchant and steals his money. The murderer experiences pangs of guilt which are accentuated when a traveling mesmerist comes to town and claims to be able to discern a person's darkest secrets. Silent with music score. **67m/B; Silent; VHS, DVD.** Lionel Barrymore; Boris Karloff; Gustav von Seyffertitz; ***D:*** James L. Young; ***W:*** James L. Young; ***C:*** L. William O'Connell.

Bells Are Ringing 🦴🦴🦴 **1960** A girl who works for a telephone answering service can't help but take an interest in the lives of the clients, especially a playwright with an inferiority complex. Based on Adolph Green and Betty Comden's Broadway musical. **126m/C; VHS, DVD, Blu-Ray.** Judy Holliday; Dean Martin; Fred Clark; Eddie Foy, Jr.; Jean Stapleton; ***D:*** Vincente Minnelli; ***W:*** Betty Comden; Adolph Green; ***C:*** Milton Krasner; ***M:*** Andre Previn.

Bells of Coronado 🦴🦴 **1950** Rogers and Evans team up to expose the murderer of the owner of a profitable uranium mine. A gang of smugglers trying to trade the ore to foreign powers is thwarted. The usual thin storyline, but filled with action and riding stunts. **67m/B; VHS, DVD.** Roy Rogers; Dale Evans; Pat Brady; Grant Withers; ***D:*** William Witney.

The Bells of Death ♪♪ *Duo hun ling; Duet wan ling* **1968** In this classic Shaw Brothers wuxia effort, Wei Fu (Yi Chang) is a simple woodcutter whose family is slaughtered by a trio of marauding bad guys. Wei undergoes extensive (i.e. years) martial arts training before chasing them down to exact his revenge. Along the way he performs various good deeds, including rescuing a young woman from a life of prostitution. While the tale of a kung fu fighter devoting his entire life to the revenge of wrongs on his loved ones is now cliche, this film was among the first to use that theme and inspired many later martial arts movie efforts. **110m/C; DVD.** *CH* Yi Chang; Ping Chin; Hsin Yen Chao; Kau Lam; ***D:*** Feng Yueh (Yue); ***W:*** Kang Chien Chiu; ***C:*** Hsueh Li Pao; ***M:*** Fu-ling Wang.

The Bells of St. Mary's ♪♪♪ 1/2 **1945** An easy-going priest finds himself in a subtle battle of wits with the Mother Superior over how the children of St. Mary's school should be raised. It's the sequel to "Going My Way." Songs include the title tune and "Aren't You Glad You're You?" Also available in a colorized version. **126m/B; VHS, DVD, Blu-Ray.** Bing Crosby; Ingrid Bergman; Henry Travers; ***D:*** Leo McCarey; ***W:*** Dudley Nichols; ***C:*** George Barnes; ***M:*** Robert Emmett Dolan; Johnny Burke; James Van Heusen. Oscars '45: Sound; Golden Globes '46: Actress--Drama (Bergman); N.Y. Film Critics '45: Actress (Bergman).

Bells of San Fernando ♪ **1947** An Irish seaman wanders into California during early Spanish rule and confronts a cruel overseer in this lackluster Western drama. Scripted by "Cisco Kid" Renaldo. **75m/B; VHS, DVD.** Donald Woods; Gloria Warren; Byron Foulger; ***D:*** Terry Morse; ***W:*** Jack DeWitt; Duncan Renaldo.

Belly ♪♪ **1998 (R)** Inner-city crime tale preaches against crime, violence and drugs while it visually glorifies the opulent benefits of them. Childhood pals Tommy (Simmons) and Sincere (Jones) are successful criminals who head down different paths. Sincere dreams of turning legit and moving his family to Africa. Tommy gets deeper into the drug biz until he is caught by feds and forced to bring down innocent black leader Reverend Saviour (Muhammed). Although the movie ends with a plea for change, it may itself be part of the problem. **95m/C; VHS, DVD.** DMX; Taral Hicks; Nasir Jones; Tionne "T-Boz" Watkins; Method Man; Tyrin Turner; Hassan Johnson; Power; Louie Rankin; Rev. Benjamin F. Muhammed; ***D:*** Hype Williams; ***W:*** Nasir Jones; Hype Williams; Anthony Bodden; ***C:*** Malik Hassan Sayeed; ***M:*** Stephen Cullo.

The Belly of an Architect ♪♪♪ 1/2 **1991 (R)** A thespian feast for the larger-than-life Dennehy as blustering American architect whose personal life and health both crumble as he obsesssively readies an exhibition in Rome. A multi-tiered, carefully composed tragicomedy from the ideosyncratic filmmaker Greenaway, probably his most accessible work for general audiences. **119m/C; VHS, DVD.** *GB IT* Brian Dennehy; Chloe Webb; Lambert Wilson; Sergio Fantoni; Geoffrey Copleston; Marino (Martin) Mase; ***D:*** Peter Greenaway; ***W:*** Peter Greenaway; ***C:*** Sacha Vierny; ***M:*** Glenn Branca; Wim Mertens.

Belly of the Beast ♪ **2003 (R)** Actor Steven Seagal sells his soul to the devil to get a chance to do an action film with HK action director Siu-Tung Ching. Not really, but there's no other way to explain how this stinker got made AND Seagal got a sex scene in it. A retiring CIA agent is on vacation in Thailand when terrorists kidnap his daughter. Worth seeing for the stunt double who does most of Seagal's fight scenes, and the fact that they occasionally dub over Steven's voice with that of a different actor for unknown reasons. **91m/C; DVD, Blu-Ray.** *CA CH GB* Steven Seagal; Byron Mann; Monica Lo; Tom Wu; Sara Malakul Lane; Patrick Robinson; Vincent Riotta; Norman Veeratum; Elidh MacQueen; Ching Siu Tung; Kevork Malikyan; Pongpat Wachirabunjong; ***D:*** Siu-Tung Ching; ***W:*** Steven Seagal; James Townsend; ***C:*** Danny Nowak; ***M:*** The Music Sculptors; Mark Sayer-Wade.

Bellyfruit ♪♪ **1999** Film, which refers to pregnancy, was inspired by the real-life stories of teen mothers in L.A. 14-year-old Shanika is living in a home for troubled girls when she's taken in by the charms of Damon, equally young Christina witnesses her mother (who had Christina when she was a teen) drug and party and decides to follow her example, while 16-year-old Aracely becomes pregnant by her boyfriend Oscar. Although he stands by her, Aracely's traditional Latin father kicks her out of the house. And when they have their babies, the teens lives just get more confused. **95m/C; VHS, DVD.** Kelly Vint; Tamara La Seon Bass; Tonatzin Mondragon; T.E. Russell; Michael Peña; Bonnie Dickenson; Kimberly Scott; James Dumant; ***D:*** Kerri Green; ***W:*** Kerri Green; Maria Bernhard; Suzannah Blinkoff; Janet Borrus; ***C:*** Peter Calvin.

Beloved ♪♪ 1/2 **1998 (R)** Sethe (Winfrey) is a middle-aged former slave in rural Ohio years after her emancipation from a Kentucky planation. She is haunted (literally) by the painful legacy of slavery in the form of a mud-covered feral child known as Beloved (Newton). Another reminder is Paul D (Glover), a former slave from the same Kentucky plantation, who stokes Sethe's embers. Metaphors abound as we wonder if Beloved really is the child Sethe killed years before. Oprah's pet project (she's owned the film rights for 10 years) is a faithful adaptation of Toni Morrison's Pulitzer Prize-winning novel. Unfortunately, the long-awaited feature can't fulfill the huge expectations. While performances are excellent, pic suffers from a sense of self-indulgence, which is accentuated by the three-hour running time. At times powerful and moving, but also slow and occasionally confusing. **172m/C; VHS, DVD.** Oprah Winfrey; Thandie Newton; Danny Glover; Kimberly Elise; Lisa Gay Hamilton; Beah Richards; Irma P. Hall; Albert Hall; Jason Robards, Jr.; Jude Ciccolella; ***D:*** Jonathan Demme; ***W:*** Akosua Busia; Richard LaGravenese; Adam Brooks; ***C:*** Tak Fujimoto; ***M:*** Rachel Portman.

Beloved ♪♪ *Les Biens-Aimes* **2011** Real-life mother/daughter Deneuve and Mastroianni play the same roles in Honore's romantic/musical drama that covers some 40 years. In 1964, young Madeleine (Sagnier) almost accidentally becomes a prostitute to live the good life. She marries, has a daughter, but doesn't leave her life of pleasure behind as she ages (Deneuve). Meanwhile, her daughter Vera (Mastroianni) is a commitment-phobe who makes impossible romantic choices. The characters also randomly express themselves in song in a manner similar to the director's 2007 film "Love Songs." French with subtitles. **139m/C; DVD.** *FR* Catherine Deneuve; Chiara Mastroianni; Ludivine Sagnier; Louis Garrel; Milos Forman; Paul Schneider; Radivoje (Rasha) Bukvic; Michel Delpech; ***D:*** Christophe Honore; ***W:*** Christophe Honore; ***C:*** Remy Chevrin; ***M:*** Alexandre Beaupain.

Beloved/Friend ♪♪ *Amigo/Amado* **1999** Everybody wants something (or someone) they can't have. Jaume (Pou) is a middleaged gay college prof who pines for his student David (Selvas), a cold-hearted stud who hustles to pay his tuition. In fact, the only way Jaume can get attention from David is to buy his services (although David has something of a father figure complex). Then, Jaume's best friend Pere (Gas) discovers that David has gotten his daughter, Alba (Montala), pregnant. David seems to be a catalyst for a lot of soul-searching but nothing much gets resolved. Spanish with subtitles. **90m/C; VHS, DVD.** *SP* Jose(p) Maria Pou; David Selvas; Mario Gas; Irene Montala; Rosa Maria Sarda; ***D:*** Ventura Pons; ***W:*** Josep Maria Benet i Jornet; ***C:*** Jesus Escosa; ***M:*** Carles Cases.

Beloved Infidel ♪♪ 1/2 **1959** Sudsy, lavish romancer, based on the book by gossip queen Sheilah Graham, about her brief romance with novelist F. Scott Fitzgerald. Fitzgerald (a badly miscast Peck) is in Hollywood trying to write screenplays when he meets young, English, aspiring writer Graham (an equally miscast Kerr). She becomes his mistress, putting up with Fitzgerald's drinking and insults, while he interferes with her career. Story is slanted towards Graham nobly trying to rescue Fitzgerald from himself (he did actually die from a heart attack while with Graham). **123m/C; DVD, Blu-Ray.** Gregory Peck; Deborah Kerr; Eddie Albert; Philip Ober; Herbert Rudley; John Sutton; Karin (Karen, Katharine) Booth; ***D:*** Henry King; ***W:*** Sy Bartlett; ***C:*** Leon Shamroy; ***M:*** Franz Waxman.

The Beloved Rogue ♪♪♪ **1927** Crosland—who gained a reputation for innovation by directing "Don Juan" and "The Jazz Singer"?mounted this well-designed and effects-laden medieval costumer with poetic license and typical excesses of the day. Barrymore is swashbuckling poet Francois Villon, who battles verbally with Louis XI (Veidt, in his first US role). Louis banishes him after a tiff with the evil Duke of Burgundy and Villon must uncover the Dukes's plans. Crosland plays fast and loose when the facts aren't fab enough, but it's great entertainment. **98m/B; Silent; DVD.** John Barrymore; Conrad Veidt; Lawson Butt; Marceline Day; Henry Victor; Slim Summerville; Mack Swain; ***D:*** Alan Crosland, Jr.; ***W:*** Paul Bern; ***C:*** Joseph August.

Beloved Sisters ♪♪♪ **2014** Charlotte and Caroline are aristocratic sisters who have been given everything they may need or want throughout their lives. When they both fall in love with a passionate writer named Friedrich, the stage is set for a traditional love triangle chamber piece, but the film transcends that archetype by remaining true to its characters. How does love destroy family? Herzsprung and Confurius are excellent in the title roles. Overly long, but worth seeing just for the debut performances from these two young actresses. **138m/C; DVD, Blu-Ray.** *GE AT* Florian Stetter; Henriette Confurius; Hannah Herzsprung; Andreas Pietschmann; ***D:*** Dominik Graf; ***W:*** Dominik Graf; ***C:*** Michael Wieswig; ***M:*** Sven Rossenbach; Florian Van Voixem.

Below ♪♪ 1/2 **2002 (R)** Nothing is certain in director David Twohy's creepy submarine thriller. The captain of World War II sub U.S.S. Manta has died under dubious circumstances, and the crew is already on edge when they rescue three survivors of a torpedoed British hospital ship. When one of these survivors is a woman (Williams), allegedly unlucky on a sub, tensions run even higher. With the Germans tracking the sub, strange events begin to occur, which could be vengeful actions of the captain's ghost, a saboteur, hallucinations caused by lack of oxygen or some combination of the three. As the disasters pile up, the crew becomes divided between acting captain Brice (Greenwood) and rebellious ensign O'Dell (Davis), who has the strangely outspoken Claire on his side. Characters are a bit one-dimensional, but the effects and acting are above average for a B movie. **103m/C; VHS, DVD, Blu-Ray.** Bruce Greenwood; Matthew Davis; Olivia Williams; Holt McCallany; Scott Foley; Zach Galifianakis; Jason Flemyng; Dexter Fletcher; Nick (Nicholas) Chinlund; Andrew Howard; Christopher Fairbank; ***D:*** David N. Twohy; ***W:*** David N. Twohy; Darren Aronofsky; Lucas Sussman; ***C:*** Ian Wilson; ***M:*** Graeme Revell.

Below the Belt ♪♪ **1980 (R)** Almost interesting tale of street-smart woman from New York City who becomes part of the blue-collar "circus" of lady wrestlers. Ex-wrestling champ Burke plays herself. **98m/C; VHS, DVD.** Regina Raff; Mildred Burke; John C. Becher; Lenny Montana; ***D:*** Robert Fowler.

Belphegor: Phantom of the Louvre ♪ 1/2 *Belphegor: Le Fantome du Louvre* **2001** Gets the extra half-bone because Marceau is such a looker. Silly French horror (remake of a 1965 miniseries that was based on a pulp novel) about a sarcophagus discovered during a renovation of the museum. A demon is unleashed and poor Lisa (Marceau) becomes its unwitting host. British archeologist Glenda Spencer (Christie) tries to find out more about the mummy inside while retired police detective Verlac (Serrault) is called in to investigate the theft of items from the Egyptology wing, which is similar to an earlier unsolved case. French with subtitles. **97m/C; DVD.** *FR* Sophie Marceau; Michel Serrault; Julie Christie; Jean-Francois Balmer; Patachou; Frederic Diefenthal; ***D:*** Jean-Paul Salome; ***W:*** Daniele Thompson; Jerome Tonnerre; Jean-Paul Salome; ***C:*** Jean-Francois Robin; ***M:*** Bruno Coulais.

Ben-Hur ♪♪♪♪ **1926** Second film version of the renowned story of Jewish and Christian divisiveness in the time of Jesus. Battle scenes and chariot races still look good, in spite of age. Problems lingered on the set and at a cost of over $4,000,000 it was the most expensive film of its time and took years to finish. A hit at the boxoffice, it still stands as the all-time silent classic. In 1931, a shortened version was released. Based on the novel by Lewis Wallace. **148m/B; Silent; VHS, DVD.** Ramon Novarro; Francis X. Bushman; May McAvoy; Betty Bronson; Claire McDowell; Carmel Myers; Nigel de Brulier; Ferdinand P. Earle; ***D:*** Fred Niblo; ***C:*** Clyde De Vinna. Natl. Film Reg. '97.

Ben-Hur ♪♪♪♪ **1959** The third film version of the Lew Wallace classic stars Heston in the role of a Palestinian Jew battling the Roman empire at the time of Christ. Won a record 11 Oscars. The breathtaking chariot race is still one of the best screen races today. Perhaps one of the greatest pictures of all time. Also available in letterbox format. **212m/C; VHS, DVD, Blu-Ray.** Charlton Heston; Jack Hawkins; Stephen Boyd; Haya Harareet; Hugh Griffith; Martha Scott; Sam Jaffe; Cathy O'Donnell; Finlay Currie; ***D:*** William Wyler; ***W:*** Karl Tunberg; ***C:*** Robert L. Surtees; ***M:*** Miklos Rozsa. Oscars '59: Actor (Heston), Art Dir./Set Dec., Color, Color Cinematog., Costume Des. (C), Director (Wyler), Film, Film Editing, Orig. Dramatic Score, Sound, Support. Actor (Griffith); AFI '98: Top 100; British Acad. '59: Film; Directors Guild '59: Director (Wyler); Golden Globes '60: Director (Wyler), Film--Drama, Support. Actor (Boyd); Natl. Film Reg. '04; N.Y. Film Critics '59: Film.

Ben Hur ♪♪ **2010** British/Canadian miniseries plays down the religious aspects of the Lew Wallace novel and the previous film versions (but there's still chariot races). Solider Messala has been assigned by Rome to safeguard the arrival of Pontius Pilate into Jersusalem. He demands his childhood friend Judah Ben Hur inform him of any plots against the new governor's life, but when Pilate comes under attack, Judah's family suffers and he wants revenge. **180m/C; DVD.** *UK CA* Joseph Morgan; Stephen Campbell Moore; Hugh Bonneville; Emily VanCamp; Kristin Kreuk; Alex Kingston; Ben Cross; Ray Winstone; ***D:*** Steve Shill; ***W:*** Alan Sharp; ***C:*** Ousama Rawi; ***M:*** Rob Lane. **TV**

Ben-Hur ♪ 1/2 **2016 (PG-13)** The epic story of Judah Ben-Hur (Huston) is told yet again complete with CGI horses and chariots. Ben-Hur is accused of treason by his jealous adopted brother Messala (Kebbell), exiled from everything he knows and loves, and forced into slavery. After years of struggle, Ben-Hur makes it back to his homeland to seek vengeance against the brother who disowned him, but an encounter with Jesus teaches him forgiveness. Clearly an attempt to appeal to faith-based audiences, this movie has no real other reason to exist--it adds nothing to the Charlton Heston classic. **125m/C; DVD, Blu-Ray.** Jack Huston; Morgan Freeman; Toby Kebbell; Rodrigo Santoro; Nazanin Boniadi; Ayelet Zurer; ***D:*** Timur Bekmambetov; ***W:*** Keith R. Clarke; John Ridley; ***C:*** Oliver Wood; ***M:*** Marco Beltrami.

Ben Is Back ♪♪ 1/2 **2018 (R)** When 19-year-old Ben (Lucas Hedges) shows up on his family's doorstep on Christmas Eve, his mom (Roberts) is torn between love for him and fear of his drug addiction. Over the next 24 hours, she gets sucked into the drama of his life, determined to save him from himself and the criminals encircling him. The latter half devolves into a crime caper, but overall Roberts gives her best performance to date. And sometimes nepotism is justified -- Lucas may be the director's son, but he knocks it out of the park with his deft and moving treatment of a troubled young man. **103m/C; DVD, Blu-Ray.** Julia Roberts; Lucas Hedges; Courtney B. Vance; Kathryn Newton; Rachel Bay Jones; ***D:*** Peter Hedges; ***W:*** Peter Hedges; ***C:*** Stuart Dryburgh; ***M:*** Dickon Hinchliffe.

Benched ♪ *Rounding Third* **2018** They're the good cop/bad cop of little league coaches: Don (McGinley) is focused on winning; his assistant Michael (Dillahunt) emphasizes fun. A generic tale of the underdog team rising from the depths while the adults make attitude adjustments learned from the other, it's just less funny or inspiring than the plethora of flicks that have used this formula before. **111m/C; DVD, Blu-Ray.** John C. McGinley; Garret Dillahunt; Brogan Hall; Kelly Lamor Wilson; Roy Oraschin; ***D:*** Robert Deaton;

George Flanigen; *W:* Richard Dresser; *C:* Maz Makhani; *M:* Jared Faber.

The Benchwarmers **2006 (PG-13)** Relentlessly stupid comedy with more than its share of gross-out moments. Gus (Schneider) was a bullied nerd in school, as were his two still-maladjusted pals, Richie (Spade) and Clark (Heder). Ex-bullied nerd-turned-billionaire Mel (a fun-loving Lovitz) offers a chance for sweet revenge by putting his trio of losers up against a Little League team of young terrors. Farting, vomiting, and booger jokes follow, and Reggie Jackson offers baseball advice. **81m/C; DVD, Blu-Ray, UMD.** Rob Schneider; David Spade; Jon Heder; Jon Lovitz; Molly Sims; Craig Kilborn; Tim Meadows; Nick Swardson; Amaury Nolasco; Dennis Dugan; Erinn Bartlett; Max Prado; Brooke Langton; Lochlyn Munro; Mary Jo Catlett; Blake Clark; Terry Crews; *Cameo(s):* Reggie Jackson; *V:* James Earl Jones; *D:* Dennis Dugan; *W:* Nick Swardson; Allen Covert; *C:* Thomas Ackerman; *M:* Waddy Wachtel.

Bend It Like Beckham **2002 (PG-13)** Sweet family comedy has girl power galore. Jesminder (Nagra) is the teenaged daughter of East Indian parents, living in a middle-class London suburb. They wish Jess would be more like her older sister Pinky (Panjabi), who is anticipating her traditional wedding. But what shy Jess wants is to play professional soccer—her hero is superstar player David Beckham—and she secretly joins a local team after befriending fellow player Juliette (Knightley). She impresses (and develops a crush on) her coach Joe (Rhys-Meyers) while trying to keep her activities from her disapproving parents. Of course, there has to be a big game, which will showcase Jess's talents. **112m/C; VHS, DVD.** *GB GE* Parminder K. Nagra; Keira Knightley; Jonathan Rhys Meyers; Shaheen Khan; Anupam Kher; Archie Panjabi; Juliet Stevenson; Frank Harper; Shaznay Lewis; *D:* Gurinder Chadha; *W:* Gurinder Chadha; Paul Mayeda Berges; Guljit Bindra; *C:* Jong Lin; *M:* Craig Pruess.

Bend of the River *Where the River Bends* **1952** A haunted, hardened guide leads a wagon train through Oregon territory, pitting himself against Indians, the wilderness and a former comrade-turned-hijacker. **91m/C; VHS, DVD, Blu-Ray.** James Stewart; Arthur Kennedy; Rock Hudson; Harry (Henry) Morgan; Royal Dano; *D:* Anthony Mann.

Bending All the Rules **2002 (R)** Kenna (Porch) prefers to keep her personal life casual so she can concentrate on her photography career. Just when she's offered her first gallery exhibition, two men make a serious play for her affections: sweet, struggling DJ Jeff (Cooper) and confident, successful businessman Martin (Gail). Of course Kenna wants to know why she can't have it all but jealousy becomes a problem. Filmed in Tampa Bay, Florida. **86m/C; DVD.** Colleen Porch; David Gail; Bradley Cooper; Kurt McKinney; James Martin Kelly; Ed Carine; *D:* Morgan Klein; Peter Knight; *W:* Morgan Klein; Peter Knight; *C:* Rob Allen; *M:* Martin Klein; Molly Knight Forde. **VIDEO**

Bending the Rules **2012 (PG-13)** A buddy action crime comedy about unlikely allies teaming up to solve a crime. The day before his birthday, Theo Gold (Kennedy) finds everything is going wrong. His wife decides to leave him and he loses a major case against Harry Blades (Copeland). Blades is an oddball detective who was being tried for corruption. Later that day, Theo finds that his most important possession—a 1956 Studebaker Goldenhawk left to him by his father—has been stolen. The only person willing to help him is Blades. As the pair looks for the car and finds a much bigger criminal enterprise, they bond through their unexpected adventures. **83m/C; DVD, Blu-Ray, Streaming, Download.** Jamie Kennedy; Adam Copeland; Jennifer Esposito; Alicia Witt; Kevin Weisman; *D:* Artie Mandelberg; *W:* Dylan Schaffer; *C:* Kenneth Zunder; *M:* Trevor Morris.

Beneath **2007 (R)** Convoluted and plodding story about creepy, depressed people having visions usually followed by someone ending up dead. Initial suspense stems from in-laws' eerie house complete with mysterious hatches, weird holes, and a monster inside the walls. Although intriguing, its eccentricities never get fully explained as the darkness and drab lead only to an anticlimatic snore. **81m/C; DVD.** Nora Zehetner; Matthew Settle; Gabrielle Rose; Carly Pope; Don S. Davis; Jessica Amlee; *D:* Dagen Merrill; *W:* Dagen Merrill; Kevin Burke; *C:* Mike Southon; *M:* John (Gianni) Frizzell; Frederik Wiedmann. **VIDEO**

Beneath **2013** Director Ketai's exploitative blend of claustrophobic drama and supernatural horror is an absolute mess. It's the last trip into the coal mine for the beloved George Marsh (Fahey) and so his daughter (Noonan) joins the gang. Of course, that's the day that a drill hits a load-bearing chunk of rock and the miners are stuck deep underground, a situation made worse by a methane link and no fans to blow it out. So they start going crazy, seeing visions of melting faces. Or are they really encountering some sort of underground supernatural force? Who cares? **89m/C; DVD.** Kelly Noonan; Jeff Fahey; Brent Briscoe; Eric Etebari; Joey Kern; *D:* Ben Ketai; *W:* Patrick Doody; Chris Valenziano; *C:* Timothy Burton; *M:* Andres Boulton.

Beneath Hill 60 **1/2 2010 (R)** True story about WWI Aussie soldiers. In 1916, mining engineer Oliver Woodward joins up with the Australian 1st Tunnellers to fight on the Western Front. Their mission is to secretly tunnel beneath the German lines in France and Belgium, packing the tunnels with explosives to destroy the enemy troops fighting above. **122m/C; DVD, Blu-Ray.** *AU* Brendan Cowell; Chris Haywood; Harrison Gilbertson; Steve LeMarquand; Gyton Grantley; Anthony Hayes; Bella Heathcote; *D:* Jeremy Sims; *W:* David Roach; *C:* Toby Oliver; *M:* Cezary Skubiszewski.

Beneath Loch Ness **2001** Laughable adventure tale finds paleontologist Case Howell (Wimmer) carrying on the work of his mentor, Professor Egan, who believed that Loch Ness was a breeding ground for ancient marine reptiles. Unfortunately, the prof disappeared while conducting research at the loch. But that isn't stopping Howell from leading another expedition to find Nessie. **95m/C; VHS, DVD, Blu-Ray.** Brian Wimmer; Patrick Bergin; Lysette Anthony; Vernon Wells; *D:* Chuck Comisky; *W:* Justin Stanley; Chuck Comisky; Shane Bitterling; *C:* Philip Timme; *M:* Richard John Baker. **VIDEO**

Beneath Still Waters **1/2** *Bajo aguas tranquilas* **2005 (R)** Two boys travel to see a town one last time before it's flooded forever by a new dam, and one of them dies accidentally, unleashing a demon. Four decades later it finally decides to get busy causing trouble. Darn lazy them critters from Hell. **92m/C; DVD.** *SP UK* Michael McKell; Patrick Gordon; Josep Maria Pou; Raquel Merono; Charlotte Salt; *D:* Brian Yuzna; *W:* Mike Hostench; Angel Sala; Zacarias De la Riva; *C:* Johnny Yebra. **VIDEO**

Beneath the Blue **1/2 2010 (PG)** Tourist Craig Morrison is vacationing in the Bahamas when he falls in love with Alyssa, who's researching dolphin communications. However Navy sonar experiments are endangering the local dolphin population and the scientists want it to stop. **93m/C; DVD.** Paul Wesley; Caitlin Wachs; David Keith; Michael Ironside; Ivana Milicevic; George Harris; *D:* Michael D. Sellers; *W:* Wendell Morris; *C:* Lila Javan; *M:* Alan Derian. **VIDEO**

Beneath the Dark *Wake* **2010 (R)** Paul and Adrienne are driving from Texas to L.A. for a wedding. A sleepy Paul nearly crashes their car and they pull into a creepy Mohave desert motel for the night. A nameless man is prodding a guilty Paul to reveal secrets from his frat boy past, which seem to involve the motel owner's promiscuous wife Sandy. **102m/C; DVD.** Josh Stewart; Jamie-Lynn Sigler; Chris Browning; Angela Featherstone; Trevor Morgan; Afemo Omilami; *D:* Chad Feehan; *W:* Chad Feehan; *C:* Jason Blount; *M:* Daniel Licht. **VIDEO**

Beneath the Darkness **1/2 2012 (R)** Quaid obviously enjoys his villainous role as a psycho mortician in a small Texas town, but the rest is simply a generic horror flick. Dysfunctional teens all seem to have recently lost a family member and start watching the creepy doings of Ely Vaughn, who likes to bury his victims alive. **96m/C; DVD, Blu-Ray.** Dennis Quaid; Tony Oiler; Aimee Teegarden; Stephen Lunsford; Devon Werkheiser; Brett Cullen; *D:* Martin Guigui; *W:* Bruce Wilkinson; *C:* Massimo Zeri; *M:* Geoff Zanelli.

Beneath the Flesh **1/2 2009** Odd horror anthology mixing live action and stop-motion animation that's about overcoming one's fears. Granted, most of the fears these people have are perfectly reasonable to have, so it's not like they're just being foolish. **72m/B; DVD.** Steve Arons; Randall Kaplan; Brandon McCluskey; Michael Whitney; Bianca Jamotte; Adair Moran; *D:* Randall Kaplan; *W:* Randall Kaplan; *C:* Leo A. Schott, III; *M:* Randall Kaplan. **VIDEO**

Beneath the Harvest Sky **2014** A familiar story of small town frustration and bad choices gets tender treatment in this indie drama. High school seniors Casper and Dominic have made a pact to escape their potato-farming Maine community after graduation but they take different paths to earn the money to get out. Honest Dom works the fields but Casper follows in the footsteps of his drug-dealing dad by smuggling prescription meds over the Canadian border--and that's before he finds out that his 15-year-old girlfriend is pregnant. Naturally, trouble thwarts their dreams. **116m/C; Blu-Ray, On Demand.** Callan McAuliffe; Emory Cohen; Aidan Gillen; Zoe Levin; Sarah Sutherland; *D:* Aron Gaudet; Gita Pullapilly; *W:* Aron Gaudet; Gita Pullapilly; *C:* Steven Capitano Calitri; *M:* Dustin Hamman.

Beneath the Mississippi **WOOF!** **2008** Crappy sound and lighting and an incoherent plot doom this indie. Documentary filmmaker Elly (Shaffer) brings her camera crew to investigate an isolated island area of the Mississippi river where hundreds of people have disappeared. She hires riverman Jack (Hazell) as their guide but the closer they get to the site, the scarier things become. **95m/C; DVD.** Ariadne Shaffer; Jon Hazell; Nick Murray; Lonnie Schuyler; *D:* Lonnie Schuyler; *W:* Jon Hazell; Lonnie Schuyler; *C:* Ken Moehn; *M:* Patrick Hazell. **VIDEO**

Beneath the Planet of the Apes **1/2 1970 (G)** In the first sequel, another Earth astronaut passes through the same warp and follows the same paths as Taylor, through Ape City and to the ruins of bomb-blasted New York's subway system, where warhead-worshipping human mutants are found. The strain of sequelling shows instantly, and gets worse through the next three films; followed by "Escape from the Planet of the Apes." **108m/C; VHS, DVD, Blu-Ray.** James Franciscus; Kim Hunter; Maurice Evans; Charlton Heston; James Gregory; Natalie Trundy; Jeff Corey; Linda Harrison; Victor Buono; Paul (E.) Richards; David Watson; Thomas Gomez; *D:* Ted Post; *W:* Paul Dehn; *C:* Milton Krasner; *M:* Leonard Rosenman.

Beneath the 12-Mile Reef **1953** Two rival groups of divers compete for sponge beds off the Florida coast. Lightweight entertainment notable for underwater photography and early Cinemascope production, as well as Moore in a bathing suit. **102m/C; DVD, Blu-Ray.** Robert Wagner; Terry Moore; Gilbert Roland; Richard Boone; Peter Graves; J. Carrol Naish; Angela (Clark) Clarke; *D:* Robert D. Webb; *W:* A(lbert) I(saac) Bezzerides; *C:* Edward Cronjager; *M:* Bernard Herrmann.

Beneath the Valley of the Ultra-Vixens **1979** Sex comedy retread directed by the man with an obsession for big. Scripted by Roger Ebert, who also scripted the cult classic "Beyond the Valley of the Dolls." Explicit nudity. **90m/C; VHS, DVD.** Francesca "Kitten" Natividad; Ann Marie; Ken Kerr; Stuart Lancaster; Steve Tracy; Henry Rowland; DeForest Covan; Aram Katcher; Candy Samples; Robert Pearson; *D:* Russ Meyer; *W:* Roger Ebert; Russ Meyer; *C:* Russ Meyer.

Beneath Us **1/2 2020 (R)** A wealthy couple hires undocumented day laborers, then traps and tortures them, eventually discarding their spent corpses beneath a secluded mansion. What's meant to be a chilling political commentary is reduced to an amateurish cliché by heavy-handedness and bad acting. **90m/C; DVD.** Lynn Collins; James Tupper; Rigo Sanchez; Roberto Sanchez; Josue Aguirre; *D:* Max Pachman; *W:* Max Pachman; Mark Mavrothalasitis; *C:* Jeff Powers; *M:* Joshua Moshier.

Benedict Arnold: A Question of Honor **2003** By-the-numbers bio of Revolutionary War general turned British Loyalist, Benedict Arnold (Quinn). By 1776, Arnold was falling out of favor with Congress amidst accusations of incompetence, although he's still supported by his friend, George Washington (Grammer). But after meeting Margaret Shippen (Montgomery), the daughter of a loyalist sympathizer, the increasingly resentful Arnold, who also needs money to stave off bankruptcy, begins to sell information to the enemy and comes up with a plan to turn over West Point to the redcoats. **100m/C; VHS, DVD.** Aidan Quinn; Kelsey Grammer; Flora Montgomery; John Light; John Kavanagh; *D:* Mikael Salomon; *W:* William Mastrosimone; *C:* Seamus Deasy; *M:* David Williams. **CABLE**

The Benefactor **2016** An uneven dramatic thriller that explores the nature of loss and the meaning of family. Franny (Gere) is a rich but eccentric philanthropist who played a role in a major tragedy that greatly impacts the life of a young girl, Olivia. Five years after the incident, the now-adult Olivia (Fanning) contacts Franny and asks for him to be in her life again. As Olivia marries Luke (James) and becomes pregnant, he ingratiates himself into their lives as their self-appointed benefactor, whether they want him to help or not, to help him re-enact his own past. **93m/C; DVD, Blu-Ray, Streaming, Download.** Richard Gere; Dakota Fanning; Theo James; Dylan Baker; Clarke Peters; *D:* Andrew Renzi; *W:* Andrew Renzi; *C:* Joe Anderson; *M:* Danny Bensi; Saunder Jurriaans.

Benefit of the Doubt **1993 (R)** Ex-con Sutherland, released from prison after 22 years, attempts to repaint his family a la Norman Rockwell. Grown-up daughter Irving, who testified against him in her mother's murder, wants to put a crimp in those plans since daddy's new vision of family fondness frankly makes her stomach turn. Aside from the sexual shenanigans, and the haunting Monument Valley backdrop, an extended chase scene would seem to be the film's only hope of salvation. Unfortunately, it fails to deliver, since it's both implausible and boring. Based on a story by Michael Lieber. **92m/C; VHS, DVD, Blu-Ray.** Donald Sutherland; Amy Irving; Christopher McDonald; Rider Strong; Graham Greene; Theodore Bikel; Gisele Kovach; Ferdinand "Ferdy" Mayne; *D:* Jonathan Heap; *W:* Jeffrey Polman; Christopher Keyser; *M:* Hummie Mann.

The Bengali Night **1988** Slow-moving romantic drama was the first starring role for Grant who plays British engineer Allan, who works in Calcutta. When he becomes ill, his employer invites Allan to recuperate at his home and lets him stay on after his recovery. But when Allan and the Sens' eldest daughter Gayatri (Pathak) become romantically involved, the culture clash leads to heartbreak. Based on a true story. **111m/C; DVD.** Hugh Grant; Shabana Azmi; Soumitra Chatterjee; John Hurt; Anne Brochet; Supriya Pathak; *D:* Nicolas Klotz; *W:* Nicolas Klotz; *C:* Jean-Claude Carriere; *M:* Emmanuel Machuel; Brij Narayan.

The Beniker Gang **1/2 1983 (G)** Five orphans, supported by the eldest who writes a syndicated advice column, work together as a family. **87m/C; VHS, DVD.** Andrew McCarthy; Jennifer (Jennie) Dundas Lowe; Danny Pintauro; Charlie (Charles) Fields; *D:* Ken Kwapis. **TV**

Benji **1974 (G)** In the loveable mutt's first feature-length movie, he falls in love with a female named Tiffany, and saves two young children from kidnappers. Kiddie classic that was a boxoffice hit when first released. Followed by "For the Love of Benji." **87m/C; VHS, DVD, Blu-Ray.** Benji; Peter Breck; Christopher Connelly; Patsy Garrett; Deborah Walley; Cynthia Smith; *D:* Joe Camp; *W:* Joe Camp; *C:* Don Reddy; *M:* Euel Box. Golden Globes '75: Song ("I Feel Love").

Benji: Off the Leash! **1/2 2004 (PG)** A generally amiable retro addition to the series that began in 1974. Colby's (Whitaker) nasty stepfather Hatchett (Kendrick) runs a puppy mill in their small Mississippi town. He plans to kill a mongrel pup, which Colby rescues and hides (and calls Puppy). Puppy (played by the latest version of Benji) befriends a smart stray named Lizard Tongue while avoiding a couple of inept dogcatchers (Newsome, Stephens) and trying to rescue his sickly mom from the mean breeder. The abuse themes (both animal and human) may scare the little ones but, of course, the dogs are cute and lovable. **97m/C; VHS, DVD, Blu-Ray.** Nick Whitaker; Nate Bynum; Chris Kendrick; Randall Newsome; Duane Stephens; Forrest Landis; Carleton Bluford; Neal Barth; Melinda Haynes; Kathleen Camp; Jeff Olson; Lincoln Hoppe; Joey Miyashima; Scott Wilkinson; Christy Summerhays; ***D:*** Joe Camp; ***W:*** Joe Camp; ***C:*** Don Reddy; ***M:*** Anthony DiLorenzo.

Benji the Hunted 1/2 **1987 (G)** The heroic canine, shipwrecked off the Oregon coast, discovers a litter of orphaned cougar cubs, and battles terrain and predators to bring them to safety. **89m/C; VHS, DVD.** Benji; Red Steagall; Frank Inn; ***D:*** Joe Camp; ***W:*** Joe Camp; ***M:*** Euel Box.

Bennett's War **2019 (PG-13)** After suffering significant injuries while serving in Afghanistan, U.S. Army sergeant Marshall Bennett (Roark) is discharged from the military. A former competitive motocross champion, Marshall also faces the end of his motorcycle riding days. Returning home to his wife Sophie (Page) and newborn child, he stays connected to motorcycles by working as a mechanic for a friend. When he starts to develop feeling in his injured foot, Marshall becomes determined to race again to help save his grandfather's (Adkins) farm--despite the concerns of his wife. A feel-good sports drama with energizing racing footage. **94m/C; DVD.** Michael Roark; Trace Adkins; Ali Afshar; Allison Paige; Hunter Clowdus; ***D:*** Alex Ranarivelo; ***W:*** Alex Ranarivelo; ***C:*** Reuben Steinberg; ***M:*** Jamie Christopherson.

Benny & Joon 1/2 **1993 (PG)** Depending on your tolerance for cute eccentrics and whimsy this will either charm you with sweetness or send you into sugar shock. Masterson is Joon, a mentally disturbed young woman who paints and has a habit of setting fires. She lives with overprotective brother Benny (Quinn). Sam (Depp) is the outsider who charms Joon, a dyslexic loner who impersonates his heroes Charlie Chaplin and Buster Keaton with eery accuracy. Depp is particularly fine with the physical demands of his role, but the film's easy dismissal of Joon's mental illness is a serious flaw. **98m/C; VHS, DVD, Blu-Ray.** Johnny Depp; Mary Stuart Masterson; Aidan Quinn; Julianne Moore; Oliver Platt; CCH Pounder; Dan Hedaya; Joe Grifasi; William H. Macy; Eileen Ryan; ***D:*** Jeremiah S. Chechik; ***W:*** Barry Berman; ***C:*** Jason Schwartzman; ***M:*** Rachel Portman.

Benny Bliss & the Disciples of Greatness **WOOF!** **2007** Stilted, stupid comedy. Benny is a crazy musician who finds enlightenment and decides to rid the world of distracting electronic gadgets that he believes are holding back human evolution. He and his band go on a cross-country road trip to spread the word and destroy the evil. Of course they drive and Benny uses a mic to reach his followers and the band plays electric guitars and has a sound system, so Benny isn't exactly a technophobe is he? **94m/C; DVD.** Martin Guigui; Courtney Gains; Michael Hateley; Norman John Cutliff, III; Corey Britz; Yvonne Delarosa; ***D:*** Martin Guigui; ***W:*** Martin Guigui; Courtney Gains; Michael Hateley; ***C:*** Massimo Zeri; ***M:*** Cody Westheimer. **VIDEO**

The Benny Goodman Story **1955** The life and music of Swing Era bandleader Benny Goodman is recounted in this popular bio-pic. Covering Benny's career from his child prodigy days to his monumental 1938 Carnegie Hall Jazz Concert, the movie's soggy plot machinations are redeemed by a non-stop music track featuring the real Benny and an all-star lineup. **116m/C; VHS, DVD.** Steve Allen; Donna Reed; Gene Krupa; Lionel Hampton; Kid Ory; Ben Pollack; Harry James; Stan Getz; Teddy Wilson; Martha Tilton; ***D:*** Valentine Davies; ***M:*** Henry Mancini.

Benny's Video 1/2 **1992** Teen Benny (Frisch) is obsessed with the violent videos he watches and makes, including the slaughter of a pig with a bolt gun, which Benny then uses in a very unfortunate manner. Heavy-handed message movie was Hanecke's second feature. German with subtitles. **105m/C; DVD.** *GE* Arno Frisch; Angela Winkler; Ulrich Muhe; Ingrid Strassner; ***D:*** Michael Haneke; ***W:*** Michael Haneke.

Bent **1997 (NC-17)** Theatre director Mathias makes his film debut with Sherman's adaptation of his 1979 play. Gay playboy Max (Owen) is enjoying the nightlife in decadent Berlin—until the Nazi crackdown. Soon, Max is in a cattle car on his way to Dachau, where he passes himself off as Jewish, thinking he'll be treated better. However Horst (Bluteau), who befriended Max on the train, is openly part of the pink triangle prisoners. Still, Max gets Horst assigned to the same meaningless hard labor and the duo fall in love—without ever being allowed to touch. Good performances (with Jagger notable in a brief role as a drag star) but the lingering staginess is to the film's detriment. An R-rated version is also available. **104m/C; VHS, DVD, Blu-Ray.** *GB* Clive Owen; Lothaire Bluteau; Ian McKellen; Brian Webber; Mick Jagger; Nikolaj Coster-Waldau; Paul Bettany; ***Cameo(s):*** Jude Law; Rupert Graves; ***D:*** Sean Mathias; ***W:*** Martin Sherman; ***C:*** Yorgos Arvanitis; ***M:*** Philip Glass.

Beowulf 1/2 **1998 (R)** Cheesy retelling of the dark ages Saxon saga that has seemingly time travelled to a vague post-apocalypse time. Wandering knight Beowulf (Lambert) battles beast Grendel, who comes each night to feed on those who live in the Outpost. Cult icon Mitra was one of the models for Lara Croft of "Tomb Raider" game fame. **92m/C; VHS, DVD.** Christopher Lambert; Rhona Mitra; Oliver Cotton; Patricia Velasquez; Goetz Otto; Layla Roberts; Brent J. Lowe; ***D:*** Graham Baker; ***W:*** Mark Leahy; David Chappe; ***C:*** Christopher Faloona; ***M:*** Ben Watkins.

Beowulf **2007 (PG-13)** Not your father's epic poem! Director Zemeckis takes the Old English classic and turns it into both a highly stylized computer-generated swordfest and a satirical take on the lit class staple. Beowulf (Winstone) battles Grendel (Glover), gets sexy with Grendel's mom (Jolie), and fights a dragon on his way to eternal heroic glory. Purists may object to the liberties taken by writers Gaiman and Avery, but they do a good job of connecting and streamlining the source material's various storylines. While still resembling a video game, Zemeckis's second attempt at the "performance capture" digital style is a dramatic improvement over his previous attempt in the lifeless "The Polar Express." **114m/C; Blu-Ray, On Demand.** ***V:*** Ray Winstone; Angelina Jolie; Crispin Glover; Anthony Hopkins; Robin Wright; John Malkovich; Alison Lohman; ***D:*** Robert Zemeckis; ***W:*** Neil Gaiman; Roger Avary; ***C:*** Robert Presley; ***M:*** Alan Silvestri.

Beowulf & Grendel **2006 (R)** Live-action adaptation of the 1000-year-old Scandanavian poem retells the story of Beowulf (Butler), the Norse warrior who helps his pal, Danish King Hrothgar (Skarsgard), rid his land of the murderous troll Grendel (Sigurdsson). Tries to appeal to modern audiences with flashy fighting, lots of blood, and awkward comedic attempts, but succeeds only in showing how beautiful Iceland is (that's where it was filmed). **102m/C; DVD, Blu-Ray.** *GB CA IC* Gerard Butler; Stellan Skarsgard; Sarah Polley; Eddie Marsan; Ingvar Sigurdsson; Tony Curran; Rory McCann; Ronan Vilbert; Martin Delaney; Olafur Darri Olafsson; Mark Lewis; Elva Osk Olafsdottir; ***D:*** Sturla Gunnarsson; ***W:*** Andrew Rai Berzins; ***C:*** Jan Kiesser; ***M:*** Hilmar Orn Hilmarsson.

Berberian Sound Studio **2012** An ode to '70s Giallos (Italian horror films) finds meek Brit sound engineer Gilderoy (Jones) brought to an Italian film studio to help finish a controversial genre flick. With a surreal style, director Strickland captures his protagonist as he creates the sound effects for a film filled with gore (that we brilliantly never actually see). As Gilderoy becomes more engrossed in the movie and the weird people making it, his sanity slides until the film truly goes off the rails in the final act, playing with film stocks, visual effects, and, of course, great sound design. English and Italian with subtitles. **92m/C; Streaming.** *UK* Toby Jones; Tonia Sotiropoulou; Susanna Cappellaro; Cosimo Fusco; ***D:*** Peter Strickland; ***W:*** Peter Strickland; ***C:*** Nicholas D. Knowland.

Bereavement **2010 (R)** Formulaic torture/slasher flick. Young Martin Bristol is kidnapped by psycho sadist Graham Sutter who keeps the boy in his family's abandoned slaughterhouse as a witness to his bloody crimes. Orphaned teenager Allison Miller comes to live with her Uncle Jonathan and his family and gets curious about their reclusive neighbor, which is a big, big mistake. **107m/C; DVD, Blu-Ray.** Alexandra Daddario; Martha Tilton; Brett Rickaby; Spencer List; John Savage; Nolan Gerard Funk; Kathryn Meisle; Peyton List; ***D:*** Stevan Mena; ***W:*** Stevan Mena; ***C:*** Marco Cappetta; ***M:*** Stevan Mena.

Berkeley 1/2 **2005 (R)** In 1968, Ben Sweet (Nick Roth) enrolls at UC Berkeley mainly to avoid the draft and is introduced to political activism, drugs, and sex. The lead actor is the director's son and the film is based on Bobby Roth's own college days although the rambling nostalgia isn't as interesting as Roth seems to believe. **88m/C; DVD.** Nick Roth; Henry Winkler; Sarah Carter; Laura Jordan; Bonnie Bedelia; Sebastian Tillinger; Jake Newton; Tom Morello; ***D:*** Bobby Roth; ***W:*** Bobby Roth; ***C:*** Steve Burns; ***M:*** Christopher Franke.

Berkeley Square 1/2 **1998** In 1902 London, three young women become nannies and grow to be friends. Tough and experienced East Ender Matty (Wilkie) goes to work for the well-bred St. Johns; country-raised Hannah (Smurfit) has an illegitimate child by her previous titled employer's son—a fact she keeps hidden from the neglectful Hutchinsons; and farm girl Lydia (Wady) is hired by the avant-garde Lamson-Scribeners, who believe in education even for servants. Naturally, the threesome become very involved in each other's lives and loves. On five cassettes. **500m/C; VHS, DVD.** *GB* Victoria Smurfit; Tabitha Wady; Clare Wilkie; Rosemary Leach; Judy Parfitt; ***D:*** Leslie Manning; Richard Signy; Martin Hutchings; Richard Holthouse. **TV**

Berlin Blues **1989 (PG-13)** A nightclub singer is torn between two men. **90m/C; VHS, Streaming.** Julia Migenes; Keith Baxter; ***D:*** Ricardo Franco.

Berlin Correspondent **1942** Briskly-paced Fox propaganda flick stars a dashing Andrews as foreign correspondent Bill Roberts, who's smuggling info on Axis plans out of Germany in bland news reports. Nazi counter-agent Karen (Gilmore) is tasked to get close and learn who's supplying Bill with his info. Turns out to be her own father (Kalser), who gets picked up by the Gestapo, leading Karen to change her alliance and ask Bill for help. **70m/B; DVD.** Dana Andrews; Virginia Gilmore; Erwin Kalser; Sig Rumann; Martin Kosleck; Mona Maris; ***D:*** Eugene Forde; ***W:*** Jack Andrews; Steve Fisher; ***C:*** Virgil Miller; ***M:*** Emil Newman.

Berlin Express 1/2 **1948** Battle of wits ensues between the Allies and the Nazis who are seeking to keep Germans divided in post-WWII Germany. Espionage and intrigue factor heavily. **86m/B; VHS, DVD.** Robert Ryan; Merle Oberon; Paul Lukas; Charles Korvin; ***D:*** Jacques Tourneur.

Berlin Job *St. George's Day* **2012** Cousins Mickey and Ray are London gangsters looking for a big payday, thanks to a cocaine shipment form the Russian mob. When the drugs go astray, the Russians give them one week to pay up, so the two set up a diamond heist in Berlin on the same day that a big soccer match between England and Germany is being held. Naturally, things don't go as planned. **109m/C; DVD, Blu-Ray.** *UK* Frank Harper; Craig Fairbrass; Charles Dance; Jamie Foreman; Sean Pertwee; Vincent Regan; Luke Treadaway; ***D:*** Frank Harper; ***W:*** Frank Harper; Urs Buehler; ***C:*** Mike Southon; ***M:*** Tim Atack.

Berlin Syndrome 1/2 **2017 (R)** In a slow burning psychological thriller, Australian photojournalist Clare (Palmer) is instantly attracted to Andi (Riemelt) when the two meet on the streets of Berlin, and they take their passion back to his apartment. The next morning, after Andi leaves to go about his day as usual, Clare discovers that she's trapped behind locked-from-the-outside doors and unbreakable windows. Palmer simmers as a woman held captive, making you wonder if she's under the influence of German-style Stockholm Syndrome or if she's quietly biding her time to escape. Based on the novel by Melanie Joosten. **116m/C; DVD.** Teresa Palmer; Max Riemelt; Matthias Habich; Emma Bading; Lucie Aron; ***D:*** Cate Shortland; ***W:*** Shaun Grant; ***C:*** Germain McMicking; ***M:*** Bryony Marks.

Berlin Tunnel 21 1/2 **1981** Based on the novel by Donald Lindquist in which five American soldiers attempt a daring Cold War rescue of a beautiful German girl. The plan is to construct a tunnel under the Berlin Wall. Better-than-average. **150m/C; VHS, Streaming.** Richard Thomas; Jose Ferrer; Horst Buchholz; ***D:*** Richard Michaels. **TV**

Berlinguer I Love You **WOOF!** *Berlinguer Ti Voglio Bene* **1977** Crude and disgustingly obnoxious comedy about a mama's-boy loser who is led to believe that his shrewish mother has died. When he returns home for her funeral, she is not happy to see him. Title refers to a popular politician of the era. Italian with subtitles. **95m/C; DVD.** *IT* Roberto Benigni; Alida Valli; Carlo Monni; ***D:*** Giuseppe Bertolucci; ***W:*** Roberto Benigni; Giuseppe Bertolucci; ***C:*** Renato Tafuri; ***M:*** Frank Coletta.

The Bermuda Depths 1/2 **1978** Made-for-TV fantasy horror involving the Bermuda Triangle, a giant sea turtle, a beautiful ghostly girl who apparently sold her soul for eternal youth, a troubled young man, and a couple of scientists. It's sorta goofy and watchable at the same time. **98m/C; DVD.** Leigh McCloskey; Connie Sellecca; Burl Ives; Carl Weathers; Julie Woodson; Ruth Attaway; ***D:*** Tom Kotani; ***W:*** William Overgard; ***C:*** Jeri Sopanen; ***M:*** Maury Laws. **TV**

Bermuda Tentacles **2014** Typical SyFy Channel creature feature goofiness. Air Force One goes down over the Bermuda Triangle but the Prez manages to get into an escape pod. Now he needs rescuing, but the Naval destroyer sent to the area is attacked by some angry tentacled killer sea critter. **90m/C; DVD, Blu-Ray.** Trevor Donovan; Linda Hamilton; Jamie Kennedy; Mya; John Savage; ***D:*** Nick Lyon; ***W:*** Geoff Mead; ***C:*** Alexander Yellen; ***M:*** Chris Ridenhour. **CABLE**

Bernadette 1/2 **1990** A French-made version of the legend of St. Bernadette, who endured persecution after claiming to have seen the Virgin Mary. Beautiful in its simplicity, but overly long. **120m/C; VHS, DVD.** *FR* Sydney Penny; Roland LeSaffre; Michele Simonnet; Bernard Dheran; Arlette Didier; ***D:*** Jean Delannoy.

Bernard and Doris **2008** Doris (Sarandon) is eccentric, cynical, lonely, aging billionaire tobacco heiress Doris Duke. Bernard Lafferty (Fiennes) is her Irish, gay, alcoholic butler. They form a delightfully odd-couple partnership where the ever-more devoted Bernard protects Doris from hangers-on (and herself)?so much so that Duke made Lafferty the executor of her will (and when he died, he left everything to her trusts). Gets the bones for the Sarandon/Fiennes combo alone even if Sarandon looks waaaaay too good as the ravaged Duke. **109m/C; DVD.** Susan Sarandon; Ralph Fiennes; James Rebhorn; Nick Rolfe; ***D:*** Bob Balaban; ***W:*** Hugh Costello; ***C:*** Mauricio Rubinstein; ***M:*** Alex Wurman. **CABLE**

Bernard and the Genie 1/2 **1991 (G)** It seems Bernard Bottle is not going to have a happy Christmas—he's been fired from his job and his girlfriend has left him. But things take a turn for the better when he discovers an antique lamp and its resident Genie. But with the Genie granting his every wish, Bernard's sudden wealth is causing some suspicions among both his greedy ex-employer and the police. Meanwhile, the Genie discovers the delights of modern-day England and poses as a department store Santa to truly fulfill a child's Christmas wish. Amusing family fare. **70m/C; VHS, DVD.** *GB* Alan Cumming; Lenny Henry; Rowan Atkinson; ***D:*** Paul Weiland.

Bernie **2012 (PG-13)** Bernie Tiede (Black) is the mortician and very well-liked resident of tiny, rural Carthage, Texas. He's an all-around good guy, sings in the church choir, is friendly to all the older ladies, and comes to the aid of anyone in need. And he is one of the few who will tolerate bitter-but-wealthy widow Marjorie Nugent (MacLaine)--so much so that the pair start taking holidays together. That is, until Bernie murders Marjorie, after which he takes great pains to create the illusion that she is still quite alive. Based on a true story, this black comedy lets Black shine. **104m/C; DVD, Blu-Ray.** Jack Black; Shirley MacLaine; Matthew McConaughey; Brady Coleman; Richard Robichaux; Rick Dial; Brandon Smith; Larry Dotson; ***D:*** Richard Linklater; ***W:*** Skip Hollandsworth; Richard Linklater; ***C:*** Dick Pope; ***M:*** Graham Reynolds.

Berserk! 1/2 **1967** A seedy traveling circus is beset by a series of murders. Not heralded as one of Crawford's best pieces. **95m/C; VHS, DVD, Blu-Ray, Streaming.** Joan Crawford; Diana Dors; Judy Geeson; Ty Hardin; ***D:*** James O'Connolly.

Bert Rigby, You're a Fool 1/2 **1989 (R)** A starstruck British coal miner finds his way to Hollywood singing old showtunes, only to be rebuffed by a cynical industry. Available with Spanish subtitles. **94m/C; VHS, DVD.** Robert Lindsay; Robbie Coltrane; Jackie Gayle; Bruno Kirby; Cathryn Bradshaw; Corbin Bernsen; Anne Bancroft; ***D:*** Carl Reiner; ***W:*** Carl Reiner; ***C:*** Jan De Bont; ***M:*** Ralph Burns.

Besieged 1/2 **1998 (R)** Fans of Bertolucci will enjoy this airy quasi-love story, but the slow pace and meandering plot will frustrate other viewers. Shandurai (Newton) moves to Rome after her husband becomes a political prisoner in Kenya. In order to put herself through medical school, she takes a job as a maid for an eccentric British musician (Thewlis). He begins to fall for his beautiful housekeeper, but she ignores his advances. To prove his love, he begins selling off his personal belongings so he can bribe officials to release her husband. **94m/C; VHS, DVD.** *IT* David Thewlis; Thandie Newton; Claudio Santamaria; ***D:*** Bernardo Bertolucci; ***W:*** Bernardo Bertolucci; Clare Peploe; ***C:*** Fabio Cianchetti; ***M:*** Alessio Vlad.

Best Defense **1984 (R)** A U.S. Army tank operator is sent to Kuwait to test a new state-of-the-art tank in a combat situation. Although the cast is popular, the movie as a whole is not funny and the story frequently is hard to follow. **94m/C; VHS, DVD.** Dudley Moore; Eddie Murphy; Kate Capshaw; George Dzundza; Helen Shaver; ***D:*** Willard Huyck; ***W:*** Willard Huyck; Gloria Katz.

The Best Exotic Marigold Hotel **2012 (PG-13)** Charmingly old-fashioned comedy-drama held together by a group of old pros and an--yes--exotic setting. Seven British retirees, in various financial and romantic circumstances, are enticed by advertisements for the restored Marigold Hotel and decide to move to less-expensive India. Only they find the former palace isn't quite what they were promised by its eager young owner Sonny. As they struggle to find their footing in a foreign land, they learn that change is still possible. Based on Deborah Moggach's novel "These Foolish Things." **124m/C; DVD, Blu-Ray.** *UK US* Dame Judi Dench; Maggie Smith; Bill Nighy; Penelope Wilton; Tom Wilkinson; Celia Imrie; Ronald Pickup; Dev Patel; Tena Desae; ***D:*** John Madden; ***W:*** Ol Parker; ***C:*** Ben Davis; ***M:*** Thomas Newman.

Best Foot Forward 1/2 **1943** Vintage musical about a movie star who agrees to accompany a young cadet to a military ball. Based on the popular Broadway show. The film debuts of Walker, Allyson, and DeHaven. **95m/C; DVD.** Lucille Ball; June Allyson; Tommy Dix; Nancy Walker; Virginia Weidler; Gloria De Haven; William Gaxton; Harry James; ***D:*** Edward Buzzell; ***W:*** Irving Brecher; ***M:*** George Bassman.

Best Friends **1975** Strange psychodrama with a lot of odd undertones, a tragedy, and an unsatisfying fade-out ending. Jess and fiancee Kathy get his best childhood friend Pat and Pat's girlfriend Jo Ella to join them in their Winnebago on a cross-country road trip. Pat gets increasingly weirded-out about losing his best bud to marriage and turns aggressive and violent to break them up. **83m/C; DVD.** Richard Hatch; Doug Chapin; Susanne Benton; Ann Noland; ***D:*** Noel Nosseck; ***W:*** Arnold Somkin; ***C:*** Stephen M. Katz; ***M:*** Richard Cunha.

Best Friends **1982 (PG)** A pair of screenwriters decide to marry after years of living and working together. Story based on the lives of screenwriters Barry Levinson and Valerie Curtin. **109m/C; VHS, DVD.** Goldie Hawn; Burt Reynolds; Jessica Tandy; Barnard Hughes; Audra Lindley; Keenan Wynn; Ron Silver; ***D:*** Norman Jewison; ***W:*** Valerie Curtin; Barry Levinson; ***C:*** Jordan Cronenweth.

Best Friends **2005** In this Lifetime cable thriller, Beth (Gallagher) doesn't realize that her longtime friend Claudia (Mink) is the source of all the sudden troubles she's having. Claudia has gone crazy, killed her own husband, and is using the secrets Beth has confided over the years to permanently get Beth out of the way so Claudia can take over her life. **90m/C; DVD.** Megan Gallagher; Claudette Mink; Barclay Hope; Liam Ranger; Brittney Wilson; Nels Lennarson; Graham Kosakoski; ***D:*** Michael Scott; ***W:*** Donna Radik; ***C:*** Adam Sliwinski; ***M:*** Terry Frewer. **CABLE**

The Best House in London **1969** Dated, silly, and vulgar Brit sex comedy. The British Home Secretary decides to clean up Victorian-era London by shooing prostitutes off the streets and into a government-run brothel. When the original manager dies suddenly, the bordello is left in the unlikely hands of social reformer Josephine, who discovers the establishment's ladies aren't so eager to change their profession. **97m/C; DVD.** *UK* David Hemmings; Joanna Pettet; Dany Robin; George Sanders; John Bird; ***D:*** Philip Saville; ***W:*** Denis Norden; ***C:*** Alex Thomson; ***M:*** Mischa Spoliansky.

Best in Show **2000 (PG-13)** Director Christopher Guest follows the successful "Waiting for Guffman" with another faux-documentary mixing improvisation and unique characters. This time, the subject is the snooty world of show dogs and the freaky, neurotic pooch-owners hoping to claim its greatest prize: Best in Show at the Mayflower Kennel Club Dog Show. The quirky dog-lovers include Meg (Posey) and Hamilton (Hitchcock), whose kinky sex life is giving their Weimaraner angst; doting gay Shih-Tzu owners Scott (Higgins) and Stefan (McKean); and seemingly tame suburbanites Gerry (Levy) and Cookie (O'Hara). Fred Willard steals the spotlight as Buck Laughlin, a sports announcer who has no knowledge of the event he's broadcasting. Worth a rental just for the bizarre one-liners fired off by the clueless commentator on such subjects as the dogs' anatomy and edibility. **89m/C; VHS, DVD, Blu-Ray.** Christopher Guest; Michael McKean; Parker Posey; Eugene Levy; Catherine O'Hara; Fred Willard; Michael Hitchcock; John Michael Higgins; Jennifer Coolidge; Trevor Beckwith; Bob Balaban; Ed Begley, Jr.; Patrick Cranshaw; Don Lake; Larry Miller; ***D:*** Christopher Guest; ***W:*** Christopher Guest; Eugene Levy; ***C:*** Roberto Schaefer; ***M:*** C.J. Vanston.

The Best Intentions 1/2 **1992** Ingmar Bergman wrote the screenplay chronicling the early years of the stormy relationship of his parents. Set in Sweden at the turn of the century, the film focuses on the class differences that divide his mother and father, while portrayal of little Bergy is limited to a bundle under his mother's maternity dress. Inspired performances and directing illuminates the emotionally complex relationship, revealing truths about the universal human condition along the way. Six-hour version was shot for TV in Europe and Japan. Director August and actress August met and married during filming. In Swedish with English subtitles. **182m/C; VHS, DVD, Blu-Ray.** *SW* Samuel Froler; Pernilla August; Max von Sydow; Ghita Norby; Mona Malm; Lena Endre; Bjorn Kjellman; ***D:*** Bille August; ***W:*** Ingmar Bergman; ***C:*** Jorgen Persson; ***M:*** Stefan Nilsson. Cannes '92: Actress (August), Film.

Best Kept Secret 1/2 **2013** Created by Samantha Buck, this documentary offers a revealing look at the struggles facing a public school in New Jersey that serves students with special education needs. Located in a rundown neighborhood in Newark, the school's faculty includes Janet Mino who teaches young men with autism. The film follows Mino and several of her students in the year and a half before graduation as she tries to find them employment or placement in a recreational center so they do not end up with no purpose or focus in life. **85m/C; DVD, Streaming, Download.** ***D:*** Samantha Buck; ***W:*** Samantha Buck; Zeke Farrow; Francisco Bello; ***C:*** Nara Garber; ***M:*** Brian Satz.

Best Laid Plans **1999 (R)** Another contemporary noir where no one and nothing is as it seems (except the overly familiar plot). Nick (Nivola) and his bud, Bryce (Brolin), are bar hopping when Bryce picks up Lissa (Witherspoon). Later, a frantic Bryce calls Nick saying Lissa is underage and accusing him of rape. Nick offers to talk to Lissa and the story flashes back to the beginnings of an elaborate scam leading all concerned to a number of ill-considered decisions. **90m/C; VHS, DVD.** Alessandro Nivola; Josh Brolin; Reese Witherspoon; Rocky Carroll; Michael G. (Mike) Hagerty; Jamie Marsh; ***D:*** Mike Barker; ***W:*** Ted Griffin; ***C:*** Ben Seresin; ***M:*** Craig Armstrong.

The Best Little Whorehouse in Texas **1982 (R)** Parton is the buxom owner of The Chicken Ranch, a house of ill-repute that may be closed down unless Sheriff-boyfriend Reynolds can think of a way out. Strong performances don't quite make up for the erratically comic script. Based on the long-running Broadway musical, in turn based on a story by Larry McMurtry. **115m/C; VHS, DVD, Blu-Ray.** Dolly Parton; Burt Reynolds; Dom DeLuise; Charles Durning; Jim Nabors; Lois Nettleton; ***D:*** Colin Higgins; ***W:*** Colin Higgins; Peter Masterson; Larry L. King; ***C:*** William A. Fraker; ***M:*** Carol Hall.

The Best Man 1/2 **1964** An incisive, darkly satiric political tract, based on Gore Vidal's play, about two presidential contenders who vie for the endorsement of the aging ex-president, and trample political ethics in the process. **104m/B; VHS, DVD.** Henry Fonda; Cliff Robertson; Lee Tracy; Margaret Leighton; Edie Adams; Kevin McCarthy; Ann Sothern; Gene Raymond; Shelley Berman; Mahalia Jackson; ***D:*** Franklin J. Schaffner; ***W:*** Gore Vidal; ***C:*** Haskell Wexler.

The Best Man 1/2 *Il Testimone dello Sposo* **1997 (PG)** It's 1899 in a small northern Italian town and beautiful Francesca (Sastre) must marry the lascivious older Edgardo Osti (Cantarelli) in order to solve her father's business problems. Francesca is revolted but does become smitten by the best man—Angelo (Abatantuono), who's returned from America, apparently with a fortune. Marriage or no, Francesca becomes obsessed with getting Angelo. Italian with subtitles. **99m/C; VHS, DVD.** *IT* Ines Sastre; Diego Abatantuono; Dario Cantarelli; Valeria (Valerie Dobson) D'Obici; Mario Erpichini; ***D:*** Pupi Avati; ***W:*** Pupi Avati; ***C:*** Pasquale Rachini; ***M:*** Riz Ortolani.

The Best Man **1999 (R)** Writer/director Malcolm D. Lee, cousin of co-producer Spike Lee, makes an impressive debut in this ensemble piece that plays like a hipper "Big Chill." Novelist Harper (Diggs) heads to New York to attend the wedding of his best friend Lance (Chestnut) and the beautiful Mia (Calhoun). Unfortunately, his soon-to-be-released first novel is a thinly disguised autobiography which alludes to an affair between Harper and the bride-to-be. As other college buddies and old flames show up for the nuptials, past issues and romantic tensions come bubbling back up to the surface. The cast gives good performances across the board, with Howard as the wisecracking and womanizing Quentin standing out in particular. **120m/C; VHS, DVD, Blu-Ray.** Taye Diggs; Monica Calhoun; Morris Chestnut; Nia Long; Melissa De Sousa; Harold Perrineau, Jr.; Terrence Howard; Sanaa Lathan; Victoria Dillard; ***D:*** Malcolm Lee; ***W:*** Malcolm Lee; ***C:*** Frank Prinzi; ***M:*** Stanley Clarke.

Best Man Down **2012 (PG-13)** Scott and Kristin have their wedding in Phoenix, away from their cold hometown of Minneapolis. Scott's best man, hard-partying Lumpy, parties too hard and dies after the reception. So, despite Kristin's obvious frustration, the cash-strapped couple cancel their honeymoon to make funeral arrangements. They take Lumpy's body back home while discovering that Scott's oldest friend had some secrets that turn the pic down some unexpectedly serious plot paths. **89m/C; DVD, Blu-Ray.** Justin Long; Jess Weixler; Tyler Labine; Addison Timlin; Shelley Long; Frances O'Connor; Evan Jones; ***D:*** Ted Koland; ***W:*** Ted Koland; ***C:*** Seamus Tierney; ***M:*** Mateo Messina.

The Best Man Holiday **2013 (R)** Fifteen years after director Lee began his career with the African-American ensemble comedy "The Best Man," he reunites the cast in this unexpectedly decent sequel. It's a typical patchwork of subplots and misunderstandings that come with holiday movies featuring several couples in one story, but the notable star power allows one to forgive a lot of storytelling miscues. These people are simply likable, a trait too often missing in characters of modern comedy. **123m/C; DVD, Blu-Ray.** Morris Chestnut; Taye Diggs; Regina Hall; Terrence Howard; Sanaa Lathan; Nia Long; Harold Perrineau, Jr.; Monica Calhoun; Melissa De Sousa; Eddie Cibrian; ***D:*** Malcolm Lee; ***W:*** Malcolm Lee; ***C:*** Greg Gardiner; ***M:*** Stanley Clarke.

Best Men 1/2 *Independence* **1998 (R)** There's a wedding, there's a would-be bank heist, and there's five men caught in the siege at the bank of Independence in this kooky crime comedy/drama. Jesse (Wilson) is heading straight from prison to his wedding to Hope (Barrymore) with his four tuxedo-clad buddies. Billy (Flanery) needs some cash before the big event and persuades the boys to stop at the bank—only his withdrawal is the illegal kind. Soon Billy's dad (Ward), who happens to be the local sheriff, is trying to contain the situation when the feds show up as does the bewildered bride-to-be. **89m/C; VHS, DVD.** Sean Patrick Flanery; Dean Cain; Luke Wilson; Andy Dick; Mitchell Whitfield; Drew Barrymore; Fred Ward; Raymond J. Barry; Brad Dourif; Art Edler Brown; Tracy Fraim; ***D:*** Tamra Davis; ***W:*** Art Edler Brown; Tracy Fraim; ***C:*** James Glennon; ***M:*** Mark Mothersbaugh.

Best Night Ever **WOOF!** **2014 (R)** There are mediocre movies, bad movies, awful movies, and then there's directors/writers Friedberg and Seltzer's stab at "Hangover"-esque hilarity in its own subcategory of horrendous. Four fun-loving, female friends (Hall, Colburn, Ritchard, Flanagan) jet off to Las Vegas for a weekend bachelorette party and attempts at hilarious hi-jinks ensue. This is straight-to-video nonsense of the worst variety with performances that are flat, at best, when they're not half-asleep. The attempts at outrageous behavior only end up as embarrassing as the film sinks deeper and deeper into fart-boy humor. **90m/C; DVD, Blu-Ray.** Desiree Hall; Samantha Colburn; Eddie Ritchard; Crista Flanagan; ***D:*** Jason Friedberg; Aaron Seltzer; ***W:*** Jason Friedberg; Aaron Seltzer; ***C:*** Shawn Maurer.

Best of Enemies **2015 (R)** The 1968 Presidential debates were an international event not just because television coverage was reaching a new peak but because of the hot-button issues of the late '60s including Vietnam and the counter-culture movement. Liberal Gore Vidal and Conservative William F. Buckley Jr. were asked to debate the issues of the day in conjunction with the candidates every night on national TV, and the result was breathtaking. This documentary deftly examines how television has influenced political conversation and debate, for better or worse. It also serves as an engrossing bio-doc about two of the most interesting political personalities of the last half-century. **88m/C; DVD, Blu-Ray, Streaming.** ***D:*** Robert Gordon; Morgan Neville; ***W:*** Robert Gordon; Morgan Neville; ***C:*** David Leonard; Mark Schwartzbard; Graham Willoughby; ***M:*** Jonathan Kirkscey.

The Best of Enemies **2019 (PG-13)** During the Civil Rights Movement in the 1960s, black activist Ann Atwater (Henson) fights for the rights of African American students to attend integrated schools. After a school fire displaces black students in East Durham, she served as co-chair with C.P. Ellis (Rockwell), a local leader of the Klu Klux Klan, of a charrette. While the local schools integration hinges on the group's vote, the significant differences between the pair and their communities are dramatized. Based on a true story, the lack of balance between the two sides' stories and factual inaccuracies undermine an important and compelling piece of history. **132m/C; DVD, Blu-Ray.** Taraji P. Henson; Sam Rockwell; Babou Ceesay; Nick Searcy; Wes Bentley; ***D:*** Robin Bissell; ***W:*** Robin Bissell; ***C:*** David Lanzenberg; ***M:*** Marcelo Zarvos.

The Best of Everything **1959** Trashy sexist soap opera about women seeking success and love in the publishing world of N.Y.C. Several stories take place, the best being Crawford's hard-nosed editor who's having an affair with a married man. Look for Evans as a philandering playboy (he went on to become the producer of "Chinatown," among others.) Based on the novel by Rona Jaffe. **121m/C; VHS, DVD, Blu-Ray.** Hope Lange; Stephen Boyd; Suzy Parker; Diane Baker; Martha Hyer; Joan Crawford; Brian Aherne; Robert Evans; Louis Jourdan; ***D:*** Jean Negulesco; ***W:*** Edith Sommer; Mann Rubin; ***C:*** William Mellor; ***M:*** Alfred Newman.

The Best of Me **2014 (PG-13)** Romance novelist Sparks gets yet another painful big screen adaptation. This time, after a near-death accident, expert mechanic and studly oil-rig worker Dawson Cole (Marsden) reunites with lost love Amanda (Monaghan). From here, the flashbacks attack. Young Dawson (Bracey) flees a troubled home to the sanctuary of a caring war veteran (McRaney), where he first meets young Amanda (Liberto). Director Hoffman crumbles under the strain of such formulaic melodrama, riddled with silly dialogue and an incredible number of loving embraces. "The Best of Me" is the worst of Nicholas Sparks. **118m/C; DVD, Blu-Ray.** Michelle Monaghan; James Marsden; Liana Liberato; Luke Bracey; Gerald McRaney; Sean Bridgers; Caroline Goodall; Clarke Peters; Jon Tenney; Sebastian Arcelus; ***D:*** Michael Hoffman; ***W:*** Will Fetters; J. Mills Goodloe; ***C:*** Oliver Stapleton; ***M:*** Aaron Zigman.

The Best of Men **1/2** **2012** Inspirational true story from the BBC. German refugee, Dr. Ludwig Guttmann, arrives at Britain's Stoke Mandeville Hospital in 1944 and is appalled to find how the paralyzed soldiers are treated. After clashing with the staff, Guttmann introduces new care and programs into the rehabilitation regime, including athletics. This leads to national wheelchair competitions and the eventual founding of the Paralympic Games. **90m/C; DVD.** *UK* Eddie Marsan; Niamh Cusack; Rob Brydon; George MacKay; Richard McCabe; ***D:*** Tim Whitby; ***W:*** Lucy Gannon; ***C:*** Matt Gray; ***M:*** Mark Russell. **TV**

Best of the Badmen **1/2** **1950** A whole bunch of outlaws, although seemingly quite nice, are brought together by an ex-Union general who is being framed. Too much talk, not enough action. **84m/B; VHS, DVD.** Robert Ryan; Claire Trevor; Jack Buetel; Robert Preston; Walter Brennan; Bruce Cabot; John Archer; Lawrence Tierney; ***D:*** William D. Russell.

Best of the Best **1/2** **1989 (PG-13)** An interracial kick-boxing team strives to win a world championship. **95m/C; VHS, DVD; Open Captioned.** Eric Roberts; Sally Kirkland; Christopher Penn; Phillip Rhee; James Earl Jones; John P. Ryan; John Dye; David Agresta; Tom Everett; Louise Fletcher; Simon Rhee; Edward (Eddie) Bunker; ***D:*** Robert Radler.

Best of the Best 2 **1/2** **1993 (R)** The Coliseum is a notorious martial-arts venue owned by the champion fighter Brackus and his manager Weldon. No rules death matches are the norm and when their friend is killed Tommy and Alex set up a grudge match with Brackus. **100m/C; VHS, DVD.** Eric Roberts; Phillip Rhee; Christopher Penn; Ralph (Ralf) Moeller; Wayne Newton; Edan Gross; Sonny Landham; Meg Foster; Simon Rhee; Claire Stansfield; Betty Carvalho; Edward (Eddie) Bunker; ***D:*** Robert Radler; ***W:*** John Allen Nelson; Max Strom; ***M:*** David Michael Frank.

Best of the Best 3: No Turning Back **1995 (R)** Asian-American Tommy Lee (Rhee) discovers a band of racist vigilantes are trying to take over the rural community of Liberty, where his sister lives. But with the help of his brother-in-law Jack (McDonald), who's also the sheriff, and school teacher Margo (Gershon), Tommy is going to fight back. **102m/C; VHS, DVD.** Phillip Rhee; Gina Gershon; Christopher McDonald; Mark Rolston; Peter Simmons; Dee Wallace; ***D:*** Phillip Rhee; ***W:*** Deborah Scott; ***C:*** Jerry Watson; ***M:*** Barry Goldberg.

Best of the Best: Without Warning **1/2** **1998 (R)** It's Russian mobsters, counterfeit money, and high tech gadgets this time around as LAPD martial arts consultant Tommy Lee (Rhee) goes after the gang who killed his best friend's daughter. **90m/C; VHS, DVD, Blu-Ray.** Phillip Rhee; Ernie Hudson; Tobin Bell; Thure Riefenstein; Chris Lemmon; Jessica Collins; ***D:*** Phillip Rhee; ***C:*** Michael D. Margulies; ***M:*** David Grant. **VIDEO**

The Best of Times **1986 (PG)** Slim story of two grown men who attempt to redress the failures of the past by reenacting a football game they lost in high school due to a single flubbed pass. With this cast, it should have been better. **105m/C; VHS, DVD.** Robin Williams; Kurt Russell; M. Emmet Walsh; Pamela Reed; Holly Palance; Donald Moffat; Margaret Whitton; Kirk Cameron; ***D:*** Roger Spottiswoode; ***W:*** Ron Shelton; ***C:*** Charles F. Wheeler; ***M:*** Arthur B. Rubinstein.

Best of Youth *La Meglio Gioventu* **2003 (R)** Sprawling modern-times epic spanning 40 years of Italy's tumultuous history through the eyes of two brothers. At close to six hours the film encapsulates the entire relationship between Nicola (Lo Cascio), an optimistic med student, wooing women worldwide before settling into a successful career as a psychiatrist, and his brother Matteo (Boni), a world-weary, brooding idealist who eventually joins the Italian police in hopes of righting the wrongs of an unfair society. History is seen with human eyes and expressed in striking passion, somehow never overindulging itself. Originally an Italian television miniseries, went on to win over the crowds and critics at Cannes. **383m/C; DVD.** *IT* Luigi Lo Cascio; Adriana Asti; Alessio Boni; Jasmine Trinca; Sonia Bergamasco; Fabrizio Gifuni; Maya Sansa; Valentina Carnelutti; Andrea Tidona; Lidia Vitale; Camilla Filippi; Greta Cavuoti; Sara Pavoncello; Claudio Gioe; ***D:*** Marco Tullio Giordana; ***W:*** Sandro Petraglia; Stefano Rulli; ***C:*** Roberto Forza. **TV**

The Best Offer **1/2** *La Migliore Offerta* **2013 (R)** Eccentric high-end auctioneer Virgil Oldman (Rush) is hired by reclusive Claire (Hoeks) to appraise the contents of the villa she's inherited. Virgil's been miscataloging art works so he can have failed artist Billy (Sutherland) buy them on the cheap and among his treasures is a collection of portraits of women. But Virgil becomes obsessed with Claire rather than her art, having fallen in love for the first time. **131m/C; DVD.** *IT* Geoffrey Rush; Sylvia Hoeks; Donald Sutherland; Jim Sturgess; ***D:*** Giuseppe Tornatore; ***W:*** Giuseppe Tornatore; ***C:*** Fabio Zamarion; ***M:*** Ennio Morricone.

Best Seller **1987 (R)** Interesting, subtext-laden thriller about a cop/bestselling author with writer's block, and the strange symbiotic relationship he forms with a slick hired killer, who wants his own story written. Dennehy is convincing as the jaded cop, and is paired well with the psychotic Woods. **112m/C; VHS, DVD, Blu-Ray; Open Captioned.** James Woods; Brian Dennehy; Victoria Tennant; Paul Shenar; Seymour Cassel; Allison Balson; George Coe; Anne Pitoniak; ***D:*** John Flynn; ***W:*** Larry Cohen; ***C:*** Fred Murphy; ***M:*** Jay Ferguson.

The Best Way **1/2** *The Best Way to Walk; La Meilleure Facon de Marcher* **1976** Two summer camp counselors discover they might be gay and desirous of each other. Miller's first film; in French with English subtitles. **85m/C; VHS, DVD.** *FR* Patrick Dewaere; Patrick Bouchitey; Christine Pascal; Claude Pieplu; ***D:*** Claude Miller; ***W:*** Claude Miller; Luc Beraud; ***C:*** Bruno Nuytten; ***M:*** Alain Jomy.

Best Worst Movie **2009** Documentary recounting the making of the infamous 1990 straight-to-video bomb "Troll 2" (stealing only the title from 1986's "Troll"). Also chronicles how it reached its pinnacle of popularity over 15 years after its debut with a rabid cult following who can recite every poorly-written line of this unquestionably and hilariously terrible movie. Lovingly written and directed by original "T2" child star Stephenson, who speaks candidly about the flick's absurd origins. Funny and insightful with appeal for horror geeks and anyone who's ever sat through a real stinker. **91m/C; On Demand.** George Hardy; Claudio; Margo Prey; Jason Steadman; Darren Ewing; ***D:*** Michael Stevenson; ***C:*** Katie Graham; Carl Indriago; ***M:*** Bobby Tahouri.

The Best Years of Our Lives **1946** Three WWII vets return home to try to pick up the threads of their lives. A film that represented a large chunk of American society and helped it readjust to the modern postwar ambience is now considered an American classic. Supporting actor Russell, an actual veteran, holds a record for winning two Oscars for a single role. In addition to his Best Supporting Actor award, Russell was given a special Oscar for bringing hope and courage to fellow veterans. Based on the novella by MacKinlay Kantor. Remade for TV as "Returning Home" in 1975. **170m/B; VHS, DVD, Blu-Ray.** Fredric March; Myrna Loy; Teresa Wright; Dana Andrews; Virginia Mayo; Harold Russell; Hoagy Carmichael; Gladys George; Roman Bohnen; Steve Cochran; Charles Halton; Cathy O'Donnell; Ray Collins; Victor Cutler; Minna Gombell; Walter Baldwin; Dorothy Adams; Don Beddoe; Ray Teal; Howland Chamberlain; ***D:*** William Wyler; ***W:*** Robert Sherwood; ***C:*** Gregg Toland; ***M:*** Hugo Friedhofer. Oscars '46: Actor (March), Director (Wyler), Film, Film Editing, Orig. Dramatic Score, Screenplay, Support. Actor (Russell); AFI '98: Top 100; British Acad. '47: Film; Golden Globes '47: Film--Drama; Natl. Bd. of Review '46: Director (Wyler); Natl. Film Reg. '89; N.Y. Film Critics '46: Director (Wyler), Film.

Bet Your Life **1/2** **2004** In 2004 NBC television had a reality gameshow called "Next Action Star", and the male and female winners of it would star opposite Billy Zane in an action film. This is that film. All things considered they're probably regretting the experience now. Sonny (Sean Carrigan) is a gambling addict who catches the attention of a perverse millionaire. He bets his entire fortune that Sonny can't stay alive for 24 hours, and Sonny promptly flees to Cleveland, Ohio. Obviously Cleveland must be some sort of impregnable fortress city that hates the rich. **90m/C; DVD.** *IN* Sean Carrigan; Corrine Van Ryck de Groot; Billy Zane; Rich Pierrelouis; Amanda Tosch; Joe Gogol; Joel Nunley; Christopher J. Quinn; Alfred Thomas Catalfo; Jeanne Brauer; Shelly Marks; ***D:*** Louis Morneau; ***W:*** Louis Morneau; Jeff Welch; ***C:*** David Litz; George Mooradian; ***M:*** Tim Truman.

Betrayal **1974** Psycho-thriller pits an unhappy widow against her seemingly innocent hired companion. Seems this girl has a boyfriend who has a plan to murder the lonely lady for her money. Routine and predictable. **78m/C; VHS, DVD.** Amanda Blake; Dick Haymes; Tisha Sterling; Sam Groom; ***D:*** Gordon Hessler; ***M:*** Ernest Gold.

Betrayal **1/2** **1978** Telefilm based on the book by Lucy Freeman and Julie Roy about a historic malpractice case involving a psychiatrist and one of his female patients. The doctor convinced the female patient that sex with him would serve as therapy. **95m/C; VHS, DVD.** Lesley Ann Warren; Rip Torn; Ron Silver; Richard Masur; Stephen Elliott; John Hillerman; Peggy Ann Garner; ***D:*** Paul Wendkos.

Betrayed *When Strangers Marry* **1944** Efficient crime drama from director Castle. Drunken conventioneer Prescott (Elliott) is murdered in his hotel room after flashing a wad of cash around a bar. Waitress Millie (Hunter) suspects her salesman hubby Paul (Jagger), whom she married after a whirlwind romance, could be involved after he admits meeting Prescott but it could also be her old flame Fred (Mitchum). **67m/B; DVD.** Dean Jagger; Kim Hunter; Robert Mitchum; Neil Hamilton; Lou Lubin; Milton Kibbee; Richard Elliott; ***D:*** William Castle; ***W:*** Philip Yordan; Dennis J. Cooper; ***C:*** Ira Morgan; ***M:*** Dimitri Tiomkin.

Betrayed **1954** Bombshell Turner and strongman Gable star in this story of WWII intrigue. Suspected of being a Nazi informer, Turner is sent back to Holland for a last chance at redemption. Her cover as a sultry nightclub performer has the Nazis drooling and ogling (can you spell h-o-t?), but her act may be blown by an informant. Can luscious Lana get out of this one intact? **107m/C; VHS, DVD.** Clark Gable; Lana Turner; Victor Mature; Louis Calhern; O.E. Hasse; Wilfrid Hyde-White; Ian Carmichael; Niall MacGinnis; Nora Swinburne; Roland Culver; ***D:*** Gottfried Reinhardt; ***C:*** Frederick A. (Freddie) Young.

Betrayed **1988 (R)** A rabid political film, dealing with an implausible FBI agent infiltrating a white supremacist organization via her love affair with a handsome farmer who turns out to be a murderous racist. Winger is memorable in her role as the FBI agent, despite the film's limitations, and admirers of Costa-Gavras's directorial work and political stances will want to see how the director botched this one. **112m/C; VHS, DVD, Blu-Ray.** Tom Berenger; Debra Winger; John Mahoney; John Heard; Albert Hall; Jeffrey DeMunn; ***D:*** Constantin Costa-Gavras; ***W:*** Joe Eszterhas; ***C:*** Patrick Blossier.

The Betrayed **1/2** **2008** When Jamie (George), the married mom of a young son, regains consciousness after a car accident, she's being held captive in an isolated warehouse. Her captor says her husband has stolen millions from a crime syndicate and if Jamie wants to keep her son safe, she must kill her husband. **99m/C; DVD.** Melissa George; Donald Adams; Christian Campbell; Scott Heindl; Ken Tremblett; Connor Christopher Levins; Roger Vernon; Blaine Anderson; ***D:*** Amanda Gusack; ***W:*** Amanda Gusack; ***M:*** Deborah Lurie. **VIDEO**

Betrayed: A Story of Three Women **1/2** **1995** The friendship of suburbanites Amanda Nelson (Baxter) and Joan Bixler (Kurtz) is destroyed when Amanda learns her lawyer husband Rob (Terry) is having an affair with his summer intern Dana (Carey), who is the widowed Joan's daughter. Lots of shouting and angst follows. **93m/C; DVD.** Swoosie Kurtz; Meredith Baxter; Clare Carey; John Terry; John Livingston; Breckin Meyer; Bill Brochtrup; ***D:*** William A. Graham; ***W:*** James Duff; ***C:*** Robert Steadman; ***M:*** Patrick Williams. **TV**

Betrayed at 17 **2011** Shy 17-year-old Lexi Ross (Bauer) is flattered to be dating football star Greg (Fischer-Price). It ends tragically when he secretly makes a sex tape and it goes viral thanks to his jealous ex, Carleigh (Gill). Lexi's widowed mother, Michelle (Paul), is determined to get justice. Lifetime teen drama. **88m/C; DVD; Closed Captioned.** Alexandra Paul; Joe Penny; Katie (Katharine) Gill; Andy Fischer-Price; Amanda Bauer; Jake Thomas; ***D:*** Doug Campbell; ***W:*** Christine Conradt; ***C:*** Robert Ballo; ***M:*** Steve Gurevitch. **CABLE**

A Bet's a Bet **1/2** *The Opposite Sex* **2014** Very mildly amusing comedy that plays like a sexed-up Hallmark Channel flick. To divorce attorney Vince winning is everything and that includes dating. When he and intensely-driven divorcee Jane meet, she and Vince make a series of bets where the loser is at the mercy of the winner and Vince begins losing all the time. **97m/C; DVD.** Geoff Stults; Mena Suvari; Josh Hopkins; Jennifer Finnigan; Kristin Chenoweth; Eric Roberts; Jonathan Silverman; ***D:*** Jennifer Finnigan; Jonathan Silverman; ***W:*** Steven Sessions; ***C:*** Jendra Jarnagin. **VIDEO**

The Betsy *Harold Robbins' The Betsy* **1978 (R)** A story of romance, money, power, and mystery centering around the wealthy Hardeman family and their automobile manufacturing business. Loosely patterned after the life of Henry Ford as portrayed in the Harold Robbins' pulp-tome. Olivier is the redeeming feature. **132m/C; VHS, DVD.** Laurence Olivier; Kathleen Beller; Robert Duvall; Lesley-Anne Down; Edward Herrmann; Tommy Lee Jones; Katharine Ross; Jane Alexander; ***D:*** Daniel Petrie; ***W:*** William Bast; Walter Bernstein; ***C:*** Mario Tosi; ***M:*** John Barry.

Betsy's Wedding **1/2** **1990 (R)** Betsy wants a simple wedding, but her father has other, grander ideas. Then there's the problem of paying for it, which Dad tries to take care of in a not-so-typical manner. Alda at his hilarious best. **94m/C; VHS, DVD, Blu-Ray.** Alan Alda; Joey Bishop; Madeline Kahn; Molly Ringwald; Catherine O'Hara; Joe Pesci; Ally Sheedy; Burt Young; Anthony LaPaglia; Julie Bovasso; Nicolas Coster; Bibi Besch; Dylan Walsh; Samuel L. Jackson; Frankie Faison; ***D:*** Alan Alda; ***W:*** Alan Alda; ***C:*** Kelvin Pike; ***M:*** Bruce Broughton.

The Better Angels **2014 (PG)** Anyone familiar with Malick's work will have some idea what to expect when he produces a B&W period piece such as this poetically rendered imagining of Abraham Lincoln's childhood. Filled with fluid shots of nature and lyrical filmmaking flourishes, this drama may frustrate those looking for a traditional narrative, but will enrapture those who like his work. Starting in Indiana in 1817, it chronicles three years in life of a young Lincoln, focusing heavily on the family tragedy that marked him forever and the two women who would be influential on his entire legacy. It's a little slight, but oh so pretty. **95m/B; DVD, Blu-Ray.** Braydon Denney; Jason Clarke; Diane Kruger; Brit Marling; Wes Bentley; Cameron Mitchell Williams; ***D:*** A.J. Edwards; ***W:*** A.J. Edwards; ***C:*** Matthew Lloyd; ***M:*** Hanan Townshend.

Better Dayz 🦴 1/2 **2002** High schooler Faye (Cargle) has her head turned by smoothie drug dealer Vaughn (Odell)?until she sees him kill a rival. When Vaughn threatens Faye, she turns to her hot-headed brother Johnny (Williams) to keep her safe. Technical flaws detract from what slowly becomes a dramatic story. **101m/C; VHS, DVD.** Erik Williams; Shantel Cargle; Rich Odell; ***D:*** Norman C. Linton; ***W:*** Norman C. Linton; ***C:*** Brenden Flint. **VIDEO**

A Better Life 🦴🦴🦴 **2011 (PG-13)** Mexican-born Carlos (Bechir) dedicates his life to working hard as a gardener in order to give his teenage son Luis (Julian) more opportunities then he had. Carlos also struggles to keep Luis away from both East L.A. gangs and immigration officials. Bechir and Julian are at the heart of this earnest but not sappy story about a father's love for his child. Director Weitz capably tells of the unrelenting struggles facing hardworking illegal immigrants while refraining from getting political on the hot topic. **110m/C; DVD, Blu-Ray, On Demand.** Demian Bechir; Jose Julian; Carlos Linares; Tom Schanley; ***D:*** Chris Weitz; ***W:*** Eric Eason; ***C:*** Javier Aguirresarobe; ***M:*** Alexandre Desplat.

Better Living Through Chemistry 🦴 1/2 **2014** Glib indie comedy with a strange voiceover narration by Fonda, playing herself. Small town milquetoast pharmacist Douglas (Rockwell) is married to ball-busting Kara (Monaghan) and owes his job to equally interfering father-in-law Walter (Howard). His life is turned upside down as he's willingly lead on a drug- and sex-fueled trip after falling for dangerously seductive trophy wife, Elizabeth (Wilde), but the pic doesn't mesh together well enough to be more than fitfully amusing. **91m/C; DVD, Blu-Ray.** Sam Rockwell; Olivia Wilde; Michelle Monaghan; Ray Liotta; Jane Fonda; Ken Howard; Norbert Lee Butz; ***D:*** Geoff Moore; David Posamentier; ***W:*** Geoff Moore; David Posamentier; ***C:*** Tim Suhrstedt; ***M:*** Andrew Feltenstein; John Nau.

Better Luck Tomorrow 🦴🦴🦴 **2002 (R)** Controversial film about Asian-American teens gone wild. Overachieving students in a wealthy Orange County suburb, they outwardly conform to the stereotype of smart, well-behaved, ambitious kids. But their extracurricular activities involve drugs and criminal activities that escalate from the petty to the serious as events spin out of their control. **98m/C; VHS, DVD.** Parry Shen; Jason J. Tobin; Roger Fan; Sung Kang; John Cho; Karin Anna Cheung; ***D:*** Justin Lin; ***W:*** Justin Lin; Ernesto M. Foronda; Fabian Marquez; ***C:*** Patrice Lucien Cochet; ***M:*** Michael J. Gonzales.

Better Off Dead 🦴🦴 1/2 **1985 (PG)** A compulsive teenager's girlfriend leaves him and he decides to end it all. After several abortive attempts, he decides instead to outski his ex-girlfriend's obnoxious new boyfriend. Uneven but funny. **97m/C; VHS, DVD, Blu-Ray.** John Cusack; Curtis Armstrong; Diane Franklin; Kim Darby; David Ogden Stiers; Dan Schneider; Amanda Wyss; Taylor Negron; Vincent Schiavelli; Demian Slade; Scooter Stevens; Elizabeth Daily; Yano Ayana; Steven Williams; ***D:*** Savage Steve Holland; ***W:*** Savage Steve Holland; ***C:*** Isidore Mankofsky; ***M:*** Rupert Hine.

Better Off Single 🦴🦴 **2016** A comedy about finding love in New York City. On one memorable day, Charlie Carroll (Tveit) quits his job and dumps his girlfriend. Though he initially feels free, his initial dating experiences leave something to be desired. Charlie soon feels that he is not capable of being single or even just living. As he embarks on a journey of self-discovery, Charlie experiences surreal hallucinations, flashbacks, and sex fantasies make him question everything about his life. **85m/C; DVD, Blu-Ray, Streaming, Download.** Aaron Tveit; Kelen Coleman; Kal Penn; Lauren Miller; Chris Elliott; ***D:*** Benjamin Cox; ***W:*** Benjamin Cox; ***C:*** Igor Kropotov; ***M:*** Kenneth Burgomaster.

The Better 'Ole 🦴 1/2 **1926** Cockney Old Bill (Chaplin) is a WWI private with the British infantry. Bill and his mate Alfie (Ackroyd) must find the traitor in their ranks who is responsible for a French town falling to the Germans. Based on cartoon characters created by Bruce Bairnsfather, with the title referring to a foxhole. Some of the humor is blunted by the passage of time, although the visual of Chaplin and Ackroyd in a horse's costume is still amusing. **97m/B; Silent; DVD.** Syd Chaplin; Jack Ackroyd; Edgar Kennedy; Charles Gerrard; Theodore Lorch; Harold Goodwin; ***D:*** Charles Reisner; ***W:*** Charles Reisner; Darryl F. Zanuck; ***C:*** Edwin DuPar.

Better Than Chocolate 🦴🦴 **1999 (R)** Sweetly touching romantic comedy follows college dropout Maggie (Dwyer), who's trying to establish her own identity, which isn't so easy when she hasn't told her flighty mother, Lila (Crewson), that she's a lesbian. But now mom is getting divorced and she and Maggie's brother Paul (Mundy) are temporarily moving in, with Maggie trying to pass off her lover Kim (Cox) as just a roommate. Meanwhile, naive Lila is confiding in Maggie's transseuxual friend, singer Judy (a stellar Outerbridge), and discovering the joys of sex toys. **101m/C; VHS, DVD.** *CA* Karyn Dwyer; Wendy Crewson; Christina Cox; Peter Outerbridge; Ann-Marie MacDonald; Kevin Mundy; Marya Delver; Jay Brazeau; Tony Nappo; ***D:*** Anne Wheeler; ***W:*** Peggy Thompson; ***C:*** Gregory Middleton; ***M:*** Graeme Coleman.

Better Than Sex 🦴🦴 1/2 **2000 (R)** Cin (Porter) meets Josh (Wenham) at a party and takes him home for the night. When things go exceptionally well, Cin agrees to Josh's staying on until he flies home to London in a couple of days. But amidst all the sex, little things like relationships, love, and commitment begin to creep in. Voiceovers from the twosome comment on the action and what they're really feeling rather than what they're telling each other. Porter and Wenham are attractive and there's (unsurprisingly) a lot of displayed skin. **85m/C; VHS, DVD.** *AU FR* David Wenham; Susie Porter; Catherine McClements; Kris McQuade; Simon Bossell; Imelda Corcoran; ***D:*** Jonathan Teplitzky; ***W:*** Jonathan Teplitzky; ***C:*** Garry Phillips; ***M:*** David Hirschfelder. Australian Film Inst. '00: Director, Film, Score (Hirschfelder).

A Better Tomorrow, Part 1 🦴🦴 1/2 *Ying Huang Boon Sik; Gangland Boss* **1986** Former hit men (Lung and Fat) team up to bring down the mob boss who double-crossed them and sent one to prison and the other to the streets. One of them also has to protect his younger brother, a cop, from the gang. Considered one of the best of Woo's Hong Kong efforts, there's plenty of his hallmark balletic action and an interesting story. In Cantonese with English subtitles. **95m/C; VHS, DVD.** *CH CH* Chow Yun-Fat; Leslie Cheung; Ti Lung; Emily Chu; Waise Lee; John Woo; ***D:*** John Woo; ***W:*** John Woo; ***C:*** Wing-Hung Wong; ***M:*** Ka-Fai Koo.

A Better Tomorrow, Part 2 🦴 1/2 *Yinghung Bunsik 2* **1988** A smooth-talking gangster, who was killed in Part I, returns in Part II as the dead man's twin brother (unmentioned in Part I). He teams up with a cop and a reformed gangster to fight the forces of evil. In Cantonese with English subtitles. **100m/C; VHS, DVD.** *CH* Chow Yun-Fat; Leslie Cheung; ***D:*** John Woo; ***W:*** John Woo; ***M:*** Joseph Koo.

A Better Tomorrow, Part 3 🦴🦴 *Love and Death in Saigon* **1989** Prequel set in 1974 finds detective Mark Gor (Fat) and his cousin (Leung) seeking to escape from Saigon. Unfortunately, they both fall for the same sultry babe (Mui), who's also a gangster's moll. Mandarin with subtitles. **114m/C; VHS, DVD.** *CH* Chow Yun-Fat; Tony Leung Ka-Fai; Anita (Yim-Fong) Mui; ***D:*** Tsui Hark.

Better Watch Out 🦴🦴 **2017 (R)** A Christmas-themed, home invasion-focused horror movie with a novel yet cheap twist. Ashley (DeJonge) is babysitting teen Luke (Miller), who longs to lose his virginity to her. Luke shares this information with friend Garrett (Oxenbould), who also wants to lose his virginity. Though Luke tries to make progress towards his goal, someone wearing a mask and a gun slip into the house without them noticing. What follows is a series of cliches, sometimes turned upside down, and incidents of terror. Unoriginal, with thin characterizations and vain attempts to push viewers' buttons. **89m/C; DVD, Blu-Ray.** Olivia DeJonge; Levi Miller; Ed Oxenbould; Aleks Mikic; Dacre Montgomery; ***D:*** Chris Peckover; ***W:*** Chris Peckover; Zack Kahn; ***C:*** Carl Robertson; ***M:*** Brian Cachia.

A Better Way to Die 🦴🦴 **2000 (R)** An ex-cop heads home to try to start a new life but is instead mistaken for a government agent who has had a contract put out on his life by a Chicago mob boss. So the cop tries to get the feds to assist him before the wiseguys get to him first. **101m/C; VHS, DVD.** Andre Braugher; Joe Pantoliano; Natasha Henstridge; Lou Diamond Phillips; Wayne Duvall; Scott Wiper; ***D:*** Scott Wiper; ***W:*** Scott Wiper. **VIDEO**

Betting on Zero **2016 99m/C; DVD, Streaming.** ***D:*** Ted Braun; ***C:*** Buddy Squires; ***M:*** Pete Anthony. **VIDEO**

Betty 🦴🦴 **1992** Sulky, drunken Betty (Trintignant) is doing her best to destroy her bourgeois life, escaping from her marriage into adultery and debasement. She meets the concerned middle-aged widow Laure (Audran), who inexplicably takes her to her hotel room, cleans her up, and spends the remainder of the movie as Betty's sounding-board. Betty's passive personality offers little to explain her appeal to either Laure or the viewer. Based on the novel by Georges Simenon. French with subtitles. **103m/C; VHS, DVD.** *FR* Marie Trintignant; Stephane Audran; Jean-Francoise Garreaud; Yves Lambrecht; Christiane Minazzoli; Pierre Vernier; ***D:*** Claude Chabrol; ***W:*** Claude Chabrol; ***M:*** Matthieu Chabrol.

Betty 🦴🦴 1/2 **1997** Betty Monday (Pollak) is a well-known actress undergoing a breakdown. So she leaves Hollywood for Palm Springs and tries out a "normal" life—at least by movie star standards. Offbeat comedy has the potential to pleasantly surprise. **88m/C; VHS, DVD.** Cheryl Pollak; Holland Taylor; Udo Kier; Ron Perlman; Stephen Gregory; ***D:*** Richard D. (R.D.) Murphy; ***W:*** Richard D. (R.D.) Murphy.

Betty & Coretta 🦴🦴 **2013** Two powerhouse women (Blige and Bassett) in the title roles can't quite overcome the stilted docudrama nature of this Lifetime effort. Ruby Dee is the onscreen narrator who fills in the details about the lives of civil rights widows, Dr. Betty Shabazz, married to Malcolm X, and Coretta Scott King, married to Martin Luther King Jr., who are brought togeher after the deaths to carry on their husbands' work and activism. **120m/C; DVD.** Mary J. Blige; Angela Bassett; Malik Yoba; Lindsay Owen Pierre; ***Nar:*** Ruby Dee; ***D:*** Yves Simoneau; ***W:*** Shem Bitterman; Ron Hutchinson; ***C:*** Guy Dufaux; ***M:*** Terence Blanchard. **CABLE**

Betty Blue 🦴🦴🦴 *37.2 le Matin; 37.2 Degrees in the Morning* **1986 (R)** A vivid, intensely erotic film about two young French lovers and how their inordinately strong passion for each other destroys them, leading to poverty, violence, and insanity. English subtitles. From the director of "Diva." Based on the novel "37.2 Le Matin" by Philippe Djian. **121m/C; VHS, DVD, Blu-Ray.** *FR* Beatrice Dalle; Jean-Hugues Anglade; Gerard Darmon; Consuelo de Haviland; Clementine Celarie; Jacques Mathou; Vincent Lindon; ***D:*** Jean-Jacques Beineix; ***W:*** Jean-Jacques Beineix; ***C:*** Jean-Francois Robin; ***M:*** Gabriel Yared.

The Betty Ford Story 🦴🦴🦴 **1987** Gena Rowlands deserved her Emmy for her strong portrayal of First Lady Betty Ford in this adaptation of Ford's autobiography "The Times of My Life." Ford earns national admiration for her candid reveal of her breast cancer and subsequent treatment but she hides her addictions to alcohol and prescription drugs. After her husband (Sommer) loses his 1976 reelection bid, her family intervenes and Betty gets clean, then decides to open her own center for substance abusers. **93m/C; DVD.** Gena Rowlands; Josef Sommer; Nan Woods; Concetta Tomei; Brian McNamara; Bradley Whitford; Daniel McDonald; Ken Tigar; ***D:*** David Greene; ***W:*** Karen Hall; ***C:*** Dennis Dalzell; ***M:*** Arthur B. Rubinstein. **TV**

Between 🦴 **2005** Allegedly spooky pic with a nonsensical plot and weak acting. Chicago lawyer Nadine Roberts (Montgomery) keeps having terrifying visions of her estranged sister Diane, who vanished in Tijuana. So Nadine heads south of the border to investigate but doesn't get much cooperation even as her nightmares worsen. Then people start calling Nadine by Diane's name and there's all this ridiculous symbolism before the surprise ending that isn't at all. **86m/C; DVD.** Poppy Montgomery; Danny Pino; Adam Kaufman; Jose Yenque; Patricia Reyes Spindola; ***D:*** David Ocanas; ***W:*** Robert Nelms; ***C:*** Rob Sweeney; ***M:*** Joel J. Richard. **CABLE**

Between God, the Devil & a Winchester 🦴 **1972** Violent western with plenty of shooting and dust. Lots of cowboys are hot on the trail of some stolen loot from a church but apparently God isn't on their side since the majority bite the dust and become a snack for the vultures. **98m/C; VHS, DVD.** Gilbert Roland; Richard Harrison; ***D:*** Dario Silvester.

Between Heaven and Hell 🦴🦴🦴 **1956** Prejudiced Southern gentleman Wagner finds how wrong his misconceptions are, as he attempts to survive WWII on a Pacific Island. Ebsen is exceptional, making this rather simplistic story a meaningful classic. **94m/C; VHS, DVD.** Robert Wagner; Terry Moore; Broderick Crawford; Buddy Ebsen; Robert Keith; Brad Dexter; Mark Damon; Ken Clark; Harvey Lembeck; Frank Gorshin; Scatman Crothers; Carl "Alfalfa" Switzer; L.Q. Jones; Tod Andrews; ***D:*** Richard Fleischer; ***W:*** Harry Brown; ***C:*** Leo Tover; ***M:*** Hugo Friedhofer.

Between Love & Goodbye 🦴 **2008** French citizen Marcel marries lesbian Sarah so he can get a green card to stay in New York with lover Kyle. Marcel and Kyle are living together when Kyle offers his troubled transgendered sister April a place to crash. Jealous of Kyle and Marcel's relationship, April sets out to break them up, which Kyle refuses to believe. The two lovers are so petulant and clueless that their romantic problems are more annoying than compelling. **87m/C; DVD.** Robert Harmon; Justin Tensen; Simon Miller; Jane Elliott; ***D:*** Casper Andreas; ***W:*** Casper Andreas; ***C:*** Jon Fordham; ***M:*** Scott Starrett.

Between Midnight and Dawn 🦴 1/2 **1950** Workmanlike crime drama. L.A. patrol car partners Dan Purvis and Rocky Barnes are the bane of gangster Ritchie Garvis, whom they put in jail. When Garvis breaks out, he's determined to eliminate the coppers. There's a minor subplot involving police dispatcher Kate, who infatuates both partners. **89m/B; DVD.** Edmond O'Brien; Gale Storm; Donald Buka; Mark Stevens; Gale Robbins; Anthony Ross; ***D:*** Gordon Douglas; ***W:*** Eugene Ling; ***C:*** George E. Diskant; ***M:*** George Duning.

Between Something & Nothing 🦴🦴 **2008** Small-town teen Joe gets into a prestigious big-city art school but he and fellow student/best friend Jennifer are constantly struggling to pay tuition and other living expenses. Then Joe meets hustler Ramon, who suggests his new bud try the sex-for-pay route and soon Joe is using his new life as inspiration for his art. **105m/C; DVD.** Tim Swain; Julia Frey; Gil Bar-Sera; ***D:*** Todd Verow; ***W:*** Todd Verow; James Dwyer; ***C:*** Todd Verow; ***M:*** Colin Owens. **VIDEO**

Between Strangers 🦴🦴 **2002 (R)** Three Toronto women suffer personal crises and contemplate changing their lives. Housewife Olivia (Loren) is debating whether to leave her abusive invalid husband (Postlethwaite); war photographer Natalia (Sorvino) is burned out trying to live up to her father's reputation and contemplates a career change; and cellist Catherine (Unger) is upset over her father's (McDowell) recent release from prison for a crime that has haunted her since childhood. Ponti's debut and his mom Loren's 100th film. **97m/C; VHS, DVD.** *US CA IT* Sophia Loren; Mira Sorvino; Deborah Kara Unger; Pete Postlethwaite; Malcolm McDowell; Klaus Maria Brandauer; Gerard Depardieu; Wendy Crewson; Andrew Tarbet; ***D:*** Edoardo Ponti; ***W:*** Edoardo Ponti; ***C:*** Gregory Middleton; ***M:*** Zbigniew Preisner.

Between the Darkness and the Dawn 🦴🦴 1/2 **1985** Abigail Foster lapses into a coma at 17 and doesn't awaken for 20 years. She (Montgomery) thinks like a teenager and has to not only adjust to being an adult but to everything that's changed in two decades. This includes her younger sister Ellen (Grassle) marrying Abigail's high school boyfriend David (Goodwin) and the worry that her conscious state may not be permanent. **96m/C; DVD.** Elizabeth Montgomery; Dorothy McGuire; Karen Grassle; Michael Goodwin; James Naughton; Robin Gammell; ***D:*** Peter Levin; ***W:*** N. Richard Nash; Dennis Turner; ***C:*** Philip H. Lathrop; ***M:*** Diana Kaproff. **TV**

Between the Lines ½ **1977 (R)** A witty, wonderfully realized ensemble comedy about the staff of a radical post-'60s newspaper always on the brink of folding, and its eventual sell-out. **101m/C; VHS, DVD, Blu-Ray.** John Heard; Lindsay Crouse; Jeff Goldblum; Jill Eikenberry; Stephen Collins; Lewis J. Stadlen; Michael J. Pollard; Marilu Henner; Bruno Kirby; ***D:*** Joan Micklin Silver; ***W:*** Fred Barron; ***M:*** Michael Kamen.

Between Truth and Lies ½ **2006** Hemingway is unconvincing as a shrink and the characters are generally unappealing in this ludicrous Lifetime movie. Dr. Claire Parker (Hemingway) encourages patient John Walters (Watton) to pursue his crush. Only she doesn't realize that it's on her teenage daughter Emily (Castle) and that he's seriously disturbed. Emily disappears sending Claire turns into action mom. **90m/C; DVD.** Mariel Hemingway; Maggie Castle; Jonathan Watton; Ted Whittall; Morgan Kelly; Conrad Coates; ***D:*** John Bradshaw; ***W:*** Paul B. Margolis; ***C:*** Russ Goozee; ***M:*** Stacey Hersh. **CABLE**

Between Two Ferns ½ **2019** Hilariously awkward Zach (Galifianakis) longs to be a network talk show host, but he is stuck interviewing, and tearing down, famous people on a low-rent show that airs on North Carolina regional cable access. One day, executive Will (Farrell) gives him a chance to be on network television, but Zach must produce 10 episodes within two weeks. Zach and his crew embark on a road trip to complete the episodes on time after a freak plumbing accident at his television station. A fun adaptation of the popular web series. **82m/C; DVD.** Zach Galifianakis; Matthew McConaughey; Rekha Shankar; Olivia Mekdara; Mo Zelof; ***D:*** Scott Aukerman; ***W:*** Scott Aukerman; ***C:*** Benjamin Kasulke; ***M:*** Alex Wurman. **VIDEO**

Between Two Women ½ **1945** Red Adams is still being romanced by Ruth, but he has two other women on his (medical) mind. Nightclub singer Edna has a serious eating disorder and Blair General's switchboard operator Sally needs an operation. Fifth in series; followed by "Dark Delusion." **83m/B; DVD.** Lionel Barrymore; Van Johnson; Marilyn Maxwell; Gloria De Haven; Marie Blake; Keye Luke; Keenan Wynn; Alma Kruger; ***D:*** Willis Goldbeck; ***W:*** Harry Ruskin; ***C:*** Harold Rosson; ***M:*** David Snell.

Between Two Worlds ½ **1944** Dreary fantasy drama. Despondent Austrian refugees Henry (Henreid) and his wife Ann (Parker) commit suicide in their London flat but awaken on a fog-shrouded cruise ship. The couple soon learns that they and their (dead) fellow passengers are awaiting judgment to either Heaven, Hell, sailing perpetually in limbo, or a second chance. Garfield overdoes his role as a cynical, blowhard reporter. Based on the play by Sutton Vane; remake of 1930's "Outward Bound." **112m/B; DVD.** Paul Henreid; Eleanor Parker; John Garfield; Sydney Greenstreet; Faye Emerson; Edmund Gwenn; George Tobias; Sara Allgood; George Coulouris; ***D:*** Edward Blatt; ***W:*** Daniel Fuchs; ***C:*** Carl Guthrie; ***M:*** Erich Wolfgang Korngold.

Between Us **2012 (R)** A dark comedy centered on the complexities of relationships based on the Off-Broadway play by Joe Hortua. Taking place over the course of two evenings two years apart, two couples who are old friends reconnect and learn their lives are not what they seem. When Grace (Stiles) and Carlo (Diggs) visit Sharyl (George) and Joel (Harbour) in the Midwest, the hosts' marriage has become destructive despite their wealth. Happier and richer two years later, Sharyl and Joel's visit to Grace and Carlo in New York finds the latter couple struggling with marriage, children, and financial issues. **90m/C; DVD.** Julia Stiles; Taye Diggs; Melissa George; David Harbour; Julia Cho; ***D:*** Dan Mirvish; ***W:*** Dan Mirvish; Joe Hortua; ***C:*** Nancy Schreiber; ***M:*** H. Scott Salinas.

Between Your Legs *Entre las Piernas* **1999** Provocatively titled sexual thriller. Receptionist Miranda (Abril) meets writer Javier (Bardem) at a group therapy session for sex addicts. He's addicted to phone sex and the married Miranda likes to have sex with strangers. While they get to know each other a murder occurs and the investigation is assigned to detective Felix (Gomez), who happens to be Miranda's husband. Soon, suspicions begin to point in Javier's direction. The triangle is strong but subplots are undeveloped and the film sinks into implausibility. Spanish with subtitles. **120m/C; VHS, DVD.** *SP FR* Victoria Abril; Javier Bardem; Carmelo Gomez; Juan Diego; Sergi Lopez; Javier Albala; ***D:*** Manuel Gomez Pereira; ***W:*** Manuel Gomez Pereira; Joaquin Oristrell; Yolanda Garcia Serrano; Juan Luis Iborra; ***C:*** Juan Amoros; ***M:*** Bernardo Bonezzi.

Beulah Land ½ **1980** Miniseries about 45 years in the lives of a Southern family, including the Civil War. Based on the novels "Beulah Land" and "Look Away, Beulah Land" by Lonnie Coleman. **267m/C; VHS, DVD.** Lesley Ann Warren; Michael Sarrazin; Don Johnson; Meredith Baxter; Dorian Harewood; Eddie Albert; Hope Lange; Paul Rudd; ***D:*** Virgil W. Vogel; Harry Falk. **TV**

The Beverly Hillbillies ½ **1993 (PG)** Big-screen transfer of the long-running TV show may appeal to fans. Ozark mountaineer Jed Clampett discovers oil, becomes an instant billionaire, and packs his backwoods clan off to the good life in California. Minimal plot finds dim-bulb nephew Jethro and daughter Elly May looking for a bride for Jed. Not that any of it matters. Everyone does fine by their impersonations, particularly Varney as the good-hearted Jed and Leachman as stubborn Granny. Ebsen, the original Jed, reprises another of his TV roles, detective Barnaby Jones. And yes, the familiar strains of the "Ballad of Jed Clampett" by Jerry Scoggins starts this one off, too. **93m/C; VHS, DVD.** Jim Varney; Erika Eleniak; Diedrich Bader; Cloris Leachman; Dabney Coleman; Lily Tomlin; Lea Thompson; Rob Schneider; Linda Carlson; Penny Fuller; Kevin Connolly; ***Cameo(s):*** Buddy Ebsen; Zsa Zsa Gabor; Dolly Parton; ***D:*** Penelope Spheeris; ***W:*** Larry Konner; Mark Rosenthal; Jim Fisher; Jim Staahl; ***C:*** Robert Brinkmann; ***M:*** Lalo Schifrin.

Beverly Hills Brats **1989 (PG-13)** A spoiled, rich Hollywood brat hires a loser to kidnap him, in order to gain his parents' attention, only to have both of them kidnapped by real crooks. **90m/C; VHS, DVD.** Martin Sheen; Burt Young; Peter Billingsley; Terry Moore; ***D:*** Dimitri Sotirakis; ***M:*** Barry Goldberg.

Beverly Hills Chihuahua **2008 (PG)** Chloe, a pampered Chihuahua living the good life in Beverly Hills, finds herself lost in Mexico with the spoiled pet-sitter during a weekend romp. Along the way Chloe must be rescued from the grips of Mexican dogfight wranglers and falls in love with Papi, a Chihuahua from the wrong side of the tracks. Light-hearted family affair with a strong Hispanic cast, as well as Barrymore as the voice of Chloe and Curtis as Chloe's wildly indulgent owner. Cute, tame, kind of lame. **86m/C; Blu-Ray.** Nick Zano; Piper Perabo; Manolo Cardona; Jose Maria Yazpik; ***V:*** Drew Barrymore; Salma Hayek; George Lopez; Andy Garcia; Jamie Lee Curtis; Marguerite Moreau; Michael Urie; Richard "Cheech" Marin; Paul Rodriguez; Placido Domingo; Edward James Olmos; Loretta Devine; Luis Guzman; ***D:*** Raja Gosnell; ***W:*** Jeffrey Bushell; Analisa LaBianco; ***C:*** Phil Mereaux; ***M:*** Hector Pereira.

Beverly Hills Chihuahua 2 ½ **2010 (G)** Mediocre sequel may have some appeal for the kiddies. Chloe and Papi are married and have become proud parents. Papi's owner Sam has learned his own parents are about to lose their house and the dogs decide to enter a dog show hoping to win some prize money. That doesn't work out and they accidentally foil a bank robbery instead, which deserves a reward. **84m/C; DVD, Blu-Ray.** Marcus Coloma; Lupe Ontiveros; Castulo Guerra; Erin Cahill; Susan Blakely; ***V:*** George Lopez; Odette Yustman Annable; Zachary Gordon; Bridgit Mendler; Ernie Hudson; Emily Osment; Mel Ferrer; ***D:*** Alex Zamm; ***W:*** Alex Zamm; Danielle Schneider; Dannah Feinglass; ***C:*** Robert Brinkmann; ***M:*** Chris Hajian. **VIDEO**

Beverly Hills Chihuahua 3: Viva La Fiesta! ½ **2012 (G)** Papi, Chloe, and their five pups move into the Langham Hotel when owners Rachel and Sam get new jobs. Tiniest pup Rosa feels neglected and Papi thinks he's losing control of his family. As the hotel struggles, Papi and his pal Pedro try to figure out if someone is sabotaging the business. **89m/C; DVD, Blu-Ray.** Marcus Coloma; Erin Cahill; Sebastien Roche; Frances Fisher; ***V:*** George Lopez; Odette Annable; Kay Panabaker; Ernie Hudson; Jake Busey; ***D:*** Lev L. Spiro; ***W:*** Dana Starfield; ***C:*** Greg Gardiner; ***M:*** Hector Pereira. **VIDEO**

Beverly Hills Cop ½ **1984 (R)** When a close friend of smooth-talking Detroit cop Axel Foley is brutally murdered, he traces the murderer to the posh streets of Beverly Hills. There he must stay on his toes to keep one step ahead of the killer and two steps ahead of the law. Better than average Murphy vehicle. **105m/C; VHS, DVD, Blu-Ray.** Eddie Murphy; Judge Reinhold; John Ashton; Lisa Eilbacher; Ronny Cox; Steven Berkoff; James Russo; Jonathan Banks; Stephen Elliott; Bronson Pinchot; Paul Reiser; Damon Wayans; Rick Overton; ***D:*** Martin Brest; ***W:*** Danilo Bach; Daniel Petrie, Jr.; ***C:*** Bruce Surtees; ***M:*** Harold Faltermeyer.

Beverly Hills Cop 2 ½ **1987 (R)** The highly successful sequel to the first profitable comedy, with essentially the same plot, this time deals with Foley infiltrating a band of international munitions smugglers. **103m/C; VHS, DVD, Blu-Ray.** Eddie Murphy; Judge Reinhold; Jurgen Prochnow; Ronny Cox; John Ashton; Brigitte Nielsen; Allen Garfield; Paul Reiser; Dean Stockwell; Chris Rock; Gil Hill; Robert Ridgely; Gilbert Gottfried; Todd Susman; Robert Pastorelli; Tommy (Tiny) Lister; Paul Guilfoyle; Hugh Hefner; ***D:*** Tony Scott; ***W:*** Larry Ferguson; Warren Skaaren; ***C:*** Jeffrey L. Kimball; ***M:*** Harold Faltermeyer. Golden Raspberries '87: Worst Song ("I Want Your Sex").

Beverly Hills Cop 3 ½ **1994 (R)** Yes, Detroit cop Axel Foley (Murphy) just happens to find another case that takes him back to his friends on the Beverly Hills PD. This time he uncovers a criminal network fronting WonderWorld, an amusement park with a squeaky-clean image. Fast-paced action, lots of gunplay, and Eddie wisecracks his way through the slow spots. Reinhold returns as the still impossibly naive Rosewood, with Pinchot briefly reprising his role as Serge of the undeterminable accent. Critically panned boxoffice disappointment relies too heavily on formula and is another disappointing followup. **105m/C; VHS, DVD, Blu-Ray.** Eddie Murphy; Judge Reinhold; Hector Elizondo; Timothy Carhart; Stephen McHattie; Theresa Randle; John Saxon; Alan Young; Bronson Pinchot; Al Green; Gil Hill; Louis Lombardi; ***D:*** John Landis; ***W:*** Steven E. de Souza; ***C:*** Mac Ahlberg; ***M:*** Nile Rodgers.

Beverly Hills Ninja ½ **1996 (PG-13)** Farley plays Haru, a pathetically inept adopted son of a ninja, who is, nevertheless, sent to Beverly Hills on a rescue mission to break up an international counterfeiting ring. There, second-time spoof siren Sheridan hires the "great white ninja" to follow her no-good boyfriend and becomes the object of Haru's desire. Farley's extraordinary gift for physical comedy is exploited to the hilt, and the increase in Haru's tripping and stumbling (and in one harrowing scene, stripping) usually coincides with the fumbling of the plot. Rock's talents are squandered on a poorly conceived bellboy character. Farley's first feature sans fellow SNL alumni Spade suffers for his absence. Director Duggan, who also helmed Adam Sandler's "Happy Gilmore," might want to start screening his calls. **88m/C; VHS, DVD.** Chris Farley; Nicolette Sheridan; Robin Shou; Nathaniel Parker; Chris Rock; Soon-Teck Oh; Francois Chau; Keith Cooke Hirabayashi; ***D:*** Dennis Dugan; ***W:*** Mark Feldberg; Mitch Klebenoff; ***C:*** Arthur Albert; ***M:*** George S. Clinton.

Beverly Hills Vamp **1988 (R)** A madame and her girls are really female vampires with a penchant for hot-blooded men. **88m/C; VHS, Streaming.** Britt Ekland; Eddie Deezen; Debra Lamb; Michelle (McClellan) Bauer; Brigitte Burdine; Tim Conway, Jr.; Jillian Kesner; Tom Shell; ***D:*** Fred Olen Ray; ***W:*** Ernest Farino; ***C:*** Stephen Blake; ***M:*** Chuck Cirino.

Beverly Lewis' The Confession ½ *The Confession* **2013** Hallmark Channel sequel to the 2011 family drama. After Katie (Leclerc) is shunned by her Amish community, she decides to be with her birth mother, Laura (Stringfield), in the outside world. Wealthy Laura is dying and her gambling addict husband, Dylan (Paul), discovers he won't inherit. So he hires actress Alyson (Whelan) to pose as long-lost Katie just when the real Katie shows up at their door. To complicate the identity mess, two different men, including Katie's childhood friend Daniel (Fisher), reach out to her. **88m/C; DVD.** Katie Leclerc; Sherry Stringfield; Adrian Paul; Julia Whelan; Cameron Deane Stewart; Michael Rupnow; ***D:*** Michael Landon, Jr.; ***W:*** Michael Landon, Jr.; Brian Bird; ***C:*** Dan Kneece; ***M:*** Lee Holdridge. **CABLE**

Beverly Lewis' The Shunning ½ *The Shunning* **2011** Hallmark Channel drama based on the first book in Lewis' trilogy. In the Amish community of Hickory Hollow, Pennsylvania, Katie Lapp (Panabaker) has somewhat reluctantly agreed to marry widower Bishop John Beiler (Jenkins) since her first love, Daniel (Topp), is presumed dead. An outsider, Laura Mayfield-Bennett (Stringfield), comes to the community looking for Katie's mother Rebecca (Van Natta) and this leads to a family secret being revealed that changes Katie's life forever. **88m/C; DVD.** Danielle Panabaker; Sherry Stringfield; Sandra Van Natta; Bill Oberst, Jr.; Burgess Jenkins; David Topp; Sarah E. Chambers; ***D:*** Michael Landon, Jr.; Chris Easterly; ***C:*** Christo Bakalov; ***M:*** Lee Holdridge. **CABLE**

Beware! Children at Play **WOOF!** **1995 (R)** Cult leader kidnaps kids and introduces them to cannibalism. Bleech! As if this didn't sound grim enough, there's also an unrated version. **90m/C; DVD.** Michael Robertson; Eric Tonken; Jamie Krause; Mik Cribben; Danny McClaughlin; ***D:*** Mik Cribben; ***C:*** Mik Cribben.

Beware of a Holy Whore *Warnung Vor Einer Heiligen Nutte* **1970** German film crew sits around a Spanish resort—complaining, drinking, and making love—as they wait for financial support from Bonn. Provocative and self-indulgently honest look at filmmaking. Filmed on location in Sorrento, Italy; German with subtitles. **103m/C; VHS, DVD.** *GE* Lou Castel; Eddie Constantine; Hanna Schygulla; Marquard Bohm; Ulli Lommel; Margarethe von Trotta; Kurt Raab; Ingrid Caven; Werner Schroeter; Rainer Werner Fassbinder; ***D:*** Rainer Werner Fassbinder; ***W:*** Rainer Werner Fassbinder; ***C:*** Michael Ballhaus; ***M:*** Peer Raben.

Beware! The Blob *Son of Blob* **1972 (PG)** A scientist brings home a piece of frozen blob from the North Pole; his wife accidentally revives the dormant gray mass. It begins a rampage of terror by digesting nearly everyone within its reach. A host of recognizable faces make for fun viewing. Post-Jeannie, pre-Dallas Hagman directed this exercise in zaniness. **87m/C; VHS, DVD, Blu-Ray.** Robert Walker, Jr.; Godfrey Cambridge; Carol Lynley; Shelley Berman; Larry Hagman; Burgess Meredith; Gerrit Graham; Dick Van Patten; Gwynne Gilford; Richard Stahl; Richard Webb; Cindy Williams; ***D:*** Larry Hagman; ***W:*** Jack Woods; Anthony Harris; ***C:*** Al Hamm; ***M:*** Mort Garson.

Bewitched **2005 (PG-13)** Instead of an actual remake of the 1964-72 hit TV show, the Ephron sisters opted for a behind-the-scenes parody. Down-and-out actor Jack Wyatt (Ferrell) hopes his new role as Darrin will magically revive his career. Not wanting to be upstaged, he picks a nose-wiggling—and unknown—Isabel (Kidman) for Samantha the witch, not knowing that she really IS one. Since she disavowed (sort of) her witchery to live a mortal life, she accepts and sees Jack as a potential worldly mate. Once his egomania becomes evident, she can't help but revert to a little voodoo to shake things up. Great cast but tale doesn't cast a spell. **100m/C; DVD, UMD.** Nicole Kidman; Will Ferrell; Shirley MacLaine; Michael Caine; Jason Schwartzman; Heather Burns; Jim Turner; David

Alan Grier; Steve Carell; Amy Sedaris; Richard Kind; Stephen Colbert; Kristin Chenoweth; Michael Badalucco; Carol(e) Shelley; Kate Walsh; ***D:*** Nora Ephron; ***W:*** Nora Ephron; Delia Ephron; ***C:*** John Lindley; ***M:*** George Fenton.

The Beyond *Seven Doors of Death; E Tu Vivrai Nel Terrore—L'aldila* **1982 (R)** A young woman inherits a possessed hotel. Meanwhile, hellish zombies try to check out. Chilling Italian horror flick that Fulci directed under the alias "Louis Fuller." **88m/C; VHS, DVD, Blu-Ray.** *IT* Katherine (Katriona) MacColl; David Warbeck; Farah Keller; Tony St. John; Al Cliver; ***D:*** Lucio Fulci; ***W:*** Lucio Fulci; Dardano Sacchetti; Giorgio Mariuzzo; ***C:*** Sergio Salvati.

Beyond **1/2 2011 (PG-13)** Police detective Jon Koski (Voight) is heading toward retirement when Chief of Police Musker (Mulroney) asks him to find his niece Amy (Lesslie), who's gone missing. The case goes cold, and Koski is contacted by a psychic (Connors) who claims to have visions of the girl. Predictable thriller. **90m/C; DVD, Blu-Ray.** Jon Voight; Julian Morris; Dermot Mulroney; Teri Polo; Ben Crowley; Brett Baker; Chloe Lesslie; Skyler Shaye; ***D:*** Josef Rusnak; ***W:*** Gregory Gieras; ***C:*** Eric Maddison; ***M:*** Mario Grigorov. **VIDEO**

Beyond a Reasonable Doubt **1956** In order to get a behind-the-scenes glimpse at the judicial system, a man plays the guilty party to a murder. Alas, when he tries to vindicate himself, he is the victim of his own folly. Not as interesting as it sounds on paper. **80m/B; VHS, DVD, Blu-Ray.** Dana Andrews; Joan Fontaine; Sidney Blackmer; Philip Bourneuf; Barbara Nichols; Shepperd Strudwick; Arthur Franz; Edward Binns; ***D:*** Fritz Lang; ***W:*** Douglas S. Morrow.

Beyond a Reasonable Doubt **2009 (PG-13)** This remake of Fritz Lang's 1956 legal thriller gets an updated treatment but loses the pacing, suspense and intrigue of the original. The magnificently coifed Martin Hunter (Douglas) is a Louisiana DA suspected by newcomer TV reporter from New York, CJ Nichols (Metcalfe) of planting evidence to pad his conviction rate. To get the goods on the DA, Nichols acts the part of accused perp of an unsolved murder, thinking he'll trap Hunter while planting bogus evidence. Things don't quite work out as planned and the film never fully explores its chance to shine a light on judicial corruption, instead skimming the surface with car chases and Hunter's super-fine hairdo. **105m/C; Blu-Ray, On Demand.** Michael Douglas; Jesse Metcalfe; Amber Tamblyn; Orlando Jones; Joel David Moore; ***D:*** Peter Hyams; ***W:*** Peter Hyams; ***C:*** Peter Hyams; ***M:*** David Shire.

Beyond All Limits **1/2 1959** Hotheaded Pepe (Armendariz) lives with his wife Magdalena (Felix) and young son Pepito in a Mexican fishing village. Slick American Jim Gatsby (Palance) comes along with an illegal shrimping scheme that could earn everyone some extra cash. Magdalena and Jim were once involved and Pepe's jealousy becomes a problem. Originally released in Spanish as "Flor de Mayo." **114m/C; DVD.** *MX* Jack Palance; Pedro Armendariz, Sr.; Maria Felix; Carlos Montalban; Paul Stewart; ***D:*** Roberto Gavaldon; ***W:*** Libertad Blasco Ibanez; ***C:*** Gabriel Figueroa; ***M:*** Gustavo Cesar Carrion.

Beyond Atlantis WOOF! 1973 (PG) An ancient underwater tribe is discovered when it kidnaps land-lubbin' women with which to mate. **91m/C; VHS, DVD, Blu-Ray.** *PH* John Ashley; Patrick Wayne; George Nader; ***D:*** Eddie Romero; ***W:*** Charles Johnson; ***C:*** Justo Paulino.

Beyond Betrayal **1994** CBS TV movie. Joanna Matthews (Dey) escapes from her police officer husband, Bradley (Anderson), after years of abuse. She makes a new life under a new identity, but violent Brad hasn't stopped searching for her. When he finds out Joanna has a boyfriend (Boutsikaris) who's separated from his crazy wife, the cop makes sure to set him up for her murder. Can Joanna find the courage to come forward with the truth? **95m/C; DVD.** Susan Dey; Richard Dean Anderson; Dennis Boutsikaris; Annie Corley; James Tolkan; ***D:*** Carl Schenkel; ***W:*** Shelley Evans; ***C:*** John S. Bartley; ***M:*** Christopher Franke. **TV**

Beyond Borders **1/2 2003 (R)** Decades-spanning romance between an overzealous doctor and a lovely do-gooder suffers from a too-earnest presentation and romantic cliches. Dashing doctor Nick (Owen) inspires American socialite Sarah (Jolie) to leave her stuffy British hubby (Roache) and really get involved in international aid relief rather than just writing a check. She follows the doc to Ethiopia and later to Cambodia and Checknya (film goes from 1984-1995), where the trouble-prone Nick has apparently been kidnapped. At least the film inspired Jolie personally since she became a goodwill ambassador for the United Nations High Commissioner for Refugees and adopted her son from Cambodia. **127m/C; VHS, DVD.** Angelina Jolie; Clive Owen; Teri Polo; Linus Roache; Yorick Van Wageningen; Noah Emmerich; Kate Ashfield; Jamie Bartlett; Timothy West; Kate Trotter; Burt Kwouk; ***D:*** Martin Campbell; ***W:*** Caspian Tredwell-Owen; ***C:*** Phil Meheux; ***M:*** James Horner.

Beyond Clueless **2014** A documentary look at the teen movie, considering more than 200 modern films in the genre. For such films as "The Craft" and "Mean Girls," the documentary examines teen angst, friendship, and sexuality. Additionally, subtext and context are offered for a number of films. As a whole, how the type and focus of teen films changed subtly changed at the turn of the twenty-first century is considered as well. **89m/C; DVD, Blu-Ray.** Fairuza Balk; ***D:*** Charlie Lyne; ***W:*** Charlie Lyne; ***M:*** Summer Camp; Elizabeth Sankey; Jeremy Warmsley.

Beyond Desire **1/2 1994 (R)** Elvis Ray (Forsythe) is released after 14 years in prison and gets picked up by corvette-driving prison groupie and Las Vegas prostitute Rita (Wuhrer) but more than sex is on both their minds. **87m/C; VHS, Streaming.** William Forsythe; Kari Wuhrer; Leo Rossi; Sharon Farrell; ***D:*** Dominique Othenin-Girard; ***W:*** Dale Trevillion; ***C:*** Sven Kirsten; ***M:*** Mark Holden.

Beyond Dream's Door **1988** A young, All-American college student's childhood nightmares come back to haunt him, making dreams a horrifying reality. **86m/C; VHS, DVD.** Nick Baldasare; Rick Kesler; Susan Pinsky; Norm Singer; ***D:*** Jay Woelfel.

Beyond Erotica *Lola* **1974** After being cut out of his father's will, a sadistic young man takes out his rage on his mother and a peasant girl. **90m/C; VHS, DVD.** David Hemmings; Alida Valli; Andrea Rau; ***D:*** Jose Maria Forque.

Beyond Evil WOOF! 1980 (R) Relatively dim-witted newlywed couple moves into an old island mansion despite rumors that the house is haunted. Sure enough, wife George becomes possessed by the vengeful spirit of a woman murdered 200 years earlier, and a reign of pointless terror begins. Poor rip-off of hybrid Amityville/Exorcist paranormality. **98m/C; VHS, DVD, Blu-Ray.** John Saxon; Lynda Day George; Michael Dante; Mario Milano; ***D:*** Herb Freed; ***W:*** Herb Freed; ***M:*** Pino Donaggio.

Beyond Fear **1/2 1993 (R)** Tipper Taylor (Lesseos) is a wilderness tour guide who's also a martial arts expert. This is going to come in handy when her tour group is stalked by two men who are after a videotape innocently filmed by someone in Tipper's group. It seems the tape shows the men committing a murder. **84m/C; VHS, DVD.** Mimi Lesseos; ***D:*** Robert F. Lyons; ***W:*** Mimi Lesseos; Robert F. Lyons; ***C:*** Bodo Holst; ***M:*** Miriam Cutler.

Beyond Honor **2005** Egyptian-American medical student Sahira tries to be a modern woman but her father Mohammad is a strict Muslim who dominates the family. When he discovers that Sahira has a boyfriend and is no longer a virgin, he enacts a brutal punishment for her dishonoring their family. **101m/C; DVD.** Jason Smith; Ruth Osuna; Wadie Andrawis; Laurel Melegrano; Ryan Izay; ***D:*** Varun Khanna; ***W:*** Varun Khanna; ***C:*** Dinesh Kampani; ***M:*** David Mann.

Beyond Justice **1992 (PG-13)** High action-adventure with the prolific Hauer starring as an ex-CIA agent who is hired to rescue the kidnapped son of a beautiful executive. **113m/C; VHS, DVD.** *IT* Rutger Hauer; Carol Alt; Omar Sharif; Elliott Gould; Kabir Bedi; David Flosi; Brett Halsey; Peter Sands; ***D:*** Duccio Tessari; ***W:*** Sergio Donati; Luigi Montefiore; ***C:*** Giorgio Di Battista; ***M:*** Ennio Morricone.

Beyond Justice *Lawless: Beyond Justice* **2001** New Zealand TV thriller with a modicum of action. Private detectives John Lawless (Smith) and Jodie Keane (Dotchin) are hired by widow Lana Vitale (Rubin) to investigate her husband's suspicious death. Lana's not exactly grieving since she's all too willing to get up close and personal with Lawless. Meanwhile, Jodie follows some clues that lead her to a porno ring. **95m/C; VHS, DVD.** *NZ* Kevin Smith; Jennifer Rubin; Angela Dotchin; Bruce Hopkins; Dean O'Gorman; ***D:*** Geoffrey Cawthorn; ***W:*** Gavin Strawhan. **TV**

Beyond Obsession *Oltre la Porta* **1982** The strange relationship between a political prisioner, his daughter, and her obsession with a mysterious American is provocatively explored. **116m/C; VHS, DVD.** *IT* Marcello Mastroianni; Elenora Giorgi; Tom Berenger; Michel Piccoli; ***D:*** Liliana Cavani; ***W:*** Liliana Cavani.

Beyond Rangoon **1/2 1995 (R)** Sisters Laura (Arquette) and Andy (McDormand) Bowman travel to Burma to unwind, only to have political unrest and a repressive regime spoil the holiday. Dr. Laura (yeah, right) loses her passport and must flee from trigger-happy soldiers with a political dissident (Ko, a real-life exiled Burmese activist) who befriends her. The search for her passport soon becomes a imperiled trek of survival and self-discovery. Tense, well-crafted action sequences hint at a potential for excitement and intrigue; too bad Arquette isn't the least bit convincing. Filmed in Malaysia. **100m/C; VHS, DVD.** Patricia Arquette; Frances McDormand; Spalding Gray; U Aung Ko; Victor Slezak; ***D:*** John Boorman; ***W:*** Alex Lasker; Bill Rubenstein; ***C:*** John Seale; ***M:*** Hans Zimmer.

Beyond Re-Animator **2003 (R)** Mad scientist Herbert West (Combs) has been in a maximum security prison for 15 years but has continued his experiments (this time on the rats in his cell). When idealistic young Howard Phillips (Barry) becomes the new prison doctor, he wants to aid West with his re-animation experiments. Of course, things still don't work out as planned and zombie mayhem ensues in this schlocky-but-fun third adventure. **95m/C; DVD, Blu-Ray.** *US SP* Jeffrey Combs; Jason Barry; Simon Andreu; Elsa Pataky; ***D:*** Brian Yuzna; ***W:*** Jose Manuel Gomez; ***C:*** Andreu Rebes; ***M:*** Xavier Capellas.

Beyond Redemption **1999 (R)** A serial killer goes after highly respected targets, crucifying his victims, and Detective Smith is in charge of catching the bad guy. It all hinges on faith—and whose is stronger. **97m/C; VHS, DVD.** *CA* Andrew McCarthy; Michael Ironside; Jayne Heitmeyer; Suzy Joachim; ***D:*** Chris Angel. **VIDEO**

Beyond Sherwood Forest **2009** Apparently what's beyond Sherwood Forrest is the realm of stupid. Syfy cable version of the Robin Hood story has Robin (Dunne), the Merry Men, and Maid Marian (Durance) battling druids and some lame CGI dragon while Malcolm (Sands), the Sheriff of Nottingham, ineffectually hunts them down as usual. **93m/C; DVD, Blu-Ray.** *CA* Robin Dunne; Erica Durance; Julian Sands; Richard de Klerk; David Richmond-Peck; David Palffy; Robert Lawrenson; ***D:*** Peter DeLuise; ***W:*** Chase Parker; ***M:*** Darren Fung. **CABLE**

Beyond Silence *Jenseits der Stille* **1996 (PG-13)** Lara (Trieb/Testud), the daughter of deaf parents, has been their guide to the outside world since childhood. When her Aunt Clarissa (Canonica) gives her a clarinet, it opens Lara's life to music and gives her the courage to move beyond the limits of her family. German with subtitles. **109m/C; VHS, DVD.** *GE* Sylvie Testud; Tatjana Trieb; Howie Seago; Emmanuelle Laborit; Sibylle Canonica; ***D:*** Caroline Link; ***W:*** Caroline Link; ***C:*** Gernot Roll; ***M:*** Niki Reiser.

Beyond Suspicion **1/2** *Auggie Rose* **2000** John C. Nolan Jr. (Goldblum) is an insurance bigshot, who stops by the neighborhood liquor store and gets caught up in an armed robbery. The store clerk, Auggie Rose (Coates), gets killed and Nolan feels responsible. He learns Auggie is fresh out of prison and is expecting to meet his prison pen pal, Lucy (Heche). John meets Lucy instead and doesn't correct her assumption that he's Auggie. In fact, John decides to just give up his old life and take up with Lucy. Film's got an intriguing premise that never develops. **108m/C; VHS, DVD.** Jeff Goldblum; Anne Heche; Timothy Olyphant; Nancy Travis; Richard T. Jones; Kim Coates; Joe Santos; Jack Kehler; Nick (Nicholas) Chinlund; ***D:*** Matthew Tabak; ***W:*** Matthew Tabak; ***C:*** Adam Kimmel; ***M:*** Don Harper; Mark Mancina. **VIDEO**

Beyond the Bermuda Triangle **1/2 1975** Unfortunate and flat TV flick. Businessman MacMurray, now retired, doesn't have enough to do. He begins an investigation of the mysterious geometric island area when his friends and fiancee disappear. Silly. **78m/C; VHS, DVD.** Fred MacMurray; Sam Groom; Donna Mills; Suzanne Reed; Dana Plato; Woody Woodbury; ***D:*** William A. Graham. **TV**

Beyond the Black Rainbow **1/2 2010 (R)** Elena (Eva Bourne) attempts to escape from the drug hazed utopia that promises happiness to the inhabitants of the future. **110m/C; DVD, Blu-Ray, Streaming.** *CA* Michael Rogers; Eva Bourne; Scott Hylands; Rondel Reynoldson; Marilyn Norry; ***D:*** Panos Cosmatos; ***W:*** Panos Cosmatos; ***C:*** Norm Li; ***M:*** Jeremy Schmidt.

Beyond the Blackboard **1/2 2011** Inspirational Hallmark Hall of Fame presentation based on Stacey Bess' memoir "Don't Love Nobody." A Salt Lake City wife, mom, and teacher, Stacey can only find a job trying to educate homeless kids in a rundown facility. Naturally, she rises to the occasion, badgering the administration for basic supplies even as she connects with her often-troubled students. **95m/C; DVD.** Emily VanCamp; Steve Talley; Treat Williams; Timothy Busfield; Liam McKanna; Paola Nicole Andino; Julio Oscar Mechoso; Nicki Aycox; ***D:*** Jeff Bleckner; ***W:*** Camille Thomasson; ***C:*** Eric Van Haren Noman; ***M:*** Jeff Beal. **TV**

Beyond the Blue Horizon **1/2 1942** A young woman is trapped in a remote jungle after her parents are killed by rampaging elephants. Eventually rescued, Tama (Lamour) expects an inheritance when she goes to San Francisco but her other relatives are doubtful of her claims. So until Tama can prove her identity, she joins a circus and falls for lion tamer Jakra (Denning). **76m/C; DVD.** Dorothy Lamour; Richard Denning; Jack Haley; Walter Abel; Helen Gilbert; Patricia Morison; ***D:*** Alfred Santell; ***W:*** Frank Butler; ***C:*** Charles P. Boyle; William Mellor.

Beyond the Call **1/2 1996 (R)** Connecticut housewife Pam O'Brien (Spacek) learns from the paper that her high-school sweetheart Russell Cates (Strathairn) is on death row in South Carolina for killing a cop and his execution has been scheduled within weeks. Pam writes Russell and then hears from his sister Fran (Wright), who urges Pam to visit her brother and get him to apply for a clemency hearing. Husband Keith (Howard) becomes angry and alarmed as Pam gets more involved with Russell and his case, which hinges on Russell's Vietnam experiences and post-traumatic shock syndrome. **101m/C; VHS, DVD.** David Strathairn; Sissy Spacek; Arliss Howard; Janet Wright; ***D:*** Tony Bill; ***W:*** Doug Magee; ***C:*** Jean Lepine; ***M:*** George S. Clinton. **CABLE**

Beyond the Call of Duty **1/2 1992 (R)** Renegade U.S. Army Commander Len Jordan (Vincent) is after a particularly deadly Vietcong enemy. Aided by the head of a special forces naval unit he tracks his quarry through the notorious Mekong River Delta. But Jordan's mission may be hindered, both personally and professionally, by a beautiful American journalist after a hot story. **92m/C; VHS, DVD.** Jan-Michael Vincent; Eb Lottimer; Jillian McWhirter; ***D:*** Cirio H. Santiago.

Beyond the Call to Duty **1/2** *Beyond the Call of Duty* **2016** An action science fiction drama about saving the world before an apocalypse takes place. When Five Spec Ops, Alpha Squad, is ordered to going on what should be an easy recon mission, things do not go as planned. They find themselves fighting for survival against a wave of undead experiments. The squad must fight to save themselves and the world. **95m/C; DVD, Streaming, Download.** Kevin Tanski; Robert Woodley; Chris Clark; Will Mutka; Mike Sarcinelli; ***D:*** Aleksandar Ivicic; ***W:*** Aleksandar Ivicic; ***C:*** Aleksandar Ivicic; ***M:*** Elias Symons. **VIDEO**

Beyond the Clouds 1/2 *Par-dela les Nuages* **1995** A wandering film director (Malkovich) muses on four stories of life and obsession, including unconsummated relationships, romantic triangles, and even violence. Based on sketches from Antonioni's book "That Bowling Alley on the Tiber." English, French, and Italian with subtitles. **109m/C; DVD.** *IT GE FR* John Malkovich; Marcello Mastroianni; Sophie Marceau; Fanny Ardant; Vincent Perez; Jean Reno; Jeanne Moreau; Irene Jacob; Peter Weller; Chiara Caselli; Ines Sastre; Kim Rossi-Stuart; ***D:*** Michelangelo Antonioni; Wim Wenders; ***W:*** Michelangelo Antonioni; Wim Wenders; Tonino Guerra; ***C:*** Robby Muller; Alfio Contini; ***M:*** Van Morrison; Lucio Dalla; Laurent Petitgand.

Beyond the Door WOOF! *Beyond Obsession; Chi Sei; The Devil within Her* **1975 (R)** San Francisco woman finds herself pregnant with a demonic child. One of the first "Exorcist" ripoffs; skip this one and go right to the sequel, "Beyond the Door 2." In Italian; dubbed. **97m/C; VHS, DVD, Blu-Ray.** *IT* Juliet Mills; Richard Johnson; David Colin, Jr.; ***D:*** Ovidio G. Assonitis; Richard Barrett; ***W:*** Ovidio G. Assonitis; Richard Barrett.

Beyond the Door 3 WOOF! 1991 (R) Fool American students in Yugoslavia board a hellish locomotive which speeds them toward a satanic ritual. Demonic disaster-movie stuff (with poor miniatures) isn't as effective as the on-location filming; Serbian scenery and crazed peasants impart an eerie pagan aura. What this has to do with earlier "Beyond the Door" movies only the marketing boys can say. Some dialogue in Serbo-Croat with English subtitles. **94m/C; VHS, DVD, Blu-Ray.** Mary Kohnert; Sarah Conway Ciminera; William Geiger; Renee Rancourt; Alex Vitale; Victoria Zinny; Savina Gersak; Bo Svenson; ***D:*** Jeff Kwitny.

Beyond the Dunwich Horror 1/2 **2008 (R)** Kenneth (Reed) goes home to Dunwich when he hears his brother has been put in an asylum. Relying on a reporter and a local eccentric, he sets out to find what's happened. **104m/C; DVD.** Jason McCormick; Jeff Dylan Graham; Sarah Nicklin; Lynn Lowry; Ruth Sullivan; ***D:*** Richard Griffin; ***W:*** Richard Griffin; ***C:*** Ricardo Rebelo; ***M:*** Tony Milano; Daniel Hildreth. **VIDEO**

Beyond the Gates **2016** A retro indie horror centered on a missing father and a perilous game. When their father is presumed dead, estranged sons Gordon (Skipper) and John (Williamson) come together to box up his video store. While staying in their father's home, they learn that the last thing he watched was Beyond the Gates, an interactive VCR board game with an all-knowing hostess (Crampton). They soon discover that the game is more than it appears, their father is a captive in its dark world, and only they can save him. An inspired genre film that excels as a nostalgic homage to B horror films. **84m/C; DVD.** Graham Skipper; Chase Williamson; Brea Grant; Barbara Crampton; Matt Mercer; ***D:*** Jackson Stewart; ***W:*** Jackson Stewart; Stephen Scarlata; ***C:*** Brian Sowell; ***M:*** Wojciech Golczewski.

Beyond the Hills 1/2 **2013** Award-winning director Mungiu examines the tug-of-war between two friends who represent secular life and religious faith in this accomplished drama. Best friends Alina and Voichita are heading down different paths. The former wants her closest partner to return with her from Romania to Germany but the latter is being pulled into a world of faith at an Orthodox convent. When reasoning with Alina fails, Voichita becomes convinced that she is possessed and seeks to exorcise that which keeps her from faith with drastic results. Mungiu's film is deliberate and slow but his excellent skill with actors and willingness to tackle complex themes is admirable. **150m/C; DVD, Blu-Ray.** *RO* Cosmina Straton; Cristina Flutur; ***D:*** Cristian Mungiu; ***W:*** Cristian Mungiu; ***C:*** Oleg Mutu.

Beyond the Law *Bloodsilver; Al Di La Della Legge* **1968** Spaghetti western with Van Cleef as the too smart bad guy. He becomes sheriff, picks up the stack of silver at the depot, and disappears. Humorous and clever, with fine location photography. **91m/C; VHS, DVD.** *IT* Lee Van Cleef; Antonio (Tony) Sabato; Lionel Stander; Bud Spencer; Gordon Mitchell; Ann Smyrner; ***D:*** Giorgio Stegani.

Beyond the Law 1/2 *Fixing the Shadow* **1992 (R)** Ex-undercover cop Danny Saxon (Sheen) is recruited by the FBI to infiltrate a biker gang involved in drugs and gun smuggling. But Saxon finds himself drawn too close into the unconventional biker lifestyle and into an uneasy friendship with leader Blood (Madsen). Clumsy and exploitative. **101m/C; VHS, DVD.** Charlie Sheen; Michael Madsen; Linda Fiorentino; Courtney B. Vance; Leon Rippy; Rip Torn; Michael Berry; ***D:*** Larry Ferguson; ***W:*** Larry Ferguson; ***C:*** Robert M. Stevens; ***M:*** John D'Andrea; Cory Lerios.

Beyond the Lights 1/2 **2014 (PG-13)** Not just another showbiz romantic drama, Prince-Bythewood's behind-the-scenes telling of the life of a pop star is the successful character piece that others wish they could be. She takes her characters seriously, avoiding cliché altogether. Noni (a phenomenal Mbatha-Raw) is a superstar singer in the vein of Rihanna or Alicia Keys. She's pulled in all directions by those who want something from her until she falls for Kaz (Parker), a cop who supports her for who she is inside instead of her level of fame. It's a smart, fascinating look at people instead of stereotypes. **102m/C; DVD, Blu-Ray.** Gugu Mbatha-Raw; Nate Parker; Minnie Driver; Danny Glover; Richard Colson Baker; Tyler Christopher; ***D:*** Gina Prince-Bythewood; ***W:*** Gina Prince-Bythewood; ***C:*** Tami Reiker; ***M:*** Mark Isham.

Beyond the Next Mountain **1987 (PG)** A missionary in China attempts to convert all those he meets. Thin plot and marginal acting will likely make viewers fall asleep. **97m/C; VHS, DVD, Streaming.** Alberto Isaac; Jon Lormer; Bennett Ohta; Richard Lineback; Edward Ashley; Barry Foster; ***D:*** James F. Collier; Rolf Forsberg.

Beyond the Poseidon Adventure **1979 (PG)** A sequel to the 1972 film in which salvage teams and ruthless looting vandals compete for access to the sunken ocean liner. Sinking ships should be abandoned. **115m/C; DVD.** Michael Caine; Sally Field; Telly Savalas; Peter Boyle; Jack Warden; Slim Pickens; Shirley Knight; Shirley Jones; Karl Malden; Mark Harmon; ***D:*** Irwin Allen; ***C:*** Joseph Biroc.

Beyond the Rocks 1/2 **1922** Sam Wood's 1922 silent film stars icons Rudolph Valentino and Gloria Swanson, and was until recently thought to have been lost forever. One surviving print was found in a Dutch archive, which has been given an impressive restoration and a new sound track. Zany rescues abound: Lord Bracondale (Valentino) rescues Theadora Fitzgerald (Swanson) after her rowboat capsizes off the British coast, and again later in the Swiss Alps after a mountaineering accident. Well worth seeing for the craft involved in creating early film. **81m/B; Silent; DVD.** Gloria Swanson; Rudolph Valentino; Edythe Chapman; Alec B. Francis; Gertrude Astor; Mabel van Buren; June Elvidge; Robert Bolder; Helen Dunbar; Raymond Blathwayt; F.R. Butler; ***D:*** Sam Wood; ***W:*** Jack Cunningham; ***C:*** Alfred Gilks.

Beyond the Sea **2004 (PG-13)** Energetic if superficial biography of Bobby Darin is the personal labor of love for director/star/producer Spacey—even if he's technically too old for the role (Darin died at 37 in 1973). His conceit is showcasing the older Darin in his own fantasy autobiography, beginning with his childhood self (Ullrich) and advancing confidently as Darin finds success crooning at the Copa, becomes a teen idol with the ditty "Splish Splash," and falls in love with teenaged golden girl actress Sandra Dee (Bosworth). This being showbiz, things eventually take a downward spiral for the insecure Darin as his smooth style becomes irrelevant in the hippie sixties before he attempts the inevitable comeback. It's Spacey's show (and he supplies his own more-than-adequate vocals) but supporting actors Hoskins, Blethyn, Aaron, and Goodman all run with their screen time. Title is taken from a 1960 Darin hit. **121m/C; VHS, DVD.** Kevin Spacey; Kate (Catherine) Bosworth; John Goodman; Bob Hoskins; Brenda Blethyn; Greta Scacchi; Caroline Aaron; Peter Cincotti; William Ullrich; Tayfun Bademsoy; ***D:*** Kevin Spacey; ***W:*** Kevin Spacey; Lewis Colick; ***C:*** Eduardo Serra; ***M:*** Christopher Slaski.

Beyond the Stars **1989** A sci-fi adventure directed by the author of "Cocoon," wherein a whiz-kid investigates the NASA cover-up of a deadly accident that occurred on the moon during the Apollo 11 landing. Unfortunately, the interesting cast can't make up for the script. **94m/C; VHS, DVD.** Martin Sheen; Christian Slater; Olivia D'Abo; F. Murray Abraham; Robert Foxworth; Sharon Stone; ***D:*** David Saperstein.

Beyond the Time Barrier 1/2 **1960** Air Force test pilot gets more than he bargained for when his high speed plane carries him into the future. There he sees the ravages of an upcoming plague, to which he must return. **75m/B; VHS, DVD.** Robert Clarke; Darlene Tompkins; Arianne Arden; Vladimir Sokoloff; ***D:*** Edgar G. Ulmer.

Beyond the Trophy **2012 (R)** Rival gangs in Los Angeles and Las Vegas vie for power while a cop works to bring them both down in this action crime drama. The gangs, led by Gino (Miano) and Cole (Madsen), both want to control these cities and nearby territories. Unknown to them, undercover LA police detective Danny (Masini) and others are working deep inside gangland to infiltrate gangland so that both gangs can be destroyed from within. During his time undercover, Danny becomes involved with Angela (Costello), who is married to Jake (Carrera) and involved with Gino. Angela has her own agenda, seeking to leave these abusive men behind for love. **99m/C; DVD, Streaming, Download.** Michael Madsen; Michael Mansini; Robert Miano; Alek Carrera; Ali Costello; ***D:*** Daniel J. Gillin; ***W:*** Daniel J. Gillin; ***C:*** Riz Story; ***M:*** Jonathan Zalben.

Beyond the Valley of the Dolls 1/2 *Hollywood Vixens* **1970 (NC-17)** Sleazy, spirited non-sequel to "Valley of the Dolls." Meyer ("Faster, Pussycat! Kill! Kill!") directed this Hollywood parody ("BVD," as it came to be known) about an all-girl rock combo and their search for stardom. Labeled the first "exploitation horror camp musical"?how can you pass that up? Screenplay by film critic Ebert, from an original story by Ebert and Meyer. Mondo trasho. **109m/C; VHS, DVD, Blu-Ray.** Dolly Reed; Cynthia Myers; Marcia McBroom; John Lazar; Michael Blodgett; David Gurian; Erica Gavin; Edy Williams; Phyllis E. Davis; Harrison Page; Duncan McLeod; James Iglehart; Charles Napier; Haji; Pam Grier; ***D:*** Russ Meyer; ***W:*** Roger Ebert; ***C:*** Fred W. Koenekamp; ***M:*** The Strawberry Alarm Clock; Stu Phillips.

Beyond the Wall of Sleep *H.P. Lovecraft's Beyond the Wall of Sleep* **2006 (R)** Ponderous, repetitive (and loose) adaptation of a Lovecraft story. In 1908, in New York's Catskill Mountains, deformed Joe Slaader (Sanderson) is confined to the Ulster County Asylum after murdering his family. But with Joe's arrival come sinister forces that seemingly infect the inmates and they begin to take over the madhouse. **84m/C; DVD.** William Sanderson; Tom Savini; Rick Dial; Fountain Yount; ***D:*** Barrett J. Leigh; Tom Maurer; ***W:*** Barrett J. Leigh; Tom Maurer; ***C:*** Bill Burton; ***M:*** Kaveh Cohen. **VIDEO**

Beyond the Walls *Hors les Murs* **2012** During a drunken evening out at a Brussels bar, Paulo meets Albanian bartender Ilir. When Paulo becomes homeless, he shows up at Ilir's who reluctantly allows him to stay. After Ilir suddenly lands in prison for drug possession, weak-willed Paulo drifts into another relationship. Ilir and Paulo have a reunion when Ilir gets out of prison but it's not a happy ending. French with subtitles. **98m/C; DVD.** *BE FR* Matila Malliarakis; Guillaume Gouix; David Salles; ***D:*** David Lambert; ***W:*** David Lambert; ***C:*** Matthieu Poirot Delpech; ***M:*** Flonja Kodheli.

Beyond Therapy 1/2 **1986 (R)** A satire on modern psychotherapy, from the play by Christopher Durang, about a confused, crazily neurotic couple and their respective, and not any saner, analysts. Unfortunately, comes off as disjointed and confused. **93m/C; VHS, DVD, Blu-Ray.** Jeff Goldblum; Tom Conti; Julie Hagerty; Glenda Jackson; Christopher Guest; ***D:*** Robert Altman; ***W:*** Robert Altman.

Beyond Tomorrow *Beyond Christmas* **1940** Young romance is guided from the spirit world during the Christmas season, as two "ghosts" come back to help young lovers. **84m/B; VHS, DVD.** Richard Carlson; Sir C. Aubrey Smith; Jean Parker; Charles Winninger; Harry Carey, Sr.; Maria Ouspenskaya; Rod La Rocque; ***D:*** Edward Sutherland; ***W:*** Adele Comandini; ***C:*** Lester White.

Beyond Valkyrie: Dawn of the Fourth Reich **2016 (R)** A World War II drama based on actual events. Near the end of the war, German military personnel weary of Adolph Hitler's rule prepare to assassinate him in in Operation Valkyrie. At the same time, an Allied special ops team makes preparations to extract a German resistance fighter who will later lead his country. When Valkyrie fails, the extraction becomes more complicated. Unexpected forces create an alliance to ensure Nazi officers do not flee to Argentina and found the Fourth Reich there. **100m/C; DVD, Streaming, Download.** Sean Patrick Flanery; Tom Sizemore; Kip Pardue; Stephen Lang; Rutger Hauer; ***D:*** Claudio Fah; ***W:*** Robert Henny; Don Michael Paul; ***C:*** Martin Chichov; ***M:*** Marcus Trumpp.

Beyond Victory **1931** Flashbacks reveal the battle experiences of American soldiers fighting for control of a French village during WWI. **70m/B; DVD.** William Boyd; Lew Cody; James Gleason; Zasu Pitts; Marion Shilling; Russell Gleason; Theodore von Eltz; ***D:*** John S. Robertson; ***W:*** James Gleason; Horace Jackson; ***C:*** Norbert Beaudine.

The BFG 1/2 **2016 (PG)** One of the most influential filmmakers in the history of family movies combines talents with one of literature's most famous voices in the genre as Steven Spielberg adapts Roald Dahl's beloved story with fun, engaging results. Using motion-capture technology, Oscar winner Mark Rylance plays the title character, the Big Friendly Giant, who befriends a young girl named Sophie, and the two head off on a series of adventures to the BFG's homeland, where he is shunned for not eating children. The somewhat-clunky CGI is forgivable because of Spielberg's whimsical, intelligent approach to the material. He never talks down to kids. **117m/C; DVD, Blu-Ray.** Mark Rylance; Ruby Barnhill; Penelope Wilton; Jemaine Clement; Rebecca Hall; ***D:*** Steven Spielberg; ***W:*** Melissa Mathison; ***C:*** Janusz Kaminski; ***M:*** John Williams.

B.F.'s Daughter 1/2 **1948** Uneasy (and now-dated) satire loosely based on the John P. Marquand novel and set in the 1930s. Independent Polly, daughter of wealthy industrialist B.F. Fulton, marries lefty-leaning economics professor Thomas Brett. When her hubby's career isn't a great success, Polly uses her father's money and influence to help Thomas prosper (unbeknownst to him) but marital strains persist. **107m/B; DVD.** Van Heflin; Barbara Stanwyck; Charles Coburn; Richard Hart; Keenan Wynn; Margaret Lindsay; Spring Byington; ***D:*** Robert Z. Leonard; ***W:*** Luther Davis; ***C:*** Joseph Ruttenberg; ***M:*** Bronislau Kaper.

Bhowani Junction **1956** A half-Indian, half-English woman is torn between her country and the British officer she loves in post-colonial India. Great cinematography. Based on a book by John Masters. **110m/C; VHS, DVD.** Ava Gardner; Stewart Granger; Bill Travers; Abraham Sofaer; Francis Matthews; Marne Maitland; Peter Illing; Edward Chapman; Freda Jackson; Lionel Jeffries; ***D:*** George Cukor; ***W:*** Ivan Moffat; ***C:*** Frederick A. (Freddie) Young; ***M:*** Miklos Rozsa.

The Bible **1966** Bloated, even by religious epic standards, Huston's drama covers the first 22 chapters of Genesis. So you get the Creation, Adam and Eve, Noah and the ark, the flood, the Tower of Babel, and Abraham, among other would-be spectacles. **174m/C; VHS, DVD, Blu-Ray.** Michael Parks; Ulla Bergryd; Richard Harris; Stephen Boyd; George C. Scott; Ava Gardner; Peter O'Toole; Franco Nero; John Huston; ***Nar:*** John Huston; ***D:***

John Huston; *W:* Christopher Fry; Vittorio Bonicelli; *C:* Giuseppe Rotunno; *M:* Toshiro Mayuzumi.

Bicentennial Man 🦴🦴 1/2 **1999 (PG)** Robin Williams is Andrew, a domestic robot of the near-future. When he's purchased by the Martin family, they notice that he's different than most robots. He exhibits compassion, as well as other human qualities. Led by Sir, the father (Niell) they help to further Andrew's growth. As time goes on, Andrew continues to develop past his programming, and eventually seeks his freedom and the pursuit of a more human form. The first hour deals mostly with a very leisurely character development, with some amusing moments. The problems occur when the film turns to the serious questions of immortality, defining humanity, and the rights of artificial entities. Director Columbus opts for sentiment and empty platitudes instead of exploring the questions the film raises. **131m/C; VHS, DVD.** Robin Williams; Embeth Davidtz; Sam Neill; Wendy Crewson; Hallie Kate Eisenberg; Oliver Platt; Stephen (Steve) Root; Lynne Thigpen; Bradley Whitford; Kiersten Warren; John Michael Higgins; George D. Wallace; *D:* Chris Columbus; *W:* Nicholas Kazan; *C:* Phil Meheux; *M:* James Horner.

Bickford Shmeckler's Cool Ideas 🦴🦴 **2006 (R)** Bickford (Fugit) is a loner college student who spends his time filing a notebook with his revelatory philosophical theories and ideas. At a party, Sarah (Wilde) steals the book, sending Bick on a wild journey to get it back, finding out in the process that it has taken on a popularity of its own among the campus "intelligensia." Mixes more big ideas than you'd expect into your basic raunchy college romp. **80m/C; DVD.** Patrick Fugit; Olivia Wilde; John Cho; Matthew Lillard; Cheryl Hines; *D:* Scott Lew; *W:* Scott Lew; *C:* Lowell Peterson; *M:* John Swihart. **VIDEO**

The Bicycle Thief 🦴🦴🦴🦴 *Ladri di Biciclette* **1948** A world classic and indisputable masterpiece about an Italian workman who finds a job, only to have the bike he needs for work stolen; he and his son search Rome for it. A simple story that seems to contain the whole of human experience, and the masterpiece of Italian neo-realism. Based on the book by Luigi Bartolini. In Italian with English subtitles. **90m/B; VHS, DVD.** *IT* Lamberto Maggiorani; Lianella Carell; Enzo Staiola; Elena Altieri; Vittorio Antonucci; Gino Saltamerenda; Fausto Guerzoni; *D:* Vittorio De Sica; *W:* Vittorio De Sica; Cesare Zavattini; *C:* Carlo Montuori; *M:* Alessandro Cicognini. Oscars '49: Foreign Film; British Acad. '49: Film; Golden Globes '50: Foreign Film; Natl. Bd. of Review '49: Director (De Sica); N.Y. Film Critics '49: Foreign Film.

Bicycling With Moliere 🦴🦴 *Cycling With Moliere; Alceste a Bicyclette* **2013** After suffering from severe depression, celebrated actor Serge Tanneur (Luchini) has retired to an isolated island cottage. He's visited by popular TV actor Gauthier Valence (Wilson) who, in a bid to be taken seriously, wants Tanneur to be part of his production of Moliere's "The Misanthrope." Tanneur decides to test Valence with a week of rehearsals at his house (and a couple of biking trips around the island). There are a couple of subplots but the focus is on the two leads discussing acting and life. French and Italian with subtitles. **104m/C; DVD.** *FR* Fabrice Luchini; Lambert Wilson; Maya Sansa; *D:* Philippe Le Guay; *W:* Philippe Le Guay; *C:* Jean-Claude Larrieu; *M:* Jorge Arriagada.

Big 🦴🦴🦴 1/2 **1988 (PG)** 13-year-old Josh makes a wish at a carnival fortune-teller to be "big." When he wakes up the next morning he finds that he suddenly won't fit into his clothes and his mother doesn't recognize him. Until he finds a cure, he must learn to live in the adult world—complete with job (in a toy firm), Manhattan apartment, and romance. Perkins is wonderful as a cynical fellow employee who warms to the new guy's naivete, while Hanks is totally believable as the little boy inside a man's body. Marshall directs with authority and the whole thing clicks from the beginning. **98m/C; VHS, DVD, Blu-Ray; Open Captioned.** Tom Hanks; Elizabeth Perkins; John Heard; Robert Loggia; Jared Rushton; David Moscow; Jon Lovitz; Mercedes Ruehl; *D:* Penny Marshall; *W:* Gary Ross; *C:* Michael Ballhaus; *M:* Howard Shore. Golden Globes '89: Actor--Mus./Comedy (Hanks); L.A. Film Critics '88: Actor (Hanks).

The Big Alligator River **WOOF!** *Il fiume del grande caimano; The Great Alligator* **1979** A tourist resort in Africa is attacked by a giant croc the local natives worship as a god. The croc eats a few of them, and they take that as a sign to unleash Hell. And that's pretty much what it would feel like sitting through this stinker. **89m/C; DVD.** *IT* Claudio Cassinelli; Mel Ferrer; Romano Puppo; Barbara Bach; Silvia Collatina; George Eastman; Richard Johnson; *D:* Sergio Martino; *W:* Sergio Martino; Cesare Frugoni; Ernesto Gastaldi; Mara Maryl; *C:* Giancarlo Ferrando; *M:* Stelvio Cipriani. **VIDEO**

Big and Hairy 🦴 1/2 **1998** When Picasso Dewlap and his family move from Chicago to a small town, the kid has trouble making friends (no wonder with that name). Then he joins the school basketball team. However, Picasso sucks. But after he meets a teen bigfoot (nicknamed Ed) who just happens to be a natural at hoops, Picasso and his hairy friend become team heroes. Based on the book by Brian Daly. **94m/C; VHS, DVD.** Richard Thomas; Donnelly Rhodes; Robert Karl Burke; Trevor Jones; Chilton Crane; *D:* Philip Spink; *C:* Peter Benison; *M:* Daryl Bennett; Jim Guttridge. **CABLE**

Big Bad John 🦴 1/2 **1990 (PG-13)** Some good ol' boys ride around in trucks as they get into a variety of shootouts. The soundtrack includes music by Willie Nelson, The Charlie Daniels Band, and others. **91m/C; VHS, DVD.** Jimmy Dean; Ned Beatty; Jack Elam; Bo Hopkins; Romy Windsor; Doug English; John Dennis Johnston; Anne Lockhart; Jeffery Osterhage; Jerry Potter; Red Steagall; *D:* Burt Kennedy; *W:* Joseph Berry; *C:* Ken Lamkin; *M:* Ken Sutherland.

Big Bad Love 🦴🦴 **2002 (R)** Howard's ambitious directorial debut is an adaptation of the short stories of Larry Brown. Vietnam vet and would-be writer Leon Barlow's (Howard), obsession with writing about his constant melancholy and getting his stories published alienates him from everything around him, especially his family, which includes his terminally ill daughter. He seems to get away with his behavior through his wry wit and some past misfortunes. Howard gives in to his most poetic and literary impulses, which results in some breathtaking scenes alongside some annoyingly self-indulgent ones. Not surprisingly, film is uneven, with some quality performances lifting the proceedings. **111m/C; VHS, DVD.** Arliss Howard; Debra Winger; Paul LeMat; Angie Dickinson; Rosanna Arquette; Michael Parks; *V:* Sigourney Weaver; *D:* Arliss Howard; *W:* Arliss Howard; Jim Howard; *C:* Dr. Paul Ryan; *M:* Tom Waits.

Big Bad Mama 🦴🦴 1/2 **1974 (R)** Tough and sexy machine-gun toting mother moves her two nubile daughters out of Texas during the Depression, and they all turn to robbing banks as a means of support while creating sharp testosterone increases among the local men. "Wild Palm" Dickinson has notable nude scene with Captain Kirk. "Big Bad Mama 2" arrived some 13 years later. **83m/C; VHS, DVD, Blu-Ray.** Angie Dickinson; William Shatner; Tom Skerritt; Susan Sennett; Robbie Lee; Sally Kirkland; Noble Willingham; Royal Dano; Dick Miller; Joan Prather; Tom Signorelli; *D:* Steve Carver; *W:* William W. Norton, Sr.; Frances Doel; *C:* Bruce Logan; *M:* David Grisman.

Big Bad Mama 2 🦴 1/2 **1987 (R)** Belated Depression-era sequel to the 1974 Roger Corman gangster film, where the pistol-packin' matriarch battles a crooked politician with the help of her two daughters. **85m/C; VHS, DVD.** Angie Dickinson; Robert Culp; Danielle Brisebois; Julie McCullough; Bruce Glover; Jeff Yagher; Jacque Lynn Colton; Ebbe Roe Smith; Charles Cyphers; *D:* Jim Wynorski; *W:* Jim Wynorski; R.J. Robertson; *C:* Robert New; *M:* Chuck Cirino.

The Big Bad Swim 🦴🦴 1/2 **2006** Needing some stress relief from work and marital problems, Amy (Brewster) decides to join an adult swim class held at a local community center. In a mixed and quirky group, Amy befriends Jordan (Weixler), a croupier and part-time stripper who has the hots for their hunky-but-insecure instructor Noah (Branson). Sharp comedy that focuses on characters rather than situations. **93m/C; DVD.** Paget Brewster; Joanna Adler; Jeff Branson; Jess Weixler; Grant Aleksander; Raviv (Ricky) Ullman; Avi Setton; Todd Sussman; Michael Mosley; *D:* Ishai Setton; *W:* Daniel Schechter; *C:* Josh Silfen; *M:* Chad Kelly. **VIDEO**

Big Bad Wolf 🦴 1/2 **2006 (R)** A kid steals the key to his father's cabin so he and his friends can get drunk and make out. Unfortunately the cabin is in the territory of a sleazy, wisecracking wolfman who enjoys offing strangers a little too much. **96m/C; DVD, Streaming.** Trevor Duke-Moretz; Richard Tyson; Christopher Shyer; Clinton Howard; David Naughton; Kimberly J. Brown; Sarah Aldrich; *D:* Lance Dreesen; *W:* Lance Dreesen; *C:* Stephen Crawford; *M:* Dana Niu. **VIDEO**

Big Bag of $ 🦴 1/2 **2009** In this modern attempt at film noir, five people (and members of the audience) have their lives sent into a spiral of destruction and misery by an unclaimed bag of cash. The main moral seems to be that if you're poor, you're always one step away from murdering other people for money if you ever get the chance. **85m/C; DVD.** Shonelle Blake; Anthony Clark; Rodney C. Cummings; Lisa Dewitt; Scott F. Evans; Eddie Goines; Lanre Idewu; Trisha Mann; Brian Marshall; Elise Matturi; Kenny McClain; Michael David Ricks; Nadirah Shakirah; Rico Simonini; Solari; Treallis; Calvin Walton; *D:* Scott F. Evans; *W:* Scott F. Evans; *C:* Scott F. Evans; *M:* Angela Burris; Stewart Hollins; Ovaciir.

The Big Bang 🦴 **2011 (R)** A Russian boxer hires L.A. PI Ned Cruz (Banderas) to find his girlfriend Lexie (Guillory)?and the millions of dollars worth of diamonds she's hiding. The job seems simple at first, but it isn't long before witnesses start turning up dead. Cruz becomes obsessed with finding Lexie, especially when the path leads him to two powerful men in the New Mexico desert plotting to destroy the world. Sounds thrilling, but without Banderas it's a complete bust. **101m/C; DVD, Blu-Ray.** Antonio Banderas; Sam Elliot; Sienna Guillory; Jimmi Simpson; Autumn Reeser; James Van Der Beek; Thomas Kretschmann; Snoop Dogg; William Fichtner; Delroy Lindo; Robert Maillet; *D:* Tony Krantz; *W:* Erik Jendresen; *C:* Shelly Johnson; *M:* Johnny Marr.

Big Bear 🦴🦴 1/2 **1998** In the 1880s, Cheif Big Bear (Tootoosis) refuses to surrender Cree ancestral lands to settlers for fear of the many broken promises made by the government. So Canadian army troops surround the Cree in order to starve them into submission. Cree warriors decide to stage an attack against the settlers that only brings the troops down on them. **190m/C; VHS, DVD.** *CA* Tantoo Cardinal; Gordon Tootoosis; Ken Charlette; *D:* Gil Cardinal. **TV**

The Big Bet 🦴🦴 **1985 (R)** High school sex comedy about a guy who is challenged by the school bully to get the gorgeous new girl into bed. Energetic romp is for adults. **90m/C; VHS, DVD.** Sylvia Kristel; Kimberly Evenson; Ron Thomas; *D:* Bert I. Gordon.

The Big Bird Cage 🦴🦴 *Women's Penitentiary 2* **1972 (R)** Prison spoof sequel to "The Big Doll House." Horny females incarcerated in a rural jail decide to defy their homosexual guards and plan an escape. They are aided by revolutionaries led by a Brooklynese expatriate and his lover. **93m/C; VHS, DVD.** Pam Grier; Sid Haig; Anitra Ford; Candice Roman; Teda Bracci; Carol Speed; Karen McKevic; Vic Diaz; *D:* Jack Hill; *W:* Jack Hill; *C:* Felipe Sacdalan; *M:* William Allen Castleman; William Loose.

The Big Blue 🦴 1/2 *Le Grand Bleu* **1988 (PG)** Vapid, semi-true tale about competing free-divers, who descend deep into the big blue without the aid of any kind of breathing apparatus. Arquette is the ditz who makes them come up for air. **122m/C; VHS, DVD.** Rosanna Arquette; Jean Reno; Jean-Marc Barr; Paul Shenar; Sergio Castellitto; Marc Duret; Griffin Dunne; *D:* Luc Besson; *W:* Luc Besson; *C:* Carlo Varini; *M:* Bill Conti. Cesar '89: Score, Sound.

Big Bluff 🦴🦴 *Worthy Deceivers* **1955** Disappointing result from an interesting premise; fatally ill woman finds love, but when she surprisingly recovers, her new husband decides to help her back along the path to death. Uneven and melodramatic. **70m/B; VHS, DVD.** *SI* John Bromfield; Martha Vickers; Robert Hutton; Rosemary Bowe; *D:* W. Lee Wilder.

The Big Boodle 🦴 1/2 **1957** Unremarkable crime drama, although Flynn puts some effort into his role as Havana casino croupier Ned Sherwood. Ned gets into trouble when he's passed some phony pesos and is accused of being a counterfeiter. This puts him on the wrong side of both the crooks and the cops, who both think he knows more than he does. **84m/B; DVD.** Errol Flynn; Rosanna Rory; Gia Scala; Pedro Armendariz, Sr.; Jacques Aubuchon; Sandro Giglio; Charles Todd; *D:* Richard Wilson; *W:* Jo Eisinger; *C:* Lee Garmes; *M:* Raul Lavista.

The Big Boss 🦴 1/2 **1941** After the death of their sheriff father, brothers Bob and Frank are separated and grow up under very different circumstances. Bob becomes a law-abiding governor and Frank turns to the criminal life. But influence peddler Jim Mahoney could bring down Bob's career because of past secrets. **70m/B; DVD.** John Litel; Otto Kruger; Don Beddoe; Robert (Fisk) Fiske; Gloria Dickson; *D:* Charles T. Barton; *W:* Howard J. Green; *C:* Benjamin (Ben H.) Kline.

The Big Bounce 🦴🦴 **1969 (R)** First adaptation of Elmore Leonard's first crime novel after years of westerns is also Ryan O'Neal's first shot at leading man status. O'Neal shows his inexperience as well as glimpes of the boxoffice star he would become as Jack Ryan (not the CIA guy), a drifter who gets mixed up with dangerous woman Nancy (Taylor-Young, also very early in her career) and her plot to swindle her married lover, who happens to be his boss. Doesn't have the spark of Leonard's later crime capers, and the flat direction, disappointing finale, and overwhelming music don't help. But the obvious chemistry between O'Neal and Taylor-Young heats up the screen. **102m/C; DVD.** Ryan O'Neal; Leigh Taylor-Young; Van Heflin; Lee Grant; James Daly; Robert Webber; Cindy Eilbacher; Noam Pitlik; *D:* Alex March; *W:* Robert Dozier; *C:* Howard Schwartz; *M:* Michael Curb.

The Big Bounce 🦴🦴 **2004 (PG-13)** Second adaptation of Elmore Leonard's first crime novel. Owen Wilson plays Jack Ryan, a small time hood who gets mixed up with Ray Ritchie, a crooked developer. Meanwhile, Ritchie's mistress Nancy (Foster) wants Ryan to steal $200,000 from Ritchie. Of course, double-crosses and deceptions ensue. Tends to meander about and lose focus, but it's somewhat enjoyable if you don't think too hard. Disappointing, considering the solid cast and the source material. **89m/C; DVD.** Owen Wilson; Morgan Freeman; Gary Sinise; Vinnie Jones; Sara Foster; Willie Nelson; Bebe Neuwirth; Charlie Sheen; Harry Dean Stanton; Andrew Wilson; Steve Jones; Anahit Minasyan; *D:* George Armitage; *W:* Sebastian Gutierrez; *C:* Jeffrey L. Kimball; *M:* George S. Clinton.

Big Boy 🦴 1/2 **1930** Based on Jolson's stage hit with Al in blackface in the minstrel tradition. Wisecracking Kentucky stablehand Gus turns jockey to ride the Bedford's horse Big Boy to victory in the Kentucky Derby despite gamblers trying to get him fired. There's a coda where Al comes out (as himself) telling the audience a Jolson film needs to end with a song so he does 'Tomorrow's Another Day.' **68m/B; DVD.** Al Jolson; Claudia Dell; Lloyd Hughes; Louise Closser Hale; Eddie (Edward) Phillips; Colin Campbell; Lew Harvey; Franklin Batie; *D:* Alan Crosland; *W:* William K. Wells; Perry Vekroff; *C:* Hal Mohr.

The Big Brass Ring 🦴🦴 1/2 **1999 (R)** Murky political drama based on an unproduced screenplay by Orson Welles. Ambitious William Blake Pellarin (Hurt) is a candidate for governor of Missouri but his ultimate goal is the presidency. However, an ugly scandal threatens his campaign, thanks to the appearance of Dr. Kimball Mennaker (Hawthorne), who's a little too close to the Pellarin family and knows about some skeletons even William isn't aware of. **104m/C; VHS, DVD.** William Hurt; Nigel Hawthorne; Miranda Richardson; Irene Jacob; Jefferson Mays; Ewan Stewart; Ron Livingston; Gregg Henry; *D:* George Hickenlooper; *W:* George Hickenlooper; F.X. Feeney; *C:* Kramer Morgenthau; *M:* Thomas Morse.

The Big Brawl ½ **1980 (R)** Chicago gangster recruits a martial arts expert to fight in a free-for-all match in Texas. **95m/C; VHS, DVD.** Jackie Chan; Jose Ferrer; Mako; Rosalind Chao; Lenny Montana; *D:* Robert Clouse; *W:* Robert Clouse; *M:* Lalo Schifrin.

The Big Broadcast of 1938 ½ **1938** Fields is the owner of an ocean liner which he enters in a race. Supposedly, the ship can convert the electricity from radio broadcasts into power for the propellers. No, it doesn't make sense, as it's just an excuse for various radio stars to show off their routines in the ship's entertainment room. Hope, in his first feature, gets to sing his Oscar-winning signature tune "Thanks for the Memories." **94m/B; VHS, DVD.** W.C. Fields; Martha Raye; Dorothy Lamour; Shirley Ross; Russell Hicks; Bob Hope; Ben Blue; Leif Erickson; *D:* Mitchell Leisen; *W:* Walter DeLeon; Francis Martin; *C:* Harry Fischbeck; *M:* Boris Morros; Ralph Rainger; Leo Robin. Oscars '38: Song ("Thanks for the Memories").

Big Brother Trouble ½ **2000 (G)** Mitch (Suchenek) has always lived in the shadow of his big brother Sean (Hart), who's the star of the soccer team. But it's Mitch to the rescue when Sean is kidnapped to insure that his team loses the City Championship game. **88m/C; VHS, DVD.** Michael Suchenek; Shad Hart; Lindsay Brooke; Mario Lopez; Bo Hopkins; Dick Van Patten; *D:* Ralph Portillo; *W:* Jeff Nimoy; Seth Walther; *C:* John Huneck; *M:* Steven Stern.

Big Brown Eyes **1936** Wisecracking hotel manicurist Eve (Bennett) is in love with detective Danny Barr (Grant). When Eve loses her job, she suddenly gets a new one working as a reporter and goes off to scope out a murder, which gets her in hot water. There's a lot of screwball complications, and the convoluted plot (which also involves a jewel heist) never does make much sense. **77m/B; DVD.** Cary Grant; Joan Bennett; Walter Pidgeon; Lloyd Nolan; Alan Baxter; Marjorie Gateson; Isabel Jewell; Douglas Fowley; Henry (Kleinbach) Brandon; *D:* Raoul Walsh; *W:* Raoul Walsh; Bert Hanlon; *C:* George T. Clemens.

Big Bully **1995 (PG)** David Leary (Moranis) is an aspiring novelist who moves back to the town where he was picked on as a kid. His son immediately starts bullying a smaller child, whose father happens to be Roscoe "Fang" Bigger (Arnold), David's former tormentor. The timid hen-pecked Roscoe's sadistic streak is awakened with the reappearance of his old prey, leading to a barrage of wet willies and indian burns. The slapstick quickly escalates to danger before all is tied up in a syrupy sweet ending. With Moranis playing the nerdy bespectacled underdog and Arnold playing the loud obnoxious guy (although that might not be acting), it may be time to call the typecasting cops. Don Knotts (looking very un-Barney-like) makes an appearance as the high school principal. **93m/C; VHS, DVD.** Tom Arnold; Rick Moranis; Julianne Phillips; Don Knotts; Carol Kane; Jeffrey Tambor; Curtis Armstrong; Faith Prince; Tony Pierce; Blake Bashoff; *D:* Steve Miner; *W:* Mark Steven Johnson; *C:* Daryn Okada; *M:* David Newman. Golden Raspberries '96: Worst Actor (Arnold).

The Big Bus **1976 (PG)** The wild adventures of the world's first nuclear-powered bus as it makes its maiden voyage from New York to Denver. Clumsy disaster-movie parody. **88m/C; VHS, DVD.** Joseph Bologna; Stockard Channing; Ned Beatty; Ruth Gordon; Larry Hagman; John Beck; Jose Ferrer; Lynn Redgrave; Sally Kellerman; Stuart Margolin; Richard Mulligan; Howard Hesseman; Richard B. Shull; *D:* James Frawley; *W:* Fred Freeman; Lawrence J. Cohen; *C:* Harry Stradling, Jr.; *M:* David Shire.

Big Business **1988 (PG)** Strained high-concept comedy about two sets of identical twins, each played by Tomlin and Midler, mismatched at birth by a near-sighted country nurse. The city set of twins intends to buy out the factory where the country set of twins work. So the country twins march up to the big city to stop the sale and destruction of their beloved home. Both set of twins stay in the Plaza Hotel and zany consequences ensue. Essentially a one-joke outing with some funny moments, but talented comediennes Midler and Tomlin are somewhat wasted. Great technical effects. **98m/C; VHS, DVD, Blu-Ray.** Bette Midler; Lily Tomlin; Fred Ward; Edward Herrmann; Michele Placido; Barry Primus; Michael Gross; Mary Gross; Daniel Gerroll; Roy Brocksmith; *D:* Jim Abrahams; *C:* Dean Cundey.

The Big Caper **1957** Gambler Frank Harber (Calhoun) gets into debt with the mob and persuades boss Flood (Gregory) to fund the heist of a small town bank that handles the payroll for a nearby army base. Flood sends Frank and his own moll Kay (Costa) to pose as a married couple to scope out the situation. Mistrust among the thieves may doom their plans and it doesn't help when Frank and Kay fall in love and want to go straight. **85m/B; DVD.** Rory Calhoun; James Gregory; Mary Costa; Robert H. Harris; Corey Allen; Paul Picerni; Roxanne Arlen; *D:* Robert Stevens; *W:* Martin Berkeley; *C:* Lionel Lindon; *M:* Albert Glasser.

The Big Cat **1949** Mountain valley in Utah is ravaged by a cougar, while two ranchers fuss and feud. Big cat, bickering, help make okay adventure. **75m/C; VHS, DVD.** Lon (Bud) McCallister; Peggy Ann Garner; Preston Foster; Forrest Tucker; *D:* Phil Karlson; *C:* William Howard Greene.

The Big Chill ½ **1983 (R)** Seven former '60s radicals, now coming upon middle age and middle-class affluence, reunite following an eighth friend's suicide and use the occasion to re-examine their past relationships and commitments. A beautifully acted, immensely enjoyable ballad to both the counter-culture and its Yuppie descendants. Great period music. Kevin Costner is the dead man whose scenes never made it to the big screen. **108m/C; VHS, DVD, Blu-Ray.** Tom Berenger; Glenn Close; Jeff Goldblum; William Hurt; Kevin Kline; Mary Kay Place; Meg Tilly; JoBeth Williams; *D:* Lawrence Kasdan; *W:* Lawrence Kasdan; Barbara Benedek; *C:* John Bailey. Writers Guild '83: Orig. Screenplay.

The Big Circus ½ **1959** Hank Twirling's (Mature) circus is failing and to get a bank loan he must put up with the presence of bank officer Sherman (Buttons) and Helen (Fleming), the publicist that Sherman hires to drum up business. But Hank has bigger problems since a saboteur is at work—letting the lions loose, starting a fire, and even causing a deadly train wreck. Fairly typical circus story featured many of the famous acts of the day. **108m/C; DVD.** Victor Mature; Red Buttons; Rhonda Fleming; Gilbert Roland; Kathryn Grant; Vincent Price; Peter Lorre; David Nelson; Joseph M. Newman; *D:* Joseph M. Newman; *W:* Irwin Allen; Charles Bennett; Irving Wallace.

Big City ½ **1937** Thoroughly ridiculous plot made palatable by Tracy's leading role. Joe works for an independent taxi company in New York that's battling with a corrupt rival firm. When the other firm's garage is bombed, Joe's pregnant, Russian immigrant wife Anna is railroaded and the D.A. orders her deported and aboard a ship in record time. So a frantic Joe takes his case to the city's ex-boxer Mayor and there's a race to the harbor to get his missus back. **80m/B; DVD.** Spencer Tracy; Luise Rainer; Charley Grapewin; Paul Harvey; Janet Beecher; Eddie Quillan; Victor Varconi; William Demarest; *D:* Frank Borzage; *W:* Hugo Butler; Dore Schary; *C:* Joseph Ruttenberg; *M:* William Axt.

Big City Blues **1999 (R)** One long night in the lives of hit men Connor (Reynolds) and Hudson (Forsythe) as they get mixed up with the plans of a hooker (Cates). **94m/C; VHS, DVD.** Burt Reynolds; William Forsythe; Georgina Cates; Giancarlo Esposito; Roger Floyd; Balthazar Getty; Arye Gross; Donovan Leitch; Roxana Zal; Amy Lyndon; Jad Mager; *D:* Clive Fleury; *W:* Clive Fleury; *C:* David Bridges; *M:* Tomas San Miguel.

The Big Clock **1948** George Stroud (Milland) is the editor of the successful Crimeways magazine, owned by tyrannical publisher Earl Janoth (Laughton). Forced to miss a vacation with his wife Georgette (O'Sullivan), George winds up spending time with lovely Pauline (Johnson), whom he inadvertently discovers is the boss' mistress. Pauline's murdered and George is quick to realize all the clues are deliberately pointed in his direction. Classic crime melodrama adapted from Kenneth Fearing's novel. Remade as "No Way Out" (1987). **95m/B; VHS, DVD, Blu-Ray.** Ray Milland; Charles Laughton; Maureen O'Sullivan; George Macready; Rita Johnson; Dan Tobin; Elsa Lanchester; Harry (Henry) Morgan; *D:* John Farrow; *W:* Jonathan Latimer; *C:* John Seitz; *M:* Victor Young.

Big Combo **1955** A gangster's ex-girlfriend helps a cop to smash a crime syndicate. Focuses on the relationship between Wilde's cop and the gangster Conte in an effective film noir, with some scenes of torture that were ahead of their time. **87m/B; DVD, Blu-Ray.** Cornel Wilde; Richard Conte; Jean Wallace; Brian Donlevy; Earl Holliman; Lee Van Cleef; Helen Walker; *D:* Joseph H. Lewis; *W:* Philip Yordan; *C:* John Alton; *M:* David Raksin.

The Big Country ½ **1958 (R)** Ex-sea captain Peck heads west to marry fiance Baker and live on her father's (Bickford) ranch. Peck immediately clashes with ranch foreman Heston and finds out there's a vicious feud with neighbor Ives. Then Peck decides he and Baker aren't meant to be and he falls for schoolmarm Simmons instead. It's too long but if you like sprawling western sagas, this one has its moments. **168m/C; VHS, DVD, Blu-Ray.** Gregory Peck; Charlton Heston; Burl Ives; Jean Simmons; Carroll Baker; Chuck Connors; Charles Bickford; *D:* William Wyler; *W:* Jessamyn West; Robert Wyler; James R. Webb; Sy Bartlett; Robert Wilder; *C:* Franz Planer; *M:* Jerome Moross. Oscars '58: Support. Actor (Ives); Golden Globes '59: Support. Actor (Ives).

Big Daddy **1999 (PG-13)** Critic-proof film for Sandler's fans—the rest won't find anything to tempt them. He's 32-year-old slacker law-school grad Sonny Koufax, who's got a big Peter Pan complex, since he's incapable of assuming any adult responsibility. However, he does want to impress women, so he decides to go for the "awww" factor by becoming the guardian of his travelling-in-China roommate Kevin's (Stewart) heretofore unknown son, five-year-old Julian (Sprouse). He teaches the kid a number of disgusting traits and winds up bonding with the tyke (they have the same emotional IQ—how hard can it be?). **95m/C; VHS, DVD, Blu-Ray, UMD.** Adam Sandler; Cole Sprouse; Dylan Sprouse; Joey Lauren Adams; Jon Stewart; Leslie Mann; Josh Mostel; Rob Schneider; Kristy Swanson; Joseph Bologna; Steve Buscemi; *D:* Dennis Dugan; *W:* Adam Sandler; Steve Franks; Tim Herlihy; *C:* Theo van de Sande; *M:* Teddy Castellucci. MTV Movie Awards '00: Comedic Perf. (Sandler); Golden Raspberries '99: Worst Actor (Sandler).

The Big Day *We Met on the Vineyard* **1999 (R)** Sara (Margulies) is supposed to be getting married. She shows up at the church but groom John (Sergei) is a no-show after his knucklehead brother Zack (Rohner) confesses to an indiscretion that leaves John with big doubts about the marriage thing. So the family starts to panic and the wedding party tries to find the groom and it's chaos everywhere you go. **88m/C; VHS, DVD.** Julianna Margulies; Ivan Sergei; Clayton Rohner; Dixie Carter; Kevin Tighe; Adrian Pasdar; Kathleen York; Andrew Buckley; Nancy Banks; *D:* Ian McCrudden; *W:* Andrew Buckley; Nancy Banks; *C:* Tony Cucchiari.

Big Deal on Madonna Street ½ *The Usual Unidentified Thieves; I Soliti Ignoti; Persons Unknown* **1958** Peppe (Gassman) is a bungling thief who leads a band of equally inept crooks who plan to make themselves very rich when they attempt to rob a jewelry store on Madonna Street. Their elaborate plans cause numerous (and hilarious) disasters. Italian with subtitles. Remade in 1984 as "Crackers." **90m/B; VHS, DVD.** *IT* Marcello Mastroianni; Vittorio Gassman; Claudia Cardinale; Renato Salvatori; Memmo Carotenuto; Toto; Rosanna Rory; *D:* Mario Monicelli; *W:* Mario Monicelli; Furio Scarpelli; Suso Cecchi D'Amico; *C:* Gianni Di Venanzo; *M:* Pierro Umiliani.

The Big Dis **1989** An interracial comedy about a young black soldier on a weekend pass who's looking for a willing sexual partner. His confidence is shattered when 12 possibilities turn him down. Feature debut of Eriksen and O'Brien. **88m/B; VHS, DVD.** Gordon Eriksen; Heather Johnston; James Haig; Kevin Haig; Monica Sparrow; *D:* Gordon Eriksen; John O'Brien; *W:* Gordon Eriksen; John O'Brien; *C:* John O'Brien.

The Big Doll House *Women's Penitentiary 1; Women in Cages; Bamboo Dolls House* **1971 (R)** Roger Corman-produced prison drama about a group of tormented female convicts who decide to break out. Features vintage Grier, and a caliber of women's-prison sleaziness that isn't equalled in today's films. **93m/C; VHS, DVD.** Judy (Judith) Brown; Roberta Collins; Pam Grier; Brooke Mills; Pat(ricia) Woodell; Sid Haig; Christiane Schmidtmer; Kathryn Loder; Jerry Frank; Charles Davis; *D:* Jack Hill; *W:* Don Spencer; *C:* Fred Conde; *M:* Les Baxter; Hall Daniels.

The Big Easy ½ **1987 (R)** A terrific thriller. Slick New Orleans detective Remy McSwain (Quaid, oozing charm and a cornball accent) uncovers a heroin-based mob war while romancing uptight assistant DA Anne Osborne (Barkin, all banked fire) who's investigating corruption on the police force. An easy, Cajun-flavored mystery, a fast-moving action-comedy, a very sexy romance, and a serious exploration of the dynamics of corruption. **101m/C; VHS, DVD.** Dennis Quaid; Ellen Barkin; Ned Beatty; John Goodman; Ebbe Roe Smith; Charles Ludlam; Lisa Jane Persky; Tom O'Brien; Grace Zabriskie; Marc Lawrence; *D:* Jim McBride; *W:* Daniel Petrie, Jr.; *C:* Affonso Beato; *M:* Brad Fiedel. Ind. Spirit '88: Actor (Quaid).

Big Eden ½ **2000 (PG-13)** Sweet-natured gay romance says you can go home again. Henry Hart (Gross) is an artist, living in New York, who returns to the small Montana town of Big Eden when his grandfather Sam (Coe) has a stroke. Henry has never admitted to anyone in his hometown that he's gay although it's pretty clear to his quirky neighbors, including the guys who hang out at the post office/general store, which is run by shy Native American Pike Dexter (Schweig), who will display some hidden talents on Henry's behalf. Henry is thrilled to discover his first crush, Dean (DeKay), is also back in town but he's looking for love in the wrong person. A happy ending is a comforting thing. **118m/C; VHS, DVD, Blu-Ray.** Arye Gross; Eric Schweig; George Coe; Tim DeKay; Louise Fletcher; Nan Martin; O'Neal Compton; Corinne Bohrer; Veanne Cox; *D:* Thomas Bezucha; *W:* Thomas Bezucha; *C:* Rob Sweeney; *M:* Joseph Conlan.

The Big Empty **1998** Lloyd Mathews (writer McManus) is a private eye who's burned out on divorce work when he's hired by a suspicious wife (Goldwasser) to find the truth about her too-good-to-be true husband (Bryan). Comparisons to Coppola's "The Conversation" are not out of place. This one's a solid sleeper. **93m/C; VHS, DVD.** James McManus; Pablo Bryant; Ellen Goldwasser; H.M. Wynant; *D:* Jack Perez; *W:* James McManus; *C:* Shawn Maurer; *M:* Jean-Michel Michenaud.

The Big Empty **2004 (R)** Struggling actor John Person (Favreau) accepts an offer to deliver a suitcase to a cowboy in a desert town for $25,000. Along the way he meets a wacky band of characters, including a bartender (Hannah) and her nympho daughter (Cook), and space aliens. Solid cast who seem to be enjoying themselves, quirky and original story, and a great soundtrack add up to an entertaining time-waster. **94m/C; VHS, DVD.** Jon Favreau; Bud Cort; Daryl Hannah; Jon(athan) Gries; Kelsey Grammer; Rachael Leigh Cook; Joey Lauren Adams; Adam Beach; Melora Walters; Sean Bean; Danny Trejo; Gary Farmer; Brent Briscoe; *D:* Steve Anderson; *W:* Steve Anderson; *C:* Chris Manley; *M:* Brian Tyler. **VIDEO**

Big Eyes **2014 (PG-13)** Tim Burton continues to trudge through the creatively flat years of his career with this surprisingly dull true story about obsession and plagiarism. So obsessed with finding fame, Walter Keane (Waltz) can't quite handle it when his new wife Margaret (Adams) proves to the better painter. As his recreations of Parisian streetsides flounder, her paintings of wide-eyed children become a literal phenomenon. Waltz chews scenery like he's in another movie while Adams does her best but often looks like she's an actress in need of a director. **105m/C; DVD, Blu-Ray.** Amy Adams; Christoph Waltz; Danny Huston; Krysten Ritter; Terence Stamp; Jason Schwartzman; Jon Polito; *D:* Tim Burton; *W:* Larry Karaszewski; Scott M. Alexander; *C:* Bruno Delbonnel; *M:*

Danny Elfman. Golden Globes '15: Actress--Mus./Comedy (Adams).

The Big Fall 🦴🦴 **1996 (R)** L.A. private investigator Blaize Rybeck (Howell) is hired by mystery babe Emma (Ward) to find her brother, Kenny, a pilot. Blaize meets some of Kenny's thrill-seeking friends at the airfield and draws the suspicious interest of FBI agent Wilcox (Applegate). Seems Kenny was mixed up in some shady dealings that get both his sister and her nosy P.I. into trouble. **94m/C; VHS, DVD.** C. Thomas Howell; Sophie Ward; Jeff Kober; Justin Lazard; Titus Welliver; William Applegate, Jr.; ***D:*** C. Thomas Howell; ***W:*** William Applegate, Jr.; ***C:*** Jurgen Baum.

Big Fan 🦴🦴 1/2 **2009 (R)** Uncomfortably odd film about an isolated man who has nothing in his life but his obsession with the New York Giants. Bottom-rung Paul (Oswalt) listens to sports radio all day and offers call-in diatribes to his favorite radio show at night. He and loser pal Sal (Corrigan) can't afford tickets so they watch the Giants on TV from the Meadowlands parking lot. A chance encounter with linebacker Quantrell Bishop (Hamm) leads to a string of bad events. **86m/C; DVD.** Patton Oswalt; Kevin Corrigan; Jonathan Hamm; Gino Cafarelli; Matt Servitto; Marcia Jean Kurtz; Michael Rapaport; ***D:*** Robert Siegel; ***W:*** Robert Siegel; ***C:*** Michael Simmonds; ***M:*** Philip Watts.

Big Fat Liar 🦴🦴 **2002 (PG)** The boy who cried wolf goes to Hollywood in search of Marty Wolf (Giamatti), the unscrupulous movie producer who stole his short story. As nobody believes his far-out tale of being ripped off by Hollywood, notorious liar Jason Shepherd (Muniz) also makes sure to bring along a witness to his pursuit, in the form of his friend Kaylee (Bynes). Pulling an array of inspired pranks, the teens zestfully set about dismantling the sanity of Wolf, to the delight, and sometimes with the aid of, some of his many enemies. Talented small-screen star Muniz and his co-star Bynes make this a likeable, though not especially inspired, broad comedy with Giamatti mugging up a storm. Their romp through Universal Studios, especially, lets you know who's really behind this mostly entertaining movie for the preteen set. **87m/C; VHS, DVD, Blu-Ray.** Frankie Muniz; Paul Giamatti; Amanda Bynes; Amanda Detmer; Donald Adeosun Faison; Lee Majors; Sandra Oh; Russell Hornsby; Christine Tucci; Sean O'Bryan; Amy Hill; Michael Bryan French; ***D:*** Shawn Levy; ***W:*** Dan Schneider; ***C:*** Jonathan Brown.

Big Fella 🦴🦴 1/2 **1937** Musical drama starring Robeson as Joe, a Marseilles dockworker (a familiar film occupation for the actor), who's asked by the police to help find a young boy (Grant) missing from an ocean liner. When Joe locates the boy, he discovers the child ran away from his wealthy family and doesn't want to return. Joe takes the boy to his cafe singer girlfriend, Miranda (Welch), and the two become his surrogate parents. Loose adapatation of the 1929 novel, "Banjo," by Claude McKay. **73m/B; VHS, DVD.** *GB* Paul Robeson; Elisabeth Welch; Eldon Grant; ***D:*** J. Elder Wills; ***W:*** Ingram D'Abbes; Fenn Sherie; ***C:*** Cyril Bristow; ***M:*** Eric Ansell.

Big Fish 🦴🦴🦴 **2003 (PG-13)** This is right up Burton's alley, as it's about a great storyteller prone to out-sized flights of fancy. Ed Bloom (Finney) is a man on his deathbed hoping to reconcile with the son (Crudup) he's alienated with the yarns he's spun about his life. When Will, who's become a journalist as a form of rebellion, returns and asks one last time for the truth, Ed again begins the familiar tall tale. This is where we learn of Ed's version of his courtship of wife Sandra, his battle with a huge catfish, his adventures with a giant in the circus, the Korean War, and an idyllic town where the residents seem content to walk around barefoot and happy. Burton is in his element with the flashback/yarn portion, but handles the delicate drama of the father-son scenes with aplomb as well. Cast is uniformly excellent, with Finney making the most of a largely sedentary role. **125m/C; DVD, Blu-Ray.** Ewan McGregor; Albert Finney; Billy Crudup; Jessica Lange; Alison Lohman; Helena Bonham Carter; Robert Guillaume; Steve Buscemi; Danny DeVito; Marion Cotillard; David Denman; Missi Pyle; Matthew McGrory; Loudon Wainwright, III; ***D:*** Tim Burton; ***W:*** John August; ***C:*** Philippe Rousselot; ***M:*** Danny Elfman.

The Big Game 🦴 1/2 *Control Factor* **1972** It's about espionage not big game hunting but it's dull in any case. Prof. Handley (Milland) designs a mind control device for the U.S. military to brainwash soldiers into becoming fighting machines. For safety's sake, the contraption is being moved via a fishing boat but the bad guys know where it's headed and plan to steal it. **90m/C; DVD.** Stephen Boyd; Cameron Mitchell; Ray Milland; France Nuyen; John Stacy; Brendon Boone; Michael Kirner; ***D:*** Robert Day; ***W:*** Robert Day; Stanley Norman; Ralph Anders; ***C:*** Mario Fioretti; ***M:*** Francesco De Masi.

Big Game 🦴 1/2 **2015 (PG-13)** After Air Force One is deliberately brought down, the president of the United States (Jackson) teams with a 13-year-old boy (Tommila) to evade kidnappers pursuing him deep in the forests of Finland. As the terrorists close in on the pre-teen and the POTUS, a group of advisors back home do their best to help. Some films never find the right balance between their B-movie origins and their desire to be more serious fare. Some of the actors in this ode to '80s action know to play their characters as over-the-top caricatures, but too much of it is played straight to work. **90m/C; DVD, Blu-Ray, Streaming.** *FI GE UK* Samuel L. Jackson; Onni Tommila; Felicity Huffman; Jim Broadbent; Jorma Tommila; Ray Stevenson; ***D:*** Jalmari Helander; ***W:*** Jalmari Helander; ***C:*** Mika Orasmaa; ***M:*** Juri Seppa; Miska Seppa.

Big Girls Don't Cry. . . They Get Even 🦴 1/2 **1992 (PG)** A teenage girl decides to run away from home after she's driven crazy by her eccentric new stepfamily. Comic confusion ensues as various family members set out to find her. Hackneyed script and annoying characters hinder this comedy. **98m/C; VHS, DVD.** Hillary Wolf; Griffin Dunne; Margaret Whitton; David Strathairn; Ben Savage; Adrienne Shelly; Patricia Kalember; ***D:*** Joan Micklin Silver.

The Big Green 🦴 1/2 **1995 (PG)** British teacher Anna Montgomery (D'Abo) blows into a small Texas town determined to give the deprived kiddies a boost of self-esteem. With help from the town sheriff (Guttenberg), Anna organizes a soccer team that's supposed to give the kids a reason to live. Problems abound when the star player disappears just before the face-off with the biggest, nastiest team in the league. Sound familiar? This is the soccer version of "The Bad News Bears," "The Little Giants," and "The Mighty Ducks." The formula is less successful in this case, but some mildly amusing moments and a few fresh performances from the kids offer minor bright spots in this tired scenario. **100m/C; VHS, DVD.** Olivia D'Abo; Steve Guttenberg; Jay O. Sanders; John Terry; Chauncey Leopardi; Patrick Renna; Billy L. Sullivan; Yareli Arizmendi; Bug Hall; ***D:*** Holly Goldberg Sloan; ***W:*** Holly Goldberg Sloan; ***C:*** Ralf Bode; ***M:*** Randy Edelman.

The Big Gundown 🦴🦴 *La Resa del Conti* **1966** Spaghetti western that's fast-paced but familiar. Texas bounty hunter Jonathan Corbett is given a temporary lawman's badge after he's hired by tycoon Brokston to hunt down Mexican Cuchillo Sanchez who's accused of raping and murdering a young white girl. Sanchez proves to be a wily adversary as he runs for the border, but Corbett eventually gets his man only to find out he's innocent. **95m/C; DVD, Blu-Ray.** *IT SP* Lee Van Cleef; Tomas Milian; Walter Barnes; Luisa Rivelli; ***D:*** Sergio Sollima; ***W:*** Sergio Sollima; Sergio Donati; ***C:*** Carlo Carlini; ***M:*** Ennio Morricone.

A Big Hand for the Little Lady 🦴🦴 1/2 *Big Deal at Dodge City* **1966** Fonda and Woodward, playing two West-headed country bumpkins, get involved in a card game in Laredo against high rollers Robards and McCarthy. Fonda risks their savings, finds himself stuck with a losing hand, and has a bit of heart trouble; that's where the little lady comes in. Fine performances and a nifty twist ending don't entirely compensate for the overly padded script (which evolved from Carroll's 48-minute TV play). **95m/C; DVD.** Henry Fonda; Joanne Woodward; Jason Robards, Jr.; Charles Bickford; Burgess Meredith; Kevin McCarthy; ***D:*** Fielder Cook; ***W:*** Sidney Carroll; ***C:*** Lee Garmes; ***M:*** David Raksin.

The Big Hangover 🦴🦴 **1950** Odd story about a man whose allergy to alcohol makes him drunk at the most inopportune moments. Johnson stars as the attorney with the peculiar problem and Taylor plays the boss' daughter who helps him overcome the allergy. Good supporting cast can't help this otherwise boring and predictable film. **82m/B; VHS, DVD.** Van Johnson; Elizabeth Taylor; Percy Waram; Fay Holden; Leon Ames; Edgar Buchanan; Selena Royle; Gene Lockhart; ***D:*** Norman Krasna; ***W:*** Norman Krasna; ***C:*** George J. Folsey.

The Big Heat 🦴🦴🦴 1/2 **1953** When detective Ford's wife (played by Jocelyn Brando, sister of Marlon) is killed in an explosion meant for him, he pursues the gangsters behind it and uncovers a police scandal. His appetite is whetted after this discovery and he pursues the criminals even more vigorously with the help of gangster moll Gloria Grahame. Definitive film noir. **90m/B; VHS, DVD, Blu-Ray.** Glenn Ford; Lee Marvin; Gloria Grahame; Jocelyn Brando; Alexander Scourby; Carolyn Jones; ***D:*** Fritz Lang; ***W:*** Sydney (Sidney) Boehm; ***C:*** Charles B(ryant) Lang, Jr. Natl. Film Reg. '11.

Big Hero 6 🦴🦴 1/2 **2014 (PG)** Disney's Oscar-winning adaptation of a relatively unknown Marvel comic is sweet and well-made, even if it doesn't quite rise to the heights of the best of the Mouse House or Pixar. When a smart teen boy's brother dies in a freak explosion, Hiro's (Potter) managed through his grief by a "Health Care Robot" named Baymax (Adsit). Joining forces with his brother's fellow science lab nerds, he plays sleuth to find his sibling's murderer, and basically forms a group of superheroes. The second half loses a bit of the charm in favor of Marvel-esque action sequences but it's still a good time. **102m/C; DVD, Blu-Ray.** ***V:*** Ryan Potter; Scott Adsit; Jamie Chung; Damon Wayans, Jr.; Genesis Rodriguez; T.J. Miller; Maya Rudolph; James Cromwell; Alan Tudyk; Stan Lee; ***D:*** Don Hall; Chris Williams; ***W:*** Robert L. Baird; Daniel Gerson; Jordan Roberts; ***M:*** Henry Jackman. Oscars '14: Animated Film.

The Big Hit 🦴🦴 1/2 **1998 (R)** Combustible mixture of extravagent stunts, cartoon violence, hip-hop soundtrack, and a colorful cast serve up an intermittently funny look at organized crime. When not executing their skills as ruthless hitmen, Melvin, Cisco, Vince, and Crunch (Wahlberg, Phillips, Sabato, Jr., and Woodbine) are regular working Joes with regular problems. For Melvin, financial and female problems force him to partner with Cisco in the kidnapping of a Chinese heiress. Said heiress turns out to be the goddaughter of their own crime boss. Much hilarity ensues. Phillips brings gusto to his flamboyant homeboy character and Wahlberg is his equal as the sappy gun for hire with a heart of gold. Big plot holes and fickle storyline, but bigger laughs make you not care so much. American directorial debut of Hong Kong import Che-Kirk Wong. **91m/C; VHS, DVD, Blu-Ray, UMD.** Mark Wahlberg; Lou Diamond Phillips; Bokeem Woodbine; Antonio Sabato, Jr.; Christina Applegate; Avery Brooks; China Chow; Lainie Kazan; Elliott Gould; Lela Rochon; Sab Shimono; ***D:*** Kirk Wong; ***W:*** Ben Ramsey; ***C:*** Danny Nowak; ***M:*** Graeme Revell.

The Big House 🦴🦴🦴 **1930** Prison melodrama at its best follows top con Beery as he plans a big breakout—and is betrayed. Life in the pen is depicted as brutal and futile, with sadistic guards and a hapless warden. Spawned numerous imitators. **80m/B; VHS, DVD.** Wallace Beery; Chester Morris; Robert Montgomery; Lewis Stone; Leila Hyams; George F. Marion, Sr.; Karl (Daen) Dane; DeWitt Jennings; ***D:*** George W. Hill; ***W:*** Frances Marion.

Big House, U.S.A. 🦴🦴 **1955** In this brutal crime drama, Jerry Barber (Meeker) lands in the big house, convicted of extortion after a kidnapping gone wrong. He buried most of the ransom money, and his cellmates come up with an escape plan to get the dough, but the FBI is ready to take 'em down. **82m/B; DVD, Blu-Ray.** Ralph Meeker; Broderick Crawford; Reed Hadley; William Talman; Lon Chaney, Jr.; Charles Bronson; ***D:*** Howard W. Koch; ***W:*** John C. Higgins; ***C:*** Gordon Avil; ***M:*** Paul Dunlap.

The Big I Am 🦴 **2010 (R)** Inexperience behind (and some in front of) the camera dooms this derivative British gangster flick. Small time London crook Mickey Skinner unexpectedly saves human trafficker/crime boss Don Barber from death at the hands of rival Frankie Stubbs. To find out who betrayed him, Barber wants to lay low so he makes bungler Mickey the temporary head of his organization. **106m/C; DVD.** *GB* Leo Gregory; Vincent Regan; Philip Davis; Beatrice Rosen; Robert Fucilla; Michael Madsen; Steven Berkoff; ***D:*** Nic Auerbach; ***W:*** Tim Cummingham; ***C:*** Shane Daly; ***M:*** James Radford.

Big Jake 🦴🦴 **1971 (PG)** An aging Texas cattle man who has outlived his time swings into action when outlaws kidnap his grandson and wound his son. He returns to his estranged family to help them in the search for Little Jake. O'Hara is once again paired up with Wayne and the chemistry is still there. **90m/C; VHS, DVD, Blu-Ray.** John Wayne; Richard Boone; Maureen O'Hara; Patrick Wayne; Chris Mitchum; Bobby Vinton; John Agar; Harry Carey, Jr.; ***D:*** George Sherman; ***C:*** William Clothier; ***M:*** Elmer Bernstein.

Big Jim McLain 🦴🦴 **1952** Wayne and Arness are federal agents working on behalf of the House Un-American Activities Committee to eliminate communist terrorism in Hawaii. And there's a suspicious psychiatrist, too: Wayne falls for a babe whose boss is a shrink who doesn't quite seem on the level. Definitely not a highpoint in the Duke's career. **90m/C; VHS, DVD.** John Wayne; Nancy Olson; James Arness; Veda Ann Borg; ***D:*** Edward Ludwig; ***C:*** Archie Stout.

The Big Kahuna 🦴🦴 1/2 **2000 (R)** Spacey produced and stars as Larry, a loudly cynical industrial lubricants salesman at a convention in Kansas. He's there with Phil (DeVito), his burned-out collegue who's going through a divorce and looking for spirituality; and Bob (Facinelli), a newlywed, devout Christian research engineer who's new to the company. They spend the night in a hospitality suite waiting for a potential client—the Big Kahuna—and discussing how work, religion, ethics, and personal life coexist. Adapted from Rueff's play "Hospitality Suite" and it feels like it. The dialogue and setting is very stagey, but the performances are excellent, especially DeVito's. **90m/C; VHS, DVD, Blu-Ray.** Kevin Spacey; Danny DeVito; Peter Facinelli; ***D:*** John Swanbeck; ***W:*** Roger Rueff; ***C:*** Anastas Michos; ***M:*** Christopher Young.

The Big Knife 🦴🦴🦴 **1955** Palance plays a Hollywood superstar who refuses to renew his studio contract, which enrages studio boss Steiger. It seems Steiger knows a very damaging secret about the star and is willing to go to any lengths to have Palance re-sign or wind up destroying himself. A ruthless, emotional look at fame and power, with excellent performances by all. Based on the play by Clifford Odets. **113m/B; DVD, Blu-Ray.** Jack Palance; Rod Steiger; Ida Lupino; Shelley Winters; Wendell Corey; Jean Hagen; Ilka Chase; Everett Sloane; Wesley Addy; Paul Langton; ***D:*** Robert Aldrich; ***C:*** Ernest Laszlo.

Big Leaguer 🦴🦴 **1953** Fictionalized sports saga about New York Giants baseball player-turned-scout Hans Lobert (Robinson). It's set at the team's Florida training camp where Lobert is eyeballing the current prospects--from a Cuban hopeful to a player who isn't sure he even likes the game. **71m/B; DVD.** Edward G. Robinson; Vera-Ellen; Richard Jaeckel; Jeff Richards; John McKee; Lalo Rios; Bill Crandall; ***D:*** Robert Aldrich; ***W:*** Herbert Baker; ***C:*** William Mellor; ***M:*** Alberto Colombo.

The Big Lebowski 🦴🦴🦴 1/2 **1997 (R)** Jeff Lebowski (Bridges), a stuck-in-the-'70s stoner who insists on being called "the Dude" and loves to go bowling, is mistaken for a wheelchair-bound millionaire of the same name, and suffers at the hands of thugs who are after money owed by the rich Lebowski's slutty wife. Dude is drawn into kidnapping, the attempted scamming of payoff money, and more bowling. While this may seem like plot-a-plenty, it's mainly a showcase for the Coen brothers' unique texturing of style and quirky-but-deep characters. Goodman is loud and funny as a quick-to-anger Vietnam vet. Turturro steals his scenes as a pervert rival bowler. The showpiece is an amazing musical-bowling-fantasy sequence that would've made Busby Berkeley proud. **117m/C; VHS, DVD, Blu-Ray, HD-DVD.** Jeff Bridges; John Goodman; Steve Buscemi; Julianne Moore; Peter Stormare; David Huddleston; Philip Seymour Hoffman; Flea; Leon Russom; Sam Elliott; John Turturro; David Thewlis; Ben Gazzara; Tara Reid; Jack Kehler; Richard Gant; Dom Irrera; Jon Polito; *D:* Joel Coen; *W:* Joel Coen; Ethan Coen; *C:* Roger Deakins; *M:* Carter Burwell. Natl. Film Reg. '14.

The Big Lift 🦴🦴 1/2 **1950** Two G.I.'s assigned to the Berlin airlift ally themselves in counter-intelligence when they discover that their mutual girlfriend is a spy. **119m/B; VHS, DVD.** Montgomery Clift; Paul Douglas; Cornell Borchers; Bruni Lobel; O.E. Hasse; *D:* George Seaton.

The Big Man: Crossing the Line 🦴🦴🦴 *Crossing the Line* **1991 (R)** Neeson shines as a down on his luck Scottish miner who loses his job during a union strike. Desperate for cash and unable to resolve his bitterness at being unable to support his family, he's enticed by a Glasgow hood to fight in an illegal bare-knuckled boxing match. What follows is an overlong and extremely brutal fight. Good performances from a talented cast overcome a rather preachy script that doesn't disguise its contempt for the Thatcher government, but also allows a glimpse into the tough times that many Brits suffered during the '80s. Based on the novel by William McIlvanney. **93m/C; VHS, DVD.** *GB* Liam Neeson; Joanne Whalley; Ian Bannen; Billy Connolly; Hugh Grant; Maurice Roeves; Rob Affleck; *D:* David Leland; *W:* Don MacPherson; *M:* Ennio Morricone.

Big Man Japan 🦴 1/2 *Dai Nipponjin; Great Japanese* **2007 (PG-13)** Weird mockumentary about a Japanese superhero with bad press. Everyman Daisato works for the Defense Department where he is routinely turned humungous, thanks to a burst of electricity, so he can battle a variety of monsters that plague Tokyo. Since they regularly destroy the city, this doesn't make the citizens too happy. Japanese with subtitles. **113m/C; DVD.** *JP* Riki Takeuchi; Ryunosuke Kamiki; Itsuji Itao; Hitoshi Matsumoto; Ua; *D:* Hitoshi Matsumoto; *W:* Hitoshi Matsumoto; Mitsuyoshi Yakasu; *C:* Hideo Yamamoto; *M:* Towa Tei.

Big Meat Eater 🦴🦴 **1985** A musical gore-comedy about extraterrestrials using radioactive butcher's discards for ship fuel. Deliberate camp that is so bad its funny! **81m/C; VHS, DVD.** *CA* George Dawson; Big Miller; Andrew Gillies; Stephen Dimopoulos; Georgina Hegedos; Ida Carnevali; Sharon Wahl; *D:* Chris Windsor; *W:* Chris Windsor; Phil Savath; Laurence Keane; *C:* Doug McKay.

Big Miracle 🦴🦴 1/2 **2012 (PG)** Based on true events, this big fish story avoids the pitfalls of sentimentality and provides a quality family movie. Small town Alaska newsman Adam (Krakowski) teams up with ex-girlfriend and Greenpeace volunteer Rachel (Barrymore) to save a family of endangered whales that are slowly being trapped by ice in the Arctic Circle. Once the story is picked up by the national media, volunteers show up to help. The do-gooders, including a slick oilman (Danson) and an Inuit leader (Pingayak), are mostly there to further their own personal agendas however. Based on Tom Rose's book "Freeing the Whales: How the Media Created the World's Greatest Non-Event." **107m/C; DVD, Blu-Ray.** John Krasinski; Drew Barrymore; Kristen Bell; Dermot Mulroney; Tim Blake Nelson; Ted Danson; Vinessa Shaw; Stephen (Steve) Root; Michael Gaston; Rob Riggle; James LeGros; John Pingayak; Kathy Baker; *D:* Ken Kwapis; *W:* Jack Amiel; Michael Begler; *C:* John Bailey; *M:* Cliff Eidelman.

Big Momma's House 🦴🦴 **2000 (PG-13)** FBI agent Lawrence is sent to Georgia to protect single mom Long and her son from her escaped con ex. Since he's a master of disguise, Lawrence passes himself off as her grandma, who's known as "Big Momma." Lawrence, like his pal Eddie Murphy, has plenty of experience with costumes, disguises, and multiple roles. So it's kind of disappointing that this isn't a better movie. Sporadic laughs are too often mined from toilet humor, and the plot doesn't allow for many quiet moments, which Lawrence needs to balance out the slapstick. **98m/C; VHS, DVD, Blu-Ray.** Martin Lawrence; Nia Long; Paul Giamatti; Terrence Howard; Anthony Anderson; Carl Wright; Ella Mitchell; Jascha Washington; Starletta DuPois; Cedric the Entertainer; *D:* Raja Gosnell; *W:* Darryl Quarles; Don Rhymer; *C:* Michael D. O'Shea; *M:* Richard Gibbs.

Big Momma's House 2 🦴🦴 **2006 (PG-13)** Hey, if you liked seeing Lawrence in a fat suit and a dress the first time, you'll probably think the sequel is okay. The plot, such as it is, has FBI agent Malcolm Turner's alter ego Hattie Mae Pierce posing as a nanny to investigate Tom Fuller (Moses), a computer expert who has created a worm that threatens national security. Long returns too, this time as Turner's suspicious pregnant missus. Be warned: the sight of Momma running along the beach in cornrows and a bright yellow bathing suit may scar the psyche for life. **98m/C; DVD, Blu-Ray.** Martin Lawrence; Nia Long; Emily Procter; Mark Moses; Kat Dennings; Chloë Grace Moretz; Marisol Nichols; Josh Flitter; Dan Lauria; Zachary Levi; Preston Shores; Trevor Shores; Lisa Arrindell Anderson; *D:* John Whitesell; *W:* Don Rhymer; *C:* Mark Irwin; *M:* George S. Clinton.

Big Mommas: Like Father, Like Son 🦴 **2011 (PG-13)** FBI agent Malcolm Turner (AKA Big Momma) and his teenage stepson Trent (AKA Charmaine) go undercover at an all-girls performing arts school to catch a killer after Trent witnesses a murder. With a complete lack of imagination from both cast and crew, jokes fall flat as either offensive, unforgivably humorless, or (most frequently) both. A tired and uninspired portrayal that pokes fun at black women, and the idea of black women having power. Lawrence would do best to hang up the fat suit and the franchise. **107m/C; Blu-Ray, On Demand.** Martin Lawrence; Brandon T. Jackson; Faizon Love; Portia Doubleday; Jessica Lucas; Michelle Ang; Emily Rios; Ken Jeong; *D:* John Whitesell; *W:* Matthew Fogel; *C:* Anthony B. Richmond; *M:* David Newman.

Big News 🦴🦴 **1929** Based on the play "For Two Cents" by George S. Brooks, this early talkie uses sound to great advantage. Fired for going after a gangster who's a big advertiser (Hardy), reporter Armstrong nevertheless keeps after the crook. When the intrepid reporter pushes too far, murder enters the picture. **75m/B; VHS, DVD.** Robert Armstrong; Carole Lombard; Tom Kennedy; Warner Richmond; Wade Boteler; Sam Hardy; Lew Ayres; *D:* Gregory La Cava.

The Big Night 🦴🦴 **1951** Coming of age drama has 17-year-old George (Barrymore) watching as his nice guy dad (Foster) is beaten by thugish sports writer Al Judge (St. John). The naive teen takes his dad's gun and goes to get revenge by trying to track Judge down in the seedier parts of town. It's a long night before George confronts his foe, with some unexpected consequences. **76m/B; DVD.** John Drew (Blythe) Barrymore, Jr.; Howard St. John; Preston Foster; Philip Bourneuf; Joan Lorring; Dorothy Comingore; *D:* Joseph Losey; *W:* Joseph Losey; Stanley Ellin; *C:* Hal Mohr; *M:* Lyn Murray.

Big Night 🦴🦴 1/2 **1995 (R)** Set in '50s New Jersey, film provides an Old World/New World look at Italian brothers Primo (Shalhoub) and Secondo (Tucci) Pilaggi and their elegant but failing restaurant. Primo is the perfectionist chef who hates compromise while Secondo wants to Americanize the place in an effort to make it a success. (He knows the customer is always right even if they can't appreciate Primo's exquisitely authentic Italian dishes). In order to get attention, Secondo arranges a special night in honor of jazz great Louis Prima, with Primo out to cook the feast of a lifetime—if they can pull it off. Another food film guaranteed to make you hungry. **109m/C; VHS, DVD.** Tony Shalhoub; Stanley Tucci; Ian Holm; Minnie Driver; Campbell Scott; Isabella Rossellini; Marc Anthony; Allison Janney; Dina Spybey; *D:* Stanley Tucci; Campbell Scott; *W:* Stanley Tucci; Joseph Tropiano; *C:* Ken Kelsch. Ind. Spirit '97: First Screenplay; Natl. Soc. Film Critics '96: Support. Actor (Shalhoub); Sundance '96: Screenplay.

Big Nothing 🦴 1/2 **2006** Now there's a title just leaving itself wide open. Well, it's more like "little nothing" anyway. Struggling writer Charlie (Schwimmer) takes a job at a call center. Co-worker Gus (Pegg) persuades Charlie to join him in blackmailing a preacher who likes kiddie-porn websites. They pick up a third partner in blonde babe Josie (Eve). **86m/C; DVD.** *GB* David Schwimmer; Simon Pegg; Alice Eve; Mimi Rogers; Natascha (Natasha) McElhone; Jon Polito; Billy Asher; Mitchell Mullen; *D:* Jean-Baptiste Andrea; *W:* Jean-Baptiste Andrea; *C:* Richard Greatrex; *M:* Alan Anton. **VIDEO**

The Big One 🦴🦴 **1998 (PG-13)** Moore once again takes his populist, CEO-baiting act on the road in search of corporate evildoers, this time on Random House's dime. Documentary lovingly follows Moore on his 1996 book promo tour, as he highlights plant closings, verbally spars with Nike boss Phil Knight, plays pranks on his "handlers," and mugs for his adoring fans. His style is still the same as in "Roger & Me," but since he's joined the celebrity ranks, Moore isn't going to sneak up on anybody. To his credit, he doesn't try, but to his discredit, he ends up haranguing the very working people he claims to be standing up for, mostly exasperated receptionists and secretaries. Corporate greed and apathy are still squarely in Moore's crosshairs, but this time his own ego prevents him from getting a clear shot at his target. **90m/C; VHS, DVD.** *Nar:* Michael Moore; *D:* Michael Moore.

The Big Parade 🦴🦴🦴🦴 **1925** Wonderful WWI silent, considered to be one of the best war flicks of all time. Gilbert and Adoree are exceptional as lovers torn apart by the conflict. Interesting and thoughtful picture of the trauma and trouble brought to men and their loved ones in wartime. Battle scenes are compelling and intense; Vidor's masterpiece. **141m/B; Silent; DVD, Blu-Ray.** John Gilbert; Renee Adoree; Hobart Bosworth; Claire McDowell; Claire Adams; Karl (Daen) Dane; Robert Ober; Tom (Thomas E.) O'Brien; Rosita Marstini; *D:* King Vidor; *W:* Harry Behn; *C:* John Arnold; *M:* William Axt; David Mendoza. Natl. Film Reg. '92.

The Big Picture 🦴🦴 1/2 **1989 (PG-13)** A hilarious, overlooked comedy by and starring a variety of Second City/National Lampoon alumni, about a young filmmaker who is contracted by a big studio, only to see his vision trampled by formula-minded producers, crazed agents, hungry starlets, and every other variety of Hollywood predator. **95m/C; VHS, DVD, Blu-Ray.** Kevin Bacon; Jennifer Jason Leigh; Martin Short; Michael McKean; Emily Longstreth; J.T. Walsh; Eddie Albert; Richard Belzer; John Cleese; June Lockhart; Stephen Collins; Roddy McDowall; Kim Miyori; Teri Hatcher; Dan Schneider; Jason Gould; Tracy Brooks Swope; *D:* Christopher Guest; *W:* Michael McKean; Christopher Guest; Michael Varhol; *M:* David Nichtern.

The Big Picture 🦴🦴 1/2 *L'homme qui voulait vivre sa vie* **2010** A successful lawyer fears his life is over after murdering his wife's lover, so he does what comes naturally: he steals the identity of the man he's killed and assumes his life. **115m/C; DVD, Blu-Ray, Streaming.** *FR* Romain Duris; Marina Fois; Niels Arestup; Branka Katic; Catherine Deneuve; *D:* Eric Lartigau; *W:* Eric Lartigau; Laurent de Bartillat; *C:* Laurent Dailland; *M:* Sacha Galperine; Evgueni Galperine.

The Big Push 🦴 1/2 *Timber Tramps* **1975 (PG)** Motley bunch of Alaskan lumberjacks get together to save a poor widow's logging camp from a pair of greedy mill owners. **98m/C; VHS, DVD.** Joseph Cotten; Claude Akins; Cesar Romero; Tab Hunter; Roosevelt "Rosie" Grier; Leon Ames; Stubby Kaye; Patricia Medina; *D:* Tay Garnett.

Big Red 🦴🦴 1/2 **1962** Set amid the spectacular beauty of Canada's Quebec Province, an orphan boy protects a dog which later saves him from a mountain lion. **89m/C; VHS, DVD.** Walter Pidgeon; Gilles Payant; *D:* Norman Tokar; *W:* Louis Pelletier; *C:* Edward Colman; *M:* Oliver Wallace; Richard M. Sherman; Robert B. Sherman.

The Big Red One 🦴🦴🦴 1/2 **1980 (PG)** Fuller's harrowing, intense semi-autobiographical account of the U.S. Army's famous First Infantry Division in WWII, the "Big Red One." A rifle squad composed of four very young men, led by the grizzled Marvin, cut a fiery path of conquest from the landing in North Africa to the liberation of the concentration camp at Falkenau, Czechoslovakia. In part a tale of lost innocence, the film scores highest by bringing the raw terror of war down to the individual level. New restored version adds about 47 minutes and sports an "R" rating. **113m/C; VHS, DVD, Blu-Ray.** Lee Marvin; Robert Carradine; Mark Hamill; Stephane Audran; Bobby DiCicco; Perry Lang; Kelly Ward; Siegfried Rauch; Serge Marquand; Charles Macaulay; Alain Doutey; Maurice Marsac; Colin Gilbert; Joseph Clark; Ken Campbell; Doug Werner; Marthe Villalonga; *D:* Samuel Fuller; *W:* Samuel Fuller; *C:* Adam Greenberg; *M:* Dana Kaproff.

The Big Scam 🦴🦴 1/2 *A Nightingale Sang in Berkeley Square; The Mayfair Bank Caper* **1979** Criminal mastermind Niven recruits ex-con Jordan to pull off a massive bank heist. **102m/C; DVD.** Richard Jordan; David Niven; Oliver Tobias; Elke Sommer; Gloria Grahame; Hugh Griffith; Richard Johnson; Joss Ackland; Alfred Molina; *D:* Ralph Thomas; *W:* Guy Elmes; *C:* John Coquillon; *M:* Stanley Myers.

Big Score 🦴 **1983 (R)** When a policeman is falsely accused and dismissed from the Chicago Police Department, he goes after the men who really stole the money from a drug bust. Script was originally intended to be a Dirty Harry flick; too bad it wasn't. **88m/C; VHS, DVD.** Fred Williamson; John Saxon; Richard Roundtree; Nancy Wilson; Ed Lauter; Ron Dean; D'Urville Martin; Michael Dante; Joe Spinell; *D:* Fred Williamson; *C:* Joao Fernandes.

The Big Short 🦴🦴🦴 **2015 (R)** McKay adapts Michael Lewis's non-fiction book about the financial meltdown of the late '00s with flair and style. Multiple characters, including ones played by Bale, Carell, Pitt, and Gosling, appear in separate plotlines that intersect just as the housing market is about to completely collapse in on itself. McKay knows that this is material that could be dry and complicated, so he punches it up whenever possible with celebrity cameos, but he never feels like he's talking down to his audience. The result is a film that's remarkably smart without ever being pretentious. **130m/C; DVD, Blu-Ray.** Ryan Gosling; Christian Bale; Steve Carell; Marisa Tomei; Hamish Linklater; *D:* Adam McKay; *W:* Adam McKay; Charles Randolph; *C:* Barry Ackroyd; *M:* Nicholas Britell. Oscars '15: Adapt. Screenplay; British Acad. '15: Adapt. Screenplay; Writers Guild '15: Adapt. Screenplay.

The Big Shot 🦴🦴 1/2 **1942** Crime potboiler from Warner Bros. that's told in flashback. Three-time loser Duke Berne (Bogart) is framed for an armored car heist by his crooked lawyer (Ridges) after Fleming finds out Duke has rekindled his romance with ex-flame Lorna (Manning), who's now Fleming's wife. Duke escapes from the big house and runs away with Lorna, but things turns out badly. **82m/B; DVD.** Humphrey Bogart; Irene Manning; Stanley Ridges; Richard Travis; Susan Peters; Minor Watson; *D:* Lewis Seiler; *W:* Abem Finkel; Bertram Millhauser; *C:* Sidney Hickox; *M:* Adolph Deutsch.

Big Shot: Confessions of a Campus Bookie 🦴🦴 1/2 **2002 (R)** Based on the true story of Brooklyn-born Benny Silman (Krumholtz) who undergoes culture shock when he begins attending Arizona State University. He takes frequent trips to Vegas and is soon running his own campus bookmaking operation but wants more. Then Benny meets hoops star Stevin Smith (Kittles) who isn't adverse to making some money on the side. So Benny hooks up with a big-time Vegas gambler (Turturro) to shave points in ASU games. **83m/C; VHS, DVD.** David Krumholtz; Nicholas Turturro; Jennifer (Jenny) Morrison; Tory Kittles; Carmine D. Giovinazzo; Alex Rocco; James LeGros; *D:* Ernest R. Dickerson; *W:* Jason Keller; *C:* Steven Bernstein; *M:* Reinhold Heil; Johnny Klimek. **CABLE**

Big Shots 🦴 **1987 (PG-13)** Two kids, one naive and white, the other black and streetwise, search for a stolen watch. **91m/C; VHS, DVD.** Ricky Busker; Darius McCrary; Robert Joy; Paul Winfield; Robert Prosky; Jerzy Skolimowski; *D:* Robert Mandel; *W:* Joe Eszterhas; *M:* Bruce Broughton.

Big Shot's Funeral 🦴 *Da Wan* **2001 (PG)** American director Don Tyler (Sutherland) is on location in Beijing when he suffers a serious health crisis and winds up in the hospital. He tells cameraman YoYo (Ge) that should he die, he wants a blow-out funeral, which YoYo promises to arrange. Since he has no money, YoYo auctions off advertising and sponsorships for the funeral but then Don begins to improve. Would-be comedy has very few laughs. English and Manderin with subtitles. **100m/C; VHS, DVD.** *CH* Donald Sutherland; Ge You; Rosamund Kwan; Da(nniel) Ying; Paul Mazursky; ***D:*** Feng Xiao Gang; ***W:*** Feng Xiao Gang; ***C:*** Li Zhang; ***M:*** San Bao.

The Big Sick 🦴🦴🦴 1/2 **2017 (R)** Based on the true romance between co-star and co-writer Kumail Nanjiani and his off-screen co-writer wife (Gordon), this rom-com charms its way over interracial, intercultural, and inter-religious hurdles. Pakistani comic Kumail hooks up with Caucasian grad student Emily (Kazan), and love blossoms, a love they keep secret from their families until Emily's medically induced coma forces Kumail to navigate the relationship landmine on his own. Director Apatow uses dry humor, touching moments, and likeable leads that will have you rooting for these two crazy kids. **120m/C; DVD, Blu-Ray.** Kumail Nanjiani; Zoe Kazan; Holly Hunter; Ray Romano; Anupam Kher; ***D:*** Michael Showalter; ***W:*** Kumail Nanjiani; Emily V. Gordon; ***C:*** Brian Burgoyne; ***M:*** Michael Andrews. Ind. Spirit '18: First Screenplay.

The Big Sleep 🦴🦴🦴🦴 **1946** Private eye Philip Marlowe, hired to protect a young woman from her own indiscretions, falls in love with her older sister while uncovering murders galore. A dense, chaotic thriller that succeeded in defining and setting a standard for its genre. The very best Raymond Chandler on film combining a witty script with great performances, especially from Bogart and Bacall. **114m/B; VHS, DVD, Blu-Ray.** Humphrey Bogart; Lauren Bacall; John Ridgely; Martha Vickers; Louis Jean Heydt; Regis Toomey; Peggy Knudsen; Dorothy Malone; Bob Steele; Elisha Cook, Jr.; ***D:*** Howard Hawks; ***W:*** William Faulkner; Jules Furthman; Leigh Brackett; ***C:*** Sidney Hickox; ***M:*** Max Steiner. Natl. Film Reg. '97.

The Big Sleep 🦴🦴 **1978 (R)** A tired remake of the Raymond Chandler potboiler about exhausted Los Angeles private dick Marlowe and his problems in protecting a wild young heiress from her own decadence and mob connections. Mitchum appears to need a rest. **99m/C; VHS, DVD, Blu-Ray.** Robert Mitchum; Sarah Miles; Richard Boone; Candy Clark; Edward Fox; Joan Collins; John Mills; James Stewart; Oliver Reed; Harry Andrews; James Donald; Colin Blakely; Richard Todd; ***D:*** Michael Winner; ***W:*** Michael Winner.

The Big Slice 🦴 1/2 **1990 (R)** Two would-be crime novelists want to improve their fiction. One masquerades as a cop, the other as a crook, and they infiltrate the underworld from both ends. Clever comedy premise, but vaudeville-level jokes fall flat. **86m/C; VHS, DVD.** Casey Siemaszko; Leslie Hope; Justin Louis; Heather Locklear; Kenneth Welsh; Nicholas (Nick) Campbell; Henry Ramer; ***D:*** John Bradshaw; ***W:*** John Bradshaw; ***M:*** Mychael Danna; Jeff Danna.

The Big Sombrero 🦴🦴 1/2 **1949** Autry takes a stand against the marriage between an unsuspecting, wealthy Mexican girl and the fortune-seeking bridegroom who wants her land. **77m/C; VHS, DVD.** Gene Autry; Elena Verdugo; Steve (Stephen) Dunne; George Lewis; ***D:*** Frank McDonald.

The Big Squeeze 🦴🦴 1/2 **1996 (R)** Married bartender Tanya (Boyle) is displeased to find out her born-again hubby Henry (Bercovici) has been holding out a large wad of cash from an insurance settlement, apparently about to donate it to a local Spanish mission. Enter Benny (Dobson), a cocky con man willing to help Tanya get her share of the dough for his own cut; sweet bartender Jesse (Nucci), who's secretly in love in Tanya; and fellow barmaid Cece (Dispina), who catches Benny's wandering eye. All get caught up in the frantic doubledealing. **100m/C; VHS, DVD.** Lara Flynn Boyle; Peter Dobson; Luca Bercovici; Danny Nucci; Teresa Dispina; Sam Vlahos; Valente Rodriguez; ***D:*** Marcus De Leon; ***W:*** Marcus De Leon; ***C:*** Jacques Haitkin; ***M:*** Mark Mothersbaugh.

Big Stan 🦴🦴 **2007 (R)** Surprisingly funny prison comedy from Schneider (who also directs) as long as you don't expect too much. Con man Stan (Schneider) gets convicted of fraud but the judge postpones his sentence for six months. Naturally worried about how he'll survive in the joint, the weakling enlists martial arts guru The Master (a deadpan Carradine) to teach him defensive skills. Stan's transformation leads to his becoming a leader among the inmates, much to the displeasure of crooked warden Gasque (Wilson). **105m/C; DVD.** Rob Schneider; Scott Wilson; David Carradine; Jennifer (Jenny) Morrison; M. Emmet Walsh; Richard Kind; Henry Gibson; Sally Kirkland; Dan Haggerty; Marcia Wallace; Kevin Gage; Bob Sapp; ***D:*** Rob Schneider; ***W:*** Josh Lieb; ***C:*** Victor Hammer; ***M:*** John Hunter.

Big Star: Nothing Can Hurt Me 🦴🦴🦴 **2013 (PG-13)** Big Star may be the most popular band that most people have never heard of. They founded a style of alternative pop music that inspired The Replacements (who even wrote a hit song about their frontman, Alex Chilton), R.E.M., The Flaming Lips, and many more. But they never really became the household name that so many music insiders thought they could and should be. DeNicola and Mori's very enjoyable documentary runs a little long (nearly two hours) but captures the adoration of a band who made it big without ever really making it famous. **113m/C; DVD, Blu-Ray.** ***D:*** Drew DeNicola; Olivia Mori; ***C:*** Drew DeNicola.

Big Steal 🦴🦴🦴 **1949** An Army officer recovers a missing payroll and captures the thieves after a tumultuous chase through Mexico. **72m/B; VHS, DVD.** Robert Mitchum; William Bendix; Jane Greer; Ramon Novarro; Patric Knowles; Don Alvarado; John Qualen; ***D:*** Donald Siegel; ***W:*** Daniel Mainwaring; Gerald Drayson Adams; ***C:*** Harry Wild; ***M:*** Leigh Harline.

Big Stone Gap 🦴🦴 1/2 **2015 (PG-13)** A romantic comedy set in small town America. In 1978, Ave Maria Mulligan (Judd) is an ordinary woman leading an ordinary life. Living with her mother, she owns a pharmacy, directs local theater, and hopes a best friendship with Jack MacChesney (Wilson) will become romantic. As she waits and waits, she turns 40 and decides that she will be a spinster and happiness is for others. Her life is changed forever when a family secret comes to light. **103m/C; DVD, Blu-Ray, Streaming, Download.** Ashley Judd; Patrick Wilson; Whoopi Goldberg; Judith Ivey; John Benjamin Hickey; ***D:*** Adriana Trigiani; ***W:*** Adriana Trigiani; ***C:*** Reynaldo Villalobos; ***M:*** John Leventhal.

Big Store 🦴🦴 1/2 **1941** Late Marx Brothers in which they are detectives in a large metropolitan department store, foiling a hostile takeover and preventing a murder. Their last MGM effort, with some good moments between the Tony Martin song numbers which include "If It's You" and the immortal "Tenement Symphony." Groucho also leads the "Sing While You Sell" number. **96m/B; VHS, DVD.** Groucho Marx; Harpo Marx; Chico Marx; Tony Martin; Margaret Dumont; Virginia Grey; Virginia O'Brien; Douglass Dumbrille; Marion Martin; Henry Armetta; ***D:*** Charles Reisner; ***W:*** Hal Fimberg; Ray Golden; Sid Kuller; ***C:*** Charles Lawton, Jr.; ***M:*** George Bassman.

Big Street 🦴🦴 1/2 **1942** A timid busboy, in love with a disinterested nightclub singer, gets to prove his devotion when she is crippled in a fall. Based on a Damon Runyon story, "Little Pinks." **88m/B; DVD.** Henry Fonda; Lucille Ball; Agnes Moorehead; Louise Beavers; Barton MacLane; Eugene Pallette; Ozzie Nelson; ***D:*** Irving Reis; ***W:*** Leonard Spigelgass; ***C:*** Russell Metty; ***M:*** Roy Webb.

Big Sur 🦴🦴 **2013 (R)** Polish's unstructured narrative, based on the 1962 autobiographical novel by Jack Kerouac (featuring his literary alter-ego Jack Duluoz). In 1960, an alcohol-ravaged Kerouac still can't deal with the public attention brought on by the success of his novel "On the Road." Writer Lawrence Ferlinghetti offers Jack his remote cabin at Big Sur for a getaway, but the writer is soon lonely and heads to San Francisco to carouse with friends, bringing them back to the cabin to party. These include Neal Casady and his mistress, Billie, with whom Kerouac is soon involved although his personal demons continue to sabotage his life. **100m/C; DVD.** Jean-Marc Barr; Josh(ua) Lucas; Kate (Catherine) Bosworth; Radha Mitchell; Anthony Edwards; Balthazar Getty; Henry Thomas; Patrick Fischler; ***D:*** Michael Polish; ***W:*** Michael Polish; ***C:*** M. David Mullen; ***M:*** Aaron Dessner; Bryce Dessner.

The Big Take 🦴🦴 1/2 **2018** When aspiring producer Vic (Holmgren) gets brushed off by famous actor Douglas Brown (McCaffery), Vic gets revenge by drugging him and making a video of him with a transgender hooker. Using the footage as blackmail, Vic gets the backing he needs for a film he wants to make with screenwriter Max (Moss-Bachrach). Max and his wife Oxana (Lada) have no idea about the blackmail, but find themselves in increasingly deeper trouble as Douglas, his agent (Sage), their private detective (Hedaya), and a hitwoman (Bell) try to end the scheme. Director Daly's debut film is a solid comedy-thriller that benefits from a strong cast. **83m/C; DVD.** James McCaffrey; Ebon Moss-Bachrach; Zoe Bell; Robert Forster; Dan Hedaya; ***D:*** Justin Daly; ***W:*** Justin Daly; ***C:*** Andreas Von Scheele.

The Big Tease 🦴🦴 **1999 (R)** Gay Glasgow hairdresser Crawford Mackenzie (Ferguson) thinks he's being asked to compete in the prestigious World Freestyle Hairdressing Championship being held in Los Angeles. So he heads to Hollywood and discovers he's just been asked to observe. Blithely self-confident, Crawford simply decides he will not only find a way to enter but he will defeat his snippy Swedish rival, Stig (Rasche). Good-natured, campy fluff. **86m/C; VHS, DVD.** *GB* Kevin Allen; Craig Ferguson; Frances Fisher; Chris Langham; Mary McCormack; Donal Logue; Larry Miller; David Rasche; Charles Napier; David Hasselhoff; Cathy Lee Crosby; Bruce Jenner; Isabella Aitken; ***D:*** Kevin Allen; ***W:*** Craig Ferguson; Sacha Gervasi; ***C:*** Seamus McGarvey; ***M:*** Mark Thomas.

Big Time Adolescence 🦴🦴 1/2 **2020 (R)** Impressionable high school student Mo (Gluck) looks up to Zeke (Davidson), a slightly older screw-up who used to date Mo's sister Kate (Arlook). The more he hangs out with Zeke and Zeke's smoking and drinking friends, the more Mo acts like Zeke to gain the popularity he desires. Though it begins with repeating Zeke's jokes, Mo later tries a crude strategy of Zeke's to get schoolmate Sophie (Laurence) to like him back before traveling further down a destructive path. The leads give this its comedic backbone, particularly Davidson, even if it's a bit rough around the edges. **91m/C; DVD.** Griffin Gluck; Emily Arlook; Michael Devine; Pete Davidson; Jon Cryer; ***D:*** Jason Orley; ***W:*** Jason Orley; ***C:*** Andrew Huebscher; ***M:*** Zachary Dawes; Nick Sena.

Big Top Pee-wee 🦴🦴 **1988 (PG)** Pee-wee's second feature film following the success of "Pee-wee's Big Adventure." This time Pee-wee owns a farm, has a girlfriend (!) and lives the good life until a weird storm blows a traveling circus onto his property. Cute, but not the manic hilarity the first one was. **86m/C; VHS, DVD.** Paul (Pee-wee Herman) Reubens; Kris Kristofferson; Susan Tyrrell; Penelope Ann Miller; ***D:*** Randal Kleiser; ***W:*** Paul (Pee-wee Herman) Reubens; ***C:*** Steven Poster; ***M:*** Danny Elfman.

Big Town 🦴🦴 1/2 **1987 (R)** A farmboy, lucky with dice, hits Chicago to claim his fortune where he meets floozies, criminals, and other streetlife. Standard '50s period underworld drama is elevated by exceptional cast's fine ensemble work. Look for Lane's strip number. **109m/C; VHS, DVD.** Matt Dillon; Diane Lane; Tommy Lee Jones; Bruce Dern; Tom Skerritt; Lee Grant; Suzy Amis; David Marshall Grant; Don Francks; Del Close; Cherry Jones; David James Elliot; Don Lake; Diego Matamoros; Gary Farmer; Sarah Polley; Lolita Davidovich; ***D:*** Ben Bolt; Harold Becker; ***W:*** Robert Roy Pool; ***C:*** Ralf Bode; ***M:*** Michael Melvoin.

The Big Trail 🦴🦴🦴 **1930** This pioneering effort in widescreen cinematography was Wayne's first feature film. A wagon train on the Oregon trail encounters Indians, buffalo, tough terrain, and romantic problems. **110m/B; DVD, Beta, Blu-Ray.** John Wayne; Marguerite Churchill; El Brendel; Tully Marshall; Tyrone Power, Sr.; Ward Bond; Helen Parrish; ***D:*** Raoul Walsh. Natl. Film Reg. '06.

Big Trees 🦴🦴🦴 **1952** A ruthless lumberman attempts a takeover of the California Redwood Timberlands that are owned by a group of peaceful homesteaders. **89m/C; VHS, DVD.** Kirk Douglas; Patrice Wymore; Eve Miller; Alan Hale, Jr.; Edgar Buchanan; ***D:*** Felix Feist.

Big Trouble 🦴🦴 **1986 (R)** An insurance broker endeavors to send his three sons to Yale by conspiring with a crazy couple in a fraud scheme that goes awry in every possible manner. Look for the cameo by screenwriter Bergman as Warren Bogle. **93m/C; VHS, DVD.** Alan Arkin; Peter Falk; Beverly D'Angelo; Charles Durning; Robert Stack; Paul Dooley; Valerie Curtin; Richard Libertini; ***Cameo(s):*** Andrew Bergman; ***D:*** John Cassavetes; ***W:*** Andrew Bergman; ***C:*** Bill Butler; ***M:*** Bill Conti.

Big Trouble 🦴🦴 **2002 (PG-13)** Fast-paced ensemble comedy based on the novel by Dave Barry packs a metric ton of narrative, not to mention characters, into a mere 84 minutes, most of which involve the clash of various characters tracking down a nuclear bomb in Miami. Suburban Anna (Russo) is trapped in a loveless marriage with unscrupulous businessman Arthur Herk (Tucci) who wants to buy a nuclear bomb, thus getting involved with some undesirable characters, most notably two hit men (Farina and Kehler). The plot kicks off when Matt (Foster), the son of divorced journalist Allen decides to snipe the Herk's daughter Jenny (Deschanel) with a high-powered squirt gun on the same night the hit men visit. Of the strong cast, Allen and Foster are the standouts. Cartoony, heavy-handed direction buries satire for which Barry is known. **84m/C; VHS, DVD, Blu-Ray.** Tim Allen; Rene Russo; Stanley Tucci; Tom Sizemore; Johnny Knoxville; Dennis Farina; Jack Kehler; Janeane Garofalo; Patrick Warburton; Ben Foster; Zooey Deschanel; Dwight "Heavy D" Myers; Omar Epps; Jason Lee; Andy Richter; Sofia Vergara; ***D:*** Barry Sonnenfeld; ***W:*** Robert Ramsey; Matthew Stone; ***C:*** Greg Gardiner; ***M:*** James Newton Howard.

Big Trouble in Little China 🦴🦴 1/2 **1986 (PG-13)** A trucker plunges beneath the streets of San Francisco's Chinatown to battle an army of spirits. An uproarious comic-book-film parody with plenty of action and a keen sense of sophomoric sarcasm. **99m/C; VHS, DVD, Blu-Ray, UMD.** Kurt Russell; Suzee Pai; Dennis Dun; Kim Cattrall; James Hong; Victor Wong; Kate Burton; ***D:*** John Carpenter; ***W:*** David Weinstein; Gary Goldman; W.D. Richter; ***C:*** Dean Cundey; ***M:*** John Carpenter; Alan Howarth.

The Big Turnaround 🦴 1/2 *Turnaround* **1988** Drug-dealing punks push their goods into Mexico via a lowly southwest town but local do-gooders led by a struggling doctor (Cranston, whose father, Joseph, serves as director and producer) and a priest (Borgnine) boldly unite to save the day in this misguided effort. **98m/C; VHS, DVD.** Mindi Miller; Michael J. Reynolds; Robert Axelrod; Robert V. Barron; Ernest Borgnine; Bryan Cranston; Luis Latino; Rick Le Fever; Ruben Castillo; Al Fleming; Stu Weltman; ***D:*** Joseph L. Cranston; ***W:*** Luis Johnston; ***C:*** Karen Grossman; ***M:*** Jasmin Larkin. **VIDEO**

The Big Wedding 🦴 **2013 (R)** Abrasively awful even by the standards of this subgenre of bad wedding comedies, director/writer Zackham's film only serves to prove the truth that a spectacular cast means nothing if the script wastes their talent. Don and Ellie Griffin (De Niro & Keaton) are forced to pretend to be a happy couple to keep their adopted son's family happy at the wedding. Sarandon, Heigl, Williams, Topher Grace, and Seyfried get sucked into a script that feels created by a computer program that started with the keyword "contrived." **89m/C; DVD, Blu-Ray.** Robert De Niro; Diane Keaton; Ben Barnes; Amanda Seyfried; Susan Sarandon; Robin Williams; Katherine Heigl; Topher Grace; Marc Blucas; Christine Ebersole; ***D:*** Justin Zackham; ***W:*** Justin Zackham; ***C:*** Jonathan Brown; ***M:*** Nathan Barr.

Big Wednesday 🦴🦴 1/2 *Summer of Innocence* **1978 (PG)** Three California surfers from the early '60s get back together after the Vietnam war to reminisce about the good old days and take on the big wave. **120m/C; VHS, DVD, Blu-Ray.** Jan-Michael Vincent; Gary Busey; William Katt; Lee Purcell; Patti D'Arbanville; ***D:*** John Milius; ***W:*** John Milius; ***M:*** Basil Poledouris.

The Big Wheel 🦴🦴 1/2 **1949** Old story retold fairly well. Rooney is young son determined to travel in his father's tracks as a race car driver, even when dad buys the farm on the oval. Good acting and direction keep this a cut above average. **92m/B; VHS, DVD.** Mickey Rooney; Thomas Mitchell; Spring Byington; Mary Hatcher; Allen Jenkins; Michael O'Shea; ***D:*** Edward Ludwig.

The Big White 🦴 1/2 **2005 (R)** A waste of talent in a lame comedy. Alaska travel agent Paul Barnell (Williams) has money problems. Then he finds a frozen body in a dumpster. Paul hopes to pass the body off as his estranged brother Raymond (Harrelson) and collect the life insurance, but agent Ted (Ribisi) is suspicious. Add in Paul's troubled wife Margaret (Hunter), the sudden return of Raymond, and a couple of wannabe kidnapper/hitmen (Nelson, Brown) and Paul's got more complications than he can handle. **105m/C; DVD, Blu-Ray.** *US CA NZ* Robin Williams; Holly Hunter; Woody Harrelson; Tim Blake Nelson; Giovanni Ribisi; W. Earl Brown; Alison Lohman; ***D:*** Mark Mylod; ***W:*** Collin Friesen; ***C:*** James Gleason; ***M:*** Mark Mothersbaugh.

The Big Year 🦴🦴 1/2 **2011 (PG)** Quirky comedy explores the offbeat world of competitive bird-watching (or "birding" as they very seriously call it). Champion birder Bostick (Wilson) neglects his wife while trying to fend off his competition. Right on his tailfeathers are stuffy CEO Stu (Martin) and goofy loser Brad (Black). The trio jet off to beautifully photographed locales in their quest to spot the most birds in one year, with alliances and friendships shifting. More pleasantly whimsical than laugh-out-loud funny, it's a family-friendly change of pace. Based on Mark Obmascik's 1998 book "The Big Year: A Tale of Man, Nature, and Fowl Obsession." **100m/C; DVD.** Steve Martin; Jack Black; Owen Wilson; Rashida Jones; Anjelica Huston; Rosamund Pike; JoBeth Williams; Brian Dennehy; Dianne Wiest; Jim Parsons; Joel McHale; Kevin Pollak; ***D:*** David Frankel; ***W:*** Howard Franklin; ***C:*** Lawrence Sher; ***M:*** Theodore Shapiro.

The Bigamist 🦴 1/2 **1953** Have you heard the one about the traveling salesman in this movie? He has one wife in Los Angeles, another in San Francisco, and they inevitably find out about each other. A maudlin soap opera with a do-it-yourself ending, only shows why bigamy was done better as farce in the later "Micki and Maude." **79m/B; DVD, Blu-Ray.** Edmond O'Brien; Joan Fontaine; Ida Lupino; Edmund Gwenn; Jane Darwell; Kenneth Tobey; ***D:*** Ida Lupino; ***W:*** Collier Young; ***C:*** George E. Diskant; ***M:*** Leith Stevens.

Bigfoot 🦴 **1970** Some bikers go hiking and find a Bigfoot partially buried in a grave. Something then beats everyone unconscious and steals the women-folk. The lesson here being let sleeping Bigfoots lie and watch out for Bigfoot's minions (yes, apparently he has furry minions). **84m/C; DVD.** John Carradine; John Mitchum; James Craig; Christopher Mitchum; Joi Lansing; Judith Jordan; ***D:*** Robert F. Slatzer; ***W:*** Robert F. Slatzer; James Gordon White; ***C:*** Wilson S. Hong; ***M:*** Richard A. Podolor. **VIDEO**

Bigfoot: The Lost Coast Tapes 🦴 1/2 *The Lost Coast Tapes* **2012 (R)** Found footage mockumentary about an attempted comeback by an investigative journalist attempting to expose hoaxes and frauds. His first target is a hunter who claims to have the world's first real Sasquatch corpse. **87m/C; DVD, Blu-Ray, Streaming.** Drew Rausch; Rich McDonald; Ashley Wood; Noah Weisberg; Frank Ashmore; ***D:*** Corey Grant; ***W:*** Brian Kelsey; Bryan O'Cain; ***C:*** Richard J. Vialet; ***M:*** Eddie Booze. **VIDEO**

Bigfoot: The Unforgettable Encounter 🦴🦴 1/2 **1994 (PG)** Young boy heads off into the woods, comes face to face with Bigfoot, and sets off a media frenzy and a band of ruthless bounty hunters determined to capture his hairy friend. **89m/C; VHS, DVD.** Zachery Ty Bryan; Matt McCoy; Barbara Willis Sweete; Clint Howard; Rance Howard; David Rasche; ***D:*** Corey Michael Eubanks; ***W:*** Corey Michael Eubanks; ***M:*** Shimon Arama.

A Bigger Splash 🦴🦴 1/2 **2015 (R)** Rock star Marianne Lane (Swinton) has retreated to a sunny Mediterranean island with her much younger boyfriend, photographer/documentarian Paul (Schoenaerts), to rest and restore her voice. They are visited by record producer Harry (Fiennes), Marianne's long-time friend and former lover, and Penelope (Johnson), the young adult daughter Harry only recently learned he had. As the days pass, the weather turns and tensions increase to a breaking point. The intense interactions of the four leads offer a riveting contrast to the beautiful cinematography in this extreme erotic thriller. **125m/C; DVD.** Tilda Swinton; Matthias Schoenaerts; Ralph Fiennes; Dakota Johnson; Aurore Clement; ***D:*** Luca Guadagnino; ***W:*** David Kajganich; ***C:*** Yorick Le Saux.

Bigger Stronger Faster 🦴🦴 1/2 **2008 (PG-13)** Director Bell grew up in the mid 1980s, an era of steroid-enhanced wrestlers and bodybuilding actors, and his commentary on how America's obsession with winning might be destroying it is filled with ambivalence towards the fate of juiced athletes, including his two brothers. Much time is spent attempting to debunk the dangers of steroids, and the rest is devoted to the idea that the ideal of winning at any cost is the real danger. **107m/C; DVD.** Chris Bell; ***D:*** Chris Bell; ***W:*** Chris Bell; Alexander Buono; Tamsin Rawady; ***C:*** Alexander Buono; ***M:*** Dave Porter. **VIDEO**

Bigger Than the Sky 🦴🦴 1/2 **2005 (PG-13)** Recently-dumped Peter (Thomas), stuck in a lousy dead-end job, decides he needs something new. He tries out for the community theatre and finds what he's looking for through company regulars Michael (Corbett) and Grace (Smart). A very mild romantic comedy that almost works. Anyone involve in small theatre will relish in the details. Features Patty Duke playing mother to her real-life son, Sean Astin. **106m/C; VHS, DVD.** Marcus Thomas; John Corbett; Amy Smart; Sean Astin; Clare Higgins; Patty Duke; Allan Corduner; Matt Salinger; Greg Germann; ***D:*** Al Corley; ***W:*** Rodney Vaccaro; ***C:*** Christine Gentet; ***M:*** Rob Cairns. **VIDEO**

The Biggest Bundle of Them All 🦴 1/2 **1968** An inept group of criminals kidnap aged mobster Cesare Celli only to discover he's broke and can't pay the ransom. He offers to cut them in on a heist, but their inexperience causes problems in this hit-or-miss crime comedy. At least Raquel Welch appears in a bikini. **105m/C; DVD.** Vittorio De Sica; Raquel Welch; Robert Wagner; Godfrey Cambridge; Davy Kaye; Francesco Mule; Edward G. Robinson; ***D:*** Ken Annakin; ***W:*** Sy Salkowitz; ***C:*** Piero Portalupi; ***M:*** Riz Ortolani.

The Biggest Fan 🦴 1/2 **2002** Silly teen romance about a fan and a boy band. Shy high school sophomore Debbie (Amariah) is the number one fan of Dream Street. Disappointed at missing their local concert, Debbie wakes up the next morning to a huge shock—she finds lead singer Chris Trousdale (playing himself) passed out in her room! Loopy from cold medicine, Chris missed the concert and stumbled around until he found a convenient place to crash. Debbie agrees to hide the dreamboat, who needs a timeout from all that squealing and screaming, but what if her parents find out? **95m/C; DVD.** Marissa Tait; Richard Moll; Noriyuki "Pat" Morita; Michael Meyer; Kaila Amariah; Chris Trousdale; Morgan Brittany; Leslie Easterbrook; Jesse McCartney; Shanelle Workman; Cindy Williams; ***D:*** Michael Criscione; ***W:*** Michael Criscione; LeeAnn Kemp; Liz Sinclair; ***C:*** Wes Llewellyn. **VIDEO**

The Biggest Little Farm 🦴🦴🦴 **2018 (PG)** The documentary follows two upper middle class professionals who leave their lives as documentary filmmaker and chef/organic food blogger behind. Moving from Los Angeles, the couple, John and Molly Chester, establishes an environmentally conscious, old-fashioned farm in Moorpark, California, dubbed Apricot Lane Farms. Chronicles the highs and lows of the Chester's efforts to create a farm that uses the principles of biodiversity to raise crops and livestock, emphasizing the difficult issues they face in everyday life on the farm. Often fascinating and insightful, it shows the hard work it takes to keep their dream alive. **91m/C; DVD, Blu-Ray.** John Chester; Molly Chester; ***D:*** John Chester; ***W:*** John Chester; Mark Monroe; ***C:*** John Chester; Mallory Cunningham; Benji Lanpher; Chris Martin; Kyle Romanek; ***M:*** Jeff Beal.

Biggie & Tupac: The Story Behind the Murder of Rap's Biggest Superstars 🦴🦴 1/2 **2002 (R)** This feature-length documentary, created by Nick Broomfield ("Kurt & Courtney"), examines the lives and untimely deaths of two rap icons: Tupac Shakur and Christopher Wallace (known as Biggie Smalls and Notorious B.I.G.). In addition to looking at the careers of both artists, Broomfield offers the theory that producer Suge Knight is responsible for the murder of both men. The documentary includes interviews with employees of Death Row Records, the authorities, and Knight himself. **108m/C; DVD, Streaming, Download.** ***D:*** Nick Broomfield; ***C:*** Joan Churchill; ***M:*** Christian Henson.

Biggles 🦴🦴 *Biggles: Adventures in Time* **1985 (PG)** Time-travel fantasy in which a young businessman from present-day New York City is inexplicably transferred into the identity of a 1917 WWI flying ace. He suddenly finds himself aboard a fighter plane over Europe during WWI. **100m/C; VHS, DVD, Blu-Ray.** *GB* Neil Dickson; Alex Hyde-White; Peter Cushing; ***D:*** John Hough.

Biker Boyz 🦴🦴 1/2 **2003 (PG-13)** Kid (Luke) is the hotshot teenager biker who challenges Smoke (Fishburne) the long-time reigning "King of Cali." Often referred to as "The Fast and the Furious" on motorcycles, but doesn't achieve the same level of entertainment. Soap opera subplots and cliched dialogue don't help. Then again, "Furious" had the same problems and managed to make a boatload of cash. The actors, however, do a good job with a so-so script, and Luke is fast becoming an actor worth noticing. **111m/C; VHS, DVD.** Laurence Fishburne; Derek Luke; Orlando Jones; Djimon Hounsou; Lisa Bonet; Brendan Fehr; Larenz Tate; Kid Rock; Rick Gonzalez; Meagan Good; Salli Richardson-Whitfield; Vanessa Bell Calloway; Eriq La Salle; Titus Welliver; Kadeem Hardison; Terrence Howard; Tyson Beckford; ***D:*** Reggie Rock Bythewood; ***W:*** Reggie Rock Bythewood; Craig Ferandez; ***C:*** Greg Gardiner; ***M:*** Camara Kambon.

Bikini Beach 🦴🦴 1/2 **1964** Surfing teenagers of the "Beach Party" series follow up "Muscle Beach Party" with a third fling at the beach and welcome a visitor, British recording star "Potato Bug" (Avalon in a campy dual role). But, golly gee, wealthy Wynn wants to turn their sandy, surfin' shores into a retirement community. What to do? Sing a few songs, dance in your bathing suits, and have fun. Classic early '60s nostalgia is better than the first two efforts; followed by "Pajama Party." **100m/C; VHS, DVD.** Annette Funicello; Frankie Avalon; Martha Hyer; Harvey Lembeck; Don Rickles; Stevie Wonder; John Ashley; Keenan Wynn; Jody McCrea; Candy Johnson; Danielle Aubry; Meredith MacRae; Dolores Wells; Donna Loren; Timothy Carey; Boris Karloff; ***D:*** William Asher; ***W:*** William Asher; Leo Townsend; Robert Dillon; ***C:*** Floyd Crosby; ***M:*** Les Baxter.

Bikini Bistro 🦴 **1994 (R)** A boring vegetarian cafe gets turned into a gourmet restaurant but, faced with an eviction notice, the female owners decide to increase business by waitressing in bikinis. Also available in an unrated version at 84 minutes. **80m/C; VHS, DVD.** Marilyn Chambers; Amy Lynn Baxter; Joan Gerardi; Isabelle Fortea; John Altamura; Joseph Pallister; ***D:*** Ernest G. Sauer; ***W:*** Matt Unger.

Bikini Bloodbath 🦴 **2006** Parody of 80s slasher movies where a group of teenage girls hold a slumber party after graduation while a serial-killing chef is on the loose. Standing between them and death is their lesbian gym teacher Miss Johnson (Rochon). **73m/C; DVD, Streaming.** Robert Cosgrove, Jr.; Russ Russo; Debbie Rochon; Sheri Lynn; Leah Ford; ***D:*** Jonathan Gorman; Thomas Edward Seymour; ***W:*** Jonathan Gorman; Thomas Edward Seymour; ***C:*** Mike Anderson; ***M:*** Tim Kulig. **VIDEO**

Bikini Bloodbath Carwash 🦴 1/2 *Bikini Bloodbath Car Wash* **2008** College girls in need of money hold a carwash, little suspecting that a killer chef is about to be resurrected from the dead as a zombie and begin harrassing them. Fortunately their house matron is Miss Johnson (Rochon), the seemingly indestructible woman who helped kill him the first time. **72m/C; DVD, Streaming.** Thomas Edward Seymour; Russ Russo; Robert Cosgrove, Jr.; Debbie Rochon; Sheri Lynn; ***D:*** Thomas Edward Seymour; Jonathan Gorman; ***W:*** Thomas Edward Seymour; Jonathan Gorman; ***C:*** Mike Anderson. **VIDEO**

Bikini Bloodbath Christmas 🦴 **2009** Miss Johnson (Rochon) returns to battle the evil zombie chef who likes killing the girls she loves so much. Apparently the filmmakers think one of the advantages of being a lesbian is immortality considering that she was killed in the previous films of this trilogy. **71m/C; DVD, Streaming.** Lloyd Kaufman; Matt Ford; Thomas Edward Seymour; Jonathan Gorman; Debbie Rochon; Sheri Lynn; ***D:*** Thomas Edward Seymour; Jonathan Gorman; ***W:*** Thomas Edward Seymour; Jonathan Gorman; ***C:*** Mike Anderson; ***M:*** Glen Gabriel. **VIDEO**

The Bikini Car Wash Company **WOOF!** *California Hot Wax* **1990 (R)** Babes in bikinis in Los Angeles. A young man is running his uncle's carwash when he meets a business major who persuades him to let her take over the business for a cut of the profits. She decides that a good gimmick would be to dress all the female employees in the tiniest bikinis possible. The story is of course secondary to the amount of flesh on display. Also available in an unrated version. **87m/C; VHS, DVD.** Joe Dusic; Neriah Napaul; Sara Suzanne Brown; Kristie Ducati; ***D:*** Ed Hansen.

The Bikini Car Wash Company 2 🦴 **1992 (R)** Entrepreneur Melissa and the other lovely ladies of the Bikini Car Wash Co. find themselves a big success, so much so that a greedy businessman wants to buy them out. In order to get money to fight the takeover, the ladies take to the airwaves of a cable-access station. Their new business adventure involves selling sexy lingerie which means the flesh quotient is as great as ever. An unrated version is also available. **94m/C; VHS, DVD.** Kristie Ducati; Sara Suzanne Brown; Neriah Napaul; Rikki Brando; Greg Raye; Larry De Russy; ***D:*** Gary Orona; ***W:*** Bart B. Gustis; ***M:*** Michael Smith.

Bikini Drive-In 🦴 1/2 **1994 (R)** Babe (Rhey) inherits grandad's decrepit drive-in, which is wanted by a mall mogul, but she refuses to sell. So to raise some cash, Rhey stages a B-movie marathon with in-person, bikini-clad scream queens. **85m/C; VHS, DVD.** Ashlie Rhey; Richard Gabai; Ross Hagen; Sara Bellomo; Steve Barkett; Conrad Brooks; ***D:*** Fred Olen Ray.

Bikini House Calls 🦴 **1996** The students of Bikini Med School love anatomy as much as they love to party. In fact, combining both activities is their idea of a perfect time. **87m/C; VHS, DVD.** Thomas Draper; Sean Abbananto; Kim (Kimberly Dawn) Dawson; Tamara Landry; ***D:*** Michael Paul Girard; ***W:*** Michael Paul Girard; ***C:*** Denis Maloney; ***M:*** Miriam Cutler. **VIDEO**

Bikini Med School 🦴 **1998** So how do med students get rid of all that nasty tension? Why they party, of course! And practice playing doctor with all the nubile lovelies they can. **87m/C; VHS, DVD.** Kim (Kimberly Dawn) Dawson; Tamara Landry; Thomas Draper; Sean Abbananto; ***D:*** Michael Paul Girard; ***W:*** Michael Paul Girard; ***C:*** Denis Maloney; ***M:*** Miriam Cutler. **VIDEO**

Bikini Summer 🦴 1/2 **1991** Laughs, music, and skin are the order of the day as two nutty guys and a few beautiful girls form an unlikely friendship on the beach. Konop was Julia Robert's "Pretty Woman" body double. Sort of the '90s version of the old '60s Frankie and Annette beach parties. **90m/C; VHS, DVD.** David Millbern; Melinda Armstrong; Jason Clow; Shelley Michelle; Alex Smith; Kent Lipham; Kelly Konop; Carmen Santa Maria; ***D:*** Robert Veze; ***W:*** Robert Veze; Nick Stone; ***M:*** John Gonzalez.

Bikini Summer 2 🦴 **1992 (R)** An eccentric family decides to stage a bikini contest to raise money to help the homeless. **94m/C; VHS, DVD, On Demand.** Jeff Conaway; Jessica Hahn; Melinda Armstrong; Avalon Anders; ***D:*** Jeff Conaway; ***M:*** Jim Halfpenny.

Bikini Summer 3: South Beach Heat 🦴 **1997 (R)** Babes in bikinis frolic on Miami's fashionable South Beach for the chance to become the spokesmodel for Mermaid Body Splash. **84m/C; VHS, DVD.** Heather-Elizabeth Parkhurst; Tiffany Turner; ***D:*** Ken Blakey.

Bilitis ½ **1977 (R)** A young girl from a private girls' school is initiated into the pleasures of sex and the unexpected demands of love. One of director Hamilton's exploitative meditations on nudity. **95m/C; VHS, DVD.** *FR* Patti D'Arbanville; Bernard Giraudeau; Mona Kristensen; ***D:*** David Hamilton.

Bill **1981** Based on a true story about a mentally retarded man who sets out to live independently after 44 years in an institution. Rooney gives an affecting performance as Bill and Quaid is strong as the filmmaker who befriends him. Awarded Emmys for Rooney's performance and the well written script. Followed by "Bill: On His Own." **97m/C; VHS, DVD.** Mickey Rooney; Dennis Quaid; Largo Woodruff; Harry Goz; ***D:*** Anthony Page. **TV**

Bill & Ted's Bogus Journey **1991 (PG)** Big-budget sequel to B & T's first movie has better special effects but about the same quota of laughs. Slain by lookalike robot duplicates from the future, the airhead heroes pass through heaven and hell before tricking the Grim Reaper into bringing them back for a second duel with their heinous terminators. Most excellent closing-credit montage. Non-fans still won't think much of it. **98m/C; VHS, DVD, Blu-Ray.** Keanu Reeves; Alex Winter; William Sadler; Joss Ackland; Pam Grier; George Carlin; Amy Stock-Poynton; Hal Landon, Jr.; Annette Azcuy; Sarah Trigger; Taj Mahal; Chelcie Ross; Roy Brocksmith; William Shatner; ***D:*** Peter Hewitt; ***W:*** Chris Matheson; Edward Solomon; ***C:*** Oliver Wood; ***M:*** David Newman.

Bill & Ted's Excellent Adventure ½ **1989 (PG)** Excellent premise: when the entire future of the world rests on whether or not two '80s dudes pass their history final, Rufus comes to the rescue in his time-travelling telephone booth. Bill and Ted share an adventure through time as they meet and get to know some of history's most important figures. Lightweight but fun. **105m/C; VHS, DVD, Blu-Ray, UMD.** Keanu Reeves; Alex Winter; George Carlin; Bernie Casey; Dan Shor; Robert V. Barron; Amy Stock-Poynton; Ted Steedman; Terry Camillieri; Rod Loomis; Al Leong; Tony Camilieri; ***D:*** Stephen Herek; ***W:*** Chris Matheson; Edward Solomon; ***C:*** Tim Suhrstedt; ***M:*** David Newman.

Bill Cunningham New York ½ **2010** Octogenarian Bill Cunningham is a New York Times fashion photographer who's obsessed with how people dress: those he sees on the street, at various society functions, and at runway shows. Director Richard Press, cinematographer Tony Cenicola, and producer Philip Gefter followed the dedicated, modest Cunningham around for two years as he offers insights about his work, while friends and colleagues tell their own stories. **84m/C; DVD, Blu-Ray.** ***D:*** Richard Press; ***C:*** Richard Press; Tony Cenicola.

Bill: On His Own **1983** Rooney is again exceptional in this sequel to the Emmy-winning TV movie "Bill." After 44 years in an institution, a mentally retarded man copes more and more successfully with the outside world. Fine supporting cast and direction control the melodramatic potential. **100m/C; VHS, DVD.** Mickey Rooney; Helen Hunt; Teresa Wright; Dennis Quaid; Largo Woodruff; Paul Leiber; Harry Goz; ***D:*** Anthony Page.

Billboard Dad ½ **1998 (G)** The Olsen twins decide it's time for their dad to remarry so they paint a personal ad on a billboard advertising his availability. Eventually, their Dad meets Brooke, who's a winner except for her bratty son who's the girls' rival. But nothing will stop the twins if it means making Dad happy. **90m/C; VHS, DVD, Streaming.** Ashley (Fuller) Olsen; Mary-Kate Olsen; Tom Amandes; Jessica Tuck; Sam Selatta; Carl Banks; ***D:*** Alan Metter; ***W:*** Maria Jacquemetton; ***C:*** Mauro Fiore; ***M:*** David Michael Frank. **VIDEO**

Billie ½ **1965** Duke stars as a tomboy athlete who puts the boys' track team to shame. Some amusing but very predictable situations, plus a few songs from Miss Duke. Based on Ronald Alexander's play "Time Out for Ginger." **86m/C; VHS, DVD.** Patty Duke; Jim Backus; Jane Greer; Warren Berlinger; Billy DeWolfe; Charles Lane; Dick Sargent; Susan Seaforth Hayes; Ted Bessell; Richard Deacon; ***D:*** Don Weis; ***W:*** Ronald Alexander.

Billion Dollar Brain *Operation Espionage* **1967** The third of five films based on the Harry Palmer spy novels by Len Deighton, this one has Michael Caine repeating his performance as British agent Harry Palmer, now a down-on-his-luck private investigator. Forced back into the espionage game, he is sent to deliver a package to an old friend, only to find him now working for a rabid right-wing Texas oil billionaire who has made a super computer running a spy ring dedicated to perpetuating the cold war and destroying the Soviet Union. Confusing and full of triple crosses, it is fairly close to the source material. **111m/C; DVD, Blu-Ray.** *GB* Michael Caine; Karl Malden; Ed Begley, Jr.; Oscar Homolka; Francoise Dorleac; Guy Doleman; Vladek Sheybal; ***D:*** Ken Russell; ***W:*** Len Deighton; John McGrath; ***C:*** Billy Williams; ***M:*** Richard Rodney Bennett.

The Billion Dollar Hobo ½ **1978 (G)** Poor, unsuspecting heir of a multimillion dollar fortune must duplicate his benefactor's experience as a hobo during the Depression in order to collect his inheritance. Slow-moving family stuff. **96m/C; VHS, DVD.** Tim Conway; Will Geer; Eric Weston; Sydney Lassick; ***D:*** Stuart E. McGowan.

A Billion for Boris ½ **1990** Boris' TV gives a sneak preview of the future and Boris plans to make some money off of it. Zany comedy in the vein of "Let It Ride." **89m/C; VHS, DVD.** Lee Grant; Tim Kazurinsky; ***D:*** Alex Grasshof; ***W:*** Mary Rogers.

Billionaire Boys Club ½ **1987** Chilling look at greed in the '80s. Nelson plays Joe Hunt, who gets together with a group of rich, preppie friends to manipulate investments in the commodities markets. When a slick con man (Silver) gets in their way he's murdered to keep their schemes intact. Based on a true story and adapted from the book by Sue Horton. The video version is considerably pared down from the original TV broadcast. **94m/C; VHS, DVD.** Judd Nelson; Frederic Lehne; Brian McNamara; Raphael Sbarge; John Stockwell; Barry Tubb; Stan Shaw; Jill Schoelen; Ron Silver; James Sloyan; James Karen; Dale Dye; ***D:*** Marvin J. Chomsky. **TV**

Billionaire Boys Club **2018 (R)** A remake of the 1987 made-for-TV movie, based on the true story of an investment scam launched by a group of snooty preppies during the 1980s. A superficial and pointless retelling that no one wanted--it made only $126 on its opening day in the United States. **108m/C; DVD.** Ansel Elgort; Taron Egerton; Emma Roberts; Kevin Spacey; Ryan Rottman; ***D:*** James Cox; ***W:*** James Cox; Captain Mauzner; ***C:*** James M. Muro; ***M:*** Joel J. Richard.

Billionaire Ransom *Take Down* **2016** An action thriller about rich kids trying to survive being kidnapped by mercenaries. After acting out, a group of privileged young adults are sent to a tough-love wilderness school by their wealthy parents. Located on a remote island off the coast of Scotland, each person has their own reason for being there. For Kyle (Sumpter) and Amy (Tonkin), they know this is their last chance to become responsible or become disinherited. The situation goes sideways when a group of mercenaries led by Billy Speck (Westwick) invade the island and hold the wildness school attendees for one billion dollars in ransom. The group must use their wilderness training to survive. **107m/C; DVD, Blu-Ray, Streaming, Download.** Jeremy Sumpter; Ed Westwick; Phoebe Tonkin; Dominic Sherwood; Sebastian Koch; ***D:*** Jim Gillespie; ***W:*** Alexander Ignon; ***C:*** Denis Crossan; ***M:*** Hybrid.

Billy Bathgate ½ **1991 (R)** Uneven but well acted drama set in 1935 New York. A street-wise young man decides getting ahead during the Depression means gaining the attention of mobster Dutch Schultz and joining his gang. As Billy becomes the confidant of the racketeer he learns the criminal life is filled with suspicion and violence; in order to stay alive he must rely on every trick he's learned. Willis has a small role as a rival mobster who gets fitted for cement overshoes. Kidman does well as Dutch's girlfriend with Hill fine as the gang's number man. Based on the novel by E.L. Doctorow. **107m/C; VHS, DVD, Blu-Ray.** Dustin Hoffman; Nicole Kidman; Loren Dean; Bruce Willis; Steven Hill; Steve Buscemi; Stanley Tucci; Tim Jerome; Billy Jaye; Katharine Houghton; Mike Starr; John A. Costelloe; Moira Kelly; ***D:*** Robert Benton; ***W:*** Tom Stoppard; ***C:*** Nestor Almendros; ***M:*** Mark Isham.

Billy Budd **1962** The classic Melville good-evil allegory adapted to film, dealing with a British warship in the late 1700s, and its struggle between evil master-at-arms and innocent shipmate. Stamp's screen debut as the naive Billy who is tried for the murder of the sadistic first mate. Well directed and acted. **123m/B; DVD, Blu-Ray; Open Captioned.** *UK* Terence Stamp; Peter Ustinov; Robert Ryan; Melvyn Douglas; Paul Rogers; John Neville; Ronald Lewis; David McCallum; John Meillon; ***D:*** Peter Ustinov; ***W:*** Peter Ustinov; Robert Rossen; ***C:*** Robert Krasker.

Billy Elliot *Dancer* **2000 (R)** Eleven-year-old Billy (Bell) is trying to survive in a Durham County town during the 1984 miners' strike that is affecting his family. His widowed dad (Lewis) wants Billy to take boxing lessons but the boy is more interested in the ballet class taught at the same gym by hard-living Mrs. Wilkinson (Walters), whose daughter Debbie (Blackwell) taunts Billy into trying to dance. Billy's natural talent is so great that Mrs. Wilkinson encourages him to audition for the Royal Ballet School in London. Of course, when his dad finds out what's been going on, there's trouble. The unfortunate rating is due to language but the film has all-around appeal and some fine performances. Stage director Daldry makes his film debut as does Bell. **111m/C; VHS, DVD.** *GB* Jamie Bell; Julie Walters; Gary Lewis; Jamie Driven; Nicola Blackwell; Jean Heywood; Stuart Wells; Adam Cooper; ***D:*** Stephen Daldry; ***W:*** Lee Hall; ***C:*** Brian Tufano; ***M:*** Stephen Warbeck. British Acad. '00: Actor (Bell), Film, Support. Actress (Walters).

Billy Galvin ½ **1986 (PG)** A bullheaded ironworker tries to straighten out the turbulent relationship he has with his rebellious son. **95m/C; VHS, Streaming.** Karl Malden; Lenny Von Dohlen; Joyce Van Patten; Toni Kalem; Keith Szarabajka; Alan North; Paul Guilfoyle; Barton Heyman; ***D:*** John Gray; ***W:*** John Gray; ***M:*** Joel Rosenbaum.

Billy Jack **1971 (PG)** On an Arizona Indian reservation, a half-breed ex-Green Beret with pugnacious martial arts skills (Laughlin) stands between a rural town and a school for runaways. Laughlin stars with his real-life wife Taylor. Features the then-hit song "One Tin Soldier," sung by Coven. The movie and its marketing by Laughlin inspired a "Billy Jack" cult phenomenon. A Spanish-dubbed version of this film is also available. Followed by a sequel in 1974, "Trail of Billy Jack," which bombed. **112m/C; VHS, DVD.** Tom Laughlin; Delores Taylor; Clark Howat; Bert Freed; Julie Webb; Victor Izay; Teresa Kelly; Lynn Baker; Stan Rice; Howard Hesseman; ***D:*** Tom Laughlin; ***W:*** Tom Laughlin; Delores Taylor; ***C:*** Fred W. Koenekamp; John Stephens; ***M:*** Mundell Lowe.

Billy Jack Goes to Washington ½ **1977** Unlike the other Billy Jack movies, this one was never theatrically released, which is probably good, as it's such a transparent rip-off of "Mr. Smith Goes to Washington." Pardoned for the trumped-up charges that sent him to prison previously, he is appointed to the U.S. Senate (wait, what?) to 'attract young voters,' and to convince the locals to get a nuke plant built. And then he finds out his predecessor is dead under odd circumstances. Of course you saw this part coming. **155m/C; DVD.** Tom Laughlin; ***D:*** Tom Laughlin; ***W:*** Tom Laughlin; Sidney Buchman; Lewis R. Foster; Delores Taylor; ***C:*** Jack Marta; ***M:*** Elmer Bernstein.

Billy Liar **1963** A young Englishman dreams of escaping from his working class family and dead-end job as an undertaker's assistant. Parallels James Thurber's story, "The Secret Life of Walter Mitty." **94m/B; VHS, DVD, Blu-Ray.** *GB* Tom Courtenay; Julie Christie; Finlay Currie; ***D:*** John Schlesinger; ***W:*** Willis Hall; Keith Waterhouse; ***C:*** Denys Coop; ***M:*** Richard Rodney Bennett.

Billy Lynn's Long Halftime Walk **2016 (R)** Billy Lynn (Alwyn) has been chosen as the face of the Army. After a harrowing battle in Iraq, the 19-year-old and his squad are paraded around the country on a goodwill tour for the military, which ends at a halftime show at a Dallas Cowboys game on Thanksgiving. That halftime is used as a ground for the flashback to what really happened to Billy in Iraq. Ang Lee's film is well-meaning but nothing feels genuine, even if it looks great, in typical Lee fashion. Based on Ben Fountain's 2012 novel. **113m/C; DVD, Blu-Ray.** Joe Alwyn; Kristen Stewart; Chris Tucker; Garrett Hedlund; Vin Diesel; ***D:*** Ang Lee; ***W:*** Jean-Christophe Castelli; ***C:*** John Toll; ***M:*** Jeff Danna; Mychael Danna.

Billy Madison ½ **1994 (PG-13)** Wealthy slacker Billy (Sandler) must prove to Dad he is capable of running the family hotel business by undertaking the obvious challenge of repeating grades 1-12 in six months. Ponder a few bodily function gags, and you'll have exhausted the humor in this lame attempt at creating a feature-length movie out of what would barely pass as a Saturday Night Live sketch. For only the most diehard fans of Sandler's silly shtick. **90m/C; VHS, DVD, Blu-Ray, HD-DVD.** Adam Sandler; Darren McGavin; Bridgette Wilson-Sampras; Bradley Whitford; Josh Mostel; Norm MacDonald; Mark Beltzman; Larry Hankin; Theresa Merritt; Chris Farley; Steve Buscemi; ***D:*** Tamra Davis; ***W:*** Adam Sandler; ***C:*** Victor Hammer; ***M:*** Randy Edelman.

Billy Rose's Jumbo *Jumbo* **1962** Better-than-average update of the circus picture. Durante and Raye are terrific, as are the Rodgers and Hart songs. Fun, with lively production numbers in the inimitable Berkeley style. **125m/C; DVD, Blu-Ray.** Doris Day; Stephen Boyd; Jimmy Durante; Martha Raye; Dean Jagger; ***D:*** Charles Walters; ***W:*** Sidney Sheldon; ***C:*** William H. Daniels.

Billy the Kid **1930** Early talkie plays fast and loose with the facts but it was filmed on location, which gives it some authenticity. During the Lincoln County, New Mexico homesteader war, Billy the Kid (Brown) vows revenge on the men who murdered his boss. Sheriff Pat Garrett (Beery) captures Billy but he escapes jail and Garrett must hunt the young outlaw down again. **95m/B; DVD.** Johnny Mack Brown; Wallace Beery; Kay Johnson; Karl (Daen) Dane; Wyndham Standing; James A. Marcus; ***D:*** King Vidor; ***W:*** Wanda Tuchock; Charles MacArthur; ***C:*** Gordon Avil.

Billy the Kid ½ **1941** Billy Bonney joins up with a group of outlaws in a Southwest town where he bumps into his old friend Jim Sherwood, now the marshal. Attempting to change his ways, he falls back into the life of a bandit when an outlaw friend is murdered. Although an entertaining western, the story bears no resemblance to the actual last days of Billy the Kid. Based on a story by Howard Emmett Rogers and Bradbury Foote, suggested by the book "The Saga of Billy the Kid" by Walter Noble Burns. **94m/C; VHS, DVD.** Robert Taylor; Brian Donlevy; Ian Hunter; Mary Howard; Gene Lockhart; Lon Chaney, Jr.; Guinn "Big Boy" Williams; Cy Kendall; Henry O'Neill; Ted Adams; Frank Puglia; Mitchell Lewis; Dick Curtis; Grant Withers; Joe Yule; Eddie Dunn; Kermit Maynard; Chill Wills; Olive Blakeney; Carl Pitti; ***D:*** David Miller; ***W:*** Gene Fowler, Sr.; ***C:*** William V. Skall; Leonard Smith; ***M:*** David Snell.

Billy the Kid Versus Dracula **1966** The title says it all. Dracula travels to the Old West, anxious to put the bite on a pretty lady ranch owner. Her fiance, the legendary outlaw Billy the Kid, steps in to save his girl from becoming a vampire herself. A Carradine camp classic. **95m/C; VHS, DVD, Blu-Ray.** Chuck Courtney; John Carradine; Melinda Plowman; Walter Janovitz; Harry Carey, Jr.; Roy Barcroft; Virginia Christine; Bing (Neil) Russell; Olive Carey; William Challee; William Forrest; ***D:*** William Beaudine; ***W:*** Carl K. Hittleman; ***C:*** Lothrop Worth; ***M:*** Raoul Kraushaar.

Billy Two Hats ½ *The Lady and the Outlaw* **1974 (PG)** Grizzled Scottish bandit Deans (Peck) teams up with young half-breed Billy (Arnaz Jr.) to pull off a robbery that results in an accidental death and Billy's capture. Deans is shot while breaking the kid out of jail and must rely on Billy to get them through, while being pursued by the law. It ain't happy. Mainly notable as the first western shot in Israel. **139m/C; VHS, DVD.** Gregory Peck; Desi Arnaz, Jr.; Jack Warden; Sian Barbara Allen; David Huddleston; ***D:*** Ted Kotcheff; ***W:*** Alan Sharp; ***C:*** Brian West; ***M:*** John Scott.

Billy's Holiday ☙☙ 1/2 **1995 (R)** Excessively offbeat Australian musical lacks the highly polished look of Hollywood's best, but given the setting and subject matter, it is probably not meant to have it. The subject is Billy Apples (Cullen), hangdog hardware owner by day, hangdog jazz musician at night. His audiences regularly fall asleep, but Kate (McQuade), owner of the beauty shop down the street, still loves him. Then one night, Billy magically receives the ability to sing just like his idol, Billie Holiday. The main attractions are the likeably middle-aged stars and a soundtrack filled with big band tunes. **92m/C; DVD.** *AU* Max Cullen; Kris McQuade; Tina Bursill; Drew Forsythe; Genevieve Lemon; Richard Roxburgh; Rachel Coopes; ***D:*** Richard Wherrett; ***W:*** Denis Whitburn; ***C:*** Roger Lanser.

Billy's Hollywood Screen Kiss ☙☙ 1/2 **1998 (R)** Very gay Billy (Hayes) is an aspiring arts photographer in L.A. who's looking for romance. He thinks he's got a hot prospect in handsome-if-sexually-confused Gabriel (Rowe), a waiter/model. Billy's latest project is recreating great film romantic scenes with drag queens and he hires Gabriel to play the male lover. But it looks as if Billy is going to get his heart broken if he expects Gabriel to carry the role over into real life. Amusing feature debut for director O'Haver and a standout performance from the witty Hayes. **92m/C; VHS, DVD.** Sean P. Hayes; Brad Rowe; Richard Ganoung; Meredith Scott Lynn; Paul Bartel; Armando Valdes-Kennedy; ***D:*** Tommy O'Haver; ***W:*** Tommy O'Haver; ***C:*** Mark Mervis; ***M:*** Alan Ari Lazar.

Biloxi Blues ☙☙ 1/2 *Neil Simon's Biloxi Blues* **1988 (PG-13)** Eugene Morris Jerome has been drafted and sent to boot camp in Biloxi, Mississippi where he encounters a troubled drill sergeant, hostile recruits, and a skillful prostitute. Walken is the drill sergeant from hell. Some good laughs from the everwry Broderick. A sequel to Neil Simon's "Brighton Beach Memoirs" and adapted by Simon from his play. Followed by "Broadway Bound." **105m/C; VHS, DVD, Blu-Ray.** Matthew Broderick; Christopher Walken; Casey Siemaszko; Matt Mulhern; Corey Parker; Penelope Ann Miller; Michael Dolan; Park Overall; ***D:*** Mike Nichols; ***W:*** Neil Simon; ***C:*** Bill Butler; ***M:*** Georges Delerue.

Bingo ☙☙ 1/2 **1991 (PG)** Mediocre spoof of hero-dog movies. The heroic title mutt roams from Denver to Green Bay in search of his absent-minded master, with numerous absurd adventures en route. Some cute moments, but sometimes Bingo is just lame-o. Good family fare. **90m/C; VHS, DVD.** Cindy Williams; David Rasche; Robert J. Steinmiller, Jr.; David French; Kurt Fuller; Joe Guzaldo; Glenn Shadix; ***D:*** Matthew Robbins; ***W:*** Jim Strain; ***M:*** Richard Gibbs.

Bingo Long Traveling All-Stars & Motor Kings ☙☙☙ **1976 (PG)** Set in 1939, this film follows the comedic adventures of a lively group of black ball players who have defected from the old Negro National League. The All-Stars travel the country challenging local white teams. **111m/C; VHS, DVD.** Billy Dee Williams; James Earl Jones; Richard Pryor; Stan Shaw; ***D:*** John Badham; ***W:*** Matthew Robbins; Hal Barwood; ***C:*** Bill Butler; ***M:*** William Goldstein.

Bio-dead ☙ **2009 (R)** Low-budget sci fi horror. After a bio-terrorist attack kills millions in Southern California, a corporation is contracted to send out a hazmat team to check for survivors and decontaminate the area. Only their safe zone turns out to be a refuge for the genetically mutated who have turned to cannibalism to survive. **84m/C; DVD.** Matthew Norton; Tony Williams; Jacob Gentry; Derek Long; Rick Hall; ***D:*** Stephen J. Hadden; ***W:*** Stephen J. Hadden; ***C:*** Manfred Drews; ***M:*** Kevin Rosen-Quan. **VIDEO**

Bio-Dome ☙ **1996 (PG-13)** Pauly Shore in a hermetically sealed environment separated from the rest of society? Great! Where do I sign? Unfortunately, it's only a movie, and a typically useless one, at that. Shore brings his lame schtick to a scientifically created "perfect environment" that he and his college (yeah, right) buddy Doyle (Baldwin) mistake for a mall and eventually destroy. In Bloom's not-too-auspicious directorial debut, bodily function jokes found in Jim Carrey's wastebasket masquerade as a script, while the supporting cast wanders aimlessly, perhaps pondering a switch in agents. **94m/C; VHS, DVD, Blu-Ray.** Pauly Shore; Stephen Baldwin; William Atherton; Henry Gibson; Joey Lauren Adams; Teresa Hill; Kylie Minogue; Jack Black; Kevin West; Denise Dowse; Dara Tomanovich; Kyle Gass; Rose McGowan; Taylor Negron; Phil LaMarr; ***D:*** Jason Bloom; ***W:*** Scott Marcano; Kip Koenig; ***C:*** Phedon Papamichael; ***M:*** Andrew Gross. Golden Raspberries '96: Worst Actor (Shore).

Bio Hazard ☙ **1985 (R)** A toxic monster needs human flesh to survive and consequently goes on a rampage. **84m/C; VHS, DVD, Blu-Ray.** Angelique Pettyjohn; Carroll Borland; Richard Hench; Aldo Ray; ***D:*** Fred Olen Ray.

Biohazard: The Alien Force ☙ 1/2 **1995 (R)** Reptilian mutant, the result of a genetic experiment gone awry, must be hunted down before it can reproduce. Sounds like a rip-off of "Species." **88m/C; VHS, DVD.** Steve Zurk; Chris Mitchum; Susan Fronsoe; Tom Ferguson; Patrick Moran; John Maynard; ***D:*** Steve Latshaw.

The Bionic Woman ☙☙ **1975** Skydiving accident leaves tennis pro Jaime Sommers crippled and near death. Her bionic buddy, Steve Austin, gets his friends to rebuild her and make her better than she was before. Pilot for the TV series. **96m/C; VHS, DVD.** Lindsay Wagner; Lee Majors; Richard Anderson; Alan Oppenheimer; ***D:*** Richard (Dick) Moder. **TV**

Bionicle 3: Web of Shadows ☙☙ **2005 (PG)** In this third animated toy commercial, the Toa return to the city of Metra Nui on a rescue mission, only to find it overrun by giant spider like fiends whose paralyzing webs transform their victims. Quickly subdued, the Toa are transformed into the Toa Hardika, odd mismatched-looking machines with new powers that will hopefully give them a chance of completing their mission. **76m/C; DVD.** Brian Drummond; Scott McNeil; ***V:*** Kathleen Barr; Paul Dobson; Brian Drummond; Alessandro Juliani; Scott McNeil; Trevor Devall; Christopher Gaze; Tabitha St. Germain; French Tickner; ***D:*** David Molina; Terry Shakespeare; ***W:*** Henry Gilroy; Bob Thompson; Bret Matthews; ***M:*** Nathan Furst.

Biozombie ☙☙ 1/2 **1998** Playing as a mixture of "Mallrats" and "Dawn of the Dead," this Hong Kong import is aimed squarely at a Generation-X audience. The film introduces us to Woody (Jordan Chan) and Bee (Sam Lee), two slackers who work at a video store. While on an errand to pick up their boss's car, they hit a strange pedestrian and take him back to the mall. This stranger turns out to be a zombie, and he soon infects several others. With the mall locked up for the night, Woody and Bee must take it upon themselves to protect the few humans remaining...while doing the least amount of work possible. The film turns into a true rollercoaster ride, as we start with the comedic opening, then move into the action-horror, and finally, a very nihilistic ending. **94m/C; DVD.** *CH* Jordan Chan; Sam Lee; ***D:*** Wilson (Wai-Shun) Yip.

Bird ☙☙☙ **1988 (R)** The richly textured, though sadly one-sided biography of jazz sax great Charlie Parker, from his rise to stardom to his premature death via extended heroin use. A remarkably assured, deeply imagined film from Eastwood that never really shows the Bird's genius of creation. The soundtrack features Parker's own solos re-mastered from original recordings. **160m/C; VHS, DVD.** Forest Whitaker; Diane Venora; Michael Zelniker; Samuel E. Wright; Keith David; Michael McGuire; James Handy; Damon Whitaker; Morgan Nagler; Peter Crook; ***D:*** Clint Eastwood; ***W:*** Joel Oliansky; ***C:*** Jack N. Green; ***M:*** Lennie Niehaus. Oscars '88: Sound; Cannes '88: Actor (Whitaker); Golden Globes '89: Director (Eastwood); N.Y. Film Critics '88: Support. Actress (Venora).

The Bird Can't Fly ☙ 1/2 **2007** Melody returns to her desolate South African diamond mining hometown for the funeral of her long-estranged daughter June. She discovers she has an eccentric 10-year-old grandson River, but her bonding efforts are thwarted by his father Scoop. The town is gradually being reclaimed by sandstorms, which delay Melody's departure and allow her the time to uncover some family secrets. **89m/C; DVD.** *GB NL SA* Barbara Hershey; Yusuf Davids; Tony Kgoroge; John Kani; ***D:*** Threes Anna; ***W:*** Threes Anna; ***C:*** Guido Van Gennep; ***M:*** Mark Killian; Paul Hepker.

The Bird Men ☙☙ *The Birder* **2013** Birding professionals vie for the same job in this comedy. Ron Spencer (Cavanagh) is struggling. A high school teacher and birding enthusiast, Ron's students disrespect him, he is being thrown out by his ex-wife, and his daughter is following her own path in birding. His only hope is gaining the job as the head of ornithology at the national park. When rival Floyd Hawkins (Spilchuk) is hired instead, Ron bonds with former student Ben (Rendall), who also loathes Floyd, to bring down Floyd and ensure that Ron gets his rightful place in bird watching. **85m/C; DVD, Streaming, Download.** Tom Cavanagh; Graham Greene; Fred Willard; Mark Rendall; Jamie Spilchuk; ***D:*** Ted Bezaire; ***W:*** Ted Bezaire; Michael Stasko; ***C:*** Arthur E. Cooper; ***M:*** Dylan Heming; Isabelle Noel; Richard Pell. **VIDEO**

Bird of Paradise ☙☙ 1/2 **1932** An exotic South Seas romance in which an adventurer is cast onto a remote Polynesian island when his yacht haphazardly sails into a coral reef. There he becomes enamored of an exotic island girl, and nature seems to disapprove. **80m/B; VHS, DVD, Blu-Ray.** Joel McCrea; Dolores Del Rio; Lon Chaney, Jr.; ***D:*** King Vidor; ***M:*** Max Steiner.

Bird of Paradise ☙ 1/2 **1951** Technicolor remake of the 1932 pic is mildly amusing for its strange casting. Frenchman Andre Laurence (Jourdan) accompanies his friend Tenga (Hunter) back to his Polynesian island and falls for Tenga's sister, Kalua (Paget). This breaks native customs (the best parts of the film) and when the local volcano erupts, Kalua vows to throw herself in to appease the gods. **100m/C; DVD.** Louis Jourdan; Debra Paget; Jeff Chandler; Everett Sloane; Maurice Schwartz; Jack Elam; ***D:*** Delmer Daves; ***W:*** Delmer Daves; ***C:*** Winton C. Hoch; ***M:*** Daniele Amfitheatrof.

Bird of Prey ☙☙ 1/2 **1995 (R)** Nick Milev (Milushev) has just been released from a Bulgarian prison for attacking Jonathan Griffith (Chamberlain), the drugs-and-arms dealer who was responsible for the death of Milev's policeman father. But Milev still wants revenge, though matters get complicated by Kily (Tilly), Griffith's naive daughter, with whom he falls in love. Plot's so-so but characters make up for some of the routiness. Filmed on location in Sofia, Bulgaria. **102m/C; VHS, DVD.** Boyan Milushev; Jennifer Tilly; Richard Chamberlain; Lenny Von Dohlen; Robert Carradine; Lesley Ann Warren; ***D:*** Temistocles Lopez; ***W:*** Boyan Milushev; ***C:*** David Knaus.

Bird on a Wire ☙☙ **1990 (PG-13)** Disappointing action-comedy finds Gibson forced to emerge from a prolonged period under the Witness Protection Program, whereupon he and ex-girlfriend Hawn are pursued by old enemies. Too little action and too little comedy add up to surprisingly dull outing, considering the cast. **110m/C; VHS, DVD.** Mel Gibson; Goldie Hawn; David Carradine; Bill Duke; Stephen Tobolowsky; Clyde Kusatsu; Joan Severance; Harry Caesar; John Pyper-Ferguson; Jeff Corey; ***D:*** John Badham; ***W:*** David Seltzer; ***C:*** Robert Primes; ***M:*** Hans Zimmer.

Bird People ☙☙ **2014** Writer/director Ferran inspired drama attempts to tell two diverging stories—one about a man who flies being ground; one about a woman who is grounded taking flight. Gary Newman's (Charles) a man who travels the world on business and decides to simply stop in Paris. He leaves his family, job, and life behind. Audrey's (Demoustier) a maid at his hotel, who climbs to the roof one day and turns into a bird. There are some interesting themes, but the movie moves in fits and starts instead of gliding gracefully. English and French with subtitles. **128m/C; DVD, Streaming.** *FR* Josh Charles; Anais Demoustier; Radha Mitchell; Roschdy Zem; ***Nar:*** Mathieu Amalric; ***D:*** Pascale Ferran; ***W:*** Pascale Ferran; Guillaume Breaud; ***C:*** Julien Hirsch; ***M:*** Beatrice Thiriet.

The Bird with the Crystal Plumage ☙☙ 1/2 *L'Ucello dalle Plume di Cristallo; The Phantom of Terror; The Bird with the Glass Feathers; The Gallery Murders* **1970 (PG)** An American writer living in Rome witnesses a murder. He becomes involved in the mystery when the alleged murderer is cleared because the woman believed to be his next victim is shown to be a psychopathic murderer. Vintage Argento mayhem. **98m/C; VHS, DVD, Blu-Ray.** *IT GE* Tony Musante; Suzy Kendall; Eva Renzi; Enrico Maria Salerno; Mario Adorf; Renato Romano; Reggie Nalder; Werner Peters; Umberto Raho; Dario Argento; ***D:*** Dario Argento; ***W:*** Dario Argento; ***C:*** Vittorio Storaro; ***M:*** Ennio Morricone.

The Birdcage ☙☙☙ *Birds of a Feather* **1995 (R)** Somewhat overlong but well-played remake of "La Cage aux Folles" features Williams suppressing his usual manic schtick to portray Armand, the subdued half of a longtime gay couple living in Miami. His partner is the ever-hysterical-but-loving drag queen Albert (Lane), whose presence provides a distinct challenge when Armand's son Val (Futterman) announces his engagement to the daughter of family values, right-wing senator Kevin Keeley (Hackman). When the Senator and family arrive for dinner, Armand tries to play it straight while Albert opts for a matronly mom impersonation (think Barbara Bush). Highlights include Armand's initial attempts to teach Albert to be butch (walk like John Wayne) and Hackman congoing in drag. **120m/C; VHS, DVD, Blu-Ray.** Robin Williams; Nathan Lane; Gene Hackman; Dianne Wiest; Hank Azaria; Dan Futterman; Christine Baranski; Calista Flockhart; Tom McGowan; ***D:*** Mike Nichols; ***W:*** Elaine May; ***C:*** Emmanuel Lubezki; ***M:*** Mark Mothersbaugh; Jonathan Tunick. Screen Actors Guild '96: Cast.

A Birder's Guide to Everything ☙☙ 1/2 **2014 (PG-13)** Sweet coming of age pic has shy, 15-year-old bird watcher David Portnoy (Smit-McPhee) still having trouble coping with his mother's death and even more trouble with his dad's (Le Gross) upcoming remarriage. Out birding, David spots what he thinks is a Labrador duck, a wild breed that's supposedly extinct. So instead of being his dad's best man, David takes off on a duck-hunting adventure with three fellow teen birders and with the help of bird expert Lawrence Konrad (Kingsley). **86m/C; DVD, Blu-Ray.** Kodi Smit-McPhee; Ben Kingsley; Katie Chang; Michael Chen; Alex Wolff; James LeGros; ***D:*** Rob Meyer; ***W:*** Rob Meyer; Luke Matheny; ***C:*** Tom Richmond; ***M:*** Jeremy Turner.

Birdman of Alcatraz ☙☙☙ **1962** Robert Stroud, convicted of two murders and sentenced to life imprisonment on the Island, becomes an internationally accepted authority on birds. Lovingly told, with stunning performance from Lancaster, and exceptionally fine work from the supporting cast. The confinement of Stroud's prison cell makes the film seem claustrophobic and tedious at times, just as the imprisonment must have been. Ritter played Stroud's mother, who never stops trying to get him out of prison. **143m/B; VHS, DVD, Blu-Ray.** Burt Lancaster; Karl Malden; Thelma Ritter; Betty Field; Neville Brand; Edmond O'Brien; Hugh Marlowe; Telly Savalas; ***D:*** John Frankenheimer; ***W:*** Guy Trosper; ***C:*** Burnett Guffey; Robert Krasker; ***M:*** Elmer Bernstein. British Acad. '62: Actor (Lancaster).

Birdman, or (The Unexpected Virtue of Ignorance) ☙☙☙ **2014 (R)** Riggan Thompson (Keaton) takes what could be his final stab at artistic credibility after years off the public radar other than nostalgia for the superhero role that made him a star (mirroring the real life of the actor himself). Thompson is adapting, directing and starring in a Broadway show, a production filled with the behind-the-scenes disasters, especially when a co-starring role is recast with the headstrong theater actor Mike (Norton), who takes an interest in Riggan's estranged daughter Sam (Stone). Filmed in a manner that makes it look like one unbroken shot, director Inarritu's pic is a surreal and sometimes overly showy drama. But it takes flight thanks to its stars and style. **119m/C; DVD, Blu-Ray.** Michael Keaton; Edward Norton; Naomi Watts; Emma Stone; Andrea Riseborough; Zach Galifianakis; Amy Ryan; ***D:*** Alejandro Gonzalez Inarritu; ***W:*** Alejandro Gonzalez Inarritu; Nicolas Giacobone; ***C:*** Emmanuel Lubezki; ***M:*** Antonio Sanchez. Oscars '14: Cinematog., Director (Inarritu), Film, Orig. Screenplay; British Acad. '14: Cinematog.; Directors Guild '14: Director (Inarritu); Golden Globes '15: Actor--Mus./Comedy (Keaton), Screenplay; Ind. Spirit '15: Actor (Keaton), Cinematog., Film; Screen Actors Guild '14: Cast.

The Birds 1/2 **1963 (PG-13)** Hitchcock attempted to top the success of "Psycho" with this terrifying tale of Man versus Nature, in which Nature alights, one by one, on the trees of Bodega Bay to stage a bloody act of revenge upon the civilized world. Only Hitchcock can twist the harmless into the horrific while avoiding the ridiculous; this is perhaps his most brutal film, and one of the cinema's purest, horrifying portraits of apocalypse. Based on a short story by Daphne Du Maurier; screenplay by novelist Evan Hunter (aka Ed McBain). **120m/C; VHS, DVD, Blu-Ray.** Rod Taylor; Tippi Hedren; Jessica Tandy; Veronica Cartwright; Suzanne Pleshette; Ethel Griffies; Charles McGraw; Ruth McDevitt; Lonny (Lonnie) Chapman; Joe Mantell; Morgan Brittany; Alfred Hitchcock; ***D:*** Alfred Hitchcock; ***W:*** Evan Hunter; ***C:*** Robert Burks; ***M:*** Bernard Herrmann. Natl. Film Reg. '16.

Birds & the Bees **1956** A millionaire falls in love with an alluring card shark, and then calls it all off when he learns of her profession, only to fall in love with her again when she disguises herself. A remake—and poor shade—of Preston Sturge's 1941 classic "The Lady Eve." **94m/C; VHS, Streaming.** Mitzi Gaynor; David Niven; George Gobel; Reginald Gardiner; Hans Conried; ***D:*** Norman Taurog; ***W:*** Sidney Sheldon.

Birds Do It **1966** Incredibly dopey comedy with Cape Kennedy janitor Melvin Byrd (Sales) in charge of keeping dust from ruining another nuclear missile project. When Melvin is unexpectedly exposed to an experiment, it gives him the ability to fly and—even sillier—makes him irresistible to women. Hunter plays a dual role as a military good guy and a lookalike spy. **88m/C; DVD.** Soupy Sales; Tab Hunter; Arthur O'Connell; Beverly Adams; Edward Andrews; Doris Dowling; ***D:*** Andrew Marton; ***W:*** Art Arthur; Arnie Kogen; ***C:*** Howard Winner; ***M:*** Samuel Matlovsky.

Birds of America **2008 (R)** College prof Morrie Tanager (Perry) and his wife Betty (Graham) lead a highly controlled life in reaction to Morrie's family history of mental instability. Just as it seems that Morrie will achieve his dreams of tenure, he's forced back into caretaker mode by his depressed, homeless brother Jay (Foster) and his promiscuous, booze-swilling sister Ida (Goodwin), who both move in. Betty's tolerance is fraying and Morrie has to decide how he's going to live his life. **85m/C; DVD.** Matthew Perry; Lauren Graham; Ben Foster; Ginnifer Goodwin; Gary Wilmes; Hilary Swank; Zoë Kravitz; ***D:*** Craig Lucas; ***W:*** Elyse Friedman; ***C:*** Yaron Orbach; ***M:*** Ahrin Mishan.

Birds of Passage *Pajaros de Verano* **2018** In the late 1960s in a remote area of Colombia populated by the indigenous Wayuu, Raypayet (Acosta) wants to marry Zaida (Reyes) but her mother Ursula (Martinez) is suspicious of him. Demanding an extensive dowry that she believes will be beyond his means, he returns with all the items and marries Zaida. He's enriched himself through the drug trade, beginning with selling marijuana from the mountains to Peace Corps volunteers. Based on actual events, it's an effective exploration of the wide impact of the drug trade on the Wayuu and their traditional way of life. Wayuu and Spanish with subtitles. **125m/C; DVD, Blu-Ray.** *CO DK MX GE SI FR* Carmina Martinez; Jose Acosta; Natalia Reyes; Jhon Narvaez; Greider Meza; ***D:*** Cristina Gallego; Ciro Guerra; ***W:*** Maria Camila Arias; Jacques Toulemonde Vidal; ***C:*** David Gallego; ***M:*** Leonardo Heiblum.

Birds of Prey **1972** Action film pits an ex-WWII army pilot against a group of kidnapping thieves in an airborne chopper chase. **81m/C; VHS, DVD.** David Janssen; Ralph Meeker; Elayne Heilveil; ***D:*** William A. Graham; ***C:*** Jordan Cronenweth. **TV**

Birds of Prey: And the Fantabulous Emancipation of One Harley Quinn 1/2 **2020 (R)** Still struggling after the end of her relationship with the Joker, Harley Quinn (Robbie) needs a new focus for her life. Quinn teams with other women in search of a new path, including sonic-voiced songstress Black Canary (Smollett-Bell), the revenge-seeking Huntress (Winstead), and former police detective Renee (Perez) after teen pickpocket Cassandra Cain (Basco) steals a valuable diamond from the lead henchman of mob boss Roman Sionis/Black Mask (McGregor). Reprising her Suicide Squad role, Robbie and her female co-stars give a charismatic performance in this enjoyable origin story. **109m/C; DVD, Blu-Ray.** Margot Robbie; Rosie Perez; Mary Elizabeth Winstead; Jurnee Smollett; Ewan McGregor; ***D:*** Cathy Yan; ***W:*** Christina Hodson; ***C:*** Matthew Libatique; ***M:*** Daniel Pemberton.

Birdsong **2012** BBC adaptation of Sebastian Faulks' 1993 novel, which is set between 1910 and 1916. In this romantic melodrama, Englishman Stephen Wraysford (Redmayne) takes a job working for Rene Azaire (Lafitte) in his French textile factory. Stephen falls in love with Rene's young, unhappy second wife, Isabelle (Poesy). The story flash-forwards to Stephen's serving in WWI in the same area, where his physical wounds are less devastating than the emotional ones shown in flashback. **165m/C; DVD, Blu-Ray.** *UK* Eddie Redmayne; Clemence Poesy; Joseph Mawle; Laurent Lafitte; Mathew Goode; Richard Madden; Marie Josee Croze; Anthony Andrews; ***D:*** Philip Martin; ***W:*** Abi Morgan; ***C:*** Julian Court; ***M:*** Nicholas Hooper. **TV**

Birdy 1/2 **1984 (R)** An adaptation of the William Wharton novel about two Philadelphia youths, one with normal interests, the other obsessed with birds, and their eventual involvement in the Vietnam War, wrecking one physically and the other mentally. A hypnotic, evocative film, with a compelling Peter Gabriel soundtrack. **120m/C; VHS, DVD, Blu-Ray.** Matthew Modine; Nicolas Cage; John Harkins; Sandy Baron; Karen Young; Bruno Kirby; ***D:*** Alan Parker; ***W:*** Jack Behr; Sandy Kroopf; ***M:*** Peter Gabriel. Cannes '85: Grand Jury Prize.

Birth **2004 (R)** Creepy psychological thriller finds widowed Anna (Kidman) finally making a commitment to marry Joseph (Huston) ten years after her husband Sean's death. That is until a strange 10-year-old, also named Sean (Bright), turns up insisting that Anna cannot remarry because he is her spouse. Sean is impervious to any suggestion otherwise and his very insistence comes to convince the emotionally fragile woman. None of this goes over well with Anna's imperious mother (Bacall) or the rest of her family, let alone her frustrated fiance. Various explanations are offered and director Glazer elegantly camouflages plot holes. Kidman, with her severe pixie haircut, somewhat resembles Mia Farrow in "Rosemary's Baby," but one thing you can be certain of is here, the devil didn't do it. **100m/C; DVD.** Nicole Kidman; Cameron Bright; Danny Huston; Lauren Bacall; Arliss Howard; Alison Elliot; Anne Heche; Peter Stormare; Ted Levine; Cara Seymour; Zoe Caldwell; Milo Addica; ***D:*** Jonathan Glazer; ***W:*** Milo Addica; Jonathan Glazer; Jean-Claude Carriere; ***C:*** Harris Savides; ***M:*** Alexandre Desplat.

The Birth of a Nation *The Clansman* **1915** Lavish Civil War epic in which Griffith virtually invented the basics of film grammar. Gish and Walthall have some of the most moving scenes ever filmed and the masterful battle choreography brought the art of cinematography to new heights. Griffith's positive attitude toward the KKK notwithstanding, this was the first feature length silent, and it brought credibility to an entire industry. Based on the play "The Clansman" and the book "The Leopard's Spots" by Thomas Dixon, it is still a rouser, and of great historical interest. Silent with music score. Also available in a 124-minute version. **175m/B; Silent; VHS, DVD, Blu-Ray.** Lillian Gish; Mae Marsh; Henry B. Walthall; Ralph Lewis; Robert "Bobbie" Harron; George Siegmann; Joseph Henabery; Spottiswoode Aitken; George Beranger; Mary Alden; Josephine Crowell; Elmer Clifton; Walter Long; Howard Gaye; Miriam Cooper; John Ford; Sam De Grasse; Maxfield Stanley; Donald Crisp; Raoul Walsh; Erich von Stroheim; Eugene Pallette; Wallace Reid; ***D:*** D.W. Griffith; ***W:*** D.W. Griffith; Frank E. Woods; ***C:*** Billy (G.W.) Bitzer; ***M:*** D.W. Griffith. AFI '98: Top 100; Natl. Film Reg. '92.

The Birth of a Nation 1/2 **2016 (R)** Nate Parker's directorial debut is an angry, passionate telling of the true story of Nat Turner, a slave who led a revolt against not just his owners but an entire village of slave owners in the antebellum South. Parker also stars as Turner, captured here as a preacher who inspired his fellow slaves to fight back against the violent, horrible oppression they faced, leading to a final act clearly inspired by Mel Gibson's "Braveheart." Parker is a better actor than director, as his rookie status as the latter shows, but there's an admirable spirit in his filmmaking, even if it's flawed. **120m/C; DVD, Blu-Ray.** Nate Parker; Armie Hammer; Penelope Ann Miller; Jackie Earle Haley; Mark Boone, Jr.; ***D:*** Nate Parker; ***W:*** Nate Parker; ***C:*** Elliot Davis; ***M:*** Henry Jackman.

Birth of the Blues 1/2 **1941** Songman Crosby starts a band in New Orleans in the midst of the jazz boom. Help from partner Martin and real-life trombonist Teagarden, with comic relief from Eddie "Rochester" Anderson, make for a fun-filled story. Plot is riddled with some unbelievable gangster scenes, but the music and laughs will keep you amused. In B&W with color segments. **76m/B; VHS, DVD.** Bing Crosby; Mary Martin; Brian Donlevy; Eddie Anderson; J. Carrol Naish; Cecil Kellaway; Warren Hymer; Horace McMahon; Carolyn Lee; Jack Teagarden; ***D:*** Victor Schertzinger; ***W:*** Harry Tugend; Walter DeLeon; ***C:*** William Mellor; ***M:*** Robert Emmett Dolan.

Birth Story: Ina May Gaskin & the Farm Wives 1/2 **2013** Created by documentarians Sara Lamm and Mary Wigmore, this feature-length documentary offers an in-depth look at counterculture figure Ina May Gaskin and the communal agricultural society she co-founded, The Farm. In 1970s, Gaskin and her friends began delivering each other's babies and, led by Gaskin, they became self-taught, skilled midwives. The Farm was an outgrowth of this experience, included self-grown food, self-built housing, and self-published books. Gaskin's approach to caring for women and their babies became a model for a generation's approach to childbirth, a movement that continues today as Gaskin works to share her knowledge and experience about childbirth. **95m/C; DVD.** ***D:*** Sara Lamm; Mary Wigmore; ***C:*** Mary Wigmore; ***M:*** Carter Little.

Birthday Girl **2002 (R)** Love story cum actioner stars Chaplin as a timid London bank clerk, John, and Kidman as Nadia, his mysterious and sexy online Russian mail-order bride with a secret. Nadia doesn't speak English, but the two begin to speak the international language anyway. Afraid, intrigued, then tickled with his Soviet missus who brings some color into his dull, drab life, John hardly has time to wallow in his new-found bliss when he's beset by Russian baddies (Frenchmen Kassovitz and Cassel) claiming to be Nadia's relatives, who show up on his doorstep one day. Kidman shows her range, however, and reportedly learned Russian for the film. Decent turn from the Butterworth clan, who also produced the hip debut film "Mojo." **93m/C; VHS, DVD.** *US GB* Nicole Kidman; Ben Chaplin; Vincent Cassel; Mathieu Kassovitz; Kate Evans; ***D:*** Jez Butterworth; ***W:*** Jez Butterworth; Tom Butterworth; ***C:*** Oliver Stapleton; ***M:*** Stephen Warbeck.

Bisbee '17 1/2 **2018** Current residents of Bisbee, Arizona, reenact a divisive and hushed-up piece of the town's history: the kidnapping and forced deportation of 1,200 immigrant miners on July 12, 1917. Told from various sides, it's an unorthodox method of making a documentary, but it compellingly captures an important part of the past, and perhaps even provides cathartic release for locals who carry the burden of century-old shame and regret. **112m/C; DVD, Blu-Ray.** Mike Anderson; Charles Bethea; Ken Boe; Benjamin Caron; Chris Dietz; ***D:*** Robert Greene; ***C:*** Jarred Alterman; ***M:*** Keegan DeWitt.

The Bishop Murder Case 1/2 **1930** Amateur sleuth Philo Vance (Rathbone) consults with New York D.A. Markham (Geldart) when college student Joseph Cochrane Robin is killed with an arrow on the grounds of scientist Bertrand Dillard's (Francis) home. A note on the body refers to the nursey rhyme "Cock Robin" and Vance has a lot of suspects to sort through. Rathbone is in one of the better adaptations of the S.S. Van Dine mysteries although this early talkie is still static in execution. **88m/B; DVD.** Basil Rathbone; Alec B. Francis; Leila Hyams; Roland Young; Clarence Geldart; James Donlan; ***D:*** Nick Grinde; ***W:*** Lenore Coffee; ***C:*** Roy F. Overbaugh.

The Bishop's Wife **1947** Episcopalian biship Henry (Niven) is praying to find the money to build a new church but his faith is shaky and his marriage to Julia (Young) even more so. But his prayers are answered (although Henry doesn't know it) in the form of angel Dudley (Grant), who's sent down to earth at Christmas to help work things out. Excellent performances by the cast make this an entertaining outing. Based on the novel by Robert Nathan. **109m/B; VHS, DVD, Blu-Ray.** Cary Grant; Loretta Young; David Niven; Monty Woolley; Elsa Lanchester; James Gleason; Gladys Cooper; Regis Toomey; ***D:*** Henry Koster; ***W:*** Leonardo Bercovici; Robert Sherwood; ***C:*** Gregg Toland; ***M:*** Hugo Friedhofer. Oscars '47: Sound.

The Bitch WOOF! **1978 (R)** High-camp follies are the rule in this lustful continuation of "The Stud" as it follows the erotic adventures of a beautiful divorcee playing sex games for high stakes on the international playgrounds of high society. A collaborative effort by the sisters Collins: written by Jackie, with sister Joan well cast in the title role. **90m/C; VHS, DVD.** *GB* Joan Collins; Kenneth Haigh; Michael Coby; Ian Hendry; Carolyn Seymour; Sue Lloyd; John Ratzenberger; ***D:*** Gerry O'Hara.

Bite **2016** Casey (Begovic) goes on a seemingly harmless bachelorette party/vacation and gets bitten by an unseen bug. What starts as an itchy, infected wound becomes something even more disturbing as Casey essentially becomes a giant bug, turning her apartment into an oozing, egg-filled cocoon, and killing anyone who dares enter. Archibald's low-budget horror flick has definite callbacks to "The Fly." It's not entirely successful but Begovic's performance is fearless and the gross-out quotient of the second half should appease horror fans looking for something different than a slasher riff. **90m/C; DVD, Blu-Ray.** Elma Begovic; Annette Wozniak; Denise Yuen; Jordan Gray; Lawrene Denkers; ***D:*** Chad Archibald; ***W:*** Jayme Laforest; ***C:*** Jeff Maher; ***M:*** Stephanie Copeland.

Bite the Bullet 1/2 **1975 (PG)** Moralistic western tells of a grueling 600-mile horse race where the participants reluctantly develop respect for one another. Unheralded upon release and shot in convincing epic style by Harry Stradling, Jr. Excellent cast. **131m/C; VHS, DVD.** Gene Hackman; James Coburn; Candice Bergen; Dabney Coleman; Jan-Michael Vincent; Ben Johnson; Ian Bannen; Paul Stewart; Sally Kirkland; Mario Arteaga; ***D:*** Richard Brooks; ***W:*** Richard Brooks; ***C:*** Harry Stradling, Jr.; ***M:*** Alex North.

Bitter Feast **2010** Horror comedy with unpleasant characters that's neither very funny nor very scary (but kinda gross). Ambitious chef Peter Grey has his career destroyed when nasty food blogger Franks runs a scathing review. He kidnaps the blogger, whisks him off to his isolated home, and gives Franks some seemingly simple food challenges. Only Grey retaliates with severe punishment for less-than-perfect results. **104m/C; DVD, Blu-Ray.** James LeGros; Joshua Leonard; Megan Hilty; Mario Batali; Amy Seimetz; Larry Fessenden; John Speredakos; ***D:*** Joe Maggio; ***W:*** Joe Maggio; ***C:*** Michael McDonough; ***M:*** Jeff Grace.

Bitter Harvest **1981** Emmy-nominated TV movie concerning a dairy farmer frantically trying to discover what is mysteriously killing off his herd. Howard is excellent as the farmer battling the bureaucracy to find the truth. Based on a true story. **98m/C; DVD.** Ron Howard; Art Carney; Tarah Nutter; Richard Dysart; Barry Corbin; Jim Haynie; David Knell; ***D:*** Roger Young. **TV**

Bitter Harvest **2017 (R)** An underwhelming historically inspired look at Soviet leader Josef Stalin's deliberate starvation of millions in the Ukraine in the 1930s. To illustrate these horrific events, it focuses on a young peasant Yuri (Irons), who loves to paint, and his long-time love interest Natalka (Barks). After Yuri moves to Kiev to study art, Soviet troops invade and crush his village. His grandfather (Stamp) does his best to fight back. In Kiev, Yuri observes ominous political changes as his professors and other leaders are liquidated and replaced by Soviets. The film feels like a television movie, but the story it tells deserves better. **103m/C; DVD.** Max Irons; Richard Brake; Terence Stamp; Samantha Barks; Aneurin Barnard; ***D:*** George Mendeluk; ***W:*** George Mendeluk; Richard Bachynsky Hoover; ***C:*** Douglas Milsome; ***M:*** Benjamin Wallfisch.

Bitter Moon **1992 (R)** Polanski effort looks promising, but ultimately disappoints. Bored British couple (Grant and Scott Thomas) meet up with sexual deviants (Coyote and Seigner, aka Mrs. Polanski) on a cruise and learn that passion and cruelty often share the same path to destruction. Masquerades as high class art, but whenever substance is lacking expect a silly, kinky sex scene. Needless to say, there isn't much substance, so erotic mischief abounds. Scott Thomas manages to hold her own, but Coyote is almost embarrassingly over the top. Based on the Pascal Bruckner novel "Lunes de Fiel." **139m/C; VHS, DVD.** Peter Coyote; Emmanuelle Seigner; Hugh Grant; Kristin Scott Thomas; Stockard Channing; Victor Banerjee; Sophie Patel; ***D:*** Roman Polanski; ***W:*** Roman Polanski; Gerard Brach; John Brownjohn; ***C:*** Tonino Delli Colli; ***M:*** Vangelis.

Bitter Rice *Riso Amaro* **1949** Mangano became a star with her sultry performance about survival in postwar Italy. She scrapes by, working in the rice fields of the Po Valley, loved by the down-to-earth Vallone, who provides her with little excitement. Gassman is the rotten-to-the-core thief who meets up with Mangano while he's running from the police. He mistreats her, she steals his money and betrays her friends, and both destroy each other. In Italian with English subtitles. **96m/C; VHS, DVD, Blu-Ray, Streaming.** *IT* Silvana Mangano; Vittorio Gassman; Raf Vallone; Doris Dowling; ***D:*** Guiseppe de Santis; ***W:*** Guiseppe de Santis; Carlo Lizzani; Gianni Puccini; ***C:*** Otello Martelli; ***M:*** Goffredo Petrassi.

Bitter Sugar *Azucar Amarga* **1996** Young, idealistic communist Gustavo (Lavan) is a Havana university student who still believes that the Castro regime can make things better. His rock musician brother Bobby (Villanueva) is a radical, defying government policies, and his psychiatrist father Tomas (Gutierrez) makes more money playing piano at a tourist hotel than in his practice. But Gustavo's eyes are opened, not only by his family situtation, but when he falls in love with cynical dancer Yolanda (Vilan), who longs to escape to Miami. Serious politics bolstered by excellent performances and sharp cinematography. Spanish with subtitles. **102m/B; VHS, DVD.** *CU* Rene Lavan; Mayte Vilan; Miguel Gutierrez; Larry Villanueva; ***D:*** Leon Ichaso; ***W:*** Leon Ichaso; Orestes Matacena; ***C:*** Claudio Chea; ***M:*** Manuel Tejada.

Bitter Sweet 1/2 **1933** Tragic tale of a woman who finally marries the man she loves, only to find that he is a compulsive gambler. Written by Coward, adapted from his operetta. **76m/B; VHS, DVD.** *GB* Anna Neagle; Fernand Gravey; Esme Percy; Clifford Heatherley; Hugh Williams; ***D:*** Herbert Wilcox; ***W:*** Noel Coward.

Bitter Sweet **1940** The second version of the Noel Coward operetta, about young romance in 1875 Vienna. Creaky and overrated, but the lush Technicolor and Coward standards help to compensate. **94m/C; VHS, DVD.** Jeanette MacDonald; Nelson Eddy; George Sanders; Felix Bressart; Ian Hunter; Sig Rumann; Herman Bing; Fay Holden; Curt Bois; Edward Ashley; ***D:*** W.S. Van Dyke; ***W:*** Lesser Samuels; Noel Coward.

Bitter Sweet **1998 (R)** Everhart spends four years in the big house after being tricked by her boyfriend into participating in a robbery. All she wants when she gets out is to get revenge on the lowlife and she gets the opportunity when approached by cop Russo, who's looking to bring down her ex-beau's gangster boss (Roberts). **96m/C; VHS, DVD.** Angie Everhart; James Russo; Eric Roberts; Brian Wimmer; ***D:*** Luca Bercovici. **VIDEO**

Bitter/Sweet **2009** Coffee expert Brian leaves his fiancee Amanda behind when he's sent to Thailand by his overbearing boss Calvert Jones to make a big purchase. The antipathy between Brian and exec Ticha, who escorts him to her family's plantation, not unexpectedly turns romantic. However, Brian gets a dual shock when both Jones and Amanda turn up. Thai/U.S. coproduction. **105m/C; DVD.** Kip Pardue; James Brolin; Napakpapha Nakrasitte; Laura Sorenson; Spencer Garrett; Kalorin Nemayothin; ***D:*** Jeff Hare; ***W:*** Jeff Hare; ***C:*** Sayombhu Mukdeeprom; Pongnarin Jonghawklang. **VIDEO**

The Bitter Tea of General Yen **1933** Stanwyck arrives in Shanghai to marry a missionary (Gordon) during the threatening days of China's civil war. Unexpectedly swept into the arms of an infamous warlord (Asher), she becomes fascinated, although his attempts to seduce her fail. She even remains with him while his enemies close in. Exotic and poetic, if melodramatic by today's standards. The interracial aspects were considered very daring for their time. Adapted from the book by Grace Zaring Stone. **89m/B; DVD, Blu-Ray.** Barbara Stanwyck; Nils Asther; Gavin Gordon; Walter Connolly; Lucien Littlefield; Toshia Mori; Richard Loo; Clara Blandick; ***D:*** Frank Capra; ***W:*** Edward Paramore.

The Bitter Tears of Petra von Kant 1/2 *Die Bitteren Traenen der Petra von Kant* **1972** Dark German story of lesbian love, the fashion world, obsession and anger. Claustrophobic settings and slow pace may frustrate some viewers. In German with English subtitles. **124m/C; VHS, DVD, Blu-Ray.** *GE* Margit Carstensen; Hanna Schygulla; Irm Hermann; Eva Mattes; ***D:*** Rainer Werner Fassbinder; ***W:*** Rainer Werner Fassbinder; ***C:*** Michael Ballhaus.

Bitter Victory **1958** Bitter psychological war drama. British Army officers Captain Leith (Burton) and Major Brand (Jurgens) are assigned to execute a commando raid on the Libyan stronghold of General Rommel and obtain some important papers. Brand learns that Leith was once involved with Brand's wife Jane (Roman) and his hatred grows when Leith also exposes his cowardice so the mission doesn't go smoothly. **97m/B; DVD.** Richard Burton; Curt Jurgens; Ruth Roman; Raymond Pellegrin; Anthony Bushnell; Christopher Lee; Alfred Burke; ***D:*** Nicholas Ray; ***W:*** Nicholas Ray; Gavin Lambert; Rene Hardy; ***C:*** Michel Kelber; ***M:*** Maurice Leroux.

Biutiful 1/2 **2010 (R)** Title is a misspelling by the young daughter of Barcelona crook Uxbal (Bardem), whose shady dealings involve trafficking Chinese sweatshop workers and Senegalese drug dealers. Uxbal is dedicated to protecting and sacrificing for his children, but he's forced to re-evaluate his life when he learns that he's dying from cancer. Bardem shines as the dark, conflicted protagonist—but cannot overcome the profound bleakness and misery of Uxbal's road to redemption. Spanish and Mandarin with subtitles. **147m/C; Blu-Ray, On Demand.** *MX SP* Javier Bardem; Maricel Alvarez; Eduardo Fernandez; Diaryatou Daff; Taisheng ("Cheng Tai Shen") Cheng; Hanaa Bouchaib; Guillermo Estrella; ***D:*** Alejandro Gonzalez Inarritu; ***W:*** Armando Bo; Nicolas Giabone; Alejandro Gonzalez Inarritu; ***C:*** Rodrigo Pireto; ***M:*** Gustavo Santaolalla.

Bizarre **1987** When a wife escapes her perverse, psychologically threatening marriage, she finds her husband still haunts her literally and figuratively, and plots psychological revenge. Dubbed. **93m/C; VHS, DVD.** *IT* Florence Guerin; Luciano Bartoli; Robert Egon Spechtenhauser; Stefano Sabelli; ***D:*** Giuliana Gamba.

Bizarre Bizarre *Drole de Drama* **1939** A mystery writer is accused of murder and disappears, only to return in disguise to try to clear his name. Along the way, a number of French comedians are introduced with a revue of comedy-farce sketches that include slapstick, burlesque, black humor, and comedy of the absurd. In French with English subtitles. **90m/B; VHS, DVD.** *FR* Louis Jouvet; Michel Simon; Francoise Rosay; Jean-Pierre Aumont; Nadine Vogel; Henri Guisol; Jenny Burnay; ***D:*** Marcel Carne; ***W:*** Jacques Prevert; ***C:*** Eugen Shufftan; ***M:*** Maurice Jaubert.

Black and Blue **2019 (R)** After serving in Afghanistan, Army veteran Alicia West (Harris) returns home to New Orleans and joins the police force. Three weeks in, she finds herself working alongside a group of officers and narcotics detectives. After Alicia witnesses a detective (Grillo) fatally shoot a drug dealer and she is shot at by another narcotics officer, she realizes her body cam captured it all. Before the bad cops catch her, she must get to police headquarters to upload the video. She enlists a local convenience store manager (Gibson) to help. Harris and Gibson make an otherwise generic genre flick worth viewing. **108m/C; DVD, Blu-Ray.** Naomie Harris; Frank Grillo; Mike Colter; Reid Scott; Tyrese Gibson; ***D:*** Deon Taylor; ***W:*** Peter A. Dowling; ***C:*** Dante Spinotti; ***M:*** Geoff Zanelli.

Black and White **1999 (R)** Director Toback attempts to investigate white kids' facsination with black hip-hop culture by creating an intriguing combination of pseudo-documentary and urban melodrama, with cameos and performances by professional celebrities alongside professional actors. In the more effective part of the film, Shields is a documentary filmmaker asking rich white kids why they're into hip-hop. This section also includes Robert Downey as her gay husband hitting on Mike Tyson (playing himself in one of the film's strongest scenes). The part that doesn't work as well is the more conventional storyline (which seems added to satisfy studio executives looking for straight narrative) involving an undercover cop (Stiller) bribing college basketball star Dean (Houston) to throw a game in an attempt to get at Dean's best friend Rich (Power), a drug kingpin turned rap mogul. While the parts don't add up to an entirely satisfying whole, the journey is worth the interesting ride. **98m/C; VHS, DVD.** Scott Caan; Robert Downey, Jr.; Stacy Edwards; Gaby Hoffman; Jared Leto; Marla Maples; Joe Pantoliano; Brooke Shields; Power; Claudia Schiffer; William Lee Scott; Ben Stiller; Eddie Kaye Thomas; Elijah Wood; Mike Tyson; James Toback; Allan Houston; Kidada Jones; Bijou Phillips; Raekwon; ***D:*** James Toback; ***W:*** James Toback; ***C:*** David Ferrara.

Black & White 1/2 **1999 (R)** Rookie cop Chris O'Brien (Cochrane) is partnered with tough veteran female officer Nora Hugosian (Gershon), who's known for both her sexiness and her ruthless style. The two begin an affair while searching for a serial killer. And then the rookie comes across some evidence that seems to implicate his partner in the crimes. **97m/C; VHS, DVD.** Gina Gershon; Rory Cochrane; Ron Silver; Alison Eastwood; Marshall Bell; ***D:*** Yuri Zeltser; ***W:*** Yuri Zeltser; Leon Zeltser; ***C:*** Phil Parmet.

Black and White in Color *La Victoire en Chantant* **1976 (PG)** Award-winning satire about a French soldier at an African outpost, who, upon hearing the news of the beginning of WWI, takes it upon himself to attack a neighboring German fort. Calamity ensues. In French, with English subtitles. **100m/C; VHS, DVD.** *FR* Jean Carmet; Jacques Dufilho; Catherine Rouvel; Jacques Spiesser; Dora Doll; Jacques Perrin; ***D:*** Jean-Jacques Annaud; ***W:*** Georges Conchon; Jean-Jacques Annaud; ***M:*** Pierre Bachelet. Oscars '76: Foreign Film.

Black Angel **1946** Catherine Bennett (Vincent) tries to clear the name of estranged husband Kirk (Phillips), who's accused of murdering his lover, blackmailing chanteuse Mavis Marlowe (Dowling). Catherine enlists the aid of Mavis' husband, drunken songwriter Martin Blair (Duryea), whom she suspects actually did the deed. Another suspect is sleazy nightclub owner Marko (Lorre), where the duo get a job to check things out. Blair falls for Catherine and goes on another bender when she rejects him, as Kirk's execution day draws ever closer. Atmospheric noir is based on the novel by Cornell Woolrich. **80m/B; VHS, DVD, Blu-Ray.** June Vincent; Dan Duryea; Peter Lorre; Broderick Crawford; John Phillips; Constance Dowling; Wallace Ford; Hobart Cavanaugh; Freddie (Fred) Steele; ***D:*** Roy William Neill; ***W:*** Roy Chanslor; ***C:*** Paul Ivano; ***M:*** Frank Skinner.

Black Arrow *Black Arrow Strikes* **1948** Original adventure film of the famous Robert Louis Stevenson novel. Upon return from 16th century's War of the Roses, a young man must avenge his father's murder by following a trail of clues in the form of black arrows. Well made and fun. **76m/B; VHS, DVD.** Louis Hayward; Janet Blair; George Macready; Edgar Buchanan; Paul Cavanagh; ***D:*** Gordon Douglas.

The Black Balloon 1/2 **2009 (PG-13)** All Thomas wants is a normal adolescence. But when he and his oddball family, including his autistic brother, Charlie, move to a new neighborhood, his vulnerabilities and familial eccentricities are exposed, specifically to Jackie, the object of his kept affections. It isn't until swimming class and mandated mouth-to-mouth practice, that their mutual feelings are exposed. Effective Aussie effort is touching without resorting to melodrama. **97m/C; DVD.** Luke Ford; Toni Collette; Erik Thomson; Rhys Wakefield; Gemma Ward; ***D:*** Elissa Down; ***W:*** Elissa Down; Jimmy Jack.

Black Beauty **1971 (G)** International remake of the classic horse story by Anna Sewell. **105m/C; VHS, DVD.** *GB GE SP* Mark Lester; Walter Slezak; ***D:*** James Hill; ***C:*** Chris Menges; ***M:*** Lionel Bart.

Black Beauty **1994 (G)** Remake of the classic Anna Sewell children's novel about an oft-sold horse whose life has its shares of ups and downs. Timeless tale still brings children and adults to tears. Six-year-old quarterhorse named Justin gives a nuanced portrayal as the Black Beauty, recalling Olivier in "Hamlet." Directorial debut of "Secret Garden" screenwriter Thompson. **88m/C; VHS, DVD, Blu-Ray.** Andrew Knott; Sean Bean; David Thewlis; Jim Carter; Alun Armstrong; Eleanor Bron; Peter Cook; Peter Davison; John McEnery; Nicholas Jones; ***D:*** Caroline Thompson; ***W:*** Caroline Thompson; ***C:*** Alex Thomson.

The Black Belly of the Tarantula *La Tarantola dal Ventre Nero* **1971** Inspector Tellini (Giannini) investigates a series of murders where the victims are first paralyzed with wasp venom before being cut open while they're still alive. And the connection between the victims seems to be a beauty spa. Italian with subtitles. **89m/C; DVD.** *IT* Giancarlo Giannini; Claudine Auger; Barbara Bouchet; Stefania Sandrelli; Barbara Bach; Rossella Falk; ***D:*** Paolo Cavara; ***W:*** Marcello Danon; Lucille Laks; ***C:*** Marcello Gatti; ***M:*** Ennio Morricone.

Black Belt **1992 (R)** A private detective is hired to protect a rock star from a fanatic Vietnam vet. **80m/C; VHS, DVD.** Don "The Dragon" Wilson; Richard Beymer; Alan Blumenfeld; Matthias Hues; ***D:*** Charles Philip Moore; ***W:*** Charles Philip Moore.

Black Belt Jones **1974 (R)** Martial arts expert fights the mob to save a school of self-defense in Los Angeles' Watts district. **87m/C; VHS, DVD.** Jim Kelly; Gloria Hendry; Scatman Crothers; ***D:*** Robert Clouse.

The Black Bird *The Blackbird* **1926** Director Browning and star Chaney teamed up for an atmospheric silent crime drama. In London's notorious Limehouse district, the crippled Bishop, who runs the local mission, tries to help the desperate inhabitants while his notorious brother, The Black Bird, preys on their weaknesses. The criminal becomes infatuated with chanteuse Fifi (Adoree), but he has a rival and his jealousy may expose an unsettling secret. **86m/B; Silent; DVD.** Lon Chaney, Sr.; Owen Moore; Renee Adoree; Doris Lloyd; ***D:*** Tod Browning; ***W:*** Tod Browning; ***C:*** Percy Hilburn.

Black Book 1/2 *Zwartboek* **2006 (R)** Wow—Verhoeven directs his first film in his native Netherlands in 20 years and comes up with an unsentimental WWII thriller with a compelling lead performance by van Houten. In 1944, Jewish Rachel has been hiding out in the country until she joins a Dutch resistance unit. After some cosmetic changes, and now renamed Ellis, she's assigned to bed Gestapo chief Ludwig Muentze

(Koch) and ferret out some Nazi secrets. What Rachel/Ellis doesn't mean to do is fall in love. The story twists and turns (eventually ending up in Israel in 1956) but is definitely worth the journey. English, Dutch, German, and Hebrew with subtitles. **145m/C; DVD, Blu-Ray.** *GB BE NL* Sebastian Koch; Thom Hoffman; Halina Reijn; Derek de Lint; Carice van Houten; Waldemar Kobus; Christian Berkel; Peter Blok; ***D:*** Paul Verhoeven; ***W:*** Paul Verhoeven; Gerard Soeteman; ***C:*** Karl Walter Lindenlaub; ***M:*** Anne Dudley.

Black Box ½ *Avarice* **2012 (R)** An offbeat science fiction exploration of greediness. A black box of unknown origins has an amazing ability to know its owner's most secret desire. Those who possess it will do anything for what is inside—what the owner most desires. As the black box changes hands, each new owner sees that he or she most desires. Each owner has a choice to resist what is wanted the most or defend what is desired in the box against an immortal assassin. As the box moves between people, each dilemma and choice is explored. **83m/C; DVD, Streaming, Download.** Kevin Sorbo; Patricia Richardson; Jason London; Brad Dourif; Tinsel Korey; ***D:*** Matthew Schilling; ***W:*** Matthew Schilling; ***C:*** Cliff Hokanson; ***M:*** Frederik Wiedmann. **VIDEO**

Black Brigade *Carter's Army* **1969** Pryor and Williams star in this low budget movie as leaders of an all-black outfit assigned to a suicide mission behind Nazi lines during WWII. Their force wreaks havoc and earns them the respect of military higher-ups. Lots of action and climactic finish. **90m/C; VHS, DVD.** Stephen Boyd; Robert Hooks; Susan Oliver; Roosevelt "Rosie" Grier; Moses Gunn; Richard Pryor; Billy Dee Williams; ***D:*** George McCowan; ***W:*** Aaron Spelling; ***M:*** Fred Steiner.

Black Butterfly ½ **2017 (R)** A home-invasion thriller centered on a reclusive writer. Writer Paul (Banderas) is an alcoholic who suffers from extreme writer's block. Living near a town where there has been a string of murders, Paul meets an unsettling drifter Jack (Rhys Meyers) at a dinner and invites him to stay at his house. Though Jack tries to help Paul write his screenplay and fix up his home, he soon shows himself to be a violent psychopath and takes Paul and his realtor Laura (Perabo) hostage. Despite uninspired performances, bland action, obvious plotting, and ineffective twists, the film retains an aura of smugness. **93m/C; DVD.** Antonio Banderas; Jonathan Rhys Meyers; Piper Perabo; Vincent Riotta; Brian Goodman; ***D:*** Brian Goodman; ***W:*** Justin Stanley; Marc Frydman; ***C:*** Jose David Montero; ***M:*** Federico Jusid.

Black Cadillac **2003** A night of partying goes awry when a bum car strands three buddies in the frigid, lonely mountains. Their luck seems to change after a deputy sheriff rescues them, but relief turns to terror as they find a mysterious black Cadillac on their tail. Effective entry in the "mysterious spooky car" genre. **92m/C; VHS, DVD.** Randy Quaid; Kiersten Warren; Shane Johnson; Josh Hammond; Jason Dohring; Adam Vernier; ***D:*** John Murlowski; ***W:*** John Murlowski; Will Aldis; ***C:*** S. Douglas Smith; ***M:*** Chris Bell. **VIDEO**

Black Caesar **1973 (R)** A small-time hood climbs the ladder to be the head of a Harlem crime syndicate. Music by James Brown. Followed by the sequel "Hell Up in Harlem." **92m/C; VHS, DVD.** Fred Williamson; Julius W. Harris; Val Avery; Art Lund; Gloria Hendry; James Dixon; ***D:*** Larry Cohen; ***W:*** Larry Cohen; ***C:*** Fenton Hamilton; James Signorelli; ***M:*** James Brown.

The Black Camel **1931** In the 2nd Charlie Chan mystery, set (and filmed) in Honolulu, the detective (Oland) investigates the murder of movie starlet Sheila Fane. Lugosi plays a psychic. Based on the Earl Derr Bigger's novel. **71m/B; DVD.** Warner Oland; Bela Lugosi; Robert Young; Victor Varconi; J.M. Kerrigan; Marjorie White; Sally Eilers; Dorothy Revier; Dwight Frye; ***D:*** Hamilton McFadden; ***W:*** Barry Connors; Philip Klein; ***C:*** Joseph August; Daniel B. Clark; ***M:*** Samuel Kaylin.

The Black Castle **1952** MacNally plays an 18th-century Austrian count whose guests tend to disappear after a visit. This happens to two of Greene's friends and he decides to investigate. Uninspired and melodramatic, not enough horror. Karloff doesn't have enough to do. **81m/B; DVD.** Richard Greene; Boris Karloff; Stephen McNally; Rita (Paula) Corday; Lon Chaney, Jr.; John Hoyt; ***D:*** Nathan "Jerry" Juran.

The Black Cat ½ *House of Doom; Vanishing Body* **1934** The first of the Boris and Bela pairings stands up well years after release. Polished and taut, with fine sets and interesting acting. Confrontation between architect and devil worshipper acts as plot, with strange twists. Worth a look. **65m/B; VHS, DVD.** Boris Karloff; Bela Lugosi; David Manners; Julie Bishop; Lucille Lund; Henry Armetta; Egon Brecher; Albert Conti; Harry Cording; John Carradine; ***D:*** Edgar G. Ulmer; ***W:*** Edgar G. Ulmer; Peter Ruric; ***C:*** John Mescall; ***M:*** Heinz Roemheld.

The Black Cat ½ **1941** Wealthy Henrietta Winslow (Loftus) has left her estate to her greedy grandchildren but only after her faithful housekeeper Abigail (Sondergaard) and all her beloved cats die. Naturally, strange and murderous events begin occurring. Not to be confused with the 1934 classic horror film of the same title. **71m/B; VHS, DVD, Blu-Ray.** Basil Rathbone; Hugh Herbert; Gale Sondergaard; Broderick Crawford; Bela Lugosi; Gladys Cooper; Anne Gwynne; Cecilia Loftus; Claire Dodd; John Eldridge; Alan Ladd; ***D:*** Albert Rogell; ***W:*** Robert Lees; Frederic Rinaldo; Eric Taylor; Robert Neville; ***C:*** Stanley Cortez.

The Black Cat WOOF! *Il Gatto Nero* **1981** Spaghetti splatter-meister Fulci, best known for his unabashed ripoffs "Zombie" and "Gates of Hell," tones down the gore this time in a vaguely Poe-ish tale of a medium with some marbles loose (Magee) whose kitty provides the temporary habitat for spirits its master calls up. The dreary English village setting and the downright myopic camera work add up to an oppressive viewing experience. **92m/C; VHS, DVD, Blu-Ray.** *IT GB* Patrick Magee; Mimsy Farmer; David Warbeck; Al Cliver; Dagmar Lassander; Geoffrey Copleston; Daniela Dorio; ***D:*** Lucio Fulci; ***W:*** Lucio Fulci; Biagio Proietti; ***C:*** Sergio Salvati; ***M:*** Pino Donaggio.

Black Cat Run **1998 (R)** Race car driver's girlfriend is abducted and then he gets involved with a psycho deputy. Lots of action. **88m/C; VHS, DVD.** Patrick Muldoon; Amelia Heinle; Russell Means; Kevin J. O'Connor; Peter Greene; Jake Busey; ***D:*** D.J. Caruso; ***W:*** Frank Darabont; Douglas Venturelli; ***C:*** Bing Sokolsky; ***M:*** Jeff Rona. **CABLE**

The Black Cauldron ½ **1985 (PG)** Disney's 25th full-length animated movie follows the adventures of pig-keeper Taran, who discovers his psychic pig Hen Wen is the key to keeping a magical cauldron out of the hands of the evil Horned King. Based on the "Chronicles of Prydain" novels by Lloyd Alexander. **82m/C; VHS, DVD.** ***V:*** Grant Bardsley; Susan Sheridan; John Hurt; Freddie Jones; Nigel Hawthorne; John Byner; Arthur Malet; ***Nar:*** John Huston; ***D:*** Ted Berman; Richard Rich; ***W:*** Ted Berman; Richard Rich; ***M:*** Elmer Bernstein.

Black Christmas ½ *Silent Night, Evil Night; Stranger in the House* **1975 (R)** A college sorority is besieged by an axe-murderer over the holidays. **98m/C; VHS, DVD, Blu-Ray.** *CA* Olivia Hussey; Keir Dullea; Margot Kidder; John Saxon; Andrea Martin; Art Hindle; ***D:*** Bob (Benjamin) Clark; ***W:*** Roy Moore; ***C:*** Reginald Morris; ***M:*** Carl Zittrer.

Black Christmas **2006 (R)** The 1974 original was an early entry in the slasher/dead teen genre. This weak remake, which takes itself way too seriously, ups the gore and adds lurid flashbacks for the killer, but so what? Sorority sisters (you may recognize a couple of faces) are stuck in their Alpha Kappa house at Christmas because of a blizzard, but the psycho killer (who lived in the sorority house when it was his family home) manages to escape the loony bin and hide out in the attic. He then terrorizes the gals before offing them, using handy holiday decorations for the most part. After seeing what he does with a cookie cutter, you may never eat Christmas cookies again. Writer/director Morgan deserves coal in his stocking. **84m/C; DVD, HD-DVD.** *US CA* Michelle Trachtenberg; Lacey Chabert; Mary Elizabeth Winstead; Andrea Martin; Katie Cassidy; Robert Mann; Oliver Hudson; Crystal Lowe; Kristen Cloke; Jessica Harmon; Dean Friss; ***D:*** Glen Morgan; ***W:*** Glen Morgan; ***C:*** Robert McLachlan; ***M:*** Shirley Walker.

Black Christmas ½ **2019 (PG-13)** Sorority sister Riley (Poots) receives mysterious, threatening text messages from someone who claims to be slave-owning college founder Calvin Hawthorne. Soon after, Riley and other sorority members are physically attacked by masked men from a fraternity whose former president, Brian (McIntire), sexually assaulted Riley. As members of Riley's sorority go missing and her fear increases, she encounters hostility and indifference from men on campus, including security guard Gil (Neilson) and frat sponsor Professor Gilson (Elwes). Director Takal's remake is drenched in feminist strength but for a horror flick it's not so scary. **92m/C; DVD, Blu-Ray.** Imogen Poots; Aleyse Shannon; Brittany O'Grady; Lily Donoghue; Caleb Eberhardt; ***D:*** Sophia Takal; ***W:*** Sophia Takal; April Wolfe; ***C:*** Mark Schwartzbard; ***M:*** Brooke Blair; Will Blair.

Black Circle Boys ½ **1997 (R)** Depressed high schooler Kyle (Bairstow) is still trying to fit in at his new school. He makes the mistake of getting involved with the "Black Circle Boys"?a clique of losers involved with drugs and the occult that's led by Shane (Mabius). The Boys enjoy malicious pranks and Kyle begins to have qualms about his participation but Shane doesn't want to let him go. Murky script gets increasingly silly as pic progresses. **100m/C; VHS, DVD.** Scott Bairstow; Eric Mabius; Heath Lourwood; Chad Lindberg; Tara Subkoff; Dee Wallace; Donnie Wahlberg; John Doe; ***D:*** Matthew Carnahan; ***W:*** Matthew Carnahan; ***C:*** Geary McLeod.

Black Cloud ½ **2004 (PG-13)** Schroder debuts as a writer/director in this formulaic but appealing drama about a Native American boxer. Black Cloud (Sparks) is an angry, out-of-control young boxer whose life outside the ring is marred by an alcoholic father, a dead mother, self-hatred, and racism. All he's got in his corner is his world-wise trainer Bud (Means) and his girlfriend Sammi (Jones). Black Cloud struggles with adversity in and out of the ring, but ultimately he's his own worst enemy. The story is strictly seen-it-before, but the strong performances (especially Sparks) balance out the predictability. **95m/C; DVD.** Eddie Spears; Russell Means; Wayne Knight; Peter Greene; Julia Jones; Rick Schroder; Nathaniel Arcand; Tim McGraw; Branscombe Richmond; ***D:*** Rick Schroder; ***W:*** Rick Schroder; ***C:*** Steve Gainer; ***M:*** John E. Nordstrom.

Black Cobra WOOF! 1983 (R) A lesbian exacts revenge for her lover's snake-bite murder by trapping the guilty party with his own snakes. **97m/C; VHS, DVD.** *IT* Laura Gemser; Jack Palance; ***D:*** Joe D'Amato.

The Black Cobra WOOF! *Cobra Nero* **1987 (R)** After photographing a psychopath in the process of killing someone, a beautiful photographer seeks the help of a tough police sergeant to protect her. The leader of the Black Cobras gang gives chase. **90m/C; VHS, DVD.** *IT* Fred Williamson; Bruno Bilotta; Eva Grimaldi; ***D:*** Stelvio Massi.

Black Cobra 2 **1989 (R)** A mismatched team of investigators tracks a notorious terrorist. They find him holding a school full of children as hostage. **95m/C; VHS, DVD.** *IT* Fred Williamson; Nicholas Hammond; Emma Hoagland; Najid Jadali; ***D:*** Stelvio Massi; ***C:*** Guglielmo Mancori; ***M:*** Aldo Salvi.

Black Cobra 3: The Manila Connection ½ **1990 (R)** Interpol turns to police lieutenant Robert Malone (Williamson) when a team of high-tech weapons thieves threatens the world. Malone attacks like a cyclone on the terrorists' jungle haven. They won't know what hit 'em! **92m/C; VHS, DVD.** Fred Williamson; Forry Smith; Debra Ward; ***D:*** Don Edwards.

Black Coffee **2014 (PG)** Romantic comedy about the difficulties of meeting your ideal woman in less than ideal circumstances. After losing his job unexpectedly, Robert's (Henson) luck changes when he meets Morgan (Dennis). Though the pair have chemistry, their young relationship faces major challenges in their former partners. Not only does Morgan's ex-husband Hill (Rucker) work to get her back, Robert's ex-girlfriend Mita (Hubbard) tries to her worm her way into his life again. Fortunately, Robert's cousin Julian (Keyes) is there to help smooth the situation over. **85m/C; DVD, Streaming, Download.** Darrin Dewitt Henson; Christian Keyes; Lamman Rucker; Gabrielle Dennis; Erica Hubbard; ***D:*** Mark Harris; ***W:*** Mark Harris; ***C:*** Adam Lee; ***M:*** John Christopher Bell.

The Black Dahlia **2006 (R)** Adaptation of James Ellroy's novel about the lurid unsolved murder features director De Palma's feverish eye for noir. Great-looking, over-stuffed, and ultimately unsatisfying production has Hollywood wannabe Elizabeth Short's (Kirshner) mutilated body discovered in a vacant lot in LA in 1947. Detective Lee Blanchard (Eckhart) becomes obsessed with the case—to the detriment of his life with blonde babe lover, Kay Lake (Johansson). Meanwhile, Lee's callow partner Buck (Hartnett) is investigating wealthy brunette Madeleine's (Swank) involvement with Short, which leads him to her lunatic clan. Fedoras, red lipstick, and cigarette smoke abound, but the glam hides plenty of dirt and corruption. **121m/C; DVD, Blu-Ray.** Josh Hartnett; Scarlett Johansson; Aaron Eckhart; Hilary Swank; Mike Starr; Fiona Shaw; John Kavanagh; Rachel Miner; Mia Kirshner; Troy Evans; Gregg Henry; Rose McGowan; Jemima Rooper; William Finley; Kevin Dunn; Ian McNeice; Pepe Serna; Patrick Fischler; ***D:*** Brian De Palma; ***W:*** Josh Friedman; ***C:*** Vilmos Zsigmond; ***M:*** Mark Isham.

The Black Dakotas ½ **1954** President Lincoln wants a peace treaty with the Sioux so the soldiers can be used to fight the Confederates. He sends an emissary with a lot of gold to sweeten the deal but the man is waylaid by southerner Brock Marsh. Stagecoach driver Mike and his girlfriend Ruth try to stop Marsh from causing more trouble. **65m/C; DVD.** Gary Merrill; Wanda Hendrix; John Bromfield; Noah Beery, Jr.; John War Eagle; Jay Silverheels; Howard Wendell; Robert F. Simon; ***D:*** Ray Nazarro; ***W:*** Ray Buffum; DeVallon Scott; ***C:*** Ellis W. Carter; ***M:*** Mischa Bakaleinikoff.

Black Dawn ½ **2005 (R)** Former CIA agent Jonathon Cold (Seagal) is working for himself now, and takes an assignment springing a terrorist from jail so he can infiltrate his group before they detonate a nuclear bomb in downtown LA. Seagal unfortunately is an action star past his prime using a stunt double that looks nothing like him to film all his fight scenes. **96m/C; DVD.** Steven Seagal; Tamara Davies; John Pyper-Ferguson; Julian Stone; Nicholas Davidoff; Warren DeRosa; Don Franklin; Timothy Carhart; Eddie Velez; Matt Salinger; Ryan Bollman; Roman Varshavsky; Noa Hegesh; David St. James; Angela Gots; ***D:*** Alexander Gruszynski; ***W:*** Darren O. Campbell; Martin Wheeler; ***C:*** Bruce McCleery; ***M:*** David Wurst; Eric Wurst.

Black Day Blue Night **1995 (R)** Rinda (Forbes) and Hallie (Sara) take a road trip from Utah to Phoenix and pick up the handsome Dodge (Bellows). Turns out he's being pursued by cop John Quinn (Walsh) as a suspect in a murder/robbery. Women-in-peril-who-help-themselves type story. **99m/C; VHS, Streaming.** Michelle Forbes; Mia Sara; Gil Bellows; J.T. Walsh; Tim Guinee; John Beck; ***D:*** J.S. Cardone; ***W:*** J.S. Cardone; ***C:*** Michael Cardone; ***M:*** Johnny Lee Schell; Joe Sublett.

Black Death **2010 (R)** Effective historical horror. In 1348, knight Ulric and his band of mercenaries accompany novice monk Osmund to an English village that is suspected of following pagan practices. Though the bubonic plague ravages the rest of the country, this village remains untouched and Ulrich is charged with capturing the leaders of a heretical cult. **101m/C; DVD, Blu-Ray, Streaming.** *GB GE* Sean Bean; Eddie Redmayne; John Lynch; Carice van Houten; Tim (McInnerny) McInnery; Andy Nyman; Kimberly Nixon; Johnny Harris; David Warner; ***D:*** Chris Smith; ***W:*** Dario Poloni; ***C:*** Sebastian Edscmid; ***M:*** Christian Henson.

Black Demons ½ *Demoni 3* **1991** College students traveling in Brazil stop at a plantation when their car breaks down. While listening to a tape of a Voodoo ritual they made in the previous town, they suddenly find themselves besieged by the zombies of the slaves who died there in what was an obviously less politically correct time. **88m/C; DVD.** *IT* Keith Van Hoven; Joe Balogh; Philip Murray; Sonia Curtis; Juliana Texeira; Maria Alves; *D:* Umberto Lenzi; *W:* Umberto Lenzi; Olga Pehar; *C:* Maurizio Dell'Orco; *M:* Franco Micalizzi. **VIDEO**

The Black Devils of Kali 🦴 *Mystery of the Black Jungle* **1955** Adventurers in the Indian jungle discover a lost race of idol-worshipping primitives. Racist garbage produced near the end of Republic Pictures' existence. Based on a novel by Emillio Salgari. **72m/B; VHS, DVD.** Lex Barker; Jane Maxwell; Luigi Tosi; Paul Muller; *D:* Ralph Murphy.

Black Dog 🦴 **1998 (PG-13)** Not since the '70s heyday of CBs and C.W. McCall have 18-wheelers been so lovingly portrayed. Too bad the rest of the characters weren't given the same attention. Swayze (resurrecting his sensitive butt-kicker persona from "Roadhouse") plays disgraced trucker Jack Crews, recently released from prison after a vehicular manslaughter rap. With no driver's license and an overdue mortgage, he agrees to an "off the books" run for his shady boss (Beckel). The cargo turns out to be guns, which attracts the attention of the FBI, ATF, and a scuzzy band of hijackers led by the Bible-quoting Red (Meatloaf). Of course, the paint-by-numbers plot puts Jack's family in harm's way, and gives him a soulful, country-croonin' ally (Travis). Avoid this mutt like three-day-old roadkill unless you're a big-rig fetishist. **88m/C; VHS, DVD, Blu-Ray.** Patrick Swayze; Randy Travis; Meat Loaf Aday; Gabriel Casseus; Graham Beckel; Stephen Tobolowsky; Charles S. Dutton; Brian Vincent; Brenda Strong; Erin Broderick; *D:* Kevin Hooks; *W:* William Mickelberry; Dan Vining; *C:* Buzz Feitshans, IV; *M:* George S. Clinton.

The Black Doll 🦴 1/2 **1938** Shady mine owner Nicholas Rood is murdered as revenge for killing his business partner. While local officials have things utterly confused, Rood's daughter's fiance, who happens to be a private detective, eventually pieces the clues together. Low-caliber installment of the "Crime Club" series. **66m/B; VHS, DVD.** Donald Woods; Nan Grey; Edgar Kennedy; Doris Lloyd; *D:* Otis Garrett; *W:* Otis Buckley. **VIDEO**

Black Dynamite 🦴🦴 1/2 **2009 (R)** Sly, satiric homage to 1970s blaxploitation films that finds heroic Black Dynamite (White) fighting all the way to Honky House (AKA Richard M. Nixon's White House) to avenge his brother's murder and prevent the destruction of his 'hood by The Man. The film looks and sounds deliberately garish with grainy film stock, a funk soundtrack, gratuitous female nudity, and a swaggering, jive-talking hero who carries a .44 Magnum and wields a mean nunchuck. These are all pluses since director/writer Sanders and writers White and Minns are complimentary to the genre rather than smug. **90m/C; DVD, Blu-Ray.** Michael Jai White; Byron Keith Minns; Kym E. Whitley; Obba Babatunde; Kevin Chapman; Tommy Davidson; Salli Richardson-Whitfield; Arsenio Hall; Cedric Yarbrough; Mykelti Williamson; Bokeem Woodbine; James McManus; Nicole Sullivan; *D:* Scott Sanders; *W:* Michael Jai White; Byron Keith Minns; Scott Sanders; *C:* Shawn Maurer; *M:* Adrian Younge.

Black Eagle 🦴🦴 **1988 (R)** Pre-Glasnost, anti-Soviet tale of two high-kicking spies. CIA and KGB agents race to recover innovative equipment in the Mediterranean. **93m/C; VHS, DVD, Blu-Ray.** Bruce Doran; Jean-Claude Van Damme; Sho Kosugi; *D:* Eric Karson; *W:* Shimon Arama; *M:* Terry Plumeri.

Black Eliminator 🦴 **1978** A black cop struggles to stop a maniacal secret agent who plans to destroy the world. **84m/C; VHS, DVD.** Jim Kelly; George Lazenby; Harold Sakata; Bob Minor; Patch MacKenzie; Aldo Ray; *D:* Al Adamson.

Black Eye 🦴🦴 **1974** Williamson goes in for some self-deprecating humor as Shep Stone, an ex-cop turned not-too-successful private eye, whose biggest case turns out to be the murder victim he finds in his own apartment. This leads Stone to a drug ring, a porn operation, a religious cult, a runaway girl, and more corpses littering the environs of Venice, California. **98m/C; DVD.** Fred Williamson; Rosemary Forsyth; Teresa Graves; Floy Dean; Richard Anderson; Richard X. Slattery; Cyril Delevanti; *D:* Jack Arnold; *W:* Mark Haggard; *C:* Ralph Woolsey; *M:* Mort Garson.

Black '47 🦴🦴 1/2 **2018 (R)** In 1847 western Ireland, the potato famine has left many Irish Catholics starving as their primary source of food is inedible. Their British rulers make the situation worse by having their soldiers attack those who cannot pay the excessive taxes and forcing locals to convert to Protestantism to receive nourishment. Some of Britain's soldiers are Irish, including Martin (Frecheville). After he is pushed too far and his family suffers major losses, he takes his murderous revenge on the British who have wronged him. A powerful thriller that capably tells an important event in Irish history. **100m/C; DVD, Blu-Ray.** Hugo Weaving; James Frecheville; Stephen Rea; Freddie Fox; Barry Keoghan; *D:* Lance Daly; *W:* Lance Daly; P. J. Dillon; Pierce Ryan; *C:* Declan Quinn; *M:* Brian Byrne.

Black Fox: Good Men and Bad 🦴🦴 1/2 **1994** Britt (Todd) accepts a job as a federal marshall while Alan (Reeve) goes after desperado Carl Glenn (Fox) and his gang. During a stagecoach robbery, the outlaws take Hallie (Rowan) hostage, thinking she's the wife of a tycoon and Alan manages to use her to get to Glenn. The third episode in the sagebrush series. **90m/C; VHS, DVD.** Christopher Reeve; David Fox; Tony Todd; Kim Coates; Kelly Rowan; *D:* Steven Hilliard Stern; *C:* Frank Tidy; *M:* Eric N. Robertson.

Black Fox: The Price of Peace 🦴🦴 1/2 **1994** Former plantation owner Alan Johnson (Reeve) and childhood friend Britt (Todd), whom he frees from slavery, try to forge a new life in 1860s Texas. But there's trouble when abusive bigot Ralph Holtz (Wiggins) threatens the peace between settlers and Indians when he goes after his wife delores (Holtz) who left him for a Kiowa warrior, Running Dog (Trujillo). Based on the novel by Matt Braun; made for TV. **90m/C; VHS, DVD.** Christopher Reeve; Raoul Trujillo; Tony Todd; Chris Wiggins; Cynthia (Cyndy, Cindy) Preston; *D:* Steven Hilliard Stern; *C:* Frank Tidy; *M:* Eric N. Robertson. **TV**

Black Friday 🦴🦴 1/2 **1940** Karloff is a surgeon who saves the life of his college professor friend (Ridges) by transplanting part of the brain of a gangster (involved in the same car crash) into the man's body. This results in a Jekyll/Hyde complex with the gangster's evil portion taking over and seeking revenge on rival mobster Lugosi. Horror stars Karloff and Lugosi never have any scenes together. **70m/B; DVD, Blu-Ray.** Boris Karloff; Stanley Ridges; Bela Lugosi; Anne Nagel; Anne Gwynne; Paul Fix; Virginia Brissac; James Craig; *D:* Arthur Lubin; *W:* Curt Siodmak; Eric Taylor; *C:* Elwood "Woody" Bredell.

Black Fury 🦴🦴🦴 **1935** A coal miner's efforts to protest working conditions earn him a beating by the company goons who also kill his friend. He draws national attention to this brutal plight of the workers when he barricades himself inside the mine. Muni's carefully detailed performance adds authenticity to this powerful drama, but it proved too depressing to command a big boxoffice. **95m/B; VHS, DVD.** Paul Muni; Barton MacLane; Henry O'Neill; John Qualen; J. Carrol Naish; *D:* Michael Curtiz.

The Black Gate 🦴 *The Darkening; Dark Encounters* **1995** Psychic investigator Scott Griffin's (Rector) vacation to a seemingly pleasant cliff-top inn is interrupted by horrific visions that lead him to an ancient object of great evil that could wreak havoc on Earth unless he can destroy it. More frightening than the lame ghost story are the poor visual effects. **81m/C; VHS, DVD.** Jeff Rector; George Philip Saunders; Rebecca Kyler Downs; Red Montgomery; Brian Carlton; *D:* William Mesa; *W:* John G. Jones; Victoria Parker; *C:* William Mesa. **VIDEO**

Black Gestapo **WOOF!** **1975 (R)** Black-exploitation film about a vigilante army taking over a Los Angeles ghetto, first to help residents, but later to abuse them. Extremely violent. **89m/C; VHS, DVD.** Rod Perry; Charles Robinson; Phil Hoover; Ed(ward) Cross; Angela Brent; Wes Bishop; Lee Frost; Charles Howerton; Uschi Digart; *D:* Lee Frost; *W:* Wes Bishop; Lee Frost; *C:* Derek Scott.

Black Girl 🦴🦴🦴🦴 *Une Noire de. . .; La Noire de. . .* **1966** The first feature-length film by Senegal's Ousmane Sembene tells the tragic, inevitable story of a young Senegalese maid's forced exile when her white employers want to use her as a servant at their home in the south of France. The film that is most often cited as marking the birth of the African cinema, it remains one of the most powerfully disturbing depictions of the dehumanizing power of racism in the history of cinema. Chilling and unforgettable. **65m/B; DVD, Blu-Ray.** Robert Fontaine; Anne-Marie Jelinek; Therese N'Bissine Diop; Momar Nar Sene; *D:* Ousmane Sembene; *W:* Ousmane Sembene; *C:* Christian Lacoste.

Black Glove 🦴 *Face the Music* **1954** A trumpet star defends himself against charges of murdering a Spanish singer by tracking down the real killer. **84m/B; VHS, DVD.** *GB* Alex Nicol; John Salew; Arthur Lane; Eleanor Summerfield; Paul Carpenter; Geoffrey Keen; Martin Boddey; Fred Johnson; *D:* Terence Fisher; *W:* Ernest Borneman; *C:* Walter J. (Jimmy W.) Harvey.

Black Godfather 🦴 **1974 (R)** The grueling story of a hood clawing his way to the top of a drug-selling mob. Features an all-black cast. **90m/C; VHS, DVD.** Rod Perry; Damu King; Don Chastain; Jimmy Witherspoon; Diane Summerfield; *D:* John Evans; *W:* John Evans; *C:* Jack Steely.

Black Gold 🦴🦴 **1962** Pilot Frank McCandless (Carey) trades in his biplane for a chance at wildcatting for oil in 1920s Oklahoma. Ruthless oil baron Chick Carrington (Aikens) doesn't take kindly to competition. **98m/B; DVD.** Phil Carey; Claude Akins; Diane McBain; James Best; Fay Spain; Dub Taylor; Iron Eyes Cody; *D:* Leslie Martinson; *W:* Bob Duncan; Wanda Duncan; *C:* Harold E. Stine; *M:* Howard Jackson.

Black Gunn 🦴 1/2 **1972 (R)** Early blaxploitation flick filled with car chases (one in a white Rolls Royce), fights, and explosions. L.A. nightclub owner Gunn (Brown) wants revenge on mobster Capelli (Landau) who order his brother Scott (Jefferson) killed. Of course, Scott was involved in ripping off a mobbed-up bookie joint to fund his militant activities but Gunn isn't cutting anyone any slack. **96m/C; DVD, Blu-Ray.** Jim Brown; Martin Landau; Brenda Sykes; Bruce Glover; Luciana Paluzzi; Herbert Jefferson, Jr.; Bernie Casey; Gary Conway; Stephen McNally; Keefe Brasselle; Vida Blue; *D:* Robert Hartford-Davis; *W:* Franklin Coen; *C:* Richard H. Kline; *M:* Tony Osborne.

Black Hawk Down 🦴🦴🦴 1/2 **2001 (R)** Producer Bruckheimer and director Scott faithfully and superbly re-create the Battle of Mogadishu of October, 1993. U.S. Army Rangers and Delta Force units are sent to apprehend Somali warlord Muhammad Farah Aidid's top staff in an Aidid-controlled section of the city. When two Black Hawk helicopters are shot down, the focus of the mission changes to rescue and defense. The usual introduction of the troops is dispensed with fairly quickly, in favor of background on the Somalian situation, and details of the impending operation. No-frills setup works perfectly with the following action, which is fierce, intense, and non-stop. Once the fighting begins, Scott's brilliance with visuals really kicks in, but nothing that happens, no matter how gruesome, seems forced or exploitative. Fine ensemble cast is nominally led by Hartnett, but no one disappoints. Based on the book by Mark Bowden. **143m/C; VHS, DVD, Blu-Ray, UMD.** Josh Hartnett; Eric Bana; Ewan McGregor; Tom Sizemore; William Fichtner; Sam Shepard; Gabriel Casseus; Kim Coates; Hugh Dancy; Ron Eldard; Ioan Gruffudd; Tom Guiry; Charlie Hofheimer; Danny Hoch; Jason Isaacs; Zeljko Ivanek; Glenn Morshower; Jeremy Piven; Brendan Sexton, III; Johnny Strong; Richard Tyson; Brian Van Holt; Steven Ford; Gregory Sporleder; Carmine D. Giovinazzo; Chris Beetem; George Harris; Ewen Bremner; Boyd Kestner; Nikolaj Coster-Waldau; Ian Virgo; Tom (Thomas) Hardy; Tac Fitzgerald; Matthew Marsden; Orlando Bloom; Kent Linville; Enrique Murciano; Michael Roof; Treva Etienne; Ty Burrell; *D:* Ridley Scott; *W:* Ken Nolan; *C:* Slawomir Idziak; *M:* Hans Zimmer. Oscars '01: Film Editing, Sound.

Black Heat 🦴 1/2 *Girls Hotel; The Murder Gang; U.S. Vice* **1976 (R)** 'Kicks' Carter (Brown) is a detective in L.A. attempting to stop a gang from using an all women's hotel as a prostitution ring. Possibly because he's supposed to be the film's hero, but equally possibly because his girlfriend of the moment happens to live there. Even as bad exploitation films go this one is pretty pointless, except for genre enthusiasts who like formulaic brutality. **90m/C; DVD.** Timothy Brown; Russ Tamblyn; Geoffrey Land; Regina Carrol; Tanya Boyd; Al Richardson; Jana Bellan; Darlene Anders; Neal Furst; J.C. Wells; *D:* Al Adamson; *W:* John D'Amato; Sheldon Lee; Bud Donnelly; *C:* Gary Graver; *M:* Paul Lewinson.

Black Heaven 🦴 1/2 *L'Autre Monde; The Other World* **2010** Gaspard and his sweet girlfriend Marion are vacationing in Marseilles when they find a cell phone and try to track down the owner. This leads to vamp Audrey who easily seduces Gaspard and draws him into the virtual reality game she plays obsessively. As it turns out, the players are a suicide club who really want to find out if there's life after death. French with subtitles. **105m/C; DVD, Blu-Ray.** *BE FR* Gregoire Leprince-Ringuet; Pauline Etienne; Louise Bourgoin; Melvil Poupaud; Pierre Niney; Ali Marhyar; *D:* Gilles Marchand; *W:* Gilles Marchand; Dominik Moll; *C:* Celine Bozon; *M:* Anthony Gonzalez; Emmanuel d'Orlando.

The Black Hole 🦴 1/2 **1979 (G)** A high-tech, computerized Disney space adventure dealing with a mad genius who attempts to pilot his craft directly into a black hole. Except for the top quality special effects, a pretty creaky vehicle. **97m/C; VHS, DVD, Blu-Ray.** Maximilian Schell; Anthony Perkins; Ernest Borgnine; Yvette Mimieux; Joseph Bottoms; Robert Forster; *D:* Gary Nelson; *W:* Gerry Day; *C:* Frank V. Phillips; *M:* John Barry.

Black Horizon 🦴 1/2 *Stranded; On Eagle's Wings; Space Station* **2001 (R)** No matter what it's called, this flick is still a less-than-exciting space opera. A Russian space station is falling apart and an international team is sent aboard a space shuttle to rescue the inhabitants. While there, the station is struck by a meteor that knocks out all communication and causes an oxygen leak, which threatens the team and crew. And on Earth, a government agent discovers that some people don't want the team to ever return. **92m/C; VHS, DVD.** Ice-T; Hannes Jaenicke; Michael Dudikoff; Yvette Nipar; Richard Gabai; Alex Veadov; Art Hindle; Larry Poindexter; Andrew Stevens; *D:* Fred Olen Ray; *W:* Steve Latshaw; *C:* Theo Angell. **VIDEO**

The Black House 🦴🦴 *Kuroi Ie* **2000** Insurance fraud is a problem in Japan, if this film is any indication. After her husband dies, a widow pesters her insurance company to pay up. An agent goes to meet her and discovers that the widow has already remarried a very odd man and her son has hanged himself. The loving parents are most interested as to when they will begin receiving insurance payments for the boy's death as well. So the insurance company has the agent meet with a psychiatrist at a strip club (of course) as a prelude to his investigation of what will be a very odd couple. **117m/C; DVD.** *JP* Machiko Washio; Daikichi Sugawara; Katsunobu Ito; Kenichi Katsura; Chikako Yuri; Toshie Kobayashi; Asako Kobayashi; *D:* Ataru Oikawa; *W:* Ataru Oikawa; Kei Oishi; Takamasa Sato; *C:* Tokushu Kikomura; *M:* John Lissauer; Masako Miyoshi.

Black House 🦴🦴 *Geomeun jip* **2007** A Korean remake of a Japanese film of the same name, about an insurance agent investigating what may be a fraudulent claim. Jeon (Hwang Jeon-min) believes his client may have faked his son's suicide for insurance money, and believes he may be out to kill his wife as well. The Korean version drops much of the black humor of the Japanese original, and relies more on gore than story to provide frights (it's often compared to Hollywood remakes of successful Asian horror films). **103m/C; DVD.** *NK* Shin-il Kang; Jeong-min Hwang; Seo-hyeong Kim; Seon Yu; Jeong-min Hwang; Yusuke Iseya; Kumiko Aso; Akira Terao; Fumiyo Kohinata; Hiroyuki Miyasako; Hidetoshi Nishijima; Susumu Terajima; Ryo; Tetsuji Tamayama; Hideji Otaki; Tatsuya Mihashi; Kanako Higuchi; Mayumi Sada; Jun Kaname; Mitsuhiro Oikawa; Toshiaki Karasawa; *D:* Terra Shin; Kazuaki Kiriya; *W:* Yusuke Kishi; Youngjong Lee; Sung-ho Kim; Kazuaki Kiriya; Dai Sato; Shotaru Suga; Tatsuo Yoshida; *C:* Ju-young Choi; Kazuaki Kiriya; *M:* Seung-hyun Choi; Shiroh Sagisu.

Black Irish 🦴🦴 1/2 **2007 (R)** Familiar family drama buoyed by strong performances. Teenager Cole McKay (Angarano) is a promising high school baseball pitcher growing up in South Boston. His dad Desmond (Gleeson) is an unemployed drinker, his mother Margaret (Leo) holds to the illusion that they are a decent Catholic family, and his older sister Kathleen (Van Camp) is unmarried and pregnant. But the biggest problem for Cole is violent elder brother Terry (Guiry), who's drifted into drugs and crime and wants to drag Cole down with him. **95m/C; DVD.** Michael Angarano; Brendan Gleeson; Tom Guiry; Melissa Leo; Emily Van Camp; Michael Rispoli; Francis Capra; Finn Curtin; *D:* Brad Gann; *W:* Brad Gann; *C:* Michael Fimognari; *M:* John (Gianni) Frizzell.

Black Jack 🦴 1/2 **1979** In brutal, 18th-century Yorkshire, young Tolly is kidnapped by criminal Black Jack, who's just survived a hanging. Black Jack becomes a highwayman, allowing the secondary story of Belle, who's being sent to Bedlam because of her supposed mental illness, to intersect. Belle and Tolly then become part of a travelling carnival, but Loach's low-budget adventure is hampered by his non-actors performances and thick accents. Adapted from the Leon Gardfield children's book. **109m/C; DVD, Blu-Ray.** *UK* Jean Franval; Stephen Hirst; Louise Cooper; Andrew Bennett; *D:* Ken Loach; *W:* Ken Loach; *C:* Chris Menges; *M:* Bob Pegg.

Black Jesus 🦴🦴 *Seduta Alla Sua Destra; Seated At His Right* **1968** Lalubi (Strode) is an African leader using passive resistance to save his people from a dictatorial regime that's supported by European colonialism. When he's betrayed by a follower, Lalubi's imprisoned and tortured, along with a thief who gains a greater understanding after contact with the leader. Film is a thinly disguised depiction of Zaire and its history. **100m/C; VHS, DVD.** *IT* Woody Strode; Jean Servais; *D:* Valerio Zurlini.

The Black King 🦴 1/2 *Harlem Hot Shot* **1932** Prejudiced propaganda based on the life of Marcus Garvey, black leader of the '20s, who advocated black superiority and a return to Africa. A black con man takes advantage of fellow blacks by organizing a phony back-to-Africa movement, enriching himself in the process. When one man's girlfriend deserts him for the bogus leader, the jilted one blows the whistle. **70m/B; VHS, DVD.** A.B. Comethiere; Vivianne Baber; Knolly Mitchell; Dan Michaels; Mike Jackson; *D:* Bud Pollard.

The Black Klansman 🦴 *I Crossed the Line* **1966** A black man masquerades as a white extremist in order to infiltrate the KKK and avenge his daughter's murder. In the interest of racial harmony, he seduces the Klan leader's daughter. As bad as it sounds. **88m/B; VHS, DVD.** Richard Gilden; Rima Kutner; Harry Lovejoy; *D:* Ted V. Mikels.

Black Knight 🦴 **2001 (PG-13)** The utterly unoriginal title should be a clue. Another remake of "A Connecticut Yankee in King Arthur's Court," and a particularly bad and formulaic one at that. Lazy, selfish Jamal (Lawrence) is transported from his minimum-wage job at theme park Medieval World to 14th century England, the real medieval world, where some life lessons await. Obvious fish-out-of-water jokes ensue, as Jamal seeks to make sense of his new surroundings, knock boots with Nubian maidens and lead a revolution against an evil king. The film's few decent gags are swallowed by lots of inane humor, a tired script and Lawrence's desperate mugging. Ironically, the story's moral message about giving up selfishness for a cause is lost on its star, who acts as if he's the only person on screen. Ye olde bore. **95m/C; VHS, DVD, Blu-Ray.** Martin Lawrence; Tom Wilkinson; Vincent Regan; Marsha Thomason; Kevin Conway; Daryl (Chill) Mitchell; Jeannette Weegar; Michael Burgess; Isabell Monk; Helen Carey; *D:* Gil Junger; *W:* Darryl Quarles; Peter Gaulke; Gerry Swallow; *C:* Ueli Steiger; *M:* Randy Edelman.

The Black Legion 🦴🦴🦴 **1937** Social drama isn't as dated as we'd like to think. Auto worker Frank Taylor (Bogart) is angry at being passed over for an expected promotion that goes to a Polish immigrant. So he's easy pickings for a Klan-like secret society that practices hatred and Frank gets in deep, eventually losing his family. His best pal, Ed (Foran), tries to get Frank out but only tragedy follows. Very grim and one of Bogart's early unsympathetic starring roles. **83m/B; DVD.** Humphrey Bogart; Dick Foran; Erin O'Brien-Moore; Helen Flint; Ann Sheridan; Henry (Kleinbach) Brandon; Robert Barrat; Joseph (Joe) Sawyer; Addison Richards; Samuel S. Hinds; John Litel; Eddie Acuff; *D:* Archie Mayo; *W:* Abem Finkel; William Wister Haines; *C:* George Barnes; *M:* Bernhard Kaun.

Black Lemons 🦴 *E venne il giorno dei limoni neri* **1970** While in prison, a convict is stalked by the Mafia because of what he knows. He eventually spills the beans to the cops, putting himself in unavoidable jeopardy. **93m/C; VHS, DVD.** *IT* Peter Carsten; Antonio (Tony) Sabato; Florinda Bolkan; *D:* Camillo Bazzoni.

Black Like Me 🦴 1/2 **1964** Based on John Howard Griffin's successful book about how Griffin turned his skin black with a drug and traveled the South to experience prejudice firsthand. Neither the production nor the direction enhance the material. **107m/B; VHS, DVD.** James Whitmore; Roscoe Lee Browne; Will Geer; Walter Mason; John Marriott; Clifton James; Dan Priest; *D:* Carl Lerner; *W:* Carl Lerner; Gerda Lerner; *C:* Victor Lukens; Henry Mueller; *M:* Meyer Kupferman.

Black Limousine 🦴 1/2 *The Land of the Astronauts* **2010 (R)** Down-on-his-luck Jack (Arquette) takes a job as a driver for a Hollywood limo service. A divorced, recovering alcoholic, Jack is trying to be a good dad and regain his former career as a film composer. Flick takes a turn for the surreal since director Colpaert likes to delve into Jack's mind but Arquette is convincing in a dramatic role. **101m/C; DVD.** David Arquette; Bijou Phillips; Nicholas Bishop; Lin Shaye; Patrick Fabian; Vivica A. Fox; *D:* Carl Colpaert; *W:* Carl Colpaert; *C:* Sero Mutarevic; *M:* Carlos Durango. **VIDEO**

Black Listed 🦴 1/2 **2003 (R)** Fed-up lawyer Alan Chambers (Townsend) compiles a list of a dozen thugs who have escaped doing time thanks to legal loopholes. It's just a way to vent his anger, until some friends take the list and turn vigilante, dragging Alan into the mess. **94m/C; DVD.** Robert Townsend; Harry J. Lennix; Vanessa Williams; Calvin Levels; Eugene "Porky" Lee; Dick Anthony Williams; Richard Lawson; Victoria Rowell; Dwight "Heavy D" Myers; *D:* Robert Townsend; *W:* Robert Townsend; *C:* Charles Mills. **VIDEO**

Black Magic 🦴🦴 1/2 **1949** Cagliostro the magician becomes involved in a plot to supply a double for Marie Antoinette. **105m/B; DVD.** Orson Welles; Akim Tamiroff; Nancy Guild; Raymond Burr; *D:* Gregory Ratoff; *W:* Charles Bennett.

Black Magic 🦴🦴 *Jiang tou; Gong tau* **2006 (R)** The first of two horror flicks by the Shaw Brothers, who were better known for martial arts films. Shan Jianmi (Feng Ku) is an evil sorcerer who terrorizes people with his powers. For the right price he makes love spells for the wealthy or the depraved. But this backfires and draws attention to him because so many different people ask for love spells that it ends up creating a mess (especially after Shan decides he wants one of the women for himself). But along with love spells, Shan can also kill with his magic, so taking him out won't be easy for his would-be assassins. **93m/C; DVD.** *CH* Lung Ti; Lieh Lo; Ni Tien; Lily Li; Feng Ku; Ping Chen; Wen Chung Ku; Wei Tu Lin; Hua Yueh; *D:* Meng Hua No; *W:* Kuang Ni; *C:* Hui-chi Tsao; *M:* Yung-Yu Chen.

Black Magic Terror 🦴 **1979** Jilted by her lover, the old queen of black magic has everybody under her spell. Trouble starts, however, when she turns her back on one of her subjects. **85m/C; VHS, DVD.** *JP* Suzanna; W.D. Mochtar; Alan Nuary; *D:* L. Sudjio.

The Black Marble 🦴🦴🦴 **1979 (PG)** A beautiful policewoman is paired with a policeman who drinks too much, is divorced, and is ready to retire. Surrounded by urban craziness and corruption, they eventually fall in love. Based on the Joseph Wambaugh novel. **110m/C; VHS, DVD.** Paula Prentiss; Harry Dean Stanton; Robert Foxworth; James Woods; Michael Dudikoff; Barbara Babcock; John Hancock; Judy Landers; Anne Ramsey; Christopher Lloyd; *D:* Harold Becker; *M:* Maurice Jarre.

Black Market Babies 🦴 1/2 **1945** Two-bit hood Eddie Condon uses drunk sawbones Jordon to help him operate a private maternity clinic that sells unwanted babies to childless couples. When a prepaid baby is stillborn, Eddie steals his sister-in-law's newborn but the baby switch leads to murder. Monogram's low-down expose based on a 1944 "Woman's Home Companion" article. **71m/B; DVD.** Kane Richmond; Ralph Morgan; George Meeker; Teala Loring; Marjorie Hoshelle; Jayne Hazard; Addison Richards; *D:* William Beaudine; *W:* George Wallace Sayre; *C:* Harry Neumann.

Black Mask 🦴🦴 1/2 *Hak Hap* **1996 (R)** Hong Kong action star Jet Li (second only to Jackie Chan in Hong Kong boxoffice success) is Tsui, a mild-mannered librarian who used to be a member of a secret, biogenetically enhanced squad of super soldiers known as the "701 Squad." These commandos, who feel no fear or pain, are out to take over Hong Kong's underworld, and are killing the crime lords in grisly fashion. Tsui, aided by his detective buddy and dressed a lot like Kato from the "Green Hornet," goes into action to stop his ex-mates. Action may be a little bloody for those not used to the Hong Kong style, but Jet Li is an exciting performer who should break out big with this one after his impressive Stateside debut in "Lethal Weapon 4." Re-dubbed from the 1996 Hong Kong release. **95m/C; VHS, DVD, Blu-Ray.** *CH* Jet Li; Karen Mok; Francoise Yip; Lau Ching Wan; *D:* Daniel Lee; *W:* Tsui Hark; Teddy Chen; *C:* Cheung Tung Leung; *M:* Ben Vaughn; Teddy Robin.

Black Mask 2: City of Masks 🦴 1/2 *Hak Hap 2; Hei xia 2* **2002 (R)** The Black Mask (Andy On) is consulting the world's leading geneticists seeking a cure for his inability to feel pain (a condition many would probably prefer). But the people he's asking for help are getting killed one by one, and he soon discovers it's being done by a group of mutant pro wrestlers whose superpowers were created by the same super computer that made him. Far more comic book-like than the original, it will appeal to fans of that genre. **101m/C; DVD.** *CH* Tobin Bell; Tyler Mane; Andrew Bryniarski; Scott Adkins; Sean Marquette; Oris Erhuero; Michael Bailey Smith; Traci Lords; Andy On; Silvio Simac; John Polito; Teresa Herrera; Rob van Dam; Robert Allan Mukes; Terence Yin; *D:* Tsui Hark; *W:* Tsui Hark; Julien Carbon; Laurent Cortiaud; Charles Cain; Jeff Black; *C:* Wing-Hung Wong; William Yim; *M:* J.M. Logan.

Black Mass 🦴🦴 1/2 **2015 (R)** Depp does his best work in years as James "Whitey" Bulger, the head of the Boston Southie mob in Cooper's examination of this amazing true story. Bulger ruled through power and fear, gaining much of the former through a relationship with an FBI agent (deftly played by Edgerton) who used him as an informant, mostly just covering up his crimes. Cooper cribs a bit from the Scorsese playbook but he's more interested in characters—focusing tightly on the faces of his key players. It's an imperfect film but it's always engaging, carried by Cooper's skills with actors. **130m/C; DVD, Blu-Ray.** Johnny Depp; Joel Edgerton; Benedict Cumberbatch; Dakota Johnson; Juno Temple; *D:* Scott Cooper; *W:* Mark Mallouk; Jez Butterworth; *C:* Masanobu Takayanagi; *M:* Junkie XL.

Black Moon 🦴🦴 **1975** A little gil escapes the harsh reality of a nebulous war between men and women by retreating into a surreal world where she lives with a strange family and a unicorn. Malle's visually stunning but incoherent experiment is definitely not for those fond of linear plotting. **100m/C; DVD, Blu-Ray.** *FR* Cathryn Harrison; Joe Dallesandro; Alexandra Stewart; Therese Giehse; *D:* Louis Malle; *W:* Louis Malle; Joyce Bunuel; Ghislain Uhry; *C:* Sven Nykvist; *M:* Diego Masson.

Black Moon Rising 🦴 1/2 **1986 (R)** Based on an idea by John Carpenter dealing with the theft of a new jet-powered car and its involvement in an FBI investigation. Solid performances and steady action enhance this routine effort. **100m/C; VHS, DVD.** Tommy Lee Jones; Linda Hamilton; Richard Jaeckel; Robert Vaughn; *D:* Harley Cokliss; *W:* John Carpenter; *C:* Misha (Mikhail) Suslov; *M:* Lalo Schifrin.

Black Mountain Side 🦴🦴 **2016** A dark horror-thriller set in remote regions of Canada. After a group of archeologists find a strange, ancient structure underneath the snow in the Canadian wilderness, strange events occur. The researchers begin to experience paranoia and mistrust, as they believe they see an unknown figure creeping nearby. They soon turn each other, though they do not know if what they think they see is real or a figment of their imaginations. They soon learn that their survival is in jeopardy because of the powerful force they have unwittingly set free in their work. **99m/C; DVD, Streaming, Download.** Shane Twerdun; Michael Dickson; Carl Tortfelt; Marc Anthony Williams; Andrew Moxham; *D:* Nick Szostakiwskyj; *W:* Nick Szostakiwskyj; *C:* Cameron Tremblay. **VIDEO**

Black Narcissus 🦴🦴🦴 1/2 **1947** A group of Anglican nuns attempting to found a hospital and school in the Himalayas confront native distrust and human frailties amid beautiful scenery. Adapted from the novel by Rumer Godden. Stunning cinematography. Crucial scenes were cut from the American release by censors. **101m/C; VHS, DVD, Blu-Ray.** *GB* Deborah Kerr; David Farrar; Sabu; Jean Simmons; Kathleen Byron; Flora Robson; Esmond Knight; Jenny Laird; Judith Furse; May Hallatt; Nancy Roberts, RN; *D:* Michael Powell; Emeric Pressburger; *W:* Michael Powell; Emeric Pressburger; *C:* Jack Cardiff; *M:* Brian Easdale. Oscars '47: Art Dir./Set Dec., Color, Color Cinematog.; N.Y. Film Critics '47: Actress (Kerr).

Black Nativity 🦴 1/2 **2013 (PG)** Good intentions notwithstanding, this adaptation of the Langston Hughes musical from adventurous director Lemmons is a drastic misfire. Poorly cast, awkwardly paced, and dramatically inert, it's the kind of TV movie special that one expects to see on basic cable during the holiday season. Troubled teen Langston, who has been raised by his single mother, travels to New York City to stay with his grandparents, one of whom is a preacher, over the holiday season. It's a coming-of-age piece about a teen who learns about family and religion, but it never connects with the viewer through dialogue, character, or song. **93m/C; DVD, Blu-Ray.** Forest Whitaker; Angela Bassett; Jennifer Hudson; Tyrese Gibson; Jacob Latimore; Mary J. Blige; Nasir Jones; Vondie Curtis-Hall; *D:* Kasi Lemmons; *W:* Kasi Lemmons; *C:* Anastas Michos; *M:* Laura Karpman.

Black Ops 🦴 1/2 *Deadwater* **2007 (R)** A WWII battleship is recommissioned and deployed to the Persian Gulf. When the ship falls into radio silence after a distress call, a Marine task force is sent in and finds most of the crew slaughtered. At first, they suspect terrorists but it turns out something else on the ship is responsible and it's so ridiculous, your jaw will drop open in disbelief. Henriksen does his usual professional job and Randolph is eye candy in a tiny tank top and a shower scene. **90m/C; DVD.** Lance Henriksen; James Russo; Katherine Randolph; Gary Stretch; Jim Hanks; D.C. Douglas; Grant Mathis; *D:* Roel Reine; *W:* Roel Reine; Ethan Wiley; *C:* Roel Reine; *M:* Joseph Bauer. **VIDEO**

Black Ops 🦴🦴 *Stairs* **2020** During an intelligence- gathering mission in Europe, the special ops squad known as "Hell's Bastards" finds themselves in a no-win scenario: they become stuck on stairs that never end. Though, they are able to jump back in time through portals along the way. But will this help them figure out how to escape? Inspired by early 1980s horror, it's high concept for sure but the repetitive time loops become a bit of a bore. **102m/C; DVD.** Shayne Ward; Bentley Kalu; Samantha Schnitzler; Alana Wallace; Toby Osmond; *D:* Tom Paton; *W:* Tom Paton; *C:* George Burt; *M:* Max Sweiry.

Black or White 🦴 1/2 **2014 (PG-13)** Hard-drinking L.A. attorney Elliot Anderson (Costner) raised his granddaughter since his daughter died during childbirth. After his wife passes, his world is rocked further when his young granddaughter's black grandmother

(Spencer) fights for custody to return her to the child's drug-addicted father. Well-intentioned but still ill-advised, writer/director Binder's commentary on race relations in the '10s doesn't quite connect. Clearly, he has more on his mind than the average family drama writer/director but it's almost worse that he takes serious issues about racial differences and the problems of black fatherhood and reduces them to a drama without nearly enough gray areas. **121m/C; DVD, Blu-Ray.** Kevin Costner; Octavia Spencer; Jillian Estell; Anthony Mackie; Andre Holland; Gillian Jacobs; Jennifer Ehle; ***D:*** Mike Binder; ***W:*** Mike Binder; ***C:*** Russ T. Alsobrook; ***M:*** Terence Blanchard.

Black Orchid 🦴🦴 1/2 **1959** A businessman and a crook's widow fall in love and try to persuade their children it can work out. **96m/B; VHS, DVD.** Sophia Loren; Anthony Quinn; Ina Balin; Peter Mark Richman; Jimmy Baird; ***D:*** Martin Ritt; ***W:*** Joseph Stefano; ***C:*** Robert Burks.

Black Orpheus 🦴🦴🦴 1/2 *Orfeu Negro* **1958** The legend of Orpheus and Eurydice unfolds against the colorful background of the carnival in Rio de Janeiro. In the black section of the city, Orfeo (Mello) is a streetcar conductor and Eurydice (Dawn), a country girl fleeing from a stranger sworn to kill her. The man has followed her to Rio and disguised himself as the figure of Death. Dancing, incredible music, and black magic add to the beauty of this film. Based on the play "Orfeu da Conceica" by De Moraes. In Portuguese with English subtitles or dubbed. **103m/C; VHS, DVD, Blu-Ray.** *BR FR PT* Breno Mello; Marpessa Dawn; Lea Garcia; Fausto Guerzoni; Lourdes De Oliveira; Adhemar Da Silva; Alexandro Constantino; Waldetar De Souza; ***D:*** Marcel Camus; ***W:*** Vinicius De Moraes; Jacques Viot; ***C:*** Jean (Yves, Georges) Bourgoin; ***M:*** Antonio Carlos Jobim; Luis Bonfa. Oscars '59: Foreign Film; Cannes '59: Film; Golden Globes '60: Foreign Film.

Black Out 🦴🦴 **2012** Stylistic Dutch comedy crime thriller follows a tense day in the life of Jos Vreeswijk (Thiry), who thought he left his life of crime behind. Waking up with a murdered man next to him on the day before his wedding, the former coke dealer finds himself immersed in race against time. Accused by gangsters of stealing 20 kilos of coke, he must find and return the drugs, protect his future wife, and make it to his wedding. In Dutch, with subtitles. **92m/C; DVD, Blu-Ray.** Raymond Thiry; Kim van Kooten; Bas Keijzer; Edmond Classen; ***D:*** Arne Toonen; ***W:*** Melle Runderkamp; ***C:*** Jeroen de Bruin; ***M:*** Jurriaan Balhuizen; Pieter Brouwer; Tom Sikkers; Koen van Baal. **VIDEO**

Black Panther 🦴🦴🦴 **2018 (PG-13)** The first (but definitely not last) solo treatment of the character introduced in *Captain America: Civil War.* T'Challa (Boseman), the newly crowned king of the technologically advanced African nation of Wakanda, must become the Black Panther to defend his country from internal enemies and resist being drawn into a world war. One of the best recent offerings by the Marvel Cinematic Universe, and important because, like the previous year's *Wonder Woman*, it breaks the mold of what a superhero is supposed to look like. **134m/C; DVD, Blu-Ray.** Chadwick Boseman; Michael B. Jordan; Lupita Nyong'o; Danai Gurira; Martin Freeman; ***D:*** Ryan Coogler; ***W:*** Ryan Coogler; Joe Robert Cole; ***C:*** Rachel Morrison; ***M:*** Ludwig Göransson. Oscars '18: Costume Des., Orig. Score, Production Design; British Acad. '18: Visual FX; Screen Actors Guild '18: Cast.

The Black Panthers: Vanguard of the Revolution 🦴🦴🦴 **2015** Stanley Nelson's documentary captures the rise and fall of one of the 20th century's most essential groups, an organization of men and women tired of asking for equal rights and ready to take them. Archival footage of The Black Panthers storming our own governments, like the legislature in California, with loaded weapons is mesmerizing, and Nelson gets some intriguing interviews from most of the key players over the history of the Panthers. They may not have the power they once did, but the Panthers still matter, and this doc successfully argues that they always will. **115m/C; DVD, Blu-Ray.** ***D:*** Stanley Nelson; ***W:*** Stanley Nelson; ***C:*** Antonio Rossi.

Black Patch 🦴🦴 **1957** New Mexico marshal Clay Morgan (Montgomery) is nicknamed "Black Patch" because he lost an eye in the Civil War. When his old friend Hank Danner (Gordon) arrives in town, so does trouble, since Danner is married to Morgan's ex-love Helen (Brewster). Danner is also accused of bank robbery so Morgan tosses him in jail and he winds up dead after an escape. Now would-be gunslinger Carl (Pittman) thinks he should avenge his friend Danner's death. **82m/B; DVD.** George Montgomery; Diane Brewster; Tom Pittman; Leo Gordon; House Peters, Jr.; Sebastian Cabot; Strother Martin; ***D:*** Allen Miner; ***W:*** Leo Gordon; ***C:*** Edward Colman; ***M:*** Jerry Goldsmith.

Black Peter 🦴🦴 1/2 *Cerny Petr; Peter and Pavla* **1963** Director Forman's first feature offers a glimpse into the struggles of a young Czech man as he copes with an oppressive father, a menial grocery store job, and first-love jitters. In Czech, with subtitles. **85m/B; VHS, DVD.** *CZ* Ladislav Jakim; Jan Vostrcil; Vladimir Pucholt; Pavla Martinkova; Pavel Sedlacek; ***D:*** Milos Forman; ***W:*** Milos Forman; Jaroslav Papousek; ***C:*** Jan Nemecek; ***M:*** Jiri Slitr.

The Black Pirate 🦴🦴🦴 *Rage of the Buccaneers; The Black Buccaneer; Gordon il Pirata Nero* **1926** A shipwrecked mariner vows revenge on the pirates who destroyed his father's ship. Quintessential Fairbanks, this film features astounding athletic feats and exciting swordplay. Silent film with music score. Also available in color. **122m/B; Silent; VHS, DVD.** *IT* Douglas Fairbanks, Sr.; Donald Crisp; Billie Dove; ***D:*** Albert Parker; ***W:*** Douglas Fairbanks, Sr.; Jack Cunningham; ***C:*** Henry Sharp; ***M:*** Mortimer Wilson. Natl. Film Reg. '93.

Black Point 🦴🦴 **2001 (R)** John Hawkins (Caruso) is a former Naval captain, down on his luck and living in the harbor town of Black Point. When he meets Natalie (Haskell), he thinks she's the woman of his dreams. He's wrong. **107m/C; VHS, DVD.** *CA* David Caruso; Susan Haskell; Thomas Ian Griffith; Gordon Tootoosis; Alex Bruhanski; ***D:*** David Mackay; ***W:*** Thomas Ian Griffith; Greg Mellott; ***C:*** Stephen McNutt; ***M:*** Terry Frewer.

Black Pond 🦴🦴 **2011** Brit black comedy indie. Tom Thompson is out walking his dog, Boy, by Black Pond when he meets and befriends eccentric loner, Blake. When Boy suddenly dies, the dysfunctional family decides to bury him (illegally) by the pond. This is only the first such burial as Blake also dies suddenly at the Thompson's dinner table. When malicious, possibly fraudulent, therapist Eric spreads the story to the tabloids, the Thompsons are labelled murderers. **83m/C; DVD.** *UK* Chris Langham; Simon Amstell; Amanda Hardingue; Helen Cripps; Anna O'Grady; Colin Hurley; Will Sharpe; ***D:*** Will Sharpe; Tom Kingsley; ***W:*** Will Sharpe; ***C:*** Simon Walton; ***M:*** Ralegh Long.

Black Rain 🦴🦴🦴 *Kuroi Ame* **1988** Erstwhile Ozu assistant Imamura directs this powerful portrait of a post-Hiroshima family five years after the bombing. Tanaka plays a young woman who, having been caught in a shower of black rain (radioactive fallout) on an ill-timed visit to Hiroshima, returns to her village to find herself ostracized by her peers and no longer considered marriage-worthy. Winner of numerous awards (including five Japanese Academy Awards). In Japanese with English subtitles. **123m/B; VHS, DVD.** *JP* Kazuo Kitamura; Yoshiko Tanaka; Etsuko Ichihara; Shoichi Ozawa; Norihei Miki; Keisuke Ishida; ***D:*** Shohei Imamura; ***W:*** Shohei Imamura; Toshiro Ishido; ***C:*** Takashi Kawamata; ***M:*** Toru Takemitsu.

Black Rain 🦴🦴 1/2 **1989 (R)** Douglas portrays a ruthless American cop chasing a Japanese murder suspect through gang-controlled Tokyo. Loads of action and stunning visuals from the man who brought you "Blade Runner." **125m/C; VHS, DVD, Blu-Ray, HD-DVD.** Michael Douglas; Andy Garcia; Kate Capshaw; Ken Takakura; Yusaku Matsuda; John Spencer; Shigeru Koyama; Stephen (Steve) Root; ***D:*** Ridley Scott; ***W:*** Craig Bolotin; Warren Lewis; ***C:*** Jan De Bont; ***M:*** Hans Zimmer.

Black Rainbow 🦴🦴🦴 **1991 (R)** Surprisingly good thriller that's relatively unknown, haunted by a menacing mood. Robards and Arquette are a father/daughter duo who perform clairvoyance scams at carnival sideshows. Suddenly, without warning, Arquette's former cons become real: she sees murder victims—before their demise. Quirky sleeper filmed on location in North Carolina. **103m/C; VHS, DVD.** Rosanna Arquette; Jason Robards, Jr.; Tom Hulce; Ron Rosenthal; John Bennes; Linda Pierce; Mark Joy; ***D:*** Mike Hodges; ***W:*** Mike Hodges.

Black Rat 🦴 1/2 *Kuronezumi* **2010** Six classmates receive an e-mail asking them back to their school from a former peer who committed suicide due to their hazing. Despite logic and common sense telling them otherwise, they show up at the appointed place, and are promptly assaulted by a girl in a rat mask screaming about revenge. **76m/C; DVD.** *JP* Hiroya Matsumoto; ***D:*** Kenta Fukasaku; ***W:*** Futoshi Fujita; ***C:*** Hiroaki Yuasa; ***M:*** Hikaru Yoshida. **TV**

Black Robe 🦴🦴🦴 1/2 **1991 (R)** In 1634 young Jesuit priest Father Laforgue (Bluteau) journeys across the North American wilderness to bring the word of God to Canada's Huron Indians. The winter journey is brutal and perilous and he begins to question his mission after seeing the strength of the Indian's native ways. Stunning cinematography, a good script, and fine acting combine to make this superb. Portrays the Indians in a realistic manner, the only flaw being that Beresford portrays the white culture with very few redeeming qualities and as the only reason for the Indian's downfall. Moore adapted his own novel for the screen. **101m/C; VHS, DVD, Blu-Ray.** *AU CA* Lothaire Bluteau; Aden Young; Sandrine Holt; August Schellenberg; Tantoo Cardinal; Billy Two Rivers; Lawrence Bayne; Harrison Liu; Marthe Tungeon; ***D:*** Bruce Beresford; ***W:*** Brian Moore; ***C:*** Peter James; ***M:*** Georges Delerue. Australian Film Inst. '92: Cinematog.; Genie '91: Director (Beresford), Film.

Black Rock 🦴🦴 **2012 (R)** Three gal pals (Aselton, Bosworth, and Bell) reunite at an old camping spot on a secluded island, only to be interrupted by three male veterans out hunting. When a romantic encounter goes horribly wrong, the hunters start stalking the girls. Actress/writer/director Aselton never succumbs to gender stereotypes and gives a strong performance herself but the film is a miss. But she does deserve credit for tackling a completely different genre than fans of her mumblecore films would expect but this thriller misses the tension. **83m/C; DVD, Blu-Ray.** Katie (Kathryn) Aselton; Kate (Catherine) Bosworth; Lake Bell; Jay Paulson; Will Bouvier; Anselm Richardson; ***D:*** Katie (Kathryn) Aselton; ***W:*** Mark Duplass; ***C:*** Hillary Spera; ***M:*** Ben Lovett.

The Black Room 🦴🦴🦴 **1935** As an evil count lures victims into his castle of terror, the count's twin brother returns to fulfill an ancient prophecy. Karloff is wonderful in his dual role as the twin brothers. **70m/B; DVD.** Boris Karloff; Marian Marsh; Robert "Tex" Allen; Katherine DeMille; John Buckler; Thurston Hall; ***D:*** Roy William Neill; ***W:*** Henry Myers; Arthur Strawn; ***C:*** Allen Siegler.

The Black Room 🦴 **1982 (R)** Couples are lured to a mysterious mansion where a brother and his sister promise to satisfy their sexual desires. Not much to recommend unless you're a fan of the vampire as psychology test case. **90m/C; VHS, DVD.** Linnea Quigley; Stephen Knight; Cassandra Gaviola; Jim Stathis; ***D:*** Norman Thaddeus Vane.

The Black Rose 🦴🦴 1/2 **1950** Technicolor action, set in the 13th century, as English Saxon Walter of Gurnie (Power) seeks to restore his fortunes by traveling in a caravan to the wilds of Cathay. Welles is the bizarre and brutal Tartan general Bayan, and pretty (and young) French actress Aubrey looks out of place as runaway concubine, Maryam, so the romance between her and Walter is sketchy at best. Based on the novel by Thomas B. Costain. **120m/C; DVD.** Tyrone Power; Orson Welles; Cecile Aubry; Jack Hawkins; Finlay Currie; Herbert Lom; Michael Rennie; Robert (Bobby) Blake; ***D:*** Henry Hathaway; ***W:*** Talbot Jennings; ***C:*** Jack Cardiff; ***M:*** Richard Addinsell.

Black Roses 🦴 **1988 (R)** A disgusting band of rockers shows up in a small town, and the local kids start turning into monsters. Coincidence? **90m/C; VHS, DVD.** Carmine Appice; Sal Viviano; Carla Ferrigno; Julie Adams; Ken Swofford; John Martin; ***D:*** John Fasano.

Black Sabbath 🦴🦴🦴 *I Tre Volti della Paura; Black Christmas; The Three Faces of Terror; The Three Faces of Fear; Les Trois Visages de la Peur* **1964** An omnibus horror film with three parts, climaxing with Karloff as a Wurdalak, a vampire who must kill those he loves. **99m/C; VHS, DVD, Blu-Ray.** *IT FR* Boris Karloff; Jacqueline Pierreux; Michele Mercier; Lidia Alfonsi; Susy Andersen; Mark Damon; Rika Dialina; Glauco Onorato; Massimo Righi; ***D:*** Mario Bava; ***W:*** Mario Bava; Marcello Fondato; Alberto Bevilacqua; ***C:*** Ubaldo Terzano; ***M:*** Les Baxter.

Black Samson **WOOF!** *Samson* **1974** A lion-owning bartender, who likes to beat Mafiosi with a staff, decides to clean the drugs out of his neighborhood in this blaxploitation classic (in the sense you just don't see films like this anymore). **87m/C; DVD.** Rockne Tarkington; William (Bill) Smith; Titos Vandis; Carol Speed; ***D:*** Charles Bail; ***W:*** Warren Hamilton, Jr.; ***C:*** Henning Schellerup; ***M:*** Allen Toussaint.

Black Samurai 🦴 **1977 (R)** When his girlfriend is held hostage, a martial arts warrior will stop at nothing to destroy the organization that abducted her. **84m/C; VHS, DVD.** Jim Kelly; Marilyn Joi; Biff Yeager; Bill Roy; Roberto Contreras; ***D:*** Al Adamson; ***W:*** B. Readick; ***C:*** Louis Horvath.

The Black Scorpion 🦴 1/2 **1957** Two geologists in Mexico unearth a nest of giant scorpions living in a dead volcano. Eventually one of the oversized arachnids escapes to wreak havoc on Mexico City. **85m/B; DVD, Blu-Ray.** Richard Denning; Mara Corday; Carlos Rivas; ***D:*** Edward Ludwig; ***W:*** Robert Blees.

Black Scorpion 🦴🦴 1/2 *Roger Corman Presents: Black Scorpion* **1995 (R)** Darcy Walker (Severance) is an ex-cop-turned-superhero (the scorpion is her symbol), who dons a mask and fetching (and tight) black vinyl to fight crime and avenge her dad's death. She's got the prerequisite sidekick—an ex-chop shop operator (Morris)?and a supervillain—the asthmatic Breathtaker (Siemaszko) who threatens to annihilate the city with toxic gas. Campy, schlock fun. **92m/C; VHS, DVD.** Joan Severance; Garrett Morris; Casey Siemaszko; Rick Rossovich; ***D:*** Jonathan Winfrey; ***W:*** Craig J. Nevius; ***C:*** Geoffrey George; ***M:*** Kevin Kiner. **CABLE**

Black Scorpion 2: Ground Zero 🦴🦴 *Black Scorpion 2: Aftershock* **1996 (R)** Fetching crimefighter Darcy Walker (Severance) returns to battle villains Gangster Prankster (Jackson) and AfterShock (Rose), who are set on destroying the City of Angels by earthquake. **85m/C; VHS, DVD.** Joan Severance; Whip Hubley; Stoney Jackson; Sherrie Rose; Garrett Morris; Laura Elena Harring; ***D:*** Jonathan Winfrey; ***W:*** Craig J. Nevius; ***C:*** Mark Kohl; ***M:*** Kevin Kiner. **CABLE**

Black Sea 🦴🦴 1/2 **2014 (R)** Workmanlike director MacDonald delivers a perfectly adequate yet ultimately forgettable submarine thriller largely through the sheer charisma of the men he cast to populate his underwater vessel. The always-good Law stars as Robinson, an ex-Navy captain who has heard the urban legends of a sunken Nazi U-boat loaded with Russian gold somewhere on the Black Sea floor. He assembles a motley crew of similarly minded treasure hunters (including great characters like Ben Mendelsohn and Scoot McNairy), but, of course, things don't go exactly as planned. They never do in submarine movies. **115m/C; DVD, Blu-Ray.** *UK* Jude Law; Ben Mendelsohn; Scoot McNairy; Grigoriy Dobrygin; Bobby Schofield; Tobias Menzies; ***D:*** Kevin MacDonald; ***W:*** Dennis Kelly; ***C:*** Christopher Ross; ***M:*** Ilan Eshkeri.

Black Shampoo **WOOF!** **1976** A black hairdresser on the Sunset Strip fights the mob with a chainsaw. **90m/C; VHS, DVD, Blu-Ray.** John Daniels; Tanya Boyd; Joe Ortiz; ***D:*** Greydon Clark.

Black Sheep 🦴 1/2 **1996 (PG-13)** Isn't there a five-day waiting period for remakes? The previously viewed copies of "Tommy

Boy" hadn't even hit the sale bin before Spade and Farley went in search of more property to destroy. The twist here? Spade is assigned to keep the oafish brother (not son) of a gubernatorial candidate (not auto parts dealer) out of trouble until after the election (not so he can save the family business). In an effort to provide humor, plot points, and character development, Farley falls out of, off of or onto every prop in sight while Spade smirks. **87m/C; DVD, Blu-Ray.** Chris Farley; David Spade; Tim Matheson; Christine Ebersole; Gary Busey; Grant Heslov; Timothy Carhart; Bruce McGill; Fred Wolf; ***D:*** Penelope Spheeris; ***W:*** Fred Wolf; ***C:*** Daryn Okada; ***M:*** William Ross.

Black Sheep **2006** Cheery gorefest. Henry (Meister) returns to the family farm in rural New Zealand, hoping to cure his aversion to sheep and get a buyout from older brother Angus (Feeney). Only Angus has been doing some genetic experimenting on the woolies that turns the placid creatures into blood-thirsty killers! **87m/C; DVD.** *NZ* Nathan Meister; Peter Feeney; Tandi Wright; Oliver Driver; Danielle Mason; Tammy Davis; ***D:*** Jonathan King; ***W:*** Jonathan King; ***C:*** Richard Buck; ***M:*** Victoria Kelly.

The Black Shield of Falworth **1/2** **1954** Typically silly '50s Technicolor swashbuckler with Curtis (and his New York accent) as Myles, the son of a disgraced knight, who's out to thwart a conspiracy against King Henry IV (Keith) and win the hand of fair maiden, Lady Anne (Leigh, Curtis' wife at the time). Loosely based on the Howard Pyle novel, "Men of Iron." **98m/C; DVD, Blu-Ray.** Tony Curtis; Janet Leigh; Ian Keith; David Farrar; Barbara Rush; Herbert Marshall; Dan O'Herlihy; Rhys Williams; Torin Thatcher; Patrick O'Neal; Craig Hill; ***D:*** Rudolph Mate; ***W:*** Oscar Brodney; ***C:*** Irving Glassberg; ***M:*** Joseph Gershenson.

Black Sister's Revenge *Emma Mae* **1976** Poorly selected video title mars this intelligent drama about a young black woman's struggle to adjust to the big city after growing up in the deep South. **100m/C; VHS, DVD.** Jerri Hayes; Ernest Williams, II; Charles D. Brook, III; Eddie Allen; ***D:*** Jamaa Fanaka; ***W:*** Jamaa Fanaka.

The Black Six **1974 (R)** Six black Vietnam veterans are out to punish the white gang who killed the brother of one of the black men. **91m/C; VHS, DVD.** Gene Washington; Carl Eller; Lem Barney; Mercury Morris; Joe "Mean Joe" Greene; Willie Lanier; Rosalind Miles; John Isenbarger; Ben Davidson; Maury Wills; Mikel Angel; Fred Scott; ***D:*** Matt Cimber; ***W:*** George Theakos; ***C:*** William Swenning; ***M:*** David Moscoe.

The Black Sleep *Dr. Cadman's Secret* **1956** Mad scientist Dr. Cadman (Rathbone) invents a drug that causes a deathlike trance and uses it to perform brain surgery on unwilling patients. Needing an assistant, Cadman frames Dr. Ramsay (Rudley) for murder and uses the drug to rescue him from the gallows. Then some of Cadman's experiments get loose and want revenge. Over-the-top hokum that wastes a who's who of horror, including Lugosi (in nearly his last role) as a mute butler. **82m/B; VHS, DVD, Blu-Ray.** Basil Rathbone; Herbert Rudley; Akim Tamiroff; Lon Chaney, Jr.; John Carradine; Bela Lugosi; Tor Johnson; Patricia Blake; ***D:*** Reginald LeBorg; ***W:*** John C. Higgins; ***C:*** Gordon Avil; ***M:*** Les Baxter.

Black Snake Moan **2007 (R)** Over-heated stew finds Jackson playing grizzled blues musician/farmer Lazarus, who's turned to religion to help him cope with his wife running off. So he's the one man ready to tackle the sex demons of abused white trash Rae (tiny Ricci in barely-there attire), even if it means chaining her inside his shack until she can control that nympho itch. Part sermon, part exploitation, wholly dull. **115m/C; DVD, Blu-Ray, HD-DVD.** Samuel L. Jackson; Christina Ricci; Justin Timberlake; S. Epatha Merkerson; John Cothran, Jr.; Kim Richards; David Banner; ***D:*** Craig Brewer; ***W:*** Craig Brewer; ***C:*** Amy Vincent; ***M:*** Scott Bomar.

The Black Stallion **1979 (PG)** A young boy and a wild Arabian Stallion are the only survivors of a shipwreck, and they develop a deep affection for each other. When rescued, they begin training for an important race. Exceptionally beautiful first half. Rooney plays a horse trainer, again. Great for adults and kids. **120m/C; VHS, DVD, Blu-Ray.** Kelly Reno; Mickey Rooney; Teri Garr; Clarence Muse; Hoyt Axton; ***D:*** Carroll Ballard; ***W:*** William D. Wittliff; Melissa Mathison; Jeanne Rosenberg; ***C:*** Caleb Deschanel; ***M:*** Carmine Coppola. Oscars '79: Sound FX Editing; L.A. Film Critics '79: Cinematog.; Natl. Film Reg. '02; Natl. Soc. Film Critics '79: Cinematog.

The Black Stallion Returns **1/2** **1983 (PG)** Sequel to "The Black Stallion" follows the adventures of young Alec as he travels to the Sahara to search for his beautiful horse, which was stolen by an Arab chieftain. Unfortunately lacks much of the charm that was present in the first film. Adapted from the stories by Walt Farley. **103m/C; VHS, DVD, Blu-Ray.** Kelly Reno; Teri Garr; Vincent Spano; Angelo Infanti; ***D:*** Robert Dalva; ***C:*** Carlo Di Palma; ***M:*** Georges Delerue.

Black Sunday *La Maschera del Demonio; The Demon's Mask; House of Fright; Revenge of the Vampire; Mask of Satan* **1960** In 1630, witch Asa (Steele) who also happens to be a vampire, is executed along with her lover Juvato (Dominici) by her own brother. Two hundred years later, they are accidentally resurrected and in revenge, Asa goes after her descendents, including her look-alike, Katia. A must see for horror fans; firsts for Steele as star and Bava as director. **83m/B; VHS, DVD, Blu-Ray.** *IT* Barbara Steele; John Richardson; Ivo Garrani; Andrea Checchi; Arturo Dominici; Antonio Pierfederici; Tino Bianchi; Clara Bindi; Enrico Olivieri; Germana Dominici; ***D:*** Mario Bava; ***W:*** Mario Bava; Ennio de Concini; Mario Serandrei; ***C:*** Mario Bava; Ubaldo Terzano; ***M:*** Les Baxter.

Black Sunday **1/2** **1977 (R)** An Arab terrorist group, with the help of a disgruntled Vietnam vet, plots to steal the Goodyear Blimp and load it with explosives. Their intent is to explode it over a Miami Super Bowl game to assassinate the U.S. president and to kill all the fans. Based on Thomas Harris' novel. **143m/C; VHS, DVD.** Robert Shaw; Bruce Dern; Marthe Keller; Fritz Weaver; Steven Keats; Michael V. Gazzo; William Daniels; Clyde Kusatsu; ***D:*** John Frankenheimer; ***W:*** Ernest Lehman; ***C:*** John A. Alonzo; ***M:*** John Williams.

The Black Swan **1942** Swashbuckling pirate film, based on the novel by Rafael Sabatini, stars Power as James Waring, compatriot of notorious buccanneer Henry Morgan (Cregar). Morgan is pardoned and sent to Jamaica as its new governor—if he can prevent his from associates from continuing their criminal ways. He enlists Waring to help him fight the renegades; meanwhile Waring falls in love with former governor's daughter Margaret (O'Hara). Lots of derring do. **85m/C; VHS, DVD, Blu-Ray.** Tyrone Power; Maureen O'Hara; Laird Cregar; Thomas Mitchell; George Sanders; Anthony Quinn; George Zucco; Edward Ashley; Fortunio Bonanova; ***D:*** Henry King; ***W:*** Ben Hecht; Seton I. Miller; ***C:*** Leon Shamroy; ***M:*** Alfred Newman. Oscars '42: Color Cinematog.

Black Swan **1/2** **2010 (R)** Harrowing tale has New York ballerina Nina (Portman) desperate to dance the lead role in the company's new production of "Swan Lake." She has an unexpected rival in newcomer Lily (Kunis), and is fighting against her own fears and paranoia. Portman does an excellent job showing Nina's descent into madness. It is a compelling and disturbing journey. Not exactly easy to watch, but well worth it for the performances. **108m/C; DVD, Blu-Ray.** Natalie Portman; Mila Kunis; Vincent Cassel; Barbara Hershey; Winona Ryder; Janet Montgomery; ***D:*** Darren Aronofsky; ***W:*** Mark Heyman; ***C:*** Matthew Libatique; ***M:*** Clint Mansell. Oscars '10: Actress (Portman); British Acad. '10: Actress (Portman); Golden Globes '11: Actress--Drama (Portman); Ind. Spirit '11: Actress (Portman), Cinematog., Director (Aronofsky), Film; Screen Actors Guild '10: Actress (Portman).

Black Swarm **2007** Cartoonish CGI wasps made for a very non-scary SciFi Channel creature feature. The sting of genetically engineered wasps creates mindless human drones of the folks of Black Stone. The wasps intend to use human innards for breeding purposes and even scientist Eli Giles (Englund) knows this is wrong. So he teams up with exterminator Devin Hall (Roberts) and sheriff Jane Kozik (Allen) to swat the flying pests permanently. **89m/C; DVD.** Sebastien Roberts; Sarah Allen; Robert Englund; Jayne Heitmeyer; Rebecca Windheim; Robert Higden; ***D:*** David Winning; ***W:*** Todd Samovitz; Ethlie Ann Vare; ***C:*** Daniel Vincelette; ***M:*** Mario Sevigny. **CABLE**

Black Thunder **1/2** **1998 (R)** An Air Force stealth jet, nicknamed "Black Thunder," is hijacked by a Libyan agent during testing. A top gun, Vince Connors (Dudikoff), is paired with hotdog pilot Rick Jannick (Hudson) to retrieve the jet. A standard actioner. **85m/C; VHS, DVD.** Michael Dudikoff; Gary Hudson; Richard Norton; Rob Madrid; Nancy Valen; Michael Cavanaugh; Robert Miranda; Frederic Forrest; ***D:*** Rick Jacobson; ***W:*** William C. Martell; ***C:*** Michael G. Wojciechowski; ***M:*** Michael Clark. **VIDEO**

Black Tight Killers *Ore Ni Sawaru to Abunaize* **1966** Imagine a Japanese Matt Helm movie with an Elvis impersonator in the lead. That's essentially what's going on in this gonzo adventure/comedy from the mid-'60s. Hondo (Kobayashi) is a combat photographer just back from Vietnam. He and his stewardess girlfriend (Matsubara) become involved with various gangsters in a fast-moving plot filled with such bizarre devices as Ninja chewing gum bullets. **84m/C; DVD.** *JP* Akira Kobayashi; Chieko Matsubara; ***D:*** Yasuharu Hasebe.

Black Tights **1/2** *Un, Deux, Trois, Quatre!* **1960** Chevalier introduces four stories told in dance by Roland Petit's Ballet de Paris company: "The Diamond Crusher," "Cyrano de Bergerac," "A Merry Mourning," and "Carmen." A keeper for dance fans. Shearer's Roxanne in "Cyrano" was her last performance before retirement. **120m/C; VHS, DVD.** *FR* Cyd Charisse; Zizi Jeanmaire; Moira Shearer; Dirk Sanders; Roland Petit; ***Nar:*** Maurice Chevalier; ***D:*** Terence Young.

Black Torment **1/2** **1964** A newly married Lord returns to the family manor only to be told he already returned a while back and has been running about killing people. Safe to say, it's probably not the honeymoon he was expecting. **115m/C; DVD.** *UK* Norman Bird; John Turner; Peter Arne; Heather Sears; Ann Lynn; ***D:*** Robert Hartford-Davis; ***W:*** Derek Ford; Donald Ford; ***C:*** Peter Newbrook; ***M:*** Robert Richards. **VIDEO**

The Black Tulip *La Tulipe Noire* **1964** During the French Revolution, a handsome aristocrat (Delon) has a dual identity as a bandit with the not-very-swashbuckling name of "The Black Tulip." Naturally, he helps the poor, bedevils the rich, and woos beautiful women. Based on the novel by Alexandre Dumas Sr. French with subtitles. **109m/C; DVD.** *FR* Alain Delon; Virna Lisi; Adolfo Marsillach; Dawn Addams; Akim Tamiroff; ***D:*** Christian-Jaque; ***W:*** Christian-Jaque; ***C:*** Henri Decae; ***M:*** Gerard Calvi.

Black Venus **WOOF!** **1983 (R)** A softcore epic, starring the former Miss Bahamas, Josephine Jacqueline Jones, about the 18th-century French aristocracy. Laughably based upon the stories of Balzac. European film dubbed in English. **80m/C; VHS, DVD, Blu-Ray.** *SP* Josephine Jacqueline Jones; Emiliano Redondo; Jose Antonio Ceinos; Monique Gabrielle; Florence Guerin; Helga Line; Mandy Rice-Davies; ***D:*** Claude Mulot; ***W:*** Gregorio Garcia Segura; Harry Alan Towers; ***C:*** Jacques Assuerus; Julio Burgos.

Black Water **2007 (R)** You'll root for the crocs to get this trio of whiners as quickly as possible in this remarkably dull creature feature. Lee (Dermody) joins her sister Grace (Glenn) and brother-in-law Adam (Rodoreda) on an ill-fated boating trip into a northern Australian mangrove swamp. A croc eats their guide and the three hustle up a tree while they try to figure out how to get back into their boat without becoming dinner. **89m/C; DVD.** *GB AU* Ben Oxenbould; Diana Glenn; Maeve Dermody; Andy Rodoreda; ***D:*** Andrew Traucki; David Nerlick; ***W:*** Andrew Traucki; David Nerlick; ***C:*** John Biggins; ***M:*** Rafael May.

Black Water **2018 (R)** A mediocre action thriller set aboard a submarine. After CIA agent Wheeler (Van Damme) is attacked, he is captured and threatened by a CIA group led by Patrick Ferris (Kilpatrick). The group wants to know the location of the files Wheeler is protecting, which include information about the CIA's active undercover agents, and Wheeler's loyalty to the United States. Wheeler is thrown into a blacksite prison on a submarine where he meets Germany spy Marco (Lundgren) and another good CIA agent Cassie (Waltz), and tries to escape with his life. Typical Van Damme fare. **104m/C; Blu-Ray, Streaming.** *CA* Jean-Claude Van Damme; Dolph Lundgren; Al Sapienza; Jasmine Waltz; Patrick Kilpatrick; ***D:*** Pasha Patriki; ***W:*** Chad Law; Tyler W. Konney; Richard Switzer; ***C:*** Pasha Patriki; ***M:*** Spencer Creaghan.

Black Water Gold **1/2** **1969** TV movie about a search for sunken Spanish gold. **75m/C; VHS, DVD.** Ricardo Montalban; Keir Dullea; Lana Wood; Bradford Dillman; France Nuyen; ***D:*** Alan Landsburg. **TV**

The Black Water Vampire **1/2** **2013 (R)** A horror film in the form of a faux documentary about an investigation in a series of murders that reveals a terrible truth. The Black Water killings were savage. A group of women were slain, mutilated, and drained of blood before being dumped in the woods. Some young documentarians decide to find the truth behind the murders and exonerate the man wrongly convicted of the crimes. When the enter the woods where these deaths took place, they find an unexpected evil who leaves them fighting for their own lives. **82m/C; DVD, Streaming, Download.** Danielle Lozeau; Andrea Monier; Anthony Fanelli; Robin Steffen; Bill Oberst, Jr.; ***D:*** Evan Tramel; ***W:*** Evan Tramel; ***M:*** Richard Figone. **VIDEO**

The Black Waters of Echo's Pond **2010 (R)** Silly horror flick has nine college students vacationing at an old home on a Maine island (Patrick is the crusty caretaker). While playing an old board game, they release a demon that possesses each student and releases their innermost ugliest impulses that also prove deadly. The students are all bland horror fodder with too much time wasted establishing the relationships between them. Get to the gore already! **92m/C; DVD, Blu-Ray.** Robert Patrick; Danielle Harris; James Duval; Mircea Monroe; Walker Howard; Sean Lawlor; Elise Avellan; Electra Avellan; M.D. Walton; Nick Mennell; ***D:*** Gabriel Bologna; ***W:*** Gabriel Bologna; Sean Clark; Michael Berenson; ***C:*** Massimo Zeri; ***M:*** Harry Manfredini.

Black Widow **1954** Rogers gets cast against type as heartless Broadway diva Lottie, who's mixed-up in the death of secretive aspiring writer Nanny (Garner). But since the gal died in the apartment of producer Peter (Heflin), he's suspect numero uno, according to Detective Bruce (Raft). And that doesn't make Peter's actress wife Iris (Tierney) too happy. **95m/C; DVD, Blu-Ray.** Ginger Rogers; Van Heflin; Gene Tierney; George Raft; Peggy Ann Garner; Reginald Gardiner; Virginia Leith; Otto Kruger; Cathleen Nesbitt; Skip Homeier; ***D:*** Nunnally Johnson; ***W:*** Nunnally Johnson; ***C:*** Charles G. Clarke; ***M:*** Leigh Harline.

Black Widow **1987 (R)** A federal agent pursues a beautiful murderess who marries rich men and then kills them, making the deaths look natural. The agent herself becomes involved in the final seduction. The two women are enticing and the locations picturesque. **101m/C; VHS, DVD, Blu-Ray.** Debra Winger; Theresa Russell; Sami Frey; Nicol Williamson; Terry O'Quinn; Dennis Hopper; D.W. Moffett; Lois Smith; Mary Woronov; Rutanya Alda; James Hong; Diane Ladd; ***Cameo(s):*** David Mamet; ***D:*** Bob Rafelson; ***W:*** Ronald Bass; ***C:*** Conrad L. Hall; ***M:*** Michael Small.

The Black Widow *Before It Had a Name* **2005** Upon the death of her lover, Eleanora (Colagrande) visits his eccentric estate known as the Rubber House, to discover more about this mysterious man. The caretaker (Defoe) is more than willing to help her discover a few secrets she herself has been hiding. Amateur attempts all around make for a directionless, awkwardly spoken tale. Dafoe might want to consider different writing partners. **99m/C; DVD.** *US IT* Giada Colagrande; Willem Dafoe; Seymour Cassel; Claudio Botosso; ***D:*** Giada Colagrande; ***W:*** Giada Colagrande; Willem Dafoe; ***C:*** Ken Kelsch; ***M:*** Gyorgy Ligeti.

Black Widow Murders: The Blanche Taylor Moore Story 🦴 1/2 **1993** Montgomery does what she can with the title role but this true crime, made-for-TV movie is predictable fare. Blanche is a smalltown North Carolina, churchgoing serial killer. Her father was an abusive alcoholic, which left Blanche hiding the hatred she feels towards men. She poisons dad, an ex-boyfriend, her first husband, and goes after her fiance before anyone gets suspicious. Adapted from "Preacher's Girl: The Life and Crimes of Blanche Taylor Moore" by Jim Schultze. **92m/C; DVD.** Elizabeth Montgomery; David Clennon; John M. Jackson; Grace Zabriskie; Bruce McGill; Mark Rolston; *D:* Alan Metzger; *W:* Judith Paige Mitchell; *C:* Geoffrey Erb; *M:* David Michael Frank. **TV**

Black Zoo 🦴 1/2 **1963** Over-the-top, teeth-nashing acting from Gough as crazy Brit Michael Conrad, who owns a private zoo and is a member of an animal-worshiping cult. He's trained his big cats to attack anyone who annoys or betrays him, including his unhappy wife Edna (Cooper), who happens to have her own traveling monkey show. **88m/C; DVD.** Michael Gough; Jeanne Cooper; Jerome Cowan; Rod Lauren; Virginia Grey; Elisha Cook, Jr.; *D:* Robert Gordon; *W:* Aben Kandel; *C:* Floyd Crosby; *M:* Paul Dunlap.

Blackbeard 🦴 1/2 *Pirates: The True Story of Blackbeard* **2006** Angus Macfayden stars as pirate Edward "Blackbeard" Teach in this miniseries made for the Hallmark channel. Not much in the way of any form of historical accuracy, or a large budget. More of a comic-book version of Blackbeard's life, geared towards those with a serious pirate fetish. **180m/C; DVD, Blu-Ray.** Angus MacFadyen; Mark Umbers; Richard Chamberlain; Stacy Keach; Rachel Ward; Anthony Green; Danny Midwinter; Patrick Regis; Alan Shearman; Dom Hetrakul; Nicholas Farrell; Nigel Terry; Steven Elder; Paul Brightwell; Kevin Connor; Bill Fellows; Jessica Chastain; Jasper Britton; Jake Curran; Robert Willox; Niko Nicotera; Christopher Clyde-Green; Wendy Mae Brown; Andrew Smith; Stuart Lounton; Ken Forge; Marion Valtas; *W:* Bryce Zabel; *C:* Alan Caso; *M:* Elia Cmiral. **TV**

Blackbeard the Pirate 🦴🦴 **1952** The 18th-century buccaneer is given the full-blooded, Hollywood treatment. **99m/C; VHS, DVD.** Robert Newton; Linda Darnell; Keith Andes; William Bendix; Richard Egan; *D:* Raoul Walsh.

Blackbeard's Ghost 🦴🦴 **1967** Disney comedy in which the famed 18th-century pirate's spirit (Ustinov) is summoned to wreak havoc in order to prevent an old family home from being turned into a casino. **107m/C; VHS, DVD, Blu-Ray.** Peter Ustinov; Dean Jones; Suzanne Pleshette; Elsa Lanchester; Richard Deacon; Joby Baker; Elliott Reid; Michael Conrad; Kelly Thordsen; *D:* Robert Stevenson; *W:* Bill Walsh; Don DaGradi; *C:* Edward Colman; *M:* Robert F. Brunner.

Blackbelt 2: Fatal Force 🦴 1/2 *Spyder* **1993 (R)** A man seeks to avenge his brother's murder by going after his killers. **83m/C; VHS, DVD.** Blake Bahner; Roxanne Baird; Michael Vlastas; *D:* Joe Mari Avellana.

Blackbird 🦴🦴 **2014 (R)** A dramatic look at young man's coming of age and understanding himself. At the age of 17, Randy (Walker) does his best to to help those around him. Because his father (Washington) has abandoned the family, Randy cares for his mentally ill mother (Mo'Nique). He also tries to be there for his friends and classmates. Inside, however, Randy has many internal struggles over his sexual identity and reconciling it with his Christian beliefs and true self. When Randy finally finds love, he comes to understand the power of self-acceptance. **99m/C; DVD, Blu-Ray, Streaming, Download.** Mo'Nique Imes; Julian Walker; Kevin Allesee; Isaiah Washington, IV; Terrell Tilford; *D:* Patrik-Ian Polk; *W:* Patrik-Ian Polk; Rikki Beadle Blair; *C:* Eun-ah Lee.

Blackboard Jungle 🦴🦴🦴 1/2 **1955** Well-remembered urban drama about an idealistic teacher in a slum area who fights doggedly to connect with his unruly students. Bill Hailey's "Rock Around the Clock" over the opening credits was the first use of rock music in a mainstream feature film. Based on Evan Hunter novel. **101m/B; VHS, DVD.** Glenn Ford; Anne Francis; Louis Calhern; Sidney Poitier; Vic Morrow; Richard Kiley; Margaret (Maggie) Hayes; John Hoyt; Warner Anderson; Paul Mazursky; Jamie Farr; Richard Deacon; Emile Meyer; *D:* Richard Brooks; *W:* Richard Brooks; *C:* Russell Harlan; *M:* Charles Wolcott. Natl. Film Reg. '16.

The Blackcoat's Daughter 🦴🦴 1/2 *February* **2017 (R)** The son of Anthony Perkins, director/writer Oz Perkins, seems to have inherited some of his father's skill with the horror genre in this daring debut film. Kat (Shipka) is a freshman at an upstate New York boarding school whose parents don't show up to take her home during winter break. Ironically, an older student named Rose (Boynton) is in the same predicament, leaving them stranded at a relatively empty school that Perkins shoots with imposing dread. And how is a strange girl named Joan (Roberts) related to all of this? A wonderfully creepy experiment in psychological horror. **93m/C; DVD, Blu-Ray.** James Remar; Emma Roberts; Kiernan Shipka; Lucy Boynton; Lauren Holly; *D:* Oz (Osgood) Perkins, II; *W:* Oz (Osgood) Perkins, II; *C:* Julie Kirkwood; *M:* Elvis Perkins.

Blackenstein **WOOF!** *Black Frankenstein* **1973 (R)** Doctor into nouveau experimentation restores a man's arms and legs. But a jealous assistant gives our man a bogus injection, causing him to become "Blackenstein," a large African American with chip on hulking shoulder who enjoys killing people and otherwise causing big trouble. Ripe blaxploitation. **87m/C; VHS, DVD, Blu-Ray.** John Hart; Ivory Stone; Andrea King; Liz Renay; Joe DeSue; Roosevelt Jackson; Nick Bolin; *D:* William A. Levey; *W:* Frank R. Saletri; *C:* Robert Caramico; *M:* Cardella Demilo; Lou Frohman.

Blackfish 🦴🦴🦴 **2013 (PG-13)** Director Cowperthaite made waves, no pun intended, at the 2013 Sundance Film Festival with this documentary about Tilikum, a notoriously aggressive killer whale who ended up killing three people, including one of the most notable whale trainers in the world. Of course, Cowperthaite's film questions whether or not animals so large, intelligent, and sometimes fierce should even be kept in captivity in the first place. She traces Tilikum's outburst back to his capture in 1983 off the coast of Iceland and notes how he was kept in dark tanks for hours. The director clearly has an agenda but makes a good argument. Documentarian Gabriela Cowperthwaite's nightmarish exposé, shedding a dark light on the harsh conditions of Sea World's whale shows. From former park employee detailing their rushed and incompetent training, to graphic accounts of a whale's suppressed killer instinct, the proof gets nasty, leading to a fatal 2010 attack against a beloved trainer. Cowperthwaite isn't just saying these animals are abused, she's also saying they are wanting to abuse. Appropriately disturbing and intelligent, this whale show is definitely not for the kiddies. **83m/C; DVD, Blu-Ray.** *D:* Gabriela Cowperthwaite; *W:* Gabriela Cowperthwaite; Eli B. Despres; *C:* Jonathan Ingalls; Chris Towey; *M:* Jeff Beal.

Blackhat 🦴🦴 1/2 **2015 (R)** Director Mann returns to the world of criminals vs. good guys, this time with a technological edge. Convicted hacker Nick Hathaway (Hemsworth) is let out of jail to put an end to a madman who's hacked into worldwide systems, including a nuclear power plant and the Mercantile Exchange. Mann's story gloriously takes Hathaway and his team, including the great Viola Davis, around the globe. Defying traditional action standards, this is about true villainy that operates not just in the shadows but electronically. Proof that people don't require weapons to commit atrocities. Frustrating but always fascinating. **133m/C; DVD, Blu-Ray.** Chris Hemsworth; Lee-hom Wang; Viola Davis; Wei Tang; Yorick Van Wageningen; Holt McCallany; Ritchie Coster; Christian Borle; *D:* Michael Mann; *W:* Morgan Davis Foehl; *C:* Stuart Dryburgh; *M:* Harry Gregson-Williams; Atticus Ross; Leopold Ross.

Blackheart 🦴🦴 **1998 (R)** A pair of con artists have their scam down—the seductive Annette (Alonso) picks up wealthy men, then Ray (Grieco) steps in, roughs them up, and takes their cash. Things get messy when they learn of a young woman (Loewi) who has yet to learn of an enormous inheritance, and Ray steps into the role of seducer. Although the film runs out of steam in the last 20 minutes, Grieco and Loewi are likeable in the lead roles. **95m/C; VHS, DVD.** Maria Conchita Alonso; Richard Grieco; Fiona Loewi; Christopher Plummer; *D:* Dominic Shiach; *W:* Brock Simpson; Brad Simpson; *C:* Ousama Rawi.

The Blackheath Poisonings 🦴🦴 1/2 **1992** The Collards and the Vandervents are toy-making families who share more than a profession—they share Albert Villa in the London suburb of Blackheath in 1894. Unhappy adults, an illicit affair, a scheming stranger—everyone has something to hide. But when a gruesome murder is committed the ensuing police inquiry will rattle both families skeletons. Based on the novel by Julian Symons. **150m/C; VHS, DVD.** *GB* Christine Kavanagh; Ian McNeice; Zoe Wanamaker; Judy Parfitt; James Faulkner; Christien Anholt; Julia St. John; Nicholas Woodeson; Ronald Fraser; Donald (Don) Sumpter; *D:* Stuart Orme; *W:* Simon Raven; *C:* Dick Pope; *M:* Colin Towns. **TV**

Blackjack 🦴🦴 1/2 **1997 (R)** Former U.S. Marshal Jack Devlin (Lundgren), who has a pathological fear of the color white, becomes the bodyguard of a young supermodel (Haskin) who's the target of a psycho killer (Mackenzie). To highlight Devlin's phobia, Woo sets one of his big action scenes in a dairy flooded with milk. **113m/C; VHS, DVD.** *CA* Dolph Lundgren; Kam Heskin; Saul Rubinek; Fred Williamson; Phillip MacKenzie; Kate Vernon; Padraigin Murphy; *D:* John Woo; *W:* Peter Lance; *C:* Bill Wong; *M:* Micky Erbe. **VIDEO**

BlacKkKlansman 🦴🦴🦴 **2018 (R)** In 1970s Colorado Springs, Ron Stallworth (Washington) becomes the first black police officer in the department. Aspiring to be an undercover detective, he escapes a miserable stint in the records room when he is asked to sneak into a black student group's rally with a former member of the Black Panthers. To cement his position, Ron infiltrates the Klu Klux Klan with the help of white detective Flip Zimmerman (Driver). Adapted from Stallworth's memoir, director Lee ties the film into events past and present, and in the process, makes a powerful statement about issues of race and justice in the United States. **135m/C; DVD, Blu-Ray.** John David Washington; Adam Driver; Laura Harrier; Topher Grace; Robert John Burke; *D:* Spike Lee; *W:* Spike Lee; Charlie Wachtel; David Rabinowitz; Kevin Willmott; *C:* Chayse Irvin; *M:* Terence Blanchard. Oscars '18: Adapt. Screenplay; British Acad. '18: Adapt. Screenplay.

Blackmail 🦴🦴🦴 **1929** This first sound film for Great Britain and director Hitchcock features an early visualization of some typical Hitchcockian themes. The story follows the police investigation of a murder, and a detective's attempts to keep his girlfriend from being involved. Look for Hitchcock's screen cameo. Made as a silent, this was reworked to become a talkie. **86m/B; VHS, DVD, Blu-Ray.** *GB* Anny Ondra; John Longden; Sara Allgood; Charles Paton; Cyril Ritchard; Donald Calthrop; Hannah Jones; Percy Parsons; Johnny Butt; Harvey Braban; Phyllis Monkman; Alfred Hitchcock; *D:* Alfred Hitchcock; *W:* Charles Bennett; Benn W. Levy; Alfred Hitchcock; Garnett Weston; *C:* Jack Cox.

Blackmale 🦴 1/2 **1999 (R)** Small-time hustlers Jimmy (Woodbine) and Luther (Pierce) bet everything on a fixed fight and lose big. Now they owe $100,000 to a loan shark. So they decide to blackmail a doctor (Rees) with an incriminating videotape and discover that their would-be mark is more dangerous than they could have imagined. **89m/C; VHS, DVD.** Bokeem Woodbine; Justin Pierce; Roger Rees; Sascha Knopf; Erik Todd Dellums; *D:* George Baluzy; Mike Baluzy. **VIDEO**

Blackout 🦴 1/2 **1950** Blind man recovers his sight and finds that the brother of his girlfriend, once thought dead, is actually alive and well and running a smuggling ring. Routine. **73m/B; VHS, DVD.** *GB* Maxwell Reed; Dinah Sheridan; Patric Doonan; Eric Pohlmann; *D:* Robert S. Baker.

Blackout 🦴🦴 *Murder by Proxy* **1954** A drunken private eye is offered a murder case, and is subsequently framed for the crime. **87m/B; VHS, DVD.** Dane Clark; Belinda Lee; Betty Ann Davies; Eleanor Summerfield; Andrew Osborn; Harold Lang; Jill Melford; Alfie Bass; *D:* Terence Fisher; *W:* Richard H. Landau; *C:* Walter J. (Jimmy W.) Harvey; *M:* Ivor Slaney.

Blackout 🦴🦴 **1978 (R)** Four killers terrorize an office building during the 1977 New York electrical blackout. Soon the police enter, confront them, and the fun starts. Comic touches provide some relief from the violence here. **86m/C; VHS, DVD, Blu-Ray.** Jim Mitchum; Robert Carradine; Ray Milland; June Allyson; Jean-Pierre Aumont; Belinda J. Montgomery; *D:* Eddy Matalon; *W:* Joseph Stefano.

The Blackout 🦴 **1997 (R)** Movie star Matty (Modine) has multiple addictions he indulges on a trip home to Miami. He proposes to pregnant girlfriend Annie (Dalle) but when he learns she's had an abortion, Matty goes on a binge and suffers a blackout. 18 months later in New York, Matty has kicked his addictions and found Susan (Schiffer) but his nightmares compel him back to Miami and the possibility that he committed murder. Sleazy and the symbolism is heavy-handed. **100m/C; VHS, DVD.** Matthew Modine; Beatrice Dalle; Claudia Schiffer; Dennis Hopper; Sarah Lassez; *D:* Abel Ferrara; *W:* Abel Ferrara; Chris Zois; Marla Hanson; *C:* Ken Kelsch; *M:* Joe Delia.

Blackout 🦴 1/2 **2007 (R)** A psycho-thriller unfairly marketed as a horror flick. Three troubled strangers are trapped in an elevator in a nearly-deserted building because of a blackout. Naturally, one of the three turns out to be a killer. Lots of flashbacks set up the clues as to who and why. Too short to wear out its welcome but not as intense as you might expect. **74m/C; DVD.** Amber Tamblyn; Aidan Gillen; Katie Stuart; Armie Hammer; *D:* Rigoberto Castaneda; *W:* Ed Dougherty; *C:* Alejandro Martinez; *M:* Reinhold Heil; Johnny Klimek. **VIDEO**

The Blackout Experiments 🦴 1/2 **2016** Rich Fox's examination of a truly odd obsession and the people who subject themselves to it might have worked as a 45-minute TV special but is too sparse as a feature documentary, raising more questions than it bothers to answer. Believe it or not, some people pay to have strangers scare them nearly to death, physically and mentally abusing them as a part of a horror experience known as Blackout. Not unlike Fincher's "The Game," people sign over control and never know when they will be assaulted, kidnapped, etc. Why? You'll never know. **78m/C; DVD.** Andrew Gallagher; Jessica Sowa; Russell Eaton; Bob Glouberman; Allison Fogarty; *D:* Rich Fox; *C:* Michael J. Pepin; *M:* James Clements.

Blackrock 🦴🦴 **1997** Cliched though dramatic saga, inspired by a true story, and adapted by Enright from his play. Uncommunicative teenager Jared (Breuls) throws a bash upon the return to town of his best surfing bud Ricko (Lyndon). The party gets out of control and Jared witnesses a group of his mates beating and raping Tracey (Novakovitch), who's discovered dead the next morning. Her death attracts rabid media attention and divides the community while Jared is filled with guilt for doing nothing to stop the act. But his conflicts increase when he realizes the extent of Ricko's involvement and he tries to decide where his loyalties lie. **100m/C; VHS, DVD.** *AU* Laurence Breuls; Simon Lyndon; Linda Cropper; Rebecca Smart; David Field; Chris Haywood; Boyana Novakovitch; *D:* Steven Vidler; *W:* Nick Enright; *C:* Martin McGrath; George Greenough; *M:* Steve Kilbey.

Blackthorn 🦴🦴 1/2 **2011 (R)** Old-fashioned, understated western takes on the mythology of Butch Cassidy. This version presumes that Butch was not killed in Bolivia in 1908, instead he's been living under the name James Blackthorn (Shepard), raising horses on his ranch. But in 1927, homesickness pushes the world-weary Blackthorn to decide to return to the States. He runs into trouble—and one last adventure—thanks to Eduardo (Noreiga), who's stolen money from the wrong man. Flashbacks to his younger days (so the Sundance Kid and Etta Place can make an appearance) and betrayal follow. English and Spanish with subtitles. **98m/C; DVD, On Demand.** *SP US* Sam Shepard; Eduardo Noreiga; Stephen Rea; Magaly Solier; Nikolaj Coster-Waldau; Padraic

Delaney; Dominique McElligott; ***D:*** Mateo Gil; ***W:*** Miguel Barros; ***C:*** Juan Ruiz Anchia; ***M:*** Lucio Godoy.

Blackwater Valley Exorcism 🦴 **2006 (R)** A daughter becomes possessed and the family calls a priest for an exorcism. Unfortunately he's not the most innocent of priests, and they aren't the most well-intentioned of families. Honestly you may end up rooting for the Devil. **90m/C; DVD, Streaming.** Cameron Daddo; James Russo; Jeffrey Combs; Randy Colton; Del Zamora; Kristin Erickson; ***D:*** Ethan Wiley; ***W:*** Ellary Eddy; ***C:*** Roel Reine; ***M:*** Joseph Bauer. **VIDEO**

Blackway 🦴🦴 *Go With Me* **2016 (R)** A vengeance thriller that lacks depth and originality. After returning to hometown, a small Oregon logging town, Lillian (Stiles) finds herself stalked by an abusive psychopath named Blackway (Liotta). Because local law enforcement refuses to take action against the former deputy turned meth dealer and motel pimp, Lillian approaches Lester (Hopkins), a retired logger who had a negative encounter with Blackway after his own daughter's death. Though the town fears Blackway, Lillian and Lester, along with Lester's friend Nate (Ludwig), scour the nearby area looking for Blackway. Though the casting seems promising, their lackluster performances match the listless script and production. **90m/C; DVD.** Anthony Hopkins; Julia Stiles; Ray Liotta; Alexander Ludwig; Lochlyn Munro; ***D:*** Daniel Alfredson; ***W:*** Joesph Gangemi; Gregory Jacobs; ***C:*** Rasmus Videbaek; ***M:*** Anders Niska; Klas Wahl.

Blackwell's Island 🦴🦴 **1939** Crime programmer from Warner Bros. stars Garfield as crusading reporter Tim Haydon and is based on a true incident from 1934. Haydon goes undercover to expose corruption at New York's notorious Blackwell's Island penitentiary. The weak warden (Bates) looks the other way as mob boss Bull Bransom (Fields) runs the show. When Bull gets suspicious of the new inmate, Haydon's in real trouble. **71m/B; DVD.** John Garfield; Stanley Fields; Rosemary Lane; Dick Purcell; Victor Jory; Granville Bates; ***D:*** William McGann; ***W:*** Crane Wilbur; ***C:*** Sidney Hickox.

Blackwoods WOOF! 2002 (R) It's just like a M. Night Shyamalan movie... only much, much worse. Uwe Boll, Germany's answer to Ed Wood, directs this pointless thriller that apes every third-act twist cliche in the book. Matt (Muldoon) and Dawn (Tracy) drive up to the "Blackwoods" to visit Dawn's hillbilly family, but after checking into a creepy motel (staffed by Clint Howard, no less), Dawn disappears and crazy axe-wielding psychos start attacking Matt. It's all leading up to one big twist that's telegraphed further than a ten-meter cattle prod. Honestly, if you can't figure out the whole movie in the first five minutes, you should put down the airplane glue and move your trailer away from the power lines. **90m/C; VHS, DVD.** *GE CA* Patrick Muldoon; Keegan Connor Tracy; Michael Paré; Clint Howard; Will Sanderson; Mathew (Matt) Walker; Anthony Harrison; Janet Wright; Sean Campbell; Ben Derrick; ***D:*** Uwe Boll; ***W:*** Robert Dean Klein; Uwe Boll; ***C:*** Mathias Neumann; ***M:*** Reinhard Besser.

Blacula 🦴🦴 **1972 (PG)** The African Prince Mamuwalde stalks the streets of Los Angeles trying to satisfy his insatiable desire for blood. Mildly successful melding of blaxploitation and horror that spawned a sequel, "Scream, Blacula, Scream." **92m/C; VHS, DVD, Blu-Ray.** William Marshall; Thalmus Rasulala; Denise Nicholas; Vonetta McGee; Gordon Pinsent; Emily Yancy; Charles Macaulay; Ted Harris; Elisha Cook, Jr.; Lance Taylor; ***D:*** William Crain; ***W:*** Raymond Koenig; Joan Torres; ***C:*** John Stevens; ***M:*** Gene Page.

Blade 🦴🦴 **1998 (R)** Action-packed gorefest that provides for high-octane escapist entertainment, with some eye-catching visuals and a pulsating techno soundtrack. Blade (Snipes) is a half-vampire/half-human, who's intent on preventing evil, ambitious Deacon Frost (Dorff) from unleashing a vampire apocalypse upon humanity so he can take over. Helping out Blade are his grizzled mentor, vampire hunter Abraham Whistler (Kristofferson), and Dr. Karen Janson (Wright), who's searching for a cure for vampirism. Adapted from the Marvel comic book character. **91m/C; VHS, DVD, Blu-Ray, UMD.** Wesley Snipes; Stephen Dorff; Kris Kristofferson; N'Bushe Wright; Donal Logue; Udo Kier; Traci Lords; Tim Guinee; Arly Jover; Sanaa Lathan; ***D:*** Stephen Norrington; ***W:*** David S. Goyer; ***C:*** Theo van de Sande; ***M:*** Mark Isham. MTV Movie Awards '99: Villain (Dorff).

Blade 2 🦴🦴 **2002 (R)** Sequel takes the more, more, more approach—more vampires, more battles, more gore. Half-vampire, half-human daywalker Blade (Snipes at his coolest) first rescues mentor Whistler (Kristofferson) from the vamps who have been holding him prisoner. Then, he's offered a truce by vampire overload Damaskinos (Kretschmann) who needs Blade to hunt an even more deadly enemy. The rat-like Reapers feed on both humans and vampires and their bite turns their victims into insatiable bloodsuckers themselves. Of course, as Blade goes a-huntin', he discovers the situation isn't as clear-cut as it seems. **116m/C; VHS, DVD, Blu-Ray.** Wesley Snipes; Kris Kristofferson; Ron Perlman; Leonor Varela; Norman Reedus; Thomas Kretschmann; Luke Goss; Matt Schulze; Donnie Yen; Danny John Jules; Daz Crawford; Karel Roden; Tony Curran; Santiago Segura; Marit Velle Kile; ***D:*** Guillermo del Toro; ***W:*** David S. Goyer; ***C:*** Gabriel Beristain; ***M:*** Marco Beltrami; Danny Saber.

Blade Boxer 🦴 *The Boxer* **1997** Police detectives go undercover to expose an illegal fight ring that has its combatants battling to the death, and equipped with deadly steel talons. **91m/C; VHS, DVD.** Kevin King; Todd McKee; Andrew Martino; Cass Magda; Dana Plato; ***D:*** Bruce Reisman.

A Blade in the Dark 🦴🦴 *La Casa con la Scala Nel Buio; House of the Dark Stairway* **1983** A young man composing a score for a horror film moves into a secluded villa and is inspired and haunted by the mysterious murder he witnesses. **104m/C; VHS, DVD.** Andrea Occhipinti; Anny Papa; Michele (Michael) Soavi; Fabiola Toledo; Valeria Cavalli; Lara Naszinsky; ***D:*** Lamberto Bava; ***W:*** Dardano Sacchetti; ***C:*** Gianlorenzo Battaglia; ***M:*** Guido de Angelis; Maurizio de Angelis.

Blade of the Immortal 🦴🦴 **1/2** *Mugen no junin* **2017 (R)** A samurai film with a twist, the 100th film by Takashi Miike and based on the manga series by Hiroaki Samura. Samurai Manji (Kimura) is immortal, which has made his long life difficult. After generations of mourning the one person he cared about and witnessing disturbing changes to the samurai code, Manji has the chance to bring meaning to his life again by helping a young girl get revenge. Rin Asano (Sugiaski) is an orphan whose parents were killed by assassins bent on changing the way of the samurai. A violent film crafted by a master of the form. Japanese with subtitles. **140m/C; DVD, Blu-Ray.** Takuya Kimura; Hana Sugisaki; Sota Fukushi; Hayato Ichihara; Erika Toda; ***D:*** Takashi Miike; ***W:*** Tetsuya Oishi; ***C:*** Nobuyasu Kita; ***M:*** Koji Endo.

Blade Runner 🦴🦴🦴 **1/2 1982 (R)** Los Angeles, the 21st century. World-weary cop tracks down a handful of renegade "replicants" (synthetically produced human slaves who, with only days left of life, search madly for some way to extend their prescribed lifetimes). Moody, beautifully photographed, dark thriller with sets from an architect's dream. Based on "Do Androids Dream of Electric Sheep" by Philip K. Dick. Director's cut, released at 117 minutes, removes Ford's narration and the last scene of the film, which Scott considered too "up," and inserts several short scenes, including a dream sequence. **122m/C; VHS, DVD, Blu-Ray, HD-DVD.** Harrison Ford; Rutger Hauer; Sean Young; Daryl Hannah; M. Emmet Walsh; Edward James Olmos; Joe Turkel; Brion James; Joanna Cassidy; William Sanderson; James Hong; ***D:*** Ridley Scott; ***W:*** Hampton Fancher; David Peoples; ***C:*** Jordan Cronenweth; ***M:*** Vangelis. L.A. Film Critics '82: Cinematog.; Natl. Film Reg. '93.

Blade Runner 2049 🦴🦴 **1/2 2017 (R)** This sci-fi classic sequel fast forwards three decades to Los Angeles in 2049, where K (Gosling) works as a Blade Runner, seeking and destroying old replicants who have gone into hiding years past their programmed lifespan. In the process, questions arise about his own past and the history of replicants, which leads him to pursue off-the-grid Blade Runner Rick Deckard (Ford) and into harm's way. Amazing cinematography by Deakins paints a vividly bleak landscape of the future, and director Villeneuve weaves together a thought-provoking—if perhaps overly long—story. Meanwhile leads Gosling and Ford show the world what real action stars should be. **164m/C; DVD, Blu-Ray, Streaming.** *CA UK US* Ryan Gosling; Harrison Ford; Ana de Armas; Sylvia Hoeks; Robin Wright; ***D:*** Denis Villeneuve; ***W:*** Hampton Fancher; Michael Green; ***C:*** Roger Deakins; ***M:*** Benjamin Wallfisch; Hans Zimmer. Oscars '17: Cinematog., Visual FX; British Acad. '17: Cinematog., Visual FX.

Blade: Trinity 🦴🦴 **2004 (R)** The last of the "Blade" trilogy (at least with the stoic Snipes), bloody actioner sticks to what it does best, this time with writer Goyer also taking on directing chores. Bitchy bloodsucker Danica (a gleeful Posey), who leads the Vampire Nation, decides to wake up Dracula, aka Drake (Purcell)?whose blood will allow them to walk in the daylight. Blade is busy doing his slaying thing when he gets involved—along with a couple of mouthy youngsters, dishy Abigail (Biel), who happens to be Whistler's (Kristofferson) daughter, and wisecracking recovered vamp Hannibal King (Reynolds). There is, of course, a final mano a mano battle between Blade and Drac, uh, Drake. The ending also leaves wiggle room for the younger actors to continue the bloodletting. **105m/C; VHS, DVD, Blu-Ray.** Wesley Snipes; Kris Kristofferson; Jessica Biel; Ryan Reynolds; Parker Posey; Dominic Purcell; John Michael Higgins; James Remar; Eric Bogosian; Patton Oswalt; Callum Keith Rennie; Natasha Lyonne; Mark Berry; Francoise Yip; Christopher Heyerdahl; Paul Anthony; ***D:*** David S. Goyer; ***W:*** David S. Goyer; ***C:*** Gabriel Beristain; ***M:*** RZA; Ramin Djawadi.

Blades 🦴 **1989 (R)** Another junk heap from Troma, dealing with the efforts of three golfers who try to stop a maniacal power mower that's been grinding duffers with regularity. **101m/C; VHS, DVD.** Robert North; Jeremy Whelan; Victoria Scott; Jon McBride; ***D:*** Thomas R. Rondinella; ***W:*** William R. Pace; ***C:*** James Hayman; ***M:*** John Hodian.

Blades of Glory 🦴🦴 **1/2 2007 (PG-13)** Lumpy Ferrell gets a mullet and stuffs himself into spandex and sparkles to play bad boy ice skater Chazz Michael Michaels, whose rival is wispy blonde peacock Jimmy MacElroy (Heder). After the two are banned from singles competition for public brawling, a loophole allows them to compete as the first male/male pairs skating team, much to the disgust of oh-so-close brother/sister skating champs, the Van Waldenbergs (real-life spouses Arnett and Poehler). The jokes are obvious, which doesn't necessarily mean they aren't funny. **93m/C; DVD, Blu-Ray, HD-DVD.** Will Ferrell; Jon Heder; Amy Poehler; Will Arnett; Jenna Fischer; Craig T. Nelson; William Fichtner; Nick Swardson; ***D:*** Will Speck; Josh Gordon; ***W:*** Jeff Cox; Craig Cox; John Altschuler; Dave Krinsky; ***C:*** Stefan Czapsky; ***M:*** Theodore Shapiro.

Blair Witch 🦴 **1/2 2016 (R)** Filmed under a different name to disguise its existence, Wingard's reboot/sequel to "The Blair Witch Project" had horror fans buzzing about what a talented young filmmaker in the new era of the genre could do for the dead franchise. It turns out not much. Perhaps it's because this spin on the saga of the found-footage classic doesn't click like the original, but this is just not scary, creative or fun, unless you find loud noises fun. The plot is merely a side note, revolving around the brother of one of the campers from the first film trying to find his sister. **89m/C; DVD, Blu-Ray.** James Allen McCune; Callie Hernandez; Corbin Reid; Brandon Scott; Wes Robinson; Valorie Curry; ***D:*** Adam Wingard; ***W:*** Simon Barrett; ***C:*** Robby Baumgartner; ***M:*** Adam Wingard.

The Blair Witch Project 🦴🦴 **1999 (R)** A Sundance Film Festival favorite, this low-budget horror film turned out to be the most successful indie ever, thanks to heavy (and savvy) market promotion. In 1994, a three-person film crew heads into the Black Hills region of Maryland to document a local legend about a demonic apparition. They vanish, but a year later their film footage is found and this amateurish, black and white footage makes up what the audience sees. Largely improvisational, the film manages a palpable sense of dread and claustrophobia, while being (deliberately) technically crude. However, the herky-jerky camera movements made a number of viewers physically sick and an equal number found the would-be theatrics boring. **87m/C; VHS, DVD, Blu-Ray.** Michael Williams; Heather Donahue; Joshua Leonard; ***D:*** Eduardo Sanchez; Daniel Myrick; ***W:*** Eduardo Sanchez; Daniel Myrick; ***C:*** Neal Fredericks; ***M:*** Tony Cora. Golden Raspberries '99: Worst Actress (Donahue).

Blaise Pascal 🦴🦴🦴 **1/2 1971** Another of Rossellini's later historical portraits, detailing the life and times of the 17th-century philosopher, seen as a man whose scientific ideas conflicted with his own religious beliefs. Italian with subtitles. **131m/C; VHS, DVD.** *IT* Pierre Arditti; Giuseppe Addobati; Christian de Sica; Rita Forzano; ***D:*** Roberto Rossellini; ***W:*** Roberto Rossellini; ***C:*** Mario Fioretti; ***M:*** Mario Nascimbene. **TV**

Blake of Scotland Yard 🦴🦴 **1/2 1936** Blake, the former Scotland Yard inspector, battles against a villain who has constructed a murderous death ray. Condensed version of the 15 episode serial (originally at 180 minutes). **70m/B; VHS, DVD.** Ralph Byrd; Herbert Rawlinson; Joan Barclay; Lloyd Hughes; ***D:*** Robert F. "Bob" Hill.

Blame 🦴🦴 **1/2 2017** After Abigail Grey (Shepherd) spends six months in a psych ward, she returns to high school and is mocked and laughed at. Despite her notoriety, she remains a shy wallflower hiding a truth about herself. After Abigail is cast in the role of Abigail in a school production of Arthur Miller's play "The Crucible," merciless Melissa (Alexander) organizes an attack on her after being cast as Abigail's understudy. Though the film explores common high school/coming of age ground and was written by Shepherd while in high school, it is unexpectedly intense with a sense of mystery. **100m/C; DVD.** Quinn Shephard; Nadia Alexander; Trieste Kelly Dunn; Chris Messina; Marcia DeBonis; ***D:*** Quinn Shephard; ***W:*** Quinn Shephard; Laurie Shephard; ***C:*** Aaron Kovalchik; ***M:*** Pierre-Philippe Côt.

Blame It on Fidel 🦴🦴 **1/2** *La Faute a Fidel* **2006** Amusing and tender film told from the point of view of nine-year-old Anna (Kervel), who becomes increasingly upset when her bourgeois parents, Fernando (Accorsi) and Marie (Depardieu, daughter of Gerard), suddenly decide to devote their time and money to various political/activist causes (it's 1970 in Paris). She and her younger brother are moved from their comfortable home to a shabby apartment and are left in the care of oddball political refugees. Anna doesn't take well to all these changes and is confused about what she hears and is told to believe. Writer/director Gavras is the daughter of political filmmaker Costas-Gavras. French with subtitles. **100m/C; DVD.** *FR IT* Julie Depardieu; Stefano Accorsi; Olivier Perrier; Nina Kremer; Benjamin Feuillet; Martine Chevallier; Marie Kremer; Marie-Noelle Bordeaux; ***D:*** Julie Gavras; ***W:*** Julie Gavras; ***C:*** Nathalie Durant; ***M:*** Armand Amar.

Blame It on Rio 🦴🦴 **1984 (R)** A middle-aged man has a ridiculous fling with his best friend's daughter while on vacation with them in Rio de Janeiro. Caine and Johnson are amusing, but the script is somewhat weak. Remake of the French film "One Wild Moment." **90m/C; VHS, DVD, Blu-Ray.** Michael Caine; Joseph Bologna; Demi Moore; Michelle Johnson; Valerie Harper; ***D:*** Stanley Donen; ***W:*** Charlie Peters; Larry Gelbart; ***C:*** Reynaldo Villalobos; ***M:*** Kenneth Wannberg.

Blame It on the Bellboy 🦴🦴 **1/2 1992 (PG-13)** Wild farce set in Venice about a hotel bellboy who confuses three similarly named visitors—sending the wrong ones to meet corporate bigwigs, date women, or even kill. The brisk pace loses it towards the end and devolves into chase scenes. **79m/C; VHS, DVD, Blu-Ray.** Dudley Moore; Bryan Brown; Richard Griffiths; Andreas Katsulas; Patsy Kensit; Alison Steadman; Bronson Pinchot; Lindsay Anderson; Penelope Wilton; ***D:*** Mark Herman; ***W:*** Mark Herman; ***M:*** Trevor Jones.

Blame It on the Night 🦴🦴 **1984 (PG-13)** A rock star gets to take care of the military cadet son he never knew after the boy's mother suddenly dies. Mick Jagger helped write the story. **85m/C; VHS, DVD, Streaming.** Nick Mancuso; Byron Thames; Leslie Ackerman; Billy Preston; Merry Clayton; ***D:*** Gene Taft.

Blanche Fury 🦴🦴 1/2 **1948** Governess Blanche (Hobson) marries her wealthy widowed cousin but the man she truly desires is the illegitimate Philip Thorn (Granger), who manages the estate for her husband. So Blanche decides to get rid of the man she doesn't love. Based on England's 19th-century Rush murder and adapted from the novel by Joseph Shearing. **95m/C; VHS, Streaming.** *GB* Valerie Hobson; Stewart Granger; Walter Fitzgerald; Michael Gough; Maurice Denham; Sybilla Binder; ***D:*** Marc Allegret; ***W:*** Hugh Mills; ***C:*** Guy Green; Geoffrey Unsworth; ***M:*** Clifton Parker.

The Blancheville Monster 🦴 1/2 *Horror* **1963** A young woman returns to the family mansion upon hearing of her father's death and that her brother has fired the staff, only to find her father alive, disfigured, and obsessed with killing her. **90m/B; DVD.** *IT SP* Gerard Tichy; Leo Anchoriz; Vanni Materassi; Paco Moran; Ombretta Colli; Helga Line; Iran Eory; ***D:*** Alberto De Martino; ***W:*** Bruno Corbucci; Sergio Corbucci; Giovanni Grimaldi; Natividad Zaro; ***C:*** Alejandro Ulloa; ***M:*** Carlo Franci; Giuseppe Piccillo. **VIDEO**

Blank Check 🦴 *Disney's Blank Check* **1993 (PG)** Parents may want to verify the whereabouts of their checkbooks after this one. Eleven-year-old Preston receives a blank check from a mobster on the run, cashes it for a million bucks, and goes on a spending orgy under an assumed name. Where are his parents? Apparently they don't have a problem with a shadowy benefactor taking their son under his wing. Sound familiar? And who thought it would be a good idea to have the little twerp mooning after a comely bank teller? Formula aside, this blatant rip-off of "Home Alone" tries to throw in an ending moral but probably won't fool the kids either. **93m/C; VHS, DVD.** Brian Bonsall; Miguel Ferrer; Michael Lerner; Tone Loc; Ric(k) Ducommun; Karen Duffy; ***D:*** Rupert Wainwright; ***W:*** Colby Carr; Blake Snyder; ***M:*** Nicholas Pike.

Blankman 🦴🦴 **1994 (PG-13)** Self-appointed superhero (Wayans), who makes up in creativity what he lacks in superpowers, fights crime in his underwear and a cape made from his grandmother's bathrobe. Life is simple, until an ambitious TV reporter (Givens) finds out about him. Silly one-joke premise is carried a little too far; didn't similar "Meteor Man" crash? Gifted comedian Wayans tries, but can't make this guy fly. **96m/C; VHS, DVD.** Damon Wayans; Robin Givens; David Alan Grier; Jason Alexander; Jon Polito; Nick(y) Corello; ***D:*** Mike Binder; ***W:*** Damon Wayans; J.F. Lawton; ***C:*** Newton Thomas (Tom) Sigel; ***M:*** Miles Goodman.

Blast 🦴🦴 1/2 **2004 (R)** Mercenaries try to detonate an electromagnetic bomb over the U.S using an oil rig. A tug boat captain (Griffin) teams with an FBI agent and computer expert in order to foil the plan. Griffin is surprisingly effective as an action hero, and the proceedings, while not breaking any new ground, provide the requisite excitement and wisecracks in the "Die Hard/Under Siege" mode. **91m/C; DVD.** Eddie Griffin; Vinnie Jones; Breckin Meyer; Vivica A. Fox; Tommy (Tiny) Lister; Anthony Hickox; ***D:*** Anthony Hickox; ***W:*** Steven E. de Souza; ***C:*** Giulio Biccari; ***M:*** Danny Saber. **VIDEO**

Blast from the Past 🦴🦴 1/2 **1998 (PG-13)** Mistaking a plane crash in his yard for an atomic bomb blast, paranoid scientist Calvin (Walken) and his pregnant wife Helen (Spacek) lock themselves in their bomb shelter. Fearful of radioactive fallout, they raise their son Adam (Fraser) in the shelter on a diet of canned goods, Perry Como music, and ballroom dancing. After 35 years, Adam is sent out for supplies and to find a nice, non-mutant wife. Plot degenerates into by-the-book romantic comedy mush after he meets cute with Eve (Silverstone), a thoroughly modern woman with a low opinion of modern men. **106m/C; VHS, DVD, Blu-Ray.** Brendan Fraser; Alicia Silverstone; Christopher Walken; Sissy Spacek; Dave Foley; Joey Slotnick; Dale Raoul; Scott Thomson; Nathan Fillion; Donovan Scott; ***D:*** Hugh Wilson; ***W:*** Hugh Wilson; Bill Kelly; ***C:*** Jose Luis Alcaine; ***M:*** Steve Dorff.

Blast of Silence 🦴🦴 **1961** Hard-boiled crime. Frank Bono (Baron) comes to Manhattan at Christmas for a contract hit for the mob. He follows his target and decides on the best place to make his shot, just waiting for the right time. When Frank makes a mistake and tries to get out of the contract, he realizes that he'll be next on the hit parade. **77m/B; DVD.** Allen Baron; Peter Clune; Larry Tucker; Molly McCarthy; ***Nar:*** Lionel Stander; ***D:*** Allen Baron; ***W:*** Allen Baron; ***M:*** Meyer Kupferman.

Blast-Off Girls 🦴 **1967** A scuzzball promoter sets out to avenge himself for being blacklisted by the rock 'n' roll industry. He discovers a fresh group, but without corporate backing he can only pay them with groovy clothes and mini-skirted girls. Trouble ensues when they unexpectedly hit the charts and want real money. **83m/C; VHS, DVD.** Ray Sager; Dan Conway; Harland "Colonel" Sanders; ***D:*** Herschell Gordon Lewis; ***W:*** Herschell Gordon Lewis.

Blaze 🦴🦴 1/2 **1989 (R)** The true story of Louisiana governor Earl Long who became involved with a stripper, Blaze Starr, causing a political scandal of major proportions. Robust, good-humored bio-pic featuring a fine character turn by Newman. **117m/C; VHS, DVD, Blu-Ray.** Paul Newman; Lolita Davidovich; Jerry Hardin; Robert Wuhl; Gailard Sartain; Jeffrey DeMunn; Richard Jenkins; Garland Bunting; ***D:*** Ron Shelton; ***W:*** Ron Shelton; ***C:*** Haskell Wexler.

Blaze 🦴🦴🦴 **2018 (R)** A biopic of Blaze Foley, a songwriter whose influence on country music is well known even if his name isn't. Benjamin Dickey, in his first acting role, gives an effortless and genuine portrayal of Foley, demonstrating his talents as well as his flaws. The film's authenticity is enhanced through Sybil Rosen, Foley's lover, who cowrote the screenplay, which in turn is based on her memoir "Living in the Woods in a Tree: Remembering Blaze Foley." **127m/C; DVD, Blu-Ray.** Ben Dickey; Alia Shawkat; Josh Hamilton; Ethan Hawke; Alynda Lee Segarra; ***D:*** Ethan Hawke; ***W:*** Ethan Hawke; Sybil Rosen; ***C:*** Steve Cosens.

Blazing Saddles 🦴🦴🦴 1/2 **1974 (R)** Wild, wacky spoof by Brooks of every cliche in the western film genre. Little is Black Bart, a convict offered a reprieve if he will become a sheriff and clean up a nasty frontier town; the previous recipients of this honor have all swiftly ended up in shallow graves. A crazy, silly film with a cast full of lovable loonies including comedy greats Wilder, Kahn, and Korman. Watch for the Count Basie Orchestra. A group writing effort, based on an original story by Bergman. Was the most-viewed movie in its first year of release on HBO cable. **90m/C; VHS, DVD, Blu-Ray, HD-DVD.** Cleavon Little; Harvey Korman; Madeline Kahn; Gene Wilder; Mel Brooks; John Hillerman; Alex Karras; Dom DeLuise; Liam Dunn; Slim Pickens; David Huddleston; Burton Gilliam; Count Basie; ***D:*** Mel Brooks; ***W:*** Mel Brooks; Norman Steinberg; Andrew Bergman; Richard Pryor; Alan Uger; ***C:*** Joseph Biroc; ***M:*** John Morris. Natl. Film Reg. '06; Writers Guild '74: Orig. Screenplay.

Blazing Stewardesses **WOOF!** *Texas Layover* **1975 (R)** The Hound salutes the distributor for truth in advertising, as they stamped this as one of the world's worst videos. Lusty, busty stewardesses relax at a western guest ranch under siege from hooded riders and the aging gags of the Ritz Brothers. **95m/C; VHS, DVD.** Yvonne De Carlo; Robert "Bob" Livingston; Donald (Don "Red") Barry; Regina Carrol; Connie Hoffman; ***Cameo(s):*** Harry Ritz; Jimmy Ritz; ***D:*** Al Adamson.

Bleach the Movie 4: Hell Verse 🦴🦴 *Bleach the Movie: Hell Verse* **2010** The fourth sequel to the long running anime and manga series finds Ichigo and his friends attempting to put down a jailbreak from Hell. **94m/C; DVD, Blu-Ray, Streaming.** *JP* ***V:*** Johnny Yong Bosch; Michelle Ruff; Travis Willington; Derek Prince; Wally Wingert; ***D:*** Noriyuki Abe; ***W:*** Natsuko Takahashi; Ookubo Masahiro; ***C:*** Toshiyuki Fukushima; ***M:*** Shiroh Sagisu. **VIDEO**

Bleading Lady **WOOF!** *Star Vehicle* **2010** Slasher/showbiz horror crapola. Movie buff Donald Cardini works as a driver for low-budget films. His latest middle-of-nowhere location is the Forest Grove Lodge for a horror flick starring his favorite scream queen Riversa Red. Don takes it upon himself to protect her from a stalker but when his volatile temper gets him fired, Don decides to make the cast and crew part of his own deadly horror show. **75m/C; DVD.** Dan Ellis; Sindy Faraguna; Nathan Durec; Nick Windebank; Mike LI; Paige Farbacher; ***D:*** Ryan Nicholson; ***W:*** Ryan Nicholson; ***C:*** Jay Gavin; ***M:*** Gianni Rossi.

Bleak House 🦴🦴 1/2 **1985** Miniseries adaptation of the Charles Dickens tome about an interminable lawsuit and the decadent, criminal ruling class of 19th-century England. **391m/C; VHS, DVD.** *GB* Denholm Elliott; Diana Rigg; Philip Franks; Peter Vaughan; T.P. McKenna; ***D:*** Ross Devenish; ***M:*** Geoffrey Burgon. **TV**

Bleak House 🦴🦴 1/2 **2005** Charles Dickens' serialized novel gets the BBC treatment in all its extended suffering. A long court case involving a disputed inheritance hides many secrets and many protagonists, including a fiendish lawyer, an icy aristocratic beauty, two innocents, and an illegitimate child, as well as obsession, madness, and murder. **510m/C; DVD, Blu-Ray.** Gillian Anderson; Charles Dance; Denis Lawson; Patrick Kennedy; Anna Maxwell Martin; Timothy West; Nathaniel Parker; Carey Mulligan; Tom Georgeson; ***D:*** Justin Chadwick; Susanna White; ***W:*** Andrew Davies; ***C:*** Kieran McGuigan; ***M:*** John Lunn. **TV**

Bleak Moments 🦴🦴 *Loving Moments* **1971** Bored secretary Sylvia (Raitt) tries to work her flirtatious charms on a repressed teacher (Allan) and an eccentric musician (Bradwell) in order to escape the pressures of caring for a mentally retarded sister. **110m/C; VHS, DVD.** *GB* Anne Raitt; Eric Allen; Mike Bradwell; Joolia Cappleman; ***D:*** Mike Leigh; ***W:*** Mike Leigh; ***C:*** Bahram Manocheri; ***M:*** Mike Bradwell.

Bleed for This 🦴🦴 **2016 (R)** It's hard to believe that the crowded based-on-a-true-story boxing genre didn't get to the saga of Vinny "The Pazmanian Devil" Pazienza before now. Teller plays the boxer who should have died in a head-on car crash. The recovery period involved years of physical therapy, but he refused to believe that his boxing career was over, and eventually rose not just to fight again but to beat champions. Teller is effective, but Eckhart actually steals the movie as his trainer. Ultimately, it's a bit too TV movie material to be quality drama. **117m/C; DVD, Blu-Ray.** Miles Teller; Aaron Eckhart; Katey Sagal; Ciaran Hinds; Ted Levine; ***D:*** Ben Younger; ***W:*** Ben Younger; ***C:*** Larkin Seiple; ***M:*** Julia Holter.

Bleeders **WOOF!** *Hemoglobin* **1997 (R)** John Struass (Dupuis), suffering from a hereditary blood disease, travels to a remote Atlantic island to research his ancestors and discovers the descendants are a grotesque clan of incestuous malformed creatures, who only emerge from their catacombs to satisfy their need for human blood and flesh. **89m/C; VHS, DVD.** *CA* Rutger Hauer; Roy Dupuis; Jackie Burroughs; Kristen Lehman; Joanna Noyes; John Dunn-Hill; Lisa Bronwyn Moore; ***D:*** Peter Svatek; ***W:*** Dan O'Bannon; Charles Adair; Ronald Shusett; ***C:*** Barry Gravelle; ***M:*** Alan Reeves. **VIDEO**

The Bleeding 🦴 **2009 (R)** Shawn Black (Matthias) comes home to find his family dead, his brother is a vampire, and he himself is some sort of "chosen one" who will save the world from evil. He could reject the power of bad movie cliches but alas he does not. **83m/C; DVD, Streaming.** Michael Madsen; Vinnie Jones; Armand Assante; William McNamara; Michael Matthias; ***D:*** Charlie Picerni; ***W:*** Lance Lane; ***C:*** Tom Priestley, Jr.; ***M:*** Justin Caine Burnett. **VIDEO**

Bleeding Heart 🦴🦴 **2015** A dramatic look at the lengths to which one sister will protect another. May (Biel) has an ideal life. She is clean-living yoga instructor with a loyal boyfriend. May's world is thrown off balance when her long-lost biological sister shows up. Shiva (Mamet) is a sex worker in an abusive relationship with a violent boyfriend. May does all she can to save her naive yet hapless new sister from the streets and her boyfriend, but finds her own calm existence become more chaotic in the process. **80m/C; DVD, Streaming, Download.** Jessica Biel; Zosia Mamet; Joe Anderson; Kate Burton; Harry Hamlin; ***D:*** Diane Bell; ***W:*** Diane Bell; ***C:*** Zak Mulligan.

Bleeding Hearts 🦴🦴 1/2 **1994** A liberal white professor falls in love with the teen-aged black student he's tutoring and then becomes aware of the vast differences between them. Their problems increase when the young woman becomes pregnant. **95m/C; VHS, DVD.** Gregory Hines; Mark Evan Jacobs; Ranjit (Chaudry) Chowdhry; Elliott Gould; Robert Levine; Peter Riegert; Lorraine Toussaint; ***D:*** Gregory Hines.

Blended 🦴 **2014 (PG-13)** Sandler and Barrymore continue to scrape the bottom of the comedy barrel in their third collaboration, a film that is slightly better than recent Happy Madison disasters, but that's like saying the flu is slightly better than pneumonia. Both suck. Jim Friedman (Sandler) and Lauren Reynolds (Barrymore) go on a bad blind date and then inexplicably end up at a family resort in Africa--yes, this is another film that exists purely to give Sandler a vacation. Cultural insensitivities, bodily humor, and more of the same nonsense; salvaged somewhat by Barrymore's unflappable charm. **117m/C; DVD, Blu-Ray.** Adam Sandler; Drew Barrymore; Bella Thorne; Emma Fuhrmann; Alyvia Alyn Lind; Braxton Beckham; Kyle Red Silverstein; Terry Crews; Kevin Nealon; Jessica Lowe; Shaquille O'Neal; ***D:*** Frank Coraci; ***W:*** Ivan Menchell; Clare Sera; ***C:*** Julio Macat; ***M:*** Rupert Gregson-Williams.

Bless Me, Ultima 🦴🦴 **2013 (PG-13)** Director Franklin plays with issues of religion, divinity, and faith in this adaptation of Rudolfo Anaya's novel. A healer known as Ultima (Colon) comes to young boy Antonio's (Ganalon) small New Mexico town in the early '40s, just as the world was succumbing to the changes brought on by WWII. The new perspectives on life that Ultima gives Antonio have a deep impact upon him. Essentially a coming-of-age story, it's rather blandly presented given its magical themes. The classic book has caused much debate since its publication in 1972 due to the intense adult topics that occur within a child's life. **106m/C; DVD.** Luke Ganalon; Miriam Colon; Benito Martinez; Dolores Heredia; Castulo Guerra; ***D:*** Carl Franklin; ***W:*** Carl Franklin; ***C:*** Paula Huidobro; ***M:*** Mark Kilian.

Bless the Beasts and Children 🦴🦴 1/2 **1971 (PG)** A group of six teenage boys at a summer camp attempt to save a herd of buffalo from slaughter at a national preserve. Treacly Kramer backwater. Based on the novel by Glendon Swarthout. **109m/C; VHS, Streaming.** Billy Mumy; Barry Robins; Miles Chapin; Darel Glaser; Bob Kramer; Ken Swofford; Jesse White; ***D:*** Stanley Kramer; ***M:*** Perry Botkin.

Bless the Child 🦴 **2000 (R)** Basinger doesn't even attempt to hide her boredom as Maggie, aunt and caretaker to a six-year-old with supernatural powers. Everyone drops the ball in this failed ripoff of "The ExorOmen's Baby's Sixth Sense." Satanist and self-help guru Stark (Sewell) wants to recruit the gifted tyke to work for the Devil, while Maggie gets an occult-expert FBI agent (Smits, perhaps making a mortgage payment) and a bunch of exposition cameos on her side. This movie's idea of thrills is showing kids getting kidnapped and later turning up dead. Not exactly the feel-good movie of the year. **110m/C; VHS, DVD.** Kim Basinger; Jimmy Smits; Rufus Sewell; Holliston Coleman; Christina Ricci; Michael Gaston; Lumi Cavazos; Angela Bettis; Ian Holm; Eugene Lipinski; Anne Betancourt; Dimitra Arlys; ***D:*** Chuck Russell; ***W:*** Thomas (Tom) Rickman; Clifford Green; Ellen Green; ***C:*** Peter Menzies, Jr.; ***M:*** Christopher Young.

Blessed Event 🦴🦴🦴 **1932** Fast-moving, entertaining film about a Broadway gossip columnist with a poison pen. Tracy has the role of a lifetime as a Walter Winchell prototype who thinks no one is exempt from his juicy column. Powell makes film debut as a crooner after a brief career as a band singer. Based on a play by Manuel Seff and Forrest Wilson. **77m/B; VHS, DVD.** Lee Tracy; Mary Brian; Dick Powell; Allen Jenkins; Ruth Donnelly; Emma Dunn; Walter Miller; Tom Dugan; Isabel Jewell; ***D:*** Roy Del Ruth; ***W:*** Howard J. Green.

The Bletchley Circle ✓✓ **2013** In this Brit miniseries, four women who worked as codebreakers at top-secret Bletchley Park find postwar Britain doesn't offer the same challenges. At least until housewife and mother Susan plays an intellectual game to find a pattern in the unsolved murders of young women found around London. As she becomes more obsessed, Susan calls on her friends Millie, Lucy, and Jean to really track down the murderer but it leads to danger as they run across a serial killer. **135m/C; DVD, Blu-Ray.** *UK* Anna Maxwell Martin; Rachael Stirling; Julie Graham; Sophie Rundle; Mark Dexter; Michael Gould; Steven Robertson; ***D:*** Andy de Emmony; ***W:*** Guy Burt; ***C:*** John Pardue; ***M:*** Nick Green. **TV**

Blind ✓✓✓ **2014** Writer Vogt makes his directorial debut with this excellent, mind-bending tale of a woman who may be going crazy as she is going blind. Ingrid (Petersen) has lost her sight as an adult and begins to lose track of her memories and perception of the real world. Writer/director Vogt also introduces us to people around Ingrid, a lonely neighbor and a woman who may be sleeping with Ingrid's husband, only to then force us to question what is real and what is in Ingrid's imagination. The result is a brilliant narrative trick; a film that forces us to question not just what we think but what we see. **96m/C; DVD.** *NO* Ellen Dorrit Petersen; Henrik Rafaelsen; Vera Vitali; Marius Kolbenstvedt; ***D:*** Eskil Vogt; ***W:*** Eskil Vogt; ***C:*** Thimios Bakatakis; ***M:*** Henk Hofstede.

Blind Corner ✓ 1/2 **1963** Routine British potboiler. Blind pop composer Paul Gregory (Sylvester) is targeted for death by his greedy wife Anne (Shelley) who persuades her lover (Davlon) to do the deed so they can inherit Paul's money. However, Paul is aware of much more than they imagine. **80m/B; DVD.** *GB* William Sylvester; Barbara Shelley; Alex Davion; Mark Eden; Elizabeth Shepherd; ***D:*** Lance Comfort; ***W:*** James Kelly; Peter Miller; ***C:*** Basil Emmott; ***M:*** Peter Hart; Brian Fahey.

Blind Date ✓ 1/2 **1984 (R)** Blind man agrees to have a visual computer implanted in his brain in order to help the police track down a psychopathic killer. Violent scenes may be disturbing to some. **100m/C; VHS, DVD, Blu-Ray.** Joseph Bottoms; Kirstie Alley; Keir Dullea; James Daughton; Lana Clarkson; Marina Sirtis; ***D:*** Nico Mastorakis; ***W:*** Nico Mastorakis.

Blind Date ✓✓ **1987 (PG-13)** A blind date between a workaholic yuppie and a beautiful blonde starts off well, but when she drinks too much at dinner, things get out of hand. In addition to embarrassing her date and destroying the restaurant, she has a jealous ex-boyfriend who must be dealt with. **95m/C; VHS, DVD, Blu-Ray.** Kim Basinger; Bruce Willis; John Larroquette; William Daniels; George Coe; Mark Blum; Phil Hartman; Stephanie Faracy; Alice Hirson; Graham Stark; Sab Shimono; ***D:*** Blake Edwards; ***W:*** Dale Launer; ***C:*** Harry Stradling, Jr.; ***M:*** Henry Mancini.

Blind Date ✓✓ **2008** The games couples play. Estranged married couple Don (Tucci) and Janna (Clarkson) place personal ads for specific role-playing dates as they struggle to reconnect in the wake of their young daughter's tragic death. Loose but loyal interpretation of a film by Dutch director Theo van Gogh, who was murdered by a Muslim extremist in 2004. Tucci's version is not as developed as the original and is a thinly veiled attempt at an homage. Shot on a single set, it would have fared better as a play but instead is an awkward mix of tragedy, comedy, and romance. **80m/C; On Demand.** Stanley Tucci; Patricia Clarkson; ***D:*** Stanley Tucci; ***W:*** Stanley Tucci; David Schechter; ***C:*** Thomas Kist; ***M:*** Evan Lurie.

Blind Dating ✓ 1/2 **2006 (PG-13)** Danny (Pine) is a young blind man, trying to decide if he should have experimental surgery that might allow him to see. Since he has no romantic experience, his sleazy brother (Kaye) has been setting him up on a series of really bad—uh—blind dates. But Danny falls for his doctor's receptionist Leeza (Jay), an Indian woman who is in an arranged engagement. But neither can quite forget about the other. **95m/C; DVD.** Chris Pine; Eddie Kaye Thomas; Jane Seymour; Anjali Jay; ***D:*** James Keach; ***W:*** Christopher Theo; ***C:*** Julio Macat; ***M:*** Hector Pereira.

Blind Eye ✓ 1/2 **2006 (R)** Volatile cop Nick Browning (Oliver) gets a call from his ex-wife when their daughter goes missing. Nick returns to his hometown, hoping to use his personal connections to get in on the investigation. When days pass without any leads, Nick realizes that something stinks and if he wants to find his daughter alive, his now-former friends are going down. **96m/C; DVD.** Nick Mancuso; Roddy Piper; Levi Oliver; Tara Goudreau; Simone Randall; Phil Babcock; Shaun Hood; Joel Hookey; ***D:*** Mark McNabb; ***W:*** Virginia Carraway; Charlie Fitzgerald; ***C:*** Paul Dunlop; ***M:*** Iain Kelso. **VIDEO**

Blind Faith ✓✓ 1/2 **1998 (R)** In 1957, John Williams (Vance) is a struggling new lawyer, living with elder sibling Charles (Dutton) and his family in a Bronx neighborhood. The first black NYPD sergeant, Charles has an uneasy relationship with his eldest son, Charlie (Whitt). The family's shocked when Charlie's accused of murdering a white boy during a robbery attempt, especially when he confesses. John thinks the cops beat the confession out of the boy and becomes determined to defend him but he gradually becomes suspicious of the story Charlie is telling him. **122m/C; VHS, DVD.** Courtney B. Vance; Charles S. Dutton; Garland Whitt; Kadeem Hardison; Lonette McKee; Karen Glave; Dan Lett; ***D:*** Ernest R. Dickerson; ***W:*** Frank Military; ***C:*** Rodney Charters; ***M:*** Ron Carter. **CABLE**

Blind Fear ✓ 1/2 **1989 (R)** A blind woman is stalked by three killers in an abandoned country inn. **98m/C; VHS, DVD.** Shelley Hack; Jack Langedijk; Kim Coates; Jan Rubes; Heidi von Palleske; ***D:*** Tom Berry; ***W:*** Sergio D. Altieri.

Blind Fury ✓✓ 1/2 **1990 (R)** A blind Vietnam vet enlists the aid of a Zen master and a sharpshooter to tackle the Mafia. Hauer works well in the lead, but unfortunately, the movie doesn't. **86m/C; VHS, DVD, Blu-Ray.** Rutger Hauer; Terry O'Quinn; Brandon Call; Lisa Blount; Randall "Tex" Cobb; Noble Willingham; Meg Foster; Sho Kosugi; Nick Cassavetes; Charles Cooper; Rick Overton; ***D:*** Phillip Noyce; ***W:*** Charles Robert Carner; ***C:*** Don Burgess; ***M:*** J. Peter Robinson.

Blind Heat ✓✓ **2000 (R)** Unfaithful hubby Jeffrey Scott (Sapienza) takes wife Adriana (Alonso) on a business trip to Mexico where she gets kidnapped. Rather than pay the ransom, Scott hires negotiator Paul Burke (Fahey) to get his wife back by force. Meanwhile, kidnapper Victor (Peck) falls for Adriana and doesn't want to kill her when their plot turns sour. **95m/C; VHS, DVD.** Maria Conchita Alonso; Jeff Fahey; J. Eddie Peck; Al Sapienza; ***D:*** Adolfo Martinez Solares; ***W:*** Adolfo Martinez Solares; Jeff O'Brien; ***C:*** Keith Holland. **VIDEO**

Blind Horizon ✓✓ 1/2 **2004 (R)** A head wound gives Frank Cavanaugh (Kilmer) a case of amnesia but he can't shake ominous flashbacks of a presidential assassination attempt—especially when he hears the president is about to visit. But trying to convince a local New Mexico sheriff (Shepard) of the imminent danger isn't so easy since he's distracted by his reelection bid. And Frank can't be sure that his fiancee Chloe (Campbell) is really who she claims to be. Subplots are overdone and memory loss is nothing new. It works well enough, though. Faye Dunaway gets a slick bit part. **99m/C; VHS, DVD.** Amy Smart; Gil Bellows; Giancarlo Esposito; Faye Dunaway; ***D:*** Michael Haussman; ***W:*** F. Paul Benz; Steve Tomlin; ***C:*** Max Malkin. **VIDEO**

Blind Husbands ✓✓✓ 1/2 **1919** An Austrian officer is attracted to the pretty wife of a dull surgeon. Controversial in its day, this lurid, sumptuous melodrama instigated many stubborn Hollywood myths, including the stereotype of the brusque, jodhpur-clad Prussian officer. This was von Stroheim's first outing as director. **98m/B; Silent; VHS, DVD.** Erich von Stroheim; Fay Wray; ***D:*** Erich von Stroheim.

Blind Justice ✓✓ 1/2 **1994 (R)** Gunfighter gets blinded in battle and rides into a small town where he's nursed back to health by an attractive lady doctor. While he recovers, he learns the town is trying to protect a cache of government silver from being stolen by bandits. **85m/C; VHS, DVD.** Armand Assante; Elisabeth Shue; Robert Davi; Adam Baldwin; Jack Black; ***D:*** Richard Spence; ***W:*** Daniel Knauf; ***C:*** Jack Conroy; ***M:*** Richard Gibbs. **CABLE**

Blind Revenge ✓ 1/2 *A Closed Book* **2010** Uneven, melodramatic thriller. Arrogant author Sir Paul (Conti) has become reclusive since being blinded and badly scarred in an accident. He hires a live-in assistant, Jane (Hannah), to help him work on his memoirs but it's apparent that she has a malevolent agenda of her own. **88m/C; DVD.** *UK* Tom Conti; Daryl Hannah; Miriam Margolyes; Simon MacCorkindale; ***D:*** Raoul Ruiz; ***W:*** Gilbert Adair; ***C:*** Ricardo Aronovich; ***M:*** Stephen Mark Barchan. **VIDEO**

Blind Side ✓ 1/2 **1993 (R)** DeMornay and Silver are a married couple whose Mexican vacation turns into trouble when they get into a hit-and-run accident which they don't report. Back home, they're frightened by the sudden appearance of Hauer, who's also just back from Mexico. They think he's after blackmail but he's really just a run-of-the-mill psycho intrigued by DeMornay, who at least keeps her character in control. Silver and Hauer have a great time chewing scenery. Also available in a 98-minute unrated version. **92m/C; VHS, DVD.** Rebecca De Mornay; Ron Silver; Rutger Hauer; ***D:*** Geoff Murphy; ***W:*** John Carlen. **CABLE**

The Blind Side ✓✓ **2009 (PG-13)** Although based on the true story of NFL football player Michael Oher (Aaron), this feel-good sports tale is dominated by Bullock's portrayal of Leigh Anne Tuohy. She is the sassy Memphis belle in charge of the family that takes the disadvantaged young Michael off of the streets. She charms and wisecracks her way past her amiable husband (McGraw), her snooty friends and every other obstacle in her crusade to help Michael fulfill his potential. The not-so-subtle story is heartwarming, but a bit over the top. Based on the book by Michael Lewis. **128m/C; Blu-Ray, On Demand.** Sandra Bullock; Tim McGraw; Quinton Aaron; Kathy Bates; Ray McKinnon; Jae Head; Lily Collins; ***D:*** John Lee Hancock; ***W:*** John Lee Hancock; ***C:*** Alar Kivilo; ***M:*** Carter Burwell. Oscars '09: Actress (Bullock); Golden Globes '10: Actress--Drama (Bullock); Screen Actors Guild '09: Actress (Bullock).

Blind Trust ✓✓ **2006** In this Lifetime crime drama, insurance adjuster Cassie Stewart (Capshaw) gets convicted of murder despite having top criminal attorney L.G. Mennick (Hindle) working the case pro bono. Cassie goes on the lam to figure out the set-up and it's no surprise who the killer is. Now she has to prove it. **90m/C; DVD.** Jessica Capshaw; Art Hindle; Chad Willett; Robin Wilcock; Sean Tucker; ***D:*** Louis Bolduc; ***W:*** Tom Gates; ***C:*** John Ashmore. **CABLE**

Blind Witness ✓✓ 1/2 **1989** Routine story about a blind woman who's the only witness to her husband's murder during a robbery. **92m/C; VHS, DVD.** Victoria Principal; Paul LeMat; Stephen Macht; Matt Clark; Tim Choate; ***D:*** Richard A. Colla; ***M:*** Robert Alcivar. **TV**

Blind Woman's Curse ✓✓ *Kaidan nobori ryu; Black Cat's Revenge; Strange Tales of a Dragon Tattoo; The Tattooed Swordswoman* **1970** Akemi (Meiko Kaji, of "Lady Snowblood" fame) is a Yakuza, and head of a group of deadly swordswomen. Attempting to kill the leader of a rival clan she blinds his daughter when the girl throws herself in front of her father. The young blind girl and her freakishly deformed henchman devote themselves to destroying Akemi by any means necessary. **85m/C; DVD, Blu-Ray.** *JP* Meiko Kaji; Makoto Sato; Toru Abe; Hideo Sunazuka; Ryohei Uchida; Hoki Tokuda; Yoshi Kato; Shiro Otsuji; Yoko Takagi; ***D:*** Teru Ishii; ***W:*** Teru Ishii; Chusei Sone; ***C:*** Shigeru Kiazumi; ***M:*** Hajime Kaburagi.

Blinded by the Light ✓✓✓ **2019 (PG-13)** In 1980s England, Javed (Kalra) lives in a small town and hides his personality and dreams from his immigrant parents. British economic struggles of the era affect the family, and Javed feels his must live up to his working class parents' expectations. After a classmate passes him copies of Bruce Springsteen's albums, Javed's worldview completely changes as he finds Springsteen's music speaking to him. Based on the memoir by Sarfraz Manzoor, the film captures the energy and joy of fandom and how music that you connect with can change your life while also exploring assimilation and tensions within immigrant families. **118m/C; DVD, Blu-Ray.** Viveik Kalra; Kulvinder Ghir; Meera Ganatra; Aaron Phagura; Dean-Charles Chapman; ***D:*** Gurinder Chadha; ***W:*** Gurinder Chadha; Paul Mayeda Berges; Sarfraz Manzoor; ***C:*** Ben Smithard; ***M:*** A.R. Rahman.

Blindness ✓ 1/2 **2008 (R)** An entire city's population is suddenly struck blind, degraded to lost souls wandering the streets, filthy, ruined, and dying. The only ones not affected by the epidemic are the inmates quarantined at prison, who descend into sheer madness from hunger, and an oppressive leader (Bernal) who wields a gun and newly-discovered sense of dictatorship. Much to her confusion, the local eye doctor's wife (Moore) also retains her vision, as well as her sense of order. The relentless allegorical suffering and way-too-artsy effects make it almost impossible to lay off the fast-forward button. Adapted from the novel by Jose Saramago. **118m/C; Blu-Ray.** *BR CA* Julianne Moore; Mark Ruffalo; Danny Glover; Gael Garcia Bernal; Alice Braga; Maury Chaykin; Don McKellar; ***D:*** Fernando Meirelles; ***W:*** Don McKellar; ***C:*** Cesar Charlone; ***M:*** Marcus Antonio Guimaraes.

Blindsight ✓✓✓ **2006 (PG)** This moving documentary follows a group of six blind Tibetan teenagers as they climb the 23,000-foot Lhakpa Ri on the north side of Mount Everest. Because Tibetan society shuns the blind and believes they are demon possessed, such children are rejected by their parents and the home communities. The teens are students at the only school for the blind in Tibet, founded by Sabriye Tenberken who personally rescued the six. After a famous blind mountain climber visits their school, they are inspired to make the climb, led by the mountain climber, over a three-week adventure documented in the film. **104m/C; DVD, Streaming, Download.** ***D:*** Lucy Walker; ***C:*** Lucy Walker; Michael Brown; Petr Cikhart; Keith Partridge; Gavin Struthers; Mahyad Tousi; ***M:*** David Christophere; Nitin Sawhney.

Blindspotting ✓✓ 1/2 **2018 (R)** An Oakland, California-set comedy-drama centered on a complicated interracial friendship. Only a few days from completing his parole, Collin (Diggs) works as a mover with his long-time best friend Miles (Casal). When Collin casually meets up with Miles one day, he witnesses Miles illegally buying a gun. As the violent Miles acts out to establish his street cred, Collin is internally tormented after witnessing the police shooting of a black man. A powerful and carefully constructed exploration of race and issues. **95m/C; DVD, Blu-Ray.** Daveed Diggs; Rafael Casal; Janina Gavankar; Jasmine Cephas Jones; Ethan (Randall) Embry; ***D:*** Carlos Lopez Estrada; ***W:*** Daveed Diggs; Rafael Casal; ***C:*** Robby Baumgartner; ***M:*** Michael Yezerski.

The Bling Ring ✓✓ **2011** Lifetime movie inspired by a true story. Zack goes to an L.A. school for troubled teens where he's befriended by risk-taker Natalie. She learns when the homes of celebrities are empty and the two break in and steal personal items like clothes and jewelry. Their friends find out and join in and their exploits are posted online, leading to attention from the media and the cops. **88m/C; DVD.** Austin Butler; Yin Chang; Tom Irwin; Sebastian Sozzi; Jennifer Grey; Wendy Makkena; ***D:*** Michael Lembeck; ***W:*** Shelley Evans; ***C:*** Ousama Rawi; ***M:*** Lawrence Shragge. **CABLE**

The Bling Ring ✓✓✓ **2013 (R)** Coppola returns to the spoiled hills of Hollywood with this excellent true crime story about the TMZ generation. In an era when a celebrity's every move is tracked by the paparazzi and the most red carpet-friendly of them amass so much wealth and property that they don't even notice when it's gone, Coppola's film dares to not demonize the kids who chose to steal from their favorite celebs but to almost ask, "Can you blame them?" With a stunning degree of directorial confidence, this dramedy takes a unique approach to a story that could have been little more than a moral message. **90m/C; DVD, Blu-Ray.** Emma Watson; Israel Broussard; Katie Chang; Claire Julien; Taissa Farmiga; Gavin Rossdale; Leslie Mann;

Cameo(s): Paris Hilton; *D:* Sofia Coppola; *W:* Sofia Coppola; *C:* Harris Savides; *M:* Brian Reitzell.

Blink 🦴🦴½ **1993 (R)** Recent corneal transplants allow blind musician Emma (Stowe) to regain her sight, but until they "settle" what she sees may not register in her mind immediately, a phenomenon the script dubs "retroactive vision." This poses a problem for Chicago cop Quinn when he falls for Emma—the only one who can recognize a sadistic killer. Average thriller has been done better before, but adds two attractive leads, enough suspense, and a unique twist to the typical woman-in-jeopardy tale to keep things interesting. The distorted images in Stowe's blurry vision were created by computer. Stowe also learned fiddle for her place as the fictional member of the real-life Irish-American band, The Drovers. **106m/C; VHS, DVD.** Madeleine Stowe; Aidan Quinn; Laurie Metcalf; James Remar; Bruce A. Young; Peter Friedman; Paul Dillon; Michael Kirkpatrick; *D:* Michael Apted; *W:* Dana Stevens; *C:* Dante Spinotti; *M:* Brad Fiedel.

Bliss 🦴½ **1996 (R)** Creepy feature-length sex-ed lecture delves deeply into sexual problems in modern society. So deeply, in fact, that it could've been called "Ouch, You're on my Hair." Clueless yuppies Joseph (Sheffer) and Maria's (Lee) sexual dysfunctions lead her to seek aid from unconventional therapist Baltazar (Stamp), who does things like compare women to violins (hint: they're not really the same. Unless you REALLY like wood). Joseph has his doubts, but soon becomes a chanting tantric goofball. Too clinical to be sexy, but too sexy to be used as an Army training film. **103m/C; VHS, DVD.** Sheryl Lee; Craig Sheffer; Terence Stamp; Casey Siemaszko; Spalding Gray; Leigh Taylor-Young; Lois Chiles; Blu Mankuma; *D:* Lance Young; *W:* Lance Young; *C:* Mike Molloy; *M:* Jan A.P. Kaczmarek.

The Bliss of Mrs. Blossom 🦴🦴🦴 **1968** Three's a crowd in this light-hearted romp through the machinations of a brassiere manufacturer (Attenborough) and his neglected wife (MacLaine). Mrs. Blossom finds sewing machine repairman Booth so appetizing that she hides him in the attic of the Blossom home. He reads books and redecorates, until, several plot twists later, Attenborough discovers the truth. Witty and wise, with fine supporting cast and excellent pacing. **93m/C; DVD.** *GB* Shirley MacLaine; Richard Attenborough; James Booth; Freddie Jones; John Cleese; *D:* Joseph McGrath.

Blithe Spirit 🦴🦴🦴½ **1945** Charming and funny adaptation of Coward's famed stage play. A man re-marries and finds his long-dead wife is unhappy enough about it to come back and haunt him. Clever supporting cast, with Rutherford exceptional as the medium. Received Oscar for its Special Effects. **96m/C; VHS, DVD.** *GB* Rex Harrison; Constance Cummings; Kay Hammond; Margaret Rutherford; Hugh Wakefield; Joyce Carey; Jacqueline Clarke; *D:* David Lean; *W:* Noel Coward; Anthony Havelock-Allan; *C:* Ronald Neame; *M:* Richard Addinsell.

Blitz 🦴½ *Killing Cars* **1985 (R)** A German car designer's pet project, a car that runs without gas, is halted by the influence of an Arab conglomerate. He nevertheless tries to complete it, and is hunted down. **104m/C; VHS, DVD.** Jurgen Prochnow; Senta Berger; William Conrad; Agnes Soral; *D:* Michael Verhoeven; *W:* Michael Verhoeven; *C:* Jacques Steyn; *M:* Michael Landau.

Blitz 🦴🦴 **2011 (R)** East London detective Tom Brant (Statham), a violence-prone loner, is teamed with gay, by-the-book Porter Nash (Considine) to find a serial killer targeting cops. Naturally, the killer likes to taunt the police, including using tabloid sleaze Dunphy (Morrissey). Tries to do a bit too much, but the cast is fine and the pace is quick even if the story is familiar. Based on novel by Ken Bruen. **97m/C; DVD, Blu-Ray.** *GB* Jason Statham; Paddy Considine; Aidan Gillen; David Morrissey; Zawe Ashton; Mark Rylance; Nicky Henson; *D:* Elliott Lester; *W:* Nathan Parker; *C:* Rob Hardy; *M:* Ilan Eshkeri.

The Blob 🦴🦴½ **1958** Sci-fi thriller about a small town's fight against a slimy jello invader from space. Slightly rebellious McQueen (in his first starring role) redeems himself when he saves the town with quick action. Low-budget, horror/teen-fantasy became a camp classic. Other names considered included "The Glob," "The Glob that Girdled the Globe," "The Meteorite Monster," "The Molten Meteorite," and "The Night of the Creeping Dead." Followed by a worthless sequel in 1972, "Son of Blob," and a worthwhile remake in 1988. **83m/C; DVD, Blu-Ray.** Steve McQueen; Aneta Corsaut; Olin Howlin; Earl Rowe; Alden "Steve" Chase; John Benson; Vincent Barbi; *D:* Irvin S. Yeaworth, Jr.; *W:* Kay Linaker; Theodore Simonson; *C:* Thomas E. Spalding; *M:* Burt Bacharach; Hal David; Ralph Carmichael.

The Blob 🦴🦴🦴 **1988 (R)** A hi-tech remake of the 1958 camp classic about a small town beset by a fast-growing, man-eating mound of glop shot into space by scientists, irradiated into an unnatural being, and then returned to earth. Well-developed characters make this an excellent tribute to the first film. **92m/C; VHS, DVD, Blu-Ray.** Kevin Dillon; Candy Clark; Joe Seneca; Shawnee Smith; Donovan Leitch; Jeffrey DeMunn; Ricky Paull Goldin; Del Close; *D:* Chuck Russell; *W:* Chuck Russell; Frank Darabont; *C:* Mark Irwin.

Block-heads 🦴🦴🦴 **1938** Twenty years after the end of WWI, soldier Stan is found, still in his foxhole, and brought back to America, where he moves in with old pal Ollie. Also includes a 1934 Charley Chase short "I'll Take Vanilla." **75m/B; VHS, DVD.** Stan Laurel; Oliver Hardy; Billy Gilbert; Patricia Ellis; James Finlayson; Charley Chase; *D:* John Blystone.

Blockers 🦴🦴 **2018 (R)** A combination of a teen coming of age comedy and heartfelt parenting comedy. Since elementary school, Julie (Newton), Kayla (Viswanathan), and Sam (Aldon) have been best friends. Their parents--Lisa (Mann), Mitchell (Cena), and Hunter (Barinholtz), respectively--also formed a friendship. As senior prom approaches, the teens decide to have sex for the first time that night, while their parents struggle with their children growing up. When the parents learn of their children's planned debauchery, they do all they can to find their kids and stop them. The talented, charismatic actors exhibit great comic timing, but the story is a bit sloppy. **102m/C; DVD, Blu-Ray.** John Cena; Leslie Mann; Kathryn Newton; Ike Barinholtz; Gideon Adlon; *D:* Kay Cannon; *W:* Brian Kehoe; Jim Kehoe; *C:* Russ T. Alsobrook; *M:* Mateo Messina.

Blockhouse WOOF! 1973 Four men are entombed in a subterranean stronghold for six years after the D-Day invasion of Normandy. Encourages claustrophobic feeling in viewer. Based on Jean Paul Clebert's novel "Le Blockhaus." **88m/C; VHS, DVD.** *GB* Peter Sellers; Charles Aznavour; Per Oscarsson; Peter Vaughan; Leon Lissek; Alfred Lynch; Jeremy Kemp; *D:* Clive Rees.

The Blonde 🦴🦴 *La Bionda* **1992** Tommasso (Rubini) is driving through the Milan streets when he knocks down a young blonde woman (Kinski). She loses her memory (apparently due to shock) and Tommasso agrees to help her—soon falling in love. One day her memory returns and Christina remembers she's involved with a drug dealer and other shady characters. She leaves Tommasso to protect him but he's got other ideas. Italian with subtitles. **100m/C; VHS, DVD.** *IT* Sergio Rubini; Nastassja Kinski; Ennio Fantastichini; Umberto Raho; Veronica Lazar; Giacomo Piperno; *D:* Sergio Rubini; *W:* Sergio Rubini; Filippo Ascione; Umberto Marino; *C:* Alessio Gelsini Torresi; *M:* Jurgen Knieper.

Blonde 🦴🦴½ **2001** Montgomery may not be as curvy as the real Marilyn Monroe, but she does well in this routine biopic about the bombshell who suffered from life-long problems with self-esteem and men. Based on the novel by Joyce Carol Oates, the miniseries covers Marilyn from her disturbing childhood/teenage Norma Jean Baker years to her transformation into a screen goddess, although it ends before her death. **240m/C; DVD.** Poppy Montgomery; Skye McCole Bartusiak; Patricia Richardson; Ann-Margret; Kirstie Alley; Eric Bogosian; Wallace Shawn; Patrick Dempsey; Jensen Ackles; Titus Welliver; Griffin Dunne; Richard Roxburgh; *D:* Joyce Chopra; *W:* Joyce Eliason; *C:* James Glennon; *M:* Patrick Williams. **TV**

Blonde Ambition 🦴½ **2007 (PG-13)** Simpson plays a clueless blonde (how's that for typecasting?) in this would-be comedy that at least has a couple of supporting performances to save it. Naive Katie heads to NY to see her boyfriend, discovers him cheating, but bucks up when she suddenly gets a job working for a bigshot CEO (Larry Miller) and begins dating Ben (a befuddled Wilson) from the mailroom. The job is a set-up by a couple of sleazy co-workers (Penelope Ann Miller, Dick) looking for a corporate takeover and the blonde must save the day. **93m/C; DVD.** Jessica Simpson; Luke Wilson; Larry Miller; Penelope Ann Miller; Andy Dick; Rachael Leigh Cook; Drew Fuller; Willie Nelson; *D:* Scott Marshall; *W:* John Cohen; *C:* Mark Irwin.

Blonde and Blonder 🦴 **2007 (PG-13)** The distaff "Dumb and Dumber" with lots of pink. Dee (Anderson) and Dawn (Richards) witness a mob hit done by pro Kat (Vaugier) and associate Kit (Ory) and then, somehow, get mistaken for the hired killers. They are offered a contract to take out Chinese gangster Mr. Wong (Mann), naturally believing that "take out" means something much less lethal, thus leading to more comic misadventure. Both blondes are getting too old to play ditzy dames even when they're in on the joke. **95m/C; DVD.** Pamela Anderson; Denise Richards; Byron Mann; Emmanuelle Vaugier; Meaghan Ory; John Farley; Kevin Farley; *D:* Dean Hamilton; *W:* Dean Hamilton; Rolfe Kanefsky; Gerry Anderson; *C:* C. Kim Miles; *M:* William Goodrum. **VIDEO**

Blonde Comet 🦴 **1941** Betsy Blake (Vale) is a famous female European race car driver who decides to try her hand at racing in America. She soon runs into a rival in the form of Jim Flynn (Kent), a racer trying to invent a new form of carburetor. The usual evil bad guy attempts to foil his inventing efforts and their budding romance. Despite Vale playing a female driver long before women drivers were allowed, don't expect her to portray a feminist—this was made in the 40s after all. **65m/B; DVD.** Virginia Vale; Robert Kent; Barney Oldfield; Vince Barnett; William (Bill) Halligan; Joey Ray; Red Knight; Diane Hughes; *D:* William Beaudine; *W:* Phillip Juergens; Robin Daniels; *C:* Jack Greenhalgh; *M:* Andrew Keresztes.

Blonde Crazy 🦴🦴½ *Larceny Lane* **1931** A charming grifter hooks up with a gorgeous blonde as he works the territory of a big wheel criminal. Escapist fare, with fun performances from Cagney and Blondell. **81m/B; DVD.** James Cagney; Joan Blondell; Louis Calhern; Ray Milland; Nat Pendleton; *D:* Roy Del Ruth; *W:* Kubec Glasmon; John Bright; *C:* Sidney Hickox.

Blonde for a Day 🦴½ **1946** Private eye Michael Shayne (Beaumont) is on the case for a newspaper reporter who finds herself in trouble when she writes articles attacking the police department for failing to solve a string of murders. She's got info about a gambling ring and the crooks are none too happy about it. Shayne's got to help the reporter and bring the crooks to justice. **68m/B; DVD.** Hugh Beaumont; Kathryn Adams; Cy Kendall; Marjorie Hoshelle; Richard Fraser; *D:* Sam Newfield; *W:* Brett Halliday; Fred Myton; *C:* Jack Greenhalgh.

Blonde Ice 🦴🦴 **1948** Cheap and fun B-movie noir. Psycho San Francisco society columnist Claire (Brooks) turns out to be a femme who's very fatale to the men she gets involved with. She just loves to see her name in the scandal rags and is even willing to frame new boyfriend Les (Paige) if it means headlines. **74m/B; DVD.** Leslie Brooks; Robert Paige; Walter Sande; John Holland; Emory Parnell; *D:* Jack Bernhard; *W:* Kenneth Gamet; *C:* George Robinson; *M:* Irving Gertz.

Blonde Venus 🦴🦴🦴½ **1932** A German cafe singer marries an Englishman, but their marriage hits the skids when he contracts radiation poisoning and she gets a nightclub job to pay the bills. Sternberg's and Dietrich's fourth film together, and characteristically beautiful, though terribly strange. Dietrich's cabaret number "Hot Voodoo," in a gorilla suit and blonde afro, attains new heights in early Hollywood surrealism. **94m/B; VHS, DVD, Blu-Ray.** Marlene Dietrich; Herbert Marshall; Cary Grant; Dickie Moore; Hattie McDaniel; Sidney Toler; *D:* Josef von Sternberg.

Blondes Have More Guns 🦴🦴 **1995 (R)** Very dumb detective Harry Bates (McGaharin) is investigating a chainsaw murder and falls for the mysterious Montana (Key), who's possibly a serial killer, or maybe it's her half-sister, Dakota (Lusiak). Spoof of "Basic Instinct" and others of that ilk, done in the usual Troma fashion. **90m/C; VHS, DVD.** Michael McGahern; Elizabeth Key; Gloria Lusiak; Richard Neil; Bennie Buttner; Romana Lisa; Andre Brazeau; *D:* George Merriweather; *W:* George Merriweather; Dan Goodman; Mary Guthrie; *C:* Maximo Munzi; *M:* Joe Renzetti.

Blondie 🦴🦴½ **1938** Chic Young's famous comic strip debuted on the big screen with Singleton in the title role, Lake as the bumbling Dagwood, and Simms as Baby Dumpling (son Alexander, when he grows up). The couple are about to celebrate their 5th wedding anniversary when Dagwood loses his job and Blondie suspects him of infidelity. The series eventually contained 28 films. **68m/B; VHS, DVD.** Penny Singleton; Arthur Lake; Larry Simms; Gene Lockhart; Ann Doran; Jonathan Hale; Gordon Oliver; Stanley Andrews; Dorothy Moore; *D:* Frank Strayer; *W:* Richard Flournoy; *C:* Henry Freulich.

Blondie Brings Up Baby 🦴🦴 **1939** Baby Dumpling is enrolled in school but on his first day he plays hooky to find Daisy who's been caught by the dogcatcher. But Blondie and Dagwood think the tyke has been kidnapped! **67m/B; VHS, DVD.** Penny Singleton; Arthur Lake; Larry Simms; Jonathan Hale; Danny Mummert; Fay Helm; Peggy Ann Garner; Irving Bacon; *D:* Frank Strayer; *W:* Richard Flournoy; Gladys Lehman; *C:* Henry Freulich.

Blondie Goes Latin 🦴🦴 **1942** Mr. Dithers invites the Bumsteads on a South American cruise and Dagwood winds up the drummer in the shipboard band while Singleton gets to show off her Broadway background in some musical numbers. **70m/B; VHS, DVD.** Penny Singleton; Arthur Lake; Jonathan Hale; Larry Simms; Ruth Terry; Tito Guizar; Danny Mummert; Irving Bacon; *D:* Frank Strayer; *W:* Richard Flournoy; Karen De Wolf; *C:* Henry Freulich.

Blondie Goes to College 🦴🦴 **1942** Actually both Bumsteads enroll but decide to pass themselves off as single, which leads to complications. Blondie draws the attentions of the school's top athlete while Dagwood's joins the rowing team and turns the head of a pretty coed. **68m/B; VHS, DVD.** Penny Singleton; Arthur Lake; Larry Simms; Jonathan Hale; Danny Mummert; Janet Blair; Larry Parks; Lloyd Bridges; *D:* Frank Strayer; *W:* Lou Breslow; *C:* Henry Freulich.

Blondie Has Trouble 🦴🦴½ *Blondie Has Servant Trouble* **1940** Mr. Dithers has a property he just can't sell because of rumors that the house is haunted. So he offers to let the Bumsteads stay in it to prove that the rumors are false. The Bumsteads also find the creepy mansion comes complete with two equally creepy servants. 6th film in the series. **70m/B; VHS, DVD.** Penny Singleton; Arthur Lake; Larry Simms; Danny Mummert; Jonathan Hale; Arthur Hohl; Esther Dale; Irving Bacon; *D:* Frank Strayer; *W:* Richard Flournoy; *C:* Henry Freulich; *M:* Leigh Harline.

Blondie in Society 🦴½ **1941** A weak entry (the ninth) in the comedic series. Dagwood brings home a pedigreed Great Dane and Blondie decides to enter the pooch in the local dog show. Then an important client of Dagwood's decides he wants the dog. **77m/B; VHS, DVD.** Penny Singleton; Arthur Lake; Larry Simms; William Frawley; Edgar Kennedy; Jonathan Hale; Danny Mummert; Chick Chandler; *D:* Frank Strayer; *W:* Karen De Wolf; *C:* Henry Freulich.

Blondie Johnson 🦴🦴 **1933** After suffering the loss of her family through poverty, smart cookie Blondie is determined to use her brains to get ahead. She takes up professionally with racketeer Danny and climbs the criminal ladder to success. There's ultimately a "crime doesn't pay" ending. **67m/B; DVD.** Joan Blondell; Chester Morris; Claire Dodd; Arthur Vinton; Allen Jenkins; Mae Busch; Sterling Holloway; Earle Foxe; *D:* Ray Enright; *W:* Earl Baldwin; *C:* Gaetano Antonio "Tony" Gaudio.

Blondie Meets the Boss 🦴🦴 **1939** Dagwood goes on a fishing trip and manages to get into trouble with Blondie when a photograph puts him in a comprising pose with another woman. Then, Blondie winds up at the office doing Dagwood's job (whatever that may be). Second in the series. **75m/B; VHS, DVD.** Penny Singleton; Arthur Lake; Larry Simms; Jonathan Hale; Dorothy Moore; Don Beddoe; Stanley Brown; Danny Mummert; Irving Bacon; ***D:*** Frank Strayer; ***W:*** Richard Flournoy; ***C:*** Henry Freulich.

Blondie On a Budget 🦴🦴 **1940** Dagwood wins 200 bucks in a contest and enlists the aid of ex-girlfriend Joan (Hayworth) to buy Blondie the fur coat she's been wanting. But Blondie wants to use the money to get Dagwood into a fishing club and misinterprets the situation. **68m/B; VHS, DVD.** Penny Singleton; Arthur Lake; Larry Simms; Rita Hayworth; Danny Mummert; Don Beddoe; Fay Helm; John Qualen; Irving Bacon; ***D:*** Frank Strayer; ***W:*** Richard Flournoy; ***C:*** Henry Freulich.

Blondie Plays Cupid 🦴🦴 **1940** The Bumsteads are traveling to visit relatives in the country when they happen across a young couple (Ford and Walters) trying to elope. So Blondie decides to help the youngsters out. **68m/B; VHS, DVD.** Penny Singleton; Arthur Lake; Larry Simms; Jonathan Hale; Glenn Ford; Luana Walters; Danny Mummert; Irving Bacon; ***D:*** Frank Strayer; ***W:*** Richard Flournoy; Karen De Wolf; ***C:*** Henry Freulich.

Blondie Takes a Vacation 🦴🦴 1/2 **1939** Third in the series of fluff films adapted from Chic Young's comic strip. After the Bumstead family is snubbed at a snobby mountain resort they move to a friendlier nearby hotel where they try to help out the owners who are in danger of losing their investment. Baby Dumpling does his bit by unleashing a skunk in the ventilation system of the competing hotel. **68m/B; VHS, DVD.** Penny Singleton; Arthur Lake; Larry Simms; Danny Mummert; Donald Meek; Donald MacBride; Thomas Ross; Robert Wilcox; Irving Bacon; ***D:*** Frank Strayer; ***W:*** Richard Flournoy; ***C:*** Henry Freulich.

Blood 🦴 *Blood: The Ultimate Death; Buraddo* **2009** Detective Hoshino (Kanji Tsuda) has been demoted to cold cases and decides to tackle the murder of a local maid before it reaches the statute of limitations. Arriving at the murder site he arrests what he assumes is a cannibal lunatic only to find that his perp is a vampire under the spell of the mansion's owner. Japanese with subtitles. **85m/C; DVD.** *JP* Aya Sugimoto; Kanji Tsuda; Jun Kaname; ***D:*** Ten Shimoyama; ***W:*** Shigenori Takechi; ***C:*** Gen Kobayashi; ***M:*** Kiyoshi Yoshikawa.

Blood Alley 🦴🦴 **1955** A seasoned Merchant Marine captain takes on a cargo of refugee Chinese to smuggle through enemy territory. Middling, mid-career Wayne vehicle. **115m/C; VHS, DVD, Blu-Ray.** John Wayne; Lauren Bacall; Paul Fix; Joy Kim; Berry Kroeger; Mike Mazurki; Anita Ekberg; ***D:*** William A. Wellman; ***C:*** William Clothier.

Blood and Black Lace 🦴 *Fashion House of Death; Six Women for the Murderer; Sei Donne per l'Assassino* **1964** Beautiful models are being brutally murdered and an inspector is assigned to the case, but not before more gruesome killings occur. Bava is, as usual, violent and suspenseful. Horror fans will enjoy this flick. **90m/C; VHS, DVD, Blu-Ray.** *IT FR GE* Cameron Mitchell; Eva Bartok; Mary Arden; Dante DiPaolo; Arianna Gorini; Lea Krugher; Harriet Medin; Giuliano Raffaelli; Thomas Reiner; Frank Ressel; Massimo Righi; ***D:*** Mario Bava; ***W:*** Mario Bava; Marcello Fondato; Joe Barilla; ***C:*** Ubaldo Terzano; ***M:*** Carlo Rustichelli.

Blood and Bone 🦴 1/2 **2009 (R)** Generic low-budget actioner with ex-con Isaiah Bone (White) getting involved in underground fighting (opposite real Mixed Martial Arts fighters) while falling for a mobster's girlfriend (Belegrin). There's at least a couple of good villains in supporting cast Sands and Walker. **94m/C; DVD.** Michael Jai White; Michelle Belegrin; Julian Sands; Eamonn Walker; Dante Basco; Nona Gaye; Bob Sapp; ***D:*** Ben Ramsey; ***W:*** Michael Andrews; ***C:*** Roy Wagner. **VIDEO**

Blood and Bones 🦴🦴 1/2 *Chi to Hone* **2004** Brutal character study of Joon-pyong Kim, a Korean immigrant to Japan who has been abused, and goes on to abuse, assault, and rape virtually every living thing he meets in return. Rising to ownership of a factory by harsh means, he swiftly graduates to loan sharking. Not for the faint of heart. **144m/C; DVD.** *JP* Takeshi "Beat" Kitano; Hirofumi Arai; Tomoko Tabata; Joe Odagiri; Kyoka Suzuki; Yutaka Matsushige; Mari Hamada; Yuko Nakamura; Kazuki Kitamura; Shuuji Kashiwabara; Susumu Terajima; Atsushi Ito; Miako Tadano; Mami Nakamura; ***D:*** Yoichi Sai; ***W:*** Yoichi Sai; Sogil Yan; Wui Sin Chong; ***C:*** Takashi Hamada; ***M:*** Taro Iwashiro.

Blood & Chocolate 🦴 1/2 **2007 (PG-13)** Interspecies dating. American Vivian (Bruckner) works in a Bucharest chocolate shop when not turning furry at the full moon. She falls for cute human artist Aiden (Dancy), who's obsessed with werewolves, but has a problem since she's betrothed to hot pack leader Gabriel (Martinez). What's a shape-shifting gal to do? Tame story from von Garnier based on the edgier teen novel by Annette Curtis Klause; the pic's ending goes for conventional romance as does the schmaltzy music. Special effects are minimal. **96m/C; DVD, Blu-Ray.** *GB RO* Agnes Bruckner; Olivier Martinez; Hugh Dancy; Bryan Dick; Katja Riemann; ***D:*** Katja von Garnier; ***W:*** Ehren Kruger; Christopher Landon; ***C:*** Brendan Galvin; ***M:*** Johnny Klimek; Reinhold Heil.

Blood & Concrete: A Love Story 🦴🦴 *Blood and Concrete* **1991 (R)** Bizarre, violent and stylish film-noir spoof, definitely not for all tastes. The innocent hero gets drawn into a maelstrom of intrigue over a killer aphrodisiac drug. Beals, an addicted punk rocker, gets to perform a few songs. **97m/C; VHS, DVD, Streaming.** Billy Zane; Jennifer Beals; Darren McGavin; James LeGros; Nicholas Worth; Mark Pellegrino; Harry Shearer; Billy Bastiani; ***D:*** Jeff Reiner; ***W:*** Jeff Reiner; Richard LaBrie; ***C:*** Declan Quinn; ***M:*** Vinnie Golia.

Blood & Donuts 🦴🦴 **1995 (R)** Hungry vampire Boya (Currie) is looking for a rat snack when he stumbles across an all-night donut shop where pretty cashier Molly (Clarkson) and friendly cabbie Earl (Louis) seek his help with a local crime boss. Mild horror mixed with comedy and limited gore. **89m/C; VHS, Streaming.** *CA* Gordon Currie; Justin Louis; Helene Clarkson; Fiona Reid; Frank Moore; ***Cameo(s):*** David Cronenberg; ***D:*** Holly Dale; ***W:*** Andrew Rai Berzins; ***C:*** Paul Sarossy.

Blood and Orchids 🦴🦴 **1986** Miniseries covers racism and lies in 1937 Hawaii. Hester (Stowe), the wife of naval officer Lloyd Murdoch (Russ), is beaten and raped by her lover (Salinger). She's found by four young Hawaiian men who take her to the hospital but flee, fearing they'll be accused of the crime. Hester's autocratic, plantation-owning mother (Alexander) insists Hester lie and the four are, indeed, arrested and put on trial. However, police captain Maddox (Kristofferson) thinks something stinks. Based on a true story; Katkov scripted from his novel. **200m/C; DVD.** Kris Kristofferson; Jane Alexander; Madeleine Stowe; William Russ; Sean Young; Jose Ferrer; Matt Salinger; James Saito; Susan Blakely; David Clennon; Richard Dysart; George Coe; ***D:*** Jerry Thorpe; ***W:*** Norman Katkov; ***C:*** Charles G. Arnold; ***M:*** Mark Snow. **TV**

Blood and Roses 🦴🦴 *Et Mourir de Plaisir* **1961** A girl who is obsessed with her family's vampire background becomes possessed by a vampire and commits numerous murders. The photography is good, but the plot is hazy and only effective in certain parts. Based on the story "Carmilla" by Sheridan Le Fanu. Later remade as "The Vampire Lovers" and "The Blood-Spattered Bride." **74m/C; VHS, Streaming.** *FR IT* Mel Ferrer; Elsa Martinelli; Annette (Stroyberg) Vadim; Marc Allegret; Jacques-Rene Chauffard; Serge Marquand; Gabriella Farinon; Alberto Bonucci; Nathalie Le Foret; ***D:*** Roger Vadim; ***W:*** Roger Vadim; Claude Martin; Roger Vailand; Claude Brule; ***C:*** Claude Renoir; ***M:*** Jean Prodromides.

Blood and Sand 🦴🦴 1/2 **1922** Vintage romance based on Vicente Blasco Ibanez's novel about the tragic rise and fall of a matador, and the women in his life. The film that made Valentino a star. Remade in 1941. Silent. **87m/B; Silent; VHS, DVD, Blu-Ray.** Rudolph Valentino; Nita Naldi; Lila Lee; Walter Long; ***D:*** Fred Niblo; ***W:*** June Mathis; ***C:*** Alvin Wyckoff.

Blood and Sand 🦴🦴🦴 **1941** Director Mamoulian "painted" this picture in the new technicolor technique, which makes it a veritable explosion of color and spectacle. Power is the matador who becomes famous and then falls when he is torn between two women, forsaking his first love, bullfighting. Based on the novel "Sangre y Arena" by Vicente Blasco Ibanez. This movie catapulted Hayworth to stardom, primarily for her dancing, but also for her sexiness and seductiveness (and of course, her acting). Remake of the 1922 silent classic; remade again in 1989. **123m/C; VHS, DVD, Blu-Ray.** Tyrone Power; Linda Darnell; Rita Hayworth; Alla Nazimova; Anthony Quinn; J. Carrol Naish; John Carradine; George Reeves; ***D:*** Rouben Mamoulian; ***W:*** Jo Swerling; ***C:*** Ernest Palmer; Ray Rennahan; ***M:*** Alfred Newman. Oscars '41: Color Cinematog.

Blood and Sand 🦴🦴 **1989 (R)** A bullfighter on the verge of super-stardom risks it all when he falls under the spell of a sexy, seductive woman. Will she destroy his one opportunity for fame? Interesting for people who actually enjoy watching the "sport" of bullfighting. Originally made in 1922 and remade in 1941. **96m/C; VHS, DVD.** Christopher Rydell; Sharon Stone; Ana Torrent; Jose-Luis De Villalonga; Simon Andreu; ***D:*** Javier Elorrieta; ***W:*** Rafael Azcona; Ricardo Franco; Thomas Fucci; ***C:*** Antonio Rios; ***M:*** Jesus Gluck.

Blood & Wine 🦴🦴 1/2 **1996 (R)** Miami wine merchant Alex (Nicholson) gets involved with terminally ill safecracker Victor (Caine) to steal a necklace worth a cool million. Meanwhile he must deal with his crumbling marriage to Suzanne (Davis) and the bitter relationship with his stepson Jason (Dorff), who has eyes for both the necklace and his Cuban mistress (Lopez). Characterizations and strong performances (particularly by Nicholson and Caine) haul the sometimes lumbering plot to its violent conclusion. Promoted as the third part of a "dysfunctional family trilogy" with "Five Easy Pieces" and "The King of Marvin's Gardens." Seventh time Nicholson has worked with director Rafelson. **100m/C; VHS, DVD.** Jack Nicholson; Michael Caine; Judy Davis; Stephen Dorff; Jennifer Lopez; Harold Perrineau, Jr.; ***D:*** Bob Rafelson; ***W:*** Nick Villiars; Allison Cross; ***C:*** Newton Thomas (Tom) Sigel; ***M:*** Stephen Cohen.

Blood Angels 🦴 *Thralls* **2005 (R)** Ashley (Baruc) left her bad home life to hang with her big sis—who, it ends up, is part of a group of half-vampire, half-human gal pals. The girls fill their human blood quota by tempting men to a club run by their oppressive master, Mr. Jones (Lamas), who won't give them full vampire powers, so they decide to use Ashley to give him the boot. **98m/C; VHS, DVD.** *CA* Lorenzo Lamas; Siri Baruc; Sonya Salomaa; Crystal Lowe; Leah Cairns; Fiona Scott; Lisa Marie Caruk; Monica Delain; ***D:*** Ron Oliver; ***W:*** Lisa Morton; Brett Thompson; ***C:*** David Pelletier. **VIDEO**

Blood Beast Terror 🦴 1/2 *The Vampire-Beast Craves Blood; Deathshead Vampire* **1967** An entomologist transforms his own daughter into a Deathshead Moth and she proceeds to terrorize and drink innocent victims' blood. **81m/C; VHS, DVD, Blu-Ray.** *GB* Peter Cushing; Robert Flemyng; Wanda Ventham; Vanessa Howard; ***D:*** Vernon Sewell; ***W:*** Peter Bryan; ***C:*** Stanley Long; ***M:*** Paul Ferris.

Blood Billz 🦴 *Urban Killas: Blood Billz* **2003 (R)** Neicy (Morris) returns to her old neighborhood only to be confronted by an old gangster trying to collect on an old debt. Trying to fix the problem on her own, her boyfriend eventually has to be drawn in to save her. **83m/C; DVD.** Krystal Morris; Lewis Powell; ***D:*** Cetre Pegues; ***W:*** Cetre Pegues; ***C:*** Sean Simmons.

Blood Brother 🦴🦴 **2018 (R)** As teenagers, four friends committed crimes from vandalism to armed robberies. By chance, they once came upon the scene of an attempted robbery of an armored truck. The friends stole $3 million in cash, but one of them killed the lone survivor among the robbers and guards and went to prison. Fifteen years later, the killer, Jake (Kesy), gets out of prison and the group's leader, current police detective Sonny (Neverson), picks him up from jail. Sonny soon learns that Jake's agenda puts everyone's life at risk. The film's interesting premise and characters are lost in its focus on violence. **85m/C; DVD, Blu-Ray.** Trey Songz; Jack Kesy; China McClain; Hassan Johnson; Fetty Wap; ***D:*** John Pogue; ***W:*** Michael Finch; Karl Gajdusek; ***C:*** Matthew Irving; ***M:*** Mark Kilian.

Blood Brothers 🦴🦴 **1993** Darryl has always looked up to older brother Sylvester. And then one day he witnesses a gang murder and Sylvester is one of the killers. The District Attorney senses Darryl knows more than he's saying and the gang bangers want to shut him up permanently, so each brother must look to his conscience and decide how best to be his brother's keeper. **91m/C; DVD.** Clark Johnson; Richard Chevolleau; Mia Korf; Richard Yearwood; Ron White; Amir Williams; Ndehru Roberts; Timothy Stickney; Bill Nunn; ***D:*** Bruce Pittman; ***W:*** Paris Qualles; ***M:*** Harold Wheeler.

Blood Brothers 🦴🦴 *Tian Tang Kou* **2007 (R)** Largely told in flashback, this sketchy underworld drama depicts three childhood buddies climbing the crime ladder in 1930s Shanghai. Feng (Wu) is the romantic, Gang (Liu) the muscle, and Gang's younger brother Hu (Yang) serves as backup. Through several coincidences, the trio begins working for kingpin Boss Hong (Sun). But eventually Kang makes his own bid for power. John Woo serves as a producer, which seems only right since director Tan was inspired by Woo's 1990 pic, "A Bullet in the Head." Chinese with subtitles. **95m/C; DVD.** *CH CH TW* Daniel Wu; Ye Liu; Tony Yang; Honglei Sun; Qi Shu; Xiaolu "Lulu" Li; Chang Chen; ***D:*** Alexi Tan; ***W:*** Tony Chan; Alexi Tan; Dan Jiang; ***C:*** Michel Taburiaux; ***M:*** Daniel Belardinelli.

Blood Creek 🦴 1/2 *Town Creek* **2009 (R)** Splatter horror with some good visuals and really stupid plot elements. In 1936, Nazi occultist Richard Wirth (Fassbinder) travels to a West Virginia farmhouse owned by German immigrants to examine a rune stone's demonic abilities. Decades pass and EMT worker Evan Marshall (Cavill) is shocked when his missing brother Victor (Purcell) suddenly turns up horribly scarred, claiming he was held hostage at the same farmhouse and they must stop what is happening there. Which involves Wirth. **90m/C; DVD.** Dominic Purcell; Henry Cavill; Michael Fassbender; Emma Booth; Rainer Winkelvoss; ***D:*** Joel Schumacher; ***W:*** David Kajganich; ***C:*** Darko Suvak; ***M:*** David Buckley. **VIDEO**

Blood Crime 🦴 1/2 **2002** No-brainer B movie. Seattle cop Daniel Pruitt (Schaech) and his wife Jessica (Lackey) take a camping trip into Oregon. While he's away, she gets attacked in the woods. When Jessica identifies her attacker, her husband beats him. Later, she changes her mind about who her assailant is but by then it's too late—the man, who turns out to be the no-good son of Sheriff McKenna (Caan)?has died. **128m/C; VHS, DVD.** James Caan; Johnathon Schaech; Elizabeth Lackey; David Field; ***D:*** William A. Graham; ***W:*** Preston A. Whitmore, II; Mark Lawrence Miller; ***C:*** Robert Steadman; ***M:*** Chris Boardman. **CABLE**

Blood Cult 🦴 **1985 (R)** A bizarre series of murder-mutilations take place on a small midwestern campus. Contains graphic violence that is not for the squeamish. This film was created especially for the home video market. **89m/C; VHS, DVD.** Chuck Ellis; Julie Andelman; Jim Vance; Joe Hardt; ***D:*** Christopher Lewis; ***M:*** Rod Slane. **VIDEO**

Blood Diamond 🦴🦴 1/2 **2006 (R)** Flawed, well-intentioned adventure-drama takes place in 1999, during the horrors of civil war in Sierra Leone. Rebels raid a village, committing mass murder and forcing the boys to become child soldiers while the men are slave labor in the diamond mines. These so-called "conflict stones" are then used to buy more weapons. Solomon Vandy (Hounsou) unearths and hides a valuable pink diamond in order to ransom his family after he escapes. But Vandy's find comes to the attention of Afrikaner smuggler Danny Archer (DiCaprio), who is looking to use the diamond to his own advantage. American journalist Maddy (Connelly) happens to be around to prick Danny's nearly non-existent conscience. The actors do well and the story is harrowing but director Zwick has a tendency to be a scold. **143m/C; DVD, Blu-Ray, HD-DVD.** Leonardo DiCaprio; Djimon Hounsou; Jennifer Connelly; Arnold Vosloo; Kagiso Kuypers; Michael Sheen; Jimi Mistry; Stephen Collins; David Harewood; Anthony Coleman;

Benu Mabhena; Basil Wallace; ***D:*** Edward Zwick; ***W:*** Charles Leavitt; ***C:*** Eduardo Serra; ***M:*** James Newton Howard.

Blood Diner **WOOF!** **1987** Two spirit-possessed, diner-owning brothers kill countless young girls for demonic rituals, and serve their corpses as gourmet food in their restaurant. Some funny moments mixed in with the requisite gore. Cult potential. Currently sold only as part of a collection. **88m/C; VHS, DVD, Blu-Ray.** Rick Burks; Carl Crew; Roger Dauer; Lisa Guggenheim; Roxanne Cybelle; Cynthia Baker; ***D:*** Jackie Kong; ***W:*** Michael Sonye; ***C:*** Jurg Walther; ***M:*** Don Preston.

Blood Done Sign My Name 1/2 **2010 (PG-13)** Straightforward, old-fashioned storytelling about a racially charged murder that happened in 1970 in Oxford, North Carolina. Black Vietnam vet Henry Marrow (Sanford) returns to a hometown virtually unchanged by the civil rights movement. Racial violence explodes after his murder when his white killers are acquitted by an all-white jury. The parallel story is that of liberal white Methodist minister Vernon Tyson (Schroder), who has been trying to foster more racial harmony, and his 10-year-old son Tim (Griffith), a witness to some of the events. The adult Tim Tyson wrote the nonfiction book on which the movie is based. **128m/C; DVD.** Rick Schroder; Nate Parker; Afemo Omilami; Gattlin Griffith; Lela Rochon; Nick Searcy; Cullen Moss; Darrin Dewitt Henson; Omar Benson Miller; Donna Biscoe; A.C Sanford; ***D:*** Jeb Stuart; ***W:*** Jeb Stuart; ***C:*** Steve Mason; David Parker; ***M:*** John Leftwich.

Blood Father **2016 (R)** Lydia (Moriarty) gets in too deep when an incident involving her drug dealer boyfriend Jonah (Luna) ends in gunfire. Jonah's crew wants her dead, so she turns to her estranged ex-con father (Gibson) to protect her. A surprisingly confident and well-made thriller at a point in its controversial star's career where it seemed like he might be done. Not only is Gibson still charismatic enough to carry a down-and-dirty drama like this one but the filmmaking is entertaining. It's the kind of no-nonsense action drama made more often in the '70s. **88m/C; DVD, Blu-Ray.** Mel Gibson; Erin Moriarty; Diego Luna; Michael Parks; William H. Macy; ***D:*** Jean-Francois Richet; ***W:*** Peter Craig; Andrea Berloff; ***C:*** Robert Gantz; ***M:*** Sven Faulconer.

Blood Feast *Feast of Flesh* **1963** The first of Lewis' gore-fests, in which a demented caterer butchers hapless young women to splice them together in order to bring back an Egyptian goddess. Dated, campy, and gross; reportedly shot in four days (it shows). **70m/C; VHS, DVD, Blu-Ray.** Connie Mason; William Kerwin; Mal Arnold; Scott H. Hall; Lyn Bolton; Toni Calvert; Ashlyn Martin; Gene Courtier; Jerome Eden; David Friedman; ***D:*** Herschell Gordon Lewis; ***W:*** Allison Louise Downe; ***C:*** Herschell Gordon Lewis; ***M:*** Herschell Gordon Lewis.

Blood Feud *Revenge* **1979 (R)** In Italy preceding Europe's entry into WWII, a young widow is in mourning over the brutal murder of her husband by the Sicilian Mafia. In the meantime she must contend with the rivalry between Mastroianni as a lawyer and Giannini as a small-time crook both vying for her affections. Dubbed. **112m/C; DVD, Streaming.** *IT* Sophia Loren; Marcello Mastroianni; Giancarlo Giannini; ***D:*** Lina Wertmuller; ***W:*** Lina Wertmuller; ***C:*** Tonino Delli Colli; ***M:*** Nando De Luca.

Blood Freak **WOOF!** *Blood Freaks* **1972** An absolutely insane anti-drug, Christian splatter film. A Floridian biker is introduced to drugs by a young woman and eventually turns into a poultry-monster who drinks the blood of junkies. Narrated by a chain smoker who has a coughing fit. Don't miss it. **86m/C; VHS, DVD.** Steve Hawkes; Dana Cullivan; Randy Grinter, Jr.; Tina Anderson; Heather Hughes; ***D:*** Steve Hawkes; Brad Grinter.

Blood from the Mummy's Tomb 1/2 **1971** The immortal spirit of Tera, Egyptian queen of evil, haunts Margaret (Leon), the daughter of an archaeologist who discovered her tomb. As a long-prophesied conjunction of stars begins to occur, Margaret finds herself enthralled by Tera's power and finds herself becoming possessed by Tera's spirit. This adaptation of Bram Stoker's "The Jewel of Seven Stars" begins well, with a wonderfully mysterious and moody first half, but it loses steam in the somewhat muddled (and tedious) second half. Coulouris (without the old age makeup) looks exactly like his Thatcher character in "Citizen Kane," 30 years earlier, but sadly is given not much to do other than roll his eyes and scream. Leon is a likable heroine but that wig and false eyelashes have got to go! Remade in post-"Omen" fashion as "The Awakening." **94m/C; VHS, DVD, Blu-Ray.** *GB* Andrew Keir; Valerie Leon; James Villiers; Hugh Burden; George Coulouris; Mark Edwards; ***D:*** Seth Holt; ***W:*** Christopher Wicking; ***C:*** Arthur Grant; ***M:*** Tristram Cary.

Blood Gnome **2002 (R)** Evil, hungry gnomes attack patrons of the local dominatrix, with a crime scene photographer as the sole spectator to the carnage. Grisly and made on the cheap, and looks it. **87m/C; VHS, DVD.** Vincent Bilancio; Stephanie Beaton; Julie Strain; Massimo Avidano; Melissa Pursley; ***D:*** John Lechago; ***W:*** John Lechago. **VIDEO**

Blood, Guts, Bullets and Octane **1999 (R)** Used-car salesmen Sid (Carnahan) and Bob (Leis) are trying to keep their failing business afloat when a broker offers then a quarter million to let a 1963 Pontiac Le Mans convertible (burgundy) stay on their lot for 48 hours. The FBI are after the car and its owners, who've left a bloody cross-country trail. And the motor-mouth duo decide to renege on the deal. Desperate lowlifes and vicious crime winds up looking very familiar. **87m/C; VHS, DVD.** Joe Carnahan; Dan Leis; Ken Rudolph; James Salter; Dan Harlan; ***D:*** Joe Carnahan; ***W:*** Joe Carnahan; ***C:*** John A. Jimenez; ***M:*** Mark Priolo; Martin Burke.

Blood Hook 1/2 **1986** A self-parodying teenage-slasher film about kids running into a backwoods fishing tournament while on vacation, complete with ghouls, cannibalism and grotesquerie. **85m/C; VHS, DVD, Blu-Ray.** Mark Jacobs; Lisa Todd; Patrick Danz; ***D:*** Jim Mallon.

Blood In . . . Blood Out: Bound by Honor 1/2 *Bound by Honor* **1993 (R)** Three-hour epic about Chicano gang culture focuses on three buddies whose lives evolve into a drug-addicted artist, a narc, and a prison regular. Written by acclaimed poet Baca, the film touches on issues such as poverty, racism, drugs, and violence as they pertain to Hispanic life. Unfortunately, the extreme violence (shootings, stabbings, and garrotings) completely overwhelms the rest of the story. Based on a story by Ross Thomas. **180m/C; VHS, DVD.** Damian Chapa; Jesse Borrego; Benjamin Bratt; Enrique Castillo; Victor Rivers; Delroy Lindo; Tom Towler; Thomas F. Wilson; ***D:*** Taylor Hackford; ***W:*** Floyd Mutrux; Jimmy Santiago Baca; Jeremy Iacone; ***C:*** Gabriel Beristain; ***M:*** Bill Conti.

Blood Island *The Shuttered Room* **1968** A couple inherits an old house on a remote New England island where the woman grew up. They discover that this old house needs more than a paint job to make it livable; seems there's something evil in them there walls. Based on an H.P. Lovecraft story. Greene, who's best known for later directing "Godspell," and the solid cast fail to animate the inert script. **100m/C; VHS, DVD.** *GB* Gig Young; Carol Lynley; Oliver Reed; Flora Robson; ***D:*** David Greene.

Blood Lake *Blood Lake: Attack of the Killer Lampreys* **2014** The Asylum presents its mockbuster of "Piranha" in the form of this cable film about lampreys infesting the water supply of a Michigan town. Even Christopher Lloyd as the evil mayor can't save this one. As seen on "Animal Planet" of all places. **90m/C; DVD.** Shannen Doherty; Jason Brooks; Zack (Zach) Ward; Christopher Lloyd; Rachel True; ***D:*** James Cullen Bressack; ***W:*** Anna Rasmussen; Delondra Williams; ***C:*** Alexander Yellen; ***M:*** Steven Bernstein. **CABLE**

Blood Legacy *Legacy of Blood* **1973 (R)** Four heirs must survive a night in a lonely country estate to collect their money; what do you think happens? Average treatment of the haunted house theme. **77m/C; VHS, DVD.** John Carradine; John Russell; Faith Domergue; Merry Anders; Richard (Dick) Davalos; Jeff Morrow; Roy Engle; ***D:*** Carl Monson; ***W:*** Eric Norden; ***C:*** Jack Beckett.

Blood Mania **1970 (R)** A retired surgeon's daughter decides to murder her father to collect her inheritance prematurely, but soon learns that crime doesn't pay as well as medicine. Low-budget, low-interest flick. **90m/C; VHS, DVD.** Peter Carpenter; Maria de Aragon; Alex Rocco; ***D:*** Robert Vincent O'Neil.

Blood Money *The Arrangement* **1998 (R)** Five dead bodies, $4 million, and one eye-witness, stripper Candy (Petty), are what remains of a drug deal gone south. Now, Detective Connor (Ironside) must protect his witness from Mob reprisals. **95m/C; VHS, DVD.** Michael Ironside; Lori Petty; Currie Graham; ***D:*** Michael Ironside. **VIDEO**

Blood Money **1999 (R)** Tony Restrelli (Bloom) is the legit member of a mob family who made his money in the stock market. Now his financial knowledge is needed by his family to fend off would-be interlopers—and he can also avenge his brother's murder. **95m/C; VHS, DVD.** Brian Bloom; Alan Arkin; Alicia Coppola; Jennifer Gatti; Bruce Kirby; Jonathan Scarfe; Gregory Sierra; Leonard Stone; ***D:*** Aaron Lipstadt. **CABLE**

Blood Money 1/2 *Misfortune* **2017 (R)** When friends Victor (Coltrane), Jeff (Artist), and Lynn (Fitzgerald) go on a rafting trip, their conflicts are pushed aside when they find the millions of dollars in loot dropped by Miller (Cusack) as he parachuted out of a plane. The trio cannot agree on what to do with the windfall. Victor wants to turn it in, but Lynn believes they should keep it and use it to finance their lives. But Miller wants his money back. With unlikable characters and poorly written dialogue, this B-movie thriller doesn't become interesting until it is too late. **100m/C; DVD, Blu-Ray, Streaming.** John Cusack; Ellar Coltrane; Willa Fitzgerald; Jacob Artist; Ned Bellamy; ***D:*** Lucky McKee; ***W:*** Jared Butler; Lars Norberg; ***C:*** Alex Vendler; ***M:*** Matt Gates.

Blood Money: The Story of Clinton and Nadine 1/2 *Clinton & Nadine* **1988** A confusing action/thriller with a good cast. Garcia is a small-time exotic bird smuggler whose gun-running brother has been murdered. He uses high-class hooker Barkin to get close to his brother's contacts, who turn out to be running guns to the Nicaraguan contras and involved in a dangerous government conspiracy. **95m/C; VHS, DVD.** Andy Garcia; Ellen Barkin; Morgan Freeman; ***D:*** Jerry Schatzberg. **CABLE**

Blood Monkey **2007** Six American grad students arrive in Africa (Thailand substituted) to study apes with Professor Hamilton (Abraham). But his studies mean investigating local rumors of a tribe of killer chimpanzees. When the students witness the carnage first-hand, they want out but neither the professor nor the chimps are willing to let them go. Not much monkey action since the budget apparently didn't stretch too far. **90m/C; DVD.** F. Murray Abraham; Amy Manson; Matt Reeves; Freishia Bomanbehram; Sebastian Armesto; Matt Ryan; Laura Aikman; ***D:*** Robert Young; ***W:*** George LaVoo; Gary Dauberman; ***C:*** Choochart Nantitanyatada; ***M:*** Charles Olins; Mark Ryder. **TV**

Blood Night: The Legend of Mary Hatchet **2009 (R)** Teen slasher with victims portrayed by actors too old to pass for teenagers and more nudity than usual. Blood Night, celebrated by the local teens, is the anniversary of the death of a local axe murderess. After Mary Mattock butchers her parents, she's sent to an insane asylum where nasty things happen to her. She's killed after another bloody rampage and now 'Mary Hatchet' is a Long Island legend. On this Blood Night it looks like Mary has been resurrected and is ready to kill again. **85m/C; DVD.** Danielle Harris; Bill Moseley; Nate Dushku; Samantha Facchi; Billy Magnussen; Anthony Marks; Alissa Dean; ***D:*** Frank Sabatella; ***W:*** Elke Blasi; ***C:*** Christopher Walters; Jarin Blaschke; ***M:*** Victor Bruno. **VIDEO**

Blood of Dracula 1/2 *Blood Is My Heritage; Blood of the Demon* **1957** They don't make 1950s rock 'n' roll girls' school vampire movies like this anymore, for which we may be grateful. Hypnotism, an amulet, and a greasepaint makeup job turn a shy female student into a bloodsucker. **71m/B; VHS, DVD.** Sandra Harrison; Louise Lewis; Gail Ganley; Jerry Blaine; Heather Ames; Malcolm Atterbury; Richard Devon; Thomas B(rowne). Henry; Don Devlin; Edna Holland; ***D:*** Herbert L. Strock; ***W:*** Aben Kandel; ***C:*** Monroe Askins; ***M:*** Paul Dunlap.

Blood of Dracula's Castle *Dracula's Castle; Castle of Dracula* **1969** Couple inherits an allegedly deserted castle, but upon moving in discover Mr. and Mrs. Dracula have settled there. The vampires keep young women chained in the dungeon for continual blood supply. Also present are a hunchback and a werewolf. Awesome Adamson production is highlighted by the presence of the gorgeous Volante. Early cinematography effort by the renowned Laszlo Kovacs. **84m/C; VHS, DVD.** John Carradine; Alexander D'Arcy; Paula Raymond; Ray Young; Vicki Volante; Robert Dix; John Cardos; Ken Osborne; ***D:*** Jean Hewitt; Al Adamson; ***W:*** Rex Carlton; ***C:*** Laszlo Kovacs.

Blood of Ghastly Horror **WOOF!** *The Fiend with the Atomic Brain; Psycho a Go Go!; The Love Maniac; The Man with the Synthetic Brain; The Fiend with the Electronic Brain* **1972** A young man thinks he has a new lease on life when he is the happy recipient of a brain transplant, but his dreams are destroyed when he evolves into a rampaging killer. This movie is so awful it hides behind numerous but rather creative aliases. **87m/C; VHS, DVD.** John Carradine; Kent Taylor; Tommy Kirk; Regina Carrol; Roy Morton; Tracey Robbins; ***D:*** Al Adamson; ***W:*** Chris Martino; Dick Poston; ***C:*** Vilmos Zsigmond.

The Blood of Heroes *The Salute of the Jugger* **1989 (R)** A post-apocalyptic action flick detailing the adventures of a battered team of "juggers," warriors who challenge small village teams to a brutal sport (involving dogs' heads on sticks) that's a cross between jousting and football. **97m/C; VHS, DVD.** Rutger Hauer; Joan Chen; Vincent D'Onofrio; Anna (Katerina) Katarina; ***D:*** David Peoples; ***W:*** David Peoples; ***C:*** David Eggby; ***M:*** Todd Boekelheide.

Blood of the Vampire 1/2 **1958** A Transylvanian doctor is executed for being a vampire and his hunchbacked assistant brings him back to life. **84m/C; VHS, DVD.** *GB* Donald Wolfit; Vincent Ball; Barbara Shelley; Victor Maddern; ***D:*** Henry Cass; ***W:*** Jimmy Sangster.

Blood on the Sun 1/2 **1945** Newspaperman in Japan uncovers plans for world dominance as propaganda, violence, and intrigue combine in this action-adventure. Also available colorized. **98m/B; VHS, DVD.** James Cagney; Sylvia Sidney; Robert Armstrong; Wallace Ford; ***D:*** Frank Lloyd; ***W:*** Lester Cole; Nathaniel Curtis; Frank Melford; ***C:*** Theodor Sparkuhl; ***M:*** Miklos Rozsa.

The Blood Oranges 1/2 **1997 (R)** Pretentious film is set in the anything-goes '70s in a tropical backwater village. Bohemian marrieds Cyril (Dance) and Fiona (Lee) believe in fulfilling every sexual fantasy but their latest exchange of marital partners comes with unexpected complications. Fiona is attracted to photographer Hugh (Lane), who resists her charms for more deviant behavior, while Hugh's wife Catherine (Robins) is easily seduced by Cyril's courtship. Dialogue is laughable and the acting equally overblown. Based on the novel by John Hawkes. **93m/C; VHS, DVD.** Charles Dance; Sheryl Lee; Colin Lane; Laila Robins; Rachael Bella; ***D:*** Philip Haas; ***W:*** Belinda Haas; Philip Haas; ***C:*** Bernard Zitzermann; ***M:*** Angelo Badalamenti.

Blood Orgy of the She-Devils **WOOF!** **1974 (PG)** Exploitative gore nonsense about female demons, beautiful witches, and satanic worship. Some movies waste all their creative efforts on their titles. **73m/C; VHS, DVD.** Lila Zaborin; Tom Pace; Leslie McRae; Ray Myles; Victor Izay; William Bagdad; ***D:*** Ted V. Mikels; ***W:*** Ted V. Mikels; ***C:*** Anthony Salinas.

Blood Out **2010 (R)** Small-town sheriff Michael Spencer sets aside his badge to go undercover as an urban gangsta when big city detectives don't pursue his brother's murder. That's because there are bad cops and a crime boss involved (although not much Kilmer or Jackson despite their billing). **89m/C; DVD, Blu-Ray.** Luke Goss; AnnaLynne McCord; Vinnie Jones; 50 Cent; Val Kilmer; Ryan Donowho; Tamer Hassan; Ed Quinn; *D:* Jason Hewitt; *W:* Jason Hewitt; *C:* Christian Herrera; *M:* Jermaine Stegall. **VIDEO**

Blood Rage WOOF! *Nightmare at Shadow Woods* **1987 (R)** A maniacal twin goes on a murderous rampage through his brother's neighborhood. AKA "Nightmare at Shadow Woods." Only for die-hard "Mary Hartman" fans. **87m/C; VHS, DVD, Blu-Ray.** Louise Lasser; Mike Soper; *D:* John Grissmer; *M:* Richard Einhorn.

Blood Red 1/2 **1988 (R)** In 1895 Northern California, an Italian immigrant and his family give bloody battle to a powerful industrialist who wants their land in wine-growing country. Watch for the scenes involving veteran Roberts and his then-newcomer sister, pretty woman Julia. **91m/C; VHS, Blu-Ray, Streaming.** Eric Roberts; Dennis Hopper; Giancarlo Giannini; Burt Young; Carlin Glynn; Lara Harris; Susan Anspach; Julia Roberts; Elias Koteas; Frank Campanella; Aldo Ray; Horton Foote, Jr.; *D:* Peter Masterson; *W:* Ron Cutler.

Blood Relations 1/2 **1987 (R)** A woman is introduced to her fiance's family only to find out that they, as well as her fiance, are murdering, perverted weirdos competing for an inheritance. **88m/C; VHS, DVD.** *CA* Jan Rubes; Ray Walston; Lydie Denier; Kevin Hicks; Lynne Adams; Sam Malkin; Steven Saylor; Carrie Leigh; *D:* Graeme Campbell.

Blood Relic 1/2 **2005 (R)** Pilot Hank Campbell (Christian) is possessed by a mysterious talisman, commits mass murder on a naval base, and winds up in the loony bin for 22 years. Upon his release, he heads back to the scene of the crime and discovers history buff Harry (Drago) is turning the base into a museum with the help of a bunch of handy young people (handy for slaughtering that is). Anyway, mayhem is likely since Campbell is determined to find his talisman again. **86m/C; DVD.** John Christian; Billy Drago; Jennifer Grant; Debbie Rochon; Joshua Park; Kelly Ray; *D:* J. Christian Ingvordsen; *W:* J. Christian Ingvordsen; Matt Howe; *C:* Matt Howe; *M:* Timo Elliston. **VIDEO**

Blood Simple 1/2 **1985 (R)** A jealous husband hires a sleazy private eye to murder his adulterous wife and her lover. A dark, intricate, morbid morality tale that deviates imaginatively from the standard murder mystery thriller. First film scripted by the Coen brothers. **96m/C; VHS, DVD, Blu-Ray.** John Getz; M. Emmet Walsh; Dan Hedaya; Frances McDormand; Samm-Art Williams; Van Brooks; Lauren Bivens; Holly Hunter; *D:* Joel Coen; *W:* Joel Coen; Ethan Coen; *C:* Barry Sonnenfeld; *M:* Carter Burwell. Ind. Spirit '86: Actor (Walsh), Director (Coen); Sundance '85: Grand Jury Prize.

Blood Sisters WOOF! **1986 (R)** Sorority babes intend to spend a giggle-strewn night in a haunted house but end up decapitated, butchered, and cannibalized. **85m/C; VHS, DVD.** Amy Brentano; Marla MacHart; Brigete Cossu; Randy Mooers; *D:* Roberta Findlay.

Blood Song *Dream Slayer* **1982** A patient (yester-decade teen throb Frankie Avalon) escapes into the night from a mental institution after murdering an attendant. He takes his only possession with him, a carved wooden flute. A young woman sees him burying his latest victim, and now he's on a hunt to play his "blood song" for her. Pretty bad, but fun to see Avalon play a less-than-squeaky-clean role. **90m/C; VHS, DVD.** Frankie Avalon; Donna Wilkes; Richard Jaeckel; Dane Clark; Antoinette Bower; Lenny Montana; *D:* Alan J. Levi; *W:* Lenny Montana.

The Blood Spattered Bride *Blood Castle; La Novia Esangrentada; Bloody Fiance; Till Death Us Do Part* **1972** Newlywed couple honeymoons in a remote castle in southern Spain. They are visited by a mysterious young woman who begins to influence the bride in the ways of lesbian bloodsucking. O.K. '70s Euro-eroti-horror based on Sheridan Le Fanu's "Carmilla." **101m/C; VHS, DVD, Blu-Ray.** *SP* Simon Andreu; Maribel Martin; Alexandra Bastedo; Dean Selmier; Rosa Ma Rodriguez; Montserrat Julio; Angel Lombarte; *D:* Vicente Aranda; *W:* Vicente Aranda; *C:* Fernando Arribas.

Blood Surf *Crocodile* **2000 (R)** A filmmaker and her crew travel to Australia to do a documentary on the extreme sport of blood surfing where thrillseekers try to out surf sharks to shore. Only the sharks aren't the problem—a giant salt-water crocodile gets to the participants first. Very silly; your enjoyment will depend on your tolerance for the fake croc. **88m/C; VHS, DVD.** Matt Borlenghi; Duncan Regehr; Kate Fischer; Taryn Reif; Joel West; Dax Miller; *D:* James D.R. Hickox; *W:* Sam Bernard; Robert L. Levy; *C:* Christopher Pearson; *M:* Jim Manzie. **VIDEO**

Blood: The Last Vampire 1/2 **2009 (R)** Tedious live-action adaptation of a 2001 anime flick that's heavy on the gore. Saya (Jeon) is a 400-year-old samurai, who looks like a 16-year-old schoolgirl (complete with kinky uniform) who is charged with hunting down the vampires and demons who plague Japan. She is ordered by a secret organization to protect the students at an American military base where her cover is blown when she must rescue general's daughter Alice (Miller) from a vampire attack. Then it all comes down to the ultimate battle between Saya and super-vamp Onigen (Koyuki). **91m/C; Blu-Ray, On Demand.** *FR CH*

Blood Thirst **1965** Obscure horror film about a woman who stays young by indulging in ritual killings and strange experiments. **73m/B; VHS, DVD.** *PH* Robert Winston; Yvonne Nielson; Vic Diaz; *D:* Newton Arnold.

Blood Tide *The Red Tide* **1982 (R)** A disgusting, flesh-eating monster disrupts a couple's vacation in the Greek isles. Beautiful scenery, good cast, bad movie. **82m/C; VHS, DVD, Blu-Ray.** James Earl Jones; Jose Ferrer; *D:* Richard Jeffries; *W:* Nico Mastorakis.

Blood Ties 1/2 **1992** Reporter Harry Martin belongs to an unusual family—modern-day vampires (who prefer to be known as Carpathian-Americans). But they have an age-old problem with a band of fanatical vampire hunters. This time around you'll root for the bloodsuckers. **90m/C; VHS, DVD.** Harley Venton; Patrick Bauchau; Kim Johnston-Ulrich; Michelle Johnson; Jason London; Bo Hopkins; Grace Zabriskie; Salvator Xuereb; *D:* Jim McBride; *W:* Richard Shapiro. **TV**

Blood Ties 1/2 **2013 (R)** Dragged-out, hackneyed crime drama, which Canet remade from 2008's "Les Liens du Sang" in which he co-starred. In 1974, 50-year-old Chris (Owen) is released from prison. His younger brother Frank (Crudup)--a Brooklyn cop--is willing to give him a second chance. Before long the career criminal is flirting with his old life--and the much-younger Natalie (Kunis)--while all Frank's sibling resentments surface. **127m/C; DVD, Blu-Ray.** *FR US* Clive Owen; Billy Crudup; Marion Cotillard; Mila Kunis; Zoe Saldana; James Caan; Lili Taylor; Matthias Schoenaerts; Noah Emmerich; *D:* Guillaume Canet; *W:* Guillaume Canet; James Gray; *C:* Christophe Offenstein.

Blood Trails 1/2 **2006 (R)** After a one-night stand with unstable bike cop Chris (Price), bike messenger Anne (Palmer) takes off with boyfriend Michael (Frederick) for a weekend of mountain biking. Guess who appears to stalk Anne? Basically a chase on two wheels and not particularly frightening. **87m/C; DVD.** Rebecca Palmer; Ben Price; Tom Frederick; *D:* Robert Krause; *W:* Robert Krause; Florian Puchert; *C:* Ralf Noack; *M:* Ben Bartlett. **VIDEO**

Blood Vows: The Story of a Mafia Wife **1987** TV's Laura Ingalls (Gilbert) leaps from the prairie to modern-day mafia in this warped Cinderella story. She meets the man of her dreams, whom she slowly finds is her worst nightmare as she becomes trapped within the confines of her new-found "family." TV soaper is way over the top in terms of melodrama. **100m/C; VHS, Streaming.** Melissa Gilbert; Joe Penny; Eileen Brennan; Talia Shire; Anthony (Tony) Franciosa; *D:* Paul Wendkos; *M:* William Goldstein. **TV**

Blood Wedding *Bodas de Sangre* **1981** A wonderfully passionate dance film from Saura and choreographed by Gades, based on the play by famed author Federico Garcia Lorca. A young bride (Hoyos) runs off with her married lover (Gades) on her wedding day and her jilted husband (Jimenez) comes after them. The film is set-up at a dress rehearsal where the dancers, led by Gades, perform upon a bare stage. If you like flamenco, there are two more: "Carmen" and "El Amor Brujo." Spanish with subtitles. **71m/C; VHS, DVD.** *SP* Antonio Gades; Cristina Hoyos; Marisol; Carmen Villena; Juan Antonio Jimenez; *D:* Carlos Saura; *W:* Antonio Gades; Carlos Saura; *C:* Teodoro Escamilla; *M:* Emillo De Diego.

Blood Work 1/2 **2002 (R)** Retired FBI profiler Terry McCaleb (Eastwood) has just had a heart transplant. But, while undergoing checkups, he's brought back to track a serial killer who apparently murdered the woman who became his donor. Clint can still do the loner detective to a T, the question is, should he? The evidence her points to "probably not." It's not that he's not good at it, it's that there's really nothing more he can do WITH it. The killer is easy to spot from a mile away, and thankfully McCaleb does, which leaves the how and when of catching him (in the gender-nonspecific sense) as the only suspense. Well done, but ultimately forgettable. Based on the novel by Michael Connelly. **111m/C; VHS, DVD, Blu-Ray.** Clint Eastwood; Anjelica Huston; Jeff Daniels; Wanda De Jesus; Paul Rodriguez; Tina Lifford; Dylan Walsh; Gerry Becker; Alix Koromzay; Mason Lucero; Rick Hoffman; *D:* Clint Eastwood; *W:* Brian Helgeland; *C:* Tom Stern; *M:* Lennie Niehaus.

Bloodbath *Sky is Falling* **1976** Drugs, sex and terrorism—Hopper is typecast as an American degenerate who, along with his expatriate friends, is persecuted by local religious cults who need sacrifices. **89m/C; VHS, DVD.** Dennis Hopper; Carroll Baker; Richard Todd; Faith Brook; Win Wells; *D:* Silvio Narizzano.

Bloodbath in Psycho Town **1989 (R)** A film crew is marked for death by a hooded man when it enters a remote little village. **87m/C; VHS, DVD.** Ron Arragon; Donna Baltron; Dave Elliott; *D:* Allessandro DeGaetano; *W:* Allessandro DeGaetano.

Bloodbrothers 1/2 **1978 (R)** Portrayal of working-class Italian men's lives—if that's possible without the benefit of Italian writers, producers, or director. Still, lots of cussing and general intensity, as Gere's character struggles between staying in the family construction business and doing what he wants to do'work with children. Re-cut for TV and re-titled "A Father's Love." **120m/C; VHS, DVD.** Richard Gere; Paul Sorvino; Tony LoBianco; Kenneth McMillan; Marilu Henner; Danny Aiello; Lelia Goldoni; Yvonne Wilder; *D:* Robert Mulligan; *C:* Robert L. Surtees; *M:* Elmer Bernstein.

Bloodfist **1989 (R)** A kickboxer tears through Manila searching for his brother's killer. A Roger Corman production. **85m/C; VHS, DVD.** Don "The Dragon" Wilson; Rob Kaman; Billy Blanks; Kris Aguilar; Riley Bowman; Michael Shaner; Joe Mari Avellana; Marilyn Bautista; *D:* Terence H. Winkless; *W:* Robert King; *C:* Ricardo Jacques Gale; *M:* Sasha Matson.

Bloodfist 2 1/2 **1990 (R)** Six of the world's toughest martial artists find themselves kidnapped and forced to do the bidding of the evil Su. The mysterious recluse stages a series of incredible fights between the experts and his own army of drugged warriors. **85m/C; VHS, DVD.** Don "The Dragon" Wilson; Maurice Smith; James Warring; Timothy Baker; Richard (Rick) Hill; Rina Reyes; Kris Aguilar; Joe Mari Avellana; *D:* Andy Blumenthal; *W:* Catherine Cyran; *C:* Bruce Dorfman; *M:* Nigel Holton.

Bloodfist 3: Forced to Fight 1/2 **1992 (R)** Just as long as nobody's forced to watch, real-life world champion kickboxer Wilson thrashes his way through another showdown-at-the-arena plot. Better-than-average fight choreography. **90m/C; VHS, DVD.** Don "The Dragon" Wilson; Richard Roundtree; Laura Stockman; Richard Paul; Rick Dean; Peter "Sugarfoot" Cunningham; *D:* Oley Sassone; *W:* Allison Burnett; *C:* Rick Bota; *M:* Nigel Holton.

Bloodfist 4: Die Trying 1/2 **1992 (R)** To rescue his daughter, a fighter must do battle with the FBI, the CIA, and an international arms cartel. **86m/C; VHS, DVD.** Don "The Dragon" Wilson; Catya (Cat) Sassoon; Amanda Wyss; James Tolkan; Liz Torres; *D:* Paul Ziller.

Bloodfist 5: Human Target 1/2 **1993 (R)** When undercover FBI agent Jim Roth (Wilson) attempts to unravel an international arms deal he's found out and left for dead. He comes to with no memory only to find himself caught between the arms dealers and the FBI, who think he's turned double-agent. Both sides want Roth dead. **84m/C; VHS, DVD.** Don "The Dragon" Wilson; Denice Duff; Yuji Okumoto; Don Stark; Danny Lopez; Steve James; Michael Yama; *D:* Jeff Yonis; *W:* Jeff Yonis; *C:* Michael G. Wojciechowski; *M:* David Wurst; Eric Wurst.

Bloodfist 6: Ground Zero 1/2 **1994 (R)** Nick Corrigan (Wilson) must battle terrorists who have a nuclear missile aimed at New York City. **86m/C; VHS, DVD.** Don "The Dragon" Wilson; Cat Sasson; Steve Garvey; *D:* Rick Jacobson; *W:* Brendan Broderick; Rob Kerchner; *C:* Michael Gallagher; *M:* John Graham.

Bloodfist 7: Manhunt **1995 (R)** Martial arts expert Jim Trudell is accused by corrupt cops of murder and is forced on the run while he tries to prove his innocence. **95m/C; VHS, DVD.** Don "The Dragon" Wilson; Jonathan Penner; Jillian McWhirter; Stephen Davies; Cyril O'Reilly; Eb Lottimer; Steven Williams; *D:* Jonathan Winfrey; *W:* Brendan Broderick; Rob Kerchner; *C:* Michael Gallagher; *M:* Elliot Anders; Mike Elliot. **VIDEO**

Bloodfist 8: Hard Way Out *Hard Way Out* **1996 (R)** Widowed teacher Rick Cowan (Wilson) turns out to have a lurid past when he and teen son Chris (White) are targeted for death. Dull dad is ex-CIA and someone is afraid their dirty secrets will get out if he's not eliminated. **78m/C; VHS, DVD.** Don "The Dragon" Wilson; John Patrick White; Warren Burton; Richard Farrell; *D:* Barry Samson; *W:* Alex Simon; *C:* John Aronson; *M:* John Faulkner.

Bloodhounds of Broadway 1/2 **1952** New York bookie Numbers Foster (Brady) heads out of town to avoid a criminal investigation and winds up in backwoods Georgia where he meets talented Tessie (Gaynor), who convinces Numbers to take her back up north with him. She finds success on Broadway and finally persuades the bookie to turn himself in. Based on a story by Damon Runyon. **90m/C; DVD.** Mitzi Gaynor; Scott Brady; Mitzie Green; Marguerite Chapman; Michael O'Shea; Wally Vernon; *D:* Harmon Jones; *W:* Sy Gomberg; *C:* Edward Cronjager; *M:* Lionel Newman.

Bloodhounds of Broadway 1/2 **1989 (PG)** A musical tribute to Damon Runyon, detailing the cliched adventures of an assortment of jazz-age crooks, flappers, chanteuses, and losers. **90m/C; VHS, DVD.** Madonna; Rutger Hauer; Randy Quaid; Matt Dillon; Jennifer Grey; Julie Hagerty; Esai Morales; Anita Morris; Josef Sommer; William S. Burroughs; Ethan Phillips; Stephen McHattie; Dinah Manoff; Googy Gress; Tony Azito; Tony Longo; Madeleine Potter; *D:* Howard Brookner; *W:* Howard Brookner; Colman DeKay; *C:* Elliot Davis; *M:* Jonathan Sheffer.

Bloodline **2019 (R)** Evan (Scott) works as a counselor for at-risk and abused teenagers. After counseling sessions, he tracks down their abusers, then interrogates and kills them. The son of an abusive father, he believes he is doing good. Evan's state of mind and carefully balanced routines are challenged when his wife Lauren (Garriga) gives birth to their son and his secretive mother Marie (Dickey) visits. Evan's activities also attract the attention of police detective Overstreet (Carroll). A stylistic revenge thriller full of potential but is ultimately unfulfilling despite a solid acting performance by Scott. **98m/C; DVD.** Seann William Scott; Mariela Garriga; Dale Dickey; Christie Herring; Raymond Alexander Cham, Jr.; *D:* Henry Jacobson; *W:* Henry Jacobson; Avra Fox-Lerner; *C:* Isaac Bauman; *M:* Trevor Gureckis.

Bloodlines 1/2 **2005** Policewoman Justine Hopkin (Pierson) finds her mother's dead body just after her dad James (McNally) is released from prison (he was in on a murder rap). She believes he's innocent and now has to prove it. **137m/C; DVD.** *GB* Kevin McNally; Robert Pugh; Kieran O'Brien; Jan Francis; Emma Pierson; Max Beesley; *D:* Philip Martin; *W:* Mike Cullen; *C:* Julian Court; *M:* Nicholas Hooper. **TV**

Bloodlust **1959** More teenagers fall prey to yet another mad scientist, who stores their dead bodies in glass tanks. Low-budget ripoff of "The Most Dangerous Game" and other such films. A must for Mike Brady (Robert Reed) fans though. **89m/B; VHS, DVD.** Wilton Graff; June Kenney; Robert Reed; Lilyan Chauvin; *D:* Ralph Brooke; *W:* Ralph Brooke.

Bloodlust: Subspecies 3 1/2 *Subspecies 3* **1993 (R)** Equally gory followup to "Bloodstone: Subspecies 2." Sadistic vampire Radu is still battling for Michelle's soul, this time against Michelle's sister Becky, aided by his disgusting Mummy and the demonic Subspecies. Castle Vladislas is awash is blood and Becky discovers more than Michelle's fate is at risk. **83m/C; VHS, DVD, Blu-Ray.** Anders (Tofting) Hove; Kevin Blair Spirtas; Denice Duff; Pamela Gordon; Ion Haiduc; Michael DellaFemina; *D:* Ted Nicolaou; *W:* Ted Nicolaou.

Bloodmoon WOOF! 1990 The setting is Australia but the sleazy story's all too familiar: an insane killer employs knives and other sharp objects to prevent sex-crazed students from getting past third base. **104m/C; VHS, DVD.** *AU* Leon Lissek; Christine Amor; Ian Patrick Williams; Helen Thomson; Hazel Howson; Craig Cronin; Anya Molina; *D:* Alec Mills; *W:* Richard Brennan; *M:* Brian May.

Bloodmoon 1/2 **1997** A New York serial killer is quite a specialist—he only kills fighters, and he kills with his bare hands. So it's up to Ken O'Hara (Daniels), who specializes in tracking murderers, to find this guy before he kills again. A good display of martial arts skills keep this one interesting. **105m/C; VHS, DVD.** Gary Daniels; Chuck Jeffreys; Darren Shahlavi; Nina Repeta; Frank Gorshin; Jeffrey Pillars; Joe Hess; *D:* Tony Leung Siu Hung; *W:* Keith W. Strandberg; *C:* Derek M.K. Wan; *M:* Richard Yuen.

Bloodmyth 1/2 **2009** Indie Brit horror with a familiar plot, but there's at least a twist to the killer's motivation. Five corporate types are forced into a team-building exercise designed by survival expert Ray. They and their two trainers have to spend a week in a woodsy campsite in Kent, but the situation goes downhill when a psycho starts picking them off. **96m/C; DVD.** Natalie Clayton; Shelley Halstead; Ben Shockley; Keith Eyles; James Payton; Ian Attfield; Jane Gull; Henry Dunn; John Rackham; *D:* John Rackham; *W:* John Rackham; *C:* John Rackham; *M:* Maria Long.

BloodRayne WOOF! 2006 (R) There are moments in this painful period vampire "epic" where you honestly have to wonder if director Uwe Boll was aware that the camera was rolling. Whatever the excuse, Boll's latest video game movie proves that even sex, gore, and violence can be boring in the hands of the right director. Rayne (Loken) is a half-vampire, half-human warrior who's out to stop her illegitimate father, Kagin (Kingsley), the king of vampires, from... sigh, bored yet? You will be. Even the cast looks half-asleep. (Madsen and Kingsley take "phoning it in" to a new and scary level.) But nothing beats the barely rehearsed fight scenes. A community theatre production of "Braveheart" would have more convincing stage combat. **95m/C; DVD.** *GE US* Kristanna Loken; Michael Madsen; Matthew Davis; Michelle Rodriguez; Ben Kingsley; Will Sanderson; Udo Kier; Meat Loaf Aday; Michael Paré; Billy Zane; Geraldine Chaplin; *D:* Uwe Boll; *W:* Guinevere Turner; *C:* Mathias Neumann; *M:* Henning Lohner.

BloodRayne 2: Deliverance WOOF! 2007 (R) Probably the worst vampire western ever made, and that's saying something. After the first "BloodRayne" bombed, Boll somehow got financing to produce this direct-to-DVD sequel. Set in the Old West, the "plot" revolves around vampire Billy the Kid (played by Scut Farkus from "A Christmas Story"), and his plans to use the railroad to help his cowboy vamp posse to take over America. (Seriously.) Enter the sexually-ambiguous warrior-woman Rayne (Malthe), a half-human/half-vampire, who fights in the name of justice with her fangs and bare midriff. Unfortunately, vampire John Ford doesn't show up to punish Boll for his crimes against the western. **95m/C; DVD.** Natassia Malthe; Zack (Zach) Ward; Brendan Fletcher; Michael Paré; Christopher Coppola; Michael Eklund; *D:* Uwe Boll; *W:* Christopher Donaldson; Neil Every; *M:* Jessica de Rooij. **VIDEO**

Bloodrayne: The Third Reich

WOOF! 2011 (R) Boll uses nudity and some soft-core sex in an attempt to hold the viewers' attention in his latest adaptation of the vampire babe videogame. In 1943, dhampir Rayne (Malthe) teams up with resistance fighters to prevent Commandant Ekart Brand (Pare) from making it to Berlin. She accidentally turned him during some fighting and Brand and evil Nazi Dr. Mangler (Howard) used his infected blood to create a serum that could make Hitler immortal. **79m/C; DVD, Blu-Ray.** Natassia Malthe; Brendan Fletcher; Michael Paré; Clint Howard; Willam Belli; Annett Culp; *D:* Uwe Boll; *W:* Michael Nachoff; *C:* Mathias Neumann; *M:* Jessica de Rooij. **VIDEO**

Bloodshot **2020 (PG-13)** In a dark future, dead soldier Ray Garrison (Diesel) has been re-animated by the evil Dr. Emil Harting (Pearce) to exact revenge on his enemies. With the technical assistance of Eric (Dhananjay), who runs Harting's simulator, Garrison is manipulated with false memories of his wife's murder so he will take brutal revenge on Harting's enemies with the help of two other similarly re-animated soldiers, KT (Gonzalez) and Dalton (Heughan). An adaptation of a comic book, the half-hearted sci-fi action feature takes many of its ideas from better, more successful films like Universal Soldier and Robocop. **109m/C; DVD.** Vin Diesel; Eiza González; Sam Heughan; Toby Kebbell; Talulah Riley; *D:* Dave Wilson; *W:* Jeff Wadlow; Eric Heisserer; *C:* Jacques Jouffret; *M:* Steve Jablonsky.

Bloodspell **1987 (R)** A student with an evil power unleashes it on those who cross his path. **87m/C; VHS, DVD.** Anthony Jenkins; Aaron Teich; Alexandra Kennedy; John Reno; *D:* Deryn Warren.

Bloodsport 1/2 **1988 (R)** American soldier Van Damme endeavors to win the deadly Kumite, an outlawed martial arts competition in Hong Kong. Lots of kick-boxing action and the sound of bones cracking. **92m/C; VHS, DVD, Blu-Ray.** Jean-Claude Van Damme; Leah Ayres; Roy Chiao; Donald Gibb; Bolo Yeung; Norman Burton; Forest Whitaker; *D:* Newton Arnold; *W:* Christopher Cosby.

Bloodsport 4: The Dark Kumite **1998 (R)** Undercover agent infiltrates a prison to find out why prisoners are disappearing and ends up forced to participate in a to-the-death tournament. Enjoyable if a steady dose of kicks to the head is your idea of intricate plotting. **100m/C; VHS, DVD.** Daniel Bernhardt; Ivan Ivanov; Lisa Stothard; Elvis Restaino; *D:* Elvis Restaino; *W:* George Saunders; *M:* Alex Wurman. **VIDEO**

The Bloodstained Shadow *Solamente Nero; Only Blackness* **1978** Stefano (Capolicchio) decides to visit his priest brother Paolo (Hill), who lives on the island of Murano near Venice. He meets the mysterious Sandra (Casini) on his journey and then witnesses a midnight murder upon his arrival. More deaths follow as Paolo and Stefano investigate. Italian with subtitles. **109m/C; DVD.** *IT* Lino Capolicchio; Craig Hill; Stefania Casini; Massimo Serato; Juliette Mayniel; *D:* Antonio Bido; *W:* Antonio Bido; Marisa Andalo; Domenico Malan; *C:* Mario Vulpiani; *M:* Stelvio Cipriani.

Bloodstalkers WOOF! 1976 Two vacationers in Florida meet up with a band of slaughtering, swamp-based lunatics. **91m/C; VHS, DVD, Blu-Ray.** Kenny (Ken) Miller; Celea Ann Cole; Jerry Albert; *D:* Robert W. Morgan.

Bloodstone **1988 (PG-13)** A couple honeymooning in the Middle East unexpectedly become involved in a jewel heist when they discover a valuable ruby amongst their luggage. Non-stop action and humor. **90m/C; VHS, DVD.** Charlie Brill; Christopher Neame; Jack Kehler; Brett Stimely; Anna Nicholas; *D:* Dwight Little; *W:* Nico Mastorakis; Curt Allen.

Bloodstone: Subspecies 2 1/2 *Subspecies 2* **1992 (R)** A gory sequel to "Subspecies" finds Radu the vampire pursuing the luscious Michelle. Radu gets some help from his ghoulish mother and yucky demonic spawn. Filmed on location in Romania. **107m/C; VHS, DVD, Blu-Ray.** Anders (Tofting) Hove; Denice Duff; Kevin Blair Spirtas; Michael Denish; Pamela Gordon; Ion Haiduc; *D:* Ted Nicolaou; *W:* Ted Nicolaou.

Bloodstorm: Subspecies 4 1/2 *Subspecies 4; Subspecies 4: Bloodstorm—The Master's Revenge* **1998 (R)** Master vampire Radu Vladislas (Hove) has awakened with an agenda. He wants to reclaim his vast wealth and recapture fledgling vamp, Michelle (Duff). Meanwhile, Radu hangs around with former protege, Ash (Morris), and Michelle is taken in by a creepy doctor (Dinvale) who's after the bloodstone. If you liked the first three, this is just more of the same. **90m/C; VHS, DVD.** Anders (Tofting) Hove; Denice Duff; Jonathan Morris; Mihai Dinvale; Floriella Grappini; *D:* Ted Nicolaou; *W:* Ted Nicolaou; *C:* Adolfo Bartoli; *M:* Richard Kosinski. **VIDEO**

The Bloodsuckers *Incense for the Damned; Doctors Wear Scarlet; The Freedom Seekers* **1970** British horror tale set on a Greek Island. An Oxford don is seduced into an ancient vampire cult. Director Michael Burrowes replaces Hartford-Davis in the credits due to a dispute over post-production editing. **90m/C; VHS, DVD.** *GB* Patrick Macnee; Peter Cushing; Patrick Mower; Edward Woodward; Alex Davion; Imogen Hassall; Madeline Hinde; Johnny Sekka; *D:* Robert Hartford-Davis; *W:* Julian More; *C:* Desmond Dickinson.

Bloodsuckers from Outer Space

WOOF! 1983 Via an alien invasion, Texas farmers becoming bloodsucking zombies. **80m/C; VHS, DVD, Blu-Ray.** Thom Meyer; Laura Ellis; Billie Keller; Kim Braden; *D:* Glenn Coburn.

Bloodsucking Bastards *Bloodsucking Bosses* **2015** A horror-comedy blend of vampire mythology with the workplace comedy works much better than it should. Evan (Kranz) is having a very bad day. He just broke up with his girlfriend (Fitzpatrick) and his high school rival (Pascal) was hired to streamline his workplace. Oh, and something weird is going on in the basement—like vampire weird. This is a low-budget, mostly clever comedy that moves quickly enough that one doesn't notice the bad acting or cheap sets. **87m/C; DVD, Blu-Ray, Streaming.** Fran Kranz; Emma Fitzpatrick; Joey Kern; Pedro Pascal; Joel Murray; Yvette Yates; *D:* Brian O'Connell; *W:* Ryan Mitts; God; *C:* Matt Mosher; *M:* Anton Sanko. **VIDEO**

Bloodsucking Freaks WOOF! *The Incredible Torture Show; The House of the Screaming Virgins* **1975 (R)** Virtually plotless Troma gagfest full of torture, cannibalistic dwarfs, and similar debaucheries, all played out on a Soho Grand Guignol stage (horror shows that allegedly contained real torture and death). Features "The Caged Sexoids," if that tells you anything (a cage of naked cannibal women tended by a dwarf). Not to mention the woman who has her brain sucked out through a straw. Filmed in "Ghoulovision" and originally rated X. Intolerable for most. **89m/C; VHS, DVD, Blu-Ray.** Seamus O'Brian; Niles McMaster; Viju Krem; Alan Dellay; Dan Fauci; *D:* Joel M. Reed; *W:* Joel M. Reed; *C:* Gerry Toll; *M:* Michael Sahl.

Bloodsucking Pharoahs of Pittsburgh WOOF! *Picking up the Pieces* **1990 (R)** Pittsburgh is plagued by crazed cannibals who think eternal life is in Pennsylvania. Two detectives on the case are mystified. **89m/C; VHS, DVD.** Jake Dengel; Joe Sharkey; Suzanne Fletcher; Beverly Penberthy; Shawn Elliott; Pat Logan; Jane Hamilton; *D:* Dean Tschetter; Alan Smithee; *W:* Dean Tschetter; *C:* Peter Reniers; *M:* Michael Melvoin.

Bloodworth **2010 (R)** Southern-fried family drama. After walking out on his family 40 years ago to pursue his music career, E.F. Bloodworth walks back into his Tennessee hometown. His ex-wife Julia is suffering from dementia and his three sons have grown up bitter and angry. Only Bloodworth's grandson Fleming is willing to give the old man a chance, probably because E.F. is sympathetic to Fleming falling in love with Raven Lee, the daughter of the local prostitute. **105m/C; DVD.** Kris Kristofferson; Frances Conroy; Dwight Yoakam; Val Kilmer; W. Earl Brown; Reece Thompson; Hilary Duff; Sheila Kelley; Barry Corbin; Hilarie Burton; *D:* Shane Dax Taylor; *W:* W. Earl Brown; *C:* Tim Orr; *M:* Patrick Warren; Randy Scruggs. **VIDEO**

Bloody Birthday 1/2 *Creeps* **1980 (R)** Three youngsters, bound together by their eerie birth during an eclipse (you know what that means), kill everyone around them that ever gave them problems. Typical "and the fun continues" ending; standard fare. **92m/C; VHS, DVD, Blu-Ray.** Susan Strasberg; Jose Ferrer; Lori Lethin; Melinda Cordell; Joe Penny; Ellen Geer; Julie Brown; Michael Dudikoff; Billy Jacoby; Elizabeth Hoy; Andy Freeman; *D:* Ed(ward) Hunt; *W:* Ed(ward) Hunt; Barry Pearson.

The Bloody Brood WOOF! 1959 Really bad flick about a drug-dealing beatnik gang who commit nasty crimes, like feeding messenger boys hamburgers filled with ground glass. Yuck. **80m/C; VHS, DVD, Blu-Ray.** *CA* Jack Betts; Barbara Lord; Peter Falk; Robert Christie; *D:* Julian Hoffman.

Bloody Homecoming 1/2 **2012** High school horror centered on revenge and homecoming. In the small Southern town of Winston, homecoming is bittersweet. Three years ago, a student tragically died at the dance in an accident. Though this class of seniors anticipates the event, homecoming becomes a bloodbath as a killer tries to get revenge for the death unless someone is able to turn the tables. **82m/C; DVD, Streaming, Download.** Jim Tavare; Rae Latt; Lexi Giovagnoli; Alex Dobrenko; Randi Lamey; *D:* Brian Weed; *W:* Jake Helgren; *C:* Yuki Noguchi; *M:* Tom Jemmott. **VIDEO**

Bloody Mama 1/2 **1970 (R)** Corman's violent, trashy story of the infamous Barker Gang of the 30s, led by the bloodthirsty and sex-crazed Ma Barker (Winters, can't you just picture it?) and backed by her four perverted sons. De Niro is the space cadet sibling, Walden the homosexual ex-con, Stroud the sadistic mama lover, and Kimbrough the lady killer. They're joined by Walden's prison lover, Dern, who also has a thing for Ma Barker. Winters is a riot in this perverse stew of crime, violence, and, of course, sentimental blood bonding (the family that slays together, stays together). First of the Corman-produced (and sometimes directed) mama movies, followed by "Big Bad Mama" and "Crazy Mama." **90m/C; VHS, DVD, Blu-Ray.** Shelley Winters; Robert De Niro; Don Stroud; Pat Hingle; Bruce Dern; Diane Varsi; Robert Walden; Clinton Kimbrough; Scatman Crothers; Pamela Dunlap; Michael Fox; Stacy Harris; *D:* Roger Corman; *W:* Robert Thom; *C:* John A. Alonzo; *M:* Don Randi.

Bloody Moon WOOF! *Die Saege des Todes* **1983** Tourists are being brutally attacked and murdered during a small Spanish village's Festival of the Moon. **84m/C; VHS, DVD, Blu-Ray.** *GE* Olivia Pascal; Christopher Brugger; Ann-Beate Engelke; Antonia Garcia; Nadja Gerganoff; Corinna Gillwald; Jasmin Losensky; Maria Rubio; Alexander Waechter; *D:* Jess (Jesus) Franco; *W:* Jess (Jesus) Franco; Rayo Casablanca; *C:* Juan Soler.

Bloody Murder WOOF! 1999 (R) Stupid teen campers in peril from maniac movie. This time the creepoid wears a hockey mask (sound familiar?) and has a chainsaw in place of his left arm. Ick. **90m/C; VHS, DVD.** Michael Stone; Jessica Morris; Peter Guillemette; Patrick Cavanaugh; Christelle Ford; Tracy Pacheco; Justin Martin; *D:* Ralph Portillo; *W:* John R. Stevenson; *C:* Keith Holland; *M:* Steven Stern. **VIDEO**

Bloody Murder 2 WOOF! 2003 (R) The sequel is no improvement over the first stinker, which was your basic teen slasher flick. Trevor Moorehorse returns after five years to slaughter a new batch of camp counselors at Camp Placid Pines. **85m/C; VHS, DVD.** Katy Woodruff; Kelly Gunning; Amanda Magarian; Lane Anderson; Benjamin Schneider; *D:* Robert Spera; *C:* David Trulli; *M:* Steven Stern. **VIDEO**

Bloody New Year *Time Warp Terror* **1987 (R)** Corpses stalk the living as a group of teens happen upon an impromptu New

Year's Eve party on a deserted island. Auld acquaintance shouldn't be forgot, just this flick. **90m/C; VHS, DVD, Blu-Ray.** Suzy Aitchison; Nikki Brooks; Colin Haeywood; Mark Powley; Catherine Roman; Julian Ronnie; ***D:*** Norman J. Warren; ***W:*** Frazer Pearce; ***C:*** John Shann; ***M:*** Nick Magnus.

The Bloody Pit of Horror 1/2 *Crimson Executioner; The Red Hangman; Il Boia Scarlatto* **1965** While wife Jayne Mansfield was in Italy filming "Primitive Love," bodybuilder Hargitay starred in this sado-horror epic. He owns a castle that is visited by a group of models for a special shoot. While in the dungeon, Hargitay becomes possessed by the castle's former owner, a sadist, and begins torturing the models. Supposedly based on the writings of the Marquis de Sade. **87m/B; VHS, DVD.** *IT* Mickey Hargitay; Louise Barrett; Walter Brandi; Moa Thai; Ralph Zucker; Albert Gordon; ***D:*** Max (Massimo Pupillo) Hunter; ***W:*** Romano Migliorini; Roberto Natale; ***C:*** Luciano Trasatti; ***M:*** Gino Peguri.

Bloody Proof **1999** A serial killer is stalking well-to-do women in Mexico. Detective Ibarra (Bauer) is assigned to the case. Rookie tabloid reporter Estela (Arizmendi) finds an important clue. The resolution of the stereotypical premise runs true to form, but the characters are treated seriously and the film is stylishly made with a few moments of abrupt, shocking violence. **99m/C; VHS, DVD.** Steven Bauer; Yareli Arizmendi; Olivia Hussey; ***D:*** Gabriel Beristain; ***W:*** M. Francesconi; Tim Hoy; ***C:*** Andres Leon Becker; ***M:*** Eduardo Gamboa.

Bloody Sunday **2001 (R)** Docudrama covers the January 30, 1972 civil rights march through Derry, Northern Ireland to protest the policy of British internment without trial. Although the majority of the marchers are Catholic, they are led by the area's Protestant MP Ivan Cooper (Nesbitt), who believes the situation can be handled peacefully. Maj. Gen. Robert Ford (Piggott-Smith) reiterates that the British Army has banned all such marches and that participants are subject to arrest. As the march splinters into factions, the Army fires on the crowd—27 civilians are wounded and 14 died. The re-creation of the event by director Greengrass is stunning at the very least. "Sunday Bloody Sunday" was eulogized in a song by U2. **110m/C; DVD.** *IR UK* James Nesbitt; Tim Pigott-Smith; Nicholas Farrell; Gerard McSorley; Kathy Kiera Clarke; Allan Gildea; Gerard Crossan; Mary Moulds; Carmel McCallion; Declan Duddy; Simon Mann; ***D:*** Paul Greengrass; ***W:*** Paul Greengrass; ***C:*** Ivan Strasburg; ***M:*** Dominic Muldowney. Berlin Intl. Film Fest. '02: Film.

Bloody Wednesday 1/2 **1987** It's sanity check-out time when a hotel caretaker is driven mad by tormentors...or is he driving himself mad? What is it about vacant hotels that make men lose their minds? If you can remove "The Shining" from yours, this flick's worthwhile. **89m/C; VHS, DVD.** Raymond Elmendorf; Pamela Baker; Navarre Perry; ***D:*** Mark Gilhuis; ***W:*** Philip Yordan; ***M:*** Albert Sendrey.

Bloom *Bl.m* **2003 (R)** Rookie director Walsh's drab take of James Joyce's revered 1922 "Ulysses" lays out the events of Leopold Bloom's (Rea) daylong journey on June 16th, 1904 in Dublin as he deals with his wife Molly's (Ball) affair and serves as young poet Stephen's (O'Conor) mentor. **108m/C; VHS, DVD.** Stephen Rea; Angeline Ball; Hugh O'Conor; Neili Conroy; Eoin McCarthy; Britta Smith; Paul Ronan; Alan Devlin; Alvaro Lucchesi; Maria Hayden; Mark Huberman; Kenneth McDonnell; Andrew McGibney; Dan Colley; Des Braiden; Donncha Crowley; Howard Jones; Russell Smith; Jimmy Keogh; Donal O'Kelly; Phelim Drew; Ronan Wilmot; Sarah Jane Drummey; Dearbhla Molloy; Jenny Maher; Ruaidhri Finnegan; Eoin MacDonagh; Peter Gaynor; Rachael Pilkington; Jamie Baker; Maria Lennon; Steve Simmonds; Colman Hanley; Conor Delaney; Charlie Bonner; Alexander Downes; Eamon Rohan; Luke Hayden; Julie Hale; Caoileann Murphy; Ciaran O'Brien; Dermot Moore; Maurice Shanahan; Seamus Walsh; Adam Fox Clarke; ***D:*** Sean Walsh; ***W:*** James Joyce; ***C:*** Ciaran Tanham; ***M:*** David Kahne. **VIDEO**

Bloomington **2010** A former child actress, 18-year-old Jackie decides to go to college in Bloomington, Indiana to escape her pushy California family. She's finding it tough to fit in since everyone just wants to talk about her old successful TV show. Jackie soon succumbs to the charms of manipulative psychology prof Catherine Stark but school gossip spreads. With a chance to resume her acting career, what will Jackie choose to do? **83m/C; DVD.** Sarah Stouffer; Allison McAtee; Katherine Ann McGregor; Ray Zupp; J. Blakemore; Erika Heidewald; Chelasea Rogers; ***D:*** Fernanda Cardoso; ***W:*** Fernanda Cardoso; ***C:*** George Feucht; ***M:*** Jermaine Stegall.

Blossoms in the Dust **1941** The true story of Edna Gladney is told as she starts the Texas Children's Home and Aid Society of Fort Worth. Major league Garson tear-jerker. **100m/B; VHS, DVD.** Greer Garson; Walter Pidgeon; Felix Bressart; Marsha Hunt; Fay Holden; Samuel S. Hinds; Kathleen Howard; ***D:*** Mervyn LeRoy.

Blow 1/2 **2001 (R)** Memorable, visually stunning, true story of cocaine entrepreneur George Jung features, at its best, stellar performances (especially from Reubens, Cruz, and Depp), and at its worst, a "Goodfellas" meets "Traffic" familiarity. Epic follows Jung (Depp) from his humble New England beginnings through his California surfer-bum days, to his rise and fall as America's biggest cocaine pipeline of the '70s and '80s without judging him or his lifestyle, although it does tend to sympathize with his family issues with mom, dad, and his own child. **124m/C; VHS, DVD.** Johnny Depp; Penelope Cruz; Jordi Molla; Franka Potente; Rachel Griffiths; Ray Liotta; Ethan Suplee; Paul (Pee-wee Herman) Reubens; Max Perlich; Clifford Curtis; Miguel (Michael) Sandoval; Kevin Gage; Jesse James; Dan Ferro; Emma Roberts; Bobcat Goldthwait; Jaime King; ***D:*** Ted (Edward) Demme; ***W:*** David McKenna; Nick Cassavetes; ***C:*** Ellen Kuras; ***M:*** Graeme Revell.

Blow Dry **2000 (R)** Comedic possibilities and family healing ensue when the National British Hairdressing Championships come to a sleepy English town. An odd assortment of Brits and Yanks populate this familiar tale, and even dependable Rickman can't save the film, whose destination is obvious from even the newspaper ads—take "The Full Monty," replace strippers with hairdressers and, voila: "Blow Dry." Written by Simon Beaufoy, author of (you guessed it) "The Full Monty." Director Breathnach fared better with his previous film, the Irish comedy "I Went Down." **91m/C; VHS, DVD.** *GB US* Alan Rickman; Natasha Richardson; Rachel Griffiths; Rachael Leigh Cook; Josh Hartnett; Bill Nighy; Warren Clarke; Rosemary Harris; Hugh Bonneville; Peter McDonald; Heidi Klum; Michael McElhatton; ***D:*** Paddy Breathnach; ***W:*** Simon Beaufoy; ***C:*** Cian de Buitlear; ***M:*** Patrick Doyle.

Blow Out **1981 (R)** When a prominent governor and presidential candidate is killed in a car crash, a sound effects engineer becomes involved in political intrigue as he tries to expose a conspiracy with the evidence he has gathered. An intricate mystery and homage to Antonioni's "Blow-Up." **108m/C; VHS, DVD, Blu-Ray.** John Travolta; Nancy Allen; John Lithgow; Dennis Franz; ***D:*** Brian De Palma; ***W:*** Brian De Palma; ***C:*** Vilmos Zsigmond; ***M:*** Pino Donaggio.

Blow The Man Down 1/2 **2019 (R)** After their mother's death, young adult sisters, sensible Priscilla (Lowe) and impulsive Mary Beth (Saylor), argue constantly though they both desperately want to leave their small coastal Maine community. Life takes an unexpected turn when Mary Beth goes home with a local low life and finds evidence of his horrific secret. When he tries to assault her, she kills him and convinces her sister to help her dispose of the body. It's drama and mystery and crime but, yes, also humor. Above all, it's a sharp look at small town life and murder with outstanding performances from the whole cast. **91m/C; DVD.** Morgan Saylor; Sophie Lowe; Margo Martindale; June Squibb; Will Brittain; ***D:*** Bridget Savage Cole; Danielle Krudy; ***W:*** Bridget Savage Cole; Danielle Krudy; ***C:*** Todd Banhazl; ***M:*** Jordan Dykstra; Brian McOmber. **VIDEO**

Blow-Up 1/2 **1966** A young London photographer takes some pictures of a couple in the park and finds out he may have recorded evidence of a murder. Though marred by badly dated 1960s modishness, this is Antonioni's most accessible film, a sophisticated treatise on perception and the film-consumer-as-voyeur, brilliantly assembled and wrought. **111m/C; DVD, Blu-Ray.** *UK IT* David Hemmings; Vanessa Redgrave; Sarah Miles; Jane Birkin; Veruschka; Peter Bowles; John Castle; Gillian Hills; Julian Chagrin; Harry Hutchinson; The Yardbirds; ***D:*** Michelangelo Antonioni; ***W:*** Michelangelo Antonioni; Tonino Guerra; ***C:*** Carlo Di Palma; ***M:*** Herbie Hancock. Cannes '67: Film; Natl. Soc. Film Critics '66: Director (Antonioni), Film.

Blowback **1999 (R)** Police officer Don Morell (Van Peebles) witnesses the execution of serial killer Claude Whitman (Remar)?or does he? Former jury members are being murdered and Morell finds cryptic bible messages at the scenes—a Whitman hallmark. So has the killer come back from the grave or has someone conspired to keep Whitman alive for their own purposes? **93m/C; VHS, DVD.** Mario Van Peebles; James Remar; Stephen Caffrey; David Groh; ***D:*** Mark L. Lester; ***W:*** Jeffrey Goldenberg; Bob Held; Randall Frakes; ***C:*** Jacques Haitkin; ***M:*** Sean Callery. **CABLE**

Blowin' Smoke *Freak Talks About Sex* **1999 (R)** Goofball stoner Freak (Zahn) lives his life (in his parents' basement) as the ultimate slacker. His best bud (besides the pot) is the equally unambitious Dave (Hamilton), who does at least have a job. Dave also has an ex-girlfriend who wants to see him again, a sweet high schooler who has a crush on him, and a family who wishes he would do something with his life. Well, at least Dave has Freak to turn to in times of stress. Based on the novel by co-writer Galvin. **88m/C; VHS, DVD.** Steve Zahn; Josh Hamilton; Heather McComb; Arabella Field; David Kinney; ***D:*** Paul Todisco; ***W:*** Paul Todisco; Michael M.B. Galvin; Peter Speakman; ***C:*** Douglas W. Shannon; ***M:*** Pete Snell.

Blown Away 1/2 **1993 (R)** Haim and Feldman are brothers working at a ski resort where Haim falls for rich teenager Eggert. She's a young femme fatale who manages to get Haim all hot and bothered but she's actually using the unsuspecting dupe in a murder plot. Also available in an unrated version at 93 minutes. **91m/C; VHS, DVD.** *CA* Nicole Eggert; Corey Haim; Corey Feldman; Jean LeClerc; Kathleen Robertson; Gary Farmer; ***D:*** Brenton Spencer; ***W:*** Robert Cooper; ***M:*** Paul Zaza.

Blown Away **1994 (R)** Boston Irish bomb-squad cop Jimmy Dove (Bridges) is after former compatriot Ryan Gaerity (Jones), an Irish radical who's taken his bombing expertise onto Jimmy's new turf. Meanwhile, Jimmy wants to keep his unsavory past from unsuspecting wife Amis. Real life dad Lloyd plays Jeff's uncle. While Jones seems adequately obsessed with making things go boom and Bridges significantly concerned that they don't, thriller moves on predictable path toward explosive climax. Special effects create the suspense, as everyday objects become lethal in Gaerity's knowledgeable hands. The final explosion was more than even the special effects coordinator desired—windows were unintentionally blown out in nearby buildings. **121m/C; VHS, DVD, Blu-Ray.** Jeff Bridges; Tommy Lee Jones; Suzy Amis; Lloyd Bridges; Forest Whitaker; ***D:*** Stephen Hopkins; ***W:*** Joe Batteer; John Rice; ***C:*** Gregory McClatchy; ***M:*** Alan Silvestri.

Blubberella **WOOF!** **2011 (R)** Boll's intentionally comic spoof is an all-around turkey--and not one served on rye. Large and in charge, half-vampire, half-human Blubberella loves eating, perfecting her cotton candy recipe, and killing Nazis, and not necessarily in that order. She hooks up with some resistance fighters and goes after her nemesis, a commandant who's also a day-walking bloodsucker. **87m/C; DVD.** Lindsay Hollister; Michael Paré; Clint Howard; Brendan Fletcher; William H. Bellis; Annett Culp; ***D:*** Uwe Boll; ***W:*** Uwe Boll; Michael Christopher; ***C:*** Mathias Neumann; ***M:*** Jessica de Rooij. **VIDEO**

Blue **1968** A dull western about an American boy (Stamp) raised by Mexicans who doesn't trust another living soul until he finds himself face to face with his former gang, led by his adoptive father (Montalban). **113m/C; VHS, DVD.** Terence Stamp; Joanna Pettet; Karl Malden; Ricardo Montalban; Joe De Santis; Sally Kirkland; ***D:*** Silvio Narizzano; ***W:*** Ronald M. Cohen; ***M:*** Manos Hadjidakis.

Blue **1993 (R)** Meditation/memoir of director Jarman's deteriorating AIDS condition consists of narration and a soundtrack set against an unvaried blue screen. Jarman ponders the associations with the color blue (sky, ocean, blindness, heaven, eternity) and his own physical problems, alternately expressed with dreamy vagueness or incendiary contempt. Limited in appeal, depending highly on boredom tolerance and ability to suspend visual expectations. **76m/C; VHS, DVD, Blu-Ray.** *GB* ***Nar:*** John Quentin; Nigel Terry; Tilda Swinton; Derek Jarman; ***D:*** Derek Jarman; ***W:*** Derek Jarman; ***M:*** Simon Fisher Turner.

The Blue and the Gray **1982** Epic miniseries about love and hate inflamed by the Civil War. Keach plays a Pinkerton's secret service agent in this loosely based historical romance. Available in uncut and 295-minute versions. **381m/C; VHS, DVD.** Gregory Peck; Lloyd Bridges; Colleen Dewhurst; Stacy Keach; John Hammond; Sterling Hayden; Warren Oates; ***D:*** Andrew V. McLaglen; ***M:*** Bruce Broughton. **TV**

The Blue Angel *Der Blaue Engel* **1930** Tale of a man stripped of his dignity. A film classic filled with sensuality and decay, which made Dietrich a European star and led to her discovery in Hollywood. When a repressed professor (Jannings) goes to a nightclub hoping to catch some of his students in the wrong, he's taken by Lola, the sultry singer portrayed by Dietrich. After spending the night with her, losing his job, and then marrying her, he goes on tour with the troupe, peddling indiscreet photos of his wife. Versions were shot in both German and English, with the German version sporting English subtitles. **90m/B; VHS, DVD, Blu-Ray.** *GE* Marlene Dietrich; Emil Jannings; Kurt Gerron; Rosa Valetti; Hans Albers; ***D:*** Josef von Sternberg; ***W:*** Robert Liebmann; Carl Zuckmayer; Karl Vollmoller; ***C:*** Gunther Rittau; ***M:*** Frederick "Friedrich" Hollander.

The Blue Bird **1940 (G)** A weird, dark fantasy about two children who search for the blue bird of happiness in various fantasy lands, but find it eventually at home. Overlooked and impressively fatalistic. **98m/C; VHS, DVD.** Shirley Temple; Gale Sondergaard; John Russell; Eddie Collins; Nigel Bruce; Jessie Ralph; Spring Byington; Sybil Jason; ***D:*** Walter Lang; ***C:*** Arthur C. Miller.

Blue Blazes Rawden **1918** Hart plays a lumberjack who gains control of a local saloon after shooting its villainous proprietor. **65m/B; Silent; VHS, DVD.** William S. Hart; Robert McKim; Maud(e) (Ford) George; Jack Hoxie; ***D:*** William S. Hart.

Blue Blood 1/2 *If I Didn't Care* **2007** Predictable thriller with Scheider channeling Columbo. Trophy husband Davis (Sage) resides in the Hamptons while his wealthy lawyer wife Janice (Beck) works in the city. Davis is fooling around with real estate agent Hadley (Misner) and the two decide to bump off the missus, although Hadley is the one who must do the actual work. Only their plan is botched, which brings in suspicious PI Linus (Scheider). **74m/C; DVD.** Bill Sage; Roy Scheider; Ronald Guttman; Susan Misner; Noelle Beck; Brian McQuillan; ***D:*** Benjamin Cummings; Orson Cummings; ***W:*** Benjamin Cummings; Orson Cummings; ***C:*** Bryan Pryzpek; ***M:*** Michael Tremante.

The Blue Butterfly **2004 (PG)** Based on a true story. Pete Carlton (Donato) is 10 and dying. His one wish is to capture the rare blue morpho butterfly. World-weary entomologist Alan Osborne (Hurt) is persuaded by Pete's mother, Teresa (Bussieres), to let them accompany his expedition into the rain forest of Costa Rica. Beautiful scenery but an overly-sappy saga. **97m/C; DVD.** *CA* William Hurt; Marc Donato; Pascale Bussieres; Steve Adams; ***D:*** Lea Pool; ***W:*** Pete McCormack; ***C:*** Michel Arcand; ***M:*** Stephen Endelman.

Blue Car 1/2 **2003 (R)** Impressive directorial debut by Moncrieff tells the story of troubled teen Meg (Bruckner) and her sad, beaten-down English teacher Mr. Auster (Strathairn). Meg's life has been turned upside down with the divorce of her parents. Her mother is distant and overworked, and her sister (Arnold, in an excellent performance) is self-destructive. When she finds solace in poetry, Auster recognizes and encourages her talent, which leads to an awkwardly closer relationship, skulkingly engineered by the teacher. Excellent script and direction, as well as stellar performances by Bruckner and Strathairn, allow the film to explore the situation without exploiting or judging. The characters are well-rounded and real, as is the dialogue, which makes the unfolding events that much more disturbing. **96m/C; VHS, DVD.** Agnes Bruckner; David Strathairn; Margaret Colin; Regan Arnold; Frances Fisher; A.J. Buckley; Sarah Beuhler; ***D:*** Karen Moncrieff; ***W:*** Karen Moncrieff; ***C:*** Rob Sweeney; ***M:*** Stuart Spencer-Nash.

Blue Chips 1/2 **1994 (PG-13)** Nolte does Bobby Knight in this saga of Western U basketball coach Pete Bell, suffering through his first losing season. What follows is a tug of war between rich alumni who want to win at any cost and his ethics as he recruits for a new season. Larger than life hoopster O'Neal's film debut. McDonnell and Woodard are merely afterthoughts, but look for cameos from many real life b-ballers, including Dick Vitale and Larry Bird. Average script is bolstered by exciting game footage, shot during real games for authenticity. **108m/C; VHS, DVD.** Nick Nolte; Shaquille O'Neal; Mary McDonnell; Ed O'Neill; J.T. Walsh; Alfre Woodard; ***Cameo(s):*** Larry Bird; Bobby Knight; Rick Pitino; ***D:*** William Friedkin; ***W:*** Ron Shelton; ***M:*** Nile Rodgers; Jeff Beck; Jed Leiber.

Blue City 1/2 **1986 (R)** A young man returns to his Florida hometown to find his father murdered, and subsequently vows to solve and avenge the matter. Based on a Ross MacDonald thriller. **83m/C; VHS, DVD, Blu-Ray.** Judd Nelson; Ally Sheedy; Paul Winfield; Anita Morris; David Caruso; Julie Carmen; Scott Wilson; ***D:*** Michelle Manning; ***W:*** Walter Hill; Lukas Heller; ***M:*** Ry Cooder.

Blue Collar **1978 (R)** Funnyman Pryor (in one of his best film roles) offers most of the laughs in this very serious drama of how three Detroit auto assembly workers (Pryor, Kotto, and Keitel), feeling the strain of family life and inflation, hatch a plan to rob their corrupt union office only to stumble into a bigger crime that later costs them dearly. Schrader makes his directorial debut in this searing study of the working class and the robbing of the human spirit, which is made memorable by the strong performances of its three leads. Filmed entirely in Detroit and Kalamazoo, Michigan. **114m/C; VHS, DVD, Blu-Ray.** Richard Pryor; Harvey Keitel; Yaphet Kotto; Ed Begley, Jr.; Lane Smith; Cliff DeYoung; ***D:*** Paul Schrader; ***W:*** Paul Schrader; Leonard Schrader; ***C:*** Bobby Byrne; ***M:*** Jack Nitzsche.

Blue Crush **2002 (PG-13)** Director John Stockwell brings back the beach/surfing genre with a story about board riding women who would kick Gidget's narrow behind. Surfer girl Anne Marie (Bosworth) moves to Hawaii, determined to win the traditionally all-male Rip Masters competition. Aided by fellow surfers Eden (Rodriguez) and Lena (Lake), she tries to mentally recover from a near-fatal accident in time for the meet. Unfortunately, the distraction of new boyfriend Matt (Davis) may cause her dreams to wipe out. Both the ripped bodies and the surfing action seem a little enhanced by science, but both are very visually stimulating. **104m/C; VHS, DVD, Blu-Ray.** Kate (Catherine) Bosworth; Michelle Rodriguez; Matthew Davis; Sanoe Lake; Mika Boorem; Faizon Love; Chris Taloa; Kala Alexander; ***D:*** John Stockwell; ***W:*** John Stockwell; Elizabeth Weiss; ***C:*** David Hennings; ***M:*** Paul Haslinger.

Blue Crush 2 **2011 (PG-13)** Underwhelming in-name-only sequel offers revealing swimwear and some other attractive scenery but a yawn of a plot. Bratty rich girl Dana leaves Malibu to follow her recently deceased mother's surfing diary along the same South African beaches. She makes friends with fellow surfer Pushy, gets a hot boyfriend in Tim, and has an unexplained rivalry with surf pro Tara. There's also an inexplicable poaching subplot that goes nowhere. **113m/C; DVD, Blu-Ray.** Sasha Jackson; Sharni Vinson; Elizabeth Mathis; Ben Milliken; Gideon Emery; Chris Fisher; ***D:*** Mike Elliott; ***W:*** Randall McCormick; ***C:*** Trevor Michael Brown; ***M:*** J. Peter Robinson. **VIDEO**

The Blue Dahlia 1/2 **1946** Classic film noir finds Navy vet Johnny Morrison (Ladd) returning home to discover his wife Helen (Dowling) has been keeping the home fires burning with Eddie Harwood (Da Silva), owner of the Blue Dahlia nightclub. After a nasty fight, Johnny takes off and is picked up by sultry blonde Joyce (Lake). The next day Johnny discovers he's wanted by the cops for the murder of his wife and decides to hide out until he can find the real killer, with Joyce's help. Very stylish and fast-paced with excellent performances; Chandler's first original screenplay. **100m/B; DVD, Blu-Ray.** Alan Ladd; Veronica Lake; William Bendix; Howard da Silva; Doris Dowling; Tom Powers; Hugh Beaumont; Howard Freeman; Don Costello; ***D:*** George Marshall; ***W:*** Raymond Chandler; ***C:*** Lionel Lindon; ***M:*** Victor Young.

Blue Desert **1991 (R)** Cox is strong in her performance as Lisa Roberts, a comic book artist who leaves New York City for small town Arizona life after surviving a traumatic rape. Once there, she's befriended by Sheffer and Sweeney, a local cop. Battersby does a good job of keeping the suspense level high (in his directorial debut) as Cox finds that there's danger in small towns, too. Fine performances keep this slightly above average. **98m/C; VHS, DVD.** D.B. Sweeney; Courteney Cox; Craig Sheffer; Philip Baker Hall; Sandy Ward; ***D:*** Bradley Battersby; ***W:*** Bradley Battersby; Arthur Collis; ***M:*** Jerry Goldsmith.

Blue-Eyed Butcher 1/2 **2012** Lifetime true crime drama. In 2003, the body of Jeffrey Wright is found buried in his suburban backyard. He was stabbed 193 times by his wife Susan, whose defense is that their seemingly perfect life was a cover for his abuse. Prosecutor Kelly Siegler thinks Susan is just a sociopath using her good looks to try to get away with murder. **89m/C; DVD.** Sara Paxton; Lisa Edelstein; Justin Bruening; Michael Gross; ***D:*** Stephen Kay; ***W:*** Michael J. Murray; Jamie Pachino; ***C:*** Jamie Barber; ***M:*** Tree Adams. **CABLE**

Blue Eyes *Alhos Azuis* **2009** On his last day before his compulsory retirement, alcoholic, bitter, and racist immigration chief Marshall humiliates legal Brazilian immigrant Nonato, leading to a tragedy for which Marshall is imprisoned. After his release, and terminally ill, Marshall travels to Brazil in an effort to find and make amends to Nonato's daughter. **110m/C; DVD.** *BR* David Rasche; Cristina Lago; Frank Grillo; Erica Gimpel; ***D:*** Jose Joffily; ***W:*** Melanie Dimantas; Paulo Halm; ***C:*** Nonato Estrela; ***M:*** Jacques Morelenbaum.

Blue Fin **1978 (PG)** When their tuna boat is shipwrecked, and the crew disabled, a young boy and his father learn lessons of love and courage as the son tries to save the ship. **93m/C; VHS, DVD.** *AU* Hardy Kruger; Greg Rowe; ***D:*** Carl Schultz; ***C:*** Geoff Burton.

Blue Fire Lady **1978** The heartwarming story of a young girl and her love of horses which endures even her father's disapproval. Good family fare. **96m/C; VHS, DVD.** *AU* Cathryn Harrison; Mark Holden; Peter Cummins; Marion Edward; Anne Sutherland; Garry Waddell; John Wood; John Ewart; ***D:*** Ross Dimsey; ***C:*** Vincent Monton; ***M:*** Mike Brady.

Blue Flame **1993 (R)** Vigilante cop is hired to track down two humanoid aliens who have escaped captivity in futuristic L.A. They evade him by time-traveling through alternate realities, infiltrating the cop's mind, and using his fantasies against him. **88m/C; VHS, DVD.** Brian Wimmer; Ian Buchanan; Kerri Green; Cecilia Peck; Jad Mager; ***D:*** Cassian Elwes; ***W:*** Cassian Elwes.

The Blue Gardenia 1/2 **1953** Seminal but rarely seen film noir. Norah Larkin (Baxter) wakes up one morning in the apartment of womanizing lout Harry Prebble (Burr). He's dead and she's labeled "The Blue Gardenia" murderess by newspaper columnist Casey Mayo (Conte). Required viewing for fans of vintage mysteries. **88m/B; DVD.** Anne Baxter; Richard Conte; Ann Sothern; Raymond Burr; George Reeves; Nat King Cole; Jeff Donnell; Richard Erdman; Ray Walker; Ruth Storey; ***D:*** Fritz Lang; ***W:*** Charles Hoffman; ***C:*** Nicholas Musuraca; ***M:*** Raoul Kraushaar.

Blue Hawaii **1962 (PG)** A soldier, returning to his Hawaiian home, defies his parents by taking a job with a tourist agency. Presley sings "Can't Help Falling in Love." For Elvis fans. **101m/C; VHS, DVD.** Elvis Presley; Angela Lansbury; Joan Blackman; Roland Winters; Iris Adrian; John Archer; Steve Brodie; Pam(ela) Austin; ***D:*** Norman Taurog; ***W:*** Hal Kanter.

Blue Hill Avenue **2001 (R)** Four childhood friends in 1970's Boston are taken under the wing of a drug dealer and taught to be gangsters. One of them, Tristan (Payne) eventually decides he has had enough and makes the inevitable betrayal of his master before the equally inevitable ensuing bloodbath. Nothing new, but still well done. **120m/C; DVD.** Allen Payne; Angelle Brooks; Michael "Bear" Taliferro; William L. Johnson; Aaron Spears; Andrew Divoff; Richard Lawson; Marlon Young; Dee Freeman; Anthony Sherwood; Gail Fulton Ross; Veronica Redd; Clarence Williams, III; William Forsythe; Myquan Jackson; Latamara Smith; William Butler; Pooch Hall; Chris Thornton; William Springfield; Martin Roach; David Julian Hirsh; Anthony Nuncio; Nichole McLean; Linette Robinson; Kenny Robinson; Nadia-Leigh Nascimento; ***D:*** Craig Ross, Jr.; ***W:*** Craig Ross, Jr.; ***C:*** Carl F. Bartels; ***M:*** William L. Johnson; Aaron Spears; Cruel Timothy; Jan Poperans.

The Blue Hour **1991** Theo is a Berlin hustler whose business is so good he can pick his clients. Marie, his next-door neighbor, lives with her boyfriend Paul until he just walks out one day. Marie is shattered and refuses to leave her apartment until Theo takes an interest in her plight. Just when it seems that the improbable couple could find true love, Paul comes back. In German with English subtitles. **87m/C; VHS, DVD.** *GE* Andreas Herder; Dina Leipzig; Cyrill Rey-Coquais; ***D:*** Marcel Gisler.

Blue Ice 1/2 **1992 (R)** Harry Anders (Caine) is an ex-spy with an eye for the ladies and a loyalty to his friends. When his friends start winding up dead, Harry decides to investigate—a very dangerous decision, especially when a mysterious woman (Young) takes an interest. **96m/C; VHS, DVD.** Michael Caine; Sean Young; Ian Bannen; Bob Hoskins; ***D:*** Russell Mulcahy; ***W:*** Ron Hutchinson; ***M:*** Michael Kamen. **CABLE**

Blue Iguana **1988 (R)** An inept bounty hunter travels south of the border to recover millions from a crooked South American bank, and meets up with sexy women, murderous thugs, and corruption. **88m/C; VHS, DVD, Blu-Ray.** Dylan McDermott; Jessica Harper; James Russo; Dean Stockwell; Pamela Gidley; Tovah Feldshuh; ***D:*** John Lafia.

Blue Iguana **2018** Ex-cons Eddie (Rockwell) and Paul (Schwartz) are working in a New York diner, when British lawyer Katherine Rookwood (Fox) comes in one day. She is being threatened by a client, shady international businessman Arkaday (Polycarpou). She owes him cash, and he is making threats. However, Arkaday will forgive her debt if she can bring him some stolen bonds. Katherine hires Eddie and Paul to go to London and do the deed. The pair take the job, but find themselves in over their heads. While it has its charms and leads do well, it doesn't quite hit the mark. **107m/C; DVD.** Sam Rockwell; Amanda Donohoe; Ben Schwartz; Simon Callow; Phoebe Fox; ***D:*** Hadi Hajaig; ***W:*** Hadi Hajaig; ***C:*** Ian Howes; ***M:*** Simon Lambros.

Blue in the Face 1/2 **1995 (R)** Wang and Auster's immediate follow-up to "Smoke," shot in five days, recycles the same Brooklyn cigar shop setting and contains a dozen fast-paced, loosely scripted or wholly improvised scenes that they couldn't cram into "Smoke," led by Reed's deadpan riff on eyewear, New York, and smoking. The action again centers around Auggie (Keitel), the shop manager, who hangs out with the mostly eccentric, and sometimes famous clientele. Jarmusch idly waxes philosophic on smoking technique, while puffing on what he claims is his last. Scenes are woven together with videotaped interviews from actual Brooklyn residents, creating a tribute to life in the borough with a documentary feel. Improv lovers will enjoy watching what sometimes seems more like outtakes than finished performances. **83m/C; VHS, DVD.** Harvey Keitel; Lou Reed; Michael J. Fox; Roseanne; Jim Jarmusch; Lily Tomlin; Mel Gorham; Jared Harris; Giancarlo Esposito; Victor Argo; Madonna; Keith David; Mira Sorvino; Malik Yoba; Michael Badalucco; Jose Zuniga; Stephen Gevedon; John Lurie; Sharif Rashed; RuPaul Charles; ***D:*** Wayne Wang; Paul Auster; ***W:*** Wayne Wang; Paul Auster.

Blue is the Warmest Color *La vie d'Adele; The Life of Adele* **2013 (NC-17)** Based on the French graphic novel "Blue Angel," this Palme d'Or winner tells the love story between French teen Adele (Exarchopoulos) and slightly older art student Emma (Seydoux), whose lives are turned upside down when they enter into a heated romance. Rarely has a film more completely captured the arc of an entire relationship--from the minute their eyes meet to its bitter end. Both actresses are remarkably honest and pure, always seeming fully in the moment and capturing something about love and romance through their genuine performances that most movies don't get anywhere near. French with subtitles. **179m/C; DVD, Blu-Ray.** *FR* Lea Seydoux; Adele Exarchopoulos; ***D:*** Abdellatif Kechiche; ***W:*** Abdellatif Kechiche; Ghalia Lacroix; ***C:*** Sofian El Fani. Ind. Spirit '14: Foreign Film.

Blue Jasmine **2013 (PG-13)** Maturing like a fine wine, Woody Allen returns to San Francisco after 40 years and brings along Blanchett to cover for him. Serious in tone, but bright and human at heart, finds fallen New York socialite Jasmine (Blanchett) heading West after losing her husband and their entire fortune. In search for a renewed life, the neurotic heroine goes from popping pills to dating diplomats. Blanchett's take on a femme Allen perfectly balances his fix for desperation with courage. Allen somehow stays relevant and Blanchett just hitting her prime here. **98m/C; DVD, Blu-Ray.** Cate Blanchett; Sally Hawkins; Alec Baldwin; Bobby Cannavale; Max Casella; Tammy Blanchard; Louis CK; Peter Sarsgaard; Andrew Silverstein; ***D:*** Woody Allen; ***W:*** Woody Allen; ***C:*** Javier Aguirresarobe. Oscars '13: Actress (Blanchett); British Acad. '13: Actress (Blanchett); Golden Globes '14: Actress--Drama (Blanchett); Ind. Spirit '14: Actress (Blanchett); Screen Actors Guild '13: Actress (Blanchett).

Blue Jay **2016** Jim Henderson (Duplass) has come back to his hometown to sell his recently deceased mother's house when he bumps into his old girlfriend Amanda (Paulson). Despite other plans, Amanda agrees to hang out with Jim and the two take a walk down memory lane, defined by regret and, now, the deeper understanding that comes with age. Both actors are fantastic, but the drama belongs to a phenomenal Paulson, who can do more with body language than most actresses can do with a monologue. **80m/B; DVD.** Mark Duplass; Sarah Paulson; Clu Gulager; ***D:*** Alexandre Lehmann; ***W:*** Mark Duplass; ***C:*** Alexandre Lehmann; ***M:*** Julian Wass.

Blue Juice 1/2 **1995 (R)** Early work from several young actors who've gone on to bigger things. Billed as Britain's first surf picture, this comedy follows the escapades of nearly 30 JC (Pertwee), a local hero of the Cornish surfing community who can't commit to his more practical girlfriend, Chloe (Zeta-Jones). Then some of JC's London buddies, Dean (McGregor), Josh (Mackintosh), and Terry (Gunn), show up for a sort of last hurrah against the boredom of acting like adults. **90m/C; VHS, DVD.** *GB* Sean Pertwee; Catherine Zeta-Jones; Ewan McGregor; Steven Mackintosh; Peter Gunn; Heathcote Williams; ***D:*** Carl Prechezer; ***W:*** Carl Prechezer; Peter Salmi; ***C:*** Richard Greatrex; ***M:*** Simon Davison.

The Blue Kite *Lan Feng Zheng* **1993** Fifteen years of political and cultural upheaval in China is shown through the eyes of young troublemaker Tietou, who certainly earns his nickname of "Iron Head" after his 1954 birth. Soon his father is sent to a labor reform camp and his mother remarries—only to be faced with more struggles as the years go by. The kite is Tietou's cherished toy, which keeps getting lost or destroyed but is always being rebuilt, offering one token of hope. Chinese with subtitles. **138m/C; VHS, DVD.** *CH* Liping Lu; Zhang Wenyao; Pu Quanxin; ***D:*** Tian Zhuangzhuang; ***W:*** Xiao Mao; ***C:*** Yong Hou; ***M:*** Yoshihide Otomo.

The Blue Lagoon **WOOF!** **1980 (R)** Useless remake of 1949 film of the same name. An adolescent boy and girl marooned on a desert isle discover love (read: sex) without the restraints of society. Not too explicit, but nonetheless intellectually offensive. Gorgeous photography of island paradise is wasted on this Shields vehicle. **105m/C; VHS, DVD, Blu-Ray.** Brooke Shields; Christopher Atkins; Leo McKern; William Daniels; ***D:*** Randal Kleiser; ***W:*** Douglas Day Stewart; ***C:*** Nestor Almendros; ***M:*** Basil Poledouris. Golden Raspberries '80: Worst Actress (Shields).

Blue Lagoon: The Awakening 🦴🦴 **2012** Lifetime remake of the 1980 pic finds teens Emma (Evans) and Dean (Thwaites) on a high school field trip in the Caribbean (it was filmed in Hawaii). Their small boat gets caught in a storm and they're stranded on a desert island where they have to survive with minimal clothing in a beautiful location. This one has several slo-mo montages and is sweetly romantic rather than sexually provocative. Atkins, who starred opposite Brooke Shields in the original, pops up as a teacher, Mr. Christiansen. **89m/C; DVD.** Indiana Evans; Brenton Thwaites; Denise Richards; Frank John Hughes; Patrick St. Esprit; Christopher Atkins; ***D:*** Mikael Salomon; ***W:*** Matt Heller; Heather Rutman; ***C:*** Denis Lenoir; ***M:*** Tree Adams. **CABLE**

The Blue Lamp 🦴🦴🦴 **1949** Action-adventure fans familiar with the hoary plot where a cop must avenge the wrongful death of his partner will appreciate this suspenseful British detective effort. It's one of the very first in the genre to explore buddy cop revenge in a very British sort of way. Also sports a concluding chase scene which has stood the test of time. Led to the long-running British TV series "Dixon of Dock Green." **84m/B; VHS, Streaming.** *GB* Dirk Bogarde; Jimmy Hanley; Jack Warner; Bernard Lee; Robert Flemyng; Patric Doonan; Bruce Seton; Frederick Piper; Betty Ann Davies; Peggy Evans; ***D:*** Basil Dearden. British Acad. '50: Film.

The Blue Light 🦴🦴🦴 *Das Blaue Licht* **1932** Fairy-tale love story, based on an Italian fable about a mysterious woman, thought to be a witch, and a painter. Riefenstahl's first film which brought her to the attention of Adolf Hitler, who requested she make films glorifying the Nazi Party. In German with English subtitles. **77m/B; VHS, DVD.** *GE* Leni Riefenstahl; Matthias Wieman; Max Holsboer; ***D:*** Leni Riefenstahl; ***W:*** Leni Riefenstahl; Bela Balazs; ***C:*** Hans Schneeberger; ***M:*** Giuseppe Becce.

Blue Like Jazz 🦴🦴 **2012 (PG-13)** This well-intentioned adaptation of Donald Miller tackles the incredibly complex issue of how teenagers from faith-heavy upbringings handle life at a liberal arts college. Don (Allman) is an incoming freshman whose understanding of religion falls apart after his youth pastor sleeps with his mother. Instead of going to a religious school, he heads for the hippie teachings of the Northwest. The characters are cliché and the story doesn't play so well on film. **108m/C; DVD, Blu-Ray; Closed Captioned.** Marshall Allman; Claire Holt; Tania Raymonde; Justin Welborn; Eric Lange; Jason Marsden; ***D:*** Steve Taylor; ***W:*** Steve Taylor; Ben Pearson; ***C:*** Ben Pearson; ***M:*** Danny Seim.

The Blue Max 🦴🦴 **1/2 1966** During WWI a young German, fresh out of aviation training school, competes for the coveted "Blue Max" flying award with other members of a squadron of seasoned flyers from aristocratic backgrounds. Based on a novel by Jack D. Hunter. **155m/C; VHS, DVD, Blu-Ray.** George Peppard; James Mason; Ursula Andress; Jeremy Kemp; Karl Michael Vogler; Anton Diffring; Harry Towb; Peter Woodthorpe; Derek Newark; Derren Nesbitt; Loni von Friedl; ***D:*** John Guillermin; ***W:*** Ben Barzman; Basilio Franchina; David Pursall; Jack Seddon; Gerald Hanley; ***C:*** Douglas Slocombe; ***M:*** Jerry Goldsmith.

Blue Moon 🦴🦴 **1/2 2000 (PG-13)** Marrieds Gazzara and Moreno take a trip to the Catskills and wish on the blue moon which, according to legend, will grant them a wish. Of course, exactly how that wish will come true may not be exactly as the couple would hope. **90m/C; VHS, DVD.** Ben Gazzara; Rita Moreno; Alanna Ubach; Brian Vincent; Heather Matarazzo; Vincent Pastore; Burt Young; Victor Argo; Lillo Brancato; ***D:*** John A. Gallagher; ***W:*** John A. Gallagher; Steve Carducci; ***C:*** Craig DiBona; ***M:*** Stephen Endelman.

Blue Murder at St. Trinian's 🦴🦴🦴 **1956** The second of the madcap British comedy series (based on cartoons by Ronald Searle) about an incredibly ferocious pack of schoolgirls. This time they travel to the European continent and make life miserable for a jewel thief. Highlight: fantasy sequence in ancient Rome showing the girls thrown to the lions—and scaring the lions. **86m/B; VHS, DVD, Streaming.** *GB* Joyce Grenfell; Terry-Thomas; George Cole; Alastair Sim; Lionel Jeffries; Thorley Walters; ***D:*** Frank Launder; ***M:*** Malcolm Arnold.

Blue Ridge Fall 🦴🦴 **1999 (R)** In the small town of Jefferson Creek, North Carolina, Danny (Facinelli) is the star high school quarterback who can do no wrong. He's befriended simple-minded Aaron (Eastman), who is driven to violent desperation by his abusive father. Danny enlists his buddies to cover up Aaron's crime but their plans quickly go wrong and things just get more desperate for them all. **99m/C; VHS, DVD.** Peter Facinelli; Rodney Eastman; Will Estes; Jay R. Ferguson; Tom Arnold; Amy Irving; Chris Isaak; Brent Jennings; Heather Stephens; Garvin Funches; ***D:*** James Rowe; ***W:*** James Rowe; ***C:*** Chris Walling; ***M:*** Greg Edmonson.

Blue River 🦴🦴 **1/2 1995 (PG-13)** Flashbacks highlight this saga of a troubled family. Successful doctor Edward Sellers (McDonough) is dismayed when his derelict older brother Lawrence (O'Connell), whom he hasn't seen in 15 years, suddenly appears on his doorstep. A gifted teenager, Lawrence once built his world around science and logic after their father deserted the family but his only purpose turns out to be getting even with everyone he feels has betrayed him. Young Edward (Stahl) tried to be the "good" son, while Mom (Dey) retreated into religion and an affair with self-righteously nasty school principal Henry Howland (Elliott). TV adaptation of the novel by Ethan Canin. **90m/C; VHS, DVD.** Jerry O'Connell; Nick Stahl; Susan Dey; Sam Elliott; Neal McDonough; Jean Marie Barnwell; Patrick Renna; ***D:*** Larry Elikann; ***W:*** Maria Nation; ***C:*** Eric Van Haren Noman; ***M:*** Lawrence Shragge.

Blue Ruin 🦴🦴🦴 **2013 (R)** Director/writer Saulnier's vengeance thriller features sudden outbursts of violence, dark humor, and clockwork precision. Blair stars as a vagrant who is forced into action when the man who murdered his parents is released from prison. Before he can even consider his actions, the victim has taken his vengeance and set into motion a new cycle of violence. The film hums along at a perfect pace, finding a great balance between tension and realism, never losing sight of its largely silent character and his fight to protect what he thinks is right. **92m/C; DVD, Blu-Ray.** Macon Blair; Amy Hargreaves; Derin Ratray; Kevin Kolack; Eve Plumb; ***D:*** Jeremy Saulnier; ***W:*** Jeremy Saulnier; ***C:*** Jeremy Saulnier; ***M:*** Brooke Blair; Will Blair.

Blue Seduction 🦴 **1/2 2009** A one-hit music wonder in the 1980s, Mikey Taylor lived the booze, drugs and sex life until he met Joyce, who sobered him up and married him. Twenty years later, Mikey is a music composer who hires sultry Matty McPherson as his demo singer and new protege. She also turns out to be his biggest (psycho) fan and is soon leading Mikey down that old decadent path. **91m/C; DVD.** Billy Zane; Estella Warren; Jane Wheeler; Bernard Robichaud; ***D:*** Timothy Bond; ***W:*** Jackie Giroux; ***C:*** Philip Hurn; ***M:*** David Wade; Richard Wade.

Blue Skies 🦴🦴🦴 **1946** Former dancer turned radio personality Astaire flashes back to his friendship with singer Crosby and the gal (Caulfield) that came between them. Flimsy plot is just an excuse for some 20 Irving Berlin songs and Astaire's split-screen dance number, "Puttin' on the Ritz." **104m/C; VHS, DVD.** Fred Astaire; Bing Crosby; Joan Caulfield; Billy DeWolfe; Olga San Juan; Frank Faylen; ***D:*** Stuart Heisler; ***W:*** Arthur Sheekman; ***C:*** Charles B(ryant) Lang, Jr.

Blue Sky 🦴🦴🦴 **1991 (PG-13)** Carly Marshall (Lange) is an irrepressible beauty, long married to adoring but uptight military scientist Hank (Jones). Things are barely in control when they're stationed in Hawaii but after Hank's transfer to a backwater base in Alabama, Carly's emotional mood swings go wildly out of control. Hell truly breaks loose when Carly attracts the attention of the camp's commander (Boothe), who's only too willing to take advantage. Set in 1962, a nuclear radiation subplot (Hank's new project) proves a minor distraction. Exceptional performance by Lange with Jones providing a quiet counterpoint as a man still deeply in love with his disturbed wife. Director Richardson's final film. Release date was delayed to 1994 due to studio Orion's financial problems. **101m/C; VHS, DVD, Blu-Ray.** Jessica Lange; Tommy Lee Jones; Powers Boothe; Carrie Snodgress; Amy Locane; Chris O'Donnell; Mitchell Ryan; Dale Dye; Richard Jones; ***D:*** Tony Richardson; ***W:*** Arlene Sarner; Jerry Leichtling; Rama Laurie Stagner; ***C:*** Steve Yaconelli; ***M:*** Jack Nitzsche. Oscars '94: Actress (Lange); Golden Globes '95: Actress--Drama (Lange); L.A. Film Critics '94: Actress (Lange).

Blue Smoke 🦴🦴 **1/2** *Nora Roberts' Blue Smoke* **2007** After her family's pizzeria is destroyed by fire when she's 11, Reena grows up to become an arson investigator. A neighborhood reunion leads her to romance with carpenter Bo, but Reena soon discovers that fire is following her. Seems an arsonist is targeting everything—and everyone—she holds dear. Lifetime original movie based on the novel by Nora Roberts. **90m/C; DVD.** Alicia Witt; Matthew Settle; Scott Bakula; Talia Shire; John Reardon; Eric Keenleyside; Chris Fassbender; Ben Ayres; ***D:*** David Carson; ***W:*** Ronni Kern; ***C:*** Nikos Evdemon; ***M:*** Chris P. Bacon; Stuart M. Thomas. **CABLE**

Blue Spring 🦴🦴 **1/2** *Aoi haru* **2001** Social commentary on violence in the Japanese school system. A school that's used as a dumping ground for rejects, quickly becomes a training ground for the Yakuza. Two friends compete to be the leader of the school, and when one wins, the other quickly grows frustrated and begins a bloody war. **83m/C; DVD.** *JP* Ryuhei Matsuda; Hirofumi Arai; Sosuke Takaoka; Yusuke Oshiba; Yuta Yamazaki; Shugo Oshinari; Eita; Onimaru; Mame Yamada; ***D:*** Toshiaki Toyoda; ***W:*** Toshiaki Toyoda; Taiyo Matsumoto; ***C:*** Norimichi Kasamatsu; ***M:*** Richiro Manabe.

Blue State 🦴 **2007 (R)** Fervently liberal John (Meyer) drunkenly proclaims that he'll move to Canada if Dubya is elected POTUS and then feels he must follow through. He finds a green card marriage website and decides to travel to Winnipeg. Needing someone to share the driving, John meets secretive Chloe (Paquin), who has her own reasons for leaving the country. Tends toward one-sided diatribes and its views on Canadians vs. Americans are stereotypical and condescending. **99m/C; DVD.** Breckin Meyer; Anna Paquin; Richard Blackburn; Adriana O'Neill; Joyce Krenz; ***D:*** Marshall Lewy; ***W:*** Marshall Lewy; ***C:*** Phil Parmet; ***M:*** Nathan Johnson.

Blue Steel 🦴🦴 **1990 (R)** Director Bigelow's much-heralded, proto-feminist cop thriller. A serious female rookie's gun falls into the hands of a Wall Street psycho who begins a killing spree. Action film made silly with over-anxious sub-text and patriarchy-directed rage. **102m/C; VHS, DVD.** Jamie Lee Curtis; Ron Silver; Clancy Brown; Louise Fletcher; Philip Bosco; Elizabeth Pena; Tom Sizemore; ***D:*** Kathryn Bigelow; ***W:*** Kathryn Bigelow; Eric Red; ***M:*** Brad Fiedel.

Blue Story 🦴🦴 **2020 (R)** In Peckham, a violent, gang-infested borough of south London, friends Timmy (Odubola) and Marco (Ward) are divided by gang allegiance and territorialism. Timmy's life changes as he falls in love and grows more compassionate towards others. Marco has a violent older brother who pulls him deeper into gang life, darkening his perspective. When tragedy occurs, a cycle of vengeance, violence, and trauma unfolds. Energetic and restless, the complex yet uneven drama moves beyond its cautionary themes into Shakespearean tragedy complete with an effective Greek chorus provided by writer/director Onwubolu. **91m/C; DVD.** Stephen Odubola; Micheal Ward; Khali Best; Karla-Simone Spence; Eric Kofi-Abrefa; ***D:*** Rapman; ***W:*** Rapman; ***C:*** Simon Stolland; ***M:*** Jonathon Deering.

Blue Streak 🦴🦴 **1999 (PG-13)** Only hardcore Martin Lawrence fans will enjoy this formulaic buddy-cop-with-a-twist action comedy. Lawrence plays jewel thief Miles Logan, who hides a gem from his latest heist at a construction site just before he's caught. Three years later and out of jail, Logan tries to retrieve his diamond only to discover the site is now a police station. While impersonating a detective in order to sneak in and grab the stash, he accidentally catches an escaping felon and is forced to continue the charade. He's saddled with rookie partner Carlson (Wilson) and begins using his criminal knowledge to catch other crooks, including his old crony Tulley (Chappelle). Lawrence gives a good effort but all of his frantic mugging can't save the lame material he's forced to work with, making this feel like a poor man's "Beverly Hills Cop." **94m/C; VHS, DVD.** Martin Lawrence; Luke Wilson; Peter Greene; Dave Chappelle; William Forsythe; Graham Beckel; Tamala Jones; Nicole Ari Parker; Robert Miranda; Olek Krupa; Anne Marie Howard; ***D:*** Les Mayfield; ***W:*** Stephen Carpenter; Michael Berry; John Blumenthal; ***C:*** David Eggby.

Blue Sunshine 🦴🦴 **1/2 1978 (R)** A certain brand of L.S.D. called Blue Sunshine starts to make its victims go insane. **94m/C; VHS, DVD, Blu-Ray.** Zalman King; Deborah Winters; Mark Goddard; Robert Walden; Charles Siebert; Ann Cooper; Ray Young; Alice Ghostley; Richard Crystal; Bill Adler; Stefan Gierasch; Brion James; ***D:*** Jeff Lieberman; ***W:*** Jeff Lieberman; ***M:*** Charles Gross.

Blue Thunder 🦴🦴 **1/2 1983 (R)** Police helicopter pilot Scheider is chosen to test an experimental high-tech chopper that can see through walls, record a whisper, and level a city block. Seems anti-terrorist supercopter is needed to ensure security during 1984 Olympics. Bothered by Vietnam flashbacks, Scheider then battles wacky McDowell in the skies over L.A. High-techy police drama with satisfying aerial combat scenes nearly crashes with story line. **110m/C; VHS, DVD, Blu-Ray.** Roy Scheider; Daniel Stern; Malcolm McDowell; Candy Clark; Warren Oates; ***D:*** John Badham; ***W:*** Dan O'Bannon; Don Jakoby; ***C:*** John A. Alonzo.

Blue Tiger 🦴🦴 **1994 (R)** Gina Hayes (Madsen) is shopping with her young son when a masked gunman enters the store and opens fire. When Gina realizes her son has been killed she becomes obsessed with finding the assailant. Her one clue—a blue tiger tattoo. **88m/C; VHS, DVD.** Virginia Madsen; Toru Nakamura; Harry Dean Stanton; Ryo Ishibashi; ***D:*** Norberto Barba; ***W:*** Joel Soisson.

The Blue Tooth Virgin 🦴 **1/2 2009 (R)** Insider Hollywood talkfest. Struggling screenwriter Sam (Peck) is working on his latest pretentious and unproduced screenplay (the title of the movie itself). He gives it to his friend David (Johnson), a successful magazine editor, to read. David thinks it's terrible and Sam can't stand the slightest hint of criticism, with their rift eventually affecting Sam's personal life. **80m/C; DVD.** Austin Peck; Lauren Stamile; Bryce Johnson; Tom Gilroy; Roma Maffia; Amber Benson; Karen Black; ***D:*** Russell Brown; ***W:*** Russell Brown; ***C:*** Marco Fargnoli; ***M:*** Karen Black.

Blue Valentine 🦴🦴 **2010 (R)** Cianfrance's flick traces the frustration, anger, and dissolution of the marriage of Dean (Gosling) and Cindy (Williams) while offering flashbacks to happier times. They are a 'normal' couple—young, romantic and optimistic at first but Dean lacks ambition and likes to drink and Cindy turns sulky over their limited life and has trust issues that crop up. The story may hit too close for some while others will find the duo merely tiresome. Viewers of the NC17-rated version should not get too hot and bothered—it's for one semi-consensual sex scene that's more emotionally violent than anything else. **120m/C; Blu-Ray, On Demand.** Ryan Gosling; Michelle Williams; Mike Vogel; John Doman; Ben Shenkman; Faith Wladyka; Jen Jones; Maryann Plunkett; ***D:*** Derek Cianfrance; ***W:*** Derek Cianfrance; Joey Curtis; Cami Delavigne; ***C:*** Andrij Parekh; ***M:*** Grizzly Bear.

Blue Valley Songbird 🦴🦴 **1/2 1999** Leanne Taylor (Parton) ran away to Nashville to find singing success but is still struggling for national recognition after 15 years, thanks to her controlling manager-boyfriend Hank (Terry). When Leanne becomes interested in new band guitarist Bobby (Dean), he tells her she has the talent to become a star but Hank is holding her back and Leanne needs to make some changes. **91m/C; DVD.** Dolly Parton; John Terry; Billy Dean; Beth Grant; Kimberley Kates; *D:* Richard A. Colla; *W:* Ken Carter, Jr.; Annette Heywood-Carter; *C:* Rob Draper; *M:* Velton Ray Bunch. **TV**

Blue Velvet **1986 (R)** Disturbing, unique exploration of the dark side of American suburbia, involving an innocent college youth who discovers a severed ear in an empty lot, and is thrust into a turmoil of depravity, murder, and sexual deviance. Brutal, grotesque, and unmistakably Lynch; an immaculately made, fiercely imagined film that is unlike any other. Mood is enhanced by the Badalamenti soundtrack. Graced by splashes of Lynchian humor, most notably the movie's lumber theme. Hopper is riveting as the chief sadistic nutcase and Twin Peaks' MacLachlan is a study in loss of innocence. **121m/C; VHS, DVD, Blu-Ray.** Kyle MacLachlan; Isabella Rossellini; Dennis Hopper; Laura Dern; Hope Lange; Jack Nance; Dean Stockwell; George Dickerson; Brad Dourif; Priscilla Pointer; Angelo Badalamenti; *D:* David Lynch; *W:* David Lynch; *C:* Frederick Elmes; *M:* Angelo Badalamenti. Ind. Spirit '87: Actress (Rossellini); L.A. Film Critics '86: Director (Lynch), Support. Actor (Hopper); Montreal World Film Fest. '86: Support. Actor (Hopper); Natl. Soc. Film Critics '86: Cinematog., Director (Lynch), Film, Support. Actor (Hopper).

Blue, White and Perfect **1/2** **1942** Shayne (Nolan) promises his marriage-minded girlfriend Merle (Hughes) that he'll leave the PI business behind and get a steady wartime job. Only the shamus soon finds himself mixed-up in the smuggling of industrial diamonds that has Shayne taking an ocean liner to Hawaii and discovering espionage and Nazis aboard ship. **74m/B; DVD.** Lloyd Nolan; Mary Beth Hughes; George Reeves; Steven Geray; Helen Reynolds; Henry Victor; Curt Bois; Mae Marsh; Arthur Loft; *D:* Herbert I. Leeds; *W:* Samuel G. Engel; *C:* Glen MacWilliams.

Bluebeard **1/2 1944** Tormented painter with a psychopathic urge to strangle his models is the basis for this effective, low-budget film. One of Carradine's best vehicles. **73m/B; VHS, DVD.** John Carradine; Jean Parker; Nils Asther; *D:* Edgar G. Ulmer; *W:* Pierre Gendron; *C:* Jock Feindel.

Bluebeard **1/2 1972 (R)** Lady killer Burton knocks off series of beautiful wives in soporific remake of the infamous story. **128m/C; VHS, DVD.** Richard Burton; Raquel Welch; Joey Heatherton; Nathalie Delon; Virna Lisi; Sybil Danning; *D:* Edward Dmytryk; *W:* Edward Dmytryk; Ennio de Concini; Maria Pia Fusco; *C:* Gabor Pogany; *M:* Ennio Morricone.

Bluebeard *Barbe Bleue* **2009** In the 1950s, Catherine insists on reading the Charles Perrault folktale of the murderous Bluebeard to her sister and as she does the viewer sees it come alive onscreen. In the story, impoverished teenaged sisters Anne and Marie-Catherine have no dowries but that doesn't matter to local squire Bluebeard (probably because his previous wives were never seen again). Marie-Catherine agrees to the marriage and he has one rule: don't open the forbidden room while he is away. Of course, she can't resist. Breillat always adds a feminist twist to her pictures and this stylized fantasy is no exception. French with subtitles. **80m/C; On Demand.** *FR* Dominique Thomas; Lola Creton; Daphne Baiwir; Marilou Lopes-Benites; Lola Giovannetti; Farida Khelfa; Isabella Lapouge; *D:* Catherine Breillat; *W:* Catherine Breillat; *C:* Vilko Filac.

Bluebeard's Eighth Wife **1938** Problematic comedy set on the French Riviera about a spoiled millionaire (Cooper) who's been married seven times and wants to go for eight with Colbert, the daughter of a destitute aristocrat. Good for a few laughs, but Coop seemed out of place in his role. Based on the play by Alfred Savoir, American version by Charlton Andrews. **86m/B; VHS, DVD, Blu-Ray.** Claudette Colbert; Gary Cooper; David Niven; Edward Everett Horton; Elizabeth Patterson; Herman Bing; William Hymer; Franklin Pangborn; *D:* Ernst Lubitsch; *W:* Charles Brackett; Billy Wilder; *C:* Leo Tover; *M:* Werner R. Heymann; Frederick "Friedrich" Hollander.

Blueberry Hill **1/2 1988 (R)** While her mother struggles with the grief over husband's death, a young girl in a small town learns about life, music, and her late father from a jazz singer. Good soundtrack. **93m/C; VHS, Streaming.** Jennifer Rubin; Carrie Snodgress; Margaret Avery; *D:* Strathford Hamilton.

Bluebird **2013** Great performances and a delicate directorial touch ably help a story that feels like something seen a few too many times before. Edmands writes and directs this harrowing piece about a bus driver (the excellent Morton) who accidentally leaves a boy on her bus overnight in the dead of winter in Northern Maine. How does one get past such a tragic mistake? Can we forgive ourselves or expect others to do so? While Edmands avoids melodrama there's a sense of indie movie familiarity here that can't be shaken, but the great cast, also including Slattery and Martindale, justify a look. **90m/C; DVD.** Amy Morton; Louisa Krause; Margo Martindale; John Slattery; Emily Meade; Adam Driver; *D:* Lance Edmands; *W:* Lance Edmands; *C:* Jody Lee Lipes; *M:* Saunder Jurriaans; Danny Bensi.

A Blueprint for Murder **1/2 1953** Low-budget but well-done noir thriller. Whitney "Cam" Cameron (Cotten) becomes suspicious of his brother's attractive widow Lynne (Peters) when his young niece dies under strange circumstances (as did his brother). An autopsy reveals poisoning and Cam is convinced that Lynne wants to become the sole inheritor to her husband's estate and is going after her stepson next. Cam chases after Lynne, who's off on an ocean voyage, in order to prove she's a cold-blooded killer despite his attraction to her. **77m/B; DVD.** Joseph Cotten; Jean Peters; Freddy Ridgeway; Gary Merrill; Catherine McLeod; Jack Kruschen; Barney (Bernard) Phillips; *D:* Andrew L. Stone; *W:* Andrew L. Stone; *C:* Leo Tover; *M:* Lionel Newman.

Blues **2008** Urban thugs Chile and Head rob a convenience store and are spotted by a couple of cops. One calls for backup while the other chases the crooks straight into Pop Boudreaux's blues club. It becomes a hostage situation with manipulative Head trying to push follower Chile into escalating the violence while Pop tries to defuse the dangerous situation. **85m/C; DVD.** Henry Sanders; Ty Hodges; Steve Connell; Marcus Folmar; Peter Gail; Ari Graynor; Sydney Tamiia Poitier; Keith Ewell; *D:* Brandon Sonnier; *W:* Brandon Sonnier; *C:* Graham Futerfas; *M:* Chris(topher) Westlake. **VIDEO**

The Blues Brothers **1980 (R)** As an excuse to run rampant on the city of Chicago, Jake (Belushi) and Elwood (Aykroyd) Blues attempt to raise $5,000 for their childhood orphanage by putting their old band back together. Good music, quotable dialogue, lots of wrecked cars, plenty of cameos. A classic. **133m/C; VHS, DVD, Blu-Ray.** John Belushi; Dan Aykroyd; James Brown; Cab Calloway; Ray Charles; Henry Gibson; Aretha Franklin; Carrie Fisher; John Candy; Kathleen Freeman; Steven Williams; Charles Napier; Stephen Bishop; Murphy Dunne; ***Cameo(s):*** Frank Oz; Steven Spielberg; Twiggy; Paul (Peewee Herman) Reubens; Steve Lawrence; John Lee Hooker; John Landis; Chaka Khan; *D:* John Landis; *W:* Dan Aykroyd; John Landis; *C:* Stephen M. Katz; *M:* Ira Newborn; Elmer Bernstein.

Blues Brothers 2000 **1998 (PG-13)** Eighteen years after the original caper, Landis, Aykroyd, and most of the original cast return to the scene of the crime. Jake's died but Elwood's (Aykroyd) still around. He gets the band back together, recruits a Blues cousin (Goodman), a half-foster-brother (Morton), and an orphan (Bonifant) in need of mentoring, and heads for a battle of the bands between New Orleans and Chicago. The music, performed by the original Blues Brothers Band as well as a rock and blues all-star lineup, is the highlight. As for the rest of the flick, watch the original instead. Did Aykroyd learn nothing from "Caddyshack 2"? **123m/C; VHS, DVD, Blu-Ray.** Dan Aykroyd; John Goodman; Joe Morton; Evan Bonifant; Nia Peeples; Kathleen Freeman; Frank Oz; Steve Lawrence; Aretha Franklin; B.B. King; James Brown; Erykah Badu; Darrell Hammond; Paul Shaffer; Murphy Dunne; *D:* John Landis; *W:* Dan Aykroyd; John Landis; *C:* David Herrington; *M:* Paul Shaffer.

Blues in the Night **1941** Unusually downbeat story about struggling musicians. Jigger (Whorf) forms a jazz/blues group with pals Nickie (Kazan), Peppi (Halop), Leo (Carson), and Leo's wife Ginger (Lane), who's their singer. They're not making any dough touring so they accept the offer of gangster Del Davis (Nolan) to play at his New Jersey roadhouse, where they're also introduced to hard-boiled dame Kay (Field), who immediately causes trouble. Whorf and Kazan later became better-known as directors. Harold Arlen and Johnny Mercer wrote the Oscar-nominated title song. **89m/B; DVD.** Richard Whorf; Priscilla Lane; Betty Field; Elia Kazan; Jack Carson; Lloyd Nolan; Billy Halop; Wallace Ford; Peter Whitney; Howard de Silva; *D:* Richard Whorf; Anatole Litvak; *W:* Elia Kazan; Robert Rossen; *C:* Ernest Haller; *M:* Heinz Roemheld.

Blume in Love **1973 (R)** An ironic comedy/drama about a man who falls hopelessly in love with his ex-wife who divorced him for cheating on her while they were married. **115m/C; VHS, DVD.** George Segal; Susan Anspach; Kris Kristofferson; Shelley Winters; Marsha Mason; *D:* Paul Mazursky; *W:* Paul Mazursky; *C:* Bruce Surtees; *M:* Bill Conti.

BMX Bandits **1983** Three adventurous Aussie teens put their BMX skills to the test when they witness a crime and are pursued by the criminals. Much big air. **92m/C; VHS, DVD.** Nicole Kidman; David Argue; John Ley; Angelo D'Angelo; *D:* Brian Trenchard-Smith; *W:* Patrick Edgeworth.

Boa **2002 (R)** A prehistoric snake, 100 feet in length, makes a reappearance beneath a maximum security prison located in Antarctic. Warden Ryan (Wasson) calls for a rescue team, which includes paleontologists Robert (Cain) and his wife Jessica (Lackey). A handful of survivors try to make it from the prison to the plane but that's one hungry snake. **95m/C; VHS, DVD.** Dean Cain; Elizabeth Lackey; Grand L. Bush; Craig Wasson; Mark A. Sheppard; *D:* Phillip J. Roth; *W:* Phillip J. Roth; Terry Neish; *C:* Todd Barron; *M:* Rich McHugh. **VIDEO**

Boa vs. Python **2004 (R)** A hunter imports a gigantic mutant python for a paid hunt for rich dilettantes outside Philly, and inevitably it runs amok. The FBI is called in since they obviously have giant-monster herding under their jurisdiction, and they 'borrow' a giant technologically enhanced snake from a local mad scientist to fight monster with monster. **92m/C; DVD, Streaming.** *BL US* David Hewlett; Jaime Bergman; Kirk B.R. Woller; Adamo Palladino; Angel Boris Reed; *D:* David Flores; *W:* Chase Parker; Sam Wells; *C:* Lorenzo Senatore; *M:* Jamie Christopherson. **CABLE**

Boarding Gate **2007 (R)** It's not a good movie by any means but there's super-confident Argento in black undies, stiletto heels, and holding a gun to keep your interest. Bad girl Sandra used to be involved in a kinky sex and business relationship with shady American financier Miles (a menacing Madsen). She's now working for a shady import firm run by dragon lady Sue (Lin) and her husband Lester (Ng) and doing drug smuggling on the side for some quick cash. Sandra's also doing Lester and when he finds out about the drug deals, he pressures her into a murder-for-hire of Miles and a quick exit to Hong Kong. Why do these plans never go as expected? English, French and Chinese with subtitles. **93m/C; DVD.** *FR* Asia Argento; Michael Madsen; Joana Preiss; Alex Descas; Kim Gordon; Kelly Lin; Carl Ng; *D:* Olivier Assayas; *W:* Olivier Assayas; *C:* Yorick Le Saux; *M:* Brian Eno.

Boarding House **1983 (R)** Residents of a boardinghouse discover sinister doings in the basement. It does not occur to any of them to move to another house. **90m/C; VHS, DVD.** Hank Adly; Kalassu; Alexandra Day; *D:* John Wintergate.

Boarding School *The Passion Flower Hotel* **1983 (R)** Basic teen sex comedy about students at a proper Swiss boarding school for girls who devise a plan to seduce the boys at a nearby school by posing as prostitutes. Kinski stars as the American girl who masterminds the caper. **100m/C; VHS, DVD.** *GE* Nastassja Kinski; *D:* Andre Farwagi.

Boarding School **1/2 2018 (R)** In 1990s Brooklyn, 12-year-old Jacob (Prael) has screaming night terrors and is caught dancing in his recently deceased grandmother's clothing. Because of his behavior, he is sent to a strange boarding school run by the disturbing Dr. Sherman (Patton) and his wife (Blanchard). There are seven other students, who also have been left there by their parents and have something odd about them. As terrifying events unfold, Jacob learns that the school is full of evil. This horror-filled coming of age story has interesting ideas that are not put together particularly well. **101m/C; DVD.** Luke Prael; Samantha Mathis; David Aaron Baker; Michael Wilkes; Barbara Kingsley; *D:* Boaz Yakin; *W:* Boaz Yakin; *C:* Mike Simpson; *M:* Lesley Barber.

Boardinghouse Blues **1948** A showbiz musical centered around a boarding house with tenant troubles. It's an excuse for popular black entertainers of the day to perform, including Lucky Millinder, Bull Moose Jackson, Una Mae Carlisle, and Stumpy and Stumpy. **90m/C; VHS, DVD.** Dusty Fletcher; Moms (Jackie) Mabley; *D:* Josh Binney.

Boardwalk **1/2 1979** Manipulative drama has elderly diner owner David Rosen (Strasberg) and his ailing wife Becky (Gordon) living in a rapidly-declining Coney Island neighborhood. Gang leader Strut (Delgado) demands protection money from the local merchants but David won't pay. Escalating threats, violence, and family problems dominate. **98m/C; DVD, Blu-Ray.** Lee Strasberg; Ruth Gordon; Janet Leigh; Kim Delgado; Eddie Barth; Joe Silver; *D:* Stephen Verona; *W:* Stephen Verona; Leigh Chapman; *C:* Billy Williams.

The Boat Is Full *Das Boot Ist Voll* **1981** A group of refugees pose as a family in order to escape from Nazi Germany as they seek asylum in Switzerland. Available in German with English subtitles or dubbed into English. **104m/C; VHS, DVD, Blu-Ray.** *SI* Tina Engel; Curt Bois; Renate Steiger; Mathias Gnaedinger; Hans Diehl; Martin Walz; Gerd David; *D:* Markus Imhoof; *W:* Markus Imhoof; *C:* Hans Liechti. Berlin Intl. Film Fest. '81: Director (Imhoof).

Boat Trip **WOOF! 2003 (R)** Isn't it about time for Gooding, Jr. to give back his Oscar? Or at least fire his agent? In this pathetic attempt at comedy, he's Jerry, a lovesick guy distraught over a failed relationship. To the rescue comes his buddy Nick (Sanz), a loud-mouth skirt chaser who suggests a singles cruise. When Nick insults the travel agent, they're sent on a gay cruise, where Jerry falls for the ship's choreographer Gabrielle (Sanchez) and must pretend to be gay to win her. Yep, it's as crappy as it sounds. Gooding, Jr. tries hard, but he can't bail out this floater, which is aimed straight at the rocks of a cliche-ridden and spectacularly unfunny script and direction that wouldn't make the cut on a third-rate sitcom. **95m/C; VHS, DVD, UMD.** Cuba Gooding, Jr.; Horatio Sanz; Roselyn Sanchez; Vivica A. Fox; Maurice Godin; Roger Moore; Lin Shaye; Victoria Silvstedt; Richard Roundtree; Will Ferrell; Artie Lange; Bob Gunton; Jennifer Gareis; *D:* Mort Nathan; *W:* Mort Nathan; William Bigelow; *C:* Shawn Maurer; *M:* Robert Folk.

The Boatniks **1/2 1970 (G)** An accident-prone Coast Guard ensign finds himself in charge of the "Times Square" of waterways: Newport Harbor. Adding to his already "titanic" problems is a gang of ocean-going jewel thieves who won't give up the ship! **99m/C; VHS, DVD, Blu-Ray.** Robert Morse; Stefanie Powers; Phil Silvers; Norman Fell; Wally Cox; Don Ameche; Kelly Thordsen; *D:* Norman Tokar; *M:* Robert F. Brunner.

Bob & Carol & Ted & Alice **1/2 1969 (R)** Two California couples have attended a trendy therapy session and, in an attempt to be more in touch with sexuality, resort to applauding one another's extramarital affairs and swinging. Wacky and well-written, this is a farce on free love and psycho-speak. Mazursky's directorial debut. **104m/C; VHS, DVD, Blu-Ray.** Natalie Wood; Robert Culp; Dyan Cannon; Elliott Gould; *D:* Paul Mazursky; *W:* Paul Mazursky; Larry Tucker; *C:* Charles B(ryant) Lang, Jr.; *M:* Quincy Jones. N.Y. Film Critics '69: Screenplay, Support. Actress (Cannon); Natl. Soc. Film Critics '69: Screenplay; Writers Guild '69: Orig. Screenplay.

Bob Funk **1/2 2009 (R)** Overly-earnest comedy. Mrs. Funk (Zabriskie) demotes eldest son Bob (Campbell) to the family futon company's janitor because his booze and broads lifestyle interferes with his work. She then hires ad exec Ms. Thorne (Cook) and depressed Bob suddenly gets a spark of interest in turning his life around. **90m/C; DVD.** Michael Leydon Campbell; Rachael Leigh Cook; Grace Zabriskie; Amy Ryan; Edward Jemison; Stephen (Steve) Root; Robert Canada; Lucy Davis; ***D:*** Craig Carlisle; ***W:*** Craig Carlisle; ***C:*** Lisa Wiegand; ***M:*** Tim Montijo. **VIDEO**

Bob le Flambeur *Bob the Gambler* **1955** Aging Bob (Duchesne) is a down-on-his-luck gambler who visits the Deauville Casino with his friend Roger (Garret), who just happens to know croupier Jean (Cerval). Informed that the casino safe is bursting with cash, Bob decides to have a final fling by robbing the casino. Low-budget, bittersweet crime comedy. French with subtitles. **97m/B; VHS, DVD, Blu-Ray.** *FR* Roger Duchesne; Isabel Corey; Daniel Cauchy; Howard Vernon; Gerard Buhr; Guy Decomble; ***D:*** Jean-Pierre Melville; ***W:*** Jean-Pierre Melville; Auguste Le Breton; ***C:*** Henri Decae; ***M:*** Jean Boyer; Eddie Barclay.

Bob Roberts **1992 (R)** Excellent pseudo-documentary satire about a 1990 Pennsylvania senatorial race between Robbins' titular right-wing folk singer/entrepreneur versus Brickley Paiste's (Vidal) aging liberal incumbent. Roberts seems like a gee-whiz kinda guy but he'll stop at nothing to get elected and he knows a lot about political dirty tricks and, even more important, manipulating the media to get what he wants. Robbins directorial debut turned out to be very timely in view of the 1992 Clinton/Bush presidential campaign. Features a number of cameos. Line to remember: "Vote first. Ask questions later." **105m/C; VHS, DVD.** Tim Robbins; Giancarlo Esposito; Ray Wise; Rebecca Jenkins; Harry J. Lennix; John Ottavino; Robert Stanton; Alan Rickman; Gore Vidal; Brian Murray; Anita Gillette; David Strathairn; Susan Sarandon; James Spader; John Cusack; Fred Ward; Pamela Reed; Jack Black; Tom Atkins; Helen Hunt; Peter Gallagher; Lynne Thigpen; Bingo O'Malley; Kathleen Chalfant; Matthew Faber; Matt McGrath; Jeremy Piven; Steve Pink; Fisher Stevens; Bob Balaban; Allan Nicholls; June Stein; Adam Simon; Ned Bellamy; Robert Hegyes; Lee Arenberg; Natalie Strong; Merilee Dale; ***D:*** Tim Robbins; ***W:*** Tim Robbins; ***C:*** Jean Lepine; ***M:*** David Robbins.

Bob the Butler ½ **2005 (PG)** Harmless fluff stars the usually obnoxious Green as perennial loser Bob Tree, who can't keep a job. His latest career attempt is attending butler school. His first placement is with neurotic Anne (Shields), who fired him when he was Bob the babysitter. Still, the single mom is desperate and hires Bob to look after her house and two exasperating children (Buechner, Smith), who decide the butler is better than mom's current boyfriend. **90m/C; DVD.** *GB CA* Tom Green; Brooke Shields; Benjamin Smith; Simon Callow; Genevieve Buechner; Rob LeBelle; ***D:*** Gary Sinyor; ***W:*** Gary Sinyor; Jane Walker Wood; Steven Manners; ***C:*** Jason Lehel; ***M:*** David A. Hughes. **VIDEO**

Bobbie Jo and the Outlaw ½ **1976 (R)** Wonderwoman Carter is a bored carhop who yearns to be a country singer. She becomes involved with Marjoe, who fancies himself as a contemporary Billy the Kid. Together, they do their Bonnie and Clyde thing, to a significantly lesser dramatic effect than the original, though a glut of violence keeps the bodies dropping. **89m/C; VHS, DVD, Blu-Ray.** Lynda Carter; Marjoe Gortner; Jesse Vint; ***D:*** Mark L. Lester.

Bobbie's Girl **2002** Meandering drama long on theatrics and short on sense. American Bailey (Peters) and her lover, Englishwoman Bobbie (Ward) run a pub in a seaside town near Dublin, assisted by Bailey's brother David (Silverman). Bobbie is diagnosed with breast cancer at the same time she learns that her estranged brother and his wife have died and their 10-year-old son, Alan (Sangster), is orphaned into Bobbie's care. Bobbie and Alan are naturally struggling to cope with their situations while eccentrics (they're both ex-actors) Bailey and David try to provide encouragement. **100m/C; VHS, DVD.** Bernadette Peters; Rachel Ward; Jonathan Silverman; Thomas Brodie-Sangster; ***D:*** Jeremy Paul Kagan; ***W:*** Samuel Bernstein; ***C:*** Ciaran Tanham; ***M:*** Bruce Broughton. **CABLE**

Bobbikins WOOF! 1959 Insufferably cute, one-joke Brit comedy. Ben Barnaby (Bygraves) gets out of the Navy and tries to resurrect his showbiz career without any luck. So toddler son Bobbikins (who only talks to Ben) gives dad some advice and then some stock tips, leading to the family's sudden wealth. Having money adversely affects Ben so the tyke decides they need to be poor again. **89m/B; DVD.** *UK* Max Bygraves; Shirley Jones; Billie Whitelaw; Barbara Shelley; Lionel Jeffries; ***D:*** Robert Day; ***W:*** Oscar Brodney; ***C:*** Geoffrey Faithfull; ***M:*** Philip Green.

Bobby ½ **2006 (R)** Writer-director Emilio Estevez uses a star-studded cast to compare turbulent events of the '60s with modern problems, with mixed results. This homage to Robert F. Kennedy uses multiple storylines and characters that revolve around L.A.'s Ambassador Hotel on the day leading up to RFK's assassination. Estevez liberally sprinkles the stories of no less than twenty-two characters surrounding the imminent tragedy, including the hotel beautician (Stone), her cheating husband (Macy) and a couple soon to be married (Lohan, Wood). The characters aren't allowed to achieve much depth, and the performances are hit and miss. The impact of the assassination drives home the trivialities of the characters and reinforces the loss of RFK, who only appears in archival footage. **119m/C; DVD.** Anthony Hopkins; Harry Belafonte; William H. Macy; Sharon Stone; Christian Slater; Freddy Rodriguez; Laurence Fishburne; Demi Moore; Martin Sheen; Helen Hunt; Lindsay Lohan; Elijah Wood; Nick Cannon; Heather Graham; Ashton Kutcher; Shia LaBeouf; Brian Geraghty; Joshua Jackson; David Krumholtz; Emilio Estevez; Mary Elizabeth Winstead; Jacob Vargas; Joy Bryant; Svetlana Metkina; ***D:*** Emilio Estevez; ***W:*** Emilio Estevez; ***C:*** Michael Barrett; ***M:*** Mark Isham.

Bobby Deerfield **1977 (PG)** Cold-blooded Grand Prix driver comes face to face with death each time he races, but finally learns the meaning of life when he falls in love with a critically ill woman. Even with race cars, soap opera stalls. **124m/C; VHS, DVD, Blu-Ray.** Al Pacino; Marthe Keller; Anny (Annie Legras) Duperey; Romolo Valli; ***D:*** Sydney Pollack; ***W:*** Alvin Sargent; ***C:*** Henri Decae; ***M:*** Dave Grusin.

Bobby Jones: Stroke of Genius ½ **2004 (PG)** Bloated homage to the late great golfer of the title starring a red-hot post-"Passion" Caviezel. Practically a natural, Jones, who still reigns as the only golfer to win all four major tournaments in a single calendar year, had to overcome a number of personal demons to become one of the greatest golfers in the world. An extremely moral man, Jones suffered from depression and sported a legendary temper that he battled in order to work his way to the top of golf world of the 1920s. After his Grand Slam coup, Jones was diagnosed with a spinal disorder and retired from golf at 28 to practice law and spend more time with wife Mary (Forlani). Historically faithful and elegant, with a fine performance by its star, but is hindered by sub-par script, formulaic plot, and undeveloped supports. **126m/C; DVD.** James (Jim) Caviezel; Claire Forlani; Jeremy Northam; Malcolm McDowell; Connie Ray; Brett Rice; Dan Albright; Larry Thompson; Paul Freeman; John Curran; Aidan Quinn; Alistair Begg; Kenny Alfonso; Tom Arcuragi; Devon Gearhart; Thomas Lewis; Hilton McRae; ***D:*** Rowdy Herrington; ***W:*** Rowdy Herrington; Tony Depaul; Bill Pryor; ***C:*** Tom Stern; ***M:*** James Horner.

Bobby Z *Let's Kill Bobby Z; The Life and Death of Bobby Z* **2007 (R)** Lots of action and limited acting required. Con Tim Kearney (Walker) agrees to DEA agent Tad Gruszka's (Fishburne) plan to pass himself off as missing surfer/drug dealer Bobby Z in order to get paroled. Seems drug lords are holding Gruszka's partner hostage and they'll trade for Bobby. Things go wrong and Kearney goes on the lam with Bobby's ex-lover (Wilde) and his young son (Villareal). Based on "The Death and Life of Bobby Z" by Don Winslow. **97m/C; DVD.** Paul Walker; Laurence Fishburne; Olivia Wilde; Joaquim Almeida; J.R. Villarreal; Jason Lewis; Jacob Vargas; Jason Flemyng; Keith Carradine; Chuck Liddell; ***D:*** John Herzfeld; ***W:*** Bob Krakower; Allen Lawrence; ***M:*** Timothy S. (Tim) Jones.

The Bobo ½ **1967** Lousy bullfighter tries to lure a gorgeous woman into romance. Filmed in Spain and Italy. **103m/C; VHS, DVD.** *GB* Peter Sellers; Britt Ekland; Rossano Brazzi; Adolfo Celi; ***D:*** Robert Parrish; ***W:*** David R. Schwartz.

Boccaccio '70 **1962** Three short bawdy/comedy/pageant-of-life films inspired by "The Decameron," each pertaining to ironically twisted sexual politics in middle class life. A fourth story, "Renzo and Luciana," by Mario Monicelli, has been cut. Dubbed. **145m/C; VHS, DVD, Blu-Ray.** *IT* Anita Ekberg; Romy Schneider; Tomas Milian; Sophia Loren; Peppino de Filippo; Luigi Gillianni; ***D:*** Vittorio De Sica; Luchino Visconti; Federico Fellini; ***W:*** Luchino Visconti; Federico Fellini; Tullio Pinelli; Ennio Flaiano; Cesare Zavattini; ***C:*** Otello Martelli; Giuseppe Rotunno; ***M:*** Nino Rota; Armando Trovajoli.

Bodied **2017 (R)** A satirical comedy about battle rap, black culture, and race relations. Calum Worthy plays Adam, a nerdy-looking white grad student writing his thesis on battle rap and the use of the n-word, who discovers an untapped talent for competing. Like the battles themselves, this award-winner is crude and offensive but ultimately entertaining and provocative. Features several real-life battle rappers, including Dizaster, Dumbfoundead, and Hollow da Don. **120m/C; DVD, Blu-Ray.** Calum Worthy; Jackie Long; Rory Uphold; Jonathan Park; Walter Perez; ***D:*** Joseph Kahn; ***W:*** Alex Larsen; ***C:*** Matt Wise; ***M:*** Bryan Kei Mantia; Melissa Reese.

Bodies, Rest & Motion **1993 (R)** Stagnant 20-something movie in which four young people basically do nothing in the sun-baked town of Enfield, Arizona. Similar to the movie "Singles," but without the Seattle grunge scene. The title's reference to Newton is fitting: "A body in rest or motion remains in that state unless acted upon by an outside force." Appealing cast is wasted in listless film that's content to just drift along. Based on the play by Roger Hedden. **94m/C; VHS, DVD.** Phoebe Cates; Bridget Fonda; Tim Roth; Eric Stoltz; Scott Frederick; Scott Johnson; Alicia Witt; Rich Wheeler; Peter Fonda; ***D:*** Michael Steinberg; ***W:*** Roger Hedden; ***C:*** Bernd Heinl; ***M:*** Michael Convertino.

The Body **2001 (PG-13)** Would-be religious thriller with wooden acting, laughable dialog, and clunky plot. In modern-day Jerusalem, Israeli archeologist Sharon Golban (Williams) checks out a tomb discovered beneath a shop and finds the skeleton of a crucified man. Could it be the remains of Jesus? When word reaches the Vatican, Cardinal Pesci (Wood) dispatches Father Matt Gutierrez (Banderas) to deal with the provocative situation. **108m/C; VHS, DVD.** Antonio Banderas; Olivia Williams; John Wood; John Shrapnel; Derek Jacobi; Jason Flemyng; Makram Khoury; Vernon Dobtcheff; Ian McNeice; ***D:*** Jonas McCord; ***W:*** Jonas McCord; ***C:*** Vilmos Zsigmond; ***M:*** Serge Colbert.

Body ½ **2015** Berk & Olsen deliver a low-budget thriller that Hitch would have liked. Three young ladies are bored over Christmas break. After hanging out and drinking a few, they go to a house that one of them claims to have access to, but she's not telling the whole truth. When they're interrupted by someone in the house, a scuffle ensues, and the man falls down the stairs. He may be dead. What do they do now? It's a tight, almost-all-one setting with strong performances from young actors and the kind of pacing needed from the best thrillers. Fun and clever. **75m/C; DVD.** Helen Rogers; Alexandra Turshen; Lauren Molina; Larry Fessenden; Adam Cornelius; ***D:*** Dan Berk; Robert Olsen; ***W:*** Dan Berk; Robert Olsen; ***C:*** Matt Mitchell; ***M:*** Luke Allen.

Body and Soul **1924** The first screen appearance of Robeson has him cast in a dual role as a conniving preacher and his good brother. The preacher preys on the heroine, making her life a misery. Objections by censors to the preacher's character caused him to be redeemed and become worthy of the heroine's love. **102m/B; Silent; VHS, DVD, Blu-Ray.** Paul Robeson; Julia Theresa Russell; Mercedes Gilbert; ***D:*** Oscar Micheaux. Natl. Film Reg. '19.

Body and Soul ½ *An Affair of the Heart* **1947** Charlie Davis (Garfield) is a Jewish boxer whose parents want him to quit the ring and get an education. Instead, he rises quickly to the top, thanks in part to gangster "protector" Roberts (Goff). After becoming a champ, Charlie starts the inevitable downward slide. One-time pro-welterweight Lee plays boxing rival Ben. A vintage '40s boxing film that defines the genre. Remade in 1981 with Leon Isaac Kennedy. **104m/B; VHS, DVD, Blu-Ray.** John Garfield; Lilli Palmer; Hazel Brooks; Anne Revere; William Conrad; Canada Lee; Joseph Pevney; Lloyd Goff; ***D:*** Robert Rossen; ***W:*** Abraham Polonsky; ***C:*** James Wong Howe; ***M:*** Hugo Friedhofer. Oscars '47: Film Editing.

Body & Soul ½ **1981 (R)** Interesting remake of 1947 gem about a boxer who loses his perspective in the world of fame, fast cars, and women. **109m/C; VHS, DVD.** Leon Isaac Kennedy; Jayne Kennedy; Peter Lawford; Muhammad Ali; Perry Lang; ***D:*** George Bowers.

Body & Soul **1993** After spending 16 years as a cloistered nun in a Welsh convent, with vows of poverty, celibacy, and obedience, Anna Gibson (Scott Thomas) must return to the outside world. Following her brother's suicide, Anna is forced to deal with his pregnant widow (Redman) and two children and her family's failing Yorkshire mill. Anna suffers a crisis of faith as both the secular and the religious exert their strong influences and she's drawn as well to two very different men—younger Hal (Mavers), the mill's supervisor, and divorced bank manager Daniel Stern (Bowe). Based on the 1991 novel by Marcelle Bernstein; British TV miniseries. **312m/C; VHS, DVD.** *GB* Kristin Scott Thomas; Amanda Redman; Gary Mavers; Anthony Valentine; Sandra Voe; John Bowe; Dorothy Tutin; Patrick Allen; ***D:*** Moira Armstrong; ***W:*** Paul Hines; ***C:*** Peter Middleton; ***M:*** Jim Parker.

Body and Soul **1998 (R)** Cliched remake of the familiar boxing saga that finds ambitious boxer Mancini and his manager Chiklis heading for a potential championship bout in Reno. Mancini might still have the boxing moves but he's certainly no amateur and his professionalism is actually a deterrent. **95m/C; VHS, DVD.** Ray "Boom Boom" Mancini; Michael Chiklis; Rod Steiger; Joe Mantegna; Jennifer Beals; Tahnee Welch; ***D:*** Sam Henry Kass; ***W:*** Sam Henry Kass; ***C:*** Arturo Smith; ***M:*** David Waters. **CABLE**

Body Armor ½ **1996 (R)** Special agent Conway (McColm) is recruited by an ex-girlfriend (Schofield) to find a missing scientist. This leads our hero to nutball virologist Dr. Krago (Perlman) who's using germ warfare for personal gain. For the action junkie (who doesn't mind a little eye candy as well). **95m/C; VHS, DVD.** Matt McColm; Ron Perlman; Annabel Schofield; Carol Alt; Clint Howard; Morgan Brittany; Shauna O'Brien; ***D:*** Jack Gill; ***W:*** Jack Gill; ***C:*** Robert Hayes; ***M:*** Mark Holden. **VIDEO**

Body Armour ½ **2007** Maybe it was a good excuse for the actors to enjoy the Spanish sunshine, because it's not much of a movie. Secret Service agent John's (Schweiger) career is ruined when the presidential nominee he's guarding gets blown up by a car bomb. Three years later, ex-agent John reluctantly accepts a bodyguard job in Barcelona and learns his client is the man responsible—international assassin Maxwell (Palminteri) who's turned on his associates and become a government witness. They want him dead (and so does John). **90m/C; DVD.** Til Schweiger; Chazz Palminteri; Lluis Homar; Gustavo Salmeron; Cristina Brondo; ***D:*** Gerry Lively; ***W:*** Ken Lamplugh; John Weidner; ***C:*** Christof Wahl; ***M:*** Jose Mora. **VIDEO**

Body at Brighton Rock ½ **2019 (R)** An amateurish attempt at a survivalist thriller. Rookie park ranger Wendy stumbles upon a dead body in the backcountry and has to guard the crime scene alone overnight. Dumdum protagonists are a hallmark of horror flicks, but Wendy here might take the cake. Dancing on the trail, poking a bear den, taking selfies on a precipice...a six-year-old Girl Scout would have better wilderness sense than this so-called pro. The directing and editing are downright bizarre, from the sitcom-style opening credits to the laughable bear scene to the unclear ending. Aside from the scenery, it's all bad, but not campy enough to be fun. **87m/C; DVD.** Karina Fontes; Casey Adams; Emily Althaus; Miranda Bailey; Martin Spanjers; ***D:*** Roxanne Benjamin; ***W:***

Roxanne Benjamin; *C:* Hannah Getz; *M:* The Gifted.

Body Bags 🦴🦴 1/2 *John Carpenter Presents Body Bags* **1993 (R)** Three gory, though humorous, stories hosted by horrormeister Carpenter as your friendly local coroner. "The Gas Station" finds the young female overnight attendent menaced by a psycho. "Hair" is about a balding yuppie who'll do anything for a full head of hair. Then he meets the sinister Dr. Lock and his magical new-hair growth treatment. The grisly "Eye" concerns a ballplayer who loses the aforementioned appendage and finds that his transplanted eyeball, taken from an executed serial killer, is subject to ghastly visions. Several fellow horror directors have cameos. **95m/C; VHS, DVD, Blu-Ray.** Alex Datcher; Robert Carradine; Stacy Keach; David Warner; Mark Hamill; Twiggy; John Agar; Deborah Harry; Sheena Easton; David Naughton; John Carpenter; ***Cameo(s):*** Wes Craven; Sam Raimi; Roger Corman; Tobe Hooper; *D:* Tobe Hooper; John Carpenter; *W:* Billy Brown; Dan Angel; *M:* John Carpenter; Jim Lang. **CABLE**

The Body Beneath WOOF! *Vampire's Thirst* **1970** A living-dead ghoul survives on the blood of innocents and is still preying on victims today. **85m/C; VHS, DVD.** Gavin Reed; Jackie Skarvellis; Susan Heard; Colin Gordon; *D:* Andy Milligan.

Body Chemistry 🦴 **1990 (R)** A married sexual-behavior researcher starts up a passionate affair with his lab partner. When he tries to end the relationship, his female associate becomes psychotic. You've seen it all before in "Fatal Attraction." And you'll see it again in "Body Chemistry 2." **84m/C; VHS, DVD.** Marc Singer; Mary Crosby; Lisa Pescia; Joseph Campanella; David Kagen; *D:* Kristine Peterson; *W:* Jackson Barr; Thom Babbes; *C:* Phedon Papamichael; *M:* Terry Plumeri.

Body Chemistry 2: Voice of a Stranger 🦴 1/2 **1991 (R)** An ex-cop (Harrison) obsessed with violent sex gets involved with a talk-radio psychologist (Pescia) whose advice could prove deadly in this erotic sequel. **84m/C; VHS, DVD.** Gregory Harrison; Lisa Pescia; Morton Downey, Jr.; Robin Riker; Jeremy Piven; John Landis; *D:* Adam Simon; *W:* Jackson Barr; Christopher Wooden; *C:* Richard Michalak; *M:* Nigel Holton.

Body Chemistry 3: Point of Seduction 🦴🦴 **1993 (R)** TV producer Alan Clay (Stevens) finds himself caught in a business and sexual triangle when he okays the making of a movie about the life of a TV sex therapist (Shattuck). Seems the lady's lovers have a nasty habit of getting murdered which doesn't prevent Clay from getting personally involved. His actress wife (Fairchild), who wants to star in the movie, is not pleased. Lives up to its title. **90m/C; VHS, DVD.** Andrew Stevens; Morgan Fairchild; Shari Shattuck; *D:* Jim Wynorski; *W:* Jackson Barr; *C:* Don E. Fauntleroy; *M:* Chuck Cirino.

Body Chemistry 4: Full Exposure 🦴 1/2 **1995 (R)** When sex psychologist Claire Archer (Tweed) is accused of murder she hires Simon Mitchell (Poindexter), the best criminal defense attorney around. But Simon becomes just a little too closely involved with his possibly psycho client and it could cost him not only his career and marriage but his life. Also available unrated. **89m/C; VHS, DVD.** Shannon Tweed; Larry Poindexter; Andrew Stevens; Chick Vennera; Larry Manetti; Stella Stevens; *D:* Jim Wynorski; *W:* Karen Kelly; *C:* Zoran Hochstatter; *M:* Paul Di Franco.

Body Count 🦴 1/2 *The 11th Commandment* **1987** A weird and wealthy family will stop at nothing, including murder and cannibalism, to enhance their fortune. Rather than bodies, count the minutes 'til the movie's over. **90m/C; VHS, Streaming.** Marilyn Hassett; Dick Sargent; Steven Ford; Greg Mullavey; Thomas Ryan; Bernie (Bernard) White; *D:* Paul Leder.

Body Count 🦴 1/2 **1995 (R)** Professional killer Makoto (Chiba) and his partner Sybil (Nielsen) seek revenge on the New Orleans cops who set them up. Opposing them are special crime unit partners, Eddie Cook (Davi) and Vinnie Rizzo (Bauer). Lots of shootouts and macho bravado. **93m/C; VHS, DVD.** Sonny Chiba; Brigitte Nielsen; Robert Davi; Steven Bauer; Jan-Michael Vincent; Talun Hsu; *D:* Talun Hsu; *W:* Henry Madden; *C:* Blake T. Evans; *M:* Don Peake.

Body Count 🦴🦴 **1997 (R)** Fiorentino and Caruso are reteamed (after "Jade") in a crime saga about a heist gone bad. There is no honor among thieves as driver Hobbs (Caruso) learns when he plans a job with some unreliable associates at the Boston Museum of Fine Arts and things go very wrong. The gang decide to drive to Miami in order to sell their ill-gotten gains, squabbling all the way. Then mystery woman Natalie (Fiorentino) comes aboard, to cause more friction between the gun-happy boys. **84m/C; VHS, DVD, Blu-Ray.** David Caruso; Linda Fiorentino; John Leguizamo; Ving Rhames; Donnie Wahlberg; Forest Whitaker; *D:* Robert Patton-Spruill; *W:* Theodore Witcher; *C:* Charles Mills; *M:* Curt Sobel. **VIDEO**

Body Count 🦴🦴 *Below Utopia* **1997 (R)** Daniel (Theroux) takes fiancee Suzanne (Milano) home to meet his wealthy family and they just happen to be out of the line of immediate mayhem when a gang of thieves (led by Ice-T) break in to steal the family art collection. Now, they're playing a very serious game of hide-and-seek in order to stay alive—only the situations isn't as clear as it seems. **88m/C; VHS, DVD.** Ice-T; Alyssa Milano; Justin Theroux; Tommy (Tiny) Lister; Jeannette O'Connor; Nicholas Walker; Eric Saiet; Marta Kristen; Ron Harper; Robert Pine; Richard Danielson; *D:* Kurt Voss; *W:* David Diamond; *C:* Denis Maloney; *M:* Joseph Williams. **VIDEO**

Body Double 🦴🦴🦴 **1984 (R)** A voyeuristic unemployed actor peeps on a neighbor's nightly disrobing and sees more than he wants to. A grisly murder leads him into an obsessive quest through the world of pornographic films. **114m/C; VHS, DVD, Blu-Ray.** Craig Wasson; Melanie Griffith; Gregg Henry; Deborah Shelton; Guy Boyd; Dennis Franz; David Haskell; Rebecca Stanley; Barbara Crampton; Mindi Miller; *D:* Brian De Palma; *W:* Brian De Palma; Robert J. Avrech; *C:* Stephen Burum; *M:* Pino Donaggio. Natl. Soc. Film Critics '84: Support. Actress (Griffith).

Body Heat 🦴🦴🦴 1/2 **1981 (R)** During a Florida heat wave, a none-too-bright lawyer becomes involved in a steamy love affair with a mysterious woman and then in a plot to kill her husband. Hurt and Turner (in her film debut) became stars under Kasdan's direction (the three would reunite for "The Accidental Tourist"). Hot love scenes supplement a twisting mystery with a suprise ending. Rourke's arsonist and Danson's soft shoe shouldn't be missed. **113m/C; VHS, DVD, Blu-Ray.** William Hurt; Kathleen Turner; Richard Crenna; Ted Danson; Mickey Rourke; J.A. Preston; Kim Zimmer; Jane Hallaren; *D:* Lawrence Kasdan; *W:* Lawrence Kasdan; *C:* Richard H. Kline; *M:* John Barry.

The Body in the Library 🦴 1/2 *Agatha Christie's Miss Marple: The Body In the Library* **1984** A Miss Marple mystery, based on Agatha Christie's 1942 novel, involving the septuagenarian detective investigating the murder of a young woman in a wealthy British mansion. **155m/C; VHS, DVD.** *GB* Joan Hickson; Gwen Watford; Valentine Dyall; Moray Watson; Frederick Jaeger; Raymond Francis; *D:* Silvio Narizzano; *W:* T.R. Bowen; *C:* John Walker; *M:* Alan Blaikley. **TV**

Body Language 🦴🦴 1/2 **1995 (R)** Criminal defense attorney Gavin St. Claire (Berenger) falls for a topless dancer (Schanz), which leads him into all sorts of trouble, including murder. **95m/C; VHS, DVD.** Tom Berenger; Heidi Schanz; Nancy Travis; *D:* George Case.

Body Melt 🦴🦴 1/2 **1993** When a crazed doctor unleashes an experimental drug on an unsuspecting town, the residents begin to literally melt away. **82m/C; VHS, DVD, Blu-Ray.** *AU* Gerard Kennedy; Andrew Daddo; Ian Smith; Vincent (Vince Gill) Gil; Regina Gaigalas; *D:* Philip Brophy; *W:* Philip Brophy; Rod Bishop; *M:* Philip Brophy.

Body of Evidence WOOF! **1992 (R)** Bad movie with pretensions takes "Basic Instinct" a step further. Instead of an ice pick and sex, sex itself is used as the weapon in a murder trial featuring Madonna as the defendant, Dafoe as her lawyer, and Mantegna as the prosecutor. The plot is, of course, secondary to the S&M sex scenes with Dafoe which feature hot wax and broken glass. Madonna's lack of performance is the least of the film's problems since everyone seems to have forgotten any acting talent they possess. Director Edel fails to direct—the film even looks bad. "Body" was the subject of another NC-17 ratings flap but this film shouldn't be seen by anybody. An unrated version is also available. **99m/C; VHS, DVD, Blu-Ray.** Madonna; Willem Dafoe; Joe Mantegna; Anne Archer; Michael Forest; Charles Hallahan; Mark Rolston; Richard Riehle; Julianne Moore; Frank Langella; Jurgen Prochnow; Stan Shaw; *D:* Uli Edel; *W:* Brad Mirman; *C:* Doug Milsome; *M:* Graeme Revell. Golden Raspberries '93: Worst Actress (Madonna).

Body of Influence 🦴🦴 **1993 (R)** A Beverly Hills psychiatrist gets overly involved with a beautiful female patient. But she not only wants his love—she wants his life. Also available in an unrated version. **96m/C; VHS, DVD.** Nick Cassavetes; Shannon Whirry; Sandahl Bergman; Don Swayze; Anna Karin; Catherine Parks; Diana Barton; Richard Roundtree; *D:* Andrew Garroni; *W:* David Schreiber.

Body of Influence 2 🦴 **1996 (R)** Shrink Dr. Benson (Anderson) finds he's using his couch for more than professional purposes with his latest patient, Leza (Fisher), whose seductive charms prove more than the doc can handle. The unrated version is 94 minutes. **88m/C; VHS, DVD.** Daniel Anderson; Jodie Fisher; Steve Poletti; Jonathan Goldstein; Pat Brennan; *D:* Brian J. Smith; *W:* Brian J. Smith; *C:* Azusa Ohno; *M:* Ron Sures.

Body of Lies 🦴🦴 1/2 **2008 (R)** Crowe packed on the pounds and sports a southern-fried accent in another collaboration with director Scott, this time as veteran CIA operative Ed Hoffman, the stateside handler of field agent Roger Ferris (DiCaprio), who's hot on the trail of a terrorist leader in Jordan and plans to infiltrate his network. But Hoffman seems to have his own agenda, leaving Ferris to wonder whom he can trust. Fraught with formulaic post-9/11, Middle Eastern terrorist v. American spy genre cliches (satellite images, chases/explosions in the local bazaar, frantic yelling into cell phones), and elements of suspense feel manufactured by heavy doses of convoluted double-crosses. Crowe's convincing portrayal of amorality, however, props up what is an otherwise pointless rehash of the evening news. Based on the 2007 novel by David Ignatius. **129m/C; Blu-Ray, On Demand.** Leonardo DiCaprio; Russell Crowe; Mark Strong; Carice van Houten; Golshifteh Farahani; Vince Colosimo; Michael Gaston; Oscar Isaac; Simon McBurney; Alon Aboutboul; *D:* Ridley Scott; *W:* William Monahan; *C:* Alexander Witt; *M:* Marc Streitenfeld.

Body Parts 🦴🦴 **1991 (R)** A crime psychologist loses his arm in an auto accident and receives a transplant from an executed murderer. Does the limb have an evil will of its own? Poorly paced horror goes off the deep end in gore with its third act. Based on the novel "Choice Cuts" by French writers Pierre Boileau and Thomas Narcejac, whose work inspired some of the greatest suspense films. **88m/C; VHS, DVD, Blu-Ray.** Jeff Fahey; Kim Delaney; Lindsay Duncan; Peter Murnik; Brad Dourif; Zakes Mokae; James Kidnie; Paul Ben-Victor; *D:* Eric Red; *W:* Eric Red; Norman Snider; Patricia Herskovic; *C:* Theo van de Sande; *M:* Loek Dikker.

Body Parts 🦴 **1994** For fans of the demented dismemberer niche. Body Parts, a sleazy skin club, loses some of its star talent when the strippers start turning up in cameo video appearances. Seems there's a psycho killer on the loose who videotapes the dismemberment of his stripper-victims. The police decide they've got to meet this guy when he sends them a sample of his work. **90m/C; VHS, DVD.** Clement von Franckenstein; Dick Monda; Johnny Mandel; Teri Marlow; *D:* Michael Paul Girard; *W:* Michael Paul Girard; *M:* Miriam Cutler.

Body Rock WOOF! **1984 (PG-13)** Brooklyn breakdancer Lamas deserts his buddies to work at a chic Manhattan nightclub. Watching Lamas as the emcee/breakdancing fool is a hoot. **93m/C; VHS, DVD.** Lorenzo Lamas; Vicki Frederick; Cameron Dye; Michelle Nicastro; Ray Sharkey; Grace Zabriskie; Carole Ita White; *D:* Marcelo Epstein.

The Body Shop WOOF! *Doctor Gore* **1972** Unorthodox love story in which a man decides to patch up his relationship with his dead wife by piecing together her dismembered body. For lovers only. Under "Doctor Gore" title the film includes an intro by horror director Herschell Gordon Lewis. **91m/C; VHS, DVD.** Pat Patterson; Jenny Driggers; Roy Mehaffey; Linda Faile; Candy Furr; *D:* Pat Patterson.

Body Shot 🦴🦴 1/2 **1993 (R)** Celebrity shutterbug Mickey Dane (Patrick) is fingered in the murder of a rock star after it turns out he did a kinky layout for a look-alike. When police find out he had an obsession for the dead woman, he employs his photographic expertise in the search for the real killer. Effective tension-builder with fast-paced chases through the seamy side of Los Angeles. **98m/C; VHS, DVD.** Robert Patrick; Michelle Johnson; Ray Wise; Jonathan Banks; Kim Miyori; Kenneth Tobey; Charles Napier; *D:* Dimitri Logothetis; *W:* Robert Strauss; *C:* Nicholas Josef von Sternberg; *M:* Cliff Magness.

Body Shots 🦴 1/2 **1999 (R)** An ensemble cast of twentysomethings explores sex and dating while traversing L.A.'s nightlife. Eight friends come to reflect on their hedonistic lifestyles when Sara (Reid) accuses macho football player Michael (O'Connell) of date rape. During the ultimate "he said/she said" battle, wafer-thin declarations on love in the '90s are made by characters who are as appealing as root canal surgery. **102m/C; VHS, DVD.** Sean Patrick Flanery; Jerry O'Connell; Amanda Peet; Tara Reid; Ron Livingston; Emily Procter; Brad Rowe; Sybil Temchen; *D:* Michael Cristofer; *W:* David McKenna; *C:* Rodrigo Garcia; *M:* Mark Isham.

Body Slam 🦴 1/2 **1987 (PG)** A small-time talent monger hits it big with a rock and roll/professional wrestling tour. Piper's debut; contains some violence and strong language. **100m/C; VHS, DVD.** Roddy Piper; Capt. Lou Albano; Dirk Benedict; Tanya Roberts; Billy Barty; Charles Nelson Reilly; John Astin; Wild Samoan; Tonga Kid; Barry J. Gordon; *D:* Hal Needham; *W:* Steven H. Burkow; *M:* John D'Andrea.

The Body Snatcher 🦴🦴🦴 1/2 **1945** Based on Robert Louis Stevenson's story about a grave robber who supplies corpses to research scientists. Set in Edinburgh in the 19th century, this Lewton production is superior. One of Karloff's best vehicles. **77m/B; VHS, DVD, Blu-Ray.** Edith Atwater; Russell Wade; Rita (Paula) Corday; Boris Karloff; Bela Lugosi; Henry Daniell; Sharyn Moffett; Donna Lee; *D:* Robert Wise; *W:* Philip MacDonald; Val Lewton; *C:* Robert De Grasse.

Body Snatchers 🦴🦴 **1993 (R)** Yet another version of "Invasion of the Body Snatchers." An innocent family arrive at an Army base which turns out to be infested with pod people. This time around the heroine is angst-ridden teenager Marti (Anwar) and the pods have something to do with a mysterious toxic spill. The 1978 remake was well done; this so-so version takes advantage of the advances in special effects (particularly in Anwar's bathtub scene) and sound technology but is slow-paced with few jolts of terror. **87m/C; VHS, DVD, Blu-Ray.** Gabrielle Anwar; Meg Tilly; Terry Kinney; Forest Whitaker; Billy Wirth; R. Lee Ermey; Reilly Murphy; *D:* Abel Ferrara; *W:* Stuart Gordon; Dennis Paoli; Nicholas St. John; *C:* Bojan Bazelli; *M:* Joe Delia.

Body Strokes 🦴 *Siren's Kiss* **1995** Blocked artist Leo Kessler (Johnston) is aroused by the wild fantasies of his beautiful models Beth (Knittle) and Claire (Weber). But it's just fantasy and it also helps get Leo's marriage back on track when manager/wife Karen (Beck) gets jealous. Also available unrated. **99m/C; VHS, DVD.** Bobby Johnston; Dixie Beck; Kristen Knittle; Catherine Weber; *D:* Edward Holzman; *W:* April Moskowitz; *C:* Kim Haun; *M:* Richard Bronskill.

Body Trouble 🦴 1/2 *Joker's Wild* **1992 (R)** After being attacked by sharks while vacationing in the Caribbean, a man washes ashore in Miami and then somehow makes his way to New York City. There he meets Vera Vin Rouge and her friends Cinnamon,

Spice, Paprika, and Johnny Zero, a gangster. Zero decides he doesn't like the man, so he chases him back to the Caribbean. Supposedly this all happens in only one day. Hmmm... **98m/C; VHS, DVD.** Dick Van Patten; Priscilla Barnes; Frank Gorshin; James Hong; Marty Rackham; Michael Unger; Jonathan Soloman; Brit Helfer; Leigh Clark; Patricia Cardell; Richie Barathy; ***D:*** Bill Milling; ***W:*** Bill Milling.

The Bodyguard 1/2 **1976 (R)** The Yakuza, Japan's mafia, and New York's big crime families face off in this martial arts extravaganza. **89m/C; VHS, DVD.** *JP* Sonny Chiba; Aaron Banks; Bill Louie; Judy Lee; Etsuko (Sue) Shihomi; ***D:*** Maurice Sarli.

The Bodyguard **1992 (R)** Buttoned-down, ex-Secret Service agent turned private bodyguard reluctantly takes on a wildly successful singer/actress as a client. Houston, in her acting debut as the over-indulged diva, doesn't have to stretch too far but acquits herself well. Costner has really bad hair day but easily portrays the tightly wound Frank. Critically trashed, a boxoffice smash, and too long. Originally scripted by producer Kasdan over a decade ago, with Steve McQueen in mind. Predictable romantic melodrama is kept moving by the occasional sharp dialog and a few action pieces. Songs include the smash hit "I Will Always Love You," written and originally performed by Dolly Parton. **130m/C; VHS, DVD.** Kevin Costner; Whitney Houston; Gary Kemp; Bill Cobbs; Ralph Waite; Tomas Arana; Michele Lamar Richards; Mike Starr; Christopher Birt; DeVaughn Nixon; Charles Keating; Robert Wuhl; ***Cameo(s):*** Debbie Reynolds; ***D:*** Mick Jackson; ***W:*** Lawrence Kasdan; ***C:*** Andrew Dunn; ***M:*** Alan Silvestri. MTV Movie Awards '93: Song ("I Will Always Love You").

The Bodyguard 1/2 **2004** Wong Kom (Pechtai Wongkamlao) is a bodyguard who is fired after his client dies. Realizing the people who murdered his client will now want to murder his son to prevent him from inheriting the family business, he places the boy in hiding while he tries to sort things out. Thai humor doesn't translate well to other nationalities, and unless you have a fairly thorough knowledge of their society, it won't make sense. Unfortunately for this film, the comedy takes precedence over the action, so many audiences will be left scratching their heads. **100m/C; DVD.** *TH* Petchthai Wongkamlao; Pumwaree Yodkamol; ***D:*** Petchthai Wongkamlao; ***W:*** Petchthai Wongkamlao; ***C:*** Nattawut Kittikhun; ***M:*** Hip-Pro.

The Bodyguard 2 **2007** In this prequel to the first film, Khumlao (Pechtai Wongkumlao) is an anti-terrorist agent posing as a singer to catch the criminal owners of a record label. Like the first film it has cameos or uses much of the crew from 'Ong-Bak'. Unlike the first one, they tried to make the humor more accessible to a non-Thai audience. **95m/C; DVD.** *TH* Petchthai Wongkamlao; Jacqueline Apitananon; Sushin Kuan-Saghuan; Surachai Sombutchareon; Janet Khiew; ***D:*** Petchthai Wongkamlao; ***W:*** Petchthai Wongkamlao; ***C:*** Jiradech Samneeyongsana; ***M:*** Lullaby Music Production.

The Bodyguard from Beijing 1/2 *The Defender; Zhong Nan Hai Bao Biao* **1994** Beijing bodyguard John Chang (Li) is hired to protect pampered rich girl Michelle (Chung), who's the witness to a murder. And John also has to deal with the revenge plans of an ex-soldier whose brother John has killed. Cantonese with subtitles. **90m/C; VHS, DVD.** *CH* Jet Li; Christy Chung; Kent Cheng; Collin Chou; ***D:*** Corey Yuen; ***W:*** Gordon Chan; Kin-Chung Chan; ***C:*** Tom Lau.

Bodywork *Body Work* **1999 (R)** Virgil Guppy (Matheson) buys a second-hand Jaguar that gives him nothing but trouble, especially when he finds a dead prostitute in the trunk of the car. Virgil goes on the run and hides out with a young woman (Coleman) who's a professional car thief. British crime caper finally has too many twists for its own good. The Winslet who plays Virgil's girlfriend is the sister of actress Kate. **93m/C; VHS, DVD.** *GB* Hans Matheson; Charlotte Coleman; Clive Russell; Beth Winslet; ***D:*** Gareth Rhys Jones; ***W:*** Gareth Rhys Jones; ***C:*** Thomas Wuthvich; ***M:*** Dusan Kojic; Srdjan Kurpjel.

Boeing Boeing 1/2 **1965** A dated but still amusing sex farce about a bachelor newspaperman (Curtis) in Paris, his three stewardess girlfriends, and the elaborate plots he resorts to in trying to keep them from finding out about each other. When the new Boeing jet makes air travel faster all Curtis' schemes may come crashing down. Ritter is fun as the exasperated housekeeper and Lewis amazingly subdued as Curtis' business rival. **102m/C; VHS, DVD, Blu-Ray.** Tony Curtis; Jerry Lewis; Dany Saval; Christiane Schmidtmer; Suzanna Leigh; Thelma Ritter; ***D:*** John Rich; ***W:*** Edward Anhalt.

Boesman & Lena 1/2 **2000** Adaptation of the apartheid-era play by Athol Fugard follows the travails of downtrodden couple, Boesman (Glover) and Lena (Bassett). Their shanty town home in Cape Town has been bulldozed by the government so they take to the dusty road with their meager belongings, constantly bickering about their plight. The couple construct a makeshift abode for the night, which attracts the attention of an old man (Jonah) even lower on the economic ladder, whom Lena allows to stay to Boesman's displeasure. Performances are outstanding. Last film for director Berry. **86m/C; VHS, DVD.** *FR* Danny Glover; Angela Bassett; Willie Jonah; ***D:*** John Berry; ***W:*** John Berry; ***C:*** Alain Choquart; ***M:*** Wally Badarou.

Bog **1984 (PG)** Boggy beast from the Arctic north awakens to eat people. Scientists mount an anti-monster offensive. **90m/C; VHS, DVD.** Gloria De Haven; Marshall Thompson; Leo Gordon; Aldo Ray; Glen Voros; Ed Clark; Carol Terry; ***D:*** Don Keeslar; ***W:*** Carl Kitt; ***C:*** Jack Willoughby; ***M:*** Bill (William) Walker.

Boggy Creek II 1/2 *The Barbaric Beast of Boggy Creek, Part II* **1983 (PG)** The continuing saga of the eight-foot-tall, 300 pound monster from Texarkana. Third in a series of low-budget movies including "The Legend of Boggy Creek" and "Return to Boggy Creek." **93m/C; VHS, DVD.** Charles B. Pierce; Cindy Butler; Serene Hedin; ***D:*** Charles B. Pierce; ***W:*** Charles B. Pierce.

Bogus **1996 (PG)** Aptly named fantasy-comedy has orphan Albert (Osment) sent to foster aunt Harriet (Goldberg) after his magician's assistant mom (Travis) dies in a car accident. He brings along an imaginary friend, the eponymous Bogus (Depardieu) to ease the transition. Harriet is your typical workaholic easterner and isn't too thrilled with the arrangement. Goldberg and Depardieu are fine, but predictability drains most of the magic. **112m/C; VHS, DVD, Blu-Ray.** Whoopi Goldberg; Gerard Depardieu; Haley Joel Osment; Nancy Travis; Andrea Martin; Denis Mercier; Ute Lemper; Sheryl Lee Ralph; Al Waxman; Fiona Reid; Don Francks; ***D:*** Norman Jewison; ***W:*** Alvin Sargent; ***C:*** David Watkin; ***M:*** Marc Shaiman.

The Bogus Witch Project **2000 (R)** In the long and ignoble history of cheap parodies, this is surely one of the cheapest. It's a series of short films—sketches and blackouts, really—that use the premise of the original "Blair Witch" film to poke fun at the movie biz. Here's the preface to one: "In August 1999, three out-of-work actors disappeared in the woods near Sherman Oaks, California, while looking for Blair Underwood to give him a script. Twenty-four hours later, their footage was found and turned into a vehicle for shameless self-promotion." The episode starring Pauly Shore is the weakest of the weak. Funnier bits appear between spoofs. **85m/C; DVD.** Pauly Shore; Michael Ian Black; ***D:*** Victor Kargan; ***M:*** Carvin Knowles.

Bohemian Girl **1936** The last of Laurel and Hardy's comic operettas finds them as guardians of a young orphan (Hood, famous for her roles in the Our Gang comedies), whom no one realizes is actually a kidnapped princess. **74m/B; VHS, DVD.** Stan Laurel; Oliver Hardy; Mae Busch; Darla Hood; Julie Bishop; Thelma Todd; James Finlayson; ***D:*** James W. Horne.

Bohemian Rhapsody 1/2 **2018 (PG-13)** A biopic of the rock band Queen and its legendary lead singer Freddie Mercury, culminating with their performance at 1985's Live Aid concert. Rami Malek absolutely embodies Mercury's vulnerability, showmanship, and dental issues. But condensing 2+ decades of a superstar band's rise and success into 2+ hours of film is challenging, which makes it all the harder to fathom why so much screentime is devoted to Mercury's hetero relationship with Mary Austin, unless it was to present Freddie as more palatable for a PG-13 audience. The film's good outweighs the bad, but just barely. **134m/C; DVD, Blu-Ray, Streaming.** *UK US* Rami Malek; Lucy Boynton; Gwilym Lee; Ben Hardy; Joseph Mazzello; ***D:*** Bryan Singer; ***W:*** Anthony McCarten; Peter Morgan; ***C:*** Newton Thomas (Tom) Sigel; ***M:*** John Ottman. Oscars '18: Actor (Malek), Film Editing, Sound, Sound FX Editing; British Acad. '18: Actor (Malek), Sound; Golden Globes '19: Actor--Drama (Malek), Film--Drama; Screen Actors Guild '18: Actor (Malek).

Boiler Room **2000 (R)** Basic plot about a greedy naive young man caught up in a situation that's out of his control gets the high testosterone treament. Seth (Ribisi) jumps at the chance to become a trainee at an up-and-coming brokerage firm filled with macho twentysomethings greedy for success. But what Seth eventually discovers is that the firm he's allied himself with runs an illegal stock-trading operation that's under investigation. Well-cast and stylish, with Affleck effective in a small role as the firm's strutting recruiter. **120m/C; VHS, DVD, Blu-Ray.** Giovanni Ribisi; Vin Diesel; Nicky Katt; Nia Long; Scott Caan; Ron Rifkin; Jamie Kennedy; Taylor Nichols; Tom Everett Scott; Ben Affleck; Jon Abrahams; Kirk Acevedo; ***D:*** Ben Younger; ***W:*** Ben Younger; ***C:*** Enrique Chediak.

Boiling Point 1/2 **1932** Lawman proves once again that justice always triumphs. **67m/B; VHS, DVD.** Hoot Gibson; Helen Foster; Wheeler Oakman; Skeeter Bill Robbins; Billy Bletcher; Lafe (Lafayette) McKee; Charles Bailey; George "Gabby" Hayes; ***D:*** George Melford; ***W:*** Donald W. Lee; ***C:*** Tom Galligan; Harry Neumann.

Boiling Point *3x Jugatsu* **1990** Masaki (Ono) is a young, inarticulate, misfit, loser gas-station attendent who even lets down his local baseball team when he tries to play ball. Then he makes the mistake of slugging a yakuza member, so he heads to Okinawa to buy a gun to defend himself and meets up with the ultimate Mr. Cool—Uehara (Kitano). Uehara is such a bad ass even the yakuza don't want anything to do with him, so who better than the master to teach Masaki how to survive. The Japanese title refers to a baseball score, which somehow seems more apt. Japanese with subtitles. **98m/C; VHS, DVD, Blu-Ray.** *JP* Takeshi "Beat" Kitano; Masahiko Ono; Hisashi Igawa; ***D:*** Takeshi "Beat" Kitano; ***C:*** Katsumi Yanagishima.

Boiling Point 1/2 **1993 (R)** Darkly flavored action drama delves into the personalities of its two main characters before setting up a final confrontation. Treasury agent Jimmy Mercer (Snipes) is trying to solve his partner's murder, relentlessly pursuing the murderers in cold and methodical fashion. Sleazy Red Diamond (Hopper), just out of prison, owes the mob and has one week to pay them back. Lawman and crook both come home to women, (Davidovich and Perrine) graduates of the Hollywood school of female martyrdom, selflessly supportive of their men. Grim but cliched. Adapted from the Gerald Petievich novel "Money Men." **93m/C; VHS, DVD.** Wesley Snipes; Dennis Hopper; Lolita Davidovich; Viggo Mortensen; Dan Hedaya; Valerie Perrine; Seymour Cassel; Jonathan Banks; Tony LoBianco; Christine Elise; James Tolkan; Paul Gleason; ***D:*** James B. Harris; ***W:*** James B. Harris; ***C:*** King Baggot; ***M:*** Cory Lerios; John D'Andrea.

Bojangles 1/2 **2001** Made-for-cable biopic of Bill "Bojangles" Robinson is strictly a by-the-numbers affair from the beginning at the funeral to the various characters who turn and address the camera to explain what they thought of the contradictory man. Gregory Hines does his usual excellent job in the lead, and the film looks very good. **101m/C; VHS, DVD.** Gregory Hines; Peter Riegert; Kimberly Elise; Savion Glover; Maria Ricossa; ***D:*** Joseph Sargent; ***W:*** Richard Wesley; Robert P. Johnson; ***C:*** Donald M. Morgan; ***M:*** Terence Blanchard. **CABLE**

The Bold Caballero 1/2 *The Bold Cavalier* **1936** Rebel chieftain Zorro overthrows oppressive Spanish rule in the days of early California. **69m/B; VHS, DVD.** Robert "Bob" Livingston; Heather Angel; Sig Rumann; Robert Warwick; ***D:*** Wells Root.

Bolero 1/2 **1982** Beginning in 1936, this international epic traces the lives of four families across three continents and five decades, highlighting the music and dance that is central to their lives. **173m/C; VHS, DVD.** James Caan; Geraldine Chaplin; Robert Hossein; Nicole Garcia; Jacques Villeret; ***D:*** Claude Lelouch; ***W:*** Claude Lelouch.

Bolero WOOF! *Bolero: An Adventure in Ecstasy* **1984 (R)** What sounds like a wet dream come true is really just a good snooze: Bo Derek plays a beautiful young woman who goes on a trip around the world in hopes of losing her virginity; in Spain, she meets a bullfighter who's willing to oblige. Too bad Bo cannot act as good as she looks. **106m/C; VHS, DVD, Blu-Ray.** Bo Derek; George Kennedy; Andrea Occhipinti; Anna (Ana Garcia) Obregon; Olivia D'Abo; ***D:*** John Derek; ***W:*** John Derek; ***M:*** Peter Bernstein; Elmer Bernstein. Golden Raspberries '84: Worst Actress (Derek), Worst Director (Derek), Worst New Star (D'Abo), Worst Picture, Worst Screenplay.

Bollywood Hero 1/2 **2009** Kattan parodies himself and his acting career. Frustrated by his lack of leading roles, he impulsively agrees to travel to India to star in a Bollywood production for a brother-sister team who are trying to revive their father's film studio. The dance numbers are bright but Kattan's character is a whiner and the story lacks surprises. **168m/C; DVD.** Chris Kattan; Pooja Kumar; Julian Sands; Ali Fazal; Rachna Shah; Neha Dhupia; ***Cameo(s):*** Maya Rudolph; Keanu Reeves; ***D:*** Bill Bennett; Ted Skillman; ***W:*** Laurie Parres; Benjamin Brand; ***C:*** Tobias Hochstein; ***M:*** David Bergeaud; Niels Bye Nielsen. **CABLE**

Bolt 1/2 **2008 (PG)** On his hit action TV series, German Shepherd Bolt (voiced by Travolta) has superpowers to crush his arch enemy, Dr. Calico, and save his owner, Penny (voiced by Cyrus). However, having spent his entire life on the studio lot, he doesn't realize that he's just another canine actor, and not a superhero. A series of accidents leaves Bolt homeless on the streets of New York, while Penny is back in Hollywood. Convinced that the evil Dr. Calico has kidnapped his owner, Bolt, along with his two new friends, the reluctant alley cat Mittens and overeager hamster Rhino, sets out for a journey across the country to save the day. The first Disney animated feature to come out since Pixar guru John Lasseter traded teams. He wisely blends smart jokes with Disney's classic animated storytelling traditions, rather than trying to one-up his former employer's spastic cool factor. **96m/C; Blu-Ray, On Demand.** Malcolm McDowell; James Lipton; Greg Germann; ***V:*** John Travolta; Susie Essman; Mark Walton; Miley Cyrus; ***D:*** Chris Williams; Byron Howard; ***W:*** Chris Williams; Dan Fogelman; ***M:*** John Powell.

Boltneck 1/2 *Big Monster on Campus; Teen Monster* **1998** When school outcast Karl becomes the victim of a hazing by jocks, nerdy Frank Stein (get it?) decides to try an experiment in re-animating the dead. But unknown to Frank, the brain he's used (which he stole from his father's lab—how convenient) is that of a mass killer and the new Karl has developed quite an attitude. **92m/C; VHS, DVD.** Justin Walker; Ryan Reynolds; Christine Lakin; Bianca Lawson; Kenny Blank; Judge Reinhold; Shelley Duvall; Charles Fleischer; Matthew Lawrence; Richard Moll; ***D:*** Mitch Marcus; ***W:*** Dave Payne; ***M:*** Roger Neill. **VIDEO**

Bomb Squad *Cold Night Into Dawn* **1997** Suicidal terrorist has a nuclear bomb small enough to fit into a suitcase and has decided to make Chicago his target. The Feds have 24-hours to find and defuse it. **91m/C; VHS, DVD.** Anthony Michael Hall; Michael Ironside; Tony LoBianco; ***D:*** Serge Rodnunsky; ***W:*** Serge Rodnunsky. **VIDEO**

Bomb the System WOOF! **2005 (R)** A trio of young artists conduct nightly "bombings" in New York City, covering available spaces with their graffiti signatures. In sync with the subculture, their paint is always stolen, although they do pay for their drugs. One of the outlaws is continually nagged by his mother to take the art scholarship he was offered in San Francisco, but he's deaf to her pleadings. There are run-ins with the law, some girlfriend situations and self-righteous speeches thrown into the mix but one never feels much sympathy toward the rebel-with-a-cause premise because truly they're just low-life druggie vandals. **93m/C; DVD.** Mark Webber; Gano Grills; Jade Yorker; Jaclyn DeSantis; Joey Dedio; Stephan Buchanana; Bonz Malone; Donna Mitchell; Al Sapienza; Kumar Pallana; ***D:*** Adam Bhala Lough; ***W:*** Adam Bhala Lough; ***C:*** Ben Kutchins; ***M:*** El-P.

Bomba and the Hidden City ♪ 1/2 **1950** In this mishmash of a plot, Bomba witnesses the assassination of the ruler of a tribal kingdom. Zita, the rightful heir, loses her memory from trauma and is raised in secret (as Leah) until evil ruler Hassan wants to marry the girl. Bomba, who's her friend, wants to put things right. 4th in the series. **71m/B; DVD.** John(ny) Sheffield; Sue England; Paul Guilfoyle; Smoki Whitfield; ***D:*** Ford Beebe; ***W:*** Carroll Young; ***C:*** William Sickner.

Bomba and the Jungle Girl ♪ 1/2 **1952** Orphaned Bomba wants to know more about his parents, which leads him to the tribe they were working with. The chief and his daughter act very suspiciously and he's secretly told they're usurpers and killed both the tribe's true chieftain and his parents! Bomba gets help finding where their bodies are buried and retrieving his dad's diary, which will reveal the truth. 8th in the series. **70m/B; DVD.** John(ny) Sheffield; Martin Wilkins; Suzette Harbin; Walter Sande; Karen Sharpe; Leonard Mudie; ***D:*** Ford Beebe; ***W:*** Ford Beebe; ***C:*** Harry Neumann; ***M:*** Raoul Kraushaar.

Bomba on Panther Island ♪ 1/2 **1949** Bomba (who's not on an island) is tracking a man-eating black panther when he's sidetracked by developer Robert Maitland and his sister, Judy, who are starting a farm. 2nd in the Monogram series. **70m/B; DVD.** John(ny) Sheffield; Allene Roberts; Harry Lewis; Charles Irwin; Smoki Whitfield; ***D:*** Ford Beebe; ***W:*** Ford Beebe; ***C:*** William Sickner.

Bomba, the Jungle Boy ♪♪ **1949** Monogram Pictures 12-pic jungle adventure series starring a teenaged Sheffield (who had outgrown his role in the "Tarzan" films), based on the books by the pseudonymous Roy Rockwood. Bomba was raised by a now-deceased naturalist in the African jungle. George Harland and his daughter Pat have come to photgraph the wildlife when Pat gets lost. Bomba finds her and then must return her to her father while surving locust swarms,dangerous animals, and other adventures. **70m/B; DVD.** John(ny) Sheffield; Peggy Ann Garner; Onslow Stevens; Charles Irwin; Smoki Whitfield; ***D:*** Ford Beebe; ***W:*** Jack DeWitt; ***C:*** William Sickner.

Bombardier ♪♪ 1/2 **1943** A group of cadet bombardiers discover the realities of war on raids over Japan during WWII. Also available colorized. **99m/B; VHS, DVD.** Pat O'Brien; Randolph Scott; Robert Ryan; Eddie Albert; Anne Shirley; Barton MacLane; ***D:*** Richard Wallace.

Bombay Mail ♪ 1/2 **1934** A great example of a Universal Studio B movie, set on the train from Calcutta to Bombay and offering a multiple murder mystery with appearances of all the usual exotic suspects, from Indian mystics to eccentric scientists to larger than life opera singers, all with witty and adroit dialogue. **70m/B; DVD.** Edmund Lowe; Shirley Grey; Onslow Stevens; Ralph Forbes; John Davidson; ***D:*** Edwin L. Marin; ***W:*** Tom Reed; Lawrence G. Blochman; ***C:*** Charles Stumar; ***M:*** Heinz Roemheld.

Bombay Talkie ♪♪ 1/2 **1970 (PG)** A bored British writer (Kendal) heads to India to gather "experiences" and becomes involved with an Indian movie actor (Kapoor). Early clash-of-cultures film from Merchant Ivory has it's dull spots; the behind-the-scenes look at the Indian film industry is more interesting than the romance. **110m/C; VHS, DVD.** *IN* Jennifer Kendal; Shashi Kapoor; Zia Mohyeddin; Aparna Sen; ***D:*** James Ivory; ***W:*** Ruth Prawer Jhabvala.

Bomber ♪♪ **2009** Bittersweet family drama. Lazy son Ross becomes the unwilling chauffeur for his aged parents' long-planned road trip to Germany where WWII vet Alistar wants to see the village on which he dropped bombs during his first RAF mission. However, Alistar is an exasperating curmudgeon and when he finds no resolution, his wife Valerie is finally fed-up and Ross must reluctantly play marriage counselor. **84m/C; DVD.** *US GB* Benjamin Whitrow; Shane Taylor; Eileen Nicholas; ***D:*** Paul Cotter; ***W:*** Paul Cotter; ***C:*** Rick Siegel; ***M:*** Stephen Coates.

Bombers B-52 ♪♪ **1957** Chuck Brennan (Malden) has worked 20 years as a ground-crew chief for the Air Force and his daughter Lois (Wood) is encouraging him to retire. While Chuck decides, he tries to discourage the budding romance between Lois and commanding officer Jim Herlihy (Zimbalist), whom he distrusts. Predictable plot is all a backdrop for the showcase of various planes, especially the B-52 Superfortress. **106m/C; DVD.** Natalie Wood; Karl Malden; Efrem Zimbalist, Jr.; Marsha Hunt; Don Kelly; Nelson Leigh; ***D:*** Gordon Douglas; ***W:*** Irving Wallace; ***C:*** William Clothier; ***M:*** Leonard Rosenman.

Bombshell ♪♪♪ *Blonde Bombshell* **1933** Wry insightful comedy into the Hollywood of the 1930s. Harlow plays a naive young actress manipulated by her adoring press agent. He thwarts her plans until she finally notices and begins to fall in love with him. Brilliant satire with Harlow turning in perhaps the best performance of her short career. **96m/B; VHS, DVD.** Jean Harlow; Lee Tracy; Pat O'Brien; Una Merkel; Sir C. Aubrey Smith; Franchot Tone; ***D:*** Victor Fleming.

Bombshell ♪♪ **1997 (R)** Scientist Buck Hogan (Thomas) discovers a deadly flaw in the world's first cancer-killing drug, which he publicly reveals, much to the dismay of the manufacturer's head honcho Donald (James). But then Hogan and his girlfriend Angeline (Amick) are abducted by a terrorist group, and Buck's implanted with a device that will kill him unless he does as they say. **95m/C; VHS, Streaming.** Henry Thomas; Frank Whaley; Madchen Amick; Brion James; Pamela Gidley; Shawnee Smith; Martin Hewitt; Michael Jace; ***D:*** Paul Wynne; ***W:*** Paul Wynne.

Bombshell ♪♪ 1/2 **2019 (R)** After cohosting Fox News' morning show for years, Gretchen Carlson (Kidman) files a sexual harassment lawsuit against network founder and former CEO Roger Ailes (Lithgow). Though Gretchen faced crushing backlash because of her claims, other women who work at the network come forward with their own tales of Ailes' harassment. Though Fox News' biggest star, anchor Megyn Kelly (Theron), initially is silent, she too reveals her own experiences with Ailes. A partially fictionalized version of true events, it captures the serious outrage related to the events of 2016 with strong leading women, but misses excellence by not digging deeper. **118m/C; DVD, Blu-Ray.** Charlize Theron; Nicole Kidman; Margot Robbie; John Lithgow; Allison Janney; ***D:*** Jay Roach; ***W:*** Charles Randolph; ***C:*** Barry Ackroyd; ***M:*** Theodore Shapiro. Oscars '19: Makeup.

Bon Cop Bad Cop ♪♪ **2006** A Canadian bilingual buddy cop movie that plays on the cultural differences between English and French-speakers. Quebec maverick David Bouchard (Huard) is paired with by-the-book Ontario detective Martin Ward (Feore) when a body is deliberately left straddling the border of the two provinces. The investigation soon involves a serial killer targeting the hockey community, and the bickering duo learns to work together and realizes what they have in common (they're both divorced but devoted dads). It's contrived and unsubtle but director Canuel seems to be clear that's the way he wanted it. **116m/C; DVD.** *CA* Patrick Huard; Colm Feore; Lucie Laurier; Sarain Boylan; Pierre Lebeau; Sarah-Jeanne Labrosse; Louis-Jose Houde; Sylvain Marcel; Rick Mercer; Patrice Belanger; ***D:*** Erik Canuel; ***W:*** Kevin Tierney; ***C:*** Bruce Chun; ***M:*** Michael Corriveau.

Bon Voyage! ♪ 1/2 **1962** A family's long-awaited European "dream" vacation turns into a series of comic misadventures in this very Disney, very family, very predictable comedy. **131m/C; VHS, DVD.** Fred MacMurray; Jane Wyman; Deborah Walley; Michael Callan; Tommy Kirk; Jessie Royce Landis; ***D:*** James Neilson.

Bon Voyage ♪♪♪ **2003 (PG-13)** Successful comedy-adventure mixes romance, espionage, murder, and melodrama amid the chaos of the Nazi occupation of France. In the role of a lifetime, Adjani is Viviane, an amoral movie star who's seeing government minister Beaufort (Depardieu) but gets humble former flame Frederic (Derangere) to do her bidding, including disposing of the body of a blackmailer (Vaude). Fred gets busted with the body, takes the rap, and winds up in jail only to escape with the help of resourceful criminal Raoul (Attal). Coyote does a turn as a spy posing as a journalist who also has a thing for the tres popular Viviane. The lives of all the characters intersect with interesting results in this not completely original but engaging and well-made romp. **114m/C; DVD.** *FR* Isabelle Adjani; Gerard Depardieu; Virginie Ledoyen; Yvan Attal; Peter Coyote; Aurore Clement; Xavier De Guillebon; Edith Scob; Michel Vuillermoz; Gregori Derangere; Jean-Marc Stehle; Nicolas Pignon; ***D:*** Jean-Paul Rappeneau; ***W:*** Jean-Paul Rappeneau; Gilles Marchand; Patrick Modiano; ***C:*** Thierry Arbogast; ***M:*** Gabriel Yared.

Bonanno: A Godfather's Story ♪♪ *Youngest Godfather* **1999** Old-fashioned storytelling seems to fit the story of an old-fashioned New York mobster—Joseph Bonanno (Landau)?thought to be the inspiration for Mario Puzo's Don Vito Corleone. The elderly Bonanno reflects on his life and how he got into criminal activity back in the Prohibition days, drawing the attention of boss Salvatore Maranzano (Olmos). From there it's just a matter of time as Joe works his way up through the ranks. Based on the autobiography of Joseph Bonanno and the book written by his son Bill. **139m/C; VHS, DVD.** Martin Landau; Bruce Ramsay; Costas Mandylor; Edward James Olmos; Tony Nardi; Zachary Bennett; Philip Bosco; Claudia Ferri; Robert Loggia; Patti LuPone; ***D:*** Michel Poulette; ***W:*** Thomas Michael Donnelly; ***C:*** Serge Ladouceur; ***M:*** Richard Gregoire. **CABLE**

Bond of Fear ♪ 1/2 **1956** Routine British programmer. John Sewell (Walsh) is packing up the car, caravan, wife and kids for a trip across the Channel to the south of France. Too bad they have an unexpected guest hiding out: escaped killer Terence Dewar (Colicos) who insists the Sewells take him to the port of Dover despite road blocks, hikers needing assistance, and other complications. **66m/B; DVD.** *GB* Anthony Pavey; Marily Baker; Dermot Walsh; John Colicos; Jane Barrett; Alan MacNaughton; Jameson Clark; ***D:*** Henry Cass; John Gilling; ***W:*** John Gilling; Norman Hudis; ***C:*** Monty Berman; ***M:*** Stanley Black.

Bond of Silence ♪♪ **2010** Lifetime drama loosely based on a true story. Neighbor Bob McIntosh (Cubitt) tries to quiet a wild teen New Year's Eve party (the parents aren't home) and winds up dead. The teens refuse to talk but Bob's shattered wife Katy (Raver) is determined to get to the truth and finally the guilt gets to one young man. **98m/C; DVD.** Kim Raver; Greg Grunberg; Charlie McDermott; David Cubitt; Haley Ramm; Rebecca Jenkins; Calum Worthy; ***D:*** Peter Werner; ***W:*** Brian D. Young; Edithe Swensen; Teena Booth; ***C:*** Attila Szalay; ***M:*** Richard (Rick) Marvin. **CABLE**

Bonded by Blood ♪♪ **2009** Brit gangster pic based on a true crime. In December 1995, drug dealers Patrick Tate, Tony Tucker, and Craig Rolfe are found murdered. A flashback to 1993 sets up the story as accused killer Darren Nicholls meets Tate in prison. Nicholls would team with ex-cons Mickey Steele and Jack Whomes and the six would partner up but a falling out between Tate and Steele leads to trouble. **96m/C; DVD.** *GB* Vincent Regan; Dave Legano; Tamer Hassan; Adam Deacon; Terry Stone; Neil Maskell; ***D:*** Sacha Bennett; ***W:*** Sacha Bennett; Graeme Muir; ***C:*** Ali Asad; ***M:*** Jason Kaye; Phillip Ryan.

The Bone Collector ♪♪ 1/2 **1999 (R)** Lincoln Rhyme (Washington) is a brilliant NYPD detective and forensics expert who was left a quadriplegic after an on-the-job accident. His suicidal thoughts are distracted by the work of a serial killer with a gruesome MO and the admirable work of hotshot young policewoman, Amelia Donoghy (Jolie). Amelia soon becomes Rhyme's surrogate investigator. The situation comes to a climax in Rhyme's apartment as he lies helpless. Thriller turns out to be predictable but Washington, as usual, turns in a fine performance. Based on the 1997 novel by Jeffrey Deaver. **118m/C; VHS, DVD, Blu-Ray, HD-DVD.** Denzel Washington; Angelina Jolie; Queen Latifah; Ed O'Neill; Michael Rooker; Mike McGlone; Leland Orser; Luis Guzman; John Benjamin Hickey; Bobby Cannavale; ***D:*** Phillip Noyce; ***W:*** Jeremy Iacone; ***C:*** Dean Semler; ***M:*** Craig Armstrong.

Bone Daddy ♪♪ **1997 (R)** Former chief medical examiner William Palmer (Hauer) turns his experiences into a best-selling novel and excites the rage of a psychopathic killer. The surgical killer, who's nicknamed "Bone Daddy" because he likes to extract the bones of his victims, is busy at work and Palmer teams up with a reluctant detective (Williams) to track the looney down. **90m/C; VHS, DVD.** Rutger Hauer; Barbara Williams; R.H. Thomson; Joseph Kell; Robin Gammell; Daniel Kash; Christopher Kelk; ***D:*** Mario Azzopardi; ***W:*** Thomas Szollosi; ***C:*** Danny Nowak; ***M:*** Christophe Beck.

Bone Dry ♪♪ **2007 (R)** Eddie (Goss) finds himself knocked out and left in the middle of the desert by a man named Jimmy (Hendriksen). Jimmy informs Eddie via walkie-talkie that he needs to head north, and should he go in any other direction a sniper rifle will put an end to him, and his wife and children will follow him into the ground quickly after. What follows is not pretty to watch. **100m/C; DVD.** Lance Henriksen; Tommy (Tiny) Lister; Dee Wallace; Luke Goss; ***D:*** Brett Hart; ***W:*** Brett Hart; ***C:*** John Darbonne; Kevin G. Ellis; ***M:*** Scott Glasgow.

Bone Eater ♪ **2007** Native Americans are protesting at a construction site that's disturbing an ancient burial ground. The workers hit a pile of bones that assembles itself into the legendary Bone Eater, which promptly destroys the crew. Sheriff Evans (Boxleitner) shows up to investigate—more people disappear—corporate greed—blah, blah, blah. It's good for a chuckle (the Bone Eater figure certainly isn't scary) but that's probably not what director Wynorski intended. **90m/C; DVD.** Bruce Boxleitner; Clara Bryant; James Storm; Gil Gerard; Veronica Hamel; Adoni Maropis; Michael Horse; Roark Critchlow; Walter Koenig; William Katt; Tom Schmid; ***D:*** Jim Wynorski; ***W:*** Jim Wynorski; ***M:*** Chuck Cirino. **CABLE**

Bone Tomahawk ♪♪ 1/2 **2015** S. Craig Zahler's debut starts as a solid, talkative Western about four very different men forced to work together by circumstance, but it turns into an equally effective horror film in the final act, upping the gore quotient. With cinematically perfect facial hair, Kurt Russell plays Sheriff Franklin Hunt, a small town lawman whose life gets turned upside down when a Native American tribe kidnaps a local woman (Lili Simmons). The woman's husband (Patrick Wilson), an out-of-towner (Matthew Fox) and the Deputy (Richard Jenkins) go to rescue her from cannibals. A lean, tight, effective thriller with a great cast. **132m/C; DVD, Blu-Ray, Streaming.** Patrick J. Wilson; Kurt Russell; Lili Simmons; Matthew Fox; David Arquette; Richard Jenkins; Sid Haig; Kathryn Morris; ***D:*** S. Craig Zahler; ***W:*** S. Craig Zahler; ***C:*** Benji Bakshi; ***M:*** Jeff Herriott; S. Craig Zahler.

The Bone Yard ♪ **1990 (R)** A weird mortuary is the setting for strange goings on when a murder is investigated. **98m/C; VHS, DVD, Blu-Ray.** Ed Nelson; Deborah Rose; Norman Fell; Jim Eustermann; Denise Young; Willie Stratford, Jr.; Phyllis Diller; ***D:*** James Cummins; ***W:*** James Cummins; ***C:*** Irl Dixon; ***M:*** Kathleen Ann Porter; John Lee Whitener.

Bones ♪♪ 1/2 **2001 (R)** Combining the best of blaxploitation and horror elements, Dickerson smartly reveals the story of benevolent pimp Jimmy Bones'(Snoop Dogg) disappearance and subsequent resurrection 22 years later as a vengeful spirit. When an entreprenuerial buppie (Kain) decides to open a dance hall in Jimmy's former digs, walls begin oozing, animals become abundant and mean, and old secrets are revealed, much to the chagrin of the kid's rich father (Davis), and a cop (Weiss). Grier shines as a neighborhood psychic, and Snoop adds miles of style and presence, keeping this one a notch above the standard-issue haunted house fare. **94m/C; VHS, DVD, Blu-Ray.** Snoop Dogg; Pam Grier; Michael T. Weiss; Clifton Powell; Ricky Harris; Bianca Lawson; Khalil Kain; Katharine Isabelle; Merwin Mondesir; Sean

Amsing; *D:* Ernest R. Dickerson; *W:* Adam Simon; *C:* Flavio Martinez Labiano; *M:* Elia Cmiral.

The Bonfire of the Vanities 🦴 ½ **1990 (R)** If you liked Tom Wolfe's viciously satirical novel, chances are you won't like this version. If you didn't read the book, you probably still won't like it. Miscast and stripped of the book's gutsy look inside its characters, the film's sole attribute is Vilmos Zsigmond's photography. Hanks is all wrong as wealthy Wall Street trader Sherman McCoy who, lost in the back streets of the Bronx, panics and accidentally kills a young black kid. Willis' drunken journalist/narrator, Griffith's mistress, and Freeman's righteous judge are all awkward and thinly written. If you're still awake, look for F. Murray Abraham's cameo as the Bronx D.A. **126m/C; VHS, DVD, Blu-Ray.** Tom Hanks; Melanie Griffith; Bruce Willis; Morgan Freeman; Alan King; Kim Cattrall; Saul Rubinek; Clifton James; Donald Moffat; Richard Libertini; Andre Gregory; Robert Stephens; ***Cameo(s):*** F. Murray Abraham; *D:* Brian De Palma; *W:* Michael Cristofer; *C:* Vilmos Zsigmond; *M:* Dave Grusin.

Bongwater 🦴🦴 **1998 (R)** David (Wilson) is a Portland pot dealer and aspiring artist who becomes roommates with Serena (Witt), although mixed signals prevents anything closer even if David is definitely lovesick. Thanks to a misunderstanding, Serena heads to New York, a bong ignites the house where David was living—burning it to the ground—and he is forced to rely on the kindness of his fellow pot buddies while Serena has her own problems in the Big Apple. However, you won't really care except Wilson is appealing in a goofy doper sort of way. **98m/C; VHS, DVD.** Luke Wilson; Alicia Witt; Amy Locane; Brittany Murphy; Jack Black; Andy Dick; Jeremy Sisto; Jamie Kennedy; Scott Caan; Patricia Wettig; *D:* Richard Sears; *W:* Nora MacCoby; Eric Weiss; *C:* Richard Crudo; *M:* Mark Mothersbaugh; Josh Mancell.

Bonjour Monsieur Shlomi 🦴🦴🦴 *Ha'Kohavim Shel Shlomi* **2003** Light-hearted human comedy about sixteen-year-old, Shlomi, a mildly slow-witted Jewish boy juggling school, love, and the family circus at home. Willing to put his own interests aside, Shlomi dedicates most of his life to caring for his senile grandfather, cooking elaborate meals for the family, and falling behind in school. His secret joys come from poetry, snooping through his older brother's explicit diary, and daydreaming about the girl next door. A surprisingly warm Israeli film that manages to avoid the usual melodramatic pitfalls of most American coming-of-age flicks. **94m/C; DVD.** Esti Zakheim; Aya Koren; Assi Cohen; Oshri Cohen; Arie Elias; Yigal Naor; Albert Illouz; Jonathan Rozen; Rotem Abuhav; Rotem Zisman; Nisso Keavia; Aya Steinovitz; *D:* Shemi Zarhin; *W:* Shemi Zarhin; *C:* Itzik Portal; *M:* Jonathan Bar-Girora.

Bonjour Tristesse 🦴🦴🦴 **1957** An amoral French girl (Seberg) conspires to break up her playboy father's (Niven) upcoming marriage to her stuffy godmother (Kerr) in order to maintain her decadent freedom. Preminger attempted, unsuccessfully, to use this soaper to catapult Seberg to stardom. Based on the novel by Francoise Sagan. **94m/B; VHS, DVD, Blu-Ray.** *FR* Deborah Kerr; David Niven; Jean Seberg; Mylene Demongeot; Geoffrey Horne; Walter Chiari; Jean Kent; *D:* Otto Preminger; *W:* Arthur Laurents; *C:* Georges Perinal.

Bonneville 🦴🦴 **2006 (PG)** On a mission to spread the ashes of a dead husband, three middle-aged women hit the open road in a 1966 Bonneville, driving from Idaho to California. Along the way they laugh about the good old days, cry about car trouble, and connect all the dots required of a formulaic road trip flick. Bates, Lange, and Allen are excellent, but ultimately wasted on a script that's lacking surprise and running on fumes from the start. **93m/C; DVD.** Jessica Lange; Kathy Bates; Joan Allen; Christine Baranski; Victor Rasuk; Tom Amandes; Tom Wopat; Tom Skerritt; *D:* Christopher Rowley; *W:* Daniel Davis; *C:* Jeffrey L. Kimball; *M:* Jeff Cardoni.

Bonnie & Clyde 🦴🦴🦴 ½ **1967** Based on the biographies of the violent careers of Bonnie Parker (Dunaway) and Clyde Barrow (Beatty), who roamed the Southwest robbing banks. In the Depression era, when any job, even an illegal one, was cherished, money, greed, and power created an unending cycle of violence and fury. Highly controversial and influential, with pronounced bloodshed (particularly the pairs balletic and bullet-ridden end) that spurred mainstream cinematic proliferation. Established Dunaway as a star; produced by Beatty in one of his best performances. **111m/C; VHS, DVD, Blu-Ray.** Warren Beatty; Faye Dunaway; Michael J. Pollard; Gene Hackman; Estelle Parsons; Denver Pyle; Gene Wilder; Dub Taylor; Evans Evans; *D:* Arthur Penn; *W:* David Newman; Robert Benton; *C:* Burnett Guffey; *M:* Charles Strouse. Oscars '67: Cinematog., Support. Actress (Parsons); AFI '98: Top 100; Natl. Film Reg. '92; N.Y. Film Critics '67: Screenplay; Natl. Soc. Film Critics '67: Screenplay, Support. Actor (Hackman); Writers Guild '67: Orig. Screenplay.

Bonnie & Clyde 🦴🦴 **2013** A somewhat conventional biopic of the Depression era crime spree of Bonnie Parker (Grainger) and Clyde Barrow (Hirsch) where the more interesting aspect of the cable drama is the manhunt conducted by Texas Ranger Frank Hamer (Hurt). Grainger plays Parker as a young woman so relentless about getting out of rural Texas and being famous that a newspaper/newsreel life of crime is a viable option as she pushes petty crook Clyde to bolder acts. **174m/C; DVD, Blu-Ray.** Holliday Grainger; Emile Hirsch; William Hurt; Sarah Hyland; Lane Garrison; Elizabeth Reaser; Holly Hunter; *D:* Bruce Beresford; *W:* Joe Batteer; John Rice; *C:* Francis Kenny; *M:* John Debney. **CABLE**

Bonnie and Clyde vs. Dracula 🦴 ½ **2008** Awkward combo of crime and horror comedy worth seeing for scream queen Shepis. Bonnie and Clyde need a place to hide out after a botched robbery and find the secluded mansion of Dr. Loveless. Hanging out in the doc's cellar is longtime guest Dracula, who really wants some fresh blood. **90m/C; DVD.** Tiffany Shepis; Trent Haaga; Allen Lowman; Russell Friend; Jennifer Friend; T. Max Graham; F. Martin Glenn; *D:* Timothy Friend; *W:* Timothy Friend; *C:* Todd Norris; *M:* Joseph Allen. **VIDEO**

Bonnie Scotland 🦴🦴 ½ **1935** Laurel & Hardy accidentally join an India-bound Scottish regiment. Laughs aplenty. **81m/B; VHS, DVD.** Stan Laurel; Oliver Hardy; James Finlayson; Daphne Pollard; June Lang; *D:* James W. Horne.

Bonnie's Kids 🦴 ½ **1973 (R)** Two sisters become involved in murder, sex, and stolen money. **107m/C; VHS, DVD, Blu-Ray.** Tiffany Bolling; Robin Mattson; Scott Brady; Alex Rocco; *D:* Arthur Marks.

Boo! 🦴🦴 **2005** Five college students decide to check out the abandoned Santa Mira Hospital on Halloween to see if rumors about it being haunted are true. They discover a vengeful spirit that wants to make sure no one gets out alive. Low-budget but inventive and sufficiently creepy for a dark and stormy night. **100m/C; DVD.** Dee Wallace; Trish Coren; M. Steven Felty; Josh Holt; Jilon Ghai; Nicole Rayburn; Michael Samluk; Dig Wayne; *D:* Anthony C. Ferrante; *W:* Anthony C. Ferrante; *C:* Carl F. Bartels. **VIDEO**

Boo 2! A Madea Halloween 🦴 *Tyler Perry's Boo 2! A Madea Halloween* **2017 (PG-13)** It's another year, which means that in the Tyler Perry universe, it's time for another Madea movie! In this one, the ever-screeching heroine and her equally annoying pals rescue teens from a Halloween party at a haunted campground. Fans of the Madea oeuvre will know what to expect: thin plot, basic jokes, and loudness. It's clearly meant to be more funny than frightening. But 10 Madea films in 12 years? That IS scary. **101m/C; DVD, Blu-Ray.** Tyler Perry; Cassi Davis; Patrice Lovely; Yousef Erakat; Diamond White; *D:* Tyler Perry; *W:* Tyler Perry; *C:* Richard J. Vialet; *M:* Philip White. Golden Raspberries '17: Worst Actress (Perry).

Boo! A Madea Halloween 🦴🦴 *Tyler Perry's Boo! A Madea Halloween* **2016 (PG-13)** When Chris Rock wrote a joke about a Madea Halloween movie in his comedy "Top Five," he couldn't have known it would actually become a reality, but don't challenge Tyler Perry to do something dumb. He'll take you up on it. Ultimately, this comedy reveals its thrown-together nature with a weak script, bad pacing, and choppy storytelling. In other words, it's a Madea movie. This one just happens to be set on Halloween, and a little darker/dirtier than these typically are. Like so many Perry movies, it's not horrible but it's far from memorable. You'll forget it before it's over. **103m/C; DVD, Blu-Ray.** Tyler Perry; Cassi Davis; Patrice Lovely; Bella Thorne; Yousef Erakat; *D:* Tyler Perry; *W:* Tyler Perry; *C:* Richard J. Vialet; *M:* Elvin Ross.

The Boogey Man 🦴🦴 **1980 (R)** Through the reflection in a mirror, a girl witnesses her brother murder their mother's lover. Twenty years later this memory still haunts her; the mirror is now broken, revealing its special powers. Who will be next? Murder menagerie; see footage from this flick mirrored in "The Boogey Man 2." **93m/C; VHS, DVD.** John Carradine; Suzanna Love; Ron James; *D:* Ulli Lommel; *W:* Suzanna Love; Ulli Lommel; *C:* Jochen Breitenstein; David Sperling; *M:* Tim Krog.

Boogey Man 2 **WOOF! 1983** The story continues; same footage, new director but with Lommel, the director of the original "Boogey Man," co-writing the script and appearing in the film. **90m/C; VHS, DVD.** John Carradine; Suzanna Love; Shannah Hall; Ulli Lommel; Sholto Von Douglas; *D:* Bruce Starr.

Boogeyman 🦴 ½ **2005 (PG-13)** Weak horror flick about monsters in the closet. Tim (Watson) returns to his hometown for his mother's (Lawless) funeral and revisits the childhood home where his father was apparently sucked into young Tim's bedroom closet by the boogeyman and killed. Naturally, Tim has an aversion to closets. He wants to prove the boogeyman is all in his imagination like his shrink says; the boogeyman has other ideas. **86m/C; DVD, UMD.** Barry Watson; Emily Deschanel; Skye McCole Bartusiak; Lucy Lawless; Philip Gordon; Aaron Murphy; Robyn Malcolm; Victoria (Tory) Mussett; Andrew Glover; Charles Mesure; Jennifer Rucker; *D:* Stephen Kay; *C:* Bobby Bukowski; *M:* Joseph LoDuca.

Boogeyman 2 🦴 ½ **2007** When Laura (Savre) and her brother (Cohen) were children, they watched their father get slaughtered by the boogeyman. Naturally, this caused a lot of trauma, so Laura decides to check herself into a local mental hospital in hopes of getting past her continuing fear. But when patients start dying, it becomes clear the creature is trolling the hospital for his next victims. **93m/C; DVD.** Tobin Bell; Renee O'Connor; Danielle Savre; Matt Cohen; *D:* Jeff Betancourt; *W:* Brian Sieve; *C:* Nelson Cragg. **VIDEO**

Boogeyman 3 🦴 ½ **2008** College sophomore Sarah Morris (Cahill) witnesses the alleged suicide of friend Audrey (Sanderson), who was terrified that the boogeyman was after her. Sarah tries to convince the other dorm inhabitants that evil does exist but they all think she's crazy until they become the next victims. A cut above most DTV horror sequels since the predictable plot does offer some scares. **92m/C; DVD.** Mimi Michaels; Matt Rippy; Kate Maberly; Erin Cahill; Chuck Hittinger; Nikki Sanderson; *D:* Gary Jones; *W:* Brian Sieve; *C:* Lorenzo Senatore; *M:* Joseph LoDuca. **VIDEO**

Boogie Boy 🦴 ½ **1998 (R)** Recently released from prison, Jesse (Dacascos) gets involved as muscle for a drug deal involving his ex-cellmate, the drug-addicted Larry (Woolvett), in order to get some quick cash. Naturally, the deal goes sour and they wind up on the lam. **110m/C; VHS, DVD, Blu-Ray.** Mark Dacascos; Emily Lloyd; Jaimz Woolvett; Traci Lords; Frederic Forrest; Joan Jett; Ben Browder; James Lew; Linnea Quigley; *D:* Craig Hamann; *W:* Craig Hamann; *M:* Tim Truman.

The Boogie Man Will Get You 🦴🦴 ½ **1942** Crazy scientist Nathaniel Billings (Karloff) has been working on creating a race of supermen in his basement. He sells his home to Bill (Parks) and Winnie (Donnell), who are turning the place into a bed and breakfast, thinking that he can use their guests as fresh subjects. Lorre plays multiple roles, including a fellow nutcase. Karloff was unavailable to reprise his role in the film version of "Arsenic and Old Lace" so he did this similar comedy instead. **66m/B; VHS, DVD.** Boris Karloff; Peter Lorre; Maxie "Slapsie" Rosenbloom; Larry Parks; Jeff Donnell; Maude Eburne; *D:* Lew Landers; *W:* Edwin Blum; *C:* Henry Freulich.

Boogie Nights 🦴🦴🦴 ½ **1997 (R)** Epic tale covering the rise and fall of porn star Eddie Adams (Wahlberg). The protege of director Jack Horner (Reynolds), 17-year-old Eddie jumps in a hot tub at an industry bash, christens himself Dirk Diggler, and goes on to become the toast of the adult entertainment industry. Brilliantly spanning the decadent disco-era 70s and the excess of the 80s, 27-year-old writer/director Anderson boldly delves into fresh, albeit dangerous, territory most successfully in this lengthy sophomore outing. What Tarantino did for Travolta, Anderson does here for Reynolds, who plays the past-his-prime but touchingly ambitious auteur with a dream to make a legitimately legendary skin flick. Wahlberg proves himself a serious and seriously good actor in his turn, surrounded by equally fine performances of the ensemble cast. Details such as wardrobe, bits of dialogue, and music are deftly used, avoiding parody. Nonstop disco and early 80s music, often with a message, and energetic camera work make you shake your booty. **155m/C; DVD, Blu-Ray.** Mark Wahlberg; Burt Reynolds; Julianne Moore; Don Cheadle; William H. Macy; Heather Graham; John C. Reilly; Luis Guzman; Philip Seymour Hoffman; Alfred Molina; Philip Baker Hall; Robert Ridgely; Joanna Gleason; Thomas Jane; Ricky Jay; Nicole Ari Parker; Melora Walters; Michael Jace; Nina Hartley; John Doe; Laurel Holloman; Robert Downey; Michael Penn; *D:* Paul Thomas Anderson; *W:* Paul Thomas Anderson; *C:* Robert Elswit; *M:* Michael Penn. Golden Globes '98: Support. Actor (Reynolds); L.A. Film Critics '97: Support. Actor (Reynolds), Support. Actress (Moore); MTV Movie Awards '98: Breakthrough Perf. (Graham); N.Y. Film Critics '97: Support. Actor (Reynolds); Natl. Soc. Film Critics '97: Support. Actor (Reynolds), Support. Actress (Moore).

Boogie Vision 🦴 *Boogievision* **1977** An aspiring filmmaker cons his girlfriend's Dad into producing his crappy science fiction film. Similar to the earlier "Groove Tube," it's a collection of skits spoofing 70's television tied together loosely by a thin plot. Except it's just not nearly as good. **84m/C; DVD.** Michael Laibson; Marlene Selsman; Bert Belant; *D:* James Bryan; *W:* James Bryan.

Boogie Woogie 🦴 ½ **2009 (R)** Flat spoof on the absurdity of the contemporary British art scene. London dealer Art Spindle is desperate to buy a Mondrian, titled "Boogie-Woogie," from its ailing owner Alfred Rhinegold, but he's being played against rival bidders. One bidder, Bob Maclestone, is having an affair with Art's ambitious employee Beth, who wants to open her own gallery and betrayal (by nearly every character) is a must. **90m/C; DVD.** *GB* Danny Huston; Heather Graham; Christopher Lee; Joanna Lumley; Stellan Skarsgard; Gillian Anderson; Jaime Winstone; Alan Cumming; Amanda Seyfried; Simon McBurney; Jack Huston; *D:* Duncan Ward; *W:* Danny Moynihan; *C:* John Mathieson; *M:* Janus Podrazik; Nigel Stone.

Book Club 🦴🦴 **2018 (PG-13)** A comedy centered on four older women and their desire for intimacy. At their book club, these new friends share their lives and gain needed support. Wealthy, commitment-shy hotel owner Vivian (Fonda) has never been married yet has a strong sex drive, while Diane (Keaton) is a recent widow seeking more from life. Though federal judge Sharon (Bergen) has not had any relationships since her divorce, she decides to try online dating. Successful restauranteur Carol (Steenburgen) is married but has lacked intimacy since her husband's retirement. The stellar cast's chemistry can't quite make up for a weak script. **104m/C; DVD, Blu-Ray, Streaming.** Diane Keaton; Jane Fonda; Candice Bergen; Mary Steenburgen; Craig T. Nelson; *D:* Bill Holderman; *W:* Bill Holderman; Erin Simms; *C:* Andrew Dunn; *M:* Peter Nashel.

The Book of Eli 🦴🦴 ½ **2010 (R)** Star/producer Washington plays Eli, a wanderer in a post-apocalyptic desert landscape who guards a mysterious book he believes will redeem mankind. In his divinely inspired trek westward, Eli shoots and slices through thieves, murderers and cannibals. Eventually, he crosses paths with Carnegie (Oldman), a warlord in a small town who covets the book and its power. Caught between the two are Carnegie's minions Claudia (Beals) and her daughter Solara (Kunis). The religious themes and surprise ending earned both scorn and praise for the Hughes brothers. This effort marks the siblings' return to filmmaking after a ten-year hiatus. **117m/C; Blu-Ray.** Denzel Washington; Gary Oldman; Mila Kunis; Ray Stevenson; Jennifer Beals; Malcolm McDowell; Michael Gambon; ***D:*** Allen Hughes; Albert Hughes; ***W:*** Gary Whitta; Anthony Peckham; ***C:*** Don Burgess; ***M:*** Atticus Ross; Leopold Ross; Claudia Sarne.

The Book of Henry **2017 (PG-13)** When Henry, a gifted 11-year-old, notices something unsettling going on between the neighbor girl and her cop stepfather, he devises a plan to help her, a step-by-step scheme detailed in a notebook. The acting is fine, particularly that of Lieberher and the always outstanding Tremblay, but the plot is so disjointed that it feels like two or three separate movies. Heed the rating: mature themes and dark twists make this unsuitable viewing for most preteens. **105m/C; DVD, Blu-Ray.** Naomi Watts; Jaeden Lieberher; Jacob Tremblay; Sarah Silverman; Dean Norris; ***D:*** Colin Trevorrow; ***W:*** Gregg Hurwitz; ***C:*** John Schwartzman; ***M:*** Michael Giacchino.

The Book of Life **2014 (PG)** Since childhood, musically-inclined bullfighter Manolo (voiced by Luna) and beefy bandit Joaquin (Tatum) have been fighting over free-spirited Maria (Saldana). After she returns to town on her 18th birthday, the love triangle heats up again. This strange, animated retelling of Mexico's Day of the Dead holiday, bookended by a museum tour guide (Applegate), looks incredible with every detail lush and vibrant. But it's a boneheaded history lesson, unwittingly lampooning every ethnic stereotype and has the nerve to inject Mariachi updates to songs like Radiohead's "Creep" and Elvis' "I Can't Help Falling in Love with You." **95m/C; DVD, Blu-Ray.** ***V:*** Diego Luna; Zoe Saldana; Channing Tatum; Kate del Castillo; Ron Perlman; Christina Applegate; Ice Cube; Hector Elizondo; Danny Trejo; ***D:*** Jorge Gutierrez; ***W:*** Jorge Gutierrez; Doug Langdale; ***M:*** Gustavo Santaolalla.

Book of Love **1991 (PG-13)** "Zany" hijinks as a teenager struggles with friendship, girls, and those all-important hormones when he moves to a new neighborhood in the mid-'50s. Average rehash of every '50s movie and TV show cliche in existence. Surprise! There's a classic rock 'n' roll soundtrack. Adapted by Kotzwinkle from his novel "Jack in the Box." **88m/C; VHS, DVD.** Chris Young; Keith Coogan; Aeryk Egan; Josie Bissett; Tricia Leigh Fisher; Danny Nucci; Michael McKean; John Cameron Mitchell; Lewis Arquette; ***D:*** Robert Shaye; ***W:*** William Kotzwinkle; ***M:*** Stanley Clarke.

Book of Love **1/2 2004 (R)** David (Baker) and Elaine's (O'Connor) childless marriage hits a lull, so the couple befriends 15-year-old Chet (Smith) to fill the void. Life for the happy wanna-be-family gets muddled up when David discovers that Chet and Elaine had a creepy and very illegal affair. **85m/C; VHS, DVD.** Frances O'Connor; Simon Baker; Gregory Edward Smith; Bryce Dallas Howard; Joanna Adler; Ari Graynor; ***D:*** Alan Brown; ***W:*** Alan Brown; ***C:*** William Rexer. **VIDEO**

The Book of Love *The Devil and the Deep Blue Sea* **2016 (PG-13)** When a film is retitled (this was once "The Devil and the Deep Blue Sea"), recut, and rescheduled over and over again, that's usually a sign that the studio knows something is wrong with and are trying to fix a gaping wound with a band-aid. Henry (a miscast Sudeikis) is an introverted architect whose life is turned upside down when his wife dies in a car accident. Not long after, he meets a homeless teenager named Millie (Williams) who he agrees to help build a raft to sail across the Atlantic. If it sounds horribly manipulative, that's because it is. **107m/C; DVD, Streaming.** Jason Sudeikis; Maisie Williams; Jessica Biel; Mary Steenburgen; Orlando Jones; ***D:*** Bill Purple; ***W:*** Bill Purple; Robbie Pickering; ***C:*** James M. Muro; ***M:*** Justin Timberlake. **VIDEO**

Book of Shadows: Blair Witch 2 **1/2** *Blair Witch 2* **2000 (R)** Thankfully, they've gotten rid of the shaky-cam (which shook more than a few viewers' stomachs), that's one plus for this sequel that finds five followers of the Blair Witch myth heading back into the woods. Unfortunately, they've also gotten rid of the scares produced by mysterious offscreen witchy shenanigans and replaced them with buckets of fake blood. This group is led by Jeff (Donovan), a townie who's decided to cash in on the Blair Witch craze by organizing tours of the sites made famous in the first movie. Grad students Tristen (Skyler) and Stephen (Turner), practicing Wiccan Erica (Leerhsen) and goth-chick Kim (Director), have fun skewering the movie and its internet movement while partying on the first night. The next day they realize they've lost five hours of their lives. They try to discover what happened, and if it has anything to do with another tour group getting disemboweled. Disappointing fictional debut from documentary director Berlinger, who filmed the truly horrific (and true) "Paradise Lost: The Child Murders at Robin Hood Hills." The townspeople of Burkittsville, Maryland were so fed up with the first film that the second was filmed elsewhere. **90m/C; VHS, DVD.** Jeffrey Donovan; Kim Director; Tristen Skylar; Stephen Barker Turner; Erica Leerhsen; ***D:*** Joe Berlinger; ***W:*** Joe Berlinger; Dick Beebe; ***C:*** Nancy Schreiber; ***M:*** Carter Burwell. Golden Raspberries '00: Worst Remake/Sequel.

The Book of Stars **1/2 1999** Penny (Masterson) is the older sister and only support for teenaged Mary (Malone), who suffers from cystic fibrosis. Penny is a jaded, pill-popping hooker while Mary, however, refuses to give up her optomistic outlook on life. With the aid of cantankerous neighbor Professor (Lindo) and a couple of new friends, Mary is determined to change Penny's views as well. Manages to skirt the subject's inherent sentimentality with some winning performances. **98m/C; VHS, DVD.** Mary Stuart Masterson; Jena Malone; Karl Geary; D.B. Sweeney; Delroy Lindo; ***D:*** Michael Miner; ***W:*** Tasca Shadix; ***C:*** Jim Whitaker; ***M:*** Richard Gibbs. **VIDEO**

The Book Thief **1/2 2013 (PG-13)** Markus Zusak's young adult novel gets a frustrating adaptation in this tonally imbalanced melodrama about a girl's coming-of-age in World War II Germany. The naturally talented Nélisse plays Liesel, an orphan who moves to a small German town with new parents (Watson & Rush) just before the start of WWII. After Liesel's new family grows by an illegal one--when they offer sanctuary to a Jew in their basement--Liesel learns a lesson or two about kindness and the importance of hope. The cast is uniformly strong but TV director Percival can't find an ounce of realism, which makes it less emotional. English and German with subtitles. **131m/C; DVD, Blu-Ray.** *US GE* Sophie Nelisse; Geoffrey Rush; Emily Watson; Roger Allam; Nico Liersch; ***D:*** Brian Percival; ***W:*** Michael Petroni; ***C:*** Florian Ballhaus; ***M:*** John Williams.

Bookies **2003 (R)** Thinking they can strike it rich the easy way, three college pals set up shop as bookies. Naturally, their hot streak abruptly ends when the local syndicate takes issue with the amateurs cutting into their cash flow. **90m/C; VHS, DVD.** Nick Stahl; Lukas Haas; Johnny Galecki; Rachael Leigh Cook; David Proval; John Diehl; Zuri Williams; ***D:*** Mark Illsley; ***W:*** Michael Bacall; ***C:*** Brendan Galvin; ***M:*** Christopher Tyng; Giuseppe Cristiano. **VIDEO**

The Bookshop **2018 (PG)** When Florence Green (Mortimer) is widowed during World War II, she opens a bookstore in an East Anglican village. Though she overcomes the dismissive attitudes of a lawyer and banker to reach her goal, Florence has an unexpected enemy in Violet Gamart (Clarkson). Violets acts as if she controls the community and informs Florence she will do whatever it takes to be rid of her. Though Florence keeps going, she faces another challenge when she sells the controversial "Lolita." Based on Penelope Fitzgerald's novel, the period British drama fails to live up to its source, cast, and promise. **113m/C; DVD.** Emily Mortimer; Bill Nighy; Hunter Tremayne; Honor Kneafsey; Michael Fitzgerald; ***D:*** Isabel Coixet; ***W:*** Isabel Coixet; ***C:*** Jean-Claude Larrieu; ***M:*** Alfonso de Vilallonga.

Booksmart **1/2 2019 (R)** On the last day of high school, type A valedictorian Molly (Feldstein) and her best friend, intelligent feminist activist Amy (Dever), are pleased that their hard work has gotten them into great colleges. When Molly learns that classmates have also gotten into great colleges despite not focusing exclusively on school, her perspective is turned upside down. Molly then convinces Amy that they should have one night of high school experiences like partying. This engaging coming-of-age comedy both acknowledges the movies that came before it while carving out its own impressive path with witty dialogue, memorable characters, and sense of fun. **102m/C; DVD, Blu-Ray.** Kaitlyn Dever; Beanie Feldstein; Jessica Williams; Jason Sudeikis; Lisa Kudrow; ***D:*** Olivia Wilde; ***W:*** Susanna Fogel; Emily Halpern; Sarah Haskins; Katie Silberman; ***C:*** Jason McCormick; ***M:*** Dan Nakamura. Ind. Spirit '20: First Feature.

Booky's Crush **1/2 2009 (G)** In Depression-era Toronto, 11-year-old Booky Thomson develops a crush on new classmate Georgie, whom she tutors in spelling. When a school dance is announced, Booky wonders how she can get Georgie to ask her to go. Based on Bernice Thurman Hunter's novels. **89m/C; DVD.** *CA* Rachel Marcus; Connor Price; Megan Fellows; Sarah White; Stuart Hughes; Dylan Everett; Marc Bendavid; ***D:*** Peter Moss; ***W:*** Tracey Forbes; ***C:*** Norayr Kasper; ***M:*** Robert Carli. **TV**

Boom Town **1/2 1940** A lively vintage comedy/drama/romance about two oil-drilling buddies competing amid romantic mix-ups and fortunes gained and lost. **120m/B; DVD.** Clark Gable; Spencer Tracy; Claudette Colbert; Hedy Lamarr; Frank Morgan; Lionel Atwill; Chill Wills; Curt Bois; ***D:*** Jack Conway; ***W:*** John Lee Mahin; ***C:*** Harold Rosson; Elwood "Woody" Bredell; ***M:*** Franz Waxman.

Boomerang **1947** Film noir based on actual events features the murder of a Connecticut clergyman and the quick arrest of vagrant John Waldron (Kennedy). Prosecuting attorney Henry Harvey (Andrews) is told by his political bosses to get an equally quick conviction to stem public outrage. The evidence seems overwhelming but Harvey begins his own investigation and suddenly switches to the defense to prove Waldron's innocence in dramatic courtroom style. Kazan filmed on location in Bridgeport, CT in a successful semi-documentary style that heightened the tension. **88m/B; VHS, DVD, Blu-Ray.** Dana Andrews; Arthur Kennedy; Lee J. Cobb; Jane Wyatt; Cara Williams; Sam Levene; Ed Begley, Sr.; Karl Malden; Taylor Holmes; Robert Keith; ***D:*** Elia Kazan; ***W:*** Richard Murphy; ***C:*** Norbert Brodine; ***M:*** David Buttolph.

Boomerang **1992 (R)** Successful, womanizing marketing exec for a cosmetics company (Murphy) meets his match when he falls for a colleague (Givens) who is as vain and sexually predatory as he is. She treats him the way he treats women (as a sex object), and he's shocked into the arms of a nice girl (Berry). Although it's refreshing to see this sexual role reversal, the typical Murphy-style humor is in play with sexist jokes and a couple of vulgar female characters. Grier and Lawrence are great as Murphy's best friends. Blaustein and Sheffield are the same guys who wrote Murphy's "Coming to America." **118m/C; VHS, DVD.** Eddie Murphy; Halle Berry; Robin Givens; David Alan Grier; Martin Lawrence; Grace Jones; Geoffrey Holder; Eartha Kitt; Chris Rock; Tisha Campbell; John Witherspoon; Melvin Van Peebles; ***D:*** Reginald (Reggie) Hudlin; ***W:*** Barry W. Blaustein; David Sheffield.

Boondock Saints **1999 (R)** Two Boston Irish-Catholic brothers, Connor (Flanery) and Murphy (Reedus) McManus, turn into unlikely local heroes after the self-defense killings of some Russian mobsters who were threatening to close down their local pub. They turn vigilante, believing they're doing God's work to rid the world of evil, which leads to more slaughter. Investigating the crimes is gay FBI agent Paul Smecker (Dafoe), who is shown reconstructing the carnage in a series of flashbacks. Stylish cult debut for writer-director Duffy is uneven but entertaining. **110m/C; VHS, DVD, Blu-Ray, UMD.** Sean Patrick Flanery; Norman Reedus; Willem Dafoe; David Della Rocco; Carlo Rota; Billy Connolly; David Ferry; Brian Mahoney; Ron Jeremy; ***D:*** Troy Duffy; ***W:*** Troy Duffy; ***C:*** Adam Kane; ***M:*** Jeff Danna.

The Boondock Saints II: All Saints Day **1/2 2009 (R)** In this second installment, Flanery and Reedus return as twin brothers Connor and Murphy, forced out of exile when they are linked to a priest's murder. Even lower-grade Tarantino rip-off than the first, this one takes racist, homophobic jokes and impossible violence to a new level of absurdity. While writer/director Duffy's 10 years between films did improve his cinematography, it didn't hone his creativity—he overcompensates what is lacking by blasting metal and techno music. If not for the original's cult status, the Boston boys and their vigilante justice would have never been reunited. **118m/C; Blu-Ray, On Demand.** Sean Patrick Flanery; Norman Reedus; Billy Connolly; Clifton (Gonzalez) Collins, Jr.; Julie Benz; Peter Fonda; Judd Nelson; ***D:*** Troy Duffy; ***W:*** Troy Duffy; Taylor Duffy; ***C:*** Miroslaw Baszak; ***M:*** Jeff Danna.

The Boost **1/2 1988 (R)** A feverish, messy melodrama about a young couple's spiraling decline from yuppie-ish wealth in a haze of cocaine abuse. **95m/C; VHS, DVD, Blu-Ray; Open Captioned.** James Woods; Sean Young; John Kapelos; Steven Hill; Kelle Kerr; John Rothman; Amanda Blake; Grace Zabriskie; ***D:*** Harold Becker; ***W:*** Darryl Ponicsan; ***C:*** Howard Atherton.

Boot Camp **1/2** *Straight Edge* **2007** Anti-social Denver teen Sophie (Kunis) hates her stepfather and causes such a ruckus that he sends her to a rehabilitation boot camp on the island of Fiji. Far from being paradise, Sophie discovers the camp uses abusive training techniques on its offenders. Sophie's boyfriend Ben (Smith) gets himself sent to the same facility so they can escape together but their impulsive plans make things worse. **99m/C; DVD.** Mila Kunis; Gregory Edward Smith; Peter Stomare; Tygh Ruyan; Regine Nehy; Barbara Wilson; Christopher Jacot; Serge Houde; ***D:*** Christian Duguay; ***W:*** Agatha Dominik; John Cox; ***C:*** Christian Duguay; ***M:*** Normand Corbeil. **VIDEO**

Boot Hill **1/2 1969 (PG)** Two guys mess with western baddies and wild women in spaghetti oater. **97m/C; VHS, DVD.** *IT* Terence Hill; Bud Spencer; Woody Strode; Victor Buono; Lionel Stander; ***D:*** Giuseppe Colizzi.

The Booth *Busu* **2006** Shogo (Ryuta Sato) is a shock jock whose radio program features people calling in with their romantic problems to be humiliated and condescended to by him. Since the company is moving to a new place, Shogo is temporarily moved to Studio 6, a run down broadcasting booth that is supposed to be haunted, and responsible for the suicide of a former DJ. And sure enough, perfectly on cue the crew begins to hear things they can't explain, especially Shogo, whose paranoia leads him to believe that the callers have found out secrets from his past. **74m/C; DVD.** *JP* Ryuta Shoto; ***D:*** Yoshihiro Nakamura; ***W:*** Yoshihiro Nakamura; ***C:*** Akihiro Kawamura; Nouaki Sasaki; ***M:*** Kyo Nakanishi.

Bootmen **2000 (R)** Young Sean must make his dance dreams come true despite a bitter, critical father and his working-class Australian surroundings. Director Dein Perry has turned his hit show "Tap Dogs" into a fictionalized and semi-autobiographical tale that combines some of the better qualities of "The Full Monty" and the standard twists and turns of so many other dance films. The "Let's put on a show" plot doesn't provide much sustenance to see the viewer through to some of the excellent choreography. Features several players from the original Tap Dogs company. **95m/C; VHS, DVD.** *AU* Adam Garcia; Sophie Lee; William Zappa; Sam Worthington; Susie Porter; ***D:*** Dein Perry; ***W:*** Steve Worland; ***C:*** Steve Mason. Australian Film Inst. '00: Cinematog., Costume Des., Score.

Booty Call **1/2 1996 (R)** Reserved Rushon (Davidson) and conservative Nikki (Jones) have been dating for a couple of months and Rushon's decided they should consummate their relationship. Nikki's more ambivalent and first sets up a double date with her vivacious best friend Lysterine (Fox) and Rushon's bragging buddy Bunz (Foxx). The duos do pair up but since the "no glove, no love" rule prevails, first the guys have to find some condoms. Raunch rules as might be expected but it's an appealing cast. **120m/C; VHS, DVD.** Jamie Foxx; Tommy Davidson; Vivica A. Fox; Tamala Jones; Art Malik; Gedde Watanabe; Scott LaRose; Ammie Sin;

Bernie Mac; David Hemblen; ***D:*** Jeff Pollack; ***W:*** Takashi Bufford; ***C:*** Ronald Orieux; ***M:*** Robert Folk.

Bopha! 1993 (PG-13) Father-son strife set against the anti-apartheid movement. In the Senior township police officer Mikah takes pride in his peaceful community, particularly in light of the growing unrest in the other townships. Son Zweli has become an activist and wife Rosie must be the family peacemaker. Then a prominent freedom movement member is arrested and two officers of the secret police make their sinister appearance. Well acted; directorial debut of Freeman. Adapted from the play by Percy Mtwa, although the hopeful ending has been changed in the movie. The title, a Zulu word, stands for arrest or detention. Filmed on location in Zimbabwe. **121m/C; VHS, DVD.** Danny Glover; Maynard Eziashi; Alfre Woodard; Malcolm McDowell; Marius Weyers; Malick Bowens; Robin Smith; Michael Chinyamurindi; Christopher John Hall; Grace Mahlaba; ***D:*** Morgan Freeman; ***W:*** Brian Bird; John Wierick; ***M:*** James Horner.

Borat: Cultural Learnings of America for Make Benefit Glorious Nation of Kazakhstan 2006 (R) British comic Sacha Baron Cohen is outrageously funny as Borat, the cheerfully ignorant and prejudiced "sixth best known reporter in Kazakhstan." The plot follows Borat's travels through America in order to bring back to his homeland two things he feels strongly about: lessons on America and Pamela Anderson. The plot is just a frame to prop up the real aim of the moviefilm, which is to allow the American public to parody and incriminate itself. Viewers will simultaneously wince and laugh as Borat's seemingly innocent Third World anti-Semitism, homophobia and misogyny are reflected in unknowing victims from both jerkwater towns and cosmopolitan cities. Critically hailed upon its release, the film was dogged with numerous lawsuits and complaints from offended parties, particularly the Kazakh government. The humor is often crude (there is a credit for "Feces provided by") and disturbing (an extended scene of graphic "dudity" when Borat and producer Azamat (Davitian) wrestle over a magazine picture), but it is genuinely funny and unsettling. **82m/C; DVD.** Sacha Baron Cohen; Pamela Anderson; Ken Davitian; Pat Haggerty; Alan Keyes; Luenell; ***D:*** Larry Charles; ***W:*** Sacha Baron Cohen; Peter Baynham; Dan Mazer; Anthony Hines; ***C:*** Luke Geissbuhler; Anthony Hardwick; ***M:*** Erran Baron Cohen. Golden Globes '07: Actor--Mus./Comedy (Baron Cohen).

The Border 1982 (R) A border guard faces corruption and violence within his department and tests his own sense of decency when the infant of a poor Mexican girl is kidnapped. Excellent cast, fine cinematography, unusual Nicholson performance. **107m/C; VHS, DVD, Blu-Ray.** Jack Nicholson; Harvey Keitel; Valerie Perrine; Warren Oates; Elpidia Carrillo; ***D:*** Tony Richardson; ***W:*** Deric Washburn; Walon Green; ***M:*** Ry Cooder.

Border Blues 1/2 2003 (R) Ex-Russian cop who tries to sneak a woman and her daughter across the U.S.-Mexico border is the primary suspect in connection with an L.A. mail-bomb scare. Painful to watch Busey and Estrada in their law enforcement roles. **86m/C; VHS, DVD.** Eric Roberts; Gary Busey; Yekaterina Rednikova; Lisa Gerstein; Erik Estrada; Rodion Nakhapetov; ***D:*** Rodion Nakhapetov; ***W:*** Rodion Nakhapetov; ***C:*** Sergei Kozlov; ***M:*** David G. Russell. **VIDEO**

Border Incident 1949 Average crime melodrama from director Mann in which federales on both sides of the border team up to prevent the exploitation and murder of illegal farm workers. Jack Bearnes (Murphy) has stolen work permits he's willing to sell to crooked rancher Owen Parkson (Da Silva) while Pablo Rodriguez (Montalban) poses as an illegal migrant, and both agents find themselves in grave danger. **94m/B; DVD.** Ricardo Montalban; George Murphy; Howard da Silva; James Mitchell; Arnold Moss; Alfonso Bedoya; Teresa Celli; Charles McGraw; Jose Torvay; John Ridgely; Arthur Hunnicutt; Sig Rumann; ***D:*** Anthony Mann; ***W:*** John C. Higgins; George Zuckerman; ***C:*** John Alton.

Border Lost 1/2 2008 (R) Typical actioner. A U.S. task force works along the Mexican border to prevent bandoleros from preying upon illegal immigrants. When one the men is killed and his girlfriend kidnapped, the other agents defy orders to cross into Mexico on a mission of rescue and revenge. **105m/C; DVD.** Chris Cleveland; Emilio Rossi; Protasio; Wes McGee; Marian Zapico; Daniel Ledesma; Kelly Noonan; Robert Vazquez; ***D:*** David Murphy; Scott Peck; ***W:*** David Murphy; Scott Peck; ***C:*** Scott Peck; ***M:*** Christopher Peck. **VIDEO**

Border Radio WOOF! 1988 A rock singer decides to steal a car and try to outrun some tough thugs hot on his trail. **88m/B; VHS, DVD.** Chris D; Luana Anders; ***D:*** Allison Anders; Kurt Voss; ***W:*** Allison Anders; Kurt Voss; ***M:*** Dave Alvin.

Border River 1/2 1947 Mexican General Calleja (Armendariz) runs Zona Libre, a small enclave at the U.S.-Mexico border. For those running from the law—or the lawless—Zona Libre offers sanctuary, for a price. New arrival Confederate officer Clete Mattson (McCrea) shows up with a cool $2 million in gold, looking to buy guns for the Confederacy. Hot tamale Carmelita (De Carlo) fancies Mattson, but the General has dibs on her, and can Mattson trust these guys at Zona Libre, anyway? Either way, trouble's a brewin'. **80m/C; DVD.** Joel McCrea; Yvonne De Carlo; Pedro Armendariz, Sr.; Howard Petrie; Erika Nordin; Alfonso Bedoya; Ivan Triesault; George Lewis; George D. Wallace; Lane Chandler; Charles Horvath; Nacho Galindo; ***D:*** George Sherman; ***W:*** William Sackheim; Louis Stevens.

Border Run *The Mule* 2012 (R) Decent enough drama although it tends to sputter along. Conservative journalist Sofie Talbert's (Stone) brother Aaron (Zane), a relief worker, goes missing in Mexico. Sofie heads south to investigate and gets caught up in illegal immigration and human trafficking along the border. A dark-haired Stone is a good lead but the one to watch is Zacarias as Juanita, the scary leader of the trafficking ring. **96m/C; DVD, Blu-Ray.** Sharon Stone; Billy Zane; Giovanna Zacarias; Rosemberg Salgado; Miguel Rodarte; ***D:*** Gabriela Tagliavini; ***W:*** Amy Kolquist; Don Fieberger; ***C:*** Andrew Strahorn; ***M:*** Emilio Kauderer. **VIDEO**

Border Shootout 1990 (PG) A trigger-happy sheriff battles a rich young cattle rustler. **110m/C; VHS, DVD.** Glenn Ford; Charlene Tilton; Jeff Kaake; Michael Horse; Russell Todd; Cody Glenn; Sergio Calderon; Michael Ansara; ***D:*** Chris T. McIntyre.

Borderland 1/2 1937 Hopalong Cassidy (Boyd) goes bad?! (He's mean to kids and drinks liquor.) Well no, he's just secretly after a bandit known as "The Fox." But the outlaw didn't get his nickname by being stupid, and he sets a trap when he realizes what Hoppy is up to. The ninth film in the series. **82m/B; DVD.** William Boyd; George "Gabby" Hayes; James Ellison; Nora Lane; Morris Ankrum; Charlene Wyatt; ***D:*** Nate Watt; ***W:*** Harrison Jacobs; ***C:*** Archie Stout.

Borderland 2007 Super-creepy and bloody, and based on a true 1989 crime. Henry (Muxworthy), Phil (Strong), and Ed (Presley) take a road trip to party in a Mexican border town. Phil doesn't make it back to the hotel and the police are no help. Henry and Ed learn that kidnappings are common and tied to a cult lead by drug dealer Santillan (Cuevas). He's convinced his followers that ritual human sacrifices will make them invulnerable and though the locals (and the cops) know what's going on, they're too terrified to do anything about it. **105m/C; DVD, Blu-Ray.** Brian Presley; Rider Strong; Jake Muxworthy; Martha Higareda; Sean Astin; Beto Cuevas; Marco Bacuzzi; ***D:*** Zev Berman; ***W:*** Zev Berman; Eric Poppen; ***C:*** Scott Kevan; ***M:*** Andres Levin.

Borderline 1950 MacMurray and Trevor play undercover agents trying to infiltrate a Mexican drug ring. With their real identities hidden, they fall for each other and make a run for the border. Although the leads work well together, they're hindered by an occasionally confusing script. Unfortunately, director Seiter never decides whether the material is of a comedic or dramatic nature. **88m/B; VHS, DVD.** Fred MacMurray; Claire Trevor; Raymond Burr; Roy Roberts; Jose Torvay; Morris Ankrum; Charles Lane; Don Diamond; Nacho Galindo; Pepe Hern; Richard Irving; ***D:*** William A. Seiter; ***C:*** Lucien N. Andriot; ***M:*** Hans J. Salter.

Borderline 1980 (PG) Bronson is a border patrol guard in pursuit of a murderer in this action flick. Meanwhile, he gets caught up in trying to help an illegal alien and her young child. **106m/C; VHS, DVD.** Charles Bronson; Wilford Brimley; Bruno Kirby; Benito Morales; Ed Harris; Kenneth McMillan; ***D:*** Jerrold Freedman.

Borderline 2002 (R) A good suspenser about obsession. Dr. Lila Colleti (Gershon) is a shrink for the criminally insane at the local prison, which may be why her ex got custody of their two daughters. Lily's troubles increase when one of her patients, Ed Baikman (Flanery), is released to a halfway house, despite his delusions that they are romantically involved. After murdering her ex on her behalf, Ed threatens Lily when she doesn't return his love and implicates her in his crime. Soon, even her detective boyfriend Macy Kobacek (Biehn) has doubts about Lily's innocence. **94m/C; VHS, DVD.** Gina Gershon; Sean Patrick Flanery; Michael Biehn; ***D:*** Evelyn Purcell; ***W:*** David Loucka; ***C:*** Michael Brierley; ***M:*** Anthony Marinelli. **CABLE**

Bordertown 1935 Poor Mexican lawyer Johnny Ramirez (Muni) loses his first case and his temper, which results in his disbarment. He takes a job as a bouncer at a bordertown nightclub where owner Charlie's (Pallette) hot-to-trot missus, Marie (Davis), makes a play that gets rejected. Johnny is stupid over slumming society dame Dale (Lindsay), and Marie gets tragically desperate in trying to get Johnny's attention. The ending borders on the absurd and Davis' performance is scaled way over-the-top throughout although Muni does his best. **80m/B; DVD.** Paul Muni; Bette Davis; Margaret Lindsay; Eugene Pallette; Gavin Gordon; ***D:*** Archie Mayo; ***W:*** Laird Doyle; Wallace Smith; ***C:*** Gaetano Antonio "Tony" Gaudio; ***M:*** Bernhard Haun.

Bordertown 1/2 2006 (R) Generic thriller based on a true story. Ambitious Chicago journalist Lauren (Lopez) is assigned to write about a series of rape/murders that have happened to young women in Juarez, Mexico. She hooks up with former colleague Alfonso (Banderas), whose persistence on covering the crimes has him in trouble with authorities. Lauren meets Eva (Zapata), who is in hiding after surviving her attack, and it is implied that the victims are all poor workers at factories making goods for the U.S. market. The politics muddies a story that, unfortunately, hasn't been compellingly told. **112m/C; DVD.** Jennifer Lopez; Antonio Banderas; Maya Zapata; Sonia Braga; Martin Sheen; ***D:*** Gregory Nava; ***W:*** Gregory Nava; ***C:*** Reynaldo Villalobos; ***M:*** Graeme Revell.

Borg vs. McEnroe *Borg McEnroe* 2017 (R) A dramatic exploration of the rivalry between tennis stars Bjorn Borg (Gudnason) and John McEnroe (LaBeouf), focusing on their 1980 showdown at Wimbledon. Though both are talented, they are polar opposites in personality. Swedish Borg disciplined and emotionless on the court, while American McEnroe is hotheaded and impulsive. Through flashbacks to their childhoods and an exploration of their current lives, it becomes clear that they have more in common than their match for the championship demonstrates. Despite an underrated performance by LaBeouf, the first feature by Danish documentarian Metz tends to tell rather than show. **107m/C; DVD, Blu-Ray.** Sverrir Gudnason; Shia LaBeouf; Stellan Skarsgard; Tuva Novotny; Scott Arthur; ***D:*** Janus Metz; ***W:*** Ronnie Sandahl; ***C:*** Niels Thastum; ***M:*** Vladislav Delay; Jon Ekstrand; Carl-Johan Sevedag; Jonas Struck.

Borgman 2013 Terrifying and mesmerizing, Alex van Warmerdam's film plays like a traditional psychological thriller told through a supernatural/biblical viewpoint. We meet the title character as he emerges from an underground bunker, bringing along a few fellow vagrants as they flee men with pitchforks and shotguns. Borgman hides in the nearby home of an upper-class family and begins to basically tear their lives apart, mostly through psychological warfare. The story is twisted and defiantly bizarre. Who is this man and what are his goals? Is he the devil? Or just a maniac? No easy answers makes for a memorable bit of storytelling. Dutch with subtitles. **113m/C; DVD, Blu-Ray.** *NL BE DK* Jan Bijvoet; Hadewych Minis; Jeroen Perceval; ***D:*** Alex Van Warmerdam; ***W:*** Alex Van Warmerdam; ***C:*** Tom Erisman; ***M:*** Vincent van Warmerdam.

Born Again 1978 Adaptation of Watergate criminal Charles Colson's biography of his becoming a born again Christian. Standard TV biopic stuff. **110m/C; VHS, DVD.** Dean Jones; Anne Francis; Dana Andrews; George Brent; ***D:*** Irving Rapper; ***W:*** Walter Bloch; ***C:*** Harry Stradling, Jr.; ***M:*** Les Baxter.

Born American *Arctic Heat* 1986 (R) Pre-Glasnost flick about teenagers vacationing in Finland who "accidentally" cross the Russian border. There they battle the Red Plague. Melodramatic and heavily politicized. Original release banned in Finland. **95m/C; VHS, DVD.** Mike Norris; Steve Durham; David Coburn; Thalmus Rasulala; Albert Salmi; ***D:*** Renny Harlin.

Born Bad 1997 (R) Teens bungle a bank robbery and hold up in the bank with hostages. The town sheriff wants to end the standoff calmly but the teens' hot-headed leader won't surrender. **84m/C; VHS, DVD.** James Remar; Corey Feldman; Taylor Nichols; Justin Walker; Heidi Noelle Lenhardt; ***D:*** Jeff Yonis. **VIDEO**

Born Bad 2011 In this remarkably nasty Lifetime movie, teenager Brooke is angry at being uprooted by her family's move to a small town and resentful of her stepmother's pregnancy. Naturally, Brooke falls for the first seemingly charming boy to look her way, although Denny quickly reveals himself to be a murderous psycho as well as the leader of a crew of home-invading scumballs. **90m/C; DVD, Blu-Ray.** Bonnie Dennison; Michael Welch; Meredith Monroe; David Chokachi; Parker Coppins; Bill Oberst, Jr.; ***D:*** Jared Cohn; ***W:*** Jared Cohn; ***C:*** Alexander Yellen; ***M:*** Chris Ridenhour. **CABLE**

Born for Hell *Naked Massacre* 1976 A maniac Vietnam vet kills nurses, leaving no clues for the police to follow. **90m/C; VHS, DVD.** Matthieu Carriere; Carole Laure; ***D:*** Denis Heroux.

Born Free 1966 The touching story of a game warden in Kenya and his wife raising Elsa the orphaned lion cub. When the cub reaches maturity, they work to return her to life in the wild. Great family entertainment based on Joy Adamson's book. Theme song became a hit. **95m/C; VHS, DVD, Blu-Ray.** Virginia McKenna; Bill Travers; ***D:*** James Hill; ***W:*** Lester Cole; ***M:*** John Barry. Oscars '66: Orig. Score, Song ("Born Free").

Born in China 1/2 *Disneynature Born in China* 2017 (G) Part of the Disneynature series, a documentary exploration of four animal family groups in China. Narrated by actor John Krasinski, the film considers the natural life cycle of Tibetan antelope, golden-snubbed nose monkeys, snow leopards, and pandas. The animals, especially the young, are cute and shown in breathtaking intimacy. Though they are found in nature far from humans, each group is anthropomorphized with names and stories that reflect human interconnectedness and familial relationships. Despite this sometimes overbearing technique, the amazing footage and extraordinary detail has wide appeal to both children and adults. **79m/C; DVD.** John Krasinski; ***D:*** Chuan Lu; ***W:*** Chuan Lu; David Fowler; Brian Leith; Phil Chapman; ***C:*** Justin Maguire; Shane Moore; Rolf Steinmann; Paul Stewart; ***M:*** Barnaby Taylor.

Born in East L.A. 1987 (R) Marin brings his Bruce Springsteen-parody song to life as he plays a mistakenly deported illegal alien who struggles to return to the U.S. Suprisingly resolute effort by the usually self-exploiting Mexican-American. Stern is the American expatriate who helps him get back and Lopez is the love interest who stalls him. **85m/C; VHS, DVD, Blu-Ray.** Richard "Cheech" Marin; Daniel Stern; Paul Rodriguez; Jan-Michael Vincent; Kamala Lopez; Tony Plana; Vic Trevino; A. Martinez; ***D:*** Richard "Cheech" Marin; ***W:*** Richard "Cheech" Marin; ***C:*** Alex Phillips, Jr.; ***M:*** Lee Holdridge.

Born in 68 *Nes en 68* 2008 Overstuffed epic traces the lives of a French family from the Paris student rebellions of

1968 to the gay rights movement in the late 1980s. Twenty-year-olds Catherine, Yves, and Herve are all involved in leftist student groups, although they eventually leave the city for a rural commune. Friendships fray and Herve tires of the pastoral life while Catherine and Yves stay to raise their two children, Boris and Ludmilla. French with subtitles. **166m/C; DVD.** *FR* Laetitia Casta; Yannick Renier; Yann Tregouet; Theo Frilet; Edouard Collin; Sabrina Seyvecou; Marc Citti; Kate Moran; ***D:*** Jacques Martineau; Olivier Ducastel; ***W:*** Jacques Martineau; Olivier Ducastel; Catherine Corsini; Guillaume Le Touze; ***C:*** Mathieu Poirot-Delpech; ***M:*** Philippe Miller.

Born Innocent 🦴 1/2 **1974** As if "The Exorcist" weren't bad enough, Blair is back for more abuse-on-film, this time as a 14-year-old runaway from a dysfunctional family who lands in a reform school for girls. There, she must struggle to be as brutal as her peers in order to survive. Fairly tame by today's standards, but controversial at its made-for-TV premiere, chiefly due to a rape scene involving a broom handle. First trip up the river for Blair. **92m/C; VHS, DVD.** Linda Blair; Joanna Miles; Kim Hunter; Richard Jaeckel; Janit Baldwin; Mitch Vogel; ***D:*** Donald Wrye; ***M:*** Fred Karlin. **TV**

Born Into Brothels: Calcutta's Red Light Kids 🦴🦴 1/2 **2004 (R)** Photojournalist Zana Briski presents the world of Calcutta prostitution through the eyes and pictures of the children who live it. Not only does she give them photography instruction as a means to help lift them from their current situation, she goes a step further in trying to place them in boarding school—much to the chagrin of the opposing parents. The subject is nothing new but her drive to make a change in these doomed lives is commendable and may hopefully inspire others. **85m/C; DVD.** *US IN* ***D:*** Zana Briski; Ross Kauffman; ***W:*** Zana Briski; Ross Kauffman; ***C:*** Zana Briski; Ross Kauffman; ***M:*** John McDowell. Oscars '04: Feature Doc.

Born Killers 🦴 *Piggy Banks* **2005 (R)** Grubby, flashback-heavy story about lowlifes. Brothers John (Muxworthy) and Michael (Mann) were raised by their sociopathic father (Sizemore), who made his living robbing and killing his victims. His sons follow in his footsteps, although Michael prefers to bed the young women who are his targets first, and he becomes fond of Archer (Garner) to the point of balking at killing her. John has his own dilemma when he discovers they have a half-sister Gertie (German), whom he immediately falls into reciprocated lust with. **87m/C; DVD.** Jake Muxworthy; Gabriel Mann; Tom Sizemore; Kelli Garner; Lauren German; ***D:*** Morgan J. Freeman; ***W:*** Kendall Delcambre; ***C:*** Nancy Schreiber; ***M:*** Jim Lang.

Born Losers 🦴🦴 **1967 (PG)** The original "Billy Jack" film in which the Indian martial arts expert takes on a group of incorrigible bikers bothering some California babes and runs afoul of the law. Classic drive-in fare. **112m/C; VHS, DVD, Blu-Ray.** Tom Laughlin; Elizabeth James; Jeremy Slate; William Wellman, Jr.; Robert Tessier; Jane Russell; Stuart Lancaster; Edwin Cook; Jeff Cooper; ***D:*** Tom Laughlin; ***W:*** Tom Laughlin; E. James Lloyd; ***C:*** Gregory Sandor.

Born of Earth 🦴 **2008 (R)** Boring horror. After his wife is murdered and his children kidnapped, Danny Kessler (Baldwin) is determined to expose the secrets of Prophet Hills, which include an ancient bloodthirsty race of underground-dwelling creatures and a cover-up. **84m/C; DVD.** Daniel Baldwin; James Russo; Brad Dourif; Shannon Zeller; Jennifer Kincer; ***D:*** Tommy Brunswick; ***W:*** Joseph Thompson; ***C:*** Michael Kudreiko. **VIDEO**

Born of Fire 🦴 1/2 **1987 (R)** A flutist investigating his father's death seeks the Master Musician; his search leads him to the volcanic (and supernatural) mountains of Turkey. **84m/C; VHS, DVD.** Peter Firth; Susan Crowley; Stephan Kalipha; ***D:*** Jamil Dehlavi; ***M:*** Colin Towns.

Born on the Fourth of July 🦴🦴🦴 1/2 **1989 (R)** A riveting meditation on American life affected by the Vietnam War, based on the real-life, bestselling experiences of Ron Kovic, though some facts are subtly changed. The film follows him as he develops from a naive recruit to an angry, wheelchair-bound paraplegic to an active antiwar protestor. Well-acted and generally lauded; Kovic co-wrote the screenplay and appears as a war veteran in the opening parade sequence. **145m/C; VHS, DVD, Blu-Ray, HD-DVD.** Tom Cruise; Kyra Sedgwick; Raymond J. Barry; Jerry Levine; Tom Berenger; Willem Dafoe; Frank Whaley; John Getz; Caroline Kava; Bryan Larkin; Abbie Hoffman; Stephen Baldwin; Josh Evans; Dale Dye; William Baldwin; Don "The Dragon" Wilson; Vivica A. Fox; Holly Marie Combs; Tom Sizemore; Daniel Baldwin; Ron Kovic; Bill Allen; ***Cameo(s):*** Oliver Stone; ***D:*** Oliver Stone; ***W:*** Oliver Stone; ***C:*** Robert Richardson; ***M:*** John Williams. Oscars '89: Director (Stone), Film Editing; Directors Guild '89: Director (Stone); Golden Globes '90: Actor--Drama (Cruise), Director (Stone), Film--Drama, Screenplay.

Born Reckless 🦴 1/2 **1959** Van Doren plays a singer working the rodeo circuit who falls for aging rider Richards. Not bad enough to be funny, however, Van Doren shows an incredible lack of talent while singing several tunes. **79m/B; DVD.** Mamie Van Doren; Jeff Richards; Arthur Hunnicutt; Carol Ohmart; Donald (Don "Red") Barry; Nacho Galindo; ***D:*** Howard W. Koch; ***W:*** Richard H. Landau; ***C:*** Joseph Biroc; ***M:*** Buddy Bregman.

Born Romantic 🦴🦴 **2000 (R)** Six lonely Londoners converge at a salsa club hoping to find a little romance. There's screwy Jocelyn (McCormack), no-nonsense Mo (Horrocks), uptight Eleanor (Williams), would-be Lothario Frank (Ferguson), awkward Eddie (Mistry), and lovelorn Fergus (Morrissey). Cabbie Jimmy (Lester) offers advice. Enjoyable (if predictable) romantic comedy. **97m/C; VHS, DVD.** *GB* Craig Ferguson; Adrian Lester; Catherine McCormack; Jimi Mistry; David Morrissey; Olivia Williams; Jane Horrocks; Hermione Norris; Ian Hart; Kenneth Cranham; Paddy Considine; ***D:*** David Kane; ***W:*** David Kane; ***C:*** Robert Alazraki; ***M:*** Simon Boswell.

Born to Be Blue 🦴🦴🦴 **2015 (R)** Legendary trumpeter Chet Baker (Hawke) fought demons, including drug addiction, and had his teeth knocked out in a fight before a comeback late in his career. Budreau's lyrical film is a unique take on the musician biopic. At times, it is a film within a film, imagining Baker making a movie about his life. And it combines real people into new characters, including a love interest played by Ejogo. Hawke gives one of his best performances, capturing Baker's struggles and true artistry in the kind subtle notes not usually seen in this genre. **97m/B; DVD.** *CA US UK* Ethan Hawke; Carmen Ejogo; Callum Keith Rennie; Stephen McHattie; Janet-Laine Green; ***D:*** Robert Budreau; ***W:*** Robert Budreau; ***C:*** Steve Cosens; ***M:*** David Braid; Todor Kobakov; Steve London.

Born to Be Wild 🦴🦴 **1938** A pair of truck drivers are commissioned to deliver a shipment of dynamite. The dynamite will be used to destroy a dam, preventing the surrounding land from falling into the hands of unscrupulous land barons. Good action picture thanks to the cast. **66m/B; VHS, DVD.** Ralph Byrd; Doris Weston; Ward Bond; Robert Emmett Keane; Bentley Hewlett; Charles Williams; ***D:*** Joseph Kane.

Born to Be Wild 🦴 1/2 **1995 (PG)** Rebellious teenager Rick (Hornoff) befriends Katie, the three-year-old gorilla his behaviorial scientist mom (Shaver) is studying. When Katie's owner (Boyle) decides she would make a better sideshow attraction than science project, Rick busts her out and they head for the Canadian border. Animal slapstick and bodily function jokes ensue as the chase continues. "Free Willy"-inspired plot and primate hijinks should keep young kids interested, but anyone over the age of nine probably won't be too impressed. **98m/C; VHS, DVD.** Wil Horneff; Helen Shaver; Peter Boyle; Jean Marie Barnwell; John C. McGinley; Marvin J. McIntyre; Thomas F. Wilson; ***D:*** John Gray; ***W:*** John Bunzel; Paul Young; ***C:*** Donald M. Morgan.

Born to Boogie 🦴🦴 *Marc Bolan and T-Rrex: Born to Boogie* **1972** A concert, a chronicle, and a tribute, "Born To Boogie" is about Marc Bolan and his band T. Rex. The film, which features concert footage from a 1972 concert at the Wembley Empire Pool in London, chronicles the glitter rock era and the next wave of British rock and roll, and pays tribute to Bolan, who died in 1977 just as he was starting a comeback. Ringo Starr and Elton John join T. Rex in the studio for "Children of the Revolution" and "Tutti-Frutti" as well as a psychadelic soiree where Bolan plays acoustic versions of his hits. This film was never released in the United States. **75m/C; VHS, DVD.** Marc Bolan; Sir Elton John; Ringo Starr; ***D:*** Ringo Starr.

Born to Dance 🦴🦴 1/2 **1936** A quintessential MGM 1930s dance musical, wherein a beautiful dancer gets a sailor and a big break in a show. Great songs by Cole Porter sung in a less than great manner by a gangly Stewart. Powell's first starring vehicle. **108m/B; DVD.** Eleanor Powell; James Stewart; Virginia Bruce; Una Merkel; Frances Langford; Sid Silvers; Raymond Walburn; Reginald Gardiner; Buddy Ebsen; ***D:*** Roy Del Ruth; ***M:*** Cole Porter; ***M:*** Cole Porter.

Born to Fight 🦴 1/2 *Kerd Ma Lui* **2007** Born to Fight is a remake in name only of a film from the 80's, both of which were done by Panna Rittikrai ("Ong-bak"). Deaw (Dan Chupong) is a cop attending a charity event sponsored by Thailands Olympic athletes of which his sister Nui (Taekwondo champion Kessarin Ektawatkul) is one. When the town the event is held in is held hostage by nuclear armed terrorists, Deaw must unite the athletes in an attempt to free the hostages. While the plot isn't complicated, all the actors (age 8 to 80) do their own stunts, some of which are incredible. **96m/C; DVD.** *TH* Nappon Gomarachun; Santisuk Promsiri; Dan Chupong; Piyapong Piew-on; Somrak Khamsing; Amornthep Waewsang; Suebsak Pansueb; Nantaway Wongwanichislip; Kessarin Ektawatkul; Rattaporn Khemtong; Chatthapong Pantanaunkal; Sasisa Jindamanee; ***D:*** Panna Rittikrai; ***W:*** Panna Rittikrai; Morakat Kaewthanek; Thanapat Taweesuk; ***C:*** Surachet Thongmee; ***M:*** Traithep Wongpaiboon.

Born to Kill 🦴🦴🦴 *Lady of Deceit* **1947** A ruthless killer marries a girl for her money. Minor tough-as-nails film noir exemplifying Tierney's stone-faced human-devil film persona. **92m/B; VHS, DVD.** Lawrence Tierney; Claire Trevor; Walter Slezak; Elisha Cook, Jr.; ***D:*** Robert Wise.

Born to Lose 🦴🦴 **1999** The Spoilers are an L.A. punk back led by singer Stevie Monroe (Rye). They're an underground success but can't break out of the music ghetto until public relations gal Lisa (Ashton) takes an interest in Stevie. Too bad she's a junkie who pulls the singer into a downward spiral that effectively destroys the band as well. Filmed in a mock-documentary style. **80m/C; VHS, DVD.** Joseph Rye; Elyse Ashton; Francis Fallon; ***D:*** Doug Cawker; ***W:*** Doug Cawker; Howard Roth; ***C:*** John Rhode; ***M:*** Greg Kuehn.

Born 2 Race 🦴🦴 **2011 (PG-13)** Solid action with a familiar story. Teen street racer Danny Krueger gets in trouble after an accident and is sent to live with his estranged father, Frank. He immediately gets involved in a local drag race, but if Danny wants to win he has to accept help from his dad--a recovering alcoholic and former NASCAR driver. **99m/C; DVD, Blu-Ray.** Joseph Cross; John Pyper-Ferguson; Sherry Stringfield; Brando Eaton; Spencer Breslin; Grant Show; ***D:*** Alex Ranarivelo; ***W:*** Alex Ranarivelo; ***C:*** Reuben Steinberg; ***M:*** Jamie Christopherson. **VIDEO**

Born to Race: Fast Track 🦴🦴 1/2 *Born 2 Race: Face Track* **2014 (PG)** The second film in the Born to Race franchise. Now 20 and still rebellious, Danny Krueger (Davern) still loves racing and has landed a scholarship to a top racing school, Fast Lane Racing Academy. There, he faces old and new competitors. Jake (Mirchoff), his small-town racing rival, is there and becomes a member of his team, while he must compete with a talented young Italian driver Enzo Lauricello (Morgado). Danny also is in a risky relationship with a new classmate Michelle (Dupont), but focuses on his primary goal of winning a rookie spot on a professional racing team. **94m/C; DVD, Blu-Ray, Download.** Brett Davern; Beau Mirchoff; Bill Sage; Sharon Lawrence; Tiffany Dupont; Diogo Morgado; ***D:*** Alex Ranarivelo; ***W:*** Steve Sarno; ***C:*** Reuben Steinberg; ***M:*** Jamie Christopherson. **VIDEO**

Born to Raise Hell 🦴 **2010 (R)** Unimpressive Seagal flick with a limited amount of martial arts action and a nonsensical title. Interpol agent Samuel Axel is assigned to a Bucharest task force targeting Russian mobster Dimitri and his ex-partner, gypsy Costel. The situation goes bad and Axel decides to get justice in his own way. **98m/C; DVD, Blu-Ray.** Steven Seagal; Dan Badarau; Darren Shahlavi; D. Neil Mark; George Remes; Claudiu Bleont; ***D:*** Lauro Chartrand; ***W:*** Steven Seagal; ***C:*** Eric Goldstein; ***M:*** Michael Neilson. **VIDEO**

Born to Ride 🦴🦴 **1991 (PG)** A biker rebel joins the Army prior to WWII in order to escape a prison term after a good ol' boy brush with the law. He shuns Army discipline, but proves himself in action as the leader of a scout troup for the Army's motorcycle cavalry brigade. Available with Spanish subtitles. **88m/C; VHS, Streaming.** John Stamos; John Stockwell; Teri Polo; Kris Kamm; ***D:*** Graham Baker.

Born to Ride **WOOF! 2011** Plot is convoluted and frequently senseless and even the actors don't seem to care. Mike (Van Dien) gets his deceased dad's classic chopper out of the garage and takes a road trip with buddy Alex (Muldoon). It soon involves money stolen from a Vietnam vet, a security tape used as blackmail against a crooked senator, and some inept, murderous goons coming after Mike and Alex. **90m/C; DVD.** Casper Van Dien; Patrick Muldoon; William Forsythe; Theresa Russell; Jack Maxwell; Branscombe Richmond; Kurt Anton; Jamison Jones; Dave Goryl; ***D:*** James Fargo; ***W:*** Mike Anthony Jones; Robert Vozza; ***C:*** Leo Napolitano; ***M:*** Ched Tolliver. **VIDEO**

Born to Win 🦴🦴 1/2 *Addict* **1971 (R)** A New York hairdresser with an expensive drug habit struggles through life in this well-made comedy drama. Excellent acting from fine cast, and interestingly photographed. Not well received when first released, but worth a look. **90m/C; VHS, DVD.** George Segal; Karen Black; Paula Prentiss; Hector Elizondo; Robert De Niro; Jay Fletcher; ***D:*** Ivan Passer; ***W:*** Ivan Passer; David Scott Milton; ***C:*** Jack Priestley; ***M:*** William S. Fisher.

Born to Win 🦴🦴 **2016** One man's quest for faith and understanding, based on a true story. While working at a school for disabled children, Leon Terblanche (Kriek) experiences a crisis of faith. By confronting his past, he learns how to believe in a higher power and inspire others as well. **104m/C; DVD, Streaming, Download.** Greg Kriek; Marie Cronje; Frans Cronje; Merline Balie; Nadia Beukes; ***D:*** Frans Cronje; ***W:*** Frans Cronje; ***C:*** Jorrie van der Walt. **VIDEO**

Born Yesterday 🦴🦴🦴 1/2 **1950** Ambitious junk dealer Harry Brock (Crawford) is in love with smart but uneducated Billie Dawn (Holliday). He hires newspaperman Paul Verrall (Holden) to teach her the finer points of etiquette. During their sessions, they fall in love and Billie realizes how she has been used by Brock. She retaliates against him and gets to deliver that now-famous line: "Do me a favor, drop dead." Holliday is a solid gold charmer as the not-so-dumb blonde, in the role she originated in Garson Kanin's Broadway play. Remade in 1993. **103m/B; VHS, DVD, Blu-Ray.** Judy Holliday; Broderick Crawford; William Holden; Howard St. John; Frank Otto; Larry Oliver; Barbara Brown; ***D:*** George Cukor; ***W:*** Albert Mannheimer; ***C:*** Joseph Walker; ***M:*** Frederick "Friedrich" Hollander. Oscars '50: Actress (Holliday); Golden Globes '51: Actress--Mus./Comedy (Holliday); Natl. Film Reg. '12.

Born Yesterday 🦴🦴 **1993 (PG)** Remake of the 1950 classic suffers in comparison, particularly Griffith, who has the thankless task of surpassing (or even meeting) Judy Holliday's Oscar-winning mark as not-so-dumb blonde Billie Dawn. Her intellectual inadequacies are glaring when she hits the political world of D.C. with obnoxious tycoon boyfriend Goodman. To save face, he hooks her up with a journalist (Johnson) willing to coach her in Savvy 101, a la Eliza Doolittle. What worked well in post-WWII America seems sadly outdated today; stick with the original. **102m/C; VHS, DVD, Blu-Ray.** Melanie Griffith; John Goodman; Don Johnson; Edward Herrmann; Max Perlich; Fred Dalton Thompson; Nora Dunn; Benjamin C. Bradlee; Sally Quinn; Michael Ensign; William Frankfather; Celeste Yarnall; Meg Wittner; ***D:*** Luis Mandoki; ***W:*** Douglas McGrath; ***C:*** Lajos Koltai; ***M:*** George Fenton.

Borough of Kings 1998 **(R)** Jimmy O'Conner (Stanek) is trying to get away from a life of crime in Brooklyn but the ties are hard to cut. Similar stories have been told dozens of times before. This little independent production has a strong spirit and commitment to the characters on its side, which outweigh its predictability. **95m/C; DVD.** Philip Bosco; Jim Stanek; Kerry Butler; Joseph Lyle Taylor; Erik Jensen; Patrick Newall; Olympia Dukakis; ***D:*** Elyse Lewin; ***W:*** Patrick Newall; ***C:*** Nils Kenaston; ***M:*** Alan Elliott.

The Borrowers 1/2 **1997 (PG)** Charming big-screen, big-budget tale about the little people who live under the floor. The British, elfin, and about four inch tall Clock family, headed by papa Pod (Broadbent) lives hidden in the walls of the home of the normal-sized American Lenders and exist by "borrowing" objects from their human's household. When an evil lawyer (Goodman), also American, threatens their happiness, the Borrowers bond with young Peter Lender (Pierce) who "discovers" them and volunteers to help them save their way of life. This remake focuses mainly on the impressive special effects, lending a modern look and appeal. Goodman is lovably evil in that wonderfully Snidely Whiplash way. Based on the children's books of Mary Norton. **86m/C; VHS, DVD.** *GB* John Goodman; Hugh Laurie; Jim Broadbent; Mark Williams; Celia Imrie; Bradley Michael Pierce; Raymond Pickard; Aden (John) Gillett; Ruby Wax; Flora Newbigin; Tom Felton; Doon Mackichan; ***D:*** Peter Hewitt; ***W:*** John Kamps; Gavin Scott; ***C:*** John Fenner; Trevor Brooker; ***M:*** Harry Gregson-Williams.

Borsalino **1970 (R)** Delon and Belmondo are partners in crime in this seriocomic film about gang warfare in 1930s Marseilles. The costumes, settings, and music perfectly capture the mood of the period. Followed by a sequel "Borsalino and Co." Based on "The Bandits of Marseilles" by Eugene Saccomano. **124m/C; VHS, DVD.** *FR* Jean-Paul Belmondo; Alain Delon; Michel Bouquet; Catherine Rouvel; Francoise Christophe; Corinne Marchand; ***D:*** Jacques Deray; ***W:*** Jacques Deray; Jean Cau; Claude Sautet; Jean-Claude Carriere; ***C:*** Jean-Jacques Tarbes; ***M:*** Claude Bolling.

Borstal Boy 1/2 **2000** Irish teen, IRA partisan, (and future writer) Brendan Behan (Hatosy) is caught smuggling dynamite into Britain and sent to reform school, known as a "borstal," in East Anglia in 1939. Naturally, he learns that all Brits aren't the devil incarnate as he befriends gay Cockney sailor Charlie (Millwall) and falls in love with fair-but-tough Warden Joyce's (York) daughter, Liz (Birthistle). Inspired by Behan's 1958 memoirs. **91m/C; VHS, DVD.** *IR GB* Shawn Hatosy; Danny Dyer; Eva Birthistle; Michael York; Lee Ingleby; Robin Laing; ***D:*** Peter Sheridan; ***W:*** Peter Sheridan; Nye Heron; ***C:*** Ciaran Tanham; ***M:*** Stephen McKeon.

The Boss **1956** Tough political drama. Ambitious WWI vet Matt Brady (Payne) returns home and becomes an increasingly corrupt political boss. He fixes elections and gets in with the mob while becoming rich and powerful. Eventually, reformers go after Brady but it's his loyalty to his only friend, Bob Herrick (Bishop) that proves to be his undoing. Blacklisted writer Trumbo used a front for his screenplay. **89m/B; DVD.** John Payne; William Bishop; Gloria McGehee; Doe Avedon; Roy Roberts; Rhys Williams; Joe Flynn; Robin Morse; ***D:*** Byron Haskin; ***W:*** Dalton Trumbo; ***C:*** Hal Mohr; ***M:*** Albert Glasser.

The Boss *Wipeout!* **1973** Di Leo's bloody gangster flick opens with mob hitman Lanzetta (Silva) eliminating most of Palermo's Attardi crime family by blowing up a porn theater with a grenade launcher. Survivor Cocchi (Capponi) puts together his own crew to get revenge in the turf war, which soon involves the kidnapping of a local boss's nympho daughter (Santilli), and more mayhem than even the mobsters want. Italian with subtitles. **100m/C; DVD.** *IT* Pier Paolo Capponi; Henry Silva; Claudio Nicastro; Antonia Santilli; Gianni "John" Garko; Richard Conte; Marino (Martin) Mase; ***D:*** Fernando Di Leo; ***W:*** Fernando Di Leo; ***C:*** Franco Villa; ***M:*** Luis Bacalov.

Boss 1/2 *The Black Bounty Killer; Boss Nigger; The Black Bounty Hunter* **1974 (PG)** Blaxploitation western parody with Williamson and Martin as a couple of bounty hunters tearing apart a town to find a fugitive. Relatively non-violent. **87m/C; VHS, DVD, Blu-Ray.** Fred Williamson; D'Urville Martin; R.G. Armstrong; William (Bill) Smith; Carmen Hayworth; Barbara Leigh; ***D:*** Jack Arnold; ***W:*** Fred Williamson.

The Boss **2016 (R)** The often-great McCarthy has made as many questionable decisions in her career as interesting ones. Consider this one of the former. She stars as Michelle Darnell, one of the most powerful women in the world, who is sent to prison for insider trading. The aggressively vile and annoying Michelle comes out of prison with the desire to change her image, but most of the world isn't ready for this brash loudmouth. Yes, McCarthy playing a jerk again. And poor Kristen Bell has to play her straight woman. **99m/C; DVD, Blu-Ray.** Melissa McCarthy; Kristen Bell; Peter Dinklage; Ella Anderson; Tyler Labine; ***D:*** Ben Falcone; ***W:*** Melissa McCarthy; Ben Falcone; Steve Mallory; ***C:*** Julio Macat; ***M:*** Christopher Lennertz.

The Boss Baby **2017 (PG)** The latest from DreamWorks Animation follows the studio's pattern of animated films that serve more as a babysitter than provide actual entertainment. Baldwin voices the title character with his typical brand of clever smarm and wit, making it more than it would have been without him, but it's still pretty thin and silly. The plot? There's been a secret war between babies and puppies for years and the lead character's new baby brother is really a secret agent in said war. A harmless film filled with jokes that kids with baby brothers will enjoy and parents will smile now and then. **97m/C; DVD, Blu-Ray.** Alec Baldwin; Steve Buscemi; Jimmy Kimmel; Lisa Kudrow; Tobey Maguire; Miles Christopher Bakshi; ***D:*** Tom McGrath; ***W:*** Michael McCullers; ***M:*** Steve Mazzaro; Hans Zimmer.

Boss of Big Town **1943** Gangsters try to infiltrate the milk industry in this standard crime drama. **65m/B; VHS, DVD.** John Litel; Florence Rice; H.B. Warner; Jean Brooks; John Miljan; Mary Gordon; John Maxwell; ***D:*** Arthur Dreifuss.

Boss of Bosses 1/2 **1999** Yet another in a long line of Mafia portrayals and betrayals but this one is flat and uninspired. Paul Castellano (Palminteri) takes organized crime into the white-collar level from the streets into legit businesses but the world is still violent, plagued by internal feuds and the feds sniffing around. Castellano wound up being the last public Mafia hit (arranged by John Gotti)?outside a New York steak house. **94m/C; VHS, DVD.** Chazz Palminteri; Daniel Benzali; Jay O. Sanders; Clancy Brown; Al Ruscio; Steven Bauer; Angela Alvarado; Sonny Marinelli; ***D:*** Dwight Little; ***W:*** Jere P. Cunningham; ***C:*** Brian Reynolds; ***M:*** John Altman. **CABLE**

The Boss of It All *Direktoren for Det Hele* **2006** Von Trier trades in polemics for a corporate comedy. Ravn (Gantzler), the director of an IT firm, decides to hire actor Kristoffer (Albinus) to portray the non-existent president of his company so he can sell out to a larger organization. But thanks to Kristoffer's overacting, the deal gets put on hold for a week and they must keep up the charade. The film was shot by Von Tier's experimental Automavision, a computer-controlled camera, and looks fairly awful. Danish with subtitles. **99m/C; DVD.** *CZ FR IT SW* Peter Gantzler; Jens Albinus; Fridrik Thor Fridriksson; Iben Hjejle; Sofie Gråbol; Benedikt Erlingsson; ***D:*** Lars von Trier; ***W:*** Lars von Trier.

The Boss' Wife **1986 (R)** A young stockbroker attempts to fix what's wrong with his life by maneuvering sexually with the boss' wife, and complications set in. **83m/C; VHS, Streaming.** Daniel Stern; Arielle Dombasle; Christopher Plummer; Martin Mull; Melanie Mayron; Lou Jacobi; ***D:*** Ziggy Steinberg; ***M:*** Bill Conti.

Bossa Nova 1/2 **1999 (R)** Sexy romantic comedy set to the beat of sultry Brazil. Middleaged American widow Mary (Irivng) teaches English in Rio and catches the romantic eye of Pedro (Fagundes), an attorney who has been dumped by his wife. Meanwhile, Mary's soccer-playing pupil Acacio (Borges) is trying to become a teacher's pet before transferring his affections to Pedro's clerk Sharon (Antonelli), who just happens to be involved with Pedro's half-brother (Cardoso). And the romantic complications just keep building. Soundtrack is filled with the songs of bossa nova composer Antonio Carlos Jobim. Based on the novel "Miss Simpson" by Sergio Sant'Anna. **95m/C; VHS, DVD.** *BR* Amy Irving; Antonio Fagundes; Alexandre Borges; Debora Bloch; Pedro Cardoso; Alberto De Mendoza; Stephen Tobolowsky; Drica Moraes; Giovanna Antonelli; Rogerio Cardoso; ***D:*** Bruno Barreto; ***W:*** Alexandre Machado; Fernanda Young; ***C:*** Pascal Rabaud; ***M:*** Eumir Deodato.

Boston Kickout **1995** A quartet of teenaged friends/losers struggle to grow up in a bleak concrete town outside London. There are neglected girlfriends, dysfunctional families, menial jobs, petty crime, emotional disasters—and some faint glimmer of hope for at least a couple of the lads. Title refers to a destructive game the boys play. **105m/C; VHS, DVD.** *GB* John Simm; Andrew Lincoln; Richard Hanson; Nathan Valente; Emer McCourt; Marc Warren; Derek Martin; Vincent Phillips; Natalie Davies; ***D:*** Paul Hills; ***W:*** Paul Hills; Diane Whitley; Roberto Troni; ***C:*** Roger Bonnici; ***M:*** Robert Hartshorne.

The Boston Strangler 1/2 **1968** Based on Gerold Frank's bestselling factual book about the deranged killer who terrorized Boston for about a year and a half. Traces events from first killing to prosecution. Curtis, going against type, is compelling in title role. **116m/C; VHS, DVD, Blu-Ray.** Tony Curtis; Henry Fonda; George Kennedy; Murray Hamilton; Mike Kellin; George Voskovec; William Hickey; James Brolin; Hurd Hatfield; William Marshall; Jeff Corey; Sally Kellerman; ***D:*** Richard Fleischer; ***W:*** Edward Anhalt.

The Boston Strangler: The Untold Story 1/2 **2008 (R)** Faustino stars as Albert De Salvo, a smalltime criminal who confesses to the serial sex killings that terrified Boston in the early 1960s. De Salvo decides to take credit for the murders while in jail on another conviction but Detective John Marsden (Divoff) isn't certain they've got the right perp or that the crimes were committed by just one man. **90m/C; DVD.** David Faustino; Andrew Divoff; Corin "Corky" Nemec; Joe Torry; Kostas Sommer; ***D:*** Michael Feifer; ***W:*** Michael Feifer; ***C:*** Hank Baumert, Jr.; ***M:*** Andres Boulton. **VIDEO**

The Bostonians 1/2 **1984 (PG)** A faith healer's daughter is forced to choose between the affections of a militant suffragette and a young lawyer in 19th Century Boston. Based on Henry James' classic novel. **120m/C; VHS, DVD.** Christopher Reeve; Vanessa Redgrave; Madeleine Potter; Jessica Tandy; Nancy Marchand; Wesley Addy; Linda Hunt; Wallace Shawn; ***D:*** James Ivory; ***W:*** Ruth Prawer Jhabvala; ***C:*** Walter Lassally. Natl. Soc. Film Critics '84: Actress (Redgrave).

Botched 1/2 **2007** Odd and not particularly successful mix of horror, comedy, and crime. American Ritchie (Dorff) must be a lousy professional thief because his jobs keep going wrong. He's sent to Moscow to steal an antique cross that's kept in a bank building and is given a couple of inept locals for backup. Naturally their getaway gets screwed and they wind up with hostages and are diverted to the building's unused 13th floor. They find out it's been abandoned for a very good reason. **94m/C; DVD.** Stephen Dorff; Sean Pertwee; Jamie Foreman; Russell Smith; Jaime Murray; Bronagh Gallagher; Edward Baker-Duly; ***D:*** Kit Ryan; ***W:*** Derek Boyle; Eamon Friel; Raymond Friel; ***C:*** Bryan Loftus; ***M:*** Tom Green. **VIDEO**

Bottle Rocket 1/2 **1995 (R)** A trio of inexperienced but aspiring criminals attempt to make their mark on the world in suburban Dallas. Newcomers Wilson, who plays the group's ambitious leader Dignan, and Anderson penned this smart ensemble piece first as a 13-minute black and white short. A subsequent showing at the Sundance Film Festival got the attention of producer James L. Brooks ("Broadcast News"). Film got the backing to go feature length with Anderson directing, and deservedly so, with its fresh dialogue and surprising warmth. **91m/C; VHS, DVD, Blu-Ray.** Owen Wilson; Luke Wilson; Robert Musgrave; Lumi Cavazos; James Caan; Andrew Wilson; Jim Ponds; Ned Dowd; ***D:*** Wes Anderson; ***W:*** Owen Wilson; Wes Anderson; ***C:*** Robert Yeoman; ***M:*** Mark Mothersbaugh. MTV Movie Awards '96: New Filmmaker (Anderson).

Bottled Up **2013 (R)** Quirk, weak dramedy with unbelievable characters and situations. Sylvie lives with mom Fay, who's enabling her daughter's painkiller addiction. When Fay meets health food store clerk Becket, she tries to set him up with her daughter but he's more interested in Fay despite their age difference. **84m/C; DVD.** Melissa Leo; Josh Hamilton; Marin Ireland; ***D:*** Enid Zentelis; ***W:*** Enid Zentelis; ***C:*** Daniel Sharnoff; ***M:*** Tim Boland; Sam Retzer.

The Bottom of the Sea **2003** Dark comedic thriller has an obsessively jealous young architect stalking his girlfriend's secret lover on one fateful night. An unexpected climax and easy-on-the-eyes actors make this Argentinean endeavor cinematically satisfying. Subtitled. **95m/C; DVD.** *AR* Dolores Fonzi; Daniel Hendler; Gustavo Garzon; Ramiro Aguero; ***D:*** Damien Szifron; ***W:*** Damien Szifron. **VIDEO**

Bottoms Up **WOOF! 2006 (R)** Bottom of the barrel is more like it. Owen (Mewes) heads to L.A. to enter a bartending contest in hopes of using the winnings to save his dad's restaurant. Things don't exactly work out and Owen's uncle (Keith) gets him a job with actor Hayden (Hallisay) and his vapid girlfriend, Lisa (a typecast Hilton). When Owen learns a few tabloid-worthy secrets, he has to decide whether to sell out his new pals for the much-needed cash. Even Mewes can't work up much enthusiasm for this mess. **89m/C; DVD.** Jason Mewes; Paris Hilton; David Keith; Phil Morris; Brian Hallisay; Jon Abrahams; Tim Thomerson; ***D:*** Erik MacArthur; ***W:*** Erik MacArthur; Nick Ballo; ***C:*** Massimo Zeri. **VIDEO**

Boudu Saved from Drowning 1/2 *Boudu Sauve des Eaux* **1932** A suicidal tramp completely disrupts the wealthy household of the man that saves him from drowning. A gentle but sardonic farce from the master filmmaker. Remade in 1986 as "Down and Out In Beverly Hills." **87m/B; VHS, DVD.** *FR* Michel Simon; Charles Granval; Jean Daste; Marcelle Hainia; Severine Lerczinska; Jacques Becker; ***D:*** Jean Renoir; ***W:*** Jean Renoir; ***C:*** Marcel Lucien.

Bought and Sold *A Jersey Tale* **2003** Coming of age tale set in Jersey City. Ray Ray Morales (Sardina) is working for minimum wage at a shoe store but really wants to buy some pawnshop turntables so he can be a DJ. So he gets a second job with local loan shark Chunks (Grifasi), who wants him to keep an eye on elderly pawnshop owner Kutty (Margulies) who owes Chunks money. Soon Ray Ray is falling for Kutty's niece, Ruby (Neshat), and getting too involved. When Kutty can't meet his payments, Ray Ray has to make some decisions about what's really important to him. **92m/C; DVD.** David Margulies; Joe Grifasi; Rafael Sardina; Marjan Neshat; Frank Harts; Christina Ablaza; Anthony Chisholm; ***D:*** Michael Tolajian; ***W:*** Michael Tolajian; ***C:*** Kip Bogdahn; ***M:*** Joe Delia.

Boulevard **2015 (R)** A drama focuses on the secret life of a husband in a marriage of convenience and features the last on-screen performance of late actor Robin Williams. At the age of 60, Nolan (Williams) is a closeted gay man married to Joy (Baker). When he finds himself in an unexpected friendship with a young charismatic hustler, Nolan goes on a journey of self-discovery. In the process, he must confront the secrets he has kept from his wife and makes a dramatic decision to rethink his identity to better the lives of both himself and his wife. **88m/C; DVD, Blu-Ray, Download.** Robin Williams; Kathy Baker; Roberto Aguire; Giles Matthey; Eleonore Hendricks; ***D:*** Dito Montiel; ***W:*** Douglas Soesbe; ***C:*** Chung-hoon Chung; ***M:*** Jimmy Haun; David Wittman.

Boulevard Nights **1979 (R)** A young Latino man tries to escape his neighborhood's streetgang violence, while his older brother is sucked into it. Music by Schifrin, known for the "Mission: Impossible" theme. **102m/C; VHS, DVD.** Richard Yniguez; Danny De La Paz; Marta DuBois; Carmen Zapata; Victor Millan; ***D:*** Michael Pressman; ***C:*** John Bailey; ***M:*** Lalo Schifrin. Natl. Film Reg. '17.

Bounce 1/2 **2000 (PG-13)** Ad exec Affleck swaps his airline ticket with a stranger who's anxious to get home to his wife. But since no good deed goes unpunished, the plane crashes and the man is killed. The guilt-stricken Affleck visits the stranger's widow (Paltrow) and winds up falling in love with her, only she doesn't know about their unfortunate connection. Okay, the plot is contrived, predictable, and a little schmaltzy, but it somehow avoids maudlin, and takes pains to make the emotions real. In this, director Roos is aided greatly by Affleck, who turns in some of his best work to date, and Paltrow, who seems less actress-y in an understated, smart performance. The two leads were said to be an item during filming. **105m/C; VHS, DVD, Blu-Ray.** Gwyneth Paltrow; Ben Affleck; Natasha Henstridge; Jennifer Grey; Tony Goldwyn; Joe Morton; David Paymer; Johnny Galecki; Alex D. Linz; Juan Garcia; Sam Robards; Julia Campbell; Michael Laskin; John Levin; David Dorfman; ***D:*** Don Roos; ***W:*** Don Roos; ***C:*** Robert Elswit; ***M:*** Mychael Danna.

The Bounce Back **2016 (PG-13)** A Los Angeles-set indie romantic comedy about finding love that is rather obvious and superficial. Self-help author Matthew Taylor (Moore) has a new best-selling book called "The Bounce Back" which encourages people to leave their past behind and reinvent themselves to achieve their romantic future. When Matthew appears on a talk show, he meets Kristin Peralta (Velazquez), a therapist who believes that understanding one's past is key to a romantic future. The pair's robust debate moves to television, and they eventually find unexpected common ground. Though the leads are good looking, the result is shallow. **104m/C; DVD.** Shemar Moore; Nadine Velazquez; Bill Bellamy; Nadja Alaya; Denise Boutte; ***D:*** Youssef Delara; ***W:*** Youssef Delara; Victor Teran; Staci Robinson; ***C:*** Ben Kufrin; ***M:*** Reza Safinia.

Bound **1996 (R)** Ex-con Corky (Gershon) is busy fixing up her new apartment after serving five years for robbery. Her next-door neighbors are Caesar (Pantoliano), a neurotic, money-laundering mobster, and his sexy girlfriend, a seemingly dumb brunette named Violet (Tilly). The femme twosome hook up (in and out of bed) and hatch a plan to steal two million freshly laundered dollars from Caesar, who goes ballistic when he discovers the money gone. It's a flashy—but not substantive—thriller. Directorial debut for the brothers Wachowski. **107m/C; VHS, DVD, Blu-Ray.** Gina Gershon; Jennifer Tilly; Joe Pantoliano; John P. Ryan; Barry Kivel; Christopher Meloni; Peter Spellos; Richard Sarafian; Mary Mara; Susie Bright; Ivan Kane; Kevin M. Richardson; Gene Borkan; ***D:*** Lilly Wachowski; Lana Wachowski; ***W:*** Lilly Wachowski; Lana Wachowski; ***C:*** Bill Pope; ***M:*** Don Davis.

Bound and Gagged: A Love Story **1993 (R)** For some reason, Elizabeth (Saltarelli), who is desperate for a husband, thinks that she might increase her chances of finding one if she kidnaps her friend Leslie (Allen) and goes on a weird wild goose chase through Minnesota with the hostage and her hopeless partner-in-crime, Cliff (Denton). Go figure. **96m/C; VHS, DVD.** Ginger Lynn Allen; Karen Black; Chris Denton; Elizabeth Saltarelli; Mary Ella Ross; Chris Mulkey; ***D:*** Daniel Appleby; ***W:*** Daniel Appleby; ***C:*** Dean Lent; ***M:*** William Murphy.

Bound by a Secret **2009** Hallmark Channel original is pure schmaltz but Warren and Baxter make for a fine sisterly match-up. Successful actress Jane (Warren) visits her uptight sister Ida Mae (Baxter), who secretly raised Jane's now-grown and married daughter Kate (White). Jane's dying and wants to reveal her secret but Ida Mae has focused her life on Kate and is afraid of losing her love. **100m/C; DVD.** Meredith Baxter; Lesley Ann Warren; Bridget Ann White; Timothy Bottoms; Holt McCallany; Ellery Sprayberry; ***D:*** David S. Cass, Sr.; ***W:*** Darrell V. Orme Mann; ***C:*** James W. Wrenn; ***M:*** Kyle Newmaster. **CABLE**

Bound by Lies 1/2 **2005** Detectives Max Garrett (Baldwin) and Eddie Fulton (Whitfield) are assigned to protect Laura (Swanson)?a sexy photographer of erotic images—when a rash of serial murders linked to her work is uncovered. But Garrett puts himself in danger by falling for her. **85m/C; VHS, DVD.** Kristy Swanson; Stephen Baldwin; Charles Malik Whitfield; Natassia Malthe; Kevin Chamberlin; Joel Brooks; Tracy Howe; ***D:*** Valerie Landsburg; ***W:*** D. Alvelo; Leland Zaitz; ***C:*** Maximo Munzi. **VIDEO**

Bound for Glory 1/2 **1976 (PG)** The award-winning biography of American folk singer Woody Guthrie set against the backdrop of the Depression. Superb portrayal of the spirit and feelings of the period featuring many of his songs encased in the incidents that inspired them. Haskell Wexler's award-winning camera work is superbly expressive. **149m/C; VHS, DVD, Blu-Ray.** David Carradine; Ronny Cox; Melinda Dillon; Randy Quaid; ***D:*** Hal Ashby; ***W:*** Robert Getchell; ***C:*** Haskell Wexler. Oscars '76: Cinematog., Orig. Song Score and/or Adapt.; L.A. Film Critics '76: Cinematog.; Natl. Bd. of Review '76: Actor (Carradine); Natl. Soc. Film Critics '76: Cinematog.

Boundaries **2018 (R)** Laura (Farmiga) has tried to set boundaries with her pothead father (Plummer), but when he gets kicked out of his retirement home, she drives him down the Pacific Coast to stay with her sister. Along the way, he enlists his grandson to help sell his huge stash of marijuana, and pushes Laura into a reunion with her ex. So much for boundaries. And so much for a decent road trip story. The "multigenerational car trip with feisty old person" theme is played out, and even Plummer's talents and charms can't make up for this flat, sometimes cringeworthy, script. **104m/C; DVD.** Vera Farmiga; Christopher Plummer; Lewis MacDougall; Christopher Lloyd; Kristen Schaal; ***D:*** Shana Feste; ***W:*** Shana Feste; ***C:*** Sara Mishara; ***M:*** Michael Penn.

The Bounty 1/2 **1984 (PG)** A new version of "Mutiny on the Bounty," with emphasis on a more realistic relationship between Fletcher Christian and Captain Bligh—and a more sympathetic portrayal of the captain, too. The sensuality of Christian's relationship with a Tahitian beauty also receives greater importance. **130m/C; VHS, DVD, Blu-Ray.** Mel Gibson; Anthony Hopkins; Laurence Olivier; Edward Fox; Daniel Day-Lewis; Bernard Hill; Philip Davis; Liam Neeson; ***D:*** Roger Donaldson; ***W:*** Robert Bolt; ***C:*** Arthur Ibbetson; ***M:*** Vangelis.

Bounty **2009 (PG-13)** Bounty hunter Nate needs money to pay off a debt or he's a dead man. But it means breaking a female outlaw out of jail and claiming the reward for himself. Story doesn't exactly hold together but for a low-budget western it's almost tolerable. **90m/C; DVD.** Michelle Acuna; Austin O'Brien; Jarret LeMaster; Bruce Isham; Rodrick Lee Goins; Steve Savage; ***D:*** Jared Isham; ***W:*** Jared Isham; ***C:*** Kenneth Yeung; ***M:*** Jason Livesay; Nolan Livesay. **VIDEO**

The Bounty Hunter 1/2 **2010 (PG-13)** Trite romantic comedy inflicts a predictable plot, grating dialogue, and a plodding pace—a multiple offender. Bounty hunter Milo (Butler) is overjoyed when he finds out his next assignment is to bring in his ex-wife Nicole (Aniston), a reporter who missed her court date to look into a suspicious suicide. The majority of the movie consists of the couple bickering and one-upping each other while evading goons trying to stop Nicole from discovering the truth. The two finally decide to work together and romance is rekindled, despite the fact that Aniston and Butler have less chemistry than a remedial science class. Watch the classic "His Girl Friday" to see how it's done correctly. **110m/C; Blu-Ray, On Demand.** Gerard Butler; Jennifer Aniston; Jason Sudeikis; Christine Baranski; Cathy Moriarty; ***D:*** Andy Tennant; ***W:*** Sarah Thorp; ***C:*** Oliver Bokelberg.

Bounty Hunters **1996 (R)** Rival bounty hunters (and ex-lovers) Jersey Bellini (Dudikoff) and B.B. Mitchell (Howard) join forces to capture bail-jumping, stolen-car king Delmos (Ratner), who's also the target of mob hitmen. Gunplay and car chases. **98m/C; VHS, DVD.** Michael Dudikoff; Lisa Howard; Benjamin Ratner; ***D:*** George Erschbamer; ***W:*** George Erschbamer; ***C:*** A.J. Vesak; ***M:*** Norman Orenstein.

Bounty Hunters 2: Hardball *Hardball* **1997 (R)** A bounty hunter and his female partner tick off the mob by foiling a heist and now must fend off hired killers looking for revenge. **97m/C; VHS, DVD, Blu-Ray.** Michael Dudikoff; Lisa Howard; Steve Bacic; Tony Curtis; ***D:*** George Erschbamer; ***W:*** George Erschbamer; Jeff Barmash; Michael Ellis; ***C:*** Brian Pearson; ***M:*** Leon Aronson. **VIDEO**

Bounty Killer 1/2 **2013 (R)** An action science fiction thriller about a post-apocalyptic future in which white collar criminals are hunted and made to pay. Two decades earlier, corporations took charge of the governments of most of the countries of the world. During their reign of terror, they focused on consolidating power and making profits which led to the worldwide corporate wars and the end of the civilization as we know it. In this dark era, the Council of Nine took control of the world and issued death warrants for all white collar criminals. A class of bounty hunters becomes the world's retributive heroes as they search for all white collar criminals and gain fame and money in the process. **92m/C; DVD, Blu-Ray, Streaming, Download.** Matthew Marsden; Kristanna Loken; Christian Pitre; Barak Hardley; Abraham Benrubi; ***D:*** Henry Saine; ***W:*** Henry Saine; Jason Dodson; Colin Ebeling; ***C:*** David Conley; ***M:*** Greg Edmonson.

The Bouquet 1/2 **2013** Terri (Swanson) ad her younger sister Mandy (Mayne) have always been opposites but they must set aside their differences when a family tragedy strikes. Terri comes home and must help Mandy and their mother, Bonnie (Cavendish), save the family's failing flower business and rediscover their family ties. **99m/C; DVD.** Kristy Swanson; Alberta Mayne; Nicola Cavendish; Danny Glover; Michael Shanks; Jermy Guilbaut; Stephen E. Miller; ***D:*** Anne Wheeler; ***W:*** Kele McGlohon; ***C:*** Paul Mitchnick; ***M:*** Stu Goldberg. **VIDEO**

The Bourne Identity **1988** Chamberlain stars as an amnesiac trying to piece together the fragments of his memory. Is he U.S. espionage agent Jason Bourne or an international terrorist? Aided by Smith (the kidnap victim who falls in love with her captor), the two traverse Europe trying to escape the spy network out to assassinate the mystery man who knows too little. Exciting miniseries adaptation of the Robert Ludlum thriller. **185m/C; VHS, DVD, Blu-Ray.** Richard Chamberlain; Jaclyn Smith; Denholm Elliott; Anthony Quayle; Donald Moffat; Yorgo Voyagis; ***D:*** Roger Young; ***W:*** Carol Sobieski. **TV**

The Bourne Identity 1/2 **2002 (PG-13)** First-rate international espionage thriller loosely based on the first book (published in 1981) of Robert Ludlum's trilogy, previously filmed as a 1988 TV miniseries starring Richard Chamberlain. A young man (Damon) gets fished out of the ocean with a couple of bullet holes and amnesia—his only clue a numbered Swiss account. This reveals he has multiple identities, including that of Jason Bourne, who has an apartment in Paris. To get there, Bourne pays free-spirited Marie (Potente) for a ride. As Bourne tries to piece his past together, he learns he's a highly efficient assassin for a covert CIA operation and his boss (Cooper) considers him a rogue operative and is trying to kill him. **118m/C; VHS, DVD, Blu-Ray, UMD, HD-DVD.** Matt Damon; Franka Potente; Chris Cooper; Brian Cox; Clive Owen; Julia Stiles; Gabriel Mann; Adewale Akinnuoye-Agbaje; Walton Goggins; Josh Hamilton; Tim Dutton; ***D:*** Doug Liman; ***W:*** Tony Gilroy; W(illiam) Blake Herron; ***C:*** Oliver Wood; ***M:*** John Powell.

The Bourne Legacy **2012 (PG-13)** Tony Gilroy, the writer of the first three films based on the Robert Ludlum series, cleverly expands on his own universe by presenting viewers with another agent, Aaron Cross (Renner), in the Bourne program. The new Bourne works much like the old Bourne although Gilroy isn't as adept at action, but he makes up for it with razor-sharp dialogue and clever plotting. It takes some time to get going but Gilroy has a gift with words--and Renner, Weisz, and Norton at delivering them--that once this Legacy takes off it doesn't look back. **125m/C; DVD, Blu-Ray.** Jeremy Renner; Rachel Weisz; Edward Norton; Joan Allen; Albert Finney; David Strathairn; Scott Glenn; ***D:*** Tony Gilroy; ***W:*** Tony Gilroy; Dan Gilroy; ***C:*** Robert Elswit; ***M:*** James Newton Howard.

The Bourne Supremacy **2004 (PG-13)** Warning! The easily-queasy should be wary of the hand-held camerawork and quick edits of the action sequences. Amnesiac CIA-trained assassin Jason Bourne (Damon) is now living quietly with girlfriend Marie (Potente) when he's targeted for death by Russian bad guys and made the patsy for a Berlin hit on a couple of agents. CIA officer Landy (Allen) and her boss (Cox) try to reel Bourne in while he tries to figure out just who wants him dead this time (and why). The non-stop action moves from India to Berlin to Amsterdam to Moscow, and while the plot eventually turns out to be simple enough, the chases are not. Damon once again proves adept as an action man while making Bourne an intelligent and oddly sympathetic character. Loosely adapted from the second book of Robert Ludlum's Bourne trilogy. **109m/C; VHS, DVD, Blu-Ray, UMD, HD-DVD.** Matt Damon; Franka Potente; Joan Allen; Brian Cox; Marton Csokas; Gabriel Mann; Karel Roden; Julia Stiles; Karl Urban; Tomas Arana; Tim Griffin; Michelle Monaghan; Tom Gallop; John Bedford Lloyd; Ethan Sandler; Oksana Akinshina; ***D:*** Paul Greengrass; ***W:*** Tony Gilroy; ***C:*** Oliver Wood; ***M:*** John Powell.

The Bourne Ultimatum 1/2 **2007 (PG-13)** In this third (and final?) chapter Jason Bourne (Damon) continues his search for clues to to his past with Treadstone, the mothballed facility where he was trained. Now CIA official Vosen (Strathairn) wants to revive the project, and assigns agent Lundy (Allen) to eliminate Bourne. Meanwhile, Bourne is outmaneuvering cops, feds, spooks, and Interpol agents in Moscow, Paris, Madrid, Tangier, London, and New York. Smart, tense, and frenetic, with excellent performances from all involved. The only drawback is the confusion- and nausea-inducing camera work during the action sequences. **111m/C; DVD, Blu-Ray, HD-DVD.** Matt Damon; Julia Stiles; Joan Allen; David Strathairn; Paddy Considine; Edgar Ramirez; Scott Glenn; Albert Finney; Tom Gallop; Corey Johnson; Daniel Brühl; Colin Stinton; Joey Ansah; ***D:*** Paul Greengrass; ***W:*** Tony Gilroy; Scott Burns; George Nolfi; ***C:*** Oliver Wood; ***M:*** John Powell. Oscars '07: Film Editing, Sound, Sound FX Editing; British Acad. '07: Film Editing, Sound.

Boutique 1/2 **2004** Window dresser at a chic boutique in Tehran steals a pair of jeans for a girl he's interested in after she says she can't afford anything at the establishment. This is the beginning of a downward spiral in his life. Thoughtfully moving film makes startling observations of Iranian society. In Farsi with English subtitles. **113m/C; DVD.** Mohammad Reza Golzar; Golshifteh Farahani; Reza Rooygari; ***D:*** Hamid Nematollah; ***W:*** Hamid Nematollah; ***C:*** Mahmoud Kalari; ***M:*** Fariborz Lachini. **VIDEO**

Bowfinger *Bowfinger's Big Thing* **1999 (PG-13)** Martin stars as wannabe Hollywood player Bobby Bowfinger, who is desperate to break into the big time. His one hope is to convince action star Kit Ramsey (Murphy) to be in a cheesy sci-fi scare flick entitled "Chubby Rain." But Ramsey and his tyrannical New Age advisor Stricter (Stamp) want nothing to do with the movie. Bowfinger gets a crew together and stalks Ramsey through the streets of L.A., filming his every movement so that the material can be used in the movie. After his tactics send Ramsey to the "relaxation home," Bowfinger hires geeky lookalike Jiff (also Murphy) to take his place. The pairing of Martin and Murphy works well, and Frank Oz is an expert at directing offbeat comedies such as this. **96m/C; VHS, DVD, Blu-Ray.** Steve Martin; Eddie Murphy; Christine Baranski; Heather Graham; Terence Stamp; Jamie Kennedy; Robert Downey, Jr.; Barry Newman; ***D:*** Frank Oz; ***W:*** Steve Martin; ***C:*** Ueli Steiger; ***M:*** David Newman.

Bowling for Columbine **2002 (R)** Moore takes on the trigger-happy American gun culture, as well as the media, the NRA, and Littleton, Colorado'the site of the Columbine High School killings—with his usual blend of satire and chutzpah. **120m/C; VHS, DVD, Blu-Ray.** ***D:*** Michael Moore; ***W:*** Michael Moore. Oscars '02: Feature Doc.; Ind. Spirit '03: Feature Doc.; Writers Guild '02: Orig. Screenplay.

The Box 1/2 **2003 (R)** Ah, it must be true love when an ex-con and an ex-stripper hook up at the local diner. But problems plague the happy pair's future like his mob connections, her psycho ex-husband, and the thugs who want their big bag of loot. **99m/C; VHS, DVD.** James Russo; Theresa Russell; Brad Dourif; Steve Railsback; Jon Polito; Michael Rooker; Joe Palese; Lee Weaver; ***D:*** Richard Pepin; ***W:*** James Russo; ***M:*** Chris Anderson. **VIDEO**

The Box **2007 (R)** Two homicide detectives question a thief and a victim of a robbery gone wrong. One detective has to face past mistakes, while the other gets an offer from the criminal behind the botched heist. **96m/C; DVD.** Gabrielle Union; Giancarlo Esposito; A. J. Buckley; Jason George; Mia Maestro; James Madio; Yul Vazquez; Brett Donowho; ***D:*** A.J. Kparr; ***W:*** A.J. Kparr; ***C:*** Sion Michel; ***M:*** James T. Sale.

The Box ½ **2009 (PG-13)** A troubled married couple, Norma and Arthur (Diaz and Marsden), is given a mysterious wooden box by a stranger who tells them if they press the button to open the box they will be given $1 million. The downside is that a person unknown to them will be murdered and they have 24 hours to decide what to do. A preposterous premise stretched to its absolute limits, but done so smoothly that somehow logic never comes into question. Director Kelly, of "Donnie Darko" cult fame, brings his usual touch of controlled confusion, loved by many and hated by just as many. Based on the Richard Matheson short story "Button, Button," also made into a Twilight Zone episode in 1986. **115m/C; Blu-Ray, On Demand.** Cameron Diaz; James Marsden; Frank Langella; Gillian Jacobs; James Rebhorn; Holmes Osborne; Sam Oz Stone; ***D:*** Richard Kelly; ***W:*** Richard Kelly; ***C:*** Steven Poster; ***M:*** Win Butler; Regine Chassagne; Owen Pallett.

Box of Moonlight **1996 (R)** Hard-working, by-the-book electrical systems engineer Al Fountain (Turturo) feels mysteriously compelled to play hookey from his family and career while on an out-of-town business trip. Lost and confused, Al meets up with the Kid, a quirky recluse played with energy and appeal by Rockwell. Through a series of mix-ups, the nice-but-stuffy Al and the wild-but-well-meaning Kid end up spending the fourth of July weekend together. Al's inability to see the point of his journey long after the audience probably has makes the film a bit predictable and stale. DeCillo's third feature was six years in the making and financed by the success of his second feature, "Living in Oblivion." **111m/C; VHS, DVD.** John Turturro; Sam Rockwell; Catherine Keener; Lisa Blount; Annie Corley; Dermot Mulroney; Alexander Goodwin; ***D:*** Tom DiCillo; ***W:*** Tom DiCillo; ***C:*** Dr. Paul Ryan; ***M:*** Jim Farmer.

Boxboarders! **2007 (PG-13)** Two goofy teen extreme sports enthusiasts with too much time on their hands find a refrigerator box in the trash and decide to mount it on a skateboard and see what happens. As they keep tinkering with their creation, they invent an unlikely new sport that draws somewhat overwhelming media attention (complete with racing footage) and unwelcome competition. **90m/C; DVD.** Austin Basis; Melora Hardin; Stephen Tobolowsky; Julie Brown; Dale Midkiff; James Immekus; Mitch Eakins; ***D:*** Rob Heddon; ***W:*** Rob Heddon; ***C:*** Matthew Williams. **VIDEO**

Boxcar Bertha ½ **1972 (R)** Scorsese's vivid portrayal of the South during the 1930s' Depression casts Hershey as a woman who winds up in cahoots with an anti-establishment train robber. Based on the book "Sister of the Road" by Boxcar Bertha Thomson. **90m/C; VHS, DVD, Blu-Ray.** Barbara Hershey; David Carradine; John Carradine; Barry Primus; Bernie Casey; Victor Argo; Martin Scorsese; John Stephens; ***D:*** Martin Scorsese; ***W:*** John W. Corrington; Joyce H. Corrington; ***M:*** Gib Guilbeau; Thad Maxwell.

The Boxer ½ **1997 (R)** Affecting, if predictable, romance set in Ulster, Northern Ireland. Having served 14 years in prison Danny Flynn (Day-Lewis) wants nothing more to do with politics and violence. But his return to his old neighborhood—where he hopes to get back to his boxing career—finds him in the thick of both. Danny manages to persuade his ex-trainer, the alcoholic Ike (Stott), to help him re-open the local gym but resentment is high. Particularly from hard-liner Harry (McSorley), who doesn't like Danny's live-and-let-live attitude and is incensed that he's interested in rekindling his lost-but-never-forgotten love for Maggie (Watson), who's the daughter of local IRA boss Joe (Cox), and the wife of another IRA prisoner. Things quickly turn ugly but the emotionally fragile Danny and Maggie continue to fight to be together against formidable odds. **113m/C; VHS, DVD, Blu-Ray.** *GB IR* Daniel Day-Lewis; Emily Watson; Brian Cox; Gerard McSorley; Ken Stott; Ciaran Fitzgerald; Kenneth Cranham; ***Cameo(s):*** Tom Bell; ***D:*** Jim Sheridan; ***W:*** Jim Sheridan; Terry George; ***C:*** Chris Menges; ***M:*** Gavin Friday; Maurice Seezer.

The Boxer and the Bombshell *The Tender Hook* **2008** It's the early 1920s in Sydney, Australia and beautiful young Iris (Byrne) is the paramour of middle-aged McHeath (Weaving). He's a gangster and shady fight promoter whose new boxing protege is Art (Le Nevez). Iris and Art are immediately attracted to one another and it all becomes a dangerous romantic mix of jealousy and violence. **100m/C; DVD.** *AU* Rose Byrne; Hugo Weaving; Pia Miranda; Matthew Le Nevez; Tyler Coppin; John Batchelor; ***D:*** Jonathan Ogilvie; ***W:*** Jonathan Ogilvie; ***C:*** Geoffrey Simpson; ***M:*** Chris Abrahams.

Boxing Helena **1993 (R)** Highly publicized as the film that cost Basinger almost $9 million in damages, the debut of director/writer Jennifer Lynch (daughter of David) explores the dark side of relationships between men and women. Sands is Dr. Nick Cavanaugh, a surgeon who becomes dangerously obsessed with the beautiful, yet unattainable Helena (Fenn). When she is hit by a car near his home, he performs emergency surgery and amputates her arms and legs, forcing her to be dependent on him. Metaphorically a situation, albeit an extreme one, that mirrors the power struggle in any sexual relationship. Problematic in some aspects, although equally fascinating as it is disturbing. **107m/C; VHS, DVD.** Julian Sands; Sherilyn Fenn; Bill Paxton; Kurtwood Smith; Betsy Clark; Nicolette Scorsese; Art Garfunkel; Meg Register; Bryan Smith; ***D:*** Jennifer Lynch; ***W:*** Jennifer Lynch; ***C:*** Bojan Bazelli; ***M:*** Graeme Revell. Golden Raspberries '93: Worst Director (Lynch).

The Boxtrolls ½ **2014 (PG)** Alan Snow's "Here Be Monsters" is very loosely adapted in the third stop-motion animation from LAIKA after hits "Coraline" and "Paranorman." The imaginative world of Cheesebridge—brought to life with a level of detail that the form hasn't seen before—features an underworld of creatures known as Boxtrolls. They happen to have one human among them, named Eggs (Wright), who fights back against the humans above ground who have demonized and hunted his friends, led by the nefarious Snatcher (Kingsley). It's not quite as ambitious as the other LAIKA films but the world creation here is breathtaking. **97m/C; DVD, Blu-Ray.** ***V:*** Isaac Hempstead-Wright; Ben Kingsley; Elle Fanning; Jared Harris; Toni Collette; Simon Pegg; Nick Frost; ***D:*** Anthony Staachi; Graham Annable; ***W:*** Irena Brignull; Adam Pava; ***C:*** John Ashlee Prat; ***M:*** Dario Marianelli.

The Boy **2016 (PG-13)** A horror-thriller about a nanny hired for a most unusual job. American woman Greta (Cohan) is hired to be a nanny for a family in a remote location in England. When she arrives to begin work, she learns the 8-year-old child she is taking care of is a life-sized doll. His parents care for the doll just like a child, having lost their own son two decades earlier. Part of the care of her charge includes a strict set of rules. When Greta violates one, the situation takes a dark turn as scary and unexplainable events begin occurring. Greta begins to believe that the doll is really living. **97m/C; DVD, Blu-Ray, Streaming, Download.** Lauren Cohan; Rupert Evans; James Russell; Jim Norton; Diana Hardcastle; ***D:*** William Brent Bell; ***W:*** Stacey Menear; ***C:*** Daniel Pearl; ***M:*** Bear McCreary.

Boy A **2007 (R)** The 24-year-old, newly renamed Jack Burridge (Garfield) has gotten out of a Manchester prison after 14 years for his involvement in the brutal murder of another youngster. His dedicated case-worker Terry (Mullan) emphasizes that Jack must not reveal his previous identity or discuss his crime or jail time. Jack hesitantly reenters society and gets an apartment, a job, and a girlfriend (Lyons), but one act of heroism backfires when media attention leads to exposure about his past. **100m/C; DVD.** *GB* Andrew Garfield; Peter Mullan; Shaun Evans; Katie Lyons; Taylor Doherty; ***D:*** John Crowley; ***W:*** Mark O'Rowe; ***C:*** Rob Hardy; ***M:*** Paddy Cunneen.

A Boy. A Girl. A Dream. ½ **2018 (R)** On election night in 2016, club promoter Cass (Hardwick) meets Frida (Good), a beautiful visitor to Los Angeles. The pair get to know each other as they travel around the city, including to and from a party in the Hollywood Hills. Most of their conversations take place in the backseats of cars. There, they learn they have different backgrounds but find common ground as discuss their hopes and dreams. Shot in one night and playing out in one take, this indie drama is a thoughtful, genuine exploration of how people relate to those they have just met. **89m/C; DVD.** Omari Hardwick; Meagan Good; Jay Ellis; Dijon Talton; Kenya Barris; ***D:*** Qasim Basir; ***W:*** Qasim Basir; Samantha Tanner; ***C:*** Steven Holleran.

A Boy and His Dog ½ **1975 (R)** In the post-holocaust world of 2024, a young man (Johnson) and his telepathic canine (McIntire supplies narration of the dog's thoughts) cohort search for food and sex. They happen upon a community that drafts Johnson to repopulate their largely impotent race; Johnson is at first ready, willing, and able, until he discovers the mechanical methods they mean to employ. Based on a short story by Harlan Ellison. The dog was played by the late Tiger of "The Brady Bunch." **87m/C; VHS, DVD, Blu-Ray.** Don Johnson; Susanne Benton; Jason Robards, Jr.; Charles McGraw; Alvy Moore; Helene Winston; Hal Baylor; L.Q. Jones; ***V:*** Tim McIntire; ***D:*** L.Q. Jones; ***W:*** L.Q. Jones; ***C:*** John Morrill; ***M:*** Tim McIntire.

Boy & the World *O Menino e o Mundo* **2015 (PG)** The conflict between rural and urban is explored through the story of Cuca, a young boy from a small village whose world is turned upside down when his father leaves for the city and the quest Cuca goes on to find him. Portuguese with subtitles. **81m/C; DVD, Blu-Ray.** Vinicius Garcia; Felipe Zilse; Ale Abreu; Lu Horta; Marco Aurelio Campos; ***D:*** Ale Abreu; ***W:*** Ale Abreu; ***M:*** Ruben Feffer; Gustavo Kurlat.

Boy Culture **2006** Money, desire, and emotional denial. X (Magyar) is a cynical hustler with a high-end and limited clientele of older men. His newest client, the urbane Gregory (Bachau), confuses X by paying for his company but refusing his sexual favors unless X is also emotionally involved. X can't even admit his attraction to his roommate Andrew (Stevens), who's unsure of his own sexuality, while their other roomie, twink Joey (Trent), openly lusts after X. Based on the novel by Matthew Rettenmund. **90m/C; DVD.** Derek Magyar; Patrick Bauchau; Darryl Stephens; John Trent; ***D:*** Q. Allan Brocka; ***W:*** Q. Allan Brocka; ***C:*** Jerusha Hess; ***M:*** Ryan Beveridge.

Boy, Did I Get a Wrong Number! **1966** A real estate agent gets more than he bargained for when he accidentally dials a wrong number. Zany comedy persists as Hope gets entangled in the life of sexy starlet Sommer. **100m/C; VHS, DVD, Blu-Ray.** Bob Hope; Phyllis Diller; Marjorie Lord; Elke Sommer; Cesare Danova; Kelly Thordsen; ***D:*** George Marshall; ***W:*** Albert Lewin; Burt Styler; ***C:*** Lionel Lindon; ***M:*** Richard LaSalle.

Boy Erased ½ **2018 (R)** After being forcibly outed to his conservative Baptist parents, 19-year-old Jared (Hedges) is given an ultimatum: attend a Christian gay-conversion program or get disowned by his family. Based on Garrard Conley's true-life horror story, this film takes us inside a program that utilizes cruelty under the guise of therapy. The acting is suberb -- Hedges will break your heart as a young man trying to please his parents and the program's leader (writer/director Edgerton) at a huge cost to himself, and Kidman and Crowe manage to elicit sympathy as loving parents who truly, but misguidedly, believe they're doing the right thing for their son. **115m/C; DVD, Blu-Ray, Streaming.** *US AU* Lucas Hedges; Nicole Kidman; Russell Crowe; Joel Edgerton; Cherry Jones; ***D:*** Joel Edgerton; ***W:*** Joel Edgerton; ***C:*** Eduard Grau; ***M:*** Danny Bensi; Saunder Jurriaans.

The Boy Friend **1971 (G)** Russell pays tribute to the Busby Berkeley Hollywood musical. Lots of charming dance numbers and clever parody of plotlines in this adaptation of Sandy Wilson's stage play. Fun! **135m/C; VHS, DVD, Blu-Ray.** *GB* Twiggy; Christopher Gable; Moyra Fraser; Max Adrian; Vladek Sheybal; Georgina Hale; Tommy Tune; ***D:*** Ken Russell; ***W:*** Ken Russell; ***C:*** David Watkin. Golden Globes '72: Actress--Mus./Comedy (Twiggy).

The Boy From Oklahoma **1954** Amiable western programmer. Law student Tom Brewster (Rogers Jr.) is in the corrupt town of Bluerock, where he's offered the job of sheriff by town boss Turlock (Caruso) who thinks the young man will be easy to control. Armed with his trusty lasso--Tom won't carry a gun--he intends to clean up the town instead. The move begat the 1957-61 TV series "Sugarfoot." **88m/C; DVD.** Will Rogers, Jr.; Nancy Olson; Lon Chaney, Jr.; Anthony Caruso; Wallace Ford; Merv Griffin; ***D:*** Michael Curtiz; ***W:*** Winston Miller; Frank Davis; ***C:*** Robert Burks; ***M:*** Max Steiner.

Boy in Blue ½ **1986 (R)** A "Rocky"-esque biography of Canadian speed-rower Ned Hanlan, who set aside lackluster pursuits to turn to rowing. **97m/C; VHS, DVD, Blu-Ray.** *CA* Nicolas Cage; Christopher Plummer; David Naughton; Cynthia Dale; Melody Anderson; James B. Douglas; ***D:*** Charles Jarrott; ***W:*** Douglas Bowie; ***C:*** Pierre Mignot; ***M:*** Roger Webb.

The Boy in the Plastic Bubble ½ **1976** Well-made, sensitive drama about a young man born with immunity deficiencies who must grow up in a specially controlled plastic environment. Travolta is endearing as the boy in the bubble. **100m/C; VHS, DVD.** John Travolta; Robert Reed; Glynnis O'Connor; Diana Hyland; Ralph Bellamy; Anne Ramsey; Vernee Watson-Johnson; P.J. Soles; John Friedrich; ***D:*** Randal Kleiser; ***W:*** Douglas Day Stewart; ***C:*** Arch R. Dalzell; ***M:*** Paul Williams; Mark Snow. **TV**

The Boy in the Striped Pajamas **2008 (PG-13)** In 1940's Germany, eight-year-old Bruno (Butterfield), the son of a Nazi prison camp commandant (Thewlis), and his family move from a comfortable home in Berlin out to the country where they will live on a "farm." Bruno questions his parents about the people working the fields he can see from his new bedroom window, wondering why they all wear striped pajamas. When his parents answers are inadequate, Bruno sneaks out to the far reaches of the farm, where he meets and befriends a boy his own age, Shmuel. Their circumstances seem equally confusing to both boys as they build a bond through the barbed wire fence. The story unfolds primarily from Bruno's perspective until the final scenes, which begin to switch to Shmuel's point of view. Poignant and timeless, the film is primarily directed at a young audience and serves to point out how easily people accept evil when they elevate some purpose above basic morality. Adapted from John Boyle's 2006 novel of the same name. **94m/C; Blu-Ray.** *US GB* David Thewlis; Vera Farmiga; David Hayman; Rupert Friend; Bruno; Shmuel; Amber Beattie; Sheila Hancock; Richard Johnson; Jim Norton; ***D:*** Mark Herman; ***W:*** Mark Herman; ***C:*** Benoit Delhomme; ***M:*** James Horner.

Boy Meets Girl **1938** Cagney and O'Brien play screenwriters whose every film is a variation on the boy meets girl theme. Trouble is they're running out of ideas and their scripts get increasingly outlandish. A fading cowboy actor is supposed to star in the duo's next film—if they can ever settle down to work. Then they get the idea to feature their friend Wilson's baby in the movie—and guess who becomes a new star. Good satire on moviemaking and movie moguls, which made fine use of the Warner studio back lots, sound stages, and offices. Based on the play by Bella and Samuel Spewack who also wrote the screenplay. **86m/B; DVD.** James Cagney; Pat O'Brien; Ralph Bellamy; Dick Foran; Marie Wilson; Frank McHugh; Bruce Lester; Ronald Reagan; Penny Singleton; James Stephenson; ***D:*** Lloyd Bacon; ***W:*** Bella Spewack; Samuel Spewack.

Boy Meets Girl 🦴🦴🦴 **1984** Alex (Lavant), a French Holden Caulfield type character, cruises the seamier side of Paris in this acclaimed film. Carax's directoral debut at age 22. Alex will return in the Carax films "Bad Blood" (1986) and "The Lovers on the Bridge" (1991). French with subtitles. **100m/B; VHS, DVD, Blu-Ray.** *FR* Denis Lavant; Mireille Perrier; Carroll Brooks; Anna Baldaccini; ***D:*** Leos Carax; ***W:*** Leos Carax; ***C:*** Jean-Yves Escoffier; ***M:*** Jacques Pinault.

The Boy Next Door 🦴 **2015 (R)** Director Cohen's erotic thriller is one of those films that most people presume they stopped making 20 years ago. High school teacher Claire (Lopez) is in the middle of a divorce when she has a one-night stand with the hunk new guy (Guzman) who lives next door. Of course, Claire has no idea that her fling is young enough to enroll at her school, nor that he's a few cards short of a full deck. When she tries to break it off, his unhealthy obsession with her blossoms because, well, there's no movie otherwise. **91m/C; DVD, Blu-Ray.** Jennifer Lopez; Ryan Guzman; Ian Nelson; John Corbett; Kristin Chenoweth; Hill Harper; ***D:*** Rob Cohen; ***W:*** Barbara Curry; ***C:*** Dave McFarland; ***M:*** Nathan Barr; Randy Edelman.

Boy Who Caught a Crook 🦴 ½ **1961** Young newsboy finds a briefcase filled with cash and shares his good fortune with his hobo friend. The kid's widowed mother wants to turn everything over to the police, especially when they learn that the money belongs to a bank robber who'll do anything to get it back. **73m/B; DVD.** Roger Mobley; Wanda Hendrix; Johnny Seven; Don Beddoe; Robert Stevenson; Bill (William) Walker; Richard Crane; ***D:*** Edward L. Cahn; ***W:*** Nathan "Jerry" Juran; ***C:*** Gilbert Warrenton; ***M:*** Richard LaSalle.

The Boy Who Could Fly 🦴🦴🦴 **1986 (PG)** After a plane crash kills his parents, a boy withdraws into a fantasy land where he can fly. The young daughter of a troubled family makes friends with him and the fantasy becomes real. A sweet film for children, charming though melancholy for adults, too. Fine cast, including Savage, Dewhurst, and Bedelia keep this from becoming sappy. **120m/C; VHS, DVD.** Lucy Deakins; Jay Underwood; Bonnie Bedelia; Colleen Dewhurst; Fred Savage; Fred Gwynne; Louise Fletcher; Jason Priestley; ***D:*** Nick Castle; ***W:*** Nick Castle; ***C:*** Steven Poster; ***M:*** Bruce Broughton.

The Boy Who Cried Werewolf 🦴🦴 ½ **2010** Harmless, cheap-looking Nickelodeon horror comedy. Shy teen Jordan Sands (Justice) and her family inherit a castle in Wolfsberg, Romania. They arrive in time to celebrate the small town festival honoring the Wolfsbeg Beast. Thanks to a lab accident, Jordan is transformed into a werewolf and it's up to her brother Hunter (Ellison) and their stern housekeeper Madame Varcolac (Shields) to get her a cure. **86m/C; DVD, Blu-Ray.** Victoria Justice; Chase Ellison; Brooke Shields; Matt Winston; Steven Grayhm; Brooke D'Orsay; ***D:*** Eric Bross; ***W:*** Douglas Sloan; ***C:*** Robert MacLachlan; ***M:*** John Van Tongeren. **CABLE**

The Boy Who Harnessed the Wind 🦴🦴 ½ **2019** In a drought-stricken Malawi village, teen William Kamkwamba (Simba) has been interested in electronics his whole life. He does radio repairs to help his farmer family financially and collects parts from the junkyard. Because of the family's struggles, he is forced to drop out of school but keeps access to its library. There, William discovers an eighth grade American textbook about energy and uses the information to help save his family and his village. Based on William's true story and published autobiography, the well-crafted film is inspiring and hopeful, largely because of the impressive work of first-time director Ejiofor and actor Simba. **113m/C; DVD.** Maxwell Simba; Chiwetel Ejiofor; Aïssa Maïga; Lily Banda; Felix Lemburo; ***D:*** Chiwetel Ejiofor; ***W:*** Chiwetel Ejiofor; ***C:*** Dick Pope; ***M:*** Antonio Pinto.

The Boy with the Green Hair 🦴🦴🦴 **1948** When he hears that his parents were killed in an air raid, a boy's hair turns green. The narrow-minded members of his community suddenly want nothing to do with him and he becomes an outcast. Thought-provoking social commentary. **82m/C; VHS, DVD.** Pat O'Brien; Robert Ryan; Barbara Hale; Dean Stockwell; ***D:*** Joseph Losey.

The Boy With the Sun in His Eyes 🦴 ½ **2009** After John's best friend Kevin commits suicide, he unexpectedly meets B-movie queen Solange at Kevin's funeral. She was big in 1980s Italian-made horror flicks and decides she needs a new personal assistant when she travels back to Italy and France. However, John finds that Solange's jet-setting, freaky lifestyle may not agree with him after all. **95m/C; DVD, Blu-Ray.** Tim Swain; Mahogany Reynolds; Josh Ubaldi; Valentin Plessy; ***D:*** Todd Verow; ***W:*** Todd Verow; Jim Dwyer; Geretta Geretta; ***M:*** Guglielmo (William) Bottin. **VIDEO**

Boy Wonder 🦴🦴 **2010 (R)** Sean grew up with an alcoholic, abusive dad and witnessed his mother's murder. He studies mug shots to allegedly find the killer but really to see which criminals have evaded justice. Homicide detective Teresa Ames suspects the emotionally volatile teen is behind a series of beatdowns of street scum and considers whether Sean is making things better or worse. **93m/C; DVD.** Caleb Steinmeyer; Zulay Henao; Bill Sage; James Russo; Tracy Middendorf; ***D:*** Michael Morrissey; ***W:*** Michael Morrissey; ***C:*** Christopher LaVasseur.

Boycott 🦴🦴🦴 ½ **2002** Superb HBO docudrama re-creates the Civil Rights movement's early days, from Rosa Parks's (Little-Thomas) refusal to give up her seat to a white man on a segregated Montgomery, Alabama, bus, through the subsequent boycott of the bus system by the city's black population, to the success of the boycott and the rise to prominence of Dr. Martin Luther King Jr. (Wright) as the movement's most eloquent and popular leader. Through the use and mix of many different visual styles, director Johnson uses artful touches to tell the story without overplaying his hand. Wright is fantastic as King, with other outstanding performances turned in by Howard as Ralph Abernathy and Pounder as boycott organizer Jo Anne Robinson. **112m/C; VHS, DVD.** Jeffrey Wright; Terrence Howard; CCH Pounder; Carmen Ejogo; Reg E. Cathey; Brent Jennings; Shawn Michael Howard; Erik Todd Dellums; Iris Little-Thomas; Whitman Mayo; E. Roger Mitchell; Mike Hodge; Clark Johnson; ***D:*** Clark Johnson; ***W:*** Timothy J. Sexton; Herman Daniel Farrell, III; ***C:*** David Hennings; ***M:*** Stephen James Taylor. **CABLE**

A Boyfriend for Christmas 🦴🦴 ½ **2004** When she was 12, Holly Grant asked Santa for a Christmas boyfriend and he promises her one—in 20 years. Now working for a nonprofit, Holly (Williams) is ticked at attorney Ryan (Muldoon), whom she's never met, when he misses an important appointment. When he turns up on her doorstep with a Christmas tree to make amends, Holly thinks he's someone else and he goes along with the charade so they can have a chance at romance. Her family thinks Holly's new guy is great but what will happen when the truth comes out? A Hallmark Channel original. **100m/C; DVD.** Kelli Williams; Patrick Muldoon; Charles Durning; Shannon Wilcox; Martin Mull; Bruce Thomas; Maeve Quinlan; Bridget Ann White; David Starzyk; ***D:*** Kevin Connor; ***W:*** Roger Schroeder; ***C:*** Amit Bhattacharya; ***M:*** Charles Syndor. **CABLE**

Boyfriends & Girlfriends 🦴🦴 ½ *My Girlfriend's Boyfriend; L'Ami de Mon Ami* **1988 (PG)** Another one of Rohmer's "Comedies and Proverbs," in which two girls with boyfriends fade in and out of interest with each, casually reshuffling their relationships. Typical, endless-talks-at-cafes Rohmer, the most happily consistent of the aging French New Wave. In French with subtitles. **102m/C; VHS, DVD.** *FR* Emmanuelle Chaulet; Sophie Renoir; Eric Viellard; Francois-Eric Gendron; Anne-Laure Meury; ***D:*** Eric Rohmer; ***W:*** Eric Rohmer; ***C:*** Bernard Lutic; ***M:*** Jean-Louis Valero.

Boyhood 🦴🦴🦴 **2014 (R)** For twelve years, writer/director Linklater assembled a small crew and cast for a few weeks every year, shooting the entire school-age arc of a young man. The result is a film that captures the ups and downs of 1st grade through high school graduation with a protagonist (Coltrane) who ages before our eyes; with great supporting turns from Hawke and Arquette as his fictional parents. The film is naturally episodic (that's part of the point) and the second half works much more than the first (as its director became a better filmmaker) but this is a stunningly ambitious piece of work. **164m/C; DVD, Blu-Ray.** Ellar Coltrane; Lorelei Linklater; Ethan Hawke; Patricia Arquette; Evie Thompson; ***D:*** Richard Linklater; ***W:*** Richard Linklater; ***C:*** Lee Daniel; Shane Kelly. Oscars '14: Actress--Supporting (Arquette); British Acad. '14: Actress--Supporting (Arquette), Director (Linklater), Film; Golden Globes '15: Actress--Supporting (Arquette), Director (Linklater), Film--Drama; Ind. Spirit '15: Actress--Supporting (Arquette), Director (Linklater); Screen Actors Guild '14: Actress--Supporting (Arquette).

The Boynton Beach Club 🦴🦴 ½ *The Boynton Beach Bereavement Club* **2005 (R)** Aged lonely hearts find support and possibly love as members of a bereavement club at a Florida "active adult" community—an unlikely but surprisingly refreshing setting for a romantic comedy. Newly widowed Marilyn (Vaccarro) joins the group after a car backs over her husband. There she meets a range of characters more interested in romance and life beyond blue hair and early-bird specials. Hotties-of-a-certain-age Cannon and Kellerman mix with master casanova Bologna and his reluctant protege Cariou to show both the funny and tender sides of the senior dating game. Plays a little sitcom-y at times, but manages to keep things dignified and unpatronizing. Director Seidelman got the idea for the movie from her mother Florence, who received a producer's credit. **105m/C; DVD.** Dyan Cannon; Brenda Vaccaro; Sally Kellerman; Joseph Bologna; Len Cariou; Michael Nouri; Renee Taylor; ***D:*** Susan Seidelman; ***W:*** Susan Seidelman; Shelly Gitlow; ***C:*** Eric Moynier; ***M:*** Marcelo Zarvos.

Boys 🦴 *The Girl You Want* **1995 (PG-13)** Seems like only yesterday we saw Haas as that big-eared, doe-eyed Amish kid from "Witness," but now, in this dry love story, he has grown into a big-eared, doe-eyed teenager lusting after older woman Ryder. John (Haas) saves Patty (Ryder) after a riding accident leaves her unconscious near his New England prep school. Immediately taken by her beauty and mystery, John decides to hide her in his dorm room and a romance blossoms between the unlikely pair. But John isn't the only one hiding something. Patty has a terrible secret from her past (gasp!), but when it's finally revealed, you'll be too bored to care. Based on the short story "Twenty Minutes" by James Salter. **86m/C; VHS, DVD, Blu-Ray.** Winona Ryder; Lukas Haas; John C. Reilly; William Sage; Skeet Ulrich; ***D:*** Stacy Cochran; ***W:*** Stacy Cochran; ***C:*** Robert Elswit; ***M:*** Stewart Copeland.

The Boys 🦴🦴 ½ *Les Boys* **1997** Popular, simply plotted French-Canadian comedy about a group of ordinary guys who play in an amateur hockey league. "Les Boys" are sponsored by local tavern-owner Stan (Girard), who's got a gambling jones and is in debt to small-time mobster, Meo (Lebeau). Meo strikes a deal pitting Stan's ragtag hockey players against his own team of thugs. If Stan's team is defeated, he loses his bar. Dirty tricks abound on both sides. French with subtitles. **107m/C; VHS, DVD.** *CA* Remy Girard; Marc Messier; Patrick Huard; Serge Theriault; Yvan Ponton; Dominic Philie; Patrick Labbe; Roc Lafortune; Pierre Lebeau; Paul Houde; ***D:*** Louis Saia; ***W:*** Christian Fournier; ***C:*** Sylvain Brault; ***M:*** Normand Corbeil.

The Boys and Girl From County Clare 🦴🦴 ½ *The Boys From County Clare* **2003** Set in the 1960s, Liverpool businessman Jimmy (Meaney) returns to his home in Ireland after 24 years to compete in the annual Celli music festival, which brings him into direct conflict with his long-estranged older brother John Joe (Hill). Soon enough the brothers are fighting about music and Maisie (Bradley), who Jimmy deserted for life in Liverpool. Meanwhile their bands are doing everything they can to sabotage each other, and Jimmy's flutist (Evans) is falling for John Joe's fiddler (Corr). Lighthearted comedy/drama uses traditional Irish music as a backdrop for an appealing but routine sibling rivalry story. **90m/C; DVD.** *GB IR GE* Bernard Hill; Colm Meaney; Charlotte Bradley; Stephen Brennan; Andrea Corr; Eamon Owens; Shaun Evans; Phil Barantini; Patrick Bergin; ***D:*** John Irvin; ***W:*** Nicholas Adams; ***C:*** Thomas Burstyn; ***M:*** Fiachra Trench.

Boys and Girls 🦴🦴 **2000 (PG-13)** Nondescript teen romance has lifelong acquaintances and most-time friends Ryan (Prinze Jr.) and Jennifer (Forlani) trying to decide if they love each other after their hormones get the better of them one night. And get this! They're complete opposites! She's carefree and live-for-the-moment. He's button-down, plan-every-second-precise. Biggs and Donahue, as the respective sidekicks, steal the movie from the leads whenever they show up. Sort of a young, poor man's "When Harry Met Sally," without the wit and insight. **94m/C; VHS, DVD.** Freddie Prinze, Jr.; Claire Forlani; Jason Biggs; Heather Donahue; Alyson Hannigan; Amanda Detmer; Lisa Eichhorn; ***D:*** Robert Iscove; ***W:*** Andrew Lowery; Andrew Miller; ***C:*** Ralf Bode; ***M:*** Stewart Copeland.

The Boys Are Back 🦴🦴 ½ *The Boys are Back in Town* **2009 (PG-13)** When Aussie sports writer Joe Warr's (Owen) wife dies from cancer, he becomes a single dad to his two sons—a six-year-old and a rebellious teen—without much of a clue as to how to proceed. Joe's philosophy degenerates into a lack of rules, which constantly puts them all on the brink of family disaster. Owens' excellent performance, combining toughness and sensitivity, saves it from sinking into melodrama. Possibly a little too picturesque with its scenic South Australian vistas, the setting doesn't always jive with the story's angst. Similarly, the glib title doesn't do justice to the emotional hardship and redemption all principal characters experience. Based on Simon Carr's 2001 memoir. **104m/C; On Demand.** *AU* Clive Owen; George MacKay; Laura Fraser; Emma Booth; Erik Thomson; Nicholas McAnulty; Emma Lung; Julia Blake; ***D:*** Scott Hicks; ***W:*** Scott Hicks; Allan Cubitt; ***C:*** Greig Fraser; ***M:*** Hal Lindes.

The Boys Club 🦴🦴 **1996 (R)** Teens-in-trouble film is given a tough core by first time director Fawcett. Excitement-craving 14-year-olds Kyle (Zamprogna), Eric (Sawa), and Brad (Stone) spend all their free time at an abandoned shack at the outskirts of their small town. Only one day they discover it occupied by gun-pointing criminal Luke Cooper (Penn), who tells the boys he's actually a good cop who's been shot and is on the run from some bad cops. The boys are willing to buy into the story at first but Cooper is quick to show his psycho colors, taking Eric hostage, and precipitating a violent finale. **92m/C; VHS, DVD.** *CA* Christopher Penn; Stuart Stone; Devon Sawa; Dominic Zamprogna; Nicholas (Nick) Campbell; Jarred Blanchard; ***D:*** John Fawcett; ***W:*** Peter Wellington; ***C:*** Thom Best; ***M:*** Michael Timmins.

Boys Don't Cry 🦴🦴🦴 **1999 (R)** Falls under the truth is stranger than fiction category. Brandon Teena (heavily awarded Swank) moves from Lincoln, Nebraska, to the small town of Falls City hoping to start over and keep his past a secret. Brandon gets a girlfriend, Lana (Sevigny), and runs afoul of the reckless John (Sarsgaard). And then Brandon's secret is discovered—he is actually a girl and the gender revelation leads to tragic consequences. Based on a true story, which is also the subject of the documentary, "The Brandon Teena Story." Pierce's version, not unexpectedly, was subjected to the charges of dramatic license, but the story is still forceful. **116m/C; VHS, DVD.** Hilary Swank; Chloë Sevigny; Peter Sarsgaard; Brendan Sexton, III; Alison Folland; Alicia (Lecy) Goranson; Matt McGrath; Rob Campbell; Jeanetta Arnette; ***D:*** Kimberly Peirce; ***W:*** Kimberly Peirce; Andy Bienen; ***C:*** Jim Denault; ***M:*** Nathan Larson. Oscars '99: Actress (Swank); Golden Globes '00: Actress--Drama (Swank); Ind. Spirit '00: Actress (Swank), Support. Actress (Sevigny); L.A. Film Critics '99: Actress (Swank), Support. Actress (Sevigny); Natl. Film Reg. '19; N.Y. Film Critics '99: Actress (Swank); Natl. Soc. Film Critics '99: Support. Actress (Sevigny); Broadcast Film Critics '99: Actress (Swank).

The Boys from Brazil 🦴🦴 ½ **1978 (R)** Based on Ira Levin's novel, a thriller about Dr. Josef Mengele endeavoring to reconstitute the Nazi movement from his Brazilian sanctuary by cloning a brood of boys from Hitler's genes. **123m/C; VHS, DVD, Blu-Ray.** Gregory Peck; James Mason; Laurence Olivier; Uta Hagen; Steve Guttenberg; Denholm Elliott; Lilli Palmer; ***D:*** Franklin J. Schaffner; ***W:*** Heywood Gould; ***C:*** Henri Decae;

M: Jerry Goldsmith. Natl. Bd. of Review '78: Actor (Olivier).

The Boys From Syracuse 🦴🦴 1/2 **1940** Musical based on Shakespeare's "A Comedy of Errors," which was first adapted for Broadway by Rodgers and Hart. In ancient Greece, wealthy Antipholus and his servant Dromio of Syracuse travel to Ephesus to find their twin brothers from whom they were separated at birth. **73m/B; DVD.** Allan Jones; Joe Penner; Irene Hervey; Martha Raye; Eric Blore; Rosemary Lane; Charles Butterworth; *D:* A. Edward Sutherland; *W:* Charles Grayson; Leonard Spigelgass; Paul Girard Smith; *C:* Joseph Valentine.

Boys in Brown 🦴 1/2 **1949** Teenaged crook Jackie (Attenborough) is arrested after a botched robbery and sentenced to three years in a Borstal (a boys reformatory). He wants to go straight but schemer Alfie (Bogarde) needs Jackie to help in an escape plan. Alfie plays on Jackie's worries that his girl Kitty (Murray) has found a new boyfriend and more trouble follows. The leads are too old for their roles and the plot is dull and earnest. **85m/B; DVD.** *UK* Richard Attenborough; Dirk Bogarde; Barbara Murray; Jack Warner; Jimmy Hanley; *D:* Montgomery Tully; *W:* Montgomery Tully; *C:* Cyril Bristow; *M:* Doreen Carwithen.

The Boys in Company C 🦴🦴 **1977 (R)** A frank, hard-hitting drama about five naive young men involved in the Vietnam War. **127m/C; VHS, DVD, Blu-Ray.** Stan Shaw; Andrew Stevens; James Canning; Michael Lembeck; Craig Wasson; R. Lee Ermey; James Whitmore, Jr.; Scott Hylands; Noble Willingham; Santos Morales; Claude Wilson; Drew Michaels; Karen Hilger; Peggy O'Neal; Stan Johns; *Cameo(s):* Rick Natkin; *D:* Sidney J. Furie; *W:* Sidney J. Furie; Rick Natkin; *C:* Godfret A. Godar; *M:* Jaime Mendoza-Nava.

The Boys in the Band 🦴🦴 1/2 **1970 (R)** A group of gay friends get together one night for a birthday party. A simple premise with a compelling depiction of friendship, expectations, and lifestyle. One of the first serious cinematic presentations to deal with the subject of homosexuality. The film was adapted from Mart Crowley's play using the original cast. **120m/C; VHS, DVD, Blu-Ray.** Frederick Combs; Cliff Gorman; Laurence Luckinbill; Kenneth Nelson; Leonard Frey; *D:* William Friedkin; *W:* Matt Crowley.

Boys Life 🦴🦴 **1994** Three shorts about gay teenagers coming of age. "Pool Days" has 17-year-old Justin (Weinstein) taking a summer job as a lifeguard at a health spa. Still clueless as to his sexual preferences, Justin is flustered when cruised by a charming male swimmer but it does get him to thinking. "A Friend of Dorothy" finds NYU student Winston (O'Connell) seeking freedom in Greenwich Village as he looks for like-minded friends (and a little romance). "The Disco Years" takes place in California during the Nixon era as casually gay-bashing high-schooler Tom (Nolan) gradually realizes his true nature. **90m/C; VHS, DVD.** Josh Weinstein; Nick Poletti; Kimberly Flynn; Richard Salamanca; Raoul O'Connell; Kevin McClatchy; Greg Lauren; Anne Zupa; Matt Nolan; Russell Scott Lewis; Gwen Welles; Dennis Christopher; *D:* Brian Sloan; Raoul O'Connell; Robert Lee King; *W:* Brian Sloan; Raoul O'Connell; Robert Lee King; *C:* W. Mott Hupfel, III; Jonathan Schell; Greg Gardiner.

The Boys Next Door 🦴🦴 1/2 **1985 (R)** Two California lads kill and go nuts during a weekend in Los Angeles. Sheen overacts as a budding psychotic, not an easy thing to do. Apparently is trying to show what a particular lifestyle can lead to. Violent. **90m/C; VHS, DVD, Blu-Ray.** Maxwell Caulfield; Charlie Sheen; Christopher McDonald; Hank Garrett; Patti D'Arbanville; Moon Zappa; *D:* Penelope Spheeris; *W:* Glen Morgan; James Wong; *C:* Arthur Albert; *M:* George S. Clinton.

The Boys Next Door 🦴🦴 1/2 **1996 (PG)** Gentle comedy/drama, based on Tom Griffin's play, about four mentally disabled men—Norman (Lane), Barry (Leonard), Arnold (Jeter), and Lucien (Vance)?who share a house under the supervision of too-dedicated social worker Jack (Goldwyn). In fact, Jack's devotion is causing enough problems in his marriage to have him consider changing careers, even as each of "the boys" struggle with their daily lives. TV movie is overly sweet but the performances are very good. **99m/C; VHS, DVD.** Nathan Lane; Tony Goldwyn; Robert Sean Leonard; Michael Jeter; Courtney B. Vance; Mare Winningham; Jenny Robertson; Elizabeth Wilson; Richard Jenkins; Lynne Thigpen; *D:* John Erman; *W:* William Blinn; *C:* Frank Tidy; *M:* John Kander. **TV**

Boys' Night Out 🦴🦴🦴 **1962** Amusing comedy about four businessmen who desperately want to escape the suburban doldrums by setting up an apartment equipped with plaything Novak. Little do they know, but Novak is a sociology student studying the American male, and they are merely her guinea pigs in an experiment beyond their control. Blair, Page, and Gabor provide comic relief. Based on a story by Marvin Worth and Arne Sultan. **113m/C; VHS, DVD.** Kim Novak; James Garner; Tony Randall; Howard Duff; Janet Blair; Patti Page; Jessie Royce Landis; Oscar Homolka; Zsa Zsa Gabor; *D:* Michael Gordon; *W:* Ira Wallach.

Boys of Abu Ghraib 🦴 1/2 **2014 (R)** Moran wrote/directed/produced/starred in this TV-movie treatment of the very complex subject matter of how power turned to torture at the detainment center in Abu Ghraib in 2003-4. The dull-as-dirt Moran plays Jack Farmer (possibly the most American name ever), the newest recruit to arrive at the camp in 2003, who quickly learns that inhumane activity is the norm in this part of the world. The interesting idea that the men tasked with guarding potential murderers could succumb to boredom and what that would lead to is discarded in favor of even more cliché when Jack makes friends with a quiet detainee (Omid Abtahi). **102m/C; DVD.** Luke Moran; Omid Abtahi; Sean Astin; Scott Patterson; Sara Paxton; John Heard; *D:* Luke Moran; *W:* Luke Moran; *C:* John Sejdinaj; *M:* Dan Marocco.

The Boys of Baraka 🦴🦴 1/2 **2005** Directors Ewing and Grady inform us that 76 percent of Baltimore's black male students do not graduate from high school. So, in 2002, 20 at-risk students are given scholarships to attend the progressive Baraka boarding school—in Kenya—which is run by American volunteers. They are supposed to stay two years, but a transformation is begun that cannot be completed when terrorists attack Nairobi and the school is forced to close. The film may not have the "feel good" ending viewers are expecting, although it seems the lives of several boys are changed for the better. **84m/C; DVD.**

The Boys of St. Vincent 🦴🦴🦴🦴 **1993** Outstanding, and heartbreaking, story of sexual abuse by Catholic clergy that was inspired by actual events. Divided into two segments, the drama begins in 1975 with 10-year-old Kevin Reevey (Morina) living at the St. Vincent orphanage in an eastern Canadian town. The orphanage is run by charismatic and terrifying Brother Lavin (Czerny), who it turns out has a special fondness for "his boy" Kevin. Nor is Brother Lavin alone—a fact eventually revealed by a police investigation, although the matter is hushed up by both the church and the government. Until 15 years later. In 1990, the case is reopened and Lavin, having married and fathered two sons, is returned to face charges. Now the young men must open wounds that have never truly healed and confront their tormentors in a court of law, amidst a blaze of publicity. Czerny gives a truly inspired performance as the self-loathing monster. The emotional agony is excruciating to watch and be forwarned that the depiction of the sexual abuse is unflinching. Made for Canadian TV; on two cassettes. **186m/C; VHS, DVD.** *CA* Henry Czerny; Johnny Morina; Sebastian Spence; Brian Dodd; David Hewlett; Jonathan Lewis; Jeremy Keefe; Phillip Dinn; Brian Dooley; Greg Thomey; Michael Wade; Lise Roy; Timothy Webber; Kristine Demers; Ashley Billard; Sam Grana; *D:* John N. Smith; *W:* Sam Grana; John N. Smith; Des Walsh; *C:* Pierre Letarte; *M:* Neil Smolar. **TV**

The Boys of 2nd Street Park 🦴🦴🦴 **2003 (R)** Drawn together for this compelling documentary, childhood buddies frankly recount the life-changing events they've confronted over the years while pining for the simpler times growing up in Brighton Beach, NY, in the 1950s. **91m/C; VHS, DVD.** *D:* Dan Klores; Ron Berger; *C:* Buddy Squires. **VIDEO**

Boys on the Side 🦴🦴 1/2 **1994 (R)** It's "Thelma & Louise" come to "Terms of Endearment" by way of "Philadelphia." Goldberg is Jane, an unemployed lesbian singer, who connects with Ms. Priss real estate agent Robin (Parker) for a road trip to California. The two become a female version of the Odd Couple as Jane tags Robin as "the whitest woman in America." They stop off to pick up addle-brain friend Holly (Barrymore) who has just knocked her drug-crazed abusive beau in the head with a baseball bat. Holly's accident turns fatal and the threesome are on the run from cops. They bond like crazy glue and become a family as they face two huge setbacks—one's pregnant, another has AIDS. Strong performances by the lead actresses and a cool soundtrack may make up for this often trite movie of the week premise. **117m/C; VHS, DVD, Blu-Ray.** Whoopi Goldberg; Mary-Louise Parker; Drew Barrymore; James Remar; Anita Gillette; Matthew McConaughey; *D:* Herbert Ross; *W:* Don Roos; *C:* Donald E. Thorin; *M:* David Newman.

Boys Town 🦴🦴🦴 1/2 **1938** Righteous portrayal of Father Flanagan and the creation of Boys Town, home for juvenile soon-to-be-ex-delinquents. **93m/B; VHS, DVD.** Spencer Tracy; Mickey Rooney; Henry Hull; Gene Reynolds; Sidney Miller; Frankie Thomas, Jr.; *D:* Norman Taurog. Oscars '38: Actor (Tracy), Story.

Boys Will Be Boys 🦴🦴 **1935** Teacher Alec Smart (Hay) works part-time at the local prison but wants to become headmaster at Narkover, which is notorious for having many of its unruly students become inmates at the same prison. Thanks to a forged letter of recommendation, Smart gets his opportunity but then must deal with a stolen diamond necklace and a climatic and chaotic rugby match. **78m/B; DVD.** *GB* Will Hay; Gordon Harker; Jimmy Hanley; David Burnaby; Norma Varden; Claude Dampier; Charles Farrell; *D:* William Beaudine; *W:* Will Hay; Robert Edmunds; *C:* Charles Van Enger; *M:* Louis Levy.

Boys Will Be Boys 🦴🦴 1/2 **1997 (PG)** With their parents away at a company party, Matt and Robbie are home alone for the first time. Expect chaos when the boys discover that their father's business rival has something nasty in store and the brothers will use anything around to defeat him. **89m/C; VHS, DVD.** Randy Travis; Julie Hagerty; Jon Voight; Michael DeLuise; Catherine Oxenberg; Mickey Rooney; Ruth Buzzi; Dom DeLuise; Charles Nelson Reilly; James Williams; Drew Winget; *D:* Dom DeLuise; *W:* Gregory Poppon; Mark Dubas; *C:* Leonard Schway; *M:* Kristopher Carter. **VIDEO**

Boystown 🦴🦴 *Chuecatown* **2007** Who'd a thought you could have a cuddly couple involved in a serial killer story? Slimy Madrid realtor Victor kills little old ladies for their apartments in a gentrifying gay neighborhood. When Rey and Leo unexpectedly inherit their next-door neighbor's apartment, the police suspect them of the crimes. Things actually get worse when Rey's hateful mother Antonia, who wants to split the couple up, takes over the disputed apartment. Too bad for her since that really interferes with Victor's plans. Spanish with subtitles. **93m/C; DVD.** *SP* Carlos Fuentes; Rosa Maria Sarda; Pablo Puyol; Pepon Nieto; Concha Valasco; Eduard Soto; *D:* Juan Flahn; *W:* Juan Flahn; Felix Sabroso; Dunia Ayaso; *C:* Juan Carlos Lausin; *M:* David San Jose; Joan Crossas.

Boyz N the Hood 🦴🦴🦴 1/2 **1991 (R)** Singleton's debut as a writer and director is an astonishing picture of young black men, four high school students with different backgrounds, aims, and abilities trying to survive L.A. gangs and bigotry. Excellent acting throughout, with special nods to Fishburne and Gooding Jr. Violent outbreaks outside theatres where this ran only proves the urgency of its passionately nonviolent, profamily message. Hopefully those viewers scared off at the time will give this a chance in the safety of their VCRs. Singleton was the youngest director ever nominated for an Oscar. **112m/C; VHS, DVD, Blu-Ray, UMD.** Laurence Fishburne; Ice Cube; Cuba Gooding, Jr.; Nia Long; Morris Chestnut; Tyra Ferrell; Angela Bassett; Whitman Mayo; *D:* John Singleton; *W:* John Singleton; *C:* Charles Mills; *M:* Stanley Clarke. MTV Movie Awards '92: New Filmmaker (Singleton); Natl. Film Reg. '02.

BPM (Beats Per Minute) 🦴🦴 1/2 *120 battements par minute* **2017** A fictitious account of ACT-UP Paris, a group of activists in the 1990s who sought to shake governmental and pharmaceutical inaction to the AIDS crisis by holding rallies, staging die-ins, and throwing fake blood. Amid the life-and-death cause, a relationship (complete with graphic sex scenes) between the group's newcomer Nathan and fiery Sean balances the movement's personal and political stakes. The film's title refers to the average number of heart beats per minute for humans. **140m/C; DVD.** Nahuel Perez Biscayart; Arnaud Valois; Adèle Haenel; Felix Maritaud; Mehdi Toure; *D:* Robin Campillo; *W:* Robin Campillo; *C:* Jeanne Lapoirie; *M:* Arnaud Rebotini.

Bra Boys 🦴 1/2 **2007 (R)** Title is an Aussie diminutive for Sydney's Maroubra Beach and refers to a notorious local working-class surfer gang. Formed around Abberton brothers Koby, Jai, and director/writer Sunny, the Bra Boys are known to the cops for turf wars and scrapes with the law while locals in the poor suburb praise the surfers for their work with troubled youth. (Don't do as I do, do as I say?) There's also lengthy coverage of a murder trial involving Jai and Koby but it's a decidedly one-sided documentary. **86m/C; On Demand.** *AU V:* Russell Crowe; *D:* Sunny Abberton; *W:* Sunny Abberton; *C:* Macario De Souza; Brooke Silvester; *M:* Jamie Holt.

Braddock: Missing in Action 3 🦴 **1988 (R)** The battle-scarred, high-kicking 'Nam vet battles his way into the jungles once more, this time to rescue his long-lost Vietnamese family. A family effort, Chuck co-wrote the script; his brother directed. **104m/C; VHS, DVD, Blu-Ray.** Chuck Norris; Aki Aleong; Roland Harrah, III; *D:* Aaron Norris; *W:* Chuck Norris; James Bruner; *C:* Joao Fernandes.

Brad's Status 🦴🦴 1/2 **2017 (R)** Who said angst was reserved for teenagers? When Troy (Abrams), a self-possessed musical prodigy, tours a couple of colleges with his dad (Stiller), it's the middle-ager who suffers inferiority and self-doubt. Recalling his own youthful aspirations and comparing his suburban, unremarkable life to those of his college pals, Brad wrestles with an existentialism that ordinarily might be annoying to watch, but Stiller's measured performance and White's frank writing/directing make Brad utterly, even uncomfortably, relatable. **102m/C; DVD, Blu-Ray.** Ben Stiller; Austin Abrams; Jenna Fischer; Michael Sheen; Jemaine Clement; Luke Wilson; *D:* Mike White; *W:* Mike White; *C:* Xavier Perez Grobet; *M:* Mark Mothersbaugh.

The Brady Bunch Movie 🦴🦴🦴 **1995 (PG-13)** Grunge and CDs may be the norm in the '90s, but the Bradys still live in the eight-track world of the '70s, where Davy Jones rocks and every day is a sunshine day. Then greedy developer McKean schemes to cash in on Mike and Carol's financial woes. (Hawaii! The Grand Canyon! What were they thinking?) Great ensemble cast capably fills the white platform shoes of the originals—Cole sounds just like Mr. Brady, Cox hilariously channels Jan's tormented middle child angst, and Taylor's self-absorbed Marcia, Marcia, Marcia is dead-on, right down to the frosty pursed lips. Look for neat-o cameos from some original Bradys and most of the Monkees. Followed by "A Very Brady Sequel." **88m/C; VHS, DVD.** Shelley Long; Gary Cole; Michael McKean; Jean Smart; Henriette Mantel; Christopher Daniel Barnes; Christine Taylor; Paul Sutera; Jennifer Elise Cox; Jesse Lee; Olivia Hack; David Graf; Jack Noseworthy; Shane Conrad; RuPaul Charles; *Cameo(s):* Ann B. Davis; Florence Henderson; Davy Jones; Barry Williams; Christopher Knight; Michael (Mike) Lookinland; Mickey Dolenz; Peter Tork; *D:* Betty Thomas; *W:* Bonnie Turner; Terry Turner; Laurice Elehwany; Rick Copp; *C:* Mac Ahlberg; *M:* Guy Moon.

Brahms: The Boy II 🦴 1/2 **2019 (PG-13)** After a violent home invasion, Sean (Yeoman) and Liza (Holmes) and their traumatized son Jude (Convery) move to a guest house on a large country estate. Jude finds a doll, known as Brahms, buried in a coffin in the woods. Though Jude has been mute since the incident, he begins to talk again after finding Brahms. As Jude's behavior becomes concerning, Liza fears Brahms is possessed and evil has taken control of her son. Forgettable and boring horror nonsense. **86m/C; DVD, Blu-Ray.** Katie Holmes; Ralph Ineson; Owain Yeoman; Christopher Convery; Anjali Jay; ***D:*** William Brent Bell; ***W:*** Stacey Menear; ***C:*** Karl Walter Lindenlaub; ***M:*** Brett Detar.

The Brain 🦴🦴 *Le Cerveau* **1969 (G)** Run of the mill comedy caper has Niven planning to heist millions from a NATO train. The caper begins when lots of other crooks decide to rob the same train. The cast holds this one together. **115m/C; DVD, Blu-Ray.** *FR* David Niven; Jean-Paul Belmondo; Andre Bourvil; Eli Wallach; Silvia Monti; Fernand Valois; ***D:*** Gerard Oury; ***W:*** Gerard Oury; Daniele Thompson; ***C:*** Vladimir Ivanov; ***M:*** Georges Delerue.

Brain Damage 🦴🦴 **1988 (R)** A tongue-in-bloody-cheek farce about a brain-sucking parasite. The parasite in question, Aylmer, addicts our dubious hero to the euphoria induced by the blue liquid the parasite injects into his brain, paving the way for the bloody mayhem that follows. Poor shadow of Henenlotter's far-superior "Basket Case." In fact, it even includes an inside-joke cameo by Van Hentenryck, reprising his "Basket Case" character; look for him on the subway. **89m/C; VHS, DVD, Blu-Ray.** Rick Herbst; Gordon MacDonald; Jennifer Lowry; Theo Barnes; Lucille Saint Peter; Kevin Van Hentenryck; Beverly Bonner; ***V:*** John Zacherle; ***D:*** Frank Henenlotter; ***W:*** Frank Henenlotter; ***C:*** Bruce Torbet; ***M:*** Gus Russo; Clutch Reiser.

Brain Dead 🦴🦴🦴 1/2 **1989 (R)** Low-budget but brilliantly assembled puzzle-film about a brain surgeon who agrees to perform experimental surgery on a psychotic to retrieve some corporately valuable data—his first mistake, which begins a seemingly endless cycle of nightmares and identity alterations. A mind-blowing sci-fi feast from ex-"Twilight Zone" writer Charles Beaumont. **85m/C; VHS, DVD, Blu-Ray.** Bill Pullman; Bill Paxton; Bud Cort; Patricia Charbonneau; Nicholas Pryor; George Kennedy; Brian Brophy; Lee Arenberg; Andy Wood; ***D:*** Adam Simon; ***W:*** Adam Simon; Charles Beaumont; ***M:*** Peter Rotter.

Brain Donors 🦴🦴 1/2 **1992 (PG)** Goofy, uneven film starring Turturro as a sleazy lawyer trying to take over the Oglethorpe Ballet Company by sweet-talking its aged patronness. He is helped by two eccentric friends, and together the three crack a lot of bad but witty jokes. The film culminates into a hilarious ballet scene featuring someone giving CPR to the ballerina playing the dying swan, an actor in a duck suit, duck hunters, and a pack of hounds. This trio reminds us of second-rate Marx Brothers (or the Three Stooges) but the movie has enough funny moments to be worth a watch. **79m/C; DVD.** John Turturro; Bob Nelson; Mel Smith; Nancy Marchand; John Savident; George de la Pena; Juli Donald; Spike Alexander; Teri Copley; ***D:*** Dennis Dugan; ***W:*** Pat Proft; ***M:*** Ira Newborn.

Brain Drain 🦴🦴 **1998** Young Argentine street kids are thieves who specialize in car radios. Their dreams of a better life are at odds with their surroundings. Things go wrong when they make false accusations against a cop and he comes after them. **92m/C; DVD.** Nicolas Cabre; Luis Quiroz; Enrique Liporace; ***D:*** Fernando Musa; ***W:*** Fernando Musa; Branko Andjic; ***C:*** Carlos Torlaschi; ***M:*** Luis Maria Serra.

The Brain from Planet Arous 🦴 **1957** Lassie meets Alien when an evil alien brain appropriates the body of a scientist in order to take over planet Earth. His plans are thwarted, however, by a good alien brain that likewise inhabits the body of the scientist's dog. High camp and misdemeanors. **80m/B; VHS, DVD.** John Agar; Joyce Meadows; Robert Fuller; Henry Travis; Bill Giorgio; Tim Graham; Thomas B(rowne). Henry; Ken Terrell; ***D:*** Nathan "Jerry" Juran; ***W:*** Ray Buffum; ***C:*** Jacques "Jack" Marquette; ***M:*** Walter Greene.

Brain of Blood **WOOF!** *The Creature's Revenge; Brain Damage* **1971** Deals with a scientist who transplants the brain of a politician into the body of a deformed idiot. The change is minimal. **107m/C; VHS, DVD, Blu-Ray.** *PH* Kent Taylor; John Bloom; Regina Carrol; Angelo Rossitto; Grant Williams; Reed Hadley; Vicki Volante; Zandor Vorkov; Richard Smedley; ***D:*** Al Adamson; ***W:*** Joe Van Rogers; ***C:*** Louis Horvath.

The Brain that Wouldn't Die 🦴🦴 1/2 *The Head that Wouldn't Die* **1963** Love is a many-splattered thing when a brilliant surgeon keeps the decapitated head of his fiancee alive after an auto accident while he searches for a suitably stacked body onto which to transplant the head. Absurd and satiric (head talks so much that Doc tapes her/its mouth shut) adding up to major entry in trash film genre; much of the gore was slashed for the video, however. **92m/B; VHS, DVD, Blu-Ray.** Herb Evers; Virginia Leith; Adele Lamont; Leslie Daniel; Bruce Brighton; Paula Maurice; ***D:*** Joseph Green; ***W:*** Joseph Green; ***C:*** Stephen Hajinal; ***M:*** Tony Restaino.

Brainjacked 🦴 **2009** A mad scentist convinces people he can cure their ills by letting him drill holes in their skulls to insert microchips. Of course he leaves out the part about the chips being used as mind control, but if you're foolish enough to trust a guy wanting to drill into your brain you probably get what you have coming. **90m/C; DVD, Streaming.** Stephen Biro; Cyndi Crotts; Rob Elfstrom; Michael Kenneth Fahr; Mark Fisher; ***D:*** Andrew Allan; ***W:*** Andrew Allan; Andy Lalino; ***C:*** Wes Pratt; ***M:*** Eddie Sturgeon. **VIDEO**

Brainscan 🦴 **1994 (R)** Teenage loner takes a trip in virtual reality and finds that murder is the first stop. Furlong ("Terminator 2") is the troubled youth whose voyage is led by Smith as Trickster, the Freddy Krueger meets David Bowie tour guide from virtual hell. Langella turns in a straight performance as a local cop hot on the trail. Hard-core horror fans will be disappointed by the lack of on-screen violence, and special effects buffs won't see anything new. Lame effort tries to appeal to a wide audience and is bland as a result. The end is left wide open, so expect a sequel or two or three. **96m/C; VHS, DVD, Blu-Ray.** Edward Furlong; Frank Langella; T. Ryder Smith; David Hemblen; Amy Hargreaves; Jamie Marsh; Victor Ertmanis; ***D:*** John Flynn; ***W:*** Andrew Kevin Walker; ***M:*** George S. Clinton.

Brainstorm 🦴🦴 1/2 **1983 (PG)** Husband-and-wife scientist team invents headphones that can record dreams, thoughts, and fantasies (VCR-style) and then allow other people to experience them by playing back the tape. Their marriage begins to crumble as the husband becomes more and more obsessed with pushing the limits of the technology; things get worse when the government wants to exploit their discovery. Special effects and interesting camera work punctuate this sci-fi flick. Wood's last film; in fact, she died before production was completed. **106m/C; VHS, DVD, Blu-Ray.** Natalie Wood; Christopher Walken; Cliff Robertson; Louise Fletcher; ***D:*** Douglas Trumbull; ***W:*** Bruce Joel Rubin; ***C:*** Richard Yuricich; ***M:*** James Horner.

Brainwaves 🦴🦴 **1982 (R)** A young woman has disturbing flashbacks after her brain is electrically revived following a car accident. Curtis is the demented doctor who jump-starts her. **83m/C; VHS, DVD.** Suzanna Love; Tony Curtis; Keir Dullea; Vera Miles; Eve Brent; ***D:*** Ulli Lommel; ***W:*** Ulli Lommel; ***C:*** Ulli Lommel; Jon Kranhouse; ***M:*** Robert O. Ragland.

Brake 🦴🦴 **2012 (R)** Dorff gives a decent performance in what is essentially a one-man show as Secret Service agent Jeremy Reins, who wakes up kidnapped in the trunk of a car. As he is psychologically and physically tortured by terrorists seeking the location of the Executive Branch's secret underground bunker, Dorff sells the complex arc of this real-time thriller. Sadly, the senseless script piles on the plot holes until it pulls out two twist endings that shatter any suspension of disbelief. **92m/C; DVD, Blu-Ray.** Stephen Dorff; Chyler Leigh; J.R. Bourne; Tom Berenger; ***V:*** Pruitt Taylor Vince; ***D:*** Gabe Torres; ***W:*** Timothy Mannion; ***C:*** James Mathers; ***M:*** Brian Tyler.

Bram Stoker's Dracula 🦴🦴 *Dracula* **1992 (R)** Coppola's highly charged view of the vampire classic is visually stunning, heavy on eroticism and violence, and weak in plot and performance. Oldman, in a number of amazing transformations, portrays the deadly bloodsucker as a lonely soul determined to reunite with his lost love, the innocent Ryder. Hopkins cheerfully chews the scenery as nemesis Van Helsing, newcomer Frost is fetching, Reeves is lightweight, and Ryder goes way over the top. Musician Waits is great as bug-eating madman Renfield. Filmed entirely on soundstages with beautiful costumes and some amazing visual effects and sets. **128m/C; VHS, DVD, Blu-Ray.** Gary Oldman; Winona Ryder; Anthony Hopkins; Keanu Reeves; Richard E. Grant; Cary Elwes; Billy Campbell; Sadie Frost; Tom Waits; Monica Bellucci; Christina (Kristina) Fulton; ***D:*** Francis Ford Coppola; ***W:*** James V. Hart; ***C:*** Michael Ballhaus. Oscars '92: Costume Des., Makeup, Sound FX Editing.

Bram Stoker's Shadowbuilder 🦴🦴 *Shadowbuilder* **1998 (R)** Silly update that apparently takes the title of the Bram Stoker short story but not much else. Shadowbuilder (Jackson) is a demonic creature that wants to unleash hell's power upon the unsuspecting town of Grand River. But he needs 12-year-old Chris (Zegers) for your basic satanic ritual, which doesn't go over well with the local priest (Rooker) and sheriff (Thompson). **101m/C; VHS, DVD, Blu-Ray.** Michael Rooker; Leslie Hope; Andrew Jackson; Kevin Zegers; Shawn Thompson; Tony Todd; Richard McMillan; ***D:*** Jamie Dixon; ***W:*** Michael Stokes; ***C:*** David Pelletier; ***M:*** Eckart Seeber. **VIDEO**

Bram Stoker's The Mummy 🦴🦴 *The Mummy; Legend of the Mummy* **1997 (R)** Modern retelling of the horror tale focuses on the savage incident that left Egyptologist Abel Trelawny (Bochner) in a coma. Now his daughter, Margaret (Locane), seeks the help of her ex-lover, Robert (Lutes), to uncover the connection between Trewlawny and an Egyptian ritual to raise a queen from her tomb. Based on Stoker's book "The Jewel of the Seven Stars." **100m/C; VHS, DVD.** Amy Locane; Eric Lutes; Louis Gossett, Jr.; Victoria Tennant; Lloyd Bochner; Mark Lindsay Chapman; Richard Karn; Mary Jo Catlett; ***D:*** Jeffrey Obrow; ***W:*** Jeffrey Obrow; ***C:*** Antonio Soriano; ***M:*** Rick Cox. **VIDEO**

Bram Stoker's Way of the Vampire 🦴 **2005 (R)** Has absolutely nothing to do with Stoker's writings. Van Helsing (Giles) goes after Dracula (Logan), leaving his wife in the care of colleague Sebastian (Beckett). Only Sebastian is actually a blood-drinker, so no more missus. Van Helsing makes a deal with God to gain immortality until the last of Dracula's kin are dead. Which leads to a showdown in present-day LA between Van Helsing and Sebastian. **81m/C; DVD.** Denise Boutte; Paul Logan; Rhett Giles; Brent Falco; ***D:*** Sara Nean Bruce; Eduardo Durao; ***W:*** Karrie Melendrez; Sherri Strain; ***C:*** Andreas Beckett; Zack Richard; ***M:*** Ralph Rieckermann.

Brand New Day 🦴 1/2 *Bran Nue Dae* **2010 (PG-13)** Set in the 1960s, bland characters and a stereotypical road trip narrative will provide little interest outside its Aussie origins. Aboriginal teen Willie (McKenzie) runs away from his Perth Catholic boarding school and its strict guardian, Father Benedictus (Rush), on a 3,000-mile odyssey to return to his family. Naturally, Willie picks up some oddball traveling companions along the way. Based on the 1990 stage musical by Aboriginal band Jimmy Chi and Kuckles. **85m/C; DVD, Blu-Ray.** *AU* Rocky McKenzie; Jessica Mauboy; Ernie Dingo; Geoffrey Rush; Magda Szubanski; ***D:*** Rachel Perkins; ***W:*** Rachel Perkins; ***C:*** Andrew Lesnie; ***M:*** Cezary Skubiszewski.

Brand New Life 🦴 **1972** A childless couple in their 40s are unexpectedly confronted by the wife's first pregnancy. Both have careers and well-ordered lives that promise to be disrupted. **74m/C; VHS, DVD.** Cloris Leachman; Martin Balsam; Wilfrid Hyde-White; Mildred Dunnock; ***D:*** Sam O'Steen; ***M:*** Billy Goldenberg. **TV**

The Brand New Testament 🦴🦴🦴 *Le tout nouveau testament* **2015** In this comedy, Ea, the daughter of God, lives with her father in Brussels, but tires of his domineering ways and does what her older brother did: leave home, find apostles, and pen her own testament. French with subtitles. **103m/C; DVD, Blu-Ray.** Pili Groyne; Benoit Poelvoorde; Catherine Deneuve; Francois Damiens; Yolande Moreau; ***D:*** Jaco Van Dormael; ***W:*** Jaco Van Dormael; Thomas Gunzig; ***C:*** Christophe Beaucarne; ***M:*** An Pierle.

Brand Upon the Brain! 🦴🦴🦴 **2006 (R)** Like most of writer/director Guy Maddin's work, this requires a deliberate viewing. A silent film in black and white sets up primarily as a flashback, possibly to the director's youth, set on an island with a lighthouse that has served as an orphanage in the past. Film moves freely through images and recollections, revealing secret longings within an utterly absurd plot for which the film is not the least diminished. Make no mistake, this is a grandly indulgent art film. But what did you expect? Most enjoyable is the narration by Isabella Rossellini. **95m/C; Silent; DVD.** *CA US* Erik Steffen Maahs; Sullivan Brown; Gretchen Krich; Maya Lawson; Todd Jefferson Moore; Katherine E. Scharhon; ***Nar:*** Isabella Rossellini; ***D:*** Guy Maddin; ***W:*** Guy Maddin; George Toles; ***C:*** Benjamin Kasulke; ***M:*** Jason Staczek.

Branded 🦴🦴 1/2 **1950** Ladd (pre-"Shane") impersonates the long-gone son of rich rancher Bickford, with unusual results. Nicely balanced action and love scenes makes this story a better-than-average western. Filmed in Technicolor. Based on the novel "Montana Rides" by Max Brand. **95m/C; VHS, DVD.** Alan Ladd; Mona Freeman; Charles Bickford; Joseph Calleia; Milburn Stone; ***D:*** Rudolph Mate.

Branded 🦴 **2012 (R)** An ad executive begins to be able to see what brands people respond to, with the ones they enjoy appearing about them as cgi figures. He immediately finds himself in a war between corporations, all trying to squash the brand recognition of their competitors. **?m/CDVD, Blu-Ray, Streaming.** *RU US* Ed Stoppard; Leelee Sobieski; Jeffrey Tambor; Ingeborga Dapkunaite; Max von Sydow; ***D:*** Jamie Bradshaw; Aleksandr Dulerayne; ***W:*** Jamie Bradshaw; Aleksandr Dulerayne; ***C:*** Rogier Stoffers; ***M:*** Eduard Artemev.

Branded to Kill 🦴🦴 *Koroshi no Rakuin* **1967** Visual tricks, including animated graphics, and a blues score highlight this gangster story, which follows No. 3 Killer, who's bungled his last hit. Now he's the target of No. 1 Killer. Japanese with subtitles. **91m/B; VHS, DVD, Blu-Ray.** *JP* Joe Shishido; Mari Annu; Koji Nambara; Isao Tamagawa; Mariko Ogawa; ***D:*** Seijun Suzuki; ***W:*** Hachiro Guryu; ***C:*** Kazue Nagatsuka; ***M:*** Naozumi Yamamoto.

Brannigan 🦴🦴 1/2 **1975 (PG)** The Duke stars in the somewhat unfamiliar role of a rough and tumble Chicago police officer. He travels across the Atlantic to arrest a racketeer who has fled the States rather than face a grand jury indictment. Humor and action abound. **111m/C; VHS, DVD, Blu-Ray.** John Wayne; John Vernon; Mel Ferrer; Daniel Pilon; James Booth; Ralph Meeker; Lesley-Anne Down; Richard Attenborough; ***D:*** Douglas Hickox; ***W:*** Michael Butler; William W. Norton, Sr.; ***C:*** Gerry Fisher; ***M:*** Dominic Frontiere.

Brass 🦴 1/2 **1985 (PG)** First post-Archie Bunker role for O'Connor, who plods through this average police drama at a snail's pace, dragging everything else down with him. Made-for-TV pilot for a series that never aired. **94m/C; VHS, Streaming.** Carroll O'Connor; Lois Nettleton; Jimmy Baio; Paul Shenar; Vincent Gardenia; Anita Gillette; ***D:*** Corey Allen. **TV**

The Brass Bottle 🦴🦴 1/2 **1963** Silly but amusing comedy that served as the inspiration for the TV series "I Dream of Jeannie," although Eden plays the girlfriend in this movie. Ives stars as jovial genie Fakrash, whose antique bottle is bought by architect Harold Ventimore (Randall). Fakrash wants nothing more than to make his new master happy but his efforts cause constant crises for the bewildered man, who'd prefer his life return to normal. Based on the novel by F. Anstey. **90m/C; DVD.** Tony Randall; Burl Ives; Barbara Eden; Edward Andrews; Ann Doran; Kamala Devi; Howard Smith; Parley Baer; ***D:*** Harry Keller; ***W:*** Oscar Brodney; ***C:*** Clifford Stine; ***M:*** Bernard Green.

The Brass Legend 🦴🦴 **1956** With the help of his fiance's 11-year-old brother, Sheriff Wade Addams (O'Brian) captures outlaw Tris Hatten (Burr). He tries to keep Clay's (MacDonald) involvement a secret for safety's sake, but it leaks out thanks to newspaperman Tatum (Sage) who implies Wade wants to keep the reward money for himself. Then Clay becomes a target for Hatten and his henchmen. **79m/B; DVD.** Hugh O'Brian; Raymond Burr; Donald MacDonald; Nancy Gates; Willard Sage; ***D:*** Gerd Oswald; ***W:*** Don Martin; ***C:*** Charles Van Enger; ***M:*** Paul Dunlap.

Brass Target ½ **1978 (PG)** Hypothetical thriller about a plot to kill George Patton in the closing days of WWII for the sake of $250 million in Nazi gold stolen by his staff. Interesting cast can't find story. **111m/C; VHS, DVD.** Sophia Loren; George Kennedy; Max von Sydow; John Cassavetes; Patrick McGoohan; Robert Vaughn; Bruce Davison; Edward Herrmann; Ed Bishop; ***D:*** John Hough; ***W:*** Alvin Boretz.

Brassed Off ½ **1996 (R)** Bittersweet tale of despair and hope in the fictional coal mining town of Grimly in Yorkshire, England. Set in 1992, when sweeping closures of British coal mines devastated the area, the sole respite of these workers is playing in the pit's brass band. Secretly suffering from black lung disease, the band's leader (Postlethwaite) dreams of winning a competition in Albert Hall. Fitzgerald plays the flugelhorn-tooting vixen who returns to the small town, inspiring the music (and virility) of the formerly all male band. She resumes her relationship with former flame MacGregor, but all is on shaky ground with the imminent closure of the mine. Fine performances brighten the generally gloomy proceedings. The band is played by the real-life Grimethorpe Colliery Brass Band. **100m/C; VHS, DVD.** *GB* Pete Postlethwaite; Ewan McGregor; Tara Fitzgerald; Jim Carter; Philip Jackson; Peter Martin; Stephen Tompkinson; ***D:*** Mark Herman; ***W:*** Mark Herman; ***C:*** Andy Collins; ***M:*** Trevor Jones. Cesar '98: Foreign Film.

Bratz WOOF! 2007 (PG) Four high school freshmen and best friends (Ramos, Browning, Parrish, and Shayne) find themselves at odds with the bossy student body president, who aims to split them up into (gasp!) separate social cliques. There's singing and dancing (like a big, long, pink, fluffy music video), and how sweetly cliche is it that these real-life Bratz are all from different ethnicities and socio-economic classes, yet still BFFs? At least these girls are (somewhat) real humans and not the creepy-faced, bubble-headed dolls (and animated characters) the movie is based on, but even your lip gloss-wearing 'tweener will roll her eyes at the mere suggestion of this film, which is cloying at best, intolerable at worst. **100m/C; DVD.** Skyler Shaye; Anneliese van der Pol; Jon Voight; Lainie Kazan; Nathalia Ramos; Janel Parrish; Logan Browning; Chelsea Staub; Stephen Lunsford; Ian Nelson; ***D:*** Sean McNamara; ***W:*** Susan Estelle Jansen; ***C:*** Christian Sebaldt; ***M:*** John Coda.

The Bravados **1958** A rough, distressing Western revenge tale, wherein a man is driven to find the four men who murdered his wife. In tracking the perpetrators, Peck realizes that he has been corrupted by his vengeance. **98m/C; VHS, DVD, Blu-Ray.** Gregory Peck; Stephen Boyd; Joan Collins; Albert Salmi; Henry Silva; Lee Van Cleef; George Voskovec; Barry Coe; ***D:*** Henry King; ***W:*** Philip Yordan; ***C:*** Leon Shamroy. Natl. Bd. of Review '58: Support. Actor (Salmi).

Brave ½ **2007** The brother of a martial artist is kidnapped, and he is told that he has to steal the credit card subscriber data from a bank in exchange for his family. He makes the switch and the pair begin to wonder who set them up for this and why, when the bank president turns up dead simultaneously. **92m/C; DVD.** *TH* Michael B.; Dean Alexandrou; Vanchart Chunsri; ***D:*** Thanapon Maliwan; Afdlin Shauki; ***W:*** Nut Nualpang; ***C:*** Amon Chunprasert.

Brave ½ **2012 (PG)** Pixar's thirteen film is also their first with a female heroine, the feisty, red-headed Scottish Princess Merida (MacDonald), a young lady who refuses to play by the traditional rules as enforced by her mother, Queen Elinor (Thompson). Merida meets a witch who gives her a spell that too literally "changes" her mother, and she discovers that true bravery involves more than mere archery or parental defiance. A sweet, beautiful film that works when compared to most animation but doesn't quite live up to the Pixar standard of storytelling. **100m/C; DVD, Blu-Ray, Streaming.** ***V:*** Kelly Macdonald; Billy Connolly; Emma Thompson; Julie Walters; Robbie Coltrane; Kevin McKidd; Craig Ferguson; ***D:*** Mark C. Andrews; Brenda Chapman; Steve Purcell; ***W:*** Mark C. Andrews; Brenda Chapman; Steve Purcell; Irene Mecchi; ***M:*** Patrick Doyle. Oscars '12: Animated Film; British Acad. '12: Animated Film; Golden Globes '13: Animated Film.

The Brave Archer *She Diao Ying Xiang Chuan; Kung Fu Warlords* **1977** Kuo Chang studies the martial arts after his father is murdered. He falls in love with Huang Yung but must pass three tests before winning her hand in marriage. Mandarin with subtitles or dubbed. **116m/C; DVD.** *CH* Sheng Fu; Niu Tien; Feng Ku; Philip Kwok; ***D:*** Cheh Chang; ***W:*** Kuang Ni; ***C:*** Mu-To Kung; ***M:*** Yung-Yu Chen.

The Brave Archer and His Mate *Shen Diao Zia Liu; Brave Archer 4* **1982** Yong Guo is tricked by crazy martial arts master Oyang Fung into believing his foster parents murdered his father. But somehow he ends up in a monastery with a bunch of other apprentices so he can be mentored by his foster father's teachers. Mandarin with subtitles or dubbed. **101m/C; DVD.** *CH* Alexander Fu Sheng; Philip Kwok; Gigi Wong; Li Wang; Siu-hou Chin; ***D:*** Cheh Chang; ***W:*** Kuang Ni; ***C:*** Hui-chi Tsao; ***M:*** Eddie Wang.

Brave New Girl ½ **2004 (PG-13)** Holly's got what it takes to get into the big-time music school and her poor-yet-resourceful mom won't let their lack of money stand in the way of her daughter's dream. But getting there is only half the ditty. Generically inspiring tale. Based on the novel "A Mother's Gift," by co-executive producers Britney and Lynne Spears. **90m/C; VHS, DVD.** Virginia Madsen; Barbara Mamabolo; Aaron Ashmore; Lindsey Haun; Jackie Rosenbaum; Joanne Boland; Nick Roth; ***D:*** Bobby Roth; ***W:*** Britney Spears; Lynne Spears; Amy Talkington; ***C:*** Eric Van Haren Noman; ***M:*** Asher Ettinger. **TV**

Brave New World **1998** In this watered down version of the novel, humanity has given up science, religion, and even individuality in pursuit of happiness. Life is now endless consumption and hedonism, run by a totalitarian elite. **90m/C; DVD, Blu-Ray.** Peter Gallagher; Leonard Nimoy; Tim Guinee; Rya Kihlstedt; Sally Kirkland; ***D:*** Leslie Libman; Larry Williams; ***W:*** Dan Mazur; David Tausik; ***C:*** Ronald Garcia; ***M:*** Daniel Licht. **TV**

The Brave One **1956** A love story between a Spanish boy and the bull who saves his life. The animal is later carted off to the bullring. Award-winning screenplay by the then-blacklisted Trumbo, credited as "Robert Rich." **100m/C; VHS, DVD, Blu-Ray.** Michel Ray; Rodolfo Hoyos; Joi Lansing; ***D:*** Irving Rapper; ***W:*** Dalton Trumbo; ***C:*** Jack Cardiff; ***M:*** Victor Young. Oscars '56: Story.

The Brave One ½ **2007 (R)** Erica Bain (Foster), the host of a radio show named "City Walk,", has spent years gushing about the wonders of life in her beloved New York City. She encounters a trio of thugs while walking with fiance David (Andrews) in Central Park. The two suffer a gruesome beating, which proves lethal for David and barely survivable for Erica, who, after months of recovery and in the throes of post-traumatic stress, acquires a hand gun. Erica suddenly and routinely witnesses violent criminal acts and begins to mete out street justice while forming a platonic relationship with Detective Mercer (Howard), who is investigating the series of vigilante-style slayings. Their interactions are a bright spot in an otherwise brutal story line. It may sound a bit (okay, a lot) like "Death Wish" but the distinction is Erica's inner turmoil, skillfully played out by Foster. Still, the overwhelming violence outweighs the attempt to humanize her character, and ultimately it fails as both an insightful psycho-thriller and as a vigilante shoot-'em-up. **119m/C; DVD, HD-DVD.** Jodie Foster; Terrence Howard; Naveen Andrews; Carmen Ejogo; Nicky Katt; Mary Steenburgen; Lenny Venito; Lenny Kravitz; ***D:*** Neil Jordan; ***W:*** Roderick Taylor; Bruce Taylor; Cynthia Mort; ***C:*** Philippe Rousselot; ***M:*** Dario Marianelli.

Braveheart ½ **1995 (R)** Producer-director-star Gibson does it all in this bold, ferocious, reasonably accurate epic about the passion and cost of freedom. Charismatic 13th century Scottish folk hero William Wallace leads his desperate and outnumbered clansmen in revolt against British oppression. Sweeping, meticulous battle scenes fit suprisingly well with moments of stirring romance and snappy wit. Among the mostly unknown (in the States, anyway) cast, Marceau and McCormack are elegant as Wallace's lady loves, and McGoohan is positively hateful as King Edward I. Gory and excessively violent (as medieval warfare tends to be) and a bit too long (as historical epics tend to be), but rewarding entertainment for those who stick it out—where else can you see the king's army get mooned en masse? Script was based on 300 pages of rhyming verse attributed to a blind poet known as Blind Harry. Gibson put up $15 million of his own money to complete the film. **178m/C; VHS, DVD, Blu-Ray.** Mel Gibson; Sophie Marceau; Patrick McGoohan; Catherine McCormack; Brendan Gleeson; James Cosmo; David O'Hara; Angus MacFadyen; Peter Hanly; Ian Bannen; Sean McGinley; Brian Cox; Stephen Billington; Barry McGovern; Alun Armstrong; Tommy Flanagan; ***D:*** Mel Gibson; ***W:*** Randall Wallace; ***C:*** John Toll; ***M:*** James Horner. Oscars '95: Cinematog., Director (Gibson), Film, Makeup; British Acad. '95: Cinematog.; Golden Globes '96: Director (Gibson); MTV Movie Awards '96: Action Seq.; Writers Guild '95: Orig. Screenplay; Broadcast Film Critics '95: Director (Gibson).

The Bravos **1972** U.S. Cavalry officer Harkness (Peppard) is in charge of remote outpost. He's trying to protect his fort and a wagon train from an Indian uprising while also searching for his missing son (Van Patten). Standard made-for-TV adventure with a familiar cast. **97m/C; DVD.** George Peppard; Pernell Roberts; Belinda J. Montgomery; L.Q. Jones; Vincent Van Patten; George Murdock; Barry Brown; Dana Elcar; Bo Svenson; ***D:*** Ted Post; ***W:*** Christopher Knopf; ***C:*** Leonard Rosenman. **TV**

Brawl in Cell Block 99 ½ **2017** Vince Vaughn sheds his doofus persona in favor of an intense, committed, downright scary performance as Bradley Thomas, a former boxer-turned mechanic-turned drug dealer who is forced to commit a violent act in prison to save his wife and their unborn child. Reminiscent of prison films of yore, this one doesn't hold back, but the violence and hardcore masculinity are kept in check by a script that elevates them above gratuitousness. **132m/C; DVD, Blu-Ray.** Vince Vaughn; Jennifer Carpenter; Don Johnson; Udo Kier; Marc Blucas; ***D:*** S. Craig Zahler; ***W:*** S. Craig Zahler; ***C:*** Benji Bakshi; ***M:*** S. Craig Zahler; Jeff Herriott.

Brazil ½ **1985 (R)** The acclaimed nightmare comedy about an Everyman trying to survive in a surreal paper-choked bureaucratic society. There are copious references to "1984" and "The Trial," fantastic mergings of glorious fantasy and stark reality, and astounding visual design. The DVD version has a 142-minute director's cut as well as a documentary. **131m/C; VHS, DVD, Blu-Ray.** *GB* Jonathan Pryce; Robert De Niro; Michael Palin; Katherine Helmond; Kim Greist; Bob Hoskins; Ian Holm; Peter Vaughan; Ian Richardson; ***D:*** Terry Gilliam; ***W:*** Terry Gilliam; Tom Stoppard; Charles McKeown; ***C:*** Roger Pratt; ***M:*** Michael Kamen. L.A. Film Critics '85: Director (Gilliam), Film, Screenplay.

Breach ½ **2007 (PG-13)** Somber true story follows ambitious FBI agent Eric O'Neill (Phillippe), who's planted by tough boss Kate Burroughs (Linney) as the new assistant to veteran agent Robert Hanssen (Cooper). She says the bureau is worried because Hanssen is a perv, but he's actually been selling info to the Russians and the feds want to catch him in the act. Hanssen starts getting suspicious, which ratchets up the tension, but there's never any clear idea of why he turned traitor, although Cooper is a creepily effective enigma. **110m/C; DVD, Blu-Ray, HD-DVD.** Chris Cooper; Ryan Phillippe; Laura Linney; Dennis Haysbert; Caroline Dhavernas; Gary Cole; Bruce Davison; Kathleen Quinlan; ***D:*** Billy Ray; ***W:*** Billy Ray; Adam Mazer; William Rotko; ***C:*** Tak Fujimoto; ***M:*** Mychael Danna.

Bread and Chocolate *Pane e Cioccolata* **1973** Uneducated Italian immigrant Manfredi works a series of odd jobs in complacently bourgeois Switzerland and tries desperately to fit in and better himself (which he fails utterly to do). Culture clash satire, with an engaging everyman lead. Italian with subtitles. **110m/C; VHS, DVD.** *IT* Nino Manfredi; Anna Karina; Johnny Dorelli; Paolo Turco; ***D:*** Franco Brusati; ***W:*** Nino Manfredi; Franco Brusati; Iaia Fiastri; ***C:*** Luciano Tovoli; ***M:*** Daniele Patrucchi. N.Y. Film Critics '78: Foreign Film.

Bread and Roses **2000 (R)** Typical Loach political polemic—this time about union organizing of janitors (many of them illegals) in Los Angeles. Maya (Padilla) is an illegal immigrant from Mexico who's working for an office cleaning company. She meets union organizer Sam (Brody) who convinces Maya to join with him, even though she not only risks her job but deportation. Things go from bad to worse for Maya but Loach never takes the easy road and his characters are flawed human beings rather than mere symbols. English and Spanish with subtitles. **106m/C; VHS, DVD.** *GB* Adrien Brody; Elpidia Carrillo; Pilar Padilla; George Lopez; Jack McGee; Alonso Chavez; ***D:*** Ken Loach; ***W:*** Paul Laverty; ***C:*** Barry Ackroyd; ***M:*** George Fenton.

Bread and Tulips *Pane e Tulipani* **2001 (PG-13)** Sweet Rosalba (Maglietta) is a much-neglected wife and mother who is accidentally left behind at a rest stop while the family is on vacation. Impulsively, Rosalba doesn't go home but hitches a ride to Venice, a city she has always longed to see. Although, she dutifully lets her husband Mimmo (Catania) know where she is, she delays her return, is befriened by waiter Fernando (Ganz), and finds a job working for a florist. Rosalba's idyll doesn't last as her loyalties pull her back to her old life but events don't work out as expected. Italian with subtitles. **105m/C; VHS, DVD.** *IT SI* Licia Maglietta; Bruno Ganz; Marina Massironi; Guiseppe Battiston; Antonio Catania; Felice Andreasi; Vitalba Andrea; ***D:*** Silvio Soldini; ***W:*** Silvio Soldini; Doriana Leondeff; ***C:*** Luca Bigazzi; ***M:*** Giovanni Venosta.

A Bread Factory, Part One *A Bread Factory, Part One: For the Sake of Gold* **2018** The long-time center of cultural life in a small upstate New York community is an arts center run by founders Dorothea (Daly) and her partner Greta (Henry). It faces a challenge from a new, bigger, more glitzy arts facility that has opened across town. While the original arts center challenges audiences with mostly locally produced work, the new one focuses on more shallow productions designed to draw in tourists. To survive, Dorothea and Greta must engage in politicking and strategizing. The first of two linked films, this ambitiously and effectively offers portraits of many colorful characters and thoughtful perspectives on art and the art economy. **122m/C; DVD, Blu-Ray.** Tyne Daly; Elisabeth Henry-Macari; James Marsters; Nana Visitor; Janeane Garofalo; ***D:*** Patrick Wang; ***W:*** Patrick Wang; ***C:*** Frank Barrera; ***M:*** Aaron Jordan; Melissa Li; Chip Taylor.

A Bread Factory, Part Two *A Bread Factory, Part Two: Walk with Me a While* **2018** In upstate New York, a community's long-running local arts center has narrowly avoided closure after nearly losing its local education grant to its newer, more flashy and shallow rival. However, the arts center and its supporters still must fight for survival. Local real estate agents urge the center's founders, Dorothea (Daly) and Greta (Henry), to stop fighting, sell part of their property, and travel the world. Including many scenes where characters act as if they are on stage or part of a musical, the second of two linked feature films offers an interesting narrative while commenting on the complex relationship between art and life. **120m/C; DVD.** Tyne Daly; Elisabeth Henry-Macari; James Marsters; Nana Visitor; Keaton Nigel Cooke; ***D:*** Patrick Wang; ***W:*** Patrick Wang; ***C:*** Frank Barrera; ***M:*** Patrick Wang; Aaron Jordan; Melissa Li; Chip Taylor; Andy Wagner.

Bread, Love and Dreams *Pane, Amore e Fantasia* **1953** Middle-aged Antonio (DeSica) is the new police chief in a small village who's looking to make sexy young Maria (Lollobrigida) his wife. But she's in love with one of his subordinates, and another woman (Merlini) is interested in Antonio instead. Followed by "Bread, Love and Jealousy" (1954). Italian with subtitles. **90m/B; DVD.** *IT* Gina Lollobrigida; Roberto Risso; Vittorio DeSica; Marisa Merlini; ***D:*** Luigi Comencini; ***W:*** Luigi Comencini; ***C:*** Arturo Gallea; ***M:*** Alessandro Cicognini.

The Bread, My Sweet 1/2 *A Wedding for Bella* **2001 (PG-13)** Corporate exec Dominic (Baio) also helps his brothers, Eddie (Mott) and Pinio (Hensley), run a bakery in an old Italian neighborhood in Pittsburgh. Their landlords (and surrogate parents) are old-fashioned immigrants Massimo (Seitz) and Bella (Prinz), who confides to Dominic that she's dying. So Dominic impulsively decides to marry their free-spirited daughter Lucca (Minter), who goes along so her marriage-minded mother can die in peace. Naturally (and unsurprisingly) the cutie twosome develop real feelings for one another. **105m/C; DVD.** Scott Baio; Kristin Minter; Rosemary Prinz; John Seitz; Billy Mott; Shuler Hensley; ***D:*** Melissa Martin; ***W:*** Melissa Martin; ***C:*** Mark Knobil; ***M:*** Susan Hartford.

The Breadwinner **2017 (PG-13)** A powerful animated film about a young girl's life in Afghanistan under the Taliban, based on Deborah Ellis's young adult novel. Eleven-year-old Parvana (Chaudry) lives in Kabul with her family. Because women are forbidden to leave their homes unaccompanied, Parvana can only go to the marketplace with her former teacher father (Badshah). After he is imprisoned, the family, which includes a sickly mother, older sister, and baby brother, struggles. To help them, Parvana cuts her hair to pass as a boy, an act that does not stave off reality forever. **94m/C; DVD, Blu-Ray.** Saara Chaudry; Soma Bhatia; Noorin Gulamgaus; Laara Sadiq; Ali Badshah; ***D:*** Nora Twomey; ***W:*** Anita Doron; Deborah Ellis; ***M:*** Jeff Danna; Mychael Danna.

The Break **1995 (PG-13)** Clumsy teen tennis hopeful Ben (Jorgensen) refuses to give up his dreams even after his bookie dad Robbins (Sheen) hires washed-up player Nick Irons (Van Patten) as a coach to show Ben the error of his game. **104m/C; VHS, DVD.** Vincent Van Patten; Martin Sheen; Ben Jorgensen; Rae Dawn Chong; Valerie Perrine; Betsy Russell; ***D:*** Lee H. Katzin; ***W:*** Vincent Van Patten; Dan Jenkins.

Break 1/2 **2009** Hitman Frank (Krueger) is hired by crime boss The Man (Everett), who has a terminal illness. Frank's okay with the contract until The Man insists Frank also kill his girlfriend (Thompson) so he won't die alone. Naturally the woman turns out to be Frank's long-lost love. Low-budget and kinda campy with its silly plot, but it does have a fair amount of action. **93m/C; DVD.** Frank Krueger; Chad Everett; Sarah Thompson; Michael Madsen; David Carradine; Charles Durning; James Russo; ***D:*** Marc Clebanoff; ***W:*** Marc Clebanoff; ***C:*** Tim Otholt; ***M:*** Peter DiStefano. **VIDEO**

Break a Leg **2003 (R)** Struggling actor Max (John Cassini) has talent but keeps losing roles to bigger names and nepotism. So he decides to literally cripple the competition, only to find out that an undercover cop (Rivera) is taking an interest in the case. **98m/C; DVD.** John Cassini; Molly Parker; Rene Rivera; Jennifer Beals; Kevin Corrigan; Sandra Oh; Danny Nucci; Eric Roberts; Frank Cassini; ***D:*** Monika Mitchell; ***W:*** John Cassini; Frank Cassini; ***C:*** Eric Goldstein; ***M:*** Roger Bellon.

Break-In 1/2 **2006** Marla and Cameron are enjoying their honeymoon at an isolated mansion on the island of San Carlos. Marla is surprised when they are joined by her sister-in-law Joani and her husband Parker. Then everyone is surprised when criminal Val and his two cohorts break into the mansion with Val claiming he is after the 10 million in cash that's in a hidden safe. And there's also a major hurricane about to hit. **90m/C; DVD.** Kelly Carlson; Eric Winter; Todd Babcock; Tessie Santiago; Marc Kudisch; Mercedes Renard; Xavier Torres; Carlos Ponce; ***D:*** Michael Nankin; ***W:*** Matt Dorff; ***C:*** Barry Stone. **CABLE**

Break of Dawn 1/2 **1988** Pedro J. Gonzalez (Chavez) is a veteran of Pancho Villa's army who takes his family and crosses into the U.S. Despite the Depression, he finds work at a radio station in L.A. and soon becomes a popular personality in the Latino community. But Gonzalez never leaves politics very far behind and his radical civil rights views lead to a political witchhunt that sends him to prison. **105m/C; VHS, DVD.** Oscar Chavez; Maria Rojo; Tony Plana; Peter Henry Schroeder; Pepe Serna; Kamala Lopez-Dawson; ***D:*** Isaac Artenstein; ***W:*** Isaac Artenstein; ***C:*** Stephen Lighthill; ***M:*** Mark Adler. **TV**

Break of Hearts 1/2 **1935** Hepburn marries Boyer, who becomes an alcoholic, and then more troubles arise. Very soapy, but well-made. **78m/B; VHS, DVD.** Katharine Hepburn; Charles Boyer; Jean Hersholt; John Beal; Sam Hardy; ***D:*** Philip Moeller; ***W:*** Victor Heerman; ***M:*** Max Steiner.

The Break Up 1/2 **1998 (R)** Predictable thriller finds Jimmy Dade (Fonda) awakening in the hospital to discover her abusive husband (Bochner) is dead and she is the prime suspect. **101m/C; VHS, DVD.** Bridget Fonda; Kiefer Sutherland; Penelope Ann Miller; Steven Weber; Hart Bochner; Tippi Hedren; ***D:*** Paul Marcus; ***W:*** Anne Amanda Opotowsky.

The Break-Up **2006 (PG-13)** Gary (Vaughn) and Brooke (Aniston) are a completely incompatible couple (he's boorish, she's high-strung) who own a Chicago condo that comes into bitter dispute when they split. Since neither will willingly leave, they seek to drive the other crazy enough so they'll bail...as everyone else must watch and suffer. There's not much romance or comedy to be seen and it's definitely NOT a date movie—unless you're planning a break-up of your own. **106m/C; DVD, Blu-Ray, HD-DVD.** Jennifer Aniston; Vince Vaughn; Joey Lauren Adams; Judy Davis; Cole Hauser; Jon Favreau; Ann-Margret; Justin Long; Vincent D'Onofrio; Jason Bateman; Peter Billingsley; John Michael Higgins; Ivan Sergei; ***D:*** Peyton Reed; ***W:*** Jeremy Garelick; Jay Lavender; ***C:*** Eric Alan Edwards; ***M:*** Jon Brion.

Breakaway 1/2 *Christmas Rush* **2002 (R)** Poorly made rip-off of the "Die Hard" series. Set in a mall at Christmas, Cornelius Morgan (Cain)--suspended by the force—swings by to get his wife (Eleniak) but a robbery/hostage situation unfolds. Strictly for those in need of a holiday explosion fix. **91m/C; DVD.** Dean Cain; Erika Eleniak; Richard Yearwood; Roman Podhora; Bernard Browne; Santino Buda; Aleks Punovic; Angelo Tsarouchas; Eric Roberts; Jack Wallace; Christopher Benson; Larry Mannell; Rothaford Gray; Jessica Smith; Brooke Palsson; Trevor Toffan; Corinne Conley; Vicki Marentette; Patricia Harras; Ed Sutton; Ernesto Griffith; David (Dave) Brown; Tommy Chang; Vince Crestejo; ***D:*** Charles Robert Carner; ***W:*** Charles Robert Carner; ***C:*** Michael Goi; ***M:*** Louis Febre. **TV**

Breakdown **1953** A boxer is set up by his girlfriend's father to take the rap for a murder. Lackluster effort. **76m/B; VHS, DVD.** Ann Richards; William Bishop; Anne Gwynne; Sheldon Leonard; Wally Cassell; Richard Benedict; ***D:*** Edmond Angelo.

Breakdown **1996 (R)** Jeff (Russell) and Amy (Quinlan) are high-falootin' Easterners on their way to San Diego when their car breaks down somewhere in the vast Southwest. When a trucker (Walsh) stops and offers to take Amy to the next stop while Jeff guards their yuppie treasure trove, they accept willingly. Inconvenience soon turns to terror when Jeff gets the car started, drives to meet his wife and finds her nowhere in sight. Spotting the truck by the side of the road, he confronts the trucker with the cops only to have him deny ever having seen them before. Thus begins the frantic hunt. Russell's descent from dismay to panic to resolve is grippingly played. You may know where it's going, but the fun is in getting there. **93m/C; VHS, DVD.** Kurt Russell; Kathleen Quinlan; J.T. Walsh; M.C. Gainey; Jack Noseworthy; Rex Linn; Ritch Brinkley; Kim Robillard; ***D:*** Jonathan Mostow; ***W:*** Jonathan Mostow; ***C:*** Doug Milsome; ***M:*** Basil Poledouris.

Breaker! Breaker! **1977 (PG)** Convoy of angry truck drivers launch an assault on the corrupt and sadistic locals of a small Texas town. Goofy entry in "mad or sex-crazed trucker armed with a CB radio" genre. **86m/C; VHS, DVD, Blu-Ray.** Chuck Norris; George Murdock; Terry O'Connor; Don Gentry; Jack Nance; ***D:*** Don Hulette; ***W:*** Terry Chambers; ***C:*** Mario DiLeo; ***M:*** Don Hulette.

Breaker Morant 1/2 **1980 (PG)** In 1901 South Africa, three Australian soldiers are put on trial for avenging the murder of several prisoners. Based on a true story which was then turned into a play by Kenneth Ross, this riveting, popular antiwar statement and courtroom drama heralded Australia's film renaissance. Rich performances by Woodward and Waters. **107m/C; VHS, DVD, Blu-Ray.** *AU* Edward Woodward; Jack Thompson; John Waters; Bryan Brown; Charles "Bud" Tingwell; Terence Donovan; Vincent Ball; Ray Meagher; Chris Haywood; Lewis Fitz-Gerald; Rod Mullinar; Alan Cassell; Rob Steele; ***D:*** Bruce Beresford; ***W:*** Bruce Beresford; Jonathan Hardy; David Stevens; ***C:*** Donald McAlpine; ***M:*** Phil Cunneen. Australian Film Inst. '80: Actor (Thompson), Film.

Breakfast at Tiffany's 1/2 **1961** Truman Capote's amusing story of an endearingly eccentric New York City playgirl and her shaky romance with a young writer. Hepburn lends Holly Golightly just the right combination of naivete and worldly wisdom with a dash of melancholy. A wonderfully offbeat romance. **114m/C; VHS, DVD, Blu-Ray.** Audrey Hepburn; George Peppard; Patricia Neal; Buddy Ebsen; Mickey Rooney; Martin Balsam; John McGiver; ***D:*** Blake Edwards; ***W:*** George Axelrod; ***C:*** Franz Planer; ***M:*** Henry Mancini. Oscars '61: Orig. Dramatic Score, Song ("Moon River"); Natl. Film Reg. '12.

The Breakfast Club **1985 (R)** Five students from different cliques at a Chicago suburban high school spend a day together in detention. Rather well done teenage culture study; these characters delve a little deeper than the standard adult view of adolescent stereotypes. One of John Hughes' best movies. Soundtrack features Simple Minds and Wang Chung. **97m/C; VHS, DVD, Blu-Ray, HD-DVD.** Ally Sheedy; Molly Ringwald; Judd Nelson; Emilio Estevez; Anthony Michael Hall; Paul Gleason; John Kapelos; ***D:*** John Hughes; ***W:*** John Hughes; ***C:*** Thomas Del Ruth; ***M:*** Gary Chang; Keith Forsey. Natl. Film Reg. '16.

Breakfast for Two 1/2 **1937** Snappy screwball comedy finds Texas heiress Valentine (Stanwyck) trying to get playboy Jonathan (Marshall) to take some responsibility for his failing steamship line. Valentine buys a controlling interest in the company to teach him a lesson, which only results in Jonathan deciding to marry his golddigger fiancee Carol (Farrell) when you just know who really suits him. Well, Butch (Blore) the valet is also smarter than his employer and that shipboard wedding runs into some problems. **68m/B; DVD.** Barbara Stanwyck; Herbert Marshall; Glenda Farrell; Eric Blore; Etienne Girardot; Frank M. Thomas, Sr.; Donald Meek; ***D:*** Alfred Santell; ***W:*** Paul Yawitz; Charles Kaufman; Viola Brothers Shore; ***C:*** J. Roy Hunt; ***M:*** George Hively.

Breakfast in Hollywood 1/2 *The Mad Hatter* **1946** Movie about the popular morning radio show of the 1940s hosted by Tom Breneman, a coast-to-coast coffee klatch. **93m/B; VHS, DVD.** Tom Breneman; Bonita Granville; Eddie Ryan; Beulah Bondi; Billie Burke; Zasu Pitts; Hedda Hopper; Spike Jones; ***D:*** Harold Schuster.

Breakfast of Champions 1/2 **1998 (R)** Messy adaptation of Kurt Vonnegut's 1973 satire on American greed and commercialism. Relentlessly upbeat salesman Dwayne Hoover (Willis) runs the most successful car dealership in middle America's Midland City. A leading citizen, who stars in his own garish TV commercials, Dwayne has alienated his tube-addicted wife, Celia (Hershey), and his aspiring lounge singer son, Bunny (Haas). Dwayne also thinks he's going nuts and his one hope for salvation lies with Kilgore Trout (Finney), an eccentric hack sci fi writer/philosopher. Oh yeah, and Nolte is around as Dwayne's sales manager Harry, who likes to wear women's lacy lingerie beneath his suits. **110m/C; VHS, DVD.** Bruce Willis; Albert Finney; Nick Nolte; Barbara Hershey; Glenne Headly; Lukas Haas; Omar Epps; Buck Henry; Vicki Lewis; Ken H. Campbell; Will Patton; Chip Zien; Owen Wilson; Alison Eastwood; Shawnee Smith; Kurt Vonnegut, Jr.; ***D:*** Alan Rudolph; ***W:*** Alan Rudolph; ***C:*** Elliot Davis; ***M:*** Mark Isham.

Breakfast on Pluto **2005 (R)** Jordan's picaresque tale is divided into a series of chapters and adventures as foundling Patrick Braden (Murphy) leaves his insular Irish community to search for his mother in 1970s London. One thing Patrick is sure of--he prefers to be called Kitten and dress like a girl. Kitten gets involved with a series of men and circumstances (including, unwittingly, with the IRA) while living life with a certain cheeky charm. Adapted from the Pat McCabe novel. **135m/C; DVD.** *UK IR* Cillian Murphy; Liam Neeson; Stephen Rea; Brendan Gleeson; Eva Birthistle; Liam Cunningham; Bryan Ferry; Gavin Friday; Ian Hart; Laurence Kinlan; Ruth McCabe; Steven Waddington; Ruth Negga; Conor McEvoy; Seamus Reilly; Sid Young; ***D:*** Neil Jordan; ***W:*** Neil Jordan; Patrick McCabe; ***C:*** Declan Quinn.

Breakfast With Scot 1/2 **2007 (PG-13)** Bland family drama that goes out of its way to avoid controversy and becomes dull instead. Ex-Maple Leafs hockey player-turned-broadcaster Eric (Cavanagh) lives with partner Sam (Shenkman), whose irresponsible brother has just dumped his 11-year-old son Scot (Bernett) with them. The flamboyantly effeminate youngster is a shocker to the conservative duo with Eric wanting to butch the boy up by teaching him to play hockey. Guess what Eric learns instead. **95m/C; DVD.** *CA* Tom Cavanagh; Ben Shenkman; Noah Bernett; Graham Greene; Fiona Reid; Colin Cunningham; Megan Follows; Dylan Everett; ***D:*** Laurie Lynd; ***W:*** Sean Reycraft; ***C:*** David Mankin; ***M:*** Robert Carli.

Breakheart Pass **1976 (PG)** A governor, his female companion, a band of cavalrymen, and a mysterious man travel on a train through the mountains of Idaho in 1870. The mystery man turns out to be a murderer. Based on a novel by Alistair MacLean. **92m/C; VHS, DVD, Blu-Ray.** Charles Bronson; Ben Johnson; Richard Crenna; Jill Ireland; Charles Durning; Ed Lauter; Archie Moore; Sally Kirkland; ***D:*** Tom Gries; ***W:*** Alistair MacLean; ***C:*** Lucien Ballard; ***M:*** Jerry Goldsmith.

Breakin' *Breakdance* **1984 (PG)** Dance phenomenon break dancing along with the hit songs that accompanied the fad. **87m/C; VHS, DVD, Blu-Ray.** Lucinda Dickey; Adolfo "Shabba Doo" Quinones; Michael "Boogaloo Shrimp" Chambers; Ben Lokey; Christopher McDonald; Phineas Newborn, III; ***D:*** Joel Silberg; ***W:*** Allen N. DeBevoise; ***C:*** Hanania Baer; ***M:*** Michael Boyd.

Breakin' 2: Electric Boogaloo *Breakdance 2: Electric Boogaloo; Electric Boogaloo "Breakin' 2"* **1984 (PG)** Breakdancers hold a benefit concert to preserve an urban community center. **94m/C; VHS, DVD, Blu-Ray.** Lucinda Dickey; Adolfo "Shabba Doo" Quinones; Michael "Boogaloo Shrimp" Chambers; Susie Bono; ***D:*** Sam Firstenberg; ***C:*** Hanania Baer.

Breakin' All The Rules 1/2 **2004 (PG-13)** Predictable romantic comedy stars Foxx as L.A. men's magazine exec Quincy Watson, who gets dumped by his fiancee Helen (Lawson) the same day his timid boss Phillip (MacNicol) wants Quincy to lay off 15% of the mag's staff. Instead, Quincy axes himself and takes his frustrations and rejections out on paper, writing what turns out to be the best-selling "Breakup Handbook." Suddenly, Quincy is Mr. Advice for Phillip, who wants to know how to avoid the gold-digging Rita (Esposito), and Quincy's playa cousin Evan (Chestnut),who wants to dump his girlfriend Nicky (Union) before she dumps him. Complications ensue when Quincy unwittingly falls for Nicky and Rita goes after Evan thinking he's Quincy. It's contrived but well done, with Foxx smirking likeably and Union lovely as always. **85m/C; VHS, DVD.** Jamie Foxx; Gabrielle Union; Morris Chestnut; Peter MacNichol; Jennifer Esposito; Bianca Lawson; Jill Ritchie; ***Cameo(s):*** Heather Headley; ***D:*** Daniel Taplitz; ***W:*** Daniel Taplitz; ***C:*** David Hennings; ***M:*** Marcus Miller.

Breaking a Monster **2016** A feature-length documentary about a young band and its first unexpected year of success. The documentary tells the story of how three grade school music loving boys from Brooklyn bonded and formed the heavy metal/speed punk band Unlocking the Truth. After the band's formation, they played on weekends in Time Square, gained attention for their talent, and made the leap into Internet fame and a deal with a record company. The film shows how these changes affect the boys as they must deal with the demands of fame, touring, managers, and success. **92m/C; DVD, Streaming, Download.** ***D:*** Luke Meyer; ***W:*** Luke Meyer; Brad Turner; ***C:*** Ethan Palmer; Hillary Spera.

Breaking and Entering 🦴🦴 **2006 (R)** Landscape architect Will (Law) and his partner Sandy (Freeman) are pioneers in the urban renewal of the crime-ridden King's Cross area in North London. However, after their office is repeatedly broken into, Will finally manages to chase the young thief long enough to discover where he lives. The thief, Miro (Gavron), is a teenaged Bosnian refugee, living with his widowed seamstress mother, Amira (Binoche). Instead of immediately ratting Miro out, Will cozies up to his attractive mum since his own home life is lacking (Wright Penn plays his depressive live-in). Law's character is a polite cipher and the dicey situations resolve themselves a little too neatly in Minghella's slice of life drama. **116m/C; DVD.** *GB* Jude Law; Juliette Binoche; Robin Wright; Martin Freeman; Ray Winstone; Vera Farmiga; Juliet Stevenson; Rafi Gavron; Poppy Rogers; ***D:*** Anthony Minghella; ***W:*** Anthony Minghella; ***C:*** Benoit Delhomme; ***M:*** Gabriel Yared.

Breaking & Exiting 🦴 **1/2 2018** Love blossoms when Harry, an aimless burglar, stumbles upon suicidal Daisy in her tub, and sticks around to develop her self-worth. The plot is farfetched, and chemistry between the couple is non-existent. A shame that the writer, Jordan Hinson, who also stars as Daisy, couldn't devise a better vehicle for either her acting or writing craft. **78m/C; DVD.** Milo Gibson; Jordan Hinson; Adam Huber; Joaquim de Almeida; Justine Wachsberger; ***D:*** Peter Facinelli; ***W:*** Jordan Hinson; ***C:*** Christopher Hamilton; ***M:*** Sacha Chaban.

Breaking Away 🦴🦴🦴 **1/2 1979 (PG)** A lighthearted coming-of-age drama about a high school graduate's addiction to bicycle racing, whose dreams are tested against the realities of a crucial race. An honest, open look at present Americana with tremendous insight into the minds of average youth; shot on location at Indiana University. Great bike-racing photography. Quaid, Barrie, and Christopher give exceptional performances. Basis for a TV series. **100m/C; VHS, DVD, Blu-Ray.** Dennis Christopher; Dennis Quaid; Daniel Stern; Jackie Earle Haley; Barbara Barrie; Paul Dooley; Amy Wright; ***D:*** Peter Yates; ***W:*** Steve Tesich; ***C:*** Matthew F. Leonetti; ***M:*** Patrick Williams. Oscars '79: Orig. Screenplay; Golden Globes '80: Film--Mus./Comedy; Natl. Bd. of Review '79: Support. Actor (Dooley); N.Y. Film Critics '79: Screenplay; Natl. Soc. Film Critics '79: Film, Screenplay; Writers Guild '79: Orig. Screenplay.

Breaking Glass 🦴🦴 **1/2 1980 (PG)** A "New Wave" musical that gives an insight into the punk record business and at the same time tells of the rags-to-riches life of a punk rock star. **94m/C; VHS, DVD, Blu-Ray.** *GB* Hazel O'Connor; Phil Daniels; Jon Finch; Jonathan Pryce; ***D:*** Brian Gibson.

Breaking In 🦴🦴🦴 **1989 (R)** A semi-acclaimed comedy about a professional thief who takes a young amateur under his wing and shows him the ropes. Under-estimated Reynolds is especially charming. Witty and innovative script, with intelligent direction from Forsyth. **95m/C; VHS, DVD; Open Captioned.** Burt Reynolds; Casey Siemaszko; Sheila Kelley; Lorraine Toussaint; Albert Salmi; Harry Carey, Jr.; Maury Chaykin; Stephen Tobolowsky; David Frishberg; ***D:*** Bill Forsyth; ***W:*** John Sayles; ***C:*** Michael Coulter; ***M:*** Michael Gibbs.

Breaking In 🦴 **1/2 2018 (PG-13)** A thriller about a mother who will do anything to protect her children. After Shawn's (Union) estranged father is killed unexpectedly, she must dispose of his estate, including selling her isolated childhood home. When Shawn takes her kids there for the weekend to prepare the home for sale, she soon discovers they are not alone. Criminals are in the house looking for a safe, hold her kids hostage, and force Shawn to take desperate action to save them. Though the film is predictable and full of plot holes, McTeigue's direction and shot selection and Union's passionate performance make it somewhat worthwhile. **88m/C; DVD, Blu-Ray, Streaming.** Gabrielle Union; Billy Burke; Richard Cabral; Ajiona Alexus; Levi Meaden; ***D:*** James McTeigue; ***W:*** Ryan Engle; ***C:*** Toby Oliver; ***M:*** Johnny Klimek.

Breaking News 🦴🦴 *Daai Si Gin* **2004** Action director To starts off with a mesmerizing 7-minute scene that follows the camera along a Hong Kong street, culminating in a shootout between crooks and cops (cops lose). Since a TV news crew got the whole debacle on tape, the humiliated department lets ambitious Inspector Rebecca Fong (Chen) equip the cops with web cams that will allow the proper spin as they hunt for the hostage-taking thieves; too bad the criminals strike back with their own video ops. Cantonese with subtitles. **90m/C; DVD.** *CH* Richie Jen; Kelly Chen; Nick Cheung; Hui Siu Hung; Lam Suet; Cheung Sui Fai; Simon Yam; You Yong; Ding Hai Feng; Le Hai Tao; Maggie Shiu; ***D:*** Johnny To; ***W:*** Chan Hing Kai; Ip Tin Shing; ***C:*** Cheng Siu Keung; ***M:*** Ben Cheung; Ching Chi Wing.

The Breaking Point 🦴🦴🦴 **1950** A somewhat more faithful adaptation of Hemingway's "To Have and Have Not" (following the 1944 Bogart flick). Garfield gives a first-rate performance as charter boat skipper Harry Morgan whose financial woes get him into bigger and bigger trouble. Shady lawyer Duncan (Ford) first gets Harry involved in a disastrous attempt to smuggle illegal Chinese immigrants and then hires him to run an escape route for some gangsters that is equally dangerous. **97m/B; DVD, Blu-Ray.** John Garfield; Phyllis Thaxter; Wallace Ford; Patricia Neal; Juano Hernandez; Ralph Dumke; Edmon Ryan; Victor Sen Yung; ***D:*** Michael Curtiz; ***W:*** Ranald MacDougall; ***C:*** Ted D. McCord; ***M:*** Ray Heindorf.

Breaking Point 🦴 **1/2 2009 (R)** One of the few reasons to watch this generic crime drama is the ferocious performance of Busta Rhymes as a murderous gangster. Former defense attorney Steven Luisi (Berenger) was brought low by drug addiction and personal tragedy. Trying to redeem himself by investigating a high-profile murder, Luisi finds his former dealer Al Bowen (Rhymnes) and corrupt DA Marty Berlin (Assante) behind the violence. **93m/C; DVD.** Tom Berenger; Armand Assante; Kirk "Sticky Fingaz" Jones; Musetta Vander; Frankie Faison; Robert Capelli, Jr.; ***D:*** Jeff Celentano; ***W:*** Vincent Campanella; ***C:*** Emmanuel Vouniozos; ***M:*** Pinar Toprak. **VIDEO**

Breaking the Bank 🦴🦴 **2014** A bank-centered comedy about a man who loses it all and tries to get it back again. Though Charles Bunbury (Grammar) knows nothing about banking, he serves as the bumbling chairman of the established London-based bank Tuftons. The institution was founded by his wife Penelope (Greig). When investment banks from the United States and Japan begin to move on the underperforming Tuftons, Charles makes a risky investment that goes bust. Forced out of the bank and his home, he makes an unlikely ally to try to work his way back into the bank and regain his wife. **105m/C; DVD, Streaming, Download.** Kelsey Grammer; Sonya Cassidy; John Michael Higgins; Tamsin Greig; Doon Mackichan; David Buckley; ***D:*** Vadim Jean; ***W:*** Roger Devlin; ***C:*** Oliver Curtis. **VIDEO**

Breaking the Surface: The Greg Louganis Story 🦴🦴 **1/2 1996** Trials and tribulations of the gold-medal winning Olympic diver, including his overbearing father, abusive lover, and his own HIV-positive status. Based on Louganis' autobiography; made for TV. **95m/C; VHS, DVD.** Mario Lopez; Michael Murphy; Jeffrey Meek; Bruce Weitz; Rosemary Dunsmore; ***D:*** Steven Hilliard Stern; ***W:*** Alan Hines. **CABLE**

Breaking the Waves 🦴🦴🦴 **1995 (R)** Sacrifical journey of shy, religious Bess (Watson), who's living in an austere northern Scotland coastal village in the '70s. Bess, who regularly talks to God, marries Jan (Skarsgard), an adventurer working on a North Sea oil rig. It must be a case of opposites attracting but the couple are happy until Jan is paralyzed from the neck down in a rig accident. Bess, who blames herself, begins sleeping around, believing her actions can somehow help Jan, and slides ever deeper into mental instability. Powerful story is divided into seven chapters and an epilogue. **152m/C; VHS, DVD, Blu-Ray.** *DK FR* Emily Watson; Stellan Skarsgard; Katrin Cartlidge; Adrian Rawlins; Jean-Marc Barr; Sandra Voe; Udo Kier; Mikkel Gaup; ***D:*** Lars von Trier; ***W:*** Lars von Trier; ***C:*** Robby Muller; ***M:*** Joachim Holbek. Cannes '96: Grand Jury Prize; Cesar '97: Foreign Film; N.Y. Film Critics '96: Actress (Watson), Cinematog., Director (von Trier); Natl. Soc. Film Critics '96: Actress (Watson), Cinematog., Director (von Trier), Film.

Breaking Up 🦴 **1/2 1997 (R)** What steamy sheet action brings together, dreary day to day living easily pulls apart. That is the basic message of this bland romantic comedy that brings nothing new to the tired genre. Typical opposites attract but can't stay together (yet can't stay apart) plot finds photographer Crowe and teacher Hayek madly in lust and impulsively marrying. Hayek had more to work with when she played this role in "Fools Rush In," and Crowe seems uncomfortable as the lackluster boyfriend. Told in a chatty style with frequent asides to the audience by the main characters and a string of flashback sequences, director Greenwald's theatre background is apparent here. Clever camera work and editing are highlights. Adapted from Michael Cristofer's Pulitzer Prize-winning play. **90m/C; VHS, DVD, Blu-Ray.** Salma Hayek; Russell Crowe; ***D:*** Robert Greenwald; ***W:*** Michael Cristofer; ***M:*** Mark Mothersbaugh.

Breaking Up Is Hard to Do 🦴 **1979** Six men leave their wives and shack up together on Malibu for a summer of partying and introspection. Made for television; edited down from its original 201 minute length. **96m/C; DVD.** Billy Crystal; Bonnie Franklin; Ted Bessell; Jeff Conaway; Tony Musante; Robert Conrad; Trish Stewart; David Ogden Stiers; George Gaynes; ***D:*** Lou Antonio; ***M:*** Richard Bellis. **TV**

Breaking Upwards 🦴 **1/2 2009** In this self-indulgent modern romance, filmmaking couple Lister-Jones and Wein portray themselves and recreate past domestic problems. After living together for four years, they become concerned that their relationship is eroding so they decide to break up their week by staying together for four days and separating for three. During their separation time the two are free to explore their independence—only they're more codependent. **89m/C; DVD.** Daryl Wein; Zoe Lister-Jones; Andrea Martin; Julie White; Peter Friedman; Olivia Thirlby; Pablo Schreiber; Ebon Moss-Bachrach; ***D:*** Daryl Wein; ***W:*** Daryl Wein; Peter Duchan; ***C:*** Alex Bergman; ***M:*** Kyle Forester.

Breaking Wind 🦴 **1/2 2012 (R)** A low-brow, satiric comedy spoof of the three films in The Twilight Saga. Beautiful Bella (Davis) faces challenges when vengeful Victoria (Collins) and her group of blood-sucking newborns threaten Bella's life. Though at odds, vampire Edward (Callero) and wolf Jacob (Pacheco) are forced to place their differences aside and work together to save the woman they both love. **82m/C; DVD, Streaming, Download.** Heather Ann Davis; Eric Callero; Frank Pacheco; Kelsey Collins; Michael Hamilton; ***D:*** Craig Moss; ***W:*** Craig Moss; ***C:*** Rudy Harbon; ***M:*** Todd Haberman.

Breakout 🦴🦴 **1975 (PG)** The wife of a man imprisoned in Mexico hires a Texas bush pilot (Bronson) to help her husband (Duvall) escape. **96m/C; VHS, DVD, Blu-Ray.** Charles Bronson; Jill Ireland; Robert Duvall; John Huston; Sheree North; Randy Quaid; ***D:*** Tom Gries; ***W:*** Howard B. Kreitsek; Marc Norman; Elliott Baker; ***C:*** Lucien Ballard; ***M:*** Jerry Goldsmith.

Breakout 🦴🦴 **1998** Zack (Carradine) has invented an environmentally friendly alternative energy source that makes him the scourge of the oil cartels. So the bad guys decide to kidnap Zack's son Joe (Bonifant) as a bargaining chip, only the kid turns out to be as smart as his old man. **86m/C; VHS, DVD, UMD.** Robert Carradine; Evan Bonifant; James Hong; Chris Chinchilla; ***D:*** John Bradshaw; ***W:*** Naomi Janzen; ***C:*** Edgar Egger; ***M:*** Gary Koftinoff. **VIDEO**

The Breaks 🦴 **1999 (R)** White Irish kid gets adopted by a black family in South Central L.A. and naturally grows up to think of himself as a homeboy. But his adoptive mom is tired of his shenanigans and gives him one simple task to do'bring home a carton of milk by supper—or else. Why isn't this as easy as it sounds ('cause it certainly is as dumb). **86m/C; VHS, DVD.** Mitch Mullany; Carl Anthony Payne, II; Paula Jai Parker; Clifton Powell; Loretta Devine; ***D:*** Eric Meza; ***W:*** Mitch Mullany; ***C:*** Carlos Gonzalez; ***M:*** Adam Hirsh. **VIDEO**

Breakthrough 🦴🦴 **1950** Focuses on one infantry platoon as they fight their way from Omaha Beach on June 6, 1944 across Normandy. The vets are led by tough Capt. Hale (Brian) and green Lt. Mallory (Agar), who'll naturally come into his own as he gains battle experience. Includes actual footage of the Allied invasion on D-Day. **91m/B; DVD.** David Brian; John Agar; Frank Lovejoy; William Campbell; Paul Picerni; Greg McClure; ***D:*** Lewis Seiler; ***W:*** Ted Sherdeman; Bernard Girard; ***C:*** Edwin DuPar; ***M:*** William Lava.

Breakthrough 🦴🦴 **2019 (PG)** Joyce (Metz) and Brian (Lucas) have been raising their now 14-year-old son John (Ruiz) since adopting him during a mission trip to Guatemala. When their typical teen son falls through the ice on a local lake, he is underwater for 15 minutes until he is saved by firefighter Tommy Shine (Colter). Though doctors pronounce John dead, his heart starts beating again after Joyce yells out a prayer. Joyce must rely on her faith as John faces overwhelming odds while receiving care in the hospital. Based on a true story, the story is quite predictable but uplifting in imparting the power of blind faith. **116m/C; DVD, Blu-Ray.** Chrissy Metz; Topher Grace; Josh(ua) Lucas; Marcel Ruiz; Dennis Haysbert; ***D:*** Roxann Dawson; ***W:*** Grant Nieporte; ***C:*** Zoran Popovic; ***M:*** Marcelo Zarvos.

The Breakup Artist 🦴🦴 **1/2 2004 (R)** A rom-com from the male point of view. Jim (Taylor) is looking for love in the Big Apple, except he can't stay focused on just one girl (hence the title). Meanwhile, sweet co-worker Teresa (Devicq) is engaged to a jerk. Of course, they're made for each other—if only Jim and Teresa can figure it out. **86m/C; DVD.** Joseph Lyle Taylor; Paula DeVicq; Sarita Choudhury; Sabrina Lloyd; Ron Mongeluzzo; ***Cameo(s):*** Edward Burns; Regis Philbin; Bobby Cannavale; ***D:*** Vincent Rubino; ***W:*** Vincent Rubino; ***C:*** Nicholas Baratta; ***M:*** Thomas DeRenzo; Paul Conte.

Breast Men 🦴🦴 **1/2 1997 (R)** A campy fictional look into the lives and careers of the two doctors who invented the silicone breast implant in 1960s Texas. Struggling Kevin Saunders (Schwimmer) is an ambitious geek who works with grumpy plastic surgeon mentor, Dr. William Larson (Cooper), to develop a prosthetic breast, made from Dow-Corning's silicone gel. It's an immediate success and the doctors become rich, successful, and ever more obnoxious. Then come the lawsuits and life is suddenly no longer so sweet. And yes, you will see a lot of naked breasts. **95m/C; VHS, DVD.** David Schwimmer; Chris Cooper; Louise Fletcher; Emily Procter; Matt Frewer; John Stockwell; Terry O'Quinn; Kathleen Wilhoite; Lisa Marie; ***D:*** Lawrence O'Neil; ***W:*** John Stockwell; ***C:*** Robert M. Stevens; ***M:*** Dennis McCarthy. **CABLE**

Breath of Scandal 🦴🦴 **1960** An American diplomat in Vienna rescues a princess when she is thrown off a horse; he falls for her like a ton o' bricks. Viennese politics complicate things. Based on a play by Molnar. **98m/C; VHS, DVD.** Sophia Loren; John Gavin; Maurice Chevalier; Angela Lansbury; ***D:*** Michael Curtiz.

Breathe 🦴🦴 **2017 (PG-13)** A drama about the struggles of a couple dealing with one member's disability, based on the true story of producer Cavendish's parents. After quickly falling in love and marrying, Robin Cavendish (Garfield) and his wife Diana (Foy) have a son. During the pregnancy, Robin is diagnosed with polio and given only a few months to live because he has irreversible paralysis. While hospitalized, Robin fights for his life and finds ways to live his life with his wife's help. Director Serkis's debut is well meaning and empathetic with strong performances, though a bit too sentimental. **117m/C; Blu-Ray, Streaming.** *UK* Andrew Garfield; Claire Foy; Diana Rigg; Miranda Raison; Dean-Charles Chapman; ***D:*** Andy Serkis; ***W:*** William Nicholson; ***C:*** Robert Richardson; ***M:*** Nitin Sawhney.

Breathe In 🦴 **1/2 2013 (R)** Writer/director Doremus falls deep into the sophomore slump chasm (after 2011's festival hit "Like Crazy") with this inert, melodrama that adds nothing new to the subgenre of overdone soap opera. Keith Reynolds (Pearce) is happily married to Megan Reynolds (Ryan) but the arrival of a beautiful foreign exchange student named Sophie (Jones) throws them all for a loop. The affair between Keith and Sophie on which the whole film hinges never once feels real, partially due to a lack of chemistry between the leads but also because Doremus can't find anything genuine buried under the bedsheets of cliché. **98m/C; DVD, Blu-Ray.** Felicity Jones; Guy Pearce; Amy Ryan; Mackenzie Davis; Matthew Daddario; Ben Shenkman; Kyle MacLachlan; Alexandra Wentworth; ***D:*** Drake Doremus; ***W:*** Drake Doremus; Ben York Jones; ***C:*** John Guleserian; ***M:*** Dustin O'Halloran.

Breathing Fire 🦴🦴 **1991 (R)** A Vietnamese teenager and his American brother find out their ex-GI father is behind an armed bank robbery and murder. They join together to protect the only eyewitness—a young girl—against the ruthless gang of criminals and their own father. Lots of kickboxing action for martial arts fans. **86m/C; VHS, DVD.** Bolo Yeung; Jonathan Ke Quan; Jerry Trimble; ***D:*** Lou Kennedy.

Breathless 🦴🦴🦴🦴 *A Bout de Souffle* **1959** Godard's first feature catapulted him to the vanguard of French filmmakers. Carefree Parisian crook, Michel (Belmondo), who emulates Humphrey Bogart, falls in love with gamine American student Patricia (Seberg) with tragic results. Wonderful scenes of Parisian life. Established Godard's Brechtian, experimental style. Belmondo's film debut. Mistitled "Breathless" for American release, the film's French title actually means "Out of Breath"; however, the fast-paced, erratic musical score leaves you breathless. French with English subtitles. Remade with Richard Gere in 1983 with far less intensity. **90m/B; VHS, DVD, Blu-Ray.** *FR* Jean-Paul Belmondo; Jean Seberg; Daniel Boulanger; Jean-Pierre Melville; Liliane Robin; ***D:*** Jean-Luc Godard; ***W:*** Jean-Luc Godard; ***C:*** Raoul Coutard; ***M:*** Martial Solal. Berlin Intl. Film Fest. '60: Director (Godard).

Breathless 🦴🦴 **1983 (R)** Car thief turned cop killer has a torrid love affair with a French student studying in Los Angeles as the police slowly close in. Glossy, smarmy remake of the Godard classic that concentrates on the thin plot rather than any attempt at revitalizing the film syntax. **105m/C; VHS, DVD, Blu-Ray.** Richard Gere; Valerie Kaprisky; Art Metrano; John P. Ryan; Lisa Jane Persky; ***D:*** Jim McBride; ***W:*** Jim McBride; L.M. Kit Carson; ***M:*** Jack Nitzsche.

Breathless 🦴 ½ **2012 (R)** Cartoonish crime thriller. Trailer-dwelling Texas housewife Lorna (Gershon) accidentally kills her lowlife husband Dale (Kilmer) after learning he wasn't going to share his loot from a bank heist. She calls her best friend Tiny (Giddish) to help get rid of the body while also trying to figure out where Dale hid the money. The local sheriff (Liotta) and a greedy PI (Duvall) show up to complicate the situation even more. **92m/C; DVD, Blu-Ray.** Gina Gershon; Kelli Giddish; Ray Liotta; Wayne Duvall; Val Kilmer; ***D:*** Jesse Baget; ***W:*** Jesse Baget; Stefania Moscato; ***C:*** Bill Otto; ***M:*** Jermaine Stegall. **VIDEO**

The Breed 🦴🦴 **2001 (R)** Set in a noirish anytime, this horror film tells the story of an FBI agent Grant (a very stiff Woodbine), who starts out searching for a serial killer and ends up teamed with Aaron Grey (Paul), who turns out to be a vampire. Seems that the vampires who walk among us are ready to come out of the closet and join society, but a political dissident in the vampire ranks is trying to start a war...or is he? Could there be crosses and double crosses afoot? Grant, a black man, is less than thrilled at being teamed with a vampire, which results in not-too-subtle moral banter about racism and the Nazis to explain the vamps' fear of the humans and condemn the human sense of self preservation. It has moments of promise, but the poor acting and choppy editing and direction make everyone look uncomfortable amid the atmospheric scenery. **91m/C; VHS, DVD.** Adrian Paul; Bai Ling; Bokeem Woodbine; Zen Gesner; Jake Eberle; ***D:*** Michael Oblowitz; ***W:*** Christos N. Gage; Ruth Fletcher. **VIDEO**

The Breed 🦴 **2006 (R)** Bad doggie flick! Two brothers inherit their uncle's remote island and decide to fly three friends to join them in a party weekend. Too bad they didn't know their uncle rented part of the island to a special canine research unit and that the genetically enhanced dogs have gone wild. Lots of plot holes, lots of genre cliches. The Hound says this one must wear the cone of shame! **87m/C; DVD, Blu-Ray.** Oliver Hudson; Hill Harper; Eric Lively; Michelle Rodriguez; Taryn Manning; ***D:*** Nick Mastandrea; ***W:*** Robert Conte; Peter Martin Wortmann; ***C:*** Giulio Biccari; ***M:*** Tom Mesmer. **VIDEO**

Breeders 🦴 ½ **1986 (R)** Ridiculous foam rubber monster attacks and impregnates women in New York. **77m/C; VHS, DVD, Blu-Ray.** Teresa Farley; Frances Raines; Amy Brentano; Lance Lewman; Natalie O'Connell; ***D:*** Tim Kincaid; ***W:*** Tim Kincaid; ***C:*** Arthur Marks.

Breeders WOOF! 1997 (R) Alien on a mating mission terrorizes a Boston womens' college. Doesn't deliver on its exploitation premise, so don't bother. **92m/C; VHS, DVD, Blu-Ray.** Todd Jensen; Samantha Janus; Kadamba Simmons; Oliver Tobias; ***D:*** Paul Matthews; ***W:*** Paul Matthews; ***M:*** Ben Heneghan.

Brenda Starr 🦴 **1986 (PG)** Amateurish adaptation of the comic strip by Dale Messick. Shields stars as girl reporter Brenda Starr, who is once again risking her life to get the scoop. She finds herself in the jungles of South America searching for a mad scientist who is creating a rocket fuel that could destroy the world. The most entertaining thing about this film is the costumes designed by Bob Mackie. **94m/C; VHS, DVD.** Brooke Shields; Timothy Dalton; Tony Peck; Diana Scarwid; Nestor Serrano; Jeffrey Tambor; June Gable; Charles Durning; Eddie Albert; Henry Gibson; Ed Nelson; ***D:*** Robert Ellis Miller; ***W:*** James David Buchanan; ***C:*** Freddie Francis; ***M:*** Johnny Mandel.

The Bretts 🦴🦴🦴 **1988** Amusing two-part British miniseries follows the egos and eccentricities of the British theatrical dynasty, the Bretts. Part 1 is set in the '20s and introduces the family heads, Charles (Rodway) and Lydia (Murray), who enjoy performing off-stage almost as well as they enjoy performing on. Also introduced are their five children and loyal (if opinionated) servants. Part 2 follows the family into the '30s with son Edwin (Yelland) having become a film star, actress daughter Martha (Lang) falling for a politician, and son Tom (Winter) continuing to write his gloomy social dramas. Each part is on six cassettes. **600m/C; VHS, DVD.** *GB* Barbara Murray; Norman Rodway; David Yelland; Belinda Lang; George Winter; Janet Maw; Tim Wylton; Bert Parnaby; Lysette Anthony; Clive Francis; Frank Middlemass; John Castle; Hugh Fraser; Patrick Ryecart; Sally Cookson; Billy Boyle; ***W:*** Rosemary Anne Sisson.

Brewster McCloud 🦴🦴🦴 ½ **1970 (R)** Altman's first picture after M*A*S*H reunites much of the cast and combines fantasy, black comedy, and satire in the story of a young man whose head is in the clouds or at least in the upper reaches of the Houston Astrodome. Brewster (Cort) lives covertly in the Dome and dreams of flying. He also has a guardian angel (Kellerman) who watches over him and may actually be killing people who give him a hard time. Murphy is a cop obsessed with catching the killer. And there's a circus allegory as well. Hard to figure what it all means and offbeat as they come, but for certain tastes, exquisite. **101m/C; VHS, DVD, Blu-Ray.** Bud Cort; Sally Kellerman; Shelley Duvall; Michael Murphy; William Windom; Rene Auberjonois; Stacy Keach; John Schuck; Margaret Hamilton; ***D:*** Robert Altman; ***W:*** Doran William Cannon; ***C:*** Jordan Cronenweth; Lamar Boren; ***M:*** Gene Page.

Brewster's Millions 🦴🦴 ½ **1945** If Brewster, an ex-GI, can spend $1 million in one year, he will inherit a substantially greater fortune. Originally a 1902 novel, this is the fifth of seven film adaptations. **79m/B; DVD.** Dennis O'Keefe; June Havoc; Eddie Anderson; Helen Walker; Gail Patrick; Mischa Auer; ***D:*** Allan Dwan; ***W:*** Charles Rodgers; Wilkie Mahoney; ***C:*** Charles Lawton, Jr.

Brewster's Millions 🦴 ½ **1985 (PG)** An aging minor league baseball player must spend $30 million in order to collect an inheritance of $300 million. He may find that money can't buy happiness. Seventh remake of the story. **101m/C; VHS, DVD, Blu-Ray.** Richard Pryor; John Candy; Lonette McKee; Stephen Collins; Jerry Orbach; Pat Hingle; Tovah Feldshuh; Hume Cronyn; Rick Moranis; Yakov Smirnoff; Joe Grifasi; Peter Jason; Grand L. Bush; Reni Santoni; Conrad Janis; Lin Shaye; ***D:*** Walter Hill; ***W:*** Herschel Weingrod; Timothy Harris; ***C:*** Ric Waite; ***M:*** Ry Cooder.

Brian Banks 🦴🦴 ½ **2018 (PG-13)** Brian Banks (Hodge) is a standout linebacker at a football powerhouse Long Beach high school when a classmate falsely accuses him of rape. Though her story is clearly untrue, Banks is forced to take a plea deal that results in an unexpectedly harsh sentence and having to register as a sex offender. During his six years in prison and after his release, he fights to clear his name so he can return to football, get a job, and resume his life. Based on a true story, the drama is well-crafted and well intentioned, and features a stand-out, engaging performance from Hodge. **99m/C; DVD, Blu-Ray.** Aldis Hodge; Greg Kinnear; Melanie Liburd; Sherri Shepherd; Tiffany Dupont; ***D:*** Tom Shadyac; ***W:*** Doug Atchison; ***C:*** Ricardo Diaz; ***M:*** John Debney.

Brian's Song 🦴🦴🦴🦴 **1971 (G)** The story of the unique relationship between Gale Sayers, the Chicago Bears' star running back, and his teammate Brian Piccolo. The friendship between the Bears' first interracial roommates ended suddenly when Brian Piccolo lost his life to cancer. Incredibly well received in its time. **74m/C; VHS, DVD.** James Caan; Billy Dee Williams; Jack Warden; Shelley Fabares; Judy Pace; Bernie Casey; ***D:*** Buzz Kulik; ***W:*** William Blinn; ***C:*** Joseph Biroc; ***M:*** Michel Legrand. **TV**

Brian's Song 🦴🦴 **2001** Unnecessary remake of the 1971 made-for-TV classic dealing with the friendship between Gale Sayers and Brian Piccolo, and Piccolo's fight against cancer heads right for the disease-of-the-week cliches with almost none of the original's charm or depth. Phifer, as Sayers, and Cale, as Joy Piccolo, along with a deeper understanding of the wives' point of view, are the main reasons to check it out. But it still can't compare to the original. **89m/C; VHS, DVD.** Mekhi Phifer; Sean Maher; Paula Cale; Elise Neal; Ben Gazzara; Aidan Devine; Dean McDermott; ***D:*** John Gray; ***W:*** John Gray; Allen Clare; William Blinn; ***C:*** James Chressanthis; ***M:*** Richard (Rick) Marvin.

The Bribe 🦴🦴 ½ **1948** Federal Agent Rigby (Taylor) is sent to a tropical isle off the coast of Central America to investigate a smuggling ring dealing in contraband war surplus airplane engines. It's run by playboy Carwood (Price) and sleazy Bealler (Laughton) along with former wartime pilot Tug (Hodiak). Tug's wife—torch singer Elizabeth (Gardner)?doesn't know about the scheme but when Rigby falls for the femme, the crooks try setting him up so Rigby will compromise his career so he can save her. **98m/B; DVD.** Robert Taylor; Ava Gardner; Vincent Price; Charles Laughton; John Hodiak; Samuel S. Hinds; ***D:*** Robert Z. Leonard; ***W:*** Marguerite Roberts; ***C:*** Joseph Ruttenberg; ***M:*** Miklos Rozsa.

Brick 🦴🦴🦴 **2006 (R)** Ever wonder what it would look like if Raymond Chandler wrote for the "Sweet Valley High" series? In his debut film, writer/director Johnson delivers one of the most impressive examples of hard-boiled noir in years, set, strangely enough, in a California high school. Gordon-Levitt brilliantly channels Humphrey Bogart as Brendan, a tough-as-nails teenaged shamus who's trying to locate his missing ex-girlfriend (de Ravin) in the seamy underbelly of drug-dealing jocks and cheerleader femme fatales. The mystery's a twisty one, peppered with Johnson's own brand of tough guy slang that will either delight or confound you. But you can't ignore the ambition of this "Miller's Crossing" meets "Breakfast Club" hybrid. **110m/C; DVD, Blu-Ray.** Joseph Gordon-Levitt; Lukas Haas; Noah Fleiss; Matt O'Leary; Nora Zehetner; Noah Segan; Meagan Good; Emilie de Ravin; Brian White; Richard Roundtree; Lucas Babin; ***D:*** Rian Johnson; ***W:*** Rian Johnson; ***C:*** Steve Yedlin; ***M:*** Nathan Johnson.

Brick Mansions 🦴 ½ **2014 (PG-13)** An unnecessary redo of the international hit "District B13" that only garners attention as Paul Walker's final film. The deceased action star appears as Damien Collier, an undercover cop in a battle against corruption that teams him up with a street kid named Lino (Belle) against drug kingpin Tremaine (RZA). Boring and poorly edited, it lacks the flair of the original, and Walker's appeal can only do so much to make it better. **90m/C; DVD.** *FR CA* Paul Walker; David Belle; RZA; Carlo Rota; ***D:*** Camille Delamarre; ***W:*** Luc Besson; ***C:*** Christophe Collette; ***M:*** Marc Bell.

Bridal Fever 🦴🦴 **2008** Hallmark Channel movie about finding old-fashioned romance in the most cliched way possible. Single Gwen (Roth) has been singed once too often and is reluctant to change her marital status until she's hired by romance author Dahlia Merchant (Burke) to edit her autobiography. The much-married Dahlia has Gwen and her friend Sandra (Deines) doing some pre-wedding visualization before they go on a serious hubby hunt. **88m/C; DVD.** Andrea Roth; Delta Burke; Gabriel Hogan; Melinda Deines; Vincent Walsh; Nigel Bennett; Richard Fitzpatrick; ***D:*** Ron Oliver; ***W:*** Karen McClellan; ***C:*** Gerald Packer. **CABLE**

The Bride 🦴 ½ **1985 (PG-13)** Re-telling of "The Bride of Frankenstein." Sting's Dr. Frankenstein has much more success in creating his second monster (Beals). She's pretty and intelligent and he may even be falling in love with her. When she begins to gain too much independence, though, the awful truth about her origins comes out. Fans of the two leads will want to see this one, but for a true classic see Elsa Lanchester's bride. **118m/C; VHS, DVD, Blu-Ray.** *GB* Sting; Jennifer Beals; Anthony (Corlan) Higgins; David Rappaport; Geraldine Page; Clancy Brown; Phil Daniels; Veruschka; Quentin Crisp; Cary Elwes; ***D:*** Franc Roddam; ***W:*** Lloyd Fonvielle; ***C:*** Stephen Burum; ***M:*** Maurice Jarre.

Bride & Prejudice 🦴🦴 **2004 (PG-13)** Bollywood meets Jane Austen in Chandha's brightly-colored confection. Will Darcy (Henderson) and chum Balraj (Andrews) arrive in Amritsar for a friend's wedding. A stuffy but wealthy businessman, Will finds himself drawn to the strikingly beautiful and headstrong Lalita (Rai) who's irritated by his arrogance. That they are meant for each other is obvious but the film must travel from India to London and L.A. and back again before it all plays out, amidst various musical numbers and family trials. **110m/C; DVD.** Aishwarya Rai; Martin Henderson; Anupam Kher; Naveen Andrews; Daniel Gillies; Indira Varma; Marsha Mason; Nadira Babbar; Namrata Shirodkar; Meghnaa; Peeya Rai Choudhuri; ***D:*** Gurinder Chadha; ***W:*** Gurinder Chadha; Paul Mayeda Berges; ***C:*** Santosh Sivan.

The Bride & the Beast WOOF! *Queen of the Gorillas* **1958** While on an African safari honeymoon, a big game hunter's new bride is carried off by a gorilla. Ludicrous jungle tale. **78m/B; VHS, DVD.** Charlotte Austin; Lance Fuller; William Justine; Johnny Roth; Jeanne Gerson; Gilbert Frye; Slick Slavin; Bhogwan Singh; ***D:*** Adrian Weiss; ***W:*** Edward D. Wood, Jr.; ***C:*** Roland Price; ***M:*** Les Baxter.

Bride by Mistake 🦴 ½ **1944** Not very successful identity switch comedy that's a remake of 1934's "The Richest Girl in the World." Wealthy Norah (Day) is annoyed by fortune hunters and uses her secretary Sylvia (Hunt) to throw them off. Since Norah is interested in convalescing fighter pilot Tony Travis (Marshal), she decides to switch places with Sylvia and see if Tony will love her for herself while she constantly throws him in the fake Norah's path. **81m/B; DVD.** Laraine Day; Alan Marshal; Marsha Hunt; Allyn Joslyn; Edgar Buchanan; Michael St. Angel; ***D:*** Richard Wallace; ***W:*** Phoebe Ephron; Henry Ephron; ***C:*** Nicholas Musuraca; ***M:*** Roy Webb.

The Bride Came C.O.D. 🦴🦴 **1941** Rough 'n' tough pilot Cagney is hired by a rich Texas oil man to prevent his daughter (the one with the Bette Davis eyes) from marrying cheesy bandleader Carson. The payoff: $10 per pound if she's delivered unwed. What a surprise when Cagney faces the timeworn dilemma of having to choose between love and money. A contemporary issue of "Time" magazine trumpeted: "Screen's most talented tough guy roughhouses one of screen's best dramatic actresses." That tells you right there it's a romantic comedy. Cagney and Davis—a likely pairing, you'd think—are essentially fish out of water, bothered and bewildered by a weak script. **92m/B; VHS, DVD.** Bette Davis; James Cagney; Stuart Erwin; Jack Carson; George Tobias; Eugene Pallette; William Frawley; Harry Davenport; ***D:*** William Keighley; ***W:*** Julius J. Epstein; Philip G. Epstein; ***C:*** Ernest Haller; ***M:*** Max Steiner.

The Bride Comes Home 🦴🦴 ½
1935 When her father's business goes bust, socialite Jeannette (Colbert) gets a job writing for a Chicago magazine thanks to smitten employee Jack Bristow (Young). However, the sparks really fly between Jeannette and her editor, Cyrus Anderson (MacMurray), although the usual romantic misunderstandings get in the way. **83m/B; DVD.** Claudette Colbert; Fred MacMurray; Robert Young; William Collier, Sr.; ***D:*** Wesley Ruggles; ***W:*** Claude Binyon; ***C:*** Leo Tover.

Bride Flight 🦴🦴 ½ **2008 (R)** Sometimes weepy romantic drama. Wanting to leave dreary postwar Holland, three women emigrate to New Zealand to meet their little-known fiances who have settled in Christchurch. Shy farm girl Ada, family-oriented Marjorie, and Jewish fashion designer Esther befriend each other on the 1953 flight and are also introduced to fellow passenger, roguish farmer Frank. Their paths will continue to cross over the years with much ensuing emotion. English and Dutch with subtitles. **130m/C; DVD, Blu-Ray.** *NL* Waldemar Torenstra; Karina Smulders; Anna Drijver; Elise Schaap; Rutger Hauer; Pleuni Touw; Willeke van Ammelrooy; Petra Laseur; Mattijn Hartemink; Marc Klein Essink; ***D:*** Ben Sombogaart; ***W:*** Marieke van der Pol; ***C:*** Piotr Kukla; ***M:*** Jeannot Sanavia.

The Bride Goes Wild 🦴🦴 ½ **1948** Prim New England schoolteacher Martha Terryton (Allyson) gets her dream opportunity to become a commercial artist when she's hired to illustrate the new book from popular children's author Uncle Bump. She heads to New York and discovers Uncle Bump is actually cynical, hard-drinking, child-hating Greg Rawlings (Johnson). An affronted Martha threatens to expose the truth and publisher McGrath (Cronyn) scams Martha with a sob story involving tough orphan Danny (Jenkins), which only complicates matters. An interrupted wedding figures into the movie's title. **98m/B; DVD.** June Allyson; Van Johnson; Jackie "Butch" Jenkins; Hume Cronyn; Una Merkel; Arlene Dahl; Richard Derr; ***D:*** Norman Taurog; ***W:*** Albert Beich; ***C:*** Ray June; ***M:*** Rudolph Kopp.

Bride of Chucky 🦴 ½ **1998 (R)** Just when you thought you had seen the last of that creepy little doll, "Chucky" returns. This fourth installment in the "Child's Play" franchise finds Chucky back on the lam after being sprung from the pen by the ex-girlfriend of his former human incarnation, serial killer Charles Lee Ray. After killing his ex, Tiffany (Tilly), Chucky transforms her soul into an equally creepy girl doll. Together, they must make their way to the very spot where he was gunned down by police in order to transfer their souls back into human forms. Aside from Chucky and both incarnations of Tiffany, the rest of the characters are undeveloped and rather useless. Fortunately, the filmmakers knew not to take themselves too seriously, and managed a few funny moments. But its really only Tilly's excellent campy-vampy performance and an occasional clever jab from the Chuckster that lift this one above a woof. **89m/C; DVD, Blu-Ray.** Jennifer Tilly; Katherine Heigl; Nick Stabile; John Ritter; Alexis Arquette; Gordon Michael Woolvett; Lawrence Dane; Kathy Najimy; ***V:*** Brad Dourif; ***D:*** Ronny Yu; ***W:*** Don Mancini; ***C:*** Peter Pau; ***M:*** Graeme Revell.

The Bride of Frank 🦴🦴 **1996** Former homeless man Frank has a temper and he's not afraid to use it on the belittling ladies who make the ill-fated gaffe of responding to his personals ad, which leads to their horrific, over-the-top, brutal demises. But, hey, he still has a sense of humor about it all. The viewer, however, might not. **89m/C; VHS, DVD.** Frank Meyer; Johnny Horizon; Steve Ballot; ***D:*** Steve Ballot; ***W:*** Steve Ballot; ***C:*** Steve Ballot. **VIDEO**

The Bride of Frankenstein 🦴🦴🦴🦴 **1935** The classic sequel to the classic original in which Dr. F. seeks to build a mate for his monster. More humor than the first, but also more pathos, including the monster's famous but short-lived friendship with a blind hermit. Lanchester plays both the bride and Mary Shelley in the opening sequence. **75m/B; VHS, DVD, Blu-Ray.** Boris Karloff; Elsa Lanchester; Ernest Thesiger; Colin Clive; Una O'Connor; Valerie Hobson; Dwight Frye; John Carradine; E.E. Clive; O.P. Heggie; Gavin Gordon; Douglas Walton; Billy Barty; Walter Brennan; ***D:*** James Whale; ***W:*** John Lloyd Balderston; William Hurlbut; ***C:*** John Mescall; ***M:*** Franz Waxman. Natl. Film Reg. '98.

Bride of Killer Nerd 🦴 **1991** Harold Kunkel, left over from the original "Killer Nerd," finds his opposite sex nirvana in the person of Thelma, also a nerd in mind, body, and soul. They relentlessly pursue revenge on the rockers who humiliate them at a campus beer bash. **75m/C; VHS, DVD.** Toby Radloff; Wayne A. Harold; Heidi Lohr; ***D:*** Mark Steven Bosko.

Bride of Re-Animator 🦴🦴 ½ *Re-Animator 2* **1989** Herbert West is back, and this time he not only re-animates life but creates life—sexy female life—in this sequel to the immensely popular "Re-Animator." High camp and blood curdling gore make this a standout in the sequel parade. Available in a R-rated version as well. **99m/C; VHS, DVD, Blu-Ray.** Bruce Abbott; Claude Earl Jones; Fabiana Udenio; Jeffrey Combs; Kathleen Kinmont; David Gale; Mel Stewart; Irene Forrest; ***D:*** Brian Yuzna; ***W:*** Brian Yuzna; Rick Fry; Woody Keith; ***C:*** Rick Fichter; ***M:*** Richard Band.

Bride of the Gorilla 🦴🦴 **1951** Burr travels to the jungle where he finds a wife, a plantation, and a curse in this African twist on the werewolf legend. Chaney is the local policeman on his trail. Burr's physical changes are fun to watch. **76m/B; VHS, DVD.** Raymond Burr; Barbara Payton; Lon Chaney, Jr.; Tom Conway; Paul Cavanagh; ***D:*** Curt Siodmak; ***W:*** Curt Siodmak.

Bride of the Monster WOOF! *Bride of the Atom* **1955** Lugosi stars as a mad scientist trying to create a race of giants. Classic Woodian badness. **68m/B; VHS, DVD.** Bela Lugosi; Tor Johnson; Loretta King; Tony McCoy; Harvey B. Dunn; George Becwar; Paul Marco; William Benedict; Dolores Fuller; Don Nagel; Bud Osborne; Conrad Brooks; ***D:*** Edward D. Wood, Jr.; ***W:*** Edward D. Wood, Jr.; Alex Gordon; ***C:*** William C. Thompson; ***M:*** Frank Worth.

Bride of the Wind 🦴 ½ **2001 (R)** Dull biopic of Alma Mahler (Wynter), a 20th-century femme who put her own musical career aside to marry composer Gustav Mahler (Pryce) in old Vienna. Alma intrigues a number of famous men, including architect Walter Gropius (Verhoeven), artist Oskar Kokoschka (Perez), and others while her marriage to the stoic Gustav suffers. Unfortunately, it's neither titillating nor interesting despite the players. **99m/C; VHS, DVD.** Sarah Wynter; Jonathan Pryce; Vincent Perez; Simon Verhoeven; August Schmolzer; Gregor Seberg; Dagmar Schwarz; Wolfgang Hubsch; Johannes Silberschneider; ***D:*** Bruce Beresford; ***W:*** Marilyn Levy; ***C:*** Peter James; ***M:*** Stephen Endelman.

The Bride Walks Out 🦴🦴 **1936** Newlywed crisis: a woman with rich taste learns how to adjust to living on her husband's poor salary, but not before she samples the life of the wealthy. Interesting in a sociological sort of way. **81m/B; VHS, DVD, Blu-Ray.** Barbara Stanwyck; Gene Raymond; Robert Young; Ned Sparks; Willie Best; Helen Broderick; Hattie McDaniel; ***D:*** Leigh Jason.

Bride Wars 🦴 ½ **2009 (PG)** Liv (Hudson) and Emma (Hathaway) are lifelong pals and soon-to-be brides who share the dream of being married at Manhattan's Plaza Hotel. But the sweet, charming women's plans of their same-season weddings hit a snag when their wedding planner's (Bergen) snafu results in the Plaza scheduling the big events on the same day. With no other openings in the schedule, the otherwise caring friends won't budge and become each other's bridezilla nightmare. Their sub-par sabotage stunts come off as childish, desperate, and downright mean, with characters that never feel real. Style over substance bittersweet confection is gorgeously shot with a beautiful cast that will likely cause producers to vow "I do" to a sequel. **90m/C; Blu-Ray, On Demand.** Anne Hathaway; Kate Hudson; Kirsten Johnson; Bryan Greenberg; Steve Howey; Chris Pratt; Candice Bergen; John Pankow; Bruce Altman; Michael Arden; ***D:*** Gary Winick; ***W:*** Casey Wilson; June Raphael; ***C:*** Frederick Elmes; ***M:*** Ed Shearmur.

The Bride with White Hair 🦴🦴 *Jiang-Hu: Between Love and Glory* **1993** Operatic martial arts fable based on a novel by Leung Yu-Sang. A young warrior revives a beautiful witch (also a champion warrior) who was killed by jealous Siamese twins. Now the duo, who have fallen in love, must battle the evil twins who rule the corrupt Mo Dynasty. Available dubbed or in Chinese with subtitles. **92m/C; VHS, DVD.** *CH* Leslie Cheung; Brigitte Lin; Nam Kit-Ying; Frances Ng; Elaine Lui; ***D:*** Ronny Yu; ***W:*** Ronny Yu; David Wu; Lan Kei-Tou; Tseng Pik-Yin; ***C:*** Peter Pau; ***M:*** Richard Yuen.

The Bride with White Hair 2 🦴🦴 *Jiang-Hu: Between Love and Glory 2* **1993** The magic saga continues with the massacre of the followers of the Eight Lineages. Powerful and obsessed with vengeance, the Bride can only be stopped by the one man who loves her. Chinese with subtitles or dubbed. **80m/C; VHS, DVD.** *CH* Brigitte Lin; Leslie Cheung; Christy Chung; ***D:*** David Wu; Ronny Yu; ***W:*** David Wu.

The Bride Wore Black 🦴🦴🦴 *La Mariee Etait en Noir* **1968** Truffaut's homage to Hitchcock, complete with Bernard Herrmann score. Young bride Julie (Moreau) exacts brutal revenge on the five men who accidentally killed her husband on the steps of the church on their wedding day. Adapted from a novel by Cornell Woolrich. **107m/C; VHS, DVD, Blu-Ray.** *FR* Jeanne Moreau; Claude Rich; Jean-Claude Brialy; Michel Bouquet; Michael (Michel) Lonsdale; Charles Denner; Daniel Boulanger; ***D:*** Francois Truffaut; ***W:*** Francois Truffaut; Jean-Louis Richard; ***C:*** Raoul Coutard; ***M:*** Bernard Herrmann.

The Bride Wore Boots 🦴🦴 **1946** Goofy marital comedy with Stanwyck as horse breeder Sally who marries writer Jeff (Cummings) despite his dislike of horses. This leads to their eventual estrangement and Jeff being beset by rapacious southern belle Mary Lou (Lynn). However, he must come to Sally's aid when the horse she's entered in a prestigious steeplechase race refuses to be ridden by anyone but Jeff. **85m/B; DVD, Blu-Ray.** Barbara Stanwyck; Robert Cummings; Diana Lynn; Patric Knowles; Peggy Wood; Robert Benchley; Natalie Wood; Willie Best; ***D:*** Irving Pichel; ***W:*** Dwight Michael Wiley; ***C:*** Stuart Thompson; ***M:*** Frederick "Friedrich" Hollander.

The Bride Wore Red 🦴🦴 **1937** Crawford stars as a cabaret singer who masquerades as a socialite in an attempt to break into the upper crust. When a wealthy aristocrat invites her to spend two weeks at a posh resort in Tyrol, Crawford plays her part to the hilt, managing to charm both a rich gentleman and the village postman. Typical "love conquers all" melodrama. **103m/B; DVD.** Joan Crawford; Franchot Tone; Robert Young; Billie Burke; Reginald Owen; Lynne Carver; George Zucco; ***D:*** Dorothy Arzner; ***C:*** George J. Folsey.

Brides of Christ 🦴🦴 ½ **1991** Set in the Australian Santo Spirito Convent during the Vatican II upheaval of the 1960s. Explores the tensions between old and new religious ideas by focusing on novices, older nuns, and the Reverend Mother of the convent as they try to cope with a changing world. TV miniseries. **300m/C; VHS, DVD.** Brenda Fricker; Sandy Gore; Josephine Byrnes; Lisa Hensley; Naomi Watts; Kym Wilson; Melissa Thomas; ***D:*** Ken Cameron; ***W:*** John Alsop; Sue Smith.

The Brides of Dracula 🦴🦴 ½ **1960** A young French woman unknowingly frees a vampire. He wreaks havoc, sucking blood and creating more of the undead to carry out his evil deeds. One of the better Hammer vampire films. **86m/C; VHS, DVD, Blu-Ray.** *GB* Peter Cushing; Martita Hunt; Yvonne Monlaur; Freda Jackson; David Peel; Mona Washbourne; Miles Malleson; Henry Oscar; Michael Ripper; Andree Melly; ***D:*** Terence Fisher; ***W:*** Peter Bryan; Edward Percy; Jimmy Sangster; ***C:*** Jack Asher.

Brides of Fu Manchu 🦴 **1966** In Lee's second outing as the villainous character, Fu Manchu kidnaps the nubile daughters of various scientists so that they will be forced to build him a weapon to take over the world. Naturally, his Scotland Yard nemesis Nayland Smith (Wilmer) will stop him. Based on the characters created by Sax Rohmer. **93m/C; DVD.** *GB* Christopher Lee; Douglas Wilmer; Tsai Chin; Joseph Furst; Marie Versini; Heinz Drache; ***D:*** Don Sharp; ***W:*** Harry Alan Towers; ***C:*** Ernest Steward; ***M:*** Bruce Montgomery.

Brides of the Beast WOOF! *Brides of Blood; Grave Desires; Island of the Living Horror* **1968** Filipino radiation monsters get their jollies by eating beautiful young naked women. Newly arrived research scientist and his bride oppose this custom. First in a series of "Blood Island" horrors. **85m/B; VHS, DVD, Blu-Ray.** *PH* John Ashley; Kent Taylor; Beverly (Hills) Powers; Eva Darren; Mario Montenegro; ***D:*** Eddie Romero; Gerardo (Gerry) De Leon; ***W:*** Eddie Romero; Gerardo (Gerry) De Leon.

Brideshead Revisited 🦴🦴🦴 **1981** The acclaimed British miniseries based on the Evelyn Waugh classic about an Edwardian young man who falls under the spell of a wealthy aristocratic family and struggles to retain his integrity and values. On six tapes. **540m/C; VHS, DVD.** *GB* Jeremy Irons; Anthony Andrews; Diana Quick; Laurence Olivier; John Gielgud; Claire Bloom; Stephane Audran; Mona Washbourne; John Le Mesurier; Charles Keating; ***D:*** Charles Sturridge; Michael Lindsay-Hogg; ***M:*** Geoffrey Burgon. **TV**

Brideshead Revisited 🦴🦴 ½ **2008 (PG-13)** It's between the world wars in England, and middle-class Charles Ryder (Goode) is enamored by the snooty lifestyle of brother and sister Sebastian (Whishaw) and Julia (Atwell) at their Brideshead estate, where they live with their mother, the devout Catholic Lady Marchmain (Thompson). At first, Charles hooks up with the boozy Sebastian but later turns his amorous attention to Julia, fueling Sebastian's jealously and Lady Marchmain's ire. Despite the lush backdrop and Thompson's icy turn, it falls short of the acclaimed 1981 British miniseries version. Adapted from the 1945 novel by Evelyn Waugh. **135m/C; Blu-Ray, On Demand.** *US GB* Matthew Goode; Ben Whishaw; Hayley Atwell; Emma Thompson; Michael Gambon; Greta Scacchi; Jonathan Cake; Patrick Malahide; ***D:*** Julian Jarrold; ***W:*** Andrew Davies; Jeremy Brock; ***C:*** Jess Hall; ***M:*** Adrian Johnston.

The Bridesmaid 🦴🦴 *La Demoiselle d'Honneur* **2004** Creepy thriller based on a novel by Ruth Rendell. Hard-working Philippe (Magimel) lives with his flirtatious mother Christine (Clement) and his two younger siblings. At his sister's wedding, he meets sultry bridesmaid Senta (Smet), who likes a lot of drama in her life. She easily seduces the uptight Philippe, who turns out to have some dark inner urges and continually tests the limits of his love. Then Senta asks, would he kill for her? French with subtitles. **111m/C; DVD.** *FR* Benoit Magimel; Laura Smet; Aurore Clement; Bernard Le Coq; Solene Bouten; Anna Mihalcea; Michel Duchaussoy; Eric Seigne; Pierre-Francois Dumeniaud; ***D:*** Claude Chabrol; ***W:*** Claude Chabrol; Peter Leccia; ***C:*** Eduardo Serra; ***M:*** Matthieu Chabrol.

Bridesmaids 🦴🦴🦴 **2011 (R)** Although her own life is falling apart, maid of honor Annie (Wiig) is determined to support her best friend Lillian (Rudolph) throughout her pre-wedding rituals. But Annie must contend with a group of wild bridesmaids and Lillian's beautiful and wealthy friend, Helen (Byrne), who seems hell-bent on replacing Annie. Features clever and gross-out humor for both sexes to enjoy, including an infamous scene where the women get food poisoning in a fancy boutique. More than that, it's a fresh, hilarious, engaging story with a heart. And writer Wiig proves to be a major star. **124m/C; Blu-Ray, On Demand.** Kristen Wiig; Maya Rudolph; Rose Byrne; Melissa McCarthy; Wendi McLendon-Covey; Jill Clayburgh; Chris O'Dowd; Jon Hamm; Ellie Kemper; ***D:*** Paul Feig; ***W:*** Kristen Wiig; Annie Mumolo; ***C:*** Robert Yeoman; ***M:*** Michael Andrews.

The Bridge 🦴🦴 *Die Brucke* **1959** In 1945, two days before the end of WWII, seven German schoolboys are drafted to defend an unimportant bridge from American tanks. Emotional anti-war film based on the autobiographical novel of Manfred Gregor.

German with subtitles. **102m/B; VHS, DVD, Blu-Ray.** *GE* Fritz Wepper; Volker Bohnet; Frank Glaubrecht; Karl Michael Balzer; Gunther Hoffman; Michael Hinz; Cordula Trantow; Wolfgang Stumpf; Volker Lechtenbrink; Gunter Pfitzmann; Edith Schultze-Westrum; Ruth Hausmeister; Eva Vaitl; ***D:*** Bernhard Wicki; ***W:*** Bernhard Wicki; Michael Mansfeld; Karl-Wilhelm Vivier; ***C:*** Gerd Von Bonen; ***M:*** Hans-Martin Majewski.

The Bridge **2000** In 1963, Mira (Bouquet) loves to go to the movies to watch "Jules et Jim" and "West Side Story." She has a 15-year-old son, but that doesn't stop her from entering into an affair with a visiting engineer (Berling) who's in her little town to build a bridge. Director Depardieu plays her husband, a builder who's working on the bridge. It's precisely the sort of material that the French handle so deftly and Depardieu proves that he's a competent craftsman behind the camera. **92m/C; DVD.** *FR* Carole Bouquet; Gerard Depardieu; Charles Berling; ***D:*** Gerard Depardieu; Frederic Auburtin; ***W:*** Francois Bupeyron; ***C:*** Pascal Ridao; ***M:*** Frederic Auburtin.

The Bridge at Remagen 1/2 **1969 (PG)** Based on the true story of allied attempts to capture a vital bridge before retreating German troops destroy it. For war-film buffs. **115m/C; VHS, DVD, Blu-Ray.** George Segal; Robert Vaughn; Ben Gazzara; Bradford Dillman; E.G. Marshall; ***D:*** John Guillermin; ***W:*** William Roberts; ***C:*** Stanley Cortez; ***M:*** Elmer Bernstein.

Bridge of Dragons **1999 (R)** Dictator Tagawa, having murdered the kingdom's rightful ruler, plots to marry the country's princess (Shane) to consolidate his power. But when the princess escapes to join the rebel forces, human killing machine Lundgren is sent to retrieve her. Only he decides to fight with her instead. Lots of explosions and high-tech gadgets. **91m/C; VHS, DVD.** Dolph Lundgren; Cary-Hiroyuki Tagawa; Gary Hudson; Scott Schwartz; Rachel Shane; ***D:*** Isaac Florentine; ***W:*** Carlton Holder; ***C:*** Yossi Wein; ***M:*** Stephen (Steve) Edwards. **VIDEO**

The Bridge of San Luis Rey **1944** A priest investigates the famous bridge collapse in Lima, Peru that left five people dead. Based upon the novel by Thornton Wilder. **89m/B; VHS, DVD.** Lynn Bari; Francis Lederer; Louis Calhern; Akim Tamiroff; Donald Woods; Alla Nazimova; Blanche Yurka; ***D:*** Rowland V. Lee; ***W:*** Howard Estabrook; Herman Weissman; ***C:*** John Boyle; ***M:*** Dimitri Tiomkin.

The Bridge of San Luis Rey **2005 (PG)** Thornton Wilder's moving, Pulitzer Prize-winning 1928 novel is disastrously adapted by director McGluckian, with stellar actors generally miscast in a stuffy costume drama. In colonial Peru in the early 18th century, Franciscan missionary Brother Juniper (Byrne) has been investigating five travelers who plunged to their deaths when the titular bridge collapsed. He's trying to determine if there's some common denominator to their fate and delivers his conclusions to a church court presided over by the Archbishop of Lima (De Niro). Flashbacks depict the lives of the victims and their survivors and the abrupt shifts in scene and character make for confusion. **120m/C; DVD.** *SP GB FR* Robert De Niro; F. Murray Abraham; Kathy Bates; Gabriel Byrne; Geraldine Chaplin; Emilie Dequenne; Adriana Dominguez; Harvey Keitel; Pilar Lopez de Ayala; John Lynch; Mark Polish; Michael Polish; ***D:*** Mary McGuckian; ***C:*** Javier Aguirresarobe; ***M:*** Lalo Schifrin.

Bridge of Spies **2015 (PG-13)** One of cinema's great historians, Steven Spielberg returns to World War II with this telling of the true story of the role attorney James B. Donovan (Tom Hanks) played in the spy game in during the height of the Cold War. When the Americans captured Russian spy Rudolf Abel (Mark Rylance), Donovan defends him and saves him from the death penalty. When the Russians capture an American pilot, an exchange is put into play, and Donovan himself travels to Berlin to conduct it. Spielberg and his team have crafted a tense, intelligent thriller that works both as history lesson and pure entertainment. **141m/C; DVD, Blu-Ray, Streaming.** Tom Hanks; Mark Rylance; Alan Alda; Amy Ryan; Scott Shepherd; Domenick Lombardozzi; ***D:*** Steven Spielberg; ***W:*** Joel Coen; Ethan Coen; Matt Charman; ***C:*** Janusz Kaminski; ***M:*** Thomas Newman. Oscars '15: Actor--Supporting (Rylance); British Acad. '15: Actor--Supporting (Rylance).

The Bridge on the River Kwai **1957** Award-winning adaptation of the Pierre Bouelle novel about the battle of wills between a Japanese POW camp commander and a British colonel over the construction of a rail bridge, and the parallel efforts by escaped prisoner Holden to destroy it. Holden's role was originally cast for Cary Grant. Memorable too for whistling "Colonel Bogey March." Because the writers were blacklisted, Bouelle (who spoke no English) was originally credited as the screenwriter. **161m/C; VHS, DVD, Blu-Ray.** *GB* William Holden; Alec Guinness; Jack Hawkins; Sessue Hayakawa; James Donald; Geoffrey Horne; Andre Morell; Ann Sears; Peter Williams; John Boxer; Percy Herbert; Harold Goodwin; Henry Okawa; Keiichiro Katsumoto; M.R.B. Chakrabandhu; ***D:*** David Lean; ***W:*** Carl Foreman; Michael Wilson; ***C:*** Jack Hildyard; ***M:*** Malcolm Arnold. Oscars '57: Actor (Guinness), Adapt. Screenplay, Cinematog., Director (Lean), Film, Film Editing, Orig. Song Score and/or Adapt.; AFI '98: Top 100; British Acad. '57: Actor (Guinness), Film, Screenplay; Directors Guild '57: Director (Lean); Golden Globes '58: Actor--Drama (Guinness), Director (Lean), Film--Drama; Natl. Bd. of Review '57: Actor (Guinness), Director (Lean), Support. Actor (Hayakawa); Natl. Film Reg. '97; N.Y. Film Critics '57: Actor (Guinness), Director (Lean), Film.

Bridge to Hell 1/2 **1987** A group of allied P.O.W.s try to make their way to the American front during WWII in Yugoslavia. A heavily guarded bridge occupied by Nazi troops stands between them and freedom. A special introduction by Michael Dudikoff doing martial arts. **94m/C; VHS, DVD.** Jeff Connors; Francis Ferre; Andy Forrest; Paky Valente; ***D:*** Umberto Lenzi.

The Bridge to Nowhere 1/2 **2009 (R)** Four blue-collar workers in Pittsburgh run minor schemes—poker games and sports betting—to make extra dough. When they meet ambitious indie prostie Jasper, they decide to start a high-end escort service that becomes a surprise success. And then it all comes crashing down. **105m/C; DVD.** Bijou Phillips; Danny Masterson; Ben Crowley; Daniel London; Sean Derry; Thomas Ian Nicholas; Alexandra Breckenridge; Ving Rhames; ***D:*** Blair Underwood; ***W:*** Chris Gutierrez; ***C:*** Keith Gruchala; ***M:*** Scott Glasgow. **VIDEO**

Bridge to Silence **1989** A young hearing-impaired mother's life begins to crumble following the death of her husband in a car crash. Her mother tries to get custody of her daughter and a friend applies romantic pressure. Melodrama features Matlin in her first TV speaking role. **95m/C; VHS, Streaming.** Marlee Matlin; Lee Remick; Josef Sommer; Michael O'Keefe; Allison Silva; Candice Brecker; ***D:*** Karen Arthur. **TV**

Bridge to Terabithia 1/2 **2007 (PG)** Katherine Paterson's popular 1977 novel isn't so much about a fantasy world (the film's CGI is limited) as it is about friendship and imagination. Jess (Hutcherson) is a bullied 10-year-old misfit with four sisters and a stern dad (Patrick). Adventurous new neighbor Leslie (Robb) turns out to be Jess' imaginative kindred soul and, between his drawings and her stories, they populate the nearby woods with their own world. For those not familiar with the book, beware—there's tragedy looming that will affect both kids and adults. **94m/C; DVD, Blu-Ray.** Josh Hutcherson; AnnaSophia Robb; Robert Patrick; Zooey Deschanel; Bailee Madison; Kate Butler; Lauren Clinton; ***D:*** Gabor Csupo; ***W:*** Jeff Stockwell; David Paterson; ***C:*** Michael Chapman; ***M:*** Aaron Zigman.

Bridge to the Sun **1961** Based on the autobiography of Gwen Terasaki, a southern belle who marries a Japanese diplomat working in DC. However, after the bombing of Pearl Harbor, Terasaki is sent back to Japan where he is stripped of his position and the family is watched by the secret police. Terasaki becomes a liaison between the two countries after peace is declared but the deprivations of the war years have taken their toll. **113m/B; DVD.** Carroll Baker; James Shigeta; James Yagi; Tetsuro Tanba; Hiroshi Tomono; ***D:*** Etienne Perier; ***W:*** Charles A. Kaufman; ***C:*** William J. Kelly; Marcel Weiss; ***M:*** Georges Auric.

A Bridge Too Far **1977 (PG)** A meticulous re-creation of one of the most disastrous battles of WWII, the Allied defeat at Arnhem in 1944. Misinformation, adverse conditions, and overconfidence combined to prevent the Allies from capturing six bridges that connected Holland to the German border. **175m/C; VHS, DVD, Blu-Ray.** *GB* Sean Connery; Robert Redford; James Caan; Michael Caine; Elliott Gould; Gene Hackman; Laurence Olivier; Ryan O'Neal; Liv Ullmann; Dirk Bogarde; Hardy Kruger; Arthur Hill; Edward Fox; Anthony Hopkins; Maximilian Schell; Denholm Elliott; Wolfgang Preiss; Nicholas (Nick) Campbell; Christopher Good; John Ratzenberger; Colin Farrell; ***D:*** Richard Attenborough; ***W:*** William Goldman; ***C:*** Geoffrey Unsworth; ***M:*** John Addison. British Acad. '77: Support. Actor (Fox); Natl. Soc. Film Critics '77: Support. Actor (Fox).

The Bridges at Toko-Ri 1/2 **1955** Based on the James A. Michener novel, the rousing war-epic about a lawyer being summoned by the Navy to fly bombing missions during the Korean War. A powerful anti-war statement. **103m/C; VHS, DVD.** William Holden; Grace Kelly; Fredric March; Mickey Rooney; Robert Strauss; Earl Holliman; Keiko Awaji; Charles McGraw; Richard Shannon; Willis Bouchey; ***D:*** Mark Robson; ***W:*** Valentine Davies; ***C:*** Loyal Griggs; ***M:*** Lyn Murray.

The Bridges of Madison County **1995 (PG-13)** Robert Kincaid (Eastwood) is on assignment in 1965 Iowa to photograph Madison County's scenic covered bridges. Only problem is he gets lost and stops for directions at Francesca Johnson's (Streep) farmhouse. There's an immediate attraction between the repressed Italian war-bride-turned-farm-wife and the charismatic world traveler, which they act on in four short days. Much of the treacle from Robert James Waller's novel has been fortunately abandoned but the mature romance remains. 64-year-old Eastwood exudes low-key sexiness while Streep (with a light Italian accent) is all earthy warmth. Fans of both book and stars should be pleased, though the leisurely paced film takes too long to get started. **135m/C; VHS, DVD, Blu-Ray.** Clint Eastwood; Meryl Streep; Victor Slezak; Annie Corley; Jim Haynie; ***D:*** Clint Eastwood; ***W:*** Richard LaGravenese; ***C:*** Jack N. Green; ***M:*** Lennie Niehaus.

Bridget Jones: The Edge of Reason 1/2 **2004 (R)** The film sequel (loosely based on Fielding's book sequel) tries too hard to be endearingly kooky, but can't go that far wrong with Zellweger, who once again packed on the pounds to play the plumpish London singleton. When we last saw Bridget, she had finally chosen steady lawyer Mark Darcy (Firth), but her insecurities get the better of her. She trashes her relationship and is soon once again with sly cad Daniel (Grant), now the host of a TV travel show. This leads Bridget and Daniel to Thailand where, in an unfortunate plot contrivance, Bridget is thrown into a Thai jail. This only serves to teach Bridget that she really loves Mark. Zellweger is subjected to many pratfalls, which she handles with good spirit, and all the supporting roles are on the money. **108m/C; VHS, DVD, Blu-Ray.** Renée Zellweger; Hugh Grant; Colin Firth; Jim Broadbent; Gemma Jones; Jacinda Barrett; James Callis; Shirley Henderson; Sally Phillips; Neil Pearson; Jessica Stevenson; Paul Nicholls; ***D:*** Beeban Kidron; ***W:*** Andrew Davies; Helen Fielding; Richard Curtis; Adam Brooks; ***C:*** Adrian Biddle; ***M:*** Harry Gregson-Williams.

Bridget Jones's Baby 1/2 **2016 (R)** This is yet another example of a sequel nobody really asked for. On her 43rd birthday, Bridget (Zellweger) is reminded that her time to have a baby is running out. Of course, she quickly has sex with two men—old flame Mark Darcy (Firth) and new beau Jack Qwant (Dempsey)—and ends up unexpectedly pregnant, so she doesn't know which one's the father! Wackiness ensues. Everyone here is up to the challenge of light romantic comedy, so it's not a horrible experience, but it's also easy to skip. **123m/C; DVD.** Renée Zellweger; Colin Firth; Patrick Dempsey; Emma Thompson; Gemma Jones; Jim Broadbent; ***D:*** Sharon Maguire; ***W:*** Emma Thompson; Helen Fielding; Dan Mazer; ***C:*** Andrew Dunn; ***M:*** Craig Armstrong.

Bridget Jones's Diary **2001 (R)** So you've got this petite, sunny-faced Texan playing a "singleton" Brit who drinks and smokes and consumes too many calories and has man trouble and is the beloved heroine of Helen Fielding's novel. No wonder the English got a little upset—not, as it turns out, for any good reason since Zellweger is fab as Bridget tries to take control of her chaotic life. Of course having a romp with your caddish, clever boss Daniel Cleaver (Grant) and ignoring the handsome but apparently stuffy Mark Darcy (Firth) isn't a good start but Bridget—bless her—does try. The movie is truncated (to the detriment of Bridget's friendships) but it still works. **115m/C; VHS, DVD, Blu-Ray.** Renée Zellweger; Hugh Grant; Colin Firth; Gemma Jones; Jim Broadbent; Embeth Davidtz; Shirley Henderson; James Callis; Sally Phillips; Lisa Barbuscia; ***D:*** Sharon Maguire; ***W:*** Richard Curtis; Andrew Davies; Helen Fielding; ***C:*** Stuart Dryburgh; ***M:*** Patrick Doyle.

Brief Encounter **1946** Based on Noel Coward's "Still Life" from "Tonight at 8:30," two middle-aged, middle-class people become involved in a short and bittersweet romance in WWII England. Intensely romantic, underscored with Rachmaninoff's Second Piano Concerto. **86m/B; VHS, DVD, Blu-Ray.** *GB* Celia Johnson; Trevor Howard; Stanley Holloway; Cyril Raymond; Joyce Carey; Everley Gregg; Margaret Barton; Dennis Harkin; Valentine Dyall; Marjorie Mars; Irene Handl; ***D:*** David Lean; ***W:*** Noel Coward; David Lean; Ronald Neame; Anthony Havelock-Allan; ***C:*** Robert Krasker. N.Y. Film Critics '46: Actress (Johnson).

Brief Interviews With Hideous Men 1/2 **2009** Brief drama based on the book by David Foster Wallace is the writing/directing debut of actor Krasinski, also featured as Ryan, who dumped Sara (Nicholson), who is now interviewing male subjects about private matters. The battle of the sexes monologues aren't terribly interesting for the most part and this seems more like a filmmaking exercise than a film. **78m/C; DVD.** John Krasinski; Julianne Nicholson; Timothy Hutton; Max Minghella; Lou Taylor Pucci; Dominic Cooper; Ben Shenkman; Chris Messina; Will Arnett; Bobby Cannavale; Josh Charles; ***D:*** John Bailey; ***C:*** John Bailey.

Brief Moment 1/2 **1933** Lackluster marital soap based on the S.N. Behrman play. Hardworking nightclub singer Abby (Lombard) marries playboy Rodney (Raymond) who would rather live off his allowance than get a job, despite her encouragement. He still spends too much time drinking and at the track, and Abby gets fed up and leaves him, which Rodney takes as a wake-up call. **70m/B; DVD.** Carole Lombard; Gene Raymond; Donald Cook; Monroe Owsley; Jameson Thomas; Arthur Hohl; ***D:*** David Burton; ***W:*** Edith Fitzgerald; Brian Marlow; ***C:*** Ted Tetzlaff.

Brigadoon **1954** The story of a magical, 18th century Scottish village which awakens once every 100 years and the two modern-day vacationers who stumble upon it. Main highlight is the Lerner and Loewe score. **108m/C; VHS, DVD, Blu-Ray.** Gene Kelly; Van Johnson; Cyd Charisse; Elaine Stewart; Barry Jones; Albert Sharpe; ***D:*** Vincente Minnelli; ***W:*** Alan Jay Lerner; ***C:*** Joseph Ruttenberg; ***M:*** Alan Jay Lerner; Frederick Loewe.

Brigands: Chapter VII 1/2 *Brigands, chapitre VII* **1997 (R)** A satiric yet witty comedy-drama created by acclaimed Georgian filmmaker Otar Iosseliani about censorship, filmmaking, and humor. The film features a framing element centered on a group of censors watching a new film to review. Because the film reels are not shown in order, the film's disjointed story moves around in time. Each reel features a different story with sex, violence, and irony. One story includes snipers shooting on unknown people. Another centers on a wealthy ancient king placing his wife in a chastity belt before going to war, without knowledge that she has a key and plans on deceiving him and gaining revenge. A third is set in current-day Paris where wealthy arms dealers live it up with beautiful women. The last is set in the Soviet Union where a young boy watches his policeman father harm innocent people. Russian,

French, and Georgian with subtitles. **149m/C; DVD.** Amiran Amiranashvili; Dato Gogibedachvili; Giorgi Tsintsadze; Nino Orjonikidze; Aleqsi Jakeli; *D:* Otar Iosseliani; *W:* Otar Iosseliani; *C:* William Lubtchansky; *M:* Nicholas Zourabichvili.

Brigham City ✂✂ 1/2 **2001 (PG-13)** Skillful murder-mystery set in the fictitious Brigham City, Utah. The townspeople mostly know each other and most are also members of the Mormon Church. Sheriff Wes Clayton (Dutcher) and his deputy Terry's (Brown) duties are usually mundane—until they discover the mutiliated body of a young female tourist at an abandoned homestead. Clayton is willing to defer to the FBI but then a second body is discovered and the media vultures descend on the formerly quiet community as their faith is all put to an unexpected test. **115m/C; VHS, DVD.** Richard Dutcher; Wilford Brimley; Matthew A. Brown; Carrie Morgan; John Enos; Tayva Patch; *D:* Richard Dutcher; *W:* Richard Dutcher; *C:* Ken Glassing; *M:* Sam Cardon.

Brigham Young: Frontiersman ✂✂ **1940** Somewhat interesting story about the pioneering Mormons and their founding of Salt Lake City. Under the leadership of Brigham Young (Jagger), they set out across the plains, battling hardships and starvation along the way. An emphasis was placed on the historical rather than the religious in an effort not to scare off moviegoers, but the picture failed at the boxoffice anyway. Based on the story by Louis Bromfield. **114m/C; VHS, DVD.** Tyrone Power; Linda Darnell; Dean Jagger; Brian Donlevy; John Carradine; Jane Darwell; Jean Rogers; Mary Astor; Vincent Price; Willard Robertson; Moroni Olsen; Marc Lawrence; Selmer Jackson; Stanley Andrews; *D:* Henry Hathaway; *W:* Lamar Trotti; Ann E. Todd; *C:* Arthur C. Miller; *M:* Cyril Mockridge; Alfred Newman.

Bright ✂✂ **2017** A high concept action fantasy film centered on reluctant cop partners. In this parallel universe version of present-day Los Angeles, fantasy creatures such as fairies and orcs have long lived alongside humans. Human officer Ward (Smith) has an orc, Jacoby (Edgerton), for a partner, but he is not trusted because of his potential divided loyalties. When Ward and Jacoby find a valuable magic wand, they team up with Tikka (Fry) to keep it out of the hands of powerful elves who lost it, corrupt cops, and the greedy feds. Awful dialogue and a derivative plot cannot be saved by the marquee cast. **117m/C; DVD.** Will Smith; Joel Edgerton; Noomi Rapace; Edgar Ramirez; Lucy Fry; *D:* David Ayer; *W:* Max Landis; *C:* Roman Vasyanov; *M:* David Sardy.

Bright Angel ✂✂ 1/2 **1991 (R)** Road movie pairs an unconventional team: George wants to visit his aunt to see if she's heard from his mother who ran off with another man; Luey is a free-spirit trying to free her brother from jail. Good performances by Mulroney, Taylor, & Pullman. Ford adapted two of his short stories, "Childern" and "Great Falls" for the gritty and uncompromising script of life in the modern west. **94m/C; VHS, DVD, Blu-Ray.** Dermot Mulroney; Lili Taylor; Sam Shepard; Valerie Perrine; Burt Young; Bill Pullman; Benjamin Bratt; Mary Kay Place; Delroy Lindo; Kevin Tighe; Sheila McCarthy; *D:* Michael Fields; *W:* Richard Ford; *M:* Christopher Young.

Bright Days Ahead ✂✂ *Les Beaux Jours* **2014** The ever-elegant Ardant stars as 60-something Caroline, who has an affair with a man 20 years her junior in this undeveloped romantic drama. Having retired from her dental practice, the long-married woman begins exploring the activities at her local senior center, which include a computer class taught by Julien (Lafitte). They're soon having a no-strings-attached sexual relationship that is quickly discovered by everyone, including Caroline's betrayed spouse, Philippe (Chesnais). French with subtitles. **94m/C; On Demand.** *FR* Fanny Ardant; Laurent Lafitte; Patrick Chesnais; Jean-Francois Stevenin; *D:* Marion Vernoux; *W:* Marion Vernoux; Fanny Chesnel; *C:* Nicolas Gaurin; *M:* Quentin Sirjacq.

Bright Eyes ✂✂ **1934 (PG)** Shirley (Temple) lives with her widowed mother Mary (Wilson), who works as a maid for the snobbish Smythe family, where only wealthy, crochety Uncle Ned (Sellon) befriends the cutie. His niece Adele (Allen) is engaged to Shirley's godfather, flyboy Loop Merritt (Dunn), who wants the tyke to live with him when her mom is killed. But Uncle Ned also wants to adopt her and there's a battle over custody. Shirley warbles "On the Good Ship Lollipop" in her usual winsome way. **84m/B; VHS, DVD.** Shirley Temple; James Dunn; Lois Wilson; Jane Withers; Judith Allen; Jane Darwell; Charles Sellon; *D:* David Butler; *W:* David Butler; Edwin J. Burke; William Conselman; *C:* Arthur C. Miller.

Bright Future ✂✂✂ *Akarui mirai* **2003** Mamoru and Yuji are best friends, co-workers, and roommates in an existentially cool and cold modern world. Dreamlike plot takes Mamoru to jail for a crime he didn't commit, but won't deny. He seems fine there, drifting in and out of reality, almost living vicariously through his pet jellyfish he entrusted with Yuji before hitting the slammer. Japanese director Kiyoshi Kurosawa's new-wave vision of art and horror are fascinating, yet alienating at once. Fans of bizarro Asian cinema will flip. Originally titled "Jellyfish Alert," a title somehow more accurately describing this movie than any review could. **92m/C; DVD.** Tadanobu Asano; Tatsuya Fuji; Joe Odagiri; Marumi Shiraishi; *D:* Kiyoshi Kurosawa; *W:* Kiyoshi Kurosawa; *C:* Takahide Shibanushi; *M:* Pacific 231.

Bright Leaf ✂✂ 1/2 **1950** In 1894, Brant Royle (Cooper) returns to his Kingsmont hometown and gets smitten brothel owner Sonia (Bacall) to become an investor in his automated cigarette-making business. His success nearly bankrupts the local tobacco tycoons, including James Singleton (Crisp) who originally ran Brant out of town for courting his daughter, Margaret (Neal). But when Margaret tries to save her family Brant ends up being used. **110m/B; DVD.** Gary Cooper; Lauren Bacall; Patricia Neal; Donald Crisp; Jack Carson; Jeff Corey; Gladys George; *D:* Michael Curtiz; *W:* Ranald MacDougall; *C:* Karl Freund; *M:* Victor Young.

Bright Lights ✂✂ *Adventures in Africa* **1930** Broadway musical star Louanne (Mackaill) is about to retire and marry into money. That's when lecherous bad guy Miguel (Beery Sr.) shows up backstage, threatening to expose her sleazy past (which includes hula dancing in South African dive bars). Then Louanne is accused of murder! Filmed in 2-strip Technicolor but only B&W prints survive. **69m/B; DVD.** Dorothy Mackaill; Noah Beery, Sr.; Frank Fay; Inez Courtney; Edmund Breese; *D:* Michael Curtiz; *W:* Humphrey Pearson; Henry McCarty; *C:* Lee Garmes.

Bright Lights, Big City ✂✂ **1988 (R)** Based on Jay McInerney's popular novel, Fox plays a contemporary yuppie working in Manhattan as a magazine journalist. As his world begins to fall apart, he embarks on an endless cycle of drugs and nightlife. Fox is poorly cast, and his character is hard to care for as he becomes more and more dissolute. Although McInerney wrote his own screenplay, the intellectual abstractness of the novel can't be captured on film. **110m/C; VHS, DVD, Blu-Ray.** Michael J. Fox; Kiefer Sutherland; Phoebe Cates; Frances Sternhagen; Swoosie Kurtz; Tracy Pollan; Jason Robards, Jr.; John Houseman; Dianne Wiest; Charlie Schlatter; William Hickey; David Warrilow; Sam Robards; Kelly Lynch; Annabelle Gurwitch; Maria Pitillo; David Hyde Pierce; Jessica Lundy; *D:* James Bridges; *C:* Gordon Willis.

Bright Road ✂✂ 1/2 **1953** Matter of fact B-movie drama from MGM. Belafonte makes his screen debut as the nameless southern school principal where 4th grade teacher Jane Richards (Dandridge) works to help troubled pupil C.T. (Hepburn). A tragedy strikes, and C.T. refuses to come to school. It takes a swarm of bees and a caterpillar's cocoon to save the day. Adapted from Mary Elizabeth Vroman's 1951 story "See How They Run." **70m/B; DVD.** Dorothy Dandridge; Harry Belafonte; Philip Hepburn; Barbara Randolph; Maidie Norman; Robert Horton; Rene Beard; *D:* Gerald Mayer; *W:* Emmet Lavery; *C:* Alfred Gilks; *M:* David Rose.

A Bright Shining Lie ✂✂ 1/2 **1998 (R)** Based on Neil Sheehan's 1988 Pulitzer Prize-winning book, which chronicles the Vietnam War as seen through the eyes of Lt. Col. John Paul Vann (Paxton). The brash Vann arrived as a military adviser to the Vietnamese Army in 1962 and eventually left that post to become part of the State Department's Civilian Aid Program, where he exposed falsified battle reports and other deceptions to newsman Steven Burnett (Logue). The complex and controversial Vann was killed in a chopper crash in 1972. **118m/C; VHS, DVD.** Bill Paxton; Donal Logue; Kurtwood Smith; Eric Bogosian; Amy Madigan; Vivian Wu; Robert John Burke; James Rebhorn; Ed Lauter; Harve Presnell; *D:* Terry George; *W:* Terry George; *C:* Jack Conroy; *M:* Gary Chang. **CABLE**

Bright Star ✂✂ 1/2 **2009 (PG)** Oh to be young and in the throes of first love! In 1818, flirty 18-year-old Fanny Brawne (Cornish) and her family live next door to brooding 23-year-old romantic poet John Keats (Whishaw) and his friend and patron, Charles Brown (Schneider). Keats is poor (and terminally ill) and fashionable seamstress Fanny knows she must meet her family's expectations and make a respectable marriage. She becomes his muse and then the object of his passionate letters. No consummation is possible so director Campion wisely makes the most of every glance, touch, and word. Title refers to the poem Keats dedicated to Fanny. **119m/C; DVD.** *GB AU* Paul Schneider; Thomas Brodie-Sangster; Ben Whishaw; Abbie Cornish; Kerry Fox; Edie Martin; Gerard Monaco; Antonia Campbell-Hughes; *D:* Jane Campion; *W:* Jane Campion; *C:* Greig Fraser; *M:* Mark Bradshaw.

Bright Young Things ✂✂ 1/2 **2003 (R)** Actor/director/writer Stephen Fry tackles literary satire with his adaptation of Evelyn Waugh's 1930 novel, "Vile Bodies." And if not precisely vile, those bodies are wicked indeed as seen through the everyman eyes of Adam (Moore), a poor aspiring novelist-turned-gossip columnist who wishes to marry superficial party girl Nina (Mortimer). Fry breezily tackles the jaded, flapper milieu of upper-class London between the wars that lends itself to glitter and eccentricity, embodied by feckless social butterflies (Woolgar) and drug-taking peers (the gentlemanly 94-year-old Sir John Mills doing a little coke in a cameo). These bored young things are bright only in the way they briefly shine before drab reality takes over. They (and the viewer) may as well enjoy it while they can. **106m/C; DVD.** Emily Mortimer; James McAvoy; Michael Sheen; David Tennant; Fenella Woolgar; Dan Aykroyd; Jim Broadbent; Simon Callow; Jim Carter; Stockard Channing; Richard E. Grant; Julia McKenzie; Peter O'Toole; Stephan Campbell Moore; *D:* Stephen Fry; *W:* Stephen Fry; *C:* Henry Braham; *M:* Anne Dudley.

Brightburn ✂✂ 1/2 **2019 (R)** In rural Kansas, Kyle (Denman) and Tori (Banks) are parents to a boy, Brandon (Dunn), they found as a baby in the wreckage of a crashed spacecraft 12 years earlier. Raised without knowledge of his alien heritage, Brandon begins behaving erratically as he matures. When crossed by someone in his small community, Brandon violently acts out, leaving bodies and a mystery for local law enforcement to solve as he comes to understand the superpowers he possesses. A unique concept that's not well executed. **90m/C; DVD, Blu-Ray.** Elizabeth Banks; David Denman; Jackson A. Dunn; Abraham Clinkscales; Christian Finlayson; *D:* David Yarovesky; *W:* Brian Gunn; Mark Gunn; *C:* Michael Dallatorre; *M:* Tim Williams.

Brightest Star ✂ 1/2 **2014** Cliché attempt at 20-something romantic comedy works too hard to pack in indie-cute dialogue and vague attempts at depth while failing to establish strong characters or plot. A charming Lowell stars as the frustratingly vague unnamed slacker at the center of the film. Dumped by his astronomy-class love, Charlotte (McIver), he sets out to prove he can grow up and get a real job. He begins dating Lita (Szohr), who doesn't think he should change at all. Her businessman father (Gregg) inexplicably gives Lowell a management job with his company, which Lowell promptly uses to try to win Charlotte's approval. **80m/C; On Demand.** Chris Lowell; Rose McIver; Jessica Szohr; Clark Gregg; Allison Janney; Peter Jacobson; *D:* Maggie Kiley; *W:* Maggie Kiley; Matthew Mullen; *C:* Chayse Irvin; *M:* Matthew Puckett.

Brighton Beach Memoirs ✂✂ 1/2 *Neil Simon's Brighton Beach Memoirs* **1986 (PG-13)** The film adaptation of the popular (and semiautobiographical) Neil Simon play. Poignant comedy/drama about a young Jewish boy's coming of age in Depression-era Brooklyn. Followed by "Biloxi Blues" and "Broadway Bound." **108m/C; VHS, DVD, Blu-Ray.** Blythe Danner; Bob (Robert) Dishy; Judith Ivey; Jonathan Silverman; Brian Drillinger; Stacey Glick; Lisa Waltz; Jason Alexander; *D:* Gene Saks; *W:* Neil Simon; *C:* John Bailey; *M:* Michael Small.

Brighton Rock ✂✂✂ *Young Scarface* **1947** Sterling performances highlight this seamy look at the British underworld. Attenborough is Pinkie Brown, a small-time hood who ends up committing murder. He manipulates a waitress to get himself off the hook, but things don't go exactly as he plans. Based on the novel by Graham Greene. **92m/B; VHS, DVD, Blu-Ray.** *GB* Richard Attenborough; Hermione Baddeley; William Hartnell; Carol Marsh; Nigel Stock; Wylie Watson; Alan Wheatley; George Carney; Reginald Purdell; *D:* John Boulting; *W:* Graham Greene.

Brighton Rock ✂✂ **2010** Another adaptation of Graham Greene's revered 1938 novel, updated to the swinging '60s. Rising hoodlum Pinkie (Riley) must court a wide-eyed waitress (Riseborough) after she becomes the only witness to link him to the murder of a thug from a rival gang. Valuing style over character sinks Joffe's debut feature, which is inferior to the original 1947 version. Hurt and Mirren thrive in their supporting roles as Rose's friends but the leads never get under the skin of these characters and the change in time period (from the '40s) proves awkward. **111m/C; DVD, Blu-Ray.** *GB* Sam Riley; Andrea Riseborough; Dame Helen Mirren; Philip Davis; Sean Harris; John Hurt; Andy Serkis; *D:* Roland Joffé; *W:* Roland Joffé; *C:* John Mathieson; *M:* Martin Phipps.

Brighty of the Grand Canyon ✂ 1/2 **1967** The spunky donkey Brighty roams across the Grand Canyon in search of adventure. He finds friendship with a gold-digging old prospector who hits pay dirt. **90m/C; VHS, DVD.** Joseph Cotten; Pat Conway; Dick Foran; Karl Swenson; *D:* Norman Foster.

Brigsby Bear ✂✂ 1/2 **2017 (PG-13)** A quirky, coming-of-age dramedy about holding on to youth, even one with a complicated backstory. Throughout his life, James adored videos of "Brigsby Bear Adventures," unaware that the TV show was created for him by his abductors. Reunited as a grown man with his birth parents, and reintroduced to the world outside his bunker, James longs for that beloved piece of his childhood, and enlists his new friends to create more episodes. Glossing over any psychological issues of trauma, this film projects an earnestness that viewers will find entertaining, moving, and supremely unique. **97m/C; DVD, Blu-Ray.** Kyle Mooney; Claire Danes; Matt Walsh; Mark Hamill; Greg Kinnear; *D:* Dave McCary; *W:* Kyle Mooney; Kevin Costello; *C:* Christian Sprenger; *M:* David Wingo.

A Brilliant Young Mind ✂✂ *X+Y* **2014 (PG-13)** Nathan Ellis (Butterfield) struggles to deal with the world around him, despite the support of a loving mother (the always-great Hawkins). Nathan takes comfort in that which he does best: math. He finds a way for his passion to inform his diminished social skills when a teacher (Spall) encourages him to join the International Math Olympiad, which takes him around the world to Taipei. Originally titled "X+Y," Matthews' coming-of-age drama was given a fittingly dull title considering it's a well-meaning but flat exercise. It's a nice, little movie with a decent cast, but does nothing special enough to make it memorable. **112m/C; DVD.** *UK* Asa Butterfield; Eddie Marsan; Rafe Spall; Sally Hawkins; Martin McCann; *D:* Morgan Matthews; *W:* James Graham; *C:* Danny Cohen; *M:* Martin Phipps.

Brimstone ✂ **2017 (R)** Some movies are about vile people; some movies are just vile. This is the latter. An epic Western (148 minutes!), this feature stars Fanning as Liz, a headstrong young woman who is being hunted by a malevolent Preacher (Pearce). This is a plodding period piece, filled with details and plot twists that are intended to be gritty, revealing the toughness of life and the strength of the film's heroine, but just make you want to take a shower when it's over. Journeys to the dark side of humanity need to have more of a positive outcome or artistic quality to make the grotesque worth experiencing. **148m/C; DVD, Blu-Ray.** Guy Pearce; Dakota Fanning; Emilia Jones; Carice van Houten; Kit Harington; ***D:*** Martin Koolhoven; ***W:*** Martin Koolhoven; ***C:*** Rogier Stoffers; ***M:*** Junkie XL.

Brimstone & Treacle **1982 (R)** Weird, obsessive psychodrama in which a young rogue (who may or may not be an actual agent of the Devil) infiltrates the home of a staid British family caring for their comatose adult daughter. **85m/C; VHS, DVD.** *GB* Sting; Denholm Elliott; Joan Plowright; Suzanna Hamilton; ***D:*** Richard Loncraine; ***W:*** Dennis Potter. Montreal World Film Fest. '82: Film.

Bring It On ½ **2000 (PG-13)** Bring on the guilty pleasure. Equal parts satire, exploitation, and earnest (if not totally successful) teen flick, the film follows cheerleader Torrence (Dunst) as she becomes captain of the Rancho Carne High Toros cheer squad, who soon after discovers her squad's championship moves have been lifted from another school, the East Compton High Clovers. All of this culminates in a showdown between the two squads, while interspersed throughout are standard teenage goings-on. No gem, by any means, but fun if you're in the mood (or spirit). But be advised: probably too raunchy for its intended young adult audience. **98m/C; VHS, DVD, Blu-Ray.** Kirsten Dunst; Eliza Dushku; Jesse Bradford; Gabrielle Union; Clare Kramer; Nicole Bilderback; Tsianina Joelson; Rini Bell; Ian Roberts; Richard Hillman; Lindsay Sloane; Cody McMains; ***D:*** Peyton Reed; ***W:*** Jessica Bendinger; ***C:*** Shawn Maurer; ***M:*** Christophe Beck.

Bring It On Again **2003 (PG-13)** College freshman Whittier (Judson-Yager) proves to be a cheerleading rival that head pom-pom girl Tina (Turner) won't tolerate. So when Whittier is cut from the squad, she decides to form a new team and challenge Tina to a cheer off. **90m/C; VHS, DVD, Blu-Ray.** Anne Judson-Yager; Bree Turner; Richard Lee Jackson; Faune A. Chambers; Kevin Cooney; Bryce Johnson; ***D:*** Damon Santostefano; ***W:*** Claudio Grazioso; ***C:*** Richard Crudo; ***M:*** Paul Haslinger. **VIDEO**

Bring It On: All or Nothing ½ **2006 (PG-13)** The plot hardly matters as long as the cheer routines astonish (which they do). Britney (Panettiere) was the cheer captain at her rich 'burb school but is just another wannabe after a move to a more urban setting. But she wins over leader Camille (Knowles-Smith) with some new routines and is ready to go up against her old squad. **99m/C; DVD, Blu-Ray.** Hayden Panettiere; Jake McDorman; Solange Knowles-Smith; Gus Carr; Marcy Rylan; ***D:*** Steve Rash; ***W:*** Alyson Fouse. **VIDEO**

Bring It On: Fight to the Finish **2009 (PG-13)** Yet another cheerleading sequel. East L.A. high school cheer captain Lina Cruz (Milian) feels her squad is a lock to win the Spirit Championships until her mother remarries and they relocate to Malibu. Lina soon learns that the Malibu Vista High Sea Lions aren't winning material until she vows to whip them into shape to knock off the award-winning rival Jaguars and their trash-talking captain, Avery (Smith). Soon Lina notices just how darn cute Avery's brother Evan (Longo) is. **103m/C; DVD.** Christina Milian; Rachele Brooke Smith; Cody Longo; Vanessa Born; Gabrielle Dennis; Nikki SooHoo; Meagan Holder; David Starzyk; ***D:*** Bille Woodruff; ***W:*** Elena Song; Alyson Fouse; ***C:*** David Claessen; ***M:*** Andrew Gross. **VIDEO**

Bring It On: In It to Win It ½ **2007 (PG-13)** It's the battle of the coastal babes as SoCal Carson (Benson) and Big Apple Brooke (Scerbo) and their cheer squads meet up at the national championships. Carson falls for Penn (Copon), who happens to be on Brooke's team, and Brooke challenges Carson to a personal cheer-off. This leads to a brawl and both teams are disqualified, but they're determined to get back into the finals. **90m/C; DVD, Blu-Ray.** Adam Vernier; Ashley Benson; Cassie Scerbo; Michael Copon; Jennifer Tisdale; Kierstin Koppell; Noel Areizaga; ***D:*** Steve Rash; ***W:*** Alyson Fouse; ***C:*** Levie Isaacks. **VIDEO**

Bring Me the Head of Alfredo Garcia **1974 (R)** Peckinpah falters in this poorly paced outing. American piano player on tour in Mexico finds himself entwined with a gang of bloodthirsty bounty hunters. Bloody and confused. **112m/C; VHS, DVD, Blu-Ray.** Warren Oates; Isela Vega; Gig Young; Robert Webber; Helmut Dantine; Emilio Fernandez; Kris Kristofferson; ***D:*** Sam Peckinpah; ***W:*** Sam Peckinpah; Gordon Dawson; ***C:*** Alex Phillips, Jr.; ***M:*** Jerry Fielding.

Bringing Ashley Home **2011** Libba Phillips' (Cook) younger sister Ashley (Morrison) is a bipolar drug addict who likes to party. When she isn't heard from, her family start searching but can't get any info on where Ashley might be. Libba refuses to give up and puts her career on hold and her marriage in jeopardy to keep searching, even founding a national organization to help families find missing adults. Lifetime drama based on a true story. **87m/C; DVD.** A.J. Cook; Jennifer (Jenny) Morrison; Patricia Richardson; Timothy Webber; John Reardon; ***D:*** Nick Copus; ***W:*** Walter Klenhard; ***C:*** Mahlon Todd Williams; ***M:*** Michael Neilson. **CABLE**

Bringing Down the House **2003 (PG-13)** Straitlaced divorced lawyer Martin makes an online date and winds up with parolee Queen Latifah, who proceeds to turn his life upside-down in her quest to get him to help her prove her innocence. Moments of inspired comedy have everything to do with the talents of Martin and Latifah, and little to do with script or direction. Levy makes the most of his sidekick role. May play better on the small screen. **105m/C; VHS, DVD, Blu-Ray.** Steve Martin; Queen Latifah; Eugene Levy; Jean Smart; Angus T. Jones; Kimberly J. Brown; Joan Plowright; Missi Pyle; Steve Harris; Michael Rosenbaum; Betty White; ***D:*** Adam Shankman; ***W:*** Jason Filardi; ***C:*** Julio Macat; ***M:*** Lalo Schifrin.

Bringing Out the Dead ½ **1999 (R)** Cage hasn't looked this haggard since his boozehound role in "Leaving Las Vegas" which could be considered a dress rehearsal for this turn as burnt out New York City paramedic Frank Pierce. Aided by Scorsese's kinetic filmmaking style, Schrader's on-tempo script, and revved up performances by Rhames and Sizemore as Pierce's partners, movie successfully convey's the day-to-day stress of emergency units. Unfortunately, Cage's sleepwalking character is a bore, and a lack of chemistry with real-life spouse Arquette as Pierce's singular ray of hope only makes you yearn for Scorsese's similarly themed masterpiece "Taxi Driver." Based on the novel by Joe Connelly. **120m/C; VHS, DVD.** Nicolas Cage; John Goodman; Tom Sizemore; Ving Rhames; Patricia Arquette; Marc Anthony; Mary Beth Hurt; Clifford Curtis; Nestor Serrano; Aida Turturro; Afemo Omilami; Arthur J. Nascarella; Cynthia Roman; Cullen Oliver Johnson; Jon Abrahams; ***D:*** Martin Scorsese; ***W:*** Paul Schrader; ***C:*** Robert Richardson; ***M:*** Elmer Bernstein.

Bringing Up Baby **1938** The quintessential screwball comedy, featuring Hepburn as a giddy socialite with a "baby" leopard, and Grant as the unwitting object of her affections. One ridiculous situation after another adds up to high speed fun. Hepburn looks lovely, the supporting actors are in fine form, and director Hawks manages the perfect balance of control and mayhem. From a story by Hagar Wilde, who helped Nichols with the screenplay. Also available in a colorized version. **103m/B; VHS, DVD.** Katharine Hepburn; Cary Grant; May Robson; Charlie Ruggles; Walter Catlett; Fritz Feld; Jonathan Hale; Barry Fitzgerald; Ward Bond; ***D:*** Howard Hawks; ***W:*** Dudley Nichols; ***C:*** Russell Metty. AFI '98: Top 100; Natl. Film Reg. '90.

Bringing Up Bobby ½ **2011 (PG-13)** Actress Janssen's directorial debut is a heavy-handed family drama that's both maudlin and foolish. Con woman Olive moves to Oklahoma with her smart-mouthed 11-year-old son Bobby after some problems with the law. She keeps up with her larcenies and smells money when Bobby has a minor mishap involving wealthy businessman Kent (Pullman). Olive is abruptly jailed for past crimes, and she asks Kent and his wife Mary, whose own son has died, to care for Bobby. **93m/C; DVD.** Milla Jovovich; Spencer List; Bill Pullman; Marcia Cross; Rory Cochrane; ***D:*** Famke Janssen; ***W:*** Famke Janssen; ***C:*** Guido van Gennep; ***M:*** Tom Holkenborg.

Brink of Life ½ *Nara Livet* **1957** Three pregnant women in a hospital maternity ward await the impending births with mixed feelings. Early Bergman; in Swedish with English subtitles. **82m/B; VHS, DVD, Blu-Ray.** *SW* Eva Dahlbeck; Bibi Andersson; Ingrid Thulin; Babro Ornas; Max von Sydow; Erland Josephson; Gunnar Sjoberg; ***D:*** Ingmar Bergman. Cannes '58: Actress (Andersson), Actress (Dahlbeck), Actress (Thulin), Director (Bergman).

Brink's Job **1978 (PG)** Re-creates the "crime of the century," Tony Pino's heist of $2.7 million from a Brink's truck. The action picks up five days before the statute of limitations is about to run out. **103m/C; VHS, DVD, Blu-Ray.** Peter Falk; Peter Boyle; Warren Oates; Gena Rowlands; Paul Sorvino; Sheldon Leonard; Allen Garfield; ***D:*** William Friedkin; ***W:*** Walon Green; ***M:*** Richard Rodney Bennett.

Britannia Hospital ½ **1982 (R)** This is a portrait of a hospital at its most chaotic: the staff threatens to strike, demonstrators surround the hospital, a nosey BBC reporter pursues an anxious professor, and the eagerly anticipated royal visit degenerates into a total shambles. **111m/C; VHS, DVD.** *GB* Malcolm McDowell; Leonard Rossiter; Graham Crowden; Joan Plowright; Mark Hamill; Alan Bates; Dave Atkins; Marsha A. Hunt; ***D:*** Lindsay Anderson; ***W:*** David Sherwin; ***C:*** Mike Flash; ***M:*** Alan Price.

Britannic **2000** The Britannic, the Titanic's sister ship, was built as a luxury liner but when WWI began the ship was turned into a hospital transport after its launch in 1914. The ship did sink off the Greek coast in 1916 (probably due to a torpedo or mine) but the filmmakers haven't let any other facts of the story stand in the way of this poor man's "Titanic" with its class difference romance and other cliches. **96m/C; VHS, DVD.** Edward Atterton; Jacqueline Bisset; John Rhys-Davies; Bruce Payne; Amanda Ryan; Ben Daniels; ***D:*** Brian Trenchard-Smith; ***W:*** Brian Trenchard-Smith; Brett Thompson; Dennis A. Pratt; ***C:*** Ivan Strasburg; ***M:*** Alan Parker. **CABLE**

British Agent **1934** In 1917, dedicated communist Elena (Francis) is saved from a street riot by English diplomat Stephen Locke (Howard). The two find romance but Stephen is wanted for anti-revolutionary activities and Elena is ordered to spy on him, although her report could mean his death. **80m/B; DVD.** Kay Francis; Leslie Howard; William Gargan; Phillip Reed; Irving Pichel; Halliwell Hobbes; Ivan Simpson; Tenen Holtz; ***D:*** Michael Curtiz; ***W:*** Laird Doyle; ***C:*** Ernest Haller.

The Brittany Murphy Story **WOOF!** **2014** Tacky and cheap Lifetime showbiz drama follows the struggles of the insecure actress who found success in the 1990s only to die suddenly in 2009 after a series of health crises--followed shortly by her controlling husband. The circumstances seem suspicious but the pic doesn't delve into any potential mystery surrounding her untimely passing preferring the usual clichés about young actresses in Hollywood. **90m/C; DVD.** Amanda Fuller; Sherilyn Fenn; Eric Petersen; Adam Hagenbuch; ***D:*** Joe Menendez; ***W:*** Peter Hunziker; Cynthia Riddle; ***C:*** Kristoffer Carrillo; ***M:*** Todd Haberman. **CABLE**

Brittany Runs a Marathon ½ **2019 (R)** When long-time party girl Brittany (Bell) receives an unexpected health-related reality check from her doctor, she changes her life by taking up running. With the help of others, including running buddy Seth (Stock), who is also out of shape, Brittany prepares for the New York City Marathon. Along the way, she confronts obstacles that include financial struggles, an annoying roommate, and trouble finding a romantic partner. The film not only works as comic exploration about fitness and weight loss but also an empathetic examination of the impact of being overweight and dealing with numerous personal insecurities. Bell is up to the task as well. **103m/C; DVD.** Jillian Bell; Michaela Watkins; Utkarsh Ambudkar; Lil Rel Howery; Micah Stock; ***D:*** Paul Downs Colaizzo; ***W:*** Paul Downs Colaizzo; ***C:*** Seamus Tierney; ***M:*** Duncan Thum.

Broadcast Bombshells **1995 (R)** TV station WSEX has a station manager who'll do anything to improve ratings, an ambitious associate producer after the weather girl's job, a sexaholic sportscaster, and lots of chaos involving a mad bomber. The barely there plot is just the excuse for a considerable display of T&A anyway. Also available unrated. **80m/C; VHS, DVD.** Amy Lynn Baxter; Debbie Rochon; Elizabeth Heyman; Joseph Pallister; ***D:*** Ernest G. Sauer.

Broadcast News ½ **1987 (R)** The acclaimed, witty analysis of network news shows, dealing with the three-way romance between a driven career-woman producer, an ace nebbish reporter and a brainless, popular on-screen anchorman. Incisive and funny, though often simply idealistic. **132m/C; VHS, DVD, Blu-Ray.** William Hurt; Albert Brooks; Holly Hunter; Jack Nicholson; Joan Cusack; Robert Prosky; Lois Chiles; John Cusack; Gennie James; ***D:*** James L. Brooks; ***W:*** James L. Brooks; ***C:*** Michael Ballhaus; ***M:*** Bill Conti; Michael Gore. L.A. Film Critics '87: Actress (Hunter); Natl. Bd. of Review '87: Actress (Hunter); Natl. Film Reg. '18; N.Y. Film Critics '87: Actress (Hunter), Director (Brooks), Film, Screenplay.

Broadway ½ **1942** Typical showbiz bio with Raft playing himself as he nostalgically remembers his early hoofing days in New York and his gangster ties. Best seen and heard for the songs and Raft dancing a particularly wild Charleston. **91m/B; DVD.** George Raft; Pat O'Brien; Broderick Crawford; Janet Blair; Anne Gwynne; Marjorie Rambeau; ***D:*** William A. Seiter; ***W:*** John Bright; Felix Jackson; ***C:*** George Barnes; ***M:*** Charles Previn.

Broadway Bill *Strictly Confidential* **1934** A man decides to abandon his nagging wife and his job in her family's business for the questionable pleasures of owning a racehorse known as Broadway Bill. This racetrack comedy was also remade by Frank Capra in 1951 as "Riding High." **90m/B; DVD.** Warner Baxter; Myrna Loy; Walter Connolly; Helen Vinson; Margaret Hamilton; Frankie Darro; ***D:*** Frank Capra; ***W:*** Robert Riskin; ***C:*** Joseph Walker; ***M:*** Howard Jackson.

Broadway Damage ½ **1998** Amateurish gay comedy whose best asset is the shopaholic (and only female) character played by Hobel, as the typical overweight fag hag roomie of aspiring New York actor Marc (Lucas). Beyond-shallow Marc is looking for a lover and only a perfect 10 will do, which means he gets dumped a lot by narcisstic manipulators. Meanwhile, his plain best friend, Robert (Williams), pines for the twit to notice him in a romantic way. **110m/C; VHS, DVD.** Michael Shawn Lucas; Aaron Williams; Mara Hobel; Hugh Panaro; ***D:*** Victor Mignatti; ***W:*** Victor Mignatti; ***C:*** Mike Mayers; ***M:*** Elliot Sokolov.

Broadway Danny Rose ½ **1984 (PG)** One of Woody Allen's best films, a hilarious, heart-rending anecdotal comedy about a third-rate talent agent involved in one of his client's infidelities. The film magically unfolds as show business veterans swap Danny Rose stories at a delicatessen. Allen's Danny Rose is pathetically lovable. **85m/B; VHS, DVD, Blu-Ray.** Woody Allen; Mia Farrow; Nick Apollo Forte; Sandy Baron; Milton Berle; Howard Cosell; ***D:*** Woody Allen; ***W:*** Woody Allen; ***C:*** Gordon Willis. British Acad. '84: Orig. Screenplay; Writers Guild '84: Orig. Screenplay.

Broadway Idiot **2013** Behind-the-scenes chronicle of "American Idiot," the squeaky-clean stage adaptation of Green Day's hugely successful pop-punk opera by the same name. The band's lead singer Billie Joe Armstrong heads a cast of otherwise young and unknown stage performers as they scramble to hit their marks and do the album justice. Bearing zero resemblance to the band's bratty roots, this surprisingly shallow documentary is nothing but smiles, giving little insight into the production's origins. Green Day would've rebelled against it 20 years ago. **80m/C; Streaming.** Billie Joe Armstrong; ***D:*** Doug Hamilton; ***C:*** Dan Krauss; ***M:*** Green Day.

Broadway Limited *The Baby Vanishes* **1941** Three aspiring actors head for the Great White Way with a baby to use as a prop. Thinking the baby kidnapped, the police make things tough for the trio. McLaglen was wasted on this one, which was apparently made to show off the considerable assets of Woodworth. **75m/B; DVD.** Victor McLaglen; Marjorie Woodworth; Dennis O'Keefe; Patsy Kelly; Zasu Pitts; Leonid Kinskey; George E. Stone; ***D:*** Gordon Douglas.

Broadway Melody 1/2 **1929** Early musical in which two sisters hope for fame on Broadway, and encounter a wily song and dance man who traps both their hearts. Dated, but still charming, with a lovely score. Considered the great granddaddy of all MGM musicals; followed by three more melodies in 1935, 1937, and 1940. **104m/B; VHS, DVD.** Bessie Love; Anita Page; Charles King; Jed Prouty; Kenneth Thomson; Edward Dillon; Mary Doran; ***D:*** Harry Beaumont; ***M:*** Nacio Herb Brown; ***M:*** Arthur Freed. Oscars '29: Film.

Broadway Melody of 1936
1935 Exceptional musical comedy with delightful performances from Taylor and Powell. Benny is a headline-hungry columnist who tries to entrap Taylor by using Powell. **110m/B; VHS, DVD.** Jack Benny; Eleanor Powell; Robert Taylor; Una Merkel; Sid Silvers; Buddy Ebsen; ***D:*** Roy Del Ruth; ***C:*** Charles Rosher; ***M:*** Nacio Herb Brown; Arthur Freed.

Broadway Melody of 1938 1/2
1937 Third entry in the melody series lacks the sparkle of "Broadway Melody of 1936" despite the all-star cast. Lots of singing and dancing without much charm. Two bright spots: a young Garland singing the now famous "Dear Mr. Gable" and the always lovely Powell's dance numbers. **110m/B; VHS, DVD.** Eleanor Powell; Sophie Tucker; George Murphy; Judy Garland; Robert Taylor; Buddy Ebsen; Binnie Barnes; ***D:*** Roy Del Ruth; ***C:*** William H. Daniels; ***M:*** Nacio Herb Brown; ***M:*** Arthur Freed.

Broadway Melody of 1940 1/2
1940 The last entry in the melody series features the only screen teaming of Astaire and Powell. The flimsy plot is just an excuse for a potent series of Cole Porter musical numbers. **103m/B; VHS, DVD.** Fred Astaire; Eleanor Powell; George Murphy; Frank Morgan; Ian Hunter; ***D:*** Norman Taurog.

Broadway Rhythm 1/2 **1944** A too-long look at Broadway behind-the-scenes. Murphy plays a Broadway producer who hopes to land a Hollywood star for his new show. She rejects his offer in favor of a show being produced by his father. Just a chance to showcase a number of popular vaudeville acts, songs, and the music of Tommy Dorsey and his orchestra. **111m/C; VHS, DVD.** George Murphy; Ginny Simms; Charles Winninger; Gloria De Haven; Nancy Walker; Ben Blue; Lena Horne; Eddie Anderson; ***D:*** Roy Del Ruth; ***W:*** Dorothy Kingsley; Harry Clork.

Broadway Serenade 1/2 **1939** Melodramatic musical in which a songwriter (Ayres) and his wife, singer MacDonald, make career choices that destroy their marriage. **114m/B; VHS, DVD.** Jeanette MacDonald; Lew Ayres; Ian Hunter; Frank Morgan; Wally Vernon; Rita Johnson; Virginia Grey; William Gargan; ***D:*** Robert Z. Leonard; ***W:*** Charles Lederer.

Brokeback Mountain 1/2 **2005 (R)** Yes, it's primarily known as the movie that inspired a million "gay cowboy" jokes, but Lee's heartbreaking drama deserves so much better. In 1963, cowhands Ennis (Ledger) and Jack (Gyllenhaal) spend the summer watching over a herd of sheep on a Wyoming mountain range and falling deeply and inexplicably in love. Terrified to admit their feelings to the outside world, Ennis and Jack try to ignore their passions by getting married to aloof women (Williams and Hathaway) and only meeting for semi-annual fishing trips. The script blends the powerful western themes of "Lonesome Dove" with a classic tragic love tale, and Ledger's outstanding lead performance carries the picture. **134m/C; DVD, Blu-Ray, HD-DVD.** Heath Ledger; Jake Gyllenhaal; Linda Cardellini; Anna Faris; Anne Hathaway; Michelle Williams; Randy Quaid; Graham Beckel; Scott Michael Campbell; Kate Mara; Roberta Maxwell; Peter McRobbie; David Harbour; ***D:*** Ang Lee; ***W:*** Larry McMurtry; Diana Ossana; ***C:*** Rodrigo Prieto; ***M:*** Gustavo Santaolalla. Oscars '05: Adapt. Screenplay, Director (Lee), Orig. Score; British Acad. '05: Adapt. Screenplay, Film, Support. Actor (Gyllenhaal); Directors Guild '05: Director (Lee); Golden Globes '06: Director (Lee), Film--Drama, Screenplay, Song ("A Love That Will Never Grow Old"); Ind. Spirit '06: Director (Lee), Film; L.A. Film Critics '05: Director (Lee), Film; Natl. Bd. of Review '05: Director (Lee), Support. Actor (Gyllenhaal); Natl. Film Reg. '18; N.Y. Film Critics '05: Actor (Ledger), Director (Lee), Film; Writers Guild '05: Adapt. Screenplay.

Brokedown Palace 1/2 **1999 (PG-13)** Danes and Beckinsale take a trip to Thailand following their high school graduation and are targeted by a smooth-talking Australian drug dealer. After he invites the pair to Hong Kong, he hides heroin in their luggage and they're busted at the airport. Accused of drug trafficking, they are sentenced to 33 years in a Thai prison. Phillips is an unfriendly DEA official, while Pullman is the expatriate American lawyer who comes to their aid. The story focuses more on the girls' relationship as friends than on their legal nightmare, however. Nevertheless, the government of Thailand was none too pleased by the script, so most of the Thai scenes were actually shot in the Phillipines. **100m/C; VHS, DVD.** Claire Danes; Kate Beckinsale; Bill Pullman; Daniel Lapaine; Lou Diamond Phillips; Jacqueline Kim; Tom Amandes; Aimee Graham; John Doe; ***D:*** Jonathan Kaplan; ***W:*** David Arata; ***C:*** Newton Thomas (Tom) Sigel; ***M:*** David Newman.

The Broken 1/2 **2008 (R)** The plot's broken too or maybe the director doesn't care that it doesn't make much sense. London radiologist Gina (Headey) glimpses her doppelganger on the street and gets obsessed. She also gets into a car crash, comes out of a coma, has flashbacks, and thinks her family and boyfriend are behaving strangely. She's paranoid at the very least. **88m/C; DVD, Blu-Ray.** *UK* Lena Headey; Richard Jenkins; Melvil Poupaud; Ulrich Thomsen; Asier Newman; Michaelle Duncan; ***D:*** Sean Ellis; ***W:*** Sean Ellis; ***C:*** Angus Hudson; ***M:*** Guy Farley.

Broken 1/2 **2013** One summer day 11-year-old British girl Skunk secretly watches in horror as a hateful neighbor (Kinnear) throws down a brutal assault on a slow-witted boy (Emms), who's been wrongly accused of rape. The violent episode sticks with her all summer, foreshadowing other violence coming down the road. Stage director Norris' pic, made for the BBC, plays up the misery of the English middle-class, but takes it too far at times, as this coming-of-age drama pushes the point past its welcome. **90m/C; On Demand.** *UK* Tim Roth; Cillian Murphy; Rory Kinnear; Robert Emms; Zana Marjanovic; ***D:*** Rufus Norris; ***W:*** Mark O'Rowe; ***C:*** Rob Hardy. **TV**

Broken Angel 1/2 **1988** Jamie seemed to be such a nice girl, with good looks and great grades—and membership in a notorious street gang. When Jamie disappears, her family discovers her secret activities and dad tries to find his wayward little girl. Melodramatic TV goo. **94m/C; VHS, Streaming.** William Shatner; Susan Blakely; Erika Eleniak; Roxann Biggs-Dawson; ***D:*** Richard T. Heffron. **TV**

Broken Arrow 1/2 **1950** A U.S. scout befriends Cochise and the Apaches, and helps settlers and Indians live in peace together in the 1870s. Acclaimed as the first Hollywood film to side with the Indians, and for Chandler's portrayal of Cochise. Based on the novel "Blood Brother" by Elliot Arnold. **93m/C; VHS, DVD, Blu-Ray.** James Stewart; Jeff Chandler; Will Geer; Debra Paget; Basil Ruysdael; Arthur Hunnicutt; Jay Silverheels; ***D:*** Delmer Daves; ***W:*** Albert (John B. Sherry) Maltz; ***C:*** Ernest Palmer.

Broken Arrow **1995 (R)** Air Force pilot Vic Deakins (Travolta) rips off a couple of nuclear weapons during a routine exercise over the Utah desert. Deakins' ex-co-pilot Riley Hale (Slater), with help from spunky park ranger Terry Carmichael (Mathis), sets out to find and retrieve the warheads before the big bang. Hong Kong action king Woo once again tries his hand at the big-budget Hollywood action extravaganza, with mixed results. Triple script whammy of cheesy dialogue, continuity problems, and predictability undercuts, but doesn't obscure, his talent for choreographing mayhem. Travolta plays the All-American Boy as creepily charming psychotic to great effect. **108m/C; VHS, DVD, Blu-Ray.** John Travolta; Christian Slater; Samantha Mathis; Delroy Lindo; Bob Gunton; Frank Whaley; Howie Long; ***D:*** John Woo; ***W:*** Graham Yost; ***C:*** Peter Levy; ***M:*** Hans Zimmer.

Broken Badge *The Rape of Richard Beck* **1985** Crenna stars as a macho, chauvinistic cop whose attitude towards rape victims changes dramatically after he himself is raped by a couple of thugs. Excellent TV movie. **100m/C; VHS, DVD.** Richard Crenna; Meredith Baxter; Pat Hingle; Frances Lee McCain; Cotter Smith; George Dzundza; Joanna Kerns; ***D:*** Karen Arthur; ***W:*** James G. Hirsch; ***M:*** Peter Bernstein.

Broken Blossoms 1/2 **1919** One of Griffith's most widely acclaimed films, about a young Chinese man in London's squalid Limehouse district hoping to spread the peaceful philosophy of his Eastern religion. He befriends a pitiful street waif who is mistreated by her brutal father, resulting in tragedy. Silent. Revised edition contains introduction from Gish and a newly recorded score. **89m/B; Silent; VHS, DVD.** Lillian Gish; Richard Barthelmess; Donald Crisp; ***D:*** D.W. Griffith; ***W:*** D.W. Griffith; ***C:*** Billy (G.W.) Bitzer; ***M:*** Louis F. Gottschalk. Natl. Film Reg. '96.

Broken Bridges 1/2 **2006 (PG-13)** Hard-drinking, washed-up country singer Bo Price returns to his Tennessee hometown when five soldiers are killed in a training accident. One is Bo's younger brother and another is the sibling of Angela Delton, whom Bo abandoned when she got pregnant. Angela returns with their 16-year-old daughter Dixie, but the Deltons prefer to keep their distance from Bo, who wants to make amends. **105m/C; DVD.** Toby Keith; Kelly Preston; Lindsey Haun; Burt Reynolds; Tess Harper; Anna Maria Horsford; ***D:*** Steven Goldman; ***W:*** Cherie Bennett; Jeff Gottesfeld; ***C:*** Patrick Cady; ***M:*** Toby Keith. **CABLE**

The Broken Circle Breakdown **2012** Sometimes heavy-handed Belgian drama that's sustained by the talented leads' unlikely devotion to American bluegrass music. Scruffy Flemish musician Didier plays in a bluegrass band. He falls for free-spirited tattoo artist, Elise, who joins as the lead singer, and a happy family emerges with the addition of daughter Maybelle. At six, tragedy strikes Maybelle, which leaves her parents grief-stricken and on the verge of tearing them apart. English and Flemish with subtitles. **111m/C; DVD.** *BE NL* Johan Heldenbergh; Veerle Baetens; ***D:*** Felix van Groeningen; ***W:*** Felix van Groeningen; Carl Joos; ***C:*** Ruben Impens; ***M:*** Bjorn Eriksson.

Broken City **2013 (R)** First solo outing from director Allen Hughes (one-half of the Hughes brothers' team). Often silly and syrupy New York mystery about a private eye (Wahlberg) hired by the city's mayor (Crowe) to follow his adulterous wife (Zeta-Jones). As with most of the predictable plot points, the detective finds not only that his sultry wife is rendezvousing with the other candidate's campaign manager, but discovers a high-profile murder along the way. A sleazy Hollywood thriller that plays like a midnight cable guilty pleasure, loaded with amusing overacting showing characters leering into windows and going on benders. **109m/C; DVD, Blu-Ray.** Mark Wahlberg; Russell Crowe; Catherine Zeta-Jones; Jeffrey Wright; Barry Pepper; Kyle Chandler; ***D:*** Allen Hughes; ***W:*** Brian Tucker; ***C:*** Ben Seresin; ***M:*** Atticus Ross; Leopold Ross; Claudia Sarne.

Broken Embraces *Los Abrazos Rotos* **2009 (R)** Director Almodovar's twisting tale of filmmaking and revenge is bursting with colors that belie the darkness of the story. One-time film director Mateo Blanco (Homar) abandons his name and career after being blinded in a car crash. As Harry Caine, he is hired by the mysterious Ray X (Ochandiano) to write a screenplay about the life of movie producer Martel (Gomez), Mateo's former partner. The common thread linking all three men is Lena (Cruz), a beautiful starlet with a checkered past. Movies within the movie and characters who change names (and personas) lend extra dimension to the serpentine plot. Almodovar also uses many clever devices to reveal his opinions about the director and his role in the movie industry. In Spanish with subtitles. **128m/C; Blu-Ray, On Demand.** *SP* Penelope Cruz; Lluis Homar; Blanca Portillo; Jose Luis Gomez; Tamar Novas; Ruben Ochandiano; Lola Duenas; ***D:*** Pedro Almodóvar; ***W:*** Pedro Almodóvar; ***C:*** Rodrigo Prieto; ***M:*** Alberto Iglesias.

Broken English 1/2 **2007 (PG-13)** Nora (Posey) is a single, moderately neurotic New Yorker working a job for which she's over-qualified, while both she and her mother wonder why she's so unlucky at love. Enter charming and perfect Julien, who seems to look past Nora's insecurities and fears in exchange for a (mostly) perfect weekend. Posey shines and Cassavetes (daughter of legendary director John) shows insight into her characters, but it's not enough to completely transcend the well-worn lonely-hearts story. **97m/C; DVD.** Parker Posey; Melvil Poupaud; Drea De Matteo; Gena Rowlands; Justin Theroux; Tim Guinee; Josh Hamilton; Michael Panes; ***D:*** Zoe Cassavettes; ***W:*** Zoe Cassavettes; ***C:*** John Pirozzi; ***M:*** Scratch Massive.

Broken Flowers **2005 (R)** Quirky, if forlorn, comedy from Jarmusch. Murray does minimalism in his portrayal of confirmed, middle-aged bachelor Don Johnston whose orderly life becomes disarrayed when he learns he fathered a son from a long-ago liaison. Only there are four potential moms (a fifth has died), so Don reluctantly goes on a road trip to re-acquaint himself with Laura (Stone), Dora (Conroy), Carmen (Lange), and Penny (Swinton). His welcome varies—not much really happens—and Murray is more Don Quixote (with Wright as his stay-at-home Sancho Panza) than Don Juan. **105m/C; DVD, Blu-Ray.** *FR US* Bill Murray; Jeffrey Wright; Sharon Stone; Frances Conroy; Jessica Lange; Tilda Swinton; Julie Delpy; Mark Webber; Chloë Sevigny; Christopher McDonald; Alexis Dziena; Larry Fessenden; Chris Bauer; Pell James; Heather Alicia Simms; Brea Frazier; ***D:*** Jim Jarmusch; ***W:*** Jim Jarmusch; ***C:*** Frederick Elmes.

Broken Harvest 1/2 **1994** Jimmy O'Leary remembers his youth in rural 1950s Ireland when a poor wheat harvest led to his family's financial demise and a feud between his father (Lane) and neighbor Josie McCarthy (O'Brien) threatened to destroy their lives. The men fought side by side for Ireland's independence, but the friendship dissolved when they took different sides during the ensuing civil war, and fought over Jimmy's mother. Strong performances and the beautiful West Cork and Wicklow location shots provide a nice balance to the uneven narrative. The black and white scenes were actually filmed in the mid-'80s when the independently financed project was begun. Adapted from O'Callaghan's own story "The Shilling." **101m/C; VHS, DVD.** *IR* Colin Lane; Niall O'Brien; Marian Quinn; Darren McHugh; Joy Florish; Joe Jeffers; Pete O'Reilly; Michael Crowley; ***D:*** Maurice O'Callaghan; ***W:*** Maurice O'Callaghan; ***C:*** Jack Conroy; ***M:*** Patrick Cassidy.

The Broken Hearts Club **2000 (R)** Talk can be cheap, but it's also what sustains the relationships in the lives of a group of gay friends in this chatty, likable film set in West Hollywood. Despite their mostly superficial (sex) conversations, the boys suspect there's more to life, and aim, hesitantly, to move beyond this dead-end topic. Witty and confident in his characters, writer/director Berlanti (co-creator of "Dawson's Creek") has put together a film about gay men that thankfully moves beyond the staleness of many of its predecessors. Good cast with notable performances by Cain (Superman in TV's "Lois and Clark") and Mahoney as the fatherly proprietor of the Broken Hearts restaurant. **94m/C; VHS, DVD.** Dean Cain; John Mahoney; Timothy Olyphant; Andrew Keegan; Nia Long; Zach Braff; Matt McGrath; Billy Porter; Justin Theroux; Mary McCormack; ***D:*** Greg Berlanti; ***W:*** Greg Berlanti; ***C:*** Paul Elliott; ***M:*** Christophe Beck.

Broken Hearts of Broadway
1923 Stories of heartbreak and success along the Great White Way. **85m/B; Silent; VHS, DVD.** Colleen Moore; Johnnie Walker; Alice Lake; Tully Marshall; Creighton Hale; ***D:*** Irving Cummings.

Broken Hill **2009 (PG)** Tommy wants to work on his music and isn't interested in the family's Australian sheep ranch.

He and newcomer Kat get into trouble and must do community service, so Tommy chooses to volunteer at the local prison and forms an inmate band. Teaching the prisoners his own musical compositions, Tommy's goal is to enter a regional competition (and impressing Kat would be a bonus). **102m/C; DVD.** Luke Arnold; Alexa Vega; Timothy Hutton; Che Timmons; Peter Lamb; Leo Taylor; ***D:*** Dagen Merrill; ***W:*** Dagen Merrill; ***C:*** Nick Remy Matthews; ***M:*** Christopher Brady. **VIDEO**

Broken Lance 1/2 **1954** Western remake of "House of Strangers" that details the dissolution of a despotic cattle baron's family. Beautifully photographed. **96m/C; VHS, DVD, Blu-Ray.** Spencer Tracy; Richard Widmark; Robert Wagner; Jean Peters; Katy Jurado; Earl Holliman; Hugh O'Brian; E.G. Marshall; ***D:*** Edward Dmytryk; ***W:*** Philip Yordan; ***C:*** Joe MacDonald; ***M:*** Leigh Harline. Oscars '54: Story.

A Broken Life 1/2 **2007** When Max Walker (Sizemore) decides to commit suicide, he hires his struggling film student friend Bud (Sevier) to record his last days. Max lets his rage out, confronting his former boss and ex-wife, as well as doing some really stupid things. As his chosen end nears, Max is shown kindness by wheelchair-bound Melinda (Kosaka) and starts rethinking his plans. **97m/C; DVD.** Tom Sizemore; Corey Sevier; Ving Rhames; Saul Rubinek; Cynthia Dale; Kris Holden-Ried; Grace Kosaka; ***D:*** Neil Coombs; ***W:*** Neil Coombs; ***C:*** Peter Benison; ***M:*** Christopher Dedrick. **VIDEO**

Broken Lullaby 1/2 **1994** Genealogist Jordan Kirkland (Harris) travels to Europe to research her orphaned Aunt Kitty's (Hyland) murky past at the time of the Russian Revolution. Her only clue is a photograph of a young girl holding a music box topped with a priceless Faberge egg. Jordan meets Hungarian art dealer Nick Rostov (Stewart), who has his own reasons for finding the same music box, but they're not the only ones searching for it. From the Harlequin Romance Series; adapted from the Laurel Pace novel. **91m/C; DVD.** *CA* Mel Harris; Rob Stewart; Oliver Tobias; Jennifer Dale; Frances Hyland; Charmion King; Vivian Reis; ***D:*** Michael Kennedy; ***W:*** Jim Henshaw; Guy Mullaly; ***C:*** Nyika Jancso; ***M:*** Claude Desjardins; Eric N. Robertson. **TV**

Broken Silence *Silencio Roto* **2001** Director Armendariz's engaging production is set in 1944 when 21-year-old Lucia (Jimenez) goes back to her homeland only to witness the dramatic and violent impact that the Spanish Civil War has had upon the people of her rustic village. Still, she finds love with Manuel (Botto), a blacksmith who is part of the resistance group, the Maquis. An uprising swells and Franco's fascist army shows up to squash it, forcing the young lovers to face the cruel realities inherent to the hostilities. In Spanish with subtitles. **110m/C; VHS, DVD.** *SP* Juan Diego Botto; Mercedes Sampietro; Lucia Jimenez; Maria Botto; Andoni Erburu; Alvaro de Luna; ***D:*** Montxo Armendariz; ***W:*** Montxo Armendariz; ***C:*** Guillermo Navarro; ***M:*** Pascal Gaigne. **VIDEO**

The Broken Star **1956** Deputy Marshal Frank Smead (Duff) claims self-defense in the killing of a Mexican rancher but it's really murder since Smead was after some hidden gold. The Sheriff is suspicious and has fellow deputy Bill Gentry (Williams) investigate further. **82m/B; DVD.** Howard Duff; Bill Williams; Addison Richards; Lita Baron; Henry Calvin; Douglas Fowley; ***D:*** Lesley Selander; ***W:*** John C. Higgins; ***C:*** William Margulies; ***M:*** Paul Dunlap.

The Broken Tower 1/2 **2011** Franco's artsy minimalist bio of early 20th century poet Hart Crane, who struggled with his middle-class upbringing, writing, sexuality, depression, and alcoholism until committing suicide in 1932. Pic is structured in chapters that reference Crane's erotic poems "Voyages." Adaptation of Paul L. Mariani's biography "The Broken Tower." **110m/B; DVD.** James Franco; David Franco; Michael Shannon; Stacey Miller; Betsy Franco; ***D:*** James Franco; ***W:*** James Franco; ***C:*** Christina Voros; ***M:*** Neil Benezra.

Broken Trail **2006** In 1898, aging cowpoke Print Ritter (Duvall) is herding 500 horses from Oregon to Wyoming with the help of his estranged nephew Tom Harte (Church). During the trip they hire on Heck (Cooper) and rescue five Chinese girls who were sold to be prostitutes in a mining camp. But this puts the horse traders at odds with madam Big Rump Kate (Schwimmer), who sends sadistic Big Ears (Mulkey) after her property. Not having enough to deal with, Print also protects good-hearted whore Nola (Scacchi) on that long, dusty trail. But everyone's in very good company. **184m/C; DVD, Blu-Ray.** Robert Duvall; Thomas Haden Church; Greta Scacchi; Chris Mulkey; Rusty Schwimmer; James Russo; Scott Cooper; Gwendoline Yeo; Van Dyke Parks; ***D:*** Walter Hill; ***W:*** Alan Geoffrion; ***C:*** Lloyd Ahern, II; ***M:*** David Mansfield. **CABLE**

Broken Trust 1/2 **1995** Municipal judge Timothy Nash (Selleck) is recruited for a sting operation, designed to ensnare fellow judges, by two slightly less-than-ethical feds (Atherton and McGovern). When Nash decides he doesn't like what's going on he discovers it's not going to be so easy to get out. Selleck's stoic, McGovern provides attractive ornamentation, and Atherton excels as the smarmy villain. From the novel "Court of Honor" by William P. Wood. **90m/C; DVD.** Tom Selleck; Elizabeth McGovern; William Atherton; Fritz Weaver; Marsha Mason; Charles Haid; Stanley DeSantis; Cynthia Martells; ***D:*** Geoffrey Sax; ***W:*** Joan Didion; John Gregory Dunne; ***C:*** Ronald Orieux; ***M:*** Richard Horowitz. **CABLE**

Broken Vessels **1998 (R)** Rent this with "Bringing Out the Dead" and you'll have a double feature that will make you take 911 off the speed dial. Both movies were released in the same year, but Scorsese's movie depicts a paramedic demented by caring too much. The ambulance drivers in "Broken Vessels" become unhinged by a cold, drug-induced indifference. Tom (London) is pulled into a downward spiral by his crazed partner Jimmy (Field), who smokes heroin and feels up unconscious girls while on break from saving lives. Clearly, things are not destined to go well for the pair, not to mention those who end up in the back of their meat wagon. Excellent debut from producer-director Scott Ziehl. **90m/C; VHS, DVD.** Todd Field; Jason London; Roxana Zal; Susan Traylor; James Hong; Patrick Cranshaw; William (Bill) Smith; Dave Baer; ***D:*** Scott Ziehl; ***W:*** Scott Ziehl; Dave Baer; John McMahon; ***C:*** Antonio Calvache.

Broken Vows 1/2 **1987** Thriller with Jones as ghetto priest Father Joseph, who has doubts about his calling. When he gives last rites to a murder victim, he decides to help the victim's girlfriend find his killers. Based on the novel "Where the Dark Secrets Go" by Dorothy Salisbury Davis. **95m/C; VHS, DVD.** Tommy Lee Jones; Annette O'Toole; M. Emmet Walsh; Milo O'Shea; David Groh; Madeline Sherwood; Jean De Baer; David Strathairn; ***D:*** Jud Taylor; ***C:*** Thomas Burstyn. **TV**

Broken Vows 1/2 **2016 (R)** A thriller about a one-night stand turned murderous stalker. Tara (Alexander) and her friends travel to New Orleans for her bachelorette party weekend. There, she has a one-night stand with handsome bartender Patrick (Bentley). After waking up with him the next day, Tara feels nothing but regret and flies home to her fiance Michael (Gigandet). Patrick becomes obsessed with Tara, flies to her home city, tries to cancel her wedding, and follows her everywhere. Becoming delusional, Patrick tries and fails to win her. The situation takes a psychotic turn when Patrick finds Tara and Michael on their honeymoon, compelling Tara to take extraordinary measures to protect all she holds dear. **90m/C; DVD, Streaming, Download.** Jaimie Alexander; Wes Bentley; Cam Gigandet; Alexandra Breckenridge; Astrid Coppens; ***D:*** Bram Coppens; ***W:*** Jim Agnew; Sean Keller; ***C:*** Kees Van Oostrum; ***M:*** David Julyan. **VIDEO**

Broken Wings *Knafayim Shvurot* **2002 (R)** Writer/director Bergman's touching feature debut about an Israeli family's inability to cope with the recent loss of patriarch David. Widow Dafna Ulman (Zilberschatz-Banai) takes up working odd shifts as a midwife for a local hospital, forcing 17-year-old daughter Maya (Maron) to put her music career on hold to care for younger siblings Ido (Daniel Magon) and Bahr (Eliana Magon). Faring little better is 16-year-old son Yair (Gvirtz), who has thrown away a potential basketball career by dropping out of school and now passes out leaflets in the subway dressed in a mouse costume. Things suddenly go from bad to worse, forcing the Ulmans into crisis mode. Simply told but very effective human drama. In Hebrew with subtitles. **83m/C; DVD.** *IS* Orly Silbersatz Banai; Maya Maron; Nitai Gaviratz; Valdimir Friedman; Dana Ivgi; Danny Niv; Daniel Magon; Eliana Magon; ***D:*** Nir Bergman; ***W:*** Nir Bergman; ***C:*** Valentin Belonogov; ***M:*** Avi Bellili.

Bronco Billy 1/2 **1980 (PG)** Eastwood stars as a New Jersey shoe clerk who decides to fulfill his dream of being a cowboy hero by becoming the proprietor of a rag-tag wild west show. Locke's one-note performance as a spoiled rich girl who joins up is a problem and the film's charm is as ragged as the acts. Good if you want to see Eastwood in something other than a shoot-'em-up. **117m/C; VHS, DVD, Blu-Ray.** Clint Eastwood; Sondra Locke; Bill McKinney; Scatman Crothers; Sam Bottoms; Geoffrey Lewis; Dan Vadis; Walter Barnes; Sierra Pecheur; ***D:*** Clint Eastwood; ***W:*** Dennis Hackin; ***C:*** David Worth; ***M:*** Steve Dorff.

Bronson **2009 (R)** Stylized Brit bio, with a ferocious performance by Hardy, about Michael Petersen, a young man jailed for armed robbery in 1974 who renames himself Charles Bronson after the tough guy American actor. Bronson eventually spends more than 30 years in solitary confinement thanks to his incorrigible glee in committing violent acts within the prison system itself. The lead in his own mental movie, Bronson speaks directly to the camera and is a media celebrity due to sheer outrageousness (the real Bronson has become an artist and writer behind bars and has published numerous books). But he's always a violent criminal, not a sympathetic character. **92m/C; Blu-Ray, On Demand.** *GB* Tom (Thomas) Hardy; Juliet Oldfield; Matt King; Hugh Ross; Jonathan Phillips; James Lance; ***D:*** Nicolas Winding Refn; ***W:*** Brock Norman Brock; Nicolas Winding Refn; ***C:*** Larry Smith.

The Bronte Sisters *Les Soeurs Bronte* **1979** A cold, bleak film from Techine that contrasts the often bleak, lonely lives of the Bronte family on those Yorkshire moors in the 1840s and the wildly romantic inner lives that produced the pseudononymous fiction of Emily, Charlotte, and Anne. The girls try escaping by becoming governesses and teachers but are drawn back home into the stern world of their father, Rev. Bronte. It's also where their would-be artist brother, Branwell, is unhappily succumbing to drink and drugs. French with subtitles. **120m/C; DVD.** *FR* Isabelle Adjani; Marie-France Pisier; Isabelle Huppert; Pascal Greggory; Patrick Magee; Xavier Depraz; ***D:*** Andre Techine; ***W:*** Andre Techine; Pascal Bonitzer; ***C:*** Bruno Nuytten; ***M:*** Philippe Sarde.

The Brontes of Haworth 1/2 **1973** The bleak moorlands and the village of Haworth are the setting for a dramatic look at the lives of writers Charlotte, Emily, and Anne Bronte, their wastral brother Branwell, and the tragedies that haunted them all. On 4 cassettes. **270m/C; VHS, DVD.** *GB* Ann Penfold; Michael Kitchen; Vickery Turner; Rosemary McHale; Alfred Burke; ***D:*** Marc Miller; ***W:*** Christopher Fry. **TV**

The Bronx Executioner **1986** Android, robot, and human interests clash in futuristic Manhattan and all martial arts hell breaks loose. Special introduction by martial arts star Michael Dudikoff. **88m/C; VHS, DVD.** Rob Robinson; Margie Newton; Chuck Valenti; Gabriel Gori; ***D:*** Bob Collins.

The Bronx Is Burning 1/2 **2007** In 1977, New York City was paralyzed by a citywide blackout, political strife, and the Son of Sam killing spree. And then there were the New York Yankees, owned by bombastic George Steinbrenner (Platt), managed by volatile, hard-drinking Billy Martin (Turturro), and with egotistical Reggie Jackson (Sunjata) as their star hitter. Nostalgic miniseries shows how the city came together as the Yanks made their bid for the World Series. **360m/C; DVD.** John Turturro; Oliver Platt; Daniel Sunjata; Erik Jensen; Michael Rispoli; Dan Lauria; Kevin Conway; Loren Dean; Charles S. Dutton; Alex Cranmer; Leonard Robinson; ***D:*** Jeremiah S. Chechik; ***W:*** James Solomon; Gordon Greisman; ***C:*** Douglas Koch; ***M:*** Tree Adams. **CABLE**

Bronx Obama **2014** This feature-length documentary examines the life and career of Louis Ortiz, a Barack Obama impersonator. Noting that after the unemployed Puerto Rican father shaved off his goatee in 2008, his uncanny resemblance to the president emerged. The film follows Ortiz and his family as he cashes in on his looks. Other themes are also considered such as his search for fame and the American dream of economic success. **92m/C; DVD, Streaming, Download.** ***D:*** Ryan Murdock; ***C:*** Ryan Murdock; ***M:*** Matt Abeysekera.

A Bronx Tale **1993 (R)** Vivid snapshot of a young Italian-American boy growing up in the '60s among neighborhood small-time wiseguys. As a nine-year-old Calogero witnesses mobster Sonny kill a man but doesn't rat to the police, so Sonny takes the kid under his wing. His upright bus-driving father Lorenzo doesn't approve but the kid is drawn to Sonny's apparent glamor and power. At 17, he's gotten both an education in school and on the streets but he needs to make a choice. Good period detail and excellent performances. Palminteri shows both Sonny's charisma and violence and De Niro handles the less-showy father role with finesse. Based on Palminteri's one-man play; De Niro's directorial debut. **122m/C; VHS, DVD.** Robert De Niro; Chazz Palminteri; Lillo Brancato; Francis Capra; Taral Hicks; Kathrine Narducci; Clem Caserta; Alfred Sauchelli, Jr.; Frank Pietrangolare; Joseph (Joe) D'Onofrio; ***Cameo(s):*** Joe Pesci; ***D:*** Robert De Niro; ***W:*** Chazz Palminteri; ***C:*** Reynaldo Villalobos; ***M:*** Butch Barbella.

The Bronx War **1990 (R)** Rival gangs take to the streets in this film from the director of "Hangin' with the Homeboys." A malicious gang leader tricks his gang into going to war over a girl he wants. Very violent; an unrated version available. **91m/C; VHS, DVD.** Joseph B. Vasquez; Fabio Urena; Charmaine Cruz; Andre Brown; Marlene Forte; Francis Colon; Miguel Sierra; Kim West; ***D:*** Joseph B. Vasquez.

The Bronze **2015 (R)** There are comedies about vile, annoying people, and there are vile, annoying comedies. This is the latter. Former Olympic bronze medal gymnast Hope (Rauch) rides that success into a degree of small-town fame that sustained her lazy lifestyle into her twenties. When asked to train an up-and-coming gymnast, this foul-mouthed creation has to put her own selfishness aside for the next generation, but can she muster enough genuine concern to do so? Rauch has decent comic timing but Hope is so unlikable that you'll want to see her hit by a bus long before her predictable redemption. **200m/C; DVD, Blu-Ray.** Melissa Rauch; Gary Cole; Thomas Middleditch; Sebastian Stan; Haley Lu Richardson; ***D:*** Bryan Buckley; ***W:*** Melissa Rauch; Winston Rauch; ***C:*** Scott Henriksen; ***M:*** Andrew Feltenstein; John Nau; Randall Poster.

The Brood 1/2 **1979 (R)** Cronenberg's inimitable biological nightmares, involving an experimentally malformed woman who gives birth to murderous demon-children that kill every time she gets angry. Extremely graphic. Not for all tastes. **92m/C; VHS, DVD, Blu-Ray.** *CA* Samantha Eggar; Oliver Reed; Art Hindle; Susan Hogan; Nuala Fitzgerald; Cindy Hinds; Robert A. Silverman; Gary McKeehan; ***D:*** David Cronenberg; ***W:*** David Cronenberg; ***C:*** Mark Irwin; ***M:*** Howard Shore.

Brooklyn 1/2 **2015 (PG-13)** Director Crowley and writer Hornby adapt Colm Toibin's lovely novel of a young Irish woman (Ronan) moving to Brooklyn in 1952. In this delicate, gorgeous coming-of-age story, heroine Eilis meets two men: a Brooklyn/Italian kid named Tony (Cohen) and, upon her return to Ireland for a visit, a nice gentleman named Jim (Gleeson). Ronan gives a perfect, balanced performance and Hornby captures something common in this very personal story. It's an old-fashioned character piece with a romantic edge that plays to multiple generations and both genders. It's one of those rare, sweet films that can truly be called beautiful. **105m/C; DVD, Blu-Ray.** Saoirse Ronan; Jim Broadbent; Emory Cohen; Domhnall Gleeson; Emily Bett Rickards; Julie

Walters; *D:* John Crowley; *W:* Nick Hornby; *C:* Yves Bélanger; *M:* Michael Brook.

Brooklyn Castle 🦴🦴🦴 ½ **2012 (PG)** Follows the chess team at Brooklyn's inner city Intermediate School 318, where the continual threats of poverty and budget cuts haven't thwarted the school from having the country's top-ranked junior high chess team. Student Rochelle aspires to be the first female African-American chess master, while Patrick finds chess helps him control his ADHD, and others face difficult pressures. Principal John Galvin and the team's teacher Elizabeth Vicary are clearly dedicated to the kids and the school. Well-played documentary balances the desperation of inner city schools and the lifeline that this opportunity gives the kids on which to dream and grow. **101m/C; DVD.** Rochelle Ballantyne; Pobo Efokoro; John Galvin; Fred Rubino; Elizabeth Vicary; *D:* Katie Dellamaggiore; *C:* Brian Schulz; *M:* Brian Satz.

The Brooklyn Heist 🦴🦴 *Capers* **2008 (PG-13)** Crazy crime caricatures shot in three distinct styles with overlapping stories. Set in Brooklyn, three criminal gangs co-exist without knowing anything about each other: the Amateurs get their look and attitude from 1970s mob flicks; the Moolies are African-Americans caught up in bad rap/gangsta videos; and the Sputniks live in a literally black-and-white world from the 1950s where the cold war hasn't ended and they constantly try to buy nuclear materials. All three gangs share the same hatred for racist pawnshop owner Connie and when she dies all plan to crack her legendary safe and all decide to do it on the same night. **86m/C; DVD.** Danny Masterson; Leon; Johnathan Hova; Dominique Swain; Aysan Celik; Michael Cecchi; Serena Reeder; Blanchard Ryan; Phyllis Somerville; Daniel Stewart Sherman; *D:* Julian mark Kheel; *W:* Julian mark Kheel; Brett Halsey; *C:* Carlo Scialla; *M:* David Poe.

Brooklyn Lobster 🦴🦴 **2005** Frank Giorgio (Aiello) is a hard-headed Sheepshead Bay lobster wholesaler whose business is about to be auctioned off and whose wife, Maureen (Curtin), has walked out on him. Son Michael (Sauli) comes home for the Christmas holidays to lend a hand, accompanied by his girlfriend Kerry (Burns), but her presence creates more problems. Aiello is especially impressive in a slice of life drama that was inspired by writer/director Jordan's own family. **90m/C; DVD.** Danny Aiello; Jane Curtin; Marisa Ryan; Heather Burns; Sam Freed; Daniel Serafini Sauli; Ian Kahn; Tom Mason; Barbara Garrick; John Rothman; Rick Aiello; *D:* Kevin Jordan; *W:* Kevin Jordan; *C:* David Tumblety; *M:* Craig Maher.

Brooklyn Rules 🦴🦴 **2007 (R)** Mild coming of age pic about three lifelong buddies, set in 1985 Brooklyn. Michael (Prinze) leaves the 'hood behind to go to law school and date an uptown girl (Suvari). Easy-going Bobby (Ferrara) plans to get married and have a steady straight job. But slickster Carmine (Caan) wants to be part of local wiseguy Cesar's (Baldwin) crew. Naturally these differing aims pull the guys apart. **99m/C; DVD.** Freddie Prinze, Jr.; Scott Caan; Mena Suvari; Alec Baldwin; Jerry Ferrara; Monica Keena; Robert Turano; Phyllis Kay; *D:* Michael Corrente; *W:* Terence Winter; *C:* Richard Crudo; *M:* Benny Rietveld.

A Brooklyn State of Mind 🦴🦴 **1997 (R)** Al (Spano) works for shady real estate developer Frank Parente (Aiello) in Brooklyn. When his Aunt Rose (King) rents a room to beautiful Gabriella (Cucinotta), who says she's working on a documentary about the neighborhood, Al is quick to succumb to her charms. But he's also suspicious—and when he finds a dossier on Frank in Gabriella's room, Al learns her father's murder is tied to his own father's death and both involve Frank. **90m/C; VHS, DVD.** Vincent Spano; Danny Aiello; Maria Grazia Cucinotta; Tony Danza; Morgana King; Abe Vigoda; *D:* Frank Rainone; *W:* Frank Rainone; Fred Stroppel; *C:* Ken Kelsch; *M:* Paul Zaza.

Brooklyn's Finest 🦴 ½ **2009 (R)** Fuqua appears to be redoing his 2001 film "Training Day" with this continuously violent story of corruption and impending doom that centers around three policemen. Burned-out veteran beat cop Eddie (Gere), about to retire, drinks too much and plans for his suicide; crooked narc Sal (Hawke) will do anything (including murder) for a big score to help his ill wife; and undercover cop Tango (Cheadle) is a little too comfortable in the thug life while needing to ensnare former major player Caz (Snipes) in order to stay on the NYPD promotional fast track. **125m/C; Blu-Ray, On Demand.** Richard Gere; Ethan Hawke; Don Cheadle; Wesley Snipes; Ellen Barkin; Will Patton; Brian F. O'Byrne; Vincent D'Onofrio; Michael K(enneth) Williams; Lili Taylor; Shannon Kane; *D:* Antoine Fuqua; *W:* Michael C. Martin; Brad Caleb Kane; *C:* Patrick Murguia; *M:* Marcelos Zavras.

Brother 🦴🦴 *Brat* **1997** Danila (Bodrov Jr.) has just gotten out of the army and needs a job so he decides to visit big brother Viktor (Sukhoroukov) in St. Petersburg. He discovers his bro is a contract killer for the Russian mob and hires on as Viktor's assistant. Danila successfully accomplishes his first assignment—the murder of a mob rival—but then has the other gangsters out for revenge. Fast-paced and gritty, with casual violence and crime the easiest options in a brokendown society. Russian with subtitles. **96m/C; VHS, DVD.** *RU* Sergei Bodrov, Jr.; Viktor Sukhorukov; Svetlana Pismitchenko; Maria Zhukova; Yuri Kouznetzov; *D:* Alexsei Balabanov; *W:* Alexsei Balabanov; *C:* Sergei Astakhov; *M:* Viatcheslav Boutoussov.

Brother 🦴🦴🦴 **2000 (R)** Kitano's films are something of an acquired taste. He mixes abrupt graphic (and usually brief) violence with prolonged scenes of introspection, and when it comes to expressing emotion, he seldom does more than twitch or take off his sunglasses. But the man is cool, and to those who accept his measured pace, his work has a hypnotic quality. In his first film set in America, he plays Yamamoto, an exiled Japanese yakuza who partners up with street hustler Denny (Epps) and takes on the local drug gangs. Yes, that's the stuff of hundreds of video premiere action flicks, but he transcends the cliches. English and Japanese dialog with subtitles. **118m/C; VHS, DVD.** *JP* Takeshi "Beat" Kitano; Omar Epps; Kuroudo Maki; Masaya Kato; Susumu Terajima; James Shigeta; *D:* Takeshi "Beat" Kitano; *W:* Takeshi "Beat" Kitano; *C:* Katsumi Yanagishima; *M:* Joe Hisaishi.

Brother Bear 🦴🦴 ½ **2003 (G)** Rather grim but ultimately heartwarming coming-of-ager invoking the far superior "The Lion King," and "Bambi." Kenai (Phoenix) is a brash Native American youth living with his two brothers in the Pacific Northwest during the end of the Ice Age. After a bear attacks and kills his brother Sitka (Sweeney), Kenai is magically transformed into a bear himself. In his new hirsute form, Kenai learns some important lessons about nature with the help of orphaned bear cub Koda (Suarez). Much needed but underdeveloped comic relief comes from Thomas and Moranis as a pair of bickering moose. Largely hand-drawn animation is lushly beautiful but overshadowed by derivative plot and heavy-handed message. Lackluster score by soft pop-meister Phil Collins. **85m/C; VHS, DVD, Blu-Ray.** *V:* Joaquin Rafael (Leaf) Phoenix; Jeremy Suarez; Jason Raize; Rick Moranis; Dave Thomas; D.B. Sweeney; Joan Copeland; Michael Clarke Duncan; Harold Gould; Estelle Harris; *D:* Aaron Blaise; Robert Walker; *W:* Tab Murphy; Lorne Cameron; David Hoselton; Steve Bencich; Ron J. Friedman; *M:* Phil Collins; Mark Mancina.

Brother Bear 2 🦴🦴 ½ **2006 (G)** Animated Disney sequel based on the 2003 release. Nita had a strong bond with Kenai when they were children (before he was turned into a bear). But if she wants to marry, Nita has to break that bond. She is told by the shaman that she and Kenai must perform a certain ritual but Kenai thinks maybe he should ask the Great Spirit if he can become human again (which he refused to do in the first film). For pure comic relief, moose buddies Rutt and Tuke are back and chasing after some moosettes. **74m/C; DVD, Blu-Ray.** *V:* Patrick Dempsey; Mandy Moore; Jeremy Suarez; Rick Moranis; Dave Thomas; Wanda Sykes; Andrea Martin; Catherine O'Hara; *D:* Ben Gluck; *W:* Rich Burns; *M:* Matthew Gerrard; Dave Metzger; Robbie Nevil. **VIDEO**

The Brother from Another Planet 🦴🦴🦴 **1984** A black alien escapes from his home planet and winds up in Harlem, where he's pursued by two alien bounty hunters. Independently made morality fable by John Sayles before he hit the big time; features Sayles in a cameo as an alien bounty hunter. **109m/C; VHS, DVD.** Joe Morton; Dee Dee Bridgewater; Ren Woods; Steve James; Maggie Renzi; David Strathairn; *Cameo(s):* John Sayles; *D:* John Sayles; *W:* John Sayles; *M:* Mason Daring.

Brother Future 🦴🦴 **1991** T.J., a black, streetsmart city kid who thinks school and helping others is all a waste of time gets knocked out in a car accident. As he's lying unconscious, he is transported back in time to a slave auction block in the Old South. There the displaced urbanite is forced to work on a cotton plantation, and watch the stirrings of a slave revolt. T.J. sees the light and realizes how much opportunity he's been wasting in his own life. He comes to just a few moments later, but worlds away from who he was before. Part of the "Wonderworks" series. **110m/C; VHS.** Phill Lewis; Frank Converse; Carl Lumbly; Vonetta McGee; Moses Gunn; *D:* Roy Campanella; *W:* Roy Campanella.

Brother John 🦴🦴🦴 **1970 (PG-13)** An early look at racial tensions and labor problems. An angel goes back to his hometown in Alabama to see how things are going. **94m/C; VHS, DVD.** Sidney Poitier; Will Geer; Bradford Dillman; Beverly Todd; Paul Winfield; *D:* James Goldstone; *M:* Quincy Jones.

Brother of Sleep 🦴🦴🦴 *Schlafes Bruder* **1995 (R)** Elias (Eisermann), the illegitimate son of the local priest, is discovered to have perfect pitch, a beautiful voice, and a special symbiosis with nature. Which does nothing to endear him to the superstitious inhabitants of his 19th-century Austrian mountain village. Elias doesn't know whether his gift is a blessing or a curse but he'd give it up if he could win the love of his cousin Elspeth (Vavrova). Schneider scripted from his 1992 novel, which has previously been adapted as a ballet and opera. German with subtitles. **133m/C; VHS, DVD.** *GE* Andre Eisermann; Dana Vavrova; Ben Becker; *D:* Joseph Vilsmaier; *W:* Robert Schneider; *C:* Joseph Vilsmaier; *M:* Norbert J. Schneider.

Brother Orchid 🦴🦴🦴 **1940** Mobster puts a henchman in charge of his gang while he vacations in Europe. Upon his return, he is deposed and wounded in an assassination attempt. Hiding out in a monastary, he plots to regain control of the gang, leading to fish outta water episodes and a change in his outlook on life. Fine cast fans through farce intelligently. **87m/B; VHS, DVD.** Edward G. Robinson; Humphrey Bogart; Ann Sothern; Donald Crisp; Ralph Bellamy; Allen Jenkins; Charles D. Brown; Cecil Kellaway; *D:* Lloyd Bacon; *C:* Gaetano Antonio "Tony" Gaudio.

Brother Rat 🦴🦴 **1938** Virginia Military Institute cadets Crawford (Reagan) and Randolph (Morris) help out their buddy Bing Edwards (Albert), who has secretly married and just learned that his wife is pregnant. They try to contain their usual hijinks and keep everything quiet until they can graduate in a few weeks. The film that introduced Reagan to future first wife Wyman, who played his love interest. **90m/B; DVD.** Wayne Morris; Ronald Reagan; Eddie Albert; Jane Wyman; Priscilla Lane; Jane Bryan; *D:* William Keighley; *W:* Jerry Wald; Richard Macaulay; *C:* Ernest Haller.

Brother Rat and a Baby 🦴 ½ **1940** In this silly sequel to the 1938 pic, Dan, Billy, and Bing have graduated from the Virginia Military Institute and are trying to settle down to real life. Knowing that Bing really wants the football coaching job at their alma mater, his buddies come up with some hare-brained schemes, including using Bing's baby son in a publicity story. **87m/B; DVD.** Ronald Reagan; Wayne Morris; Eddie Albert; Jane Bryan; Priscilla Lane; Jane Wyman; *D:* Ray Enright; *W:* Jerry Wald; *C:* Charles Rosher; *M:* Heinz Roemheld.

Brother Sun, Sister Moon 🦴🦴 ½ **1973 (PG)** Post-'60s costume epic depicting the trials of St. Francis of Assisi as he evaluates his beliefs in Catholicism. **120m/C; DVD.** *UK IT* Graham Faulkner; Judi Bowker; Alec Guinness; Leigh Lawson; Kenneth Cranham; Lee Montague; Valentina Cortese; *D:* Franco Zeffirelli; *W:* Franco Zeffirelli; *C:* Ennio Guarnieri; *M:* Donovan.

Brother to Brother 🦴🦴 ½ **2004** Ambitious debut effort ties the personal plight of a modern African-American painter to the artistic turmoil of the Harlem Renaissance. Perry (Mackie) is thrown out of his house once his father discovers that he is homosexual. Embittered, Perry rails against the antigay hostility within the black community and his college classrooms. After he meets a homeless man, Bruce Nugent (Robinson), in a local shelter, Perry realizes that Bruce was once a noted poet during the Harlem Renaissance. We then flash back to the 1930s to witness Bruce interacting with such luminaries as Langston Hughes and Zora Neale Hurston. Evans effectively shows how issues of politics and sexuality transcend time, but the film lapses into didacticism once too often. **94m/C; DVD.** Anthony Mackie; Roger Robinson; Larry (Lawrence) Gilliard, Jr.; Aunjanue Ellis; Duane Boutte; Daniel Sunjata; Alex Burns; *D:* Rodney Evans; *W:* Rodney Evans; *C:* Harlan Bosmajian; *M:* Marc Anthony Thompson; Bill Coleman.

The Brotherhood 🦴🦴 ½ **1968** Two hot-headed brothers in a Mafia syndicate clash over old vs. new methods and the changing of the Family's guard. **96m/C; DVD.** Kirk Douglas; Alex Cord; Irene Papas; Luther Adler; Susan Strasberg; Murray Hamilton; *D:* Martin Ritt; *W:* Lewis John Carlino; *C:* Boris Kaufman; *M:* Lalo Schifrin.

Brotherhood 🦴🦴 **2010 (R)** A fraternity hazing turns nasty when prez Frank (Foster) demands the pledges jump out of the van and rob various convenience stores. Each store has a fellow brother to prevent the joke from going too far, until one clerk acts too quickly and shoots. From here, the wounded pledge is kept in secrecy as the brothers try to cover their tracks. An effectively tense low-budget affair with decent performances from a generally unknown cast. First-time director Canon keeps the action popping and highlights the idiocy of human nature but has a severe lack of humor or irony. **79m/C; Blu-Ray.** Jon Foster; Trevor Morgan; Arlen Escarpeta; Lou Taylor Pucci; Jennifer Sipes; Luke Sexton; Chad Halbrook; Jesse Steccato; *D:* Will Canon; *W:* Will Canon; Douglas Simon; *C:* Michael Fimognari; *M:* Dan Marocco.

Brotherhood 2: The Young Warlocks **WOOF! 2001** Luke is a new kid at a private school who decides to recruit a group of fellow outcast kids for a coven he's starting. Laughably bad in all regards except that some of the cast are hotties. **85m/C; VHS, DVD.** Sean Faris; Forrest Cochran; Stacey Scowley; Noah Frank; Julie Briggs; Justin Allen; C.J. Thomason; *D:* David DeCoteau. **VIDEO**

The Brotherhood 3: The Young Demons **WOOF! 2002** Teenagers heavily into a role-playing wizard and warriors game gather every Friday to perform faux ceremonies complete with costumes and weaponry. When they find a real book of magic, they can't resist chanting a few spells, which conjures up some medieval horrors. **82m/C; VHS, DVD.** Kristopher Turner; Paul Andrich; Ellen Wieser; Julie Pedersen; *D:* David DeCoteau. **VIDEO**

Brotherhood of Blood 🦴 ½ **2008** The world's best vampire slayer (a comely young blonde) has been captured by the King of Vampires and languishes in his dungeons while her compatriots attempt to find a way in to release her. Meanwhile the King must somehow figure out how to stop the coming of a vampiric demon, who may end up making the world a hell on earth. The team-up between himself and his imprisoned enemy to stop this is inevitable, and surprisingly not so exciting. **90m/C; DVD.** Victoria Pratt; Sid Haig; Ken Foree; Jason Connery; Wes Ramsey; Jeremy James Kissner; Rachel Grant; William Snow; *D:* Michael Roesch; Peter Scheerer; *W:* Michael Roesch; Peter Scheerer; *C:* River O'Mahoney Hagg; *M:* Ralph Rieckermann; Tom Bimmerman. **VIDEO**

Brotherhood of Death 🦴 ½ **1976 (R)** Three black Vietnam veterans return to their southern hometown to get even with the Klansmen who slaughtered all of the townspeople. **85m/C; VHS, DVD, Blu-Ray.** Roy Jefferson; Larry Jones; Mike Bass; Le Tari; Haskell V. Anderson; *D:* Bill Berry.

Brotherhood of Justice 🦴🦴 **1986** Young men form a secret organization to rid their neighborhood of drug dealers and violence. As their power grows, their propriety weakens, until all are afraid of the "Brotherhood of Justice." **97m/C; VHS, DVD.** Keanu Reeves; Kiefer Sutherland; Billy Zane; Joe Spano; Darren Dalton; Evan Mirand; Don Michael Paul; ***D:*** Charles Braverman; ***M:*** Brad Fiedel. **TV**

Brotherhood of Murder **1999** Based on the book by Thomas Martinez and John Gunther that depicts the rise and fall of the white supremacist group known as "The Order." Martinez (Baldwin) is a struggling family man who falls in with charismatic Bob Mathews (Gallagher) and his hate group—until the shooting starts. **93m/C; VHS, DVD.** William Baldwin; Peter Gallagher; Kelly Lynch; Joel S. Keller; Zack (Zach) Ward; Vincent Gale; ***D:*** Martin Bell; ***W:*** Robert J. Avrech; ***C:*** James R. Bagdonas; ***M:*** Laura Karpman. **CABLE**

The Brotherhood of Satan **½ 1971 (PG)** In an isolated southern town, a satanic coven persuades children to join in their devil-may-care attitude. Worthwhile. **92m/C; VHS, DVD, Blu-Ray.** Strother Martin; L.Q. Jones; Charles Bateman; Ahna Capri; Charles Robinson; Alvy Moore; Geri Reischl; Helene Winston; ***D:*** Bernard McEveety; ***W:*** William Welch; ***C:*** John Morrill.

The Brotherhood of the Rose **½ 1989 (PG-13)** Too many twists and turns mar the otherwise mediocre plot of this murky adaption of a book by David (First Blood) Morrell. Strauss and Morse are the C.I.A. agents marked for death and running for their lives after uncovering their boss's (Mitchum) plot of world domination. Though almost every scene takes place in a different country, the movie was in fact filmed entirely in New Zealand. Convoluted and frustratingly difficult to follow. **103m/C; VHS, DVD.** Robert Mitchum; Peter Strauss; Connie Sellecca; James B. Sikking; David Morse; M. Emmet Walsh; James Hong; ***D:*** Marvin J. Chomsky.

Brotherhood of the Wolf *Le Pacte des Loups* **2001 (R)** Based on the French legend about the Beast of Gevaudan, a wolf-like creature that killed more than 100 people in the 1760s. In 1765, in a remote province, a mysterious creature is savagely killing women and children throughout the countryside. Naturalist Gregoire de Fronsac (Le Bihan) and his Iroquis blood brother Mani (Dacascos) are sent by King Louis XV to kill and stuff the beast for posterity. But what they finally discover is quite unexpected. Flamboyantly entertaining adventure. French with subtitles. **143m/C; DVD.** *FR* Samuel Le Bihan; Mark Dacascos; Vincent Cassel; Emilie Dequenne; Jeremie Renier; Monica Bellucci; Jean Yanne; Edith Scob; Jean-Francois Stevenin; Hans Meyer; Jacques Perrin; Philippe Nahon; Eric Prat; Johan Leysen; Bernard Fresson; Bernard Farcy; Virginie Darmon; ***D:*** Christophe Gans; ***W:*** Christophe Gans; Stephane Cabel; ***C:*** Dan Laustsen; ***M:*** Joseph LoDuca.

Brotherly Love **½ 1985** Good twin/bad twin made-for-TV mystery about an escaped psychopath who's out to get his businessman twin brother (Hirsch in both roles). **94m/C; DVD.** Judd Hirsch; Karen Carlson; George Dzundza; Barry Primus; Lori Lethin; ***D:*** Jeff Bleckner; ***W:*** Ernest Tidyman; ***C:*** Bradford May; ***M:*** Jonathan Tunick.

The Brothers **2001 (R)** A chain reaction of male introspection is set off as four successful, young African-American men navigate the tricky waters of serious relationships in modern Los Angeles. All the bases are covered: there is the womanizing lawyer, Brian (Bellamy); the one night stand-weary physician, Jackson (Chestnut); the just-engaged Terry (Shemar); and the unhappily married Derrick (Hughley). Not quite as strong as its female counterpart, the much-praised "Waiting to Exhale," but novelist Hardwick's first film is well managed and funny, and he never lets his capable comic actors veer too far away from the exploration of modern sexual politics. **101m/C; VHS, DVD.** Morris Chestnut; D.L. Hughley; Bill Bellamy; Shemar Moore; Gabrielle Union; Tamala Jones; Susan Dalian; Angelle Brooks; Jenifer Lewis; Clifton Powell; Marla Gibbs; Tatyana Ali; Julie Benz; ***D:*** Gary Hardwick; ***W:*** Gary Hardwick; ***C:*** Alexander Grusynski.

Brothers *Brodre* **2004 (R)** Michael is a husband and father in the Danish military deployed to Afghanistan. When his helicopter crashes he is presumed dead. In his absence his younger "screw-up" brother steps up to the plate to help Michael's wife and children cope with life in his absence. However, Michael was not dead, but captured by guerrilla fighters and forced to commit a barbaric act. When he finally returns home he is a different man. Great narrative drive, emotionally explosive and brutally honest. In Danish with English subtitles. **110m/C; DVD.** Connie Nielsen; Ulrich Thomsen; Nikolaj Lie Kaas; ***D:*** Suzanne (Susanne) Bier; ***W:*** Anders Thomas Jensen; ***C:*** Morten Soborg; ***M:*** Johan Soderqvist.

Brothers **2009 (R)** All-American Marine Capt. Sam Cahill (Maguire) is presumed dead during a tour of duty in Afghanistan, leaving a wife, Grace (Portman), and two young daughters. Trying to fill in for his responsibilities is his brother, Tommy (Gyllenhaal), a troubled ex-con. When Sam, held prisoner by the Taliban, finally returns, the trauma he's endured is made worse when it seems that the formerly unreliable Tommy has replaced him. A remake of Susanne Blier's 2004 Danish film, it occasionally rises to the original's depth but mostly misses the mark, opting for overstatement and melodrama instead. **110m/C; Blu-Ray, On Demand.** Tobey Maguire; Jake Gyllenhaal; Natalie Portman; Sam Shepard; Mare Winningham; Patrick Flueger; Carey Mulligan; ***D:*** Jim Sheridan; ***W:*** David Benioff; ***C:*** Frederick Elmes; ***M:*** Thomas Newman.

The Brothers Bloom **2009 (PG-13)** Orphans Stephen (Ruffalo) and his younger brother Bloom (Brody) spent their troubled youth perfecting their natural-born con artist abilities. Now grown up, the moody Bloom decides he's had enough of the game but a persuasive Stephen gets him to do one last con. Enter eccentric heiress Penelope (Weisz) who's looking for a little excitement in life but of course Bloom complicates things by falling hard for their mark. A familiar farce that's still appealing enough, just as is its cast—Weisz, especially—with a gorgeous European backdrop. But writer/director Johnson makes it a little too hyper and witty for its own good. **109m/C; Blu-Ray, On Demand.** Adrien Brody; Mark Ruffalo; Rachel Weisz; Maximilian Schell; Rinko Kikuchi; Robbie Coltrane; Ricky Jay; ***Nar:*** Ricky Jay; ***D:*** Rian Johnson; ***W:*** Rian Johnson; ***C:*** Steve Yedlin; ***M:*** Nathan Johnson.

The Brothers Grimm **½ 2005 (PG-13)** Rather grim indeed is this ill-conceived fairytale from Gilliam that had a rocky and delayed production (it was filmed in 2003). Wilhelm (Damon) and Jacob (Ledger) are 18th century German con men fleecing credulous country folk who believe in the supernatural. But in order to save their own skins, the brothers must investigate the disappearance of a number of young women who have vanished into a truly enchanted forest that is the domain of the Mirror Queen (Bellucci). The film looks good but it's really all an illusion. **118m/C; DVD, Blu-Ray, UMD.** *US CZ* Matt Damon; Heath Ledger; Monica Bellucci; Jonathan Pryce; Lena Headey; Peter Stormare; Jan Unger; ***D:*** Terry Gilliam; ***W:*** Ehren Kruger; ***C:*** Newton Thomas (Tom) Sigel; ***M:*** Dario Marianelli.

The Brothers Grimsby **½** *Grimsby* **2016 (R)** For those who love Sasha Baron Cohen's brand of comedy, read on. The rest...move on. Here he plays simple Englishman Nobby, who has a seemingly content and happy life with his wife and 11 children. But he's spent nearly 30 years looking for his long-lost brother Sebastian (Strong). Little does he know Sebastian is a MI6 agent. Naturally the pair gets thrust into saving the world. At least the 83-minute runtime is merciful. **83m/C; DVD, Blu-Ray, Streaming.** *AU UK* Sacha Baron Cohen; Mark Strong; Isla Fisher; Penelope Cruz; Rebel Wilson; ***D:*** Louis Leterrier; ***W:*** Sacha Baron Cohen; Phil Johnston; Peter Baynham; ***C:*** Oliver Wood; ***M:*** David Buckley; Erran Baron Cohen.

Brother's Justice **½ 2011** In this showbiz mockumentary, comedian Dax Shepard decides to change his image by getting a martial arts/adventure pic greenlit. It will star himself, though Dax has no martial arts training (or ability) and no script. Best friend Nate is the wannabe producer and they pitch the dismal project relentlessly to various biz friends with predictable (and only mildly comedic) results. **86m/C; DVD, Blu-Ray.** Dax Shepard; Nate Tuck; Tom Arnold; Bradley Cooper; David Koechner; Jon Favreau; ***D:*** Dax Shepard; David Palmer; ***W:*** Dax Shepard; ***C:*** David Palmer; ***M:*** Julian Wass. **VIDEO**

The Brothers Karamazov *Karamazov; The Murderer Dmitri Karamazov; Der Morder Dimitri Karamasoff* **1958** Hollywood adaptation of the classic novel by Dostoyevsky, in which four 19th-Century Russian brothers struggle with their desires for the same beautiful woman and with the father who brutalizes them. Incredible performances from every cast member, especially Cobb. Long and extremely intense, with fine direction from Brooks. Marilyn Monroe tried desperately to get Schell's part. **147m/C; VHS, DVD.** Yul Brynner; Claire Bloom; Lee J. Cobb; William Shatner; Maria Schell; Richard Basehart; ***D:*** Richard Brooks; ***W:*** Richard Brooks; ***C:*** John Alton.

Brother's Keeper **1992** Filmmakers Berlinger and Sinofsky document the story of the eccentric and reclusive Ward brothers, four bachelor dairy farmers who shared the same two-room shack for more than 60 years in rural New York. When Bill Ward dies, brother Delbert is accused of murder and goes to trial. The film covers a year's span in preparation for the trial and how the media attention changed the Ward's lives. **104m/C; VHS, DVD.** ***D:*** Joe Berlinger; Bruce Sinofsky; ***C:*** Douglas Cooper. Directors Guild '92: Documentary Director (Berlinger), Documentary Director (Sinofsky); Natl. Bd. of Review '92: Feature Doc.; N.Y. Film Critics '92: Feature Doc.; Sundance '92: Aud. Award.

Brother's Keeper *My Brother's Keeper* **2002 (R)** After police detective Lucinda Pond (Tripplehorn) screwed up and let a killer get away, she left the force to run a fishing boat and start drinking. Ex-partner/lover Travis (Orser) shows up when his current homicide case turns out to be identical to the incident that ended Lucinda's career. She unofficially agrees to help but solving the case may lead her close to home and her crazy brother Ellis (Nemec). **86m/C; VHS, DVD.** Jeanne Tripplehorn; Corin "Corky" Nemec; Leland Orser; Evan Dexter Parke; ***D:*** John Badham; ***W:*** Steven Baigelman; Glen Gers; ***C:*** Ron Stannett; ***M:*** John Ottman; John Willett. **CABLE**

A Brother's Kiss **1997 (R)** Growing up in an East Harlem neighborhood with an alcoholic mother (Moriarty), two brothers are set on different paths that strain their brotherly love. Lex (Chinlund) is a never-was ex-basketball player with a bad marriage and an even worse drug problem. Mick (Raynor) is a tightly wound, obsessive, and sexually dysfunctional cop. Both of their problems stem from a childhood trauma that neither is able or willing to discuss with the other. Starts out strong but runs out of energy by the second half. Expanded from a one-act play by director Rosenfeld. **92m/C; VHS, DVD.** Nick (Nicholas) Chinlund; Michael Raynor; Justin Pierce; Cathy Moriarty; Rosie Perez; Marisa Tomei; Joshua Danowsky; John Leguizamo; Michael Rapaport; Frank Minucci; Adrian Pasdar; ***D:*** Seth Zvi Rosenfeld; ***W:*** Seth Zvi Rosenfeld; ***C:*** Fortunato Procopio; ***M:*** Frank London.

The Brothers McMullen **1994 (R)** Slice of life drama finds three Irish-American brothers suddenly living under the same Long Island roof for the first time since childhood. Eldest brother Jack (Mulcahy) is a stolid high-school basketball coach married to teacher Molly (Britton) who's pressing him to have children. Cynical middle brother Barry (Burns), a writer, has just broken up with free-spirited Ann (McKay), and earnest young Patrick (McGlone) is engaged to Jewish girlfriend Susan (Albert). All three find their romantic relationships, as well as their belief in each other, tested. Generally good performances and dialogue, with Burns proving himself a triple threat as actor/writer/director. **98m/C; VHS, DVD, Blu-Ray.** Edward Burns; Jack Mulcahy; Mike McGlone; Connie Britton; Shari Albert; Elizabeth P. McKay; Maxine Bahns; Jennifer Jostyn; Catharine Bolt; Peter Johansen; ***D:*** Edward Burns; ***W:*** Edward Burns; ***C:*** Dick Fisher; ***M:*** Seamus Egan. Ind. Spirit '96: First Feature; Sundance '95: Grand Jury Prize.

Brothers of the Head **2006 (R)** Bizzare mockumentary a la "This Is Spinal Tap," only without the humor, tells the fictional story of British conjoined twins who are sold by their father to an unsavory music promoter who turns them into a freak-show punk band. The flashback-documentary style shows the rapid rise and fall of the band due to the usual rock and roll excesses. Pic gets a half bone for recreating an authentic 1970s British art/rock scene that makes an otherwise creepy flick watchable. Based on the 1977 illustrated novel by Brian Aldiss. **120m/C; DVD.** *GB* Sean Harris; Jonathan Pryce; John Simm; Jane Horrocks; Harry Treadaway; Luke Treadway; Bryan Dick; Elizabeth Rider; Howard Attfield; Luke Wagner; Anna Nygh; Ed Hogg; Thomas Sturridge; Barbara Ewing; ***Cameo(s):*** Ken Russell; ***D:*** Keith Fulton; Louis Pepe; ***W:*** Tony Grisoni; ***C:*** Anthony Dod Mantle; ***M:*** Clive Langer.

Brothers O'Toole **1973 (G)** The misadventures of a pair of slick drifters who, by chance, ride into a broken-down mining town in the 1890s. **94m/C; VHS, DVD.** John Astin; Steve Carlson; Pat Carroll; Hans Conried; Lee Meriwether; ***D:*** Richard Erdman.

The Brothers Rico **1957** Eddie (Conte) left the mob life behind, got married, and has a successful business, but his two brothers remained in the rackets. Unbeknownst to Eddie, they are targeted by mob boss Kubik (Gates) who uses Eddie's family loyalty to track them down. When Eddie discovers his brothers have been rubbed out, he decides to turn informer. Based on a novella by Georges Simenon. **92m/B; DVD.** Richard Conte; James Darren; Paul Picerni; Dianne Foster; Kathryn Grant; Larry Gates; Lamont Johnson; Argentina Brunetti; ***D:*** Phil Karlson; ***W:*** Lewis Meltzer; Ben L. Perry; ***C:*** Burnett Guffey; ***M:*** George Duning.

The Brothers Solomon **½ 2007 (R)** Dean (Forte) and John (Arnett) decide to grant their father's (Majors) last wish before he slipped into a coma: a grandchild. Unfortunately, they were raised in the Arctic, have no social skills, and are, well, idiots. Along comes surrogate Janine (Wiig), who is willing to bear the child for a price. Mostly, though, it's just a set up for an endless series of gags based on how stupid and out of touch the brothers are. Arnett and Forte's "even dumber than dumberer" act, as directed by Odenkirk, is exhausting and the occasional splashes of sweetness don't make up for what is basically a one-joke extended sketch comedy skit. **93m/C; DVD, Blu-Ray.** Will Arnett; Will Forte; Chi McBride; Jenna Fischer; Kristen Wiig; Malin Akerman; David Koechner; Lee Majors; ***D:*** Bob Odenkirk; ***W:*** Will Forte; ***C:*** Tim Suhrstedt; ***M:*** John Swihart.

Brothers Three **½ 2007 (R)** Dysfunctional family 101. College-educated businessman Peter (Wilson) receives an urgent message from his hot-tempered outdoorsman brother Rick (McDonough) to join him and their mentally-challenged younger brother Norman (Campbell) at the family's remote, run-down cabin. Once there, Peter learns that their shifty father (Heard) has recently died a violent death. The brothers then spend their time drinking and offering up confessions that reveal dark secrets (through some confusing flashbacks). **102m/C; DVD.** Patrick Wilson; Neal McDonough; Scott Michael Campbell; John Heard; Melora Walters; ***D:*** Paul Kampf; ***W:*** Paul Kampf; ***C:*** Henryk Cymerman.

The Brown Bunny **½ 2003** After his film's trashing as the worst movie in the history of the Cannes Film Festival, director/writer/star Gallo slashed nearly a half-hour from this story of a forlorn motorcycle racer's long, lonely coast-to-coast journey from a New Hampshire competition to his home in L.A., where he eventually meets up with true love Daisy (Sevigny). An infamously graphic oral sex scene ensues, which leads to a funky final plot twist. Curiosity, about the Cannes hubbub and the sex scene, will be rewarded by an interesting, sometimes poignant, homage to the maverick filmmaking of the 1970s. **93m/C; DVD.** Vincent Gallo; Chloë Sevigny; Cheryl Tiegs; Elizabeth Blake; Anna Vareschi; Mary Morasky; ***D:*** Vincent Gallo; ***W:*** Vincent Gallo; ***C:*** Vincent Gallo.

Brown Sugar **½ 2002 (PG-13)** Using the world of hip-hop music as its background, this romantic comedy succeeds in breathing life into a rather tired formula. Record producer Dre (Diggs) and music journalist Sidney (Lathan) are childhood friends who are drawn together by their shared love of the music. Although they think that romance is out of the question for them, everyone else knows that they're wrong, especially Sidney's friend Francine (Latifah). Unfortunately, Sidney doesn't figure it out until Dre becomes engaged to lovely lawyer Reese (Parker). She rebounds with suave basketball player Kelby (Kodjoe). Mos Def steals scenes as the shy, rapping cabbie who has a crush on Francine. **109m/C; VHS, DVD.** Taye Diggs; Sanaa Lathan; Mos Def; Nicole Ari Parker; Queen Latifah; Wendell Pierce; Boris Kodjoe; Erik Weiner; Reggi Wyns; ***D:*** Rick Famuyiwa; ***W:*** Rick Famuyiwa; Michael Elliot; ***C:*** Enrique Chediak; ***M:*** Robert Hurst.

The Browning Version 1/2 **1951** A lonely, unemotional classics instructor at a British boarding school realizes his failure as a teacher and as a husband. From the play by Terrence Rattigan. **89m/B; VHS, DVD.** *GB* Michael Redgrave; Jean Kent; Nigel Patrick; Wilfrid Hyde-White; Bill Travers; ***D:*** Anthony Asquith. Cannes '51: Actor (Redgrave).

The Browning Version 1/2 **1994 (R)** Mediocre remake of the Terence Rattigan play, previously filmed in 1951. Austere classics professor (Finney) at prestigious British boys school is disillusioned with both his floundering career and marriage. His emotional chill drives his younger wife (Scacchi) into an affair with a visiting American science teacher (Modine). Unfortunately updated to contemporary times, which can't hide apparent mustiness. Worth seeing for Finney's superb work as the out-of-touch prof. **97m/C; VHS, DVD.** Albert Finney; Greta Scacchi; Matthew Modine; Michael Gambon; Julian Sands; Ben Silverstone; Maryam D'Abo; ***D:*** Mike Figgis; ***W:*** Ronald Harwood; ***M:*** Mark Isham.

Brown's Requiem 1/2 **1998 (R)** Ex-cop and ex-drunk Fritz Brown (Rooker) is a sometime L.A. private eye and repo man. He's hired by the aptly named Freddie "Fat Dog" Baker (Sasso) to check out Solly K (Gould), at whose manse Baker's kid sister Jane (Blair) is living. Solly's involved with ex-cop Cathcart (James), with whom Fritz has a longstanding beef, and the P.I. uncovers various lowlifes and a scam. Based on James Ellroy's Chandleresque detailed and dialogue-heavy first novel, which was published in 1981. **97m/C; VHS, DVD.** Michael Rooker; Brion James; Harold Gould; Selma Blair; Kevin Corrigan; Tobin Bell; Jack Conley; Brad Dourif; Will Sasso; Valerie Perrine; Barry Newman; ***D:*** Jason Freedland; ***W:*** Jason Freedland; ***C:*** Sead Muhtarevic; ***M:*** Cynthia Millar.

Brubaker **1980 (R)** A sanctimonious drama about a reform warden who risks his life to replace brutality and corruption with humanity and integrity in a state prison farm. Powerful prison drama. **131m/C; VHS, DVD, Blu-Ray.** Robert Redford; Jane Alexander; Yaphet Kotto; Murray Hamilton; David Keith; Morgan Freeman; Matt Clark; M. Emmet Walsh; Everett McGill; ***D:*** Stuart Rosenberg; ***W:*** W.D. Richter; Arthur Ross; ***M:*** Lalo Schifrin.

Bruce Almighty 1/2 **2003 (PG-13)** No, it's not a Springsteen documentary, it's an enjoyable, if slight, Jim Carrey comedy. Carrey is Bruce Nolan, a TV reporter stuck with the fluff stories and longing to be taken seriously. He gets his chance when God (Freeman) decides to turn over the reins for a day and gives Bruce his divine powers. The comedy set-pieces are well done, and Carrey can do a lot with a little (at least in his comedies), but the overall effect is less laugh-out-loud funny than fans of the earlier Carrey-Shadyac pairings would expect. Aniston's not given much to do, but Carrell and Freeman stand out among the supporting cast. **101m/C; VHS, DVD, Blu-Ray, HD-DVD.** Jim Carrey; Jennifer Aniston; Morgan Freeman; Lisa Ann Walter; Philip Baker Hall; Catherine Bell; Nora Dunn; Steve Carell; ***D:*** Tom Shadyac; ***W:*** Steve Oedekerk; Steve Koren; Mark O'Keefe; ***C:*** Dean Semler; ***M:*** John Debney.

Bruce Lee Fights Back from the Grave **1976 (R)** Bruce Lee returns from the grave to fight the Black Angel of Death with his feet and to wreak vengeance on the evil ones who brought about his untimely demise. **84m/C; VHS, DVD.** Bruce Le; Deborah Chaplin; Anthony Bronson; ***D:*** Umberto Lenzi.

Bruiser 1/2 **2000** First film from horror icon Romero in more than seven years offers a great central premise, but little else. Henry Creedlow (Flemyng) is a nice guy who gets used by everyone around him. His cheating wife, his overbearing boss, and his dishonest stock broker all push Henry around, but he never stands up for himself. That is, until the day that he wakes up to find that his face has been replaced by a blank white mask. Being "faceless" allows Henry to assert himself and get revenge. The film is boring and filled with many unlikable characters, the worst of which is Henry. The last act is simply absurd and one can't help but wonder what has happened to the once great Romero. **99m/C; VHS, DVD.** Jason Flemyng; Peter Stormare; Leslie Hope; Nina Garbiras; Tom Atkins; Jeff Monahan; ***D:*** George A. Romero; ***W:*** George A. Romero; ***C:*** Adam Swica; ***M:*** Donald Rubinstein.

Bruno **2009 (R)** Really, did Baron Cohen actually think this character was funny or was he merely being smug and cynical? After "Borat," it's time to retire this shtick of a ridiculously stupid—or in this case, flamboyant and stupid—staged character intersecting with 'real' people and situations. Over-the-top gay Austrian fashionista Bruno heads to L.A. to become a 'superstar' though, like some reality TV show participant, he lacks any talent except that of relentless self-promotion. The sexual content is constantly crude rather than provocative. Erratic, nausea-inducing, and takes a turn for the nasty. **83m/C; DVD.** Sacha Baron Cohen; ***D:*** Larry Charles; ***W:*** Sacha Baron Cohen; ***M:*** Erran Baron Cohen.

Brush with Fate **2003** Mousy teacher Cornelia (Close) is in possession of a 300-year-old Dutch painting called "Girl in Hyacinth Blue." It's possibly a Vermeer but Cornelia is afraid to find out since she may not be the legal owner. Still Cornelia would like new art professor Richard (Gibson) to give her his opinion. But the painting's history (told in flashbacks) has caused its previous owners trouble as well. Based on the novel by Susan Vreeland. **100m/C; VHS, DVD.** Glenn Close; Thomas Gibson; Ellen Burstyn; Phyllida Law; Kelly Macdonald; Patrick Bergin; ***D:*** Brent Shields; ***W:*** Richard Russo; ***C:*** Eric Van Haren Noman; ***M:*** Lawrence Shragge. **TV**

Brutal Massacre: A Comedy **2007 (R)** Horror director Harry Penderecki's (Naughton) career has been plagued by boxoffice bombs and critical disdain and he hasn't had a money-maker in years. Harry's trying to shoot his low-budget comeback film, "Brutal Massacre," but the mishaps keep increasing, leaving him teetering on the edge while every move is being recorded by reporter Bert Campbell (Butta) for a behind-the-scenes documentary. **95m/C; DVD.** David Naughton; Brian O'Halloran; Ellen Sandweiss; Ken Foree; Gunnar Hansen; Gerry Bednob; Vincent Butta; ***D:*** Stevan Mena; ***W:*** Stevan Mena; ***C:*** Brendan Flynt.

The Brutal Truth **1999 (R)** Group of high school friends get together for a 10-year reunion at a secluded mountain cabin for a weekend of fun, but then learn that one of the gang, Emily (Applegate), has committed suicide. This leads to arguments and secrets revealed. **89m/C; VHS, DVD.** Christina Applegate; Justin Lazard; Johnathon Schaech; Moon Zappa; Paul Gleason; Molly Ringwald; Leslie Horan; ***D:*** Cameron Thor.

Brute 1/2 **1997** Schweiger is doing humanitarian work in Eastern Europe when he discovers a group of orphans who are being abused by institute director Postlethwaite. So he tries to come to their rescue. Based on a true story. English and Polish with subtitles. **90m/C; DVD.** *GE PL* Til Schweiger; Pete Postlethwaite; John Hurt; Polly Walker; Ida Joblonska; ***D:*** Maciej Dejczer; ***W:*** Cezary Harasimowicz; ***C:*** Paul Prokop; Arthur Reinhart; ***M:*** Michael Lorenc.

Brute Force 1/2 **1947** Lancaster (in a star-making turn) is Joe, an inmate in an overcrowded prison lorded over by sadistic guard Munsey (Cronyn). When Munsey pushes the prisoners too far, Joe leads a daring prison break attempt. While some see this intense drama as heavy-handed (all of the inmates are victims of circumstance), the portrayals are compelling, and the story is first-rate noir. **102m/B; DVD.** Burt Lancaster; Ann Blyth; Ella Raines; Yvonne De Carlo; Hume Cronyn; Charles Bickford; Whit Bissell; Howard Duff; Jeff Corey; ***D:*** Jules Dassin; ***W:*** Richard Brooks; ***C:*** William H. Daniels; ***M:*** Miklos Rozsa.

The Brylcreem Boys **1996 (PG-13)** In September, 1941, Canadian pilot Miles Keogh (Campbell) and his crew are forced to bail out of their plane. They land in neutral southern Ireland, where they're interned in the local POW camp run by Sean O'Brien (Byrne). The camp holds both Allies and Germans—separated by only a thin wire fence. Keogh figures it's his patriotic duty to try to escape as does German officer Rudolph von Stegenbeck (Macfadyen), and problems compound when both soldiers are let out on day-release passes and, naturally, fall for the same lovely local colleen, Mattie (Butler). It's pleasant but unmemorable. **105m/C; VHS, DVD.** *GB* Billy Campbell; Angus MacFadyen; William McNamara; Gabriel Byrne; Jean Butler; Joe McGann; Oliver Tobias; Gordon John Sinclair; ***D:*** Terence Ryan; ***W:*** Terence Ryan; Jamie Brown; ***C:*** Gerry Lively; ***M:*** Richard Hartley.

BTK Killer WOOF! **2006 (R)** Nonsensical and loathsome flick purportedly about Dennis Rader, the Wichita serial killer who wasn't caught for 30 years. The initials stand for Rader's methods: Bind. Torture. Kill. For some unknown reason, hack director Lommel pads things out by including non-related animal slaughter scenes. **82m/C; DVD.** Gerard Griesbaum; ***D:*** Ulli Lommel; ***W:*** Ulli Lommel; ***C:*** Bianco Pacelli; ***M:*** Robert Walsh. **VIDEO**

Bubba Ho-Tep **2003 (R)** Elvis and JFK team up to battle the dark forces of Egypt, who threaten the residents of their East Texas convalescent home. Believable plot aside, director Coscarelli's delightfully wacky cult-concept comedy still manages to take the whole thing seriously, especially with an inspired performance from Campbell, playing it totally straight. In addition to the presumed-dead celebrities and world leaders, the small town of Mud Creek also attracts an Egyptian mummy known as Bubba Ho-Tep, who terrorizes the aged Texans. The feisty King and former Prez gleefully open a king-sized can of whoop-ass on the ancient terror. While flawed, it's still solid campy fun. Adapted from a short story by Joe Lansdale. **92m/C; VHS, DVD, Blu-Ray.** Bruce Campbell; Ossie Davis; Ella Joyce; Reggie Bannister; Bob Ivy; Larry Pennell; Heidi Marnhout; ***D:*** Don A. Coscarelli; ***W:*** Don A. Coscarelli; ***C:*** Adam Janeiro; ***M:*** Brian Tyler.

The Bubble *Ha Buah* **2006** The westernized district of Sheikin St. in Tel Aviv seems far removed from the racial and religious conflicts plaguing the area. Lulu (Wircer) shares her apartment (and life) with two gay men: Yali (Firedmann) and Noam (Knoller), who is in love with Palestinian Ashraf (Sweid). Ashraf is living and working in the city illegally and his abrupt return to his home in Nablus leads to a last act that strains credibility. Hebrew and Arabic with subtitles. **117m/C; DVD.** *IS* Ohad Knoller; Yousef (Joe) Sweid; Alon Friedmann; Daniela Wircer; Roba Blal; Shredy Jabarin; ***D:*** Eytan Fox; ***W:*** Eytan Fox; Gal Uchovsky; ***C:*** Yaron Sharf; ***M:*** Ivri Lider.

Bubble **2006 (R)** Soderbergh's uneven, low-budget experiment features a non-professional cast portraying blue-collar workers at a small Midwestern doll factory. Overweight, middle-aged Martha's (Doebereiner) life consists of caring for her sick, elderly father and fussing over young, shy co-worker Kyle (Ashley). The boring predictability of their lives is shaken by a new co-worker, outgoing single mom Rose (Wilkins), and Martha baby-sits when Rose asks Kyle out on a date. Then one of the three is murdered and there's an investigation. It's all as minimalist and banal as the lives it depicts. Besides directing, Soderbergh shot the film under the pseudonym Peter Andrews. **73m/C; DVD.** Debbie Doebereiner; Dustin Ashley; Misty Wilkins; K. Smith; ***D:*** Steven Soderbergh; ***W:*** Coleman Hough; ***C:*** Steven Soderbergh; ***M:*** Robert Pollard.

Bubble Boy **2001 (PG-13)** Disney has finally jumped on the crude and offensive humor bandwagon, with a simplistic storyline involving the journey of Jimmy (Gyllenhaal), a naive guy born with an immune system deficiency that requires him to live in a germ-free environment, as he races across the country to stop his sweetheart (Shelton) from marrying a jerk. Jimmy constructs a mobile bubble and hits the road. Along the way, the alleged jokes manage to offend Christians, Hindus, Jews, Republicans, Latinos, Asians and circus freaks while still wallowing in boner humor. That'd be almost forgivable if the "humor" was actually funny. **84m/C; VHS, DVD.** Jake Gyllenhaal; Swoosie Kurtz; Marley Shelton; Danny Trejo; John Carroll Lynch; Stephen Spinella; Verne Troyer; Dave Sheridan; Brian George; Patrick Cranshaw; Fabio; ***D:*** Blair Hayes; ***W:*** Ken Daurio; Cinco Paul; ***C:*** Jerzy Zielinski; ***M:*** John Ottman.

The Buccaneer **1958** A swashbuckling version of the adventures of pirate Jean LaFitte and his association with President Andrew Jackson during the War of 1812. Remake of Cecille B. DeMille's 1938 production. **121m/C; VHS, DVD, Blu-Ray.** Yul Brynner; Charlton Heston; Claire Bloom; Inger Stevens; Charles Boyer; Henry Hull; E.G. Marshall; Lorne Greene; ***D:*** Anthony Quinn; ***C:*** Loyal Griggs; ***M:*** Elmer Bernstein.

The Buccaneers **1995** Lavish adaptation of the Edith Wharton novel follows the adventures of four American girls in 1870s society. Nouveaux riche, the young ladies are unable to crack New York snobbery and, after vivacious Brazilian Conchita (Sorvino) manages to snag Lord Richard (Vibert), the others are encouraged by English governess Laura Testvalley (Lunghi) to try their luck in London. There, Virginia (Elliott), sister Nan (Gugino), their friend Lizzy (Kihlstedt), and Conchita all find hope and heartbreak among the English aristocracy. Wharton's novel was unfinished at her death and, though she left story notes, scripter Wadey concedes to changes. Made for TV. **288m/C; VHS, DVD.** *GB* Carla Gugino; Mira Sorvino; Alison Elliott; Rya Kihlstedt; Cherie Lunghi; Connie Booth; Mark Tandy; Ronan Vibert; Jenny Agutter; Richard Huw; Greg Wise; James Frain; Michael Kitchen; Sheila Hancock; Rosemary Leach; Elizabeth Ashley; Conchata Ferrell; Peter Michael Goetz; James Rebhorn; E. Katherine Kerr; ***D:*** Philip Saville; ***W:*** Maggie Wadey; ***C:*** Maggie Wadey; ***M:*** Colin Towns. **TV**

Buccaneer's Girl 1/2 **1950** Charming swashbuckler. Pirate Frederick Baptiste (Friend) only attacks the ships of evil Narbonne (Douglas) as revenge for his father's death. During one of his raids, New Orleans entertainer Deborah (De Carlo) stows away and falls for the sea-faring Robin Hood. However, hoping to marry into money, Deborah sets her sights on an aristocrat, only to figure out that Baptiste has been leading a double life. **77m/C; DVD.** Yvonne De Carlo; Philip Friend; Robert Douglas; Elsa Lanchester; Andrea King; Norman Lloyd; Jay C. Flippen; ***D:*** Fred de Cordova; ***W:*** Joseph Hoffman; Harold Shumate; ***C:*** Russell Metty; ***M:*** Walter Scharf.

Buchanan Rides Alone 1/2 **1958** Loner Buchanan (Scott) befriends young Mexican Juan (Rojas) in a California border town run by the bickering Agry family. Juan kills a bullying Agry in self-defense, but he and Buchanan both wind up in the pokey. However, Buchanan manages to pit the Agrys against each other. **89m/C; DVD.** Randolph Scott; Craig Stevens; Barry Kelley; Peter Whitney; Manuel Rojas; Tol Avery; L.Q. Jones; ***D:*** Budd Boetticher; ***W:*** Charles Land; ***C:*** Lucien Ballard.

Buck **2011 (PG)** An engrossing look at Buck Brannaman, the real man behind (and consultant for) "The Horse Whisperer" as played by Robert Redford in the 1998 film (adapted from Nicholas Evans' 1996 novel). Overcoming the physical abuse inflicted upon him by his father as a child, Buck becomes an inspirational, unassuming, and tenderhearted horseman who gently but firmly trains his animals. Rookie director Meehl tags along with Buck as he crosses the country with the arduous task of helping both troubled horses and their often equally troubled owners. **88m/C; On Demand.** Buck Brannaman; Robert Redford; ***D:*** Cindy Meehl; ***C:*** Luke Geissbuhler; Guy Mossman; ***M:*** David Robbins.

Buck and the Preacher 1/2 **1972 (PG)** A trail guide and a con man preacher join forces to help a wagon train of former slaves who are seeking to homestead out West. Poitier's debut as a director. **102m/C; VHS, DVD.** Sidney Poitier; Harry Belafonte; Ruby Dee; Cameron Mitchell; Denny Miller; ***D:*** Sidney Poitier.

Buck Benny Rides Again 1/2 **1940** Radio performer Benny (playing himself) boasts he's a regular cowboy type with a ranch in Nevada—claims challenged by rival Fred Allen. So Benny is forced to travel west, where he makes a fool of himself before accidentally capturing two outlaws while romancing singer Joan (Drew). Rochester is there to assist as well as others from the Benny program. **82m/B; DVD.** Jack Benny; Ellen Drew; Virginia Dale; Eddie Anderson; Andy Devine; Phil Harris; Dennis Day; ***D:*** Mark Sandrich; ***W:*** Edmund Beloin; William Morrow; ***C:*** Charles Lang.

Buck Privates 1/2 *Rookies* **1941** Abbott and Costello star as two dim-witted tie salesmen, running from the law, who become buck privates during WWII. The duo's first great success, and the film that established the formula for each subsequent film. **84m/B; VHS, DVD, Blu-Ray.** Bud Abbott; Lou Costello; Shemp Howard; Lee Bowman; Alan Curtis; Andrews Sisters; ***D:*** Arthur Lubin; ***W:*** Arthur T. Horman; John Grant; ***C:*** Milton Krasner; ***M:*** Charles Previn.

Buck Privates Come Home *Rookies Come Home* **1947** Abbott and Costello return to their "Buck Privates" roles as two soldiers trying to adjust to civilian life after the war. They also try to help a French girl sneak into the United States. Funny antics culminate into a wild chase scene. **77m/B; VHS, DVD.** Bud Abbott; Lou Costello; Tom Brown; Joan Shawlee; Nat Pendleton; Beverly Simmons; Don Beddoe; Don Porter; Donald MacBride; ***D:*** Charles T. Barton; ***W:*** John Grant; Frederic Rinaldo; Robert Lees; ***C:*** Charles Van Enger; ***M:*** Walter Schumann.

Buck Rogers Conquers the Universe **1939** The story of Buck Rogers, written by Phil Nolan in 1928, was the first science-fiction story done in the modern superhero space genre. Many of the "inventions" seen in this movie have actually come into existence—spaceships, ray guns (lasers), anti-gravity belts—a testament to Nolan's almost psychic farsightedness. **91m/B; VHS, DVD.** Buster Crabbe; Constance Moore; Jackie Moran; ***D:*** Ford Beebe; Saul Goodkind.

Buck Rogers in the 25th Century **1979 (PG)** An American astronaut, preserved in space for 500 years, is brought back to life by a passing Draconian flagship. Outer space adventures begin when he is accused of being a spy from Earth. Based on the classic movie serial. TV movie that began the popular series. Additional series episodes are available. **90m/C; VHS, DVD.** Gil Gerard; Pamela Hensley; Erin Gray; Henry Silva; ***V:*** Mel Blanc; ***D:*** Daniel Haller. **TV**

The Bucket List 1/2 **2007 (PG-13)** Yes, that's as in "kick the bucket." Cliched sitcom finds cancer patients Edward Cole (Nicholson) and Carter Chambers (Freeman) getting the bad news that their time is very limited. Since Edward is a self-satisfied gazillionaire estranged from his family, he decides to indulge his every last whim and takes fellow patient Carter, a working-class married father, on their own buddy road trip 'round the world. Nicholson's crazy, Freeman's serious, and the scenery seems to be all computer-generated. **97m/C; DVD, Blu-Ray.** Jack Nicholson; Morgan Freeman; Sean P. Hayes; Beverly Todd; Alfonso Freeman; Rowena King; Rob Morrow; ***D:*** Rob Reiner; ***W:*** Justin Zackham; ***C:*** John Schwartzman; ***M:*** Marc Shaiman.

A Bucket of Blood **1959** Cult favorite Dick Miller stars as a sculptor with a peculiar "talent" for lifelike artwork. Corman fans will see thematic similarities to his subsequent work, "Little Shop of Horrors" (1960). "Bucket of Blood" was made in just five days, while "Little Shop of Horrors" was made in a record breaking two days. Corman horror/spoof noted for its excellent beatnik atmosphere. **66m/B; VHS, DVD, Blu-Ray.** Dick Miller; Barboura Morris; Antony Carbone; Julian Burton; Ed Nelson; Bert Convy; Judy Bamber; John Brinkley; Myrtle Domerel; John Herman Shaner; Bruno VeSota; ***D:*** Roger Corman; ***W:*** Charles B. Griffith; ***C:*** John Marquette; ***M:*** Fred Katz.

Buckskin 1/2 **1968** Slowmoving western about a marshall protecting townspeople from a greedy, land-grabbing cattle baron. **98m/C; VHS, Streaming.** Barry Sullivan; Wendell Corey; Joan Caulfield; Lon Chaney, Jr.; John Russell; Barbara Hale; Barton MacLane; Bill Williams; ***D:*** Michael D. Moore.

Buckskin Frontier 1/2 **1943** Story is built around Western railroad construction and cattle empires in the 1860s. Cobb tries to stop the railroad from coming through by hiring Jory to do his dirty work. **75m/B; VHS, DVD.** Richard Dix; Jane Wyatt; Lee J. Cobb; Albert Dekker; Victor Jory; Lola Lane; Max Baer, Sr.; ***D:*** Lesley Selander.

Bucktown 1/2 **1975 (R)** A black man who reopens his murdered brother's bar fights off police corruption and racism in a Southern town. **95m/C; VHS, DVD, Blu-Ray.** Fred Williamson; Pam Grier; Bernie Hamilton; Thalmus Rasulala; Art Lund; Robert (Skip) Burton; Carl Weathers; ***D:*** Arthur Marks; ***W:*** Bob Ellison; ***C:*** Robert Birchall; ***M:*** Johnny Pate.

Bucky Larson: Born to Be a Star WOOF! *Born to Be a Star* **2011 (R)** The most notable achievement of Swardson's first starring vehicle may be that it can now be referenced as one of the worst movies ever made?"Well, at least it wasn't as bad as Bucky Larson!" Bucky's an exaggerated hick who learns that his parents were once porn stars, so he takes off for Hollywood to pursue the family "business." A rare film that's so horrendous it seems purposeful given that it's hard to believe any producers or writers (Swardson, Sandler, and Covert) thought the crude humor worked somehow. Even the decent work of Ricci and Johnson can't overcome this atrocity. **97m/C; DVD, Blu-Ray.** Nick Swardson; Stephen Dorff; Christina Ricci; Edward Herrmann; Don Johnson; Ido Mosseri; Kevin Nealon; Miriam Flynn; ***D:*** Tom Brady; ***W:*** Nick Swardson; Adam Sandler; Allen Covert; ***C:*** Michael Barrett; ***M:*** Waddy Wachtel.

The Buddha of Suburbia **1992** Satire set in late '70s suburban London follows the coming of age adventures of Karim (Andrews), the handsome son of an Indian father and English mother. His gleeful father Haroon (Seth) exploits the vogue for eastern philosophies he knows nothing about with lectures to the upper-middle classes while he carries on with devotee Eva (Fleetwood). When his mother finds out, Karim and his father move into central London with Eva, where Karim decides to take up acting in fringe theatre and sex while his friend, Eva's son Charlie (Mackintosh), experiments with the punk music scene. TV miniseries adapted by Kureishi from his novel. **220m/C; VHS, DVD.** *GB* Naveen Andrews; Roshan Seth; Susan Fleetwood; Steven Mackintosh; Brenda Blethyn; John McEnery; Janet Dale; David Bamber; Donald (Don) Sumpter; Jemma Redgrave; David Bradley; ***D:*** Roger Michell; ***W:*** Hanif Kureishi; Roger Michell; ***C:*** John McGlashan; ***M:*** David Bowie. **TV**

Buddy 1/2 **1997 (PG)** Animals run amok in the Lintz household. Mother hen Gertrude Lintz (Russo) raises just about everything from mischievous chimps to impressionable parrots on her estate. A baby gorilla (named Buddy, short for Budha) becomes part of the family, but as he grows in size, so does the difficulty in caring for him. Amiable tale of one woman's motherly bond with a gorilla includes convincing performances by Russo and an animatronic gorilla courtesy of Jim Henson's Creature Shop. Well-paced and very touching at moments, children will definitely enjoy the zany animal antics, and adults should be moved by the unusual relationship. Based on the book by Lintz. **84m/C; VHS, DVD.** Rene Russo; Robbie Coltrane; Irma P. Hall; Alan Cumming; Paul (Pee-wee Herman) Reubens; ***D:*** Caroline Thompson; ***W:*** Caroline Thompson; ***C:*** Steve Mason; ***M:*** Elmer Bernstein.

Buddy Boy 1/2 **1999 (R)** Isolated by the need to care for his ailing mother (Tyrell), shy Francis (Gillen) begins a voyeuristic relationship with his sexy neighbor (Seigner). Strange but captivating film provides some gothic creepiness as well as commentary on the toll of enforced isolation. **105m/C; DVD.** Aidan Gillen; Emmanuelle Seigner; Susan Tyrrell; Mark Boone, Jr.; Hector Elias; Harry Groener; ***D:*** Mark Hanlon; ***W:*** Mark Hanlon; ***C:*** Hubert Taczanowski; ***M:*** Graeme Revell; Brian Eno; Michael Brook.

The Buddy Holly Story 1/2 **1978 (PG)** An acclaimed biography of the famed 1950s pop star, spanning the years from his meteoric career's beginnings in Lubbock to his tragic early death in the now famous plane crash of February 3, 1959. Busey performs Holly's hits himself. **113m/C; VHS, DVD, Blu-Ray.** Gary Busey; Don Stroud; Charles Martin Smith; Conrad Janis; William Jordan; Albert "Poppy" Popwell; ***D:*** Steve Rash; ***W:*** Robert Gittler; ***C:*** Stevan Larner; ***M:*** Joe Renzetti. Oscars '78: Orig. Song Score and/or Adapt.; Natl. Soc. Film Critics '78: Actor (Busey).

Buena Vista Social Club **1999 (G)** American musician Ry Cooder assembled a number of aging Cuban musicians and singers, informally known as the Buena Vista Social Club, to record an album in Havana. The success of that 1997 venture led director Wenders to record this documentary as the group reunites for a concert tour that culminates in a 1998 performance at Carnegie Hall. **106m/C; VHS, DVD, Blu-Ray.** Ry Cooder; ***D:*** Wim Wenders. L.A. Film Critics '99: Feature Doc.; Natl. Bd. of Review '99: Feature Doc.; N.Y. Film Critics '99: Feature Doc.; Natl. Soc. Film Critics '99: Feature Doc.

Buffalo Bill **1944** A light, fictionalized account of the life and career of Bill Cody, from frontier hunter to showman. **89m/C; VHS, DVD.** Joel McCrea; Maureen O'Hara; Linda Darnell; Thomas Mitchell; Edgar Buchanan; Anthony Quinn; Moroni Olsen; Sidney Blackmer; ***D:*** William A. Wellman; ***C:*** Leon Shamroy.

Buffalo Bill & the Indians *Sitting Bull's History Lesson* **1976 (PG)** A perennially underrated Robert Altman historical pastiche, portraying the famous Wild West character as a charlatan and shameless exemplar of encroaching imperialism. Great all-star cast amid Altman's signature mise-en-scene chaos. **135m/C; VHS, DVD, Blu-Ray.** Paul Newman; Geraldine Chaplin; Joel Grey; Will Sampson; Harvey Keitel; Burt Lancaster; Kevin McCarthy; ***D:*** Robert Altman; ***W:*** Robert Altman; Alan Rudolph; ***M:*** Richard Baskin.

Buffalo Bill Rides Again 1/2 **1947** With an Indian uprising on the horizon, Buffalo Bill is called in. Mr. Bill finds land swindlers pitting natives against ranchers, but there's precious little action or interest here. **68m/C; VHS, DVD.** Richard Arlen; Jennifer Holt; Edward Cassidy; Edmund Cobb; Charles Stevens; ***D:*** Bernard B. Ray; ***W:*** Barney A. Sarecky; ***C:*** Robert E. Cline.

Buffalo Girls 1/2 **1995** Western saga, set in the 1870s, tells of the lifelong friendship between hard-drinking, hard-living Calamity Jane (Huston—who's not exactly any plain Jane) and buxom, soft-hearted madam Dora DuFran (Griffith). Dora's in love (but refuses to marry) rancher Teddy Blue (Byrne) while Calamity has a daughter by Wild Bill Hickok (Elliott) that she gives up for adoption. There's lots of rambling and commiserating over the changing and civilizing of the west and various man trouble. Based on the novel by Larry McMurty; originally a two-part TV miniseries. **180m/C; VHS, DVD.** Anjelica Huston; Melanie Griffith; Gabriel Byrne; Peter Coyote; Jack Palance; Sam Elliott; Reba McEntire; Floyd "Red Crow" Westerman; Tracey Walter; Russell Means; Charlaine Woodard; John Diehl; Liev Schreiber; Andrew Bicknell; Kathryn Witt; ***D:*** Rod Hardy; ***W:*** Cynthia Whitcomb; ***C:*** David Connell; ***M:*** Lee Holdridge.

Buffalo Jump *Getting Married in Buffalo Jump* **1990** An independent woman, working as a lounge singer in Toronto, returns to her home in Alberta when her father dies. To her surprise he has left her the family ranch and, to the surprise of everyone else, she decides to stay and run it. She hires a good-looking local man to help her out and they both discover that they want more than a working relationship. However, the fireworks really start when he proposes a marriage of convenience. Engaging performances and beautiful scenery help raise this romantic tale of opposites above the average. **97m/C; VHS, DVD.** *CA* Wendy Crewson; Paul Gross; Marion Gilsenan; Kyra Harper; Victoria Snow; ***D:*** Eric Till.

Buffalo 66 **1997** Billy Brown (Gallo) is a loser of epic proportions. He's named after the Buffalo Bills, notorious losers of Super Bowls. After he loses $10,000 on one of those Super Bowls, he turns to a life of crime and promptly lands in prison. He gets out of jail as a man with a mission. Stumbling into a dance studio, Billy kidnaps the nubile Layla (Ricci) and forces her to pose as his wife for a visit to his parents. He had explained his five-year absence to them by saying that he was working for the CIA overseas with his new bride. His father Jimmy (Gazzara), a bitter ex-lounge singer, barely hides his disdain for Billy, and mother Janet (Huston) is too obsessed with the Bills to interact with him. They both like Layla instantly, and she seems to take unexpected glee in playing her part. Former artist and rock musician Gallo also directed, co-wrote and composed the music for the film. **112m/C; VHS, DVD, Blu-Ray.** Vincent Gallo; Christina Ricci; Anjelica Huston; Ben Gazzara; Kevin Corrigan; Mickey Rourke; Rosanna Arquette; Jan-Michael Vincent; ***D:*** Vincent Gallo; ***W:*** Vincent Gallo; Alison Bagnall; ***C:*** Lance Acord; ***M:*** Vincent Gallo. Natl. Bd. of Review '98: Support. Actress (Ricci).

Buffalo Soldiers **1997** Post-Civil War western concerns the all-black Cavalry troops, created by Congress in 1866 to patrol the west. They received their nickname from the Indians, who thought the black soldiers on horseback looked like buffalo. A former slave and by-the-book Army man, Sgt. Washington Wyatt (Glover) leads the chase for Apache warrior Victorio (Lowe) across the New Mexico Territory while trying tp deal with the common degradation suffered by his troops at the hands of white officers. Lots of cruelty and explicit violence. **120m/C; VHS, DVD.** Danny Glover; Carl Lumbly; Bob Gunton; Tom Bower; Harrison Lowe; Glynn Turman; Michael Warren; Mykelti Williamson; Timothy Busfield; Gabriel Casseus; ***D:*** Charles Haid; ***W:*** Frank Military; Susan Rhinehart; ***C:*** William Wages; ***M:*** Joel McNeely. **CABLE**

Buffalo Soldiers 1/2 **2001 (R)** Darkly satiric look at the military revolves around a supply unit of an American Army base in 1989 Germany. Leader of the pack is the bored, amoral Elwood (Phoenix) who gets his kicks and a few extra bucks by dabbling in the black market, dealing in heroin and illegal weapons, and other equally illicit activities. Soon, the newly prosperous Elwood is basically running things at the base until a new Top Sergeant (Glenn) cracks down. Elwood retaliates by dating Sarge's daughter (Paquin) but finds he's actually falling for her. Premiered at the Toronto Film Festival in 2001, then waited for a more appropriate release date, which never actually came (it's not exactly complimentary to the military). Based on a novel by Robert O'Connor. **98m/C; VHS, DVD.** *US GB GE* Joaquin Rafael (Leaf) Phoenix; Scott Glenn; Anna Paquin; Ed Harris; Leon Robinson; Dean Stockwell; Elizabeth McGovern; Gabriel Mann; Shiek Mahmud-Bey; Michael Peña; Glenn Fitzgerald; Brian Delate; Jimmie Ray Weeks; ***D:*** Gregor Jordan; ***W:*** Gregor Jordan; Eric Weiss; Nora MacCoby; ***C:*** Oliver Stapleton; ***M:*** David Holmes.

Buffaloed 1/2 **2020** After serving time in prison for scalping counterfeit Buffalo Bills tickets, hustler Peg Dahl (Deutch) returns to her native Buffalo and lives with her mother (Greer). Looking for a new job, Peg finds her skills are useful in the shady debt collection industry. Working for an agency run by the sleazy Wizz (Courtney), Peg not only learns the ropes but bests her coworkers, all men, at their own game. The situation grows more complicated when she founds her own debt collecting company. The comedy showcases Deutch's fascinating take on Peg and the screenwriter's love letter to his native upstate New York city. **95m/C; DVD, Blu-Ray.** Zoey Deutch; Jai Courtney; Judy Greer; Jermaine Fowler; Noah Reid; ***D:*** Tanya Wexler; ***W:*** Brian Sacca; ***C:*** Guy Godfree; ***M:*** Matthew Margeson.

Buffet Froid 1/2 **1979** Surreal black comedy about a group of bungling murderers. First rate acting and directing makes this film a hilarious treat. From the director of "Menage." In French with English subtitles. **95m/C; VHS, DVD, Blu-Ray.** *FR* Gerard Depardieu; Bernard Blier; Jean Carmet; Genevieve Page; Denise Gence; Carole Bouquet; Jean Benguigui; Michel Serrault; ***D:*** Bertrand Blier; ***W:*** Bertrand Blier; ***C:*** Jean Penzer; ***M:*** Philippe Sarde. Cesar '80: Writing.

Buffy the Vampire Slayer **1992 (PG-13)** Funny, near-camp teen genre spoof. Buffy is a typical mall gal concerned with shopping and cheerleading, until the mysterious Sutherland proclaims it her destiny to slay the vampires who have suddenly infested Los Angeles. Like, really. Buffy requires some convincing, but eventually takes up the challenge, fighting off the vamps and their seductive leader Hauer, aided by perpetual guy-in-distress Perry. "Pee-wee" Reubens is unrecognizable and terribly amusing as the vampire king's sinister henchman, engaging in one of the longer death scenes of film history. Check out Cassandra (Wagner), Natalie Wood's daughter. **98m/C; VHS, DVD, Blu-Ray.** Kristy Swanson; Donald Sutherland; Luke Perry; Paul (Pee-wee Herman) Reubens; Rutger Hauer; Michele Abrams; Randall Batinkoff; Hilary Swank; Paris Vaughan; David Arquette; Candy Clark; Natasha Gregson Wagner; Stephen (Steve) Root; Ben Affleck; Mark DeCarlo; Thomas Jane; Ricki Lake; ***D:*** Fran Rubel Kuzui; ***W:*** Joss Whedon; ***C:*** James Hayman; ***M:*** Carter Burwell.

Bug WOOF! **1975 (PG)** The city of Riverside is threatened with destruction after a massive earth tremor unleashes a superrace of ten-inch mega-cockroaches that belch fire, eat raw meat, and are virtually impervious to Raid. Produced by gimmick-king William Castle, who wanted to install windshield wiper-like devices under theatre seats that would brush against the patrons' feet as the cockroaches crawled across the screen; unfortunately, the idea was squashed flat. **100m/C; VHS, DVD, Blu-Ray.** Bradford Dillman; Joanna Miles; Richard Gilliland; Jamie Smith-Jackson; Alan Fudge; Jesse Vint; Patty McCormack; Brendan Dillon, Jr.; Frederic Downs; William Castle; ***D:*** Jeannot Szwarc; ***W:*** William Castle; Thomas Page; ***C:*** Michel Hugo; ***M:*** Charles Fox.

Bug 🦴🦴 **2006 (R)** Girl (Judd) meets boy (Shannon). Girl and boy have one night stand. Boy goes insane and takes girl with him (maybe). Thriller based on a play and marketed as a horror film because its director is famous for "The Exorcist." If you like dark psychological movies shot almost entirely in one room where people talk and slowly lose their minds, this film is for you. If you were expecting a gory traditional horror movie, you will likely be disappointed. But you'll probably be somewhat happy that Ashley Judd briefly gets naked. **101m/C; DVD.** Ashley Judd; Michael Shannon; Harry Connick, Jr.; Lynn Collins; Brian F. O'Byrne; ***D:*** William Friedkin; ***W:*** Tracy Letts; ***C:*** Michael Grady; ***M:*** Brian Tyler.

Bug Buster 🦴🦴 **1999 (R)** The Griffins, dad (Kopell), mom (Lockhart) and daughter Shannon (Heigl) move to scenic Mountainview to flee the stress of city life. But they didn't bargain for the giant creature "unknown to science" that's attacking people and leaving giant bug larvae in 'em. Mutant insects overrun the town, leaving the survivors one last hope, in the form of ex-military man-turned-uberexterminator General George (Quaid). Plenty of gore and over-the-top acting, plus Scotty and Mr. Sulu, give this one late-night cult potential. **93m/C; VHS, DVD.** Randy Quaid; Katherine Heigl; Meredith Salenger; Bernie Kopell; Anne Lockhart; George Takei; James Doohan; Ty O'Neal; Julie Brown; Brenda Doumani; David Lipper; ***D:*** Lorenzo Doumani; ***W:*** Malick Khoury; ***C:*** Hanania Baer; ***M:*** Sidney James.

Bugged! 🦴 **1996 (PG-13)** Flesh-eating insects attack a beautiful homemaker and a group of bumbling exterminators are her only hope. **90m/C; VHS, DVD.** Ronald K. Armstrong; Priscilla Basque; Jeff Lee; Derek C. Johnson; Billy Graham; ***D:*** Ronald K. Armstrong; ***W:*** Ronald K. Armstrong; ***C:*** S. Torriano Berry; ***M:*** Boris Elkis.

Bugs 🦴 **2003** A cop chasing a bad guy through an unfinished subway tunnel is eaten by a huge scorpion-like prehistoric insect whose nest he disturbed. FBI agent Matt Pollack (Sabato Jr.) and insect expert Emily Foster (Everhart) investigate, but they (along with a SWAT team) are soon trapped in the bug-infested tunnel. A Sci-Fi Channel original. **85m/C; DVD.** Antonio Sabato, Jr.; Angie Everhart; R.H. Thomson; Karl Pruner; Duane Murray; Romano Orzari; ***D:*** Joseph Conti; ***W:*** Robinson Young; Patrick Doody; Chris Valenziano; ***C:*** Richard Wincenty; ***M:*** William T. Stromberg. **CABLE**

A Bug's Life 🦴🦴🦴 **1998 (G)** Computer animated feature by Pixar, the makers of "Toy Story," takes a cutesy look into the world of insects. Flik (Foley) is an ant who must help defend his colony after he messes up a tribute to a bullying group of grasshoppers led by Hopper (Spacey). He recruits a crew of misfits from a flea circus, including a male ladybug with gender issues (Leary), a prissy stick bug (Pierce), and an obese caterpillar (Ranft). Together they form a plan to keep the grasshoppers away, but still must confront Hopper in order to ensure lasting peace. Amazing animation, from the blades of grass down to the facial expressions of the bugs, along with dozens of sight gags keep this family feature flying. Competed with fellow computer animated insect feature "Antz" on its release. **94m/C; VHS, DVD, Blu-Ray.** ***V:*** Dave Foley; Kevin Spacey; Julia Louis-Dreyfus; Phyllis Diller; Richard Kind; David Hyde Pierce; Joe Ranft; Denis Leary; Jonathan Harris; Madeline Kahn; Bonnie Hunt; Michael McShane; John Ratzenberger; Brad Garrett; Roddy McDowall; Edie McClurg; Hayden Panettiere; Alex Rocco; David Ossman; ***D:*** John Lasseter; Andrew Stanton; ***W:*** Joe Ranft; Donald McEnery; Bob Shaw; Andrew Stanton; ***C:*** Sharon Calahan; ***M:*** Randy Newman.

Bugsy 🦴🦴🦴 1/2 **1991 (R)** Beatty is Benjamin "Bugsy" Siegel, the 40s gangster who built the Flamingo Hotel in Las Vegas when it was still a virtual desert, before it became a gambling mecca. Bening is perfect as Bugsy's moll, Virginia Hill, who inspired him to carry out his dream of building the Flamingo (which was her nickname). Beatty and Bening heat up the screen and their off-screen relationship was no different. Fans anticipated their seemingly imminent marriage almost as much as the release of this movie. Almost nothing mars this film which Toback adapted from a novel by Dean Jennings, "We Only Kill Each Other: The Life and Bad Times of Bugsy Siegel." **135m/C; VHS, DVD.** Warren Beatty; Annette Bening; Harvey Keitel; Ben Kingsley; Elliott Gould; Joe Mantegna; Richard Sarafian; Bebe Neuwirth; Wendy Phillips; Robert Beltran; Bill Graham; Lewis Van Bergen; Debrah Farentino; ***D:*** Barry Levinson; ***W:*** James Toback; ***C:*** Allen Daviau; ***M:*** Ennio Morricone. Oscars '91: Art Dir./Set Dec., Costume Des.; Golden Globes '92: Film--Drama; L.A. Film Critics '91: Director (Levinson), Film, Screenplay; Natl. Bd. of Review '91: Actor (Beatty).

Bugsy Malone 🦴🦴 1/2 **1976 (G)** Delightful musical features an all-children's cast highlighting this spoof of 1930s' gangster movies. **94m/C; VHS, DVD.** *GB* Jodie Foster; Scott Baio; Florrie Augger; John Cassisi; Martin Lev; ***D:*** Alan Parker; ***W:*** Alan Parker; ***C:*** Peter Biziou; ***M:*** Paul Williams. British Acad. '76: Screenplay.

Bull Durham 🦴🦴🦴 1/2 **1988 (R)** Lovable American romantic comedy, dealing with a very minor minor-league team and three of its current constituents: aging baseball groupie Annie Savoy (Sarandon) who beds one player each season; a cocky, foolish new pitcher, Ebby Calvin "Nuke" LaLoosh (Robbins); and older, weary catcher Crash Davis (Costner), who's brought in to wise the rookie up. The scene in which Annie tries poetry out on the banal rookie (who has more earthly pleasures in mind) is a hoot. Highly acclaimed, the film sears with Sarandon and Costner's love scenes and some clever dialogue. **107m/C; VHS, DVD, Blu-Ray.** Kevin Costner; Susan Sarandon; Tim Robbins; Trey Wilson; Robert Wuhl; Jenny Robertson; ***D:*** Ron Shelton; ***W:*** Ron Shelton; ***C:*** Bobby Byrne; ***M:*** Michael Convertino. L.A. Film Critics '88: Screenplay; N.Y. Film Critics '88: Screenplay; Natl. Soc. Film Critics '88: Screenplay; Writers Guild '88: Orig. Screenplay.

Bulldance 🦴 *Forbidden Son* **1988** At a gymnastic school in Crete, a girl's obsession with Greek mythological ritual leads to murder. **105m/C; VHS, DVD.** Lauren Hutton; Cliff DeYoung; Renee Estevez; ***D:*** Zelda Barron.

Bulldog Drummond Comes Back 🦴🦴 **1937** Drummond, aided by Colonel Nielson, rescues his fiancee from the hands of desperate kidnappers. **119m/B; VHS, DVD.** John Howard; John Barrymore; Louise Campbell; Reginald Denny; Guy Standing; ***D:*** Louis King.

Bulldog Drummond Escapes 🦴🦴 **1937** Drummond, aided by his side-kick and valet, rescues a beautiful girl from spies. He then falls in love with her. **67m/B; VHS, DVD.** Ray Milland; Heather Angel; Reginald Denny; Guy Standing; Porter Hall; E.E. Clive; ***D:*** James Hogan; ***W:*** Edward T. Lowe; ***C:*** Victor Milner.

Bulldog Drummond's Bride 🦴🦴 **1939** Ace detective Bulldog Drummond has to interrupt his honeymoon in order to pursue a gang of bank robbers across France and England. The last of the Bulldog Drummond film series. **69m/B; VHS, DVD.** John Howard; Heather Angel; H.B. Warner; E.E. Clive; Reginald Denny; Eduardo Ciannelli; Elizabeth Patterson; John Sutton; ***D:*** James Hogan; ***W:*** Garnett Weston; ***C:*** Harry Fischbeck.

Bulldog Drummond's Peril 🦴🦴 **1938** Murder and robbery drag the adventurous Drummond away from his wedding and he pursues the villains until they are behind bars. One in the film series. **77m/B; VHS, DVD.** John Barrymore; John Howard; Louise Campbell; Reginald Denny; E.E. Clive; Porter Hall; ***D:*** James Hogan.

Bullet 🦴 1/2 **1994 (R)** Butch (Rourke) gets released from prison and immediately returns to his old drug and burglary ways on New York's mean streets. And he's got a score to settle with crazy drug kingpin Tank (Shakur). Has little to recommend it, except to those who like violence, with lackluster performances and a dull script. **96m/C; VHS, DVD.** Mickey Rourke; Tupac Shakur; Ted Levine; Adrien Brody; John Enos; ***D:*** Julien Temple; ***W:*** Bruce Rubenstein; ***C:*** Crescenzo G.P. Notarile.

Bullet Down Under 🦴 *Signal One* **1994 (R)** Cop Atkins joins Australian police and gets involved with a crime syndicate and a female killer. **95m/C; VHS, DVD.** *AU* Christopher Atkins; Mark "Jacko" Jackson; Virginia Hey; ***W:*** Karl Schiffman; ***C:*** Martin McGrath; ***M:*** Art Phillips.

A Bullet for Joey 🦴 1/2 **1955** Fifties red scare flick. American physicist Carl Macklin (Dolenz) is teaching in Montreal. Gangster Joey Victor (Raft) has been hired to kidnap Macklin, unaware that the commies are behind the snatch. A couple of murders bring Inspector Raoul Leduc (Robinson) onto the scene and he soon tags Joey, who turns patriotic when he discovers he's being used by reds. **85m/B; DVD, Blu-Ray.** Edward G. Robinson; George Raft; Peter Van Eyck; Joseph (Joe) Vitale; George Dolenz; Audrey Trotter; Bill Bryant; John Cliff; ***D:*** Lewis Allen; ***W:*** Daniel Mainwaring; A(lbert) I(saac) Bezzerides; ***C:*** Harry Neumann; ***M:*** Harry Sukman.

Bullet for Sandoval 🦴🦴 **1970 (PG)** An ex-Confederate renegade loots and pillages the north Mexican countryside on his way to murder the grandfather of the woman he loves. **96m/C; VHS, DVD.** *SP IT* Ernest Borgnine; George Hilton; ***D:*** Julio Buchs.

A Bullet for the General 🦴 *Quien Sabe?* **1968** An American mercenary joins with rebel forces during the Mexican Revolution. **95m/C; VHS, DVD, Blu-Ray.** *IT* Martine Beswick; Lou Castel; Gian Marie Volonte; Klaus Kinski; ***D:*** Damiano Damiani; ***W:*** Salvatore Laurani; Franco Solinas; ***C:*** Antonio Secchi; ***M:*** Luis Bacalov.

Bullet Head 🦴🦴 **2017 (R)** A crime thriller about heist gone bad. After failing to complete a robbery of a big box store, Gage (Culkin), Stacy (Brody), and Walker (Malkovich) crash their getaway vehicle in an empty industrial complex. Hiding out in a warehouse, the trio finds a vicious, wounded fighting dog, De Niro, that has been left for dead. Escaping him, the trio tells stories about previous jobs while dodging Mr. Blue (Banderas), who has come for the loot left from previous dog fights, and a policeman investing a break-in. The labored plot does not give the film's veteran cast enough to work with. **93m/C; DVD, Blu-Ray.** Adrien Brody; John Malkovich; Antonio Banderas; Rory Culkin; Alexandra Dinu; ***D:*** Paul Solet; ***W:*** Paul Solet; ***C:*** Zoran Popovic; ***M:*** Austin Wintory.

A Bullet in the Head 🦴🦴🦴 *Die Xue Jie Tou* **1990** Violent (no surprise there) tale of friendship finds Frank (Cheung), Ben (Leung), and Paul (Lee) heading out of 1967 Hong Kong for Saigon, where they hope to make money selling contraband goods in the city. They wind up on the wrong side of the Vietnamese Army, steal a fortune in gold from a local crime lord, and end up the prisoners of the Viet Cong. There's betrayal and death and a final moral reckoning and—did we mention lots and lots of (over-the-top) violence? Chinese with subtitles. **85m/C; VHS, DVD.** *CH* Tony Leung Chiu-Wai; Jacky Cheung; Waise Lee; Simon Yam; Fennie Yuen; Yolinda Yam; John Woo; ***D:*** John Woo; ***W:*** Janet Chun; Patrick Leung; John Woo; ***C:*** Wilson Chan; Ardy Lam; Chai Kittikum Som; Wing-Hung Wong; ***M:*** Romeo Diaz; James Wong.

A Bullet Is Waiting 🦴🦴 **1954** A diligent sheriff finally catches his man only to be trapped in a blinding snowstorm with the hardened criminal. **83m/C; VHS, DVD.** Jean Simmons; Rory Calhoun; Stephen McNally; Brian Aherne; ***D:*** John Farrow.

Bullet to the Head 🦴🦴 **2012 (R)** Stallone's comeback sans his "Expendables" crew proves as further evidence to why the '80s star needs a comeback in the first place. Stuck in a persona long ago deemed irrelevant by modern audiences, Sly is in full beefcake mode as New Orleans hitman Jimmy Bobo, a tough guy forced to team with D.C. cop Taylor Kwon (Kang) to take down crime lord Morel (Akkinuoye-Agbaje). Director Hill--an '80s icon himself--returns to the genre he used to do so well and does it in a disappointingly routine, by-the-numbers fashion. **92m/C; DVD, Blu-Ray.** Sylvester Stallone; Sung Kang; Jason Momoa; Sarah Shahi; Adewale Akinnuoye-Agbaje; Christian Slater; Holt McCallany; Jon Seda; ***D:*** Walter Hill; ***W:*** Alessandro Camon; ***C:*** Lloyd Ahern, II; ***M:*** Steve Mazzaro.

Bulletproof 🦴 **1988 (R)** An unstoppable ex-CIA agent battles to retrieve a high-tech nuclear tank from terrorist hands. **93m/C; VHS, DVD.** Gary Busey; Darlanne Fluegel; Henry Silva; Thalmus Rasulala; L.Q. Jones; R.G. Armstrong; Rene Enriquez; ***D:*** Steve Carver; ***W:*** Steve Carver.

Bulletproof 🦴 **1996 (R)** Desperately trying to be a male buddy bonding movie, "Bulletproof" fails miserably in every respect. Keats (Wayans) and Moses (Sandler) are an unlikely pair of car thieves with an equally unlikely bond to each other. Turns out Keats is really undercover cop Jack Carter, who is trying to infiltrate a drug cartel via his pal Moses. When the bust goes bad, Carter must bring Moses in unharmed to testify. Meanwhile the two rejuvenate their tainted relationship amid many homoerotic innuendoes. It's an embarrassment all around, especially for ex-Spike Lee cinematographer Dickerson on his first directing outing. **85m/C; VHS, DVD, Blu-Ray, HD-DVD.** Damon Wayans; Adam Sandler; James Caan; Kristen Wilson; James Farentino; Bill Nunn; Mark Roberts; Xander Berkeley; Allen Covert; Jeep Swenson; Larry McCoy; ***D:*** Ernest R. Dickerson; ***W:*** Joe Gayton; Lewis Colick; ***C:*** Steven Bernstein; ***M:*** Elmer Bernstein.

Bulletproof Heart 🦴🦴🦴 *Killer* **1995 (R)** Mick (LaPaglia), a hit man with a severe case of burnout, is assigned to kill Fiona (Rogers), a beautiful socialite who, conveniently, wants to die. Despite being warned by his boss (Boyle) that Fiona has a habit of making men weak, he falls in love and can't bring himself to kill her. First-time director Malone takes great care to establish the noir look and feel, capitalizing on the all-in-one-night timeframe to raise the tension level. LaPaglia and Rogers turn in riveting performances, but can't stop the film from losing momentum when it becomes self-consciously melodramatic near the end. **95m/C; VHS, Streaming.** Anthony LaPaglia; Mimi Rogers; Peter Boyle; Matt Craven; Monica Schnarre; Joseph Maher; ***D:*** Mark Malone; ***W:*** Gordon Melbourne; Mark Malone; ***C:*** Tobias Schliessler; ***M:*** Graeme Coleman.

Bulletproof Monk 🦴🦴 1/2 **2003 (PG-13)** Chow-Yun Fat is the monk with no name, chosen to protect The Scroll of the Ultimate, which gives the power to shape the world to the person who reads it aloud. Each monk can only protect the scroll for 60 years, so the new chosen one must be found. An unlikely candidate emerges in a New York pickpocket named Kar, after a chance meeting between the two. Adding a definite "Indiana Jones" vibe are Jade, a mysterious "bad girl" who catches Kar's eye, and the villains, a Nazi who tried to steal the scroll years earlier, and his icy granddaughter. Plot holes abound if you look too closely, but the action sequences are nicely timed to distract you from them, and Chow-Yun Fat's cool persona adds a touch of grace. Scott makes a nice first step from teen comedy doofus to action hero. **103m/C; VHS, DVD, Blu-Ray.** Chow Yun-Fat; Seann William Scott; Jaime King; Karel Roden; Victoria Smurfit; Mako; Roger Yuan; Marcus Jean Pirae; ***D:*** Paul Hunter; ***W:*** Ethan Reiff; Cyrus Voris; ***C:*** Stefan Czapsky; ***M:*** Éric Serra.

Bullets or Ballots 🦴🦴🦴 **1938** Tough New York cop goes undercover to join the mob in order to get the goods on them. Old-fashioned danger and intrigue follow, making for some action-packed thrills. **82m/B; VHS, DVD.** Edward G. Robinson; Humphrey Bogart; Barton MacLane; Joan Blondell; Frank McHugh; Louise Beavers; ***D:*** William Keighley; ***W:*** Seton I. Miller; ***C:*** Hal Mohr.

Bullets over Broadway 🦴🦴🦴 1/2 **1994 (R)** Mediocre playwright David Shayne (Cusack, in the Allen role) talks up the virtues of artistic integrity to his pretentious hothouse contemporaries, then sells out to a gangster who agrees to finance his latest play provided his no-talent, brassy moll (Tilly) gets a part. And it's her hit-man bodyguard's (Palminteri) unexpected artistic touches that redeem Shayne's otherwise lousy work. Wiest as the eccentric diva, Ullman as the aging ingenue, Reiner as the Greenwich Village sage, and Broadbent as the increasingly plump matinee idol lead a collection of delicious, over-the-top performances in this smart and howlingly funny tribute to Jazz Age New York City that showcases Woody at his self-conscious best. **106m/C; VHS, DVD.** Dianne Wiest; John Cusack; Jennifer Tilly; Rob Reiner; Chazz Palminteri; Tracey Ullman; Mary-Louise Parker; Joe (Johnny) Viterelli; Jack Warden; Jim Broadbent; Harvey Fierstein; Annie-Joe Edwards; ***D:*** Woody Allen; ***W:*** Woody Allen; Douglas McGrath; ***C:*** Carlo Di Palma. Oscars '94: Support. Actress (Wiest); Golden Globes '95: Support. Actress (Wiest); Ind. Spirit '95: Support. Actor (Palminteri), Support. Actress (Wiest); L.A. Film Critics '94: Support. Actress (Wiest); N.Y. Film Critics '94: Support. Actress (Wiest); Natl. Soc. Film Critics '94: Support. Actress (Wiest); Screen Actors Guild '94: Support. Actress (Wiest).

Bullfighter & the Lady 🦴🦴 1/2 **1950** An American goes to Mexico to learn the fine art of bullfighting in order to impress a beautiful woman. **87m/B; VHS, Blu-Ray, Streaming.** Robert Stack; Gilbert Roland; Virginia Grey; Katy Jurado; ***D:*** Budd Boetticher.

Bullhead 🦴🦴 *Rundskop* **2011 (R)** Ambitious first film from writer/director Roskam is a complex and intense crime drama. Steroid-fueled farmer Jacky works in the family cattle business, which uses a steady supply of illegal growth hormone supplied by a shady vet. Jacky's encouraged to make a deal to sell beef to a new client—a hormone trafficker who had a federal investigator killed. He doesn't want to get involved but unexpected ties to his past drag Jacky down a dangerous road. Dutch and French with subtitles. **124m/C; DVD, Blu-Ray.** *BE* Matthias Schoenaerts; Sam Louwyck; Jeroen Perceval; Jeanne Dandoy; Barbara Sarafian; Frank Lammers; ***D:*** Michael R. Roskam; ***W:*** Michael R. Roskam; ***C:*** Nicolas Karakatsanis; ***M:*** Raf Keunen.

Bullies WOOF! 1986 (R) A woodland-transplanted young man decides to fight back against an ornery mountain clan who have raped his mother, tortured his father, and beat up his girlfriend. Brutal and unpalatable. **96m/C; VHS, DVD.** *CA* Janet-Laine Green; Dehl Berti; Stephen Hunter; Jonathan Crombie; Olivia D'Abo; ***D:*** Paul Lynch.

Bullitt 🦴🦴🦴 **1968 (PG)** A detective assigned to protect a star witness for 48 hours senses danger; his worst fears are confirmed when his charge is murdered. Based on the novel, "Mute Witness" by Robert L. Pike, and featuring one of filmdom's most famous car chases. **105m/C; VHS, DVD, Blu-Ray, HD-DVD.** Steve McQueen; Robert Vaughn; Jacqueline Bisset; Don Gordon; Robert Duvall; Norman Fell; Simon Oakland; ***D:*** Peter Yates; ***W:*** Alan R. Trustman; ***C:*** William A. Fraker; ***M:*** Lalo Schifrin. Oscars '68: Film Editing; Natl. Film Reg. '07; Natl. Soc. Film Critics '68: Cinematog.

Bullseye! 🦴 1/2 **1990 (PG-13)** Knockabout farce is a letdown considering the talents involved. Shady scientists (Moore and Caine) pursue/are pursued by lookalike con-artists (Caine and Moore), who are pursued in turn by international agents. Full of inside jokes and celebrity cameos, but nothing exceptional. **95m/C; DVD, Streaming.** Michael Caine; Roger Moore; Sally Kirkland; Patsy Kensit; Jenny Seagrove; John Cleese; Lee Patterson; Deborah Maria Moore; Mark Burns; Deborah Leng; Alexandra Pigg; ***Cameo(s):*** Lynn Nesbitt; Steffanie Pitt; ***D:*** Michael Winner; ***W:*** Michael Winner; Leslie Bricusse; ***M:*** John Du Prez.

Bullshot 🦴🦴 1/2 **1983 (PG)** Zany English satire sends up the legendary Bulldog Drummond. In the face of mad professors, hapless heroines, devilish Huns and deadly enemies, our intrepid hero remains distinctly British. **84m/C; VHS, DVD.** *GB* Alan Shearman; Diz White; Ron House; Frances Tomelty; Michael Aldridge; Ron Pember; Christopher Good; ***D:*** Dick Clement; ***M:*** John Du Prez.

Bully 🦴 **2001** Director Clark continues his cinematic theme (announced in "Kids") of amoral and hedonistic young adults with this adaptation of the true story of a 1993 murder by a group of teens in Florida. Bobby (Stahl) is a dominating scumbag who pushes his best friend Marty (Renfro) around and pressures him into unwanted sexual and narcotic experimentation. When Marty meets and begins dating Lisa (Miner), Bobby forces himself into their sexual encounters. After Bobby rapes Lisa's friend Ali (Phillips), Lisa decides that the only solution is to kill Bobby. Inexperienced in such things, the homicidal posse gets some advice from a hit man (Fitzpatrick) who's barely older than they are. Filling the screen with graphic scenes of drug use and joyless sex, Clark doesn't seem to have any message other than "Look how bad these kids are. Now look at them naked." No psychological depth is given to the characters, although the actors do their best with what they've got. Also available in an R-rated version at 107 minutes. **113m/C; VHS, DVD.** Brad Renfro; Nick Stahl; Bijou Phillips; Rachel Miner; Michael Pitt; Kelli Garner; Daniel Franzese; Leo Fitzpatrick; ***Cameo(s):*** Larry Clark; ***D:*** Larry Clark; ***W:*** Zachary Long; Roger Pullis; ***C:*** Steve Gainer.

Bully 🦴🦴🦴 *The Bully Project* **2011 (PG-13)** Director Hirsch's documentary looks at the personal anguish of the bullying of students by their peers in American schools through the experiences of five students and their families. Two students committed suicide (the interviews are with their families), one is in a reformatory for brandishing a gun on a school bus after being tormented, one star athlete comes out as a lesbian and is immediately ostracized, and a young middle-schooler is repeatedly subjected to taunts and physical violence. The ineptitude and indifference of the educators when presented with the evidence is almost as shocking. **98m/C; DVD, Blu-Ray.** ***D:*** Lee Hirsch; ***W:*** Lee Hirsch; Cynthia Lowen; ***C:*** Lee Hirsch; ***M:*** Michael Furjanic; Justin Rice; Christian Rudder.

Bulworth 🦴🦴🦴 **1998 (R)** No-holds barred look at the political process. Senator John Jay Bulworth (Beatty), bored and disillusioned by the banality of his own political career, hires a hitman to end his misery. During his last days on earth fulfilling reelection duties, and with nothing to loose, he starts spewing the truth about politics and big business, much to the dismay of his constituents and assistants. Morphing into a hip-hop political phrophet, he becomes entranced and invigorated by beautiful South Central resident Nina (Berry). Beatty (in an engaging and funny performance) tackles his fiery subject matter of dwindling racial harmony and corporate deceit with a brazen and winning sense of humor lost in contemporary films. Fine script and enjoyable supporting performances by Platt as Bulworth's panic-stricken aide and Cheadle as an enterprising drug lord. **107m/C; VHS, DVD.** Warren Beatty; Halle Berry; Oliver Platt; Paul Sorvino; Don Cheadle; Jack Warden; Christine Baranski; Isaiah Washington, IV; Joshua Malina; Richard Sarafian; Amiri Baraka; Sean Astin; Laurie Metcalf; Wendell Pierce; Michele Morgan; Ariyan Johnson; Graham Beckel; Nora Dunn; Jackie Gayle; ***D:*** Warren Beatty; ***W:*** Warren Beatty; Jeremy Pikser; ***C:*** Vittorio Storaro; ***M:*** Ennio Morricone. L.A. Film Critics '98: Screenplay.

Bumblebee 🦴🦴🦴 **2018 (PG-13)** A prequel that redefines the *Transformers* franchise, replacing its garish cacophony with heart, humor, and fully developed human characters. In 1987, 18-year-old Charlie (Steinfeld) salvages a yellow VW from a junkyard, and discovers that Bumblebee is no mere car. Director Knight and screenwriter Hodson collaboratively deliver a cocktail of joy and sci-fi action in the vein of 1980s-era Steven Spielberg. **114m/C; DVD, Blu-Ray, Streaming.** Hailee Steinfeld; Jorge Lendeborg, Jr.; John Cena; John Ortiz; ***V:*** Dylan O'Brien; ***D:*** Travis Knight; ***W:*** Christina Hodson; ***C:*** Enrique Chediak; ***M:*** Dario Marianelli. **TV**

The Bumblebee Flies Anyway 🦴🦴 1/2 **1998 (PG-13)** Amnesiac Barney Snow (Wood) is residing at a facility where all the other youths are terminally ill. As the doctors try to help Barney remember his past, Barney and the other patients go through the usual bonding rituals. Ordinary story at least has some winning performers to get past the maudlin aspects. Based on the novel by Robert Cormier. **95m/C; VHS, DVD.** Elijah Wood; Janeane Garofalo; Rachael Leigh Cook; Roger Rees; Joe Perrino; George Gore, III; Chris Petrizzo; ***D:*** Martin Duffy; ***W:*** Jennifer Sarja; ***C:*** Stephen Kazmierski; ***M:*** Christopher Tyng.

Bummer WOOF! 1973 (R) Rock band's wild party turns into tragedy when the bass player goes too far with two groupies. It's a bad scene, man. **90m/C; VHS, DVD.** Kipp Whitman; Dennis Burkley; Carol Speed; Connie Strickland; ***D:*** William Allen Castleman; ***W:*** Alvin L. Fast.

Bunco Squad 🦴 1/2 **1950** L.A. Bunco squad detective Steve Johnson (Sterling) goes after con man Wells (Cortez) who runs phony seances and is trying to bilk wealthy widow Jessica Royce (Risdon). Steve enlists his actress girlfriend Grace (Dixon) to pose as a phony medium to set-up the bad guys. **67m/B; DVD.** Robert Sterling; Joan Dixon; Ricardo Cortez; Elisabeth Risdon; Douglas Fowley; Marguerite Churchill; ***D:*** Herbert I. Leeds; ***W:*** George Callahan; ***C:*** Henry Freulich; ***M:*** Paul Sawtell.

Bundle of Joy 🦴🦴 1/2 **1956** Salesgirl who saves an infant from falling off the steps of a foundling home is mistaken for the child's mother. Remake of 1939's "Bachelor Mother." **98m/C; VHS, DVD.** Debbie Reynolds; Eddie Fisher; Adolphe Menjou; ***D:*** Norman Taurog.

Bundy: A Legacy of Evil WOOF! *Bundy: An American Icon* **2008 (R)** Limp, low-budget serial killer flick hits all the usual points about Bundy's life of crime, which marginally improves when Ted gets to killing. The subsequent capture, trial, and Bundy's imprisonment are equally dull. **92m/C; DVD.** Corin "Corky" Nemec; Jen Nikolaisen; David DeLuise; Shannon Pierce; Kane Hodder; ***D:*** Michael Feifer; ***C:*** Roberto Schein; ***M:*** Andres Boulton. **VIDEO**

B.U.S.T.E.D. 🦴🦴 *Everybody Loves Sunshine* **1999 (R)** Gangmates and cousins Terry (Goldie) and Ray (Goth) are just out of prison. Violent Terry is looking to re-take control from efficient Bernie (Bowie), who's been looking after the business. Ray decides he wants to go legit and falls for lovely Clare (Shelley). But Terry wants his coz with him and kidnaps Clare to force Ray's hand—a bad move since Ray decides love is thicker than blood. The leads are caricatures and American audiences will be hampered by the regional Brit slang but Bowie's cool intensity is worth watching. **97m/C; VHS, DVD.** *GB* Goldie; Andrew Goth; David Bowie; Rachel Shelley; Clint Dyer; Sarah Shackleton; ***D:*** Andrew Goth; ***W:*** Andrew Goth; ***C:*** Julian Morson; ***M:*** Nicky Matthew.

Bunny and the Bull 🦴 1/2 **2009** Ambitious kinda comedic effort from writer/director King was filmed entirely in the studio and places its cast against animated and drawn backgrounds. Flashbacks depict what turned neurotic, introverted Stephen (Hogg) into an agoraphobic after a disastrous trek across Europe with his drunken, womanizing, gambling-addicted friend Bunny (Farnaby) that ended in Spain. **101m/C; DVD.** *GB* Ed Hogg; Simon Farnaby; Veronica Echegui; Julian Barratt; Noel Fielding; ***D:*** Paul King; ***W:*** Paul King; ***C:*** John Sorapure; ***M:*** Ralfe Band.

Bunny Lake Is Missing 🦴🦴 **1965** Director Preminger dismissed his 'little' picture, but this psycho-thriller has become a cult fave. Neurotic American single mom Ann Lake (Lynley) has relocated to London with her 4-year-old daughter Bunny. She takes the child to her first day of nursery school but when Ann returns, Bunny is missing and the staff claims never to have seen her. Ann and Bunny have always lived with Ann's possessive older brother Stephen (Dullea), but when Scotland Yard Superintendent Newhouse (Olivier) investigates, he starts believing that Bunny never existed. A hysterical Ann tries to convince him otherwise. **107m/B; DVD, Blu-Ray.** *GB* Carol Lynley; Laurence Olivier; Keir Dullea; Noel Coward; Martita Hunt; Anna Massey; Clive Revill; Finlay Currie; Lucie Mannheim; ***D:*** Otto Preminger; ***W:*** John Mortimer; Penelope Mortimer; ***C:*** Denys Coop; ***M:*** Paul Glass.

Bunny Whipped 🦴 **2006 (R)** Where's a killer rabbit when you need one? Bob (Powell) is looking to change his life and finds it when rapper Cracker Jack is murdered. Bob transforms himself into a cartoonish vigilante ("The Whip") and the media attention gets Bob a call from ex-girlfriend Ann (Adams), an animal rights activist, who wants Bob's help in saving some lab rabbits. But his rapper case doesn't go away as it seems Bob's suspect, rival rapper Kenny Kent (Alonso), doesn't want this goof poking into his business. Just all-around lame-but gets a bone for having honey Adams in the cast. **91m/C; DVD.** Esteban Louis Powell; Joey Lauren Adams; Laz Alonso; Rebecca Gayheart; Amanda Noret; Brande Roderick; ***D:*** Rafael Riera; ***W:*** Rafael Riera; ***C:*** Bob Brill; ***M:*** Jessika Zen. **VIDEO**

Bunraku 🦴 **2010** Post-apocalyptic pulp action fantasy, shot completely in the studio, that's all artifice and little sense. Guns have been banished but violence is common as a Drifter comes to town with a revenge plan against local big shot Nicola. The Drifter teams up with sword-wielding Yoshi to lead the fight against Nicola and his henchmen. **124m/C; DVD, Blu-Ray.** Josh Hartnett; Ron Perlman; Gackt; Demi Moore; Woody Harrelson; Jordi Molla; Kevin McKidd; ***D:*** Guy Moshe; ***W:*** Guy Moshe; ***C:*** Juan Ruiz-Anchia; ***M:*** Terence Blanchard.

The 'Burbs 🦴 1/2 **1989 (PG)** A tepid satire about suburbanites suspecting their creepy new neighbors of murderous activities. Well-designed and sharp, but light on story. **101m/C; VHS, DVD, Blu-Ray.** Tom Hanks; Carrie Fisher; Ric(k) Ducommun; Corey Feldman; Brother Theodore; Bruce Dern; Gale Gordon; Courtney Gains; ***D:*** Joe Dante; ***W:*** Dana Olsen; ***C:*** Robert M. Stevens; ***M:*** Jerry Goldsmith.

Burden of Dreams 🦴🦴🦴 1/2 **1982** The landmark documentary chronicling the berserk circumstances behind the scenes of Werner Herzog's epic "Fitzcarraldo." Stuck in the Peruvian jungles, the film crew was subjected to every disaster imaginable while executing Herzog's vision, including disease, horrendous accident, warring local tribes and the megalomaniacal director himself. Considered better than "Fitzcarraldo," although both films discuss a man's obsession. **94m/C; VHS, DVD.** Klaus Kinski; Mick Jagger; Jason Robards, Jr.; Werner Herzog; ***D:*** Les Blank.

Bureau of Missing Persons 🦴🦴 1/2 **1933** Comedy-drama about big-city bureau of missing persons, in which the hardened Stone is in charge. O'Brien plays a tough cop who is transferred to the bureau and Davis stars as the mystery woman with whom he gets involved. Although fast-paced and intriguing, the film is somewhat confusing and never stays in one direction for very long. **75m/B; VHS, DVD.** Bette Davis; Lewis Stone; Pat O'Brien; Glenda Farrell; Allen Jenkins; Ruth Donnelly; Hugh Herbert; ***D:*** Roy Del Ruth; ***W:*** Robert Presnell, Sr.; ***C:*** Barney McGill; ***M:*** Bernhard Kaun.

The Burglar 🦴🦴 **1957** David Goodis adapted his own novel for this pulp noir that reeks of sexual tension amidst its crime trappings. Thief Nat Harbin (Duryea) and his team score big after stealing a valuable diamond necklace. Trouble comes as they wait to fence the piece in Atlantic City. A crooked cop is involved as is Gladden (Mansfield), the femme member of their crew who willfully ignores Nat's plans and causes grief for them all. **90m/B; DVD.** Dan Duryea; Jayne Mansfield; Peter Capell; Mickey Shaughnessy; Stewart Bradley; Martha Vickers; ***D:*** Paul Wendkos; ***W:*** David Goodis; ***C:*** Don Malkames; ***M:*** Sol Kaplan.

Burglar **1987 (R)** A cat burglar moves to the right side of the law when she tries to solve a murder case. Whoopi's always a treat, but this movie's best forgotten; Goldberg's fans should watch "Jumpin' Jack Flash" again instead. Co-star Goldthwait elevates the comedic level a bit. **103m/C; VHS, DVD.** Whoopi Goldberg; Bobcat Goldthwait; Lesley Ann Warren; John Goodman; G.W. Bailey; James Handy; Anne DeSalvo; ***D:*** Hugh Wilson; ***W:*** Hugh Wilson; ***C:*** William A. Fraker; ***M:*** Sylvester Levay; Bernard Edwards.

Burglar *Vzlomschik* **1987** Not to be confused with the Whoopi Goldberg vehicle, this Russian film relates a story no less American than apple pie and teenage angst. Senka and would-be punk star Kostya are two neglected and disaffected brothers whose father is a drunken womanizer best known for absentee paternalism. When Howmuch, a serious heavy metalloid, pressures Kostya to steal a synthesizer, brother Senka steps in to steal the Community Center's property himself. In Russian with English subtitles, the solid performances hold their own against the heavy musical content. **89m/C; VHS, DVD.** *RU* Konstantin Kinchev; Oleg Yelykomov; ***D:*** Valery Orgorodnikov.

Burial Ground *Burial Ground: Night of Terrors* **1985** A classically grisly splatter film in which the hungry dead rise and proceed to kill the weekend denizens of an isolated aristocratic mansion. **85m/C; VHS, DVD, Blu-Ray.** Karen Well; Peter Bark; ***D:*** Andrea Bianchi.

Burial of the Rats **1/2** *Roger Corman Presents Burial of the Rats; Bram Stoker's Burial of the Rats* **1995 (R)** Based on a short story by Bram Stoker, this cable campiness features young Bram (Alber) himself being kidnapped while traveling in Eastern Europe. He's taken to the "Queen of Vermin" (Barbeau), who heads a bloodthirsty cult that hate men, worship rats, and live by violence. Fortunately, the Queen decides to spare Bram so he can write of their exploits and he falls for the fleshy charms of rat-woman Madeleine (Ford). **85m/C; VHS, DVD.** Adrienne Barbeau; Maria Ford; Kevin Alber; ***D:*** Dan Golden.

Buried **2010 (R)** A claustrophobic nightmare in real-time with director Cortes shrewdly increasing the tension to almost unbearable effect. Civilian truck driver Paul Conroy's (Reynolds) convoy is ambushed by insurgents in Iraq. He's kidnapped, buried alive, and held for ransom. Conroy has a lighter, a pen, a pocketknife, and a cell phone to contact the outside world (with his captors able to contact him) and finds neither his employer nor the State Department are willing to help. **95m/C; Blu-Ray.** *SP* Ryan Reynolds; Stephen Tobolowsky; Samantha Mathis; Erik Palladino; Robert Paterson; Jose Luis Garcia-Perez; ***D:*** Rodrigo Cortés; ***W:*** Chris Sparling; ***C:*** Eduard Grau; ***M:*** Victor Reyes.

Buried Alive **1939** A man is sent to prison on trumped up charges. Only the prison nurse believes he is innocent as a crooked politician strives to keep him behind bars. **74m/B; DVD.** Beverly Roberts; Robert Wilcox; George Pembroke; Ted Osborn; Paul McVey; Alden "Steve" Chase; ***D:*** Victor Halperin.

Buried Alive **1981** Director d'Amato reaps his finest gore-fest to date, incorporating the well-established taxidermist gone loony motif in his repertoire of appalling bad taste. Not for the squeamish, this bloodier-than-thou spaghetti spooker is chock full of necrophilia, cannibalism, and more. **90m/C; VHS, DVD.** *IT* Kieran Canter; Cinzia Monreale; Franca Stoppi; ***D:*** Joe D'Amato.

Buried Alive **1989 (R)** Once Ravenscroft Hall was an asylum for the incurably insane. Now, the isolated mansion is a school for troubled teenage girls, run by a charismatic psychiatrist. Captivated by his charm, a young woman joins the staff. Soon, she is tormented by nightmare visions of the long-dead victims of a nameless killer. When the students begin to disappear, she realizes he still lives...and she may be his next victim. Carradine's last role. **97m/C; VHS, DVD.** Robert Vaughn; Donald Pleasence; Karen Witter; John Carradine; Ginger Lynn Allen; ***D:*** Gerard Kikoine.

Buried Alive **1/2 1990 (PG-13)** One of the many horror flicks entitled "Buried Alive," this one is not bad, injecting a bit of levity into the time-worn genre. Schemestress Leigh and her paramour poison her husband. Or so they think, only to discover that he's not quite dead. **93m/C; DVD.** Tim Matheson; Jennifer Jason Leigh; William Atherton; Hoyt Axton; ***D:*** Frank Darabont; ***W:*** Mark Patrick Carducci; Jake Clesi; ***M:*** Michel Colombier. **CABLE**

Burke & Hare **2010** Old-fashioned horror comedy based (loosely) on the true story of 19th-century body-snatchers William Burke (Pegg) and William Hare (Serkis) who illegally supplied cadavers to Edinburgh medical schools. Only since their new profession is so lucrative, they decide to help a number of live bodies along rather than just relying on stealing corpses. Pegg and Serkis obviously relish their roles, with some slapstick and a touch of moral uncertainty (after all they are mass murderers) thrown in. **91m/C; DVD, Blu-Ray.** *GB* Simon Pegg; Andy Serkis; Tom Wilkinson; Tim Curry; Isla Fisher; Jessica Hynes; Ronnie Corbett; Hugh Bonneville; ***D:*** John Landis; ***W:*** Piers Ashworth; Nick Moorcraft; ***C:*** John Mathieson; ***M:*** Joby Talbot.

Burlesque **1/2 2010 (PG-13)** Small town Iowa waitress Ali (Aguilera) moves to L.A. and lands at the Burlesque Lounge, run by former headliner Tess (Cher). Ali's got big dreams and works her way onto the stage via a jaw-dropping audition for Tess. Since Cher's face and Aguilera's acting are both stiff, this winds up as more of a two-hour music video. Tucci shines as gay stage manager Sean, who is naturally the only one who can go toe-to-toe with the mega divas. Fans of the genre will have a blast with the outrageous dancing, singing and costuming—just don't expect great acting, quality script writing or much of a plot. **100m/C; Blu-Ray, On Demand.** Cher; Kristen Bell; Christina Aguilera; Julianne Hough; Cam Gigandet; Stanley Tucci; Alan Cumming; Eric Dane; Peter Gallagher; ***D:*** Steve Antin; ***W:*** Steve Antin; ***C:*** Bojan Bazelli; ***M:*** Christophe Beck. Golden Globes '11: Song ("You Haven't Seen the Last of Me").

The Burmese Harp *Harp of Burma; Birumano Tategoto* **1956** At the end of WWII, a Japanese soldier is spiritually traumatized and becomes obsessed with burying the masses of war casualties. A searing, acclaimed anti-war statement, in Japanese with English subtitles. Remade by Ichikawa in 1985. **115m/B; VHS, DVD.** *JP* Shoji Yasui; Rentaro Mikuni; Tatsuya Mihashi; Tanie Kitabayashi; Yunosuke Ito; ***D:*** Kon Ichikawa; ***W:*** Natto Wada; ***C:*** Minoru Yokoyama; ***M:*** Akira Ifukube.

Burn! **1/2** *Quemimada!* **1970 (PG)** An Italian-made indictment of imperialist control by guerrilla-filmmaker Pontecorvo, depicting the efforts of a 19th century British ambassador to put down a slave revolt on a Portuguese-run Caribbean island. Great Brando performance. **112m/C; VHS, DVD.** *FR IT* Marlon Brando; Evarist Marquez; Renato Salvatori; Norman Hill; Dana Ghia; Giampiero Albertini; Tom Lyons; ***D:*** Gillo Pontecorvo; ***W:*** Giorgio Arlorio; Franco Solinas; ***C:*** Marcello Gatti; ***M:*** Ennio Morricone.

Burn **1/2 2012** Tom Putnam and Brenna Sanchez spent a year in a Detroit firehouse and came away with a striking documentary about one of the most dangerous professions in the world. Not only does it capture personalities well, it becomes a socio-cultural commentary on a city that's being burned down as it's being abandoned. And, most importantly, the people left behind willing to fight to keep it standing. Executive produced by Denis Leary, the film has the power of his fictional TV series "Rescue Me," although every minute of it is real. **86m/C; DVD, Blu-Ray.** Donald Austin; Brendan Doogie Milewski; Craig Dougherty; Terrell Hardaway; Dennis Hunter; ***D:*** Tom Putnam; Brenna Sanchez; ***C:*** Mark Eaton; Nicola Marsh; Matt Pappas.

Burn After Reading **1/2 2008 (R)** Two greedy and none-too-smart gym employees (Pitt, McDormand) attempt to sell a disk containing the memoirs of an ousted CIA agent (Malkovich) with unpleasant consequences. Swinton and Clooney, who are re-teamed after "Michael Clayton," play the agent's unhappy wife and her scheming lover. Swinton looks like she's still in that movie, while Clooney gets into Coen brothers mode effortlessly and is a highlight. Convoluted plot takes a back seat to excellent dialogue and pleasantly over the top characters. Pitt looks like he's having a blast with his dim-bulb workout junkie. Simmons and Jenkins shine in limited roles as bosses trying to figure out what the hell is going on. **96m/C; Blu-Ray, On Demand.** Brad Pitt; George Clooney; John Malkovich; Tilda Swinton; Frances McDormand; Richard Jenkins; J.K. Simmons; David Rasche; Olek Krupa; Jeffrey DeMunn; Elizabeth Marvel; ***D:*** Joel Coen; Ethan Coen; ***W:*** Joel Coen; Ethan Coen; ***C:*** Emmanuel Lubezki; ***M:*** Carter Burwell.

Burn, Witch, Burn! **1/2** *Night of the Eagle* **1962** Creepy psycho-horror. Oblivious college prof Norman Taylor (Wyngarde) doesn't believe in the occult and is furious when he finally discovers his wife Tansy (Blair) has been a practitioner since their days in Jamaica. He makes her destroy her protection charms and their lives take a decided turn for the worse. Adaptation of the 1943 novel "Conjure Wife" by Fritz Leiber Jr. **89m/B; VHS, DVD, Blu-Ray.** *UK GB* Peter Wyngarde; Janet Blair; Margaret Johnston; Colin Gordon; Anthony Nicholls; Kathleen Byron; Reginald Beckwith; Jessica Dunning; Norman Bird; Judith Scott; ***D:*** Sidney Hayers; ***W:*** Charles Beaumont; Richard Matheson; George L. Baxt; ***C:*** Reginald Wyer; Reg Wyer; ***M:*** William Alwyn.

The Burning **1982 (R)** Story of macabre revenge set in the dark woods of a seemingly innocent summer camp. **90m/C; VHS, DVD, Blu-Ray.** Brian Matthews; Leah Ayres; Brian Backer; Larry Joshua; Jason Alexander; Ned Eisenberg; Garrick Glenn; Carolyn Houlihan; Fisher Stevens; Lou David; Holly Hunter; ***D:*** Tony Maylam; ***W:*** Bob Weinstein; Peter Lawrence; ***C:*** Harvey Harrison; ***M:*** Rick Wakeman.

Burning *Beoning* **2018** A slow-burning, psychological thriller with an ending you won't see coming. Jong-su becomes romantically entangled with an old friend, Hae-mi, who later introduces the mysterious and wealthy Ben as her new boyfriend. When Hae-mi suddenly vanishes, secrets and true characters are revealed. Based on the short story "Barn Burning" by Haruki Murakami, this film was South Korea's official submission for the 91st Academy Awards in 2019. **148m/C; DVD, Blu-Ray.** Ah-In Yoo; Steven Yeun; Jong-seo Jeon; Soo-Kyung Kim; Seung-ho Choi; ***D:*** Chang-dong Lee; ***W:*** Chang-dong Lee; Jungmi Oh; ***C:*** Kyung-Pyo Hong; ***M:*** Mowg.

The Burning Bed **1/2 1985** Dramatic expose (based on a true story) about wife-beating. Fawcett garnered accolades for her performance as the battered wife who couldn't take it anymore. Highly acclaimed and Emmy-nominated. **95m/C; VHS, DVD, Blu-Ray.** Farrah Fawcett; Paul LeMat; Penelope Milford; Richard Masur; ***D:*** Robert Greenwald. **TV**

Burning Blue **1/2 2014 (R)** Well-intentioned but stilted gay melodrama that Greer adapted from his 1992 play. Three fatal flight accidents aboard an aircraft carrier lead to an NCIS investigation. It turns into a witch hunt focusing on some closeted gay Naval fliers in the era of 'don't ask, don't tell'. Filmed in 2011. **96m/C; DVD.** Trent Ford; Rob Mayes; Morgan Spector; Michael Sirow; Tammy Blanchard; William Lee Scott; Cotter Smith; Michael Crumpsty; ***D:*** D.M.W. Greer; ***W:*** D.M.W. Greer; Helene Kvale; ***C:*** Frederic Fasano; ***M:*** James Lavino. **VIDEO**

Burning Cane **1/2 2019** Devout widow Helen (Livers) has many difficulties in her life. In addition to owning a dog with mange, her unemployed son Daniel (McClellan) is a resentful alcoholic who beats his working wife Sherry (Crutchfield). Daniel is their son's (Kelly) loving caretaker but he struggles with his father's violent legacy. The minister at Helen's church, Reverend Tillman (Pierce), also is an alcoholic struggling with personal issues as he condemns secular America from the pulpit. Teenage filmmaker Youman has created a powerful debut that thoughtfully looks at faith and family in a small Louisiana community. **78m/C; DVD.** Wendell Pierce; Karen Kaia Livers; Dominique McClellan; Braelyn Kelly; Emyri Crutchfield; ***D:*** Phillip Youmans; ***W:*** Phillip Youmans; ***C:*** Phillip Youmans; ***M:*** Kevin Gullage.

The Burning Court **1/2** *La Chambre Ardente* **1962** Unusual horror film involving occultism, possession, and family curses. Dubbed into English. Based on a story by John Dickson Carr. **102m/C; VHS, DVD.** *IT FR* Nadja Tiller; Jean-Claude Brialy; Edith Scob; Perette Pradier; Claude Rich; ***D:*** Julien Duvivier.

Burning Daylight **1928** Alaskan real estate baron loses everything to a group of San Francisco sharpies. Based on the story by Jack London. **72m/B; Silent; VHS, DVD.** Milton Sills; Arthur Stone; Doris Kenyon; Guinn "Big Boy" Williams; ***D:*** Richard A. Rowland.

Burning Daylight **1/2 2010** An anthology of films, based on three Jack London stories, set in 1920s New York. 1) Just Meat: Two thieves enjoy a big score from a jewel heist until conflicts arise between them. 2) To Kill a Man: Unexpected mind games occur between a manipulative wealthy woman and a poor thief she believes is stupid. 3) Burning Daylight: Three Wall Street bankers think they can outwit a Klondike millionaire. **102m/C; DVD.** Robert Knepper; Paul Calderon; Adrian Cowan; Sanzhar Sultanov; ***D:*** Sanzhar Sultanov; ***W:*** Sanzhar Sultanov; ***C:*** Pasha Patriki; ***M:*** Steve Cupani. **VIDEO**

Burning Down the House **2001 (R)** Desperate director Jake Selling (Savage) has his next story all lined up but no money to pursue his ambitions until he crosses paths with B-movie producer Arnie Green (Wilder). They figure out the only way to raise money is to burn down Jake's house for the insurance. Only Jake's ex—actress Brenda Goodman (Baron)?catches the scam on film and demands to be in the movie. And the insurance investigator turns out to be a wannabe actor as well whom they may also have to placate. **84m/C; VHS, DVD.** John Savage; James Wilder; Joanne Baron; William Atherton; Arye Gross; Rene Auberjonois; Orson Bean; John Ales; C. Thomas Howell; Luca Bercovici; David Keith; ***Cameo(s):*** Mick Fleetwood; ***D:*** Philippe Mora; ***W:*** Michael Cole Dinelli; ***C:*** Dan Gillham; ***M:*** Jeff Marsh.

The Burning Hills **1/2 1956** Unexceptional cow flick based on a Louis L'Amour novel. Hunter hides from cattle thieves in a barn and, eventually, in the arms of a half-breed Mexican girl (Wood). Tedious and unsurprising. **94m/C; VHS, DVD.** Tab Hunter; Natalie Wood; Skip Homeier; Eduard Franz; Earl Holliman; Claude Akins; Ray Teal; Frank Puglia; ***D:*** Stuart Heisler; ***W:*** Irving Wallace; ***C:*** Ted D. McCord; ***M:*** David Buttolph.

A Burning Hot Summer **1/2** *Un Ete Brulant* **2011** Bland and boring drama. Rich artist Frederic (Louis Garrel) dies. This happens in the first scenes and it takes the rest of writer/director Philippe Garrel's languid pic to find out why he crashes his car. Frederic lives with his actress wife Angele (Bellucci) in Rome where he is increasingly unhappy. He strikes up a friendship with Paul (Robart) and his actress girlfriend Elisabeth (Sallette) and they talk a lot--apparently about why their lives have no purpose. French with subtitles. **95m/C; DVD.** *FR* Louis Garrel; Monica Bellucci; Jerome Robart; Celine Sallette; ***D:*** Philippe Garrel; ***W:*** Philippe Garrel; Marc Cholodenko; ***C:*** Willy Kurant; ***M:*** John Cale.

Burning Life **1/2 1994** In the eastern states of a recently reunified Germany, Anna and Lisa become punk folk heroines after a series of bank robberies. One of the most unbelievable aspects is that these not-too-bright amateurs continue to elude the efficient East German police, who are made to look like bumpkins. German with subtitles. **105m/C; DVD.** *GE* Anna Thalbach; Maria Schrader; Max Tidof; Jaecki Schwarz; Andreas Hoppe; Dani Levy; ***D:*** Peter Welz; ***W:*** Stefan Kolditz; ***C:*** Michael Schaufert; ***M:*** Neil Quinton.

Burning Man **1/2 2011** Nonlinear narrative (with rather a lot of nudity) finds Sydney restaurant chef Tom (Goode) losing control of his life to his anger even as he struggles to be a caring dad to his young son. Flashbacks reveal that his wife Sarah's recent death from breast cancer has left Tom unable to cope with his grief except by lashing out. Goode's capable but the character is so unlikeable that not even tragedy seems a justification for his behavior. **109m/C; DVD.** *AU* Matthew Goode; Bojana Novakovic; Essie Davis; Kerry Fox; Rachel Griffiths; *D:* Jonathan Teplitzky; *W:* Jonathan Teplitzky; *C:* Garry Phillips; *M:* Lisa Gerrard.

The Burning Plain 1/2 **2008 (R)** An elaborate mishmash of stories and characters that covers 20-some years and travels between Oregon and New Mexico before the inevitable reveal. Married New Mexico mom Gina (Basinger) has an affair with married father Nick (de Almeida) that ends in their deaths and haunts both their families. Twenty years later, unhappy, promiscuous Sylvia (Theron) is being pestered by Carlos (Yazpik) about the past. Then there's the plight of young Maria (La), whose father has just died and who was—not so coincidentally—a friend of Carlos' who takes Maria in until they can find her other relatives. **111m/C; Blu-Ray, On Demand.** Charlize Theron; Kim Basinger; Joaquim de Almeida; Danny Pino; Jose Maria Yazpik; Brett Cullen; J.D. Pardo; John Corbett; Robin Tunney; Rachel Ticotin; Tessa Ia; Jennifer Lawrence; *D:* Guillermo Arriaga; *W:* Guillermo Arriaga; *C:* Robert Elswit; *M:* Hans Zimmer; Omar Rodrguez Lopez.

Burning Rage **1984** A blazing, abandoned coal mine threatens to wreak havoc in the Appalachians. The government sends geologist Mandrell to help prevent a disaster. **100m/C; VHS, DVD.** Barbara Mandrell; Tom Wopat; Bert Remsen; John Pleshette; Carol Kane; Eddie Albert; *D:* Gilbert Cates. **TV**

Burning Sands 1/2 **2017** Zurich (Jackson) is a headstrong pledge in the middle of Hell Week at an all-black college. With his fellow frat brothers, he's put through nightmarish torture, and he starts to question what he's doing it for. Gerard McMurray's drama gains added cultural weight by factoring race into its narrative, but in a very subtle way. It's impossible not to look at young African-American men being branded by superiors at a frat and not think about racial history. And Zurich too wonders why he's submitting to something his ancestors fought to free themselves from. A tough but interesting drama. **96m/C; DVD.** Trevor Jackson; Alfre Woodard; Trevante Rhodes; Steve Harris; DeRon Horton; *D:* Gerard McMurray; *W:* Gerard McMurray; Christine Berg; *C:* Isiah Donté Lee; *M:* Kevin Lax.

Burnt **2015 (R)** A stunning waste of talent and time, this drama should be returned to the chef. John Wells directs a script from Steven Knight about a recovering addict named Adam Jones (Cooper), who finds purpose in his life through cooking. Can he lead a London restaurant to a third Michelin star or will his own demons and self-confidence overcome him? It's almost impossible to care. Cooper is typically good and the supporting cast is filled with talented people who should have known better, but the movie is the typical White Male Redemption story we've seen a thousand times. There's nothing new. **101m/C; DVD, Blu-Ray, Streaming.** Bradley Cooper; Sienna Miller; Daniel Brühl; Emma Thompson; Uma Thurman; *D:* John Wells; *W:* Steven Knight; *C:* Adriano Goldman; *M:* Ron Simonsen.

Burnt by the Sun *Outomlionnye Solntsem* **1994 (R)** Masterful evocation of '30s Stalinist Russia, covering a day in the life of Soviet revolutionary hero Serguei (Mikhalkov) and his family, far from the purges and gulags. Enjoying a country existence with wife Moroussia (Dapkounaite) and daughter Nadia (played by Mikhalkov's daughter), his idyll is disturbed by mystery man Dimitri (Menchikov), and Serguei realizes their fates are bound by the difference between their Communist dreams and reality. Symbolism is a little heavy but film delivers emotionally. Russian with subtitles. **134m/C; VHS, DVD.** *RU FR* Nikita Mikhalkov; Ingeborga Dapkounaite; Oleg Menshikov; Nadia Mikhalkov; Andre Oumansky; Viatcheslav Tikhonov; Svetlana Krioutchkova; Vladimir Ilyine; *D:* Nikita Mikhalkov; *W:* Nikita Mikhalkov; Rustam Ibragimbekov; *C:* Vilen Kalyuta; *M:* Eduard Artemyev. Oscars '94: Foreign Film; Cannes '94: Grand Jury Prize.

Burnt Money *Plata Quemada* **2000** Based on a 1965 true crime story set in Argentina and Uruguay. Twentysomething lovers Nene (Sbaraglia) and the unstable Angel (Noriega), nicknamed the Twins, are stickup men hired by veteran criminal Fontana (Bartis) for a big money heist in Buenos Aires. They're paired with young, pill-popping getaway driver Cuervo (Echarri) but things go wrong when the Twins become cop killers. The foursome flee with the money to a squalid apartment in Montevideo where they wait for new identity papers. The young trio begin to unravel amidst a lot of drinking, drugs (who knew cocaine was so popular in the '60s?), and boredom, leading to a lethal confrontation with authorities. Title refers to what happens to the heist cash. Spanish with subtitles. **125m/C; VHS, DVD.** *AR* Leonardo Sbaraglia; Eduardo Noriega; Ricardo Bartis; Pablo Echarri; Leticia Bredice; Dolores Fonzi; *D:* Marcelo Pineyro; *W:* Marcelo Figueras; *C:* Alfredo Mayo; *M:* Osvaldo Montes.

Burnt Offerings **1976 (PG)** A family rents an old mansion for the summer and they become affected by evil forces that possess the house. Based on the novel by Robert Marasco. **116m/C; VHS, DVD, Blu-Ray.** Oliver Reed; Karen Black; Bette Davis; Burgess Meredith; Eileen Heckart; Lee Montgomery; Dub Taylor; *D:* Dan Curtis; *W:* Dan Curtis.

The Burnt Orange Heresy 1/2 **2020 (R)** In Italy, an art critic (Bang) and his new lover are enticed by a powerful art collector (Jagger) to steal a painting from a reclusive artist (Sutherland), but their once-simple art heist devolves into more serious crimes. This adaptation of Charles Willeford's 1971 neo-noir novel is intriguing at first (even though the main character is smarmy and unlikeable) but makes a sharp turn into absurdity in the third act. **99m/C; DVD.** Elizabeth Debicki; Donald Sutherland; Claes Bang; Mick Jagger; Rosalind Halstead; *D:* Giuseppe Capotondi; *W:* Scott B. Smith; *C:* David Ungaro; *M:* Chris Armstrong.

Burnzy's Last Call **1995** Sal (McCaffrey) tends bar at Eppy's, a Manhattan joint where Burnzy (Gray), a retired newspaperman, is a regular. The film is an ensemble piece that focuses on the various colorful characters who drift in and out of the place. **88m/C; VHS, DVD.** Sam Gray; David Johansen; James McCaffrey; Chris Noth; Sherry Stringfield; Roger Robinson; Tony Todd; *D:* Michael de Avila; *W:* George Gilmore; *C:* Scott St. John.

Burton and Taylor 1/2 **2013** The leads are too young for their famous leads but they have the talent to pull off this BBC TV production without impersonation. The still tempestuous relationship of Elizabeth Taylor (Bonham Carter) and Richard Burton (West) is played out through their ill-fated reunion in 1982 when they appear onstage together in a New York revival of Noel Coward's "Private Lives." Rumors swirl as everyone looks for paralells between their characters and their own private lives while an ill Burton tries to deal with his unprepared ex, whom he suspects is abusing alcohol and drugs. **90m/C; DVD.** *UK* Dominic West; Helena Bonham Carter; Stanley Townsend; William Hope; Sarah Hadland; Lenora Crichlow; Cassie Raine; *D:* Richard Laxton; *W:* William Ivory; *C:* David Katznelson; *M:* John Lunn. **TV**

Bury Me an Angel **1971** A female biker sets out to seek revenge against the men who killed her brother. **85m/C; VHS, DVD.** Dixie Peabody; Terry Mace; Clyde Ventura; Dan Haggerty; Stephen Whittaker; Gary Littlejohn; Dave Atkins; Marie Denn; Alan DeWitt; *D:* Barbara Peeters; *C:* Sven Walnum; *M:* Richard Hieronymous.

Bury My Heart at Wounded Knee **2007** Loose adaptation of the 1970 Dee Brown book. This oversimplified version concentrates on the experiences of the Sioux from Little Big Horn to the Wounded Knee massacre. It follows Charles Eastman (Beach)?who's not in Brown's book, by the way—who grew up among the Sioux (he's a quarter white on his mother's side) until his Christianized father claims him. Eastman is educated in the East and becomes a doctor at Pine Ridge, aided by his white wife (Paquin). The story is given over to various confrontations and philosophical differences. **?m/CDVD.** Adam Beach; Aidan Quinn; Anna Paquin; August Schellenberg; J.K. Simmons; Shawn Johnston; Gordon Tootoosis; Wes Studi; Eric Schweig; Colm Feore; Fred Dalton Thompson; *D:* Yves Simoneau; *W:* Daniel Giat; *C:* David Franco; *M:* George S. Clinton. **CABLE**

Burying the Ex **2015 (R)** The mighty Joe Dante falls in ways that most fans never thought he could with this truly regrettable horror-comedy that offers nothing new and features such bland, personality-less filmmaking that it's nearly impossible to believe the director of "Gremlins" helmed it. Max (Yelchin) has a manipulative girlfriend named Evelyn (Green), with whom he's afraid to break up. She dies. He starts a new relationship with Olivia (Daddario). Evelyn comes back from the dead as a zombie and wants to rekindle her relationship with Max. You'll wish you were dead. It's not funny, it's poorly made and it's depressingly boring. **89m/C; DVD, Blu-Ray, Streaming.** Anton Yelchin; Ashley Greene; Alexandra Daddario; Oliver Cooper; *D:* Joe Dante; *W:* Alan Trezza; *C:* Jonathan Hall; *M:* Joseph LoDuca. **VIDEO**

Bus Driver **2016** An action film in which a wrong turn leads to a stand-off and, perhaps, death. Traveling by bus to a retreat, five troubled students, their over-the-top gym teacher chaperone, and the bus driver find their journey coming to an unexpected halt when the bus blows out a tire. Stopping for help at the closest ranch, they find themselves in unfriendly territory as the ranch houses criminals with a drug operation. Though the students and gym teacher may be easily killed by the criminals, the bus driver proves to have unexpected skills which just might save them all. **75m/C; DVD, Streaming, Download.** Steven Chase; Steve Daron; Holly Dignard; Robert Forster; Michael Bailey Smith; *D:* Brian Herzlinger; *W:* Brian Herzlinger; Jay Black; *C:* Matt Fore; *M:* Matthew Dahan. **VIDEO**

Bus Stop *The Wrong Kind of Girl* **1956** Murray plays a naive cowboy who falls in love with Monroe, a barroom singer, and decides to marry her without her permission. Considered by many to be the finest performance by Marilyn Monroe; she sings "That Old Black Magic" in this one. Very funny with good performances by all. Based on the William Inge play. **96m/C; VHS, DVD, Blu-Ray.** Marilyn Monroe; Arthur O'Connell; Hope Lange; Don Murray; Betty Field; Max (Casey Adams) Showalter; Hans Conried; Eileen Heckart; *D:* Joshua Logan; *W:* George Axelrod; *C:* Milton Krasner; *M:* Cyril Mockridge; Alfred Newman.

The Bushido Blade 1/2 *The Bloody Bushido Blade* **1980** An action-packed samurai thriller of adventure and betrayal set in medieval Japan. **92m/C; VHS, DVD.** *JP* Richard Boone; James Earl Jones; Frank Converse; *D:* Tom Kotani.

Bushido: The Cruel Code of the Samurai *Bushido zankoku monogatari; Bushido, Samurai Saga; Cruel Story of the Samurai's Way; Cruel Tales of Bushido; The Oath of Obedience* **1963** Susumu (Kinnosuke Nakamura) chronicles the history of his family while attending to his dying fiance who has attempted suicide. Beginning at the 17th century his Samurai ancestor follows his lord into death, declaring that his family will forever honor the code of Bushido, which stresses loyalty to one's master. Each succeeding generation has an ever more horrifying and humiliating request placed upon them by their master, which they follow to remain loyal. Directed by Tadashi Imai, it is his response to the propaganda films he was forced to author in WWII imploring the Japanese workers to sacrifice their lives for their leaders' goals. **119m/B; DVD.** *JP* Kinnosuke Nakamura; Eijiro Tono; Kyoko Kishida; Masayuki Mori; Shinjiro Ebara; Yoshiko Mita; Ineko Arima; Isao (Ko) Kimura; *D:* Tadashi Imai; *W:* Norio Nanjo; Naoyuki Suzuki; Yoshikata Yoda; *C:* Makoto Tsuboi; *M:* Toshiro Mayuzumi.

Bush's Brain **2004** Election year investigation of the role Karl Rove played in crafting Dubyah into a president. Yet another volley in the political documentary war of 2004. Interesting exploration of behind-the-scenes political dirty work. Though based largely on hearsay, film will surely outrage democrats everywhere. **80m/C; VHS, DVD.** *D:* Michael Shoob; Joseph Mealey; *C:* Joseph Mealey; *M:* David Friedman; Michelle Shocked.

The Bushwackers 1/2 *The Rebel* **1952** Ireland plays a veteran of the Confederate army who wishes only to put his violent past behind him. He is forced to reconsider his vow when old-west bullies threaten his family. **70m/B; VHS, DVD.** Dorothy Malone; John Ireland; Wayne Morris; Lawrence Tierney; Jack Elam; Lon Chaney, Jr.; Myrna Dell; *D:* Rod Amateau.

Bushwhacked 1/2 *Tenderfoots; The Tenderfoot* **1995 (PG-13)** Crude, rude, dim-witted, kid-hating Max Grabelski (Stern) is falsely accused of murder and forced to become a fugitive. While not to be confused with Harrison Ford, he is mistaken for the leader of a group of Cub Scouts out on their maiden camping trip and soon finds himself in an unlikely partnership with the boys. Together they encounter everything from grizzly bears to whitewater rapids. Lighthearted, goofy comedy continues Stern's tendency toward kid-intensive, family-oriented fare in the "Rookie of the Year" vein. **85m/C; VHS, DVD.** Daniel Stern; Jon Polito; Brad Sullivan; Ann Dowd; Anthony Heald; Tom Wood; *D:* Greg Beeman; *W:* Tommy Swerdlow; Michael Goldberg; John Jordan; Danny Byers; *M:* Bill Conti.

Bushwick **2017** Five city blocks never felt so vast. When Lucy emerges from the subway onto the Brooklyn streets, she's terrified to discover that Texas secessionists are taking over the neighborhood of Bushwick, so she partners with a war veteran to reach safety beyond the bloody battle. The budget is low, the acting merely adequate, and the dialogue somewhat artificial, but extended takes and first-person-adjacent perspectives lend this thriller a video game's ability to insert you into the action. **94m/C; DVD, Blu-Ray.** Dave Bautista; Brittany Snow; Arturo Castro; Christian Navarro; Jeff Lima; *D:* Cary Murnion; *W:* Nick Damici; Graham Reznick; *C:* Lyle Vincent; *M:* Aesop Rock.

The Business **2005 (R)** The sunny, tacky setting makes this Cockney crime flick, set amid the conspicuous consumption of the 1980s, at least a little different though the plot is ordinary enough. Young Frankie (Dyer) heads to the criminal haven of Spain's Costa del Sol and gets a job driving for flashy Charlie (Hassan) and his psycho partner Sammy (Bell). Then Frankie starts running drugs for Charlie and multiple betrayals are set in motion. **92m/C; DVD.** *GB* Danny Dyer; Tamer Hassan; Geoff Bell; Georgina Chapman; Linda Henry; Eddie Weber; *D:* Nick Love; *W:* Nick Love; *C:* Damian Bromley; *M:* Ivor Guest.

A Business Affair 1/2 *D'Une Femme a L'Autre* **1993 (R)** Kate Swallow (the ravishing Bouquet), the neglected wife of tempermental author Alex Bolton (Pryce), begins an affair with his flamboyant American publisher Vanni Corso (Walken). While the men posture between themselves for her affections, Kate, who has literary aspirations, decides to strike out on her own. Based on the romantic triangle of British writers Barbara Skelton and Cyril Connolly and his publisher George Weidenfeld and taken from Skelton's memoirs "Tears Before Bedtime" and "Weep No More." **102m/C; VHS, DVD.** Carole Bouquet; Jonathan Pryce; Christopher Walken; Sheila Hancock; *D:* Charlotte Brandstrom; *W:* William Stadiem; *C:* Willy Kurant; *M:* Didier Vasseur.

Business is Business 1/2 *Diary of a Hooker; Any Special Way* **1971** Verhoeven's first feature film (after his television work) is a sex comedy about a couple of prostitutes who are apartment neighbors in Amsterdam. Nel's got an abusive boyfriend she just can't shake despite the efforts of her friend Blonde Greet. BG decides they should become partners (she's got a lot of fetish clients) but she gets put-out when Nel finds a nice, boring guy who wants to marry her and take her out of the life. Especially since Blonde Greet's special guy is already hitched. A slight and surprisingly timid story considering Verhoeven's later work but everyone's gotta start somewhere. Dutch with subtitles. **89m/C; DVD.** *NL* Ronnie Bierman; Sylvia De Leur; Piet Romer; Jules Hamel; Bernard Droog; Henk Molenberg; Albert Mol; *D:* Paul Verhoeven; *W:* Gerard Soeteman; *C:* Jan De Bont; *M:* Mulius Steffaro.

The Business of Fancydancing **2002** Seymour (Adams) is a gay Native American who has left the reservation, gone to college, and now uses his heritage to achieve literary fame as a poet. He hasn't been back to the rez in years but returns for the funeral of onetime friend Mouse (Kanim). Seymour's return is awkward as it triggers the frustrated resentment of another boyhood pal Aristotle (Tagaban) as well as a confrontation with his college girlfriend Agnes (St. John) who is now Aristotle's lover. **103m/C; VHS, DVD.** Evan Adams; Michelle St. John; Gene Tagaban; Swil Kanim; Rebecca Carroll; Cynthia Geary; Leo Rossi; Kevin Phillip; Elaine Miles; ***D:*** Sherman Alexie; ***W:*** Sherman Alexie; ***C:*** Holly Taylor.

The Business of Strangers 🦴🦴 **2001 (R)** Julie Styron (Channing) is a tough, middleaged executive for a software company who is having a bad day at an out-of-town meeting. She worries she's about to be fired and then fires her young assistant Paula (Stiles) for missing the meeting and ruining Julie's presentation. Instead, Julie gets a promotion and decides to rehire Paula after they diss men over drinks at the hotel bar. When Paula spots corporate headhunter Nick (Weller), she tells Julie that he raped a friend of hers and it's payback time. But since the two women have been playing mind games, is this the truth or not? **83m/C; VHS, DVD.** Stockard Channing; Julia Stiles; Frederick Weller; Marcus Giamatti; ***D:*** Patrick Stettner; ***W:*** Patrick Stettner; ***C:*** Teodoro Maniaci; ***M:*** Alexander Lasarenko.

Buster 🦴🦴 1/2 **1988 (R)** The story of Buster Edwards, the one suspect in the 1963 Great Train Robbery who evaded being captured by police. Collins makes his screen debut as one of Britain's most infamous criminals. Collins also performs on the film's soundtrack, spawning two hit singles, "Two Hearts" and "Groovy Kind of Love." **102m/C; VHS, DVD.** *GB* Phil Collins; Julie Walters; Larry Lamb; Stephanie Lawrence; Ellen Beaven; Michael Atwell; Ralph Brown; Christopher Ellison; Sheila Hancock; Martin Jarvis; Anthony Quayle; ***D:*** David Green; ***M:*** Anne Dudley.

Buster's Mal Heart 🦴 1/2 **2017** An intricate dramatic thriller about three parts of a troubled man's life. Before Y2K, Jonah (Malek) is a mild-mannered husband and father employed at a remote mountain hotel as a concierge and married to a drug addict turned Christian Mary (Sheil). After the mysterious Brown (Qualls) shares information about a forthcoming cataclysmic event, the film shows Jonah, now known as Buster, living as a hermit and finding shelter by breaking into empty vacation homes. The final thread finds Jonah wallowing in loneliness. The emotionally complex film shows how heartbreak can literally break someone apart. **96m/C; DVD.** Rami Malek; DJ Qualls; Kate Lyn Sheil; Toby Huss; Lin Shaye; ***D:*** Sarah Adina Smith; ***W:*** Sarah Adina Smith; ***C:*** Shaheen Seth.

Bustin' Loose 🦴🦴🦴 **1981 (R)** A fast-talking ex-con reluctantly drives a bus load of misplaced kids and their keeper cross-country. **94m/C; VHS, DVD.** Richard Pryor; Cicely Tyson; Robert Christian; George Coe; Bill Quinn; ***D:*** Oz Scott; ***W:*** Richard Pryor; Lonnie Elder, III; ***C:*** Dennis Dalzell; ***M:*** Roberta Flack; Mark Davis.

Busting 🦴🦴 1/2 **1974 (R)** Gould and Blake play a pair of slightly off-the-wall L.A. cops. The pair are forced "to bust" local addicts and prostitutes instead of the real crime bosses because much of the police department is on the take. Plenty of comedy and action as well as highly realistic drama. **92m/C; VHS, DVD.** Elliott Gould; Robert (Bobby) Blake; Allen Garfield; Antonio Fargas; Michael Lerner; Sid Haig; Cornelia Sharpe; ***D:*** Peter Hyams; ***W:*** Peter Hyams; ***M:*** Billy Goldenberg.

The Busy Body 🦴🦴 **1967** A plethora of sixties comedians enliven this mild flick from Castle, who's probably better-known for schlock film promotions. Bumbling smalltime crook George (Caesar) is suspected of pilfering mob money by his gangland boss Charley Baker (Ryan). If he doesn't want to wind up wearing cement overshoes, George had better find the real thief and the corpse that's buried in a suit lined with the stolen moolah. Adapted from a Donald E. Westlake novel. **102m/C; DVD.** Sid Caesar; Robert Ryan; Anne Baxter; Kay Medford; Jan Murray; Richard Pryor; Bill Dana; Ben Blue; Dom DeLuise; Godfrey Cambridge; Marty Ingels; George Jessel; Charles McGraw; Arlene Golanka; ***D:*** William Castle; ***W:*** Ben Starr; ***C:*** Michael Reed; Harold E. Stine; ***M:*** Vic Mizzy.

But I'm a Cheerleader 🦴🦴 **1999 (R)** Broad satire falls flat. Megan (Lyonne) is a peppy high school cheerleader who is suspected of being a lesbian by her rigid parents, who send her off to a rehabilitation camp designed to turn adolescent homosexuals into straight members of society. Megan (who's naively unaware of her true nature) goes along with the program until she befriends rebellious Graham (DuVall) and discovers that, golly, she really does like girls. **81m/C; VHS, DVD.** Natasha Lyonne; Clea DuVall; Cathy Moriarty; RuPaul Charles; Bud Cort; Mink Stole; Julie Delpy; Eddie Cibrian; ***D:*** Jamie Babbit; ***W:*** Jamie Babbit; Brian Wayne Peterson; ***C:*** Jules Labarthe; ***M:*** Pat Irwin.

But the Flesh Is Weak 🦴 1/2 **1932** Novello adapted his play "The Truth Game" for this dated romantic comedy about father/son gigolos. Max (Montgomery) and Florian (Smith) Clement prefer to live off the generosity of wealthy women and Max sets his sights on marrying Lady Joan Culver (Thatcher). Instead, he falls for widow Rosine Brown (Gregor), who's looking for a moneyed suitor. Florian incurs a huge gambling debt and Max tries again with Lady Joan. He still makes a romantic mistake when Rosine comes back into the picture since she's an Austrian drip. **77m/B; DVD.** Robert Montgomery; Sir C. Aubrey Smith; Nora Gregor; Heather Thatcher; Eva Moore; Edward Everett Horton; Nils Asther; ***D:*** Jack Conway; ***W:*** Ivor Novello; ***C:*** Oliver Marsh.

Butch and Sundance: The Early Days 🦴🦴 1/2 **1979 (PG)** Traces the origins of the famous outlaw duo. It contains the requisite shoot-outs, hold-ups, and escapes. A "prequel" to "Butch Cassidy and the Sundance Kid." **111m/C; VHS, DVD, Blu-Ray.** Tom Berenger; William Katt; John Schuck; Jeff Corey; Jill Eikenberry; Brian Dennehy; Peter Weller; ***D:*** Richard Lester; ***W:*** Allan Burns.

Butch Cassidy and the Sundance Kid 🦴🦴🦴🦴 **1969 (PG)** Two legendary outlaws at the turn of the century take it on the lam with a beautiful, willing ex-school teacher. With a clever script, humanly fallible characters, and warm, witty dialogue, this film was destined to become a classic. Featured the hit song "Raindrops Keep Falling on My Head" and renewed the buddy film industry, as Newman and Redford trade insult for insult. Look for the great scene where Newman takes on giant Ted Cassidy in a fist fight. **110m/C; VHS, DVD, Blu-Ray.** Paul Newman; Robert Redford; Katharine Ross; Jeff Corey; Strother Martin; Cloris Leachman; Kenneth Mars; Ted Cassidy; Henry Jones; George Furth; Sam Elliott; ***D:*** George Roy Hill; ***W:*** William Goldman; ***C:*** Conrad L. Hall; ***M:*** Burt Bacharach. Oscars '69: Cinematog., Orig. Score, Song ("Raindrops Keep Fallin' on My Head"), Story & Screenplay; AFI '98: Top 100; British Acad. '70: Actor (Redford), Actress (Ross), Director (Hill), Film, Screenplay; Golden Globes '70: Score; Natl. Film Reg. '03; Writers Guild '69: Adapt. Screenplay.

The Butcher 🦴🦴 **2007** A group of snuff film producers kidnap four people (two of which are husband and wife), strap cameras to their heads, and then force them to endure inhumane punishments in a game designed to murder them as grotesquely as possible. **75m/C; DVD, Blu-Ray.** *NK* Dong-Hun You; Sung-Il Kim; ***D:*** Jin-Won Kim; ***W:*** Jin-Won Kim; ***C:*** Sang-hyeon Lee.

The Butcher 🦴 1/2 **2007** Mob enforcer Merle Hench (Roberts) is set-up to take the fall for a bigtime heist on a rival mob boss. Surviving the trap, and grabbing a piece of the take, Merle decides being betrayed after 20 years of loyalty deserves payback. **113m/C; DVD.** Eric Roberts; Robert Davi; Keith David; Geoffrey Lewis; Michael Ironside; Bokeem Woodbine; ***D:*** Jesse Johnson; ***W:*** Jesse Johnson; ***C:*** Robert Hayes; ***M:*** Marcello De Francisci. **VIDEO**

The Butcher Boy 🦴🦴🦴 **1997 (R)** Offbeat, black comedy takes a disturbing look into the madness of 12-year old Francie Brady (Owens) in Ireland in the 1960s. An alcoholic father and a mentally strained mother makes Francie escape into a world populated by voices in his head, comic books, and his one childhood friend. When his homelife becomes unbearable, Frankie's demons catapult him into a climatic and destructively criminal breakdown. Newcomer Owens is electrifying as the red-haired dynamo whose lost childhood turns him into a monster and Stephen Rea (a regular in any Jordan film) provides stern support as Francie's loser father and film's narrator. The rural Irish town is recreated with stunning detail, with light touches of kitsch that may put off some looking for a serious treatment of main character's plight. Still a daring movie, with pop star O'Connor as the Virgin Mary. Based on the novel by Peter McCabe. **105m/C; VHS, DVD.** Eamon Owens; Stephen Rea; Fiona Shaw; Sinead O'Connor; Aisling O'Sullivan; Alan Boyle; Ian Hart; Andrew Fullerton; Patrick McCabe; Sean McGinley; Brendan Gleeson; Milo O'Shea; ***D:*** Neil Jordan; ***W:*** Neil Jordan; Patrick McCabe; ***C:*** Adrian Biddle; ***M:*** Elliot Goldenthal. L.A. Film Critics '98: Score.

The Butcher's Wife 🦴🦴 **1991 (PG-13)** Charming tale of a young psychic (Moore) who brings romance to a Greenwich Village neighborhood that never quite gets off the ground. Moore stars as the clairvoyant whose mystical powers bring magic into the lives of everyone around her, including the local psychiatrist (Daniels), who falls under her spell. Talented cast is virtually wasted with a script that is lightweight; excepting Steenburgen and Dzundza who shine. **107m/C; VHS, DVD.** Demi Moore; Jeff Daniels; George Dzundza; Frances McDormand; Margaret Colin; Mary Steenburgen; Max Perlich; Miriam Margolyes; Christopher Durang; Diane Salinger; ***D:*** Terry Hughes; ***W:*** Ezra Litwack; Marjorie Schwartz; ***C:*** Frank Tidy; ***M:*** Michael Gore.

Butter 🦴🦴 **2012 (R)** A rather smug and inert satire with an undeniably talented cast that gets sucked into a morass of bad behavior. Ambitious Laura Pickler (Garner) is a control freak determined to carry on her retired husband Bob's (Burrell) winning streak in the annual Iowa butter-carving competiton. But Laura's unexpected (and unlikely) competitor is 11-year-old black foster child Destiny (Shahidi).The pic ends up being too direct and in-your-face with its pretty misanthropic viewpoint of friendly competition among not-so-friendly people. **90m/C; DVD, Blu-Ray.** Jennifer Garner; Ty Burrell; Yara Shahidi; Olivia Wilde; Rob Corddry; Hugh Jackman; Ashley Greene; Alicia Silverstone; ***D:*** Jim Field Smith; ***W:*** Jason A. Micallef; ***C:*** Jim Denault; ***M:*** Mateo Messina.

The Buttercup Chain 🦴 1/2 **1970** First cousins France (Bennett) and Margaret (Asher) are fighting incestuous feelings so France decides they should both get involved with others: he chooses Swedish student Fred (Taube) for Margaret and free-spirited American Manny (Taylor-Young) for himself. But it's Manny and Fred who marry and move away; when France and Margaret eventually visit, they discover the marriage is unhappy. **95m/C; DVD.** *GB* Hywel Bennett; Leigh Taylor-Young; Jane Asher; Sven-Bertil Taube; Clive Revill; Roy Dotrice; ***D:*** Robert Ellis Miller; ***W:*** Peter Draper; ***C:*** Douglas Slocombe; ***M:*** Richard Rodney Bennett.

Butterfield 8 🦴🦴🦴 **1960** A seedy film of the John O'Hara novel about a prostitute that wants to go straight and settle down. Taylor won an Oscar, perhaps because she was ill and had lost in the two previous years in more deserving roles. **108m/C; VHS, DVD.** Elizabeth Taylor; Laurence Harvey; Eddie Fisher; Dina Merrill; Mildred Dunnock; Betty Field; Susan Oliver; Kay Medford; ***D:*** Daniel Mann; ***W:*** John Michael Hayes; Charles Schnee; ***C:*** Joseph Ruttenberg. Oscars '60: Actress (Taylor).

Butterflies Are Free 🦴🦴🦴 **1972 (PG)** Fast-paced humor surrounds the Broadway play brought to the big screen. Blind youth Albert is determined to be self-sufficient. A next-door-neighbor actress helps him gain independence from his over-protective mother (Heckart). **109m/C; VHS, DVD.** Goldie Hawn; Edward Albert; Eileen Heckart; Michael Glaser; ***D:*** Milton Katselas; ***C:*** Charles B(ryant) Lang, Jr.; ***M:*** Robert Alcivar. Oscars '72: Support. Actress (Heckart).

Butterfly 🦴 1/2 **1982 (R)** Based on James M. Cain's novel about an amoral young woman (Pia, who'd you think?) who uses her beauty and sensual appetite to manipulate the men in her life, including her father. Set in Nevada of the 1930s, father and daughter are drawn into a daring and forbidden love affair by their lust and desperation. **105m/C; VHS, DVD.** Pia Zadora; Stacy Keach; Orson Welles; Edward Albert; James Franciscus; Lois Nettleton; Stuart Whitman; June Lockhart; Ed McMahon; ***D:*** Matt Cimber; ***W:*** Matt Cimber; ***M:*** Ennio Morricone. Golden Raspberries '82: Worst Actress (Zadora), Worst New Star (Zadora), Worst Support. Actor (McMahon).

Butterfly 🦴🦴🦴 ***La Lengua de las Mariposas; Butterfly's Tongue*** **1998 (R)** Young Moncho (Lozano) grows up in 1935 Galicia, Spain and is guided by his leftist teacher Don Gregorio (Gomez). But their lives are soon torn apart by the politics of the Spanish Civil War. This kind of languidly paced coming-of-age story is almost never found in American theatrical releases these days. Europeans tend to treat the material with more seriousness. Director Jose Cuerda's work is solidly in the tradition of Fellini and Truffaut. Based on the stories of Manuel Riva; Spanish with subtitles. **94m/C; VHS, DVD.** *SP* Fernando Fernan-Gomez; Manuel Lozano; Uxia Blanco; ***D:*** Jose Luis Cuerda; ***W:*** Rafael Azcona; ***C:*** Javier Salmones; ***M:*** Alejandro Amenabar.

Butterfly Affair 🦴 1/2 **1971 (PG)** Beautiful singer, involved in a scheme to smuggle $2 million worth of gems, plots to double-cross her partners in crime. **75m/C; VHS, DVD.** Claudia Cardinale; Henri Charriere; Stanley Baker; ***D:*** Jean Herman.

Butterfly Ball 🦴 **1976** Retelling of the 19th century classic combines the rock music of Roger Glover, live action and animation by Halas and Batchelor. Only for the brain-cell depressed. **85m/C; VHS, DVD.** *GB* Twiggy; Ian Gillian; David Coverdale; ***Nar:*** Vincent Price; ***D:*** Tony Klinger.

Butterfly Collectors 🦴🦴 **1999** While investigating a murder, DI John McKeown (Postlethwaite) develops an unlikely friendship with 17-year-old suspect Dex (Draven), who is raising his younger siblings. But as McKeown gets closer to the family, his suspicions grow, and not just about Dex's involvement in the original crime. **150m/C; DVD.** *GB* Pete Postlethwaite; Crissy Rock; Jamie Draven; Alison Newman; ***D:*** Jean Stewart; ***W:*** Paul Abbott; ***C:*** Cinders Forshaw; ***M:*** Philip Appleby; Jocelyn Pook. **TV**

The Butterfly Effect 🦴 1/2 **2004 (R)** Kutcher takes time out from his usual dumb pretty-boy roles and tries his hand at a thriller. He plays Evan Treborn, a college psych major with a troubled past. He discovers that he can go back in time and change childhood events, which he does, to save himself and a group of friends from childhood traumas. Unfortunately, when he returns to the present, he finds his actions have changed everything that has happened since then, and not always for the better. There's a strong "ick" factor, touching on several rather disturbing topics. Kutcher acquits himself admirably, but not enough to save this jumbled mess. **113m/C; DVD, Blu-Ray, UMD.** Ashton Kutcher; Amy Smart; Eric Stoltz; William Lee Scott; Elden (Ratliff) Henson; Logan Lerman; Irene Gorovaia; Jesse James; Melora Walters; Ethan Suplee; John Patrick Amedori; Kevin G. Schmidt; ***D:*** Eric Bress; J. Mackye Gruber; ***W:*** Eric Bress; J. Mackye Gruber; ***C:*** Matthew F. Leonetti; ***M:*** Michael Suby.

The Butterfly Effect 2 🦴 1/2 **2006 (R)** Nick (Lively) loses control of his car, resulting in an accident that kills his girlfriend Julie (Durance) and two friends. Still traumatized after a year, Nick realizes that he feels a power whenever he looks at the photos of their last trip and can actually travel back in time to that particular moment. But when Nick returns to the present, he doesn't always like the changes that occurred as he tries to save Julie's life. An overly-complicated execution ruins the suspense factor. **92m/C; DVD, Blu-Ray.** Eric Lively; Gina Holden; J.R. Bourne; Erica Durance; Dustin Milligan; ***D:*** John R. Leonetti; ***W:*** Michael D. Weiss; ***C:*** Brian Pearson; ***M:*** Michael Suby. **VIDEO**

The Butterfly Effect 3: Revelation 🦴🦴 **2009 (R)** This low-budget DTV sequel is a cut above the last effort, thanks to Miner's fine performance as Jenna, jumper Sam's (Carmack) fragile sister. Sam is working with Detroit police, getting a paycheck by helping solve cold cases. When he time-travels back to ID his own girlfriend's killer, Sam changes his past and his efforts to fix one mistake result in him becoming the prime suspect in a series of murders. **90m/C; DVD, Blu-Ray.** Chris Carmack; Rachel Miner; Richard Wilkinson; *D:* Seth Grossman; *W:* Holly Brix; *C:* Dan Stoloff; *M:* Adam Balzacs. **VIDEO**

Butterfly Kiss 🦴🦴 **1994** Strange psychodrama/road tale finds drifter Eunice (Plummer) wandering the motorways of northern England. At one service station she meets Miriam (Reeves)?the two, immediately drawn together, make love at Miriam's that night. When Eunice hitches a ride with a trucker next morning, Miriam decides to follow and discovers Eunice with the truck and the driver's dead body. It's soon not the only dead body Miriam encounters as she discovers Eunice is a serial killer—not that this seems to worry Miriam a great deal as she herself gets into the spirit of their crimes. Grim all the way 'round. **90m/C; VHS, DVD.** *GB* Amanda Plummer; Saskia Reeves; Paul Bown; Des McAleer; Ricky Tomlinson; *D:* Michael Winterbottom; *W:* Frank Cottrell-Boyce; *C:* Seamus McGarvey; *M:* John Harle.

Butterfly Sword 🦴🦴 *San lau sing woo dip gim; Xin liu xing hu die jian; Comet, Butterfly and Sword* **1993 (R)** Bizarre, over-the-top bloody wire-fu action, as a group of eunuchs attempting to overthrow the Ming Dynasty are challenged by hired killers Meng Sing Wan (Tony Leung Chiu Wai) and Sister Ko (Michelle Yeoh). Complicating their fight is Meng's wife who is unaware he is an assassin, a drunken swordsman who is in love with Ko, and Ko's secret love for Meng. The original ending was considered to be too upsetting for Hong Kong audiences, so buyers should make sure the version they get has it intact (which may require getting a non-Chinese version). Otherwise the films pre-emptive ending will make little sense. **87m/C; DVD.** *CH* Michelle Yeoh; Jimmy Lin; Tony Leung Chiu Wai; Joey Wang; Donnie Yen; Chung Hua Tou; Elvis Tsui; Chaun Chen Yeh; *D:* Michael Mak; *W:* John Chong; *M:* Chin Yung Shing.

BuyBust 🦴🦴 **2018** Tough, rebellious narcotics officer Manigan (Curtis) believes that her commanding officers, Dela Cruz (Rodriguez) and Alvarez (Buencamino), are sending her into an ambush. She leads her team into a raid of the labyrinth-like home of major drug dealer Biggie Chen (Atayde), where they try to both bring him to justice and find the mole that put the whole team in danger. Though this siege drama has moments of engaging action and Curtis is solid, it's plot is too by-the-numbers and cliché-heavy. Filipino and Tagalog with subtitles. **127m/C; DVD, Blu-Ray.** Anne Curtis; Brandon Vera; Victor Neri; Arjo Atayde; Levi Ignacio; *D:* Erik Matti; *W:* Erik Matti; Anton C. Santamaria; *C:* Neil Bion; *M:* Malek Lopez; Erwin Romulo.

Buying the Cow 🦴 **1/2 2002 (R)** Commitment-phobe David (O'Connell) is being pressured by long-time girlfriend Sarah (Wilson) to get married. Cliched romantic comedy. **88m/C; VHS, DVD.** Jerry O'Connell; Bridgette Wilson-Sampras; Ryan Reynolds; Bill Bellamy; Annabeth Gish; Ron Livingston; *D:* Walt Becker; *W:* Walt Becker; Peter W. Nelson; *C:* Nancy Schreiber; *M:* Andrew Gross.

Buying Time 🦴 **1989 (R)** Two teenagers are arrested when they try to pry their money away from a dishonest bookie, and the police use their connections to solve a drug-related murder. **97m/C; VHS, Streaming.** Dean Stockwell; Jeff Schultz; Michael Rudder; Tony De Santis; Leslie Toth; Laura Cruickshank; *D:* Mitchell Gabourie.

Buzzard 🦴🦴🦴 **2015** Joel Potrykus' dark comedy about a man living on the edge of society, scrounging for whatever small advantages he can find, is a clever bit of social commentary buried in what first looks like another tale of a quirky loser. Marty Jackitansky (Burge) is the kind of guy who empties his checking account and then tries to re-open a new one with the same clerk to get the new account bonus. And he works for the bank. When a bigger scam involving check fraud crosses his desk, he takes the chance, but he may have gone too far this time. **97m/C; DVD.** Joshua Burge; Joel Potrykus; Teri Ann Nelson; Jason Roth; Joe Anderson; *D:* Joel Potrykus; *W:* Joel Potrykus; *C:* Adam Minnick.

By Dawn's Early Light 🦴🦴 **1989** Thriller about two Air Force pilots who must decide whether or not to drop the bombs that would begin WWIII. **100m/C; VHS, DVD; Open Captioned.** Powers Boothe; Rebecca De Mornay; James Earl Jones; Martin Landau; Rip Torn; Darren McGavin; *D:* Jack Sholder; *M:* Trevor Jones. **CABLE**

By Dawn's Early Light 🦴🦴 **1/2 2000** Aging Colorado cowboy Ben (Crenna) is pleased when his grandson Mike (Olivero) comes to stay for the summer. Until he realizes that Mike is a sullen teen given to pranks that backfire. After one such episode, Ben decides Mike needs some discipline and decides they should go on an 800-mile trip—by horseback. **105m/C; VHS, DVD.** Richard Crenna; Chris Olivero; David Carradine; Stella Stevens; Ben Cardinal; *D:* Arthur Allan Seidelman; *W:* Jacqueline Feather; David Seidler. **CABLE**

By Love Possessed 🦴🦴 **1/2 1961** Can a seemingly typical, quiet, New England town stay quiet when Lana Turner is your neighbor? Vintage romantic melodrama about an attorney who is drawn into an affair when he realizes his home life is not all it could be. **115m/C; VHS, DVD.** Lana Turner; Efrem Zimbalist, Jr.; Jason Robards, Jr.; George Hamilton; Thomas Mitchell; *D:* John Sturges; *C:* Russell Metty; *M:* Elmer Bernstein.

By the Gun 🦴 **2014 (R)** Monotonous Boston-set crime flick. Criminal Nick finally proves himself to aging mafioso Sal, much to the disgust of his own dad. Naturally Nick learns that being a made man isn't everything he thought. **110m/C; DVD, Blu-Ray.** Ben Barnes; Harvey Keitel; Leighton Meester; Paul Ben-Victor; Toby Jones; Ritchie Coster; *D:* James Mottern; *W:* Emilio Mauro; *C:* Jimmy Lindsey; *M:* Nathan Whitehead. **VIDEO**

By the Light of the Silvery Moon 🦴🦴 **1/2 1953** The equally old-fashioned sequel to "On Moonlight Bay" finds Day engaged to MacRae, who's just returned from Army service in WWI. He wants to postpone their marriage until he gets financially secure and the waiting causes some jealous misunderstandings (naturally resolved by movie's end). Based on Booth Tarkington's "Penrod" stories. **101m/C; VHS, DVD.** Doris Day; Gordon MacRae; Leon Ames; Billy Gray; Rosemary DeCamp; Mary Wickes; Russell Arms; Maria Palmer; *D:* David Butler; *W:* Robert O'Brien; Irving Elinson; *M:* Max Steiner.

By the Sea 🦴 **1/2 2015 (R)** Vanessa (Jolie Pitt) and Roland (Pitt) are a dissatisfied married couple on the edge of crisis. They're traveling in France in the 1970s when they stop in a seaside town for a rest and, hopefully, a bit or reconciliation. Unexpectedly, they become obsessed with their fellow hotel residents, especially another couple. There's so much here with which to play, especially given how much the real-life couple at the center of it have to understand being the obsession of others. Sadly, Jolie Pitt, directing for the third time, seems to have no idea what to do with the material. **122m/C; DVD, Blu-Ray.** Brad Pitt; Angelina Jolie; Melanie Laurent; Melvil Poupaud; Niels Arestrup; *D:* Angelina Jolie; *W:* Angelina Jolie; *C:* Christian Berger; *M:* Gabriel Yared.

By Way of the Stars 🦴🦴 **1/2 1992 (PG)** Young man is pursued by a killer while he searches for his father on the 19th-century Canadian frontier. Made for TV. **150m/C; VHS, DVD.** *CA* Zachary Bennett; Tantoo Cardinal; Gema Zamprogna; Jan Rubes; Michael Mahonen; *D:* Allan King. **TV**

Bye-Bye 🦴🦴 **1996** Ismael (Bouajila), 25, and his 14-year-old brother Mouloud (Embarek) are French-born Arabs whose parents have abruptly returned to their Tunisian homeland after a family tragedy. The brothers have travelled from Paris to stay with their uncle (Ahourari) and his family in the port city of Marseilles. Their cousin Rhida (Mammeri), a petty criminal involved with drugs, takes the innocent Mauloud under his wing and hides him away so the boy won't be sent back to his parents. Ismael desperately roams the city trying to find his brother while he also struggles to make a fresh start amidst much societal hostility. French and Arabic with subtitles. **105m/C; VHS, DVD.** *FR* Sami Bouajila; Ouassini Embarek; Benhaissa Ahourari; Sofiane Mammeri; Jamila Darwich-Farah; Nozha Khouadra; *D:* Karim Dridi; *W:* Karim Dridi; *C:* John Mathieson; *M:* Jimmy Oihid; Steve Shehan.

Bye Bye Baby 🦴 **1988 (R)** Two luscious young women cavort amid lusty Italian men on various Mediterranean beaches. **80m/C; VHS, DVD.** *IT* Carol Alt; Brigitte Nielsen; Jason Connery; Luca Barbareschi; *D:* Enrico Oldoini; *M:* Manuel De Sica.

Bye, Bye, Birdie 🦴🦴🦴 **1963** Energized and sweet film version of the Broadway musical about a teen rock and roll idol (Pearson doing Elvis) coming to a small town to see one of his fans before he leaves for the army. The film that made Ann-Margret a star. **112m/C; VHS, DVD, Blu-Ray.** Dick Van Dyke; Janet Leigh; Ann-Margret; Paul Lynde; Bobby Rydell; Maureen Stapleton; Ed Sullivan; Trudi Ames; Jesse Pearson; *D:* George Sidney; *W:* Irving Brecher; *C:* Joseph Biroc; *M:* Johnny Green.

Bye Bye Birdie 🦴🦴 **1/2 1995 (G)** TV adaptation of the Broadway musical (previously filmed in 1963) about an Elvis-like singer, about to be inducted into the Army, who causes havoc when he visits fans in a small town. **135m/C; VHS, DVD, Blu-Ray.** Jason Alexander; Vanessa L(ynne) Williams; Chynna Phillips; George Wendt; Tyne Daly; Marc Kudisch; *D:* Gene Saks. **TV**

Bye Bye Braverman 🦴 **1/2 1967** Cliched character study of four New York Jewish men, all of whom are writers, mourning the death of their friend Braverman. They attempt to travel from Greenwich Village to Brooklyn to attend his funeral but run into a number of delays. **95m/C; DVD.** George Segal; Jack Warden; Joseph Wiseman; Jessica Walter; Phyllis Newman; Zohra Lampert; Godfrey Cambridge; Sorrell Booke; *D:* Sidney Lumet; *W:* Herbert Sergent; *C:* Boris Kaufman; *M:* Peter Matz.

Bye Bye Brazil 🦴🦴 **1/2 1979** A changing Brazil is seen through the eyes of four wandering gypsy minstrels participating in a tent show traveling throughout the country. Lots of Brazilian charm. In Portuguese with English subtitles. **115m/C; VHS, DVD.** *BR* Jose Wilker; Betty Faria; Fabio Junior; Zaira Zambello; *D:* Carlos Diegues; *W:* Carlos Diegues; *M:* Chico Buarque.

Bye Bye, Love 🦴🦴 **1/2 1994 (PG-13)** Forty-eight hours in the lives of three divorced buddies starts at the local Mickey D's for the biweekly exchange of their kids. The dads don't offer any surprises: Donny (Reiser) still loves his ex, Vic (Quaid) hates his, and Dave (Modine) loves anything in a skirt. Sometimes witty, but just as often sadly poignant, the plot is as shallow as a TV sitcom, with an easy answer for every difficult question about divorce. The three leads are likeable enough, but Garofalo is the gem in an otherwise dull flick. She looks like she's having a blast, stealing scenes with abandon as Vic's blind date from hell. **107m/C; VHS, DVD.** Matthew Modine; Randy Quaid; Paul Reiser; Rob Reiner; Janeane Garofalo; Ed Flanders; Lindsay Crouse; Johnny Whitworth; Maria Pitillo; Amy Brenneman; Ross Malinger; Eliza Dushku; Wendell Pierce; Cameron Boyd; Mae Whitman; Jayne Brook; Dana Wheeler-Nicholson; Amber Benson; Stephen (Steve) Root; Danny Masterson; Jack Black; Brad Hall; *D:* Sam Weisman; *W:* Gary David Goldberg; Brad Hall; *M:* J.A.C. Redford.

The Bye Bye Man 🦴 **2017 (PG-13)** Three college students (Douglas Smith, Lucien Laviscount, Cressida Bonas) move into a new house off campus. Guess what? It's haunted. This haunting is by the title creature, played well by the great Doug Jones, who is essentially a riff on the Slenderman riff of an all-powerful boogeyman. This one gains power when you think about him. It's more jump-scare, hyper-edited garbage that fails even basic filmmaking tests. **97m/C; DVD, Blu-Ray, Streaming.** Cressida Bonas; Lucien Laviscount; Doug Jones; Carrie-Anne Moss; Faye Dunaway; *D:* Stacy Title; *W:* Jonathan Penner; *C:* James Kniest; *M:* The Newton Brothers.

Byleth: The Demon of Incest 🦴 **1972** In 19th-century Italy, the demon Byleth (who's also the king of hell) punishes Lionello by possessing him and making him lust after his sister Barbara. Less Italian horror than softcore sex and lots of nudity. Italian with subtitles. **81m/C; DVD, Blu-Ray.** *IT* Mark Damon; Claudia Gravy; Aldo Bufi Landi; Silvana Pompili; *D:* Leopoldo Savona; *W:* Leopoldo Savona; *C:* Giovanni Crisci; *M:* Vasil Kojukaroff.

Byron 🦴🦴 **1/2 2003** Byron as poet comes in second to Byron as scandalous lover in this BBC production that depicts the price of fame. Byron's (Miller) romantic style includes radical politics and adventure after the aristocrat becomes famous in 1812. His marriage to the pious Annabella (Cox) is a disaster and he's forced into exile when Byron's alleged love affair with half-sister Augusta (Little) becomes society gossip. Miller is both sympathetic and self-aware in the title role. **150m/C; DVD.** *GB* Johnny Miller; Philip Glenister; Natasha Little; Vanessa Redgrave; Julie Cox; Camilla Power; Sally Hawkins; Oliver Dimsdale; *D:* Julian Farino; *W:* Nick Dear; *C:* David Odd; *M:* Adrian Johnston. **TV**

Byzantium 🦴🦴 **2012 (R)** "Interview with the Vampire" director Jordan returns to the world of the bloodsucker in this tale of two female vampires (Arterton and Ronan) on the run for centuries from the male establishment that considers their very existence against their rules. They move from town to town and even start up a brothel in one coastal village before being discovered by both humans and the immortals chasing them. Jordan nails the atmosphere of the piece but even he seems bored by this overly familiar tale that brings nothing new to the genre. It's another example of talented people working with a truly subpar script. **118m/C; DVD, Blu-Ray.** *UK US IR* Saoirse Ronan; Gemma Arterton; Caleb Landry Jones; Sam Riley; Jonny Lee Miller; *D:* Neil Jordan; *W:* Moira Buffini; *C:* Sean Bobbitt; *M:* Javier Navarrete.

The C-Man 🦴🦴 **1949** Customs agent Jagger finds work isn't so dull after all. Murder and theft on an international scale make for a busy week as he follows jewel smugglers from Paris to New York. Docu-style though routine crime story. **75m/B; VHS, DVD.** Dean Jagger; John Carradine; Harry Landers; Rene Paul; *D:* Joseph Lerner.

Cabaret 🦴🦴🦴 **1/2 1972 (PG)** Hitler is rising to power, racism and anti-Semitism are growing, and the best place to hide from it all is the Berlin cabaret. With dancing girls, an androgynous master of ceremonies (Grey), and American expatriate singer Sally Bowles (Minnelli), you can laugh and drink and pretend tomorrow will never come. Sally does just that. Face to face with the increasing horrors of Nazism, she persists in the belief that the "show must go on." Along for the ride is Englishman Brian Roberts (York, in a role based on Christopher Isherwood's own experiences), who serves both as participant and observer. Based on the John Kander's hit Broadway musical (and Isherwood's stories), the film is impressive, with excellent direction and cinematography. **119m/C; VHS, DVD, Blu-Ray.** Liza Minnelli; Joel Grey; Michael York; Marisa Berenson; Helmut Griem; Fritz Wepper; Elisabeth Neumann-Viertel; *D:* Bob Fosse; *W:* Jay Presson Allen; *C:* Geoffrey Unsworth; *M:* Ralph Burns. Oscars '72: Actress (Minnelli), Art Dir./Set Dec., Cinematog., Director (Fosse), Film Editing, Orig. Song Score and/or Adapt., Sound, Support. Actor (Grey); British Acad. '72: Actress (Minnelli), Director (Fosse), Film; Golden Globes '73: Actress--Mus./Comedy (Minnelli), Film--Mus./Comedy, Support. Actor (Grey); Natl. Bd. of Review '72: Director (Fosse), Support. Actor (Grey), Support. Actress (Berenson); Natl. Film Reg. '95; Natl. Soc. Film Critics '72: Support. Actor (Grey); Writers Guild '72: Adapt. Screenplay.

Cabaret Balkan 🦴🦴 *The Powder Keg; Bure Baruta* **1998 (R)** Acerbicly cruel and frequently physically brutal comedy is set in Belgrade one winter night and features characters whose stories turn out to be interrelated and are bookended by the comments of sneering nightclub M.C. Boris (Ristanovski). There are betrayals, feuds, random acts of violence, and various absurdities set in a war-torn country where the veneer of civilization has long-since disappeared. Based on the play "Bure Baruta" by Dukovski. Serbo-Croatian with subtitles. **102m/C; VHS, Streaming.** *YU* Miki (Predrag) Manojlovic; Nikola Ristanovski; Nebojsa Glogovac; Marko Urosevic; Bogdan Diklic; *D:* Goran Paskalyevic;

W: Goran Paskalyevic; Dejan Dukovski; *C:* Milan Spasic; *M:* Zoran Simjanovic.

Cabeza de Vaca **1990 (R)** In 1528, a Spanish expedition shipwrecks in unknown territory off the Florida coast. Only survivor Cabeza de Vaca is captured by the Iguase Indian tribe and made a slave to their shaman. He's later freed, but leaves with respect for their culture. Spanish soldiers find him and want his help in capturing the natives, but he is outraged by their cruelty and must confront his own people. Strong visual style easily brings the audience deeply into this uncharted world. Based on Cabeza de Vaca's book "Naufragios." Director Echevarria's feature film debut. Spanish and Indian with subtitles. **111m/C; VHS, DVD.** *MX SP* Juan Diego; Daniel Gimenez Cacho; Roberto Sosa; Carlos Castanon; Gerardo Villarreal; Roberto Cobo; Jose Flores; Ramon Barragan; *D:* Nicolas Echevarria; *W:* Guillermo Sheridan; Nicolas Echevarria; *C:* Guillermo Navarro; *M:* Mario Lavista.

Cabin Boy **WOOF! 1994 (PG-13)** Obnoxious "fancy lad" Elliott mistakenly boards the wrong boat and becomes the new cabin boy for a ridiculous bunch of mean, smelly sailors. Fish out of water saga is so bad it's—bad, a blundering attempt at parody that's just plain stupid. Surprisingly produced by Tim Burton, this effort will disappoint even diehard fans. Look for Chris' real life dad Bob as the lad's dad; good friend Letterman appears briefly as nasty "Old Salt," but uses the alias Earl Hofert in the final credits. As usual, the acerbic Letterman gets the best line, "Man, oh, man do I hate them fancy lads." We know how you feel, Dave. **80m/C; VHS, DVD, Blu-Ray.** Chris Elliott; Ann Magnuson; Ritch Brinkley; James Gammon; Brian Doyle-Murray; Russ Tamblyn; Brion James; Ricki Lake; Bob Elliott; Andy Richter; ***Cameo(s):*** David Letterman; *D:* Adam Resnick; *W:* Adam Resnick; *C:* Amy Barrett; *M:* Steve Bartek.

Cabin by the Lake **2000** Screenwriter Stanley (Nelson) takes his work a little too seriously when he does research on a story about a serial killer who kidnaps and drowns his female victims. Stanley has his own garden of victims until one young woman escapes and a trap is laid for the killer. **91m/C; VHS, DVD.** Judd Nelson; Hedy Burress; Michael Weatherly; Bernie Coulson; Susan Gibney; *D:* Po-Chih Leung; *W:* C. David Stephens; *C:* Philip Linzey; *M:* Frankie Blue; Daniel Licht. **CABLE**

Cabin Fever **2003 (R)** Scattershot horror/comedy with a twist has five teenagers rent a cabin in the woods for a week contend with a very deadly and very gross virus. A bloody man who appears in the woods is the harbinger of doom for the appropriately sex- and booze-crazed archetypical horror movie teens. They are soon knee-deep in local weirdos and rednecks as well as appropriate amounts of blood and gore. Though not outstanding, pic boasts enough gore to satisfy the most hard-core horror fans. **94m/C; VHS, DVD, Blu-Ray, UMD.** Jordan Ladd; Rider Strong; James DeBello; Cerina Vincent; Joey Kern; Arie Verveen; Giuseppe Andrews; Eli Roth; *D:* Eli Roth; *W:* Eli Roth; Randy Pearlstein; *C:* Scott Kevan; *M:* Nathan Marr.

Cabin Fever 2: Spring Fever **WOOF! 2008 (R)** The flesh-eating virus that infected the water supply in the 2003 flick is back. The water bottling plant delivers contaminated water bottles to the local high school just in time for prom night. Over-the-top gore and grossness with no redeeming humor. Director West disowned this mess, saying re-shoots and the ending were none of his doing, which still leaves him responsible for the rest of the ick. **86m/C; DVD.** Judah Friedlander; Marc Senter; Giuseppe Andrews; Michael Bowen; Mark Borchardt; Rider Strong; Alexi Wasser; Noah Segan; Rusty Kelley; *D:* Ti West; *W:* Joshua Malkin; *C:* Eliot Rockett; *M:* Ryan Shore. **VIDEO**

Cabin in the Sky **1943** A poor woman fights to keep her husband's soul out of the devil's clutches. Based on a Broadway show and featuring an all-Black cast. Lively dance numbers and a musical score with contributions from Duke Ellington. Minnelli's first feature film. **99m/C; VHS, DVD.** Ethel Waters; Eddie Anderson; Lena Horne; Rex Ingram; Louis Armstrong; Duke Ellington; *D:* Vincente Minnelli; *M:* Duke Ellington; Harold Arlen; E.Y. Harburg; George Bassman.

The Cabin in the Woods **2012 (R)** Writers Whedon and Goddard deconstruct what horror fans love about the genre with this brilliant comedy-driven gore-fest that feeds our need for the gruesome and the grotesque. With razor wit and vivid pacing, it tells the story of five average college kids who travel to the so-named location only to become unwitting experiments in...well, to say more would spoil things. Perfectly cast, it goes against the usual expectations of a horror movie about beautiful people in a dangerous place. **95m/C; DVD, Blu-Ray, Streaming; Closed Captioned.** Kristen Connolly; Chris Hemsworth; Anna Hutchison; Fran Kranz; Jesse Williams; Richard Jenkins; Bradley Whitford; Brian White; Amy Acker; *D:* Drew Goddard; *W:* Drew Goddard; Joss Whedon; *C:* Peter Deming; *M:* David Julyan.

The Cabinet of Dr. Caligari *Das Cabinet des Dr. Caligari; Das Kabinett des Doktor Caligari* **1919** A pioneering film in the most extreme expressionistic style about a hypnotist in a carnival and a girl-snatching somnambulist. Highly influential in its approach to lighting, composition, design and acting. Much imitated. Silent. **92m/B; Silent; VHS, DVD, Blu-Ray.** *GE* Conrad Veidt; Werner Krauss; Lil Dagover; Hans von Twardowski; Rudolf Klein-Rogge; Friedrich Feher; Rudolf Lettinger; *D:* Robert Wiene; *W:* Carl Mayer; Hans Janowitz; *C:* Willy Hameister.

Cabiria **1/2 1914** The pioneering Italian epic about a Roman and a slave girl having a love affair in Rome during the Second Punic War. Immense sets and set-pieces; an important influence on Griffith and DeMille. Silent. **123m/B; Silent; VHS, DVD.** *IT* Lidia Quaranta; Bartolomeo Pagano; Umberto Mozzato; *D:* Giovanni Pastrone; *W:* Giovanni Pastrone; Gabriele D'Annunzio; *C:* Segundo de Chomon.

The Cable Guy **1/2 1996 (PG-13)** Carrey's first $20 million paycheck finds cable subscriber Broderick in for a comedic nightmare when he accepts the offer of free movie channels. The overeager installer (Carrey, naturally) turns his life upside down. A little darker humor than Carrey fans may be used to, and don't expect any bodily ventriloquism. Carrey (did we mention he's in it?) gets to act with real life people. Director Stiller does a nice job of reining in his more manic impulses when necessary. Broderick holds his own as the reluctant pal. Original scripter Holtz won a Writer's Guild arbitration for sole writing credit from producer-writer Judd Apatow. **95m/C; VHS, DVD, Blu-Ray.** Jim Carrey; Matthew Broderick; Leslie Mann; George Segal; Diane Baker; Jack Black; Janeane Garofalo; Andy Dick; Charles Napier; Ben Stiller; Bob Odenkirk; David Cross; Owen Wilson; Joel Murray; Kathy Griffin; Sean M. Whalen; Annabelle Gurwitch; Conrad Janis; Alex D. Linz; *D:* Ben Stiller; *W:* Judd Apatow; Lou Holtz, Jr.; *C:* Robert Brinkmann; *M:* John Ottman. MTV Movie Awards '97: Comedic Perf. (Carrey), Villain (Carrey).

Cabo Blanco **1981 (R)** A bartender and a variety of other characters, including an ex-Nazi and a French woman searching for her lover, assemble in Peru after WWII. Nazi Robards controls police chief Rey, while American Bronson runs the local watering hole and eyes French woman Sanda. Hey, this sounds familiar. Everyone shares a common interest: finding a missing treasure of gold, lost in a ship wreck. Remaking "Casablanca" via "The Treasure of Sierra Madre" is never easy. **87m/C; VHS, DVD, Blu-Ray.** Charles Bronson; Jason Robards, Jr.; Dominique Sanda; Fernando Rey; Gilbert Roland; Simon MacCorkindale; *D:* J. Lee Thompson; *W:* Morton S. Fine; Milton S. Gelman; *C:* Alex Phillips, Jr.; *M:* Jerry Goldsmith.

Cactus **1/2 1986** Melodrama about a young French woman, separated from her husband, who faces the reality of losing her sight after a car accident. She experiences a growing relationship with a blind man and contemplates the thought of risky surgery which may improve her eyesight or cause complete blindness. Countering all that blindness and tangled romance is a camera that pans lush Australian landscapes and humorously focuses on the small telling details of daily life. **95m/C; VHS, DVD.** *AU* Isabelle Huppert; Robert Menzies; Monica Maughan; Sheila Florance; Norman Kaye; Banduk Marika; *D:* Paul Cox; *W:* Norman Kaye; Paul Cox; Bob Ellis; *C:* Yuri Sokol; *M:* Giovanni Pergolese; Yannis Markopolous; Elsa Davis.

Cactus Flower **1969 (PG)** Good cast doesn't quite suffice to make this adaptation of a Broadway hit work. A middle-aged bachelor dentist gets involved with a kookie mistress, refusing to admit his real love for his prim and proper receptionist. Hawn's big leap to stardom. **103m/C; VHS, DVD, Blu-Ray.** Walter Matthau; Goldie Hawn; Ingrid Bergman; Jack Weston; Rick Lenz; *D:* Gene Saks; *W:* I.A.L. Diamond; *C:* Charles B(ryant) Lang, Jr.; *M:* Quincy Jones. Oscars '69: Support. Actress (Hawn); Golden Globes '70: Support. Actress (Hawn).

The Caddy **1953** Lewis plays frantic caddy prone to slapstick against Martin's smooth professional golfer with a bent toward singing. Mostly a series of Martin and Lewis sketches that frequently land in the rough. Introduces several songs, including a classic Martin and Lewis rendition of "That's Amore." Look for cameos by a host of professional golfers. **95m/C; DVD.** Dean Martin; Jerry Lewis; Donna Reed; Barbara Bates; Joseph Calleia; Marshall Thompson; Fred Clark; ***Cameo(s):*** Ben Hogan; Sam Snead; Byron Nelson; Julius Boros; Jimmy Thomson; Harry E. Cooper; *D:* Norman Taurog; *W:* Danny Arnold.

Caddyshack **1/2 1980 (R)** Inspired performances by Murray and Dangerfield drive this sublimely moronic comedy onto the green. The action takes place at Bushwood Country Club, where caddy Danny (O'Keefe) is bucking to win the club's college scholarship. Characters involved in various sophomoric set pieces include obnoxious club president Judge Smails (Knight), playboy Ty Webb (Chase), who is too laid back to keep his score, loud, vulgar, and extremely rich Al Czernik (Dangerfield), and filthy gopher-hunting groundskeeper Carl (Murray). Occasional dry moments are followed by scenes of pure (and tasteless) anarchy, so watch with someone immature. Does for golf what "Major League" tried to do for baseball. **99m/C; VHS, DVD, Blu-Ray, HD-DVD.** Chevy Chase; Rodney Dangerfield; Ted (Edward) Knight; Michael O'Keefe; Bill Murray; Sarah Holcomb; Cindy Morgan; Brian Doyle-Murray; Scott Colomby; Dan Resin; Henry Wilcoxon; Elaine Aiken; *D:* Harold Ramis; *W:* Harold Ramis; Brian Doyle-Murray; Doug Kenney; *C:* Stevan Larner; *M:* Johnny Mandel.

Caddyshack 2 **1/2 1988 (PG)** Obligatory sequel to "Caddyshack," minus Bill Murray, who wisely avoided further encroachment of gopher holes, and director Ramis who opted for the screenwriting chore. Mason is the star of the show as a crude self-made millionaire who tangles with the snobs at the country club. Although it occasionally earns a chuckle, "Shack 2" has significantly fewer guffaws than the original, proving once again that funny guys are always undone by lousy scripts and weak direction. **103m/C; VHS, DVD.** Jackie Mason; Chevy Chase; Dan Aykroyd; Dyan Cannon; Robert Stack; Dina Merrill; Randy Quaid; Jessica Lundy; Jonathan Silverman; Chynna Phillips; *D:* Allan Arkush; *W:* Harold Ramis; Peter Torokvei; *C:* Harry Stradling, Jr.; *M:* Ira Newborn. Golden Raspberries '88: Worst Song ("Jack Fresh"), Worst Support. Actor (Aykroyd).

Cadence **1989 (PG-13)** The directorial debut of actor Martin Sheen, this fitful melodrama stars son Charlie as an unruly trooper on a 1960s army base. Placed in an all-black stockade for punishment, he bonds with his brother prisoners by defying the hardcase sergeant (played by Sheen the elder). Characters and situations are intriguing but not rendered effectively. Based on the novel "Count a Lonely Cadence" by Gordon Weaver. **97m/C; VHS, DVD.** Charlie Sheen; Martin Sheen; Laurence Fishburne; Michael Beach; Ramon Estevez; *D:* Martin Sheen; *M:* Georges Delerue.

Cadillac Man **1990 (R)** Williams is the quintessential low-life car salesman in this rather disjointed comedy. A lesser comedic talent might have stalled and been abandoned, but Williams manages to drive away despite the flat script and direction. One storyline follows his attempt to sell 12 cars in 12 days or lose his job, while another follows his confrontation with a gun-toting, mad-as-hell cuckolded husband. Williams and Robbins are often close to being funny in a hyperkinetic way, but the situations are dumb enough to rob most of the scenes of their comedy. Watch for a movie-stealing bit by the spunky waitress at the local Chinese restaurant. **95m/C; VHS, DVD, Blu-Ray.** Robin Williams; Tim Robbins; Pamela Reed; Fran Drescher; Zack Norman; Annabella Sciorra; Lori Petty; Paul Guilfoyle; Tristen Skylar; *D:* Roger Donaldson; *W:* Ken Friedman; *C:* David Gribble; *M:* J. Peter Robinson.

Cadillac Ranch **1/2 1996 (R)** CJ (Amis), Frances (Feeney), and Mary Katharine (Humphrey) Crowley are three squabbling Texas sisters who have reunited to celebrate Mary K.'s upcoming marriage. CJ works in a strip club owned by greedy ex-Texas Ranger Wood (Lloyd), who sent their long-gone daddy, Travis (Metzler), to prison for a heist Wood was involved in. When CJ gets fired, the threesome steal a key from Wood that will supposedly access money from the heist and the vengeful Wood goes after them. **104m/C; VHS, DVD.** Suzy Amis; Renee Humphrey; Caroleen Feeney; Christopher Lloyd; Jim Metzler; Linden Ashby; Charles Solomon, Jr.; *D:* Lisa Gottlieb; *W:* Jennifer Cecil; *C:* Bruce Douglas Johnson; *M:* Christopher Tyng.

Cadillac Records **2008 (R)** Chronicles the rise and fall of legendary Chicago blues label Chess Records in the 1950s and 1960s, which began with Muddy Waters (Wright) and later featured Chuck Berry (Mos Def), Etta James (Knowles, also serving as executive producer), and Howlin' Wolf (Walker). Founded by brothers Leonard and Phil Chess, Polish immigrants who rose from poverty, the film ignores Phil and focuses only on Leonard (Brody). Packed with the great sounds of an era that led to the birth of rock and roll, writer-director Martin showcases the singers more than the story. The fact that the actors did their own performances gives it a natural feel though, led by Knowles, whose powerful voice captures the spirit of the passionate and troubled James. **108m/C; Blu-Ray, On Demand.** Emmanuelle Chriqui; Adrien Brody; Gabrielle Union; Beyonce Knowles; Mos Def; Jeffrey Wright; Eamonn Walker; Cedric the Entertainer; Tammy Blanchard; Columbus Short; Eric Bogosian; *D:* Darnell Martin; *W:* Darnell Martin; *C:* Anastas Michos; *M:* Terence Blanchard.

Caesar and Cleopatra **1/2 1946** Based on the classic George Bernard Shaw play. Caesar meets the beautiful Cleopatra in ancient Egypt and helps her gain control of her life. Remains surprisingly true to Shaw's adaptation, unlike many other historical films of the same era. **135m/C; VHS, DVD.** *GB* Claude Rains; Vivien Leigh; Stewart Granger; Flora Robson; Francis L. Sullivan; Cecil Parker; *D:* Gabriel Pascal; *C:* Robert Krasker.

Caesar the Conqueror *Giulio Cesare, il conquistatore delle Gallie* **1963** Based (incredibly loosely) on a book supposed to be Julius Caesar's autobiography, covers the Roman leader's battles against Gaul. Coincidentally, marketing this film probably also took incredible gall at the time. Disappointing even for diehard fans of Italian Sword and Sandal costume dramas from the 1960s. **103m/C; DVD.** *IT* Cameron Mitchell; Rick (Rik) Battaglia; Dominique Wilms; Ivica Pajer; Raffaella Carra; Carlo Tamberlani; Giulio Donnini; Cesare Fontani; Carla Calo; Nerio Bernardi; Bruno Tocci; Aldo Pini; Lucia Randi; Enzo Petracca; *D:* Tanio Boccia; *W:* Gaius Julius Caesar; Nino Scolaro; Arpad DeRiso; George Higgins 2; *C:* Romolo Garroni; *M:* Guido Robuschi; Gian Stellari.

Cafe **2010** A Philadelphia cafe is the center of the local community as various customers and employees interact. There's a couple of low-level drug dealers, laptop geeks, friends-with-no-benefits, and would-be romances. One of the geeks is involved in a virtual reality world with a cyber girl who insists the geek isn't real, leading to some ridiculous fantasy sequences he's supposedly watching online. **95m/C; DVD.** Jennifer Love Hewitt; Jamie Kennedy; Richard Short; Alexa Vega; Madeline Carroll; Hubbel Palmer; *D:* Marc Erlbaum; *W:* Marc Erlbaum; *C:* Joseph White; *M:* Christopher Brady. **VIDEO**

Cafe au Lait *Metisse* **1994** Actor/director/writer Kassovitz scores in his debut feature about an interracial menage a trois.

Beautiful mulatto Lola (Mauduech) is pregnant but she's not sure by which of her two contrasting lovers (who don't yet know about each other). It could be white, Jewish, easygoing bicycle messenger Felix (Kassovitz) or stuffy, wealthy, black Moslem student Jamal (Kounde). Both men desire the fatherhood role and both move in with Lola to share responsibility. This is not without complications. Generally light and frothy without ignoring racial tensions. French with subtitles. **94m/C; VHS, DVD.** *FR* Mathieu Kassovitz; Julie Mauduech; Hubert Kounde; Vincent Cassel; Tadek Lokcinski; Jany Holt; ***D:*** Mathieu Kassovitz; ***W:*** Mathieu Kassovitz; ***C:*** Pierre Aim; ***M:*** Marie Daulne; Jean-Louis Daulne.

Cafe Express ✓✓ 1/2 **1983** A con artist (he sells coffee illegally aboard an Italian train) stays one step ahead of the law as he raises money to help his ailing son. As in "Bread and Chocolate," Manfredi is again the put-upon working class hero comedically attempting to find a better way of life in this bittersweet tale. **90m/C; VHS, DVD.** *IT* Nino Manfredi; Gigi Reder; Adolfo Celi; Vittorio Mezzogiorno; ***D:*** Nanni Loy.

Cafe Lumiere ✓ 1/2 *Kohi jikou* **2005** Taiwanese director Hou dedicates his homage to Japanese master Yasujiro Ozu with a narrative about loneliness, isolation, and modern urban life. In Tokyo, Yoko (pop star Hitoto in her debut) announces to her father and stepmother that she's pregnant but has no intention of marrying. Her best friend is bookseller Hijame (Asano). She is doing research on composer Jiang Wen-Ye (whose work is used on the soundtrack); he's doing a computer art project about the city's commuter trains, which mean you see a lot of the subway system. It's understated to the point of inertia. Japanese with subtitles. **104m/C; DVD.** ***D:*** Hou Hsiao-hsien; ***W:*** Tien-wen Chu; ***C:*** Lee Ping-Bing; ***M:*** Jiang Wen.

Cafe Metropole ✓✓ **1937** Parisian restauranteur Victor Lombard (Menjou) gets into money trouble and thinks he's getting out when he wins at baccarat. Too bad the check he gets from impecunious American Alexander Brown (Power) is rubber. Lombard blackmails Brown into pretending to be Russian royalty to romance heiress Laura (Young). Naturally, Brown falls in love so Lombard then tells Laura's protective daddy that Brown is a fraud. It's a romantic comedy so things work out for practically everyone. **84m/B; DVD.** Adolphe Menjou; Tyrone Power; Loretta Young; Charles Winninger; Gregory Ratoff; Helen Westley; ***D:*** Edward H. Griffith; ***W:*** Jacques Deval; ***C:*** Lucien N. Andriot; ***M:*** Louis Silvers.

Cafe Society ✓✓ 1/2 **1997 (R)** The fictional nightclub El Casbah is the setting for director De Felitta's debut take on a 1952 New York prostitution scandal. Wealthy young playboy Mickey Jelke (Whaley) prefers to mix with lowlifes rather than high society. Newcomer Jack Kale (Gallagher) is working the scene and turns out to be an undercover cop investigating a prostiution ring operating out of the clubs. Jack befriends both Mickey and his latest girlfriend, in-the-know Patricia Ward (Boyle), who's not above selling her favors. Then patsy Jelke gets indicted as a pimp and all cafe society's tawdriness is exposed. **104m/C; VHS, DVD.** Peter Gallagher; Frank Whaley; Lara Flynn Boyle; John Spencer; Anna Thomson; David Patrick Kelly; Paul Guilfoyle; ***D:*** Raymond De Felitta; ***W:*** Raymond De Felitta; ***C:*** Mike Mayers; ***M:*** Chris Guardino.

Café Society ✓✓ 1/2 **2016 (PG-13)** Woody Allen digs again into his obsession with nostalgia with mixed results in this dramedy set in the golden age of Hollywood. In the 1930s, Bobby Dorfman (Eisenberg, doing a bit of a Woody impression, per the usual in these films) moves to Hollywood to work for his Uncle Phil (Carell). He quickly falls in love with Phil's secretary Vonnie (Stewart), but she's torn between him and a married man who she's seeing, who happens to be Uncle Phil. Allen's latest looks amazing with gorgeous costume design and a gorgeous capturing of luxurious Hollywood, but it's a little thin. Stewart steals the movie. **96m/C; DVD, Blu-Ray.** Jesse Eisenberg; Kristen Stewart; Steve Carell; Jeannie Berlin; Blake Lively; ***D:*** Woody Allen; ***W:*** Woody Allen; ***C:*** Vittorio Storaro.

Caffeine ✓✓ **2006** Intermittently amusing workplace comedy, set in London, about the denizens of the Black Cat Cafe. Manager Rachel fires boyfriend/chef Charlie for cheating on her and leaves ill-prepared waiter Tom in charge of the kitchen; waiter Dylan is waiting to hear if his novel is going to be published; waitress Vanessa must bring her crazy grandmother Lucy to work for the day; and the customers have an equal number of problems, including bad blind dates, jealous boyfriends, and cross-dressing secrets. **88m/C; DVD.** Marsha Thomason; Callum Blue; Breckin Meyer; Mena Suvari; Mark Pellegrino; Katherine Heigl; Daz Crawford; Mike Vogel; Roz Witt; Andrew Lee Pitts; Sonya Walger; Orlando Seale; ***D:*** John Cosgrove; ***W:*** Dean Craig; ***C:*** Shawn Maurer; ***M:*** David Kitay.

The Cage ✓ **1989 (R)** Gangsters enlist a brain-damaged Vietnam vet played by Ferrigno to participate in illegal "cage fights," enclosed wrestling matches fought to the death. Crude and annoying. **101m/C; VHS, DVD.** Lou Ferrigno; Reb Brown; Michael Dante; Mike Moroff; Marilyn Tokuda; James Shigeta; Al Ruscio; ***D:*** Hugh Kelley.

The Cage ✓✓✓ **1990** Sent to prison for murdering his girlfriend, Jive has no idea what the pen has in store for him. The inmates stage a mock trial, the defendant is found guilty and the sentence is too horrible to imagine. From a stage play by the San Quentin Drama Workshop and co-starring Hayes, author of "Midnight Express." **90m/C; VHS, DVD.** Rick Cluchey; William Hayes; ***D:*** Rick Cluchey; ***W:*** Rick Cluchey.

Cage of Evil ✓✓ 1/2 **1960** Average B-movie crime drama. Police detective Harper is passed over for promotion yet again, he's susceptible to the blandishments of Holly, whose boyfriend is a diamond thief Harper is investigating. Holly easily persuades Harper to bump off her beau and take her and the gems to Mexico. Only Harper's partner Kearns is suspicious. **71m/B; DVD.** Ron Foster; Patricia Blair; Harp McGuire; John Maxwell; Preston Hanson; ***D:*** Edward L. Cahn; ***W:*** Orville H. Hampton; ***C:*** Maury Gertsman; ***M:*** Paul Sawtell.

Caged ✓✓✓ **1950** Innocent Marie Allen (Parker) is sent to prison as an accomlice to her husband's fatal armed robbery attempt because she was in the car. Once inside, the frightened, pregnant widow encounters reform-minded warden Benton (Moorehead) and vicious matron Harper (Emerson), who fight for her soul, along with a varied cast of fellow inmates. Harper's vicious treatment of the inmates eventually turns Allen into a hardened con. A classic, which shouldn't be lumped in with later exploitation examples of the genre. Excellent performances and scripting make it a fine representation of noir. **96m/B; DVD.** Eleanor Parker; Agnes Moorehead; Hope Emerson; Ellen Corby; Betty Garde; Jan Sterling; Lee Patrick; Olive Deering; Sheila MacRae; Jane Darwell; Gertrude Michael; Don Beddoe; Edith Evanson; Gertrude Hoffman; ***D:*** John Cromwell; ***W:*** Bernard C. Schoenfeld; Virginia Kellogg; ***C:*** Carl Guthrie; ***M:*** Max Steiner.

Caged Animal ✓ 1/2 *The Wrath of Cain* **2010 (R)** Violent and predictable. Crime kingpin Miles 'Cain' Skinner is sentenced to life in prison at the same penitentiary as his lifelong rival Redfoot. As they prepare to battle for supremacy behind bars, Cain learns his son is following too closely in his criminal footsteps and may also spend his life in the joint unless Cain can prevent it. **78m/C; DVD, Blu-Ray.** Ving Rhames; Robert LaSardo; Robert Patrick; Nipsey Hussle; Erick Nathan; ***D:*** Ryan Combs; ***W:*** Ryan Combs; Kevin Carraway; Lawrence Sara; ***C:*** Mario Signore; ***M:*** Cody Westheimer. **VIDEO**

Caged Fury ✓ **1980 (R)** American women being held captive in Southeast Asia are brainwashed into becoming walking time bombs. Yes, that dame's gonna blow. Made in the Philippines with the best of intentions. **90m/C; VHS, DVD.** *PH* Bernadette Williams; Taaffe O'Connell; Jennifer Laine; ***D:*** Cirio H. Santiago.

Caged Fury ✓ **1990** Two Los Angeles women allegedly commit sexual crimes and are sent to prison. Cheap, exploitive women's prison rehash. **85m/C; VHS, DVD, Blu-Ray.** Erik Estrada; Richie Barathy; Roxanna Michaels; Paul Smith; James Hong; Greg Cummins; Mindi Miller; ***D:*** Bill Milling.

Caged Hearts ✓ **1995 (R)** Chicks-behind-bars flick finds Kate (Genzel) and Sharon (McClure) framed for murder by a shady organization called "The Shield." Cliches abound. **87m/C; VHS, DVD.** Tane McClure; Carrie Genzel; Taylor Leigh; Nick Wilder; ***D:*** Henri Charr.

Caged Heat ✓✓ *Renegade Girls; Caged Females* **1974 (R)** Low-budget babes-behind-bars film touted as the best sexploitation film of the day. Demme's directorial debut is a genre-altering installment in Roger Corman's formulaic cellblock Cinderella cycle. Recycled plot—innocent woman is put behind bars, where she loses some of her innocence—boasts an updated treatment. These babes may wear hot pants and gratuitously bare their midriffs, but they're not brainless bimbos. They're strong individuals who work together to liberate themselves. Reached cult status. Cult diva Steele returned to the big screen after six years to play the wheelchair-ridden prison warden, written specifically for her. **83m/C; VHS, DVD.** Juanita Brown; Erica Gavin; Roberta Collins; Barbara Steele; Ella Reid; Cheryl "Rainbeaux" Smith; John Aprea; Amy Barrett; Gary Goetzman; ***D:*** Jonathan Demme; ***W:*** Jonathan Demme; ***C:*** Tak Fujimoto; ***M:*** John Cale.

Caged Terror **WOOF!** **1972** Two urbanites hit the countryside for a weekend and meet a band of crazy rapists who ravage the wife and set the husband raging with bloodthirsty revenge. Squalid stroll through the ruins. **76m/C; VHS, DVD.** Percy Harkness; Elizabeth Suzuki; Leon Morenzie; ***D:*** Barry McLean.

Caged Women ✓ *Women's Penitentiary 4* **1984 (R)** Undercover journalist enters a women's prison and gets the usual eyeful. Mattei used the pseudonym Vincent Dawn. **97m/C; VHS, DVD.** *FR IT* Laura Gemser; Gabriele Tinti; Lorraine (De Sette) De Selle; Maria Romano; ***D:*** Bruno Mattei.

Cahill: United States Marshal ✓✓ **1973 (PG)** The aging Duke in one of his lesser moments, portraying a marshal who comes to the aid of his sons. The boys are mixed up with a gang of outlaws, proving that no matter how good a parent you are, sometimes the kids just lean toward the wayward. Turns out, though, that the boys harbor a grudge against the old man due to years of workaholic neglect. Will Duke see the error of his ways and reconcile with the delinquent boys? Will he catch the outlaw leader? Will he go on to star in other Duke vehicles? **103m/C; VHS, DVD, Blu-Ray.** John Wayne; Gary Grimes; George Kennedy; Neville Brand; Marie Windsor; Harry Carey, Jr.; Clay O'Brien; Walter Barnes; ***D:*** Andrew V. McLaglen; ***M:*** Elmer Bernstein.

Cain and Mabel ✓✓ 1/2 **1936** Would-be musical comedy star (and ex-waitress) Mabel O'Dare (Davies) and heavyweight boxer Larry Cain (Gable) are promoted as a couple to boost their careers although they can't stand each other. Of course that changes but when the duo decide to ditch their time in the limelight for marriage and regular jobs it causes consternation among their handlers. Davies, a little too mature for such naivety, did best with the comedic portion of her role while Gable is most notable for being mustache-less per director Bacon's insistence. **89m/B; DVD.** Marion Davies; Clark Gable; Allen Jenkins; Roscoe Karns; Walter Catlett; Ruth Donnelly; Pert Kelton; Robert Paige; Hobart Cavanaugh; ***D:*** Lloyd Bacon; ***W:*** Laird Doyle; ***C:*** George Barnes.

The Caine Mutiny ✓✓✓✓ **1954** A group of naval officers revolt against a captain they consider mentally unfit. Bogart is masterful as Captain Queeg, obsessed with cleanliness while onboard and later a study in mental meltdown during the court-martial of a crew member who participated in the mutiny. Based on the Pulitzer-winning novel by Herman Wouk, the drama takes a close look at the pressure-filled life aboard ship during WWII. **125m/C; VHS, DVD, Blu-Ray.** Humphrey Bogart; Jose Ferrer; Van Johnson; Fred MacMurray; Lee Marvin; Claude Akins; E.G. Marshall; Robert Francis; May Wynn; Tom Tully; Arthur Franz; Warner Anderson; Katherine Warren; Jerry Paris; Steve Brodie; Whit Bissell; Robert Bray; Ted Cooper; ***D:*** Edward Dmytryk; ***W:*** Stanley Roberts; Michael Blankfort; ***C:*** Franz Planer; ***M:*** Max Steiner.

The Caine Mutiny Court Martial ✓✓✓ **1988 (PG)** A young lieutenant is up for a court-martial after taking control of the USS Caine in the midst of a typhoon. In order to save him, his lawyer must discredit the paranoid Commander Queeg. As the events of the mutiny unfold, it becomes clear that Queeg's obsession with discipline had become a threat to everyone aboard. Good performances, particularly by Bogosian as the lawyer. Based on the novel by Pulitzer prize-winner Herman Wouk. **100m/C; VHS, DVD.** Jeff Daniels; Eric Bogosian; Brad Davis; Peter Gallagher; Michael Murphy; Kevin J. O'Connor; Daniel H. Jenkins; ***D:*** Robert Altman. **TV**

Cain's Cutthroats ✓ *Cain's Way; The Blood Seekers; Justice Cain* **1971 (R)** A former Confederate army captain and a bounty hunting preacher team up to settle the score with soldiers on a gang-raping, murdering spree. **87m/C; VHS, DVD.** Scott Brady; John Carradine; Robert Dix; Don Epperson; Adair Jamison; Darwin Joston; Bruce (Kemp) Kimball; Russ McCubbin; Valda Hansen; ***D:*** Kent Osborne; ***W:*** Wilton Denmark; ***C:*** Ralph Waldo; ***M:*** Harley Hatcher.

Cairo ✓✓ **1942** War correspondent Young lands in Cairo where he is supposed to pass along classified information to a Nazi spy posing as a Brit. He meets and falls in love with American movie queen thought to be enemy agent (MacDonald) and a race across the desert follows when Young is trapped in a pyramid. Catchy tunes can't save this cheesy WWII spy spoof that marked the end of MacDonald's MGM contract. **101m/B; DVD.** Jeanette MacDonald; Robert Young; Ethel Waters; Reginald Owen; Grant Mitchell; Lionel Atwill; Eduardo Ciannelli; Mitchell Lewis; ***D:*** W.S. Van Dyke; ***W:*** John McClain; ***M:*** Herbert Stothart.

Cairo Time ✓✓ **2009** Old-fashioned romance about a middle-aged woman set free by her experiences in Cairo (both with the city and a particular man). Juliette (Clarkson) travels to Egypt to spend some time with her hubby Mark (McCamus) who's working at a Gaza refugee camp. But when he can't get away, Mark asks former colleague Tareq (Siddig) to serve as Juliette's tour guide, which leads to a certain attraction between the two. **88m/C; DVD.** *CA IR* Patricia Clarkson; Alexander Siddig; Tom McCamus; Elena Anaya; Ruba Nadda; ***C:*** Luc Montpellier; ***M:*** Niall Byrne.

Cake ✓✓ **2005 (R)** Happily single with no interest in married life, travel writer Pippa (Graham) is thrown for a loop when her ill publisher father puts her in charge of his wedding publication. As her day-to-day work causes her to face her marital phobias, her fling with her usual studly-type guy (Diggs) is complicated by her feelings for her more grounded mentor (Sutcliffe)at the magazine. **94m/C; DVD.** Heather Graham; David Sutcliffe; Taye Diggs; Sandra Oh; Cheryl Hines; Sarah Chalke; Reagan Pasternak; Kate Kelton; Bruce Grey; Sabrina Grdevich; Suzanne Cyr; ***D:*** Nisha Ganatra; ***W:*** Tassie Cameron; ***C:*** Gregory Middleton; ***M:*** Andrew Lockington. **VIDEO**

Cake ✓ 1/2 **2014 (R)** Claire Simmons (Aniston) is in constant pain. She is one of those movie creations that uses biting criticisms of others to hide her own skeletons. Turning the tables on this anti-hero and asking us to root for her as she deals with the root causes of her real internal agony, Aniston deserves praise for working outside of her traditional box. She scowls confidently and appropriately. But it is at the behest of a melodrama that's too purposefully designed to win awards and garner attention that it forgets to be realistic or entertaining. **102m/C; DVD.** Jennifer Aniston; Sam Worthington; Adriana Barraza; Anna Kendrick; Mamie Gummer; Felicity Huffman; Chris Messina; William H. Macy; ***D:*** Daniel Barnz; ***W:*** Patrick Tobin; ***C:*** Rachel Morrison; ***M:*** Christophe Beck.

Cake: A Wedding Story ✓✓ **2007** Lovers Juliet and Felix are planning to elope until their families take over and insist on a lavish county club wedding instead. Things get out of hand and the fed-up bride-to-be makes other arrangements and bolts before the ceremony. The confused would-be groom has inadvertently missed her message though. **93m/C; DVD.** Catherine Anderson Martin; Adam Green; William Zabka; Thomas Calabro; G.W. Bailey; Ann Cusack; Joe Estevez; Becky Jane Romine; Mary Ellen Trainor; William Wallace; *D:* William Wallace; *W:* George Langworthy; Iain Weatherby; *C:* Kirk Douglas; *M:* Thomas Dawson, Jr.

The Cake Eaters 🦴🦴 1/2 **2007 (R)** It's not a happy family reunion. Unsuccessful indie rocker Guy (Bartok) is in the doghouse with younger bro Beagle (Stanford) when he finally returns home after their mother's death. With his dad Easy (Dern) abdicating responsibility, Beagle was forced into being the family caretaker. Now he's attracted to terminally ill but fiercely determined teen Georgia (Stewart), whose family is more closely involved with Beagle's than he realizes. Meanwhile Guy has decided to make a play for ex-fiancee Stephanie (Shor) who's involved with another guy. Directorial debut of Masterson. **86m/C; DVD.** Aaron Stanford; Kristen Stewart; Jayce Bartok; Bruce Dern; Talia Balsam; Elizabeth Ashley; Melissa Leo; Miriam Shor; Jesse L. Martin; *D:* Mary Stuart Masterson; *W:* Jayce Bartok; *C:* Peter Masterson; *M:* Duncan Sheik.

The Calamari Wrestler WOOF! *Ika resuraa* **2004** A surreal satire of "Rocky" (and similar sports films) and the Buddhist concept of Reincarnation, a former champion pro wrestler is comes back as a giant squid and retakes his former championship while trying to rekindle his romance with his human girlfriend. Various rivals reincarnate themselves as sea life as well, and rubber monster fights abound. **86m/C; DVD.** *JP* Kana Ishida; Osamu Nishimura; Miho Shiraishi; Yoshihiro Takayama; *D:* Minoru Kawasaki; *W:* Minoru Kawasaki; Masakazu Migita.

Calamity Jane 🦴🦴🦴 **1953** In one of her best Warner musicals, Day stars as the rip-snortin', gun-totin' Calamity Jane of Western lore, in an on-again, off-again romance with Wild Bill Hickok. **101m/C; VHS, DVD, Blu-Ray.** Doris Day; Howard Keel; Allyn Ann McLerie; Dick Wesson; *D:* David Butler; *W:* James O'Hanlon; *C:* Wilfred M. Cline; *M:* Sammy Fain; *M:* Paul Francis Webster. Oscars '53: Song ("Secret Love").

Calcutta 🦴 1/2 **1947** Pals Neale Gordon (Ladd) and Pedro Blake (Bendix) are cargo pilots routing flights between Chungking and Calcutta. When their pal Bill is murdered, they become suspicious of his former fiancee, Virginia. **83m/B; DVD.** Alan Ladd; Gail Russell; William Bendix; June Duprez; Lowell Gilmore; *D:* John Farrow; *W:* Seton I. Miller.

Calendar 🦴🦴🦴 **1993** A Canadian photographer (Egoyan) is hired to take pictures of ancient Armenian churches for a calendar. His wife (Egoyan's real-life spouse Khanjian) accompanies him, serving as a translator, and they hire a driver (Adamian) who turns out to be an architectural expert. Told in flashback, the film gradually reveals a romantic triangle—with the photographer becoming so caught up in his work that he fails to realize his wife, increasingly drawn to her ethnic heritage, and their driver are having an affair. This romantic puzzle also includes the photographer, having returned to Canada wifeless and apparently seeking a replacement, having dinner with a series of women he's meet through the personals. In English and Armenian. **73m/C; VHS, DVD.** *CA* Atom Egoyan; Arsinee Khanjian; Ashot Adamian; *D:* Atom Egoyan; *W:* Atom Egoyan; *C:* Norayr Kasper.

Calendar Girl Murders 🦴🦴 1/2 **1984** Minor mystery about the murder of some girlie magazine pinups. **104m/C; VHS, DVD.** Robert Culp; Tom Skerritt; Barbara Parkins; Sharon Stone; *D:* William A. Graham; *M:* Brad Fiedel. **TV**

Calendar Girls 🦴🦴 1/2 **2003 (PG-13)** The local members of the Women's Institute club in Yorkshire decide to pose nude for a calendar in order to raise money for leukemia research. The calendar, surprisingly, is a hit, even though the models are a little older than your usual calendar pinup girls. Enjoyable for the right audience (read: fans of veddy understated British humor that is secondary to the drama), but starts losing cohesiveness near the end. Loosely based on a true story. **108m/C; VHS, DVD.** *GB* Dame Helen Mirren; Julie Walters; John Alderton; Linda Bassett; Annette Crosbie; Philip Glenister; Ciaran Hinds; Celia Imrie; Geraldine James; Penelope Wilton; George Costigan; Graham Crowden; John Fortune; *Cameo(s):* Jay Leno; *D:* Nigel Cole; *W:* Juliette Towhidi; Tim Firth; *C:* Ashley Rowe; *M:* Patrick Doyle.

Caliber 9 🦴🦴 *Milano Calibro 9; The Contract* **1972** Violent crime thriller from Di Leo where loyalty has little meaning in relation to survival. Paroled ex-con Ugo (Moschin) is targeted by both his mobster boss Americano (Stander) and the cops who believe he's been hiding loot from a botched robbery. Ugo won't say anything so he's given a job to keep him close by but he has his own agenda. Scene-stealing Adorf plays criminal Rocco, whose ruthlessness escalates the violence. Italian with subtitles. **88m/C; DVD.** *IT* Gastone Moschin; Lionel Stander; Mario Adorf; Phillippe LeRoy; Barbara Bouchet; Luigi Pistilli; Ivo Garrani; Frank Wolff; *D:* Fernando Di Leo; *W:* Fernando Di Leo; *C:* Franco Villa; *M:* Luis Bacalov.

California 🦴🦴 **1963** Historical adventure set in 1841. Mexican general Francisco Hernandez (Pate) pits his troops against his half-brother, Michael O'Casey (Mahoney), and Michael's revolutionaries who want California to become part of the United States. **76m/B; DVD.** Jock Mahoney; Michael Pate; Faith Domergue; Susan Seaforth Hayes; Rodolfo Hoyos; Nestor Paiva; *D:* Hamil Petroff; *W:* James West; *C:* Eddie (Edward) Fitzgerald; *M:* Richard LaSalle.

California 🦴🦴 1/2 *California addio; Lo chiamavano California* **1977** At the end of the Civil War a newly released POW seeks revenge on a band of Union renegades for the murder of his friend. Currently only available as part of the 'Westerns Unchained' collection. **98m/C; Blu-Ray.** *IT SP* Giuliano Gemma; William Berger; Miguel Bose; Chris Avram; Paola Dominguin; *D:* Michele Lupo; *W:* Roberto Leoni; Franco Bucceri; Nico Ducci; Mino Roli; *C:* Alejandro Ulloa; *M:* Gianni Ferrio. **VIDEO**

California Dreamin' 🦴🦴 **2007** In 1999, a platoon of American Marines escort a NATO train traveling through Romania. They lack the proper paperwork and get sidelined in a remote area where local leader Doiaru, who's the railway station manager, refuses to let them continue as he ignores messages from officials at the capitol for his own reasons. Director Nemescu died shortly after the film shoot and it could use some editing but the movie deftly juggles various plots into a dark comedy that's based on a true story. English and Romanian with subtitles. **156m/C; DVD.** *RO* Razvan Vasilescu; Armand Assante; Jamie Elman; Maria Dinulescu; Ion Sapdaru; Alex Margineanu; Andi Vasluianu; *D:* Cristian Nemescu; *W:* Cristian Nemescu; Catherine Linstrum; Tudor Voican; *C:* Liviu Marghidan.

California Dreaming 🦴🦴 **1979 (R)** Nerdy young man heads west to California where he tries to fit in with the local beach crowd. Reminiscent of the popular beach movies of the '60s. **93m/C; VHS, Streaming.** Dennis Christopher; Tanya Roberts; Glynnis O'Connor; John Calvin; Seymour Cassel; *D:* John Hancock.

California Dreaming *Out of Omaha* **2007** Stu (Foley) and Ginger (Thompson) Gainer seem like the typical married suburban couple: they have jobs, they have a house, they have two kids and a dog. Control freak Ginger thinks it would be fun to rent an RV and take a family vacation from their Omaha home to California. Naturally, it's the road trip from heck (the pic is rated PG after all). **?m/CDVD.** Dave Foley; Lea Thompson; Patricia Richardson; Ethan Phillips; Vicki Lewis; Lindsay Seim; David Kalis; Melissa Jarecke; Nicholas Fackler; Ethan Philips; *D:* Linda Voorhees; *W:* Linda Voorhees; *C:* James Bartle.

California Girls 🦴 **1984** Radio station stages a beauty contest and three sexy ladies prove to be tough competition. Features women in little swimsuits, minimal plot, and a soundtrack by the Police, Kool & the Gang, Blondie, Queen, and 10cc. **83m/C; VHS, DVD.** Al Music; Mary McKinley; Alicia Allen; Lantz Douglas; Barbara Parks; *D:* Rick Wallace; *C:* Gil Hubbs.

The California Kid 🦴🦴 **1974** A sadistic small town sheriff (Morrow) deals with speeders by ramming their car and sending them over a cliff. Eventually a relative of one of his victims (Sheen) shows up to find out what happened to his brother. He is unhappy to say the least. And what better way to show your unhappiness than to challenge the sheriff to a deadly mountain race? **75m/C; DVD.** Martin Sheen; Vic Morrow; Michelle Phillips; Nick Nolte; Janit Baldwin; Gary Morgan; Frederic Downs; Don Mantooth; Joe Estevez; Britt Leach; Norman Bartold; Barbara Collentine; Gavan O'Herlihy; Michael Richardson; Jack McCulloch; Ken Johnson; Monika Henreid; Sandy Brown Wyeth; *D:* Richard T. Heffron; *W:* Richard Compton; *C:* Terry Meade; *M:* Luchi De Jesus.

California Solo 🦴 1/2 **2012** Contrived character study though Carlyle does well by his embittered, self-destructive character. Former '90s Britpop rocker Lachlan is now working on an organic farm in LA. A drunk driving arrest reveals an old drug conviction that could get him deported and Lachlan is forced to deal with what he's done with his life. **94m/C; DVD.** Robert Carlyle; Alexia Rasmussen; Danny Masterson; Kathleen Wilhoite; Michael Des Barres; William Russ; *D:* Marshall Lewy; *W:* Marshall Lewy; *C:* James Laxton; *M:* T. Griffin.

California Straight Ahead 🦴🦴 **1925** Denny—whose niche in the '20s was silent action comedies, and who had teamed with director Pollard earlier in the decade to produce "The Leatherpushers" series—stars in this silent actioner which features a cross-country road trip, zoo animals-on-a-rampage, and a car-racing conclusion (sounds like an action formula ahead of its time). Audiences didn't realize until the talkies that the All-American manly man was in fact played by a Brit. For those who revel in trivia, Denny appeared in the 1961 "Batman." **77m/B; Silent; VHS, DVD.** Reginald Denny; Gertrude (Olmstead) Olmsted; Tom Wilson; Lucille Ward; John Steppling; *D:* Harry A. Pollard.

California Suite 🦴🦴🦴 **1978 (PG)** The posh Beverly Hills Hotel is the setting for four unrelated Neil Simon skits, ranging from a battling husband and wife to feuding friends. Smith is notable as a neurotic English actress in town for the Oscar awards while Caine is effectively low-key in the role of her bisexual husband. Simonized dialogue is crisp and funny. **103m/C; VHS, DVD.** Alan Alda; Michael Caine; Bill Cosby; Jane Fonda; Walter Matthau; Richard Pryor; Maggie Smith; Elaine May; *D:* Herbert Ross; *W:* Neil Simon; *C:* David M. Walsh; *M:* Claude Bolling. Oscars '78: Support. Actress (Smith); Golden Globes '79: Actress--Mus./Comedy (Smith).

The California Trail 🦴 1/2 **1933** The corrupt mayor of La Loma, California, is attempting to force the peons to deed over their land by starving them out with the help of his brother, the commander of the local troops. Santa Fe Stewart is hired to bring in food relief and gets into big trouble with the crooked authorities. **65m/B; DVD.** Buck Jones; George Humbert; Luis Alberni; Helen Mack; Chris-Pin (Ethier Crispin Martini) Martin; Charles Stevens; Carlos Villarias; Emile Chautard; *D:* Lambert Hillyer; *W:* Lambert Hillyer; *C:* Benjamin (Ben H.) Kline.

Caligula WOOF! 1980 Infamous, expensive, extremely graphic, and sexually explicit adaptation of the life of the mad Roman emperor, Caligula. Scenes of decapitation, necrophilia, rape, bestiality, and sadomasochism abound. Biggest question is why Gielgud, O'Toole, and McDowell lent their talents to this monumentally abhorred film (not to mention Gore Vidal on the writing end, who didn't want the credit). Adult magazine publisher Bob Guccione coproduced and didn't particularly want to release it. Also available in a censored, "R" rated version. **143m/C; VHS, DVD.** *IT* Malcolm McDowell; John Gielgud; Peter O'Toole; Dame Helen Mirren; Theresa-Ann Savoy; John Steiner; Paolo Bonacelli; Adriana Asti; *D:* Tinto Brass; *W:* Gore Vidal; *C:* Tinto Brass; Silvano Ippoliti; *M:* Paul Clemente.

The Call 🦴🦴 *The Hive* **2013 (R)** Jordan Turner (Berry) is a 911 operator still suffering the emotional scars of a mishandled call when she takes over a cry for help from kidnapped teen Casey Welson (Breslin), who is reaching out from the trunk of a car. An old-fashioned and effective thriller, director Anderson's film falls apart in the final act but he works wonders cutting back and forth between Berry and Breslin before then. His talent at crafting well-made thrillers helps boost a disappointingly generic script. **94m/C; DVD, Blu-Ray.** Halle Berry; Abigail Breslin; Morris Chestnut; Michael Imperioli; Michael Eklund; Justina Machado; Roma Maffia; David Otunga; *D:* Brad Anderson; *W:* Richard D'Ovidio; *C:* Tom Yatsko; *M:* John Debney.

Call Her Savage 🦴 1/2 **1932** Pre-Code melodrama finds Texan Nasa (a scantily-clad Bow) causing all kinds of trouble to spite her family before being sent off to finishing school where she gets involved with the wrong man (Owsley). She ends up walking the streets to make some dough, all the while drinking and drugging too much. Eventually, she returns home and learns her mother had an affair and her real dad is an Indian and it's her half-breed blood that made her act so wild. Definitely not for the PC crowd, although since Nasa likes to use a bullwhip on a would-be beau, you could have guessed that. **88m/B; DVD.** Clara Bow; Monroe Owsley; Gilbert Roland; Thelma Todd; Estelle Taylor; *D:* John Francis Dillon; *W:* Edwin J. Burke; *C:* Lee Garmes.

Call Him Mr. Shatter 🦴 *Shatter* **1974 (R)** A hired killer stalks a tottering Third World president and becomes embroiled in international political intrigue. **90m/C; VHS, DVD.** *GB* Stuart Whitman; Peter Cushing; Anton Diffring; *D:* Michael Carreras.

Call It a Day 🦴🦴 1/2 **1937** The first day of spring makes everyone in the conservative British Hilton family go a little silly in strange ways, including having several unexpected romantic dalliances thwarted. De Havilland gets top billing as the family's lovesick daughter although she has a smaller role than Hunter and Inescort, who play her parents. **89m/B; DVD.** Olivia de Havilland; Ian Hunter; Frieda Inescort; Anita Louise; Alice Brady; Roland Young; Bonita Granville; Peter Willes; Walter Woolf King; Peggy Wood; Marcia Ralston; *D:* Archie Mayo; *W:* Casey Robinson; *C:* Ernest Haller.

Call Me Bwana 🦴 1/2 **1963** Pure cornpone with Hope as a bumbling explorer sent with CIA agent Adams to track down a lost American space capsule in deepest Africa. Enemy agents Ekberg and Jeffries try to make things difficult. **103m/C; VHS, DVD.** Bob Hope; Edie Adams; Anita Ekberg; Lionel Jeffries; Percy Herbert; Paul Carpenter; Orlando Martins; *D:* Gordon Douglas; *W:* Nate Monaster; Johanna Harwood.

Call Me by Your Name 🦴🦴🦴 **2017 (R)** A gorgeous romance that captures the uplifting and heartbreaking duality of love. Set in 1983 Italy, 17-year-old Elio (Chalamet) grows increasingly attracted to his father's live-in intern Oliver (Hammer), and the pair explore a romance they must keep secret from their female lovers and Elio's parents. A love story about more than sex, taboos, and even bi- or homosexuality, this adaptation of Andre Aciman's novel captures the ecstasy and agony of first love, underlined by a monologue by Elio in the final act that's sure to touch everyone's heart. **132m/C; DVD, Blu-Ray.** Armie Hammer; Timothée Chalamet; Michael Stuhlbarg; Amira Casar; Esther Garrel; *D:* Luca Guadagnino; *W:* James Ivory; *C:* Sayombhu Mukdeeprom. Oscars '17: Adapt. Screenplay; British Acad. '17: Adapt. Screenplay; Ind. Spirit '18: Actor (Chalamet), Cinematog.; Writers Guild '17: Adapt. Screenplay.

Call Me Claus 🦴🦴 **2001** Goldberg mugs her way through her role as a TV shopping network producer with Scrooge-like tendencies. Hawthorne is the good-natured St. Nick who wants to retire and have her replace him at the yuletide gig. Might rate a few chuckles if you've seen all the good Christmas movies twice already. **90m/C; VHS, DVD.** Whoopi Goldberg; Nigel Hawthorne; Taylor Negron; Brian Stokes Mitchell; Victor Garber; Gregory Bernstein; Brian Bird; *D:* Peter Werner; *W:* Sarah Bernstein; *M:* Garth Brooks. **TV**

Call Me Crazy 🦴🦴 1/2 **2013** Lifetime anthology of five short films about mental illness. "Lucy" follows a young woman who's institutionalized for her schizophrenia when she stops taking her meds. "Grace" tries to look after her bipolar mother. "Allison" comes home for the holidays, but is resentful when her mentally ill sister causes trouble. "Eddie" is a comedian who struggles with severe clinical depression. "Maggie" is a returning war vet who suffers from PTSD. **88m/C; DVD.** Brittany Snow; Sarah Hyland; Sofia Vassilieva; Mitch Rouse; Jennifer Hudson; ***D:*** Laura Dern; Bryce Dallas Howard; Bonnie Hunt; Ashley Judd; Sharon Maguire; ***W:*** Stephen Godchaux; Howard J. Morris; Deirdre O'Connor; Jan Oxenberg; Erin Cressida Wilson; ***C:*** Dermott Downs; Andre Lascaris; Karl Walter Lindenlaub; Gale Tattersall; ***M:*** Alex Wurman. **CABLE**

Call Me Lucky **2015** Goldthwait shifts gears yet again for a heartbreaking and inspiring documentary about infamous stand-up comedian Barry Crimmins, who was a clear influence on modern stars like Denis Leary and Lewis Black, but essentially disappeared when it comes to mainstream fame. As dozens of comedy greats discuss how fantastic Crimmins was on-stage and off, one wonders why he isn't a household name. And then Bobcat turns the film into something entirely unexpected, detailing how personal revelations sent Crimmins on a different path. It's both entertaining and unexpectedly moving at the same time. **105m/C; DVD, Blu-Ray.** Margaret Cho; David Cross; Mike Donovan; Tom Kenny; Patton Oswalt; ***D:*** Bobcat Goldthwait; ***C:*** Bradley Stonesifer; ***M:*** Charlyne Yi.

Call Me Mister 1/2 **1951** Kay Hudson (Grable) arrives in Tokyo to put on a show for the troops and discovers her estranged hisband Shep (Dailey) has finagled his way into being the director so he can woo her back. Mild musical though the Dailey/Grable numbers (choreographed by Busby Berkeley) are worth watching. **96m/C; DVD.** Betty Grable; Dan Dailey; Danny Thomas; Dale Robertson; Richard Boone; Jeffrey Hunter; ***D:*** Lloyd Bacon; ***W:*** Albert Lewin; Burt Styler; ***C:*** Arthur E. Arling; ***M:*** Leigh Harline.

Call Me Mrs. Miracle 1/2 *Debbie Macomber's Call Me Mrs. Miracle* **2010** Hallmark Channel sequel to 2009's "Mrs. Miracle." The possibly angelic Emily Merkle (Roberts), better-known as Mrs. Miracle, takes a job at the failing Finley department store during the Christmas season. With Mrs. Miracle around, the season starts looking bright for both the Finleys and their customers. **90m/C; DVD.** Doris Roberts; Jewel Staite; Lauren Holly; Eric Johnson; Quinn Lord; Tom Butler; ***D:*** Michael M. Scott; ***W:*** Nancey Silvers; ***C:*** Adam Sliwinski; ***M:*** James Jandrisch. **CABLE**

Call Me: The Rise and Fall of Heidi Fleiss 1/2 **2004** Stale made-for-TV flick follows the real story of Heidi Fleiss (Sigler) as she leaves behind her posh family life to take over a call-girl business for the rich and famous Hollywood crowd. Her time to revel in the excess is cut short, and Tinseltown's movers-and-shakers fear exposure from the publicity of Heidi's little black book. Interestingly, DiScala is said to have shunned most of the sex scenes. **84m/C; VHS, DVD.** Jamie-Lynn Sigler; Saul Rubinek; Emmanuelle Vaugier; Ian Tracey; Natassia Malthe; Corbin Bernsen; Brenda Fricker; Robert Davi; Lisa Marie Caruk; Missy Peregrym; ***D:*** Charles McDougall; ***W:*** Norman Snider; ***C:*** David Franco; ***M:*** Ryan Shore. **VIDEO**

Call Northside 777 1/2 *Calling Northside 777* **1948** Hard-boiled Chicago reporter McNeal (Stewart) finds himself in the crux of a decade-old murder investigation when he follows up a newspaper ad offering $5,000 for any information leading to the arrest and conviction of a police killer. The cunning reporter discovers police coverups and missing evidence pointing to an imprisoned man's innocence. Powerful performance from Stewart directs this docu-drama based on the real-life story of Chicago's Joe Majczek, unjustly imprisoned for 11 years, and the Pulitzer Prize winning reporter Jim McGuire who, through a clever investigation, found enough evidence to have the case re-opened. **111m/B; VHS, DVD.** James Stewart; Richard Conte; Lee J. Cobb; Helen Walker; Betty Garde; Moroni Olsen; E.G. Marshall; Howard Smith; John McIntire; Paul Harvey; George Tyne; Michael Chapin; Addison Richards; Richard Rober; Eddie Dunn; Charles Lane; Walter Greaza; William Post, Jr.; George Melford; Charles F. Miller; Lionel Stander; Jonathan Hale; Freddie (Fred) Steele; ***D:*** Henry Hathaway; ***W:*** Jerome Cady; Jay Dratler; ***C:*** Joe MacDonald; ***M:*** Alfred Newman.

Call of Heroes **2016** Set in the warlord era of Chinese history, this action film centers on one village's quest for justice. The son of a powerful general, Cao (Koo) was indulged as a child and became a vicious commandant as an adult. One rural village, Puncheng, accuses Cao of killing three innocent people and is set to put the depraved man on trial. Though Cao's father swears he will destroy the community if his son is found guilty and sentenced to death, the residents prepare for the outfall that will come from punishing the guilty man. Cantonese with subtitles. **120m/C; DVD, Blu-Ray, Streaming, Download.** Louis Koo; Ching-Wan Lau; Eddie Peng; Jing Wu; ***D:*** Benny Chan; ***C:*** Chor Keung Chan; ***M:*** Kin-wai Wong. **VIDEO**

Call of the Canyon 1/2 **1942** A crooked agent for a local meat packer won't pay a fair price, so Gene goes off to talk to the head man to set him straight. **71m/B; VHS, DVD.** Gene Autry; Smiley Burnette; Ruth Terry; Thurston Hall; Pat Brady; ***D:*** Joseph Santley.

Call of the Coyote **WOOF!** **1934** Carlyle may not be quite Ed Wood bad but this amateur, extremely low budget western was deservedly forgotten. Cowboy Don Adios finds the body of murdered prospector Jim Barrett and must protect Barrett's young daughter from harm. **80m/B; DVD.** Pat Carlyle; Merrill McCormick; Marie Bracco; Charles Stevens; ***D:*** Pat Carlyle; ***W:*** Robert Emmett Tansey; ***C:*** Irvin Akers.

Call of the Forest 1/2 **1949** Bobby makes friends with a beautiful wild black stallion which is captured and tamed by his father. The father has found a goldmine, also desired by an villain, and Bobby and his horse must come to his father's aid. Black Diamond (the horse) has the best role. **74m/B; VHS, DVD.** Robert Lowery; Ken Curtis; Martha Sherrill; Chief Thundercloud; Charles Hughes; ***D:*** John F. Link.

The Call of the Wild **1935** Not much remains from the Jack London novel although the adventure drama is expertly done and leads Gable and Young have a lot of chemistry. Prospector Jack Thornton (Gable) and his pal Shorty (Oakie) head into the Alaskan wilderness to search for gold accompanied by Thornton's sled dog Buck. Buck's literally a lifesaver but he's secondary to the romance that develops between Jack and Claire (Young), the wife of a missing prospector. **95m/B; DVD.** Clark Gable; Loretta Young; Jack Oakie; Frank Conroy; Reginald Owen; Sidney Toler; Katherine DeMille; ***D:*** William A. Wellman; ***W:*** Gene Fowler, Sr.; Leonard Praskins; ***C:*** Charles Rosher; ***M:*** Alfred Newman.

Call of the Wild **1972 (PG)** Jack London's famous story about a man whose survival depends upon his knowledge of the Alaskan wilderness almost comes to life. Filmed in Finland. **105m/C; VHS, DVD.** Charlton Heston; Michele Mercier; George Eastman; ***D:*** Ken Annakin; ***W:*** Harry Alan Towers; Hubert Frank; ***C:*** John Cabrera; ***M:*** Carlo Rustichelli.

Call of the Wild 1/2 **1993** Another of Jack London's survival tales is dramatized for TV. John Thornton (Schroder) is a rich greenhorn seeking adventure during the 1897 Klondike gold rush. Buck is a German shepherd, sold as a sled dog, who finds adventures of his own in the frozen North until man and dog are united to search for a legendary gold mine. The book is more exciting but the film is more violent. Filmed on location in British Columbia. **97m/C; VHS, DVD.** ***IT*** Rick Schroder; Gordon Tootoosis; Mia Sara; Duncan Fraser; Richard Newman; Brent Stait; Allan Lysell; Tom Heaton; Eric McCormack; Vince Metcalfe; ***D:*** Alan Smithee; Michael Toshiyuki Uno; ***C:*** David Geddes; ***M:*** Lee Holdridge. **TV**

Call of the Wild 1/2 *Jack London's Call of the Wild* **2004** Filmed for the Animal Planet network, and based very loosely on the novel, this is the first film in a series. Fifteen-year-old Miles Challenger (Meier) has his life change after meeting a heroic dog named Buck. Very family-oriented, and not quite as dark as the novel. **100m/C; DVD.** Shane Meier; Nick Mancuso; Rachel Hayward; Kathleen Duborg; Mark Hildreth; Crystal Buble; Harvey Dumansky; George Josef; ***D:*** Brenton Spencer; David Winning; Zale Dalen; Jorge Montesi; ***W:*** David Fallon; Tim John; David Assael; Michael Sloan; Madeline Sunshine; ***C:*** Wade Ferley; Stephen McNutt; Tony Westman; ***M:*** Hal Beckett.

The Call of the Wild 1/2 **2020 (PG)** Buck, a carefree St. Bernard mix, is dognapped from his California home and taken to Alaska to serve as a sled dog during the 1890s Klondike Gold Rush before ultimately returning to his ancestral roots in a wolf pack. This latest adaptation of Jack London's classic tale took the "wild" out of the title -- the animals, including our canine hero, are computer-generated, and it shows. Still, the adventure and life lessons about courage will appeal to young viewers. **100m/C; DVD, Blu-Ray.** Harrison Ford; Omar Sy; Cara Gee; Dan Stevens; Bradley Whitford; ***D:*** Chris (Christopher) Sanders; ***W:*** Michael Green; ***C:*** Janusz Kaminski; ***M:*** John Powell.

Call of the Wild 3D 1/2 **2009 (PG)** Modern take on the Jack London adventure story has nine-year-old Bostonian Ryan visiting her grandpa Bill in Montana. She finds and cares for wounded wild dog/wolf Buck and makes new friends by trying to train Buck to run in the annual sled race. **87m/C; DVD.** Ariel Gade; Christopher Lloyd; Veronica Cartwright; Timothy Bottoms; Joyce DeWitt; Wes Studi; Aimee Teegarden; Devon Graye; Jaleel White; ***D:*** Richard Gabai; ***W:*** Leland Douglas; ***C:*** Scott Peck; ***M:*** Deeji Mincey; Boris Zelkin. **VIDEO**

Call of the Wilderness 1/2 *Trailing the Killer* **1932** Humans aren't very important in this animal adventure. Half-wolf hunting dog Lobo is accused of being a sheep killer but his fur trapping master Pierre knows it's not true. A mountain lion is the real culprit and, while they're tracking the animal, it kills Pierre. This crime is also blamed on Lobo, who now has to protect his mate and pups from bounty hunters and the mountain lion. **57m/B; DVD.** Francis McDonald; Heinie Conklin; Joe de la Cruz; Tom London; ***D:*** Herman C. Raymaker; ***W:*** Jackson Richards; ***C:*** Pliny Goodfriend; ***M:*** Oscar Potoker.

Call of the Yukon 1/2 **1938** A female writer and her various animal companions travel to a remote Alaskan Eskimo village in search of inspiration for her new novel. Unfortunately the Eskimos are fleeing the oncoming winter, and the leader of a vicious wolf pack named Swift Lightning. When winter sets in, the entire group gets trapped in a cabin and love triangles among humans and animals ensue. Likeable for diehard fans of 1930s cinema but tedious otherwise. **70m/B; DVD.** Richard Arlen; Beverly Roberts; Lyle Talbot; Mala; Garry Owen; Ivan Miller; Al "Fuzzy" St. John; ***D:*** John T. Coyle; B. Reeves Eason; ***W:*** Gertrude Orr; Bill Peet; ***C:*** Ernest Miller; ***M:*** Alberto Colombo.

Callas Forever **2002** Cinematic tribute by Zeffirelli to his longtime friend, opera diva Maria Callas who died in 1977. His own alter ego is British impresario Larry Kelly (Irons), Callas's former manager. Callas (Ardant) is living in isolation in her Paris apartment, mourning the loss of both her voice and her great love, Aristotle Onassis. Kelly and journalist friend Sarah (Plowright) persuade the singer to come out of retirement to lip-synch to a film version of "Carmen," one of her best roles. She agrees and the film shoot revives her but what happens when the filming stops? Ardant may not resemble the real Callas but she has a commanding charisma that enhances her portrayal. **108m/C; Blu-Ray.** Fanny Ardant; Jeremy Irons; Joan Plowright; Jay Rodan; Gabriel Garko; ***D:*** Franco Zeffirelli; ***W:*** Franco Zeffirelli; Martin Sherman; ***C:*** Ennio Guarnieri; ***M:*** Alessio Vlad.

The Caller **1987 (R)** A strange man enters the house of a lone woman and sets off a long night of suspense and an almost longer evening of inept movie-making. **90m/C; VHS, DVD.** Malcolm McDowell; Madolyn Smith; ***D:*** Arthur Allan Seidelman; ***M:*** Richard Band.

The Caller 1/2 **2008 (PG-13)** Distancing and talky drama that goes nowhere. Jimmy (Langella), an exec at an international energy firm, blows the whistle on their illegal practices and knows he's now a target. So he secretly hires PI Frank (Gould) to document his every move over a two-week period before his probable murder. Frank doesn't realize the guy he's shadowing is the guy who hired him. There's also something about Jimmy wanting to make peace with some childhood trauma that took place in 1940s France. **92m/C; DVD.** Frank Langella; Elliott Gould; Laura Elena Harring; Anabel Sosa; ***D:*** Richard Ledes; ***W:*** Richard Ledes; ***C:*** Stephen Kazmierski; ***M:*** Robert Miller.

The Caller **2011 (R)** Throw the phone away! Divorcee Mary moves into a rundown San Juan apartment after getting away from her abusive ex. The apartment has a rotary phone that rings constantly; the caller is a woman named Rose looking for her boyfriend. Mary eventually realizes Rose is calling from 1979 and is some kind of evil spirit who starts influencing Mary's present. **91m/C; DVD.** Rachelle Lefevre; Ed Quinn; Stephen Moyer; Luis Guzman; ***V:*** Lorna Raver; ***D:*** Matthew Parkhill; ***W:*** Sergio Casci; ***C:*** Alexander Melman; ***M:*** Aidan Lavelle. **VIDEO**

Callie and Son *Rags to Riches* **1981** Details the sordid story of a waitress who works her way up to become a Dallas socialite and her obsessive relationship with her illegitimate son. **97m/C; VHS, DVD.** Lindsay Wagner; Dabney Coleman; Jameson Parker; Andrew Prine; James Sloyan; Michelle Pfeiffer; ***D:*** Waris Hussein; ***M:*** Billy Goldenberg.

The Calling 1/2 **2014 (R)** Tough-talking Canadian detective Hazel Micallef (Sarandon) can crack any case, but adapting to everyday society has always been her blind spot. Still living at home with her mother (Burstyn) and a loner otherwise, Micallef is tasked with investigating a nasty batch of murders, much to the chagrin of mom. Turning to a rookie cop (Grace) and an astute priest (Sutherland) to track down a killer hell-bent on twisted Biblical interpretation sounds hackneyed, but an excellent cast breathes life into an otherwise stiff story. Dark, atmospheric, though probably better suited as a TV series. **108m/C; DVD.** Susan Sarandon; Christopher Heyerdahl; Gil Bellows; Topher Grace; Ellen Burstyn; Donald Sutherland; ***D:*** Jason Stone; ***W:*** Scott Abramovitch; ***C:*** David Robert Jones; ***M:*** Grayson Matthews.

Calling Dr. Gillespie 1/2 **1942** After the success of the "Dr. Kildare" movies, MGM continued with a six-film series starring Barrymore as cranky senior surgeon/mentor Dr. Leonard Gillespie at Blair General. In this unexpectedly dark and violent first effort, Gillespie's new assistant is Dutch refuge Dr. Gerniede, who is also studying psychiatry. That comes in handy since patient Roy Todwell turns out to be a homicidal maniac who is out to kill Gillespie for wanting to have him committed. Followed by "Dr. Gillespie's New Assistant." **84m/B; DVD.** Lionel Barrymore; Philip Dorn; Phil Brown; Donna Reed; Nat Pendleton; Alma Kruger; Mary Nash; ***D:*** Harold Bucquet; ***W:*** Willis Goldbeck; Harry Ruskin; ***C:*** Ray June; ***M:*** Daniele Amfitheatrof.

Calling Dr. Kildare **1939** Working at a street clinic, Dr. Kildare (Ayres) treats young Nick (Offerman) for gunshot wounds. He thinks the accused murderer is innocent and insists on helping Nick's sister, Rosalie (Turner), find the real criminal. Second in the MGM series. **86m/B; DVD.** Lew Ayres; Lionel Barrymore; Laraine Day; Lana Turner; George Offerman, Jr.; Nat Pendleton; Lynne Carver; ***D:*** Harold Bucquet; ***W:*** Willis Goldbeck; Harry Ruskin; ***C:*** Alfred Gilks; ***M:*** David Snell.

Calvary **2014** Father James (career-best work from Gleeson) is in confessional in his small Irish town when the man on the other side tells him he has a week to live. The confessor was abused by a priest and, even though Father James is a good man, the scales must be balanced. Over the next several days, James discusses faith, philosophy, and religion with his fellow townspeople and director/writer McDonagh's film becomes a stunning conversation-starter about the decreasing importance of church in the modern world. A daring, complex script that won't hit you until it's over; not unlike an effective sermon. **100m/C; DVD, Blu-Ray.** ***UK IR*** Brendan Gleeson; Chris O'Dowd; Gary Lydon; Aidan Gillen; Kelly Reilly; Domhnall Gleeson; M. Emmet Walsh; Dylan Moran; Marie Josee Croze; ***D:*** John Michael McDonagh; ***W:*** John Michael McDonagh; ***C:*** Larry Smith; ***M:*** Patrick Cassidy.

Calvin Marshall 1/2 **2009 (R)** Calvin (Frost) excels on the local softball team though he doesn't have the ability for junior college baseball. Still, he's so persistent and hopeful that cynical Coach Little (Zahn), a former minor leaguer, is reluctant to cut him. But Calvin must make a decision about his seemingly unattainable dreams to find his true strengths. Pic focuses on character and coming of age rather than its sports aspects. **95m/C; DVD.** Alex Frost; Steve Zahn; Michelle Lombardo; Cynthia Watros; Jeremy Sumpter; Jane Adams; Diedrich Bader; Abraham Benrubi; ***D:*** Gary Lundgren; ***W:*** Gary Lundgren; ***C:*** Patrick Neary; ***M:*** John Askew.

Cambridge Spies 1/2 **2003** Semi-fictional and romanticized account of the friendship of longtime British spies Harold Philby (Stephens), Guy Burgess (Hollander), Anthony Blunt (West), and Donald Maclean (Penry-Jones), which began in the 1930s while the quartet was at Cambridge University and continued for more than 30 years (Philby defected to Moscow in 1964). **240m/C; DVD.** *GB* Toby Stephens; Samuel West; Tom Hollander; Rupert Penry-Jones; Anthony Andrews; Imelda Staunton; Stuart Laing; Patrick Kennedy; James Fox; Anna-Louise Plowman; John Light; ***D:*** Tim Fywell; ***W:*** Peter Moffatt; ***C:*** David Higgs; ***M:*** John Lunn. **TV**

Camel Spiders **2011** Syfy Channel flick, with sucky CGI, that was executive produced by Roger Corman. An Army platoon in Iraq is attacked by venomous camel spiders and some hitch a ride in the body of a dead soldier. After the body is returned home to some small desert town, the spiders (who have multiplied) escape. They first attack a group of partying teens and then crawl their way to terrorize the rest of the locals. **84m/C; DVD, Blu-Ray.** Brian Krause; C. Thomas Howell; Melissa Brasselle; Michael Swan; ***D:*** Jim Wynorski; ***W:*** Jim Wynorski; ***C:*** Andrea V. Rossotto; ***M:*** Chuck Cirino. **CABLE**

Camelot **1967** The long-running Lerner and Loewe Broadway musical about King Arthur, Guinevere, and Lancelot was adapted from T.H. White's book, "The Once and Future King." Redgrave and Nero have chemistry as the illicit lovers, Harris is strong as the king struggling to hold together his dream, but muddled direction undermines the effort. **150m/C; VHS, DVD, Blu-Ray.** Richard Harris; Vanessa Redgrave; David Hemmings; Franco Nero; Lionel Jeffries; ***D:*** Joshua Logan; ***W:*** Alan Jay Lerner; ***C:*** Richard H. Kline; ***M:*** Frederick Loewe; ***M:*** Alan Jay Lerner. Oscars '67: Adapt. Score, Art Dir./Set Dec., Costume Des.; Golden Globes '68: Actor--Mus./Comedy (Harris), Score, Song ("If Ever I Should Leave You").

Camera Buff *Amator* **1979** Satire on bureaucracy finds a factory worker buying a home-movie camera to film his new baby but becoming obsessed with his new toy. So he begins recording everything he sees—even things the authorities don't want shown. Polish with subtitles. **108m/C; VHS, DVD.** *PL* Jerzy Stuhr; Malgorzata Zajaczkowska; Ewa Pokas; Krzysztof Zanussi; ***D:*** Krzysztof Kieslowski; ***W:*** Jerzy Stuhr; Krzysztof Kieslowski; ***M:*** Krzysztof Knittel.

The Cameraman **1928** After moving to MGM, Keaton made his first feature with a major studio, giving up the artistic control he had enjoyed in his previous films. Spared from the vilification of studio politics (not the case with later Keaton films) "The Cameraman" enjoyed both critical and popular success. Keaton's inept tintype portrait-maker has a heart that pitter-patters for an MGM office girl. He hopes to impress her by joining the ranks of the newsreel photographers. Fortuitously poised to grab a photo scoop on a Chinese tong war, he is forced to return empty-handed when an organ-grinder's monkey absconds with his firsthand footage. Silent with a musical score. **78m/B; Silent; VHS, DVD.** Buster Keaton; Marceline Day; Harold Goodwin; Harry Gribbon; Sidney Bracy; Edward Brophy; Vernon Dent; William Irving; ***D:*** Edward Sedgwick. Natl. Film Reg. '05.

Cameraperson **2016** People who look for absolute truth in documentary filmmaking don't understand that the minute a camera is placed on a subject, the "truth" of the situation changes. No film has ever expressed this as brilliantly as Kirsten Johnson's stunning documentary about her own career. After working as a documentarian for a quarter-century, Johnson looks back at her own footage, examining the objectivity and interference of her camera on the people she filmed. It's an examination of the very form of documentary filmmaking—its strengths and its flaws—and it's one of the best films of its kind in years. **102m/C; DVD, Blu-Ray.** Kirsten Johnson; ***D:*** Kirsten Johnson; ***C:*** Kirsten Johnson.

Cameron's Closet 1/2 **1989 (R)** Every child's nightmare comes true. A young boy is convinced that a monster lives in his closet due to his perverse father's psychological tortures. Only this time the monster is real! **86m/C; VHS, DVD.** Cotter Smith; Mel Harris; Scott Curtis; Chuck McCann; Leigh McCloskey; Kim Lankford; Tab Hunter; ***D:*** Armand Mastroianni; ***W:*** Gary Brandner; ***C:*** Russell Carpenter.

Camila **1984** The true story of the tragic romance between an Argentinean socialite and a Jesuit priest in 1847. The two lovers escape to a small provincial village where they live together as man and wife. Eventually they are recognized and condemned to death. Available in Spanish with English subtitles or dubbed into English. **105m/C; VHS, DVD.** *AR SP* Susu Pecoraro; Imanol Arias; Hector Alterio; Elena Tasisto; ***D:*** Maria-Luisa Bemberg.

Camilla 1/2 **1994 (PG-13)** Tandy is delightful in her last starring role as a former violinist on the run with frustrated musician Fonda. Oafish son (Chaykin) and insensitive husband (Koteas) just don't understand, so its time to head to Toronto, site of a fondly, if perhaps incorrectly, remembered triumph. Sort of a May-December female-bonding roadtrip with lots of conversation and comic asides. An inevitably poignant pairing of Tandy and real-life husband Cronyn offers the chance to experience one of America's greatest acting teams one last time. Lack of stereotyping and fairly novel twist on the road movie keep this one on the highway. **91m/C; VHS, DVD.** Jessica Tandy; Bridget Fonda; Hume Cronyn; Elias Koteas; Maury Chaykin; Graham Greene; ***D:*** Deepa Mehta; ***W:*** Paul Quarrington; ***M:*** Daniel Lanois.

Camille 1/2 **1936** Marguerite (Garbo) has found success as Parisian courtesan "La Dame aux Camille" but has never found love. Until she unwisely falls for a handsome but innocent, young aristocrat, Armand (Taylor). Still, Camille agrees to give him up, realizing her scandalous past will jeopardize his future. Oh yes, then she contracts TB and fades away beautifully in gowns by Adrian. This classic Alexandre Dumas story somehow manages to escape the cliches and stands as one of the most telling monuments to Garbo's unique magic and presence on film. **108m/B; VHS, DVD.** Greta Garbo; Robert Taylor; Lionel Barrymore; Henry Daniell; Elizabeth Allan; Rex O'Malley; Lenore Ulric; Laura Hope Crews; ***D:*** George Cukor; ***W:*** Frances Marion; James Hilton; Zoë Akins; ***C:*** William H. Daniels; ***M:*** Herbert Stothart. N.Y. Film Critics '37: Actress (Garbo).

Camille 1/2 **1984** Filmed in Paris, this pretty version of Alexandre Dumas' "La Dame aux Camelias" was a Hallmark Hall of Fame presentation. Beautiful courtesan Marguerite (Scacchi) is willing to give up her scandalous profession for the love of young Armand (Firth). She is convinced by his father that their union would be ruinous and sends Armand away although their love remains amidst later tragedy. **100m/C; DVD.** Greta Scacchi; Colin Firth; Ben Kingsley; John Gielgud; Denholm Elliott; Rachel Kempson; Lila Kaye; Ronald Pickup; Patrick Ryecart; Billie Whitelaw; ***D:*** Desmond Davis; ***W:*** Blanche Hanalis; ***C:*** Jean Tournier; ***M:*** Allyn Ferguson. **TV**

Camille **2007 (PG-13)** Now this is one weird romance. Ever-optimistic Camille (Miller) marries thief Silas (Franco), who was forced into the match by Camille's sheriff uncle (Glenn) since it was either that or jail. They get into a terrible car accident while driving to their Niagara Falls honeymoon, which kills the bride (this is no big revelation). But as far as Camille is concerned being dead is no reason not to keep going. **94m/C; DVD.** Sienna Miller; James Franco; Scott Glenn; David Carradine; Ed Lauter; ***D:*** Gregory Mackenzie; ***W:*** Nick Pustav; ***C:*** Sharone Meir; ***M:*** Mark Mancina.

Camille Claudel **1989 (R)** A lushly romantic version of the art world in the late 19th century, when art was exploding in new forms and independence for women was unheard of. Young sculptor Claudel's (Adjani) tragic love for art, Auguste Rodin (the larger-than-life Depardieu), and independence clash, costing her sanity and her confinement to an insitution for the last 30 years of her life. Very long, it requires an attentive and thoughtful viewing. In French with English subtitles. **149m/C; VHS, DVD, Blu-Ray.** *FR* Isabelle Adjani; Gerard Depardieu; Laurent Grevill; Alain Cuny; Madeleine Robinson; Katrine Boorman; Daniele Lebrun; ***D:*** Bruno Nuytten; ***W:*** Bruno Nuytten; Marilyn Goldin; ***C:*** Pierre Lhomme; ***M:*** Gabriel Yared. Cesar '89: Actress (Adjani), Art Dir./Set Dec., Cinematog., Costume Des., Film.

Camille 2000 1/2 **1969** Dumas meets Debbie Does Rome in this artier than thou mess. Unreasonably well endowed Marguerite (Gaubert) spends much horizontal time with Rome's decadent society denizens while pining pitifully for tru luv Armand (Castelnuovo). She dies a horrible death in the end, but her disease's initials aren't TB. **115m/C; VHS, DVD.** Daniele Gaubert; Nino Castelnuovo; Eleanora Rossi-Drago; Silvana Venturelli; Massimo Serato; ***D:*** Radley Metzger; ***W:*** Michael DeForrest; ***C:*** Ennio Guarnieri; ***M:*** Piero Piccioni.

The Camomile Lawn 1/2 **1992** In August 1939, various young cousins gather at their uncle's house on the Cornish coast for a last holiday before the inevitable war changes all their lives. Thirty years later, they return to the house for a funeral and the chance to look back on their frequently risque behavior. Naughty adaptation of the novel by Mary Wesley. **264m/C; DVD.** *GB* Jennifer Ehle; Tara Fitzgerald; Toby Stephens; Felicity Kendal; Rebecca Hall; Paul Eddington; Oliver Cotton; Claire Bloom; Rosemary Harris; Richard Johnson; Virginia McKenna; Nicholas Le Prevost; ***D:*** Peter Hall; ***W:*** Kenneth Taylor; ***C:*** Ernest Vincze; ***M:*** Stephen (Steve) Edwards. **TV**

Camouflage 1/2 **2000 (R)** Dumb, blond but likeable actor Marty Mackenzie (Munro) wants to perfect his tough-guy persona so he decides to apprentice with old-timer PI Jack Potter (Nielsen). But the routine surveillance case that Jack assigns Marty to turns out to be the tip of a deadly iceberg. It's a goof but don't expect "Naked Gun" type humor. **98m/C; VHS, DVD.** Leslie Nielsen; Lochlyn Munro; Vanessa Angel; William Forsythe; ***D:*** James Keach; ***W:*** Tom Epperson; Billy Bob Thornton; ***C:*** Glen MacPherson. **VIDEO**

Camp 1/2 **2003 (PG-13)** Wanna-be teenage thesps flock to Camp Ovation-the summertime equivalent of the "Fame" school—where they can sing, dance and generally be nerdy to their heart's content. First-time director/writer Graff, who in real life was a counselor at a performing arts camp, assembles a cast of typical misfit kids drawn to the stage: budding transvestite Michael (de Jesus), tomboy Ellen (Chilcoat), and the good-looking, seemingly straight Vlad (Letterle), shepherded into adult theaterhood by the cynical, alcoholic musical-theater pro (Dixon). Story follows the ups and downs of these hopefuls, as well as other fringe characters but especially focuses on the sexual preference of Vlad. Despite uneven acting and stereotypical scenarios, flick is an indie with integrity and heart, while also boasting some rousing musical numbers. **114m/C; VHS, DVD.** Daniel Letterle; Joanna Chilcoat; Robin De Jesus; Tiffany Taylor; Sasha Allen; Alana Allen; Anna Kendrick; Don Dixon; ***D:*** Todd Graff; ***W:*** Todd Graff; ***C:*** Kip Bogdahn; ***M:*** Stephen Trask.

Camp Cucamonga: How I Spent My Summer Vacation **1990** Zany antics at summer camp abound when Camp Cucamonga's owner mistakes the new handyman for the camp inspector. Well-known stars from TV's "Cheers," "The Jeffersons," "The Wonder Years," and "The Love Boat" are featured in this silly flick. **100m/C; VHS, DVD.** John Ratzenberger; Sherman Hemsley; Josh Saviano; Danica McKellar; Chad Allen; Dorothy Lyman; Lauren Tewes; G. Gordon Liddy; ***D:*** Roger Duchowny. **TV**

Camp Dread **2014** A horror movie/reality TV spoof that's a slasher horror film all in itself. During the 1980s, the three Summer Camp horror flicks were popular with audiences. The triology's director/screenwriter, Julian Barrett (Roberts), wants to revitalize his career by reviving the trilogy. To that end, he uses a reality show to land a cast and funding. After some former cast members, young reality show wannabes, and Barrett get together, the director is sure he will be successful again. Unfortunately, people starting getting killed, derailing his plans and leaving his career—and life—in jeopardy. **94m/C; DVD, Streaming, Download.** Eric Roberts; Danielle Harris; Felissa Rose; Joe Raffa; Montana Marks; ***D:*** Harrison Smith; ***W:*** Harrison Smith; ***C:*** Charlie Anderson; ***M:*** John Avarese. **VIDEO**

Camp Hell *Camp Hope* **2010 (R)** Bait-and-switch from its title to its box cover art and non-horror plot. Camp Hope is a summer camp in the New Jersey woods run by Father Phineas McAllister who's on the evangelical/traditionalist end of the Christian scale. The priest is just a little too interested in preaching about temptation and sins of the flesh to the point that hormonal teen Tommy begins suffering from nightmares. McAllister thinks they're the work of the devil but Tommy's been sneaking out to fool around with girlfriend Melissa so it's more likely a guilty conscience. **99m/C; DVD.** Will Denton; Bruce Davison; Valentina de Angelis; Dana Delany; Andrew McCarthy; Connor Paolo; Christopher Denham; James McCaffrey; Spencer Treat Clark; Jesse Eisenberg; ***D:*** George Vanbuskirk; ***W:*** George Vanbuskirk; ***C:*** Michael McDonough.

Camp Nowhere **1994 (PG)** Video fodder for the juniors in the household as kids turn tables on parents. Instead of trudging off to summer camp for the umpteenth time, a group of upscale kids create their own with the help of laid-off drama teacher Lloyd, who must first con their parents into believing that Camp Nowhere is legit. What follows is that very special summer camp in the Hollywood tradition with lots of junk food, video games galore, and of course, no rules. Camp beserko formula good for a few laughs. **106m/C; VHS, DVD, Blu-Ray.** Christopher Lloyd; Wendy Makkena; M. Emmet Walsh; Peter Scolari; Peter Onorati; Ray Baker; Kate Mulgrew; Jonathan Jackson; Romy Walthall; Maryedith Burrell; Thomas F. Wilson; Nathan Cavaleri; Andrew Keegan; Melody Kay; Joshua Gibran Mayweather; John Putch; Devin Oatway; Burgess Meredith; Marne(tte) Patterson; Jessica Alba; ***D:*** Jonathan Prince; ***W:*** Andrew Kurtzman; Eliot Wald; ***C:*** Sandi Sissel.

Camp Rock 1/2 **2008** Think Cinderella as a wannabe pop star in this Disney Channel original. Bubbly teenager Mitchie (Lovato) is desperate to attend a prestigious rock camp her family can't afford. So her mom gets a job as the camp cook, which means Mitchie can be a student if she works part-time in the kitchen. Embarrassed, Mitchie pretends to be as wealthy and popular as her new friends. Then she's overheard singing (but not seen) by celebrity camp instructor and troubled teen heartthrob Shane Gray (Joe Jonas), who wants to know who the voice belongs to. But can Mitchie come clean about her deception? Jonas brothers Nick and Kevin also appear. Filmed at Kilcoo Camp in Ontario. **90m/C; DVD, Blu-Ray.** Alyson Stoner; Demi Lovato; Joe Jonas; Maria Canals-Barrera; Meaghan Jette Martin; Jasmine Richards; Anna Maria Perez de Tagle; ***D:*** Matthew Diamond; ***W:*** Karin Gist; Regina Hicks. **CABLE**

Camp Rock 2: The Final Jam 1/2 **2010** Sequel to the 2008 Disney Channel teen musical finds successful brother band Connect 3 taking a summer break so lead singer Shane (Joe Jonas) can spend time with girlfriend Mitchie (Lovato). However, Camp Rock is in financial trouble thanks to a new rival, Camp Star, so the campers need to win a televised competition to save the day. It's all just adorable fun (and that's not a knock on the flick). **90m/C; DVD, Blu-Ray.** Demi Lovato; Joe Jonas; Kevin Jonas; Nick Jonas; Chloe Bridges; Alyson Stoner; Meaghan Jette Martin; Daniel Fathers; Daniel Kash; Frankie Jonas; ***D:*** Paul Hoen; ***W:*** Daniel Berendsen; Karin Gist; Regina Hicks; ***C:*** David Makin; ***M:*** Christopher Lennertz. **CABLE**

Camp X-Ray **2014 (R)** Army Private First Class Amy Cole (Stewart) escaped a small-town life she hated to serve her country. Thinking she'd go into combat, she's surprised to find herself in Guantanamo Bay as a guard at Camp Delta, where she's ostracized by male soldiers and uncertain of her role. She befriends a detainee named Ali Amir (Maadi), who only adds to her crisis of conscience. This Sundance drama is well-intentioned and well-performed, but overly familiar and way too long. Stewart is quite good but it's a script with an agenda more than characters. **117m/C; Blu-Ray, Streaming.** Kristen Stewart; Payman Moaadi; John Carroll Lynch; Lane Garrison; ***D:*** Peter Sattler; ***W:*** Peter Sattler; ***C:*** James Laxton; ***M:*** Jess Stroup.

The Campaign 🦴🦴 1/2 **2012 (R)** Long-time North Carolina congressman Cam Brady (Ferrell) has run unopposed for years but he faces his greatest political challenge when a pair of CEOs convinces timid Marty Huggins (Galifianakis) to run. They have undeniably strong comic timing and make excellent verbal sparring partners. Going for the crude joke instead of the smart one, director Roach's political comedy has more hits than misses. But it misses its potential of being the great one it could have been. **85m/C; DVD, Blu-Ray.** Will Ferrell; Zach Galifianakis; Jason Sudeikis; Dylan McDermott; Katherine LaNasa; Sarah Baker; John Lithgow; Dan Aykroyd; Brian Cox; ***D:*** Jay Roach; ***W:*** Chris Henchy; Shawn Harwell; ***C:*** Jim Denault; ***M:*** Theodore Shapiro.

Campbell's Kingdom 🦴🦴 1/2 **1957** Average adventure yarn. Bruce Campbell (Bogarde) inherits property in the Canadian Rockies from his grandfather, who was always certain it held oil. Shady contractor Owen Morgan (Baker) wants Campbell to sell the valley so he can flood it as part of his hydroelectric dam project, but Campbell says no. This results in sabotage on both sides. **100m/C; DVD.** *GB* Dirk Bogarde; Stanley Baker; Barbara Murray; Michael Craig; James Robertson Justice; Athene Seyler; Robert Brown; John Laurie; ***D:*** Ralph Thomas; ***W:*** Robin Estridge; ***C:*** Ernest Steward; ***M:*** Clifton Parker.

Campfire Tales 🦴🦴 **1998 (R)** Four teens get lost in the woods and are terrorized by a maniac. **103m/C; VHS, DVD.** James Marsden; Kim Murphy; Christine Taylor; Jay R. Ferguson; Christopher K. Masterson; Ron Livingston; Jennifer MacDonald; Hawthorne James; Alex McKenna; Glenn Quinn; Erick Fleeks; Amy Smart; Rick Lawrence; Suzanne Goddard; ***D:*** David Semel; Martin Kunert; Matt Cooper; ***W:*** Martin Kunert; Matt Cooper; Eric Manes; ***C:*** John Peters; ***M:*** Andrew Rose.

The Campus Corpse 🦴 **1977 (PG)** Young man stumbles into deadly college frat hazing and discovers he and rest of cast are utterly devoid of acting ability. **92m/C; VHS, DVD.** Charles Martin Smith; Jeff East; Brad Davis; ***D:*** Douglas Curtis.

Campus Man 🦴 **1987 (PG)** An entrepreneurial college student markets a beefcake calendar featuring his best friend, until the calendar's sales threaten his friend's amateur athletic status. **94m/C; VHS, DVD.** John Dye; Steve Lyon; Kim Delaney; Miles O'Keeffe; Morgan Fairchild; Kathleen Wilhoite; ***D:*** Ron Casden; ***W:*** Geoffrey Baere; ***M:*** James Newton Howard.

Campus Rhythm 🦴🦴 1/2 **1943** Popular Joan is tired of singing radio jingles for Crunchy-Wunchy cereal and refuses to sign a new contract. Instead, she sneaks off and enrolls in a small college under an assumed name and becomes active in the coed life. Only Joan's radio sponsors launch a big publicity campaign to get her back and her secret doesn't stay secret for long. **61m/B; DVD.** Gale Storm; Johnny Downs; Robert Lowery; Douglas Leavitt; Herbert (Hayes) Heyes; Claudia Drake; GeGe Pearson; ***D:*** Arthur Dreifuss; ***W:*** Charles Marion; ***C:*** Mack Stengler; ***M:*** Edward Kay; Edward Cherkose.

Can-Can 🦴🦴 **1960** Lackluster screen adaptation of the Cole Porter musical bears little resemblance to the stage version. MacLaine is a cafe owner who goes to court to try and get the "Can-Can," a dance considered risque in gay Paree at the end of the 19th century, made legal. Love interest Sinatra happens to be a lawyer. **131m/C; VHS, DVD.** Frank Sinatra; Shirley MacLaine; Maurice Chevalier; Louis Jourdan; Juliet Prowse; Marcel Dalio; Leon Belasco; ***D:*** Walter Lang; ***C:*** William H. Daniels.

Can I Do It. . . Till I Need Glasses? **WOOF! 1977** More to the point, can you stay awake till the end? Prurient juvenile junk. Brief Williams footage was grafted to this mess during 15 minutes of Mork fame. **72m/C; VHS, DVD.** Robin Williams; Roger Behr; Debra Klose; Moose Carlson; Walter Olkewicz; ***D:*** I. Robert Levy.

Can She Bake a Cherry Pie? 🦴🦴 **1983** Two offbeat characters meet and fall in love in an odd sort of way. Slow-moving and talky but somewhat rewarding. One of Black's better performances. **90m/C; VHS, DVD.** Karen Black; Michael Emil; Michael Margotta; Frances Fisher; Martin Frydberg; ***D:*** Henry Jaglom; ***W:*** Henry Jaglom; ***M:*** Karen Black.

Can You Ever Forgive Me? 🦴🦴🦴 **2018 (R)** In early 1990s New York City, biographer Lee Israel (McCarthy) is facing professional failure. This situation leads to financial stress as she gets an eviction notice and her favorite cat becomes ill. To pay her bills, she uses her skills as a writer to create fake letters and sells them for hefty sums. With the help of her charming friend Jack Hock (Grant), Lee tries to keep her fraud going as the FBI closes in on her crime. Based on a true story, McCarthy's performance is layered and sympathetic, and she and Grant have great on-screen rapport. **106m/C; DVD, Blu-Ray.** Melissa McCarthy; Richard E. Grant; Jane Curtin; Ben Falcone; Stephen Spinella; ***D:*** Marielle Heller; ***W:*** Nicole Holofcener; Jeff Whitty; ***C:*** Brandon Trost; ***M:*** Nate Heller. Ind. Spirit '19: Actor--Supporting (Grant), Screenplay; Writers Guild '18: Adapt. Screenplay.

Can You Keep a Secret? 🦴 1/2 **2019** When Emma (Daddario) panics during airplane turbulence, she fears death and shares her secrets with the handsome stranger (Hoechlin) sitting next to her. Among them is fake friendships with her stuck-up coworkers, her sometimes lax work ethic, and that she's never been in love. At work the next day, she finds the stranger, Jack Harper, there because he owns the company (shocking!). As an embarrassed Emma tries to play it cool with Jack, he shares his own secrets with her. An uninspiring adaptation of Sophie Kinsella's novel. **95m/C; DVD.** Alexandra Daddario; Tyler Hoechlin; Laverne Cox; Kimiko Glenn; Sunita Mani; ***D:*** Elise Duran; ***W:*** Peter Hutchings; ***C:*** Autumn Eakin; ***M:*** Jeff Cardoni.

The Canadian 🦴 1/2 **1926** Predictable silent melodrama. Would-be homesteader Frank Taylor is working on his friend Ed Marsh's Alberta farm until he can afford a place of his own. Ed's prim sister Nora arrives from London and soon clashes with her sister-in-law, resulting into her agreeing to a marriage of convenience to Frank. However, Nora hates life on the prairie and it takes a natural disaster to give her a change of heart about both farm life and Frank. **80m/B; Silent; DVD.** Thomas Meighan; Mona Palma; Wyndham Standing; Dale Fuller; Charles Winninger; ***D:*** William Beaudine; ***W:*** J. Clarkson Miller; Howard Emmett Rogers; ***C:*** Alvin Wyckoff.

Canadian Bacon 🦴 1/2 **1994 (PG)** Regrettably amateurish satire (with some sharp observations) serves as the feature film debut for Moore, who irritated many with "Roger & Me." Title refers to the military code name for a campaign to whip up anti-Canadian hysteria and justify a U.S. invasion of its neighbor to the north. Evil political advisor Pollak convinces well-meaning but inept President Alda that it's just the thing to get the presidential popularity up and those defense industries humming. Ugly Americans abound, at expense of polite Canadians, eh? Filmed in Toronto, which is shown to good advantage. Candy in one of last roles is the superpatriotic sheriff of Niagara Falls, New York. **110m/C; VHS, DVD.** Alan Alda; Kevin Pollak; John Candy; Rhea Perlman; Rip Torn; Bill Nunn; Kevin J. O'Connor; Steven Wright; G.D. Spradlin; James Belushi; Wallace Shawn; Dan Aykroyd; ***Cameo(s):*** Michael Moore; ***D:*** Michael Moore; ***W:*** Michael Moore; ***C:*** Haskell Wexler; ***M:*** Elmer Bernstein; Peter Bernstein.

The Canal 🦴 1/2 **2014** In this horror film, David (Evans), a film archivist, believes his wife Alice (Hoekstra) is having an affair with Alex (Shaaban). He also becomes convinced that his home--where a horrific murder took place in 1902--has an evil presence. When his wife disappears, David believes the home's dark forces are besetting him, leading him to lunacy. **92m/C; DVD, Streaming, Download.** Antonia Campbell-Hughes; Rupert Evans; Steve Oram; Hannah Hoekstra; Kelly Byrne; Carl Shaaban; ***D:*** Ivan Kavanagh; ***W:*** Ivan Kavanagh; ***C:*** Piers McGrail; ***M:*** Ceiri Torjussen.

Canal Zone 🦴 1/2 **1942** Hard-nosed Hardtack Hamilton is the training officer for pilots flying Army bombers from the Panama Canal to Africa. Reckless newcomer, Harley Ames, immediately clashes with Hamilton and makes it worse by making a play for his girl, Susan. Naturally, he redeems himself during a rescue mission. **79m/B; DVD.** Chester Morris; John Hubbard; Harriet Hilliard Nelson; Larry Parks; Forrest Tucker; Lloyd Bridges; ***D:*** Lew Landers; ***W:*** Robert Lee Johnson; ***C:*** Franz Planer.

Cancel Christmas 🦴 1/2 **2011** In this predictable Hallmark Channel holiday flick, Santa is appalled when the Christmas Board of Directors threatens to cancel the holiday forever unless Santa and his head elf can make it less commercial. First job is to get some over-privileged kiddies to help out a boy in a wheelchair and his single mom. Expect sap. , Santa is appalled in this predictable Hallmark Channel comedy when the Christmas Board of Directors threatens to cancel the holiday if Santa and his head elf can't find a way to get over-privileged kiddies to help the less fortunate. A single mom and a boy in a wheelchair are involved so expect some sap. **88m/C; DVD.** Judd Nelson; Justin Landry; Sante Scaletta; Natalie Brown; Connor Price; ***D:*** John Bradshaw; ***W:*** David Alexander; ***C:*** John Dyer; ***M:*** Stacey Hersh. **CABLE**

Cancel My Reservation 🦴 **1972 (G)** New York talk show host Hope sets out for a vacation on an Arizona ranch, but winds up in trouble due to a mysterious corpse, a rich rancher, and an enigmatic mystic. Even more muddled than it sounds. Based on the novel "Broken Gun" by Louis L'Amour, with pointless cameos by Crosby, Wayne, and Wilson. **99m/C; VHS, DVD.** Bob Hope; Eva Marie Saint; Ralph Bellamy; Anne Archer; Forrest Tucker; Keenan Wynn; Flip Wilson; Noriyuki "Pat" Morita; Chief Dan George; ***Cameo(s):*** John Wayne; Bing Crosby; Doodles Weaver; ***D:*** Paul Bogart; ***W:*** Arthur Marx; ***C:*** Russell Metty.

The Candidate 🦴🦴🦴 **1972 (PG)** Realistic, satirical look at politics and political campaigning. Bill McKay (Redford) is a telegenic, idealistic lawyer whose father (Douglas) was once governor of California. Uninterested in politics, Bill is eventually persuaded to run for the Senate against bluff incumbent Jarman (Porter). Bill refuses to follow the party line but discovers the lure of political power when he begins to gain in the polls. Director Ritchie also worked with Redford on "Downhill Racer." **105m/C; VHS, DVD.** Robert Redford; Peter Boyle; Don Porter; Allen Garfield; Karen Carlson; Melvyn Douglas; Michael Lerner; ***D:*** Michael Ritchie; ***W:*** Jeremy Larner; ***C:*** John Korty; Victor Kemper; ***M:*** John Rubinstein. Oscars '72: Story & Screenplay; Writers Guild '72: Orig. Screenplay.

Candlelight in Algeria 🦴🦴 1/2 **1944** British spy Thurston (Mason) is sent to the Vichy colony of Algiers to retrieve a camera containing film showing the meeting location of some Allied chiefs. Nazi Muller (Rilla) is tailing Thurston but a couple of femmes come to the Brit's aid in the Casbah. Loosely based on an actual Allied meeting to plan out Operation Torch. **81m/B; DVD.** *GB* James Mason; Carla Lehmann; Walter Rilla; Pamela Stirling; Raymond Lovell; Enid Stamp-Taylor; ***D:*** George King; ***W:*** Brock Williams; Katherine (Kay) Strueby; ***C:*** Otto Heller; ***M:*** James Turner; Roy Douglas.

Candles at Nine 🦴 1/2 **1944** An innocent showgirl must spend a month in her late uncle's creepy mansion in order to inherit it, much to the malevolent chagrin of the rest of the family who want the place and the loot for themselves. Uninspired. **84m/B; VHS, DVD.** *GB* Jessie Matthews; John Stuart; Reginald Purdell; ***D:*** John Harlow.

Candleshoe 🦴🦴 **1978 (G)** A Los Angeles street urchin poses as an English matron's long lost granddaughter in order to steal a fortune hidden in Candleshoe, her country estate, where Niven butlers. Somewhat slapschticky Disney fare. **101m/C; VHS, DVD.** Vivian Pickles; Helen Hayes; David Niven; Jodie Foster; Leo McKern; ***D:*** Norman Tokar; ***W:*** Rosemary Anne Sisson; David Swift; ***C:*** Paul Beeson; ***M:*** Ronald Goodwin.

Candy 🦴🦴 **1968 (R)** Sexual satire, based on the book by Terry Southern and Mason Hoffenberg, can't sustain its simple premise. The teenaged nubile, blonde, and naive title character (Aulin) sets out to discover her sexual awakening and gets chased by every kook she meets, including guru Brando, alcohlic poet Burton, gardener Starr, general Matthau, hunchback Aznavour, surgeon Coburn, and even her own dad, Astin. Very much of part of its psychedelic age. **124m/C; VHS, DVD, Blu-Ray.** *FR IT* Ewa Aulin; Marlon Brando; Charles Aznavour; Richard Burton; Ringo Starr; James Coburn; Walter Matthau; John Huston; John Astin; Elsa Martinelli; Anita Pallenberg; "Sugar Ray" Robinson; ***D:*** Christian Marquand; ***W:*** Buck Henry; ***C:*** Giuseppe Rotunno.

Candy 🦴🦴 **2006 (R)** Heroin chic. Handsome Dan (Ledger) is a would-be poet wooing lovely artist Candy (Cornish). He's already shooting heroin and Candy (who sniffs the stuff) demands he let her needle up. A near-overdose doesn't dim Candy's enthusiasm, especially when their fatherly dealer Casper (Rush) is such a reliable supplier. Pic naturally descents into druggie hell as the two turn to crime to help pay for their habits, with intermittent efforts to get clean. Typical junkie fare, although much less harrowing than a lot of addiction flicks. **108m/C; DVD, Blu-Ray.** *AU* Heath Ledger; Abbie Cornish; Geoffrey Rush; Tony (Anthony) Martin; Noni Hazlehurst; ***W:*** Neil Armfield; Luke Davies; ***C:*** Garry Phillips; ***M:*** Paul Charlier.

Candy Stripe Nurses 🦴 *Sweet Candy* **1974 (R)** Even hard-core Roger Corman fans might find his final installment in the nursing comedy pentad to be a lethargic exercise in gratuitous "sexual situations." Bet those uniforms don't meet hospital standards. The previous films in the series are: "The Student Nurses," "Private Duty Nurses," "Night Call Nurses," and "The Young Nurses." **80m/C; VHS, DVD.** Candice Rialson; Robin Mattson; Maria Rojo; Kimberly Hyde; Dick Miller; Stanley Ralph Ross; Monte Landis; Tom Baker; Don Keefer; Sally Kirkland; Rick Gates; ***D:*** Allan Holleb.

Candy Tangerine Man 🦴 **1975** Respectable businessman leads a double life as loving father and LA pimp. **88m/C; VHS, DVD, Blu-Ray.** John Daniels; Tom Hankerson; Eli Haines; Marva Farmer; George "Buck" Flower; ***D:*** Matt Cimber.

Candyman 🦴🦴 **1992 (R)** Terrifying tale from horror maven Clive Barker is an effective combination of American gothic, academia, and urban squalor. A search for dissertation material leads graduate student Helen Lyle (Madsen) into gang-infested housing. There she encounters the urban myth of Candyman, the son of a former slave who was lynched and is now back with a hook and a vendetta. Filled with the appropriate amount of yucky stuff, yet successfully employs subtle scare tactics and plausible characters. **98m/C; DVD, Blu-Ray.** Virginia Madsen; Tony Todd; Xander Berkeley; Kasi Lemmons; Vanessa L(ynne) Williams; DeJuan Guy; Michael Culkin; Gilbert Lewis; Stanley DeSantis; ***D:*** Bernard Rose; ***W:*** Bernard Rose; ***C:*** Anthony B. Richmond; ***M:*** Philip Glass.

Candyman 2: Farewell to the Flesh 🦴 **1994 (R)** Explains the origins of the urban bogeyman called Candyman—the man, the hook, and the bees. Rehashes the same old scare tactics from previous and better horror movies and uses cheesy special effects. The sensual background of New Orleans during Mardi Gras can't help this stale sequel. Embrace this "Farewell" from a distance. Based on stories by Clive Barker. **99m/C; VHS, DVD, Blu-Ray.** Tony Todd; Kelly Rowan; Veronica Cartwright; Timothy Carhart; William O'Leary; Bill Nunn; Fay Hauser; Joshua Gibran Mayweather; ***D:*** Bill Condon; ***W:*** Rand Ravich; Mark Kruger; ***C:*** Tobias Schliessler; ***M:*** Philip Glass.

Candyman 3: Day of the Dead 🦴🦴 **1998 (R)** The Candyman (Todd) haunts an L.A. descendent (D'Errico), framing her for murder, in the hopes that she will join him. **93m/C; VHS, DVD.** Tony Todd; Donna D'Errico; Jsu Garcia; Lupe Ontiveros; ***D:*** Turi Meyer; ***W:*** Turi Meyer; Al Septien; ***C:*** Michael G. Wojciechowski. **VIDEO**

Cannery Row ½ **1982 (PG)** Baseball has-been Nolte lives anonymously among the downtrodden in the seamy part of town and carries on with working girl girlfriend Winger. Based on John Steinbeck's "Cannery Row" and "Sweet Thursday." **120m/C; VHS, DVD.** Nick Nolte; Debra Winger; Audra Lindley; M. Emmet Walsh; Frank McRae; James Keane; Lloyd "Sunshine" Parker; ***Nar:*** John Huston; ***D:*** David S. Ward; ***W:*** David S. Ward; ***C:*** Sven Nykvist; ***M:*** Jack Nitzsche.

Cannes Man **1996 (R)** Features legendary Hollywood producer Sy Lerner (Cassel), who vows to make unknown cabbie/screenwriter Frank Rhinoslavsky (Quinn) a star, all while being schmoozed at Cannes by stars who want to be in his latest epic, while he tries to find backers for his unwritten script. **88m/C; VHS, DVD.** Seymour Cassel; Francesco Quinn; Rebecca Broussand; ***D:*** Richard Martini.

Cannibal Apocalypse **WOOF!** *Cannibals in the Streets; Savage Apocalypse; The Slaughterers; Cannibals in the City; Virus; Invasion of the Flesh Hunters* **1980** Group of tortured Vietnam veterans returns home carrying a cannibalistic curse with them. Smorgasbord of gore and sensationalism is not for discriminating tastes. **96m/C; VHS, DVD, Blu-Ray.** *IT* John Saxon; Elizabeth Turner; Giovanni Lambardo Radice; Tony King; ***D:*** Anthony M. Dawson; ***W:*** Anthony M. Dawson; Dardano Sacchetti; Jimmy Gould; ***C:*** Fernando Arribas; ***M:*** Alexander Blonksteiner.

Cannibal Campout **1988** Crazed orphans with eating disorders make square meal of coed babes getting back to nature. **89m/C; VHS, DVD.** Carrie Lindell; Richard Marcus; Amy Chludzinski; Jon McBride; ***D:*** Jon McBride; Tom Fisher.

Cannibal Holocaust *Ruggero Deodato's Cannibal Holocaust* **1980** Ostensibly a social commentary on the evils of mass media, one of the most brutal films ever made follows a scholar's trek into the jungle a year after a group of celebrity documentary filmmakers have disappeared. He finds their cameras, and the lost footage is infinitely disturbing: apparently his predecessors, unable to find anything interesting to film (except a tribe of cannibals), massacred most of the village to film the aftermath and have something "newsworthy." The tribe's revenge isn't pretty. **96m/C; DVD, Blu-Ray.** Robert Kerman; Luca Barbareschi; Salvatore Basile; Francesca Ciardi; Perry Pirkanen; Ricardo Fuentes; Carl Gabriel Yorke; ***D:*** Ruggero Deodato; ***W:*** Gianfranco Clerici; ***C:*** Sergio d'Offizi; ***M:*** Riz Ortolani. **VIDEO**

Cannibal Man *The Apartment on the 13 Floor; La Semana del Asesino; Week of the Killer* **1971** Slaughterhouse worker Marcos (Parra) accidentally kills a man in a fight and then covers up the incident with more killings. Then he's got to get rid of all those dead bodies and what better place than at the butcher's where he works. **98m/C; VHS, DVD, Blu-Ray.** *SP* Vicente Parra; Emma Cohen; Eusebio Poncela; ***D:*** Eloy De La Iglesia; ***W:*** Eloy De La Iglesia.

Cannibal! The Musical **1996 (R)** Only those wacky people at Troma could offer a horror/musical about a group of 1883 gold miners who get lost in the Colorado Rockies, have some strange adventures, and eventually wind up as dinner to cannibal Alferd Packer (who's telling his version of the story to a female reporter while in prison). Seven rather tedious musical numbers lead up to the gore-splashed finale. From director Trey Parker, who also repulses (and amuses us) with TV's "South Park." **105m/C; VHS, DVD, UMD.** Ian Hardin; Jason McHugh; Matt Stone; Trey Parker; Juan Schwartz; ***D:*** Trey Parker; ***W:*** Trey Parker.

Cannibal Women in the Avocado Jungle of Death ½ **1989 (PG-13)** Tongue-in-cheek cult classic features erstwhile playmate Tweed as feminist anthropologist who searches with ditzy student and mucho macho male guide for lost tribe of cannibal women who dine on their mates. Lawton directed under the alias "J.D. Athens." **90m/C; VHS, DVD, Blu-Ray.** Shannon Tweed; Adrienne Barbeau; Karen Mistal; Barry Primus; Bill Maher; Jim MacKrell; Brett Stimely; Paul Ross; ***D:*** J.F. Lawton; J.D. Athens; ***W:*** J.F. Lawton; J.D. Athens; ***C:*** Robert Knouse; ***M:*** Carl Dante.

Cannon for Cordoba ½ **1970** In 1912, Mexican revolutionary Hector Cordoba (Vallone) steals cannon from an army fort along the Texas/Mexico border. Captain Rod Douglas (cigar-chomping Peppard) and various misfit recruits are sent by General John J. Pershing (Russell) to bring back the cannon and Cordoba. **104m/C; DVD, Blu-Ray.** Raf Vallone; George Peppard; Giovanna Ralli; Peter Duel; Don Gordon; Gabriele Tinti; John Larch; John Russell; ***D:*** Paul Wendkos; ***W:*** Stephen Kandel; ***C:*** Antonio Macasoli; ***M:*** Elmer Bernstein.

Cannonball *Carquake* **1976 (PG)** Assorted ruthless people leave patches of rubber across the country competing for grand prize in less than legal auto race. Not top drawer New World but nonetheless a cult fave. Inferior to Bartel's previous cult classic, "Death Race 2000." Most interesting for plethora of cult cameos, including Scorsese, Dante, and grandmaster Corman. **93m/C; VHS, DVD.** *CH* David Carradine; Bill McKinney; Veronica Hamel; Gerrit Graham; Robert Carradine; Jonathan Kaplan; Martin Scorsese; Belinda Balaski; Roger Corman; Judy Canova; Joe Dante; Carl Gottlieb; Archie Hahn; Dick Miller; Sylvester Stallone; Paul Bartel; Mary Woronov; ***D:*** Paul Bartel; ***W:*** Paul Bartel; Donald Stewart; ***C:*** Tak Fujimoto; ***M:*** David A. Axelrod.

Cannonball Run ½ **1981 (PG)** So many stars, so little plot. Reynolds and sidekick DeLuise disguise themselves as paramedics to foil cops while they compete in cross-country Cannonball race. Shows no sign of having been directed by an ex-stuntman. One of 1981's top grossers—go figure. Followed by equally languid sequel "Cannonball Run II." **95m/C; VHS, DVD, Blu-Ray.** Burt Reynolds; Farrah Fawcett; Roger Moore; Dom DeLuise; Dean Martin; Sammy Davis, Jr.; Jack Elam; Adrienne Barbeau; Peter Fonda; Molly Picon; Bert Convy; Jamie Farr; ***D:*** Hal Needham; ***W:*** Brock Yates; ***C:*** Michael C. Butler; ***M:*** Al Capps.

Cannonball Run 2 **1984 (PG)** More mindless cross-country wheel spinning with gratuitous star cameos. Director Needham apparently subscribes to the two wrongs make a right school of sequels. **109m/C; VHS, DVD.** Burt Reynolds; Dom DeLuise; Jamie Farr; Marilu Henner; Shirley MacLaine; Jim Nabors; Frank Sinatra; Sammy Davis, Jr.; Dean Martin; Telly Savalas; Susan Anton; Catherine Bach; Jack Elam; Sid Caesar; Ricardo Montalban; Charles Nelson Reilly; Henry Silva; Tim Conway; Don Knotts; Molly Picon; Jackie Chan; ***D:*** Hal Needham; ***W:*** Harvey Miller; ***C:*** Nick McLean; ***M:*** Steve Dorff.

Cannonball Run Europe: The Great Escape ½ **2005** Documentary following legendary Cannonball racer Tim 'Maverick' Porter, as he and his fellow Cannonballers begin in London and set out to race across Europe. More notable for the cast of incredibly eccentric driving teams than racing action (after all they can't really film most of the illegal stuff). **135m/C; DVD.** *GB* ***D:*** Rupert Bryan.

Can't Buy Me Love ½ **1987 (PG-13)** Unpopular high school nerd Dempsey buys a month of dates with teen babe Peterson for $1000 in order to win friends and influence people. Semi-amusing and earnest in a John Hughes Lite kind of way. Previously known as "Boy Rents Girl." **94m/C; VHS, DVD.** Patrick Dempsey; Amanda Peterson; Dennis Dugan; Courtney Gains; Seth Green; Katrina Caspary; Sharon Farrell; Darcy Demoss; Devin Devasquez; Eric Bruskotter; Gerardo Mejia; Ami Dolenz; Max Perlich; ***D:*** Steve Rash; ***W:*** Michael Swerdlick; ***C:*** Peter Lyons Collister; ***M:*** Robert Folk.

Can't Hardly Wait *The Party* **1998 (PG-13)** Writer-directors Kaplan and Elfont attempt to reheat the John Hughes 80s teen-party-and-angst casserole for the kids of the 90s. Unfortunately, it's lost its flavor. All of your favorite high school cardboard cut-ups are here. Jock-jerk Mike (Facinelli) dumps teen queen Amanda (Hewitt) on the eve of a graduation blowout. Shy, sensitive Preston (Embry), who believes himself linked to Amanda by fate and their mutual love of toaster pastry, decides this is his opportunity to finally tell her how he feels. Frolicking in the background are your stereotypical foreign exchange students, stoners, geeks, metal heads, jocks and bimbos herded around by the ever-present Girl Whose Party It Is. Wavers between (unsuccessfully) trying to be thoughtful like "American Graffiti" and thoughtless like "Animal House." **101m/C; VHS, DVD, Blu-Ray.** Ethan (Randall) Embry; Jennifer Love Hewitt; Peter Facinelli; Charlie Korsmo; Seth Green; Jerry O'Connell; Lauren Ambrose; Jenna Elfman; Michelle Brookhurst; Erik Palladino; Steve Monroe; ***D:*** Harry Elfont; Deborah Kaplan; ***W:*** Harry Elfont; Deborah Kaplan; ***C:*** Lloyd Ahern, II; ***M:*** David Kitay; Matthew Sweet.

Can't Help Singing ½ **1945** In 1849, willful heiress Caroline (Durbin) ignores her senator father's (Collins) wishes and heads west to marry her Army sweetheart (Bruce). But on the wagon train she falls for wagon master Lawlor (Paige), who's a better guy anyway. Durbin's first color musical. **90m/C; VHS, DVD.** Deanna Durbin; Robert Paige; David Bruce; Akim Tamiroff; Leonid Kinskey; Ray Collins; June Vincent; Thomas Gomez; ***D:*** Frank Ryan; ***W:*** Frank Ryan; Lewis R. Foster; ***C:*** Elwood "Woody" Bredell; William Howard Greene; ***M:*** Hans J. Salter; Jerome Kern; ***M:*** E.Y. Harburg.

Can't Stop the Music **WOOF!** **1980 (PG)** Retired model invites friends from Greenwich Village to a party to help the career of her roommate, an aspiring composer. Disco inferno that nearly reaches heights of surreal ineptness. Put it in a time capsule and let the people of the future decide what the heck was going on in the '70s. Features two of the top hits by the Village People. **120m/C; VHS, DVD, Blu-Ray.** Valerie Perrine; Bruce Jenner; Steve Guttenberg; Paul Sand; Leigh Taylor-Young; Village People; ***D:*** Nancy Walker; ***W:*** Allan Carr; Bronte Woodard; ***C:*** Bill Butler; ***M:*** Jacques Morali. Golden Raspberries '80: Worst Picture, Worst Screenplay.

A Canterbury Tale **1944** Writer-director team Powell and Pressburger have loosely modeled a retelling of Chaucer's famous tale of a pilgrimage to the cathedral in Canterbury. Set in Nazi-threatened Britain in 1944, the story follows the pilgrimage of three Brits and an American GI to the eponymous cathedral. Strange, effective, worth looking at. The 95-minute American version, with added footage of Kim Hunter, is inferior to the 124-minute original. **124m/B; DVD.** *UK* Eric Portman; Sheila Sim; Dennis Price; Esmond Knight; Charles Hawtrey; Hay Petrie; ***D:*** Michael Powell; Emeric Pressburger; ***W:*** Michael Powell; Emeric Pressburger; ***C:*** Erwin Hillier; ***M:*** Allan Gray.

The Canterbury Tales *I Racconti di Canterbury* **1971** Four Chaucer tales, most notably "The Merchant's Tale" and "The Wife of Bath," are recounted by travelers, with director Pasolini as the bawdy poet. Deemed obscene by the Italian courts, it's the second entry in Pasolini's medieval "Trilogy of Life," preceded by "The Decameron" and followed by "The Arabian Nights." In Italian with English subtitles. **109m/C; VHS, DVD, Blu-Ray.** *IT* Laura Betti; Ninetto Davoli; Pier Paolo Pasolini; Hugh Griffith; Josephine Chaplin; Michael Balfour; Jenny Runacre; ***D:*** Pier Paolo Pasolini; ***W:*** Pier Paolo Pasolini; ***C:*** Tonino Delli Colli; ***M:*** Ennio Morricone. Berlin Intl. Film Fest. '72: Golden Berlin Bear.

The Canterville Ghost ½ **1944** Laughton, a 300-year-old ghost with a yellow streak, is sentenced to spook a castle until he proves he's not afraid of his own shadow. American troops stay at the castle during WWII, and, as luck would have it, soldier Young is distantly related to spunky young keeper of the castle O'Brien, ghost Laughton's descendant. Once Young is acquainted with his cowardly ancestor, he begins to fear a congenital yellow streak, and both struggle to be brave despite themselves. Vaguely derived from an Oscar Wilde tale. **95m/B; VHS, DVD.** Charles Laughton; Robert Young; Margaret O'Brien; William Gargan; Reginald Owen; Rags Ragland; Una O'Connor; Peter Lawford; Mike Mazurki; ***D:*** Jules Dassin; ***W:*** Edwin Blum; ***M:*** George Bassman.

The Canterville Ghost ½ **1986** An American family inherits an English castle and must deal with a disgruntled 300-year-old ghost. Loose adaptation of the Oscar Wilde story with Gielgud (as the ghost) and Milano (as the teen daughter) playing charmingly off each other; however Wass (as the dad) acts as if he's in a TV sitcom. **98m/C; DVD.** John Gielgud; Ted Wass; Alyssa Milano; Andrea Marcovicci; Harold Innocent; Lila Kaye; Celia Breckon; ***D:*** Paul Bogart; ***W:*** George Zalesio; ***C:*** Bob Edwards; ***M:*** Howard Blake. **TV**

The Canterville Ghost ½ **1996 (PG)** Stewart is the highlight of this updated TV version of the Oscar Wilde short story. He's the cursed Elizabethan spirit of Sir Simon de Canterville, doomed to haunt the family mansion until a prophecy is fulfilled. But he's not happy with a family of American intruders, until teenager Virginia (Campbell) discovers Sir Simon and realizes she may hold the key to freeing the unhappy ghost. **91m/C; VHS, DVD.** Patrick Stewart; Neve Campbell; Ed Wiley; Cherie Lunghi; Donald Sinden; Joan Sims; Leslie Phillips; Ciaran Fitzgerald; Daniel Betts; Raymond Pickard; ***D:*** Syd Macartney; ***W:*** Robert Benedetti; ***C:*** Denis Lewiston; ***M:*** Ernest Troost.

Canvas ½ **2006 (PG-13)** Convincing performances help out a somewhat familiar plot about mental illness. Ten-year-old Chris (Gearhart) returns home after a stay with relatives. His mom, Mary (Harden), was hospitalized for schizophrenia and her sanity is still in question, despite the best efforts of hard-working hubby John (Pantoliano). Countless problems inundate their lives as Mary becomes more disruptive and an embarrassment Chris finds hard to bear. **101m/C; DVD.** William Morrissey; Marcia Gay Harden; Joe Pantoliano; Devon Gearhart; Marcus Johns; Sophia Bairley; ***D:*** Joseph Greco; ***W:*** Joseph Greco; ***C:*** Rob Sweeney; ***M:*** Joel Goodman.

The Canyon **2009 (R)** Nick and Lori go to the Grand Canyon on their honeymoon. They want to take a mule tour but their plans are thwarted because they don't have permits. Then grizzled Henry offers to be their guide. He has some odd ideas, gets them lost, and the newlyweds are left to fend for themselves amidst rattlesnakes, scorpions, vultures, and wolves. **91m/C; DVD.** Yvonne Strahovski; Eion Bailey; Will Patton; ***D:*** Richard Harrah; ***W:*** Steve Allrich; ***C:*** Nelson Cragg; ***M:*** Hector Pereira.

Canyon Passage **1946** Riproarin' western set in the Oregon Territory in 1856. Stuart (Andrews) is a former scout turned store owner who falls for Lucy (Hayward), who happens to be the fiance of banker/gambler Camrose (Donlevy). Camrose gets into money troubles, there's a villain named Bragg (Bond), and a pretty spectacular Indian attack. Carmichael serves as the wandering minstrel to the action, singing four songs. Director Tourneur was best known for his horror films. **92m/C; VHS, DVD, Blu-Ray.** Dana Andrews; Brian Donlevy; Susan Hayward; Ward Bond; Hoagy Carmichael; Lloyd Bridges; Andy Devine; Patricia Roc; ***D:*** Jacques Tourneur; ***W:*** Ernest Pascal; ***C:*** Edward Cronjager; ***M:*** Frank Skinner.

Canyon River ½ **1956** Typical oater has Wyoming rancher Steve Patrick (Montgomery) and his foreman Bob Andrews (Graves) traveling to Oregon to bring back some breeding stock to improve his herd. Too bad Andrews has plotted with rancher Maddox (Sande) to kill Patrick and steal the herd instead. **80m/C; DVD.** George Montgomery; Peter Graves; Walter Sande; Marcia Henderson; Richard Eyer; Robert J. Wilke; Alan Hale, Jr.; ***D:*** Harmon Jones; ***W:*** Daniel Ullman; ***C:*** Ellsworth Fredricks; ***M:*** Marlin Skiles.

The Canyons **2013** Nearly experimental in its awfulness, director Schrader's controversial film earned more headlines for the reportedly difficult behavior of leading lady Lohan. But this laughable drama is awful for reasons other than its cast. Writer Bret Easton Ellis spews another inert story of spoiled people in the Hollywood Hills as Lohan plays the girlfriend of a manipulative jerk (porn star Deen) who is convinced she's having an affair in between their own extreme sexual three- and foursomes. He's right. There's no reason to care about the infidelity, jealousy, or spoiled nature of these irredeemable jerks. **99m/C; Blu-Ray, Streaming.** Lindsay Lohan; James Deen; Nolan Gerard Funk; Amanda Brooks; Gus Van Sant; Tenille Houston; ***D:*** Paul Schrader; ***W:*** Bret Easton Ellis; ***C:*** John DeFazio; ***M:*** Brendan Canning.

Cape Fear 🦴🦴🦴 ½ **1961** Small-town lawyer Peck and his family are plagued by the sadistic attentions of criminal Mitchum, who just finished a six year sabbatical at the state pen courtesy of witness Peck. Taut and creepy; Mitchum's a consummate psychopath. Based on (and far superior to) John MacDonald's "The Executioners." Don't pass this one up in favor of the Scorsese remake. **106m/B; VHS, DVD, Blu-Ray.** Gregory Peck; Robert Mitchum; Polly Bergen; Martin Balsam; Telly Savalas; Jack Kruschen; John McKee; Lori Martin; ***D:*** J. Lee Thompson; ***C:*** Sam Leavitt; ***M:*** Bernard Herrmann.

Cape Fear 🦴🦴🦴 **1991 (R)** Scorsese takes on this terrifying tale of brutality and manipulation (previously filmed in 1961) and cranks it up a notch as a paroled convict haunts the lawyer who put him away. Great cast, a rollercoaster of suspense. Note the cameos by Mitchum, Peck, and Balsam, stars of the first version. Original source material was "The Executioners" by John D. MacDonald. Breath-taking rollercoaster of a film. Elmer Bernstein adapted the original score by Bernard Herrmann. **128m/C; VHS, DVD, Blu-Ray.** Robert De Niro; Nick Nolte; Jessica Lange; Juliette Lewis; Joe Don Baker; Robert Mitchum; Gregory Peck; Martin Balsam; Illeana Douglas; Fred Dalton Thompson; ***D:*** Martin Scorsese; ***W:*** Wesley Strick; ***C:*** Freddie Francis; ***M:*** Elmer Bernstein.

Cape of Good Hope 🦴🦴 ½ **2004 (PG-13)** A Cape Town animal rescue shelter is the link for numerous characters and their stories. Kate (Brown) runs the shelter and is the object of attraction for a shy vet (Visser). She befriends young Thabo (Masilo), whose widowed mother, Lindiwe (Moshesh), is being pressured to marry an elderly, wealthy minister, but refugee Jean Claude (Ebouaney), who works at the shelter, loves her. Meanwhile, Kate's friend and co-worker Sharifa (Adams) is having marital trouble. Director Bamford doesn't ignore poverty and racism in a post-apartheid South Africa but his focus remains on how this group deals with ordinary, everyday life. **107m/C; DVD.** Eriq Ebouaney; Nthati Moshesh; David Isaacs; Nick Boraine; Debbie Brown; Morné Visser; Quanita Adams; Kamo Masilo; ***D:*** Mark Bamford; ***W:*** Mark Bamford; Suzanne Kay; ***C:*** Larry Fong; ***M:*** J.B. Eckl.

Capernaum 🦴🦴🦴 *Capharnaüm* **2018 (R)** Choosing homelessness over the abuse and neglect that his parents heap on him and his many siblings, young Zain escapes to the streets of Beirut. He befriends Rahil, an undocumented Egyptian woman, at first babysitting her infant son, then becoming sole caregiver after tragedy strikes. Later sent to prison for stabbing someone, Zain sues his parents for bringing him into this crummy world. Needless to say, this isn't a laugh riot. It will gut you. Labaki shot it with handheld cameras and utilized non-actors whose lives paralleled their characters', giving it a documentary-style realism. **121m/C; DVD, Blu-Ray.** *US LB* Fadi Yousef; Zain Al Rafeea; Yordanos Shiferaw; Boluwatife Treasure Bankole; Kawther Al Haddad; ***D:*** Nadine Labaki; ***W:*** Nadine Labaki; Jihad Hojeily; Michelle Keserwany; ***C:*** Christopher Aoun; ***M:*** Khaled Mouzannar.

Capitaine Conan 🦴🦴🦴 *Captain Conan* **1996** On the Bulgarian border in 1918, during the last clashes of WWI, Conan (Torreton) is a fearless, impulsive warrior, reserving his respect only for his men. Although armistice is finally declared, the troops stationed in the Balkans are not demobilized and become increasingly fractious. This causes a rift between Conan and his educated friend Norbert (Le Bihan), who's been appointed a military legal representative. They are warily reunited in defense of a soldier (Val) charged with desertion, while still dealing with the ravages of the long conflict. Adapted from the book by Roger Vercel; French with subtitles. **129m/C; VHS, DVD.** *FR* Philippe Torreton; Samuel Le Bihan; Bernard Le Coq; Francois Berleand; Claude Rich; Catherine Rich; Pierre Val; ***D:*** Bertrand Tavernier; ***W:*** Bertrand Tavernier; Jean Cosmos; ***C:*** Alain Choquart; ***M:*** Oswald D'Andrea. Cesar '97: Actor (Torreton), Director (Tavernier), Film.

Capital 🦴 ½ *Le Capital* **2012 (R)** A dull chronicle of morally bankrupt executive Marc (Elmaleh), who rises to power after the CEO of his company dies and then tries to thwart a takeover by an equally unethical company run by Dittmar (Byrne). Director Costa-Gavras unfortunately doesn't make us care who gets what. **114m/C; DVD, Blu-Ray, Streaming.** *FR* Gad Elmaleh; Gabriel Byrne; Natacha Regnier; Celine Sallette; Liya Kebede; Hippolyte Girardot; ***D:*** Constantin Costa-Gavras; ***W:*** Constantin Costa-Gavras; Karim Boukercha; Jean-Claude Grumberg; ***C:*** Eric Gautier; ***M:*** Armand Amar.

Capital Games 🦴 ½ **2013** Low-budget gay indie. Former LA cop Steve now works for an ad agency. Hyper-competitive, Steve is upset that new hire, Brit Mark Richfield, is drawing all his colleagues' attention as they compete for the same new campaign. On a company retreat to Santa Fe, the two men become lost in the desert, resulting in a night of sex. Mark insists he's actually straight and also engaged, but Steve doesn't believe him. Based on the G.A. Hauser novel. **97m/C; DVD.** Eric Presnall; Gregor Cosgrove; Shane Keough; Corinne Fox; ***D:*** Ilo Orleans; ***W:*** Wendell Lu; ***C:*** Peter Borosh; ***M:*** Leandro Gaetan. **VIDEO**

Capital Punishment 🦴 ½ **1996** Martial arts expert James Thayer (Daniels) is recruited by the DEA to go undercover and stop Nakata (Yamashita), the supplier of a new illegal drug. His operation turns up a corrupt police chief (Carradine), who frames him for murder, and lots of action. **90m/C; VHS, DVD.** Gary Daniels; Tadashi Yamashita; David Carradine; Mel Novak; Ian Jacklin; Ava Fabian; ***D:*** David Hue; ***W:*** David Hue; ***C:*** David Swett.

Capitalism: A Love Story 🦴🦴 ½ **2009 (R)** Loud-mouthed provocateur Moore's documentary on the global financial crisis and the meltdown of the U.S. economy during the transition from the Bush to the Obama administrations. Moore's belief is that capitalism rewards greed and that corporations and financial institutions exploit (and deliberately confuse) the majority of Americans with their practices. Moore likes to grandstand but he's not afraid to tackle big subjects that can (and should) be up for debate. **120m/C; Blu-Ray, On Demand.** Michael Moore; ***D:*** Michael Moore; ***W:*** Michael Moore; ***C:*** Jayme Roy; Daniel Marracino; ***M:*** Jeff Gibbs.

The Capitol Conspiracy 🦴 ½ *The Prophet* **1999 (R)** CIA agents Jarrid Maddox (Wilson) and Vicki Taylor (Keith) uncover evidence that links government officials with illegal mind-control experiments. The duo become targets of a hit squad determined to keep the information secret. Very familiar actioner. **83m/C; VHS, DVD.** Don "The Dragon" Wilson; Alexander Keith; Paul Michael Robinson; Arthur Roberts; Barbara Steele; ***D:*** Fred Olen Ray; ***C:*** Gary Graver. **VIDEO**

Capone 🦴🦴 ½ *The Revenge of Al Capone* **1989 (R)** Story of the gangster after Elliot Ness put him in a Chicago jail. That didn't stop Capone from running his crime empire until a single FBI agent worked to sent the crime boss to Alcatraz, where his power would be useless. Exuberant performances from Sharkey and Carradine. **96m/C; VHS, DVD.** Ray Sharkey; Keith Carradine; Debrah Farentino; Jayne Atkinson; Bradford English; Marc Figueroa; Neil Giuntoli; Charles Haid; Nicholas Mele; Scott Paulin; Alan Rosenberg; ***D:*** Michael Pressman; ***W:*** Tracy Keenan Wynn; ***C:*** Tim Suhrstedt; ***M:*** Craig Safan. **TV**

Capone 🦴🦴 **2020 (R)** As once-feared gangster Al Capone (Hardy) reaches the end of his life, he is falling apart mentally and physically. The self-involved Capone is surrounded by those who are loyal to him, including wife Mae (Cardellini), sister Rosie (Narducci), and right hand man (Dillon), but struggles to get through each day. The psychological drama revolves around Hardy's challenging character study, including a highly stylized vocal style, with the rest of the cast essentially reacting to him instead of telling a story. Though the film has been crafted with care, the result is as uneven as Hardy's interpretation. **103m/C; DVD.** Tom (Thomas) Hardy; Linda Cardellini; Matt Dillon; Al Sapienza; Kathrine Narducci; ***D:*** Josh Trank; ***W:*** Josh Trank; ***C:*** Peter Deming; ***M:*** El-P.

Capote 🦴🦴🦴 **2005 (R)** Based on the book "Capote" by Gerald Clark. Enigmatic Truman Capote (an outstanding Hoffman) was a celebrated author and a member of elite New York society. Biopic sheds light on Capote's obsessive research into the killers behind the startling murders of a Kansas family, which formed the groundwork for his "In Cold Blood," an obsession that ultimately led to Capote's own demise, spiraling into obesity, alcoholism and ouster from the intellectual elite. Hoffman nails his portrayal of the self-absorbed man at his manipulative best. **114m/C; DVD.** Philip Seymour Hoffman; Catherine Keener; Chris Cooper; Bruce Greenwood; Bob Balaban; Amy Ryan; Mark Pellegrino; Clifton (Gonzalez) Collins, Jr.; ***D:*** Bennett Miller; ***W:*** Dan Futterman; ***C:*** Adam Kimmel; ***M:*** Mychael Danna. Oscars '05: Actor (Hoffman); British Acad. '05: Actor (Hoffman); Golden Globes '06: Actor--Drama (Hoffman); Ind. Spirit '06: Actor (Hoffman), Screenplay; L.A. Film Critics '05: Actor (Hoffman), Screenplay, Support. Actress (Keener); Natl. Bd. of Review '05: Actor (Hoffman); N.Y. Film Critics '05: First Feature; Natl. Soc. Film Critics '05: Actor (Hoffman), Film; Screen Actors Guild '05: Actor (Hoffman); Broadcast Film Critics '05: Actor (Hoffman).

Caprica 🦴🦴 ½ **2009** Prequel to the "Battlestar Galatica" series, set 58 years before those events, and intended as the pilot episode for another series. Robotics expert Daniel Graystone (Stoltz) is disturbed by his failing marriage and his rebellious daughter Zoe (Toressani). A robotics whiz herself, Zoe has created a virtual world (and a virtual avatar) where she and her friends can discuss their monotheistic beliefs vs. Caprica's polytheistic society. When Zoe is killed in a terrorist bombing, Daniel discovers he can use her avatar to create an artificial life and thus the Cylons are born. Daniel isn't the only one to suffer: mobbed-up lawyer Joseph Adama (Morales), an immigrant from the Tauron colony, has lost his wife and daughter and is raising son William alone, but he regards Daniel's experiment as an abomination. **93m/C; DVD.** Eric Stoltz; Esai Morales; Paula Malcomson; Polly Walker; Alessandra Toressani; Magda Apanowicz; Sasha Roiz; ***D:*** Jeff Reiner; ***W:*** Ronald D. Moore; ***C:*** Joel Ransom; ***M:*** Bear McCreary. **CABLE**

Caprice 🦴 **1967** Truly awful comedy, best left to Day fans only. The middle-aged actress is still playing wide-eyed and primly sunny, even as industrial spy Patricia Fowler. Pat is trying to get something on a rival cosmetics company, which leads her to mystery man Christopher White (Harris), her would-be rescuer and love interest. Actually, the only interesting thing is how Day's costumes are frequently coordinated to their settings. With material like this, no wonder she retired from movies in 1968. **98m/C; DVD.** Doris Day; Richard Harris; Ray Walston; Jack Kruschen; Edward Mulhare; Lilia Skala; Michael J. Pollard; Irene Tsu; ***D:*** Frank Tashlin; ***W:*** Frank Tashlin; ***C:*** Leon Shamroy; ***M:*** Frank DeVol.

Capricorn One 🦴🦴🦴 **1978 (R)** Astronauts Brolin, Simpson and Waterston follow Mission Controller Holbrook's instructions to fake a Mars landing on a soundstage when their ship is discovered to be defective. When they find out they're supposed to expire in outer space so that the NASA scam won't become public knowledge, they flee to the desert, while reporter Gould sniffs out the cover up. Based on a pseudonymous novel by Ken Follett. **123m/C; VHS, DVD, Blu-Ray.** Elliott Gould; James Brolin; Brenda Vaccaro; O.J. Simpson; Hal Holbrook; Sam Waterston; Karen Black; Telly Savalas; ***D:*** Peter Hyams; ***W:*** Peter Hyams; ***C:*** Bill Butler; ***M:*** Jerry Goldsmith.

Captain America 🦴🦴 *The Return of Captain America* **1944** Captain America battles a mad scientist in this 15-episode serial based on the comic book character. **240m/B; VHS, DVD.** Dick Purcell; Adrian Booth; Lionel Atwill; ***D:*** John English; ***W:*** Elmer Clifton.

Captain America 🦴 ½ **1979** Marvel Comic character steps into feature film and flounders. The patriotic superhero son of WWII hero fights bad guy with contraband nuclear weapon. **98m/C; VHS, DVD.** Reb Brown; Len Birman; Heather Menzies; Steve Forrest; Robin Mattson; Joseph Ruskin; Michael McManus; ***D:*** Rod Holcomb. **TV**

Captain America 🦴 ½ **1989 (PG-13)** Based on the Marvel Comics superhero. It's 1941 and Steve Rogers has just been recruited to join a top secret experimental government program after flunking his army physical. Injected with a serum, Steve becomes super strong, fast, and smart but is matched in all three by an evil Nazi counterpart, Red Skull. The two battle to a WWII standstill and while Red Skull goes on with his evil plots, the next 40 years finds Captain America fast frozen in the Alaskan tundra. Finally, our hero is thawed in time to do a final battle with his evil nemesis. This one is ridiculous even by comic book standards but it may amuse the kids. **103m/C; VHS, DVD, Blu-Ray.** Matt Salinger; Scott Paulin; Ronny Cox; Ned Beatty; Darren McGavin; Melinda Dillon; ***D:*** Albert Pyun; ***W:*** Stephen Tolkin.

Captain America: Civil War 🦴🦴🦴 **2016 (PG-13)** The third Captain America film could really be looked at as the third Avengers film given how many of that franchise's character appear. It suffers a bit from overcrowding, but its well-choreographed and executed action saves it from CGI overload. It also helps that Evans seems to get better with each film. His Cap faces off against Iron Man when the two disagree over international oversight over superheroes. The two charismatic leaders get other heroes on their sides, leading to appearances by a dozen or so MCU icons, including a new Spider-Man (Holland). It's fun, but not quite as memorable as it should be. **147m/C; DVD, Blu-Ray.** Chris Evans; Robert Downey, Jr.; Scarlett Johansson; Sebastian Stan; Anthony Mackie; ***D:*** Anthony Russo; Joe Russo; ***W:*** Christopher Markus; Stephen McFeely; ***C:*** Trent Opaloch; ***M:*** Henry Jackman.

Captain America: The First Avenger 🦴🦴 ½ *Captain America* **2011 (PG-13)** An old-fashioned action/adventure film dressed up like a modern superhero movie that primarily serves as a prologue for next year's Avengers film and just barely stands on its own without that context. The Marvel Comics icon Captain America (Evans) is finally given an origin story of his own as Steve Rogers transforms from skinny wannabe to super soldier. Comic book movie regular Evans (Fantastic Four, Scott Pilgrim, and The Losers) is charismatic enough and the piece is well-paced but a bit too retro in tone to avoid being dull. Moderately entertaining yet ultimately not memorable. **121m/C; Blu-Ray.** Chris Evans; Hayley Atwell; Hugo Weaving; Sebastian Stan; Toby Jones; Dominic Cooper; Tommy Lee Jones; Stanley Tucci; Neal McDonough; Richard Armitage; Samuel L. Jackson; ***D:*** Joe Johnston; ***W:*** Christopher Markus; Stephen McFeely; ***C:*** Shelly Johnson; ***M:*** Alan Silvestri.

Captain America: The Winter Soldier 🦴🦴🦴 **2014 (PG-13)** Finally, a superhero movie that doesn't feel like empty spectacle. The best Marvel movie since The Avengers features the return of Steve Rogers aka Captain America (Evans) as the wisecracking, square-jawed hero, who teams up with Nick Fury (Jackson), Black Widow (Johansson) and Sam Wilson (Mackie) to defeat the title bad guy. The film wisely and somewhat brilliantly plays as a '70s political thriller, recognizing that the hero we need may be the guy who can get to the bottom of government corruption. Fun, smart, and consistently clever, it's one of the best Marvel flicks. **136m/C; DVD, Blu-Ray.** Chris Evans; Scarlett Johansson; Samuel L. Jackson; Sebastian Stan; Robert Redford; Cobie Smulders; Anthony Mackie; Frank Grillo; ***D:*** Anthony Russo; Joe Russo; ***W:*** Christopher Markus; Stephen McFeely; ***C:*** Trent Opaloch; ***M:*** Henry Jackman.

Captain America 2: Death Too Soon 🦴 **1979** Terrorists hit America where it hurts, threatening to use age accelerating drug. Sequelized superhero fights chronic crow lines and series dies slow, painful death. **98m/C; VHS, DVD.** Reb Brown; Connie Sellecca; Len Birman; Christopher Lee; Katherine Justice; Lana Wood; Christopher Carey; ***D:*** Ivan Nagy. **TV**

Captain Apache **1971** Union intelligence officer Van Cleef investigates murder of Indian commissioner and discovers fake Indian war landscam. As clever as the title. **95m/C; VHS, DVD.** Lee Van Cleef; Carroll Baker; Stuart Whitman; ***D:*** Alexander Singer; ***W:*** Philip Yordan.

Captain Blood **1/2 1935** Sabatini adventure story launched then unknown 26-year-old Flynn and 19-year-old De Havilland to fame in perhaps the best pirate story ever. Exiled into slavery by a tyrannical governor, Irish physician Peter Blood is forced into piracy but ultimately earns a pardon for his swashbuckling ways. Love interest De Havilland would go on to appear in seven more features with Flynn, who took the part Robert Donat declined for health reasons. Cleverly budgeted using ship shots from silents, and miniature sets when possible. First original film score by composer Korngold. Also available colorized. **120m/B; VHS, DVD.** Errol Flynn; Olivia de Havilland; Basil Rathbone; J. Carrol Naish; Guy Kibbee; Lionel Atwill; Ross Alexander; ***D:*** Michael Curtiz; ***W:*** Casey Robinson; ***C:*** Hal Mohr; ***M:*** Erich Wolfgang Korngold.

Captain Boycott **1/2 1947** In 1880 Ireland, Boycott (Parker) is the despised rent collector for an aristocratic English landlord. When the poor tenant farmers can't pay, he's quick to throw them off the land. The farmers then band together to get rid of Boycott. Granger and Ryan are the prerequisite young lovers. Adapted from the novel by Philip Rooney. **94m/B; VHS, On Demand.** *GB* Cecil Parker; Stewart Granger; Kathleen Ryan; Niall MacGinnis; Robert Donat; Mervyn Johns; Alastair Sim; Noel Purcell; Maurice Denham; ***D:*** Frank Launder; ***W:*** Frank Launder; Wolfgang Wilhelm; ***C:*** Wilkie Cooper; Oswald Morris; ***M:*** William Alwyn.

Captain Calamity **1/2** *Captain Hurricane* **1936** Bill Jones (Houston) is known better as 'Captain Calamity' due to his penchant for getting into fights and trouble. When he pays for his supplies in gold the locals assume he's found a hidden treasure somewhere, and the local pirates immediately begin to chase him down. Pretty much bad news for Bill and the young woman whose mission of revenge he has just agreed to help. It's not quite as good as the plot sounds. **65m/B; DVD.** George Houston; Marion (Marian) Nixon; Vince Barnett; Juan Torena; Movita; Crane Wilbur; George Lewis; Roy D'Arcy; Matthew Irving; Barry Norton; Louis Natheaux; Lloyd Ingraham; Alberto Gandero; Harold Howard; Charles Moyer; ***D:*** John Reinhardt; ***W:*** Gordon Ray Young; ***C:*** Mack Stengler.

Captain Carey, U.S.A. **1950** Muddled spy mystery, best remembered for its Academy Award-winning song, "Mona Lisa," sung by Nat King Cole. Former OSS agent Webster Carey (Ladd) is drifting after the war when a painting catches his eye. Knowing it was last hidden away in an Italian castle, Carey returns to the village to find who smuggled the piece out and if it's the same person who betrayed his unit to the Nazis. **82m/B; DVD, Blu-Ray.** Alan Ladd; Wanda Hendrix; Francis Lederer; Celia Lovsky; Frank Puglia; Joseph Calleia; ***D:*** Mitchell Leisen; ***W:*** Robert Thoeren; ***C:*** John Seitz; ***M:*** Hugo Friedhofer. Oscars '50: Song ("Mona Lisa").

Captain Corelli's Mandolin **2001 (R)** Based on the novel by Louis de Bernieres, the film is set on the Greek island of Cephallonia during WWII. After numerous scenes of hearty Greek peasant life, the island is occupied by an aria-singing Italian army troop, led by mandolin strumming Captain Corelli (Cage). He moves into the local doctor's (Hurt) place and quickly falls for his daughter Pelagia (Cruz). The problem is that she's engaged to fisherman Mandras (Bale), a Greek partisan. Cage's over-done accent makes him sound like he's trying to sell you a pizza, but it matches the overwrought tone. Director Madden was signed late in preproduction after scheduled director Roger Michell suffered a heart attack. **127m/C; VHS, DVD, Blu-Ray.** *GB US* Nicolas Cage; Penelope Cruz; Christian Bale; John Hurt; David Morrissey; Irene Papas; Patrick Malahide; ***D:*** John Madden; ***W:*** Shawn Slovo; ***C:*** John Toll; ***M:*** Stephen Warbeck.

Captain Fantastic **2016 (R)** For a movie about breaking the rules and living off the grid, director/writer Ross' drama is a surprisingly predictable and routine. Ben Cash (Mortensen) raised his family completely away from society in the woods of the Pacific Northwest. After his wife dies, he takes the family of seven on a road trip to New Mexico to honor her wishes regarding the disposal of her body, over the objections of his father-in-law (Langella). It's earnest, and Mortensen gives it more than it deserves, but the script is nonsense, mistaking idealism for family values. **118m/C; DVD, Blu-Ray.** Viggo Mortensen; Frank Langella; Kathryn Hahn; Missi Pyle; Steve Zahn; ***D:*** Matt Ross; ***W:*** Matt Ross; ***C:*** Stephane Fontaine; ***M:*** Alex Somers.

Captain from Castile **1947** Exciting saga finds 16th-century Spanish nobleman Pedro De Vargas (Power) forced to flee the wrath of Inquisition chief De Silva (Sutton). He takes peasant girl Cantana (Peters), who's helped him, and joins Cortez's expedition to Mexico and the search for Aztec riches. Lots of adventures and old-fashioned pageantry. Peters' screen debut. **141m/C; VHS, DVD, Blu-Ray.** Tyrone Power; Jean Peters; Cesar Romero; Lee J. Cobb; John Sutton; Antonio Moreno; Thomas Gomez; Alan Mowbray; ***D:*** Henry King; ***W:*** Lamar Trotti; ***C:*** Charles G. Clarke; Arthur E. Arling; ***M:*** Alfred Newman.

The Captain Hates the Sea **1/2 1934** Last film for Gilbert who plays the uncomfortably close-to-home role of Steve, an alcoholic who takes a cruise to try to dry out. He commiserates with Captain Helquist (Connolly), who says how much he hates his job, which is complicated by Steve's PI friend Junius (McLaglen), who's after criminals hiding stolen bonds aboard ship. There are also a number of other subplots to keep the comedy sailing along. **93m/B; DVD.** John Gilbert; Walter Connolly; Victor McLaglen; Helen Vinson; Alison Skipworth; Fred Keating; Leon Errol; Walter Catlett; ***D:*** Lewis Milestone; ***W:*** Wallace Smith; ***C:*** Joseph August.

Captain Horatio Hornblower **1951** A colorful drama about the life and loves of the British sea captain during the Napoleonic wars. Peck is rather out of his element as the courageous, swashbuckling hero (Errol Flynn was originally cast) but there's enough fast-paced derring-do to make this a satisfying saga. Based on the novel by C.S. Forester. **117m/C; VHS, DVD.** *GB* Gregory Peck; Virginia Mayo; Robert Beatty; Denis O'Dea; Christopher Lee; ***D:*** Raoul Walsh; ***W:*** Ivan Goff; ***C:*** Guy Green.

Captain Jack **1/2** *An Inch Over the Horizon* **1998** Sentimental, old-fashioned story about eccentric sea captain Jack (Hoskin) who dreams of sailing the same journey as Captain Scoresby made in 1791—from Whitby in northern England to the Arctic. But his misfit crew is a group of novices and his vessel is deemed unseaworthy by authorities. Nevertheless, Jack and his group set sail. **96m/C; VHS, DVD.** *GB* Bob Hoskins; Peter McDonald; Sadie Frost; Gemma Jones; Anna Massey; Maureen Lipman; Robert Addie; Trevor Bannister; ***D:*** Robert M. Young; ***W:*** Jack Rosenthal; ***C:*** John McGlashan; ***M:*** Richard Harvey.

Captain January **1/2 1936 (G)** Crusty old lighthouse keeper rescues little orphan girl with curly hair from drowning and everyone breaks into cutesy song and dance, interrupted only when the authorities try to separate the two. Also available colorized. **81m/B; VHS, DVD.** Shirley Temple; Guy Kibbee; Buddy Ebsen; Slim Summerville; Jane Darwell; June Lang; George Irving; Si Jenks; ***D:*** David Butler.

Captain Kidd **1/2 1945** Laughton huffs and puffs and searches for treasure on the high seas, finds himself held captive with rest of cast in anemic swashbuckler. **83m/B; VHS, DVD.** Charles Laughton; John Carradine; Randolph Scott; Reginald Owen; Gilbert Roland; Barbara Britton; John Qualen; Sheldon Leonard; ***D:*** Rowland V. Lee; ***W:*** Norman Reilly Raine; ***C:*** Archie Stout.

Captain Kidd and the Slave Girl **1954** Swashbuckling adventure. The Earl of Bellomont saves Captain Kidd from the gallows in order to get Kidd's hidden treasure. He sends pampered Judith Duvall, disguised as a slave girl, to seduce the pirate. Instead, after a lot of bickering, Judith falls in love with Kidd and threatens the Earl's plans. **82m/C; DVD.** Anthony Dexter; Eva Gabor; James Seay; Alan Hale, Jr.; Sonia Sorrell; Richard Karlan; Lyle Talbot; Michael Ross; ***D:*** Lew Landers; ***W:*** Jack Pollexfen; Aubrey Wisberg; ***C:*** Charles Van Enger; ***M:*** Paul Sawtell.

Captain Kronos: Vampire Hunter *Kronos; Vampire Castle* **1974 (R)** Captain Kronos fences thirsty foes in Hammer horror hybrid. Artsy, atmospheric and atypical, it's written and directed with tongue firmly in cheek by Clemens, who penned many an "Avengers" episode. **91m/C; VHS, DVD, Blu-Ray.** *GB* Horst Janson; John Carson; Caroline Munro; Ian Hendry; Shane Briant; Wanda Ventham; John Cater; Lois Daine; William Hobbs; Robert James; Elizabeth Dear; ***D:*** Brian Clemens; ***W:*** Brian Clemens; ***C:*** Ian Wilson; ***M:*** Laurie Johnson.

Captain Lightfoot **1955** In 1815, Irish patriot Michael Martin (Hudson) joins with rebel leader John Doherty (Morrow-)?known as Captain Thunderbolt—to fight the British dragoons while also falling in love with Doherty's daughter Aga (Rush). As second-in-command Captain Lightfoot, Martin gets into trouble after Doherty is captured and he tries to free him from prison. Sirk's swashbuckler was filmed on location in Ireland. **91m/C; DVD.** Rock Hudson; Barbara Rush; Jeff Morrow; Finlay Currie; Kathleen Ryan; Denis O'Dea; ***D:*** Douglas Sirk; ***W:*** Oscar Brodney; W.R. Burnett; ***C:*** Irving Glassberg; ***M:*** Heinz Roemheld.

Captain Marvel **2019 (PG-13)** Training as a warrior on the Kree planet of Hala, Captain Marvel (Larson) is taken prisoner during a battle with the Skrulls, escapes, and ends up in early 1990s Los Angeles. Though Marvel does not remember fully remember her past, she does have flashes including training with an older pilot (Benning) and crashing. As Marvel slowly remembers her life as pilot Carol Danvers, she teams up with young S.H.I.E.L.D. agent Nick Fury (Jackson) to find a glowing space cube. Part of the broader Marvel Comics universe, the film is both an exercise in 90s nostalgia and an effective vehicle for an engaging female superhero. **123m/C; DVD, Blu-Ray.** Brie Larson; Samuel L. Jackson; Ben Mendelsohn; Jude Law; Annette Bening; ***D:*** Anna Boden; Ryan Fleck; ***W:*** Anna Boden; Ryan Fleck; Geneva Robertson-Dworet; ***C:*** Ben Davis; ***M:*** Pinar Toprak.

Captain Nemo and the Underwater City **1/2 1969** A dull use of the Jules Verne characters in this would-be adventure story. Capt. Nemo (Ryan) uses his submarine the Nautilus to rescue the survivors of a sinking sailing ship. He takes them to his fabulous domed underwater city of Templemer but then doesn't want to let them go, fearing they'll reveal his secrets to the world and destroy his utopia. Naturally, they still plan an escape. **105m/C; DVD.** *GB* Robert Ryan; Chuck Connors; Nanette Newman; Luciana Paluzzi; Bill Fraser; Kenneth Connor; John Turner; ***D:*** James Hill; ***W:*** Robert W(right) Campbell; Jane Barker; Pip Barker; ***C:*** Alan Hume; ***M:*** Angela Morley.

Captain Newman, M.D. **1/2 1963** Three army guys visit stiff shrink Peck during the final months of WWII in VA ward for the mentally disturbed. Much guilt and agonizing, with comic relief courtesy of Curtis. Peck is sub par, the direction flounders and there's something unsettling about quicksilver shifts from pathos to parody. Nonetheless touching with fine performance from Darin as guilt ridden hero. Based on the novel by Leo Rosten. **126m/C; VHS, DVD.** Gregory Peck; Bobby Darin; Tony Curtis; Angie Dickinson; Eddie Albert; James Gregory; Jane Withers; Larry Storch; Robert Duvall; ***D:*** David Miller.

Captain Phillips **2013 (PG-13)** Hanks shines in this adaptation of the true story of the hijacking of an American cargo ship in Somali waters. He plays the title character as the only hope for his crew and cargo when four Somali pirates board the ship and end up taking Phillips hostage. Director Greengrass creates a relentless tension in closed quarters while Hanks and co-star Barkhad Adbi--as the lead hijacker--give the film much-needed humanity, grounding the non-stop action with unforgettable characters. **134m/C; DVD, Blu-Ray.** Tom Hanks; Barkhad Adbi; Michael Chernus; Catherine Keener; David Warshofsky; ***D:*** Paul Greengrass; ***W:*** Billy Ray; ***C:*** Barry Ackroyd; ***M:*** Henry Jackman. British Acad. '13: Actor--Supporting (Adbi); Writers Guild '13: Adapt. Screenplay.

Captain Ron **1/2 1992 (PG-13)** Harried couple Short and Place inherit a large boat and, with their two smart-mouthed kids, go to the Caribbean to sail the boat back to the U.S. Of course they know nothing about sailing, so they hire Captain Ron (Russell), a one-eyed, Long John Silver-talking boat captain. From there, numerous mishaps occur. Amusing sounding premise sinks like a stone. Russell looks great in his teeny-weeny bikini, and the scenery is beautiful, but that's about it. **104m/C; VHS, DVD.** Kurt Russell; Martin Short; Mary Kay Place; Meadow Sisto; Benjamin Salisbury; Dan E. Butler; ***D:*** Thom Eberhardt; ***W:*** Thom Eberhardt.

Captain Salvation **1927** Silent melodrama. In 1840, New Englander Anson Campbell (Hanson) is torn between his love of the sea and studying for the ministry. When he takes pity on fallen woman Bess Morgan (Starke), he's condemned by everyone he knows and so Anson signs on to work aboard a sailing ship. It turns out to be a convict ship with Bess, who's vowed to reform, also on board and fighting off the advances of the lecherous Captain (Torrence). There's tragedy and repentance and redemption (check out that title). **88m/B; Silent; DVD.** Lars Hanson; Pauline Starke; Ernest Torrence; Marceline Day; George Fawcett; Sam De Grasse; Jay Hunt; ***D:*** John S. Robertson; ***W:*** Jack Cunningham; ***C:*** William H. Daniels.

Captain Scarlett **1/2 1953** Formulaic swashbuckler has nobleman Greene and highway guy Young fighting nasty French Royalists who've been putting the pressure on impecunious peasants. Runaway Spanish damsel in distress courtesy of Amar. Most novel aspect of the production is that the post-Napoleon French terrain has that vaguely south of the border feel. **75m/C; VHS, DVD.** Richard Greene; Leonora Amar; Isobel Del Puerto; Nedrick Young; Manolo Fabregas; ***D:*** Thomas Carr.

Captain Sinbad **1/2 1963** Captain Sinbad must destroy the evil El Kerim, but first he must tackle a many-headed ogre, man-eating fish and crocodiles, a large fist clad in a spiked glove, an invisible monster, and more. To kill the villain, Sinbad must destroy his heart, which is kept in a tower with no entrance. A huge, witty, epic production with lots of special effects. This one is fun. **85m/C; VHS, DVD.** Guy Williams; Heidi Bruhl; Pedro Armendariz, Sr.; Abraham Sofaer; Bernie Hamilton; Helmuth Schneider; ***D:*** Byron Haskin; ***W:*** Ian McLellan Hunter; Guy Endore.

Captain Underpants: The First Epic Movie **1/2 2017 (PG)** A delightful animated romp that remains true to the bestselling children's books. Pranksters George and Harold hypnotize their principal into believing he's an exuberant superhero named Captain Underpants, then have to stop him from hurting his mortal self while trying to save the world. Children will love the cheery animation and nod to friendship and teamwork; adults will dig the subversive humor. **89m/C; DVD, Blu-Ray.** ***V:*** Kevin Hart; Ed Helms; Nick Kroll; Thomas Middleditch; Jordan Peele; ***D:*** David Soren; ***W:*** Nicholas Stoller; ***M:*** Theodore Shapiro.

Captains Courageous **1937** Rich brat Bartholomew takes a dip sans life jacket while leaning over an ocean liner railing to relieve himself of the half dozen ice cream sodas imprudently consumed at sea. Picked up by a Portugese fishing boat, he at first treats his mandatory three month voyage as an unscheduled cab ride, but eventually, through a deepening friendship with crewman Tracy, develops a hitherto unheralded work ethic. The boy's filial bond with Tracy, of course, requires that the seaman meet with watery disaster. Based on the Rudyard Kipling novel. Director Fleming went on to "Gone With the Wind" and "The Wizard of Oz." **116m/B; VHS, DVD.** Spencer Tracy; Lionel Barrymore; Freddie Bartholomew; Mickey Rooney; Melvyn Douglas; Charley Grapewin; John Carradine; Bobby Watson; Jack La Rue; ***D:*** Victor Fleming. Oscars '37: Actor (Tracy).

Captains Courageous 1/2 **1995** TV adaptation of the 1897 novel by Rudyard Kipling finds pampered rich kid Vadas learning to become a man at the hands of stalwart sea captain Urich. **93m/C; VHS, DVD.** Robert Urich; Kenny Vadas; Kaj-Erik Eriksen; Robert Wisden; Duncan Fraser; ***D:*** Michael Anderson, Sr.; ***W:*** John McGreevey; ***C:*** Glen MacPherson; ***M:*** Eric N. Robertson; Claude Desjardins.

Captains of the Clouds 1/2 **1942** Unabashedly patriotic film starring Cagney as a daredevil, independent Canadian bush pilot who makes his own flying rules. When WWII begins he joins the Royal Canadian Air Force but washes out when he can't follow orders. However, he finds a way to prove himself a hero as a civilian pilot ferrying a bomber to England. Cagney's first Technicolor film. **113m/C; DVD.** James Cagney; Dennis Morgan; Brenda Marshall; Alan Hale; George Tobias; Reginald Gardiner; Reginald Denny; Russell Arms; Paul Cavanagh; Charles Halton; ***D:*** Michael Curtiz; ***W:*** Arthur T. Horman; Richard Macaulay; Norman Reilly Raine; ***C:*** Wilfred M. Cline; Sol Polito; ***M:*** Max Steiner.

Captain's Paradise **1953** Golden Fleece captain Guinness chugs between wives in Gibraltar and North Africa, much to the adulation of chief officer Goldner. While Gibraltar's little woman Johnson is homegrown homebody, little woman de Carlo is paint the town red type, allowing Guinness to have cake and eat it too, it seems, except that he's inconveniently positioned in front of a firing squad at movie's start. **89m/B; VHS, DVD, Blu-Ray.** *GB* Alec Guinness; Yvonne De Carlo; Celia Johnson; Miles Malleson; Nicholas Phipps; Ferdinand "Ferdy" Mayne; Sebastian Cabot; ***D:*** Anthony Kimmins; ***W:*** Nicholas Phipps; Alec Coppel; ***C:*** Edward (Ted) Scaife; ***M:*** Malcolm Arnold.

The Captain's Table **1960** Former cargo vessel captain Gregson is given luxury liner to command, and fails to revise his cargo captain style to fit new crew and clientele. British cast saves unremarkable script from mediocrity. **90m/C; DVD.** *UK* John Gregson; Peggy Cummins; Donald Sinden; Nadia Gray; ***D:*** Jack Lee.

Captive 1/2 **1987 (R)** Spoiled heiress is kidnapped by terrorist trio and brainwashed into anti-establishment Hearst-like creature. **98m/C; VHS, DVD.** Oliver Reed; Irina Brook; Xavier DeLuc; Hirofumi Arai; ***D:*** Paul Mayersberg.

Captive **1998** All too-familiar evil doctor/mental hospital/terrified patient plot. Samantha (Eleniak) attempts suicide after her cop husband is killed on their wedding day and becomes a patient at a mental hospital with questionable practices and employees. Then she finds she can't leave. **92m/C; VHS, DVD.** *CA* Erika Eleniak; Michael Ironside; Catherine Colvey; Noel Burton; Stewart Bick; Adrienne Ironside; Laurel Paetz; ***D:*** Roger Cardinal; Rodney Gibbons; ***W:*** Richard Stanford; Rodney Gibbons; Richard Stamford; ***C:*** Bruno Philip; ***M:*** David Findlay; David Finley. **VIDEO**

The Captive 1/2 **2014** Eight years ago, a girl named Cassandra disappeared, shattering the lives of her parents, Matthew (Reynolds) and Tina (Enos). Now, evidence has surfaced that she may still be alive, sending Matthew into an emotional tailspin as he tries to atone for the role he feels he played in her disappearance and solve the crime. Egoyan's divisive film has been incorrectly lumped in with his recently disappointing work, but it's a solid thriller with good work from Reynolds. It may not be as breakthrough as Egoyan's best, but it works on its own. **112m/C; DVD, Blu-Ray.** *CA* Ryan Reynolds; Mireille Enos; Scott Speedman; Rosario Dawson; Kevin Durand; Alexia Fast; ***D:*** Atom Egoyan; ***W:*** Atom Egoyan; David Fraser; ***C:*** Paul Sarossy; ***M:*** Mychael Danna.

Captive **2015 (PG-13)** Two good actors are trapped in a bad movie in this moral-message thriller produced by a faith-based organization and targeted at that loyal audience. Ashley Smith (Mara) is a drug addict, struggling to keep her life together. Brian Nichols (Oyelowo) is the criminal who takes her hostage after breaking out of jail and murdering the judge assigned to his case. Of course, Ashley and Brian both have some healing and learning to do. You'll wish someone could save you from watching this movie. Based on a true story. **97m/C; DVD, Blu-Ray.** Kate Mara; David Oyelowo; Michael K(enneth) Williams; Mimi Rogers; Leonor Varela; ***D:*** Jerry Jameson; ***W:*** Brian Bird; Reinhard Denke; ***C:*** Luis David Sansans; ***M:*** Lorne Balfe.

The Captive City 1/2 **1952** Crusading newspaper editor Jim Austin (Forsythe) is preparing his testimony for the Kefauver Committee on organized crime after discovering that a gambling syndicate has taken over Kennington. Mob boss Murray Sirak (Sutherland) uses his police connections to intimidate Austin and his wife (Camden) who head to DC with the bad guys in pursuit. Senator Estes Kefauver appears in an epilogue in Wise's pic, which was filmed in a semi-documentary style. **91m/B; DVD, Blu-Ray.** John Forsythe; Ray Teal; Victor Sutherland; Hal K. Dawson; Joan Camden; Harold J. Kennedy; Marjorie Crossland; Victor Romito; Martin Milner; ***D:*** Robert Wise; ***W:*** Karl Kamb; Alvin Josephy; ***C:*** Lee Garmes; ***M:*** Jerome Moross.

Captive Heart **1947** Czech soldier Redgrave assumes the identity of a dead British officer in order to evade Nazis in WWII. Captured and imprisoned in camp reserved for British POWs, his stalagmates think they smell a spy, but he manages to convince them he's an OK Joe. Meanwhile, he's been writing letters home to the little missus, which means he's got a little explaining to do when he's released from prison. Especially fine Redgrave performance. **86m/B; VHS, DVD, Blu-Ray.** *GB* Michael Redgrave; Basil Radford; Jack Warner; Jimmy Hanley; Rachel Kempson; Mervyn Johns; ***D:*** Basil Dearden.

Captive Hearts **1987 (PG)** Well frayed story holds cast captive in sushi romance. Two American flyers are shot down and taken prisoner in isolated Japanese mountain village, and one is shot by Cupid's arrow. **97m/C; VHS, Streaming.** Noriyuki "Pat" Morita; Michael Sarrazin; Chris Makepeace; ***D:*** Paul Almond; ***M:*** David Benoit.

Captive Planet **1978** Bargain basement FX and really atrocious acting hold audience captive in routine earth on the verge of obliteration yarn. **95m/C; VHS, DVD.** Sharon Baker; Chris Auram; Anthony Newcastle; ***D:*** Al (Alfonso Brescia) Bradley.

Captive State **2019 (PG-13)** Nearly a decade after an alien invasion of Earth, the governments of the world surrender and the aliens have ultimate control. The parents of Gabriel (Sanders) were killed in the initial invasion and his older brother Rafe (Majors) allegedly later died while trying to attack the aliens. Though Gabriel has a girlfriend and a job, and is watched over by his police officer father's former partner William Mulligan (Goodman), he becomes part of a larger plot to fight against the alien forces and remove them from Earth. An interesting concept, but this thriller falls short in keeping the Hound interested. **109m/C; DVD, Blu-Ray.** John Goodman; Ashton Sanders; Jonathan Majors; Vera Farmiga; Kevin Dunn; ***D:*** Rupert Wyatt; ***W:*** Rupert Wyatt; Erica Beeney; ***C:*** Alex Disenhof; ***M:*** Rob Simonsen.

Captives 1/2 **1994 (R)** Middle-class dentist Rachel Clifford (Ormond), recently separated from her husband, takes a part-time job at a local prison where she becomes attracted to her patient, Cockney charmer Philip Chaney (Roth). He's coming to the end of a 10-year sentence and the lusty duo manage to consummate their relationship during one of Philip's day-releases. Only problem is fellow con Towler (Salmon) notices what's happening and blackmails and threatens Rachel—leading to a violent confrontation. Roth and Ormond click believably as opposites-attract partners though the script has some weak elements. **100m/C; VHS, DVD.** *GB* Tim Roth; Julia Ormond; Colin Salmon; Keith Allen; Siobhan Redmond; Peter Capaldi; Richard Hawley; Annette Badland; Jeff Nuttal; ***D:*** Angela Pope; ***W:*** Frank Deasy; ***C:*** Remi Adefarasin; ***M:*** Colin Towns.

Captivity WOOF! **2007 (R)** The kazillionth contribution to the relatively new subgenre known as torture-porn. Yeah, they keep coming—only by now anything shocking, original, or smart has been milked. Generic fashion model Jennifer (Cuthbert) has been drugged and abducted for the purpose of sporting torture and mutilation. Forced by her captor to endure one indignity after another as she pleads for her life, Jennifer somehow strikes up an unlikely romance with dungeon mate and hot guy Gillies. Way too grisly to sit through, not even the pretty people can save it. **85m/C; DVD.** *US RU* Elisha Cuthbert; Daniel Gillies; Laz Alonso; Pruitt Taylor Vince; Michael Harney; ***D:*** Roland Joffé; ***W:*** Larry Cohen; Joseph Tura; ***C:*** Daniel Pearl; ***M:*** Marco Beltrami.

The Capture **1950** Above-average story told in flashback has Ayres hiding out in Mexico because he thought he killed an innocent man. He seeks out the widow to question her about him and they wind up marrying. When he finds the real culprit, the man is killed and the evidence points to Ayres. Ayres and Wright are great, as is the native Mexican musical score. **67m/B; VHS, DVD.** Lew Ayres; Teresa Wright; Victor Jory; Jacqueline White; Jimmy Hunt; Duncan Renaldo; William "Billy" Bakewell; ***D:*** John Sturges.

The Capture of Bigfoot **1979 (PG)** Barefoot monster tracks footprints around town after 25 years of peace, and evil businessman attempts to capture creature for personal gain. **92m/C; VHS, DVD.** Stafford Morgan; Katherine Hopkins; Richard Kennedy; Otis Young; George "Buck" Flower; John Goff; ***D:*** Bill Rebane.

The Capture of the Green River Killer 1/2 **2008** This Lifetime miniseries, based on King County task force member David Reichert's book, is part plodding and part pathos. The fictional character of teenage runaway Helen (Davidson) serves as narrator and typical prostitute victim of the serial killer who was active in Washington State from 1982 to 1998. The long investigation takes its increasingly frustrating toll on Reichert (Cavanagh), both professionally and personally. **180m/C; DVD.** Tom Cavanagh; Amy Davidson; John Pielmeier; Jessica Harmon; Currie Graham; Ingrid Rogers; Sharon Lawrence; James Russo; James Marsters; ***D:*** Norma Bailey; ***W:*** John Pielmeier; David Reichert; ***C:*** Mathias Herndl; ***M:*** Christopher Ward. **CABLE**

Captured **1999 (R)** Car thief picks the wrong auto to boost when he gets locked inside a special high-tech Porsche, which is maneuvered by a remote control in the hands of its sadistic owner. Who decides the thief needs to be taught a lesson. **95m/C; VHS, DVD.** Andrew Divoff; Nick Mancuso; Linda Hoffman; Michael Mahonen; ***D:*** Peter Paul Liapis. **VIDEO**

Capturing the Friedmans **2003** Disturbing documentary follows the lives of the Friedman family of Great Neck, Long Island. On Thanksgiving of 1987, police raid the Friedman home and find child pornography belonging to father Arthur, who's a high school science and computer teacher. The police allege that Arthur and youngest son, Jesse (then 18), molested dozens of boys. There is a rash of conflicting testimony as the case goes to trial (both are convicted, though Jesse's guilt is called into question). Shows excerpts from some 50 hours of home movies, much of which eldest son David filmed, and which the family permitted director Jarecki to use. He also conducted present-day interviews with a number of figures involved in the case. **107m/C; DVD.** ***D:*** Andrew Jarecki; ***C:*** Adolfo Doring; ***M:*** Andrea Morricone. Sundance '03: Feature Doc.

The Car **1977 (PG)** Driverless black sedan appears out of nowhere to terrorize the residents of a small New Mexico town. And it's up to Sheriff Wade Parent (Brolin) to stop the demonic auto. **96m/C; VHS, DVD, Blu-Ray.** James Brolin; Kathleen Lloyd; John Marley; Ronny Cox; John Rubinstein; R.G. Armstrong; Elizabeth Thompson; Roy Jenson; Robert Phillips; ***D:*** Elliot Silverstein; ***W:*** Dennis Shryack; Michael Butler; ***C:*** Gerald Hirschfeld; ***M:*** Leonard Rosenman.

Car Babes **2006 (PG-13)** A very misleading title since you're probably expecting a flick about scantily-clad ladies purring over automobiles. Wrong kind of comedy. Owing his dad money, recent college grad Ford Davis (Savage) must take a job at the family's used car lot and figures out it means more than just a paycheck. He makes friends with the usual group of wacky salesmen and then is forced into action when the business is threatened by a rival dealership. **90m/C; DVD.** Ben Savage; Carolina Garcia; Jon(athan) Gries; Marshall Manesh; Blake Clarke; Kevan Blackton; Donnell Rawlings; David Shackelford; John Campo; ***D:*** Christopher Wolf; Nick Fumia; ***W:*** Christopher Wolf; Nick Fumia; Blake Dirickson; ***C:*** Oden Roberts; ***M:*** Dino Campanella. **VIDEO**

Car 54, Where Are You? **1994 (PG-13)** Exceedingly lame remake of the exceedingly lame TV series, which ran for only two seasons, 1961-63. This time, Toody (Johansen) and Muldoon (McGinley) are protecting a mafia stool pigeon (Piven), while vampy Velma Velour (Drescher) sets her sights on Muldoon. Not many laughs and a waste of a talented cast. Sat on the shelf at Orion for three years (with good reason). **89m/C; VHS, DVD.** David Johansen; Fran Drescher; Rosie O'Donnell; John C. McGinley; Nipsey Russell; Al Lewis; Daniel Baldwin; Jeremy Piven; ***D:*** Bill Fishman; ***W:*** Ebbe Roe Smith; Erik Tarloff; Peter McCarthy; Peter Crabbe; ***M:*** Bernie Worrell; Pray for Rain. Golden Raspberries '94: Worst Support. Actress (O'Donnell).

Car Trouble 1/2 **1986** Dull Gerald Spong loves his new Jaguar much more than his neglected wife Jacqueline. When Jacqueline borrows the car, she accidentally gets trapped in the two-seater with an amorous car salesman, resulting in the police having to cut apart the Jag to free them. An incensed Gerald decides only Jacqueline's death will now satisfy him. **93m/C; DVD.** Ian Charleston; Julie Walters; Stratford Johns; Hazel O'Connor; Vincent Riotta; ***D:*** David Green; ***W:*** A.J Tipping; James Whaley; ***C:*** Mike Garfath.

Car Wash 1/2 **1976 (PG)** L.A. carwash provides a soap-opera setting for disjointed comic bits about owners of dirty cars and people who hose them down for a living. Econo budget and lite plot, but serious comic talent. A sort of disco carwash version of "Grand Hotel." **97m/C; VHS, DVD, Blu-Ray.** Franklin Ajaye; Sully Boyar; Richard Brestoff; George Carlin; Richard Pryor; Melanie Mayron; Ivan Dixon; Antonio Fargas; ***D:*** Michael A. Schultz; ***W:*** Joel Schumacher; ***C:*** Frank Stanley; ***M:*** Norman Whitfield.

Caracara *The Last Witness* **2000 (R)** Ornithologist Rachel Sutherland (Henstridge) agrees to allow the FBI to use her apartment for a stakeout and falls for agent David MacMillan (Schaech). Then she learns she's been duped—her "guests" are actually assassins planning to kill Nelson Mandela. **93m/C; VHS, DVD.** Natasha Henstridge; Johnathon Schaech; David McIlwraith; Lauren Hutton; ***D:*** Graeme Clifford; ***W:*** Craig Smith; ***C:*** Bill Wong. **CABLE**

Caramel *Sukkar Banat* **2007 (PG)** Modernity collides with custom as five women, portrayed mostly by local nonprofessionals, lament on issues involving sex, religion, and family at a beauty salon in Beirut, Lebanon (where apparently the titular sticky-sweet treat is used to remove unwanted hair). Even when it gets a bit soapy, actor/writer/director Labaki (a stunner both in front of and behind the camera) deftly winds the personal and cultural impact of each woman's dilemma into a story of universal sisterhood. The result is a cut above most Western chick-flickery, with a refreshing lack of Hollywood gloss. **95m/C; On Demand.** *FR* Nadine Labaki; Yasmine Al Masri; Joanna Moukarzel; Gisele Aouad; Sihame Haddad; Aziza Semaan; ***D:*** Nadine Labaki; ***W:*** Nadine Labaki; Jihad Hojeily; Rodney Al Haddad; ***C:*** Yves Schnaoui; ***M:*** Khaled Mouzanar.

Carancho 1/2 **2010** Disbarred, middle-aged lawyer Sosa shows up on the streets after car accidents, running an insurance/lawsuit scam. He meets young, overworked doctor Lujan, who's trying to help the injured, and thinks she can be his salvation into an ethical life. When Sosa stages an accident so a friend can claim a payout, things go very, very wrong. Spanish with subtitles. **107m/C; DVD.** *AR* Ricardo Darin; Martina Gusman; Carlos Weber; Jose Luis Arias; Fabio Ronzano; Loren Acuna; ***D:*** Pablo Trapero; ***W:*** Pablo Trapero; Alejandro Fadel; ***C:*** Julian Apezteguia.

Carandiru **2003 (R)** Hellish fact-based prison drama based on events leading up to the 1992 San Paolo massacre in which

111 inmates died. A nameless doctor (Vasconcelos) arrives at the city's infamous House of Detention because of an AIDS epidemic. As he tests and treats the inmates of the severely overcrowded facility, he learns about their lives on the outside (shown in flashbacks) and about the prison's codes, which are enforced by the inmates and not the guards or warden. Viewers are lulled into a false sense of normalcy before the horror begins. Based on "Carandiru Station," the fictionalized account of Dr. Drauzio Varella's experiences. Portuguese with subtitles. **148m/C; DVD.** *BR* Luiz Carlos Vasconcelos; Milhem Cortaz; Milton Goncalves; Ivan de Almeida; Ailton Graca; Maria Luisa Mendonca; Aida Leiner; Rodrigo Santoro; Gero Camilo; Caio Blat; Wagner Moura; ***D:*** Hector Babenco; ***W:*** Hector Babenco; Victor Nava; Fernando Bonassi; ***C:*** Walter Carvalho; ***M:*** Andre Abujamra.

Caravaggio **1986** Controversial biography of late Renaissance painter Caravaggio (Terry), famous for his bisexuality, fondness for prostitute models, violence and depravity. The painter divides his time between two street models, Ranuccio (Bean) and his lover Lena (Swinton), the decadent cardinals who commission his religious works, and Caravaggio's young assistant (Leigh), who cares for the artist as he lies dying. Photography by Gabriel Beristain reproduces the artist's visual style. **97m/C; VHS, DVD.** *GB* Nigel Terry; Sean Bean; Tilda Swinton; Spencer Leigh; Michael Gough; Nigel Davenport; Robbie Coltrane; Jack Birkett; ***D:*** Derek Jarman; ***W:*** Derek Jarman; ***C:*** Gabriel Beristain; ***M:*** Simon Fisher.

Caravaggio **2007** Entertaining made-for-Italian-TV bio of the controversial Renaissance artist. Violent and lusty (and openly bisexual), Caravaggio preferred using live models from the streets, including prostitutes, for his earthy biblical scenes. He also attracted patrons and enemies with equal ease, leading to a deadly brawl. Italian with subtitles. **211m/C; DVD.** *IT* Alessio Boni; Claire Keim; Jordi Molla; Benjamin Sadler; Elena Sofia Ricci; Paolo Briguglia; Sarah Felberbaum; ***D:*** Angelo Longoni; ***W:*** James Carrington; Andrea Purgatori; ***C:*** Vittorio Storaro; ***M:*** Luis Bacalov. **TV**

Caravan 1/2 **1946** In Regency England, poor writer Richard Darrell (Granger) is in love with upper-class Oriana (Crawford) and thinks he can get the money to marry her by transporting a valuable necklace to Spain. However, Richard's evil aristocratic rival, Sir Francis (Price), has henchman Wycroft (Helpmann) attack Richard though he only manages to wound him. Now suffering from amnesia, Richard's nursed to health by gypsy beauty Rosal (Kent). She loves him, but Oriana still manages to interfere in their romance. **122m/B; DVD.** *GB* Stewart Granger; Anne Crawford; Jean Kent; Dennis Price; Robert Helpmann; Gerard Heinz; ***D:*** Arthur Crabtree; ***W:*** Roland Pertwee; ***C:*** Stephen Dade; ***M:*** Bretton Byrd.

Carbide and Sorrel 1/2 *Karbid und Sauerampfer* **1963** To rebuild a Dresden cigarette factory destroyed by bombing in WWII, workers need carbide for welding torches. So Kalle travels to Wittenberg to buy seven barrels of the rationed material and then must find a way to get them home while dodging Soviet soldiers, mines, and other various hazards. German with subtitles. **80m/B; DVD.** *GE* Erwin Geschonneck; Marita Bohme; Kurt Rackelmann; Margot Busse; ***D:*** Frank Beyer; ***W:*** Frank Beyer; Hans Oliva; ***C:*** Gunter Marczinkowski; ***M:*** Joachim Werzlau.

Carbine Williams 1/2 **1952** Director Thorpe tells an uncomplicated story in flashback as bootlegger David 'Marsh' Williams (Stewart) winds up on a brutal North Carolina prison farm. Fascinated by firearms, he secretly begins working on a new kind of rifle in the machine shop. Warden People (Corey) allows Marsh to continue when he says its intended use is for the U.S. military. His creation becomes the M1 carbine used in WWII, which will earn Marsh an early parole and a new life on the straight and narrow. **93m/B; DVD.** James Stewart; Wendell Corey; Jean Hagen; Paul Stewart; Carl Benton Reid; James Arness; ***D:*** Richard Thorpe; ***W:*** Art Cohn; ***C:*** William Mellor; ***M:*** Conrad Salinger.

Carbon Copy *Time of the Wolves; The Last Shot; The Heist; Le Temps des Loups; Dillinger 70* **1969** A criminal with a split personality (Hossein) has renamed himself Dillinger because he patterns his crimes after the legendary gangster. As he and his gang strike, an Inspector (Aznavour) tries to bring him down. Dubbed. **105m/C; VHS, DVD.** *FR IT* Robert Hossein; Charles Aznavour; Virna Lisi; Marcel Bozzuffi; ***D:*** Sergio Gobbi; ***W:*** Andre Tabet; Sergio Gobbi; ***C:*** Daniel Diot; ***M:*** Georges Garvarentz.

Carbon Copy **1981 (PG)** Successful white executive has life turned inside out when his 17-year-old illegitimate son, who happens to be black, decides it's time to look up dear old dad. Typical comedy-with-a-moral. **92m/C; VHS, DVD, Blu-Ray.** George Segal; Susan St. James; Jack Warden; Paul Winfield; Dick Martin; Vicky Dawson; Tom Poston; Denzel Washington; ***D:*** Michael A. Schultz; ***W:*** Stanley Shapiro; ***M:*** Bill Conti.

Cardboard Boxer **2016** Willie (Thomas Hayden Church) is a homeless man lured into fighting other homeless men for cheap cash. He regains some of his drive upon discovering the lost diary of a 9-year-old girl and seeks to discover what became of her. While a brutal portrait of street life, its grittiness is undermined by its sentimentality. **89m/C; DVD, Blu-Ray, Streaming.** Thomas Haden Church; Terrence Howard; Boyd Holbrook; Rhys Wakefield; Macy Gray; ***D:*** Knate Gwaltney; ***W:*** Knate Gwaltney; ***C:*** Peter Holland; ***M:*** Jess Stroup. **VIDEO**

Cardiac Arrest **1974 (PG)** Lunatic eviscerates victims in trolley town. They left their hearts in San Francisco. **95m/C; VHS, DVD.** Garry Goodrow; Mike Chan; Max Gail; ***D:*** Murray Mintz.

The Cardinal 1/2 **1963** Priestly young Tryon rises through ecclesiastical ranks to become Cardinal, struggling through a plethora of tests of faith, none so taxing as the test of the audience's patience. Had Preminger excised some 60 minutes of footage, he might have had a compelling portrait of faith under fire, but as it stands, the cleric's life is epic confusion. Fine acting, even from Tryon, who later went on to bookish fame, and from Huston who's normally on the other side of the camera. McNamara's final performance. Based on the Henry Morton Robinson novel. **175m/C; VHS, DVD.** Tom Tryon; Carol Lynley; Dorothy Gish; Maggie McNamara; Cecil Kellaway; John Huston; John Saxon; Burgess Meredith; ***D:*** Otto Preminger; ***C:*** Leon Shamroy. Golden Globes '64: Film--Drama, Support. Actor (Huston).

Cardinal Richelieu **1935** Typical fictionalized biopic of the manipulative, power-hungry Cardinal Richelieu (Arliss), the power behind the 17th-century French throne of ineffectual King Louis XIII (Arnold). Arliss' last American film. **82m/B; DVD.** George Arliss; Edward Arnold; Violet Kemble-Cooper; Francis Lister; Maureen O'Sullivan; Cesar Romero; Douglass Dumbrille; Halliwell Hobbes; ***D:*** Rowland V. Lee; ***W:*** Maude Howell; W.P. Lipscomb; ***C:*** J. Peverell Marley; ***M:*** Alfred Newman.

Career 1/2 **1959** An overwrought, depressing drama about the trials and tribulations of an actor trying to make it on Broadway. He'll try anything to succeed. Good direction, but so-so acting. **105m/B; VHS, Streaming.** Dean Martin; Anthony (Tony) Franciosa; Shirley MacLaine; Carolyn Jones; Joan Blackman; Robert Middleton; Donna Douglas; ***D:*** Joseph Anthony; ***C:*** Joseph LaShelle. Golden Globes '60: Actor--Drama (Franciosa).

Career Girl 1/2 **1944** Typical showbiz musical with Joan leaving Kansas City and her boyfriend James for New York and a chance on Broadway. She moves into a theatrical boarding house and Joan and her new friends pool their resources with Joan eventually getting a lead in a musical revue. Then James shows up insisting Joan marry him and return home. **69m/B; DVD.** Frances Langford; Iris Adrian; Edward Norris; Craig Woods; Ariel Heath; Linda Brent; Alec Craig; ***D:*** Wallace Fox; ***W:*** Sam Neuman; ***C:*** Gus Peterson.

Career Girls **1997 (R)** Two young women, the caustic acid-tongued Hannah (Cartlidge) and shy eczema-scarred Annie (Steadman), are introduced in a flashback sequence as they meet and become college roommates. They reunite for a weekend visit six years after they graduate. Both have become career women and have smoothed out their rough edges. In their wanders around London, they coincidentally run into people they knew back in the day, including a smarmy real estate agent (Tucker) who dated them both and a despondent schizophrenic (Benton) who pursued Annie. Excellent performances from a largely unknown cast. **87m/C; VHS, DVD.** Katrin Cartlidge; Lynda Steadman; Kate Byers; Mark Benton; Andy Serkis; Joe Tucker; Margo Stanley; Michael Healy; ***D:*** Mike Leigh; ***W:*** Mike Leigh; ***C:*** Dick Pope; ***M:*** Marianne Jean-Baptiste; Tony Remy.

Career Opportunities 1/2 **1991 (PG-13)** "Home Alone" clone for teenagers from John Hughes' factory. Whaley is an unsuccessful con-artist who finally gets a job as the night janitor of the local department store. He fools around at company expense until he finds the town's beauty (Connelly) asleep in a dressing room. The pair then play make-believe until its time to thwart some small-time thieves. Unexciting and unrealistic in the worst way; no wonder Candy isn't billed—he probably didn't want to be. **83m/C; VHS, DVD.** Frank Whaley; Jennifer Connelly; Dermot Mulroney; Kieran Mulroney; John M. Jackson; Jenny O'Hara; Noble Willingham; Barry Corbin; Denise Galik; William Forsythe; John Candy; ***D:*** Bryan Gordon; ***W:*** John Hughes; ***C:*** Donald McAlpine; ***M:*** Thomas Newman.

Career Woman **1936** Idealistic young lawyer Carroll Aiken (Trevor) returns to her small hometown to defend downtrodden Gracie Clay (Jewell) on a charge of murdering her abusive dad. Carroll's flamboyant partner Barry Conant (Whalen) alienates the jury with his condescension and grandstanding and it looks like they'll lose the case. **75m/B; DVD.** Claire Trevor; Michael Whalen; Isabel Jewell; Sterling Holloway; Eric Linden; Virginia Field; Guinn "Big Boy" Williams; ***D:*** Lewis Seiler; ***W:*** Lamar Trotti; ***C:*** Robert Planck; James Van Trees.

Carefree **1938** Dizzy radio singer Rogers can't make up her mind about beau Bellamy, so he sends her to analyst Astaire. Seems she can't even dream a little dream until shrink Astaire prescribes that she ingest some funny food, which causes her to dream she's in love with the Fredman. Au contraire, says he, it's a Freudian thing, and he hypnotically suggests that she really loves Bellamy. The two line up to march down the aisle together, and Fred stops dancing just long enough to realize he's in love with Ginger. A screwball comedy with music. **83m/B; VHS, DVD.** Fred Astaire; Ginger Rogers; Ralph Bellamy; Jack Carson; Franklin Pangborn; Hattie McDaniel; ***D:*** Mark Sandrich; ***M:*** Irving Berlin.

Careful **1992** Butler-in-training Neale courts Neville in an alpine mountain village where silence is golden, or at least being quiet will lessen the chance of an avalanche. Dig a little deeper and you find incest, repression and other nasty things. Highly individualistic black comedy parodies German Expressionism and Freudian psychology to the point of absurdity, dealing with snow, sex, sleep, spirits, and obsessive/compulsive personality disorders. Third film from Canadian cult director Maddin is awash in vivid primary colors when it suits the scene's mood and employs between-scenes titles in a homage to cinematic antiquity. **100m/C; VHS, DVD.** Kyle McCulloch; Gosia Dobrowolska; Jackie Burroughs; Sarah Neville; Brent Neale; Paul Cox; Victor Cowie; Michael O'Sullivan; Vince Rimmer; Katya Gardner; ***D:*** Guy Maddin; ***W:*** Guy Maddin; George Toles; ***C:*** Guy Maddin; ***M:*** John McCulloch.

Careful, He Might Hear You **1984 (PG)** Abandoned by his father, six-year-old P.S. becomes a pawn between his dead mother's two sisters, one working class and the other wealthy, and his worldview is further overturned by the sudden reappearance of his prodigal father. Set in Depression-era Australia, Schultz's vision is touching and keenly observed, and manages a sort of child's eye sense of proportion. Based on a novel by Sumner Locke Elliott. **113m/C; VHS, DVD.** *AU* Nicholas Gledhill; Wendy Hughes; Robyn Nevin; John Hargreaves; ***D:*** Carl Schultz; ***W:*** Michael Jenkins; ***C:*** John Seale; ***M:*** Ray Cook. Australian Film Inst. '83: Actress (Hughes), Film.

Careless 1/2 **2007 (R)** Meandering dramedy that only fitfully maintains interest. Mild-mannered mystery bookstore employee Wiley Roth (Hanks) is shocked to find a severed finger on his kitchen floor. He stows the digit in the freezer and enlists his oddball father (Shalhoub) and best bud Mitch (Kranz) to track down the finger's owner. When Wiley meets Rachel (Blanchard) at a party, he can't help noticing her bandaged hand but she doesn't want to talk about her injury. **90m/C; DVD.** Colin Hanks; Tony Shalhoub; Fran Kranz; Rachel Blanchard; ***D:*** Peter Spears; ***W:*** Eric Laster; ***C:*** Byron Shah; ***M:*** John (Gianni) Frizzell.

The Careless Years **1957** Arthur Hiller's first feature is a well-played teen drama. Working-class Jerry and wealthy Emily fall in love and the starry-eyed twosome immediately want to get married. They face strong opposition from both families, who want the teens to stop and think about their futures. Instead, the lovebirds decide to elope to Mexico. **70m/B; DVD.** Dean Stockwell; Natalie Trundy; Barbara Billingsley; John Stephenson; John Larch; Virginia Christine; Alan Dineheart, III; Maureen Cassidy; ***D:*** Arthur Hiller; ***W:*** John Howard Lawson; Mitch Lindemann; ***C:*** Sam Leavitt; ***M:*** Leith Stevens.

Caresses *Caricies* **1997** Eleven short scenes confront the lack of tenderness in the restless lives of a big city's inhabitants over the course of one night, until the film circles back to where it began—with the domestic argument between a young man and woman who no longer love each other. Adaptation of Belbel's play. Spanish with subtitles. **94m/C; VHS, DVD.** *SP* Julieta Serrano; Augustin Gonzalez; Sergi Lopez; David Selvas; Laura Conejero; Montserrat Salvador; Naim Thomas; Merce Pons; Jordi Dauder; Roger Coma; Rosa Maria Sarda; ***D:*** Ventura Pons; ***W:*** Ventura Pons; Sergi Belbel; ***C:*** Jesus Escosa; ***M:*** Carles Cases.

The Caretaker **2008 (R)** Barely tolerable slasher flick. Three teenagers leave a Halloween dance with their dates in order to play a trick involving a grapefruit orchard and a local legend that turns out to be true. Bloody but not exactly menacing what with rolling grapefruits serving as distractions and a mechanical fruit picker involved. **82m/C; DVD.** Andrew St. John; James Immekus; Diego Torres; Victoria Vande Vegte; Jennifer Freeman; Kira Verrastro; Will Stiles; Lola Davidson; Jennifer Tilly; Judd Nelson; ***D:*** Bryce Olson; ***W:*** Jackie Olson; ***C:*** Vern Nobles; ***M:*** Jim Lang. **VIDEO**

The Caretaker 1/2 **2016** A horror thriller centered on one young woman's discovery of her family's dark past. Birdie (Blake) is elderly and ill, but well enough to drive off all her caretakers. When no one else will help, her granddaughter Mallorie (Warner) is forced to take the job. When Mallorie moves into Birdie's large Victorian home, she soon finds herself sleepwalking and seeing spirits. As she tries and fails to find a proper caretaker for Birdie, Mallorie must face her family's deep, untenable secrets before the evil in the house drives her into insanity. **80m/C; DVD, Streaming, Download.** Meegan Warner; Sondra Blake; Sean Martini; Barry Jenner; Sadie Stratton; ***D:*** Jeff Prugh; ***W:*** Jeremy Robinson; ***C:*** Jesse Eisenhardt; ***M:*** Darrell Raby.

The Caretakers 1/2 **1963** Lorna (Bergen) blames herself for the death of her child, has a breakdown, and is admitted to an overcrowded state mental hospital. New doctor MacLeod (Stack) tries progressive, experimental therapy on Lorna and his other patients but his efforts are undercut by conservative head nurse Terry (Crawford). Crawford is over-the-top and the flick gets maudlin. **97m/B; DVD.** Robert Stack; Polly Bergen; Joan Crawford; Janis Paige; Barbara Barrie; Ellen Corby; Diane McBain; Susan Oliver; Van Williams; Herbert Marshall; Robert Vaughn; ***D:*** Hall Bartlett; ***W:*** Henry Greenberg; ***C:*** Lucien Ballard; ***M:*** Elmer Bernstein.

The Carey Treatment 1/2 **1972** Botched mystery that director Edwards and the screenwriters disowned because of MGM's interference. Unorthodox playboy pathologist Peter Carey (Coburn) comes to Boston, working for chief of staff Dr. Randall (O'Herlihy). Randall's teenage daughter Karen dies from an illegal abortion and fellow doc David Tao (Hong) is quickly arrested. Carey doesn't believe it so he starts his own investigation, which leads him to hospital drug thefts and a sinister masseur. Based on the Michael Crichton novel (written under a pseudonym) "A Case of Need." **101m/C;**

DVD. James Coburn; Dan O'Herlihy; James Hong; Jennifer O'Neill; Pat Hingle; Skye Aubrey; Alex Dreier; Elizabeth Allen; John Fink; ***D:*** Blake Edwards; ***W:*** Irving Ravetch; John D.F. Black; Harriet Frank, Jr.; ***C:*** Frank Stanley; ***M:*** Roy Budd.

Caribe ½ **1987** Caribbean travelogue masquerades as spy thriller. Arms smuggling goes awry, and neither voodoo nor bikinied blondes can prevent audience from dozing. Never released theatrically. **96m/C; VHS, DVD.** John Savage; Kara Glover; Stephen McHattie; Sam Malkin; ***D:*** Michael Kennedy.

Carjacked **2011 (R)** Insecure divorced mom Lorraine and her young son Chad are carjacked by bank robber Roy, who holds them as hostages as he heads to Mexico. Lorraine manages to screw up every chance at escape, either through fear or stupidity, and Bello can't make this character believable though that's hardly this pic's only problem. **89m/C; DVD, Blu-Ray.** Maria Bello; Connor Hill; Stephen Dorff; Joanna Cassidy; Jeff Joslin; ***D:*** John Bonito; ***W:*** Michael Compton; Sherry Compton; ***C:*** Theo van de Sande; ***M:*** Bennett Salvay. **VIDEO**

Carla's Song **1997** Left-leaning director Loach sets his sometimes gripping, sometimes over-bearing political/love story in war torn Nicaragua in the late 1980s. George (Carlyle) is a Glasgow bus driver who helps out passenger Carla (Cabezas), a Nicaraguan emigre who raises money for the Sandanista cause. George falls in love with Carla and decides that the only way she can get on with her life is to confront her former lover Antonio, who was maimed by the contras and has disappeared. The two lovers go to Nicaragua, where George is totally out of his environment. Shot (with great difficulty) on location in Nicaragua. **127m/C; VHS, DVD, Blu-Ray.** Robert Carlyle; Oyanka Cabezas; Gary Lewis; Scott Glenn; Subash Sing Pall; ***D:*** Ken Loach; ***W:*** Paul Laverty; ***C:*** Barry Ackroyd; ***M:*** George Fenton.

Carlito's Way **1993 (R)** Puerto Rican crime czar Carlito Brigante (Pacino) has just gotten out of jail and wants to go straight. But his drug underworld cohorts don't believe he can do it. Penn (barely recognizable) is great as a sleazy coked-out lawyer who's way out of his league. Remarkably subdued violence given DePalma's previous rep—it's effective without being gratuitous, especially the final shootout set in Grand Central Station. Pacino's performance is equally subdued, with controlled tension and lots of eye contact rather than grandiose emotions. Based on the novels "Carlito's Way" and "After Hours" by Edwin Torres. Pacino and DePalma previously teamed up for "Scarface." **145m/C; VHS, DVD, Blu-Ray, HD-DVD.** Al Pacino; Sean Penn; Penelope Ann Miller; Luis Guzman; John Leguizamo; Ingrid Rogers; James Rebhorn; Viggo Mortensen; Jorge Porcel; Joseph Siravo; Adrian Pasdar; Jon Seda; Vincent Pastore; ***D:*** Brian De Palma; ***W:*** David Koepp; ***C:*** Stephen Burum; ***M:*** Patrick Doyle.

Carlito's Way: Rise to Power **2005 (R)** Depicts the early years of Puerto Rican drug dealer Carlito Brigante (Hernandez), who wants to become the crime kingpin of New York's Spanish Harlem in the '70s. Carlito is drawn into an alliance with numbers runner Earl (Van Peebles) and mobster Rocco (Kelly) despite Harlem boss Hollywood Nicky (Combs) and various crooked cops. Hernandez does what he can with Pacino's shadow looming over him but this is familiar territory. Adapted from a book by Edwin Torres. **100m/C; DVD, UMD, HD-DVD.** Jay Hernandez; Mario Van Peebles; Sean (Puffy, Puff Daddy, P. Diddy) Combs; Michael Kelly; Luis Guzman; Jaclyn DeSantis; Giancarlo Esposito; Burt Young; Domenick Lombardozzi; Juan Carlos Hernandez; Mtume Gant; Tony Cucci; ***D:*** Michael Scott Bregman; ***W:*** Michael Scott Bregman; ***C:*** Adam Holender; ***M:*** Joe Delia. **VIDEO**

Carlos **2010** Originally produced for French television, Assayas' detailed and ambitious drama traces the rise and fall of the image-conscious, charismatic 1970s and 80s terrorist known as Carlos (AKA Carlos the Jackal). In 1973, Venezuelan-born Ilich Ramirez Sanchez joins the militant Popular Front for the Liberation of Palestine and several missions make him into a notorious celebrity. As the years pass, Carlos forms his own revolutionary group but finds allies abandon him as the political landscape changes. Assayas effectively intersperses actual news footage of various bombings and other atrocities into his dramatization. English, French, Spanish, Japanese, German, Arabic, Russian, and Hungarian with subtitles. **330m/C; Blu-Ray, On Demand.** *FR GE* Edgar Ramirez; Alexander Scheer; Nora von Waldstatten; Ahmad Kaabour; Christoph Bach; Rodney Ed-Haddad; Julia Hummer; Rami Farah; Zeid Hamdan; ***D:*** Olivier Assayas; ***W:*** Olivier Assayas; Dan Franck; ***C:*** Yorick Le Saux; Denis Leconte.

Carlton Browne of the F.O. ½ *Man in a Cocked Hat* **1959** Bumbling Brit diplomat Thomas visits tiny Pacific island of Gallardia, forgotten by the mother country for some 50 years, to insure tenuous international agreement after the island's king dies. Not sterling Sellers but some shining moments. **88m/C; VHS, DVD.** *GB* Peter Sellers; Terry-Thomas; Luciana Paluzzi; Ian Bannen; ***D:*** Roy Boulting; Jeffrey Dell; ***W:*** Roy Boulting; ***M:*** John Addison.

Carmen **1983 (R)** Choreographer casts Carmen and finds life imitates art when he falls under the spell of the hotblooded Latin siren. Bizet's opera lends itself to erotically charged flamenco context. Well acted, impressive scenes including cigarette girls' dance fight and romance between Carmen and Don Jose. In Spanish with English subtitles. **99m/C; VHS, DVD.** *SP* Antonio Gades; Laura Del Sol; Paco de Lucia; Cristina Hoyos; ***D:*** Carlos Saura; ***W:*** Antonio Gades; Carlos Saura; ***C:*** Teodoro Escamilla. British Acad. '84: Foreign Film.

Carmen **2003** The screenwriters use Prosper Merimee's original 1845 novel rather than George Bizet's 1875 opera, although the plot is certainly familiar. Sultry gypsy Carmen (Vega) toys with the affections of military officer Jose (Sbaraglia) until his obsession leads to disgrace, murder, and execution. This version is told by Jose to Prospero (Benedict) in flashbacks. Vega is a looker (and not shy about disrobing) but she doesn't have a lot of chemistry with the various actors in the lurid story. **119m/C; DVD.** *SP GB IT* Paz Vega; Leonardo Sbaraglia; Jay Benedict; Antonio Dechent; Joan Crosas; Joe Mackay; Josep Linuesa; ***D:*** Vicente Aranda; ***W:*** Vicente Aranda; Joaquin Jorda; ***C:*** Paco Femenia; ***M:*** Jose Nieto.

Carmen: A Hip Hopera ½ **2001 (PG-13)** Modernized and urban set version of Bizet's tragic opera, originally made for MTV. Carmen (Knowles) is the femme fatale who seduces straight-laced cop Derek Hill (Phifer) to keep herself out of jail. He abandons everything to follow her to California, where, naturally, Carmen wants to break into show biz. But she tires of Derek's devotion and becomes interested in an up-and-coming rapper. Surprisingly effective and the cast does a fine job. **88m/C; VHS, DVD.** Beyonce Knowles; Mekhi Phifer; Mos Def; Rah Digga; Bow Wow; Nelust Wyclef Jean; Troy Winbush; ***Nar:*** Da Brat; ***D:*** Robert Townsend; ***W:*** Michael Elliot; ***C:*** Geary McLeod; ***M:*** Kip Collins. **CABLE**

Carmen, Baby ½ **1966** Metzger's erotic modern update of Bizet's opera "Carmen." Spanish prostitute Carmen (Levka) becomes the object of obsession for a local cop (Ringer) and things wind up badly because of his jealousy. **90m/C; VHS, DVD.** Uta Levka; Claus Ringer; Barbara Valentin; Walter Wilz; ***D:*** Radley Metzger; ***W:*** Jesse Vogel; ***C:*** Hans Jura; ***M:*** Daniel Hart.

Carmen Jones **1954** Bizet's tale of fickle femme fatale Carmen heads South with an all black cast and new lyrics by Hammerstein II. Soldier Belafonte falls big time for factory working belle Dandridge during the war, and runs off with miss thang after he kills his C.O. and quits the army. Tired of prettyboy Belafonte, Dandridge's eye wanders upon prize pugilist Escamillo, inspiring ex-soldier beau to wring her throaty little neck. Film debuts of Carroll and Peters. More than a little racist undertone to the direction. Actors' singing is dubbed. **105m/C; VHS, DVD, Blu-Ray.** Dorothy Dandridge; Harry Belafonte; Pearl Bailey; Roy Glenn; Diahann Carroll; Brock Peters; ***D:*** Otto Preminger; ***W:*** Harry Kleiner; ***C:*** Sam Leavitt; ***M:*** Oscar Hammerstein; Georges Bizet. Golden Globes '55: Film--Mus./Comedy; Natl. Film Reg. '92.

Carnage **1984** Hungry house consumes inhabitants. **91m/C; VHS, DVD.** Leslie Den Dooven; Michael Chiodo; Deeann Veeder; ***D:*** Andy Milligan.

Carnage **2002** Okay, this film is about a dead bull and its various body parts. Said bull gores a matador during a bullfight and is subsequently killed and butchered. It's various parts go to various people throughout Spain and France, including a young girl named Winnie who gets a bull bone for her Great Dane, a taxidermist who gets the animal's horns, steaks that wind up in a restaurant, etc. There's a lot of obscure symbolism about how life and death are connected. You may not care. Spanish and French with subtitles. **130m/C; VHS, DVD.** *FR SP BE SI* Chiara Mastroianni; Angela Molina; Lucia Sanchez; Bernard Sens; Esther Gorintin; Jacques Gamblin; Feodor Atkine; Marilyne Even; Clovis Cornillac; Raphaelle Molinier; Lio; ***D:*** Delphine Gleize; ***W:*** Delphine Gleize; ***C:*** Crystal Fournier; ***M:*** Eric Neveux.

Carnage ½ **2011 (R)** The controversial director Polanski, accustomed to telling tales with only a few characters in limited locations, adapts the award-winning play by Yasmine Reza ("God of Carnage") with less-than-memorable results. A disagreement at a park leads to one adolescent boy swinging a stick at another and the parents of the aggressor (Waltz, Winslet) spend a day at the apartment of the injured child's parents (Foster, Reilly) and basically realize none of them like each other over cobbler, conversation, and alcohol. More about the dialogue, the acting quartet does what it can to create a tense setting. **79m/C; DVD, Blu-Ray.** Jodie Foster; Kate Winslet; Christoph Waltz; John C. Reilly; ***D:*** Roman Polanski; ***W:*** Roman Polanski; Yasmina Reza; ***C:*** Pawel Edelman; ***M:*** Alexandre Desplat.

Carnage Park **2016** Keating tries to imitate the grindhouse pics of the '70s with dull, plodding results in this wannabe horror-thriller that's neither scary nor thrilling. Bell plays Vivian Fontaine, a woman kidnapped by two bank robbers who happen to stumble upon a remote piece of land in California owned by a lunatic named Wyatt Moss (Healy, the only possible reason to see the film). The trio learns that Moss is basically a fan of "The Most Dangerous Game," hunting them across this barren landscape. Keating's film creates little tension and there's nary a reason to care. **90m/C; DVD, Blu-Ray.** Ashley Bell; Pat Healy; James Landry Hébert; Michael Villar; Alan Ruck; ***D:*** Mickey Keating; ***W:*** Mickey Keating; ***C:*** Mac Fisken; ***M:*** Giona Ostinelli.

Carnal Crimes ½ **1991 (R)** Well-acted upscale softcore trash about a sensuous woman, ignored by her middle-aged lawyer husband and drawn to a young stud photographer with a shady past and S&M tendencies. Available in a sexy unrated version also. **103m/C; VHS, DVD.** Martin Hewitt; Linda Carol; Rich Crater; Alex Kubik; Yvette Stefens; Paula Trickey; ***D:*** Alexander Gregory (Gregory Dark) Hippolyte; ***W:*** Jon Robert Samsel; ***C:*** Paul Desatoff; ***M:*** Matthew Ross; Jeff Fishman.

Carnal Innocence ½ *Nora Roberts' Carnal Innocence* **2011** Lifetime drama based on the Nora Roberts novel. Violinist Caroline Waverly has a professional setback, suffers a breakdown, and decides to spend some quiet time in Innocence, Mississippi where she spent her childhood summers. She meets Tucker Longstreet, who immeduately sets out to charm Caroline. But he may be a literal ladykiller since authorities suspect Tucker is behind a series of murders since the victims have all been his former flames. **87m/C; DVD.** Gabrielle Anwar; Colin Egglesfield; Shirley Jones; Ed Lauter; Brad Rowe; Pancho Demmings; ***D:*** Peter Markle; ***W:*** Donald Martin; ***C:*** Mark Irwin; ***M:*** Tree Adams. **CABLE**

Carnal Knowledge **1971 (R)** Carnal knowledge of the me generation. Three decades in the sex-saturated lives of college buddies Nicholson and Garfunkel, chronicled through girlfriends, affairs, and marriages. Controversial upon release, it's not a flattering anatomy of Y-chromosome carriers. Originally written as a play. Kane's debut. **96m/C; VHS, DVD.** Jack Nicholson; Candice Bergen; Art Garfunkel; Ann-Margret; Rita Moreno; Carol Kane; ***D:*** Mike Nichols; ***W:*** Jules Feiffer; ***C:*** Giuseppe Rotunno. Golden Globes '72: Support. Actress (Ann-Margret).

Carnegie Hall ½ **1947** Widowed Irish-American Nora (Hunt) gets a job at Carnegie Hall and raises her son Tony to be a talented pianist. But the adult Tony (Prince) develops an interest in jazz and popular music that his ma despises. They have a rift, Tony goes on the road with a band, marries singer Ruth (O'Drsicoll), and becomes a famous jazz pianist. After years pass, Ruth decides it's about time to reunite mother and son and Carnegie Hall plays a big part in her scheme. Schmaltzy story showcases a number of big musical stars of the day. **134m/B; VHS, DVD.** Marsha Hunt; William Prince; Martha O'Driscoll; Frank McHugh; ***D:*** Edgar G. Ulmer; ***W:*** Karl Kamb; ***C:*** William J. Miller.

Carnera: The Walking Mountain ½ **2008 (R)** Standard biopic about Italian heavyweight boxing legend Prima Carnera (Iaia). Moving from his impoverished childhood, bellicose Carnera becomes a circus strongman and goes into boxing with shady promoters Leon See (Abraham) and Lou Soresi (Young) as Martinelli twists the facts to serve his dully-presented situations. Italian with subtitles or dubbed. **125m/C; DVD.** *IT* Andrea Iaia; Burt Young; F. Murray Abraham; Anna Valle; Paolo Seganti; Antonio Cupo; Kasia Smutniak; ***D:*** Renzo Martinelli; ***W:*** Renzo Martinelli; Alessandro Gassman; Franco Ferrini; ***C:*** Saverio Guarna; ***M:*** Pivio de Scalzi; Aldo De Scalzi.

Carnival in Costa Rica **1947** In this colorful musical Pepe (Romero) and Luisa (Vera-Ellen) are supposed tyo go along with the marriage arranged by their fathers. But Pepe loves nightclub singer Celeste (Holm) and Luisa is eyeing coffee buyer Jeff (Haymes). **96m/C; DVD.** Cesar Romero; Vera-Ellen; Dick Haymes; Celeste Holm; J. Carrol Naish; Pedro de Cordoba; ***D:*** Gregory Ratoff; ***W:*** Samuel Hoffenstein; John Larkin; Elizabeth Reinhardt; ***C:*** Harry Jackson.

Carnival of Blood *Death Rides a Carousel* **1971 (PG)** Boring talky scenes punctuated by Coney Island murder mayhem followed by more boring talky scenes. Young's debut, not released for five years. The question's not why they delayed release, but why they bothered at all. A carnival of cliches. **80m/C; VHS, DVD.** Earle Edgerton; Judith Resnick; Martin Barlosky; John Harris; Burt Young; Kaly Mills; Gloria Spivak; ***D:*** Leonard Kirtman; ***W:*** Leonard Kirtman; ***C:*** David Howe.

Carnival of Crime **1962** Tedious crime/mystery set in Brazil. Mike returns home from a trip and finds his chronically unfaithful wife Lynn is missing. He starts searching, she turns up murdered, and he becomes the prime suspect. Dubbed. **90m/B; DVD.** *BR* Jean-Pierre Aumont; Alix Talton; Tonia Carrero; Luis Davila; ***D:*** George Cahan; ***W:*** Bill Barret; ***C:*** Americo Hoss; ***M:*** Luis Bonfa.

Carnival of Souls **1962** Cult-followed zero budget zombie opera has young Hilligoss and girlfriends take wrong turn off bridge into river. Mysteriously unscathed, Hilligoss rents room and takes job as church organist, but she keeps running into dancing dead people, led by director Harvey. Spooky, very spooky. **72m/B; VHS, DVD, Blu-Ray.** Candace Hilligoss; Sidney Berger; Frances Feist; Stan Levitt; Art Ellison; Bill de Jarnette; Steve Boozer; Pamela Ballard; Harold (Herk) Harvey; ***D:*** Harold (Herk) Harvey; ***W:*** John Clifford; ***C:*** Maurice Prather; ***M:*** Gene Moore.

Carnival of Souls WOOF! *Wes Craven Presents Carnival of Souls* **1998 (R)** A young girl witnesses the brutal murder of her mother by a circus clown. As an adult she has nightmares about the circus, which intensify when the carnival hits town. Craven's "remake" has nothing much in common with the original except the title. Boring, disjointed waste of time. **87m/C; VHS, DVD.** Bobbie Phillips; Larry Miller; Paul Johansson; Cleavant Derricks; Sidney Berger; Shawnee Smith; ***D:*** Adam Grossman; ***W:*** Adam Grossman; ***M:*** Andrew Rose.

Carnival of Wolves ½ **1996** Four friends who have only their unemployed status in common decide that it would be a good idea to rob the local casino. Which happens to be owned by the easily angered boss of a Chinese Triad (who is a Caucasian male in a bit of a weird moment). Unfortunately the casino has security cameras (oops!), and the guys very soon have a large problem. **103m/C; DVD.** Mike Norris; Stoney Jackson; Forrest Montegomery; *D:* Takeshi Watanabe; *W:* Eric P. Sherman; *C:* Kaz Tanaka; Kazunari Tanaka.

Carnival Rock 1/2 **1957** Story of love triangular in seedy nightclub. Club owner Stewart loves chanteuse Cabot who loves card playin' Hutton. Who cares? Maybe hardcore Corman devotees. Good tunes from the Platters, the Blockbusters, Bob Luman, and David Houston. **80m/B; VHS, DVD.** Susan Cabot; Brian Hutton; David J. Stewart; Dick Miller; Iris Adrian; Jonathan Haze; Ed Nelson; Bob Luman; Frankie Ray; Bruno VeSota; *D:* Roger Corman; *W:* Leo Lieberman; *C:* Floyd Crosby; *M:* Buck Ram.

Carnival Story 1/2 **1954** Yet another melodramatic cliche about love triangular under the big top. German girl joins American-owned carnival and two guys start acting out unbecoming territorial behavior. Filmed in Germany. **94m/C; DVD.** Anne Baxter; Steve Cochran; Lyle Bettger; George Nader; Jay C. Flippen; *D:* Kurt Neumann; *W:* Kurt Neumann; Hans Jacoby; *C:* Ernest Haller; *M:* Willy Schmidt-Gentner.

Carnosaur **1993 (R)** Straight from the Corman film factory, this exploitive quickie about dinosaurs harkens back to '50s-style monster epics. Predictable plot with extremely cheap effects. Genetic scientist Dr. Jane Tiptree (Ladd) is hatching diabolic experiments with chickens when things go awry. The experiments result in a bunch of lethal prehistoric creatures wrecking havoc among the community. **82m/C; VHS, DVD.** Diane Ladd; Raphael Sbarge; Jennifer Runyon; Harrison Page; Clint Howard; Ned Bellamy; *D:* Adam Simon; *W:* Adam Simon; *C:* Keith Holland; *M:* Nigel Holton.

Carnosaur 2 1/2 **1994 (R)** Technicians investigating a power shortage at a secret military mining facility encounter deadly dinos. Entertaining schlock. **90m/C; VHS, DVD.** John Savage; Cliff DeYoung; Arabella Holzbog; Ryan Thomas Johnson; *D:* Louis Morneau; *C:* John Aronson; *M:* Ed Tomney; Michael Palmer.

Carnosaur 3: Primal Species 1/2 **1996** Terrorists get big surprise when the cargo they hijack turns out to be three very hungry dinos who make snacks of them all. Then it's up to commando Valentine, scientist Gunn, and some soldiers to get rid of the beasts. **82m/C; VHS, DVD.** Scott Valentine; Janet Gunn; Rick Dean; Rodger Halston; Tony Peck; *D:* Jonathan Winfrey; *C:* Andrea V. Rossotto; *M:* Kevin Kiner.

Carny **1980 (R)** Hothead carnival bozo Busey and peacemaker Robertson experience friendship difficulties when runaway Foster rolls in hay with one and then other. Originally conceived as a documentary by "Derby" filmmaker Kaylor, it's a candid, unsavory, behind-the-scenes anatomy. Co-written by "The Band" member Robertson. **102m/C; VHS, DVD.** Gary Busey; Robbie Robertson; Jodie Foster; Meg Foster; Kenneth McMillan; Elisha Cook, Jr.; Craig Wasson; Tim Thomerson; Bill McKinney; Bert Remsen; Tina Andrews; Fred Ward; *D:* Robert Kaylor; *W:* Robbie Robertson; Thomas Baum; *C:* Harry Stradling, Jr.; *M:* Alex North.

Carny 1/2 **2009** A part of the "Maneater" series from the Syfy Channel that uses the urban legend of the Jersey Devil. A traveling carnival shows up in a small town with a nasty new acquisition, a winged gargoyle-like creature that has a taste for human blood. When it escapes, the sheriff must save the locals. Usual low-budget predictable plot with weak CGI. **87m/C; DVD.** Lou Diamond Phillips; Alan C. Peterson; Vlasta Vrana; Simone-Elise Girard; Dominic Cuzzocrea; Joe Cobden; *D:* Sheldon Wilson; *W:* Douglas Davis; *C:* Danny Nowak. **CABLE**

Caro Diario *Dear Diary* **1993** Three offbeat chapters from director Moretti's own life. "On My Vespa" has the director taking off on a personal tour of Rome, including its cinemas and their influence on him. In "Islands" Moretti and friend Gerardo travel to a series of island communities, including Salina, dominated by only children to whom their parents defer obsessively. "Doctors" finds Moretti experiencing a misdiagnosed medical crisis. Lots of charm and a certain shameless romanticism. Italian with subtitles. **100m/C; VHS, Streaming.** *IT* Nanni Moretti; Renato Carpentieri; *D:* Nanni Moretti; *W:* Nanni Moretti; *C:* Giuseppe Lanci; *M:* Nicola Piovani. Cannes '94: Director (Moretti).

Carol 1/2 **2015 (R)** Adapting Patricia Highsmith's "The Price of Salt," writer/director Haynes affirms his status as one of his generation's most impressive filmmakers. The auteur tells the story of Therese (Mara), a sweet, shy shopgirl who meets an older, confident woman named Carol (Blanchett), and falls in love with her. Therese is uncertain of her emotions and sexual longing while Carol knows this still unacceptable in her world, especially to her ex-husband (Chandler), who wants custody of their daughter. With sumptuous design elements, one of the most beautiful scores you'll ever hear, and a breathtaking attention to detail, this one gets under your skin. **118m/C; DVD, Blu-Ray.** Cate Blanchett; Rooney Mara; Kyle Chandler; Jake Lacy; Sarah Paulson; *D:* Todd Haynes; *W:* Phyllis Nagy; *C:* Edward Lachman; *M:* Carter Burwell. Ind. Spirit '16: Cinematog.

Carolina 1/2 **2003 (PG-13)** Carolina (Stiles) and her two sisters, Georgia (Skye) and Maine (Boorem), were raised by their eccentric grandma (McLaine) since dad (Quaid) kept skipping out of their lives. Carolina works for a reality matchmaking TV show in L.A. though, naturally, she doesn't have a love-life of her own since she doesn't realize her longtime best friend Albert (Nivola) is actually in love with her but too shy to make a move. **98m/C; DVD.** Julia Stiles; Shirley MacLaine; Alessandro Nivola; Edward Atterton; Randy Quaid; Azura Skye; Mika Boorem; Jennifer Coolidge; Alan Thicke; *D:* Marleen Gorris; *W:* Katherine Fugate; *C:* John Peters; *M:* Steve Bartek.

Carolina Blues 1/2 **1944** Wartime musical has bandleader Kay Kyser agreeing to perform at a southern defense plant. Kyser's vocalist has quit and he's persuaded to hire the daughter of one of the plant's owners as his new songbird. Really it's just an excuse to show off a variety of musical numbers and dance acts popular at the time. **81m/B; DVD.** Kay Kyser; Ann Miller; Victor Moore; Jeff Donnell; Howard Freeman; *D:* Leigh Jackson; *W:* Joseph Hoffman; *C:* Franz Planer.

Carolina Moon 1/2 *Nora Roberts' Carolina Moon* **2007** Psychic Tory returns to her hometown to confront the terrible memories of her past—the night her friend Hope was murdered. But Tory discovers that Hope's was only the first in a series of deaths and that the killer has been waiting patiently for Tory's return. Can Hope's older brother Cade help Tory save herself before she becomes the next victim? Lifetime original movie based on the novel by Nora Roberts. **90m/C; DVD.** Claire Forlani; Oliver Hudson; Jacqueline Bisset; Jonathan Scarfe; Josie Davis; Chad Willet; Greg Lawson; *D:* Stephen Tolkin; *W:* Stephen Tolkin; *C:* Derick Underschultz; *M:* Steve Porcaro. **CABLE**

Carolina Skeletons **1992 (R)** As a child in a small southern town, Gossett watched as his brother was accused of a vicious double murder and quickly tried and executed. Thirty years later, the ex-Green Beret returns home to find the real killer and clear his brother's name. But there are those in the town who will do anything to stop their secrets from being revealed. **94m/C; VHS, DVD.** Louis Gossett, Jr.; Bruce Dern; Melissa Leo; Paul Roebling; G.D. Spradlin; Bill Cobbs; Henderson Forsythe; Clifton James; *D:* John Erman; *W:* Tracy Keenan Wynn; *C:* Tony Imi; *M:* John Morris.

Carousel **1956** Much-loved Rodgers & Hammerstein musical based on Ferenc Molnar's play "Liliom" (filmed by Fritz Lang in 1935) about a swaggering carnival barker (MacRae) who tries to change his life after he falls in love with a good woman. Killed during a robbery he was reluctantly involved in, he begs his heavenly hosts for the chance to return to the mortal realm just long enough to set things straight with his teenage daughter. Now indisputably a classic, the film lost $2 million when it was released. **128m/C; VHS, DVD.** Gordon MacRae; Shirley Jones; Cameron Mitchell; Gene Lockhart; Barbara Ruick; Robert Rounseville; Richard Deacon; Tor Johnson; *D:* Henry King; *W:* Henry Ephron; Phoebe Ephron; *C:* Charles G. Clarke; *M:* Richard Rodgers; *M:* Oscar Hammerstein.

The Carpenter **1989 (R)** Post-nervous breakdown woman receives nightly visits from guy who builds stuff with wood. Very scary stuff. Also available in slightly longer unrated version. **85m/C; VHS, DVD.** *CA* Wings Hauser; Lynne Adams; Pierce Lenoir; Barbara Ann Jones; Beverly Murray; *D:* David Wellington; *W:* Doug Taylor; *C:* David Franco.

The Carpetbaggers **1964 (PG)** Uncannily Howard Hughesian Peppard wallows in wealth and women in Hollywood in the 1920s and 1930s. Spayed version of the Harold Robbins novel. Ladd's final appearance. Followed by the prequel "Nevada Smith." Introduced by Joan Collins. **150m/C; DVD.** George Peppard; Carroll Baker; Alan Ladd; Elizabeth Ashley; Lew Ayres; Martha Hyer; Martin Balsam; Robert Cummings; Archie Moore; Audrey Totter; Leif Erickson; Tom Lowell; *D:* Edward Dmytryk; *W:* John Michael Hayes; *C:* Joe MacDonald; *M:* Elmer Bernstein. Natl. Bd. of Review '64: Support. Actor (Balsam).

Carpool **1996 (PG)** Dumb but amiable comedy finds harried dad Daniel Miller stuck driving a minivan filled with kids to school. Too bad he gets sidetracked and hijacked by bumbling would-be bank robber Franklin Laszlo (Arnold) who takes them hostage and on a really wild ride through the streets and shopping malls of Seattle (except it's filmed in Vancouver). **92m/C; DVD.** Tom Arnold; David Paymer; Rhea Perlman; Rod Steiger; Kim Coates; Rachael Leigh Cook; Mikey Kovar; Micah Gardener; Blake Warkol; *D:* Arthur Hiller; *W:* Don Rhymer; *C:* David M. Walsh; *M:* John Debney. Golden Raspberries '96: Worst Actor (Arnold).

Carpool Guy 1/2 **2005 (PG-13)** If you're a soap opera fan, your pleasure may derive from seeing familiar actors in other roles 'cause there's not much else to recommend this comedy. Ad exec Joel (Hearst) wants that newly-vacated corner office but may lose out because he's always late for work thanks to L.A.'s horrendous traffic. So he hires homeless guy Oliver (Geary) to ride with him, making Joel eligible to drive in the carpool lane. But Oliver also has some unexpected business smarts that Joel can use. **118m/C; DVD.** Rick Hearst; Anthony Geary; Sean Kanan; Kristoff St. John; Lauralee Bell; Jeanne Cooper; Corbin Bernsen; *D:* Corbin Bernsen; *W:* Pete Soldinger; *C:* Mike Jones; *M:* Adam Barber. **VIDEO**

Carrie **1952** In a part turned down by Cary Grant, Olivier plays a married American who self destructs as the woman he loves scales the heights to fame and fortune. The manager of a posh epicurean mecca, Olivier deserts wife Hopkins and steals big bucks from his boss to head east with paramour Jones, a country bumpkin transplanted to Chicago. Once en route to thespian fame in the Big Apple, Jones abandons her erstwhile beau, who crumbles pathetically. Adapted from Theodore Dreiser's "Sister Carrie," it's mega melodrama, but the performances are above reproach. **118m/B; VHS, DVD.** Laurence Olivier; Jennifer Jones; Miriam Hopkins; Eddie Albert; Basil Ruysdael; Ray Teal; Barry Kelley; Sara Berner; William Reynolds; Mary Murphy; Charles Halton; *D:* William Wyler; *C:* Victor Milner.

Carrie **1976 (R)** Overprotected by religious fanatic mother Laurie and mocked by the in-crowd, shy, withdrawn high school girl Carrie White is asked to the prom. Realizing she's been made the butt of a joke, she unleashes her considerable telekinetic talents. Travolta, Allen, and Irving are teenagers who get what they deserve. Based on the Stephen King novel. **98m/C; VHS, DVD, Blu-Ray.** Sissy Spacek; Piper Laurie; John Travolta; William Katt; Amy Irving; Nancy Allen; Edie McClurg; Betty Buckley; P.J. Soles; Sydney Lassick; Stefan Gierasch; *D:* Brian De Palma; *W:* Lawrence D. Cohen; *C:* Mario Tosi; *M:* Pino Donaggio. Natl. Soc. Film Critics '76: Actress (Spacek).

Carrie 1/2 **2002** This remake (broadcast on NBC) of King's first novel was stretched to three hours (with commercials) by introducing new characters and using flashbacks. Face it, what you want to see is the outcast Carrie (Bettis) getting her telekinetic revenge on all her tormentors at the high school prom. That's about the last half-hour, so just fast-forward to the good stuff. **132m/C; VHS, DVD, Blu-Ray.** Angela Bettis; Patricia Clarkson; Rena Sofer; Tobias Mehler; Kandyse McClure; Emilie de Ravin; Katharine Isabelle; David Keith; Jasmine Guy; *D:* David Carson; *W:* Bryan Fuller; *C:* Victor Goss; *M:* Laura Karpman. **TV**

Carrie 1/2 **2013 (R)** Pierce deftly updates the classic Stephen King tale of the awkward girl with telekinetic powers for an era of viral videos and bullying, amply assisted by fiery performances from Moretz and Moore. Moretz plays the title character (and Moore her demented, overly religious mother), a shy teen who is publicly embarrassed when she gets her period in the showers after gym class. When the head bully is denied prom privileges after the incident, vengeance is planned but Carrie has a deadly secret of her own. Doesn't replace the Brian De Palma version but works on its own terms for a new generation. **100m/C; DVD, Blu-Ray.** Chloë Grace Moretz; Julianne Moore; Portia Doubleday; Gabriella Wilde; Judy Greer; Ansel Elgort; Alex Russell; Zoe Belkin; *D:* Kimberly Peirce; *W:* Roberto Aguirre-Sacasa; *C:* Steve Yedlin; *M:* Marco Beltrami.

Carrie Pilby **2017** Based on the bestselling novel of the same name, Powley plays the title character in this coming-of-age dramedy with a great cast but overly familiar template. Pilby is a teen genius, someone who graduated Harvard at age 18. She may be book smart, but she's still young when it comes to dealing with the world, and she withdraws into her apartment. Her shrink (Lane) gives her a checklist of things to do between Thanksgiving and the end of the year in an effort to teach her about adult human dynamics. It's fine but unremarkable. **98m/C; DVD.** Bel Powley; Nathan Lane; Gabriel Byrne; Vanessa Bayer; Colin O'Donoghue; *D:* Susan Johnson; *W:* Kara Holden; *C:* Gonzalo Amat; *M:* Michael Penn.

Carried Away 1/2 *Acts of Love* **1995 (R)** Exposing his middle-aged bod, as well as the myth that he can play only psycho toughs, Hopper, as the Midwestern teacher Joseph, is seduced by a 17-year-old student (Locane) in their small conservative town. Based on Harrison's novel "Farmer," it's a sexually active slice of life with the injured Joseph limping through the care of his dying mother, the fate of the small country school where he teaches and his relationship with longtime lover Rosealee (Amy Irving). Hopper's not the only one playing against type, as Irving turns in a fine performance as the widowed schoolmarm. Director Barreto (and Irving's husband) pushes the envelope with full frontal nudity. **107m/C; VHS, DVD.** Dennis Hopper; Amy Irving; Amy Locane; Gary Busey; Julie Harris; Hal Holbrook; Christopher Pettiet; Priscilla Pointer; Gail Cronauer; *D:* Bruno Barreto; *W:* Ed Jones; *C:* Declan Quinn; *M:* Bruce Broughton.

Carriers 1/2 **2009 (PG-13)** An unspecified plague that turns infected citizens into red-faced ghouls leaves some tough survivors, including four in the rural Southwest: Brian (Pine), Bobby (Perabo), Danny (Pucci), and Kate (VanCamp). When a man (Meloni) asks for help for his apparently infected daughter (Shipka), Brian initially refuses but of course the story doesn't end there with a nasty twist to come. Rating means there's more chills than outright grossness but that's definitely in the flick's favor. **84m/C; DVD.** Chris Pine; Piper Perabo; Christopher Meloni; Lou Taylor Pucci; Emily VanCamp; Kiernan Shipka; *D:* Alex Pastor; David Pastor; *W:* Alex Pastor; David Pastor; *C:* Benoît Debie; *M:* Peter Nashel; Brick Garner.

Carrie's War 1/2 **2004** 14-year-old Carrie (Fawcett) and her younger brother Nick (Stanley) are sent to live in the country to escape the London bombings during WWII. Naturally, they must cope with a variety of characters both pleasant and strict. Based on the Nina Bawden novel. **90m/C; DVD.** *GB* Jack Stanley; Lesley Sharp; Alun Armstrong; Geraldine McEwan; Keeley Fawcett; Pauline Quirke; Eddie Cooper; Jamie Boddard; *D:* Coky Giedroyc; *W:* Michael Crompton; *C:* Julian Court; *M:* Nick Bicat. **TV**

Carrington 🦴🦴 1/2 **1995 (R)** England's artistic Bloomsbury group is examined through the eccentric relationship of artist Dora Carrington (Thompson) and her love for homosexual Lytton Strachey (Pryce), celebrated author of "Eminent Victorians." There's many a menage as the duo live together with Carrington's husband (Waddington), on whom Strachey has a crush, and both their various amours (though Carrington's heart is reserved for Lytton). Film is distractingly divided into titled segments (from 1915 to 1932) and, while Pryce gives a bravura performance, Thompson is merely enigmatic. Based on Michael Holroyd's biography "Lytton Strachey." Hampton's directorial debut. **120m/C; VHS, DVD, Blu-Ray.** *FR GB* Emma Thompson; Jonathan Pryce; Steven Waddington; Samuel West; Rufus Sewell; Penelope Wilton; Jeremy Northam; Peter Blythe; Janet McTeer; Alex Kingston; Sebastian Harcombe; Richard Clifford; ***D:*** Christopher Hampton; ***W:*** Christopher Hampton; ***C:*** Denis Lenoir; ***M:*** Michael Nyman. Cannes '95: Actor (Pryce), Special Jury Prize; Natl. Bd. of Review '95: Actress (Thompson).

Carry Me Home 🦴🦴 **2004 (PG-13)** As Harriet (Miller) suffers through the loss of her husband from his WWII tour of duty, her tomboy daughter Carrie (Orr) deals with the pain by angrily shutting her mom out, particularly when Harriet moves on with the high-brow Bernard (Basche) causing Carrie to seek comfort from Charlie (Anderson), a mentally-challenged and troubled local farmhand. Showtime cable coming-of-age drama feels more like a tearjerker-of-the-week Lifetime channel show. **97m/C; VHS, DVD.** Penelope Ann Miller; Kevin Anderson; David Alan Basche; Ashley Rose Orr; Jane Alexander; Leo Burmester; Nicholas Braun; ***D:*** Jace Alexander; ***W:*** Christopher Fay; ***C:*** David Herrington; ***M:*** Bill Elliott. **CABLE**

Carry On Abroad 🦴 1/2 **1972** British tourists arrive for a cheap packaged holiday at the Spanish town of Elsbels to find the weather is terrible, the hotel is unfinished, and apparently there is only one person on staff. The 23rd entry in the series. **89m/C; DVD.** *GB* Kenneth Williams; Sidney James; Joan Sims; Charles Hawtrey; Bernard Bresslaw; Peter Butterworth; Kenneth Connor; Barbara Windsor; June Whitfield; Hattie Jacques; ***D:*** Gerald Thomas; ***W:*** Talbot Rothwell; ***C:*** Alan Hume; ***M:*** Eric Rogers.

Carry On Admiral 🦴 1/2 *The Ship was Loaded* **1957** Weak British comedy about two friends who get drunk and decide it would be fun to switch identities. One has an easy job as a public relations exec but the other is supposedly the captain of a ship. His lack of sea knowledge causes wacky catastrophes. Unrelated to the "Carry On" series of comedies. **85m/B; VHS, DVD.** *GB* David Tomlinson; Brian Reece; Peggy Cummins; Eunice Gayson; A.E. Matthews; Lionel Murton; Joan Sims; ***D:*** Val Guest; ***W:*** Val Guest.

Carry On Again Doctor 🦴🦴 **1969** Disgraced doctor Jimmy Nookey (Dale) leaves England to practice medicine on a remote tropical isle. Fellow worker Gladstone Screwer (James) has learned how to make a native weight-loss potion, and Nookey takes the formula back to England, where he establishes a successful weight-loss clinic, but some of his fellow doctors want him taken down a peg. The 18th film in the series follows the usual pattern of innuendo and slapstick. **86m/C; DVD.** *GB* Jim Dale; Sidney James; Kenneth Williams; Charles Hawtrey; Joan Sims; Barbara Windsor; Hattie Jacques; Patsy Rowlands; ***D:*** Gerald Thomas; ***W:*** Talbot Rothwell; ***C:*** Ernest Steward; ***M:*** Eric Rogers.

Carry On at Your Convenience 🦴 1/2 *Carry On 'Round the Bend* **1971** Williams, who played in the original ("Carry On Sergeant"), and Carry On regulars (charpei-mugged James and ever-zaftig Jacques) go 'round the bend in yet another installment of the British spoof in and around a toilet factory. **86m/C; VHS, Streaming.** *GB* Sidney James; Kenneth Williams; Charles Hawtrey; Joan Sims; Kenneth Cope; Hattie Jacques; ***D:*** Gerald Thomas.

Carry On Behind 🦴🦴 **1975** "Carry On" crew heads for archeological dig and find themselves sharing site with holiday caravan. **95m/C; VHS, Streaming.** *GB* Sidney James; Kenneth Williams; Elke Sommer; Joan Sims; ***D:*** Gerald Thomas.

Carry On Cabby 🦴🦴 **1963** The seventh entry in the series is a little sharper-edged than usual. Charlie Hawkins (James) is so busy running the Speedee Cab Company that he forgets his wedding anniversary. In retaliation, neglected wife Peggy (Jacques) starts Glamcabs, where all the drivers are beautiful women in skimpy uniforms. Charlie is upset about losing business to his new rival (not knowing his wife is the boss) and vows to get even. **91m/B; DVD.** *GB* Sidney James; Hattie Jacques; Kenneth Connor; Charles Hawtrey; Esma Cannon; Oskar Karlweis; Bill Owen; Milo O'Shea; Jim Dale; ***D:*** Gerald Thomas; ***W:*** Talbot Rothwell; ***C:*** Alan Hume; ***M:*** Eric Rogers.

Carry On Camping 🦴 1/2 **1971** Another entry in the silly series finds James and Bresslaw trying to persuade their girlfriends to go on a camping trip to what the men hope is a nudist colony. They don't find nudists but they do find a group of sex-starved schoolgirls. Part of the Carry On Double Feature, Vol. 3. **88m/C; VHS, DVD.** *GB* Sidney James; Bernard Bresslaw; Kenneth Williams; Joan Sims; Charles Hawtrey; Barbara Windsor; ***D:*** Gerald Thomas; ***W:*** Talbot Rothwell.

Carry On Cleo 🦴🦴 1/2 **1965** "Carry On" spoof of Shakespeare's "Antony and Cleopatra." The film used some of the sets from the budget-busting 1963 disaster "Cleopatra." **91m/C; VHS, DVD.** *GB* Sidney James; Amanda Barrie; Kenneth Williams; Kenneth Connor; Jim Dale; Charles Hawtrey; Joan Sims; ***D:*** Gerald Thomas.

Carry On Columbus 🦴 **1992** A lame effort to revive the franchise after 1978's "Carry on Emmannuelle." This 30th entry finds a befuddled Christopher Columbus (Dale) searching for a new route to India in order to bypass the greedy Sultan of Turkey (Mayall) and winding up in the Americas, where the natives speak with Brooklyn accents and call him Columbo. **91m/C; DVD.** *GB* Jim Dale; Bernard Cribbins; Rik Mayall; Leslie Phillips; June Whitfield; Maureen Lipman; Peter Richardson; Larry Miller; Charles Fleischer; Alexei Sayle; Sara Crowe; ***D:*** Gerald Thomas; ***W:*** David Freeman; ***C:*** Alan Hume; ***M:*** John Du Prez.

Carry On Constable 🦴🦴 **1960** In the fourth film of the series a flu epidemic results in no-nonsense Sgt. Frank Wilkins (James) having to work with a trio of oddball new recruits who bumble every assignment. Then they have to track down and arrest a criminal gang who robbed a payroll truck without mucking it up. **86m/B; DVD.** *GB* Sidney James; Leslie Phillips; Kenneth Williams; Kenneth Connor; Charles Hawtrey; Hattie Jacques; Eric Barker; Shirley Eaton; Joan Sims; Joan Hickson; ***D:*** Gerald Thomas; ***W:*** Norman Hudis; ***C:*** Edward (Ted) Scaife; ***M:*** Bruce Montgomery.

Carry On Cowboy 🦴🦴 *Rumpo Kid* **1966** "Carry On" Western parody of "High Noon." **91m/C; VHS, DVD.** *GB* Sidney James; Kenneth Williams; Jim Dale; Joan Sims; Charles Hawtrey; Angela Douglas; Peter Butterworth; Bernard Bresslaw; Percy Herbert; Davy Kaye; ***D:*** Gerald Thomas; ***W:*** Talbot Rothwell; ***C:*** Alan Hume; ***M:*** Eric Rogers.

Carry On Cruising 🦴 **1962** "Carry On" gang attacks sailing world with low humor and raunchiness. **89m/C; VHS, DVD.** Sidney James; Kenneth Williams; Liz Fraser; ***D:*** Gerald Thomas.

Carry On Dick 🦴🦴 **1975** What made the seemingly endless "Carry On" series of super-low-budget British farces such a hit is a mystery not to be solved. Low production values, scripts that peter out midway, and manifest humor don't normally a classic make; and yet the gang has its following. "Dick," a spoof on highwayman Dick Turpin, was preceded by some 20-odd carryings on; suffice it to say that the series, which began in 1958 with "Carry on Sergeant," has not improved with age in subsequent incarnations. Currently only available as part of a collection. **95m/C; VHS, DVD.** *GB* Sidney James; Joan Sims; ***D:*** Gerald Thomas.

Carry On Doctor 🦴🦴🦴 **1968** British series continues as characters of questionable competence join the medical profession. **95m/C; VHS, Streaming.** *GB* Frankie Howerd; Kenneth Williams; Jim Dale; Barbara Windsor; ***D:*** Gerald Thomas.

Carry On Emmanuelle 🦴 **1978** Emmanuelle, the wife of the French Ambassador to England, uses bedroom diplomacy to foster international relations. Part of the British "Carry On" series. **104m/C; VHS, DVD.** *GB* Suzanne Danielle; Kenneth O'Connor; Kenneth Williams; Beryl Reid; ***D:*** Gerald Thomas.

Carry On England 🦴 **1976** Mercifully, the gang didn't carry on much beyond this entry, in which a WWII anti-aircraft gun battery crew bumbles through the usual pranks and imbroglios. **89m/C; VHS, Streaming.** *GB* Kenneth Connor; Patrick Mower; Judy Geeson; ***D:*** Gerald Thomas.

Carry On Henry VIII 🦴 1/2 **1971** Slapstick sex humor with Henry marrying the French Marie of Normandie and having to deal with both her addiction to garlic and the fact that she's pregnant by her lover. **88m/C; VHS, Streaming.** *GB* Sidney James; Kenneth Williams; Joan Sims; Charles Hawtrey; Barbara Windsor; Kenneth Connor; Julian Holloway; ***D:*** Gerald Thomas; ***W:*** Talbot Rothwell.

Carry On Jack 🦴🦴 *Carry On Venus* **1963** The eighth in the film series is a spoof of seafaring/Horatio Hornblower yarns with innocent Midshipman Albert Poop-Decker (Cribbins) losing his uniform to sultry Sally (Mills) and sailing with sea-hating, misnamed Captain Fearless (Williams), battling pirates and mutineers ala "Mutiny on the Bounty." **91m/C; DVD.** *GB* Bernard Cribbins; Juliet Mills; Percy Herbert; Cecil Parker; Kenneth Williams; Charles Hawtrey; Donald Huston; Jim Dale; ***D:*** Gerald Thomas; ***W:*** Talbot Rothwell; ***C:*** Alan Hume; ***M:*** Eric Rogers.

Carry On Loving 🦴 1/2 **1970** The 20th entry is rife with the usual sight gags and sexual innuendo as Sidney Bliss (James) runs a fake lonely hearts agency designed to unite the love-starved in a series of bumbling blind dates. **90m/C; DVD.** *GB* Sidney James; Hattie Jacques; Kenneth Williams; Charles Hawtrey; Joan Sims; Terry Scott; Joan Hickson; ***D:*** Gerald Thomas; ***W:*** Talbot Rothwell; ***C:*** Ernest Steward; ***M:*** Eric Rogers.

Carry On Matron 🦴 1/2 **1972** In the 24th entry in the series (another hospital spoof), a group of thieves plan to steal a shipment of contraceptive pills from Finisham Maternity Hospital. But they are continually thwarted by oblivious head doctor Cutting (Williams) and Matron (Jacques). **89m/C; DVD.** *GB* Kenneth Williams; Hattie Jacques; Terry Scott; Charles Hawtrey; Barbara Windsor; Joan Sims; Kenneth Connor; Sidney James; Bernard Bresslaw; Kenneth Cope; ***D:*** Gerald Thomas; ***W:*** Talbot Rothwell; ***C:*** Ernest Steward; ***M:*** Eric Rogers.

Carry On Nurse 🦴🦴 **1959** Men's ward in a British hospital declares war on nurses and the rest of the hospital. The second of the "Carry On" series. **86m/B; VHS, DVD.** *GB* Shirley Eaton; Kenneth Connor; Hattie Jacques; Wilfrid Hyde-White; ***D:*** Gerald Thomas.

Carry On Regardless 🦴🦴 **1961** A series of slapstick sketches tied together with the flimsiest of plots. Bert Handy (James) hires a bunch of incompetents for his employment agency to work a variety of odd jobs, including baby-sitters, bouncers, models, and house cleaners (or wreckers in this case). Fifth in the series. **90m/B; DVD.** *GB* Sidney James; Kenneth Connor; Charles Hawtrey; Joan Sims; Kenneth Williams; Liz Fraser; Bill Owen; Esma Cannon; Joan Hickson; Stanley Unwin; ***D:*** Gerald Thomas; Ralph L. (R.L.) Thomas; ***W:*** Tony Lo Bianco; ***C:*** Alan Hume; ***M:*** Bruce Montgomery.

Carry On Screaming 🦴🦴 **1966** "Carry On" does horror. A pair of goofy detectives trail monsters suspected in kidnapping. **97m/C; VHS, DVD.** *GB* Harry H. Corbett; Kenneth Williams; Fenella Fielding; Joan Sims; Charles Hawtrey; Jim Dale; Angela Douglas; Jon Pertwee; ***D:*** Gerald Thomas.

Carry On Sergeant 🦴🦴 **1958** The first in the long-running comedy series chronicles the misadventures of Sergeant Grimshawe (Hartnett) and his latest batch of recruits doing their National Service. Grimshawe is due to retire and wants to leave a success so he takes the bet of rival Sgt. O'Brien (Scott) that he will have the championship platoon. Then he meets the bumblers he must whip into shape. Based on the book "The Bull Boys" by R.F. Delderfield. The title was deliberately used to cash in on the success of 1957's "Carry On Admiral," which had nothing to do with the subsequent films. **81m/B; DVD.** *GB* William Hartnell; Kenneth Williams; Eric Barker; Charles Hawtrey; Terence Longdon; Norman Rossington; Kenneth Connor; Hattie Jacques; Terry Scott; Bob Monkhouse; Shirley Eaton; ***D:*** Gerald Thomas; ***W:*** Peter Hennessy; ***C:*** Norman Hudis; ***M:*** Bruce Montgomery.

Carry On Spying 🦴🦴 **1964** The "Carry On" gang does a spoof of spy films with their silly names, villains, and gadgets. Top-secret chemical Formula X has been stolen by STENCH and it's up to gullible, inexperienced Desmond (Williams), an agent of BOSH, to get it back, assisted by toothsome Daphne Honeybutt (Windsor). The ninth in the series. **87m/C; DVD.** *GB* Kenneth Williams; Barbara Windsor; Eric Pohlmann; Bernard Cribbins; Charles Hawtrey; Judith Furse; Eric Barker; Jim Dale; Victor Maddern; ***D:*** Gerald Thomas; ***W:*** Sid Colin; Talbot Rothwell; ***C:*** Alan Hume; ***M:*** Eric Rogers.

Carry On Up the Jungle 🦴 1/2 **1970** The 19th entry in the series is in the intrepid explorer/Tarzan mode as ornithologist Inigo Tinkle (Howerd) searches for a rare bird while Lady Bagley (Sims) looks for her long-lost son. Meanwhile, they're beset by cannibals, a female tribe from Aphrodisia looking for mates, and an amorous gorilla. **89m/C; DVD.** *GB* Frankie Howerd; Sidney James; Joan Sims; Charles Hawtrey; Terry Scott; Kenneth Connor; Bernard Bresslaw; ***D:*** Gerald Thomas; ***W:*** Talbot Rothwell; ***C:*** Ernest Steward; ***M:*** Eric Rogers.

Carry On Up the Khyber 🦴 1/2 **1968** In this 16th entry, the gang mangles the heroic "Brits defending the Empire" epic. The men of the Third Foot and Mouth regiment are sent to the Khyber Pass to prevent the revolting Burpas, led by Khasi of Kalabar (Williams), from discovering what's beneath the kilts of the fearsome Scottish Devil's Regiment. (Hint: it's not regulation wear.) **87m/C; DVD.** *GB* Sidney James; Kenneth Williams; Charles Hawtrey; Joan Sims; Bernard Bresslaw; Terry Scott; Roy Castle; Angela Douglas; Peter Butterworth; ***D:*** Gerald Thomas; ***W:*** Talbot Rothwell; ***C:*** Ernest Steward; ***M:*** Eric Rogers.

Cars 🦴🦴🦴 **2006 (G)** Brightly-colored animated adventure from those Pixar folks about automobiles. Arrogant rookie racecar Lightning McQueen (Wilson) is detoured to the sleepy town of Radiator Springs on his way to a big race. Forced to perform community service, Lightning gets a lesson in humility and figures out that fame isn't everything, thanks to such new friends as Sally Carrera (Hunt), a hot 2002 Porsche 911; gruff Doc (Newman), the 1951 Hudson Hornet; and Mater (Larry the Cable Guy), a goofy, good-natured tow truck. Just as heartwarming and funny as you'd expect a Pixar feature to be. **118m/C; DVD, Blu-Ray.** Larry the Cable Guy; ***V:*** Owen Wilson; Paul Newman; Bonnie Hunt; Paul Dooley; Joe Ranft; George Carlin; Katherine Helmond; Michael Keaton; Richard "Cheech" Marin; John Ratzenberger; Tony Shalhoub; Richard Petty; Guido Quaroni; Jenifer Lewis; Michael Wallis; ***D:*** John Lasseter; ***W:*** Joe Ranft; John Lasseter; Dan Fogelman; Kiel Murray; Phil Lorin; Jorgen Klubien; ***C:*** Jean-Claude Kalache; ***M:*** Randy Newman. Golden Globes '07: Animated Film.

Cars 2 🦴🦴 1/2 **2011 (G)** Disney/Pixar's 3D sequel is a fast-track caper comedy that has racecar Lightning McQueen (Wilson) and his best bud, tow truck Mater (Larry the Cable Guy), heading overseas for the first World Grand Prix. Racing takes a back seat when naive Mater is mistakenly pulled into a top-secret, international spy mission that involves sabotaging the race. Newcomers include the oh-so-cool British spies Finn McMissile (Caine) and Holly Shiftwell (Mortimer) as well as zipping through Tokyo, Paris, London, and the Italian Riviera. Doesn't quite live up to the ultra-high Pixar standard, but entertaining nonetheless. **113m/C; DVD, Blu-Ray.** ***V:*** Owen Wilson; Larry the Cable Guy; Michael Caine; Emily Mortimer; Jason Isaacs; Joe Mantegna; Thomas Kretschmann; Bonnie Hunt; Cheech Marin; Tony

Shalhoub; Michael Keaton; John Ratzenberger; Eddie Izzard; John Turturro; *D:* John Lasseter; Brad Lewis; *W:* Ben Queen; *M:* Michael Giacchino.

Cars 3 **2017 (G)** This third installment recaptures the heart of the first and dazzles with Pixar animation. On the verge of being considered a "classic car," Lightning McQueen (Wilson) shifts from simply outracing to outsmarting Jackson Storm (Hammer) and the next generation of cocky, technologically-advanced vehicles. A better-than-middle-of-the-road final lap for the franchise. **102m/C; DVD, Blu-Ray.** *V:* Owen Wilson; Cristela Alonzo; Chris Cooper; Nathan Fillion; Larry the Cable Guy; Armie Hammer; *D:* Brian Fee; *W:* Keil Murray; Bob Peterson; Mike Rich; *M:* Randy Newman.

The Cars That Ate Paris *The Cars That Eat People* **1974 (PG)** Parasitic town in the Parisian (Australia) outback preys on car and body parts generated by deliberate accidents inflicted by wreck-driving wreckless youths. Weir's first film released internationally, about a small Australian town that survives economically via deliberately contriving car accidents and selling the wrecks' scrap parts. A broad, bitter black comedy with some horror touches. **91m/C; VHS, DVD.** *AU* Terry Camillieri; Kevin Miles; John Meillon; Melissa Jaffer; *D:* Peter Weir; *W:* Peter Weir; *M:* Bruce Smeaton.

Carson City **½** **1952** Silent Jeff Kincaid (Scott) is a construction engineer hired by Carson City banker William Sloan (Keating) to build a railway line between Carson City and Virginia City, Nevada. Sloan is tired of the stagecoach being constantly robbed but the locals (and the bandits) try to prevent the rail line from going through. The bandits cause a landslide (which results in several deaths) and then steal a shipment of gold bullion until Jeff can set things right. **87m/C; DVD.** Randolph Scott; Raymond Massey; Richard Webb; James Millican; Lucille Norman; Larry Keating; George Cleveland; Don Beddoe; *D:* Andre de Toth; *W:* Winston Miller; Sloan Nibley; Eric Jonsson; *C:* John Boyle; *M:* David Buttolph.

Cartel **WOOF!** **1990 (R)** O'Keeffe, "B" actor extraordinaire, plays the wrong man to pick on in this rancid dope opera. Hounded by drug lord Stroud and framed for murder, pilot O'Keeffe decides the syndicate has gone too doggone far when they kill his sister. Exploitive and otherwise very bad. **106m/C; VHS, DVD.** Miles O'Keeffe; Don Stroud; Crystal Carson; William (Bill) Smith; *D:* John Stewart; *W:* Moshe Hadar; *C:* Thomas Callaway; *M:* Rick Krizman.

Carter High **2015 (PG-13)** Based on real events, the true story of football players dealing with adversity as their team pursues greatness. In Dallas, Texas, in the late 1980s, Carter High School had a strong football program led by Coach James (Dutton). On the path to the state championship in 1988, the coach tries to guide his student athletes on and off the field to overcome adversity. Four friends, however, ignore this message, commit petty crimes, and endure their life lessons changed their course of their lives. **110m/C; DVD, Streaming, Download.** Charles S. Dutton; Vivica A. Fox; Pooch Hall; John West, Jr.; David Banner; *D:* Arthur Muhammad; *W:* Arthur Muhammad; *C:* Ron Gonzalez; *M:* Giona Ostinelli.

Carthage in Flames *Cartagine in Fiamme; Carthage en Flammes* **1960** A graphic portrayal of the destruction of ancient Carthage in a blood and guts battle for domination of the known world. A tender love story is a welcome aside in this colorful Italian-made epic. **96m/C; VHS, DVD.** *IT* Anne Heywood; Jose Suarez; Pierre Brasseur; *D:* Carmine Gallone.

Cartier Affair **1984** A beautiful TV actress unwittingly falls in love with the man who wants to steal her jewels. Collins designed her own wardrobe. **120m/C; VHS, DVD.** Joan Collins; David Hasselhoff; Telly Savalas; Ed Lauter; Joe La Due; *D:* Rod Holcomb; *C:* Hanania Baer. **TV**

Cartouche *Swords of Blood* **1962** A swashbuckling action-comedy set in 18th-century France. Belmondo plays a charming thief who takes over a Paris gang, aided by the lovely Cardinale. When he is captured, she sacrifices her life to save him and Belmondo and his cohorts vow to have their revenge. Based on a French legend and a well-acted combination of tragedy, action, and farce. In French with English subtitles. **115m/C; VHS, DVD.** *FR IT* Jean-Paul Belmondo; Claudia Cardinale; Odile Versois; Philippe Lemaire; *D:* Philippe de Broca; *W:* Philippe de Broca; *M:* Georges Delerue.

Carve Her Name with Pride **½** **1958** The true story of Violette Szabo who at age 19 became a secret agent with the French Resistance in WWII. **119m/B; VHS, DVD.** *GB* Virginia McKenna; Paul Scofield; Jack Warner; Denise Grey; Alan Saury; Maurice Ronet; Anne Leon; Nicole Stephane; Sydney Tafler; Avice Landone; *D:* Lewis Gilbert; *W:* Lewis Gilbert; Vernon Harris; *C:* John Wilcox; *M:* William Alwyn.

Carver's Gate **1996** Thanks to an environmental disaster, earth is in big trouble and its inhabitants take refuge in a virtual reality game called Afterlife. But when an engineer tries to improve the game by heightening its reality, the game's computer-generated demons get loose and it's up to cybercop Pare to stop them by traveling between virtual reality and the actual world. **97m/C; VHS, DVD.** Michael Paré; Kevin Stapleton; Marian Skretas; Tara Maria Manuel; Peter Wylde; Pamela Keyes; *D:* Sheldon Inkol; *W:* Sheldon Inkol; *C:* Jonathan Freeman; *M:* Donald Quan.

Caryl of the Mountains **½ 1936** Rin Tin Tin helps the Mounties track an embezzler who also killed the fur trapper uncle of the title character. **68m/B; DVD.** Ralph Bushman; Earl Dwire; Lois Wilde; Josef Swickard; *D:* Bernard B. Ray; *W:* Tom Gibson; *C:* William (Bill) Hyer.

Cas & Dylan **½ 2015** Dr. Cas Pepper (a timeless Dreyfuss) has just discovered he has a terminal brain tumor. An unusual sequence of events leads to a road trip with 22-year-old Dylan (Maslany)...that leads to a clichéd melodrama which wastes the talents of its leads. Do you love when rebellious young people teach dying old people how to really value their last days on Earth? Yeah, neither does the Hound. Director Priestley starts on shaky ground and then just allows his characters to drive to sentimental-ville before the whole thing crashes and burns. **90m/C; DVD.** Tatiana Maslany; Richard Dreyfuss; Aaron Poole; Jayne (Jane) Eastwood; Eric Peterson; *D:* Jason Priestley; *W:* Jessie Gabe; *C:* Gerald Packer; *M:* Michael Brook.

Casa de los Babys **2003 (R)** Sayles's quiet, insightful look at adoption, poverty, politics and international trade as five diverse American women wait (and wait) at a local motel nicknamed Casa de Los Babys to adopt children in an unnamed South American country. Each has a particular reason for adoption: Fitness freak Skipper (Hannah) has had three miscarriages while Jennifer (Gyllenhaal) hopes adoption will help her ailing marriage. Rounding out the gang of expectant mothers are the hard-need single-mom to be Leslie (Taylor); Steenburgen's alcoholic Gayle; and the extremely disagreeable Nan (Harden). Memorably poignant scene as the Irish Eileen and the Latina Asuncion (Lynch and Martinez, respectively) bond over heartfelt exchanges in a language that neither can understand. **95m/C; VHS, DVD.** Maggie Gyllenhaal; Marcia Gay Harden; Daryl Hannah; Susan Lynch; Mary Steenburgen; Lili Taylor; Rita Moreno; Vanessa Martinez; *D:* John Sayles; *W:* John Sayles; *C:* Mauricio Rubinstein; *M:* Mason Daring.

Casa de mi Padre **2012 (R)** Not unlike a "Funny or Die" or "Saturday Night Live" sketch stretched far past its creative breaking point, this truly bizarre comedy earns points for originality and commitment, but can't quite justify its existence. Ferrell plays Armando Alvarez, a ranch worker in Mexico who falls for his brother's (Luna) fiancee Sonia (Rodriguez) and plunges the entire family into a battle with a nefarious drug lord (Bernal). Having Ferrell lead a film that is entirely in Spanish and pitched like a telenovela allows for some unique comedy possibilities, but just not enough for a feature film. In Spanish, with subtitles. **84m/C; DVD, Blu-Ray.** Will Ferrell; Gael Garcia Bernal; Diego Luna; Genesis Rodriguez; Pedro Armendariz, Jr.; Nick Offerman; Efren Ramirez; Adrian Martinez; *D:* Matt Piedmont; *W:* Andrew Steele; *C:* Ramsay Nickell; *M:* Beacon Street Studios.

Casablanca **1942 (PG)** Can you see George Raft as Rick? Jack Warner did, but producer Hal Wallis wanted Bogart. Considered by many to be the best film ever made and one of the most quoted movies of all time, it rocketed Bogart from gangster roles to romantic leads as he and Bergman (who never looked lovelier) sizzle on screen. Bogart runs a gin joint in Morocco during the Nazi occupation, and meets up with Bergman, an old flame, but romance and politics do not mix, especially in Nazi-occupied French Morocco. Greenstreet, Lorre, and Rains all create memorable characters, as does Wilson, the piano player to whom Bergman says the oft-misquoted, "Play it, Sam." Without a doubt, the best closing scene ever written; it was scripted on the fly during the end of shooting, and actually shot several ways. Written from an unproduced play. See it in the original black and white. **102m/B; VHS, DVD, Blu-Ray, HD-DVD.** Humphrey Bogart; Ingrid Bergman; Paul Henreid; Claude Rains; Peter Lorre; Sydney Greenstreet; Conrad Veidt; S.Z. Sakall; Dooley Wilson; Marcel Dalio; John Qualen; Helmut Dantine; Madeleine LeBeau; Joy Page; Leonid Kinskey; Curt Bois; Oliver Blake; Monte Blue; Martin Garralaga; Ilka Gruning; Ludwig Stossel; Frank Puglia; *D:* Michael Curtiz; *W:* Julius J. Epstein; Philip G. Epstein; Howard Koch; *C:* Arthur Edeson; *M:* Max Steiner. Oscars '43: Director (Curtiz), Film, Screenplay; AFI '98: Top 100; Natl. Film Reg. '89.

Casablanca Express **1989** Nazi commandos hijack Churchill's train in this action-adventure drama. **90m/C; VHS, DVD.** Glenn Ford; Donald Pleasence; Jason Connery; *D:* Sergio Martino.

Casanova **2005** The elderly Giacomo Casanova (O'Toole) has been exiled from Venice and is working as a librarian in a crumbling castle. Depressed, he finds new vigor relating his lustful adventures as a young man to his maid, Edith (Byrne). The younger Casanova (Tennant) was a reckless bon vivant willing to risk everything, especially for the love of noblewoman Henriette (Fraser). Wonderful romp; both O'Toole and Tennant sparkle. **182m/C; DVD.** *GB* Peter O'Toole; David Tennant; Rose Byrne; Laura Fraser; Rupert Penry-Jones; Nina Sosanya; Nickolas Grace; *D:* Sheree Folkson; *W:* Russell T. Davies; *C:* Anthony Radcliffe; *M:* Murray Gold. **TV**

Casanova **2005 (R)** Set in Venice and loosely based on the legendary life of the 18th century womanizer. Casanova (Ledger) is running from the Roman Inquisitor Pucci (Irons) who wants to try him for heresy, which sets up an excuse for drama and disguise resulting in an unlikely clandestine relationship with Francesca (Miller), who may be Venice's first feminist writer. Don't look for a naughty glimpse of the legendary exploits of Casanova. Here he is forced posthumously to figure out that a woman's true value is her intellect...um...et tu, Casanova? If you love romantic costume comedies set in Venice and you're house-bound for the weekend, you could do worse. **108m/C; DVD.** Heath Ledger; Sienna Miller; Jeremy Irons; Oliver Platt; Lena Olin; Omid Djalili; Stephen Greif; Ken Stott; Charlie Cox; Tim (McInnerny) McInnery; Phil Davies; Paddy Ward; Helen McCrory; Leigh Lawson; Natalie Dormer; *D:* Lasse Hallstrom; *W:* Jeffrey Hatcher; Kimberly Simi; *C:* Oliver Stapleton; *M:* Alexandre Desplat.

Casanova Brown **½ 1944** Lighthearted comedy about a shy English professor (Cooper) who learns that his recent ex-wife (Wright) has had a baby (guess whose). When Cooper learns Wright has decided to give their daughter up for adoption he kidnaps the tyke and attempts fatherhood in a hotel room. When Wright finds out where he is, the twosome (who have really been in love all along) decide to remarry and be a family. Cooper, with baby and surrounded by diapers, makes a comedic sight. Based on the play "The Little Accident" by Floyd Dell and Thomas Mitchell. **94m/B; VHS, DVD, Blu-Ray.** Gary Cooper; Teresa Wright; Frank Morgan; Anita Louise; Patricia Collinge; Edmund Breon; Jill Esmond; Emory Parnell; Isobel Elsom; Mary Treen; Halliwell Hobbes; *D:* Sam Wood; *W:* Nunnally Johnson; *M:* Arthur Lange.

Casanova '70 **½ 1965** Mastroianni plays a handsome soldier who has a knack for enticing liberated women in this comic rendition of the much-cinematized legendary yarn. Trouble is, he's in the mood only when he believes that he's in imminent danger. In Italian with English subtitles. **113m/C; VHS, DVD, Blu-Ray.** *IT* Marcello Mastroianni; Virna Lisi; Michele Mercier; Guido Alberti; Margaret Lee; Bernard Blier; Liana Orfei; *D:* Mario Monicelli; *W:* Tonino Guerra.

Casanova's Big Night **½ 1954** Classic slapstick comedy stars Hope masquerading as Casanova to test Fontaine's virtue before her marriage to a duke. The all-star cast provides one hilarious scene after another in this dated film. Price has a cameo as the "real" Casanova. Based on a story by Aubrey Wisberg. **85m/C; VHS, DVD.** Bob Hope; Joan Fontaine; Audrey Dalton; Basil Rathbone; Hugh Marlowe; Vincent Price; John Carradine; Raymond Burr; *D:* Norman Z. McLeod; *W:* Hal Kanter; Edmund L. Hartmann; *C:* Lionel Lindon.

The Case Against Brooklyn **1958** Based on a true story of corruption. A cop task force is given the go-ahead by the D.A. to smash a violent Brooklyn betting syndicate. Rookie Pete Harris (McGavin) goes undercover but learns that his superiors are actually working with the racketeers. **80m/B; DVD, Blu-Ray.** Darren McGavin; Warren Stevens; Margaret (Maggie) Hayes; Peggy McCay; Tol Avery; Emile Meyer; Nestor Paiva; Robert Osterloh; Joe Turkel; Brian Hutton; Joe De Santis; *D:* Paul Wendkos; *W:* Bernard Gordon; *C:* Fred H. Jackman, Jr.; *M:* Mischa Bakaleinikoff.

The Case for Christ **2017 (PG)** A drama based on the true story of how reporter Lee Strobel (Vogel) went from atheist to Christ follower. In 1980, Lee was working at the Chicago Tribune when his wife Leslie (Christensen) becomes a born again Christian. Using his investigative skills to prove to her that Christianity is malarkey and God that does not exist, Lee consults experts in medicine, psychiatry, archaeology, and religion. Though Leslie is patient with him as their marriage flounders, Lee struggles with what he learns and questions his own beliefs. Though faith affirming and appealing for fans of author Strobel, the film is uneven and sometimes overly sentimental. **112m/C; DVD.** Mike Vogel; Erika Christensen; Faye Dunaway; Frankie Faison; Robert Forster; *D:* Joe Gunn; *W:* Brian Bird; *C:* Brian Shanley; *M:* Will Musser.

The Case for Christmas **2011** As a kid, Braxton Bennett (Flatman) was always on Santa's naughty list; now a disgruntled adult, Braxton sues Santa (Buza) for emotional distress for not getting the gifts he wanted. Santa requires a lawyer and hires widowed dad Michael Silverman (Cain), who needs some holiday spirit himself. Hallmark Channel movie. **87m/C; DVD.** Dean Cain; George Buza; Barry Flatman; Rachel Blanchard; Helen Colliander; Alan C. Peterson; *D:* Timothy Bond; *M:* Stacey Hersh. **CABLE**

The Case of the Black Cat **½ 1936** Cortez assumed the role of Perry Mason for one film that conveniently forgot about Perry and Della getting married in the previous pic. Perry's called to change the will of invalid Peter Laxter, who winds up murdered. Perry represents the accused killer. Original director Alan Crosland died during production and William McGann took over. **66m/B; DVD.** Ricardo Cortez; June Travis; Jane Bryan; Carlyle Moore, Jr.; Garry Owen; Bill "Wild Bill" Elliott; Harry Davenport; *D:* William McGann; *W:* F. Hugh Herbert; *C:* Allen Siegler.

The Case of the Bloody Iris *Perche Quelle Strane Gocce di Sangre sul Corpo di Jennifer?; What Are Those Strange Drops of Blood on the Body of Jennifer?* **1972** Models and friends Jennifer (French) and Marilyn (Quattrini) move into an apartment building where two women have already been killed. The police suspect Andrea Barto (Hilton), who not only owns the apartment building but a modeling agency, and who knew both women. Soon, Jennifer realizes she is being stalked but there are several candidates, including her estranged husband who belongs to a weird sex cult. Italian with subtitles. **94m/C; DVD.** *IT* Edwige Fenech; George Hilton; Giampiero Albertini; Paola Quattrini; Jorge (George) Rigaud; *D:* Giuliano Carnimeo; *W:* Ernesto Gastaldi; *C:* Stelvio Massi; *M:* Bruno Nicolai.

The Case of the Curious Bride 𝒿𝒿 **1935** Rhoda, a former flame of Perry Mason's, asks his advice when her cad of a first husband, who was presumed dead, turns up alive. He's also demanding a payoff since Rhoda has remarried into money. The louse winds up dead, and Mason defends Rhoda on a murder charge. Errol Flynn has the bit role of the murdered Moxley. Besides Della, Mason also gets a familiar sidekick--Paul Drake--here known as "Spudsy." Second in the series. **80m/B; DVD.** Warren William; Margaret Lindsay; Claire Dodd; Allen Jenkins; Donald Woods; Errol Flynn; *D:* Michael Curtiz; *W:* Tom Reed; *C:* David Abel; *M:* Bernhard Kaun.

The Case of the Frightened Lady 𝒿 *The Frightened Lady* **1939** A homicidal family does its collective best to keep its dark past a secret in order to collect some inheritance money. Watch, if you're still awake, for the surprise ending. **80m/B; VHS, DVD.** *GB* Marius Goring; Helen Haye; Penelope Dudley Ward; Felix Aylmer; Patrick Barr; *D:* George King.

The Case of the Howling Dog 𝒿𝒿 ½ **1934** The first of six films in Warner Bros. "Perry Mason" series based on the Erle Stanley Gardner novel. Jittery Arthur Cartwright comes to Mason's office complaining about his neighbor's dog but also to have Perry draw up a new will. Cartwright becomes a murder victim and the attorney is left with a confusing case that involves the dog and its owner. Warren William would play Mason for the first four films. **74m/B; DVD.** Warren William; Mary Astor; Helen Trenholme; Grant Mitchell; Gordon Westcott; Russell Hicks; Allen Jenkins; *D:* Alan Crosland; *W:* Ben Markson; *C:* William Rees.

The Case of the Lucky Legs 𝒿 ½ **1935** The third in the Warner Bros. series. Perry Mason is a high-living, interminably hungover tippler who winces and wisecracks as he unravels the case of the corpse of a crooked con man. William, who left after the fourth film, when the series was downgraded to "B" status, plays the esquire; Tobin is, once again, his smart-mouthed secretary Della, and Ellis is the tomato suspected of murder. **76m/B; DVD.** Warren William; Genevieve Tobin; Patricia Ellis; Porter Hall; Allen Jenkins; Lyle Talbot; Barton MacLane; Peggy Shannon; *D:* Archie Mayo; *W:* Brown Holmes; Ben Markson; *C:* Tony Gaudio.

The Case of the Scorpion's Tail 𝒿𝒿 *La Coda dello Scorpione* **1971** A series of murders follows a million-dollar insurance settlement, which brings investigator Peter Lynch (Hilton) looking into the situation. Reporter Cleo Dupont (Strindberg) helps out and becomes a potential victim. Set in Athens. Italian with subtitles. **90m/C; DVD, Blu-Ray.** *IT* George Hilton; Anita Strindberg; Alberto De Mendoza; Ida Galli; Janine Reynaud; Luigi Pistilli; *D:* Sergio Martino; *W:* Ernesto Gastaldi; Sauro Scavolini; Eduardo Brochero; *C:* Emilio Foriscot; *M:* Bruno Nicolai.

The Case of the Stuttering Bishop 𝒿 ½ **1937** Woods took over from Cortez in the sixth and last pic in the Perry Mason series. Two women (both named Janice) claim to be the heir to a fortune, an Australian Bishop asks Mason to clear a woman of an old manslaughter charge, and there's a murder. **70m/B; DVD.** Donald Woods; Ann Dvorak; Anne Nagel; Linda Perry; Gordon Oliver; Joseph Crehan; Mira McKinney; *D:* William Clemens; *W:* Kenneth Gamet; *C:* Rexford Wimpy.

A Case of You 𝒿 ½ **2013 (R)** Bland indie rom com with an annoying lead character. Work-for-hire Brooklyn writer Sam (Long) falls for free-spirit barista Birdie (Wood) and studies her Facebook profile so he can become her ideal guy. He arranges an 'accidental' meeting but then tries too hard until you wonder why Birdie would be interested in a guy so obviously insecure. Co-writer Long must have called on his friends since lots of familiar faces pop in for a scene or two. **91m/C; DVD, Blu-Ray.** Justin Long; Evan Rachel Wood; Keir O'Donnell; Vince Vaughn; Sam Rockwell; Brendan Fraser; Peter Dinklage; Busy Philipps; Sienna Miller; Peter Billingsley; *D:* Kat Coiro; *W:* Justin Long; Keir O'Donnell; Christian Long; *C:* Doug Chamberlain; *M:* Mateo Messina.

Case 39 𝒿 ½ **2010 (R)** Shot in 2006, this silly-not-frightening killer kiddie pic finds social worker Emily Jenkins (Zellweger) needing a foster care family for troubled 10-year-old Lilith (Ferland) after her parents try to kill her. But they obviously know more about the little horror than Emily does, although she's going to learn the hard way when she foolishly decides to take Lilith in herself. Even more disturbing then little Lillith's evilness is the reason why this was released after sitting around for four years. **109m/C; Blu-Ray, On Demand.** Renée Zellweger; Jodelle Ferland; Ian McShane; Bradley Cooper; Callum Keith Rennie; Adrian Lester; Cynthia Stevenson; Georgia Craig; Kerry O'Malley; *D:* Christian Alvart; *W:* Christian Alvart; Ray Wright; *C:* Hagen Bogdanski; *M:* Michi Britsch.

Casey's Shadow 𝒿𝒿 **1978 (PG)** The eight-year-old son of an impoverished horse trainer raises a quarter horse and enters it in the world's richest horse race. **116m/C; VHS, DVD.** Walter Matthau; Alexis Smith; Robert Webber; Murray Hamilton; *D:* Martin Ritt; *C:* John A. Alonzo.

Ca$h 𝒿 ½ *Bullets, Blood & a Fistful of Cash* **2006 (R)** If you looking for a lot of brutal mayhem then this crime pic is for you, cliches and all. In one busy and bloody day (shown with various time shifts), ex-con bank robber Cash is left for dead after being double-crossed by his partners, who are all involved in a turf war. Cash himself wants revenge on kingpin Hector Gonzales, who murdered Cash's wife. **115m/C; DVD.** Tom Doty; Jerry Lloyd; Roy Stanton; Rodrigo DeMedeiros; Phil Randoy; Toan Le; Thi Nguyen; Dex Manley; Kori K. Just; *D:* Sam Akina; *W:* Sam Akina; *C:* Sam Akina; *M:* Jahn Titterness. **VIDEO**

Cash 𝒿𝒿 **2008** Slick caper flick with a lot of twists. When Cash's brother is killed by a rival during a botched scam, he teams up with various criminals to get revenge in a series of elaborate heists and schemes set in Paris and Monaco. French with subtitles. **100m/C; DVD.** *FR* Jean Dujardin; Jean Reno; Valeria Golino; Alice Taglioni; Francois Berleand; Caroline Proust; Jocelyn Quivrin; Ciaran Hinds; Clovis Cornillac; *D:* Eric Besnard; *W:* Eric Besnard; *C:* Gilles Henry; *M:* Jean-Michel Bernard.

Cash Crop 𝒿𝒿 ½ *Harvest* **1998 (R)** Kids try to protect their farmer parents who decided to grow marijuana in order to pay off big debts. The DEA shows up, coming into conflict with the local sheriff, who's sympathetic to the farmers' plight. Fairly even-handed treatment, confounding expectations of an easy stoner comedy. **96m/C; VHS, DVD.** Mary McCormack; John Slattery; James Van Der Beek; Jeffrey DeMunn; Wil Horneff; Frederick Weller; Paula Garces; Julianne Nicholson; Lisa Emery; Josh(ua) Lucas; Evan Handler; *D:* Stuart Burkin; *W:* Stuart Burkin; James Bieberman; David A. Korn; *C:* Oliver Bokelberg; *M:* Paul Rabjohns. **VIDEO**

Cash McCall 𝒿𝒿 ½ **1960** McCall (Garner) is a corporate raider who just loves making money. But problems come in when he falls for the lovely daughter (Wood) of his latest takeover target, failing businessman Jagger. Based on the novel by Cameron Hawley. **116m/C; VHS, DVD.** James Garner; Natalie Wood; Dean Jagger; Nina Foch; E.G. Marshall; Henry Jones; Otto Kruger; Roland Winters; Parley Baer; Dabbs Greer; *D:* Joseph Pevney; *W:* Lenore Coffee; Marion Hargrove; *C:* George J. Folsey; *M:* Max Steiner.

Cash on Demand 𝒿𝒿 **1961** Claustrophobic crime caper from Hammer studios. Criminal Hepburn (Morell) kidnaps the wife and son of stuffy bank manager Fordyce (Cushing) to ensure his aid in robbing the joint, passing himself off as an insurance company detective. However, Fordyce's employees get suspicious and he must plead with them to not inform the police, who are actually already aware of the situation. **84m/B; DVD.** *GB* Peter Cushing; Andre Morell; Richard Vernon; Norman Bird; Kevin Stoney; Vera Cook; Barry Lowe; *D:* Quentin Lawrence; *W:* David Chantler; Lewis Greifer; *C:* Arthur Grant; *M:* Wilfred Josephs.

Cashback 𝒿𝒿 **2006 (R)** After a painful break-up, art student Ben Willis develops insomnia. So he decides to get a job working the late shift at the supermarket, where he becomes interested in checkout girl Sharon. Ben can freeze time—so he does, and wanders around the store, mostly stripping down unsuspecting women, drawing them, and then re-dressing them. It sounds sleazier than it actually is, but still. Ick. **90m/C; DVD.** *UK* Sean Biggerstaff; Emilia Fox; Shaun Evans; Michael Dixon; Michelle Ryan; Stuart Goodman; Marc Pickering; Michael Lambourne; *D:* Sean Ellis; *W:* Sean Ellis; *C:* Angus Hudson; *M:* Guy Farley.

Casino 𝒿𝒿𝒿 **1995 (R)** Final part of the Scorsese underworld crime trilogy that began with "Mean Streets" and continued in "GoodFellas." Casino boss Sam "Ace" Rothstein (De Niro), his ex-hustler wife Ginger (Stone), and his loose-cannon enforcer pal Nicky (Pesci) are the principals in this lengthy, fictionalized account of how the mob lost Las Vegas in a haze of drugs, sex, coincidence, and betrayal. Flashy, intricate, and unflinchingly violent account of mob-run '70s Vegas clicks when exploring the inner workings of a major casino and its hierarchy. Although Stone shines as a hedonistic money chaser, visuals are great and the soundtrack is a killer, storyline suffers from deja vu. Pileggi again adapted the screenplay from his own book. **177m/C; VHS, DVD, Blu-Ray, HD-DVD.** Robert De Niro; Joe Pesci; Sharon Stone; James Woods; Don Rickles; Alan King; Kevin Pollak; L.Q. Jones; Dick Smothers; John (Joe Bob Briggs) Bloom; Frankie Avalon; Steve Allen; Jayne Meadows; Jerry Vale; *D:* Martin Scorsese; *W:* Nicholas Pileggi; Martin Scorsese; *C:* Robert Richardson. Golden Globes '96: Actress--Drama (Stone).

Casino Jack 𝒿𝒿 ½ *Bagman* **2010 (R)** Bio-pic of Washington DC superlobbyist Jack Abramoff (Spacey) shows how Abramoff, with help from his unscrupulous partner Michael Scanlon (Pepper), became the wealthiest, best-connected lobbyist on Capitol Hill during W's presidency. The pair ostensibly bilked hundreds of millions from Native American casino operators and spent it on influence, votes, a brilliant wardrobe and lavish lifestyle. Accurate portrayal of the excesses of greed and ego that lead to their downfall and Spacey shines in the final scene as Abramoff melts down in a tirade while answering questions during a Congressional hearing investigating corruption. **108m/C; Blu-Ray, On Demand.** Kevin Spacey; Kelly Preston; Jon Lovitz; Barry Pepper; Yannick Bisson; Eric Schweig; Christian Campbell; Maury Chakin; *D:* George Hickenlooper; *W:* Norman Snider; *C:* Adam Swica; *M:* Jonathan Goldsmith.

Casino Jack and the United States of Money 𝒿𝒿 **2010 (R)** Documentary on convicted Washington, DC political lobbyist Jack Abramoff. The superstar Republican lobbyist fell victim to hubris, got involved in a number of increasingly notorious influence-peddling political scandals, and pled guilty to fraud and bribery charges and to tax evasion in January 2006. His tactics also had some politicians resigning (former Majority Leader Tom DeLay) or also convicted (former Ohio Congressman Robert Ney). Abramoff was still in prison and not allowed to participate on camera in Gibney's film, though he was interviewed by the director. **123m/C; On Demand.** *D:* Alex Gibney; *W:* Alex Gibney; *C:* Maryse Alberti; *M:* John McCullough.

The Casino Job 𝒿𝒿 **2008 (R)** Scumbag casino owner Barry Kaylin (Mauro) rents four strippers for an evening and forces himself on one of them. The police won't arrest him, so the strippers plot revenge by stealing his money. Described by some as 'a porn film without the sex,' the movie is somewhat impressive given its incredibly low budget. **81m/C; DVD.** Amylia Joiner; Dean Munro; Iisa Martinez; Jay Antony Franke; Irina Voronina; Curtis Joe Walker; Deanna Minerva; Julia Beatty; Mokis Zavros; Warren Thomas; Barry Sharp; Kerry M. Shahan; Paul Joseph; Ken Kupstis; Brian H. Scott; Clint Wilder; Christopher J. Buzzell; *D:* Christoper Robin Hood; *W:* Nick Murphy; *C:* Jeffrey Mahon; *M:* George Dare.

The Casino Murder Case 𝒿 ½ **1935** Lukas and his Hungarian accent are problematic for his role as American sleuth Philo Vance in this contrived mystery. Vance gets word that a member of the wealthy Llewellyn family will be murdered at their casino but the poison kills someone else instead. Russell, as private secretary Doris, is the most fun to watch. **82m/B; DVD.** Paul Lukas; Alison Skipworth; Rosalind Russell; Donald Cook; Arthur Byron; Ted Healy; *D:* Edwin L. Marin; *W:* Florence Ryerson; Edgar Allan Woolf; *C:* Charles G. Clarke.

Casino Royale 𝒿 **1967** The product of five directors, three writers and a mismatched cast of dozens, this virtually plotless spoof of James Bond films can stand as one of the low-water marks for 1960s comedy. And yet, there are some marvelous bits within, in scenes of bizarre hilarity. Welles and Sellers literally couldn't stand the sight of one another, and their scenes together were filmed separately, with stand-ins. **130m/C; VHS, DVD.** David Niven; Woody Allen; Peter Sellers; Ursula Andress; Orson Welles; Jacqueline Bisset; Deborah Kerr; Peter O'Toole; Jean-Paul Belmondo; Charles Boyer; Joanna Pettet; John Huston; William Holden; George Raft; Kurt Kasznar; Terence Cooper; Barbara Bouchet; Anna Quayle; Geoffrey Bayldon; Duncan MacRae; Burt Kwouk; David Prowse; Caroline Munro; *D:* John Huston; Ken Hughes; Robert Parrish; Val Guest; Joseph McGrath; *W:* Wolf Mankowitz; John Law; Michael Sayers; *C:* Jack Hildyard; *M:* Burt Bacharach.

Casino Royale 𝒿𝒿𝒿 **2006 (PG-13)** Bond is back and Craig does not destroy the franchise as the whiners would have you believe. Based on Fleming's first (1953) novel, Bond has just achieved 007 status and is still learning his way. He may be blond(ish) but he's brutal, ruthless, and arrogant (and he bleeds). Story revolves around a high-stakes poker game with a Eurotrash banker (Mikkelsen) to terrorists and the Bond babe is Vesper Lynd (Green), a sexy, cool accountant. Dench returns as M, and she and Bond share some of the best moments as she tries to keep her "blunt instrument" in line. It's a little too long but Craig proves he can wear a tux, say "Bond...James Bond," and kill, which is what true aficionados require. **144m/C; DVD, Blu-Ray.** *GB US CZ GE* Daniel Craig; Eva Green; Mads Mikkelsen; Dame Judi Dench; Jeffrey Wright; Giancarlo Giannini; Caterina Murino; Isaach de Bankole; Simon Abkarian; Ivana Milicevic; Tobias Menzies; Claudio Santamaria; Jesper Christensen; Sebastien Foucan; *D:* Martin Campbell; *W:* Paul Haggis; Neal Purvis; Robert Wade; *C:* Phil Meheux; *M:* David Arnold. British Acad. '06: Sound.

Casper 𝒿𝒿𝒿 **1995 (PG)** World's friendliest ghost appears on the big screen with outstanding visual trickery (from Industrial Light and Magic) and a lively, if hokey, story. Evilish Carrigan Crittenden (Moriarty) inherits ghost-infested Whipstaff Manor and hires scatterbrained "ghost therapist" Dr. Harvey (Pullman) to get rid of its unwanted occupants. His daughter Kat (Ricci) is soon the object of Casper's friendly attention while the good doc must contend with Casper's mischievous uncles—Stinkie, Fatso, and Stretch. Exec producer Spielberg shows his influence with numerous topical gags and screen references that help amuse the adults while the ghosts work their magic on the kiddies. Silberling's directorial debut; based on the comic-book and TV cartoon character created more than 30 years ago. **95m/C; VHS, DVD, Blu-Ray.** Christina Ricci; Bill Pullman; Cathy Moriarty; Eric Idle; Amy Brenneman; Ben Stein; *Cameo(s):* Don Novello; Rodney Dangerfield; Clint Eastwood; Mel Gibson; Dan Aykroyd; *V:* Malachi Pearson; Joe Nipote; Joe Alaskey; Brad Garrett; *D:* Brad Silberling; *W:* Sherri Stoner; Deanna Oliver; *C:* Dean Cundey; *M:* James Horner.

Casque d'Or 𝒿𝒿𝒿 *Golden Marie* **1952** Crime passionnel in turn-of-the-century Paris as an honest carpenter (Reggiani) gets drawn into the netherworld of pimps and thieves. He's finally driven to murder—all for love of gangster's moll Marie (a very sultry Signoret). French with subtitles. **96m/B; VHS, DVD.** *FR* Serge Reggiani; Simone Signoret; Claude Dauphin; Raymond Bussieres; Gaston Modot; *D:* Jacques Becker; *W:* Jacques Becker; Jacques Companeez; *C:* Robert Lefebvre; *M:* Georges Van Parys.

Cass Timberlane 𝒿𝒿 ½ **1947** Scandalous story of a May-December romance set in a small Midwestern town. Tracy stars as Cass Timberlane, a widowed judge who falls for a voluptuous young girl from the wrong side of the tracks (Turner). They marry and experience problems when she is shunned by his snobbish friends. Good performances, especially from the supporting cast, dominate this fairly predictable film. Based on the novel by Sinclair Lewis. **119m/B; VHS, DVD.** Spencer Tracy; Lana Turner; Zachary Scott; Tom Drake; Mary Astor; Albert Dekker; Margaret Lindsay; John Litel; Mona Barrie; Josephine Hutchinson; Rose Hobart; Selena Royle; ***Cameo(s):*** Walter Pidgeon; ***D:*** George Sidney; ***W:*** Donald Ogden Stewart.

The Cassandra Crossing 1/2 **1976 (R)** A terrorist with the plague causes havoc on a transcontinental luxury train. Turgid adventure filmed in France and Italy. **129m/C; VHS, DVD, Blu-Ray.** *GB* Sophia Loren; Richard Harris; Ava Gardner; Burt Lancaster; Martin Sheen; Ingrid Thulin; Lee Strasberg; John Phillip Law; Lionel Stander; O.J. Simpson; Ann Turkel; Alida Valli; ***D:*** George P. Cosmatos; ***W:*** George P. Cosmatos; Tom Mankiewicz; ***C:*** Ennio Guarnieri; ***M:*** Jerry Goldsmith.

Cassanova Was a Woman 1/2 **2015** A comedy that explores issues related to one woman's sexuality and her identity as a Latino woman. A blonde-haired, blue-eyed Cuban American, Cassanova Canto (Montero) is a struggling as an actress but has a complicated personal life. Though still married to man, she has fallen in love with a woman. While pondering this dilemma in her life, she must manager her famous Spanish soap star mother, her anti-gay sister, and a naked guy. Through it all, she wonders what is the truth about her free-spirited self. **113m/C; DVD, Blu-Ray, Streaming, Download.** Jezabel Montero; Margo Singaliese; Paolo Andino; Chaz Mena; Jessica Blank; ***D:*** Kevin Arbouet; ***W:*** Jezabel Montero; ***C:*** Eric Hales; John Mcclung; ***M:*** Tyler Westen. **VIDEO**

Casshern 1/2 *Kasshan* **2004 (R)** Adapted from the comic (and later anime series from the 1970s) "Shinzo Ningen Kyashan." After 50 years of war between Europe and Asia, the land and people are failing quick, thanks to radiation, pollution, and manufactured diseases. A doctor believes he may have a revolutionary medical treatment that can save humanity, but ends up creating a race of superhuman mutants instead. They waste no time in reviving a robot army to go out and take over the world. In desperation the doc uses the same treatment to resurrect his dead son, and sends him out alone to stop them. Anime and video-game fans will love it for the sparse but over-the-top action scenes. **136m/C; DVD.** *JP* Yosuke Iseya; Kumiko Aso; Akira Terao; Kanako Higuchi; ***D:*** Kazuaki Kiriya; ***W:*** Kazuaki Kiriya; ***C:*** Kazuaki Kiriya; ***M:*** Shiroh Sagisu.

Cast a Dark Shadow **1955** Bogarde is the charmer who decides to reap his reward by marrying and murdering elderly women for their fortunes. But Bogarde meets his match when he plots against his latest intended (Lockwood). Tidy thriller with effective performances. Based on the play "Murder Mistaken" by Janet Green. **82m/B; VHS, DVD.** *GB* Dirk Bogarde; Margaret Lockwood; Mona Washbourne; Kay Walsh; Kathleen Harrison; Robert Flemyng; Walter Hudd; ***D:*** Lewis Gilbert; ***W:*** John Cresswell.

Cast a Giant Shadow **1966** Follows the career of Col. David "Mickey" Marcus, an American Jew and WWII hero who helped turn Israel's army into a formidable fighting force during the 1947-48 struggle for independence. **138m/C; VHS, DVD, Blu-Ray.** Kirk Douglas; Senta Berger; Angie Dickinson; John Wayne; James Donald; Topol; Frank Sinatra; Yul Brynner; ***D:*** Melville Shavelson; ***W:*** Melville Shavelson; ***C:*** Aldo Tonti; ***M:*** Elmer Bernstein.

Cast a Long Shadow 1/2 **1959** A minor B-western. A drifter (Murphy) inherits a ranch from a man who may have been his father, but the property is deeply in debt. In order to save his new home, Matt organizes a cattle drive. **82m/B; DVD.** Audie Murphy; Terry Moore; John Dehner; James Best; Denver Pyle; Ann Doran; ***D:*** Thomas Carr; ***W:*** John McGreevey; Martin Goldsmith; ***C:*** Wilfred M. Cline; ***M:*** Gerald Fried.

Cast Away 1/2 **2000 (PG-13)** Hanks first gained, and then lost, 40 pounds for his role as FedEx employee Chuck Noland, who gets marooned on a South Pacific island for four years. He does an excellent job of showing Chuck's desperation, isolation, and finally, resignation, and for a good chunk of the movie, does it without saying a single word (although later he does get to "talk" to a volleyball named Wilson). Zemeckis does his part with amazing visuals and a restrained approach to the score, which he uses sparingly. **143m/C; VHS, DVD, Blu-Ray.** Tom Hanks; Helen Hunt; Nick Searcy; Michael Forest; Viveka Davis; Chris Noth; Geoffrey Blake; Jenifer Lewis; David Allan Brooks; Nan Martin; Steve Monroe; ***D:*** Robert Zemeckis; ***W:*** William Broyles, Jr.; ***C:*** Don Burgess; ***M:*** Alan Silvestri. Golden Globes '01: Actor--Drama (Hanks).

Castaway 1/2 **1987 (R)** Based on the factual account by Lucy Irvine. The story of Michael Wilmington, who placed an ad for a young woman to spend a year on a Pacific atoll with him, and the battle of the sexes that followed. **118m/C; VHS, Streaming.** *GB* Oliver Reed; Amanda Donohoe; Tony Rickards; Georgina Hale; Frances Barber; Todd Rippon; ***D:*** Nicolas Roeg; ***W:*** Allan Scott; ***C:*** Harvey Harrison; ***M:*** Stanley Myers.

The Castaway Cowboy **1974 (G)** Shanghaied Texas cowboy Lincoln Constain (Garner) jumps ship in Hawaii and becomes partners with widowed Henrieatta MacAvoy (Miles) when she turns her potato farm into a cattle ranch. That means turning the islanders into cowpokes and dealing with both a local witch doctor and Henrieatta's suitor. **91m/C; VHS, DVD.** James Garner; Robert Culp; Vera Miles; ***D:*** Vincent McEveety; ***M:*** Robert F. Brunner.

The Castilian 1/2 *Valley of the Swords* **1963** Some very odd casting in this historical tale of heroism and swordplay about a Spanish nobleman who leads his followers against the invading Moors and their evil king (Crawford). Based on a 13th century poem. **128m/C; DVD.** Cesar Romero; Broderick Crawford; Alida Valli; Frankie Avalon; Espartaco (Spartaco) Santoni; Fernando Rey; Jorge (George) Rigaud; ***D:*** Javier Seto; ***W:*** Sidney W. Pink.

The Castle **1997 (R)** The Kerrigans are a working class clan who happily live directly adjacent to Melbourne's Tullamarine airport. But when the airport decides to expand, their house is subject to a compulsory acquisition order. However, Daryl Kerrigan (Caton) decides to fight and takes their case all the way to the High Court in Canberra. It's a David vs. Goliath comedy with an Aussie disdain for authority figures. Cultural references may not travel overseas but the film was a hit on its home turf. **93m/C; VHS, DVD.** *AU* Michael Caton; Charles "Bud" Tingwell; Sophie Lee; Anne Tenney; Eric Bana; Stephen Curry; Anthony Simcoe; Wayne Hope; Tiriel Mora; ***D:*** Rob Sitch; ***W:*** Rob Sitch; Santo Cilauro; Tom Gleisner; Jane Kennedy; ***C:*** Miriana Marusic; ***M:*** Craig Harnath. Australian Film Inst. '97: Orig. Screenplay.

Castle Freak **1995 (R)** Italian countess leaves her creepy haunted castle to her American nephew and his family. They find an unwelcome surprise lurking in the cellar. **90m/C; VHS, DVD, Blu-Ray.** Jeffrey Combs; Barbara Crampton; Jonathan Fuller; Jessica Dollarhide; ***D:*** Stuart Gordon; ***W:*** Dennis Paoli; ***C:*** Mario Vulpiani; ***M:*** Richard Band.

Castle Keep **1969** One of the most bizarre war films ever made. Eight battle-weary American soldiers, led by a randy one-eyed major (Lancaster), make a defiant last stand in a fairytale medieval castle against the German assault on the Ardennes in WWII. Loopy surreal parable pushes past every boundary of good taste and stays enjoyable to the end. Full of great memorable characters and silly over-the top moments that almost always work, such as an impotent count (Aumont) pimping out his wife to German and American alike to keep the dynasty going, and a soldier (Falk) who takes over the local village bakery, waxing poetically about the superiority of bread to war. The whole film is absurdly done up in full sixties regalia and topped off with a loungy Michel Legrand soundtrack. A forgotten camp treasure. **105m/C; VHS, DVD.** Burt Lancaster; Patrick O'Neal; Jean-Pierre Aumont; Peter Falk; Astrid Heeren; Scott Wilson; Tony Bill; Bruce Dern; Al Freeman, Jr.; James Patterson; Michael Conrad; Caterina Boratto; Olga Bisera; Harry Baird; Ernest Clark; ***D:*** Sydney Pollack; ***W:*** David Rayfiel; Daniel Taradash; ***C:*** Henri Decae; ***M:*** Michel Legrand.

Castle of Blood *Castle of Terror; Coffin of Terror; Danza Macabra; Dimensions in Death; Terrore* **1964** Staying overnight in a haunted castle, a poet is forced to deal with a number of creepy encounters. Cult favorite Steele enhances this atmospheric chiller. Dubbed in English. **85m/B; VHS, DVD.** *IT FR* Barbara Steele; George Riviere; Margrete Robsahm; Henry Kruger; Silvano Tranquilli; Sylvia Sorente; ***D:*** Anthony M. Dawson; ***W:*** Jean (Giovanni Grimaldi) Grimaud; ***C:*** Riccardo (Pallton) Pallottini; ***M:*** Riz Ortolani.

The Castle of Cagliostro **1980** Animated Japanese adventure tale featuring a hero named Wolf, who's a thief. Wolf infiltrates the suspicious country of Cagliostro, whose one industry is conterfeiting money, and winds up rescuing a princess. Lots of violence to go with the action. In Japanese with English subtitles. **100m/C; VHS, DVD.** *JP* ***V:*** David Hayter; Bridget Hoffman; Dorothy Elias-Fahn; Kirk Thornton; ***D:*** Hayao Miyazaki; ***C:*** Hirokata Takahashi; ***M:*** Yuji Ono.

The Castle of Fu Manchu *Assignment: Istanbul; Die Folterkammer des Dr. Fu Manchu* **1968 (PG)** The final chapter in a series starring Lee as the wicked doctor. This time, Lee has developed a gadget which will put the earth into a deep freeze, and at his mercy. To fine tune this contraption, he enlists the help of a gifted scientist by abducting him. However, the helper/hostage has a bad ticker, so Lee must abduct a heart surgeon to save his life, and thus, the freezer project. Most critics felt this was the weakest installment in the series. **92m/C; VHS, DVD, Blu-Ray.** *GE SP IT GB* Christopher Lee; Richard Greene; Howard Marion-Crawford; Tsai Chin; Gunther Stoll; Rosalba Neri; Maria Perschy; Werner Abrolat; Jose Martin; ***D:*** Jess (Jesus) Franco; ***W:*** Harry Alan Towers; ***C:*** Manuel Merino; ***M:*** Gert Wilden.

Castle of the Creeping Flesh **WOOF! 1968** A surgeon's daughter is brutally murdered. Vowing to bring her back he begins ripping out the organs of innocent people and transplanting them into her body. Has the dubious honor of being one of the few movies to sport actual open heart surgery footage. So bad it's...just bad. **85m/C; VHS, DVD, Streaming.** Adrian Hoven; Janine Reynaud; Howard Vernon; ***D:*** Percy G. Parker.

Castle of the Living Dead *Il Castello de Morti Vivi* **1964** Evil Count Drago's hobbies include mummifying a traveling circus group visiting his castle. Lee is as evil as ever, but be sure to look for Sutherland's screen debut. In a dual role, he plays not only the bumbling inspector, but also a witch, in drag. **90m/B; VHS, DVD.** *IT FR* Christopher Lee; Gaia Germani; Phillippe LeRoy; Jacques Stanislawsky; Donald Sutherland; ***D:*** Herbert Wise.

Castle on the Hudson **1940** This Warner Bros. prison saga is a remake of 1933's "20,000 Years in Sing Sing" with Garfield taking on Spencer Tracy's role. Cocky jewel thief Tommy Gordon gets sent to the big house but thinks his friends will get him off. Instead he's looking at a long stretch of time unless his girlfriend Kay (Sheridan) can get shifty lawyer Crowley (Cowan) to get Tommy paroled. Kay winds up in serious difficulties and there's more trouble brewing. **71m/B; DVD.** John Garfield; Ann Sheridan; Pat O'Brien; Jerome Cowan; Burgess Meredith; Guinn "Big Boy" Williams; Henry O'Neill; John Litel; ***D:*** Anatole Litvak; ***W:*** Brown Holmes; Seton I. Miller; Courtney Terrett; ***C:*** Arthur Edeson.

Casual Encounters **2016 (R)** A comedy about the quirky world of online dating. Justin (Killam) is humiliated when his girlfriend breaks up with him in public. His friends from his office convince him to try online dating in the form of a website called Casual Encounters, and Justin has odd experiences among with women also seeking a connection. A female office mate, Laura (Decker), shows him there may be a better way of finding true love again. **82m/C; DVD, Streaming, Download.** Taran Killam; Brooklyn Decker; David Krumholtz; Mark Boone, Jr.; David Arquette; ***D:*** Zackary Adler; ***W:*** Sebastian J. Michael; Erik Steinmetz; ***C:*** Peter Holland; ***M:*** Devon Culiner. **VIDEO**

Casual Sex? 1/2 **1988 (R)** Two young women, looking for love and commitment, take a vacation at a posh resort where they are confronted by men with nothing on their minds but sex, be it casual or the more formal black-tie variety. Supposedly an examination of safe sex in a lightly comedic vein, though the comic is too light and the morality too limp. Adapted from the play by Wendy Goldman and Judy Toll. **87m/C; VHS, DVD, Blu-Ray.** Lea Thompson; Victoria Jackson; Stephen Shellen; Jerry Levine; Mary Gross; Andrew Silverstein; ***D:*** Genevieve Robert; ***W:*** William Goldman; Judy Toll; ***C:*** Rolf Kestermann; ***M:*** Van Dyke Parks.

Casualties **1997 (R)** Annie's (Goodall) got very unfortunate luck with men. Her abusive husband Bill's (Gries) a cop and she can't safely get away from home. Then she meets a seemingly nice guy, Tommy (Harmon), at her cooking class, who offers to help Annie out. But when Tommy's behavior becomes erratic (turns out he's a hitman), Annie figures she just has to rely on herself. **86m/C; VHS, Streaming.** Mark Harmon; Caroline Goodall; Michael Beach; Jon(athan) Gries; John Diehl; ***D:*** Alex Graves; ***W:*** Alex Graves.

Casualties of War **1989 (R)** A Vietnam war morality play about army private Fox in the bush who refuses to let his fellow soldiers and commanding sergeant (Penn) skirt responsibility for the rape and murder of a native woman. Fox achieves his dramatic breakthrough. Based on the true story by Daniel Lang. **120m/C; VHS, DVD, Blu-Ray.** Sean Penn; Michael J. Fox; Don Harvey; Thuy Thu Le; John Leguizamo; Sam Robards; John C. Reilly; Erik King; Dale Dye; ***D:*** Brian De Palma; ***W:*** David Rabe; ***C:*** Stephen Burum; ***M:*** Ennio Morricone.

CAT. 8 **2013** Reelz Channel doomsday miniseries where the 'science' is, as usual, laughable. Physicist Michael Ranger abandons his idea about harnessing the sun's energy through solar flares when the Pentagon wants to use the breakthrough as a weapon. That doesn't stop his former assistant going head and the situation getting completely out of control with the government trying for a cover-up as Earth is (again) threatened with destruction. **180m/C; DVD, Blu-Ray.** *CA* Matthew Modine; Maxim Roy; Ted Whitfall; Alain Goulem; Susan Hogan; ***D:*** Kevin Fair; ***W:*** Donald Martin; ***C:*** Brian Couture; ***M:*** Michel Corriveau. **CABLE**

The Cat and the Canary **1927** A group of greedy relatives gather on a stormy night in a creepy mansion for the reading of a 20-year-old will. But before anyone can claim the money, they must spend the night in the manor—and an escaped lunatic is at large! Remade twice, once in 1939 and again in 1979. **81m/B; Silent; VHS, DVD, Blu-Ray.** Laura La Plante; Creighton Hale; Tully Marshall; Gertrude Astor; Arthur Edmund Carewe; Lucien Littlefield; ***D:*** Paul Leni; ***W:*** Robert F. "Bob" Hill; Alfred A. Cohn; ***C:*** Gilbert Warrenton.

The Cat and the Canary 1/2 **1939** In this 'old dark house' comic mystery, lawyer Crosby (Zucco) gathers the prospective heirs of an eccentric millionaire at the deceased Bayou mansion. Spineless, wisecracking Wally (Hope) tries to protect beautiful Joyce (Goddard), the main beneficiary, from being driven crazy (she loses the money if declared insane) amidst trap doors, hidden passageways, swiveling bookcases, and a spooky housekeeper (Songergaard) and her black cat. **72m/B; DVD.** Bob Hope; Paulette Goddard; John Beal; Douglass Montgomery; Gale Sondergaard; George Zucco; Elizabeth Patterson; ***D:*** Elliott Nugent; ***W:*** Walter DeLeon; Lynn Starling; ***C:*** Charles B(ryant) Lang, Jr.; ***M:*** Ernst Toch.

The Cat and the Canary **1979 (PG)** A stormy night, a gloomy mansion, and a mysterious will combine to create an atmosphere for murder. An entertaining remake of the 1927 silent film. **96m/C; VHS, DVD.** *GB* Carol Lynley; Michael Callan; Wendy Hiller; Olivia Hussey; Daniel Massey; Honor Blackman; Edward Fox; Wilfrid Hyde-White; Beatrix Lehmann; Peter McEnery; ***D:*** Radley Metzger; ***W:*** Radley Metzger; ***C:*** Alex Thomson.

The Cat and the Fiddle 🦴🦴🦴 **1934** Lovely Jerome Kern-Oscar Hammerstein operetta in which Novarro plays a struggling composer who forces his affections on MacDonald. She sings in response to his romantic proposals. The final sequence is in color. **90m/B; DVD.** Ramon Novarro; Jeanette MacDonald; Frank Morgan; Charles Butterworth; Jean Hersholt; Vivienne Segal; Frank Conroy; Henry Armetta; Adrienne D'Ambricourt; Joseph Cawthorn; ***D:*** William K. Howard; ***W:*** Bella Spewack; Samuel Spewack; Jerome Kern; ***C:*** Charles G. Clarke; Ray Rennahan; Harold Rosson; ***M:*** Herbert Stothart; Jerome Kern.

Cat Ballou 🦴🦴🦴 **1/2 1965** At the turn of the century, a schoolmarm turns outlaw with the help of a drunken gunman. Marvin played Kid Shelleen and his silver-nosed evil twin Tim Strawn in this cheery spoof of westerns. Cole and Kaye sing the narration in a one of a kind Greek chorus. **96m/C; VHS, DVD, Blu-Ray.** Jane Fonda; Lee Marvin; Michael Callan; Dwayne Hickman; Reginald Denny; Nat King Cole; Stubby Kaye; Robert Phillips; ***D:*** Elliot Silverstein; ***W:*** Frank Pierson; ***C:*** Jack Marta; ***M:*** Frank DeVol. Oscars '65: Actor (Marvin); Berlin Intl. Film Fest. '65: Actor (Marvin); British Acad. '65: Actor (Marvin); Golden Globes '66: Actor--Mus./Comedy (Marvin); Natl. Bd. of Review '65: Actor (Marvin).

Cat Chaser 🦴🦴 **1990** Weller walks listlessly through the role of an ex-soldier in Miami who has an affair with the wife of an exiled—but still lethal—military dictator. Surprisingly low-key, sometimes effective thriller that saves its energy for sex scenes, also available in a less steamy, 90-minute "R" rated version. Based on an Elmore Leonard novel. **97m/C; VHS, DVD.** Kelly McGillis; Peter Weller; Charles Durning; Frederic Forrest; Tomas Milian; Juan Fernandez; ***D:*** Abel Ferrara; ***W:*** Elmore Leonard; Jim Borrelli; ***M:*** Chick Corea.

Cat City 🦴 **1/2 2008 (R)** Predictable thriller has lawyer Victoria Compton learning from PI Harold that her horndog real estate developer hubby Nick had an affair with her law partner. Nick has bigger problems since the financing for a planned casino in Cathedral City has gone bust and he has a particularly aggressive investor wanting his money back. **90m/C; DVD.** Rebecca Pidgeon; Julian Sands; Brian Dennehy; Shawn Huff; Alano Massi; Edward Kerr; William Shockley; ***D:*** Brent Huff; ***W:*** Brent Huff; Douglas Walton; ***C:*** Rudy Harbon; ***M:*** Tor Hyams. **VIDEO**

The Cat from Outer Space 🦴🦴 **1978 (G)** An extraterrestrial cat named Jake crashes his spaceship on Earth and leads a group of people on endless escapades. Enjoyable Disney fare. **103m/C; VHS, DVD.** Ken Berry; Sandy Duncan; Harry (Henry) Morgan; Roddy McDowall; McLean Stevenson; ***D:*** Norman Tokar; ***W:*** Ted Key; ***C:*** Charles F. Wheeler; ***M:*** Lalo Schifrin.

A Cat in Paris 🦴🦴 **1/2 2011** In this old-school animated adventure that's something of a spoof of the crime/thriller genre, French kitty Dino leads a double life: by day he's the pet of seven-year-old Zoe and by night he assists burglar Nico. When Dino comes home with a bracelet Zoe's cop mom Jeanne recognizes as stolen property, Zoe follows her cat and it leads her to sinister gangster Victor Costa. French with subtitles. **65m/C; DVD, Blu-Ray.** *FR BE* ***V:*** Oriane Zani; Dominique Blanc; Bruno Salomone; Jean Benguigui; Bernard Bouillon; Bernadette LaFont; ***D:*** Jean-Loup Felicioli; Alain Gagnol; ***W:*** Alain Gagnol; Jacques-Remy Girerd; ***M:*** Serge Besset.

Cat in the Cage 🦴 **1/2 1968** A young man finds many things have changed at home while he was in a mental institution. Dad has remarried, the housekeeper is practicing witchcraft, the chauffeur is after his mistress, and the cat is gone. So where'd that cat go? **96m/C; VHS, DVD.** Colleen Camp; Sybil Danning; Mel Novak; Frank De Kova; ***D:*** Tony Zarin Dast.

The Cat o' Nine Tails 🦴 **1971 (PG)** A blind detective and a newsman team up to find a sadistic killer. A gory murder mystery. **112m/C; VHS, DVD, Blu-Ray.** *GE FR IT* Karl Malden; James Franciscus; Catherine Spaak; Cinzia de Carolis; Carlo Alighiero; ***D:*** Dario Argento; ***W:*** Dario Argento; ***C:*** Erico Menczer; ***M:*** Ennio Morricone.

Cat on a Hot Tin Roof 🦴🦴🦴 **1/2 1958** Tennessee Williams' powerful play about greed and deception in a patriarchal Southern family. Big Daddy (Ives) is dying. Members of the family greedily attempt to capture his inheritance, tearing the family apart. Taylor is a sensual wonder as Maggie the Cat, though the more controversial elements of the play were toned down for the film version. Intense, believable performances from Ives and Newman. **108m/C; VHS, DVD, Blu-Ray.** Paul Newman; Burl Ives; Elizabeth Taylor; Jack Carson; Judith Anderson; ***D:*** Richard Brooks; ***W:*** Richard Brooks; James Poe; ***C:*** William H. Daniels.

Cat on a Hot Tin Roof 🦴🦴 **1/2 1984** Showtime/PBS co-production of the Tennesse Williams classic about alcoholic exjock Brick (Jones) and his sultry wife Maggie (Lange) and their desires. This version uses a script revised by Williams to revive some of the sexual frankness watered down in other productions. **122m/C; VHS, DVD.** Tommy Lee Jones; Jessica Lange; Rip Torn; Kim Stanley; David Dukes; Penny Fuller; ***D:*** Jack Hofsiss; ***W:*** Tennessee Williams. **TV**

Cat People 🦴🦴🦴 **1942** Irena (Simon) is an immigrant from the Balkans who believes in a curse that will change her into a deadly panther who must kill to survive. So she won't consummate her marriage to Oliver (Smith). When he confides her troubles to co-worker Alice (Randolph), Irena's jealousy precipitates her transformation as she stalks Alice. A classic among the horror genre with unrelenting terror from beginning to end, especially since the metamorphosis is only suggested. First horror film from RKO producer Val Lewton. **73m/B; VHS, DVD, Blu-Ray.** Simone Simon; Kent Smith; Jane Randolph; Jack Holt; Elizabeth Russell; Alan Napier; Tom Conway; ***D:*** Jacques Tourneur; ***W:*** DeWitt Bodeen; ***C:*** Nicholas Musuraca; ***M:*** Roy Webb. Natl. Film Reg. '93.

Cat People 🦴🦴 **1/2 1982 (R)** A beautiful young woman learns that she has inherited a strange family trait—she turns into a vicious panther when sexually aroused. The only person with whom she can safely mate is her brother, a victim of the same genetic heritage. Kinski is mesmerizing as the innocent, sensual woman. Remake of the 1942 film. **118m/C; VHS, DVD, Blu-Ray, HD-DVD.** Nastassja Kinski; Malcolm McDowell; John Heard; Annette O'Toole; Ruby Dee; Ed Begley, Jr.; John Larroquette; ***D:*** Paul Schrader; ***W:*** Alan Ormsby; ***C:*** John Bailey; ***M:*** Giorgio Moroder.

Cat Run 🦴 **1/2 2011 (R)** Inconsequential action-comedy. High-priced hooker Catalina makes off with a surveillance disc containing footage of American politician Krebb accidentally killing an escort during their liaison. He wants the evidence back at all costs, which means hiring ladylike-but-lethal assassin Helen to retrieve it. Cat has a couple of would-be PIs as her bodyguards as they dash around Eastern Europe trying to figure out what to do (kinda like the flick). **107m/C; DVD, Blu-Ray.** Paz Vega; Janet McTeer; Alphonso McAuley; Scott Mechlowicz; Christopher McDonald; Karel Roden; D.L. Hughley; ***D:*** John Stockwell; ***W:*** Nick Ball; John Niven; ***C:*** Jean-Francois Hensgens; ***M:*** Devin Powers.

Cat Women of the Moon 🦴🦴 *Rocket to the Moon* **1953** Scientists land on the moon and encounter an Amazon-like force of skimpily attired female chauvinists. Remade as "Missile to the Moon." Featuring the Hollywood Cover Girls as various cat women. Available in its original 3-D format. **65m/B; VHS, DVD.** Sonny Tufts; Victor Jory; Marie Windsor; Bill Phipps; Douglas Fowley; Carol Brewster; Suzanne Alexander; Susan Morrow; Ellye Marshall; Bette Arlen; Judy W; Roxann Delman; ***D:*** Arthur Hilton; ***W:*** Roy Hamilton; ***C:*** William F. Whitley; ***M:*** Elmer Bernstein.

Cataclysm 🦴🦴 **1/2** *Satan's Supper* **1981 (R)** A swell flick about a sadistic demon who spends his time either finding people willing to join him or killing the people who won't. **94m/C; VHS, DVD.** Cameron Mitchell; Marc Lawrence; Faith Clift; Charles Moll; ***D:*** Tom McGowan; Gregg Tallas; Philip Marshak.

Catacombs 🦴 **1/2** *The Woman Who Wouldn't Die* **1964** Raymond blackmails his crippled, wealthy wife Ellen's unscrupulous attorney Corbett into helping murder her so he can inherit her fortune and get involved with her pretty niece Alice. After the crime is committed, Raymond starts believing Ellen is haunting him. **85m/B; DVD.** *GB* Gary Merrill; Georgina Cookson; Neil McCallum; Jane Merrow; Rachel Thomas; Frederick Piper; ***D:*** Gordon Hessler; ***W:*** Daniel Mainwaring; ***C:*** Arthur Lavis; ***M:*** Carlo Martelli.

Catacombs 🦴 **2007** The running and screaming turns out to be remarkably boring. Nervous Victoria (Sossamon) heads to Paris to visit her naughty sister Caroline (Moore) who insists on taking her to a secret rave held in the catacombs, the limestone tunnels that run for miles under the city and that house the bones of the dead. Carolyn's friends scare Victoria with a legend about a satanic cult and a flesh-eating beast and when she's separated from the group, Victoria's convinced something is stalking her. **92m/C; DVD.** Shannyn Sossamon; Alecia Moore; Emil Hostina; Mihai Stanescu; Sandi Dragoi; Cabral Ibacka; Cain Manoli; ***D:*** Tomm Coker; ***W:*** David Elliot; Tomm Coker; ***C:*** Maxime Alexandre; ***M:*** Yoshiki Hayashi. **VIDEO**

The Catamount Killing 🦴 **1/2 1974 (PG)** The story of a small town bank manager and his lover. They decide to rob the bank and run for greener pastures only to find their escape befuddled at every turn. **82m/C; VHS, DVD, Streaming.** *GE* Horst Buchholz; Ann Wedgeworth; ***D:*** Krzysztof Zanussi.

Catch a Fire 🦴🦴 **1/2 2006 (PG-13)** Fierce political drama centering on the Apartheid-era terrorism in South Africa during the early '80s. Patrick Chamusso (Luke) is an unassuming oil refinery foreman wrongly accused, imprisoned, and tortured for a plant bombing. The injustice transforms the apolitical worker into a radicalized insurgent, who then carries out his own successful sabotage mission. Robbins plays the Security Branch Colonel on Chamusso's case. A decent script and good performances, but the dated material lacks a sense of urgency and importance. **101m/C; DVD.** *US GB SA* Derek Luke; Tim Robbins; Bonnie Henna; Mncedisi Shabangu; Malcolm Purkey; ***D:*** Phillip Noyce; ***W:*** Shawn Slovo; ***C:*** Ron Fortunato; Garry Phillips; ***M:*** Philip Miller.

Catch and Release 🦴🦴 **2007 (PG-13)** Kevin Smith is cuddly. But fortunately, he's not the rebound romance for the ever-appealing Garner because that would really make heads spin. Garner plays Gray, a one-of-the-guys kinda gal whose fiance Grady died before the wedding. Crushed, Gray (who seems to have no family or girlfriends) becomes roomies with his buds Sam (Smith) and Dennis (Jaeger), who was also Grady's partner in a fly-fishing venture. Frisky Fritz (Olyphant), will eventually console Gray, who finds out some secrets about Grady that involve a ditzy single mom, played too weirdly by Lewis. Grant's directorial debut veers uncertainly between tragedy and comedy. **110m/C; DVD, Blu-Ray.** Jennifer Garner; Timothy Olyphant; Kevin Smith; Juliette Lewis; Sam Jaeger; Fiona Shaw; Joshua Friesen; ***D:*** Susannah Grant; ***W:*** Susannah Grant; ***C:*** John Lindley; ***M:*** BT (Brian Transeau); Tommy Stinson.

Catch Me a Spy 🦴 **1/2** *To Catch a Spy* **1971** A foreign agent attempts to lure an innocent man into becoming part of a swap for an imprisoned Russian spy. **94m/C; VHS, DVD.** *GB FR* Kirk Douglas; Tom Courtenay; Trevor Howard; Marlene Jobert; Bernard Blier; Patrick Mower; Bernadette LaFont; ***D:*** Dick Clement; ***W:*** Dick Clement; Ian La Frenais; ***M:*** Claude Bolling.

Catch Me If You Can 🦴🦴 **1/2 2002 (PG-13)** Spielberg's lightweight, entertaining, but overly lengthy flick follows the exploits of Frank Abagnale Jr. (DiCaprio), who, starting at age 16, eluded the FBI (in the person of Carl Hanratty, played by Hanks) while passing bad checks in the guise of airline pilot, doctor, lawyer, and college professor in the early '60s. Frank's journey starts when his perfect suburban life is turned upside-down by the divorce of his parents and his dad's (Walken) trouble with the IRS. DiCaprio is chameleon-like in his portrayal of Frank, as befits the role, but takes it further by looking every age he's supposed to be. Hanks make the most of what could've been a thankless role as Frank's workaholic pursuer/father figure, but Walken stands out as the broken father who, with more chutzpah and luck, might've been what Junior became. Based on the real Frank Abagnale, Jr's memoirs. **140m/C; VHS, DVD, Blu-Ray.** Leonardo DiCaprio; Tom Hanks; Christopher Walken; Nathalie Baye; Martin Sheen; Amy Adams; James Brolin; Jennifer Garner; Frank John Hughes; Steve Eastin; Chris Ellis; John Finn; Brian Howe; ***D:*** Steven Spielberg; ***W:*** Jeff Nathanson; ***C:*** Janusz Kaminski; ***M:*** John Williams. British Acad. '02: Support. Actor (Walken); Natl. Soc. Film Critics '02: Support. Actor (Walken); Screen Actors Guild '02: Support. Actor (Walken).

Catch That Kid 🦴🦴 **2004 (PG)** One part kid caper to one part heist movie, equals a real klunky movie. Maddy (Stewart), a 12-year-old adventurous (and apparently morally flexible) tomboy, decides to pull off a $250,000 bank robbery so the family can afford an operation for her father (Robards), who is paralyzed. The worst crime here is the lackluster writing and uninspired direction. Adapted from the Danish film "Klatretosen." **92m/C; VHS, DVD.** Kristen Stewart; Corbin Bleu; Max Thieriot; Jennifer Beals; Sam Robards; John Carroll Lynch; James LeGros; Michael Des Barres; Kevin G. Schmidt; Stark Sands; Grant Hayden Scott; Shane Avery Scott; ***D:*** Bart Freundlich; ***W:*** Michael Brandt; Derek Haas; ***C:*** Julio Macat; ***M:*** George S. Clinton.

Catch the Heat 🦴 *Feel the Heat* **1987 (R)** Alexandra is an undercover narcotics agent sent to infiltrate Steiger's South American drug operation. **90m/C; VHS, DVD.** Tiana Alexandra; David Dukes; Rod Steiger; ***D:*** Joel Silberg; ***W:*** Stirling Silliphant; ***M:*** Tom Chase; Steve Rucker.

Catch-22 🦴🦴🦴 **1970 (R)** Buck Henry's adaptation of Joseph Heller's black comedy about a group of fliers in the Mediterranean during WWII. A biting anti-war satire portraying the insanity of the situation in both a humorous and disturbing manner. Perhaps too literal to the book's masterfully chaotic structure, causing occasional problems in the "are you following along department?" Arkin heads a fine and colorful cast. **121m/C; VHS, DVD.** Alan Arkin; Martin Balsam; Art Garfunkel; Jon Voight; Richard Benjamin; Buck Henry; Bob Newhart; Paula Prentiss; Martin Sheen; Charles Grodin; Anthony Perkins; Orson Welles; Jack Gilford; Bob Balaban; Susanne Benton; Norman Fell; Austin Pendleton; Peter Bonerz; Jon Korkes; Collin Wilcox-Paxton; John Brent; Richard Libertini; Bruce Kirby; Elizabeth Wilson; Liam Dunn; ***D:*** Mike Nichols; ***W:*** Buck Henry; ***C:*** David Watkin.

Catch.44 🦴 **2011 (R)** Murky crime drama with too many pointless conversations and flashbacks. Tes, Kara, and Dawn screwed up their last assignment for crime boss Mel but he's apparently giving them a second chance by sending them to rural Louisiana to intercept a drug deal. When they get to their diner rendezvous it looks like there's been a doublecross. **93m/C; DVD, Blu-Ray.** Malin Akerman; Nikki Reed; Deborah Ann Woll; Bruce Willis; Forest Whitaker; Brad Dourif; Michael Rosenbaum; Shea Whigham; ***D:*** Aaron Harvey; ***W:*** Aaron Harvey; ***C:*** Jeff Cutter. **VIDEO**

The Catcher 🦴 **1/2 1998** After being released from an insane asylum, a man returns to the ballfield where he murdered his father and begins hanging around the minor-league stadium in order to finish off various players and managers. **90m/C; VHS, DVD.** David Heavener; Monique Parent; Joe Estevez; Sean Dillingham; ***D:*** Guy Crawford; Yvette Hoffman. **VIDEO**

The Catcher Was a Spy 🦴🦴 **2018 (R)** War drama about a professional baseball player turned intelligence operative, based on a true story. Newark-raised Morris "Moe" Berg graduates from Princeton despite anti-Semitism and takes his skills as a catcher to teams such as the Boston Red Sox. In the mid-1930s, he travels to Japan as part of a players group and lays the ground for a spying career. During World War II, Moe joins the Office of Strategic Services (later then CIA), and takes part in critical war missions. Rudd does his part but the movie falls flat. **98m/C; Streaming.** Paul Rudd; Mark Strong; Sienna Miller; Jeff Daniels; Guy Pearce; ***D:*** Ben Lewin; ***W:*** Robert Rodat; ***C:*** Andrij Parekh; ***M:*** Howard Shore.

Catching Faith 🦴🦴 **1/2 2015** Faith-centered drama about the power of sport, family, and personal strength. The Taylors seem like the perfect family with a well-crafted social image. John (Moslemi) is the CFO of a start up, and he and his wife Alexa (York) have a strong marriage and two teenagers. Beau (Westton) is a high school football star, while Ravyn (Peterson) is a strong student. Their world is shattered when Alexa's father dies and Beau is caught consuming alcohol. Not only his place on the football team in jeopardy, his future is on the line and the community is turning away from the Taylors. The family comes together and embraces a sense of faith to learn what is truly important in life. **88m/C; DVD, Blu-Ray, Streaming, Download.** Lorena Segura York; Garrett Weston; Bethany Peterson; Dariush Moslemi; Bill Engvall; ***D:*** John K.D. Graham; ***W:*** John K.D. Graham; Alexandra Boylan; Andrea Polnaszek; ***C:*** Richard Galli; ***M:*** Benjamin Stanton. **VIDEO**

Category 7: The End of the World 🦴🦴 **2005** Delightfully inept disaster pic finds FEMA head Judith Carr (sexy Gershon) trying to pinpoint the cause of deadly weather that's causing worldwide havoc. She turns to ex-beau and discredited scientist Ross (Daddo) for answers while fighting the bureaucrats. Meanwhile, scientist Faith (Doherty) teams up with Tornado Tommy (Quaid) to track the storms up close and personal. The subplots are especially lame, although Brolin as an evangelist is a hoot. **169m/C; DVD.** Gina Gershon; Cameron Daddo; Shannen Doherty; Randy Quaid; James Brolin; Swoosie Kurtz; Robert Wagner; Sebastian Spence; Nicholas Lea; Tom Skerritt; James Kirk; ***D:*** Dick Lowry; ***W:*** Christian Ford; Roger Soffer; ***C:*** Neil Roach; ***M:*** Joseph Williams. **TV**

Category 6: Day of Destruction 🦴🦴 **2004** Amusingly cheesy disaster flick with lots of predictable subplots and bad CGI. Hackers shut down the Chicago power company's computers during a heatwave, just as a super tornado is heading to that toddlin' town to make one major headache for all involved. Followed by "Category 7: The End of the World." **174m/C; DVD.** Thomas Gibson; Nancy McKeon; Chandra West; Brian Markinson; Nancy Sakovich; Randy Quaid; Dianne Wiest; Brian Dennehy; Andrew Jackson; Christopher Shyer; Ari Cohen; ***D:*** Dick Lowry; ***W:*** Matt Dorff; ***C:*** Neil Roach; ***M:*** Jeff Rona; Joseph Williams. **TV**

The Catered Affair 🦴🦴🦴 *Wedding Breakfast* **1956** Davis, anti-typecast as a Bronx housewife, and Borgnine, as her taxi-driving husband, play the determined parents of soon-to-be-wed Reynolds set on giving her away in a style to which she is not accustomed. Based on Paddy Chayefsky's teleplay, the catered affair turns into a familial trial, sharing the true-to-life poignancy that marked "Marty," the Oscar-winning Chayefsky drama of the previous year. **92m/B; VHS, DVD.** Bette Davis; Ernest Borgnine; Debbie Reynolds; Barry Fitzgerald; Rod Taylor; Robert F. Simon; ***D:*** Richard Brooks; ***W:*** Gore Vidal; ***C:*** John Alton; ***M:*** Andre Previn.

Caterina in the Big City 🦴🦴 *Caterina va in citta* **2003** Caterina (Teghil) is a small town teenager who experiences a nasty case of culture shock when her family moves to Rome. Frustrated, ambitious school teacher dad Giancarlo (Castellitto) is glad to be out of the sticks and back to the big city but Caterina is soon pulled between two high school cliques—lead by rebellious bohemian Margherita (Iaquaniello) and spoiled debutante Daniela (Sbrenna). Meant to be seen (in a cynical comedic way) as a microcosm of Italian society with the middle-class caught between the strident, communist left and the elitist, conservative right. Italian with subtitles. **106m/C; DVD.** *IT* Alice Teghil; Sergio Castellitto; Margherita Buy; Carolina Iaquaniello; Federica Sbrenna; Claudio Amendola; ***D:*** Paolo Virzi; ***W:*** Paolo Virzi; Francesco Bruni; ***C:*** Arnaldo Catinari; ***M:*** Paolo Virzi.

Catfight 🦴🦴 **1/2 2017** Veronica (Oh) is a well-to-do wine lover who runs into Ashley (Heche), an old friend from college with whom she has lost touch. They attend the same birthday party, and start throwing nasty verbal barbs at each other, which lead to actual, all-out combat. Sort of a satire on what really hides beneath many relationships—a desire to beat the crap out of each other. Onur Turkel's jet-black comedy is dark and daring enough to almost come together, but it runs out of ideas before it's over. Oh and Heche commit completely to what becomes a physically challenging slice of lunacy. **95m/C; DVD, Blu-Ray.** Sandra Oh; Anne Heche; Alicia Silverstone; Amy Hill; Damian Young; ***D:*** Onur Tukel; ***W:*** Onur Tukel; ***C:*** Zoe White.

Catfish 🦴🦴 **1/2 2010 (PG-13)** What happens when a user gets too caught up in an online posting on a social network? Twenty-four-year-old Yaniv 'Nev' Schulman has a photo published in the "New York Sun" and begins receiving messages via Facebook from young admirer Abby Pierce. A naive Nev pursues his online involvement with Abby and her family and finally decides to take a road trip from New York to Michigan to meet them but something's not quite right. Unexpectedly compelling real-life tale was filmed by Nev's brother Ariel Schulman and Henry Joost in late 1997. **86m/C; Blu-Ray.** ***D:*** Ariel Schulman; Henry Joost; ***C:*** Ariel Schulman; Henry Joost; Yaniv Schulman.

Catfish in Black Bean Sauce 🦴🦴 **1/2 2000 (PG-13)** While serving in Vietnam, African-American Harold Williams (Winfield) saved the lives of Vietnamese Mai (Tom) and her young brother Dwayne (Lo) and he and wife Dolores (Alice) adopted the duo. Dwayne acts black and has a black girlfriend, Nina (Lathan), but married Mai has never forgotten her roots and announces to the stunned family that she has located her birth mother, Thanh (Chinh), and the woman is coming not only to visit but to live with her. But Thanh turns out to be a critical schemer, unreasonably jealous of the Williams', and determined to reclaim her grown children, no matter what the cost. **111m/C; VHS, DVD.** Chi Muoi Lo; Lauren Tom; Kieu Chinh; Paul Winfield; Mary Alice; Sanaa Lathan; Tzi Ma; Tyler Christopher; ***D:*** Chi Muoi Lo; ***W:*** Chi Muoi Lo; ***C:*** Dean Lent; ***M:*** Stanley A. Smith.

Catherine Cookson's Colour Blind 🦴🦴 **1/2** *Colour Blind* **1998** In post-WWI England, Bridget McQueen comes to stay with her sprawling, poor family with her new husband and their baby daughter. But Bridget has neglected to tell her family that her husband is black. This not only stirs up a lot of trouble but more tribulations follow as Bridget's mixed-race daughter grows up. On two cassettes. **150m/C; VHS, DVD, Blu-Ray.** *GB* Niamh Cusack; Carmen Ejogo; Art Malik; Tony Armatrading; ***D:*** Alan Grint; ***W:*** Gordon Hann. **TV**

Catherine Cookson's The Black Candle 🦴🦴 **1/2 1992** Mill owner is caught up in a murder case that involves the father of her child, her husband (not the same guy), her husband's brother, and many aristocratic machinations. Well-done story boasts an excellent cast. Based on the novel by Catherine Cookson; made for British TV. **103m/C; VHS, DVD.** *GB* Nathaniel Parker; James Gaddas; Bob Smeaton; Brian Hogg; Cathy Sandford; Samantha Bond; Tara Fitzgerald; Denholm Elliott; ***D:*** Roy Battersby; ***W:*** Gordon Hann; ***C:*** Ken Morgan; ***M:*** Dominic Muldowney. **TV**

Catherine Cookson's The Black Velvet Gown 🦴🦴 **1/2** *The Black Velvet Gown* **1992** Riah Millican (McTeer) is a poor miner's widow living in rural 1834 England with her three children. She finds work as a housekeeper to the reclusive Miller (Peck), who agrees to educate her children and even gives Riah the titular gown, which was once his mother's. Now educated out of their working-class, the Millican's lives provide unexpected love and tragedy for all concerned. Based on the novel by Catherine Cookson; made for British TV. **103m/C; VHS, DVD.** *GB* Janet McTeer; Bob Peck; Geraldine Somerville; ***D:*** Norman Stone; ***W:*** Gordon Hann; ***C:*** Ken Westbury; ***M:*** Carl Davis. **TV**

Catherine Cookson's The Cinder Path 🦴🦴 **1/2** *The Cinder Path* **1994** Coming-of-age story begins in 1913 with unassuming Charlie MacFell (Owen) forced to take over the family farm. Charlie (who needs a spine transplant) also goes along with an arranged marriage to local lovely Victoria (Zeta-Jones), a disaster since she's little more than a well-bred tart and it's her younger sister Nellie (Miles) who's really in love with Charlie anyway. As if Charlie didn't have enough to cope with, he's soon an army soldier as WWI begins and up against vindictive Ginger (Byrne), a former farmhand who resents the monied classes Charlie represents. Based on the novel by Catherine Cookson. **145m/C; VHS, DVD.** *GB* Lloyd Owen; Catherine Zeta-Jones; Maria Miles; Antony Byrne; Tom Bell; ***D:*** Simon Langton; ***W:*** Alan Seymour; ***M:*** Barrington Pheloung. **TV**

Catherine Cookson's The Dwelling Place 🦴🦴 **1/2** *The Dwelling Place* **1994** Sixteen-year-old Cissie (Whitwell) struggles to hold her family together after the death of their parents in 1830's England. But her situation turns tragic when she's raped and left pregnant but drunken young aristocrat Clive (Rawle-Hicks), eventually giving the baby to be raised by Clive's father (Fox). Based on a novel by Catherine Cookson. **145m/C; VHS, DVD.** *GB* Tracy Whitwell; James Fox; Edward Rawle-Hicks; ***D:*** Gavin Millar; ***W:*** Gordon Hann; ***C:*** John Hooper; ***M:*** Colin Towns. **TV**

Catherine Cookson's The Fifteen Streets 🦴🦴 **1/2** *The Fifteen Streets* **1990** Kind-hearted dock worker John O'Brien (Teale) is the quiet one in a boozing, brawling Irish family living in near poverty in late-Victorian England. He meets well-bred schoolteacher Mary Llewellyn (Holman) and the two fall in love but bigotry, scandal, and tragedy challenge their chances at happiness. Based on a novel by Catherine Cookson. **108m/C; VHS, DVD.** *GB* Owen Teale; Clare Holman; Sean Bean; Billie Whitelaw; Ian Bannen; Jane Horrocks; Anny Tobin; Leslie Schofield; ***D:*** David Wheatley; ***W:*** Rob Bettinson; ***C:*** Ken Morgan; ***M:*** Colin Towns. **TV**

Catherine Cookson's The Gambling Man 🦴🦴 **1/2** *The Gambling Man* **1998** Rent collector Rory O'Connor is ambitious to escape his humble past and his talent at gambling leads him to winning a fortune. But a lie and a tragedy return to haunt him. Based on a book by Catherine Cookson. **150m/C; VHS, DVD.** *GB* Robson Green; Sylvestria Le Touzel; Bernard Hill; Stephanie Putson; Anne Kent; ***D:*** Norman Stone; ***W:*** T.R. Bowen; ***C:*** Doug Hallows; ***M:*** David Ferguson. **TV**

Catherine Cookson's The Girl 🦴🦴 **1/2** *The Girl* **1996** Illegitimate Hannah Boyle is simply called "The Girl" by her jealous stepmother, who forces her into a disastrous marriage. But Hannah is willing to fight to regain her freedom and the man she truly loves. TV adaptation of the novel by Catherine Cookson. **148m/C; VHS, DVD.** *GB* Siobhan Flynn; Malcolm Stoddard; Jonathan Cake; Jill Baker; Mark Benton; ***D:*** David Wheatley; ***W:*** Gordon Hann; ***C:*** Doug Hallows; ***M:*** Colin Towns. **TV**

Catherine Cookson's The Glass Virgin 🦴🦴 **1/2** *The Glass Virgin* **1995** In 1859, young Annabella Lagrange (Mortimer) discovers that her spendthrift father, Edmund (Haver), has been hiding the secrets surrounding her birth. These revelations force Annabella to find her own way in a new life. Based on a novel by Catherine Cookson. **150m/C; VHS, DVD.** *GB* Emily Mortimer; Nigel Havers; Brendan Coyle; Christine Kavanagh; Sylvia Syms; Samantha Glenn; Jan Graveson; ***D:*** Sarah Hellings; ***W:*** Alan Seymour; ***C:*** Doug Hallows; ***M:*** Christopher Gunning. **TV**

Catherine Cookson's The Man Who Cried 🦴🦴 **1/2** *The Man Who Cried* **1993** Abel Mason (Hinds) is an unhappily married man with a vindictive wife (Walsh) and a young son he's desperate to provide for. When an affair with a married woman ends in murder, Mason and his son travel in search of a new life. Desperate for a home, Mason enters into a bigamous marriage with a widow—only to find himself falling in love with her sister. Based on the novel by Catherine Cookson. Set in the years between England's depression and WW2. **156m/C; VHS, DVD.** *UK* Ciaran Hinds; Amanda Root; Kate Buffery; Angela Walsh; Daniel Massey; ***D:*** Michael Whyte; ***W:*** Gordon Hann; ***C:*** Fred Tammes; ***M:*** Richard Hartley. **TV**

Catherine Cookson's The Moth 🦴🦴 **1/2** *The Moth* **1996** Robert Bradley leaves the shipyards to work in his uncle's furniture business but soon finds himself at odds with the old man. So he becomes a servant for the destructive Thormans, and falls for the lady of the house, Sarah. But in 1913 this upstairs/downstairs romance can only lead to disaster. TV movie based on the novel by Catherine Cookson. **150m/C; VHS, DVD.** *GB* Jack Davenport; Juliet Aubrey; David Bradley; Justine Waddell; ***D:*** Roy Battersby; ***W:*** Gordon Hann; ***C:*** Alec Mills; ***M:*** Colin Towns. **TV**

Catherine Cookson's The Rag Nymph 🦴🦴 **1/2** *The Rag Nymph* **1996** Aggie Winkowski finds 10-year-old Millie Forrester abandoned on the streets. Knowing how dangerous the child's life could become, Aggie decides to take Millie in. TV movie based on the novel by Catherine Cookson. **150m/C; VHS, DVD.** *GB* Honeysuckle Weeks; Val McLane; Perdita Weeks; Alec Newman; Crispin Bonham Carter; ***D:*** David Wheatley; ***W:*** T.R. Bowen; ***C:*** Alec Mills; ***M:*** Colin Towns. **TV**

Catherine Cookson's The Secret 🦴🦴🦴 *The Secret* **2000** Complex historical thriller is based on Catherine Cookson's "The Harrogate Secret." In 19th-century England, Freddie Musgrave (Buchanan) has to work through secrets hidden in his own past as a runner and messenger for criminals. Anonymous letters, diamonds, and the like are involved. **156m/C; DVD.** *GB* Colin Buchanan; June Whitfield; Stephen Moyer; Hannah Yelland; Clare Higgins; ***D:*** Alan Grint; ***W:*** T.R. Bowen; ***C:*** Allan Pyrah; ***M:*** Colin Towns. **TV**

Catherine Cookson's The Tide of Life 🦴🦴 **1/2** *The Tide of Life* **1996** TV adaptation of Catherine Cookson's novel finds young Emily Kennedy entering service as a maid to the McGilby family and weathering various tragedies, romantic and otherwise. **156m/C; VHS, DVD.** *GB* Gillian Kearney; Ray Stevenson; John Bowler; James Purefoy; Diana Hardcastle; ***D:*** David Wheatley; ***W:*** Gordon Hann; ***C:*** Doug Hallows; ***M:*** Colin Towns.

Catherine Cookson's The Wingless Bird 🦴🦴 **1/2** *The Wingless Bird* **1997** Agnes Conway (Skinner) is the strong-minded daughter of a Newcastle shop-owner in class-conscious England in December, 1913. Managing her unhappy father's store, Claire waits on two members of the wealthy Farrier family and is soon drawn into their lives when the younger Farrier son, Charles (Atterton), falls in love with her, despite their class differences. But the Conway's have their own class problems—Agnes' younger sister Jessie becomes pregnant by a lower-class lad and her father's fury is murderous. Still as Agnes' love for Charlie grows, she must also deal with the outbreak of WWI, which will bring changes for all concerned. **156m/C; VHS, DVD.** *GB* Claire Skinner; Edward Atterton; Julian Wadham; Frank Grimes; Moira Redmond; Elspet Gray; Dinsdale Landen; Anne Reid; ***D:*** David Wheatley; ***W:*** Alan Seymour; ***M:*** Colin Towns. **TV**

Catherine Cookson's Tilly Trotter 🦴🦴 **1/2** *Tilly Trotter* **1999** Tilly lives in rural England in the 1830s where the young woman is envied for her beauty by the local ladies and lusted after because of that same beauty by the local gentlemen. Accused of witchcraft, Tilly is rescued by a married farmer but there's another romance on the horizon as well. **210m/C; VHS, DVD.** *GB* Carli Norris; Simon Shepherd; Gavin Abbott; Madelaine Newton; Rosemary Leach; Basil Moss; Amelia Bullmore; Richard Dempsey; ***D:*** Alan Grint; ***W:*** Ray Marshall; ***C:*** Robin Vidgeon; ***M:*** Colin Towns. **TV**

Catherine the Great 🦴🦴 **1/2** *The Rise of Catherine the Great* **1934** Slow but lavish and engrossing British dramatization of the tortured and doomed love affair between Catherine, Empress of Russia, and her irrational, drunken husband Peter. **88m/B; VHS, DVD.** *GB* Douglas Fairbanks, Jr.; Elisabeth Bergner; Flora Robson; ***D:*** Paul Czinner; ***C:*** Georges Perinal.

Catherine the Great 🦴🦴 **1/2 1995** Teenaged German princess Sophia (Zeta-Jones) marries into Russian royalty in 1744 when she weds Peter (Jaenicke), nephew of the Empress Elizabeth (Moreau), and has a name change when she's crowned Catherine II. The marriage is a disaster and with the help of her lover Gregory Orlov (McGann), Catherine eventually gets rid of Peter and is crowned Empress and Czarina of all the Russias as she struggles to drag her medieval empire into the modern world. Typically lavish and simplistic historical retelling. Originally released as a two-part miniseries. **100m/C; VHS, DVD.** *GE* Catherine Zeta-Jones; Paul McGann; Ian Richardson; Jeanne Moreau; Mark McGann; Hannes Jaenicke; Mel Ferrer; Omar Sharif; John Rhys-Davies; Brian Blessed; ***D:*** Marvin J. Chomsky; ***W:*** John Goldsmith; ***C:*** Elemer Ragalyi; ***M:*** Laurence Rosenthal. **TV**

Catholics 🦴🦴🦴 *The Conflict* **1973** A sensitive exploration of contemporary mores and changing attitudes within the Roman Catholic church. Sheen is sent by the Pope to Ireland to reform some priests. Based on Brian Moore's short novel. **86m/C; VHS, DVD.** Martin Sheen; Trevor Howard; ***D:*** Jack Gold; ***M:*** Carl Davis. **TV**

Cathy's Curse 🦴 *Cauchemares* **1977** The spirit of her aunt, who died as a child, possesses a young girl in this Canadian-French collaboration. Tries to capitalize on the popularity of "The Exorcist," but falls seriously short. **90m/C; VHS, DVD, Blu-Ray.** *FR CA* Alan Scarfe; Beverly Murray; ***D:*** Eddy Matalon.

Catlow 🦴🦴 **1/2 1971 (PG-13)** A comedic western with Brynner aiming to steal $2 million in gold from under the nose of his friend, lawman Crenna. Based on the novel by Louis L'Amour. **103m/C; VHS, DVD.** Yul Brynner; Richard Crenna; Leonard Nimoy; JoAnn Pflug; Jeff Corey; Michael Delano; David Ladd; Bessie Love; ***D:*** Sam Wanamaker; ***W:*** Scot (Scott) Finch; J.J. Griffith.

The Cats 🦴 **1/2** *The Bastards; Sons of Satan* **1968** Ridiculously lurid Eurotrash family/crime drama. Adam (Kinski) arranges heists while younger brother Jason (Gemma) does the actual thefts. They quarrel over the goods from a jewel robbery and Adam leaves his brother for dead. Hayworth chews the scenery as their alcoholic mom. **93m/C; DVD.** *IT GE* Klaus Kinski; Giuliano Gemma; Rita Hayworth; Margaret Lee; Claudine Auger; Serge Marquand; ***D:*** Duccio Tessari; ***W:*** Duccio Tessari; Ennio de Concini; Mario di Nardo; ***C:*** Carlo Carlini; ***M:*** Carlo Rustichelli.

Cats 🦴 **2019 (PG)** When cat Victoria (Hayward) is abandoned by her owners, she is adopted by a group of street cats known as the Jellicle cats. The Jellicle cats and others compete in a talent competition for a trip to Heaven, where the chosen cat gets a new life. The wise elderly cat Old Deuteronomy, (Dench) serves as the master of ceremonies, while malicious Macivity (Elba) tries to wreck the acts of others. Though based on an extremely popular Broadway musical and featuring a gifted all-star cast, it lacks the magic of the stage production, is overproduced, and includes disturbing-looking humans in cat suits. **?m/C; DVD, Blu-Ray.** Jennifer Hudson; Dame Judi Dench; Taylor Swift; Robbie Fairchild; Jason Derulo; Francesca Hayward; Rebel Wilson; James Corden; ***D:*** Tom Hooper; ***W:*** Tom Hooper; Lee Hall; ***C:*** Christopher Ross; ***M:*** Andrew Lloyd Webber. Golden Raspberries '19: Worst Director (Hooper), Worst Picture, Worst Screenplay, Worst Support. Actor (Corden), Worst Support. Actress (Wilson).

Cats & Dogs 🦴🦴 **2001 (PG)** Mix of live-action and animatronics as the secret war between cats and dogs is exposed in your neighborhood. It seems the latest cat plot is to destroy a vaccine that would prevent all human allergies to dogs and the dogs, of course, must keep that from happening. The human actors are upstaged at every turn (naturally) and the plot showcases some inconsistent pacing, but the kids should enjoy it (unless they like cats) and adults won't hate it until, say, the sixth or seventh viewing. **87m/C; VHS, DVD, Blu-Ray.** Jeff Goldblum; Elizabeth Perkins; Miriam Margolyes; Alexander Pollock; ***V:*** Glenn Ficarra; Tobey Maguire; Sean P. Hayes; Alec Baldwin; Joe Pantoliano; Susan Sarandon; Michael Clarke Duncan; Jon Lovitz; Charlton Heston; Salome Jens; ***D:*** Lawrence (Larry) Guterman; ***W:*** John Requa; Glenn Ficarra; ***C:*** Julio Macat; ***M:*** John Debney.

Cats & Dogs: The Revenge of Kitty Galore 🦴 **2010 (PG)** Absolutely dreadful late sequel, in which household pets are somehow high-tech super spies. This time around Kitty Galore (voiced by Midler), a "radical felinist," has gone rogue from spy organization MEOW and plans to unleash a signal that will cause dogs to turn on their human masters. MEOW hires a disgraced police dog (voiced by Marsden) to lead a band of cats, dogs, and humans against Galore. Cringe-worthy puns and lame jabs add up to a boring time for kids and adults alike. **82m/C; Blu-Ray.** Chris O'Donnell; Jack McBrayer; Paul Rodriguez; Roger Moore; Sean P. Hayes; Christina Applegate; Nick Nolte; Katt Micah Williams; ***V:*** Bette Midler; Michael Clarke Duncan; Joe Pantoliano; Alec Baldwin; James Marsden; Neil Patrick Harris; ***D:*** Brad Peyton; ***W:*** Ron J. Friedman; Steve Bencich; ***C:*** Steven Poster; ***M:*** Christopher Lennertz.

Cats Don't Dance 🦴🦴 **1997 (G)** Animated musical/comedy finds Danny (Bakula) a hoofer wanna-be trying to break into '30s Hollywood. Only problem is that he's a cat and can't understand why he only gets parts playing animals. He gets into trouble with bratty human star Darla Dimple (Peldon) and nearly sees his chance at a career vanish. Combines "Singin' in the Rain" and "Who Framed Roger Rabbit," with some showbiz cynicism from "The Player" to create a cartoon that will most likely sail over the heads of its target audience. Most of the time, as in the old Warner Bros. classics, that's a good thing. Not in this case, however. **77m/C; VHS, DVD.** ***V:*** Scott Bakula; Jasmine Guy; Ashley Peldon; Kathy Najimy; John Rhys-Davies; George Kennedy; Rene Auberjonois; Hal Holbrook; Don Knotts; Frank Welker; Natalie Cole; David Johansen; ***D:*** Mark Dindal; ***W:*** Cliff Ruby; Roberts Gannaway; Elana Lesser; Theresa Pettengill; ***M:*** Steve Goldstein; ***M:*** Randy Newman.

Cat's Eye 🦴🦴 *Stephen King's Cat's Eye* **1985 (PG-13)** An anthology of three Stephen King short stories connected by a stray cat who wanders through each tale. **94m/C; VHS, DVD, Blu-Ray.** Drew Barrymore; James Woods; Alan King; Robert Hays; Candy Clark; Kenneth McMillan; James Naughton; Charles S. Dutton; ***D:*** Lewis Teague; ***W:*** Stephen King; ***C:*** Jack Cardiff; ***M:*** Alan Silvestri.

The Cat's Meow 🦴🦴 **1/2 2001 (PG-13)** Bogdanovich takes on an old Hollywood scandal in this period drama. In 1924 publishing tycoon William Randolph Hearst (Herrmann) and his much-younger mistress, actress Marion Davies (Dunst), invite a group of partygoers aboard Hearst's yacht for a weekend. Producer/director Thomas Ince (Elwes) dies—but how is in question (heart attack? murder?)?and there's a coverup. Did Hearst mistakenly kill Ince while aiming for guest Charlie Chaplin (Izzard), whom Hearst suspected of carrying on with Davies? Film looks terrific, has a talented cast, and the story shows that little has changed in Hollywood regarding sex, scandal, ambition, and power. **112m/C; VHS, DVD.** *GB GE* Edward Herrmann; Kirsten Dunst; Cary Elwes; Eddie Izzard; Joanna Lumley; Jennifer Tilly; Victor Slezak; James Laurenson; Ronan Vibert; Claudia Harrison; ***D:*** Peter Bogdanovich; ***W:*** Steven Peros; ***C:*** Bruno Delbonnel.

Cat's Play 🦴🦴 *Mascskajatek* **1974** A widowed music teacher makes a ceremonial occasion of a weekly dinner with an old flame. Then an old friend from her youth suddenly reappears and begins an affair with the gentleman, causing self-destructive passions to explode. In Hungarian with English subtitles. **115m/C; VHS, DVD.** *HU* Margit Dayka; Margit Makay; Elma Bulla; ***D:*** Karoly Makk.

Cattle King 🦴🦴 *Guns of Wyoming* **1963** In 1883 Wyoming, cattle baron Clay Matthews (Middleton) is doing his worst to grab land to establish a national cattle trail from Texas to Canada. Rancher Sam Brassfield (Taylor) knows the days of open grazing are over, so he'll fight to keep his property and stop a range war. Routine western was Taylor's last contract film for MGM. **88m/C; DVD.** Robert Taylor; Robert Middleton; Joan Caulfield; Robert Loggia; Larry Gates; William Windom; ***D:*** Tay Garnett; ***W:*** Thomas Thompson; ***C:*** William E. Snyder; ***M:*** Paul Sawtell; Bert Shefter.

Cattle Queen of Montana 🦴🦴 **1/2 1954** Reagan stars as an undercover federal agent investigating livestock rustlings and Indian uprisings. **88m/C; VHS, DVD.** Ronald Reagan; Barbara Stanwyck; Jack Elam; Gene Evans; Lance Fuller; Anthony Caruso; ***D:*** Allan Dwan; ***W:*** Robert Blees.

Cattle Town 🦴 **1/2 1952** Texas ranchers are displaced by nesters when Northerner Judd Hastings (Teal) starts buying up their grazing land in the post-Civil War depression. Mike McCann (Morgan) is sent in by the governor to play peacemaker between the two groups although there's a stampede before order is restored. Morgan does find the time to sing four forgettable ditties in between the action. **70m/B; DVD.** Dennis Morgan; Ray Teal; Amanda Blake; Phil Carey; Rita Moreno; Paul Picerni; Jay Novello; George O'Hanlon; Robert J. Wilke; Charles Meredith; ***D:*** Noel Mason Smith; ***W:*** Tom Blackburn; ***C:*** Ted D. McCord; ***M:*** William Lava.

Catwoman 🦴 **2004 (PG-13)** Halle Berry is Patience Phillips, an artist in the ad department of a cosmetics company who overhears a discussion about side effects of their newest product. Soon she and the scientist who discovered the problem are disposed of. Luckily, a few cats are around to revive our heroine and dress her in a tight leather catsuit to take her revenge. Unfortunately, Berry's talents and wardrobe are not enough to carry a movie that, while it will undoubtedly have an extended shelf-life as a camp classic, is a mess. Director Pitof saturates every frame with his presence and revels in drawing attention to flamboyant visuals and frenetic editing rather than focusing on characterization or good, old-fashioned storytelling. Wooden characters and a laughable storyline make this arguably one of the worst comic book adaptations ever made. **91m/C; VHS, DVD.** Halle Berry; Sharon Stone; Benjamin Bratt; Lambert Wilson; Alex Borstein; John Cassini; Frances Conroy; Byron Mann; Michael Massee; Kim Smith; Christopher Heyerdahl; Peter Wingfield; ***D:*** Pitof; ***W:*** John Brancato; Michael Ferris; John Rogers; ***C:*** Thierry Arbogast; ***M:*** Klaus Badelt. Golden Raspberries '04: Worst Actress (Berry), Worst Director (Pitof), Worst Picture, Worst Screenplay.

Caught 🦴🦴🦴 **1949** A woman marries for wealth and security and is desperately unhappy. She runs away and takes a job with a struggling physician, and falls in love with him. Her husband finds her, forcing her to decide between a life of security or love. **90m/B; VHS, Blu-Ray, Streaming.** James Mason; Barbara Bel Geddes; Robert Ryan; Curt Bois; Natalie Schafer; Art Smith; ***D:*** Max Ophuls; ***C:*** Lee Garmes.

Caught 🦴🦴 **1996 (R)** Homeless Irishman Nick (Verveen) winds up in the New Jersey fish shop run by Joe (Olmos) and his wife Betty (Alonso). Betty takes a liking to the good-looking young man and encourages Joe to offer him a job and even invites Nick to stay with them in departed son Danny's (Schub) old room. Soon, room and board isn't all the spicy Betty is offering and Nick's willing to please, especially since Joe turns a blind eye. Too bad cocaine-addicted Danny, a failed comedian, returns home and immediately becomes jealous of the interloper. He's also too willing to drag secrets out into the open, whatever the cost. Based on Pomerantz's novel "Into It." **109m/C; VHS, DVD.** Edward James Olmos; Maria Conchita Alonso; Arie Verveen; Steven Schub; Bitty Schram; Shawn Elliot; Joseph (Joe) D'Onofrio; ***D:*** Robert M. Young; ***W:*** Edward Pomerantz; ***C:*** Michael Barrow; ***M:*** Chris Botti.

Caught in the Act 🦴🦴 **2004** Amusing if a little too southern-fried cliched. Married Tennessee mom Jodie Colter (Holly) has just uncovered all her cheating husband Buck's (Martini) lies. When a new friend, whose husband was also unfaithful, is murdered, Jodie decides to put her snooping skills to practical use by becoming a domestic private eye and solving the case. **90m/C; DVD.** Lauren Holly; Maximillian Martini; Brian McNamara; Madeleine Potter; Eddie Marsan; ***D:*** Jeff Reiner; ***W:*** Cynthia Whitcomb; ***C:*** Feliks Parnell; ***M:*** Marty Stuart. **CABLE**

Caught in the Crossfire 🦴 **1/2 2010 (R)** Detectives Briggs and Shepherd are transporting gang police informant Tino when they come to the assistance of officers under fire. The perps all die and it may turn out be a case of bad cops getting rid of their criminal partners. The detectives' bosses don't like the attention and want to know what really went on. **85m/C; DVD.** Chris Klein; Adam Rodriguez; 50 Cent; Richard T. Jones; Michael Matthias; Lyle Kanouse; Christine Lakin; ***D:*** Brian A. Miller; ***W:*** Brian A. Miller; ***C:*** William Eubank; ***M:*** Erin Davis. **VIDEO**

Caught in the Draft 🦴🦴🦴 **1941** Hope's funniest role has him as a Hollywood star trying to evade the draft in WW II, but he ends up accidentally enlisting himself. Lamour plays the daughter of a colonel in the Army whom Hope plans to marry, thinking it will get him out of the service. Very funny military comedy and one of Hope's best. Based on a story by Harry Tugend. **82m/B; VHS, DVD.** Bob Hope; Dorothy Lamour; Lynne Overman; Eddie Bracken; Clarence (C. William) Kolb; Paul Hurst; Ferike Boros; Irving Bacon; ***D:*** David Butler; ***W:*** Harry Tugend.

Caught Plastered 🦴 **1/2 1931** Mother Talley expects to be forced into an old folks home when bootlegger Harry tries to take over her failing drugstore to use as a front. But vaudevillians Tommy and Egbert pay off the mortgage first and then have to face off against the bad guys with their usual gags and banter. **68m/B; DVD.** Bert Wheeler; Robert Woolsey; Dorothy Lee; Lucy Beaumont; Jason Robards, Sr.; ***D:*** William A. Seiter; ***W:*** Ralph Spence; Eddie Welch; ***C:*** Jack MacKenzie; ***M:*** Victor Schertzinger.

Caught Up 🦴🦴 **1998 (R)** Directorial debut for Darin Scott follows the luckless path of ex-con Daryl (Woodbine). After serving five years as an unwitting accomplice to a bank robbery, he meets Vanessa (Williams) who is a dead ringer for his ex-girlfriend. She gets him a job as a limo driver that caters to thugs and gangsters. Unfortunately for Daryl, Vanessa has stolen some diamonds from a Rastafarian, so Daryl gets tangled up violence and deceit. He is also tangled in a plot that twists and turns a little too much for its own good. Director Scott tries a few too many fancy tricks, although some of them work reasonably well. Cameos from Snoop Doggy Dog and LL Cool J. **95m/C; VHS, DVD.** Bokeem Woodbine; Cynda Williams; Snoop Dogg; Joseph Lindsey; Clifton Powell; Basil Wallace; Tony Todd; LL Cool J; Jeffrey Combs; Damon Saleem; Shedric Hunter, Jr.; ***D:*** Darin Scott; ***W:*** Darin Scott; ***C:*** Thomas Callaway; ***M:*** Marc Bonilla.

Cause Celebre 🦴🦴🦴 **1987** Absorbing true crime drama set in Britain during the '30s. Alma Rattenbury (Mirren) is in a dull marriage to an aging and ill husband (Andrews) and is beset by financial and domestic difficulties. Then Alma hires 18-year-old George Bowman (Morrissey) as a family servant/chauffeur and, despite their age difference, the two are soon lovers. When her husband is bludgeoned to death, both Alma and George are swiftly arrested and on trial. But just who committed the crime and who is covering up? **105m/C; VHS, DVD.** *GB* Dame Helen Mirren; David Morrissey; David Suchet; Harry Andrews; Norma West; Oliver Ford Davies; Geoffrey Bayldon; Gillian Martell; ***D:*** John Gorrie; ***W:*** Kenneth Taylor; ***C:*** Malcolm Harrison; Trevor Vaisey; ***M:*** Richard Harvey. **TV**

Cause for Alarm 🦴🦴 **1/2 1951** A jealous husband recovering from a heart attack begins to lose his mind. He wrongly accuses his wife of having an affair and attempts to frame her for his own murder. A fast-paced thriller with a nifty surprise ending. **74m/B; VHS, DVD.** Loretta Young; Barry Sullivan; Bruce Cowling; Margalo Gillmore; Irving Bacon; Carl "Alfalfa" Switzer; ***D:*** Tay Garnett; ***M:*** Andre Previn.

Cause of Death 🦴 **1/2 1990 (R)** After the accidental death of his brother, Colombian drug lord Manuel Ramirez is lured to L.A. to collect his millions in blood money. **90m/C; VHS, DVD.** Michael Barak; Sydney Coale Phillips; Daniel Martine; ***D:*** Philip Jones.

Cause of Death 🦴🦴 **2000 (R)** Taylor Lewis (Bergin) is a prosecutor in Baltimore, who is assigned to a seemingly open-and-shut murder in which Angela Carter (Severance) has murdered her corrupt businessman husband to collect on his large insurance policy. But Lewis is cautious because of a past mistake and then he starts getting very close to the beautiful widow. Is Angela guilty or is someone in power pulling the strings? **95m/C; VHS, DVD.** Patrick Bergin; Joan Severance; Maxim Roy; Michael Ironside; Larry Day; ***D:*** Marc S. Grenier; ***W:*** Les Weldon; ***C:*** Yves Bélanger. **VIDEO**

Cavalcade 🦴🦴🦴 **1933** Traces the lives of the British Marryot family from the death of Queen Victoria, through WWI, the Jazz Age, and the Depression. A wistful adaptation of the hit play by Noel Coward with its touching portrayal of one family trying to weather good times and bad together. **110m/B; VHS, Blu-Ray.** Diana Wynyard; Clive Brook; Herbert Mundin; Una O'Connor; Ursula Jeans; Beryl Mercer; Merle Tottenham; Frank Lawton; John Warburton; Margaret Lindsay; Billy Bevan; ***D:*** Frank Lloyd; ***C:*** Ernest Palmer. Oscars '33: Director (Lloyd), Film.

Cavalcade of the West 🦴🦴 **1936** Typical western with two brothers, separated by a kidnapping, growing up on opposite sides of the law. Much later they meet, and the question is: will the outlaw be reformed and reunited with his happy family? **70m/B; VHS, DVD.** Hoot Gibson; Rex Lease; Marion Shilling; Earl Dwire; ***D:*** Harry Fraser.

Cavalier of the West 🦴 **1931** An Army captain is the only negotiating force between the white man and a primitive Indian tribe. **66m/B; VHS, DVD.** Harry Carey, Sr.; Kane Richmond; George "Gabby" Hayes; ***D:*** John P. McCarthy.

Cavalry Charge 🦴🦴 1/2 *The Last Outpost* **1951** Vance Britton (Reagan) is the captain of a brigade of Confederate troops wreaking havoc on Union outposts. His brother Jeb (Bennett) is a Union soldier sent to the western frontier to take care of the Confederate problem. Vance's former fiance Julie (Fleming) is also living in the territories with her new husband. All three converge when the Union fort, where Julie is living and Jeb is defending, is attacked by Apaches. Brother Vance rides to the rescue. Lots of action. **72m/C; VHS, DVD.** Ronald Reagan; Bruce Bennett; Rhonda Fleming; Noah Beery, Jr.; Bill Williams; Peter Hansen; Hugh Beaumont; John Ridgely; Lloyd Corrigan; James Burke; Richard Crane; Ewing Mitchell; ***D:*** Lewis R. Foster; ***W:*** Daniel Mainwaring; George Worthing Yates; Winston Miller; ***C:*** Loyal Griggs.

Cavalry Command 🦴 1/2 *Cavalleria Commandos* **1963** Good will and integrity characterize the U.S. soldiers called into a small village to quiet a guerrilla rebellion. **77m/C; VHS, DVD.** John Agar; Richard Arlen; Myron Healey; Alicia Vergel; William Phipps; Eddie Infante; ***D:*** Eddie Romero; ***W:*** Eddie Romero.

Cavalry Scout 🦴 1/2 **1951** Union cavalry scout Kirby Frye is sent to the Montana Territory to find stolen Gatling guns. The government is worried that the guns will be sold to Indian tribes who are about to go on the warpath. **78m/C; DVD.** Rod Cameron; James Millican; Jim Davis; Audrey Long; James Arness; John Doucette; ***D:*** Lesley Selander; ***W:*** Daniel Ullman; ***C:*** Harry Neumann; ***M:*** Marlin Skiles.

The Cave 🦴 **2005 (PG-13)** Cut from the same cloth as the hundred or so other films you've seen that were called "The (insert scary place or thing here)." All of the essential stereotypes are present, so everyone gets a character to relate to, hate, or both. Explorers Jack (Hauser) and Tyler (Cibrian) assemble a team of cavers, divers and scientists to explore a massive network of caves beneath a medieval Romanian church. As they descend into the cave it becomes clear that they have company in the form of hideous flying monsters. **97m/C; DVD, UMD.** Cole Hauser; Morris Chestnut; Eddie Cibrian; Marcel Iures; Daniel Dae Kim; Lena Headey; Piper Perabo; Rick Ravanello; Kieran Darcy-Smith; ***D:*** Bruce Hunt; ***W:*** Michael Steinberg; Tegan West; ***C:*** Emery Ross; ***M:*** Johnny Klimek; Reinhold Heil.

The Cave 🦴🦴🦴 **2019 (PG-13)** In an area near Damascus, Syria, evacuees find refuge from war in a series of underground tunnels and passages located under what was their neighborhood. A last resort hospital known as The Cave also operates down there. Though the hospital provides care for those trying to survive airstrikes and starvation above and below ground, it suffers from supply and staff issues. Despite these difficulties, the staff of The Cave, including its determined manager, pediatrician Dr. Amani Ballour, do their best with what they have. The beautifully shot documentary captures the urgency of the situation while sharing very human stories and emotions. Arabic with subtitles. **107m/C; DVD.** ***D:*** Feras Fayyad; ***W:*** Feras Fayyad; Alisar Hasan; ***C:*** Salama Abdo; Mohammad Eyad; Samer Qweder; Muhammed Khamir Al Shami; Muhammed Khamir Al Shami; Ammar Suleiman; ***M:*** Matthew Herbert.

Cave Girl WOOF! *Cavegirl* **1985 (R)** After falling through a time-warp during a high-school field trip, a social pariah makes a hit with a pre-historic honey. Sexist teen exploitation film, with few original ideas and a not-so-hot cast. **85m/C; VHS, DVD.** Daniel Roebuck; Cindy Ann Thompson; Saba Moor; Jeff Chayette; ***D:*** David Oliver; ***W:*** David Oliver; ***C:*** David Oliver; ***M:*** Jon St. James.

Cave-In! 🦴 **1979** TV disaster flick from producer Irwin Allen. Various folks get trapped after a collapse at the popular Five Mile Caverns tourist attraction. Among them is fugitive Tom Arlen (Olson), who plans on using one of the group as a hostage should they make it to the surface. Although made in 1979, the flick didn't even get a broadcast showing until 1983, which says something about its tediousness and predictability. **98m/C; DVD.** Dennis Cole; James Olson; Julie Sommars; Leslie Nielsen; Susan Sullivan; Ray Milland; Lonny (Lonnie) Chapman; Sheila Larken; ***D:*** Georg Fenady; ***W:*** Norman Katkov; ***C:*** John M. Nickolaus, Jr.; ***M:*** Richard LaSalle. **TV**

Cave of Forgotten Dreams 🦴🦴🦴 1/2 **2011 (G)** Director Herzog captivatingly explores the majestic views of a remarkable limestone cave in Southern France that was unearthed in 1994, which contains the oldest known manmade visual art, likely dating back about 32,000 years. Poetic in his narration, this is also a visual gem and why 3-D was created in the first place—to allow access to a place where few humans will ever be permitted. In English and French with English subtitles. **95m/C; DVD, Blu-Ray.** Dominique Baffier; Jean Clottes; Jean-Michel Geneste; Carole Fritz; Gilles Tosello; ***Nar:*** Werner Herzog; ***D:*** Werner Herzog; ***W:*** Werner Herzog; ***C:*** Peter Zeitlinger; ***M:*** Ernst Reijseger.

The Cave of the Silken Web 🦴 1/2 *Pan si dong; Pun see dung* **1967** In the late 1960s the Shaw Brothers did a series of four films based on the Chinese epic fable "Journey to the West" about the Monkey King (also inspiration for the anime series "Dragon Ball"). In this third film in the series, the Seven Spider Sisters kidnap the Tang Monk as he journeys to India, intending to devour him to gain immortality. Working to save him are the Monkey King, Pig, and Sand. Unintentional comedy, martial arts choreography, and flamboyant costumed dance numbers abound. **82m/C; DVD.** *CH* Chien Yu; Liang Hua Liu; Fan Ho; Peng Peng; Lung Chang Chou; Shun Tien; Ekin Cheng; Josie Ho; George Lam; Candy Lo; Bey Logan; Shawn Tam; Chapman To; Kenneth Tsang; Andy Hui; Yi Huang; Clarence Hui; Kar Yan Lam; Hacken Lee; ***D:*** Meng Hua Ho; Chun-Chun Wong; ***W:*** Kang Cheng; Chun-Chun Wong; Lawrence Cheng; Cindy Tang; ***C:*** Kuo-Hsiang Lin; ***M:*** Fu-ling Wang; Ken Chan.

Cave Women on Mars 🦴🦴 **2008** Campy spoof of 50s movie in which Earth achieves space travel in 1987. Promptly arriving on Mars, they find a lush forest world inhabited by squabbling tribes of cave women. **73m/B; DVD, Streaming.** Daniel Sjerven; Josh Craig; Brook Lemke; Alana Bloom; Emma Danbury; ***D:*** Christopher R. Mihm; ***W:*** Christopher R. Mihm; ***C:*** Christopher R. Mihm. **VIDEO**

Caveman 🦴🦴 **1981 (PG)** Starr stars in this prehistoric spoof about a group of cavemen banished from different tribes who band together to form a tribe called "The Misfits." **92m/C; VHS, DVD, Blu-Ray.** Ringo Starr; Barbara Bach; John Matuszak; Dennis Quaid; Jack Gilford; Shelley Long; Cork Hubbert; Avery Schreiber; ***D:*** Carl Gottlieb; ***W:*** Carl Gottlieb; Rudy DeLuca; ***C:*** Alan Hume; ***M:*** Lalo Schifrin.

The Caveman's Valentine 🦴 1/2 **2001 (R)** Jackson plays a homeless schizophrenic who finds a dead body outside his cave in Central Park and must pull his faltering mental faculties together enough to play Sherlock Holmes and solve the who-done-it. Plot points stretch well beyond the bounds of believability and venture into the territory of the ridiculous as the Caveman conveniently infiltrates every realm of society he wishes in order to follow up on his suspicions. Granted, he used to be a master pianist before his mental downfall, but come on. Director Lemmons's second feature film, the first being "Eve's Bayou." Based on the Edgar Award-winning 1994 novel by George Dawes Green. **105m/C; VHS, DVD.** Samuel L. Jackson; Aunjanue Ellis; Colm Feore; Ann Magnuson; Rodney Eastman; Tamara Tunie; Anthony Michael Hall; Jay Rodan; ***D:*** Kasi Lemmons; ***W:*** George Dawes Green; ***C:*** Amy Vincent; ***M:*** Terence Blanchard.

The Cavern 🦴 1/2 *Within* **2005 (R)** An eight-person team exploring a newly discovered cavern in Kyzl Kum Desert in Central Asia run into big trouble when they find themselves trapped. Too familiar story and not very frightening. **81m/C; DVD.** *AU* Sybil Temtchine; Mustafa Shakir; Ogy Durham; Andrew Caple-Shaw; Danny A. Jacobs; Andres Saenz-Hudson; Johnnie Colter; Neno Pervan; ***D:*** Olatunde Osunsanmi; ***W:*** Olatunde Osunsanmi; ***C:*** Yasu Tanida; ***M:*** Bryan Galvez.

CB4: The Movie 🦴 1/2 **1993 (R)** Falling somewhere between a serious attempt and parody, CB4 tries to do both and succeeds at neither. Written in the key of "Wayne's World" by "Saturday Night Live's" Rock, it starts out as a "rockumentary" (please refer to "This is Spinal Tap"), but quickly turns into a sitcom after two gangsta rap friends assume the identity of a local club owner when he is in jail. Hartman, also of SNL, appears as a right-wing city councilman. Chock full of violence, sexism, and profanity tucked into a wandering plot. **83m/C; VHS, DVD.** Chris Rock; Allen Payne; Deezer D; Phil Hartman; Charlie (Charles Q.) Murphy; Khandi Alexander; Art Evans; Chris Elliott; Willard Pugh; Theresa Randle; ***D:*** Tamra Davis; ***W:*** Chris Rock; Nelson George; Robert Locash; ***M:*** John Barnes.

CBGB 🦴 **2013 (R)** Gratingly banal and perfunctory pastiche. In 1973, eccentric Hilly Kristal (a morose Rickman) opens a club on New York's Lower East Side for country, bluegrass, and blues that turns into a showcase for the burgeoning punk rock scene. Hilly has no financial acumen and his jam-packed club is always on the verge of bankruptcy (it would close in 2006). The draw should be the music, but the lip-synched performances vary as the actors portray such seminal performers as Patti Smith, The Ramones, The Dead Boys, Iggy Pop, and Blondie. Stick to the originals. **101m/C; DVD, Blu-Ray.** Alan Rickman; Donal Logue; Justin Bartha; Mickey Sumner; Joel David Moore; Malin Akerman; Ashley Greene; Rupert Grint; Stana Katic; Josh Zuckerman; Taylor Hawkins; Kyle Gallner; Johnny Galecki; ***D:*** Randall Miller; ***W:*** Randall Miller; Jody Savin; ***C:*** Mike Ozier.

C.C. & Company 🦴 *Chrome Hearts* **1970 (R)** Rebel biker rescues a buxom gal from a fate worse than death, than vies for control of the gang. Laughable, with Namath hopeless in his film debut. Redeemed only by Ann-Margret in continual disarray. **91m/C; VHS, DVD.** Joe Namath; Ann-Margret; William (Bill) Smith; Jennifer Billingsley; Teda Bracci; Greg Mullavey; Sid Haig; Bruce Glover; ***D:*** Seymour Robbie; ***W:*** Roger Smith; ***C:*** Charles F. Wheeler; ***M:*** Lenny Stack.

Cecil B. Demented 🦴🦴 1/2 **2000 (R)** Waters returns to a more hard-edged satire with this indictment against the studio system. Dorff is Cecil B. Demented, indie auteur who, along with his band of cinema terrorists, wreack havoc on Hollywood. They kidnap A-list actress Honey Whitlock (Griffith) and force her to appear in their film—in doing so, making her the poster child for their cause. Punish bad film! No English-language remakes of foreign film! Death to those who are cinematically incorrect! Will appeal more to fans of Waters's very early work than to those who enjoyed "Serial Mom" or "Hairspray." **88m/C; VHS, DVD.** Stephen Dorff; Melanie Griffith; Jack Noseworthy; Alicia Witt; Larry (Lawrence) Gilliard, Jr.; Adrian Grenier; Patty (Patricia Campbell) Hearst; Ricki Lake; Mink Stole; Maggie Gyllenhaal; Eric M. Barry; Zenzele Uzoma; Erika Lynn Rupli; Harriet Dodge; Eric Roberts; ***D:*** John Waters; ***W:*** John Waters; ***C:*** Robert M. Stevens; ***M:*** Basil Poledouris; Zoe Poledouris.

Cedar Rapids 🦴🦴🦴 **2011 (R)** There's remarkable generosity, and excellent performances, amidst the raunch of Arteta's comedy. Sincere small town insurance salesman Tim (Helms) is chosen to represent his conservative firm at his first professional convention, which is being held in Cedar Rapids, Iowa. But Tim's morality is tested after being taken in hand by three convention veterans (Reilly, Heche, Whitlock Jr.) who regard the weekend as a chance to let loose by drinking too much and indulging in sexual peccadilloes. **86m/C; Blu-Ray, On Demand.** Ed Helms; John C. Reilly; Anne Heche; Isiah Whitlock, Jr.; Stephen (Steve) Root; Kurtwood Smith; Alia Shawkat; Thomas Lennon; Sigourney Weaver; Rob Corddry; Michael O'Malley; ***D:*** Miguel Arteta; ***W:*** Philip Johnston; ***C:*** Chuy Chavez; ***M:*** Christophe Beck.

The Celebration 🦴🦴 *Festen* **1998 (R)** Danish patriarch Helge (Moritzen) is turning 60 and a black-tie bash is being given to celebrate the event. But the celebration turns into a rancid display when all the family skeletons coming rattling out of their closets. Everyone's got a score to settle and is more than happy to air the family's dirty linen. Danish with subtitles. The film was shot with a hand-held video camera in available light and sound according to the tenets of Dogma 95—a Danish filmmaking collective Vinterberg belongs to. **105m/C; VHS, DVD.** *DK* Henning Moritzen; Ulrich Thomsen; Thomas Bo Larsen; Paprika Steen; Lene Laub Olsen; Helle Dolleris; Gbatokai Dakinah; ***D:*** Thomas Vinterberg; ***W:*** Thomas Vinterberg; Mogens Rukov; ***C:*** Anthony Dod Mantle. Ind. Spirit '99: Foreign Film; L.A. Film Critics '98: Foreign Film; N.Y. Film Critics '98: Foreign Film.

Celebrity 🦴🦴🦴 **1998 (R)** Woody examines the phenomenon of celebrity with his usual sarcastic and semi-autobiographical perspective. Lee Simon (Branaugh) is a hack celebrity journalist who attempts to enter the glitz and glam world of the famous people he follows and writes about. In true Allen fashion, bitter irony abounds as Simon loses sight of his pathetic reality while those around him acquire what he so desperately seeks. DiCaprio steals his 15 minutes of screen time playing a hedonistic, hotel-trashing, spoiled young film star with amazing ease and conviction (Coincidence? Perhaps...). The writing is among Allen's best, but watching Branaugh, and Judy Davis as Lee's estranged wife, do their best Woody Allen impressions grates on the nerves. Although it's redundant, nobody plays Woody like Woody. **113m/B; VHS, DVD.** Kenneth Branagh; Judy Davis; Hank Azaria; Leonardo DiCaprio; Joe Mantegna; Famke Janssen; Winona Ryder; Melanie Griffith; Michael Lerner; Charlize Theron; Bebe Neuwirth; Dylan Baker; Patti D'Arbanville; Kate Burton; Gretchen Mol; Allison Janney; Aida Turturro; Jeffrey Wright; J.K. Simmons; Polly Adams; ***Cameo(s):*** Greg Mottola; Isaac Mizrahi; Andre Gregory; Donald Trump; ***D:*** Woody Allen; ***W:*** Woody Allen; ***C:*** Sven Nykvist.

Celeste & Jesse Forever 🦴🦴 **2012 (R)** Jones proves to be a capable leading lady as Celeste, a woman who is travelling the murky waters after her divorce from Jesse (Samberg). She wants to stay friends, wants to get ahead at work, and might even want romance in her future. Co-written by Jones and co-star McCormick, this unfocused dramedy has multiple elements that work, including charming performances from most of the cast members, but never becomes the sum of its notable parts. **92m/C; DVD, Blu-Ray.** Rashida Jones; Andy Samberg; Chris Messina; Ari Gaynor; Will McCormack; Elijah Wood; Rebecca Dayan; Rafi Gavron; ***D:*** Lee Toland Krieger; ***W:*** Rashida Jones; Will McCormack; ***C:*** David Lazenberg; ***M:*** Sunny Levine; Zach Cowie.

Celestial Clockwork 🦴🦴 1/2 *Mecaniques Celestes* **1994** Runaway Venezuelan bride Ana (Gil), an aspiring opera singer, takes off for Paris clutching her Maria Callas poster. God must protect the innocent because she meets a friendly cabbie, immediately finds a place to live, and gets the perfect singing teacher, a cranky Russian emigre named Grigorief (Debrane). In fact, the only problem in this Cinderella's life is jealous would-be star Celeste (Dombasle), who wants the same lead theatrical role that Ana is also interested in. French with subtitles. **85m/C; VHS, DVD.** *FR* Ariadna Gil; Arielle Dombasle; Evelyne Didi; Frederic Longbois; Lluis Homar; Michel Debrane; ***D:*** Fina Torres; ***W:*** Fina Torres; ***C:*** Ricardo Aronovich; ***M:*** Michel Musseau; Francois Farrugia.

The Celestine Prophecy 🦴 **2006 (PG)** Pure hokum and clumsy in narrative, dialog, and character development. John

Woodson (Settle) impulsively travels to Peru after a friend alerts him to the discovery of ancient scrolls said to reveal universal life truths. But when John arrives he discovers that both the church and the government want to suppress the find and stop those involved from talking. Based on the metaphysical novel by James Redfield, who co-scripted. **99m/C; DVD.** Matthew Settle; Thomas Kretschmann; Annabeth Gish; Hector Elizondo; Sarah Wayne Callies; Jurgen Prochnow; Obba Babatunde; Joaquim Almeida; ***D:*** Armand Mastroianni; ***W:*** Dan Gordon; James Redfield; Barnet Bain; ***C:*** R. Michael Givens; ***M:*** Nuno Malo.

Celine **2008 (PG-13)** Riddled with errors and dull to boot. This unauthorized bio of Canadian super-singer Celine Dion starts with her childhood in Quebec (although basically ignoring the fact that she's French-Canadian and started her career singing in French) and then marches through her climb up the showbiz ladder, including her meeting with manager Rene Angelil. In what passes for scandal, Dion has to hide her romantic involvement with the married Rene until he gets a divorce; after that, the flick hurries through various career highlights including her successful showcase in Las Vegas. **90m/C; DVD.** *CA* Jodelle Ferland; Enrico Colantoni; Grant Nickalls; Peter MacNeill; Christine Ghawi; Louise Pitre; ***D:*** Jeff Woolnough; ***W:*** Donald Martin; ***C:*** Miroslaw Baszak; ***M:*** Jack Lenz. **CABLE**

The Cell 1/2 **2000 (R)** Psychotherapist Catherine (Lopez) is involved in breakthrough research that allows her access into a patient's mind. Desperate FBI agent Novak (Vaughn) asks her to invade the mind of a comatose serial killer (D'Onofrio) in order to save his latest victim. As you'd expect, the mind of a serial killer is not an exactly pleasant place to be, and Catherine (and the audience) encounters some pretty creepy and disturbing stuff. Feature debut of music video director Tarsem (REM's "Losing My Religion") is long on dazzling visual effects, trippy images, and style, but short on real suspense and cohesive plotting. Narrative is not the main focus here, however, so the faint of heart and the plot-dependent are forewarned. **110m/C; VHS, DVD, Blu-Ray.** Jennifer Lopez; Vince Vaughn; Vincent D'Onofrio; Marianne Jean-Baptiste; Dylan Baker; Jake Weber; Patrick Bauchau; James Gammon; Tara Subkoff; Gareth Williams; Colton James; Catherine Sutherland; Dean Norris; Pruitt Taylor Vince; ***D:*** Tarsem Singh; ***W:*** Mark Protosevich; ***C:*** Paul Laufer; ***M:*** Howard Shore.

Cell 1/2 **2016 (R)** Stephen King's 2006 novel was already a little dated when it came out, so the decade-later adaptation suffers greatly from missing its cultural mark. A signal is broadcast around the world that turns cellphone users into rabid maniacs—it's his warning on the power of technology wrapped in a zombie concept. Cusack phones it in as the protagonist Clay Riddell, one of the few remaining survivors trying to find safety. The dialogue here is flat and the action is stunningly unengaging. It's as if everyone involved here is trapped by a contractual obligation. **98m/C; DVD, Blu-Ray.** John Cusack; Samuel L. Jackson; Isabelle Fuhrman; Clark Sarullo; Ethan Andrew Casto; Owen Teague; Stacy Keach; ***D:*** Tod Williams; ***W:*** Adam Alleca; Stephen King; ***C:*** Michael Simmonds; ***M:*** Marcelo Zarvos.

The Cell 2 **2009 (R)** Another one of those in-name-only sequels. Serial killer "The Cusp" tortures his victims by letting them flatline and then reviving them over and over again. His first victim, Maya (Santiago), managed to escape and developed psychic powers after recovering from her ordeal. Now she's recruited by the FBI to get the madman. **94m/C; DVD.** Chris Bruno; Frank Whaley; Bart Johnson; Tessie Santiago; ***D:*** Tim Iacofano; ***W:*** Lawrence Silverstein; Alex Barder; ***C:*** Geno Salvatori; ***M:*** John Massari. **VIDEO**

Cell 2455, Death Row **1955** Based on the autobiography of "Lover's Lane Bandit," Caryl Chessman. Thief and rapist Whit Whittier (Campbell) is sent to San Quentin's death row where he studies law, successfully representing himself in numerous appeals to fend off his execution. Flashbacks show how Whit started his life of crime. The real Chessman was executed in 1960. **77m/B; DVD.** William Campbell; Marian Carr; Kathryn Grant; Vince Edwards; Harvey Stephens; Robert W(right) Campbell; Allen Nourse; Diane DeLaire; ***D:*** Fred F. Sears; ***W:*** Jack DeWitt; ***C:*** Fred H. Jackman, Jr.; ***M:*** Mischa Bakaleinikoff.

Cell 211 **2009** Powerful prison drama. Juan Oliver arrives a day early for his new job as a prison guard to get a tour of the facility. He's knocked unconscious by some falling debris and placed in empty cell 211 when the guards are called to quell a riot. Juan wakes up and figures out what's happening and passes himself off as a new prisoner to survive, which means getting in good with suspicious riot leader Malamadre. Spanish with subtitles. **111m/C; DVD.** *SP* Luis Tosar; Antonio Resines; Marta Etura; Alberto Ammann; Carlos Bardem; Manuel Moron; ***D:*** Daniel Monzon; ***W:*** Daniel Monzon; Jorge Guerricaechevarria; ***C:*** Carlos Gusi; ***M:*** Roque Baños.

Cell 213 1/2 **2011 (R)** A young attorney (Balfour) is framed for the murder of his incarcerated client and ends up in the very same prison cell. As a bonus, it's haunted by something that likes messing with people. Offers a few scares but it mostly falls short on substance. **109m/C; DVD, Streaming.** *CA* Bruce Greenwood; Eric Balfour; Michael Rooker; Deborah Valente; ***D:*** Stephen Kay; ***W:*** Maninder Chana; ***C:*** Luc Montpellier; ***M:*** Jonathan Goldsmith. **VIDEO**

Cellblock Sisters: Banished Behind Bars 1/2 **1995 (R)** Biker babe Harris reunites with college girl sis Wood to off their disgusting stepfather who separately sold them to adoptive families after killing their junkie mom. Harris does the crime but Wood does the time—until her guilty sibling deliberately gets thrown behind bars in order to protect her. Has all the standard jail chicks elements. **95m/C; VHS, DVD.** Gail Harris; Annie Wood; Ace Ross; ***D:*** Henri Charr.

Cellmates 1/2 **2012** Bizarre racial comedy. Set in 1976, a KKK Grand Dragon (Sizemore) is forced to share a cell with illegal Mexican immigrant Emilio (Jimenez). While the two first butt heads, they get closer when the blatant racist falls for the Hispanic maid who cleans the warden's office. The clichéd material displays both Sizemore's wasted star power and inability to get leading roles in worthwhile modern projects. **85m/C; Streaming.** Tom Sizemore; Hector Jimenez; Stacy Keach; Kevin Farley; Olga Segura; ***D:*** Jesse Baget; ***W:*** Jesse Baget; Stefania Moscato; ***C:*** Bill Otto; ***M:*** Jim Lang.

Cello 1/2 **2005 (R)** Confusing Korean ghost story—or maybe the main character is just nuts. Cello teacher Mi-Ju (Seong) barely survived a car accident that ruined her professional career and killed her best friend. Now Mi-Ju is being threatened by one of her students and thinks she's haunted by a ghost. Korean with subtitles. **93m/C; DVD.** *NK* Heyon-a Seong; Ho-bin Jeong; Da-an Park; ***D:*** Woo-cheol Lee; ***W:*** Woo-cheol Lee.

Cellular 1/2 **2004 (PG-13)** Efficient little thriller wastes no time. Science teacher Jessica Martin (Basinger) is kidnapped and locked in a grungy attic. Head bad guy Ethan (Statham) smashes the wall phone but Jessica hears a dial tone and manages to connect the wires and randomly gets the cell phone of beach bum Ryan (Evans), who naturally thinks it's a prank. Finally convinced, Ryan also figures out if he loses the call, the lady is lost, which leads to a number of realistic obstacles as he races to warn her husband and son, who are also targets. Veteran actor Macy plays veteran LAPD desk sergeant Mooney, who's about to retire when this case lands in his lap. The story is by Larry Cohen, who was also into phones as the screenwriter of 2002's "Phone Booth." **94m/C; VHS, DVD, Blu-Ray.** Kim Basinger; Chris Evans; Jason Statham; Eric Christian Olsen; Matt McColm; Noah Emmerich; William H. Macy; Brendan Kelly; Caroline Aaron; Richard Burgi; Rick Hoffman; Eric Etebari; Adam Taylor Gordon; Jessica Biel; ***D:*** David R. Ellis; ***W:*** Larry Cohen; Chris Morgan; ***C:*** Gary Capo; ***M:*** John Ottman.

The Celluloid Closet 1/2 **1995 (R)** Terrific documentary on how Hollywood films have depicted homosexual characters, subliminally and otherwise. Working chronologically and in an historical context, beginning with silent films, there are clips from more than 100 films, along with interviews from writers and actors. (Notable is writer Gore Vidal's comments on the gay subtext in 1959's "Ben-Hur"). Based on Vito Russo's 1981 book. **102m/C; VHS, DVD.** ***Nar:*** Lily Tomlin; ***D:*** Robert Epstein; Jeffrey Friedman; ***W:*** Armistead Maupin; ***C:*** Nancy Schreiber; ***M:*** Carter Burwell.

Celtic Pride **1996 (PG-13)** Mike O'Hara (Stern) and Jimmy Flaherty (Aykroyd) are the worst kind of crazy. They're sports nuts. They are so consumed with passion for their beloved Celtics that they kidnap foul-mouthed superstar Lewis Scott (Wayans) of the Utah Jazz before game seven of the NBA finals. If this sounds far fetched, well. . .it is, unless you have an ESPN junkie in your life. There's not as much court action as you would expect, since most of the story revolves around intermittent trash-talking and escape attempts. If you're a Celtic hater, stick around for the end, when the Boston Garden is demolished using special effects. **90m/C; VHS, DVD, Blu-Ray.** Damon Wayans; Daniel Stern; Dan Aykroyd; Gail O'Grady; Christopher McDonald; Paul Guilfoyle; Adam Hendershott; Deion Sanders; Gus Williams; Ted Rooney; Vladimir Cuk; Darrell Hammond; ***Cameo(s):*** Larry Bird; Bill Walton; ***D:*** Tom DeCerchio; ***W:*** Judd Apatow; ***C:*** Oliver Wood; ***M:*** Basil Poledouris.

Cement 1/2 **1999 (R)** Intense performances in a nasty crime story told via flashbacks. Hollywood vice detectives Holt (Penn) and Nin (Wright) have crossed the line between the cops and the criminals. When violent Holt catches his gal (Fenn) with a local wiseguy (DeSando), he buries him in a cement freeway and the mob is out for revenge. Pasdar's directorial debut. **100m/C; VHS, DVD.** Christopher Penn; Jeffrey Wright; Sherilyn Fenn; Anthony De Sando; Henry Czerny; ***D:*** Adrian Pasdar; ***W:*** Justin Monjo; ***C:*** Geary McLeod; ***M:*** Doug Caldwell.

The Cement Garden **1993** Fatherless 15-year-old Jack (Robertson) and 16-year-old sister Julie (Gainsbourg) are afraid that they and their two younger siblings Sue (Coulthard) and Tom (Birkin) will be taken into foster care after their mother dies at home. So to keep their secret, they bury her in the basement and try to assume a normal family life. Not that this works for long—Jack and Julie give into an incestuous fascination and the household slowly sinks into chaotic squalor around them. Gainsbourg is the director's niece and the young Birkin is his son. Based on Ian McEwan's 1978 novel. **105m/C; VHS, DVD.** *FR GE GB* Charlotte Gainsbourg; Andrew Robertson; Alice Coulthard; Ned Birkin; Sinead Cusack; Hanns Zischler; Jochen Horst; ***D:*** Andrew Birkin; ***W:*** Andrew Birkin; ***C:*** Stephen Blackman; ***M:*** Ed Shearmur.

The Cemetery Club 1/2 **1993 (PG-13)** Story of three Jewish widows who make weekly visits to their husband's graves while attempting to cope with their lives. Doris (Dukakis) is loyal to the memory of her husband and acts as the moral conscience of the trio. Lucille (Ladd) is a merry widow who wears clothes more suitable for younger women, but she also harbors a painful secret. Esther (Burstyn) struggles with her loneliness until a widowed cab driver begins to woo her. Commendably, the characters are given more dimension than Hollywood usually grants women of a certain age. Based on the play "The Cemetary Club" by Menchell, who also wrote the screenplay. **114m/C; VHS, DVD, Blu-Ray.** Ellen Burstyn; Olympia Dukakis; Diane Ladd; Danny Aiello; Lainie Kazan; Christina Ricci; Bernie Casey; Alan Mason; Sam Schwartz; Jeff Howell; Robert Costanzo; Wallace Shawn; Louis Guss; ***D:*** Bill Duke; ***W:*** Ivan Menchell; ***C:*** Steven Poster; ***M:*** Elmer Bernstein.

Cemetery High **1989** Beautiful high school girls decide to lure the local boys into a trap and kill them. **80m/C; VHS, DVD.** Debi Thibeault; Karen Nielsen; Lisa Schmidt; Ruth (Coreen) Collins; Simone; Tony Kruk; David Coughlin; Frank Stewart; ***D:*** Gorman Bechard; ***W:*** Gorman Bechard; Carmine Capobianco.

Cemetery Junction **2010 (R)** A familiar coming of age story about wanting to escape the dull and predictable. It's 1973 and working-class mates Freddie, Bruce, and Snork live in the dreary south England suburb of Cemetery Junction where the main activities seem to be drinking and fighting. Neither the characters nor the situations are original or particularly interesting. **95m/C; DVD.** *GB* Christian Cooke; Tom Hughes; Jack Doolan; Matthew Goode; Ralph Fiennes; Emily Watson; Felicity Jones; Ricky Gervais; ***D:*** Ricky Gervais; Stephen Merchant; ***W:*** Ricky Gervais; Stephen Merchant; ***C:*** Remi Adefarasin; ***M:*** Tim Attack.

Cemetery Man *Dellamorte Dellamore; Of Death, of Love* **1995 (R)** Grotesque little saga about zombies and necrophilia set in a small Italian cemetery. Thanks to a weird post-death plague the corpses refuse to stay quietly in their graves, forcing watchman Francisco Dellamorte (Everett) and mute gravedigger Gnaghi (Hadji-Lazaro) to split their heads open. But when Francisco's dead sweetheart (Falchi) rises from her grave, he's a little slow to rebury the still-active corpse. Based on the Italian graphic novel "Dellamorte Dellamore," from the "Dylan Dog" series by Tiziano Sclavi. **100m/C; VHS, DVD.** *IT* Rupert Everett; Anna Falchi; Francois Hadji-Lazaro; Mickey Knox; ***D:*** Michele (Michael) Soavi; ***W:*** Gianni Romoli; ***C:*** Mauro Marchetti; ***M:*** Manuel De Sica.

Cemetery of Splendor *Rak ti Khon Khaen* **2015** Soldiers with a mysterious sleeping sickness lay in a clinic in an abandoned school. A woman named Jenjira cares for them, talking to them for the brief moments they wake, and wandering the grounds, still haunted by generations of soldiers. Thai director Apichatpong Weerasethakul blurs the line between life and death. The result is an expressive, haunting film about nature and history and how we are tied to the past and the world around us. **122m/C; DVD, Blu-Ray, Streaming.** *TH UK GE FR ML SK US MX NO* Jenjira Pongpas; Banlop Lomnoi; Jarinpattra Rueangram; Petcharat Chaiburi; Tuwatchai Buawat; ***D:*** Apichatpong Weerasethakul; ***W:*** Apichatpong Weerasethakul; ***C:*** Diego Garcia.

Centennial **1978** Epic 12-part TV miniseries, based on the 1974 novel by James Michener, about the building of the Rocky Mountain town of Centennial, Colorado, from 1795 to the present. There are trappers and Indians, immigrants and cattlemen, soldiers, conservationists, and politicians all with their own stories to tell. **1258m/C; DVD.** Robert Conrad; Richard Chamberlain; Raymond Burr; Sally Kellerman; Barbara Carrera; Michael Ansara; Gregory Harrison; Stephanie Zimbalist; Christina Raines; Stephen McHattie; Kario Salem; Chad Everett; Alex Karras; Mark Harmon; Dennis Weaver; Timothy Dalton; Richard Crenna; Cliff DeYoung; Glynn Turman; Brian Keith; Les Lannom; Rafael Campos; Anthony Zerbe; Doug McKeon; Lynn Redgrave; William Atherton; A. Martinez; Lois Nettleton; David Janssen; Robert Vaughn; Andy Griffith; Sharon Gless; ***D:*** Virgil W. Vogel; Harry Falk; Paul Krasny; Bernard McEveety; ***W:*** John Wilder.

Center of the Web **1992 (R)** John Phillips is a victim of mistaken identity—someone thinks he's a professional hit man. After surviving an apparent mob attempt on his life, Phillips is persuaded by a CIA operative to go along with the deception in order to capture a potential political assassin. At least that's what Phillips is told, but he soon realizes that the deeper he gets into his new role, the deadlier the plot becomes. Davi is one of the best bad guys around and the fast-paced stunts and plot twists make this watchable. **88m/C; VHS, DVD.** Ted Prior; Robert Davi; Tony Curtis; Charlene Tilton; Bo Hopkins; Charles Napier; ***D:*** David A. Prior.

The Center of the World **2001** Put this one strongly in the love it or hate it category. Richard (Sarsgaard) is a wealthy dot.com geek who offers stripper Florence (Parker) a lot of dough to spend a few days with him in Vegas. She makes some strict rules about what she will and won't do for him—which she promptly breaks. They're both immature and vulnerable and inclined to play humiliating mind games with each other. The sex show turns out to be nothing to get hot and bothered about and the leads give as credible performances as the narrowness of their characters allow. Shot in digital video; the screenwriters used the pseud. "Ellen Benjamin Wong." **86m/C; VHS, DVD.** Peter

Sarsgaard; Molly Parker; Carla Gugino; Balthazar Getty; Mel Gorham; *D:* Wayne Wang; *W:* Wayne Wang; *C:* Mauro Fiore.

Center Stage **2000 (PG-13)** How familar does this sound? Newcomers enrolled at the American Ballet Academy vie for places in the professional company. Meanwhile, former dancer/company director Jonathan (Gallagher) has to contend with his insolent star dancer Cooper (Stiefel), whose ambitions are growing by leaps and bounds. There's also the usual love connections to be made (and unmade). The professional dancers in the cast have limited acting ability and aren't served particularly well by most of the choreography. **116m/C; VHS, DVD.** Peter Gallagher; Ethan Stiefel; Amanda Schull; Sascha Radetsky; Susan May Pratt; Ilia Kulik; Donna Murphy; Zoe Saldana; Debra Monk; Julie Kent; Eion Bailey; Shakiem Evans; Victor Anthony; Elizabeth Hubbard; Priscilla Lopez; *D:* Nicholas Hytner; *W:* Carol Heikkinen; *C:* Geoffrey Simpson; *M:* George Fenton.

Center Stage: Turn It Up ½ **2008 (PG-13)** A predictable but fun "fight for your dreams" flick. Self-taught dancer Kate heads to New York to audition for the American Academy of Ballet. No big surprise when she doesn't meet the school's rigid and traditional standards, but Kate isn't giving up. She spends some time working on her moves at a popular hip-hop club, partnered with Tommy, an ex-hockey player turned dancer. (Now there's a career change.) **95m/C; DVD.** Peter Gallagher; Ethan Stiefel; Rachele Brooke Smith; Kenny Wormald; Sarah Jayne Jensen; *D:* Steven Jacobson; *W:* Karen Bloch; *C:* Dino Parks; *M:* Laura Karpman. **VIDEO**

The Centerfold Girls **WOOF! 1974 (R)** Microscopic story line involves a deranged man who is determined to kill all the voluptuous young women who have posed nude for a centerfold. **93m/C; VHS, DVD, Blu-Ray.** Andrew Prine; Tiffany Bolling; Aldo Ray; Jeremy Slate; Ray Danton; Francine York; *D:* John Peyser.

Centerstage: On Pointe **2016 (PG)** The third entry in the Center Stage series finds one young girl's dance dreams coming true. At the American Ballet Academy, Jonathan Reeves (Gallagher) has been told to bring in more contemporary styles into the school. To find the right talent, he sends his best choreographers to locate dancers to compete at a camp and win a spot at the academy. One such dancer is Bella Parker (Munoz), who has always been overshadowed by her successful ballet dancer sister. Competition at the camp is tough, but Bella is determined to win her own spot in the limelight. **92m/C; DVD, Download.** Nicole Munoz; Peter Gallagher; Kenny Wormald; Barton Cowperthwaite; Rachele Brooke Smith; *D:* Director X.; *W:* Nisha Ganatra; *M:* Patric Caird.

Centipede **WOOF! 2005 (PG-13)** A party of spelunkers encounter, yup, you guessed it, killer centipedes. But the caves are so dark that the actors and centipedes are rarely seen. When the creatures do show up, they look like killer sock-puppets. Too goofy and takes itself too seriously. **90m/C; DVD.** George Foster; Larry Casey; Margaret Cash; Trevor Murphy; Matthew Pohlson; Danielle Kirlin; Steve Herd; *D:* Gregory Gieras; *W:* Gregory Gieras; *C:* Ajayan Vincent; *M:* Tom Batoy; Franco Tortora. **CABLE**

Central Airport **1933** Daredevil pilot Jim Blaine (Barthelmess) and parachute-jumper Jill Collins (Eilers) are part of a flying carnival. Jim says marriage isn't for him so sweetheart Jill rebounds by marrying Jim's steady younger brother Neil (Brown) and the siblings have a falling out. An air rescue in Havana figures into the story, which has some good flying sequences. Get a glimpse of John Wayne as the co-pilot of a downed plane. **75m/B; DVD.** Richard Barthelmess; Sally Eilers; Tom Brown; James Murray; Grant Mitchell; Claire McDowell; *D:* William A. Wellman; *W:* Rian James; James Seymour; *C:* Sidney Hickox.

Central Intelligence ½ **2016 (PG-13)** Calvin Joyner (Hart) may have been the most popular kid in his high school, but he's grown up to be a relatively depressed accountant, stuck in the rut of thirtysomething life. When his 20th high school anniversary approaches, he's contacted by old classmate Bob Stone (Johnson), who was so miserably mocked in high school that he dropped out. It turns out that Bob has changed as much as Calvin, and now works for the CIA. Or does he? As Calvin and Bob head off on a mission, the remarkable charm of Hart and Johnson get the script over some bumpy patches and clichés. **107m/C; Blu-Ray, Download.** Dwayne "The Rock" Johnson; Kevin Hart; Amy Ryan; Danielle Nicolet; Jason Bateman; *D:* Rawson Marshall Thurber; *W:* Rawson Marshall Thurber; Ike Barinholtz; David Stassen; *C:* Barry Peterson; *M:* Ludwig Göransson; Theodore Shapiro.

The Central Park Five ½ **2012** A media frenzy ensued after a white, female jogger in Central Park was horrifically raped, beaten, and left for dead in 1989; five black and Latino teens from Harlem spent years in prison after confessing (and then recanting) before a serial rapist's admission of guilt freed them. Based on Sarah Burns' book and co-directed by her husband, David McMahon and father, famed filmmaker Ken Burns, no stone is left unturned in depicting the real story of the coercion leading to the boys' conviction amidst a fearful public. Archival footage helps tell the story, set against a gritty backdrop of 1980's crime-ridden New York. **119m/C; DVD, Blu-Ray.** Ed Koch; David Dinkins; Craig Steven Wilder; Calvin O. Butts, III; Jim Dwyer; *D:* Ken Burns; Sarah Burns; David McMahon; *W:* Ken Burns; Sarah Burns; David McMahon; *C:* Anthony Savini; Buddy Squires; *M:* Doug Wamble.

Central Station *Central Do Brasil* **1998 (R)** Dora (Montenegro) is a bitter, aging woman who makes a living writing letters for the illiterate at a stand located in Rio de Janeiro's central railway station. One of her customers sends letters to her 9-year-old son Josue's (de Oliveira) father, who lives in northern Brazil and who has never seen the boy. When Josue's mother is killed in an accident, Dora reluctantly takes the homeless boy in and reluctantly decides they must locate his father. Their road trip turns out to have some unexpected consequences. Portuguese with subtitles. **110m/C; VHS, DVD.** *BR* Fernanda Montenegro; Vinicius de Oliveira; Marilia Pera; Othon Bastos; *D:* Walter Salles; *W:* Joao Emmanuel Carneiro; Marcos Bernstein; *C:* Walter Carvalho; *M:* Antonio Pinto; Jaques Morelembaum. British Acad. '98: Foreign Film; Golden Globes '99: Foreign Film; L.A. Film Critics '98: Actress (Montenegro); Natl. Bd. of Review '98: Actress (Montenegro), Foreign Film.

Centurion ½ **2010 (R)** Lots of bloody action as native Picts seek revenge on Roman soldiers, who are fighting on the edge of the British Roman Empire (Scotland, where much of the pic was shot). After their fort is destroyed, the fleeing Ninth Legion fall into a trap and then the few survivors are hunted, including protagonist Quintus Dias (Fassbender). **97m/C; Blu-Ray, On Demand.** *GB* Michael Fassbender; Dominic West; J.J. Feild; Lee Ross; David Morrissey; Ulrich Thomsen; Paul Freeman; Olga Kurylenko; Liam Cunningham; Noel Clarke; Demitri Leonidas; Rizwan Ahmed; Imogen Poots; *D:* Neil Marshall; *W:* Neil Marshall; *C:* Sam McCurdy; *M:* Ilan Eshkeri.

Cerberus ½ **2005 (R)** In this nonsensical effort from the SciFi Channel, Attila the Hun makes a pact with Satan that causes whoever holds his sword to be invincible. Surprisingly somehow Attila still dies, and the monster Cerberus becomes his guardian. Fast forward to the modern day when an Asian nutcase with a stockpile of nukes hires unsuspecting Americans to steal Attila's breastplate in order to get the sword because he needs it to threaten the world. **88m/C; DVD.** Garret Sato; Bodan Uritescu; Greg Evigan; *D:* John Terlesky; *W:* Raul Inglis; *C:* Viorel Sergovici, Jr.; *M:* Aldo Shllaku; Neal Acree.

The Ceremony **1963** Harvey made his directorial debut with this routine crime drama. Sean McKenna (Harvey) is a scapegoat for a murder in Tangiers and is in prison awaiting execution. His girlfriend Catherine (Miles) and brother Dominic (Walker Jr.) break him out of jail but Sean learns they've been having an affair, which complicates the situation. **107m/B; DVD.** Laurence Harvey; Sarah Miles; Robert Walker, Jr.; John Ireland; Ross Martin; Lee Patterson; Fernando Rey; *D:* Laurence Harvey; *W:* Ben Barzman; *C:* Oswald Morris; *M:* Gerard Schurmann.

Ceremony ½ **2010 (R)** Awkward coming-of-age comedy with immature 20-something Sam (Angarano) crashing the wedding weekend of his 30-something ex-girlfriend Zoe (Thurman). The aspiring children's book author obsessively pursues Zoe at the posh Long Island estate where she's soon to wed, pushing that she swap her kind, reliable fiance Whit (Pace) for his brand of wild zaniness. As unlikable as he may be and as silly as it may sound, she considers it. Director Winkler's absurd premise is candy-coated with obligatory downbeat quirk. Sporadically funny, but ultimately shallow. **89m/C; Blu-Ray, On Demand.** Michael Angarano; Uma Thurman; Lee Pace; Reece Thompson; Jake M. Johnson; Rebecca Mader; Brooke Bloom; Harper Dill; *D:* Max Winkler; *W:* Max Winkler; *C:* William Rexer; *M:* Eric Johnson.

A Certain Justice ½ **1999** Adam Dalgleish's (Marsden) latest case of murder involves barrister Venetia Aldridge (Downie), who is found bizarrely costumed and stabbed to death in her chambers. It turns out a number of people had a reason to dislike Venetia and prying the truth from a group of lawyers proves to be a challenge even for Scotland Yard's eminent Commander. **180m/C; VHS, DVD.** *GB* Roy Marsden; Penny Downie; Ricci Harnett; Flora Montgomery; Frederick Treves; Matthew Marsh; Ian McNeice; Sarah Winman; Richard Huw; Ken Jones; Britta Smith; Miles Anderson; Philip Stone; *D:* Ross Devenish; *W:* Michael Russell. **TV**

Certain Prey *John Sandford's Certain Prey* **2011** USA Network movie adapted from the 10th novel in John Sandford's crime series. Lucas Davenport (Harmon) likes women, nice suits, fast cars, and the fortune he made designing computer simulations. But he also likes his day job as the Deputy Chief of Police of Minneapolis and the challenges it holds. This time a murder brings in the FBI after they link the crime to hit woman Clara Rinker. Lucas follows his own lead to high-powered attorney Carmel Loan (Glaudini) but neither woman is going to escape Lucas's desire for justice. **85m/C; DVD.** Mark Harmon; Lola Glaudini; Tatiana Maslany; Art Hindle; *D:* Chris Gerolmo; *W:* Chris Gerolmo; *C:* Steve Cosens; *M:* Tom Third. **CABLE**

Certain Women **2016 (R)** The great Kelly Reichardt delivers her most star-studded ensemble but arguably her most independent and deliberately slow film to date. Adapting stories by Maile Meloy, the writer/director tells three loosely connected narratives about an attorney (Dern), mother (Williams), and teacher (Stewart). As she has before, Reichardt focuses on the natural flow of the world, stopping off with people that filmmakers often ignore. She draws fantastic performances throughout, particularly from newcomer Lily Gladstone as a solitary ranch hand who finds herself mournfully attracted to Stewart's teacher. It's a film of quiet dignity and unexpected grace. It's slow but haunting. **107m/C; DVD, Blu-Ray.** Laura Dern; Kristen Stewart; Michelle Williams; James LeGros; Jared Harris; Lily Gladstone; *D:* Kelly Reichardt; *W:* Kelly Reichardt; *C:* Christopher Blauvelt; *M:* Jeff Grace.

Certified Copy *Copie Conforme* **2010** A volatile nameless French antiques dealer (Binoche) and cool British art historian and author James (Shimell) meet during his book tour, become curious about each other, and wind up driving through the Tuscan countryside since she volunteers to be his tour guide. When they are mistaken for a long-married couple they try on the new personas and soon become a bickering duo. Now their playacting doesn't seem so frivolous. English, French, and Italian with subtitles. **106m/C; DVD, Blu-Ray.** *FR IT BE* Juliette Binoche; William Shimell; *D:* Abbas Kiarostami; *W:* Abbas Kiarostami; *C:* Luca Bigazzi.

Cesar **1936** This is the third and most bittersweet part of Pagnol's famed trilogy based on his play depicting the lives and loves of the people of Provence, France. Marius returns after a 20-year absence to his beloved Fanny and his now-grown son, Cesariot. The first two parts of the trilogy are "Marius" and "Fanny" and were directed by Alexander Korda and Marc Allegret respectively. In French with English subtitles. **117m/B; VHS, DVD, Blu-Ray.** *FR* Raimu; Pierre Fresnay; Orane Demazis; Charpin; Andre Fouche; Alida Rouffe; *D:* Marcel Pagnol; *W:* Marcel Pagnol; *M:* Vincent Scotto.

Cesar & Rosalie **1972 (PG)** Acclaimed French comedy depicts the love triangle between a beautiful divorcee, her aging live-in companion and a younger man. Engaging portrait of how their relationship evolves over time. In French with English subtitles. **110m/C; VHS, DVD.** *FR* Romy Schneider; Yves Montand; Sami Frey; Umberto Orsini; *D:* Claude Sautet; *W:* Claude Sautet; Jean-Loup Dabadie; Claude Neron; *C:* Jean Boffety; *M:* Philippe Sarde.

Cesar Chavez ½ **2014 (PG-13)** An important subject does not automatically make for a successful film. While actor Diego Luna's directorial effort to shed light on the history of Cesar Chavez (Pena) can be commended in theory, the result is a soft, TV-movie version of reality. This broad, shallow documentary of the farm worker organizer and union activist only puts him up on a pedestal, rather than getting anywhere near to the human side of a man who is already an icon in certain circles. Only a few solid performances, particularly by Pena and John Malkovich, save it from complete disaster. **102m/C; DVD, Blu-Ray.** *US MX* Michael Peña; America Ferrera; Rosario Dawson; Eli Vargas; John Malkovich; Yancey Arias; Wes Bentley; Jack Holmes; *D:* Diego Luna; *W:* Keir Pearson; Timothy J. Sexton; *C:* Enrique Chediak; *M:* Michael Brook.

Chad Hanna ½ **1940** In the 1840s, farm boy Chad Hanna (Fonda) runs away to join the circus after falling for bareback rider, Albany (Lamour). Circus owner Huguenine (Kibbee) is threatened by larger rival Shepley (North), who then steals Albany away to work for him. She's replaced by young lovely, Caroline (Darnell), who marries Chad, but continuing clashes between the two outfits leads to trouble. The finale involves an elephant. **88m/C; DVD.** Henry Fonda; Dorothy Lamour; Linda Darnell; Guy Kibbee; Jane Darwell; Ted North; John Carradine; *D:* Henry King; *W:* Nunnally Johnson; *C:* Ernest Palmer; *M:* David Buttolph.

Chain Gang ½ **1950** Newshound Cliff Roberts goes undercover as a prison guard assigned to a chain gang so he can expose the brutal conditions. But when his cover is blown, he nearly becomes another victim, dodging attack dogs and bullets. **70m/B; DVD.** Douglas Kennedy; Emory Parnell; Marjorie Lord; Thurston Hall; Bill (William) Phillips; *D:* Lew Landers; *W:* Howard J. Green; *C:* Ira Morgan.

Chain Gang Girls *Kuga no ori: Nami dai-42 zakkyobo* **2008** Yet another women-in-prison film, this one re-using the set from "Female Prisoner Sigma." Nami (Yuka Kosaka) is framed for the murder of her boyfriend's pregnant significant other—even worse, he's a prosecutor with jurisdiction over the prison she's sent to and tells the warden to make life hell for her. The prisoners outnumber the guards 100 to 1, making the odds of a riot higher with each passing day. **75m/C; DVD.** *JP* Jae-yong Lee; Ju-hyeon Lee; Ju-Bong Gi; Yun-shik Baek; *D:* Sasuke Sasuga; *W:* Bakuto Ijuin.

Chain Gang Women **WOOF! 1972 (R)** Sordid violence. Two escaped convicts plunder, rob, and rape until a victim's husband comes looking for revenge. **85m/C; VHS, DVD.** Robert Lott; Barbara Mills; Michael Stearns; Linda York; Wes Bishop; Phil Hoover; Chuck Wells; *D:* Lee Frost.

Chain Letter **WOOF! 2010 (R)** Introducing the most passive-aggressive serial killer in horror history. A mysterious chain letter is e-mailed and texted—yay! technology!?to six teens with deadly results for those not following its instructions. The oh-so-cleverly-christened Chain Man (B-list horror vet Bailey Smith) dishes out disturbing torture to this group of high schoolers (played by actors 10 years out of high school) using, as if the gimmick hadn't been pushed enough, chains. This muddled mess looks patched together from rejected clips of "Saw" and "Hostel," with arguably the silliest premise since the U.S. version of "One Missed Call."

86m/C; Blu-Ray, On Demand. Nikki Reed; Keith David; Brad Dourif; Bai Ling; Betsy Russell; Matt Cohen; Noah Segan; Cody Kasch; *D:* Deon Taylor; *W:* Deon Taylor; Michael J. Pagan; Diana Erwin; *C:* Philip Lee; *M:* Vincent Gillioz.

Chain Lightning **1950** Bogart stars as a bomber pilot who falls in love with a Red Cross worker (Parker) while fighting in Europe in 1943. They lose touch after the war until Bogie goes to work as a test pilot for the same shady airplane manufacturer (Massey) where Parker works. He is given the chance to test a new plane, which has already cost the life of one of his friends. Bogart has more success, along with rekindling the flames of romance. Average script but the flying sequences are well-done. **94m/B; VHS, DVD.** Humphrey Bogart; Eleanor Parker; Raymond Massey; Richard Whorf; *D:* Stuart Heisler; *W:* Liam O'Brien; Vincent B. Evans.

Chain Link 1/2 **2008** In this first time effort by director Dylan Reynolds, Anthony (Irvingsen) is a con just released from prison struggling to make ends meet, get a job, and bond with his son without having to resort to his old habits to survive. Not quite as cliche as it sounds, since it doesn't portray the lead as a misunderstood guy. **98m/C; DVD.** Mark Irvingsen; Jody Jaress; David Kallaway; Peter Looney; Luciano Rauso; Jim Round; Jim Storm; Yassmin Alers; Lelia Goldoni; *D:* Dylan Reynolds; *W:* Jim Storm; *C:* Matt Gulley.

Chain of Command **1995 (R)** Anti-terrorist agent Merrill Ross (Dudikoff) goes up against hired mercenaries trying to overthrow the government of the oil-rich Republic of Qumir. Then Ross realizes he's being manipulated and it could be by any number of players. **97m/C; VHS, DVD.** Michael Dudikoff; R. Lee Ermey; Todd Curtis; Keren Tishman; *D:* David Worth; *W:* Christopher Applegate; Ben Jonson Handy; *C:* Avi Koren; *M:* Gregory King.

Chain of Command **2000 (R)** Agent Mike Connelly (Muldoon) must protect the President's (Scheider) briefcase-sized computer that holds the nuclear codes. But when one of Connelly's colleagues betrays them, a nuclear winter could be as close as a madman's command. **96m/C; VHS, DVD.** Patrick Muldoon; Roy Scheider; Michael Biehn; Maria Conchita Alonso; Ric Young; William R. Moses; Michael Mantell; Pat Skipper; *D:* John Terlesky. **VIDEO**

Chain of Command *Echo Effect* **2015 (R)** A dramatic action thriller centering on murder, government corruption, and one man's efforts to expose the truth. Soon after returning home from military duty, Special Operative James Webster (White) sees his brother killed in front of him. As Webster tries to find who did the crime, he learns of government secrets and a deadly conspiracy. He is also being trailed by a skilled government assassin, Ray Peters (Austin). Webster does all he can to expose the corrupt officials before he loses his own life. **88m/C; DVD, Blu-Ray, Streaming, Download.** Michael Jai White; Max Ryan; Steve Austin; Ian Short; Allen Yates; *D:* Kevin Carraway; *W:* Kevin Carraway; Lawrence Sara; *C:* Curtis Petersen; *M:* Steve Yeaman. **VIDEO**

Chain of Fools 1/2 **2000 (R)** Suicidal barber Zahn comes into possession of a stolen treasure and falls for detective Hayek, who's assigned to the case. Director Traktor is actually a six-person Swedish filmmaking collective. **98m/C; DVD.** Steve Zahn; Salma Hayek; Jeff Goldblum; Elijah Wood; David Cross; Tom Wilkinson; Orlando Jones; Kevin Corrigan; David Hyde Pierce; Lara Flynn Boyle; Michael Rapaport; Craig Ferguson; John Cassini; *D:* Traktor.

Chain of Souls **WOOF!** **2000** Cult finds self-fulfillment through murder, luring wannabe actresses to fake auditions. One victim has a sister who worries when she doesn't hear from her sibling so she hightails it to Hollywood to find out what happened. Sound familiar? **105m/C; VHS, DVD.** Joe Decker; Eric Chaikin; Denise Gossett; Suzanne Talhouk; Deborah Joy Vinall; Stephanie Kane; *D:* Steve Jarvis; *W:* Dennis Devine; *C:* Dennis Devine; *M:* Michael Kelley. **VIDEO**

Chain Reaction 1/2 *Nuclear Run* **1980** When a nuclear scientist is exposed to radiation after an accident at an atomic power plant, he must escape to warn the public of the danger. **87m/C; VHS, DVD.** Steve Bisley; Ross Thompson; *D:* Ian Barry; *C:* Russell Boyd.

Chain Reaction 1/2 *Dead Drop* **1996 (PG-13)** Government/scientific conspiracy chase story finds Chicago lab tech Eddie Kasalivich (Reeves) a member of a research team that's discovered the formula for cheap, pollution-free energy. This doesn't sit well with someone since the team's leader is murdered and the lab destroyed in an explosion. Eddie and scientist Lily Sinclair (Weisz) become prime suspects and are pursued by the feds as they try to find the real culprits. Old pro Freeman, as money man Paul Shannon, is the best reason to watch (as usual). Davis did "The Fugitive," so he knows his tension-filled chases but this is just more same old-same old. **107m/C; VHS, DVD, Blu-Ray, UMD.** Keanu Reeves; Morgan Freeman; Rachel Weisz; Fred Ward; Brian Cox; Kevin Dunn; Joanna Cassidy; Chelcie Ross; Tzi Ma; Nicholas Rudall; Peter J. D'Noto; *D:* Andrew Davis; *W:* J.F. Lawton; Michael Bortman; *C:* Frank Tidy; *M:* Jerry Goldsmith.

Chained 1/2 **1934** Crawford and Gable star in this love triangle that somehow never sizzles. Crawford, in love with married businessman Kruger, takes a South American cruise to get away from it all, meets Gable, and of course falls in love. Seems simple enough, but wait! Crawford goes back to New York City and marries Kruger (his wife grants him a divorce) and is miserable. But then Gable shows up, further complicating matters. Choices, choices. Predictable script was not helped by half-hearted performances. **73m/B; VHS, DVD.** Joan Crawford; Clark Gable; Otto Kruger; Stuart Erwin; Una O'Connor; *D:* Clarence Brown; *C:* George J. Folsey.

Chained for Life **WOOF!** **1951** Daisy and Violet Hilton, real life Siamese twins, star in this old-fashioned "freak" show. When a gigolo deserts one twin on their wedding night, the other twin shoots him dead. The twins go on trial and the judge asks the viewer to hand down the verdict. Exploitative and embarrassing to watch. **81m/B; VHS, DVD, Blu-Ray.** Daisy Hilton; Violet Hilton; Allen Jenkins; Sheldon Leonard; *D:* Harry Fraser; *W:* Nat Tanchuck.

Chained Heat **1983 (R)** Seamy tale of the vicious reality of life for women behind bars. Naive Blair is imprisoned again (after another bad jailhouse gig in "Born Innocent") and has usual assortment of negative experiences with domineering prisoners, degenerative guards, and the creepy warden who maintains a prison bachelor pad equipped with hot tub. Needless to say, she grows up in a hurry. Trashifying, archetypal women-in-prison effort that aims to satisfy full range of low-quality audience demands. Sequel to 1982 "Concrete Jungle." **97m/C; VHS, DVD.** *GE* Linda Blair; Stella Stevens; Sybil Danning; Tamara Dobson; Henry Silva; John Vernon; Nita Talbot; Louisa Moritz; Sharon Hughes; Robert Miano; Kendal Kaldwell; *D:* Paul Nicholas; *W:* Paul Nicholas; Vincent Mongol; *C:* Mac Ahlberg; *M:* Joseph Conlan. Golden Raspberries '83: Worst Support. Actress (Danning).

Chained Heat 2 1/2 **1992 (R)** Another sordid tale of women behind bars. Nielsen stars as the psychotic stiletto-heeled warden of an infamous prison, complete with sadistic heroin-smuggling guards. This drug ring also deals in prostitution, which results in two imprisoned sisters (innocent, naturally) being separated from one another. One sister is determined to find true justice. **98m/C; VHS, DVD.** Brigitte Nielsen; Paul Koslo; Kari Whitman; Kimberley Kates; *D:* Lloyd A. Simandl; *W:* Chris Hyde.

Chained Heat 3: Hell Mountain 1/2 *Chained Heat 3: The Horror of Hell Mountain; Chained Heat 3* **1998 (R)** Future Earth is a barren wasteland where survivors are forced to work in the mines of overlord Stryker. Each year, young women are taken to the mines on Hell Mountain but this time Kal is determined to save his girlfriend and destroy Stryker. **97m/C; VHS, DVD.** Bentley Mitchum; Kate Rodger; Christopher Clarke; Karel Augusta; Noelle Balfour; Jack Scalia; Sarah Douglas; *D:* Mike Rohl; *W:* Chris Hyde; *C:* David Frazee; *M:* Peter Allen. **VIDEO**

Chains *Catene* **1949** Endless suffering plagues the Aniello family in Matarazzo's convoluted melodrama. Rosa is happily married to mechanic Guglielmo when her ex-fiance, gangster Emilio, turns up. He wants her back and tries to blackmail Rosa with some amorous letters she wrote to him. All that gets him is dead and Rosa's life then gets really complicated. Italian with subtitles. **90m/B; DVD.** *IT* Amedeo Nazzari; Yvonee Sanson; Aldo Nicodemi; Teresa Franchini; Gianfranco Magalotti; Rosalia Randazzo; Aldo Silvani; *D:* Raffaello Matarazzo; *W:* Aldo De Benedetti; Nicola Manzari; *C:* Carlo Montuori; *M:* Gino Campase.

Chains of Gold **1992 (R)** Kind social worker (Travolta) befriends teen who wants to get out of the crack-dealing gang in which he's involved. He infiltrates the gang and risks his life helping the boy get out. **95m/C; VHS, DVD.** John Travolta; Marilu Henner; Bernie Casey; Hector Elizondo; Joseph Lawrence; *D:* Rod Holcomb; *M:* Trevor Jones. **CABLE**

The Chairman *Most Dangerous Man in the World* **1969 (PG)** Typically bizarre 60s spy thriller involving a scientist unknowingly carrying a bomb in his head trying to steal crop research from China. A relic of cold-war paranoia that will seem odd to modern audiences (its title is a reference to Mao Zedong), it's still interesting to watch Gregory Peck in the lead. **102m/C; DVD, Blu-Ray.** *GB* Gregory Peck; Anne Heywood; Arthur Hill; Alan Dobie; Conrad Yama; Zienia Merton; Eric Young; Francesca Tu; Ori Levy; Burt Kwouk; Keye Luke; Helen Horton; J. Lee Thompson; *D:* J. Lee Thompson; *W:* J. Lee Thompson; Ben Maddow; Jay Richard Kennedy; *C:* John Wilcox; Ted Moore; *M:* Jerry Goldsmith.

Chairman of the Board **WOOF!** **1997 (PG-13)** Some studio executive decided to take a bad prop comic named after a vegetable and give him a major motion picture. If this movie accomplishes one thing, it may be the abolition of Friday afternoon 12-martini lunches in Hollywood. Carrot Top plays Edison, a wacky surfer/inventor who befriends an old eccentric man. After the old guy heads for the big wave in the sky, it turns out that he was fabulously wealthy and left his company to Edison. This doesn't sit well with the conniving Bradford (Miller). Courtney Thorne-Smith plays Natalie (although this does not stop Mr. Top from calling her Courtney in one scene) as the standard love interest. Also appearing are Jack Warden, Raquel Welch and M. Emmet Walsh. Why? That's what they're asking their agents. Rent it only if every single video, including the instructional mime section, is already out. **95m/C; VHS, DVD.** Carrot Top; Courtney Thorne-Smith; Larry Miller; Raquel Welch; Jack Warden; Estelle Harris; Bill Erwin; M. Emmet Walsh; Jack McGee; Glenn Shadix; Fred Stoller; Mystro Clark; Jack Plotnick; *D:* Alex Zamm; *W:* Al Septien; Turi Meyer; Alex Zamm; *C:* David Lewis; *M:* Chris Hajian.

Chalet Girls 1/2 **2011** Predictable but exuberant romantic comedy for the younger crowd. Teenager Kim looks after her impractical dad Bill since the accidental death of her mother, even though it meant giving up a promising pro-am skateboarding career. Working-class Kim gets a housekeeping job for the posh Madsen family at their Austrian Alps winter vacation lodge. Their son Jonny takes a liking to Kim and appreciates her efforts on the slopes even as she gets a chance to compete again when she learns to snowboard. English and German with subtitles. **97m/C; DVD.** *UK GE AT* Felicity Jones; Ed Westwick; Bill Nighy; Bill Bailey; Brooke Shields; Sophia Bush; Tamsin Egerton; Ken Duken; *D:* Phil Traill; *W:* Tom Williams; *C:* Ed Wild; *M:* Christian Henson.

Chalk 1/2 **2006 (PG-13)** Dark comedic look at the frustrations endured by a group of high school teachers over a typical school year. Assistant principal Reddell (Haragan) finds administrative duties are even worse than teaching; vain Mr. Stroope (Mass) is determined to be popular with his students so he can be named teacher of the year; tough gym coach Ms. Webb (J. Schremmer) is tired of everyone assuming she's a lesbian; and shy rookie Mr. Lowrey (T. Schremmer) can't manage his unruly students. **84m/C; DVD.** Chris Mass; Shannon Haragan; Janelle Schremmer; Troy Schremmer; *D:* Mike Akel; *W:* Chris Mass; Mike Akel; *C:* Steven Schaefer; *M:* Chris Jagich.

The Chalk Garden **1964** A woman with a mysterious past takes on the job of governess for an unruly 14-year-old girl, with unforseen consequences. An excellent adaptation of the Enid Bagnold play although not as suspenseful as the stage production. **106m/C; DVD.** *UK* Deborah Kerr; Hayley Mills; Edith Evans; John Mills; Elizabeth Sellars; Felix Aylmer; *D:* Ronald Neame; *W:* John Michael Hayes; *M:* Malcolm Arnold. Natl. Bd. of Review '64: Support. Actress (Evans).

The Challenge **1938** Story of the courageous party of explorers who conquered the Matterhorn. Incredible avalanche scenes. **77m/B; VHS, DVD.** *GB* Luis Trenker; Robert Douglas; Joan Gardner; Mary Clare; Frank Birch; Geoffrey Wardwell; Lyonel (Lionel) Watts; Fred Groves; Lawrence (Laurence) Baskcomb; Ralph Truman; *D:* Luis Trenker; Milton Rosmer; *W:* Milton Rosmer; Patrick Kirwan; *C:* Albert Benitz; Georges Perinal; *M:* Allan Gray; Muir Mathieson.

Challenge of the Gladiator *Il Gladiatore che Sfido l'Impero* **1965** Typically bad dubbing and nonsensical plot. Evil Roman senator Quintilius (Serato) journeys to Thrace in search of a legendary treasure. He has ex-gladiator Terenzius (Barnes) posing as the Emperor Nero so the locals won't be any trouble, but that plan backfires when word comes that the real Nero has died back in Rome. Local governor Metellus (Lulli) is peeved and joins with rebellious Spartacus (Lupus using the wonderful nom de film "Rock Stevens") to defeat the traitors. **90m/C; DVD.** *IT* Peter Lupus; Massimo Serato; Pierro Lulli; Walter Barnes; Livio Lorenzon; Maria Fie; *D:* Domenico Paolella; *W:* Domenico Paolella; *C:* Raffaele Masciocchi; *M:* Giuseppe Piccillo.

Challenge To Be Free *Mad Trapper of the Yukon* **1976 (G)** Action adventure geared toward a young audience depicting the struggles of a man being pursued by 12 men and 100 dogs across a thousand miles of frozen wilderness. The last film directed by Garnett, who has a cameo as Marshal McGee. Produced in 1972, the release wasn't until 1976. **90m/C; VHS, DVD.** Mike Mazurki; Jimmy Kane; ***Cameo(s):*** Tay Garnett; *D:* Tay Garnett.

Challenge to White Fang 1/2 **1986 (PG)** A courageous dog prevents a scheming businessman from taking over an old man's gold mine. **89m/C; VHS, DVD.** Harry Carey, Jr.; Franco Nero; *D:* Lucio Fulci.

The Chamber **1996 (R)** Dull retelling of yet another John Grisham legal thriller fails to engross. White supremacist Sam Cahall (Hackman) is on Mississippi's death row for killing two Jewish boys in a 1967 bombing. Young Chicago lawyer Adam Hall (O'Donnell), looking to find out more about his family's odious past, volunteers to work on his grandfather's case and win a stay of execution. Sam's an unrepentent racist but there's some question about whether he was the only culprit. Hackman and Dunaway (as his alcoholic daughter) are their usual professional selves while the charming O'Donnell seems out of his depth. Co-screenwriter Robinson used the pen name Chris Reese. **113m/C; VHS, DVD, Blu-Ray.** Gene Hackman; Chris O'Donnell; Faye Dunaway; Lela Rochon; Robert Prosky; Raymond J. Barry; Bo Jackson; David Marshall Grant; Millie Perkins; *D:* James Foley; *W:* Phil Alden Robinson; William Goldman; *C:* Ian Baker; *M:* Carter Burwell.

Chamber of Horrors 1/2 *The Door with Seven Locks* **1940** A family is brought together at an English castle to claim a fortune left by an aristocrat. However, there's a catch—seven keys may open the vault with the fortune, or leave the key turner dead. Based on the work by Edgar Wallace. **80m/B; VHS, DVD, Blu-Ray.** *GB* Leslie Banks; Lilli Palmer; *D:* Norman Lee.

The Chambermaid 1/2 *La camarista* **2019** In a posh hotel in Mexico City, Eve (Cartol) works as a maid, cleaning up messy rooms with efficiency. She works hard to improve her lot in life and care for her young son. She takes advantage of the hotel's equivalent of high school equivalency classes and only buys cheap snacks in the cafeteria to save money. At the same time, she is kind and generous to those around her, and sometimes gets taken advantage of. Though Eve's work negatively affects her self-worth, she finds ways to make the job interesting. A moving observational drama, highlighted by Cartol's subtle performance. **102m/C; DVD.** Gabriela Cartol; Teresa Sanchez; ***D:*** Lila Aviles; ***W:*** Lila Aviles; Juan Carlos Marquez; ***C:*** Carlos Rossini.

The Chambermaid on the Titanic *La Femme de Chambre du Titanic; The Chambermaid* **1997** French foundry worker Horty (Martinez) wins a strongman contest and his prize is a trip to Southampton to see the launch of the Titanic. There he (platonically) shares a hotel room with maid Maria (Sanchez-Gijon), who says she has a job aboard the ship. After returning home and learning about the Titanic's sinking, Horty regales his friends with stories of his night with Maria—gradually beginning to believe his own lies about his passionate escapade. Based on the novel by Didier Decoin. French with subtitles. **96m/C; VHS, Streaming.** *FR SP* Olivier Martinez; Aitana Sanchez-Gijon; Romane Bohringer; Didier Bezace; Aldo Maccione; ***D:*** Bigas Luna; ***W:*** Bigas Luna; Cuca Canals; ***C:*** Patrick Blossier; ***M:*** Alberto Iglesias.

Chameleon Street **1989 (R)** Entertaining fact-based account of William Douglas Street, a Detroit man who successfully impersonated, among others, a Time magazine reporter and a surgeon until he was caught and sent to prison. He escaped and went to Yale, faked his identity as a student, and then returned to Michigan to impersonate a lawyer for the Detroit Human Rights Commission. Harris wrote and directed this insightful look into the man who fooled many people, including the mayor of Detroit, Coleman A. Young, who appears briefly as himself. **95m/C; VHS, DVD.** Wendell B. Harris, Jr.; Angela Leslie; Amina Fakir; Paula McGee; Mano Breckenridge; David Kiley; Anthony Ennis; ***Cameo(s):*** Coleman A. Young; ***D:*** Wendell B. Harris, Jr.; ***W:*** Wendell B. Harris, Jr.; ***C:*** Daniel S. Noga; ***M:*** Peter S. Moore. Sundance '90: Grand Jury Prize.

The Champ **1932** A washed up boxer dreams of making a comeback and receives support from no one but his devoted son. Minor classic most notorious for jerking the tears and soiling the hankies, this was the first of three Beery/Cooper screen teamings. **87m/B; VHS, DVD.** Wallace Beery; Jackie Cooper; Irene Rich; Roscoe Ates; Edward Brophy; Hale Hamilton; Jesse Scott; Marcia Mae Jones; ***D:*** King Vidor; ***W:*** Frances Marion. Oscars '32: Actor (Beery), Story.

The Champ **½ 1979 (PG)** An ex-fighter with a weakness for gambling and drinking is forced to return to the ring in an attempt to keep custody of his son. Excessive sentiment may cause cringing. Remake of the 1931 classic. **121m/C; VHS, DVD.** Jon Voight; Faye Dunaway; Rick Schroder; Jack Warden; Arthur Hill; Strother Martin; Joan Blondell; Elisha Cook, Jr.; ***D:*** Franco Zeffirelli; ***C:*** Fred W. Koenekamp; ***M:*** Dave Grusin.

Champagne **1928** A socialite's father fakes bankruptcy to teach his irresponsible daughter a lesson. Early, silent endeavor from Hitchcock is brilliantly photographed. **93m/B; Silent; VHS, DVD, Blu-Ray.** *GB* Betty Balfour; Gordon Harker; Ferdinand von Alten; Clifford Heatherley; Jack Trevor; ***D:*** Alfred Hitchcock; ***W:*** Alfred Hitchcock.

Champagne for Caesar **1950** The laughs keep coming in this comedy about a self-proclaimed genius-on-every-subject who goes on a TV quiz show and proceeds to win everything in sight. The program's sponsor, in desperation, hires a femme fatale to distract the contestant before the final program. Wonderful spoof of the game-show industry. **99m/B; VHS, DVD.** Ronald Colman; Celeste Holm; Vincent Price; Art Linkletter; Barbara Britton; ***D:*** Richard Whorf.

Champion **½ 1949** An ambitious prizefighter alienates the people around him as he desperately fights his way to the top. When he finally reaches his goal, he is forced to question the cost of his success. From a story by Ring Lardner. Certainly one of the best films ever made about boxing, with less sentiment than "Rocky" but concerned with sociological correctness. **99m/B; DVD, Blu-Ray.** Kirk Douglas; Arthur Kennedy; Marilyn Maxwell; Ruth Roman; Lola Albright; Paul Stewart; ***D:*** Mark Robson; ***W:*** Carl Foreman; ***C:*** Franz Planer; ***M:*** Dimitri Tiomkin. Oscars '49: Film Editing.

Champions **1984** Moving but cliched story of Bob Champion, a leading jockey who overcame cancer to win England's Grand National Steeplechase. A true story, no less. **113m/C; VHS, DVD.** *GB* John Hurt; Gregory Jones; Mick Dillon; Ann Bell; Jan Francis; Peter Barkworth; Edward Woodward; Ben Johnson; Kirstie Alley; Alison Steadman; ***D:*** John Irvin; ***W:*** Evan Jones; ***M:*** Carl Davis.

Champions: A Love Story **½ 1978** Shameless TV movie tearjerker. Driven figure skater Carrie Harlich (LeDuc) is constantly having partner problems (does this sound familiar?). Her new coach Alan (Lo Bianco) teams her with ex-hockey player Peter (McNichol) and the two eventually get friendly on and off the ice. Then tragedy strikes. LeDuc and McNichol were doubled by Ice Follies stars Susan Bevens and Rick Turley. **98m/C; DVD.** Jimmy (James Vincent) McNichol; Tony Lo Bianco; Shirley Knight; Richard Jaeckel; Jennifer Warren; Joy LeDuc; ***D:*** John A. Alonzo; ***W:*** John Sacret Young; ***C:*** John A. Alonzo; ***M:*** John Rubenstein. **TV**

Champs **2015** A sports documentary that looks at the lives of several famous boxers as a means of achieving the American Dream. Through interviews and their own words, boxers Mike Tyson, Evander Holyfield, and Bernard Hopkins discuss their lives and careers. The boxers discuss their origins in poverty and violence, their periods of fame and fortune, and their years of self-destruction and self-discovery. The film also includes classic bouts and interviews with journalists, educators, and famous boxing fans. **91m/C; DVD, Streaming, Download.** ***D:*** Bert Marcus; ***W:*** Bert Marcus; ***C:*** John Tipton; ***M:*** Tom Caffey.

Chan Is Missing **1982** Two cab drivers try to find the man who stole their life savings. Wry, low-budget comedy filmed in San Francisco's Chinatown was an art-house smash. The first full-length American film produced exclusively by an Asian-American cast and crew. **80m/B; VHS, DVD.** Wood Moy; Marc Hayashi; Laureen Chew; Judy Mihei; Peter Wang; Presco Tabios; Frankie Allarcon; Virginia Cerenio; Roy Chan; George Woo; Emily Yamasaki; Ellen Yeung; ***D:*** Wayne Wang; ***W:*** Wayne Wang; Terrel Seltzer; Isaac Cronin; ***C:*** Michael G. Chin; ***M:*** Robert Kikuchi-Yngojo. Natl. Film Reg. '95.

Chance **½ 1989** With over $1 million in diamonds missing, Haggerty and Jacobs throw out all the stops to recover them in this action thriller. **90m/C; VHS, DVD.** Dan Haggerty; Lawrence-Hilton Jacobs; Addison Randall; Roger Rudd; Charles Gries; Pamela Dixon; ***D:*** Addison Randall; Charles Kanganis.

Chance at Heaven **½ 1933** Ambitious gas station owner Blacky Gorman (McCrea) dumps faithful girlfriend Marje (Rogers) to marry smitten socialite Glory Franklyn (Nixon). Glory moves into Blacky's modest home and attempts to be a housewife (with Marje's help) but soon realizes the working-class life is not for her. Pre-Code flick allowed Glory both an abortion and a divorce without any moral consequences. **71m/B; DVD.** Joel McCrea; Ginger Rogers; Marion (Marian) Nixon; Andy Devine; Virginia Hammond; Ann Shoemaker; Lucien Littlefield; George Meeker; ***D:*** William A. Seiter; ***W:*** Julien Josephson; Sarah Y. Mason; ***C:*** Nicholas Musuraca.

Chances Are **1989 (PG)** After her loving husband dies in a chance accident, a pregnant woman remains unmarried, keeping her husband's best friend as her only close male companion. Years later, her now teenage daughter brings a friend home for dinner, but due to an error in heaven, the young man begins to realize that this may not be the first time he and this family have met. A wonderful love-story hampered only minimally by the unbelievable plot. **108m/C; VHS, DVD, Blu-Ray.** Cybill Shepherd; Robert Downey, Jr.; Ryan O'Neal; Mary Stuart Masterson; Josef Sommer; Christopher McDonald; Joe Grifasi; James Noble; Susan Ruttan; Fran Ryan; ***D:*** Emile Ardolino; ***W:*** Perry Howze; Randy Howze; ***C:*** William A. Fraker; ***M:*** Maurice Jarre.

Chandler **½ 1971** Uninspired contemporary noir with a confusing plot. Tough guy PI Chandler (Oates) is hired to guard Frenchwoman Katherine (Caron) who's reluctantly returned to L.A. The former mistress of a mobster, Katherine is supposed to be a state's witness—if Chandler can keep her alive. **88m/C; DVD.** Warren Oates; Leslie Caron; Alex Dreier; Gloria Grahame; Mitchell Ryan; Charles McGraw; Richard Loo; Gordon Pinsent; Scatman Crothers; ***D:*** Paul Magwood; ***W:*** John Sacret Young; ***C:*** Alan Stensvold; ***M:*** George Romanis.

Chandu on the Magic Island **1934** Chandu the Magician takes his powers of the occult to the mysterious lost island of Lemuri to battle the evil cult of Ubasti. Sequel to "Chandu the Magician" and just as campy. **67m/B; VHS, DVD.** Bela Lugosi; Maria Alba; Clara Kimball Young; ***D:*** Ray Taylor.

Chandu the Magician **1932** Bad guy searches desperately for the secret of a powerful death ray so he can (surprise!) destroy civilization. Not well received in its day, but makes for great high-camp fun now. One of Lugosi's most melodramatic performances. **70m/B; VHS, DVD, Blu-Ray.** Edmund Lowe; Bela Lugosi; Irene Ware; Henry B. Walthall; ***D:*** William Cameron Menzies; Marcel Varnel; ***C:*** James Wong Howe.

Chang: A Drama of the Wilderness **½ 1927** A farmer and his family has settled a small patch of ground on the edge of the jungle and must struggle for survival against numerous wild animals. The climatic elephant stampede is still thrilling. Shot on location in Siam. **67m/B; VHS, DVD.** ***D:*** Merian C. Cooper; Ernest B. Schoedsack; ***W:*** Merian C. Cooper; Ernest B. Schoedsack; ***C:*** Ernest B. Schoedsack.

Change My Life *Change Moi Ma Vie* **2001** Nina is a middle-aged actress who has long been unemployed. In despair, she takes an overdose of tranquilizers and collapses on a Paris street, where she is found by a passerby. Algerian immigrant Sami saves Nina and she is determined to find and thank him. When she does, Nina discovers Sami working as a transvestite prostitute and the two lonely souls vow to support each other and make changes in their lives. French with subtitles. **101m/C; DVD.** *FR* Fanny Ardant; Roschdy Zem; Fanny Cottencon; Sami Bouajila; Olivier Cruveiller; ***D:*** Liria Begeja; ***W:*** Jerome Beaujour; Francois Olivier Rousseau; Liria Begeja; ***C:*** Laurent Machuel.

Change of Habit **1969 (G)** Three novitiates undertake to learn about the world before becoming full-fledged nuns. While working at a ghetto clinic a young doctor forms a strong, affectionate relationship with one of them. Presley's last feature film. **93m/C; VHS, DVD.** Elvis Presley; Mary Tyler Moore; Barbara McNair; Ed Asner; Ruth McDevitt; Regis Toomey; Jane Elliot; Leora Dana; Robert Emhardt; Richard Carlson; William (Bill) Elliott; ***D:*** William A. Graham; ***W:*** Eric Bercovici; John Joseph; ***C:*** Russell Metty; ***M:*** Billy Goldenberg.

A Change of Heart **½ 1998** Smart is always good in wronged woman roles and she's got a doozy in this weepie. Elaine Marshall (Smart) thinks she and husband Jim (Terry) are doing okay marriage-wise. They've been together 20 years, have a couple of kids, two good careers, and apparent happiness. Then Elaine realizes Jim's having an affair. The real shocker for Elaine comes when she finds out her husband's lover is another man. **112m/C; VHS, DVD, Streaming.** Jean Smart; John Terry; Gretchen Corbett; Phillip Geoffrey Hough; Shawna Waldron; Dorian Harewood; ***D:*** Arvin Brown; ***W:*** Aaron Mendelsohn; ***C:*** John J. Campbell; ***M:*** Patrick Williams. **CABLE**

A Change of Place **½ 1994** Identical twins Kate and Kim (Roth) lead completely different lives. Kate is known as fashion model Domenique in Paris wile Kim is a shy grad student. Kate is also a drunk and when Kim checks her into rehab, Kate pleads with her sister to take her place at the fashion house. Too bad Kate didn't warn Kim that she is suspected of stealing designs by Philippe (Springfield). Can Kim quietly clear her sister's name or should she reveal the truth to the man she's falling in love with? From the Harlequin Romance Series; adapted from the Tracy Sinclair novel. **91m/C; DVD.** *CA* Andrea Roth; Rick Springfield; Stephanie Beacham; Geordie Johnson; Ian Richardson; ***D:*** Donna Deitch; ***W:*** Jim Henshaw; Rosemary Anne Sissons; ***C:*** Nyika Jancso; ***M:*** Brent Barkman; Carl Lennox. **TV**

Change of Plans *La Code a Change* **2009** In this crowded Parisian comedy, writer/director Thompson looks at the lives of eight middle-aged, middle-class dinner party guests and their complicated love lives, including multiple infidelities, family ties, employment decisions, and emotional traumas. And then the story moves forward a year to see what's transpired. French with subtitles. **100m/C; DVD.** *FR* Dany Boon; Marina Hands; Emmanuelle Seigner; Karin Viard; Pierre Arditti; Patrick Bruel; Patrick Chesnais; Marina Fois; Blanca Li; Laurent Stocker; Christopher Thompson; ***D:*** Daniele Thompson; ***W:*** Christopher Thompson; Daniele Thompson; ***C:*** Jean-Marc Fabre; ***M:*** Nicola Piovani.

A Change of Seasons **1980 (R)** One of them so-called sophisticated comedies that look at the contemporary relationships and values of middle-class, middle-aged people who should know better. The wife of a college professor learns of her husband's affair with a seductive student and decides to have a fling with a younger man. The situation reaches absurdity when the couples decide to vacation together. **102m/C; VHS, DVD.** Shirley MacLaine; Bo Derek; Anthony Hopkins; Michael Brandon; Mary Beth Hurt; ***D:*** Richard Lang; ***W:*** Erich Segal; ***M:*** Henry Mancini.

The Change-Up **½ 2011 (R)** Married workaholic Dave (Bateman) switches souls with his slacker single buddy Mitch (Reynolds) and the Freaky Friday-ish transfer allows ample opportunity for jokes involving baby poop and awkward sex. The typically-restrained Bateman gets to let his angry side out and his ace comic timing works. But the best efforts of its talented stars can't make up for a gross-out script that turns this played-out body switch comedy into an uncomfortable, unfunny affair. **112m/C; Blu-Ray.** Jason Bateman; Ryan Reynolds; Olivia Wilde; Leslie Mann; Mircea Moore; ***D:*** David Dobkin; ***W:*** Jon Lucas; Scott Moore; ***C:*** Eric Alan Edwards; ***M:*** John Debney; Matt Aberly.

The Changeling **½ 1980 (R)** A music teacher moves into an old house and discovers that a young boy's ghostly spirit is his housemate. The ghost wants revenge against the being that replaced him upon his death. Scary ghost story with some less than logical leaps of script. **114m/C; VHS, DVD, Blu-Ray.** *CA* George C. Scott; Trish Van Devere; John Russell; Melvyn Douglas; Jean Marsh; John Colicos; Barry Morse; Roberta Maxwell; James B. Douglas; ***D:*** Peter Medak; ***W:*** William Gray; Diana Maddox; ***C:*** John Coquillon. Genie '80: Film.

Changeling **½ 2008 (R)** In 1928, single mother Christine Collins (Jolie) comes home from work to discover her 10-year-old son Walter missing. When the LAPD returns a boy to her months later, Christine insists that he's not her son—and she's not the only one to say so, as political and police corruption and cover-ups lead down some very disturbing paths. Eastwood creates another superb film in yet another genre (horror for adults), showcasing an Oscar-worthy performance by Jolie, who flaunts her acting chops more than her beauty, while Malkovich is typically intense and captivating, further elevating this harrowing story to the cinematic stratosphere. Loosely based on the crimes known as the "Wineville Chicken Murders." **141m/C; Blu-Ray, On Demand.** Angelina Jolie; John Malkovich; Jeffrey Donovan; Michael Kelly; Colm Feore; Jason Butler Harner; Eddie Alderson; Amy Ryan; Denis O'Hare; Peter Gerety; Gattlin Griffith; ***D:*** Clint Eastwood; ***W:*** J. Michael Straczynski; ***C:*** Tom Stern; ***M:*** Clint Eastwood.

Changing Habits **½ 1996 (R)** Starving artist Soosh (Kelly) moves into a nunnery, in exchange for doing chores, in order to save money. She's so broke, she's taken to stealing art supplies, but salesman Felix

(Walsh) is more interested in romancing Soosh than turning her in. Dull, dull, dull, and a waste of a talented cast. **92m/C; VHS, DVD.** Moira Kelly; Christopher Lloyd; Teri Garr; Shelley Duvall; Dylan Walsh; Marissa Ribisi; Frances Bay; Bob Gunton; Anne Haney; Eileen Brennan; *D:* Lynn Roth; *W:* Scott Davis Jones; *C:* Mike Mayers; *M:* David McHugh.

Changing Lanes ♂♂♂ **2002 (R)** A fender-bender on the FDR pits two harried New Yorkers in an escalating battle of revenge. Banek (Affleck), a privileged Wall Street lawyer, and Gipson (Jackson), a recovering-alcoholic insurance man, both need to get to court on time. Banek to file documents crucial to his firm's success, and Gipson, to prove he's fit to retain joint custody of his two kids. Because of the accident, neither gets quite what he wants. When Gipson finds that he has the vital document, after having been stranded by Banek (and subsequently late to the custody hearing), he begins the battle. Throughout the back and forth, the plot (and many of its excesses), gives way to a fully realized character study and thoughtful pondering of motivations, corruption, and desperation, powered by dialogue not usually seen in a "revenge" flick. Michell deftly brings out the best in every member of a talented cast. **98m/C; VHS, DVD, Blu-Ray.** Ben Affleck; Samuel L. Jackson; Toni Collette; Sydney Pollack; William Hurt; Amanda Peet; Richard Jenkins; Kim Staunton; John Benjamin Hickey; Jennifer (Jennie) Dundas Lowe; Dylan Baker; Matt Malloy; Pamela Hart; *D:* Roger Michell; *W:* Michael Tolkin; Chap Taylor; *C:* Salvatore Totino; *M:* David Arnold.

Changing Times ♂♂ *Les Temps Qui Changent* **2004** Sucessful engineer Antoine (Depardieu) has spent the last three decades pining for Cecile (Deneuve), the love of his life, who left France for Morocco more than 30 years ago, and has since moved on with her life. Antoine volunteers for a job in Tangiers and promptly tracks down Cecile (and her much younger doctor-husband) in order to win her back, as he informs them both. Layers of heady complications follow, including the appearance of Cecile's son, who drops by with his girlfriend despite his being gay, Cecile's own deteriorating marriage, and cultural clashes between French and Moroccan characters and their values. Pic is a reunion of French legends Deneuve, Depardieu and director Andre Techine and will appeal to Francophiles and probably few others. **98m/C; DVD.** *FR* Catherine Deneuve; Gerard Depardieu; Gilbert Melki; Malik Zidi; Lubna Azabal; Tanya Lopert; Nabila Baraka; Idir Elomri; Nadem Rachati; Jabir Elomri; *D:* Andre Techine; *W:* Andre Techine; Pascal Bonitzer; Laurent Guyot; *C:* Julien Hirsch; *M:* Juliette Garrigues.

The Chant of Jimmie Blacksmith ♂♂♂ **1978 (R)** Intense, ultrviolent true story set in 19th century Australia follows aborigine Jimmie as he is brutalized by white civilization and reponds in kind. Shocking violence perpetrated by and to Jimmie is not for the faint of heart, and is not softened in the least by the superb performances by the excellent cast. **120m/C; VHS, DVD, Blu-Ray.** *AU* Tommy (Tom E.) Lewis; Bryan Brown; Ray Barrett; Elizabeth (Liz) Alexander; Jack Thompson; Peter Carroll; Liddy Clark; Ruth Cracknell; Arthur Dignam; Ian Gilmour; John Jarratt; Ray Meagher; Kevin Miles; Robyn Nevin; Angela Punch McGregor; Peter Sumner; *D:* Fred Schepisi; *W:* Fred Schepisi; *C:* Ian Baker; *M:* Bruce Smeaton.

Chaos ♂♂ **2001** Workaholic Parisian businessman Paul (Lindon) and his wife Helene (Frot) are driving to dinner when a frantic young Algerian immigrant, Noemie (Brakni), begs them to let her in as thugs grab and beat her before their eyes. Paul refuses to get involved and abandons the girl, which sets in motion a domestic crisis for Helene. Guilt-ridden and disgusted by her husband's indifference, Helene tracks the severly-injured Noemie to a hospital and abandons her family to assume responsibility for Noemie and her rehabilitation, which includes protecting her from her abusers. French with subtitles. **109m/C; VHS, DVD.** *FR* Catherine Frot; Vincent Lindon; Rachida Brakni; Line Renaud; Wojciech Pszoniak; Aurelien Wilk; *D:* Coline Serreau; *W:* Coline Serreau; *C:* Jean-Francois Robin; *M:* Ludovic Navarre.

Chaos WOOF! **2005 (NC-17)** Repulsive, exploitative horror flick features a group of psycho-sickos, led by the Manson-like Chaos (Gage), who torture and finally murder two female college students. Atrocious in every imaginable way. **78m/C; DVD, Blu-Ray.** Kevin Gage; Sage Stallone; Kelly K. C. Quann; Stephen Wozniak; *D:* David DeFalco; *W:* David DeFalco; *C:* Brandon Trost.

Chaos & Cadavers ♂♂ ½ **2003** Newlyweds Edward (Moran) and Samantha (Hawes) have their honeymoon at a remote hotel disrupted by rowdy conventioneers attending an undertakers' conference. But when the head of the funeral director's association is found dead under suspicious circumstances, they decide to find out whodunit. **90m/C; DVD.** *GB* Nick Moran; Keeley Hawes; Steve Huison; John Bennett; Ian McNeice; Hugh Fraser; Rick Mayall; *D:* Niklaus Hilber; *W:* Niklaus Hilber; Drew Bird; *C:* Tony Imi; *M:* Warren Bennett.

The Chaos Experiment ♂ ½ *The Steam Experiment* **2009 (R)** Crazy ex-professor James Pettis (Kilmer) wants to prove his theory of the effects of global warming so he traps six people in a Tampa bathhouse. He vows to turn up the heat on his hostages until his theories get published on the front page of the newspaper. This isn't torture porn so the steambath stuff quickly gets dull and it may be all a delusion on Pettis' part, which is what Detective Mancini (Assante) has to figure out. **96m/C; DVD.** Val Kilmer; Armand Assante; Eric Roberts; Patrick Muldoon; Megan Brown; Eve Mauro; Quinn Duffy; Cordelia Reynolds; *D:* Philippe Martinez; *W:* Robert Malkani; *C:* Erik Curtis; *M:* Don MacDonald. **VIDEO**

Chaos Factor ♂♂ **2000 (R)** Jack Poynt (Sabato Jr.) is an Army Intelligence officer working in Cambodia. He discovers evidence linking the death of American soldiers to high-ranking officials and becomes the target of a deadly coverup by the Defense Department. **102m/C; VHS, DVD.** Antonio Sabato, Jr.; Fred Ward; Kelly Rutherford; Sean Kanan; R. Lee Ermey; *D:* Terry Cunningham. **VIDEO**

Chaos Theory ♂♂ **2008 (PG-13)** Motivational speaker and efficiency expert Frank Allen (Reynolds) has driven wife Susan (Mortimer) nuts with their micromanaged lifestyle. (Frank really lives what he preaches.) Susan resets their clocks, making Frank late for a conference and throwing his organized world into chaos, which he decides to embrace when he can't seem to get it back under control. But his new attitude leads to Frank and Susan splitting up and just causing a whole different set of problems. Reynolds is likeable (Mortimer less so) but it's a rather odd rom-com entry until it heads into happy ending territory. **86m/C; DVD.** Ryan Reynolds; Emily Mortimer; Stuart Townsend; Sarah Chalke; Mike Erwin; Constance Zimmer; Elisabeth Harnois; Damon; Jocelyne Loewen; *D:* Marcos Siega; *W:* Daniel Taplitz; *C:* Ramsay Nickell; *M:* Gilad Benamram.

Chapayev ♂♂♂ **1934** Striking propagandist drama dealing with the exploits of a legendary Red Army commander during the 1919 battle with the White Russians. Stunning, and carefully choreographed, battle scenes. Adapted from a biographical novel by Dmitri Furmanov. In Russian with English subtitles. **101m/B; VHS, DVD.** *RU* Boris Babochkin; Leonid Kmit; Boris Chirkov; Varvara Myasnikova; Illarian Pevzov; Stephan Shkurat; Boris Blinov; Vyacheslav Volkov; Nikolai Simonov; Georgi Zhzhenov; *D:* Sergei Vassiliev; Georgy Vassiliev; *W:* Sergei Vassiliev; Georgy Vassiliev; *C:* Aleksander Sigayev; Alexander Xenofontov; *M:* Gavriil Popov.

The Chaperone ♂ ½ **2011 (PG-13)** Goofy crime/family comedy starring wrestler Paul Levesque. Getaway driver Ray Bradstone is determined to go straight after getting out of prison so he can reunite with his teen daughter Sally and make amends to his ex-wife Lynne. He rejects an offer from his former crew to do one last job and becomes a chaperone for Sally's museum class field trip instead. The heist goes wrong and boss Larue comes after Ray. **90m/C; DVD, Blu-Ray.** Paul Levesque; Ariel Winter; Annabeth Gish; Kevin Corrigan; Jose Zuniga; Enrico Colantoni; Kevin Rankin; *D:* Stephen Herek; *W:* S.J. Roth; *C:* Kenneth Zunder; *M:* James Alan Johnston. **VIDEO**

Chaplin ♂♂♂ **1992 (PG-13)** The life and career of "The Little Tramp" is chronicled by director Attenborough and brilliantly portrayed by Downey, Jr as Chaplin. A flashback format traces his life from its poverty-stricken Dickensian origins in the London slums through his directing and acting career, to his honorary Oscar in 1972. Slow-moving at parts, but captures Chaplin's devotion to his art and also his penchant towards jailbait. In a clever casting choice, Chaplin's own daughter from his fourth marriage to Oona O'Neill, Geraldine Chaplin, plays her own grandmother who goes mad. **135m/C; VHS, DVD, Blu-Ray.** *GB* Robert Downey, Jr.; Dan Aykroyd; Geraldine Chaplin; Kevin Dunn; Anthony Hopkins; Milla Jovovich; Moira Kelly; Kevin Kline; Diane Lane; Penelope Ann Miller; Paul Rhys; John Thaw; Marisa Tomei; Nancy Travis; James Woods; David Duchovny; Deborah Maria Moore; Bill Paterson; John Standing; Robert Stephens; Peter Crook; *D:* Richard Attenborough; *W:* Bryan Forbes; William Boyd; William Goldman; *C:* Sven Nykvist; *M:* John Barry. British Acad. '92: Actor (Downey).

The Chaplin Revue ♂♂ ½ **1958** The "Revue," put together by Chaplin in 1958, consists of three of his best shorts: "A Dog's Life" (1918), the WWI comedy "Shoulder Arms" (1918), and "The Pilgrim," in which a convict hides out in a clerical guise (1922). Chaplin added self-composed score, narration, and some documentary on-the-set material. **121m/B; Silent; VHS, DVD.** Charlie Chaplin; Edna Purviance; Syd Chaplin; Mack Swain; *D:* Charlie Chaplin.

The Chapman Report ♂ ½ **1962** Tame and tacky melodrama based on the Irving Wallace bestseller. The facade of L.A.'s smug suburbia is exposed when four women become part of a scientific survey about their sex lives, which reveals their hangups. **125m/C; DVD.** Jane Fonda; Shelley Winters; Glynis Johns; Claire Bloom; Efrem Zimbalist, Jr.; Andrew Duggan; Ray Danton; Ty Hardin; *D:* George Cukor; *W:* Wyatt Cooper; Don Mankiewicz; *C:* Harold Lipstein; *M:* Leonard Rosenman.

Chappaquiddick ♂♂ ½ **2017 (PG-13)** A dramatic look at a defining incident in Edward Kennedy's (Clarke) life, which occurred on the evening of July 18, 1969. After spending the evening with veterans of his brother Bobby's 1968 presidential campaign, Kennedy gives a ride to an attendee, young political strategist Mary Jo Kopechne (Mara). The intoxicated Kennedy drives his car off a bridge into shallow water, escapes, and allows Mary Jo to drown without attempting to save her life. Calling his father before the authorities, Kennedy focuses on protecting his image after the accident. Clarke is a convincing Kennedy, and the film effectively explores thorny ethical issues. **107m/C; DVD, Blu-Ray.** Jason Clarke; Ed Helms; Jim Gaffigan; Kate Mara; Bruce Dern; *D:* John Curran; Taylor Allen; *W:* Andrew Logan; *C:* Maryse Alberti; *M:* Garth Stevenson.

Chappie ♂ **2015 (R)** Once-heralded director Blomkamp (of "District 9" fame) fails spectacularly here with a ridiculous, boring riff on the moral gray area of the potential development of AI. In the near future, robots are a mechanized police force, but one of them is stolen and reprogrammed to think and feel for himself. Naturally, that leads to problems. Blomkamp not only presents something seen before and done better, but displays a shocking lack of filmmaking skills in this bloated, incoherent mess. There are no interesting characters, the science in the sci-fi is nonsensical, and the action is boring. **119m/C; DVD, Blu-Ray.** *US MX* Sharlto Copley; Dev Patel; Ninja; Yo-Landi Visser; Jose Pablo Cantillo; Hugh Jackman; *D:* Neill Blomkamp; *W:* Neill Blomkamp; Terri Tatchell; *C:* Trent Opaloch; *M:* Hans Zimmer.

Chapter 27 ♂ ½ **2007 (R)** Leto gained more than 60 pounds for this?! Well, he's starring as tubby, delusional Mark David Chapman, the killer of John Lennon. Writer/director Schafer covers the three days leading up to the murder, from Chapman's arrival in New York from Hawaii to his staking out the Dakota. There's not much room for anyone else in the story (although Lohan pops up as Beatles fan Jude) but there's nothing particularly new to view. **84m/C; DVD.** Jared Leto; Lindsay Lohan; Judah Friedlander; Ursula Abbott; *D:* Jarrett Schaefer; *W:* Jarrett Schaefer; *C:* Tom Richmond; *M:* Anthony Marinelli.

Chapter Two ♂♂ **1979 (PG)** Loosely based on Neil Simon's marriage to Mason and his Broadway hit of the same name. A writer, grief-stricken over the death of his first wife, meets the woman who will become his second. Witty dialogue in first half deteriorates when guilt strikes. **124m/C; VHS, DVD.** James Caan; Marsha Mason; Valerie Harper; Joseph Bologna; *D:* Robert Moore; *W:* Neil Simon.

Character ♂♂ *Karakter* **1997 (R)** Based on the 1938 novel by F. Bordewijk, which follows the troubled relationship of young lawyer Jacob Willem Katadreuffe (van Huet) and his overbearing father in 1920s Rotterdam. Dreverhaven (Decleir) is a powerful baliff who has an illegitimate son with his servant, Joba (Schuurman), who turns down his marriage proposal. Still, Dreverhaven is determined to control his son's life, even if it means ruining him first. No wonder the old man gets murdered. Dark and unsentimental. Dutch with subtitles. **114m/C; VHS, DVD.** *NL* Fedja Van Huet; Jan Decleir; Betty Schuurman; Victor Low; Tamar van den Dop; Hans Kestig; *D:* Mike van Diem; *W:* Mike van Diem; *C:* Rogier Stoffers; *M:* Paleis Van Boem. Oscars '97: Foreign Film.

Charade ♂♂ **1953** Mason and wife Pamela star in this trilogy of love and violence. "Portrait of a Murderer" has a young artist sketching the picture of the man who'unknown to her—has just murdered her girlfriend. "Duel at Dawn" concerns an 1880s Austrian officer who steals a woman from another officer and is then challenged to a duel. "The Midas Touch" revolves around a successful but dissatisfied man who abandons his riches to find the meaning of life. Mason himself had said he hoped "this curiosity" would disappear. **83m/B; VHS, DVD.** James Mason; Pamela Mason; Scott Forbes; Paul Cavanagh; Bruce Lester; Sean McClory; Vince Barnett; *D:* Roy Kellino.

Charade ♂♂♂ ½ **1963** After her husband is murdered, a young woman finds herself on the run from crooks and double agents who want the $250,000 her husband stole during WWII. Hepburn and Grant are charming and sophisticated as usual in this stylish intrigue filmed in Paris. Based on the story "The Unsuspecting Wife" by Marc Behm and Peter Stone. **113m/C; VHS, DVD, Blu-Ray.** Cary Grant; Audrey Hepburn; Walter Matthau; James Coburn; George Kennedy; *D:* Stanley Donen; *W:* Peter Stone; *C:* Charles B(ryant) Lang, Jr.; *M:* Henry Mancini. British Acad. '64: Actress (Hepburn).

Charge of the Lancers ♂♂ **1954** Technicolor adventure. During the 1850s Crimean War, the British develop a new cannon in order to destroy the Russian naval base at Sebastopol. Through the usual contrivances, French officer Capt. Evoir (Aumont), who's working with the Brits, teams up with lovely gypsy Tanya (Goddard) to prevent the Russians from learning too much about the new weapon. **73m/C; DVD.** Jean-Pierre Aumont; Paulette Goddard; Richard Wyler; Ben Astar; Karin (Karen, Katharine) Booth; Charles Irwin; Lester Matthews; *D:* William Castle; *W:* Robert E. Kent; *C:* Henry Fruelich.

The Charge of the Light Brigade ♂♂♂ **1936 (PG-13)** A British army officer stationed in India deliberately starts the Balaclava charge to even an old score with Surat Khan, who's on the other side. Still an exciting film, though it's hardly historically accurate. De Havilland is along to provide the requisite romance with Flynn. Also available colorized. **115m/B; VHS, DVD.** Errol Flynn; Olivia de Havilland; David Niven; Nigel Bruce; Patric Knowles; Donald Crisp; C. Henry Gordon; J. Carrol Naish; Henry Stephenson; E.E. Clive; Scotty Beckett; G.P. (Tim) Huntley, Jr.; Robert Barrat; Spring Byington; George Regas; *D:* Michael Curtiz; *W:* Michael Jacoby; Rowland Leigh; *C:* Sol Polito; *M:* Max Steiner.

The Charge of the Light Brigade ♂♂ ½ **1968 (PG-13)** Political indictment of imperialistic England in this revisionist retelling of the notorious British defeat by the Russians at Balaclava. Battle scenes are secondary to this look at the stupidity of war. Fine cast; notable animation sequences by Richard Williams. **130m/C; VHS, DVD.** *GB* Trevor Howard; John Gielgud; David Hemmings; Vanessa Redgrave; Harry Andrews; Jill Bennett; Peter Bowles; Mark Burns; Alan Dobie; T.P. McKenna; Corin Redgrave; Norman Rossington; Rachel Kempson; Donald Wolfit; Howard Marion-Crawford; Mark Dignam; Ben Aris; Peter Woodthorpe; Roger Mutton; Joely Richardson; ***D:*** Tony Richardson; ***W:*** Charles Wood; ***C:*** David Watkin; ***M:*** John Addison.

Charge of the Model T's 🦴 ½ **1976 (G)** Comedy about a WWI German spy who tries to infiltrate the U.S. army. **90m/C; VHS, DVD.** Louis Nye; John David Carson; Herb Edelman; Carol Bagdasarian; Arte Johnson; ***D:*** Jim McCullough, Sr.; ***W:*** Jim McCullough, Sr.

Chariots of Fire 🦴🦴🦴 ½ **1981 (PG)** A lush telling of the parallel stories of Harold Abraham and Eric Liddell, English runners who competed in the 1924 Paris Olympics. One was compelled by a hatred of anti-Semitism, the other by the love of God. Outstanding performances by the entire cast. **123m/C; VHS, DVD, Blu-Ray.** *GB* Ben Cross; Ian Charleson; Nigel Havers; Ian Holm; Alice Krige; Brad Davis; Dennis Christopher; Patrick Magee; Cheryl Campbell; John Gielgud; Lindsay Anderson; Nigel Davenport; ***D:*** Hugh Hudson; ***W:*** Colin Welland; ***C:*** David Watkin; ***M:*** Vangelis. Oscars '81: Costume Des., Film, Orig. Score, Orig. Screenplay; British Acad. '81: Film, Support. Actor (Holm); Golden Globes '82: Foreign Film; N.Y. Film Critics '81: Cinematog.

Charles & Diana: A Palace Divided 🦴🦴 ½ **1993** Trashy scandalous tale of the disintegration of the fairytale romance and marriage of Prince Charles and Princess Diana. Oxenberg stars as Princess Di, a role she played a decade ago in "The Royal Romance of Charles and Diana," and Rees does a fine job playing the conservative Prince Charles. Although the film covers all of the couple's highly publicized troubles, it's such a quick superficial treatment that it's often hard to follow. Nonetheless, it's a flashingly inviting look into the privileged House of Windsor. **92m/C; VHS, DVD.** Roger Rees; Catherine Oxenberg; Benedict Taylor; Tracy Brabin; Amanda Walker; David Quilter; Jane How; ***D:*** John Power.

Charley and the Angel 🦴🦴 ½ **1973 (G)** Touching story of a man who changes his cold ways with his family when informed by an angel that he hasn't much time to live. Amusing Disney movie set in the Great Depression. **93m/C; VHS, DVD, Streaming.** Fred MacMurray; Cloris Leachman; Harry (Henry) Morgan; Kurt Russell; Vincent Van Patten; Kathleen (Kathy) Cody; Kelly Thordsen; ***D:*** Vincent McEveety.

Charley Varrick 🦴🦴🦴 **1973 (PG)** Matthau, a small-town hood, robs a bank only to find out that one of its depositors is the Mob. Baker's the vicious hit-man assigned the job of getting the loot back. A well-paced, on-the-mark thriller. **111m/C; VHS, DVD, Blu-Ray.** Walter Matthau; Joe Don Baker; Felicia Farr; John Vernon; Sheree North; Norman Fell; Andrew (Andy) Robinson; Jacqueline Scott; Albert "Poppy" Popwell; ***D:*** Donald Siegel; ***W:*** Dean Riesner; ***M:*** Lalo Schifrin.

Charley's Aunt 🦴🦴🦴 **1941** Benny's at his comedic best in this amusing farce. Lord Fancourt "Babbs" Babberly (Benny) and his Oxford roommates Jack Chesney (Ellison) and Charley Wyckeham (Haydn in his film debut) must find a proper escort so their lady friends (Whelan, Baxter) will agree to visit. Babbs dons drag to impersonate Charley's maiden aunt (from Brazil—where the nuts come from) but finds himself fending off the romantic overtures of a couple of codgers (Cregar, Gwenn). Based on the play by Brandon Thomas. **80m/B; VHS, DVD.** Jack Benny; Kay Francis; James Ellison; Richard Haydn; Arleen Whelan; Anne Baxter; Laird Cregar; Edmund Gwenn; Reginald Owen; ***D:*** Archie Mayo; ***W:*** George Seaton; ***C:*** J. Peverell Marley; ***M:*** Alfred Newman.

Charlie 🦴🦴 **2004 (R)** Based on the actual events of South London's "Torture Gang" leader Charlie Richardson's (Goss) barbaric 1960s underworld reign. Dramatizes the gang's 1966 trial after Richardson is caught doing shady deals with a South African diamond baron. Director Needs' dizzying flashbacks are intense but also question whether the group was really to blame. **94m/C; DVD.** Luke Goss; Steven Berkoff; Marius Weyers; Anita Dobson; Leslie Grantham; ***D:*** Malcolm Needs; ***W:*** Malcolm Needs. **VIDEO**

Charlie & Me 🦴🦴 **2008** Keep the tissues handy for this sentimental family drama from the Hallmark Channel. Aging jazz aficionado Charlie Baker (Bosley) is felled by a heart attack, which makes him more determined to bond with his feisty 12-year-old granddaughter Casey (Benattar) and her widowed father, Charlie's workaholic son, Jeffrey (Gallanders). **88m/C; DVD.** Tom Bosley; Jordy Benattar; James Gallanders; Barclay Hope; Hannah Fleming; Tyler Stentiford; ***D:*** David Weaver; ***W:*** Karen Struck; ***C:*** Francois Dagenais; ***M:*** Ron Ramin. **CABLE**

Charlie and the Chocolate Factory 🦴🦴🦴 **2005 (PG)** Unlike 1971's "Willy Wonka & the Chocolate Factory," this is not a musical, although the Oompa Loompas still sing. And Burton does a more faithful adaptation of the 1964 book by Roald Dahl. Poor boy Charlie Bucket (Highmore) is one of five winners of a golden ticket that allows him to tour the mysterious Willy Wonka's (Depp) chocolate factory. Fans of the original may have qualms, but this one has a little more depth and heart, great visuals, and the cooperation of Dahl's widow, an exec producer. Depp is brilliantly quirky and Highmore shines. **115m/C; DVD, Blu-Ray, UMD, HD-DVD.** *US GB* Johnny Depp; Freddie Highmore; David Kelly; AnnaSophia Robb; Deep Roy; Christopher Lee; Helena Bonham Carter; Noah Taylor; James Fox; Missi Pyle; Julia Winter; Jordan Fry; Philip Wiegratz; Franziska Troegner; Harry Taylor; Adam Godley; Eileen Essell; Liz Smith; David Morris; ***Nar:*** Geoffrey Holder; ***D:*** Tim Burton; ***W:*** John August; ***C:*** Philippe Rousselot; ***M:*** Danny Elfman.

Charlie Bartlett 🦴🦴🦴 **2007 (R)** Troubled teen Charlie (Yelchin) is forced to attend the local public high school after getting the boot from a private academy, and he soon realizes his years of therapy will serve him well with his new mixed-up, angst-ridden school mates. Before long he's set up shop in the boys room handing out sage advice along with fistfulls of the meds his psychs dispense to him. Charlie begins to work his docs for all manner of drugs, and the line to the bathroom grows exponentially with his popularity, much to the chagrin of school officials, especially Principal Gardner (Downey Jr.), whose daughter (Dennings) is Charlie's new galpal. Newcomer Yelchin is super charming, and the film puts the whole pop psych Dr. Phil culture on a humorous skewer while calling to mind classic John Hughes teen flicks. Smart viewing. **96m/C; DVD.** Anton Yelchin; Kat Dennings; Robert Downey, Jr.; Hope Davis; Tyler Hilton; Mark Rendall; Jake Epstein; Megan Park; Ishan Dave; Jonathan Malen; ***D:*** Jon Poll; ***W:*** Gustin Nash; ***C:*** Paul Sarossy; ***M:*** Christophe Beck.

Charlie Chan and the Curse of the Dragon Queen 🦴 ½ **1981 (PG)** The famed Oriental sleuth confronts his old enemy the Dragon Queen, and reveals the true identity of a killer. **97m/C; VHS, DVD, Blu-Ray.** Peter Ustinov; Lee Grant; Angie Dickinson; Richard Hatch; Brian Keith; Roddy McDowall; Michelle Pfeiffer; Rachel Roberts; ***D:*** Clive Donner; ***W:*** David Axelrod; Stanley Burns.

Charlie Chan at Monte Carlo 🦴🦴 **1937** Chan (Oland) is gambling in Monaco when two murders occur. One is a two-bit gangster working as a hotel bartender and the other is a casino messenger who was traveling to Paris with a million bucks in bonds that has disappeared. Now Chan has to tie the cases together to solve the crimes. A good portion of the dialog is in French and much is made of the language difficulties of Chan and company. This was Oland's last appearance as the sleuth; he died in 1938. 16th in the series. **71m/B; DVD.** Warner Oland; Keye Luke; Virginia Field; Sidney Blackmer; Harold Huber; Kay Linaker; Robert Kent; ***D:*** Eugene Forde; ***W:*** Jerome Cady; Charles Belden; ***C:*** Daniel B. Clark; ***M:*** Samuel Kaylin.

Charlie Chan at the Circus 🦴🦴 ½ **1936** On vacation, Chan takes his wife and 12 (!) children to the circus. When one of the owners is murdered, Chan investigates with the help of some of the performers. Filmed at the Al G. Barnes Circus. 11th in the series. **72m/B; DVD.** Warner Oland; Keye Luke; Shirley Deane; John McGuire; Francis Ford; J. Carrol Naish; George Brasno; Olive Brasno; Maxine Reiner; Drue Leyton; ***D:*** Harry Lachman; ***W:*** Robert Ellis; Helen Logan; ***C:*** Daniel B. Clark; ***M:*** Samuel Kaylin.

Charlie Chan at the Olympics 🦴🦴 ½ **1937** Chan's (Oland) son Lee (Luke) is a member of the American swim team at the Berlin Olympics. When an experimental auto pilot device is stolen, Chan is called in (arriving by blimp) and suspects German spies. Since Lee is busy training, Charlie Chan Jr. (Tom Jr.) steps in to help his pop, but when Lee is kidnapped they may have to stop their investigation to save his life. Newsreel shots of the actual 1936 Olympics add to the atmosphere. 14th in the series. **71m/B; DVD.** Warner Oland; Keye Luke; Katherine DeMille; Pauline Moore; Layne Tom, Jr.; Allan "Rocky" Lane; C. Henry Gordon; ***D:*** Tom Krause; ***W:*** Robert Ellis; Helen Logan; ***C:*** Daniel B. Clark; ***M:*** Samuel Kaylin.

Charlie Chan at the Opera 🦴🦴🦴 **1936** The great detective investigates an amnesiac opera star (Karloff) who may have committed murder. Considered one of the best of the series. Interesting even to those not familiar with Charlie Chan. **66m/B; VHS, DVD.** Warner Oland; Boris Karloff; Keye Luke; Charlotte Henry; Thomas Beck; Nedda Harrigan; William Demarest; ***D:*** H. Bruce Humberstone.

Charlie Chan at the Race Track 🦴🦴 **1936** Chan (Oland) is traveling by ship from Honolulu to L.A. with some racehorses after his friend, the owner of a champion, is murdered. He and number one son Lee (Luke) tie the death into the Santa Anita race track where Chan figures out that gamblers have substituted a nag for a winning horse in order to cash in on the betting action. 12th in the series. **70m/B; DVD.** Warner Oland; Keye Luke; Helen Wood; Thomas Beck; Alan Dinehart; Gavin Muir; ***D:*** H. Bruce Humberstone; ***W:*** Robert Ellis; Helen Logan; Edward T. Lowe; ***C:*** Harry Jackson; ***M:*** Samuel Kaylin.

Charlie Chan at Treasure Island 🦴🦴 **1939** Chan (Toler) investigates the alleged suicide of a writer friend, aided by Fred Radini (Romero), an illusionist at the Treasure Island theater at the San Francisco International Exposition. The trail leads them to phony mystic Dr. Zodiac (Mohr), whose predictions always involve blackmail. 19th entry in series. **72m/B; DVD.** Sidney Toler; Victor Young; Cesar Romero; Gerald Mohr; Pauline Moore; Douglas Fowley; June Gale; Douglass Dumbrille; Sally Blane; Louis Jean Heydt; Donald MacBride; ***D:*** Norman Foster; ***W:*** John Larkin; ***C:*** Virgil Miller; ***M:*** Samuel Kaylin.

Charlie Chan in City of Darkness 🦴 ½ **1939** Chan (Toler) travels to Paris for a reunion of his WWI buddies and finds himself investigating the murder of a munitions manufacturer (Dumbrille) with unsavory clients. Notably preachy entry that reflects the distrust of appeasement and the Munich pact. 20th entry in series. **75m/B; DVD.** Sidney Toler; Lynn Bari; Richard Clarke; Douglass Dumbrille; Harold Huber; Leo G. Carroll; Lon Chaney, Jr.; C. Henry Gordon; Dorothy Tree; Noel Madison; Pedro de Cordoba; ***D:*** Herbert I. Leeds; ***W:*** Helen Logan; Robert Ellis; ***C:*** Virgil Miller.

Charlie Chan in Egypt 🦴🦴 **1935** Charlie Chan (Oland) is at a dig in Egypt where an archeologist has disappeared. An X-ray reveals that the body in a pharaoh's sarcophagus is that of the missing man. Is there a curse on the team for desecrating the ruler's tomb? 8th in the series. **72m/B; DVD.** Warner Oland; Thomas Beck; Rita Hayworth; James Thomas; Pat Paterson; Frank M. Thomas, Sr.; Stepin Fetchit; ***D:*** Louis King; ***W:*** Robert Ellis; Helen Logan; ***C:*** Daniel B. Clark; ***M:*** Samuel Kaylin.

Charlie Chan in Honolulu 🦴🦴 **1938** Toler makes his first appearance as Chan, who discovers a murder aboard a cruise ship docked at Honolulu and refuses to let the liner leave until the case is solved. Sons Jimmy (Yung) and Willie (Tom Jr.) try to help out. 17th entry in the series. **67m/B; DVD.** Sidney Toler; Phyllis Brooks; Victor Young; Layne Tom, Jr.; Eddie Collins; John "Dusty" King; Claire Dodd; George Zucco; Robert Barrat; ***D:*** H. Bruce Humberstone; ***W:*** Charles Belden; ***C:*** Charles G. Clarke.

Charlie Chan in London 🦴🦴 **1934** Pamela (Leyton) pleads with Chan (Oland) to help her brother Paul (Walton), who is about to be hanged for murder. Chan follows Pamela to the country home of Geoffrey Richmond (Mowbray) and tries to reconstruct the crime, nearly getting himself killed in the process. 6th in the series. **72m/B; DVD.** Warner Oland; Alan Mowbray; Douglas Walton; Ray Milland; Drue Leyton; Mona Barrie; ***D:*** Eugene Forde; ***W:*** Philip MacDonald; ***C:*** L. William O'Connell; ***M:*** Samuel Kaylin.

Charlie Chan in Panama 🦴 ½ **1940** Charlie (Toler) uncovers a spy plot to destroy part of the Panama Canal just as the American naval fleet is passing through. 23rd entry in the series. **66m/B; DVD.** Sidney Toler; Victor Sen Yung; Jack LaRue; Frank Puglia; Jean Rogers; Lionel Atwill; Chris-Pin (Ethier Crispin Martini) Martin; Mary Nash; Kane Richmond; Lionel Royce; ***D:*** Norman Foster; ***W:*** Lester Ziffren; John Larkin; ***C:*** Virgil Miller.

Charlie Chan in Paris 🦴🦴 ½ **1935** Chan scours the city of lights to track down a trio of counterfeiters. Top-notch plot and plenty of suspense will please all. **72m/B; VHS, DVD.** Warner Oland; Mary Brian; Thomas Beck; Erik Rhodes; John Miljan; Minor Watson; John Qualen; Keye Luke; Henry Kolker; ***D:*** Lewis Seiler.

Charlie Chan in Shanghai 🦴🦴 **1935** Chan (Oland) is called in by the Chinese government to investigate a murder that is tied to an opium ring and he's aided by number one son Lee (Luke). Pretty standard fare is ninth in the series. **70m/B; DVD.** Warner Oland; Keye Luke; Irene Hervey; Jon Hall; Russell Hicks; Halliwell Hobbes; ***D:*** James Tinling; ***W:*** Edward T. Lowe; Gerald Fairlie; ***C:*** Barney McGill; ***M:*** Samuel Kaylin.

Charlie Chan on Broadway 🦴🦴 **1937** Fellow ocean liner passenger Billie Bronson (Henry) hides her diary in Chan's (Oland) luggage for safekeeping. Seems Billie is wanted as a material witness in a gangster scandal (the diary names names) and upon her return to New York, she's soon murdered. The diary disappears and Chan has to hit the city's nightspots to investigate. 15th entry in the series. **68m/B; DVD.** Warner Oland; Keye Luke; Joan Marsh; J. Edward Bromberg; Louise Henry; Douglas Fowley; Harold Huber; Leon Ames; Joan Woodbury; Jerome Cady; ***D:*** Eugene Forde; ***W:*** Charles Belden; ***C:*** Harry Jackson; ***M:*** Samuel Kaylin.

Charlie Chan's Murder Cruise 🦴 ½ **1940** Scotland Yard Inspector Duff is strangled before revealing to his friend Charlie Chan (Toler) how he intended to trap a killer aboard a cruise ship heading from Honolulu to San Francisco. Chan joins the cruise and tries to unmask the killer before too many passengers also die. 21st in the series. **70m/B; DVD.** Sidney Toler; Victor Sen Yung; Marjorie Weaver; Lionel Atwill; Cora Witherspoon; Robert Lowery; Don Beddoe; Leo G. Carroll; Kay Linaker; Leonard Mudie; ***D:*** Eugene Forde; ***W:*** Lester Ziffren; Robertson White; ***C:*** Virgil Miller.

Charlie Chan's Secret 🦴🦴 **1935** Chan must solve the murder of the heir to a huge fortune. A good, logical script with plenty of suspects to keep you guessing. **72m/B; VHS, DVD, Blu-Ray.** Warner Oland; Rosina Lawrence; Charles Quigley; Henrietta Crosman; Edward Trevor; Astrid Allwyn; ***D:*** Gordon Wiles.

Charlie Countryman 🦴 *The Necessary Death of Charlie Countryman* **2013 (R)** Fumbling debut from Bond is a dreary, strained mix of genres. Charlie is depressed after the death of his mom until she comes to him in a vision, saying he should travel to Bucharest. This first in a series of inexplicable acts then finds the grubby American fulfilling the last wish of his Romanian seat-mate, who dies on the flight. That means visiting the man's depressed daughter, Gabi, who has lousy taste in men since they're gangsters after some videotape that dad was supposedly bringing home. Charlie doesn't know anything about it, but gets beaten up (a lot) anyway. And you won't care. **103m/C; Blu-Ray, On Demand.** *US RO* Shia LaBeouf; Evan

Rachel Wood; Mads Mikkelsen; Til Schweiger; Rupert Grint; Melissa Leo; ***Nar:*** John Hurt; ***D:*** Fredrik Bond; ***W:*** Matt Drake; ***C:*** Roman Vasyanov; ***M:*** Christophe Beck.

Charlie St. Cloud 🦴 1/2 **2010 (PG-13)** Sniffle-inducing, melancholy drama based on Ben Sherwood's 2004 novel "The Death and Life of Charlie St. Cloud." When Charlie (handsome-but-bland Efron) survives the car crash that kills his beloved younger brother Sam (Tahan), he puts his college plans on hold and becomes the caretaker of the local cemetery. Every day Sam shows up to play ball with his guilt-stricken brother until Charlie can figure out a way to move on—maybe with high school friend Tess (Crew). **109m/C; Blu-Ray.** Zac Efron; Charlie Tahan; Amanda Crew; Augustus Prew; Donal Logue; Ray Liotta; Kim Basinger; ***D:*** Burr Steers; ***W:*** Craig Pearce; Lewis Colick; ***C:*** Enrique Chediak; ***M:*** Rolfe Kent.

Charlie the Lonesome Cougar 🦴🦴 1/2 **1967** A classic Disney family movie filmed in the style of a wilderness documentary, this is the story of Jess Bradley (Brown) who adopts an orphaned baby cougar that quickly becomes the mascot of his logging camp. But as the cat grows older, his behavior begins to cause problems, and it quickly becomes apparent he will have to be reintroduced to the wild. **75m/C; DVD.** Ron Brown; Brian Russell; ***Nar:*** Rex Allen; ***D:*** Rex Allen; ***W:*** Winston Hibler; ***C:*** William W. Bacon, III; Lloyd Beebe; Charles L. Draper; ***M:*** Franklyn Marks.

Charlie White WOOF! 2004 Charlie White is a self-destructive party boy with more money than brains, trying to get noticed on the London scene. Charlie takes it badly when someone else steals the limelight but you won't care at all about these upper-class twits. Big yawn. **85m/C; DVD.** *GB* Alex McGettigan; Danny George; Alex Besley; Lucy McCall; Hamish Jenkinson; ***D:*** Samuel P. Abrahams; ***W:*** Samuel P. Abrahams; ***C:*** Samuel P. Abrahams; Oliver Campbell; ***M:*** Philip Zikking.

Charlie Wilson's War 🦴🦴 **2007 (R)** In the "truth is stranger than fiction" category, Charlie Wilson (Hanks) is a hard-drinking, pleasure-loving Democratic congressman from East Texas who's also resourceful and interested in foreign affairs. Houston socialite Joanne Herring (Roberts in big hair) is a power broker who convinces Charlie that they can help end the cold war by arming the Afghan mujahideen so they can defeat the invading Russkies. (It's set in the 1980s.) Charlie heads off to Afghanistan to check things out and is given assistance by renegade CIA op Gust Avrakotos (Hoffman), which leads back to some D.C. maneuvering. A big story (based on the bestseller by George Crile) that's packed into a brief running time, so things seem just a little hurried, with Hanks and Hoffman vying to see who can steal the picture. **97m/C; Blu-Ray, On Demand.** Tom Hanks; Julia Roberts; Philip Seymour Hoffman; Amy Adams; Ned Beatty; Emily Blunt; Om Puri; Ken Stott; John Slattery; Denis O'Hare; Peter Gerety; Brian Markinson; ***D:*** Mike Nichols; ***W:*** Aaron Sorkin; ***C:*** Stephen Goldblatt; ***M:*** James Newton Howard.

Charlie's Angels 🦴🦴 1/2 **2000 (PG-13)** Seventies TV jigglefest finally gets a belated big screen treatment that has the trio (Barrymore, Diaz, Liu) saving Charlie (Forsythe reprises his voice role) from assassination and thwarting bad guy Roger Corwin (Curry). Merchant-Ivory it ain't (yay!), but it is everything a summer movie's supposed to be: loud, flashy, and fun. Matt LeBlanc, Tom Green, and Luke Wilson are around as nominal romantic interests but it's the women who run the show. Everyone seems to be having a good time, especially Murray as Bosley and Diaz as "perky" angel, Natalie. **99m/C; VHS, DVD, Blu-Ray, UMD.** Drew Barrymore; Cameron Diaz; Lucy Liu; Bill Murray; Tim Curry; Sam Rockwell; Kelly Lynch; Crispin Glover; Matt LeBlanc; LL Cool J; Tom Green; Luke Wilson; Sean M. Whalen; Alex Trebek; Michael (Mike) Papajohn; ***V:*** John Forsythe; ***D:*** McG; ***W:*** John August; Ryan Rowe; Ed Soloman; ***C:*** Russell Carpenter; ***M:*** Ed Shearmur.

Charlie's Angels 🦴🦴 **2019 (PG-13)** Gifted engineer Elena (Scott) has invented a revolutionary energy-generating device that has the potential to make the world a better place but could also be used as a weapon by criminal forces. When Elena's boss (Faxon) wants to sell it on the world market, she teams up with bad girl heiress Sabrina (Stewart) and former MI6 agent Jane (Balinska) to expose the plan and prevent the worst case scenario. An assassin (Tucker) tries to prevent the women from succeeding. The latest reboot of the 1970s series brings new energy and balances the escapist fun of the series with a contemporary feminist point of view. **118m/C; DVD, Blu-Ray.** Kristen Stewart; Naomi Scott; Ella Balinska; Elizabeth Banks; Patrick Stewart; ***D:*** Elizabeth Banks; ***W:*** Elizabeth Banks; ***C:*** Bill Pope; ***M:*** Brian Tyler.

Charlie's Angels: Full Throttle 🦴🦴 **2003 (PG-13)** The Angels investigate murders linked to the theft of a Witness Protection database. Enough about plot. Murray's been replaced by Bernie Mac, Demi Moore returns to the screen as a former Angel gone bad, and a good time is still had by all. McG and the girls amp up the "boom" quotient, but some of the breezy fun of the original feels a bit forced this time around. **105m/C; VHS, DVD, Blu-Ray.** Drew Barrymore; Cameron Diaz; Lucy Liu; Bernie Mac; Demi Moore; Luke Wilson; Matt LeBlanc; Crispin Glover; Robert Patrick; John Cleese; Shia LaBeouf; Jaclyn Smith; Justin Theroux; Rodrigo Santoro; Ja'net DuBois; Robert Forster; Eric Bogosian; Carrie Fisher; ***Cameo(s):*** Alecia Moore; Ashley (Fuller) Olsen; Mary-Kate Olsen; ***V:*** John Forsythe; ***D:*** McG; ***W:*** John August; Marianne S. Wibberley; Cormac Wibberley; ***C:*** Russell Carpenter; ***M:*** Ed Shearmur. Golden Raspberries '03: Worst Remake/Sequel, Worst Support. Actress (Moore).

Charlie's Ghost: The Secret of Coronado 🦴🦴 1/2 *Charlie's Ghost Story* **1994 (PG)** Kid who has trouble fitting in is befriended by the ghost of a Spanish conquistador. **92m/C; VHS, DVD.** Richard "Cheech" Marin; Trenton Knight; Anthony Edwards; Linda Fiorentino; Daphne Zuniga; ***D:*** Anthony Edwards.

Charlotte Gray 🦴🦴 **2001 (PG-13)** Uninvolving WWII romantic drama based on the 1998 novel by Sebastian Faulks. Scottish Charlotte (Blanchett) is living in London when she meets dashing RAF pilot Peter Gregory (Penry-Jones). After learning that Peter has been shot down over France, Charlotte (who speaks perfect French) volunteers for British Special Operations and is sent to work with the Resistance in Vichy. Charlotte's contacts are Levade (Gambon) and his handsome son Julian (Crudup). Naturally, there are supposed to be sparks between the two but the romance fizzles rather than sizzles as does the film itself. Chameleon Blanchett and gruff Gambon are the main reasons to watch. **118m/C; VHS, DVD.** *GB AU* Cate Blanchett; Billy Crudup; Michael Gambon; Rupert Penry-Jones; Anton Lesser; James Fleet; Ron Cook; Jack Shepherd; Nicholas Farrell; Helen McCrory; Abigail Cruttenden; Charlie Condou; David Birkin; ***D:*** Gillian Armstrong; ***W:*** Jeremy Brock; ***C:*** Dion Beebe; ***M:*** Stephen Warbeck.

Charlotte Rampling: The Look 🦴🦴 *The Look* **2011** This feature-length documentary is an insightful biographical look at the life and career of actress Charlotte Rampling. Her life story is told through conversations she held with artist friends and collaborators she worked with throughout her career, including Paul Auster and Juergen Teller. The documentary also includes footage from the best known films of Rampling's, such as "Babylon A.D." and "Swimming Pool." **90m/C; DVD, Streaming, Download.** Charlotte Rampling; ***D:*** Angelina Maccarone; ***W:*** Angelina Maccarone; ***C:*** Judith Kaufmann; Bernd Meiners.

Charlotte Sometimes 🦴🦴 1/2 **2002 (R)** Michael manages his Aunt Margie's (Hoshi) duplex and runs the family auto repair business. He has a crush on tenant Lori (Yuan), who has a boyfriend, Justin (Westmore), although she frequently turns to the diffident Michael for friendly companionship. Then Michael meets the mysterious Darcy (Kim) at the local bar. She is sexually agressive, while insisting that she's only in town for a few days. But Darcy seems overly interested in the relationship between Michael and Lori and it turns out the two women have a history than neither wants Michael to discover. **85m/C; VHS, DVD.** Michael Idemoto; Jacqueline Kim; Eugenia Yuan; Matt Westmore; Shizuko Hoshi; Kimberly Rose; ***D:*** Eric Byler; ***W:*** Eric Byler; ***C:*** Robert Humphreys; ***M:*** Michael Brook.

Charlotte's Web 🦴🦴 1/2 **1973 (G)** E.B. White's classic story of a friendship between a spider and a pig is handled only adequately by Hanna-Barbera studios. Some okay songs. **94m/C; VHS, DVD.** ***V:*** Debbie Reynolds; Agnes Moorehead; Paul Lynde; Henry Gibson; Pamelyn Ferdin; Danny Bonaduce; ***Nar:*** Rex Allan; ***D:*** Charles A. Nichols; Iwao Takamoto; ***W:*** Earl Hamner; ***M:*** Irwin Kostal.

Charlotte's Web 🦴🦴🦴 **2006 (G)** Faithful to E.B. White's timeless 1952 children's novel about a young girl, Fern (played graciously by Fanning, just barely young enough for the role), who rescues runt pig Wilbur from the smokehouse. Wilbur is later aided by Charlotte, a sophisticated spider (Roberts) whose "some pig" artwork awes the masses. Though the animals' mouths move thanks to CG effects, the animals and action are the real deal, as are the appealing gaggle of celebrities. Sticks to the book's gentle nature, but things get a bit sluggish at times. **96m/C; DVD, Blu-Ray.** Dakota Fanning; Kevin Anderson; Essie Davis; Gary Basaraba; Siobhan Fallon Hogan; Beau Bridges; ***V:*** Julia Roberts; Steve Buscemi; John Cleese; Dominic Scott Kay; Oprah Winfrey; Cedric the Entertainer; Kathy Bates; Reba McEntire; Robert Redford; Thomas Haden Church; Andre Benjamin; Sam Shepard; Abraham Benrubi; ***D:*** Gary Winick; ***W:*** Susannah Grant; Karey Kirkpatrick; ***C:*** Seamus McGarvey; ***M:*** Danny Elfman.

Charly 🦴🦴🦴 **1968** A retarded man becomes intelligent after brain surgery, then romances a kindly caseworker before slipping back into retardation. Moving account is well served by leads Robertson and Bloom. Adapted from the Daniel Keyes novel "Flowers for Algernon." **103m/C; VHS, DVD, Blu-Ray.** Cliff Robertson; Claire Bloom; Lilia Skala; Leon Janney; Dick Van Patten; William Dwyer; ***D:*** Ralph Nelson; ***W:*** Stirling Silliphant. Oscars '68: Actor (Robertson); Golden Globes '69: Screenplay; Natl. Bd. of Review '68: Actor (Robertson).

The Charmer 🦴🦴 1/2 **1987** Havers stars as Ralph Gorse, a charming but amoral con man who uses any means to get what he wants. This includes using the affection (and money) of an older woman, blackmail, and even murder. Set in the late '30s. Made for British TV miniseries. **312m/C; VHS, DVD.** *GB* Nigel Havers; Rosemary Leach; Bernard Hepton; Fiona Fullerton; Abigail McKern; George Baker; Judy Parfitt; ***D:*** Alan Gibson; ***W:*** Allan Prior. **TV**

Charming Billy 🦴🦴 **1998** Living a life of quiet desperation finally proves to be too much for Billy Starkman (Hayden) and he goes postal—sniping at passersby from the top of a rural water tower. Flashbacks show how Billy got to that desperate point in his life. **80m/C; VHS, DVD.** Michael Hayden; Sally Murphy; Tony Mockus, Sr.; Chelcie Ross; ***D:*** William R. Pace; ***W:*** William R. Pace; ***C:*** William Newell; ***M:*** David Barkley.

Charms 🦴 *Hex; The Shrieking* **1973** A group of WWI vets turned bikers tour the states looking for something they can't explain and inexplicably decide to get stoned and force themselves on a pair of vengeful witch twins instead. But then, one of them is played by Gary Busey. **101m/C; DVD, Streaming.** Keith Carradine; Mike Combs; Scott Glenn; Gary Busey; Robert Walker, Jr.; Cristina Raines; Hilary Thompson; ***D:*** Leo Garen; ***W:*** Leo Garen; Stephen Katz; Vernon Zimmerman; Doran William Cannon; ***C:*** Charles Rosher, Jr.; ***M:*** Charles Bernstein; Patrick Williams. **VIDEO**

Charms for the Easy Life 🦴🦴 1/2 **2002** Southern matriarch and holistic healer, Miss Charlie Kate (Rowlands) has definite opinions—she loathes her no-account son-in-law and won't set foot in her daughter Sophie's (Rogers) house. Fortunately, he eventually dies and Miss Charlie moves in to help look after granddaughter Margaret (Pratt). Miss Charlie has a generally low opinion of men since her husband ran off but the more fragile Sophie is pleased to have a suitor (Johnson) and teen Margaret also finds a boy (Mitchell) who thinks she's neat. Set in the mid-1940s; based on Kaye Gibbon's 1993 novel. Graceful and charming and all three actresses keep the sentimental excess to a minimum. **111m/C; VHS, DVD.** Gena Rowlands; Mimi Rogers; Susan May Pratt; Geordie Johnson; Kenneth Mitchell; ***D:*** Joan Micklin Silver; ***W:*** Angela Shelton; ***C:*** Jean Lepine; ***M:*** Van Dyke Parks. **CABLE**

Charro! 🦴 **1969 (G)** Presley in a straight role as a reformed bandit hounded by former gang members. Western fails on nearly all accounts, with Presley hopelessly acting outside the bounds of his talent. Furthermore, he sings only one song. **98m/C; VHS, DVD.** Elvis Presley; Ina Balin; Victor French; Lynn Kellogg; Barbara Werle; Paul Brinegar; James B. Sikking; ***D:*** Charles Marquis Warren; ***W:*** Charles Marquis Warren; ***M:*** Hugo Montenegro.

Charulata 🦴🦴 *The Lonely Wife* **1964** Charulata is a loyal and dutiful wife taken for granted by her husband. But when his young cousin Amal comes to live with them, Charulata glimpses what true love could be. Adapted from the novella by Rabindranath Tagore. Bengali with subtitles. **117m/B; VHS, DVD, Blu-Ray.** *IN* Madhabi Mukherjee; Soumitra Chatterjee; Shailan Mukherjee; Shyamal Ghoshal; Gitali Roy; Bholanath Koyal; Suku Mukherjee; Dilip Bose; Joydeb; Bankim Ghosh; Subrata Sensharma; ***D:*** Satyajit Ray; ***W:*** Satyajit Ray; ***C:*** Subrata Mitra; ***M:*** Satyâjit Ray; Rabindranath Tagore.

The Chase 🦴🦴 1/2 **1946** Not realizing that his boss-to-be is a mobster, Cummings takes a job as a chauffeur. Naturally, he falls in love with the gangster's wife (Morgan), and the two plan to elope. Somewhat miffed, the cuckolded mafioso and his bodyguard (Lorre) pursue the elusive couple as they head for Havana. The performances are up to snuff, but the story's as unimaginative as the title, with intermittent bouts of suspense. **86m/B; VHS, DVD, Blu-Ray.** Robert Cummings; Michele Morgan; Peter Lorre; Steve Cochran; Lloyd Corrigan; Jack Holt; Don Wilson; ***D:*** Arthur Ripley; ***W:*** Philip Yordan.

The Chase 🦴🦴 1/2 **1966** Southern community is undone when rumors circulate of a former member's prison escape and return home. Excellent cast only partially shines. Brando is outstanding as the beleaguered, honorable sheriff, and Duvall makes a splash in the more showy role of a cuckold who fears the escapee is returning home to avenge a childhood incident. Reliable Dickinson also makes the most of her role as Brando's loving wife. Fonda, however, was not yet capable of fashioning complex characterizations, and Redford is under-utilized as the escapee. Adapted from the play by Horton Foote. Notorious conflicts among producer, director, and writer kept it from being a winner. **135m/C; VHS, DVD, Blu-Ray.** Marlon Brando; Robert Redford; Angie Dickinson; E.G. Marshall; Jane Fonda; James Fox; Janice Rule; Robert Duvall; Miriam Hopkins; Martha Hyer; ***D:*** Arthur Penn; ***W:*** Lillian Hellman; Horton Foote; ***M:*** John Barry.

The Chase 🦴🦴 **1991 (PG-13)** Routine actioner in which an ex-con killer leads a ruthless cop and a TV news team on a wild chase. Loosely based on a true story. **93m/C; VHS, DVD.** Ben Johnson; Casey Siemaszko; Gerry Bamman; Robert Beltran; Barry Corbin; Ricki Lake; Megan Follows; Sheila Kelley; Gailard Sartain; ***D:*** Paul Wendkos; ***W:*** Guerdon (Gordon) Trueblood; ***C:*** Chuck (Charles G.) Arnold; ***M:*** W.G. Snuffy Walden. **TV**

The Chase 🦴🦴 1/2 **1993 (PG-13)** Heiress Natalie Voss (Swanson) is in the wrong place at the wrong time when she's carjacked by escaped con Jack Hammond (Sheen) who uses a Butterfinger for his weapon. Frantic chases ensues as it turns out that Daddy Voss is a media hungry millionaire and he's followed by not only the cops but the media as well. One-dimensional characters aren't helped by a one-dimensional script, but slick filmmaking and a little charm helps. Skewers the media hype that surrounds crime, taking on news programs that offer immediate coverage and reality based shows with glee. **87m/C; VHS, DVD.** Kristy Swanson; Charlie Sheen; Josh Mostel; Ray Wise; Henry Rollins; Flea; Joao Fernandes; ***D:*** Adam Rifkin; ***W:*** Adam Rifkin; ***M:*** Richard Gibbs.

Chase a Crooked Shadow 🦴🦴 1/2 **1958** In this suspenser, diamond heiress Kimberly Prescott (Baxter) fears for her sanity, her diamonds, and her life. She returns to the family estate in Barcelona after the deaths of her father and brother in South Africa. Then a stranger (Todd) shows up, claiming to be her dead brother and, despite Kim's protests, he's soon accepted as part of the family by sinister Uncle Chandler (Knox) and the locals. **87m/B; DVD.** *UK* Anne Baxter; Richard Todd; Alexander Knox; Herbert Lom; ***D:*** Michael Anderson, Sr.; ***W:*** David Osborn; Charles Sinclair; ***C:*** Erwin Hillier; ***M:*** Matyas Seiber.

Chasers ✐✐ **1994 (R)** Gruff Navy petty officer Rock Reilly (Berenger) and his conniving partner Eddie Devane (McNamara) are stuck escorting maximum security prisoner Toni Johnson (Eleniak) to a Charleston naval base. Imagine their surprise when Toni turns out to be a beautiful blonde whose one purpose is to escape her jail-sentence for going AWOL. Considering how dumb her jailers are this shouldn't be too difficult. Lots of sneering, leering, and macho posturing. **100m/C; VHS, DVD.** Tom Berenger; William McNamara; Erika Eleniak; Gary Busey; Crispin Glover; Dean Stockwell; Seymour Cassel; Frederic Forrest; Marilu Henner; Dennis Hopper; ***D:*** Dennis Hopper; ***W:*** Joe Batteer; John Rice; Dan Gilroy; ***C:*** Ueli Steiger; ***M:*** Dwight Yoakam; Pete Anderson.

Chasing Amy ✐✐ **1/2 1997 (R)** Holden (Affleck) and best friend Banky (Lee), New Jersey comic book artists, attend a convention in New York where Holden is immediately attracted to fellow artist Alyssa (Adams). His ego is quickly deflated when Alyssa lets him know she's a lesbian. They try for friendship, head into a rocky romance, and then Holden discovers Alyssa's had a wild (and heterosexual) past, which pushes all his emotional buttons. Writer/director Smith supplies his trademark sharp dialogue, and the leads all contribute fine performances. Jay (Mewes) and Silent Bob (Smith), from Smith's earlier pics, make another appearance and supply the story that gives the film its title. **113m/C; VHS, DVD, Blu-Ray.** Ben Affleck; Joey Lauren Adams; Jason Lee; Dwight Ewell; Jason Mewes; Kevin Smith; Matt Damon; Carmen (Lee) Llywelyn; Ethan Suplee; Brian O'Halloran; Guinevere Turner; ***D:*** Kevin Smith; ***W:*** Kevin Smith; ***C:*** David Klein; ***M:*** David Pirner. Ind. Spirit '98: Screenplay, Support. Actor (Lee).

Chasing Christmas ✐ **2005 (PG)** Bahhumbug. Bitter divorcee Jack Cameron (Arnold) is a holiday Scrooge who comes to the attention of the Bureau of Yuletide Affairs. It's decided to "Dickens" him with the ghosts of Christmas Past, Present, and Future, only when peevish Past (Jordan) takes Jack back to his 1965 boyhood, he decides to take a sudden vacation and leaves Jack stranded. This means Present (Roth) has to fix the timeline and get Jack to see the error of his ways. Lame holiday humor, although seeing Arnold tied to a chair with Christmas lights is kinda funny. **90m/C; DVD.** Tom Arnold; Andrea Roth; Leslie Jordan; Jed Rees; Brittney Wilson; ***D:*** Ron Oliver; ***W:*** Todd Berger; ***C:*** C. Kim Miles; ***M:*** John Sereda. **CABLE**

Chasing Destiny ✐✐ **1/2 2000 (PG-13)** Once famous as a '60s rock 'n' roller, Jet James (Lloyd) is in debt and has a collector (Van Dien) at his door. But when his pretty daughter (Graham) comes to visit, Jet thinks getting the two young people together could be his way out of financial crisis. **90m/C; VHS, DVD.** Christopher Lloyd; Casper Van Dien; Lauren Graham; Roger Daltrey; Justin Henry; Stuart Pankin; Deborah Van Valkenburgh; ***D:*** Tim Boxell. **VIDEO**

Chasing Freedom ✐✐ **1/2 2004** After escaping the brutal Taliban rule in Afghanistan in 2004, Meena (Alizada) must battle to remain in the United States or face death in her native country if deported. Pro bono lawyer Libby (Lewis), a cocky corporate counselor is been ordered to take on her case. An original drama by cable channel Court TV. **89m/C; VHS, DVD.** Juliette Lewis; Brian Markinson; Bruce Gray; Layla Alizada; Gail Hanrahan; ***D:*** Don McBrearty; ***W:*** Barbara Samuels. **CABLE**

Chasing Ghosts ✐ **1/2 2005** Derivative cop caper. Kevin Harrison (Madsen) is about to retire and is trying to get through a complicated murder case while breaking in new partner Davies (Large). But Harrison is also guilt-ridden over the death of cop Mark Spencer (Rooker), which happened because Harrison has been bought and paid for by mobster Alfiri (Busey). Soon the investigation is leading in directions Harrison doesn't want it to go. **114m/C; DVD.** Michael Madsen; Michael Rooker; Meat Loaf Aday; Gary Busey; Corey Large; Shannyn Sossamon; Lochlyn Munro; Sean M. Whalen; Danny Trejo; James Duval; ***D:*** Kyle Dean Jackson; ***W:*** Alan Pao; ***C:*** Andrew Huebscher; ***M:*** Scott Glasgow. **VIDEO**

Chasing Ghosts ✐✐ **2014** A moving family comedy-drama about learning to live after the death of a loved one. Eleven-year-old Lucas Simons (Nichols) is a young filmmaker coping with the passing of his brother. In the wake of his brother's death, Lucas becomes more and more interested in death. This fascination unexpectedly leads to fame after he captures a mysterious entity on film, posts his footage on YouTube, and it goes viral. The pressures of this situation compel Lucas to live in the spotlight, but also help him learn to fully appreciate being alive. **89m/C; DVD, Streaming, Download.** Toby Nichols; Tim Meadows; Robyn Lively; W. Earl Brown; Frances Conroy; ***D:*** Josh Shreve; ***W:*** Josh Chesler; ***C:*** Jeff Steinborn; ***M:*** Matthew Perryman Jones; Michael Whittaker. **VIDEO**

Chasing Holden ✐ **1/2 2001 (R)** Cliched teen angst comedy/drama does refer to Holden Caulfield of "Catcher in the Rye." 19-year-old Neal (Qualls) is back at prep school after a two-year stay in a mental hospital. His English teacher Alex (Kanan) assigns his students an essay on what happened to Holden after the end of the Salinger novel. Neal decides the best way to find out is to visit the reclusive author—accompanied by his one friend, T.J. (Blanchard). **101m/C; VHS, DVD.** DJ Qualls; Rachel Blanchard; Sean Kanan; ***D:*** Malcolm Clarke; ***W:*** Sean Kanan. **VIDEO**

Chasing Ice ✐✐✐ **2012 (PG-13)** Visually beautiful and thoughtful documentary from National Geographic Films that follows photographer/scientist James Balog's adventures (beginning in 2007) studying glaciers and the effects of climate change. With a team of experts, Balog launches the Extreme Ice Survey, which sets up cameras in icy regions that automatically capture glacial formations throughout the year, providing inescapable proof of their extreme rate of shrinkage. **80m/C; DVD, Blu-Ray.** ***D:*** Jeff Orlowski; ***W:*** Mark Monroe; ***C:*** Jeff Orlowski; ***M:*** J. Ralph.

Chasing Liberty ✐✐ **1/2 2004 (PG-13)** Singer Moore is restless and rebellious First Daughter Anna, who chafes under the scrutiny of the Secret Service. Mayhem and romance ensues when Anna tags along on a friend's travels across Europe and meets up with a cutie Brit (Goode). While Moore has better acting chops than your average pop singer turned movie actor, this isn't much more than a decaffeinated version of "Roman Holiday." Even so, it should please its target audience of pre-adolescent girls. **110m/C; DVD.** Mandy Moore; Matthew Goode; Mark Harmon; Caroline Goodall; Jeremy Piven; Annabella Sciorra; Stark Sands; Miriam Margolyes; Beatrice Rosen(blatt); ***D:*** Andy Cadiff; ***W:*** Derek Guiley; David Schneiderman; ***C:*** Ashley Rowe; ***M:*** Christian Henson.

Chasing Mavericks ✐✐ *Of Men and Mavericks* **2012 (PG)** An oddly inert movie given its subject matter, Curtis Hanson's film tells the true story of Jay Moriarty (Weston), a 15-year-old surfing phenom who makes it his goal to surf the legendary Mavericks surf break. Jay enlists the help of a local old timer named Frosty (Butler) and the two practice in order to be able to survive the legendary wave. Films about young talents working with veterans to accomplish a remarkable feat are a dime a dozen and Hanson's work here does nothing to justify the existence of this sweet but ultimately boring tale of men who ride the waves. **115m/C; DVD, Blu-Ray.** Jonny Weston; Gerard Butler; Elisabeth Shue; Leven Rambin; Abigail Spencer; Scott Eastwood; ***D:*** Curtis Hanson; Michael Apted; ***W:*** Kario Salem; ***C:*** Oliver Euclid; Bill Pope; ***M:*** Chad Fischer.

Chasing Papi ✐✐ **2003 (PG-13)** Hottie L.A. ad exec Tomas Fuentes (Verastegui) travels a lot for his work and makes friends wherever he goes—girlfriends, that is. There's dancer Cici (Vergara) in Miami, attorney Lorena (Sanchez) in Chicago, and heiress Patricia in New York (Velasquez). But the pressure is getting to this lothario and his doctor (Gomez) prescribes tranquilizers and abstinence. Then, Tomas's three ladies all decide to pay him surprise visits. Naturally, the surprise is on them. There's an odd subplot about stolen money and an FBI agent (Vidal) but it's what the threesome discover about themselves—girl power-!?that's important. Everyone involved is very, very attractive. **92m/C; VHS, DVD, Blu-Ray.** Eduardo Verastegui; Roselyn Sanchez; Sofia Vergara; Jaci Velasquez; Lisa Vidal; Freddy Rodriguez; D.L. Hughley; Maria Conchita Alonso; Ian Gomez; ***D:*** Linda Mendoza; ***W:*** Steve Antin; Laura Angelica Simon; Alison Balian; Elizabeth Sarnoff; ***C:*** Xavier Perez Grobet; ***M:*** Emilio Estefan, Jr.

Chasing Rainbows ✐✐ **1930** Standard musical comedy from MGM. A traveling theatrical troupe has its share of adventure, overseen by jaded stage manager Eddie Rock (Benny). The most prominent is the vaudeville team of Semour and Fay since Carlie Semour (Love) is in love with her oblivious partner Terry Fay (King), who is currently romancing their leading lady Daphne (Martan). Some musical numbers and the final sequence were shot in Technicolor but they have been lost. **90m/B; DVD.** Bessie Love; Charles King; Jack Benny; Nita Martan; Marie Dressler; Polly Moran; George K. Arthur; Gwen Lee; ***D:*** Charles Reisner; ***W:*** Bess Meredyth; Wells Root; ***C:*** Ira Morgan.

Chasing Sleep ✐✐ **2000 (R)** College prof. Ed Saxon (Daniels) worries when his wife doesn't return from work. The cops find her car but that's all. Meanwhile, pill-popping insomniac Ed discovers his wife's diary, which reveals she was having an affair with a neighbor. Then he keeps having to deal with strange household plumbing problems. Ed becomes increasingly disoriented, so is he hallucinating the whole thing or has something terrible really happened? Daniels gives an effective off-center performance but the story loses its momentum. **104m/C; VHS, DVD.** Jeff Daniels; Emily Bergl; Gil Bellows; Zach Grenier; Julian McMahon; Ben Shenkman; Molly Price; ***D:*** Michael Walker; ***W:*** Michael Walker; ***C:*** Jim Denault.

Chasing the Green ✐✐ **1/2 2009** In the 1990s, twenty-something entrepreneur Ross gets his brother Andy to go into partnership in the transaction-credit card processing industry through their marketing of electronic terminals. The brothers become rich but their lack of business experience shows when they ignore Federal Trade Commission warnings. The FTC starts investigating alleged complaints but something stinks since the Commission gets involved at the behest of the brothers' industry competitors. Andy finds solace from their corporate woes through his golf obsession while Ross tries to keep their business from collapsing. Based on a true story. **102m/C; DVD.** Jeremy London; Ryan Hurst; Heather McComb; William Devane; Robert Picardo; Larry Pine; Dan Grimaldi; ***D:*** Russ Emanuel; ***W:*** Craig Frankel; Emilio Iasiello; ***C:*** Seth Melnick; ***M:*** Jason Lively; Neil Agro. **VIDEO**

Chasing 3000 ✐✐ **1/2 2007** While taking his kids to a Pittsburgh Pirates game, Mickey (Liotta) regales them with the story of how he and his muscular-dystrophy-stricken younger brother Roger were determined to see Roberto Clemente make his 3,000th career hit during the 1972 baseball season. The teens are particularly unhappy when their single mom Marilyn (Holly) moves them to L.A., so when she's away on a business trip, Mickey (Morgan) decides to take her car and drive back to Pittsburgh. Neither of the brothers realizes how sick Roger (Culkin) truly is as they encounter both trouble and kindness along their route. **102m/C; DVD.** Ray Liotta; Trevor Morgan; Rory Culkin; Jay Karnes; Lauren Holly; Seymour Cassel; Keith David; Chuck Ireland; Ricardo Chavira; Lori Petty; Tania Raymonde; Willa Holland; Kevin Gage; ***D:*** Gregory J. Lanesey; ***W:*** Gregory J. Lanesey; Bill Mikita; Cris D'Annunzio; ***C:*** Denis Maloney; ***M:*** Lawrence Shragge.

The Chateau ✐✐ **1/2 2001 (R)** Naif geek Graham (Rudd) and his black entrepreneurial adoptive brother Allen (Malco) unexpectedly inherit a crumbling chateau in the French countryside. The servants seemed surprised by their arrival and even more shocked when the brothers say they intend to sell the property. They conspire to make the sale as difficult as possible until they can outsmart (which isn't hard) these uncouth Americans and save their home and jobs. English and French with subtitles. **92m/C; VHS, DVD.** Paul Rudd; Romany Malco; Sylvie Testud; Didier Flamand; Philippe Nahon; Maria Verdi; Nathalie Jouen; Donal Logue; ***D:*** Jesse Peretz; ***W:*** Jesse Peretz; Thomas Bidegain; ***C:*** Tom Richmond; ***M:*** Nathan Larson; Patrik Bartosch; Nina Persson.

The Chateau Meroux ✐✐ **1/2 2011 (PG-13)** Pleasant, occasionally diverting rom com. Wendy's inherited her estranged father's debt-ridden Napa Valley winery. She knows nothing about the business and is being pressured to sell by another local owner, Nathan. While Wendy's dithering, attractive winemaker Chris offers his help. **94m/C; DVD.** Marla Sokoloff; Barry Watson; Christopher Lloyd; Amanda Righetti; Jeffrey Weissman; ***D:*** Bob Fugger; ***W:*** Adam Morrison; Tim Carter; ***C:*** Ricardo Jacques Gale; ***M:*** Alec Puro. **VIDEO**

Chato's Land ✐✐ **1/2 1971 (PG)** An Indian is tracked by a posse eager to resolve a lawman's death. Conventional violent Bronson vehicle is bolstered by presence of masterful Palance. **100m/C; VHS, DVD, Blu-Ray.** Charles Bronson; Jack Palance; Richard Basehart; James Whitmore; Simon Oakland; Richard Jordan; Ralph Waite; Victor French; Lee Patterson; ***D:*** Michael Winner; ***W:*** Gerald Wilson; ***C:*** Robert Paynter; ***M:*** Jerry Fielding.

Chatroom ✐ **2010 (R)** Clunky, shrill thriller has troubled teens meeting online (shown as a virtual hotel room) and in actual London locations as they go about their lives. Disturbed cyber-bully William manipulates the others to reveal their darkest secrets and then pushes them to act out their violent impulses. Adapted by Enda Walsh from his play. **91m/C; DVD.** *GB* Aaron Taylor-Johnson; Imogen Poots; Hannah Murray; Daniel Kaluuya; Matthew Beard; Megan Dodds; Jacob Anderson; Rebecca McLintock; Richard Madden; ***D:*** Hideo Nakata; ***W:*** Enda Walsh; ***C:*** Benoit Delhomme; ***M:*** Kenji Kawai.

Chattahoochee ✐✐ **1/2 1989** A man suffering from post-combat syndrome lands in a horrifying institution. Strong cast, with Oldman fine in the lead, and Hopper memorable in extended cameo. Fact-based film is, unfortunately, rather conventionally rendered. **97m/C; VHS, DVD, Blu-Ray; Open Captioned.** Gary Oldman; Dennis Hopper; Frances McDormand; Pamela Reed; Ned Beatty; M. Emmet Walsh; William De Acutis; Lee Wilkof; Matt Craven; Gary Klar; ***D:*** Mick Jackson; ***W:*** James Cresson.

Chatterbox ✐✐ **1976** A starlet's life and career are severely altered when her sex organs begin speaking. So why didn't they warn her about movies like this? Plenty of B-queen Rialson on view. Good double bill with "Me and Him." **73m/C; VHS, DVD.** Candice Rialson; Larry Gelman; Jean Kean; Perry Bullington; ***D:*** Tom De Simone.

The Chatterley Affair ✐✐ **1/2 2006** In October of 1960, D.H. Lawrence's scandalous novel "Lady Chatterley's Lover" is brought before a British jury in a famous (and landmark) obscenity trial. But jurors Keith (Spall) and Helena (Delamere) soon find themselves more enthralled with each other than the court proceedings. **90m/C; DVD.** *GB* Rafe Spall; Louise Delamere; Karl Johnson; Kenneth Cranham; Mary Healey; Claire Bloom; ***D:*** James Hawes; ***W:*** Andrew Davies; ***C:*** James Aspinall; ***M:*** Nicholas Hooper. **TV**

Che ✐✐ **2008** Soderbergh's ambitious, generally straightforward, and overlong biography of iconic revolutionary, Argentinian-born Ernesto "Che" Guevara. It starts with Che (Del Toro) meeting Fidel Castro (Bichir) in 1955 and then moves through the Cuban revolution, Che's speech at the United Nations, his desire to spread Marxism in Central and South America, and his fatal misadventures in Bolivia. Released as both a single film (with an intermission) and in two parts: "The Argentine" and "Guerrilla." Soderbergh seems determined not to be overly-dramatic, but instead he's boring and Del Toro's Che (though a fine performance) seems almost a bystander to his own story. English and Spanish with subtitles. **258m/C; Blu-Ray.**

Benicio Del Toro; Demian Bichir; Santiago Cabrera; Elvira Minguez; Jorge Perugorria; Edgar Ramirez; Victor Rasuk; Catalina Sandino Moreno; Rodrigo Santoro; Carlos Bardem; Joaquim de Almeida; Jordi Molla; Julia Ormond; Lou Diamond Phillips; Franka Potente; Armando Riesco; ***Cameo(s):*** Matt Damon; ***D:*** Steven Soderbergh; ***W:*** Peter Buchman; ***C:*** Steven Soderbergh; ***M:*** Alberto Iglesias.

The Cheap Detective ♂♂♂ **1978 (PG)** Neil Simon's parody of the "Maltese Falcon" gloriously exploits the resourceful Falk in a Bogart-like role. Vast supporting cast—notable Brennan, DeLuise, and Kahn—equally game for fun in this consistently amusing venture. **92m/C; VHS, DVD.** Peter Falk; Ann-Margret; Eileen Brennan; Sid Caesar; Stockard Channing; James Coco; Dom DeLuise; Louise Fletcher; John Houseman; Madeline Kahn; Fernando Lamas; Marsha Mason; Phil Silvers; Vic Tayback; Abe Vigoda; Paul Williams; Nicol Williamson; ***D:*** Robert Moore; ***W:*** Neil Simon; ***C:*** John A. Alonzo.

Cheap Thrills ♂♂ **2014** Violet (Paxton) and Colin (Koechner) are rich and bored. Craig (Healy) and Vince (Embry) are broke and desperate. It's a dangerous double date one night at a seedy bar when Violet & Colin start offering their new friends more money for more dangerous behavior. Do a shot for $50, smack a stranger for $200; how much to cut off your pinkie? The final act could have been tighter but it's an undeniably good time for those drawn to this dark subgenre. Twisted, delectable fun of the ilk that fans of "Tales From the Crypt" or "The Twilight Zone" will love. **88m/C; DVD, Blu-Ray.** Pat Healy; Ethan (Randall) Embry; David Koechner; Sara Paxton; Amanda Fuller; ***D:*** E.L. Katz; ***W:*** Trent Haaga; David Chirchirillo; ***C:*** Andrew Wheeler; ***M:*** Mads Heldtberg.

Cheaper by the Dozen ♂♂♂ **1950** Turn-of-the-century family comedy based on the book by Frank B. Gilbreth Jr., and Ernestine Gilbreth Carey, which chronicled life in the expansive Gilbreth household—12 children, efficiency expert father Frank (Webb), and psychologist mother Lillian (Loy). Stern dad likes to test his theories on the family (and have everything his own way) while nuturing mom easily manages him as well as their large household. There are various family crises (times 12) but it's all very heartwarming. Followed by "Belles on Their Toes." **85m/C; VHS, DVD.** Clifton Webb; Myrna Loy; Jeanne Crain; Edgar Buchanan; Mildred Natwick; Sara Allgood; Betty Lynn; Barbara Bates; Norman Ollestad; ***D:*** Walter Lang; ***W:*** Lamar Trotti; ***C:*** Leon Shamroy; ***M:*** Cyril Mockridge.

Cheaper by the Dozen ♂♂ ½ **2003 (PG)** Has little in common with the 1950 original, except the title and the number of kids. Mom (Hunt) and Dad (Martin) and the 12 kids have to cope with moving to Chicago while Mom goes on a book tour and Dad ponders a higher-profile coaching gig. A rather perky, old-fashioned lot, this is a brood for which the term "family values" was presumably invented. Cute in a harmless, antiseptic kind of way. Martin adds his usual bemused charm, and the kids should enjoy the sibling-induced highjinks. **98m/C; VHS, DVD, UMD.** Steve Martin; Bonnie Hunt; Piper Perabo; Tom Welling; Hilary Duff; Ashton Kutcher; Kevin J. Edelman; Alyson Stoner; Jacob Smith; Liliana Mumy; Paula Marshall; Alan Ruck; Richard Jenkins; Holmes Osborne; Vanessa Bell Calloway; Rex Linn; Amy Hill; Morgan York; Forrest Landis; Blake Woodruff; Brent Kinsman; Shane Kinsman; Steven Anthony Lawrence; ***Cameo(s):*** Regis Philbin; Kelly Ripa; ***D:*** Shawn Levy; ***W:*** Sam Harper; Joel Cohen; Alec Sokolow; ***C:*** Jonathan Brown; ***M:*** Christophe Beck.

Cheaper by the Dozen 2 ♂♂ **2005 (PG)** Another in the rather endless string of lazy, mediocre family slapstick comedies. Dad Tom Baker (Martin) and wife Kate (Hunt) are still trying to manage their motley crew, but now a few are older and about to leave the family nest. The solution? One last family vacation to Lake Winnetka, Wisconsin. Only the beloved lakefront property is a bit decrepit, and Baker's arch-rival (Levy)?who has eight kids of his own AND a hot new wife (Electra)?has built a mansion across the lake. Lots of harmless silliness. Martin, Levy, and Hunt have all done much better work elsewhere, and they're obviously just picking up a paycheck. **94m/C; DVD.** Steve Martin; Eugene Levy; Bonnie Hunt; Tom Welling; Piper Perabo; Carmen Electra; Jaime King; Hilary Duff; Alyson Stoner; Jonathan Bennett; Jacob Smith; Liliana Mumy; Morgan York; Kevin G. Schmidt; Forrest Landis; Taylor Lautner; ***D:*** Adam Shankman; ***W:*** Sam Harper; ***C:*** Peter James; ***M:*** John Debney.

The Cheat ♂♂ **1931** Elsa (Bankhead) loses a fortune gambling and tries to keep the news from her husband Jeffrey (Stephens) by embezzling money from a charity fund and speculating on the stock market. When Elsa loses that too, she accepts dough from sleazy admirer Livingston (Pichel), but she's not willing to accept his repayment terms. There's a courtroom climax. Remake of a 1915 silent. **65m/B; DVD.** Tallulah Bankhead; Harvey Stephens; Irving Pichel; Williard Dashiell; Edward (Ed Kean, Keene) Keane; Robert Strange; Jay Fassett; ***D:*** George Abbott; ***W:*** Harry Hervey; ***C:*** George J. Folsey.

The Cheaters ♂ **1976 (R)** A young gambler runs away with his boss's son's girlfriend, and is pursued therein. **91m/C; VHS, DVD.** *IT* Dayle Haddon; Luc Merenda; Lino Troisi; Enrico Maria Salerno; ***D:*** Sergio Martino.

Cheaters ♂ ½ **1984** Two middle class couples are having affairs with each other's spouses. Complications arise when their respective children decide to marry each other. **103m/C; VHS, DVD.** Peggy Cass; Jack Kruschen.

Cheaters ♂♂ ½ **2000 (R)** Students at Chicago's run-down Steinmetz High School don't have a prayer of winning the state Academic Decathalon championship until they stumble across a copy of the test and decide that winning is everything—encouraged by their teacher/coach Gerald Plecki (Daniels), who helps them cheat, believing his intentions are good. Based on a true story. **106m/C; VHS, DVD.** Jeff Daniels; Jena Malone; Paul Sorvino; Luke Edwards; Blake Heron; ***D:*** John Stockwell; ***W:*** John Stockwell; ***C:*** David Hennings; ***M:*** Paul Haslinger. **CABLE**

Cheaters' Club ♂ ½ **2006** Shrink Roberta Adler (Anderson) prescribes a controversial therapy for her unhappily married female patients: a no-strings affair. But after taking her own advice, tragedy strikes the doctor and her lover and now Linda (Carpenter), Meredith (Bridges), and Cindy (Gardner) are worried that the investigation will not only reveal their adultery but that their actions have put them in danger. **90m/C; DVD.** Charisma Carpenter; Katya Gardner; Krista Bridges; Wendy Anderson; Kate Trotter; Tim Campbell; Andrew Kraulis; Jeff Pangman; Rogue Johnston; ***D:*** Steve DiMarco; ***W:*** Kevin Commins; ***C:*** Alwyn Kumst; ***M:*** Stacey Hersh. **CABLE**

Cheatin' Hearts ♂♂ ½ **1993 (R)** Kirkland is a woman beset by woe: she's about to lose her house, her philandering husband (Brolin) wanders back to town with his latest bimbo in tow, and her daughter's getting married. This should be a good thing, except hubby makes a fool of himself at the wedding and nearly ruins everything. Well, at least local rancher Kristofferson is around to lift a woman's spirits. And yes, there's a (predictably) happy ending. **88m/C; VHS, DVD.** Sally Kirkland; James Brolin; Kris Kristofferson; Pamela Gidley; Laura Johnson; ***D:*** Rod McCall.

Check & Double Check ♂ **1930** Radio's original Amos 'n' Andy (a couple of black-faced white guys) help solve a lover's triangle in this film version of the popular radio series. Interesting only as a novelty. Duke Ellington's band plays "Old Man Blues" and "Three Little Words." **85m/B; VHS, DVD.** Freeman Gosden; Charles Correll; Duke Ellington; ***D:*** Melville Brown; ***M:*** Max Steiner.

The Checkered Flag ♂ **1963** Lame auto-racing drama about an aging, millionaire race car driver with an alcoholic wife who would like nothing more than to see him dead. She talks a young rookie into helping her dispose of hubby. Plans go awry—with horrifying results. Racing scenes overshadow incredibly weak script and performances. **110m/C; VHS, DVD.** Joe Morrison; Evelyn King; Charles G. Martin; Peggy Vendig; ***D:*** William Grefe; ***W:*** William Grefe.

Checking Out ♂ ½ **1989 (R)** Black comedy about a manic hypochondriac who is convinced that his demise will soon occur. You'll pray that he's right. Daniels can't make it work, and supporters Mayron and Magnuson also have little chance in poorly conceived roles. **95m/C; VHS, DVD; Open Captioned.** Jeff Daniels; Melanie Mayron; Michael Tucker; Kathleen York; Ann Magnuson; Allan Havey; Jo Harvey Allen; Felton Perry; Alan Wolfe; ***D:*** David Leland; ***W:*** Joe Eszterhas; ***M:*** Carter Burwell.

Cheech and Chong: Still Smokin' ♂ ½ *Still Smokin'* **1983 (R)** Not really. More like still trying to make a buck. Veteran marijuana-dazed comedy duo travel to Amsterdam to raise funds for a bankrupt film festival group by hosting a dope-a-thon. Lots of concert footage used in an attempt to hold the slim plot together. Only for serious fans of the dopin' duo. **91m/C; VHS, DVD.** Richard "Cheech" Marin; Thomas Chong; ***D:*** Thomas Chong; ***W:*** Richard "Cheech" Marin; Thomas Chong; ***C:*** Harvey Harrison; ***M:*** George S. Clinton.

Cheech and Chong: Things Are Tough All Over ♂♂ **1982 (R)** Stoner comedy team are hired by two rich Arab brothers (also played by Cheech and Chong in acting stretch) and unwittingly drive a car loaded with money from Chicago to Las Vegas. Tired fourth in the series. **87m/C; VHS, DVD.** Richard "Cheech" Marin; Thomas Chong; Shelby Fiddis; Rikki Marin; Evelyn Guerrero; Rip Taylor; ***D:*** Tom Avildsen; ***W:*** Richard "Cheech" Marin; Thomas Chong.

Cheech & Chong's Animated Movie! ♂ ½ **2013 (R)** Nostalgic stoner fun as the comedy duo of Cheech and Chong decide to redo many of their classic skits in animated form, along with nine new songs. **120m/C; DVD, Blu-Ray, Streaming.** ***V:*** Cheech Marin; Tommy Chong; ***D:*** Branden Chambers; Eric Chambers; ***W:*** Cheech Marin; Tommy Chong; ***M:*** Dominic Kelly. **VIDEO**

Cheech and Chong's Next Movie ♂♂ **1980 (R)** A pair of messed-up bumblers adventure into a welfare office, massage parlor, nightclub, and flying saucer, while always living in fear of the cops. Kinda funny, like. Sequel to "Up in Smoke." **95m/C; VHS, DVD, Blu-Ray.** Richard "Cheech" Marin; Thomas Chong; Evelyn Guerrero; Edie McClurg; Paul (Pee-wee Herman) Reubens; Phil Hartman; ***D:*** Thomas Chong; ***W:*** Richard "Cheech" Marin; Thomas Chong.

Cheech and Chong's Nice Dreams ♂♂ **1981 (R)** The spaced-out duo are selling their own "specially mixed" ice cream to make cash and realize their dreams. Third in the series. **97m/C; VHS, DVD.** Richard "Cheech" Marin; Thomas Chong; Evelyn Guerrero; Stacy Keach; Paul (Pee-wee Herman) Reubens; Sab Shimono; Sandra Bernhard; Linnea Quigley; Michael Winslow; ***Cameo(s):*** Timothy Leary; ***D:*** Thomas Chong; ***W:*** Richard "Cheech" Marin; Thomas Chong; ***C:*** Charles Correll; ***M:*** Harry Betts.

Cheech and Chong's The Corsican Brothers **WOOF!** **1984 (PG)** Wretched swashbuckler features the minimally talented duo in a variety of worthless roles. Dumas would vomit in his casket if he knew about this. Fifth in the series. **91m/C; VHS, DVD, Blu-Ray.** Richard "Cheech" Marin; Thomas Chong; Roy Dotrice; Rae Dawn Chong; Shelby Fiddis; Rikki Marin; Edie McClurg; ***D:*** Thomas Chong; ***W:*** Richard "Cheech" Marin; Thomas Chong; ***C:*** Harvey Harrison.

Cheech and Chong's Up in Smoke ♂♂ ½ *Up in Smoke* **1979 (R)** A pair of free-spirited burn-outs team up for a tongue-in-cheek spoof of sex, drugs, and rock and roll. First and probably the best of the dopey duo's cinematic adventures. A boxoffice bonanza when released and still a cult favorite. **87m/C; VHS, DVD, Blu-Ray.** Richard "Cheech" Marin; Thomas Chong; Stacy Keach; Tom Skerritt; Edie Adams; Strother Martin; Cheryl "Rainbeaux" Smith; ***D:*** Lou Adler; ***W:*** Richard "Cheech" Marin; Thomas Chong; ***C:*** Gene Polito.

Cheerful Weather for the Wedding ♂ **2012 (PG)** The weather might be cheerful but the bride isn't in this shallow costume fare adapted from Julia Strachey's 1932 novella. Bride Dolly is hiding upstairs in the family's country manor, drinking and wondering if she's making a mistake marrying dry stick Owen. It seems her former flame Joseph has turned up and is determined to get Dolly back as chaos reigns downstairs while everyone awaits her decision. **92m/C; DVD.** *UK* Felicity Jones; James Norton; Luke Treadaway; Ellie Kendrick; Elizabeth McGovern; Julian Wadham; Zoe Tapper; ***D:*** Donald Rice; ***W:*** Donald Rice; Mary Henely-Magill; ***C:*** John Lee; ***M:*** Michael Price.

Cheerleader Camp **WOOF!** *Bloody Pom Poms* **1988 (R)** Nubile gals are stalked by a psychopath while they cavort semi-clad at summer camp. **89m/C; VHS, DVD.** Betsy Russell; Leif Garrett; Lucinda Dickey; Lorie Griffin; George "Buck" Flower; Teri Weigel; Rebecca Ferratti; Travis McKenna; Kathryn Litton; ***D:*** John Quinn; ***W:*** David Lee Fein; R.L. O'Keefe; ***C:*** Bryan England; ***M:*** Joel Hamilton; Muriel Hodler-Hamilton.

The Cheerleaders **WOOF!** **1972 (R)** Dim-witted exploitation effort has the usual suspects—moronic jocks and lamebrained gals—cavorting exuberantly. Followed by "Revenge of the Cheerleaders." **84m/C; VHS, DVD, Blu-Ray.** Stephanie Fondue; Denise Dillaway; Jovita Bush; Debbie Lowe; Sandy Evans; ***D:*** Paul Glickler.

Cheerleaders' Wild Weekend **WOOF!** **1985 (R)** Group of cheerleaders are held captive by a disgruntled former football star. Pom poms wave. **87m/C; VHS, DVD.** Jason Williams; Kristine DeBell; ***D:*** Jeff Werner.

Cheers for Miss Bishop ♂♂ ½ **1941** The story of a woman who graduates from college then teaches at the same institution for the next 50 years. Somewhat moving. Based on Bess Streeter Aldrich's novel. **95m/B; VHS, DVD, Blu-Ray.** Martha Scott; William Gargan; Edmund Gwenn; Sterling Holloway; Rosemary DeCamp; ***D:*** Tay Garnett; ***M:*** Edward Ward.

Cheetah ♂♂ **1989 (G)** Two California kids visiting their parents in Kenya embark on the adventure of their lives when, with the help of a young Masai, they adopt and care for an orphaned cheetah. Usual Disney kids and animals story. **80m/C; VHS, DVD.** Keith Coogan; Lucy Deakins; Collin Mothupi; ***D:*** Jeff Blyth; ***W:*** John Cotter; ***C:*** Thomas Burstyn.

The Cheetah Girls ♂ ½ **2003 (G)** This Disney Channel original is made for undiscriminating tween girls. New York teens Galleria (Raven-Symone), Chanel (Bailon), Aqua (Williams), and Dorinda (Bryan) form a pop group for the school talent show. They get a professional chance when record producer Jackal Johnson (Corazza) hears their music, but Jackal's aptly named when he wants to give them a makeover. However, the girls have another problem when their success turns Galleria into a diva, which isn't "cheetah-licious." (Yes, they have their own catch phrase.) **93m/C; DVD.** Raven; Vincent Corazza; Lynn Whitfield; Kyle Schmid; Sandra Caldwell; Adrienne Bailon; Kiely Williams; Sabrina Bryan; ***D:*** Oz Scott; ***W:*** Alison Taylor; ***C:*** Derick Underschultz; ***M:*** John Van Tongeren. **CABLE**

The Cheetah Girls 2 ♂ ½ **2006 (G)** In this Disney Channel sequel, Galleria (Raven-Symone) enters the Cheetah Girls in a talent competition/music festival being held in Barcelona, Spain. When the girls arrive, they're so interested in everything else going on (boys, sightseeing, shopping) that they neglect their music, which frustrates Galleria because they have a real rival in local teen queen Marisol (Peregrin). **96m/C; DVD.** Raven; Adrienne Bailon; Sabrina Bryan; Kiely Williams; Abel Folk; Lynn Whitfield; Belinda Peregrin; Lori Alter; Golan Yosef; Kim Manning; ***D:*** Kenny Ortega; ***W:*** Alison Taylor; Bethesda Brown; ***C:*** Daniel Aranyo; ***M:*** David Lawrence. **CABLE**

The Cheetah Girls: One World ♂♂ ½ **2008 (G)** Galleria is off to college so only Chanel, Dorinda, and Aqua appear in this third colorful music extravaganza. The girls head to India after being cast in a Bollywood flick only to learn the producer actually wants just one of them and they will have to compete for the part. But are the Cheetah Girls willing to risk their friendships or can they find a way to make the situation work? **88m/C; DVD.** Adrienne Bailon; Sabrina Bryan; Kiely Williams; Roshan Seth; Michael Steger; Kunal Sharma; Rupak Ginn; Deepti Daryanani; ***D:*** Paul Hoen; ***W:*** Nisha Ganatra; ***C:*** Donald Duncan; ***M:*** David Lawrence. **CABLE**

Chef 1/2 **2014 (R)** Favreau climbs down from Mount Marvel to deliver something more intimate and personal in this dramedy about a Miami-born chef (Favreau himself) who crashes and burns in L.A. but returns to family in Florida to find his culinary passion again. The idea of a man who goes from trying to scale the top of his profession to finding his true joy in a "smaller project" of a food truck has to be read as somewhat autobiographical for Favreau himself, but he injects the film with enough light-hearted energy and joy that it doesn't feel too self-conscious or over-written. **114m/C; DVD, Blu-Ray.** Jon Favreau; Emjay Anthony; Sofia Vergara; John Leguizamo; Robert Downey, Jr.; Dustin Hoffman; Oliver Platt; ***D:*** Jon Favreau; ***W:*** Jon Favreau; ***C:*** Kramer Morgenthau.

A Chef in Love *Les Mille et Une Recettes du Cuisinier Amoureux; The Cook in Love* **1996 (PG-13)** In 1920, Parisian Pascal Ishac (Richard) meets Georgian Princess Cecilia (Kirtadze) while travelling and decides to stay and open a French restaurant in the capital of Tbilisi. When the capital is invaded by the Red Army in 1921, communist leader Zigmund (Kahmhadze) forces Cecilia to marry him and shuts down Pascal's eatery. With his great love and his restaurant both gone, Pascal writes a master cookbook and memoir that is later discovered and translated by Cecilia's son Anton (Gautier), who also discovers that Pascal is his father. French, Russian and Georgian with subtitles. **95m/C; VHS, DVD.** *FR* Pierre Richard; Nino Kirtadze; Temur Kahmhadze; Jean-Yves Gautier; Micheline Presle; ***D:*** Nana Dzhordzadze; ***W:*** Irakli Kvirikadze; ***C:*** Georgi Beridze; ***M:*** Goran Bregovic.

Chef's Special *Fuera de Carta* **2008** Overwhelmed Madrid chef Maxi is trying to keep his restaurant afloat while waiting for an important review that could make his career. Then his personal life implodes when his ex-wife dies and the self-absorbed man is forced to raise his two estranged children. And find romance with the gorgeous soccer superstar who just came out of the closet (and moved into an apartment down the hall). Lots of silly situations. Spanish with subtitles. **111m/C; DVD.** *SP* Javier Camara; Lola Duenas; Fernando Tejero; Benjamin Vicuna; Chus (Maria Jesus) Lampreave; Luis Varela; ***D:*** Nacho G. Velilla; ***W:*** Nacho G. Velilla; Antonia Sanchez; David Sanchez; Oriol Capel; ***C:*** David Omedes; ***M:*** Juanjo Javierre.

Chelsea Walls **2001 (R)** Hawke's directorial debut features wife Thurman as one of the would-be artists living at the legendary (and seedy) Chelsea Hotel. There's a variety of struggling writers, musicians, and artists who all have romantic dilemmas and substance abuse problems as well. Lots of chatter and atmosphere but the characters are all walking cliches. **108m/C; VHS, DVD.** Kris Kristofferson; Uma Thurman; Vincent D'Onofrio; Natasha Richardson; Tuesday Weld; Rosario Dawson; Mark Webber; Kevin Corrigan; Robert Sean Leonard; Steve Zahn; Frank Whaley; ***D:*** Ethan Hawke; ***W:*** Nicole Burdette; ***C:*** Tom Richmond; ***M:*** Jeff Tweedy.

Cheri **2009 (R)** Exquisite-looking, if bloodless, melodrama about doomed love. Lea (Pfeiffer) is a still beautiful, middle-aged courtesan in Belle Epoque Paris, now retired from her very successful career. She exchanges barbs and gossip with former colleague Charlotte (Bates), who has a louche teenaged son nicknamed Cheri (Friend), and Charlotte decides Lea should give him some seasoning. Six years later the mismatched lovers are still together, refusing to recognize any of the deep emotions they have for each other. Then Charlotte makes other plans for Cheri's future, and Lea plays at not caring. Based on two novels by Colette. **92m/C; On Demand.** *GB FR GE* Michelle Pfeiffer; Kathy Bates; Rupert Friend; Felicity Jones; Iben Hjejle; Bette Bourne; Anita Pallenberg; Frances Tomelty; Harriet Walter; Nichola McAuliffe; ***Nar:*** Stephen Frears; ***D:*** Stephen Frears; ***W:*** Christopher Hampton; ***C:*** Darius Khondji; ***M:*** Alexandre Desplat.

Cherish **2002 (R)** Zoe (Tunney) is a nervous San Francisco dot.commer who, under convoluted circumstances, winds up accused of vehicular manslaughter while driving under the influence. She winds up under house arrest wearing an electronic surveillance anklet with deputy Daly (Blake) to check up on her. She gets to make friends with her neighbors and convinces Daly to help her find the stalker who's the cause of all her misery. Confusing blend of genres with a good soundtrack. **99m/C; VHS, DVD.** Robin Tunney; Tim Blake Nelson; Jason Priestley; Nora Dunn; Brad Hunt; Liz Phair; Lindsay Crouse; Stephen Polk; Ricardo Gil; Kenny Kwong; ***D:*** Finn Taylor; ***W:*** Finn Taylor; ***C:*** Barry Stone; ***M:*** Mark De Gil Antoni.

Chernobyl Diaries **2012 (R)** A group of tourists head out on an "extreme" adventure to the city left a ghost town by the Chernobyl nuclear disaster in Russia. After their van is sabotaged and night falls, the horror begins. While some of the beats are expected, director Parker has a strong visual eye, a confident sense of pacing, and a unique sensibility. Far from perfect (especially in its rushed, abominable final ten minutes) but more original than many of the films inspired by the found footage craze. Heading up the script is Peli of "Paranormal Activity" fame. **88m/C; DVD, Blu-Ray.** Jonathan Sadowski; Jesse McCartney; Devin Kelley; Olivia Taylor Dudley; Ingrid Bolso Berdal; Nathan Phillips; Dimitri Diatchenko; ***D:*** Bradley Parker; ***W:*** Oren Peli; Carey Van Dyke; Shane Van Dyke; ***C:*** Morten Soborg; ***M:*** Diego Stocco.

The Cherokee Kid 1/2 **1996 (PG-13)** Western/comedy about a novice gunslinger (Sinbad) avenging his family. There's a corrupt banker (Coburn), a bounty hunter (Hines), a Mexican freedom fighter (Martinez), and a gang of bankrobbing nuns to keep things interesting while the Kid learns his outlaw ways. **91m/C; VHS, DVD.** Sinbad; James Coburn; Burt Reynolds; Gregory Hines; A. Martinez; Ernie Hudson; ***D:*** Paris Barclay; ***W:*** Tim Kazurinsky; Denise DeClue; ***M:*** Stanley Clarke. **CABLE**

Cherry Blossoms *Cherry Blossoms: Hanami; Kirschbluesten-Hanami* **2008** Hausfrau Trudi (Elsner) is fascinated by Japan and wants her overbearing husband Rudi (Wepper) to agree to visit their son who has a job in Tokyo. Instead, Rudi insists they see their other children who live nearby in Berlin. Trudi dies suddenly and the aimless widower decides to honor his wife by finally visiting Japan, where he meets a teenage Butoh dancer in Tokyo and makes a pilgrimage to Mount Fuji. Unhurried drama about loss and acceptance. German and Japanese with subtitles. **127m/C; On Demand.** *GE* Hannelore Elsner; Nadja Uhl; Maximilian Bruckner; Birgit Minichmayr; Felix Eitner; Floriane Daniel; Elmar Weper; Aya Irizuki; ***D:*** Doris Doerrie; ***W:*** Doris Doerrie; ***C:*** Hanno Lentz; ***M:*** Claus Bantzer.

Cherry Crush 1/2 **2007 (R)** Dull noir wannabe. Prep school student Jordan Wells (Tucker) is expelled after taking naughty pics of female classmates. Now enrolled in public school, Jordan is putty for wrong side of the tracks Shay (Reed), even when things turn deadly. Reed's more petulant than provocative. **89m/C; DVD.** Jonathan Tucker; Nikki Reed; Frank Whaley; Michael O'Keefe; Julie Gonzalo; Dennis Boutsikaris; Haviland (Haylie) Morris; ***D:*** Nicholas DiBella; ***W:*** Nicholas DiBella; Paul Root; ***C:*** Tim Wainwright; ***M:*** Joe Kaltenbach. **VIDEO**

Cherry Falls 1/2 **2000 (R)** The small town of Cherry Falls is plagued by a serial killer who only kills teenaged virgins, so naturally every teen there is out to do it and save themselves. However Sheriff Marken (Biehn) has no intention of letting daughter Jody (Murphy) go to such extremes. This one is an amusing parody of slasher flicks, teen sex comedies, and suburban nightmares. **100m/C; VHS, DVD, Blu-Ray.** Jay Mohr; Michael Biehn; Brittany Murphy; Candy Clark; Gabriel Mann; Keram Malicki-Sanchez; Jesse Bradford; ***D:*** Geoffrey Wright; ***W:*** Ken Selden; ***C:*** Anthony B. Richmond; ***M:*** Walter Werzowa.

Cherry Hill High WOOF! 1976 (R) Five teen girls compete for former-virgin status. Pass on this one. **92m/C; VHS, DVD.** Linda McInerney; Carrie Olsen; Nina Carson; Lynn Hastings; Gloria Upson; Stephanie Lawlor; ***D:*** Alex E. Goiten.

The Cherry Orchard 1/2 **1999** Underwhelming and tedious adaptation of the Chekov play. A broke Russian aristocrat can't cope with the changing times and refuses to sell her beloved cherry orchard to upstart developers despite needing the money to continue living on the family estate. **137m/C; DVD.** *FR GR* Charlotte Rampling; Alan Bates; Katrin Cartlidge; Owen Teale; Michael Gough; Tushka Bergen; Xander Berkeley; Gerard Butler; Andrew Howard; Melanie Lynskey; Ian McNeice; Frances de la Tour; ***D:*** Michael Cacoyannis; ***W:*** Michael Cacoyannis; ***C:*** Aris Stavrou.

Cherry 2000 **1988 (PG-13)** Futuristic flick concerns a man who short-circuits his sex-toy robots and embarks on a search for replacement parts across treacherous territory, only to meet a real female—Griffith. Offbeat, occasionally funny. **94m/C; VHS, DVD, Blu-Ray.** Melanie Griffith; David Andrews; Ben Johnson; Tim Thomerson; Michael C. Gwynne; Pamela Gidley; ***D:*** Steve DeJarnatt; ***W:*** Michael Almereyda; ***C:*** Jacques Haitkin; ***M:*** Basil Poledouris.

The Chess Player *Le Joueur d'Echecs* **1927** In 1776, Polish nobleman Boleslas Vorowski heads a secret movement to free his country from Russian control. When Vorowski is wounded in battle, his mentor, inventor Baron von Kempelen, constructs a chess-playing automaton named Turk that conceals Vorowski in order to smuggle him to safety. When Catherine the Great learns of Turk's chess prowess, she commands the automaton be brought to Russia for a royal match. From the novel by Henri Dupuy-Mazuel, which is based on the real 18th-century machine. **133m/B; Silent; VHS, DVD.** *FR* Pierre Blanchar; Edith Jehanne; Charles Dullin; Camille Bert; Pierre Batcheff; ***D:*** Raymond Bernard; ***W:*** Raymond Bernard; ***C:*** Joseph-Louis Mundwiller; Willy; Marc Bujard; ***M:*** Henri Rabaud.

Chesty Anderson USN *Anderson's Angels* **1976** Ultra-lame sexploitation about female naval recruits. Minimal nudity. **90m/C; VHS, DVD.** Shari Eubank; Dorri Thompson; Rosanne Katon; Marcie Barkin; Scatman Crothers; Frank Campanella; Fred Willard; ***D:*** Ed Forsyth.

Chevalier 1/2 **2016** Six men are on a fishing trip in the middle of the Aegean Sea. To pass the time, they start a series of games, a competition that will result in one winner. Of course, this leads to conflict and outbursts of overheated masculinity. Athina Rachel Tsangari's festival hit is sometimes a clever commentary on macho competition, but it's more often playful and fun than it is self-serious. A brilliant set-up and first half doesn't quite get the follow-through it deserves in the conclusion, but this is still an enjoyable journey on the open seas of testosterone. Greek with subtitles. **105m/C; DVD.** Sakis Rouvas; Yorgos Pirpassopoulos; Makis Papadimitriou; Panos Koronis; Vangelis Mourikis; ***D:*** Athina Rachel Tsangari; ***W:*** Athina Rachel Tsangari; Efthymis Filippou; ***C:*** Christos Karamanis.

Cheyenne 1/2 **1947** Gambler and fast gun James Wylie (Morgan) gets into trouble but is offered a way out by Wells Fargo detective Yancey (MacLane). Wylie is to go undercover and find out the real identity of a stagecoach-robbing bandit known as 'The Poet.' He heads to Cheyenne and gets involved with tempestuous Ann Kinkaid (Wyman) along the way. **99m/B; DVD.** Dennis Morgan; Jane Wyman; Janis Paige; Bruce Bennett; Alan Hale, Jr.; Arthur Kennedy; Barton MacLane; ***D:*** Raoul Walsh; ***W:*** Alan LeMay; ***C:*** Sidney Hickox; ***M:*** Max Steiner.

Cheyenne Autumn 1/2 **1964** The newly restored version of the ambitious, ultimately hit-and-miss western epic about three hundred Cheyenne Indians who migrate from Oklahoma to their Wyoming homeland in 1878. The cavalry, for once, are not the good guys. Widmark is strong in the lead. Stewart is memorable in his comic cameo as Wyatt Earp. Last film from genre master Ford, capturing the usual rugged panoramas. Based on a true story as told in the Mari Sandoz novel. **156m/C; VHS, DVD.** Richard Widmark; Carroll Baker; Karl Malden; Dolores Del Rio; Sal Mineo; Edward G. Robinson; Ricardo Montalban; Gilbert Roland; Arthur Kennedy; John Carradine; Victor Jory; Mike Mazurki; George O'Brien; John Qualen; ***Cameo(s):*** James Stewart; ***D:*** John Ford; ***C:*** William Clothier; ***M:*** Alex North.

The Cheyenne Social Club **1970 (PG)** Stewart inherits a brothel and Fonda helps him operate it. Kelly directs, sort of. Some laughs, but this effort is beneath this trio. **103m/C; VHS, DVD.** Henry Fonda; James Stewart; Shirley Jones; Sue Ane Langdon; Elaine Devry; Arch Johnson; Dabbs Greer; Jackie Joseph; Richard Collier; Charles Tyner; Robert J. Wilke; Warren Kemmerling; John Dehner; James Lee Barrett; ***D:*** Gene Kelly; ***C:*** William Clothier; ***M:*** Walter Scharf.

Cheyenne Warrior 1/2 **1994 (PG)** Pregnant young bride Rebecca heads west with a husband who soons winds up dead, leaving her stranded at an isolated trading post. She takes in a wounded Cheyenne warrior, nurses him back to health, and he tries to convince her to let his tribe care for her. Respectable performances if unexciting. **90m/C; VHS, DVD.** Kelly Preston; Pato Hoffmann; Bo Hopkins; Dan Haggerty; Charles Powell; Rick Dean; Clint Howard; ***D:*** Mark Griffiths; ***W:*** Michael B. Druxman.

Chi-raq **2015 (R)** Spike Lee delivers his most passionate fictional film in over a decade with this loose adaptation of "Lysistrata," re-imagined as a commentary on race, violence, gun control and class in the '10s. Parris plays Lysistrata, the gorgeous girlfriend of South Side Chicago gang leader Chi-Raq (Cannon). When a child is killed in a drive-by, Lysistrata leads a daring charge, demanding that all of the women currently sleeping with gang members give up sex. As the tagline says, "No Peace, No Piece." Lee throws various styles at the wall from comedy to musical to satire to drama, and the result is a stunning call to action. **127m/C; DVD, Blu-Ray.** Nick Cannon; Teyonah Parris; Wesley Snipes; Angela Bassett; Samuel L. Jackson; ***D:*** Spike Lee; ***W:*** Spike Lee; Kevin Willmott; ***C:*** Matthew Libatique; ***M:*** Terence Blanchard.

Chicago **1927** In this cynical first version of the 1926 Maurine Dallas Watkins play, married gold-digger Roxie Hart (Haver) is unrepentant over shooting her fed-up sugar daddy, Rodney Casley (Pallette). A good-looking gal can sell a lot of newspapers, especially when she's so cooperative and has equally scheming lawyer William Flynn (Edeson) to turn her trial into showbiz. **98m/B; Silent; DVD.** Phyllis Haver; Victor Varconi; Robert Edeson; Eugene Pallette; Virginia Bradford; May Robson; Julia Faye; T. Roy Barnes; Warner Richmond; ***D:*** Frank Urson; ***W:*** Lenore Coffee; ***C:*** J. Peverell Marley.

Chicago 1/2 **2002 (R)** The first Oscar-winning musical since the 1970s celebrates the unlikely themes of murder, adultery and greed with winning results. Heroine Roxie Hart (Zellweger) in jail for offing her two-timing boyfriend, finally finds the fame she craved. Ditto for Zeta-Jones' Velma Kelly, who's also in stir for popping her old man. The hot-headed beauties share the same slick lawyer, Billy Flynn (Gere). Reilly is Zellweger's simpleton husband, the sole spot of earnestness in an otherwise cynical film. Deftly directed, with musical numbers done as fantasy segments. Zeta-Jones and Latifah are the ones with the pipes for the genre, while lesser singer/dancers Gere and Zellweger score with appealing performances. Big-screen version of the award-winning musical by John Kander, Fred Ebb, and Bob Fosse. **113m/C; VHS, DVD, Blu-Ray.** Renée Zellweger; Catherine Zeta-Jones; Richard Gere; Queen Latifah; John C. Reilly; Christine Baranski; Lucy Liu; Taye Diggs; Colm Feore; Dominic West; ***D:*** Rob Marshall; ***W:*** Bill Condon; ***C:*** Dion Beebe; ***M:*** Danny Elfman; John Kander; ***M:*** Fred Ebb. Oscars '02: Art Dir./Set Dec., Costume Des., Film, Film Editing, Sound, Support. Actress (Zeta-Jones); British Acad. '02: Sound, Support. Actress (Zeta-Jones); Directors Guild '02: Director (Marshall); Golden Globes '03: Actor--Mus./Comedy (Gere), Actress--Mus./Comedy (Zellweger), Film--Mus./Comedy; Screen Actors Guild '02: Actress (Zellweger), Cast, Support. Actress (Zeta-Jones).

Chicago Cab *Hellcab* **1998 (R)** This checkered sketch piece about a cab driver (Dillon) and the assorted passengers he picks up during a "normal" day never really pulls away from the curb. Despite cameos from actors such as John Cusack, Gillian Anderson and Laurie Metcalf, the passengers are nasty obnoxious stereotypes drawn to prove the point that other people are irritating. Will Kern adapted the screenplay from his original play "Hellcab." **96m/C; VHS, DVD.** Paul Dillon; Gillian Anderson; John Cusack; Julianne Moore; Michael Ironside; John C. Reilly; Laurie Metcalf; Matt Roth; Shulle Cowen; Philip Van Lear; Michael Shannon; ***D:*** Mary Cybulski; John Tintori; ***W:*** Will Kern; ***C:*** Hubert Taczanowski; ***M:*** Page Hamilton.

Chicago Calling **1952** Unemployed alcoholic Bill Cannon's (Duryea) wife Mary (Anderson) has left him and taken their daughter Nancy (Plowman) with her to Chicago. Just when Bill's phone is about to be repossessed for nonpayment, he learns they have both been hospitalized after a serious accident. He desperately tries to raise the money to pay the overdue bill and finds some unexpected kindness as he waits for a long-distance call telling him their fate. **70m/B; DVD.** Dan Duryea; Mary Anderson; Melinda Plowman; Ross Elliot; Marsha Jones; ***D:*** John Reinhardt; ***W:*** John Reinhardt; Peter Berneis; ***C:*** Robert De Grasse; ***M:*** Heinz Roemheld.

Chicago Confidential **1/2 1957** Cheap crime expose. Honest union president Arthur Blane (Foran) is framed for murder by mobsters. Disbarred mob attorney Dixon (Garden) uses ambitious D.A. Jim Fremont (Keith) to get Blane a death row conviction despite conflicting evidence. Blane's gal Laura (Garland) insists he's innocent and Fremont finally decides something stinks and reopens the case despite increasing mob violence. **73m/B; DVD.** Brian Keith; Dick Foran; Beverly Garland; Gavin Gordon; Douglas Kennedy; Elisha Cook, Jr.; Paul Langton; Beverly Tyler; Buddy Lewis; ***D:*** Sidney Salkow; ***W:*** Bernard Gordon; ***C:*** Kenneth Peach, Sr.; ***M:*** Emil Newman.

Chicago Joe & the Showgirl **1990 (R)** A London-based GI befriends a loopy showgirl and helps her in various crimes during WWII. Appealing Lloyd overwhelms Sutherland, who shows only limited acting ability here. Kensit and Pigg are fine in smaller roles. **105m/C; VHS, DVD.** *GB* Emily Lloyd; Kiefer Sutherland; Patsy Kensit; Keith Allen; Liz Fraser; Alexandra Pigg; Ralph Nossek; Colin Bruce; ***D:*** Bernard Rose; ***M:*** Hans Zimmer.

Chicago Overcoat **1/2 2009 (R)** A compelling performance from lead Vincent helps this familiar gangland story. Aging Lou's (Vincent) glory days as a hitman for a Chicago crime syndicate are long past. He sees an opportunity for one last big payday when boss D'Agnostino (Assante) needs three witnesses in a tax fraud trial whacked. Only street boss Galante (Starr) doesn't want Lou interfering and a couple of longtime detectives (Goldring, Keach) are dogging his every move. Title is slang for a coffin. **94m/C; DVD.** Frank Vincent; Armand Assante; Mike Starr; Danny Goldring; Stacy Keach; Katherine Naducci; Gina D'Ercoli; Tim Gamble; Martin Shannon; ***D:*** Bryan Caunter; ***W:*** Bryan Caunter; John Bosher; Josh Staman; Andrew Dowd; ***C:*** Kevin Moss; ***M:*** Gregory Nicolett.

Chicago 10 **1/2 2007 (R)** A unique blend of archival footage, vocal reenactment, and rotoscope animation recounts the infamous trial of eight anti-war protesters following the 1968 Democratic National Convention, along with the chaos surrounding the case. An unconventional and fresh take on the documentary form, almost as radical as its subjects. Rather than being set to the music of the heroes of the day, like Dylan or CSN, contemporary artists provide the soundtrack, going as far as having Rage Against the Machine covering "Kick Out the Jams" during footage of the MC5 performing the original live during the protests. **103m/C; DVD, Streaming.** ***V:*** Hank Azaria; Dylan Baker; Nick Nolte; Mark Ruffalo; Roy Scheider; Liev Schreiber; Jeffrey Wright; Amy Ryan; Debra Eisenstadt; ***D:*** Brett Morgen; ***W:*** Brett Morgen; ***M:*** Jeff Danna.

El Chicano **2019 (R)** When a vicious cartel on the streets of L.A. murders his twin brother, Detective Diego Hernandez exacts vengeance by adopting the masked persona of El Chicano, the legendary grim reaper of the ghetto. It gets props as Hollywood's first Latino superhero movie, but it's a bloody and humorless foray into the genre. **107m/C; DVD, Blu-Ray.** Raúl Castillo; Aimee Garcia; Jose Pablo Cantillo; David Castaneda; George Lopez; ***D:*** Ben Hernandez Bray; ***W:*** Ben Hernandez Bray; Joe Carnahan; ***C:*** Juanmi (Juan Miguel) Azpiroz; ***M:*** Mitch Lee.

Chicken Every Sunday **1948** After 20 years of marriage, Emily (Holm) opts to divorce her foolish husband Jim (Dailey). She's been keeping a boarding house to make ends meet since all Jim's get-rich-quick schemes fail and she's had enough. Their friends and family work to get them back together. Set in Tucson, circa 1910; based on Rosemary Taylor's memoirs. **91m/B; DVD.** Celeste Holm; Dan Dailey; Colleen Townsend; Natalie Wood; Alan Young; William Frawley; Veda Ann Borg; Whit Bissell; ***D:*** George Seaton; ***W:*** George Seaton; Valentine Davies; ***C:*** Harry Jackson; ***M:*** Alfred Newman.

Chicken Little **1/2 2005 (G)** Disney's first solo (without Pixar) foray into CG animation won't please everyone, but the intended audience of grade-schoolers probably won't notice. Chicken Little (Braff) causes a panic and big trouble for himself when he thinks the sky is falling and sounds the alarm. He spends most of his time trying to live the incident down and build a good relationship with his pop (Marshall) a former athletic hero. When a piece of the "sky" falls on him again, it's up to him and his pals to convince everyone that it really happened, especially when an alien kid gets stranded in town, almost prompting an invasion. Lacks the originality, verve, and adult-pleasing inside humor of the Pixar collaborations, but not a bad first try. **82m/C; DVD, Blu-Ray.** ***V:*** Zach Braff; Garry Marshall; Joan Cusack; Steve Zahn; Amy Sedaris; Don Knotts; Harry Shearer; Patrick Stewart; Wallace Shawn; Fred Willard; Catherine O'Hara; Adam West; Patrick Warburton; ***D:*** Mark Dindal; ***W:*** Steve Bencich; Ron J. Friedman; Ron Anderson; ***M:*** John Debney.

Chicken People **1/2 2016** A feature-length documentary on the wild world of show chickens and their humans. At the Ohio National Poultry Show—the chicken equivalent to the Westminster Dog Show—people invest all they can in breeding the best birds to compete in the largest national poultry competition. Following three of the top competitors in the year between shows, the documentary considers how the chickens are raised and prepared for the competition amidst the personal lives of the breeders. The film shows the passion of the breeders with humor while relating an uplifting story. **83m/C; DVD, Streaming, Download.** ***D:*** Nicole Lucas Haimes; ***C:*** Martina Radwan; ***M:*** Michael Hearst.

Chicken Run **1/2 2000 (G)** It's a prisoner-of-war escape movie with chickens. This Claymation wonder is a comedy set on a failing 1950s Yorkshire chicken farm, where the hens realize their necks are literally on the chopping block when greedy farm wife, Mrs. Tweedy (Richardson), decides to go into the chicken pie business. So chicken leader, Ginger (Sawalha), tries to find a workable mass escape plan. And then daredevil Yankee rooster Rocky (Gibson) literally drops into the barnyard and Ginger believes he can teach all the hens to fly out. Chickens are just funny and you'll be amazed at what the animators have managed to make them do and how expressive they are. **86m/C; VHS, DVD, Blu-Ray.** *GB* ***V:*** Mel Gibson; Julia Sawalha; Miranda Richardson; Jane Horrocks; Tony Haygarth; Timothy Spall; Imelda Staunton; Phil Daniels; Benjamin Whitrow; Lynn Ferguson; ***D:*** Nick Park; Peter Lord; ***W:*** Karey Kirkpatrick; ***M:*** John Powell; Harry Gregson-Williams.

Chicken Tikka Masala **2005** Jimi Chopra (Bisson) is from an Anglo-Hindi family and is expected to go along with his arranged marriage to Simran (Mahal). Except he's gay and living with his boyfriend Jack (Ash), though obviously Jimi hasn't the courage to tell his family. So he tries to convince them that he's already involved with Jack's sister Vanessa (Bankes). The ruse is hopeless as is the entire film, with its weak script, timid storytelling, and risible acting. **92m/C; DVD.** *GB* Chris Bisson; Saeed Jaffrey; Zohra Sehgal; Sally Bankes; Peter Ash; Jinder Mahal; Jamila Massey; ***D:*** Hormage Singh Kalirai; ***W:*** Roopesh Parekh; ***C:*** Mike Muschamp.

Chicken With Plums *Poulet aux Prunes* **2011 (PG-13)** In the late-1950s in Tehran, musician Nasser Ali has a fight with his wife and she breaks his beloved violin. He can't find an instrument that pleases him and takes to his bed to die. Since this magical realism folktale, based on Santrapi's graphic novel, is narrated by the Angel of Death and is told in flashback, you can guess Nasser's fate. French with subtitles. **91m/C; DVD.** *FR* Mathieu Amalric; Edouard Baer; Maria De Medeiros; Chiara Mastroianni; ***D:*** Marjane Satrapi; Vincent Paronnauel; ***W:*** Marjane Satrapi; Vincent Paronnauel; ***C:*** Christophe Beaucarne; ***M:*** Olivier Bernet.

Chicklit **2016** A comedy-drama about the unexpected power of literature. In the British city of Holt, four men are regulars at their local pub. When they learn that it will be closing unless a significant amount of funding can be raised, they write an exotic novel in the style of "Fifty Shades of Grey" and make up a female author's name. To their surprise, it is published, and they hire an out of work actress to play their author. She becomes the star of the adaptation of the film. Though they save the pub, the situation they have created grows out of control as the actress holds the power and makes them write more sex novels. **96m/C; DVD, Blu-Ray, Streaming, Download.** Christian McKay; Dakota Blue Richards; Caroline Catz; David Troughton; Miles Jupp; ***D:*** Tony Britten; ***W:*** Tony Britten; Oliver Britten; ***C:*** Phil Wood. **VIDEO**

Chicks, Man **1999** Boring, man. Rod and Jack are a couple of clueless, mopey Gen-Xers who don't understand the ladies. Jack gets dumped and then tries rebound dating while Rod macks on Heather at a party and is later beaten up by Heather's boyfriend for taking liberties. There's much whining—not least by unwary viewers of this tedious pic. **93m/C; DVD.** Aaron Priest; Robia LaMorte; Krista Gano; Nick Wechsler; Scott Roberts; Renee Humphrey; ***D:*** Jeremy Wagener; ***W:*** Jeremy Wagener; ***C:*** Michael J. Bruggemeyer; ***M:*** David Stout.

Chico & Rita **1/2 2010** The soundtrack of Cuban jazz is the best thing about this unflatteringly stylized Spanish/British animated feature. Piano player Chico meets singer Rita in a pre-Castro Cuba and would-be romance, separation, and music follows them to Paris, New York, Hollywood, and Vegas over the ensuing decades. English and Spanish with subtitles. **94m/C; DVD, Blu-Ray.** *UK SP* ***V:*** Eman Xor Ona; Liamara Meneses; Mario Guerra; ***D:*** Fernando Trueba; Javier Mariscal; Tono Errando; ***W:*** Fernando Trueba; Ignacio Martinez de Pison; ***M:*** Bebo Waldes.

Chihwaseon: Painted Fire **2002** Artist bio fouses on the years 1882-1897 in the life of the commoner Korean artist known as Ohwon. With his country in turmoil--caught politically between China and Japan--and the beginning of a peasant uprising, the mercurial Ohwon struggles to find his own style and be accepted on his own terms. Korean with subtitles. **117m/C; DVD.** *SK* Min-Sik Choi; Sung-Ki Ahn; Ho-Jeong You; Yeo-Jim Kim; Ye-Jin Son; Myoung-Gu Han; ***D:*** Kwon Taek Im; ***W:*** Kwon Taek Im; Young-Oak Kim; ***C:*** Il Sung Jung.

The Child *Kill and Go Hide* **1976 (R)** Low-budget horror-quickie combining elements of "The Bad Seed," "The Omen," and "Night of the Living Dead," that attempts to cash in on the fright-film craze of the early '70s. What we get is a poorly dubbed film that makes little sense, but does offer some interesting shocks. A young woman returns to her hometown to be the nanny for a disturbed girl, Rosalie (Cole), who has a bad habit of killing neighbors and talking to zombies in the local graveyard, all the way harping on her mother's mysterious death. This is one of those movies where everyone acts very eccentric, but said behavior doesn't add anything to the plot. The finale offers some excitement, but overall the film is more of a curiosity than a "must-see." **95m/C; VHS, DVD, Blu-Ray.** Laurel Barnett; Rosalie Cole; Frank Janson; Richard Hanners; Ruth Ballan; ***D:*** Robert Voskanian; ***W:*** Ralph Lucas; ***C:*** Mori Alavi; ***M:*** Rob Wallace.

The Child *L'Enfant* **2005 (R)** Amoral, 20-year-old petty criminal Bruno (Renier) and his younger girlfriend Sonia (Francois) have just had a baby boy. Unprepared for fatherhood, he casually sells the child to a black market adoption ring. Bruno discovers his thoughtless actions have consequences when Sonia becomes hysterical and wants her son back. This turns out to be less easy than the original transaction. French with subtitles. **95m/C; DVD.** *BE FR* Jeremie Renier; Fabrizio Rongione; Olivier Gourmet; Deborah Francois; Jeremie Segard; Samuel de Ryck; Mireille Bailly; ***D:*** Jean-Pierre Dardenne; Luc Dardenne; ***W:*** Jean-Pierre Dardenne; Luc Dardenne; ***C:*** Alain Marcoen.

Child Bride of Short Creek **1/2 1981** A young Korean war veteran returns to his community where polygamy is allowed, to find that his father intends to marry again, this time to a 15-year-old. Conflict ensues. Based on an actual event that occurred in the 1950s. **100m/C; VHS, DVD.** Diane Lane; Conrad Bain; Christopher Atkins; Kiel Martin; Helen Hunt; ***D:*** Robert Lewis. **TV**

Child 44 **1/2 2015 (R)** In Stalin-era Soviet Union in the 1950s, belief in communism dictates that crime does not exist. Of course, that means that disgraced Ministry of State Security Agent Leo Demidov (Hardy) is baffled when he stumbles on a series of child murders. There can't be a serial killer in a perfect community. Based on the hit mystery novel, director Epsinosa's inert thriller is a fascinating curiosity, given the amazing talent on screen (Hardy, Rapace, Oldman, Cassel, and Clarke) and their complete inability to overcome the boring script and flat direction. Hardy is expectedly great but even his charisma can't compensate for this slog. **137m/C; DVD, Blu-Ray.** Xavier Atkins; Mark Lewis Jones; Tom (Thomas) Hardy; Joel Kinnaman; Fares Fares; Noomi Rapace; Paddy Considine; Gary Oldman; Vincent Cassel; Charles Dance; ***D:*** Daniel Espinosa; ***W:*** Richard Price; ***C:*** Oliver Wood; ***M:*** Jon Ekstrand.

Child in the House **1/2 1956** When her mother is hospitalized, 11-year-old Elizabeth is sent to London to stay with her childless, wealthy aunt and uncle. Lonely, the girl secretly meets with her estranged, criminal father Stephen, who's on the run from the law. Aunt Evelyn pries Stephen's whereabouts out of Elizabeth and calls the police, which just causes more family trauma. **90m/B; DVD.** *GB* Mandy Miller; Stanley Baker; Phyllis Calvert; Eric Portman; Dora Bryan; Joan Hickson; Victor Maddern; Percy Herbert; ***D:*** Cy Endfield; ***W:*** Cy Endfield; ***C:*** Otto Heller; ***M:*** Mario Nascimbene.

Child of Glass **1978 (G)** A young boy's family moves into a huge New Orleans mansion, and soon after encounters a young girl's ghost and lost treasure from the Civil War. A Disney made for TV movie. **93m/C; VHS, DVD.** Barbara Barrie; Biff McGuire; Anthony Zerbe; Nina Foch; Steve (Steven) Shaw; Katy Kurtzman; Olivia Barash; ***D:*** John Erman. **TV**

Child of God **1/2 2014 (R)** Franco continues to diversify his resume, adapting Cormac McCarthy's first novel for the screen with, at best, mixed results. He seems obsessed with the ugly elements of McCarthy's story, portraying protagonist Lester Ballard (Haze) as an animal more than a man. Ballard lives WAY off the grid in the mountains of Tennessee, and his special brand of crazy gets him into an increasing amount of trouble in his small community. Haze is fearless but Franco seems more in love with his "art" than telling a story at this point in his directorial career. Too self-conscious and pretentious by half. **104m/C; DVD, Blu-Ray.** Scott Haze; Tim Blake Nelson; Jim Parrack; James Franco; ***D:*** James Franco; ***W:*** James Franco; Vince Jolivette; ***C:*** Christina Voros; ***M:*** Aaron Embry.

Child Star: The Shirley Temple Story **1/2 2001** TV biopic that charts the rise to Depression-era fame of little Shirley Temple (with an entertaining performance by Orr). Shirley's mom Gertrude (Britton) is around to see that big bad studio mogul Darryl Zanuck (Vidler) doesn't take advantage of her little darling. The best parts are the faithful re-creations of some of Temple's most famous song-and-dance numbers, including those with Bill (Bojangles) Robinson, here played by Battle. **88m/C; VHS, DVD.** Ashley Rose Orr; Connie Britton; Steven Vidler; Colin Friels; Emily Anne

Hart; Hinton Battle; *D:* Nadia Tass; *W:* Joe Wiesenfeld; *C:* David Parker; *M:* Bill Elliot. **TV**

The Child Stealer 🦴 1/2 **1979** ABC TV movie. Jan has custody of her two daughters and a restraining order against her ex-husband, David. It means nothing when he kidnaps the girls and Jan can't get any help from the authorities. She goes after her children on her own. **96m/C; DVD.** Blair Brown; Beau Bridges; Christina Raines; Eugene Roche; Marj Dusay; Tracey Gold; Lauri Hendler; *D:* Mel Damski; *W:* Sue Milburn; *C:* Robert Moreno; *M:* Jimmie Haskell. **TV**

The Childhood of a Leader 🦴🦴 **2016** A stylish but subtle coming-of-age domestic drama about a budding sociopath in early twentieth century Europe and the debut feature for filmmaker Brady Corbet. In turbulent France during and after World War I, American diplomat (Cunningham) has brought his family abroad with him as he helps negotiate the Treaty of Versailles. His young son shows his dark tendencies as he learns to manipulate the adults that surround him. As Charles matures in a monstrous adult, his life and actions take a parallel path to the rise of fascism and dictators in Europe. **115m/C; DVD, Streaming, Download.** Robert Pattinson; Stacy Martin; Berenice Bejo; Liam Cunningham; Tom Sweet; *D:* Brady Corbet; *W:* Brady Corbet; Mona Fastvold; *C:* Lol Crawley; *M:* Scott Walker.

The Children WOOF! **1980 (R)** Familiar nuclear leak leads to monster mutants done to a novel (though extremely low-budget) turn: after a school bus passes through radioactive fog, the kiddies inside assume the ability to incinerate whoever they hug. They also assume a certain zombie-like demeanor and sport black fingernails. None of this is noted by their uncaring and less-than-observant parents, many of whom are enticed into a very warm hug. This may be intended as social satire. Not only are the little microwaves extremely dangerous, the only way to kill them is to chop off their hands, leading to a wild limbless finale. **89m/C; VHS, DVD, Blu-Ray.** Martin Shaker; Gale Garnett; Gil Rogers; *D:* Max Kalmanowicz.

The Children 🦴🦴 **2008 (R)** Low-budget horror about killer kiddies. Elaine (Birthistle) and hubby Jonah (Campbell Moore) take their kids to spend the Christmas holidays with her sister Chloe (Shelley), Chloe's husband Robbie (Shefield), and their brood. At a remote country house of course. Almost before the first 'ho-ho-ho' the kids go on an unexplainable violent rampage. **84m/C; DVD, Blu-Ray.** *GB* Eva Birthistle; Stephen Campbell; Rachel Shelley; Jeremy Sheffield; Hannah Tointon; Raffiella Brooks; Jake Hathaway; William Howes; Eva Sayer; *D:* Tom Shankland; *W:* Tom Shankland; *C:* Nanu Segal; *M:* Steve Hilton.

The Children Act 🦴🦴 1/2 **2018 (R)** A family court judge in London, Fiona May (Thompson) struggles with the extreme pressures that come with her position. At home, her sexless marriage to Jack (Tucci) is strained in part because of the stresses of her job through she finds solace in playing a baby grand piano. After Fiona makes a ruling in a difficult case about young cancer patient Adam (Whitehead), the teen becomes infatuated and inserts himself in her life. Sophisticated and challenging, the film considers serious themes related to family, religion, marriage, and law. Thompson's excellent performance adds depth to this adaptation of an Ian McEwan novel. **105m/C; DVD.** Emma Thompson; Stanley Tucci; Ben Chaplin; Fionn Whitehead; Angela Holmes; *D:* Richard Eyre; *W:* Ian McEwan; *C:* Andrew Dunn; *M:* Stephen Warbeck.

The Children Are Watching Us 🦴🦴🦴 *The Little Martyr; I Bambini Ci Guardano* **1944** Sobering drama of a family dissolution as seen by a child. A four-year-old boy drifts unloved by his suicidal father and by his mother, who's only interested in her own love affair. Worthy example of Italian neo-realism marks the first collaboration between Zavattini and De Sica. In Italian with subtitles. **92m/B; VHS, DVD.** *IT* Luciano de Ambrosis; Isa Pola; Emilio Cigoli; *D:* Vittorio De Sica; *W:* Cesare Zavattini; Vittorio De Sica.

Children in the Crossfire 🦴🦴 1/2 **1984** When youngsters from war-torn Northern Ireland spend a summer in America with children from the Republic of Ireland, both sides find their nationalistic prejudices falling away. But a great challenge awaits them when they return home from their summer of fun. Nicely done drama. **96m/C; VHS, DVD.** Charles Haid; Karen Valentine; Julia Duffy; David Huffman; *D:* George Schaefer; *M:* Brad Fiedel. **TV**

The Children Nobody Wanted 🦴🦴🦴 **1981** Inspirational CBS movie is a true story. In 1959, college freshman Tom Butterfield (Lehne) is working at an adult mental asylum in Missouri and encounters children who have been orphaned or abandoned. Without foster homes, they are left in unsuitable, and sometimes dangerous, institutional care. After young Joey is attacked, Tom fights to become his foster parent and begins his lifelong dedication to changing child care laws, establishing the Butterfield Youth Ranches. Pfeiffer plays Tom's supportive girlfriend, Jennifer. **92m/C; DVD.** Frederic Lehne; Michelle Pfeiffer; Matt Clark; Noble Willingham; Barbara Barrie; *D:* Richard Michaels; *W:* Lee Hutson; *C:* Reynaldo Villalobos; *M:* Barry De Vorzon. **TV**

Children of a Lesser God 🦴🦴🦴 1/2 **1986 (R)** Based upon the play by Mark Medoff, this sensitive, intelligent film deals with an unorthodox speech teacher at a school for the deaf, who falls in love with a beautiful and rebellious ex-student. Inarguably romantic; the original stage production won the Best Play Tony in 1980. Hurt and Matlin reportedly continued their romance off-screen as well. **119m/C; VHS, DVD.** William Hurt; Marlee Matlin; Piper Laurie; Philip Bosco; E. Katherine Kerr; *D:* Randa Haines; *W:* Hesper Anderson; Mark Medoff; *C:* John Seale; *M:* Michael Convertino. Oscars '86: Actress (Matlin); Golden Globes '87: Actress--Drama (Matlin).

Children of Dune 🦴🦴 **2003** The continuation of the 2000 miniseries "Dune" is based on the second and third novels of Frank Herbert's series and may be confusing to the uninitiated. It's now 12 years since Paul Atreides (Newman) has become emperor of Arrakis, which has a monopoly on the precious commodity Spice, but his ascension to the throne has caused a holy war across the universe. It has also caused rivalry with the deposed royal family led by scheming Princess Wensicia (Sarandon). Paul's children, Leto (McAvoy) and Ghanima (Brooks), who are being groomed to rule, soon come to realize they must destroy their father's legacy in order to save their world. **266m/C; VHS, DVD.** Alec Newman; Susan Sarandon; James McAvoy; Jessica Brooks; Alice Krige; Edward Atterton; Steven Berkoff; Julie Cox; Barbara Kodetova; Ian McNeice; P. H. Moriarty; *D:* Greg Yaitanes; *W:* John Harrison; *C:* Arthur Reinhart; *M:* Brian Tyler. **CABLE**

Children of Hannibal 🦴🦴 *Figli de Annibale* **1998** Unemployed sad-sack Domenico (Orlando) decides to rob a Turin bank and head north to Switzerland, but he bungles the job and winds up with businessman Tommaso (Abatantuono) as a hostage. However, Tommaso has his own money troubles—nearly bankrupt, he persuades Domenico to head south with the loot and get help from Tommaso's friend, Orfeo (Insinni), who just happens to be a cop and Tommaso's lover. Then, Tommaso's daughter Rita (Cervi) decides to join their strange road trip. Italian with subtitles. **93m/C; VHS, DVD.** *IT* Diego Abatantuono; Silvio Orlando; Valentina Cervi; Flavio Insinna; Ugo Conti; *D:* Davide Ferrario; *W:* Davide Ferrario; *C:* Giovanni Cavallini; *M:* Damiano Rota.

Children of Heaven 🦴🦴 1/2 **1998 (PG)** When nine-year-old Ali (Hashemian) discovers that his younger sister Zahra's (Seddiqi) shoes have somehow been lost, he keeps the information from his parents who are already desperately struggling to provide for them. They share Ali's tattered sneakers so that both children can still go to school. Then Ali learns of a race where one of the prizes is a pair of running shoes and he becomes determined to win them. Story is simple enough that kids may enjoy watching other kids even in a foreign film. Farsi with subtitles. **88m/C; VHS, DVD.** *IA* Amir Farrokh Hashemian; Bahareh Seddiqi; Amir Naji; *D:* Majid Majidi; *W:* Majid Majidi; *C:* Parviz Malek-zadeh; *M:* Keivan Jahanshahi.

The Children of Huang Shi 🦴🦴 **2008 (R)** A humanitarian wartime adventure weepie based on the story of British reporter George Hogg (Rhys-Meyers). He's reporting on the Sino-Japanese War and the Japanese invasion of Nanking in 1937 when he's wounded and taken by Australian nurse Lee (Mitchell) to recover in a remote orphanage for boys. It's not remote enough, however, to escape the war. As the Japanese army approaches, George, Lee, and Communist rebel Chen (Chow) lead 60 boys on a 700-mile trip across the mountains to a safer haven. English, Chinese, and Japanese with subtitles. **114m/C; DVD, Blu-Ray.** *AU CH GE* Jonathan Rhys Meyers; Radha Mitchell; Chow Yun-Fat; Michelle Yeoh; David Wenham; Li Guang; *D:* Roger Spottiswoode; *W:* James MacManus; Jane Hawksley; *C:* Xiaoding Zhao; *M:* David Hirschfelder.

Children of Invention 🦴🦴 **2009** Boston single mom Elaine Cheng struggles when her ex-husband returns to Hong Kong without paying any spousal or child support. She tries a series of questionable jobs to care for her young children, but things go awry forcing Raymond to grow up too quickly. **96m/C; DVD.** Cindy Cheung; Michael Chen; *D:* Crystal Chiu; Tze Chun; *W:* Crystal Chiu; Tze Chun; *C:* Chris Teague; *M:* T. Griffin.

Children of Men 🦴🦴🦴 **2006 (R)** The future's never fun. It's 2027 and there's global infertility and worldwide chaos, which doesn't matter much to British bureaucratic drone Theo Faron (Owen), until he's pulled into an activist group headed by his ex, Julian (Moore). Seems she needs Faron to take illegal refugee Kee (Ashitay), who's pregnant with the first child conceived in 18 years, to safety. This involves a long, strange, and dangerous trip—and a stop at Theo's pothead friend Jasper's (a raucous Caine) cottage. Dark and dreary yet oddly fascinating. Loosely based on the 1993 novel by P.D. James. **108m/C; DVD, Blu-Ray, HD-DVD.** Clive Owen; Julianne Moore; Michael Caine; Chiwetel Ejiofor; Charlie Hunnam; Pam Ferris; Danny Huston; Peter Mullan; Clare-Hope Ashitey; *D:* Alfonso Cuarón; *W:* Alfonso Cuarón; Timothy J. Sexton; *C:* Emmanuel Lubezki. British Acad. '06: Cinematog.

Children of Paradise 🦴🦴🦴🦴 *Les Enfants du Paradis* **1944** Considered by many to be the greatest film ever made, certainly one of the most beautiful. In the Parisian theatre district of the 1800s an actor falls in love with a seemingly unattainable woman. Although circumstances keep them apart, their love never dies. Produced in France during WWII right under the noses of Nazi occupiers; many of the talent (including the writer, poet Jacques Prevert) were active resistance fighters. In French with English subtitles. **188m/B; VHS, DVD, Blu-Ray.** *FR* Jean-Louis Barrault; Arletty; Pierre Brasseur; Maria Casares; Albert Remy; Leon Larive; Marcel Herrand; Pierre Renoir; Gaston Modot; Jane (Jeanne) Marken; Louis Salou; *D:* Marcel Carne; *W:* Jacques Prevert; *C:* Roger Hubert; *M:* Maurice Thiriet; Joseph Kosma.

Children of Sanchez 🦴🦴 **1979 (PG)** Mexican man attempts to provide for his family with very little except faith and love. U.S./Mexican production based on Oscar Lewis' novel. **103m/C; VHS, DVD.** *MX* Anthony Quinn; Dolores Del Rio; Katy Jurado; Lupita Ferrer; *D:* Hall Bartlett; *W:* Hall Bartlett; *M:* Chuck Mangione.

Children of the Century 🦴🦴 *Les Enfants du Siecle* **1999** Antenuated costumer depicting the volatile affair between the Baroness Dudevant, soon to be known as writer George Sand (Binoche), and the younger (and dissolute) poet, Alfred de Musset (Magimel). To escape his wealthy family's disapproval, the lovers travel to Venice where Alfred's continued dissipation leads to illness and the services of Dr. Pagello (Dionisi), with whom a fed-up Sands soon begins a romance. Musset returns to Paris and when Sands follow later, the duo try to rekindle their romantic ardor. Musset's fictionized version of their affair was entitled "Confessions of a Child of the Century." French with subtitles. **137m/C; VHS, DVD.** *FR* Juliette Binoche; Benoît Magimel; Stefano Dionisi; Robin Renucci; Karin Viard; Isabelle Carre; Denis Podalydes; *D:* Diane Kurys; *W:* Diane Kurys; Murray Head; Francois Olivier Rousseau; *C:* Vilko Filac; *M:* Luis Bacalov.

Children of the Corn 🦴 **2009** In 1975, Vietnam vet Burt and his wife Vicki constantly bicker their way on a cross-country road trip until an accident brings them into the grim community of Gatlin, Nebraska. Boy preacher Isaac and his teenage enforcer Malachi have killed all the adults and now two more sacrifices have just shown up. Based on the Stephen King short story but the author was not involved in this unsatisfying Syfy Channel remake of the 1984 flick. **92m/C; DVD, Blu-Ray.** David Anders; Kandyse McClure; Preston Bailey; Daniel Newman; Alexa Nikolas; *D:* Donald P. Borchers; *W:* Donald P. Borchers; *C:* Jamie Thompson; *M:* Jonathan Elias. **CABLE**

Children of the Corn 🦴 1/2 **1984 (R)** Young couple lands in a small Iowa town where children appease a demon by murderously sacrificing adults. Time to move or dispense with some major spankings. Infrequently scary. Another feeble attempt to translate the horror of a Stephen King book to film. **93m/C; VHS, DVD, Blu-Ray, UMD.** Peter Horton; Linda Hamilton; R.G. Armstrong; John Franklin; Courtney Gains; Robbie Kiger; *D:* Fritz Kiersch; *W:* George Goldsmith; *C:* Raoul Lomas; *M:* Jonathan Elias.

Children of the Corn 2: The Final Sacrifice 🦴 1/2 **1992 (R)** Reporter working for a tabloid paper gets more than he bargained for when he decides to do a story on the adults murdered in the town of Gatlin, Nebraska. Gatlin's surviving children, who killed their parents in the first film, are now living in a neighboring town and free to kill again. This youthful satanic cult does in authority figures in a number of sacrifical ways, working ever more smartly to create the prime attraction—blood flow. Not based on anything written by Stephen King. **93m/C; VHS, DVD.** Terence Knox; Paul Scherrer; Rosalind Allen; Christie Clark; Ned Romero; Ryan Bollman; Ted Travelstead; *D:* David F. Price; *W:* A.L. Katz; Gilbert Adler.

Children of the Corn 3: Urban Harvest 🦴🦴 **1995 (R)** Joshua (Melendez) and younger brother Eli (Cerny) are adopted by a wealthy couple and transplanted from Nebraska to Chicago's suburbia. But when Eli grows a corn patch that resurrects an evil force, only Joshua can stop his reign of terror. Contrived premise but lots of nifty special effects. **103m/C; VHS, DVD, Blu-Ray.** Daniel Cerny; Ron Melendez; Mari Morrow; Duke Stroud; Jim Metzler; Nancy Lee Grahn; *D:* James D.R. Hickox; *W:* Dode Levenson; *M:* Daniel Licht.

Children of the Corn 4: The Gathering 🦴 *Deadly Harvest* **1996 (R)** Medical student Grace Rhodes (Watts) seeks to free the children of her Nebraska hometown from a mysterious plague and a shadowy figure. **85m/C; VHS, DVD, Blu-Ray.** Naomi Watts; Brent Jennings; Jamie Renee Smith; William Windom; Karen Black; *D:* Greg Spence; *W:* Stephen Berger; Greg Spence; *C:* Richard Clabaugh; *M:* David Williams.

Children of the Corn 5: Fields of Terror 🦴 1/2 **1998 (R)** Alison (Galina), Greg (Arquette), Tyrus (Vaughan), and Kir (Mendez) have traveled to Divinity Falls to bury the cremated remains of Kir's recently deceased boyfriend. That's when they run into the local cult of murderous children and Alison realizes that her long-lost brother, Jacob (Buzzotta), is one of them. She's determined to get him away but the evil force that leads the children has other ideas. **85m/C; VHS, DVD, Blu-Ray.** Alexis Arquette; Greg Vaughan; Stacy Galina; Eva Mendes; Adam Wylie; Dave Buzzotta; David Carradine; Fred Williamson; *D:* Ethan Wiley; *W:* Ethan Wiley; *C:* David Lewis; *M:* Paul Rabjohns. **VIDEO**

Children of the Corn 666: Isaac's Return 🦴 1/2 **1999 (R)** Hannah Martin (Ramsey) is traveling to Nebraska in search of her birth mother but when she arrives in the small town of Gatlin, she finds the residents want to keep their secrets. **82m/C; VHS, DVD, Blu-Ray.** Natalie Ramsey; John Franklin; Stacy Keach; Alix Koromzay; Nancy Allen; *D:* Keri Skogland. **VIDEO**

Children of the Corn: Revelation 🦴🦴 **2001** Jamie (Mink) is looking for her missing grandma at the condemned Hampton Arms where the remaining residents are meeting grisly fates. She and detective Armbrister (Cassie) are informed by a mysterious priest (Ironside) that the condos were built on the site of a tent revival fire that killed a number of children. Of course the kids turn out to be the Gatlin killer-kiddie cult and they return to reclaim their land. Some decent shockers in this 7th installment of the series. **81m/C; VHS, DVD.** Claudette Mink; Michael Ironside; Troy Yorke; Sean Smith; Kyle Cassie; Michael Rogers; Taylor Hobbs; Jeff(rey) Ballard; Crystal Lowe; ***D:*** Guy Magar. **VIDEO**

Children of the Corn: Genesis
WOOF! 2011 (R) In this unbelievably lame and unnecessary 7th sequel, Tim and Allie have car trouble and get stranded in the desert. They are reluctantly given shelter by Preacher, who warns them not to wander around his compound. When a pregnant Allie hears crying, she finds an imprisoned child whom Preacher says is an evil seed and bad things happen. **95m/C; DVD, Blu-Ray.** Kelen Coleman; Tim Rock; Billy Drago; Barbara Nedeljakova; Duane Whitaker; ***D:*** Joel Soisson; ***W:*** Joel Soisson; ***C:*** Alexandre Lehmann; ***M:*** Jacob Yoffee. **VIDEO**

Children of the Damned **1963** Six children, who are a sample of what man will evolve to in a million years, are born all around the world with genius IQs, ray-gun eyes, and murderous dispositions. Two investigators bring the children together, and while they are being examined by scientists they escape. The children hide out in a church, but they are doomed because their destiny is to be destroyed to teach a lesson to modern man. A sequel to "Village of the Damned" based loosely on the novel "The Midwich Cuckoos" by John Wyndham. **90m/B; VHS, DVD.** *GB* Ian Hendry; Alan Badel; Barbara Ferris; Alfred Burke; Sheila Allen; Clive Powell; Frank Summerscales; Mahdu Mathen; Gerald Delsol; Roberta Rex; Franchesca Lee; Harold Goldblatt; Ralph Michael; Martin Miller; Lee Yoke-Moon; ***D:*** Anton Leader; ***W:*** John Briley; ***C:*** Davis Boulton.

Children of the Living Dead
WOOF! 2000 (R) Standard ". . .of the Living Dead" fare has only producer John Russo as a connection to the original. One of the worst of these seemingly endless low-budget horrors. The voice dubbing sounds exceptionally unnatural; lighting is amateurish with the odd flash when someone behind the camera mishandles a mirror; acting is poor. Story is the same old same old. **90m/C; DVD.** Tom Savini; A. Barrett Worland; Jamie McCoy; ***D:*** Tor Ramsey; ***W:*** Karen Wolf.

Children of the Night **1985** TV movie based on a true story. Ph.D. sociology candidate Lois Lee wants to interview runaway teen girls working in Hollywood's sex trade. Her distress over their plight leads her to found a non-profit organization to rescue kids forced into prostitution. **94m/C; DVD.** Kathleen Quinlan; Mario Van Peebles; Lar Park-Lincoln; Wallace (Wally) Langham; Marta Kober; Nicholas (Nick) Campbell; Eddie Velez; ***D:*** Robert Markowitz; ***W:*** Robert Guenette; Vickie Patik; ***C:*** Gil Hubbs; ***M:*** Miles Goodman. **TV**

Children of the Night **1/2 1992 (R)** Allburg seems like a typically quiet small town far removed from any danger—until a vampire is released from an underground crypt and decides to make the town his bloodthirsty target. When a teacher, whose girlfriend is visiting Allburg, learns of the supernatural goings on he decides to investigate, which may be a deadly mistake. **92m/C; VHS, DVD.** Peter DeLuise; Karen Black; Ami Dolenz; Maya McLaughlin; Evan Mackenzie; David Sawyer; Garrett Morris; ***D:*** Tony Randel; ***W:*** Nicolas Falacci; ***C:*** Richard Michalak.

Children of the Revolution
1995 (R) Mockumentary covering 45 years of Australian history and politics, beginning in 1951 when the conservative Prime Minister attempts to ban the Australian Communist Party. Party member (and Stalin admirer) Joan Fraser (Davis) helps to prevent the ban, bringing her to the Russian leader's attention, and she's invited to Moscow. There, Joan winds up in bed with Stalin (Abraham) and comes home pregnant. Eventually, son Joe (Rush) makes an entry into the Australian political scene, resulting in chaos. There's almost too much more for the film to handle, although the actors don't seem to have any problems. **101m/C; VHS, DVD.** *AU* Judy Davis; Sam Neill; Richard Roxburgh; Rachel Griffiths; Geoffrey Rush; F. Murray Abraham; ***D:*** Peter Duncan; ***W:*** Peter Duncan; ***C:*** Martin McGrath; ***M:*** Nigel Westlake. Australian Film Inst. '96: Actress (Davis), Art Dir./Set Dec., Costume Des.

Children of the Wild **1/2** *Killers of the Wild* **1937** Adventure story about a pack of dogs surviving in the Rocky Mountain wilderness. Splendid scenery and some interesting sequences. **65m/B; VHS, DVD.** Patsy Moran; Joan Valerie; James Bush; Leroy Mason; ***D:*** Charles (Hutchison) Hutchinson; Vin Moore; ***W:*** Hilda May Young; ***C:*** Robert Doran; ***M:*** Edward Kilenyi.

The Children of Theatre Street **1977** Absorbing documentary follows three children attending the renowned Kirov Ballet School. A show for all ages that may be especially enjoyed by kids who are interested in ballet. Kelly's last film appearance. **92m/C; VHS, DVD.** *RU* Angelina Armeiskaya; Alec Timoushin; Lena Voronzova; Michaela Cerna; Galina Messenzeva; Konstantin Zaklinsky; ***Nar:*** Grace Kelly; ***D:*** Robert Dornhelm; ***W:*** Beth Gutcheon; ***C:*** Karl Kofler.

The Children of Times Square **1986** A mother pursues her son who has fled home and joined a gang of drug dealers in N.Y.C.'s seedy Times Square. Ordinary film despite strong casting of Cassidy and Rollins. **95m/C; VHS, Streaming.** Joanna Cassidy; Howard E. Rollins, Jr.; Brandon Douglas; David Ackroyd; Griffin O'Neal; Danny Nucci; Larry B. Scott; Jacob Vargas; De'voreaux White; Joe Spinell; Jason Bernard; R.D. Call; John Capodice; Ami Dolenz; Courtney Gains; ***D:*** Curtis Hanson; ***W:*** Curtis Hanson; ***M:*** Patrick Gleeson. **TV**

Children On Their Birthdays **1/2 2002 (PG)** Based on a short story by Truman Capote and set in small Medda, Alabama in 1947, which is where 13-year-old Billy Bob Murphy (Pichler) lives with his widowed mother Elinore (Lee). His best bud is Preacher (Plemons) but the two are soon vying for the affections of the new girl in town—Lilly Jane Bobbit (Raymonde). Meanwhile, romance is in the air for Elinore and sheriff/mechanic Speedy (McDonald) to Billy Bob's dismay. And there's even more excitement over the shady dealings of smooth-talking Lionel Quince (Arnold). **102m/C; VHS, DVD.** Joe Pichler; Jesse Plemons; Sheryl Lee; Tania Raymonde; Phyllis Frelich; Christopher McDonald; Tom Arnold; ***D:*** Mark Medoff; ***W:*** Douglas J. Sloan; ***C:*** Steve (Steven) Shaw; ***M:*** James D. Hinton; Ross Vannelli.

Children Shouldn't Play with Dead Things **1/2** *Revenge of the Living Dead* **1972** A band of foolhardy hippie filmmakers on an island cemetary skimp on special effects by using witchcraft to revive the dead. The plan works. Soon the crew has an island full of hungry ghouls to contend with. Film strives for yucks, frequently succeeds. A late night fave, sporting some excellent dead rising from their grave scenes as well as a selection of groovy fashions. Screenwriter/star Ormsby went on to write the remake of "Cat People," while director Clark would eventually helm "Porky's." **85m/C; VHS, DVD, Blu-Ray.** Alan Ormsby; Valerie Mamches; Jeff Gillen; Anya Ormsby; Paul Cronin; Jane Daly; Roy Engelman; Robert Philip; Bruce Solomon; Alecs Baird; Seth Sklarey; ***D:*** Bob (Benjamin) Clark; ***W:*** Alan Ormsby; Bob (Benjamin) Clark; ***C:*** Jack McGowan; ***M:*** Carl Zittrer.

The Children's Hour *The Loudest Whisper* **1961** The teaching careers of two women are ruined when girls begin circulating vicious rumors. Only an occasionally taut drama despite forceful handling of a lesbian theme. Updated version of Lillian Hellman's play (adapted by Hellman) is more explicit, but less suspenseful in spite of excellent performances from the talented cast. Remake of Wyler's own "These Three." **107m/C; VHS, DVD, Blu-Ray.** Shirley MacLaine; Audrey Hepburn; James Garner; Miriam Hopkins; Veronica Cartwright; Fay Bainter; ***D:*** William Wyler; ***W:*** John Michael Hayes; ***M:*** Alex North.

Child's Play **1/2 1972** Plodding, claustrophic adaptation of the play by Robert Marasco. Former student Paul Reis (Bridges) returns to his Catholic boys boarding school as the new gym teacher. He discovers that the longtime rivalry between Latin instructor Jerome Malley (Mason) and literature professor Joseph Dobbs (Preston) is worse than ever. It's affecting the students as they participate in increasingly violent hazing rituals. The devil didn't make them do it as the flick is psychological rather than supernatual. **100m/C; DVD, Blu-Ray.** James Mason; Robert Preston; Beau Bridges; Ron Weyand; ***D:*** Sidney Lumet; ***W:*** Leon Prochnik; ***C:*** Gerald Hirschfeld; ***M:*** Michael Small.

Child's Play **1/2 2019 (R)** Tween Andy (Bateman) has problems making friends, so his single mother Karen (Plaza) buys him a "Buddi" doll. Though Andy does not like the doll and insists he is too old for it, he finds himself bonding with it, dubbed Chucky. Soon, Chucky is helping Andy make friends with neighborhood kids. However, when people make Andy unhappy, the doll turns deadly to protect Andy. As more people die, Andy tries to get someone to believe him about Chucky's violent acts. A reboot of the Chucky horror movies, the film retains the series' weird, creepy edge but is also playful and funny. **90m/C; DVD, Blu-Ray.** Aubrey Plaza; Mark Hamill; Gabriel Bateman; Brian Tyree Henry; Tim Matheson; ***D:*** Lars Klevberg; ***W:*** Tyler Burton Smith; ***C:*** Brendan Uegama; ***M:*** Bear McCreary.

Child's Play **1/2 1988 (R)** A boy discovers that his new doll named Chucky is actually the embodiment of a deranged killer. His initially skeptical mom and a police officer come around after various killings. Exciting, if somewhat moronic, fare, with fine special effects. Followed by "Child's Play 2." **95m/C; VHS, DVD, Blu-Ray.** Catherine Hicks; Alex Vincent; Chris Sarandon; Dinah Manoff; Brad Dourif; Tommy Swerdlow; Jack Colvin; ***D:*** Tom Holland; ***W:*** Tom Holland; Don Mancini; John Lafia; ***C:*** Bill Butler; ***M:*** Joe Renzetti.

Child's Play 2 WOOF! 1990 (R) Chucky lives. Basic doll-on-a-rampage story, a metaphor for the Reagan years, lives on in the sequel (you remember: somehow guy-doll Chucky made it past the quality control people with a highly inflammable temper). A little dotty from playing with dolls, young Vincent finds himself fostered by two new parents, and plagued by an obnoxious and very animated doll that fosters ill will toward all. What's worse is the doll is transmigratory, craving the boy's body as his next address. Chef d'effects Kevin Yagher's new toy is bad, real bad, and so are the other part two FX. Little Chucky's saga, however grows a tad tiresome. A bad example for small children. **84m/C; VHS, DVD, Blu-Ray.** Alex Vincent; Jenny Agutter; Gerrit Graham; Christine Elise; Grace Zabriskie; ***V:*** Brad Dourif; ***D:*** John Lafia; ***W:*** Don Mancini; ***C:*** Stefan Czapsky; ***M:*** Graeme Revell.

Child's Play 3 **1991 (R)** Possessed doll Chucky returns to life again in search of a new child to control, and luckily finds his old pal (Whalin) at a military school filled with the usual stereotypes. Gory sequel in a mostly awful series. "Don't F?- with the Chuck" was its catch phrase; that should indicate the level of this junk. **89m/C; VHS, DVD, Blu-Ray.** Justin Whalin; Perrey Reeves; Jeremy Sylvers; Peter Haskell; Dakin Matthews; Travis Fine; Dean Jacobson; Matthew (Matt) Walker; Andrew (Andy) Robinson; ***V:*** Brad Dourif; ***D:*** Jack Bender; ***W:*** Don Mancini; ***M:*** Cory Lerios; John D'Andrea.

Chill **1/2 2006 (R)** Struggling writer Sam (Calabro) takes a job at a small L.A. grocery store to pay the bills. The owner, Dr. Munoz (Kurtz), is a former scientist who claims that his strange skin condition requires freezing temperatures but Sam discovers that Munoz has been dead a long time and has made an occult pact to keep going. Now he expects Sam to help him or become his next victim. Based on the H.P. Lovecraft story "Cool Air." **86m/C; DVD.** Thomas Calabro; Ashley Laurence; James Russo; Shaun Kurtz; ***D:*** Serge Rodnunsky; ***W:*** Serge Rodnunsky; ***C:*** Serge Rodnunsky. **VIDEO**

Chill Factor **1990 (R)** A TV reporter for an investigative news show uncovers evidence of an international conspiracy. Plot twists abound. **95m/C; VHS, DVD.** Paul Williams; Patrick Macnee; Andrew Prine; Carrie Snodgress; Patrick Wayne; Gary Crosby; ***D:*** David L. Stanton.

Chill Factor **1/2 1999 (R)** Stealing every plot device and cliche in the action thriller genre, this is indeed one unoriginal cold turkey. After accidentally blowing up a platoon of soldiers while testing a chemical weapon codenamed "Elvis" and pinning the blame on cranky general Brynner (Firth), scientist Dr. Long (Paymer) moves to Montana to take up fly-fishing while continuing his research. He befriends diner clerk Tim (Ulrich), but only until the general is released from prison with a grudge to settle. The general has plans to sell the weapon to the highest bidder, but Long manages to get Elvis out of the building. The canister can't get hotter than 50 degrees, or Elvis will become a hunka hunka burnin' Armageddon. Tim hijacks an ice cream truck and its driver Arlo (Gooding), and the pair are chased and shot at until the movie is mercifully over. **102m/C; VHS, DVD.** Skeet Ulrich; Cuba Gooding, Jr.; Peter Firth; David Paymer; Daniel Hugh-Kelly; Kevin J. O'Connor; Judson Mills; Hudson (Heidi) Leick; Jim Grimshaw; ***D:*** Hugh Johnson; ***W:*** Drew Gitlin; Mike Cheda; ***C:*** David Gribble; ***M:*** Hans Zimmer; John Powell.

Chillers **1988** Travellers waiting for a bus are besieged by carnivorous zombies and voracious vampires. How this is different from the standard bus trip is unclear. **90m/C; VHS, DVD.** Jesse Emery; Marjorie Fitzsimmons; Laurie Pennington; Jim Wolfe; David Wohl; ***D:*** Daniel Boyd; ***W:*** Daniel Boyd.

The Chilling WOOF! *Gamma 693* **1989 (R)** Corpses preserved in a deep freeze come alive and plague Kansas City as flesh-chomping zombies. Utterly worthless film doesn't even provide convincing effects. **91m/C; VHS, DVD.** Linda Blair; Dan Haggerty; Troy Donahue; Jack A. De Rieux; Ron Vincent; ***D:*** Deland Nuse; Jack A. Sunseri.

Chilly Dogs WOOF! *Kevin of the North* **2001 (PG-13)** A woofer that deserves to be buried. Slacker Kevin Manley (Ulrich) learns he's inherited land in Alaska from his grandfather. But in order to collect he must compete in the 1,000 mile dog sled race between Anchorage and Nome, Alaska. Babe Bonnie (Nestridge) is willing to help the tenderfoot out while sneaky lawyer Thornton (Nielsen) is among those trying to undermine Kevin's every chance. At least the similarly themed "Snow Dogs" had a certain amount of kiddie humor to sustain it. **102m/C; VHS, DVD, On Demand.** *CA* Skeet Ulrich; Natasha Henstridge; Leslie Nielsen; Rik Mayall; Lochlyn Munro; Jay Brazeau; ***D:*** Bob Spiers; ***W:*** William Osborne; ***M:*** Harvey Summers.

Chimera Strain **2019 (R)** When scientist Quint's (Cusick) children develop a disease that will kill them, he puts them in a cryonic ametabolic state to preserve them while he works on a cure. Quint then obsessively explores gene modifications that would allow them to regenerate in a fashion similar to the immortal Turritopsis jellyfish. Because his research requires human embryonic stem cells, he makes a deal with the shadowy Masterson (Quinlan) by promising to cure someone for her in exchange for cells. Though intriguing, the story drags and its low budget makes it low quality. **80m/C; DVD.** Henry Ian Cusick; Kathleen Quinlan; Erika Ervin; Jenna Harrison; Karishma Ahluwalia; ***D:*** Maurice Haeems; ***W:*** Maurice Haeems; ***C:*** David Kruta; ***M:*** Aled Roberts.

Chimes at Midnight *Falstaff; Campanadas a Medianoche* **1967** Classic tragedy—derived by Welles from five Shakespeare plays—about a corpulent blowhard and his friendship with a prince. Crammed with classic sequences, including a battle that is both realistic and funny. The love scene between massive Welles and a nonetheless willing Moreau also manages to be both sad and amusing. Great performances all around, but Welles understandably dominates. The film's few flaws (due to budget problems) are inconsequential before considerable strengths. This one ranks among Welles', and thus the entire cinema's, very best. **115m/B; VHS, DVD, Blu-Ray.** *SP SI* Orson Welles; Jeanne Moreau; Margaret Rutherford; John Gielgud; Marina Vlady; Keith Baxter; Fernando Rey; Norman Rodway; ***Nar:*** Ralph Richardson; ***D:*** Orson Welles; ***W:*** Orson Welles; ***C:*** Edmond Richard; ***M:*** Angelo Francesco Lavagnino.

Chimpanzee 1/2 **2012 (G)** Tim Allen narrates the heartbreaking and heartwarming true story of Oscar, an Ivory Coast chimpanzee, who loses his parents in a brutal fashion. Left to care for himself, the baby chimp seeks acceptance into a new group of chimps from its Alpha Male. This latest admirable--though at times a bit cheesy--effort from the Disneynature brand has gorgeous cinematography as it tells a story of triumph over tragedy that transcends species. **78m/C; DVD, Blu-Ray.** ***Nar:*** Tim Allen; ***D:*** Alastair Fothergill; Mark Linfield; ***W:*** Alastair Fothergill; Mark Linfield; ***C:*** Martyn Colbeck; Bill Wallauer; ***M:*** Nicholas Hooper.

China 1/2 **1943** David Jones (Ladd) is an unfeeling profiteer who's making money off the Japanese invading China (it's 1941). But he and buddy Johnny Sparrow (Bendix) have their truck hijacked by a group of Chinese guerrillas, lead by China-born American teacher Carolyn Grant (Young), who need a group of schoolgirls driven to safety through enemy lines. Naturally, Jones has a change of heart (and sides) and battles the Japanese troops. Typically fervent propaganda film. Based on the play by Archibald Forbes. **79m/B; DVD.** Alan Ladd; Loretta Young; William Bendix; Philip Ahn; Victor Sen Yung; Marianne Quon; Richard Loo; ***D:*** John Farrow; ***W:*** Frank Butler; ***C:*** Leo Tover.

China Clipper 1/2 **1936** Fictionalized version of Pan American Airways' first trans-Pacific commercial flight as Dave Logan (O'Brien) puts his aviation dreams before his marriage and friends. Includes newsreel footage of the actual seaplane. **88m/B; DVD.** Pat O'Brien; Ross Alexander; Humphrey Bogart; Marie Wilson; Beverly Roberts; ***D:*** Ray Enright; ***W:*** Frank Wead; ***C:*** Arthur Edeson.

China Cry 1/2 **1991 (PG-13)** Based on the true story of Sung Negn Yee who escaped from Communist China to the freedom of Hong Kong in the early '60s. Fine portrayal of the young woman from a privileged background who witnessed some of the atrocities of Mao's government policies. **103m/C; VHS, DVD.** Julia Nickson-Soul; Russell Wong; James Shigeta; France Nuyen; ***D:*** James F. Collier.

China Gate **1957** A band of multinational troops follows a French officer against a communist stronghold in Indochina. Conventional fare bolstered considerably by director Fuller's flair for action. Weak male leads, but Dickinson shines. **97m/B; DVD, Blu-Ray.** Gene Barry; Angie Dickinson; Nat King Cole; Paul Dubov; Lee Van Cleef; George Givot; Marcel Dalio; Gerald Milton; Neyle Morrow; Maurice Marsac; Warren Hsieh; Paul Busch; Sasha Hardin; James Hong; Walter Soo Hoo; Weaver Levy; ***D:*** Samuel Fuller; ***W:*** Samuel Fuller; ***C:*** Joseph Biroc; ***M:*** Max Steiner; Victor Young.

China Girl 1/2 **1942** The plot's all over the place in this wartime melodrama. American newsreel photog Johnny (Montgomery) is working in Mandalay, where he falls for Eurasian beauty Haoli (Tierney). Johnny's got some Japanese military info and a couple of spies are sent to retrieve it. Johnny also tries to help Haoli and her dad return to the Chinese village where they have an orphanage before the Japanese invade. **95m/B; DVD.** George Montgomery; Gene Tierney; Lynn Bari; Victor McLaglen; Sig Rumann; Robert (Bobby) Blake; ***D:*** Henry Hathaway; ***W:*** Ben Hecht; ***C:*** Lee Garmes; ***M:*** Hugo Friedhofer.

China Heat 1/2 *Zhing hua jing hua* **1990** Captain Tie Hua (Hu) leads a three-woman Chinese police task force en route to New York City to track down an infamous drug lord fleeing mainland China. Cheesy acting, bizarre stunts, and pretty decent kung fu ensue. Cheesy B-movie with some good fights and lots of "what the...!" moments. **90m/C; DVD.** *CH* Michael Depasquale, Jr.; Sibelle Hu; ***D:*** William Cheung; Yang Yang.

China Moon 1/2 **1991 (R)** Convoluted police thriller, set in Florida, about beautiful Rachel (Stowe), who's married to rich-but-abusive Rupert (Dance). Kyle (Harris) is the lonely homicide detective who's besotted by Rachel and conveniently helps her dispose of her murdered husband's body. Kyle's problems increase when his rookie partner (Del Toro) turns out to be smarter than anyone thinks. Good performances but the suspense is only average. **99m/C; VHS, DVD, Blu-Ray.** Ed Harris; Madeleine Stowe; Benicio Del Toro; Charles Dance; ***D:*** John Bailey; ***W:*** Roy Carlson; ***C:*** Willy Kurant; ***M:*** George Fenton.

China O'Brien 1/2 **1988 (R)** Gorgeous police officer with martial arts expertise returns home for a little R&R, but finds she has to kick some major butt instead. Violent, dim-witted action drama proves only that cleavage can be macho too. **90m/C; VHS, DVD.** Cynthia Rothrock; Richard Norton; Patrick Adamson; David Blackwell; Steven Kerby; Robert Tiller; Lainie Watts; Keith Cooke; ***D:*** Robert Clouse; ***W:*** Robert Clouse; ***C:*** Kent Wakeford; ***M:*** Paul Antonelli.

China Seas **1935** The captain of a commercial steamship on the China route has to fight off murderous Malay pirates, a spurned woman, and a raging typhoon to reach port safely. Fast-moving romantic action taken from Crosbie Garstin's novel. **89m/B; VHS, DVD.** Clark Gable; Jean Harlow; Wallace Beery; Rosalind Russell; Lewis Stone; Sir C. Aubrey Smith; Dudley Digges; Robert Benchley; William Henry; Lillian Bond; Edward Brophy; Hattie McDaniel; Akim Tamiroff; ***D:*** Tay Garnett; ***W:*** Jules Furthman; James Kevin McGuinness; ***C:*** Ray June; ***M:*** Herbert Stothart.

The China Syndrome 1/2 **1979 (PG)** A somewhat unstable executive at a nuclear plant uncovers evidence of a concealed accident and takes drastic steps to publicize the incident. Lemmon is excellent as the anxious exec, while Fonda and Douglas are scarcely less distinguished as a sympathetic TV journalist and camera operator, respectively. Tense, prophetic thriller that ironically preceded the Three Mile Island accident by just a few months. Produced by Douglas. **123m/C; VHS, DVD, Blu-Ray.** Jane Fonda; Jack Lemmon; Michael Douglas; Scott Brady; James Hampton; Peter Donat; Wilford Brimley; James Karen; ***D:*** James Bridges; ***W:*** James Bridges; Mike Gray; T.S. Cook; ***C:*** James A. Crabe. British Acad. '79: Actor (Lemmon), Actress (Fonda); Cannes '79: Actor (Lemmon); Writers Guild '79: Orig. Screenplay.

Chinatown **1974 (R)** Private detective Jake Gittes (Nicholson) finds himself overwhelmed in a scandalous case involving the rich and powerful of Los Angeles. Gripping, atmospheric mystery excels in virtually every aspect, with strong narrative drive and outstanding performances from Nicholson, Dunaway, and Huston. Director Polanski also appears in a suitable unsettling cameo. Fabulous. A sneaky, snaking delight filled with seedy characters and plots-within-plots. Followed more than 15 years later by "The Two Jakes." **131m/C; VHS, DVD, Blu-Ray.** Jack Nicholson; Faye Dunaway; John Huston; Diane Ladd; John Hillerman; Burt Young; Perry Lopez; Darrell Zwerling; Roman Polanski; Joe Mantell; James Hong; ***D:*** Roman Polanski; ***W:*** Robert Towne; ***C:*** John A. Alonzo; ***M:*** Jerry Goldsmith. Oscars '74: Orig. Screenplay; AFI '98: Top 100; British Acad. '74: Actor (Nicholson), Director (Polanski), Screenplay; Golden Globes '75: Actor--Drama (Nicholson), Director (Polanski), Film--Drama, Screenplay; Natl. Film Reg. '91; N.Y. Film Critics '74: Actor (Nicholson); Natl. Soc. Film Critics '74: Actor (Nicholson); Writers Guild '74: Orig. Screenplay.

The Chinatown Kid **1978** Tan Tung escapes from Red China on a ship bound for San Francisco. There he becomes involved in a local extortion racket and he'll need all his martial arts skills to overcome the two gangs fighting for power. **115m/C; VHS, DVD.** Alexander Fu Sheng; Sun Chein; Shirley Yu; Shaw Yin-Yin; ***D:*** Chen Chen.

The Chinatown Murders: Man against the Mob *Man Against the Mob: The Chinatown Murders* **1989 (R)** A tough cop is up against the Chinese mafia and his own corrupt police force as he tries to stay alive and find some justice. **96m/C; VHS, DVD.** George Peppard; Charles Haid; Richard Bradford; Ursula Andress; Jason Beghe; Julia Nickson-Soul; James Pax; Sandy Ward; ***D:*** Michael Pressman; ***C:*** Tim Suhrstedt.

Chinese Box 1/2 **1997** Hong Kong's return to Chinese rule is the backdrop for Wang's story of a dying British journalist (Irons) and a former bar girl turned nightclub owner (Li). In the months before the 1997 handover, business writer John learns he is dying of leukemia and decides to pursue Vivian, the woman he has secretly loved for some time. He also sets out to discover the "meaning" of Hong Kong itself. This quest is personified by Jean (Cheung), a street hustler with stories to tell. Metaphors abound as Wang tries to convey the everyday chaos and impenetrability of Hong Kong life. Striking visuals provide cues and clues to the not-always-subtle symbolism. Mandarin and English dialogue. **109m/C; VHS, DVD.** *FR JP* Jeremy Irons; Gong Li; Maggie Cheung; Ruben Blades; Michael Hui; ***D:*** Wayne Wang; ***W:*** Wayne Wang; Jean-Claude Carriere; Larry Gross; Paul Theroux; ***C:*** Vilko Filac; ***M:*** Graeme Revell.

The Chinese Cat **1944** Poorly scripted formula mystery has the younger Chan smitten with a girl who needs the elder Chan's detective skills in finding her father's killer. **65m/B; VHS, DVD.** Sidney Toler; Benson Fong; Mantan Moreland; Weldon Heyburn; Joan Woodbury; Ian Keith; Sam Flint; ***D:*** Phil Rosen.

Chinese Connection 1/2 *Fist of Fury; The Iron Hand; Jing Wu Men* **1973 (R)** A martial arts expert tracks sadistic brutes who slew his instructor. Wild action sequences provide a breathtaking view of Lee's skill. Dubbed. **90m/C; VHS, DVD, Blu-Ray.** *CH* Bruce Lee; James Tien; Robert Baker; ***D:*** Lo Wei; ***W:*** Lo Wei; ***C:*** Chen Ching Chu; ***M:*** Fu-ling Wang.

Chinese Connection 2 *Fistful of the Dragon; Fists of Fury 2; Jie Quan Ying Zhao Gong* **1977 (R)** A martial-arts expert learns that the school where he trained is now run by an unappealing master. Conflict ensues. Bruce Li is not Bruce Lee (who, to make things more confusing, is shown in flashbacks since he started in the first film), but he is fairly good in action portions of this otherwise dull, sloppy venture. **96m/C; VHS, DVD.** *CH* Bruce Li; Bruce Lee; Lieh Lo; Quin Lee; ***D:*** Tso Nam Lee.

Chinese Odyssey 2002 **2002** Lau's broad genre spoof of kung fu epics. The Emperor and his princess sister try to escape the confines of the Forbidden City but only she is successful in getting away (disguised as a man). The Princess winds up in the same town as restaurant owner Bully, who decides the confusingly attractive newcomer should marry his sister Phoenix. Eventually, the Emperor (in disguise) appears and more crazy things happen. Cantonese with subtitles. **105m/C; DVD.** *CH* Chen "Chang Chen" Chang; Faye Wong; Tony Leung Chiu-wai; Vicki Zhao; Rebecca Pan; ***D:*** Jeff Lau; ***W:*** Jeff Lau; ***C:*** Peter Ngor; ***M:*** Frankie Chan; Roel A. Garcia.

Chinese Puzzle 1/2 *Casse-Tete Chinois* **2013 (R)** The final installment of director Cédric Klapisch's trilogy, following the 2002 dramedy, "L'Auberge Espagnole", and 2005's "Russian Dolls", continues to follow bumbling novelist Xavier's (Duris), now older and worn out. His estranged wife has fled with the kids to New York, forcing him to follow along. Complicating the shtick further, his ex-girlfriend Martine (Tatou) searches him out, stepping on his toes as he sets out to make a new life and stick around for the kids. Unfortunately, this final act lacks the charm and playfulness of its predecessors. **117m/C; DVD, Blu-Ray.** *FR* Romain Duris; Audrey Tautou; Kelly Reilly; Peter Hermann; Cecile de France; Sandrine Holt; ***D:*** Cedric Klapisch; ***W:*** Cedric Klapisch; ***C:*** Natasha Braier; ***M:*** Loik Dury.

The Chinese Ring **1947** The 41st film in the series is the first for Winters as Charlie Chan. It's also a remake of 1939's "Mr. Wong in Chinatown" as written by the same screenwriter. In San Francisco, Chinese Princess Mei Ling (Wong) is killed by a poison dart in Chan's home after handing him the ring of the title and scrawling the initial 'K' on a scrap of paper. This leads the detective in various directions. **67m/B; DVD.** Roland Winters; Victor Sen Yung; Mantan Moreland; Warren Douglas; Louise Currie; Philip Ahn; Thayer Roberts; Byron Foulger; Barbara Jean Wong; ***D:*** William Beaudine; ***W:*** Scott Darling; ***C:*** William Sickner.

Chinese Roulette 1/2 **1986** A host of unappealing characters convene at a country house for sexual shenanigans and a cruel game masterminded by a sadistic crippled girl. Cold effort from German master Fassbinder. In German with English subtitles. **82m/C; VHS, DVD.** *GE* Anna Karina; Margit Carstensen; Ulli Lommel; Brigitte Mira; Macha Meril; Andrea Schober; Volker Spengler; ***D:*** Rainer Werner Fassbinder; ***W:*** Rainer Werner Fassbinder; ***C:*** Michael Ballhaus.

Chino *Valdez the Half Breed; The Valdez Horses* **1975 (PG)** A half-Indian horse rancher struggles to maintain his livelihood in this spaghetti western. Not among Bronson's stronger—that is, more viscerally effective—films. Adapted from Lee Hoffman's novel. **97m/C; VHS, DVD.** *IT* Charles Bronson; Jill Ireland; Vincent Van Patten; ***D:*** John Sturges; ***W:*** Massimo De Rita; Clair Huffaker; Arduino (Dino) Maiuri; ***C:*** Armando Nannuzzi; ***M:*** Guido de Angelis; Maurizio de Angelis.

CHIPS **2017 (R)** Shepard stars and directs this comedy that tries to do for the Erik Estrada cult classic what "21 Jump Street" did for that TV franchise. To say he fails would be an understatement. Shepard and Pena play Jon Baker and Ponch, respectively, in this action-comedy hybrid. Partnered up for the first time, Jon is the former pro trying to play it straight while Ponch is the cocky undercover Federal agent investigating an inside job. It's all just an excuse for waves of sexist, homophobic, and deeply unfunny scenes. Takes unfunny to a new level. **100m/C; DVD, Blu-Ray.** Dax Shepard; Michael Peña; Jessica McNamee; Adam Brody; Ryan Hansen; ***D:*** Dax Shepard; ***W:*** Dax Shepard; ***C:*** Mitchell Amundsen; ***M:*** Fil Eisler.

Chisum 1/2 **1970 (G)** Cattle baron faces various conflicts, including a confrontation with Billy the Kid. Lame Wayne vehicle contributes nothing to exhausted western genre. **111m/C; VHS, DVD, Blu-Ray.** John Wayne; Forrest Tucker; Geoffrey Deuel; Christopher George; Ben Johnson; Bruce Cabot; Patric Knowles; Richard Jaeckel; Glenn Corbett; John Agar; ***D:*** Andrew V. McLaglen; ***W:*** Andrew J. Fenady; ***C:*** William Clothier.

Chitty Chitty Bang Bang **1968 (G)** An eccentric inventor spruces up an old car and, in fantasy, takes his children to a land where the evil rulers have forbidden children. Poor special effects and forgettable score stall effort. Loosely adapted by Roald Dahl and Hughes from an Ian Fleming story. **142m/C; VHS, DVD, Blu-Ray.** *GB* Dick Van Dyke; Sally Ann Howes; Lionel Jeffries; Gert Frobe; Anna Quayle; Benny Hill; ***D:*** Ken Hughes; ***W:*** Ken Hughes; Roald Dahl; ***C:*** Christopher Challis; ***M:*** Richard M. Sherman; Robert B. Sherman.

Chloe 1/2 **2009 (R)** Catherine (Moore) suspects her popular college professor husband David (Neeson) may be cheating so she hires escort Chloe (Seyfried) to try to seduce him. Only Chloe is a liar, spinning tales of her encounters that have Catherine becoming increasingly volatile. Seyfried is a looker but out of her league with heavy hitters Neeson and Moore in this overheated melodrama. Remake of Anne Fontaine's 2003 film "Nathalie." **96m/C; Blu-Ray.** *CA FR* Julianne Moore; Liam Neeson; Amanda Seyfried; Max Thieriot; R.H. Thomson; Nina Dobrev; ***D:*** Atom Egoyan; ***W:*** Erin Cressida Wilson; ***C:*** Paul Sarossy; ***M:*** Mychael Danna.

Chloe & Theo 1/2 **2015 (PG-13)** A quirky drama about one man's quest to save the world and create a better future. Charged by Inuit elders with spreading a message related to the world's survival to world leaders, Theo (Ikummaq), an Inuit himself, is sent to New York City. There, he meets Chloe (Johnson), a homeless woman who embraces life, is obsessed with Bruce Lee, and suffers from some delusions. The pair become friends and with the assistance of a lawyer, Monica (Sorvino), Theo's story is heard before the United Nations. **81m/C; DVD, Streaming, Download.** Theo Ikummaq; Dakota Johnson; Ashley Springer; Andre De

Shields; Mira Sorvino; *D:* Ezna Sands; *W:* Ezna Sands; *C:* Luke Geissbuhler; Aaron Krummel; Peter Zeitlinger; *M:* The Newton Brothers.

Chloe in the Afternoon 🦴🦴🦴 *L'Amour l'Apres-midi* **1972 (R)** A married man finds himself inexplicably drawn to an ungainly young woman. Sixth of the "Moral Tales" series is typical of director Rohmer's talky approach. Not for all tastes, but rewarding for those who are drawn to this sort of thing. In French with English subtitles. **97m/C; VHS, DVD.** *FR* Bernard Verley; Zouzou; Francoise Verley; Daniel Ceccaldi; Malvina Penne; Babette Ferrier; Suze Randall; Marie-Christine Barrault; *D:* Eric Rohmer; *W:* Eric Rohmer; *C:* Nestor Almendros; *M:* Arie Dzierlatka.

Chlorine 🦴 ½ **2013** Heavy-handed family drama. Schlub Roger Lent is stuck in a dead-end job that can't pay for wife Georgie's keeping-up-with-the-neighbors lifestyle in their upscale New England suburb. A flashy new real estate development seems to be the get-rich-quick opportunity they're looking for, but it's too good to be true and sparks an unlikely moral crisis. **93m/C; DVD.** Vincent D'Onofrio; Kyra Sedgwick; Flora Cross; Ryan Donowho; Jordan Belfi; Tom Sizemore; Elisabeth Rohm; Rhys Coiro; *D:* Jay Alaimo; *W:* Jay Alaimo; Matthew Fiorello; *C:* Jamie Kirkpatrick; *M:* Jay Lifton.

Chocolat 🦴🦴🦴 ½ **1988 (PG-13)** A woman recalls her childhood spent in French West Africa and the unfulfilled sexual tension between her mother and black servant. Vivid film provides a host of intriguing characters and offers splendid panoramas of rugged desert landscapes. Profound, if somewhat personal filmmaking from novice director Denis. In French with English subtitles. **105m/C; VHS, DVD.** Mireille Perrier; Emmet Judson Williamson; Cecile Ducasse; Giulia Boschi; Francois Cluzet; Isaach de Bankole; Kenneth Cranham; *D:* Claire Denis; *W:* Claire Denis; Jean-Pol Fargeau.

Chocolat 🦴🦴🦴 **2000 (PG-13)** Free-spirited Vianne (Binoche) and her young daughter Anouk (Thivisol) are literally blown into the dull French town of Lansquenet in the late 1950s. Before the scandalized eyes of the Comte de Reynaud (Molina), the community's moral arbitrator, the unmarried hussy opens a chocolaterie—during Lent! While the Comte tries to rally the residents to boycott the establishment, Vianne's delicacies are setting the townspeople's pulses racing, as she becomes intrigued by gypsy vagabond Roux (Depp). Sweetly predictable if overly chastising against religion and conventional morality. Binoche is radiant as usual (and have some chocolate handy when you watch). Based on the novel by Joanne Harris. **121m/C; VHS, DVD, Blu-Ray.** *FR* Juliette Binoche; Victorie Thivisol; Johnny Depp; Alfred Molina; Dame Judi Dench; Lena Olin; Peter Stormare; Carrie-Anne Moss; John Wood; Hugh O'Conor; Leslie Caron; Aurelien Parent Koenig; *D:* Lasse Hallstrom; *W:* Robert Nelson Jacobs; *C:* Roger Pratt; *M:* Rachel Portman. Screen Actors Guild '00: Support. Actress (Dench).

The Chocolate Soldier 🦴 **1941** Dull musical in which an opera star tests his wife's fidelity. Lovers of the musical genre will find that this one has too much talking, not enough singing. Lovers of fine films will realize that more singing would hardly improve things. Based loosely on Molnar's play "The Guardsman." **102m/B; DVD.** Nelson Eddy; Rise Stevens; Nigel Bruce; Florence Bates; Dorothy Gilmore; Nydia Westman; *D:* Roy Del Ruth; *C:* Karl Freund.

The Chocolate War 🦴🦴🦴 **1988 (R)** An idealistic student and a hardline headmaster butt heads at a Catholic boys' school over an unofficial candy business in this tense, unsettling drama. Glover is notable in his familiar villain role, and Gordon is effective in his first effort as director. Based on the Robert Cormier novel. **95m/C; DVD.** John Glover; Jenny Wright; Wallace (Wally) Langham; Bud Cort; Ilan Mitchell-Smith; Adam Baldwin; *D:* Keith Gordon; *W:* Keith Gordon.

The Choice 🦴 **2016 (PG-13)** The Nicholas Sparks romantic drama machine keeps spinning with diminishing results. Long past its heyday with films like The Notebook, this "franchise" keeps turning out manipulative soap operas, typically scheduled around a Valentine's Day release. In this one, neighbors (Walker & Palmer) fall in love but she's got a man (Welling) overseas. A traditional love triangle gets "Sparks-ed" when she gets into a car accident, forcing another "choice" as her husband has to decide whether or not to turn off life support. These movies have become so cheesy and formulaic that they almost write themselves. **111m/C; DVD, Blu-Ray.** Benjamin Walker; Teresa Palmer; Maggie Grace; Alexandra Daddario; Tom Wilkinson; *D:* Ross Katz; *W:* Bryan Sipe; *C:* Alar Kivilo; *M:* Marcelo Zarvos.

Choice of Weapons 🦴🦴 *A Dirty Knight's Work; Trial by Combat* **1976** Ex-cop trying to solve murders focuses on a curious group of 20th-century men who live within a 12th-century fantasy—jousting for sport and chivalrous honor. Offbeat lance thruster notable for incongruity and all-star cast. **88m/C; VHS, DVD.** *GB* David Birney; Peter Cushing; Donald Pleasence; Barbara Hershey; John Mills; Margaret Leighton; *D:* Kevin Connor; *W:* Julian Bond.

Choices 🦴 ½ **1981** A hearing-impaired athlete suffers alienation when banned from the football squad. What? Controversial covergirl Moore is a supporting player in this, her first film. **90m/C; VHS, DVD.** Paul Carafotes; Victor French; Lelia Goldoni; Val Avery; Dennis Patrick; Demi Moore; *D:* Rami Alon; *W:* Rami Alon; *C:* Hanania Baer; *M:* Christopher L. Stone.

Choices 🦴🦴 ½ **1986** Scott is a 62-year-old man with a lovely second wife (Bisset) and a rebellious grown daughter (Gilbert), who announces she's pregnant and is getting an abortion. Meanwhile, his wife also discovers she's pregnant and wants the child, although Scott is adamantly opposed to raising a second family at his age. Family strife carried by fine performances. **95m/C; VHS, DVD.** George C. Scott; Jacqueline Bisset; Melissa Gilbert; *D:* David Lowell Rich. **TV**

Choices of the Heart: The Margaret Sanger Story 🦴🦴 ½ **1995** In 1914, New York nurse Margaret Sanger (Delaney) writes a booklet on birth control to provide women information on family planning. This places her in opposition to city moralist Anthony Comstock (Steiger) whose office forbids the dissemination of contraception information. Sanger went on to help establish the first birth control clinic in 1916 and became one the founders of Planned Parenthood in 1925. **83m/C; DVD.** Dana Delaney; Rod Steiger; Henry Czerny; Julie Khaner; Tom McCamus; Kenneth Welsh; *Nar:* Jason Priestley; *D:* Paul Shapiro; *W:* Matt Dorff; *C:* Alar Kivilo; *M:* Jonathan Goldsmith. **TV**

The Choirboys 🦴 **1977 (R)** Thoroughly mediocre production about overbearing L.A. cops and their off-hours handling of job stress. Few of the strong cast emerge unscathed. Based on the Joseph Wambaugh novel. **120m/C; VHS, Streaming.** Charles Durning; Louis Gossett, Jr.; Perry King; Clyde Kusatsu; Stephen Macht; Tim McIntire; Randy Quaid; Chuck Sacci; Don Stroud; James Woods; Burt Young; Robert Webber; Barbara Rhoades; Vic Tayback; Blair Brown; Charles Haid; Jim Davis; *D:* Robert Aldrich; *C:* Joseph Biroc.

Choke 🦴 ½ **2000 (R)** Weak thriller with dumb dialogue. Shady businessman Harry (Hopper) is trying to cover up his daughter's deadly drunken hit-and-run accident when he's threatened by a con man who knows about the crime. Then Harry just makes the situation worse by accepting the help of a killer (Madsen) who knows how to get rid of troublesome bodies. **95m/C; VHS, DVD.** Dennis Hopper; Michael Madsen; L.P. Brown, III; Chelsy Reynolds; Roy Tate; *D:* John Sjogren. **VIDEO**

Choke 🦴🦴 ½ **2008 (R)** Sex addict Victor Mancini (Rockwell) supplements his modest income as a historical re-enactor at a colonial village theme park by conning upscale restaurant patrons into believing he is choking and then preying on their sympathies and fat wallets, a scam that helps him keep his crazy mother Ida (Huston) in an expensive private mental hospital. His vacant life takes a turn when, in a rare lucid moment, his mother reveals his father's shocking identity, giving him cause to reflect on his pathetic, single-track life. Graphic sex scenes border on gratuitous, but Rockwell makes an otherwise detestable character somewhat sympathetic and likeable while pitching black dark comedy. Will either strongly offend or greatly entertain, depending on a tolerance of Oedipal complexes and kink as comedy. Based on the novel by "Fight Club" author Chuck Palahniuk, and directorial debut of Gregg, who also has a role. **89m/C; On Demand.** Sam Rockwell; Anjelica Huston; Kelly Macdonald; Bijou Phillips; Brad William Henke; Clark Gregg; Gillian Jacobs; *D:* Clark Gregg; *W:* Clark Gregg; *C:* Tim Orr; *M:* Nathan Larson.

C.H.O.M.P.S. 🦴 ½ **1979 (PG)** Comedy in which a youthful inventor and a popular robot guard dog become the target of a business takeover. Harmless but unfunny and unfun. **90m/C; VHS, DVD.** Jim Backus; Valerie Bertinelli; Wesley Eure; Conrad Bain; Chuck McCann; Red Buttons; *D:* Don Chaffey.

Choose Connor 🦴🦴 **2007** Idealistic 15-year-old Owen Norris (Linz) gets a summer job working on the senate campaign of Congressman Connor (Weber), who's eager to use Owen as his youth spokesman. However, Owen is soon disillusioned by how self-serving and corrupt politics can be. There's also a disturbing subplot involving Connor's adopted teenaged nephew, Caleb (Holloway), who has both physical and emotional scars, and his burgeoning relationship to Owen. **109m/C; DVD.** Alex D. Linz; Steven Weber; Diane Delano; John Rubinstein; Erik Avari; Christopher Marquette; Escher Holloway; *D:* Luke Eberl; *W:* Luke Eberl; *C:* Jim Timperman; *M:* Kaz(imir) Boyle.

Choose Me 🦴🦴🦴 ½ **1984 (R)** Comedy-drama about sad, lonely, and often quirky characters linked to an unlikely L.A. radio sex therapist. Moody, memorable fare features especially strong playing from Bujold as a sexually inexperienced sex therapist and Warren as one of her regular listeners. Typically eccentric fare from director Rudolph. **106m/C; VHS, DVD.** Keith Carradine; Genevieve Bujold; Lesley Ann Warren; Rae Dawn Chong; John Larroquette; John Considine; Patrick Bauchau; *D:* Alan Rudolph; *W:* Alan Rudolph; *C:* Jan Kiesser; *M:* Phil Woods.

Chopper 🦴🦴 ½ **2000** Biopic of famous Aussie criminal Mark "Chopper" Read is highlighted by Bana's extraordinary performance in the title role. Dominik's directorial debut follows Read's career from prison, where he murders one inmate, forces another to cut off his ears, and generally makes hardened criminal fear for their lives, to his old haunts, where he seeks revenge for past wrongs. Full of gore and ultraviolence, it's not for the sqeamish, but it does make its point about society's preoccupation with the "celebrity criminal." Read didn't participate in the production, but it was based on his nine bestsellers, and he did suggest Bana for the lead. **94m/C; DVD.** *AU* Eric Bana; Vince Colosimo; Simon Lyndon; David Field; Daniel Wyllie; Bill Young; Garry Waddell; Kate Beahan; Kenny Graham; *D:* Andrew Dominik; *W:* Andrew Dominik; *C:* Geoffrey Hall; *M:* Mick Harvey. Australian Film Inst. '00: Actor (Bana), Director (Dominik), Support. Actor (Lyndon).

Chopper Chicks in Zombietown 🦴🦴 **1991 (R)** Tough but sexy Chopper Chicks show up in that American vacation mecca, Zombietown, for a little rest and relaxation. Little do they know that a mad mortician has designs on turning our hot heroines into mindless zombie slaves. Can the buxom biker babes thwart the evil embalmer before it's too late, or will they abandon their Harleys to shuffle about in search of human flesh? From the Troma Team, featuring Oscar-winner Billy Bob Thornton as "Donny." **86m/C; VHS, DVD.** Jamie Rose; Catherine Carlen; Lycia Naff; Vicki Frederick; Kristina Loggia; Gretchen Palmer; Whitney Reis; Nina Peterson; Ed Gale; David Knell; Billy Bob Thornton; Don Calfa; Martha Quinn; *D:* Dan Hoskins; *W:* Dan Hoskins; *C:* Tom Fraser; *M:* Daniel May.

The Choppers 🦴 **1961** Naw, not a fable about false teeth. Teen punk Hall operates a car theft ring made up of fellow punksters. Rock'n'roll tunes by the Hall-meister include the much-overlooked "Monkey in my Hatband." **66m/B; VHS, DVD.** Arch Hall, Jr.; Marianne Gaba; Robert Paget; Tom Brown; Rex Holman; Bruno VeSota; *D:* Leigh Jason; *W:* Arch (Archie) Hall, Sr.; *C:* Clark Ramsey; *M:* Al Pellegrini.

Chopping Mall 🦴 ½ *Killbots* **1986 (R)** A freak electric storm unleashes killer security robots on a band of teens trapped inside the mall. Nobody shops. Premise undone by obscure humor, lack of flair, action, or horror. Updated imitation of the 1973 TV movie "Trapped." **77m/C; VHS, DVD, Blu-Ray.** Kelli Maroney; Tony O'Dell; Suzee Slater; Russell Todd; Paul Bartel; Mary Woronov; Dick Miller; Karrie Emerson; Barbara Crampton; Nick Segal; John Terlesky; Gerrit Graham; Mel Welles; *D:* Jim Wynorski; *W:* Jim Wynorski; Steve Mitchell; *C:* Tom Richmond; *M:* Chuck Cirino.

The Chorus 🦴🦴 *Les Choristes* **2004 (PG-13)** Two childhood friends, drawn together again by personal tragedy, reflect on the role of an old mentor who elevated their lives through song. Story of saintly teacher is told in flashback from his point of view. Very schmaltzy retread that has been made so many times before. Tired and predictably inspiring. **95m/C; DVD.** Gerard Jugnot; Francois Berleand; Jacques Perrin; Marie Bunel; Kad Merad; Jean-Baptiste Maunier; Didier Flamand; Jean-Paul Bonnaire; Phillippe Du Janerand; Maxence Perrin; *D:* Christophe Barratier; *W:* Christophe Barratier; Philippe Lopes-Curval; *C:* Carlo Varini; *M:* Bruno Coulais.

A Chorus Line 🦴🦴 **1985 (PG-13)** A range of performers reveal their insecurities and aspirations while auditioning before a hardnosed director in this adaptation of the popular, overblown Broadway musical. Singing and dancing is rarely rousing. Director Attenborough probably wasn't the right choice for this one. **118m/C; VHS, DVD, Blu-Ray.** Michael Douglas; Audrey Landers; Gregg Burge; Alyson Reed; Janet Jones; Michael Blevins; Terrence Mann; Cameron English; Vicki Frederick; Nicole Fosse; Michelle Johnson; *D:* Richard Attenborough; *W:* Arnold Schulman; *M:* Marvin Hamlisch; Ralph Burns.

A Chorus of Disapproval 🦴 ½ **1989 (PG)** Adaptation of prolific Alan Ayckbourn's play about a withdrawn, somewhat dim-witted British widower who attempts social interaction by joining community theatre, then finds himself embroiled in romantic shenanigans and theatrical intrigue. Irons is fine in the lead, but Hopkins sparkles in the more spectacular role of the musical production's demanding but beleaguered director. Seagrove is impressive as an amoral sexpot. Sharper focus from director Winner would have improved this one, but the film is fun even when it isn't particularly funny. **105m/C; VHS, Streaming.** *GB* Jeremy Irons; Anthony Hopkins; Jenny Seagrove; Lionel Jeffries; Patsy Kensit; Gareth Hunt; Prunella Scales; Sylvia Syms; Richard Briers; Barbara Ferris; *D:* Michael Winner; *W:* Michael Winner; Alan Ayckbourn; *M:* John Du Prez.

The Chosen **WOOF!** *Holocaust 2000* **1977 (R)** Executive of a nuclear power facility located in the Sahara Desert realizes that his son is the Anti-Christ bent on the world's destruction. This truly horrible film provides nothing in terms of entertainment. It's rarely even laughably bad. **102m/C; VHS, DVD, Blu-Ray.** Kirk Douglas; Simon Ward; Agostina Belli; Anthony Quayle; Virginia McKenna; Alexander Knox; *D:* Alberto De Martino; *M:* Ennio Morricone.

The Chosen 🦴🦴🦴 **1981** Set in 1940s Brooklyn about the friendship between two teenagers—Benson, the Hassidic son of a rabbi, and Miller, whose father is a Zionist professor. Based on the novel by Chaim Potok. **108m/C; VHS, DVD.** Robby Benson; Barry Miller; Maximilian Schell; Rod Steiger; Hildy Brooks; Ron Rifkin; Val Avery; *D:* Jeremy Paul Kagan; *M:* Elmer Bernstein.

Chosen 🦴🦴 **2016 (R)** A World War II drama set based on actual events. When the military forces of Nazi Germany take over a Hungarian village in 1943, they kill people including the wife of unassuming lawyer Sonson (Keitel). The lawyer quietly works to undermine the Nazis and becomes a leader of the opposition to the regime. Through such acts as posing as an SS officer to help free a group of female resistance fighters, Sonson becomes a hero. **105m/C; DVD, Streaming, Download.** Luke Mably; Ana Ularu; Harvey Keitel; Ioana Flora; Paul Ipate; *D:* Jasmin Dizdar; *W:* Gabriel De Mercur; *C:* Balazs Bolygo; *M:* Philip Sheppard. **VIDEO**

The Chosen One: Legend of the Raven 🦴🦴 **1998 (R)** McKenna Ray ("Baywatch" babe Electra) wants payback after her sister is murdered and is transformed into a superheroine avenger (guided by her shaman father) so she can rid the world of scum. Electra has a provocative costume but the nude scenes are courtesy of a body-double. **105m/C; VHS, DVD.** Carmen Electra; Michael Stadvec; Dave Oliver; Shauna Sand; *D:* Lawrence Lanoff; *W:* Sam Rappaport; Khara Bromiley; *C:* Robert New; *M:* Keith Arem.

Chow Bella 1/2 **1998** Everyone's a critic and for David Felder that turns out to be a big mistake. Substitute food critic David writes a really bad review for a restaurant that turns out to be mob owned. Sensitive gangster Anthony doesn't take kindly to David's words and decides (after kidnapping him) to make sure that David changes his mind. **90m/C; DVD.** Arye Gross; Paul Provenza; Carolyn Feeney; Clint Howard; *D:* Gavin Grazer; *W:* Gavin Grazer; *C:* Peter-Kowalski; *M:* Eric Lundmark.

Chris & Don: A Love Story **2007** This insightful, feature-length documentary examines the lives of and relationship between British writer Christopher Isherwood and American portrait painter Don Barchady. Despite a three-decade age difference, the couple met in 1950s in Malibu and formed a lasting bond. Individual successes of both men are also identified, and their story is told through interviews and rare home movies. **90m/C; DVD, Streaming, Download.** Michael York; *D:* Tina Mascara; Guido Santi; *C:* Ralph Q. Smith; *M:* Miriam Cutler.

Christ Stopped at Eboli *Eboli; Cristo si e fermato a Eboli* **1979** Subdued work about an anti-Fascist writer exiled to rural Italy in the 1930s. Excellent performances from the lead Volonte and supporting players Papas and Cuny. Slow, contemplative film is probably director Rosi's masterpiece. Adapted from Carlo Levi's book. In Italian with English subtitles. **118m/C; VHS, DVD.** *IT FR* Gian Marie Volonte; Irene Papas; Paolo Bonacelli; Francois Simon; Alain Cuny; Lea Massari; *D:* Francesco Rosi; *W:* Francesco Rosi; *C:* Pasqualino De Santis. British Acad. '82: Foreign Film.

Christabel **1989** Condensed version of the BBC miniseries based on the true-life WWII exploits of Christabel Bielenberg, a British woman who battled to save her German husband from the horrors of the Ravensbruck concentration camp. **148m/C; VHS, DVD.** *GB* Elizabeth Hurley; Stephen (Dillon) Dillane; Nigel le Vaillant; Geoffrey Palmer; Ann Bell; Ralph Brown; John Burgess; Suzan Crowley; Eileen Maciejewska; Hugh Simon; Nicola Wright; *D:* Adrian Shergold; *W:* Dennis Potter; *C:* Remi Adefarasin; *M:* Stanley Myers. **TV**

Christian the Lion 1/2 **1976 (G)** The true story of Christian, a lion cub raised in a London zoo, who is transported to Africa to learn to live with other lions. With the principals from "Born Free." **87m/C; VHS, DVD.** *GB* Virginia McKenna; Bill Travers; George Adamson; James Hill; *D:* Bill Travers.

Christiane F. **1982 (R)** Gripping, visually impressive story of a bored German girl's decline into drug use and prostitution. Based on a West German magazine article. Sobering and dismal look at a milieu in which innocence and youth have run amok. The film's impact is only somewhat undermined by poor dubbing. Bowie appears in a concert sequence. **120m/C; VHS, DVD.** *GE* Natja Brunkhorst; Thomas Haustein; David Bowie; *D:* Uli Edel; *M:* David Bowie.

Christie's Revenge 1/2 **2007** In this Lifetime cable movie, 16-year-old Christie Colton (Kind) comes home to discover her father has committed suicide. As Christie remembers it, he badly needed a loan and was refused by his doctor brother Ray (Shipp). Three years later, with her mother remarried, Christie finagles her way into living with Uncle Ray and his family, determined to destroy his life as her father's was destroyed. But is what Christie remembers what actually happened? **90m/C; DVD.** Danielle Kind; John Wesley Shipp; Cynthia Gibb; James McGowan; Annie Bovaird; Anastasia Phillips; *D:* Douglas Jackson; *W:* Christine Conradt; *C:* Bert Tougas; *M:* Steve Gurevitch. **CABLE**

Christina **2010** Troubling drama confined to three actors and one Berlin apartment. In the waning days of World War II, Christina is hoping to escape to a new life in America with her G.I. fiance Billy. Police inspector Edgar Reinhardt shows up and forces her to confront her past and a decision Christina won't willingly acknowledge. **94m/C; DVD.** Nicki Aycox; Jordan Belfi; Stephen Lang; *D:* Larry Brand; *W:* Larry Brand; *C:* Kees Van Oostrum; *M:* David C. Williams. **VIDEO**

Christina's House **1999** Teen learns she's likely to be the next victim of a murderous stalker who's hiding within her own home. **97m/C; VHS, DVD.** *CA* Brendan Fehr; Brad Rowe; John Savage; Allison Lange; Lorne Stewart; *D:* Gavin Wilding. **VIDEO**

Christine 1/2 **1984 (R)** Unassuming teen gains posession of a classic auto equipped with a murderous will. Then it's the car doing the possessing. The car more than returns the care and consideration its owner provides it. Are you listening GMC? Better than average treatment of Stephen King's work features a creepy performance by Gordon. **110m/C; VHS, DVD, Blu-Ray.** Keith Gordon; John Stockwell; Alexandra Paul; Robert Prosky; Harry Dean Stanton; Kelly Preston; Christine Belford; Roberts Blossom; William Ostrander; David Spielberg; Robert Darnell; *D:* John Carpenter; *W:* Bill (William) Phillips; *C:* Donald M. Morgan; *M:* John Carpenter; Alan Howarth.

Christine **2016 (R)** Rebecca Hall shines in Antonio Campos' telling of the tragic tale of Christine Chubbuck, but the film gets away from the filmmaker uncertain of the story he's trying to tell. Chubbuck was a depressed, lonely news anchor who pulled out a gun on the 5 o'clock news in Florida in 1974 and shot herself in the head. Too much of Campos' film feels like an "explanation" for such a truly unexplainable act of violence. There is no answer to "why" she did it. However, Hall finds depth in this tragic figure and it's her performance that nearly salvages an unfocused film. **115m/C; DVD.** Rebecca Hall; Michael C. Hall; Tracy Letts; Maria Dizzia; J. Smith-Cameron; *D:* Antonio Campos; *W:* Craig Shilowich; *C:* Joe Anderson; *M:* Danny Bensi; Saunder Jurriaans.

The Christine Jorgensen Story **1970** Based (with the usual showbiz liberties) on the autobiography of transsexual Christine Jorgensen. Suffering a gender identity crisis since childhood, George finally goes to Copenhagen in 1952 to have a sex-change operation. (No, he actually wasn't the first to have such surgery.) Unfortunately, the flick is stilted, campy, and Hansen is unconvincing as a woman. **98m/C; DVD.** Quinn (K.) Redeker; John Hansen; Joan Tompkins; John Himes; Oscar Beregi; Rod McCary; Ellen Clark; *D:* Irving Rapper; *W:* Robert E. Kent; Ellis St. Joseph; *C:* Jacques Marquette; *M:* Bert Shefter; Paul Sawtell.

Christmas, Again 1/2 **2015** Noel (Audley) is the kind of gentle, quiet soul who occupies street corners in major cities like New York City every holiday season selling Christmas trees. He's hardly memorable, but Poekel's film captures the unique hybrid of melancholy and joy in which these men linger, watching tree buyers come in and out of their life for brief periods of time. Noel meets a young lady named Lydia (Gross) in need of his assistance. The two form a tenuous bond, slightly more romantic but more just in need of some sort of kindness and companionship. This is a delicate, human movie. **80m/C; DVD.** Kentucky Audley; Hannah Gross; Oona Roche; Ben Webster; Sam Stillman; *D:* Charles Poekel; *W:* Charles Poekel; *C:* Sean Price Williams.

Christmas Angel 1/2 **2009 (PG)** Ashley Matthews is a struggling single gal whose day starts off badly and goes downhill when she loses her cell phone and misses out on a new job. Fortunately, her phone is returned by cutie Will and her neighbor Nick hires Ashley to become his 'Secret Santa' assistant to help the needy. A former foster child, Ashley has a bah humbug attitude but finds her generous spirit with Nick and Will's help. **90m/C; DVD, Blu-Ray.** Bruce Davison; Kari Hawker; K.C. Clyde; *D:* Brian Brough; *W:* Scott Champion; Brittany Wiscombe; *C:* John Lyde; *M:* Michael Shumway. **VIDEO**

Christmas Angel 1/2 *My Angel* **2011** Brit holiday TV movie. 15-year-old Eddie and his older brother Stewart are trying to fend for themselves after their mother is seriously injured in a car accident. Eddie dreams his mother asks him to find an angel's halo to save her life and, when Stewart scoffs, Eddie turns to grumpy Mr. Lambert to help with his Christmas miracle. **90m/C; DVD.** *UK* Joseph Phillips; Timothy Spall; Angus Harrison; Brenda Blethyn; Janet Dibley; *D:* Stephen Cookson; *W:* Stephen Cookson; *C:* Ollie Downey; *M:* Vince Pope. **TV**

Christmas at Water's Edge 1/2 **2004** Leila Turner is from a wealthy family but she helps out at a home for troubled teens. However, the building is about to be demolished, thanks to one of her father's development projects. Leila and her friend Tre discover some of the teens can sing and they decide to hold a fund-raising concert that's helped by some heavenly influence. **87m/C; DVD.** Keisha Knight Pulliam; Richard Lawson; Tom Bosley; Earl Billings; Pooch Hall; Ray J. Norwood; *D:* Lee Davis; Janet Hubert; *W:* Riley Weston; Mike Watts. **CABLE**

The Christmas Blessing 1/2 **2005** Weepy, heartfelt sequel to "The Christmas Shoes." The now grown-up Nathan Andrews (Harris) is a medical resident, but when a young patient dies, he's in crisis and decides to move back home to think things over. Volunteering at the local school, Nathan falls for teacher Meagan (Gayheart) but he needs a Christmas miracle when both her life and that of a young boy (Jones) are in danger. **90m/C; DVD.** Neil Patrick Harris; Rebecca Gayheart; Angus T. Jones; Rob Lowe; Hugh Thompson; Wanda Cannon; Shaun Johnston; *D:* Karen Arthur; *W:* Wesley Bishop; *M:* Lawrence Shragge. **TV**

The Christmas Box 1/2 **1995** Tearjerking Christmas drama based on Richard Paul Evans' surprising 1992 bestseller, which started out as a story for the author's children. Richard (Thomas) and Keri (O'Toole) Evans have money troubles so they and their five-year-old daughter Jenna (Mulrooney) move into the mansion of elderly widow Mary Parkin (O'Hara) as caretakers. Richard keeps seeing an angel in a recurring dream and hears a familiar tune—all of which leads to a music box hidden in the attic, a series of love letters, and Mary's unhappy past. **92m/C; VHS, DVD.** Maureen O'Hara; Richard Thomas; Annette O'Toole; Kelsey Mulrooney; *D:* Marcus Cole; *W:* Greg Taylor; *C:* John Newby.

Christmas Caper **2007 (PG)** Typical "true meaning of Christmas" cable comedy. Thief Cate Dove (Doherty) hides out in her quaint hometown of Comfort, Connecticut, when her partner Clive (Coates) double-crosses her. Since her sister (Salomaa) and brother-in-law (Lewis) are delayed out of town, Cate the grinch is left caring for her niece and nephew and uses the time to plan her next heist for Christmas Eve. But the season softens even the hardest heart, especially since Cate's hunky ex-beau Hank (Olsson), now the town's sheriff, is taking an interest. **88m/C; DVD.** Shannen Doherty; Ty Olsson; Conrad Coates; Stefanie von Pfetten; Sonya Salomaa; David Lewis; Natasha Calis; Josh Hayden; *D:* David Winkler; *W:* April Blair. **CABLE**

The Christmas Card 1/2 **2006** Career solider Cody Cullen (Newton) is touched by the strangers who have sent Christmas cards to his unit in Afghanistan. He saves one special card from Faith Spelman (Evans) and when Cody gets leave, he impulsively decides to visit her small hometown. Faith and her father (Asner) welcome Cody and he soon feels part of their family but as Cody and Faith get closer, he needs to decide where his future lies. **84m/C; DVD.** Alice Evans; Ed Asner; Lois Nettleton; Peter Jason; Ben Weber; *D:* Stephen Bridgewater; *W:* Joany Kane; *C:* Maximo Munzi; John Newton; *M:* Roger Bellon; Brian Robinson. **CABLE**

A Christmas Carol **1938** An early version of Dickens' classic tale about miser Scrooge, who is instilled with the Christmas spirit after a grim evening with some ghosts. Good playing from Owen as Scrooge and Lockhart as the hapless Bob Cratchit. Scary graveyard sequence too. **70m/B; VHS, DVD, Blu-Ray.** Reginald Owen; Gene Lockhart; Terence (Terry) Kilburn; Leo G. Carroll; Lynne Carver; Ann Rutherford; *D:* Edwin L. Marin.

A Christmas Carol *Scrooge* **1951** A fine retelling of the classic tale about a penny-pinching holiday hater who learns appreciation of Christmas following a frightful, revealing evening with supernatural visitors. Perhaps the best rendering of the Dickens classic. "And God bless Tiny Tim!" **86m/B; VHS, DVD, Blu-Ray.** *GB* Alastair Sim; Kathleen Harrison; Jack Warner; Michael Hordern; Patrick Macnee; Mervyn Johns; Hermione Baddeley; Clifford Mollison; George Cole; Carol Marsh; Miles Malleson; Ernest Thesiger; Hattie Jacques; Peter Bull; Hugh Dempster; *D:* Brian Desmond Hurst; *W:* Noel Langley; *C:* C.M. Pennington-Richards; *M:* Richard Addinsell.

A Christmas Carol **1984 (PG)** Excellent TV adaptation of the Dickens Christmas classic features a memorable Scott as miserly misanthrope Ebenezer Scrooge, who gets a scary look at his life thanks to a Christmas Eve visit from the ghosts of Christmas Past, Present, and Future. Terrific supporting cast; filmed on location in Shrewsbury, England. **100m/C; VHS, DVD, Blu-Ray.** George C. Scott; Nigel Davenport; Edward Woodward; Frank Finlay; Lucy Gutteridge; Angela Pleasence; Roger Rees; David Warner; Susannah York; *D:* Clive Donner; *W:* Roger O. Hirson; *C:* Tony Imi; *M:* Nick Bicat.

A Christmas Carol 1/2 **1999** Oft-told tale does have the advantage of Stewart (who has a one-man stage production of the Dickens saga as well as recording an audiobook) as the miserly Scrooge. It also has a strong supporting cast and special effects that enhance but don't overwhelm. **120m/C; VHS, DVD.** Patrick Stewart; Richard E. Grant; Joel Grey; Saskia Reeves; Desmond Barrit; Bernard Lloyd; Tim Potter; Ben Tibber; Dominic West; Trevor Peacock; Liz Smith; Elizabeth Spriggs; Laura Fraser; Celia Imrie; *D:* David Hugh Jones; *W:* Peter Barnes; *C:* Ian Wilson; *M:* Stephen Warbeck. **CABLE**

A Christmas Carol 1/2 *Disney's A Christmas Carol* **2009 (PG)** Disney again taps director Zemeckis, this time to create a high-tech, animated 3-D version of the Dickens' Christmas classic with Carrey the voice of miser Ebenezer Scrooge (as well as the three Ghosts who help show him the true meaning of the season). Using the stop-motion technique he employed in "The Polar Express," the overdose of CGI however overshadows excellent, expressive performances from Carrey and Oldham (as Bob Cratchit, Jacob Marley, and Tiny Tim) as well as the holiday tale itself. Though it does faithfully maintain the storyline and Victorian England era setting. But much like an overloaded Christmas tree, the techno-bling is pretty to look at but things are bound to go awry. **96m/C; DVD, Blu-Ray.** *V:* Jim Carrey; Gary Oldman; Colin Firth; Bob Hoskins; Robin Wright; Lesley Manville; Daryl Sabara; *D:* Robert Zemeckis; *W:* Robert Zemeckis; *C:* Robert Presley; *M:* Alan Silvestri.

Christmas Child **2003** Typical seasonal heart-tugger based on a short story by Max Lucado. Troubled journalist Jack (Moses) is on his way to Dallas when a mystery photo catches his eye and detours him to the small town of Clearwater. He's intrigued by the town's living nativity scene and finds out his Christmas birthday is somehow related to the annual celebration. **96m/C; DVD.** William R. Moses; Megan Follows; Steve Chapman; Tonya Bordeaux; Vicki Taylor Ross; *D:* William Ewing; *W:* Andrea Jobe; Eric Newman; *C:* Fernando Argelles; *M:* Phil Marshall. **CABLE**

The Christmas Choir 1/2 **2008** Hallmark Channel holiday fare about workaholic accountant Peter Brockman (Gedrick) who finds unexpected rewards when he decides to volunteer at a men's homeless shelter run by cantankerous Sister Agatha (Perlman). After hearing some of the musical talents of the guys, Peter's encouraged to form a choir. **85m/C; DVD.** Jason Gedrick; Rhea Perlman; Michael Sarrazin; Tyrone Benskin; Luis Oliva; Marianne Farley; Claudia Ferri; Cindy Sampson; *D:* Peter Svatek; *W:* Donald Martin; *C:* Eric Cayla; *M:* James Gelfand. **CABLE**

The Christmas Clause ♪♪ *The Mrs. Clause* **2008** Lawyer, wife, and mother of three, Sophie Kelly is feeling overwhelmed when she takes her brood to see Santa at the mall. She impulsively makes her own plea to Santa, wishing for a different life. Sophie then wakes up single, rich, and a ruthless exec with her own law firm. However, Sophie realizes that this new life isn't what she wants after all but she only has until Christmas Day to figure out how to change things back. **90m/C; DVD.** *CA* Lea Thompson; Andrew Airlie; Laura Mennell; Rachel Hayward; Rick Ravanello; Doug Abrahams; ***D:*** George Erschbamer; ***W:*** Sheri Elwood; ***C:*** Cliff Hokanson; ***M:*** Stu Goldberg. **TV**

Christmas Comes Home to Canaan ♪♪ **2011** Hallmark Channel sequel to 2009's "Christmas in Canaan." Daniel's (Cyrus) son Bobber (James) is seriously injured in a car accident, and former foster son Rodney (Freeman) tells them to come to San Francisco for treatment. Bobber really likes his therapist Briony (Holden) and, when the Burtons head back to Texas, she's invited to spend Christmas with the family. Only daughter Sarah (Tennant) isn't happy with how well widower Daniel and Briony get along. **87m/C; DVD, Blu-Ray.** Billy Ray Cyrus; Gina Holden; Liam James; Matt Ward; Emily Tennant; Jacob Blair; ***D:*** Neill Fearnley; ***W:*** Donald Davenport; ***M:*** John Sereda. **CABLE**

Christmas Comes to Willow Creek ♪♪ **1987** Mutually antagonistic brothers are enlisted to deliver Christmas gifts to an isolated Alaskan community. Can brotherly love be far off? Two leads played together in the rowdy TV series "Dukes of Hazzard." This is hardly an improvement. **96m/C; VHS, DVD.** John Schneider; Tom Wopat; Hoyt Axton; Zachary Ansley; Kim Delaney; ***D:*** Richard Lang; ***M:*** Charles Fox.

The Christmas Consultant ♪ 1/2 **2012** Lifetime holiday cheesefest with Hasselhoff going all out wth the zany. Workaholics Maya and Jack Fletcher hire consultant Owen to get their family through the holidays. Owen takes over in ways Maya doesn't expect, and the would-be supermom gets jealous. **96m/C; Streaming.** David Hasselhoff; Caroline Rhea; Barclay Hope; Jessica McLeod; ***D:*** John Bradshaw; ***W:*** Brian Sawyer; Gregg Rossen; ***C:*** Paul Mitchnick; ***M:*** Christopher Nickel. **CABLE**

The Christmas Cottage ♪♪ *Thomas Kinkade's The Christmas Cottage; Thomas Kinkade's Home for Christmas* **2008 (PG)** How the inspirational artist got his start. College student Thomas Kinkade (Padalecki) comes home for Christmas and discovers the family home is about to go into foreclosure. So with the help of mentor Glenn (O'Toole), Thomas accepts a commission to paint a mural of his hometown and realizes his true calling. **96m/C; DVD, Blu-Ray.** Jared Padalecki; Marcia Gay Harden; Peter O'Toole; Kiersten Warren; Gina Holden; Aaron Ashmore; Richard Burgi; Richard Moll; ***D:*** Michael Campus; ***W:*** Ken LaZebnik; ***C:*** Robert Brinkmann. **VIDEO**

Christmas Cupid ♪ 1/2 **2010** In this ABC Family movie (that's not so family-oriented), self-centered Hollywood publicist Sloane is visited by the ghost of her infamous and recently-deceased client Caitlin who serves as the would-be cupid of the title. It's a contemporary version of Dickens "A Christmas Carol" as Caitlin is determined Sloane find true love by visiting her past, present, and future boyfriends. **90m/C; DVD.** Christina Milian; Ashley Benson; Chad Michael Murray; Jackee; Burgess Jenkins; ***D:*** Gil Junger; ***W:*** Amy Wallington; ***C:*** Dave Perkal. **CABLE**

Christmas Do-Over ♪ 1/2 **2006** Think "Groundhog Day" only at Christmas. Grumpy Kevin (Mohr) isn't happy to be spending the holiday with his ex-wife Jill (Zuniga) and his in-laws but he does want to see his cute-as-a-button son Ben (Grove). Ben wishes to have Christmas every day and Kevin is stuck reliving the holiday until he understands this is his last chance to get his old life back. Except Kevin is such a selfish whiner you know why Jill dumped him, which spoils the whole fantasy. **90m/C; DVD.** Jay Mohr; Daphne Zuniga; Adrienne Barbeau; Logan Grove; Tim Thomerson; David Millbern; Ruta Lee; ***D:*** Catherine Cyran; ***W:*** Trevor Reed Cristow; Jacqueline David; ***C:*** Ken Blakey; ***M:*** Andrew Gross. **CABLE**

Christmas Eve ♪♪ 1/2 **2015 (PG)** A Christmas comedy-drama about the unexpected impact of a power outage. In Manhattan on Christmas Eve, an unexpected power outage hits the city and traps groups of people in six different elevators. In one, a real estate tycoon (Stewart) is trapped alone, while in another, an atheist surgeon (Cole) is stuck with his dying patient. While members of an orchestra are trapped in a small elevator together, the residents and guests of an apartment building end up spending the night in an elevator together sharing and arguing. **95m/C; DVD, Streaming, Download.** Patrick Stewart; Gary Cole; Roxanne Cook; James Roday; Jon Heder; ***D:*** Mitch Davis; ***W:*** Mitch Davis; Tyler McKellar; ***C:*** Ty Arnold; ***M:*** Christian Davis.

Christmas Evil ♪ 1/2 *Terror in Toyland; You Better Watch Out* **1980 (R)** Once again a knife-wielding lunatic dresses as Santa Claus to strike terror and death into the hearts of children. **92m/C; VHS, DVD, Blu-Ray.** Brandon Maggart; Jeffrey DeMunn; Dianne Hull; Scott McKay; Peter Friedman; Joe Jamrog; Rutanya Alda; Raymond J. Barry; Andy Fenwick; Sam Gray; Patricia Richardson; ***D:*** Lewis Jackson; ***W:*** Lewis Jackson; ***C:*** Ricardo Aronovich.

The Christmas Hope ♪♪ 1/2 **2009** In this Lifetime family drama, social worker Patti has shut herself off emotionally after the death of her teenage son. This includes pushing away her husband Mark who is spending a lot of time away from home. Patti's reluctant to temporarily take in young Emily, whose single mom is hospitalized. Based on the Donna Van Liere novel. **86m/C; DVD.** Madeleine Stowe; James Remar; Tori Barban; Devon Weigel; Ian Ziering; Rebecca Gibson; Phillip Jarrett; ***D:*** Norma Bailey; ***W:*** Wesley Bishop; ***C:*** Mathias Herndl; ***M:*** Lawrence Shragge. **CABLE**

A Christmas Horror Story ♪♪ **2015** Festively Christmas-themed horror anthology! Set on Christmas Eve, the four interwoven stories are related by a radio host. In one story, a family brings home a Christmas tree but finds it comes with something unexpected. In another, students making a documentary explore a high school basement where a massacre took place. The other two stories focus on the Christmas spirit known as Krampus terrorizes a local family and a Santa who must fight zombie elves. **99m/C; DVD, Blu-Ray, Streaming, Download.** William Shatner; George Buza; Rob Archer; Zoe De Grand Maison; Alex Ozerov; ***D:*** Grant Harvey; Steven Hoban; Brett Sullivan; ***W:*** James Kee; Sarah Larsen; Doug Taylor; Pascal Trottier; ***C:*** Gavin Smith; ***M:*** Alex Khaskin. **VIDEO**

Christmas in Boston ♪♪ **2005** ABC Family original. Gina and Seth became pen pals in the 6th grade but they've always exchanged photos of their better-looking friends Ellen and Matt. When Seth goes to Boston for a convention it seems the perfect first time to meet with Gina but there's still that big identity problem to resolve. **94m/C; DVD.** Marla Sokoloff; Patrick J. Adams; Lindy Booth; Jonathan Cherry; Shawn Lawrence; Art Hindle; ***D:*** Neill Fearnley; ***W:*** Stephanie Baxendale; ***C:*** Russ Goozee; ***M:*** Robert Carli. **CABLE**

Christmas in Canaan ♪♪ 1/2 **2009** Widower Daniel Burton (Cyrus) is struggling to hold his family and farm together in 1960s Texas in this Hallmark Channel family drama. Daniel is upset when racism enters into a school fight between his 10-year-old son DJ and black classmate Rodney. So Daniel and Rodney's grandmother Miss Eunice team up to set the boys straight. Eventually, one Christmas turns out to be particularly memorable (as you might guess from the title). Adapted from the book by Kenny Rogers and Donald Davenport. **96m/C; DVD.** Billy Ray Cyrus; Candus Churchill; Jaishon Fisher; Zak Ludwig; Matt Ward; Jacob Blair; Jessica McLeod; Darien Provost; Tom Heaton; ***D:*** Neill Fearnley; ***W:*** Donald Davenport; ***C:*** Michael Balfry; ***M:*** John Sereda. **CABLE**

Christmas in Compton ♪♪ 1/2 **2012 (PG-13)** Likable family/holiday comedy. Big Earl (David) runs a Christmas tree lot and is a longtime neighborhood mentor and supporter. He's running out of patience with his would-be music producer son Derrick (Gooding), who has no business sense. His latest act is ripped off by record exec Tommy Maxwell (Roberts), and Derrick tries returning the insult and things get complicated. **90m/C; DVD.** Keith David; Omar Gooding; Eric Roberts; Sheryl Lee Ralph; Miguel A. Nunez, Jr.; ***D:*** David Raynr; ***W:*** David Raynr; Suzanne Broderick; Robert Fedor; ***C:*** Sandra Valde-Hansen. **VIDEO**

Christmas in Connecticut ♪♪♪ *Indiscretion* **1945** Lightweight comedy about a housekeeping magazine's successful columnist who isn't quite the expert homemaker she presents herself to be. When a war veteran is invited to her home as part of a publicity gimmick, she must master the ways of housekeeping or reveal her incompetence. Stanwyck is winning in the lead role. Also available in a colorized version. **101m/B; VHS, DVD, Blu-Ray.** Barbara Stanwyck; Reginald Gardiner; Sydney Greenstreet; Dennis Morgan; S.Z. Sakall; Una O'Connor; Robert Shayne; Joyce Compton; ***D:*** Peter Godfrey.

Christmas in Connecticut ♪♪ **1992** Cannon hosts a weekly TV show as America's favorite homemaker/hostess. A local forest ranger (Kristofferson) becomes a hero by saving a little boy's life and her network stages a media event by inviting him to her home for a traditional Christmas dinner. There's only one problem: she can't cook. Schwarzenegger's directorial debut lacks challenge in this fluffy remake. See the original instead. **93m/C; VHS, DVD.** Dyan Cannon; Kris Kristofferson; Tony Curtis; Richard Roundtree; Kelly Cinnante; Gene Lithgow; Vivian Bonnell; ***D:*** Arnold Schwarzenegger; ***W:*** Janet Brownell. **CABLE**

Christmas In Conway ♪ 1/2 **2013** Garcia overdoes the grump factor in this tearjerking Hallmark Hall of Fame drama. Duncan Mayor refuses help in caring for his beloved, dying wife Suzy (Parker) but is finally forced to accept live-in hospice nurse Natalie (Moore). He then works to fulfill Suzy's last wish--to once again ride the Ferris wheel where Duncan proposed marriage. He buys a decrepit ride and starts reassembling the wheel in his backyard, upsetting his social-climbing neighbor (Oteri) who tries to stop the project. Parker's the only one to make a memorable impression. **90m/C; DVD.** Andy Garcia; Mary-Louise Parker; Mandy Moore; Riley Smith; Cheri Oteri; Ric Reitz; ***D:*** John Kent Harrison; ***W:*** Luis Ugaz; Stephen P. Lindsey; ***C:*** James Chressanthis; ***M:*** Geoff Zanelli. **TV**

Christmas in July ♪♪♪ 1/2 **1940** A young man goes on a spending spree when he thinks he's won a sweepstakes. Things take a turn for the worse when he finds out that it was all a practical joke. Powell provides a winning performance in this second film from comic master Sturges. **67m/B; VHS, DVD, Blu-Ray.** Dick Powell; Ellen Drew; Raymond Walburn; William Demarest; Franklin Pangborn; ***D:*** Preston Sturges.

Christmas in Paradise ♪♪ 1/2 **2007** A holiday cruise to San Juan is supposed to ease Christmas memories for widowed Dana Marino (Ross) and her two sons. Dan Casey (Ferguson) and his two daughters are also having problems since wife and mom Madeline (Martin) ran off with another man. The families start mingling and just when it looks like it will be a happy holiday, the unexpected happens. **90m/C; DVD.** Colin Ferguson; Charlotte Ross; Devon Werkheiser; Kenton Duty; Aria Wallace; Josie Loren; Martha Martin; ***D:*** Sheldon Larry; ***W:*** Matt Dorff; ***C:*** P.J. Lopez; ***M:*** David Resnik; Luis Marin. **CABLE**

Christmas in the Clouds ♪♪ 1/2 **2001 (PG)** Fun, screwball comedy set in a very upscale Native-American owned resort. The main characters all seem to bring a peculiar little twist to the story line. A writer from a prestigious travel guide publication is expected to make a surprise visit. Joe Clouds on Fire (Vlhos) has secretly been writing love letters to a pen pal, Tina (Tosca), who shows up to spy on her suitor only to be mistaken for the hotel critic. The actual critic, Stu O'Malley (Walsh), is a disheveled half-drunk grouch, and is shuffled to a small, cramped room. Very funny farce filmed in Utah's Sundance Resort. **97m/C; DVD.** Sam Vlahos; M. Emmet Walsh; Graham Greene; Sheila Tousey; Rosalind Ayres; Tim Vahle; MariAna Tosca; Jonathan Joss; ***D:*** Kate Montgomery; ***W:*** Kate Montgomery; ***C:*** Steven Bernstein; ***M:*** Rita Coolidge.

Christmas in Wonderland ♪♪ **2007 (PG)** The Saunders family has just moved to a new city and have no money, no friends, and no Christmas spirit. Then 12-year-old Brian and 6-year-old Mary find a bag of money at the mall and go on a shopping spree. Only the cash is counterfeit and the crooks want it back. **70m/C; DVD.** Patrick Swayze; Tim Curry; Chris Kattan; Carmen Electra; Preston Lacey; Matthew Knight; Amy Schlagel; Zoe Schlagel; ***D:*** James Orr; ***W:*** James Orr; Jim Cruickshank; ***C:*** Duane Manwiller; ***M:*** Terry Frewer. **VIDEO**

Christmas Lodge ♪♪ *Thomas Kinkade Presents: Christmas Lodge* **2011 (G)** A few too many coincidences hinder this faith-based family story. Mary Tole takes a trip with boyfriend Kent to the mountains and discovers the lodge where she spent childhood family holidays is now a dilapidated shell. Single dad Jack, whose family built the lodge, is struggling to rebuild and Mary just happens to do historical restoration and the Toles are in construction. Mary hopes to fulfill her grandfather's Christmas wish to celebrate at the lodge once again. **90m/C; DVD.** Erin Karpluk; Michael Shanks; Victoria Banks; Michelle Creber; Peter Benson; ***D:*** Terry Ingram; ***W:*** Renee de Roche; ***C:*** Anthony C. Metchie; ***M:*** Stu Goldberg. **VIDEO**

Christmas Magic ♪♪ **2011** Well, doesn't this sound like a Hallmark Channel holiday downer: New Yorker Carrie Bishop suffers head trauma in a nasty car accident and wakes up in Central Park with old-timer Henry telling her he's Carrie's guide into heaven. but to earn her wings, event planner Carrie needs to help widowed restaurant owner Scott save his business. Soon Carrie's falling for Scott and his cute-as-a-button young daughter but time isn't on her side. **87m/C; DVD.** Lindy Booth; Paul McGillion; Derek McGrath; Kiara Glasco; ***D:*** John Bradshaw; ***W:*** Joany Kane; Rickie Castaneda; ***C:*** Russ Goozee; ***M:*** Stacey Hersh. **CABLE**

Christmas Mail ♪♪ *We've Got Christmas Mail* **2010** Predictable but not unappealing Christmas fare. Officious postal boss Mr. Fuller is suspicious of new employee Kristi, who's been hired to answer children's letters to Santa. Disillusioned postman Matt, who's caring for his young niece Emily, is told by Fuller to keep an eye on Kristi. Emily writes to Santa and Matt becomes curious about Kristi's efforts to make the girl's wishes come true and her own secret (which is very easy to figure out). **90m/C; DVD.** Ashley Scott; A.J. Buckley; Lochlyn Munro; Piper Mackenzie Harris; Vanessa Lee Evigan; Ron Rogge; ***D:*** John Murlowski; ***W:*** Steven Palmer Peterson; ***C:*** Justin Duval. **VIDEO**

The Christmas Miracle of Jonathan Toomey ♪♪ 1/2 **2007** Reclusive woodcarver Jonathan Toomey (Berenger) is hired by widowed Susan McDowell (Richardson) to carve a replica of a nativity set (now lost) that was given to her son Thomas (Ward-Wilkinson) by his late father. But the work and the approaching holiday bring up painful memories for everyone that they must overcome in order to find hope in the season. **97m/C; DVD.** *GB* Tom Berenger; Joely Richardson; Ronald Pickup; Saoirse Ronan; Luke Ward-Wilinson; ***D:*** Bill Clark; ***W:*** Bill Clark; ***C:*** Emmanuel (Manu) Kadosh; ***M:*** Guy Farley. **VIDEO**

Christmas on Mars ♪ 1/2 **2008** Bizarre arthouse film based around the music of the Flaming Lips. The leader of a martian colony slowly goes insane while trying to keep up morale as the birth of the colonies' first child comes ever closer. **90m/C; DVD.** Steven Drozd; Wayne Coyne; Steve Burns; ***D:*** Wayne Coyne; Bradley Beesely; George Salisbury; ***W:*** Wayne Coyne; ***C:*** Bradley Beesely. **VIDEO**

The Christmas Ornament ♪♪ 1/2 **2013** Hallmark Channel drama. Widowed Kathy isn't interested in celebrating Christmas though she decides to continue her cookie baking and giving tradition. When Kathy meets shop owner Tim, he gives her a special ornament symbolizing hope and she tries to decide what her future holds. **90m/C; DVD.** Kellie Martin; Cameron Mathison; Jewel Staite; ***D:*** Mark Jean; ***W:*** J.B. White; ***C:*** Mathias Herndl; ***M:*** Michael Richard Plowman. **CABLE**

The Christmas Pageant 🦴🦴 ½ **2011** In this Hallmark Channel movie, overbearing Broadway director Vera Parks (Gilbert) gets fired (again) and can only find a job with a smalltown Christmas pageant. Turns out former fiance Jack (Mailhouse) recommended her and Vera discovers those romantic sparks rekindling. **87m/C; DVD.** Melissa Gilbert; Robert Mailhouse; Lennon Wynn; Edward Herrmann; Candice Azzara; ***D:*** David S. Cass, Sr.; ***W:*** Mark Valenti; ***C:*** James W. Wrenn; ***M:*** Nathan Wang. **CABLE**

A Christmas Proposal 🦴🦴 **2008 (PG)** Two lawyers fight over a proposal to turn a quaint mountain ski community into an all-year resort. Then they discover they were childhood sweethearts and when big city lawyer Rick has a car accident and is forced to stick around, the small town plus Lisa's presence finds him changing his mind about his current case. **90m/C; DVD.** Nicole Eggert; David O'Donnell; Tom Arnold; David DeLuise; Shannon Sturges; Sarah Thompson; Patty McCormack; ***D:*** Michael Feifer; ***W:*** Peter Sullivan; ***C:*** Mark Ritchie; ***M:*** Andres Boulton. **VIDEO**

The Christmas Shoes 🦴🦴 ½ **2002** Lawyer Robert Layton (Lowe) isn't feeling any Christmas cheer as his work commitments keep him from his family, including daughter Lily's (Marshall) choir concerts. Choir director Maggie Andrews (Williams) is terminally ill and her son Nathan (Morrow) wants to buy his mother a special pair of red shoes. Naturally, Robert and Nathan's lives will overlap to make the spirit of the season meaningful for them all. Still, this is a flick about a dying mom so it may be too sad for the youngest members of the family to view. Based on the novel by Donna Van Lieve. **100m/C; DVD.** Rob Lowe; Kimberly Williams; Max Morrow; Maria Del Mar; Hugh Thompson; Dorian Harewood; Shirley Douglas; Amber Marshall; ***D:*** Andy Wolk; ***W:*** Wesley Bishop; ***C:*** John Berrie; ***M:*** Lawrence Shragge. **TV**

A Christmas Story 🦴🦴🦴🦴 **1983 (PG)** Unlikely but winning comedy of Ralphie's (Billingsley) single-minded obsession to acquire a Red Ryder BB-gun for Christmas, and the obstacles that everyday life in 1940s Indiana can throw his way. Particularly great sequence involving an impatient department-store Santa. Fun for everyone. Based on "In God We Trust, All Others Pay Cash," an autobiographical story by Shepherd. Followed by "My Summer Story" in 1994, also from Shepherd's book. **95m/C; VHS, DVD, Blu-Ray, HD-DVD.** *CA US* Peter Billingsley; Darren McGavin; Melinda Dillon; Ian Petrella; Bob (Benjamin) Clark; Zack (Zach) Ward; Leslie (Les) Carlson; Scott Schwartz; R.D. Robb; Tedde Moore; Yano Ayana; ***Cameo(s):*** Jean Shepherd; ***Nar:*** Jean Shepherd; ***D:*** Bob (Benjamin) Clark; ***W:*** Bob (Benjamin) Clark; Leigh Brown; Jean Shepherd; ***C:*** Reginald Morris; ***M:*** Paul Zaza; Carl Zittrer. Genie '84: Director (Clark); Natl. Film Reg. '12.

A Christmas Story 2 🦴 **2012 (PG)** Derivative and cheap sequel to the 1983 holiday classic rightly went straight to video. Ralphie is almost 16 and dreams of owning a car. An accident means he needs a part-time job, which he gets during the holiday rush at Higbee's department store. Ralphie predicts disaster--and he's right. **85m/C; DVD, Blu-Ray.** Braeden Lemasters; Daniel Stern; Stacey Travis; David W. Thompson; David Buehrle; Valin Shinyei; ***D:*** Brian Levant; ***W:*** Nat Mauldin; ***C:*** Jan Kiesser; ***M:*** David Newman. **VIDEO**

A Christmas Tale 🦴🦴🦴 *Un Conte de Noel* **2008** When matriarch Junon is diagnosed with leukemia she uses the opportunity of the Christmas holiday to invite her bickering family home for a reunion in hopes one of them will be a match for a bone marrow transplant. Not exactly your typical warm and fuzzy American holiday fare; that's because it's French and is as dark as it sounds. Despite the premise, pic is buoyed by wit, humor (albeit dark) and excellent performances, namely from the legendary Deneuve. French with subtitles. **150m/C; Blu-Ray, On Demand.** *FR* Catherine Deneuve; Jean-Paul Roussillon; Mathieu Amalric; Chiara Mastroianni; Hippolyte Girardot; Anne Consigny; Melvil Poupaud; Emmanuelle Devos; Francoise Bertin; Emile Berling; Laurent Capelluto; ***D:*** Arnaud Desplechin; ***W:*** Arnaud Desplechin; Emmanuel Bourdieu; ***C:*** Eric Gautier; ***M:*** Gregoire Hetzel.

The Christmas That Almost Wasn't 🦴 ½ *Il Natale Che Quasi Non Fu* **1966 (G)** Loathsome humbug decides to destroy Christmas forever by removing Santa Claus from the North Pole. Crude Italian-made children's film nonetheless remembered fondly by a generation of kids. **95m/C; VHS, DVD.** *IT* Rossano Brazzi; Paul Tripp; Lidia Brazzi; Sonny Fox; Mischa Auer; ***D:*** Rossano Brazzi.

Christmas Town 🦴🦴 **2008 (G)** A week before Christmas, no-nonsense single mom Liz and her 9-year-old son Mason visit her estranged father who lives in a holiday-bedecked town that's amped up with the Christmas spirit. Her former banker dad is surprisingly working as a cook at the local cafe that's owned by Kevin, who seems to have been chosen by the community to be Liz's special gift. Meanwhile, Mason insists that Santa is actually living inside the local Christmas-themed corporation, North Pole, Inc., and he's determined to see the workshop, the elves, and Santa himself. **90m/C; DVD.** Nicole de Boer; Patrick Muldoon; Gig Morton; Garry Chalk; ***D:*** George Erschbamer; ***W:*** Ron McGee; ***M:*** Peter Allen. **VIDEO**

A Christmas Tree Miracle 🦴🦴 ½ **2013** The George family has always lived a life of suburban excess and self-involvement. Even after dad David loses his job, the family doesn't control their spending and eventually finds themselves homeless just before the holidays. Repaying a kindness, eccentric tree farmer Henry takes the family in and shows them the true meaning of the season. **102m/C; DVD.** Kevin Sizemore; Claudia Esposito; Barrett Carnahan; Emily Capehart; Siomha Kenney; Terry Kiser; ***D:*** J.W. (John Wayne) Myers; ***W:*** Ty DeMartino; ***C:*** Ryan Schlagbaum. **VIDEO**

A Christmas Wedding 🦴🦴 **2006** Pure holiday schmaltz. Emily (Paulson) and Ben (Mabius) met on Christmas Day, became engaged on Christmas Day, and are determined to be married on Christmas Day. Only perfectionist Emily must go away on a business trip and leave the wedding plans in the hands of procrastinating Ben. Naturally she gets stranded trying to get home and Ben finds everything bewildering (bridesmaids' shoes?) and falling apart around him. **90m/C; DVD.** Sarah Paulson; Eric Mabius; Dean Cain; Richard Blackburn; Reagan Pasternak; Art Hindle; Louise Pitre; Mimi Kuzyk; ***D:*** Michael Zinberg; ***W:*** Richard Cray; ***C:*** Derick Underschultz; ***M:*** David Schwartz. **CABLE**

A Christmas Wedding Tail 🦴🦴 ½ **2011** Sweet Hallmark Channel flick with a couple of talking dogs. Widowed mom Susan is trying to start a new life for her, her three sons, and their Labrador Rusty in a small California town. Rusty falls for poodle Cheri, owned by Jake, the local winery owner and a single dad of two girls. The dogs play matchmaker and a Christmas wedding is planned, but blending the families proves to be a challenge. **82m/C; DVD.** Jennie Garth; Brad Rowe; Tom Arnold; Catherine Hicks; Caia Coley; Bobbie Eakes; John Colton; ***V:*** Jay Mohr; Nikki Cox; ***D:*** Michael Feifer; ***W:*** Peter Sullivan; ***C:*** Hank Baumert, Jr. **CABLE**

The Christmas Wife 🦴🦴 ½ **1988** A lonely man pays a woman to be his holiday companion at a mountain retreat. Sturdy performances by Robards and Harris manage to keep this one from going to the dogs. Based on a story by Helen Norris. **73m/C; VHS, DVD.** Jason Robards, Jr.; Julie Harris; Don Francks; Patricia Hamilton; Deborah Grover; James Eckhouse; ***D:*** David Hugh Jones. **CABLE**

A Christmas Wish 🦴🦴 ½ **2011** Hallmark Channel holiday fare about hope and family. Martha Evans' wandering husband Cal takes off again, leaving her broke and homeless. She and their kids hit the road and after the car breaks down in a small town Martha moves them into a motel and begs diner owner Trudy to hire her as a waitress. They begin to settle in, and Martha catches the eye of handsome sheriff Joe, when Cal finds them and declares he wants his family back (again). **90m/C; DVD.** Kristy Swanson; Bart Johnson; Tess Harper; K.C. Clyde; Edward Herrmann; Kirstin Dorn; Kevin Herring, III; Danielle Chuchran; ***D:*** Craig Clyde; ***W:*** Craig Clyde; ***C:*** Brandon Christensen. **CABLE**

Christmas with Holly 🦴🦴 **2012** Sweet Hallmark Hall of Fame adaptation of "Christmas Eve at Friday Harbor" by Lisa Kleypas. Six-year-old Holly's mother died and left her in the care of her overwhelmed young Uncle Mark who takes her to live with his two brothers, Alex and Scott, in his hometown of Friday Harbor, where he runs a coffee shop. There he meets Maggie who, having been jilted at the altar, finally follows her heart and opens up a toy store on Main Street. Think Maggie, Mark, and Holly will all bond? **90m/C; DVD; Closed Captioned.** Sean Faris; Eloise Mumford; Daniel Eric Gold; Dana Watkins; Lucy Gallina; Alex Paxton-Beesley; ***D:*** Allan Arkush; ***W:*** P'nenah Goldstein; ***C:*** Charles Minsky; ***M:*** Nathan Wang. **TV**

Christmas With the Kranks 🦴 **2004 (PG)** After the two "Santa Clause" movies, Allen sticks with the holiday in this crass, slapstick comedy based on John Grisham's 2001 novel "Skipping Christmas." That is what Luther (a game Allen) and wife Nora (the ill-used Curtis) intend to do when their only daughter, Blair (Gonzalo), announces she won't be coming home to suburban Chicago for the holiday. Mr. Krank decides a nice Caribbean cruise is in order, but the duo find themselves the recipients of neighborhood scorn when they refuse to get in the seasonal spirit. That changes when Blair suddenly decides to return, accompanied by her brand-new fiance, and the Kranks cave in to Christmas commercialism with zealous glee. Pic is dedicated to the late Alan King, who was cast in a small role as Allen's boss. **98m/C; VHS, DVD, UMD.** Tim Allen; Jamie Lee Curtis; Dan Aykroyd; Erik Per Sullivan; Jake Busey; M. Emmet Walsh; Elizabeth Franz; Rene Lavan; Austin Pendleton; Patrick Breen; Felicity Huffman; Julie Gonzalo; Richard "Cheech" Marin; Kevin Chamberlain; Caroline Rhea; Arden Myrin; ***D:*** Joe Roth; ***W:*** Chris Columbus; ***C:*** Don Burgess; ***M:*** John Debney.

A Christmas Without Snow 🦴🦴 ½ **1980** A lonely divorced woman finds communal happiness within a local church choir led by a crusty choir master. **96m/C; VHS, DVD.** Michael Learned; John Houseman; Ramon Bieri; James Cromwell; Valerie Curtin; Ruth Nelson; Beah Richards; Calvin Levels; ***D:*** John Korty; ***M:*** Ed Bogas. **TV**

Christopher and His Kind 🦴🦴🦴 **2011** Excellently acted adaptation of Isherwood's memoir about his arrival in Berlin in the early 1930s, joining his friend and fellow writer W.H. Auden in the German capital of hedonism. Christopher (Smith) was eager to explore the gay underground (quite explicitly) while remaining self-involved and trying to ignore the rise of Nazism. Isherwood would fictionalize his experiences in the "Goodbye to Berlin" stories with fellow roominghouse boarder Jean Ross (Poots) transformed into cabaret singer Sally Bowles among others. **90m/C; DVD.** *GB* Matt Smith; Pip Carter; Toby Jones; Imogen Poots; Alexander Doetsch; Douglas Booth; Tom Wlashchiha; Lindsay Duncan; Perry Millward; ***D:*** Geoffrey Sax; ***W:*** Kevin Elyot; ***C:*** Kieran McGuigan; ***M:*** Dominik Scherrer. **TV**

Christopher Columbus 🦴🦴 ½ **1949** Step-by-step biography of the 15th-century explorer, his discovery of America, the fame that first greeted him, and his last days. **103m/C; VHS, DVD, Streaming.** *GB* Fredric March; Florence Eldridge; Francis L. Sullivan; ***D:*** David MacDonald.

Christopher Robin 🦴🦴 ½ **2018 (PG)** While Winnie the Pooh (Cummings) and friends happily live in the Hundred Acre Wood, an adult Christopher Robin (McGregor) resides in London and has a miserable job in a factory. The workaholic Christopher also has a strained relationship with his wife (Atwell) and daughter (Carmichael) and has not thought about Pooh in decades. That is, until the bear shows up to ask Christopher's help in finding Piglet (Mohammed), Eeyore (Garrett), and other friends. Christopher returns Pooh to his home, where he connects with his past and gains insight about his present. Despite memorable comic moments, the nostalgic film is rather dark for a family-oriented entertainment. **120m/C; DVD.** Ewan McGregor; Hayley Atwell; Bronte Carmichael; Mark Gatiss; Oliver Ford Davies; ***D:*** Marc Foster; ***W:*** Alex Ross Perry; Tom McCarthy; Allison Schroeder; ***C:*** Matthias Koenigswieser; ***M:*** Jon Brion; Geoff Zanelli.

Christopher Strong 🦴🦴 ½ **1933** Interesting Hepburn turn as a daredevil aviatrix who falls in love with a married British statesman. **77m/B; VHS, DVD.** Katharine Hepburn; Billie Burke; Colin Clive; Helen Chandler; ***D:*** Dorothy Arzner; ***M:*** Max Steiner.

Christy 🦴🦴 ½ **1994** Pilot movie for the TV series finds 19-year-old Christy Huddleston (Martin) leaving her privileged Southern life to teach school in the Great Smoky Mountains. It's 1912 in Cutter Gap, Tennessee, and her students are literally dirt poor, with ignorance and supersitition the norm. Christy's inspiration in Miss Alice (Daly), a middle-aged Quaker who runs the mission school. And Christy needs encouragement as she struggles to cope with her new life and responsibilities. Based on the novel by Catherine Marshall, which is a fictional biography of her mother. **90m/C; VHS, DVD.** Kellie Martin; Tyne Daly; Tess Harper; Randall Batinkoff; Annabelle Price; Stewart Finlay-McLennan; ***D:*** Michael Rhodes; ***M:*** Ron Ramin. **TV**

Chrome and Hot Leather 🦴 ½ **1971 (PG)** A Green Beret is out for revenge after vicious bikers kill his fiance. Conventional, tasteless genre fare notable only as Gaye's first film. **91m/C; VHS, DVD.** William (Bill) Smith; Tony Young; Michael Haynes; Peter Brown; Marvin Gaye; Michael Stearns; Kathrine Baumann; Wes Bishop; Herbert Jeffries; ***D:*** Lee Frost.

ChromeSkull: Laid to Rest 2 🦴🦴 **2011** Slasher sequel to 2009's "Laid to Rest." You can't keep a serial killer down, even when he's been shot and burned. Somewhat the worse for wear, ChromeSkull is back for more victims as he finds follower Preston has taken to tidying up the loose ends—and really enjoys the work. Gorehounds will again delight in the bloody mayhem. **93m/C; DVD, Blu-Ray.** Brian Austin Green; Thomas Dekker; Owain Yeoman; Nick Principe; Danielle Harris; Gail O'Grady; Mimi Michaels; Johnathon Schaech; ***D:*** Robert Hall; ***W:*** Robert Hall; ***C:*** Amanda Treyz; ***M:*** Leon Bradford; Lance Warlock. **VIDEO**

Chronic 🦴🦴 **2016 (R)** Tim Roth gives one of the best performances of his career, but this drama lets him down with a disastrously stupid final scene. Roth plays a caregiver to people literally on death's door. He's willing to do that which most people are not, including round-the-clock physical care for his dying patients. With excruciating detail and tenderness, we become attached to this man who we learn is punishing himself for perceived sins. Then the film pulls it all out with a twist ending. Turn it off 60 seconds before the end and it's a whole star higher. **93m/C; DVD.** Tim Roth; Elizabeth Tulloch; Michael Cristofer; Nailea Norvind; Sarah Sutherland; ***D:*** Michel Franco; ***W:*** Michel Franco; ***C:*** Yves Cape.

Chronically Unfeasible 🦴🦴 *Cronicamente Inviavel* **2000** Social satire takes on the Brazilian middleclass as six disparate characters meet in a restaurant in Sao Paulo, struggling with political, class, sexual, and economic issues. Portuguese with subtitles. **101m/C; VHS, DVD.** *BR* Patrick Alencar; Leonardo Vieira; Umberto Magnani; Betty Gofman; Daniel Dantas; Dira Paes; Dan Stulbach; Cecil Thire; ***D:*** Sergio Bianchi; ***W:*** Sergio Bianchi; Gustavo Steinberg; ***C:*** Marcelo Coutinho; Antonio Penido.

Chronicle 🦴🦴🦴 **2012 (PG-13)** Taking the trend of handheld camera cinematography to a new genre, director Trank's debut examines the lives of a group of teenagers who develop superhuman powers. Andrew (DeHaan), Matt (Russell), and Steve (Jordan) make a discovery that grants the average teenagers very non-average abilities, including the power to move things with their minds. Of course, as in most superhero tales, with great power comes great responsibility, and the actions of one member of the trio leads to intense drama. Surprisingly tight and well-made—a genre success given its limited aspirations. **83m/C; DVD, Blu-Ray.** Dane DeHaan; Alex Russell; Michael B. Jordan; Michael Kelly; Ashley Hinshaw; ***D:*** Josh Trank; ***W:*** Max Landis; ***C:*** Matthew Jensen.

Chronicle of a Boy Alone 🦴🦴 *Chronicle of a Lonely Child; Cronica de un Nino Solo* **1964** Eleven-year-old Polin is abandoned by his family and sent to live in a state-run orphanage where well-meaning administrators succeed in destroying the childrens' lives. Spanish with subtitles. **86m/C; VHS, DVD.** *AR* Oscar Espindola; Beto Gianola; Victoriano Moreira; Leonardo Favio; *D:* Leonardo Favio; *W:* Leonardo Favio; *C:* Ignacio Souto.

Chronicle of an Escape *Cronica de una Fuga; Buenos Aires, 1977* **2006 (R)** This brutal look at Argentina's "dirty war" is based on a true story. Soccer player Claudio Tamburrini (de la Serna) is falsely accused of being part of a liberal activist underground. Kidnapped off the streets in Buenos Aires by military thugs, he's taken to a secret government facility that holds dozens of people suspected of anti-government activities. Interrogated and tortured, Claudio realizes his death is a certainty unless he can escape. Spanish with subtitles. **104m/C; DVD.** *AR* Rodrigo de la Serna; Pablo Echarri; Nazareno Casero; Martin Urruty; Lautaro Delgado; Matias Marmorato; *D:* Adrian Caetano; *W:* Adrian Caetano; Esteban Student; Julian Loyola; *C:* Julian Apezteguia; *M:* Ivan Wyszogrod.

Chronicle of the Raven *Jennifer's Shadow* **2004 (R)** Fairly atmospheric horror flick finds Jennifer (Phillips) traveling to Buenos Aires after she inherits the house of her recently deceased twin. Her sinister grandmother, Mary Ellen (a theatrical Dunaway), who also lives there, doesn't want Jennifer to sell the place. Suddenly, Jennifer begins having nightmares about being attacked by flesh-eating ravens and discovers strange wounds when she wakes up. Seems Granny isn't above killing her kin to get her way. **90m/C; DVD.** *US AR* Gina Philips; Faye Dunaway; Duilio Marzio; Hilda Bernard; Nicolas Pauls; *D:* Daniel De La Vega; Pablo Pares; *W:* Daniel De La Vega; Pablo Pares; *C:* Monty Rowan; Robin Melhuish; *M:* Micha Liberman.

The Chronicles of Narnia **1989** Exceptional BBC production of the C.S. Lewis fantasy about four brave children who battle evil in a mythical land where the animals talk and strange creatures roam the countryside. In three volumes; aired on PBS as part of the "Wonderworks" family movie series. **180m/C; VHS, DVD.** *GB* Barbara Kellerman; Jeffrey S. (Jeff) Perry; Richard Dempsey; Sophie Cook; Jonathan Scott; Sophie Wilcox; David Thwaites; Tom Baker; *D:* Alex Kirby. **TV**

The Chronicles of Narnia: Prince Caspian **2008 (PG)** As is often the case with sequels, this one is darker and more conventional. The Pevensie siblings (Henley, Keynes, Moseley, Popplewell) are transported from war-torn 1940s London to war-torn Narnia some 1300 years after they left. They discover that the Telmarines have conquered the original Narnians and their ruthless ruler, King Miraz (Castellitto), has driven the survivors, including his nephew, Prince Caspian (Barnes), the rightful heir, into the woods. Caspian and the sibs rally the denizens, and some big (albeit PG-rated) battles ensue, while lion Aslan (voiced by Neeson) turns up, offering bits of wise counsel. The series' religious allegories have been toned down even farther and the CGI visual effects heightened while events are set up for the next installment. **140m/C; Blu-Ray, On Demand.** Georgie Henley; Skander Keynes; William Moseley; Anna Popplewell; Sergio Castellitto; Pierfrancesco Favino; Peter Dinklage; Warwick Davis; Ben Barnes; Tilda Swinton; *V:* Liam Neeson; Eddie Izzard; *D:* Andrew Adamson; *W:* Andrew Adamson; Christopher Markus; Stephen McFeely; *C:* Karl Walter Lindenlaub; *M:* Harry Gregson-Williams.

The Chronicles of Narnia: The Lion, the Witch and the Wardrobe 1/2 **2005 (PG)** "Shrek" director Adamson turns C.S. Lewis' children's classic into a "Lord of the Rings" meets "Veggie Tales" adventure-allegory for kids. The four Pevensie siblings stumble into a magical wardrobe that transports them to the wonderful world of Narnia, a fairy tale kingdom torn between the evil White Witch (Swinton, in the film's best role) and the messianic lion Aslan (Neeson). Adamson stays faithful to the book, but bolsters the eye candy factor with lots of PG-friendly battles between fauns, unicorns, and giants. Fun stuff for seven-year-olds, but if you're a grown-up, you'll be rolling your eyes at the heavy-handed religious allusions and cut-rate CGI effects. **139m/C; DVD, Blu-Ray, UMD.** Tilda Swinton; Anna Popplewell; James McAvoy; Jim Broadbent; James Cosmo; Judy McIntosh; Elizabeth Hawthorne; Georgie Henley; Skander Keynes; William Moseley; Kiran Shah; *V:* Liam Neeson; Ray Winstone; Dawn French; Rupert Everett; Sim Evan-Jones; Cameron Rhodes; Philip Steuer; Jim May; *D:* Andrew Adamson; *W:* Andrew Adamson; Ann Peacock; Christopher Markus; Stephen McFeely; *C:* Donald McAlpine; *M:* Harry Gregson-Williams. Oscars '05: Makeup; British Acad. '05: Makeup.

The Chronicles of Narnia: The Voyage of the Dawn Treader **2010 (PG)** The third trip back to Narnia for Edmund, Lucy, now in their mid-teens, and their young cousin Eustace. This time around they find themselves dangerously entering the magical world through a painting of the Dawn Treader out at sea. Captain Caspian (Barnes) explains that Narnia is threatened by forces from the mysterious Dark Island, and that seven lost swords representing the Lords of Telmar must be found again to break an evil spell. New director Apted successfully disguises a slightly incoherent storyline with a skilled eye for the mystical landscape and terrific 3D special effects. Loads of swashbuckling adventure, but skimps on character here and there. **113m/C; Blu-Ray, On Demand.** Georgie Henley; Skander Keynes; Will Poulter; Ben Barnes; Gary Sweet; Bruce Spence; William Moseley; Anna Popplewell; *V:* Liam Neeson; Simon Pegg; *D:* Michael Apted; *W:* Christopher Markus; *C:* Dante Spinotti; *M:* David Arnold.

The Chronicles of Riddick *Pitch Black 2: Chronicles of Riddick* **2004 (PG-13)** Riddick (of "Pitch Black" fame) is back in this overstuffed compilation of cliched space shenanigans. The fascist Necromongers, led by Lord Marshall (Feore), have one edict: join us or we destroy your planet. Dame Judi Dench goes slumming as an ethereal prophetess named Aereon, who predicts that Riddick (Diesel again) will once again (if reluctantly) be a big hero. Diesel scowls a lot and then goes about saving the galaxy with a lot of big battles but not much gore given the MPAA rating. All acting is subordinate to the action anyway, but Newton swans about nicely as a devious wife who thinks her hubby (Urban) should be head creep. **119m/C; VHS, DVD, Blu-Ray, UMD, HD-DVD.** Vin Diesel; Dame Judi Dench; Thandie Newton; Colm Feore; Karl Urban; Linus Roache; Nick (Nicholas) Chinlund; Keith David; Alexa Davalos; Yorick Van Wageningen; *D:* David N. Twohy; *W:* David N. Twohy; *C:* Hugh Johnson; *M:* Graeme Revell.

Chrysalis **2007 (PG-13)** Hard-boiled French Police Detective David Hoffman (Dupontel) watches as his wife and partner are killed by notorious human trafficker Dimitry Nikolov (Figlarz). Years later while investigating the death of an illegal immigrant, he is led to the doors of a plastic surgery clinic whose lead surgeon is researching human memory and identity. He also has links to Dimitry, and Detective Hoffman finds there are worse things than simple human trafficking as he begins his quest for revenge. **91m/C; DVD.** *FR* Albert Dupontel; Marie Guillard; Marthe Keller; Mélanie Thierry; Claude Peron; Alain Figlarz; Smadi Wolfman; Patrick Bauchau; Guy Lecluyse; Cyril Lecomte; Francis Renaud; Manon Chevallier; Estelle Lefebure; *D:* Julien Leclercq; *W:* Franck Philipon; *C:* Thomas Hardmeier; *M:* Jean-Jacques Hertz; Francois Roy.

Chubasco 1/2 **1967** Wayward title character (Jones) chooses to work aboard a San Diego tuna boat rather than go to jail. Back home, protective father Sebastian (Egan) isn't pleased about Chubasco's romance with his innocent daughter Bunny (Strasberg). Both Strasberg and Jones, who were married at the time, look too old for their teenager roles in this routine troubled youth drama. **100m/C; DVD.** Christopher Jones; Susan Strasberg; Richard Egan; Ann Sothern; Simon Oakland; Audrey Totter; Edward Binns; *D:* Allen Miner; *W:* Allen Miner; *C:* Louis Jennings; Paul Ivano; *M:* William Lava.

Chuck 1/2 **2017 (R)** The true story of Chuck "The Bayonne Bleeder" Wepner, whose bout with Muhammad Ali was Sylvester Stallone's inspiration for Rocky Balboa. Set in the 1970s, this flick chronicles Chuck's rise to fame, thanks to the movie *Rocky*, and his subsequent fall from it when he's unable to keep himself relevant in the boxing world. Schreiber delivers a knock-out performance as the warm, funny, and empathetic lead. **98m/C; DVD.** Liev Schreiber; Naomi Watts; Elisabeth Moss; Ron Perlman; Jim Gaffigan; *D:* Philippe Falardeau; *W:* Liev Schreiber; Jeff Feuerzeig; Jerry Stahl; Michael Cristofer; *C:* Nicolas Bolduc; *M:* Corey A. Jackson.

Chuck & Buck 1/2 **2000 (R)** In the mood for a pseudo-comedy about a stalking homosexual idiot man-child? Buck (White), the childhood friend from hell, attempts to latch back onto former pal Chuck (Chris Weitz) after a reunion at the funeral of Buck's mother. Apparently, Chuck and Buck shared a furtive moment of experimental sexuality as kids, and Buck never advanced emotionally beyond this point. So when Chuck (who, being an adult, prefers being called Charles) and his fiancee Carlyn (Colt) casually invite Buck to their home in L.A., he drops everything in order to rekindle his imagined affair with the poor guy. After Chuck tells him to stay away, Buck writes and produces an uncomfortably transparent play titled "Hank & Frank" about their relationship, hiring a Chuck look-alike (Paul Weitz, brother of the lead) as his love interest. White manages to keep a sense of innocence in portraying Buck, but the overwhelming creepiness of the plot overrides any sense of subtlety in the performances. **99m/C; VHS, DVD.** Mike White; Chris Weitz; Paul Weitz; Lupe Ontiveros; Paul Sand; Beth Colt; Maya Rudolph; Mary Wigmore; Gino Buccola; *D:* Miguel Arteta; *W:* Mike White; *C:* Chuy Chavez; *M:* Joey Waronker. Natl. Bd. of Review '00: Support. Actress (Ontiveros).

Chuck Berry: Hail! Hail! Rock 'n' Roll **1987 (PG)** Engaging, energetic portrait of one of rock's founding fathers, via interviews, behind-the-scenes footage and performance clips of Berry at 60. Songs featured: "Johnny B. Goode," "Roll Over Beethoven," "Maybelline," and more. Appearances by Keith Richards, Eric Clapton, Etta James, John and Julian Lennon, Roy Orbison, Linda Ronstadt, Bo Diddley and Bruce Springsteen among others. **121m/C; VHS, DVD.** Chuck Berry; Eric Clapton; Etta James; Robert Cray; Julian Lennon; Keith Richards; Linda Ronstadt; John Lennon; Roy Orbison; Bo Diddley; Jerry Lee Lewis; Bruce Springsteen; Kareem Abdul-Jabbar; *D:* Taylor Hackford.

C.H.U.D. WOOF! **1984 (R)** Cannibalistic Humanoid Underground Dwellers are what it's about. Exposed to toxic wastes, a race of flesh-craving, sewer-dwelling monstrosities goes food shopping on the streets of New York. Don't be fooled by the presence of real actors, this one is inexcusable. Followed by a sequel. **90m/C; VHS, DVD, Blu-Ray.** John Heard; Daniel Stern; Christopher Curry; Kim Greist; John Goodman; Jay Thomas; Eddie Jones; Sam McMurray; Justin Hall; Cordis Heard; Michael O'Hare; Vic Polizos; *D:* Douglas Cheek; *W:* Parnell Hall; *C:* Peter Stein; *M:* David A. Hughes.

Chuka 1/2 **1967** A gunfighter tries to resolve a conflict between Indians and unlikeable troops while simultaneously romancing the fort's beautiful occupant. Pedestrian western features convincing playing from the always reliable Taylor. **105m/C; DVD.** Rod Taylor; Ernest Borgnine; John Mills; Luciana Paluzzi; James Whitmore; Angela Dorian; Louis Hayward; Michael Cole; Hugh Reilly; *D:* Gordon Douglas; *W:* Richard Jessup; *C:* Harold E. Stine; *M:* Leith Stevens.

The Chumscrubber 1/2 **2005 (R)** The unfortunate title refers to a videogame avenger who appears a la the creepy rabbit in "Donnie Darko" throughout this smug satire. Brooding SoCal teen Dean (Bell)?yes, think James—fails to tell anyone that his best friend, Troy (Janowicz), has hung himself in his bedroom. Problem is, Troy was the local drug supplier and when word does get out, his fellow high school scuzzballs expect Dean to find Troy's stash or else. Depiction of self-satisfied suburbia and teen angst has been better told elsewhere. **102m/C; DVD.** Jamie Bell; Camilla Belle; Justin Chatwin; Glenn Close; Rory Culkin; Tim DeKay; William Fichtner; Ralph Fiennes; Caroline Goodall; John Heard; Lauren Holly; Jason Isaacs; Allison Janney; Carrie-Anne Moss; Lou Taylor Pucci; Rita Wilson; Thomas Curtis; Richard Gleason; Josh Janowicz; *D:* Arie Posin; *W:* Zac Stanford; *C:* Lawrence Sher; *M:* James Horner.

Chungking Express *Hong Kong Express; Chongqing Senlin* **1995 (PG-13)** Director Kar-wai presents two quirky tales of loneliness and love, loosely linked by a snack bar in the tourist section of Hong Kong. Cops and drugs are still a part of the storyline, but this is no chop-socky action movie. Both male protagonists are cops, identified only by their badge numbers, who have recently been dumped by their girlfriends. One has a fixation for canned pineapple and expiration dates, the other talks to the inanimate objects in his apartment. The women they eventually fall for are a blonde-wigged heroin dealer and a shy counter girl who bops to "California Dreaming" after breaking in and cleaning the cop's apartment without his knowledge. Shot commando-style in 23 days during the hiatus of Wong's "Ashes of Time" without permits or professional lighting. The high energy is reflected in the pacing and acting performances. Chosen by Quentin Tarantino as the first release of his Miramax-backed Rolling Thunder imprint. **102m/C; VHS, DVD, Blu-Ray.** *CH* Brigitte Lin; Takeshi Kaneshiro; Tony Leung Chiu-Wai; Faye Wong; Valerie Chow; Piggy Chan; *D:* Wong Kar-Wai; *W:* Wong Kar-Wai; *C:* Christopher Doyle; Lau Wai-Keung; *M:* Frankie Chan; Roel A. Garcia.

Chunhyang 1/2 **2000** Romance based on a 13th-century folktale of forbidden love. Chunhyang (Lee) is the educated daughter of a courtesan who is expected to be a plaything for wealthy gentlemen. Instead, she falls in love and secretly marries the higher-caste Mongryong (Cho), who leaves his bride to complete his studies in Seoul. Chunhyang is soon beset by advances from the new governor and, when she refuses, he sentences her to death. Korean with subtitles. **120m/C; VHS, DVD.** *NK* Hyo Jung Lee; Seung Woo Cho; Jung Hun Lee; Sung Nyu Kim; *D:* Kwon Taek Im; *W:* Myoung Kon Kim; *C:* Il Sung Jung; *M:* Jung Gil Kim.

Chupacabra Terror 1/2 *Chupacabra: Dark Seas* **2005 (R)** A mythical beast, the Chupacabra, is caught in the Caribbean by cryptozoologist Dr. Pena, who somehow figures that transporting the evil brute on a cruise ship is a good idea. Carnage ensues for everyone on-board upon its escape. **88m/C; VHS, DVD.** John Rhys-Davies; Giancarlo Esposito; Dylan Neal; Paula Shaw; Chelan Simmons; David Millbern; Steve Jankowski; *D:* John Shepphird; *W:* John Shepphird; Steve Jankowski. **VIDEO**

Chupacabra vs. the Alamo **2013** Syfy Channel silliness. DEA agent Carlos Seguin finds drug cartel corpses with their throats ripped out and he and his partner, Tracy Taylor, discover that the legendary chupacabra are using the drug tunnels to make their way from Mexico to San Antonio. So Carlos, Tracy, Carlos' estranged son, Tommy, and some of his street gang make a stand against the bloodthirsty creatures at the Alamo. **88m/C; DVD.** Erik Estrada; Julia Benson; Jorge Vargas; Zak Santiago; Aleks Paunovic; *D:* Terry Ingram; *W:* Peter Sullivan; *C:* Anthony C. Metchie; *M:* Stu Goldberg. **CABLE**

The Church *La Chiesa* **1998** Italian thrill-meister Argento scripted and produced this ecclesiastical gorefest. A gargoyle-glutted gothic cathedral which happens to stand on the site of a gruesome mass murder is renovated, and the kirk-cleaning turns into a special-effects loaded demonic epiphany. It'll have you muttering your pater noster. Unrated, it's also available in an R-rated version. **102m/C; VHS, DVD.** *IT* Tomas Arana; Hugh Quarshie; Feodor Chaliapin, Jr.; Barbara Cupisti; Antonella Vitale; Asia Argento; *D:* Michele (Michael) Soavi; *W:* Dario Argento; Michele (Michael) Soavi; Franco Ferrini; *C:* Renato Tafuri; *M:* Keith Emerson.

The Church Mouse 1/2 **1934** Lively British comedy with a Cinderella plot. Betty Miller (La Plante) is hired by prominent banker Jonathan Steele (Hunter) as his secretary because she's efficient but dowdy and he tends to fall for his female staff. But eventually Betty gets a makeover and oh, my! **75m/B; DVD.** *GB* Laura La Plante; Ian Hunter; Jane Carr; Edward Chapman; Clifford Heatherley; Montague (Monty) Banks; John Batten; *D:* Montague (Monty) Banks; *W:* Scott Darling; Tom Geraghty; *C:* Basil Emmett.

Churchill 🦴🦴 1/2 **2017 (PG)** A behind-the-scenes study of British Prime Minister Winston Churchill in the days before the D-Day landings in Normandy in June 1944. Churchill, plagued by depression, self-doubt, and obsession over his legacy, clashes with other Allied leaders over the impending military campaign, which he fears will be a repeat of World War I's disastrous Battle of Gallipoli. Cox delivers a convincing performance as the often-unlikable titular character, as does Richardson as his rock-steady wife, but von Tunzelmann's dialogue is alternatingly simplistic and grandiose, undercutting the gravitas of the events at play. **105m/C; DVD.** Brian Cox; Miranda Richardson; John Slattery; Julian Wadham; Richard Durden; *D:* Jonathan Teplitzky; *W:* Alex von Tunzelmann; *C:* David Higgs; *M:* Lorne Balfe.

Chutney Popcorn 🦴🦴 1/2 **1999** Amusing and touching comedy about family ties and cultural differences. Reena (Ganatra) is a New York photographer from a very traditional East Indian immigrant family. Her mother Meenu (Jaffrey) is already upset because her daughter is a lesbian but Reena has a chance to get in her good graces when she impulsively agrees to act as a surrogate for her married older sister Sarita (Jaffrey), who is infertile. But the plan upsets Reena's girlfriend Lisa (Hennessy) and then Sarita has her own change of heart, even though Reena is now pregnant. **93m/C; VHS, DVD.** Nisha Ganatra; Jill(ian) Hennessey; Madhur Jaffrey; Sakina Jaffrey; Nick (Nicholas) Chinlund; Cara Buono; Ajay Naidu; Priscilla Lopez; *D:* Nisha Ganatra; *W:* Nisha Ganatra; Susan Carnival; *C:* Erin King; *M:* Karsh Kale.

C.I.A.: Code Name Alexa 🦴 1/2 **1992 (R)** Alexa is the beautiful and deadly protege of Victor, who heads an international crime ring. A CIA agent decides the best way to stop Victor is to turn Alexa against her boss. Lots of action and violence. **93m/C; VHS, DVD.** Kathleen Kinmont; Lorenzo Lamas; Alex Cord; O.J. Simpson; Stephen Quadros; Pamela Dixon; Michael Smith; *D:* Joseph Merhi.

C.I.A. 2: Target Alexa 🦴🦴 **1994** When a nuclear guidance system is stolen from a government facility CIA agent Mark Graver (Lamas) reteams with former terrorist Alexa (Kinmont) to retrieve the system from international terrorist Franz Klug (Savage). Complicating things are ex-CIA agent Straker (Ryan), who now heads his own commando army and wants to sell the device to the highest bidder. **90m/C; VHS, DVD.** Lorenzo Lamas; Kathleen Kinmont; John Savage; John P. Ryan; Pamela Dixon; Larry Manetti; *D:* Lorenzo Lamas; *W:* Michael January.

A Ciambra 🦴🦴 1/2 **2017** A dramatic exploration of the life of a teenage Romani gypsy on the brink of manhood. Living with his large extended family, Pio (Amato) spends much of his time in bars and nightclubs. Rarely having fun, he tries to pull off scams like his hardened older brother, who steals cars for a local crime boss. Pio's criminal enterprises rarely result in much money, but demonstrate that he has few choices in life. Featuring non-actors using their real names and playing semi-fictionalized versions of themselves, the film's sure-handed director finds depth in Pio's story and expressively uses his camera to add local color. **118m/C; Blu-Ray, Streaming.** *BR FR GE IT SW US* Pio Amato; Koudous Seihon; Damiano Amato; *D:* Jonas Carpignano; *W:* Jonas Carpignano; *C:* Tim Curtin; *M:* Dan Romer.

Ciao, Professore! 🦴🦴 1/2 *Io Speriamo Che Me La Cavo* **1994 (R)** Okay comedy about conventional teacher Marco Sperelli (Villaggio), from northern Italy, who is mistakenly sent to a ramshackle village school in Naples, populated by poor, wily, unruly students. Both, of course, manage to learn from each other. Humor derived from northern vs. southern Italian culture clash may bypass most viewers although the cast of amateur kid actors provide charm. Italian with subtitles. **91m/C; VHS, DVD.** *IT* Paolo Villaggio; Isa Danieli; Ciro Esposito; *D:* Lina Wertmuller; *W:* Leonardo Benvenuti; Piero De Bernardi; Alessandro Bencivenni; Domenico Saverni; Lina Wertmuller.

The Cider House Rules 🦴🦴🦴 **1999 (PG-13)** Homer Wells (Maguire) grows up in the St. Clouds, Maine orphanage, with his mentor, Dr. Larch (Caine), teaching Homer everything about caring for the children, delivering babies, and performing (illegal) abortions (which Homer refuses to do). But, in 1943, when flyboy Wally (Rudd) shows up with girlfriend Candy (Theron), Homer gets his chance to see something of the world. He winds up as an apple picker and, when Wally returns to the war, Candy's new beau. But Homer has a lot of lessons to learn about making—and living by—your own rules. Irving wrote his first screenplay from his novel. Old-fashioned, coming of age story with excellent performances. **125m/C; VHS, DVD.** Tobey Maguire; Charlize Theron; Michael Caine; Delroy Lindo; Paul Rudd; Erykah Badu; Kathy Baker; Jane Alexander; Kieran Culkin; Kate Nelligan; K. Todd Freeman; Dwight "Heavy D" Myers; J.K. Simmons; Erik Per Sullivan; Evan Dexter Parke; ***Cameo(s):*** John Irving; *D:* Lasse Hallstrom; *W:* John Irving; *C:* Oliver Stapleton; *M:* Rachel Portman. Oscars '99: Adapt. Screenplay, Support. Actor (Caine); Screen Actors Guild '99: Support. Actor (Caine).

Cider with Rosie 🦴🦴 1/2 **1999** Adaptation of Laurie Lee's 1959 story about his Cotswolds childhood. Set in 1918, in the Slad Valley, disorganized Annie Lee (Stevenson) has been left to raise nine children on her own. Laurie's childhood consists of school, church, village festivals, eccentric relations and neighbors, and the usual childhood tribulations. Lee himself provided narration before his death at 82 in 1997. **120m/C; VHS, DVD.** *GB* Juliet Stevenson; Emily Mortimer; Joe Roberts; Dashiell Reece; David Troughton; Robert Lang; Hugh Lloyd; *D:* Charles Beeson; *W:* John Mortimer; *C:* Rex Maidment; *M:* Geoffrey Burgon. **TV**

The Cigarette Girl of Mosselprom 🦴🦴 1/2 **1924** A lowly cigarette girl is thrust into the world of moviemaking in this sharp Russian satire. Silent with orchestral score. **78m/B; Silent; VHS, DVD, Streaming.** *RU* Yulia Solntseva; Igor Ilyinsky; Nikolai Tseretelli; Anna Dmokhovskaya; Leonid Baratov; M. Tsybulsky; *D:* Yuri Zhelyabuzhsky; *W:* Aleksey Fajko; Fedor Ozep; *C:* Yuri Zhelyabuzhsky.

Cimarron 🦴🦴 **1931** Hopelessly overblown saga of an American frontier family from 1890 to 1915. Hokey, cliched, with only sporadic liveliness. How did this one win an Oscar? An adaptation of Edna Ferber's novel, featuring Dunne in an early major role. Remade in 1960. **130m/B; VHS, DVD.** Richard Dix; Irene Dunne; Estelle Taylor; Nance O'Neil; William "Buster" Collier, Jr.; Roscoe Ates; George E. Stone; Stanley Fields; Edna May Oliver; Dennis O'Keefe; *D:* Wesley Ruggles; *M:* Max Steiner. Oscars '31: Adapt. Screenplay, Art Dir./Set Dec., Art Dir./Set Dec. (Ree), Film.

Cimarron 🦴🦴 1/2 **1960** Director Mann's remake of the 1931 Academy Award-winning film about frontier life in Oklahoma. This version features Ford as a carefree survivor of the Old West with an extreme case of wanderlust. Schell plays his civilizing wife. Based on Edna Ferber's novel. **140m/C; VHS, DVD, Blu-Ray.** Glenn Ford; Maria Schell; Anne Baxter; Arthur O'Connell; Russ Tamblyn; Mercedes McCambridge; Vic Morrow; Robert Keith; Charles McGraw; *D:* Anthony Mann; *W:* Arnold Schulman; *M:* Franz Waxman.

The Cincinnati Kid 🦴🦴 1/2 **1965** Gambler "The Cincinnati Kid" (McQueen) is hustling card games in New Orleans when he comes up against the veteran cardshark Lancey Howard (Robinson). During a marathon card game, Kid notices dealer Shooter (Malden) is throwing the game his way but he only wants to win fair and square. Conventional fare, with Ann-Margaret around for some conventional romance, helped along by serviceable performances and some stunning cinematography. **104m/C; VHS, DVD, Blu-Ray.** Steve McQueen; Edward G. Robinson; Ann-Margret; Tuesday Weld; Karl Malden; Joan Blondell; Rip Torn; Jack Weston; Cab Calloway; *D:* Norman Jewison; *W:* Ring Lardner, Jr.; Terry Southern; *C:* Philip H. Lathrop; *M:* Lalo Schifrin. Natl. Bd. of Review '65: Support. Actress (Blondell).

Cinderella 🦴🦴🦴 1/2 **1950** Classic Disney animated fairytale about the slighted beauty who outshines her evil stepsisters at a royal ball, then returns to her grim existence before the handsome prince finds her again. Engaging film, with a wicked stepmother, kindly fairy godmother, and singing mice. **76m/C; VHS, DVD, Blu-Ray.** *V:* Ilene Woods; William Phipps; Verna Felton; James MacDonald; *D:* Wilfred Jackson. Natl. Film Reg. '18; Venice Film Fest. '50: Special Jury Prize.

Cinderella 🦴🦴 1/2 **1964** Charming musical version of the fairy tale as scored by Rodgers and Hammerstein. Warren is lovely as Cinderella, Damon is a handsome prince, and Holm is a perfect fairy godmother. **83m/C; VHS, DVD.** Lesley Ann Warren; Ginger Rogers; Walter Pidgeon; Stuart Damon; Celeste Holm; *D:* Charles S. Dubin; *W:* Joseph Schrank; *M:* Richard Rodgers. **TV**

Cinderella 🦴🦴 1/2 *Rodgers & Hammerstein's Cinderella* **1997** Disney does some multiracial casting in this lavish, latest TV version of the fairytale. Norwood is sweetly sincere in the title role, with Houston as her diva-like Fairy Godmother. Peters camps as wicked stepmama, Goldberg's the Prince's mother, and the Prince is handsome newcomer Montalban. And Alexander gets the role of comic relief as the princely confidante, Lionel. The Rodgers and Hammerstein score, written for the 1957 TV version, has been augmented with other Richard Rodgers tunes. **92m/C; VHS, DVD.** Brandy Norwood; Whitney Houston; Paolo Montalban; Jason Alexander; Bernadette Peters; Whoopi Goldberg; Victor Garber; *D:* Robert Iscove; *W:* Robert Freedman. **TV**

Cinderella 🦴 1/2 *Cinderella 3D; Cendrillon au Far West* **2012 (PG)** A bizarre retelling of the classic tale set in a faux Wild West full of funny animal people and gorilla pirates. **81m/C; DVD, Blu-Ray, Streaming.** *FR V:* Alexandra Lamy; Yolande Moreau; Isabelle Nanty; Antoine de Caunes; Michel Boujenah; *D:* Pascal Herold; *W:* Pascal Herold; *M:* Zagaraf. **VIDEO**

Cinderella 🦴🦴 1/2 **2015 (PG)** Disney continues to mine their own history for updates of their most famous characters with this live-action riff on the princess with the missing shoe. The film is remarkably old-fashioned and arguably dull (why not just watch the classic cartoon?) but director Branagh brings some class, taking it seriously as a costume drama more than a kid's film. It certainly helps to have the always-great Blanchett as the Wicked Stepmother and James makes a Cinderella who is easy to root for. In the end, it's not awful but the slipper doesn't quite fit. **105m/C; DVD, Blu-Ray.** Cate Blanchett; Lily James; Richard Madden; Helena Bonham Carter; Sophie McShera; Holliday Grainger; Derek Jacobi; *D:* Kenneth Branagh; *W:* Chris Weitz; *C:* Haris Zambarloukos; *M:* Patrick Doyle.

Cinderella III: A Twist in Time 🦴🦴 **2007 (G)** Cinderella must fight to regain her prince when her evil stepmother uses magic to turn back time and reset events. **74m/C; DVD, Blu-Ray, Streaming.** *V:* Jennifer Hale; Susanne Blakeslee; Tress MacNeille; Christopher Daniel Barnes; Russi Taylor; *D:* Frank Nissen; *W:* Daniel Berendsen; Margaret Heidenry; Colleen Millea Ventimilia; Eddie Guzelian; *M:* Joel McNeely. **VIDEO**

Cinderella Liberty 🦴🦴🦴 **1973 (R)** Bittersweet romance in which a kindly sailor falls for a brash hooker with a son. Sometimes funny, sometimes moving, with sometimes crude direction overcome by truly compelling performances from Caan and Mason. Story written by Darryl Ponicsan from his novel. **117m/C; DVD, Blu-Ray.** James Caan; Marsha Mason; Eli Wallach; Kirk Calloway; Burt Young; Bruno Kirby; Dabney Coleman; Sally Kirkland; Allyn Ann McLerie; Allan Arbus; David Proval; Don Calfa; *D:* Mark Rydell; *W:* Darryl Ponicsan; *C:* Vilmos Zsigmond; *M:* John Williams. Golden Globes '74: Actress--Drama (Mason).

Cinderella Man 🦴🦴🦴 1/2 **2005 (PG-13)** Taken from the true story of heavyweight boxer Jim Braddock (Crowe) whose promising career was stalled by an injury, winless streak, and a revoked license. Despite his fall from glory, wife Mae (Zellweger) and their children remain unwavering in their devotion while Braddock labors on the Jersey docks during the Depression. Out of shape after a year, he finds himself back in the ring and winning again, which leads to a title bout in 1935 against the (fictitiously) vicious Max Baer (well-played by Bierko). Just as in the Oscar-winning "A Beautiful Mind," Crowe and Howard connect, with Crowe pounding out another stellar portrayal while Howard easily blends the fierceness of the boxing ring with the plain-spoken goodness of family-man Braddock. **144m/C; DVD, Blu-Ray, HD-DVD.** Russell Crowe; Renée Zellweger; Paul Giamatti; Craig Bierko; Paddy Considine; Bruce McGill; Ron Canada; David Huband; Connor Price; Ariel Waller; Patrick Louis; Rosemarie DeWitt; Linda Kash; Nicholas (Nick) Campbell; Gene Pyrz; *D:* Ron Howard; *W:* Cliff Hollingsworth; Akiva Goldsman; *C:* Salvatore Totino; *M:* Thomas Newman. Screen Actors Guild '05: Support. Actor (Giamatti); Broadcast Film Critics '05: Support. Actor (Giamatti).

A Cinderella Story 🦴 **2004 (PG)** A movie designed for tweenies who worship the chirpy Duff. This trifle finds Valley teen Samantha (Duff) bereft after the death of her father and stuck slaving for pea-brained stepmom Fiona (Coolidge) and her vicious twin daughters. Sam's only consolation is an email flirtation with a poetic soul who's actually the school's hottie football star Austin (Murray). Thanks to fairy godmother Rhonda (King), the cute twosome hook up at the Halloween dance but, alas, Sam slips out before revealing her true identity to hunk boy (although she does leave behind her cell phone). Of course, it's all so sugary that anyone who's not a 12-and-under girl will probably gag. **96m/C; VHS, DVD.** Hilary Duff; Jennifer Coolidge; Chad Michael Murray; Dan Byrd; Regina King; Julie Gonzalo; Lin Shaye; Madeline Zima; Andrea Avery; Mary Pat Gleason; Paul Rodriguez; Whip Hubley; Kevin Kilner; Erica Hubbard; Simon Helberg; Brad Bufanda; J.D. Pardo; Kady Cole; Hannah Robinson; *D:* Mark Rosman; *W:* Leigh Dunlap; *C:* Anthony B. Richmond; *M:* Christophe Beck.

A Cinderella Story: Once Upon a Song 🦴🦴 1/2 **2011 (PG)** Generally innocuous ABC Family movie finds 17-year-old Katie living with her monster stepmom Gail and her equally obnoxious stepsiblings Bev and Victor. Katie and Bev attend the prestigious Wellesley Academy, where Katie befriends newcomer Luke, whose dad is record mogul Guy Morgan. Katie's the one with the singing talent but it's no-talent Bev who passes herself off as the songbird. Will Katie ever be strong enough to tell the truth and realize her dream? **85m/C; DVD.** Lucy Kate Hale; Missi Pyle; Megan Park; Matthew Lintz; Freddie Stroma; *D:* Damon Santostefano; *W:* Erik Patterson; Jessica Scott; *C:* Dkran Tulaine; John Peters; *M:* Braden Kimball. **CABLE**

Cinderella 2000 🦴🦴 **1978 (R)** Softcore musical version of the classic fairy tale. It's the year 2047 and sex is outlawed, except by computer. Strains of Sugarman's score, including "Doin' Without" and "We All Need Love," set the stage for Erhardt's Cinderella to meet her Prince Charming at that conventional single prince romance venue, a sex orgy. Trouble is, it wasn't a shoe Cinderella lost before she fled, and the charming one must interface, as it were, with the local pretenders to the throne in order to find his lost princess. Touching. **86m/C; VHS, DVD.** Catharine Erhardt; Jay B. Larson; Vaughn Armstrong; *D:* Al Adamson; *M:* Sparky Sugarman.

Cinderfella 🦴🦴 1/2 **1960** This twist on the classic children's fairy tale features Lewis as the hapless buffoon guided by his fairy godfather. Somewhat overdone, with extended talking sequences and gratuitous musical interludes. Lewis, though, mugs effectively. **88m/C; VHS, DVD.** Jerry Lewis; Ed Wynn; Judith Anderson; Anna Maria Alberghetti; Henry Silva; Count Basie; Robert Hutton; *D:* Frank Tashlin; *W:* Frank Tashlin.

Cinema Paradiso 🦴🦴🦴 *Nuovo Cinema Paradiso* **1988** Memoir of a boy's life working at a movie theatre in small-town Italy after WWII. Film aspires to both majestic sweep and stirring poignancy, but only occasionally hits its target. Still manages to move the viewer, and it features a suitably low-key performance by the masterful Noiret. Autobiographically inspired script written by Tornatore. The version shown in America is approximately a half-hour shorter than the original Italian form. **123m/C; VHS, DVD, Blu-Ray.** *IT* Philippe Noiret; Jacques Perrin; Salvatore Cascio; Marco Leonardi; Agnes Nano; Leopoldo Trieste; *D:* Giuseppe Tornatore; *W:* Giuseppe Tornatore; *C:* Blasco Giurato; *M:* Ennio

Morricone. Oscars '89: Foreign Film; British Acad. '90: Actor (Noiret), Foreign Film, Orig. Screenplay, Support. Actor (Cascio); Cannes '89: Grand Jury Prize; Golden Globes '90: Foreign Film.

Cinema Verite 2011 Reasonably sympathetic portrait of the making of the pioneering 12-part 1973 PBS program, "An American Family," a depiction of the Loud family of Santa Barbara, California. A precursor to reality TV, producer Craig Gilbert (Gandolfini) pushed and manipulated, but apparently didn't quite realize just how open the Louds would be about their private crises, which include father Bill's (Robbins) infidelity, homemaker mom Pat's (Lane) increasing independence, and gay eldest son Lance's (Dekker) flamboyance. **90m/C; DVD, Blu-Ray.** Diane Lane; Tim Robbins; James Gandolfini; Thomas Dekker; Patrick Fugit; Shanna Collins; Kathleen Quinn; Lolita Davidovich; James Urbaniak; Kaitlyn Dever; Nick Eversman; Caitlin Custer; ***D:*** Shari Springer Berman; Robert Pulcini; ***W:*** David Seltzer; ***C:*** Affonso Beato; ***M:*** Rolfe Kent. **CABLE**

Circadian Rhythm ½ 2005 Killer babe in lingerie. Sarah (Miner) wakes up in a bare room with no idea where she is or—more importantly—who she is. Soon she's wondering why people are trying to kill her and how she knows how to defend herself. Of course, it's one of those government conspiracy plots. **82m/C; DVD.** Rachel Miner; Seymour Cassel; Sarah Wynter; David Anders; Robert Berson; ***D:*** Rene Besson; ***W:*** James Portolese; ***C:*** Nick Hay; ***M:*** Jason Nesmith. **VIDEO**

The Circle *Dayereh* 2000 Arezou (Almani) and Nargess (Mamizadeh) have just been released from an Iranian prison. Arezou apparently prostitutes herself (you don't see anything) in order to get the money for Nargess to travel back to her village, only because of Iranian law the girl can't travel without permission from a male. Nargress leads to two other former inmates who suffer because of their female identity and eventually everything circles back to the prison again. The film was banned in Iran because it makes the ceaseless difficulties of being born female in such a society very clear. Farsi with subtitles. **91m/C; VHS, DVD.** *IA* Mariam Palvin Almani; Nargess Mamizadeh; Fereshteh Sadr Orfani; Fatemeh Naghavi; Monir Arab; Elham Saboktakin; Mojhan Faramarzi; ***D:*** Jafar Panahi; ***W:*** Kambuzia Partovi; ***C:*** Bahram Badakhshami. Venice Film Fest. '00: Film.

Circle ½ 2010 U.S. Marshal Richard is teamed with FBI agent Kathy to recapture Greek mythology-obsessed killer James Bennett. He's escaped from a prison mental hospital and is headed back to his childhood home just as a group of criminology students have arrived to study the making-of-a-psycho's surroundings. **88m/C; DVD.** Peter Onorati; Kinsey Packard; Silas Weir Mitchell; Gail O'Grady; Erin Reese; Michael DeLuise; America Olivo; Jason Thompson; ***D:*** Michael W. Watkins; ***W:*** Brad Tiemann; ***C:*** Alan Jacoby; ***M:*** Gunnard Doboze. **VIDEO**

The Circle 2017 (PG) A great cast and interesting premise are wasted in this techno-thriller/satire that lacks both. Mae (Watson) thinks she's hit the jackpot when she lands a job at The Circle, a tech firm headed by charming Eamon Bailey (Hanks). She's persuaded to model the company's newest gadget, a camera that lets the world see, and comment on, her whole life in real time, presumably ushering in the age of "living transparently" and ending the expectation of any privacy. The bad guys are so, ahem, transparently evil, that any suspense disappears, while the satire is undercut by the ham-fisted script. Hanks brings charisma to the villain role, and Paxton adds some depth in his final role as Mae's MS-afflicted dad. **110m/C; DVD, Blu-Ray.** Emma Watson; Tom Hanks; John Boyega; Karen Gillan; Ellar Coltrane; ***D:*** James Ponsoldt; ***W:*** James Ponsoldt; Dave Eggers; ***C:*** Matthew Libatique; ***M:*** Danny Elfman.

Circle of Deceit ½ 1994 SAS officer John Neil (Waterman) is called back into service in Belfast two years after his wife and child were killed by terrorists. His assignment is to assume the identity of recently deceased IRA soldier Jackie O'Connell and learn about an arms shipment headed for Northern Ireland. But can his disguise hold against local IRA commander Liam McAuley (Vaughan)? Made for British TV. **103m/C; VHS, DVD.** *GB* Dennis Waterman; Peter Vaughan; Derek Jacobi; Clare Higgins; ***W:*** Jean-Claude Carriere. **TV**

Circle of Fear ½ 1989 (R) An ex-hitman who worked for the Mob upends the black market for sex and drugs in the Philippines while looking for his daughter who was sold into a sex slave ring. El cheapo exploiter. **90m/C; VHS, DVD.** *PH* Patrick Dollaghan; Welsey Pfenning; Joey Aresco; Vernon Wells; ***D:*** Clark Henderson.

Circle of Friends ½ 1994 (PG-13) Nostalgic Irish coming-of-ager focuses on three friends and the trials and tribulations they face when hearts and hormones conflict with a strict Catholic upbringing. Small-town teenager Benny (Driver), overweight and slightly awkward, reunites with her friends at university in Dublin. Benny begins a romance with gentle, doe-eyed Jack Foley (O'Donnell) and endures the humorous but sometimes painful passage from adolescence to womanhood. Sentimental moments can be too sticky-sweet at times, but humor, disappointment, and small triumphs are convincingly portrayed, offering a universal appeal. Adapted from the Maeve Binchy novel. **96m/C; VHS, DVD.** Chris O'Donnell; Minnie Driver; Geraldine O'Rawe; Saffron Burrows; Colin Firth; Alan Cumming; Aidan Gillen; Mick (Michael) Lally; ***D:*** Pat O'Connor; ***W:*** Andrew Davies; ***C:*** Kenneth Macmillan; ***M:*** Michael Kamen.

Circle of Friends 2006 Maggie (Benz) returns to her upstate New York hometown to dedicate a scholarship in her late husband's name. She becomes suspicious that his death is connected to the deaths of some high school classmates, which leads back to a camping trip where someone died. Made for Lifetime. **96m/C; DVD.** Julie Benz; Chris Kramer; Venus Terzo; Paula Costain; Adrianne Richards; Peter Michael Dillon; ***D:*** Stefan Pleszczynski; ***W:*** Joyce Heft Brotman; ***C:*** Daniel Villeneuve; ***M:*** Martin Roy; Vincent Rehel. **CABLE**

Circle of Iron ½ *The Silent Flute* 1978 (R) Plenty of action and martial arts combat abound in this story of one man's eternal quest for truth. Originally co-written by and intended for Bruce Lee as a rib-crunching vehicle, until he died before production began and was replaced by Kung-Fu Carradine. A cut above most chop-socky actioners. Filmed in Israel. **102m/C; VHS, DVD, Blu-Ray.** *GB* Jeff Cooper; David Carradine; Roddy McDowall; Eli Wallach; Christopher Lee; ***D:*** Richard Moore; ***W:*** Bruce Lee; James Coburn; Stirling Silliphant; ***M:*** Bruce Smeaton.

Circle of Love 1964 Episodic melodrama drifts from romance to romance in contemporary Paris. A somewhat pretentious remake of Ophuls classic "La Ronde," which was in turn adapted from Arthur Schnitzler's play. Credible performers are undone by Vadim's strained direction. **110m/C; VHS, DVD.** *FR* Jane Fonda; Francine Berge; Marie DuBois; Jean-Claude Brialy; Catherine Spaak; Claude Giraud; ***D:*** Roger Vadim; ***W:*** Jean Anouilh.

Circle of Passion *Never Ever* 1997 (R) Devoted hubby Thomas Murray (Finch) works for his father-in-law at a London bank. But when Thomas is transferred to Paris and his socialite wife (March) refuses to go with him, devotion falls by the wayside when he falls in love with the free-spirited Katherine (Bonnaire). Now Thomas has to choose between money and love. **94m/C; VHS, Streaming.** Charles Finch; Sandrine Bonnaire; Jane March; Julian Sands; James Fox; ***D:*** Charles Finch.

Circle of Two 1980 (PG) A platonic friendship between an aging artist and a young girl is misunderstood by others. Well, of course they do meet in a porno theatre. Pedestrian fare adapted from a story by Marie Therese Baird. **90m/C; VHS, DVD.** *CA* Richard Burton; Tatum O'Neal; Kate Reid; ***D:*** Jules Dassin.

Circuit ½ 2002 Sexual hedonism is alive and well in West Hollywood in this would-be cautionary tale of a small town Midwesterner who comes to the big, bad city. John (Drahos) gets introduced to the party circuit of casual gay sex and lots of drugs but vows to keep his distance. This doesn't last and John sinks ever deeper into the self-destructive pursuit of pleasure. **90m/C; VHS, DVD.** Jonathan Wade Drahos; Daniel Kucan; Andre Khabbazi; Brian Lane Green; Kiersten Warren; William Katt; ***D:*** Dirk Shafer; ***W:*** Dirk Shafer; Gregory Hinton; ***C:*** Joaquin Sedillo; ***M:*** Tony Moran.

The Circuit ½ 2008 ABC Family movie finds pro racecar track circuit driver Al Shines (Campbell) getting fired by his shady sponsor Robin Cates (Rae). While Al tries to start his own team, Cates hires Al's resentful, inexperienced daughter Kylie (Trachtenberg) in a marketing ploy. Kylie sets out to prove herself to her widowed dad as well as reigning champ Kid Walker (Fuller) with whom she begins a troublesome romance. **89m/C; DVD.** Michelle Trachtenberg; Billy Campbell; Drew Fuller; Paul Rae; Tommy Lioutas; Maurice Dean Wint; ***D:*** Peter Werner; ***W:*** Bill Hanley; Quinton Peeples; ***C:*** Neil Roach; ***M:*** Danny Lux. **CABLE**

The Circuit 2 *The Circuit 2: The Final Punch* 2002 (R) Dirk Longstreet (Gruner) goes a bit nuts after bad guys rape his reporter girlfriend and leave her for dead as she's investigating a prison where it's rumored the inmates are dying. Cue the inevitable "ah shall have mah revenge!" speech as Dirk goes undercover in the prison (despite not being a cop) to find out what happened and beat down everyone responsible. Even diehard action fans will be disappointed. **98m/C; DVD.** Olivier Gruner; Jalal Merhi; Lorenzo Lamas; Michael Blanks; Gary Hudson; Gail Harris; ***D:*** Jalal Merhi; ***W:*** Glen G. Doyle; ***C:*** Curtis Petersen; ***M:*** Varouje. **VIDEO**

Circuitry Man ½ 1990 (R) Post-apocolyptic saga of future American life as a woman tries to deliver a briefcase full of computer chips to the underground Big Apple. Along the way she runs into Plughead, a humanoid with electrical outlets that allow him to "plug in" to other people's fantasies. Intelligent retelling of a standard tale with an inspired soundtrack by Deborah Holland. Witty and original. **85m/C; VHS, DVD.** Jim Metzler; Dana Wheeler-Nicholson; Lu Leonard; Vernon Wells; Barbara Alyn Woods; Dennis Christopher; ***D:*** Steven Lovy; ***W:*** Steven Lovy; Robert Lovy; ***C:*** Jamie Thompson; ***M:*** Deborah Holland.

Circumstance ½ *Sharayet* 2011 (R) Iranian melodrama has Tehrani teens Atafeh and Shireen falling in love. The girls try to live as modern lives as possible, knowing their way around gatherings in private homes and warehouse dance clubs. The film starts falling apart with the return of Atafeh's long-absent brother Mehran, a former drug addict who suddenly becomes an Islamic fundamentalist who spies (literally with hidden cameras) on his liberal-leaning family for the country's morality police. Persian with subtitles. **106m/C; DVD.** *IA* Nikohl Boosheri; Sarah Kazemy; Reza Sixo Safai; Nasrin Pakkho; Soheil Parsa; ***D:*** Maryam Keshavarz; ***W:*** Maryam Keshavarz; ***C:*** Brian Rigney Hubbard; ***M:*** Gingger Shankar.

Circumstantial Evidence 1935 Newspaper reporter (Chandler) goes to extremes for a story and nearly dies as a result. Chandler sets it up to look like he's murdered a colleague, and he's tried and convicted on, you guessed it, circumstantial evidence. The colleague's then supposed to come forward but there's a problem. **69m/B; VHS, DVD.** Chick Chandler; Shirley Grey; Dorothy Revier; Arthur Vinton; ***D:*** Charles Lamont; ***W:*** Ewart Adamson.

The Circus ½ 1928 Classic comedy silent details the tramp's exploits as a member of a traveling circus, including a romance with the bareback rider. Hilarious, less sentimental than most of Chaplin's feature films. Chaplin won a special Academy Award for "versatility and genius in writing, acting, directing and producing" for this one. Outrageous final scenes. **105m/B; Silent; VHS, DVD.** Charlie Chaplin; Merna Kennedy; Allan Garcia; ***D:*** Charlie Chaplin; ***W:*** Charlie Chaplin; ***C:*** Roland H. Totheroh; ***M:*** Charlie Chaplin.

Circus 2000 (R) British gambler/con man Leo Garfield (Hannah) is being pressured by gang boss Bruno (Conley) to manage his Brighton casino. But Leo and his equally shady American wife Lily (Janssen) have some double-crossing ideas of their own, involving Bruno's brother Caspar (Burfield), his accountant Julius (Stormare), Julius' unfaithful wife Gloria (Donohue), and well, things get even more complicated but the film doesn't have the flair to pull off all the plots. It does make an interesting attempt, though. **95m/C; VHS, DVD.** *GB* John Hannah; Famke Janssen; Peter Stormare; Brian Conley; Eddie Izzard; Fred Ward; Amanda Donohoe; Ian Burfield; Tommy (Tiny) Lister; Neil Stuke; ***D:*** Rob Walker; ***W:*** David Logan; ***C:*** Ben Seresin; ***M:*** Simon Boswell.

Circus of Fear ½ *Psycho-Circus* 1967 A travelling troupe is stalked by a murderer. The unedited version is occasionally scary. **92m/C; VHS, DVD, Blu-Ray.** *GB GE* Christopher Lee; Leo Genn; Anthony Newlands; Heinz Drache; Eddi Arent; Klaus Kinski; Margaret Lee; Suzy Kendall; ***D:*** John Llewellyn Moxey.

Circus of Horrors ½ 1960 Nip 'n' tuck horror about a plastic surgeon who takes over a circus to escape a disfigured patient bent on revenge. The circus is staffed by former patients with new faces who, one by one, fall victim in fine circus style. A bloody one-ring extravaganza. **92m/C; VHS, DVD, Blu-Ray.** *GB* Donald Pleasence; Anton Diffring; Erika Remberg; Yvonne Monlaur; Jane Hylton; Kenneth Griffith; Colette Wilde; Charla Challoner; ***D:*** Sidney Hayers; ***W:*** George L. Baxt; ***C:*** Douglas Slocombe; ***M:*** Muir Mathieson.

Circus World ½ *The Magnificent Showman* 1964 A circus boss tries to navigate a reckless, romancing crew through a European tour while searching for aerialist he loved 15 years before and whose daughter he has reared. Too long and too familiar, but nonetheless well done with an excellent finale. **132m/C; VHS, DVD.** John Wayne; Rita Hayworth; Claudia Cardinale; Lloyd Nolan; Richard Conte; ***D:*** Henry Hathaway; ***W:*** Ben Hecht; James Edward Grant; Julian Zimet; ***C:*** Jack Hildyard. Golden Globes '65: Song ("Circus World").

Cirque du Freak: The Vampire's Assistant ½ *The Vampire's Assistant* 2009 (PG-13) Static and muddled adaptation of the young adult fantasy series by Darren Shan that features a teenager named—wait for it—Darren Shan (a disappointingly bland Massoglia). Darren and rebellious best friend Steve (Hutcherson) meet florid Larten Crepsley (Reilly) at a freak show. Darren is sure Crepsley is a vampire and, thanks to youthful bad judgment and the theft of a spider, Darren is soon a half-vampire, joining the Cirque du Freak on the road after unwittingly breaking a 200-year-old truce between warring vampire factions. **108m/C; Blu-Ray, On Demand.** Chris Massoglia; Josh Hutcherson; Salma Hayek; John C. Reilly; Jane Krakowski; Ray Stevenson; Patrick Fugit; Ken(saku) Watanabe; Orlando Jones; Frankie Faison; Willem Dafoe; Michael Cerveris; Jessica Carlson; ***D:*** Paul Weitz; ***W:*** Paul Weitz; Brian Helgeland; ***C:*** J.(James) Michael Muro; ***M:*** Stephen Trask.

Cirque du Soleil: Worlds Away 2012 (PG) Little more than a commercial for the various stage versions of Cirque du Soleil that play across Las Vegas (the film was shot at five casino shows), this quasi-documentary is almost like a concert film in the way it tries to capture something that is best experienced live. Director Adamson brings a bit of visual panache to the piece but one can't help but wish they were seeing the aerial acrobatics and glorious costume design in person instead of projected digitally, even if the 3-D does its best to recreate the experience of being there. **91m/C; DVD, Blu-Ray.** Erica Linz; Igor Zaripov; Lutz Halbhubner; John Clarke; Dallas Barnett; ***D:*** Andrew Adamson; ***W:*** Andrew Adamson; ***C:*** Brett Turnbull; ***M:*** Benoit Jutras.

The Cisco Kid ½ 1994 The Cisco Kid and his sidekick Pancho went from O. Henry's short story, to silent movies, talkies, a '50s TV series, and now this made for TV movie. Benito Juarez is leading an uprising to overthrow the French-backed Emperor Maximilian in 1867 Mexico. Cisco's (Smits) supplying the rebels with guns while carrying on romantic escapades (watch for the tango). Meanwhile, true-believer Pancho tries to convince his friend to become a revolutionary. Light-hearted with pedestrian action shots. Filmed on location in Mexico. **96m/C; DVD.** Jimmy Smits; Richard "Cheech" Marin; Sadie Frost; Tim Thomerson; Bruce Payne; ***D:*** Luis Valdez; ***W:*** Luis Valdez; Michael Kane; ***C:*** Guillermo Navarro; ***M:*** Joseph Julian Gonzalez. **TV**

The Cisco Kid and the Lady 🦴🦴 1/2 **1939** In this lively western, Romero takes on the title role for the first of his six outings for Fox. The Cisco Kid and his sidekick Gordito come to the aid of a gold prospector who's been ambushed by a claim jumper. He asks them to make sure his claim goes to his now-orphaned baby and Cisco takes the tyke to pretty schoolmarm Julie Lawson. He still needs to catch the killer, but lovesick dancehall gal, Billie, proves helpful. **73m/B; DVD.** Cesar Romero; Chris-Pin (Ethier Crispin Martini) Martin; Robert Barrat; Marjorie Weaver; Virginia Field; George Montgomery; ***D:*** Herbert I. Leeds; ***W:*** Frances Hyland; ***C:*** Barney McGill; ***M:*** Samuel Kaylin.

The Citadel 🦴🦴🦴 **1938** From the A.J. Cronin novel, the intelligent and honest Hollywood drama about a young British doctor who is morally corrupted by his move from a poor mining village to a well-off practice treating wealthy hypochondriacs. Somewhat hokey but still consistently entertaining, with Donat fine in the lead. **114m/C; VHS, DVD.** *GB* Robert Donat; Rosalind Russell; Rex Harrison; Ralph Richardson; Emlyn Williams; Penelope Dudley Ward; ***D:*** King Vidor; ***C:*** Harry Stradling, Sr. N.Y. Film Critics '38: Film.

Citadel 🦴🦴 **2012 (R)** After helplessly witnessing the deadly savage attack of his pregnant wife, Tommy (Barnard) is an emotional wreck as he cares for their newborn daughter. Trying to get his life back on track, social worker Marie (Mosaku) suggests he forgives her killers. Which is hard to do when they reappear and come after his child--forcing a confrontation in the very building where it all began--the Citadel. Irish director/writer Foy's feature debut is effectively bleak though a little farfetched, and Barnard is convincing as a man trying to overcome overwhelming fear to protect his family. **84m/C; DVD, Blu-Ray, Streaming.** *UK IR* Aneurin Barnard; James Cosmo; Wunmi Mosaku; Jake Wilson; Amy Shiels; ***D:*** Ciaran Foy; ***W:*** Ciaran Foy; ***C:*** Tim Fleming; ***M:*** tomandandy.

Citizen Cohn 🦴🦴 **1992 (R)** An appallingly fascinating look at a human monster. Told in hallucinatory flashbacks, as he lays dying from AIDS, Roy Cohn is a lawyer and power broker, probably best-remembered as the malevolent sidekick to Communist-hunting Senator Joseph McCarthy. But his contempt also extended to antisemitism and gay-bashing (though Cohn was both homosexual and Jewish), and his past comes, literally, back to haunt him. Woods does an exceptional job in bringing this sociopathic heel to wretched life. Adapted from the biography by Nicholas von Hoffman. **112m/C; VHS, DVD.** James Woods; Joe Don Baker; Joseph Bologna; Ed Flanders; Frederic Forrest; Lee Grant; Pat Hingle; ***D:*** Frank Pierson; ***W:*** David Franzoni; ***C:*** Paul Elliott. **CABLE**

Citizen Duane 🦴 1/2 **2006 (PG-13)** Limp Canadian comedy finds geeky high schooler Duane deciding to run for mayor of his small town in order to best his nemesis Chad, whose grandmother, the incumbent, would be Duane's opponent. **90m/C; DVD.** *CA* Douglas Smith; Donal Logue; Nicholas Carella; Rosemary Dunsmore; Jane McGregor; Alberta Watson; Devon Bostick; Vivica A. Fox; ***D:*** Michael Mabbott; ***W:*** Jonathan Sobol; Robert DeLeskie; ***C:*** Adam Swica; ***M:*** Michael Shields.

Citizen Gangster 🦴🦴 *Edwin Boyd* **2011** Low-key true crime drama. In Toronto in the early 1950s, WWII vet Edwin Boyd (Speedman) is struggling to support his family, so he takes his failed acting dream and turns it into bank robbing. He gets caught, escapes from prison with some more experienced cons, and returns to an increasingly violent life. **104m/C; DVD.** *CA* Scott Speedman; Kelly Reilly; Kevin Durand; Joseph Cross; William Mapother; Brendan Fletcher; Brian Cox; Charlotte Sullivan; ***D:*** Nathan Morlando; ***W:*** Nathan Morlando; ***C:*** Steve Cosens; ***M:*** Max Richter.

Citizen Jane 🦴🦴 **2009** True crime drama from the Hallmark Channel. Jane Alexander teams up with detective Jack Morris after her aunt is murdered. She wants justice but the killer turns out to be someone Jane thought she knew very well. Based on the book "Citizen Jane" by James Dalessandro, who also wrote the teleplay. **89m/C; DVD.** Ally Sheedy; Sean Patrick Flanery; Meat Loaf Aday; Patty McCormick; Nia Peeples; Chuck McCann; Jon Polito; ***D:*** Armand Mastroianni; ***W:*** James Dalessandro; ***C:*** Dane Peterson; ***M:*** Rob Mounsey. **CABLE**

Citizen K 🦴🦴 1/2 **2019** A documentary look at post-Soviet Russia, focusing on oligarch Mikhail Khodorkovsky and his contentious relationship with Vladimir Putin. When he began his career, Khodorkovsky admits he was greedy and opportunistic as he built an oil empire. He developed some empathy when he had to cut salaries and lay off workers to stay in business. Khodorkovsky's perspective changes when Putin takes power and imprisons him for a decade for not giving up his business as he demanded. Living in exile in London, Khodorkovsky now focuses on fighting corruption in his native country. It's a fascinating documentary features memorable footage. Russian with subtitles. **126m/C; DVD.** Alex Gibney; ***D:*** Alex Gibney; ***W:*** Alex Gibney; ***C:*** Mark Garrett; Denis Sinyakov; ***M:*** Ivor Guest; Robert Logan.

Citizen Kane 🦴🦴🦴🦴 **1941** Extraordinary film is an American tragedy of a newspaper tycoon (based loosely on William Randolph Hearst) from his humble beginnings to the solitude of his final years. One of the greatest films ever made—a stunning tour-de-force in virtually every aspect, from the fragmented narration to breathtaking, deep-focus cinematography; from a vivid soundtrack to fabulous ensemble acting. Welles was only 25 when he co-wrote, directed, and starred in this masterpiece. Watch for Ladd and O'Connell as reporters. **119m/B; VHS, DVD, Blu-Ray.** Orson Welles; Joseph Cotten; Everett Sloane; Dorothy Comingore; Ruth Warrick; George Coulouris; Ray Collins; William Alland; Paul Stewart; Erskine Sanford; Agnes Moorehead; Alan Ladd; Gus Schilling; Philip Van Zandt; Harry Shannon; Sonny Bupp; Arthur O'Connell; ***D:*** Orson Welles; ***W:*** Orson Welles; Herman J. Mankiewicz; ***C:*** Gregg Toland; ***M:*** Bernard Herrmann. Oscars '41: Orig. Screenplay; AFI '98: Top 100; Natl. Film Reg. '89; N.Y. Film Critics '41: Film.

Citizen Ruth 🦴🦴 1/2 *Precious; Meet Ruth Stoops* **1996 (R)** Glue-sniffing, pregnant Ruth Stoops (Dern) has already borne four children and been declared an unfit mother. In trouble again, Ruth's quietly told it's in her best interests to get an abortion but a couple (Smith and Place) from the pro-life community bail her out and give her a place to stay, while the group uses her as a propaganda symbol. Added to the commotion is a smarmy televangelist (Reynolds) and tough pro-choice Diane (Kurtz), who manages to get Ruth to stay with her while Ruth ineffectually tries to get some control over her wayward life. Doesn't take sides—both the pro-choice and pro-life camps are tweaked, with neither willing to compromise. **104m/C; VHS, DVD.** Laura Dern; Swoosie Kurtz; Mary Kay Place; Kurtwood Smith; Kelly Preston; Burt Reynolds; M.C. Gainey; Kenneth Mars; Kathleen Noone; David Graf; Tippi Hedren; Alicia Witt; Diane Ladd; ***D:*** Alexander Payne; ***W:*** Alexander Payne; Jim Taylor; ***C:*** James Glennon; ***M:*** Rolfe Kent. Montreal World Film Fest. '95: Actress (Dern).

Citizen Soldier 🦴🦴 1/2 **2016 (R)** A documentary about the war in Afghanistan from the perspective of American soldiers. Focusing on the Oklahoma Army National Guard's 45th Infantry Brigade Combat Team, the film shows their experiences in Afghanistan during the surge. Including footage from helmet cameras, a personal view of the war in the most dangerous parts of Afghanistan shows the chaos, bravery, and valor of the soldiers involved. **105m/C; DVD, Blu-Ray, Streaming, Download.** ***D:*** David Salzberg; Christian Tureaud; ***M:*** Michael Trella.

Citizen Toxie: The Toxic Avenger 4 **WOOF! 2001** As gleefully offensive as always, this sequel comes 12 years after part 3. An explosion in Tromaville creates a parallel universe in which Toxie and his evil twin, Noxie AKA Noxious Offender (who lives in Amortville), change places. Noxie promptly terrorizes the community while Toxie goes on with his good deeds in his new dimension. Meanwhile, a coalition of other superheroes try to eliminate the evil Noxie from their midst. **100m/C; DVD, Blu-Ray.** David Mattey; Heidi Sjursen; Paul Kyrmse; Dan Snow; ***D:*** Lloyd Kaufman; ***W:*** Lloyd Kaufman; Gabriel Friedman; Trent Haaga; ***C:*** Brendan Flynt; ***M:*** Wesly Nagy.

Citizen X 🦴🦴🦴 **1995 (R)** Based on the true story of '80s Russian serial killer Andrei Chikatilo (DeMunn) and his 52 victims. Viktor Burakov (Rea) is a beleagured rural forensics expert who is blatantly told by party officials that the Soviet state does not have serial killers—in spite of a rising body count. His only ally is Col. Fetisov (Sutherland), who's adept at political maneuvering, but it takes the duo eight frustrating years to bring the grisly killer to justice. Fine performances highlight a literate script from Robert Cullen's book "The Killer Department." Filmed on location in Budapest, Hungary. **100m/C; VHS, DVD.** Stephen Rea; Donald Sutherland; Jeffrey DeMunn; John Wood; Joss Ackland; Max von Sydow; Ralph Nossek; Imelda Staunton; Radu Amzulrescu; Czeskaw Grocholski; Ion Caramitru; Andras Balint; Tusse Silberg; ***D:*** Chris Gerolmo; ***W:*** Chris Gerolmo; ***C:*** Robert Fraisse; ***M:*** Randy Edelman. **CABLE**

Citizenfour 🦴🦴🦴 **2014** Laura Poitras found herself in the middle of one of the stories of the new century when she began communicating with a young man named Edward Snowden right in the middle of the NSA spying scandal. As we all know, Snowden had quite a story to tell, and Poitras' film plays like a thriller more than a documentary by placing viewers right in the middle of the revelations, secrets, and international intrigue. Her film doesn't just capture what happened before but what's happening right in front of her camera. It's a riveting piece of work that places the viewer in history. **114m/C; DVD, Blu-Ray.** *US GE* Edward Snowden; Glenn Greenwald; ***D:*** Laura Poitras; ***C:*** Kirsten Johnson; Katy Scoggin; Trevor Paglen. Oscars '14: Feature Doc.; British Acad. '14: Feature Doc.; Directors Guild '14: Documentary Director, Documentary Director (Poitras); Ind. Spirit '15: Feature Doc.

Citizens Band 🦴🦴🦴 *Handle With Care* **1977 (PG)** Episodic, low-key comedy about people united by their CB use in a midwestern community. Notable performance from Clark as a soft-voiced guide for truckers passing through. Demme's first comedy is characteristically idiosyncratic. **98m/C; VHS, Streaming.** Paul LeMat; Candy Clark; Ann Wedgeworth; Roberts Blossom; Charles Napier; Marcia Rodd; Bruce McGill; Ed Begley, Jr.; Alix Elias; ***D:*** Jonathan Demme; ***W:*** Paul Brickman; ***C:*** Jordan Cronenweth; ***M:*** Bill Conti. Natl. Soc. Film Critics '77: Support. Actress (Wedgeworth).

City Beneath the Sea 🦴🦴 1/2 **1971** Irwin Allen TV pilot movie has Admiral Mike Matthews (Whitman) forced to return to his former command in the undersea city of Pacifica where his old crew doesn't trust him. The city is about to store a highly-unstable radioactive explosive, which must be surrounded by the USA's gold reserves for safety's sake. Naturally, an asteroid is headed towards earth and thieves want to get to the gold when Matthews' orders an evacuation of the city. **93m/C; DVD.** Stuart Whitman; Robert Colbert; Robert Wagner; Rosemary Forsyth; Susan Miranda; Richard Basehart; Joseph Cotten; James Darren; Whit Bissell; Burr de Benning; ***D:*** Irwin Allen; ***W:*** John Meredyth Lucas; ***C:*** Kenneth Peach, Sr.; ***M:*** Richard LaSalle. **TV**

City Boy 🦴🦴🦴 **1993** At the turn of the century the orphaned Nick makes his way from Chicago to the Pacific Northwest in search of his natural father. He takes a job guarding Limberlost, a valuable old-growth forest, from thieves and is torn between the ideals of two new friends. His mentor Tom sees the forest as timber that will build homes and provide jobs, while Angelica sees the forest as an irreplaceable sanctuary. Filmed on location in Vancouver, British Columbia. Adaptation of "Freckles" by Gene Stratton Porter. **120m/C; VHS, DVD.** *GB CA* Christian Campbell; James Brolin; Sarah Chalke; Wendel Meldrum; Christopher Bolton; ***D:*** John Kent Harrison; ***W:*** John Kent Harrison.

City by the Sea 🦴🦴 1/2 **2002 (R)** Pitch-black drama starring De Niro as NYC homicide detective La Marca, an absentee father trying to find his son Joey (Franco), a junkie on the lam for murder. Though he's not exactly a model son, La Marco is convinced Joey is not the perp who popped a loathsome drug dealer. Events force him to revisit the title's run-down Long Island city, where he must confront his bitter ex (LuPone) and the troubled past he fled 14 years ago. McDormand appears as La Marca's trusty sometime-girlfriend. Suffers from overwrought, lengthy exposition, mostly via De Niro (not exactly his specialty). Overacting only exposes a depressing, overcooked script. Loosely based on a true story. **108m/C; VHS, DVD.** Robert De Niro; James Franco; Frances McDormand; Eliza Dushku; William Forsythe; George Dzundza; Patti LuPone; Anson Mount; John Doman; Brian Tarantina; Nestor Serrano; Leo Burmester; ***D:*** Michael Caton-Jones; ***W:*** Ken Hixon; ***C:*** Karl Walter Lindenlaub; ***M:*** John Murphy.

City for Conquest 🦴🦴🦴 **1940** Two lovers go their separate ways to pursue individual careers. He attempts to become a boxing champ, but is blinded in the ring and ends up selling newspapers. She takes a shot at a dancing career but hooks up with an unscrupulous partner. Will the ill-fated pair find happiness again? **101m/B; VHS, DVD.** James Cagney; Ann Sheridan; Frank Craven; Donald Crisp; Arthur Kennedy; Frank McHugh; George Tobias; Anthony Quinn; Blanche Yurka; Elia Kazan; Bob Steele; ***D:*** Anatole Litvak; ***W:*** John Wexley; ***C:*** James Wong Howe; ***M:*** Max Steiner.

City Girl 🦴🦴 1/2 *Our Daily Bread* **1930** Friedrich Murnau, who directed the silent vampire classic "Nosferatu," was removed from the director's chair before "City Girl" was completed and it shows. But so do the marks of his inimitable camera direction. The story concerns a Minnesota grain grower who visits the Windy City and returns with a waitress as his wife. Frustratingly inconsistent, leading you to wonder what could have been had Murnau remained behind the camera (he died the following year). Silent. **90m/B; Silent; VHS, DVD.** Charles Farrell; Mary Duncan; ***D:*** F.W. Murnau.

City Hall 🦴🦴🦴 **1995 (R)** Investigating the deaths of a heroic cop, a drug dealer, and six-year old boy in a shoot-out, idealistic deputy mayor Cusack uncovers a web of corruption and deceit in the Big Apple. Pacino excels as charismatic mayor John Pappas by showing the crafty string-puller behind the glossy image of the modern politico. Supporting cast is also strong, including Aiello as a Rodgers and Hammerstein-loving Brooklyn boss, and Fonda as the police union lawyer and standard issue love interest. Screenplay was conceived by Ken Lipper, who was once deputy mayor under Ed Koch, but the involvement of three other scripters causes confusion over what type of picture it's aiming to be. Cash-strapped New York rented its actual city hall out for filming at a price of $50,000. **111m/C; VHS, DVD.** Al Pacino; John Cusack; Bridget Fonda; Danny Aiello; David Paymer; Martin Landau; Anthony (Tony) Franciosa; Lindsay Duncan; Nestor Serrano; Mel Winkler; Richard Schiff; ***D:*** Harold Becker; ***W:*** Paul Schrader; Nicholas Pileggi; Bo Goldman; Ken Lipper; ***C:*** Michael Seresin; ***M:*** Jerry Goldsmith.

City Heat 🦴🦴 1/2 **1984 (PG)** A hard-nosed cop and a plucky private eye berate each other while opposing the mob in this overdone comedy. Both Eastwood and Reynolds spoof their screen personas, but the results are only slightly satisfactory. Good back-up, though, from Alexander and Kahn as the dames. Screenplay written by Blake Edwards under the pseudonym Sam O. Brown. **98m/C; VHS, DVD, Blu-Ray.** Clint Eastwood; Burt Reynolds; Jane Alexander; Irene Cara; Madeline Kahn; Richard Roundtree; Rip Torn; Tony LoBianco; William Sanderson; ***D:*** Richard Benjamin; ***W:*** Blake Edwards; ***M:*** Lennie Niehaus.

City in Panic 🦴 **1986** A detective and radio talk show host try to catch a psychotic mass murderer busy offing homosexuals throughout the city. Violent with no redeeming social qualities. **85m/C; VHS, DVD.** Dave Adamson; Ed Chester; Leeann Westegard; ***D:*** Robert Bouvier.

City Island 🦴🦴 1/2 **2009 (PG-13)** De Felitta helms a rather sweet farce about the Rizzos, a working-class family in the Bronx's

City Island, whose numerous secrets all get revealed. Prison guard Vince (Garcia) recognizes new inmate Tony (Strait) as his illegitimate son. Deciding Tony needs a second chance, he has him paroled into his custody and takes him home to his family (without explaining the blood ties). Vince is already hiding the secret that he's taking acting classes in Manhattan, while his increasingly suspicious wife Joyce (Margulies) thinks he's having an affair. Their kids are hiding things too: daughter Vivian (Garcia-Lorido) has become a stripper to pay for college and teenaged son Vinnie (Miller) has a sexual kink for overweight women he finds on the Internet. There's lots of yelling and hugging too. **100m/C; Blu-Ray.** Andy Garcia; Julianna Margulies; Alan Arkin; Emily Mortimer; Steven Strait; Ezra Miller; Dominik Garcia-Lorido; ***D:*** Raymond De Felitta; ***W:*** Raymond De Felitta; ***C:*** Vanja Cernjul; ***M:*** Jan A.P. Kaczmarek.

City Lights **1931** Masterpiece that was Chaplin's last silent film. The "Little Tramp" falls in love with a blind flower seller. A series of lucky accidents permits him to get the money she needs for a sight-restoring surgery. One of the most eloquent movies ever filmed, due to Chaplin's keen balance between comedy and tragedy. **86m/B; Silent; VHS, DVD, Blu-Ray.** Charlie Chaplin; Virginia Cherrill; Florence Lee; Hank Mann; Harry C. (Henry) Myers; Henry Bergman; Jean Harlow; ***D:*** Charlie Chaplin; ***W:*** Charlie Chaplin; ***C:*** Roland H. Totheroh; Gordon Pollock; ***M:*** Charlie Chaplin; Alfred Newman. AFI '98: Top 100; Natl. Film Reg. '91.

City Limits **1985 (PG-13)** In a post-apocalyptic city, gangs of young people on choppers clash. **85m/C; VHS, DVD.** John Stockwell; Kim Cattrall; Darrell Larson; Rae Dawn Chong; Robby Benson; James Earl Jones; Jennifer Balgobin; ***D:*** Aaron Lipstadt.

City of Angels 1/2 **1998 (PG-13)** Weepy American remake of Wim Wenders' "Wings of Desire" finds guardian angel Seth (Cage) falling in love with heart surgeon Maggie (Ryan) and then trying to decide whether he wants to become mortal in order to join her. Subtle, it is not. Cage does his doe-eyed best to convey Seth's longing and innocence to earthly ways, and the chemistry with Ryan really clicks. Overly sappy and sentimental, especially near the end, but that won't stop the intended audience from loving it. Big Hollywood flick that wears its art-house aspirations on its sleeve. **117m/C; VHS, DVD, Blu-Ray.** Nicolas Cage; Meg Ryan; Andre Braugher; Dennis Franz; Colm Feore; Robin Bartlett; Joanna Merlin; ***D:*** Brad Silberling; ***W:*** Dana Stevens; ***C:*** John Seale; ***M:*** Gabriel Yared.

City of Bad Men **1953** Outlaw Brett Stanton (Robertson) is just one of several bad guys heading to Carson City with a plan to steal the receipts from an upcoming title prize fight. Sheriff Gifford (Sanders) tries to swear the outlaws in as deputies to protect the loot, but Brett is the only one to take him up on the job. It's all because he's rekindled a romance with former sweetheart Linda (Crain) and wants to go straight but it won't be easy. **81m/C; DVD.** Dale Robertson; Jeanne Crain; Richard Boone; Lloyd Bridges; Hugh Sanders; Carl Betz; ***D:*** Harmon Jones; ***W:*** George F. Slavin; George W. George; ***C:*** Charles G. Clarke; ***M:*** Lionel Newman.

City of Ember 1/2 **2008 (PG)** The end of humanity, death of a civilization, dwindling resources, a race against time and corrupt authorities—all in a family-friendly fantasy setting! Imperiled humans built the underground city of Ember to provide a safe haven for 200 years. But time is up, and the generator that powers the city has broken. Now, teenagers Lina and Doon are on a secret mission to save the inhabitants from certain death. Original and visually impressive, with a relevant "green" theme, but the funhouse-like setting and general weirdness detract from the story. **95m/C; On Demand.** Saoirse Ronan; Harry Treadaway; Bill Murray; Tim Robbins; Martin Landau; Mackenzie Crook; Mary Kay Place; Toby Jones; Marianne Jean-Baptiste; ***D:*** Gil Kenan; ***W:*** Caroline Thompson; ***C:*** Xavier Perez Grobet; ***M:*** Andrew Lockington.

City of Fear 1/2 **1959** Escaping from a prison hospital, con Ryker (Edwards) steals a canister he thinks contains pharmaceutical heroin. Instead, it's radioactive material (in powdered form) and the container is leaking. The authorities rush to capture Ryker even as he's dying of radiation poisoning. **75m/B; DVD.** Vince Edwards; Lyle Talbot; John Archer; Patricia Blair; Steven Ritch; ***D:*** Irving Lerner; ***W:*** Steven Ritch; Robert Dillon; ***C:*** Lucien Ballard; ***M:*** Jerry Goldsmith.

City of Ghosts 1/2 **2003 (R)** Dillon makes his directorial debut (as well as starring and co-writing the screenplay) with this overly-ambitious effort. Jimmy Creemins (Dillon) works for a shady New York insurance agency. His boss (and Jimmy's mentor), Marvin (Caan), has cleaned out the firm's offshore accounts and the feds think Jimmy was in on the scam. Jimmy discovers Marvin is holed up in Phnom Penh and he heads to Cambodia to join him at the Belleville Hotel, the usual sort of seedy Euro-dive, which is run by Frenchman Emile (Depardieu). Soon Jimmy is caught up in further unsavory activities, with various unsavory characters, a damsel-in-distress (McElhone), and more sideline plots. **117m/C; VHS, DVD.** Matt Dillon; James Caan; Natascha (Natasha) McElhone; Gerard Depardieu; Sereyvuth Kem; Chalee Sankhavesa; Stellan Skarsgard; Rose Byrne; Christopher Curry; Shawn Andrews; ***D:*** Matt Dillon; Matthew Heineman; ***W:*** Matt Dillon; Barry Gifford; ***C:*** Jim Denault; ***M:*** Tyler Bates. Directors Guild '17: Documentary Director (Heineman).

City of God 1/2 *Cidade de Deus* **2002 (R)** A long and generally lively chronicle (covering the late sixties to the early eighties) of the drug trade and gang warfare in the slums of Rio. Taken from Paulo Lins novel, the narrator is budding photographer Rocket (Rodrigues), a kid from the projects observing the violence and trying to stay out of its grip. He observes the rise to gang power of the ruthless Little Ze (da Hora), who will eventually go up against his rival, amateur boxer Knockout Ned (Jorge), who has a personal as well as professional grudge. Portuguese with subtitles. **130m/C; DVD, Blu-Ray.** *BR* Alexandre Rodrigues; Leandro Firmino da Hora; Phellipe Haagensen; Matheus Nachtergaele; Seu Jorge; Johnathan Haagensen; ***D:*** Fernando Meirelles; Katia Lund; ***W:*** Braulio Mantovani; ***C:*** Cesar Charlone; ***M:*** Antonio Pinto; Ed Cortes. N.Y. Film Critics '03: Foreign Film.

City of Gold **2016 (R)** A feature-length documentary look at the life, work, and influence of Pulitzer Prize-winning food critic Jonathan Gold. In the documentary, Gold explains how food can enact change and food writing can provide unexpected insights into how communities are experienced. Gold offers insights into this cultural movement through his perspectives on Los Angeles, sharing his knowledge of culinary geography there. He shows that ethnic cooking is a means sharing the depths of a city and makes a wider statement on the possibilities in America. **96m/C; DVD.** ***D:*** Laura Gabbert; ***W:*** Laura Gabbert; ***C:*** Jerry Henry; Goro Toshima; ***M:*** Bobby Johnston.

City of Hope **1991 (R)** The picture that "Bonfire of the Vanities" wanted to be, an eventful few days in the fictional metropolis of Hudson: an ugly racial incident threatens to snowball, the corrupt mayor pushes a shady real-estate deal, and a botched robbery has profound implications. Some of the subplots resolve too easily, but this cynical, crazy-quilt of urban life is worthy of comparison with "American Graffiti" and "Nashville" as pure Americana. **132m/C; VHS, Streaming.** Vincent Spano; Tony LoBianco; Joe Morton; Todd Graff; David Strathairn; Anthony John (Tony) Denison; Barbara Williams; Angela Bassett; Gloria Foster; Lawrence Tierney; John Sayles; Maggie Renzi; Kevin Tighe; Chris Cooper; Jace Alexander; Frankie Faison; Michael Mantell; Josh Mostel; Joe Grifasi; Louis Zorich; Gina Gershon; Rose Gregorio; Bill Raymond; Maeve Kinkead; Ray Aranha; ***D:*** John Sayles; ***W:*** John Sayles; ***C:*** Robert Richardson; ***M:*** Mason Daring. Ind. Spirit '92: Support. Actor (Strathairn).

City of Industry **1996 (R)** Efficient contemporary noir that doesn't always live up to its promise. Old pro thief Roy Egan (Keitel), now retired, is drawn into the final jewel heist of his younger brother, Lee (Hutton), who's also vowed to get out of the game. Unfortunately for him, Lee's picked one wrong partner in volatile wheelman Skip Kovich (Dorff). When the violent Skip decides he doesn't want to share the goods it starts an elaborate cat-and-mouse hunt through the seedier sides of L.A. **97m/C; VHS, DVD, Blu-Ray.** Harvey Keitel; Stephen Dorff; Famke Janssen; Timothy Hutton; Michael Jai White; Wade Dominguez; Reno Wilson; Lucy Liu; Dana Barron; Elliott Gould; ***D:*** John Irvin; ***W:*** Ken Solarz; ***C:*** Thomas Burstyn; ***M:*** Stephen Endelman.

City of Joy **1992 (PG-13)** Disillusioned American heart surgeon Swayze flees to India after losing a patient. In Calcutta he is beaten by a street gang and loses his money and passport, but finds help from a farmer (Puri) who takes him to a nearby clinic in the City of Joy, one of Calcutta's poorest areas. Collins runs the clinic and recruits the reluctant doctor, who undergoes a life-changing transformation. The squalor of Calcutta is shown, but the city's portrayal as a magical place where problems miraculously disappear is unrealistic. Swayze lacks the emotional range for his part, but Collins and Puri are excellent in their roles. Adapted from the book by Dominique Lapierre. **134m/C; VHS, DVD.** *GB FR* Patrick Swayze; Pauline Collins; Om Puri; Shabana Azmi; Art Malik; Ayesha Dharker; Santu Chowdhury; Imran Badsah Khan; Shyamanand Jalan; ***Cameo(s):*** Sam Wanamaker; ***D:*** Roland Joffé; ***W:*** Mark Medoff; ***C:*** Peter Biziou; ***M:*** Ennio Morricone.

City of Life and Death *Nanjing! Nanjing!* **2009 (R)** Wrenching historical drama, partially filmed in black and white that focuses on the 1937-38 massacre in Nanking, China by Japanese troops. Director Lu uses a few archetypal characters to showcase human behavior, both good and bad, during the atrocities that affect the citizens and soldiers. English, Japanese, and Mandarin with subtitles. **132m/B; DVD, Blu-Ray.** *CH CH* Ryu Kohata; John Paisley; Yuko Miyamoto; Yiyan Jiang; Ye Liu; ***D:*** Chuan Lu; ***W:*** Chuan Lu; ***C:*** Yu Cao; ***M:*** Tong Liu.

The City of Lost Children *La Cite des Enfants Perdus* **1995 (R)** Weird not-for-the-kiddies fairytale finds crazed inventor Krank (Emilfork) getting his evil one-eyed minions, the appropriately named Cyclops, to kidnap local children so that he can steal their dreams (because Krank himself is incapable of dreaming). The latest victim is young Denree (Lucien), the adopted brother of sideshow strongman One (Perlman), who single-mindedly pursues a way to get Denree back—aided by nine-year-old feral child Miette (Vittet) and a band of orphan thieves. Freaks galore with avant-garde designer Jean-Paul Gaultier in charge of costumes. French with subtitles or dubbed. **114m/C; VHS, DVD, Blu-Ray.** *FR* Ron Perlman; Daniel Emilfork; Joseph Lucien; Judith Vittet; Dominique Pinon; Jean-Claude Dreyfus; Odile Mallet; Genevieve Brunet; Mireille Mosse; Marc Caro; ***V:*** Jean-Louis Trintignant; ***D:*** Jean-Pierre Jeunet; Marc Caro; ***W:*** Jean-Pierre Jeunet; Marc Caro; Gilles Adrien; ***C:*** Darius Khondji; ***M:*** Angelo Badalamenti. Cesar '96: Art Dir./Set Dec.

City of M *Ciudad de M* **2001** M (Magill) lives on the streets and has no job prospects, but he's happy enough since he can still party with his girlfriend and the guys. Then, he's offered the chance to become a drug courier to Miami. It's the only opportunity he's got but is the risk worth his future? Spanish with subtitles. **102m/C; VHS, DVD.** *PV* Santiago Magill; Christian Meier; Vanessa Robbiano; ***D:*** Felipe Degregori; ***W:*** Giovanna Pollarolo; ***C:*** Micaela Cajhuaringa.

City of Men 1/2 *Cidade des Homens* **2007 (R)** Two teenage friends, Ace and Wallace, struggle to grow up in a gang-ridden Brazilian shantytown, where much of their thoughts drift to the idea of fatherhood. Ace's father was gunned down at an early age, and he's now become a new father himself. Wallace, about to turn 18 and needing an ID card, must track down his long-lost deadbeat dad to get a necessary signature. The fight to connect with his father is touching and plagued with danger as the two friends scurry from the neighborhood to neighborhood, dodging gang warfare along the way. Based on the Brazilian television series of the same name, and loosely follows Meirelles' earlier gangster epic "City of God," using some of the same actors, but taking a more emotional and mature approach to the themes. **110m/C; DVD, Blu-Ray.** *BR* Douglas Silva; Darlan Cunha; Johnathan Haagensen; Camila Monteiro; Rodrigo dos Santos; Eduardo BR Piranha; ***D:*** Paulo Morelli; ***W:*** Elena Soarez; ***C:*** Adriano Goldman; ***M:*** Antonio Pinto.

City of the Walking Dead *Nightmare City; Nightmare; Incubo Sulla Citta Contaminata* **1980** Eco-misery as a community must contend with prowling, radiation-zapped zombies who enjoy chewing through human flesh. **92m/C; VHS, DVD, Blu-Ray.** *IT SP* Mel Ferrer; Hugo Stiglitz; Laura Trotter; Francisco Rabal; ***D:*** Umberto Lenzi; ***W:*** Antonio Corti; Luis Maria Delgado; Piero Regnoli; ***C:*** Hans Burman; ***M:*** Stelvio Cipriani.

The City of Violence 1/2 *Jjakpae* **2006** Tae-su (Doo-hong Jung) returns to his hometown to attend the funeral of an old friend who has been murdered. Being a cop, Tae-su is a little suspicious of events, and soon discovers an old acquaintance is responsible for the assassination, and he and his old partner decide to get revenge personally. It's a style-over-substance film, but the fights and musical score do well to make up for its shortcomings in plot. Besides, it's a revenge movie with the prerequisite amounts of massive butt kickin'. **92m/C; DVD.** *NK* Doo-hong Jung; Seung-wan Ryoo; Kil-Kang Ahn; Seok-yong Jeng; Beom-su Lee; ***D:*** Seung-wan Ryoo; ***W:*** Seung-wan Ryoo; Jeong-min Kim; Won-jae Lee; ***C:*** Yeong-cheol Kim; ***M:*** Jun-Seok Bang.

City of Women *La Citte delle Donne* **1981 (R)** Visually stunning, but otherwise thin fantasy/drama about a man smothered with women. A journalist wanders through a feminist theme park replete with a roller rink and screening room. Some worthwhile adventures are mixed in with rather dull stretches. Not among the best from either Mastroianni, who is under utilized, or Fellini, who here seems incapable of separating good ideas from bad. Plenty of buxom babes, but otherwise undistinguished. In Italian with English subtitles. **140m/C; VHS, DVD, Blu-Ray.** *IT* Marcello Mastroianni; Ettore Manni; Anna Prucnal; Bernice Stegers; ***D:*** Federico Fellini; ***W:*** Federico Fellini; ***C:*** Giuseppe Rotunno; ***M:*** Luis Bacalov.

The City of Your Final Destination **2009 (R)** Genteel adaptation of Peter Cameron's 2002 novel that's best enjoyed by fans of Merchant/Ivory productions. Doctoral student Omar's (Metwally) university career is in jeopardy when his request to write an authorized biography of writer Jules Gund is turned down by Gund's heirs. So Omar travels to the Gund estate in Ochos Rios, Uruguay to persuade Gund's brittle widow Caroline (Linney), mistress Arden (Gainsbourg), and older brother Adam (Hopkins) to let him do the work after all. The lush-looking pic, with a generally accomplished cast (Metwally's character is weak) and lots of cosmopolitan conversation, is nonetheless enervating and unfocused. **118m/C; Blu-Ray, On Demand.** Omar Metwally; Anthony Hopkins; Laura Linney; Charlotte Gainsbourg; Hiroyuki (Henry) Sanada; Alexandra Maria Lara; Norma Aleandro; Kate Burton; ***D:*** James Ivory; ***W:*** Ruth Prawer Jhabvala; ***C:*** Javier Aguirresarobe; ***M:*** Jorge Drexler.

City on Fire 1/2 **1987** Ko Chow (Chow Yun-Fat) is an undercover cop who just wants out so he can marry his girl and forget about his past. He agrees to do one more job for his uncle, an aging inspector being forced out by an ambitious newcomer. He infiltrates a violent crew (one that's already killed a cop who had gotten in with them) that's planning a jewel heist. Like most Hong Kong cops-and-gangs flicks, it goes heavy on the action, but it also delves into Chow's character, sometimes to the detriment of the pacing. Most people know this as the inspiration for Tarantino's "Reservior Dogs." **98m/C; VHS, DVD.** *CH* Chow Yun-Fat; Sun Yueh; Danny Lee; Carrie Ng; Roy Cheung; ***D:*** Ringo Lam; ***W:*** Ringo Lam; Tommy Sham; ***C:*** Wai Keung (Andrew) Lau; ***M:*** Teddy Robin Kwan.

City Park **1934** Homeless and hungry, Rose (Blane) gets herself arrested so she can have shelter and food. Her plight is noticed by Col. Henry Ransome (Walthall) and his park bench cronies who decide to help her. Henry poses as a relative to get Rose released into his custody but his actual family isn't happy with his altruism. **72m/B;**

DVD. Sally Blane; Henry B. Walthall; Lafe (Lafayette) McKee; Wilson Benge; Matty Kemp; Hale Hamilton; *D:* Richard Thorpe; *W:* Karl Brown; *C:* M(ilton) A(rthur) Anderson.

City Slickers 1991 **(PG-13)** Three men with mid-life crises leave New York City for a cattle-ranch vacation that turns into an arduous, character-building stint. Many funny moments supplied by leads Crystal, Stern, and Kirby, but Palance steals the film as a salty, wise cowpoke. Slater is fetching as the lone gal vacationer on the cattle drive. Boxoffice winner notable for a realistic calf birthing scene, one of few in cinema history. From an idea by Crystal, who also produced. Palance stole the show from Oscar ceremonies host Crystal a second time when he accepted his award and suddenly started doing one-arm pushups, startling the audience into laughter. **114m/C; VHS, DVD, Blu-Ray.** Billy Crystal; Daniel Stern; Bruno Kirby; Patricia Wettig; Helen Slater; Jack Palance; Noble Willingham; Tracey Walter; Josh Mostel; David Paymer; Bill Henderson; Jeffrey Tambor; Phill Lewis; Kyle Secor; Yeardley Smith; Jayne Meadows; *D:* Ron Underwood; *W:* Lowell Ganz; Babaloo Mandel; *C:* Dean Semler; *M:* Marc Shaiman. Oscars '91: Support. Actor (Palance); Golden Globes '92: Support. Actor (Palance); MTV Movie Awards '92: Comedic Perf. (Crystal).

City Slickers 2: The Legend of Curly's Gold ½ 1994 **(PG-13)** Mid-life crisis meets the wild west, part deux. Crystal and his fellow urban dudes discover a treasure map in the hat of departed trail boss Curly and decide to go a-huntin'. Palance is back as Curly's seafarin,' equally cantankerous, twin brother. Lovitz occupies the screen as Crystal's ne'er-do-well brother, replacing sidekick Bruno Kirby. A bit of a rehash, formulaic and occasionally straining for a punchline, it's still pretty darn funny, especially when the boys start to improvise. **116m/C; VHS, DVD.** Billy Crystal; Daniel Stern; Jon Lovitz; Jack Palance; Patricia Wettig; Pruitt Taylor Vince; Bill McKinney; Lindsay Crystal; Noble Willingham; David Paymer; Josh Mostel; *D:* Paul Weiland; *W:* Billy Crystal; Lowell Ganz; Babaloo Mandel; *M:* Marc Shaiman.

City Streets 1938 Pathos and tragedy abound as immigrant shopkeeper Joe Carmine (Carillo) becomes the guardian of orphaned, crippled Winnie (Fellows). He struggles to find a doctor to help the girl while keeping his business going. More bad times follow. **88m/B; DVD.** Leo Carillo; Edith Fellows; Mary Gordon; Tommy "Butch" Bond; Helen Jerome Eddy; *D:* Albert Rogell; *W:* Lou Breslow; Fred Niblo, Jr.; *C:* Allen Siegler.

City Unplugged *Darkness in Tallinn* **1995** Heist film with some twists. $970 million in gold, in Paris for safekeeping since WWII, has been returned to the treasury in the newly independent Republic of Estonia. The thieves, who belong to the Russian mob, plan to cut all electricity in the capital city of Tallinn, break into the bank, and move the gold to a nearby cigarette factory where it can be melted down and repackaged as cigarettes. The mob's use of local electrician Toivo proves to be their undoing in a comedy of errors. Estonian with subtitles. **99m/C; VHS, Streaming.** Peter Oja; Ivo Uukkivi; Milena Gulbe; Monika Mager; *D:* Ilkka Jarvilaturi; *W:* Paul Kolsby; *C:* Rein Kotov.

City Without Men ½ **1943** Melodramatic story about a boarding house near a prison where the women tenants await the release of their imprisoned men. Little plot, no suspense. **75m/B; VHS, DVD.** Linda Darnell; Sara Allgood; Michael Duane; Edgar Buchanan; Leslie Brooks; Glenda Farrell; Margaret Hamilton; Sheldon Leonard; *D:* Sidney Salkow.

Civic Duty ½ **2006 (R)** Terry Allen (Krause) has lost his job, and now spends his days at home while his wife goes to work. Eventually he begins obsessing over a middle-eastern looking neighbor who he begins to believe is a terrorist. Soon he's driving off his wife, annoying the FBI, and watching media hype about the 'terrorist threat' to our country. And stalking his neighbor, who may or may not be what he seems. Take it seriously and you may begin to wonder what those gophers in your yard are up to... **98m/C; DVD.** Peter Krause; Richard Schiff; Kari Matchett; Ian Tracey; Khaled Abol Naga; Mark Brandon; Val Cole; Brenda Crichlow; Agam Darshi; P. Lynn Johnson; *D:* Jeff Renfroe; *W:* Andrew Joiner; *C:* Dylan MacLeod; *M:* Terry Huud; Eli Krantzberg.

A Civil Action ½ **1998 (PG-13)** Low-key courtroom thriller doesn't contain many thrills. Travolta is Jan Schlichtmann, a flashy lawyer who freely admits that he's an ambulance chasing weasel. When a grieving mother (Quinlan) approaches him with a case accusing two corporate conglomerates of causing an outbreak of leukemia among children, Jan smells a big payoff. As the case drags on (and his firm falls deeper into debt pursuing it), his perspective changes and he begins to seek justice for the lost children. Robert Duvall steals the show as the homespun Harvard lawyer representing one of the companies. Based on a true story. **115m/C; VHS, DVD.** John Travolta; Robert Duvall; Kathleen Quinlan; Tony Shalhoub; Zeljko Ivanek; John Lithgow; William H. Macy; Bruce Norris; Sydney Pollack; Peter Jacobson; James Gandolfini; *D:* Steven Zaillian; *W:* Steven Zaillian; *C:* Conrad L. Hall; *M:* Danny Elfman. Screen Actors Guild '98: Support. Actor (Duvall).

Civil Brand ½ **2002 (R)** Minority inmates stage a bloody revolt against abuse and exploitation. Melodrama quickly boils over the top and doesn't lose its charge. Notable performances by rappers MC Lite, Da Brat, and Mos Def. Neema Barnette makes good use of her low budget but scrimps on attention to pertinent civil issues. **95m/C; DVD.** LisaRaye; Mos Def; N'Bushe Wright; Monica Calhoun; Da Brat; M.C. Lyte; Clifton Powell; Lark Voorhies; Tichina Arnold; Reed McCants; *D:* Neema Barnette; *W:* Joyce Renee Lewis; Preston A. Whitmore, II; *C:* Yuri Neyman; *M:* Mandrill.

Civilization **1916** A silent epic about the horrors and immorality of war as envisioned by the ground-breaking film pioneer Ince, who was later murdered. Famous scene involves Christ walking through body-ridden battlefields. **80m/B; Silent; VHS, DVD.** Howard Hickman; Enid Markey; Lola May; *D:* Thomas Ince; Reginald Barker; Raymond B. West. Natl. Film Reg. '99.

Cjamango ½ **1967** Gunslinger Cjamango was robbed of his fortune in gold and left for dead. He tracks his money to a town controlled by bandit El Tigre and steals it back but El Tigre learns that Cjamango's weakness is a young orphan he's caring for and demands the gold be returned. Dubbed spaghetti western. **90m/C; DVD.** *IT* Ivan Rassimov; Mickey Hargitay; Pierro Lulli; Livio Lorenzon; Helene Chanel; Pedro Sanchez; Giusva (Gilda) Fioravanti; *D:* Edoardo Mulargia; *W:* Fabio Piccioni; *C:* Vitaliano Natalucci; *M:* Felice Di Stefano.

The Claim ½ **2000 (R)** Winterbottom, who already adapted Thomas Hardy's "Jude the Obscure," takes on Hardy's "The Mayor of Casterbridge," transporting the story to California during the gold rush. Miner Dillon (Mullan) sells his wife Elena (Kinski) and baby daughter for gold and uses the money to establish his own town. But his sins come back to haunt him when his dying wife and grown daughter Hope (Polley) arrive, as does railway surveyor Dalglish (Bentley). Now Dillon's very future is threatened. There's more than the winter weather that's chilly about the film, which never reaches the tragic dimensions it should. **120m/C; VHS, DVD.** *GB CA* Peter Mullan; Nastassja Kinski; Sarah Polley; Wes Bentley; Milla Jovovich; Sean McGinley; Julian Richings; *D:* Michael Winterbottom; *W:* Frank Cottrell-Boyce; *C:* Alwin Kuchler; *M:* Michael Nyman.

Claire Dolan **1997** Irish immigrant Claire (Cartlidge), a hooker, decides to relocate after her mother dies and she leaves town owing her pimp, Roland (Meaney), a lot of money. She moves to Newark, gets a job as a beautician, and begins a romance with Elton (D'Onofrio). Then Roland finds her and forces Claire back into business to pay off her debt. Bleak but well-acted. **95m/C; VHS, DVD.** Katrin Cartlidge; Vincent D'Onofrio; Colm Meaney; *D:* Lodge Kerrigan; *W:* Lodge Kerrigan; *C:* Teodoro Maniaci; *M:* Simon Fisher Turner.

Claire of the Moon **1992** Famous satirist Claire goes to a women writers retreat in the Pacific Northwest where she's assigned a room with Noel, a solemn sex therapist. Noel's recovering from a disastrous love affair while Claire is promiscuous and unwilling to commit. Inspite of their differences, the two women find themselves drawn together. Too many philosophical debates slow the story down but the gentle romance works well. **102m/C; VHS, DVD.** Trisha Todd; Karen Trumbo; Faith McDevitt; Damon Craig; *D:* Nicole Conn; *W:* Nicole Conn; *M:* Michael Allen Harrison.

Claire's Knee ½ *Le Genou de Claire* **1971** A grown man about to be married goes on a holiday and develops a fixation on a young girl's knee. Another of Rohmer's Moral Tales exploring sexual and erotic obsessions. Lots of talk, little else. You'll either find it fascinating or fail to watch more than 10 minutes. Most, however, consider it a classic. Sophisticated dialogue, lovely visions of summer on Lake Geneva. In French with English subtitles. **105m/C; VHS, DVD, Blu-Ray.** *FR* Jean-Claude Brialy; Aurora Cornu; Beatrice Romand; Laurence De Monaghan; Gerard Falconetti; *D:* Eric Rohmer; *W:* Eric Rohmer; *C:* Nestor Almendros. Natl. Soc. Film Critics '71: Film.

Clambake **1967** Noxious Elvis vehicle about a rich man's son who wants success on his own terms, so he trades places with a water-skiing teacher. Inane, even in comparison to other Elvis ventures. **98m/C; VHS, DVD, Blu-Ray.** Elvis Presley; Shelley Fabares; Bill Bixby; James Gregory; Gary Merrill; Will Hutchins; Harold (Hal) Peary; Suzie Kaye; Angelique Pettyjohn; *D:* Arthur Nadel; *W:* Arthur Browne, Jr.; *C:* William Margulies; *M:* Jeff Alexander.

The Clan of the Cave Bear ½ **1986 (R)** A scrawny cavegirl is taken in by Neanderthals after her own parents are killed. Hannah is lifeless as a primitive gamine, and the film is similarly DOA. Ponderous and only unintentionally funny. Based on the popular novel by Jean M. Auel. **100m/C; DVD.** Daryl Hannah; James Remar; Pamela Reed; John Doolittle; Thomas G. Waites; *D:* Michael Chapman; *W:* John Sayles; *C:* Jan De Bont; *M:* Alan Silvestri.

Clancy in Wall Street ½ **1930** Clancy (Murray) and MacIntosh (Littlefield) are longtime partners in a plumbing business. But their friendship goes through a rocky patch after Clancy suddenly gets wealthy from stock investments and starts living extravagantly. Then he loses everything in the crash. Murray and Littlefield had a longtime vaudeville act and this is a creaky filmed version of their typical humor. **76m/B; DVD.** Charles Murray; Lucien Littlefield; Miriam Seegar; Edward J. Nugent; *D:* Ted Wilde; *W:* William Francis Dugan; *C:* Harry Jackson.

Clancy Street Boys ½ **1943** Muggs McGinnis (Gorcey) recruits his pals to pose as his siblings to fool wealthy Pete, a visiting friend of his late father's, who has been giving the family financial aid under the mistaken impression the McGinnis' had seven children. But a local thug hears about the scam and tries to horn in. Part of the "East Side Kids" series. **89m/B; DVD.** Leo Gorcey; Huntz Hall; Bobby Jordan; Amelita Ward; Noah Beery, Sr.; Martha Wentworth; Bennie Bartlett; *D:* William Beaudine; *W:* Harvey Gates; *C:* Mack Stengler.

Clapham Junction **2007** Shown on British TV's Channel 4 to mark the 40th anniversary of the decriminalization of homosexual acts in England. Five separate stories (of varying interest and success) are set in South London during a 36-hour period: lovers celebrate their commitment ceremony, a couple hosts a quarrelsome dinner party, a young teenager gets interested in an older neighbor, young men go cruising, and a gay bashing occurs on Clapham Common. **120m/C; DVD.** *GB* Tom Beard; Stuart Bunce; Rupert Graves; James Wilby; Samantha Bond; Rachael Blake; Richard Lintern; Joseph Mawle; Paul Nicholls; *D:* Adrian Shergold; *W:* Kevin Elyot; *C:* Tony Slater-Ling; *M:* Martin Phipps. **TV**

The Clapper **2018 (R)** Eddie (Helms) makes his living as a clapper, someone who is hired to applaud or ask planned questions in infomercials. With fellow clapper Chris (Morgan), Eddie travels from studio lot to studio lot to make his living. Eddie's life changes forever after late night host Jayme Stillerman (Peters) creates a bit out of Eddie's appearances on his show and manufactures a manhunt, complete with billboards, looking for Eddie's true identity. Adapted by director Montiel from his 2007 novel, the comedy tries to make a statement about the celebrity culture but sadly there's nothing much here to clap about. **89m/C; DVD.** Ed Helms; Amanda Seyfried; Tracy Morgan; Adam Levine; Russell Peters; *D:* Dito Montiel; *W:* Dito Montiel; *C:* Michael Barrett; *M:* Jimmy Haun; David Wittman.

Clara **2019** A bummed-out astronomy professor (Adams) and a dreamy artist (Bellisario) bond over a shared fascination in life beyond our planet, and collaborate in a quest to discover a planet similar to Earth. The cosmic visuals are gorgeous and the science holds water, but despite excellent acting, the love story is predictable and hampered by shallow characterizations, particularly of the titular character. **105m/C; DVD.** *CA US* Patrick J. Adams; Troian Bellisario; Ennis Esmer; Kristen Hager; R.H. Thomson; *D:* Akash Sherman; *W:* Akash Sherman; *C:* Nick Haight; *M:* Jonathan Kawchuk.

Clara's Heart **1988 (PG-13)** A Jamaican maid enriches the lives of her insufferable, bourgeois employers and their particularly repellent son. A kinder, gentler waste of film and Goldberg; sentimental clap-trap which occasionally lapses into comedy. **108m/C; VHS, DVD.** Whoopi Goldberg; Michael Ontkean; Kathleen Quinlan; Neil Patrick Harris; Spalding Gray; Beverly Todd; Hattie Winston; *D:* Robert Mulligan; *W:* Mark Medoff; *M:* Dave Grusin.

Clarence, the Cross-eyed Lion **1965** Follows the many adventures of a cross-eyed lion and his human compatriots. Great family viewing from the creator of "Flipper." **98m/C; VHS, DVD.** Marshall Thompson; Betsy Drake; Richard Haydn; Cheryl Miller; Rockne Tarkington; Maurice Marsac; *D:* Andrew Marton; *W:* Alan Caillou.

Clarissa ½ **1991** Clarissa Harlowe (Wickham) is a wealthy heiress famed for her virtue who is badgered by her family to marry a nobleman, which leads her to rebellion and into the arms of the handsome rake Lovelace (Bean). His seductive tactics are foiled by Clarissa's strength of character and his own heart, leading him down a path of self-destruction. Fabulous period costumes, gorgeous settings and stellar acting. **156m/C; DVD.** Saskia Wickham; Sean Bean; Lynsey Baxter; Sean Pertwee; Jonathan Phillips; Jeffrey Wickham; Cathryn Harrison; Shirley Henderson; *D:* Robert Bierman; *W:* Janet Barron; David Nokes; *C:* John McGlashan; *M:* Colin Towns. **VIDEO**

Clash by Night ½ **1952** A wayward woman marries a fisherman, then beds his best friend. Seamy story line is exploited to the hilt by master filmmaker Lang. An utterly unflinching melodrama. Early Monroe shines in a supporting role too. Based on the Clifford Odets play. **105m/B; DVD.** Barbara Stanwyck; Paul Douglas; Marilyn Monroe; Robert Ryan; J. Carrol Naish; *D:* Fritz Lang; *W:* Alfred Hayes; *C:* Nicholas Musuraca; *M:* Roy Webb.

Clash of the Titans WOOF! **1981 (PG)** Mind-numbing fantasy derived from Greek legends about heroic Perseus, who slays the snake-haired Medusa and rescues a semi-clad maiden from the monstrous Kraken. Wooden Hamlin plays Perseus and fares better than more accomplished Olivier and Smith, who seem in need of enemas as they lurch about Mt. Olympus. Only Bloom seems truly godlike in a supporting role. Some good, some wretched special effects from pioneer Harryhausen. **118m/C; VHS, DVD, Blu-Ray.** *GB* Laurence Olivier; Maggie Smith; Claire Bloom; Ursula Andress; Burgess Meredith; Harry Hamlin; Sian Phillips; Judi Bowker; *D:* Desmond Davis; *W:* Beverley Cross; *C:* Ted Moore.

Clash of the Titans ½ **2010 (PG-13)** Loving but ultimately empty remake of the campy 1981 fantasy-adventure. Perseus (Worthington) must embrace his own destiny as the son of an Olympic god (though he was raised as a man) when vengeful Hades (Fiennes) tries usurping Zeus' (paycheck-cashing Neeson) power to unleash hell on earth. Movie retains the basic storyline of the original, but none of its charm, exchanging distinctive stop-motion special effects for bland, often indecipherable CGI action. The only thing left is the hammy performances, and even those seem like a chore. **106m/C; Blu-Ray, On Demand.** Sam Worthington; Liam Neeson; Ralph Fiennes; Danny Huston; Izabella Miko; Mads Mikkelsen; Jason Flemyng; Gemma Arterton; Alexa Davalos; Tine Stapelfeldt; ***D:*** Louis Leterrier; ***W:*** Phil Hay; Matt Manfredi; Travis Beacham; ***C:*** Peter Menzies, Jr.; ***M:*** Ramin Djawadi; Mike Higham.

Class ♪♪ **1983 (R)** A prep school student discovers that his mother is the lover whom his roommate has bragged about. Lowe is serviceable as the stunned son of sexy Bisset, who woos McCarthy, even in an elevator. Too ludicrous to be enjoyed, but you may watch just to see what happens next. **98m/C; VHS, DVD, Blu-Ray.** Jacqueline Bisset; Rob Lowe; Andrew McCarthy; Cliff Robertson; John Cusack; Stuart Margolin; Casey Siemaszko; ***D:*** Lewis John Carlino; ***W:*** Jim Kouf; David Greenwalt; ***C:*** Ric Waite; ***M:*** Elmer Bernstein.

The Class ♪♪ ½ *Entre les Murs; Between the Walls* **2008 (PG-13)** A school year in the life of the 14- and 15-year-old students and their teacher in one high school classroom in Paris. Based on his own 2006 novel, Begaudeau plays a variation of himself—humorous, self-aware, dedicated teacher Francois Marin. His classroom is a cultural and intellectual mix of the diligent and the troubled with director Cantet rejecting a clear narrative in favor of fly-on-the-wall dialogue and situations. French with subtitles. **128m/C; Blu-Ray, On Demand.** *FR* Francois Begaudeau; Esmeralda Oeurtaini; Rachel Regulier; Franck Keita; Wei Huang; ***D:*** Laurent Cantet; ***W:*** Laurent Cantet; Robin Campillo; Francois Begaudeau; ***C:*** Pierre Milon; Catherine Pujol; Georgi Lazarevski. Ind. Spirit '09: Foreign Film.

Class Act ♪♪ ½ **1991 (PG-13)** Rappers Kid 'N' Play team up once again in this role reversal comedy. A straight-laced brain and a partying, macho bully find their school records and identifications switched when they enroll in a new high school. This turns out to be good for the character of both young men, as the egghead learns to loosen up and the bully learns what it feels like to be respected for his ideas rather than a fierce reputation. Comedy is very uneven but the duo are energetic and likable. **98m/C; VHS, DVD.** Christopher Reid; Christopher Martin; Meshach Taylor; Karyn Parsons; Doug E. Doug; Ric(k) Ducommun; Rhea Perlman; ***D:*** Randall Miller; ***M:*** Vassal Benford.

Class Action ♪♪♪ **1991 (R)** 1960s versus 1990s ethics clash when a father and daughter, both lawyers, wind up on opposing sides of a litigation against an auto manufacturer. Hackman and Mastrantonio give intense, exciting performances, almost surmounting the melodramatic script. **110m/C; VHS, DVD.** Mary Elizabeth Mastrantonio; Gene Hackman; Joanna Merlin; Colin Friels; Laurence Fishburne; Donald Moffat; Jan Rubes; Matt Clark; Fred Dalton Thompson; Jonathan Silverman; Dan Hicks; ***D:*** Michael Apted; ***W:*** Samantha Shad; Christopher Ames; ***M:*** James Horner.

Class of '44 ♪ ½ **1973 (PG)** The sequel to "Summer of '42" finds insufferable boys becoming insufferable men at military school. Worse than its predecessor, and notable only in that it is Candy's film debut. **95m/C; VHS, DVD.** Gary Grimes; Jerry Houser; Oliver Conant; Deborah Winters; William Atherton; Sam Bottoms; John Candy; ***D:*** Paul Bogart; ***M:*** David Shire.

Class of 1984 **WOOF! 1982 (R)** Teacher King must face a motley crew of teenagers in the classroom. Ring leader and student psychopath Van Patten leads his groupies on a reign of terror through the high school halls, stopping to gang rape King's wife. Teacher attempts revenge. Bloody and thoughtless update of "Blackboard Jungle." Early Fox appearance. Followed by "Class of 1999." **93m/C; VHS, DVD, Blu-Ray.** *CA* Perry King; Roddy McDowall; Timothy Van Patten; Michael J. Fox; Merrie Lynn Ross; Stefan Arngrim; Al Waxman; Lisa Langlois; ***D:*** Mark L. Lester; ***W:*** Mark L. Lester; Tom Holland; ***C:*** Albert J. Dunk; ***M:*** Lalo Schifrin.

Class of 1999 ♪ **1990 (R)** Freewheeling sci-fi set in the near future where teen gangs terrorize seemingly the entire country. A high school principal determines to enforce law and order by installing human-like robots with rocket launchers for arms. Violent, crude entertainment. Class dismissed. Sequel to "Class of 1984" and available in an unrated version. **98m/C; VHS, DVD.** Bradley Gregg; Traci Lind; Malcolm McDowell; Stacy Keach; Patrick Kilpatrick; Pam Grier; John P. Ryan; Darren E. Burrows; Joshua John Miller; ***D:*** Mark L. Lester; ***W:*** C. Courtney Joyner.

Class of 1999 2: The Substitute ♪ ½ **1993 (R)** High school in 1999 is filled with violent gangs who murder at random. Enter substitute teacher John Bolen, who has his own ideas of discipline—leading to an even higher body count. John just doesn't seem human and when a CIA agent starts investigating, school may never be the same. **90m/C; VHS, DVD.** Sasha Mitchell; Nick Cassavetes; Caitlin Dulany; Jack Knight; Gregory West; Richard (Rick) Hill; ***D:*** Spiro Razatos; ***W:*** Mark Sevi.

Class of Nuke 'Em High ♪ ½ **1986 (R)** Team Troma once again experiments with the chemicals, with violent results. Jersey high school becomes a hotbed of mutants and maniacs after a nuclear spill occurs. Good teens Chrissy and Warren succumb, the school blows, life goes on. High camp, low budget, heavy gore. Followed by "Class of Nuke 'Em High Part 2." **84m/C; VHS, DVD.** Janelle Brady; Gilbert Brenton; Robert Prichard; R.L. Ryan; Theo Cohan; Diana De Vries; Brad Dunker; Gary Schneider; ***D:*** Richard W. Haines; Lloyd Kaufman; ***W:*** Richard W. Haines; Lloyd Kaufman; Mark Rudnitsky; Stuart Strutin.

Class of Nuke 'Em High 2: Subhumanoid Meltdown ♪ **1991 (R)** The Troma team brings us back into the world of the strange. In this adventure, the evil Nukamama Corporation holds secret experiments at their "college" and create subhumanoids as slave labor, swelling unemployment and wrecking the economy. This does not fare too well with the rest of society, including our heroes Roger the reporter, Professor Holt, and the scantily clad sub-humanoid Victoria. **96m/C; VHS, DVD, Blu-Ray.** Lisa Gaye; Brick Bronsky; Leesa Rowland; Michael Kurtz; Scott Resnick; ***D:*** Eric Louzil; ***W:*** Eric Louzil; Lloyd Kaufman; ***C:*** Ron Chapman; ***M:*** Bob Mithoff.

Class of Nuke 'Em High 3: The Good, the Bad and the Subhumanoid **WOOF! 1994 (R)** Revisit Tromie the nuclear rodent and the other disaster-prone denizens of Tromaville, USA. Admire the classic good twin vs. evil subhumanoid twin plot as they battle against each other, aided by chicks with guns and tin undergarments. Supposedly inspired by Shakespeare's "Comedy of Errors." Tip: stick to the BBC production for your senior thesis. **95m/C; VHS, DVD, Blu-Ray.** Brick Bronsky; Lisa Gaye; Lisa Star; John Tallman; Albert Rear; Phil Rivo; ***D:*** Eric Louzil; ***W:*** Lloyd Kaufman; ***C:*** Ron Chapman; ***M:*** Bob Mithoff.

Class Reunion Massacre **WOOF!** *The Redeemer* **1977 (R)** Typically lame-brained horror about the mysterious deaths of former school jerks who've reconvened for the 10-year reunion. Worthless flick stars someone named Finkbinder. Contains graphic violence that is not for the squeamish. **87m/C; VHS, DVD.** T.K. Finkbinder; Damien Knight; Nick Carter; Jeanetta Arnette; Christopher Flint; ***D:*** Constantine S. Gochis; ***W:*** William Vernick.

Classe Tous Risque ♪♪♪ *The Big Risk* **1960** Classic crime thriller deserves to be rediscovered. Aging French gangster Abel Davos (Ventura) has been hiding out in Italy for years with his wife and sons. Deciding he wants to move back to Paris, Davos agrees to pull off a payroll heist with an old pal in order to finance his return, but the getaway is botched. So Davos tries calling in some favors from his former gang, who are reluctant to disturb their own lives. Instead, they hire Erik (Belmondo) to handle things, though Davos is wary of the respectful new kid. French and Italian with subtitles. **100m/B; DVD.** *FR IT* Lino Ventura; Jean-Paul Belmondo; Marcel Dalio; Sandra Milo; Claude Cerval; Michele Meritz; Michel Ardan; Simone France; Stan Krol; ***D:*** Claude Sautet; ***W:*** Claude Sautet; Jose Giovanni; Pascal Jardin; ***C:*** Ghislan Cloquet; ***M:*** Georges Delerue.

Claudelle Inglish ♪ **1961** Sleazy southern gothic based on the Erskine Caldwell novel. Beautiful-but-poor Georgia sharecropper's daughter Caludelle (McBain) is betrayed by the young man she thought loved her. Then, apparently to get even on the rest of the cads panting after her, she decides to become the town tramp. **99m/B; DVD.** Diane McBain; Arthur Kennedy; Constance Ford; Chad Everett; Claude Akins; Will Hutchins; ***D:*** Gordon Douglas; ***W:*** Leonard Freeman; ***C:*** Ralph Woolsey; ***M:*** Howard Jackson.

Claudia ♪♪ ½ **1943** McGuire, in her screen debut, recreated her stage role from the play by Rose Franken. Immature new bride Claudia is having a difficult time getting used to married life. She and hubby David (Young) have moved to a farm in Connecticut and Claudia misses their life in Manhattan as well as her mother (Claire). However, the young woman is forced to grow up quickly when she learns her mother is fatally ill. **91m/B; DVD.** Dorothy McGuire; Robert Young; Ina Claire; Reginald Gardiner; Olga Baclanova; ***D:*** Edmund Goulding; ***W:*** Morrie Ryskind; ***C:*** Leon Shamroy; ***M:*** Alfred Newman.

Claudia and David ♪♪ **1946** Sequel to 1943's "Claudia" finds the young couple still trying to cope with married life in Connecticut as well as becoming parents. Claudia (McGuire) still seems to get into a tizzy over the least thing and lets her imagination run wild, certain that every mishap is a disaster. When attractive neighbor Elizabeth (Astor) asks for David's (Young) advice, Claudia is immediately jealous even though she doesn't realize that another neighbor (Sutton) is making a play for her. **78m/B; DVD.** Dorothy McGuire; Robert Young; Mary Astor; John Sutton; Rose Hobart; Gail Patrick; ***D:*** Walter Lang; ***W:*** Rose D. Franken; Vera Caspary; William Brown Meloney; ***C:*** Joseph LaShelle; ***M:*** Cyril Mockridge.

Clawed: The Legend of Sasquatch ♪ ½ *The Unknown* **2005 (R)** A group of bear poachers are found brutally mauled on Echo Mountain and many in the nearby town of Pine Creek believe a grizzly was to blame—or maybe the mountain's lurid legend has resurfaced. A Native American forest ranger sets out to investigate and so do four teen campers. **90m/C; DVD.** Miles O'Keeffe; Nathaniel Arcand; Jack Conley; Chelsea Hobbs; Dylan Purcell; Brandon Henschel; David "Shark" Fralick; Casey LaBow; ***D:*** Karl Kozak; ***W:*** Karl Kozak; Don J. Rearden; ***C:*** Victor Lou; ***M:*** Lawrence Nash Groupe. **VIDEO**

Clay Pigeons ♪♪ ½ **1998 (R)** Bodies are mysteriously piling up in a sleepy Montana town after strange cowboy trucker Lester (Vaughn) shows up. Clay Birdwell (Phoenix) finds himself a prime suspect after a series of bizarre twists stemming from his affair with his best friend's wife. After crossing paths, Clay and Lester quickly become best buddies. When they discover a body while fishing, Clay begins to link unsolved murders elsewhere in the state to his new pal. Problem is, the FBI has just shown up to investigate the disappearance of Clay's best friend and his wife, while Lester has disappeared, leaving Clay to take the heat. Features outstanding performances by Phoenix and Vaughn. Vaughn is given free reign, and goes near, but never over, the top. Second half is slower and less fun than the first half. Still, the original story and clever twists keep it interesting. **104m/C; VHS, DVD.** Vince Vaughn; Joaquin Rafael (Leaf) Phoenix; Janeane Garofalo; Scott Wilson; Georgina Cates; Phil Morris; Vince Vieluf; Nikki Arlyn; Monica Moench; Joseph D. Reitman; Gregory Sporleder; ***D:*** David Dobkin; ***W:*** Matthew Healy; ***C:*** Eric Alan Edwards; ***M:*** John Lurie.

Clean ♪♪ **2004 (R)** Emily (Cheung) and her common-law husband Lee Hauser (Johnston) are heroin addicts who abandoned their young son to Lee's parents. Lee, a faded 80s rocker, dies of an overdose, and Emily is sent to jail, where she tries to get clean. After her release, Emily wants to reconnect with her son, but grandma Rosemary (Henry) hates her; grandpa Albrecht (Nolte) is more willing to give Emily a chance. Emily struggles to keep off drugs while attempting to find work and mend fences but the character is so prickly and self-centered that she garners little sympathy. **110m/C; VHS, DVD.** *CA GB FR* Maggie Cheung; Nick Nolte; Beatrice Dalle; Jeanne Balibar; Don McKellar; Martha Henry; James Johnston; Remi Martin; James Dennis; Laetitia Spigarelli; ***Cameo(s):*** David Roback; ***D:*** Olivier Assayas; ***W:*** Olivier Assayas; ***C:*** Eric Gautier; ***M:*** David Roback; Brian Eno.

Clean and Sober ♪♪♪ ½ **1988 (R)** A drug addict hides out at a rehabilitation clinic and actually undergoes treatment. A serious, subtle, and realistic look at the physical/emotional detoxification of an obnoxious, substance-abusing real estate broker; unpredictable and powerful without moralizing. Keaton is fine in unsympathetic lead, with both Baker and Freeman excelling in lesser roles. Not for all tastes, but it's certainly a worthwhile work. Caron, creator of TV's "Moonlighting," debuts here as director. **124m/C; VHS, DVD.** Michael Keaton; Kathy Baker; Morgan Freeman; M. Emmet Walsh; Claudia Christian; Pat Quinn; Ben Piazza; Brian Benben; Luca Bercovici; Tate Donovan; Henry Judd Baker; Mary Catherine Martin; ***D:*** Glenn Gordon Caron; ***W:*** Tod Carroll; ***C:*** Jan Kiesser; ***M:*** Gabriel Yared. Natl. Soc. Film Critics '88: Actor (Keaton).

Clean, Shaven ♪♪ **1993** Schizophrenic Peter Winter (Greene in a stunning performance) is searching bleak Miscou Island, off the New Brunswick coast, for the young daughter his mother put up for adoption after Peter was institutionalized and his wife died. Peter's being tailed by Detective McNally (Albert), who suspects him of a child's murder, and his tenuous hold on reality slowly disintegrates into torment and self-mutilation. Debut for director/writer Kerrigan. **80m/C; VHS, DVD.** Peter Greene; Robert Albert; Jennifer MacDonald; Megan Owen; Molly Castelloe; ***D:*** Lodge Kerrigan; ***W:*** Lodge Kerrigan; ***C:*** Teodoro Maniaci; ***M:*** Hahn Rowe.

Clean Slate ♪♪ **1994 (PG-13)** Private-eye Maurice Pogue (Carvey) sustains injuries that cause a rare type of amnesia making every day seem like the first day of his life. As the only witness to a crime, he bumbles through mix-ups with the mob and his job as a bodyguard. Lightweight comedy fare is good for a few yuks but doesn't work as well as the similar "Groundhog Day." Barkley the sight-impaired dog steals nearly every scene he's in. **106m/C; VHS, DVD, Blu-Ray.** Dana Carvey; Valeria Golino; James Earl Jones; Kevin Pollak; Michael Murphy; Michael Gambon; Jayne Brook; Vyto Ruginis; Olivia D'Abo; Peter Crook; Bob Odenkirk; ***D:*** Mick Jackson; ***W:*** Robert King; ***M:*** Alan Silvestri.

Cleaner ♪♪ **2007 (R)** Disappointingly lackluster thriller. Former New Jersey cop Tom Carver (Jackson) now makes his living cleaning up crime scenes. But Tom is shocked to discover that his recent clean-up of a shooting has erased evidence, which points to a cover-up and maybe Tom becoming the fall guy for murder. **91m/C; DVD.** Samuel L. Jackson; Ed Harris; Robert Forster; Luis Guzman; Marc Macaulay; Eva Mendes; Keke Palmer; Jose Pablo Cantillo; Maggie Lawson; ***D:*** Renny Harlin; ***W:*** Matthew Aldrich; ***C:*** Scott Kevan; ***M:*** Richard Gibbs. **VIDEO**

Cleanskin ♪♪ **2012** Violent, gritty action-thriller. British secret service agent Ewan (Bean) goes off the grid to find a radical terrorist group in London. This means out-witting British-born Ash (Galeya), a student turned extremist. Flashbacks detail how the young Muslim, who doesn't fit the usual profile (hence the pic's title), got to his present situation. **108m/C; DVD, Blu-Ray.** *UK* Sean Bean; Abhin Galeya; Charlotte Rampling; Tuppence Middleton; James Fox; Tom Burke; ***D:*** Hadi Hajaig; ***W:*** Hadi Hajaig; ***C:*** Ian Howes; ***M:*** Simon Lambros.

Clear All Wires! ♪♪ **1933** In this fast-pased comic adventure, unethical Moscow foreign correspondent Buckley Joyce Thomas (Tracy) has been fired. He schemes to get his job back by staging an assassination attempt on a Russian prince and writing the big scoop. Based on the play by Bela and Samuel Spewack, who also wrote the screenplay. **78m/B; DVD.** Lee Tracy; Una Merkel; James Gleason; Benita Hume; Alan Edwards; Eugene Sigaloff; ***D:*** George W. Hill; ***W:*** Bella Spewack; Samuel Spewack; ***C:*** Norbert Brodine; ***M:*** William Axt.

Clear and Present Danger ♪♪ ½ **1994 (PG-13)** Ford returns for a second go at CIA agent Jack Ryan in the third installment of Tom Clancy's bestselling adventures. With the Cold War over, the U.S. government is the bad guy as Ryan discovers a link between a South American drug cartel and a Presidential advisor. Viewers will also finally get an answer to that nagging question at the end of "Patriot Games:" is it a boy or a girl? Archer's back as Ryan's annoying wife, and Birch and Jones also return. Keep alert for complex plot twists in lieu of tons of action, though there's enough to keep action fans happy. **141m/C; VHS, DVD, Blu-Ray.** Harrison Ford; Anne Archer; James Earl Jones; Willem Dafoe; Thora Birch; Henry Czerny; Harris Yulin; Raymond Cruz; Joaquim de Almeida; Miguel (Michael) Sandoval; Donald Moffat; Theodore (Ted) Raimi; Dean Jones; ***D:*** Phillip Noyce; ***W:*** John Milius; Donald Stewart; Steven Zaillian; ***C:*** Donald McAlpine; ***M:*** James Horner. Blockbuster '95: Action Actor, T. (Ford); Blockbuster '96: Action Actor, V. (Ford).

The Clearing 🦴🦴🦴 **2004 (R)** Rich businessman Redford is kidnapped from his driveway by frustrated former employee Dafoe. As Dafoe leads Redford through the woods towards an appointed meeting spot with the other kidnappers, Redford tries to talk Dafoe into letting him go free. His wife (Mirren), meanwhile, finally notices his prolonged absence and calls in family and FBI. Redford talks to Dafoe about his wife; Mirren talks to an understanding agent about her husband. As the tension builds around them, the two reflect upon their importance to one another. Quietly suspenseful and full of interesting, fully fleshed characters, with a deliberate pace, beautiful acting, and a rewarding twist at the end. **91m/C; DVD.** Robert Redford; Willem Dafoe; Dame Helen Mirren; Matt Craven; Alessandro Nivola; Melissa Sagemiller; Wendy Crewson; Larry Pine; Diana Scarwid; Elizabeth Ruscio; ***D:*** Pieter Jan Brugge; ***W:*** Justin Haythe; ***C:*** Denis Lenoir; ***M:*** Craig Armstrong.

The Clearstream Affair 🦴🦴 ½ *L'enquete* **2015** A French thriller centered on a journalist's quest to reveal corruption in banking and government. Though journalist Denis Robert (Lellouche) creates a firestorm of controversy by denouncing the underhanded dealings of the banking firm Clearstream, he continues his investigation into learning the truths about the secretive world of multinational banking. In the process, he joins forces with a judge conducting his own growing anti-corruption investigation. What they find is both political and financial intrigue that encompasses both the French government and wider European concerns. French, Mandarin, and Luxembourgish with subtitles. **106m/C; DVD.** Gilles Lellouche; Charles Berling; Laurent Capelluto; Florence Loiret Caille; Christian Kmiotek; ***D:*** Vincent Garenq; ***W:*** Vincent Garenq; Stephane Cabel; ***C:*** Renaud Chassaing; ***M:*** Erwann Kermorvant. **VIDEO**

Cleaverville 🦴🦴 **2007** When Grace Flynn's (Carradine) con goes wrong, she's on the run from mobsters with a bag full of diamonds. Grace heads to her estranged mother Kay's (Rose) house but Kay's first priority is protecting Grace's teen daughter Laura (Savasta) whom she's raised. But the three generations of women soon realize they have to work together if they're going to stay alive. **90m/C; DVD.** Ever Carradine; Gabrielle Rose; Leela Savasta; Scott Hylands; Zak Santiago; Susan Hogan; ***D:*** Jorge Montesi; ***W:*** Lisanne Sarter; ***M:*** Hal Beckett. **CABLE**

Clemency 🦴🦴 ½ **2019 (R)** Long-time prison warden Bernandine (Woodard) has become a shell of a person who leaves a part of herself at the prison each night when she goes home to her husband Anthony (Pierce). Though she wants to be a whole person again, the difficulties of her position have left her lonely and struggling. Anthony (Hodge), a prisoner on death row who claims innocence but faces a looming execution date, has similar feelings though he embraces optimism as hopes for clemency. A gripping drama that delves into the effects of the criminal justice system on both the incarcerated and those who work there. **112m/C; DVD.** Aldis Hodge; Alfre Woodard; Richard Schiff; Vernee Watson-Johnson; Wendell Pierce; ***D:*** Chinonye Chukwu; ***W:*** Chinonye Chukwu; ***C:*** Eric Branco; ***M:*** Kathryn Bostic.

Cleo from 5 to 7 🦴🦴🦴 ½ *Cleo de 5 a 7* **1961** A singer strolls through Paris for 90 minutes, and reconsiders her life while awaiting the results of medical tests for cancer. Typical documentary-like effort from innovative filmmaker Varda, who constructed the film in real time. Look for a brief appearance of master director Jean-Luc Godard. In French with English subtitles. **90m/B; VHS, DVD.** ***FR*** Corinne Marchand; Antoine Bourseiller; Dorothee Blanck; Michel Legrand; Jean-Claude Brialy; Jean-Luc Godard; Anna Karina; Eddie Constantine; Sami Frey; ***D:*** Agnes Varda; ***W:*** Agnes Varda; ***C:*** Jean Rabier.

Cleopatra 🦴🦴 **1934** Early Hollywood DeMille version of the Egyptian temptress's lust for Marc Antony after Julius Caesar's death. Intermittently interesting extravaganza. Colbert seems to be enjoying herself in the lead role in this hokey, overdone epic. Includes the original theatrical trailer on laser-track 2. Remade in 1963. **100m/B; VHS, DVD, Blu-Ray.** Claudette Colbert; Henry Wilcoxon; Warren William; Gertrude Michael; Joseph Schildkraut; Sir C. Aubrey Smith; ***D:*** Cecil B. DeMille; ***C:*** Victor Milner. Oscars '34: Cinematog.

Cleopatra 🦴 **1963** And we thought DeMille's version was extravagant. After the death of Julius Caesar, Cleopatra, Queen of Egypt, becomes infatuated with Mark Antony. Costly four-hour epic functions like a blimp-sized, multi-colored sleeping tablet. Historical characters are utterly dwarfed by the film's massive scope, and audiences are benumbed by a spectacle of crowd scenes and opulent, grotesque interiors. Taylor looks and often acts like a sex bomb ruler, while Harrison has some notion of Caesar's majesty. Burton, however, is hopelessly wooden. Hard to believe this came from director Mankiewicz. **246m/C; VHS, DVD, Blu-Ray.** Elizabeth Taylor; Richard Burton; Rex Harrison; Roddy McDowall; Martin Landau; Pamela Brown; Michael Hordern; Kenneth Haigh; Andrew Keir; Hume Cronyn; Carroll O'Connor; ***D:*** Joseph L. Mankiewicz; ***W:*** Joseph L. Mankiewicz; ***C:*** Leon Shamroy; ***M:*** Alex North. Oscars '63: Art Dir./Set Dec., Color, Color Cinematog., Costume Des. (C), Visual FX; Natl. Bd. of Review '63: Actor (Harrison).

Cleopatra 🦴🦴 **1999** Lavishly trashy TV miniseries about the infamous Egyptian queen and her Roman lovers. Young royal, Cleopatra (Varela), wants to rule Egypt but she needs the power of Rome to make things happen. When Julius Caesar (Dalton) comes to Egypt, she seduces the conqueror to gain a kingdom. But after Caesar's murder, Cleopatra pins her hopes on rash Marc Antony (Zane) and things don't turn out so well. Based on the book by Margaret George. **139m/C; VHS, DVD.** Leonor Varela; Timothy Dalton; Billy Zane; Rupert Graves; Art Malik; John Bowe; Nadim Sawalha; Owen Teale; Daragh O'Malley; Sean Pertwee; Bruce Payne; Caroline Langrishe; ***D:*** Franc Roddam; ***W:*** Stephen Harrigan; Anton Diether; ***C:*** David Connell; ***M:*** Trevor Jones. **TV**

Cleopatra Jones 🦴🦴 **1973 (PG)** Lean and lethal government agent with considerable martial arts prowess takes on loathsome drug lords. Dobson is fetching as the lead performer in this fast-paced, violent flick. Followed by "Cleopatra Jones and the Casino of Gold." **89m/C; VHS, DVD, Blu-Ray.** Tamara Dobson; Shelley Winters; Bernie Casey; Brenda Sykes; Albert "Poppy" Popwell; ***D:*** Jack Starrett; ***W:*** Max Julien; Sheldon Keller; ***C:*** David M. Walsh; ***M:*** J.J. Johnson.

Cleopatra Jones & the Casino of Gold 🦴🦴 **1975 (R)** Dobson returns as the lethal, physically imposing federal agent to Hong Kong to take on a powerful druglord in this sequel to "Cleopatra Jones." Watch for sexy Stevens as the Dragon Lady. **96m/C; VHS, DVD.** Tamara Dobson; Stella Stevens; Norman Fell; Albert "Poppy" Popwell; ***D:*** Charles "Chuck" Bail.

Cleopatra's Second Husband 🦴🦴 **2000 (R)** Let's play master and servant. Whiny, selfish yuppie couple Robert (Hipp) and Hallie (Schram) Marrs go on vacation and need housesitters for their fabulous L.A. pad. They accept a recommendation from friends to employ sexy Zack (Kestner) and Sophie (Mitchell). Some friends—when the Marrs return early, their housesitters ask to stay on a little longer and proceed to take over. Hallie takes off after Robert gets it on with Sophie but the sexual/mind games are just beginning. **92m/C; VHS, DVD.** Paul Hipp; Boyd Kestner; Radha Mitchell; Bitty Schram; Alexis Arquette; Jonathan Penner; ***D:*** Jonathan Reiss; ***W:*** Jonathan Reiss; ***C:*** Matt Faw; ***M:*** Cary Berger.

Clerks 🦴🦴🦴 **1994 (R)** "What kind of convenience store do you run here?" Day in the life of a convenience store clerk is an often hilarious lesson in the profane from first time writer/director Smith (who has a cameo as Silent Bob). Twenty-two-year-old Dante Hicks (O'Halloran) is a disaffected New Jersey Quick Stop employee who spends most of his time bored and dealing with borderline crazies. The next-door video store is clerked by his best friend Randal (Anderson), who derives equal delight from tormenting his customers and debating absolutely anything (especially anything sexual). Nothing much actually happens but the very low-budget ($27,575) production has a decidedly scuzzy charm and a cult following. Based on the director's four years of clerking at the Quick Stop and shot on location. **89m/B; VHS, DVD, Blu-Ray, UMD.** Brian O'Halloran; Jeff Anderson; Marilyn Ghigliotti; Lisa Spoonhauer; Jason Mewes; ***Cameo(s):*** Kevin Smith; ***D:*** Kevin Smith; ***W:*** Kevin Smith; ***C:*** David Klein; ***M:*** Scott Angley. Natl. Film Reg. '19; Sundance '94: Filmmakers Trophy.

Clerks 2 🦴🦴🦴 **2006 (R)** Writer/director/actor Kevin Smith revisits the New Jersey suburban landscape that put him and his recurring characters on the map 12 years ago. Little has changed in the lives or ambitions of clerks Dante (Brian O'Halloran) and Randal (Jeff Anerson)?they still pass the time with Smith's signature debates and diatribes on such topics as beastiality, "The Man," and the virtues of "Star Wars" vs. "Lord of the Rings"?while harassing the occasional, unfortunate customer. The same semi-professional, low-budget charm of its predecessor makes for a strong follow-up. Simply put, if you liked "Clerks," you'll like "Clerks II"; if you were offended by the first, you'll be horrified by this one. **98m/C; DVD, HD-DVD.** Brian O'Halloran; Jeff Anderson; Jason Mewes; Rosario Dawson; Kevin Smith; Jennifer Schwalbach Smith; Jason Lee; Ethan Suplee; Trevor Fehrman; Kevin Weisman; Wanda Sykes; ***Cameo(s):*** Ben Affleck; ***D:*** Kevin Smith; ***W:*** Kevin Smith; ***C:*** David Klein; ***M:*** James L. Venable.

Click 🦴🦴 **2006 (PG-13)** Workaholic family man Michael Newman (Sandler) needs a universal remote to simplify at least one thing in his life. Salesclerk Morty (Walken) hands over a special device that allows Michael to pause, mute, fast-forward, and rewind his actual life. Naturally, this is not the blessing that Michael first imagines it to be. Sandler does some more of his disgruntled man-child shtick, Walken is benignly crazy, and Beckinsale is nagging and hot. **98m/C; DVD, Blu-Ray.** Adam Sandler; Kate Beckinsale; Christopher Walken; Sean Astin; David Hasselhoff; Henry Winkler; Julie Kavner; Jennifer Coolidge; Lorraine Nicholson; Jonah Hill; Rob Schneider; Rachel Dratch; Katie Cassidy; Nick Swardson; Tatum McCann; ***D:*** Frank Coraci; ***W:*** Mark O'Keefe; Steve Koren; ***C:*** Dean Semler; ***M:*** Rupert Gregson-Williams.

The Client 🦴🦴 ½ **1994 (PG-13)** Another legal thriller from the Grisham factory. Reggie Love (Sarandon) is a troubled attorney hired by 11-year-old Mark (Renfro), who witnessed the suicide of a Mafia attorney and now knows more than he should. Ambitious federal prosecutor Foltrigg's (Jones) willing to risk the boy's life in exchange for career advancement. Lacks the mega-big Hollywood names of "The Firm" and "The Pelican Brief" but gains solid acting in return with Renfro a find in his film debut. No frills, near-faithful adaptation by Schumacher basically travels down the path of least resistance. Filmed on location in Memphis. **121m/C; VHS, DVD, Blu-Ray.** Susan Sarandon; Tommy Lee Jones; Brad Renfro; Mary-Louise Parker; Anthony LaPaglia; Bradley Whitford; Anthony Edwards; Ossie Davis; Walter Olkewicz; J.T. Walsh; Will Patton; Anthony Heald; William H. Macy; Ron Dean; ***D:*** Joel Schumacher; ***W:*** Robert Getchell; Akiva Goldsman; ***C:*** Tony Pierce-Roberts; ***M:*** Howard Shore. British Acad. '94: Actress (Sarandon).

The Client List 🦴 ½ **2010** In this Lifetime drama, unemployed small town Texas wife and mother Samantha Horton (Hewitt) becomes desperate after her husband Rex (Sears) loses his job. The former massage therapist applies for work at a spa but discovers the massages are particularly intimate. Samantha turns out to be successful in her new profession until the cops raid the joint. Not the weepy you might imagine, although the humor could be unintentional. **95m/C; DVD.** Jennifer Love Hewitt; Teddy Sears; Cybill Shepherd; Sonja Bennett; Lynda Boyd; Chelah Horsdal; ***D:*** Eric Laneuville; ***W:*** Suzanne Martin; ***C:*** Tony Westman; ***M:*** Richard (Rick) Marvin. **CABLE**

Client 9: The Rise and Fall of Eliot Spitzer 🦴🦴 **2010 (R)** Yet another scandal about a politician caught with his pants down. In this case it was New York Governor Eliot Spitzer who resigned (in March 2008) after being linked as a VIP patron of the escort service Emperor's Club. Though not negating Spitzer's actions (and hubris), director Gibney also interviews various politicians, power brokers, and businessmen whom Spitzer investigated as the state's attorney general, suggesting that payback played a part in Spitzer's downfall. **117m/C; DVD, Blu-Ray.** ***D:*** Alex Gibney; ***W:*** Alex Gibney; ***C:*** Maryse Alberti; ***M:*** Peter Nashel.

Cliffhanger 🦴🦴🦴 **1993 (R)** Action-packed thriller. Expert climber Gabe Walker (Stallone) faces his greatest challenge when criminal mastermind Lithgow and his henchman appear on the scene. Turner plays fellow climber and love interest. Lithgow makes a particularly convincing, if not downright chilling, murderous thief. Filmed in the Italian Alps with a budget of $70 million-plus; boasts stunning cinematography and breathtaking footage of the Dolomite mountain range. Harlin's expert pacing and direction combine to produce maximum thrills and suspense. The hit Stallone's been waiting for, placing eighth on the list of top 1993 boxoffice grossers. **113m/C; VHS, DVD, Blu-Ray.** Sylvester Stallone; John Lithgow; Michael Rooker; Janine Turner; Rex Linn; Caroline Goodall; Leon; Paul Winfield; Ralph Waite; Craig Fairbrass; Michelle Joyner; Max Perlich; ***D:*** Renny Harlin; ***W:*** Sylvester Stallone; Michael France; ***C:*** Alex Thomson; ***M:*** Trevor Jones.

Clifford WOOF! **1992 (PG)** Short plays a 10-year-old in an effort delayed by Orion's financial crisis. Creepy little Clifford's uncle Martin (Grodin) rues the day he volunteered to babysit his nephew to prove to his girlfriend (Steenburgen) how much he likes kids. Clifford terrorizes Grodin in surprisingly nasty ways when their plans for visiting Dinosaurworld fall through, although Grodin sees to well-deserved revenge. Not just bad in the conventional sense, but bad in a bizarre sort of alien fashion that raises questions about who was controlling the bodies of the producers. To create the effect of Short really being short, other actors stood on boxes and sets were built slightly larger. **90m/C; VHS, DVD.** Martin Short; Charles Grodin; Mary Steenburgen; Dabney Coleman; Sonia Jackson; ***D:*** Paul Flaherty; ***W:*** Bobby Von Hayes; Jay Dee Rock; Steven Kampmann; Will Aldis; ***C:*** John A. Alonzo; ***M:*** Richard Gibbs.

Clifford's Really Big Movie 🦴🦴 ½ **2004 (G)** Animated tale of TV's lovably oversized canine hero, Clifford (Ritter), and normal-sized friends Cleo the poodle (Summer) and T-Bone the mutt (Mitchell) who take to the road after the Big Red Dog mistakenly thinks his large appetite is causing his owners to go broke. The trio join up with a traveling carnival populated by plenty of child-delighting characters. Clifford revives the struggling show and becomes a star, all in the hope that the act will help him win a lifetime supply of his fave snack Tummy Yummies. Mildly evil doggie-treat tycoon (Goodman) has other plans for Clifford, however, and plots to kidnap the dog. Extremely gentle story and nice message especially suitable for younger viewers; older watchers won't find much here. **73m/C; VHS, DVD.** ***V:*** John Ritter; Wayne Brady; Jenna Elfman; John Goodman; Kel Mitchell; Judge Reinhold; Kath Soucie; Cree Summer; Grey DeLisle; Wilmer Valderrama; Earl Boen; Teresa Ganzel; Jess Harnell; Ernie Hudson; Oren Williams; Cam(eron) Clarke; ***D:*** Robert Ramirez; ***W:*** Robert Ramirez; Rhett Reese; ***M:*** Jody Gray.

Cliffs of Freedom 🦴 ½ **2019 (R)** During the 19th century Greek War of Independence, most of the Turkish occupiers of Greece take pleasure in acting sadistically towards locals. Only Colonel Tariq (Uddin) argues that they should not be treated brutality, mostly because of the influence of his Greek tutor and mentor (Plummer). Tariq is also challenged by Christina (Raymonde), whom he saved when she was a child and who has grown into a freedom fighter and revolutionary symbol. Despite their differences, Tariq and Christina experience serious attraction. The historical epic was made with limited resources, and it shows. **137m/C; DVD.** Tania Raymonde; Jan Uddin; Raza Jaffrey; Patti LuPone; Christopher Plummer; ***D:*** Van Ling; ***W:*** Van Ling; Marianne Metropoulos; Kevin Bernhardt; ***C:*** Cory Geryak; ***M:*** George Kallis.

Climates ✓✓✓ *Iklimler* **2006** A Turkish couple's decision to call things off spans not only their native countryside but also several seasons. Beginning in summer, the distant 40ish professor Isa and his much-younger TV art director girlfriend Bahar break up, though the reasons are never given. In fact, not much is said throughout, though their feelings are usually obvious. Moving along to fall, Isa has a manic sex encounter with Serap (Kesal)?a possible culprit in Isa and Bahar's troubles—even though, in winter, Serap tells Isa where to find Bahar. Writer-director-lead actor Nuri Bilge Ceylan (Isa) is the real-life husband of Ebru Ceylan (Bahar). In Turkish with subtitles. **97m/C; DVD.** *FR TU* Nuri Bilge Ceylan; Ebru Ceylan; Nazan Kirilmis; Mehmet Eryilmaz; Arif Asci; Can Ozbatur; ***D:*** Nuri Bilge Ceylan; ***W:*** Nuri Bilge Ceylan; ***C:*** Gokhan Tiryaki.

The Climax ✓✓ ½ **1944** Technicolor highlights this horror saga of obsession. House physician for Vienna's Royal Theatre, Dr. Hohner (Karloff) kills opera singer Marcellina (Vincent) when she rejects him. Twenty years later, Hohner hears the beautiful voice of Angela (Foster), a near duplicate of Marcellina's, and hypnotizes her to prevent her singing. Now, it's up to Angela's composer friend Franz (Bey) to overcome the doctor's evil influence. Adapted from a play by Edward Locke. Waggner directed this "The Phantom of the Opera" clone using the same sets as the 1943 "Phantom" remake. **86m/C; DVD, Blu-Ray.** Boris Karloff; Susanna Foster; Turhan Bey; Gale Sondergaard; Thomas Gomez; June Vincent; Jane Farrar; Scotty Beckett; ***D:*** George Waggner; ***W:*** Curt Siodmak; Lynn Starling; ***C:*** Hal Mohr; William Howard Greene; ***M:*** Edward Ward.

Climax ✓✓ **2018 (R)** In 1996 France, a multicultural group of talented dancers prepare for an American tour by rehearsing in a community center in a rural area. After a run-through of a powerful dance that showcases each performer's strength and personality, the dancers socialize in the common room and drink from a bowl of sangria. It becomes clear that the sangria was laced with acid, with horrifying effects. As the members try to figure out who spiked the punch, they endure hallucinations and paranoia. Though the film is unique, especially the camerawork, the graphic sex and violence can be hard to watch. **97m/C; DVD, Blu-Ray.** *FR BE US* Sofia Boutella; Romain Guillermic; Souheila Yacoub; Kiddy Smile; Claude Gajan Maull; ***D:*** Gaspar Noé; ***W:*** Gaspar Noé; ***C:*** Benoit Debie.

The Climb ✓✓ ½ **1997 (PG-13)** In late '50s Baltimore, 12-year-old Danny (Smith) is the target of bullies and humiliated by the fact that his dad Earl (Strathairn) is accused of cowardice because he's not a vet. So Danny decides to prove his own courage by climbing the local, soon-to-be-demolished 203-foot radio tower. Danny is unexpected aided by his crochety neighbor, Chuck Langer (Hurt), a hard-drinking grump dying of cancer. But when Danny gets into trouble, it's his dad who comes to the rescue. Nostalgic family fare. **94m/C; VHS, DVD.** *FR NZ* Gregory Edward Smith; John Hurt; David Strathairn; Stephen McHattie; Seth Smith; Sarah Buxton; ***D:*** Bob Swaim; ***W:*** Vince McKewin; ***C:*** Allen Guilford; ***M:*** Greco Casadeus.

The Climbers ✓✓ *Pan deng zhe* **2019** Fang Wuzhou (Wu) leads the first Chinese group to Mount Everest's summit via the north face in 1960 but loses most of his team in an avalanche. This climb is later invalidated due to lack of photographic evidence. Though Fang sets aside his goal to reach this summit because of the Cultural Revolution, he does not lose sight of it. In the mid-1970s, Fang, other surviving members, and newcomers form another climbing team to take another shot at reaching the summit. Based on a true story, the action-adventure has a blockbuster feel but misses out on the emotional connection. Mandarin and Tibetan with subtitles. **125m/C; DVD.** Jing Wu; Ziyi Zhang; Boran Jing; Yi Zhang; Jackie Chan; ***D:*** Daniel Lee; ***W:*** Daniel Lee; Alai Ying Shang; ***C:*** Tony Cheung.

Climbing High ✓✓ ½ **1938** Madcap Brit rom com. Amiable, wealthy Nicky (Redgrave) is involved in a pedestrian vs. car accident with penniless model Diana (Matthews). Immediately smitten, Nicky's afraid his money will prejudice Diana against him, so he pretends to be poor. She learns the truth and dumps him for lying to her and Nicky unhappily rebounds with a snooty aristocrat (Vyner) until the expected conclusion, which happens in the Swiss Alps. **79m/B; DVD.** *UK* Michael Redgrave; Jessie Matthews; Margaret Vyner; Alastair Sim; Noel Madison; ***D:*** Carol Reed; ***W:*** Marion Dix; Lesser Samuels; ***C:*** Mutz Greenbaum.

The Clinic ✓ **2010 (R)** Despite the sensationalism and gore, this Aussie pic is more thriller than horror.Set in 1979, pregnant Beth and her husband Cameron are traveling in the Outback when she's abducted. Beth awakens in a warehouse and her fetus has been stolen. She stumbles across several other women whose babies are also gone and then more craziness happens. Pic moves along but never amkes much sense. **94m/C; DVD.** *AU* Tabrett Bethell; Freya Stafford; Clare Bowen; Andy Whitfield; ***D:*** James Rabbitts; ***W:*** James Rabbitts; ***C:*** Brad Shield. **VIDEO**

Clip ✓✓ ½ *Klip* **2013** A dramatic exploration of one teen girl's out-of-control life. Living in the dreary suburbs of Belgrade, Serbia, disillusioned teen Jasna (Simijonovic) has a messy family life. Her father is terminally ill and her mother struggles to keep going. Jasna has one outlet. She uses her camera phone to make videos of everything around her, including her family, friends, and the boy she has a crush on, Djole (Jasnic). As Jasna starts to drink and party, she talks to Djole and the pair begin a sexual relationship. When Djole realizes that he has power over her, she does anything, including skipping school and drugs, to be accepted by him. Jasna must decide if everything is worth gaining Djole's affections and who she wants to be. Serbian with subtitles. **102m/C; DVD, Blu-Ray, Streaming, Download.** Isidora Simijonovic; Vukasin Jasnic; Sanja Mikitisin; Jovo Maksic; Monja Savic; ***D:*** Maja Milos; ***W:*** Maja Milos; ***C:*** Vladimir Simic.

The Clique ✓✓ ½ **2008 (PG)** Based on the book series by Lisa Harrison for tweens too young for "Gossip Girl." Gawky Claire Lyons has just moved with her family to New York City from Florida. She's starting classes at Octavian Country Day school and it's obvious Claire doesn't fit in with the popular clique of mean girls. But will she let them bully her or change her? **87m/C; DVD.** Ellen Marlow; Elizabeth McLaughlin; Samantha Boscarino; Sophie Anna Everhard; Bridgit Mendler; Elizabeth Keifer; Neal Matarazzo; ***D:*** Michael Lembeck; ***W:*** Liz Tigelaar; ***C:*** Michael Weaver; ***M:*** George S. Clinton. **VIDEO**

Clive Barker's Book of Blood ✓✓ *Book of Blood* **2008 (R)** Adapted from two 1984 framing stories by Barker: "Book of Blood" and "On Jerusalem Street." Paranormal investigator Mary Florescu (Ward) and her skeptic partner Reg Fuller (Blair) examine an old gothic Edinburgh mansion that Mary believes is used as an intersecting road for transporting souls into the afterlife. Mary recruits her student Simon (Armstrong) to assist with dire consequences. **100m/C; DVD, Blu-Ray.** Sophie Ward; Paul Blair; Jonas Armstrong; Doug Bradley; Romana Abercromby; Simon Bramford; ***D:*** John Harrison; ***W:*** John Harrison; Darin Silverman; ***C:*** Philip Robertson; ***M:*** Guy Farley. **VIDEO**

Clive of India ✓✓ **1935** Typically noble biopic of Robert Clive (Colman), a clerk with the East India Company in the 18th century. Clive believes it's Britain's destiny to rule India by any means necessary, which involves mutinies and bloody battles (most of which are talked about and not shown), when he becomes a military leader. The real Clive suffered a sad fate back in London but the Hollywood version has a happier ending. **92m/B; DVD.** Ronald Colman; Loretta Young; Colin Clive; Francis Lister; Sir C. Aubrey Smith; Cesar Romero; Montagu Love; ***D:*** Richard Boleslawski; ***W:*** W.P. Lipscomb; R.J. Minney; ***C:*** J. Peverell Marley; ***M:*** Alfred Newman.

Cloak and Dagger ✓✓ **1946** An American physicist joins the secret service during WWII and infiltrates Nazi territory to release a kidnapped scientist who is being forced to build a nuclear bomb. Disappointing spy show with muted anti-nuclear tone. **106m/B; DVD, Blu-Ray.** Gary Cooper; Lilli Palmer; Robert Alda; James Flavin; Vladimir Sokoloff; J. Edward Bromberg; Marc Lawrence; Ludwig Stossel; ***D:*** Fritz Lang; ***W:*** Ring Lardner, Jr.; Albert (John B. Sherry) Maltz; ***C:*** Sol Polito; ***M:*** Max Steiner.

Cloak & Dagger ✓✓ ½ **1984 (PG)** A young boy, last seen befriending E.T., depends upon his imaginary super-friend to help him out when some real-life agents are after his video game. Coleman is particularly fun as both dad and fantasy hero in an interesting family adventure. **101m/C; VHS, DVD.** Dabney Coleman; Henry Thomas; Michael Murphy; John McIntire; Jeannette Nolan; ***D:*** Richard Franklin; ***W:*** Tom Holland; ***M:*** Brian May.

The Clock ✓✓✓ *Under the Clock* **1945** Appealing romance about an office worker who meets and falls in love with a soldier on two-day leave in NYC. Charismatic Walker and likeable Garland make a fine screen couple, and Wynn is memorable as the drunk. **91m/B; VHS, DVD.** Judy Garland; Robert Walker; James Gleason; Marshall Thompson; Keenan Wynn; ***D:*** Vincente Minnelli; ***C:*** George J. Folsey; ***M:*** George Bassman.

Clockers ✓✓✓ **1995 (R)** Strike (Phifer), leader of a group of bottom-feeding drug dealers ("clockers"), engages in a power struggle with his boss (Lindo), his do-the-right-thing brother Victor (Washington), and his own conscience. He's also suspected of murder by relentless narcotics cop Rocco Klein (Keitel). Supported by an excellent cast, first-timer Phifer surprises with a fierce and powerful performance. Lindo, in particular, stands out as the paternally evil Rodney. Aggressively edited, with Turturro's performance mostly lost on the cutting room floor. Critically lauded cinematography is marred by the occasional boom shot. Poignant and compelling street drama is based on the Richard Price novel. Lee took over after Scorsese and De Niro dropped out to make "Casino." **128m/C; VHS, DVD, Blu-Ray.** Mekhi Phifer; Harvey Keitel; John Turturro; Delroy Lindo; Keith David; Isaiah Washington, IV; Lisa Arrindell Anderson; Kirk "Sticky Fingaz" Jones; ***D:*** Spike Lee; ***W:*** Spike Lee; Richard Price; ***C:*** Malik Hassan Sayeed; ***M:*** Terence Blanchard.

The Clockmaker ✓✓✓ ½ *L'Horloger de Saint-Paul* **1973** Contemplative drama about a clockmaker whose life is shattered when his son is arrested as a political assassin. Tavernier regular Noiret excels in the lead. In French with English subtitles. **105m/C; VHS, DVD.** *FR* Philippe Noiret; Jean Rochefort; Jacques Denis; William Sabatier; Christine Pascal; ***D:*** Bertrand Tavernier; ***W:*** Bertrand Tavernier; Jean Aurenche; Pierre Bost; ***C:*** Sylvain Rougerie; ***M:*** Philippe Sarde.

Clockstoppers ✓✓ ½ **2002 (PG)** Amusing kid fare has heroes Zak (Bradford) and Venezuelan exchange student Francesca (Garces) zipping around in speeded-up "hypertime" to rescue Zak's scientists dad Dr. Gibbs (Thomas) from time-traveling baddies, headed by corporate bigwig Henry Gates (Biehn). It seems the wristwatch/time machine Gibbs invented needs tweaking, so Gibbs and top grad student Dopler (Stewart) are kidnaped to fix the snag by the evil QT corporation, which wants to use the device to, what else, conquer the world. The teen duo must do their rescuing, however, before they all prematurely age in hypertime (one of the snags). No stranger to sci-fi, director Frakes (Riker on "Star Trek: Next Generation") makes the most of the inherent FX. **94m/C; VHS, DVD.** Jesse Bradford; French Stewart; Michael Biehn; Paula Garces; Robin Thomas; Julia Sweeney; Linda Kim; Garikayi Mutambirwa; ***D:*** Jonathan Frakes; ***W:*** Rob Hedden; J. David Stem; David N. Weiss; ***C:*** Tim Suhrstedt; ***M:*** Jamshield Sharifi.

Clockwatchers ✓ ½ **1997 (PG-13)** Decent cast gets wasted in a slice of life story that goes nowhere. Meek temp Iris's (Collette) new assignment is at a big, faceless credit company. Iris is taken in hand by fellow temps Margaret (Posey), Paula (Kudrow), and Jane (Ubach), who like to complain about how badly they're treated by management. Things gets worse when the company makes an announcement about a rash of petty thefts and the temps get blamed. That's it. **105m/C; VHS, DVD.** Toni Collette; Parker Posey; Lisa Kudrow; Alanna Ubach; Stanley DeSantis; Jamie Kennedy; David James Elliott; Kevin Cooney; Bob Balaban; Paul Dooley; ***D:*** Jill Sprecher; ***W:*** Jill Sprecher; Karen Sprecher; ***C:*** Jim Denault.

Clockwise ✓✓ ½ **1986 (PG)** Monty Python regular Cleese is a teacher preoccupied by punctuality. His neurosis proves his undoing when he falls victim to misadventure while traveling to deliver a speech. Cleese is acceptable, dialogue and story is less so, though sprinkled with a fair amount of humor. **96m/C; VHS, DVD.** *GB* John Cleese; Penelope Wilton; Alison Steadman; Stephen Moore; Sharon Maiden; ***D:*** Christopher Morahan; ***W:*** Michael Frayn; ***C:*** John Coquillon; ***M:*** George Fenton.

A Clockwork Orange ✓✓✓✓ **1971 (R)** In the Britain of the near future, a sadistic punk leads a gang on nightly rape and murder sprees, then is captured and becomes the subject of a grim experiment to eradicate his violent tendencies in this extraordinary adaptation of Anthony Burgess's controversial novel. The film is an exhilarating experience, with an outstanding performance by McDowell as the funny, fierce psychopath. Many memorable, disturbing sequences, including a rape conducted while assailant McDowell belts "Singing in the Rain." Truly outstanding, provocative work from master filmmaker Kubrick. **137m/C; VHS, DVD, Blu-Ray, HD-DVD.** *GB* Malcolm McDowell; Patrick Magee; Adrienne Corri; Michael Bates; Warren Clarke; Aubrey Morris; James Marcus; Steven Berkoff; John Clive; David Prowse; Carl Duering; Miriam Karlin; ***D:*** Stanley Kubrick; ***W:*** Stanley Kubrick; ***C:*** John Alcott; ***M:*** Walter (Wendy) Carlos. AFI '98: Top 100; N.Y. Film Critics '71: Director (Kubrick), Film.

Clone ✓ **2005** Humanity is dying as radioactive fallout has rendered everyone infertile. The remnants are fighting over the one person whose genes can activate dormant clones and thus either save humanity or doom it to be run by a militant dictator. **109m/C; DVD, Streaming.** *UK US* Jeff St. Clair; Gary Skiba; James Kisicki; Bill Caco; Valerie Law; ***D:*** Jason J. Tomaric; ***W:*** Jason J. Tomaric; ***C:*** Jason J. Tomaric; ***M:*** Christopher First. **VIDEO**

Clone Hunter ✓ *Clonehunter* **2009 (R)** In the future the wealthy have achieved immortality by transferring their brains to younger clones of themselves. Unfortunately sometimes the clones gain mutant psychic powers and take planets hostage, and that's where the clone hunters come in. **86m/C; DVD, Streaming.** Tzaddi Allick; Jeff Betz; Gregg Oliver Bodine; H. R. Britton; ***D:*** Andrew Bellware; ***W:*** Eric Steele; ***C:*** Andrew Bellware; ***M:*** Sam Reising. **VIDEO**

The Clonus Horror ✓ ½ *Clonus; Parts: The Clonus Horror* **1979** A scientist discovers a government plot to clone prominent citizens for spare parts. The clones are kept isolated and not told of their true origins or purpose, but one (Donnelly) escapes. This causes problems for him, his clone girlfriend, and, basically anyone he comes in contact with in the "real world." Muddled and cheesy in a late-70s kind of way. **90m/C; VHS, DVD.** Tim Donnelly; Eileen Dietz; Keenan Wynn; Paulette Breen; Peter Graves; Dick Sargent; Frank Ashmore; Paulette Breen; ***D:*** Robert S. Fiveson; ***W:*** Robert S. Fiveson; Ron Smith; Bob Sullivan; Myrl A. Schreibman; ***C:*** Max Beaufort; ***M:*** Hod David Schudson. **VIDEO**

Close ✓✓ **2019** Sam (Rapace) is a respected private security expert hired to guard wealthy teenager Zoe (Nelisse). Struggling with depression after the recent death of her mining company CEO father, Zoe is now the company's majority stockholder and under the threat of kidnapping, if not murder, because of a potential merger. Sam keeps Zoe out of danger while helping her through her personal crisis. Loosely based on bodyguard

Jacquie Davis's career, the no-nonsense female-led thriller features well-done action scenes, an outstanding performance by Rapace, and a memorable heroine in Sam. But it gets bogged down in overexplaining her motivation. **94m/C; DVD.** Noomi Rapace; Olivia Jewson; Abdellatif Chaouqi; Sophie Nelisse; Huw Parmenter; *D:* Vicky Jewson; *W:* Vicky Jewson; Rupert Whitaker; *C:* Malte Rosenfeld; *M:* Marc Canham. **VIDEO**

Close Encounters of the Third Kind **1977 (PG)** Middle-American strangers become involved in the attempts of benevolent aliens to contact earthlings. Despite the sometimes mundane nature of the characters, this Spielberg epic is a stirring achievement. Studded with classic sequences; the ending is an exhilarating experience of special effects and peace-on-earth feelings. Dreyfuss and Dillon excel as friends who are at once bewildered and obsessed by the alien presence, and French filmmaker Truffaut is also strong as the stern, ultimately kind scientist. **152m/C; VHS, DVD, Blu-Ray.** Richard Dreyfuss; Teri Garr; Melinda Dillon; Francois Truffaut; Bob Balaban; Cary Guffey; J. Patrick McNamara; *D:* Steven Spielberg; *W:* Steven Spielberg; *C:* Vilmos Zsigmond; *M:* John Williams. Oscars '77: Cinematog., Sound FX Editing; AFI '98: Top 100; Natl. Film Reg. '07.

Close My Eyes **1991 (R)** Insecure Natalie (Reeves) is newly married to wealthy and garrulous entrepreneur Sinclair (Rickman) when she reunites with her long-estranged younger brother, Richard (Owen). Richard has just taken a job as a city planner in London and is suddenly Natalie's confidante and soon much more. The simmering sexual tension between the two finally explodes into a volatile relationship that becomes an obsession to Richard. And when Natalie decides to break off their affair, he's determined to stop her. Reeves's character is somewhat whiny and unappealing so it's up to the men to carry the movie, which they do with aplomb. **105m/C; VHS, DVD.** *GB* Alan Rickman; Clive Owen; Saskia Reeves; Karl Johnson; Lesley Sharp; *D:* Stephen Poliakoff; *W:* Stephen Poliakoff; *C:* Witold Stok; *M:* Michael Gibbs.

Close Range **2015** An action crime-thriller centered on one man's efforts to ensure his family's safety. Colton MacReady (Adkins)—once a rogue soldier now working outside the law—gained the wrath of a powerful drug cartel after he rescued his niece from them. Because Colton took back his kidnapped relation, the cartel has surrounded his out-of-the-way ranch in a quest for revenge. Though the cartel has the support of corrupt law enforcement, Colton does all he can without help to protect himself, his property, and his family from the relentless assault of those who seek his demise. **80m/C; DVD, Blu-Ray, Streaming, Download.** Scott Adkins; Nick (Nicholas) Chinlund; Caitlin Keats; Jake La Botz; Tony Perez; *D:* Isaac Florentine; *W:* Chad Law; Shane Dax Taylor; *C:* Tal Lazar; *M:* Stephen (Steve) Edwards.

Close to Leo *Tout Contre Leo* **2002** Uneven-but-intimate family drama finds 20-year-old Leo (Mignard), the eldest of four sons, revealing to his family that he is HIV-positive. His parents decide that their youngest, 12-year-old Marcel (Lespert), is too young to hear the news, although the kid is bright enough to realize something serious is going on and resentful that he is being left out. Honore adapted and directed from his own 1996 novel. French with subtitles. **90m/C; DVD.** *FR* Pierre Mignard; Yannis Lespert; Marie Bunel; Dominic Gould; Rodolphe Pauly; Jeremie Lippmann; *D:* Christophe Honore; *W:* Christophe Honore; Diasteme; *C:* Remy Chevrin; *M:* Alexandre Beaupain. **TV**

Close to My Heart **1/2 1951** Family melodrama. Newspaperman Brad Sheridan (Milland) and his wife Midge (Tierney) are dismayed by the long adoption process so when Brad learns a baby has been abandoned at the police station, he and Midge offer to care for the tyke. Brad gets obsessed with finding out about the boy's parentage, which doesn't put him in a good light with adoption supervisor Mrs. Morrow (Bainter) and Midge may lose the baby she's come to love. **90m/B; DVD.** Ray Milland; Gene Tierney; Fay Bainter; Howard St. John; Mary Beth Hughes; James Seay; Ann Morrison; *D:* William Keighley; *W:* James R. Webb; *C:* Robert Burks; *M:* Max Steiner.

Close-Up **1/2 1948** Mundane B-movie thriller. New York newsreel photographer Phil Sparr (Baxter) unwittingly films Martin Beaumont (Kollmar), a wanted Nazi thought to have been killed in the war. The fugitive will stop at nothing to get back the evidence of his existence and eliminate any witnesses. Most interesting aspect of the flick is the location shooting. **76m/B; DVD.** Alan Baxter; Richard Kollmar; Virginia Gilmore; Loring Smith; Phillip Huston; *D:* Jack Donohue; *W:* John Bright; Max Wilk; *C:* William Miller; *M:* Jerome Moross.

Close Your Eyes **1/2** *Hypnotic; Dr. Sleep* **2002 (R)** Psychic hypnotist Michael Strother (Visnjic) has limited himself to curing smokers after an unsavory event in the U.S. caused him to flee to the UK. When Janet (Henderson), who also happens to be a British cop, comes to Michael hoping to kick her cigarette habit, Michael has a vision which reluctantly brings about his involvement in the highly publicized "tattoo murderer" case and the serial killer's only living victim, Heather. After hypnotizing the now-mute Heather to find some answers, Michael is knee deep in the case against the wishes of his pregnant wife (Otto). He teams up with Janet, who bucks traditional police methods to go with her gut. Not quite a horror film, this overly elaborate, stale supernatural thriller boasts interesting locales, suitably moody climate, and decent performances. **108m/C; DVD.** *GB* Goran Visnjic; Shirley Henderson; Miranda Otto; Paddy Considine; Claire Rushbrook; Fiona Shaw; Corin Redgrave; Sophie Stuckey; *D:* Nick Willing; *W:* Nick Willing; William Brookfield; *C:* Peter Sova; *M:* Simon Boswell.

Closed Circuit **2013 (R)** A bomb goes off in a busy London market and a suspect is arrested but the chain of evidence against him reveals the structure of the war on terrorism. The Attorney General (Broadbent) appoints a Special Advocate (Hall), who actually has a past relationship with the defense attorney (Bana). Writer Knight's cluttered script doesn't know if it's a legal drama, a terrorism thriller, or a commentary on modern technology. Director Crowley's dramatic thriller is surprisingly tame as it attempts to expose how the government's constant surveillance impacts the general public's everyday life. We're better left in the dark. **96m/C; DVD, Blu-Ray.** *UK US* Eric Bana; Rebecca Hall; Ciaran Hinds; Riz Ahmed; Anne-Marie Duff; Kenneth Cranham; Julia Stiles; Jim Broadbent; Denis Moschitto; *D:* John Crowley; *W:* Steven Knight; *C:* Adriano Goldman; *M:* Joby Talbot.

Closed Curtain *Parde* **2013** Iranian filmmaker Panahi is forced into exile in his own home by a government that doesn't exactly take kindly to freedom of expression or creative thought. Serving a totalitarian version of home arrest, Panahi hasn't given up his filmmaking aspirations, making a documentary called "Five Broken Cameras" and this quasi-fictional film about a man trapped in his own home that blurs the line between fiction and non-fiction. It's a clever, engaging piece of work from a talented filmmaker unable to keep those talents hidden even if it sometimes feels a bit too self-aware to be entertaining to mainstream audiences. **106m/C; DVD.** *IA* Kambuzia Parton; Maryam Moqadam; Hadi Saeedi; Jafar Panahi; *D:* Kambuzia Parton; Jafar Panahi; *W:* Jafar Panahi; *C:* Mohamad Reza Jahanpanah.

Closely Watched Trains **1/2** *Ostre Sledovane Vlaky* **1966** A novice train dispatcher attempts to gain sexual experience in German-occupied Czechoslovakia during WWII. Many funny scenes in this film regarded by some as a classic. Based upon the Czech novel by Bohumil Hrabal. In Czech with English subtitles. **89m/B; VHS, DVD.** *CZ* Vaclav Neckar; Jitka Bendova; Vladimir Valenta; Josef Somr; *D:* Jiri Menzel; *W:* Jiri Menzel; *C:* Jaromir Sofr; *M:* Jiri Sust. Oscars '67: Foreign Film.

Closer **2004 (R)** Love stinks. Especially in this caustic adaptation by Marber of his 1997 drama. Waifish stripper Alice (Portman) enchants writer Dan (Law) after they meet cute in London. Dan later writes a novel about his life with Alice and indulges in a flirtation with successful photographer Anna (Roberts). Dan then decides to impersonate Anna during an Internet sex chat and arranges to meet dermatologist Larry (a ferocious performance by Owen), who does meet, and eventually marries, the real Anna. Dan has an affair with Anna, which Larry finds out about (in a laceratingly brutal verbal scene), and Larry meets the abandoned Alice without knowing about their secondhand connection. Marber changed Alice's fate from his play and made both female characters American to accommodate his leads. Owen played the role of Dan in the original National Theatre production. **101m/C; DVD, HD-DVD.** Julia Roberts; Jude Law; Natalie Portman; Clive Owen; *D:* Mike Nichols; *W:* Patrick Marber; *C:* Stephen Goldblatt; *M:* Steven Patrick Morrissey. British Acad. '04: Support. Actor (Owen); Golden Globes '05: Support. Actor (Owen), Support. Actress (Portman).

Closer and Closer **1/2 1996** Cable thriller finds author Kate Sander (Delaney) paralyzed after being stalked by someone resembling the stalker character in her last book "Gargoyle." Kate works with wheelchair-bound personal trainer B.J. Connors (York) to regain her strength, which she'll need as she writes "Gargoyle 2." This time Kate's decided to kill off her stalker/serial killer and soon real murders begin to occur. **93m/C; VHS, DVD.** Kim Delaney; John J. York; Peter Outerbridge; Peter MacNeill; Scott Craft; Anthony Sherwood; *D:* Fred Gerber; *W:* Matt Dorff. **CABLE**

The Closet **1/2** *Le Placard* **2000 (R)** Francois Pignon (Auteuil) is a dull everyguy accountant who learns he's about to be fired after 20 years (from his job at a condom factory). His new (gay) neighbor Belone (Aumont) makes a unique suggestion—he will send doctored photos, showing Pignon at a gay bar, to Pignon's company and they will be forced to back down or be accused of sexual discrimination. Francois protests he can't pass as gay but he doesn't have to his bosses and co-workers believe the rumors and make their own assumptions, including the homophobic personnel director Felix (Depardieu) who fears for his own job if he's not especially nice to Francois. Balances neatly between slapstick and sentiment. French with subtitles. **86m/C; VHS, DVD.** *FR* Daniel Auteuil; Gerard Depardieu; Thierry Lhermitte; Michel Aumont; Michele Laroque; Jean Rochefort; Alexandra Vandernoot; *D:* Francis Veber; *W:* Francis Veber; *C:* Luciano Tovoli; *M:* Vladimir Cosma.

Closet Monster **1/2 2016** Talented young actor Connor Jessup carries this unique dramedy about a young man who retreats into his own imagination to avoid the stress of the real world. Oscar Madly (Jessup) is an average young man who has an above-average amount of creativity and a sizable degree of sexual confusion. To deal with the issues surrounding him as well as a high dose of loneliness, he imagines a vibrant world around him, including a talking hamster voiced by Isabella Rossellini. Stephen Dunn's debut film is a daring, strange dramedy. **90m/C; DVD, Blu-Ray.** Connor Jessup; Aaron Abrams; Joanne Kelly; Aliocha Schneider; Jack Fulton; *D:* Stephen Dunn; *W:* Stephen Dunn; *C:* Bobby Shore; *M:* Todor Kobakov; Maya Postepski.

Closing the Ring **2007 (R)** Schmaltzy drama begins in the 1990s with Ethel (MacLaine) burying her unloved husband. She's surprised when their old friend Jack (Plummer) comes to the funeral. Meanwhile in Ireland, Quinlan (Postlethwaite) digs around a WWII B-17 bomber crash site and finds a ring engraved with the names Ethel and Teddy. Flashbacks lead to the 1940s romance of Ethel (Barton) and her first husband Teddy (Amell), which also involved his best friends Chuck (Alpay) and Jack (Smith). **118m/C; DVD.** *CA GB* Shirley MacLaine; Christopher Plummer; Pete Postlethwaite; Mischa Barton; Gregory Edward Smith; David Alpay; Neve Campbell; Martin McCann; Brenda Fricker; Stephen Amell; *D:* Richard Attenborough; *W:* Peter Woodward; *C:* Roger Pratt; *M:* Jeff Danna.

Closure **WOOF!** *Straightheads* **2007 (R)** Cheap, violent, and nasty. Alice and Adam are brutally attacked by a group of hunters while driving home from a country party. A chance meeting leads Alice to the identity of the attackers and she forces the guilt-ridden Adam to go along with her plan for revenge. **80m/C; DVD, Blu-Ray.** *GB* Gillian Anderson; Danny Dyer; Ralph Brown; *D:* Dan Reed; *W:* Dan Reed; *C:* Chris Seager; *M:* Ilan Eshkeri.

Cloud Atlas **1/2 2012 (R)** Tykwer and the Wachowski siblings adapt David Mitchell's daringly ambitious novel with an approach that both delights and maddens, often in the same scene. With dozens of characters spread across six stories (most of them played by the same core group of actors--Hanks, Berry, Grant, and Broadbent), the film of this oft-considered unfilmable book never stops moving but too often underlines and highlights themes that Mitchell allowed readers to interpret themselves. At its core, it explores how so many lives can interweave and affect one another and the impact this can have on society. Aspires for more, but nonetheless disappointing. **164m/C; DVD, Blu-Ray.** Tom Hanks; Halle Berry; Hugh Grant; Jim Broadbent; Hugo Weaving; Jim Sturgess; Susan Sarandon; Keith David; *D:* Lilly Wachowski; Lana Wachowski; Tom Tykwer; *W:* Lilly Wachowski; Lana Wachowski; Tom Tykwer; *C:* Frank Griebe; John Toll; *M:* Tom Tykwer; Reinhold Heil; Johnny Klimek.

Cloudburst **1951** Dark revenge story. Former WWII codebreaker John Graham (Preston) has resettled in London with his pregnant wife Carol (Sellars) and is working for the Foreign Office. Carol is killed in a hit-and-run by criminals fleeing a crime scene and Graham uses his wartime skills to track them down while staying ahead of Scotland Yard Inspector Davis' (Tapley) investigation. **83m/B; DVD.** *GB* Robert Preston; Elizabeth Sellars; Colin Tapley; Sheila Burrell; Harold Lang; Mary Germaine; Lyn Evans; *D:* Francis Searle; *W:* Francis Searle; *C:* Walter J. (Jimmy W.) Harvey; *M:* Frank Spencer.

Cloudburst **2011** Good-hearted (and raunchy) rom com with a couple of great performances from the leading ladies. Surly Stella (Dukakis) and sweet Dot (Fricker) have been a couple for more than 30 years. After the nearly-blind Dot is slightly injured in a mishap, her disapproving granddaughter Molly (Booth) puts her in an extended care facility. Fearing that they will be separated for good, Stella springs Dot and they head out on a road trip from Maine to Nova Scotia where they can be legally married in the hopes this will give them some standing to stay together. **93m/C; DVD.** *CA US* Olympia Dukakis; Brenda Fricker; Ryan Doucette; Kristin Booth; John Dunsworth; *D:* Thom Fitzgerald; *W:* Thom Fitzgerald; *C:* Tom Harting; *M:* Jason Michael MacIsaac; Warren Robert.

Clouds of Sils Maria **1/2 2015 (R)** Olivier Assayas explores the intersection of fame and reality in this story of an aging actress (Binoche) who returns to the play that her famous two decades ago, this time in the role opposite the one she created. As she rehearses her lines with an assistant (the phenomenal Stewart), the lines between the play and reality begin to blur. After meeting the actual actress who will take on the role (Moretz), a surprising third act twist places the entire piece in a new context. Binoche and Stewart are so fantastic that they make Assayas' thin Hollywood satire easier to swallow. **124m/C; DVD, Blu-Ray.** Juliette Binoche; Kristen Stewart; Chloë Grace Moretz; Lars Eidinger; Johnny Flynn; *D:* Olivier Assayas; *W:* Olivier Assayas; *C:* Yorick Le Saux.

Cloudstreet **2011** Australian miniseries set around Perth from 1943-63. It follows the lives of the hard-working Lamb and the equally hard-luck Pickles clans, who end up sharing a ramshackle house that gambler Samuel Pickles has inherited. He decides to rent some of it out and, because of family difficulties, the Lambs leave their failing farm and move into the city. Tim Winton adapted from his popular novel. **365m/C; DVD.** *AU* Stephen Curry; Essie Davis; Geoff Morrell; Kerry Fox; Emma Booth; *D:* Matthew Saville; *W:* Tim Winton; *C:* Mark Wareham; *M:* Bryony Marks. **TV**

Cloudy with a Chance of Meatballs **1/2 2009 (PG)** Wildly irreverent 3D animated fantasy based on the children's book by Judi and Ron Barrett. Would-be inventor Flint Lockwood's gadgets tend not to work as planned but he's still hoping to impress his dad by helping the depressed economy of their island home of Swallow Falls by turning water into food. It turns out to be gigantic food that falls from the sky (orange juice showers, mashed potato snow...) that has the mayor changing the town's name to Chew and Swallow and making it a tourist destination. But it isn't as much fun as you might think (and quite messy) when the weather takes a turn for the worse. **81m/C; Blu-Ray, UMD, On Demand.** ***V:*** Bill Hader; Anna Faris; Andy Samberg; Mr. T; James Caan; Bruce Campbell; Neil Patrick Harris; Lauren Graham; Bobb'e J. Thompson; Benjamin Bratt; ***D:*** Christopher Miller; Phil Lord; ***W:*** Christopher Miller; Phil Lord; Judi Barrett; Ron Barrett; ***M:*** Mark Mothersbaugh.

Cloudy with a Chance of Meatballs 2 🦴🦴 ½ **2013 (PG)** Visually striking for sure but less satisfying than its smarter predecessor. Too much of the sequel to the 2009 hit relies on jokes repeated from the original or the characters responding to visual cues with oohs and aahs. Character, romance, and identifiable themes have been replaced by taking strawberries as Flint (Hader) and the rest of the gang goes back to Swallow Falls to save it from a "Lost World" of food-animal hybrids. The film has a few undeniably clever riffs on its concept (mostly of the pun variety) but feels more shallow than the surprise hit that came before it. **95m/C; DVD, Blu-Ray.** ***V:*** Bill Hader; Anna Faris; James Caan; Will Forte; Andy Samberg; ***D:*** Cody Cameron; Kris Pearn; ***W:*** John Francis Daley; Jonathan M. Goldstein; Erica Rivinoja; ***M:*** Mark Mothersbaugh.

Cloverfield 🦴🦴 ½ **2008 (PG-13)** Rob (Stahl-David) and friends are enjoying his going-away party in Manhattan on the night before he is to leave for Japan. Pal Hud (Miller) is filming the party, complete with mushy goodbyes and confessions of things undone—and one might get drowsy here if not for the dizzying effect of Hud's camera-work—when there's a terrifying rattle. Thinking an earthquake hit, the friends rush to the roof only to realize it's no earthquake and the city's in total chaos, evidenced by screams and fireballs and Lady Liberty's head (yes, the statue) rolling down a city street. Not to spoil the fun, but it's an old-fashioned monster movie. The "Blair Witch" generation will be nonplussed by the jumpy, hyperactive filming (the unfolding tragedy is all captured courtesy of Hud's digital video cam), and others will appreciate the nod to monster flicks of the past. A fun romp with a scary monster and a little love story tossed in—mix up and enjoy. **90m/C; DVD, Blu-Ray.** Lizzy Caplan; Jessica Lucas; Michael Stahl-David; Mike Vogel; T.J. Miller; Odette Annable; ***D:*** Matt Reeves; ***W:*** Drew Goddard; ***C:*** Michael Bonvillain.

The Clown 🦴🦴 **1953** Tearjerker remake of 1931's "The Champ" with a showbiz setting. Gambling and booze have reduced the once-great Ziegfeld star Dodo Delwyn (Skelton) to clowning on fairgrounds. Dodo is still a hero to his eight-year-old son Dink (Considine) who encourages his pop to make a comeback by doing a variety show on TV. **91m/B; DVD.** Red Skelton; Tim Considine; Jane Greer; Philip Ober; Loring Smith; Lou Lubin; ***D:*** Robert Z. Leonard; ***W:*** Martin Rackin; ***C:*** Paul Vogel; ***M:*** David Rose.

Clown 🦴 ½ **2016 (R)** Buried for a couple years and only really unearthed because director Watts had a minor hit with Cop Car, this odd horror film has its moments but can't quite fulfill its unique premise. Kent (Andy Powers) stumbles upon an old clown suit and puts it on when the child's entertainer he hired for his son's birthday doesn't show up. Funny thing is, he can't take it off. And then he gets hungry—for the blood of children of course. A horror film based on the eternal fear of clowns always has some power but this is an idea in search of a movie. **100m/C; DVD, Blu-Ray.** Andy Powers; Laura Allen; Peter Stormare; Christian Distefano; Chuck Shamata; ***D:*** Jon Watts; ***W:*** Jon Watts; Christopher Ford; ***C:*** Matthew Santo; ***M:*** Matt Veligdan.

Clown Murders 🦴 ½ **1983** Posh Halloween party is undone when a cruel group fakes a kidnapping to ruin a too-prosperous pal's business deal. Awkward thriller boasts little suspense. Candy plays it straight, mostly, in this one. **94m/C; VHS, DVD.** John Candy; Al Waxman; Susan Keller; Lawrence Dane; ***D:*** Martyn Burke.

Clownhouse 🦴 **1988 (R)** Young brothers are stalked in their home by three murderous clowns. **95m/C; VHS, DVD.** Nathan Forrest Winters; Brian McHugh; Sam Rockwell; Viletta Skillman; Timothy Enos; Tree; ***D:*** Victor Salva.

The Clowns 🦴🦴🦴 ½ **1971 (G)** An idiosyncratic documentary about circus clowns. Director Fellini has fashioned an homage that is sincere, entertaining, and personal. Contains some truly poignant sequences. Made for Italian TV with English subtitles. **90m/C; VHS, DVD, Blu-Ray.** *IT* ***D:*** Federico Fellini; ***W:*** Federico Fellini; Bernardino Zapponi; ***C:*** Dario Di Palma; ***M:*** Nino Rota. **TV**

The Club 🦴🦴🦴 *Players* **1981 (PG)** A soccer coach tries to train and motivate a mediocre squad into one worth playing for—and perhaps even winning—the league cup. Conventional sports story is significantly improved by Thompson's rendering of the coach. **99m/C; VHS, DVD.** *AU* Jack Thompson; Graham Kennedy; John Howard; Alan Cassell; ***D:*** Bruce Beresford; ***W:*** David Williamson.

The Club 🦴🦴🦴 *El Club* **2016** Pablo Larrain's pitch-black dramedy about pedophilic priests is an indictment of a process that not only protects criminals who have abused their power but, in doing so, fails to instill a sense in these people that they have done anything wrong. In a small Chilean beach town, a group of Priests accused of horrible crimes are forced into seclusion, although the real world is starting to notice. When a man abused by a religious figure is killed in front of the house, the curtains come down. Larrain's film is a complex, stark examination of how human nature demands community, even when communal trust has been broken. **98m/C; DVD, Blu-Ray.** Alfredo Castro; Robert Farias; Antonia Zegers; Marcelo Alonso; Jaime Vadell; ***D:*** Pablo Larrain; ***W:*** Pablo Larrain; Guillermo Calderon; Daniel Villalobos; ***C:*** Sergio Armstrong; ***M:*** Carlos Cabezas.

Club Dread 🦴 *Broken Lizard's Club Dread* **2004 (R)** Fresh off spoofing highway patrolmen in Super Troopers, the Broken Lizard crew takes on beach vacation slasher movies, to lousy results. There's a killer on the loose at an island resort run by Jimmy Buffet wanna-be Coconut Pete (Paxton), interrupting the party. Stupidity ensues. Plot takes a backseat to lame gags, nudity, and slasher pic gore. Vacation elsewhere, because this club is a waste of time. **103m/C; DVD.** Bill Paxton; Jay Chandrasekhar; Kevin Heffernan; M.C. Gainey; Jordan Ladd; Lindsay Price; Michael Weaver; Samm Levine; Dan Montgomery, Jr.; Steve Lemme; Paul Soter; Erik Stolhanske; Brittany Daniel; Nat Faxon; Elena Lyons; Tanja (Tanya) Reichert; ***D:*** Jay Chandrasekhar; ***W:*** Jay Chandrasekhar; Kevin Heffernan; Steve Lemme; Paul Soter; Erik Stolhanske; ***C:*** Lawrence Sher; ***M:*** Nathan Barr.

Club Fed 🦴 ½ **1990 (PG-13)** A rigid prison warden's plot to impose greater discipline is undone by inmate highjinks. Crude laughs and one-dimensional play from a cast of recognizable names and faces. **93m/C; VHS, DVD.** Judy Landers; Sherman Hemsley; Karen Black; Burt Young; Rick Schmidt; Allen Garfield; Joseph Campanella; Lyle Alzado; Mary Woronov; Debbie Lee Carrington; ***D:*** Nathaniel Christian; ***C:*** Arledge Armenaki.

Club Med 🦴🦴 **1986** ABC TV movie filmed Club Med's Ixtapa, Mexico location. Single mom Kate leaves Boston for a vacation at Club Med only to find old flame O'Shea is running the place and he's going to do his best to win her back. Meanwhile, French runaway Simone sneaks into the resort with the help of stuffy British widower Gilbert Anthony Page and teenager Danny is dealing with some personal issues. Gloria Estefan and the Miami Sound Machine are the resort band and Sinbad is the club's comedian. **94m/C; DVD.** Linda Hamilton; Jack Scalia; Traci Lind; Patrick Macnee; Bill Maher; Timothy Williams; ***D:*** Bob Giraldi; ***W:*** Jeff Freilich; ***C:*** Robert E. (Bob) Collins; ***M:*** Peter Bernstein. **TV**

Club Paradise 🦴🦴 ½ **1986 (PG-13)** A Chicago fireman flees the big city for a faltering tropical resort and tries to develop some night life. Somewhat disappointing with Williams largely playing the straight man. Most laughs provided by Martin, particularly when she is assaulted by a shower, and Moranis, who gets lost while windsurfing. **96m/C; VHS, DVD.** Robin Williams; Peter O'Toole; Rick Moranis; Andrea Martin; Jimmy Cliff; Brian Doyle-Murray; Twiggy; Eugene Levy; Adolph Caesar; Joanna Cassidy; Mary Gross; Carey Lowell; Robin Duke; Simon Jones; ***D:*** Harold Ramis; ***W:*** Brian Doyle-Murray; Harold Ramis; ***M:*** David Mansfield; Van Dyke Parks.

Club Vampire 🦴 **1998 (R)** Vampire Zero (Savage) wants to bite stripper Corri (Andreff) but Laura (Frank) gets there first and Corri starts to transform. Vampire leader Aiko (Parris) doesn't want any new converts and sends Zero to kill her. But Zero has other plans. A bore. **77m/C; VHS, DVD.** John Savage; Starr Andreeff; Diana Frank; Michael J. Anderson; Marriam Parris; Ross Malinger; ***D:*** Andy Ruben; ***W:*** Andy Ruben; ***C:*** Steve Gainer; ***M:*** Michael Elliott. **VIDEO**

Clubhouse Detectives 🦴🦴 ½ **1996 (PG)** When Billy witnesses a crime at a neighbor's no one believes him—except his friends, so the clubhouse detectives decide to investigate. **85m/C; VHS, DVD.** Michael Ballem; Michael Galeota; Jimmy Galeota; Suzanne Barnes; ***D:*** Eric Hendershot.

Clue 🦴🦴 ½ **1985 (PG)** The popular boardgame's characters must unravel a night of murder at a spooky Victorian mansion. The entire cast seems to be subsisting on sugar, with wild eyes and frantic movements the order of the day. Butler Curry best survives the uneven script and direction. Warren is appealing too. The theatrical version played with three alternative endings, and the video version shows all three successively. **96m/C; VHS, DVD, Blu-Ray.** Lesley Ann Warren; Tim Curry; Martin Mull; Madeline Kahn; Michael McKean; Christopher Lloyd; Eileen Brennan; Howard Hesseman; Lee Ving; Jane Wiedlin; Colleen Camp; Bill Henderson; ***D:*** Jonathan Lynn; ***W:*** Jonathan Lynn; John Landis; ***C:*** Victor Kemper; ***M:*** John Morris.

Clueless 🦴🦴🦴 *I Was a Teenage Teenager; No Worries* **1995 (PG-13)** Watch out "Beverly Hills 90210," here comes Cher. No, not the singer Cher, but ultra-filthy-rich brat Cher, who's out to make over her classmates and teachers, specifically flannel-shirted transfer student Tai (Murphy). Aerosmith vamp Silverstone stars as the teenage manipulator who knows all too well how to spend her trust fund. The only person who can match her wits is disapproving stepbrother Josh (Rudd). (Ah, love.) Loosely based on Jane Austen's "Emma," Heckerling, of "Fast Times at Ridgemont High" fame, knows this territory and directs a bright, surprisingly satirical romp. **113m/C; VHS, DVD, Blu-Ray.** Alicia Silverstone; Stacey Dash; Paul Rudd; Brittany Murphy; Donald Adeosun Faison; Julie Brown; Jeremy Sisto; Dan Hedaya; Wallace Shawn; Breckin Meyer; Elisa Donovan; Aida Linares; ***D:*** Amy Heckerling; ***W:*** Amy Heckerling; ***C:*** Bill Pope; ***M:*** David Kitay. MTV Movie Awards '96: Female Perf. (Silverstone), Most Desirable Female (Silverstone); Natl. Soc. Film Critics '95: Screenplay; Blockbuster '96: Female Newcomer, T. (Silverstone).

The Clutching Hand 🦴🦴 **1936** The Clutching Hand seeks a formula that will turn metal into gold and detective Craig Kennedy is out to prevent him from doing so. A serial in 15 chapters on three cassettes. **268m/B; VHS, DVD.** Jack Mulhall; Rex Lease; Mae Busch; William Farnum; Robert Frazer; Reed Howes; Marion Shilling; ***D:*** Al(bert) Herman.

Coach 🦴 ½ **1978 (PG)** Sexy woman is unintentionally hired to coach a high school basketball team and mold rookies into lusty young champions. Low-grade roundball fever. **100m/C; VHS, DVD.** Cathy Lee Crosby; Michael Biehn; Keenan Wynn; Sidney Wicks; ***D:*** Bud Townsend.

Coach 🦴🦴 ½ **2010 (PG-13)** Predictable but sweet romance/sports comedy. Trust fund baby Nick (Dancy) is drifting aimlessly while his friends move on into adulthood. In an effort to find some direction, soccer-loving Nick decides to coach the local youth team, bonding with 13-year-old star player Hector (Gutierrez). This also garners Nick the attention of doctor Gabrielle (Balaban), who's so far been unimpressed by Nick's lazy lifestyle. **87m/C; DVD.** Hugh Dancy; Liane Balaban; Mamie Gummer; David Zayas; Gillian Jacobs; Jonathan Gutierrez; ***D:*** Will Frears; ***W:*** Jason Pugatch; ***C:*** Harlan Bosmajian. **VIDEO**

Coach Carter 🦴🦴🦴 **2005 (PG-13)** Based on a true story of a coach who benched his entire team until their grades improved. Coach Carter (Jackson) is a self-made sporting goods businessman who decides to take a basketball coaching job at his alma mater Richmond High. Carter is a strict disciplinarian and makes it clear that the boys must follow a certain set of rules to play for him, and each student is required to sign a contract to maintain a grade point average of 2.3. Despite the familiar plot of inspirational teacher making a difference, the movie rises above due to a good supporting cast and a great performance by Jackson, making excellent use of his commanding screen presence. **137m/C; DVD, Blu-Ray, UMD.** Samuel L. Jackson; Robert Ri'chard; Debbi (Deborah) Morgan; Rick Gonzalez; Antwon Tanner; Denise Dowse; Rob Brown; Ashanti; Nana Gbewonyo; Channing Tatum; Texas Battle; ***D:*** Thomas Carter; ***W:*** Mark Schwahn; John Gatins; ***C:*** Sharone Meir; ***M:*** Trevor Rabin.

Coal Miner's Daughter 🦴🦴🦴 **1980 (PG)** Strong bio of country singer Loretta Lynn, who rose from Appalachian poverty to Nashville riches. Spacek is perfect in the lead, and she even provides acceptable rendering of Lynn's tunes. Band drummer Helm shines as Lynn's father, and Jones is strong as Lynn's downhome husband. Uneven melodrama toward the end, but the film is still a good one. **125m/C; VHS, DVD, Blu-Ray.** Sissy Spacek; Tommy Lee Jones; Levon Helm; Beverly D'Angelo; ***D:*** Michael Apted; ***C:*** Ralf Bode. Oscars '80: Actress (Spacek); Golden Globes '81: Actress--Mus./Comedy (Spacek), Film--Mus./Comedy; L.A. Film Critics '80: Actress (Spacek); Natl. Bd. of Review '80: Actress (Spacek); Natl. Film Reg. '19; N.Y. Film Critics '80: Actress (Spacek); Natl. Soc. Film Critics '80: Actress (Spacek).

The Coalition 🦴 **2013 (R)** Four jilted women conspire to get revenge on their pro-athlete boyfriends who have tossed them aside for someone else. **100m/C; DVD, Blu-Ray, Streaming.** Ricardo Alvarado; Adrienne Bailon; Ingrid Clay; Michelle Cohrt; ***D:*** Monica Mingo; ***W:*** Monica Mingo; Terrell Suggs; ***C:*** Sant'e Andrews; Hilton Carter; ***M:*** George J. Fontenette. **VIDEO**

Coast of Skeletons 🦴 ½ **1963** Insurance investigator Sanders learns unscrupulous Magnus is looting sunken ships whose contents belong to Sanders' employers. Barely passable reworking of Edgar Wallace novel "Sanders of the Rivers." **90m/C; DVD.** *GB* Richard Todd; Dale Robertson; Heinz Drache; Elga Andersen; Marianne Koch; Derek Nimmo; ***D:*** Robert Lynn; ***W:*** Anthony Scott Veitch; ***C:*** Stephen Dade; ***M:*** Christopher Whelen.

Coast to Coast 🦴🦴 **2004 (R)** An older married couple isn't sure they want to stay together anymore but luckily they have loads of time to figure things out cruising from Connecticut to L.A. to see their son tie the knot. **107m/C; VHS, DVD.** Richard Dreyfuss; Judy Davis; Selma Blair; Maximilian Schell; Fred Ward; Saul Rubinek; John Salley; Paul Mazursky; Kate Lynch; Richard Fitzpatrick; Clare Coulter; Catherine Disher; James Kee; Nancy Sakovich; David Julian Hirsh; Owen Rotharmel; Rick Mota; Angela Asher; Catherine Burdon; Lyssa J. Caster; Laura Catalano; Paul Essiembre; Dominic Fung; Paula Garrido; Chris Gillett; Carolyn Goff; Lindsay Leese; Richard Partington; Les Porter; Krista Sutton; Joreen Todd; ***D:*** Paul Mazursky; ***W:*** Frederic Raphael; ***C:*** Jean Lepine; ***M:*** Bill Conti. **TV**

Coastlines 🦴🦴 **2002 (R)** Pulp noir in the Florida panhandle. Sonny (Olyphant) took the fall for his drug partners Fred (Forsythe) and Eddie (Lucas) Vance. Out of prison, he wants the $200K they owe him and to be left alone. The Vances would like Sonny gone permanently, which brings in Sonny's best bud, Dave (Brolin), who's the local sheriff, and his unsatisfied wife Ann (Wynter), immediately leading to a familiar and not very exciting triangle. Unfortunately, this is a mix of crime and sex that never successfully meshes together. **110m/C; DVD.** Timothy Olyphant; Josh Brolin; Sarah Wynter; Scott Wilson; Angela Bettis; Josh(ua) Lucas; Robert Wisdom; Daniel von Bargen; Blake Lindsley; Bob Glaudini; Edwin Hodge; Abigail Mavity; Elizabeth Caity; ***D:*** Victor Nunez; ***W:*** Victor Nunez; ***C:*** Virgil Marcus Mirano; ***M:*** Charles Engstrom.

Cobain: Montage of Heck 🦴🦴🦴🦴 **2015** An in-depth biographical documentary look at the life, work, and influence of Kurt

Cobain, the lead singer, guitarist, and songwriter of Nirvana. Created by filmmaker Morgen with the blessing of Cobain's estate, this looks at the whole of Cobain's existence from his earliest days to his suicide in the early 1990s. In addition to interviews with family, friends, and peers, the film features Cobain's own home movies, home recordings, artwork, animation, photography, and journals. **145m/C; DVD.** ***D:*** Brett Morgen; ***W:*** Brett Morgen; ***C:*** Eric Edwards; Jim Whitaker; Nicole Hirsch; ***M:*** Nirvana.

Cobb 🦴🦴🦴 **1994 (R)** Biography of Ty Cobb (Jones), the universally acknowledged "most hated man in baseball" who, near the end of his life, realizes he doesn't want to be remembered in that way. So he hires sportswriter Al Stump (Wuhl) to ghostwrite (read: sugarcoat) his life story. As seen through Stump's eyes, Cobb is an unrelenting, petty, bigoted, hateful, paranoid, drunken, and yet compelling man. They form an uneasy bond as Stump duly records the fiction Cobb is feeding him, secretly deciding to write the truth after the legend's death. Jones is at his scene-chewing, antagonistic best, while Wuhl seems both overwhelmed and overshadowed as the embattled Stump. Shelton has something to say about American hero worship and a celebrity's desire for posterity, but with the focus intent on portraying Cobb's meanness, it's hard to say what. Surprisingly little baseball action for a baseball bio. Based on Stump's "Cobb: A Biography." **128m/C; VHS, DVD.** Tommy Lee Jones; Robert Wuhl; Lolita Davidovich; ***D:*** Ron Shelton; ***W:*** Ron Shelton; ***C:*** Russell Boyd.

The Cobbler WOOF! 2014 A horrendously misguided and offensive comedy-fairy tale about a man (Sandler) who discovers an enchanted shoe repair machine that allows him to literally become other people by stepping into their shoes. The result is a film that bizarrely argues that you can judge a book by its cover. It starts off purely mediocre and gets worse and worse, before a final act twist that stands among the dumbest screenwriting decisions of all time. A huge stumble for talented writer/director McCarthy. **99m/C; DVD, Blu-Ray.** Adam Sandler; Steve Buscemi; Ellen Barkin; Dustin Hoffman; Dascha Polanco; ***D:*** Thomas (Tom) McCarthy; ***W:*** Thomas (Tom) McCarthy; Paul Sado; ***C:*** W. Mott Hupfel, III; ***M:*** John Debney; Nick Urata.

Cobra 🦴 **1925** To pay off the debts incurred by his profligate playboyance, Valentino takes a job with an antique dealer, falls for the dealer's secretary and arranges an assignation with the dealer's wife, who is inconveniently killed at the designated rendezvous. Complications abound as Valentino finds himself Sheik out of luck. Lesser Valentino effort was released a year before the famous heartthrob's untimely death and enjoyed a rather acrid critical reception. Which isn't to say the public didn't flock to see the Italian stallion flare his nostrils. **75m/B; Silent; VHS, DVD.** Rudolph Valentino; Nita Naldi; Casson Ferguson; Gertrude (Olmstead) Olmsted; ***D:*** Joseph Henabery.

The Cobra 🦴 *Il Cobra; El Cobra* **1968** A tightlipped U.S. agent ogles a voluptuous siren when not fighting opium smugglers from the Middle East. A must for all admirers of Ekberg. **93m/C; VHS, DVD.** Dana Andrews; Anita Ekberg; ***D:*** Mario Sequi.

Cobra 🦴 **1986 (R)** A cold-blooded cop protects a model from a gang of deranged killers. Low-brow, manipulative action fare void of feeling. Truly exploitive, with little expression from the leads. Highlight is the extended chase sequence. Based on the Paula Gosling novel "Fair Game," which was remade under the book's title (and in a more faithful adaptation) in 1995. **87m/C; VHS, DVD, Blu-Ray.** Sylvester Stallone; Reni Santoni; Brigitte Nielsen; Andrew (Andy) Robinson; ***D:*** George P. Cosmatos; ***W:*** Sylvester Stallone; ***C:*** Ric Waite; ***M:*** Sylvester Levay.

Cobra Verde 🦴🦴 *Slave Coast* **1988** Even by Herzog/Kinski standards, their last collaboration was one wild trip. Kinski is a 19th-century Brazilian bandit, known as Cobra Verde, who finds work as a slave overseer on a sugar plantation. When he impregnates all three of the owner's daughters, he's sent on an impossible mission to re-open the slave trade with a mad African king. Discovering he's being cheated, Cobra Verde trains an army of women to overthrow the king, so he can control the slave trade himself. Based on the novel "The Viceroy of Ouidah" by Bruce Chatwin. German with subtitles. **110m/C; VHS, DVD, Blu-Ray.** ***GE*** Klaus Kinski; Peter Berling; Jose Lewgoy; Salvatore Basile; ***D:*** Werner Herzog; ***W:*** Werner Herzog; ***C:*** Viktor Ruzicka; ***M:*** Popul Vuh.

Cobra Woman 🦴🦴 ½ **1944** Technicolor adventure fantasy about the jungle queen (Montez) of a cobra-worshipping cult and her evil twin sister who wants the throne for herself. **70m/C; VHS, DVD, Blu-Ray.** Maria Montez; Jon Hall; Sabu; Edgar Barrier; Lois Collier; Lon Chaney, Jr.; Mary Nash; Samuel S. Hinds; Moroni Olsen; ***D:*** Robert Siodmak; ***W:*** Richard Brooks; Gene Lewis; ***C:*** William Howard Greene; ***M:*** Edward Ward.

The Cobweb 🦴🦴 **1955** Shady goings on are uncovered at a psychiatric ward run by a bunch of neurotic administrators. A strong cast, director and producer do not add much to this dull outing. **125m/C; DVD.** Lauren Bacall; Richard Widmark; Gloria Grahame; Charles Boyer; Lillian Gish; John Kerr; Susan Strasberg; Oscar Levant; Tommy Rettig; Paul Stewart; Adele Jergens; Bert Freed; Sandy Descher; Fay Wray; Virginia Christine; ***D:*** Vincente Minnelli; ***C:*** George J. Folsey.

The Coca-Cola Kid 🦴🦴🦴 ½ **1984 (R)** Smug U.S. sales exec Becker (Roberts) treks to Australia to improve regional sales and becomes embroiled in sexual and professional shenanigans. He gets involved with free-spirited secretary Terri (sexy Scacchi) and discovers that a soft drink locally brewed by eccenric McDowall (Kerr) is his determined competition. Roberts is strong in the difficult lead role, and Scacchi is compelling in an awkwardly constructed part. Ambitious satire is somewhat scattershot, with more storylines than it needs. Still, filmmaker Makavejev is usually capable of juggling the entire enterprise. **94m/C; VHS, DVD.** ***AU*** Eric Roberts; Greta Scacchi; Bill Kerr; Chris Haywood; Kris McQuade; Max Gilles; ***D:*** Dusan Makavejev; ***W:*** Frank Moorhouse; ***C:*** Dean Semler; ***M:*** William Motzing.

Cocaine and Blue Eyes 🦴 **1983** TV pilot movie fails badly as a would-be hard-boiled crime story with a stiff performance by Simpson as San Francisco detective Michael Brennen. He's hired by lowlife Joey Crawford to find Joey's missing blue-eyed girlfriend, Dani Anatole. Brennen stays on the case after Joey is killed in a car crash that's not accidental and when he looks into Dani's family, Brennen finds out they're longtime mobsters involved in a cocaine-smuggling operation. **96m/C; DVD.** O.J. Simpson; Cliff Gorman; Candy Clark; Eugene Roche; Tracy Reed; Irena Ferris; Cindy Pickett; Keye Luke; ***D:*** E.W. Swackhamer; ***W:*** Kendelle Blair; ***C:*** Richard C. Glouner; ***M:*** Morton Stevens. **TV**

Cocaine Angel 🦴🦴 **2006** Taking place over the course of one week in the unrelenting Jacksonville, Florida, this drama follows Scott (Lahey) as he deals with tragedies and downfalls in his life from losing his job to trying to see his daughter. A cocaine addict with an empty existence, he comes to terms with the remnants of the dreams and hopes that once gave him a reason to live. **75m/C; DVD.** Brenda Benfield; Adonis Boyd; Jamie Dawson; Richard Dawson; Kelly Forester; Blanca Franco; Anne Knowles; Damian Lahey; Charley Riley; Christina Ward; ***D:*** Michael Tully; ***W:*** Damian Lahey; ***C:*** Shawn Lewallen; ***M:*** Brian Jenkins. **VIDEO**

Cocaine Cowboys 🦴 ½ **1979 (R)** Lame rockers support themselves between gigs by peddling drugs then find out they've run afoul of the mob. Palance is the only worthwhile aspect of this rambling venture produced at Andy Warhol's home. **90m/C; VHS, DVD.** Jack Palance; Andy Warhol; Tomas D. Sullivan; Suzanna Love; Richard Young; ***D:*** Ulli Lommel; ***W:*** Tomas D. Sullivan; Ulli Lommel; Victor Bockris; ***C:*** Jochen Breitenstein; ***M:*** Elliot Goldenthal.

Cocaine Cowboys 2: Hustlin' with the Godmother 🦴🦴 **2008** A documentary sequel to acclaimed documentary "Cocaine Cowboy," this film follows the highs and lows of Charles Cosby's relationship with so-called Cocaine Godmother Griselda Blanco. A small-time dealer in the Bay Area, Charles writes a fan letter to Griselda in federal prison. Within months, he becomes her lover, is put in charge of her cocaine empire, and a millionaire in his own right. However, Griselda has a reputation for jealousy and killing men after she has ended her relationship with them. Obsessed with proving his faithfulness, Charles becomes increasingly aware that his life is out of control and tries to take appropriate action. **97m/C; DVD, Streaming, Download.** ***D:*** Billy Corben; ***C:*** David Cypkin; Jorge Valdes-Iga. **VIDEO**

Cocaine Fiends 🦴🦴 *The Pace That Kills* **1936** Drug use leads siblings into a squalid life of addiction, crime, prostitution, and eventually suicide. Ostensibly straight morality tale functions better as loopy camp. Features memorable slang. **74m/B; VHS, DVD.** Lois January; Noel Madison; Willy Castello; Dean Benton; Lois Lindsay; Sheila Mannors; ***D:*** William A. O'Connor.

Cocaine: One Man's Seduction 🦴🦴 ½ **1983** Documents one man's degeneration into drug addiction. Weaver snorts convincingly in lead. **97m/C; VHS, Streaming.** Dennis Weaver; Karen Grassle; Pamela Bellwood; David Ackroyd; ***D:*** Paul Wendkos; ***M:*** Brad Fiedel. **TV**

Cock & Bull Story 🦴🦴 *Southside* **2003** Gritty examination of the machismo world of boxing and homophobia in a depressed working-class environment. Up-and-coming boxer Travis (Roberts) is the last hope for aging manager/trainer Pascoe (Mullavey). Pascoe (and everyone else) disapproves of the inseparable friendship between Travis and unemployed screw-up Jacko (Green). Rumors begin to circulate about Travis's sexuality and Jacko's own volatility makes matters worse. Of course, on the night of Travis's biggest fight, matters come to a head between the two men. Adapted from the play by Richard Crowe and Richard Zajdlic. **102m/C; DVD.** Bret Roberts; Brian Austin Green; Greg Mullavey; Wendy Fowler; Darin Heames; ***D:*** Billy Hayes; ***W:*** Billy Hayes; ***C:*** Ben Kufrin; ***M:*** Pierpaolo Tiano.

Cockfighter 🦴🦴🦴 *Gamblin' Man; Born to Kill; Wild Drifters* **1974 (R)** A unique, grim portrait of a cockfighting trainer. Oates, in the lead, provides voiceover narrations, but the film otherwise remains silent until the end. Strong support from Stanton. Interesting, violent fare. **84m/C; VHS, DVD.** Warren Oates; Harry Dean Stanton; Richard B. Shull; Troy Donahue; Millie Perkins; Robert Earl Jones; Warren Finnerty; Ed Begley, Jr.; Charles Willeford; ***D:*** Monte Hellman; ***W:*** Charles Willeford; ***C:*** Nestor Almendros; ***M:*** Michael Franks.

Cocktail 🦴🦴 ½ **1988 (R)** A smug young man finds fame and fortune as a proficient, flashy bartender, charming the ladies with his bottle and glass juggling act. Slick, superficial film boasts a busy soundtrack and serviceable exchanges between male leads Cruise and Brown. There's less chemistry between Cruise and love interest Shue. Filmed in a high-tech rock video style. **103m/C; VHS, DVD, Blu-Ray.** Tom Cruise; Bryan Brown; Elisabeth Shue; Lisa Banes; Laurence Luckinbill; Kelly Lynch; Gina Gershon; Ron Dean; Paul Benedict; ***D:*** Roger Donaldson; ***W:*** Heywood Gould; ***C:*** Dean Semler; ***M:*** J. Peter Robinson. Golden Raspberries '88: Worst Picture, Worst Screenplay.

Coco 🦴🦴🦴 **2017 (PG)** A Pixar classic that celebrates Mexican culture. Though the Rivera family has been forbidden from music for generations, tween Miguel (Gonzalez) has secretly taught himself to play guitar by studying the songs of singer Ernesto de la Cruz (Bratt). Before Miguel can take part in a local talent show, his family discovers his musical secret and destroys his guitar. After he steals Ernesto's guitar from his mausoleum, Miguel must overcome a curse and make things right in the Land of the Dead. Full of colorful customs and folklore from the Dia de Muertos, the entertaining film relates a classic family-friendly story. **109m/C; DVD, Blu-Ray.** Edward James Olmos; Benjamin Bratt; Alanna Ubach; Gael Garcia Bernal; John Ratzenberger; ***D:*** Lee Unkrich; Adriana Molina; ***W:*** Lee Unkrich; Adriana Molina; Matthew Aldrich; ***M:*** Michael Giacchino. Oscars '17: Animated Film, Orig. Song Score and/or Adapt. ("Remember Me"); British Acad. '17: Animated Film; Golden Globes '18: Animated Film.

Coco Before Chanel 🦴🦴 *Coco avant Chanel* **2009 (PG-13)** Biopic of French fashion designer Gabrielle "Coco" Chanel from her humble upbringing to the height of the international fashion world and popular culture. The orphaned Gabrielle (Tautou) is working as a seamstress and cabaret singer when she meets millionaire roue Etienne Balsan (Poelvoorde), who makes her his mistress. Given the time, money, and opportunity, Chanel begins to experiment with simplifying the era's overly-fussy clothing and making herself both financially and sexually independent. Too much of the focus is wasted on a dull romance, giving little insight into Chanel's business savvy approach to becoming the icon of her day. Tautou's performance, unfortunately, takes a back seat to the extravagant fashions on parade. French with subtitles. **105m/C; Blu-Ray, On Demand.** ***FR*** Audrey Tautou; Benoit Poelvoorde; Alessandro Nivola; Marie Gillain; Emmanuelle Devos; ***D:*** Anne Fontaine; ***W:*** Anne Fontaine; Camille Fontaine; Edmonde Charles-Roux; ***C:*** Christophe Beaucarne; ***M:*** Alexandre Desplat.

Coco Chanel 🦴🦴 **2008** Lavish—if melodramatic—biopic of the French fashion designer (played by Boblova and MacLaine). Story begins in 1954 with the aged Chanel seemingly irrelevant after a disastrous comeback attempt. Then it flashes back to the 1910s when the young Coco leaves the orphanage for work as a seamstress. Brashly appealing, Chanel is soon persuading her wealthy male admirers to fund her fashion ambitions as she negotiates two world wars and various romantic dilemmas. **139m/C; DVD.** Shirley MacLaine; Barbara Bobulova; Sagamore Stevenin; Olivier Sitruk; Malcolm McDowell; Valetino Lodovini; ***D:*** Christian Duguay; ***W:*** Enrico Medioli; ***C:*** Fabrizio Lucci; ***M:*** Andrea Guerra. **CABLE**

Coco Chanel & Igor Stravinsky 🦴 ½ **2009 (R)** With little background info, the 1920s affair between iconic fashion designer Chanel (Mouglalis) and avant-garde composer Stravinsky (Mikkelsen) never matters much, especially out of the bedroom. Chanel offers financial assistance to the displaced, impoverished Russian and his family and they both apparently find some creative inspiration. Pic is actually at its best recreating Stravinsky's controversial 1913 Paris debut of "The Rite of Spring," which Chanel attended. French and Russian with subtitles. **118m/C; DVD, Blu-Ray.** ***FR*** Mads Mikkelsen; Anna Mouglalis; Elena Morozova; Anatole Taubman; Natacha Lindinger; Grigori Manoukov; ***D:*** Jan Kounen; ***W:*** Jan Kounen; Carol de Boutiny; Chris Greenhalgh; ***C:*** David Ungaro; ***M:*** Gabriel Yared.

The Cocoanuts 🦴🦴 ½ **1929** In their film debut, the Marx Brothers create their trademark, indescribable mayhem. Stagey, technically crude comedy nonetheless delights with zany, free-for-all exchanges, antics. Includes famous "viaduct" exchange. **96m/B; VHS, DVD, Blu-Ray.** Groucho Marx; Chico Marx; Harpo Marx; Zeppo Marx; Margaret Dumont; Kay Francis; Oscar Shaw; Mary Eaton; Cyril Ring; Basil Ruysdael; ***D:*** Robert Florey; Joseph Santley; ***W:*** George S. Kaufman; Morrie Ryskind; ***C:*** George J. Folsey; ***M:*** Irving Berlin.

Cocoon 🦴🦴🦴 **1985 (PG-13)** Humanist fantasy in which senior citizens discover their fountain of youth is actually a breeding ground for aliens. Heartwarming, one-of-a kind drama showcases elderly greats Ameche, Brimley, Gilford, Cronyn, and Tandy. A commendable, recommendable venture. Based on David Saperstein's novel and followed by "Cocoon: The Return." **117m/C; VHS, DVD.** Wilford Brimley; Brian Dennehy; Steve Guttenberg; Don Ameche; Tahnee Welch; Jack Gilford; Hume Cronyn; Jessica Tandy; Gwen Verdon; Maureen Stapleton; Tyrone Power, Jr.; Barret Oliver; Linda Harrison; Herta Ware; Clint Howard; ***D:*** Ron Howard; ***W:*** Tom Benedek; ***M:*** James Horner. Oscars '85: Support. Actor (Ameche), Visual FX.

Cocoon: The Return 🦴🦴 **1988 (PG)** Old timers who left with aliens in "Cocoon" return to earth and face grave problems. Less compelling sequel misses guiding hand of earlier film's director, Ron Howard. Still, most of cast from the original is on board here, and the film has its moments. **116m/C; VHS, DVD.** Don Ameche; Wilford Brimley; Steve Guttenberg; Maureen Stapleton; Hume Cronyn; Jessica Tandy; Gwen Verdon; Jack Gilford; Tahnee Welch; Courteney Cox; Brian Dennehy; Barret Oliver; *D:* Daniel Petrie; *C:* Tak Fujimoto; *M:* James Horner.

The Code 🦴 1/2 *Thick as Thieves* **2009 (R)** Bad heist movie that telegraphs its twists. Ripley (Freeman), a criminal indebted to the Russian mob, recruits thief Jack (Banderas) to help him pull off a heist of Faberge eggs. Only things aren't what they seem—except for the actors not being very interested in what's going on. **103m/C; DVD, Blu-Ray.** Morgan Freeman; Antonio Banderas; Robert Forster; Radha Mitchell; Rade Serbedzija; *D:* Mimi Leder; *W:* Ted Humphrey; *C:* Julio Macat; *M:* Atli Orvarsson. **VIDEO**

The Code Conspiracy 🦴 **2001 (PG-13)** In this laughably bad mix of thrillers and religion, a professor discovers a hidden formula while working on the Dead Sea scrolls that not only unlocks all known computer encryption but gives mathematical proof of the existence of God. Obviously every government and large corporation has to kill him to prevent this from getting out and they immediately set about doing so. Worth noting only for its actors who usually do better films, and are probably praying to their respective deities this film doesn't haunt their careers. **97m/C; DVD.** Jim Fitzpatrick; Maria Conchita Alonso; *D:* Hank Whetstone; *W:* Hank Whetstone; *C:* Mark Woods; *M:* Christopher L. Stone. **VIDEO**

Code 46 🦴🦴 1/2 **2003 (R)** Stylish, sci-fi noir explores the not-too-distant future where, in order to travel from city to cloistered city, people need "papelles," a combination visa, passport and genetic ID code. Evidently, excessive cloning has led to DNA protected zones that require strict policing. Robbins is William Geld, an investigator who has been infected with an empathy virus that enables him to read minds. Geld is tracking forged papelles, which leads him to Shanghai and the suspect Maria (Morton), a Shanghai factory worker. Geld, however falls for Maria and they enter into an intense love affair. Some provocative ideas and good premise are compromised by lack of chemistry between Robbins and Morton. **92m/C; DVD, Blu-Ray.** *GB* Tim Robbins; Samantha Morton; Jeanne Balibar; Om Puri; Essie Davis; Shelley King; David Fahm; *D:* Michael Winterbottom; *W:* Frank Cottrell-Boyce; *C:* Alwin Kuchler; Marcel Zyskind; *M:* David Holmes.

Code Hunter 🦴 1/2 *Storm Watch; Virtual Storm* **2002 (R)** Nick (Cornish) is a reformed hacker being blackmailed into stealing a file from an unknown computer network that just happens to belong to a contractor trying to sell the U.S. government on its weather control machine. Unfortunately the A.I. running said machine becomes sentient and decides to wipe out humanity by creating monstrous hurricanes. **100m/C; DVD.** Nick Cornish; Adrian Paul; Coolio; Tone Loc; Vanessa Marcil; Bai Ling; *D:* Terry Cunningham; *W:* Terry Cunningham; Steve Latshaw; Flavia Carrozzi; *C:* Jacques Haitkin; *M:* Sean Murray. **VIDEO**

Code Name: Dancer 🦴🦴 *Her Secret Life* **1987** A retired spy leaves her peaceful life, husband, and family to take care of business in Cuba. **93m/C; VHS, DVD.** Kate Capshaw; Jeroen Krabbe; Gregory Sierra; Cliff DeYoung; Valerie Mahaffey; James Sloyan; *D:* Buzz Kulik; *M:* Georges Delerue. **TV**

Code Name: Emerald 🦴 **1985 (PG)** WWII drama in which an American agent must stop an enemy spy with knowledge of impending D-Day invasion. Conventional TV fare boasts a fine performance by von Sydow, but Stolz is hopelessly miscast as an adult. Perhaps the only film featuring both Buchholz and Berger. First feature film by NBC-TV network. **95m/C; VHS, DVD.** Ed Harris; Max von Sydow; Eric Stoltz; Horst Buchholz; Helmut Berger; Cyrielle Claire; Patrick Stewart; Graham Crowden; *D:* Jonathan Sanger; *W:* Ronald Bass; *M:* John Addison.

Code Name: The Cleaner 🦴 1/2 **2007 (PG-13)** Low-brow action-comedy for Mr. The Entertainer's fans. Jake wakes up in a hotel room with no memory, next to a dead FBI agent and a lot of cash. Va-voomish Diane (Sheridan) picks him up, says they're married, and takes Jake to a grandiose mansion. Jake has flashbacks that convince him he's a secret agent and Diane is after a computer chip. When Jake runs into waitress Gina (Liu), she tells him he's actually a janitor and head trauma is causing his delusions. Ah, but there's more to the story (a lot of it extremely silly). Still, Liu is sexy in leather and the pic is nothing if not good-natured. **91m/C; DVD.** Cedric the Entertainer; Lucy Liu; Nicolette Sheridan; Mark Dacascos; Callum Keith Rennie; Niecy Nash; Will Patton; DeRay David; *D:* Les Mayfield; *W:* Robert Adetuyi; George Gallo; *C:* David Franco; *M:* George S. Clinton.

Code Name: Wild Geese 🦴 1/2 *Geheimecode Wildganse* **1984 (R)** A group of mercenaries is hired to destroy an opium plant somewhere in the jungles of Thailand and cause explosions along the way. It's worth noting for the horribly animated (and physically impossible) chase sequence in which a man drives his car sideways along a tunnel wall. **101m/C; DVD.** *IT GE* Lewis Collins; Lee Van Cleef; Ernest Borgnine; Klaus Kinski; *D:* Anthony M. Dawson; *W:* Michael Lester; *C:* Peter Baumgartner.

Code Name: Zebra 🦴 1/2 **1984** The Zebra Force helps the cops put bad guys away. When the bad guys get out, they want revenge. The result: lots of violence and action. Wasn't released theatrically. **96m/C; VHS, DVD.** Jim Mitchum; Mike Lane; Timothy Brown; Joe Dante; Deana Jurgens; Frank Sinatra, Jr.; Robert Z'Dar; *D:* Joe Tornatore.

Code of Honor 🦴 *Kill Squad* **1982** Prominent businessman embarks on mission of revenge when police fail to apprehend his wife's rapist. No surprise here. You either enjoy this sort of thing or you find a reasonably fulfilling life. **90m/C; VHS, DVD.** Cameron Mitchell; Mark Sabin; Frank Ramirez; Jeff Risk; Jean Glaude; Jerry Johnson; *D:* Patrick G. Donahue; *W:* Patrick G. Donahue; *C:* Christopher W. Strattan; *M:* Joseph Conlan.

Code of Honor 🦴🦴 1/2 *Sweet Revenge* **1984** A young woman vows revenge on the military commanders who caused her brother's demise. Neatly made psychological thriller is surprisingly good for a TV movie. **105m/C; VHS, DVD.** Kevin Dobson; Wings Hauser; Alec Baldwin; Merritt Butrick; Kelly McGillis; Alfre Woodard; Savannah Smith; Helen Hunt; Dana Elcar; *D:* David Green.

Code of Honor 🦴🦴 **2016 (R)** A formulaic vigilante action film starring Steven Seagal. After his loved ones are murdered in a drive-by shooting, Robert Sikes (Seagal) feels he must act. Drawing on skills gained while a special-ops operative, Robert decide that he will cleanse his city of all criminals—including street gangs, mobsters, and politicians—on his own. FBI Agent William Porter (Sheffer), Robert's former protege, and a witness to the shooting, Keri Green (Mattsson), try to stop Robert before the police bring him to justice or he is caught by those who would like to see him dead. **106m/C; DVD, Blu-Ray, Streaming, Download.** Steven Seagal; Craig Sheffer; James Russo; Helena Mattsson; *Cameo(s):* Louis Mandylor; *D:* Michael Winnick; *W:* Michael Winnick; *C:* Anthony J. Rickert-Epstein; *M:* Michael John Mollo.

Code of Silence 🦴🦴 **1985 (R)** A police loner must contend with both a gang war and police department corruption. Hectic, violent action-drama with some wild stunts. **100m/C; VHS, DVD, Blu-Ray.** Chuck Norris; Henry Silva; Bert Remsen; Molly Hagan; Nathan Davis; Dennis Farina; *D:* Andrew Davis; *W:* Michael Butler; Mike Gray; *C:* Frank Tidy; *M:* David Michael Frank.

Code Two 🦴 1/2 **1953** B-movie crime drama of some interest because of its now-vintage motorcycles. Chuck, Harry, and Russ all pass the training program and join the LAPD. Before long they're bored by their routine assignments and transfer to the motorcycle squad. A routine traffic stop leads to tragedy and to truckers involved in a hijacking ring. **70m/B; DVD.** Ralph Meeker; Robert Horton; Jeff Richards; Keenan Wynn; James Craig; Elaine Stewart; Sally Forrest; *D:* Fred M. Wilcox; *W:* Marcy (Marcel) Klauber; *C:* Ray June; *M:* Alberto Colombo.

Code Unknown 🦴🦴 *Code Unknown: Incomplete Tales of Several Journeys; Code Inconnu: Recit Incomplet De Divers Voyages* **2000** Teeanger Jean (Hamidi) has run away from the farm work his father (Bierbichler) expects from him. He goes to see his brother Georges (Neuvic), a war photographer, in Paris. Although Georges is frequently away, Jean stays with Georges' lover Anne (Binoche) in their apartment. On the street, Jean insults Romanian beggar Maria (Gheorghiu) and gets into a scuffle with young black teacher Amadou (Yenke) over Jean's lack of respect. The characters lives continue to interact in random ways. French and Romanian with subtitles. **118m/C; VHS, DVD, Blu-Ray.** *FR* Juliette Binoche; Alexandre Hamidi; Thierry Neuvic; Sepp Bierbichler; Ona Lu Yenke; Luminita Gheorghiu; *D:* Michael Haneke; *W:* Michael Haneke; *C:* Jurgen Jurges; *M:* Giba Goncalves.

Codename: Icarus 🦴🦴 **1985** A young mathematical genius, enrolled at a special school for accelerated study, uncovers evil government plots to use the students for espionage. **106m/C; VHS, DVD.** *GB* Barry Angel; Jack Galloway; *D:* Marilyn Fox. **TV**

Codename: Jaguar 🦴🦴 *Sublet* **1998 (R)** Stuart (Nucci) moves to New York to accept a newspaper job, and happily sublets an apartment from the beautiful Daphne (Sanchez). Unknown to him, the apartment is actually owned by 'The Jaguar', a world-class assassin whose face no one knows. Rumor has it he's in town to kill the Russian president, and everyone from the CIA to the local underworld to the increasingly mysterious Daphne believes that Stuart is the hitman. **105m/C; DVD.** *CA* Danny Nucci; Victoria Sanchez; David Carradine; Serge Houde; Mark Camacho; *D:* John Hamilton; *W:* Tim Kring; *C:* Bert Tougas; *M:* Daniel Scott.

Codename: Wildgeese 🦴 1/2 *Geheimecode Wildganse* **1984 (R)** The big-name cast of this meandering mercenary macho-rama probably wish they'd been credited under code names; solid histrionics cannot a silly script save. A troop of commandos-for-hire are engaged by the Drug Enforcement Administration to obliterate an opium operation in Asia's infamous Golden Triangle, and much mindless agitation ensues. **101m/C; VHS, DVD.** *IT GE* Lewis Collins; Lee Van Cleef; Ernest Borgnine; Klaus Kinski; Mimsy Farmer; *D:* Anthony M. Dawson.

A Coeur Joie 🦴🦴 *Two Weeks in September* **1967** Beautiful 30-something Cecile is married to a much older Englishman. She's content with her peaceful life until she meets a young man who rekindles her passions. Will Cecile run off with her new lover or stay with the man who makes her secure? French with subtitles. **96m/C; VHS, DVD.** *GB FR* Brigitte Bardot; Laurent Terzieff; Jean Rochefort; James Robertson Justice; Michael Sarne; Murray Head; *D:* Serge Bourguignon; *W:* Serge Bourguignon; Pascal Jardin.

Coffee and Cigarettes 🦴🦴🦴 **2003 (R)** Director/writer Jarmusch returns after a five-year absence with these 11 short films inspired by or having to do with the two addictions of the title. Shot in black and white, the short vignettes feature a wide range of talent from Cate Blanchett to Steven Wright. Jarmusch filmed the shorts over a period of 17 years between projects, and while some of the episodes are better than others there are more hits than misses. The highlight is "Somewhere in California" featuring Tom Waits and Iggy Pop. Jarmusch again demonstrates why he is the king of independent film makers today. **96m/B; DVD, Blu-Ray.** Iggy Pop; Tom Waits; Cate Blanchett; Steve Buscemi; Alfred Molina; RZA; Steve Coogan; Jack White; Roberto Benigni; Joie Lee; Steven Wright; Cinque Lee; Alex Descas; Isaach de Bankole; Michael Hogan; Meg White; Joe Rigano; Vinnie Vella; Vinnie Vella, Jr.; Renee French; E.J. Rodriguez; Bill Rice; Taylor Mead; Katy Hansz; GZA; *Cameo(s):* Bill Murray; *D:* Jim Jarmusch; *W:* Jim Jarmusch; *C:* Tom DiCillo; Frederick Elmes; Ellen Kuras; Robby Muller.

Coffee Date 🦴🦴 **2006** Generally sweet romantic comedy has straight-laced Todd's (Bray) loser brother Barry (Silverman) decides to hook him up with an online date. Only Barry places the ad in the "men seeking men" section. Todd chats with Kelly (Cruz) online, they arrange to meet for coffee, and—whoops—Kelly's a guy! The two become friends and everyone assumes divorced Todd is gay—and maybe Todd isn't quite as upset as he thinks he should be. **93m/C; DVD.** Wilson Cruz; Jonathan Silverman; Sally Kirkland; Leigh Taylor-Young; Jonathan Bray; Jason Stuart; Elaine Hendrix; Deborah Gibson; *D:* Stuart Wade; *W:* Stuart Wade; *C:* Howard Wexler; *M:* Eban Schletter.

Coffin 🦴 **2011** Stock low-budget wannabe thriller. Jack (Barnitt) arrives home to be greeted by masked baddie Trick (Alonso) who shows him live video feed of his wife Rona (Doench) and her lover Sean (Sorbo) whom he's buried alive with 75 minutes of oxygen. Amidst too much yapping, the kidnapper makes his demands but Jack has problems delivering the ransom. **95m/C; DVD.** Patrick Barnitt; Johnny Alonso; Sunny Doench; Kevin Sorbo; Bruce Davison; Kipp Tribble; Derek Wingo; *D:* Kipp Tribble; Derek Wingo; *W:* Kipp Tribble; *C:* Keiko Nakahara; *M:* Jason Gaines; Roger Ryan. **VIDEO**

Coffy 🦴🦴 **1973 (R)** A beautiful woman feigns drug addiction to discover and destroy the evil dealers responsible for her sister's death. Grler is everything in this exploitative flick full of violence and nudity. **91m/C; VHS, DVD, Blu-Ray.** Pam Grier; Booker Bradshaw; Robert DoQui; Allan Arbus; William (Bill) Elliott; Sid Haig; *D:* Jack Hill; *W:* Jack Hill; *C:* Paul Lohmann; *M:* Roy Ayers.

C.O.G. 🦴 1/2 **2013 (R)** Ineffectual, uneasy mix of satire and soul-searching is an adaptation of a David Sedaris essay. Self-absorbed Yale grad student David (Goff) leaves college to find his inner everyman by taking a job on an Oregon apple farm. Calling himself Samuel, the dilettante is resented by the migrant workers and humiliated by the farm's surly owner (Stockwell). A trip to town introduces closeted David to troubled, born-again "child of God" Jon (O'Hare), who takes him in when a flirtation with blue-collar stud Curly (Stoll) goes awry. But David can't manage any equilibrium between his sexuality and Jon's anti-gay diatribes. **88m/C; DVD, Streaming.** Jonathan Groff; Denis O'Hare; Corey Stoll; Dean Stockwell; Troian Bellisario; *D:* Kyle Patrick Alvarez; *W:* Kyle Patrick Alvarez; *C:* Jas Shelton; *M:* Steve Reich; Joe Berry.

Cohen and Tate 🦴🦴 **1988 (R)** Two antagonistic mob hitmen kidnap a nine-year-old who witnessed his parent's recent murder by the mob. In order to survive, the boy begins to play one psycho off the other. **113m/C; VHS, DVD, Blu-Ray.** Roy Scheider; Adam Baldwin; Harley Cross; Cooper Huckabee; *D:* Eric Red; *W:* Eric Red; *M:* Bill Conti.

Coherence 🦴🦴 **2013** Eight friends get together for a nice dinner on the same night that a comet is coming dangerously close to the planet. The power goes out. They venture outside, only to see that there's one house in the distance that looks like it has power. A few guys go to check it out and see the same group of friends at a dinner party. Alternate universes have gone off their parallel tracks and now share the same space. What is real? Who is real? Byrkit didn't give his actors the entire script, making their fearful responses enjoyably genuine. **89m/C; DVD.** Nicholas Brendon; Lorene Scafaria; Emily Foxler; Maury Sterling; Hugo Armstrong; Elizabeth (Ward) Gracen; Alex Manugian; Lauren Maher; *D:* James Ward Byrkit; *W:* James Ward Byrkit; *C:* Nic Sadler; Arlene Muller; *M:* Kristin Ohrn Dyrud.

Cold and Dark 🦴 1/2 **2005** Muddled Brit frightener finds young copper John Dark (Goss) being mentored by experienced detective Mortimer Shade (Howarth) as they investigate a series of strange murders. Dark eventually realizes that his partner is committing the crimes; having been taken over by an alien parasite, Shade needs fresh blood to survive. But Dark worries (as well he should!) when he realizes that Shade is becoming more monster and less human each time he kills. **94m/C; DVD.** *GB* Luke Goss; Kevin Howarth; Cassandra Bell; Michael Culkin; Matt Lucas; Carly Jane Turnbull; Steven Elder; *D:* Andrew Goth; *W:* Joanne Reay; *C:* Sam McCurdy; *M:* Lauren Yason.

Cold Around the Heart 🦴🦴 **1997 (R)** Familiar crime/road movie finds sensitive jewel thief Ned (Caruso) partnering up (both in and out of the sack) with tough cookie Jude (Lynch). Only in their latest heist, Jude takes off with the diamonds and Ned's in pursuit across the southwest but, nice guy that Ned is, he stops to help out pregnant, black hitchhiker Bec (Dash). If you don't expect much, you won't be disappointed. **96m/C; VHS, DVD.** David Caruso; Kelly Lynch; Stacey Dash; Chris Noth; John Spencer; *D:* John

Ridley; *W:* John Ridley; *C:* Malik Hassan Sayeed; *M:* Mason Daring.

Cold Blood 🦴 1/2 *Das Amulett des Todes* **1975 (R)** A pair of kidnap victims turn the tables on their captors. **90m/C; VHS, DVD.** *GE* Rutger Hauer; Vera Tschechowa; Horst Frank; Gunther Stoll; *D:* Ralf Gregan; Gunter Vaessen; *W:* Gunter Vaessen; *C:* Michael Ballhaus; *M:* Rolf Bauer.

Cold Blooded 🦴🦴 **2000 (R)** Reporter suspects a cover-up when the police dismiss the death of a young woman as a suicide. He thinks she's another victim of a serial killer who has already killed 12 and isn't done yet. **94m/C; VHS, DVD.** Michael Moriarty; Patti LuPone; John Kapelos; Gloria Reuben; *D:* Randy Bradshaw; *W:* Ian Adams; *C:* Dean Bennett; *M:* Tim McCauley. **VIDEO**

Cold Brook 🦴🦴 1/2 **2018** College maintenance workers and friends Ted (Fichtner) and George (Coates) are working in the school's art museum after hours when they encounter a man (Perrineau) standing near an exhibit of Civil War-era items. The duo chases him off, leading to a viral video shot by students and praise from the community. Some supernatural oddities begin happening to them, which make the men look at the situation – and their own lives-- differently. Fichtner's enjoyable directorial debut is proof that sometimes less is more when it comes to good storytelling. **100m/C; DVD.** William Fichtner; Harold Perrineau, Jr.; Robin Weigert; Kim Coates; Mary Lynn Rajskub; *D:* William Fichtner; *W:* William Fichtner; *C:* Edd Lukas; *M:* Michael Deragon.

Cold Case Hammarskjöld 🦴🦴🦴 *The Secret Lives of Pigs* **2019** In 1961, UN Secretary General Dag Hammarskjold died in a plane crash. A Swedish aristocrat who had been the UN head since 1953, he was especially interested in helping newly independent African countries become free from their colonizers. Though Hammarskjold's death was ruled accidental, foul play was suspected because he had made powerful enemies. The documentary looks at the case for murder, with filmmaker Brugger and Swedish private investigator Goran Bjorkdahl conducting related interviews in Europe and Africa. Though the gripping film is a documentary, it unfolds like a thriller as it explores issues like the Cold War and the decolonization of Africa. **128m/C; DVD.** Mads Brügger; Göran Björkdahl; Dag Hammarskjöld; *D:* Mads Brügger; *W:* Mads Brügger; *C:* Tore Vollan; *M:* John Erik Kaada.

Cold Comes the Night 🦴🦴 **2014 (R)** Single mom Chloe (Eve) is the manager of a skeevy highway stop motel. Needing money to move somewhere better in order to keep her young daughter, Chloe unwillingly becomes the new driver for nearly-blind career criminal Topo (Cranston), who needs to retrieve a bag of cash hidden in a car that was confiscated by the cops after a killing at the motel. The plot gets more complicated, but director Chun knows how to ratchet up the tension in his still low-key thriller. **90m/C; DVD, Blu-Ray.** Alice Eve; Bryan Cranston; Logan Marshall-Green; Leo Fitzpatrick; Erin Cummings; *D:* Tze Chun; *W:* Tze Chun; Oz (Osgood) Perkins, II; Nick Simon; *C:* Noah Rosenthal; *M:* Jeff Grace.

Cold Comfort Farm 🦴🦴🦴 **1994 (PG)** Stella Gibbons classic 1932 comedic novel is brought to life in this TV adaptation, which finds orphaned London lass Flora Poste (Beckinsdale) trying to take charge of the lives of her very odd country cousins, the Starkadders. The rowdy family and their dilapidated farm are putty in practical Flora's hands as she works to make everybody happy (including herself). Terrific ensemble cast, with a fast pace and wicked humor. **104m/C; VHS, DVD.** *GB* Kate Beckinsale; Eileen Atkins; Ian McKellen; Sheila Burrell; Rufus Sewell; Maria Miles; Freddie Jones; Ivan Kaye; Miriam Margolyes; Joanna Lumley; Stephen Fry; Christopher Bowen; *D:* John Schlesinger; *W:* Malcolm Bradbury; *C:* Chris Seager; *M:* Robert Lockhart. **TV**

Cold Creek Manor 🦴🦴 1/2 **2003 (R)** How is it that Michael Douglas isn't involved with this? This is just the kind of yuppie nightmare thriller for which he was the go-to guy for much of the 1980s and '90s. Quaid does an admirable job filling his shoes, however, as an NYC-based documentary filmmaker who, along with his business hotshot wife (Stone), decides to chuck the rat race of the city for a nice, quiet life in the country. Oops. They buy a big, creepy house "for a steal" and find it comes with some secrets, and a redneck caretaker (Dorff) who strangely attracts the missus, but creeps out the kids, especially daughter Kristen. Not much new is brought to the genre, but it has some truly creepy moments, and Figgis ads some much-needed subtle satire. Top-notch cast helps, as well. **118m/C; VHS, DVD, Blu-Ray.** Dennis Quaid; Sharon Stone; Stephen Dorff; Juliette Lewis; Kristen Stewart; Christopher Plummer; Ryan Wilson, MS III; Dana Eskelson; *D:* Mike Figgis; *W:* Richard Jefferies; *C:* Declan Quinn; *M:* Mike Figgis.

A Cold Day in Hell **WOOF!** **2011 (PG-13)** Strictly amateur time (and not even competent amateurs) with the prominently-featured Madsen in little more than a cameo. In 1887, sharpshooter William Drayton has isolated himself in the Sierra Nevada mountains when his long-lost daughter Elizabeth shows up. She needs his help fighting Drayton's former boss, banker Horace Scarsdale, who's using any means necessary to build his railroad empire. **95m/C; DVD.** Jim Hilton; Heather Clark; Dave Long; Stan Fink; Michael Madsen; *D:* Christopher Forbes; *W:* Jim Hilton; Christopher Forbes; *C:* Michael G. Hennessy; *M:* Christopher Forbes; W. Clay Lee. **VIDEO**

Cold Dog Soup 🦴 **1989** A dead dog in a garbage bag is the subject of this unfunny comedy. Michael is invited to Sarah's for dinner and maybe some nookie if he can pass muster with her eccentric mother and ancient family pet Jasper. Too bad Jasper drops dead and the women insist Michael bury him immediately at his favorite spot in the park. Michael's then subjected to the ramblings of the crazy cabbie who picks him up and insists there's money to be made from a dog carcass even if the Chinese restaurant won't put ole Jasper on the menu (hence the title). **87m/C; DVD.** Frank Whaley; Randy Quaid; Christina Harnos; Sheree North; Nancy Kwan; Seymour Cassel; *D:* Alan Metter; *W:* Tom Pope; *C:* Frederick Elmes; *M:* Michael Kamen.

The Cold Equations 🦴🦴 **1996** Lt. John Barton (Campbell) is sent on an emergency mission to deliver a vaccine to a distant mining colony. His spacecraft has been precisely calibrated to hold him and the medicine so the discovery of stowaway Lee (Montgomery) and her added weight puts everything in jeopardy and Barton's superiors have a harsh solution. Adapted from Tom Godwin's 1954 short story. **93m/C; DVD.** Billy Campbell; Poppy Montgomery; Daniel Roebuck; William R. Moses; John Prosky; *D:* Peter Geiger; *W:* Peter Geiger; Norman Plotkin; Stephen Berger; *C:* Chris Walling; *M:* Paul Rabjohns. **TV**

Cold Eyes of Fear 🦴 **1970** A man and his girlfriend are besieged by a raving convict whom his uncle, a judge, had put away years before. Shades of "Cape Fear" on a low budget. **88m/C; VHS, DVD, Blu-Ray.** Fernando Rey; Frank Wolfe; Karin Schubert; *D:* Enzo G. Castellari; *W:* Enzo G. Castellari; Tito Carpi; Leo Anchoriz; *C:* Antonio Ballesteros; *M:* Ennio Morricone.

Cold Feet 🦴🦴 1/2 **1989 (R)** Modern-day western in which a trio of loopy desperados smuggle jewels inside a racehorse's stomach. Quirky comedy offers wild performances from Waits and sex-bomb Kirkland, but could use a few more laughs. Filmed largely on McGuane's ranch. **94m/C; VHS, DVD.** Keith Carradine; Tom Waits; Sally Kirkland; Rip Torn; Kathleen York; Bill Pullman; Vincent Schiavelli; Jeff Bridges; *D:* Robert Dornhelm; *W:* Thomas McGuane; Jim Harrison; *C:* Bryan Duggan; *M:* Tom Bahler.

Cold Harvest 🦴🦴 **1998 (R)** A comet strikes the earth, killing a great portion of the population and then disaster strikes again when a deadly disease runs unchecked, killing those who become infected. A bounty hunter and his partner seek to find one of the seven people who carry the antibody to the disease. **93m/C; VHS, DVD.** Gary Daniels; Barbara Crampton; Bryan Genesse; *D:* Isaac Florentine; *W:* Frank Dietz; *C:* David Varod; *M:* Stephen (Steve) Edwards. **VIDEO**

Cold Hearts 🦴🦴 1/2 **1999** Charles is the head of a group of young vampires who take over a small New Jersey town. But best friends Viktoria and Alicia want to escape from Charles' influence and turn to a stranger for help. Low-budget vamp flick is surprisingly professional and watchable. **88m/C; VHS, DVD.** Marisa Ryan; Amy Jo Johnson; Christopher Wiehl; Robert Floyd; *D:* Robert Masciantonio. **VIDEO**

Cold Heaven 🦴 1/2 **1992 (R)** Alex and Marie Davenport are on vacation when an accident occurs and Alex dies—or does he? The next day his body disappears and his unfaithful wife begins to have paranoid delusions that he is returning to exact retribution for her affair. But these aren't her only visions, for during the past year Marie has also had religious visions she believes are part of a personal battle with God. Harmon does what he can with his role as the alleged corpse but Russell is uncharacteristically whiny and bland. Convoluted story of marriage, death, and spirituality; doesn't pan out on any accounts. Based on a novel by Brian Moore. **103m/C; VHS, Streaming.** Theresa Russell; Mark Harmon; James Russo; Talia Shire; Will Patton; Richard Bradford; *D:* Nicolas Roeg; *W:* Allan Scott.

Cold in July 🦴🦴🦴 **2014** A split-second decision to commit an act of violence opens a door into a dark world in Mickle's genre-jumping adaptation of the Joe Lansdale novella. Richard Dane's (Hall) a man who wakes one night to find an intruder in his house. Grabbing the gun from the dresser, Richard shoots the man in the head but his world really collapses when the thug's father Ben (a perfect Shepard) comes to the Dane home seeking vengeance. And then Mickle's narrative jumps again. Drama-thriller-comedy-action-horror, it's a pulp fiction novel in film form, and that's meant in the best way possible. **109m/C; DVD, Blu-Ray.** Michael C. Hall; Sam Shepard; Don Johnson; Vinessa Shaw; Wyatt Russell; Nick Damici; *D:* Jim Mickle; *W:* Nick Damici; Jim Mickle; *C:* Ryan Samul; *M:* Jeff Grace.

The Cold Lands 🦴🦴 **2013** Eleven-year-old Atticus (Yelich) has long lived on the edge of society with his single mother (Taylor). When she passes away, he's left completely on his own to eat and survive in an increasingly dangerous world in which the meth addicts may get you before the animals do. Atticus runs into a drifter (Scanavino) and director/writer Gilroy's coming-of-age tale takes on a bittersweet tone about what is lost when young boys are forced to turn into men at far too young an age. It's a confident, engaging drama even if the central performance doesn't quite click like one hopes it would. **100m/C; DVD.** Silas Yelich; Peter Scanavino; Lili Taylor; *D:* Tom Gilroy; *W:* Tom Gilroy; *C:* Wyatt Garfield; *M:* Hahn Rowe.

The Cold Light of Day 🦴 1/2 **2012 (PG-13)** Out for a secret briefcase, intelligence agents kidnap the family of unassuming Wall Street stock trader, Will (Cavill), while on a sailing trip in Spain. Will must then hunt down and outwit the operatives responsible. What appears to be a big budget action flick is unfortunately a generic, paycheck job for its big stars. Cavill is bland while head villain Weaver comes across as silly--spouting off a plethora of cliched lines. Willis plays the brief role of dad Martin, who seemingly isn't an innocent in the events. A cold, sluggish mess. **93m/C; DVD, Blu-Ray.** Bruce Willis; Henry Cavill; Caroline Goodall; Jim Piddock; Sigourney Weaver; Roschdy Zem; Oscar Jaenada; *D:* Mabrouk El Mechri; *W:* Scott Wiper; John Petro; *C:* Remi Adefarasin; *M:* Lucas Vidal.

Cold Mountain 🦴🦴🦴 1/2 **2003 (R)** Minghella's excellent adaptation of Charles Frazier's dense and challenging novel has Inman (Law) attempting to return home, "Odyssey"-style, to North Carolina after his friends are all killed in the disastrous battle at Petersburg, Virginia in 1864. Inman sees no point in continuing the fight and begins his journey so he can continue the brief, chaste, tentative courtship he had begun with the sophisticated Ada (Kidman) before the war. Ada has also seen hardship during their separation. Her father has died, leaving her unprepared to tend the farm until neighbor Ruby (Zellweger) is sent to help. All the actors are superb, with Zellweger stealing every scene she's in, and Minghella strikes the perfect balance between the two stories, thanks to some expert editing. **155m/C; DVD, Blu-Ray.** *GB RO IT* Jude Law; Nicole Kidman; Renée Zellweger; Donald Sutherland; Eileen Atkins; Brendan Gleeson; Philip Seymour Hoffman; Natalie Portman; Giovanni Ribisi; Ray Winstone; Kathy Baker; James Gammon; Charlie Hunnam; Jack White; Ethan Suplee; Jena Malone; Melora Walters; Lucas Black; Taryn Manning; Tom Aldredge; James Rebhorn; *D:* Anthony Minghella; *W:* Anthony Minghella; *C:* John Seale; *M:* Gabriel Yared. Oscars '03: Support. Actress (Zellweger); British Acad. '03: Score, Support. Actress (Zellweger); Golden Globes '04: Support. Actress (Zellweger); Screen Actors Guild '03: Support. Actress (Zellweger).

Cold Prey II 🦴🦴 *Fritt vilt II* **2008** The last survivor from the first film is found and taken to a hospital where she reveals her tale of woe. Skeptical police investigate, and bring the somehow still living killer to the hospital where he is revived and immediately begins leaving a trail of destruction. **86m/C; DVD.** *NO* Ingrid Bolso Berdal; Marthe Snorresdotter Rovik; Kim Wifladt; Johanna Merck; Fridtjov Saheim; *D:* Mats Stenberg; *W:* Thomas Moldestad; Martin Sundland; Roar Uthaug; *C:* Anders Flatland; *M:* Magnus Beite. **VIDEO**

Cold Pursuit 🦴🦴 1/2 **2019 (R)** In wintery Kehoe, Colorado, Nels Coxman (Neeson) is a locally respected snowplow driver whose life changes forever when his son Kyle (Richardson) is murdered by members of a local drug cartel because he mishandled a cocaine shipment during his duties as an airport baggage handler. The killers made Kyle's death look like a heroin overdose though he did not use drugs. Nels then vows revenge on his son's killers. Based on a Norweigan film that was also directed by Moland, this revenge film gets a bit murky at times but it's bolstered by dark humor, Western motifs, and creative deaths. **119m/C; DVD, Blu-Ray.** Liam Neeson; Laura Dern; Micheal Richardson; Michael Eklund; Bradley Stryker; *D:* Hans Petter Moland; Frank Baldwin; *C:* Philip Ogaard; *M:* George Fenton.

Cold River 🦴🦴 1/2 **1981 (PG)** An experienced guide takes his two children on an extended trip through the Adirondacks. For the children, it's a fantasy vacation until their father succumbs to a heart attack in the chilly mountains. "Cold River" is a journey of survival, and an exploration of human relationships. **94m/C; VHS, DVD.** Pat Petersen; Richard Jaeckel; Suzanne Weber; Brad Sullivan; Robert Earl Jones; Elizabeth Hubbard; Augusta Dabney; *D:* Fred G. Sullivan.

Cold Room 🦴 1/2 *The Prisoner* **1984** College student on vacation with her father in East Berlin discovers the horrors hidden in an antiquated hotel room next to hers. From the novel by Jeffrey Caine. **95m/C; VHS, DVD.** George Segal; Renee Soutendijk; Amanda Pays; Warren Clarke; Anthony (Corlan) Higgins; *D:* James Dearden; *M:* Michael Nyman. **CABLE**

Cold Showers 🦴🦴 *Doches Froides* **2005** Mickael (Libereau) is 17 and proud of his judo skills and hot squeeze Vanessa (Stevenin). He becomes friends with judo-club member Clement (Perrier) and the trio briefly become a menage although Mickael's jealousy soon surfaces. Slight story includes nudity and sex scenes (remember it's French). French with subtitles. **102m/C; DVD.** *FR* Salome Stevenin; Florence Thomassin; Jean-Philippe Ecoffey; Johan Libereau; Pierre Perrier; *D:* Anthony Cordier; *W:* Anthony Cordier; *C:* Nicolas Gaurin; *M:* Nicolas Lemercier.

Cold Skin 🦴 1/2 **2018** Shortly before World War I begins, an unnamed Irish soldier (Oakes) has become disillusioned while fighting for Irish independence. Seeking solitude, he takes a position on an isolated island near Antarctica for one year. Though warned about the danger and finding his predecessor is missing, the soldier stays. The only other person on the island is a seemingly insane older man Gruner (Stevenson). The soldier learns that creatures attack each night, and he must team with Gruner to survive. Based on a 2002 novel, this thriller has an artful look but ultimately is another ho-hum monster flick. **108m/C; DVD.** Ray Stevenson; David Oakes; Aura Garrido; Winslow Iwaki; John Benfield; *D:* Xavier Gens; *W:* Jesus Olmo; Eron Sheean; *C:* Daniel Aranyo; *M:* Victor Reyes.

Cold Souls 🦴🦴 **2009 (PG-13)** Paul Giamatti plays an anxiety-ridden version of himself as the actor struggles with his stage role in Chekov's "Uncle Vanya." A magazine article offers a solution: Dr. Flintstein (Strathairn) specializes in 'soul storage,' which temporarily removes the soul and its emotional burdens. The only problem is that without his soul, Giametti can't act and so Flintstein loans him the soul of a Russian poet. Complications ensue when Russian Nina (Korzun), who deals in black-market souls, borrows Giamatti's stored soul, which then sends the actor to St. Petersburg so he can get it back. **101m/C; On Demand.** Paul Giamatti; Dina Korzun; Katheryn Winnick; David Strathairn; Emily Watson; Lauren Ambrose; Boris Kievsky; ***D:*** Sophie Barthes; ***W:*** Sophie Barthes; ***C:*** Andrij Parekh; ***M:*** Dickon Hinchliffe.

Cold Steel 1/2 **1987 (R)** Standard revenge drama about a hardnosed Los Angeles cop tracking his father's disfigured psycho-killer. Cast includes the always intense Davis, ex-pop star Ant, and screen scorch-stress Stone. Still it's predictable, low-grade fare. **91m/C; VHS, DVD.** Brad Davis; Jonathan Banks; Adam Ant; Sharon Stone; ***D:*** Dorothy Ann Puzo.

Cold Sweat *L'Uomo Dalle Due Ombre; De la Part des Copains* **1971 (PG)** A brutal drug trader takes his ultra-violent revenge after his wife is captured by a drug boss' moronic henchmen. Typical Bronson flick boasts superior supporting cast of Ullmann and Mason. Writing and direction, however, are mediocre. Based on the Richard Matheson novel "Ride the Nightmare." **94m/C; VHS, DVD, Blu-Ray.** *IT FR* Charles Bronson; Jill Ireland; Liv Ullmann; James Mason; ***D:*** Terence Young; ***W:*** Albert Simonin; Shimon Wincelberg; ***C:*** Jean Rabier; ***M:*** Michel Magne.

Cold Sweat **1993 (R)** A professional hit man (Cross) is literally haunted by the ghost of his last victim (who happens to be female and usually appears naked), so he decides his next assignment will be his last. A ruthless businessman suspects his very sexy wife (Tweed) has been unfaithful but she has lots of other secrets to hide. **93m/C; VHS, DVD.** Ben Cross; Shannon Tweed; Adam Baldwin; Dave Thomas; ***D:*** Gail Harvey; ***W:*** Richard Beattie.

Cold Turkey **1971 (PG)** Often witty satire about what happens when an entire town tries to stop smoking for a contest. Van Dyke is fine as the anti-smoking minister; newscasters Bob and Ray are riotous; oldtimer Horton's swansong. Wholesome, somewhat tame fare. **99m/C; VHS, DVD, Blu-Ray.** Dick Van Dyke; Pippa Scott; Tom Poston; Bob Newhart; Vincent Gardenia; Barnard Hughes; Jean Stapleton; Graham Jarvis; Edward Everett Horton; ***D:*** Norman Lear; ***W:*** Norman Lear; ***M:*** Randy Newman.

Cold Turkey **2013** A Thanksgiving turkey indeed. Am affluent, dysfunctional family gathers to celebrate the holiday, including the return of estranged daughter Nina (Witt, the one bright spark). Poppy (Bogdanovich) is morose, stepmom Deborah (Hines) is smug, and the adult children continue to whine about childhood slights. This self-absorbed bunch guarantees indigestion. **84m/C; On Demand.** Peter Bogdanovich; Alicia Witt; Sonya Walger; Ashton Holmes; Cheryl Hines; ***D:*** Will Slocombe; ***W:*** Will Slocombe; ***C:*** Lucas Lee Graham; ***M:*** William C. White.

Cold War *Zimna wojna* **2018 (R)** During the Cold War in the 1950s, singer Zula (Kulig) and musical director Wiktor (Kot) are bound to each other in a passionate yet turbulent relationship for over a decade. Shot in beautiful and nostalgic black and white, with the music itself cluing the audience in to the changing expectations and limitations of Communism, this romance is loosely based on Pawlikowski's parents, who split up several times yet were irresistibly drawn together. **88m/B; DVD, Blu-Ray.** Joanna Kulig; Tomasz Kot; Borys Szyc; Agata Kulesza; Cedric Kahn; ***D:*** Pawel Pawlikowski; ***W:*** Pawel Pawlikowski; Janusz Glowacki; ***C:*** Lukasz Zal.

Cold War Killers 1/2 **1986 (PG)** Soviet and British agents vie for control of prized cargo plane recently retrieved from the sea floor. **85m/C; VHS, DVD.** *GB* Terence Stamp; Mike Lane; Robin Sachs; Peter Ivatts; Martin Dale; ***D:*** William Brayne; ***W:*** Murray Smith; ***C:*** Mike Blakely; ***M:*** Christopher Gunning.

Coldblooded 1/2 **1994 (R)** Minor mob flunky (and dim bulb) Cosmo (Priestley) is unwillingly promoted to the position of hit man by his mobster boss. He's tutored by the organization's primo professional (Riegert) and finds out he has a real knack for murder. More sophomoric than satiric and a waste of Riegert's talents; Williams is attractive as Priestley's clueless girlfriend. Directorial debut of Wolodarsky. **92m/C; VHS, Streaming.** Jason Priestley; Peter Riegert; Kimberly Williams; Robert Loggia; Janeane Garofalo; Josh Charles; David Anthony Higgens; Doris Grau; ***Cameo(s):*** Talia Balsam; Michael J. Fox; ***D:*** M. Wallace Wolodarsky; ***W:*** M. Wallace Wolodarsky; ***C:*** Robert Yeoman; ***M:*** Steve Bartek.

Coldfire 1/2 **1990** Two rookie cops work to undo the havoc unleashed on the streets of LA because of a deadly new drug sought for its powerful high. Not many surprises here. **90m/C; VHS, DVD.** Wings Hauser; Kamar De Los Reyes; Robert Viharo; Gary Swanson; ***D:*** Wings Hauser.

Colditz: Escape of the Birdmen 1/2 *Escape of the Birdmen; The Birdmen* **1971** ABC TV movie inspired by a WWII true story. Major Harry Cook is sent to Norway to aid in the defection of scientist Halden Brevik, who's been working on an atomic bomb. Both men are captured and sent as POWs to Colditz Castle on the German-Swiss border. Cook convinces some other prisoners to help him and Brevik, who's imprisoned under another name, make a two-person glider they can fly into neutral Switzerland before the Gestapo can discover Brevik's true identity. **85m/C; DVD.** Doug McClure; Rene Auberjonois; Richard Basehart; Chuck Connors; Max Baer, Jr.; Tom Skerritt; Greg Mullavey; Don Knight; ***D:*** Philip Leacock; ***W:*** David Kidd; ***C:*** Jack Marta; ***M:*** David Rose. **TV**

The Colditz Story 1/2 **1955** Prisoners of war from the Allied countries join together in an attempt to escape from Colditz, an allegedly escape-proof castle-prison deep within the Third Reich. **93m/B; VHS, DVD, Blu-Ray.** John Mills; Eric Portman; Lionel Jeffries; Bryan Forbes; Ian Carmichael; Anton Diffring; ***D:*** Guy Hamilton.

Coldwater **2014** A very promising set-up is destroyed in the end in director/writer Grashaw's drama about abuse in juvenile reform camps. Newcomer Boudousqué stars as Brad Lunders, a kid stuck in a society that doesn't know how to deal with troubled teens. After a tragedy (revealed in flashback), Brad gets sent to the titular juvenile reform camp, a place that thinks Army training techniques are the way to correct bad behavior. The first hour works but a plot twist feels fake when one of Brad's cohorts gets to Coldwater and all Hell breaks loose. **104m/C; DVD.** P.J. Boudousque; James C. Burns; Chris Petrovski; Octavius J. Johnson; ***D:*** Vincent Grashaw; ***W:*** Vincent Grashaw; Mark Penney; ***C:*** Jayson Crothers; ***M:*** Chris Chatham; Mark Miserocchi.

Cole Younger, Gunfighter 1/2 **1958** A typical low-budget western that has nothing to do with the actual Younger's life. Kit Caswell (Best) becomes friends with the desperado (Lovejoy) and they join up with a cattle drive. Frank (Merlin) wants Kit's gal Lucy (Dalton) for himself so he accuses Kit of murder and the cowpoke is arrested and goes on trial. Cole knows the truth but will he risk his own freedom to save an innocent man? The last film for Lovejoy who finished his career on TV. **78m/C; DVD.** Frank Lovejoy; James Best; Abby Dalton; Jan Merlin; Douglas Spencer; ***D:*** R.G. Springsteen; ***W:*** Daniel Mainwaring; ***C:*** Harry Neumann; ***M:*** Marlin Skiles.

Colewell 1/2 **2019** In a small rural Pennsylvania community, Nora (Allen) operates the local post office. Other than postal worker Charles (O'Connor), who brings her the mail to distribute each day, Nora's community is primarily the locals who use the post office as a gathering place. Nora's life is turned upside down when the decision is made to close it. Though she can retire or transfer, Nora fights to keep it open but the effort makes her feel hopeless. Allen dominates in this intimate exploration of social and economic issues in contemporary America. **79m/C; DVD.** Karen Allen; Kevin J. O'Connor; Hannah Gross; Catherine Kellner; Craig Walker; ***D:*** Tom Quinn; ***W:*** Tom Quinn; ***C:*** Paul Yee; ***M:*** Dara Taylor.

Collapse **2009** Talking-head analysis from independent writer and researcher Michael Ruppert who spreads his doomsday scenario that our industrial civilization is collapsing and global capitalism is finished. In 2006, Ruppert predicted the 2009 economic collapse in his self-published newsletter. Director Smith intersperses Ruppert's conversation with archival footage. **82m/C; On Demand.** Michael Ruppert; ***D:*** Chris Smith; ***C:*** Max Malkin; Edward Lachman; ***M:*** Didier Leplae; Joe Wong.

Collateral **2004 (R)** Vincent (Cruise) is a contract killer as cool and sleek as his gray-haired, gray-suited appearance suggests. He's got a busy schedule to keep in nighttime L.A.--five hits and out on the 6 A.M. flight. Fortunately, he's got the perfect cabbie, 12-year veteran Max (Foxx), who can get anywhere in the least possible time. Naturally, there's time to talk, and as Vincent shares his advice on how to adapt and improvise, Max gets some ideas on how he's going to survive. It's basically a two-handed drama and both actors give nuanced performances; Mann is also at the top of his game. Also notable is the high-def digital video of cinematographers Beebe and Cameron that makes the city another character in the drama. **119m/C; DVD, Blu-Ray.** Tom Cruise; Jamie Foxx; Mark Ruffalo; Irma P. Hall; Jada Pinkett Smith; Bruce McGill; Bodhi (Pine) Elfman; Javier Bardem; Peter Berg; Barry (Shabaka) Henley; Debi Mazar; ***D:*** Michael Mann; ***W:*** Stuart Beattie; ***C:*** Dion Beebe; Paul Cameron; ***M:*** James Newton Howard; Antonio Pinto; Tom Rothrock. British Acad. '04: Cinematog.

Collateral Beauty **2016 (PG-13)** Movies don't get much more offensively manipulative than this piece of grief porn about a man trying to deal with the death of his child. Howard Inlet (Smith) is an advertising executive about to lose his business when his partners (Norton, Winslet, Pena) hire a private investigator to get dirt on Howard. She discovers he's been writing letters to Love, Time, and Death, so the partners hire actors (Knightley, Latimore, Mirren) to "play" the three concepts. And it gets way more ridiculous from there, if you can believe it. **97m/C; DVD, Blu-Ray.** Will Smith; Edward Norton; Kate Winslet; Michael Peña; Dame Helen Mirren; Naomie Harris; Keira Knightley; ***D:*** David Frankel; ***W:*** Allan Loeb; ***C:*** Maryse Alberti; ***M:*** Theodore Shapiro.

Collateral Damage **2002 (R)** Revenge drama pits Ah-nuld against the Columbian terrorists whose actions caused the death of his wife and child. When investigators come up short, nothing-left-to-lose fireman Gordy Brewer (Schwarzenegger) takes matters into his own hands and sets out to catch "The Wolf," the rebel leader of Columbia's civil war and the one responsible for his family's demise. In Columbia, he meets Selena (Neri) and her son Mauro (Posey) and his instinct to protect and serve them kicks into action, giving him renewed purpose. Highlights are Leguizamo as Felix, the Columbian drug producer, and Turturro as an exiled Canadian working as a mechanic. Mexico subs for Columbia in this unbelievable and formulaic actioner for genre and Arnold fans only. **109m/C; VHS, DVD, Blu-Ray.** Arnold Schwarzenegger; Elias Koteas; Francesca Neri; Clifford Curtis; John Leguizamo; John Turturro; Miguel (Michael) Sandoval; Harry J. Lennix; Lindsay Frost; Jsu Garcia; ***D:*** Andrew Davis; ***W:*** David Griffiths; Peter Griffiths; ***C:*** Adam Greenberg; ***M:*** Graeme Revell.

The Collection **2012 (R)** Pointless sequel to 2009's "The Collector." Elena (Fitzpatrick) and her friends go to a secretive dance party, but it's not a dance party, it's a slasher fest and she's the "lucky" one to survive. The crazed masked serial killer known as "The Collector" (how very catchy and clever!) abducts her. Elena's rich folks hire mercenaries to save her and they convince Arkin (Stewart), the only person who has escaped the Collector's torturous maze, to help. **82m/C; DVD, Blu-Ray.** Josh Stewart; Christopher Macdonald; Navi Rawat; Randall Archer; Emma Fitzpatrick; ***D:*** Marcus Dunstan; ***W:*** Marcus Dunstan; Patrick Melton; ***C:*** Sam McCurdy; ***M:*** Charlie Clouser.

The Collector 1/2 **1965** Compelling adaptation of the John Fowles novel about a withdrawn butterfly collector who decides to add to his collection by kidnapping a beautiful girl he admires. He locks her in his cellar hoping she will fall in love with him. Chilling, unsettling drama with Stamp unnerving, yet sympathetic in lead. **119m/C; VHS, DVD, Blu-Ray.** *GB* Terence Stamp; Samantha Eggar; Maurice Dallimore; Mona Washbourne; ***D:*** William Wyler; ***W:*** John Kohn; Stanley Mann; ***C:*** Robert Krasker; Robert L. Surtees; ***M:*** Maurice Jarre. Cannes '65: Actor (Stamp), Actress (Eggar); Golden Globes '66: Actress--Drama (Eggar).

The Collector **2009 (R)** Seen "Saw"? Then you've seen this, since Dunstan and Melton were also writers of some of that franchise's lamer sequels. Ex-jewel thief turned handyman Arkin (Stewart) is trying to go straight, but only after he robs the home of the Chase family (he's got a good reason, of course). The family is supposed to be on vacation, but Arkin finds the house has been booby-trapped by a masked sicko and the family is unfortunately at home. Various cringe-making tortures abound. **88m/C; Blu-Ray.** Josh Stewart; Michael Reilly Burke; Andrea Roth; Karley Scott Collins; Madeline Zima; Juan Fernandez; ***D:*** Marcus Dunstan; ***W:*** Marcus Dunstan; Patrick Melton; ***C:*** Brandon Cox; ***M:*** Jerome Dillon.

The Collectors **1999 (R)** Mob boss sends hit men Ray (Van Dien) and A.K. (Fox) to collect a big debt that's owed but they would rather take the payoff and get out of New York—preferably alive. **97m/C; VHS, DVD.** Casper Van Dien; Rick Fox; Catherine Oxenberg; Daniel Pilon; ***D:*** Sidney J. Furie. **VIDEO**

Collector's Item **1989** Two lovers reunite after 16 years and a flurry of memories temporarily rekindles their passion, which comes dangerously close to obsession. Casting of the physically bountiful Antonelli helps this effective erotic drama. **99m/C; VHS, DVD.** *IT* Tony Musante; Laura Antonelli; Florinda Bolkan; ***D:*** Giuseppe Patroni-Griffi.

Colleen **1936** The final collaboration between Powell and Keeler is a weak musical romance. Wealthy eccentric Cedric Ames (Herbert) buys gold-digging Minnie (Blondell) a dress shop where Colleen Reilly (Keeler) is also working. Cedric's suspicious nephew Donald (Powell) eventually persuades him to close the shop, even though Donald has fallen for Colleen. The family lawyer pays off Minnie but Colleen doesn't want their dough and gets a job on an ocean liner bound for Europe. Guess who turns out to be a passenger? **89m/B; DVD.** Dick Powell; Ruby Keeler; Joan Blondell; Hugh Herbert; Jack Oakie; Addison Richard; Louise Fazenda; ***D:*** Alfred E. Green; ***W:*** F. Hugh Herbert; Sid Herzig; Peter Milne; ***C:*** Byron Haskin; Sol Polito.

College WOOF! **2008 (R)** After being dumped by his girlfriend, a high school senior nerd and his two nerdier friends head to the college in an attempt to escape their otherwise pathetic lives and party like, well, freshmen. Attempts to rise to the stratospheric heights of such cinematic masterpieces as "Porky's," "Revenge of the Nerds," and even "American Pie," but offers little more than a deluge of low-brow, gross-out, t & a humor as the dorks get smashed, hit on hot girls way out of their league, and vomit. Not even an appearance by thespian Troyer can salvage a passing grade. **94m/C; On Demand.** Drake Bell; Andrew Caldwell; Haley Bennett; Nick Zano; Ryan Pinkston; Verne Troyer; Kevin Covais; Camille Mana; Nathalie Walker; Alona Tal; ***D:*** Deb Hagan; ***W:*** Dan Callahan; Adam Ellison; ***C:*** Dan Stoloff; ***M:*** Transcenders.

College Humor 1/2 **1933** Early musical comedy for Crosby finds him a college prof, Frederick Danvers, who attracts the attentions of pretty coed Barbara (Carlisle). Only Barbara's crush is leaving her football star boyfriend Mondrake (Arlen) in a jealous rage just before the big game. Fortunately, Barbara's brother Barney (Oakie) fills in. Burns and Allen appear as caterers. **80m/B; VHS, DVD.** Bing Crosby; Jack Oakie; Richard Arlen; Mary Carlisle; Mary Kornman; Joseph (Joe) Sawyer; George Burns; ***D:*** Wesley Ruggles; ***W:*** Claude Binyon; Frank Butler; ***C:*** Leo Tover; ***M:*** Arthur Johnston; Sam Coslow.

College Road Trip **2008 (G)** The good news is that a G rating ensures worry-free family viewing. The bad news is that instead of eliciting the universal road trip lament, "Are we there yet?" most parents will be asking, "Is it over yet?" Suburban Chicago police chief and over-protective dad James Porter (Lawrence) and high-school senior daughter Melanie (Symone) clash about her choice of colleges, so they set off on a road trip to visit the campus. Even with the cute little brother (Draper) and pet pig along for the ride, the overdone gags fall flat, especially the multiple encounters with another college-bound girl and her Cheez-Wiz dad Doug (Osmond). Sorry, Disney: creepily overprotective dads just aren't funny. **83m/C; DVD, Blu-Ray.** Martin Lawrence; Raven; Donny Osmond; Brenda Song; Will Sasso; Kym E. Whitley; Margo Harshman; Eshaya Draper; Vincent Pastore; Lucas Grabeel; ***D:*** Roger Kumble; ***W:*** Ken Daurio; ***C:*** Theo van de Sande; ***M:*** Ed Shearmur; Lisa Brown.

College Swing 1/2 *Swing, Teacher, Swing* **1938** Lightweight, lackluster musical about Allen inheriting a small town college which she turns into a hangout for her vaudeville pals. Top cast is basically wasted performing many forgettable songs and familiar routines. Based on an adaptation by Frederick Hazlitt Brennan from a story by Ted Lesser. **86m/B; VHS, DVD.** George Burns; Gracie Allen; Martha Raye; Bob Hope; Edward Everett Horton; Ben Blue; Betty Grable; Jackie Coogan; John Payne; ***D:*** Raoul Walsh; ***W:*** Walter DeLeon; Francis Martin; ***C:*** Victor Milner; ***M:*** Boris Morros; Hoagy Carmichael; Burton Lane; Frank Loesser.

Collide **2017 (PG-13)** Casey (Hoult) is a low-level employee for a German drug dealer named Geran (Kingsley). When he meets the lovely Juliette (Jones), he vows to get out of the dangerous business, but her sudden need for a kidney transplant forces him to try one last job before he changes his life. The job requires that Casey pull off a drug theft from the biggest drug dealer in Germany, Hagen (Hopkins). How so many talented people got involved in something so dumb is the real mystery here folks. It's not just mindless entertainment; it's mind-numbing. **99m/C; DVD, Blu-Ray.** Nicholas Hoult; Felicity Jones; Marwan Kenzari; Ben Kingsley; Anthony Hopkins; ***D:*** Eran Creevy; ***W:*** Eran Creevy; F. Scott Frazier; ***C:*** Ed Wild; ***M:*** Ilan Eshkeri.

Collier & Co.: Hot Pursuit 1/2 **2006 (PG)** Down-on-his-luck J.R. Collier (Schneider) wants to go legit and start his own car dealership to win back his estranged wife and daughter. He decides to sell the cars he wins street racing but a Dodge Charger has something in its glovebox that some goofy bad guys want back. Harmless family fun and a family affair since Schneider cast his own wife and daughter as his onscreen family too. He also cast The General Lee from his "Dukes of Hazzard" days, although not with the signature paint job. **107m/C; DVD.** John Schneider; Rex Smith; Karis Schneider; Elly Castle; ***D:*** John Schneider; ***W:*** John Schneider; ***M:*** Bob Boykin. **VIDEO**

Collision **2009** Rather plodding Brit miniseries about a deadly highway crash outside London that's investigated by DI John Tolin (Henshall), who has his own past road tragedy to overcome. Each of the occupants of the ten vehicles involved get their own backstory, which can get confusing as they shift around. Some of the stories veer into melodrama with corporate espionage, murder, and smuggling as well as the usual family and romantic dilemmas. Best appreciated for the recognizable actors involved in the workmanlike production. **210m/C; DVD.** *GB* Douglas Henshall; Kate Ashfield; Dean Lennox Kelly; Craig Kelly; David Bamber; Richard Reeves; Philip Davis; Claire Rushbrook; Jo Woodcock; Nicholas Farrell; Sylvia Syms; Lucy Griffiths; Lenora Crichlow; Anwar Lynch; ***D:*** Marc Evans; ***W:*** Anthony Horowitz; Michael A. Walker; ***C:*** Christopher Ross; ***M:*** Daniel Giorgetti. **TV**

Collision 1/2 *Intersections* **2013 (R)** While on their honeymoon in Morocco, Scott and Taylor Dolan take a road trip into the desert and get involved in a multi-car accident that leaves them stranded. They set off to get help with some other survivors, but wealthy Scott better watch out since Taylor isn't such a loving bride. **101m/C; DVD, Blu-Ray.** Frank Grillo; Jaimie Alexander; Charlie Bewley; Roschdy Zem; Marie Josee Croze; Moussa Maaskri; ***D:*** David Marconi; ***W:*** David Marconi; ***C:*** Thomas Hardmeier; ***M:*** Richard Horowitz. **VIDEO**

Collision Course **1989 (PG)** A wisecracking cop from Detroit teams up with Japan's best detective to nail a ruthless gang leader. Release was delayed until 1992 due to a lawsuit, but it was resolved in time to coordinate the release with Leno's debut as the host of "The Tonight Show." Pretty marginal, but diehard fans of Leno may appreciate it. Filmed on location in Detroit. **99m/C; VHS, DVD.** Noriyuki "Pat" Morita; Jay Leno; Chris Sarandon; Al Waxman; ***D:*** Lewis Teague.

Collision Course **2012** Banal, unbelievable melodrama. Wendy Parks is flying home after a book tour promoting her bestseller about the attempted coverup of her husband's death in a plane crash. A solar flare hits the plane, the pilot and co-pilot are either dead or incapacitated, and the electronics are fried. Naturally, it's now up to Wendy and flight attendent Jake to take charge and land the plane. **84m/C; DVD.** Tia Carrere; David Chokachi; Tim Abell; Dee Wallace; Dylan Vox; ***D:*** Fred Olen Ray; ***W:*** Fred Olen Ray; Jason Bourque. **VIDEO**

Collision Earth 1/2 **2011** The planet Mercury is thrown out of its orbit and is headed for Earth but Dr. James Preston (Acevedo) can't get anyone to listen to his plan to stop the collision. Except for a couple of college kids who happen to be in touch with Preston's astronaut wife, Victoria (Farr), who's on the Mercury mission that got into trouble. Uh, yeah, it's from the Syfy Channel so it's not supposed to make any sense but Acevedo sells his role for all it's worth. **90m/C; DVD, Blu-Ray.** Kirk Acevedo; Diane Farr; Andrew Airlie; Chad Krowchuk; Jessica Parker Kennedy; ***D:*** Paul Ziller; ***W:*** Ryan Landels; ***C:*** Tom Harting; ***M:*** Michael Neilson. **VIDEO**

Colombian Love 1/2 *Ahava Colombianit* **2004** Light-hearted Israeli romantic comedy about three buddies coping with adulthood and amore. Womanizing Zydane is surprised when he begins obsessing over his Colombian ex-girlfriend; Omer is newly married and already having problems handling his added responsibilities; and Uri is caught between his independent girlfriend Tali and his domineering father. Hebrew with subtitles. **96m/C; DVD.** *IS* Assi Cohen; Mili Avital; Nir Levy; Italy Barnea; Elinor Ben Haim; Shmil Ben Ari; Osnat Hakim; ***D:*** Shai Kannot; ***W:*** Regev Levy; Reshef Levy; ***C:*** Ofer Harari; ***M:*** Asaf Amdurski.

Colombiana **2011 (PG-13)** Another Besson-produced action piece about a relatively-silent killer seeking revenge in as stylish a way as possible, although this one is more shameful and tedious than its predecessors. Cataleya (Saldana) has grown up training herself as a killer to avenge the murder of her parents at the hands of government-protected Colombian drug lord, leading up to the action-packed finale for which the film basically exists. Getting there is a chore—Saldana struggles to pull off the sexy killer act and the script saddles her with a useless romance (with Vartan) and nonsensical motivations. **107m/C; Blu-Ray.** Zoe Saldana; Jordi Molla; Beto Benites; Lennie James; Clifford Curtis; Michael Vartan; Amandla Stenberg; Maximillian Martini; Jesse Borrego; Graham McTavish; Callum Blue; ***D:*** Olivier Megaton; ***W:*** Luc Besson; Robert Mark Kamen; ***C:*** Romain Lacourbas; ***M:*** Nathaniel Mechaly.

Colonel Effingham's Raid 1/2 *Man of the Hour* **1945** A retired army colonel uses military tactics to keep an old historical courthouse open, while defeating some crooked politicians in the process. **70m/B; DVD.** Joan Bennett; Charles Coburn; William Eythe; Donald Meek; Allyn Joslyn; Elizabeth Patterson; Frank Craven; Thurston Hall; Cora Witherspoon; Emory Parnell; Henry Armetta; Steve (Stephen) Dunne; Roy Roberts; Charles Trowbridge; ***D:*** Irving Pichel; ***W:*** Kathryn Scola; ***C:*** Edward Cronjager; ***M:*** Cyril Mockridge.

Colonel Redl **1984 (R)** Absorbing, intricately rendered psychological study of an ambitious officer's rise and fall in pre-WWI Austria. Brandauer is excellent as the vain, insecure homosexual ultimately undone by his own ambition and his superior officer's smug loathing. Muller-Stahl and Landgrebe are particularly distinguished among the supporting players. The second in the Szabo/Brandauer trilogy, after "Mephisto" and before "Hanussen." In German with English subtitles. **142m/C; VHS, DVD.** *GE HU* Klaus Maria Brandauer; Armin Mueller-Stahl; Gudrun Landgrebe; Jan Niklas; Hans-Christian Blech; Laszlo Mensaros; Andras Balint; ***D:*** Laszlo Szabo; ***W:*** Laszlo Szabo; Peter Dobai; ***C:*** Lajos Koltai; ***M:*** Zdenko Tamassy. British Acad. '85: Foreign Film; Cannes '85: Special Jury Prize.

The Colony 1/2 **1995 (PG-13)** "The Colony" is a luxurious and exclusive gated community owned by secretive billionaire developer Phillip Denning (Linden). Newest residents, security expert Rick Knowlton (Ritter), wife Leslie (Keller) and their two children, find out things are just too good to be true—and that trying to leave could be the very last thing they'll ever do. **93m/C; VHS, DVD.** John Ritter; Hal Linden; Mary Page Keller; Marshall Teague; Frank Bonner; Michelle Scarabelli; June Lockhart; Todd Jeffries; Alexandra Picatto; Cody Dorkin; ***D:*** Rob Hedden; ***W:*** Rob Hedden; ***C:*** David Geddes.

The Colony 1/2 **1998 (R)** Aliens planning an earth invasion decide to test humankind by abducting four people and observing their survival skills. **94m/C; VHS, DVD.** Isabella Hofmann; Michael Weatherly; Cristi Conaway; Eric Allen Kramer; Jeff Kober; James Avery; Clare Salstrom; ***D:*** Peter Geiger; ***W:*** Peter Geiger; Richard Kletter; ***C:*** Zoltan David; ***M:*** Paul Rabjohns. **CABLE**

Colony: The Endangered World of Bees 1/2 *Colony* **2011** The insightful documentary chronicles the crisis among honeybees centered on the phenomenon known as Colony Collapse Disorder. Because of the disorder, bees are dying, empty beehives are common in the United States, and the world's food supply is threatened. As the search for a cause continues, the documentary looks at the crisis from the perspectives of a veteran beekeeper and two young brothers who are becoming beekeepers at this time. All three faces challenges related to both beekeeping and a world economy that is falling apart. **85m/C; DVD, Streaming, Download.** ***D:*** Carter Gunn; Ross McDonnell; ***C:*** Carter Gunn; Ross McDonnell. **VIDEO**

Color Me Blood Red WOOF! *Model Massacre* **1964** Artist decides that the red in his paintings is best rendered with human blood. He even manages to continue his art career—when not busy stabbing and mutilating the unsuspecting citizenry. Short and shoddy. **74m/C; VHS, DVD, Blu-Ray.** Don Joseph; Candi Conder; Elyn Warner; Scott H. Hall; Jerome Eden; Patricia Lee; James Jackel; ***D:*** Herschell Gordon Lewis; ***W:*** Herschell Gordon Lewis; ***C:*** Herschell Gordon Lewis.

Color Me Kubrick 1/2 **2005** Malkovich swans about in outrageous attire and attitude as con man Alan Conway, who made his way to London in the early 1990s and passed himself off as reclusive director Stanley Kubrick despite knowing nothing about filmmaking. The con man was after money and sex, which he was given by the flattered and gullible who were too embarrassed to press charges when they'd discovered they'd been had (much to the real Kubrick's frustration). A bit of silly fluff. **86m/C; DVD.** *GB FR* John Malkovich; Jim Davidson; Richard E. Grant; Luke Mably; Terence Rigby; James Dreyfus; Peter Bowles; Leslie Phillips; William Hootkins; ***D:*** Brian Cook; ***W:*** Anthony Frewin; ***C:*** Howard Atherton; ***M:*** Bryan Adams.

Color of a Brisk and Leaping Day **1995** While living in L.A. at the end of WWII, Chinese-American John Lee (Alexander) learns that the Yosemite Valley Railroad is being scrapped and he becomes determined to save it—in part as a homage to his grandfather who emigrated to work as a railroad laborer. A romantic train fanatic himself, Lee arranges financing from wealthy businessman Pinchot (Diehl) but must make the railroad pay within a year—unlikely as the automobile rapidly takes over as preferred transportation. Well-captures a '40s atmosphere but pacing and dialogue are uneven. **87m/B; VHS, DVD.** Peter Alexander; Jeri Arredondo; Henry Gibson; Michael Stipe; John Diehl; David Chung; Diana Larkin; Bok Yun Chon; ***D:*** Christopher Munch; ***W:*** Christopher Munch; ***C:*** Rob Sweeney. Sundance '96: Cinematog.

The Color of Freedom 1/2 *Goodbye Bafana* **2007 (R)** In 1968, Afrikaaner James Gregory (Fiennes) takes a job at Robben Island where Nelson Mandela (Haysbert) is a political prisoner. A firm believer in apartheid, Gregory becomes one of Mandela's principal guards because he can speak Xhosa and thus censor his prisoner's communications. But over a 20-year period, Gregory begins to change his views. Static storytelling, adapted from Gregory's memoirs, that's too noble to retain interest. **118m/C; DVD.** *GB SA* Joseph Fiennes; Dennis Haysbert; Diane Kruger; ***D:*** Bille August; ***W:*** Greg Latter; ***C:*** Robert Fraisse; ***M:*** Dario Marianelli.

The Color of Lies *Au Coeur du Mensonge* **1999** French crime drama that never adds up to more than a workmanlike effort from director Chabrol. A young girl from a Breton fishing village is found raped and murdered. New chief inspector Lesage makes artist Rene Sterne her prime suspect since the girl took art lessons from him and he was the last to see her alive. Then townsfolk begin to shun Rene, who's supported by his wife Vivianne, although she's also attracted to newcomer Desmot, a smarmy celebrity journalist. French with subtitles. **113m/C; DVD, Blu-Ray.** *FR* Valeria Bruni-Tedeschi; Jacques Gamblin; Sandrine Bonnaire; Antoine de Caunes; Bernard Verley; Pierre Martot; ***D:*** Claude Chabrol; ***W:*** Claude Chabrol; Odile Barski; ***C:*** Eduardo Serra; ***M:*** Matthieu Chabrol.

The Color of Magic 1/2 *Terry Pratchett's The Color of Magic* **2008** Based on the first two books in Pratchett's Discworld fantasy series. Discworld is supported on the backs of four elephants that stand on the back of the Great A'Tuin (a giant turtle) that floats through space. Only the turtle has suddenly decided to move towards a fiery red star that will cause Discworld's destruction. In order to save the day, naive tourist Twoflower (Astin) and incompetent wizard Rinceweed (Jason) must collect eight spells that are all part of an elaborate game. **137m/C; DVD, Blu-Ray.** *GB* Sean Astin; David Jason; Tim Curry; Jeremy Irons; David Bradley; James Cosmo; Janet Suzman; Karen Shenaz David; ***V:*** Christopher Lee; ***Nar:*** Brian Cox; ***D:*** Vadim Jean; ***W:*** Vadim Jean; ***C:*** Gavin Finney; ***M:*** Paul Francis; David A. Hughes. **TV**

The Color of Money 1/2 **1986 (R)** Flashy, gripping drama about former pool hustler Fast Eddie Felsen (Newman) who, after years off the circuit, takes a brilliant but immature pool shark (Cruise) under his wing. Strong performances by Newman as the grizzled veteran, Cruise as the showboating youth, and Mastrantonio and Shaver as the men's worldly girlfriends. Worthy sequel to "The Hustler." **119m/C; VHS, DVD, Blu-Ray.** Paul Newman; Tom Cruise; Mary Elizabeth Mastrantonio; Helen Shaver; John Turturro; Forest Whitaker; ***D:*** Martin Scorsese; ***W:*** Richard Price; ***C:*** Michael Ballhaus; ***M:*** Robbie Robertson. Oscars '86: Actor (Newman); Natl. Bd. of Review '86: Actor (Newman).

Color of Night 1/2 **1994 (R)** Psychologist Dr. Bill Capa (Willis) takes over a murdered colleague's therapy group hoping to find out the killer's identity. Then he meets temptress Rose (March) and gets involved in a hot affair, but she's not what she seems—nor is anyone else. Preposterous thriller fails to deliver necessary suspense although the eroticism could spark some interest, particularly in the director's cut, which puts the sex back in the sex scenes between Willis and March (and is 15 minutes longer than the theatrical release). **136m/C; VHS, DVD, Blu-Ray.** Bruce Willis; Jane March; Scott Bakula; Ruben Blades; Lesley Ann Warren; Lance Henriksen; Kevin J. O'Connor; Andrew Lowery; Brad Dourif; Eriq La Salle; Jeff Corey; Shirley Knight; Kathleen Wilhoite; ***D:*** Richard Rush; ***W:*** Matthew Chapman; Billy Ray; Richard Rush; ***C:*** Dietrich Lohmann; ***M:*** Dominic Frontiere. Golden Raspberries '94: Worst Picture.

The Color of Paradise *Rang-e Khoda* **1999 (PG)** Mohammad is an eight-year-old blind boy who is regarded as a burden by his recently widowed and hard-working father. His father hopes to remarry but thinks his son will be an obstacle and sends him to live with a carpenter, who is also blind, so that the boy can learn a trade. Of course, it is the father who must truly learn to see, since Mohammad already appreciates everything surrounding him. Farsi with subtitles. **90m/C; VHS, DVD.** *IA* Mohsen Ramezani; Hossein Mahjoub; ***D:*** Majid Majidi; ***W:***

Majid Majidi; *C:* Mohammad Davudi; *M:* Alireza Kohandairy.

The Color of Pomegranates 🦴🦴🦴 *Sayat Nova; Tsvet Granata* **1969** Paradjanov's depiction of the life of Armenian poet Arutiun Sayadin, known as Sayat Nova, who rises from carpet weaver to court minstrel to archbishop. Eloquent imagery and symbols are derived from Armenian paintings, poetry and history. In Armenian with English subtitles. Also includes "Hagop Hovnatanian," a 12-minute short on the artist. **80m/C; VHS, DVD, Blu-Ray.** *RU* Sofiko Chiaureli; M. Aleksanian; V. Galstian; *D:* Sergei Paradjanov; *W:* Sergei Paradjanov; *C:* A. Samvelyan.

Color Out of Space 🦴🦴 ½ **2019** The Gardner family has left the big city for a remote home in rural Massachusetts. While Theresa (Richardson) recovers from breast cancer, her husband Nathan (Cage) is trying farming, while their three children have their own issues caused by the isolation. One night, the sky turns a shade of fuchsia and a meteorite crashes in their yard. Afterwards, odd things start to happen on the land, with electronics, and among those who live on the property. An adaptation of a famous H.P. Lovecraft story, the science fiction/horror film is stylish and weird, but also weirdly delightful. **111m/C; DVD.** Nicolas Cage; Joely Richardson; Madeleine Arthur; Elliot Knight; Tommy Chong; *D:* Richard Stanley; *W:* Richard Stanley; Scarlett Amaris; *C:* Steve Annis; *M:* Colin Stetson.

The Color Purple 🦴🦴🦴 ½ **1985 (PG-13)** Celie is a poor black girl who fights for her self-esteem when she is separated from her sister and forced into a brutal marriage. Spanning 1909 to 1947 in a small Georgia town, the movie chronicles the joys, pains, and people in her life. Adaptation of Alice Walker's acclaimed book features strong lead from Goldberg (her screen debut), Glover, Avery, and talk-show host Winfrey (also her film debut). It's hard to see director Spielberg as the most suited for this one, but he acquits himself nicely, avoiding the facileness that sometimes flaws his pics. Brilliant photography by Allen Daviau and musical score by Jones (who co-produced) compliment this strong film. **154m/C; VHS, DVD.** Whoopi Goldberg; Danny Glover; Oprah Winfrey; Margaret Avery; Adolph Caesar; Rae Dawn Chong; Willard Pugh; Akosua Busia; *D:* Steven Spielberg; *W:* Menno Meyjes; *C:* Allen Daviau; *M:* Chris Boardman; Quincy Jones. Directors Guild '85: Director (Spielberg); Golden Globes '86: Actress--Drama (Goldberg); Natl. Bd. of Review '85: Actress (Goldberg).

The Color Wheel 🦴 **2011** A micro-budgeted, black-and-white mumblecore road trip from hell with a deliberately unlikeable, vapid, and self-involved brother-sister duo. Alienating JR (Altman) manages to browbeat her useless brother Colin (Perry) into driving with her to pick up her things from the professor she briefly lived with. It's an uncomfortable, annoying trip for everyone concerned, including the viewer. **83m/B; Streaming.** Carlen Altman; Alex Ross Perry; Bob Byington; Ry Russo-Young; *D:* Alex Ross Perry; *W:* Carlen Altman; Alex Ross Perry; *C:* Sean Price Williams; *M:* Preston Spurlock.

Colorado Serenade 🦴🦴 **1946** Standard oater has Dean, Sharpe and Ates trying to prevent a young outlaw from bullying the local citizenry. Sharpe shows off his athletic prowess, and King provides some laughs. Other than that, it's pretty routine stuff. **68m/C; VHS, DVD.** Eddie Dean; David Sharpe; Roscoe Ates; Forrest Taylor; Dennis Moore; Warner Richmond; Bob Duncan; Charles "Blackie" King; *D:* Robert Emmett Tansey.

Colorado Sundown 🦴 **1952** A conniving brother and sister attempt to cheat a man out of his inheritance. **67m/B; VHS, DVD.** Rex Allen; Mary Ellen Kay; Slim Pickens; June Vincent; Koko; *D:* William Witney.

Colorado Territory 🦴🦴 ½ **1949** Outlaw Wes McQueen (McCrea) breaks out of jail, vowing to go straight. Instead, he winds up back with his old partner Rickard (Ruysdael). He agrees to a last job railroad heist with Rickard's new gang, which includes former dance-hall dame Colorado (Mayo), and the chivalrous Wes decides to protect Colorado from his shifty cohorts. **94m/B; DVD.** Joel McCrea; Virginia Mayo; Dorothy Malone; Henry Hull; Basil Ruysdael; John Archer; James Mitchell; Harry Woods; Morris Ankrum; *D:* Morris Ankrum; Raoul Walsh; *W:* Edmund H. North; John Twist; *C:* Sidney Hickox; *M:* David Buttolph.

Colorful: The Motion Picture 🦴🦴🦴 *Colourful; Karafuru* **2010** The soul of a suicidal man is informed he has a second chance at life: He will inhabit the body of another suicidal boy, and has a limited amount of time to figure out what brought both of them to end their existence, and what his greatest mistakes were in his former life. **126m/C; DVD, Blu-Ray.** *JP V:* Greg Ayres; Luci Christian; Clint Bickham; Emily Neves; Brittney Karbowski; *D:* Keiichi Hara; *W:* Miho Maruo; *C:* Koichi Yanai; *M:* Kou Otani. **VIDEO**

Colors 🦴🦴🦴 ½ **1988 (R)** Vivid, realistic cop drama pairs sympathetic veteran Duvall and trigger-tempered rookie Penn on the gang-infested streets of East Los Angeles. Fine play from leads is one of the many assets in this controversial, unsettling depiction of deadly streetlife. Colorful, freewheeling direction from the underrated Hopper. Rattling rap soundtrack too. Additional footage has been added for video release. **120m/C; VHS, DVD, Blu-Ray.** Sean Penn; Robert Duvall; Maria Conchita Alonso; Trinidad Silva; Randi Brooks; Grand L. Bush; Don Cheadle; Rudy Ramos; Glenn Plummer; Sy Richardson; Damon Wayans; Fred Asparagus; Sherman Augustus; R.D. Call; Seymour Cassel; Nick(y) Corello; Virgil Frye; Courtney Gains; Clark Johnson; Leon; Tina Lifford; Micole Mercurio; Jack Nance; Tony Todd; Gerardo Mejia; *D:* Dennis Hopper; *W:* Michael Schiffer; *C:* Haskell Wexler; *M:* Herbie Hancock.

Colorz of Rage 🦴🦴 ½ **1997** Story of an interracial relationship between Tony (Resteghini) and Debbie (Richards) covers familiar ground, but the New York locations have a gritty feel that's accentuated by the rough production values. **91m/C; DVD.** Dale Resteghini; Nicki Richards; Cheryl "Pepsii" Riley; Don Wallace; *D:* Dale Resteghini; *W:* Dale Resteghini; *C:* Martin Ahlgren; *M:* Tony Prendatt.

Colossal 🦴🦴 ½ **2017 (R)** Gloria (Hathaway), a dissolute party girl, heads back to her depressed hometown after getting kicked out of her New York home and relationship by her fed-up boyfriend. While settling back into drinking with pals led by Sudeikis, she discovers that she is strangely connected to a giant monster terrorizing Seoul, South Korea. The plot and execution don't lend themselves to easy classification or anticipation of where it's going. That is a good thing. Director Vigalondo manages to keep you guessing without getting frustrated, keeps the tone and pacing balanced, and doesn't fall into the easy traps of the many genres he samples. Hathaway and Sudeikis are both excellent. **109m/C; DVD, Blu-Ray.** Anne Hathaway; Jason Sudeikis; Austin Stowell; Dan Stevens; *D:* Nacho Vigalondo; *W:* Nacho Vigalondo; *C:* Eric Kress; *M:* Bear McCreary.

Colossus and the Amazon Queen 🦴 ½ *La Regina delle Amazzoni; Colossus and the Amazons* **1960** Who the heck is Colossus? Maybe just a convenient nickname for one of the slabs of beefcake in this Italian sword-and-sandal pic that may (or may not) be meant as a comedy. Greek warriors Glauco and Pirro find themselves on the island of the Amazons where the men are slaves. There's some trouble since a couple of the Amazons would like to depose their current queen—at least until a band of pirates threaten all the island's inhabitants. **84m/C; VHS, DVD.** *IT* Rod Taylor; Ed Fury; Dorian Gray; Daniela Rocca; Gianna Maria Canale; *D:* Vittorio Sala; *W:* Vittorio Sala; *C:* Bitto Albertini; *M:* Roberto Nicolosi.

Colossus of New York 🦴 ½ **1958** A mad scientist and a giant robot in a '50s sci fi message flick. Scientist and humanitarian Jeremy Spensser is killed in an accident and his demented surgeon father William reveals to younger son Henry that he's removed Jerry's brain. He enlists Henry's help in building a giant robot to contain the brain but Jerry's once-gentle personality has been corrupted and the United Nations becomes a target for destruction. **70m/B; DVD.** Otto Kruger; Ross Martin; John Baragrey; Mala Powers; Charles Herbert; Robert Hutton; *D:* Eugene Lourie; *W:* Thelma Schnee; *C:* John F. Warren; *M:* Nathan Van Cleave.

The Colossus of Rhodes 🦴 ½ *Il Colosso di Rodi* **1961** Leone's first credited directorial effort is a hambone sword-and-sandal adventure. The colossus is the great bronze statue straddling Rhodes' harbor, which allows fighters to dump burning oil and fire catapults of molten lead on their enemies. It also serves as a secret torture chamber, so war hero Darios leads a slave revolt against the city's rulers. (A convenient earthquake also helps out the good guys.) **128m/C; DVD, Blu-Ray.** *IT SP* Rory Calhoun; Lea Massari; Georges Marchal; Conrado San Martin; Roberto Carmardiel; *D:* Sergio Leone; *W:* Sergio Leone; *C:* Antonio Ballesteros; *M:* Angelo Francesco Lavagnino.

Colossus of the Arena 🦴🦴 *Maciste, Il Gladiatore piu Forte del Monte* **1962** In 4th century Rome, Forest plays a mighty gladiator who uncovers a plot to imprison a beautiful princess. Through an incredible series of feats and combats, he exposes an evil duke as a traitor. **98m/C; VHS, DVD, Streaming.** *IT* Mark Forest; Scilla Gabel; *D:* Michele Lupo; *W:* Lionello De Felice; Ernesto Guida; *M:* Francesco De Masi.

Colossus: The Forbin Project 🦴🦴🦴 *The Forbin Project* **1970** A computer designed to manage U.S. defense systems teams instead with its Soviet equal and they attempt world domination. Wire-tight, suspenseful film seems at once dated yet timely. Based on the novel by D.F. Jones. **100m/C; VHS, DVD, Blu-Ray.** Eric Braeden; Susan Clark; Gordon Pinsent; William Schallert; Georg Stanford Brown; *D:* Joseph Sargent; *W:* James Bridges; *C:* Gene Polito; *M:* Michel Colombier.

Colt Comrades 🦴🦴 **1943** A bad guy's monopoly on water rights is jeopardized when Boyd and Clyde strike water while drilling for oil. Nothing really notable here, except for Bob (Robert) Mitchum and George ("Superman") Reeves in minor roles. **67m/B; VHS, DVD.** William Boyd; Andy Clyde; Jay Kirby; George Reeves; Gayle Lord; Earle Hodgins; Victor Jory; Douglas Fowley; Herbert Rawlinson; Robert Mitchum; *D:* Lesley Selander.

Columbo: Murder by the Book 🦴🦴 ½ *Columbo: The Complete First Season* **1971** The rumpled, cigar-smoking TV detective investigates the killing of a mystery writer. Scripted by Bochco of "Hill Street Blues" and "L.A. Law" fame. **79m/C; VHS, DVD.** Peter Falk; Jack Cassidy; Rosemary Forsyth; Martin Milner; *D:* Steven Spielberg; *W:* Steven Bochco.

Columbo: Prescription Murder 🦴🦴 ½ **1967** Falk's debut as the raincoat-clad lieutenant who always has just one more question. In the TV series pilot he investigates the death of a psychiatrist's wife. Rich with subplots. Good mystery fare. **99m/C; VHS, DVD.** Peter Falk; Gene Barry; Katherine Justice; William Windom; Nina Foch; Anthony James; Virginia Gregg; *D:* Richard Irving; *W:* Richard Levinson; William Link. **TV**

Columbus 🦴🦴🦴 **2017** Writer/director Kogonada offers a moving and visually stunning debut, with buildings used not as backdrop but as emotional components. When his father, an architecture scholar, falls into a coma in the small Indiana city of Columbus, Jin (Cho) reluctantly stays with him, and meets Casey (Richardson), an architecture enthusiast with similarly conflicted feelings about her recovering addict mother. As their friendship develops, Casey shows Jin Columbus's architectural treasures, where straight lines and hard edges contrast with their messy and unstable parental relationships. **104m/C; DVD.** John Cho; Haley Lu Richardson; Parker Posey; Rory Culkin; Michelle Forbes; *D:* Kogonada; *W:* Kogonada; *C:* Elisha Christian; *M:* Hammock.

Columbus Circle 🦴 ½ **2010 (PG-13)** Lackluster, predictable thriller. After Abigail received her substantial inheritance on her 18th birthday, she became a paranoid recluse in her Manhattan penthouse for the next 20 years. An elderly neighbor dies and a homicide cop insists on interviewing her and the neighbor's apartment is swiftly occupied by Charles and Lillian. Abigail sees Lillian being abused by her husband and tries to help but things may not be what they seem. **86m/C; DVD, Blu-Ray.** Selma Blair; Giovanni Ribisi; Amy Smart; Jason Lee; Beau Bridges; Robert Guillaume; Kevin Pollack; *D:* George Gallo; *W:* Kevin Pollack; George Gallo; *C:* Anastas Michos; *M:* Brian Tyler.

Columbus Day 🦴 ½ **2008 (R)** Thief John Cologne (Kilmer) is determined to go straight so he can reunite with his ex-wife and daughter. He pulls off one last job—involving a briefcase full of diamonds—and has to fence the goods ASAP, which is how he winds up in a public park on Columbus Day yakking with some kid (Thompson). Garbled story. **90m/C; DVD.** Val Kilmer; Ashley Johnson; Bobb'e J. Thompson; Wilmer Valderrama; Marg Helgenberger; Lobo Sebastian; Richard Edson; Michael Muhney; *D:* Charles Burmeister; *W:* Charles Burmeister; *C:* Julio Macat; *M:* Michael A. Levine.

Coma 🦴🦴🦴 **1978 (PG)** A doctor discovers murder and corpse-nabbing at her Boston hospital, defies her male bosses, and determines to find out what's going on before more patients die. Exciting, suspenseful fare, with Bujold impressive in lead. Based on the novel by Robin Cook. **113m/C; VHS, DVD, Blu-Ray.** Genevieve Bujold; Michael Douglas; Elizabeth Ashley; Rip Torn; Richard Widmark; Lois Chiles; Hari Rhodes; Tom Selleck; Ed Harris; *D:* Michael Crichton; *W:* Michael Crichton; *C:* Victor Kemper; Gerald Hirschfeld; *M:* Jerry Goldsmith.

Coma 🦴🦴 **2012** A&E miniseries leaves out much of the ethical questions from Robin Cook's medical thriller novel as well as the jolts of the 1978 movie but there's enough creepiness to keep watching. Susan (Ambrose) is a med student at an Atlanta hospital who quickly becomes suspicious over the abnormally high number of patients who lapse into comas after routine procedures. Especially since the bodies are sent to the high-tech Jefferson Institute, where Susan uncovers a lot of sinister doings involving hospital personnel. **160m/C; DVD; Closed Captioned.** Lauren Ambrose; Steven Pasquale; Geena Davis; James Woods; Richard Dreyfuss; Ellen Burstyn; James Rebhorn; Joe Morton; Michael Weston; *D:* Mikael Salomon; *W:* John J. McLaughlin; *C:* Ben Nott; *M:* David Buckley. **CABLE**

Comanche Moon 🦴 ½ **2008** Disappointing adaptation of McMurtry's 1997 novel, which falls second in terms of "The Lonesome Dove" timeframe, set mostly in the 1850s. Best friends Gus (Zahn) and Call (Urban) are Texas Rangers hunting Comanches, including leader Buffalo Hump (Studi). When their eccentric captain, Inish Scully (Kilmer), goes after a horse thief, they are left in charge. Kilmer spends a lot of time stuck in a pit and going crazy after Inish is captured by a Mexican bandito (Lopez). Back in town, Gus pines for Clara (Cardellini) while Call struggles with his feelings for Maggie (Banks), and Inish's wife Inez (Griffiths) spreads her charms amongst the Rangers. Oh yeah, and the Comanches attack. Disjointed storyline, stilted dialogue, and poor (miscast) performances doom this effort. **284m/C; DVD.** Steve Zahn; Karl Urban; Val Kilmer; Linda Cardellini; Elizabeth Banks; Rachel Griffiths; Wes Studi; Sal Lopez; Ryan Merriman; Adam Beach; James Rebhorn; Jake Busey; Melanie Lynskey; Floyd "Red Crow" Westerman; *D:* Simon Wincer; *W:* Larry McMurtry; Diana Ossana; *C:* Alan Caso; *M:* Lennie Niehaus. **TV**

Comanche Station 🦴🦴 ½ **1960** Loner Jefferson Cody (Scott) agrees to rescue Mrs. Lowe (Gates), a senator's wife who's been captured by the Comanches. After Cody achieves her rescue, they fall in with outlaw Ben Lane (Akins) and his two young proteges, who insist on accompanying them back to the Lowe homestead, saying that they'll need additional protection. But Cody soon realizes that Lane is after the reward money and is planning an ambush. **73m/C; VHS, DVD.** Randolph Scott; Nancy Gates; Claude Akins; Skip Homeier; Richard Rust; Rand Brooks; *D:* Budd Boetticher; *W:* Burt Kennedy; *C:* Charles Lawton, Jr.

The Comancheros 🦴🦴🦴 **1961** Texas Ranger Wayne and his prisoner fight with the Comancheros, an outlaw gang who is supplying guns and liquor to the dreaded Comanche Indians. Musical score adds flavor. Last film by Curtiz. **108m/C; VHS, DVD, Blu-Ray.** John Wayne; Ina Balin; Stuart Whitman; Nehemiah Persoff; Lee Marvin; Bruce Cabot; ***D:*** Michael Curtiz; ***C:*** William Clothier; ***M:*** Elmer Bernstein.

Combat Shock *American Nightmares* **1984 (R)** A Vietnam veteran returns home and can't cope with the stresses of modern life, including the lowlifes who have been taking over the streets. So he goes after some scum who have been trying to kill him, succeeds, but things don't end well. Familiar plot handled in a conventional manner. **85m/C; VHS, DVD, Blu-Ray.** Ricky Giovinazzo; Nick Nasta; Veronica Stork; Mitch Maglio; Asaph Livni; ***D:*** Buddy Giovinazzo; ***W:*** Buddy Giovinazzo; ***C:*** Stella Varveris; ***M:*** Ricky Giovinazzo.

Combination Platter 1/2 **1993** Anxious young immigrant Robert (Lau), newly arrived from Hong Kong, becomes a waiter at the Szechuan Inn in Queens, New York, where he gets a crash course in American culture and romance (as well as tipping). Gentle comedy works best with little details that ring true: overheard customer conversations, staff banter, the kitchen scenes. Lau's earnest, but effort feels like a series of small vignettes rather than a complete story. Still, a worthy first effort for the then 24-year-old Chan, who directed on a $250,000 budget, using his parents restaurant after hours for a set. **84m/C; VHS, DVD.** Jeff Lau; Coleen O'Brien; Lester Chan; Thomas S. Hsiung; David Chung; Colin Mitchell; Kenneth Lu; Eleonara Kihlberg; James DuMont; ***D:*** Tony Chan; ***W:*** Tony Chan; Edwin Baker; ***C:*** Yoshifumi Hosoya; ***M:*** Brian Tibbs. Sundance '93: Screenplay.

Come and Find Me **2016 (R)** A romantic drama that fails to be an effective thriller as well. Graphic designer David (Paul) is in love with his girlfriend Claire (Wallis) of one year when she suddenly disappears. As he reflects on their relationship through flashbacks, it becomes clear that she was living a double life. However, David's efforts to find out what happened to her is undermined by the misinformation he is given. Only a roll of underdeveloped film might hold the key to what happened. Though good ideas abound in the film's concept, its problems include underwhelming scripting and a lack of chemistry between the leads. **112m/C; DVD.** Annabelle Wallis; Aaron Paul; Garret Dillahunt; Chris Chalk; Enver Gjokaj; ***D:*** Zack Whedon; ***W:*** Zack Whedon; ***C:*** Sean Stiegemeier; ***M:*** Nate Walcott.

Come and Get It *Roaring Timber* **1936** A classic adaptation of the Edna Ferber novel about a lumber king battling against his son for the love of a woman. Farmer's most important Hollywood role. **99m/B; VHS, DVD.** Frances Farmer; Edward Arnold; Joel McCrea; Walter Brennan; Andrea Leeds; Charles Halton; ***D:*** William Wyler; Howard Hawks; ***W:*** Jules Furthman; Jane Murfin; ***C:*** Rudolph Mate; Gregg Toland; ***M:*** Alfred Newman. Oscars '36: Support. Actor (Brennan).

Come and See *Idi i Smotri; Go and See* **1985** Harrowing, unnerving epic which depicts the horrors of war as a boy soldier roams the Russian countryside during the Nazi invasion. Some overwhelming sequences, including tracer-bullets flashing across an open field. War has rarely been rendered in such a vivid, utterly grim manner. Outstanding achievement from Soviet director Klimov. In Russian with English subtitles. **137m/C; VHS, DVD.** *RU* Alexei Kravchenko; Olga Mironova; Lubomiras Lauciavicus; Vladas Bagdonas; Viktor Lorents; Juris Lumiste; Kazimir Rabetsky; Yevgeni Tilicheyev; ***D:*** Elem Klimov; ***W:*** Elem Klimov; Alex Adamovich; ***C:*** Alexei Rodionov; ***M:*** Oleg Yanchenko.

Come as You Are 1/2 **2005** Quickly sinking dotcom entrepreneur Craig (Sterling) hosts a reunion for his old college chums so they can meet Kellie (Fixx), his knockout fiancee. Little do they know, their buddy is desperately launching a new business. After a series of contrived events occur, a hostile porn director, crew, and cast show up to the rental house to start filming a sex video, causing Craig to fess up to his new smut-meister gig. Mostly unknown cast plays out matters of the heart and groin commendably. **83m/C; DVD.** Maury Sterling; James Russo; Michelle Harrison; James Marshall; Barbara Fixx; ***D:*** Chuck Rose; ***W:*** Chuck Rose; ***C:*** Lawrence Schweich; ***M:*** Nathan Wang; John Abella. **VIDEO**

Come As You Are 1/2 **2020** A paraplegic from birth, rapper Scotty (Rosenmeyer) lives with his helicopter mom Liz (Garofalo) in Colorado. At his physical therapy center, the often disgruntled Scotty connects with another client, Matt (Szeto), a former athlete who is now wheelchair bound. When Scotty learns of a brothel in Montreal that services special needs people, they take a road trip there with Mo (Patel), a blind employee of the center, and driver Sam (Sidibe), a feisty nurse. Based on real events, this lively comedy-drama transcends the sex comedy genre by taking an honest look at the unmet sexual needs of the disabled. **106m/C; DVD.** Grant Rosenmeyer; Hayden Szeto; Ravi Patel; Gabourey Sidibe; Janeane Garofalo; ***D:*** Richard Wong; ***W:*** Erik Linthorst; ***C:*** Richard Wong; ***M:*** Jeremy Turner.

Come Back, Little Sheba 1/2 **1952** Unsettling drama about a worn-out housewife, her abusive, alcoholic husband and a comely boarder who causes further marital tension. The title refers to the housewife's despairing search for her lost dog. Booth, Lancaster, and Moore are all excellent. Based on the play by William Inge, this film still packs an emotional wallop. **99m/B; VHS, DVD.** Burt Lancaster; Shirley Booth; Terry Moore; Richard Jaeckel; Philip Ober; Lisa Golm; Walter Kelley; ***D:*** Daniel Mann; ***C:*** James Wong Howe. Oscars '52: Actress (Booth); Cannes '53: Actress (Booth); Golden Globes '53: Actress--Drama (Booth); N.Y. Film Critics '52: Actress (Booth).

Come Blow Your Horn **1963** Neil Simon's first major Broadway success is a little less successful in its celluloid wrapper, suffering a bit from a familiar script. Sinatra's a playboy who blows his horn all over town, causing his close-knit New York Jewish family to warp a bit. Dad's not keen on his son's pledge of allegiance to the good life, and kid brother Bill would like to be his sibling's understudy in playboyhood. **115m/C; VHS, DVD, Blu-Ray.** Frank Sinatra; Lee J. Cobb; Tony Bill; Molly Picon; Barbara Rush; Jill St. John; ***D:*** Bud Yorkin; ***W:*** Norman Lear; ***C:*** William H. Daniels.

Come Dance at My Wedding **2009** Seriously schmaltzy Hallmark Channel movie about a family reconciliation (and dancing and a wedding). Cyd Merriman (Nevin) wants to sell the family dance studio she inherited from her mother so she can marry Zach (Jacot) and make a career change. Then her lawyer informs Cyd that the father she always assumed was dead is not only alive but co-owns the studio and must sign off on the sale. Tanner Grey (Schneider) never knew he had a daughter and comes to town to get to know Cyd. He also turns out to be quite a hoofer himself. **88m/C; DVD.** Brooke Nevin; John Schneider; Christopher Jacot; Roma Downey; ***D:*** Mark Jean; ***W:*** J.B. White; ***C:*** Mathias Herndl. **CABLE**

Come Dance With Me 1/2 **2012** Hallmark Channel holiday rom com. Jack hopes that dating Demi Clayton, the boss's daughter, will get him a promotion. To further impress, Jack signs up for dance lessons to make smooth moves at the Clayton's Christmas soiree. But he doesn't intend to fall for his instructor, Christine. **90m/C; DVD.** Andrew McCarthy; Michelle Nolden; Stephanie Mills; Chris Gillett; Jane Moffat; ***D:*** John Bradshaw; ***W:*** Kevin Commins; ***C:*** Russ Goozee; ***M:*** Stacey Hersh. **CABLE**

Come Die With Me 1/2 **1975** Frumpy housekeeper Mary (Brennan) knows she doesn't attract her handsome boss Walter (Maharis) so when she realizes he murdered his brother, Mary decides to blackmail him into marriage. A twist ending in this average made-for-TV movie. **68m/C; DVD.** Eileen Brennan; George Maharis; Charles McCauley; Kathryn Leigh Scott; Philip Sterling; Alan Napier; ***D:*** Burt Brinckerhoff; ***M:*** Robert Cobert. **TV**

Come Drink with Me *Da zui xia; Great Drunken Hero* **1965** Credited with inspiring both "Kill Bill" and "Crouching Tiger, Hidden Dragon" and directed by veteran filmmaker King Hu for the Shaw Brothers, this flick features equally legendary Chinese actress Cheng Pei-Pei as Golden Swallow, a female warrior disguised as a man hired to find the governor's kidnapped son. After a bar fight, she is joined in her quest by a kung fu master called the Drunken Cat, who has business of his own with the kidnappers. While it isn't the nonstop action film many classic kung fu movies are, Cheng Pei-Pei is a far more accomplished martial artist than some actors of the time. **91m/C; DVD.** *CH* Jackie Chan; Pei-pei Ching; Hua Yueh; Hung Lieh Chen; Yunzhong Li; Chih-Ching Yang; ***D:*** King Hu; ***W:*** King Hu; Yang Erh; ***C:*** Tadashi Nishimoto; ***M:*** Lan-Ping Chow.

Come Early Morning 1/2 **2006 (R)** Lucy Fowler (Judd) lives two lives in her Arkansas community: she's very efficient at her day contractor job while raising hell as a hard-drinking, one-night-stand kinda gal in the evening. Maybe she's just emulating her womanizing, alcoholic pop (Wilson). Courtly newcomer Cal (Donovan) refuses to let her use him and leave, but even Cal may not be able to overcome Lucy's self-destructiveness. Adams does well with her slice-of-life tale—her writing/directing debut—as does surrogate Judd (Adams once intended to play the lead herself). **97m/C; DVD.** Ashley Judd; Jeffrey Donovan; Tim Blake Nelson; Laura Prepon; Stacy Keach; Scott Wilson; Diane Ladd; Pat Corley; ***D:*** Joey Lauren Adams; ***W:*** Joey Lauren Adams; ***C:*** Tim Orr; ***M:*** Alan Brewer.

Come Hell or High Water 1/2 *One-Eyed Horse* **2008 (R)** Former Confederate soldier Justin Gatewood has just been released from prison where he was held for the attempted murder of Union soldier William Curry, whom Justin blames for the death of his brother. It's now 1887 but Justin travels back to Hadley, Missouri, with revenge on his mind and the violence entangles the daughters of both men. **90m/C; DVD.** Richard Cutting; Mark Redfield; Michael Hagan; Jennifer Rouse; Kelly Potchak; Jason Brown; ***D:*** Wayne Shipley; ***W:*** Wayne Shipley; ***C:*** Jeff Herberger. **VIDEO**

Come Live With Me **1940** Austriah political refugee Johnny Jones (Lamarr) is going to be deported until she makes a green card marriage to broke writer Bill Smith (Stewart). They won't live together and Johnny says she'll pay Bill a stipend while he writes his novel. When Johnny asks for a divorce, Bill tells her no unless she agrees to spend a weekend with him in the country. However, they're confronted there by Johnny's married lover Barton (Hunter). Naturally Lamarr is gorgeous and Stewart is charming. **86m/B; DVD.** Hedy Lamarr; James Stewart; Ian Hunter; Verree Teasdale; Donald Meek; Barton MacLane; Adeline de Walt Reynolds; ***D:*** Clarence Brown; ***W:*** Patterson McNutt; ***C:*** George J. Folsey; ***M:*** Herbert Stothart.

Come See the Paradise **1990 (R)** Jack McGurn (Quaid) takes a job at a movie theatre in Los Angeles' Little Tokyo and falls for owner's daughter Lily (Tomita). They marry, but after the bombing of Pearl Harbor all Japanese-Americans are interned. Told in flashback, the story offers a candid look at the racism implicit in the relocations and the hypocrisy that often lurks beneath the surface of the pursuit of liberty and justice for all. Sometimes melodramatic script indulges a bit too much in the obvious, but the subject is worthwhile, one that has not yet been cast into the vast bin of Hollywood cliches. The cast, apart from Quaid's misguided attempt at seriousness, is excellent. **135m/C; VHS, DVD.** Dennis Quaid; Tamlyn Tomita; Sab Shimono; Shizuko Hoshi; Stan(ford) Egi; Ronald Yamamoto; Akemi Nishino; Naomi Nakano; Brady Tsurutani; Pruitt Taylor Vince; Joe Lisi; ***D:*** Alan Parker; ***W:*** Alan Parker; ***M:*** Randy Edelman.

Come September 1/2 **1961** American business tycoon Robert Talbot (Hudson) maintains a holiday villa on the Italian Riveria. But the only time he uses the place is the month of September, so when Talbot arrives in July he discovers his enterprising major domo Maurice (Slezak) has been managing the place as a hotel the rest of the year. Talbot finds his home filled with tourists and, to make matters worse, discovers his Italian lover Lisa (Lollobrigida) about to get married. Darin and Dee are the film's romantic ingenues and wound up getting married after filming wrapped; his screen debut. **114m/C; VHS, DVD.** Rock Hudson; Gina Lollobrigida; Sandra Dee; Bobby Darin; Walter Slezak; Joel Grey; Brenda de Banzie; ***D:*** Robert Mulligan; ***W:*** Stanley Shapiro; Maurice Richlin; ***C:*** William H. Daniels; ***M:*** Hans J. Salter.

Come to Daddy 1/2 **2020 (R)** When Norval (Wood) was five years old, his father, Gordon (McHattie) left his family. Three decades later, Norval receives a letter from Gordon asking him to visit. Norval travels to Gordon's remote beach house, but the reunion is stressful. While Norval shares his story of alcohol dependence, mental health struggles, and music industry success, alcoholic Gordon goes out of his way to embarrass his son. The situation grows more weird and uncomfortable, leading Norval to fear for his life. Clever and strange horror flick with tension created by increasingly bad events. **96m/C; DVD.** Elijah Wood; Stephen McHattie; Garfield Wilson; Madeleine Sami; Martin Donovan; ***D:*** Ant Timpson; ***W:*** Toby Harvard; ***C:*** Daniel Katz; ***M:*** Karl Steven.

Come to the Stable **1949** Warm, delightful story about two French nuns, Young and Holm, who arrive in New England and set about building a children's hospital. Although Catholic in intent, pic demonstrates that faith and tenacity can move mountains. (This film must have been Fox's response to Paramount's "Going My Way" and "The Bells of Saint Mary's.") Based on a story by Clare Boothe Luce. **94m/B; DVD.** Loretta Young; Celeste Holm; Hugh Marlowe; Elsa Lanchester; Regis Toomey; Mike Mazurki; ***D:*** Henry Koster; ***W:*** Oscar Millard; Sally Benson; ***C:*** Joseph LaShelle; ***M:*** Cyril Mockridge.

Come Undone *Presque Rien* **2000** A matter of fact coming of age tale about a French teenager, Mathieu (Elkaim), who acknowledges his sexuality when he falls in love with the slightly older Cedric (Rideau). Mathieu and his younger sister Sarah (Legrix) are stuck at their summer house in a coastal resort town with their depressed mother (Reymond) and their aunt (Matheron) who's serving as a nurse/housekeeper. The emotional Mathieu finds sex and solace with the volatile Cedric but their affair doesn't work out as expected. Film is non-linear and the viewer must piece together what has happened from the various scenes, which can be confusing. French with subtitles. **98m/C; VHS, DVD.** *FR* Jeremie Elkaim; Stephane Rideau; Marie Matheron; Laetitia Legrix; Dominique Reymond; Nils Ohlund; Rejane Kerdaffrec; Guy Houssier; ***D:*** Sabastien Lifshitz; ***W:*** Sabastien Lifshitz; Stephane Bouquet; ***C:*** Pascal Paoucet; ***M:*** Perry Blake.

The Comeback *The Day the Screaming Stopped* **1977** A singer attempting a comeback in England finds his wife murdered. **100m/C; VHS, DVD, Blu-Ray.** *GB* Jack Jones; Pamela Stephenson; David Doyle; Bill Owen; Sheila Keith; Richard Johnson; ***D:*** Pete Walker.

Comeback 1/2 **1983** The story of a disillusioned rock star, played by Eric Burdon (the lead singer of the Animals), who gives up his life in the fast lane and tries to go back to his roots. **105m/C; VHS, DVD.** Eric Burdon; ***D:*** Christel Bushmann; ***M:*** Eric Burdon.

The Comebacks **2007 (PG-13)** Truly lame spoof of sports flicks. Losing football coach Lambeau Fields (Koechner) gets a last chance when he's hired at Heartland State U. So he moves his family, including limber hottie daughter Michelle (Nevin), to Texas to whip a bunch of losers into shape. The climatic game is called the Toilet Bowl—yea, those are the jokes, folks, in another "spoof everything and something might be funny" outing. **84m/C; DVD.** David Koechner; Melora Hardin; Brooke Nevin; Carl Weathers; Matthew Lawrence; Nick Searcy; Jermaine Williams; Jesse Garcia; George Back; Eric Christian Olsen; Will Arnett; Bradley Cooper; Dax Shepard; Jackie Long; Robert Ri'chard; Martin Spanjers; Jon(athan) Gries; Andy Dick; Kerri Kenney; Dennis Rodman; Frank Caliendo; Finesse Mitchell; Noureen DeWulf; ***Cameo(s):*** John Salley; Lawrence Taylor; Eric Dickerson; Michael Irvin; ***D:*** Tom Brady; ***W:*** Ed Yeager; Joey Gutierrez; ***C:*** Anthony B. Richmond; ***M:*** Christopher Lennertz.

The Comedian 1/2 **2016 (R)** Renowned director Hackford and beloved actor De Niro working together on a dramedy about an aging insult comic sounds like a recipe for at least goodness, possibly even greatness. Try bland-ness. The biggest prob-

Paul De Meo; ***C:*** Martin Chichov; ***M:*** Frederik Wiedmann. **VIDEO**

The Company of Wolves 🦴🦴🦴 **1985 (R)** Thirteen-year-old Rosaleen (Patterson) lives with her parents (Warner, Silberg) on the outskirts of a forbidding forest. The girl, who's on the verge of womanhood, listens to her grandmother (Lansbury) tell fairy tales and dreams of a medieval fantasy world inhabited by men who turn into wolves. An adult "Little Red Riding Hood" that's heavy on dreamy visuals and Freudian symbolism. **95m/C; VHS, DVD.** Angela Lansbury; David Warner; Stephen Rea; Tusse Silberg; Sarah Patterson; Brian Glover; Danielle Dax; Graham Crowden; Micha Bergese; Kathryn Pogson; Georgia Slowe; ***D:*** Neil Jordan; ***W:*** Neil Jordan; Angela Carter; ***C:*** Bryan Loftus; ***M:*** George Fenton.

The Company You Keep 🦴🦴 ½ **2012 (R)** Fictional round-up of a sect of the infamous '70s radical protest group, the Weather Underground. Nearly four decades later, the members are living happy, productive lives, but pressure mounts when new details emerge connecting the group to a bloody 1981 bank robbery. Quickly, Sharon (Sarandon) turns herself in, prompting hungry young reporter Ben (LaBeouf) to sniff out the rest of the gang. The remaining members at large confront the ethical dilemmas associated with such a past. Though it stumbles at times, solid performances from a sure-fire ensemble cast, lead by director Redford, make for a tight political thriller. Adapted from Neil Gordon's 2003 novel. **125m/C; DVD, Blu-Ray.** Robert Redford; Shia LaBeouf; Terrence Howard; Julie Christie; Richard Jenkins; Brendan Gleeson; Sam Elliott; Susan Sarandon; ***D:*** Robert Redford; ***W:*** Lem Dobbs; ***C:*** Adriano Goldman; ***M:*** Cliff Martinez.

The Competition 🦴🦴🦴 **1980 (PG)** Two virtuoso pianists meet at an international competition and fall in love. Will they stay together if one of them wins? Can they have a performance career and love too? Is he trying to distract her with sex, so he can win? Dreyfuss and Irving are fine (they practiced for four months to look like they were actually playing the pianos), and Remick's character has some interesting insights into the world of art. **125m/C; VHS, Download.** Richard Dreyfuss; Amy Irving; Lee Remick; Sam Wanamaker; Joseph Cali; Ty Henderson; Priscilla Pointer; James B. Sikking; ***D:*** Joel Oliansky; ***M:*** Lalo Schifrin.

Complete Unknown 🦴 **2016 (R)** It's rare to see two incredibly talented, charismatic actors as wasted as Weisz and Shannon are in this ho-hum, pretentious drama. The great Shannon plays Tom, a quiet gentleman who crosses paths with Weisz's Alice at a party, and he's convinced he's met her before. Alice is an identity thief, jumping across the country changing lives at a whim. Tom becomes fascinated with Alice and her willingness to do whatever she feels in the moment, but there's no joy or suspense in Marston's film. **90m/C; DVD.** Rachel Weisz; Michael Shannon; Danny Glover; Kathy Bates; Chris Lowell; ***D:*** Joshua Marston; ***W:*** Joshua Marston; Julian Sheppard; ***C:*** Christos Voudouris; ***M:*** Danny Bensi; Saunder Jurriaans.

Compliance 🦴🦴🦴 ½ **2012 (R)** Zobel's controversial drama pulls no punches in this remarkable telling of a disturbing true story that forces viewers to question not only what they would do in the same situation but how they would judge those who did wrong. In 2004, a prank caller phoned fast food restaurants and pretended to be a police officer. He convinced a manager to not only hold one of her employees, who's allegedly a thief, in a back room but strip search her and leave her to be monitored by complete strangers. With stunning performances and strikingly realistic direction, this drama is one haunting film. **90m/C; DVD, Blu-Ray.** Ann Dowd; Dreama Walker; Pat Healy; Bill Camp; Philip Ettinger; James McCaffrey; ***D:*** Craig Zobel; ***W:*** Craig Zobel; ***C:*** Adam Stone; ***M:*** Heather McIntosh.

Compulsion 🦴🦴🦴 ½ **1959** Artie Strauss (Dillman) is a mother-dominated sadist who, along with submissive friend Judd Steiner (Stockwell), plan and execute a cold-blooded murder. Flamboyant lawyer Jonathan Wilk (brilliantly portrayed by Welles) knows he has no defense so he attacks the system and establishment, seeking to at least save his clients from death. A suspenseful shocker with taut direction and a tight script. Based on the notorious 1924 Leopold and Loeb murder trial, also filmed as "Rope" and "Swoon." **103m/B; VHS, DVD, Blu-Ray.** Orson Welles; Bradford Dillman; Dean Stockwell; Diane Varsi; E.G. Marshall; Martin Milner; Richard Anderson; Robert F. Simon; Edward Binns; Robert Burton; Wilton Graff; Gavin MacLeod; Wendell Holmes; ***D:*** Richard Fleischer; ***W:*** Richard Murphy; ***C:*** William Mellor.

Compulsion 🦴 ½ **2008** Clumsy erotic thriller with a plot that defies credibility. Fifty-something Don Flowers (Winstone) is the longtime chauffeur for a wealthy Indian family living in London. The family's over-indulged daughter Anjika (Nagra) is appalled when her traditional father brokers an arranged marriage and Don agrees to help her—if she'll sleep with him. Don's behavior already borders on stalking but after doing the deed, Anjika isn't the only one with a compulsion to keep the unlikely sex thing going. **94m/C; DVD.** *GB* Ray Winstone; Parminder K. Nagra; Ben Aldridge; Bhasker Patel; Veena Sood; James Floyd; ***D:*** Sarah Harding; ***W:*** Joshua St. Johnston; ***M:*** Jennie Muskett. **TV**

Compulsion 🦴 ½ **2013 (R)** Claustrophobic crime mystery that's a remake of the 1995 Korean pic "301/302." Saffron's (Moss) an abused former child star who's become an anorexic recluse. Amy (Graham), her next door apartmenrt neighbor, idolized Saffron when she was on television and is obsessed with cooking and having her own TV show herself. Now, she pushes her attentions on her depressed neighbor to an unhealthy extent. When Saffron goes missing, Detective Reynolds (Mantegna) interviews Amy and soon realizes just how unstable she is. **88m/C; DVD.** Heather Graham; Carrie-Anne Moss; Joe Mantegna; Kevin Dillon; ***D:*** Egidio Coccimiglio; ***W:*** Floyd Byars; ***C:*** Vilmos Zsigmond; ***M:*** Jonathan Goldsmith. **VIDEO**

Computer Chess 🦴🦴 **2013** Shot on an old-school video cameras, this early '80s mockumentary focuses on a fictional tournament pitting human against computer in a John Henry-like chess tournament. The bitter Buescher (Wiggins), cocky upstart Papageorge (Paige), and wallflower Bishton (Riester) emerge as the stand-out personalities, debating, perhaps too often, the future of artificial intelligence and gawk at the lone nerd female. Mumblecore pioneer Buljaski crafts a pitch-perfect portrait of the dawn of home computers, but any trace of actual story is just as clunky and frustrating as its chess machines. **92m/B; DVD.** Gerald Peary; Wiley Wiggins; Myles Paige; Patrick Riester; Robin Schwartz; ***D:*** Andrew Bujalski; ***W:*** Andrew Bujalski; ***C:*** Matthias Grunsky.

Computer Wizard 🦴 *Where's Willie?* **1977 (G)** Boy genius builds a powerful electronic device. His intentions are good, but the invention disrupts the town and lands him in big trouble. Not the "Thomas Edison Story." **91m/C; VHS, DVD.** Henry Darrow; Kate Woodville; Guy Madison; Marc Gilpin; ***D:*** John Florea.

The Computer Wore Tennis Shoes 🦴 ½ **1969 (G)** Disney comedy (strictly for the kids) about a slow-witted college student who turns into a genius after a "shocking" encounter with the campus computer. His new brains give the local gangster headaches. Sequel: "Now You See Him, Now You Don't." **87m/C; VHS, DVD, Blu-Ray.** Kurt Russell; Cesar Romero; Joe Flynn; William Schallert; Alan Hewitt; Richard Bakalyan; ***D:*** Robert Butler; ***M:*** Robert F. Brunner.

Comrade X 🦴🦴 ½ **1940** Gable is an American correspondent in Moscow who is blackmailed into marrying die-hard Communist Lamarr in this comedic spinoff of "Ninotchka." The two stars failed to create any sparks as a love duo, although their previous film "Boom Town" was a hit. Based on a story by Walter Reisch. **87m/B; VHS, DVD.** Clark Gable; Hedy Lamarr; Oscar Homolka; Felix Bressart; Eve Arden; Sig Rumann; Natasha Lytess; Vladimir Sokoloff; ***D:*** King Vidor; ***W:*** Ben Hecht; Charles Lederer.

Con Air 🦴🦴🦴 **1997 (R)** Producer Bruckheimer flies solo for the first time, and has a very successful flight. Cage re-ups as former Ranger Cameron Poe, jailed for manslaughter, who gets paroled just in time to catch a ride home aboard a plane filled with the worst of America's criminals. Led by Cyrus "The Virus" Grissom (Malkovich), the first-class psycho passengers take over the plane, and Cameron must save the day. Among the snappy one-liners, chases, shoot-outs, and stuff blowin' up real good, comes Federal Marshal Larkin (Cusack) to help Poe from the ground. Cusack can't shake his indie-film, quirky-kid image enough to really pass as an action hero, but he gives it his all. Flick supplies everything you'd expect from a summer blockbuster actioner, but it's best seen on a big-screen with surround sound to get the full effect. **105m/C; VHS, DVD, Blu-Ray.** Nicolas Cage; John Malkovich; John Cusack; Mykelti Williamson; Ving Rhames; Steve Buscemi; Colm Meaney; Rachel Ticotin; Dave Chappelle; M.C. Gainey; Danny Trejo; Nick (Nicholas) Chinlund; Jesse Borrego; Angela Featherstone; Monica Potter; John Roselius; Renoly; Landry Allbright; Jose Zuniga; ***D:*** Simon West; ***W:*** Scott Rosenberg; ***C:*** David Tattersall; ***M:*** Mark Mancina; Trevor Rabin.

The Con Artist 🦴🦴 ½ **2010 (R)** Amusing crime comedy with Sutherland father and son in the lead roles. Car thief Vince has just been paroled and wants to go straight. He owes his ex-boss Kranski money and Kranski expects him to return to stealing cars. Vince is a metal sculptor in his spare time and, through contrived but funny circumstances, his work comes to the attention of art dealer Belinda, who wants to make him the next big thing. Vince thinks he can pay Kranski back through legit means but it's not that simple. **87m/C; DVD.** *CA* Rossif Sutherland; Donald Sutherland; Rebecca Romijn; Sarah Roemer; Russell Peters; ***D:*** Risa Bramon Garcia; ***W:*** Michael Melsi; Collin Friesen; ***C:*** Derek Rogers.

The Con Artists 🦴 ½ *The Con Man* **1980** After con man Quinn is sprung from prison, he and his protege set up a sting operation against the beautiful Capucine. Not clever or witty enough for the caper to capture interest. **86m/C; VHS, DVD.** *IT* Anthony Quinn; Adriano Celentano; Capucine; Corinne Clery; ***D:*** Sergio Corbucci.

Con Games 🦴 ½ **2002 (R)** John Woodrow (Thomas) goes undercover in a maximum security California prison to investigate the murder of a senator's grandson. The prison is ruled by corrupt guard Hopkins (Roberts) and Woodrow's life expectency takes a nosedive when Hopkins learns his true identity. **90m/C; VHS, DVD.** Eric Roberts; Martin Kove; Tommy Lee Thomas; Jody Nolan; ***D:*** Jefferson Edward Donald; ***W:*** Tommy Lee Thomas; Jefferson Edward Donald; ***C:*** John Lazear. **VIDEO**

Conagher 🦴🦴 ½ *Louis L'Amour's Conagher* **1991** A lyrical, if poorly plotted Western about a veteran cowboy who takes the whole movie to decide to end up in the arms of the pretty widow lady. Cable adaptation of Louis L'Amour's novel doesn't have much intensity, though Elliott captures his character well. **94m/C; VHS, DVD.** Sam Elliott; Katharine Ross; Barry Corbin; Buck Taylor; Dub Taylor; Daniel Quinn; Anndi McAfee; Billy Green Bush; Ken Curtis; ***D:*** Reynaldo Villalobos. **CABLE**

Conan O'Brien Can't Stop 🦴🦴 **2011 (R)** After a messy parting of the ways with NBC and "The Tonight Show" in 2010, Conan O'Brien goes on a two-month, 32-city, comedy/music/variety tour he called "The Legally Prohibited from Being Funny on Television Tour." Contractually barred (through a buyout) to host another television show for six months, O'Brien appears everywhere from the glitz of Las Vegas to Radio City Music Hall and a tent at the Bonnaroo music festival in Tennessee. Onstage shtick is contrasted with tour and backstage demands and duties, including fans and celebrity guests and well-wishers. **89m/C; DVD, Blu-Ray.** Conan O'Brien; Andy Richter; ***D:*** Rodman Flender; ***C:*** Rodman Flender.

Conan the Barbarian 🦴🦴🦴 **1982 (R)** A fine sword and sorcery tale featuring brutality, excellent production values, and a rousing score. Conan's (Arnie, who else) parents are killed and he's enslaved. But hardship makes him strong, so when he is set free he can avenge their murder and retrieve the sword bequeathed him by his father. Sandahl Bergman is great as The Queen of Thieves, and Schwarzenegger maintains an admirable sense of humor throughout. Jones is dandy, as always, this time as bad guy Thulsa Doom. Based on the character created by Robert E. Howard. Sequel: "Conan the Destroyer." **115m/C; VHS, DVD, Blu-Ray.** Arnold Schwarzenegger; James Earl Jones; Max von Sydow; Sandahl Bergman; Mako; Ben Davidson; Valerie Quennessen; Cassandra Gaviola; William (Bill) Smith; ***D:*** John Milius; ***W:*** John Milius; Oliver Stone; ***C:*** Duke Callaghan; John Cabrera; ***M:*** Basil Poledouris.

Conan the Barbarian 🦴 **2011 (R)** Based on Robert E. Howard's mythic conqueror, previously (and memorably) played by Arnold Schwarzenegger in 1982. This version by director Nispel is more faithful to its pulp origins as Conan (Momoa) makes his way across Hyboria to avenge the murder of his father (Perlman) and the destruction of his village by King Khalar Zym (Lang). Besides an unabashed reveling in obscene amounts of bloody violence (particularly lurid in 3D) and abhorrent dialogue, Khalar's long-clawed-goth-witch-daughter Marique offers McGowan a chance to be truly horrible. Momoa is studlier than Schwarzenegger though not as funny. **113m/C; DVD, Blu-Ray.** Jason Momoa; Rose McGowan; Stephen Lang; Ron Perlman; Rachel Nichols; ***D:*** Marcus Nispel; ***W:*** Joshua Oppenheimer; Sean Hood; Thomas Dean Donnelly; ***C:*** Thomas Kloss; ***M:*** Tyler Bates.

Conan the Destroyer 🦴🦴 ½ **1984 (PG)** Conan is manipulated by Queen Tamaris into searching for a treasure. In return she'll bring Conan's love Valeria back to life. On his trip he meets Jones and Chamberlain, who later give him a hand. Excellent special effects, good humor, camp fun, somewhat silly finale. Sequel to the better "Conan the Barbarian." **101m/C; VHS, DVD, Blu-Ray.** Arnold Schwarzenegger; Grace Jones; Wilt Chamberlain; Sarah Douglas; Mako; Jeff Corey; Olivia D'Abo; Tracey Walter; ***D:*** Richard Fleischer; ***W:*** Stanley Mann; ***C:*** Jack Cardiff; ***M:*** Basil Poledouris. Golden Raspberries '84: Worst New Star (D'Abo).

Concealed Weapon 🦴 ½ **1994 (R)** A struggling actor gets the part of a lifetime but then becomes the prime suspect in a brutal crime. **80m/C; VHS, DVD.** Daryl Haney; Suzanne Wouk; Monica Simpson; Mark Driscoll; Karen Stone; ***D:*** Dave Payne; Milan Zivkovich.

Conceiving Ada 🦴🦴 **1997** Experimental film is a homage to Lady Ada Lovelace (Swinton), daughter of Lord Byron, a 19th-century mathematician who developed what is now considered the first computer programming language. Ada is regarded by contemporary computer scientist Amy Coer (Faridany) as her spiritual mentor and Amy becomes obsessed with devising a method to actually communicate with the long-deceased Ada, whose life uncannily paralells her own. **85m/C; VHS, DVD.** Tilda Swinton; Francesca Faridany; Karen Black; John E. O'Keefe; J.D. Wolfe; Timothy Leary; John Perry Barlow; Owen Murphy; ***D:*** Lynn Hershman Leeson; ***W:*** Lynn Hershman Leeson; Eileen Jones; ***C:*** Hiro Narita.

Concerning Violence 🦴🦴 ½ *Om vald* **2014** Exploring the mid- to late twentieth century process of decolonization as described in Frantz Fanon's "The Wretched of the Earth," this documentary uses archival footage to examine and highlight bold moments in the quest for freedom by colonized territories. Using footage from the archives of Swedish television, the documentary features footage of anti-imperialist liberation movements. The documentary also considers how Fanon's book illuminates present-day neocolonialism activities. English, French, Portuguese, and Swedish with subtitles. **88m/C; DVD, Streaming, Download.** Lauryn Hill; ***D:*** Goran Olsson; ***W:*** Goran Olsson; ***C:*** Lis Asklund; Bo Bjelfvenstam; Ingrid Dahlberg; Lars Hjelm; Roland Hjelte; Stig Holmqvist; Per Kallberg; Lennart Malmer; Ingela Romare; Leyla Assaf Tengroth.

The Concert 🦴🦴 **2009 (PG-13)** Russian conductor Andrei Filipov (Guskov) lost his job with the Bolshoi in the 1980s after championing Jewish musicians. Long-reduced to being the hall's janitor, he sees a second chance when he intercepts a desperate request from Paris theater director Olivier (Berleand) to have the orchestra step in for a cancelled performance. So Andrei recruits his own group of ragtag musicians, travels to Paris, and then insists on engaging young, beautiful French violinist Anne-Marie (Laurent), whose connection to the Russians is gradually revealed. French and Russian with subtitles. **120m/C; DVD, Blu-Ray.** *FR RO BE IT* Melanie Laurent; Francois Berleand; Miou-Miou; Lionel Abelanski; Aleksei Guskov; Dmitri Nazarov; Valeriy Barinov; ***D:*** Radu Mihaileanu; ***W:*** Radu Mihaileanu; Matthew Robbins; Alain-Michel Blanc; ***C:*** Laurent Dailland; ***M:*** Armand Amar.

The Concorde: Airport '79 🦴 *Airport '79* **1979 (PG)** A supersonic film in the "Airport" tradition has the Concorde chased by missiles and fighter aircraft before it crashes in the Alps. Incredibly far-fetched nonsense with an all-star cast doesn't fly. **103m/C; VHS, DVD, Blu-Ray.** Alain Delon; Susan Blakely; Robert Wagner; Sylvia Kristel; John Davidson; Charo; Sybil Danning; Jimmie Walker; Eddie Albert; Bibi Andersson; Monica Lewis; Andrea Marcovicci; Martha Raye; Cicely Tyson; Mercedes McCambridge; George Kennedy; David Warner; ***D:*** David Lowell Rich; ***W:*** Eric Roth; ***M:*** Lalo Schifrin.

Concrete Cowboys 🦴 **1/2** *Ramblin' Man* **1979** In this old TV movie pilot, Jerry Reed and Tom Selleck are a pair of drifters who head out to Nashville to find fame and fortune when Morgan Fairchild mistakes them for a pair of private detectives. Obviously a great deal of thought was put into the script. Pretty soon the inevitable car chases and slapstick ensue. **100m/C; DVD.** Jerry Reed; Tom Selleck; Morgan Fairchild; Claude Akins; Roy Acuff; Barbara Mandrell; Ray Stevens; Gene Evans; Randy Powell; Grace Zabriskie; Bob Hannah; Joseph Burke; ***D:*** Bert Kennedy; ***W:*** Eugene Price; Jimmy Sangster; ***C:*** Alan Stensvold; Vincent Saizis.

Concussion 🦴 **1/2 2013 (R)** Unsympathetic lead does little to make Passon's relationship drama believable or interesting. Stay-at-home mom Abby gets beaned by a baseball and, after recovering from her blow to the head, suddenly becomes consumed with upending her life. She resolves the lack of affection in her marriage to divorce lawyer Kate by going to a prostitute and then suddenly decides to become one herself. **97m/C; Streaming.** Robin Weigert; Maggie Siff; Johnathan Tchaikovsky; Julie Fain Lawrence; Ben Shenkman; ***D:*** Stacie Passon; ***W:*** Stacie Passon; ***C:*** David Kruta; ***M:*** Barb Morrison.

Concussion 🦴🦴 **2015 (PG-13)** What Dr. Bennet Omalu (Smith) learned about the impact of brain damage on professional football players is still impacting the game so much of the world loves. And Smith does a solid, workmanlike job of capturing a complex man, someone scared to take down an institution. The problem with Landesman's film is that to get the names of actual teams they had to give the NFL script approval. And so there's so much story left untold, including how much the NFL knew about the brain damage and when they knew it. The result is a decent but unsatisfying film. Based on real events. **123m/C; DVD, Blu-Ray.** Will Smith; Alec Baldwin; Albert Brooks; Gugu Mbatha-Raw; Eddie Marsan; Adewale Akinnuoye-Agbaje; ***D:*** Peter Landesman; ***W:*** Peter Landesman; ***C:*** Salvatore Totino; ***M:*** James Newton Howard.

The Condemned 🦴 **2007 (R)** Violent grade-D actioner does exactly what it's supposed to and no more. Media slime Ian (Mammone) hits on a new reality concept: drop ten death-row inmates onto a remote island and tell them that the last survivor earns freedom and a paycheck while Internet subscribers pay to watch a live feed. Probably the only recognizable faces are former WWE wrestler Austin and Brit soccer star turned screen villain Jones but everyone is pretty much dead meat. **113m/C; DVD, Blu-Ray.** Steve Austin; Vinnie Jones; Robert Mammone; Victoria (Tory) Mussett; Masa Yamaguchi; Manu Bennett; Marcus Johnson; Christopher Baker; Rick Hoffman; Luke Pegler; Samantha Healy; Madeleine West; Emelia Burns; Nathan Jones; Angie Milliken; ***D:*** Scott Wiper; ***W:*** Scott Wiper; Rob Hedden; ***C:*** Ross Emery.

Condemned 🦴 **1/2 2015** Squatting takes a deadly turn in this pathogen-centered horror flick. After Maya (Penn) escapes her difficult family life, she decides to live with her boyfriend in his Manhattan home. He lives as a squatter in a condemned building, among drug abusers and degenerates. The situation grows dire when a virus emerges in the building, forming in its waste and garbage. As the virus infects each person living there, everyone becomes a determined killer with bloodlust and the squat a place that must be survived. **83m/C; DVD, Blu-Ray, Streaming, Download.** Dylan Penn; Michel Gill; Johnny Messner; Jon Abrahams; Ronen Rubinstein; ***D:*** Eli Morgan Gesner; ***W:*** Eli Morgan Gesner; ***C:*** Richard Henkels; ***M:*** Daniel A. Davies; Sebastian Robertson.

The Condemned 2 🦴🦴 **2016 (R)** The action-filled sequel to The Condemned finds bounty hunter Will Tanner (Orton) a target himself. When Tanner fails to capture Cyrus Merrick (Studi), the head of a deadly gambling ring, he finds himself the human target in a game of survival known as Condemned. All contestants—nearly all convicts—in this publicly broadcast game must kill or be killed while high stakes bettors place money on who will survive. During the tournament, Tanner, his father Frank Tanner (Roberts), and other members of his team wage war against the man behind the game Raul Quezada (Baccaro) with the goal of defeating him in time. **90m/C; DVD, Download.** Randy Orton; Eric Roberts; Wes Studi; Steven Michael Quezada; Bill Stinchcomb; ***D:*** Roel Reine; ***W:*** Alan B. McElroy; ***C:*** Roel Reine; ***M:*** Trevor Morris; Ted Reedy.

Condemned to Live 🦴🦴 **1935** Mild-mannered doctor Ralph Morgan and his fiancee Maxine Doyle seem like your average early 20th Century Middle-European couple...but the doctor's hunchbacked servant Mischa Auer is a tipoff that this is a horror movie of some sort. Like many men, the doctor has suffered from a vampire curse all his life. And, like many men, he is unaware of his blood-sucking habit, thanks to the concealment efforts of his loyal (hunchback) servant. Doyle discovers her fiance's sanguine secret, but not before she finds out she really loves Gleason, anyway. Answers the question: just how do you jilt a vampire? **68m/B; VHS, DVD.** Ralph Morgan; Maxine Doyle; Russell Gleason; Pedro de Cordoba; Mischa Auer; Lucy Beaumont; Carl Stockdale; ***D:*** Frank Strayer.

Condition Red 🦴🦴 **1995 (R)** Philadelphia prison guard Dan Capelli's (Russo) illicit involvement with inmate Gidell (Williams) turns into big trouble and double-crosses thanks to her drug-dealing boyfriend Angel (Calderon). **85m/C; VHS, DVD.** James Russo; Cynda Williams; Paul Calderon; ***D:*** Mika Kaurismaki; ***W:*** Andre Degas; ***C:*** Ken Kelsch; ***M:*** Mauri Sumen.

Condorman 🦴🦴 **1/2 1981 (PG)** Woody Wilkins, an inventive comic book writer, adopts the identity of his own character, Condorman, in order to help a beautiful Russian spy defect. A Disney film, strictly for the small fry. **90m/C; VHS, DVD.** Michael Crawford; Oliver Reed; Barbara Carrera; James Hampton; Jean-Pierre Kalfon; Dana Elcar; ***D:*** Charles Jarrott; ***W:*** Glenn Gordon Caron; ***C:*** Charles F. Wheeler; ***M:*** Henry Mancini.

Conduct Unbecoming 🦴🦴 **1/2 1975 (PG)** Late 19th-century India is the setting for a trial involving the possible assault of a British officer's wife. Ambitious production based on a British stage play suffers from claustrophobic atmosphere but is greatly redeemed by the first rate cast. **107m/C; VHS, DVD.** *GB* Michael York; Richard Attenborough; Trevor Howard; Stacy Keach; Christopher Plummer; Susannah York; James Faulkner; Michael Culver; Persis Khambatta; ***D:*** Michael Anderson, Sr.

Conductor 1492 🦴🦴 **1/2 1924** In Hines' amusing comedy (he wrote and starred), Irish immigrant Terry O'Toole saves the life of Bobby Connelly (Sage) and is rewarded with a job at the Connelly's streetcar company. Terry then falls in love with the boss's daughter Noretta (May) and seeks to ensure both his work and romance by defending the company against a hostile takeover with some help from his father Mike (Mason). **84m/B; Silent; DVD.** Johnny Hines; Doris May; Dan Mason; Ruth Renick; Fred Esmelton; Byron Sage; Robert Cain; Michael Dark; ***D:*** Charles Hines; Frank Griffin; ***W:*** Johnny Hines; ***C:*** Charles E. Gilson.

Coneheads 🦴🦴 **1/2 1993 (PG)** Comedy inspired by once popular characters from "Saturday Night Live" coasts in on the coattails of "Wayne's World." Aykroyd and Curtin reprise their roles as Beldar and Prymaat, the couple from the planet Remulak who are just trying to fit in on Earth. Newman, who created the role of teenage daughter Connie, appears as Beldar's sister, while Thomas takes over as Connie (toddler Connie is Aykroyd's daughter, in her film debut). One-joke premise is a decade late and a dime short, though cast of comedy all-stars provides a lift. **86m/C; VHS, DVD.** Dan Aykroyd; Jane Curtin; Laraine Newman; Jason Alexander; Michelle Rene Thomas; Chris Farley; Michael Richards; Lisa Jane Persky; Sinbad; Shishir Kurup; Michael McKean; Phil Hartman; David Spade; Dave Thomas; Jan Hooks; Chris Rock; Adam Sandler; Julia Sweeney; Danielle Aykroyd; ***D:*** Steven Barron; ***W:*** Dan Aykroyd; Tom Davis; Bonnie Turner; Terry Turner; ***C:*** Francis Kenny; ***M:*** David Newman.

Coney Island 🦴🦴🦴 **1943** Delightful Technicolor musical stars Grable as flashy Coney Island singer Kate Farley who's working for Joe Rocco (Romero). Rocco's friendly rival, Eddie Johnson (Montgomery), thinks Kate can be classed-up and turned into a Broadway star, which happens amidst various romantic misunderstandings. **93m/C; DVD, Blu-Ray.** Betty Grable; George Montgomery; Cesar Romero; Phil Silvers; Charles Winninger; Matt Briggs; ***D:*** Walter Lang; ***W:*** George Seaton; ***C:*** Ernest Palmer; ***M:*** Alfred Newman.

Confess 🦴🦴 **2005 (R)** Former hacker Terell (Byrd) is ticked off when the surveillance technology he developed is stolen, so he takes compromising footage (via spycams) of those who slighted him and puts it on the Internet. Then Terrell decides to go big-time and he and accomplice Olivia (Larter) start targeting CEOs, politicians, and others of the power elite. He becomes a front-page anti-hero but the feds are calling Terrell a cyber-terrorist and want him brought to justice. Terrell's got bigger problems when imitators take his idea to a violent extreme. **87m/C; DVD.** Eugene Byrd; Ali Larter; William Sadler; Melissa Leo; Glenn Fitzgerald; ***D:*** Stefan C. Schaefer; ***W:*** Stefan C. Schaefer; ***C:*** Leland Krane; ***M:*** Scott Jacoby. **VIDEO**

The Confession 🦴🦴 **1/2 1920** A priest hears a killer's confession and must protect the sanctity of the confessional, even as his own brother is being convicted of the murder. When Father Bartlett's brother Tom escapes from prison, he tries to persuade the killer to finally do the right thing. **78m/B; Silent; DVD.** Henry B. Walthall; Francis McDonald; William H. Clifford; Margaret McWade; Margaret Landis; ***D:*** Bertram Bracken; ***W:*** Franklin Hall; ***C:*** Walter L. Griffin.

The Confession 🦴🦴 **1/2 1998 (R)** Slick lawyer Roy Bleakie (Baldwin) suffers a crisis of conscience with his latest case—the one he expects will hand him the District Attorney's office. Harry Fertig (Kingsley) has killed the three people he regards as responsible for the death of his young son. He's confessed to the crime and wants to plead guilty and accept responsiblity—for his own ambitions Roy wants Harry to plead temporary insanity. But it turns out there's more to the case than even Roy knows. Good performances in what could be just another courtroom melodrama. **114m/C; VHS, DVD.** Alec Baldwin; Ben Kingsley; Amy Irving; Jay O. Sanders; Kevin Conway; Anne Twomey; Christopher Lawford; Boyd Gaines; Chris Noth; ***D:*** David Hugh Jones; ***W:*** David Black; ***C:*** Mike Fash; ***M:*** Mychael Danna.

The Confessional 🦴 *House of Mortal Sin* **1975 (R)** A mad priest unleashes a monster from his confessional to wreak havoc upon the world. Pray for your VCR. **108m/C; VHS, DVD, Blu-Ray.** *GB* Anthony Sharp; Susan Penhaligon; Stephanie Beacham; Norman Eshley; Sheila Keith; ***D:*** Pete Walker.

Confessions of a Dangerous Mind 🦴🦴 **1/2 2002 (R)** Clooney makes his directorial debut in this uneven but ultimately enjoyable biopic of TV game show producer Chuck Barris (Rockwell), who claimed in his "unauthorized" biography to be a CIA assassin during the height of his success. Clooney sometimes gets a little self-consciously "arty," but doesn't go overboard, and it actually fits with the absurdist tone of Kaufman's script. It's Rockwell who stands out here, with a breakout performance that showcases his range. **113m/C; VHS, DVD, Blu-Ray.** Sam Rockwell; Drew Barrymore; Rutger Hauer; George Clooney; Julia Roberts; Maggie Gyllenhaal; Kristen Wilson; Jennifer Hall; Michael Cera; Michael Ensign; Richard Kind; ***Cameo(s):*** Chuck Barris; Brad Pitt; Matt Damon; Jaye P. Morgan; ***D:*** George Clooney; ***W:*** Charlie Kaufman; ***C:*** Newton Thomas (Tom) Sigel; ***M:*** Alex Wurman. Natl. Bd. of Review '02: Screenplay.

Confessions of a Driving Instructor 🦴 **1/2 1976** The third in the low-brow, bawdy Brit comedy series finds Tim and brother-in-law Sid involved in yet another money-making scheme when they buy a failing driving school. However, most of the female students seem more interested in back seat romps and the usual misadventures ensue. **90m/C; DVD.** *UK* Robin Askwith; Anthony Booth; Sheila White; Bill Maynard; Doris Hare; Liz Fraser; Irene Handl; Windsor Davies; ***D:*** Norman Cohen; ***W:*** Christopher Wood; ***C:*** Ken Hodges; ***M:*** Ed Welch.

Confessions of a Nazi Spy 🦴🦴 **1939** Propaganda film from Warner Bros. based on the 1937 trials of several German-American Nazi sympathizers who were arrested for espionage. British intelligence uncovers a Nazi spy network that extends into New York and informs the FBI, who send agent Ed Renard (Robinson) to ferret out its members. Actual newsreel footage is included, which enhances director Litvak's semi-documentary film style. **89m/B; DVD.** Edward G. Robinson; Francis Lederer; George Sanders; Paul Lukas; Dorothy Tree; Lya Lys; Joseph (Joe) Sawyer; Henry O'Neill; ***D:*** Anatole Litvak; ***W:*** John Wexley; Milton Krims; ***C:*** Sol Polito; ***M:*** Max Steiner.

Confessions of a Pit Fighter 🦴 **1/2 2005 (R)** Ex-con Eddie is struggling to go straight but then his younger brother is murdered during a bout at an illegal fight club and Eddie wants revenge. **99m/C; DVD.** Armand Assante; James Russo; John Savage; Hector Echavarria; Flavor Flav; Richard Medina, Jr.; Quinton 'Rampage' Jackson; ***D:*** Art Camacho; ***W:*** Art Camacho; R. Ellis Frazier; ***C:*** Curtis Petersen; ***M:*** Geoff Levin; Ricardo Veiga. **VIDEO**

Confessions of a Police Captain 🦴🦴 **1972 (PG)** A dedicated police captain tries to wipe out the bureaucratic corruption that is infecting his city. Balsam gives a fine performance in a heavy-going tale. **104m/C; VHS, DVD.** *IT* Martin Balsam; Franco Nero; Marilu Tolo; ***D:*** Damiano Damiani; ***W:*** Damiano Damiani; Salvatore Laurani; ***C:*** Claudio Ragona; ***M:*** Riz Ortolani.

Confessions of a Shopaholic 🦴🦴 **2009 (PG)** Spendthrift, debt-ridden fashionista New Yorker Rebecca Bloomwood (Fisher) ironically becomes a celebrity after getting a job as the advice columnist for a new financial magazine. But her intemperate ways threaten both her new career and new romance. It doesn't bode well for a pic to be on the losing end of a comparison to *Sex and the City*, but that about sums up this popcorn puff piece. A mindless chick-flick that banks on unbridled, inconspicuous spending as humor would be a tough sell on a good day but during a recession it's downright insulting. Fisher is easy on the eyes but everything else is utterly painful. Based on the chick lit series by Sophie Kinsella. **104m/C; Blu-Ray.** Isla Fisher; Hugh Dancy; Krysten Ritter; Joan Cusack; John Goodman; Kristin Scott Thomas; Leslie Bibb; Lynn Redgrave; Julie Hagerty; Wendie Malick; Clea Lewis; Christine Ebersole; John Lithgow; Fred Armisen; Robert Stanton; ***D:*** P.J. Hogan; ***W:*** Tim Firth; Tracey Jackson; Kayla Alpert; ***C:*** Jo Willems; ***M:*** James Newton Howard.

Confessions of a Sociopathic Social Climber 🦴🦴 **2005 (R)** Katya Livingston (Hewitt) is a bad girl—a bitchy, self-serving but successful ad exec who is desperate to be invited to the San Francisco social event of the year. Unfortunately for her, Katya previously insulted the hostess. But that won't stop her angling for an invite, even if it causes problems for her dreamboat beau, Charles (Ferguson). **85m/C; DVD.** Jennifer Love Hewitt; Colin Ferguson; Natassia Malthe; Daniel Roebuck; Joseph Lawrence; James Kirk; ***D:*** Dana Lustig; ***W:*** Eric Charmelo; Nicole Snyder; ***C:*** Luc Montpellier; ***M:*** Phil Marshall. **CABLE**

Confessions of a Teenage Drama Queen **2004 (PG)** Hip 15-year-old Lola (Lohan)--who decides her real name, Mary, isn't cool enough—is totally bumming when her divorced mom (Headly) grows weary of Manhattan's big city lifestyle and banishes her to a quaint New Jersey suburb. To make matters worse she is snubbed by the popular set at her new high school and decides to take action, which includes vying against ultra-popular Carla (Fox) for the lead in the school play. Along the way there's ample opportunity to witness the self-absorbed, shallow, and materialistic behaviors that drown out any positive messages for the 'tweener target group. Mediocre Disney production is based on Dyan Sheldon's successful book. **89m/C; VHS, DVD.** Lindsay Lohan; Adam Garcia; Glenne Headly; Alison Pill; Carol Kane; Eli Marienthal; Sheila McCarthy; Tom McCamus; Megan Fox; Richard Fitzpatrick; ***D:*** Sara Sugarman; ***W:*** Gail Parent; ***C:*** Stephen Burum; ***M:*** Mark Mothersbaugh.

Confessions of a Vice Baron **1942** Vice Baron Lombardo makes it big as a drug dealer and flesh peddler, then loses it all when he falls in love. Sleazy exploitation. **70m/B; VHS, DVD.** Willy Castello; ***D:*** John Melville.

Confessions of a Window Cleaner ½ **1974** Low-brow Brit sex comedy. Naïve Tim goes to work for his lazy brother-in-law, Sid, as a window washer and discovers some of his female customers expect more than a clean shine. He gets involved in some sexual shenanigans while unexpectedly proposing to his girlfriend Liz, although their wedding day (and night) doesn't turn out as expected. **90m/C; DVD.** *UK* Robin Askwith; Anthony Booth; Linda Hayden; Sheila White; Dandy Nichols; Bill Maynard; John Le Mesurier; Joan Hickson; ***D:*** Val Guest; ***W:*** Val Guest; Christopher Wood; ***C:*** Norman Warwick; ***M:*** Sam Sklair.

Confessions of an American Bride ½ **2005** Ad exec Samantha finally finds the perfect fiance in Ben. Sam also wants the perfect wedding but various problems immediately arise—they're different religions, they have family problems, and a work promotion is taking up all Sam's energy. Tied into work is her new client, Luke, who happens to be her (still tempting) college crush. With Sam's neuroses getting the best of her, Ben may just call the whole thing off. **90m/C; DVD.** Shannon Elizabeth; Eddie McClintock; Geoff Stults; Alan Van Sprang; Carolyn Scott; Mark Melymick; Chris Gillett; Roz Michaels; ***D:*** Douglas Barr; ***W:*** Edward Kitsis; Adam Horowitz; ***C:*** Peter Benison; ***M:*** Eric Allaman. **CABLE**

Confessions of an Opium Eater *Souls for Sale* **1962** Cheap, enjoyable exploitation complete with opium-induced hallucinations. Mercenary Gilbert De Quincey (Price) returns to San Francisco and gets caught up in a Tong war in Chinatown. He tries to break up a human trafficking ring where the women are auctioned for opium. **85m/B; DVD.** Vincent Price; Philip Ahn; Linda Ho; Richard Loo; June Kyoto Lu; ***D:*** Albert Zugsmith; ***W:*** Robert Hill; ***C:*** Joseph Biroc; ***M:*** Albert Glasser.

Confessions of Sorority Girls ½ **1994 (PG-13)** Sometime in the early '60s, wicked Sabrina (Luner) shows up at college and takes it by storm. Will she steal Rita's (Milano) beau? That's the least of her schemes. The villainy is played strictly for campy laughs and the film is never as trashy as its title suggests. Originally made as part of Showtime's "Rebel Highway" series and a remake of Roger Corman's 1957 "Sorority Girl." **83m/C; VHS, DVD.** Jamie Luner; Alyssa Milano; Bette Rae; Brian Bloom; Natalija Nogulich; ***D:*** Uli Edel; ***C:*** Jean De Segonzac. **CABLE**

The Confessor ½ *The Good Shepherd* **2004 (PG-13)** Worldly Father Daniel Clemens (Slater) is shocked when a parish priest (Flores) is arrested for the murder of a young street hustler and apparently commits suicide in jail. Clemens is convinced the priest was innocent and sets out to find out whodunit with the aid of journalist (and ex-flame) Madeline (Parker). Predictable story with huge plot holes. **90m/C; DVD.** *CA* Christian Slater; Molly Parker; Stephen Rea; Gordon Pinsent; Von Flores; Nancy Beatty; ***D:*** Lewin Webb; ***W:*** Brad Mirman; ***C:*** Curtis Petersen; ***M:*** Gary Koftinoff. **VIDEO**

Confetti **2006 (R)** Over the top Brit romantic comedy about three would-be weddings. Bridal magazine Confetti is sponsoring a contest for the year's most original wedding. The three finalists are: competitive yuppies Josef (Mangan) and Isabelle (MacNeill) who choose a tennis theme; Matt (Freeman) and Sam (Stevenson) who want a musical extravaganza, though neither of them can sing or dance; and nudists Michael (Webb) and Joanna (Colman) who want a clothes-free ceremony, to the consternation of Confetti editor Vivien (Montagu). Meltdowns occur as the big finale approaches for one overwhelmed couple. **100m/C; DVD.** *GB* Martin Freeman; Jessica Stevenson; Robert Webb; Stephen Mangan; Meredith MacNeill; Olivia Colman; Marc Wootton; Vincent Franklin; Jason Watkins; ***D:*** Debbie Isitt; ***C:*** Dewald Aukema; ***M:*** Paul Englishby.

The Confidant ½ **2010** College football star Nigel is going to sign a big pro contract when a fight leads to an accidental death. Somehow Nigel persuades childhood friend Daniel to take the rap and go to prison. Daniel expects to be compensated on his release but Nigel is now an ex-player with a gambling addiction who doesn't want the truth revealed. **90m/C; DVD.** Boris Kodjoe; David Banner; Kenya Moore; Billy Zane; Richard Roundtree; Bai Ling; ***D:*** Alton Glass; ***W:*** Alton Glass; ***C:*** Matt Steinauer; ***M:*** Kurt Oldman. **VIDEO**

Confidence ½ **2003 (R)** That would be "confidence" as in manner and game. Jake Vig (Burns) and his cronies are smalltime con artists who scam the wrong man—an accountant for L.A. crime boss King (Hoffman). To forestall any further unpleasantness, Jake goes to King and agrees to repayment by performing an elaborate con on King's rival. Let's just say that there's always another scam and things are hardly ever what they seem. Hoffman, with king-sized tics and quirks, veers into territory usually reserved for Walken or Pacino, but at least he's having fun. The movie could use a little more of that. Gritty and dark at times, this one's still an enjoyable entry in the scam/heist genre. **98m/C; VHS, DVD.** Edward Burns; Dustin Hoffman; Rachel Weisz; Andy Garcia; Paul Giamatti; Donal Logue; Luis Guzman; Brian Van Holt; Franky G.; Morris Chestnut; Robert Forster; Leland Orser; Louis Lombardi; Tommy (Tiny) Lister; John Carroll Lynch; ***D:*** James Foley; ***W:*** Doug Jung; ***C:*** Juan Ruiz-Anchia.

Confidential Agent ½ **1945** Gloomy, muddled espionage story adapted from a Graham Greene thriller. Luis Denard (Boyer) is working as an agent for the Loyalist cause during the Spanish Civil War. He's sent to London to negotiate for coal supplies and to prevent Fascist Licata (Francen) from getting the contract instead. Denard is aided by sympathetic socialite Rose (Bacall in her second film) but must protect himself from various (and murderous) Fascist villains. **118m/B; DVD.** Charles Boyer; Lauren Bacall; Victor Francen; Katina Paxinou; Peter Lorre; George Coulouris; John Warburton; Holmes Herbert; ***D:*** Herman Shumlin; ***W:*** Robert Buckner; ***C:*** James Wong Howe; ***M:*** Franz Waxman.

Confidentially Connie ½ **1953** A dated comedy that revolves around meat. Pregnant housewife Connie Bedloe (Leigh) craves steak but they can't afford meat on her husband Joe's (Johnson) meager salary as a college professor in Maine. Joe's Texas cattle rancher dad Opie (Calhern) visits and comes up with a scheme involving the local butcher (Slezak) to get Joe to leave academia and take over the family business. **72m/B; DVD.** Janet Leigh; Van Johnson; Louis Calhern; Walter Slezak; Gene Lockhart; Kathleen Lockhart; ***D:*** Edward Buzzell; ***W:*** Max Shulman; ***C:*** Harold Lipstein; ***M:*** David Rose.

Confidentially Yours *Vivement Dimanche!; Finally, Sunday* **1983 (PG)** Truffaut's homage to Hitchcock, based on Charles Williams' "The Long Saturday Night." A hapless small-town real estate agent is framed for a rash of murders and his secretary, who is secretly in love with him, tries to clear his name. Truffaut's last film is stylish and entertaining. In French with English subtitles. **110m/B; VHS, DVD.** *FR* Fanny Ardant; Jean-Louis Trintignant; Philippe Morier-Genoud; Philippe Laudenbach; Caroline Sihol; ***D:*** Francois Truffaut; ***W:*** Francois Truffaut; Suzanne Schiffman; Jean Aurel; ***C:*** Nestor Almendros; ***M:*** Georges Delerue.

Confined ½ **2010** Victoria (Caulfield) and Michael (Elliott) Peyton move from the city to the 'burbs with their daughter Eva (Papalia) after Victoria suffers an apparent mental breakdown. With nothing to do but watch the neighbors, Victoria becomes convinced that next-door neighbor Fritz (Hogan) is actually holding a girl captive in his basement. **90m/C; DVD.** Emma Caulfield; David James Elliot; Michael Hogan; Karen Austin; Erica Carroll; Paul McGillion; Melanie Papalia; ***D:*** Andrew C. Erin; ***W:*** Kraig Wenman; ***C:*** Mahlon Todd Williams; ***M:*** Kevin Blumenfeld. **CABLE**

Confirm or Deny **1941** American foreign correspondent Mitch Mitchell (Ameche) is in London covering the blitz but teletype operator, Jennifer Carson (Bennett), works for the Ministry of Information and has to make certain Mitch doesn't send out anything inappropriate. Mitch's frustrated by the censorship but grows to like Jennifer just fine. **73m/B; DVD.** Don Ameche; Joan Bennett; Roddy McDowall; John Loder; Raymond Walburn; Eric Blore; ***D:*** Archie Mayo; ***W:*** Jo Swerling; ***C:*** Leon Shamroy.

The Confirmation ½ **2016 (PG-13)** A comedy about the unexpected connections found between a father and son. When Bonnie (Bello) and her new husband Kyle (Modine) go out of town for the weekend, eight-year-old Anthony (Lieberher) spends the time with his father Walt (Owens). Walt is an alcoholic but a a talented carpenter, and is unsure about taking care of his son. Despite a rocky start—which includes a stolen tool box, a broken down truck, and being locked out of his house—Walt and Anthony bond as they work through each challenge and find compassion and hope in each other. **101m/C; DVD, Blu-Ray, Streaming, Download.** Clive Owen; Jaeden Lieberher; Maria Bello; Patton Oswalt; Matthew Modine; ***D:*** Bob Nelson; ***W:*** Bob Nelson; ***C:*** Terry Stacey; ***M:*** Jeff Cardoni.

Conflict **1945** Bogart falls for his sister-in-law and asks his wife for a divorce. She refuses, he plots her murder, and thinks up the alibi. When the police fail to notify him of her death, Bogart is forced to report his wife missing. But is she dead? Her guilty husband smells her perfume, sees her walking down the street, and discovers the body is missing from the scene of the crime. Suspenseful thriller also features Greenstreet as a psychologist/family friend who suspects Bogart knows more than he's telling. **86m/B; DVD.** Humphrey Bogart; Alexis Smith; Sydney Greenstreet; Rose Hobart; Charles Drake; Grant Mitchell; ***D:*** Curtis Bernhardt.

Conflict of Interest ½ **1992 (R)** Gideon (Nelson) is a thug who runs stolen cars, drugs, and women from his heavy-metal club on the wrong side of town. Mickey Flannery (McDonald) is the new cop determined to get Gideon behind bars, especially after Gideon kills Mickey's wife, sets up his son on a phony murder rap, and kidnaps his son's girlfriend. Now it's personal and Mickey will stop at nothing to get his revenge. Over-the-top performance by Nelson will have the viewer hoping he gets it soon and puts the film out of its misery. **88m/C; VHS, Streaming.** Judd Nelson; Christopher McDonald; Alyssa Milano; Dey Young; Gregory Alan Harris; ***D:*** Gary Davis; ***W:*** Gregory Miller; Michael Angeli; ***C:*** Bryan England.

The Conformist *Il Conformista* **1971 (R)** Character study of young Italian fascist, plagued by homosexual feelings, who must prove his loyalty by killing his old professor. Decadent and engrossing story is brilliantly acted. Based on the novel by Alberto Moravia. **108m/C; VHS, DVD, Blu-Ray.** *IT FR GE* Jean-Louis Trintignant; Stefania Sandrelli; Dominique Sanda; Pierre Clementi; Gastone Moschin; Pasquale Fortunato; ***D:*** Bernardo Bertolucci; ***W:*** Bernardo Bertolucci; ***C:*** Vittorio Storaro; ***M:*** Georges Delerue. Natl. Soc. Film Critics '71: Cinematog. (Storaro), Director (Bertolucci).

Confusion of Genders *La Confusion des Genres* **2000** Bisexual fortyish lawyer Alain (Greggory) wallows in various sexual relationships without committing emotionally to anyone in this provocative but ultimately tiresome farce, whose characters are all slick surface. The narcissist has a vague interest in having a family and has reluctantly agreed to marry longtime law partner Laurence (Richard), who is pregnant by him. Meanwhile, there's the lustful teenage brother, Christophe (Thouvenin), of one of Alain's ex-girlfriends and Alain's own interest in one of his incarcerated clients, Marc (Martinez). Marc is willing to trade sex with Alain for a jailhouse meeting with his girlfriend Babette (Gayet), whom Alain also gets involved with. And so it continues. French with subtitles. **94m/C; DVD.** *FR* Pascal Greggory; Nathalie Richard; Julie Gayet; Vincent Martinez; Cyrille Thouvenin; Alain Bashung; ***D:*** Ilan Duran Cohen; ***W:*** Ilan Duran Cohen; Philippe Lasry; ***C:*** Jeanne Lapoirie; ***M:*** Jay-Jay Johanson.

Congo **1995 (PG-13)** Communications company supervisor jets off to the African jungle along with a primatologist to search for a lost city's priceless diamonds, and to return Amy, a gorilla who communicates with sign language to her natural habitat. Why she would want to return to volcanoes and bloodthirsty mutant gray gorillas is anybody's guess. This appropriately technology-laden adaptation of Michael Crichton's novel delivers all the cliches of the old B-movie jungle flicks, but none of the thrills or fun of other Crichton adaptations. **109m/C; VHS, DVD, Blu-Ray.** Dylan Walsh; Laura Linney; Ernie Hudson; Mary Ellen Trainor; Tim Curry; Grant Heslov; Joe Don Baker; ***D:*** Frank Marshall; ***W:*** John Patrick Shanley; ***C:*** Allen Daviau; ***M:*** Jerry Goldsmith.

Congo Maisie ½ **1940** Maisie (Sothern) stows away on a steamer to escape a hotel bill and ends up in West Africa. She gets work at a hospital on a rubber plantation, flirts with Dr. Michael Shane (Carroll), and saves everyone from a native attack. Adapted from Wilson Collison's novel "Congo Landing." Second in the MGM series. **70m/B; DVD.** Ann Sothern; John Carroll; Rita Johnson; Shepperd Strudwick; J.M. Kerrigan; E.E. Clive; ***D:*** H.C. Potter; ***W:*** Mary C. McCall; ***C:*** Charles Lawton, Jr.; ***M:*** Edward Ward.

Congratulations ½ **2013** Jim (Dietzen) has his marriage proposal rejected by girlfriend Bridget (Miller) as they're driving to see his recently widowed mom, Nancy (Rupp). Too bad Jim had already spoken about his plans and his mom is thrilled about the 'engagement.' Being a decent sort, Bridget agrees to pretend for the weekend but the lie quickly falls apart as Jim and Bridget discover they aren't at the same place in their romance. **95m/C; Streaming.** Brian Dietzen; Abby Miller; Debra Jo Rupp; Kevin Rankin; ***D:*** Juan Cardarelli; Eric M. Levy; ***W:*** Brian Dietzen; Abby Miller; Juan Cardarelli; Eric M. Levy; ***C:*** Matt Garrett; ***M:*** Kim Carroll.

A Congregation of Ghosts ½ **2009** In 1931, eccentric Rev. Frederick Densham (Woodward's last role) is assigned to a rural parish in Cornwall, England. A former missionary in India, Densham alienates his conservative congregation and is ostracized. Even after his death, the community denies his last wish to be buried in the churchyard. When the abandoned rectory is bought in 1967, the Baxters come to believe that the reverend's ghost haunts the premises. Based on a true story. **93m/C; DVD.** *UK* Edward Woodward; Nicholas Gleaves; Susannah Doyle; Natasha Little; ***D:*** Mark Collicott; ***W:*** Mark Collicott; ***C:*** Ray Coates; ***M:*** Luke Phillips.

The Congress ½ **2013** A live-action/animation hybrid about identity, celebrity, and the way we allow our pop culture to define us. In the not-too-distant future, Hollywood won't need actors or actresses, as technology allows them to recreate the likeness of whomever they choose. So Robin Wright, playing a thinly-veiled version of herself, signs away the rights to "Robin Wright." Then director/writer Folman jumps to the future, offering an animated vision of a universe in which everything we are, watch, and want blends into one twisted landscape. The first half is stronger, but the second half is remarkably ambitious. **122m/C; DVD, Blu-Ray.** *IS* Robin Wright; Danny Huston; Harvey Keitel; Kodi Smit-McPhee; Paul Giamatti; *V:* Jon Hamm; *D:* Ari Folman; *W:* Ari Folman; *C:* Michael Englert; *M:* Max Richter.

The Congressman 1/2 **2016 (R)** A political drama about a congressman trying to overcome a set of difficult circumstances. Though Charlie Winship (Williams) is proud to represent Maine in the House of the Representatives, he has created a set of challenging circumstances for himself. Video has caught him failing to stand and take part in the pledge of allegiance, and he has knocked out a fellow member of the House. Not only is he criticized in the media, he is forced to confront his angry ex-wife. Despite his life spiraling out of control, he takes a meaningful journey to a remote island in the Atlantic to investigate the battle between the residents over fishing rights. Through this experience and seeing a very different way of life, Charlie is reminded who he truly serves. **98m/C; DVD, Streaming, Download.** Treat Williams; Elizabeth Marvel; Ryan Merriman; Chris Conroy; George Hamilton; *D:* Jared Martin; Robert Mrazek; *W:* Robert Mrazek; *C:* Joe Arcidiacono; *M:* David Carbonara.

Conjurer 1/2 **2008 (PG-13)** Shawn (Bowen) and his wife Helen (Bahns) move into her brother Frank's (Schneider) old farmhouse after suffering a tragedy. Helen feels at home but Shawn is uneasy, especially when he's around an old cabin on the property that has a nasty legend about a conjurer (witch) and a curse. Shawn becomes convinced that the place is haunted and ghosts are out to destroy his family but it may be all in his troubled mind. **88m/C; DVD.** Andrew Bowen; Maxine Bahns; John Schneider; Tom Nowicki; Brett Rice; *D:* Clint Hutchison; *W:* Clint Hutchison; *C:* Ken Blakey; *M:* Dana Niu. **VIDEO**

The Conjuring **2013 (R)** Hit horror director Wan goes old school with this ghost tale based, as almost all of them claim to be, on a true story. It is 1971 when Carolyn (Taylor) and Roger Perron (Livingston) move into a dilapidated old farmhouse and discover they're not its only residents. When husband and wife poltergeist investigators Ed (Wilson) and Lorraine Warren (Farmiga) are brought in for an exorcism, they learn the true depth of the haunting at the Perron home. Old-school scares dominate the action here, leading to a scary film that feels both nostalgic to ghost stories yet completely fresh. **112m/C; DVD, Blu-Ray.** Lili Taylor; Ron Livingston; Vera Farmiga; Patrick Wilson; Joey King; *D:* James Wan; *W:* Carey Hayes; Chad Hayes; *C:* John R. Leonetti; *M:* Joseph Bishara.

The Conjuring 2 1/2 **2016 (R)** Sequel to the 2013 horror hit. In the late '70s, a poor family on the outskirts of London was traumatized by a haunting, especially in the manner in which it took over one of the family's young girls. Notorious ghost hunters Ed and Lorraine Warren (Wilson & Farmiga) travel to England to either debunk the haunting as a hoax or save a family from demonic possession. Director Wan's dynamic filmmaking overcomes some relative storytelling weakness and a bloated running time. **134m/C; DVD, Blu-Ray.** Patrick Wilson; Vera Farmiga; Madison Wolfe; Frances O'Connor; Lauren Esposito; *D:* James Wan; *W:* James Wan; Carey Hayes; Chad Hayes; David Leslie Johnson; *C:* Don Burgess; *M:* Joseph Bishara.

A Connecticut Yankee in King Arthur's Court 1/2 *A Yankee in King Arthur's Court* **1949** A pleasant version of the famous Mark Twain story about a 20th century man transported to Camelot and mistaken for a dangerous wizard. This was the third film version of the classic, which was later remade as "Unidentified Flying Oddball," a TV movie, and an animated feature. **108m/C; VHS, DVD.** Bing Crosby; Rhonda Fleming; William Bendix; Cedric Hardwicke; Henry Wilcoxon; Murvyn Vye; Virginia Field; *D:* Tay Garnett; *C:* Ray Rennahan.

The Connection 1/2 **1961** The Living Theatre's ground-breaking performance of Jack Gelber's play about heroin addicts waiting for their connection to arrive, while a documentary filmmaker hovers nearby with his camera. **105m/B; VHS, DVD, Blu-Ray.** Warren Finnerty; Carl Lee; William Redfield; Roscoe Lee Browne; Garry Goodrow; James Anderson; Jackie McLean; *D:* Shirley Clarke.

The Connection 1/2 *La French* **2015 (R)** Based on real events, The Connection explores the criminal activity depicted in The French Connection (1971) from the European perspective. Magistrate Pierre Michel (Dujardin) goes to extraordinary lengths to destroy the French Connection, the biggest drug smuggling ring in France, risking his career and family in the process. It's a little long, but the action is tight, the cinematography is gorgeous, and the period recreation pops. French with subtitles. **135m/C; DVD.** Jean Dujardin; Gilles Lellouche; Celine Sallette; Melanie Doutey; Benoît Magimel; *D:* Cedric Jimenez; *W:* Cedric Jimenez; Audrey Diwan; *C:* Laurent Tangy; *M:* Guillaume Roussel.

Connie and Carla 1/2 **2004 (PG-13)** "Victor/Victoria" meets "Some Like it Hot" in this train wreck. Writer Vardalos and Colette are Connie and Carla, who have been a singing team since childhood and who perform medleys in an airport lounge where, despite being has-beens that never were, the two still dream of stardom. In an unlikely turn of events, the two witness a mob hit and are forced to go on the lam to L.A., where they pretend to be female impersonators. The girls pretending to be boys pretending to be girls act is a surprise hit, allowing minor celebrity and close calls with the mob to ensue. Duchovney is the inferior sub-plot love interest who adds nothing to this unfunny, forced comedy filled with extremely cliched, stereotypical gay humor. **98m/C; DVD.** Nia Vardalos; Toni Collette; David Duchovny; Stephen Spinella; Ian Gomez; Nick Sandow; Dash Mihok; Robert John Burke; Alec Mapa; Chris(topher) Logan; Robert Kaiser; Boris McGiver; Babz Chula; Linda Darlow; ***Cameo(s):*** Debbie Reynolds; *D:* Michael Lembeck; *W:* Nia Vardalos; *C:* Richard Greatrex; *M:* Randy Edelman.

Connor's War 1/2 **2006 (R)** After CIA special agent Connors (Treach) is blinded during a mission, he asks hot doctor Amanda (Peeples) to help him out while he takes down his former boss, Brooks (Mankuma), who's gone rogue. Treach does well in this routine actioner. **90m/C; DVD.** Treach; Nia Peeples; Blu Mankuma; *D:* Nick Castle; *W:* D. Kyle Johnson; *C:* Suki Medencevic. **VIDEO**

The Conqueror WOOF! *Conqueror of the Desert* **1956** Wayne in pointed helmet and goatee is convincingly miscast as Genghis Khan in this woeful tale of the warlord's early life and involvement with the kidnapped daughter of a powerful enemy. Rife with stilted, unintentionally funny dialogue, Oriental western was very expensive to make (with backing by Howard Hughes), and is now listed in the "Fifty Worst Films of All Time." No matter; it's surreal enough to enable viewer to approximate an out-of-body experience. Even those on the set suffered; filming took place near a nuclear test site in Utah and many members of the cast and crew eventually developed cancer. **111m/C; DVD.** John Wayne; Susan Hayward; William Conrad; Agnes Moorehead; Lee Van Cleef; Pedro Armendariz, Sr.; Thomas Gomez; John Hoyt; Ted de Corsia; Leslie Bradley; *D:* Dick Powell; *W:* Oscar Millard; *C:* Joseph LaShelle; William E. Snyder; Leo Tover; Harry Wild; *M:* Victor Young.

The Conqueror Worm *Witchfinder General; Edgar Allan Poe's Conqueror Worm* **1968** Price turns in a fine performance portraying the sinister Matthew Hopkins, a real-life 17th-century witchhunter. No "ham" in this low-budget, underrated thriller, based on Ronald Bassett's novel. The last of three films from director Reeves, who died from an accidental overdose in 1969. **95m/C; VHS, DVD, Blu-Ray.** *GB* Vincent Price; Ian Ogilvy; Hilary Dwyer; Rupert Davies; Robert Russell; Patrick Wymark; Wilfrid Brambell; Nicky Henson; Bernard Kay; Tony Selby; *D:* Michael Reeves; *W:* Michael Reeves; Louis M. Heyward; Tom Baker; *C:* John Coquillon; *M:* Paul Ferris.

The Conquerors **1932** Obvious, though well-done, story intended to show that perseverance can overcome any obstacle (including the Depression). The Standish family leaves New York after the financial collapse of 1873 and eventually makes their home in Fort Allen, Nebraska. Roger (Dix) opens a bank and establishes a banking dynasty over the next 55 years while enduring both prosperity and hard times. **84m/B; DVD.** Richard Dix; Ann Harding; Edna May Oliver; Guy Kibbee; Julie Haydon; Donald Cook; *D:* William A. Wellman; *W:* Robert Lord; *C:* Edward Cronajer; *M:* Max Steiner.

Conquest *Marie Walewska* **1937** Garbo, as the Polish countess Marie Walewska, tries to persuade Napoleon (Boyer) to free her native Poland from the Russian Tsar. Garbo, Boyer, and Ouspenskaya are outstanding, while the beautiful costumes and lavish production help, but the script is occasionally weak. A boxoffice flop in the U.S., which ended up costing MGM more than any movie it had made up until that time. **115m/B; VHS, DVD.** Greta Garbo; Charles Boyer; Reginald Owen; Alan Marshal; Henry Stephenson; Leif Erickson; May Whitty; Maria Ouspenskaya; Vladimir Sokoloff; Scotty Beckett; *D:* Clarence Brown; *C:* Karl Freund.

Conquest 1/2 **1983 (R)** Sword and sorcery tale of two mighty warriors against an evil sorceress who seeks world domination. Excellent score. **92m/C; VHS, DVD, Blu-Ray.** *IT SP MX* Jorge (George) Rivero; Andrea Occhipinti; Violeta Cela; Sabrina Siani; *D:* Lucio Fulci; *M:* Claudio Simonetti.

Conquest of Cochise **1953** Mediocre oater about a cavalry officer who must stop the war between the Apache and Comanche tribes and a group of Mexicans in the Southwest of the 1850s. **70m/C; VHS, DVD.** John Hodiak; Robert Stack; Joy Page; *D:* William Castle.

Conquest of Mycene 1/2 *Ercole Contro Molock; Hercules vs. the Moloch* **1963** The Prince of Mycene (who becomes Hercules thanks to dubbing) battles evil queen Neri and her equally evil son, Moloch. Typical muscleman fodder. **102m/C; VHS, DVD.** *IT FR* Gordon Scott; Rosalba Neri; Jany Clair; Alessandra Panaro; Michel Lemoine; *D:* Giorgio Ferroni; *W:* Giorgio Ferroni; Remigio del Grosso; *C:* Augusto Tiezzi; *M:* Carlo Rustichelli.

Conquest of Space 1/2 **1955** A spaceship sets off to explore Mars in spite of the commander's attempts to sabotage the voyage. He believes the flight is an heretical attempt to reach God. An uneasy mixture of religion and space exploration detracts from the nifty special effects which are the only reason to watch. **81m/C; VHS, DVD.** Walter Brooke; Eric Fleming; Mickey Shaughnessy; Phil Foster; William Redfield; William Hopper; Benson Fong; Ross Martin; *D:* Byron Haskin; *C:* Lionel Lindon.

Conquest of the Normans *Normanni, I; Attack of the Normans* **1962** During the Norman invasion of England, Oliver is accused of kidnapping the King. To save his life, Oliver must find the true identity of the abductors. With so much plot, there should have been some suspense. **83m/C; VHS, DVD.** *IT* Cameron Mitchell; *D:* Giuseppe Vari; *W:* Nino Stresa.

Conquest of the Planet of the Apes 1/2 **1972 (PG)** The apes turn the tables on the human Earth population when they lead a revolt against their cruel masters in the distant year of 1990. Sure, there's plenty of cliches—but the story drags you along. The 4th film in the series. Followed by "Battle for the Planet of the Apes." **87m/C; VHS, DVD, Blu-Ray.** Roddy McDowall; Don Murray; Ricardo Montalban; Natalie Trundy; Severn Darden; Hari Rhodes; Asa Maynor; Gordon Jump; John Randolph; H.M. Wynant; Lou Wagner; *D:* J. Lee Thompson; *W:* Paul Dehn; *C:* Bruce Surtees; *M:* Tom Scott.

The Conrad Boys **2006** After his mother dies, 19-year-old Charlie Conrad (Lo) must put off his own plans in order to care for his young brother Ben (Stewart). Their alcoholic father (Shay) has been out of the picture for years but suddenly re-enters their lives, sober and wanting to make amends. Charlie has more troubles than just his family—he's succumbed to drifter Jordan (Bartzen), who has charmed his way into the Conrad home and Charlie's bed. Lo's ambitious and the gay aspects are taken matter-of-factly but the story seems overly familiar. **93m/C; DVD.** Booboo Stewart; Barry Shay; Nick Bartzen; Justin Lo; *D:* Justin Lo; *W:* Justin Lo; *C:* Oktay Ortabasi; *M:* Charles A. Lo.

Consenting Adults **1992 (R)** Cookie-cutter thriller capitalizes on popular "psycho-destroys-your-normal-life" theme. Average yuppie couple (Kline and Mastrantonio) are startled and then seduced by the couple moving in next door (Spacey and Miller), who conduct a considerably less-restrained lifestyle. Wife-swapping leads to murder and an innocent man is framed. Plot and characters are underdeveloped yet manage to hold interest through decent performances. **100m/C; VHS, DVD, Blu-Ray.** Kevin Kline; Mary Elizabeth Mastrantonio; Kevin Spacey; Rebecca Miller; Forest Whitaker; E.G. Marshall; Billie Neal; *D:* Alan J. Pakula; *W:* Matthew Chapman.

Consinsual **2010 (R)** Terrence is a button-downed faithful husband who finally gives in to his wife Angelica's kinkier sexual requests. Then she accuses him of marital rape, but the subsequent investigation leads to questions. **98m/C; DVD.** Keena Ferguson; Siaka Massaquoi; Kathryn Taylor; Alexis Zibolis; Bryan Keith; *D:* Paul D. Hannah, Jr.; *W:* Paul D. Hannah, Jr.; *C:* Larking Seiple; *M:* Jaebon Hwang. **VIDEO**

Conspiracy 1/2 **2001 (R)** Another in HBO's long line of excellent movies based on real-life events. This one covers the January, 1942 meeting of high-ranking Nazi SS and civilian government leaders to decide what to do about "the Jewish question." Led by SS Geneal Reinhard Heydrich (Branagh, in a riveting performance) and set up by SS Col. Adolf Eichmann (Tucci), this conference was conducted like a board meeting, and that's where the power of the movie comes from, because the outcome of the conference was implementation of the "final solution," the attempted extermination of the Jewish population of Europe. While every man in the room is a villain, they aren't the kind of Nazi villain we're used to. They are bureaucrats who offer administrative and logistical objections, but only token moral dissent (which is dispensed with rather quickly and completely). **96m/C; VHS, DVD, Blu-Ray.** Stanley Tucci; Kenneth Branagh; Colin Firth; Barnaby Kay; Ben Daniels; David Threlfall; Jonathan Coy; Brendan Coyle; Ian McNeice; Owen Teale; Nicholas Woodeson; Ewan Stewart; Kevin McNally; Brian Pettifer; *D:* Frank Pierson; *W:* Loring Mandel; *C:* Stephen Goldblatt. **CABLE**

Conspiracy **2008 (R)** William Macpherson was forced to retire as a sniper after an injury. Bored with civilian life, he's eager to help out fellow Iraq War vet Miguel Silva with his new ranch in Lukeville, Arizona. Except when Macpherson arrives, Silva has disappeared and no one in town will admit to knowing anything. Macpherson discovers the town is controlled by ruthless John Rhodes, but Rhodes learns that Macpherson can't be intimidated. **90m/C; DVD.** Val Kilmer; Gary Cole; Jennifer Esposito; Greg Serano; Bob Rumnock; Adam Marcus; Jay Jablonski; *D:* Debra Sullivan; *W:* Debra Sullivan; *C:* Ben Weinstein; *M:* Sujin Nam. **VIDEO**

Conspiracy of Fear **1996 (R)** After his father's strange death, Chris discovers he's being followed by a sadistic stalker and double agents who believe he has a package that everybody wants. Chris teams with a thief to solve both the mystery of the package and his father's death. **112m/C; VHS, DVD.** Christopher Plummer; Geraint Wyn Davies; Leslie Hope; Andrew Lowery; Ken Walsh; Don Francks; *D:* John Eyres; *W:* Roy Sallows; *C:* Peter Benison; *M:* Stephen (Steve) Edwards.

Conspiracy of Hearts **1960** A convent of nuns hide Jewish children in 1943 Italy despite threats to their personal safety. Suspenseful tale despite the familiar plot. **113m/B; VHS, DVD.** *GB* Lilli Palmer; Yvonne Mitchell; Sylvia Syms; Ronald Lewis; *D:* Ralph Thomas; *W:* Robert Presnell, Jr.

Conspiracy of Silence 1/2 **2003** A desperately unbiased Irish drama about the troubles arising from priests required to take the vow of celibacy. Director John Deery is very obviously claiming that these otherwise good men are forced into a life of quiet lust and despair, leading to suicide and disturbing homosexual relations. Although well-acted, Deery's characters are presented in such sharp black or white, good or bad, friend or enemy, that it's kind of like watching a man argue with himself. **84m/C; DVD.** *GB* Jason

Barry; Brenda Fricker; Hugh Bonneville; John Lynch; Jim Norton; Sean McGinley; James Ellis; Hugh Quarshie; Fintan McKeown; Jonathan Forbes; Catherine Cusack; Catherine Walker; Patrick Casey; Owen McDonnell; ***Cameo(s):*** Gay Byrne; ***D:*** John Deery; ***W:*** John Deery; ***C:*** Jason Lehel; ***M:*** Stephen Parsons; Francis Haines.

Conspiracy: The Trial of the Chicago Eight 1987 Courtroom drama focuses on the rambunctious trial of the Chicago Eight radicals, charged with inciting a riot at the Democratic National Convention of 1968. Dramatized footage mixed with interviews with the defendants. Imaginative reconstruction of history. **118m/C; VHS, DVD.** Peter Boyle; Elliott Gould; Robert Carradine; Martin Sheen; David Clennon; David Kagen; Michael Lembeck; Robert Loggia; ***D:*** Jeremy Paul Kagan.

Conspiracy Theory 1997 (R) Whacked-out New York cabbie Jerry Fletcher (Gibson) writes a newsletter on conspiracy theories, which he finds in every possible place and situation. Naturally, he doesn't keep his thoughts to himself and exasperated Justice Department attorney Alice Sutton (Roberts) is stuck listening to the lovestruck fool. But as the saying goes just because you're paranoid doesn't mean they're not out to get you. Sure enough, one of Jerry's conspiracies turns out to be true and suddenly he and Alice are being pursued by CIA shrink Dr. Jonas (Stewart), who's not what he seems to be either. Gibson's more geek than hero but appealing regardless, as is heroine Roberts. Another successful, enjoyable, and highly profitable, teaming of Donner, Gibson and producer Joel Silver. **135m/C; VHS, DVD, Blu-Ray.** Mel Gibson; Julia Roberts; Patrick Stewart; Cylk Cozart; Terry Alexander; ***D:*** Richard Donner; ***W:*** Brian Helgeland; ***C:*** John Schwartzman; ***M:*** Carter Burwell.

Conspirator 1/2 1949 Somewhat engrossing drama about a beautiful young girl who discovers that her new husband, a British army officer, is working with the Communists. Elizabeth Taylor stars as the naive American wife and Robert Taylor plays her Russkie agent husband. Although madly in love with his wife, he is given orders to kill her. Picture falls apart at end due to weak script. Based on the novel by Humphrey Slater. **85m/B; VHS, DVD.** *GB* Robert Taylor; Elizabeth Taylor; Robert Flemyng; Harold Warrender; Honor Blackman; Marjorie Fielding; Thora Hird; ***D:*** Victor Saville; ***W:*** Sally Benson; Gerald Fairlie; ***C:*** Frederick A. (Freddie) Young.

The Conspirator 2010 (PG-13) Courtroom drama based on the true story of Mary Surratt (a genuine Wright), who owned the boarding house where John Wilkes Booth and his fellow conspirators met. After President Lincoln's assassination, Mary is also charged as a co-conspirator. As the country, led by Secretary of War Edwin Stanton (Kline), seeks justice, young Union soldier and uneager attorney Frederick Aiken (McAvoy) holds her life in his hands during a military tribunal. An interesting moment in American history, to be sure, but not always engaging enough for most viewers—this one's more for the history buffs. **122m/C; Blu-Ray, On Demand.** Robin Wright; James McAvoy; Kevin Kline; Evan Rachel Wood; Danny Huston; Justin Long; Colm Meaney; Tom Wilkinson; Toby Kebbell; Johnny Simmons; ***D:*** Robert Redford; ***W:*** James Solomon; ***C:*** Newton Thomas (Tom) Sigel; ***M:*** Mark Isham.

The Conspirators 1/2 1944 Henreid is dreary but Lamarr is perfectly cast as the mysterious Irene Von Mohr in director Negulesco's film noir. Vincent (Henreid) escapes from the Netherlands after committing an act of sabotage against the Nazis. Hiding out in neutral Lisbon, he works with the resistance and their leader Ricardo (Greenstreet), who wants Vincent to uncover a traitor. This involves getting cozy with secretive beauty Irene. **101m/B; DVD.** Paul Henreid; Hedy Lamarr; Sydney Greenstreet; Peter Lorre; Victor Francen; Joseph Calleia; Steven Geray; ***D:*** Jean Negulesco; ***W:*** Leo Rosten; Vladimir Pozner; ***C:*** Arthur Edeson; ***M:*** Max Steiner.

The Constant Gardener 2005 (R) Multi-faceted, multi-layered tale hits all the buttons of a great thriller: sex, love, murder, intrigue, exotic (if underprivileged) locale, and international politics, all mixed with a topical bent ripped from today's headlines. Justin (Fiennes) and Tessa (Weisz) plunge headfirst from passion into marriage, hardly knowing a thing about each other. He's an official in the British government; she's an activist; together they end up in Kenya where she witnesses foul play by drug companies who use the locals as guinea pigs for drug testing. The film starts with Tessa's brutal murder, and we follow along with Justin as he uncovers the mysteries of her life and death. Adapted from the 2001 novel by John le Carre. **129m/C; DVD, Blu-Ray.** *GB* Ralph Fiennes; Rachel Weisz; Danny Huston; Bill Nighy; Pete Postlethwaite; Richard McCabe; Donald (Don) Sumpter; Juliet Aubrey; Hubert Kounde; Archie Panjabi; Gerard McSorley; ***D:*** Fernando Meirelles; ***W:*** Jeffrey Caine; ***C:*** Cesar Charlone; ***M:*** Alberto Iglesias. Oscars '05: Support. Actress (Weisz); British Acad. '05: Film Editing; Golden Globes '06: Support. Actress (Weisz); Screen Actors Guild '05: Support. Actress (Weisz).

The Constant Nymph 1943 Sentimental romantic melodrama. Teenaged Tessa (Fontaine) and her family are friends with poor-but-gifted composer Lewis Dodd (Boyer). Lewis marries Tessa's sophisticated cousin Florence (Smith) and, when her father dies, Tessa and her sisters are sent off to boarding school courtesy of Florence, which Tessa doesn't appreciate. She rebels and shows up at their London home, where she becomes Lewis' muse as Florence's jealousy grows. Based on Margaret Kennedy's 1925 novel. **112m/B; DVD.** Charles Boyer; Joan Fontaine; Alexis Smith; Charles Coburn; Peter Lorre; Brenda Marshall; May Whitty; Jean Muir; Montagu Love; Joyce Reynolds; Joan Blair; Doris Lloyd; ***D:*** Edmund Goulding; ***W:*** Kathryn Scola; ***C:*** Gaetano Antonio "Tony" Gaudio; ***M:*** Erich Wolfgang Korngold.

Constantine 1/2 2005 (R) Freelance exorcist and all-around surly loner John Constantine (Reeves) stalks the divide between good and evil, playing the forces of Heaven and Hell against themselves, all for his own benefit. When a policewoman, Angela (Weisz), seeks out the chain-smoking ghostbuster to help solve her twin sister's mysterious suicide, Constantine acts as her guide into LA's supernatural underworld, revealing a plot involving the Spear of Destiny, rogue angels, and a scheme to unleash Hell on earth. Director Lawrence creates a nifty neo-noir atmosphere, but confusing exposition and an over-reliance on CGI scares hurts the final product. Based on DC's "Hellblazer" comic. **120m/C; VHS, DVD, Blu-Ray, UMD, HD-DVD.** Keanu Reeves; Rachel Weisz; Djimon Hounsou; Max Baker; Pruitt Taylor Vince; Tilda Swinton; Peter Stormare; Shia LaBeouf; Gavin Rossdale; Jose Zuniga; Larry Cedar; ***D:*** Francis Lawrence; ***W:*** Kevin Brodbin; Frank Cappello; ***C:*** Philippe Rousselot; ***M:*** Brian Tyler; Klaus Badelt.

Consuming Passions 1/2 1988 (R) A ribald, food-obsessed English comedy about a young idiot who rises within the hierarchy of a chocolate company via murder. You'll never guess what the secret ingredient in his wonderful chocolate is. Based on a play by Michael Palin and Terry Jones (better known as part of the Monty Python troupe), the film is sometimes funny, more often gross, and takes a single joke far beyond its limit. **95m/C; VHS, DVD.** *GB* Vanessa Redgrave; Jonathan Pryce; Tyler Butterworth; Freddie Jones; Prunella Scales; Sammi Davis; Thora Hird; John Wells; William Rushton; Timothy West; ***D:*** Giles Foster; ***W:*** Michael Palin; Andrew Davies; Paul Zimmerman.

Contact 1/2 1997 (PG) Thought-provoking (if overlong) drama rather than sci-fi spectacular (though it has its fair share of special effects). Radio astronomer Dr. Ellie Arroway (Foster) discovers signals being transmitted from the distant star Vega. When they're deciphered, the signals turn out to be blueprints for a craft that will take its occupant into space and a first meeting with aliens. Ellie fights to become that first spokesperson for Earth's inhabitants. More philosophical than the usual sci-fi alien encounter epic, but the excellent cast, led by Foster, pulls it off nicely. Based on the novel by Carl Sagan. **150m/C; VHS, DVD.** Jodie Foster; Matthew McConaughey; James Woods; Tom Skerritt; Angela Bassett; John Hurt; David Morse; Rob Lowe; Jake Busey; William Fichtner; Geoffrey Blake; Jena Malone; ***D:*** Robert Zemeckis; ***W:*** Michael Goldenberg; ***C:*** Don Burgess; ***M:*** Alan Silvestri.

Contagion 2011 (PG-13) The great Soderbergh perfectly crafts a multi-character, multi-location, complex cautionary tale about a lethal airborne virus' impact and its swift and destructive powers. Opening with the stateside return and death of an average woman (Paltrow), the disease she brings back to the U.S. quickly makes its way through a star-studded ensemble. As citizens (including Damon and Law) just try to survive, the focus lies heavily upon the men and women (including Fishburne, Ehle, Cotillard, and Winslet) who work to find a cure. As easy to follow as it is powerful. **106m/C; DVD, Blu-Ray.** Marion Cotillard; Matt Damon; Laurence Fishburne; Jude Law; Gwyneth Paltrow; Kate Winslet; Bryan Cranston; Jennifer Ehle; John Hawkes; Elliott Gould; Demetri Martin; Enrico Colantoni; Sanaa Lathan; Monique Gabriela Curnen; Luis van Rooten; ***D:*** Steven Soderbergh; ***W:*** Scott Burns; ***C:*** Steven Soderbergh; ***M:*** Cliff Martinez.

Contaminated Man 1/2 *Contagion* **2000 (R)** Joseph Muller (Weller) is an entry level worker at a toxic waste facility fired after being there several decades. Apparently he wasn't the greatest of workers. He's also been contaminated with an experimental pesticide that causes an immediate and fatal allergic reaction within many people who come in contact with him, and the NSA quickly believes he's some sort of bio-terrorist. TV movie dull beyond belief. Peter Weller getting to do an eccentric Olivier-like turn as the Russian-accented, bald Muller is the only fun in the whole film. **100m/C; DVD.** *GB GE* William Hurt; Natascha (Natasha) McElhone; Peter Weller; Katja Woywood; Michael Brandon; Hendrick Haese; Nikolett Barabas; Desiree Nosbuch; Geraldine McEwan; Mari Nagy; Virag Ambrus; ***D:*** Anthony Hickox; ***W:*** John Penney; John Pinney; ***C:*** Bruce Douglas Johnson; ***M:*** Michael Hoenig. **TV**

Contempt 1/2 *Le Mepris; Il Disprezzo* **1964** A film about the filming of a new version of "The Odyssey," and the rival visions of how to tell the story. Amusing look at the film business features Fritz Lang playing himself, Godard as his assistant. Bardot is pleasant scenery. Adapted from Moravia's "A Ghost at Noon." **102m/C; VHS, DVD, Blu-Ray.** *IT FR* Brigitte Bardot; Jack Palance; Fritz Lang; Georgia Moll; Michel Piccoli; Jean-Luc Godard; Linda Veras; ***D:*** Jean-Luc Godard; ***W:*** Jean-Luc Godard; ***C:*** Raoul Coutard; ***M:*** Georges Delerue.

The Contender 1/2 **2000 (R)** An excellent cast propels this political potboiler, although the plot contains some hot air. After the sitting Veep dies, downhome Prez Evans (Bridges) nominates Sen. Laine Hanson (Allen) for the post. Although principled and experienced, she also happens to be a woman with a past. Evans's oily conservative rival Runyon (Oldman) takes advantage by digging up photos of the senator being the life of a college fraternity party. Hanson refuses to answer questions about her youthful indiscretions, arguing that her sexual history is nobody's business. As in real politics, much speechifying ensues and not much is accomplished. Allen shines in a role that was written expressly for her. Reports filtered out after the film's release that exec producer Oldman, a conservative himself, was unhappy about the editing and portrayal of his character, who he thought was the hero of the movie. **127m/C; VHS, DVD.** Joan Allen; Gary Oldman; Jeff Bridges; Sam Elliott; Christian Slater; William L. Petersen; Philip Baker Hall; Saul Rubinek; ***D:*** Rod Lurie; ***W:*** Rod Lurie; ***C:*** Denis Maloney; ***M:*** Lawrence Nash Groupe.

Contest 1/2 **2013 (PG)** A teen drama that explores what happens when a bully suddenly tries to become friends with his target. For much of his life, Tommy (Flaherty) has been bullied. Now in high school, he is bullied most by popular student-athlete Matt (Duty) and his teammates. One day, Matt decides to befriend Tommy. Though Tommy wonders about Matt's true motivations, he must accept the friendship so he can take part in a cooking contest that comes with a big prize. As the contest becomes more tense, Tommy's crush Sarah (McNamara) believes there is a conspiracy and Tommy himself wonders if Matt's friendship is real or a joke. **87m/C; DVD, Streaming, Download.** Danny Flaherty; Kenton Duty; Mary Beth Peil; Katherine McNamara; Kyle Massey; ***D:*** Anthony Joseph Giunta; ***W:*** Anthony Joseph Giunta; ***C:*** Giacomo Belletti; ***M:*** Robert J. Cornejo. **VIDEO**

Continental Divide 1981 (PG) A hard-nosed political columnist takes off for the Colorado Rockies on an "easy assignment"?interviewing a reclusive ornithologist, with whom he instantly falls in love. A city slicker, he first alienates her, but she eventually falls for him, too. But it's not exactly a match made in heaven. Story meanders to a conclusion of sorts. Probably the most normal Belushi ever was on screen. **103m/C; VHS, DVD.** John Belushi; Blair Brown; Allen Garfield; Carlin Glynn; Val Avery; Tony Ganios; Tim Kazurinsky; ***D:*** Michael Apted; ***W:*** Lawrence Kasdan; ***C:*** John Bailey.

Contraband 1/2 *Blackout* **1940** Danish sea captain Andersen (Veidt) and the mysterious Mrs. Sorenson (Hobson) are kidnapped by a cell of Nazi spies operating in London in the early days of WWII. They manage to turn the tables on the bad guys. Story takes place under blackout conditions lending a lot of atmosphere to this early thriller. **88m/B; VHS, DVD.** *GB* Conrad Veidt; Valerie Hobson; Esmond Knight; Hay Petrie; Raymond Lovell; Harold Warrender; Charles Victor; ***D:*** Michael Powell; ***W:*** Michael Powell; ***C:*** Frederick A. (Freddie) Young.

Contraband 1/2 *Luca il Contrabbandiere* **1980** The leader of a smuggling gang escapes from an ambush in which his brother was murdered. He searches for a haven of safety while his cronies seek brutal revenge. Average crime yarn lacks much excitement. Dubbed into English. **95m/C; VHS, DVD.** *IT* Fabio Testi; Ivana Monti; Guido Alberti; Venantino Venantini; Ajita Wilson; Marcel Bozzuffi; Saverio Marconi; Enrico Maisto; Giordano Falzoni; Giulio Farnese; Ofelia Meyer; Ferdinando Murolo; Tommaso Palladino; Cintia Lodetti; Rita Frei; Aldo Massasso; ***D:*** Lucio Fulci; ***W:*** Lucio Fulci; Gianni Di Chiara; Ettore Sanzo; Giorgio Mariuzzo; ***C:*** Sergio Salvati; ***M:*** Fabio Frizzi.

Contraband 1/2 **2012 (R)** Gritty, solid B-movie actioner set in New Orleans, Panama City, and the high seas. Security guard Chris Farraday (Wahlberg) used to be a successful contraband smuggler who went straight for the sake of his family. His doofus brother-in-law Andy (Jones) gets into trouble with ruthless, crazy drug lord Tim Briggs (Ribisi) and Chris agrees to one last job involving counterfeit cash and a merchant ship to repay the debt. However, he finds the criminal game is still filled with violence and betrayal. Based on the 2008 Icelandic pic "Reykjavik-Rotterdam." **110m/C; DVD, Blu-Ray.** Mark Wahlberg; Ben Foster; Giovanni Ribisi; Caleb Landry Jones; Kate Beckinsale; Lukas Haas; Diego Luna; J.K. Simmons; William Lucking; ***D:*** Baltasar Kormakur; ***W:*** Aaron Guzikowski; ***C:*** Barry Ackroyd; ***M:*** Clinton Shorter.

The Contract 1998 (R) Former black ops specialist Luc (Imbault) is now making a living as a pro assassin and is teaching the trade to daughter Hannah (Black). When dad gets killed in a set-up, Hannah wants revenge against the man behind the deed. It's Presidential candidate J. Harmon (Williams), who wants his own black ops past to stay hidden—but Hannah has other ideas. **90m/C; VHS, DVD.** Billy Dee Williams; Johanna Black; Laurent Imbault; ***D:*** K.C. Bascombe. **VIDEO**

The Contract 2007 (R) Frank Carden (Freeman) is a freelance hitman who gets arrested by some Washington state cops and is turned over to the feds for transport. Carden escapes into the woods with the help of some cronies, only to be re-captured by Ray Keene (Cusack), a former cop who is hiking with his teenaged son Chris (Anderson). Keene forces Carden to hike towards the authorities while his guntoting associates come searching. **96m/C; DVD, Blu-Ray, HD-DVD.** Morgan Freeman; John Cusack; Jamie Anderson; Alice Krige; Megan Dodds; Corey Johnson; Jonathan Hyde; Bill Smitrovich; Ned Bellamy; ***D:*** Bruce Beresford; ***W:*** Stephen Katz; John Darrouzet; ***C:*** Dante Spinotti; ***M:*** Normand Corbeil. **VIDEO**

Contract Killer 1/2 *Sat sau ji wong; The Hitman* **1998 (R)** Fu (Li) is a down-on-his-luck ex-soldier who needs money, and sees opportunity when a $1 million bounty is offered on the head of the assassin of a Japanese businessman. He can't get into the assassins meeting though until con man Lo (Tsang) acts as his manager. Once inside they can't back out, even after Fu realizes he may not have what it takes to kill someone. Begs one to ask the question: How is it you were in the military and thought being a hitman would be a good idea for money if you can't kill people? **103m/C; DVD.** *CH* Jet Li; Eric Tsang; Simon Yam; Gigi Leung; Keiji Sato; Paul Rapovski; John Ching; *D:* Wei Tung; *W:* Hing Kai Chan; Vincent Kok; Domonic Muir; Kam Fu Cheng; *C:* Arthur Wong; *M:* Jussi Tegelman.

Contract Killers ½ **2008** CIA assassin Jane plans to retire but her unhappy employers try framing her for the murder of her husband. However, they picked the wrong femme to mess with as Jane discovers a rogue CIA plot to ruin the Federal Reserve and decides to shut it down to get even. **86m/C; DVD.** Frida Show; Nick Mancuso; Rhett Giles; Christian Willis; *D:* Justin B. Rhodes; *W:* Justin B. Rhodes; *C:* Andre Lascaris; *M:* Michael Mouracade. **VIDEO**

Contract on Cherry Street **1977** In this made-for-TV movie, Deputy Inspector Frank Hovannes (Sinatra) is in charge of a special unit battling organized crime. But when restrictions and legalities hamper him, Hovannes goes vigilante with several like-minded officers. **145m/C; DVD.** Frank Sinatra; Martin Balsam; Henry Silva; Verna Bloom; Martin Gabel; Michael Nouri; Harry Guardino; James Luisi; Joe De Santis; *D:* William A. Graham; *W:* Edward Anhalt; *C:* Jack Priestley; *M:* Jerry Goldsmith. **TV**

Contract to Kill **2016 (R)** An overwrought Steven Seagal action film. Shocking, right?! Skilled assassin Harmon (Seagal) has been called back into service by the CIA to protect the United States from a serious terrorist threat. Harmon is charged with identifying and killing key figures in an Islamic plot that involves entering the United States through tunnels used by Mexican drug cartels. Harmon is assisted in this fight of good versus evil by FBI agent Zara Hayek (Dallender) and drone expert Mathew Sharp (Wong). While the film may appeal serious Seagal fans, it lacks a strong script, looks cheaply made, and features a phoned-in performance by Seagal. **90m/C; DVD.** Steven Seagal; Russell Wong; Jemma Dallender; Mircea Drambareanu; Sergiu Costache; *D:* Keoni Waxman; *W:* Keoni Waxman; *C:* Liviu Pojoni, Jr.; *M:* Michael Richard Plowman.

Contracted ½ **2013** Townsend gives a daring performance as Samantha, a heartbroken lesbian who ends up having a one-night stand after a party. She wakes up the next morning and her body essentially starts to fall apart. It starts with heavy menstrual bleeding and moves on to teeth falling out and bloodshot eyes. Then it gets really gross. Did she contract a sexual disease or something more sinister? Director/writer England draws a great performance from Townsend but doesn't craft a memorable story. **78m/C; DVD.** Najarra Townsend; Caroline Williams; Alice MacDonald; Katie Stegeman; Matt Mercer; *D:* Eric England; *W:* Eric England; *C:* Mike Testin; *M:* Kevin Riepl.

The Contractor **2007 (R)** Routine would-be thriller has retired CIA assassin James Dial (Snipes) called in for one last job. Suddenly he's on the lam when the killing of a terrorist mastermind in London leads to a double-cross. James is befriended by 12-year-old Emma (Bennett), a witness who wants to help him prove his innocence. **105m/C; DVD, Blu-Ray.** Wesley Snipes; Lena Headey; Eliza Bennett; Charles Dance; Ralph Brown; Gemma Jones; *D:* Josef Rusnak; *W:* Robert Foster; Joshua Michael Stern; *C:* Wendigo von Schultzendorff; *M:* Nicholas Pike. **VIDEO**

Control **2007 (R)** Corbijn makes his directorial debut in this compelling B&W bio of Ian Curtis (Riley), frontman for British post-punk band "Joy Division." Epileptic and suffering from depression, Curtis is torn between a conventional life—a teenage marriage, child, and steady job—and the excitement and temptations of the music world. Although Curtis committed suicide in 1980 at the age of 23 this isn't the typical live fast/die young rock fantasy, but a thoughtful depiction of young man who couldn't reconcile competing impulses. Based on the memoir "Touching from the Distance" by Deborah Curtis. **121m/B; Blu-Ray.** *GB AU JP* Samantha Morton; Alexandra Maria Lara; Joe Anderson; James Anthony Pearson; Sam Riley; Craig Parkinson; Toby Kebbell; Harry Treadaway; Andrew Sheridan; Robert Shelly; *D:* Anton Corbijn; *W:* Matt Greenhalgh; Deborah Curtis; *C:* Martin Ruhe; *M:* New Order.

Control Alt Delete **2008 (R)** It's 1999, and computer programmer Lewis (Labine) is trying to debug his company's Y2K software while dealing with being dumped by longtime girlfriend Sarah (Bertram) when she got tired of his online porn fixation. Now Lewis has developed this sexual fetish for desktop computers (the computer itself not visiting websites). The fetish is icky enough (okay it's funny for awhile in a perverted way) and seeing Labine naked, especially for an extended length of time, is not flick highlight. **93m/C; DVD.** Tyler Labine; Sonja Bennett; Keith Dallas; Laura Bertram; Kevin James; *D:* James Liston; *W:* James Liston; *M:* Tygh Runyan. **VIDEO**

Control Room **2004** Shot days prior to the Iraq War, director Noujaim provides a fly on the wall account of the goings on at Al Jazeera, the leading news service for Arab-speaking viewers and also at Centcom, a makeshift media village set up by the U.S. military for the purpose of holding and briefing journalists from around the world. Your certainties will be scrambled and your assumptions shaken, if you think you can believe everything you hear on your news broadcasts. Presented in a surprisingly unbiased manner, provocative critique strongly questions the notion of journalistic objectivity. **85m/C; VHS, DVD.** *D:* Jehane Noujaim; *W:* Jehane Noujaim; Julia Bacha; *C:* Jehane Noujaim; *M:* Hani Salama; Thomas DeRenzo.

The Convent **1995** Idiosyncratic saga of Paris-based American scholar Michael Padovic (Malkovich) and his French wife Helene (Deneuve) who travel to an ancient Portuguese monastery so Michael may do research at their library. The convent's guardian is the charming and sinister Baltar (Cintra), who flirts with neglected Helene, while playing Mephistopheles to Michael's Faust. Lots of mysticism and religious iconography. Portuguese, French, and English dialogue. **90m/C; VHS, DVD.** *PT FR* John Malkovich; Catherine Deneuve; Luis Miguel Cintra; Leonor Silveira; *D:* Manoel de Oliveira; *W:* Manoel de Oliveira; *C:* Mario Barroso.

The Convent **2000 (R)** In 1960, a young woman enters a church, shoots several nuns and a priest, and then torches the place. Jump ahead to the present, as a group of college kids enter the now-condemned convent to perform a fraternity prank. Elsewhere in the dilapidated convent, amateur Satanists perform a ritual, releasing the evil spirits held captive in the sanctuary. From this point on, the movie becomes a monster mash, as each character is either possessed, killed, or both. The only hope for the trapped youngsters is the now-grown girl who started all of this in 1960. The film is creatively shot by director Mendez, and the demon makeup is unusual, but the action owes too much to "Night of the Demons 2," "The Church," and the "Goth Talk" skit from "Saturday Night Live." Horror aficionados will feel as if they've seen it all before. **79m/C; VHS, DVD.** Adrienne Barbeau; Coolio; Bill Moseley; Joanna Canton; Megahn Perry; Dax Miller; David Gunn; *D:* Mike Mendez; *W:* Chaton Anderson; *C:* Jason Lowe; *M:* Joseph Bishara.

Convention Girl ½ *Atlantic City Romance* **1935** Cynthia "Babe" Laval (Hobart) is an aging lady of the evening who has become Atlantic City's most influential madam, controlling almost every call girl in town. Her real aim is to meet the man of her dreams, but she's caught between her desire for Wade Hollister (Rawlinson), a dull soap company executive, and the decidedly more dangerous Bill Bradley (Heyburn), who runs an illicit gambling joint. The two suitors clash, and Bradley gets nasty when he thinks he may be cut out of Babe's future plans. The plot is thin but classic Atlantic City attractions play a co-starring role. **66m/B; DVD.** Rose Hobart; Weldon Heyburn; Sally O'Neil; Herbert Rawlinson; Shemp Howard; *D:* Luther Reed; *W:* George Boyle; *C:* Nick Rogelli.

Conventioneers **2005** During the Republican National Convention in New York City in 2004, a liberal Democrat, Lea (Koons) attends on a mission of protest. There, she runs into a college acquiantance, Dave Massey (Mabe), a Republican delegate. The pair unexpectedly fall in love but have difficulties with their political differences. Shot at the actual 2004 Republican convention, the film also considers the political divide in the United States and its wider impact. **95m/C; DVD, Streaming.** Matthew Mabe; Woodwyn Koons; Alek Friedman; Alicia Harding; Jennifer Brown; *D:* Mora Stephens; *W:* Mora Stephens; Joel Viertel; *C:* Andreas Burgess; Brian O'Carroll; *M:* Danny Manor; H. Scott Salinas. **VIDEO**

The Conversation ½ **1974 (PG)** Freelance surveillance expert Harry Caul (Hackman) is becoming increasingly uneasy about his current job for a powerful businessman (Duvall). He and assistant Stan (Cazale) are watching a young couple (Williams, Forrest) when Harry begins to suspect that they are murder targets. Powerful statement about privacy, responsibility and guilt. One of the best movies of the '70s. **113m/C; VHS, DVD, Blu-Ray.** Gene Hackman; John Cazale; Frederic Forrest; Allen Garfield; Cindy Williams; Robert Duvall; Teri Garr; Michael Higgins; Elizabeth McRae; Harrison Ford; *D:* Francis Ford Coppola; *W:* Francis Ford Coppola; *C:* Bill Butler; *M:* David Shire. Cannes '74: Film; Natl. Bd. of Review '74: Actor (Hackman), Director (Coppola); Natl. Film Reg. '95; Natl. Soc. Film Critics '74: Director (Coppola).

Conversation Piece *Violence et Passion; Gruppo di Famiglia in un Interno* **1975 (R)** An aging art historian's life is turned upside down when a Countess and her daughters rent out the penthouse in his estate. Sometimes-talky examination of scholarly pretensions. **112m/C; VHS, DVD, Blu-Ray.** *IT FR* Burt Lancaster; Silvana Mangano; Helmut Berger; Claudia Cardinale; Claudia Marsani; *D:* Luchino Visconti; *W:* Luchino Visconti; Suso Cecchi D'Amico; Enrico Medioli; *C:* Pasqualino De Santis; *M:* Franco Mannino.

Conversations with Other Women ½ **2005 (R)** Arty romantic-suspenser in which a man (Eckhart) and a woman (Bonham Carter) meet at a wedding reception and end up in bed, but as the night progresses it's revealed that they are possibly not strangers. Clever split-screen style shows each character separately navigating their encounter over the course of the evening, a technique that provides both emotional weight and insight to their backstory and motives as much as it illustrates the theme of perception-is-reality. Chemistry and fine acting turn a he said/she said one-night stand story into an examination of the passage of time, regret, and knowing better. **84m/C; DVD.** Helena Bonham Carter; Aaron Eckhart; Brian Geraghty; Olivia Wilde; Brianna Brown; Thomas Lennon; Nora Zehetner; *D:* Hans Canosa; *W:* Gabrielle Zevin; *C:* Steve Yedlin; *M:* Star Parodi; Jeff Eden Fair.

Convict Cowboy ½ **1995 (R)** Hardbitten professional rodeo cowboy Ry Weston (Voight) killed a man and now works the Montana prison rodeo circuit. Newcomer greenhorn Clay Treyton (Chandler) wants to get out of kitchen duty and decides Ry is the perfect ridin' and ropin' teacher. Only Ry isn't interested in wasting his time (at first). It's a predictable bonding experience in a melodramatic movie. **106m/C; VHS, Streaming.** Jon Voight; Kyle Chandler; Ben Gazzara; Marcia Gay Harden; Glenn Plummer; Stephen McHattie; *D:* Rod Holcomb; *C:* James L. Carter. **CABLE**

Convict 762 ½ **1998 (R)** Zagarino and Drago are survivors of a remote penal colony who are rescued by the all-female crew of a cargo ship. But it turns out one of the duo is a murderer who begins to kill again. **100m/C; VHS, DVD.** Frank Zagarino; Billy Drago; Shannon Sturges; *D:* Luca Bercovici; *W:* J. Reifel; *C:* Steven Wacks. **VIDEO**

Convict Women *Thunder County; Cell Block Girls; Swamp Fever; Women's Penitentiary XI* **1974 (PG)** Four women are bored and decide to break out of prison and go for a skip through the local swamp after angering the local rednecks and heroin dealers. Yes that's a bit sarcastic, but the script has to be spiffed up somehow. **90m/C; DVD, Streaming.** Mickey Rooney; Ted Cassidy; Carol Locatell; Chris Robinson; *D:* Chris Robinson; *C:* Jack Beckett; *M:* Jaime Mendoza-Nava. **VIDEO**

Convicted ½ **1950** Joe Hufford (Ford) is convicted of manslaughter after his lawyer botches his case. Sympathetic DA George Knowland (Crawford) becomes the new warden at the prison where Joe is doing his time. He makes Joe a trustee and puts him on the track for parole. Joe's bad luck continues until the contrived happy ending. Remake of 1931's "The Criminal Code." **91m/B; DVD.** Glenn Ford; Broderick Crawford; Dorothy Malone; Millard Mitchell; Frank Faylen; Will Geer; *D:* Henry Levin; *W:* William Bowers; Fred Niblo, Jr.; Seton I. Miller; *C:* Burnett Guffey; *M:* George Duning.

Convicted ½ *Return to Sender* **2004 (R)** A deceitful former attorney (Quinn) makes some quick bucks selling off his letters with death row prisoners until he falls for convicted child killer Charlotte (Nielsen) and struggles to help clear her once new evidence surfaces. Decent as a message movie but stoops to stale action-movie-type twists toward the end. **108m/C; VHS, DVD.** Connie Nielsen; Kelly Preston; Aidan Quinn; Timothy Daly; Mark Holton; *D:* Bille August; *W:* Neal Purvis; Robert Wade; *C:* Dirk Bruel; *M:* Harry Gregson-Williams. **VIDEO**

Conviction **2002 (R)** Philadelphia-born Carl Upchurch (Epps) drops out of school at nine and into a life of crime that leads to various prison sentences. A man with a violent temper, he's no one to mess with but he also wants more from his life. This leads to his mentoring by Quaker prison instructor Martha (Delany) and Carl's goal to save other inner-city youth from a life of violence and imprisonment. Based on Upchurch's autobiography. **100m/C; VHS, DVD.** Omar Epps; Dana Delany; Charles S. Dutton; Treach; Bentley Mitchum; *D:* Kevin Rodney Sullivan; *W:* Jon Huffman; Carl Upchurch; *C:* Miroslaw Baszak; *M:* Jeff Beal. **CABLE**

Conviction ½ **2010 (R)** Earnest and straightforward portrayal by Swank in an inspirational family drama based on a true story. When her wild brother Kenny (Rockwell) is sentenced to life in prison for murder in 1983, homemaker Betty Anne Waters (Swank) is convinced of his innocence. So she puts herself through high school and college, eventually earning a law degree, in an 18-year quest to get his conviction overturned. **96m/C; Blu-Ray.** Hilary Swank; Sam Rockwell; Minnie Driver; Melissa Leo; Clea DuVall; Juliette Lewis; Loren Dean; Peter Gallagher; Ari Graynor; Conor Donovan; Owen Campbell; John Pyper-Ferguson; Karen Young; Bailee Madison; Tobias Campbell; *D:* Tony Goldwyn; *W:* Pamela Gray; *C:* Adriano Goldman; *M:* Paul Cantelon.

Convoy ½ **1940** Life aboard a convoy ship in the North Sea during WWII. The small cruiser is picked on by a German U-Boat. Will a rescuer appear? Noted for technical production values. **95m/B; VHS, DVD.** Clive Brook; John Clements; Edward Chapman; Judy Campbell; Edward Rigby; Stewart Granger; Michael Wilding; George Benson; *D:* Pen Tennyson.

Convoy **1978 (R)** A defiant trucker leads an indestructible truck convoy to Mexico to protect high gasoline prices. Lightweight stuff was inspired by the song "Convoy" by C.W. McCall. **106m/C; VHS, DVD, Blu-Ray.** Kris Kristofferson; Ali MacGraw; Ernest Borgnine; Burt Young; Madge Sinclair; Franklin Ajaye; Cassie Yates; *D:* Sam Peckinpah; *C:* Harry Stradling, Jr.

Coogan's Bluff **1968 (PG)** An Arizona deputy sheriff (Eastwood) travels to New York in order to track down a killer on the loose. First Eastwood/Siegel teaming is tense actioner. The TV series "McCloud" was based on this film. **100m/C; VHS, DVD, Blu-Ray.** Clint Eastwood; Lee J. Cobb; Tisha Sterling; Don Stroud; Betty Field; Susan Clark; Tom Tully; Albert "Poppy" Popwell; *D:* Donald Siegel; *W:* Dean Riesner; *M:* Lalo Schifrin.

The Cook, the Thief, His Wife & Her Lover ½ **1990 (R)** An exclusive restaurant houses four disturbing characters. Greenaway's powerful vision of greed, love, and violence may be too strong for some tastes. Available in several different versions: the standard unrated theatrical release, the unrated version in a letterboxed format, and an R-rated cut which runs half an hour shorter. **123m/C; VHS, DVD.** *GB* Richard Bohringer; Michael Gambon; Dame Helen Mirren; Alan Howard; Tim Roth; *D:* Peter Greenaway; *W:* Peter Greenaway; *C:* Sacha Vierny; *M:* Michael Nyman.

Cookie 1/2 **1989 (R)** Light comedy about a Mafia don's daughter trying to smart mouth her way into the mob's good graces. A character-driven vehicle, this plot takes a backseat to casting. Wiest is superb as Falk's moll. **93m/C; VHS, DVD.** Emily Lloyd; Peter Falk; Dianne Wiest; Jerry Lewis; Brenda Vaccaro; Ricki Lake; Lionel Stander; Michael V. Gazzo; Adrian Pasdar; Bob Gunton; Rockets Redglare; G. Anthony "Tony" Sirico; *D:* Susan Seidelman; *W:* Alice Arlen; Nora Ephron; *M:* Thomas Newman.

Cookie's Fortune 1/2 **1999 (PG-13)** Neal is Jewel Mae "Cookie" Orcutt, the matriarch of a Mississippi family with its share of female eccentrics. When Cookie offs herself to join her deceased husband, her officious, scandal-fearing spinster neice Camille (Close) destroys the suicide note, setting up the family's loyal, good-natured handyman (Dutton) for the fall. At the same time, she's directing practically the whole town in a church performance of "Salome." Excellent script by Rapp allows more characterization than usual for Altman, as well as a pleasantly leisurely pace. Flawless ensemble work (another Altman hallmark) is highlighted by the performances of Neal, Close, and Dutton. **118m/C; VHS, DVD.** Charles S. Dutton; Glenn Close; Patricia Neal; Liv Tyler; Chris O'Donnell; Julianne Moore; Ned Beatty; Courtney B. Vance; Donald Moffat; Lyle Lovett; Matt Malloy; Rufus Thomas; Danny Darst; Randle Mell; Niecy Nash; Ruby Wilson; Preston Strobel; *D:* Robert Altman; *W:* Anne Rapp; *C:* Toyomichi Kurita; *M:* David A. Stewart. Natl. Bd. of Review '99: Support. Actress (Moore).

The Cookout **2004 (PG-13)** Lowbrow, slack-paced comedy debut from Rivera is filled with stereotypes. Todd Anderson (Storm P) takes advantage of being the NBA's No. 1 draft pick by letting his greedy girlfriend Brittany (Good) talk him into buying an ostentatious mansion in a gated community, among other perks. His distrustful mom (Lewis) insists he keep to his down-home ways by hosting the big annual cookout for family and friends, which brings all the hangers-on into the backyard. Queen Latifah has what's basically an extended cameo as a zealous community security guard. **88m/C; VHS, DVD.** Tim Meadows; Jenifer Lewis; Meagan Good; Jonathan Silverman; Ja Rule; Storm P; Farrah Fawcett; Frankie Faison; Eve; Danny Glover; Rita Owens; Marci Reed; Ruperto Vanderpool; Queen Latifah; *Cameo(s):* Marv Albert; Elton Brand; Baron Davis; Mark Cuban; *D:* Lance Rivera; *W:* Laurie B. Tuner; Ramsey Gbelawoe; Jeffrey Brian Holmes; *C:* Tom Houghton; *M:* Camara Kambon; Keir Gist.

Cool and the Crazy **1994 (R)** High school sweethearts Michael (Leto) and Roslyn (Silverstone) are now in a troubled marriage. Apparently dissatisfied by hubby's sexual performance, Roslyn decides to take a walk on the wide side with hoodlum Joey (Flint). Michael finds out and decides to have his own extramarital fling with a beatnik coworker (it's set in the 50s). But there's even more trouble ahead. Rather than "cool" and "crazy," it's amateurish and nonsensical. **90m/C; VHS, DVD.** Alicia Silverstone; Jared Leto; Jennifer Blanc; Matthew Flint; Bradford Tatum; Christina Harnos; Tuesday Knight; *D:* Ralph Bakshi; *W:* Ralph Bakshi; *C:* Roberto Schaefer; *M:* Hummie Mann. **CABLE**

Cool As Ice **1991 (PG)** "Rapper" Vanilla Ice makes his feature film debut as a rebel with an eye for the ladies, who motors into a small, conservative town. Several so-so musical segments. For teenage girls only. **92m/C; VHS, DVD.** Vanilla Ice; Kristin Minter; Michael Gross; Sydney Lassick; Dody Goodman; Naomi Campbell; Candy Clark; *D:* David Kellogg; *C:* Janusz Kaminski; *M:* Stanley Clarke. Golden Raspberries '91: Worst New Star (Vanilla Ice).

Cool Blue 1/2 **1988 (R)** An unsuccessful painter meets the woman of his dreams, has a brief affair, then tries to locate her in the greater Los Angeles metro area. Good luck. Watch for Penn's cameo. **93m/C; VHS, Streaming.** Woody Harrelson; Hank Azaria; Ely Pouget; John Diehl; *Cameo(s):* Sean Penn; *D:* Mark Mullin; Richard Shepard.

Cool Breeze **1972** Messy blaxploitation heist remake of 1950's "The Asphalt Jungle." Recently released con Sidney Lord Jones (Rasulala) gathers a disparate crew to pull off a jewel heist. It's all for a noble cause since Jones intends to sell the loot and use the proceeds to start a bank that will support black businesses. **103m/C; DVD.** Thalmus Rasulala; Judy Pace; James Watkins; Lincoln Kilpatrick; Raymond St. Jacques; Wally Taylor; Rudy Challenger; Royce Wallace; Margaret Avery; Pam Grier; *D:* Barry Pollack; *W:* Barry Pollack; *M:* Solomon Burke.

A Cool, Dry Place 1/2 **1998 (PG-13)** Basically a variation on "Kramer vs. Kramer." Russ Durrell (Vaughn) was a hotshot Chicago lawyer with a five-year old son, Calvin (Moat), when wife Kate (Potter) took a hike. So Russ moves to small town Kansas to make a go of single fatherhood in a slower-paced world. Eventually, he begins dating Beth (Adams) and when things start to get serious, guess who turns up and decides she wants back into her son's life? Vaughn does fine as the dad but Potter is stuck with a dopey, inarticulate character. **97m/C; VHS, DVD.** Vince Vaughn; Monica Potter; Joey Lauren Adams; Bobby Moat; Devon Sawa; *D:* John N. Smith; *W:* Matthew McDuffie; *C:* Jean Lepine; *M:* Curt Sobel.

Cool Hand Luke 1/2 **1967** One of the last great men-in-chains films. A man (Newman) sentenced to sweat out a term on a prison farm refuses to compromise with authority. Martin shines in his supporting role as the oily warden, uttering that now-famous phrase, "What we have here is a failure to communicate." Kennedy's performance as leader of the chain gang won him an Oscar. Based on the novel by Donn Pearce. **126m/C; VHS, DVD, Blu-Ray.** Paul Newman; George Kennedy; J.D. Cannon; Strother Martin; Dennis Hopper; Anthony Zerbe; Lou Antonio; Wayne Rogers; Harry Dean Stanton; Ralph Waite; Joe Don Baker; Richard (Dick) Davalos; Jo Van Fleet; Robert Drivas; Clifton James; Morgan Woodward; Luke Askew; Robert Donner; Warren Finnerty; James Gammon; Rance Howard; Buck Kartalian; John McLiam; Charles Tyner; Donn Pearce; Marc Cavell; Charles Hicks; James Jeter; Robert Luster; John Pearce; Eddie Rosson; *D:* Stuart Rosenberg; *W:* Frank Pierson; Donn Pearce; *C:* Conrad L. Hall; *M:* Lalo Schifrin. Oscars '67: Support. Actor (Kennedy); Natl. Film Reg. '05.

The Cool Ones 1/2 **1967** Music industry spoof is silly--if dated--fun. Eccentric record producer Tony (MacDowell) pairs ambitious teenaged TV go-go dancer Hallie (Watson) with one-hit wonder Cliff (Peterson) and plans to make them a top-of-the-charts duo. **95m/C; DVD.** Roddy McDowall; Debbie Watson; Gil Peterson; Phil Harris; Nita Talbot; Robert Coote; George Furth; *D:* Gene Nelson; *W:* Gene Nelson; Robert Kaufman; *C:* Floyd Crosby; *M:* Ernie Freeman.

Cool Runnings 1/2 **1993 (PG)** Bright, slapstick comedy based on the true story of the Jamaican bobsled team's quest to enter the 1988 Winter Olympics in Calgary. Candy is recruited to coach four unlikely athletes who don't quite exemplify the spirit of the Games. He accepts the challenge not only because of its inherent difficulty but because he needs to reconcile himself to past failures as a former sledder. When our heroes leave their sunny training ground for Calgary, their mettle is tested by serious sledders from more frigid climes who pursue the competition with a stern sense of mission. An upbeat story which will appeal to children, its target audience. **98m/C; VHS, DVD, Blu-Ray.** Leon; Doug E. Doug; John Candy; Marco Brambilla; Malik Yoba; Rawle Lewis; Raymond J. Barry; Peter Outerbridge; Larry Gilman; Paul Coeur; *D:* Jon Turteltaub; *W:* Tommy Swerdlow; Lynn Siefert; Michael Goldberg; *C:* Phedon Papamichael; *M:* Hans Zimmer.

The Cool Surface **1992 (R)** Sex and ambition, Hollywood style. Dani, a wannbe actress, and Jarvis, an aspiring screenwriter become lovers. Jarvis turns their hot affair into a sizzling novel and then a script. Dani may have inspired the lead role but that doesn't mean she'll get the part. But it won't be for lack of trying (anything). **88m/C; VHS, DVD.** Robert Patrick; Teri Hatcher; Matt McCoy; Cyril O'Reilly; Ian Buchanan; *D:* Erik Anjou; *W:* Erik Anjou; *M:* Dave Kopplin.

Cool World **1992 (PG-13)** Underground cartoonist Jack Deebs enters his own adult cartoon "Cool World," lured by his sex-kitten character "Holli Would," who needs him to leave her animated world and become human. Holli's plan is opposed by the only other human to occupy Cool World, a slick detective whose main job is to prevent noids (humans) and doodles (cartoons) from having sex and destroying the balance between the two existences. A mixture of live-action and wild animation. Director Bakshi's creations are not intended for children but this is less explicit than usual, which may be one of the problems. Little humor and a flat script leave this film too uninvolving. **101m/C; VHS, DVD.** Gabriel Byrne; Kim Basinger; Brad Pitt; Michele Abrams; Deirdre O'Connell; Carrie Hamilton; Frank Sinatra, Jr.; Michael David Lally; William Frankfather; *D:* Ralph Bakshi; *W:* Michael Grais; Mark Victor; *C:* John A. Alonzo; *M:* Mark Isham.

The Cooler **2003 (R)** Bernie Lootz (Macy) is a Las Vegas gambler with a nasty losing streak. After getting into debt to casino manager Shelly Kaplow (Baldwin), Bernie finds himself indentured as a "cooler," a walking bad luck charm sent to cool off the winning streaks simply by sitting next to the gamblers. Bernie's luck begins to change about a week before he's finished paying off. He meets and falls for Natalie (Bello), a casino waitress, and it seems his perennial bad luck begins to disappear (but of course, there are complications). Great cast provides sterling performances all around. Most notable is Macy, who hits the jackpot playing a loser. **101m/C; VHS, DVD.** William H. Macy; Alec Baldwin; Maria Bello; Shawn Hatosy; Ron Livingston; Paul Sorvino; Estella Warren; Arthur J. Nascarella; M.C. Gainey; Ellen Greene; Joey Fatone; Tony Longo; *D:* Wayne Kramer; *W:* Wayne Kramer; Frank Hannah; *C:* Jim Whitaker; *M:* Mark Isham. Natl. Bd. of Review '03: Support. Actor (Baldwin).

Cooley High **1975 (PG)** Black high school students in Chicago go through the rites of passage in their senior year during the '60s. Film is funny, smart, and much acclaimed. Great soundtrack featuring Motown hits of the era is a highlight. Basis for the TV series "What's Happening." **107m/C; VHS, DVD, Blu-Ray.** Glynn Turman; Lawrence-Hilton Jacobs; Garrett Morris; Cynthia Davis; *D:* Michael A. Schultz; *W:* Eric Monte.

Cooties **2014** "Recess of the Living Dead" takes place on the day a new substitute teacher (a game Wood) reports for his first day at the grade school that he attended when he was a child. A chicken nugget gone very wrong turns the youngest children in this small-town elementary school into rabid, brain-eating maniacs, forcing the faculty (which also includes Wilson and Pill) to fend for their lives. The set-up is brilliant and the make-up effects are great but the follow-through is lackluster in the way that the writers waste the opportunity for gory fun by focusing on an uninteresting love triangle. **96m/C; DVD, Blu-Ray.** Elijah Wood; Rainn Wilson; Alison Pill; Jack McBrayer; Cooper Roth; Armani Jackson; Leigh Whannell; *D:* Cary Murnion; Jonathan Milott; *W:* Leigh Whannell; Ian Brennan; *C:* Lyle Vincent.

Cop 1/2 **1988 (R)** Left by his wife and child, a ruthless and work-obsessed detective goes after a twisted serial killer. Woods' exceptional ability to play sympathetic weirdos is diluted by a script—based on James Ellroys's novel "Blood on the Moon"?that warps the feminist theme, is violent, and depends too heavily on coincidence. **110m/C; VHS, DVD, Blu-Ray.** James Woods; Lesley Ann Warren; Charles Durning; Charles Haid; Raymond J. Barry; Randi Brooks; Annie McEnroe; Victoria Wauchope; *D:* James B. Harris; *W:* James B. Harris; *M:* Michel Colombier.

Cop and a Half 1/2 **1993 (PG)** Streetwise eight-year-old (Golden) accidentally witnesses a murder and then bullies police into letting him join the force (for a day) when he withholds key information. Enter his partner for the day—hard-edged detective Reynolds, who claims to hate kids, but who we know will learn to love them. Meanwhile, the outlaw (Sharkey) knows Devon saw him and is trying to silence him permanently. Predictable fantasy may appeal to kids, but will make most adults yawn. One of Sharkey's last roles. **87m/C; VHS, DVD, Blu-Ray.** Norman D. Golden, II; Burt Reynolds; Ruby Dee; Ray Sharkey; Holland Taylor; Frank Sivero; Marc Macaulay; Rocky Giordani; Sammy Hernandez; *D:* Henry Winkler; *W:* Arne Olsen; *C:* Bill Butler; *M:* Alan Silvestri. Golden Raspberries '93: Worst Actor (Reynolds).

Cop Au Vin 1/2 *Poulet au Vinaigre* **1985** Chabrol's crime thriller is set in a corrupt provincial town. Possessive wheelchair-bound widow Madame Cuno (Audran) and her bullied son, postman Louis (Belvaux), are in danger of losing their home to local land speculators who won't take Madame's refusal to sell for an answer. Thanks to Louis reading their mail, the Cunos find out some dirty secrets and people go missing and then turn up dead. This shifts the focus and brings in cynical detective Levardin (Poiret) to investigate. French with subtitles. **100m/C; DVD.** *FR* Stephane Audran; Jean Poiret; Lucas Belvaux; Jean Topart; Michel Bouquet; Caroline Cellier; Pauline Lafont; Jean-Claude Bouillaud; *D:* Claude Chabrol; *W:* Claude Chabrol; *C:* Jean Rabier; *M:* Matthieu Chabrol.

Cop Car **2015 (R)** Writer/director Watts can't quite stretch his 20 minutes of concept into 88 minutes of filmmaking, even if some of this Coen-esque thriller is occasionally inspired, especially a fun performance by a mustachioed Kevin Bacon. The legendary star is a small town sheriff with many secrets, which are threatened with exposure after a couple of kids just looking for a way to kill time find his car, and steal it. The kids go joy riding through the middle of nowhere, stumbling into a very dangerous situation. Watts' ride is a bumpy, but promising debut. **88m/C; DVD, Blu-Ray.** Kevin Bacon; James Freedson-Jackson; Hays Wellford; Camryn Manheim; Shea Whigham; *D:* Jon Watts; *W:* Jon Watts; Christopher Ford; *C:* Matthew Lloyd; Larkin Seiple; *M:* Phil Mossman.

Cop Dog 1/2 **2008 (PG)** Teenager Robby withdraws after his cop dad is killed in the line of duty. Then Robby befriends his dad's four-legged former partner Marlowe, who chases after the criminals Robby's dad was after. When Marlowe dies in a hit-and-run, Robby is bereft again until Marlowe comes back as a ghost dog determined to catch the bad guys. **90m/C; DVD.** Billey Unger; Cassi Thomson; Stephanie Michels; Alexander Chapman; Corin "Corky" Nemec; *D:* John Murlowski; *W:* Steven Palmer Peterson; *C:* John Murlowski; *M:* Ted Masur. **VIDEO**

Cop Hater 1/2 **1958** During a heatwave, two detectives of the 87th Precinct are gunned down and Steve Carella (Loggia) and Mike Maguire (O'Loughlin) are assigned to the case. Maguire is also murdered and Carella drunkenly shoots off his mouth about the killer's possible identity to reporter Hank Miller (Miller) putting Carella's deaf-mute girlfriend Teddy (Parker) in danger. Based on the first of Ed McBain's 87th Precinct crime novels. **75m/B; DVD.** Robert Loggia; Gerald S. O'Loughlin; Ellen Parker; Gene Miller; Russell Hardie; William Neff; Shirley Ballard; Hal Riddle; Jerry Orbach; Vincent Gardenia; *D:* William Berke; *W:* Henry Kane; *C:* J. Burgi Contner; *M:* Albert Glasser.

Cop in Blue Jeans **1978** Undercover cop goes after a mob kingpin in this violent, badly dubbed crime yarn. **92m/C; VHS, DVD.** Tomas Milian; Jack Palance; Maria Rosaria Omaggio; Guido Mannari; *D:* Bruno Corbucci.

Cop Killers **WOOF! 1973 (R)** Two men desperate for an easy way to make money embark on a murderous shooting spree. Mostly blanks. **93m/C; VHS, DVD, Blu-Ray.** Jason Williams; Bill Osco; *D:* Walter R. Cichy; *W:* Walter R. Cichy; *C:* Howard Ziehm; *M:* Hal Yoergler.

Cop Land *Copland* **1997 (R)** Partially deaf sheriff (Stallone), whose small New Jersey town is home to a number of New York cops, has divided loyalties when a criminal investigation could implicate his department and the cops he idolizes. Stallone wanted to put "actor" back on his resume, and made the ultimate sacrifice of his physique for the role by gaining some 35 pounds and letting his muscles go. Writer-director Mangold, who grew up in an upstate New York town populated by NYC cops and firemen, pairs his earnest morality tale with a Western feel to provide the excellent cast a chance to do what they do best. Welcome departure from the usual summer bombast. **105m/C; VHS, DVD, Blu-Ray.** Sylvester Stallone; Robert De Niro; Annabella Sciorra; Harvey Keitel; Peter Berg; Janeane Garofalo; Michael Rapaport; Ray Liotta; Cathy Moriarty; Robert Patrick; Noah Emmerich; John Spencer; Malik Yoba; Frank Vincent; Arthur J. Nascarella; Edie Falco; Deborah Harry; ***D:*** James Mangold; ***W:*** James Mangold; ***C:*** Eric Alan Edwards; ***M:*** Howard Shore.

Cop Out 🦴 *A Couple of Dicks* **2010 (R)** Two awkwardly paired cops (Willis and Morgan) track down a stolen baseball card, rescue a babe, and deal with gangsters and laundered drug money in this send-up of cop buddy movies that manages to be worse than the movies it is trying to mock. Not entirely without laughs, but the sheer number of failed jokes?-most of the poo-poo variety—more than overshadows the successes. Notable for being the first movie Smith directed that he did not also write, there are occasional signs of his unique wit but he shows little skill at working with someone else's material. **107m/C; Blu-Ray.** Bruce Willis; Tracy Morgan; Seann William Scott; Adam Brody; Kevin Pollak; Jason Lee; Michelle Trachtenberg; Mark Consuelos; ***D:*** Kevin Smith; ***W:*** Robert Cullen; Marc Cullen; ***C:*** David Klein; ***M:*** Harold Faltermeyer.

Copacabana 🦴🦴 **1947** A shady theatrical agent (Groucho) books a nightclub singer into two shows at the same time at New York's ritzy nightclub. Lots of energy spent trying to enliven a routine script. Also available colorized. **91m/B; DVD, Blu-Ray.** Groucho Marx; Carmen Miranda; Steve Cochran; Gloria Jean; Andy Russell; ***Cameo(s):*** Earl Wilson; ***D:*** Alfred E. Green; ***W:*** Allen Boretz; Laszlo Vadnay; ***C:*** Bert Glennon.

Copper Canyon 🦴🦴 ½ **1950** Milland plays a Confederate Army officer who heads West after the Civil War, meets up with Lamarr, and sparks a romance. Good chemistry between the leads in this otherwise standard western. **84m/B; VHS, DVD.** Ray Milland; Hedy Lamarr; MacDonald Carey; Mona Freeman; Harry Carey, Jr.; Frank Faylen; Taylor Holmes; Peggy Knudsen; ***D:*** John Farrow.

Copperhead 🦴 ½ **2013 (PG-13)** Ernest but dull Civil War family drama takes place in a small upstate New York community. Abner Beech is opposed to slavery but also to the war because he's a pacifist and wants his sons safe at home. His neighbors don't feel the same and rabble-rousing preacher Jee Hagadorn turns the community against Abner. Complicating the matter is the romance between Abner's son Jeff and Jee's daughter Esther, especially when Jeff decides to join the Union Army to prove his love. Based on the Harold Frederic novel. **119m/C; Blu-Ray, Streaming.** Billy Campbell; Angus MacFadyen; Lucy Boynton; Casey Thomas Brown; François Arnaud; Augustus Prew; Peter Fonda; ***D:*** Ronald F. Maxwell; ***W:*** Bill Kauffman; ***C:*** Kees Van Oostrum; ***M:*** Laurent Eyquem.

Cops and Robbers 🦴🦴 ½ **1973 (PG)** Two cops use a Wall Street parade for returning astronauts as a cover for a multi-million dollar heist. Exceptional caper film thanks to the likable leads and genuine suspense. **89m/C; VHS, DVD, Blu-Ray.** Joseph Bologna; Dick Ward; Shepperd Strudwick; John P. Ryan; Ellen Holly; Dolph Sweet; Joe Spinell; Cliff Gorman; ***D:*** Aram Avakian; ***W:*** Donald E. Westlake.

Cops and Robbersons 🦴 **1994 (PG)** Bored, dim-witted dad Chase, a TV cop-show junkie, wishes his life had a little more danger and excitement. How lucky for him when hard-nosed cop Palance sets up a command post in his house to stake out the mobster living next door (Davi). Predictable plot isn't funny and drags Chase's bumbling idiot persona on for too long; Wiest and Davi are two bright spots, but their talents are wasted, while Palance does little more than reincarnate his "City Slickers" character. Poor effort for otherwise notable director Ritchie. **93m/C; DVD.** Chevy Chase; Jack Palance; Dianne Wiest; Robert Davi; Jason James Richter; Fay Masterson; Miko Hughes; Richard Romanus; David Barry Gray; Jack Kehler; ***D:*** Michael Ritchie; ***W:*** Bernie Somers; ***C:*** Gerry Fisher; ***M:*** William Ross.

Cops vs. Thugs 🦴🦴 ½ *Kenkei tai soshiki boryoku* **1975** Director Kinji Fukasawa is best known in America for the film "Battle Royale" (which is incidentally difficult to get here legally), but got his start as the director of Yakuza films. Set in Kurashima City in 1963, two rival Yakuza gangs share control of the city's underworld. When the boss of one is sent to prison, the other sees opportunity and soon the streets are covered in blood and bullets. Outnumbered, one of the gangs appeals to the cops for help and surprisingly some of them agree. **101m/C; DVD, Blu-Ray.** *JP* Bunta Sugawara; Hiroki Matsukata; Mikio Narita; Tatsuo Umemiya; ***D:*** Kinji Fukasaku; ***W:*** Kazuo Kasahara; ***C:*** Shigeru Akatsuka; ***M:*** Toshiaki Tsushima.

Copycat 🦴🦴 **1995 (R)** Crowded serial killer genre yields crooner Connick as southern psychopath stuck on murder. Soon he's in jail, advising the police in their hunt for another serial killer who imitates the murders of other infamous serial killers. Agoraphobic, boozing criminal psychologist Helen Hudson (Weaver), still suffering the after effects of an attack by sicko subject Darryl Lee Cullum (Connick), is enlisted to help detective M.J. Monahan (Hunter) catch the homage specialist. Weaver and Hunter bring sparks to the usually testosterone-laden formula, helping mask the preponderance of serial killer cliches and giant holes in the script. Connick's turn as a nut-job killer won't make you forget Anthony Hopkins, or even Frank Sinatra. Exploitative and imitative, and always faithful to the formula. **124m/C; VHS, DVD, Blu-Ray.** Sigourney Weaver; Holly Hunter; Dermot Mulroney; Harry Connick, Jr.; William McNamara; Will Patton; John Rothman; David Michael Silverman; ***D:*** Jon Amiel; ***W:*** Ann Biderman; David Madsen; ***C:*** Laszlo Kovacs; ***M:*** Christopher Young.

Cora Unashamed 🦴🦴 ½ **2000** Adaptation of the Langston Hughes short story that finds racism and tragedy in a small Iowa town in the 1930s. Cora Jenkins (Taylor) and her mother (Pounder) are the only blacks in the community. Cora works as a housekeeper for the Studevant family and becomes strongly attached to the family's daughter, Jessie (Graham). This bond is resented by Jessie's mother, selfish and cold Lizbeth (Jones), whose exaggerated sense of propriety brings about disaster. **95m/C; VHS, DVD.** Regina Taylor; Cherry Jones; CCH Pounder; Michael Gaston; Arlen Dean Snyder; Molly Graham; Ellen Muth; Kohl Sudduth; ***D:*** Deborah Pratt; ***W:*** Ann Peacock; ***C:*** Ernest Holzman; ***M:*** Patrice Rushen. **TV**

Coraline 🦴🦴🦴 **2009 (PG)** A stop-motion animated fantasy based on the novel by Neil Gaiman. Young Coraline Jones (Fanning), not a particularly nice little girl, discovers a secret door in her family's new home that leads to a bizarre, alternate version of her own life. Threatened by her new, strange parents to trap her in this "Alice in Wonderland" nightmare forever, she must then plan her escape. Director Selick suggests this creepy chiller is intended for "brave children." Shot in stereoscopic 3-D, which unfortunately doesn't translate well off the big screen. **100m/C; Blu-Ray.** ***V:*** Dakota Fanning; Teri Hatcher; Ian McShane; Keith David; Jennifer Saunders; Dawn French; John Hodgman; Robert Bailey, Jr.; ***D:*** Henry Selick; ***W:*** Henry Selick; ***C:*** Pete Kozachik; ***M:*** Bruno Coulais.

The Core 🦴🦴 ½ **2003 (PG-13)** The molten-hot magma goo at the Earth's core has stopped spinning (?!), bringing about the end of the world...unless a team of scientists and pilots can drill to the center of the planet and detonate an atomic device to get it going again in this unabashedly silly popcorn flick. Led by scruffy geophysicist Josh Keyes (Eckhart), the multi-ethnic, multi-talented crew sets off on their preposterous mission, knowing full-well that the whole thing is ridiculous. This self knowledge, agreeing that it's all absurd, and not taking itself to seriously, is what gets this disaster flick by. Everybody has a good time playing their characters' assigned quirks, especially Tucci as a smug, smarmy geophysicist. **135m/C; VHS, DVD.** Aaron Eckhart; Hilary Swank; Delroy Lindo; Stanley Tucci; DJ Qualls; Richard Jenkins; Tcheky Karyo; Bruce Greenwood; Alfre Woodard; ***D:*** Jon Amiel; ***W:*** John Rogers; Cooper Layne; ***C:*** John Lindley; ***M:*** Christopher Young.

Coriolanus 🦴🦴🦴 **2011 (R)** Fiennes makes his directorial debut and stars in this Shakespearian adaptation updated for modern audiences as the titular Roman general, a man first lauded as a savior of his people but shortly exiled after losing the support of his base. To get revenge, he allies himself with his former enemy Tullius Aufidis (Butler). Despite a macho tone, actresses Chastain and Redgrave hold their own. Well-staged and noble but Fiennes doesn't quite yet have the eye for composition to get past the relatively stale story. There's a reason this hasn't been one of the Bard's most-adapted works. **122m/C; DVD, Blu-Ray.** Ralph Fiennes; Gerard Butler; Vanessa Redgrave; Brian Cox; Jessica Chastain; James Nesbitt; John Kani; Paul Jesson; ***D:*** Ralph Fiennes; ***W:*** John Logan; ***C:*** Barry Ackroyd; ***M:*** Ilan Eshkeri.

Corky 🦴 **1972** MGM hack job with a thoroughly unlikeable title character. Ambitious, reckless rural Texas mechanic Corky Curtiss is certain he can make it as a winner on the stock car racing circuit if only he didn't have these problems with other people--like his wife and kids, his boss, and the other drivers. Corky ditches everything to try his luck, which is all bad. Features cameos by various NASCAR stars, including Cale Yarborough, Buddy Baker and Bobby and Donnie Allison. **88m/C; DVD.** Robert (Bobby) Blake; Charlotte Rampling; Patrick O'Neal; Christopher Connelly; Ben Johnson; ***D:*** Leonard Horn; ***W:*** Eugene Price; ***C:*** David M. Walsh; ***M:*** Jerry Styner.

Corky of Gasoline Alley 🦴 ½ **1951** Hope's drifter cousin Elwood shows up to mooch off her and Corky, causing havoc at home and work and for their friends as well. The second in the film series following "Gasoline Alley." Based on the Frank O. King comic strip. **80m/B; DVD.** Scotty Beckett; Susan Morrow; Gordon Jones; Don Beddoe; James Lydon; Dick Wessel; Pat Brady; ***D:*** Edward L. Bernds; ***W:*** Edward L. Bernds; ***C:*** Henry Freulich.

Corky Romano 🦴 **2001 (PG-13)** Remember when ex-SNL cast members made good movies? Yeah, neither do they. Kattan is the title character—a spastic, twitchy veterinary assistant, estranged from his mob family, who's so naive, he thinks his Pops (Falk) is actually a landscaping mogul. He is talked into infiltrating the FBI to retrieve evidence against the family by gruff henchman Leo (Ward), the actual stool pigeon talking to the feds. His frantic bumbling is mistaken for genius by his FBI superior Schuster (Roundtree) and hottie special agent Kate (Shaw). The plot is just dressing for Kattan's "funny-looking rubbery guy knocks everything over" routine, and he plays it like Jerry Lewis without the subtlety. First "Night at the Roxbury," then "Monkeybone" and now this? Can someone get Kattan a script consultant? Please? **85m/C; VHS, DVD.** Chris Kattan; Vinessa Shaw; Peter Falk; Peter Berg; Christopher Penn; Fred Ward; Richard Roundtree; Mathew Glave; Dave Sheridan; Roger Fan; ***D:*** Rob Pritts; ***W:*** David Garrett; Jason Ward; ***C:*** Steven Bernstein; ***M:*** Randy Edelman.

Corn 🦴🦴 **2004 (PG)** The locals don't put much stock in Emily's word when the unmarried, pregnant college dropout starts carrying on about the dangers of some "genetically enhanced" corn crops even though a bunch of folks suddenly aren't feeling so good. What is it about corn that makes small towns go all crazy in the movies, anyway? **97m/C; VHS, DVD.** Jena Malone; Pamela Gray; Peter McRobbie; Jamie Harrold; Libby Langdon; Don Harvey; John Hartmann; Brian Dykstra; David Matthew Feldman; Denise Grayson; John Quincy Lee; Rick Lyon; Adrian Martinez; ***D:*** Dave Silver; ***W:*** Dave Silver; ***C:*** H. Michael Otano; ***M:*** Craig Snyder. **VIDEO**

The Corn Is Green 🦴🦴🦴 **1945** Touching story of a school teacher in a poor Welsh village who eventually sends her pet student to Oxford. Davis makes a fine teacher, though a little young, while the on-site photography provides atmosphere. Based on the play by Emlyn Williams. Remade in 1979. **115m/B; DVD.** Bette Davis; John Dall; Nigel Bruce; Joan Lorring; Arthur Shields; Mildred Dunnock; Rhys Williams; Rosalind Ivan; ***D:*** Irving Rapper; ***M:*** Max Steiner.

The Corn Is Green 🦴🦴🦴 **1979** Excellent TV adaptation of the Emlyn Willimas play has Hepburn as dedicated teacher Lilly Moffat, determined to bring education to a small Welsh mining village. She finds and mentors a student she believes can escape the mines with the power of his intellect. Cukor overcomes the limitations of television in his last collaboration with Hepburn. **93m/C; VHS, DVD.** Katharine Hepburn; Bill Fraser; Anna Massey; Patricia Hayes; Dorothy Phillips; ***D:*** George Cukor; ***W:*** Ivan Davis; ***M:*** John Barry. **TV**

Cornbread, Earl & Me 🦴🦴 **1975 (R)** A high school basketball star from the ghetto is mistaken for a murderer by cops and shot, causing a subsequent furor of protest and racial hatred. Superficial melodrama. **95m/C; VHS, DVD, Blu-Ray.** Moses Gunn; Rosalind Cash; Bernie Casey; Tierre Turner; Madge Sinclair; Keith Wilkes; Antonio Fargas; Laurence Fishburne; ***D:*** Joseph Manduke; ***W:*** Leonard Lamensdorf; ***C:*** Jules Brenner; ***M:*** Donald Byrd.

The Corner 🦴🦴 ½ **2000** This HBO miniseries was adapted from reporter David Simon's book "The Corner: A Year in the Life of an Inner-City Neighborhood" that neighborhood being Fayette Street in Baltimore. This corner is the local hub of drug activity that draws in members of the same family: Fran Boyd (Alexander) and Gary McCullough (Carter), who are both addicts, as well as their 15-year-old son DeAndre (Nelson). His parents are losing the battle to keep DeAndre away from drugs, gangs, and other trouble but when Fran learns that DeAndre's equally young girlfriend is pregnant, it spurs her into rehab and the hope of making something right. **376m/C; DVD.** Khandi Alexander; T.K. Carter; Sean Nelson; Glenn Plummer; Clarke Peters; Tyra Ferrell; Tasha Smith; Toy Connor; ***D:*** Charles S. Dutton; ***W:*** David Mills; ***C:*** Ivan Strasburg; ***M:*** Henry Butler; Corey Harris. **CABLE**

Cornered 🦴🦴🦴 **1945** Tough Powell plays an airman released from a German prison camp who pursues a Nazi war criminal to avenge the death of his wife and child. **102m/B; VHS, DVD.** Dick Powell; Walter Slezak; Micheline Cheirel; Luther Adler; ***D:*** Edward Dmytryk.

Cornered! 🦴 ½ **2009 (R)** Slow-paced, low-budget slasher/horror with an obvious killer. A late-night poker game in a seedy L.A. convenience store has the players talking about the masked serial killer targeting such stores and what they would do. The killer shows up and puts all their talk to the test. **87m/C; DVD.** Steve Guttenberg; James Duval; Ellia English; Elizabeth Nicole; Eduardo Antonio Garcia; Peter Story; ***D:*** Daniel Maze; ***W:*** Darrin Grimwood; ***C:*** Keith Dunkerloy; ***M:*** Konstantinos Zacharopoulos. **VIDEO**

Coronado 🦴 ½ **2003 (R)** Claire Winslow (Datillo) lives a life of ease in Beverly Hills until she follows her boyfriend to Switzerland on a whim. Not only is his business trip there a fib, she finds out he's really in some third world country called Coronado. Flying there she finds out he may have been kidnapped by local revolutionaries trying to overthrow the country's corrupt government. Just once wouldn't it be nice to see a movie about a non-corrupt third world government? **84m/C; DVD.** *GE* Michael Lowry; David Earl Waterman; Byron Quiros; David Purdham; Aline Mayagoitia; Elizabeth Beckwith; Kristin Dattilo-Hayward; Clayton Rohner; John Rhys-Davies; Daniel Zacapa; Carlos Cervantes; ***D:*** Claudio Fah; ***W:*** Volker Engel; Marc Weigart; Claudio Fah; ***C:*** Anna Foerster; Jaime Reynoso; S. Douglas Smith; ***M:*** Ralf Weinrich.

The Coroner 🦴🦴 **1998 (R)** Dr. Leon Urasky (St. Louis) is both a coroner and a serial killer. He chooses lawyer Emma Santiago (Longenecker) as a victim, but she is no pushover. Horror/thriller has some humor, a few nice moments, but mostly tedious. **75m/C; DVD.** Jane Longenecker; Dean St. Louis; Rebecca Gray; ***D:*** Juan A. Mas; ***W:*** Geralyn Ruane; ***C:*** Charles "Chip" Schner.

Corporate Affairs 🦴🦴 **1990 (R)** A ruthless business woman climbing her way to the top literally seduces her boss to death. **92m/C; VHS, DVD.** Peter Scolari; Mary Crosby; Chris Lemmon; Ken Kercheval; ***D:*** Terence H. Winkless; ***W:*** Terence H. Winkless; Geoffrey Baere.

Corporate Affairs 🦴 **2007 (R)** Lame flick that can't make up its mind whether to be a morality tale or an office sex comedy. Ted

(Meyer) is married to Cassie (Harris) and they live in the 'burbs with their kids. Ted enjoys being a computer programmer for a software company but can't turn down a big promotion to management because the pay is too good, but unfortunately Ted's a techno geek, not a schmoozer of clients. He starts to travel a lot for business and soon realizes that managers employ hookers as perks (for themselves and the clients), and Ted isn't man enough to resist. **99m/C; DVD.** Breckin Meyer; Laura Harris; George Coe; Bess Armstrong; Adam Scott; Monica Keena; Melinda Page Hamilton; ***D:*** Dan Cohen; ***W:*** Dan Cohen; ***C:*** Ian Mcglocklin. **VIDEO**

Corporate Animals 🦴 1/2 **2019 (R)** Petty boss Lucy (Moore) takes her long-suffering tech company team on a team-building trip to a dangerous cave. Once they arrive, the situation grows complicated when an earthquake traps them in the cave and kills their guide, Brandon (Helms). Forced to survive on their own, Lucy's cruelties and selfishness affects their efforts to escape. A satire of corporate America and start-up culture, the film never moves beyond its comedic premise. Instead, the energy of the ensemble cast is wasted on a miserable story and random pop culture references. **85m/C; DVD.** Demi Moore; Ed Helms; Jessica Williams; Karan Soni; Isiah Whitlock, Jr.; ***D:*** Patrick Brice; ***W:*** Sam Bain; ***C:*** Tarin Anderson; ***M:*** Michael Yezerski.

The Corpse Grinders WOOF! 1971 (R) Low-budget bad movie classic in which a cardboard corpse-grinding machine makes nasty cat food that makes cats nasty. Sets are cheap, gore effects silly, and cat attacks ridiculous. **73m/C; VHS, DVD, Blu-Ray.** Sean Kenney; Monika Kelly; Sandford Mitchell; Byron J. Foster; Warren Ball; Ann Noble; ***D:*** Ted V. Mikels; ***W:*** Ted V. Mikels; Arch Hall, Jr.; Joseph L. Cranston; ***C:*** Bill Anneman.

Corpse Mania 🦴🦴 *Si yiu; Shi yao* **1981** A disturbing Chinese version of the Italian Giallo genre, we find a man kindly taking sick prostitutes off the streets to care for them. Unknown to these women he is a secret necrophiliac who needs women to be dead to 'romance' them. Coincidentally many of the local prostitutes are being graphically murdered, and the police have little in the way of suspects but a recently released mental patient (who is the aforementioned necrophile). But he claims to be incapable of killing, and many of the locals seem to have a secret or two to hide. **78m/C; DVD.** *CH* Ni Tien; Yung Wang; Tsui Ling Yu; Siu-Kwan Lau; Erik Chan Ka Kei; ***D:*** Chih-Hung Kuei; ***W:*** Chih-Hung Kuei; On Szeto; ***C:*** Hsin Yeh Li; ***M:*** Eddie Wang.

Corpus Christi 🦴🦴🦴 *Boze Cialo* **2019 115m/C; DVD.** Bartosz Bielenia; Aleksandra Konieczna; Eliza Rycembel; Tomasz Zietek; Leszec Lichota; ***D:*** Jan Komasa; ***W:*** Mateusz Pacewicz; ***C:*** Piotr Sobocinski, Jr.; ***M:*** Evgueni Galperine; Sacha Galperine.

Corregidor 🦴🦴 **1943** A love triangle develops between doctors treating the wounded during the WWII battle. A poor propaganda piece which contains only shaky stock footage for its "action" sequences. **73m/B; VHS, DVD.** Otto Kruger; Elissa Landi; Donald Woods; Rick Vallin; Frank Jenks; Wanda McKay; Ian Keith; ***D:*** William Nigh.

Corridors of Blood 🦴🦴 1/2 *The Doctor from Seven Dials* **1958** Karloff is a doctor, in search of a viable anesthetic, who accidently becomes addicted to drugs, then turns to grave robbers to support his habit. Karloff plays usual threatening doctor to perfection. **86m/C; VHS, DVD.** *GB* Boris Karloff; Betta St. John; Finlay Currie; Christopher Lee; Francis Matthews; Adrienne Corri; Nigel Green; ***D:*** Robert Day; ***W:*** Jean Scott Rogers; ***C:*** Geoffrey Faithfull; ***M:*** Buxton Orr.

Corrina, Corrina 🦴🦴 1/2 **1994 (PG)** Newly widowed jingle-writer Liotta needs someone to care for his withdrawn eight-year-old daughter. Enter Whoopi, as housekeeper and eventual love interest. Sweet, nostalgic romance set in the 1950s. Goldberg also found off-screen romance (again), this time with the film's union organizer Lyle Trachtenberg. Last role for Ameche. **115m/C; VHS, DVD.** Whoopi Goldberg; Ray Liotta; Don Ameche; Tina Majorino; Wendy Crewson; Jenifer Lewis; Larry Miller; Erica Yohn; Anita Baker; ***D:*** Jessie Nelson; ***W:*** Jessie Nelson; ***C:*** Bruce Surtees; ***M:*** Rick Cox; Thomas Newman.

Corrupt 🦴🦴🦴 *Order of Death; Cop Killers* **1984 (PG)** Bad narcotics cop goes after murderer, but mysterious Lydon gets in the way. An acquired taste, best if you appreciate Lydon, better known as Johnny Rotten of the Sex Pistols. **99m/C; VHS, DVD.** *IT* Harvey Keitel; John (Johnny Rotten) Lydon; Sylvia Sidney; Nicole Garcia; Leonard Mann; ***D:*** Roberto Faenza; ***W:*** Roberto Faenza; Ennio de Concini; Hugh Fleetwood; ***C:*** Guiseppe Pinori; ***M:*** Ennio Morricone.

Corrupt 🦴 1/2 **1999 (R)** Corrupt (Ice-T) is the drug lord who holds the South Bronx but he has would-be competition from some up-and-coming homeboys. However, one ex-gang banger (Silkk the Shocker) wants out of the 'hood to make a new life for himself and his girl. Only Corrupt and his posse stand in the way. **72m/C; VHS, DVD.** Ice-T; Ernie Hudson; silkk the Shocker; Karen Dyer; ***D:*** Albert Pyun. **VIDEO**

Corrupted Hands 🦴🦴 *Dastha-ye aloode* **2000** An Iranian comedy about a pair of friends who use marriage as means of making money, both legally and illegally. Wedding photographer Siamak (Pour-Arab) and his close friend Nader (Hayayi) have a business that puts weddings on, with the help of Diba (Tehrani), Siamak's romantic interest, and Roya (Imani), Nader's fiancee. The friends use the wedding service as means of robbing their clients. The ruse works until Siamak finds himself falling in love with Nasrin (Badiie). Not only is Diba jealous, but Nasrin's father is suspicious of Siamak and hires a detective to spy on him. In the meantime, the focused Siamak wants to rob his own wedding and the detective wants in on the deal. **100m/C; DVD.** Abolfazl Poorarab; Hediyeh Tehrani; Asal Badii; Amin Hayayee; Elham Imani; ***D:*** Sirus Alvand; ***W:*** Sirus Alvand; Tirdad Sakhai; ***C:*** Ali Allahyari; ***M:*** Babak Bayat. **VIDEO**

Corrupted Minds 🦴🦴 *Detroit; Panic in Detroit* **2006 (R)** The lives of four groups of people who come into Michigan from Canada to visit Detroit are on display. The result is a revoltingly prejudicial display of Detroit as a city, where angry people have degrading sex and African-Americans kill each other with gleeful abandon. Despite the low budget and rampant use of cliches, it's not a bad effort for a first-time low budget flick. **85m/C; DVD.** Derek Denham; Candace Poluzny; Deirdre Tracey; Dale Reynolds; Mark Brock; ***D:*** Brian Lawrence; ***W:*** Brian Lawrence; ***C:*** Lon Stratton; ***M:*** Gary Haverkate; Dan Kolton.

Corruption 🦴 1/2 **1933** A corrupt political machine put new mayor Tim Butler in office but when he decides to change his ways and clean up the city Tim's framed for the murder of a political boss. His secretary Ellen and reporter Charlie team up to clear Tim's name. **67m/B; DVD.** Preston Foster; Evalyn Knapp; Charles Delaney; Tully Marshall; Natalie Moorhead; Mischa Auer; Warner Richmond; Huntley Gordon; ***D:*** Charles E. Roberts; ***W:*** Charles E. Roberts; ***C:*** Robert E. Cline.

The Corruptor 🦴🦴🦴 **1999 (R)** Slick crime thriller starring Wahlberg as Danny, a young Caucasian cop assigned to New York's Chinatown precinct and partnered with shrewd veteran Chen (Chow Yun-Fat). The two men are drawn into a web of deception and betrayal as they try to stop a war between rival underworld factions. Chow finally receives a Hollywood role that showcases the talents that made him an international star in Asia, although the action segments suffer in comparison to his work with John Woo. The plot and performances are excellent, and there's enough shoot-'em-up to satisfy the average appetite for destruction. **110m/C; VHS, DVD, Blu-Ray.** Chow Yun-Fat; Mark Wahlberg; Ric Young; Paul Ben-Victor; Brian Cox; Byron Mann; Kim Chan; Tovah Feldshuh; Jon Kit Lee; Andrew Pang; Elizabeth Lindsey; Bill MacDonald; Susie Trinh; ***D:*** James Foley; ***W:*** Robert Pucci; ***C:*** Juan Ruiz-Anchia; ***M:*** Carter Burwell.

Corsair 🦴🦴 **1931** Actioner about a gorgeous debutante and a handsome gangster who find themselves caught up with a gang of bootlegging pirates. Todd is always worth watching. **73m/B; VHS, DVD.** Chester Morris; Thelma Todd; Frank McHugh; Ned Sparks; Mayo Methot; ***D:*** Roland West.

The Corsican Brothers 🦴🦴 1/2 **1942** Siamese-twins Mario and Lucien are separated by Dr. Paoli (Warner) shortly before their parents are murdered by evil Colonna (Tamiroff). One boy is sent to Paris and the other grows up in the Corsican mountains. Reunited as adults (and dashingly played by Faribanks Jr.), the twins plot revenge. Entertaining swashbuckler based on a novel by Alexandre Dumas. **111m/B; VHS, DVD.** Douglas Fairbanks, Jr.; Akim Tamiroff; Ruth Warrick; J. Carrol Naish; H.B. Warner; Henry Wilcoxon; Veda Ann Borg; ***D:*** Gregory Ratoff; ***W:*** George Bruce; ***C:*** Harry Stradling, Sr.; ***M:*** Dimitri Tiomkin.

Corvette Summer 🦴 *The Hot One* **1978 (PG)** After spending a semester restoring a Corvette in his high school shop class, an L.A. student must journey to Las Vegas to recover the car when it is stolen. There he meets a prostitute, falls in love, and steps into the "real world" for the first time. Potts is intriguing as the low-life love interest, but she can't save this one. **104m/C; VHS, DVD, Blu-Ray.** Mark Hamill; Annie Potts; Eugene Roche; Kim Milford; Richard McKenzie; William (Bill) Bryant; ***D:*** Matthew Robbins; ***W:*** Matthew Robbins; Hal Barwood.

Cosh Boy WOOF! *The Slasher; Killer's Delight* **1952** Vicious male youths stalk women on the streets of London in this low-budget Jack the Ripper rip-off. **90m/B; VHS, DVD, Blu-Ray.** *GB* Joan Collins; James Kennedy; Hermione Baddeley; ***D:*** Lewis Gilbert; ***W:*** Lewis Gilbert.

Cosi 🦴🦴🦴 *Caught in the Act* **1995 (R)** Amiable Lewis (Mendelsohn) is hired to help with drama therapy at the local Sydney mental institution. Pressured by long-term patient Roy (Otto), Lewis finds himself agreeing to stage a production of Mozart's opera "Cosi Fan Tutte" though none of the patients can speak Italian or sing. Rehearsals prove a challenge, there are numerous setbacks, and then it's show time. Fine ensemble cast delivers; adapted from Nowra's play. Friels stepped into the role of security guard Errol when Bruno Lawrence died before filming was completed; pic is dedicated to Lawrence. **100m/C; VHS, DVD.** *AU* Ben Mendelsohn; Barry Otto; Aden Young; Toni Collette; Rachel Griffiths; Colin Friels; Paul Chubb; Pamela Rabe; Jacki Weaver; David Wenham; Colin Hay; Tony Llewellyn-Jones; Kerry Walker; ***Cameo(s):*** Greta Scacchi; Paul Mercurio; ***D:*** Mark Joffe; ***W:*** Louis Nowra; ***C:*** Ellery Ryan; ***M:*** Stephen Endelman. Australian Film Inst. '96: Adapt. Screenplay, Support. Actress (Collette).

The Cosmic Eye 🦴🦴🦴 **1971** Animated tale of three musicians from outer space who come to earth to spread the message of worldwide peace and harmony. A variety of cultural perspectives about the origins and destiny of the Earth are offered. Rather moralizing but the animation is impressive. **71m/C; VHS, DVD.** ***V:*** Dizzy Gillespie; Maureen Stapleton; Benny Carter; ***D:*** Faith Hubley.

The Cosmic Man 🦴 1/2 **1959** An alien arrives on Earth with a message of peace and restraint. He is regarded with suspicion by us nasty Earthlings. Essentially "The Day the Earth Stood Still" without the budget, but interesting nonetheless. **72m/B; VHS, DVD.** Bruce Bennett; John Carradine; Angela Greene; Paul Langton; Scotty Morrow; ***D:*** Herbert Greene; ***W:*** Arthur C. Pierce; ***C:*** John F. Warren; ***M:*** Paul Sawtell; Bert Shefter.

Cosmopolis 🦴🦴🦴 **2012 (R)** Director and co-writer Cronenberg adapts Don DeLillo's novella with mixed results as Pattinson plays young corporate mogul Eric who basically exists only in the back of his customized stretch limousine as the world around him collapses. With death threats and potential riots outside his bulletproof windows, Eric can barely find a reason to care beyond a potential financial loss. Cronenberg's devotion to the thin source material turns out to be a major flaw. But Pattinson delivers as does the supporting cast including dazzling actors like Binoche and Giamatti and that makes this journey easier to bear. **109m/C; DVD, Blu-Ray.** *CA FR* Robert Pattinson; Juliette Binoche; Sarah Gadon; Mathieu Amalric; Jay Baruchel; Kevin Durand; Samantha Morton; Paul Giamatti; ***D:*** David Cronenberg; ***W:*** David Cronenberg; ***C:*** Peter Suschitzky; ***M:*** Howard Shore.

Cosmos 🦴🦴 1/2 **2016** World renowned Polish director/writer Andrzej Zulawski's final film (he passed in early 2016) further shows the director's willingness to stretch the boundaries. Based on the book by Witold Gombrowicz, this is the story of two young men (Jonathan Geot and Johan Libereau) who retreat to a family guest house after some bumps in the road of life. There they meet a pair of women, one of whom Witold falls in love with. Until the end, Zulawski was more interested in creating a feeling in his viewers, or merely disorienting them, than telling a story. **103m/C; DVD, Blu-Ray.** Sabine Azema; Jean-Francois Balmer; Jonathan Genet; Johan Libereau; Victoria Guerra; ***D:*** Andrzej Zulawski; ***W:*** Andrzej Zulawski; ***C:*** Andre Szankowski; ***M:*** Andrzej Zulawski.

Cosmos: War of the Planets WOOF! *Cosmo 2000: Planet Without a Name; War of the Planets* **1980 (PG)** The ultimate battle for survival is fought in outer space, though not very well and on a small budget. Special effects especially laughable. **90m/C; VHS, DVD.** *IT* Katia Christine; West Buchanan; John Richardson; Yanti Somer; ***D:*** Al (Alfonso Brescia) Bradley.

The Cost of Love 🦴 1/2 **2011** Dale is a successful escort in London who's secretly in love with his best buddy Raj, who's just announced that he's getting married. Dale turns to another friend, rebellious drag artist Sean, for comfort without realizing that Sean is in love with him. **90m/C; DVD.** *GB* Christopher Kelham; Michael Joyce; Valmike Rampersad; Frank Jakeman; ***D:*** Carl Medland; ***W:*** Carl Medland; ***C:*** Amarjeet Singh; ***M:*** Ram Khatabaksh.

Cote d'Azur 🦴🦴 *Crustaces et Coquillages; Cockles and Muscles* **2005** Silly sex farce set on the sunny French Riviera. Marrieds Beatrix and Marc take their daughter Laura, son Charly, and Charly's best pal Martin for a summer beach holiday. Laura promptly disappears with a new beau and Charly has his own reasons for not correcting his parents' misconception that he and the openly gay Martin are sexually involved. Meanwhile, Beatrix's city lover shows up to surprise her and Marc has a secret involving boyhood friend Didier. French with subtitles. **93m/C; DVD.** *FR* Valeria Bruni-Tedeschi; Gilbert Melki; Jean-Marc Barr; Jacques Bonnaffe; Romain; Edouard Collin; Sabrina Seyvecou; ***D:*** Olivier Ducastel; Jacques Martineau; ***W:*** Olivier Ducastel; Jacques Martineau; ***C:*** Mathieu Poirot-Delpech; ***M:*** Philippe Miller.

Cottage Country 🦴 1/2 **2013** Todd plans to propose to his pushy girlfriend at the family cabin, only to be thwarted by his jerk of a brother who turns the place into party central. Accidentally murdering his bro in a fit of pique, he is shocked to discover his fiancé has no problem hiding the body. **91m/C; DVD, Blu-Ray.** Malin Akerman; Tyler Labine; Lucy Punch; Dan Petronijevic; Jim Annan; ***D:*** Peter Wellington; ***W:*** Jeremy Boxen; ***C:*** Luc Montpellier; ***M:*** Ansher Lenz; Stephen Skratt. **VIDEO**

Cottage to Let 🦴 1/2 *Bombsight Stolen* **1941** Propaganda thriller about a Nazi plot to kidnap the inventor of a new bombsight. Focused cast struggles with lackluster script. **90m/B; DVD, Streaming.** *UK* Leslie Banks; Alastair Sim; John Mills; Jeanne de Casalis; Carla Lehmann; George Cole; Michael Wilding; Frank Cellier; Wally Patch; Catherine Lacey; ***D:*** Anthony Asquith; ***W:*** Anatole de Grunwald; ***C:*** Jack Cox.

Cotter 🦴 **1972** A Native American rodeo clown feels responsible for a cowboy's death, returns home to reflect on his life. Fair story, best at the small town feeling. **94m/C; VHS, DVD.** Don Murray; Carol Lynley; Rip Torn; Sherry Jackson; Christopher Knight; ***D:*** Paul Stanley; ***W:*** William D. Gordon; ***C:*** Alan Stensvold.

The Cotton Club 🦴🦴🦴 **1984 (R)** With $50 million in his pocket, Francis reaches for an epic and delivers: handsome production, lots of dance, bit of singing, confused plot, uneven performances, tad too long. A musician playing at The Cotton Club falls in love with gangster Dutch Schultz's girlfriend. A black tap dancer falls in love with a member of the chorus line who can pass for white. These two love stories are told against a background of mob violence and music. Excellent performances by Hoskins and Gwynne. **121m/C; VHS, DVD.** Diane Lane; Richard Gere; Gregory Hines; Lonette McKee; Bob Hoskins; Fred Gwynne; James Remar; Nicolas Cage; Lisa Jane Persky; Allen Garfield; Gwen Verdon; Joe Dallesandro; Jennifer Grey; Tom Waits; Diane Venora; Robert Earl Jones; ***D:*** Francis Ford Coppola; ***W:*** Francis Ford Coppola; William Kennedy; Mario Puzo; ***C:*** Stephen Goldblatt; ***M:*** John Barry.

Cotton Comes to Harlem 𝒥𝒥𝒥 **1970 (R)** Cambridge and St. Jacques star as Harlem plainclothes detectives Grave Digger Jones and Coffin Ed Johnson in this successful mix of crime and comedy. They're investigating a suspicious preacher's back-to-Africa scheme which they suspect is a swindle. Directorial debut of Davis. Filmed on location in Harlem, New York. Based on the novel by Chester Himes. Followed by a weak sequel, "Come Back, Charleston Blue." **97m/C; VHS, DVD, Blu-Ray.** Godfrey Cambridge; Raymond St. Jacques; Calvin Lockhart; Judy Pace; Redd Foxx; John Anderson; Emily Yancy; J.D. Cannon; Teddy Wilson; Eugene Roche; Cleavon Little; Lou Jacobi; ***D:*** Ossie Davis; ***W:*** Ossie Davis; ***C:*** Gerald Hirschfeld; ***M:*** Galt MacDermot.

Cotton Mary 𝒥𝒥 **1999 (R)** Lily (Scacchi) is the lonely wife of reporter John (Wilby), living in India in 1954. She cannot nurse her newborn daughter and turns to the ministrations of bossy Anglo-Indian nurse Mary (Jaffrey), who is soon living in their household and having the child fed by her own sister, Blossom (Gupta). Meanwhile, the philandering John eyes Mary's niece, Rosie (Sakina Jaffrey), while Lily sinks into depression, and an increasingly mad Mary ruthlessly takes over their home. **124m/C; VHS, DVD.** *GB* Madhur Jaffrey; Greta Scacchi; James Wilby; Neena Gupta; Sakina Jaffrey; Gemma Jones; Sarah Badel; Joanna David; Riyu Bajaj; Prayag Raj; ***D:*** Ismail Merchant; ***W:*** Alexandra Viets; ***C:*** Pierre Lhomme; ***M:*** Richard Robbins.

The Couch 𝒥 1/2 **1962** Deeply disturbed Charles Campbell's therapy isn't doing him much good since he's a homicidal maniac who likes calling and taunting the cops before committing his murders. **100m/B; DVD.** Grant Williams; Shirley Knight; Onslow Stevens; Simon Scott; William Leslie; Anne Helm; ***D:*** Owen Crump; ***W:*** Robert Bloch; ***C:*** Harold E. Stine; ***M:*** Frank Perkins.

A Couch in New York 𝒥𝒥 *Un Divan a New York* **1995 (R)** Limp romantic comedy features that old standby—opposites attracting. French dancer Beatrice (Binoche) responds to an ad for a temporary Paris-New York apartment switch placed by a stuffy psychoanalyst, Henry Harriston (Hurt). Henry's patients presume Beatrice is his replacement (he works at home) and the free-spirit begins giving them ad hoc advice. Meanwhile, in Paris, Henry's plagued by all Beatrice's heartsick boyfriends and decides to come back early. When he arrives unannounced, she assumes he's a new patient and he's intrigued enough to go along. Lots of yakking, not too many sparks, and a strained artificiality make for a dull mix. **104m/C; VHS, DVD.** *FR BE GE* William Hurt; Juliette Binoche; Paul Guilfoyle; Stephanie Buttle; Richard Jenkins; Kent Broadhurst; Henry Bean; Barbara Garrick; ***D:*** Chantal Akerman; ***W:*** Chantal Akerman; Jean-Louis Benoit; ***C:*** Dietrich Lohmann; ***M:*** Paolo Conte; Sonia Atherton.

The Couch Trip 𝒥 1/2 **1987 (R)** Aykroyd is an escapee from a mental institution who passes himself off as a radio psychologist and becomes a media sensation. There are a few laughs and some funny characters but for the most part this one falls flat. **98m/C; VHS, DVD, Blu-Ray.** Dan Aykroyd; Walter Matthau; Charles Grodin; Donna Dixon; Richard Romanus; Arye Gross; David Clennon; Mary Gross; ***D:*** Michael Ritchie; ***W:*** Will Aldis; Steven Kampmann; ***M:*** Michel Colombier.

Cougar Club 𝒥 1/2 **2007** Usual sex comedy about horny guys. Two recent college grads are dismayed to find that their dream jobs at an upscale law firm consist of menial and demeaning tasks. So they decide to open an exclusive dating club for young men like themselves who are interested in fulfilling their fantasies with experienced older women. Soon their day jobs and their night-time escapades are overlapping. **99m/C; DVD.** Joe Mantegna; Kaley Cuoco; Izabela Scorupco; Joan Laurer; Jason Jurman; Warren Kole; Jon Polito; Loretta Devine; ***Cameo(s):*** Faye Dunaway; Carrie Fisher; ***D:*** Christopher Duddy; ***W:*** Chris Mancuso; ***C:*** Dennis Laine; ***M:*** Steve Porcaro.

Cougar Hunting 𝒥 1/2 **2011 (R)** Horny 20-somethings Tom, Dick, and Tyler head to Aspen and get a job at a resort where they hope to find some rich, older women to play sugar mamas. Only recently-dumped Tyler disappoints his buds by making eyes at his contemporary Penelope instead. **103m/C; DVD.** Matt Prokop; Jareb Dauplaise; Randy Wayne; Jillian Murray; Vanessa Angel; Lara Flynn Boyle; ***D:*** Robin Blazak; ***W:*** Robin Blazak; ***C:*** Dan Stoloff; ***M:*** William Goodrum. **VIDEO**

Cougars, Inc. 𝒥 1/2 **2010 (R)** Sam's mom can't continue to pay his private school tuition so the teen decides to start an escort service. He recruits his horny friends to entertain the attractive mature women who are interested in younger men, but they all get a little more than they bargained for. **81m/C; DVD.** Kyle Gallner; Kathryn Morris; Rebecca Mader; Denise Richards; Sarah Hyland; Ryan Pinkston; James Belushi; ***D:*** K. Asher Levin; ***W:*** K. Asher Levin; ***C:*** Harris Charalambous. **VIDEO**

Counsellor-at-Law 𝒥𝒥𝒥 **1933** One of Barrymore's best. He stars as Jewish lawyer George Simon, who has climbed to the top of his profession in New York from a poverty-stricken past that continues to haunt him. His constant struggles in the elitist law community are taking their toll and his personal life is no better when George discovers that his gentile wife Cora (Kenyon) has been unfaithful. But his secretary Regina (Daniels), who has always loved him, remains loyal. Rice adapted from his own play. Director Wyler dumped the musical score except for what's heard over the opening and closing credits. **80m/B; VHS, DVD.** John Barrymore; Bebe Daniels; Doris Kenyon; Onslow Stevens; Isabel Jewell; Melvyn Douglas; Thelma Todd; Mayo Methot; ***D:*** William Wyler; ***W:*** Elmer Rice; ***C:*** Norbert Brodine.

The Counselor 𝒥 1/2 **2013 (R)** With an A-list cast working from the first script written directly for the screen by McCarthy and direction by Scott, expectations were high for this dark thriller about an attorney (Fassbender) who gets caught up in a very deadly world when he decides to increase his wealth by financing a drug run. Those expectations were not met. Too self-conscious and unbelievable, the result is a film that's never thrilling because the characters don't exist in the real world. The cast looks lost in all the philosophy masquerading as entertainment. **117m/C; DVD, Blu-Ray.** Michael Fassbender; Penelope Cruz; Javier Bardem; Cameron Diaz; Brad Pitt; ***D:*** Ridley Scott; ***W:*** Cormac McCarthy; ***C:*** Dariusz Wolski; ***M:*** Daniel Pemberton.

Count Dracula 𝒥𝒥 1/2 *Bram Stoker's Count Dracula; Il Conte Dracula; Dracula 71; Nachts wenn Dracula Erwacht; The Nights of Dracula* **1971 (R)** Passable version of the Dracula legend (based on the novel by Bram Stoker) has Lee as the thirsty count on the prowl for fresh blood. Starts out as one of the most faithful adaptations, but loses momentum because Franco was running out of money. **90m/C; VHS, DVD, Blu-Ray.** *SP GE IT* Christopher Lee; Herbert Lom; Klaus Kinski; Frederick Williams; Maria Rohm; Soledad Miranda; Paul Muller; ***D:*** Jess (Jesus) Franco; ***W:*** Jess (Jesus) Franco; Augusto Finocchi; Harry Alan Towers; Milo G. Cuccia; Carlo Fadda; ***C:*** Manuel Merino.

Count Dracula 𝒥𝒥 1/2 **1977** Three-part BBC adaptation of the Bram Stoker novel with French actor Jourdan naturally seductive and aloof in the vampire role. The pace is leisurely and there's more plot development but it's still not a completely faithful accounting, although only purists will probably be annoyed. **150m/C; DVD.** *GB* Louis Jourdan; Judi Bowker; Bosco Hogan; Frank Finley; Susan Penhaligon; Mark Burns; Richard Barnes; Jack Shepherd; ***D:*** Philip Saville; ***W:*** Gerald Savory; ***C:*** Peter Hall; ***M:*** Kenyon Emrys Roberts. **TV**

The Count of Monte Cristo 𝒥𝒥 1/2 **1912** One of the first full-length features starring popular stage stars of the day. The first truly American feature, it was based on the classic tale of revenge by Alexander Dumas. Silent. Remade many times. Lead actor O'Neill was the father of famed American playwright, Eugene O'Neill, who covered his father's success in this role in his own family drama "Long Day's Journey Into Night." **90m/B; Silent; VHS, DVD.** James O'Neill; ***D:*** Edwin S. Porter.

The Count of Monte Cristo 𝒥𝒥𝒥 **1934** A true swashbuckling revenge tale about Edmond Dantes (Donat), who unjustly spends years in prison. After escaping and retrieving a pirate treasure from the island of Monte Cristo, he gains ever so sweet and served quite cold revenge. Adaptation of the Alexandre Dumas classic. **114m/B; VHS, DVD.** Robert Donat; Elissa Landi; Louis Calhern; Sidney Blackmer; Irene Hervey; Raymond Walburn; O.P. Heggie; ***D:*** Rowland V. Lee; ***W:*** Rowland V. Lee; Philip Dunne; ***C:*** J. Peverell Marley; ***M:*** Alfred Newman.

The Count of Monte Cristo 𝒥𝒥 1/2 *Le Comte de Monte Cristo* **1999** It seems only fitting that French TV produced this zestful miniseries version of the 1844 novel by Dumas pere. Depardieu obviously is enjoying himself in the lead role of Edmond Dantes, who is unjustly imprisoned for 20 years. After his escape, he discovers a fortune and uses it to get revenge as he adopts a fictional identity as the Count of Monte Cristo. Overwrought, over-the-top and lots of fun. Depardieu's daughter Julie and son Guillaume both have roles. French with subtitles. **480m/C; VHS, DVD.** *FR* Gerard Depardieu; Ornella Muti; Sergio Rubini; Guillaume Depardieu; Pierre Arditti; Jean Rochefort; Florence Darel; Julie Depardieu; Naike Rivelli; Jean-Claude Brialy; Ines Sastre; Helene Vincent; Christopher Thompson; Stanislas Merhar; Constanze Engelbrecht; Georges Moustaki; ***D:*** Josee Dayan; ***W:*** Didier Decoin; ***C:*** Willy Stassen; ***M:*** Bruno Coulais. **TV**

The Count of Monte Cristo 𝒥𝒥 1/2 **2002 (PG-13)** Yet another remake of the Dumas classic revenge tale with some beautiful cinematography by Dunn to distinguish it. Hero Edmond Dantes (Caviezel) is betrayed by best friend Fernand Mondego (Pearce), who wants his girlfriend Mercedes (Dominczyk) among other things, and unjustly imprisoned. Dantes learns of a great treasure from fellow inmate Abbe Faria (Harris), eventually escapes, finds said treasure, and seeks his revenge under the disguise of—well, you know. Pearce has fun as the foppish villain and Caviezel is suitably heroic. **131m/C; VHS, DVD.** James (Jim) Caviezel; Guy Pearce; Richard Harris; Dagmara Dominczyk; Luis Guzman; James Frain; Albie Woodington; Henry Cavill; Michael Wincott; Alex Norton; Freddie Jones; ***D:*** Kevin Reynolds; ***W:*** Jay Wolpert; ***C:*** Andrew Dunn; ***M:*** Ed Shearmur.

Count Yorga, Vampire 𝒥𝒥 1/2 *The Loves of Count Yorga, Vampire* **1970 (PG-13)** The vampire Count Yorga is practicing his trade in Los Angeles, setting up a coven and conducting seances. Good update of the traditional character, with Quarry suitably solemn and menacing. Followed by "The Return of Count Yorga." **93m/C; VHS, DVD, Blu-Ray.** Robert Quarry; Roger Perry; Michael Murphy; Michael Macready; Donna Anders; Judith Lang; Marsha Jordan; Julie Conners; Paul Hansen; ***D:*** Bob Kelljan; ***W:*** Bob Kelljan; ***C:*** Arch Archambault; ***M:*** Bill Marx.

Countdown 𝒥𝒥 1/2 **1968** Documentary-type fictional look at the first moon mission and its toll on the astronauts and their families. Timely because the U.S. was trying to send a man to the moon in 1968. Interesting as a look at the developing Altman style. **102m/C; VHS, DVD.** James Caan; Robert Duvall; Michael Murphy; Ted (Edward) Knight; Joanna Moore; Barbara Baxley; Charles Aidman; Steve Ihnat; Robert Altman; ***D:*** Robert Altman.

Countdown 𝒥𝒥 **2016 (R)** An action film featuring two popular WWE entertainers. After the death of his young son, Ray Fitzpatrick (Ziggler) is deeply moved by any danger to children. The officer's traumatization plays a big role in his efforts to save a boy has been kidnapped by an insane man and rigged with explosives. Ignoring the orders of his captain, Ray does all he can to rescue the boy. **90m/C; DVD, Blu-Ray, Streaming, Download.** Dolph Ziggler; Glenn Jacobs; Katharine Isabelle; Josh Blacker; Alexander Kalugin; ***D:*** John Stockwell; ***W:*** Michael Finch; Richard Wenk; ***C:*** Cliff Hokanson; ***M:*** Claude Foisy. **VIDEO**

Countdown 𝒥 1/2 **2019 (PG-13)** When hospital nurse Quinn Harris (Lail) downloads an app that allegedly reveals when you will die, she learns she has less than two days. After her drunken boyfriend dies suspiciously at the time the app predicted, she believes its powers are real and that she will die soon unless she, her sister (Bateman), and friend Matt (Calloway) can figure out what makes the app tick and how to beat it. The low-grade horror film is a poor excuse of a knock-off of the "Final Destination" films. **90m/C; DVD, Blu-Ray.** Elizabeth Lail; Jordan Calloway; Talitha Eliana Bateman; Peter Facinelli; Dillon Lane; ***D:*** Justin Dec; ***W:*** Justin Dec; ***C:*** Maxime Alexandre; ***M:*** Danny Bensi; Saunder Jurriaans.

Countdown: Jerusalem 𝒥 **2009** A journalist searches for her missing daughter who's actually been kidnapped by her CIA operative dad (the journalist's ex) and taken to Jerusalem because....well, really who knows because the plot never makes any sense. However there is something about a series of disasters that are pushing society towards global war. Sound positively apocalyptic. **90m/C; DVD.** Kim Little; Clint Browning; Russell Reynolds; Audrey Latt; Mark Hengst; April Wade; ***D:*** Adam Silver; ***W:*** Jose Prendes; David Michael Latt; ***C:*** Adam Silver; ***M:*** Joseph Trapanese. **VIDEO**

Countdown to Zero 𝒥𝒥 **2010 (PG)** Documentary contains interviews, archival and other footage of nuclear weapons and discusses the current issue of nuclear power, proliferation, disarmament, and the potential for a devastating nuclear event to happen. Director Walker shows how easy it is to buy black-market uranium and delves into past (near-) misses with nuclear devices. **90m/C; DVD, Blu-Ray.** ***Nar:*** Gary Oldman; ***D:*** Lucy Walker; ***C:*** Robert Chappell; Gary Clarke; Bryan Donnell; Nick Higgins; ***M:*** Peter Golub.

Counter-Attack 𝒥𝒥 **1945** In 1942, Russian paratrooper Alexei Kulkov (Muni) is trapped inside a bombed-out building alongside fellow Russian Lisa Elenko (Chapman) and some German soldiers in a small Nazi-held town. Kulkov and German officer Ernemann (Meller) then try to get information that can be passed on to his own army, depending on who rescues them first. **90m/B; DVD.** Paul Muni; Marguerite Chapman; Harro Meller; Larry Parks; Erik Rolf; Ludwig Donath; Roman Bohnen; George Macready; Philip Van Zandt; Rudolph Anders; ***D:*** Zoltan Korda; ***W:*** John Howard Larson; ***C:*** James Wong Howe; ***M:*** Louis Gruenberg.

Counter Attack 𝒥 1/2 **1984** Story of murder and insurance fraud takes place on the back lots of the Hong Kong film industry. As good as these get. **105m/C; VHS, DVD.** Bruce Li; Dan Inosanto; John Ladalski; Young Kong; ***D:*** Bruce Li.

Counter Clockwise 𝒥 1/2 **2016** After Ethan (Michael Kopelow) accidentally invents time travel, he ends up 6 months in the future. Elated with success, he returns to find his lab is gone, his wife and sister are dead, and everyone who sees him calls the cops. Instead of trying to fix things in the present, he decides to go back into the past to figure out what happened. Fans of black comedy will like this, but beware, for it comes with the usual convoluted plot common to time travel movies. **91m/C; DVD, Blu-Ray, Streaming. VIDEO**

Counter-Espionage 𝒥 1/2 **1942** The Lone Wolf (William) is after Nazi spies in London, but Scotland Yard thinks he's the baddie. Set during the Blitz; the seventh in the series. **71m/B; DVD.** Warren William; Eric Blore; Hillary Brooke; Thurston Hall; Matthew Boulton; Fred Kelsey; Forrest Tucker; Morton Lowry; ***D:*** Edward Dmytryk; ***W:*** Aubrey Wisberg; ***C:*** Philip Tannura.

Counter Measures 𝒥𝒥 **1999 (R)** Zach Silver (Dudikoff) and the USS Springfield are deployed to hunt the Odessa, a Russian nuclear submarine that's been hijacked by terrorists. **93m/C; VHS, DVD.** Michael Dudikoff; James Horan; Alexander Keith; Scott Marlowe; Tracy Brooks Swope; Cliff (Potter) Potts; Robert F. Lyons; ***D:*** Fred Ray Olen; ***W:***

Steve Latshaw; ***C:*** Thomas Callaway; ***M:*** Eric Wurst; David Wurst. **VIDEO**

Counter Punch 🦴🦴 ½ *Ripped Off; The Boxer; Uomo Dalla Pelle Dura; Murder in the Ring; Tough Guy* **1971 (R)** Blake is a boxer framed for the murder of his manager who sets out to clear his name by finding the killers. Fair rendition of a familiar plot. **72m/C; VHS, DVD.** *IT* Robert (Bobby) Blake; Ernest Borgnine; Gabriele Ferzetti; Catherine Spaak; Tomas Milian; ***D:*** Franco Prosperi.

Counterblast 🦴🦴 *The Devil's Plot* **1948** A Nazi spy assumes the role of a British scientist in order to gain classified information for the Fatherland. The trouble begins when he refuses to carry out an order to execute a pretty young assistant. Appealing performances distract from the somewhat confusing plot. **99m/B; VHS, DVD.** *GB* Robert Beatty; Mervyn Johns; Nova Pilbeam; Margaretta Scott; Sybilla Binder; Marie Lohr; Karel Stepanek; Alan Wheatley; ***D:*** Paul Stein.

The Counterfeit Plan 🦴 ½ **1957** After escaping from a French prison, ruthless murderer Max Brandt (Scott) sets up in the English country home of former partner Louis Bernard (Johns), whom Brandt forces back into counterfeiting. Then Louis' lovely daughter, Carol (Castle), comes home and is suspicious of her dad's lecherous friend. **80m/B; DVD.** *UK* Zachary Scott; Mervyn Johns; Peggie Castle; Sydney Tafler; Lee Patterson; ***D:*** Montgomery Tully; ***W:*** James Eastwood; ***C:*** Phil Grindrod.

The Counterfeit Traitor 🦴🦴🦴 ½ **1962** Suspense thriller with Holden playing a double agent in Europe during WWII. Based on the true adventures of Eric Erickson, the top Allied spy of WW II, who was captured by the Gestapo but escaped. **140m/C; DVD.** William Holden; Lilli Palmer; Hugh Griffith; Werner Peters; Eva Dahlbeck; ***D:*** George Seaton; ***W:*** George Seaton; ***C:*** Jean (Yves, Georges) Bourgoin.

The Counterfeiters 🦴🦴🦴 ½ *Die Falscher* **2007 (R)** Russian-Jewish counterfeiter Salomon "Sally" Sorowitsch (Markovics) is arrested and winds up in a concentration camp in 1944 Berlin, where he's not only marked as Jewish, but designated as a habitual criminal, alienating him from the general prisoner population. There he's placed in charge of a secret counterfeiting unit with other prisoners, all of whom are afforded special privileges like clean sheets and cigarettes. Even with the "luxuries," there's no doubt about where they are—the screams penetrate the walls and their new clothes are from the victims. Sally and the others are forced to confront the morality of their situation (aid those who imprison them or rebel at the ultimate cost) as well as confronting their individual demons. Darkly provocative alternative to the more common heroic stories of camp survivorship. In German with subtitles. **98m/C; DVD.** *AT GE* Karl Markovics; August Diehl; August Zirner; Marie Baumer; Dolores Chaplin; David Striesow; Martin Zirner; ***D:*** Stefan Ruzowitzky; ***W:*** Stefan Ruzowitzky; ***C:*** Benedict Neuenfels; ***M:*** Marius Ruhland. Oscars '07: Foreign Film.

Counterplot 🦴 ½ **1959** Brock goes on the lam after thinking he's committed murder, thanks to his double-dealing lawyer. He leaves New York for Puerto Rico and aims to get evidence to clear his name, with the help of girlfriend Connie and local Manuel. Director Neumann's last film is a low-grade crime drama of little interest. **77m/B; DVD.** Forrest Tucker; Allison Hayes; Jackie Wayne; Gerald Milton; Charlie (Charles) Gibb; ***D:*** Kurt Neumann; ***W:*** Richard Blake; ***C:*** Karl Struss; ***M:*** Paul Sawtell; Bert Shefter.

Counterpoint 🦴 ½ **1967** Heston's an odd casting choice as a conductor whose orchestra is captured by the Nazis when they're on a USO tour in Belgium in 1944. Gen. Schiller insists they play a concert to boost his soldiers' morale and Lionel Evans agrees while trying to come up with a plan to save themselves from certain death. **107m/C; DVD.** Charlton Heston; Maximilian Schell; Anton Diffring; Leslie Nielsen; Kathryn Hays; Linden Chiles; ***D:*** Ralph Nelson; ***W:*** James H. Lee; Joel Oliansky; ***C:*** Russell Metty; ***M:*** Bronislau Kaper.

Counterspy Meets Scotland Yard 🦴 **1950** Sleuth David Harding (St. John) wants to track down the killer of one of his agents so he teams up with Scotland Yard detective Simon Langton (Randell), who poses as the dead man. Based on the radio series. **67m/B; DVD.** Howard St. John; Ron Randell; Amanda Blake; June Vincent; Fred F. Sears; John Dehner; ***D:*** Seymour Friedman; ***W:*** Harold Greene; ***C:*** Philip Tannura.

Counterstrike 🦴🦴 ½ **2003 (PG-13)** Typical escapist cable fare finds a couple of secret service-type brothers (Estes, Lando) called into action when a group of Taiwanese nationalists decide to press their claim for independence from China by threatening to assassinate the presidents of the U.S. and China unless their demand is met by the U.N. Of course, the two heads of state just happen to be aboard the QE2 for a series of summit talks to make things easy. **96m/C; DVD.** Rob(ert) Estes; Joe Lando; Marie Matiko; Carmen Duncan; Rachel Blakely; Christopher Lawford; Ron Lee; ***D:*** Jerry London; ***W:*** J.B. White; ***C:*** Ben Nott. **CABLE**

The Countess 🦴 **2009 (R)** Outlandish historical drama with Delpy out of her depth as star, co-composer, writer, and director. After 16th-century German Countess Erzebet Bathory's husband dies, she becomes something of a merry widow by beginning an affair with handsome, much-younger Istvan. His father, Count Thurzo, disapproves and sends his son away and Erzebet doesn't know why she was abandoned. Fearing her age is showing, the "Blood Countess" takes to drastic measures to regain a youthful appearance. English and French with subtitles. **99m/C; DVD.** *FR GE* Julie Delpy; Daniel Brühl; William Hurt; Anamaria Marinca; Sebastian Blomberg; Charly Hubner; ***D:*** Julie Delpy; ***W:*** Julie Delpy; ***C:*** Martin Ruhe; ***M:*** Julie Delpy.

A Countess from Hong Kong 🦴 **1967 (G)** Very bad romantic comedy features impoverished Russian countess Natasha (would you believe Loren is Russian?) stowing away in the luxury liner suite of stuffy American diplomat Ogden Mears (equally miscast Brando). The ship is sailing from Hong Kong to Honolulu and Natasha has until then to persuade Ogden to assist her. Chaplin's final film. **108m/C; VHS, DVD, Blu-Ray.** Marlon Brando; Sophia Loren; Syd Chaplin; Tippi Hedren; Patrick Cargill; Michael Medwin; Oliver Johnston; Margaret Rutherford; ***D:*** Charlie Chaplin; ***W:*** Charlie Chaplin; ***C:*** Arthur Ibbetson; ***M:*** Charlie Chaplin.

Country 🦴🦴🦴 **1984 (PG)** Strong story of a farm family in crisis when the government attempts to foreclose on their land. Good performances all around and an excellent portrayal of the wife by Lange. "The River" and "Places in the Heart," both released in 1984, also dramatized the plight of many American farm families in the early 1980s. **109m/C; VHS, DVD, Blu-Ray.** Jessica Lange; Sam Shepard; Wilford Brimley; Matt Clark; Therese Graham; Levi L. Knebel; ***D:*** Richard Pearce; ***W:*** William D. Wittliff.

The Country Bears 🦴🦴 **2002 (G)** Fresh out of new ideas, Disney apparently saw gold in a few of their amusement park rides and decided to make movies out of them. This tale of talking, singing bears is the first installment. When Beary (voice of Osment) finds out that he's adopted, and not actually part of the human family that raised him, he decides to take a journey to visit Country Bear Hall in order to find his roots. Unfortunately, the hall is slated for demolition by evil banker Reed Thimple (Walken). Beary attempts to reunite the Country Bears, the legendary band that made the hall famous, in order to save it. Standard Disney fare, which means nothing objectionable except the attempt to make you buy more of their toys. **88m/C; VHS, DVD.** Christopher Walken; Daryl (Chill) Mitchell; Diedrich Bader; Alex Rocco; Stephen Tobolowsky; M.C. Gainey; Meagen Fay; Eli Marienthal; Queen Latifah; ***V:*** Diedrich Bader; Haley Joel Osment; James Gammon; Brad Garrett; Candy Ford; Toby Huss; Kevin M. Richardson; Stephen (Steve) Root; ***D:*** Peter Hastings; ***W:*** Mark Perez; ***C:*** C. Mitchell Anderson; ***M:*** Christopher Young; John Hiatt.

Country Girl 🦴🦴🦴 ½ **1954** In the role that completely de-glamorized her (and won her an Oscar), Kelly plays the wife of alcoholic singer Crosby who tries to make a comeback with the help of director Holden. One of Crosby's four dramatic parts, undoubtedly one of his best. Seaton won an Oscar for his adaptation of the Clifford Odets play. Remade in 1982. **104m/B; VHS, DVD.** Bing Crosby; Grace Kelly; William Holden; Gene Reynolds; Anthony Ross; ***D:*** George Seaton; ***W:*** George Seaton. Oscars '54: Actress (Kelly), Screenplay; Golden Globes '55: Actress--Drama (Kelly); Natl. Bd. of Review '54: Actress (Kelly); N.Y. Film Critics '54: Actress (Kelly).

Country Life 🦴🦴 **1995 (PG-13)** Down Under adaptation of Chekov's "Uncle Vanya," has Blakemore returning to Aussie farm roots after 22-year stint as unsuccessful London theatre critic. His bored young wife (Scacchi) upsets the business-as-usual life of her husband's brother-in-law (Hargreaves) and abandoned daughter, Sally (Fox), who is also jealous of the attention paid the beautiful Deborah by both her uncle and longtime crush, Dr. Askey (Neill). Exchanges Chekov's emotional exploration for a light comedy of manners and a message of Australian independence from England. **107m/C; VHS, DVD.** *AU* Sam Neill; Greta Scacchi; Kerry Fox; John Hargreaves; Googie Withers; Patricia Kennedy; Michael Blakemore; ***D:*** Michael Blakemore; ***W:*** Michael Blakemore; ***C:*** Stephen F. Windon; ***M:*** Peter Best.

Country Strong 🦴🦴 **2010 (PG-13)** Beautifully shot and well-acted backstage melodrama about talented but volatile superstar country singer Kelly Canter (Paltrow) who, following a too-brief stay in rehab for drug and alcohol abuse, is pushed to tour by her husband and manager James (McGraw). The two are joined on the road by Chiles (Meester), a pageant queen turned singer and the handsome Beau (Hedlund), recruited from the rehab center. The romantic tensions, conflicts and relapses are as predictable as they are cliche, but Paltrow manages to steal the show with her surprisingly good singing. **112m/C; Blu-Ray, On Demand.** Gwyneth Paltrow; Tim McGraw; Garrett Hedlund; Leighton Meester; ***D:*** Shana Feste; ***W:*** Shana Feste; ***C:*** John Bailey; ***M:*** Michael Brook.

The Country Teacher 🦴🦴 *Venkovsky Ucitel* **2008** Shy, closeted teacher Petr leaves Prague hoping to find a new life by taking a job at a small school in the country. Despite the conservative community, Petr is soon accepted, especially by widow Marie who offers Petr a room at her farm. She believes her romantic overtures are rejected because she is older than Petr but little does she suspect that Petr has developed a crush on Marie's straight, 17-year-old son Lada. Problems occur when Petr's boorish ex-boyfriend makes a surprise appearance. Czech with subtitles. **113m/C; DVD.** *CZ* Pavel Liska; Marek Daniel; Zuzana Bydzovska; Ladislav Sedivy; ***D:*** Bohdan Slama; ***W:*** Bohdan Slama; ***C:*** Divis Marek; ***M:*** Vladimir Godar.

Countryman 🦴🦴 **1983 (R)** A dope-smuggling woman crashes her plane in Jamaica and is rescued by Countryman, a rasta super hero. Not very good, but at least there's great music by Bob Marley and others. **103m/C; VHS, DVD.** Hiram Keller; Kristine Sinclair; ***D:*** Dickie Jobson.

Coup de Grace 🦴🦴 ½ **1978** Engaging political satire about a wealthy aristocratic woman in Latvia during the 1919-20 Civil War, and how she attempts to maintain her lifestyle as German soldiers are housed on her estate. Her unrequited love for a German officer adds to her troubles. In German with English subtitles. Co-written by von Trotta and based on the novel by Marguerite Yourcenar. **96m/B; DVD.** *GE FR* Margarethe von Trotta; Matthias Habich; Rudiger Kirschstein; Matthieu Carriere; ***D:*** Volker Schlondorff; ***W:*** Margarethe von Trotta.

Coup de Torchon 🦴🦴🦴 *Clean Slate* **1981** Set in 1938 French West Africa, Noiret plays corrupt police chief Lucien Cordier who is consistently harrassed by his community, particularly by the town pimp. He usually overlooks the pimp's crimes, but when Cordier catches him and a friend shooting at plague victims' bodies floating down the river he decides to murder them in cold blood. Based on the novel "POP 1280" by Jim Thompson. In French with English subtitles. **128m/C; VHS, DVD.** *FR* Philippe Noiret; Isabelle Huppert; Guy Marchand; Stephane Audran; Eddy Mitchell; Jean-Pierre Marielle; Irene Skobline; ***D:*** Bertrand Tavernier; ***W:*** Bertrand Tavernier; ***C:*** Pierre William Glenn; ***M:*** Philippe Sarde.

Coupe de Ville 🦴🦴 ½ **1990 (PG-13)** Three brothers are forced by their father to drive mom's birthday present from Detroit to Florida in the summer of '63. Period concerns and music keep it interesting. **98m/C; VHS, DVD.** Patrick Dempsey; Daniel Stern; Arye Gross; Joseph Bologna; Alan Arkin; Annabeth Gish; Rita Taggart; James Gammon; ***D:*** Joe Roth; ***W:*** Mike Binder; ***M:*** James Newton Howard.

Couples Retreat 🦴 ½ **2009 (PG-13)** Troubled Midwestern marrieds Jason (Bateman) and Cynthia (Bell) persuade three pairs of friends to join them at the Eden Resort in Bora Bora where they can work on their relationship in a series of workshops while the others have fun in the sun. Upon arrival, their couples counselor Marcel (Reno) informs them that all four couples must participate (willingly or not—mostly not), leading to generally mainstream comedic moments. The scenery impresses more than the script or the acting, which are both bland. **107m/C; Blu-Ray, On Demand.** Vince Vaughn; Jon Favreau; Jason Bateman; Faizon Love; Kristin Davis; Malin Akerman; Kristen Bell; Kali Hawk; Jean Reno; Ken Jeong; Temuera Morrison; Tasha Smith; Carlos Ponce; John Michael Higgins; Amy Hill; Peter Serafinowicz; Charlotte Cornwell; ***D:*** Peter Billingsley; ***W:*** Vince Vaughn; Jon Favreau; Dana Fox; ***C:*** Eric Alan Edwards; ***M:*** A.R. Rahman.

Courage 🦴🦴🦴 **1986** Based on fact, about a Hispanic mother in NYC who, motivated by her drug-troubled children, goes undercover and exposes a multimillion-dollar drug ring. Loren is great in a decidedly non-glamorous role. **141m/C; VHS, DVD.** Sophia Loren; Billy Dee Williams; Hector Elizondo; Val Avery; Dan Hedaya; Ron Rifkin; Jose Perez; ***D:*** Jeremy Paul Kagan. **TV**

Courage 🦴 ½ **2009** Faith-based family film. Troubled author Robert (Priestley) decides to take his second wife Teresa (Roth) and 16-year-old daughter Megan (Buechner) on a weekend boating trip. They crash their boat in a storm and are stranded on a small, rocky island in the midst of the torrential river. With Robert injured, Teresa and Megan must set aside their differences to survive. **90m/C; DVD.** *CA* Jason Priestley; Andrea Roth; Genevieve Buechner; Gabrielle Rose; ***D:*** George Erschbamer; ***W:*** Jack Nasser; Luis Cruz; ***M:*** Stu Goldberg. **VIDEO**

Courage Mountain 🦴 **1989 (PG)** If you're looking for a good sequel to Johanna Spyri's classic "Heidi" this isn't it. Europe is on the brink of WWI when teenage Heidi leaves her beloved mountain for an exclusive boarding school in Italy. Not surprisingly in a war zone, the military takes over and the kids are sent to an orphanage run by nasties (see also "Oliver!"). The girls escape to the mountains and are saved by none other than Sheen as Heidi's pal Peter (who cast the 20-something Sheen as a teenager? Bad mistake.) Ridiculous sequel to the classic tale will appeal to kids despite what the critics say. **92m/C; VHS, DVD.** Juliette Caton; Joanna Clarke; Nicola Stapleton; Charlie Sheen; Jan Rubes; Leslie Caron; Jade Magri; Kathryn Ludlow; Yorgo Voyagis; Laura Betti; ***D:*** Christopher Leitch; ***W:*** Weaver Webb; ***M:*** Sylvester Levay.

Courage of Lassie 🦴🦴 ½ *Blue Sierra* **1946** Fourteen-year-old Taylor is the heroine in this girl loves dog tale. In this case, the dog is actually called Bill, not Lassie, in spite of the film's title. Bill is found wounded by Taylor and she nurses him back to health. He proves to be loving, loyal, and useful, so much so that, through a complicated plotline, he winds up in the Army's K-9 division and returns home with the doggie version of shell-shock. Taylor's still there to nurse him back to his old kind self again. **93m/C; DVD.** Elizabeth Taylor; Frank Morgan; Tom Drake; Selena Royle; Harry Davenport; Arthur Walsh; ***D:*** Fred M. Wilcox; ***W:*** Lionel Houser; ***C:*** Leonard Smith.

The Courage to Love 🦴🦴 ½ **2000 (PG-13)** Real-life portrayal of Henriette Dellille who, as the product of an affair between a white plantation owner and an African-American woman, shunned family and societal pressures to devote her life to caring for the underprivileged through her group the Sisters of the Holy Family in 19th-century New Orleans. **90m/C; VHS, DVD.** Vanessa L(ynne) Williams; Gil Bellows; Lisa Bronwyn

Moore; David La Haye; Cynda Williams; Diahann Carroll; Stacy Keach; Eddie Bo Smith, Jr.; Kevin Jubinville; Jean-Louis Roux; Lise Roy; Mariah Inger; Paul-Antoine Taillefer; Chris(topher) Williams; Karen Williams; Graeme Somerville; Susannah Hoffman; Raven Dauda; Sylvia Stewart; Heather Hale; ***D:*** Keri Skogland; ***W:*** Toni Johnson; ***C:*** Jonathan Freeman; ***M:*** Christopher Dedrick. **TV**

Courage Under Fire 🦴🦴🦴 **1996 (R)** Army Lt. Col. Nat Serling (Washington) is unexpectedly assigned to review the candidacy of Capt. Karen Emma Walden (Ryan, seen only in flashbacks) to receive the posthumous Medal of Honor for bravery in combat. A Gulf War Medevac pilot, Walden would be the first woman awarded the honor if Serling can figure out the truth from her surviving crew's wildly conflicting reports. Ironically, Serling's dealing with a guilt complex since four members of his tank unit died in the war under friendly fire. Stellar performances, including a frightening one by Phillips. Based on the novel by Duncan, who also did the screenplay; Washington and director Zwick previously worked together on "Glory." **120m/C; VHS, DVD, Blu-Ray.** Denzel Washington; Meg Ryan; Matt Damon; Lou Diamond Phillips; Michael Moriarty; Scott Glenn; Bronson Pinchot; Seth Gilliam; Sean Astin; Regina Taylor; Tim Guinee; Ken Jenkins; Kathleen Widdoes; Zeljko Ivanek; Tim Ransom; Ned Vaughn; ***D:*** Edward Zwick; ***W:*** Patrick Sheane Duncan; ***C:*** Roger Deakins; ***M:*** James Horner.

Courageous 🦴🦴 **2011 (PG-13)** Faith-based indie drama about four buddy cops and a tragedy that has Adam (Kendrick) making a decision that will affect his personal and professional life, especially as a dad to his teen son Dylan (Martin). He asks his friends to sign a pledge to follow God's guidance as parents, but one of their foursome isn't quite so morally upright. Writer/director/actor Alex Kendrick and his writer/producer brother Stephen are the pastors of the Sherwood Baptist Church in Albany, Georgia. **130m/C; DVD.** Alex Kendrick; Kevin Downes; Ben Davies; Ken Bevel; Eleanor Brown; Matt Hardwick; Rusty Martin; Lauren Etchells; Robert Amaya; Angelica Nelsom; ***D:*** Alex Kendrick; ***W:*** Alex Kendrick; Stephen Kendrick; ***C:*** Bob Scott; ***M:*** Mark Willard.

Courageous Dr. Christian 🦴🦴 **1940** Dr. Christian is faced with an epidemic of meningitis among the inhabitants of a shanty town. Typical entry in the "Dr. Christian" series. **66m/B; VHS, DVD.** Jean Hersholt; Dorothy Lovett; Tom Neal; Robert Baldwin; Maude Eburne; ***D:*** Bernard Vorhaus; ***C:*** John Alton.

The Courier 🦴 **2012 (R)** Some decent fight sequences can't overcome wooden acting and a risible plot that's a rip-off of "The Transporter." The courier (Morgan) will deliver any package, anywhere. Trouble strikes when this particular item comes with a delivery deadline and belongs to a hit man (Rourke). **97m/C; DVD, Blu-Ray.** Jeffrey Dean Morgan; Mickey Rourke; Josie Ho; Lili Taylor; Miguel Ferrer; Til Schweiger; Mark Margolis; ***D:*** Hany Abu-Assad; ***W:*** Pete Dris; ***C:*** Antonio Calvache; ***M:*** Nima Fakhrara. **VIDEO**

The Courier 🦴 **1/2 2019 (R)** One of the world's most powerful bad men, Ezekiel Mannings (Oldman) is seen killing an associate by the naive, fearful Nick (Shah). The only living witness to a crime committed by Mannings, Nick is kept under heavy guard ahead of testimony in London. The leader of these guards is Interpol agent Simmonds (Agneson), a turncoat with links to Mannings. When an attempt is made on Nick's life, he is saved by an unnamed motorcycle courier (Kurylenko) and the pair are stuck fighting for their lives in a parking garage. It tries to be a slick action-thriller but fails, miserably. **97m/C; DVD, Blu-Ray.** Olga Kurylenko; Gary Oldman; Amit Shah; Alicia Agneson; Greg Orvis; ***D:*** Zackary Adler; ***W:*** Zackary Adler; James Edward Barker; Andy Conway; Nicky Tate; ***C:*** Michel Abramowicz; ***M:*** James Edward Barker; Tim Despic.

The Court Jester 🦴🦴🦴 **1/2 1956** Swashbuckling comedy stars Danny Kaye as a former circus clown who teams up with a band of outlaws trying to dethrone a tyrant king. Kaye poses as the court jester so he can learn of the evil king's intentions. Filled with more color, more song, and more truly funny lines than any three comedies put together, this is Kaye's best performance. **101m/C; DVD.** Danny Kaye; Glynis Johns; Basil Rathbone; Angela Lansbury; Cecil Parker; John Carradine; Mildred Natwick; Robert Middleton; ***D:*** Melvin Frank; Norman Panama; ***W:*** Norman Panama; ***C:*** Ray June; ***M:*** Sammy Cahn; Sylvia Fine; Vic Schoen. Natl. Film Reg. '04.

The Court Martial of Billy Mitchell 🦴🦴🦴 *One-Man Mutiny* **1955** Terrific courtroom drama depicts the secret trial of Billy Mitchell, head of the Army Air Service in the 1920s, who predicted the role of airpower in subsequent warfare and the danger of war with Japan. Mitchell incurred the wrath of the military by publicly faulting the lack of U.S. preparedness for invasion. Steiger is outstanding as the attorney; Cooper is great as Mitchell. Debut for Montgomery. **100m/C; VHS, DVD, Blu-Ray.** Gary Cooper; Charles Bickford; Ralph Bellamy; Rod Steiger; Elizabeth Montgomery; Fred Clark; James Daly; Jack Lord; Peter Graves; Darren McGavin; Robert F. Simon; Jack Perrin; Charles Dingle; ***D:*** Otto Preminger; ***C:*** Sam Leavitt.

The Courtesans of Bombay 🦴🦴🦴 **1985** Gritty docudrama, set in Pavanpul, the poverty-stricken brothel section of Bombay, looks at how the impoverished women support themselves through a combination of prostitution and performing. **74m/C; VHS, DVD.** *GB* Kareem Samar; Zohra Sehgal; Saeed Jaffrey; ***D:*** Ismail Merchant; James Ivory; Ruth Prawer Jhabvala. **TV**

Courtship 🦴🦴🦴 **1987** From renowned playwright Horton Foote comes this touching story about a sheltered, upper-crust young girl who shocks her family and friends by eloping with a traveling salesman. **84m/C; VHS, DVD.** Hallie Foote; William Converse-Roberts; Amanda Plummer; Rochelle Oliver; Michael Higgins; ***D:*** Howard Cummings. **TV**

The Courtship of Andy Hardy 🦴🦴 **1/2 1942** In the 13th film in the series, Judge Hardy is overseeing a bitter custody battle. Melodie, the teen caught in the middle, has become sullen and withdrawn, so Judge Hardy asks Andy to take the girl out. Andy's in trouble (again) so he reluctantly goes along even though he thinkg Melodie is a no-fun frump (he'll learn differently). Meanwhile, Marian's new boyfriend, Jeff, drinks too much. **94m/B; DVD.** Lewis Stone; Mickey Rooney; Donna Reed; Frieda Inescort; Harvey Stephens; Cecilia Parker; William Lundigan; Fay Holden; Sara Haden; ***D:*** George B. Seitz; ***W:*** Agnes Christine Johnston; ***C:*** Lester White; ***M:*** David Snell.

The Courtship of Eddie's Father 🦴🦴🦴 **1962** A clever nine-year-old boy plays matchmaker for his widowed dad in this rewarding family comedy-drama (the inspiration for the TV series). Some plot elements are outdated, but young Howard's performance is terrific; he would later excel at direction. Based on the novel by Mark Toby. **117m/C; DVD.** Glenn Ford; Shirley Jones; Stella Stevens; Dina Merrill; Ron Howard; Jerry Van Dyke; Roberta Sherwood; ***D:*** Vincente Minnelli; ***W:*** John Gay; ***C:*** Milton Krasner; ***M:*** George Stoll.

Cousin Bette 🦴🦴 **1/2 1997 (R)** Lange plays a mean game of Old Maid in this adaptation of Honore Balzac's novel, set in 1840s Paris. Always outshone by her more beautiful cousin Adeline (Chaplin), Bette is considered plain and not very bright by her aristocratic family. When Adeline's husband Hector (Laurie) asks her to become his housekeeper instead of his wife after Adeline dies, there is no doubt what she means when she hisses she will "take care of everyone." She uses her family's own baser instincts to bring about their downfall. Lange's performance as the cold and manipulative Bette is worth the price of a rental by itself. Big screen debut for theatrical director McAnuff. **112m/C; VHS, DVD.** Jessica Lange; Elisabeth Shue; Aden Young; Bob Hoskins; Kelly Macdonald; Hugh Laurie; Geraldine Chaplin; Toby Stephens; John Sessions; ***D:*** Des McAnuff; ***W:*** Lynn Siefert; Susan Tarr; ***C:*** Andrzej Sekula; ***M:*** Simon Boswell.

Cousin, Cousine 🦴🦴🦴 **1/2 1976 (R)** Pleasant French comedy about distant cousins who meet at a round of family parties, funerals, and weddings and become friends, but their relationship soon becomes more than platonic. Remade in the U.S. in 1989 as "Cousins." In French with English subtitles. **95m/C; VHS, DVD.** *FR* Marie-Christine Barrault; Marie-France Pisier; Victor Lanoux; Guy Marchand; Ginette Garcin; Sybil Maas; ***D:*** Jean-Charles Tacchella; ***W:*** Jean-Charles Tacchella; ***C:*** Georges Lendi; ***M:*** Gerard Anfosso. Cesar '76: Support. Actress (Pisier).

The Cousins 🦴🦴🦴 *Les Cousins* **1959** Set against the backdrop of Parisian student life, two very different cousins (one twisted, the other saintly) vie for the hand of Mayniel. This country mouse, city mouse adult fable ultimately depicts the survival of the fittest. Chabrol's lovely but sad second directorial effort. **112m/B; VHS, DVD.** *FR* Jean-Claude Brialy; Gerard Blain; Juliette Mayniel; Claude Cerval; Genevieve Cluny; Stephane Audran; ***D:*** Claude Chabrol; ***W:*** Claude Chabrol.

Cousins 🦴🦴🦴 **1/2 1989 (PG-13)** An American remake of "Cousin, Cousine," in which two distant cousins-by-marriage meet at a wedding and, due to their respective spouses' infidelities, fall into each other's arms. A gentle love story with a humorous and biting look at the foibles of extended families. **110m/C; VHS, DVD.** Isabella Rossellini; Sean Young; Ted Danson; William L. Petersen; Norma Aleandro; Lloyd Bridges; Keith Coogan; ***D:*** Joel Schumacher; ***W:*** Stephen Metcalfe; ***C:*** Ralf Bode; ***M:*** Angelo Badalamenti.

The Cove 🦴🦴 **2009 (PG-13)** Richard O'Barry went from 1960s dolphin trainer on the "Flipper" TV show to dolphin rescuer. O'Barry is especially incensed by the mass harpooning of dolphins by fishermen that occurs in the port town of Tajii, Japan, where dolphins are lured into the titular cove. O'Barry has been arrested for trying to free the captive dolphins and barred from entering the cove. All photography and recording is banned so activists and divers must slip past security to plant cameras for their disturbing night footage in this compelling documentary. **92m/C; DVD, Blu-Ray.** Hayden Panettiere; Richard O'Barry; Louie Psihoyos; ***D:*** Louie Psihoyos; ***W:*** Mark Monroe; ***C:*** Brook Aitken; ***M:*** J. Ralph. Oscars '09: Feature Doc.; Writers Guild '09: Documentary Screenplay.

The Covenant 🦴 **2006 (PG-13)** Dull and dopey horror story focuses on the sons of Ipswich, four young studs who attend private Spenser Academy and have inherited supernatural powers from their spooky Massachusetts ancestors. Caleb (Strait) will come into his full powers on his 18th birthday but the more he uses them, the faster he'll age. This will be a problem since new transfer student Chase (Stan) is challenging Caleb for top warlock status. Can't even be considered cheesy fun, although the spider scene is pretty nasty. **97m/C; DVD, Blu-Ray.** Steven Strait; Laura Ramsey; Wendy Crewson; Sebastian Stan; Taylor Kitsch; Toby Hemingway; Jessica Lucas; Chace Crawford; ***D:*** Renny Harlin; ***W:*** J.S. Cardone; ***C:*** Pierre Gill; ***M:*** tomandandy.

A Covenant With Death 🦴 **1/2 1967** Warner Bros. backlot courtroom melodrama set in the 1920s. Bryan Talbot (Holliman) is wrongly convicted of murdering his wife and sentenced to hang. The real killer confesses to the murder just as Bryan accidentally kills the hangman at his execution. Judge Ben Lewis (Maharis) must determine whether Bryan acted in self-defense or should be tried for murder. **97m/C; DVD.** George Maharis; Earl Holliman; Laura Devon; Katy Jurado; Sidney Blackmer; Gene Hackman; Whit Bissell; ***D:*** Lamont Johnson; ***W:*** Lawrence B. Marcus; ***C:*** Robert Burks; ***M:*** Leonard Rosenman.

Cover 🦴 **2008 (PG-13)** Screechy and simplistic morality tale. Church-going wife and mother Valerie (Ellis) is outraged when she's questioned about a murder. The problem stems from her family's recent move to Philly and distant hubby Dutch's (Adoti) taking up with some old college friends. Shady goings-on and infidelity turn out to be the least of the problems. **98m/C; DVD.** Aunjanue Ellis; Louis Gossett, Jr.; Raz Adoti; Roger Guenveur Smith; Leon; Clifton Davis; Paula Jai Parker; Vivica A. Fox; Mya; Patti LaBelle; Obba Babatunde; ***D:*** Bill Duke; ***W:*** Aaron Rashaan Thomas; ***C:*** Francis Kenny; ***M:*** Kurt Farquhar.

Cover Girl 🦴🦴🦴 **1944** A vintage wartime musical about a girl who must decide between a nightclub career and a future as a cover model. Hayworth is beautiful, Kelly dances like a dream, and Silvers and Arden are hilarious. **107m/C; VHS, DVD.** Rita Hayworth; Gene Kelly; Phil Silvers; Otto Kruger; Lee Bowman; Jinx Falkenberg; Eve Arden; Edward Brophy; Anita Colby; ***D:*** Charles Vidor; ***C:*** Rudolph Mate; ***M:*** Ira Gershwin; Jerome Kern. Oscars '44: Orig. Dramatic Score.

Cover Girl Models 🦴 **1975** An action-packed '70s adventure in which beautiful models are forced to fight for survival. **82m/C; VHS, DVD.** Lindsay Bloom; Pat Anderson; John Kramer; Rhonda Leigh Hopkins; Mary Woronov; ***D:*** Cirio H. Santiago.

Cover Up 🦴🦴 **1/2 1949** Insurance investigator Sam Donovan heads to a Midwestern town after a policy holder apparently commits suicide. It's really a murder, but even the sheriff isn't interested in investigating although Sam has some help from lovely local, Anita. Takes place at Christmas, but no one has the yuletide spirit as they try to make the cover up stick until the contrived ending. **82m/B; DVD, Blu-Ray.** Dennis O'Keefe; Barbara Britton; William Bendix; Art Baker; Ann E. Todd; Virginia Christine; Russell Arms; ***D:*** Alfred E. Green; ***W:*** Dennis O'Keefe; Jerome Odlum; ***C:*** Ernest Laszlo; ***M:*** Hans J. Salter.

Cover-Up 🦴 **1/2 1991 (R)** Terrorist attacks on U.S. military bases in Israel are just a smokescreen for a greater threat. The below-par actioner stands out only for the hokey religious symbolism in its Good Friday climax. **89m/C; VHS, DVD.** Dolph Lundgren; Louis Gossett, Jr.; John Finn; ***D:*** Manny Coto.

Covert Assassin 🦴🦴 **1994 (R)** Anti-terrorist specialist is hired by wealthy widow to avenge her husband's murder. Adapted from the novel "Wild Justice" by Wilbur Smith. **114m/C; VHS, DVD.** Roy Scheider; Sam Wanamaker; Ted McGinley; Christopher Buchholz; ***D:*** Tony Wharmby.

Cow Belles 🦴🦴 **1/2 2006 (G)** Frothy tween fare from the Disney Channel. Teen sisters Courtney and Taylor are well-provided for thanks to daddy's dairy business. But the girls have grown up selfish and irresponsible, so their fed-up father makes them work in the dairy over the summer. The girls get their "a-ha!" moment when dad is out of the country and the company's finances are suddenly in big trouble, which means the sisters must figure out a way to save the family business. **90m/C; DVD.** Jack Coleman; Sheila McCarthy; Alyson Michalka; Amanda (A.J.) Michalka; Michael Trevino; ***D:*** Francine McDougall; ***W:*** Stu Krieger; ***C:*** Tony Westman; ***M:*** Kenneth Burgomaster. **CABLE**

Cow Town 🦴🦴 **1950** A range war results when ranchers begin fencing in their land to prevent cattle rustling. Autry's 72nd film has some good songs and a dependable cast. **70m/B; VHS, DVD.** Gene Autry; Gail Davis; Jock Mahoney; Harry Shannon; ***D:*** John English.

Coward of the County 🦴🦴 **1/2 1981** A devout pacifist is put to the test when his girlfriend is raped. Good performances by all concerned. Based on the lyrics of Kenny Rogers's hit song of the same name. **115m/C; VHS, DVD.** Kenny Rogers; Frederic Lehne; Largo Woodruff; Mariclare Costello; Ana Alicia; Noble Willingham; ***D:*** Dick Lowry. **TV**

Cowboy 🦴🦴🦴 **1958** Western roundup based on the memoirs of tenderfoot-turned-cowpoke Frank Harris. Harris (Lemmon) is a Chicago hotel clerk who meets cattle boss Tom Reece (Ford) who's in the city on business. Losing his money in a poker game, Reece reluctantly accepts a loan from Harris in exchange for a piece of his cattle business. So Harris and Reece hit the dusty trail on a cattle drive that takes them into Mexico where Harris falls in love with Maria (Kashfi), the daughter of a wealthy rancher, and gradually turns from city slicker into hardened trail boss. Good cast, no fuss. From the book "Reminiscences As a Cowboy" by Harris. **92m/C; VHS, DVD, Blu-Ray.** Jack Lemmon; Glenn Ford; Anna Kashfi; Brian Donlevy; Dick York; Victor Manuel Mendoza; Richard Jaeckel; King Donovan; ***D:*** Delmer Daves; ***W:*** Edmund H. North; ***C:*** Charles Lawton, Jr.; ***M:*** George Duning.

The Cowboy and the Lady 🦴🦴 **1/2 1938** Oberon plays a madcap heiress who is deposited by her politician father on their

Florida estate to keep her out of trouble while he seeks the Presidential nomination. She is bored and decides to go to a local rodeo where she meets cowboy Cooper. Both are instantly smitten and marry on impulse. Cooper doesn't know about her wealth and when her father finds out about the marriage he's appalled that his daughter has married beneath her. Since this is a comedy all comes out right in the end. Good cast, weak story. **91m/B; VHS, DVD.** Gary Cooper; Merle Oberon; Patsy Kelly; Walter Brennan; Fuzzy Knight; Mabel Todd; Henry Kolker; Harry Davenport; ***D:*** H.C. Potter; ***C:*** Gregg Toland. Oscars '38: Sound.

Cowboy from Brooklyn 🦴🦴 ½ **1938** City slicker Elly Jordan (Powell) is on his way to Hollywood when he winds up on Jane Hardy's (Lane) dude ranch instead. Elly is terrified of all animals but he can sing and when he's heard by a couple of talent agents, they pass him off as singing cowboy Wyoming Steve Gibson. His secret may be exposed when Elly is pushed into performing in a rodeo at Madison Square Garden. **77m/B; DVD.** Dick Powell; Pat O'Brien; Priscilla Lane; Ann Sheridan; Ronald Reagan; Dick Foran; Johnnie Davis; ***D:*** Lloyd Bacon; ***W:*** Earl Baldwin; ***C:*** Arthur Edeson.

Cowboy Millionaire 🦴🦴 ½ **1935** An Englishwoman comes to an American dude ranch and falls in love with one of the ranch hands. Entertaining Western comedy. **65m/B; VHS, DVD.** George O'Brien; Evalyn Bostock; Edgar Kennedy; Alden "Steve" Chase; ***D:*** Edward F. (Eddie) Cline.

Cowboy Up 🦴🦴 *Ring of Fire* **2000 (PG-13)** Hank (Sutherland) is a rodeo clown while younger brother Ely (Thomas) is a bullrider. They clash when barrel rider Celia (Hannah) comes into the picture, which causes Ely to take some dangerous chances to win a bull-riding championship. The film's original title, which was changed for the video release, comes from the Johnny Cash song. **105m/C; VHS, DVD.** Kiefer Sutherland; Marcus Thomas; Daryl Hannah; Melinda Dillon; Molly Ringwald; Russell Means; Bo Hopkins; Pete Postlethwaite; Al Corley; ***D:*** Xavier Koller; ***W:*** James Redford; ***C:*** Andrew Dintenfass; ***M:*** Daniel Licht.

The Cowboy Way 🦴 ½ **1994 (PG-13)** A mess from start to finish made somewhat watchable by cowpoke charm of the leads and one good horse chase. Two rodeo stars (Harrelson and Sutherland) from New Mexico ride into New York City to avenge a buddy's death, with Hudson as a mounted NYC cop who always yearned to be a cowboy. Great premise is overcome by tasteless humor and a patched-up plot shot full of holes. Good for a gander is the 90-foot Times Square billboard of Harrelson's character as a Calvin Klein underwear model, which stopped traffic even in jaded New York. **106m/C; VHS, DVD.** Woody Harrelson; Kiefer Sutherland; Dylan McDermott; Ernie Hudson; Cara Buono; Marg Helgenberger; Tomas Milian; Joaquin Martinez; ***Cameo(s):*** Travis Tritt; ***D:*** Gregg Champion; ***W:*** William D. Wittliff; Rob Thompson; ***C:*** Dean Semler; ***M:*** David Newman.

The Cowboys 🦴🦴🦴 **1972 (PG)** Wayne stars as a cattle rancher who is forced to hire 11 schoolboys to help him drive his cattle 400 miles to market. Clever script makes this one of Wayne's better Westerns. Carradine's film debut. Inspired the TV series. **128m/C; VHS, DVD, Blu-Ray, HD-DVD.** John Wayne; Roscoe Lee Browne; A. Martinez; Bruce Dern; Colleen Dewhurst; Slim Pickens; Robert Carradine; Clay O'Brien; Nicolas Beauvy; ***D:*** Mark Rydell; ***W:*** Harriet Frank, Jr.; Irving Ravetch; ***C:*** Robert L. Surtees; ***M:*** John Williams.

Cowboys & Aliens 🦴🦴 **2011 (PG-13)** The pitch is right there in the title as cowboys (Craig, Ford, Rockwell) battle creatures from outer space in 1875's New Mexico territories. But the combined megapowers of James Bond, Indiana Jones, and the man who directed Iron Man, strain to overcome a humdrum script (despite the multitude of credited writers who pieced it together). The stars and the action might be a hoot for some, while others might find rolling tumbleweed more appealing. Loosely based on Scott Mitchell Rosenberg's 2006 graphic novel. **118m/C; Blu-Ray.** Daniel Craig; Harrison Ford; Olivia Wilde; Sam Rockwell; Adam Beach; Paul Dano; Keith Carradine; Abigail Spencer; Clancy Brown; Walton Goggins; Buck Taylor; ***D:*** Jon Favreau; ***W:*** Alex Kurtzman; Mark Fergus; Damon Lindelof; Roberto Orci; Hawk Ostby; ***C:*** Matthew Libatique; ***M:*** Harry Gregson-Williams.

Cowboys and Angels 🦴🦴 ½ **2000 (PG)** Danny (Trese) gets dumped by his fiancee on the eve of their wedding (in favor of his best friend) and isn't sure he'll ever love again. So Danny decides to make some changes—he'll follow his dream of becoming a cowboy. Then, the bubbly Jo Jo (Mitchell) comes into his life. However, Jo Jo has a secret (let's put it this way—she's the second half of the title) and tries to steer Danny's affections in the direction of the receptive Candace (Kirshner). **97m/C; VHS, DVD.** Adam Trese; Radha Mitchell; Mia Kirshner; Hamilton von Watts; Carmen (Lee) Llywelyn; ***D:*** Gregory C. Haynes; ***W:*** Gregory C. Haynes; ***C:*** Kramer Morgenthau; ***M:*** Stephen (Steve) Edwards.

Cowboys & Angels 🦴🦴🦴 **2004 (PG)** Shane (Legge), a straight-laced 20-year-old decides to break away from his family and move to the city on his own. He takes an apartment with Vincent (Leech), a charismatic gay art student. They strike up a friendship, and Shane develops the confidence to create a new life for himself, with its fresh possibilities and dangers. Hip, appealing Irish coming-of-age film with a great, unknown cast. Notable for its portrait of a healthy gay/straight friendship. **90m/C; DVD.** Michael Legge; Allen Leech; Frank Kelly; David Murray; Amy Shiels; ***D:*** David Gleeson; ***W:*** David Gleeson; ***C:*** Volker Tittel; ***M:*** Stephen McKeon.

Cowboys Don't Cry 🦴🦴 **1988** When a modern cowboy's wife is killed in an automobile accident, he must change his immature ways and build a solid future with his teenage son or perish in loneliness. **96m/C; VHS, DVD.** Rebecca Jenkins; Ron White; Janet-Laine Green; ***D:*** Anne Wheeler.

Cowboys vs Dinosaurs 🦴 ½ **2015** An absurd action-science fiction thriller that explores the response of one town to a dinosaur invasion. When there is an unintended explosion at a mine in the small western town of Livingston, Montana, dinosaurs come out from the rubble. The community fights back against these supposedly extinct creatures, led by a local band of gunslingers. The battle for control of Livingston, and life itself, that ensues is truly cowboys versus dinosaurs. **89m/C; DVD, Streaming, Download.** Eric Roberts; Rib Hillis; Vernon Wells; John Freeman; Sara Malakul Lane; ***D:*** Ari Novak; ***W:*** Anthony Fankhauser; Rafael Jordan; ***C:*** Stuart Brereton; ***M:*** Chris(topher) Cano.

Cowgirls 'n Angels 🦴🦴 ½ **2012 (PG)** Good family fare. Ida Clayton's (Madison) single mom Elaine (Witt) never mentions her absent dad, but the 12-year-old learns he once worked the rodeo. She checks out the local Oklahoma circuit and joins a team of female trick riders coached by Terence Parker (Cromwell). Ida convinces herself that if she becomes a top rodeo star, her dad will find out and want to meet her. **91m/C; DVD, Blu-Ray.** Bailee Madison; James Cromwell; Alicia Witt; Jackson Rathbone; Dora Madison Burge; ***D:*** Timothy Armstrong; ***W:*** Timothy Armstrong; ***C:*** John Barr; ***M:*** Alan Williams. **VIDEO**

Coyote Ugly 🦴 ½ **2000 (PG-13)** Producer Bruckheimer revisits the "Flashdance" formula for this tale of a young innocent songwriter (Perabo) who ends up slingin' drinks and barin' her navel in the eponymous bar while seeking fame and fortune in New York. The plot is as naive and wide-eyed as the main character, leaving no room for surprise twists, but allowing for a movie-saving performance by John Goodman as the concerned dad and a discovery in Aussie Garcia as the love interest. The rest of the cast consists of jiggly window dressing, but the PG-13 rating guarentees disappointment for a large segment of the audience. It's bad, but not in a career-destroying, "Showgirls" kind of way. **94m/C; VHS, DVD, UMD.** Piper Perabo; Maria Bello; Tyra Banks; John Goodman; Melanie Lynskey; Ellen Cleghorne; Bud Cort; Izabella Miko; Bridget Moynahan; Adam Garcia; Del Pentacost; Michael Weston; ***D:*** David McNally; ***W:*** Todd Graff; Kevin Smith; Gina Wendkos; ***C:*** Amir M. Mokri; ***M:*** Trevor Horn.

Coyote Waits 🦴🦴 ½ **2003** Another adaptation of a Tony Hillerman novel, following "Skinwalker," about Navaho policemen Jim Chee (Beach) and Joe Leaphorn (Studi). Chee discovers the dead body of a fellow officer near some caves and finds drunken suspect Ashie Pinto (Herman) wandering the roads with a bottle and a gun. Since Leaphorn's wife Emma (Tousey) and Pinto are kin, she requests her husband investigate while Chee also has some questions. Pinto told legends involving Butch Cassidy to a local professor, who believed the outlaw survived Bolivia, only to die on the Navaho reservation. A Vietnamese immigrant with ties to the CIA and Native American mysticism all play their part but the slow-paced story is sometimes confusing. **105m/C; VHS, DVD.** Wes Studi; Adam Beach; Sheila Tousey; Jimmy Herman; Keith Carradine; Graham Greene; Alex Rice; Bodhi (Pine) Elfman; Long Nguyen; ***D:*** Jan Egleson; ***W:*** Lucky Gold; ***C:*** Roy Wagner; ***M:*** B.C. Smith. **TV**

CQ 🦴🦴 **2001 (R)** It's 1969 and film editor Paul (Davies) is in Paris working on an arty futuristic thriller for egotistical director Andrezej (Depardieu) while filming his own black and white personal documentary. When the film's producer, Enzo (Giannini), fires the director, Paul winds up with the gig and has to come up with the slam-bang ending Enzo is demanding. Also demanding is leading lady Valentine (Lindvall), who is paying extra attention to her new director, which distracts Paul from the film and his French girlfriend Marlene (Bouchoz). Paul's a dull character and the film suffers for it but it's not bad for a first effort from Coppola (son of Francis and brother of Sofia). **92m/C; VHS, DVD.** Jeremy Davies; Elodie Bouchez; Angela Lindvall; Gerard Depardieu; Giancarlo Giannini; Massimo Ghini; Jason Schwartzman; Billy Zane; John Phillip Law; Dean Stockwell; ***D:*** Roman Coppola; ***W:*** Roman Coppola; ***C:*** Robert Yeoman.

Crack House 🦴🦴 **1989 (R)** A man seeks revenge for the murder of a relative by drug dealers. Average exploitation flick. **91m/C; VHS, DVD.** Jim Brown; Richard Roundtree; Anthony Geary; Angel Tompkins; Greg Gomez Thomsen; Clyde Jones; Cheryl Kay; ***D:*** Michael Fischa; ***C:*** Arledge Armenaki.

A Crack in the Floor 🦴 ½ **2000 (R)** Three couples go on a weekend hiking trip in the mountains and run into the deranged local folk. But their nightmare really begins when they make camp in a seemingly abandoned cabin that's not so empty after all. **90m/C; VHS, DVD.** Gary Busey; David Naughton; Mario Lopez; Tracy Scoggins; Bo Hopkins; Rance Howard; Justine Priestley; ***D:*** Sean Stanek; Corbin Timbrook; ***W:*** Sean Stanek. **VIDEO**

Crack in the World 🦴🦴 ½ **1965** Terminally ill scientist Stephen Sorenson (Andrews) insists on going ahead with his risky experiment to drill through the Earth's crust to harness geothermal energy. A crack appears and causes global disasters and the only way to contain it seems to be a nuclear explosion. **96m/C; DVD.** Dana Andrews; Jenette Scott; Kieron Moore; Alexander Knox; Peter Damon; ***D:*** Andrew Marton; ***W:*** Jon Manchip White; Julian Zimet; ***C:*** Manuel Berenguer; ***M:*** Johnny Douglas.

Crack-Up 🦴🦴 ½ **1946** Largely ignored at the time of its release, this tense tale is now regarded as a minor classic of film noir. An art expert suffers a blackout while investigating a possible forgery and must piece together the missing hours to uncover a criminal conspiracy. **70m/B; VHS, DVD.** Pat O'Brien; Claire Trevor; Herbert Marshall; Ray Collins; Wallace Ford; Damian O'Flynn; Erskine Sanford; ***D:*** Irving Reis.

Cracked Nuts 🦴 ½ **1931** To impress his fiancee's Aunt Minnie, Wendell buys a revolution in El Dorania to become its king. Then he discovers his childhood chum, Zander, has already won the kingdom in a craps game, so Wendell plans a coup involving a bomb. The explosion succceeds but not in the way that he intended (fortunately). **65m/B; DVD.** Bert Wheeler; Robert Woolsey; Edna May Oliver; Dorothy Lee; Stanley Fields; Leni Stengel; Boris Karloff; ***D:*** Edward F. (Eddie) Cline; ***W:*** Ralph Spence; Al Boasberg; ***C:*** Nicholas Musuraca; ***M:*** Max Steiner.

Cracker: Brotherly Love 🦴🦴🦴 **1995** Everyone carries lots of emotional baggage in this entry of the British series. Detective Jane Penhaligon (Somerville) is still suffering from the aftereffects of rape, which she believes was by colleague Jimmy Beck (Cranitch), who's just returned to duty following a breakdown. Meanwhile, Fitz's (Coltrane) mother has died bringing him into contact with his stodgy brother Danny (Russell). And yes, there are murders to investigate—a killer who likes prostitutes to dress up as little girls. **150m/C; VHS, DVD.** *GB* Robbie Coltrane; Geraldine Somerville; Lorcan Cranitch; Ricky Tomlinson; Barbara Flynn; Clive Russell; Kieran O'Brien; Tessa Thompson; Brid Brennan; David Calder; Mark Lambert; ***D:*** Roy Battersby; ***W:*** Jimmy McGovern. **TV**

Cracker: Men Should Weep 🦴🦴 ½ **1994** Fitz's skills are called into play when he must deal with a serial rapist (Aggrey). However, things become personal when Detective Jane Penhaligon (Somerville) is raped. **150m/C; VHS, DVD.** *GB* Robbie Coltrane; Geraldine Somerville; Lorcan Cranitch; Graham Aggrey; ***D:*** Jean Stewart; ***W:*** Jimmy McGovern. **TV**

Cracker: The Big Crunch 🦴🦴 ½ **1994** The leader of a Christian fundamentalist sect has an affair with a schoolgirl and then plots her murder to avoid a scandal. But what he can't avoid is Fitz (Coltrane). **150m/C; VHS, DVD.** *GB* Robbie Coltrane; Jim Carter; Samantha Morton; James Fleet; Cherith Mellor; ***D:*** Julian Jarrold; ***W:*** Jimmy McGovern; Ted Whitehead. **TV**

Cracker: To Be a Somebody 🦴🦴 **1994** The murder of an Asian shopkeeper first prompts the Manchester police to look for their suspect in the violent world of skinheads. But when the professor helping to profile the killer is murdered, the cops are forced to call in irascible forensic psychologist "Fitz" Fitzgerald (Coltrane) to aid in their investigation. Made for TV. **150m/C; VHS, DVD.** *GB* Robbie Coltrane; Robert Carlyle; Barbara Flynn; Christopher Eccleston; Geraldine Somerville; Lorcan Cranitch; ***D:*** Tim Fywell; ***W:*** Jimmy McGovern. **TV**

Crackerjack 🦴🦴 *The Man With 100 Faces* **1938** Jack Drake (Walls) is a gentleman thief with a heart as the infamous Crackerjack. He thwarts an American gang's heist at a London hotel but gets blamed for the murder they committed. His old flame, the Baroness (Palmer), mistakenly gets involved with the American crooks and a trap for Crackerjack is planned. **80m/B; DVD.** *UK* Tom Walls; Lilli Palmer; Noel Madison; Leon M. Lion; Edmund Breon; Jack Lester; Charles Heslop; ***D:*** Albert de Courville; ***W:*** Michael Pertwee; A.R. Rawlinson; Basil Mason; ***C:*** Jack Cox; ***M:*** Louis Levy.

Crackerjack 3 🦴🦴 **2000 (PG-13)** Jack Thorn (Svenson) is an ex-Navy S.E.A.L. and the current director of the CIA's covert ops. He's planning to retire when he discovers his would-be replacement, Marcus Clay (Gruner), wants to cause a worldwide economic catastrophe. So Jack gathers together some fellow old-timers and tries to cope with high tech in order to save the world. **97m/C; VHS, DVD.** Bo Svenson; Olivier Gruner; Leo Rossi; Amy Weber; ***D:*** Lloyd A. Simandl; ***M:*** Peter Allen. **VIDEO**

Crackers 🦴🦴 **1984 (PG)** The offbeat story of two bumbling thieves who round up a gang of equally inept neighbors and go on the wildest crime spree you have ever seen. A would-be comic remake of "Big Deal on Madonna Street." **92m/C; VHS, DVD, Streaming.** Donald Sutherland; Jack Warden; Sean Penn; Wallace Shawn; Larry Riley; Trinidad Silva; Christine Baranski; Charlaine Woodard; Tasia Valenza; ***D:*** Louis Malle.

Crackie 🦴 ½ **2009** Dismal drama finds Newfoundland teen Mitsy (Greeley) daydreaming about a better life after having been abandoned by her drug addict, prostitute mother Gwennie (Wells) and raised by her equally hardened grandma Bride (Walsh). Even Mitsy's new puppy can't help those no-one-loves-me feelings when Gwennie returns. **94m/C; DVD.** *CA* Meghan Greeley; Mary Walsh; Cheryl Wells; Joel Hynes; ***D:*** Sheryl White; ***W:*** Sheryl White; ***C:*** Stephen Reizes; ***M:*** Duane Andrews.

Cracking Up 🦴 ½ *Smorgasbord* **1983 (PG)** Accident-prone misfit's mishaps on the road to recovery create chaos for everyone he meets. Lewis plays a dozen characters in this overboard comedy with few laughs. **91m/C; VHS, DVD.** Jerry Lewis; Herb Edelman; Foster Brooks; Milton Berle; Sammy Davis, Jr.; Zane Buzby; Dick Butkus; Buddy Lester; *D:* Jerry Lewis.

Cracks 2009 Debut feature for Jordan Scott (daughter of director Ridley) goes off the deep end in more than one way. It's 1934 and Miss G is the diving teacher at an isolated all-girls boarding school located on an island off the British coast. She basks in the adoration of her adolescent charges, especially teacher's pet Di. That changes when aristocratic and independent Spanish transfer student Flamma draws everyone's attention, including Miss G who becomes obsessed with the girl—much to Di's jealous rage. **94m/C; DVD.** *GB* Eva Green; Maria Valverde; Juno Temple; Imogen Poots; Sinead Cusack; Ellie Nunn; Clemmie Dugdale; Zoe Carroll; Adele McCann; *D:* Jordan Scott; *W:* Jordan Scott; Ben Court; Caroline Ip; *C:* John Mathieson; *M:* Javier Navarrete.

The Cradle ½ 2006 Frank (Haas) is hoping a change of scene will help the postpartum depression of his wife Julie (Hampshire) so he moves them to an isolated new home. Too bad the house comes with its own ghost—the vengeful spirit of a murdered child—and soon Frank is having hallucinations about danger for his infant son Sam. **107m/C; DVD.** Lukas Haas; Emily Hampshire; Amanda Smith; *D:* Timothy Brown; *W:* Timothy Brown; *C:* Candace Sparks; *M:* Marcus Elliott. **VIDEO**

The Cradle of Courage 1920 Crook-turned-soldier Square Kelly (Maynard) returns from WWI to his San Francisco hometown and becomes a cop. This miffs his old gang and leader Tierney (Santschi) shoots Kelly's brother Jim (Thorwald) so Kelly tries to get revenge through legal means. **67m/B; Silent; DVD.** William S. Hart; Thomas Santschi; Ann Little; Francis (Frank) Thorwald; Gertrude Claire; *D:* William S. Hart; Lambert Hillyer; *W:* Lambert Hillyer; *C:* Joseph August.

Cradle of Lies ½ 2006 Jack (Neal) and Haley (Sturges) are excited about her pregnancy until Haley learns that she's having a girl. Jack is on a time limit and needs a son to inherit the family fortune, which is apparently news to oblivious Haley. He has a younger woman (Brown) lined up and becomes a seriously crazy threat to both mom and unborn daughter. **90m/C; DVD.** Shannon Sturges; Dylan Neal; Natalie Brown; Martin Roach; Philip Craig; *D:* Oley Sassone; *W:* Oley Sassone; David DuBos; *C:* Malcolm Cross; *M:* David Christal. **CABLE**

Cradle 2 the Grave ½ 2003 (R) Jewel theif Fait (DMX) steals some black diamonds that draw attention from many factions, including Li's Taiwanese government agent Su and some oily, world-domination types led by Su's former partner and friend Ling (Dacascos), who isn't above kidnapping Fait's daughter to get what he wants. DMX is pretty good at looking all cool and bad-ass, but runs into trouble when acting is called for. Li, the only real reason to bother with this flick, provides all the martial arts action you'd expect, but looks kinda bored doing it. Anderson and Arnold are around for comic relief (take that info as warning or praise, depending on your tolerance for both). **100m/C; VHS, DVD, Blu-Ray.** Jet Li; DMX; Anthony Anderson; Kelly Hu; Tom Arnold; Mark Dacascos; Gabrielle Union; Michael Jace; Chi McBride; Paolo Seganti; Drago; Paige Hurd; *D:* Andrzej Bartkowiak; *W:* John O'Brien; *C:* Daryn Okada; *M:* John (Gianni) Frizzell; Damon Blackman.

The Cradle Will Rock ½ 1999 (R) An exuberant if not always successful attempt by Robbins to capture the artistic/political fervor of New York in the '30s. Theatrical collaborators Orson Welles (Macfadyen) and John Houseman (Elwes) agree to produce Marc Blitzstein's (Azaria) new political musical "The Cradle Will Rock" for their Federal Theater company in 1937. Right-wing political interference closes the theater on opening night but Welles leads his company to another venue in Manhattan where the actors (because of their union) must perform the piece from the audience—the dramatic circumstances offering a unique success and a place in theatre history. **133m/C; VHS, DVD, Blu-Ray.** Angus MacFadyen; Cary Elwes; Hank Azaria; Cherry Jones; Ruben Blades; Joan Cusack; John Cusack; Philip Baker Hall; Bill Murray; Vanessa Redgrave; Susan Sarandon; Jamey Sheridan; John Turturro; Emily Watson; Bob Balaban; Paul Giamatti; Barnard Hughes; Barbara Sukowa; John Carpenter; Gretchen Mol; Harris Yulin; Dominic Chianese; Jack Black; Kyle Gass; Lee Arenberg; Daniel H. Jenkins; Peter Jacobson; *D:* Tim Robbins; *W:* Tim Robbins; *C:* Jean-Yves Escoffier; *M:* David Robbins.

The Craft ½ 1996 (R) Call it "Heathers" with hexes. Troubled 17-year-old Sarah (Tunney) moves to L.A. and begins her senior year at St. Benedict's Academy. She takes up with three rebels—Nancy (Balk), Bonnie (Campbell), and Rochelle (True)?who like to dabble in witchcraft. Now, with the addition of would-be witch Sarah, these black magic women start slinging spells at their uppity classmates. Works best when concentrating on the girls and their problems, but degenerates into a special effects barrage toward the end. Alas, no one is turned into a newt. **100m/C; VHS, DVD, Blu-Ray.** Robin Tunney; Fairuza Balk; Neve Campbell; Rachel True; Skeet Ulrich; Helen Shaver; Cliff DeYoung; Christine Taylor; Assumpta Serna; *D:* Andrew Fleming; *W:* Andrew Fleming; Peter Filardi; *C:* Alexander Grusynski; *M:* Graeme Revell. MTV Movie Awards '97: Fight (Fairuza Balk/Robin Tunney).

The Craigslist Killer ½ 2011 Lifetime true crime movie is a bland, predictable portrayal of Philip Markoff's double life that focuses as much on his fiance Megan's shock as she discovers he's a killer. Med student Philip uses online ads placed in the erotic services section of Craigslist to find his masseuse victims, whom he robs and kills. He's actually not too bright and is quickly caught and jailed so there's not much suspense. **87m/C; DVD.** Jake McDorman; Agnes Bruckner; William Baldwin; Joshua Close; Julia Campbell; Kevin Kilner; *D:* Stephen Kay; *W:* Donald Martin; Stephen Tolkin; *C:* Jamie Barber; *M:* Tree Adams. **CABLE**

The Cranes Are Flying ½ *Letyat Zhuravit* 1957 When her lover goes off to fight during WWII, a girl is seduced by his cousin. Touching love story is free of politics. Filmed in Russia; English subtitles. **91m/B; VHS, DVD, Blu-Ray.** *RU* Tatyana Samoilova; Alexei Batalov; Vasily Merkuryev; A. Shvorin; *D:* Mikhail Kalatozov; *W:* Viktor Rozov; *C:* Sergei Urusevsky; *M:* Moisej Vajnberg. Cannes '58: Film.

Cranford ½ 2008 Cranford is a seemingly quaint and quiet English village in 1842 that's about to undergo a profound upheaval, thanks to the expansion of the railroad. Its society is held in check by the local widows and spinsters who know everyone and gossip about everything. There's a number of accidents, deaths, would-be romances, engagements, misunderstandings, financial hardships, and societal changes for everyone to endure and overcome as at least some of the inhabitants find longed-for happiness. Based on the novel by Elizabeth Gaskell. **295m/C; DVD.** *GB* Dame Judi Dench; Simon Woods; Imelda Staunton; Julia McKenzie; Barbara Flynn; Francesca Annis; Julia Sawalha; Emma Fielding; Philip Glenister; Jim Carter; John Bowe; Greg Wise; Joseph McFadden; Michael Gambon; Eileen Atkins; Lisa Dillon; Kimberly Nixon; Alex Etel; Alex Jennings; *D:* Simon Curtis; Steve Hudson; *W:* Heidi Thomas; *C:* Ben Smithard; *M:* Carl Davis. **TV**

Crank ½ 2006 (R) Mindlessly enjoyable "B" pic and proud of it. Freelance assassin Chev Chelios (Statham) learns his rival Ricky (Cantillo) has injected him with a toxin that kills if his heart rate drops too low. The only way Chev can fight the toxin is to continuously pump up his adrenaline, which leads him to rampage through LA in search of revenge, an antidote, and thrills of any kind. The premise is a variation on the 1950 noir "D.O.A." and it actually works if you don't think about it. **87m/C; DVD, Blu-Ray.** Jose Pablo Cantillo; Jason Statham; Amy Smart; Efren Ramirez; Dwight Yoakam; Carlos Sanz; Reno Wilson; *D:* Mark Neveldine; Brian Taylor; *W:* Mark Neveldine; Brian Taylor; *C:* Adam Biddle; *M:* Paul Haslinger.

Crank: High Voltage *Crank 2: High Voltage* 2009 (R) Picking up right where the first movie left off, Chev (Statham) survives a climactic plunge to his most certain death on the streets of Los Angeles, only to be kidnapped by a mysterious Chinese mobster. Three months later, he wakes up to discover his nearly indestructible heart has been surgically removed and replaced with a battery-operated ticker that requires regular jolts of electricity in order to work. While he attends to that, he's also on a chase through L.A. to get his heart back. Takes over-the-top to a new level, as only the narrowest of target audiences will find the unrelenting violence, blood, nudity, and impossible action sequences the least bit entertaining. **96m/C; Blu-Ray, On Demand.** Jason Statham; Corey Haim; Amy Smart; Bai Ling; Efren Ramirez; Dwight Yoakam; Clifton (Gonzalez) Collins, Jr.; *D:* Mark Neveldine; Brian Taylor; *W:* Brian Taylor; *C:* Brandon Trost.

Crash 1995 (NC-17) You can always expect surreal kinkiness from Cronenberg and this film, awarded a Special Jury Prize at Cannes for "daring, originality, and audacity," won't prove the exception. It's "auto" erotica taken to the max, with car crashes and bodily injury turned into fetishes. James (Spader) lands in the hospital after an accident, which injured Helen (Hunter), a passenger in the other car. Helen and James' shared experience soon leads to a sexual relationship, which doesn't bother James' wife, Catherine (Unger). Then there's Vaughan (Koteas) and his group, who like to reenact famous auto crashes (like those of James Dean and Jayne Mansfield). Oh yes, there's lots more sex (in various combinations). Based on J.G. Ballard's 1973 cult novel. An R-rated version clocks in at 90 minutes. **98m/C; VHS, DVD.** *CA* James Spader; Holly Hunter; Elias Koteas; Deborah Kara Unger; Rosanna Arquette; Peter MacNeill; *D:* David Cronenberg; *W:* David Cronenberg; *C:* Peter Suschitzky; *M:* Howard Shore. Cannes '96: Special Jury Prize; Genie '96: Adapt. Screenplay, Cinematog., Director (Cronenberg), Film Editing.

Crash ½ 2005 (R) From the writer of "Million Dollar Baby" comes this racially charged ensemble piece, which follows numerous lives intersecting over a 36-hour period in the volatile melting pot of L.A. Opening with a car-jacking, a central event that connects most of the characters, Haggis' drama meditates on the levels of class conflict between cops, criminals, showbiz types, and various ethnic and racial groups. A bit preachy at times, but the cast is so uniformly strong and the characters so multi-layered, you won't care. Cheadle, as always, stands out, but even the ensemble's typically bland Hollywood actors (Bullock, Fraser, Phillippe) acquit themselves nicely. **100m/C; DVD, Blu-Ray, UMD.** Chris Bridges; Sandra Bullock; Don Cheadle; Matt Dillon; Jennifer Esposito; William Fichtner; Brendan Fraser; Terrence Howard; Thandie Newton; Ryan Phillippe; Larenz Tate; Nona Gaye; Michael Peña; Beverly Todd; Keith David; Shaun Toub; Loretta Devine; *D:* Paul Haggis; *W:* Paul Haggis; Robert Moresco; *C:* J.(James) Michael Muro; *M:* Mark Isham. Oscars '05: Film, Film Editing, Orig. Screenplay; British Acad. '05: Orig. Screenplay, Support. Actress (Newton); Ind. Spirit '06: First Feature, Support. Actor (Dillon); Natl. Bd. of Review '05: Breakthrough Perf. (Howard); Screen Actors Guild '05: Cast; Writers Guild '05: Orig. Screenplay.

Crash and Burn ½ 1990 (R) Rebels in a repressive future police state reactivate a huge, long-dormant robot to battle the establishment's army of powerful androids. Special effects by David Allen make the mayhem interesting. **85m/C; VHS, DVD.** Ralph Waite; Paul Ganus; Eva LaRue; Bill Moseley; Jack McGee; *D:* Charles Band; *W:* J.S. Cardone; *M:* Richard Band.

Crash and Burn ½ 2007 Pretty much what this dull crime actioner does. Car thief Kevin (Palladino) delivers his latest ride to L.A. choppers Hill (Moscow) and Winston (Jason), who work for crime boss Vincent (Madsen). Kevin runs into ex-squeeze Penny (Marsden), who's unhappy Kev's still a criminal. But really Kevin is working undercover for the FBI, not only to bust Vincent but a rival gang of carjackers who have turned to murder to protect their turf. **85m/C; DVD.** Erik Palladino; Michael Madsen; Heather Marie Marsden; David Moscow; Peter Jason; Lobo Sebastian; Anthony John (Tony) Denison; Owen Beckman; Tom O'Keefe; *D:* Russell Mulcahy; *W:* Frank Hannah; Jack LoGiudice; *C:* Maximo Munzi; *M:* Jeff Rona. **TV**

Crash & Byrnes ½ 1999 Jack "Crash" Riley (Larson) is a retired CIA agent who is reluctantly called back into service to bring down a bioterrorist. A by-the-book kinda guy, Crash is, of course, paired with loose cannon DEA agent Roman Byrnes (Ellis). If the two can ever figure out a way to work together, they may just accomplish their mission. Standard fare in the wannabe "Lethal Weapon" mold. **92m/C; VHS, DVD.** *CA* Wolf Larson; Greg Ellis; Joanna Pacula; Steven Williams; Sandra Lindquist; Terry Chen; Melanie Angel; *D:* Jon Hess; *W:* Wolf Larson; *C:* Anthony C. Metchie; *M:* Ken Williams.

Crash Course ½ *A Mother's Fight for Justice* 2000 Terry Stone's (Baxter) college student son Terry (Lively) is critically injured in a car crash and suffers from severe brain trauma. Since the accident was caused by a drunk driver, Terry seeks justice while Andrew struggles to regain his life. Based on a true story. **91m/C; VHS, DVD.** Meredith Baxter; Alan Rosenberg; Eric Lively; *D:* Thomas (Tom) Rickman. **CABLE**

Crash Dive ½ 1943 WWII glory film provides comic relief in the form of romance. Second-in-command Power falls hopelessly in love with school teacher Baxter, only to find out later that she is Lt. Commander Andrews' fiance. Once this little tidbit of information is disclosed, the two officers embark on a mission to destroy a Nazi U-Boat responsible for laying mines in the North Atlantic. Fantastic special effects and sound. Based on the story by W.R. Burnett. **105m/B; VHS, DVD.** Tyrone Power; Anne Baxter; Dana Andrews; James Gleason; May Whitty; Harry (Henry) Morgan; Ben Carter; Frank Conroy; Florence Lake; John Archer; Minor Watson; Kathleen Howard; Stanley Andrews; Thurston Hall; Trudy Marshall; Charles Tannen; Chester Gan; *D:* Archie Mayo; *W:* Jo Swerling; W.R. Burnett; *C:* Leon Shamroy; *M:* David Buttolph.

Crash Dive 1996 (R) An atomic submarine is taken hostage by Richter (Schone) and his band of terrorists, who demand $1 billion in gold or Washington D.C. will become a nuclear disaster. Naturally, there's one hero'sub designer James Carter (Dudikoff)?who manages to sneak aboard and plots to save the day. Fast pace and top special effects make this one watchable. **90m/C; VHS, DVD.** Michael Dudikoff; Reiner Schone; Frederic Forrest; Jay Acovone; *D:* Andrew Stevens; *W:* William C. Martell; *C:* Michael Slovis; *M:* Eric Wurst; David Wurst. **VIDEO**

Crash Landing 1958 Cliched disaster flick. A New York-bound Trans-Atlantic flight develops engine trouble and is likely to crash into the ocean. Boring flashbacks then focus on how the passengers and crew came to be on the flight. **76m/B; DVD.** Gary Merrill; Nancy Davis; Roger Smith; Irene Hervey; Bek Nelson; Jewell Lain; Richard Keith; Sheridan Comerate; *D:* Fred F. Sears; *W:* Fred Freiberger; *C:* Benjamin (Ben H.) Kline; *M:* Mischa Bakaleinikoff.

Crash Pad 2017 (R) The directorial debut of longtime film editor Kevin Tent lacks the comic timing to make its premise work. When his fling with married Morgan (Applegate) ends, romantic slacker Stensland (Gleeson) has a broken heart. He responds by binge-watching Dawson's Creek and trying to blackmail Morgan. Stensland's situation changes when he receives an offer from Morgan's husband Grady (Church) to move in together to make Morgan jealous. The roomies also try to get over their hurt feelings with other women and cheap booze. Despite decent performances by Applegate and Church, the script is wordy and unnatural, and the characters somewhat unsympathetic. **91m/C; DVD.** Domhnall Gleeson; Nina Dobrev; Christina Applegate; Thomas Haden Church; Aliyah O'Brien; *D:* Kevin Tent; *W:* Jeremy Catalino; *C:* Seamus Tierney; *M:* Rolfe Kent.

Crashing 2007 (R) Richard McMurray (Scott) was once a successful writer with a trophy wife and a house in Malibu. Now he's middle-aged, divorced, homeless, and suffering from extended writer's block. While guest-lecturing in a college writing class, he casually mentions his lack of a bed and is offered the couch in lithesome Jacqueline's

(Caplan) and Kristin's (Miko) tiny apartment. Soon they're involved in a breezy menage a trois and all are using their new arrangement to ignite their literary aspirations. No one seems conflicted, which makes a nice change from angsty musings on morality and sex. **80m/C; DVD.** Campbell Scott; Lizzy Caplan; Izabella Miko; Alex Kingston; ***D:*** Gary Walkow; ***W:*** Gary Walkow; ***C:*** Andrew Huebscher; ***M:*** Ernest Troost.

The Crater Lake Monster WOOF! 1977 (PG) The dormant egg of a prehistoric creature hatches after a meteor rudely awakens the dozing dino. He's understandably miffed and begins a revenge campaign. Prehistoric yawner. **85m/C; VHS, DVD.** Richard Cardella; Glenn Roberts; Mark Siegel; Bob Hyman; Kacey Cobb; ***D:*** William R. Stromberg; ***C:*** Paul Gentry.

The Craving 𝒮 *Return of the Wolfman; El Retorno del Hombre-Lobo; Night of the Werewolf* **1980 (R)** Naschy (AKA Jacinto Molina) returns as El Hombre Lobo for the umpteenth time and once again battles a female vampire (see "Werewolf vs. the Vampire Woman"). Although continental Europe's biggest horror star, this film was such a boxoffice disaster that Naschy went bankrupt. He was then forced to turn to Japan for financing (see "The Human Beasts"). Naschy/Molina directed under the pseudonym "Jack" Molina. Sold as 'Night of the Werewolf'. **93m/C; VHS, DVD, Blu-Ray.** *SP* Paul Naschy; Julie Saly; Silvia Aquilar; Azucena Hernandez; Beatriz Elorietta; Pilar Alcon; ***D:*** Paul Naschy.

Cravings 𝒮𝒮 *Daddy's Girl* **2006 (R)** Disturbing Brit psycho-horror. Widowed shrink Stephen (whose own wife committed suicide by slashing her wrists) gets a new patient in disturbed teen Nina, who cut her wrists and then drank the blood. Her mother, Liz, thinks Stephen treating Nina isn't a good idea since she's easily fixated. Stephen and Liz soon become sexually involved. **90m/C; DVD.** *GB* Richard Harrington; Jaime Winstone; Louise Delamere; Ifan Huw Dafydd; Mark Lewis Jones; Katie Owen; ***D:*** D.J. Evans; ***W:*** D.J. Evans; ***C:*** Jonathan Bloom; ***M:*** Owen Powell; Rob Reed.

Crawl 𝒮𝒮 **1/2 2019 (R)** When a Category 5 hurricane hits Florida, a town in the southwestern part of the state is particularly hard hit. Because of the deluge, professional swimmer Haley (Scodelario) checks in on her estranged father Dave (Pepper) after not hearing from him for a while. At his home, she looks in the overflowing basement, which is dirty and rat infested. What she encounters is an unforgiving alligator that attacks and attempts to eat her. Though Haley survives and others try to rescue her, the alligator relentlessly seek their next meal. Nothing new, but undeniably joyful mindless action and humor. **87m/C; DVD, Blu-Ray.** Kaya Scodelario; Barry Pepper; Morfydd Clark; Ross Anderson; Jose Palma; ***D:*** Alexandre Aja; ***W:*** Michael Rasmussen; Shawn Rasmussen; ***C:*** Maxime Alexandre; ***M:*** Max Aruj; Steffen Thum.

The Crawling Eye 𝒮𝒮 *The Trollenberg Terror* **1958** Hidden in a radioactive fog on a mountaintop, the crawling eye decapitates its victims and returns these humans to Earth to threaten mankind. Average acting, but particularly awful special effects. Based on a British TV series. **87m/B; VHS, DVD.** *GB* Forrest Tucker; Laurence Payne; Janet Munro; Jennifer Jayne; Warren Mitchell; ***D:*** Quentin Lawrence; ***W:*** Jimmy Sangster; ***M:*** Stanley Black.

The Crawling Hand WOOF! 1963 An astronaut's hand takes off without him on an unearthly spree of stranglings. Silly stuff is a hands-down loser. **98m/B; VHS, DVD.** Kent Taylor; Peter Breck; Rod Lauren; Sirry Steffen; Alan Hale, Jr.; Richard Arlen; Allison Hayes; Arline Judge; ***D:*** Herbert L. Strock; ***W:*** Herbert L. Strock; ***C:*** Willard Van der Veer.

Crawlspace 𝒮 **1986 (R)** Beautiful girls lease rooms from a murdering, perverted doctor who spies on them, then kills. You may find Kinski amusing but not terrifying. **86m/C; VHS, DVD, Blu-Ray.** Klaus Kinski; Talia Balsam; Joyce Van Patten; Sally Brown; Barbara Whinnery; ***D:*** David Schmoeller; ***W:*** David Schmoeller; ***M:*** Pino Donaggio.

Craze 𝒮𝒮 *The Infernal Idol; Demon Master* **1974 (R)** Toungue-in-cheek tale of a crazed antique dealer who slays a number of women as sacrifices to an African idol named Chuku. **96m/C; VHS, DVD.** Jack Palance; Diana Dors; Julie Ege; Suzy Kendall; Michael Jayston; Edith Evans; Hugh Griffith; Trevor Howard; ***D:*** Freddie Francis.

The Crazies 𝒮𝒮 *Code Name: Trixie* **1973 (R)** A poisoned water supply makes the residents of a small town go on a chaotic, murderous rampage. When the army is called in to quell the anarchy, a small war breaks out. Message film about the military is muddled and derivative. **103m/C; VHS, DVD, Blu-Ray.** Lane Carroll; Will MacMillan; Harold W. Jones; Lloyd Hollar; Lynn Lowry; Richard France; Richard Liberty; Will Disney; Harry Spillman; ***D:*** George A. Romero; ***W:*** George A. Romero; ***C:*** Bill (William Heinzman) Hinzman; ***M:*** Bruce Roberts.

The Crazies 𝒮𝒮 **2009 (R)** A biological weapon makes its way into the water supply of a small town, causing the townsfolk to lose their minds in a violent rage and die. Sheriff Dutton (Olyphant) and crew must defend themselves from the crazed masses, while the government responds by shutting the town off from the rest of the world. A remake of the George Romero classic, the movie offers up great screams, thrills, and other key elements of the horror genre, but misses Romero's social satire and mistrust of authority that provided the original such unique tension. **101m/C; DVD, Blu-Ray, On Demand.** Timothy Olyphant; Radha Mitchell; Joe Reegan; Joe Anderson; Danielle Panabaker; ***D:*** Breck Eisner; ***W:*** Ray Wright; Scott Kosar; ***C:*** Maxime Alexandre; ***M:*** Mark Isham.

Crazy 𝒮𝒮 **2008 (R)** Basic country showbiz bio (with the usual inaccuracies) based on the life of busy 1950s session guitarist Hank Garland. Garland's life was ruled by his music obsessions (including his interest in jazz), temper, womanizing ways, and his frequent clashes with the Nashville establishment. His career was cut short by a devastating car crash. Musician Payne does as well as the script allows in the lead role with Larter in a stereotypical role as Garland's sexy, troubled wife Evelyn. **106m/C; DVD.** Waylon Malloy Payne; Ali Larter; Lane Garrison; David Conrad; Scott Michael Campbell; Mandy Barnett; Jason Alan Smith; Brian Jones; Shawn Colvin; ***D:*** Rick Bieber; ***W:*** Rick Bieber; Brent Boyd; Jason Ehles; ***C:*** Craig Haagensen; ***M:*** Larry Klein. **VIDEO**

Crazy as Hell 𝒮𝒮 **1/2 2002 (R)** Eriq La Salle makes his feature directorial debut in this uneven swirl of psychiatric and metaphysical themes. Renowned psychiatrist Dr. Adams (Beach) arrives at a mental hospital to treat a group of patients using his controversial methods. Fueling his already robust superiority complex, his efforts are being filmed by weaselly documentary maker Parker (McGinley). When a seemingly rational man admits himself into the hospital claiming to be Satan (La Salle), Adams begins to lose control of his patients and his own sanity. Worthwhile for La Salle's performance but seems to drag when he's not on screen. **113m/C; VHS, DVD.** Eriq La Salle; Michael Beach; Ronny Cox; John C. McGinley; Tia Texada; Sinbad; Tracy Pettit; ***D:*** Eriq La Salle; ***W:*** Erik Jendresen; Jeremy Leven; Butch Robinson; ***C:*** George Mooradian; ***M:*** Billy Childs.

crazy/beautiful 𝒮𝒮 **1/2 2001 (PG-13)** Cultural clash and teen relationship troubles all set in the affluent neighborhood of Pacific Palisades. Latino Carlos (Hernandez), from the wrong-side-of-the tracks in East L.A., is going to the rich high school in order to better himself. Nicole (Dunst) is the self-destructive wealthy chick (and congressman's daughter) who shows him that money doesn't buy happiness because she's got troubles, man. Familiar teen flick redeemed somewhat by the lead performances with handsome newcomer Hernandez appealing as a decent guy who's intrigued by willful, misunderstood hottie Dunst. **99m/C; VHS, DVD.** Kirsten Dunst; Jay Hernandez; Taryn Manning; Rolando Molina; Bruce Davison; Lucinda Jenney; Soledad St. Hilaire; ***D:*** John Stockwell; ***W:*** Phil Hay; Matt Manfredi; ***C:*** Shane Hurlbut; ***M:*** Paul Haslinger.

Crazy Eights 𝒮 **2006 (R)** You don't expect Oscar-caliber work in a cheap horror flick but it would be nice if the plot was at least semi-coherent. Six childhood friends reunite after 20 years for a friend's funeral. In his will said friend requests that they open the trunk they buried as kids. In the trunk, they find the decayed corpse of a young girl. Somehow the group then becomes trapped in an abandoned psychiatric hospital where the girl's ghost starts killing them off. So they have to figure out their past connection to the hospital and the dead girl. **80m/C; DVD, Blu-Ray.** Traci Lords; Dina Meyer; Gabrielle Anwar; Frank Whaley; George Newbern; Dan DeLuca; ***D:*** James Koya Jones; ***W:*** Dan DeLuca; James Koya Jones; ***C:*** Stephen M. Lyons; ***M:*** Olivier Glissant.

Crazy Eyes 𝒮 **2012** Cynical, mopey drama set in L.A. Self-destructive playboy Zach (Haas) is a wealthy, womanizing alcoholic. His latest would-be conquest is Rebecca (Zima)--whom he nicknames 'crazy eyes'--who's only interested in being his drinking and not bed buddy, which makes Zach crazy. Zack's drug-dealing bartender Dan (Busey) serves as his confidante. **95m/C; DVD.** Lukas Haas; Madeline Zima; Jake Busey; Tania Raymonde; Ray Wise; Valerie Mahaffey; ***D:*** Adam Sherman; ***W:*** Adam Sherman; Rachel Hardisty; ***C:*** Sharone Meir; ***M:*** Bobby Johnston.

Crazy Fat Ethel II WOOF! *Criminally Insane 2* **1985** A fat, hungry, homicidal female psychopath gets released from the asylum and goes on a cannabilistic rampage. Offensive junk. Sequel to "Criminally Insane." Currently sold under the the title 'Criminally Insane 2' in collection only. **90m/C; VHS, DVD.** Priscilla Alden; Michael Flood; Robert Copple; ***D:*** Nick (Steve Millard) Phillips.

Crazy for Christmas 𝒮𝒮 **2005** Single mom Shannon (Roth) would rather be home with her son Trevor (Spevack) on Christmas Eve but the limo driver is hired by lonely, wealthy eccentric Fred Nickells (Hesseman) to take him all around town as he hands out hundred dollar bills. Fred's generosity comes to the attention of reporter Peter (Bisson) and you can tell where this plot is going without any help from Santa's elves. **90m/C; DVD.** Andrea Roth; Howard Hesseman; Yannick Bisson; Jason Spevack; Daniel Fathers; Karen LeBlanc; Mark Wilson; ***D:*** Eleanor Lindo; ***W:*** Michael A. Simpson; Rick Bitzelberger; ***C:*** Alwyn Kumst; ***M:*** John McCarthy. **CABLE**

Crazy from the Heart 𝒮𝒮𝒮 **1991** Sweet cable romance finds Charlotte Bain (Lahti), the straitlaced high school principal in a small south Texas town, changing her ways. Charlotte surprises herself by agreeing to a date with the school's new janitor, Ernesto (Blades), and what's even more shocking to them both is how much they enjoy each other's company over one wild weekend. Strong, nuanced performances from Lahti and Blades make this chestnut of a story work beautifully, with able help from supporting actors. **104m/C; DVD.** Christine Lahti; Ruben Blades; Mary Kay Place; Brent Spiner; William Russ; Louise Latham; Tommy Muntz; Robin (Robyn) Lively; Bibi Besch; Kamala Lopez; ***D:*** Thomas Schlamme; ***W:*** Linda Voorhees; ***C:*** Stevan Larner; ***M:*** Arthur B. Rubinstein. **CABLE**

Crazy Heart 𝒮𝒮 **1/2 2009 (R)** The plot is a country & western cliche but Bridges' vanity-free performance elevates the film above it. A physical and financial wreck, Bad Blake still has the charm and loves the music but he's a has-been reduced to croaking at bowling alley venues thanks to too much hard living. Sympathetic—and much younger—Santa Fe journalist/single mom Jean Craddock (Gyllenhaal) offers an unexpected lifeline as does Bad's very successful protege Tommy Sweet (Farrell) who gives him an opening act gig and the push to write some new songs. And yep, Bridges and Farrell are solid doing their own singing. Based on the 1987 novel by Thomas Cobb. **112m/C; Blu-Ray.** Jeff Bridges; Maggie Gyllenhaal; Robert Duvall; Colin Farrell; Tom Bower; James Keane; William Marquez; ***D:*** Scott Cooper; ***W:*** Scott Cooper; ***C:*** Barry Markowitz; ***M:*** T-Bone Burnett; Stephen Bruton. Oscars '09: Actor (Bridges), Song ("The Weary Kind"); Golden Globes '10: Actor--Drama (Bridges), Song ("The Weary Kind"); Ind. Spirit '10: Actor (Bridges), First Feature; Screen Actors Guild '09: Actor (Bridges).

Crazy Horse 𝒮𝒮𝒮 **2012** Legendary documentarian Frederick Wiseman takes his cameras to Le Crazy Horse de Paris, a place that has claimed to have "the best nude dancing show in the world" since 1951 and chronicles the behind-the-scenes machinations that are required to put on a show. More than a mere French strip club, the Crazy Horse sees itself more as an elaborate spectacle not unlike Cirque du Soleil or a Broadway show. Wiseman approaches his subject in a way that may surprise viewers who see French cabaret as nothing more than a high-budget girlie show. **134m/C; DVD, Blu-Ray.** Philippe Decoufle; Naamah Alva; Daizy Blu; Philippe Katerine; ***D:*** Frederick Wiseman.

Crazy Horse and Custer: "The Untold Story" 𝒮 **1990 (R)** Long before Little Big Horn, two legendary enemies find themselves trapped together in deadly Blackfoot territory. George Armstrong Custer and Crazy Horse are forced to form a volatile alliance in their life-or-death struggle against the murderous Blackfoot Tribe. History takes a back seat to Hollywood scriptwriting. **120m/C; VHS, DVD.** Slim Pickens; Wayne Maunder; Mary Ann Mobley; Michael Dante; ***D:*** Norman Foster; ***C:*** Harold E. Stine; ***M:*** Leith Stevens.

Crazy in Alabama 𝒮 **1/2 1999 (PG-13)** If they greenlighted this southern fried mess, they're crazy in Hollywood, too. Lucille (Griffith) is an unbalanced aging southern belle who decapitates her husband and heads off to fulfill her dream of becoming a Hollywood star. She also takes his severed noggin with her, although it is a little talkative. Woven through this bizarre storyline is another that focuses on Lucille's nephew Peejoe back home in Alabama as he stands up to a bigoted sheriff, helps protest for civil rights and meets Martin Luther King. Banderas' directoral debut is fine technically, but veers wildly all over the road as far as content goes. **111m/C; VHS, DVD.** Melanie Griffith; David Morse; Lucas Black; Cathy Moriarty; Meat Loaf Aday; Rod Steiger; Richard Schiff; John Beasley; Robert Wagner; Noah Emmerich; Sandra Seacat; Paul Ben-Victor; Brad Beyer; Fannie Flagg; Elizabeth Perkins; Linda Hart; Paul Mazursky; William Converse-Roberts; Holmes Osborne; David Speck; ***D:*** Antonio Banderas; ***W:*** Mark Childress; ***C:*** Julio Macat; ***M:*** Mark Snow.

Crazy in Love 𝒮𝒮 **1/2 1992** Three generations of women live on an island in the home that has been in their family for years. Hunter is wildly in love with her husband, but misses (and doesn't quite trust) him when he is away on business. Enter Sands, who showers her with affection and fills the void in her life. The supporting cast fleshes out the story nicely and illustrates the reasons behind Hunter's insecurity. Enjoyable romantic comedy doesn't throw out anything heavy. Adapted from the novel by Luanne Rice; made for TNT. **93m/C; DVD.** Holly Hunter; Gena Rowlands; Bill Pullman; Julian Sands; Frances McDormand; Herta Ware; Joanne Baron; ***D:*** Martha Coolidge; ***W:*** Gerald Ayres; ***C:*** Johnny E. Jensen; ***M:*** Cynthia Millar. **CABLE**

Crazy Kind of Love 𝒮𝒮 **2012 (R)** Charming, if cliched, and well-acted family comedy/drama. After her cheating husband leaves, depressed Angela takes to her bed while her sons Henry and Matthew try to hold the family together. They're not doing so well until Henry's outspoken new girlfriend Bette moves in and promptly takes charge. Based on April Stevens' 1995 novel "Angel Angel." **90m/C; DVD.** Virginia Madsen; Graham Rogers; Zach Gilford; Amanda Crew; Sam Trammell; Madeline Zima; Anthony LaPaglia; ***D:*** Sarah Siegel-Magness; ***W:*** Karen McCullah; ***C:*** Dean Cundey; ***M:*** Mario Grigorov.

Crazy Like a Fox 𝒮 **1/2 2004 (PG-13)** No, just crazy. Irresponsible Nat Banks (Rees) is the 8th generation to live on his now-impoverished family farm in Virginia. Forced to sell, Nat makes what he thinks is a deal with some northern land speculators to save the property and allow him and his family to continue to live on it. Instead, the Yankee carpetbaggers plan to turn the farm into a subdivision. So Nat retaliates by putting on a (no doubt original) Confederate uniform, hiding out in a cave, and practicing some guerilla warfare. Probably plays best south of the Mason-Dixon line. **99m/C; DVD.** Roger Rees; Mary McDonnell; Robert Wisdom; Mark Joy; Paul Fitzgerald; Christina Rouner; ***D:*** Richard Squires; ***W:*** Richard Squires; ***C:*** Gary Grieg; ***M:*** David Kane; Richard Squires.

Crazy Little Thing 𝒮𝒮 **1/2** *The Perfect You* **2002 (R)** That "thing" would be love, of course. But reporter Whitney (McCarthy), newly arrived in New York, tells her friend Dee (de Matteo) that she's only looking for sex. So Dee sends her to a certain bar where Whitney can hire a male escort for the evening. Meanwhile, waiter Jimmy (Eigeman) is also hoping to get lucky and happens to turn up at the same bar. Whitney thinks Jimmy knows the score but after a night of wild sex, Jimmy turns out to want more than a one-night stand. **90m/C; VHS, DVD.** Christopher Eigeman; Jenny McCarthy; Drea De Matteo; Paul Dooley; Alanna Ubach; ***D:*** Matthew Miller; ***W:*** Matthew Miller; ***C:*** Michael Barrett; ***M:*** Adam Dorn.

Crazy Love **2007 (PG-13)** Documentary tells of the bizarre romance of Bronx-born ambulance-chasing attorney Burt Pugach and a stunning younger woman, Linda Riss, who breaks things off when she discovers he is married. Her departure pushes the obsessive Pugach over the edge, and he contracts three wiseguys to throw acid in her face, disfiguring and partially blinding her. Somehow the strength of attraction wins out, unthinkably bringing Burt and Linda together again. The film includes interviews with the couple, old friends, and reporters who covered the case as well as news footage and photographs. This is way too weird to be made up. **92m/C; DVD.** Burt Pugach; Lisa Riss Pugach; ***D:*** Dan Klores; ***C:*** Wolfgang Held; ***M:*** Douglas J. Cuomo. Ind. Spirit '08: Feature Doc.

Crazy Mama **1/2 1975 (PG)** Three women go on a crime spree from California to Arkansas, picking up men and having a hoot. Crime and comedy in a campy romp. Set in the 1950s and loaded with period kitsch. **81m/C; VHS, DVD.** Cloris Leachman; Stuart Whitman; Ann Sothern; Jim Backus; Linda Purl; Donny Most; Sally Kirkland; Dick Miller; Bill Paxton; ***D:*** Jonathan Demme; ***W:*** Robert Thom; ***C:*** Bruce Logan.

Crazy on the Outside **1/2 2010 (PG-13)** Unfortunately, Allen's directorial debut (in which he also stars) is a weak and generic comedy that doesn't appear worthy of a big screen. Tommy (Allen) was in the big house for video piracy. After being released, the ex-con moves in with his over-protective sister Vicky (Weaver) and her skeptical husband Ed (Simmons) and tries to start over. First he gets a job in a pirate-themed fast food joint, then he meets up with former flame Christy (Bowen), and then Tommy finds that he's actually attracted to his single-mom parole officer, Angela (Tripplehorn). Too bad his old partner-in-crime Gray (Liotta) wants Tommy in on his latest scheme. The female roles are mostly one-note and some of the acting gets sitcom cartoonish. **96m/C; Blu-Ray, On Demand.** Tim Allen; Julie Bowen; Sigourney Weaver; Ray Liotta; Jeanne Tripplehorn; Kelsey Grammer; J.K. Simmons; Jon(athan) Gries; Helen Slayton-Hughes; Malcolm Goodwin; Kenton Duty; ***D:*** Tim Allen; ***W:*** Judd Pillot; John Peaslee; ***C:*** Robbie Greenberg; ***M:*** David Newman.

Crazy People **1/2 1990 (R)** Advertising exec Emory Leeston (Moore) writes commercials that describe products with complete honesty, and is committed to a mental hospital as a result. He meets a variety of characters at the hospital, including Hannah, with whom he falls in love. Tepid boxoffice blunder sounds funnier than it is. We give half a bone for the ad slogans, the funniest part of the movie. Our favorite: "Most of our passengers arrive alive" for an airline. **91m/C; VHS, DVD.** Dudley Moore; Daryl Hannah; Paul Reiser; Mercedes Ruehl; J.T. Walsh; Ben Hammer; Richard (Dick) Cusack; Alan North; David Paymer; Danton Stone; Doug Yasuda; Bill Smitrovich; Paul Bates; Floyd Vivino; ***D:*** Tony Bill; ***W:*** Mitch Markowitz; ***M:*** Cliff Eidelman.

Crazy Rich Asians **2018 (PG-13)** This contemporary romantic comedy, based on a global bestseller, follows native New Yorker Rachel Chu to Singapore to meet her boyfriend's zillionaire family. In many ways, it's a typical rom-com, albeit higher on the opulence meter, featuring beautiful people, romantic hurdles, and screwball gags. What makes it noteworthy is that it's the first Hollywood flick since 1993's *The Joy Luck Club* to feature an all-Asian cast. **120m/C; DVD, Blu-Ray.** Constance Wu; Henry Golding; Michelle Yeoh; Gemma Chan; Nora Lum; ***D:*** Jon M. Chu; ***W:*** Peter Chiarelli; Adele Lim; ***C:*** Vanja Cernjul; ***M:*** Brian Tyler.

Crazy Six **1/2 1998 (R)** In a futuristic Europe, organized crime families vie for control of the underground arms trade and the black market. **94m/C; VHS, DVD, Blu-Ray.** Rob Lowe; Burt Reynolds; Ice-T; Mario Van Peebles; ***D:*** Albert Pyun.

The Crazy Stranger *Gadjo Dilo* **1998** The third film in director Gatlif's Gypsy trilogy following "Latcho Drom" and "Mondo." In order to honor his late father, Parisian Stephane (Duris) travels to Romania to track down and record the music of his father's favorite Gypsy singer. He's taken in by village headman, Isidor (Serban), whose own son has just been sent to prison. Isidor and the villagers make their living as musicians and Stephane is drawn ever deeper into their lives until tragedy forces him to make a choice. In French and Romany with subtitles. **97m/C; VHS, DVD.** *FR* Romain Duris; Isidor Serban; Rona Hartner; Florin Moldovan; ***D:*** Tony Gatlif; ***W:*** Tony Gatlif; ***C:*** Eric Guichard; ***M:*** Tony Gatlif.

Crazy, Stupid, Love. **2011 (PG-13)** An incredibly talented ensemble elevates a sometimes-cliched script beyond its grand statements on the crazy nature of one of Hollywood's favorite subjects, love. Gosling proves to have ace comic timing to match his proven dramatic abilities, adding three-dimensionality to what could have been a cartoonish player who teaches the unlucky-in-love Cal (Carell) how to find his confidence again after his cheating wife (Moore) decides to leave him. Ably supported by a strong female ensemble (including Stone, Tomei, and newcomer Tipton), this rom-com defies the current dire state of the genre by being both romantic and actually funny. **117m/C; Blu-Ray.** Steve Carell; Ryan Gosling; Julianne Moore; Emma Stone; Kevin Bacon; Marisa Tomei; Analeigh Tipton; Jonah Bobo; Joey King; Josh Groban; ***D:*** John Requa; Glenn Ficarra; ***W:*** Dan Fogelman; ***C:*** Andrew Dunn; ***M:*** Christophe Beck; Nick Urata.

Crazy Wisdom: The Life & Times of Chogyam Trungpa Rinpoche **1/2** *Crazy Wisdom* **2011** This revealing documentary looks at Chogyam Trungpa, who was a key figure in bringing Tibetan Buddhism to the United States. Known as the bad boy of Buddhism, Tungpa came to the United States in 1970 after fleeing Tibet when China invaded. Though he was well-known for translating ancient Buddhist concepts into information packets palatable to Westerners, Tungpa also behaved outrageously for a religious leader including having sexual relations with his students. Yet years after his death, his teaching are regarded as authentic and profound though his behavior remains controversial. The difference between the man and the myth are a highlight of the film. **86m/C; DVD.** ***D:*** Johanna Demetrakas; ***C:*** Pablo Bryant; Patrick Selvage; ***M:*** Sean Callery.

Crazylove **2005 (R)** Letty Mayer is happy with her teaching job, happy with her attorney boyfriend, and happy about her sister's upcoming wedding. But stress and her need for perfection drive Letty into a nervous breakdown and a stay in a mental institution. There she meets charming schizophrenic Michael. They decide to pursue their newfound passion when both are released, although Letty seems purposefully unaware of the severity of Michael's condition, especially when he's off his meds. **99m/C; DVD.** Reiko Aylesworth; Bruno Campos; Marla Sokoloff; Meat Loaf Aday; JoBeth Williams; David Alan Basche; Greg Germann; K. Callan; ***D:*** Ellie Kanner; ***W:*** Carol Watson; ***C:*** Matthew Heckerling; ***M:*** Brad Segal.

The Crazysitter **1/2 1994 (PG-13)** Edie (D'Angelo), a petty thief recently released from jail, is hired as a sitter to the twins-from-hell. So, she decides to sell the little monsters. **92m/C; VHS, DVD.** Beverly D'Angelo; Ed Begley, Jr.; Carol Kane; Phil Hartman; Brady Bluhm; Rachel Duncan; Nell Carter; Steve Landesberg; ***D:*** Michael James McDonald; ***W:*** Michael James McDonald; ***C:*** Christopher Baffa; ***M:*** David Wurst; Eric Wurst.

Creation **2009 (PG-13)** Amiel's melodrama about Charles Darwin focuses not on the intellectual aspects of his writing but on its spiritual and personal consequences. Set in 1858, Darwin (Bettany) has been writing for 20 years but is still hesitant to complete and publish his work, "The Origin of Species," since he's reluctant to deal with the controversy he knows it will cause. Constantly brooding over the death of his favorite child Annie, Darwin is also unwilling to further upset his devout Christian wife Emma (Connelly) while his friends encourage him to publish for the sake of science. **108m/C; Blu-Ray, On Demand.** *GB* Paul Bettany; Jennifer Connelly; Jeremy Northam; Toby Jones; Benedict Cumberbatch; Jim Carter; Martha West; ***D:*** Jon Amiel; ***W:*** John Collee; ***C:*** Jess Hall; ***M:*** Christopher Young.

Creation of the Humanoids *Ewvolt of the Humanoids* **1962** When society's birth rates begin falling after a nuclear war, mankind creates humanoid robots to serve them as laborers, and subsequently freak out when their creations get a little too human. **75m/C; DVD.** Don Megowan; Erica Elliott; Frances McCann; Don Doolittle; David Cross; ***D:*** Wesley Barry; ***W:*** Jay Simms; ***C:*** Hal Mohr; ***M:*** Edward Kay.

Creator **1985 (R)** A Frankenstein-like scientist plans to clone a being based on his wife, who died 30 years ago. As his experiments begin to show positive results, his romantic attention turns towards his beautiful lab assistant. O'Toole as the deranged scientist almost saves this one. Based on a novel by Jeremy Leven. **108m/C; VHS, DVD.** Peter O'Toole; Mariel Hemingway; Vincent Spano; Virginia Madsen; David Ogden Stiers; John Dehner; Karen Kopins; Jeff Corey; ***D:*** Ivan Passer; ***W:*** Jeremy Leven; ***C:*** Robbie Greenberg; ***M:*** Sylvester Levay.

Creature *Titan Find* **1985 (R)** A two thousand-year-old alien life form is killing off astronauts exploring the planet Titan. "Alien" rip-off has its moments, but not enough of them. Kinski provides some laughs. **97m/C; VHS, DVD, Blu-Ray.** Klaus Kinski; Stan Ivar; Wendy Schaal; Lyman Ward; Annette McCarthy; Diane Salinger; ***D:*** William Malone; ***M:*** Tom Chase; Steve Rucker.

Creature **WOOF! 2011 (R)** Inept, completely predictable Deep South, swamp monster horror. Three couples traveling to New Orleans mistakenly make a pit stop in some backwoods, inbred bog community and then decide wouldn't it be fun to check out a local legend about some half-gator/half-human creature. They are too stupid to live--and most don't survive for long. **93m/C; DVD.** Mehcad Brooks; Serinda Swan; Amanda Fuller; Dillon Casey; Lauren Schneider; Aaron Hill; Pruitt Taylor Vince; Sid Haig; ***D:*** Fred M. Andrews; ***W:*** Fred M. Andrews; ***C:*** Christopher Faloona; ***M:*** Kevin Haskins.

Creature from Black Lake **1976 (PG)** Two anthropology students from Chicago travel to the Louisiana swamps searching for the creature from Black Lake. Predictably, they find him. McClenny, incidentally, is Morgan Fairchild's sister. **95m/C; VHS, DVD.** Jack Elam; Dub Taylor; Dennis Fimple; John David Carson; Bill (Billy) Thurman; Catherine McClenny; ***D:*** Joy Houck, Jr.; ***W:*** Jim McCullough, Jr.

Creature from the Black Lagoon **1954** An anthropological expedition in the Amazon stumbles upon the Gill-Man, a prehistoric humanoid fish monster who takes a fancy to fetching Adams, a coed majoring in "science," but the humans will have none of it. Originally filmed in 3-D, this was one of the first movies to sport top-of-the-line underwater photography and remains one of the most enjoyable monster movies ever made. Sequels: "Revenge of the Creature" and "The Creature Walks Among Us." **79m/B; VHS, DVD, Blu-Ray.** Richard Carlson; Julie Adams; Richard Denning; Antonio Moreno; Whit Bissell; Nestor Paiva; Ricou Browning; Ben Chapman; Bernie Gozier; ***D:*** Jack Arnold; ***W:*** Arthur Ross; Harry Essex; ***C:*** William E. Snyder; Charles S. Welbourne; ***M:*** Hans J. Salter; Henry Mancini.

Creature from the Haunted Sea **1960** Monster movie satire set in Cuba shortly after the revolution and centering around an elaborate plan to loot the Treasury and put the blame on a strange sea monster. Corman comedy is predictably low budget but entertaining. "Wain" is really Robert Towne, winner of an Oscar for screenwriting. Remake of "Naked Paradise." **76m/B; VHS, DVD.** Antony Carbone; Betsy Jones-Moreland; Beach Dickerson; Edward (Robert Towne) Wain; Edmundo Rivera Alvarez; Robert Bean; Sonya Noemi Gonzalez; ***Cameo(s):*** Roger Corman; ***D:*** Roger Corman; Monte Hellman; ***W:*** Charles B. Griffith; ***C:*** Jacques "Jack" Marquette; ***M:*** Fred Katz.

Creature of Darkness **1/2 2009 (R)** Cheesy and brainlessly entertaining low-budget sci-fi horror. Andrew has had nightmares even since his late uncle told him about an alien creature called The Catcher that collects humans for an outer space museum. When Andrew and some friends go off-roading in a remote desert location, he recognizes the terrain from his nightmares and everyone soon learns that The Catcher is real. **90m/C; DVD.** Devon Sawa; Dan(iel) White; Fernanda Romero; Siena Goines; Sanoe Lake; Matthew Lawrence; ***D:*** Mark Stouffer; ***C:*** Tom Camarda. **VIDEO**

Creature of Destruction **1967** A beautiful young woman is hypnotized and inadvertantly reverted to her past life as a hideous sea monster. Buchanan's remake of his own 1956 production, "The She Creature." **80m/B; VHS, DVD.** Les Tremayne; Aron Kincaid; Pat Delaney; Neil Fletcher; Ann McAdams; Scott McKay; ***D:*** Larry Buchanan; ***C:*** Robert C. Jessup.

The Creature Walks among Us **1/2 1956** Sequel to "Revenge of the Creature" has the Gill-Man once again being captured by scientists for studying purposes. Through an accidental lab fire, the creature's gills are burned off and he undergoes surgery in an attempt to live out of water. Final entry in the Creature series has little magic of the original. Also shot in 3-D. **79m/B; VHS, DVD, Blu-Ray.** Jeff Morrow; Rex Reason; Leigh Snowden; Gregg (Hunter) Palmer; Ricou Browning; Don Megowan; Maurice Manson; Frank Chase; Larry Hudson; Paul Fierro; ***D:*** John Sherwood; ***W:*** Arthur Ross; ***C:*** Maury Gertsman; ***M:*** Henry Mancini; Joseph Gershenson.

Creature with the Blue Hand **1970** A German horror film based on a passable Edgar Wallace story about a man unjustly convicted of murders actually committed by a lunatic. Dubbed. **92m/C; VHS, DVD.** *GE* Klaus Kinski; Harald Leopold; Hermann Leschau; Diana Kerner; Carl Lange; Ilse Page; ***D:*** Alfred Vohrer.

Creatures from the Abyss **1/2** *Plankton* **1994** After being stranded on a raft, five young people board an abandoned yacht, which is actually an oceanographic research vessel where very strange fish were being studied. The youngsters decide to make the yacht their party-place, but things get nasty once they realize that killer fish are running wild on board the ship. As if that weren't bad enough, exposure to these aquatic nasties causes humans to mutate into monsters! On the surface (?!), this looks like the average Italian thriller, with bad acting, atrocious dubbing, and lackluster pacing, but the odd plot concerning mutant plankton and the fact that the movie consistently crosses the line with its disturbing special effects make it stand out. The timid will find the last act revolting, but those looking for a throwback to the gore-soaked '80s will love it. **86m/C; DVD.** *IT*

Creatures from the Pink Lagoon **2007** B-movie spoof that sets-up '50s monsters and gay stereotypes. A group of gay friends gather at a beach cottage for a birthday party in 1967. They learn a nearby lagoon is overrun with zombies, who are man-eaters in more ways than one. **71m/B; DVD.** Phillip Clarke; Nick Garrison; Lowell Deo; Evan Mosher; Vincent Kovar; ***D:*** Chris Diani; ***W:*** Chris Diani; ***C:*** Peter Torr; ***M:*** David Moddux. **VIDEO**

Creatures the World Forgot **WOOF! 1970** A British-made bomb about two tribes of cavemen warring over power and a cavewoman. No special effects, dinosaurs, or dialogue. **96m/C; VHS, DVD, Streaming.** Julie Ege; Robert John; Tony Bonner; Rosalie Crutchley; Sue Wilson; ***D:*** Don Chaffey; ***W:*** Michael Carreras.

Creed 𝒱𝒱𝒱 **2015 (PG-13)** Who would have guessed that there would be an excellent Rocky film in 2015? Jordan plays Adonis Johnson Creed, the son of Apollo, who wants to follow in his father's footsteps and become a legendary boxer in his own right. He finds a new father figure and mentor in Rocky himself (a career-best performance from Stallone). Director Coogler and star Jordan didn't just make a sequel to the saga of the Philly boxer, they made a drama that fights its own battles. In the process they crafted a riveting character study. **132m/C; DVD, Blu-Ray.** Michael B. Jordan; Sylvester Stallone; Tessa Thompson; Phylicia Rashad; Graham McTavish; ***D:*** Ryan Coogler; ***W:*** Ryan Coogler; Aaron Covington; ***C:*** Maryse Alberti; ***M:*** Ludwig Göransson. Golden Globes '16: Actor--Supporting (Stallone).

Creed II 𝒱𝒱 ½ **2018 (PG-13)** Adonis Creed (Jordan), cocky as the newly crowned light heavyweight champion, accepts a challenge to fight Viktor Drago (Munteanu), son of the Russian boxer who killed Adonis's father Apollo in 1985. The battles are waged both inside and outside of the ring: Adonis and Rocky face foes from their past while weighing the cost to their relationships in the present, and the Dragos seek redemption from the loser status they have in their home country. The training montages and fight scenes are glorious, and the character explorations elevate this from a mere rock-em/sock-em fight flick. **130m/C; DVD, Blu-Ray, Streaming.** Michael B. Jordan; Sylvester Stallone; Tessa Thompson; Phylicia Rashad; Dolph Lundgren; Florian Munteanu; ***D:*** Steven Caple, Jr.; ***W:*** Sylvester Stallone; Cheo Hodari Coker; Sascha Penn; Juel Taylor; ***C:*** Kramer Morgenthau; ***M:*** Ludwig Göransson.

Creep 𝒱𝒱 **2015 (R)** A horror-thriller about a job that turns out to be more than it seems for one unlucky man. Desperate for work, Aaron (Brice) answers an online ad to do filming for a day in a remote mountain town. There, he meets Josef (Duplass), who seems sincere and focused on his project. As Aaron films, he realizes that Josef is not who he says he is and his intentions are more sinister. The interplay of the pair grows more and more complex as the truth reaches the light. **77m/C; DVD, Streaming, Download.** Patrick Brice; Mark Duplass; ***D:*** Patrick Brice; ***W:*** Patrick Brice; Mark Duplass; ***C:*** Christopher Donlon; ***M:*** Kyle Field; Eric Andrew Kuhn.

Creepers 𝒱𝒱 ½ *Phenomena* **1985 (R)** A young girl talks to bugs and gets them to follow her instructions, which comes in handy when she battles the lunatic who is killing her school chums. Argento weirdness—and graphic gore—may not be for all tastes. **82m/C; VHS, DVD, Blu-Ray.** *IT* Jennifer Connelly; Donald Pleasence; Daria Nicolodi; Elenora Giorgi; Dalia di Lazzaro; Patrick Bauchau; Fiore Argento; Federica Mastroianni; Michele (Michael) Soavi; Gavin Friday; ***D:*** Dario Argento; ***W:*** Dario Argento; Franco Ferrini; ***C:*** Romano Albani; ***M:*** Simon Boswell.

The Creeping Flesh 𝒱𝒱 ½ **1972 (PG)** A scientist decides he can cure evil by injecting his patients with a serum derived from the blood of an ancient corpse. Some truly chilling moments will get your flesh creeping. **89m/C; VHS, DVD.** *GB* Peter Cushing; Christopher Lee; Lorna Heilbron; George Benson; Kenneth J. Warren; Duncan Lamont; Harry Locke; Hedger Wallace; Michael Ripper; Jenny Runacre; ***D:*** Freddie Francis; ***W:*** Peter Spenceley; Jonathan Rumbold; ***C:*** Norman Warwick.

Creeping Terror **WOOF!** *The Crawling Monster; Dangerous Charter* **1964** Gigantic alien carpet monster (look for the tennis shoes sticking out underneath) devours slow-moving teenagers. Partially narrated because some of the original soundtrack was lost, with lots of bad acting, a worse script, laughable sets, and a ridiculous monster. Beware of the thermometer scene. **81m/B; VHS, DVD, Blu-Ray.** Vic Savage; Shannon O'Neal; William Thourlby; Louise Lawson; Robin James; Byrd Holland; Jack King; Art J. Nelson; ***D:*** Art J. Nelson; ***W:*** Robert Silliphant; ***C:*** Andrew Janczak.

Creepozoids 𝒱 **1987** In the near future, a monster at an abandoned science complex stalks army deserters hiding out there. Violent nonsense done better by others. **72m/C; DVD, Blu-Ray.** Linnea Quigley; Ken Abraham; Michael Aranda; ***D:*** David DeCoteau.

The Creeps 𝒱𝒱 **1997 (PG-13)** A horror-film obsessed scientist, Dr. Winston Berber, steals the original manuscript of Mary Shelley's "Frankenstein" and librarian Anna (Griffin) hires detective David Rawley (Lauer) to get it back. Then Berber returns to steal Bram Stoker's original "Dracula" and kidnaps Anna to use in his wacky experiment as well. He decides to reanimate his four favorite movie monsters but when David rescues Anna before the experiment is complete, Dracula (Fondacaro), the Mummy (Smith), the Wolfman (Simanton), and Frankenstein's Monster (Wellington) wind up only three feet tall. Not pleased by their diminutive size, the creeps work to restore themselves to the proper height (and cause a little mayhem as well). **80m/C; VHS, DVD, Blu-Ray.** Phil Fondacaro; Rhonda Griffin; Justin Lauer; Bill Moynihan; Kristin Norton; Jon Simanton; Joe Smith; Thomas Wellington; ***D:*** Charles Band; ***W:*** Benjamin Carr; ***C:*** Adolfo Bartoli; ***M:*** Carl Dante. **VIDEO**

Creepshow 𝒱𝒱 ½ **1982 (R)** Stephen King's tribute to E.C. Comics, those pulp horror comic books of the 1950s that delighted in grisly, grotesque, and morbid humor. The film tells five horror tales, and features King himself in one segment, as a none-too-bright farmer who unknowingly cultivates a strange, alien-origin moss. With despicable heroes and gory monsters, this is sure to delight all fans of the horror vein. Those easily repulsed by cockroaches beware! **120m/C; VHS, DVD, Blu-Ray.** Hal Holbrook; Adrienne Barbeau; Viveca Lindfors; E.G. Marshall; Stephen King; Leslie Nielsen; Carrie Nye; Fritz Weaver; Ted Danson; Ed Harris; John Amplas; Tom Savini; ***D:*** George A. Romero; ***W:*** Stephen King; ***C:*** Michael Gornick; ***M:*** John Harrison.

Creepshow 2 𝒱 ½ **1987 (R)** Romero adapted three Stephen King stories for this horror anthology which presents gruesome looks at a hit-and-run driver, a wooden Indian, and a vacation gone wrong. Gory and childish stuff from two masters of the genre. Look for King as a truck driver. **92m/C; VHS, DVD, Blu-Ray.** Lois Chiles; George Kennedy; Dorothy Lamour; Tom Savini; Domenick John; Frank S. Salsedo; Holt McCallany; David Holbrook; Page Hannah; Daniel Beer; Stephen King; Paul Satterfield; Jeremy Green; Tom Wright; ***D:*** Michael Gornick; ***W:*** George A. Romero; ***C:*** Richard Hart; Tom Hurwitz; ***M:*** Les Reed; Rick Wakeman.

Creepshow III 𝒱 **2006 (R)** The final incarnation of the horror anthology series has five tales to offer, including serial killers, evil remote controls, radios that talk, and dead hobos. Sadly without the influence of Stephen King and George Romero it's not nearly as good as the original. **104m/C; DVD.** Stephanie Pettee; AJ Bowen; Elina Madison; Ryan Carty; Emmet McGuire; Pablo C. Pappano; ***D:*** Ana Clavell; James Glenn Dudelson; ***W:*** Ana Clavell; James Glenn Dudelson; Scott Frazelle; Alex Ugelow; ***C:*** James M. LeGoy; ***M:*** Chris Anderson. **VIDEO**

Creepy 𝒱𝒱𝒱 *Kurîpî: Itsuwari no rinjin* **2016** Internationally renowned auteur Kiyoshi Kurosawa returns to the genre of horror that made him a superstar although he brings a dramatist's edge to this, well, creepy tale of a serial killer living in plain sight. Profiler Koichi Takakura (Hidetoshi Nishijima) is trying to unwind after a tragedy at his workplace when insanity moves in next door. One night, the girl who lives next door to Koichi and his wife Yasuko jumps through their window and tells them that the man they met is not really her father. And then things get really dark. Some of the twists aren't believable but the filmmaking is exceptional. **130m/C; DVD.** Hidetoshi Nishijima; Yuko Takeuchi; Teruyuki Kagawa; Haruna Kawaguchi; Masahiro Higashide; ***D:*** Kiyoshi Kurosawa; ***W:*** Kiyoshi Kurosawa; Chihiro Ikeda; ***M:*** Yuri Habuka.

Cremains 𝒱𝒱𝒱 **2000** Anthology centers on a mortician (Chester Delacruz) who is being investigated for cremating two bodies at once. As he is questioned by an unseen panel of inquisitors, he relates three stories. In the first, a young woman (Plimmer) makes the mistake of driving through a small town famous for its ritual sacrifices. In the next story, a serial killer (Williams) captures a hitchhiker and then the mind-games begin. The third story features a woman (Cole) who seeks out the help of a horror author (Smith), as she's convinced that a female vampire is after her. The final segment returns to the mortician and the macabre results of his double-cremation. The stories are good; while they aren't incredibly original, they all have that "urban legend" feel, which makes them accessible. Howeverm the film is way too long, and all of the segments feel padded. Not perfect, but actually better than some studio horror films released lately. **107m/C; DVD.** Chester Delacruz; Wanda Plimmer; Christopher (David) Williams; Kimberly Lynn Cole; R.W. Smith; ***D:*** Steve Sessions; ***W:*** Steve Sessions. **VIDEO**

The Cremators **WOOF!** **1972** A meteorite carrying an alien lands at a seaside resort and everyone begins bursting into flames. Low budget effort from the scripter of "It Came from Outer Space." **90m/C; VHS, DVD, Blu-Ray.** Marvin Howard; Maria de Aragon; ***D:*** Harry Essex.

Crescendo 𝒱 **1969** Generally unimpressive Hammer psycho-thriller. American student Susan (Powers) is writing her thesis on a recently deceased composer and travels to the south of France where she is invited to stay in the creepy family mansion by his widow (Scott). Everyone is crazy, including the composer's wheelchair-bound, drug addict son (Olson), the hired help, and whoever is confined to the attic. **95m/C; DVD.** *GB* Stefanie Powers; James Olson; Margaretta Scott; Jane Lapotaire; Joss Ackland; ***D:*** Alan Gibson; ***W:*** Jimmy Sangster; Alfred Shaughnessy; ***C:*** Paul Beeson; ***M:*** Malcolm Williamson.

Crest of the Wave 𝒱 ½ *Seagulls Over Sorrento* **1954** Dry and lacking much action. Royal Navy scientists and sailors, stationed on a Scottish island, have died trying to engineer a new torpedo (it keeps blowing up). The Admiralty sends in some Yank help, which isn't appreciated by the British group, since neither side seems much interested in cooperation. **91m/B; DVD.** *UK* Gene Kelly; John Justin; Bernard Lee; Jeff Richards; Sidney James; David Orr; ***D:*** Roy Boulting; John Boulting; ***W:*** Roy Boulting; Frank Harvey; ***C:*** Gilbert Taylor; ***M:*** Miklos Rozsa.

The Crew 𝒱𝒱 **1995 (R)** Sometimes it doesn't pay to be a good samaritan—as a boatload of pleasure cruisers discover when they rescue two psychopaths from a burning boat in the Bahamas. **99m/C; VHS, Streaming.** Viggo Mortensen; Jeremy Sisto; Pamela Gidley; Donal Logue; Laura Del Sol; Grace Zabriskie; John Philbin; ***D:*** Carl Colpaert; ***W:*** Carl Colpaert.

The Crew 𝒱𝒱 **2000 (PG-13)** Dreyfuss, Hedaya, Reynolds, and Cassel are a quartet of retired wiseguys who hatch a plan to save their South Beach Miami retirement home with a fake mob hit. Complications arise when the body turns out to be a South American druglord's missing father. Occasionally funny but overly plotted script was written by former "Golden Girls" writer Fanaro, and the sitcom lineage is obvious. **88m/C; VHS, DVD, Blu-Ray.** Richard Dreyfuss; Burt Reynolds; Dan Hedaya; Seymour Cassel; Carrie-Anne Moss; Jennifer Tilly; Lainie Kazan; Miguel (Michael) Sandoval; Jeremy Piven; Casey Siemaszko; Matt Borlenghi; Jeremy Ratchford; Mike Moroff; Billy Jayne Young; Jose Zuniga; Louis Lombardi; Allan Nicholls; Ron Karabatsos; Frank Vincent; Fyvush Finkel; ***D:*** Michael Dinner; ***W:*** Barry Fanaro; ***C:*** Juan Ruiz-Anchia; ***M:*** Steve Bartek.

The Crew 𝒱𝒱 **2008** British gangster flick set in Liverpool. Old-fashioned gang leader Ged wants to invest in a legit property development scheme but he needs to do one last job to get enough money. Meanwhile, his ambitious younger bro Ratter is working in the drug trade (to Ged's disgust) while other baddies try muscling in on Ged's action. Adapted from Kevin Sampson's 2001 novel "Outlaws." **100m/C; DVD, Blu-Ray.** *GB* Kenny Doughty; Cordelia Bugeja; Rosie Fellner; Scot Williams; Raza Jaffrey; Rory McCann; Stephen Graham; ***D:*** Adrian Vitoria; ***W:*** Adrian Vitoria; Ian Brady; ***C:*** Mark Hamilton; ***M:*** James Edward Barker.

Cria Cuervos 𝒱𝒱𝒱 ½ **1976** Moving freely between reality and fantasy, Saura portrays the complexities of childhood emotions through the grief of 8-year-old Ana (Torrent), who lives in Madrid and conjures her mother's ghost (Chaplin), as well as the struggles of Spain's middle class under fascist rule. Well-scripted, beautifully written and acted, the title is derived from the Spanish proverb: "Raise ravens and they'll peck out your eyes." Spanish with subtitles. **109m/C; DVD.** *SP* Syd Chaplin; Monica Randall; Ana Torrent; Florinda Chico; Hector Alterio; German Cobos; Mirta Miller; ***D:*** Carlos Saura; ***W:*** Carlos Saura; ***C:*** Teodoro Escamilla; ***M:*** Federico Mompou.

Cries and Whispers 𝒱𝒱𝒱 *Viskingar Och Rop* **1972 (R)** As a woman dies slowly of tuberculosis, three women care for her: her two sisters, one sexually repressed, the other promiscuous, and her servant. The sisters remember family love and closeness, but are too afraid to look death in the face to aid their sister. Only the servant can touch her in her dying and only the servant believes in God and his will. Beautiful imagery, focused through a nervous camera, which lingers on the meaningless and whisks away from the meaningful. Absolute mastery of cinematic art by Bergman. **91m/C; VHS, DVD, Blu-Ray.** *SW* Harriet Andersson; Ingrid Thulin; Liv Ullmann; Kari Sylway; Erland Josephson; Henning Moritzen; ***D:*** Ingmar Bergman; ***W:*** Ingmar Bergman; ***C:*** Sven Nykvist. Oscars '73: Cinematog.; Natl. Bd. of Review '73: Director (Bergman); N.Y. Film Critics '72: Actress (Ullmann), Director (Bergman), Film, Screenplay; Natl. Soc. Film Critics '72: Cinematog., Screenplay.

Cries in the Dark 𝒱 ½ **2006** When her nine-months-pregnant sister Elle (Sullivan) goes missing, cop Carrie Macklin (LaRue) first suspects her brother-in-law Scott (Harrington). When Elle is found murdered and the newborn has been taken, Carrie discovers Scott had a one-nighter with Rosa (Chiarelli), a psycho with her own agenda. **90m/C; DVD.** Eva LaRue; Adam Harrington; Gina Chiarelli; Camille Sullivan; Adrian Holmes; Anthony Harrison; Linda Darlow; ***D:*** Paul Schneider; ***W:*** Kraig Wenman; ***C:*** Pascal Jean Provost; ***M:*** Brent Belke. **CABLE**

A Crime 𝒱𝒱 **2006 (R)** Vincent's wife is murdered in their home and the killer is never found, though Vincent suspected a flashy cab driver he saw in the area. Three years later, Vincent hasn't realized that his beautiful NY apartment neighbor Alice wants him and she decides if someone takes the fall for the murder, Vincent will move on but her plans go awry. **98m/C; DVD.** *FR* Harvey Keitel; Emmanuelle Beart; Norman Reedus; Joe Grifasi; Lily Rabe; Kim Director; Brian Tarantina; Patrick Collins; ***D:*** Manuel Pradal; ***W:*** Manuel Pradal; Tonino Benacquista; ***C:*** Yorgos Arvanitis; ***M:*** Ennio Morricone.

Crime & Passion 𝒱 ½ **1975 (R)** Two scheming lovers plan to get rich by having the woman marry a multimillionaire and sue for a quick divorce. The multimillionaire is no patsy, however, and seeks a deadly revenge. Three scripts by six writers were combined to create this story. That explains the many problems. **92m/C; VHS, DVD.** Omar Sharif; Karen Black; Joseph Bottoms; Bernhard Wicki; ***D:*** Ivan Passer.

Crime and Punishment 𝒱𝒱 **1970** Ponderous, excruciatingly long adaptation of the Dostoyevski classic involving a haunted murderer and the relentless policeman who seeks to prove him guilty. In Russian with English subtitles. **200m/B; VHS, DVD.** *RU* Georgi Taratorkin; Victoria Fyodorova; ***D:*** Lev Kulijanov; ***W:*** Lev Kulijanov.

Crime and Punishment in Suburbia 𝒱 ½ **2000 (R)** Dostoyevsky heads to the mall in this suburban gloomfest very loosely based on the classic Russian novel. Roseanne (Keena) is a pretty, popular teen whose family life is screwed up beyond repair. Her father Fred (Ironside) is an abusive monster and her mother Maggie (Barkin) is a drunken floozy. She hopes that she can endure the situation until she graduates, but Fred's reaction to an affair by Maggie causes her to contemplate killing her father. With the help of her boyfriend Jimmy (DeBello), Roseanne murders her old man. When her mother is arrested for the crime and she becomes an outcast at school, she turns to mysterious classmate Vincent (Kartheiser) for solace, not knowing he's been lurking in the shadows and observing everything. The themes explored in this grim view of suburbia were better served up in "American Beauty." **98m/C; VHS, DVD.** Monica Keena; Vincent Kartheiser; Ellen Barkin; Michael Ironside; Jeffrey Wright; James DeBello; Conchata Ferrell; Marshall Teague; Brad Greenquist; Lucinda Jenney; ***D:*** Rob Schmidt; ***W:*** Larry Gross; ***C:*** Bobby Bukowski; ***M:*** Michael Brook.

Crime and Punishment, USA 1/2 **1959** Modern update of the Dostoyevsky novel set in a seedy Southern California milieu. Law student Robert Cole (Hamilton) murders a pawnbroker and comes under the suspicious gaze of Lt. Porter (Silvera). **96m/B; DVD.** George Hamilton; Frank Silvera; Mary Murphy; Marian Seldes; John Harding; ***D:*** Denis Sanders; ***W:*** Walter Newman; ***C:*** Floyd Crosby; ***M:*** Herschel Burke Gilbert.

Crime Boss *New Mafia Boss; The Mafia Terminator; I familiari delle vittime non sarrano avvertiti* **1972** Antonio Mancuso (Sabato) is a small time country Mafioso called to the city to do a favor for crime lord Don Vincenzo (Savalas). He befriends the Don but when Vincenzo starts having heart problems and begins to show signs of weakness he decides it may be time to assume the Don's position. Low budget rip-off of "The Godfather" filmed the same year. **90m/C; DVD.** *IT* Telly Savalas; Antonio (Tony) Sabato; Paola Tedesco; Guido Lollobrigida; Nino Dal Fabbro; Teodoro Corra; Sergio Rossi; Sergio Tramonti; Carlo Gaddi; Giuliano Persico; ***D:*** Alberto De Martino; ***W:*** Alberto De Martino; Lucio Battistrada; ***C:*** Joe D'Amato; ***M:*** Francesco De Masi.

Crime Broker **1994** A respected judge (Bisset) decides to experience life on the other side of the bench for a change. So she hooks up with a handsome partner to execute a series of high-profile robberies of bank vaults and museums. Implied sex so don't look for this under erotic thrillers. **93m/C; VHS, DVD.** Jacqueline Bisset; Masaya Kato; Gary Day; ***D:*** Ian Barry; ***W:*** Tony Morphett; ***C:*** Dan Burstall; ***M:*** Roger Mason.

Crime Busters 1/2 **1978 (PG)** Two guys attempt to pull off a bank heist but accidentally join the Miami police force instead. Hill and Spencer are enjoyable as usual but the film suffers from poor dubbing. Remake of "Two Supercops." **114m/C; VHS, DVD.** *IT* Terence Hill; Bud Spencer; Laura Gemser; Luciano Catenacci; David Huddleston; ***D:*** E.B. (Enzo Barboni) Clucher.

Crime in the Streets **1956** Typical low-budget '50s juvie drama. Well-meaning social worker Ben Wagner (Whitmore) tries to help the local juvenile delinquents overcome their slum lives. He's got trouble with violent Hornets gang leader Frankie Dane (Cassavetes) who vows to murder a neighbor who ratted to the cops. However, most of the Hornets want no part of Frankie's plan so he only has psycho Lou (Rydell) and wannabe gang member Baby (Mineo) willing to help him out. **91m/B; DVD.** James Whitmore; John Cassavetes; Sal Mineo; Mark Rydell; Peter Votrian; Virginia Gregg; Will Kuluva; Malcolm Atterbury; Denise Alexander; ***D:*** Donald Siegel; ***W:*** Reginald Rose; ***C:*** Sam Leavitt; ***M:*** Franz Waxman.

The Crime of Father Amaro *El Crimen del Padre Amaro* **2002 (R)** Eca de Queiroz's 1875 Portuguese novel is transplanted to modern-day Mexico, confronting a number of controversies surrounding the Catholic Church, including abortion, celibacy, and corruption. Young cleric Padre Amaro (Bernal) is the protege of Bishop Ernesto (Gomez Cruz) who sends him to the provinces to learn church politics from the seasoned Padre Benito (Gracia). Benito has had a longtime affair with Sanjuanera (Aragon) whose beautiful young daughter Amelia (Talancon) becomes infatuated with the handsome young priest. Amaro is soon learning to justify his less than priestly behavior with Amelia, which leads him down increasingly precarious moral paths. Spanish with subtitles. **120m/C; VHS, DVD.** *MX* Gael Garcia Bernal; Sancho Gracia; Ana Claudia Talancon; Damian Alcazar; Angelica Aragon; Pedro Armendariz, Jr.; Luisa Huertas; Ernesto Gomez Cruz; ***D:*** Carlos Carrera; ***W:*** Vicente Lenero; ***C:*** Guillermo Granillo; ***M:*** Rosino Serrano.

The Crime of Monsieur Lange *Le Crime de Monsieur Lange* **1936** Charming French socialist fantasy where workers at a publishing company turn the business into a thriving cooperative while their evil boss is gone. When he returns, worker Lefevre plots to kill him. Rather talky, but humorous. In French with subtitles. French script booklet also available. **90m/B; VHS, DVD.** *FR* Rene Lefevre; Jules Berry; Florelle; Sylvia Bataille; Jean Daste; Nadia Sibirskaia; Henri Guisol; ***D:*** Jean Renoir; ***W:*** Jean Renoir; Jacques Prevert; ***C:*** Jean Bachelet; ***M:*** Jean Wiener; Joseph Kosma.

Crime of Passion 1/2 **1957** Stanwyck plays a femme fatale whose ambitions for detective hubby lead to murder. Good performances from Stanwyck, Hayden, and Burr make this an above-average, although outlandish, crime-drama. **85m/B; VHS, DVD, Blu-Ray.** Barbara Stanwyck; Sterling Hayden; Raymond Burr; Fay Wray; Royal Dano; Virginia Grey; Dennis Cross; Robert E. (Bob) Griffin; Jay Adler; Malcolm Atterbury; S. John Launer; Brad Trumbull; Skipper McNally; Jean Howell; Peg La Centra; Nancy Reynolds; Marjorie Owens; Robert Quarry; Joe Conley; Stuart Whitman; ***D:*** Gerd Oswald; ***W:*** Jo Eisinger; ***C:*** Joseph LaShelle; ***M:*** Paul Dunlap.

Crime School 1/2 **1938** Underwhelming Dead End Kids entry with the juvies ending up in reformatory hell thanks to a corrupt and brutal warden. When deputy corrections commissioner Braden (Bogart) makes a surprise inspection things turn around and the Kids return the favor when Braden lands in political hot water. **90m/B; DVD.** Billy Halop; Bobby Jordan; Huntz Hall; Leo Gorcey; Bernard Punsley; Gabriel Dell; Humphrey Bogart; Gale Page; Charles Trowbridge; Crane Wilbur; ***D:*** Lewis Seiler; Vincent Sherman; Crane Wilbur; Terry Morse; ***W:*** Crane Wilbur; ***C:*** Arthur L. Todd; ***M:*** Max Steiner.

Crime Spree 1/2 *Wanted* **2003 (R)** After bungling a Paris heist, Daniel (Depardieu), Julien (Freiss), and Raymond (Dray) are sent by their boss, Laurent (Bohringer), to Chicago for a diamond heist. Joined by Marcel (Hallyday), Zero (Renaud), and Sami (Taghmaoui), the group manages to rob the wrong house—that of Chicago hood Frankie Zammeti (Keitel). Frankie has been staked out by the FBI, who want an audio cassette the French hoods have also taken, which incriminates his boss Giancarlo (Vigoda). Equal opportunity stereotypes abound with the bad guys—French, Italian, Latino, and blacks—but this aging buddy cast is so self-confident that they can carry this caper a long way. English and some French with subtitles. **99m/C; VHS, DVD.** *CA GB* Gerard Depardieu; Johnny Hallyday; Renaud; Harvey Keitel; Richard Bohringer; Said Taghmaoui; Stephane Freiss; Albert Dray; Abe Vigoda; ***D:*** Brad Mirman; ***W:*** Brad Mirman; ***C:*** Derek Rogers; ***M:*** Rupert Gregson-Williams.

Crime Story *Hard to Die* **1993 (R)** Police Inspector Eddie Chan (Chan) tries to crack a kidnapping case and discovers his partner, Detective Hung (Cheng), is not on the up-and-up. Usual arobatic stunts from Chan and company. Cantonese with subtitles. **104m/C; VHS, DVD, Blu-Ray.** *CH* Jackie Chan; Kent Cheng; Law Hang Kang; Christine Ng; ***D:*** Kirk Wong; ***C:*** Arthur Wong Ngok Tai; Ardy Lam.

Crime Wave **1954** Cons break out of San Q and then botch a gas-station robbery. They head for the home of ex-cellmate Steve Lacey (Nelson), who's married Ellen (Kirk), gone straight, and doesn't want the trouble landing at his door. Steve's willing to cooperate with hard-boiled detective Sims (Hayden) but Penny (de Corsia) and Hastings (Bronson) take Ellen hostage and threaten Steve unless he helps them in a bank job. Nelson was better known as a song-and-dance man, but he's good in this noir role, and the toothpick-chewing Hayden can snarl with the best of them. **73m/B; DVD.** Sterling Hayden; Gene Nelson; Phyllis Kirk; Ted de Corsia; Charles Bronson; Jay Novello; Nedrick Young; Timothy Carey; ***D:*** Andre de Toth; ***W:*** Bernard Gordon; Crane Wilbur; Richard Wormser; ***C:*** Bert Glennon; ***M:*** David Buttolph.

Crimebroker **1993 (R)** Australian judge Holly McPhee (Bisset) has a sideline—she devises criminal blueprints and then anonymously hires the rabbles that come before the bench to carry out the crime. But things get complicated when Japanese criminologist Jin Okazaki (Kato) figures out what's going on. **93m/C; DVD.** *AU JP* Jacqueline Bisset; Masaya Kato; John Bach; Ralph Cotterill; ***D:*** Ian Barry; ***W:*** Tony Morphett; ***C:*** Dan Burstall; ***M:*** Roger Mason.

Crimebusters 1/2 **1979 (PG)** A man exacts revenge against a government conspiracy that kidnapped his loved ones. **90m/C; VHS, DVD.** Henry Silva; Antonio (Tony) Sabato; ***D:*** Michael Tarantini.

Crimes & Misdemeanors **1989 (PG-13)** One of Allen's most mature films, exploring a whole range of moral ambiguities through the parallel and eventually interlocking stories of a nebbish filmmaker—who agrees to make a profile of a smug Hollywood TV comic and then sabotages it—and an esteemed ophthalmologist who is being threatened with exposure by his neurotic mistress. Intriguing mix of drama and comedy few directors could pull off. Look for Daryl Hannah in an unbilled cameo. **104m/C; VHS, DVD, Blu-Ray.** Martin Landau; Woody Allen; Alan Alda; Mia Farrow; Joanna Gleason; Anjelica Huston; Jerry Orbach; Sam Waterston; Claire Bloom; Jenny Nichols; Caroline Aaron; Daryl Hannah; Nora Ephron; Jerry Zaks; ***D:*** Woody Allen; ***W:*** Woody Allen; ***C:*** Sven Nykvist. Natl. Bd. of Review '89: Support. Actor (Alda); N.Y. Film Critics '89: Support. Actor (Alda); Writers Guild '89: Orig. Screenplay.

Crimes at the Dark House **1939** In this campy, melodramatic adaptation of Wilkie Collins's novel "The Woman in White," a man kills his rich wife and puts a disguised mental patient in her place. Later remade using the book's title. **69m/B; VHS, DVD, Blu-Ray.** *GB* Tod Slaughter; Hilary Eaves; Sylvia Marriott; Hay Petrie; Geoffrey Wardwell; Elsie Wagstaff; David Keir; David Horne; Rita Grant; Margaret Yarde; ***D:*** George King; ***W:*** Frederick Hayward; Edward Dryhurst; H.F. Maltby; ***C:*** Hone Glendinning.

Crimes of Dr. Mabuse 1/2 *The Testament of Dr. Mabuse; The Last Will of Dr. Mabuse* **1932** Supernatural horror classic about the evil Dr. Mabuse controlling an underworld empire while confined to an insane asylum. The third, and only sound, Mabuse film by Lang. German with subtitles. **120m/B; VHS, DVD.** *GE* Rudolf Klein-Rogge; Otto Wernicke; Gustav Diesl; Karl Meixner; ***D:*** Fritz Lang.

Crimes of Fashion 1/2 **2004** ABC Family comedy finds hard-working Brooke (Cuoco), who grew up in foster homes, about to realize her dream of becoming a fashion designer. Until the grandfather she never knew dies and leaves her his business—a trying-to-go legit crime syndicate. George (Chianese), who was Gramps' second-in-command, insists that Brooke become 'Godmother' even though the FBI has an ongoing investigation and an agent who's closer than Brooke knows. **90m/C; DVD.** Kaley Cuoco; Dominic Chianese; Pat Kelly; Megan Fox; Chuck Shamata; Louis Di Bianco; Raymond Miller; Serena Lee; ***D:*** Stuart Gillard; ***W:*** David Mickel; ***C:*** Manfred Guthe; ***M:*** Michael Wandmacher. **CABLE**

Crimes of Passion **1984** Vintage whacked-out Russell, not intended for the kiddies. A business-like fashion designer becomes a kinky prostitute at night. A disturbed street preacher makes her the heroine of his erotic fantasies. A dark terrifying vision of the underground sex world and moral hypocrisy. Sexually explicit and violent, with an extremely black comedic center. Turner's portrayal is honest and believable, Perkins overacts until he nearly gets a nosebleed, but it's all for good effect. Cut for "R" rating to get it in the theatres; this version restores some excised footage. Also available in rated version. **101m/C; VHS, DVD, Blu-Ray.** Kathleen Turner; Anthony Perkins; Annie Potts; John Laughlin; Bruce Davison; Norman Burton; Ian Petrella; Gerald S. O'Loughlin; ***D:*** Ken Russell; ***W:*** Barry Sandler; ***C:*** Dick Bush; ***M:*** Rick Wakeman. L.A. Film Critics '84: Actress (Turner).

The Crimes of Stephen Hawke *Strangler's Morgue* **1936** The world knows Stephen Hawke as a bighearted money lender. What they don't know is his favorite hobby is breaking peoples' spines. An entertaining thriller set in the 1800s. **65m/B; VHS, DVD.** *GB* Tod Slaughter; Marjorie Taylor; D.J. Williams; Eric Portman; Ben Soutten; ***D:*** George King.

Crimes of the Heart 1/2 **1986 (PG-13)** Based on Beth Henley's acclaimed play. A few days in the lives of three very strange Southern sisters, one of whom has just been arrested for calmly shooting her husband after he chased her black lover out of town. Spacek as the suicidal sister is a lark. A tart, black comedy that works better as a play than a film. **105m/C; VHS, DVD.** Sissy Spacek; Diane Keaton; Jessica Lange; Sam Shepard; Tess Harper; Hurd Hatfield; ***D:*** Bruce Beresford; ***W:*** Beth Henley; ***C:*** Dante Spinotti; ***M:*** Georges Delerue. Golden Globes '87: Actress--Mus./Comedy (Spacek); N.Y. Film Critics '86: Actress (Spacek).

Crimes of the Past 1/2 **2009 (R)** Predictable pic about father/daughter issues that tosses in some post-spy problems as well. In the 1980s, CIA op Thomas Sparrow (Rasche) has a money-drop go wrong (the money disappears and he's badly injured). He then has an altercation with his unfaithful wife and drops out of young daughter Josephine's life. After his retirement, 25 years later, Thomas tries to make amends and finds Josephine (Rohm) is a troubled single mom with a drinking problem. And his CIA past has Russian mobsters after Thomas too. **86m/C; DVD.** David Rasche; Elisabeth Rohm; Eric Roberts; Chad Lindberg; John Aylward; Cynthia Geary; Grant Goodeve; ***D:*** Garrett Bennett; ***W:*** Steve Edmiston; ***C:*** Julio Ribeyro; ***M:*** Kyle Porter. **VIDEO**

Crimetime 1/2 **1996 (R)** Silly thriller has actor Bobby (Baldwin) finding unexpected success portraying a serial killer in a crime re-enactment TV show called "Crimetime." Meanwhile, Sydney (Postlethwaite), who's the real killer Bobby's character is based on, becomes seduced by the media frenzy surrounding the crimes and seeing them re-enacted on television. He goes on killing, so the show can literally go on. **118m/C; VHS, DVD.** Stephen Baldwin; Pete Postlethwaite; Sadie Frost; Geraldine Chaplin; Karen Black; James Faulkner; ***Cameo(s):*** Marianne Faithfull; ***D:*** George Sluizer; ***W:*** Brendan Somers; ***C:*** Jules Van Den Steenhoven.

The Criminal **2000 (R)** Unemployed musician Jasper (Mackintosh) thinks he's gotten lucky when he meets sultry Sarah (Little) at the pub and she agrees to go home with him. But before anything intimate happens, Sarah's killed by intruders in Jasper's flat. A grumpy detective (Hill) and his smart woman partner (Aird) are certain of Jasper's guilt while Jasper tries to elude both the cops and Sarah's killers. **96m/C; VHS, DVD.** *GB* Steven Mackintosh; Natasha Little; Bernard Hill; Holly Aird; Eddie Izzard; Yvan Attal; Andrew Tiernan; ***D:*** Julian Simpson; ***W:*** Julian Simpson; ***C:*** Nic Morris; ***M:*** Tolga Kashif; Mark Sayer-Wade.

Criminal 1/2 **2004 (R)** Experienced con man takes a novice under his wing to help bilk a rich collector. But like most con/heist flicks, everything is not what it seems. Complex and enjoyable remake of Argentine filmmaker Fabian Bielinski's "Nine Queens." Reilly and Luna give great performances, as do Gyllenhaal and Mullan. Fun in the vein of "Matchstick Men", full of twists and turns with a terrific payoff. **87m/C; DVD.** John C. Reilly; Diego Luna; Maggie Gyllenhaal; Jonathan Tucker; Peter Mullan; ***D:*** Gregory Jacobs; ***W:*** Gregory Jacobs; Steven Soderbergh; ***C:*** Chris Menges; ***M:*** Alex Wurman.

Criminal **2016 (R)** Bill Pope (Reynolds) is a CIA agent who is killed while trying to track down a hacker named "The Dutchman." Because it's a movie, his memories get transplanted into a dangerous convict with the awesome name of Jericho Stewart (Costner). Will the convict chase the hacker? How much did Gary Oldman and Tommy Lee Jones get paid to star in this? Costner continues his failed quest to find a little of that action movie money that Liam Neeson found later in life with another gritty performance in a garbage movie. **113m/C; DVD, Blu-Ray.** Kevin Costner; Gary Oldman; Tommy Lee Jones; Ryan Reynolds; Jordi Molla; ***D:*** Ariel Vromen; ***W:*** Douglas Cook; David Weisberg; ***C:*** Dana Gonzales; ***M:*** Keith Power; Brian Tyler.

Criminal Act 1/2 *Tunnels* **1988** A newspaper editor hits the street to prove she's still a tough reporter, but uncovers a dangerous scandal in the process. **94m/C; VHS, DVD.** Catherine Bach; Charlene Dallas; Nicholas Guest; John Saxon; Vic Tayback; ***D:*** Mark Byers.

Criminal Activities 𝅘𝅥 𝅘𝅥 1/2 **2015** Fast-paced, mostly fun crime drama/thriller about a deal gone bad. When a former classmate dies, four young men are reunited at the funeral. One of these men claims to have insider knowledge on a stock that will make them all instantly rich. All four sign up, but soon face difficulties as the deal goes bad and their money disappears. The situation grows from bad to worse when it is revealed that one of them borrowed his funds from a ruthless mobster. To pay back the debt, the mobster demands they commit a kidnapping or pay with their lives. **94m/C; DVD, Blu-Ray, Streaming, Download.** Michael Pitt; Dan Stevens; Christopher Abbott; Rob Brown; Edi Gathegi; ***D:*** Jackie Earle Haley; ***W:*** Robert Lowell; ***C:*** Seamus Tierney; ***M:*** Keefus Ciancia.

The Criminal Code 𝅘𝅥 𝅘𝅥 1/2 **1931** Aging melodrama about a young man who's jailed for killing in self-defense. His life worsens at the hands of a prison warden when the head guy's daughter falls for him. Remade as "Penitentiary" and "Convicted." **98m/B; DVD.** Walter Huston; Phillips Holmes; Boris Karloff; Constance Cummings; Mary Doran; DeWitt Jennings; John Sheehan; ***D:*** Howard Hawks; ***W:*** Fred Niblo, Jr.; Seton I. Miller; ***C:*** James Wong Howe; Ted Tetzlaff.

Criminal Desire 𝅘𝅥 1/2 *Lovers and Liars* **1998** Street savvy P.I. Darrel Chisum (Faustino of 'Married with Children' fame—seriously) is hired to find the daughter of a fashion industry billionaire. Working his way into a position to mingle with the ad executives of the modeling agency she worked at, he soon discovers everyone there is guilty of something (the missing daughter included) and they're all stabbing each other in the back. Typical P.I. 'everyone is evil' genre movie. **96m/C; DVD.** Michael York; David Faustino; Chris Conrad; Robin Joi Brown; Jamie Anderson; David Carradine; Micheal Bays; Kerri Marrone; Amy Alexander; Alice Arden; Jack Fugett; Ron Robbins; Dale Clemmons; Matt Felmlee; David Fuggett; Christian Demijohn; Joe Lacoco; Rusty Meyers; ***D:*** Mark Freed; ***W:*** Mark Freed; Dave Tedder; ***C:*** Ken Stipe.

Criminal Intent 𝅘𝅥 **2005** Well there's a lot that doesn't make sense so be prepared to scoff. After a bitter divorce, Devon Major (Spence) becomes the prime suspect when he's found hovering over his ex-wife Angela's dead body. Devon calls Angela's divorce attorney Susan Grace (Angel) to defend him and when she talks to D.A. Kirsten Sorensen (Purl), Susan learns that Treasury agent Mark Fairfield (Palffy) is investigating Devon's business for money laundering. **90m/C; DVD.** Sebastian Spence; Vanessa Angel; Linda Purl; David Palffy; Ingrid Torrance; Tom Pickett; Sarah Deakins; ***D:*** George Erschbamer; ***W:*** George Erschbamer; Peter Layton; ***C:*** C. Kim Miles; ***M:*** John Sereda. **CABLE**

Criminal Justice 𝅘𝅥 𝅘𝅥 **2008** British miniseries. Young Ben Coulter is in prison, awaiting trial for a murder he very likely didn't commit (heavy drinking, sex with a stranger, and waking up next to a dead body is suspicious though). He's assigned a slovenly lawyer who seems rather cavalier about Ben's predicament, although the detective in charge of the investigation questions Ben's guilt as well. But being accused of a crime may be the least of Ben's troubles. **285m/C; DVD.** *GB* ***D:*** Luke Watson; ***W:*** Peter Moffatt; ***C:*** Eric Maddison; ***M:*** John Lunn. **TV**

Criminal Law 𝅘𝅥 𝅘𝅥 **1989 (R)** An ambitious young Boston lawyer gets a man acquitted for murder, only to find out after the trial that the man is guilty and renewing his killing spree. Realizing he's the only one privy to the killer's trust, the lawyer decides to stop him himself. A white-knuckled thriller burdened by a weak script. **113m/C; VHS, DVD, Blu-Ray; Open Captioned.** Kevin Bacon; Gary Oldman; Karen Young; Joe Don Baker; Tess Harper; ***D:*** Martin Campbell; ***W:*** Mark Kassen; ***C:*** Phil Meheux; ***M:*** Jerry Goldsmith.

Criminal Lawyer 𝅘𝅥 1/2 **1951** Successful attorney James Regan (O'Brien) isn't above using unethical means to win cases. His tactics hold him back from the judgeship he covets, so Regan turns to the bottle until his loyal bodyguard Moose (Mazurki) is accused of murder and Regan must step up to defend him. **72m/B; DVD.** Pat O'Brien; Mike Mazurki; Jane Wyatt; Carl Benton Reid; Jerome Cowan; Mary Castle; Robert Shayne; ***D:*** Seymour Friedman; ***W:*** Harold Greene; ***C:*** Philip Tannura.

The Criminal Life of Archibaldo de la Cruz 𝅘𝅥 𝅘𝅥 𝅘𝅥 *Ensayo de un Crimen; Rehearsal for a Crime* **1955** Seeing the death of his governess has a lasting effect on a boy. He grows up to be a demented cretin whose failure with women leads him to conspire to kill every one he meets, a task at which he also fails. Hilarious, bitter Bunuelian diatribe. In Spanish with English subtitles. **95m/B; VHS, DVD.** *MX SP* Ernesto Alonso; Ariadne Welter; Rita Macedo; Rodolfo Landa; Andrea Palma; Miroslava Stern; ***D:*** Luis Bunuel; ***W:*** Luis Bunuel; ***C:*** Augustin Jimenez; ***M:*** Jorge Perez.

Criminal Lovers 𝅘𝅥 𝅘𝅥 *Les Amants Criminels* **1999** Aggressive 17-year-old Alice (Regnier) persuades her ambivalent boyfriend Luc (Renier) to kill their classmate Said, after telling Luc that Said got his friends to rape her. They drive the body into the woods to bury it but then become lost and seek refuge in a ramshackle cottage that happens to belong to a hermit (Manojlovic) who witnessed the burial. He tosses them in his cellar but soon releases Luc to satisfy his own pleasures (and those of the sexually confused boy). Eventually the duo escape, only to find the police on their trail. French with subtitles. **96m/C; VHS, DVD.** *FR* Natacha Regnier; Jeremie Renier; Miki (Predrag) Manojlovic; Salim Kechiouche; ***D:*** Francois Ozon; ***W:*** Francois Ozon; ***C:*** Pierre Stoeber; ***M:*** Philippe Rombi.

Criminal Ways 𝅘𝅥 1/2 *The Wannabes* **2003 (R)** Danny dreams of a showbiz career while teaching dance classes. He's hired by thug Marcus and his crew to show them how to entertain at a kiddie birthday party, not realizing the crooks plan to rob the place. Through a series of silly circumstances, Danny joins in, the job gets bungled, but the 'entertainers' are a hit as a children's musical group and find themselves on the road to stardom. Broadly-done Australian farce. **92m/C; DVD.** *AU* Isla Fisher; Tony Nikolakopoulos; Ryan Thomas Johnson; Nick Giannopoulos; Russell Dykstra; Costas Kilias; Michael Carmen; Lena Cruz; ***W:*** Chris Anastassiades; Ray Boseley; ***C:*** Dan Burstall; ***M:*** David Hirschfelder.

Criminals Within 𝅘𝅥 *Army Mystery* **1941** A scientist working on a top secret formula is murdered and a detective tries to nail the spy ring responsible. Very confusing, poor usage of some fine female cast members. **67m/B; VHS, DVD.** Eric Linden; Ann Doran; Constance Worth; Donald Curtis; Weldon Heyburn; Ben Alexander; ***D:*** Joseph H. Lewis.

The Crimson Code 𝅘𝅥 1/2 **1999 (R)** FBI agents Chandler (Muldoon) and Dobson (Moriarty) discover a serial killer who goes after other serial killers. Then Chandler is offered a chance to circumvent that pesky legal thing by joining a covert ops that takes retribution as it sees fit. Just one cliche after another. **90m/C; VHS, DVD.** Patrick Muldoon; Cathy Moriarty; C. Thomas Howell; Fred Ward; Tim Thomerson; ***D:*** Jeremy Haft; ***W:*** Alex Metcalf; ***C:*** Ian Elkin; ***M:*** Ken Williams. **VIDEO**

The Crimson Cult 𝅘𝅥 *The Crimson Altar; Curse of the Crimson Altar* **1968 (PG)** Eden and his girlfriend are invited to a mysterious mansion. They discover that Lee is out to enact revenge as his ancestor was burned for witchcraft by Eden's. An all-star horror disaster. Karloff was 80 and confined to a wheelchair. Despite ads claiming this as his last film, he made four more in Mexico. Highlights include the scantily clad Steele in sado-masochistic sequences and a psychedelic party with strippers and body painters. **87m/C; VHS, Blu-Ray, Streaming.** *GB* Boris Karloff; Christopher Lee; Mark Eden; Barbara Steele; Virginia Wetherell; Michael Gough; Rupert Davies; ***D:*** Vernon Sewell.

Crimson Force 𝅘𝅥 **2005** How many ways can you deride yet another lame, low-budget Sci-Fi Channel original? The crew of the first manned mission to Mars has traveled to the big red planet in order to locate a new source of energy to use at home. What they discover is a Martian civilization in the midst of a civil war and the winners intend to invade Earth next. **90m/C; DVD.** C. Thomas Howell; David Chokachi; Tony Amendola; Julia Rose; Terasa Livingstone; Jeff Gimble; Richard Gnolfo; ***D:*** David Flores; ***W:*** Rob Mecarini; ***C:*** Lorenzo Senatore; ***M:*** Chris Walden; Matthias Weber. **CABLE**

Crimson Gold 𝅘𝅥 𝅘𝅥 1/2 *Talaye Sorgh* **2003** Hussein (Emadeddin) is a simple, war-veteran-turned-pizza-deliveryman, but the opening sequence shows him in the midst of a botched jewelry-store robbery that ends abruptly and grimly—resulting in tragedy. What follows are flashbacks (compelling yet often slow-paced) that attempt to define his behavior and the social rejection that led him down his destructive path. Set in Tehran and based on a true story, this has—like other Panahi films—been banned in Iran. Farsi with subtitles. **95m/C; DVD.** *IA* Hossain Emadeddin; Kamyar Sheisi; Azita Rayeji; Shahram Vaziri; Ehsan Amani; Pourang Nakhael; Kaveh Najmabadi; Saber Safael; ***D:*** Jafar Panahi; ***W:*** Abbas Kiarostami; ***C:*** Hossain Djafarian; ***M:*** Peyman Yazdanian.

The Crimson Kimono 𝅘𝅥 𝅘𝅥 **1959** Fuller's look at interracial romance and jealousy is tied up in a not-too-interesting murder investigation. Friends since the Korean War, Bancroft (Corbett) and Kojaku (Shigeta) work homicide in L.A. They're assigned a stripper's murder, which is how they meet artist Christine (Shaw) and both fall for her. She prefers gentlemanly Kojaku and Bancroft gets jealous although they set aside their differences for the sake of the case, which takes them into Little Tokyo. **81m/B; DVD, Blu-Ray.** Glenn Corbett; James Shigeta; Victoria Shaw; Anna Lee; Paul Dubov; Neyle Morrow; Jaclynne Greene; Gloria Pall; ***D:*** Samuel Fuller; ***W:*** Samuel Fuller; ***C:*** Sam Leavitt; ***M:*** Harry Sukman.

Crimson Peak 𝅘𝅥 𝅘𝅥 𝅘𝅥 **2015 (R)** Guillermo Del Toro brings another one of his nightmares to cinematic life in this luscious Gothic Horror story, a film that captures its creator's brilliant craftsmanship and limitless creativity. Edith Cushing (Wasikowska) has always believed in ghosts. After a mysterious, handsome man named Thomas (Hiddleston) enters her life, she ditches the reliable boyfriend (Hunnam) and jets off with him to his titular estate. His sister (Chastain) is less than welcome and Crimson Peak houses a few secrets of its own. It may be narratively thin, but Guillermo Del Toro's technical accomplishment is remarkable. It's a gorgeous, vibrant, old-fashioned ghost story. **119m/C; DVD, Blu-Ray, Streaming.** Jessica Chastain; Charlie Hunnam; Mia Wasikowska; Tom Hiddleston; Burn Gorman; ***D:*** Guillermo del Toro; ***W:*** Guillermo del Toro; Matthew Robbins; ***C:*** Dan Laustsen; ***M:*** Fernando Velazquez.

The Crimson Petal and the White 𝅘𝅥 𝅘𝅥 **2012** Graphically sexual Brit miniseries based on Michel Faber's 2002 novel set in Victorian-era London. Expensive whore Sugar (Garai) works in Mrs. Castaway's (Anderson) brothel and is contemptuous of her clients. She attracts the attention of privileged William Rackham (O'Dowd) whose wife Agnes (Hale) is mentally ill. Rackham buys Sugar away, first setting her up in a flat as his mistress before moving her into his own home as governess to his lonely daughter Sophie (Watt). The fates of William, the women, and even Sophie are intertwined to an unfortunate degree. **245m/C; DVD.** *UK* Romola Garai; Chris O'Dowd; Amanda Hale; Richard E. Grant; Isla Watt; Mark Gatiss; Shirley Henderson; Gillian Anderson; ***D:*** Marc Munden; ***W:*** Lucinda Coxon; ***C:*** Lol Crawley; ***M:*** Cristobal Tapia de Veer. **TV**

Crimson Pirate 𝅘𝅥 𝅘𝅥 𝅘𝅥 1/2 **1952** An 18th-century buccaneer pits his wits and brawn against the might of a ruthless Spanish nobleman. Considered by many to be one of the best swashbucklers, laced with humor and enthusiastically paced. Showcase for Lancaster and Cravat's acrobatic talents. **104m/C; VHS, DVD.** *GB* Burt Lancaster; Eva Bartok; Torin Thatcher; Christopher Lee; Nick Cravat; Charles Farrell; ***D:*** Robert Siodmak.

The Crimson Rivers 𝅘𝅥 𝅘𝅥 *Les Rivieres Pourpres* **2001 (R)** Audacious and gruesome thriller set in the French Alps. A librarian from the local private university is found horribly mutilated on a mountain slope and Parisian investigator Pierre Niemans (Reno) is called in. Before long, there's more than one victim, all of whom have ties to the university, and Niemans has a young, aggressive partner in provincial policeman Max Kerkerian (Cassel). French with subtitles or dubbed. **105m/C; VHS, DVD.** *FR* Jean Reno; Vincent Cassel; Nadia Fares; Dominique Sanda; Laurent Avare; Jean-Pierre Cassel; Didier Flamand; ***D:*** Mathieu Kassovitz; ***W:*** Mathieu Kassovitz; Jean-Christophe Grange; ***C:*** Thierry Arbogast; ***M:*** Bruno Coulais.

Crimson Rivers 2: Angels of the Apocalypse 𝅘𝅥 1/2 *Les Rivieres Pourpres II: Les Anges de L'apocalypse* **2005** A series of religious-related murders puts Parisian detective Pierre Niemans (Reno) on the case. He's paired with police captain Reda (Magimel)--who has stumbled upon a man resembling Jesus Christ—to solve the mystery and contend with a dark, deadly organization bent on razing Europe. Fans of the original should be pleased, though the story needs an oar and compass to find its way to shore. In French, with English subtitles or dubbed. **99m/C; VHS, DVD.** *FR GB IT* Jean Reno; Benoît Magimel; Christopher Lee; Johnny Hallyday; Camille Natta; Augustin Legrand; ***D:*** Olivier Dahan; ***W:*** Jean-Christophe Grange; Luc Besson; ***C:*** Alex Lamarque; ***M:*** Colin Towns. **VIDEO**

Crimson Romance 𝅘𝅥 𝅘𝅥 **1934** Two unemployed American pilots in Europe decide to join the German airforce for want of anything better to do. Conflicts revolve around a warmongering Commandant and his pilot. **70m/B; VHS, DVD.** Ben Lyon; Sari Maritza; James Bush; Erich von Stroheim; Jason Robards, Sr.; Herman Bing; Vince Barnett; ***D:*** David Howard.

Crimson Tide 𝅘𝅥 𝅘𝅥 𝅘𝅥 **1995 (R)** Mutiny erupts aboard the submarine USS Alabama as Captain Ramsey (Hackman) and his Executive Officer Hunter (Washington) clash over the validity of orders to launch the sub's missiles. Ramsey, who wants to fire the missiles, and Hunter, who refuses to comply until the message is verified, battle for control of the sub. Suspenseful and well-paced thriller lets Hackman and Washington show off their considerable screen presence, while Bruckheimer, Simpson, and Scott show that they haven't lost any of their trademark big-budget, testosterone-laden flash. Original screenplay went under the knife of a number of script doctors, most notably Quentin Tarantino. **116m/C; VHS, DVD, Blu-Ray, UMD.** Gene Hackman; Denzel Washington; George Dzundza; Viggo Mortensen; James Gandolfini; Matt Craven; Lillo Brancato; Danny Nucci; Steve Zahn; Rick Schroder; Vanessa Bell Calloway; Rocky Carroll; ***Cameo(s):*** Jason Robards, Jr.; ***D:*** Tony Scott; ***W:*** Michael Schiffer; Richard P. Henrick; ***C:*** Dariusz Wolski; ***M:*** Hans Zimmer.

The Crippled Masters 𝅘𝅥 𝅘𝅥 **1982 (R)** After Li Ho's (Shum) arms are cut off by an evil warlord, he wanders the countryside facing ridicule until he teams up with disfigured Dax Oh Jen (Conn). Helped by an elderly yoga master, the duo unite to seek revenge. Features kung-fu masters with real-life disabilities. **90m/C; VHS, DVD.** Frankie Shum; Jack Conn; ***D:*** Joe Law.

Crisis 𝅘𝅥 1/2 **1950** Heavy-handed and dull political melodrama. Brain surgeon Eugene Ferguson (Grant) and his wife Helen (Raymond) are vacationing in some South American country that's suddenly beset by a revolution. However, dictator Farrago (Ferrer) needs an operation and makes sure the Fergusons can't leave. Revolutionary leader Gonzalez (Roland) wants Ferguson to botch the operation and holds Helen as a hostage for leverage. **95m/B; DVD.** Cary Grant; Jose Ferrer; Paula Raymond; Gilbert Roland; Signe Hasso; Ramon Novarro; Leon Ames; ***D:*** Richard Brooks; ***W:*** Richard Brooks; ***C:*** Ray June; ***M:*** Miklos Rozsa.

Criss Cross 𝅘𝅥 𝅘𝅥 𝅘𝅥 **1948** A classic grade-B film noir, in which an armored car driver is suckered into a burglary by his ex-wife and her hoodlum husband. Multiple back-stabbings and double-crossings ensue. **98m/B; VHS, DVD, Blu-Ray.** Burt Lancaster; Yvonne De Carlo; Dan Duryea; Stephen McNally; Richard Long; Tony Curtis; Alan Napier; ***D:*** Robert Siodmak; ***W:*** Daniel Fuchs; ***C:*** Franz Planer; ***M:*** Miklos Rozsa.

Crisscross 🦴🦴 ½ *Alone Together* **1992 (R)** It's 1969 and Tracy Cross is a divorced mom whose ex-husband is a traumatized Vietnam vet who has left her alone to raise their 12 year-old son Chris during some hard times. She works two jobs, as a waitress and, unbeknownst to her son, as a stripper in a local club. When Chris sneaks into the club and sees her act he takes drastic measures to help out—by selling drugs. Film is sluggish and relies too much on voice-overs to explain thoughts but Hawn gives a convincing and restrained performance as the mother. **107m/C; VHS, DVD.** Goldie Hawn; David Arnott; Arliss Howard; James Gammon; Keith Carradine; J.C. Quinn; Steve Buscemi; Paul Calderon; ***D:*** Chris Menges; ***M:*** Trevor Jones.

Critical Care 🦴 ½ **1997 (R)** Spader is a doctor in a high-tech intensive care unit dealing with the ethics of modern health care, such as insurance scams, euthanasia, and a drunken administrator (Brooks) whose only concern is the hospital's profits. Two sisters (Sedgwick and Martindale) fight over the fate of their terminally ill, near-vegetable father. Spader finds his career on the line after bedding Sedgwick and backing her attempts to pull the plug. Given the meatiness of the subject, director Lumet could have made a much more scathing satire. Schwartz's script is lame even for a first-time effort, and the usually interesting Shawn falls horribly flat with an embarrassing bit of dialogue. Occasional laughs (this was supposed to be a dark comedy) and good performances from Brooks and Mirren can't keep this one from flatlining. Watch an episode of "ER" instead. **105m/C; VHS, DVD.** James Spader; Albert Brooks; Kyra Sedgwick; Dame Helen Mirren; Margo Martindale; Jeffrey Wright; Wallace Shawn; Anne Bancroft; Philip Bosco; Edward Herrmann; Colm Feore; James Lally; Al Waxman; Harvey Atkin; ***D:*** Sidney Lumet; ***W:*** Steven S. Schwartz; ***C:*** David Watkin; ***M:*** Michael Convertino.

Critical Condition 🦴 **1986 (R)** During a blackout, a criminal masquerades as a doctor in a city hospital. Limp comedy embarrassing for Pryor. **99m/C; VHS, DVD.** Richard Pryor; Rachel Ticotin; Ruben Blades; Joe Mantegna; Kate McGregor-Stewart; ***D:*** Michael Apted; ***C:*** Ralf Bode; ***M:*** Alan Silvestri.

Critical Mass 🦴🦴 **2000 (R)** This one will seem very familiar. Terrorist Samson (Kier) and his crew steal nuclear material and retreat to a deserted nuclear power plant in southern California in order to build a bomb. Only the power plant isn't so deserted and security guard Mike (Williams), aided by babe Janine (Loughlin), work to thwart Samson's nefarious plan. **95m/C; VHS, DVD.** Treat Williams; Udo Kier; Lori Loughlin; Blake Clark; Andrew Prine; ***D:*** Fred Olen Ray; ***C:*** Theo Angell; ***M:*** Neal Acree. **VIDEO**

Critic's Choice 🦴🦴 **1963** Tedious adaptation of Ira Levin's insider play that's likely to only be appreciated by Ball and/or Hope fans. Angela Ballantine (Ball) is an aspiring playwright whose first effort is about to open on Broadway. And it's going to be reviewed by her theater critic husband, Parker (Hope), who would rather be doing anything else. Like having a few drinks with his consoling ex-wife Ivy (Maxwell). Parker stumbles into the theater, drunk and the center of unwelcome attention, especially from the current Mrs. Ballantine, who's not pleased. Edith Head did the costumes. **100m/C; DVD.** Bob Hope; Lucille Ball; Marilyn Maxwell; Rip Torn; Jessie Royce Landis; John Dehner; Jim Backus; Rick Kelman; Marie Windsor; Joseph (Joe) Gallison; Richard Deacon; Jerome Cowan; Donald Losby; Soupy Sales; ***D:*** Don Weis; ***W:*** Jack Sher; ***C:*** Charles B(ryant) Lang, Jr.; ***M:*** George Duning.

Critters 🦴🦴 ½ **1986 (PG-13)** A gang of furry, razor-toothed aliens escapes from its prison ship to Earth with their bounty hunters right behind them. They make it to a small town in Kansas where they begin to attack anything that moves. Not just a thrill-kill epic, but a sarcastic other-worldly thrill-kill epic. **86m/C; VHS, DVD, Blu-Ray.** Dee Wallace; M. Emmet Walsh; Billy Green Bush; Scott Grimes; Nadine Van Der Velde; Terrence Mann; Billy Zane; Don Opper; ***D:*** Stephen Herek; ***W:*** Stephen Herek; Domonic Muir; ***C:*** Tim Suhrstedt; ***M:*** David Newman.

Critters 2: The Main Course 🦴🦴 **1988 (PG-13)** Sequel to the hit horror-comedy, wherein the voracious alien furballs return in full force to Grovers Bend, Kansas, from eggs planted two years before. Occasionally inspired "Gremlins" rip. **93m/C; VHS, DVD, Blu-Ray.** Scott Grimes; Liane (Alexandra) Curtis; Don Opper; Barry Corbin; Terrence Mann; ***D:*** Mick Garris; ***W:*** Mick Garris; David N. Twohy; ***C:*** Russell Carpenter.

Critters 3 🦴🦴 **1991 (PG-13)** The not-so-loveable critters are back, terrorizing the occupants of a tenement building. **86m/C; VHS, DVD, Blu-Ray.** Frances Bay; Aimee Brooks; Leonardo DiCaprio; Don Opper; ***D:*** Kristine Peterson; ***W:*** David J. Schow.

Critters 4 🦴🦴 **1991 (PG-13)** The ghoulish critters are back, and this time a strain of genetically engineered mutant critters (what's the difference?) wants to take over the universe. **94m/C; VHS, DVD, Blu-Ray.** Don Opper; Paul Whitthorne; Angela Bassett; Brad Dourif; Terrence Mann; ***D:*** Rupert Harvey; ***W:*** David J. Schow.

Croc 🦴 ½ **2007** There's a lot of unnecessary story added to this killer croc movie but here goes: ex-pat American Jack McQuade (Tuinstra) has a failing croc attraction at a Thai beach resort. His land is coveted by his competition so when locals go missing, Jack gets blamed since his star attraction, Delilah, is also absent. Jack and his pals decide to track Delilah, which means venturing into the most dangerous swampland in the area. **90m/C; DVD.** Michael Madsen; Elizabeth Healey; Peter Tuinstra; Tawon Sawtang; Sherry Phungprasert; ***D:*** Stewart Raffill; ***W:*** Ken Solarz; ***C:*** Choochart Nantitanyatada; ***M:*** Charles Olins; Mark Ryder. **TV**

Crocodile WOOF! **1981 (R)** Giant crocodile attacks a beach town, killing and devouring dozens of people. The locals sit around trying to figure a way to stop the critter. Special effects include rear-projected croc. Lots of blood but lacking humor of "Alligator." Filmed in Thailand and Korea. **95m/C; VHS, DVD.** *NK* Nat Puvanai; Tany Tim; Angela Wells; Kirk Warren; ***D:*** Sompote Sands.

Crocodile 🦴 ½ **2000 (R)** Cheesy special effects doom this low-budget horror. College students spend spring break on a houseboat and are terrorized by a giant crocodile who regards them as a new snack food. **94m/C; VHS, DVD.** Chris Solari; Mark McLaughlin; Caitlin Martin; Julie Mintz; Sommer Knight; ***D:*** Tobe Hooper; ***W:*** Michael D. Weiss; Adam Gierasch; Jace Anderson; ***C:*** Eliot Rockett. **VIDEO**

Crocodile 2: Death Swamp WOOF! **2001 (R)** Airliner crashes into a Mexican swamp and the survivors get picked off by big hungry crocodile. This one is too boring to even be bad fun. **90m/C; VHS, DVD.** Heidi Lenhart; Steve Moreno; Joe Sklaroff; Martin Kove; Darryl Theirse; ***D:*** Gary Jones; ***W:*** Jace Anderson; Adam Gierasch; ***C:*** Rasool Ellore; ***M:*** Bill Wandel. **VIDEO**

Crocodile Dundee 🦴🦴🦴 ½ **1986 (PG-13)** New York reporter Sue Charlton (Kozlowski) is assigned to the Outback to interview living legend Mike Dundee (Hogan). When she finally locates the man, she is so taken with him that she brings him back to New York with her. There, the naive Aussie wanders about, amazed at the wonders of the city and unwittingly charming everyone he comes in contact with, from high-society transvestites to street hookers. One of the surprise hits of 1986. **98m/C; VHS, DVD, Blu-Ray.** *AU* Paul Hogan; Linda Kozlowski; John Meillon; David Gulpilil; Mark Blum; ***D:*** Peter Faiman; ***W:*** Paul Hogan; John Cornell; ***C:*** Russell Boyd; ***M:*** Peter Best. Golden Globes '87: Actor--Mus./Comedy (Hogan).

Crocodile Dundee 2 🦴🦴 ½ **1988 (PG)** In this sequel Mike Dundee, the loveable rube, returns to his native Australia looking for new adventure, having "conquered" New York City. He finds trouble when Colombian drug lords kidnap his woman (Kozlowski again) and later track the couple to the Australian Outback. Lacks the charm and freshness of the first film. **110m/C; VHS, DVD, Blu-Ray.** Paul Hogan; Linda Kozlowski; Kenneth Welsh; John Meillon; Ernie Dingo; Juan Fernandez; Charles S. Dutton; Stephen (Steve) Root; Jace Alexander; Luis Guzman; Colin Quinn; ***D:*** John Cornell; ***W:*** Paul Hogan; ***C:*** Russell Boyd; ***M:*** Peter Best.

Crocodile Dundee in Los Angeles 🦴 ½ **2001 (PG)** Mick is back, for no good reason other than Hogan and Kozlowski probably needed the dough. The happy couple return to the States so Sue (Kozlowski) can investigate a movie studio that may be involved in a smuggling ring and, even worse, keeps cranking out dumb sequels. Where DO they come up with these ideas? Meanwhile, Dundee introduces their son (Cockburn) to life in the big city while working as an extra on the suspicious studio lot. It looks and feels like a real movie, but something's missing. What is it? Hmmmm-m......Oh, yeah! A point! Unless the previous two installments left too many unanswered questions, you can probably skip this one. **95m/C; VHS, DVD.** Paul Hogan; Linda Kozlowski; Jere Burns; Jonathan Banks; Paul Rodriguez; Alec Wilson; Serge Cockburn; Aida Turturro; Kaitlin Hopkins; ***Cameo(s):*** Mike Tyson; ***D:*** Simon Wincer; ***W:*** Matthew Berry; Eric Abrams; ***C:*** David Burr; ***M:*** Basil Poledouris.

The Crocodile Hunter: Collision Course 🦴🦴 ½ **2002 (PG)** Nature show hosts Steve Irwin and his wife Terri take their "The Crocodile Hunter" TV shtick to the big screen in this far-fetched story about a croc who swallows a top secret U.S. satellite beacon. Irwin attempts to protect the animal from a gun-toting farmer and some secret agents he mistakes for poachers. The story is just an excuse for Irwin to round up and irritate some of the world's most dangerous animals, presumably while Terri is checking his life insurance coverage. Kids who like the show will love the movie. **89m/C; VHS, DVD.** *AU US* Steve Irwin; Terri Irwin; Magda Szubanski; David Wenham; Aden Young; Kenny Ransom; Lachy Hulme; Kate Beahan; Steven Vidler; Steve Bastoni; ***D:*** John Stainton; ***W:*** Holly Goldberg Sloan; ***C:*** David Burr; ***M:*** Mark McDuff.

Crocodile Tears 🦴🦴 **1998** Gay art teacher Simon (Sod) makes a devil's bargain (literally) when he learns he's HIV-positive. Sinister Mr. Cheseboro (Salyers) offers the gift of health if Simon will become a straight stand-up comic who specializes in racist, sexist, and homophobic humor. Simon becomes a huge success but can he live with the consequences? Outrageous if heavy-handed. **84m/C; VHS, DVD.** Ted Sod; William Salyers; Dan Savage; Jeanne L. Klein; ***D:*** Ann Coppel; ***W:*** Ted Sod.

Croczilla 🦴 ½ *Million Dollar Crocodile* **2012 (PG-13)** The owner of a crocodile farm falls on hard times and is forced to sell his prize 36 footer named Amao to a gangster hungry to eat croc meat. Unfortunately Amao escapes and swallows a bag with a million yuan in the proces. Shenanigans swiftly ensue as all of the locals compete to catch the giant and get the money without somehow being eaten. **87m/C; DVD, Streaming.** *CH* Tao Guo; Barbie Tsu; Suet Lam; ***D:*** Li Sheng Lin; ***W:*** Li Sheng Lin; ***C:*** Xi Li. **VIDEO**

Cromwell 🦴🦴 ½ **1970 (G)** A lavish British-made spectacle about the conflict between Oliver Cromwell and Charles I, and the British Civil War. History is twisted as Cromwell becomes the liberator of the oppressed. Harris gives a commanding performance and the battle scenes are stunners. **139m/C; VHS, DVD.** *GB* Richard Harris; Alec Guinness; Robert Morley; Frank Finlay; Patrick Magee; Timothy Dalton; ***D:*** Ken Hughes; ***W:*** Ken Hughes; ***C:*** Geoffrey Unsworth. Oscars '70: Costume Des.

Cronicas 🦴🦴 **2004 (R)** Manolo Bonilla (Leguizamo) is an ambitious Miami TV tabloid reporter who heads to an Ecuadorian village that has been targeted by a serial child rapist and killer. Bible salesman Vinicio (Alcazar) accidentally runs over a victim's brother, is set upon by a mob, and saved by Bonilla. In return, Vinicio promises to reveal the killer's identity, claiming they met on his travels. But is Vinicio, himself, the killer or is he stringing Manolo along in order to stay alive? And just how far will Manolo go to get his story? Runs out of steam but Leguizamo gives an intense performance. **111m/C; DVD.** *MX* John Leguizamo; Leonor Watling; Damian Alcazar; Alfred Molina; Jose Maria Yazpik; ***D:*** Sebastian Cordero; ***W:*** Sebastian Cordero; ***C:*** Enrique Chediak; ***M:*** Antonio Pinto.

Cronos 🦴🦴 *Chronos* **1994 (R)** Stylish Mexican variation of the vampire tale. Aged antiques dealer Jesus Gris (Luppi) comes across the mysterious title object—a 14th century golden egg possessing magical powers to grant eternal life. But can its possessor stand the consequences, which include a developing taste for blood? Another problem is Gris isn't the only one to know about the device. First feature for writer/director del Toro. Spanish with subtitles. **92m/C; VHS, DVD, Blu-Ray.** *MX* Federico Luppi; Ron Perlman; Claudio Brook; Tamara Shanath; Margarita Isabel; ***D:*** Guillermo del Toro; ***W:*** Guillermo del Toro; ***C:*** Guillermo Navarro; ***M:*** Javier Alvarez.

The Croods 🦴🦴 ½ **2013 (PG)** The latest from DreamWorks Animation has a plot that is simple enough--animated cavemen. Grug (Cage) leads a prehistoric family on a road trip where they encounter a nomad named Guy (Reynolds) and go on an adventure into the brave new world around them. The themes of family unity against the scary world of the new are common but the script is smart enough. Not ambitious enough to be truly memorable, but it does provide enough visual razzle-dazzle to keep families entertained and doesn't insult the intelligence of their parents at the same time. **98m/C; DVD, Blu-Ray.** ***V:*** Nicolas Cage; Emma Stone; Ryan Reynolds; Catherine Keener; Cloris Leachman; Clark Duke; Randy Thom; Chris (Christopher) Sanders; ***D:*** Chris (Christopher) Sanders; Kirk De Micco; ***W:*** Chris (Christopher) Sanders; Kirk De Micco; ***C:*** Yong Duk Jhun; ***M:*** Alan Silvestri.

Crooked 🦴 *Soft Target* **2005 (R)** Two cops who can't stand each other must team up to protect a woman who has seen the face of a hitman who's been killing witnesses in the witness protection program. Supposedly he's a police detective and as soon as the trio arrives at the safe house they're attacked. The plot is cliched, with bad acting (with the possible exception of Gary Busey), choreography, editing, script, dialogue, and direction. But other than that, it's fine. **92m/C; DVD.** Don "The Dragon" Wilson; Olivier Gruner; Gary Busey; Fred Williamson; Martin Kove; Michael Cavalieri; Bret Roberts; Mark Parra; Maurice Lamont; Diana Kauffman; Michael R. Thayer; Jerry Airola; Vince Melocchi; Lorraine Farris; Suzanne Von Schaack; Rick Almada; Eric Rutherford; T. J. Hart; Nick Di Brizzi, Jr.; ***D:*** Art Camacho; ***W:*** William C. Martell; ***C:*** Curtis Petersen; Andrea V. Rossotto; Kim Kroonenburg; ***M:*** Kenny Meriedeth.

Crooked Arrows 🦴 **2012 (PG-13)** Low-budget and amateurish sports drama about a Native American high school lacrosse team and their reluctant coach. Mixed-blood Joe Logan (Routh) is trying to convince the tribal council to allow a casino expansion on the upstate New York reservation. The council will only agree if Joe coaches their terrible high school lacrosse team and gets them ready to face a hated rival. About as cliched as you can imagine. **105m/C; Blu-Ray, Download.** Brandon Routh; Gil Birmingham; Chelsea Ricketts; Crystal Allen; Tom Kemp; ***D:*** Steve Rash; ***W:*** Todd Baird; Brad Riddell; ***C:*** Daniel Stoloff; ***M:*** Brian Ralston.

The Crooked Circle 🦴 ½ **1932** More comedy than mystery as slapstick policeman Gleason goes under cover as a swami. Not helped at all by a weak script and poor photography. **68m/B; VHS, DVD, Blu-Ray.** Ben Lyon; Zasu Pitts; James Gleason; C. Henry Gordon; Raymond Hatton; Roscoe Karns; ***D:*** H. Bruce Humberstone.

Crooked Hearts 🦴🦴 **1991 (R)** Dysfunctional family drama means well but lays it on too thick, as a father/son rivalry threatens to sunder the tight-knit Warrens. Based on a novel by Robert Boswell. **113m/C; VHS, DVD.** Peter Coyote; Jennifer Jason Leigh; Peter Berg; Cindy Pickett; Vincent D'Onofrio; Noah Wyle; Juliette Lewis; Wendy Gazelle; Marg Helgenberger; ***D:*** Michael Bortman; ***W:*** Michael Bortman; ***C:*** Tak Fujimoto; ***M:*** Mark Isham.

The Crooked Road 🦴 ½ **1965** Journalist Richard Ashley (Ryan) wants to prove that the Duke of Orgagna (Granger) is misusing American funds to bolster his anti-Communist stance in upcoming elections somewhere in the Balkans. Ashley's ex-lover, Cosima (Gray), happens to be the Duke's missus, but he has more than romance to worry about when he's framed for murder to keep him quiet. **93m/B; DVD.** Robert Ryan; Stewart Granger; Nadia Gray; Marius Goring; ***D:*** Don Chaffey; ***W:*** Don Chaffey; Joy Garrison; ***C:*** Stephen Dade; ***M:*** Bojan Adamic.

A Crooked Somebody 1/2 **2018 (R)** Michael Vaughn (Sommer) is a successful traveling psychic, holding group events where he claims to talk to the dead loved ones of folks in the audience. When an event is not going well, his partner (Froggatt) pretends to be someone who wants to communicate with someone beyond the grave to rouse other attendees. Things get wacky when impressed audience member Nathan (Collins) kidnaps Michael later that night to connect with someone he killed. This mix of thriller and satire succeeds thanks to a superb cast, which is only marred by an overly polished ending. **102m/C; DVD.** Ed Harris; Amanda Crew; Michael Mosley; Gillian Vigman; Joanne Froggatt; ***D:*** Trevor White; ***W:*** Andrew Zilch; ***C:*** Robert Lam; ***M:*** Andrew Hewitt.

The Crooked Web **1955** Slow, far-fetched crime drama. Ex-GI Stan (Lovejoy) is willing to listen to a deal proposed by Frank (Denning), the brother of his girlfriend Joanie (Blanchard). Frank spins a yarn about gold from WWII hidden in Berlin, but the fake siblings are actually undercover agents after Stan for a wartime murder. **77m/B; DVD, Blu-Ray.** Frank Lovejoy; Mari Blanchard; Richard Denning; Harry Lauter; John (Jack) Mylong; ***D:*** Nathan "Jerry" Juran; ***W:*** Lou Breslow; ***C:*** Henry Freulich; ***M:*** Mischa Bakaleinikoff.

Crooklyn **1994 (PG-13)** Director Lee turns from the life of Malcolm X to the early lives of Generation X in this profile of an African-American middle-class family growing up in 1970s Brooklyn. Lee's least politically charged film to date is a joint effort between him and sibs Joie and Cinque, and profiles the only girl in a family of five children coming of age. Tender and real performances from all, especially newcomer Harris, propel the sometimes messy, music-laden trip to nostalgia land. **112m/C; VHS, DVD, Blu-Ray.** Alfre Woodard; Delroy Lindo; Zelda Harris; David Patrick Kelly; Carlton Williams; Sharif Rashed; Tse-March Washington; Christopher Knowings; Jose Zuniga; Isaiah Washington, IV; Ivelka Reyes; N. Jeremi Duru; Frances Foster; Norman Matlock; Patriece Nelson; Joie Lee; Vondie Curtis-Hall; Tiasha Reyes; Spike Lee; RuPaul Charles; ***D:*** Spike Lee; ***W:*** Joie Lee; Cinque Lee; ***C:*** Arthur Jaffa; ***M:*** Terence Blanchard.

Cropsey **2010** The title refers to the urban myth name of the Staten Island boogeyman who lurked on the grounds of the abandoned Willowbrook State School for the mentally handicapped. For directors and Staten Island natives, Zeman and Brancaccio it also surrounds the case of Andre Rand, a former attendant at the school, who was convicted of the kidnapping and murder of one of five children who went missing between 1972 and 1987. Includes archival news footage and interviews. **84m/C; On Demand.** ***D:*** Joshua Zeman; Barbara Brancaccio; ***W:*** Joshua Zeman; ***C:*** Chad Davidson; ***M:*** Alexander Lasarenko.

Cross 1/2 **2011 (R)** Crazy fantasy-action with an equally crazy plot. Callan (Green) was given a Celtic cross that bestows super powers. He and his band of vigilantes are roaming the streets of L.A. looking for kidnapped babes being used in a nefarious plot by immortal Gunnar (Jones). Gunnar wants to make and release a mystic potion that will finally allow him to die, even though there'll be lots of collateral deaths. Gunnar has his own band of thugs, headed by Erlk (Duncan), to help him out. **105m/C; DVD.** Brian Austin Green; Vinnie Jones; Michael Clarke Duncan; Jake Busey; C. Thomas Howell; Tom Sizemore; Robert Carradine; William Zabka; Lori Heuring; ***D:*** Patrick Durham; ***W:*** Patrick Durham; Tanner Willey; Jonathan Sachar; ***C:*** Massimo Zeri; ***M:*** Peter Carl Ganderup. **VIDEO**

The Cross & the Switchblade 1/2 **1972 (PG)** An idealistic priest tries to bring the message of religion to the members of a vicious street gang. They don't wanna listen. Spanish language version available. **105m/C; VHS, DVD.** Pat Boone; Erik Estrada; Jackie Giroux; Jo-Ann Robinson; ***D:*** Don Murray.

Cross Creek 1/2 **1983 (PG)** Based on the life of Marjorie Kinnan Rawlings, author of "The Yearling," who, after 10 years as a frustrated reporter/writer, moves to the remote and untamed Everglades. There she meets colorful local characters and receives the inspiration to write numerous bestsellers. Well acted though overtly sentimental at times. **120m/C; VHS, DVD.** Mary Steenburgen; Rip Torn; Peter Coyote; Dana Hill; Alfre Woodard; Malcolm McDowell; ***D:*** Martin Ritt; ***W:*** Dalene Young; ***C:*** John A. Alonzo; ***M:*** Leonard Rosenman.

Cross Mission **1989 (R)** Predictable actioner about a photographer and a soldier who are captured by the enemy. Packed with a bit of ninja, ammo, and occult. **90m/C; VHS, DVD.** Richard Randall; ***D:*** Al (Alfonso Brescia) Bradley.

Cross My Heart **1988 (R)** Light comedy about two single people with complicated, post-divorce lives who go on a date and suffer accordingly. Will true love prevail? **91m/C; VHS, DVD.** Martin Short; Annette O'Toole; Paul Reiser; Joanna Kerns; ***D:*** Armyan Bernstein; ***W:*** Armyan Bernstein; ***M:*** Bruce Broughton.

Cross of Iron 1/2 *Steiner—Das Eiserne Kreuz* **1976 (R)** During WWII, two antagonistic German officers clash over personal ideals as well as strategy in combatting the relentless Russian attack. Followed by "Breakthrough." **120m/C; VHS, DVD, Blu-Ray.** *GB GE* James Coburn; Maximilian Schell; James Mason; David Warner; Senta Berger; Klaus Lowitsch; Vadim Glowna; Roger Fritz; Dieter Schidor; Burkhard Driest; Fred Stillkrauth; Michael Nowka; Veronique Vendell; Arthur Brauss; ***D:*** Sam Peckinpah; ***W:*** Julius J. Epstein; Walter Kelley; James Hamilton; ***C:*** John Coquillon; ***M:*** Ernest Gold.

The Cross of Lorraine 1/2 **1943** Violent wartime propaganda about POWs in a Nazi camp in France in 1940. Victor Labiche (Kelly) is a former cab driver held in solitary confinement for defying authority. Part of a POW escape, Victor's will to fight is rekindled by the courage of the other escapees and the resistance fighters who help them. **90m/B; DVD.** Gene Kelly; Jean-Pierre Aumont; Cedric Hardwicke; Peter Lorre; Richard Whorf; Joseph Calleia; Hume Cronyn; ***D:*** Tay Garnett; ***W:*** Michael Kanin; Ring Lardner, Jr.; ***C:*** Sidney Wagner; ***M:*** Bronislau Kaper.

A Cross to Bear 1/2 **2012** After many difficult life experiences, a woman finds hope and redemption at a shelter. Erica Moses (Deadwyler) wanted a bright life, but instead had a series of failed relationships, addiction issues, homelessness, and the death of a child. When she finds a woman's shelter that helps women find second chances, Erica finds forgiveness, redemption, and family. **89m/C; DVD, Streaming, Download.** Danielle Deadwyler; Parris Fluellen; Kim Fields; Malinda Williams; Jackie Long; ***D:*** Tandria Potts; ***W:*** Cas Sigers; ***C:*** Samm Wallace; ***M:*** Kenneth Lampl. **VIDEO**

Crossbar **1979** Aaron Kornylo is determined to reach Olympic qualifications in the high jump despite having only one leg. Inspired by a true story, this program dramatically shows how far determination and work can take a person. **77m/C; VHS, DVD.** John Ireland; Brent Carver; Kate Reid; ***D:*** John Trent.

Crossfire 1/2 **1947** A Jewish hotel guest is murdered and three soldiers just back from Europe are suspected of the crime. The first Hollywood film that explored racial bigotry. Due to the radical nature of its plot, the director and the producer were eventually black-listed for promoting "un-American" themes. Loosely based on Richard Brooks' "The Brick Foxhole." **86m/B; DVD.** Robert Young; Robert Mitchum; Robert Ryan; Gloria Grahame; Paul Kelly; ***D:*** Edward Dmytryk; ***W:*** John Paxton; ***C:*** J. Roy Hunt; ***M:*** Roy Webb.

Crossfire Trail **2001** Cowboy Rafe Covington (Selleck) promises his dying friend that he will look out for the man's wife, Ann (Madsen), and their Wyoming spread. Rafe heads to town with his sidekicks (Brimley, O'Hara, Kane) and discovers the widow is already being courted by ruthless Bruce Barkow (Harmon), who wants the ranch since there's oil on the land. Naturally, Barkow has a hired gun (Johnson) and the sheriff (Corbin) in his pocket. Accomplished cast, straight forward direction, lush scenery (it's Calgary, Alberta), and a little humor. Based on Louis L'Amour's 1954 novel. **100m/C; VHS, DVD.** Tom Selleck; Virginia Madsen; Mark Harmon; Wilford Brimley; David O'Hara; Christian Kane; Barry Corbin; Brad Johnson; William Sanderson; Joanna Miles; Ken Pogue; Rex Linn; ***D:*** Simon Wincer; ***W:*** Charles Robert Carner; ***C:*** David Eggby; ***M:*** Eric Colvin. **CABLE**

The Crossing 1/2 **2000** No, General George Washington did not cross the Delaware river standing in his boat as Emanuel Leutze's famous painting shows. But this historical story is still pretty darn exciting. On Christmas Day in 1776, it seems the American Revolution is destined for failure. Washington (Daniels) has only 2000 troops left and the Continental Army has continually been defeated by the British. But Washington wants to make a final push—a surprise attack on the Hessian garrison at Trenton. Adapted by Howard Fast from his novel. **100m/C; VHS, DVD.** Jeff Daniels; Roger Rees; Sebastien Roche; Steven McCarthy; John Henry Canavan; Ned Vukovic; ***D:*** Robert Harmon; ***W:*** Howard Fast. **CABLE**

Crossing Delancey **1988 (PG)** Jewish woman (Bozyk), in old world style, plays matchmaker to her independent 30-something granddaughter. Charming modern-day New York City fairy tale deftly manipulates cliches and stereotypes. Lovely performance from Irving as the woman whose heart surprises her. Riegert is swell playing the gentle but never wimpy suitor. Perfectly cast Bozyk was a star on the Yiddish vaudeville stage; this is her film debut. Appealing music by the Roches, with Suzzy Roche giving a credible performance as Irving's friend. Adapted for the big screen by Sandler from her play of the same name. **97m/C; VHS, DVD.** Amy Irving; Reizl Bozyk; Peter Riegert; Jeroen Krabbe; Sylvia Miles; Suzzy Roche; George Martin; John Bedford Lloyd; Rosemary Harris; Amy Wright; Claudia Silver; David Hyde Pierce; ***D:*** Joan Micklin Silver; ***W:*** Susan Sandler.

The Crossing Guard **1994 (R)** Nicholson headlines as Freddy Gale, a revenge-minded father who hunts down a drunk driver (Morse), who killed his daughter five years previous. Story focuses on dual emotions of the two men: Gale seeks an end to his grief and rage; Booth attempts to deal with guilt and regret. Writer Penn pairs one-time lovers Nicholson and Huston (playing ex-spouses here) in his sophomore directorial effort with explosive results. Focus is, accordingly, on emotional performances while narrative and directorial finesse take a back seat. Dedicated to the late chronicler of the curbside, Charles Bukowski. **111m/C; VHS, DVD, Blu-Ray.** Jack Nicholson; Anjelica Huston; David Morse; Robin Wright; Robbie Robertson; Piper Laurie; Richard Bradford; John Savage; Priscilla Barnes; Kari Wuhrer; Jennifer Leigh Warren; Richard Sarafian; Jeff Morris; Joe (Johnny) Viterelli; Eileen Ryan; Ryo Ishibashi; Michael Ryan; Nicky Blair; Gene Kirkwood; Jason Kristofer; Hadda Brooks; ***D:*** Sean Penn; ***W:*** Sean Penn; ***C:*** Vilmos Zsigmond; ***M:*** Jack Nitzsche.

Crossing Over **2009 (R)** Bland multi-narrative melodrama about various U.S. immigration cases. Brit Gavin Kossef (Sturgess) and Aussie Claire Sheperd (Eve) have outstayed their visas; he keeps his status secret at his new job and she decides to trade sex with sleazy Cole Frankel (Liotta) for a chance at a green card. Meanwhile, Cole's wife Denise (Judd) is an immigration attorney who wants to adopt a Nigerian orphan. Ford's a good-guy immigration agent who takes a paternal interest in a young Mexican mother who's about to be deported and there's also a couple of subplots involving a Bangladeshi teenager writing a naive essay on terrorism and a Korean teen caught up in gang life. The coincidences seem forced and director Kramer wraps things up tidily—unlike real life. **140m/C; Blu-Ray, On Demand.** Harrison Ford; Clifford Curtis; Ashley Judd; Sean Penn; Ray Liotta; Alice Braga; Alice Eve; Jim Sturgess; Summer Bishil; Justin Chon; Hamid Baraheri; ***D:*** Wayne Kramer; ***W:*** Wayne Kramer; ***C:*** Jim Whitaker; ***M:*** John Murphy; Mark Isham.

Crossing the Bridge **1992 (R)** An after high-school tale of three buddies and their restless lives as they take their uncertain steps towards adulthood. It's 1975 in Detroit and Mort, Danny, and Tim cling to high-school memories as they pass time on petty jobs, drinking, and cruising across the Ambassador Bridge to check out the Canadian strip joints. Their big moment—for better or worse—comes when they are offered the chance to make a lot of quick cash if they'll smuggle hash from Toronto to Detroit. Directorial debut of Binder. **105m/C; VHS, DVD, Blu-Ray.** Josh Charles; Jason Gedrick; Stephen Baldwin; Cheryl Pollak; Jeffrey Tambor; Rita Taggart; Richard Edson; Ken Jenkins; Abraham Benrubi; David Schwimmer; Hy Anzell; Bob Nickman; James Krag; Rana Haugen; Todd Tidgewell; ***D:*** Mike Binder; ***W:*** Mike Binder; ***C:*** Newton Thomas (Tom) Sigel; ***M:*** Peter Himmelman.

Crossing the Line **1990 (R)** Two motocross racers battle it out for the championship. **90m/C; VHS, DVD.** Jon Stafford; Rick Hearst; Paul Smith; Cameron Mitchell; Vernon Wells; Colleen Morris; John Saxon; ***D:*** Gary Graver.

Crossover **2006 (PG-13)** So why are streetballers playing their game in an abandoned Detroit train station? Too cold outside? Not enough grunge atmosphere? A dopey and cliched sports soap opera, with very few actual basketball sequences, which has studious Cruise (Jonathan) getting a b-ball scholarship to an LA college while his best bud, dropout Tech (Mackie), just wants to beat local rival Jewelz (Champion). There's also a slick wannabe sports agent (Brady) and a couple of hotties (one good and one a gold-digger). This amateur night don't got game. **95m/C; DVD.** Anthony Mackie; Wesley Jonathan; Wayne Brady; Kristen Wilson; Lil' J.J.; Phillip Champion; Eva Pigford; Alecia Fears; ***D:*** Preston A. Whitmore, II; ***W:*** Preston A. Whitmore, II; ***C:*** Christian Sebaldt; ***M:*** Matthias Weber.

Crossover Dreams 1/2 **1985** Actor and musician Blades moves this old story along. Sure that he has at last made the international Big Time, a salsa artist becomes a self-important back-stabber after cutting an album. Great music. Blades's first film. **86m/C; VHS, DVD.** Ruben Blades; Shawn Elliott; Elizabeth Pena; Virgilio Marti; Tom Signorelli; Frank Robles; Joel Diamond; Amanda Barber; John Hammil; ***D:*** Leon Ichaso; ***W:*** Ruben Blades; Leon Ichaso; Manuel Arce; ***M:*** Mauricio Smith.

Crossroads **1942** David Talbot (Powell) is a rising French diplomat, living in 1935 Paris with his bride Lucienne (Lamarr). David suddenly starts receiving blackmail letters, accusing him of being wanted criminal Jean Pelletier. The bewildered man goes to the police who trap Carlos Le Duc (Sokloff) who's then put on trial. When Henri Sarrou (Rathbone) testifies on David's behalf, David finds his intentions are insincere leaving him baffled. Hollywood remake of the 1938 French thriller "Carrefour." **84m/B; DVD.** William Powell; Hedy Lamarr; Basil Rathbone; Claire Trevor; Felix Bressart; Sig Rugman; Vladimir Sokoloff; Margaret Wycherly; ***D:*** Jack Conway; ***W:*** Guy Trosper; ***C:*** Joseph Ruttenberg; ***M:*** Bronislau Kaper.

Crossroads 1/2 **1986 (R)** A blues-loving young white man, classically trained at Juilliard, befriends an aging black blues-master. After helping the old man escape from the nursing home, the two hop trains to the South where it's literally a duel with the devil. Fine performances by Macchio, Gertz, Seneca, and Morton. Wonderful score by Ry Cooder, with some help from Steve Vai in the final showdown. **100m/C; VHS, DVD.** Ralph Macchio; Joe Seneca; Jami Gertz; Joe Morton; Robert Judd; Harry Carey, Jr.; Steve Vai; ***D:*** Walter Hill; ***W:*** John Fusco; ***C:*** John Bailey; ***M:*** Steve Vai; Ry Cooder.

Crossroads 1/2 **2002 (PG-13)** Underwhelming teen buddy road pic has pop tart Spears debut as Lucy, a virginal, small-town high school senior who hits the road to L.A. with childhood buds Kit (Saldana) and Mimi (Manning), with depressing results. Lucy's searching for her real mom (Cattrall); Kit, a no-good boyfriend; and Mimi trying to get to an open audition as a singer. Convenient cute love interest for Lucy is driver Ben (Mount), who may harbor a dangerous secret. Most laughable scene features Lucy scribbling "poetry" (actually lyrics to one of her soundtrack songs) while Ben "composes" the music for it. Spears is likeable and harmless while Manning is the real stand-out. One notch up from "Glitter," quality competed with quantity (of wardrobe) as lowest priority.

94m/C; VHS, DVD. Britney Spears; Taryn Manning; Zoe Saldana; Anson Mount; Kim Cattrall; Dan Aykroyd; Justin Long; Beverly Johnson; Kool Moe Dee; Richard Voll; *D:* Tamra Davis; *W:* Shonda Rhimes; *C:* Eric Alan Edwards; *M:* Trevor Jones. Golden Raspberries '02: Worst Actress (Spears), Worst Song ("I'm Not a Girl, Not Yet a Woman").

Crossworlds ✗✗ **1996 (PG-13)** All dimensions of the universe collide in the mystical valley of Crossworlds. When alien night riders attack Joe Talbolt (Charles), he escapes with girlfriend Laura (Roth) and they meet up with mercenary A.T. (Hauer). Turns out the crystal pendant Joe's father left him is one of the keys that unlock the boundaries between the worlds. Along with a scepter, they give the owner unlimited power. So the trio enter Crossworlds to fight a battle between good and evil. **91m/C; VHS, DVD.** Rutger Hauer; Josh Charles; Andrea Roth; Stuart Wilson; Jack Black; *D:* Krishna Rao; *W:* Raman Rao; Krishna Rao; *C:* Chris Walling; *M:* Christophe Beck. **CABLE**

Crouching Tiger, Hidden Dragon ✗✗✗ 1/2 **2000** Two veteran Wudan fighters (Yun-Fat and Yeoh) in 19th-century China recognize their passion for each other while tracking down a vengeful master criminal (Pei-Pei) and her protege (the exciting Ziyi). A martial arts love story that satisfies on both accounts. The emotional impact of the romance is as real and true as the choreographed fight scenes are spectacular and graceful. The film's overt feminism flies (literally) in the face of its patriarchal setting, yet doesn't seem a bit out of place. The extraordinary battle scenes were choreographed by Yuen Wo-Ping, who performed the same duties for "The Matrix." Mandarin with subtitles. **120m/C; VHS, DVD, Blu-Ray, UMD.** Chow Yun-Fat; Michelle Yeoh; Ziyi Zhang; Chen "Chang Chen" Chang; Cheng Pei-Pei; Sihung Lung; *D:* Ang Lee; *W:* James Schamus; Wang Hui Ling; Tsai Kuo Jung; *C:* Peter Pau; *M:* Tan Dun. Oscars '00: Art Dir./Set Dec., Cinematog., Foreign Film, Orig. Score; Australian Film Inst. '01: Foreign Film; British Acad. '00: Director (Lee), Foreign Film, Score; Directors Guild '00: Director (Lee); Golden Globes '01: Director (Lee), Foreign Film; Ind. Spirit '01: Director (Lee), Film; L.A. Film Critics '00: Cinematog., Film, Score; Natl. Bd. of Review '00: Foreign Film; N.Y. Film Critics '00: Cinematog.; Broadcast Film Critics '00: Foreign Film.

Crouching Tiger, Hidden Dragon: Sword of Destiny ✗✗ *Wo hu cang long 2: Qing ming bao jian* **2016 (PG-13)** Long overdue to the point that many questioned why even bother, the sequel to Ang Lee's 2000 Oscar winner nevertheless assembled an impressive crew in front of and behind the camera, led by the fight choreographer from the first film, Yuen Woo-ping, in the director's chair. The timeless Michelle Yeoh returns as Yu Shu Lien, a warrior forced into combat after enemies seek the titular legendary weapon, which also reunites her with an old flame played by the great Donnie Yen. The "Wire Fu" sequences are well-staged and the movie flows, but it lacks the magic of the original. **96m/B; DVD.** *CH US* Donnie Yen; Michelle Yeoh; Harry Shum, Jr.; Natasha Liu Bordizzo; Jason Scott Lee; *D:* Woo-ping Yuen; *W:* John Fusco; *C:* Newton Thomas (Tom) Sigel; *M:* Carlo Siliotto; Shigeru Umebayashi.

Croupier ✗✗✗ **1997** Director Hodges scored a hit with the 1971 British crime thriller "Get Carter." And after some rocky followups, he scores another with this cool casino neo-noir. A cynical South African, now living in London, Jack Manfred (Owen) is trying to escape the reach of his con man dad. The would-be writer (his detective character Jake does the film's narrative) takes a job as a casino dealer where he can observe life at his preferred distance—that is until a fellow South African, sulty gambling beauty Jani (Kingston), talks him into a shady scheme that provides fodder for Jack's writing. Owen is especially watchable in the title role. **91m/C; VHS, DVD, Blu-Ray.** *GB* Clive Owen; Alex Kingston; Kate Hardie; Gina McKee; Nicholas Ball; Nick Reding; *D:* Mike Hodges; *W:* Paul Mayersberg; *C:* Mike Garfath; *M:* Simon Fisher Turner.

The Crow ✗✗ 1/2 **1993 (R)** Revenge-fantasy finds Eric Draven (Lee) resurrected on Devil's Night, a year after his death, in order to avenge his own murder and that of his girlfriend. 90% of the scenes are at night, in the rain, or both, and it's not easy to tell what's going on (a blessing considering the violence level). Very dark, but with good performances, particularly from Lee, in his last role before an unfortunate on set accident caused his death. That footage has been destroyed, but use of a stunt double and camera trickery allowed for the movie's completion. Film was dedicated to Lee and his fiance Eliza. Based on the comic strip by James O'Barr. The video release includes Brandon Lee's final interview. **100m/C; VHS, DVD, UMD.** Brandon Lee; Ernie Hudson; Michael Wincott; David Patrick Kelly; Rochelle Davis; Angel David; Michael Massee; Bai Ling; Laurence Mason; Bill Raymond; Marco Rodriguez; Anna Thomson; Sofia Shinas; Jon Polito; Tony Todd; *D:* Alex Proyas; *W:* David J. Schow; John Shirley; *C:* Dariusz Wolski; *M:* Graeme Revell. MTV Movie Awards '95: Song ("Big Empty").

The Crow 2: City of Angels ✗✗ **1996 (R)** James O'Barr's cult graphic-novel "hero" returns in a new incarnation. It's eight years later (in film time) and the setting's changed from Detroit to L.A. but the horror remains. Ashe (Perez) and his young son witness a murder and are killed themselves by scumbags working for drug lord Judah (Brooks). So the Crow brings back Ashe to get revenge. Also involved is Sarah (Kirshner), who retains her role as story narrator but is now a grown-up tattoo artist who falls in love with Ashe. Lots of kink and flash—no substance—and confusing as well. The eerie sepia-toned look is created with sodium lighting. **93m/C; VHS, DVD, Blu-Ray.** Vincent Perez; Mia Kirshner; Iggy Pop; Richard Brooks; Ian Dury; Thuy Trang; Thomas Jane; Vincent Castellanos; Tracey Ellis; *D:* Tim Pope; *W:* David S. Goyer; *C:* Jean-Yves Escoffier; *M:* Graeme Revell.

The Crow Road ✗✗ **1996** Prentice Hogan comes back to his hometown for his grandmother's funeral. Old conflicts surface and Prentice becomes determined to solve the disappearance of his Uncle Rory, who's been missing seven years. As he reads his uncle's unpublished novel, Prentice discovers some very disturbing family secrets. Based on the novel by Iain Banks. **210m/C; DVD.** *GB* Joseph McFadden; Peter Capaldi; Dougray Scott; Bill Paterson; Stella Gonet; Valerie Edmond; David Robb; *D:* Gavin Millar; *W:* Bryan Eisley; *C:* John Else; *M:* Colin Towns. **TV**

The Crow: Salvation ✗✗ **2000 (R)** Third in the series of films based on James O'Barr's comic book finds Alex Corvis (Mabius) wrongly convicted of murdering girlfriend Lauren Randall (O'Keefe). He's executed on his 21st birthday but returns as the Crow to seek revenge on those who wronged him. Alex convinces Erin (Dunst), Lauren's teenaged sister, of his innocence and they team up. Rather than revitalizing the franchise, this one basically got dumped by the studio, although the performances and the production are worth your time. **102m/C; VHS, DVD.** Eric Mabius; Kirsten Dunst; Fred Ward; Jodi Lyn O'Keefe; William Atherton; Dale Midkiff; Grant Shaud; *D:* Bharat Nalluri; *W:* Chip Johannessen; *C:* Carolyn Chen; *M:* Marco Beltrami.

The Crow: Wicked Prayer ✗✗ **2005 (R)** A satanic gang murders a juvenile delinquent (Furlong) and his mystical girlfriend (Chriqui) so that their leader (Boreanaz) can become a powerful demon. Instead, the kid becomes The Crow and returns for vengeance against the gang. Not a whole lot to recommend to non-fans of the franchise, although Hopper scores in his campy cameo. **99m/C; DVD, Blu-Ray.** Edward Furlong; Emmanuelle Chriqui; David Boreanaz; Tara Reid; Dennis Hopper; Macy Gray; Danny Trejo; Marcus Chong; Yuji Okumoto; *D:* Lance Mungia; *W:* Lance Mungia; Sean Hood; *C:* Kurt Brabbee; *M:* Jason Christopherson. **VIDEO**

The Crowd Roars ✗✗ **1932** Champion auto racer Joe Greer (Cagney) returns to his Indianapolis hometown for a race and his younger brother Eddie (Linden) wants to follow in his footsteps. Joe is free with a lot of unasked for advice and the siblings have a falling out. Joe loses his nerve after a crash, and Eddie becomes a star but the brothers aren't done yet. Shooting on location at the Indianapolis and Ascot Motor speedways and the Ventura Raceway up the action authenticity amidst the family drama. **70m/B; DVD.** James Cagney; Eric Linden; Joan Blondell; Ann Dvorak; Guy Kibbee; Frank McHugh; *D:* Howard Hawks; *W:* John Bright; Niven Busch; *C:* Sidney Hickox.

The Crowd Roars ✗✗ 1/2 **1938** Typical '30s sports melodrama with a convincing performance from lead Taylor. Young boxer, Tommy 'Killer' McCoy, has some problems and winds up owing mobster/gambler James Carson (Arnold). Carson poses as Tommy's manager under the alias Jim Cain because he doesn't want his sweet daughter Sheila (O'Sullivan) to learn what he really does for a living. And since Tommy's in love with Sheila, he's not going to tell her. The situation gets messier when Tommy's supposed to take a dive in a big fight. Remade as 1947's "Killer McCoy." **92m/B; DVD.** Robert Taylor; Maureen O'Sullivan; Edward Arnold; Frank Morgan; William Gargan; Lionel Stander; Jane Wyman; *D:* Richard Thorpe; *W:* Thomas Lennon; George Bruce; George Oppenheimer; *C:* John Seitz; *M:* Edward Ward.

The Crowded Sky ✗✗ **1960** A commercial jet and a Navy plane with defective navigation equipment and no radio are on a collision course. Flashbacks depict personal moments of the crew and passengers of the airliner who don't realize they're in imminent danger, unlike the Naval pilot who must make a terrible choice. **105m/C; DVD.** Dana Andrews; Efrem Zimbalist, Jr.; Troy Donahue; Rhonda Fleming; John Kerr; Anne Francis; Keenan Wynn; Patsy Kelly; *D:* Joseph Pevney; *W:* Charles Schnee; *C:* Harry Stradling, Sr.; *M:* Leonard Rosenman.

Crown Heights ✗✗ 1/2 **2002 (R)** An orthodox Rabbi and an African-American community leader join forces to save their racially-fractured neighborhood from more violence. Inspired by real-life events after the 1991 Brooklyn riots that were triggered by a Jewish man accidentally running down a black child. **93m/C; VHS, DVD.** Jeremy Blackman; Jason Blicker; Daniel Kash; Judah Katz; Mpho Koaho; Michael Yarmush; *D:* Jeremy Paul Kagan; *W:* Michael D'Antonio; Toni Johnson; *C:* Rudolf Blahacek; *M:* Aaron Zigman. **TV**

Crown Heights ✗✗ **2017 (R)** The true story of Colin Warner (Stanfield), an 18-year-old from the Brooklyn neighborhood of Crown Heights, who was identified by a child witness in a 1980 murder. Carl "KC" King (newcomer Asomugha) devotes his life to proving the innocence of his childhood friend, even to the detriment of his own family. Adapted from a "This American Life" segment, it's a tale of friendship and determination, with commentary on criminal (in)justice and racial inequality, that needs to be told, even if its ultimate delivery is flatter than the fine performances of its leads. **94m/C; DVD.** Lakeith Stanfield; Nnamdi Asomugha; Natalie Paul; Amari Cheatom; Marsha Stephanie Blake; *D:* Matt Ruskin; *W:* Matt Ruskin; *C:* Ben Kutchins; *M:* Mark De Gli Antoni.

The Crown Prince ✗✗ 1/2 *Kronprinz Rudolf* **2006** In the late 1880s, Crown Prince Rudolf, heir to the Austro-Hungarian Empire, enters into an unhappy marriage of convenience to try to please his controlling father, Emperor Franz-Joseph. Progressive for his time, Rudolf finds his suggestions for political alliances and reforms shunned and he seemingly has nothing better to do than fall obsessively in love with the beautiful Baroness Mary Vetsera, whom he takes to his castle at Mayerling. Rudolf's father does not approve; things don't end well. Based on a true story that has been filmed before, notably as 1969's "Mayerling." **181m/C; DVD.** *AT GE* Omar Sharif; Christian Clavier; Klaus Maria Brandauer; Sandra Ceccarelli; Max von Thun; Victoria Puccini; Alexandra Vandernoot; Birgit Minichmayr; *D:* Robert Dornhelm; *W:* Didier Decoin; Klaus Lintschinger; *C:* Michael Riebl; *M:* Ludwig Eckmann; Joerg Magnus Pfeil. **TV**

Crows and Sparrows ✗✗✗ *Wuya Yu Maque* **1949** Poor tenants of a Shanghai boardinghouse are about to lose their home when their greedy landlord decides to sell and move to Taiwan. But the advancing Red Army causes a change in plans and they're saved! Sounds politically turgid but isn't, thanks to naturalistic acting and dialog. Completed just before the revolution, the film was censored by the Nationalist Kuomintang government but cuts were restored when the Communists came to power. Mandarin with subtitles. **108m/B; VHS, DVD.** *CH* Zhao Dan; Wu Yin; Wei Heling; Daolin Sun; Li Tianji; Ouyang Yunzhu; *D:* Zheng Junli; *W:* Zhao Dan; Zheng Junli; *C:* Miao Zhenhua; Hu Zhenhua; *M:* Wang Yunjie.

Crows Zero ✗✗ 1/2 *Crows: Episode Zero; Kurozu Zero* **2007** Based on the Japanese comic "Crows," and directed by Takashi Miike (without his usual over the top violence and freakishness) this is the story of Suzuran High School, one of the most brutal schools in the nation. Its students spend more time fighting for supremacy in their gangs than learning anything. Newcomer Genji Takaya (Oguri) intends to make his own gang and conquer the school to gain the respect of his Yakuza father. Which obviously won't set well with the other gangs. **129m/C; DVD.** *JP* Shun Oguri; Meisa Kuroki; Takayuki Yamada; Kenichi Endo; Goro Kishitani; Kyosuke Yabe; Sansei Shiomi; *D:* Takashi Miike; *W:* Hiroshi Takahashi; Shogo Muto; *C:* Takumi Furuya; *M:* Naoki Otsubo.

The Crucible ✗✗✗ **1996 (PG-13)** Mass hysteria reigns in 17th century Salem, Mass., when a group of teenaged girls, caught performing heathen rituals in the woods, concoct an elaborate story to exonerate themselves by whipping the town into a witch-hunting frenzy. Chief liar is Abigail Williams (Ryder), who was cast aside by married farmer John Proctor (Day-Lewis), for whom she still lusts. The deranged lass puts her dubious talents into getting Proctor's wife (Allen) out of the picture. Director Hytner demanded authentic period reproduction, down to the finest detail. Impressive cast does justice to the story, especially Scofield's delightfully odious Judge Danforth. Based on Miller's 1953 play which, not so coincidentally, opened during the communist witch hunts of the early 1950s. Screenwriter Miller willingly slashed dialogue from his original work for cinematic purposes. Filmed at the remote wildlife sanctuary of Hog Island, Massachusetts. **123m/C; VHS, DVD, Blu-Ray.** Daniel Day-Lewis; Winona Ryder; Paul Scofield; Joan Allen; Bruce Davison; Jeffrey Jones; Rob Campbell; Peter Vaughan; Karron Graves; Charlaine Woodard; Frances Conroy; Elizabeth Lawrence; George Gaynes; *D:* Nicholas Hytner; *W:* Arthur Miller; *C:* Andrew Dunn; *M:* George Fenton. British Acad. '96: Support. Actor (Scofield); Broadcast Film Critics '96: Support. Actress (Allen).

Crucible of Horror ✗✗ *Velvet House; The Corpse* **1969** Chilling story of a terrorized wife, who, along with her daughter, plots to murder her sadistic husband to end his abusive treatment of them. However, he isn't yet ready to die and comes back to drive them mad. **91m/C; VHS, DVD, Blu-Ray.** *GB* Michael Gough; Yvonne Mitchell; Sharon Gurney; David Butler; Simon Gough; Nicholas Jones; Olaf Pooley; Mary Hignett; *D:* Viktors Ritelis; *W:* Olaf Pooley; *C:* John Mackey.

Crucible of Terror **WOOF!** **1972** Mad sculptor covers beautiful models with hot wax, then imprisons them in a mold of bronze. **95m/C; VHS, DVD.** *GB* Mike Raven; Mary Maude; James Bolam; John Arnatt; Ronald Lacey; Judy Matheson; Me Me Lai; Melissa Stribling; Beth Morris; *D:* Ted Hooker; *W:* Ted Hooker; Tom Parkinson; *C:* Peter Newbrook.

The Crucifer of Blood ✗ 1/2 **1991** A disappointing Sherlock Holmes yarn. Heston is adequate as the Baker Street sleuth, but the mystery—about two retired British soldiers who share an accursed secret and a vengeful comrade—unreels clumsily in the form of flashbacks that give away most of the puzzle from the start. Interesting only in that Dr. Watson has a love affair, more or less. Adapted from a play (and looking like it) by Paul Giovanni, inspired by Arthur Conan Doyle's "The Sign of Four." **105m/C; VHS, DVD.** Charlton Heston; Richard Johnson; Susannah Harker; John Castle; Clive Wood; Simon Callow; Edward Fox; *D:* Fraser Heston. **CABLE**

Crude: The Real Price of Oil ✗✗ 1/2 **2009** Created by award-winning filmmaker Joe Belinger, this feature-length documentary provides the backstory to the biggest oil-related environmental lawsuit ever to be brought at $27 billion. Focusing on a controversial case known as the

"Amazon Chernobyl," this environmental disaster took place in the rainforests of Ecuador. The disaster and the case are explored from many angles, including the environmental aspect, global politics, celebrity activism, human rights, the media, corporate power, human suffering, and indigenous culture. **100m/C; DVD.** ***D:*** Joe Berlinger; ***C:*** Joe Berlinger; Pocho Alvarez; Michael Bonfiglio; Juan Diego Perez; ***M:*** Wendy Blackstone.

Cruel and Unusual *Watchtower* **2001 (R)** Adam Turrell (Berenger) comes to stay in a quiet Oregon fishing town, introducing himself as an English professor working on a first novel. He befriends sister and brother Kate (Hayward) and Mike (Runyan) O'Connor whose father has recently died. But their friendship takes a terrifying turn since Adam isn't at all what he seems. **100m/C; VHS, DVD.** Tom Berenger; Rachel Hayward; Tygh Runyan; Mitchell Kosterman; ***D:*** George Mihalka; ***W:*** Robert Geoffrion; Rod Browning; Dan Witt; ***C:*** Peter Benison; ***M:*** Michel Cusson. **VIDEO**

Cruel Intentions 1/2 **1998 (R)** Fourth film adaptation of Choderlos de Loclos's 1782 novel "Les Liaisons Dangereuses" takes the tale of seduction and intrigue from the 18th century French court to a modern Manhattan prep school. Think "I Know Who You Did Last Summer." Gellar plays teen vamp Kathryn, who bets her stepbrother Sebastian (Phillipe) a night of passion against his car that he can't deflower the virginal Annette (Witherspoon). The overall effect is like the characters' lives: full of guilty pleasures. **95m/C; VHS, DVD, Blu-Ray, UMD.** Sarah Michelle Gellar; Ryan Phillippe; Reese Witherspoon; Selma Blair; Joshua Jackson; Eric Mabius; Louise Fletcher; Swoosie Kurtz; Christine Baranski; Sean Patrick Thomas; ***D:*** Roger Kumble; ***W:*** Roger Kumble; ***C:*** Theo van de Sande; ***M:*** Ed Shearmur. MTV Movie Awards '00: Female Perf. (Gellar), Kiss (Sarah Michelle Gellar/Selma Blair).

Cruel Intentions 2 *Manchester Prep* **1999 (R)** A prequel to the 1998 release finds a rather precocious 16-year-old Sebastian deciding to become a one-woman guy—in this case to naive Danielle, the high school headmaster's daughter. However, his new stepsister Katherine has other adventures in mind. This was intended as the pilot to a TV series (based on the film) that was cancelled before it aired. **87m/C; VHS, DVD.** Amy Adams; Mimi Rogers; Robin Dunne; Sarah Thompson; Keri Lynn Pratt; David McIlwraith; ***D:*** Roger Kumble; ***W:*** Roger Kumble; ***C:*** James R. Bagdonas. **TV**

Cruel Intentions 3 1/2 **2004 (R)** Gratuitous, rehashed third version in which the scene has shifted to an exclusive southern California college. All-new fiendish players Cassidy (Anapau), Jason (Smith), and Patrick (Wetherington) use their considerable free time plotting and pursuing sexual conquests with others and among themselves. **85m/C; VHS, DVD.** Kerr Smith; Natalie Ramsey; Tom Parker; Kristina Anapau; Nathan Wetherington; Melissa Yvonne Lewis; ***D:*** Scott Ziehl; ***W:*** Rhett Reese; ***C:*** Thomas Callaway; ***M:*** David Reynolds. **VIDEO**

Cruel Restaurant *Zankoku Hoten* **2008** Ms. Lin's (Mihiro Taniguchi) dumpling restaurant is the darling of the town and people will do anything to get them. When people start dying or going nuts, the local restaurant reviewer and cops think she's behind the murders and that the secret ingredient is actually people. Despite sounding like a horror mystery, it's actually supposed to be something of an erotic comedy and the female lead is naked for most of the film. **75m/C; DVD.** Mihiro; Sakae Yamazaki; Katsuya Naruse; Yusuke Iwata; Miho Funatsu; Toshiyuki Teranaka; Chihiro Koganezaki; Kesuke; ***D:*** Koji Kawano; ***W:*** Satoshi Owada; Koji Kawano.

The Cruel Sea **1953** Well-made documentary-like account of a Royal Navy corvette on convoy duty in the Atlantic during WWII. **121m/B; VHS, DVD.** *GB* Jack Hawkins; Stanley Baker; Denholm Elliott; Virginia McKenna; ***D:*** Charles Frend; ***W:*** Eric Ambler.

Cruel World **WOOF!** **2005 (R)** Grubby and stupid. Philip (Furlong) goes psycho over being dumped by Catherine (Pressly in an extended cameo) on the finale of their reality TV show. So he decides to create his own show, using an isolated mansion and enticing a group of college kids who don't realize that the elimination round is literal and permanent. **92m/C; DVD, Blu-Ray.** Edward Furlong; Andrew Keegan; Susan Ward; Joel Michaely; Sanoe Lake; Brian Geraghty; Daniel Franzese; Laura Ramsey; Jaime Pressly; ***D:*** Kelsey T. Howard; ***W:*** Eugene Hess; Paul Lawrence; Paul T. Murray; ***C:*** Ward Russell. **VIDEO**

Cruise **2018** In the summer of 1987 in Queens, New York, Gio (Boldman) is a working class, Italian American bad boy who commits petty thefts and competes in drag races. His world is turned upside down when he meets Jessica (Ratajkowski). She is an upper class Jewish good girl who attends Brown University. Their differences initially keep them apart, but Gio goes to extraordinary lengths to get them together. This exercise in nostalgia faithfully captures a time and place, but the story it tells does not have the same attention to detail nor does it explore the relationship between Gio and Jessica in a meaningful way. **90m/C; DVD.** Emily Ratajkowski; Kathrine Narducci; Sebastian Maniscalco; Spencer Boldman; Noah Robbins; ***D:*** Robert Siegel; ***W:*** Robert Siegel; ***C:*** Noah Greenberg; ***M:*** Jay Wadley.

Cruising **1980 (R)** Rookie cop Pacino is deep undercover investigating the bizarre murders of homosexuals in New York's West Village by delving into leather bars and underground clubs. Sexually explicit but less than suspenseful mystery. Release was sensationalized, with many gay rights groups voicing loud disapproval of the sordid gay characterization, while others feared copy-cat crimes. Excellent NYC cinematography. **102m/C; DVD, Blu-Ray.** Al Pacino; Paul Sorvino; Karen Allen; Powers Boothe; Richard Cox; James Remar; Mike Starr; Don Scardino; Joe Spinell; Ed O'Neill; Barton Heyman; William Russ; ***D:*** William Friedkin; ***W:*** William Friedkin; ***C:*** James A. Contner; ***M:*** Jack Nitzsche.

Crumb **1994 (R)** Countercultural documentary looking at the life of underground cartoonist Robert Crumb?'60s satirist and social misfit who created such drug and sex characters as Fritz the Cat and Mr. Natural. Crumb's extraordinarily dysfunctional family play a significant role, with his mother and two brothers, elder brother Charles and younger brother Max, also interviewed as well as Crumb's friends and current and former wives. The dead abusive father also plays a part. Director Zwigoff spent six years filming his material, and gained wider distribution for his work after taking the Grand Jury prize at Sundance. **119m/C; VHS, DVD, Blu-Ray.** Robert Crumb; ***D:*** Terry Zwigoff; ***C:*** Maryse Alberti. Directors Guild '95: Documentary Director (Zwigoff); Natl. Soc. Film Critics '95: Feature Doc.; Sundance '95: Cinematog., Grand Jury Prize.

Crusade: A March through Time *Crusade in Jeans* **2006 (PG)** Fifteen-year-old Dolf Vega's (Flynn) mother (Watson) works at a research center testing an actual time machine. When Dolf blows his soccer team's championship by missing a goal, Dolf thinks it would be easy to go back a few hours for a do-over. Oopsy! An error sends him back to the year 1212 instead! Dolf is rescued from bandits by Jenne (Leonidas), who is part of the Children's Crusade to Jerusalem, but a betrayal will put the pilgrimage in danger. **100m/C; DVD.** *GE* Joe Flynn; Stephanie Leonidas; Emily Watson; Michael Culkin; Benno Furmann; ***D:*** Ben Sombogaart; ***W:*** Bill Haney; ***C:*** Reinier van Brummelen; ***M:*** Jurre Haanstra.

The Crusader 1/2 **1932** The title character is crusading District Attorney Phillip Brandon (Warner), who's giving the local crooks fits. They first try blackmail because Brandon's wife Tess (Brent) is a woman with a past. When a murder is committed, Tess's ex-sweetheart, bootlegger Jimmie (Cody), unexpectedly comes to the rescue. Creaky early talkie is pre-Production Code with a liberal use of salty language. **65m/B; DVD.** H.B. Warner; Evelyn Brent; Marceline Day; Lew Cody; Ned Sparks; Walter Byron; ***D:*** Frank Strayer; ***W:*** Edward T. Lowe.

The Crusades 1/2 **1935** Typical DeMille extravaganza, loosely based on the Third Crusade, which finds Richard the Lionheart (Wilcoxon) and the armies of Europe battling Saladin and the Mahammedan horde in order to reclaim Jerusalem. Meanwhile, Richard marries by proxy in order to gain supplies for his men—something that enrages his bride Berengaria (Young). Once he realizes how beautiful she is, Richard tries to win her love. Obviously, not historically accurate and it's all secondary to the battle scenes, anyway. Based on the Harold Lamb book "The Crusade: Iron Men and Saints." **126m/B; DVD.** Henry Wilcoxon; Loretta Young; Sir C. Aubrey Smith; Ian Keith; Katherine DeMille; Joseph Schildkraut; Alan Hale; C. Henry Gordon; George Barbier; Lumsden Hare; William Farnum; Hobart Bosworth; Montagu Love; Pedro de Cordoba; Mischa Auer; ***D:*** Cecil B. DeMille; ***W:*** Waldemar Young; Dudley Nichols; Harold Lamb; ***C:*** Victor Milner; ***M:*** Rudolph Kopp.

Crush **1993** Christina is a local New Zealand literary critic on her way to interview Colin, a reclusive novelist. Along for the ride is her seductive American friend Lane who manages to crash the car but walk away with hardly a scratch. Christina appears to be dead and Lane abandons her, finding her way to the home Colin shares with his teenage daughter Angela. Lane promptly sets out to seduce Colin, making Angela jealous, (oh, and Christina's not dead after all). Poor script finds the characters actions baffling and why Lane is so wildly attractive is never apparent. **97m/C; VHS, DVD.** *NZ* Marcia Gay Harden; Donough Rees; William Zappa; Caitlin Bossley; ***D:*** Alison Maclean; ***W:*** Alison Maclean; Anne Kennedy; ***C:*** Dion Beebe.

The Crush 1/2 **1993 (R)** Wealthy 14-year-old temptress Silverstone (in her debut) develops an obsessive crush on handsome 28-year-old Elwes, who rents her family's guest house. In an attempt to win his heart, she rewrites his poorly composed magazine articles. This doesn't convince him they should mate for life, so she sabotages his apartment to vent her rage. Sound familiar? The plot's lifted right out of "Fatal Attraction" and Shapiro doesn't offer viewers anything inventively different. He does manage to substitute new methods for the spurned lover to snare her prey. Limp plot would have been exciting if we hadn't seen it so many times before. **89m/C; VHS, DVD, Blu-Ray.** Cary Elwes; Alicia Silverstone; Jennifer Rubin; Kurtwood Smith; Gwynyth Walsh; Amber Benson; ***D:*** Alan Shapiro; ***W:*** Alan Shapiro; ***C:*** Bruce Surtees; ***M:*** Graeme Revell. MTV Movie Awards '94: Breakthrough Perf. (Silverstone), Villain (Silverstone).

Crush **2002 (R)** A "with friends like these, who needs enemies" movie that leaves a sour aftertaste. Kate (MacDowell), Janine (Staunton), and Molly (Chancellor) are three professional women in their 40s who live in a small English town and meet weekly to drink and commiserate about their lousy love lives. That is, until sexily repressed American headmistress Kate sets off sparks with hottie twentysomething Jed (Doughty), an organist and former pupil. Her friends are outraged and turn distinctly nasty trying to break up the happy twosome. Maybe they're jealous that Kate is having great sex and they're not. **115m/C; VHS, DVD.** *GB* Andie MacDowell; Imelda Staunton; Anna Chancellor; Kenny Doughty; Bill Paterson; ***D:*** John McKay; ***W:*** John McKay; ***C:*** Henry Braham; ***M:*** Kevin Sargent.

Crush 1/2 **2009 (R)** Psycho-thriller with some supernatural elements. American Julian (Egan) is in Perth on a student visa when he gets a house-sitting job at a spectacular mansion. Also in residence is the owner's provocative niece Anna (Lung) who rapidly becomes obsessed with Julian, causing his life to unravel. **82m/C; DVD.** *AU* Christopher Egan; Emma Lung; Brooke Harmon; Christian Clark; Jenna Lind; ***D:*** John V. Soto; Jeffrey Gerritsen; ***W:*** John V. Soto; ***C:*** Richard Malins; ***M:*** Jamie Blanks.

Crush 1/2 **2013 (PG-13)** The shy new girl in town develops an obsessive crush on a local sports star in what looks like 'Fatal Attraction' remade for the teen set. **94m/C; DVD, Blu-Ray, Streaming.** Sarah Bolger; Holt McCallany; Lucas Till; Crystal Reed; Isaiah Mustafa; ***D:*** Malik Bader; ***W:*** Sonny Mallhi; ***C:*** Scott Kevan; ***M:*** Julian Boyd. **VIDEO**

Crusoe 1/2 **1989 (PG-13)** A lushly photographed version of the Daniel Defoe classic. Crusoe is an arrogant slave trader stranded on a desert island populated by unfriendly natives. Themes of prejudice, fear, and choice appear in this never-padded, thoughtful film. Quinn gives an excellent performance as the stranded slave-trader. **94m/C; VHS, DVD; Open Captioned.** Aidan Quinn; Ade Sapara; Jimmy Nail; Timothy Spall; Colin Bruce; Michael Higgins; Shane Rimmer; Hepburn Grahame; ***D:*** Caleb Deschanel; ***W:*** Walon Green; Christopher Logue; ***M:*** Michael Kamen.

Crutch 1/2 **2004 (R)** Sixteen-year-old David (Gordon) must deal with his alcoholic mom Katie (Walsh), who's forced into rehab after an accident. This leaves David vulnerable to the predatory desires of his 30-something drama teacher, Kenny (Moretti), who also introduces the impulsive, lonely teen to drugs. Unsettling story based on Moretti's own experiences. **88m/C; DVD.** Rob Moretti; Eben Gordon; Juanita Walsh; James Earley; ***D:*** Rob Moretti; ***W:*** Rob Moretti; Paul Jacks; ***C:*** Brian Fass; ***M:*** Ben Goldberg.

Cry-Baby **1990 (PG-13)** An homage and spoof of '50s teen-rock melodramas by the doyen of cinematic Bad Taste, involving a terminal bad-boy high schooler who goes with a square blond and starts an inter-class rumble. Musical numbers, throwaway gags and plenty of knee-bending to Elvis, with a weak story supported by offbeat celeb appearances. **85m/C; VHS, DVD, Blu-Ray.** Johnny Depp; Amy Locane; Polly Bergen; Traci Lords; Ricki Lake; Iggy Pop; Susan Tyrrell; Patty (Patricia Campbell) Hearst; Kim McGuire; Darren E. Burrows; Troy Donahue; Willem Dafoe; David Nelson; Mink Stole; Joe Dallesandro; Joey Heatherton; Robert Walsh; Mary Vivian Pearce; ***D:*** John Waters; ***W:*** John Waters; ***C:*** David Insley; ***M:*** Patrick Williams.

Cry Blood, Apache **1970 (R)** An old man (Joel McCrae) remembers when, as a young man (Jody McCrae), he and his sadistic friends massacred a group of Apaches and were hunted by the husband of one of their victims. It's violent but not as sadistic as some. **90m/C; DVD.** Joel McCrea; Jody McCrea; Robert Tessier; Marie Gahva; Don Henley; ***D:*** Jack Starrett; ***W:*** Sean McGregor; ***C:*** Bruce Scott; ***M:*** Elliot Kaplan.

Cry Danger **1951** A falsely imprisoned man is released from jail, and he searches for those who framed him. **80m/B; DVD, Blu-Ray.** Dick Powell; Rhonda Fleming; William Conrad; Richard Erdman; Regis Toomey; ***D:*** Robert Parrish; ***W:*** William Bowers; ***C:*** Joseph Biroc; ***M:*** Emil Newman; Paul Dunlap.

Cry Freedom 1/2 **1987 (PG)** A romantic look at the short life of South African activist Steven Biko, and his friendship with the white news editor, Donald Woods. The film focuses on Woods' escape from Africa while struggling to bring Biko's message to the world. Based on a true story. **157m/C; VHS, DVD.** Kevin Kline; Denzel Washington; Penelope Wilton; Kevin McNally; John Thaw; Timothy West; John Hargreaves; Alec McCowen; Zakes Mokae; Ian Richardson; Juanita Waterman; ***D:*** Richard Attenborough; ***W:*** John Briley; ***C:*** Ronnie Taylor; ***M:*** George Fenton; Jonas Gwangwa.

A Cry from the Streets **1957** Drama about the plight of orphan children and dedicated social workers in England. **100m/C; VHS, DVD.** *GB* Max Bygraves; Barbara Murray; Kathleen Harrison; Colin Petersen; ***D:*** Lewis Gilbert; ***M:*** Larry Adler.

Cry Havoc 1/2 **1943** A different look at WWII with an all-female cast. In 1942 on the Bataan Peninsula, Army head nurse Lt. Mary Smith (Sullavan) is in charge of an inexperienced staff of civilian volunteers who do the best they can to aid G.I. casualties. The pic primarily takes place in the women's quarters as they talk about their lives and the war, especially when the Japanese start bombing and an invasion of the island will soon commence. Based on the play by Allan Kenward. **97m/B; DVD.** Margaret Sullavan; Joan Blondell; Ann Sothern; Fay Bainter; Marsha Hunt; Ella Raines; Frances Gifford; Diana Lewis; Connie Gilchrist; ***D:*** Richard Thorpe; ***W:*** Paul Osborn; ***C:*** Karl Freund; ***M:*** Daniele Amfitheatrof.

A Cry in the Dark 1/2 *Evil Angels* **1988 (PG-13)** Tight film story of the infamous Australian murder trial of Lindy Chamberlain (Streep), who was accused of killing her own baby, mostly because of the intensely adverse public opinion, aroused by vicious press, that surrounded the case. Chamberlain blamed the death on a wild dingo dog, which dragged off the baby from where the family was camped. Near-documentary style, with Streep excellent as the religious, unknowable mother. Based on the book "Evil Angels" by John Bryson. This case was also detailed in the film "Who Killed Baby Azaria?" **120m/C; VHS, DVD.** *AU* Meryl Streep; Sam Neill; Bruce Myles; Charles "Bud" Tingwell; Nick (Nicholas) Tate; Neil Fitzpatrick; Maurice Fields; Lewis Fitz-Gerald; Tony (Anthony) Martin; ***D:*** Fred Schepisi; ***W:*** Fred Schepisi; Robert Caswell; ***C:*** Ian Baker; ***M:*** Bruce Smeaton. Australian Film Inst. '89: Actor (Neill), Actress (Streep), Film; Cannes '89: Actress (Streep); N.Y. Film Critics '88: Actress (Streep).

A Cry in the Wild 🦴🦴🦴 **1990 (PG)** A 14-year-old boy must find his way back to civilization when he's the lone survivor of an airplane crash. Strong acting from Rushton, excellent nature photography make this well used story work again. **93m/C; VHS, DVD.** Jared Rushton; Ned Beatty; Pamela Sue Martin; Stephen Meadows; ***D:*** Mark Griffiths; ***W:*** Catherine Cyran; ***C:*** Gregg Heschong; ***M:*** Arthur Kempel.

The Cry: La Llorona 🦴 ½ **2007 (R)** Overly-ambitious horror story that's a retelling of the Mexican folktale about a woman who drowns her children and then haunts other mothers to do the same. The story is relocated to NYC where detectives Scott (Carmargo) and Perez (Leon) are assigned to a series of child murders and disappearances. Scott is also still dealing with the trauma of his own son being drowned by his late wife. Meanwhile, single mom Maria (Dominguez) has visions and keeps sketching pictures of the missing kids. Afraid for her own son, she whisks him off to Central Park after leaving a cryptic message for the detectives. The various strands of the story don't come together very well and the plot falls completely apart in the last act. **80m/C; DVD.** Carlos Leon; Adriana Dominguez; Miriam Colon; Christian Carmargo; ***D:*** Bernadine Santistevan; ***W:*** Bernadine Santistevan; Monique Salazar; ***C:*** Richard Lopez; ***M:*** Dean Parker. **VIDEO**

Cry of a Prostitute: Love Kills 🦴 **1972 (R)** Former prostitute joins with a professional assassin in an effort to pacify rival gangsters in Italy. **86m/C; VHS, DVD, Blu-Ray.** Henry Silva; Barbara Bouchet; ***D:*** Andrea Bianchi.

Cry of Battle 🦴🦴 ½ *To Be a Man* **1963** Anxious for the challenges of manhood, a well-heeled young man joins a guerrilla militia in the Philippines. **99m/B; VHS, DVD.** Van Heflin; Rita Moreno; James MacArthur; ***D:*** Irving Lerner.

Cry of the Banshee 🦴🦴 ½ **1970 (PG)** Witch-hunter Price and family are tormented by Satanic powers seeking revenge. Superior horror period piece. **87m/C; VHS, DVD, Blu-Ray.** *GB* Vincent Price; Elisabeth Bergner; Essy Persson; Hugh Griffith; Hilary Dwyer; Sally Geeson; Patrick Mower; Marshall Jones; Michael Elphick; Pamela Fairbrother; Robert Hutton; ***D:*** Gordon Hessler; ***W:*** Christopher Wicking; Tim Kelly; ***C:*** John Coquillon; ***M:*** Les Baxter.

Cry of the City 🦴🦴 ½ *The Chair for Martin Rome* **1948** Detective Landella (Victor Mature) confronts his bedridden nemesis Martin Rome (Richard Conte), trying to figure out if Rome is responsible for a jewel heist gone wrong. As usual with film-noir, things are definitely not black and white. **95m/B; DVD, Blu-Ray.** Victor Mature; Richard Conte; Shelley Winters; Debra Paget; Fred Clark; ***D:*** Robert Siodmak; ***W:*** Richard Murphy; Ben Hecht; ***C:*** Lloyd Ahern; ***M:*** Alfred Newman.

Cry of the Innocent 🦴🦴🦴 **1980** An action-packed thriller about a Vietnam veteran who is out to find a group of Irish terrorists that killed his family. **93m/C; VHS, DVD.** Cyril Cusack; Alexander Knox; Rod Taylor; Joanna Pettet; Nigel Davenport; ***D:*** Michael O'Herlihy.

The Cry of the Owl 🦴🦴 *Le Cri du Hibou* **1987** Robert (Malavoy) has divorced the dreadful Veronique (Thevenet) and struck up a friendship with Juliette (May). He admires the way her life seems so satisfied and orderly but Juliette decides she doesn't like this idea of herself and impulsively drops her swinish fiance Patrick (Penot) and pursues Robert instead. But Robert is only interested in friendship, leading to some very twisted revenge plots. Suspenseful look at what obsessions can drive people to do. Adapted from the novel by Patricia Highsmith. In French with English subtitles. **102m/C; VHS, DVD.** *FR IT* Christophe MaLavoy; Mathilda May; Virginie Thevenet; Jacques Penot; Jean-Pierre Kalfon; Patrice Kerbrat; ***D:*** Claude Chabrol; ***W:*** Claude Chabrol; Odile Barski; ***C:*** Jean Rabier; ***M:*** Matthieu Chabrol.

The Cry of the Owl 🦴 **2009 (R)** Depressed and recently divorced Robert Forrester (Considine) moves to a small town in search of peace. He suddenly takes to peeping in the kitchen window of Jenny (Stiles), who befriends Robert when she catches him looking. That's 'cause Jenny is kinda weird and has just broken up with her boyfriend Greg (Gilbert). And then Robert's manipulative ex Nickie (Dhavernas) gets into the mix. The interactions between the characters seem forced and clumsy and the movie isn't nearly as well-thought out as its source material—the 1962 novel by Patricia Highsmith. **99m/C; DVD.** *CA* Paddy Considine; Julia Stiles; Caroline Dhavernas; James Gilbert; Karl Pruner; Gordon Rand; ***D:*** Jamie Thraves; ***C:*** Luc Montpellier; ***M:*** Jeff Danna. **VIDEO**

Cry of the Penguins 🦴🦴 ½ *Mr. Forbush and the Penguins* **1971** Womanizing biologist Forbush (Hurt) heads off on an Antartic expedition to study penguins when his would-be romance with Tara (Mills) comes to naught. Beautiful photography, shallow story. Adapted from the novel "Mr. Forbush and the Penguins" by Graham Billing. Note the similarities with "Never Cry Wolf." **105m/C; VHS, DVD.** *GB* John Hurt; Hayley Mills; Dudley Sutton; Tony Britton; Thorley Walters; Judy Campbell; Joss Ackland; Nicholas Pennell; ***D:*** Albert T. Viola; ***W:*** Anthony Shaffer; ***M:*** John Addison.

Cry Panic 🦴🦴 **1974** A man is thrown into a strange series of events after accidentally running down a man on a highway. **74m/C; VHS, DVD.** John Forsythe; Anne Francis; Earl Holliman; Claudia McNeil; Ralph Meeker; ***D:*** James Goldstone. **TV**

Cry Rape! 🦴🦴 **1973** Starts off strong then sharply changes direction into a wrong man story. Betty Jenner (Marcovicci) is raped and then further victimized by the cops and the court. She identifies her attacker in a lineup but subsequent badgering by the defense has Betty questioning whether the accused is the right man. **73m/C; DVD.** Andrea Marcovicci; Peter Coffield; Greg Mullavey; Joseph Sirola; James Luisi; Robert Hogan; Whit Bissell; ***D:*** Corey Allen; ***W:*** Will Lorin; ***C:*** Jack Woolf. **TV**

Cry Terror! 🦴🦴 **1958** Jim Molner's (Mason) electronics expertise is exploited by ex-Army buddy and demolitions expert Paul Hoplin (Steiger). He's planted a bomb aboard a plane and is demanding a ransom not to detonate it while holding Jim and his family hostage to get his way. The FBI is onto everyone involved and the twisted story ends in a New York subway. **96m/B; DVD.** James Mason; Rod Steiger; Inger Stevens; Angie Dickinson; Neville Brand; Jack Klugman; Terry Ann Ross; Kenneth Tobey; Jack Kruschen; Carleton Young; ***D:*** Andrew L. Stone; ***W:*** Andrew L. Stone; ***C:*** Walter Strenge; ***M:*** Howard Jackson.

Cry, the Beloved Country 🦴🦴🦴 **1995 (PG-13)** Alan Paton's classic South African apartheid novel (first filmed in 1951) depicts a Zulu Christian pastor and a wealthy white farmer finding common ground through personal loss—both of their sons were killed in regional violence. Rural black minister Stephen Kumalo (Jones), travels to Johannesburg only to discover his sister (Kente) is a prostitute, his younger brother John (Dutton) no longer believes in Christianity and his son is in prison for the murder of a white man. That man turns out to be the son of rich farmer James Jarvis (Harris), from Kumalo's own village. Both Jones and Harris turn in wonderfully understated performances in this hopeful tale of potential racial harmony. **120m/C; VHS, DVD.** *SA* James Earl Jones; Richard Harris; Charles S. Dutton; Leleti Khumalo; Dambisa Kente; Vusi Kunene; Eric Miyeni; Ian Robers; ***D:*** Darrell Roodt; ***W:*** Ronald Atwood; ***C:*** Paul Gilpin; ***M:*** John Barry.

Cry Uncle 🦴 ½ **1971 (R)** Comic account of a private eye who investigates a blackmailing case involving a film of orgies in which, much to his chagrin, he participated. **85m/C; VHS, DVD.** Allen Garfield; Paul Sorvino; Devin Goldenberg; Madeleine Le Roux; ***D:*** John G. Avildsen; ***W:*** David Odell; ***C:*** John G. Avildsen; ***M:*** Harper Mckay.

Cry Wolf 🦴🦴 **1947** Weak mystery thriller places Stanwyck in creepy environs when she goes to claim her inheritance from her late husband's estate. Based on the novel by Marjorie Carleton. **83m/B; VHS, DVD.** Errol Flynn; Barbara Stanwyck; Richard Basehart; Geraldine Brooks; Jerome Cowan; John Ridgely; Patricia Barry; ***D:*** Peter Godfrey; ***W:*** Catherine Turney.

Cry Wolf 🦴🦴 **2005 (PG-13)** Bored trust-funders at a boarding school start up an internet game of spreading stories and rumors. The game turns serious when someone makes up a story about a serial killer and people start turning up dead. Twisty plot goes for sleight-of-hand and visceral thrills, and doesn't completely fail. But it's all only mildly effective. Typical slasher fare might keep you entertained but won't register past the final credits. **90m/C; DVD.** Lindy Booth; Jared Padalecki; Kristy Wu; Paul James; Julian Morris; Sandra McCoy; Jon Bon Jovi; Gary Cole; Jesse Janzen; Anna Deavere Smith; ***D:*** Jeff Wadlow; ***W:*** Jeff Wadlow; Beau Bauman; ***C:*** Romeo Tirone; ***M:*** Michael Wandmacher.

The Crying Game 🦴🦴🦴 ½ **1992 (R)** PR lesson in how to launch a small movie into the hypersphere and ensure critical silence on salient characterization. Jordan's gritty drama is on par with his best, a complex blend of violence, love, betrayal, guilt, and redemption and is not about what it seems to be about much of the time. Wonderful performances by all, including Rea as the appealing, conscience-stricken Fergus; Richardson as the cold, violent IRA moll Jude; and Davidson, in a film debut, as the needy, charismatic Dil. Whitaker is terrific in his 15 minutes of intense screen time. Filled with definite surprises and unexpected pleasures. Title is taken from a top-5 British hit of 1964, three versions of which are heard. **112m/C; VHS, DVD.** *IR* Stephen Rea; Jaye Davidson; Miranda Richardson; Forest Whitaker; Adrian Dunbar; Jim Broadbent; Ralph Brown; Breffini McKenna; Joe Savino; Birdy Sweeney; Andre Bernard; ***D:*** Neil Jordan; ***W:*** Neil Jordan; ***C:*** Ian Wilson; ***M:*** Anne Dudley. Oscars '92: Orig. Screenplay; Australian Film Inst. '93: Foreign Film; Ind. Spirit '93: Foreign Film; L.A. Film Critics '92: Foreign Film; N.Y. Film Critics '92: Screenplay, Support. Actress (Richardson); Natl. Soc. Film Critics '92: Actor (Rea); Writers Guild '92: Orig. Screenplay.

Crypt of Dark Secrets 🦴 **1976 (R)** Vietnam veteran recovering from wounds in the Louisiana swamps encounters a friendly Indian spirit who saves him from death. **100m/C; VHS, DVD.** Maureen Chan; Ronald Tanet; Wayne Mack; Herbert G. Jahncke; ***D:*** Jack Weis.

Crypt of the Living Dead WOOF! **1973 (PG)** An undead woman from the 13th century makes life miserable for visitors on Vampire Island. **75m/C; VHS, DVD, Blu-Ray.** Andrew Prine; Mark Damon; Teresa Gimpera; Patty (Patti) Shepard; Francisco (Frank) Brana; ***D:*** Ray Danton.

Crypto 🦴🦴 **2019 (R)** Martin Duran (Knapp), is a New York City-based cybersecurity agent who distanced himself from his farmer father (Russell) and veteran brother (Hemsworth) after the death of his mother a decade ago. After a conflict with his NYC superiors, he is assigned to a branch in his upstate New York hometown. Connecting with cryptocurrency-supporting childhood friend Earl (Harris), Martin learns about potential fraud and money laundering through a local business, and draws the attention of the Russian mafia. Though the thriller has a brand name cast and focuses on cryptocurrency, most of the high profile actors have only small roles and has a predictable plot. **105m/C; DVD, Blu-Ray.** Beau Knapp; Alexis Bledel; Luke Hemsworth; Kurt Russell; Jeremie Harris; ***D:*** John Stalberg, Jr.; ***W:*** Carlyle Eubank; David Frigerio; ***C:*** Pieter Vermeer; ***M:*** Nima Fakhrara.

Crystal Fairy & the Magical Cactus 🦴🦴 **2013** After money ran out on another production that Cera and Silva were making in Chile (Magic Magic), the guys made this lark of a road trip movie while waiting for the cash on their other production to come in. The result is a "hey, let's make a movie!" in the haphazard approach to storytelling. But that risk-taking can be sometimes infectious, especially in the charming performance from Hoffman as the girl who won't leave Cera's against-type jerk and his travelling buddies alone. Secrets are revealed, drugs are taken, and the whole thing sometimes gets as annoying as being on a real road trip gone awry would be. **98m/C; DVD, Blu-Ray.** *CL* Michael Cera; Gaby Hoffman; Juan Andres Silva; Jose Miguel Silva; Augustin Silva; Sebastian Silva; ***D:*** Sebastian Silva; ***W:*** Sebastian Silva; ***C:*** Cristian Petit-Laurent; ***M:*** Pedro Subercaseaux.

Crystal Heart 🦴 **1987 (R)** A medically isolated songwriter with an incurable disease falls in love with a lovely rock singer. **103m/C; VHS, DVD.** Lee Curreri; Tawny Kitaen; Lloyd Bochner; ***D:*** Gil Bettman; ***M:*** Joel Goldsmith.

Crystal River 🦴🦴 ½ **2008** Doesn't take the obvious road when examining love and friendship. Davie Nance (Carpenter) is a sweet, respected member of her community with a charitable heart, which is why she looks out for her crotchety elderly neighbor Olin Arrendal (Manson). However, after Davie suffers her fourth miscarriage, she feels lost and estranged from her husband Paul (Pralgo). When Olin's grandson Clay (Flanery), fleeing his own disappointments, comes to stay, Davie finds him easy to talk to, but their budding friendship causes town tongues to wag. **102m/C; DVD.** Sean Patrick Flanery; Ted Manson; Karla Droege; Emily Carpenter; Robert Pralgo; Daniel Burnley; Brandon O'Dell; ***D:*** Brett Levner; ***C:*** Edwin Myers; ***M:*** Woody Pak.

Crystal Swan 🦴🦴🦴 *Khrustal* **2020** In 1996 Minsk, Velya (Nasibullina) works as a DJ and aspires to move to Chicago to work where House music was born. Though her mother is dismissive of her ambitions, Velya tries to get her visa even though she does not have the required steady job. Velya's schemes to work around this truth results in mishaps. The debut film by Zhuk is a delight, full of bold colors, interesting music, and a suspenseful story. Russian with subtitles. **95m/C; DVD.** Alina Nasibullina; Ivan Mulin; Yuriy Borisov; Svetlana Anikey; Ilya Kapanets; ***D:*** Darya Zhuk; ***W:*** Darya Zhuk; Helga Landauer; ***C:*** Carolina Costa. **VIDEO**

Crystalstone 🦴🦴 **1988 (PG)** A wooden cross leads a pair of orphans on a dangerous search for the legendary Crystalstone. **103m/C; VHS, DVD.** Frank Grimes; Kamlesh Gupta; Laura Jane Goodwin; Sydney Bromley; ***D:*** Antonio Pelaez.

CSA: The Confederate States of America 🦴🦴 ½ **2004** Mockumentary ponders the history of the past 150 years had the Confederacy won the Civil War and slavery endured. Told via a faux British public network Ken Burns-type series and presented by Spike Lee. Purposely unsettling, with images like a black-faced Lincoln in hiding as Harriet Tubman helps him to escape to Canada, the picky attention to historical details falls short by presuming such modern events as JFK's presidency and assassination, and the Vietnam War would have really taken place in such a world. **89m/C; DVD.** Charles Frank; Evamarii Johnson; Rupert Pate; Larry J. Peterson; ***C:*** Matthew Jacobson; ***M:*** Kelly Werts.

Cthulhu 🦴 **2008 (R)** An unpronounceable title is just the first problem with this feeble supernatural thriller based on the works of H.P. Lovecraft. Russell March returns to his island home for his mother's funeral. His family consists of various crackpots, including his religious father whose cult-like church believes saving mankind means returning to the sea. Russell's also gay and there are some subplots about an old flame and a female friend, both with sexual designs on Russ, but the whole production is fairly unhinged. **109m/C; DVD.** Cara Buono; Tori Spelling; Greg Michaels; Jason Cottle; Scott Patrick; Dennis Kleinsmith; Nancy Stark; Ian Geoghegan; ***D:*** Daniel Gildark; ***W:*** Grant Cogswell; ***C:*** Sean Kirby; ***M:*** Willy Greer.

Cuba 🦴🦴🦴 **1979 (R)** Cynical, satirical adventure/love story. Mercenary soldier rekindles an old affair during the Castro revolution. Charismatic cast and good direction make for an entertaining, if overlooked, Connery vehicle. **121m/C; VHS, DVD, Blu-Ray.** Sean Connery; Brooke Adams; Jack Weston; Hector Elizondo; Denholm Elliott; Chris Sarandon; Lonette McKee; ***D:*** Richard Lester; ***W:*** Charles Wood; ***C:*** David Watkin; ***M:*** Patrick Williams.

Cuban Blood 🦴🦴 1/2 *Dreaming of Julia* **2003 (PG-13)** Director Gerard's nostalgic semi-autobiographical tale centers around a nameless 8-year-old boy (Mendez) who lives in the town of Holguin, Cuba, in 1958. The boy loves the movies but in the middle of watching the thriller "Julie" (with Doris Day), guerrillas cut the power, foreshadowing the revolution about to take place. This situation eventually leads to a meeting between the boy and a beautiful blonde American woman (Hjejle) who has some unexpected ties to his grandfather, Che (Keitel). **109m/C; DVD.** Harvey Keitel; Iben Hjejle; Gael Garcia Bernal; Andhy Mendez; Diana Bracho; ***V:*** Tony Plana; ***D:*** Juan Gerard; ***W:*** Juan Gerard; Letvia Arza-Goderich; ***C:*** Kramer Morgenthau; ***M:*** Jose Padilla; Edesio Alejandro.

Cuban Fury 🦴🦴 **2014 (R)** Frost gets his first leading role in this mediocre comedy with a likable cast but not much of a script. The regular Simon Pegg collaborator stars as Bruce, the unlikely comeback kid in the world of salsa dancing. O'Dowd is always funny and continues to do good work as Bruce's nemesis, and you can't get two women much more pleasant than Jones and Colman in the supporting cast. So what went wrong? There's a bit of a mean-spirited edge to the humor, even misogynistic, that often leaves a bad taste, but it's mostly just not funny enough to remember. **98m/C; DVD, Blu-Ray.** *UK* Nick Frost; Rashida Jones; Chris O'Dowd; Olivia Colman; Rory Kinnear; Ian McShane; Kayvan Novak; ***D:*** James Griffiths; ***W:*** Jon Brown; ***C:*** Dick Pope; ***M:*** Daniel Pemberton.

Cube 🦴 1/2 **1998 (R)** Claustrophobic sci-fi thriller about six people who inexplicably wake up chained together in a bare room attached to other bare rooms that are fiendishly booby-trapped. They are forced to work together in order to escape. The fact that the bizarro force holding these people hostage is never explained may escape you; since your senses will be dulled by the bad acting and lack of plot. Not as much fun as spending an hour and a half in a refrigerator box. **90m/C; VHS, DVD.** *CA* Maurice Dean Wint; Nicole de Boer; David Hewlett; Wayne Robson; Andrew Miller; Nicky Guadagni; Julian Richings; ***D:*** Vincenzo Natali; ***W:*** Graeme Manson; Vincenzo Natali; Andre Bijelic; ***C:*** Derek Rogers; ***M:*** Mark Korven.

Cube 2: Hypercube 🦴 1/2 *Hypercube* **2002 (R)** The sequel's basically a carbon copy of the first film with a couple more hostages. This time eight people find themselves trapped in a paranormal cube made up of deadly chambers. They struggle to escape and discover their would-be leader, Kate (Matchett), has her own agenda. Yawn. **94m/C; VHS, DVD.** *CA* Kari Matchett; Geraint Wyn Davies; Matthew Ferguson; Neil Crone; Barbara Gordon; Lindsey Connell; Grace Lynn Kung; Greer Kent; ***D:*** Andrzej Sekula; ***W:*** Sean Hood; ***M:*** Norman Orenstein.

Cube: Zero 🦴 1/2 **2004 (R)** Third flick in the series is actually a story prequel that stays pretty close to the formula. Cube tech Wynn (Bennett) falls for Rain (Moore), an unwilling prisoner of the maze. Since Wynn has some idea of what's happening—and is a rebel—he enters the cube to try and rescue her. **94m/C; DVD.** *CA* Zachary Bennett; Stephanie Moore; David Huband; Martin Roach; Michael Riley; Richard McMillan; ***D:*** Ernie Barbarash; ***W:*** Ernie Barbarash; ***C:*** Francois Dagenais; ***M:*** Norman Orenstein.

Cuck 🦴🦴 **2019** Thirtysomething misfit Ronnie (Sherman) lives at home, is underemployed, and has few friends. He is smothered by his overbearing mother (Kirkland) and spends most of his time on alt-right propaganda websites. Ronnie finds his purpose when he goes viral for his right-wing vlog rants. At the same time, he becomes sexually involved with neighbor Candy (Parent), is convinced to appear in homemade porn with her and her druggie husband (Murphy), and gains another type of internet fame. A low budget drama-thriller with a black comedy touch, Lambert's debut has its moments but mostly tries too hard. **115m/C; DVD, Blu-Ray.** Zachary Ray Sherman; Sally Kirkland; Timothy V. Murphy; Monique Parent; David Diaan; ***D:*** Rob Lambert; ***W:*** Rob Lambert; Joe Varkle; ***C:*** Nick Remy Matthews; ***M:*** Room8.

The Cuckoo 🦴🦴 1/2 *Kushka* **2002 (PG-13)** It's not a joke but the film does have its humorous moments: a Russian, a Finn, and a Lapp are drawn together in 1944. That was the year the Nazis, who occupied Finland, pulled out, leaving behind Finns who had been pressed into service against the advancing Russians. One of these Finns is reluctant sniper Veiko (Haapasalo). The Russian is Ivan (Bychkov), wounded and found by the Lapp—young war widow Anni (Juuso-)?who is caring for him in her hut. Veiko also stumbles upon the hut. None speak the other's language, which doesn't prevent a lot of conversation and misunderstandings as well as desire. In Finnish, Russian, and Sami (the Lapp language) with subtitles. **104m/C; DVD.** *RU* Villie Haapsalo; Anni-Kristina Usso; Vikter Bychkov; ***D:*** Alexander Rogozhkin; ***W:*** Alexander Rogozhkin; ***C:*** Andrei Zhegalov; ***M:*** Dmitri Pavlov.

Cujo 🦴🦴 **1983 (R)** Bad doggie!! A rabid St. Bernard goes berserk and attacks mom Donna (Wallace Stone) and her five-year-old son Tad (Pintauro), who are trapped inside a broken-down Pinto. Frighteningly realistic film is based on Stephen King's bestseller. **94m/C; DVD, Blu-Ray.** Dee Wallace; Daniel Hugh-Kelly; Danny Pintauro; Ed Lauter; Christopher Stone; Kaiulani Lee; Mills Watson; Jerry Hardin; Billy Jacoby; Sandy Ward; ***D:*** Lewis Teague; ***W:*** Lauren Currier; Don Carlos Dunaway; ***C:*** Jan De Bont; ***M:*** Charles Bernstein.

Cul de Sac 🦴🦴🦴 **1966** A macabre, psychological thriller set in a dreary castle on a small island off the British coast. Pleasence is an eccentric, middle-aged hermit living acrimoniously with his young, nympho wife (Dorleac) when their home is invaded by two wounded gangsters (Stander and MacGowran), who proceed to hold the couple hostage. MacGowran soon dies of his wounds, leaving Stander and Pleasence to fight it out, encouraged by the luscious Dorleac, who finds her fun where she can. A bleak, sinister film considered one of Polanski's best. **111m/C; VHS, DVD, Blu-Ray.** *GB* Donald Pleasence; Francoise Dorleac; Lionel Stander; Jack MacGowran; Jacqueline Bisset; ***D:*** Roman Polanski; ***W:*** Roman Polanski; Gerard Brach.

Culpepper Cattle Co. 🦴🦴 1/2 **1972 (PG)** A young, starry-eyed yokel wants to be a cowboy and gets himself enlisted in a cattle drive, where he learns the harsh reality of the West. **92m/C; VHS, DVD.** Gary Grimes; Billy Green Bush; Bo Hopkins; Charles Martin Smith; Geoffrey Lewis; ***D:*** Dick Richards; ***M:*** Jerry Goldsmith.

Cult 🦴 1/2 **2007** Dumb college horror. While researching a class project, co-ed Mindy (Miner) becomes obsessed with a Chinese legend about a murdered young girl who took a magical jade amulet to her grave. The amulet has been recovered by a cult leader who is using ritual sacrifice to harness its power. **90m/C; DVD.** Rachel Miner; Taryn Manning; Joel Michaely; Glenn Dunk; Myke Michaels; ***D:*** Joe Knee; ***W:*** Benjamin Oren; ***C:*** Dave McFarland; ***M:*** Tung Thanh Tran. **VIDEO**

Cult of the Cobra 🦴🦴 **1955** Mysterious horror film that became minor camp classic. It seems ex-servicemen are being killed by exotic snake-lady Domergue. Cheesy film that can be fun. Based on a story by Jerry Davis. **75m/B; DVD.** Faith Domergue; Richard Long; Marshall Thompson; William Reynolds; Jack Kelly; Kathleen Hughes; ***D:*** Francis D. Lyon; ***W:*** Jerry Davis.

Cunningham 🦴🦴 1/2 **2019 (PG)** Documentary celebrating the life and work of renowned New York choreographer Merce Cunningham. Besides providing background about his life, it tells his story primarily through his out-of-this world dance works. Featuring footage of Cunningham and members of his last company, it focuses on his creative peak from 1942 to 1972, though he continued to work until 2009, the year he died at age 90. As artistic as the film's subject in his approach, filmmaker Koygan balances information about Cunningham with a creative blend of music, dance, poetry, sound, and action. **93m/C; DVD.** ***D:*** Alla Kovgan; ***W:*** Alla Kovgan; ***C:*** Mko Malkhasyan; ***M:*** Volker Bertelmann.

The Cup 🦴🦴 1/2 *Phorpa* **1999 (G)** Tibetan teenager Orgyen arrives at a monastery in the Himalayan foothills where he is to join the religious life. But Orgyen is soccer-mad and obsessed with the World Cup (he wears a soccer shirt under his robes) and sneaks out to watch the games. Eventually, the monastery's abbott agrees to allow the monks to have a satellite dish to watch the finals—if they can raise the money to obtain it. Bhutanese with subtitles. **94m/C; VHS, DVD.** *AU* Jamyang Lodro; Orgyen Tobgyal; Lama Chonjor; ***D:*** Khyentse Norbu; ***W:*** Khyentse Norbu; ***C:*** Paul Warren; ***M:*** Douglas Mills.

The Cup 🦴🦴 1/2 **2011 (PG)** Heartwarming sports drama based on a true story. Talented jockey Damien Oliver gets the chance to ride a top horse in the 2002 Melbourne Cup, a premier race. His brother Jason is killed in a riding accident just days before the big event, and Damien doesn't know if he can set aside his grief to compete. **99m/C; DVD.** *AU* Stephen Curry; Daniel MacPherson; Brendan Gleeson; Colleen Hewett; Tom Burlinson; ***D:*** Simon Wincer; ***W:*** Simon Wincer; Eric O'Keefe; ***C:*** David Burr; ***M:*** Bruce Rowland.

Cup Final 🦴🦴 1/2 *G'mar Giviya* **1992** The similarities and contradictions in war and sports, where passions and competition run high, are depicted in this emotional drama. Set in 1982 during Israel's invasion of Lebanon. Cohen is an Israeli soldier passionately interested in the World Cup soccer tournament. When he is taken prisoner by the PLO he discovers his captor Ziad shares his interest in the Italian national team. This common interest brings the two antagonists reluctantly together. In Hebrew and Arabic with English subtitles. **107m/C; VHS, DVD.** *IS* Moshe Ivgi; Muhamad (Mohammed) Bakri; Suheil Haddad; ***D:*** Eran Riklis; ***W:*** Eyal Halfon; ***M:*** Raviv Gazil.

Cupid 🦴🦴 1/2 **2012** Hallmark Channel rom com offers some amusing physical moments from lead Fisher. Workaholic TV show host Eve Lovett is certain she'll never find true love when Vernon Gart (Kennedy) suddenly shows up on set, claiming to work for Cupid, Inc. As the perfect Valentine's Day promo, Vernon is booked as a love expert with Eve matchmaking couples and promised a chance at finding her own lasting romance. **86m/C; DVD.** Joely Fisher; Roark Critchlow; Jamie Kennedy; Christine Estabrook; ***D:*** Ron Oliver; ***W:*** Judd Parkin; ***C:*** James W. Wrenn; ***M:*** Nathan Wang. **CABLE**

Cupid & Cate 🦴🦴 1/2 **2000** Cate De Angelo (Parker) is the quirky owner of a failing D.C. vintage clothing store. The youngest in a large Italian/Irish American family, Cate is still trying to deal with her alcoholic mother's death and an ongoing feud with her overbearing father, Dominic (Bosco). She has a reliable relationship with dull Philip (Lansbury) but doesn't realize the passion she's been missing until she meets handsome Harry (Gallagher) the lawyer. Stereotypes abound as do too many subplots but the leads are endearing. Based on Christina Bartolomeo's novel "Cupid and Diana." **95m/C; VHS, DVD.** Mary-Louise Parker; Peter Gallagher; Philip Bosco; David Lansbury; Bebe Neuwirth; Joanna Going; Brenda Fricker; Kurt McKinney; Rebecca Luker; ***D:*** Brent Shields; ***W:*** Jennifer Miller; Ron Raley; ***C:*** Kees Van Oostrum; ***M:*** Mark Adler. **TV**

Cupid's Mistake 🦴 **2001** No-budget video feature about unrequited love that's set in Venice Beach. Actress Susan is in love with aspiring filmmaker Gil who's in love with Korean-American model Toya who's in love with Japanese-American bodybuilder Ken—and they are all so self-absorbed that you won't care about any of them. **70m/C; DVD.** Susan Petry; Everardo Gil; Toya Cho; Ken Yasuda; ***D:*** Young Man Kang; ***W:*** Young Man Kang; ***C:*** Doo H. Lee; ***M:*** Oliver Lyons.

Curdled 🦴🦴 1/2 **1995 (R)** And you thought your job sucked. Tarantino-funded dark comedy arouses interest with that tag line alone. Gore-obsessed Gabriela (Jones) gets her dream job cleaning up blood and guts with the Post-Forensic Cleaning Service and becomes obsessed with serial killer to the rich Paul (Baldwin), who is keeping her company hopping with one beheading after another. Cultishly violent pic culminates in a tango by the gruesome twosome around a murder scene. Tarantino spotted student Jones, starring in Braddock's original student short, while touring with "Reservoir Dogs" and borrowed her for "Pulp Fiction," only to return the favor by exec producing this interesting feature debut. Soundtrack adds spice to the formaldehyde flavor. **87m/C; VHS, DVD.** Angela Jones; William Baldwin; Mel Gorham; Barry Corbin; Bruce Ramsay; Daisy Fuentes; Lois Chiles; Carmen Lopez; ***D:*** Reb Braddock; ***W:*** John Maass; Reb Braddock; ***C:*** Steven Bernstein; ***M:*** Joseph Julian Gonzalez.

The Cure 🦴🦴 1/2 **1995 (PG-13)** Erik (Renfro), the neighborhood bad kid, befriends Dexter (Mazzello), a boy with AIDS. As Dexter's health weakens, Erik decides they must go on a quest for a cure, Huck Finn style, by floating along the Mississippi River to New Orleans. Despite film's preposterous plot, the performances of the two young leads do inspire a level of sentiment. **99m/C; VHS, DVD.** Brad Renfro; Joseph Mazzello; Annabella Sciorra; Diana Scarwid; Bruce Davison; Renee Humphrey; ***D:*** Peter Horton; ***W:*** Robert Kuhn; ***C:*** Andrew Dintenfass; ***M:*** Dave Grusin.

Cure 🦴🦴🦴 1/2 *The Cure; Kyua* **1997** A detective must solve a series of murders that all end with the victims having an "X" slashed in their throat. Eventually he discovers a young drifter who has no memory or self-identity, but somehow seems able to bring out the worst repressed desires in anyone he meets (they all end up killing people). **111m/C; DVD.** *JP* Koji Yakusho; Masato Hagiwara; Anna Nakagawa; Yoriko Douguchi; Tsuyoshi Ujiki; Yukihiro Hotaru; Denden; Ren Osugi; Shin Nakazawa; Shogo Suzuki; Masahiro Toda; Akira Otaka; ***D:*** Kiyoshi Kurosawa; ***W:*** Kiyoshi Kurosawa; ***C:*** Tokusho Kikumura; ***M:*** Gary Hashiya.

A Cure for Wellness 🦴🦴 **2017 (R)** A company sends their newest employee, Lockhart (Dane Dehaan), to retrieve their CEO from a "wellness center" in the Swiss Alps to sign off on a merger. When Lockhart gets there, he discovers that all is not as it seems, of course. Director Verbinski's visual strengths and storytelling weaknesses collide in this epic horror film that wants to play German expressionism but just wears out its welcome before it gets interesting. The whole thing looks great, but at nearly 150 minutes there's a version that works that's an hour shorter. **146m/C; DVD, Blu-Ray.** Dane DeHaan; Jason Isaacs; Mia Goth; Ivo Nandi; Adrian Schiller; ***D:*** Gore Verbinski; ***W:*** Justin Haythe; ***C:*** Bojan Bazelli; ***M:*** Benjamin Wallfisch.

The Cured 🦴🦴 **2018 (R)** A horror film exploring what happens after a cure is found for a zombie virus. After receiving the cure, Senan (Keeley) has been released into the public. Though some of the cured are rejected by their families, Senan is welcomed by family members and has a job in a facility where the scientist who developed the cure works on a new version for victims who were not cured by the first version. The resistant will be wiped out by the government if a cure for them is not found in time. The debut feature by Freyne is impressive in its premise and execution. **95m/C; DVD.** Ellen Page; Sam Keeley; Tom Vaughan-Lawlor; Stuart Graham; Hilda Fay; ***D:*** David Freyne; ***W:*** David Freyne; ***C:*** Piers McGrail; ***M:*** Rory Friers; Niall Kennedy.

Curfew 🦴🦴 **1988 (R)** A young woman rushes home so she doesn't break her curfew, only to find two killers with time on their hands waiting for her. Violent. **86m/C; VHS, DVD.** John Putch; Kyle Richards; William Wellman, Jr.; Bert Remsen; ***D:*** Gary Winick.

The Curfew Breakers 🦴 **1957** Dim teen-exploitation/message-movie finds a pair of community workers investigating the murder of a gas station attendent by a drug-crazed youth. **78m/B; VHS, DVD.** Regis Toomey; Paul Kelly; Cathy Downs; Marilyn Madison; Sheila Urban; ***D:*** Alex Wells.

The Curiosity of Chance 🦴 1/2 **2006** Inspired by John Hughes' teen flicks, this deliberately campy comedy/drama finds openly gay teen and army brat Chance Marquis (Hilgenbrink) the new kid at yet another school (this one in some unnamed place in Europe). Chance (who wears a top hat and bow tie) is immediately persecuted by jock Brad (Maes) and befriended by a couple of fellow outcasts. He gets some good advice from a drag queen, so Chance decides to be himself (and go after the hunk next door). **99m/C; DVD.** Tad Hilgenbrink; Brett Chukerman; Chris Mulkey; Maxim Maes; Aldevina Da Silva; Pieter van Nieuwenhuyze; Magali Uytterhaegen; *D:* Russell P. Marleau; *W:* Russell P. Marleau; *C:* Jack Messitt; *M:* Willie Aron; Josef Peters. **VIDEO**

The Curious Case of Benjamin Button 🦴🦴🦴 1/2 **2008 (PG-13)** As Hurricane Katrina bears down on New Orleans in 2005, daughter Caroline (Ormond) reads from her mother Daisy's (Blanchett) book as she lay dying, not realizing it's the story of Daisy's life, and of Benjamin Button (Pitt)?a man who was born a wrinkly-skinned senior citizen who goes through life aging backwards. Raised by Queenie (Henson) after being abandoned as a newborn by his father Thomas (Flemyng) in 1918, Benjamin sees the other old-timers who surround him at the old folks' home where his adoptive mother works pass on while he becomes more virile. While many adventures ensue, the focus is on Daisy and Benjamin's relationship, which begins while both are "young" (with Fanning as Daisy), even though Benjamin looks old and their friendship inappropriate but later blossoms when the pair meet in their prime. Loosely taken from F. Scott Fitzgerald's 1922 fantasy short story of the same name, the lead actors are golden in this endearing, though lengthy, tale. **167m/C; Blu-Ray, On Demand.** Brad Pitt; Cate Blanchett; Tilda Swinton; Julia Ormond; Taraji P. Henson; Elias Koteas; Jason Flemyng; Jared Harris; Mahershala Ali; Phyllis Somerville; Elle Fanning; Madisen Beaty; *D:* David Fincher; *W:* Eric Roth; *C:* Claudio Miranda; *M:* Alexandre Desplat. Oscars '08: Art Dir./Set Dec., Makeup, Visual FX; British Acad. '08: Makeup, Visual FX.

The Curious Dr. Humpp 🦴 **1970** A mad scientist (Barbero) kidnaps exotic dancers and extracts their libidos to preserve his youth. Under the guise of research, he encourages his victims to engage in trysts so that their carnal energies will increase. Everything is hunky dory until a reporter (Bauleo) starts snooping around the laboratory, discovering Dr. Humpp observing multiple couplings via closed-circuit TV. Boldly exploitative, the American distributor added about 10 minutes of raunchy hard-core footage of exotic dance routines. **87m/B; VHS, DVD.** *AR* Ricardo Bauleo; Aldo Barbero; Gloria Prat; Susan Beltran; *D:* Emilio Vieyra; *W:* Emilio Vieyra; Raul Zorrilla; *C:* Anibal Gonzalez Paz; *M:* Victor Buchino.

Curious George 🦴🦴 1/2 **2006 (G)** The cute, mischievous chimp and The Man in the Yellow Hat (Ferrell) take a pleasant trip to the big screen. The New York museum where TMitYH works is having financial trouble, so he ventures to Africa to find a lost idol that will bring in the crowds. Along the way he meets George, who has been having fun with his jungle playmates. George takes a liking to The Man after a game of peek-a-boo and manages to follow him back to NYC. George's playful and curious nature gets The Man in trouble with the museum owner's son, who wants to close the museum and build a parking garage. The animation and story are simplistic, but that's just fine with the target audience of pre-schoolers and elementary-agers. The adults will find a few chuckle-worthy gags here and there, as well. **86m/C; DVD, Blu-Ray.** *V:* Will Ferrell; Drew Barrymore; David Cross; Eugene Levy; Dick Van Dyke; Frank Welker; Joan Plowright; Clint Howard; Ed O'Ross; *D:* Matthew O'Callaghan; *W:* Ken Kaufman; *C:* Julie Rogers; *M:* Hector Pereira.

Curly Sue 🦴🦴 **1991 (PG)** Adorable, homeless waif Porter and her scheming, adoptive father Belushi plot to rip off single, career-minded female attorney Lynch in order to take in some extra cash. Trouble is, all three heartstrings are tugged, and the trio develop a warm, caring relationship. A throwback to the Depression era's Shirley Temple formula films met with mixed reviews. Undiscriminating younger audiences should have a good time, though. **102m/C; VHS, DVD.** James Belushi; Kelly Lynch; Alison Porter; John Getz; Fred Dalton Thompson; *D:* John Hughes; *W:* John Hughes; *M:* Georges Delerue.

Curly Top 🦴🦴 1/2 **1935 (G)** Orphan Temple helps land a husband for her beautiful sister. Along the way, she sings "Animal Crackers in My Soup." Remake of the silent "Daddy Long Legs," which was remade again in 1955. **74m/B; VHS, DVD.** Shirley Temple; John Boles; Rochelle Hudson; Jane Darwell; Esther Dale; Arthur Treacher; Rafaela (Rafael, Raphaella) Ottiano; *D:* Irving Cummings.

The Current War: Director's Cut 🦴🦴 1/2 **2019 (PG-13)** In late nineteenth century America, arrogant inventor Thomas Edison (Cumberbatch) is on the cusp of lighting up Manhattan with his direct current electricity technology. Though he is often unpleasant, his relationship with his wife Mary (Middleton) brings balance to his life. Edison's position for electric world dominance is challenged by the more affable industrialist George Westinghouse (Shannon), who promotes what he believes is the safer alternating current. A reworked version of a drama that premiered in 2017, this portrayal accurately reflects the more balanced intentions of the director. Still, the output is less than energizing. **102m/C; DVD.** Benedict Cumberbatch; Michael Shannon; Nicholas Hoult; Stanley Townsend; Tuppence Middleton; *D:* Alfonso Gomez-Rejon; *W:* Michael Mitnick; *C:* Chung-hoon Chung; *M:* Danny Bensi; Saunder Jurriaans.

The Curse 🦴 *The Farm* **1987 (R)** After a meteorite lands near a small farming community and contaminates the area, a young boy tries to prevent residents from turning into slime-oozing mutants. Remake of "Die, Monster, Die." **92m/C; VHS, DVD, Blu-Ray.** Wil Wheaton; Claude Akins; Malcolm Danare; Cooper Huckabee; John Schneider; David Keith; Amy Wheaton; David Chaskin; Kathleen Jordan Gregory; *D:* David Keith; *W:* David Chaskin; *C:* Robert D. Forges.

Curse 2: The Bite 🦴 **1988 (R)** Radiation affected snakes are transformed into deadly vipers whose bites change their unsuspecting victims into horrible creatures. **97m/C; VHS, DVD, Blu-Ray.** Jill Schoelen; J. Eddie Peck; Jamie Farr; Savina Gersak; Bo Svenson; Sydney Lassick; Marianne Muellerleile; Terrence Evans; *D:* Fred Goodwins; *W:* Fred Goodwins; Susan Zelouf; *C:* Roberto D'Ettorre Piazzoli.

Curse of Chucky 🦴🦴 **2013 (R)** Set after the Seeds of Chucky, another clunky entry in the Chucky horror series. After attending her mother's funeral, the wheelchair-bound Nica (Dourif) must manage her divided family including sister Barb (Bisutti), brother in law Ian (Elliott), and young niece. As these events unfold, Nica receives a package with a creepy doll—Chucky (Dourif). People around Nica begin to die under odd circumstances, and Nica soon realizes the doll is not what he seems. **97m/C; DVD, Blu-Ray, Streaming, Download.** Brad Dourif; Chantal Quesnelle; Fiona Dourif; Danielle Bisutti; Brennan Elliott; *D:* Don Mancini; *W:* Don Mancini; *C:* Michael Marshall; *M:* Joseph LoDuca. **VIDEO**

The Curse of Downers Grove 🦴 1/2 **2015** Based on the novel by Michael Hornburg, this dramatic thriller-mystery is centered on a small town that seems cursed. In the community of Downers Grove, a high school senior has died in bizarre fashion right before graduation every year for the past eight years. As high school graduation again approaches, senior Chrissie Swanson (Heathcote) believes that she will be the one to die. When she goes to a party, she nearly loses her life to a man intent on sexually assaulting her, must evade him to stay alive, and break the curse. **90m/C; DVD, Blu-Ray, Download.** Bella Heathcote; Lucas Till; Helen Slater; Penelope Mitchell; Mark L. Young; *D:* Derick Martini; *W:* Derick Martini; Bret Easton Ellis; *C:* Frank Godwin; *M:* Pinar Toprak.

The Curse of Frankenstein 🦴🦴 1/2 **1957** Young Victor Frankenstein reenacts his father's experiments with creating life from the dead resulting in a terrifying, hideous creature. The first in Hammer's Frankenstein series and followed by "Revenge of Frankenstein." From the Shelley story. Make-up by Jack Pierce, who also created the famous make-up for Universal's Frankenstein monster. **83m/C; VHS, DVD.** *GB* Peter Cushing; Christopher Lee; Hazel Court; Robert Urquhart; Valerie Gaunt; Noel Hood; *D:* Terence Fisher; *W:* Jimmy Sangster; *C:* Jack Asher; *M:* James Bernard.

The Curse of King Tut's Tomb 🦴 1/2 **2006** Originally made for the Hallmark network, this film (well miniseries really) attempts to be somewhere between "The Mummy" and "Raiders of the Lost Ark." Attempts is the operative word here. Danny Fremont (Van Dien) is an archaeologist who believes the Emerald Tablet of Egyptian King Tutankhamen holds the power to rule the world, but the only ones who believe him are evil bad guys who want to use it to summon the evil god Set. Cue the usual race against each other to see who gets it first. **170m/C; DVD, Blu-Ray.** Casper Van Dien; Jonathan Hyde; Leonor Varela; Steven Waddington; Brendan Patricks; Malcolm McDowell; Simon Callow; Parvin Dabas; Niko Nicotera; Tat Whalley; Patrick Toomey; Thomas Alter; Rajesh Balwani; Robin Das; Vir Das; Suvarchala Narayanan; Tony Mirchandani; Theron D'Souza; Francisco Bosch; Rajesh Kumar; Ulhas Tayad; *D:* Russell Mulcahy; *W:* David Titcher; *C:* Chris Manley; *M:* Nathan Furst. **TV**

The Curse of La Llorona 🦴🦴 **2019 (R)** In 1973 Los Angeles, Anna (Cardellini) is a widow raising her two kids and working as a social worker. When she comes across a mother, Patricia (Velsquez), who has kept her two young sons locked in the closet to protect them from evil, the boys are quickly placed in foster care and found drowned within hours. Though Patricia is blamed, the real killer is an evil spirit, La Llorona (Ramirez), whom Patricia then calls upon to take revenge on Anna. Part of The Conjuring universe, the film has too few scares and moments of suspense. **93m/C; DVD, Blu-Ray.** Linda Cardellini; Roman Christou; Jaynee-Lynne Kinchen; Raymond Cruz; Marisol Ramirez; *D:* Michael Chaves; *W:* Mikki Daughtry; Tobias Iaconis; *C:* Michael Burgess; *M:* Joseph Bishara.

Curse of the Cat People 🦴🦴🦴 **1944** A young sensitive girl is guided by the vision of her dead mother and bonds with an eccentric neighbor with family issues of her own. Dad and new wife Alice are understandably concerned. Sequel to "Cat People" doesn't come close to measuring up to the original. Available in a colorized version. **70m/B; VHS, DVD, Blu-Ray.** Simone Simon; Kent Smith; Jane Randolph; Elizabeth Russell; Ann Carter; *D:* Robert Wise; Gunther Von Fritsch.

Curse of the Demon 🦴🦴🦴 1/2 *Night of the Demon; The Haunted* **1957** A famous psychologist investigates a colleague's mysterious death and enters a world of demonology and the occult, climaxing in a confrontation with a cult's patron demon. Superb thriller based upon the story "Casting the Runes" by M.R. James. **81m/B; VHS, DVD.** *GB* Dana Andrews; Peggy Cummins; Niall MacGinnis; Maurice Denham; Athene Seyler; Liam Redmond; Reginald Beckwith; Ewan Roberts; Peter Elliott; Brian Wilde; Rosamund Greenwood; *D:* Jacques Tourneur; *W:* Charles Bennett; Hal E. Chester; *C:* Edward (Ted) Scaife; *M:* Clifton Parker.

Curse of the Devil 🦴 1/2 *El Retorno de la Walpurgis* **1973 (R)** This time Naschy is turned into a werewolf by annoyed gypsies whose ancestors were slain by his. **73m/C; VHS, DVD.** *MX SP* Paul Naschy; Maria Silva; Patty (Patti) Shepard; Fay Falcon; Fabiola Falcon; Mariano Vidal Molina; Ines Morales; *D:* Carlos Aured; *W:* Paul Naschy; *C:* Francisco Sanchez.

Curse of the Faceless Man 🦴 1/2 **1958** An archeological dig at Pompeii uncovers the now-faceless stone body of Etruscan gladiator Quintillus. Italian archeologist Carlo Fiorillo and American medical researcher Paul Mallon debate whether the body could still contain some spark of life but since Quintilius' remains keep disappearing and they keep finding fresh dead bodies, Carlo may be right. Mallon's fiancee Tina starts having dreams of a past life before the eruption of Vesuvius that involve the gladiator. **66m/C; DVD, Blu-Ray.** Richard Anderson; Elaine Edwards; Bob Bryant; Luis van Rooten; Adele Mara; Gar Moore; Felix Locher; Jan Arvan; *D:* Edward L. Cahn; *W:* Jerome Bixby; *C:* Kenneth Peach, Sr.; *M:* Gerald Fried.

Curse of the Golden Flower 🦴🦴 *Man Cheng Jin Dai Huang Jin Jia* **2006 (R)** Zhang's tale, set in the 10th-century Tang Dynasty, is a sumptuous, convoluted saga of family mayhem. The Emperor (Chow) has returned home from a long battle, just before the annual chrysanthemum festival (the flower of the title). The emperor is having the royal doctor poison his unloved empress (Gong), who is having an affair with Crown Prince Wan, her stepson, who is actually in love with the doctor's daughter, Chan. The doctor's wife warns the empress about the poison; she turns out to be the emperor's ex-wife, and the mother of Wan (who thought she was dead) and Chan. There's some martial arts stuff between the imperial factions and it's all very operatic, including the elaborate corseted, bosom-lifting costumes the empress wears. Mandarin with subtitles. **114m/C; DVD, Blu-Ray.** *CH* Gong Li; Liu Ye; Chow Yun-Fat; Jay Chou; Qin Junjie; Man Li; Ni Dahong; Chen Jin; *D:* Yimou Zhang; *W:* Yimou Zhang; Wu Nan; Bian Zhihong; *C:* Xiaoding Zhao; *M:* Shingeru Umebayashi.

Curse of the Headless Horseman 🦴 **1972** The headless horseman rides again, bringing terror to all who cross his path! **80m/C; VHS, DVD.** Don Carrara; Claudia Dean; B.G. Fisher; Margo Dean; Lee Byers; Joe Cody; *D:* John Kirkland.

The Curse of the Jade Scorpion 🦴🦴 1/2 **2001 (PG-13)** Where can a 65-year-old guy who looks like Woody Allen bag a babe like Helen Hunt? In a Woody Allen movie, that's where. Hunt plays efficiency expert Betty Ann Fitzgerald, who's hired to update the offices of a Manhattan insurance agency where C.W. Briggs (Allen) is the chief investigator, so he and "Fitz" develop an immediate mutual dislike. After several increasingly tedious games of verbal darts, the two are mesmerized by nightclub hypnotist Voltan (Stiers) into believing that they're in love. He also uses hypnotic cues to have C.W. unknowingly pull off jewel heists of his own clients. After a mystery woman (Theron) shows up, C.W. begins to question where he's been and who he's been with late at night and enlists the help of the Coopersmith Brothers (Mulheren and Linari) to help crack the case. Lighter and shallower than most of Allen's work, it's still mostly fun to watch. Soundtrack is chock full of Allen's beloved 40s era jazz and Big Band tunes. **103m/C; VHS, DVD.** Woody Allen; Helen Hunt; Dan Aykroyd; Elizabeth Berkley; Charlize Theron; Wallace Shawn; David Ogden Stiers; John Schuck; Brian Markinson; Michael Mulheren; Peter Linari; Prof. Irwin Corey; Peter Gerety; *D:* Woody Allen; *W:* Woody Allen; *C:* Fei Zhao.

Curse of the Living Corpse 🦴 **1964** A millionaire comes back to rotting life to kill his negligent relatives. Scheider's first film. **84m/C; VHS, DVD.** Candace Hilligoss; Roy Scheider; Helen Warren; Margot Hartman; *D:* Del Tenney.

Curse of the Pink Panther 🦴🦴 **1983 (PG)** Clifton Sleigh, an inept New York City detective played by Wass, is assigned to find the missing Inspector Clouseau. His efforts are complicated by an assortment of gangsters and aristocrats who cross paths with the detective. So-so attempt to keep popular series going after Seller's death. Niven's last film. **110m/C; VHS, DVD, Blu-Ray.** Ted Wass; David Niven; Robert Wagner; Herbert Lom; Joanna Lumley; Capucine; Robert Loggia; Harvey Korman; Leslie Ash; Denise Crosby; Ed Parker; *D:* Blake Edwards; *W:* Blake Edwards; *C:* Dick Bush; *M:* Henry Mancini.

Curse of the Puppet Master: The Human Experiment 🦴 1/2 **1998 (R)** The little guys have been taking a break since 1994's "Puppet Master 5" but they're baaaack. This time they're trying to prevent their new master, evil Dr. Magrew, from transforming more victims into living dolls. The director, "Victoria Sloan," is actually DeCoteau. **90m/C; VHS, DVD, Blu-Ray.** George Peck; Emily Harrison; Michael Guerin; Robert Donovan; *D:* David DeCoteau; *W:* Benjamin

Carr; *C:* Howard Wexler; *M:* Richard Band. **VIDEO**

Curse of the Queerwolf **1987** A man is bitten on the butt by gay werewolf and transforms into the title character. Filmed in Santa Barbara in 8mm; some funny moments. From the director of "A Polish Vampire in Burbank." **90m/C; VHS, DVD.** Michael Palazzolo; Kent Butler; Taylor Whitney; Darwyn Carson; Sergio Bandera; Mark Pirro; Forrest J Ackerman; Conrad Brooks; *D:* Mark Pirro; *W:* Mark Pirro; *M:* Gregg Gross.

Curse of the Starving Class **1994 (R)** Ineffective adaptation of Sam Shepard's 1977 play exploring family disintegration. Weston (Woods) is the alcoholic, irresponsible patriarch of a decaying farm. His unhappy wife, Ella (Bates), wants to sell out to land speculator Taylor (Quaid) and move to Paris while rebellious teenager Emma (Fiorella) plans to run off to Mexico and sullen older brother Wesley (Thomas) desires to stay and make a go of things. One-dimensional characterizations don't translate well from stage to screen. **102m/C; VHS, Streaming.** James Woods; Kathy Bates; Henry Thomas; Kristin Fiorella; Randy Quaid; Louis Gossett, Jr.; *D:* Michael McClary; *W:* Bruce Beresford; *C:* Dick Quinlan.

Curse of the Swamp Creature **1966** A mad scientist in the Everglades attempts to create half human/half alligator monsters. In turn, a geologic expeditionary force attempts to stop his experimentation. Low budget thrills courtesy of Larry Buchanan. **80m/C; VHS, DVD.** John Agar; Francine York; Shirley McLine; Bill (Billy) Thurman; Jeff Alexander; *D:* Larry Buchanan.

The Curse of the Werewolf ½ **1961** Horror film about a 19th-century European werewolf that is renowned for its ferocious departure from the stereotypical portrait of the beast. **91m/C; VHS, DVD, Blu-Ray.** *GB* Oliver Reed; Clifford Evans; Yvonne Romain; Catherine Feller; Anthony Dawson; Michael Ripper; Peter Sallis; *D:* Terence Fisher; *W:* John (Anthony Hinds) Elder; *C:* Arthur Grant.

Curse of the Witching Tree **2015** Indie psychological horror exploration whose premise is perhaps better than its overall plot and effect. A single mom and her two children moves into a house and come face to face with what is buried in its troubled past. Centuries ago, a woman is accused of murdering her son. Though she is innocent, she labeled a witch and hung. She takes revenge by cursing a tree, a house nearby, and all the children who every play around tree. Over the years, cursed children are buried around the home, newly occupied by the small family. The family is also haunted by many restless spirits of the murdered children and soon learn the truth about their home. **90m/C; DVD, Streaming, Download.** Sarah Rose Denton; Lucy Clarvis; Lawrence Weller; Danielle Bux; Jon Campling; *D:* James Crow; *W:* James Crow; *C:* James Crow; *M:* Pete Coleman. **VIDEO**

Cursed ½ **2004 (PG-13)** Writer Williamson and director Craven were much more successful with their "Scream" franchise than with this obvious werewolf horror. Los Angelenos Ellie (Ricci) and her geeky brother Jimmy (Eisenberg) encounter a nasty beastie after a car accident. They get bitten and start developing werewolf-like tendencies. Ellie doesn't want to accept the truth as her girlfriends are becoming beastie fodder. Rick Baker did better effects back in 1981 with "An American Werewolf in London." Film lives up to its title as it was rewritten, recast, reshot, and recut before it finally making it into the multiplex. **97m/C; VHS, DVD, Blu-Ray.** Christina Ricci; Joshua Jackson; Jesse Eisenberg; Judy Greer; Milo Ventimiglia; Kristina Anapau; Portia de Rossi; Shannon Elizabeth; Mya; Michelle Krusiec; *Cameo(s):* Scott Baio; *D:* Wes Craven; *W:* Kevin Williamson; *C:* Robert McLachlan; *M:* Marco Beltrami.

Curtain at Eight **1933** An elderly detective has a lot of suspects when an unpopular stage actor is murdered although it's clear to see whodunit. Unfortunately, it's not the monkey (who's part of the play's cast). **90m/B; DVD.** Dorothy Mackaill; Sir C. Aubrey Smith; Paul Cavanagh; Sam Hardy; Russell Hopton; Marion Shilling; *D:* E. Mason Hopper; *W:* Edward T. Lowe; *C:* Ira Morgan.

Curtain Call **1997 (PG-13)** Publishing exec Stevenson Lowe (Spader) movies into a brownstone that is haunted by the ghosts of bickering theatrical marrieds Max (Caine) and Lily (Smith). Unfortunately for him, Stevenson is the only one who can see the duo, so his girlfriend Julia (Walker) thinks he's nuts. She has a problem with her commitment-phobe beau anyway and it's up to Max and Lily to see the duo stay together. **94m/C; VHS, DVD.** James Spader; Polly Walker; Michael Caine; Maggie Smith; Buck Henry; Sam Shepard; Todd Alcott; Susan Berman; Marcia Gay Harden; Valerie Perrine; Frances Sternhagen; Frank Whaley; *D:* Peter Yates; *W:* Todd Alcott; *C:* Sven Nykvist; *M:* Richard Hartley. **VIDEO**

Curtains WOOF! **1983 (R)** Director has a clash of wills with a film star that spells "Curtains" for a group of aspiring actresses gathered together at a haunted house for an audition. Hamfest with no thrills, chills, gore, or gratuitous skin. No wonder why director Richard Ciupka hides behind pseudonym Stryker. **90m/C; DVD, Blu-Ray.** *CA* John Vernon; Samantha Eggar; Linda Thorson; Lynne Griffin; Michael Wincott; Maury Chaykin; *D:* Richard Ciupka; *W:* Robert Guza, Jr.; *C:* Robert Paynter; *M:* Paul Zaza.

The Curve *Dead Man's Curve* **1997 (R)** Think "Dead Man on Campus" since you've got basically the same premise. College roomies Tim (Lillard), Rand (Batinkoff), and Chris (Vartan) learn that student myth is true at their small university. Should a roomie commit suicide, the survivors receive an automatic 4.0 for the semester. So Tim offs Rand and has Chris help him cover things up. Naturally this doesn't work out entirely as expected. Not nearly as clever as it tries to be. **90m/C; VHS, DVD.** Matthew Lillard; Michael Vartan; Randall Batinkoff; Keri Russell; Dana Delany; Tamara Craig Thomas; Anthony Griffin; Bo Dietle; Kevin Huff; Henry Strozier; *D:* Dan Rosen; *W:* Dan Rosen; *C:* Joey Forsyte.

Curve **2016 (R)** Picking up a stranger proves harmful in this thriller. Heading to Denver to get married, Mallory Rutledge (Hough) decides to make a quick detour to see the Grand Canyon. When her truck stops unexpectedly, she has no cell service and allows drifter Christian Laughton (Sears) to fix her car. When Mallory gives him a ride after the repair, he shows his true colors, pulls a knife, and tells her to go to a motel. To rid herself of him, she throws the truck off the road in a curve. It does not go as planned, and Mallory's leg gets trapped in the overturned vehicle. Though Christian disappears, Mallory is left alone with no way out and a psychotic man seemingly her only hope. **81m/C; DVD, Streaming, Download.** Julianne Hough; Teddy Sears; Penelope Mitchell; Madalyn Horcher; Drew Rausch; *D:* Iain Softley; *W:* Kimberly Lofstrom Johnson; Lee Patterson; *C:* Brad Shield; *M:* Ed Shearmur. **VIDEO**

Curveball ½ **2015** A teen/sports drama exploring the temptations of youth and the impact of life choices. After his father was killed in front of him as a child and the early death of his mother, Nolan (McMurtry) struggled to fit in and feel less alone in the world. Nolan finds his vistas opened by Sam (Aalderks), a neighborhood troublemaker who shares Nolan's love of baseball. Though Sam helps make Nolan into a star pitcher, he also leads Nolan down a path of life lived on the fast track with more freedom than most teens can handle. As Nolan's future becomes threatened by the trouble brought by Sam, Nolan's mother Sharon (Christian) tries to ensure her son has a positive future from beyond the grave. **96m/C; DVD, Streaming, Download.** Jean-Luc McMurtry; Adam Aalderks; Cheri Christian; Paul Chappell; Rockmond Dunbar; *D:* Brandon Thaxton; *W:* Linton "Buddy" Barnett, III; *C:* German Valle; *M:* Daeus Cannon. **VIDEO**

Custer's Last Stand ½ **1936** Feature-length version of the Mascot serial recounting the last days of the famous General. **70m/B; VHS, DVD.** Frank McGlynn; Rex Lease; Nancy Caseell; Lona Andre; William Farnum; Reed Howes; Jack Mulhall; Josef Swickard; Ruth Mix; *D:* Elmer Clifton.

Cut **2000 (R)** In this instance the title can be taken literally since a killer is knocking off those involved in a low-budget horror film. It seems that a group of film students want to finish a film that was shut down 15 years earlier after it's female director (Minogue) was murdered on the set. The students manage to get Vanessa (Ringwald), the star of the original, to reprise her role but is the film cursed or is someone giving their efforts a critical thumbs down? **82m/C; VHS, DVD.** *AU* Molly Ringwald; Jessica Napier; Simon Bossell; Sarah Kants; Stephen Curry; Geoff Revell; Frank Roberts; Sam Lewis; *Cameo(s):* Kylie Minogue; *D:* Kimble Rendall; *W:* Dave Warner; *C:* David Foreman; *M:* Guy Gross. **VIDEO**

Cut and Run *Inferno in Diretta; Amazon: Savage Adventure; Straight to Hell* **1985 (R)** Two journalists follow a lead to the former South American home of Jim Jones, and are instantly captured by local guerrillas. **91m/C; VHS, DVD, Blu-Ray.** *IT* Lisa Blount; Leonard Mann; Willie Aames; Richard Lynch; Michael Berryman; Karen Black; Eriq La Salle; *D:* Ruggero Deodato; *W:* Cesare Frugoni; *C:* Alberto Spagnoli; *M:* Claudio Simonetti.

Cut Bank ½ **2015 (R)** Again, we learn that the Coen Brothers' balance of dark humor and deep philosophy is much harder to pull off than it looks in the latest riff on "No Country For Old Men" with a cast too talented for this script. Hemsworth plays a young man who accidentally films a murder, sending the naïve sheriff (Malkovich) on an investigation that involves a corrupt mailman (Dern) and a sociopathic loner (Stuhlbarg). The film never figures out if it's funny or thrilling. Hemsworth doesn't cut it as the lead while Stuhlbarg easily steals the thunder. **93m/C; DVD, Blu-Ray.** Liam Hemsworth; Teresa Palmer; John Malkovich; Billy Bob Thornton; Oliver Platt; *D:* Matt Shakman; *W:* Roberto Patino; *C:* Ben Richardson; *M:* James Newton Howard.

Cut Off ½ *Taking Charge* **2006** Patricia Burton (Brooks) is a whiny spoiled brat, who decides to get her drug-addicted boyfriend to help her knock over a check-cashing store when her wealthy father cuts her off. The boyfriend is hurt, and she accidentally kills a guard, prompting her to make the further bad decision of hijacking an ambulance carrying a wounded drug dealer who is none too happy about it. Don't let the box cover that looks like "Sin City" fool you. Roberto Rodriguez-style wackiness this isn't. **88m/C; DVD.** Amanda Brooks; Thomas Ian Nicholas; Kurupt; Malcolm McDowell; Faye Dunaway; Anne Archer; *D:* Dick Fisher; Gino Cabanas; *W:* Myer Grovic; Brian Mazo; *C:* Michael Goi; *M:* Vincent Gillioz.

Cutaway ½ **2000 (R)** Vic Cooper (Baldwin) is a customs agent who goes undercover to infiltrate a group of drug dealers who deliver their goods via skydiving. He discovers the sport gives him a bigger adrenaline rush than his job, so which one will he choose? **104m/C; VHS, DVD.** Tom Berenger; Stephen Baldwin; Dennis Rodman; Maxine Bahns; Casper Van Dien; Ron Silver; *D:* Guy Manos; *W:* Guy Manos; Greg Manos; *C:* Gerry Lively. **VIDEO**

Cutie and the Boxer **2013 (R)** Unions between artists are often perfectly attuned to documentary films about them but rarely has a movie taken on the quirky tones of its subjects like director Heinzerling's debut piece about Noriko & Ushio Shinohara. The couple has been together for four decades and Ushio is a prominent, well-known painter who literally throws himself into his work, ending most sessions covered in paint. His wife Noriko has been by his side for years but seeks an identity of her own from her larger-than-life husband. It's interesting to watch such vibrant personalities at an advanced age and the filmmaker incorporates their passion into his style. **82m/C; DVD, Blu-Ray.** *D:* Zachary Heinzerling; *C:* Zachary Heinzerling; *M:* Yasuahi Shimizu.

The Cutter ½ **2005 (R)** Hang around the Internet long enough and you'll be told that Chuck Norris is a deity who can do no wrong, kill you with his eyelashes, is the second coming of Jesus, and has never made a bad film. This film runs contrary to all of that. Detective John Shepherd (Norris) is hired to find a kidnapped jewel cutter, despite the fact that the daughter of his last client died. Nothing looks good on a resume like "50 percent of my clients have survived the John Shepherd experience." **92m/C; DVD.** Chuck Norris; Joanna Pacula; Daniel Bernhardt; Bernie Kopell; Todd Jensen; Marshall Teague; Tracy Scoggins; Curt Lowens; Daron McBee; Dean Cochran; Mark Ivanir; Aaron Norris; Dennis Kleinsmith; Eli Danker; Elsa Raven; *D:* William (Bill) Tannen; *W:* Bruce Haskett; *C:* Peter Moss; *M:* Elia Cmiral.

Cutter's Way ½ *Cutter and Bone* **1981 (R)** An embittered and alcoholic disabled Vietnam vet and his small-time crook/gigolo friend wrestle with justice and morality when the drifter uncovers a murder but declines to get involved. An unusually cynical mystery from the novel by Newton Thorburg. **105m/C; VHS, DVD, Blu-Ray.** Jeff Bridges; John Heard; Lisa Eichhorn; Ann Dusenberry; Stephen Elliott; Nina Van Pallandt; George Dickerson; *D:* Ivan Passer; *W:* Jeffrey Alladin Fiskin; *C:* Jordan Cronenweth; *M:* Jack Nitzsche.

Cutthroat Island ½ **1995 (PG-13)** Big-budget swashbuckling adventure—long on action and short on plot and character. Female pirate captain Morgan Adams (Davis) is left part of a treasure map by her father and "persuades" educated slave/thief William Shaw (Modine), who has lots of charm and no morals, to assist her. Her scurvy Uncle Dawg (despically well-played by Langella) also has a portion of the map and is willing to let Morgan find the treasure—on Cutthroat Island—before taking it for himself. Director Harlin likes lots of big, noisy explosions (when he doesn't know what else to do) but Davis' exuberance for her pirate queen role is appealing. **123m/C; VHS, DVD, Blu-Ray.** Geena Davis; Matthew Modine; Frank Langella; Patrick Malahide; Stan Shaw; Maury Chaykin; Harris Yulin; George Murcell; *D:* Renny Harlin; *W:* Robert King; Marc Norman; *C:* Peter Levy; *M:* John Debney.

Cutting Class **1989 (R)** Murders proliferate in a high school, where a student with a history of mental illness is number one on the suspect list. Tongue-in-cheek mayhem. **91m/C; VHS, DVD, Blu-Ray.** Jill Schoelen; Roddy McDowall; Donovan Leitch; Martin Mull; Brad Pitt; *D:* Rospo Pallenberg.

The Cutting Edge ½ **1992 (PG)** Spoiled figure skater's lifelong quest for Olympic gold is seriously hampered by her inability to be nice to her partners. In a final effort to snag the medal she teams up with a cocky guy who thinks the only sport on ice is hockey, but whose own dreams of NHL stardom were cut short by an injury. Saddled with a predictable and thin plot, it sometimes looks and feels like a TV movie. So why bother? Because the chemistry between photogenic leads Kelly and Sweeney is terrific. Add half a bone for the flying sparks and snappy dialogue, sit back, and enjoy. **101m/C; VHS, DVD, Blu-Ray.** D.B. Sweeney; Moira Kelly; Roy Dotrice; Terry O'Quinn; Dwier Brown; Rachelle Ottley; Jo Jo Starbuck; *D:* Paul Michael Glaser; *W:* Tony Gilroy; *C:* Elliot Davis; *M:* Patrick Williams.

The Cutting Edge 3: Chasing the Dream **2008 (PG-13)** Same basic plot only with a role reversal. Medal-winning figure skater Zack Conroy (Lanter) drops his partner (literally) and her injury takes her out of competition. Needing a replacement in a hurry, Zack heads to the ice rink and recruits feisty amateur hockey player Alexandra Delgado (Raisa). There's the usual training montage, jeering rivals, and misunderstandings that all lead up to the big championship moment. At least Lanter and Raisa are cute eye candy. **92m/C; DVD.** Christy Carlson Romano; Alycia Purrott; Matt Lanter; Francia Raisa; Sarah Gordon; Luis Oliva; Stefan Colacitti; Ben Hollingsworth; *D:* Stuart Gillard; *W:* Randall Badat; *C:* Pierre Jodoin; *M:* Robert Duncan. **CABLE**

The Cutting Edge: Fire and Ice ½ **2010** The ABC Family Channel sports romance is the fourth in the series. Alex Delgado turns to teaching when her pairs partner retires after an injury and also ends their romantic relationship. Bad boy speed skater James Mckinsey is banned from the national team and persuades Alex to partner with him as pairs skaters. Their tempestuous relationship—on and off the ice—threatens their chances to win. **90m/C; DVD.** Francia Raisa; Brendan Fehr; Russell Yuen; Stephen Amell; *D:* Stephen Herek; *W:* Holly Brix; *C:* Pierre Jodoin; *M:* Bennett Salvay. **CABLE**

The Cutting Edge: Going for the Gold ½ *The Cutting Edge 2: Going for the Gold* **2005 (PG-13)** Kate (Kramer) and

Doug (Thompson) got married and their baby girl Jackie (Romano) is now a teenager following in their skate tracks as a promising figure skater who'like her mom way back when—is forced to pair up with a new partner, inline skater Alex (Thomas), and they face the same problems that Jackie's folks had. Major point deductions for the lifeless banter of this sequel, which might explain why original cast members Sweeney and Kelly decided to skip it. **99m/C; DVD.** Christy Carlson Romano; Ross Thomas; Scott Thompson Baker; Stephanie Kramer; Kim Kindrick; ***D:*** Sean McNamara; ***W:*** Tony Gilroy; Daniel Berendsen. **VIDEO**

Cyber Bandits 🦴 1/2 **1994 (R)** In a future society, navigator Jack Morris (Kemp) has just sailed a pleasure craft to the island city of Pacifica. His passengers included wealthy Morgan Wells (Hays), whose scientists have developed a deadly virtual reality weapon, and Wells' mistress Rebecca (Paul). Rebecca steals the plans for the weapon and seduces Jack into having the data digitally transferred onto his back in the form of a tattoo. Then Rebecca disappears and Jack finds himself in big trouble. **86m/C; VHS, DVD.** Martin Kemp; Alexandra Paul; Robert Hays; Adam Ant; Grace Jones; ***D:*** Erik Fleming; ***W:*** James Robinson; Winston Beard; ***M:*** Steve Hunter.

Cyber Seduction: His Secret Life **WOOF! 2005** Laughably ridiculous family drama. Sixteen-year-old star swimmer Justin Petersen (Sumpter) gets so obsessed with internet porn that he has problems concentrating on either school or athletics. He gets kicked off the swim team, his disgusted girlfriend leaves, his mom has hysterics, and he consumes way too many energy drinks. **90m/C; DVD.** Jeremy Sumpter; Kelly Lynch; John Robinson; Jake Scott; Lyndsy Fonseca; Kyle Schmid; Benz Antoine; ***D:*** Tom McLoughlin; ***W:*** Wesley Bishop; Richard Kletter; ***C:*** Rudolf Blahacek; ***M:*** Louis Febre. **CABLE**

Cyber-Tracker 🦴 1/2 **1993 (R)** In the judicial system of the future androids hunt down vicious criminals and execute them immediately. When secret service agent Eric Phillips is framed for murder, he's also marked for death. His only chance is to link up with rebels fighting the mechanized monsters. **91m/C; VHS, DVD.** Don "The Dragon" Wilson; Richard Norton; Joseph Ruskin; Abby Dalton; John Aprea; ***D:*** Richard Pepin; ***W:*** Jacobsen Hart; ***C:*** Ken Blakey; ***M:*** Bill Montei; Lisa Popeil.

Cyber-Tracker 2 🦴 1/2 **1995 (R)** An international weapons dealer has gotten control of the cybertracker technology and created cyborg lookalikes of secret agent Eric Phillips (Wilson) and his newscaster wife Connie (Foster). When the cyborgs commit murder on live TV, the human duo become fugitives who must expose the real killers. **97m/C; VHS, DVD, On Demand.** Don "The Dragon" Wilson; Stacie Foster; Steve (Stephen) Burton; ***D:*** Richard Pepin; ***W:*** Richard Preston, Jr.

Cyberbully 🦴🦴 **2011** In this ABC Family Movie, 17-year-old Taylor Hillridge is dealing with her parents' divorce and high school issues by trying to make new friends on a popular social website. Instead, she becomes the victim of online bullying and it gets so bad that Taylor attempts suicide. Her mother, Kris, then takes on the school and state legislators to make certain that such abhorrent behavior is taken seriously and maybe criminally. **87m/C; DVD.** Emily Osment; Kelly Rowan; Kay Panabaker; Meaghan Rath; Jon McLaren; ***D:*** Charles Biname; ***W:*** Teena Booth; ***C:*** Pierre Gill; ***M:*** James Gelfand. **CABLE**

Cybercity 🦴 1/2 *The Shepherd* **1999 (R)** When mercenary Howell's family is murdered by virtual prophet Piper, who's trying to take over the world, Howell tries for revenge with the aid of assassin von Palleske. **86m/C; VHS, DVD.** C. Thomas Howell; Roddy Piper; Heidi von Palleske; David Carradine; ***D:*** Peter Hayman; ***W:*** Nehu Ghiran; ***C:*** Graeme Mears; ***M:*** Donald Quan. **VIDEO**

Cybergeddon 🦴🦴 **2012** Middling thriller that was originally a web miniseries. Ex-hacker Chloe Jocelyn is now an FBI agent working cybercrimes. Her big fish is Gustov, an international cyber terrorist who's escaped prison and is already planning his next job. First, he frames Chloe to get her out of the way, so she goes rogue to clear her name and bring Gustov down. **95m/C; DVD.** Missy Peregrym; Olivier Martinez; Manny Montana; Kick (Christopher) Gurry; Tonya Lee Williams; ***D:*** Diego Velasco; ***W:*** Miles Chapman; ***C:*** Samy Inayeh; ***M:*** Freddy Sheinfeld. **VIDEO**

Cybermutt 🦴🦴 *Rex: Le cyber chien* **2002 (PG)** Eccentric scientist Nelson implants a computer chip into the dog that saved him from a car accident. The chip enables the dog to communicate with other computers and draws the attention of technospies who naturally want to use the bionic pup for their own nefarious purposes. Of course a boy who has befriended the dog is enperiled long the way. Adults won't find much worth sitting through, but kids will enjoy the feats of the canine star. **86m/C; VHS, DVD.** *CA* Judd Nelson; Michelle Nolden; Ryan Cooley; Paulina Mielech; Tonio Arango; ***D:*** George Miller; ***W:*** Kevin Commins; Gerald Sanford; ***C:*** Gerald R. Goozie. **TV**

Cybernator 🦴 **1991 (R)** In 2010 the economy and government falls, and as the military takes over society reverts to the late 1980's. Officer Brent McCord (Lonnie Schuyler) is asked to put down cyborgs assassinating the locals in L.A. Which sucks for him because there are no cyborgs on the police force to back him up. **85m/C; DVD.** Lonnie Schuyler; Jeff Jenkins; Christina Peralta; Jack Senior; ***D:*** Robert Rundle; ***W:*** Robert Rundle; Edward Sanchez; ***C:*** Jimmy Williams; ***M:*** Keith Bilderbeck. **VIDEO**

Cyberstalker 🦴 1/2 *The Digital Prophet* **1996** Detective twosome must track down a serial killer who uses the Internet to select his victims. **96m/C; VHS, DVD.** Blake Bahner; Jeffrey Combs; Annie Biggs; Schnele Wilson; ***D:*** Christopher Romero; ***W:*** Annie Biggs; Tony Brownrigg.

The Cyberstalking 🦴 1/2 **1999** Aspiring singer Holly Moon (Kelly) wants to appear in the same futuristic techno club as her diva idol Samantha (Wilde). What Holly doesn't know is that the setup is part of a secret computer program that uses the imagination of a real person to create a virtual reality. Holly is that person for now but a flaw in the program could prove deadly. **90m/C; DVD.** Jean Louisa Kelly; Noah Huntley; Claudine Wilde; ***D:*** Brian Grant; ***W:*** Joe Gannon; ***C:*** Richard Wincenty; ***M:*** Donald Quan. **TV**

Cyborg 🦴 **1989 (R)** In a deathly, dirty, post-holocaust urban world, an able cyborg battles a horde of evil mutant thugs. Poorly made action flick. **85m/C; VHS, DVD, Blu-Ray.** Jean-Claude Van Damme; Deborah Richter; Vincent Klyn; Dayle Haddon; Alex Daniels; Terrie Batson; Janice Graser; Jackson "Rock" Pinckney; ***D:*** Albert Pyun; ***W:*** Kitty Chalmers; ***C:*** Philip Alan Waters; ***M:*** Kevin Bassinson.

Cyborg 2 🦴🦴 *Cyborg 2: Glass Shadow* **1993 (R)** In the year 2074 cyborgs have replaced humans at all levels. A devious company which manufactures cyborgs decides to get rid of its chief competition by literally killing them off. They plan to inject cyborg Cash Reese (Jolie) with a liquid explosive that will detonate her and everything else in sight. Tech-master Mercy (Palance) clues Cash in and she escapes with the help of the human Colton (Koteas) but they've become prey to a group of ruthless hunters. **99m/C; VHS, DVD.** Angelina Jolie; Elias Koteas; Jack Palance; Billy Drago; ***D:*** Michael Schroeder; ***W:*** Michael Schroeder; Mark Geldman; Ron Yanover; ***C:*** Jamie Thompson; ***M:*** Peter Allen.

Cyborg 3: The Recycler 🦴🦴 **1995 (R)** Female cyborg has been programmed to become a creator—essentially making mankind useless. **90m/C; VHS, DVD.** Khrystyne Haje; Zach Galligan; Andrew Bryniarski; Richard Lynch; Malcolm McDowell; ***D:*** Michael Schroeder; ***W:*** Barry Victor; Troy Bolotnick.

Cyborg Conquest 🦴 1/2 *Chrome Angels* **2009** An evil genius wants to use his deadly robot creations to rule the world. The only thing standing in his way are a group of biker chicks who spend their hours robbing banks and beating up people. **90m/C; DVD, Streaming.** Stacey Dash; Frida Farrell; Monti Domingue; Jessika Brodosi; Eliza Swensen; ***D:*** Leigh Scott; ***W:*** Leigh Scott; ***C:*** Steven Parker; ***M:*** Miles Hankins. **VIDEO**

Cyborg Soldier 🦴🦴 1/2 *Cyborg Cop 2* **1994 (R)** Loose cannon cop Jack Ryan (Bradley) is up against psycho killer Starkraven (Hunter) who gets turned into a new-model cyborg by your basic suspicious government agency. But when the cyborg decides to go on an unplanned human killing spree, Ryan gets to break out the heavy artillery to mow him down. Also available in an unrated version. **96m/C; VHS, DVD.** David Bradley; Morgan Hunter; Jill Pierce; ***D:*** Sam Firstenberg; ***W:*** Jon Stevens.

Cyborg Soldier 🦴 1/2 *Weapon* **2008 (PG-13)** Isaac (Franklin) takes border patrol agent Lindsey Rearden (Thiessen) hostage after escaping from a military research facility. The former death row inmate was used as a scientific experiment and genetically reconstructed by robotics engineer Simon Hart (Greenwood) as a prototype super-weapon. Isaac wants to expose the military group behind the program and expects Lindsey to help him do that. **84m/C; DVD.** Tiffani(-Amber) Thiessen; Richard Franklin; Bruce Greenwood; Aaron Abrams; Jim Annan; Wendy Anderson; ***D:*** John Stead; ***W:*** Christopher Warre Smets; John Flock; ***C:*** David Mitchell. **VIDEO**

Cycle Psycho **WOOF!** *Numbered Days; Savage Abduction* **1972 (R)** Serial killer blackmails the businessman whose wife he was contracted to kill into bringing him young girls to slaughter. The businessman hires out the job to sleazy motorcycle gang. **80m/C; VHS, DVD.** Joe Turkel; Tom Drake; Stephen Oliver; ***D:*** John Lawrence; ***W:*** John Lawrence.

Cyclo 🦴🦴 *Xich Lo* **1995** An orphaned 18-year-old (Van Loc), known only by by his profession of cyclo (pedal-taxi) driver, struggles on the streets of Ho Chi Minh City. When his vehicle is stolen, he's forced by his boss to repay its value and takes small-time jobs from local crime boss, The Poet (Leung), who, unbeknownst to the cyclo, is also his sister's (Yen-Khe) pimp. The deeper the young man gets into the criminal world, the closer he also gets to tragedy. Vietnamese with subtitles. **123m/C; VHS, DVD.** *VT* Le Van Loc; Lee Van Loc; Tran Nu Yen-Khe; Tony Leung Chiu Wai; Tony Leung Chiu-Wai; Nguyen Nhu Quynh; ***D:*** Anh Hung Tran; Tran Anh Hung; ***W:*** Anh Hung Tran; Tran Anh Hung; ***C:*** Benoit Delhomme; Laurence Tremolet; ***M:*** Ton That Tiet.

Cyclone 🦴🦴 **1987 (R)** The girlfriend of a murdered scientist must deliver a secretly devised motorcycle into righteous government hands, much to the dismay of evil agents and corrupt officials. Good fun, sparked by a stellar "B" cast. **89m/C; VHS, DVD.** Heather Thomas; Jeffrey Combs; Ashley Ferrare; Dar Robinson; Martine Beswick; Robert Quarry; Martin Landau; Huntz Hall; Troy Donahue; Michael Reagan; Dawn Wildsmith; Bruce Fairbairn; Russ Tamblyn; ***D:*** Fred Olen Ray; ***C:*** Paul Elliott.

The Cyclone Ranger 🦴 1/2 **1935** Bill Cody is the white-hated sometime hero in this low-budget western from Spectrum Pictures. The cattle-rustling Pecos Kid does a good deed for blind Dona Castelar, the mother of his deceased friend Juan, by saving her ranch from his former gang. **65m/B; DVD.** Bill Cody; Soledad Jiminez; Donald Reed; Nina Quartero; Eddie Gribbon; Earle Hodgins; Colin Chase; ***D:*** Robert F. "Bob" Hill; ***W:*** Oliver Drake; ***C:*** Donald Biddle Keyes.

Cyclops 🦴🦴 **1956** When an expedition party searches throughout Mexico for a woman's long lost fiance, they are shocked when they find out that radiation has turned him into a one-eyed monster. **72m/B; VHS, DVD, Blu-Ray.** Tom Drake; Gloria Talbott; Lon Chaney, Jr.; James Craig; ***D:*** Bert I. Gordon.

Cyclops 🦴🦴 **2008** Evil Roman Emperor Tiberius (Roberts) sends centurion Marcus (a bland Stapleton) to capture the Cyclops terrorizing the countryside. When the monster is safely in the dungeons, Marcus becomes embroiled in a slave revolt and is declared a traitor. He's forced into the arena to fight the Cyclops but they become allies to overthrow Tiberius instead. Cheese from the Sci-Fi Channel that comes across as a throwback to those old Italian-made gladiator flicks. **88m/C; DVD.** Eric Roberts; Kevin Stapleton; Frida Show; Craig Archibald; Mike Straub; ***D:*** Declan O'Brien; ***W:*** Frances Doel; ***C:*** Emil Topuzov; ***M:*** Tom Hiel. **CABLE**

Cymbeline 🦴 1/2 **2015 (R)** Flashy, contemporary retelling of the problematic late Shakespeare play. Drug kingpin Cymbeline heads the Britons motorcycle club. His daughter, Imogen, has secretly married Posthumus, whom Cymbeline kicks to the curb. Cymbeline's devious current wife wants her son Cloten to take over and thinks getting Cymbeline in trouble with the local corrupt cops will speed things along. Meanwhile, idiot Posthumus accepts a bet from cocky Iachimo that he can seduce Imogen, whom Posthumus has been talking up as the perfect babe. It didn't make sense when Shakespeare told it either. **98m/C; DVD, Blu-Ray.** Ed Harris; Dakota Johnson; Penn Badgley; Ethan Hawke; Milla Jovovich; Anton Yelchin; John Leguizamo; Vondie Curtis-Hall; ***D:*** Michael Almereyda; ***W:*** Michael Almereyda; ***C:*** Tim Orr; ***M:*** David Ludwig.

Cynthia 🦴🦴 1/2 **1947** Trifle starring teen Elizabeth Taylor in the title role. Fifteen-year-old Cynthia has always been considered frail by her over-protective parents but the young woman is tired of sitting on the sidelines. She joins the high school choir (Taylor's singing voice is dubbed), starts a chaste romance with fellow student Ricky (Lydon) who gives Cynthia her first kiss, and goes to the prom while her parents struggle to get used to her newfound independence. **98m/B; DVD.** Elizabeth Taylor; Mary Astor; George Murphy; James Lydon; S.Z. Sakall; Gene Lockhart; Spring Byington; ***D:*** Robert Z. Leonard; ***W:*** Charles Kaufman; Harold Buchman; ***C:*** Charles E. Schoenbaum; ***M:*** Bronislau Kaper.

Cypher 🦴🦴🦴 **2002 (R)** Somewhat convoluted but intriguing sci-fi thriller. Milquetoast businessman Morgan Sullivan (Northam) hopes for a more exciting life when he applies for a job at multinational Digicorp. He's put to work as a corporate spy under the alias Jack Thursby and sent to a number of conventions to record the speeches that are made. Morgan/Jack doesn't understand the purpose of this until he meets mystery femme Rita (Liu), who informs Morgan that he has been brainwashed. She convinces him to turn double-agent and work for rival Sunway Systems but this only makes his life more confusing until a final assignment and shocking revelation. **96m/C; DVD.** Jeremy Northam; Lucy Liu; Nigel Bennett; Timothy Webber; David Hewlett; Kari Matchett; ***D:*** Vincenzo Natali; ***W:*** Brian King; ***C:*** Derek Rogers; ***M:*** Michael Andrews.

Cypress Edge 🦴🦴 1/2 **1999 (R)** The murder of Louisiana Senator Woodrow McCammon's (Steiger) daughter brings her estranged family back together. The motive is clear—an $18 million estate—and the benefactors are the usual suspects. **90m/C; VHS, DVD.** Rod Steiger; Damian Chapa; Brad Dourif; Ashley Laurence; Charles Napier; ***D:*** Serge Rodnunsky; ***W:*** Serge Rodnunsky; ***M:*** Carl Dante.

Cyrano de Bergerac 🦴🦴🦴 **1925** Silent version of Edmond Rostand's novel about romantic Cyrano who fears to reveal his love to Roxanne because he feels his enormous nose makes him unattractive. So, he serves as a surrogate lover by encouraging another man's attentions to her. Colortinted. **114m/C; Silent; VHS, DVD.** *IT FR* Pierre Magnier; Linda Moglia; Angelo Ferrari; ***D:*** Augusto Genina; ***M:*** Carlo Moser.

Cyrano de Bergerac 🦴🦴🦴🦴 **1950** Edmund Rostand's famous story of a large-nosed yet poetic cavalier, who finds himself too ugly to be loved. He bears the pain of his devotion to Roxanne from afar, and helps the handsome but tongue-tied Christian to romance her. Ferrer became famous for this role, which won him an Oscar. Based on Brian Hooke's translation of the play. Also available colorized. **113m/B; DVD, Blu-Ray.** Jose Ferrer; Mala Powers; William Prince; Elena Verdugo; Morris Carnovsky; ***D:*** Michael Gordon; ***W:*** Carl Foreman; ***C:*** Franz Planer; ***M:*** Dimitri Tiomkin. Oscars '50: Actor (Ferrer); Golden Globes '51: Actor--Drama (Ferrer).

Cyrano de Bergerac 🦴🦴🦴🦴 **1990 (PG)** Depardieu brings to exhilarating life Rostand's well-loved play about the brilliant but grotesque-looking swordsman/poet, afraid of nothing—except declaring his love to the beautiful Roxanne (Brochet). But

Cyrano expresses his own feelings by helping handsome (but tongue-tied) fellow soldier Christian (Perez) woo Roxanne instead. One of France's costliest modern productions, a multi-award winner for its cast, costumes, music and sets. English subtitles (by Anthony Burgess) are designed to capture the intricate rhymes of the original French dialogue. **135m/C; VHS, DVD.** *FR* Gerard Depardieu; Jacques Weber; Anne Brochet; Vincent Perez; Roland Bertin; Josiane Stoleru; Philippe Volter; Philippe Morier-Genoud; Pierre Maguelon; ***D:*** Jean-Paul Rappeneau; ***W:*** Jean-Claude Carriere; Jean-Paul Rappeneau; ***C:*** Pierre Lhomme; ***M:*** Jean-Claude Petit. Oscars '90: Costume Des.; Cannes '90: Actor (Depardieu); Cesar '91: Actor (Depardieu), Art Dir./Set Dec., Cinematog., Costume Des., Director (Rappeneau), Film, Score, Sound, Support. Actor (Weber); Golden Globes '91: Foreign Film.

Cyrus **2010 (R)** Tomei wins the hot mom/inappropriate behavior award in this queasy, cartoonish comedy. Middle-aged, divorced schlub John (Reilly) meets cute with vibrant single mom Molly (Tomei) whose baggage is 21-year-old doughboy son Cyrus (Hill). The duo has an overly-attentive relationship and hostile Cyrus is deeply resentful that John is taking any of his mom's attention away from himself so he tries to ensure the romance fails. **91m/C; DVD, Blu-Ray.** Jonah Hill; John C. Reilly; Marisa Tomei; Catherine Keener; Matt Walsh; Tim Guinee; ***D:*** Jay Duplass; Mark Duplass; ***W:*** Jay Duplass; Mark Duplass; ***C:*** Jas Shelton; ***M:*** Michael Andrews.

Cyxork 7 **2006** The title refers to the name of the tired sci-fi franchise and its last gasp sequel currently being filmed by ambitious director Angela LaSalle (Smith). She has some artistic pretensions that clash with Rex Anderson (Wise), the aging actor typecast in the lead role who's just after a paycheck. When their arguments lead to the plug getting pulled, the two decide to brazen it out and finish the shoot, using a predicted L.A. earthquake to cheaply film their special effects shots and as a publicity hook. A Troma release. **93m/C; DVD.** Ray Wise; Beata Pozniak; Joseph Culp; Paget Brewster; Greg Proops; Cassandra Creech; Rebecca Corry; ***D:*** John Huff; ***W:*** John Huff; Andreas Kossak; ***C:*** Michael Negrin. **VIDEO**

D-Day, the Sixth of June *The Sixth of June* **1956** An American soldier has an affair with a Englishwoman weeks before D-Day, where he unhappily finds himself fighting side by side with her husband. Based on the novel by Lionel Shapiro. **106m/C; VHS, DVD.** Richard Todd; Dana Wynter; Robert Taylor; Edmond O'Brien; John Williams; Jerry Paris; Richard Stapley; ***D:*** Henry Koster; ***C:*** Lee Garmes.

The D Train **1/2 2015 (R)** Jack Black is at his most annoying as abrasive jerk Dan who decides that his life went off the rails in high school. To fix it, he tracks down Oliver Lawless (Marsden), the most popular guy from his school who's now a commercial actor, to the upcoming reunion. He forms a strange friendship with the guy, and maybe even something more. The modern blend of sexuality and how we never really leave our high school cliques should work but Black is so aggressively unlikable that you'd rather see him get hit by a bus than figure out his life. **101m/C; DVD.** Jack Black; James Marsden; Kathryn Hahn; Jeffrey Tambor; Henry Zebrowski; ***D:*** Andrew Mogel; Jarrad Paul; ***W:*** Andrew Mogel; Jarrad Paul; ***C:*** Giles Nuttgens; ***M:*** Andrew Dost.

D2: The Mighty Ducks *The Mighty Ducks 2* **1994 (PG)** When an injury forces Gordon (Estevez) out of the minor leagues, he is tapped by promotor Tibbles (Tucker) to coach Team U.S.A. in the Junior Goodwill Games. Upon arriving in LA, the coach's head is turned by the money to be made in endorsements, and he soon gets a lesson in character-building (hey, it's Disney). The duck redux premise is lame, but kids will want ice time to see more of the hockey action that made the first a hit. **107m/C; VHS, DVD, Blu-Ray.** Emilio Estevez; Michael Tucker; Jan Rubes; Kathryn Erbe; Shaun Weiss; Kenan Thompson; Ty O'Neal; ***Cameo(s):*** Kristi Yamaguchi; Kareem Abdul-Jabbar; Wayne Gretzky; ***D:*** Sam Weisman; ***W:*** Steven Brill; ***M:*** J.A.C. Redford.

D3: The Mighty Ducks **1996 (PG)** Estevez proves that he'll quack for a dollar in the latest redux of the Disney franchise. This time the members of the rag-tag team are drafted by an exclusive prep school where, once again, they don't fit in. Go figure! Although billed as the star, Estevez only appears briefly at the beginning and end of the movie, leaving team captain Charlie (Jackson) as the focus of the story. Facing off against the new coach and the snooty elitist varsity team, the players learn lessons about maturity, responsibility and whacking people with sticks. In all probability, Disney will not be happy with just the hat trick, so don't be surprised if you see "D4: Mighty Old to Still Be Playing Kids" in a theatre near you soon. Cameo from professional Mighty Duck and fellow Disney employee Paul Kariya. **104m/C; VHS, DVD, Blu-Ray.** Emilio Estevez; Jeffrey Nordling; Joshua Jackson; David Selby; Heidi Kling; Joss Ackland; Elden (Ratliff) Henson; Shaun Weiss; Matt Doherty; Michael Cudlitz; Vincent A. Larusso; Colombe Jacobsen; Aaron Lohr; Christopher Orr; ***D:*** Robert Lieberman; ***W:*** Steven Brill; Jim Burnstein; ***C:*** David Hennings; ***M:*** J.A.C. Redford.

Da 5 Bloods **1/2 2020 (R)** While serving in the Vietnam War, five African American soldiers, Melvin (Whitlock), Otis (Peters), Eddie (Lewis), Paul (Lindo), and Norman (Boseman), find a trunk of gold bars in a downed CIA plane and bury it in the jungle. Decades later, the group, minus deceased Norman, returns to Vietnam to retrieve the gold under the guise of exhuming Norman's body. As they do so, they revisit issues related to race, the war, and trauma. Spike Lee's is a potent combination of war drama and heist film that offers both critiques of and homages to older genre films. **156m/C; DVD.** Delroy Lindo; Jonathan Majors; Clarke Peters; Norm Lewis; Isiah Whitlock, Jr.; ***D:*** Spike Lee; ***W:*** Spike Lee; Danny Bilson; Paul De Meo; Kevin Willmott; ***C:*** Newton Thomas (Tom) Sigel; ***M:*** Terence Blanchard. **VIDEO**

Da Hip Hop Witch **2000 (R)** Not so much a parody of "Blair Witch Project" as a collection of rap artists' unscripted monologues about a woman who is doing terrible things to them. It also marks the return to the screen of Vanilla Ice, last seen in the abominable "Cool As Ice." **93m/C; VHS, DVD.** Stacii Jae Johnson; Dale Resteghini; Pras; Killah Priest; Spliff Star; Mobb Deep; Eminem; Rock; Colleen (Ann) Fitzpatrick; ***D:*** Dale Resteghini; ***W:*** Dale Resteghini.

Da Sweet Blood of Jesus **2014** Working as low budget as he has in years, writer/director Spike Lee adapts a '70s Blaxploitation era vampire film called "Ganja and Hess" for a new generation with decidedly mixed results. Dr. Hess Greene (Williams) has been cursed by a mysterious artifact that forces him to crave the nourishment of blood. It's a vampire drama with the unique, socio-cultural angle that Lee brings to everything he does. The problems come in the dull story and unengaging performances. **123m/C; DVD, Blu-Ray.** Stephen Tyrone Williams; Zaraah Abrahams; Elvis Nolasco; Rami Malek; Nate Bova; ***D:*** Spike Lee; ***W:*** Spike Lee; ***C:*** Daniel Patterson; ***M:*** Bruce Hornsby.

The Da Vinci Code **2006 (PG-13)** Dan Brown's controversial mega-bestseller hits the big screen with Howard and Hanks reuniting for their first feature since "Apollo 13." The murder of a Louvre curator leads to a conspiracy and a secret that has been protected by the Catholic Church since its beginnings. Cryptologist Sophie Neveu (Tautou) and Harvard symbiologist Robert Langdon (Hanks) team up to puzzle out the clues that are hidden in the works of Leonardo Da Vinci. Naturally, there are those who will protect the secret from being revealed at any cost. Solid performances by great cast generally overcomes Howard's faithful recreation of the novel's talkiness, which doesn't always make for an abundance of thrills. **149m/C; DVD, Blu-Ray.** Tom Hanks; Audrey Tautou; Ian McKellen; Alfred Molina; Paul Bettany; Jean Reno; Jurgen Prochnow; Etienne Chicot; Jean-Pierre Marielle; ***D:*** Ron Howard; ***W:*** Akiva Goldsman; ***C:*** Salvatore Totino; ***M:*** Hans Zimmer.

The Da Vinci Treasure **2006 (R)** Asylum is well known for its low budget rip-offs of more mainstream films, and it's pretty obvious which Tom Hanks vehicle they're 'paying homage' to here. Thomas Howell plays an archeologist who must unlock the code hidden in the works of Leonardo Da Vinci in order to find a treasure that could change Christianity forever. **96m/C; DVD.** C. Thomas Howell; Lance Henriksen; Nicole Sherwin; Alexis Zibolis; Jason S. Gray; Elvis Naumovski; Antonio Jaramillo; Tim Casto; Rocky Hart; A.J. Castro; ***D:*** Peter Mervis; ***W:*** Carlos De Los Rios; David Michael Latt; Peter Mervis; Paul Bales; ***C:*** Steven Parker; ***M:*** Mel Lewis.

Dad **1/2 1989 (PG)** Hoping to make up for lost time, a busy executive rushes home to take care of his father who has just had a heart attack. What could have easily become sappy is made bittersweet by the convincing performances of Lemmon and Danson. Based on the novel by William Wharton. **117m/C; VHS, DVD, Blu-Ray.** Jack Lemmon; Ted Danson; Ethan Hawke; Olympia Dukakis; Kathy Baker; Zakes Mokae; J.T. Walsh; Kevin Spacey; Chris Lemmon; ***D:*** Gary David Goldberg; ***W:*** Gary David Goldberg; ***M:*** James Horner.

A Dad for Christmas **1/2** *Me and Luke* **2006** Well the legalities don't bear looking at (the custody matters are wrong) but it's still somewhat inspiring. Teenaged father Matt (Turner) learns his girlfriend has made arrangements for their newborn son to be adopted. Instead, Matt smuggles baby Luke out of the hospital and they settle in at his eccentric grandma's (Fletcher) house until Matt decides to fight for custody. **90m/C; DVD.** Kristopher Turner; Louise Fletcher; Jack Shepard; Lindsay Ames; Sean McCann; ***D:*** Eleanor Lindo; ***W:*** Alan Hines; ***C:*** Russ Goozee. **CABLE**

Dad On the Run *Cours Toujours* **2000** In the summer of 1997, the Pope's visit to Paris has the city in an uproar, which makes things even more chaotic for new Jewish father Jonas (Sibony). Custom demands that after their son's bris, Jonas bury the foreskin within three days. He suffers a series of complications in his task, involving religious pilgrims and a truck filled with fish. French with subtitles. **92m/C; VHS, DVD.** *FR* Clement Sibony; Rona Hartner; Isaac Sharry; Marie Desgranges; Emmanuelle Devos; Gilbert Levy; Francois Chattot; Francoise Bertin; ***D:*** Dante Desarthe; ***W:*** Dante Desarthe; Agnes Desarthe; Fabrice Guez; ***C:*** Laurent Machuel; ***M:*** Krishna Levy.

Dad Savage **1997 (R)** Strange British crime pic told in flashbacks. Dad Savage (Stewart) is an East Anglia gangster who grows tulips and has a fondness for country music and dressing like a cowboy. His son Sav (Wood) works for him and his right-hand man is H (McKidd). H tells fellow criminals Vic (Warren) and Bob (McFadden) that Dad has a stash of cash buried in a deserted house in the nearby woods. Dad finds out his workers are double-crossing him and there's hell to pay for everyone concerned. **104m/C; VHS, Streaming.** *GB* Patrick Stewart; Kevin McKidd; Joseph McFadden; Jake Wood; Marc Warren; Helen McCrory; ***D:*** Betsan Morris-Evans; ***W:*** Steven Williams; ***C:*** Gavin Finney; ***M:*** Simon Boswell.

Daddy & Them **1/2 1999 (R)** Part romance, part dysfunctional family comedy, Thornton's followup to "Sling Blade" is set in Little Rock, Arkansas. Claude (Thornton) and wife Ruby (Dern) decide to head back home after they learn that Claude's Uncle Hazel (Varney) is in jail, convicted of a petty crime. But the homecoming with Claude's extended family is chaotic to say the least. The constant family bickering gets annoying and the film's minimal charm tires quickly. **101m/C; VHS, DVD.** Billy Bob Thornton; Laura Dern; Ben Affleck; Jamie Lee Curtis; Kelly Preston; Diane Ladd; Brenda Blethyn; Andy Griffith; Jim Varney; Walton Goggins; ***D:*** Billy Bob Thornton; ***W:*** Billy Bob Thornton; ***C:*** Barry Markowitz; ***M:*** Marty Stuart.

Daddy Day Camp **2007 (PG)** Is it still a sequel if the cast is nearly all new? In this sequel to "Daddy Day Care," Charlie Hinton (Gooding, Jr.) and buddy Phil (Rae) have finished their second year as owners of Daddy Day Care. Charlie's son Ben (Bridges) is about to attend summer day camp, but Charlie's trauma from his own childhood camp experience makes him put the kibosh on Ben's plans for uber-cool Camp Canola. Yep, Ben will relive his dad's past at scrappy Camp Driftwood—except the long-neglected Driftwood is about to be put to rest. It's daddies to the rescue as Camp Driftwood is resurrected (sort-of) and the bumbling pops try not to make a flop of their kids' summers (trying equally hard not to kill anyone in the process). Embarrassing and dreadfully predictable. **93m/C; DVD, Blu-Ray.** Cuba Gooding, Jr.; Lochlyn Munro; Richard Gant; Spencir Bridges; Paul Rae; Josh McLerran; Tamala Jones; Brian Doyle-Murray; Talon G. Ackerman; ***D:*** Fred Savage; ***W:*** David N. Weiss; Geoff Rodkey; J. David Stern; ***C:*** Geno Salvatori; ***M:*** James Dooley. Golden Raspberries '07: Worst Sequel/Prequel.

Daddy Day Care **2003 (PG)** Laid-off coworkers (Murphy, Garlin) become stay-at-home dads and caregivers and come up with the idea of opening their own unconventional day-care center. This puts them in direct competition with the director (Huston) of the expensive Chapman Academy. The new Murphy's Law seems to be that for every success, he'll have four disasters. This one is definitely one of the latter, as even in his usually-successful family-friendly mode, he merely mugs amid the chaos. The script is ridiculous and unfunny, and the talented adult cast is wasted as foils for the ankle-biter inmates running the asylum. Sure they're cute, but it shouldn't be their job to carry an Eddie Murphy vehicle. Pre-school set may be amused by the antics of their on-screen peers, but their parents won't enjoy anything but the 93 minutes of quiet while their progeny zone out. **92m/C; VHS, DVD, UMD.** Eddie Murphy; Steve Zahn; Jeff Garlin; Regina King; Anjelica Huston; Lacey Chabert; Sloane Momsen; Kevin Nealon; Jonathan Katz; Khamani Griffin; Michelle Krusiec; ***D:*** Steve Carr; ***W:*** Geoff Rodkey; ***C:*** Steven Poster; ***M:*** David Newman.

Daddy Issues **2020** British stand-up comedian Henrietta (Datnow) desperately needs validation from the men she dates because she lacks the approval of her father. After his death, Henrietta fulfills his dying wish to inherit his Los Angeles estate while making sure his business interests remain intact. Once there, she serves on the business's board of directors despite her lack of qualifications. At the same time, she must deal with her father's former employee, Nolan (Rittenhouse), who is living in the dead man's home. The indie romantic comedy has its charms and Datnow is appealing but it's otherwise one to avoid. **82m/C; DVD.** Jo Ashe; Rachel Barry; Kimia Behpoornia; Francis Lloyd Corby; Max Crandall; ***D:*** Laura Holliday; ***W:*** Laura Holliday; John Cox; ***C:*** Dylan Dugas; Jaryl Lim; ***M:*** Jessica Dannheisser.

Daddy Long Legs **1/2 1919** Judy (Pickford), the eldest inhabitant of a dreary orphanage, comes to the attention of a mysterious benefactor who sends her to college. She eventually discovers the identity of her guardian, falls in love, and marries him. Based on a play by Jean Webster. **94m/B; Silent; VHS, DVD.** Mary Pickford; Milla Davenport; Mahlon Hamilton; Lillian Langdon; Marshall Neilan; ***D:*** Marshall Neilan; ***W:*** Agnes Christine Johnston; ***C:*** Charles Rosher; Henry Cronjager.

Daddy Long Legs **1955** Far from the great musicals, but enjoyable. An eccentric millionaire glimpses a French orphan and becomes her anonymous benefactor. Her musing over his identity spawns some surreal (often inexplicable) dance numbers, but love conquers all, even lesser Johnny Mercer songs. From a story by Jean Webster, also done in 1919 with Mary Pickford, 1931 with Janet Gaynor and 1935 with Shirley Temple as "Curly Top." **126m/C; VHS, DVD, Blu-Ray.** Fred Astaire; Leslie Caron; Terry Moore; Thelma Ritter; Fred Clark; Charlotte Austin; Larry Keating; ***D:*** Jean Negulesco; ***W:*** Phoebe Ephron; Henry Ephron; ***C:*** Leon Shamroy; ***M:*** Alex North.

Daddy Nostalgia *These Foolish Things; Daddy Nostalgie* **1990** Birkin plays the estranged daughter of Bogarde, who rushes from her home in England to France to be with her seriously ill father. She must come to terms with her feelings for him just as Bogarde must deal with his own mortality. Wonderful performances, with Bogarde a charming and dominating presence. In French with English subtitles. **105m/C; VHS, DVD.** *FR* Dirk Bogarde; Jane Birkin; Odette Laure; ***D:*** Bertrand Tavernier; ***W:*** Colo Tavernier O'Hagan; ***C:*** Denis Lenoir; ***M:*** Antoine Duhamel.

Daddy's Dyin'. . . Who's Got the Will? **1/2 1990 (PG-13)** Based on the critically acclaimed play, this bittersweet comedy stars Bridges and D'Angelo as two members of the spiteful Turnover clan. When Daddy is on his deathbed, the entire family uses the opportunity to stab each other in the back. Non-stop humor and deep-hearted honesty carries this delightful adaptation quickly from beginning to end. **95m/C; VHS, DVD.** Beau Bridges; Beverly D'Angelo; Tess Harper; Judge Reinhold; Amy Wright; Keith Carradine; Patrika Darbo; Molly McClure; Bert Remsen; ***D:*** Jack Fisk; ***W:*** Del Shores; ***C:*** Paul Elliott; ***M:*** David McHugh.

Daddy's Girl 1/2 **1996 (R)** When adopted Jody's new family is threatened she'll stop at nothing to protect herself and them. **95m/C; VHS, Streaming.** William Katt; Michele Greene; Roxana Zal; Mimi (Meyer) Craven; Whip Hubley; Gabrielle Boni; ***D:*** Martin Kitrosser; ***W:*** Steve Pesce.

Daddy's Gone A-Hunting **1969 (PG)** It's an eye for an eye, a baby for a baby in this well-done psychological thriller. A happily married woman is stalked by her deranged ex-boyfriend, whose baby she aborted years before. Now he wants the life of her child as just compensation for the loss of his. **108m/C; VHS, DVD.** Carol White; Paul Burke; Scott Hylands; Rachel Ames; Mala Powers; James B. Sikking; ***D:*** Mark Robson; ***W:*** Larry Cohen; ***C:*** Ernest Laszlo; ***M:*** John Williams.

Daddy's Home 1/2 **2015 (PG-13)** Wahlberg and Ferrell fail to recapture the comedy gold they found in "The Other Guys" in this tepid, boring comedy about modern male roles in society, especially when it comes to fatherhood. Brad Whitaker (Ferrell) is a nice, white-collar family man just trying to forge a bond with his new brood as their stepfather. When their biological father, Dusty Mayron (Wahlberg), rides in on a motorcycle, a bit of alpha-male posturing begins. Dusty is the opposite of Brad in that he's all macho and cool to his kids. The cast and concept is fine, but someone forgot to write funny material. **96m/C; DVD, Blu-Ray.** Will Ferrell; Mark Wahlberg; Linda Cardellini; Thomas Haden Church; Scarlett Estevez; Eric Kissack; ***D:*** Sean Anders; ***W:*** Sean Anders; Brian Burns; John Morris; ***C:*** Julio Macat; ***M:*** Michael Andrews.

Daddy's Home 2 1/2 **2017 (PG-13)** A more engaging sequel to the original features smarter humor and more complex family dynamics. In this outing, cool dad Dusty (Wahlberg) and wimpy stepdad Brad (Ferrell) find their alliance to co-parent Dusty's children with Brad's wife Sarah (Cardellini) challenged by the appearance of their fathers near the holidays. While Dusty's ex-astronaut father Kurt (Gibson) tries to undermine their parenting arrangement and acts aggressively, Brad's wimpy dad Don (Lithgow) is a non-stop talker. Tensions played for laughs are also increased by Dusty's pretentious new wife Karen (Ambrosio) and stepdaughter. **100m/C; DVD, Blu-Ray.** Will Ferrell; Mark Wahlberg; Mel Gibson; John Lithgow; Linda Cardellini; ***D:*** Sean Anders; ***W:*** Sean Anders; John Morris; ***C:*** Julio Macat; ***M:*** Michael Andrews. Golden Raspberries '17: Worst Support. Actor (Gibson).

Daddy's Little Girls 1/2 *Tyler Perry's Daddy's Little Girls* **2007 (PG-13)** This isn't really about the little girls as much as it is about Monty (Elba) overcoming all obstacles to be a good father. He's a hard-working mechanic who loses custody to his greedy ex (Smith), thanks to some problems in his own past. This also leads to trouble in his growing relationship with his uptown lawyer, Julia (Union). Perry's characters tend to be two-dimensional but he's never less than sincere, and it's an uplifting story. **95m/C; DVD, Blu-Ray.** Idris Elba; Gabrielle Union; Louis Gossett, Jr.; Tasha Smith; Malinda Williams; Tracee Ellis Ross; Gary Sturgis; Sierra McClain; China McClain; Lauryn McClain; Craig Robinson; ***D:*** Tyler Perry; ***W:*** Tyler Perry; ***C:*** Toyomichi Kurita; ***M:*** Brian McKnight.

Dad's Army 1/2 **2016** A sadly inferior reboot of the beloved British television series. The Home Guard (older men unable to serve in WWII) are Britain's last defense against the Nazis invading, and keep an ever watchful eye for bad guys. At least they do until the Nazi scum send a beautiful spy posing as a reporter. **100m/C; DVD, Streaming.** *UK* Catherine Zeta-Jones; Michael Gambon; Bill Nighy; Toby Jones; Mark Gatiss; Tom Courtenay; ***D:*** Oliver Parker; ***W:*** Hamish McColl; ***C:*** Christopher Ross; ***M:*** Charlie Mole. **VIDEO**

The Dagger of Kamui *Kamui No Ken; Revenge of the Ninja Warrior* **1985** The only family Jiro has ever known is killed and he is accused of the crime. The evil Tenkai promises to take him to the real killer, but Jiro does not realize until later how cruelly he has been tricked. Then Jiro goes on a quest to find his past, all the while being manipulated by a vast and complex political machine. Watching this and Jiro's reactions make this anime more than a simple adventure or coming of age story. Whatever their motivations, Jiro's travels take him as far as America and into the paths of some characters as familiar to Western viewers as the historical figures in his homeland are to anyone knowledgeable of Japanese history. Based on the novels by Tetsu Yano. **132m/C; VHS, DVD.** *JP* Michio Hazama; ***D:*** Taro Rin.

Dagora, the Space Monster WOOF! *Dagora; Space Monster Dagora; Uchudai Dogora; Uchu Daikaiiju Dogora* **1965** Giant, slimy, pulsating mass from space lands on Earth and begins eating everything in sight. Scientists join together in a massive effort to destroy the creature. Believe it or not, it's sillier than most of the Japanese sci-fi genre. **80m/C; VHS, DVD.** *JP* Yosuke Natsuki; Yoko Fujiyama; Akiko Wakabayashi; Hiroshi Koizumi; ***D:*** Inoshiro Honda; ***W:*** Shinichi Sekizawa; ***C:*** Hajime Koizumi.

D'Agostino WOOF! 2012 Aimless, incoherent, and frustrating sci-fi drama. Wealthy exec Allan (Roenke) leaves his girlfriend behind when he heads to Greece to check out some inherited property. On the premises is the feral D'Agostino (Angels), a clone intended for medical uses, who has been shipwrecked. Allan trains D'Agostino in a master/slave relationship until an unbelievable horror ending. **117m/C; DVD, Blu-Ray.** *GR US* Keith Roenke; Michael Angels; Jorge Ameer; ***D:*** Jorge Ameer; ***W:*** Jorge Ameer; ***C:*** Zach Voytas; ***M:*** Keith Roenke.

Daguerreotypes **1975** An insightful documentary by Agnes Verda focusing on a microcosm the community in which she had spent most of her life. In the film, she creates an intimate portrait of the ordinary shopkeepers and shops that are found on the Rue Daguerre in Paris, France, in the 1970s. Each shopkeeper shares his or her life story. In the process, she reveals much about her city and a way of life no longer in existence. **80m/C; DVD.** ***D:*** Agnes Varda; ***W:*** Agnes Varda; ***C:*** Nurith Aviv; William Lubtchansky.

Dahmer **2002 (R)** That would be Dahmer as in serial killer Jeffrey who murdered, dismembered, and even munched on some 15 young men whom he killed in his Milwaukee, Wisconsin apartment. Although the story is sensationalistic, the film is surprisingly restrained and Renner gives a spooky performance as a psycho whose psychosis can never be explained. **101m/C; VHS, DVD.** Jeremy Renner; Artel Kayaru; Bruce Davison; Matt Newton; ***D:*** David Jacobson; ***W:*** David Jacobson; ***C:*** Chris Manley.

The Dain Curse *Dashiell Hammett's The Dain Curse* **1978** In 1928, private eye Hamilton Nash must recover stolen diamonds, solve a millionaire's suicide, avoid being murdered, and end a family curse. Miniseries based on the novel by Dashiell Hammett. **138m/C; VHS, DVD.** James Coburn; Jason Miller; Jean Simmons; Beatrice Straight; Hector Elizondo; Nancy Addison; ***D:*** E.W. Swackhamer. **TV**

Daisy Kenyon 1/2 **1947** Daisy (Crawford) finally gets fed up when married lover Dan (Andrews) keeps breaking his promises. She decides to move on with kind war vet Peter (Fonda) and they get married. Despite this, Dan stays in touch with Daisy, and his wife (Warwick) finally figures things out and gets a divorce. Now a free man, Dan wants Daisy for himself but does she go to him or stay with the decent guy? Crawford can suffer with the best of 'em but Andrews' character is pretty much a heel. **99m/C; DVD, Blu-Ray.** Joan Crawford; Dana Andrews; Henry Fonda; Peggy Ann Garner; Ruth Warwick; Martha Stewart; Connie Marshall; Nicholas Joy; ***D:*** Otto Preminger; ***W:*** David Hertz; ***C:*** Leon Shamroy; ***M:*** David Raskin.

Daisy Miller 1/2 **1974 (G)** Shepherd portrays the title character in this adaptation of the Henry James novella about a naive young American woman travelling through Europe and getting a taste of the Continent during the late 19th century. Though it is intelligently written and has a good supporting cast, the film seems strangely flat, due in large part to Shepherd's hollow performance. **93m/C; VHS, DVD.** Cybill Shepherd; Eileen Brennan; Cloris Leachman; Mildred Natwick; ***D:*** Peter Bogdanovich; ***W:*** Frederic Raphael.

Dakota **1945** Fine cast becomes embroiled in railroad land dispute. In the meantime, love strikes The Duke. Standard Wayne western saga never quite gets on track. **82m/B; DVD, Blu-Ray.** John Wayne; Vera Hruba Ralston; Walter Brennan; Ward Bond; Ona Munson; ***D:*** Joseph Kane.

Dakota **1988 (PG)** A troubled half-breed teenager works for a rancher, romances his daughter, and befriends his crippled 12-year-old son. A well-meaning, but predictable drama. **96m/C; VHS, DVD.** Lou Diamond Phillips; Dee Dee Norton; Eli Cummins; Herta Ware; Jordan Burton; ***D:*** Fred Holmes; ***C:*** James W. Wrenn.

Dakota Incident **1956** Decent western about stagecoach passengers travelling through Dakota Territory who must defend themselves against an Indian attack. **88m/C; VHS, Streaming.** Dale Robertson; Ward Bond; Linda Darnell; John Lund; ***D:*** Lewis R. Foster.

Daleks—Invasion Earth 2150 A.D. 1/2 *Invasion Earth 2150 A.D.* **1966** A sequel to "Dr. Who and the Daleks," wherein the popular British character endeavors to save the Earth from a robotic threat. **81m/C; VHS, DVD.** *GB* Peter Cushing; Andrew Keir; Jill Curzon; Ray Brooks; ***D:*** Gordon Flemyng.

Dallas Buyers Club **2013 (R)** The true story of a man forced to work around the pharmaceutical system and the law to get the drugs he needs to extend the 30-day life sentence his doctors give him when he's diagnosed with AIDS. In 1985 in Dallas, AIDS drugs are still in testing phases, but hard-living Ron Woodruff (McConaughey) finds ways around the system and crafts an unlikely friendship with fellow sufferer Rayon (Leto), a transsexual. Before long, Woodruff is setting up a monthly subscription club to sell the needed drugs. Great cast, despite some script problems. **117m/C; DVD, Blu-Ray.** Matthew McConaughey; Jared Leto; Jennifer Garner; Denis O'Hare; Steve Zahn; Dallas Roberts; Kevin Rankin; Griffin Dunne; ***D:*** Jean-Marc Vallee; ***W:*** Craig Borten; Melisa Wallack; ***C:*** Yves Bélanger. Oscars '13: Actor (McConaughey), Actor--Supporting (Leto), Makeup; Golden Globes '14: Actor--Drama (McConaughey), Actor--Supporting (Leto); Ind. Spirit '14: Actor (McConaughey), Actor--Supporting (Leto); Screen Actors Guild '13: Actor (McConaughey), Actor--Supporting (Leto).

The Dallas Connection **1994 (R)** Three of the four scientists working on a satellite weapons system are assassinated by a trio of sexy but lethal females. Now the remaining scientist is under federal protection in Dallas while he continues his work. Lots of T&A. **90m/C; VHS, DVD, Blu-Ray.** Julie Strain; Samantha (Sam) Phillips; Julie K. Smith; Wendy Hamilton; ***D:*** Andy Sidaris.

Dallas 362 **2003 (R)** Rusty (Hatosy) and Dallas (Caan) waste away their lives in a cycle of drinking, bar fights, and minor arrests—always to be bailed out by Rusty's mother Mary (Lynch). Mary puts her son in therapy and through unconventional methods he starts to see a better life for himself, though Dallas hurtles further toward the dark side. The subplot romance between the mother and therapist (Goldblum) is engaging but lacks depth. Conclusion provides a surprise emotional tug. **100m/C; DVD.** Scott Caan; Jeff Goldblum; Shawn Hatosy; Kelly Lynch; Dwight "Heavy D" Myers; Bob Gunton; Marley Shelton; Selma Blair; Isla Fisher; Freddy Rodriguez; James Caan; ***D:*** Scott Caan; ***W:*** Scott Caan; ***C:*** Phil Parmet.

The Dalmarian Chronicles 1/2 **2003** Animated sci-fi flick. The Dalmarians are beginning to lose their decades-long war against their alien enemies and send a group of sentient robots to find them a new home-world to replace the old one that is crumbling. After two years without any further contact the robots assume their creators have not survived, and create their own civilization. Eighty years later the Dalmarians suddenly return, and demand their robots come back to serve them, leaving them in a bit of an emotional quandary. **85m/C; DVD.** ***V:*** Jeff Haas; Scott Anderson; Joe Buckner; Bryan French; Lynne Haas; Doyle McPherson; Fred Wade, Jr.; ***D:*** Jeff Haas; ***W:*** Jeff Haas.

The Dalton Girls **1957** The four Dalton sisters take up bank and stagecoach robbing after their brothers are killed or incarcerated. Holly and Rose are unrepentant outlaws but younger Marigold and Columbine begin to rethink their criminal ways, especially when Columbine falls for gambler Illinois Grey. The sisters are pursued by Det. Hiram Parsh and it doesn't look like it'll be a happy ending. **71m/B; DVD.** Merry Anders; Lisa Davis; Penny Edwards; Sue George; John Russell; Ed Hinton; Glenn Dixon; ***D:*** Reginald LeBorg; ***W:*** Maurice Tombragel; ***C:*** Carl Guthrie; ***M:*** Les Baxter.

Daltry Calhoun **2005 (PG-13)** Debut feature from Bronson stars Knoxville as the slick sod salesman of the title. Daltry hightailed it out of Ducktown, Tennessee, leaving behind his teenaged girlfriend and baby daughter. Fourteen years later, May (Banks) is dying of some mystery illness and needs Daltry to take responsibility for June (Traub). There are quirky townsfolk and quirky situations and quirky, annoying narration from June. And an intrusive soundtrack. **100m/C; DVD.** Johnny Knoxville; Juliette Lewis; Elizabeth Banks; Kick (Christopher) Gurry; David Koechner; Sophie Traub; Andrew Prine; ***D:*** Katrina Holden Bronson; ***W:*** Katrina Holden Bronson; ***C:*** Matthew Irving; ***M:*** John Swihart.

Dalva 1/2 **1995** Dull TV movie finds restless Dalva Northridge (Fawccett) deciding to search for the son she was forced to give up for adoption some 20 years before. But she gets sidetracked juggling two love affairs—with Sam Creekmouth (Boothe), whose Indian heritage is tied to Dalva's family, and alcoholic university professor Michael (Coyote) who wants the Northridge family diaries for his research on the Great Plains. Based on the novel by Jim Harrison. **96m/C; VHS, DVD.** Farrah Fawcett; Powers Boothe; Peter Coyote; Rod Steiger; Carroll Baker; ***D:*** Ken Cameron; ***W:*** Jim Harrison; ***C:*** Tony Imi. **TV**

Dam Busters 1/2 **1955** Well-done and exciting film details the efforts of British scientists trying to devise a method of destroying a strategic dam in Nazi Germany during WWII. Definitely one of the better in the war movie genre. **119m/B; VHS, DVD, Blu-Ray.** *GB* Michael Redgrave; Richard Todd; Ursula Jeans; Basil Sydney; ***D:*** Michael Anderson, Sr.

Damage **1992 (R)** The elegant Irons portrays Stephen, a middle-aged, married British politican who has always been completely in control of his life, especially where his feelings are concerned. Then he meets Anna (Binoche), his son's less-than-innocent fiance, and immediately begins an obsessive, wildly sexual affair with her. Stephen should have listened to Anna's warning about herself "Damaged people are dangerous, they know they can survive," because their passion leads to betrayal and tragedy. Binoche is more icon than human being but the film still hypnotizes as an exploration of passion. Based on the novel by Josephine Hart. An unrated version is also available. **111m/C; VHS, DVD.** *GB FR* Jeremy Irons; Juliette Binoche; Rupert Graves; Miranda Richardson; Ian Bannen; Leslie Caron; Peter Stormare; Gemma Clark; Julian Fellowes; ***D:*** Louis Malle; ***W:*** David Hare; ***C:*** Peter Biziou; ***M:*** Zbigniew Preisner. British Acad. '92: Support. Actress (Richardson); L.A. Film Critics '92: Score.

Dames **1934** A millionaire with fanatically religious beliefs tries to stop the opening of a Broadway show. In the last of the grand budget-breaking spectacles before the "production code" came into being, distinguished choreographer Busby Berkeley took his imagination to the limit: watch for the dancing clothes on an ironing board and dancing girls with puzzle pieces on their backs which form the real Keeler. **95m/B; VHS, DVD.** Dick Powell; Joan Blondell; Ruby Keeler; Zasu Pitts; Guy Kibbee; Busby Berkeley; ***D:*** Ray Enright; ***W:*** Delmer Daves; ***C:*** George Barnes.

Damien: Omen 2 🦴🦴 **1978 (R)** Sequel to "The Omen" about Damien, a young boy possessed with mysterious demonic powers, who kills those people who anger him. Followed by "The Final Conflict." **110m/C; VHS, DVD, Blu-Ray.** William Holden; Lee Grant; Lew Ayres; Robert Foxworth; Sylvia Sidney; Lance Henriksen; Jonathan Scott-Taylor; Nicholas Pryor; Allan Arbus; Meshach Taylor; ***D:*** Don Taylor; ***W:*** Mike Hodges; ***C:*** Bill Butler; ***M:*** Jerry Goldsmith.

Damn the Defiant 🦴🦴🦴 *HMS Defiant* **1962** Adventure abounds when Guinness, as captain of the HMS Defiant during the Napoleonic wars, finds himself up against not only the French but his cruel second-in-command (Bogarde) and a mutinous crew as well. In the end, both a fleet-wide mutiny and a French invasion of England are avoided. Much attention is paid to period detail in this well-crafted film. **101m/C; VHS, DVD.** *GB* Alec Guinness; Dirk Bogarde; Maurice Denham; Anthony Quayle; ***D:*** Lewis Gilbert; ***W:*** Nigel Kneale; Edmund H. North; ***C:*** Christopher Challis; ***M:*** Clifton Parker.

Damn Yankees 🦴🦴🦴 *What Lola Wants* **1958** Musical feature adapted from the Broadway hit. A baseball fan frustrated by his team's lack of success makes a pact with the devil to become the team's new star. Verdon is dynamite as the devil's accomplice. Great Bob Fosse choreography. **110m/C; VHS, DVD.** Gwen Verdon; Ray Walston; Tab Hunter; Jean Stapleton; Russ Brown; ***D:*** George Abbott; Stanley Donen.

Damnation Alley 🦴 1/2 **1977 (PG)** A warrior, an artist, and a biker jump in tank and set off in search of civilization after Armageddon. They go to Albany instead. So-so attempt to revive the post-nuclear holocaust genre which was more successfully accomplished by the "Mad Max" series. Adapted from Roger Zelazny's novel. **87m/C; VHS, DVD.** George Peppard; Jan-Michael Vincent; Paul Winfield; Dominique Sanda; Jackie Earle Haley; ***D:*** Jack Smight; ***W:*** Alan Sharp; Lukas Heller; ***C:*** Harry Stradling, Jr.; ***M:*** Jerry Goldsmith.

The Damned 🦴🦴 1/2 **1969 (R)** Depicts the Nazi takeover of a German industrialist family and their descent into greed, lust, and madness. Comes in dubbed or subtitled formats. **146m/C; VHS, DVD.** *IT GE* Dirk Bogarde; Ingrid Thulin; Helmut Griem; Charlotte Rampling; Helmut Berger; ***D:*** Luchino Visconti; ***M:*** Maurice Jarre.

The Damned 🦴 **2006 (R)** Cheap, dull urban horror (with a thankfully brief runtime) about some Latino vampires moving into the 'hood. The guys next door discover their new neighbors are bloodsuckers and team up with a weary PI (Bridges) to get rid of the fanged threat. **76m/C; DVD.** Todd Bridges; Elias Castillo; Victor Zaragoza; Chris Angelo; Raul Martinez; Jose Roseto; ***D:*** Eduardo Quiroz; Jose Quiroz; ***W:*** Eduardo Quiroz; Jose Quiroz; ***C:*** Eduardo Quiroz; Jose Quiroz; ***M:*** Eduardo Quiroz. **VIDEO**

The Damned Don't Cry 🦴🦴 1/2 **1950** Crawford is a small-town girl who leaves her family to climb the social ladder to the top of organized crime as a boss's moll by using her looks and guile. Melodrama, in the vein of Crawford's "Mildred Pierce," mixes with a noirish atmosphere to create an interesting crime drama/character study. **103m/C; DVD.** Joan Crawford; David Brian; Steve Cochran; Kent Smith; Hugh Sanders; Selena Royle; Jacqueline DeWit; Morris Ankrum; Edith Evanson; Richard Egan; Jimmy Moss; Eddie Marr; ***D:*** Vincent Sherman; ***W:*** Harold Medford; ***C:*** Ted D. McCord; ***M:*** Daniele Amfitheatrof.

Damned River 🦴 1/2 **1989 (R)** Four friends take a guided tour down Zimbabwe's Zambezi River, only to find midway down that their guide is a murderous psycho. Survival becomes a priority. **93m/C; VHS, Streaming.** Stephen Shellen; Lisa Aliff; John Terlesky; Marc Poppel; Bradford Bancroft; ***D:*** Michael Schroeder; ***W:*** John Crowther.

The Damned United 🦴🦴 1/2 **2009 (R)** Fact and fiction mix in Hooper's bio of 70s-era football team manager Brian Clough (Sheen) who goes from successfully remaking Derby County into a winner to lead their archrivals Leeds United, where he quickly alienates both players and management. Follows typical rise-and-fall-of-the-rebel theme but Sheen kicks it up a notch (in fact, the role was reportedly written for him). More focused on Clough's hyper-competitive personality than the actual sport. **97m/C; Blu-Ray, On Demand.** *GB* Michael Sheen; Timothy Spall; Colm Meaney; Henry Goodman; Maurice Roeves; Jim Broadbent; Stephen Graham; Brian McCardie; David Roper; Jimmy Reddington; ***D:*** Tom Hooper; ***W:*** Peter Morgan; ***C:*** Ben Smithard; ***M:*** Robert (Rob) Lane.

Damon and Pythias 🦴 *Il Tiranno di Siracusa; The Tyrant of Syracuse* **1962** Dull Italian sword-and-sandal flick. Syracuse tyrant Dionysus (Foa) wants to make an example of rabble-rousing Athenian Pythias (Burnett) and condemns him to death. His best friend Damon (Williams) offers himself as a hostage so Pythias can go home to see his sick wife. Dionysus agrees because he's sure Pythias won't return. **99m/C; DVD.** *IT* Guy Williams; Don Burnett; Arnoldo Foa; Ilaria Occhini; Liana Orfei; ***D:*** Curtis Bernhardt; ***W:*** Samuel Marx; Franco Riganti; ***C:*** Aldo Tonti; ***M:*** Angelo Francesco Lavagnino.

Damsel 🦴🦴 **2018 (R)** Pattinson plays Samuel Alabaster, a wealthy but naïve pioneer who sets off through the Wild West to marry his true love, Penelope (Wasikowska). As it turns out, though, Penelope's not exactly onboard with that plan. Although its billed as a quirky comedy in the vein of the Coen brothers, it lacks their wit and flair, making it more a weird western with a few slightly humorous gags. **113m/C; DVD.** Robert Pattinson; Mia Wasikowska; David Zellner; Nathan Zellner; Joseph Billingiere; ***D:*** David Zellner; Nathan Zellner; ***W:*** David Zellner; Nathan Zellner; ***C:*** Adam Stone.

A Damsel in Distress 🦴🦴🦴 **1937** Astaire falls for an upper-class British girl, whose family wants her to have nothing to do with him. Features memorable songs from the Gershwins. **101m/B; VHS, DVD.** Fred Astaire; Joan Fontaine; George Burns; Gracie Allen; Ray Noble; Montagu Love; Reginald Gardiner; ***D:*** George Stevens; ***M:*** George Gershwin; George Bassman; ***M:*** Ira Gershwin.

Damsels in Distress 🦴🦴 1/2 **2011 (PG-13)** Writer/director Stillman delivers his first dramedy since 1998 with this indie romp about an East Coast college dominated by a male-driven culture. A trio of new girl students (Gerwig, Echikunwoke, MacLemore) tries to change the landscape of the school through atypical girl power means. The men in their life (Brody, Becker, Metcalf, Magnussen) can only hope to keep up. Funny, smart, and engaging, it makes one realize how rare Stillman's gift at dialogue is and how much it's been missed. **99m/C; DVD, Blu-Ray, Streaming.** Greta Gerwig; Carrie Maclemore; Megalyn Echikunwoke; Analeigh Tipton; Billy Magnussen; Ryan Metcalf; Jermaine Crawford; Caitlin FitzGerald; Hugo Becker; Adam Brody; ***D:*** Whit Stillman; ***W:*** Whit Stillman; ***C:*** Doug Emmett; ***M:*** Mark Suozzo.

Dan Candy's Law 🦴 1/2 *Alien Thunder* **1973** A Canadian mountie becomes a driven hunter, and then desperate prey, when he tries to track down the Indian who killed his partner. **90m/C; VHS, DVD.** *CA* Donald Sutherland; Gordon Tootoosis; Chief Dan George; Kevin McCarthy; ***D:*** Claude Fournier; ***M:*** Georges Delerue.

Dan in Real Life 🦴🦴 1/2 **2007 (PG-13)** Gee, a romantic comedy that features age-appropriate adults who actually act like grown-ups! Who knew? Likeable (if baffled) widower Dan (Carell) is trying to raise three daughters and write his family advice newspaper column (of course none of his advice works for him). Dan's not even thinking about dating until he takes his brood to a family reunion and meets beautiful, friendly Marie (Binoche), who happens to be his younger bro Mitch's (Cook) new love. Dan tries to suppress his feelings, which results in a number of amusing moments for Carell that don't go over the top. Engaging if predictable. **98m/C; DVD.** Steve Carell; Juliette Binoche; Dane Cook; Dianne Wiest; John Mahoney; Emily Blunt; Alison Pill; Brittany Robertson; Marlene Lawston; Norbert Lee Butz; Amy Ryan; ***D:*** Peter Hedges; ***W:*** Peter Hedges; Pierce Gardner; ***C:*** Lawrence Sher; ***M:*** Sondre Lerche.

Dance Flick 🦴 1/2 **2009 (PG-13)** Clumsy genre spoof of teen/dance flicks from the Wayans brothers with ballet meeting hip-hop. Suburban white girl Megan (Bush) is rejected by Juilliard but finds Thomas (Wayans Jr.), the most non-threatening gangbanger in existence. He's also the brother of Megan's new bestie at Music High School, single mom Charity (Atkins). Thomas and his street dance crew owe money to super-size bad guy Sugar Bear (Grier, hilarious in a fat suit) and a dance-off is the answer to his woes. **83m/C; DVD, Blu-Ray.** Marlon Wayans; Shawn Wayans; Keenen Ivory Wayans; Amy Sedaris; Christina Murphy; Essence Atkins; David Alan Grier; Chris Elliott; Shoshana Bush; Damon Wayans, Jr.; Brennan Hillard; Craig Wayans; ***D:*** Damien Dante Wayans; ***W:*** Marlon Wayans; Shawn Wayans; Keenen Ivory Wayans; Damien Dante Wayans; Craig Wayans; ***C:*** Mark Irwin.

Dance Fools Dance 🦴🦴🦴 **1931** Fast-paced drama has Crawford and Bakewell as a pair of spoiled rich kids who are forced to face poverty when the stock market crashes. He meets up with Gable, who's producing liquor illegally, while she gets a job at a newspaper. When Gable arranges something akin to the St. Valentine's Day Massacre, Bakewell's investigative reporting of the situation produces fatal results. The Hays Office had a problem with Crawford and friends appearing in their underwear. Cast notes: Gable was just starting out at MGM, which is why he was billed sixth; the William Holden here is not THE William Holden, and Edwards went on to provide the voice of Jiminy Cricket in "Pinocchio." **82m/B; VHS, DVD.** Joan Crawford; Lester Vail; Cliff Edwards; William "Billy" Bakewell; Clark Gable; ***D:*** Harry Beaumont; ***C:*** Charles Rosher.

Dance, Girl, Dance 🦴🦴 **1940** The private lives and romances of a wartime nightclub dance troupe. Standard Hollywood potpourri of dance, drama, comedy. **88m/B; VHS, DVD, Blu-Ray.** Maureen O'Hara; Louis Hayward; Lucille Ball; Virginia Field; Ralph Bellamy; Maria Ouspenskaya; Mary Carlisle; Katherine Alexander; Edward Brophy; Walter Abel; Harold Huber; ***D:*** Dorothy Arzner; ***W:*** Frank Davis; Tess Slesinger; ***C:*** Russell Metty; ***M:*** Edward Ward. Natl. Film Reg. '07.

Dance Hall 🦴 1/2 **1941** A Pennsylvania dance hall owner is propelled into romantic confusion with the introduction of a sultry blond dancer into his club. **73m/B; VHS, DVD.** Cesar Romero; Carole Landis; William Henry; June Storey; Charles Halton; ***D:*** Irving Pichel.

Dance Me Outside 🦴🦴 1/2 **1995 (R)** Native Canadian teens look for some excitement on their Northern Ontario reservation and find themselves cut off from their tradition-bound parents in this slice of life drama. Friends Silas and Blackie plot revenge against a white who murdered a native girl while Silas' sister Illianna comes to visit from Toronto, with her Yuppie lawyer husband, just as her ex-boyfriend returns from a prison stint. Based on the novel by W.P. Kinsella. **91m/C; VHS, DVD.** *CA* Ryan Black; Adam Beach; Michael Greyeyes; Lisa Lacroix; ***D:*** Bruce McDonald; ***W:*** Bruce McDonald; Don McKellar; John Frizzell. Genie '95: Film Editing.

Dance of Death WOOF! *House of Evil; Macabre Serenade* **1968** Just before his death, Karloff agreed to appear in footage for four Mexican cheapies that were practically thrown together (Karloff actually filmed his scenes in Los Angeles). If they had mixed the footage instead of matched it, the flicks couldn't be any worse. This one concerns a lunatic toy-maker whose toys kill and maim his heirs. **89m/C; VHS, DVD.** *MX* Boris Karloff; Julissa; Andres Garcia; Jack Hill; ***D:*** Juan Ibanez.

The Dance of Reality 🦴🦴 1/2 *La Danza de la Realidad* **2014** Cult director Jodorowsky aims to challenge his audience and his fans will be happy to hear that his 28-year hiatus hasn't softened him up. Only on the surface is there an actual story, focusing on feminine and sensitive Alejandro (Herskovits), a boy growing up in 1930s coastal Chile with a comically tyrant father (Jodorowsky) and a mother who communicates only with song (Flores). Sure enough, the proceedings quickly spin into mysticism, racial taboos, and a dog show thrown in for good measure. For all its inspired imagery and surrealism, there's still a lack of inspiration, feeling like the director is often simply trying to be weird for weirdness's sake. **130m/C; DVD, Blu-Ray.** *CL FR* Brontis Jodorowsky; Pamela Flores; Jeremias Herskovits; Alejandro Jodorowsky; ***D:*** Alejandro Jodorowsky; ***W:*** Alejandro Jodorowsky; ***C:*** Jean-Marie Drevjou; ***M:*** Adan Jodorowsky.

Dance of the Dead 🦴🦴 **2008** The obstacles of a good prom night are many: Getting the money for the dress, tux, and limo. Scoring the booze. Getting your date buzzed enough to agree to give it up. And, of course, escaping the hordes of flesh-eating zombies running down the street at top speed, kicking butt and stealing cars as they go. Oh, to be a teenager again, spending time gleefully shooting the undead while trying to seduce cheerleaders. **95m/C; DVD.** Jared Kusnitx; Greyson Chadwick; Chandler Darby; Carissa Capobianco; Randy McDowell; Michael V. Mammoliti; Mark Lynch; Justin Welborn; Mark Oliver; Blair Redford; Lucas Till; Hunter Pierce; Jonathon Spencer; Stephen Caudill; J. Jacob Adelman; ***D:*** Gregg Bishop; ***W:*** Joe Ballarini; ***C:*** George Feucht; ***M:*** Kristopher Carter. **VIDEO**

A Dance to the Music of Time 🦴🦴 1/2 **1997** Explores the social, political, and artistic fortunes and foibles of upper-class Brits from the 1920s through the '60s from the viewpoint of everyman Nicholas Jenkins (D'Arcy and Purefoy) and his journey from schooldays to old age. Richardson is sexy man-eater Pamela Flitton and Beale is the unremarkable but ambitious and lucky Widmerpool among a cast of hundreds. Based on Anthony Powell's 12-volume series. **480m/C; DVD.** *GB* James Purefoy; Miranda Richardson; Simon Russell Beale; James D'Arcy; Paul Rhys; Jonathan Cake; Claire Skinner; Alan Bennett; John Gielgud; Zoe Wanamaker; Edward Fox; Michael Williams; Eileen Atkins; ***D:*** Alvin Rakoff; Christopher Morhan; ***W:*** Hugh Whitemore; ***C:*** Chris Seager; ***M:*** Carl Davis. **TV**

Dance with a Stranger 🦴🦴🦴 1/2 **1985 (R)** The engrossing and factual story of Ruth Ellis (Richardson) who gained notoriety as the last woman hanged in Great Britain in 1955. This emotional and sometimes violent film mirrors the sensationalism and class conflicts of 1950s British society. The film follows single mom Ellis's pre-trial life as a tawdry nighclub hostess, struggling to maintain her independence, while becoming obsessively involved with immature cas/upper-class playboy David Blakely (Everett) whom she murders when he finally rejects her. **101m/C; VHS, DVD.** *GB* Miranda Richardson; Rupert Everett; Ian Holm; Joanne Whalley; Mathew Carroll; Tom Chadbon; Jane Bertish; David Troughton; Paul Mooney; Stratford Johns; Susan Kyd; Lesley Manville; Sallie-Anne Field; Martin Murphy; Michael Jenn; Daniel Massey; ***D:*** Mike Newell; ***W:*** Shelagh Delaney; ***C:*** Peter Hannan; ***M:*** Richard Hartley. Cannes '85: Film.

Dance with Death 🦴 **1991 (R)** When strippers turn up brutally murdered, a young journalist goes undercover to solve the case. **90m/C; VHS, DVD.** Maxwell Caulfield; Barbara Alyn Jones; Martin Mull; Drew Snyder; Catya (Cat) Sassoon; ***D:*** Charles Philip Moore.

Dance with Me 🦴🦴 1/2 *Shut Up and Dance* **1998 (PG)** Cuban emigre Rafael (Chayanne) winds up in Houston, teaching at the fading Excelsior Dance Studio, which is owned by a friend of his late mother's, John Burnett (Kristofferson). Instructor (and single mom) Ruby (Williams) is looking for a partner who can help her enter the competitive ballroom dance world but she's not looking for love. But at the World Open Dance Championships in Las Vegas, she may find both. Hot salsa music and dancing, as well as the charm of the two leads, make this one worth watching for any dancer fever fan. **126m/C; VHS, DVD.** Vanessa L(ynne) Williams; Chayanne; Kris Kristofferson; Joan Plowright; Jane Krakowski; Beth Grant; ***D:*** Randa Haines; ***W:*** Daryl Matthews; ***C:*** Fred Murphy; ***M:*** Michael Convertino.

Dance with Me, Henry 🦴 1/2 **1956** When Lou becomes involved with Bud's gambling debts and the local district attorney turns up dead, Lou's not only wanted by the law, but by the mafia as well. This was the great comedy duo's last picture together and it's clear the pair are not happy about working with each other, even on this mediocre effort. **90m/B; VHS, DVD, Blu-Ray.** Bud Abbott; Lou Costello; Gigi Perreau; Rusty Hamer; Mary Wickes; Ted de Corsia; ***D:*** Charles T. Barton.

Dance with the Devil *Perdita Durango* **1997 (R)** Prostitute Perdita (Perez) and witch doctor/drug dealer Romeo (Bardem) meet at the Mexican border and soon become lovers and criminal partners. They get a kinky job hijacking human fetuses for a Vegas mob boss and, since Romeo believes in human sacrifice before starting a new endeavor, they kidnap a cute teen couple as the victims. Then Romeo discovers his expartner, Shorty (Segura), isn't so ex—and there's lots more that's very weird and bloody. Based on the novel "59 and Raining: The Story of Perdita Durango" by Barry Gifford. **126m/C; VHS, DVD.** *MX SP* Rosie Perez; Javier Bardem; Harley Cross; Aimee Graham; Don Stroud; James Gandolfini; Santiago Segura; Screamin' Jay Hawkins; Alex Cox; Carlos Bardem; ***D:*** Alex de la Iglesia; ***W:*** Alex de la Iglesia; Barry Gifford; Jorge Guerricaechevarria; David Trueba; ***C:*** Flavio Martinez Labiano; ***M:*** Simon Boswell.

Dancehall Queen **1997** Single mom Marcia is barely scraping together a living as a Kingston street vendor. So she decides to disguise herself and enter a dancehall contest to try to win some cash as well as solve some other personal problems. **96m/C; DVD.** *JM* Audrey Reid; Carl Davis; Paul Campbell; Cherine Anderson; ***D:*** Don Letts; Rick Elgood; ***W:*** Suzanne Fenn; Don Letts; ***C:*** Louis Mulvey; ***M:*** Wally Badarou.

Dancer in the Dark **1999 (R)** A love it or hate it production from Danish provocateur Von Trier. Czech immigrant Selma (Bjork) is a single mom working in a small factory, where her best friend is another immigrant, Kathy (Deneuve). Selma is also close to her landlords Bill and Jean (Morse, Seymour) but tells no one that she's going blind, a fate her son will also suffer unless he gets an expensive operation. Then the money Selma has been saving is stolen and she accuses the bankrupt Bill, leading to tragedy. It sounds clear enough but mixed up in the story is Selma's participation in an amateur production of "The Sound of Music" and her numerous musical fantasies. Exteriors were filmed in Sweden and interiors in a Danish studio, although it's set in rural America. **141m/C; VHS, DVD.** *DK SW FR* Bjork; Catherine Deneuve; David Morse; Peter Stormare; Cara Seymour; Joel Grey; Vincent Paterson; Vladica Kostic; Jean-Marc Barr; Udo Kier; Zeljko Ivanek; ***D:*** Lars von Trier; ***W:*** Lars von Trier; ***C:*** Robby Muller; ***M:*** Bjork. Cannes '00: Actress (Bjork), Film; Ind. Spirit '01: Foreign Film.

Dancer, Texas—Pop. 81 **1998 (PG)** Four buddies have to decide if they're going to fulfill the pact they made when they were 11 to leave the eponymous town upon graduating from high school. Each one has a reason to consider sticking around: Keller (Meyer) tkaes care of his widowed grandfather; Terrell Lee (Facinelli) is expected to join the family's failing oil business; Squirrel (Embry) thinks he should care for his alcoholic father; and John (Mills) is a natural at cattle ranching. Coming-of-age comedy deals in honest emotion and humor, and doesn't resort to syrupy sentiment or small-town stereotyping. Texas-born writer-director McCanlies' feature debut. **95m/C; VHS, DVD.** Breckin Meyer; Peter Facinelli; Eddie Mills; Ethan (Randall) Embry; Ashley Johnson; Patricia Wettig; Michael O'Neill; Eddie Jones; Alexandra Holden; ***D:*** Tim McCanlies; ***W:*** Tim McCanlies; ***C:*** Andrew Dintenfass; ***M:*** Steve Dorff.

The Dancer Upstairs **1/2** **2002 (R)** Politics and romance once again make strange bedfellows in this adaptation of Shakespeare's 1995 novel. In an unidentified Latin American country (filmed in Ecuador), idealistic lawyer Agustin Rejas (Bardem) abandons the law to pursue justice by joining the police. He's been assigned to track down Ezequiel (Folk), a terrorist who's behind a series of executions of government leaders. Rejas dotes on his young daughter, who takes ballet lessons from the lovely Yolanda (Morante), with whom he becomes infatuated. But his interest leads to him learning of a connection between the teacher and his quarry. Malkovich's directorial debut. **128m/C; VHS, DVD.** *US SP* Javier Bardem; Laura Morante; Juan Diego Botto; Elvira Minguez; Oliver Cotton; Luis Miguel Cintra; Abel Folk; Alexandra Lencastre; ***D:*** John Malkovich; ***W:*** Nicholas Shakespeare; ***C:*** Jose Luis Alcaine; ***M:*** Alberto Iglesias.

Dancers **1/2 1987 (PG)** During the filming of the ballet "Giselle" in Italy, a famous, almost-over-the-hill dancer (Baryshnikov, ten years after his role in "The Turning Point") coaches a young, inexperienced starlet. He hopes to revitalize his life and his dancing. Features dancers from the Baryshnikov-led American Ballet Theatre. **99m/C; VHS, DVD.** Mikhail Baryshnikov; Leslie Browne; Julie Kent; Mariangela Melato; Alessandra Ferri; Lynn Seymour; Victor Barbee; Tommy (Thomas) Rall; ***D:*** Herbert Ross; ***M:*** Pino Donaggio.

Dances with Wolves **1/2 1990 (PG-13)** The story of a U.S. Army soldier, circa 1870, whose heroism in battle allows him his pick of posts. His choice, to see the West before it disappears, changes his life. He meets, understands and eventually becomes a member of a Lakota Sioux tribe in the Dakotas. Costner's first directorial attempt proves him a talent of vision and intelligence. This sometimes too objective movie lacks a sense of definitive character, undermining its gorgeous scenery and interesting perspective on the plight of Native Americans. Lovely music and epic proportions. Adapted by Blake from his novel. **181m/C; VHS, DVD, Blu-Ray.** Kevin Costner; Mary McDonnell; Graham Greene; Rodney A. Grant; Floyd "Red Crow" Westerman; Tantoo Cardinal; Robert Pastorelli; Charles Rocket; Maury Chaykin; Jimmy Herman; Nathan Lee Chasing His Horse; Wes Studi; ***D:*** Kevin Costner; ***W:*** Michael Blake; ***C:*** Dean Semler; ***M:*** John Barry. Oscars '90: Adapt. Screenplay, Cinematog., Director (Costner), Film, Film Editing, Orig. Score, Sound; AFI '98: Top 100; Directors Guild '90: Director (Costner); Golden Globes '91: Director (Costner), Film--Drama, Screenplay; Natl. Bd. of Review '90: Director (Costner); Natl. Film Reg. '07; Writers Guild '90: Adapt. Screenplay.

Dancing at Lughnasa **1998 (PG-13)** Kate (Streep) is the eldest of five lonely unwed sisters living together on a farm in 1930s Ireland. Their brother Father Jack (Gambon) returns home, fresh from a stint as a missionary in Africa, and Gerry (Ifans), who fathered a son with sister Christina, turns up as well. The reunion and resulting emotions are the main elements in this anecdotal tale, but unfortunately most of the episodes are lacking energy and fun. Streep gives her usual impeccably accented performance, McCormack is sensual as Christina, but it's Ifans who delivers the only gusto as he readies to go to war in Spain. Adapted from the Tony Award-winning stage play by Brian Friels. Title refers to a pagan ritual the town engages in annually, and one would think just the dance alone should have led to a more energetic outing. **92m/C; VHS, DVD.** *IR GB* Meryl Streep; Michael Gambon; Catherine McCormack; Rhys Ifans; Brid Brennan; Kathy Burke; Sophie Thompson; Lorcan Cranitch; Darrell Johnston; Peter Gowen; Dawn Bradfield; Marie Mullen; ***D:*** Pat O'Connor; ***W:*** Frank McGuinness; ***C:*** Kenneth Macmillan; ***M:*** Bill Whelan.

Dancing at the Blue Iguana **1/2 2000 (R)** These "dancers" are strippers at the titular San Fernando Valley club and their interwoven stories comprise the plot. Stormy (Kelley) is the tough veteran with the questionable past; Angel (Hannah) is sweet but dumb; Jo (Tilly) must deal with an unplanned pregnancy; Jasmine (Oh) is an aspiring poet; and Jesse (Ayanna) is an over-eager newcomer. Eddie (Wisdom) presides over the establishment and has his own demons. Much of the film was improvised in workshops and rehearsals. **123m/C; VHS, DVD.** Sheila Kelley; Daryl Hannah; Sandra Oh; Jennifer Tilly; Charlotte Ayanna; Robert Wisdom; Elias Koteas; Vladimir Mashkov; W. Earl Brown; Chris Hogan; Rodney Rowland; Kristin Bauer van Straten; ***D:*** Michael Radford; ***W:*** David Linter; Michael Radford; ***C:*** Ericson Core; ***M:*** Tal Bergman; Renato Neto.

Dancing Co-Ed **1/2 1939** In this MGM musical, press agent Joe Drew (Karns) comes up with a stunt to find a new dancing star for a movie by holding auditions on college campuses. The contest is rigged though since starlet Patty Marlow (Turner) already has the gig but she enrolls at a Midwestern college to make it look legit. Only college newspaper editor Pug Braddock (Carlson) smells something fishy. **80m/B; DVD.** Lana Turner; Richard Carlson; Ann Rutherford; Roscoe Karns; Lee Bowman; Leon Errol; Monty Woolley; Thurston Hall; Artie Shaw; ***D:*** S. Sylvan Simon; ***W:*** Albert Mannheimer; ***C:*** Alfred Gilks; ***M:*** Edward Ward; David Snell.

Dancing in September **1/2 2000 (R)** Black writer Tomasina "Tommy" Crawford (Parker) has just lost her job on a sitcom so she has nothing to lose by pitching a black issues comedy to George (Washington), a slick exec looking to make a name for himself at a startup network. Tommy also discovers the show's lead—former gangbanger and single dad James (Shannon). The three gain success but come under fire from the black community for being sellouts as they reevaluate their personal and professional aspirations. **106m/C; VHS, DVD.** Nicole Ari Parker; Isaiah Washington, IV; Vicellous Shannon; Malinda Williams; Jay Underwood; Michael Cavanaugh; Chi McBride; James Avery; LeVar Burton; Peter Onorati; Kadeem Hardison; Jenifer Lewis; Anna Maria Horsford; ***D:*** Reggie Rock Bythewood; ***W:*** Reggie Rock Bythewood; ***C:*** Bill Dill. **CABLE**

Dancing in the Dark **1/2 1986 (PG-13)** An interesting but slow-moving Canadian film about the perfect housewife who learns that after 20 years of devotion to him, her spouse has been unfaithful. Realizing how her life has been wasted she murders her husband and, in the end, suffers a mental breakdown. **93m/C; VHS, DVD.** *CA* Martha Henry; Neil Munro; Rosemary Dunsmore; Richard Monette; ***D:*** Leon Marr; ***W:*** Leon Marr. Genie '87: Actress (Henry).

Dancing in Twilight **2005 (PG-13)** Houston businessman Madhav Singh (Evari) can barely function after the unexpected death of his wife (Patel). His loneliness is amplified when his estranged son Sam (Penn) comes home for a visit, accompanied by his girlfriend (Sheth). Now Madhav realizes he must make a decision about moving on with his life. **90m/C; DVD.** Erik Avari; Kal Penn; Mimi Rogers; Louise Fletcher; Sheetal Sheth; Artee Patel; ***D:*** Bob Rose; ***W:*** Rishi Vij; ***C:*** Robert Steadman; ***M:*** Scott Szabo.

Dancing Lady **1/2 1933** Rarely seen film is MGM's answer to "42nd Street," with Crawford as a small-time hoofer trying to break into Broadway. The screen debuts of Astaire and Eddy. Look for none other than the Three Stooges as stage hands. **93m/B; VHS, DVD.** Clark Gable; Joan Crawford; Fred Astaire; Franchot Tone; Nelson Eddy; Ted Healy; Moe Howard; Curly Howard; Larry Fine; May Robson; Robert Benchley; Eve Arden; ***D:*** Robert Z. Leonard; ***W:*** P.J. Wolfson; Allen Rivkin; Zelda Sears; ***C:*** Oliver Marsh; ***M:*** Richard Rodgers; Burton Lane; Jimmy McHugh.

Dancing Mothers **1/2 1926** A fast-living woman becomes involved with her mother's roguish boyfriend in this silent film with accompanying musical score. **85m/B; Silent; VHS, DVD.** Clara Bow; Alice Joyce; Conway Tearle; Donald Keith; ***D:*** Herbert Brenon; ***W:*** Forrest Halsey; ***C:*** J. Roy Hunt.

Dancing Pirate **1936** A Boston dance instructor is kidnapped by pirates and jumps ship in Mexico, where he romances a mayor's daughter. The silly story boasts some Rodgers and Hart tunes, plus the early use of Technicolor, exploited here for all it was worth and then some. **83m/C; VHS, DVD.** Charles Collins; Frank Morgan; Steffi Duna; Luis Alberni; Victor Varconi; Jack La Rue; ***D:*** Lloyd Corrigan.

Dandy in Aspic **1/2 1968 (R)** A double-agent is assigned to kill himself in this hard to follow British spy drama. The film is based on Derek Marlowe's novel. Mann died midway through shooting and Harvey finished direction. **107m/C; VHS, DVD.** *GB* Laurence Harvey; Tom Courtenay; Lionel Stander; Mia Farrow; Harry Andrews; Peter Cook; Per Oscarsson; ***D:*** Anthony Mann; ***M:*** Quincy Jones.

Danger Beneath the Sea **2002** What appears to be a made-for-TV adventure trots out every known submarine movie cliche. The massively jawed Van Dien is Capt. Sheffield, who's been given command of the Lansing, much to the dismay of many of the boat's officers. A nuclear incident occurs while the sub is in the China Sea, and he must deal with uncertainties about a possible war and a mutinous crew. The pace moves along nicely and production values are on the high side. **93m/C; VHS, DVD.** Casper Van Dien; Gerald McRaney; Shane Daly; Stewart Bick; ***D:*** Jon Cassar; ***W:*** Lucien K. Truscott, IV; ***C:*** Derick Underschultz; ***M:*** Norman Orenstein.

Danger Close **1/2** *Danger Close: The Battle of Long Tan* **2019 (R)** Major Harry Smith (Fimmel) is full of resentment when he given the assignment of commanding Delta Company. Once a special forces commando, Smith is now in charge of fresh, young troops under the age of 21 from Australia and New Zealand. Smith immediately clashes with cocky private Paul Large (Webber). Their relationship evolves as Smith and his men become involved in difficult, rain-soaked battles against more experienced North Vietnamese troops in what becomes known as the Battle of Long Tan. Though clearly inspired by previous war movies, the suspenseful Vietnam War drama is well crafted. **118m/C; DVD.** Travis Fimmel; Richard Roxburgh; Luke Bracey; Daniel Webber; Nicholas Hamilton; ***D:*** Kriv Stenders; ***W:*** Stuart Beattie; James Nicholas; Karel Segers; Paul Sullivan; Jack Brislee; ***C:*** Ben Nott; ***M:*** Caitlin Yeo.

Danger: Diabolik *Diabolik* **1968 (PG-13)** A superthief called Diabolik (Law) continuously evades the law while performing his criminal antics. **99m/C; VHS, DVD, Blu-Ray.** *IT* John Phillip Law; Marisa Mell; Michel Piccoli; Terry-Thomas; Adolfo Celi; ***D:*** Mario Bava; ***W:*** Mario Bava; Arduino (Dino) Maiuri; Adriano Barracio; Brian Degas; Tudor Gates; ***C:*** Antonio Rinaldi; ***M:*** Ennio Morricone.

Danger Lights **1/2 1930** Depicts the railroads and the railroad men's dedication to each other and their trains. **73m/B; VHS, DVD.** Jean Arthur; Louis Wolheim; Robert Armstrong; ***D:*** George B. Seitz.

Danger: Love at Work **1/2 1937** Screwball comedy has New York lawyer Henry (Haley) sent to a small town to close an important land purchase. But the owners are the eccentric Pemberton family and they cause Henry problems until he and (sane) daughter Toni (Sothern) fall for each other. **84m/B; DVD.** Jack Haley; Ann Sothern; Mary Boland; John Carradine; Edward Everett Horton; ***D:*** Otto Preminger; ***W:*** Ben Markson; James Edward Grant; ***C:*** Virgil Miller.

Danger on the Air **1938** A radio program sponsor—a much-despised misogynist—is murdered, and the sound engineer attempts to solve the mystery. Features Cobb in one of his earliest roles; Garrett also directed "Lady in the Morgue" that year. **70m/B; VHS, DVD.** Donald Woods; Nan Grey; Berton Churchill; Jed Prouty; William Lundigan; Richard "Skeets" Gallagher; Edward Van Sloan; George Meeker; Lee J. Cobb; Johnny Arthur; Linda Hayes; Louise Stanley; ***D:*** Otis Garrett.

Danger UXB **1/2 1981** During the 1940 London blitz, "Danger UXB" was scrawled wherever there was—or thought to be—an unexploded German bomb. This miniseries covers the exploits of the Royal Engineers whose job it was, with little training and lots of nerve, to defuse the bombs. Based on the memoirs of Major A.B. Hartley of the Royal Engineers. **660m/C; VHS, DVD.** *GB* Anthony Andrews; Judy Geeson; Maurice Roeves; Kenneth Cranham; Jeremy Sinden; Iain Cuthbertson; George Innes; Norman Chappell; Kenneth Farrington; Gordon Kane; Ken Kitson; Robert Longden; Robert Pugh; Deborah Watling; ***D:*** Roy Ward Baker; Douglas Camfield; Ferdinand Fairfax; Henry Herbert; Simon Langton; Jeremy Summers. **TV**

Danger Zone **1995 (R)** American mining expert Rick Morgan (Zane) uncovers a worldwide nuclear plot when he's lured to East Africa to supposedly contain a toxic spill. Instead, he's being used to recover a load of plutonium. **92m/C; VHS, DVD.** Billy Zane; Ron Silver; Robert Downey, Jr.; Cary-Hiroyuki Tagawa; ***D:*** Allan Eastman; ***W:*** Jeff Albert; ***C:*** Yossi Wein.

Dangerous **1/2 1935** Davis won her first Oscar for her rather overdone portrayal of a has-been alcoholic actress reformed by a smitten architect who recognizes her from her days as a star. **79m/B; VHS, DVD.** Bette Davis; Franchot Tone; Margaret Lindsay; John Eldredge; Alison Skipworth; George Irving; Dick Foran; ***D:*** Alfred E. Green; ***W:*** Laird Doyle; ***C:*** Ernest Haller; ***M:*** Bernhard Kaun. Oscars '35: Actress (Davis).

A Dangerous Age ½ **1957** A young girl, hoping to marry her lover, runs away from boarding school. **70m/C; VHS, DVD.** Ben Piazza; Ann Pearson; ***D:*** Sidney J. Furie; ***W:*** Sidney J. Furie; ***C:*** Herbert S. Alpert.

Dangerous Appointment *One in a Million* **1934** Story of an innocent store clerk accused of theft and attempted murder. **66m/B; VHS, DVD.** Charles Starrett; Dorothy Wilson; Guinn "Big Boy" Williams; Holmes Herbert; ***D:*** Frank Strayer; ***W:*** Karl Brown; Robert Ellis; ***C:*** M(ilton) A(rthur) Anderson.

Dangerous Beauty *The Honest Courtesan; Indiscretion; Venice; Courtesan* **1998 (R)** In 16th-century Venice, poor but beautiful Veronica (McCormack) gains wealth and power by becoming a sought after courtesan. The bewigged, bewitched and bewildered heads of state fall as hard for the comely courtesan as victims to the plague that strikes Venice later in the film. The one man she wants, however, Marco Venier (Sewell), comes from a wealthy family that looks down on the common Veronica. Director Herskovitz mixes the strong feminist messages with humor and a modern sensibility that sometimes make you forget you're watching a period film. Based on the biography of the real Veronica Franco by Margaret Rosenthal. **112m/C; VHS, DVD.** Catherine McCormack; Rufus Sewell; Moira Kelly; Jacqueline Bisset; Oliver Platt; Fred Ward; Naomi Watts; Jeroen Krabbe; Joanna Cassidy; Daniel Lapaine; Jake Weber; Simon Dutton; Michael Culkin; Peter Eyre; ***D:*** Marshall Herskovitz; ***W:*** Jeannine Dominy; ***C:*** Bojan Bazelli; ***M:*** George Fenton.

Dangerous Cargo **1996** Alexander (Lucas) is a Russian expatriate living in L.A. who is being blackmailed by the Russian Mob to help smuggle U.S. money back to Russia with the help of an older woman he has become infatuated with. The loans she takes out come due, and she grabs some guns and takes a girlfriend to journey there to seize the shipment of winter coats the money is held in. Since when do middle aged house fraus have the ability to outshoot trained killers? Only available as part of a collection. **91m/C; DVD, Blu-Ray.** Margaux Hemingway; Nicholas Worth; Peter J. Lucas; Rosemarie Belden; Joey Travolta; Hudson (Heidi) Leick; Robert Z'Dar; Olga Vodin; Laurel King; Leeza Vinnichenko; Pierre Dulat; Victor Rylkov; Jordan Nacchio; ***D:*** Eric Louzil; ***C:*** Mark Melville; ***M:*** Juan J. Colomer.

Dangerous Charter ½ **1962** A group of fishermen discover a deserted yacht and man its helm. But their good fortune takes a decided turn for the worst as they become caught in mob-propelled danger. **76m/C; VHS, DVD.** Chris Warfield; Sally Fraser; Richard Foote; Peter Foster; Wright King; ***D:*** Robert Gottschalk.

Dangerous Child ½ **2001** Sixteen-year-old Jack Cambridge (Merriman) is one angry kid. He lives with his divorced mom Sally (Burke), who tries to make allowances for his temper, even when he starts hitting her, because she doesn't want Jack taken away from her. But it's only a matter of time before the situation gets worse. Scarily good performance by Merriman. **95m/C; VHS, DVD.** Delta Burke; Ryan Merriman; Marc Donato; ***D:*** Graeme Campbell; ***W:*** Karen Stillman; ***C:*** Nikos Evdemon. **CABLE**

Dangerous Corner **1983** BBC TV adaptation of J.B. Priestley's 1932 play. Freda and Robert Caplan invite friends to their country home for the weekend. A careless remark by a guest causes unforeseen consequences relating to a suicide and the theft of a large sum of money. There's also a last-act plot twist. **90m/C; DVD.** *UK* Susan Fleetwood; David Robb; Daniel Day-Lewis; Judi Bowker; Sarah Badel; Anthony Valentine; Elvi Hale; ***D:*** James Ormerod. **TV**

Dangerous Crossing **1953** Crain's lovely but this is a B-list film noir. Ruth Bowman (Crain) is enjoying her transatlantic honeymoon cruise until her new spouse John (Betz) disappears. The only problem is the passenger list says Ruth is traveling alone and no one admits to seeing the couple together. Only sympathetic ship's doctor Paul Manning (Rennie) is willing to help out the bewildered bride. **75m/B; DVD.** Jeanne Crain; Michael Rennie; Carl Betz; Max (Casey Adams) Showalter; Mary Anderson; Willis Bouchey; Yvonne Peattie; Marjorie Hoshelle; ***D:*** Joseph M. Newman; ***W:*** Leo Townsend; ***C:*** Joseph LaShelle; ***M:*** Lionel Newman.

Dangerous Curves ½ **1988 (PG)** Two friends are assigned to deliver a new Porsche to a billionaire's daughter—one of them talks the other into taking a little detour, and the trouble begins. **93m/C; VHS, Streaming.** Robert Stack; Tate Donovan; Danielle von Zerneck; Robert Klein; Elizabeth Ashley; Leslie Nielsen; ***D:*** David Lewis. **VIDEO**

Dangerous Curves **1999 (R)** Handsome attorney decides to track down a former lover. This is always a mistake. **85m/C; VHS, DVD.** Robert Carradine; David Carradine; Maxine Bahns; Marina Carradine; ***D:*** Jeremiah Cullinane; ***W:*** Christopher Wood; ***C:*** Laurence Manly; ***M:*** Siobhan Cleary. **VIDEO**

Dangerous Evidence: The Lori Jackson Story ½ **1999** Whitfield stars in this true story as Lori Jackson, a 1980s civil rights activist who takes on the case of Marine Corporal Lindsay Scott (Yearwood), the only black in the battalion, who is falsely accused of raping a white officer's wife. When he is convicted on circumstantial evidence, Jackson secures a new trial, which exacts a high price on her own life. Based on the book "Dangerous Evidence" by Ellis A. Cohen. **90m/C; VHS, DVD.** Lynn Whitfield; Richard Lineback; Richard Yearwood; Peter MacNeill; Erica Luttrell; Barbara Mamabolo; Geordie Johnson; Bruce Gray; ***D:*** Sturla Gunnarsson; ***W:*** Sterling Anderson; ***M:*** Jonathan Goldsmith. **CABLE**

Dangerous Game ½ **1990 (R)** A computer hacker leads his friends through a department store's security system, only to find they can't get out until morning. They soon discover they are not alone when one of the group turns up dead. **102m/C; VHS, DVD.** Miles Buchanan; Sandy Lillingston; Kathryn Walker; John Polson; ***D:*** Stephen Hopkins.

Dangerous Game *Snake Eyes* **1993 (R)** Abrasive filmmaker Eddie Israel's (Keitel) new movie is about a couple's disintegrating marriage turning violent. Stars Sarah (Madonna) and Francis (Russo) find the on-camera violence spilling over into their tangled private lives while Eddie finds his personal traumas intruding more and more into the fictional material. Very raw movie within a movie features volatile Keitel (who also worked with Ferrera on "Bad Lieutenant") and suitably histrionic Russo; Madonna manages to hold her own in the least showy role, a cinematic first. Eddie's betrayed and bewildered wife is sympathetically portrayed by Ferrara, director Abel's wife. Also available in an unrated version. **107m/C; VHS, DVD, Blu-Ray.** Harvey Keitel; James Russo; Madonna; Nancy Ferrara; ***D:*** Abel Ferrara; ***W:*** Nicholas St. John.

Dangerous Ground **1996 (R)** Hackneyed thriller has expatriate South African Vusi (Cube) returning to his homeland to find his younger brother Steven, who has double-crossed the head of a drug cartel. Since Vusi's departure 12 years ago, apartheid's been replaced by gangs and drugs, and while combing the dangerous streets of Johannesburg, the graduate student implausibly turns into a gun-wielding hero. Rhames's sinister drug lord Muki is pic's best character. Lead Cube shows just how limited his acting ability is while Hurley displays the picture's clearly limited wardrobe budget. Interracial relationships are glossed over, while South Africa's sociological problems are used as plot devices and then ignored. Filmed on location in South Africa, this shoot-em-up's locale could easily be Anytown, USA. **92m/C; VHS, DVD.** Ice Cube; Elizabeth Hurley; Ving Rhames; Eric Miyeni; Sechaba Morojele; ***D:*** Darrell Roodt; ***W:*** Darrell Roodt; Greg Latter; ***C:*** Paul Gilpin; ***M:*** Stanley Clarke.

Dangerous Liaisons *Les Liaisons Dangereuses; Dangerous Love Affairs* **1960** A couple take each other to the brink of destruction via their insatiable desire for extra-marital affairs. Vadim attempted to repeat his success with Brigitte Bardot by featuring wife Annette as a new sex goddess, but lightning didn't strike twice. **111m/B; VHS, DVD, Blu-Ray.** *FR IT* Gerard Philipe; Jeanne Moreau; Jeanne Valerie; Annette (Stroyberg) Vadim; Simone Renant; Jean-Louis Trintignant; Nicolas Vogel; ***D:*** Roger Vadim; ***W:*** Roger Vadim; ***C:*** Marcel Grignon.

Dangerous Liaisons **1988 (R)** Stylish and absorbing, this adaptation of the Laclos novel and the Christopher Hampton play centers around the relationship of two decadent members of 18th-century French nobility. The Marquise de Merteuil (Close) and the Vicomte de Valmont (Malkovich) spend their time testing and manipulating the loves of others. Merteuil wishes Valmont to deflower teenager Cecile (Thurman) while Valmont himself is after the virtuous married Madame de Tourvel (Pfeiffer). They find love often has a will of its own. Interesting to comparison-view with director Milos Forman's version of this story, 1989's "Valmont." **120m/C; VHS, DVD.** John Malkovich; Glenn Close; Michelle Pfeiffer; Uma Thurman; Keanu Reeves; Swoosie Kurtz; Mildred Natwick; Peter Capaldi; ***D:*** Stephen Frears; ***W:*** Christopher Hampton; ***C:*** Philippe Rousselot; ***M:*** George Fenton. Oscars '88: Adapt. Screenplay, Art Dir./Set Dec., Costume Des.; British Acad. '89: Adapt. Screenplay, Support. Actress (Pfeiffer); Cesar '90: Foreign Film; Writers Guild '88: Adapt. Screenplay.

Dangerous Liaisons ½ *Les Liaisons dangereuses* **2003** French miniseries of the oft-remade story moves the treachery to 1960s Paris high society. Deneuve and Everett head a fine cast, and they all perform well in the luscious, if overdone, adaptation. **200m/C; DVD.** *FR* Catherine Deneuve; Rupert Everett; Nastassja Kinski; Leelee Sobieski; Danielle Darrieux; Francoise Brion; Cyrille Thouvenin; Andrzej Zulawski; Lynne Adams; ***D:*** Josee Dayan; ***W:*** Eric-Emmanuel Schmitt; ***M:*** Angelo Badalamenti. **TV**

Dangerous Liaisons *Wei Xian Guan Xi* **2012** Pierre Choderlos de Laclos' novel is moved from 18th-century France to 1930s Shanghai on the eve of the Japanese invasion. Cynical playboy Yifan (Jang) meets his country cousin, beautiful widow Fengyu (Zhang). He makes a sexual bet with ambitious Jieyu (Cheung), who wants him to seduce her ex-lover's virginal teenage fiancee (Wang), and Yifan offers to seduce the demure widow as well. However, he doesn't expect the emotional response that both of them feel. English and Mandarin with subtitles. **110m/C; DVD, Blu-Ray.** *SG CH* Dong-gun Jang; Ziyi Zhang; Cecilia Cheung; Candy Wang; ***D:*** Jin-ho Hur; ***W:*** Geling Yan; ***C:*** Byung-seo Kim; ***M:*** Sung-woo Jo.

The Dangerous Lives of Altar Boys **2002 (R)** Don't let the title keep you away from this innovative coming-of-ager set in the '70s. Rebellious Catholic schoolmates Francis (Hirsch) and Tim (Culkin) seek love and chaos, respectively, while attending St. Agatha Parochial school, run by iron-fisted, wooden-legged nun Foster and hard-drinking priest D'Onofrio. While Francis falls for a girl with a secret past (Malone), Tim fantasizes about staging a coup against the sadistic Sister. The boys channel their boredom into increasingly dangerous pranks and a sacrilegious comic book called "The Atomic Trinity," which stars motorcycle-riding witch Nunzilla (Foster's nun rides a moped). Inventive directorial debut by Care with animated fantasy segments deftly directed by Spawn creator Todd McFarlane. Based on the 1994 novel by Chris Fuhrman. **105m/C; VHS, DVD.** Kieran Culkin; Emile Hirsch; Jena Malone; Jodie Foster; Vincent D'Onofrio; Jake Richardson; Tyler Long; ***D:*** Peter Care; ***W:*** Jeff Stockwell; Michael Petroni; ***C:*** Lance Acord; ***M:*** Marco Beltrami; Joshua Homme. Ind. Spirit '03: First Feature.

A Dangerous Man: Lawrence after Arabia **1991** At the 1919 Paris Peace Conference, T.E. Lawrence serves as the liaison to the Hashemite delegation in an effort to have the Allies agree to Arab independence. He finds the diplomatic fields more treacherous than anything he encountered during WWI. Fiennes does well in the difficult role of the reluctant, ambivalent hero. **104m/C; VHS, DVD.** *GB* Ralph Fiennes; Denis Quilley; Alexander Siddig; Nicholas Jones; Roger Hammond; Peter Copley; Paul Freeman; Polly Walker; ***D:*** Christopher Menaul; ***W:*** Tim Rose Price. **TV**

A Dangerous Method ½ **2011 (R)** Filmmaker Cronenberg has long been curious about the complexities of human sexuality and psychosis and so turns to the men who helped define it as he tells the story of psychoanalysts Sigmund Freud (Mortensen) and Carl Jung (Fassbender), two geniuses who inspired and often infuriated each other. The focus is on their dynamic with Sabina Spielrein (Knightley), who is at first a patient of Jung's and later a lover and even a colleague. The cast is uniformly great, but the film is remarkably safe, especially for a director who has been so dangerous in the past. Vincent Cassel appears in a small-but-superior performance. **99m/C; DVD, Blu-Ray.** Viggo Mortensen; Michael Fassbender; Keira Knightley; Sarah Gadon; Vincent Cassel; ***D:*** David Cronenberg; ***W:*** Christopher Hampton; ***C:*** Peter Suschitzky; ***M:*** Howard Shore.

Dangerous Minds ½ *My Posse Don't Do Homework* **1995 (R)** Based on the autobiography of LouAnne Johnson (Pfeiffer), a 10-year Marine turned inspirational inner-city high school English teacher. Naturally, Johnson has to take on the establishment educational system to fight for her kids. If you can buy Pfeiffer as an ex-jarhead, a tough teacher should be no problem. A subplot romance involving Pfeiffer and Andy Garcia was cut from the film to focus on the teacher/student byplay (which seems a real shame); Elaine May did a uncredited script rewrite. Kinda squishy and surprisingly successful. **99m/C; VHS, DVD.** Michelle Pfeiffer; George Dzundza; Courtney B. Vance; Robin Bartlett; Renoly Santiago; Lorraine Toussaint; John Neville; ***D:*** John N. Smith; ***W:*** Ronald Bass; ***C:*** Pierre Letarte. Blockbuster '96: Drama Actress, T. (Pfeiffer).

Dangerous Money ½ **1946** In this 37th film in the series, Charlie Chan (Toler), son Jimmy (Sen Yung), and chauffeur Chattanooga Brown (Best) are all aboard a ship traveling to Pago Pago in order to expose a gang of thieves. But Chan finds himself also investigating the murder of a federal agent that's tied into stolen art and smuggled currency. **66m/B; DVD.** Sidney Toler; Victor Sen Yung; Willie Best; Joseph Crehan; Gloria Warren; Joseph Allen; Elaine Lange; Emmett Vogan; Amira Moustafa; Rick Vallin; ***D:*** Terry Morse; ***W:*** Miriam Kissinger; ***C:*** William Sickner.

Dangerous Moves *La Diagonale du Fou* **1984 (PG)** A drama built around the World Chess championship competition between a renowned Russian master and a young, rebellious dissident. The chess game serves as both metaphor and background for the social and political tensions it produces. With English subtitles. **96m/C; VHS, DVD.** *SI* Liv Ullmann; Michel Piccoli; Leslie Caron; Alexandre Arbatt; ***D:*** Richard Dembo; ***W:*** Richard Dembo; ***C:*** Raoul Coutard. Oscars '84: Foreign Film.

Dangerous Orphans ½ **1986 (R)** Not completely awful tale of three brothers, orphaned as boys when their father is murdered before their very eyes, and the vendetta they have against the killer. **90m/C; VHS, DVD.** *NZ* Peter Stevens; Peter Bland; Ian Mune; Ross Girven; Jennifer Ward-Lealand; ***D:*** John Laing.

Dangerous Passion ½ **1995** Ruthless Lou (Williams) kills an intruder and tries to force his mechanic, Kyle (Weathers), to take the fall for him. But instead Kyle escapes with Lou's mistreated wife (and Kyle's lover) Meg (McKee), with Lou's henchman Frank (Boswell) on their tail. **94m/C; VHS, DVD.** Billy Dee Williams; Carl Weathers; Lonette McKee; Charles Boswell; Elpidia Carrillo; Tony DiBenedetto; Dan Ziskie; ***D:*** Michael Miller; ***W:*** Brian Taggert; ***C:*** Steve (Steven) Shaw; ***M:*** Rob Mounsey.

A Dangerous Place ½ **1994 (R)** Teenaged Ethan (Roberts) joins a karate team to prove his older brother's death was not a suicide. But the Scorpion's leader (Feldman) has a definite mean streak. **97m/C; VHS, DVD.** Ted Jan Roberts; Corey Feldman; Mako; Erin Gray; Dick Van Patten; ***D:*** Jerry P. Jacobs.

A Dangerous Profession 1949 Bail bondsman Vince Kane turns into a sap and uses his own dough when his former flame Lucy can't raise all the money needed to get her husband Claude out of jail on a securities theft beef. Claude gets himself murdered and Vince starts snooping around shady nightclub owner Jerry McKay. **79m/B; DVD.** George Raft; Ella Raines; Roland Winters; Pat O'Brien; Jim Backus; Bill Williams; ***D:*** Ted Tetzlaff; ***W:*** Warren Duff; Martin Rackin; ***C:*** Robert De Grasse; ***M:*** Frederick "Friedrich" Hollander.

Dangerous Pursuit 1989 A woman discovers that a man she slept with years ago is an assassin. Knowing too much, she finds herself next on his hit list. Decent psycho-thriller that was never released theatrically. **95m/C; VHS, DVD.** Gregory Harrison; Alexandra Powers; Scott Valentine; Brian Wimmer; Elena Stiteler; ***D:*** Sandor Stern.

Dangerous Relations 1/2 *Father & Son: Dangerous Relations* **1993 (PG-13)** Made-for-TV drama with Gossett as a tough convict at the end of 15-year prison sentence whose authority is challenged by young punk prisoner Underwood. Imagine his surprise when the old con realizes the punk is the son he hasn't seen since he started his time behind bars. Things don't improve (well, not at first) when they are paroled into each other's custody. **93m/C; VHS, DVD.** Louis Gossett, Jr.; Blair Underwood; Rae Dawn Chong; Clarence Williams, III; Rigg Kennedy; ***D:*** Georg Stanford Brown; ***W:*** Walter Halsey Davis; ***C:*** James Chressanthis. **TV**

Dangerous Summer *The Burning Man* **1982** In Australia, an American businessman building a resort is the victim of elaborate arson/murder insurance schemes. **100m/C; VHS, DVD.** *AU* Tom Skerritt; James Mason; Ian Gilmour; Wendy Hughes; ***D:*** Quentin Masters; ***W:*** David Ambrose; ***C:*** Peter Hannan.

Dangerous Touch 1/2 **1994 (R)** A very charming sociopath seduces a radio host/therapist into a willing, if kinky, sexual relationship. But everything she values is put at risk when he threatens to show an incriminating video tape if she doesn't continue to do as he demands. An unrated version is also available. **101m/C; VHS, DVD.** Lou Diamond Phillips; Kate Vernon; ***D:*** Lou Diamond Phillips.

Dangerous When Wet 1953 A typical Williams water-musical. A farm girl dreams of fame by swimming the English Channel. One famous number pairs Williams with cartoon characters Tom & Jerry in an underwater frolic. **96m/C; VHS, DVD.** Esther Williams; Fernando Lamas; Charlotte Greenwood; William Demarest; Jack Carson; ***D:*** Charles Walters; ***M:*** Arthur Schwartz; Johnny Mercer.

Dangerously We Live 1/2 **1941** Spy thriller, filled with plot holes, that benefitted from wartime paranoia. After a taxi accident, British agent Jane (Coleman) feigns amnesia while under the care of intern Michael Lewis (Garfield). A man (Olsen) claiming to be Jane's father appears at the hospital and insists on taking her home under the care of shrink Dr. Ingersoll (Massey). Michael accompanies them and he and Jane are soon captives of a Nazi spy ring. **77m/B; DVD.** John Garfield; Nancy Coleman; Raymond Massey; Moroni Olsen; Lee Patrick; Esther Dale; ***D:*** Robert Florey; ***W:*** Marion Parsonnet; ***C:*** L. William O'Connell.

Daniel 1/2 **1983 (R)** The children of a couple who were executed for espionage (patterned after the Rosenbergs) struggle with their past in the dissident 1960s. So-so adaptation of E.L. Doctorow's "The Book of Daniel." **130m/C; VHS, DVD, Blu-Ray.** Timothy Hutton; Amanda Plummer; Mandy Patinkin; Lindsay Crouse; Ed Asner; Ellen Barkin; ***D:*** Sidney Lumet; ***C:*** Andrzej Bartkowiak.

Daniel & Ana 2009 Unsettling psychological drama set in Mexico City. Upper-class Ana is out shopping with her teenage brother Daniel when they are kidnapped by a gang who isn't after ransom. They are forced to have sex on camera (based on a true story) for showing to a porn subculture. Much emotional fallout follows. Spanish with subtitles. **90m/C; DVD.** *MX* Marimar Vega; Dario Yazbek Bernal; Chema Torre; Jose Maria Torre; Montserrat Ontiveros; Luis Miguel Lombana; ***D:*** Michel Franco; ***W:*** Michel Franco; ***C:*** Chuy Chavez.

Daniel Boone 1/2 **1934** Daniel Boone guides a party of settlers from North Carolina to the fertile valleys of Kentucky, facing Indians, food shortages and bad weather along the way. O'Brien turns in a fine performance as the early American frontier hero. **75m/B; VHS, DVD.** George O'Brien; Heather Angel; John Carradine; ***D:*** David Howard.

Daniel Boone: Trail Blazer 1/2 **1956** Low-budget, though surprisingly well-acted rendition of the frontiersman's heroics, filmed in Mexico. **75m/B; VHS, DVD.** Bruce Bennett; Lon Chaney, Jr.; Faron Young; Damian O'Flynn; Fred Kohler, Jr.; Claudio Brook; Kem Dibbs; ***D:*** Ismael Rodriguez; Albert C. Gannaway; ***W:*** John Patrick; Tom Hubbard; ***C:*** Jack Draper; ***M:*** Raul Lavista.

Daniel Deronda 1/2 **2002** Daniel Deronda (Dancy) is the handsome, upright young ward of Sir Hugo Malinger (Fox), who dreams of doing something with his life in 1875 Victorian England. Two women will influence his decisions. The first is the headstrong Gwendolen Harleth (Garai), who will make a devil's bargain when she agrees to marry the wealthy and possessive Henleigh Grandcourt (Bonneville) to rescue her family from penury. The second is Jewess Mira Lapidoth (May), whom Daniel saves from drowning. He aids her singing career and helps her search for her family—a search that will lead to revelations about Daniel's own past. Last novel by George Eliot. **210m/C; VHS, DVD.** *GB* Hugh Dancy; Romola Garai; Hugh Bonneville; Jodhi May; Edward Fox; Barbara Hershey; Amanda Root; Greta Scacchi; Celia Imrie; David Bamber; Daniel Evans; Allan Corduner; Jamie Bamber; ***D:*** Tom Hooper; ***W:*** Andrew Davies; ***M:*** Robert (Rob) Lane. **TV**

Daniella by Night 1961 French model Daniella (Sommer) gets a contract to work for an Italian fashion house in Rome and she's soon attracting a lot of attention, including some that involves a spy plot. This leads to a chase through a Paris cabaret and a nude scene of Sommer, so how much does the story really matter, anyway. French with subtitles. **83m/B; VHS, DVD.** *FR* Elke Sommer; Ivan Desny; ***D:*** Max Pecas; ***W:*** Grisha Dabat; Wolfgang Steinhardt; ***C:*** Andre Germain; ***M:*** Charles Aznavour; Georges Garvarentz.

Danielle Steel's Changes 1/2 *Changes* **1991** Ladd is a successful, divorced New York TV anchorwoman who turns her life upside-down when she marries an equally successful, widowed Los Angeles surgeon (Nouri). Can they overcome their bicoastal careers to make things work? What do you think? **96m/C; VHS, DVD.** Cheryl Ladd; Michael Nouri; Christopher Gartin; Randee Heller; Charles Frank; James Sloyan; Cynthia Bain; ***D:*** Charles Jarrott. **TV**

Danielle Steel's Daddy 1/2 *Daddy* **1991** Ad exec Oliver Watson (Duffy) is happily married to Sarah (Mulgrew) and living the good life with their three kids—or so he thinks. Then Sarah announces she's leaving and Oliver's left to cope with family crisis as a single parent. A move to a new job in LA finds Oliver falling for an actress (Carter) and wondering if his family can ever be put back together again. **95m/C; VHS, DVD.** Patrick Duffy; Lynda Carter; Kate Mulgrew; ***D:*** Michael Miller. **TV**

Danielle Steel's Fine Things 1/2 *Fine Things* **1990** Bernie Fine thinks everything will be dandy now that he has a beautiful new bride and a cute stepdaughter. Then his wife dies and his stepdaughter's unreliable father wants sole custody. What's a nice guy to do? Based on the novel by Danielle Steel. **145m/C; VHS, DVD.** D.W. Moffett; Tracy Pollan; Judith Hoag; Cloris Leachman; Noley Thornton; ***D:*** Tom (Thomas R.) Moore; ***W:*** Peter Lefcourt. **TV**

Danielle Steel's Heartbeat 1/2 *Heartbeat* **1993** Shameless soap opera with Draper as Adrian Townsend, an L.A. TV-news producer with a self-involved ad-exec hubby (Kilner) who never wants children because of his own lousy childhood. When Adrian gets preggers the louse dumps her and she's left to weep prettily. That is until lovable divorced dad Bill Grant (Ritter) comes along to dry her tears. Predictable and glossy adaptation of the Steel best-seller. **95m/C; VHS, DVD.** Polly Draper; John Ritter; Kevin Kilner; Michael Lembeck; Nancy Morgan; Victor Dimattia; Christian Cousins; ***D:*** Michael Miller; ***W:*** Jan Worthington. **TV**

Danielle Steel's Kaleidoscope 1/2 *Kaleidoscope* **1990** Three sisters are separated in childhood, after the mysterious deaths of their parents. Then a detective is hired to reunite the adult siblings. But Hilary, the eldest, has secrets she doesn't want her sisters to share. **96m/C; VHS, DVD.** Jaclyn Smith; Perry King; Colleen Dewhurst; Donald Moffat; ***D:*** Jud Taylor. **TV**

Danielle Steel's Palomino 1/2 *Palomino* **1991** Bittersweet romance with Frost as an ambitious photojournalist who gets involved with a headstrong cowboy (Horsley). Their differences drive them apart and tragedy strikes when Frost becomes a paraplegic after a horse-riding accident. This leads her to new goals and the eventual return of her old flame. Between the palomino's blond mane and the equally impressive blond locks of Frost, there's a lot of streaming in the wind hair shots. Horsley's merely tall, dark, and handsome. **90m/C; VHS, DVD.** Lindsay Frost; Lee Horsley; Eva Marie Saint; Rod Taylor; Michele Greene; Beau Gravitte; ***D:*** Michael Miller; ***W:*** Karol Ann Hoeffner; ***C:*** Lloyd Ahern, II; ***M:*** Dominic Frontiere. **TV**

Danielle Steel's Star 1/2 *Star* **1993** Garth is the country girl with big dreams of a singing career but an unhappy love life. She falls for an idealist lawyer (Bierko) but their romance is put on hold by career ambitions. She goes to Hollywood and gets discovered, becoming a singing/acting sensation who's under the thumb of her increasingly obsessed manager, Wass. Meanwhile, Bierko's trapped in a miserable marriage to the wealthy, influential Farrell. Do the true lovers get together? (Take a guess.) Although the story spans 15 years and lots of tribulations the young Garth never ages a day. **90m/C; VHS, DVD.** Jennie Garth; Craig Bierko; Ted Wass; Terry Farrell; Penny Fuller; Mitchell Ryan; Jim Haynie; ***D:*** Michael Miller; ***W:*** Claire Labine. **TV**

Daniel's Daughter 2008 In this Hallmark Channel flick, successful magazine editor Cate (Leighton) returns to her tiny Massachusetts hometown after her father's death. She's still resentful over being sent away as a child after her mother died, but a chance to reexamine the past and then meeting a handsome attorney (Spence) bring some unexpected compensations. **88m/C; DVD.** Laura Leighton; Sebastian Spence; Barry Flatman; Derek McGrath; Martin Doyle; Kelli Fox; Brandon Firla; Brad Borbridge; ***D:*** Neill Fearnley; ***W:*** Tracy Rosen; ***C:*** Francois Dagenais; ***M:*** Ian Thomas. **CABLE**

The Danish Girl **2015 (R)** When one looks up "Oscar Bait" in the dictionary, they may see the poster for Tom Hooper's inert period drama about the first known recipient of sexual reassignment surgery. Lili Elbe (Redmayne) is a painter who discovers that he was born in the wrong body and works to become a woman, much to the surprise of his wife Gerda (Vikander, whose subtle, Oscar-award winning performance steals the film). This story sat in the Hollywood pipeline for years and time hasn't been kind. Calculated and flat, it means well but is easily forgotten by the time the credits are over. Based on the novel by David Ebershoff. **120m/C; DVD, Blu-Ray.** Alicia Vikander; Eddie Redmayne; Amber Heard; Emerald Fennell; Ben Whishaw; Matthias Schoenaerts; ***D:*** Tom Hooper; ***W:*** Lucinda Coxon; ***C:*** Danny Cohen; ***M:*** Alexandre Desplat. Oscars '15: Actress--Supporting (Vikander); Screen Actors Guild '15: Actress--Supporting (Vikander).

Danny 1/2 **1979 (G)** Charming story of a lonely young girl who receives an injured horse that was no longer fit for the spoiled daughter of the rich owners. **90m/C; VHS, DVD.** Rebecca Page; Janet Zarish; Barbara Jean Earhardt; Gloria Maddox; George Luce; ***D:*** Gene Feldman.

Danny Boy 1/2 **1946** Veteran dog, returning from the war, has difficulty adjusting to life back home. Things get worse for him and his young master when Danny Boy is assumed to be shell-shocked and dangerous. One of the few shell-shocked dog stories ever filmed. **67m/B; DVD, Streaming.** Robert "Buzzy" Henry; Ralph Lewis; Sybil Merritt; ***D:*** Terry Morse; ***W:*** Raymond L. Schrock; ***C:*** Jack Greenhalgh; ***M:*** Walter Greene.

Danny Boy *Angel* **1982 (R)** Takes place in Ireland where a young saxaphonist witnesses a murder and, in an effort to understand it, sets out to find the killer. Thought-provoking film is meant to highlight the continuing struggles in Ireland. **92m/C; VHS, DVD.** *IR* Stephen Rea; Veronica Quilligan; Honor Heffernan; Alan Devlin; Peter Caffrey; Ray McAnally; ***D:*** Neil Jordan; ***W:*** Neil Jordan; ***C:*** Chris Menges.

Danny Collins 1/2 **2015 (R)** This inspired-by-a-true story drama is surprisingly effective, carried by a game-winning performance from Pacino. The legendary actor plays the title character, an aging rocker who was kind of a big deal in the 1970s. His manager (Plummer) discovers a 40-year-old letter written to Collins by the legendary John Lennon, encouraging him to never give up. The inspiration sends Collins on the road to rediscover his passion in life, get his family back together, and find true love. It's all a bit cheesy and unrealistic but Pacino gives his most likable performance in years. **106m/C; DVD, Blu-Ray.** Annette Bening; Al Pacino; Jennifer Garner; Melissa Benoist; Bobby Cannavale; Nick Offerman; Christopher Plummer; ***D:*** Dan Fogelman; ***W:*** Dan Fogelman; ***C:*** Steve Yedlin; ***M:*** Ryan Adams; Theodore Shapiro.

Danny Deckchair **2003 (PG-13)** Danny Morgan (Ifans), an eccentric dreamer and cement-truck driver, has just discovered his realtor girlfriend Trudy (Clarke) is dating one of her clients. Well, as any young man faced with this knowledge would do, he attaches giant helium balloons to a lawn chair and flies away. Faster than you can say "99 Luftballoons" he crashes in the backyard of Glenda (Otto), a small town parking cop who is lonely and frustrated with love. Typical of such premises, they fall in love in an endearing fashion. Despite unoriginal script and enormous plot holes, Aussie comedy is mainly watchable due to its two romantic leads. **99m/C; VHS, DVD.** *AU* Rhys Ifans; Miranda Otto; Justine Clarke; Rhys Muldoon; Rod Zuanic; Maggie Dence; Jeanette Cronin; Frank Magree; Andrew Phelan; Andrew Batchelor; Jules Sobotta; Alan Flower; Michelle Boyle; Jane Beddows; Alex Mann; ***D:*** Jeff Balsmeyer; ***W:*** Jeff Balsmeyer; ***C:*** Martin McGrath; ***M:*** David Donaldson; Janet Roddick; Steve Roche.

Danny Roane: First Time Director 1/2 **2006 (R)** One-time sitcom star Danny Roane (Dick) has been blacklisted in Hollywood because of his infamous partying. After sobering up, Danny tries to make a comeback by directing his own autobiographical movie. But after Danny goes on a bender, he decides to suddenly turn his production into a musical and winds up in deep trouble. Your tolerance for Dick's antics will determine if you enjoy the flick. **83m/C; DVD.** Andy Dick; Michael Hitchcock; Bob Odenkirk; Anthony Rapp; James Van Der Beek; Maura Tierney; Jack Black; Mo Collins; Danny Trejo; Sara Rue; Kevin Farley; Paul Henderson; ***Cameo(s):*** Ben Stiller; ***D:*** Andy Dick; ***W:*** Andy Dick; ***C:*** Ben Gamble; ***M:*** Jason Miller. **CABLE**

Dante 01 **2008 (R)** Dank and disturbing space hell (yes, the title symbolism is deliberate). A shuttle delivers prisoner Saint Georges (Lambert) and new doctor Elisa (Pham) to the prison space station. Since the station is controlled by a pharmaceutical company, the violent inmates are used as guinea pigs in new technology trials. However, Saint Georges is apparently possessed by an alien entity that allows him to miraculously cure the inmates and a prison revolt is started. French with subtitles. **82m/C; DVD.** *FR* Lambert Wilson; Linh Dan Pham; Dominique Pinon; Francois Levantal; Simona Maicanescu; Gerald Laroche; ***D:*** Marc Caro; ***W:*** Pierre Bordage; ***C:*** Jean Poissoon; ***M:*** Raphael Elig; Eric Wenger.

Dante's Inferno 1/2 **1935** Ambitious Jim Carver (Tracy) gets a job as a carnival barker for Pop McWade's (Walthall) sideshow, which depicts scenes of Hell from Dante's "Inferno." (Heavy-handed symbolism alert!) He marries McWade's daughter, Betty (Trevor), to get ahead and then ignores his family in order to get rich. Carver's greed leads to an amusement pier collapse, a trial, and somewhere along the way, redemption. If not for Tracy's intensity, it would be all sap. **88m/B; DVD.** Spencer Tracy; Claire Trevor; Henry B. Walthall; Alan Dinehart; Willard Robertson; ***D:*** Harry Lachman; ***W:*** Robert Yost; Philip Klein; ***C:*** Rudolph Mate.

Dante's Peak ✌✌ 1/2 **1997 (PG-13)** Northwest volcano serves up a smorgasbord of molten disaster in the second most desirable town in the U.S.?the titular Dante's Peak. Brosnan is the intuitive scientist who comes to Washington to match wits with the conical adversary and joins forces with the town's tres femme mayor Wando (Hamilton). Ashes fall like snow in January, computer generated lava flows profusely, poisonous gases leak out and water turns to acid, all with desired nail-biting effect. Wando's two kids, dog and grandma lend folksy charm and the requisite loved-ones-in-grave-danger, but this heated disaster flick is not exactly for the whole family. Cliched and predictable, flick runs the Disaster Movie Playbook page by page as plot takes a backseat to nonstop action. **112m/C; VHS, DVD, Blu-Ray, HD-DVD.** Pierce Brosnan; Linda Hamilton; Charles Hallahan; Grant Heslov; Elizabeth Hoffman; Jamie Renee Smith; Arabella Field; Tzi Ma; Jeremy Foley; Brian Reddy; Kirk Trutner; ***D:*** Roger Donaldson; ***W:*** Leslie Bohem; ***C:*** Andrzej Bartkowiak; ***M:*** John (Gianni) Frizzell.

Danton ✌✌✌✌ **1982 (PG)** A sweeping account of the reign of terror following the French Revolution. Focuses on the title character (wonderfully portrayed by Depardieu) and is directed with searching parallels to modern-day Poland by that country's premier filmmaker, Andrzej Wajda. Well-done period sets round out a memorable film. In French with English subtitles. **136m/C; DVD.** *PL FR* Gerard Depardieu; Wojciech Pszoniak; Patrice Chereau; Angela Winkler; Boguslaw Linda; ***D:*** Andrzej Wajda; ***W:*** Jean-Claude Carriere; Agnieszka Holland; Boleslaw Michalek; Jacek Gasiorowski; Andrzej Wajda. British Acad. '83: Foreign Film; Cesar '83: Director (Wajda); Montreal World Film Fest. '83: Actor (Depardieu).

Daphne ✌ 1/2 **2007** Lifeless look at a seven-year period in the 1940s that depicts the two great loves of English author Daphne Du Maurier. Repressing her sexuality for marriage and motherhood, Daphne (Somerville) fell into an unrequited romance with Ellen (McGovern), the wife of her publisher Nelson Doubleday (Malcolm). This leads to her writing about forbidden longing in the play "September Tide," which introduces Daphne to bisexual actress Gertrude Lawrence (McTeer). Director Beavan used Du Maurier's letters and memoirs but it's still dull. **88m/C; DVD.** *GB* Geraldine Somerville; Elizabeth McGovern; Janet McTeer; Christopher Malcolm; ***D:*** Clare Beavan; ***W:*** Amy Jenkins; ***C:*** Christopher Titus King. **TV**

Darby O'Gill & the Little People ✌✌✌ 1/2 **1959 (G)** Set in Ireland, roguish old story teller Darby O'Gill (Sharpe), whose also the caretaker of a large estate, tumbles into a well and visits the land of leprechauns who give him three wishes in order to rearrange his life. When he tries to tell his friends what happened, they think that it is only another one of his stories. Connery plays the youhg man who takes Darby's job and courts his daughter (Munro) as well. A wonderful Disney production (despite its disappointing boxoffice performance) with wit, charm and an ounce or two of terror. **93m/C; VHS, DVD.** Albert Sharpe; Janet Munro; Sean Connery; Estelle Winwood; Kieron Moore; Jimmy O'Dea; ***D:*** Robert Stevenson; ***W:*** Lawrence Edward Watkin; ***C:*** Winton C. Hoch.

Darby's Rangers ✌✌ 1/2 *Young Invaders* **1958** WWII pot-boiler with Garner as the leader of a commando team put together for covert operations in North Africa and Italy. Successful battle sequences combine with slow-paced romantic scenes as the soldiers chase women when not chasing the enemy. **122m/B; VHS, DVD.** James Garner; Jack Warden; Edd Byrnes; Peter Brown; Stuart Whitman; David Janssen; Etchika Choureau; Venetia Stevenson; Torin Thatcher; Joan Elan; Corey Allen; Murray Hamilton; ***D:*** William A. Wellman; ***W:*** Guy Trosper; ***C:*** William Clothier; ***M:*** Max Steiner.

Dare ✌✌ **2009** This sexually charged coming-of-age tale takes the standard Hollywood teen comedy in unexpected directions. Alexa (Rossum) is a good-girl drama student who seduces popular jock Johnny (Gilford) after being ripped as inexperienced by a local actor (Cumming). Meanwhile, her sexually confused childhood friend Ben (Springer) is also making moves on Johnny. The story unfolds in three sections featuring each member of the triangle, with Gilford standing out as the surprisingly sensitive Johnny. Good performances all the way around help roughen the edges of this story that seems aimed at the art house crowd. **90m/C; Blu-Ray, On Demand.** Ashley Springer; Rooney Mara; Emmy Rossum; Zach Gilford; Ana Gasteyer; Sandra Bernhard; Alan Cumming; Cady Huffman; ***D:*** Adam Salky; ***W:*** David Brind; ***C:*** Michael Fimognari; ***M:*** David Poe; Duncan Sheik.

Daredevil ✌✌ **2003 (PG-13)** Daredevil made his appearance in Marvel Comics in 1964. Having lost his sight in an industrial accident when he was a kid, his remaining senses are enhanced but he's basically still human. Too bad the movie isn't. It's flashy and loud but uninvolving. Lawyer Matt Murdock (Affleck) turns vigilante and dons red leather and a goofy mask when one too many criminals goes free. The big (literally) bad guy is Kingpin (an avuncular Duncan) who keeps flashy assassin Bullseye (Farrell) on the payroll. Meanwhile, Matt is trying to make time with heiress Electra (Garner) who thinks Daredevil killed her father—putting a crimp in the potential romance. Garner looks great in leather and refines the butt-kicking skills she uses in her TV series "Alias" to good effect. Affleck's sorta lightweight since Daredevil has lots of issues; he's better at sarcasm than angst. **114m/C; VHS, DVD, Blu-Ray.** Ben Affleck; Jennifer Garner; Michael Clarke Duncan; Colin Farrell; Joe Pantoliano; Jon Favreau; David Keith; Erik Avari; Paul Ben-Victor; Derrick O'Connor; Leland Orser; Scott Terra; Kevin Smith; ***Cameo(s):*** Stan Lee; ***D:*** Mark Steven Johnson; ***W:*** Mark Steven Johnson; ***C:*** Ericson Core; ***M:*** Graeme Revell. Golden Raspberries '03: Worst Actor (Affleck).

Darfur Now ✌✌ 1/2 **2007 (PG)** Documentary attempts to bring the complex, tribal-based Darfur (Sudan) conflict and its accompanying genocide to American audiences. Director Braun focuses on six individuals—three in the midst of the horror (a refugee camp leader, a mother who joins a guerilla group after the death of her son, and a food aid worker), and three trying to affect change from the outside (an activist advocating divestment of Sudanese stock, the UN prosecutor preparing a case against those responsible for the genocide, and actor Cheadle, who is committed to raising awareness about the conflict). Cheadle and fellow American Sterling are noble, but their stories are significantly less interesting than the others, especially Argentinian-born prosecutor Moreno-Ocampo, who has already lived through a brutal dictatorship in his homeland, and is committed to bringing justice to Darfur. **99m/C; On Demand.** ***D:*** Theodore Braun; ***W:*** Theodore Braun; ***C:*** Kirsten Johnson; ***M:*** Graeme Revell.

Daring Dobermans ✌✌ **1973 (PG)** In this sequel to "The Doberman Gang," the barking bank-robbers have a new set of crime-planning masters. A young Indian boy who loves the dogs enters the picture and may thwart their perfect crime. **88m/C; VHS, DVD.** Charles Robinson; Tim Considine; David Moses; Claudio Martinez; Joan Caulfield; ***D:*** Byron Ross Chudnow.

The Daring Young Man ✌ 1/2 **1935** Competing reporters find their rivalry turning romantic. At least until Martha (Clarke) gets left at the altar when Don's (Dunn) big scoop means he has to immediately go undercover in prison to get his story. **76m/B; DVD.** James Dunn; Mae Clarke; Neil Hamilton; Sidney Toler; Arthur Treacher; Raymond Hatton; ***D:*** William A. Seiter; ***W:*** Sam Hellman; William Hurlbut; Glenn Tryon; ***C:*** Merritt B. Gerstad.

Dario Argento's Trauma ✌✌ *Trauma* **1993 (R)** When a teenage girl's parents are decapitated, she and an artist friend start following the clues to a psychotic killer known as "The Headhunter." Trademark horror work for Italian cult director Argento with high suspense quotient and equally high gore. An unrated version is also available. **106m/C; VHS, DVD.** Christopher Rydell; Asia Argento; Laura Johnson; James Russo; Brad Dourif; Frederic Forrest; Piper Laurie; ***D:*** Dario Argento; ***W:*** Dario Argento; T.E.D. Klein.

The Darjeeling Limited ✌✌✌ **2007 (R)** Brothers Francis (Wilson), Peter (Brody), and Jack (Schwartzman) seek spiritual healing after their father's death on a cross-Asia trip aboard the Darjeeling Limited. Along the way, the three men struggle with each other and their own problems, including a (possibly intentional) accident that's left Francis's head in bandages, Peter's desertion of his pregnant wife, and Jack's recent breakup (chronicled in the companion short film "Hotel Chevalier"), until Francis reveals that their trip is taking them to their estranged mother (Huston), now a nun living in India. Anderson manages to capture the absurdity and humanity of the brothers while exploring the crises that have shaped their individual struggles for meaning and purpose, while infusing the film with his traditional detail-obsessed style. He and co-screenwriters Schwartzman and Coppola penned the film while traveling across India by, of course, train. **91m/C; DVD.** Owen Wilson; Adrien Brody; Jason Schwartzman; Amara Karan; Wally Wolodarsky; Anjelica Huston; ***D:*** Wes Anderson; ***W:*** Jason Schwartzman; Wes Anderson; Roman Coppola; ***C:*** Robert Yeoman.

The Dark ✌ 1/2 *The Mutilator* **1979 (R)** A supernatural beast commits a string of gruesome murders. **92m/C; VHS, DVD.** William Devane; Cathy Lee Crosby; Richard Jaeckel; Keenan Wynn; Vivian Blaine; Biff (Elliott) Elliot; Warren Kemmerling; Casey Kasem; John Bloom; ***D:*** John Cardos; ***W:*** Stanford Whitmore; ***C:*** John Morrill.

Dark and Stormy Night ✌✌ **2009** Comic mystery spoof set in the 1930s (in black and white no less) of the 'old dark house' genre. A group of family, friends, reporters, and passersby gather in the mansion of the late Sinas Cavinder for a reading of his will. As a storm rages outside, the lights go out, the family lawyer is murdered, and death threatens those who remain. **93m/B; DVD.** Larry Blamire; Jennifer Blaire; Daniel Roebuck; Jim Beaver; Betty Garrett; James Karen; Tom Reese; ***D:*** Larry Blamire; ***W:*** Larry Blamire; ***C:*** Anthony J. Rickert-Epstein; ***M:*** Christopher Caliendo.

Dark Angel: The Ascent ✌ 1/2 **1994 (R)** She-devil gets tired of hell and decides to get a look at the world upstairs. She also decides to turn vigilante and dispatch some bad guy souls to her former home. Part of the 'Full Moon Classics, Vol. 2' collection. **80m/C; VHS, DVD, Blu-Ray.** Charlotte Stewart; Daniel Markel; Michael C. Mahon; Nicholas Worth; Milton James; Angela Featherstone; ***D:*** Linda Hassani; ***W:*** Matthew Bright; ***M:*** Fuzzbee Morse.

Dark Asylum ✌✌ **2001 (R)** Shrink Maggie Bleham (Porizkova) is called on to examined a serial killer (Drake) who's so dangerous that authorities have brought him to an abandoned asylum to be evaluated. Naturally, the nutball gets loose and kills his guards with the doc next on his list. Only she's got other ideas. **96m/C; VHS, DVD.** Paulina Porizkova; Larry Drake; Judd Nelson; Jurgen Prochnow; ***D:*** Gregory Gieras; ***W:*** Gregory Gieras; ***C:*** Viorel Sergovici, Jr. **VIDEO**

The Dark Backward ✌ 1/2 **1991 (R)** A dark, subversive comedy about a garbage man who dreams of making it big in show biz as a stand-up comedian. He's terrible until a third arm starts growing out of his back and the sheer grotesqueness of his situation makes him a temporary star. Caan and Newton are interestingly cast, but young, first-time director Rifkin's foray into David Lynch territory was not well received by critics. **97m/C; VHS, DVD.** Judd Nelson; Bill Paxton; Wayne Newton; Lara Flynn Boyle; James Caan; Rob Lowe; Claudia Christian; King Moody; Adam Rifkin; ***D:*** Adam Rifkin; ***W:*** Adam Rifkin; ***C:*** Joey Forsyte; ***M:*** Marc David Decker.

Dark Blue ✌✌✌ **2003 (R)** Another James Ellroy L.A. cop novel comes to life in this powerful tale of deep-seated corruption set against the Rodney King verdict and its aftermath. Veteran cop Eldon Perry (Russell) is part of the elite Special Investigations Squad, a brutal, corrupt, and racist unit run by Jack Van Meter (Gleeson). Partnered with Van Meter's green nephew Bobby (Speedman), Eldon is assigned to steer a homicide investigation away from the two snitches who did it. Standing in his way is the black deputy chief (Rhames) who has vowed to shut down the SIS. Russell's outstanding performance anchors the proceedings, which gets somewhat muddled by the pairing of Ayers's hard-boiled script with Shelton's more reflective bent. Ellroy's original first draft was set against the 1965 Watts riots, and Ayers wrote "Training Day" at about the same time he was adapting "Blue." **116m/C; VHS, DVD, Blu-Ray.** Kurt Russell; Ving Rhames; Scott Speedman; Brendan Gleeson; Michael Michele; Lolita Davidovich; Dash Mihok; Kurupt; Khandi Alexander; Master P; ***D:*** Ron Shelton; ***W:*** David Ayer; ***C:*** Barry Peterson; ***M:*** Terence Blanchard.

Dark Blue Almost Black ✌ 1/2 *Azulo Scuro Casi Negro* **2006** Overstuffed debut drama about personal ambition vs. responsibility and family obligation. Jorge is forced to put his life on hold after his father suffers a severe stroke. He takes over his father's janitorial job while continuing his studies at night and coping with other personal issues, including an imprisoned brother and a gay best friend. Spanish with subtitles. **105m/C; DVD.** *SP* Quim Gutierrez; Antonio de la Torre; Hector Colome; Marta Etura; Raul Arevalo; Eva Pallares; ***D:*** Daniel Sanchez Arevalo; ***W:*** Daniel Sanchez Arevalo; ***C:*** Juan Carlos Gomez; ***M:*** Pascal Gaigne.

Dark Blue World ✌✌ 1/2 *Trmavomodry Svet* **2001 (R)** Told in flashbacks, this is an old-fashioned WWII epic about heroism and romance. In 1950 in Czechoslovakia, Franta (Vetchy) is imprisoned by the Communists who fear the war hero's previous contacts with democracy. After the Nazis invaded his country in 1939, Franta fled to England, where he joins the RAF and befriends younger Czech pilot Karel (Hadek). But the duo have a falling out over a local woman, Susan (Fizgerald), who favors the mature Franta. Czech, German, and English dialogue. **115m/C; VHS, DVD.** *CZ GB* Ondrej Vetchy; Tara Fitzgerald; Krystof Hadek; Oldrich Kaiser; Charles Dance; Linda Rybova; Hans-Jorg Assmann; Anna Massey; ***D:*** Jan Sverak; ***W:*** Zdenek Sverak; ***C:*** Vladimir Smutny; ***M:*** Ondrej Soukup.

Dark Breed ✌✌ **1996 (R)** Ewww, yuck, it's sci-fi infestation time once again as Nick Saxon (Scalia) is assigned to find the bodies of six astronauts whose top secret space craft has mysteriously crashed. He discovers that the bodies are playing host to reptilian parasites with designs on world domination. **104m/C; VHS, DVD.** Jack Scalia; Jonathan Banks; Robin Curtis; Donna W. Scott; ***D:*** Richard Pepin.

Dark City ✌✌ **1950** Businessman Arthur Winant (DeFore) loses money that's not his in a crooked poker game and commits suicide. Card hustler Danny Haley (Heston) doesn't realize what kind of trouble this makes until Arthur's nutzo brother Sidney (Mazurki) starts bumping off anyone involved in the scam. **98m/B; DVD, Blu-Ray.** Charlton Heston; Mike Mazurki; Don DeFore; Viveca Lindfors; Lizabeth Scott; Dean Jagger; Harry (Henry) Morgan; Jack Webb; Ed Begley, Sr.; ***D:*** William Dieterle; ***W:*** Larry Marcus; ***C:*** Victor Milner; ***M:*** Franz Waxman.

Dark City ✌✌ *Dark Empire; Dark World* **1997 (R)** Brooding city of gloom floats in a sunless world, with skylines nightmarishly changing as its residents sleep. The city seems to belong to no era, looking at times like a neo-goth music video and at others like a work of German expressionism. Sometimes it just looks like '60s Cleveland. Director Proyas seems to have wanted to make a futuristic film noir like "Blade Runner," but gets lost somewhere along the way. He does however, keep the style. Disfigured Dr. Schreber (Sutherland) is forced by a dying race of pasty-faced long-coated aliens to use humans as guinea pigs in an attempt to find out what makes them tick. John Murdoch (Sewell) wakes up in a hotel room with a dead body and no memory of his life. Searching for his past, he wanders through one incredible set after another, but is it real or is it hypodermically injected? Hurt is a detective who only wants to stop the grisly murders. Garbled story rewards persistence at the end. **103m/C; VHS, DVD, Blu-Ray.** Kiefer

Sutherland; William Hurt; Rufus Sewell; Richard O'Brien; Jennifer Connelly; Ian Richardson; Colin Friels; Frank Gallacher; Bruce Spence; John Bluthal; Mitchell Butel; Melissa George; *D:* Alex Proyas; *W:* Alex Proyas; Lem Dobbs; David S. Goyer; *C:* Dariusz Wolski; *M:* Trevor Jones.

Dark Command 🦴🦴🦴 **1940** The story of Quantrell's Raiders who terrorized the Kansas territory during the Civil War until one man came along to put a stop to it. Colorful and talented cast add depth to the script. Also available colorized. **95m/B; VHS, DVD, Blu-Ray.** John Wayne; Walter Pidgeon; Claire Trevor; Roy Rogers; Marjorie Main; George "Gabby" Hayes; *D:* Raoul Walsh.

Dark Corner 🦴🦴🦴 **1946** Private detective Bradford Galt (Stevens) is framed and suspects his ex-partner Jardine (Kreuger) is the culprit. But then Jardine winds up dead. Then there's a guy in a white suit (Bendix) who keeps dogging him and sinister wealthy art dealer Hardy Cathcart (Webb) seems to be pulling everyone's strings. It's a good thing Galt's loyal secretary Kathleen (Ball) believes in the lug. Gripping, intricate film noir. **99m/B; VHS, DVD.** Mark Stevens; Clifton Webb; William Bendix; Lucille Ball; Cathy Downs; Reed Hadley; Constance Collier; Kurt Kreuger; *D:* Henry Hathaway; *W:* Jay Dratler; Bernard C. Schoenfeld; Leo Rosten; *C:* Joe MacDonald; *M:* Cyril Mockridge.

Dark Corners 🦴 **2006** Writer/director Gower plays mind games with his audience and then leaves us confused and dissatisfied. Karen Clark (Birch), a suburban housewife undergoing fertility treatments, begins having horrific nightmares about a woman who looks just like her. Disturbed mortuary assistant Susan Hamilton (yep, Birch again) has blackouts. Both women learn that people they know are victims of a serial killer. Ah, if only the plot were actually that simple. **92m/C; DVD.** *GB* Thora Birch; Christien Anholt; Toby Stephens; Oliver Price; Ray Charleson; Joanna Hole; *D:* Ray Gower; *W:* Ray Gower; *C:* Paul Sadourian; *M:* Andrew Pearce. **VIDEO**

Dark Country 🦴🦴 **2009 (R)** Richard (Jane) and Gina (German) impulsively married in Vegas and are now driving through a nighttime Nevada desert to begin their honeymoon. They spot an unconscious man injured in a car accident and decide to take him to a hospital. The man suddenly awakens but tragedy occurs. Then the newlyweds realize they are lost and left in unimaginable circumstances. Jane's directorial debut. **88m/C; DVD.** Lauren German; Ron Perlman; Thomas Jane; *D:* Tab Murphy; *W:* Tab Murphy; *C:* Geoff Boyle; *M:* Eric Lewis. **VIDEO**

Dark Crimes 🦴 1/2 *True Crimes* **2016 (R)** An action crime thriller about a Polish policeman solving a murder using clues found in a fictional work, based on a true story. After a woman is killed in an underground sex club, put-upon police detective Tadek (Carrey) is forced to free the prime suspect Kozlow (Csokas). After his release, Kozlow lies about how he was treated while in police custody and claims his rights were violated. Convinced of Kozlow's guilt, the detective pursues the killer outside of the law to get justice. This cat-and-mouse includes pursuing Kozlow's girlfriend (Gainsbourg). Though Carrey gives his all, the film is muddled. **92m/C; DVD, Blu-Ray, Streaming.** *PL UK US* Jim Carrey; Marton Csokas; Charlotte Gainsbourg; Agata Kulesza; Kati Outinen; *D:* Alexandros Avranas; *W:* Jeremy Brock; *C:* Michael Englert; *M:* Richard Patrick. **VIDEO**

The Dark Crystal 🦴🦴🦴 **1982 (PG)** Jen and Kira, two of the last surviving Gelflings, attempt to return a crystal shard (discovered with the help of a sorceress) to the castle where the Dark Crystal lies, guarded by the cruel and evil Skeksis. Designed by Brian Froud. From the creators of the Muppets. **93m/C; VHS, DVD, Blu-Ray, UMD.** *V:* Jim Henson; Frank Oz; Kathryn Mullen; Dave Goetz; *D:* Jim Henson; Frank Oz; *W:* David Odell; *C:* Oswald Morris; *M:* Trevor Jones.

Dark Days 🦴 1/2 **2000** Director Singer's documentary on the homeless men and women, many of them former and current crack addicts, who formed a community in an underground Amtrak railroad tunnel in Manhattan. Singer filmed for more than two years before Amtrak had the squatters evicted. **84m/B; DVD.** *D:* Marc Singer; *C:* Marc Singer; *M:* DJ Shadow.

Dark Delusion 🦴 1/2 **1947** The sixth and last entry in the MGM series goes out with a whimper and with Dr. Gillespie taking a decidedly secondary role. His latest protégé is stubborn Dr.Tommy Coalt, who lacks any bedside manner. To keep him out of trouble, Gillespie sends Tommy to a small town to cover for a vacationing doctor. But Tommy finds lots of trouble when he refuses to sign commitment papers for troubled socialite Cynthia, because he thinks her condition is medical not mental. **90m/B; DVD.** James Craig; Lucille Bremer; Lionel Barrymore; Lester Matthews; Keye Luke; Alma Kruger; *D:* Willis Goldbeck; *W:* Harry Ruskin; Jack Andrews; *C:* Charles Rosher; *M:* David Snell.

Dark Descent 🦴 *Descent into Darkness* **2002 (R)** A corporation mining the underwater Mariana Sea Trench sends an investigator after an accident kills several workers. But all is not what it seems to be. A poor ripoff of "Outland" and Cain is no Sean Connery. **96m/C; DVD.** *BL US* Scott Wiper; Biliana Petrinska; Maxim Gentchev; Art Mendelson; *D:* Daniel Knauf; *W:* Daniel Knauf; Phillip J. Roth; *C:* Todd Barron; *M:* Richard McHugh. **VIDEO**

Dark Diamond 🦴🦴 *Dark Inclusion; Diamant Noir* **2016** A heist thriller that has echoes of contemporary noir. Pier (Schneider) believes his father led a tragic life and had a tragic death because of the family's diamond business and his extended family involved in the business. To get revenge and destroy the business, he worms his way into the family enterprise. Once he begins working in the business, Pier gets dragged into the conflict over power between his uncle Joseph (Cloos) and his cousin Gabi (Diehl). Pier's plan is compromised by his attraction to another cousin Luisa (Godin). **115m/C; DVD.** Niels Schneider; August Diehl; Hans Peter Cloos; Raphaele Godin; Hafed Benotman; *D:* Arthur Harari; *W:* Arthur Harari; Agnes Feuvre; Vincent Poymiro. **VIDEO**

Dark Fields 🦴 1/2 *The Rain* **2009 (R)** The farming community of Perseverance has been plagued by a Native American curse for generations. When the crops dry up, a lethal sickness also literally dries up the people. Then they must sacrifice a child (drawn by lottery) to save the community. The story is told in three time periods: the 1880s, the 1950s, and the present day. Carradine's 1880s character is the most effective (and the creepiest). **111m/C; DVD, Blu-Ray.** David Carradine; Dee Wallace; Richard Lynch; Ellen Sandweiss; Derek Brandon; Kristen Jarzembowski; Tiren Jhames; Paula Ciccone; Colin Crenshaw; William Giordano; *D:* Douglas Schulze; *W:* Douglas Schulze; Kurt Eli Mayry; *C:* Lon Stratton; *M:* David Bateman.

Dark Forces 🦴🦴 *Harlequin* **1983 (PG)** A faith-healer promises to help a senator's dying son and finds the politician's wife also desires his assistance. This Australian film is uneven and predictable. Though rated "PG," beware of two rather brief, but explicit, nudity scenes. **96m/C; VHS, DVD, Blu-Ray.** *AU* Robert Powell; David Hemmings; Broderick Crawford; Carmen Duncan; *D:* Simon Wincer.

Dark Habits 🦴🦴 1/2 *Entre Tinieblas* **1984** An early Almodovar farce about already-demented nuns in a failing convent trying to raise funds with the help of a nightclub singer who is on the run. Although certainly irreverant, it doesn't quite have the zing of his later work. In Spanish with subtitles. **116m/C; VHS, DVD.** *SP* Carmen Maura; Christina Pascual; Julieta Serrano; Marisa Paredes; *D:* Pedro Almodóvar; *W:* Pedro Almodóvar; *C:* Angel Luis Fernandez.

The Dark Half 🦴🦴 **1991 (R)** Flawed chiller based on a Stephen King novel. Thad Beaumont's serious novels have been failures, but writing as George Stark, he's had phenomenal success with grisly horror stories. In a publicity stunt Thad kills off and publicly buries George (who doesn't want to stay dead). Soon everyone who's crossed Thad is brutally murdered. Hutton acquits himself well in a change of pace dual role. Otherwise, the psychological thrills are few and the gore is plentiful. Pittsburgh serves as location double for King's usual New England territory. Film's release was delayed due to Orion's bankruptcy problems. **122m/C; VHS, DVD, Blu-Ray.** Timothy Hutton; Amy Madigan; Michael Rooker; Julie Harris; Robert Joy; Kent Broadhurst; Beth Grant; Rutanya Alda; Tom Mardirosian; Chelsea Field; Royal Dano; *D:* George A. Romero; *W:* George A. Romero; *C:* Tony Pierce-Roberts; *M:* Christopher Young.

Dark Harbor 🦴🦴 **1998 (R)** A wealthy married couple, traveling to their vacation home off the coast of Maine, stop to help an injured young man. A series of coincidences leads the threesome to spend the weekend together in the couple's isolated retreat, where sexual attraction makes the situation very volatile. **89m/C; VHS, DVD.** Alan Rickman; Polly Walker; Norman Reedus; *D:* Adam Coleman Howard; *W:* Adam Coleman Howard; Justin Lazard; *C:* Walt Lloyd; *M:* David Mansfield.

Dark Hazard 🦴 1/2 **1934** Packs a lot of story into a brief run time with Robinson in an atypical role. Compulsive gambler Jim Turner swears off gambling after marrying Marge. But his eventual management of a dog track has him placing bets again and she leaves him. Turner then takes a chance on rehabilitating the injured racing dog of the title who becomes a winner although Turner still winds up a loser. **72m/B; DVD.** Edward G. Robinson; Genevieve Tobin; Glenda Farrell; Robert Barrat; George Meeker; *D:* Alfred E. Green; *W:* Brown Holmes; Ralph Block; *C:* Sol Polito.

Dark Heart 🦴 1/2 **2006 (R)** Matt Taylor (Joelson) returns to his economically depressed mill hometown after a tour in Iraq. Swapping lies at a bar with old friend Bobby (Howe), Matt tells him a (probably apocryphal) story about an outfit that found millions in U.S. dollars hidden in Baghdad. The tale catches the attention of four desperate mill workers and they kidnap Matt, taking him to a remote cabin in hopes he'll confess to where the money is. **100m/C; DVD.** R.D. Call; Brian Howe; Huntley Ritter; Sam Scarber; Greg Joelson; Darcy Halsey; William Dennis Hurley; Larry Weissman; Mageina Tovah; *D:* Kevin Lewis; *W:* Kevin Lewis; *C:* Marco Cappetta; *M:* Michael P. Bondies; Dax Pierson. **VIDEO**

Dark Hearts 🦴 1/2 **2012** Struggling artist Colson takes younger brother Sam to an underground club where Colson is immediately attracted to singer Fran. Too bad she has a jealous lover in gangster Armand. Not that it stops either Colson or Fran, leading to betrayal and murder and Colson deciding to paint with human blood. More muddled cheap noir than horror. **84m/C; DVD.** Kyle Schmid; Sonja Kinski; Lucas Till; Goran Visnjic; Rachel Blanchard; Juliet Landau; *D:* Rudolf Buitendach; *W:* Christian Piers Betley; *C:* Kees Van Oostrum; *M:* Guy Theaker. **VIDEO**

Dark Honeymoon 🦴 1/2 **2008** Paul (Cornish) apparently marries Kathryn (Booth) because of the great sex even though he doesn't really know anything about her. When they honeymoon along the Oregon coast, he finds out a lot about his bride he probably doesn't want to know. Like why there seems to be dead bodies wherever she's been. **94m/C; DVD.** Nick Cornish; Lindy Booth; Roy Scheider; Tia Carrere; Daryl Hannah; Eric Roberts; Wes Ramsey; *D:* David O'Malley; *W:* David O'Malley; *C:* Matt Molitor; *M:* Juan J. Colomer. **VIDEO**

Dark Horse 🦴🦴 1/2 **1992 (PG)** Meyers is a young woman distraught over the death of her mother. She gets into trouble and is assigned to do community service work at a horse farm where she finds herself caring for a prize-winning horse. **98m/C; VHS, Streaming.** Ari Meyers; Mimi Rogers; Ed Begley, Jr.; Donovan Leitch; Samantha Eggar; *D:* David Hemmings.

Dark Horse 🦴🦴 1/2 **2011** Avid toy collector Abe (Gelber) is not any kind of catch--overweight, firmly stuck back in his puberty days, living with mom and pop (Farrow and Walken), and generally unhappy. A chance meeting with troubled girl Miranda (a somber yet engaging Blair) leads to a bizarre relationship--there is no other kind in director Solondz's universe. While it could be argued that Solondz is spinning his wheels a bit by delivering another tragic comedy, he finds dark beauty in the people often ignored by society. **88m/C; DVD, Blu-Ray.** Jordan Gelber; Selma Blair; Mia Farrow; Christopher Walken; Justin Bartha; Donna Murphy; Aasif Mandvi; *D:* Todd Solondz; *W:* Todd Solondz; *C:* Andrij Parekh.

The Dark Horse 🦴🦴🦴 **2014 (R)** Based on a true story, a drama about a Maori champion chess player's life and struggle with mental illness. As a child, Genesis "Gen" Potini (Curtis) was a child chess prodigy who attacked the game with energy. Because of his sever bipolar disorder, he is repeatedly hospitalized, institutionalized, and imprisoned. Upon his release, he is put in the custody of his elder brother Ariki (Hapi). Ariki is a brutal gang leader who cannot wait to initiate his reluctant son Mana (Rolleston). Despite the challenges of family and community, Gen finds new purpose in his life when he offers to teach chess to a local chess club. **124m/C; DVD, Streaming, Download.** Clifford Curtis; James Rolleston; Kirk Torrance; Miriama McDowell; Wayne Hapi; *D:* James Napier Robertson; *W:* James Napier Robertson; *C:* Denson Baker; *M:* Dana Lund.

Dark Horse 🦴🦴 1/2 **2016 (PG)** Louise Osmond's telling of the story of the Dream Alliance is what modern viewers call a hybrid film in that it's mostly a documentary but the director employs techniques of the fictional drama to tell her true story as well. The winner of an audience award at Sundance, it's the story of a group of friends working at a racing club who decide to try and breed a racehorse themselves. Of course, the horse becomes a symbol for not just the individual underdog but the Welsh city, one that has been beaten down by economic collapse. **85m/C; DVD.** *D:* Louise Osmond; *W:* Louise Osmond; *C:* Benjamin Kracun.

The Dark Hour 🦴 1/2 **1936** Two detectives team up to solve a murder in which multiple suspects are involved. Based on Sinclair Gluck's "The Last Trap." **72m/B; VHS, DVD.** Ray Walker; Irene Ware; Berton Churchill; Hedda Hopper; Hobart Bosworth; E.E. Clive; *D:* Charles Lamont.

Dark House 🦴 1/2 **2009 (R)** Routine and gimmick-ridden slasher pic. As a child, Claire witnessed the murder of several children by her crazy foster mother, Miss Darrode, who then killed herself. She is still plagued by nightmares, so her shrink tells Claire she should return to the scene of the crime to unlock those repressed memories. Conveniently, Claire's drama class has been hired as part of a haunted horror attraction in the massacre house. **85m/C; DVD.** Meaghan Ory; Diane Salinger; Jeffrey Combs; Bevin Prince; Matt Cohen; Shelly Cole; Danso Gordon; Rylan Melander; Ian Reed Kesler; Scott Whyte; *D:* Darin Scott; *W:* Darin Scott; *C:* Philip Lee; *M:* Vincent Gillioz.

Dark House 🦴 *Haunted* **2014 (R)** Typical horror suspense fare helmed by director Salva (of Jeepers Creepers fame). Possessing the gift of fortelling how people are going to die, Nick Di Santo (Kleintank) finds himself reliving what he thought was a childhood dream when he takes a road trip to an abandoned manson that has been waiting for his return. The house not only enhances Nick's ability but also holds secrets from the past. Along the way he learns his presumed deceased father is still alive and that his ability might be passed on to his unborn child. **102m/C; DVD, Blu-Ray.** Luke Kleintank; Alex McKenna; Lacey Anzelc; Ethan S. Smith; Lesley-Anne Down; Tobin Bell; *D:* Victor Salva; *W:* Victor Salva; Charles Agron; *C:* Don E. FauntLeRoy; *M:* Bennett Salvay. **VIDEO**

Dark Journey 🦴🦴🦴 *The Anxious Years* **1937** WWI Stockholm is the setting for a love story between a double agent and the head of German Intelligence. Clever, sophisticated production; Leigh is stunning. **82m/B; DVD, Blu-Ray.** *UK* Vivien Leigh; Conrad Veidt; Joan Gardner; Anthony Bushell; Ursula Jeans; *D:* Victor Saville; *W:* Lajos Biro; *C:* Georges Perinal; Harry Stradling, Sr.; *M:* Richard Addinsell.

Dark Justice 🦴🦴 1/2 **1991** Judge by day, avenger by night, in this actioner created from three episodes of the late-night TV series. Judge Nicholas Marshall is disgusted by the criminals sprung on legal loopholes and backroom deals, so he decides to take justice into his own hands. **99m/C; VHS, DVD.** Ramy Zada; Dick O'Neill; Clayton Prince; Begona Plaza. **TV**

Dark Justice 🦴🦴 *Yup-Yup Man* **2000** Thirty years after Robert (Bumiller) sees his homeless dad murdered on the LA streets, he's still traumatized—wandering around and muttering to himself (hence the alternate film title). Robert's personal hero is vigilante comic book star Dark Justice. In fact, he decides to emulate his hero by taking on real street criminals, except Robert kills them instead of turning them in to the cops. **89m/C; DVD.** William Bumiller; David Bowe; Jocelyn Seagrave; Matt Gallini; Chase Mackenzie Bebak; *D:* Glenn Klinker; *W:* Glenn Klinker; *C:* Yoram Astrakhan; *M:* Sharon Farber.

Dark Kingdom: The Dragon King 1/2 *Curse of the Ring; Ring of the Nibelungs; Die Nibelungen; Sword of Xanten* **2004** Inspired by the legend of Siegfried and Fafnir the Dragon, this modern adaptation of the Das Nibelungenlied was originally a three-hour miniseries on German television. Somewhere between there and its DVD release it lost almost an hour in length. It's the usual story of a young boy with a destiny unknown to him who will one day rise to great fame. This version isn't sanitized from the myths for modern audiences though, so it's a little darker than most fantasy films. If you can view Region 2 or PAL DVDs, look for the German version which also has an English soundtrack. **132m/C; DVD.** Benno Furmann; Kristanna Loken; Alicia Witt; Julian Sands; Samuel West; Max von Sydow; Robert Pattinson; Mavie Horbiger; Aletta Bezuidenhout; Sean Higgs; Goetz Otto; Ralph (Ralf) Moeller; Tamsin MacCarthy; Dean Slater; *D:* Uli Edel; *W:* Uli Edel; Diane Duane; Peter Morwood; *C:* Elemer Ragalyi; *M:* Ilan Eshkeri. **TV**

The Dark Knight **2008 (PG-13)** Batman (Bale), along with Lt. Gordon (Oldman) has been cleaning up the streets of Gotham, and the criminal underworld wants him gone, along with crusading DA Harvey Dent (Eckhard). Along comes the grotesque and psychotic Joker (Ledger, in a tour de force performance, his last) to wreak havok for the pure sport of it. Nolan's masterpiece destroys the preconceptions of what a superhero movie can be, presenting a deep, thoughtful, action-packed, and VERY dark film. He also stretches the limits of the PG-13 rating to the breaking point. The cast is uniformly excellent (including Gyllenhaal, taking over the Rachel Dawes role from Katie Holmes), but Ledger surpasses them all in what should be an Oscar-winning performance. **152m/C; Blu-Ray, On Demand.** Christian Bale; Heath Ledger; Aaron Eckhart; Maggie Gyllenhaal; Gary Oldman; Michael Caine; Eric Roberts; Cillian Murphy; Morgan Freeman; Anthony Michael Hall; Monique Gabriela Curnen; Nestor Carbonell; Michael Jai White; Melinda McGraw; William Fichtner; Joshua Harto; Colin McFarlane; Ron Dean; Ritchie Coster; Nathan Gamble; Tommy (Tiny) Lister; Chin Han; *D:* Christopher Nolan; *W:* Christopher Nolan; Jonathan Nolan; *C:* Wally Pfister; *M:* Hans Zimmer; James Newton Howard. Oscars '08: Sound FX Editing, Support. Actor (Ledger); British Acad. '08: Support. Actor (Ledger); Screen Actors Guild '08: Support. Actor (Ledger).

The Dark Knight Rises **2012 (PG-13)** The last of the Nolan/Bale/DC Comics trilogy introduces Hathaway as Catwoman and Hardy as Bane. Batman has taken the hit for Harvey Dent's crimes, making him persona non grata in Gotham City. But, eight years later, terrorist Bane and his crew arrive to take over the city and Batman has to resurface and become a hero again. Nolan's Batman swan song retains the grit and spectacle, and ups the stakes for all the characters. Satisfying conclusion showcases excellent performances by Gordon-Levitt and Hathaway, even if no one quite matches Ledger's legendary Joker. **165m/C; DVD, Blu-Ray.** Christian Bale; Tom (Thomas) Hardy; Anne Hathaway; Marion Cotillard; Joseph Gordon-Levitt; Michael Caine; Gary Oldman; Morgan Freeman; Juno Temple; Matthew Modine; Alon Aboutboul; Ben Mendelsohn; Burn Gorman; Daniel Sunjata; Cillian Murphy; Nestor Carbonell; Liam Neeson; Brett Cullen; Thomas Lennon; Tom Conti; William Devane; Tomas Arana; *D:* Christopher Nolan; *W:* Christopher Nolan; Jonathan Nolan; *C:* Wally Pfister; *M:* Hans Zimmer.

Dark Matter **2007 (R)** Based on a true story that happened at the University of Iowa in 1991. Ambitious Chinese student Xing Liu (Liu) is honored to be studying for his PhD in America, especially when he becomes the protege of cosmology prof Jacob Reiser (Quinn). However, when Liu challenges Reiser's own ideas about dark matter, he's betrayed by school politics and it leads him to violence. Streep plays a university patron enamored of Chinese culture. Structured in five acts in accordance to the five elements of energy in Chinese philosophy. **90m/C; DVD, Blu-Ray.** Ye Liu; Aidan Quinn; Meryl Streep; Erik Avari; Blair Brown; *D:* Shi-Zheng Chen; *W:* Billy Shebar; *C:* Oliver Bokelberg; *M:* Van Dyke Parks.

Dark Metropolis *The Next Race* **2010** Inept sci-fi indie. After humans mistreat the race of genetically engineered soldiers they created, the Ghen rebel, leading to a 300-year war that ultimately leave them in charge. The few human survivors are forced into surface ghettos and are ravaged by plague but a Ghen politician wants to eliminate the remaining humans as part of his campaign promises. **97m/C; DVD.** Eric Scott Woods; Bailey Chase; Pamela Clay; *D:* Stewart St.John; *W:* Stewart St.John; *C:* Seamus Tierney; *M:* Ludek Drizhal. **VIDEO**

Dark Mirror **1946** A psychologist and a detective struggle to determine which twin sister murdered a prominent physician. Good and evil siblings finely acted by de Havilland. **85m/B; DVD, Blu-Ray.** Olivia de Havilland; Lew Ayres; Thomas Mitchell; Garry Owen; *D:* Robert Siodmak; *C:* Milton Krasner.

Dark Mirror **2007** Truly haunted house or truly haunted mind? Photographer Deborah (Vidal), her husband Jim (Chisum), and their young son Ian (Pelegrin) move into a creepy house that's filled with glass panels and mirrors. Deborah comes to believe that everyone she sees in the glass—or photographs—dies but maybe she's just going crazy. **89m/C; DVD.** Lisa Vidal; David Chisum; Joshua Pelegrin; Christine Lakin; Lupe Ontiveros; Jim Storm; *D:* Pablo Proenza; *W:* Pablo Proenza; Matthew Reynolds; *C:* Armando Salas; *M:* Pieter A. Schlosser; Isaac Sprintis.

The Dark Myth 1/2 *Anokoku Shinwa* **1990** Susanoo was the god of the storms and sea in the Japanese Shinto religion, and in this anime has somehow become the god of darkness and the underworld. The time for his reappearance is at hand, and a young boy shows signs he may reincarnate as one of the Buddhas to oppose him. Basically an exploration of the two main Japanese religions, which will make it pretty confusing for any viewers not well-versed in either (especially viewing the dubbed version). **110m/C; DVD.** *JP V:* Peter Marinker; Blair Fairman; Alan Myers; Jay Harper; John Baddeley; Larissa Murray; John Bennet; Daniel Flynn; *D:* Takashi Anno; *W:* Takashi Anno; Daijiro Morohoshi; *C:* Hitoshi Kaneko; Akio Saito; *M:* Kenji Kawai.

Dark Night 1/2 **2017** Director/writer Sutton's controversial drama works very loosely from the 2012 shooting in an Aurora, Colorado theater during a screening of "The Dark Knight Rises." Although this is in a no way a traditional true story film. Rather, it's a thought-provoking piece on the doldrums of suburban life and the commonality of violence and mental illness. It presents multiple, fictional characters in everyday life, only ending with someone walking through the back door of a theater. The result is striking, revealing how what happened in Aurora could happen absolutely anywhere. **85m/C; DVD.** Robert Jumper; Aaron Purvis; Anna Rose Hopkins; Eddie Cacciola; Rosie Rodriguez; Karina Macias; *D:* Tim Sutton; *W:* Tim Sutton; *C:* Helene Louvart; *M:* Maica Armata.

Dark Night of the Scarecrow 1/2 **1981** Thriller with a moral. Prejudiced townspeople execute a retarded man who was innocently befriended by a young girl. After his death unusual things begin to happen. Slow to start but effective. **100m/C; VHS, DVD.** Charles Durning; Tanya Crowe; Larry Drake; *D:* Frank De Felitta. **TV**

Dark Obsession *Diamond Skulls* **1990 (R)** Byrne portrays a husband who lives out his dark erotic fantasies with his wife (Donohoe), and is involved in a hit-and-run accident. Driven by guilt, madness slowly begins to take him. Ugly and depressing. Based on a true scandal. Available in an "NC-17" rated version. **87m/C; VHS, DVD.** Gabriel Byrne; Amanda Donohoe; Michael Hordern; Judy Parfitt; Douglas Hodge; Sadie Frost; Ian Carmichael; Peter Allen; *D:* Nick Broomfield; *W:* Tim Rose Price; *C:* Michael Coulter; *M:* Hans Zimmer.

Dark Odyssey **1957** Metzger's first feature tells the tragic tale of a young Greek seaman who jumps ship in New York in order to avenge his sister's rape. He finds himself conflicted between his masculine sense of family honor and love when he falls for a Greek-American woman. Director's cut includes the original theatrical trailer. **85m/B; VHS, DVD.** David Hooks; Edward Brazier; Jeanne Jerrems; *D:* William Kyriakis; Radley Metzger; *W:* William Kyriakis; Radley Metzger; *C:* Peter Erik Winkler; *M:* Laurence Rosenthal.

Dark of the Sun 1/2 *The Mercenaries* **1968 (PG)** Lots of action; routine plot. Taylor is a tough mercenary hired to retrieve a supply of uncut diamonds from a beseiged town in the Congo during the 1950s rebellion. Oh, and if he can help out the town's inhabitants, that's okay too. Based on the novel by Wilbur A. Smith. **101m/C; VHS, DVD, Blu-Ray.** *GB* Rod Taylor; Jim Brown; Yvette Mimieux; Kenneth More; Peter Carsten; Calvin Lockhart; Andre Morell; *D:* Jack Cardiff; *W:* Quentin Werty; Adrian Spies; *M:* Jacques Loussier.

Dark Passage 1/2 **1947** Bogart plays a convict who escapes from San Quentin to prove he was framed for the murder of his wife. He undergoes plastic surgery and is hidden and aided by Bacall as he tries to find the real killer. Stars can't quite compensate for a far-fetched script and so-so direction. **107m/B; VHS, DVD, Blu-Ray.** Humphrey Bogart; Lauren Bacall; Agnes Moorehead; Bruce Bennett; Tom D'Andrea; *D:* Delmer Daves.

Dark Phoenix *X-Men: Dark Phoenix* **2019 (PG-13)** Raised by Professor Charles Xavier (McAvoy) after the death of her parents, Jean Grey (Turner) learns to control her psychic powers and joins the X-Men. When the team goes on a mission to save a space shuttle crew, Jean takes the brunt of a powerful interstellar force that then lives inside her. Dubbed the Phoenix because she cheated death, Jean struggles to come to terms with her past and her new, uncontrollable powers, and turns to the dark side. A bland effort to what could have been a meaningful send-off to longtime characters in the X-Men series. **113m/C; DVD, Blu-Ray.** James McAvoy; Michael Fassbender; Jennifer Lawrence; Nicholas Hoult; Sophie Turner; Jessica Chastain; *D:* Simon Kinberg; *W:* Simon Kinberg; *C:* Mauro Fiore; *M:* Hans Zimmer.

Dark Places 1/2 **2015 (R)** This thriller based on another novel by Gillian Flynn contains all of the twists of "Gone Girl" but none of the directorial style. Paquet-Brenner helms this adaptation with a lead foot, making a morose, unfocused piece out of a relatively strong book. Theron plays Libby Day, a woman famous for surviving the brutal murder of her family decades earlier. She agrees to discuss the tragedy for the first time with the head of a true crime club (Hoult), but quickly learns he has a different theory of the crime. It's a boring, depressing slog. **114m/C; DVD, Blu-Ray.** Charlize Theron; Sterling Jerins; Nicholas Hoult; Christina Hendricks; Corey Stoll; *D:* Gilles Paquet-Brenner; *W:* Gilles Paquet-Brenner; *C:* Barry Ackroyd; *M:* BT (Brian Transeau).

Dark Planet **1997 (R)** In the year 2636 Earth is in the middle of WW6 and it's up to rebel commander Hawke (Mercurio) to search for the Dark Planet and complete a secret assignment that is humanity's last hope. **99m/C; VHS, DVD.** Paul Mercurio; Harley Jane Kozak; Michael York; Maria Ford; Ed O'Ross; *D:* Albert Magnoli; *W:* S.O. Lee; *C:* William MacCollum.

The Dark Power **1985** Ex-cowboy LaRue and his trusty whip provide this flick with its only excitement. As sheriff, he must deal with the dead Mexican warriors who rise to wreak havoc when a house is built on their burial ground. **87m/C; VHS, DVD.** Lash LaRue; Anna Lane Tatum; *D:* Phil Smoot.

Dark Remains **2005 (R)** Scary little indie horror flick. Allen and Julie are devastated when their young daughter Emma is murdered in her bed. They rent a remote mountain cabin hoping the distance will help them heal, but photographer Julie sees Emma's ghostly image in the pictures she's taking. Seems the cabin has been the spot of numerous suicides and Emma is trying to warn her parents to get out. **91m/C; DVD.** Greg Thompson; Cheri Christian; Rachel Jordan; Jeff Evans; Scott Hodges; *D:* Brian Avenet-Bradley; *W:* Brian Avenet-Bradley; *C:* Laurence Avenet-Bradley; *M:* Benedikt Bryden.

The Dark Ride 1/2 *Killer's Delight* **1978** Lunatic picks up women with the intention of raping and killing them. Ugly thriller based on the evil deeds of serial murderer Ted Bundy. **83m/C; VHS, DVD.** James Luisi; Susan Sullivan; Martin Speer; *D:* Jeremy Hoenack.

Dark River **2018** Raised in an abusive home in Ireland, Alice (Wilson) left it as a teen. Fifteen years later, Alice goes back to help save the family farm as she struggles to overcome the traumas of her childhood. Upon her return, her brother Joe (Stanley), who has been managing the farm and their ailing father (Bean), is not pleased and the pair clash over control of the land and livestock. Though the film is based on the popular Rose Tremain book and features a superb performance by Wilson, the story is poorly developed. **91m/C; DVD, Blu-Ray.** Ruth Wilson; Mark Stanley; Sean Bean; Esme Creed-Miles; Aiden McCullough; *D:* Clio Barnard; *W:* Clio Barnard; *C:* Adriano Goldman; *M:* Harry Escott.

Dark Secrets **1995 (R)** Reporter Claire (Parent) wants to get a hot story on sex club mogul Justin DeVille (Carroll) and winds up falling prey to his charms. But Justin's not the trusting kind and sets up some loyalty tests for Claire. The unrated version is 99 minutes. **90m/C; VHS, DVD.** Monique Parent; Julie Strain; Justin Carroll; *D:* John Bowen; *W:* Steve Tymon; *C:* Keith Holland; *M:* Efrem Bergman.

Dark Shadows 1/2 **2012 (PG-13)** Inspired director Burton has yet again shown that he is merely a shadow of his former self as he fails to get a grip on this bizarre material that mixes soap opera, horror, and fish-out-of-water into a stew of bland nothing. Depp and Green shine as immortals (a vampire and witch, respectively) who rekindle their heated battle in the 1970s, hundreds of years after it began. Depp's Barnabas Collins is trying to get used to a world with TV and cars, but Burton's revival of the popular TV series (1966-71)--while pretty to look at--leaves us feeling drained. Marked the last movie by producer Richard D. Zanuck (1934-2012). **113m/C; DVD, Blu-Ray, Streaming.** Johnny Depp; Michelle Pfeiffer; Helena Bonham Carter; Eva Green; Jackie Earle Haley; Jonny Lee Miller; Bella Heathcote; Chloë Grace Moretz; Gulliver McGrath; *D:* Tim Burton; *W:* John August; Seth Grahame-Smith; *C:* Bruno Delbonnel; *M:* Danny Elfman.

Dark Side *Darkness Falling* **2002 (R)** While investigating the suicide of her twin sister Jane, corporate lawyer Megan (Kidder) discovers that Jane was involved with the lurid underworld of kinky sex and a mysterious lover. **85m/C; VHS, DVD.** *CA GB* Janet Kidder; Jason Priestley; Patsy Kensit; Paul Johansson; *D:* Dominic Shiach; *W:* Sheldon Inkol; *C:* Harry Makin.

The Dark Side of Love **2012** Undeveloped indie (with some undeveloped performances) about family ties. Waiter Julian, who's gay, has to deal with his estranged drug addict brother Michael after their mother's death as making funeral arrangements brings up all their past resentments. Added in are Julian's new friend Steven and Michael's girlfriend Chanel. **87m/C; DVD.** Carlos Salas; Jason Susag; Harsha First; Raquel Rosser; *D:* Jorge Ameer; *W:* Jorge Ameer; *C:* Xavier Henselmann.

Dark Side of Midnight 1/2 *The Creeper* **1986 (R)** A super-detective tracks down a psychopathic killer. **108m/C; VHS, DVD.** James Moore; Wes Olsen; Sandy Schemmel; Dave Bowling; *D:* Wes Olsen; *W:* Wes Olsen; *C:* Wes Olsen.

The Dark Side of the Heart *El Lado Oscuro del Corazon* **1992** Magic realism features in this story of struggling Buenos Aires poet Oliverio (Grandinetti) who falls in love with prostitute Ana (Ballesteros). She wants to keep things businesslike but when a man finds a woman whose lovemaking causes them to actually levitate, he's not about to make things easy. Spanish with subtitles. **127m/C; VHS, DVD.** *CA AR* Dario Grandinetti; Sandra Ballesteros; Nacha Guevara; ***D:*** Eliseo Subiela; ***W:*** Eliseo Subiela; ***C:*** Hugo Colace; ***M:*** Osvaldo Montes. Montreal World Film Fest. '92: Film.

The Dark Side of the Sun ✗✗ **1988 (R)** Pitt stars as a dying young man, traveling the world in search of a cure, who meets the woman of his dreams. Pitt's feature film debut. **107m/C; VHS, DVD.** Brad Pitt; Cheryl Pollak; Guy Boyd.

Dark Skies ✗ 1/2 **2013 (PG-13)** Daniel and Lacey Barrett (Hamilton and Russell) experience weird, unexplainable activities in their formerly safe home. Is it ghosts? Nope, this time it's aliens, although the producers of Paranormal Activity barely alter the formula, resulting in another hackneyed sci-fi/horror flick. The talented and underutilized Russell does her best to elevate the material, and there are some stylish set pieces that should work for the genre audience. The end result is about as memorable as a SyFy Original Movie, maybe even less so, especially with its stupid closing minutes. **97m/C; DVD, Blu-Ray.** Keri Russell; Josh Hamilton; Dakota Goyo; Kaden Rockett; J.K. Simmons; L.J. Benet; ***D:*** Scott Charles Stewart; ***W:*** Scott Charles Stewart; ***C:*** David Boyd; ***M:*** Joseph Bishara.

Dark Spirits WOOF! **2008** Lousy horror (set in Prague) with an inept, confusing plot. Eva has a vision of her sister Tereza being murdered but her sibling won't listen. After Tereza is killed under mysterious circumstances, Eva is haunted by continuing visions and eventually realizes that the evil is coming for her. **99m/C; DVD.** Milka Minichova; Vlastina Svatkova; Jan Budar; Marco Igonda; ***D:*** Huck Keppler; ***W:*** Huck Keppler; ***C:*** Nicolas Loir; ***M:*** David N. Jahn. **VIDEO**

Dark Star ✗✗✗ **1974 (G)** John Carpenter's directorial debut is a low-budget, sci-fi satire which focuses on a group of scientists whose mission is to destroy unstable planets. During their journey, they battle their alien mascot (who closely resembles a walking beach ball), as well as a "sensitive" and intelligent bombing device which starts to question the meaning of its existence. Enjoyable early feature from John "Halloween" Carpenter and Dan "Aliens" O'Bannon. Fun, weird, and unpredictable. **95m/C; VHS, DVD, Blu-Ray.** Dan O'Bannon; Brian Narelle; Dre Pahich; Cal Duniholm; ***D:*** John Carpenter; ***W:*** Dan O'Bannon; John Carpenter; ***C:*** Douglas Knapp; ***M:*** John Carpenter.

Dark Streets ✗ **2008 (R)** Musical film noir turns out to be an unsuccessful mix that's not helped by the wooden acting (although the elaborate production numbers are well-staged). Set in the 1930s, nightclub owner Chaz Davenport (Mann) is having financial woes (he owes money to the mob) and dumps his singer girlfriend (Phillips) for another talented babe (Miko). Then there's some stuff about Davenport's dad, who maybe didn't commit suicide, and corporate corruption with the family firm but it doesn't add up to much. Based on the 2004 stage musical "The City Club" by Glenn M. Stewart. **83m/C; On Demand.** Gabriel Mann; Bijou Phillips; Izabella Miko; Elias Koteas; Michael Fairman; Toledo Diamond; ***D:*** Rachel Samuels; ***W:*** Wallace King; ***C:*** Sharone Meir; ***M:*** George Acogny.

Dark Tide ✗ **2012 (PG-13)** Berry looks great in a bikini but that's about all worth noting in this chaotic underwater adventure. Shark whisperer Kate Mathieson and her boyfriend Jeffrey (Martinez) are filming a documentary about great whites when a friend becomes shark food. Guilt-stricken Kate loses her courage, livelihood, and lover (temporarily) until arrogant, wealthy businessman William Brady (Brown) makes her a lucrative offer for a dangerous dive and it all goes bad. **94m/C; DVD, Blu-Ray.** Halle Berry; Olivier Martinez; Ralph Brown; Luke Tyler; Mark Elderkin; ***D:*** John Stockwell; ***W:*** Amy Sorlie; Ronnie Christensen; ***C:*** Jean-Francois Hensgens; ***M:*** Mark Sayfritz. **VIDEO**

The Dark Tower ✗ 1/2 **2017 (PG-13)** A bad guy (McConaughey) wants to topple a tower joining Earth with another world, thereby unleashing a hellish dimension, so a lone gunslinger (Elba) and his junior sidekick try to stop him. Could be a plausible plot for an episode of "Buffy the Vampire Slayer," but it's another crummy film adaption of Stephen King's work. The tagline should read, "There are other movies than this." **95m/C; DVD, Blu-Ray.** Matthew McConaughey; Idris Elba; Tom Taylor; Dennis Haysbert; Ben Gavin; ***D:*** Nikolaj Arcel; ***W:*** Nikolaj Arcel; Akiva Goldsman; Jeff Pinkner; Anders Thomas Jensen; ***C:*** Rasmus Videbaek; ***M:*** Junkie XL.

Dark Town ✗ **2004 (R)** Low-budget vampire flick that rarely makes sense although it really doesn't need a plot. A slumlord gets turned into a bloodsucker, goes homes to the 'burbs, and infects his family during a convenient blackout. Apparently, the only two not to succumb are a lesbian daughter (yeah, there's some gratuitous girl-on-girl action) and a black gang banger who wants revenge on the slumlord. Or something. Lots of blood and gore. **88m/C; DVD.** Joe King; Janet Martin; Delpano Willis; Sarah Horvath; Meghan Stansfield; Curtis Nysmith; ***D:*** Desi Scarpone; ***W:*** David J. Burke; ***C:*** Adam Tash; ***M:*** Mark Fontana. **VIDEO**

A Dark Truth ✗ *The Truth* **2012 (R)** Environmentally-conscious melodrama focuses on ex-CIA operative Jack Begosian (Garcia), turned talk radio host, traveling to Ecuador to seek justice. Jack pursues the aid of revolutionary leader Francis (Whitaker) and his wife Mia (Longoria) in overthrowing the evil head of a Canadian water-filtration company who goes to extremes in covering up the disease caused by their botched practices. A good cast is wasted in this cheap conspiracy thriller, flooded with amateurish dialogue and clunky action sequences. The message is clear and constantly preached by these cardboard-thin characters: mega-corporations are bad, trees are good. It's somewhere between "An Inconvenient Truth" and "Birdemic." **106m/C; DVD, Streaming.** Andy Garcia; Forest Whitaker; Eva Longoria; Deborah Kara Unger; Kim Coates; ***D:*** Damian Lee; ***W:*** Damian Lee; ***C:*** Bobby Shore; ***M:*** Jonathan Goldsmith.

Dark Universe ✗ 1/2 **1993 (R)** An alien terror wants to conquer the Earth and make its inhabitants their new food source. **83m/C; VHS, DVD.** Blake Pickett; Cherie Scott; Bently Tittle; John Maynard; Paul Austin Saunders; Tom Ferguson; Steve Barkett; Joe Estevez; Patrick Moran; ***D:*** Steve Latshaw; ***W:*** Patrick Moran.

Dark Victory ✗✗✗ 1/2 **1939** A spoiled young heiress discovers she is dying from a brain tumor. She attempts to pack a lifetime of parties into a few months, but is rescued by her doctor, with whom she falls in love. Classic final scene with Davis at the top of her form. Bogart plays an Irish stable hand, but not especially well. Also available in a colorized version. **106m/B; VHS, DVD, Blu-Ray.** Bette Davis; George Brent; Geraldine Fitzgerald; Humphrey Bogart; Ronald Reagan; Henry Travers; ***D:*** Edmund Goulding; ***W:*** Casey Robinson; ***C:*** Ernest Haller; ***M:*** Max Steiner.

Dark Water ✗✗ **2002 (PG-13)** Dahlia Williams' (Connelly) soon-to-be ex-husband tells her she's nuts and she wonders if he might be right when she moves with her five-year-old daughter Ceci (Gabe) into a dilapidated and perhaps, yes, haunted Roosevelt Island apartment that is plagued by creepy noises from a supposedly vacant flat upstairs. Then there's that little-but-quickly-expanding water stain on the ceiling that seems a little...alive. Tries to be spooky but is just all wet. Based on Hideo Nakata's 2002 Japanese horror film of the same name. **120m/C; DVD, Blu-Ray, UMD.** Ariel Gade; Jennifer Connelly; John C. Reilly; Tim Roth; Pete Postlethwaite; Dougray Scott; Camryn Manheim; Perla Haney-Jardine; Debra Monk; Elina Lowensohn; Jennifer Baxter; ***D:*** Walter Salles; ***W:*** Rafael Yglesias; ***C:*** Affonso Beato; ***M:*** Angelo Badalamenti.

Dark Water ✗✗ *Honogurai mizu no soko kara* **2002 (PG-13)** Yoshimi Matsubara is in the middle of a brutal divorce and custody battle. Normally the case would weigh heavily in her favor because of the Japanese Court's preference for letting children be raised by the mother. But Yoshimi has a history of mental imbalance due to a problematic childhood. The stress of the divorce and her conversion to a working single mother is weighing on her heavily. When she moves into a new apartment with her young daughter, bizarre frightening occurrences begin; she initially believes her husband is trying to make her crack to get sole custody. But then a small girl begins appearing and disappearing inside the apartment. **100m/C; DVD.** *JP* Hitomi Kuroki; Fumiyo Kohinata; Yu Tokui; Isao Yatsu; Kiriko Shimizu; Rio Kanno; Mirei Oguchi; Asami Mizukawa; Shigemitsu Ogi; Maiko Asano; Yukiko Ikari; Shinji Nomura; Teruko Hanahara; Youko Yatsuda; Kono Tarou Suwa; Shichiro Gou; Sachiko Hara; Toru Shinagawa; Chihiro Otsuka; Takashige Ichise; Yoshihiro Nakamura; ***D:*** Hideo Nakata; ***W:*** Hideo Nakata; Koji Suzuki; Kenichi Suzuki; ***C:*** Junichiro Hayashi; ***M:*** Kenji Kawai; Shikao Suga.

Dark Waters ✗✗ **1944** The drowning death of her parents has left a young woman mentally unstable. She returns to her family home in the backwaters of Louisiana with her peculiar aunt and uncle to serve as guardians. It eventually becomes apparent that someone is trying to drive her insane. This one tends to be rather murky and it's not simply due to the plentiful scenes of misty swampland. **93m/B; VHS, DVD.** Merle Oberon; Franchot Tone; Thomas Mitchell; Fay Bainter; Elisha Cook, Jr.; John Qualen; Rex Ingram; ***D:*** Andre de Toth; ***W:*** Joan Harrison; Marian Cockrell; ***C:*** Archie Stout; John Mescall; ***M:*** Miklos Rozsa.

Dark Waters ✗ **2003 (R)** In this SciFi channel original, an oil rig is attacked by bio-engineered sharks that look suspiciously like bad CGI effects. Fortunately the military can kidnap and blackmail several divers turned con artists/gigolos to kill the evil bad guy sharks with horrible acting and incomprehensible dialogue. Whatever happened to the good old days when even bad B movies made an odd kind of sense? **93m/C; DVD.** Lorenzo Lamas; Simmone MacKinnon; Bruce Gray; Ross Manarchy; Stefan Lysenko; Robert Zachar; Jeffrey Corman; Rodrigo Abed; P.K. Ewing; ***D:*** Phillip J. Roth; ***W:*** Phillip J. Roth; Brett Orr; ***C:*** Todd Baron; ***M:*** Christopher Holden. **TV**

Dark Waters ✗✗✗ **2019 (PG-13)** Corporate attorney Robert Billott (Ruffalo) works for a company that represents major firms like powerful chemical manufacturer DuPont. Through personal connections, he helps West Virginia cattle farmer Wilbur Tennant (Camp) who believes that DuPont has poisoned the local water supply because his cows have been getting sick, acting crazy, and dying at a rapid rate. Despite the protests of Robert's legal colleagues, he sets out to prove the connection and hold DuPont liable. Based on a true story, director Haynes rivetingly captures the draining process of an ethical crusader taking on a corrupt corporation, led by Ruffalo's determined performance. **126m/C; DVD, Blu-Ray.** Mark Ruffalo; Anne Hathaway; Tim Robbins; Bill Pullman; William Jackson Harper; ***D:*** Todd Haynes; ***W:*** Matthew Michael Carnahan; Mario Correa; ***C:*** Edward Lachman; ***M:*** Marcelo Zarvos.

The Dark Wind ✗ 1/2 **1991 (R)** The first of Tony Hillerman's popular Native American mysteries comes to the screen in a lame adaptation. Phillips stars as the Navaho cop investigating a murder on a New Mexico Indian reservation. Since the Navaho believe a "dark wind" enters a man's soul when he does evil, expect some "spirited" goings-on as well. **111m/C; VHS, DVD.** Lou Diamond Phillips; ***D:*** Errol Morris; ***W:*** Eric Bergren.

Dark World ✗ 1/2 **2008 (R)** The ex factor. Ex-L.A. cop Harry Boyd (Pare) teams up with his ex-partner Bob (Berg) to solve a series of missing person cases. Then Grace (Graham), the niece of Harry's ex-wife Nicole (Russell), goes missing, so Nicole and her boyfriend Rick (Bauer) travel from Vegas to help out. And soon everyone is suspected of something. **90m/C; DVD.** Michael Paré; Theresa Russell; Steven Bauer; Julie St. Claire; Charles Arthur Berg; James Russo; Jen Graham; Trevor Stevens; ***D:*** Zia Mojabi; ***W:*** Zia Mojabi; ***C:*** Tom Hejda; ***M:*** P. Daniel Newman. **VIDEO**

Darkdrive ✗✗ 1/2 **1998 (R)** In the near future, the Zircon Corporation has created a virtual prison where the minds of criminals are held in isolation. Naturally, something's gone wrong and it's up to special operations officer Steven Falcon (Olandt) to risk his mind and solve the problem. **100m/C; VHS, DVD.** Ken Olandt; Julie Benz; Claire Stansfield; Carlo Scandiuzzi; ***D:*** Phillip J. Roth; ***W:*** Alec Carlin; ***C:*** Andres Garreton; ***M:*** Jim Goodwin. **VIDEO**

The Darkest Corner of Paradise ✗ **2010** A young graduate moves to the big city to take a job in accounting, only to fail horribly in a bad economy. To make it worse for him he witnesses a murder and suddenly finds himself a reactive protagonist in events beyond his control in a plot which may sound eerily familiar. **71m/B; DVD.** Patrick O'Driscoll; Kato Buss; John Schmor; Lorien Emmerich; Richard Leebrick; ***D:*** Henry Weintraub; ***W:*** Henry Weintraub; Michael Burgner; ***C:*** Henry Weintraub; ***M:*** Zac Sawyer. **VIDEO**

The Darkest Hour ✗ **2011 (PG-13)** A group of Americans (including former next-big-things Hirsch, Thirlby, and Minghella) travel to Moscow just in time for another Hollywood alien invasion. These interstellar killers play with perception as they are largely invisible but can be detected by power surges in nearby bulbs. The script for this creatively bankrupt venture could have used a bit more power or perhaps should have just been left in the dark. **89m/C; DVD, Blu-Ray.** Olivia Thirlby; Emile Hirsch; Max Minghella; Rachael Taylor; Joel Kinnaman; Veronika Vernadskaya; Dato Bakhtadze; Gosha Kutsenko; ***D:*** Chris Gorak; ***W:*** Jon Spaihts; ***C:*** Scott Kevan; ***M:*** Tyler Bates.

Darkest Hour ✗✗✗ **2017 (PG-13)** A captivating historical drama about Winston Churchill (a superb Oldman) that is as engaging as any fictional thriller. Centering on one key month in the spring of 1940 which Britain faced the real possibility of being invaded by Nazi Germany, Churchill gives two of his most important speeches about the war and becomes prime minister at a grave moment in his country's history. Comprehending the depth of Hitler's threat, Churchill rallies Britain to fight Nazi Germany instead of making a deal to stem the conflict. **125m/C; DVD, Blu-Ray.** Gary Oldman; Lily James; Ben Mendelsohn; Kristin Scott Thomas; Stephen (Dillon) Dillane; ***D:*** Joe Wright; ***W:*** Anthony McCarten; ***C:*** Bruno Delbonnel; ***M:*** Dario Marianelli. Oscars '17: Actor (Oldman), Makeup; British Acad. '17: Actor (Oldman), Makeup; Golden Globes '18: Actor--Drama (Oldman); Screen Actors Guild '17: Actor (Oldman).

The Darkest Minds ✗✗ **2018 (PG-13)** An adaptation of Alexandra Bracken's dystopian YA novel. Humanity is changed forever when an unknown illness kills nearly all children and brings out superpowers in some of the survivors. Adults put all the young survivors into internment camps, segregated or slaughtered depending upon their ability. When Ruby (Stenberg) shows telepathic powers, sympathetic doctor Cate (Moore) helps her escape. With three other escapees, Ruby hopes to find the promised land where kids like her can be free. Despite Stenberg's strong performance, the film is more melodramatic than gripping. **104m/C; DVD, Blu-Ray.** Amandla Stenberg; Mandy Moore; Bradley Whitford; Harris Dickinson; Patrick Gibson; ***D:*** Jennifer Yuh Nelson; ***W:*** Chad Hodge; ***C:*** Kramer Morgenthau; ***M:*** Benjamin Wallfisch.

Darklight ✗ **2004 (R)** Really, waifish Shiri Appleby as some kind of formerly evil immortal? No wonder it's claptrap (from the Sci-Fi Channel of course). Lilith was the first woman created but is damned after rejecting God. One of those secret religious societies subdues her, wipes her memory, and has her living as a human. A disillusioned member of the society transforms himself into some creature called Demonicus and only Lilith, using her previously-hidden Darklight power, can stop the apocalypse. **89m/C; DVD.** Shiri Appleby; David Hewlett; Richard Burgi; John de Lancie; Ross Manarchy; ***D:*** Bill Platt; ***W:*** Bill Platt; Chris Regina; ***C:*** Lorenzo Senatore; ***M:*** John Dickson. **CABLE**

Darkman ✗✗✗ **1990 (R)** Raimi's disfigured-man-seeks-revenge suspenser is comicbook kitsch cross-pollinated with a strain of gothic horror. Neeson plays a scientist who's on the verge of discovering the key to cloning body parts; brutally attacked by the henchmen of a crooked politico, his lab is destroyed and he's left for dead. Turns out he's not dead—just horribly disfigured and a wee bit chafed—and he stalks his deserving victims from the shadows, using his lab know-how to disguise his rugged bad looks. Exquisitely violent. Montage by Pablo Ferro. **96m/C; VHS, DVD, Blu-Ray, HD-DVD.** Liam Neeson; Frances McDormand; Larry Drake; Colin Friels; Nelson Mashita; Jenny Agutter; Rafael H. Robledo; Nicholas Worth; Theodore (Ted) Raimi; John Landis; William Lustig; Scott Spiegel; Bruce Campbell; ***D:*** Sam Raimi; ***W:*** Sam Raimi; Ivan Raimi; Daniel Goldin; Joshua Goldin; Chuck Pfarrer; ***C:*** Bill Pope; ***M:*** Danny Elfman.

Darkman 2: The Return of Durant 1/2 **1994 (R)** The first in a series of direct-to-video adventures about disfigured scientist Peyton "Darkman" Westlake (now played by Vosloo), who's continuing his liquid skin research in the hopes of transforming his grotesque appearance. He finds an ally in scientist David Brinkman but Westlake's nemesis, crime boss Robert G. Durant (Drake), wants the property where Brinkman's lab is located. And what Durant wants, he takes. Sam Raimi, who directed the original film, is one of the series producers. **93m/C; VHS, DVD, Blu-Ray.** Arnold Vosloo; Larry Drake; Kim Delaney; Renee O'Connor; Rod Wilson; ***D:*** Bradford May; ***W:*** Steven McKay; Chuck Pfarrer; ***C:*** Bradford May; ***M:*** Randy Miller. **VIDEO**

Darkman 3: Die Darkman Die 1/2 **1995 (R)** The second direct-to-video Darkman saga finds Dr. Peyton Westlake (Vosloo) disrupting the drug-dealing activities of underworld boss Peter Rooker (Fahey). The obsessed Rooker is determined to figure out the secret to Darkman's enormous strength, employing the feminine wiles of his mistress, Dr. Bridget Thorne (Fluegel). Then Westlake/Darkman finds himself drawn to Rooker's neglected wife and young daughter. Our hero suffers a lot (as usual) and there's lots of action (as usual). **87m/C; VHS, DVD, Blu-Ray.** Arnold Vosloo; Jeff Fahey; Darlanne Fluegel; Nigel Bennett; Roxann Biggs-Dawson; ***D:*** Bradford May; ***W:*** Mike Werb; Michael Colleary; ***C:*** Bradford May; ***M:*** Randy Miller.

Darkness **2002 (PG-13)** Spanish director Balaguero follows up his debut feature, "The Nameless," with a haunted house chiller that fails its fright quotient. Americans Mark (Glen), his wife Maria (Olin), and their kids Regina (Paquin) and Paul (Enquist) relocate to a rural house somewhere in Spain. Various paranormal experiences begin to occur, which Regina's parents ignore. Her little brother develops unexplained bruises and becomes afraid of the dark. Regina finds out the house has a disturbing history involving children who disappeared. Should have been more scary. **102m/C; DVD, Blu-Ray.** Lena Olin; Iain Glen; Giancarlo Giannini; Fele Martinez; Anna Paquin; Fermi Reixach; Stephen Enquist; ***D:*** Jaume Balaguero; ***W:*** Jaume Balaguero; Fernando de Felipe; ***C:*** Xavi Gimenez; ***M:*** Carles Cases.

The Darkness **2016 (PG-13)** Another disposable horror film that uses the same clichés increasingly ineffective ends. Even hardcore, forgiving genre fans won't care about this at all. A family (led by Bacon and Mitchell) visits the Grand Canyon and brings home a supernatural force. Yes, it's the ghost of the Grand Canyon. There is literally nothing here that you haven't seen before, done better, making it one of those films that fails to justify its existence. **92m/C; DVD.** Jennifer (Jenny) Morrison; Radha Mitchell; Kevin Bacon; Ming Na; Lucy Fry; ***D:*** Greg McLean; ***W:*** Greg McLean; Shayne Armstrong; Shane Krause; ***C:*** Toby Oliver; ***M:*** Johnny Klimek.

Darkness Falls **1998 (R)** John Barrett (Winstone) is looking for revenge. His adulterous wife Jane (McCaffrey) was critically injured in a car crash from which her lover escaped. So John goes to the Driscoll home and decides to terrorize Jane's boyfriend Mark (Dutton) and his unsuspecting wife Sally (Fenn). Filmed on the Isle of Man, which may be the most interesting thing about this routine thriller. **91m/C; VHS, DVD.** Sherilyn Fenn; Ray Winstone; Tim Dutton; Robin McCaffrey; Oliver Tobias; Michael Praed; ***D:*** Gerry Lively; ***W:*** John Howlett; ***C:*** Adam Santelli; ***M:*** Guy Farley.

Darkness Falls 1/2 **2003 (PG-13)** In the small New England town of Darkness Falls (aren't you asking for trouble when you name a town that?), young Kyle Walsh witnesses his mother's murder by a ghost who was wrongfully hanged 150 years earlier. Known as the Tooth Fairy, the spirit takes her revenge on the children of the town after they lose the last of their baby teeth. Twelve years later, Kyle is living in Las Vegas, psychologically scarred and paranoid from his encounter. Knowing that the ghost only comes in the dark, he surrounds himself with light. Caitlin (Caulfield), his childhood girlfriend, asks him to come back and help her younger brother, who's starting to have the same nightmares that Kyle use to have. Genuinely scary moments overcome some obvious plot devices. Wisely, the movie is restrained and delivers on spooky atmosphere. **85m/C; VHS, DVD, Blu-Ray.** Chaney Kley; Emma Caulfield; Lee Cormie; Grant Piro; Sullivan Stapleton; Steve Mouzakis; Peter Curtin; ***D:*** Jonathan Liebesman; ***W:*** John Fasano; James Vanderbilt; Joe Harris; ***C:*** Dan Laustsen; ***M:*** Brian Tyler.

Darkness Falls *Anderson Falls* **2020** The wife of homicide detective Jeff (Ashmore) is murdered by two intruders (Cole and Harmon) who stage her death to look like she committed suicide. Grief-stricken Jeff does not believe she took her own life and investigates the case. He learns that a father and son are killing prominent women and making their deaths look like suicides. As Jeff gathers evidence, he finds that people do not accept his theories, including his own mother (Shaye). Endlessly clichéd and this wannabe can't be saved despite the cast's best efforts. **84m/C; DVD.** Shawn Ashmore; Gary Cole; Daniella Alonso; Richard Harmon; Judah Mackey; ***D:*** Julien Seri; ***W:*** Giles Daoust; ***C:*** Shan Liljestrand; ***M:*** Sacha Chaban.

Darkroom 1/2 **1990** An unstable young man devises a scheme to photograph his father in bed with his mistress, and then use the pics to blackmail dear ol' dad. **90m/C; VHS, DVD, Blu-Ray.** Jill Pierce; Jeffrey Allen Arbaugh; Sara Lee Wade; Aaron Teich; ***D:*** Terrence O'Hara. **VIDEO**

The Darkside 1/2 **1987 (R)** In this frightening drama, a young prostitute and an innocent cabbie attempt to escape the clutches of a maniacal film producer with a secret he won't let them reveal. **95m/C; VHS, DVD.** Tony Galati; Cynthia (Cyndy, Cindy) Preston; ***D:*** Constantino Magnatta.

Darkwolf 1/2 **2003 (R)** A werewolf (Hodder) is stalking Los Angeles in search of newbie Josie (Armstrong) so they can mate and perpetuate the species. Detective Steve Turley (Alosio) wants to protect her from the big bad beast. Limited special effects and an overly confusing plot for the genre. **94m/C; VHS, DVD.** Samaire Armstrong; Kane Hodder; Ryan Alosio; Tippi Hedren; Steven Williams; Jaime Bergman; Alexis Cruz; ***D:*** Richard Friedman; ***W:*** Geoffrey Alan Holliday; ***C:*** Stuart Asbjornsen; ***M:*** Geoff Levin. **VIDEO**

Darling 1/2 **1965** Amoral young model Diana Scott (Christie) tries to hold boredom at bay by having a number of love affairs. She moves from intellectual Robert (Bogarde) to playboy Miles (Harvey) and eventually joins the international jet set and manages to reach the top of European society by marrying a prince. Diana then learns what an empty life she has. Christie won an Oscar for her portrayal of the disillusioned, cynical young woman. **122m/B; VHS, DVD.** *GB* Julie Christie; Dirk Bogarde; Laurence Harvey; Jose-Luis De Villalonga; Roland Curram; ***D:*** John Schlesinger; ***W:*** Frederic Raphael; ***C:*** Ken Higgins; ***M:*** John Dankworth. Oscars '65: Actress (Christie), Costume Des. (B&W), Story & Screenplay; British Acad. '65: Actor (Bogarde), Actress (Christie), Screenplay; Golden Globes '66: Foreign Film; Natl. Bd. of Review '65: Actress (Christie), Director (Schlesinger); N.Y. Film Critics '65: Actress (Christie), Director (Schlesinger), Film.

Darling Companion 1/2 **2012 (PG-13)** Mild-mannered, predictable drama of little consequence. Beth (Keaton) is unhappy in her longtime marriage to her distant surgeon spouse, Joseph (Kline). After she and daughter Grace (Moss) rescue a stray dog, Beth insists on keeping the pooch. The appropriately-named Freeway becomes Beth's furry lifeline and when Joseph loses the dog at their vacation home in the Rockies, Beth enlists friends and family into search parties that show Freeway isn't the only one who's lost. **103m/C; DVD, Blu-Ray.** Diane Keaton; Kevin Kline; Richard Jenkins; Elisabeth Moss; Mark Duplass; Dianne Wiest; Sam Shepard; Ayelet Zurer; Jay Ali; ***D:*** Lawrence Kasdan; ***W:*** Lawrence Kasdan; Meg Kasdan; ***C:*** Michael McDonough; ***M:*** James Newton Howard.

Darling Lili 1/2 **1970** Big-budget WWI spy comedy/musical with Andrews as a German agent posing as an English music hall performer, who falls in love with squadron leader Hudson and finds she can't betray him. A critical flop when first released, film has its charms though director Edwards did much better for Andrews in "Victor/Victoria." **136m/C; VHS, DVD.** Julie Andrews; Rock Hudson; Jeremy Kemp; Jacques Marin; Michael Witney; Vernon Dobtcheff; ***D:*** Blake Edwards; ***W:*** Blake Edwards; William Peter Blatty; ***M:*** Henry Mancini; ***M:*** Johnny Mercer. Golden Globes '71: Song ("Whistling Away the Dark").

The Darwin Awards 1/2 **2006 (R)** Lumpy, leaden comedy. The Darwin Awards are given (posthumously) to those who die in the most stupid and preventable ways. Michael (Fiennes), a former San Francisco forensic detective-turned-insurance profiler, is paired up with claims investigator Siri (Ryder) and a film student (Valderrama) who's taping their investigations as they try to identify possible victims and prevent their demise (thus saving the insurance firm lots of pay-outs). There's also a serial killer (Nelson), who previously escaped Michael, that figures in the plot. Last role for Chris Penn. **90m/C; DVD.** Joseph Fiennes; Winona Ryder; Wilmer Valderrama; Tim Blake Nelson; David Arquette; Ty Burrell; Alessandro Nivola; Tom Hollander; Julianna Margulies; Christopher Penn; David Perlich; ***D:*** Finn Taylor; ***W:*** Finn Taylor; ***C:*** Hiro Narita; ***M:*** David Kitay.

Darwin's Darkest Hour **2009** Charles Darwin (Cusick) has been writing his evolutionary opus "On the Origins of Species" for 20 years, fretting over completing his controversial work. But in 1858, Darwin receives a letter from naturalist Alfred Russell Wallace (Bevan-John) that shows similar conclusions. So Darwin must decide whether to publish—and knowingly take on religious opposition—or let others present their theories first. **104m/C; DVD.** *GB* Henry Ian Cusick; Frances O'Connor; Alfred Russell Wallace; ***D:*** John Bradshaw; ***W:*** John Goldsmith; ***C:*** Christopher Ball; ***M:*** Charles Bernstein. **TV**

Darwin's Nightmare 1/2 **2004** Compelling documentary probing the traumatic economic and social effects on the people of Tanzania by the 1960s introduction of the non-native Nile perch fish to Lake Victoria, which has since depleted the lake of over 200 natural species. Without the guidance of voiceovers, director/writer Sauper depicts the local citizens' poor living conditions, as they don't benefit from the country's Nile perch industry—in fact, most struggle to survive on little food (the fish are too costly) and small wages (even with the highly hazardous nature of fishing on Victoria) despite the great profits that perch shipments to Europe and Russia bring to the government. **107m/C; DVD.** ***D:*** Hubert Sauper; ***W:*** Hubert Sauper; ***C:*** Hubert Sauper.

D.A.R.Y.L. **1985 (PG)** The little boy found by the side of the road is too polite, too honest and too smart. His friend explains to him the necessity of imperfection (If you don't want the grown-ups to bother you too much) and he begins to become more like a real little boy. But the American military has a top-secret interest in this child, since he is in fact the combination of a cloned body and a computer brain. More interesting when it's involved with the human beings and less so when it focuses on science. **100m/C; DVD.** Mary Beth Hurt; Michael McKean; Barret Oliver; Colleen Camp; Danny Corkill; ***D:*** Simon Wincer; ***W:*** David Ambrose; Allan Scott; Jeffery Ellis; ***C:*** Frank Watts; ***M:*** Marvin Hamlisch.

Das Boot *The Boat* **1981 (R)** Superb detailing of life in a German U-boat during WWII. Intense, claustrophobic atmosphere complemented by nail-biting action provides a realistic portrait of the stressful conditions that were endured on these submarines. Excellent performances, especially from Prochnow. In German with subtitles. From the novel by Lothar-Guenther Buchheim. Originally a six-hour special made for German TV. **210m/C; VHS, DVD, Blu-Ray.** *GE* Jurgen Prochnow; Herbert Gronemeyer; Klaus Wennemann; Hubertus Bengsch; Martin Semmelrogge; Bernd Tauber; Erwin Leder; Martin May; Heinz Honig; Uwe Ochsenknecht; Claude-Oliver Rudolph; Jan Fedder; Ralph Richer; Joachim Bernhard; Oliver Stritzel; Konrad Becker; Lutz Schnell; Martin Hemme; Rita Cadillac; ***D:*** Wolfgang Petersen; ***W:*** Wolfgang Petersen; ***C:*** Jost Vacano; ***M:*** Klaus Doldinger. **TV**

Date and Switch **2013 (R)** Amiable, though self-conscious, comedy. Friends since they were kids, high school seniors Michael (Braun) and Matty (Cope) made a pact to score and lose their virginity before prom. Only Matty finally informs Michael he's gay and not finding it so easy to hook-up with the right dude, while a confused Michael turns to mutual friend Em (Johnson) for advice. **91m/C; DVD, Blu-Ray.** Nicholas Braun; Hunter Cope; Zach Cregger; Dakota Johnson; Nick Offerman; Gary Cole; Megan Mullally; ***D:*** Chris Nelson; ***W:*** Alan Young; ***C:*** David Robert Jones; ***M:*** Eric D. Johnson.

Date Bait **1960** When a teen couple decides—much to their parents' chagrin—to elope, they find themselves on a date with danger when their post-nuptuals are plagued by pushers and assorted other bad guys. **71m/B; VHS, DVD.** Gary Clarke; Marlo Ryan; Richard Gering; Danny Logan; D'Oale Ireland.

Date Movie 1/2 **2006 (PG-13)** Shameless mockery of romantic movies such as "My Big Fat Greek Wedding" and "Meet the Fockers" can't make it to first base. Obese Julia (Hannigan) is looking for love and freedom from her overbearing African-American "Greek" dad (Griffin) when she meets handsome Brit Grant Funckyerdoder and seeks the aid of a "Hitch"-like date doctor (Cox) to shape up. Penned by two of the "Scary Movie" series writers. **83m/C; DVD, UMD.** Alyson Hannigan; Eddie Griffin; Fred Willard; Jennifer Coolidge; Adam Campbell; Sophie Monk; Meera Simhan; Marie Matiko; Judah Friedlander; Carmen Electra; Tony Cox; Valery Ortiz; ***D:*** Aaron Seltzer; ***W:*** Aaron Seltzer; Jason Friedberg; ***C:*** Shawn Maurer; ***M:*** David Kitay. Golden Raspberries '06: Worst Support. Actress (Electra).

Date Night **2010 (PG-13)** A suburban married couple (Carell and Fey) try to enliven thier dinner-and-a-movie date night when they take another couple's dinner reservation, leading to run-ins with all kinds of unsavory characters and more "excitement" than they bargained for. Excellent cast is the only reason this one works as well as it does. **88m/C; DVD, Blu-Ray.** Tina Fey; Steve Carell; James Franco; Leighton Meester; Taraji P. Henson; Kristen Wiig; Ray Liotta; Mila Kunis; Common; Mark Ruffalo; ***D:*** Shawn Levy; Josh Klausner; ***W:*** Tina Fey; Josh Klausner; ***C:*** Dean Semler; ***M:*** Christophe Beck.

Date with an Angel 1/2 **1987 (PG)** When aspiring musician Knight fishes a beautiful angel out of the swimming pool, he is just trying to rescue her. But the beauty of the angel overwhelms him and he finds himself questioning his upcoming wedding to Cates, a cosmetic mogul's daughter. Sickeningly cute and way too sentimental, though Beart's beauty is other-wordly. **105m/C; VHS, DVD.** Emmanuelle Beart; Michael E. Knight; Phoebe Cates; David Dukes; Bibi Besch; Albert Macklin; David Hunt; Michael Goodwin; Charles Lane; ***D:*** Tom McLoughlin; ***W:*** Tom McLoughlin; ***C:*** Alex Thomson; ***M:*** Randy Kerber.

A Date With Darkness **2003** Andrew Luster (Gedrick), the heir to the Max Factor fortune, is a sociopathic sexual predator who drugs and rapes women he meets in bars. When Connie (Sokoloff) realizes what has happened to her, she presses charges and two more women come forward at Luster's trial. But his conviction on multiple charges isn't the end of the story. **90m/C; DVD.** Jason Gedrick; Marla Sokoloff; Sarah Carter; Stefanie von Pfetten; Lisa Edelstein; Winston Rekert; Samantha Ferris; Kevin McNulty; Robert Wisden; ***D:*** Bobby Roth; ***W:*** Christopher Canaan; ***C:*** Eric Van Haren Noman; ***M:*** Christopher Franke. **CABLE**

A Date with Judy **1948** Standard post-war musical dealing with teenage mix-ups in and around a big high school dance. Choreography by Stanley Donen. **114m/C; VHS, DVD.** Jane Powell; Elizabeth Taylor; Carmen Miranda; Wallace Beery; Robert Stack;

Xavier Cugat; Selena Royle; Leon Ames; *D:* Richard Thorpe; *C:* Robert L. Surtees.

A Date With the Falcon 🦴🦴 1/2
1942 The second film in the mystery series has Gay Lawrence (Sanders) standing up new fiance Helen (Barrie)?whom he met in 1941's "The Gay Falcon"?to find a kidnapped scientist who's developed a valuable formula for synthetic diamonds. There's a shady lady (Maris) and the Falcon gets captured by the bad guys. **63m/B; DVD.** George Sanders; Wendy Barrie; Allen Jenkins; James Gleason; Mona Maris; Victor Kilian; Edward (Ed) Gargan; Eddie Dunn; Frank Moran; *D:* Irving Reis; *W:* Lynn Root; Frank Fenton; *C:* Robert De Grasse; *M:* Paul Sawtell.

The Daughter 🦴🦴 1/2 **2015** This reworking of Henrik Ibsen's "The Wild Duck" is a confident drama that nonetheless feels a little flat and lackluster when compared to more subtle works. Christian Nielsen (Schneider) comes back to his family home in Australia for the wedding of his father Henry (Rush) to his own, much younger, housekeeper Anna (Torv). While home, he discovers that Henry had an affair years earlier that led to the birth of a daughter named Hedvig (Young). The soap opera plotting isn't embraced enough, making everything a little bland, but the cast keeps it interesting. **96m/C; DVD, Blu-Ray, Streaming.** *AU* Geoffrey Rush; Ewen Leslie; Paul Schneider; Miranda Otto; Anna Torv; *D:* Simon Stone; *W:* Simon Stone; *C:* Andrew Commis; *M:* Mark Bradshaw.

Daughter of Death 🦴 *Julie Darling*
1982 (R) A little mentally off-center since she witnessed the gruesome rape and murder of her mother, a teenage girl doesn't bond well with her new mom when dad remarries. **100m/C; VHS, DVD, Blu-Ray.** *CA GE* Anthony (Tony) Franciosa; Isabelle Mejias; Sybil Danning; Cindy Girling; Paul Hubbard; Benjamin Schmoll; *D:* Paul Nicholas.

The Daughter of Dr. Jekyll 🦴 1/2
1957 The doc's daughter believes she may have inherited her father's evil curse when several of the locals are found dead. Originally released in theaters on a double bill with "Dr. Cyclops." **71m/B; VHS, DVD.** John Agar; Arthur Shields; John Dierkes; Gloria Talbott; *D:* Edgar G. Ulmer; *W:* Jack Pollexfen; *C:* John F. Warren; *M:* Melvyn Lenard.

Daughter of Keltoum 🦴🦴 **2001** Rallia is 19 and has been raised by adoptive parents in Switzerland. She returns to her birthplace, a remote Berber settlement in Algeria, in order to learn from her mother Keltoum why she was abandoned as a baby. But when Rallia discovers that Keltoum is working in a luxury hotel in the city, she decides to travel there, accompanied by her Aunt Nedjma. The road trip opens Rallia's eyes to the harshness of Algerian life and finally meeting her mother leads to other revelations. French and Arabic with subtitles. **101m/C; DVD.** *FR TU* Cylia Malki; Baya Belal; Deborah Lamy; Brahim Ben Salah; *D:* Mehdi Charef; *W:* Mehdi Charef; *C:* Alain Levent; *M:* Bernardo Sandoval.

The Daughter of Rosie O'Grady 🦴🦴 **1950** Minor Warner Bros. musical set in the Gay '90s. Trolley driver Dennis O'Grady (Barton) is determined that none of his three daughters will follow his late wife (and himself) into show business. But Patricia (Haver) is determined and is hired for Tony Pastor's (MacRae) vaudeville review, much to her father's displeasure. To complicate matters further, Patricia then falls in love with Pastor. **105m/C; DVD.** June Haver; Gordon MacRae; James Barton; Debbie Reynolds; Marcia Mae Jones; S.Z. Sakall; Gene Nelson; Sean McClory; Jane Darwell; *D:* David Butler; *W:* Jack Rose; Melville Shavelson; Peter Milne; *C:* Wilfred M. Cline; *M:* David Buttolph.

A Daughter's Conviction 🦴 1/2 **2006** Though estranged from her much-married mother Maureen, college student Joanne is convinced she didn't murder her newspaper editor husband Jack McBride. While Maureen is in jail, Joanna does some investigating on her own and learns that Jack may not have been the great guy everyone is making him out to be. **90m/C; DVD.** Brooke Nevin; Kate Jackson; Keegan Connor; John Furey; Steve Francis; Sean Rogerson; Reg Tupper; *D:* David Winkler; *W:* Becca Doten; Mark Doten; *C:* Michael Balfry; *M:* Hal Beckett. **CABLE**

Daughters Courageous 🦴🦴 1/2
1939 Not really a sequel to Warner Bros. successful 1938's "Four Daughters" since, although the same cast appears, they play a different family. After 20 years, footloose dad Jim Masters (Rains) returns to his abandoned ex-wife Nancy (Bainter) and his four daughters just as Nan is about to marry steady Samuel Sloane (Crisp). The gals are all outraged until some familial bonding occurs but dad recognizes that young Buff's (Lane) fiance Gabriel (Garfield) is a wandering type and likely to break her heart. In the next film, 1939's "Four Wives," the story returns to the Lemp family. **106m/B; DVD.** Priscilla Lane; Rosemary Lane; Lola Lane; Gale Page; Fay Bainter; Claude Rains; John Garfield; Donald Crisp; May Robson; Jeffrey Lynn; Dick Foran; Frank McHugh; *D:* Michael Curtiz; *W:* Julius J. Epstein; Philip G. Epstein; *C:* James Wong Howe; *M:* Max Steiner.

Daughters of Darkness 🦴🦴🦴 *Le Rouge aux Levres; Blut an den Lippen; Erzebeth; The Promise of Red Lips; The Red Lips* **1971 (R)** Newlyweds on their way to England stop at a posh French hotel. There they meet a beautiful woman whom the hotel owner swears had been there 40 years ago, even though she hasn't aged a bit. When she introduces herself as Countess of Bathory (the woman who bathed in the blood of virgins to stay young) folks begin to wonder. A really superb erotic vampire film charged with sensuality and a sense of dread. **87m/C; VHS, DVD.** *BE GE IT FR* Delphine Seyrig; John Karlen; Daniele Ouimet; Andrea Rau; Paul Esser; Georges Jamin; Joris Collet; Fons Rademakers; *D:* Harry Kumel; *W:* Harry Kumel; Pierre Drouot; Jean Ferry; *C:* Eddy van der Enden; *M:* Francois de Roubaix.

Daughters of Satan 🦴🦴 **1972 (R)** Selleck, in an early role as a virile museum buyer, antagonizes a coven of witches when he purchases a painting. His wife, played by Grant, becomes a target of the witches' revenge and salacious shenanigans ensue. **96m/C; VHS, DVD, Blu-Ray.** Tom Selleck; Barra Grant; Paraluman; Tani Phelps Guthrie; *D:* Hollingsworth Morse.

Daughters of the Dust 🦴🦴🦴 1/2
1991 Five women of a Gullah family living on the Sea Islands off the Georgia coast in 1902 contemplate moving to the mainland in this emotional tale of change. The Gullah are descendants of West African slaves and their isolation has kept their superstitions and native dialect (a mixture of Western African, Creole, and English) intact. Family bonds and memories are celebrated with a quiet narrative and beautiful cinematography in Dash's feature-film directorial debut. **113m/C; VHS, DVD, Blu-Ray.** Cora Lee Day; Barbara O; Alva Rogers; Kaycee Moore; Cheryl Lynn Bruce; Adisa Anderson; Eartha D. Robinson; Bahni Turpin; Tommy Redmond Hicks; Malik Farrakhan; Cornell (Kofi) Royal; Vertamae Grosvenor; Umar Abdurrahman; Sherry Jackson; Rev. Ervin Green; *D:* Julie Dash; *W:* Julie Dash; *C:* A. Jafa Fielder; *M:* John Barnes. Natl. Film Reg. '04; Sundance '91: Cinematog.

Daughters of the Sun 🦴🦴 *Dakhtaran-e Khorshid* **2000** Amanagol (Taghani) is the eldest of six daughters from a poor rural family. In order to get money to support them and help her ill mother, Amanagol's father cuts her hair and disguises her as a boy named Aman, sending her to a distant village as an apprentice weaver. But her employer is dishonest—keeping her earnings instead of sending them to Aman's family. Then Aman learns her mother has died because of her employer's deception. Persian with subtitles. **92m/C; VHS, DVD.** *IA* Altinay Ghelich Taghani; *D:* Mariam Shahriar; *W:* Mariam Shahriar; *C:* Homayun Payvar; *M:* Hosein Ali-Zadeh.

Dave 🦴🦴🦴 **1993 (PG-13)** Regular guy Dave Kovic (Kline) is a dead ringer for the President, launching him into the White House after the prez suffers a stroke in embarrassing circumstances. Seamless comedy prompts lots of hearty laughs and the feel-good faith that despite the overwhelming odds, everything will turn out just fine. Political cameos abound: look for real-life Senators Alan Simpson, Paul Simon, Howard Metzenbaum, Tom Harkin, and Christopher Dodd as well as the commentators from TV's "The McLaughlin Group," and Stone, poking fun at himself on "Larry King Live," as he tries to convince the public there's a conspiracy going on. **110m/C; VHS, DVD, Blu-Ray.** Kevin Kline; Sigourney Weaver; Frank Langella; Kevin Dunn; Ving Rhames; Ben Kingsley; Charles Grodin; Faith Prince; Laura Linney; Bonnie Hunt; Parley Baer; Stefan Gierasch; Anna Deavere Smith; Bonnie Bartlett; Ben Stein; Stephen (Steve) Root; Dan E. Butler; ***Cameo(s):*** Jay Leno; Larry King; Oliver Stone; Arnold Schwarzenegger; *D:* Ivan Reitman; *W:* Gary Ross; *C:* Adam Greenberg; *M:* James Newton Howard.

Dave Chappelle's Block Party 🦴🦴🦴 **2006 (R)** Comedian Chapelle is followed from his Ohio home to the free all-day concert he stages on a Brooklyn street on September 18, 2004. He impulsively hands out tickets and buses to the concertgoers while keeping the lineup a secret until such performers as Kanye West, Mos Def, the reunited Fugees, Dead Prez, Erykah Badu, Jill Scott, and Ohio's Central State University marching band take the stage. **100m/C; DVD.** Dave Chappelle; *D:* Michel Gondry; *C:* Ellen Kuras.

David 🦴🦴 1/2 **1997** TNT's Old Testament biblical series continues with the story of shepherd boy David (Turner) who succeeds Saul (Pryce) to become king over the tribes of Israel. When King David (Parker) becomes smitten with the married Bathsheba (Lee), he sends her husband into battle, soon leaving her a comely widow (although not for long). And there's also subplots involving three of David's children: Absalom (Rowan), Amnon (Hall), and Tamar (Bellar). Lots of action. **190m/C; VHS, DVD.** Nathaniel Parker; Sheryl Lee; Jonathan Pryce; Leonard Nimoy; Dominic Rowan; Edward Hall; Clara Bellar; Marco Leonardi; Franco Nero; Ben Daniels; Maurice Roeves; Gina Bellman; Gideon Turner; *D:* Robert Markowitz; *W:* Larry Gross; *C:* Raffaele Mertes; *M:* Carlo Siliotto. **CABLE**

David and Bathsheba 🦴🦴🦴 **1951**
The Bible story comes alive in this lush and colorful Fox production. Peck and Hayward are great together and Peck is properly concerned about the wrath of God over his transgressions. Terrific costumes and special effects, lovely music and a fine supporting cast keep this a notch above other Biblical epics. **116m/C; VHS, DVD.** Gregory Peck; Susan Hayward; Raymond Massey; Kieron Moore; James Robertson Justice; Jayne Meadows; John Sutton; Dennis Hoey; Francis X. Bushman; George Zucco; *D:* Henry King; *W:* Philip Dunne; *C:* Leon Shamroy.

David and Goliath 🦴 *David e Golia*
1961 The story of David and Goliath is well-known, since it's pretty widely taught in churches. What should also be known is that when a movie proudly says it was 'freely adapted' from the Bible, that means "We kind of sort of maybe used some parts of it for inspiration for our god-awful movie adaptation starring a few famous guys and lots of cleavage." **95m/C; DVD.** *IT* Orson Welles; Ivica Pajer; Hilton Edwards; Massimo Serato; Eleanora Rossi-Drago; Giulia Rubini; Pierre Cressoy; Furio Meniconi; Luigi Tosi; Ugo Sasso; Kronos; Dante Maggio; Umberto Fiz; *D:* Orson Welles; Ferdinando Baldi; Richard Pottier; *W:* Gino Mangini; Ambrogio Molteni; Emmimo Salvi; Umberto Scarpelli; *C:* Bitto Albertini; Carlo Fiore; *M:* Carlo Innocenzi.

David & Layla 🦴🦴 1/2 **2007** Earnest-if-cliched culture clash romantic comedy. Jewish Brooklynite David (Moscow) falls for lovely Kurdish Muslim refugee Layla (Rose), much to the dismay and disapproval of both their families. Layla also has immigration problems that could be solved if she marries an American citizen but David would have to convert to Islam to satisfy Layla and her relatives. Good performances by the leads. **106m/C; DVD.** David Moscow; Shiva Rose; Callie (Calliope) Thorne; Peter Van Wagner; Polly Adams; Will Janowitz; Ed Chemaly; Anna George; Tibor Feldman; *D:* Jay Jonroy; *W:* Jay Jonroy; *C:* Harlan Bosmajian; *M:* Richard Horowitz; John Lissauer.

David and Lisa 🦴🦴🦴 **1962** Director Perry was given an Oscar for this sensitive independently produced film. Adapted from Theodore Isaac Rubin's true case history novel concerning a young man and woman who fall in love while institutionalized for mental illness. Dullea and Margolin are excellent in the title roles of this sleeper. **94m/B; VHS, DVD, Blu-Ray.** Keir Dullea; Janet Margolin; Howard da Silva; Neva Patterson; Clifton James; *D:* Frank Perry; *W:* Eleanor Perry; *C:* Leonard Hirschfield; *M:* Mark Laurence.

David Copperfield 🦴🦴🦴🦴 **1935** Superior adaptation of Charles Dickens' great novel. An orphan grows to manhood in Victorian England with a wide variety of help and harm. Terrific acting by Bartholomew, Fields, Rathbone, and all the rest. Lavish production, lovingly filmed. **132m/B; VHS, DVD.** Lionel Barrymore; W.C. Fields; Freddie Bartholomew; Maureen O'Sullivan; Basil Rathbone; Lewis Stone; Frank Lawton; Madge Evans; Roland Young; Edna May Oliver; Lennox Pawle; Elsa Lanchester; Una O'Connor; Arthur Treacher; *D:* George Cukor; *W:* Howard Estabrook; Hugh Walpole; *M:* Herbert Stothart.

David Copperfield 🦴🦴 1/2 **1970** This British made-for-TV production is more faithful to the Dickens classic than any of its predecessors. The added material, however, fails to highlight any one character as had the successful 1935 MGM version. Still, the exceptional (and largely stage-trained) cast do much to redeem the production. **118m/C; VHS, DVD.** Richard Attenborough; Cyril Cusack; Edith Evans; Pamela Franklin; Susan Hampshire; Wendy Hiller; Ron Moody; Laurence Olivier; Robin Phillips; *D:* Delbert Mann; *M:* Malcolm Arnold. **TV**

David Copperfield 🦴🦴 1/2 **1999** Lavish and traditional retelling of the Dickens saga, which concerns the hard-knock life, from birth to maturity, of the title character. Hoskins' Mr. Micawber and Smith's Aunt Betsey Trotwood are particular standouts in a large cast. **210m/C; VHS, DVD.** *GB* Daniel Radcliffe; Ciaran McMenamin; Bob Hoskins; Maggie Smith; Ian McKellen; Nicholas Lyndhurst; Pauline Quirke; Emilia Fox; Trevor Eve; Zoe Wanamaker; Alun Armstrong; Imelda Staunton; Amanda Ryan; Ian McNeice; Joanna Page; ***Nar:*** Tom Wilkinson; *D:* Simon Curtis; *W:* Adrian Hodges; *C:* Andy Collins; *M:* Robert (Rob) Lane. **TV**

David Crosby: Remember My Name 🦴🦴 1/2 **2019 (R)** Through revealing interviews with iconic musician David Crosby, the documentary explores his life, work, and influence with honesty and forthrightness. The son of a respected Hollywood cinematographer, Crosby joined the L.A. music scene that emerged after the mid-1960s British invasion. It follows him through his time with the Byrds, including his firing after the 1967 Monterey Pop Festival, and quick rebound with his more famous supergroup, Crosby, Stills and Nash. It takes an earnest look at the complexities of the 1960s—both the sex, drugs, and rock and roll as well as the price paid by those who overindulged—through the life of Crosby. **95m/C; DVD.** David Crosby; *D:* A.J. Eaton; *C:* Ian Coad; Edd Lukas; *M:* Marcus Eaton; Bill Laurance; Joey Singer.

David Harding, Counterspy 🦴 1/2
1950 Covert spymaster David Harding sends Naval officer Jerry Baldwin into a munitions factory to protect torpedo plans. Harding suspects the plant has been infiltrated by enemy agents, who killed Baldwin's predecessor. Set in WWII. Based on the radio series. **71m/B; DVD.** Howard St. John; Willard Parker; Audrey Long; Raymond Greenleaf; Alex Gerry; *D:* Ray Nazarro; *W:* Tom Reed; Clint Johnson; *C:* George E. Diskant.

David Harum 🦴🦴 1/2 **1934** Rogers plays the philosophical title character, a small-town banker, confirmed bachelor, and horse trader in the 1890s. Young bank teller John (Taylor) places a large bet on a horse race so he can afford to marry rich girl Ann (Venable) and Harum provides encouragement. **83m/B; DVD.** Will Rogers; Louise Dresser; Kent Taylor; Evelyn Venable; Stepin Fetchit; Noah Beery, Sr.; Roger Imhof; Charles Middleton; Frank Melton; *D:* James Cruze; *W:* Walter Woods; *C:* Hal Mohr.

David Holzman's Diary 🦴🦴🦴 **1967** Director McBride helmed this fake underground movie, a legendary put-on focusing on film student pretensions. Holzman is a sincere geek who seeks the meaning of life by filming his own existence in oh-so-chic grainy black-and-white verite. He learns reality is more important than film. Drolly captures the state of the art in late '60s America. **71m/B; VHS, DVD, Blu-Ray.** L.M. Kit Carson; *D:* Jim McBride; *W:* L.M. Kit Carson; Jim McBride. Natl. Film Reg. '91.

David Searching 🦴🦴 **1997** Aspiring documentary filmmaker David (Rapp) is broke and boyfriendless in his two-bedroom apartment. He needs a roomie to help with the rent and comes up with newly separated Gwen (Mannheim). She's equally in search of romance (or sex, as the case may be). Oh, and David stills needs to find that elusive job. Series of vignettes do feature some talented actors but the film never goes anywhere. **103m/C; VHS, DVD.** Anthony Rapp; Camryn Manheim; Joseph Fuqua; Julie Halston; Stephen Spinella; John Cameron Mitchell; David Drake; Kathleen Chalfant; David Courier; *D:* Leslie L. Smith; *W:* Leslie L. Smith; *C:* John P. Scholz.

David's Birthday 🦴🦴 *Il Compleanno* **2009** Diego and Shary are sharing a summer home with best friends Matteo and Francesca when they are surprised by their 20-something son David suddenly joining them. Matteo is more surprised to find some long-suppressed emotions surfacing, especially when David seems to return his interest. Italian with subtitles. **106m/C; DVD.** *IT* Massimo Poggio; Thyago Alves; Maria De Medeiros; Alessandro Gassman; Michela Cescon; Christo Jivkov; Piera Degli Esposti; *D:* Marco Filiberti; *W:* Marco Filiberti; Deborah De Furia; *M:* Andrea Chenna.

DaVinci's War 🦴🦴 **1992 (R)** Frank DaVinci's sister is murdered and he wants revenge. So he hooks up with a professional killer and a bunch of Vietnam vets and gets the firepower he needs to blow the bad guys away. **94m/C; VHS, DVD.** Joey Travolta; Michael Nouri; Vanity; Richard Foronjy; Branscombe Richmond; Sam Jones; Jack Bannon; Brian Robbins; James Russo; Kamar De Los Reyes; *D:* Raymond Martino; *W:* Raymond Martino; *M:* Jeff Lass.

Davy Crockett and the River Pirates 🦴🦴 ½ **1956 (G)** Another Disney splice and dice of two episodes from the TV series, chronicling the further adventures of our frontier hero. Davy meets up with Mike Fink, the King of the Ohio River, and the two engage in a furious keelboat race, and then unite to track down a group of thieves masquerading as Indians and threatening the peace. **81m/C; VHS, DVD, Blu-Ray.** Fess Parker; Buddy Ebsen; Jeff York; *D:* Norman Foster; *M:* George Bruns.

Davy Crockett, Indian Scout 🦴 ½ **1950** In 1848, namesake cousin Davy Crockett (Montgomery) is a military scout assigned to protect wagon trains from Indian attacks. Crockett suspects someone is a spy and passing on information. Suspicion first falls on his friend and fellow scout Red Hawk (Reed) and then on half-Kiowa schoolteacher Frances Oatman (Drew). Low-budget western uses stock footage from producer Edward Small's 1940 flick "Kit Carson." **71m/B; DVD.** George Montgomery; Phillip Reed; Ellen Drew; Noah Beery, Jr.; Paul Guilfoyle; Robert Barrat; Addison Richards; Erik Rolf; John Hamilton; *D:* Lew Landers; *W:* Richard Schayer; *C:* George E. Diskant; John Mescall; *M:* Paul Sawtell.

Davy Crockett, King of the Wild Frontier 🦴🦴🦴 **1955 (PG)** Three episodes of the popular Disney TV series are blended together here to present the life and some of the adventures of Davy Crockett, including his days as an Indian fighter and his gallant stand in defense of the Alamo. Well-done by a splendid cast, the film helped to spread Davy-mania among the children of the 1950s. **93m/C; VHS, DVD, Blu-Ray.** Fess Parker; Buddy Ebsen; Hans Conried; Ray Whiteside; Pat Hogan; William "Billy" Bakewell; Basil Ruysdael; Kenneth Tobey; *D:* Norman Foster; *M:* George Bruns. **TV**

Dawg 🦴🦴 *Bad Boy* **2002 (R)** Following 2001's "Double Whammy," Leary and Hurley also teamed up for this romantic comedy. The aptly named Doug "Dawg" Munford (Leary) stands to inherit a fortune but only if the love 'em and leave 'em lothario finds and apologizes to the many women he's used and dumped. And they have to forgive him. Estate attorney Anna Lockheart (Hurley) will tag along to make sure Dawg doesn't make a mess. **83m/C; VHS, DVD.** Denis Leary; Elizabeth Hurley; Vanessa Bell Calloway; Alex Borstein; Mia Cottet; *D:* Victoria Hochberg; *W:* Ken Hastings; *C:* Steven Finestone; *M:* Jason Frederick.

Dawn at Socorro 🦴 ½ **1954** Predictable western with flashbacks showing how gunslinger Brett Wade (Calhoun) hung up his six-shooters. Brett falls for dancehall girl Rannah (Laurie) and wants to get her away from her sleazy boss, Braden (Brian). Braden has his hired gun Rapp (Nicol) challenge Brett to a showdown to stop his interferring. **80m/C; DVD.** Rory Calhoun; Piper Laurie; David Brian; Alex Nicol; Edgar Buchanan; *D:* George Sherman; *W:* George Zuckerman; *C:* Carl Guthrie.

Dawn of the Dead 🦴🦴🦴 ½ *Zombi; Zombie; Zombies* **1978** Romero's gruesome sequel to his "Night of the Living Dead." A mysterious plague causes the recently dead to rise from their graves and scour the countryside for living flesh. Very violent, gory, graphic, and shocking, yet not without humor. Gives interesting consideration to the violence created by the living humans in their efforts to save themselves. **126m/C; VHS, DVD, Blu-Ray.** David Emge; Ken Foree; Gaylen Ross; Scott H. Reiniger; David Crawford; David Early; Daniel Dietrich; Richard France; Tom Savini; Howard K. Smith; George A. Romero; *D:* George A. Romero; *W:* George A. Romero; *C:* Michael Gornick; *M:* Dario Argento.

Dawn of the Dead 🦴🦴🦴 **2004 (R)** The dead are rising from their graves yet again in this remake of the 1978 classic, except now the zombies move around much faster (no waddling allowed!). To level the playing field, Snyder (making his feature film directorial debut) includes more survivors to fight 'em off. The result is still lots of gory fun, but the biting humor so vital to the original is lacking. **100m/C; DVD, Blu-Ray, UMD, HD-DVD.** Sarah Polley; Ving Rhames; Jake Weber; Mekhi Phifer; Ty Burrell; Michael Kelly; Kevin Zegers; Dr. Michael Barry; Lindy Booth; Jayne (Jane) Eastwood; Boyd Banks; Matt Frewer; R.D. Reid; Justin Louis; Kim Poirier; Tom Savini; *D:* Zack Snyder; *W:* James Gunn; *C:* Matthew F. Leonetti; *M:* Tyler Bates.

Dawn of the Mummy WOOF! **1982** Lousy plot and bad acting—not to mention gore galore—do this one in. A photographer and a bevy of young fashion models travel to Egypt for a special shoot. They unwittingly stumble upon an ancient tomb, teeming with vengeance-minded mummies. **93m/C; VHS, DVD.** Brenda King; Barry Sattels; George Peck; Joan Levy; *D:* Frank Agrama.

Dawn of the Planet of the Apes 🦴🦴🦴 ½ **2014 (PG-13)** An impressive follow-up to the successful 2011 reboot finds Caesar (once again perfectly rendered through motion capture by Serkis) the leader of a growing community of primates deep in the San Francisco redwoods. The few remaining humans left in the world after a plague (introduced in the first movie) decimated the population are running out of resources and the apes happen to be camping out on a hydroelectric dam that could solve their problems. What starts as a peaceful dynamic evolves into war--not only between the apes and the humans but among the apes--in this brilliant analogy for the way civilizations are formed through violence as much as peace. Wildly entertaining and so, so smart. **130m/C; DVD, Blu-Ray.** Gary Oldman; Jason Clarke; Andy Serkis; Toby Kebbell; Keri Russell; Kodi Smit-McPhee; Kirk Acevedo; Judy Greer; Enrique Murciano; *D:* Matt Reeves; *W:* Rick Jaffa; Amanda Silver; Mark Bomback; *C:* Michael Seresin; *M:* Michael Giacchino.

The Dawn Patrol 🦴🦴🦴 *The Flight Commander* **1930** Director Hawks made his somewhat stilted talkie debut with this anti-war WWI story. Unruly ace pilots Dick Courtney (Barthelmess) and Douglas Scott (Fairbanks Jr.) criticize their leader, Major Brand (Hamilton), who's appalled at the death rate of the raw recruits of the 59th British Squadron. Courtney gets promoted and realizes the burden of command when he must send young fliers to certain death. Warner Bros. reused the aerial footage for the 1938 remake. **108m/B; DVD.** Richard Barthelmess; Douglas Fairbanks, Jr.; Neil Hamilton; William Janney; Frank McHugh; *D:* Howard Hawks; *W:* Howard Hawks; Seton I. Miller; Dan Totheroh; *C:* Ernest Haller. Oscars '30: Writing.

Dawn Patrol 🦴🦴🦴 **1938** Flynn plays a flight commander whose nerves are shot in this story of the British Royal Flying Corps during WWI. The focus is on the effects that the pressures and deaths have on all those concerned. Fine performances from all in this well-done remake of the 1930 film. **103m/B; VHS, DVD.** Errol Flynn; David Niven; Basil Rathbone; Donald Crisp; Barry Fitzgerald; Melville Cooper; Carl Esmond; Peter Willes; Morton Lowry; Michael Brooke; James Burke; Stuart Hall; *D:* Edmund Goulding; *W:* Seton I. Miller; Dan Totheroh; *C:* Gaetano Antonio "Tony" Gaudio; *M:* Max Steiner.

Dawn Rider 🦴 ½ **2012 (R)** Poor remake of the 1935 John Wayne western. Slater is miscast as gunslinger John Mason, whose father was killed by bandits. He wants revenge but this involves John in a romantic triangle with his friend Rudd (Munro) over Alice (Hennessy). **94m/C; DVD, Blu-Ray.** Christian Slater; Jill Hennessy; Donald Sutherland; Lochlyn Munro; Adrian Hough; *D:* Terry Miles; *W:* Joseph Nasser; *C:* Norm Li; *M:* Jim Guttridge; Sean Hosein. **VIDEO**

The Dawning 🦴🦴 ½ **1988** An Irish revolutionary in the 1920s draws a young woman into his dangerous world of romance, intrigue, and death. Howard's last film. Based on the novel "Old Jest" by Jennifer Johnston. **97m/C; VHS, DVD.** *GB* Anthony Hopkins; Jean Simmons; Trevor Howard; Rebecca Pidgeon; Hugh Grant; Tara MacGowran; *D:* Robert Knights.

Dawning 🦴 **2009** Siblings Chris and Aurora arrive at the family cabin in the Northern Minnesota woods to spend the weekend with their estranged alcoholic father Richard and stepmother Laura. A bleeding, gun-wielding man shows up babbling about evil and holds the family hostage as they wait for whatever is out there to appear. There's more dull domestic drama than terror with an abruptly disappointing ending. **80m/C; DVD, Blu-Ray.** Jonas Goslow; Najarra Townsend; David Coral; Christine Kellogg-Darrin; Daniel Jay Salmen; *D:* Gregg Holtgrewe; *W:* Gregg Holtgrewe; Matthew Wilkins; *C:* Thomas Schwingle; *M:* Nathaniel Levisay. **VIDEO**

The Day 🦴 ½ **2011 (R)** Brutally violent post-apocalyptic film following 5 people who can't bring themselves to trust each other, possibly because of the local cult of cannibals stalking them. **84m/C; DVD, Blu-Ray, Streaming.** Shawn Ashmore; Brianna Barnes; Ashley Bell; Brayden Edwards; Michael Eklund; *D:* Douglas Aarniokoski; *W:* Luke Pasmore; *C:* Boris Mojsovski; *M:* Rock Mafia. **VIDEO**

The Day After 🦴🦴🦴 **1983** Powerful drama graphically depicts the nuclear bombing of a midwestern city and its after-effects on the survivors. Made for TV, and very controversial when first shown, gathering huge ratings and vast media coverage. **122m/C; VHS, DVD, Blu-Ray.** Jason Robards, Jr.; JoBeth Williams; John Lithgow; Steve Guttenberg; John Cullum; *D:* Nicholas Meyer. **TV**

The Day After Tomorrow 🦴🦴 ½ **2004 (PG-13)** It was more fun watching the good guys battle aliens in Emmerich's "Independence Day" than this bunch of mopes who try to survive global warming. Paleoclimatologist Jack Hall (Quaid) predicts a new ice age and, sure enough, there's suddenly softball-sized hail blanketing Tokyo, L.A. gets leveled by tornadoes, New York is buried under ice and snow, and most of the northern hemisphere is wiped out just for fun. Jack's intrepid son Sam (Gyllenhaal)is trapped in Manhattan, riding out the weather with some friends in the New York Public Library and flirting with classmate Laura (Rossum). Meanwhile, Dad decides to snowshoe it from D.C. to NYC to rescue his boy. If you like watching familiar monuments destroyed (poor Lady Liberty), this special effects melodrama is for you. **123m/C; DVD, Blu-Ray, UMD.** Dennis Quaid; Jake Gyllenhaal; Sela Ward; Emmy Rossum; Ian Holm; Dash Mihok; Jay O. Sanders; Tamlyn Tomita; Austin Nichols; Arjay Smith; Kenneth Welsh; Glenn Plummer; Nestor Serrano; Adrian Lester; Sheila McCarthy; Perry King; *D:* Roland Emmerich; *W:* Roland Emmerich; Jeffrey Nachmanoff; *C:* Ueli Steiger; *M:* Harald Kloser. British Acad. '04: Visual FX.

Day at the Beach 🦴🦴 ½ **1998** Jimmy (Veronis) works in a mob-fronted New York ravioli factory while trying to make a film—a gangster movie that features his fellow pasta workers. But when one of his buddies, John (Fitzgerald), tosses a briefcase over a river bridge for a scene, the heavy case accidently kills a passing fisherman. Now Jimmy's got a guilt-racked John to deal with and numerous other problems—all eventually leading to the palatial home of wealthy (and connected) Antonio Gintolini (Ragno). **93m/C; VHS, DVD.** Nick Veronis; Patrick Fitzgerald; Neal Jones; Robert Maisonett; Catherine Kellner; Jane Adams; Joe Ragno; Ed Setrakian; *D:* Nick Veronis; *W:* Nick Veronis; *C:* Nils Kenaston; *M:* Tony Saracene.

A Day at the Races 🦴🦴🦴 ½ **1937** Though it seems labored at times, the brilliance of the brothers Marx still comes through in this rather weak tale of a patient in a sanitorium who convinces horse doctor Groucho to take on running the place. **111m/B; VHS, DVD.** Groucho Marx; Harpo Marx; Chico Marx; Sig Rumann; Douglass Dumbrille; Margaret Dumont; Allan Jones; Maureen O'Sullivan; Leonard Ceeley; Esther Muir; *D:* Sam Wood; *W:* Robert Pirosh; George Seaton; George Oppenheimer; *C:* Joseph Ruttenberg; *M:* George Bassman; Bronislau Kaper; Walter Jurmann.

Day for Night 🦴🦴🦴🦴 *La Nuit Americaine* **1973 (PG)** Director Ferrand (Truffaut) is working on a mediocre romantic melodrama with sullen actor Alphonse (Leaud) who falls for his married co-star Julie (Bissset) in just one of the off-screen stories that's more interesting than what's being filmed. A wryly affectionate look at the profession of moviemaking—its craft, character, and the personalities that interact against the performances commanded by the camera. In French with English subtitles. **116m/C; VHS, DVD, Blu-Ray.** *FR* Jean-Pierre Leaud; Jacqueline Bisset; Jean-Pierre Aumont; Valentina Cortese; Alexandra Stewart; Dani; Nathalie Baye; Francois Truffaut; *D:* Francois Truffaut; *W:* Suzanne Schiffman; Jean-Louis Richard; Francois Truffaut; *C:* Pierre William Glenn; *M:* Georges Delerue. Oscars '73: Foreign Film; British Acad. '73: Director (Truffaut), Film, Support. Actress (Cortese); N.Y. Film Critics '73: Director (Truffaut), Film, Support. Actress (Cortese); Natl. Soc. Film Critics '73: Director (Truffaut), Film, Support. Actress (Cortese).

A Day for Thanks on Walton's Mountain 🦴🦴 **1982** Many of the original television-show cast members returned for this sentimental Thanksgiving reunion on Walton's Mountain. **97m/C; VHS, DVD.** Ralph Waite; Ellen Corby; Judy Norton-Taylor; Eric Scott; Jon Walmsley; Robert Wightman; Mary (Elizabeth) McDonough; David W. Harper; Kami Cotler; Joe Conley; Ronnie Clair Edwards; Richard Gilliland; Melinda Naud; *Nar:* Earl Hamner; *D:* Harry Harris. **TV**

The Day He Arrives 🦴🦴 ½ *Book chon bang hyang* **2011** A former filmmaker travels to Seoul to visit a friend. When his friend doesn't appear he begins to wander the city night after night, spending time with a woman who looks very much like his ex. Each day resembles the last, but less new, less enjoyable. A witty and good-natured take on Bill Murray's "Groundhog Day." **79m/B; DVD.** *SK* Jun-sang Yu; Sang Jung Kim; Seon-mi Song; Bo-kyung Kim; *D:* Sang-soo Hong; *W:* Sang-soo Hong; *C:* Hyung-ku Kim; *M:* Young-jin Jeong.

A Day in October 🦴🦴 ½ **1992 (PG-13)** 1943, Copenhagen, Denmark. There are signs the Jewish population is in danger from occupying Nazi officials and the resistance movement is active. Wounded resistance fighter Sweeney is rescued by the Jewish Sara (Wolf), and their relationship deepens as the realities of WWII change their lives. Based on historical fact, but there's little explanation of the politics or the fierce nationalism and intense loyalty most Danes felt towards their fellow countrymen, a loyalty that ultimately saved most of the Danish Jews from the Holocaust. Good performances, particularly Benzali as Sara's father, help overcome the script weaknesses. Filmed on location in Denmark. **96m/C; VHS, DVD.** D.B. Sweeney; Kelly Wolf; Tovah Feldshuh; Daniel Benzali; Ole Lemmeke; Kim Romer; Anders Peter Bro; Lars Oluf Larsen; ***D:*** Kenneth Madsen; ***W:*** Damian F. Slattery; ***M:*** Jens Lysdal.

A Day in the Death of Joe Egg **1971 (R)** Based on the Peter Nichols play, an unlikely black comedy about a British couple trying to care for their retarded/autistic child, nearly destroying their marriage in the process. They begin to contemplate euthanasia as a solution. Well-acted, but potentially offensive to some. **106m/C; VHS, DVD.** *GB* Alan Bates; Janet Suzman; Elizabeth Robillard; Peter Bowles; Joan Hickson; Sheila Gish; ***D:*** Peter Medak; ***W:*** David Deutsch.

A Day in the Life **1/2 2009 (R)** Stick is part of the New York gangsta life but wants to go straight for the sake of his girlfriend. Then his family is targeted by rivals and he gets pulled back in. All the dialogue is rapped rather than spoken. **90m/C; DVD.** Kirk "Sticky Fingaz" Jones; Mekhi Phifer; Omar Epps; Faizon Love; Michael Rapaport; Fredro Starr; Malinda Williams; Michael K(enneth) Williams; Bokeem Woodbine; Ray J; ***D:*** Kirk "Sticky Fingaz" Jones; ***W:*** Kirk "Sticky Fingaz" Jones; ***C:*** Erik Voake; ***M:*** Kirk "Sticky Fingaz" Jones. **VIDEO**

The Day It Came to Earth **WOOF!** **1977 (PG)** Completely silly and unbelievable sci-fi flick has meteor crashing into the watery grave of a mobster. The decomposed corpse is revived by the radiation and plots to take revenge on those who fitted him with cement shoes. **89m/C; VHS, DVD.** Roger Manning; Wink Roberts; Bob Ginnaven; Rita Wilson; Delight de Bruine; ***D:*** Harry Z. Thomason.

A Day Late and a Dollar Short **1/2 2014** Lifetime family drama based on the Terry McMillan novel. Viola Price (Goldberg) has learned that her health issues are now terminal. With an estranged husband (who's got a young girlfriend) and four adult, squabbling children, Viola decides to keep her diagnosis a secret while working to restore some harmony to her family. The plot's overstuffed, but the cast is great. **90m/C; DVD.** Whoopi Goldberg; Ving Rhames; Anika Noni Rose; Tichina Arnold; Kimberly Elise; Mekhi Phifer; Lyriq Bent; Arnold Pinnock; ***D:*** Stephen Tolkin; ***W:*** Shernold Edwards; ***C:*** David (Robert) A. Greene; ***M:*** Jeff Beal. **CABLE**

The Day My Parents Ran Away **1/2 1993 (PG)** Rebellious 16-year-old gets a tough lesson in responsibility when his parents get tired of his antics and decide to leave home in search of a new life. He finds out things aren't so easy on your own. **95m/C; VHS, DVD.** Matt Frewer; Bobby Jacoby; Brigid Brannagh; Blair Brown; Martin Mull; ***D:*** Martin Nicholson; ***W:*** Handel Glassberg; ***M:*** J. Peter Robinson.

Day Night Day Night **2006** Luisa Williams plays a nameless young woman who at the story's outset is holed up in a shabby motel receiving instruction from black-hooded men. While few clues are given about her motivation, her intention is clearly to become a suicide bomber in Times Square. Once on the streets of New York, her scenes are filmed with handheld cameras in daylight amid the unwitting masses of Manhattan. The film raises many issues, leaving most unresolved and leaving viewers to contemplate the very real possibility of terrorism close to home. **94m/C; On Demand.** *US GE* Luisa Williams; ***D:*** Julia Loktev; ***W:*** Julia Loktev; ***C:*** Benoît Debie.

Day of Reckoning **1933** And the reckoning is steep for all concerned. Middle-class Dorothy Day's (Evans) extravagance gets her doting husband John (Dix) arrested for embezzlement. Dorothy's sleazy admirer George Hollins (Tearle) has his equally sleazy lawyer bungle John's case so he gets a prison sentence. Dorothy abandons her children to the care of maid Mamie (Merkel) so she can openly fool around with George and the situation actually gets worse. **69m/B; DVD.** Madge Evans; Richard Dix; Conway Tearle; Isabel Jewell; Una Merkel; George "Spanky" McFarland; Stuart Erwin; Raymond Hatton; ***D:*** Charles Brabin; ***W:*** Zelda Sears; Eve Greene; ***C:*** Ted Tetzlaff.

Day of the Animals *Something Is Out There* **1977 (PG)** Nature gone wild. It seems a depleted ozone layer has exposed the animals to the sun's radiation, turning Bambi and Bugs into brutal killers. A group of backpackers trek in the Sierras, unaware of the transformation. Far-fetched and silly (we hope). **95m/C; VHS, DVD, Blu-Ray.** Christopher George; Leslie Nielsen; Lynda Day George; Richard Jaeckel; Michael Ansara; Ruth Roman; Jon Cedar; Susan Backlinie; Andrew Stevens; Gil Lamb; ***D:*** William Girdler; ***W:*** William W. Norton, Sr.; ***C:*** Robert Sorrentino; ***M:*** Lalo Schifrin.

Day of the Cobra **1/2 1984** A corrupt narcotics bureau official hires an ex-cop to find a heroin kingpin on the back streets of Genoa, Italy. **95m/C; VHS, DVD.** *IT* Franco Nero; Sybil Danning; Mario Maranzana; Licinia Lentini; William Berger; ***D:*** Enzo G. Castellari.

Day of the Dead **1/2 1985** The third in Romero's trilogy of films about flesh-eating zombies taking over the world. Romero hasn't thought up anything new for the ghouls to do, and the humans are too nasty to care about this time around. For adult audiences. **91m/C; VHS, DVD, Blu-Ray.** Lori Cardille; Terry Alexander; Joe Pilato; Jarlath Conroy; Richard Liberty; ***D:*** George A. Romero; ***W:*** George A. Romero; ***C:*** Michael Gornick; ***M:*** John Harrison.

The Day of the Dolphin **1973 (PG)** Research scientist, after successfully working out a means of teaching dolphins to talk, finds his animals kidnapped; espionage and assassination are involved. Dolphin voices by Henry, who also wrote the screenplay. **104m/C; VHS, DVD, Blu-Ray.** George C. Scott; Trish Van Devere; Paul Sorvino; Fritz Weaver; Jon Korkes; John Dehner; Edward Herrmann; Severn Darden; ***V:*** Buck Henry; ***D:*** Mike Nichols; ***W:*** Buck Henry; ***M:*** Georges Delerue.

Day of the Evil Gun **1/2 1968** Workmanlike western. Gunslinger Lorn Warfield (Ford) returns home after three years and discovers that Apaches have kidnapped his wife Angie (Babcock) and their children. He joins forces with rancher Owen Forbes (Kennedy), who loves Angie, but there's a personality switch in the men as they get deeper into their quest. **94m/C; DVD.** Glenn Ford; Arthur Kennedy; Barbara Babcock; Dean Jagger; Harry Dean Stanton; John Anderson; Paul Fix; ***D:*** Jerry Thorpe; ***W:*** Eric Bercovici; Charles Marquis Warren; ***C:*** W. Wallace Kelley; ***M:*** Jeff Alexander.

Day of the Falcon **1/2** *Black Gold* **2011 (R)** Historical drama set in the 1930s in the Arabian desert about two warring princes: Emir Nesib (Banderas) and Sultan Amar (Strong). Making peace after years of war, the two declare a large swath of land between the two a no man's land to preserve that peace. A peace that lasts right up until America discovers oil in the neutral zone. **125m/C; DVD, Blu-Ray.** *FR IT QA TN* Mark Strong; Antonio Banderas; Freida Pinto; Riz Ahmed; Tahar Rahim; ***D:*** Jean-Jacques Annaud; ***W:*** Jean-Jacques Annaud; Menno Meyjes; Alain Godard; ***C:*** Jean-Marie Dreujou; ***M:*** James Horner.

The Day of the Jackal **1/2 1973 (PG)** Frederick Forsyth's best-selling novel of political intrigue is splendidly brought to the screen by Zinnemann. A brilliant and ruthless assassin hired to kill Charles de Gaulle skirts the international intelligence pool, while intuitive police work try to stop him. Tense, suspenseful, beautiful location photography. Excellent acting by Fox, Cusack and Britton. **142m/C; VHS, DVD, Blu-Ray.** Edward Fox; Alan Badel; Tony Britton; Derek Jacobi; Cyril Cusack; Olga Georges-Picot; Michael (Michel) Lonsdale; ***D:*** Fred Zinnemann; ***W:*** Kenneth Ross; ***C:*** Jean Tournier; ***M:*** Georges Delerue.

The Day of the Locust **1/2 1975 (R)** Compelling adaptation of Nathaniel West's novel concerning the dark side of 1930s' Hollywood. A no-talent amoral actress's affair with a meek accountant leads to tragedy and destruction. Told from the view of a cynical art director wise to the ways of Hollywood. **140m/C; VHS, DVD.** Donald Sutherland; Karen Black; Burgess Meredith; William Atherton; Billy Barty; Bo Hopkins; Richard Dysart; Geraldine Page; ***D:*** John Schlesinger; ***C:*** Conrad L. Hall; ***M:*** John Barry.

Day of the Maniac **1/2 1977 (R)** Psychotic drug addict will stop at nothing to support his growing habit. **89m/C; VHS, DVD.** George Hilton; Nieves Navarro; ***D:*** Sergio Martino.

Day of the Mummy **1/2 2014** A mummy wrecks havoc in this Egypt-set horror film. When Jack Wells (McNamara) travels to Egypt with a group of archaeologists, he is on a quest for an The Codex Stone. This well-known diamond has been lost in time. During his search, Jack ends up in the tomb of King Neferu (deSpain). The cursed Neferu is awakened from his eternal rest by greedy humans looking for the diamond and rises from the dead. As the titular mummy, Neferu takes out his fury on the living humans he encounters during a new reign of terror. **81m/C; DVD, Streaming, Download.** Danny Glover; William McNamara; Anthony Fanelli; Andrea Monier; Brandon deSpain; ***D:*** Johnny Tabor; ***W:*** Garry Charles; ***C:*** Ryan Valdez.

The Day of the Outlaw **1/2 1959** Bleak wintry western. Wounded Jack Bruhn (Ives) and his gang take over the remote town of Bitter, Wyoming. Cattleman Blaise Starrett (Ryan) ignores the town's plight since he's upset that the settlers are stringing up barbed wire and his young love Helen (Louise) has married another. But finally Starrett's decency gets the better of him and he decides to take a stand against Bruhn. **92m/B; DVD, Blu-Ray.** Robert Ryan; Burl Ives; Tina Louise; Alan Marshal; Nehemiah Persoff; Jack Lambert; Venetia Stevenson; David Nelson; Elisha Cook, Jr.; Dabbs Greer; ***D:*** Andre de Toth; ***W:*** Philip Yordan; ***C:*** Russell Harlan; ***M:*** Alexander Courage.

Day of the Panther **1/2 1988** The Panthers?-the world's most formidable martial artists?-are mighty torqued when panther-Linda is pithed, and they're not known to turn the other cheek. Much chop-socky kicking and shrilling. **86m/C; VHS, DVD.** John Stanton; Eddie Stazak; ***D:*** Brian Trenchard-Smith.

Day of the Triffids **1963** The majority of Earth's population is blinded by a meteor shower which also causes plant spores to mutate into giant carnivores. Well-done adaptation of John Wyndham's science fiction classic; Philip Yordan acknowledged "fronting" for blacklisted screenwriter Gordon, who finally received credit in 1996. **94m/C; VHS, DVD.** *GB* Howard Keel; Janette Scott; Nicole Maurey; Kieron Moore; Mervyn Johns; Alison Leggatt; Ewan Roberts; Janina Faye; Gilgi Hauser; Carol Ann Ford; ***D:*** Steve Sekely; Freddie Francis; ***W:*** Bernard Gordon; Philip Yordan; ***C:*** Ted Moore.

Day of the Warrior **1996 (R)** Babes who belong to a paramilitary law-and-order group infiltrate crime lord, the Warrior's, smuggling operations, strip joints and porn palaces. **96m/C; VHS, DVD.** Julie Strain; Marcus Bagwell; ***D:*** Andy Sidaris; ***W:*** Andy Sidaris.

The Day of the Wolves **1/2 1971** Seven nameless, bearded criminals are hired to loot an isolated town by first cutting off all outside communication. The town's former sheriff tries to stop them. There's a not-bad twist at the end but otherwise it's strictly a low-budget B-movie. **95m/C; DVD.** Richard Egan; Martha Hyer; Jan Murray; Frankie Randall; Andre Marquis; Rick Jason; Zaldy Zschornack; Henry Capps; Smokey Roberts; ***D:*** Ferde Grofe, Jr.; ***W:*** Ferde Grofe, Jr.; ***C:*** Ric Waite; ***M:*** Sean Bonniwell.

Day of Wrath *Vredens Dag* **1943** An involving psychological thriller based on records of witch trials from the early 1600s. Young Anne (Movin) is married to the much older and puritannical widower, Absalon (Roose) but falls in love with his son Martin (Lerdorff). She wishes aloud for her husband's death and when he does dies, Anne is accused of witchcraft. Grim and unrelentingly pessimistic, moving from one horrific scene to another, director Dreyer creates a masterpiece of terror. Based on a play by Hans Wiers Jenssen. In Danish with English subtitles. **110m/B; VHS, DVD.** *DK* Thorkild Roose; Sigrid Neiiendam; Lisbeth Movin; Preben Lerdorff; Anna Svierker; ***D:*** Carl Theodor Dreyer; ***W:*** Carl Theodor Dreyer; ***C:*** Karl Andersson; ***M:*** Poul Schierbeck.

Day of Wrath **1/2 2006 (R)** Pretty much of a snorer. 16th-century sheriff Ruy de Mendoza (Lambert) investigates the gruesome murders of several nobles during the Spanish Inquisition, only to discover family ties that put his life in peril. **101m/C; DVD.** *GB HU* Christopher Lambert; Brian Blessed; James Faulkner; Phyllida Law; Blanca Marsillach; Ben O'Brien; ***D:*** Adrian Rudomin; ***W:*** Adrian Rudomin; ***C:*** Tamas Lajos; ***M:*** David Schweitzer. **VIDEO**

Day One **1989** Vivid re-creation of one of the most turbulent periods of American history—the WWII race to build the atomic bomb. Chronicles the two year top-secret efforts of the Manhattan Project, with General Leslie Groves (Dennehy) having to supervise the project and contain the scientific rivalries. Outstanding cast, with Strathairn notable as physicist J. Robert Oppenheimer. Adapted from "Day One: Before Hiroshima and After" by Peter Wyden. **141m/C; VHS, DVD.** Brian Dennehy; David Strathairn; Michael Tucker; Hume Cronyn; Richard Dysart; Barnard Hughes; Hal Holbrook; David Ogden Stiers; John McMartin; ***D:*** Joseph Sargent; ***W:*** David W. Rintels; ***M:*** Mason Daring. **TV**

The Day Reagan Was Shot **2001 (R)** Recalls March 30, 1981 when President Reagan (Crenna) lay critically wounded in George Washington University hospital after having been shot by John W. Hinckley Jr. The administration is in chaos and power struggles break out between Secretary of State Alexander Haig (Dreyfuss) and Secretary of Defense Caspar Weinberger (Feore). Cable drama seems to be more satire than fact. **95m/C; VHS, DVD.** Richard Crenna; Richard Dreyfuss; Colm Feore; Holland Taylor; Kenneth Welsh; Leon Pownall; Michael Murphy; Jack Jessop; ***D:*** Cyrus Nowrasteh; ***W:*** Cyrus Nowrasteh; ***C:*** Michael McMurray. **CABLE**

The Day Shall Come **1/2 2019** Moses (Davis) is a somewhat delusional preacher with a tiny following and revolutionary plans that include overthrowing the government one day in the future. His Miami-based self-sufficiency organization, the Star of Six, has serious financial issues but he still manages to spread his message via Facebook Live. A group of FBI agents, including Kendra (Kendrick), seeking personal glory try to lure Moses into an illegal arms scheme to further their careers. though the well-shot political satire could have been more amusing, it uses its humorous situation to highlight bold truths about the FBI and its tactics. **88m/C; DVD.** Marchánt Davis; Danielle Brooks; Anna Kendrick; Denis O'Hare; Jim Gaffigan; ***D:*** Christopher Morris; ***W:*** Christopher Morris; Jesse Armstrong; ***C:*** Marcel Zyskind; ***M:*** Christopher Morris; Sebastian Rochford; Jonathan Whitehead.

The Day the Earth Caught Fire **1/2 1961** The earth is knocked out of orbit and sent hurtling toward the sun when nuclear testing is done simultaneously at both the North and South Poles. Realistic and suspenseful, this is one of the best of the sci-fi genre. **95m/B; VHS, DVD.** Janet Munro; Edward Judd; Leo McKern; ***D:*** Val Guest; ***W:*** Val Guest; Wolf Mankowitz; ***C:*** Harry Waxman; ***M:*** Stanley Black. British Acad. '61: Screenplay.

The Day the Earth Froze **1959** Witch steals the sun because she couldn't have a magical mill that produced grain, salt, and gold. Everything on Earth freezes. Based on a Finnish epic poem. **67m/B; VHS, DVD.** *FI RU* Nina Anderson; Jon Powers; Ingrid Elhardt; Paul Sorenson; ***Nar:*** Marvin Miller; ***D:*** Gregg Sebelious.

The Day the Earth Stood Still **1/2 1951** A gentle alien lands on Earth to deliver a message of peace and a warning against experimenting with nuclear power. He finds his views echoed by a majority of the population, but not the ones who are in control. In this account based loosely on the story of Christ, Rennie is the visitor backed by the mighty robot Gort. One of the greatest science fiction films of all time. **92m/B; VHS, DVD, Blu-Ray.** Michael Rennie; Patricia Neal; Hugh Marlowe; Sam Jaffe; Frances Bavier; Lock Martin; Billy Gray; Edith Evanson; Frank Conroy; Drew Pearson; ***D:*** Robert Wise; ***W:*** Edmund H. North; ***C:*** Leo Tover; ***M:*** Bernard Herrmann. Natl. Film Reg. '95.

The Day the Earth Stood Still **2008 (PG-13)** Subpar and bland reworking of the 1951 sci-fi classic is not out of this world, but maybe should be sent there. Alien Klaatu (Reeves) arrives in Central Park with another warning for earthlings—humankind must change the way they treat the environment or else be doomed. Klaatu's companion metal robot Gort is inexplicably less mighty than in the original, a poor excuse given the technology available. Wasted are the talents of: Connelly as microbiologist Helen Benson who is among a group of scientists the government forcibly gathers; Bates of the U.S. Department of Defense; and Cleese, an "Important Scientist." **103m/C; Blu-Ray.** Keanu Reeves; Jennifer Connelly; Jon Hamm; John Cleese; Jaden Smith; Kathy Bates; Kyle Chandler; Robert Knepper; James Hong; ***D:*** Scott Derrickson; ***W:*** David Scarpa; ***C:*** David Tattersall; ***M:*** Tyler Bates.

The Day the Earth Stopped **2008 (R)** Naked alien babe. After massive intergalactic robots land on Earth and take over the capitol cities worldwide, this naked chick walks out of some woods around L.A. She is taken by military man Josh Myron (Howell) to an Army base where she tells them that the robots are giving earthlings an ultimatum: prove the value of human civilization or be destroyed. **90m/C; DVD.** C. Thomas Howell; Sinead McCafferty; Darren Dalton; Judd Nelson; Bug Hall; Cameron Bender; ***D:*** C. Thomas Howell; ***W:*** Darren Dalton; Carey Van Dyke; Shane Van Dyke; ***C:*** Adam Silver; ***M:*** Guillermo J. Silberstein; Mauricio Yazigi. **VIDEO**

The Day the Sky Exploded ½ *Death From Outer Space; La Morte Viene Dalla Spazio; Le Danger Vient de l'Escape* **1957** Sci-fi disaster drama doesn't live up to the grandiose title, as a runaway rocket ship hits the sun, unleashing an asteroid shower that threatens Earth with tidal waves, earthquakes, heat waves and terrible dialogue. The highlight of this Franco-Italian effort is the cinematography by horror director Mario Bava. **80m/B; VHS, DVD.** *FR IT* Paul (Christian) Hubschmid; Madeleine Fischer; Fiorella Mari; Ivo Garrani; Dario Michaelis; ***D:*** Richard Benson; ***C:*** Mario Bava.

Day the World Ended **1955** The first science-fiction film of exploitation director Roger Corman. Five survivors of nuclear holocaust discover a desert ranch house fortress owned by a survivalist (Birch) and his daughter (Nelson). With relatively abundant supplies, they fatuously wallow in false misery until a disfigured visitor, wasting away from radiation, stumbles into their paradise. His mutation into an alien being confronts them with the horror that lurks outside. **79m/B; VHS, DVD.** Paul Birch; Lori Nelson; Adele Jergens; Raymond Hatton; Paul Dubov; Richard Denning; Mike Connors; Paul Blaisdell; Jonathan Haze; ***D:*** Roger Corman; ***W:*** Lou Rusoff; ***C:*** Jockey A. Feindel; ***M:*** Ronald Stein.

The Day the World Ended ½ **2001 (R)** Shrink Dr. Jennifer Stillman (Kinski) leaves New York for a small town as the school district's new therapist. Her first patient, Ben (Edner), is a young outsider whose adoptive father is the town doctor (Quaid). Jennifer realizes Ben is hiding something about his mother's mysterious death, which involves a coverup by the town. When several locals are brutally murdered, Jennifer becomes a suspect but Ben blames his biological father—a space alien. This cable remake has nothing to do with the 1955 original and even the title seems off. **90m/C; VHS, DVD.** Nastassja Kinski; Randy Quaid; Debra Christofferson; Bobby Edner; Stephen Tobolowsky; Lee DeBroux; David Getz; Alexander Gould; ***D:*** Terence Gross; ***W:*** Annie de Young; Max Enscoe; ***C:*** Mark Vargo; ***M:*** Charles Bernstein. **CABLE**

The Day They Robbed the Bank of England **1960** Crime drama based on a true story. In 1901, Irish-American mining engineer Charles Norgate (Ray) agrees to help the IRA fund its activities by robbing the Bank of England's vault of its gold. He befriends guard Fitch (O'Toole) to get information and then proceeds to tunnel in through the sewers, but Fitch's suspicious are finally aroused. **85m/B; DVD.** *UK* Aldo Ray; Peter O'Toole; Hugh Griffith; Elizabeth Sellars; Kieron Moore; Albert Sharpe; ***D:*** John Guillermin; ***W:*** Howard Clewes; Richard Maibaum; ***C:*** Georges Perinal; ***M:*** Edwin Astley.

Day Time Ended *Vortex; Timewarp* **1980** A pair of glowing UFO's streaking across the sky and an alien mechanical device with long menacing appendages are only two of the bizarre phenomena witnessed from a lone house in the desert. Good special effects. Also released as "Time Warp" (1978). **80m/C; VHS, DVD, Blu-Ray.** Chris Mitchum; Jim Davis; Dorothy Malone; ***D:*** John Cardos; ***W:*** David Schmoeller; J. Larry Carroll; ***M:*** Richard Band.

Day-Time Wife **1939** Some questionable moral choices managed to sneak past the Hays Production Code in this marital drama. Exec Ken Norton (Power) calls his beautiful wife Jane (Darnell) and tells her he's working late and he's going to miss their second anniversary. He's working alright—making time with secretary Kitty (Barrie). Jane suspects and decides she wants to know why men fall for their secretaries so she takes a job (without Ken knowing) with womanizing architect Bernard Dexter (William). While out to dinner with Dexter, Jane spies Ken with Kitty. Will this married couple ever decide who they're meant to be with? **71m/B; DVD.** Tyrone Power; Linda Darnell; Warren William; Wendy Barrie; Binnie Barnes; Joan Valerie; Joan Davis; Leonid Kinskey; ***D:*** Gregory Ratoff; ***W:*** Art Arthur; Robert Harari; ***C:*** J. Peverell Marley; ***M:*** Cyril Mockridge.

Day Watch *Dnevnoi Dozor: Mel Sudbi* **2006 (R)** Vampires, chases, explosions, "Matrix"-style fight scenes, and just a touch of post-Communist allegory make this an incoherent but fun ride. Two factions of Moscow vampires ("Darks" and "Lights") struggle to manage an uneasy truce as an inevitable conflict rises. Good-guy vamp Anton (Khabensky) is torn between two rising powers: his lover Svetlana (Poroshina) on one side and his increasingly evil son Yegor (Martynov) on the other. Non-stop action sequences make up for the thin plot but what really stands out is the creative characterization and innovative direction. Sequel to 2004's "Night Watch." **132m/C; DVD.** *RU* Konstantin Khabensky; Maria Poroshina; Vladimir Menshov; Viktor Verzhbitsky; Galina Tyunina; Alexsei Chadov; Dima Martinov; Valery Zolotukhin; ***D:*** Timur Bekmambetov; ***W:*** Timur Bekmambetov; Sergey Lukyanenko; Aleksandr Talal; ***C:*** Sergei Trofimov; ***M:*** Yuri Potyeyenko.

A Day Without a Mexican ½ *Un dia sin mexicanos* **2004 (R)** One morning, the state of California wakes up to find the entire Latino population has disappeared. The consequences are huge. Fields remain unharvested, cars are abandoned, schools are closed and the poor Anglos are left holding the bag. Without cheap laborers and migrant workers, the economy falls into a hopeless shambles. The lone Latino survivor is Lila Rodriguez (Arizmendi, who also co-scripted), a reporter who becomes the center of intense scrutiny. Amusingly shot as a mockumentary, but what could have been a biting critique suffers from lack of focus and overly broad scope. **97m/C; VHS, DVD.** *US MX* Yareli Arizmendi; John Getz; Maureen Flannigan; Muse Watson; Caroline Aaron; Melinda Allen; Eduardo Palomo; Bru Muller; Rick Najera; ***D:*** Sergio Arau; ***W:*** Sergio Arau; Sergio Guerrero; ***C:*** Alan Caudillo; ***M:*** Juan J. Colomer.

Day Zero ½ **2007 (R)** In this slightly futuristic fare, the U.S. military draft has been reinstated because of increasing terrorist acts. Three New York friends are called up and react to the news in different ways: lawyer George (Klein) asks his wealthy dad to help him wriggle out; insecure writer Aaron (Wood) thinks the military can make him a man; and cabdriver James (Bernthal) is patriotic and willing to serve. Overly self-important and formulaic. **96m/C; DVD.** Chris Klein; Elijah Wood; Ginnifer Goodwin; Elisabeth Moss; Jon Bernthal; Ally Sheedy; Sofia Vassilieva; ***D:*** Bryan Gunnar Colé; ***W:*** Rob Makani; ***C:*** Matthew Clark; ***M:*** Erin O'Hara.

Daybreak ½ **1993 (R)** In the near future America has been decimated by a nameless, sexually transmitted disease (read AIDS parable) and public policy is to quarantine the infected in concentration camp-like prisons. This leads to a quasi-official group of green-shirted thugs roaming the streets and imprisoning or killing anyone they suspect has the disease. A small resistance movement is lead by Torch (Gooding Jr.), who happens to fall in love with Blue (Kelly), the sister of one of the fascist leaders. Based on Alan Bowne's play "Beirut, Daybreak." **91m/C; VHS, DVD.** Cuba Gooding, Jr.; Moira Kelly; Omar Epps; Martha Plimpton; Alice Drummond; David Eigenberg; John Savage; ***Cameo(s):*** Phil Hartman; ***D:*** Stephen Tolkin; ***W:*** Stephen Tolkin. **CABLE**

Daybreak ½ **2001 (R)** A throwback to the cheesy disaster flicks of the '70s, which isn't necessarily a bad thing. An L.A. subway train is stuck in a tunnel after an earthquake and it's up to subway supervisor Dillan Johansen (McGinley) to find a way to save himself and the passengers from fire, water, and toxic chemicals. **93m/C; VHS, DVD.** Ted McGinley; Roy Scheider; Adam Wylie; Ursula Brooks; Jaime Bergman; ***D:*** Jean Pellerin. **VIDEO**

Daybreakers **2009 (R)** In 2017, a plague has turned most humans into vampires, and blood's running out. As the vampire society slowly declines into a world where the rich get blood and the poor turn into rabid, starving animals, researcher Edward (Hawke) works to develop a blood substitute for a nasty corporate CEO (Neill). When he meets human rebel Elvis (an energetically over-the-top Dafoe), who claims to have found a cure for vampirism, Edward has to figure out where his loyalties lie with the future of humanity in his hands. Creates a beautifully realized, detailed world of vampire society and serves up some early thrills, but the story quickly settles into standard horror film gear and never aspires to aim higher than big explosions and corny dialogue. Fun, but fails to live up to its wickedly smart premise. **98m/C; Blu-Ray, On Demand.** *US AU* Willem Dafoe; Ethan Hawke; Sam Neill; Vince Colosimo; Claudia Karvan; Isabel Lucas; Michael Dorman; ***D:*** Michael Spierig; Peter Spierig; ***W:*** Michael Spierig; Peter Spierig; ***C:*** Ben Nott; ***M:*** Christopher Gordon.

Daydream Nation ½ **2010 (R)** Smart, bored, and brazen Caroline (an appealingly flip Dennings) is appalled when her widowed dad moves them to a backwater town where the high schoolers spend their time getting high. She determinedly seduces troubled teacher Barry Anderson (Lucas) but also has stoner classmate Thurston (Thompson) in her lovestruck orbit. The males get jealous and Caroline isn't quite as confident as she likes to appear. **98m/C; DVD.** *CA* Kat Dennings; Reece Thompson; Josh(ua) Lucas; Andie MacDowell; Rachel Blanchard; Natasha Calis; Landon Liboiron; Ted Whittall; Luke Camilleri; Quinn Lord; Calum Worthy; ***D:*** Michael Goldbach; ***W:*** Michael Goldbach; ***C:*** Jon Joffin; ***M:*** Ohad Benchetrit.

The Daydreamer ½ *Absent-Minded; Le Distrait* **1970** Actor/director/writer Richard stars as a bumbling fool let loose in the French corporate world with comical results. In French with subtitles. **90m/C; VHS, DVD.** *FR* Pierre Richard; Bernard Blier; Maria Pacome; Marie-Christine Barrault; ***D:*** Pierre Richard; ***W:*** Pierre Richard; ***M:*** Vladimir Cosma.

Daylight **1996 (PG-13)** After a massive explosion seals both ends of New York's Holland Tunnel (The Tunneling Inferno?), a small band of stock disaster flick survivors are trapped under the waters of the Hudson River. Fortunately, a cab driver with a really square jaw who, conveniently, is an ex-emergency rescue worker AND who knows the entire layout of the tunnel happens to be driving toward the tunnel at the exact moment of the disaster. Coincidence? Nope, just Hollywood. Kit Latura (Stallone) leads the survivors through cave-ins, floods, fire, rats, and poison gas (The Poison-Hiding Adventure!) only to discover to their dismay that they have emerged in New Jersey. Long on special effects but short on character development, this nod to the catastrophe movies of the '70s is still enjoyable for those who like to watch things go boom. **109m/C; VHS, DVD, Blu-Ray, HD-DVD.** Sylvester Stallone; Viggo Mortensen; Amy Brenneman; Stan Shaw; Claire Bloom; Renoly Santiago; Sage Stallone; Dan Hedaya; Jay O. Sanders; Karen Young; Vanessa Bell Calloway; Colin Fox; Danielle Harris; Jo Anderson; Mark Rolston; Rosemary Forsyth; Barry Newman; ***D:*** Rob Cohen; ***W:*** Leslie Bohem; ***C:*** David Eggby; ***M:*** Randy Edelman.

Daylight's End **2016** Low-budget action science fiction horror about a dark future in which the survival of humanity is threatened by vampire/zombie-like creatures. In the years following the outbreak of a plague which destroyed most of the planet, most of humanity has been turned into the creatures that only want blood. One man, Thomas Rourke (Strong), survives as a rogue drifter. After he saves Sam Sheridan (Edmundson) from being sexually assaulted by criminals, he takes her back to her group which has found hiding a police station. After he meets them, Thomas agrees to help them kill The Alpha (Soszynski), the leader of a creature group, and escape to a safer sanctuary. **105m/C; DVD, Streaming, Download.** Johnny Strong; Chelsea Edmundson; Krzysztof Soszynski; Lance Henriksen; Louis Mandylor; ***D:*** William Kaufman; ***W:*** Chad Law; ***C:*** Kelly Riemenschneider; ***M:*** Johnny Strong.

Days ½ *Giorni* **2002** Caludio (Trabacchi) is a workaholic mid-30s bank exec in Rome. HIV-positive, he's stayed healthy with a rigid regime of drugs and exercise. Claudio also has a longtime lover, Andrea (Salerno), and they are supposed to be moving to Milan together. Except Claudio is suddenly reluctant—could this have anything to do with his encounter with handsome young waiter Dario (Bechini)? (What do you think.) Suddenly, uptight Claudio is acting very recklessly. He begins an affair with Dario, goes off his meds, sloughs off his job, and can't make up his mind about either man. Claudio's not the most likeable guy around but he's very, very real and you'll even understand why both his lovers still around to see what happens next. Italian with subtitles. **90m/C; VHS, DVD.** *IT* Thomas Trabacchi; Riccardo Salerno; Davide Bechini; ***D:*** Laura Muscardin; ***W:*** Laura Muscardin; Francesco Montini; David Oserio; Jane Ruhm; ***C:*** Sabrina Varani; ***M:*** Ivan Iusco.

Days and Clouds *Giorni e Nuvole* **2007** Elsa is fulfilling her dream of getting an advanced degree in art restoration. After she graduates, her husband Michele confesses that he lost his job months ago and has been unsuccessful finding employment so they will have to drastically downsize their lives. Elsa goes into crisis mode and finds an office job to support them while Michele's apathy and depression get the best of him and their 20-year-old daughter Alice remains resolutely oblivious to the family's problems. Italian with subtitles. **115m/C; DVD.** *IT* Margherita Buy; Antonio Albanese; Alba Rohrwacher; Guiseppe Battiston; Carla Signoris; Fabio Troiano; ***D:*** Silvio Soldini; ***W:*** Silvio Soldini; Doriana Leondeff; Francesco Piccolo; Federica Pontremoli; ***C:*** Ramiro Civita; ***M:*** Giovanni Venosta.

Days and Nights ½ **2014** Tepid, dreary take on Chekov's "The Seagull," set in 1984 rural New England. Actress Elizabeth takes her younger director lover Peter with her to the family home over Memorial Day weekend. It's not happy times for anyone on the estate: her brother Herb is dying, her neglected son Eric makes an experimental film starring neighbor Eva that's a disaster, and a nesting bald eagle (in place of the seagull) is killed. **92m/C; DVD.** Allison Janney; William Hurt; Ben Whishaw; Juliet Rylance; Katie Holmes; Mark Rylance; Jean Reno; Michael Nyqvist; Cherry Jones; Christian Camargo; ***D:*** Christian Camargo; ***W:*** Christian Camargo; ***C:*** Steve Cosens. **VIDEO**

Days of Being Wild *A Fei jing juen; A Fei zheng zhuan; Ah Fei's Story* **1991** Yuddy (Leslie Cheung) learns his mom is an ex-prostitute who raised him when he was abandoned by his real mother. He is so stunned by the revelation he can't even make a decision between the two women fighting for him, even though they have other men fighting for them as well. When his adopted mother won't confess the identity of his real mother, Yuddy goes in search of her. Winner of many trophies at the Hong Kong Film Awards. **89m/C; DVD.** *CH* Leslie Cheung; Maggie Cheung; Andy Lau; Carina Lau; Rebecca Pan; Jacky Cheung; Tony Leung Chiu-wai; Mei-Mei Hung; ***D:*** Kar-Wai Wong; ***W:*** Kar-Wai Wong; ***C:*** Christopher Doyle.

Days of Glory ½ **1943** Peck's screen debut finds him as a Russian peasant bravely fighting the Nazi blitzkrieg almost single-handedly. **86m/B; VHS, DVD.** Tamara Toumanova; Gregory Peck; Alan Reed; Maria Palmer; Lowell Gilmore; Hugo Haas; ***D:*** Jacques Tourneur; ***C:*** Gaetano Antonio "Tony" Gaudio.

Days of Glory *Indigenes* **2006 (R)** Issue-based WWII drama caused a furor as it brought up the shabby treatment received by

North African colonial recruits who fought for France as second-class citizens. Poorly trained, they bravely battle on while being unjustly treated and degraded by their superior officers. The Moroccans are more mouthpieces than individuals but the actors work well as an ensemble, and director Bouchareb keeps his drama to human scale. French and Arabic with subtitles. **123m/C; DVD.** *AL BE FR* Jamel Debbouze; Roschdy Zem; Sami Bouajila; Mathieu Simonet; Samy Naceri; Bernard Blancan; Benoit Giros; ***D:*** Rachid Bouchareb; ***W:*** Rachid Bouchareb; Olivier Lorelle; ***C:*** Patrick Blossier; ***M:*** Armand Amar.

Days of Heaven 1/2 **1978 (PG)** Drifter Gere, his younger sister, and a woman he claims is his sister become involved with a Texas sharecropper. Told through the eyes of the younger girl, this is a sweeping vision of the U.S. before WWI. Loss and loneliness, deception, frustration, and anger haunt these people as they struggle to make the land their own. Deservedly awarded an Oscar for breathtaking cinematography. **95m/C; VHS, DVD.** Richard Gere; Brooke Adams; Sam Shepard; Linda Manz; Stuart Margolin; ***D:*** Terrence Malick; ***W:*** Terrence Malick; ***C:*** Nestor Almendros; ***M:*** Ennio Morricone. Oscars '78: Cinematog.; Cannes '79: Director (Malick); L.A. Film Critics '78: Cinematog.; Natl. Film Reg. '07; N.Y. Film Critics '78: Director (Malick); Natl. Soc. Film Critics '78: Cinematog., Director (Malick), Film.

Days of Thunder **1990 (PG-13)** "Top Gun" in race cars! Cruise follows the same formula he has followed for several years now (with the notable exception of "Born on the Fourth of July.") Cruise and Towne co-wrote the screenplay concerning a young kid bursting with talent and raw energy who must learn to deal with his mentor, his girlfriend, and eventually the bad guy. First film that featured cameras that were actually on the race cars. If you like Cruise or race cars then this is the movie for you. **108m/C; VHS, DVD, Blu-Ray.** Tom Cruise; Robert Duvall; Randy Quaid; Nicole Kidman; Cary Elwes; Michael Rooker; Fred Dalton Thompson; John C. Reilly; ***D:*** Tony Scott; ***W:*** Tom Cruise; Robert Towne; ***C:*** Ward Russell; ***M:*** Hans Zimmer.

Days of Wine and Roses 1/2 **1958** The original "Playhouse 90" TV version of J.P. Miller's story which was adapted for the big screen in 1962. An executive on the fast track and his young wife, initially only social drinkers, find themselves degenerating into alcoholism. A well-acted, stirring drama. **89m/B; VHS, DVD.** Cliff Robertson; Piper Laurie; ***D:*** John Frankenheimer. **TV**

Days of Wine and Roses 1/2 **1962** A harrowing tale of an alcoholic advertising man who gradually drags his wife down with him into a life of booze. Big screen adaptation of the play originally shown on TV. **138m/B; VHS, DVD, Blu-Ray.** Jack Lemmon; Lee Remick; Charles Bickford; Jack Klugman; Jack Albertson; ***D:*** Blake Edwards; ***W:*** J(ames) P(inckney) Miller; ***M:*** Henry Mancini; ***M:*** Johnny Mercer. Oscars '62: Song ("Days of Wine and Roses"); Natl. Film Reg. '18.

The Daytrippers 1/2 **1996** Happily married Eliza D'Amico is living on Long Island while husband Louis (Tucci) goes to work in Manhattan. That is she's happy until she finds what appears to be a love letter addressed to her husband. Frantic, Eliza runs to aggressive mom Rita (Meara), who decides that her daughter should immediately confront her possibly erring husband at his office. So Eliza, her mom and dad (McNamara), sarcastic younger sister Jo (Posey), and Jo's pretentious boyfriend Carl (Schreiber) all pile into the family station wagon and head into the city. Only Louis isn't at his office and they scour Manhattan to track him down. **88m/C; VHS, DVD, Blu-Ray.** Hope Davis; Anne Meara; Parker Posey; Liev Schreiber; Pat McNamara; Stanley Tucci; Campbell Scott; Marcia Gay Harden; Andy Brown; ***D:*** Greg Mottola; ***W:*** Greg Mottola; ***C:*** John Inwood.

Dazed and Confused **1993 (R)** A day in the life of a bunch of high schoolers should prove to be a trip back in time for those coming of age in the '70s. Eight seniors facing life after high school have one last year long hurrah, as they search for Aerosmith tickets and haze the incoming freshmen. Keen characterization by writer/director Linklater captures the spirit of a generation shaped by Watergate, the Vietnam War, feminism, and marijuana. Groovy soundtrack features Alice Cooper, Deep Purple, KISS, and Foghat. **97m/C; VHS, DVD, Blu-Ray, HD-DVD.** Jason London; Rory Cochrane; Sasha Jenson; Wiley Wiggins; Michelle Rene Thomas; Adam Goldberg; Anthony Rapp; Marissa Ribisi; Parker Posey; Joey Lauren Adams; Ben Affleck; Milla Jovovich; Cole Hauser; Matthew McConaughey; Christin Hinojosa; ***D:*** Richard Linklater; ***W:*** Richard Linklater; ***C:*** Lee Daniel.

DC 9/11: Time of Crisis *The Big Dance* **2004 (R)** Retelling of the horrific terrorist attacks in New York City and Washington D.C. while providing a supposed behind-the-scenes view of the reaction of President Bush (played by Bottoms) and his administration. Undoubtedly will cause debates between those who see this as a vehicle to inflate the president's image and combat Michael Moore's flogging in "Fahrenheit 9/11" and others who consider it as fact. Let's remember it's a made for TV flick. **127m/C; VHS, DVD.** Timothy Bottoms; John Cunningham; James Carroll; Greg Ellwand; Lawrence Pressman; Stephen Macht; Gregory Itzin; Penny Johnson; Myron Natwick; Andrew Gillies; Bobby Johnston; Debra McGrath; David McIlwraith; Brian Rhodes; Allan Royal; Greg Spottiswood; George Takei; Roger Barnes; Geoffrey Bowes; Dom(enico) Fiore; Chris Gillet; Thomas Hauff; Howard Jerome; Doug Lennox; Gerry Mendicino; Mary Gordon Murray; David Wolos-Fonteno; ***D:*** Brian Trenchard-Smith; ***W:*** Lionel Chetwynd; ***C:*** Ousama Rawi; ***M:*** Lawrence Shragge. **TV**

D.C. Cab 1/2 **1984 (R)** A rag-tag group of Washington, D.C. cabbies learn a lesson in self-respect in this endearing comedy. Though not without flaws, it's charming all the same. **100m/C; VHS, DVD.** Mr. T; Leif Erickson; Adam Baldwin; Charlie Barnett; Irene Cara; Anne DeSalvo; Max Gail; Gloria Gifford; Gary Busey; Jill Schoelen; Marsha Warfield; ***D:*** Joel Schumacher; ***W:*** Joel Schumacher; Topper Carew; ***C:*** Dean Cundey.

De-Lovely *She's De Lovely* **2004 (PG-13)** Biopic of songwriter Cole Porter (Kline) is played as if Porter himself were directing a musical about his life. Focuses on his adultery-ridden marriage to put-upon wife Linda (Judd), who puts up with everything for as long she can. Dreary film is brightened by oddly updated covers of his tunes done by contemporary pop stars such as Elvis Costello, Alanis Morissette, and Sheryl Crow, but the story contains no real nods to Porter's artistic genius or creative struggles. Contrived staging is stolen from better films like "All That Jazz" and "Cabaret." Solid cast is very good, especially Judd, but story is deadly dull and glum. **125m/C; DVD.** Kevin Kline; Ashley Judd; Jonathan Pryce; Keith Allen; Natalie Cole; Elvis Costello; Kevin McNally; Allan Corduner; Sandra Nelson; James Wilby; Kevin McKidd; Richard Dillane; Peter Polycarpou; Edward Baker-Duly; ***D:*** Irwin Winkler; ***W:*** Jay Cocks; ***C:*** Tony Pierce-Roberts.

De Palma **2016 (R)** Baumbach and Paltrow, both acknowledged directors in their own right, deliver what is essentially a love letter to one of the most controversial filmmakers of the '70s and '80s, Brian De Palma. The filmmaker behind "Carrie," "Blow Out," and "The Untouchables," among many others, was once considered one of the most creatively elite of the Hollywood establishment. However, the last few decades haven't been as kind. In extensive interviews, he lets the viewer into his process and how his star rose and fell over the course of a career that was always distinctly his own. **107m/C; DVD, Blu-Ray.** Brian De Palma; ***D:*** Noah Baumbach; Jake Paltrow; ***C:*** Jake Paltrow.

Deacon Brodie **1998** William Deacon Brodie (Connolly) is one of Edinburgh's most respected citizens in 1788. So his trial and conviction for defrauding the city is doubly shocking—until his secret life of gambling, drinking, and wenching is exposed. **90m/C; VHS, DVD.** *GB* Billy Connolly; Patrick Malahide; Catherine McCormack; Lorcan Cranitch; ***D:*** Philip Saville; ***W:*** Simon Donald; ***C:*** Ivan Strasburg; ***M:*** Simon Boswell. **TV**

The Dead 1/2 **1987 (PG)** The poignant final film by Huston, based on James Joyce's short story from "Dubliners." At a Christmas dinner party in 1904 Dublin, Gabriel Conroy (McCann) discovers how little he knows about his wife Gretta (Angelica Huston) when a song reminds her of a cherished lost love. Beautifully captures the spirit of the story while providing Huston an opportunity to create a last lament on the fickle nature of time and life. **82m/C; VHS, DVD.** *GB* Anjelica Huston; Donal McCann; Marie Kean; Donal Donnelly; Dan O'Herlihy; Helen Carroll; Frank Patterson; ***D:*** John Huston; ***W:*** Tony (Walter Anthony) Huston; ***C:*** Fred Murphy; ***M:*** Alex North. Ind. Spirit '88: Director (Huston), Support. Actress (Huston); Natl. Soc. Film Critics '87: Film.

The Dead 2 **2013 (R)** This sequel to "The Dead" finds the zombie apocalypse reaching a new country with bigger consequences. The infectious epidemic that turns people into zombies is nearing India, and an American engineer Nicholas (Millson) there on a work contract learns that his pregnant girlfriend is stuck near Mumbai. He crosses 300 miles of zombie wasteland to reach the city, where he finds more flesh eaters, all to find and save his girlfriend and their unborn child. **98m/C; DVD, Blu-Ray, Download.** Joseph Millson; Meenu Mishra; Anand Goyal; Sandip Datta Gupta; Poonam Mathur; ***D:*** Howard Ford; Jonathan Ford; ***W:*** Howard Ford; Jonathan Ford; ***C:*** Jonathan Ford; ***M:*** Imran Ahmad. **VIDEO**

Dead Again 1/2 **1991 (R)** Branagh's first film since his brilliant debut as the director/star of "Henry V" again proves him a visionary force on and off camera. Smart, cynical L.A. detective Mike Church (Branagh) is hired to discover the identity of a beautiful but mute woman (Thompson) whom he calls Grace. With the help of hypnotist Franklyn Madson (Jacobi) Mike finds that he's apparently trapped in a nightmarish cycle of murder begun years before, involving a jealous conductor and his concert pianist wife. Literate, lovely to look at, suspenseful, with a sense of humor to match its high style. **107m/C; VHS, DVD.** Kenneth Branagh; Emma Thompson; Andy Garcia; Lois Hall; Richard Easton; Derek Jacobi; Hanna Schygulla; Campbell Scott; Wayne Knight; Christine Ebersole; ***Cameo(s):*** Robin Williams; ***D:*** Kenneth Branagh; ***W:*** Scott Frank; ***C:*** Matthew F. Leonetti; ***M:*** Patrick Doyle.

Dead Air **2008** Paranoid radio talk show host Logan Burnhardt tries to use the airwaves to get the message out that terrorists have used a bio weapon to target L.A. and turn its inhabitants into flesh-eating maniacs. (They're not really zombies 'cause they're alive-but-infected but they act like zombies, so let's call 'em zombies.) **97m/C; DVD.** David Moscow; Patricia Tallman; Dan Lauria; Larry Drake; Corbin Bernsen; Bill Moseley; Lakshmi Manchu; ***D:*** Corbin Bernsen; ***W:*** Kenny Yakkel; ***C:*** Eric Gustavo Petersen. **VIDEO**

Dead Alive *Braindead* **1993** This outrageously over-the-top horror flick from New Zealand is a gore aficionado's delight (think "Evil Dead" movies for comparison). Set in 1957 and satirizing the bland times, the "plot" has the mom of a nerdy son getting bitten by an exotic monkey, which promptly turns her into a particularly nasty ghoul. This condition is apparently contagious (except for her son who tries to hide the fact mom is literally a monster) and calls for lots of spurting blood and body parts which take on lives of their own. For those with strong stomachs and senses of humor. Also available in an 85-minute R-rated version. **97m/C; VHS, DVD.** *NZ* Timothy Balme; Elizabeth Moody; Diana Penalver; Ian Watkin; Brenda Kendall; Stuart Devenie; Peter Jackson; Forrest J Ackerman; ***D:*** Peter Jackson; ***W:*** Peter Jackson; Fran Walsh; Stephen Sinclair; ***C:*** Murray Milne; ***M:*** Peter Dasent.

Dead and Buried 1/2 **1981 (R)** Farentino is the sheriff who can't understand why the victims of some pretty grisly murders seem to be coming back to life. Eerily suspenseful. **95m/C; VHS, DVD, Blu-Ray.** James Farentino; Jack Albertson; Melody Anderson; Lisa Blount; Bill Quinn; Michael Pataki; Robert Englund; Barry Corbin; Lisa Marie; ***D:*** Gary Sherman; ***W:*** Dan O'Bannon; Ronald Shusett; ***C:*** Steven Poster; ***M:*** Joe Renzetti.

Dead Are Alive 1/2 **1972** Alcoholic archaeologist Jason (Cord) has come to Italy to search for Etruscan ruins near the home of orchestral conductor Nicos (John Marley) and his wife Myra (Samantha Eggar), Jason's ex-lover. Soon after he opens an Etruscan tomb, a series of violent murders begin. The above-average giallo shocker and is much better than director Crispino's more popular "Autopsy." **103m/C; DVD, Blu-Ray.** *IT* Alex Cord; Samantha Eggar; John Marley; Nadja Tiller; Horst Frank; Enzo Tarascio; ***D:*** Armando Crispino; ***W:*** Armando Crispino; Lucio Battistrada; ***C:*** Erico Menczer; ***M:*** Riz Ortolani.

Dead Awake 1/2 *Dead of Night; Wild Awake* **2001** A bizarre mix of film noir and black comedy, this is the story of Desmond Caine (Baldwin), a modest financial whiz and insomniac who sleeps at his job with his eyes open and spends his nights wandering or in a local blue collar diner. Eventually he witnesses a murder he's promptly blamed for and must deal with an attorney more interested in the movie rights to his story than in helping him. **100m/C; DVD.** Stephen Baldwin; Macha Grenon; Michael Ironside; Edward Yankie; Janet Kidder; Maxim Roy; Claudia Ferri; Karen Elkin; Frank Schorpion; Conrad Pla; Lorne Brass; Rachelle Lefevre; Gillian Ferrabee; Michelle Lipper; Donovan Reiter; Kevin Ryder; Holly O'Brien; ***D:*** Marc S. Grenier; ***W:*** Terry Abrahamson; ***C:*** David Franco; ***M:*** E.P. Bergen.

Dead Bang 1/2 **1989 (R)** A frustrated cop uncovers a murderous white supremacist conspiracy in L.A. Frankenheimer's deft directorial hand shapes a somewhat conventional cop plot into an effective vehicle for Johnson. **102m/C; VHS, DVD; Open Captioned.** Don Johnson; Bob Balaban; William Forsythe; Penelope Ann Miller; Tim Reid; Frank Military; Michael Higgins; Michael Jeter; Evans Evans; Tate Donovan; ***D:*** John Frankenheimer; ***W:*** Robert Foster; ***C:*** Gerry Fisher; ***M:*** Gary Chang; Michael Kamen.

Dead Beat 1/2 **1994 (R)** Teen love and lust—and murder—all set in Albuquerque, New Mexico, circa 1965. Womanizer Kit (Ramsey) will use any tale to score with his dates—and is happy to pass on tips to adoring disciple Rudy (Getty). When Kit meets up with rebellious rich girl Kirsten (Wagner), she demands proof of his love and he confides he once murdered a girl. Kirsten tries to tighten her stranglehold on Kit with this info and force Rudy from his life but Kit's dark side doesn't stay hidden either. **94m/C; VHS, Streaming.** Bruce Ramsay; Natasha Gregson Wagner; Balthazar Getty; Meredith Salenger; Sara Gilbert; Deborah Harry; Max Perlich; Alex Cox; ***D:*** Adam Dubov; ***W:*** Adam Dubov.

Dead Birds **2004 (R)** In 1863 Alabama, a group of Confederate soldiers, led by William (Thomas), rob a bank of its gold bullion—leaving a lot of dead bodies behind—and plan to head to Mexico. But first, they spend the night in an abandoned plantation house that apparently isn't so abandoned. They hear noises, see strange creatures, and start to get very spooked indeed. **91m/C; DVD.** Henry Thomas; Patrick Fugit; Nicki Aycox; Michael Shannon; Muse Watson; Mark Boone, Jr.; Isaiah Washington, IV; ***D:*** Alex Turner; ***W:*** Simon Barrett; ***C:*** Steve Yedlin; ***M:*** Peter Lopez.

Dead Bodies 1/2 **2003** Premise strains credulity. After an argument, slacker Tommy (Scott) discovers that whiny ex-girlfriend Jean (Davis) has accidentally died. So Tommy decides to bury the body in the woods, only to find the one patch of dirt that already contains a dead body—a woman missing for 8 years. So the police find 2 dead bodies and Tommy is in deep muck. **84m/C; DVD.** *IR* Andrew Scott; Kelly Reilly; Sean McGinley; Gerard McSorley; Darren Healy; Katy Davis; ***D:*** Robert Quinn; ***W:*** Derek Landy; ***C:*** Donal Gilligan; ***M:*** Ray Harman.

Dead Broke **1999 (R)** Lying witnesses make it hard for detective Sam (Glover) to solve a murder that happens outside a Brooklyn debt collection agency, whose employees are all suspicious characters. Hits all the film noir cliches but you're never quite sure if this is intended as a spoof or not. **98m/C; DVD.** John Glover; Paul Sorvino; Jill(ian) Hennessey; Tony Roberts; Justin Theroux; Patricia Scanlon; Nela Wagman; Cheryl Rogers; ***D:*** Edward Vilga; ***W:*** Edward Vilga; ***C:*** Joaquin Baca-Asay; ***M:*** Edward Bilous.

Dead by Dawn **1998** Regular-guy Tim and his wife get drawn into the glitzy life of Tim's high-school friend Don, only to find themselves embroiled in blackmail, insurance fraud, and murder. Exploitation disguised as a cautionary tale about temptation, with noir-ish aspirations. **91m/C; VHS, DVD.** Shannon Tweed; Ted Prior; Jodie Fisher; Bill Ferrell; ***D:*** James Salisbury; ***W:*** Stephen J. Downing; ***C:*** Pierre Chemaly; ***M:*** David Grant. **VIDEO**

Dead by Sunset ✗✗ **1995** NBC miniseries based on a novel by Ann Rule. Dr. Sara Gordon (Frost) thinks Brad Cunningham (Olin) is charming even in the midst of an ugly divorce. She stands by him after his wife is murdered and he's the prime suspect, but only discovers he's a lying psycho after she marries him herself. But when Brad's finally put on trial for murder will Sara find the courage to testify against him? **180m/C; DVD.** Lindsay Frost; Ken Olin; Annette O'Toole; John Terry; ***D:*** Karen Arthur; ***W:*** Wesley Bishop; ***C:*** Thomas Neuwirth; ***M:*** David Michael Frank. **TV**

A Dead Calling ✗ ½ **2006 (R)** Familiar horror storyline has a few frights. Reporter Rachel (Holden) has returned home after a personal tragedy and joined the local TV station. She's given a fluff assignment to investigate the town's historic homes but runs into trouble with the Sullivan place. That's where Frank Sullivan (Oman) butchered his family and escaped custody. And when Rachel enters the house, the ghosts of the slain family plead for her help to find their eternal rest. Except Frank has other ideas. **90m/C; DVD.** Alexandra Holden; Bill Moseley; Sid Haig; Leslie Easterbrook; Timothy Oman; John Burke; Caia Coley; ***D:*** Michael Feifer; ***W:*** Michael Feifer; ***C:*** Hank Beaumert, Jr.; ***M:*** Glenn Morrisette. **VIDEO**

Dead Calm ✗✗✗ **1989 (R)** A taut Australian thriller based on a novel by Charles Williams. A young married couple is yachting on the open seas when they happen upon the lone survivor of a sinking ship. They take him on board only to discover he's a homicidal maniac. Makes for some pretty suspenseful moments that somewhat make up for the weak ending. **97m/C; VHS, DVD.** *AU* Sam Neill; Billy Zane; Nicole Kidman; Rod Mullinar; ***D:*** Phillip Noyce; ***W:*** Terry Hayes; ***C:*** Dean Semler; ***M:*** Graeme Revell.

Dead Cert ✗ ½ **2010** British gangster flick with a twist that still doesn't make it very exciting. Former gangster Freddy is making a more-or-less honest living with his London nightclub and some underground fights. He bets the club on what he thinks is a sure thing but loses it to mysterious Romanian Livenko. Turns out Livenko and his minions cheated because they are vampires, which doesn't stop Freddy for very long. **92m/C; DVD, Blu-Ray.** *GB* Craig Fairbrass; Billy Murray; Steven Berkoff; Dexter Fletcher; Jason Flemyng; Andrew Tiernan; Lisa McAllister; Danny Dyer; ***D:*** Steven Lawson; ***W:*** Ben Shillito; ***C:*** James Friend; ***M:*** Tim Atack.

Dead Certain ✗ **1992 (R)** A "Silence of the Lambs" rip-off. Dourif (again specializing in weirdos) is the jailed serial killer providing tantalizing clues to the identity of a new killer on the loose. **93m/C; VHS, DVD.** Brad Dourif; Francesco Quinn; Karen Russell; Joel Kaiser; ***D:*** Anders Palm; ***W:*** Anders Palm.

Dead Collections ✗ ½ **2012** When Sara (Caitlyn Fletcher) loses everything and moves in with her uncle she quickly begins to believe his house is haunted. Unfortunately, the effects are limited by a small budget. **110m/C; Blu-Ray.** Caitlyn Fletcher; Roberto Lombardi; Edward Young; Jerry Ross; Suzi Lorraine; ***D:*** John Orrichio; ***W:*** John Orrichio; Romberto Lombardi; ***C:*** John Orrichio; Ira Goldberg; ***M:*** John Orrichio; Romberto Lombardi; Anthony Belluscio. **VIDEO**

Dead Cool ✗✗ **2004 (R)** Self-absorbed 15-year-old David (Geller) has yet to come to terms with his father Josh's (Callis) death and frequently talks to his ghost. He and his younger brother (Johnson) are upset when their mother Henny (Stubbs) decides to move them in with her divorced boyfriend Mark (Calf). To complicate the situation further, Mark's ex-wife Deirdre (Arquette), a self-help author, lives around the corner with the couple's two daughters. Since Deirdre has just written a book about stepfamilies, she decides they should all practice what she's preached. **103m/C; DVD.** *GB* Stephen Geller; Imogen Stubbs; Anthony Calf; Rosanna Arquette; James Callis; Aaron Taylor-Johnson; Liz Smith; Gemma Lawrence; Olivia Wedderburn; ***D:*** David Cohen; ***W:*** David Cohen; ***C:*** Jean-Paul Seresin; ***M:*** Andy Richards; Mike Higham.

Dead Creatures ✗ **2001** A close-knit group of British twentysomething women travels around the dingy areas outside of London satiating their need for human flesh with saran-wrapped body parts they carry in their luggage. The girls are all suffering from a kind of zombie-disease that is inflicted by a bite and eventually results in the victim's literal decomposition. The dreary tone of the film echoes that of lower-class British TV dramas: heavy grainy images, squalid locations with minimal lighting and makeup. Parkinson directs this low-key horror drama without the usual female nudity prevalent in today's micro-budgeted horror films, but the lack of a thriller element or traditional genre structure works against it. Without anywhere to go with the story, this one peters out around the halfway mark. The gore effects, though used minimally, are repugnant and truly nauseating. **89m/C; DVD.** Beverly Wilson; Antonia Beamish; Brendan Gregory; ***D:*** Andrew Parkinson; ***W:*** Andrew Parkinson; ***C:*** Jack Shepherd; ***M:*** Andrew Parkinson.

Dead Dog ✗✗ **2000** Tom and Perri's dog gets mowed down by a hit-and-run driver on the streets of NYC. Tormented, Tom's life unravels causing Perri to worry about the possible fallout from his urge for vengeance. **90m/C; VHS, DVD.** Jeremy Sisto; Paige Turco; Emily Cline; Julianne Nicholson; Lisa Bowman; Christopher Cousins; Jay O. Sanders; Adrienne Shelly; David Thornton; ***D:*** Christopher Goode; ***W:*** Grant Morris; ***C:*** Eric Schmidt; ***M:*** John M. Davis. **VIDEO**

The Dead Don't Die ✗✗ ½ **2019 (R)** In Centerville, New York, the local police chief Cliff Robertson (Murray), officer Ronnie Petersen (Driver), and officer Mindy Morrison (Sevigny) must deal with profound changes as the Earth has spun off its axis. These changes include longer days, messed up electronic systems, and the dead awakening and becoming zombies. The locals struggle with these events in their own way—funeral home undertaker Zelda (Swinton) uses her skills with a sword to great effect—as they prepare for their dark future. Featuring Jarmusch's distinctive style and sense of humor imposed on a zombie movie, the film also includes strong performances by the leads. **104m/C; DVD, Blu-Ray.** Bill Murray; Adam Driver; Tom Waits; Chloë Sevigny; Steve Buscemi; ***D:*** Jim Jarmusch; ***W:*** Jim Jarmusch; ***C:*** Frederick Elmes.

Dead Drop ✗ **2013 (R)** Generic, slow-moving crime-actioner has former CIA operative Michael left for dead by his supposed friend Santiago, who's part of a Mexican drug cartel. Naturally, dude wants revenge. **89m/C; DVD.** Luke Goss; Nestor Carbonell; Cole Hauser; ***D:*** R. Ellis Frazier; ***W:*** Benjamin Budd; ***C:*** Anthony J. Rickert-Epstein; ***M:*** Larry Groupe. **VIDEO**

Dead End ✗✗✗ ½ *Cradle of Crime* **1937** Sidney Kingsley play, adapted for the big screen by Lillian Hellman, traces the lives of various inhabitants of the slums on New York's Lower East Side as they try to overcome their surroundings. Gritty drama saved from melodrama status by some genuinely funny moments. Film launched the Dead End Kids. **92m/B; VHS, DVD.** Sylvia Sidney; Joel McCrea; Humphrey Bogart; Wendy Barrie; Claire Trevor; Allen Jenkins; Marjorie Main; Billy Halop; Huntz Hall; Bobby Jordan; Gabriel Dell; Leo Gorcey; Charles Halton; Bernard Punsley; Minor Watson; James Burke; ***D:*** William Wyler; ***W:*** Lillian Hellman; ***C:*** Gregg Toland; ***M:*** Alfred Newman.

Dead End ✗✗ ½ **1998 (R)** Police sargeant Henry Smolenski (Roberts) gains custody of his troubled 16-year-old son Adam (Tierney) after his ex-wife's death. Then he learns that the death is being investigated as a murder and Adam is the primary suspect. When Adam takes off, Henry searches for him and winds up becoming a suspect himself. Soon the estranged father and son are teaming up to discover who's out to frame them. Roberts gets to play a likable, caring character for a change of pace. **93m/C; VHS, DVD.** *CA* Eric Roberts; Jacob Tierney; Jayne Heitmeyer; Eliza Roberts; Jack Langedijk; Frank Schorpion; ***D:*** Douglas Jackson; ***W:*** Karl Schiffman; ***C:*** Georges Archambault; ***M:*** Milan Kymlicka. **VIDEO**

Dead End Drive-In ✗✗ **1986 (R)** In a surreal, grim future a man is trapped at a drive-in theatre-cum-government-run concentration camp, where those considered to be less than desirable members of society are incarcerated. **92m/C; VHS, DVD, Blu-Ray.** *AU* Ned Manning; Natalie McCurry; Peter Whitford; ***D:*** Brian Trenchard-Smith.

Dead End Kids: Little Tough Guy ✗✗ *Little Tough Guy* **1938** Johnny Boylan (Halop) is drawn into a life of crime by his gang of friends to support his family after his father is imprisoned for a murder. It's an oddly dark entry in the Dead End Kids series, considering later entries were slapstick comedies. Although it was the Great Depression so a little bit of downcast emotions are to be expected. **84m/B; DVD.** Robert Wilcox; Helen Parrish; Marjorie Main; Jackie Searl; Peggy Stewart; Helen MacKellar; Olin Howland; Edward Pawley; Pat C. Flixx; Billy Halop; Huntz Hall; Gabriel Dell, Jr.; Bernard Punsley; Hal E. Chester; David Gorcey; ***D:*** Harold Young; ***W:*** Gilson Brown; Brenda Weisberg; ***C:*** Elwood "Woody" Bredell; ***M:*** Charles Henderson; Frank Skinner; Hans J. Salter.

Dead End Street ✗ ½ *Kvish L'Lo Motzah* **1983** Young prostitute attempts to change her self-destructive lifestyle. It's not easy. **86m/C; VHS, DVD.** *IS* Anat Atzmon; Yehoram Gaon; ***D:*** Yaky Yosha; ***W:*** Yaky Yosha; Eli Tavor.

Dead Evidence ✗✗ *Lawless: Dead Evidence* **2000 (R)** Young P.I. Jodie Keane (Dotchin) teams up with ex-cop John Lawless (Smith) to track a serial killer by offering herself as the next potential victim. **94m/C; VHS, DVD.** *NZ* Kevin Smith; Angela Dotchin; C. Thomas Howell; Bruce Hopkins; Geoff Dolan; Andrew Binns; ***D:*** Charlie Haskell; ***W:*** Gavin Strawhan; ***C:*** Mark Olsen; ***M:*** Peter Blake. **TV**

Dead Eyes of London ✗✗ ½ *Dark Eyes of London; Die Toten Augen von London* **1961** Blind old German men are dying to lower their premiums in this geriatric thriller: someone (perhaps the director of the home for the blind?) is killing off the clientele for their insurance money, and a Scotland Yard inspector aims to expose the scam. Relatively early vintage Kinski, it's a remake of the eerie 1939 Lugosi vehicle, "The Human Monster" (originally titled "Dark Eyes of London"), adapted from Edgar Wallace's "The Testament of Gordon Stuart." **95m/B; VHS, DVD, Blu-Ray.** *GE* Joachim Fuchsberger; Karin Baal; Dieter Borsche; Ady Berber; Klaus Kinski; Eddi Arent; Wolfgang Lukschy; ***D:*** Alfred Vohrer.

Dead Fire ✗✗ **1998** A space substation has been in orbit around earth for the past 50 years trying to regenerate the planet's poisoned atmosphere. But now a shipboard traitor is trying to destroy the operation. **105m/C; VHS, DVD.** Matt Frewer; C. Thomas Howell; Monica Schnarre; ***D:*** Robert Lee; ***M:*** Peter Allen. **VIDEO**

Dead Fish ✗ **2004 (R)** Despite the cast, it stinks like week-old dead fish too. Contract killer Lynch (Oldman) runs into trouble when he helps out Abe (Potts) and his pregnant girlfriend Mimi (Anaya) with a would-be thief. His and Abe's cell phones accidentally get switched and Lynch falls inexplicably and instantly in love with Mimi despite the fact that he's on the way to his next hit. **94m/C; DVD.** *GB* Gary Oldman; Elena Anaya; Robert Carlyle; Karel Roden; Terence Stamp; Andrew Lee Potts; Billy Zane; Jimi Mistry; ***D:*** Charley Stadler; ***W:*** David Mitchell; Adam Kreutner; ***C:*** Fraser Taggart; ***M:*** Andrew Cato.

Dead for a Dollar ✗ ½ *T'ammazzo! Raccomandati a Dio* **1970** A Colonel, a con man, and a mysterious woman team up in the Old West to search for the $200,000 they stole from a local bank. **92m/C; VHS, DVD.** John Ireland; George Hilton; Piero Vida; Sandra Milo; ***D:*** Osvaldo Civirani.

The Dead Girl ✗✗ **2006 (R)** Moncrieff's troubling drama showcases one victim of a serial killer from five female perspectives. The title character is runaway druggie hooker Krista (Murphy), whose body is found by downtrodden Arden (Collette). Forensic student Leah (Byrne) first thinks the body is that of her missing sister, while enabling wife Ruth (Hurt) suspects her husband (Searcy) is the killer. Then Melora (Harden) rounds out the story when Krista is identified and the grieving mom is forced to confront how her daughter was living. **93m/C; DVD.** Toni Collette; Rose Byrne; Mary Beth Hurt; Marcia Gay Harden; Brittany Murphy; Kerry Washington; Giovanni Ribisi; Nick Searcy; Piper Laurie; Josh Brolin; James Franco; Mary Steenburgen; Bruce Davison; ***D:*** Karen Moncrieff; ***W:*** Karen Moncrieff; ***C:*** Michael Grady; ***M:*** Adam Gorgoni.

Dead Gorgeous ✗✗ ½ **2002** Antonia Ashton (McCrory) is a brazen hussy and a consummate schemer. She's married to boring business tycoon Hector (Cook) while carrying on with hunky professor Vic (Owen). She wants out of her marriage—by murder if necessary. Mousy Rose Bell (Ripley) wishes she could get rid of her drunken, philandering spouse as well. Antonia and Rose—old friends from the war—meet again in a gray 1946 London. Antonia has a plan—she'll see that Rose's husband has an "accident" and Rose will do the same with Hector. Antonia carries through but a grateful Rose is more cautious. Some unexpected twists in this variation of "Strangers on a Train." From the 1989 novel, "On the Edge," by Peter Lovesey. **100m/C; VHS, DVD.** *GB* Fay Ripley; Helen McCrory; Ron Cook; Lloyd Owen; Jonathan Phillips; Dermot Crowley; Michael Mueller; ***D:*** Sarah Harding; ***W:*** Andrew Payne; ***C:*** Simon Kossoff; ***M:*** Jennie Muskett. **TV**

The Dead Hate the Living ✗✗ **1999 (R)** Young filmmakers sneak into an abandoned medical research facility to make a low-budget horror feature about a scientist who raises the dead to be his zombie slaves. Little do they know that the facility was abandoned after a scientist's experiments to revive the dead through alchemical means went horribly wrong. When they discover the scientist's body, they decide to go use what they've found to add to the film's production value and accidentally manage to open a rift into the dimension of the dead. The script is a patchwork of influences. Effects are impressive, with many spectacular (and gruesome) zombies. **90m/C; DVD.** Eric Clawson; Jamie Donahue; Brett Beardslee; Wendy Speake; ***D:*** Dave Parker; ***W:*** Dave Parker; ***C:*** Tom Calloway; ***M:*** Jared DePasquale.

Dead Heart ✗✗✗ **1996** Culture clash story set in the 1930s is highlighted by a terrific lead performance by Brown. He's cop Ray Lorkin, whose territory is the tiny community of Wala Wala in Australia's outback. This remote spot just happens to be a focal point for the local aboriginals, who regard the area as a spiritual place. Trouble erupts when an aboriginal prisoner (Pederson), who just happened to be having an affair with the schoolteacher's white wife (Mikkiken) is found hanged in his cell. Tradition demands revenge—from there every other situation in the community just gets worse. First-timer Parsons directs from his stage play. **106m/C; VHS, DVD.** *AU* Bryan Brown; Ernie Dingo; Angie Milliken; Aasron Pedersen; Lewis Fitz-Gerald; John Jarratt; Anne Tenney; Gnarnayarrahe Waitaire; Lafe Charlton; ***D:*** Nick Parsons; ***W:*** Nick Parsons; ***C:*** James Bartle; ***M:*** Stephen Rae.

Dead Heat ✗ ½ **1988 (R)** Some acting talent and a few funny moments unfortunately don't add up to a fine film, though they do save it from being a complete woofer. In this one even the cops are zombies when one of them is resurrected from the dead to help his partner solve his murder and rid the city of the rest of the undead. **86m/C; VHS, DVD, Blu-Ray.** Joe Piscopo; Treat Williams; Lindsay Frost; Darren McGavin; Vincent Price; Keye Luke; Clare Kirkconnell; ***D:*** Mark Goldblatt; ***W:*** Terry Black; ***C:*** Robert Yeoman; ***M:*** Ernest Troost.

Dead Heat ✗✗ ½ *I Fought the Law* **2001 (R)** Pally Lamarr (Sutherland) is a suicidal ex-cop with a drinking problem. His shady stepbrother Ray (LaPaglia) persuades Pally to purchase a long-shot racehorse with a jockey (Bluteau) who's an ex-con gambling addict. Things get even worse when a mobster (Benzali), who also wanted the horse, gets involved. Plot has too many holes but the two leads are worth watching. **97m/C;**

VHS, DVD. *CA* Kiefer Sutherland; Anthony LaPaglia; Radha Mitchell; Lothaire Bluteau; Daniel Benzali; *D:* Mark Malone; *W:* Mark Malone; *M:* Patric Caird.

Dead Heat on a Merry-Go-Round **1966 (R)** Coburn turns in a great performance as the ex-con who masterminds the heist of an airport safe. Intricately woven plot provides suspense and surprises. The film is also notable for the debut of Ford in a bit part (he has one line as a hotel messenger). **108m/C; VHS, DVD.** James Coburn; Camilla Sparv; Aldo Ray; Nina Wayne; Robert Webber; Rose Marie; Todd Armstrong; Marian Moses; Severn Darden; Harrison Ford; Vic Tayback; *D:* Bernard Girard; *W:* Bernard Girard; *C:* Lionel Lindon; *M:* Stu Phillips.

Dead Heist **1/2 2007** Four friends pick the wrong night for a bank heist and end up trapped by vampire zombie townsfolk. Were it not for Hunter (Kane), a mysteriously shady bloke familiar with creature extermination, they might never get away with their loot or their lives. A giddy attempt, seriously lacking in horror. **80m/C; DVD.** Big Daddy Kane; D.J. Naylor; E-40; Bone Crusher; *D:* Bo Webb; *W:* Anghus Houvouras; Eric Tomosunas; *C:* Matt Malloy; Patrick Borowiak; *M:* Jim McKeever. **VIDEO**

Dead in a Heartbeat **2002** Veteran bomb squad cop Royko (Reinhold) teams up with heart surgeon Dr. Hayes (Miller) to find the mad bomber who's blowing people up via their pacemakers. Mediocre TV movie features a cliched plot that telegraphs all the twists. The leads do what they can with what they're given. **91m/C; VHS, DVD.** *CA* Judge Reinhold; Penelope Ann Miller; Fulvio Cecere; Timothy Busfield; Matthew (Matt) Walker; Jeff(rey) Ballard; Sarah Jane Redmond; *D:* Paul Antier; *W:* Mark Rosman; Richard Ades; *C:* Danny Nowak; *M:* Louis Febre. **TV**

Dead in the Water **1/2 1991 (PG-13)** Brown is Charlie Deegan, a big-time lawyer with a rich wife that he'd rather see dead. Charlie and his mistress plot the perfect murder to dispose of his spouse and collect her money. When plans go awry, he ends up as a suspect for the wrong murder in this story of infidelity and greed. **90m/C; VHS, DVD.** Bryan Brown; Teri Hatcher; Anne DeSalvo; Veronica Cartwright; *D:* Bill Condon; *W:* Eleanor Gaver; Robert Seidenberg; Walter Klenhard.

Dead in the Water **2001 (R)** Wealthy hot babe Gloria (Swain) takes her boyfriend (Bairstow), their buddy (Thomas), and Marcos, the son of her father's business partner on the family cabin cruiser for a day of fun. Only tensions rise and violence erupts when Gloria gets too involved with the wrong guy. **89m/C; VHS, DVD.** Dominique Swain; Henry Thomas; Scott Bairstow; Renata Fronzi; Sebastian DeVincente; *D:* Gustavo Lipzstein. **VIDEO**

Dead in the Water **2006 (R)** Arriving for a weekend retreat at the family cabin, Tiffany, Jen and their boyfriends find the cabin void of parents, cell phone reception, or a running vehicle. As night falls, zombies begin their attack. Instead of running like deer through the woods, the foursome decides to seek refuge in a boat out on the lake. Bad move, fairly decent movie. **78m/C; DVD.** Alissa Bailey; Megan Renne Burgess; Mike Parrish; Bill Zasadil; *D:* Marc Buhmann; *W:* David Moore; *C:* Fred Miller; *M:* Piernicola Di Muro. **VIDEO**

Dead Leaves **1/2 1998** After a young girl falls to her death her unstable boyfriend steals the body and embarks on a trip from New York to West Virginia, stopping along the way to perform strange rituals to preserve her beauty. As she increasingly decays physically so does he emotionally and mentally. Art-house flick has hypnotic music, long frames of rainy highways, deserted hotels, gloomy urban landscapes topped with narratives of dark poetry to portray the mood and feeling of a mad love. Not much in the way of dialogue, as the conversations tend to be a little one-sided. **80m/C; DVD, UMD, On Demand.** Haim Abramsky; Beth Gondek; *D:* Constantin Werner; *W:* Constantin Werner; *C:* Mindaugas Blaudziunas. **VIDEO**

Dead Lenny **1/2 2006** Low-level LA mobster Lenny Long (Bauer) goes missing, along with the five million bucks he was supposed to deliver to NY wiseguy Tony Thick (Assante). Thick sends associate Shady (Baker) to straighten things out, only he finds a lot of crazy people who want a cut of any cash that turns up. Unsatisfying mob comedy. **89m/C; DVD.** Armand Assante; Nicole Eggert; Stephen Baker; Steven Bauer; John Heard; Joe Piscopo; Whitney Able; *D:* Serge Rodnunsky; *W:* Serge Rodnunsky; *C:* Serge Rodnunsky; *M:* Greg Manning. **VIDEO**

Dead Letter Office **1/2 1998** Lonely Alice (Otto) gets a job at the dead letter office of the postal system. Her boss is Frank (DelHoyo), a political refugee from Chile, who lost his family to the junta. Frank and Alice seem destined to hit it off but not before a few obstacles get in their path. Otto's father Barry has a brief scene as Alice's irresponsible dad. More distinctive than the story might indicate, thanks to the performances and tart comedy. **95m/C; VHS, DVD.** *AU* Miranda Otto; George DelHoyo; Nicholas Bell; Syd Brisbane; Georgina Naidu; Vanessa Steele; Barry Otto; *D:* John Ruane; *W:* Deb Cox; *C:* Ellery Ryan; *M:* Roger Mason.

Dead Man **1995 (R)** Depp wanders throughs the 19th-century American west as William Blake, an Ohio accountant who runs afoul of the law. Hooking up with a Native American named Nobody (Farmer), who envisions Blake as the famous English poet, the two try to stay one step ahead of the hired guns and lawmen out to get them. Action is sporadic and pace is all over the road in this offbeat and long-winded western, while Farmer's performance and Jarmusch's polished visuals are high points. **121m/B; VHS, DVD, Blu-Ray.** Johnny Depp; Gary Farmer; Lance Henriksen; Michael Wincott; Mili Avital; Crispin Glover; Gabriel Byrne; Iggy Pop; Billy Bob Thornton; Jared Harris; Jimmie Ray Weeks; Mark Bringleson; John Hurt; Alfred Molina; Robert Mitchum; *D:* Jim Jarmusch; *W:* Jim Jarmusch; *C:* Robby Muller; *M:* Neil Young. N.Y. Film Critics '96: Cinematog.; Natl. Soc. Film Critics '96: Cinematog.

Dead Man Down **1/2 2013 (R)** A pair of beautiful people seeks revenge in this generic thriller weighed down with stupid dialogue and character decisions that defy disbelief. Victor (Farrell) wants Alphonse (Howard) to pay for the deaths of his wife and child while Beatrice blackmails Victor into helping her get revenge against a drunk driver who disfigured her. What should have been a twisted modern noir becomes little more than a cut-rate thriller as Oplev's direction isn't stylish enough and the script annoys more than it entertains. Farrell, Howard, and Rapace do their best to elevate the B-movie material but can't lift it up. **118m/C; DVD, Blu-Ray.** Colin Farrell; Noomi Rapace; Terrence Howard; Isabelle Huppert; Dominic Cooper; Armand Assante; F. Murray Abraham; *D:* Niels Arden Oplev; *W:* J.H. (Joel Howard) Wyman; *C:* Paul Cameron; *M:* Jacob Groth.

Dead Man on Campus **1997 (R)** Failing college freshmen Scott and Gosselaar learn that if your roomie commits suicide, you get a straight-A average for the year. So they decide to find a new roommate who's on the edge and make certain to push him over. Anyone who's ever done time in the dorms has heard this rumor, so it was only a matter of time before someone turned it into a screenplay. The wait wasn't long enough. One-joke premise can't sustain a whole movie, and Gosselaar goes a long way toward duplicating "Saved By the Bell" co-star Elizabeth Berkley's "Showgirls" um, success. **94m/C; VHS, DVD.** Tom Everett Scott; Mark-Paul Gosselaar; Alyson Hannigan; Poppy Montgomery; Lochlyn Munro; Randy Pearlstein; Mari Morrow; Jason Segel; Linda Cardellini; John Aprea; *D:* Alan Cohn; *W:* Michael Traeger; Mike White; *C:* John Thomas; *M:* Mark Mothersbaugh.

Dead Man Running **1/2 2009 (R)** Fast pace can't quite hide the recycled Brit crime cliches. Ex-con Nick is trying to go straight and set up a travel biz with his mate Bing. But he owes vicious loan shark Mr. Thigo 100 grand and is given only 24 hours to pay. **92m/C; DVD.** *GB* Tamer Hassan; Danny Dyer; 50 Cent; Brenda Blethyn; Monet Mazur; Philip Davis; Blake Ritson; *D:* Alex de Rakoff; *W:* Alex de Rakoff; *C:* Ali Asad; *M:* Mark Sayfritz.

Dead Man Walking **1/2 1995 (R)** True story of a nun whose anti-death penalty beliefs put her in moral crisis with grieving victims when she becomes the spiritual advisor to a death-row murderer. Based on the book by Sister Helen Prejean, Sarandon stars as the nun who develops a relationship of understanding with inmate Poncelet (Penn), unwavering in her Christian beliefs even though Penn's character shows little or no remorse for the two young lovers he was accused of murdering. Penn offers one of the best performances (but worst hair-dos) of his career, while writer/director Robbins presents both sides of the death-penalty issue mingled with simple human compassion. **122m/C; VHS, DVD, Blu-Ray.** Susan Sarandon; Sean Penn; Robert Prosky; Raymond J. Barry; R. Lee Ermey; Celia Weston; Lois Smith; Scott Wilson; Roberta Maxwell; Margo Martindale; Barton Heyman; Larry Pine; Jon Abrahams; Jack Black; *D:* Tim Robbins; *W:* Tim Robbins; *C:* Roger Deakins; *M:* David Robbins. Oscars '95: Actress (Sarandon); Ind. Spirit '96: Actor (Penn); Screen Actors Guild '95: Actress (Sarandon).

Dead Man's Bounty **1/2** *Summer Love* **2006 (R)** A Polish-made art house spaghetti western that's big on visuals but not much else. A nameless stranger rides into town with a dead outlaw. After collecting the bounty, he loses all the money in a card game with the sheriff and then considers reclaiming the body. Kilmer plays the dead guy. **94m/C; DVD.** *PL* Boguslaw Linda; Karel Roden; Kasia (Katarzyna) Figura; Val Kilmer; *D:* Piotr Uklanski; *W:* Piotr Uklanski; *C:* Jacek Petrycki.

Dead Man's Burden **2012** Impressive debut feature from Moshe is an intense family western set on an isolated New Mexico homestead after the Civil War. Martha Kirkland and her husband Heck bury her father and now she's prepared to sell off the marginal land to a copper mining company and move. Then Martha's estranged brother Wade, whom she thought killed in the war, suddenly returns and is easily swayed by a neighbor's suspicion that their father's death wasn't accidental. He doesn't want to sell and Wade's interference causes rising family tensions. **93m/C; DVD.** Barlow Jacobs; Clare Bowen; David Call; Joseph Lyle Taylor; Richard Riehle; *D:* Jared Moshe; *W:* Jared Moshe; *C:* Robert Hauer; *M:* H. Scott Salinas.

Dead Man's Eyes **1/2 1944** Artist Chaney is accidentally blinded but may get a second chance through an eye operation. His father-in-law offers his own eyes after he dies—and then he's murdered. Based on radio's "The Inner Sanctum Mysteries." **130m/B; VHS, DVD.** Lon Chaney, Jr.; Brenda Joyce; George Cleveland; Clara Blandick; Paul Kelly; Jean Parker; George Meeker; Acquanetta; J. Edward Bromberg; Rosalind Ivan; Wilton Graff; Bernard B. Thomas; *D:* Wallace Fox; Reginald LeBorg; *W:* George Bricker; Dwight V. Babcock.

Dead Man's Revenge **1/2 1993 (PG-13)** Ruthless railroad mogul Payton McCay (Dern) doesn't let anyone stand in his way—even if it means framing innocent homesteader Hatcher (Ironside) in order to get his land. Hatcher escapes from jail and goes after McCay, trailed by bounty hunter Bodeen (Couloris). But Bodeen's not what he seems and has his own plans on getting even with the villainous McCay. **92m/C; VHS, DVD.** Bruce Dern; Michael Ironside; Keith Coulouris; Randy Travis; *D:* Alan J. Levi; *W:* Jim Byrnes; David Chisholm.

Dead Man's Shoes **2004** Grungy revenge thriller has disturbed ex-soldier Richard (Considine) returning to his hometown in England's Midlands to get payback on the yabbos who tormented his mentally retarded younger brother Anthony (Kebbell). Things get quite bloody. **86m/C; DVD.** *GB* Paddy Considine; Gary Stretch; Toby Kebbell; *D:* Shane Meadows; *W:* Shane Meadows; *C:* Danny Cohen.

Dead Mate **1988** A woman marries a mortician after a whirlwind romance only to discover that, to her husband, being an undertaker is not just a job, it's a way of life. **93m/C; VHS, DVD.** Elizabeth Mannino; David Gregory; Lawrence Bockus; Adam Wahl; *D:* Straw Weisman.

Dead Men Can't Dance **1997 (R)** CIA agent Victoria Ellis (York) gets sent to South Korea to train with a women-only group of Army Rangers. Meanwhile, Vic's boyfriend Hart (Biehn) and his buddy Shooter (Paul) are in the demilitertized zone where Hart learns Shooter is out to steal nuclear detonators on behalf of crazy Senator Fowler (Ermey), who wants to revive the Cold War. Things go bad and the women are forced to take things into their own more than capable hands. Lots of action. **97m/C; VHS, Streaming.** Kathleen York; Michael Biehn; Adrian Paul; R. Lee Ermey; Grace Zabriskie; *D:* Steve (Stephen M.) Anderson; *W:* Mark Sevi; Bill Kerby; Paul Sinor; *C:* Levie Isaacks; *M:* Richard (Rick) Marvin.

Dead Men Don't Die **1/2 1991 (PG-13)** An anchorman is slain by criminals but resurrected as a shambling voodoo zombie. Few viewers notice the difference in this inoffensive but repetitious farce. The living-dead Gould appears to be having a lot of fun. **94m/C; VHS, DVD.** Elliott Gould; Melissa Anderson; Mark Moses; Philip Bruns; Jack Betts; Mabel King; *D:* Malcolm Marmorstein; *W:* Malcolm Marmorstein.

Dead Men Don't Wear Plaid **1/2 1982 (PG)** Martin is hilarious as a private detective who encounters a bizarre assortment of suspects while trying to find out the truth about a scientist's death. Ingeniously interspliced with clips from old Warner Bros. films. Features Humphrey Bogart, Bette Davis, Alan Ladd, Burt Lancaster, Ava Gardner, Barbara Stanwyck, Ray Milland, and others. Its only flaw is that the joke loses momentum by the end of the film. **89m/B; VHS, DVD, Blu-Ray.** Steve Martin; Rachel Ward; Reni Santoni; George Gaynes; Francis X. (Frank) McCarthy; Carl Reiner; *D:* Carl Reiner; *W:* Steve Martin; Carl Reiner; *C:* Michael Chapman; *M:* Miklos Rozsa.

Dead Men Walk *Creatures of the Devil* **1943** A decent, albeit low budget, chiller about twin brothers (Zucco in a dual role); one a nice, well-adjusted member of society, the other a vampire who wants to suck his bro's blood. Sibling rivalry with a bite. **65m/B; VHS, DVD.** George Zucco; Mary Carlisle; Dwight Frye; Nedrick Young; Al "Fuzzy" St. John; Fern Emmett; Robert Strange; *D:* Sam Newfield; *W:* Fred Myton; *C:* Jack Greenhalgh; *M:* Leo Erdody.

Dead Mine **2012** Treasure hunters look for gold in an old WWII bunker in Indonesia. Standing in their way are cliche Japanese soldiers who don't accept the war is over, and who happen to be zombies. **91m/C; DVD, Blu-Ray.** *ID* Miki Mizuno; Sam Hazeldine; Ario Bayu; Les Loveday; Carmen Soo; *D:* Steven Sheil; *W:* Steven Sheil; Ziad Semaan; *C:* John Radel; *M:* Charlie Mole. **VIDEO**

The Dead Next Door **1989** Eerily reminiscent of "Night of the Living Dead." A scientist manufactures a virus which inhabits corpses and multiplies while replacing the former cells with its own. But the newly living corpses need human flesh to survive. In response, the government creates "The Zombie Squad" who do heroic battle with the stiffs. When a bizarre cult whose goal is the eradication of the human race befriend the dead, the battle gets ugly. **84m/C; VHS, DVD, Blu-Ray.** Pete Ferry; Bogdan Pecic; Michael Grossi; Len Kowalewich; Jolie Jackunas; Robert Kokai; Scott Spiegel; J.R. Bookwalter; *D:* J.R. Bookwalter; *W:* J.R. Bookwalter; *M:* J.R. Bookwalter.

Dead of Night **1945** The template for episodic horror films, this suspense classic, set in a remote country house, follows the individual nightmares of five houseguests. Redgrave turns in a chillingly convincing performance as a ventriloquist terrorized by a demonic dummy. Not recommended for light-sleepers. Truly spine-tingling. **102m/B; VHS, DVD, Blu-Ray.** *GB* Michael Redgrave; Mervyn Johns; Sally Ann Howes; Basil Radford; Naunton Wayne; Roland Culver; Googie Withers; Frederick Valk; Antony Baird; Judy Kelly; Miles Malleson; Ralph Michael; Mary Merrall; Renee Gadd; Michael Allan; Robert Wyndham; Esme Percy; Peggy Bryan; Hartley Power; Elisabeth Welch; Magda Kun; Garry Marsh; *D:* Alberto Cavalcanti; Charles Crichton; Basil Dearden; Robert Hamer; *W:* T.E.B. Clarke; John Baines; Angus MacPhail; *C:* Stanley Pavey; Douglas Slocombe; *M:* Georges Auric.

Dead of Night **1/2 1977** This trilogy features Richard Matheson's tales of the Supernatural: "Second Chance," "Bobby," and "No Such Thing As a Vampire," all served up by your hostess, Elvira. **76m/C; VHS, DVD.** Joan Hackett; Ed Begley, Jr.; Patrick Macnee; Anjanette Comer; ***D:*** Dan Curtis.

Dead of Night 🦴 *Lighthouse* **1999 (R)** Leo Rook (Adamson) is a psycho who collects the severed heads of his victims as trophies. He's aboard the prison ship Hyperion, which is transporting criminals to a remote island off the northern English coast. Leo steals a lifeboat and escapes to desolate Gehenna Rocks just before the ship runs aground. Then the few survivors are subjected to Leo's stalking and slashing. Crude and gory. **95m/C; VHS, DVD.** *GB* Chris(topher) Adamson; James Purefoy; Rachel Shelley; Paul Brooke; Don Warrington; Chris Dunne; Bob Goody; Pat Kelman; ***D:*** Simon Hunter; ***W:*** Simon Hunter; ***C:*** Tony Imi; ***M:*** Debbie Wiseman.

Dead of Winter 🦴🦴🦴 **1987 (R)** A young actress is suckered into a private screen test for a crippled old director, only to find she is actually being remodeled in the guise of a murdered woman. Edge-of-your-seat suspense as the plot twists. **100m/C; VHS, DVD, Blu-Ray.** Mary Steenburgen; Roddy McDowall; Jan Rubes; Ken Pogue; William Russ; ***D:*** Arthur Penn; ***W:*** Mark Shmuger; Mark Malone; ***M:*** Richard Einhorn.

The Dead One 🦴🦴 **2007 (PG-13)** Diego (Valderrama) outfits himself in a zombie mariachi costume for the Mexican Day of the Dead parties but he's killed before he gets to do any celebrating. His restless spirit becomes a slave to the Atzec god of death, who has captured his soul. Diego is returned to the living to battle the death god for the soul of his girlfriend Maria (Cepeda) among others. Flashy-looking and fairly mild horror (note the rating) based on the comic book, "El Muerto." **88m/C; DVD.** Wilmer Valderrama; Joel David Moore; Tony Plana; Maria Conchita Alonso; Angie Cepeda; Michael Parks; Tony Amendola; Billy Drago; ***D:*** Brian Cox; ***W:*** Brian Cox; ***C:*** Steve Yedlin; ***M:*** Tony Humecke. **VIDEO**

Dead or Alive 🦴🦴 *Dead or Alive: Hanzaisha* **2000** With director Miike it should be obvious this will not be a normal Japanese Yakuza film. Ryuuichi (Takeuchi) is an ethnic Chinese born in Japan, meaning he's permanently persona non grata in both countries (so he has no problem starting a mob war between the Yakuza and the Triads). Detective Jojima (Aikawa) is assigned to solve whatever the heck is going on and it quickly becomes personal between him and Ryuuichi. Filled with filth and perversion and is more of a black comedy than a serious mob film. **104m/C; DVD, Blu-Ray.** *JP* Riki Takeuchi; Sho Aikawa; Renji Ishibashi; Hitoshi Aizawa; Shingo Tsurumi; Kaoru Sugita; ***D:*** Takashi Miike; ***W:*** Ichiro Ryu; ***C:*** Hideo Yamamoto; ***M:*** Koji Endo.

Dead or Alive 🦴 **2002** Parris Bally is a bounty hunter who alone can defeat an international terrorist, but his wife wants him to quit the business. Standard "one-last-job" actioner. **90m/C; DVD.** Lowry Brooks, Jr.; Simeon Ndi; Gregory Dorsey; Veronica Pitts; Linda Floyd; Brian Horsey; ***D:*** Lowry Brooks, Jr.; ***W:*** Lowry Brooks, Jr.; ***C:*** Dominic Desantis; ***M:*** Gabriel Holden. **VIDEO**

Dead or Alive 2 🦴🦴 *Dead or Alive 2: Birds; Dead or Alive 2: The Birds; Dead or Alive 2: Tobosha; Dead or Alive 2: Runaway* **2000** Sho Aikawa and Riki Takeuchi return from the first film as different characters in Miike's trilogy. This time around they play two orphans separated at childhood who have both become hitmen as adults. They decide to team up and use their money from killing people to buy vaccines for third world children in some odd moment of nostalgia. It's much lighter in tone than the first movie and without the perversion. **97m/C; DVD, Blu-Ray.** *JP* Sho Aikawa; Riki Takeuchi; ***D:*** Takashi Miike; ***W:*** Masa Nakamura; ***C:*** Kazunari Tanaka; ***M:*** Chu Ishikawa.

Dead or Alive: Final 🦴 ½ **2002** Several years in the future Yokohama is now a mix of immigrants around the world ruled by a gay tyrannical mayor who has outlawed procreation as he believes only gay love can possibly be true. Anyone refusing to take the pill is rounded up by his agent Honda (Takeuchi) and exiled. Standing in his way are a ragtag group of rebels and a replicant named Ryo (Aikawa). If the word replicant brings to mind the film "Blade Runner," the association was intentional though unlike that movie this is about as bizarre as cyberpunk films get. **88m/C; DVD, Blu-Ray.** *JP* Sho Aikawa; Maria Chen; Josie Ho; Richard Chen; Riki Takeuchi; Terence Yin; Tony Ho; Don Tai; ***D:*** Takashi Miike; ***W:*** Hitoshi Ishikawa; Ichiro Ryu; Yoshinobu kamo; ***C:*** Kazunari Tanaka; ***M:*** Koji Endo.

Dead Pet 🦴🦴 ½ **2001** Kevin Coetteleer follows in the footsteps of Adam Sandler as a likeable, slightly geeky nice guy. He plays Jake Thompson who comes home from college to find that his repulsive parents have forgotten to pick him up at the airport and they've spent the rest of his education fund on an operation for their beloved poodle. From there, the comedy is nicely deadpan and inventive. **93m/C; DVD.** Kevin Cotteleer; Gina Doctor; Brian Sostek; ***D:*** Kevin Cotteleer; ***W:*** Kevin Cotteleer; ***C:*** Dan Ming.

Dead Pigeon on Beethoven Street 🦴🦴 ½ **1972 (PG)** Sandy (Corbett) is a detective whose partner gets murdered while investigating blackmailers who take compromising pictures of international big-wigs. So Sandy goes undercover and joins the gang. Cheeky paranoia from Fuller. **92m/C; VHS, DVD, Blu-Ray.** *GE* Glenn Corbett; Christa Lang; Anton Diffring; Alexander D'Arcy; ***D:*** Samuel Fuller; ***W:*** Samuel Fuller; ***C:*** Jerzy Lipman.

Dead Pit WOOF! **1989 (R)** Leave this one in the pit it crawled out of. Twenty years ago a mad scientist was killed as a result of horrible experiments he was conducting on mentally ill patients at an asylum. A young woman stumbles across his experiments, awakening him from the dead. **90m/C; VHS, DVD, Blu-Ray.** Jeremy Slate; Steffen Gregory Foster; ***D:*** Brett Leonard.

Dead Poets Society 🦴🦴🦴 ½ **1989 (PG)** An idealistic English teacher inspires a group of boys in a 1950s' prep school to pursue individuality and creative endeavor, resulting in clashes with school and parental authorities. Williams shows he can master the serious roles as well as the comic with his portrayal of the unorthodox educator. Big boxoffice hit occasionally scripted with a heavy hand in order to elevate the message. The ensemble cast is excellent. **128m/C; VHS, DVD; Open Captioned.** Robin Williams; Ethan Hawke; Robert Sean Leonard; Josh Charles; Gale Hansen; Kurtwood Smith; James Waterson; Dylan Kussman; Lara Flynn Boyle; Melora Hardin; Alexandra Powers; ***D:*** Peter Weir; ***W:*** Tom Schulman; ***C:*** John Seale; ***M:*** Maurice Jarre. Oscars '89: Orig. Screenplay; British Acad. '89: Film; Cesar '91: Foreign Film.

The Dead Pool 🦴 ½ **1988 (R)** Dirty Harry Number Five features a new twist on the sports pool: a list of celebrities is distributed and bets are placed on who will be first to cross the finish line, literally. Unfortunately someone seems to be hedging their bet by offing the celebs themselves. When Harry's name appears on the list, he decides to throw the game. **92m/C; VHS, DVD, Blu-Ray.** Clint Eastwood; Liam Neeson; Patricia Clarkson; Evan C. Kim; David Hunt; Michael Currie; Michael Goodwin; Jim Carrey; Louis Giambalvo; Justin Whalin; ***D:*** Buddy Van Horn; ***M:*** Lalo Schifrin.

Dead Presidents 🦴🦴 ½ **1995 (R)** Sophomore release for the Hughes brothers falls short of impact of "Menace II Society," but not for lack of ambition. Combination coming of age tale, war story, period piece and caper film follows Anthony ("Menace" veteran Tate) from his Bronx neighborhood in 1968 to Vietnam (for "Platoon" adventures in the wilds of Florida) and then back to the 'hood, where his life continues to spiral downward. Desperate to escape, he becomes involved in an armoured car heist to grab some cash (the "dead presidents"). Supported by hard-edged and effective acting, the Hughes continue to develop their control of cinematic imagery, displaying genius for staging violent, confrontational scenes. But the script, based on a story by the brothers, fails to live up to the vision, with characterization and dialogue lagging. Pounding period soundtrack with contributions by Curtis Mayfield, James Brown, and Marvin Gaye keeps things humming. **120m/C; VHS, DVD.** Larenz Tate; Keith David; Chris Tucker; Freddy Rodriguez; N'Bushe Wright; Bokeem Woodbine; Rose Jackson; Clifton Powell; Kirk "Sticky Fingaz" Jones; ***D:*** Albert Hughes; Allen Hughes; ***W:*** Michael Henry Brown; ***C:*** Lisa Rinzler; ***M:*** Danny Elfman.

Dead Reckoning 🦴🦴🦴 **1947** Bogart and Prince are two WWII veterans en route to Washington when Prince disappears. Bogart trails Prince to his Southern hometown and discovers he's been murdered. Blackmail and more murders follow as Bogie tries to uncover the truth. Suspenseful with good performances from all, especially Bogart. **100m/B; VHS, DVD.** Humphrey Bogart; Lizabeth Scott; Morris Carnovsky; Charles Cane; Wallace Ford; William Prince; Marvin Miller; Matthew "Stymie" Beard; William Forrest; ***D:*** John Cromwell; ***W:*** Steve Fisher; Allen Rivkin; Oliver H.P. Garrett; ***C:*** Leo Tover; ***M:*** Marlin Skiles; Hugo Friedhofer.

Dead Ringer 🦴🦴 ½ **1964** Bette Davis plays twins; Margaret, who's rich and recently widowed, and Edith, who's poor and feels that Margaret won her hubby unfairly (they were rivals for his affection). Edith kills Margaret and takes over her life, only to discover that the grass isn't always greener. Solid thriller showcases Davis in one of the better of her mystery/suspense roles of the 1960s. **115m/B; VHS, DVD.** Bette Davis; Karl Malden; Peter Lawford; Phil Carey; Jean Hagen; George Macready; Estelle Winwood; George Chandler; Cyril Delevanti; Bert Remsen; Monika Henreid; ***D:*** Paul Henreid; ***W:*** Albert Beich; Oscar Millard; ***C:*** Ernest Haller; ***M:*** Andre Previn.

Dead Ringers 🦴🦴🦴 **1988 (R)** A stunning, unsettling chiller, based loosely on a real case and the bestseller by Bari Wood and Jack Geasland. Irons, in an excellent dual role, is effectively disturbing as the twin gynecologists who descend into madness when they can no longer handle the fame, fortune, drugs, and women in their lives. Bujold is the actress/patient bedded by both brothers but jealouly loved by Beverly. Acutely upsetting film made all the more so due to its graphic images and basis in fact. **117m/C; VHS, DVD, Blu-Ray.** *CA* Jeremy Irons; Genevieve Bujold; Heidi von Palleske; Barbara Gordon; Shirley Douglas; Stephen Lack; Nick Nichols; ***D:*** David Cronenberg; ***W:*** David Cronenberg; Norman Snider; ***C:*** Peter Suschitzky; ***M:*** Howard Shore. Genie '89: Actor (Irons), Director (Cronenberg), Film; L.A. Film Critics '88: Director (Cronenberg), Support. Actress (Bujold); N.Y. Film Critics '88: Actor (Irons).

Dead Rising: End Game 🦴🦴 **2016** An action-horror zombie flick centered on one man's quest to save humanity. As zombie hordes ravage their way through an abandoned city, investigative reporter Chase Carter (Metcalfe) considers himself luck that he barely escaped a zombie quarantine. However, he feels guilty about leaving a trusted work ally behind. Returning to the quarantine to expose the government conspiracy behind the outbreak, he uncovers a dark secret. To save humanity, he allies himself with an unlikely group of misfit allies to make their way through the zombies and reveal the truth. **96m/C; DVD, Blu-Ray, Streaming, Download.** Jesse Metcalfe; Marie Avgeropoulos; Keegan Connor Tracy; Dennis Haysbert; Jessica Harmon; ***D:*** Pat Williams; ***W:*** Tim Carter; Michael Ferris; ***M:*** Rich Walters.

Dead Sexy 🦴 ½ **2001 (R)** Detective Kate McBain (Tweed) is investigating the murders of four L.A. high-price hookers. Of course, she becomes more than a little interested in one of her suspects, charming Blue (Enos), but is Kate willing to die to find out the truth? **89m/C; VHS, DVD.** Shannon Tweed; John Enos; Kenneth White; Sam Jones; Eric Keith; ***D:*** Robert Angelo; ***W:*** Anthony Laurence Greene; Elroy Canton; ***C:*** Kazuo Minami; ***M:*** Nicholas Rivera. **VIDEO**

Dead Silence 🦴🦴 ½ **1996 (R)** Three escaped convicts, including ruthless Ted Handy (Coates), have hijacked a busload of deaf children and their teacher (Matlin) and are holding them hostage in an abandoned slaughterhouse. Veteran FBI agent John Cooper (Garner) is called in but he not only has to deal with a tense and possibly tragic situation but with a grandstanding politician (Smith) who's criticizing his every action and the last-minute arrival of another hostage negotiator (Davidovich). Based on the novel "A Maiden's Grave" by Jeffery Deaver. **105m/C; VHS, DVD.** James Garner; Kim Coates; Marlee Matlin; Charles Martin Smith; Lolita Davidovich; Kenneth Welsh; James Villemaire; Gary Basaraba; Vanessa Vaughan; Blu Mankuma; Mimi Kuzyk; Scott Speedman; John Bourgeois; Barry Pepper; ***D:*** Daniel Petrie, Jr.; ***W:*** Donald Stewart; ***C:*** Thomas Burstyn; ***M:*** Jonathan Goldsmith. **CABLE**

Dead Silence 🦴 ½ *Wilbur Falls* **1998** Renata (Edwards) decides on a simple plan of revenge against Jeff (Newmark) who humiliated her at their junior-high prom five years before. Only her plans backfire and he accidentally dies. That should be the plot but it's surrounded by so many other storylines that it gets lost in the telling, which is a shame since Edwards does a good job. **95m/C; VHS, DVD.** Shanee Edwards; Danny Aiello; Sally Kirkland; Suzanne Cryer; Charles Newmark; ***Cameo(s):*** Maureen Stapleton; ***D:*** Juliane Glantz; ***W:*** Juliane Glantz; ***C:*** Kurt Brabbee; ***M:*** Jim Halfpenny.

Dead Silence 🦴 ½ **2007 (R)** Did you know that automatonophobia is the fear of ventriloquist dummies? Well, they're usually pretty creepy even though this retro-looking flick isn't. Jamie (Kwanten) receives a vintage wooden dummy in the mail and then his wife gets murdered. He actually realizes that there's a connection between the two events and travels to his hometown of Ravens Fair, where ventriloquist Mary Shaw (Roberts) was murdered and her dummies buried with her. Except they're not staying in the ground and Mary's using them to get her revenge. **90m/C; DVD, Blu-Ray, HD-DVD.** Ryan Kwanten; Donnie Wahlberg; Amber Valletta; Michael Fairman; Bob Gunton; Judith Roberts; Laura Regan; Joan Heney; ***D:*** James Wan; ***W:*** Leigh Whannell; ***C:*** John R. Leonetti; ***M:*** Charlie Clouser.

Dead Silent 🦴🦴 **1999 (R)** Doctor Julia Kerrbridge (Stewart) must care for her traumatized young niece whose parents were killed by the mob. But the girl, who has become mute, also has information that the bad guys will do anything to keep secret. Then there's Julia's new neighbor Kevin Finney (Lowe)?is he really a nice guy? Or a potential killer? **95m/C; VHS, DVD, On Demand.** Catherine Mary Stewart; Rob Lowe; Peter Colvey; Larry Day; Sean Devine; Allen Altman; Mark Camacho; ***D:*** Roger Cardinal; ***W:*** Ed Fitzgerald; Paul Koval; ***C:*** Bruno Philip; ***M:*** David Findlay. **VIDEO**

Dead Simple 🦴🦴 *Viva Las Nowhere* **2001 (R)** Frank Jacobs (Stern) and his nagging wife Helen (Richardson) owe a failing motel in dusty nowhere Kansas. Frank dreams of being a C&W singer and he hooks up with lounge performer Julie (Kohl), who has an abusive manager, has-been Roy Baker (Caan). Then there's Helen's twin sister Wanda (Richardson again), barmaid Marguerite (Stringfield), and the motel's garden, which gets a lot of unexpected fertilizer. Black comedy can't sustain its edge. **98m/C; VHS, DVD.** Daniel Stern; James Caan; Patricia Richardson; Sherry Stringfield; Lacey Kohl; Tim Abell; ***D:*** Jason Bloom; ***W:*** Richard Uhlig; Steve Seitz; ***C:*** James Glennon; ***M:*** Andrew Gross.

Dead Sleep 🦴🦴 **1991 (R)** A nurse discovers that comatose patients at a private clinic have been used as guinea pigs by an overzealous doctor. This minor-league chiller from Down Under is said to have been inspired by an actual medical scandal. **95m/C; VHS, DVD.** Linda Blair; Tony Bonner; ***D:*** Alec Mills.

Dead Snow 🦴🦴 **2009** Frozen Nazi zombies. Over their Easter break, seven medical students travel to a friend's remote cabin in northern Norway and are warned of evil in the woods. Turns out the area's one-time Nazi occupiers never left, they just became (hungry) zombies instead. Lots of gore and played for horror humor. Norwegian with subtitles. **91m/C; DVD.** *NO* Bjorn Sundquist; Vegar Hoel; Stig Frode Henriksen; Charlotte Frogner; Jenny Skavlan; Jeppe Laursen; Lasse Valdal; Evy Kasseth Rosten; Orjan Gamst; Ane Dahl Torp; Tommy Wirkola; ***D:*** Tommy Wirkola; ***W:*** Tommy Wirkola; ***C:*** Matthew Weston; ***M:*** Christian Wibe.

Dead Snow: Red vs. Dead 🦴🦴🦴 **2014** Director Wirkola picks up immediately where his last Nazi zombie horror-comedy left off and turns the volume up to eleven, resulting in one of the bloodiest, brashest, and best of the "gore with laughs" subgenre. Martin (Hoel), the only survivor of the last film, descends to the village at the mountain's base and the zombie SS follows, forcing Martin to call on the help of the Zombie Squad (led by a pitch-perfect Starr). Nazi zombies, Russian zombies, more uses for undead intestines than previously imagined, Wirkola knows how to deliver for his twisted fans. Norwegian with subtitles. **100m/C; DVD, Blu-Ray.** *NO* Vegar Hoel; Stig Frode Henriksen; Orjan Gamst; Martin Starr; Jocelyn DeBoer; Ingrid Haas; ***D:*** Tommy Wirkola; ***W:*** Vegar Hoel; Stig Frode Henriksen; Tommy Wirkola; ***C:*** Matthew Weston; ***M:*** Christian Wibe.

Dead Space 🦴 **1990 (R)** Dead space lay between the ears of whoever thought we needed this remake of 1982's "Forbidden World." At a lab on a hostile planet an experimental vaccine mutates into a prickly puppet monster who menaces the medicos. Needed: a vaccine against cheapo "Alien" ripoffs. **72m/C; VHS, DVD.** Marc Singer; Laura Tate; Bryan Cranston; Judith Chapman; ***D:*** Fred Gallo.

Dead Tone 🦴 *7eventy 5ive* **2007 (R)** Cheap thrills slasher flick for the undemanding. Stupid college students come up with a telephone prank game that requires keeping their callers on the line for 75 seconds. They annoy the wrong person who takes his objections out in a very bloody and permanent manner when the group celebrates the end of finals at the remote mansion of a rich student. **100m/C; DVD.** Brian Hooks; Antwon Tanner; Aimee Garcia; Judy Tylor; Cherie Johnson; Wil Horneff; Rutger Hauer; Gwendoline Yeo; Jonathan Chase; German Legarreta; ***D:*** Brian Hooks; Deon Taylor; ***W:*** Brian Hooks; Deon Taylor; Vashon Nutt; ***C:*** Philip Lee; ***M:*** Vincent Gillioz. **VIDEO**

Dead Water 🦴 **1/2 2019 (R)** Wealthy, gregarious orthopedic surgeon John (Van Dien) is best friends with the hot-headed Coop (Furst), an Afghan war veteran with a temper. One weekend, John invites Coop and his beautiful television news reporter wife Vivian (Davis) on his yacht for a cruise to the Virgin Islands. Tension between John and Coop emerges during the trip, but the situation grows more dire when the boat engine unexpectedly dies. When Coop uses the dinghy to find help, he comes across a boat with pirate McLean (Nelson) aboard. Despite the presence of Van Dien and Nelson, it's not a very thrilling thriller. **90m/C; DVD.** Casper Van Dien; Judd Nelson; Brianne Davis; Griff Furst; ***D:*** Chris Helton; ***W:*** Jason Usry; ***C:*** Josh Pickering; ***M:*** John Avarese.

Dead Waters 🦴🦴 *Dark Waters* **1994** Elizabeth (Salter) travels to a remote Russian island to visit her sister, Theresa (Phipps), who resides at the convent there. But Theresa is murdered after witnessing an occult ritual and Elizabeth finds strange references to "The Beast" in the convent library and realizes the nuns are trying to raise the demonic creature. **94m/C; VHS, DVD, Blu-Ray.** *IT RU GB* Louise Salter; Venera Simmons; Maria Kapnist; Anna Rose Phipps; ***D:*** Mariano Baino; ***W:*** Mariano Baino; Andrew Bark; ***C:*** Alex Howe; ***M:*** Igor Clark.

Dead Waves 🦴🦴 *Shiryoha* **2006** Hiroshi Ishui (Kanji Furutachi) is the producer of a hit tv show about exorcisms. But the ratings are falling amid accusations that the exorcisms he films are just mentally ill people, and that teenage suicides have increased almost 25% since his show first aired. He decides to soldier on, going to a house where a man has accuses his younger sister of being possessed. But on arriving, the brother appears to have serious mental problems, and his sister appears perfectly normal. But when the footage shot at the house is played back, the crew sees things in it that weren't there when they shot it. **166m/C; DVD.** *JP* Toshihiro Wada; Shigenori Yamazaki; Tsuyoshi Nagao; Shihori Kanjiya; ***D:*** Yoichiro Hayama; ***W:*** Yoichiro Hayama; Kayo Kano; ***C:*** Masahito Nakao; ***M:*** Hajime Yamane.

Dead Women in Lingerie WOOF! 1990 (R) When beautiful models are turning up dead, a detective is called in to solve the mystery. Perhaps they committed suicide to avoid being in this picture any longer than necessary. Title sounds like the next episode of "Geraldo." **87m/C; VHS, DVD.** June Lockhart; Lyle Waggoner; John Romo; Jerry Orbach; Maura Tierney; Laura Elena Harring; ***D:*** Erika Fox.

Dead Zone 🦴🦴🦴 **1983 (R)** Diffident teacher Johnny Smith (Walken) gains extraordinary psychic powers following a near-fatal car accident and a five-year coma. He has developed the ability to foresee a person's future by touching their hands—and when he shakes the hand of presidential candidate Greg Stillson (Sheen), he foresees a holocaust. So Johnny decides to use his "gift" to save mankind from impending evil. A good adaptation of the Stephen King thriller. **104m/C; VHS, DVD.** Christopher Walken; Brooke Adams; Tom Skerritt; Martin Sheen; Herbert Lom; Anthony Zerbe; Colleen Dewhurst; ***D:*** David Cronenberg; ***W:*** Jeffrey Boam; ***C:*** Mark Irwin; ***M:*** Michael Kamen.

The Dead Zone 🦴🦴 **1/2 2002 (R)** Pilot film for the cable series, which is based on the characters and story from the Stephen King novel. Johnny Smith (Hall) was in a coma for six years after a car crash. When he regains consciousness, he discovers he has psychic abilities that allow him to see into the lives of those he touches. **87m/C; VHS, DVD.** Anthony Michael Hall; Nicole de Boer; David Ogden Stiers; Chris Bruno; ***D:*** Robert Lieberman; ***W:*** Michael Piller. **CABLE**

The Deadbeat Club 🦴 **2004** Misfit teens in a small Texas town try to help a man whose family died in a fire. The actors look too old for their teen roles and virtue turns out to be really boring. **113m/C; DVD.** Daphne Khoury; Brandon Dixon; Jennifer Wetter; Nicole Cook; Jason Magee; ***D:*** Israel Luna; ***W:*** Israel Luna; ***C:*** Brad Walker; ***M:*** Philip Kappaz.

Deadbolt 🦴🦴 **1992 (R)** Divorced med student Marty Hiller (Bateman) desperately needs a roommate and Alec Danz (Baldwin) seems perfect. Soon they're sharing more than the rent, until Danz kills her friends and imprisons her in the apartment (equipped of course with soundproof walls and bulletproof glass—one wonders why she doesn't bang on the floor to gain attention.) Predictable and silly would-be thriller attempts to capitalize on the roommate-from-hell theme that started with "Single White Female," but isn't nearly as effective. Went straight to video and showed up on network TV several months later. **95m/C; VHS, Streaming.** Justine Bateman; Adam Baldwin; Michelle Scarabelli; Chris Mulkey; Cyndi Pass; Isabelle Truchon; ***D:*** Douglas Jackson. **VIDEO**

Deadfall 🦴🦴 **1/2 1993 (R)** Father/son grifters plan an elaborate scam that goes wrong when son Joe (Biehn) inadvertently kills dear old dad (Coburn). When Joe is going through his father's effects he finds out about an unknown twin uncle, who also turns out to be a racketeer. Along with Uncle Lou's mistrustful henchman Eddie (Cage), they plan another con but swindles and vendettas abound. **99m/C; VHS, DVD.** Michael Biehn; Sarah Trigger; Nicolas Cage; James Coburn; Charlie Sheen; Peter Fonda; ***D:*** Christopher Coppola; ***W:*** Christopher Coppola; David Peoples; ***C:*** Maryse Alberti; ***M:*** Jim Fox.

Deadfall 🦴🦴 **2012 (R)** With a twisted edge that attempts to replicate the noir comedy of Joel & Ethan Coen or David Lynch's Wild at Heart, this odd hybrid never comes together. Bana is miscast as a hardened criminal who ends up on the run after a heist with his sister (Wilde). The two are split up and sis teams up with a troubled soul named Jay (Hunnam) as the whole thing comes to a bloody head at the most bizarre Thanksgiving dinner of the year as Jay's parents. The central cast, which also includes Kate Mara & Treat Williams, is impressive even if the script and tonally awkward direction is not. **95m/C; DVD, Blu-Ray.** Eric Bana; Olivia Wilde; Charlie Hunnam; Sissy Spacek; Kris Kristofferson; ***D:*** Stefan Ruzowitsky; ***W:*** Zach Dean; ***C:*** Shane Hurlbut; ***M:*** Marco Beltrami.

Deadgirl WOOF! 2008 (R) Must be some kind of gross teen boy fantasy or the filmmakers are serious sickos. Teen losers J.T. and Rickie cut class to break into the local abandoned mental hospital. While exploring, they find a naked zombie girl tied to a gurney. Since she's pretty, J.T. wants to use her as his personal sex slave. Apparently he's forgotten that zombies feed on human flesh. **101m/C; DVD.** Noah Segan; Shiloh Fernandez; Jenny Spain; Candice Accola; ***D:*** Gadi Harel; Marcel Sarmiento; ***W:*** Trent Haaga; ***C:*** Harris Charalambous; ***M:*** Joseph Bauer. **VIDEO**

Deadlands 2: Trapped WOOF! 2008 Ugarek basically remade his first movie only this time he found someone beside his friends (and himself) to act in it and acquired more technical skills but it's still bad, unless you really like lame zombie flicks. The government secretly quarantines a small Maryland town to test a nerve gas that turns its citizens into zombies. Only six residents are not infected and they hide out in a movie multiplex to escape the horror. **85m/C; DVD.** Jim Krut; Joseph D. Durbin; Christopher L. Clark; Josh Davidson; Ashley Young; Corrine Brush; ***D:*** Gary Ugarek; ***W:*** Gary Ugarek; ***C:*** Krystian Ramlogan; ***M:*** Gary Ugarek. **VIDEO**

Deadlier Than the Male 🦴🦴 **1967** In this swinging '60s update on the '20s British hero, Bulldog Drummond (Johnson) is now a suave London insurance investigator after industrialist Carl Petersen (Green). It seems Petersen uses his own sexy assassins, Irma (Sommer) and Penelope (Koscina), to get rid of business partners and the competition. Gadgetry, exotic locations, and bikinied babes in a James Bond knockoff. **95m/C; VHS, DVD.** *GB* Richard Johnson; Nigel Green; Elke Sommer; Sylva Koscina; Suzanna Leigh; Steve Carlson; ***D:*** Ralph Thomas; ***W:*** Jimmy Sangster; Liz Charles-Williams; David Osborn; ***C:*** Ernest Steward; ***M:*** Malcolm Lockyer.

Deadline 🦴🦴 **1987 (R)** Walken is a cynical American journalist assigned to cover the warring factions in Beirut. He finds himself becoming more and more involved in the events he's supposed to report when he falls in love with a German nurse who is aiding the rebel forces. Tense, though sometimes murky drama. **110m/C; VHS, DVD.** *GE* Christopher Walken; Hywel Bennett; Marita Marschall; ***D:*** Nathaniel Gutman.

Deadline 🦴🦴 **2000 (R)** The publisher of a leading Chicago newspaper is murdered following his hostile takeover of said paper and the leading suspect is the paper's editor (but he's the wrong guy). Formulaic thriller. **94m/C; VHS, DVD.** Patrick Bergin; Bruce Dinsmore; Annie Dufresne; Alex Ivonovic; Edward Yankie; ***D:*** Robbie Ditchburn; ***W:*** Ron Base; Michael Stokes; ***C:*** Daniel Valdilleneuve. **VIDEO**

Deadline 🦴🦴 **2009 (R)** After suffering a breakdown, writer Alice retreats to a remote Victorian house to concentrate on finishing her screenplay so she can meet her deadline. Hearing and seeing strange things, Alice fears her imagination is in overdrive until she explores the house's creepy attic and discovers a box of videotapes that have her investigating what became of the couple shown on them. **89m/C; DVD, Blu-Ray.** Brittany Murphy; Thora Birch; Marc Blucas; Tammy Blanchard; ***D:*** Sean McConville; ***W:*** Sean McConville; ***C:*** Ross Richardson; ***M:*** Carlos Alvarez. **VIDEO**

Deadline 🦴 **2012 (PG-13)** Cliched, self-righteous thriller. Newspaper reporter Matt Harper (Talley) joins with smalltown Alabama local Trey Hall (Jenkins) to look into the 20-year-old unsolved murder of an African-American teenager when a white cop is killed on the same spot. Trey thinks the two crimes are related but the locals just want the past to stay buried. **95m/C; DVD.** Steve Talley; Lauren Jenkins; Eric Roberts; David Dwyer; J.D. Souther; ***D:*** Curt Hahn; ***W:*** Mark Ethridge; ***C:*** Paul Marschall; ***M:*** Dave Perkins.

Deadline at Dawn 🦴🦴 **1946** Hayward is an aspiring actress who tries to help a sailor (Williams) prove that he is innocent of murder. Based on a novel by Cornell Woolrich. **82m/B; VHS, DVD.** Bill Williams; Susan Hayward; Lola Lane; Paul Lukas; Joseph Calleia; ***D:*** Harold Clurman; ***W:*** Clifford Odets.

Deadlock 🦴🦴 **1/2 1991 (R)** Hauer and Rogers star as inmates in a prison of the future. This prison has no walls, no fences and no guards—and no one EVER escapes. Each prisoner wears an explosive collar that is tuned to the same frequency as one of the other prisoner's. Should the two separate by more than 100 yards, the collars explode. When Rogers convinces Hauer that they are on the same frequency, the two escape. Trouble is, they are being pursued not only by the police, but by Hauer's former partners in crime as well. Can the two find the freedom they are looking for—without losing their heads? **103m/C; VHS, DVD.** Rutger Hauer; Mimi Rogers; Joan Chen; James Remar; Stephen Tobolowsky; Basil Wallace; ***D:*** Lewis Teague. **CABLE**

Deadlocked 🦴🦴 **2000** Demond Doyle (Jonz) is convicted of rape and murder and prosecutor Ned Stark (Caruso) wants the death penalty. Demond's father, Jacob (Dutton), is convinced that his son is innocent, so he takes the jury hostage. He tells Stark that he has 24 hours to find the evidence that will clear his son or the captives start dying. Compelling leads in a contrived story. Made for TNT. **100m/C; DVD.** David Caruso; Charles S. Dutton; John Finn; Jo D. Jonz; Malcolm Stewart; Tom Butler; Diego Wallraff; Michael Tomlinson; ***D:*** Michael Watkins; ***W:*** David Rosenfelt; Erik Jendresen; ***C:*** Thomas Burstyn; ***M:*** B.C. Smith. **CABLE**

Deadly Advice 🦴🦴 **1993 (R)** Meek bookseller Jodie (Horrocks) and her sister are constantly humiliated by their overbearing mother (Fricker), who also objects to Jodie's romance with the local doctor (Pryce). As life becomes increasingly unbearable, Jodie discovers a book on infamous killers and is visited by their ghosts, including Jack the Ripper, who is happy to suggest ways to get rid of mom. **91m/C; VHS, DVD.** Jane Horrocks; Imelda Staunton; Brenda Fricker; Jonathan Pryce; ***D:*** Mandie Fletcher.

Deadly Bet 🦴 **1/2 1991 (R)** A made-for-video saga of a kickboxer who loses his money and his girl when he loses the big match. Lots of fight sequences as he works to regain his career. **93m/C; VHS, DVD, Streaming.** Jeff Wincott; Charlene Tilton; Steven Leigh; ***D:*** Richard W. Munchkin.

Deadly Blessing 🦴🦴 **1981 (R)** A young, recently widowed woman is visited in her rural Pennsylvania home by some friends from the city. Something's not quite right about this country life and they become especially suspicious after meeting their friend's very religious in-laws. **104m/C; VHS, DVD, Blu-Ray.** Maren Jensen; Susan Buckner; Sharon Stone; Ernest Borgnine; Jeff East; Lisa Hartman Black; Lois Nettleton; Colleen Riley; Douglas Barr; Michael Berryman; ***D:*** Wes Craven; ***W:*** Wes Craven; Glenn Benest; Matthew F. Barr; ***C:*** Robert C. Jessup; ***M:*** James Horner.

Deadly Breed 🦴 **1/2 1989** Beware your friendly neighborhood cop. A band of white supremacists has infiltrated the local police force, intent on causing violence, not keeping the peace. **90m/C; VHS, DVD.** William (Bill) Smith; Addison Randall; Blake Bahner; Joe Vance; ***D:*** Charles Kanganis.

Deadly Companions 🦴🦴 **1/2 1961** Keith is an ex-gunslinger who agrees to escort O'Hara through Apache territory in order to make up for inadvertently killing her son. Director Peckinpah's first feature film. **90m/C; DVD.** Maureen O'Hara; Brian Keith; Chill Wills; Steve Cochran; ***D:*** Sam Peckinpah; ***W:*** A.S. (Albert Sidney) Fleischmann; ***C:*** William Clothier; ***M:*** Marlin Skiles.

Deadly Daphne's Revenge 🦴 **1/2 1993** Gory story of rape and revenge from the Troma Team. Hitchhiker Cindy is beaten and raped by Charlie Johnson. When she seeks justice via the local police, Johnson makes plans to have her snuffed out. Meantime, another of his victims escapes from the asylum she's been in and comes looking for him with murder on her mind. **98m/C; VHS, DVD, Blu-Ray.** Anthony Holt; Laurie Tait Partridge; John Suttle; Alan Levy; Richard Harding Gardner; ***D:*** Richard Harding Gardner; ***W:*** Richard Harding Gardner; Tim Bennett; ***C:*** Vern Virlene; ***M:*** John Banning.

Deadly Encounter 🦴🦴🦴 **1972** Thrilling actioner in which Hagman portrays a helicopter pilot—a former war ace—who allows an old flame to talk him into helping her escape from the mobsters on her trail. Terrific edge-of-your-seat aerial action. **90m/C; VHS, DVD.** Larry Hagman; Susan Anspach; James Gammon; ***D:*** William A. Graham.

A Deadly Encounter 🦴 *Over the Edge* **2004** Single mom Joanne accidentally cuts off another car on the highway while driving home late at night. The man suffers an extreme case of road rage and begins stalking Joanne who behaves very, very stupidly even when his criminal actions escalate. **90m/C; DVD.** Laura Leighton; Daniel Magder; Alain Goulem; Frank Schorpion; Anthony Lemke; Larry Day; Catherine Colvey; ***D:*** Richard Roy; ***W:*** Duane Poole; ***C:*** Daniel Vincelette; ***M:*** Carl Bastien; Martin Roy. **CABLE**

Deadly Fieldtrip 1/2 **1974** Four female students and their teacher are abducted by a biker gang and held hostage on a deserted farm. **91m/C; VHS, DVD.** Zalman King; Brenda Fogarty; Robert Porter; ***D:*** Earl Barton.

Deadly Friend **1986 (R)** A well-meaning horror flick? That's what Wes Craven has tried to provide for us. When the girlfriend of a lonely teenage genius is accidentally killed, he decides to insert his robot's "brain" in her body, though the results aren't entirely successful. The same can be said for the film which was based on Diana Henstell's more effective novel "Friend." **91m/C; VHS, DVD.** Matthew Laborteaux; Kristy Swanson; Michael Sharrett; Anne Twomey; Richard Marcus; Anne Ramsey; ***D:*** Wes Craven; ***W:*** Bruce Joel Rubin; ***C:*** Philip H. Lathrop; ***M:*** Charles Bernstein.

Deadly Game **1977** Griffith reprises his role from 1977's "The Girl in the Empty Grave" as resort town police chief Abel Marsh. A dangerous chemical spill by an Army convoy traveling through the community may not have been an accident. Filmed on location in Big Bear, CA. **90m/C; DVD.** Andy Griffith; James Cromwell; Dan O'Herlihy; Morgan Woodward; Rebecca Balding; Sharon Spelman; Fran Ryan; Eddie Foy, Jr.; Mitzi Hoag; ***D:*** Lane Slate; ***W:*** Lane Slate; ***C:*** Gayne Rescher; ***M:*** Mundell Lowe. **TV**

Deadly Game *Catch Me If You Can* **1998** Nathan is a 12-year-old runaway with an attitude who witnesses some mob business and winds up stealing a lot of mob cash. He decides to live it up on his ill-gotten gains until a down-on-his-luck cop (Matheson) catches up with Nathan and tries to protect him from the goons' revenge. **120m/C; VHS, DVD.** Tim Matheson; Carol Alt; William Katt; Ryan DeBoer; Catherine Oxenberg; Ed Marinaro; Eddie Mekka; ***D:*** Jeff Reiner; ***W:*** Lorne Cameron; David Hoselton; ***C:*** Jonathan Freeman; ***M:*** Christopher Brady. **TV**

Deadly Harvest **1972 (PG)** Scientists' worst fears have been realized—due to ecological abuse and over-development of the land, food has become extremely scarce. This in turn has caused people to become a bit savage. They are particularly nasty to a farmer and his family. Not a bad plot, but a poorly acted film. **86m/C; VHS, DVD.** Clint Walker; Nehemiah Persoff; Kim Cattrall; David G. Brown; Gary Davies; ***D:*** Timothy Bond.

Deadly Hero **1975 (R)** Gripping tale of a young woman who becomes the prey of a New York City cop after questioning the brutal methods he employed while saving her from being assaulted, ultimately killing her attacker. Williams makes film debut in this chilling suspenser. **102m/C; VHS, DVD, Blu-Ray.** Don Murray; James Earl Jones; Diahn Williams; Lilia Skala; Conchata Ferrell; George S. Irving; Treat Williams; Josh Mostel; ***D:*** Ivan Nagy; ***C:*** Andrzej Bartkowiak; ***M:*** Brad Fiedel.

Deadly Honeymoon **2010** A dead spouse crime drama from Lifetime. After marrying in Hawaii, Lindsey and Trevor take a cruise to Tahiti. Bad boy Trevor continues his hard partying ways onboard, befriending some suspicious passengers, but Lindsey is hardly the model for newlywed bliss. Trevor goes missing, and the cruise ship's captain tells vacationing FBI agent Gwen Merced that Trevor could have fallen overboard--or been pushed. Gwen can't wait to investigate. **90m/C; Streaming.** Summer Glau; Chris Carmack; Zoe McLellan; Erik Palladino; Mark Harelik; Emily Foxler; Peter Katona; ***D:*** Paul Shapiro; ***W:*** Ron McGee; ***C:*** Michael Lohmann; ***M:*** Joseph Conlan. **CABLE**

Deadly Impact 1/2 **1984** Las Vegas casinos are targeted for rip-off by means of a computer. Svenson and Williamson give good performances, but that's not enough to save this one. De Angelis used the pseudonym Larry Ludman. **90m/C; VHS, DVD.** *IT* Bo Svenson; Fred Williamson; Marcia Clingan; Giovanni Lambardo Radice; Vincent Conti; ***D:*** Fabrizio de Angelis.

Deadly Impact **2009** Deadly dull and interchangeable with numerous other so-called action-thrillers. Albuquerque cop Tom Armstrong (Flanery) is after serial bomber/killer The Lion (Pantoliano) who forces Tom to kill his own wife to prevent a bigger tragedy. Naturally this sends Tom to the booze until FBI agent Isabel (Serano) persuades Tom to help them get the scuzzball who's upped the ante on his bombing threats. **96m/C; DVD.** Sean Patrick Flanery; Joe Pantoliano; Carmen Serano; Amanda Wyss; David House; ***D:*** Robert Kurtzman; ***W:*** Alexander Vesha; ***C:*** Paul Elliot; ***M:*** Steve Gutheinz. **VIDEO**

Deadly Intent **1988** The widow of a murdered archeologist becomes the target of fortune hunters when they try to get their hands on the priceless jewel her husband brought back from a dig. **83m/C; VHS, DVD, Streaming.** Lisa Eilbacher; Steve Railsback; Maud Adams; Lance Henriksen; Fred Williamson; Persis Khambatta; ***D:*** Nigel Dick.

Deadly Isolation **2005** Widow Susan is at her isolated Maine summer home to grieve over husband Ron when his old college buddy Jeff turns up. Except Jeff is really an escaped con who partnered with Ron to steal $20 million in diamonds and he's sure that Susan knows where Ron hid them. **90m/C; DVD.** Sherilyn Fenn; Nicholas Lea; Andreas Apergis; Marcel Jeannin; Sara Bradeen; ***D:*** Rodney Gibbons; ***W:*** David Rosenfelt; ***C:*** Daniel Vincelette; ***M:*** Marc Ouellette. **CABLE**

The Deadly Mantis 1/2 *The Incredible Praying Mantis* **1957** A gigantic praying mantis lies in a million-year-old sleep in the frozen reaches of the Arctic. Then a volcanic eruption releases the critter and the flying beastie does it's destructive best on Washington, D.C., and New York City until the military can gas it into oblivion. Typically silly '50s sci-fi with decent special effects. **79m/B; DVD, Blu-Ray.** Craig Stevens; William Hopper; Alix Talton; Pat Conway; Donald Randolph; ***D:*** Nathan "Jerry" Juran; ***W:*** Martin Berkeley.

Deadly Mission 1/2 *Inglorious Bastards* **1978 (R)** Five soldiers in WWII France are convicted of crimes against the Army, only to escape from lock-up and become focal points in a decisive battle. **99m/C; VHS, DVD, Blu-Ray.** *IT* Bo Svenson; Peter Hooten; Fred Williamson; ***D:*** Enzo G. Castellari; ***W:*** Alessandro Continenza; Sergio Grieco; Romano Migliorini; Laura Toscano; Franco Marotta.

Deadly Neighbor **1991** New neighbor moves in, dead neighborhood housewives move out. Another neighbor becomes suspicious and investigates. **90m/C; VHS, DVD.** Don Leifert; George Stover; Lydia Laurans; ***D:*** Donald M. Dohler.

Deadly Reckoning 1/2 **2001 (R)** Ernest Grey (Zagarino) is a former military commando turned spy who has since retired to run a bookstore when terrorists blow it up and kidnap his daughter. Seems he imprisoned their leader back in the old days and he's finally gotten out and wants revenge. Sounds nice, but really is a low budget direct to video spy film. **90m/C; DVD.** Matthias Hues; Robert Vaughan; Frank Zabarino; Elizabeth Giordino; ***D:*** Art Camacho.

Deadly Recruits 1/2 **1986** The Russians did it! The Russians did it! Stamp is convinced that the downfall of several top students at Oxford, amid scandal and rumor, is due to a KGB conspiracy. **92m/C; VHS, DVD.** *GB* Terence Stamp; Michael Culver; Carmen (De Sautoy) Du Sautoy; Robin Sachs; ***D:*** Roger Tucker.

Deadly Relations 1/2 **1993** Controlling dad Leonard Fagot (Ulrich) loses it when his four daughters grow up and want to leave home to get married. Leonard goes to deadly extremes to keep them safe since no man is good enough for his little girls. Based on a true crime; an ABC TV movie. **91m/C; DVD.** Robert Urich; Shelley Fabares; Gwyneth Paltrow; Georgia Emelin; Jillian Boyd; Joy Farmer; Matthew Perry; ***D:*** Bill Condon; ***W:*** Dennis Nemec; ***C:*** Stephen Katz; ***M:*** Philip Griffin. **TV**

Deadly Sanctuary **WOOF!** **1968** Censors stopped production of this film several times. The Marquis de Sade's writings provided the inspiration (though there's nothing inspired about it) for this tale of two recently orphaned young women who get caught up in prostitution, an S&M club, and murder. **92m/C; VHS, DVD.** Jack Palance; Mercedes McCambridge; Sylva Koscina; Klaus Kinski; Akim Tamiroff; Romina Power; ***D:*** Jess (Jesus) Franco.

Deadly Shift 1/2 *Polar Opposites* **2008 (PG-13)** When scientist David Terran's unconventional theories about the Earth's magnetic fields are laughed at, he retreats into isolation. However, underground nuclear testing by the Iranian government causes a spike in solar radiation and sets off a chain of earthquakes. Now David may be the only one able to find a solution to the disaster. **90m/C; DVD.** Charles Shaughnessy; Tracy Nelson; Ken Barnett; Beth Grant; Kieren Hutchison; Clive Revill; ***D:*** Fred Olen Ray; ***W:*** Paolo Mazzucato; ***C:*** Theo Angell; ***M:*** Chuck Cirino. **VIDEO**

Deadly Stranger *Border Heat* **1988** Fluegel's talents could have been put to much better use than as the selfish mistress of a plantation owner who is taking advantage of the migrant workers toiling on his land. Moore is a drifter and hired hand who rallies the workers to stand up to the owner. **93m/C; VHS, Streaming.** Darlanne Fluegel; Michael J. Moore; John Vernon; Ted White; ***D:*** Max Kleven.

Deadly Target 1/2 **1994 (R)** Detective Charles Prince (Daniels) is sent to L.A. to return a notorious Chinese gangster to Hong Kong for trial. But Prince finds out his would-be prisoner's escaped and soon he's involved in martial arts mayhem. **90m/C; VHS, DVD.** Gary Daniels; Kenneth McLeod; Max Gail; Susan Byun; ***D:*** Charla Driver; ***W:*** Michael January; James Adelstein; ***C:*** Richard Pepin; ***M:*** Michael Lewis.

Deadly Thief *Shalimar* **1978** A former jewel thief comes out of retirement to challenge those who are now tops in the profession to try and steal the world's most precious ruby from him. Of course all they have to lose is their lives. What could have been an exciting adventure is made curiously boring. **90m/C; VHS, DVD.** *IN* Rex Harrison; John Saxon; Sylvia Miles; Dharmendra; Zenat Aman; Shammi Kapoor; ***D:*** Krishna Shah.

The Deadly Trackers **1973 (PG)** If gorey oaters are your thing, this one's definitely for you; if not, make tracks. Harris plays a spiteful sheriff who heads south of the border to get his pound of flesh from the outlaws who slew his family in a bank robbery. Overlong revenge-o-rama based on Samuel Fuller's short story, "Riata"; might have been bearable if Fuller hadn't been bumped from the director's chair (as it is, he and other contributors refused to be listed in the credits). **104m/C; VHS, DVD, Blu-Ray.** Richard Harris; Rod Taylor; Al Lettieri; Neville Brand; William (Bill) Smith; Paul Benjamin; Pedro Armendariz, Jr.; ***D:*** Barry Shear.

Deadly Voyage 1/2 **1996 (R)** In 1992, nine Ghanaian dockworkers are discovered hiding aboard a Ukrainian freighter bound for New York. Since each stowaway would cost the shipping company a hefty fine, sadistic first officer Ion (Pertwee) orders them killed. Only one, Kingsley (Epps), manages to survive and reveal the truth. **92m/C; VHS, DVD.** Omar Epps; Sean Pertwee; Joss Ackland; David Suchet; Jean LaMarre; Andrew Divoff; ***D:*** John MacKenzie; ***C:*** Stuart Urban; ***M:*** John Scott. **CABLE**

Deadly Weapons **1970 (R)** Chesty Morgan, she of the 73-inch bustline, takes on the mob using only her God-given abilities. One of Joe Bob Brigg's "Sleaziest Movies in the History of the World" series, and he is welcome to it. **90m/C; VHS, DVD, Blu-Ray.** Chesty Morgan; Harry (Herbert Streicher) Reems; Greg Reynolds; Saul Meth; Phillip Stahl; Mitchell Fredericks; Denise Purcell; John McMohon; ***D:*** Doris Wishman; ***W:*** J.J. Kendall; ***C:*** Juan Fernandez.

Deadpool 1/2 **2016 (R)** The long-awaited, R-rated adaptation of the Marvel hit series tries so hard to please by "being edgy and different" that it could be depressing how many of the standard superhero movie beats it hits along the way. But Ryan Reynolds is the best thing about the film, giving a brash, charismatic performance that makes outdated jokes, cheap effects and desperate one-liners a good thing. Remarkably memorable...who knew being so wrong could be so right? **108m/C; DVD, Blu-Ray, Streaming.** *CA US* Ryan Reynolds; Karan Soni; Ed Skrein; Michael Benyaer; Kyle Cassie; ***D:*** Tim Miller; ***W:*** Rhett Reese; Paul Wernick; ***C:*** Ken Seng; ***M:*** Junkie XL.

Deadpool 2 1/2 **2018 (R)** The much anticipated, more dramatic sequel to the cliche-bending superhero hit. After Deadpool/Wade Wilson (Reynolds) suffers a tremendous personal loss, his grief nearly consumes him. Deadpool's quest for revenge includes a visit to the X-Men mansion, where he becomes involved in helping Domino (Beetz) and Colossus (Kapicic). The X-Men and Deadpool go to extremes to protect a rebellious teen mutant, Firefist (Dennison), from mercenary Matthew Cable (Brolin). The sense of irreverent, dark humor, endlessly relevant pop culture references, and another strong performance by the incomparable Reynolds make this must-see for genre fans. **119m/C; DVD, Blu-Ray, Streaming.** Ryan Reynolds; Josh Brolin; Morena Baccarin; Julian Dennison; Zazie Beetz; ***D:*** David Leitch; Michael McCusker; ***W:*** Ryan Reynolds; Rhett Reese; Paul Wernick; ***C:*** Jonathan Sela; ***M:*** Tyler Bates.

Deadtime Stories 1/2 **1986** Mother Goose it's not. Fairy tales "Little Red Riding Hood" and "Goldilocks and the Three Bears," among others, are presented like you've never before seen them—as low-budget horror tales. **93m/C; VHS, DVD, Blu-Ray.** Michael Mesmer; Brian DePersia; Scott Valentine; Phyllis Craig; Melissa Leo; Nicole Picard; ***D:*** Jeffrey Delman.

Deadwood 1/2 **1965** In the untamed West, a young cowboy is mistaken for the notorious Billy the Kid. **100m/C; VHS, DVD.** Arch Hall, Jr.; Jack Lester; Liz Renay; Robert Dix; ***D:*** James Landis; ***C:*** Vilmos Zsigmond.

The Deal **2005 (R)** It's the near future, the U.S. is at war with the 'Confederation of Arab States' and gas is $6 a gallon and rising. A Wall Street hotshot, Tom Grover (Slater), is called in to help seal a $20-billion deal with a Russian oil conglomerate called Black Star which is most likely a Russian Mafia 'oil-laundering' operation. Young Harvard grad, and new hire (Blair) acts as Grover's investigative partner and lust interest. Early portions of Epstein's script contain copious amounts of intriguing industrial data but once Angie Harmon enters the scene with her laughable Russian accent it becomes a corporate espionage thriller spoof. **107m/C; DVD.** Christian Slater; Selma Blair; John Heard; Angie Harmon; Kevin Tighe; Francoise Yip; Colm Feore; Robert Loggia; Philip Granger; Jim Thorburn; Ruth Epstein; ***D:*** Harvey Kahn; ***C:*** Adam Sliwinski; ***M:*** Christopher Lennertz.

Deal 1/2 **2008 (PG-13)** Alex (Harrison) taught himself poker via online tournaments and he attracts the attention of retired pro Tommy (Reynolds), who offers to teach Alex the details that will get him into big money games. When Alex hits the World Poker Tournament in Vegas, their partnership falters and Tommy winds up across the table from his former protege. Reynolds projects the right air of world-weariness but Harrison is too callow a foil and there's nothing about the plot that'll be a surprise. **86m/C; DVD.** Burt Reynolds; Bret Harrison; Shannon Elizabeth; Charles Durning; Jennifer Tilly; Gary Grubbs; Maria Mason; ***D:*** Gil Cates, Jr.; ***W:*** Gil Cates, Jr.; Marc Weinstock; ***C:*** Thomas M. (Tom) Harting; ***M:*** Peter Rafelson.

The Deal 1/2 **2008 (R)** This is one deal you won't have any trouble passing up. Suicidal Hollywood producer Charlie Berns (Macy) decides to play the system, turning a snoozer script into a buzzworthy go project set to shoot in South Africa. Development exec Deidre Hearn (Ryan) sees the scam but goes along with the studio deal—at least until demanding lead actor Bobby Mason (LL Cool J) gets kidnapped; then Charlie and Deidre are all about covering their assets. **98m/C; DVD, Blu-Ray.** William H. Macy; Meg Ryan; LL Cool J; Elliott Gould; Jason Ritter; ***D:*** Steven Schachter; ***W:*** Steven Schachter; ***C:*** Paul Sarossy; ***M:*** Jeff Beal.

Deal of a Lifetime **1999 (PG)** It's a deal that's too good to be true, of course. Loser teen Henry (Goorjian) is tempted to sell his soul to the Devil's agent, Jerry (Pollak), in order to get a date with the school's most popular babe (Appleby). **95m/C; VHS, DVD.** Kevin Pollak; Michael Goorjian; Shiri Appleby; Jennifer Rubin; ***D:*** Paul Levine; ***W:*** Katharine R. Sloan; ***C:*** Denise Brassard; ***M:*** Amotz Plessner. **VIDEO**

Deal of the Century **1983 (PG)** A first-rate hustler and his cohorts sell second-rate weapons to third-world nations; unfortunately, their latest deal threatens to blow up in their faces—literally. **99m/C; DVD.** Chevy Chase; Sigourney Weaver; Gregory Hines; Richard Libertini; Wallace Shawn; ***D:*** William Friedkin; ***W:*** Paul Brickman.

Dealers ½ **1989 (R)** Two money-hungry stock traders mix business and pleasure, then set their sights on one final all or nothing score. **92m/C; VHS, DVD.** *GB* Rebecca De Mornay; Paul McGann; Derrick O'Connor; Paul Guilfoyle; ***D:*** Colin Bucksey; ***W:*** Andrew Maclear; ***C:*** Peter Sinclair.

Dealing: Or the Berkeley-to-Boston Forty-Brick Lost-Bag Blues **1972** Counterculture time-capsule about hippies, drugs, and the Ivy League. Harvard Law student Peter (Lyons) goes to Berkeley to buy pot to bring back to Boston and falls for hippie chick Susan (Hershey). Peter convinces campus drug dealer John (Lithgow) to let Susan bring in another shipment but she gets busted by corrupt cop Murphy (Durning) and there's more trouble involving Cuban mobsters. Uh, yeah, the drug dealers are the good guys. **88m/C; DVD.** John Lithgow; Ellen Barber; ***D:*** Paul Williams; ***W:*** David Odell.

Dean **2017 (PG-13)** Dean (Demetri Martin) avoids dealing with his mom's death by escaping his New York life for Los Angeles, while his dad (Kline) takes a more pragmatic approach to loss, namely selling the family home. Martin's directorial debut offers a thoughtful, humorous treatment of grief, father-and-son connection, and hope. **94m/C; DVD.** Demetri Martin; Kevin Kline; Gillian Jacobs; Rory Scovel; Ginger Gonzaga; ***D:*** Demetri Martin; ***W:*** Demetri Martin; ***C:*** Mark Schwartzbard; ***M:*** Mark Noseworthy; Orr Rebhun.

Dean Koontz's Black River *Black River* **2001 (PG)** Novelist/screenwriter Bo Aikens (Mohr) is in need of a little creative inspiration and leaves Hollywood for the bucolic friendliness of the small town of Black River. Then Bo discovers the town is monitored by video cameras and he begins to get weird phone calls and notices an SUV tailing him. He can't escape unless he figures out the community's sinister secrets (which unfortunately turn out to be lame-o). **87m/C; VHS, DVD.** Jay Mohr; Lisa Edelstein; Ann Cusack; Ron Canada; Stephen Tobolowsky; ***D:*** Jeff Bleckner; ***W:*** Daniel Taplitz; ***C:*** John Bartley. **TV**

Dean Koontz's Intensity *Intensity* **1997** TV mini-series, which originally aired on the Fox network, lives up to its name. Troubled waitress Chyna Shepherd (Parker) is after serial killer Edgler Foreman Vess (McGinley), who murdered her best friend. He kidnapped teenager Ariel (Paul) and Chyna is determined to rescue her while Vess is equally determined to play a deadly game of cat-and-mouse. **181m/C; DVD.** Molly Parker; John C. McGinley; Piper Laurie; Tori Paul; Blu Mankuma; ***D:*** Yves Simoneau; ***W:*** Stephen Tolkin; ***C:*** David Franco; ***M:*** George S. Clinton. **TV**

Dean Koontz's Mr. Murder *Mr. Murder* **1998 (R)** Marty Stillwater (Baldwin) is a successful mystery writer and family man who discovers that he has a killer clone. Seems industrialist Drew Oslett Jr. (Church) managed to screwup in the biotech lab and now there's a bloodthirsty Marty lookalike named Alfie, who decides he wants Marty's life. Meanwhile, everyone thinks Marty is going crazy. **132m/C; VHS, DVD.** Stephen Baldwin; Thomas Haden Church; Julie Warner; Bill Smitrovich; James Coburn; Don Hood; Dan Lauria; ***D:*** Dick Lowry; ***W:*** Stephen Tolkin; ***C:*** Greg Gardiner; ***M:*** Louis Febre. **TV**

Dear Brigitte **1965** A young American kid ("Lost in Space" tyke Mumy) writes a love letter to Brigitte Bardot and travels to Paris to meet her in person. Based on the novel "Erasmus with Freckles" by John Haase. **100m/C; VHS, Streaming.** James Stewart; Billy Mumy; Glynis Johns; Fabian; Cindy Carol; John Williams; Jack Kruschen; Brigitte Bardot; Ed Wynn; Alice Pearce; ***D:*** Henry Koster; ***W:*** Hal Kanter.

Dear Dead Delilah ½ **1972** Moorehead is Delilah, the matriarch of a southern family, who is on her deathbed. Her heirs are fighting to the bitter—and bloody—end to be the first to find Delilah's money, buried somewhere on her land. **90m/C; VHS, DVD, Blu-Ray.** Agnes Moorehead; Will Geer; Michael Ansara; Patricia Carmichael; Dennis Patrick; ***D:*** John Farris.

Dear Dictator ½ **2018** A high-concept, coming-of-age comedy that examines what happens when a teenage girl befriends a dictator. Tatiana (Rush) is unhappy with her life, her peers, teachers, and mother Darlene (Holmes). Tatiana is particularly resentful of Darlene because her mother is romantically attached to an immature, married dentist Charles (Green) who will not leave his wife. One day, Tatiana starts a pen-pal correspondence with Anton Vincent (Caine), a Fidel Castro-like fascist dictator. The pair become fast friends, with hilarious honesty, as they affect each other's lives. Great performances, well-timed jokes, and a sense of warmth eventually lose out to the cliches. **90m/C; DVD, Blu-Ray.** Michael Caine; Odeya Rush; Katie Holmes; Seth Green; Jason Biggs; ***D:*** Lisa Addario; Joe Syracuse; ***W:*** Lisa Addario; Joe Syracuse; ***C:*** Wyatt Troll; ***M:*** Sebastian Kauderer.

Dear Dumb Diary ½ **2013** Hallmark Channel family movie based on the book series by Jim Benton, who co-wrote the script. 11-year-old middle-schooler Jamie daydreams about her life in vivid musical productions, including her crush on the school's cutest boy, Hudson Rivers. She shares everything in her diary, which goes missing just as Jamie decides to impress Hudson by winning the school's Jump-a-Thon fundraiser to save the arts program. **86m/C; DVD, Blu-Ray.** Emily Alyn Lind; David Mazouz; Mary-Charles Jones; Sterling Griffith; Laura Bell Bundy; ***D:*** Kristin Hanggi; ***W:*** Kristin Hanggi; Jim Benton; ***C:*** Anka Malatynska; ***M:*** Steven Argila. **CABLE**

Dear Eleanor **2016 (PG-13)** 1960s teen road trip movie. As the Cuban missile crisis simmers in 1962, two teen girls--Max (Fuhrman) and Ellie Potter (Liberato)--travel from their rural home town in California to New York. Sneaking away in the convertible owned by Ellie's father Bob (Wilson), their goal is to find and meet the former First Lady of the United States Eleanor Roosevelt. Along the way, they met a series of unusual people, some of whom join their cross-country car adventure as they try to stay ahead of Ellie's father and the police. **89m/C; DVD, Streaming, Download.** Isabelle Fuhrman; Liana Liberato; Luke Wilson; Ione Skye; Jessica Alba; ***D:*** Kevin Connolly; ***W:*** Cecilia Contreras; Amy Garcia; ***C:*** Steven Fierberg; ***M:*** Aaron Zigman. **VIDEO**

Dear Frankie **2004 (PG-13)** Scottish tearjerker about a woman, her deaf son, and the guy she pays to pretend to be Dad. Lizzie (Mortimer) has raised 9-year-old Frankie (McElhone) to believe that the father he doesn't remember is a member of a cargo ship crew, when in reality he was an abusive jerk that Lizzie left years ago. Of course, this means that she has to come up with a fake father on the spot, and finds a stranger (Butler) to fill the role, with the standard mom-falls-for-fake-dad, fake-dad-learns-to-like-his-fake-family results. Solid performances by all fail to make up for a bland, manipulative story. **102m/C; DVD.** *GB* Emily Mortimer; Jack McElhone; Sharon Small; Cal Macaninch; Mary Riggans; Sophie Main; Katy Murphy; Gerard Butler; ***D:*** Shona Auerbach; ***W:*** Andrea Gibb; ***M:*** Alex Heffes.

Dear God **1996 (PG)** TV vets Marshall (director) and Kinnear team up for a sappy and predictable "Miracle on Melrose," a little piece of Capra-corn that feels like it lodged in your tooth. Cynical con man Tom (Kinnear) goes to work for the post office and gets stuck with a group of misfits at the Dead Letter Office, sorting mail for the likes of Elvis, Santa, and God. Even though he's merely working the ultimate angle for easy cash, the oddball team of postal workers think he's on a mission from the Lord and joins him in aiding the needy. Most unbelievable is the premise that single mom and love interest Gloria (Pitillo) can give the hardened criminal an instant psychological makeover. Broadly characterized supporting cast, including Conway and Metcalf, suffer at the hands of script. Strictly a star vehicle for Kinnear's budding movie career, it won't help. It also won't do anything for Marshall's downward-spiraling reputation. Ironic cameo from Christopher Darden as a reporter outside the courtroom, and Marshall himself as Postmaster General. **112m/C; VHS, DVD.** Greg Kinnear; Laurie Metcalf; Maria Pitillo; Hector Elizondo; Tim Conway; Roscoe Lee Browne; Jon Seda; Anna Maria Horsford; Donal Logue; Nancy Marchand; Larry Miller; Rue McClanahan; Toby Huss; Jack Klugman; ***Cameo(s):*** Garry Marshall; ***D:*** Garry Marshall; ***W:*** Ed Kaplan; Warren Leight; ***C:*** Charles Minsky.

Dear Heart **1964** Top-notch performances in an unconventional romantic story. Middle-aged small town postmistress Evie Jackson (Page) has a bright outlook on life despite her own loneliness. While she's at a New York convention, she meets roguish traveling salesman, Harvey (Ford), who's just decided he should settle down. So he's become engaged to persuasive widow, Phyllis (Lansbury). Naturally, Harvey and Evie hit it off despite their differences and Harvey realizes he's about to commit to the wrong gal. Title song was Oscar nominated. **114m/B; DVD.** Glenn Ford; Geraldine Page; Angela Lansbury; Michael Anderson, Jr.; Barbara Nichols; Patricia Barry; Richard Deacon; ***D:*** Delbert Mann; ***W:*** Tad Mosel; ***C:*** Russell Harlan; ***M:*** Henry Mancini.

Dear John **2010 (PG-13)** Anyone who has read a Nicholas Sparks novel (or knows what the term "Dear John letter" means) knows that this tearjerker likely won't end well. John (Tatum) is a soldier on leave who meets the vacationing Savannah (Seyfried) in the spring of 2001. They immediately fall in love, as tragic romantics are prone to do. They promise to write each other letters until they can reunite. After the 9/11 attacks, John is compelled to re-enlist over and over. Plot lines involving autism and cancer are also thrown in just in case things aren't sad enough for the viewer. Tatum and Seyfried perform well, but this is really only for those looking for a good cry. **105m/C; Blu-Ray, On Demand.** Channing Tatum; Amanda Seyfried; Henry Thomas; Keith D. Robinson; Richard Jenkins; D.J. Cotrona; Cullen Moss; Gavin McCulley; ***D:*** Lasse Hallstrom; ***W:*** Jamie Linden; ***C:*** Terry Stacey; ***M:*** Deborah Lurie.

Dear Lemon Lima ½ **2009 (PG-13)** Quirky, 13-year-old, half-Eskimo Vanessa Lemor lives in Fairbanks, Alaska and has an imaginary confidante she writes to in her diary. Snobbish ex-boyfriend Philip attends a private school and Vanessa manages to get a scholarship so she can win him back. Instead, she's cast with the social misfits, eventually accepting the challenge of captaining her new friends in the school's snow survival competition—against Philip's team. **87m/C; DVD.** Meaghan Jette Martin; Savanah Wiltfong; Shayne Topp; Zane Huett; Elaine Hendrix; Melissa Leo; Eleanor Hutchins; Beth Grant; ***C:*** Sarah Levy; ***M:*** Sasha Gordon.

Dear Me: A Blogger's Tale **2008** Samantha suffers from a social anxiety disorder that has prevented her from her dream job in advertising. Then she discovers blogging and conveying her anxieties online helps put her in control and obtain a copywriting job. Samantha then falls for VP Desmond and everything is going well until a jealous coworker discovers her blog and it becomes an office sensation—unbeknownst to Samantha. **97m/C; DVD.** Sarah Thompson; David O'Donnell; David DeLuise; Felecia Day; Dan Lauria; Michael Bowen; Jessica Anderson; Caia Coley; Zach Roerig; ***D:*** Michael Feifer; ***W:*** David Hirschmann; Steven Weiss-Smith; ***C:*** Matt Steinauer; ***M:*** Evan Beigel. **VIDEO**

Dear Mr. Prohack ½ **1949** One-joke comedy, based on the Arnold Bennett novel, flounders. Middleclass treasury official Arthur Prohack is a whiz at managing government money as Great Britian is deep in postwar austerity but proves fallible when he unexpectedly inherits a fortune. The windfall causes trouble as he makes unwise investments and his family goes on a spending spree and the fortune proves to be a burden. **90m/B; DVD.** *UK* Cecil Parker; Hermione Baddeley; Dirk Bogarde; Sheila Sim; Glynis Johns; Denholm Elliott; ***D:*** Thornton Freeland; ***W:*** Ian Dalrymple; Donald Bull; ***C:*** H.E. (Henry Edward) Fowle; ***M:*** Temple Abady.

Dear Santa *Secret Santa* **1998 (G)** Unspeakably sappy seasonal supernatural comedy is a low-budget version of "The Santa Claus." Used-car salesman Gordon (Green) is transformed into the red-suited "jolly old elf" and then must fulfill his duties. **87m/C; DVD.** D.L. Green; Debra Rich; Harrison Myers; Richard Gabai; ***D:*** Stewart Peter; ***W:*** Hamilton Underwood; ***C:*** Theo Angell.

Dear Santa **2011** L.A. shopaholic party girl Crystal has until Christmas to change her aimless, frivolous ways or her wealthy parents are going to cut her off financially. When she finds 7-year-old Olivia's letter to Santa asking him to find her widowed dad Derek a new wife, Sarah investigates. Socially-conscious Derek runs a soup kitchen and Sarah volunteers to make herself look good and maybe gain a new beau. Derek's current lady friend Jilian really doesn't like the competition. **90m/C; DVD.** Amy Acker; David Haydn-Jones; Emma Duke; Gina Holden; Brooklynn Proulx; ***D:*** Jason Priestley; ***W:*** Barbara Kymlicka; ***C:*** Dave Vernerey; ***M:*** Mitch Lee. **VIDEO**

Dear Viola ½ **2014** When the advice columnist of her small town newspaper suddenly retires, shy accountant Kate Miner becomes the anonymous 'Dear Viola.' But she gets into trouble when she counsels widower Russ to start dating again and then realizes she's fallen for him herself. **90m/C; DVD.** Kellie Martin; Jefferson Brown; Arnold Pinnock; Adamo Ruggiero; ***D:*** Laurie Lynd; ***W:*** Kathleen McGhee-Anderson; Lee Rose; ***C:*** Russ Goozee. **VIDEO**

Dear Wendy **2005** A misfit gang of teens form, call themselves the Dandies, meet in a dingy mine with their guns and profess their vows of non-violence. Dick thinks Wendy is a toy gun at first, but she's not—and she's got some kind of hold on him. As if things aren't odd enough from the start, the only African American member of the Dandies has a thing for Wendy, making Dick jealous. Is all this going anywhere? Um-...Sure. It all leads to pacifist misfit teens brandishing their beloved handguns. Artsy, unraveling presentation of bizarre images and lost messages. **100m/C; DVD.** *DK FR GE GB* Jamie Bell; Bill Pullman; Michael Angarano; Novella Nelson; Chris Owen; Alison Pill; Mark Webber; Danso Gordon; ***D:*** Thomas Vinterberg; ***W:*** Lars von Trier; ***C:*** Anthony Dod Mantle; ***M:*** Benjamin Wallfisch.

Dear White People **2014 (R)** Simien's satirical drama adds to the conversation about race in unexpected ways. Pushing buttons and hitting issues in a way that's reminiscent of early Spike Lee, the writer/director is one to watch. Four Black students at a fictional Ivy League college deal with a group of white students who throw an "African American" party. The way that racial perception influences behavior has rarely been this interestingly captured. The film isn't perfect but it asks big, hard questions without feeling like it has an agenda. **108m/C; DVD, Blu-Ray.** Tessa Thompson; Brandon Bell; Teyonah Parris; Tyler James Williams; Kyle Gallner; Dennis Haysbert; Peter Syversten; ***D:*** Justin Simien; ***W:*** Justin Simien; ***C:*** Topher Osborn; ***M:*** Kathryn Bostic. Ind. Spirit '15: First Screenplay.

Dear Zachary: A Letter to a Son About His Father **2008** A moving documentary about the power of love and family even in the face of an unexpected death. Medical resident Andrew Bagby is murdered in 2001. Shortly thereafter, his ex-girlfriend, with whom he had broken up right before before his demise and who was his killer, finds out she is pregnant. A close friend of Bagby, filmmaker Kurt Kuenne begins making this film to share Bagby's life with his son, Zachary. The film follows the trial of Bagby's killer, the reaction of his parents to the trial and grandson, and their quest to gain custody of the child amidst a miscarriage of justice. **95m/C; DVD, Blu-Ray.** ***D:*** Kurt Kuenne; ***W:*** Kurt Kuenne; ***C:*** Kurt Kuenne; ***M:*** Kurt Kuenne.

Death Among Friends 🦴 1/2 **1975** Someone doesn't like shady financier Ham Russell Buckner (Balsam) or the people who hang out at his estate. This is apparent to LAPD detective Shirley Ridgeway (Reid) when she has to investigate a murder there and has a lot of suspects to choose from. NBC TV movie that plays like a failed series pilot. **78m/C; DVD.** Kate Reid; Martin Balsam; John Anderson; Jack Cassidy; Lynda Day George; Paul Henreid; William (Bill) Smith; ***D:*** Paul Wendkos; ***W:*** Stanley Ralph Ross; ***C:*** Terry Meade; ***M:*** Jim Helms. **TV**

Death and Cremation 🦴 **2010** Slow-moving horror. Aging recluse Stan (Dourif) lives in a funeral home and offers cremation services. He's actually a sociopath who hates bullies and befriends mistreated misfit teen Jarod (Sumpter), who is prone to making mistakes. A series of disappearances brings Detective Fairchild (Elrod) too close to the truth of just who's being cremated. **93m/C; DVD.** Brad Dourif; Jeremy Sumpter; Scott Elrod; Debbon Ayer; Daniel Baldwin; ***D:*** Justin Steele; ***W:*** Justin Steele; ***C:*** Akis Konstantakopoulos; ***M:*** Keith E. Waggoner. **VIDEO**

Death and Desire 🦴🦴 *Illicit Dreams 2* **1997 (R)** Fashion photographer Jeff Reed isn't tempted by the beautiful models he shoots because he's happily married. But when his wife is killed in an accident, the vulnerable Jeff becomes the target of fashion mag editor, Lynn, who desperately wants to offer him comfort. Too desperately. Soon Lynn's obsessed and Jeff's fighting for his life. Unrated version runs 88 minutes. **84m/C; VHS, DVD.** Tane McClure; Tim Abell; Jennifer Burton; ***D:*** Fred Olen Ray; ***W:*** Steve Armogida; ***C:*** Gary Graver; ***M:*** Bob Kulick. **VIDEO**

The Death and Life of John F. Donovan 🦴 1/2 **2019** Adult Rupert (Schnetzer) relates his fascinating story of his childhood friendship with a star to a reporter (Newton). In flashbacks, these events unfold. Young Rupert (Tremblay) has moved to London with his mother (Portman). The lonely child struggles to fit in and writes a letter one day to his favorite television actor, John F. Donovan (Harrington). John replies and they exchange letters for years as they find common ground and John influences the course of Rupert's life. The first English language film by Dolan features a strong performance by Tremblay and interesting themes but it's a bit messy at its core. **123m/C; DVD.** Natalie Portman; Emily Hampshire; Kit Harington; Jacob Tremblay; Sarah Gadon; ***D:*** Xavier Dolan; ***W:*** Xavier Dolan; ***C:*** Andre Turpin; ***M:*** Gabriel Yared. **VIDEO**

Death and the Maiden 🦴🦴🦴 **1994 (R)** Former political prisoner and torture victim (Weaver) turns the tables on the man she believes was her tormentor 15 years before. Pressing her civil rights lawyer husband (Wilson) into duty as defense attorney, she becomes prosecutor, judge, and jury. The accused (Kingsley) learns the dangers of picking up stranded motorists, as he is bound, gagged, and roughed up by the now empowered and vengeful Paulina. Tense, claustrophobic political thriller features a talented ensemble both on screen and behind the scenes. From the Ariel Dorfman play. **103m/C; VHS, DVD.** Sigourney Weaver; Ben Kingsley; Stuart Wilson; ***D:*** Roman Polanski; ***W:*** Rafael Yglesias; Ariel Dorfman; ***C:*** Tonino Delli Colli; ***M:*** Wojciech Kilar.

Death at a Funeral 🦴🦴 **2007 (R)** Ridiculous situations arise at the funeral of the patriarch of a dysfunctional British family, which brings about a reunion of estranged brothers Daniel (Macfayden) and Robert (Graves). They are also confronted by a blackmailer who's determined to give the family's dirty laundry a good airing, unless they can find a way to stop him. **90m/C; DVD.** *US NL GE* Rupert Graves; Peter Dinklage; Alan Tudyk; Daisy Donovan; Matthew Macfadyen; Ewen Bremner; Peter Vaughan; Keeley Hawes; Andy Nyman; Jane Asher; Kris Marshall; Peter Egan; ***D:*** Frank Oz; ***W:*** Dean Craig; ***C:*** Oliver Curtis; ***M:*** Murray Gold.

Death at a Funeral 🦴🦴 **2010 (R)** A nearly scene-by-scene American remake of the 2007 British comedy does a good job translating the original's absurd, screwball high-jinx for an American audience—though that doesn't translate into funny. The deceased's son, Aaron (Rock), tries to keep his head straight while holding the funeral for his father at home. The cadaver has as many misadventures as the oddball guests (a misused wide array of well-known and talented actors). Shocking family secrets are eventually exposed, leading to blackmail and a missing corpse. **92m/C; Blu-Ray, On Demand.** Chris Rock; Tracy Morgan; Martin Lawrence; Loretta Devine; Ron Glass; Danny Glover; Regina Hall; James Marsden; Zoe Saldana; Columbus Short; Kevin Hart; Luke Wilson; Peter Dinklage; Keith David; ***D:*** Neil LaBute; ***W:*** Chris Rock; Dean Craig; ***C:*** Rogier Stoffers; ***M:*** Christophe Beck.

Death at Love House 🦴 1/2 **1975** A screenwriter becomes obsessed when he is hired to write the life story of a long dead silent movie queen. Filmed at the Harold Lloyd estate. **74m/C; VHS, DVD.** Robert Wagner; Kate Jackson; Sylvia Sidney; Joan Blondell; John Carradine; ***D:*** E.W. Swackhamer. **TV**

Death Becomes Her 🦴🦴🦴 **1992 (PG-13)** Aging actress Streep will do anything to stay young and beautiful, especially when childhood rival Hawn shows up, 200 pounds lighter and out to revenge the loss of her fiance, Streep's henpecked hubby. Doing anything arrives in the form of a potion that stops the aging process (and keeps her alive forever). Watch for the hilarious party filled with dead celebrities who all look as good as the day they died. Great special effects and fun performances by Streep and Hawn playing their glamour-girl roles to the hilt add merit to this biting commentary on Hollywood's obsession with beauty and youth. **105m/C; VHS, DVD, Blu-Ray.** Meryl Streep; Bruce Willis; Goldie Hawn; Isabella Rossellini; Sydney Pollack; Michael Caine; Ian Ogilvy; Adam Storke; Nancy Fish; Alaina Reed Hall; Michelle Johnson; Mimi Kennedy; Jonathan Silverman; Mary Ellen Trainor; ***Cameo(s):*** Fabio; ***D:*** Robert Zemeckis; ***W:*** Martin Donovan; David Koepp; ***C:*** Dean Cundey; ***M:*** Alan Silvestri. Oscars '92: Visual FX.

Death Before Dishonor 🦴 1/2 **1987 (R)** Formula actioner stars Dryer as a tough Marine sergeant who battles ruthless Middle Eastern terrorists after they slaughter his men and kidnap his commanding officer (Keith). **95m/C; VHS, DVD.** Fred (John F.) Dryer; Brian Keith; Joanna Pacula; Paul Winfield; ***D:*** Terry J. Leonard; ***W:*** John Gatliff; ***C:*** Don Burgess; ***M:*** Brian May.

Death Blow 🦴 1/2 **1987 (R)** The victims of a violent rapist team together to stop the criminal after he repeatedly skirts conviction. **90m/C; VHS, DVD.** Martin Landau; Frank Stallone; Jerry Van Dyke; Terry Moore; Henry Darrow; Jack Carter; Peter Lapis; Don Swayze; Donna Denton; ***D:*** Raphael Nussbaum.

Death by Dialogue 🦴 **1988 (R)** Muddled story of some teenagers who discover an old film script from a project never produced because it was haunted by tragic accidents. **90m/C; VHS, DVD.** Laura Albert; Ken Sagoes; ***D:*** Tom Dewier.

Death Collector 🦴 1/2 **1989 (R)** In the future when insurance companies run the world, if you don't pay your premium, you die. **90m/C; VHS, DVD.** Daniel Chapman; Ruth (Coreen) Collins; ***D:*** Tom Gniazdowski.

Death Comes to Pemberley 🦴🦴 1/2 **2013** TV adaptation of the P.D. James mystery that's a continuation of Jane Austen's "Pride & Prejudice." Six years into their marriage, Darcy and Elizabeth are confronted by a murder occurring in the nearby woods. The accused killer is caddish brother-in-law George Wickham, who expects Darcy to make certain he doesn't hang. Secrets prevail and tensions cause a strain on the Darcy's marriage. Darcy's pompous, Elizabeth's bedraggled, and the story is surprisingly dull until its last moments. **180m/C; DVD, Blu-Ray.** *UK* Matthew Rhys; Anna Maxwell Martin; Matthew Goode; Eleanor Tomlinson; Jenna-Louise Coleman; Trevor Eve; Tom Ward; James Norton; ***D:*** Daniel Percival; ***W:*** Juliette Towhidi; ***C:*** Steve Lawes. **TV**

The Death Curse of Tartu WOOF! **1966** Another aspiring cult classic. (Read: A low-budget flick so bad it's funny). Students accidentally disturb the burial ground of an Indian medicine man who comes to zombie-like life with a deadly prescription. **84m/C; VHS, DVD.** Fred Pinero; Doug Hobart; Babette Sherrill; Mayra Christine; Bill Marcos; Sherman Hayes; Gary Holtz; Frank Weed; ***D:*** William Grefe; ***W:*** William Grefe; ***C:*** Julio Chavez; ***M:*** Al Greene; Al Jacobs.

Death Defying Acts 🦴🦴 1/2 **2007 (PG)** Famed magician Harry Houdini (Pearce) is touring Edinburgh in 1926, offering a large monetary incentive to any medium who can channel his late mother. Mary McGarvie (Zeta-Jones) and her tomboy daughter Benji (Ronan) fake a music-hall psychic act and she wants the dough, despite knowing Houdini is an expert at exposing fakes. However, Harry becomes romantically interested in the attractive Mary and she starts developing a conscience. The leads look good but don't have much romantic chemistry. **97m/C; DVD.** *GB AU* Guy Pearce; Catherine Zeta-Jones; Saoirse Ronan; Timothy Spall; ***D:*** Gillian Armstrong; ***W:*** Tony Grisoni; Brian Ward; ***C:*** Haris Zambarloukos; ***M:*** Cezary Skubiszewski.

Death Do Us Part 🦴🦴 **2014 (R)** This psychological horror explores what happens when a pre-wedding party takes a very dark turn. Before the nuptials of Ryan Harris (Benson) and Kennedy Jamieson (Benson), the best man Chet (Cassie) hosts a combined bachelor/bachelorette party at a remote cabin. Though the weekend should be fun, events take a more negative turn when secrets and taboos reach the light of day resulting in the ruining of many friendships. The weekend takes a deadly turn when an unknown killer starts killing each party goer by turn, further making what should be a memorable celebration into a nightmare. **89m/C; DVD, Blu-Ray, Download.** Julia Benson; Peter Benson; Emilie Ullerup; Christine Chatelain; Kyle Cassie; ***D:*** Nicholas Humphries; ***W:*** Julia Benson; Peter Benson; Ryan Copple; ***C:*** Christopher Charles Kempinski; ***M:*** Kim Oxlund. **VIDEO**

Death Feud 🦴 **1989** A man tries to save the woman he loves from her former pimp. Not much to recommend this one, unless you like relatives of more famous actors. **98m/C; VHS, DVD.** Karen Mayo-Chandler; Chris Mitchum; Frank Stallone; ***D:*** Carl Monson.

Death Force 🦴 1/2 **1978 (R)** When a Vietnam veteran comes to New York City, he becomes a hitman for the Mafia. **90m/C; VHS, DVD.** Jayne Kennedy; Leon Isaac Kennedy; James Iglehart; Carmen Argenziano; ***D:*** Cirio H. Santiago.

Death from a Distance 🦴 1/2 **1936** A reporter and a detective put the moves on a group of astronomers who may be responsible for a murder. **73m/B; VHS, DVD.** Russell Hopton; Lola Lane; George F. Marion, Sr.; John St. Polis; Lee Kohlmar; Lew Kelly; Wheeler Oakman; Robert Frazer; Cornelius Keefe; ***D:*** Frank Strayer.

Death Game 🦴 1/2 *The Seducers* **1977 (R)** George Manning (Cassel) has just turned 40, and his wife and kids have left town for the weekend. Two crazed lesbian teenagers immediately descend on his house, offer him sex, then go psycho and trash the place after tying him up and threatening to murder him at dawn. One has to wonder if they arrived as random coincidence or if George should be a little more suspicious of his wife. **92m/C; DVD.** Sondra Locke; Colleen Camp; Seymour Cassel; Beth Brickell; ***D:*** Peter S. Traynor; ***W:*** Anthony Overman; ***C:*** David Worth; ***M:*** Jimmie Haskell.

Death Games 🦴 1/2 *Final Cut* **1980** Two young men shooting a documentary about an influential music promoter ask too many wrong questions, causing the powers-that-be to want them out of the picture for good. **78m/C; VHS, DVD.** Lou Brown; David Clendenning; Jennifer Cluff; ***D:*** Ross Dimsey; ***W:*** Ross Dimsey; ***C:*** Ron Johanson; ***M:*** Howard J. Davidson.

Death Games 🦴🦴 **2002** Killer (Barry) leaves behind his native Ireland and tours Europe with a 'heavy metal circus' that relies on gladiatorial events including chainsaw-wielding bikers. He falls in love with one of the performers and would like to settle down with her, but first they have to get the tyrannical circus boss' permission to do so. Interestingly, the filmmakers compare it to a modern interpretation of "Romeo & Juliet." **85m/C; DVD.** Jason Barry; Peter Lohmeyer; Phelim Drew; Tara Lynn O'Neill; Donncha Crowley; Ned Dennehy; Lindsey Harris; Tommy O'Neill; Caitriona Ni Mhurchu; Jay Ledesama; Elvis Sebastian; Colm O'Maonlai; Michelle Bibbi; Emma Lowe; ***D:*** Geraldine Creed; ***W:*** Geraldine Creed; ***C:*** Markus Fraunholz; ***M:*** David A. Stewart; Stephen McLaughlin.

Death Has a Bad Reputation 🦴 1/2 **1990** Terrorist Carlos the Jackal is spotted in Rome by journalist Julia Latham. British agent Sam McCready is particularly interested since his son Nick was badly injured in one of the Jackal's bombings and Sam wants him captured or dead. Based on a Frederick Forsyth story. **98m/C; DVD.** *UK* Alan Howard; Elizabeth Hurley; Tony Lo Bianco; Gottfried John; Guy Scantlebury; ***D:*** Lawrence Gordon Clark; ***W:*** Murray Smith; ***C:*** Cristiano Pogany; ***M:*** Paul Chihara. **TV**

Death House 🦴 1/2 **1988** Derek Keillor is on Death Row at Townsend State Prison when he discovers a plot to use inmates for scientific experiments in biological warfare. He decides the best way to get out is to volunteer, which means convincing the man who put him in prison that they're now on the same side. **92m/C; VHS, DVD.** Dennis Cole; Anthony (Tony) Franciosa; Michael Pataki; John Saxon; ***D:*** John Saxon.

Death Hunt 🦴🦴 **1981 (R)** A man unjustly accused of murder pits his knowledge of the wilderness against the superior numbers of his pursuers. **98m/C; VHS, DVD, Blu-Ray.** Charles Bronson; Lee Marvin; Ed Lauter; Andrew Stevens; Carl Weathers; Angie Dickinson; ***D:*** Peter Hunt; ***W:*** Mark Victor; Michael Grais.

A Death in California 🦴🦴 **1985** Hope Masters (Ladd) is a Beverly Hills mom, with a co-dependent personality, who is raped and threatened by sociopath Jordan Williams (Elliott). She is then manipulated into believing his lies so that he becomes part of her life which eventually leads to their arrest and trial for her fiance's murder. Elliott's vain would-be charmer is chilling but the behavior of Ladd's character is generally inexplicable and you're left with more questions than answers. Based on a true story; adapted from the Joan Barthel book. **188m/C; DVD.** Cheryl Ladd; Sam Elliott; Alexis Smith; Fritz Weaver; John Aston; Barry Corbin; Jim Haynie; Kerrie Keane; Granville Van Dusen; ***D:*** Delbert Mann; ***W:*** E. Jack Neuman; ***C:*** Joseph Biroc; ***M:*** John Cacavas. **TV**

Death in Love 🦴 1/2 **2008 (R)** Don't you hate it when the writer/director makes his characters into some weird archetypes that can't even have names? A young Jewish woman in a concentration camp survives by having a sexual relationship with a Nazi doctor that warps her for life. Immigrating to the United States, she turns into a harpy (Bisset) who emotionally stunts her two sons. The elder (Lucas) is promiscuous and is involved in sado/masochistic sex with his boss while the younger (Haas) isolates himself in his apartment. Everything feels very stagy and awkward. English, French, and German with subtitles. **97m/C; DVD.** Jacqueline Bisset; Josh(ua) Lucas; Lukas Haas; Emma Bell; Adam Brody; Carrington Vilmont; Vanessa Kai; ***D:*** Boaz Yakin; ***W:*** Boaz Yakin; ***C:*** Frederik Jacobi; ***M:*** Lesley Barber.

Death in Small Doses 🦴 1/2 **1957** Drab, matter-of-fact crime drama. FDA agent Tom Kayler (Graves) goes undercover to bust an amphetamine operation involving long-haul trucking. Kayler's doped-up partner Mink (Connors) takes him to his dealer and that leads to murder. **79m/B; DVD.** Peter Graves; Chuck Connors; Merry Anders; Mala Powers; ***D:*** Joseph M. Newman; ***W:*** John McGreevey; ***C:*** Carl Guthrie; ***M:*** Emil Newman.

A Death in the Family 🦴🦴 1/2 **2002** Adaptation of James Agee's Pulitzer Prize-winning novel, set in Knoxville in 1915. Title tells you the tragedy that's about to befall the loving family of May (Gish) and Jay (Slattery) Follet when Jay is killed in an auto accident. It's up to the grieving May to cope and to tell their 7-year-old son Rufus (Wolff) that his father is dead. **90m/C; VHS, DVD.** Annabeth Gish; John Slattery; James Cromwell; Austin Wolff; Kathleen Chalfant; Bill Raymond; David Alford; Christopher Strand; ***D:*** Gilbert Cates; ***W:*** Robert W. Lenski; ***C:*** Stephen M. Katz; ***M:*** Charles Fox. **TV**

Death in the Garden 🦴🦴 *La Mort en Ce Jardin; Evil Eden* **1956** Surreal film, filled with symbolism, about a group of French people, living in a South American settlement, who must flee a riot between soldiers and striking miners. Local adventurer, Chark (Marchal), agrees to lead them to safety but their trek through the jungle is fraught with peril (and not just from the animal life). French with subtitles. **90m/C; VHS, DVD, Blu-Ray.** *MX FR* Georges Marchal; Simone Signoret; Charles Vanel; Michele Girardon; Michel Piccoli; Tito Junco; ***D:*** Luis Bunuel; ***W:*** Luis Bunuel; Luis Alcoriza; Raymond Queneau; ***C:*** Jorge Stahl, Jr.; ***M:*** Paul Misraki.

Death in Venice 🦴🦴🦴 1/2 *Morte a Venezia* **1971 (PG)** A lush, decadent adaptation of the Thomas Mann novella about a aging, jaded, and dying composer Gustav von Aschenbach (Bogarde)?here suggested to be Gustav Mahler—who is plagued by fears that he can no longer feel anything. Instead, he becomes tragically obsessed with ideal beauty as personified in the young boy, Tadzio (Andresen). Visconti uses Mahler's 3rd and 5th symphonies to haunting effect. **124m/C; VHS, DVD, Blu-Ray.** *IT* Dirk Bogarde; Mark Burns; Bjorn Andresen; Marisa Berenson; Silvana Mangano; ***D:*** Luchino Visconti; ***W:*** Luchino Visconti; Nicola Badalucco; ***C:*** Pasqualino De Santis.

Death is Nimble, Death is Quick 🦴🦴 *Kommissar X-Drei gelbe Katzen* **1967** Currently only available as part of a collection, this Eurospy take on the James Bond films present a pair of American agents hired to protect a wealthy woman from bad guys in the jungle. Along the way you get to see karate fights, jungle animals, and mad scientists experimenting with diseases. **95m/C; DVD.** *AT FR IT* Tony Kendall; Brad Harris; Ann Smyrner; Dan Vadis; Siegfried Rauch; Philippe Lemaire; Erno Crisa; Rudolf Zehetgruber; H.D. Kulatunga; Michele Mahaut; A. Jayarati; Paul Beckmann; Joe Abey; Chandrika "Champa" Liyanage; ***D:*** Rudolf Zehetgruber; Gianfranco Parolini; ***W:*** Rudolf Zehetgruber; Paul Alfred Muller; ***C:*** Klaus Von Rautenfeld; ***M:*** Gino Marinuzzi, Jr.

Death Journey 🦴 1/2 **1976 (R)** Producer and director Williamson portrays private eye Jesse Crowder, hired by the New York D.A. to escort a key witness cross-country. A regular Williamsonfest. **90m/C; VHS, DVD.** Fred Williamson; D'Urville Martin; Bernie Kuby; Heidi Dobbs; Stephanie Faulkner; ***D:*** Fred Williamson.

Death Kappa 🦴 **2010** Terrorists trying to create bio-engineered aquatic super soldiers based on the legendary Kappa draw the attention of an actual Kappa, and the giant monster fight is on. **90m/C; DVD, Blu-Ray.** *JP* Hideaki Anno; ***D:*** Tomoo Haraguchi; ***W:*** Masakazu Migita; ***C:*** Yoshihito Takahashi. **VIDEO**

The Death Kiss 🦴🦴 1/2 **1933** Creepy thriller about eerie doings at a major Hollywood film studio where a sinister killer does away with his victims while a cast-of-thousands movie spectacular is in production. **72m/B; VHS, DVD, Blu-Ray.** Bela Lugosi; David Manners; Adrienne Ames; Edward Van Sloan; Vince Barnett; ***D:*** Edwin L. Marin.

Death Kiss 🦴 1/2 **1974 (R)** When a man hires a psychopath to murder his wife, his plan doesn't proceed exactly as expected. **90m/C; VHS, DVD.** *GR* Larry Daniels; Dorothy Moore; ***D:*** Costas Karagiannis.

Death Machine 🦴 1/2 **1995 (R)** New company exec Hayden Cale (Pouget) uncovers questionable scientific project at weapons technology company and scientist in charge Jack Dante (Dourif) decides to get even by testing his death machine, which works by sensing fear, in corporate headquarters. **99m/C; VHS, DVD.** Brad Dourif; Ely Pouget; William Hootkins; ***D:*** Stephen Norrington; ***W:*** Stephen Norrington; ***C:*** John de Borman.

Death Machines 🦴 1/2 **1976 (R)** Young karate student must face the "Death Machines," a team of deadly assassins who are trained to kill on command. **93m/C; VHS, DVD, Blu-Ray.** Ron Marchini; Michael Chong; Joshua Johnson; ***D:*** Paul Kyriazi.

Death Mask 🦴🦴 1/2 **1998** Screenwriter, executive producer, and star James Best plays Wilbur Johnson, a vengeful carnival worker who was abused and disfigured as a child. He becomes friends with Angel (Linnea Quigley), a sideshow dancer. After hearing Wilbur's story, she takes him to the swamp, where he meets a witch (Brigitte Hill), who gives him the titular "Death Mask." It causes violent and painful death to Wilbur's enemies when he dons the mask, so Wilbur goes on a killing spree. Then it's up to Angel to convince him to stop. Best hams it up in every scene and Quigley proves that she's still willing to take her clothes off whenever necessary. The film doesn't aim to be anything more than campy fun, and on that point, it delivers. **97m/C; DVD.** James Best; Linnea Quigley; Brigitte Hill; ***D:*** Steve Latshaw; ***W:*** James Best.

The Death Merchant 🦴 **1991** Foundering attempt at a nuclear thriller. A modern mad man hopes to sell a computer chip to third world countries but is thwarted by a secret agent. Confusing, illogical plot highlighted by mediocre performances. **90m/C; VHS, DVD.** Lawrence Tierney; Martina Castle; Melody Munyan; Monica Schnarre; ***D:*** James R. Winburn; ***W:*** Kari Holman.

Death Merchants 🦴 *Tod eines Fremden; Death of a Stranger; The Execution; The Mad Killers; The Death Merchants; The Spy Who Never Was* **1973** Arthur Hersfeld (Kruger) is a Jew of German descent who is mistaken for an Israeli secret agent by Arab terrorists while on a business trip. They assign an agent named Amina (Almagor) to track him, and she ends up dating him to make it easier. Just about the time they fall in love her superiors order her to execute him, proving that once again the greatest obstacle to a successful relationship is your significant other's family. **92m/C; DVD.** *GE IS* Hardy Kruger; Jason Robards, Sr.; Gila Almagor; ***D:*** Reza Badiyi; Uri Massad; ***W:*** Carjen Alexis; Paule Hennge; ***C:*** Tomislav Pinter; ***M:*** Hans-Martin Majewski.

Death Note 🦴🦴🦴 *Desu Noto* **2006** The God of Death has become bored with eternal existence, and has given the Death Note (a book that kills anyone whose name is written in it) to a mortal boy named Light Yagami (Fujiwara). An aspiring law student, Light immediately goes off the deep-end and uses the book to kill all the criminals in the world, earning him the displeasure of the police. They use a detective code named L (Ken'ichi Matsuyama) to track him down, hoping that he can find out who Light is before Light discovers L's true identity. **125m/C; DVD.** *JP* Tatsuya Fujiwara; Ken'ichi Matsuyama; Asako Seto; Shigeki Hosokawa; Erika Toda; Shunji Fujimura; Takeshi Kaga; Yu Kashii; ***V:*** Shusuke (Shu) Kaneko; Shiro Nakamura; ***W:*** Tsugumi Oba; Takeshi Obata; Tetsuya Oishi; ***C:*** Hiroshi Takase; ***M:*** Kenji Kawai.

Death Note 2: The Last Name 🦴🦴 1/2 *Death Note The Last Name; Desu Noto: The Last Name* **2007** Set directly after the events of the first movie, Light (Fujiwara) slides into darkness, using the Death Note to kill whomever he pleases as opposed to criminals. Even worse, another Death God has appeared and given a second Death Note to an emotionally unstable television personality who happens to be a fan of his killings, and she has volunteered to help him find L once and for all. Purists will be upset that this film deviates from the manga and anime a bit. **139m/C; DVD.** *JP* Shin Shimizu; Shigeki Hosokawa; Tatsuya Fujiwara; Ken'ichi Matsuyama; Erika Toda; Takeshi Kaga; ***V:*** Shiro Nakamura; ***D:*** Shusuke (Shu) Kaneko; ***W:*** Tsugumi Oba; Takeshi Obata; Tetsuya Oishi; ***C:*** Kenji Takama; ***M:*** Kenji Kawai.

Death Note 3: L Change the World 🦴 1/2 *L Change the World* **2008** Detective L (Matsuyama) has finally solved his case, but as a result of events in the second film, his time has grown short. He has a mere 23 days to stop a bio-terrorist from destroying the world by unleashing a horrible virus. It's a departure from the Death Note comics and anime storyline, and unfortunately not a good one though it's also not a stand-alone storyline, so viewers who haven't seen the first two films will be lost. **129m/C; DVD.** *JP* Tatsuya Fujiwara; Ken'ichi Matsuyama; Asako Seto; Shigeki Hosokawa; Erika Toda; Takeshi Kaga; Shunji Fujimura; Sota Aoyama; Hirohoshi Kobayashi; ***V:*** Shiro Nakamura; ***D:*** Hideo Nakata; ***W:*** Tsugumi Oba; Hideo Nakata; Takeshi Obata; Kiyomi Fujii; Hirohoshi Kobayashi; ***C:*** Tokusho Kikumura; ***M:*** Kenji Kawai.

Death of a Centerfold 🦴🦴 **1981** Drama based on the life and tragic death of Playboy model and actress Dorothy Stratten. More effectively handled in Bob Fosse's "Star 80." **96m/C; VHS, DVD.** Jamie Lee Curtis; Bruce Weitz; Robert Reed; Mitchell Ryan; Bibi Besch; ***D:*** Gabrielle Beaumont.

Death of a Gunfighter 🦴🦴 **1969 (PG)** A western town courting eastern investors and bankers seeks a way to kill their ex-gunslinger sheriff. **94m/C; VHS, DVD.** Richard Widmark; Lena Horne; Carroll O'Connor; John Saxon; Larry Gates; David Opatoshu; Kent Smith; Dub Taylor; Jacqueline Scott; Darleen Carr; Morgan Woodward; Michael McGreevey; Royal Dano; Kathleen Freeman; Harry Carey, Jr.; Victor French; ***D:*** Robert Totten; Donald Siegel; ***W:*** Joseph Calvelli; ***C:*** Andrew Jackson.

Death of a Nation 🦴 1/2 **2018 (PG-13)** A provocative documentary by conservative commentator D'Souza that argues that President Donald J. Trump is the modern-day equivalent of President Abraham Lincoln. Focusing specifically on slavery and the Civil War, the filmmaker asserts that the Democrats are responsible for both and that their ideas influenced Adolf Hitler. The film also explores the 2016 presidential election, D'Souza's belief that Republicans are the true anti-racists, unlike their Democratic counterparts, and that such truths about history are being kept from the American people. Full of reenactments and interviews, the film's quality is as misguided as the arguments it makes. **108m/C; DVD.** Dinesh D'Souza; ***D:*** Dinesh D'Souza; Bruce Schooley; ***W:*** Dinesh D'Souza; Bruce Schooley; ***M:*** Dennis McCarthy.

Death of a Salesman 🦴🦴🦴 **1951** Screen adaptation of Arthur Miller's Pulitzer Prize-winning play has Fredric March superbly playing the failure and lament of Loman along with a first-rate supporting cast. Classic must see cinema. **115m/B; VHS, DVD.** Fredric March; Mildred Dunnock; Kevin McCarthy; Cameron Mitchell; ***D:*** Laszlo Benedek; ***W:*** Stanley Roberts; ***C:*** Franz Planer; ***M:*** Alex North. **VIDEO**

Death of a Salesman 🦴🦴🦴 1/2 **1986** A powerful adaptation of the famous Arthur Miller play. Hoffman won an Emmy (as did Malkovich) for his stirring portrayal of Willy Loman, the aging salesman who realizes he's past his prime and tries to come to grips with the life he's wasted and the family he's neglected. Reid also turns in a fine performance as his long-suffering wife. **135m/C; VHS, DVD, Blu-Ray.** Dustin Hoffman; John Malkovich; Charles Durning; Stephen Lang; Kate Reid; Louis Zorich; ***D:*** Volker Schlondorff; ***C:*** Michael Ballhaus; ***M:*** Alex North. **TV**

Death of a Scoundrel 🦴🦴 1/2 *Loves of a Scoundrel* **1956** A womanizing stock market speculator is murdered and the culprit could be any one of his many jealous romantic conquests. Excellent pacing and cinematography, and a solid performance by lead Sanders, help cover for a tiny budget. **119m/B; VHS, DVD.** George Sanders; Zsa Zsa Gabor; Yvonne De Carlo; Victor Jory; Nancy Gates; Coleen Gray; John Hoyt; Werner Klemperer; ***D:*** Charles Martin; ***W:*** Charles Martin; ***C:*** James Wong Howe; ***M:*** Max Steiner.

The Death of Adolf Hitler 🦴🦴 1/2 **1984** Depicts Hitler's last ten days in an underground bunker. Drug-addled, suicidal, and Eva Braun-haunted, he receives the news of the fall of the Third Reich. While the film avoids cliche, it lacks emotional depth. **107m/C; VHS, DVD.** *GB* Frank Finlay; Caroline Mortimer; ***D:*** Rex Firlin. **TV**

The Death of Dick Long 🦴🦴 1/2 **2019 (R)** After band practice, three friends, Zeke (Abbott), Earl (Hyland), and Dick (Scheinert), have fun in their small Alabama town by drinking and setting off fireworks. Events take a turn, and panicked Zeke and Earl drive a blood-covered Dick to the hospital and dump him without his wallet. Dick dies of his horrific injuries, setting off an investigation by the local sheriff (Cochrane) and making Zeke and Earl maniacally paranoid as they try to control their fates. The situation is absurd but the hilarity is complex making this agreeable viewing in its own special way. **100m/C; DVD, Blu-Ray.** Michael Abbott, Jr.; Virginia Newcomb; Andre Hyland; Sarah Baker; Jess Weixler; ***D:*** Daniel Scheinert; ***W:*** Billy Chew; ***C:*** Ashley Connor; ***M:*** Andy Hull; Robert McDowell.

The Death of Mr. Lazarescu 🦴🦴 *Moartea Domnului Lazarescu* **2005 (R)** The title character (Fiscutenau) is a grubby 62-year-old widower living in a shabby apartment with a lot of cats. After suffering head and stomach pains all day, he finally calls for help. Medic Mioara (Gheorghiu) and the ambulance driver eventually arrive and the dying man is trundled from one over-crowded hospital to another to be seen by one over-worked and/or indifferent doctor after another. He gets sicker and weaker until someone finally pays attention. This all takes a very, very long time and the message seems to be don't get seriously sick in Bucharest. Inspired by an actual 1997 incident; Romanian with subtitles. **154m/C; DVD.** *RO* Luminita Gheorghiu; Ion Fiscuteanu; Gabriel Spahiu; Doru Ana; Dana Dogaru; Florin Zamfirescu; ***D:*** Cristi Puiu; ***W:*** Cristi Puiu; Razvan Radulescu; ***C:*** Oleg Mutu; ***M:*** Andreea Paduraru.

The Death of Richie 🦴🦴 *Richie* **1976** Gazzara does a fine job as a father driven to kill his drug-addicted teenage son, portrayed by Benson. Occasionally lapses into melodrama, but all-in-all a decent adaptation of Thomas Thompson's book "Richie," which was based on a true story. **97m/C; VHS, DVD.** Ben Gazzara; Robby Benson; Eileen Brennan; Clint Howard; ***D:*** Paul Wendkos. **TV**

The Death of Stalin 🦴🦴🦴 *La Morte de Staline* **2017 (R)** A hilarious satire about the death of Soviet dictator Joseph Stalin and the subsequent jockeying for power among his scheming cronies. An ensemble cast and witty script deliver an intelligent and delightful farce lambasting government bureaucracy. Based on Fabien Nury's 2010 graphic novel of the same name. **106m/C; DVD, Streaming.** *BE FR UK* Steve Buscemi; Jeffrey Tambor; Simon Russell Beale; Paddy Considine; Rupert Friend; ***D:*** Armando Iannucci; ***W:*** Armando Iannucci; David Schneider; Ian Martin; ***C:*** Zac Nicholson; ***M:*** Christopher Willis.

The Death of the Heart 🦴 **1987** Dreary Granada TV adaptation of the Elizabeth Bowen novel set in 1937 London. Orphaned 16-year-old Portia is sent to live with her barely known half-brother Thomas and his brittle wife Anna. The sophisticated Anna is bored by the naïve, awkward Portia and takes to reading her diary to figure the girl out. This leads to mistaken assumptions and social faux pas on Portia's part, resulting in a broken heart. An abrupt ending doesn't help with plot confusion. **109m/C; DVD.** *UK* JoJo Cole; Patricia Hodge; Nigel Havers; Daniel Chatto; Wendy Hiller; Robert Hardy; Jonathan Hyde; Miranda Richardson; ***D:*** Peter Hammond; ***W:*** Derek Mahon; ***C:*** Ray Goode; ***M:*** Geoffrey Burgon. **TV**

Death of the Incredible Hulk 🦴 1/2 **1990** Scientist David Banner's new job just may provide the clues for stopping his transformation into the monstrous Incredible Hulk. But first there are terrorists after the Hulk who need to be defeated and Banner's new romance to contend with. **96m/C; VHS, DVD.** Bill Bixby; Lou Ferrigno; Elizabeth (Ward) Gracen; Philip Sterling; ***D:*** Bill Bixby. **TV**

Death on the Nile 🦴🦴 1/2 **1978 (PG)** Agatha Christie's fictional detective, Hercule Poirot, is called upon to interrupt his vacation to uncover who killed an heiress aboard a steamer cruising down the Nile. Ustinov's first stint as the Belgian sleuth. Anthony Powell's costume design won an Oscar. **135m/C; VHS, DVD.** *GB* Peter Ustinov; Jane Birkin; Lois Chiles; Bette Davis; Mia Farrow; David Niven; Olivia Hussey; Angela Lansbury; Jack Warden; Maggie Smith; George Kennedy; Simon MacCorkindale; Harry Andrews; Jon Finch; ***D:*** John Guillermin; ***W:*** Anthony Shaffer; ***C:*** Jack Cardiff; ***M:*** Nino Rota. Oscars '78: Costume Des.; Natl. Bd. of Review '78: Support. Actress (Lansbury).

Death on the Set 🦴 1/2 **1935** Complicated B-thriller. Gangster Cayley Morden (Kendall) is posing as his double, alcoholic film director Charlie Marsh, in order to commit crimes. When Inspector Burford (Marsh) gets too close, Morden murders Marsh and pins the crime on Lady Blanche (Stuart), Marsh's ex-lover whom Morden has been blackmailing over incriminating love letters. The plan goes bad when Morden's moll Laura (Gray) is strangled and Burford is ready to arrest the hood. **72m/B; DVD.** *GB* Henry Kendall; Garry Marsh; Eve Gray; Jeanne Stuart; Adrienne Wilkinson; Robert Nainby; ***D:*** Leslie Hiscott; ***W:*** Michael Barringer; ***C:*** William Luff; Ernest Palmer.

Death Proof 🦴🦴 1/2 *Quentin Tarantino's Death Proof; Grindhouse: Death Proof* **2007** Tarantino's half of the "Grindhouse" double bill features the best and worst of his creative impulses. Q creepily indulges foot and cheerleader fetishes, and overdoses on the dialogue-heavy scenes that have become his stock-in-trade, but in this instance just delay the action that everyone came to see. He pays homage to the slasher drive-in flicks of his youth with this tale of Stuntman Mike (Russell), who stalks his (always female) victims using his souped-up and reinforced muscle cars. The extended, and exciting chase scene that closes the film comes ohsoclose to making up for Tarantino's transgressions that led up to it. It is, in fact, one of the best car chase sequences put to film. **120m/C; DVD, Blu-Ray.** Kurt Russell; Rosario Dawson; Vanessa Ferlito; Sydney Tamiia Poitier; Zoe Bell; Tracie Thoms; Rose McGowan; Jordan Ladd; Mary Elizabeth Winstead; Eli Roth; Omar Doom; Michael Bacall; Jonathan Loughran; Melissa Arcaro; Michael Parks; James Parks; Marley Shelton; Nicky Katt; Quentin Tarantino; ***D:*** Quentin Tarantino; ***W:*** Quentin Tarantino; ***C:*** Quentin Tarantino.

Death Race 🦴 1/2 **2008 (R)** Contrary to its title and theme, not quite a remake of the 1975 cult classic "Death Race 2000," which was great campy, popcorn fun. This time around, in the grim future of 2012, ex-racecar driver and steelworker Jenson Aimes (Statham) is wrongly accused of murdering his wife and is ultimately sentenced to a Death Race, a race to win his freedom or die trying, in which each participant drives souped-up assault vehicles around the prison yard, trying to take out the other guy and avoid booby traps along the way. Looks like a video game, feels like a video game, and surprise, surprise, directed by video-game-to-screen veteran Anderson. The non-stop action would be fun if it weren't so serious. **105m/C; Blu-Ray, On Demand.** Jason Statham; Tyrese Gibson; Ian McShane; Joan Allen; Nathalia Martinez; Max Ryan; Jason Clarke; Frederick Koehler; Jacob Vargas; Justin Mader; Robert LaSardo; ***D:*** Paul W.S. Anderson; ***W:*** Paul W.S. Anderson; ***C:*** Scott Kevan.

Death Race 2 🦴🦴 **2010 (R)** Predictable but high-octane prequel/origin story for mysterious racer Frankenstein. Cop killer Carl Lucas is sent to for-profit prison Terminal Island just as ruthless TV producer September Jones needs a new network reality show. She comes up with a death-match of prisoners driving lethally-equipped vehicles, with the survivor getting his freedom, and Lucas is coerced into driving. **96m/C; DVD, Blu-Ray.** Luke Goss; Lauren Cohan; Sean Bean; Ving Rhames; Danny Trejo; Frederick Koehler; Patrick Lyster; Tanit Phoenix; ***D:*** Roel Reine; ***W:*** Tony Giglio; ***C:*** John McKay; ***M:*** Paul Haslinger. **VIDEO**

Death Race 2000 🦴🦴 1/2 **1975 (R)** In the 21st century, five racing car contenders challenge the national champion of a cross country race in which drivers score points by killing pedestrians. Gory fun. Based on the 1956 story by Ib Melchior, and followed by "Deathsport." **80m/C; VHS, DVD, Blu-Ray.** David Carradine; Simone Griffeth; Sylvester Stallone; Mary Woronov; Roberta Collins; Martin Kove; Louisa Moritz; John Landis; Don Steele; ***D:*** Paul Bartel; ***W:*** Charles B. Griffith; Robert Thom; ***C:*** Tak Fujimoto; ***M:*** Paul Chihara. **TV**

Death Race 3: Inferno 🦴 1/2 *Death Race: Inferno* **2012 (R)** Straight-up action flick that plays like a video game. Convicted killer Carl Lucas (Goss) is the best driver on the prison Death Race circuit. One more win means freedom for himself and his pit crew but everything is stacked against them in a cross-country race across South Africa's Kalahari Desert. **105m/C; DVD, Blu-Ray.** Luke Goss; Ving Rhames; Dougray Scott; Danny Trejo; Frederick Koehler; Tanit Phoenix; ***D:*** Roel Reine; ***W:*** Tony Giglio; ***C:*** Wayne Shields; ***M:*** Trevor Morris. **VIDEO**

Death Racers 🦴 1/2 **2008 (R)** A remake of the old film "Death Race," the Asylum did their typical own version with far more gore, nudity, and profanity than the official remake, "Death Race 2000," and starring hip hop group Insane Clown Posse. A California convict has taken over a prison built on a water treatment plant and has threatened to contaminate the nation's water supply with sarin. Instead of just blowing the place up, the governor sends in four teams of crazed criminals to race them to the death. **90m/C; DVD.** Elissa Dowling; Elina Madison; Jason Ellefson; Damien Puckler; Violent J; Shaggy 2 Dope; Scott Levy aka Raven; Stephen Blackheart; Jonathan Nation; Jennifer Keith; Dustin Fitzsimmons; Caroline Attwood; Koco Limbevski; Monique La Barr; Dean Kreyling; Jesse Pate; Robert Pike Daniel; Mark Hengst; Krystle Connor; John Karyus; Paolo Carascon; Michael R. Rabanera; ***D:*** Roy Knyrim; ***W:*** Roy Knyrim; Andrew Helm; Patrick Tantalo; ***C:*** David Conley.

Death Rage 🦴 1/2 **1977 (R)** A hitman comes out of retirement to handle the toughest assignment he has ever faced: search for and kill the man who murdered his brother. He finds out he's the victim of a Mafia double-cross. **92m/C; VHS, DVD, Blu-Ray.** *IT* Yul Brynner; Martin Balsam; ***D:*** Anthony M. Dawson.

Death Ray 2000 🦴 1/2 *T.R. Sloane* **1981** Bondian superspy T.R. Sloane must search out the whereabouts of a stolen military device that could kill all life on Earth. TV pilot for the series "A Man Called Sloane." **100m/C; VHS, DVD.** Robert F. Logan; Ann Turkel; Maggie Cooper; Dan O'Herlihy; ***D:*** Lee H. Katzin. **TV**

Death Rides a Horse 🦴 1/2 *Da Uomo a Uoma; As Man to Man* **1969** Spaghetti western. As a child, Bill (Law) witnessed his family's murder at the hands of four thieves. It takes 15 years but he's finally riding to get his revenge when Bill crosses paths with gunslinger Ryan (Van Cleef). Ryan's just out of prison after being double-crossed by his partners. Think there's a connection? **114m/C; DVD, Blu-Ray.** *IT* Lee Van Cleef; John Phillip Law; Luigi Pistilli; Mario Brega; Jose Torres; Anthony Dawson; Carla Cassola; ***D:*** Giulio Petroni; ***W:*** Luciano Vincenzoni; ***C:*** Carlo Carlini; ***M:*** Ennio Morricone.

Death Ring 🦴 **1993 (R)** Basic action/martial arts tale about three men who must battle the bad guys to ensure their own survival. **91m/C; VHS, DVD.** Mike Norris; Chad McQueen; Don Swayze; Billy Drago; Isabel Glasser; ***D:*** Robert J. Kizer; ***W:*** George T. LeBrun.

Death Sentence 🦴 1/2 *Murder One* **1974** When a woman juror on a murder case finds out that the wrong man is on trial, she is stalked by the real killer. **74m/C; VHS, DVD.** Cloris Leachman; Laurence Luckinbill; Nick Nolte; William Schallert; ***D:*** E.W. Swackhamer; ***M:*** Laurence Rosenthal. **TV**

Death Sentence 🦴 1/2 **2007 (R)** Nick Hume (Bacon) is a suited exec with a seemingly picture-perfect life: beautiful wife (Preston), two sons, comfortable suburban digs. Out for an evening hockey game, Nick and oldest son Brendan (Lafferty) stop for gas in a seedy neighborhood and, in the blink of an eye, find themselves part of a gang initiation that ends in Brendan's brutal murder at the hands of gangbanger wannabe Joe Darly (O'Leary). Joe's caught, but Nick has his own idea of justice for Joe and his gang, and it doesn't involve a jail cell. Unfortunately the film can't decide if it wants to be a thoughtful melodrama or an overly-violent action thriller, so it misses both targets. Missed opportunities for redemption and social commentary make this just another vigilante shoot-em-up. **105m/C; DVD.** Kevin Bacon; Garrett Hedlund; Kelly Preston; Aisha Tyler; John Goodman; Matt O'Leary; Jordan Garrett; Stuart Lafferty; ***D:*** James Wan; ***W:*** Ian Mackenzie Jeffers; ***C:*** John R. Leonetti; ***M:*** Charlie Clouser.

Death Sport 🦴🦴 **1978 (R)** Another offering from Corman and Carradine follows, but isn't really a sequel of "Death Race 2000." Carradine is Kaz Oshay, leading a band of rebels against organized society. Upon capture Kaz participates in Death Sport, resulting in a show of fighting and motorcycle stunt work. Doesn't live up to the cult hit, but seems to fit into the genre. **83m/C; VHS, DVD.** David Carradine; Claudia Jennings; Richard Lynch; William (Bill) Smithers; Will Walker; David McLean; Jesse Vint; ***D:*** Allan Arkush; Nicholas Niciphor; ***W:*** Donald Stewart; Nicholas Niciphor; ***C:*** Gary Graver; ***M:*** Andrew Stein.

Death Squad WOOF! *2047: Sights of Death* **2014** This all-around embarrassment--lacking any discernible talent behind the camera and just a paycheck for those in front--finds the tyrannical Confederate Central Government controlling the planet. Naturally, there's a rebel agent going to expose them if he can stay alive with their mercenaries hunting him. **89m/C; DVD.** Stephen Baldwin; Rutger Hauer; Daryl Hannah; Michael Madsen; Danny Glover; ***D:*** Alessandro Capone; ***W:*** Tommaso Agnese; Luca D'Alisera; ***C:*** Davide Manca. **VIDEO**

Death Takes a Holiday 🦴🦴🦴 **1934** Death (March) is bored and wonders why humans fear him so much. He takes on human form, pretending to be the handsome Prince Sirki, and becomes a guest of Italian nobleman, Duke Lambert (Standing). He bewilders most, except the lovely Grazia (Venable), who falls in love with him. And when she does, nothing dies because Death is also in love and not attending to business. But Death is also afraid to reveal his true self for fear of repelling her. Based on Alberto Casella's play and the inspiration for the bloated "Meet Joe Black." **79m/B; DVD, Blu-Ray.** Fredric March; Evelyn Venable; Guy Standing; Katherine Alexander; Gail Patrick; Helen Westley; Kent Taylor; Edward Van Sloan; ***D:*** Mitchell Leisen; ***W:*** Maxwell Anderson; Gladys Lehman; Walter Ferris; ***C:*** Charles B(ryant) Lang, Jr.

Death to Smoochy 🦴 **2002 (R)** DeVito-directed dark comedy follows a clash of the clowns: one good and one evil. Rainbow Randolph (Williams), is the corrupt, alcoholic star of a kiddie show fired over a bribery scandal and replaced by his polar opposite: Barney-esque purple rhino good-guy, Smoochy (Norton). Keener is the ruthless Kidsnet exec who takes orders from her fetid network boss (Stewart). Director DeVito doubles as a loathsome agent. Although Norton is proficient as the cloying, wide-eyed kiddie magnet and Williams clearly revels in ranting, this over-the-top to the point of ugliness revenge comedy's one note joke wears thin and behind the scenes kiddie show satire is way less subtle than it needs to be. **109m/C; VHS, DVD.** Robin Williams; Edward Norton; Catherine Keener; Danny DeVito; Jon Stewart; Harvey Fierstein; Michael Rispoli; Pam Ferris; Danny Woodburn; Vincent Schiavelli; ***D:*** Danny DeVito; ***W:*** Adam Resnick; ***C:*** Anastas Michos; ***M:*** David Newman.

Death Toll 🦴 1/2 **2007 (R)** Despite DMX and Lou Diamond Phillips receiving top billing, neither is in this film for more than a few minutes, even though DMX is supposed to be playing a legendary New Orleans drug dealer that a spree of gang killings is being blamed on. The entire plot can be summed up in that sentence. **80m/C; DVD.** Lou Diamond Phillips; Keisha Knight Pulliam; Leila Arcieri; DMX; ***D:*** Phenomenon; ***W:*** Anthony Faia; Dan Garcia; Jason Hewitt; Evan Scott; ***C:*** Michael Campbell.

Death Trance 🦴🦴 1/2 **2005 (R)** In an "unknown place and time" (it appears to be feudal Japan but people have bazookas and motorcycles) a master swordsman searches for the ultimate battle, as no one appears to be able to challenge him anymore. He hears tales of a mysterious coffin holding the body of the Goddess of Destruction who will bring about the Armageddon if she is released. Intrigued, he swipes the coffin, and it quickly becomes a free-for-all as everyone tries to take it from him while he tries to figure out how to open it. You'd think the whole concept of Armageddon would make everyone think twice, but sadly they seem oblivious. **90m/C; DVD, Blu-Ray.** *JP* Tak Sakaguchi; Yuko Takeuchi; Yoko Fujita; Kentaro Seagal; Takamasa Suga; Osamu Takahashi; ***D:*** Yuji Shimomura; ***W:*** Yuji Shimomura; Seiji Chiba; Shinichi Fujita; Junya Kato; ***M:*** Rui Ogawa.

Death Tunnel 🦴 1/2 **2005 (R)** A college freshman initiation gag goes horribly wrong for five women when they are trapped inside a deserted—and haunted—asylum with the only route to safety being an underground tunnel through which scores of deceased patients had once traveled. Filmed at the actual site of the Waverly Hills Sanatorium, which was built in the early 1900s and housed patients suffering from tuberculosis; many local residents were offended about the content of the film. **97m/C; DVD.** Steffany Huckaby; Melanie Lewis; Yolanda Pecoraro; Kristin Novak; Annie Burgstede; ***D:*** Philip Adrian Booth; ***W:*** Philip Adrian Booth; Christopher Saint Booth. **VIDEO**

Death Valley 🦴 1/2 **1981 (R)** Good cast, lousy plot. Youngster (Billingsley) gets caught up with a psycho cowpoke while visiting mom in Arizona. **90m/C; VHS, DVD, Blu-Ray.** Paul LeMat; Catherine Hicks; Peter Billingsley; Wilford Brimley; Edward Herrmann; Stephen McHattie; ***D:*** Dick Richards; ***C:*** Stephen Burum.

Death Valley 🦴 1/2 *Mojave* **2004 (R)** Mindless badass action. Josh (Olsen) is talked into going to a weekend techno rave in the desert by three buddies. But the pals manage to get on the wrong side of the local biker gang and its odious leader Dom (Mihok) and Josh seems to be the only one with the cojones to survive. **95m/C; DVD.** Eric Christian Olsen; Rider Strong; Dash Mihok; Vince Vieluf; Bumper Robinson; Brendan Fletcher; Genevieve Cortese; Wayne Young; ***D:*** David Kebo; Rudi Liden; ***W:*** David Kebo; Rudi Liden; ***C:*** Thomas M. (Tom) Harting; ***M:*** Nathan Barr.

Death Valley: The Revenge of Bloody Bill 🦴 **2004 (R)** Several college students on a road trip are carjacked by drug dealer Earl (Bastien) who takes them to the ghost town of Sunset Valley in search of his missing partner. Seems the town is haunted by the spirit of vengeful Confederate soldier "Bloody Bill" Anderson (Bouvet), who uses zombies to make his guests feel at home. **88m/C; DVD.** Scott Carson; Chelsea Jean; Jeremy Bouvet; Gregory Bastien; Denise Boutte; Matt Marraccini; Steven Glinn; Kandis Erickson; ***D:*** Byron Werner; ***W:*** John Yuan; Matt Yuan; ***C:*** Byron Werner; ***M:*** Ralph Rieckermann.

Death Warmed Up 🦴 1/2 **1985** A crazed brain surgeon turns ordinary people into bloodthirsty mutants, and a small group of young people travel to his secluded island to stop him. **83m/C; VHS, DVD, Blu-Ray.** Michael Hurst; Margaret Umbers; David Letch; ***D:*** David Blyth.

Death Warrant 🦴🦴 **1990 (R)** Van Damme whams and bams a little less than usual in this cop-undercover-in-prison testosterone fest. As a Royal Canadian Mountie undercover in prison—where inmates are perishing under mysterious circumstances—the pectoral-perfect Muscles from Brussels is on the brink of adding two plus two when an inmate transferee threatens his cover. Contains the requisite gratuitous violence, prison bromide, and miscellaneous other Van Dammages. **111m/C; VHS, DVD, Blu-Ray.** Jean-Claude Van Damme; Robert Guillaume; Cynthia Gibb; George Dickerson; Patrick Kilpatrick; ***D:*** Deran Sarafian; ***W:*** David S. Goyer; ***C:*** Russell Carpenter; ***M:*** Gary Chang.

Death Watch 🦴🦴🦴 **1980 (R)** In the future, media abuse is taken to an all time high as a terminally ill woman's last days are secretly filmed by a man with a camera in his head. Intelligent, adult science fiction with an excellent cast. **128m/C; DVD, Blu-Ray.** *FR GE* Romy Schneider; Harvey Keitel; Harry Dean Stanton; Max von Sydow; ***D:*** Bertrand Tavernier; ***W:*** Bertrand Tavernier; David Rayfiel.

Death Will Have Your Eyes 🦴 *La Moglie Giovane; Savage City* **1974** You'll be willing to temporarily give up your sight if it means you don't have to watch this turgid, confusing Italian flick. Newcomer Louisa can't make ends meet in Rome and becomes a hooker who grows to like the money and gifts. A chauffeur sees something he shouldn't have and starts blackmailing her. Italian with subtitles. **97m/C; DVD.** *IT* Marisa Mell; Farley Granger; Helga Line; Riccardo Salvino; ***D:*** Giovanni d'Eramo; ***W:*** Giovanni d'Eramo; ***C:*** Francisco Sempere; ***M:*** Stelvio Cipriani.

Death Wish 🦴🦴 **2018 (R)** A remake of the 1974 Charles Bronson classic that recaptures the macho archetype of vengeful vigilante. Willis plays a gentle surgeon whose wife and daughter are attacked in their home, so he buys a Glock, learns to shoot from YouTube videos, and takes down bad guys in the streets of Chicago. Although its release was delayed by several months following the Las Vegas shootings in October 2017, it's not making any political statement or apologizing for what it is: a satisfying, bloody, revenge flick. **107m/C; DVD, Blu-Ray.** Bruce Willis; Vincent D'Onofrio; Elisabeth Shue; Camila Morrone; Dean Norris; ***D:*** Eli Roth; ***W:*** Joe Carnahan; ***C:*** Rogier Stoffers; ***M:*** Ludwig Göransson.

Death Wish ½ **1974 (R)** Paul Kersey (Bronson) is a middle-aged businessman who turns vigilante after his wife and daughter are raped and left for dead by a gang of hoodlums (one is Goldblum in his film debut). He stalks the streets of New York seeking revenge on other muggers, pimps, and crooks, making the neighborhood safer for those less macho. Brosnan's his usual stoic self and the violence could be deemed excessive—certainly Brian Garfield, whose novel the film is based on, thought so. **93m/C; VHS, DVD, Blu-Ray.** Charles Bronson; Vincent Gardenia; William Redfield; Hope Lange; Jeff Goldblum; Stuart Margolin; Olympia Dukakis; ***D:*** Michael Winner; ***W:*** Wendell Mayes; ***C:*** Arthur Ornitz; ***M:*** Herbie Hancock.

Death Wish 2 WOOF! 1982 (R) Bronson re-creates the role of Paul Kersey, an architect who takes the law into his own hands when his family is victimized once again. Extremely violent sequel to the successful 1974 movie. Followed by "Death Wish 3" (1985) and 4 (1987) in which Bronson continues to torture the street scum and the viewers as well. **89m/C; VHS, DVD, Blu-Ray.** Charles Bronson; J.D. Cannon; Jill Ireland; Vincent Gardenia; Anthony (Tony) Franciosa; Laurence Fishburne; ***D:*** Michael Winner; ***C:*** Richard H. Kline; ***M:*** Jimmy Page.

Death Wish 3 ½ **1985 (R)** Once again, Charles Bronson blows away the low lifes who have killed those who were dear to him and were spared in the first two films. **100m/C; VHS, DVD, Blu-Ray.** Charles Bronson; Martin Balsam; Deborah Raffin; Ed Lauter; Alex Winter; Marina Sirtis; ***D:*** Michael Winner; ***M:*** Jimmy Page.

Death Wish 4: The Crackdown **1987 (R)** The four-times-weary urban vigilante hits crack dealers this time, hard. **100m/C; VHS, DVD, Blu-Ray.** Charles Bronson; John P. Ryan; Kay Lenz; Danny (Daniel) Webb; ***D:*** J. Lee Thompson.

Death Wish 5: The Face of Death WOOF! 1994 (R) Paul Kersey (Bronson) returns to vigilantism when his clothing manufacturer fiancee Olivia (Downs) has her business threatened by mobsters, one of whom turns out to be her sadistic ex (Parks). Bronson looks bored with the rehashed material. Lots of explicit and grisly violence. **95m/C; VHS, DVD.** Charles Bronson; Lesley-Anne Down; Michael Parks; Kenneth Welsh; ***D:*** Allan Goldstein; ***W:*** Allan Goldstein; ***C:*** Curtis Petersen; ***M:*** Terry Plumeri.

Deathdream ½ *Dead of Night; Night Walk; The Veteran; The Night Andy Came Home* **1972** In this reworking of the "Monkey's Paw" tale, a mother wishes her dead son would return from Vietnam. He does, but he's not quite the person he used to be. Gripping plot gives new meaning to the saying, "Be careful what you wish for—it might come true." One of Tom Savini's earliest F/X assignments. **98m/C; VHS, DVD, Blu-Ray.** *CA* John Marley; Richard Backus; Lynn Carlin; Alan Ormsby; ***D:*** Bob (Benjamin) Clark; ***W:*** Alan Ormsby; ***C:*** Jack McGowan; ***M:*** Carl Zittrer.

Deathgasm **2015** Jason Lei Howden's zom-rom-com debut gets a bit repetitive and stupid before it gets over, but it has enough gorey wit to make it worth a look for horror hounds and metal heads. Brodie (Milo Cawthorne) hates the new small town to which he's been forced to move but finds a soulmate in fellow metalhead Zakk (James Blake). He also falls for the charming Medina (Kimberley Crossman) but she's dating his obnoxious cousin. Everything changes when Brodie and Zakk end up playing a really heavy song that brings forth "The Blind One," a demonic entity that plunges their entire hood into bloody chaos. **86m/C; DVD, Blu-Ray, Streaming.** *NZ* Milo Cawthorne; James Blake; Kimberley Crossman; Daniel Cresswell; Stephen Ure; ***D:*** Jason Lei Howden; ***W:*** Jason Lei Howden; ***C:*** Simon Raby.

Deathlands: Homeward Bound ½ **2003** By 2084 the Earth has been decimated by war and disaster and civilization has devolved into feudal states, with the USA simply called the Deathlands. Eyepatch-wearing Ryan Cawdor (Spano) leads a band of nomadic scavengers. Ryan decides it's time to return to his home in Front Royale, which has been ruled by his evil brother (Peterson) and his evil stepmother (Lords) ever since they offed his pops and took control. Ryan wants revenge. Sci-Fi Channel flick is adapted from the fifth book in James Axler's "Deathlands" series. **86m/C; DVD.** Vincent Spano; Traci Lords; Jenya Lano; Alan C. Peterson; Colin Fox; Cliff Saunders; Nathan Carter; ***D:*** Joshua Butler; ***W:*** Gabrielle Stanton; Harry Werksman, Jr.; ***C:*** Bruce Worrall; ***M:*** Christopher Lennertz. **CABLE**

The Deathless Devil WOOF! *Yilmayan seytan; Yilmayan Adam; Deathless Man* **2005** A Turkish remake of an old serial called "The Mysterious Dr. Satan", this film could be called odd at best. On one side you have a spy/masked wrestler/superhero called Copperhead, some chick with big hair, and an annoying sidekick whose theme song is stolen from the original "Pink Panther" film. On the other is Dr. Seytan, an army of mind controlled minions, and a cardboard robot. If Ed Wood directed a film starring El Santo fighting a Klingon with a bad 70's wardrobe, it would be this movie. Please note this comparison possibly was not meant as a compliment. **84m/C; DVD.** *TU* Kunt Tulgar; Mine Mutlu; Muzaffer Tema; Erol Gunaydin; Yalin Tolga; Tijen Doray; Erol Tas; ***D:*** Yilmaz Atadeniz; ***W:*** Orhan Atadeniz; ***C:*** Sertac Karan.

Deathrow Gameshow ½ **1988** Condemned criminals can either win their freedom or die in front of millions on a new TV show that doesn't win the host many friends. **78m/C; VHS, DVD, Blu-Ray.** John McCafferty; Robin Bluthe; Beano; Mark Lasky; ***D:*** Mark Pirro; ***W:*** Mark Pirro.

The Deaths of Ian Stone ½ **2007 (R)** Ian Stone (Vogel) is hunted by demons who kill him over and over and then watch as he's resurrected into a new life. His stalkers feed off of human fear but why did they choose Ian to die? The character isn't so compelling that you'll care but there are a few good frights. **87m/C; DVD.** *GB* Mike Vogel; Jaime Murray; Christina Cole; Michael Feast; Michael Dixon; Charlie Anson; ***D:*** Dario Piana; ***W:*** Brendan William Hood; ***C:*** Stefano Morcaldo; ***M:*** Elia Cmiral.

Deathstalker WOOF! *El Cazador de la Muerte* **1983 (R)** Deathstalker sets his sights on seizing the evil wizard Munkar's magic amulet so he can take over Munkar's castle. The only excuse for making such an idiotic film seems to have been to fill it with half-naked women. Filmed in Argentina and followed by two sequels that were an improvement. **80m/C; VHS, DVD, Blu-Ray.** Richard (Rick) Hill; Barbi Benton; Richard Brooker; Victor Bo; Lana Clarkson; ***D:*** John Watson; ***W:*** Howard R. Cohen; ***C:*** Leonardo Solis; ***M:*** Oscar Cardozo Ocampo.

Deathstalker 2: Duel of the Titans **1987 (R)** Campy fantasy comically pits the lead character against an evil wizard. Sword-and-sorcery spoof doesn't take itself too seriously. **85m/C; VHS, DVD, Blu-Ray.** John Terlesky; Monique Gabrielle; John Lazar; Toni Naples; Maria Socas; Deanna (Dee) Booher; ***D:*** Jim Wynorski; ***W:*** Jim Wynorski; ***C:*** Leonardo Solis; ***M:*** Chuck Cirino.

Deathstalker 4: Match of Titans **1992 (R)** The sword and sorcery epic continues, with our hero revealing yet more musculature in his efforts to defeat an evil queen and her legion of stone warriors. **85m/C; VHS, DVD.** Richard (Rick) Hill; Maria Ford; Michelle Moffett; Brett (Baxter) Clark; ***D:*** Howard R. Cohen.

Deathtrap **1982 (PG)** A creatively blocked playwright, his ailing rich wife, and a former student who has written a sure-fire hit worth killing for, are the principals in this compelling comedy-mystery. Cross and double-cross are explored in this film based on the Broadway hit by Ira Levin. **118m/C; VHS, DVD, Blu-Ray.** Henry Jones; Michael Caine; Christopher Reeve; Dyan Cannon; Irene Worth; ***D:*** Sidney Lumet; ***W:*** Jay Presson Allen; ***C:*** Andrzej Bartkowiak; ***M:*** Johnny Mandel.

Deathwatch ½ **2002 (R)** After an intensely bloody World War I battle, nine soldiers get off-track inside a massive labyrinth of deserted German trenches filled with mounds of the deceased and packed with a mother lode of rats. Further complicating matters is a deadly unearthly force that pits the men against one another while picking them off one at a time. Bassett nicely blends frightful atmosphere with a disturbingly realistic backdrop that somewhat atones for the uninspired dialogue. **95m/C; VHS, DVD.** Jamie Bell; Ruaidhri Conroy; Laurence Fox; Dean Lennox Kelly; Kris Marshall; Hans Matheson; Hugh O'Conor; Matthew Rhys; Andy Serkis; Hugo Speer; Mike Downey; Roman Horak; ***D:*** Michael J. Bassett; ***W:*** Michael J. Bassett; ***C:*** Hubert Taczanowski; ***M:*** Curt Cress; Chris Weller. **VIDEO**

Debbie Macomber's Trading Christmas *Trading Christmas* **2011** Widowed Emily (Ford) surprises daughter Heather (Lahana) at her Boston college for Christmas so she arranges a house swap with prof Charles (Cavanagh). The thing is, Heather is out of town with her boyfriend (without telling mom) and the one surprised is Emily, especially by Charles' brother Ray (Bellows). Emily's best friend Faith (Miller) wants to surprise her too and walks in on Charles instead! A Hallmark Channel movie. **87m/C; DVD.** Faith Ford; Tom Cavanagh; Gil Bellows; Gabrielle Miller; Emma Lahana; ***D:*** Michael Scott; ***W:*** Bruce Graham; ***C:*** Adam Sliwinski; ***M:*** James Jandrisch. **CABLE**

D.E.B.S. ½ **2004 (PG-13)** Low-budget riot grrl send-up of "Charlie's Angels" begs the question "Why parody something that never took itself seriously in the first place?" A secret government agency known as the D.E.B.S. recruits nubile teenage girls through trick questions in the S.A.T. that identify their willingness to lie, cheat, and kill. After the team monitors supervillian Lucy Diamond (Brewster) during her blind date with assassin Ninotchka (Cauffiel), leader Amy (Foster) gets a crush on Lucy, which jeopardizes the whole team. Even with the lesbianism added for extra taboo, Robinson can't elevate her material beyond its one-joke premise. Pretty anemic comedy, but plenty for schoolgirl fetishists to be happy about. **91m/C; DVD.** Sara Foster; Jordana Brewster; Meagan Good; Devon Aoki; Jill Ritchie; Holland Taylor; Michael Clarke Duncan; Jimmi Simpson; Jessica Cauffiel; Geoff Stults; ***D:*** Angela Robinson; ***W:*** Angela Robinson; ***C:*** M. David Mullen; ***M:*** Steven Stern.

The Debt *Back to Even* **1998 (R)** Printing press operator Mitch's (Lamas) gambling problems get him deeply in debt to local wiseguy Danny Boyle (Pare) who gets Mitch to help him in a counterfeiting operation. Usual gangster cliches but the action moves along. **92m/C; VHS, DVD.** Lorenzo Lamas; Michael Paré; Heidi Thomas; Angela Jones; Herb Mitchell; ***D:*** Rod Hewitt; ***W:*** Rod Hewitt; ***C:*** Garrett Fisher. **VIDEO**

The Debt ½ **2003** Safecracker Geoff Dresner (Clarke) has left his criminal past behind until his stupid son-in-law Terry (Freeman) fails to repay a dangerous loan shark. In order to protect his family, Geoff agrees to do one last job, which goes horribly wrong. **110m/C; DVD.** Warren Clarke; Martin Freeman; Hugo Speer; Lee Williams; Orla Brady; Barbara Marten; Amanda Abbington; ***D:*** Jon Jones; ***W:*** Richard McBrien; ***C:*** John Pardue; ***M:*** Martin Phipps. **TV**

The Debt **2007** Thirty years after the fact, former Mossad agent Rachel has a successful book out about her part in the death of Nazi Max Rainer. A man in Ukraine claims to be Max and this sends Rachel and another former agent, Uhud, on a hunt to cover up the past. Flashbacks reveal a younger Rachel, Ehud, and fellow agent Zvi first undertaking their mission in 1965. This Israeli film was remade in 2010. **97m/C; DVD.** *IS* Gila Almagor; Oded Teomi; Alex Peleg; Neta Garty; Itay Tiran; Yehezkel Lazrov; Edgar Selge; ***D:*** Assaf Bernstein; ***W:*** Assaf Bernstein; Ido Rosenblum; ***C:*** Giora Bejach; ***M:*** Jonathan Bar-Giora.

The Debt **2010 (R)** In this tense, though conventional, adaptation of the 2007 Israeli film "Ha-Hov," retired Mossad agents confront their pasts and the secrets and regrets that drove them apart. In 1966, Rachel (Chastain), Stephan (Csokas), and David (Worthington) are sent to East Berlin to kidnap infamous Nazi doctor Dieter Vogel (Christensen), smuggling him out of the country and to justice in Israel. Their plan goes badly awry although what actually happened only comes out 30 years later when Rachel (Mirren) and Stephan's (Wilkinson) daughter writes a heroic version of the event. **114m/C; DVD, Blu-Ray.** *US GB* Dame Helen Mirren; Ciaran Hinds; Tom Wilkinson; Jessica Chastain; Sam Worthington; Marton Csokas; Jesper Christensen; Romi Aboulafia; ***D:*** John Madden; ***W:*** Matthew Vaughn; Jane Goldman; Peter Straughan; ***C:*** Benjamin Davis; ***M:*** Thomas Newman.

A Decade Under the Influence ½ **2002 (R)** Filmmakers LaGravenese and Demme chronicle the rise of new, independent filmmakers from the ashes of the old Hollywood studio system, beginning in 1967 with such films as "The Graduate" and "Bonnie & Clyde" and ending in 1977 with "Star Wars." Contains extensive film clips and interviews with diretors, actors, writers, and producers. Originally a three-part series shown on the Independent Film Channel; a theatrical version was released at 108 minutes. **180m/C; DVD.** ***D:*** Richard LaGravenese; Ted (Edward) Demme; ***C:*** Clyde Smith; Anthony Janelli; ***M:*** John Kimbrough.

The Decalogue ½ **1988** Originally produced for Polish TV, Kieslowski's 10-hour epic offers moments from the lives of residents of a late-Communist era Warsaw apartment complex. Each of the segments is a modern retelling of the Ten Commandments as the individuals confront morality, ethics, betrayal, and a variety of human frailities and crises. Polish with subtitles. **584m/C; VHS, DVD.** *PL* Krystyna Janda; Aleksander Bardini; Maja Komorowska; Daniel Olbrychski; Janusz Gajos; Maria Pakulnis; Jerzy Stuhr; Zbigniew Zamachowski; Boguslaw Linda; Artur Barcis; Henryk Baranowski; ***D:*** Krzysztof Kieslowski; ***W:*** Krzysztof Kieslowski; Krzysztof Piesiewicz; ***C:*** Wieslaw Zdort; Edward Klosinski; Krysztof Pakulski; Slawomir Idziak; Witold Adamek; Dariusz Kuc; Andrzej Jaroszewicz; Piotr Sobocinski; Jacek Blawut; ***M:*** Zbigniew Preisner. **TV**

The Decameron ½ *Il Decameron* **1970 (R)** Pasolini's first epic pageant in his "Trilogy of Life" series. An acclaimed, sexually explicit adaptation of a handful of the Boccaccio tales. In Italian with English subtitles. **111m/C; VHS, DVD, Blu-Ray.** *FR IT GE* Franco Citti; Ninetto Davoli; Angela Luce; Patrizia Capparelli; Jovan Jovanovich; Silvana Mangano; Pier Paolo Pasolini; ***D:*** Pier Paolo Pasolini; ***W:*** Pier Paolo Pasolini; ***C:*** Tonino Delli Colli; ***M:*** Ennio Morricone. Berlin Intl. Film Fest. '71: Silver Prize.

Decameron Nights ½ **1953** Story of Boccaccio's pursuit of a recently widowed young women is interwoven amongst the three of the 14th century Italian writer's bawdy tales. **87m/C; VHS, DVD, Streaming.** *GB* Louis Jourdan; Joan Fontaine; Binnie Barnes; Joan Collins; Marjorie Rhodes; ***D:*** Hugo Fregonese.

Deceit **2004** Slow-moving Lifetime crime drama. When Ellen McCarthy's husband Grove is lost at sea in his new boat, it appears to be an accident. Then Ellen learns Grove apparently embezzled from his company and all she's left with are debts. As Det. Hal Kazin and lawyer Sam Penney investigate, it appears that whatever happened was no accident and there's more than one suspect. **91m/C; DVD.** Marlo Thomas; Vondie Curtis-Hall; Brett Cullen; William Devane; ***D:*** John Sacret Young; ***W:*** John Sacret Young; ***C:*** Johnny Jensen; ***M:*** David M. Hamilton. **CABLE**

Deceit **2006** Dave (Long), his best friend Brian (Mably), and Brian's girlfriend Emily (Chriqui) are recent college grads. Before Dave heads to law school, he and Emily have an alcohol-influenced one-nighter. Five years later, Brian is a millionaire and he and Emily are unhappily married. Dave returns home to settle his dad's estate and finds himself drawn to Emily again, which is not a good idea. **92m/C; DVD.** Emmanuelle Chriqui; Matt Long; Luke Mably; Pell James; Jon Abrahams; Joe Pantoliano; *D:* Michael Cole Weiss; *W:* Michael Cole Weiss; *C:* Ruben O'Malley; *M:* Dan Silver. **CABLE**

Deceived ♪♪ 1/2 **1991 (PG-13)** A successful career woman with a passionate husband and a young daughter feels she has it all until her husband is apparently killed in a bizarre tragedy. But just how well did she know the man she married? Who was he really and what secrets are hidden in his past? As she struggles to solve these mysteries, her own life becomes endangered in this psychological thriller. **115m/C; VHS, DVD, Blu-Ray.** Goldie Hawn; John Heard; Ashley Peldon; Jan Rubes; Amy Wright; Maia Filar; Robin Bartlett; Tom Irwin; Beatrice Straight; Kate Reid; *D:* Damian Harris; *W:* Mary Agnes Donoghue; Derek Saunders; *C:* Jack N. Green; *M:* Thomas Newman.

Deceiver ♪♪ *Liar* **1997 (R)** Contrived psychological thriller starts out with the requisite dead prostitute (Zellwegger, in a questionable career move) and the rounding up of the usual suspects, settling on disturbed but brainy Princeton grad Wayland (indie film icon Roth). Wayland uses his superior I.Q. and penchant for mind games to send head detectives Kennesaw and Braxton (Rooker and Penn) into a tailspin of deceit and lies, turning the investigation around on the gritty cops. Flashy camera work only adds to the tangled mayhem. Fine performances from talented cast bring this up a notch. Twin directors Jonas and Joshua Pate's convoluted spin on a noirish murder mystery follows up their 1996 debut, "Grave." **102m/C; VHS, DVD.** Renée Zellweger; Tim Roth; Christopher Penn; Michael Rooker; Ellen Burstyn; Rosanna Arquette; *D:* Jonas Pate; Josh Pate; *W:* Jonas Pate; Josh Pate; *C:* Bill Butler; *M:* Harry Gregson-Williams.

The Deceivers ♪♪ **1988 (PG-13)** Brosnan stars as a British officer sent on a dangerous unercover mission in 1820s India. He's to infiltrate the notorious Thuggee cult, known for robbing and murdering unwary travelers. Interesting premise falters due to slow pacing and Brosnan's lack of believability. **112m/C; VHS, DVD.** *IN GB* Pierce Brosnan; Saeed Jaffrey; Shashi Kapoor; Keith Michell; *D:* Nicholas Meyer; *C:* Walter Lassally.

December ♪♪ **1991 (PG)** Four prep-school students in New Hampshire must confront the reality of war when the Japanese bomb Pearl Harbor. A touching story of courage and friendship that takes place in one night during the suprise-attack. **92m/C; VHS, DVD.** Wil Wheaton; Chris Young; Brian Krause; Balthazar Getty; Jason London; *D:* Gabe Torres; *W:* Gabe Torres.

December Boys ♪ 1/2 **2007 (PG-13)** The four "December Boys"? named so because they were all born in December—Sparks (Byers), Spit (Fraser), Misty (Cormie) and Maps (Radcliffe—yep, Harry Potter) are tight friends, and all orphans in Australia in the 60s. The teens get to leave the orphanage for a seaside holiday on the coast, where they learn that a couple down the beach may be interested in adopting one of them. Three of the four jostle for the attention of the would-be parents while Maps, having given up ever having his own family, pursues the local hot girl (Palmer). The boys get to live it up on the outside of the orphanage, but there's just nothing special in this uninspired and occasionally sappy plot. The breathtaking scenery of Australia's south coast, with its shoreline, caves, and rock formations, is interesting. **105m/C; DVD.** Daniel Radcliffe; Lee Cormie; Teresa Palmer; Victoria Hill; Christin Byers; James Fraser; Sullivan Stapleton; Jack Thompson; Kris McQuade; Frank Gallacher; *D:* Rod Hardy; *W:* Marc Rosenberg; *C:* David Connell; *M:* Carlo Giacco.

December Bride ♪♪ 1/2 **1991** Determined young woman (Reeves) becomes the housekeeper to two taciturn Irish farmer/brothers (Hinds and McCann) and proceeds to bully them into prosperity in early 20th century rural Ireland. She also scandalizes the community by sleeping with both men and refusing to marry either—even after she becomes pregnant. Based on the novel by Sam Hanna Bell. **88m/C; VHS, DVD.** *IR* Saskia Reeves; Ciaran Hinds; Donal McCann; Patrick Malahide; Brenda Bruce; *D:* Thaddeus O'Sullivan; *W:* David Rudkin; *C:* Bruno de Keyzer; *M:* Jurgen Knieper.

December 7th: The Movie ♪♪ 1/2 **1991** Banned for 50 years by the U.S. Government, this planned Hollywood explanation to wartime audiences of the Pearl Harbor debacle offers such "offensive" images as blacks fighting heroically alongside whites, loyal Japanese-Americans, and Uncle Sam asleep on the morning of the attack. The Chief of Naval Operations confiscated the original film, claiming it demeaned the Navy. The battle scenes were so realistic they fooled even documentarians. This isn't the most incisive video on the event—just an unforgettable snapshot. **82m/B; VHS, DVD.** Walter Huston; Harry Davenport; *D:* John Ford; *M:* Alfred Newman.

A Decent Proposal ♪ 1/2 **2006** Career woman Tia (Tuck) is pregnant when her lover Nick (Rochfort) dies while mountain climbing somewhere remote. Her wealthy boss John (Airlie) offers to marry Tia and raise the baby as his own and she agrees, only to have John apparently more interested in work than his new family until a turn of events put everything into question. **90m/C; DVD.** Jessica Tuck; Spencer Rochfort; Andrew Airlie; Jennifer Spence; Hrothgar Mathews; *D:* Neill Fearnley; *W:* Debra Gendel; Morgan Gendel; *C:* Larry Lynn; *M:* Clinton Shorter. **CABLE**

Deception ♪♪♪ **1946** Davis is a pianist torn between two loves: her intensely jealous sponsor (Rains) and her cellist boyfriend (Henreid). Plot in danger of going over the melodramatic edge is saved by the very effective performances of the stars. **112m/B; VHS, DVD.** Bette Davis; Paul Henreid; Claude Rains; John Abbott; Benson Fong; *D:* Irving Rapper.

Deception ♪ 1/2 *Ruby Cairo* **1992 (PG-13)** Talented cast is wasted in an old-fashioned mystery that lacks a coherent script. MacDowell is married to Mortensen, the owner of an aircraft salvage company. He's supposedly killed in a plane crash but she thinks he's just pulled a fast one and sets off to find him. Tracking her hubby's secret bank accounts takes her all over the world, and finally to Cairo, Egypt where she meets Neeson. Together they discover Mortensen's scam involves smuggling poison gas and the duo then try to outwit the hoods on their trail. Film was originally released at 110 minutes. **90m/C; VHS, DVD, Blu-Ray.** Andie MacDowell; Liam Neeson; Viggo Mortensen; Jack Thompson; Jeff Corey; Miriam Reed; Luis Cortes; Paco Mauri; *D:* Graeme Clifford; *W:* Robert Dillon; Michael Thomas; *M:* John Barry.

Deception ♪ 1/2 **2008 (R)** McGregor is a milquetoast accountant, Jackman is a silky snake, and Williams is a blonde seductress. If you can buy the leads in these roles you may possibly find some enjoyment in this transparent thriller. Corporate numbers-cruncher Jonathan (McGregor) is led on a journey into NYC's anonymous sex underground by lawyer Wyatt (Jackman). Among the women Jonathan meets is the mysterious S (Williams), who soon disappears. The sex is all a set-up for something much more dangerous but—as the title blatantly proclaims—nothing is what it seems. **108m/C; DVD, Blu-Ray.** Ewan McGregor; Hugh Jackman; Michelle Williams; Maggie Q; Rachael Taylor; Natasha Henstridge; Lisa Gay Hamilton; Charlotte Rampling; Margaret Colin; Paz de la Huerta; *D:* Marcel Langenegger; *W:* Mark Bomback; *C:* Dante Spinotti; *M:* Ramin Djawadi.

Deceptive Practice: The Mysteries and Mentors of Ricky Jay ♪♪ **2012** Bernstein's documentary on legendary magician and actor Ricky Jay offers little insight into the personal life of the notoriously private man but instead illuminates his craft and the seriousness with which he takes it by focusing on the people who trained him and to whom he passes down his craft. With an amazing amount of archival footage of not just Jay's performances but numerous other magic practitioners, Bernstein's film has a cumulative power that allows us to get just as close to Jay as he wants us to be. The magician is always in control. **88m/C; DVD.** Ricky Jay; *D:* Molly Bernstein; *C:* Edward Marritz.

Deceptive Practice: The Mysteries and Mentors of Ricky Jay ♪♪♪ **2013** This biographical documentary focuses on Ricky Jay, an acclaimed magician who has the ability to impress even the most doubtful audience. Also an author, historian, and actor, the documentary explores Jay's influences and relationship to magic which began when he was an apprentice to his grandfather as a small child. The film also includes early footage from television appearances and other performances as well as an exploration of the small, insular world of magic and its practitioners. **88m/C; DVD.** Dick Cavett; Olivier Manchon; *D:* Molly Bernstein; *C:* Edward Marritz; *M:* Clare Manchon.

Decision at Sundown ♪♪ 1/2 **1957** Gunman Bart Allison (Scott) is obsessed with killing Tate Kimbrough (Carroll), whom he blames for the suicide of his wife Mary after she was seduced by Kimbrough. He gets in a lot of trouble after riding into a town controlled by Kimbrough and remains true to his deadly intentions even after learning the truth about his missus. But the final showdown doesn't go exactly as expected. **77m/C; DVD.** Randolph Scott; John Carroll; Karen Steele; Valerie French; Noah Beery, Jr.; Andrew Duggan; John Archer; *D:* Budd Boetticher; *W:* Charles B(ryant) Lang, Jr.; *C:* Burnett Guffey; *M:* Heinz Roemheld.

Decision Before Dawn ♪♪ 1/2 **1951** In late 1944, German POW Karl Maurer, codename 'Happy' (Werner), agrees to work with the Americans to shorten the war. Parachuting behind enemy lines along with his cynical partner, 'Tiger' (Blech), and their American handler, Lt. Rennick (Basehart), Maurer is sent to track the movements of a Panzer Corp. But the would-be spies aren't trusted by either side. Litvak filmed in a semi-documentary style on location in a war-scarred Germany. Based on a true story and adapted from George Howe's novel "Call It Treason." **119m/B; DVD.** Richard Basehart; Gary Merrill; Oskar Werner; Hans-Christian Blech; Hildegarde Knef; O.E. Hasse; Dominique Blanchar; *D:* Anatole Litvak; *W:* Peter Viertel; *C:* Franz Planer; *M:* Franz Waxman.

Decisions ♪ **2010 (R)** Uninspired crime drama where the plot threads are frayed and the end twist doesn't help hold it together. Friends decide a heist will solve their money troubles. They steal from the wrong people and get in deeper than intended when a crooked LAPD detective and a crime syndicate bad guy want the money back within 24 hours. Haim's final role before his 2010 death. **89m/C; DVD.** Corey Haim; Anthony Vitale; Matt Madrano; Cisco Reyes; Yeniffer Behrens; Mike Foy; *D:* Jensen LeFlore; *W:* Anthony Vitale; Julius LeFlore; *C:* Jon Myers; *M:* Zenon Kesik. **VIDEO**

Deck the Halls ♪ 1/2 **2006 (PG)** Joyless holiday fare pumped out by the studio to scrooge a few dollars from the Christmas mall crowd. Steven (Broderick) is the smug, self-appointed "Christmas guy" of a sleepy New England town, making sure the holidays are celebrated tastefully. His crass neighbor Buddy (DeVito) wants to put enough lights on his house so that it can be seen from space. A war of childish pranks erupts between the two until a forced lesson on the "true meaning of Christmas" is tacked onto the ending. File this one in the Bastard Children of "Christmas Vacation" folder. **93m/C; DVD, Blu-Ray.** Danny DeVito; Matthew Broderick; Kristin Davis; Kristin Chenoweth; Alia Shawkat; Jorge Garcia; Dylan Blue; Kelly Aldridge; Sabrina Aldridge; *D:* John Whitesell; *W:* Don Rhymer; Matt Corman; Chris Ord; *C:* Mark Irwin; *M:* George S. Clinton.

The Decks Ran Red ♪ 1/2 **1958** Overwrought adventure drama. Former first mate Edwin Rummill (Mason) wants to prove himself on his first command aboard an old freighter heading out of New Zealand. But psychotic Henry Scott (Crawford) and some crewmembers stage a violent mutiny with the intention of sinking the ship and collecting the insurance payment. Rummill survives in a lifeboat and is determined to retake command. Dandridge, as the cook's wife, adds some exoticness and tension. **84m/B; DVD.** James Mason; Broderick Crawford; Dorothy Dandridge; Stuart Whitman; Jack Kruschen; John Gallaudet; *D:* Andrew L. Stone; *W:* Andrew L. Stone; *C:* Meredith Nicholson.

Declaration of War ♪♪ *La Guerre est Declaree* **2011** Reckless lovers Juliette and Romeo are parents to baby boy Adam whose constant ill health is eventually diagnosed as a cancerous brain tumor. It's not as downbeat as it sounds because Donzelli is a lively, unsentimental filmmaker despite--or maybe because of--the autobiographical nature of her story. French with subtitles. **100m/C; DVD.** *FR* Valerie Donzelli; Jeremie Elkaim; Elina Lowensohn; Michele Moretti; *D:* Valerie Donzelli; *W:* Valerie Donzelli; Jeremie Elkaim; *C:* Sebastien Buchmann.

Decline and Fall...of a Birdwatcher ♪ 1/2 **1968** Lightweight comedy that has little to do with Evelyn Waugh's social satire novel as it follows the misadventures of naïve Oxford University student Paul Pennyfeather (Phillips). He gets expelled, teaches at an unsavory boys' boarding school, becomes a tutor and is seduced by the lady of the house (Page), and is later convicted of white slavery as he stumbles from one experience to the next. **113m/C; DVD.** *UK* Robin Phillips; Genevieve Page; Colin Blakely; Leo McKern; Donald Wolfit; *D:* John Krish; *W:* Ivan Foxwell; *C:* Desmond Dickinson; *M:* Ronald Goodwin.

The Decline of the American Empire ♪♪♪ 1/2 *Le Declin De L'Empire Americain* **1986 (R)** The critically acclaimed French-Canadian film about eight academic intellectuals who spend a weekend shedding their sophistication and engaging in intertwining sexual affairs. Examines the differing attitudes of men and women in regards to sex and sexuality. In French with English subtitles. **102m/C; VHS, DVD.** *CA* Dominique Michel; Dorothee Berryman; Louise Portal; Genevieve Rioux; Gabriel Arcand; *D:* Denys Arcand; *W:* Denys Arcand. Genie '87: Director (Arcand), Film, Support. Actor (Arcand), Support. Actress (Portal); N.Y. Film Critics '86: Foreign Film; Toronto-City '86: Canadian Feature Film.

Decoding Annie Parker ♪♪ **2013 (R)** Uneven drama with parallel narratives that's based on a true story. Toronto housewife and mother Annie Parker is struggling with her third bout of breast cancer, certain there is some family connection since her mother and sister died of the disease. Geneticist Mary-Claire King is equally certain there's a link between cancer and DNA but her research study is constantly underfunded and dismissed by her male colleagues. (King would discover the BRCA1 gene mutation.) **91m/C; DVD, Blu-Ray.** Samantha Morton; Helen Hunt; Aaron Paul; Alice Eve; Maggie Grace; Rashida Jones; Corey Stoll; *D:* Steven Bernstein; *W:* Steven Bernstein; Adam Bernstein; Michael Moss; *C:* Ted Hayash; *M:* Steven Bramson.

Decommissioned ♪ 1/2 **2016 (R)** An action-thriller in which a former CIA agent is being framed. John Niles (Messner) has retired from the CIA and built a new life that is focused on his family. Unbeknown to him, certain members of the CIA, including David Marino (Remar), is planning to assassinate the president and blaming him for the crime. Marino goes as far as to kidnap Niles' family to keep him in line. To save his family and his president, Niles works with Michael Price (Jones) and detective Tom Watson (Pare) to stop the plot in time. **80m/C; DVD, Streaming, Download.** Johnny Messner; Vinnie Jones; James Remar; Michael Paré; Estella Warren; *D:* Timothy Woodward, Jr.; *W:* Sean Ryan; *C:* Jonathan Mariande; *M:* Sid De La Cruz. **VIDEO**

Deconstructing Harry ♪♪ 1/2 **1997 (R)** Interesting idea has Allen as a successful author, Harry Block, whose thinly veiled autobiographical fiction spills the beans on his ex-wives, lovers, friends, and family, thereby pissing them all off. Toggles back and forth between Harry's "real" life and scenes from his books, giving characters and situations two versions: one slanted to suit Harry and one more real than Harry wants or knows how to deal with. Infidelity, divorce, and art all get their usual treatment. Another not bad, but not great project by Allen that may be too self-absorbed for most. Features an elaborate, star-studded cast, mostly delegated to minor roles. **96m/C; VHS, DVD.** Woody Allen; Billy Crystal; Judy Davis; Elisabeth Shue; Kirstie Alley; Caroline Aaron; Bob Balaban; Richard

Benjamin; Eric Bogosian; Mariel Hemingway; Amy Irving; Julie Kavner; Eric Lloyd; Julia Louis-Dreyfus; Tobey Maguire; Demi Moore; Stanley Tucci; Robin Williams; Philip Bosco; Gene Saks; Hazelle Goodman; *D:* Woody Allen; *W:* Woody Allen; *C:* Carlo Di Palma.

Decoration Day **1990 (PG)** Garner plays reclusive retired Southern judge Albert Sidney Finch who aids an angry black childhood friend, Gee (Cobbs), who has refused to accept his long-overdue Medal of Honor. Investigating the past leads to a decades-old mystery and a tragic secret that has repercussions for everyone involved. Based on the novel by John William Corrington. A Hallmark Hall of Fame presentation. **99m/C; VHS, DVD.** James Garner; Bill Cobbs; Judith Ivey; Ruby Dee; Laurence Fishburne; Jo Anderson; *D:* Robert Markowitz; *W:* Robert W. Lenski. **TV**

Decoy **1/2 1946** Ooooooh—bad girl flick! Margot (Gillie) is the heartless moll of death row gangster Olins (Armstrong) who won't reveal where he hid $400K. So Margot gets rival gangster Vincent (Norris) to agree to help her remove Olin's body from the gas chamber and force prison doc Craig (Rudley) to revive him with a special drug. The plan works—sorta—Olin revives, hands Margot a map, Vincent kills him for real, and they take the doc hostage as they go for the dough. But Margot doesn't want to split the loot, see, so she just happens to run over Vincent several times. There's also a prime double cross as Margot relates her "crime doesn't pay" tale to a cop (Leonard). **76m/B; DVD.** Edward Norris; Herbert Rudley; Robert Armstrong; Sheldon Leonard; Jean Gillie; Philip Van Zandt; *D:* Jack Bernhard; *W:* Nedrick Young; *C:* L. William O'Connell; *M:* Edward Kay.

The Decoy Bride **1/2 2011 (PG)** Predictable but sweet Brit rom com. American film star Lara (Eve) and English author James (Tennat) have their wedding plans sabotaged by the media. They relocate to a remote Scottish island and hire Katie (MacDonald) as a decoy to fool the paparazzi. Only the joke appears to be on the engaged couple who find out three's a crowd, especially when the would-be groom is more sympatico with the fake bride than his diva fiance. **89m/C; DVD, Blu-Ray.** *UK* David Tennant; Kelly Macdonald; Alice Eve; Federico Castelluccio; Michael Urie; Dylan Moran; Maureen Beattie; *D:* Sheree Folkson; *W:* Sally Phillips; Neil Jaworski; *C:* Nanu Segal; *M:* Julian Nott.

Decoys **1/2 2004 (R)** Goofy Canadian combo of a teen sex comedy with sci-fi horror. College freshman roommates Luke (Sevier) and Roger (Toufexis) are looking to get laid, preferably by their blonde bombshell neighbors Lilly (von Pfetten) and Constance (Poirier). Then a drunken Luke happens to witness the gals sprouting tentacles and comes to the conclusion that these alien babes are responsible for the flash-freezing deaths of horny frat boys. Naturally, everyone thinks Luke has had one too many brewskis. **96m/C; DVD.** *CA* Corey Sevier; Kim Poirier; Stefanie von Pfetten; Meaghan Ory; Nicole Eggert; Elias Toufexis; Ennis Esmer; *D:* Matthew Hastins; *W:* Tom Berry; Matthew Hastins; *C:* Daniel Villeneuve; *M:* Daryl Bennett; Jim Guttridge.

Decoys: The Second Seduction *Decoys 2: Alien Seduction* **2007 (R)** Takes a dip on the ole quality meter although it's essentially the same movie. Grad student Luke (Sevier) has moved on to a new university but hasn't escaped his old alien babe problem since Constance (Poirier) has also returned. She's posing as a doctor in charge of student health services so she and her slutty cohorts have first pick of lusty lads for mating purposes. Have sex and die seems to be the alien way. **94m/C; DVD.** *CA* Corey Sevier; Kim Poirier; Dina Meyer; Tobin Bell; Sam Easton; Tyler Johnston; Kailin See; *D:* Jeffrey Scott Lando; *W:* Miguel Tejada-Flores; *C:* John Spooner; *M:* Steve London. **VIDEO**

Dedication **2007 (R)** Henry Roth (Crudup), the most neurotic, compulsive children's book writer on the planet, finds himself without an illustrator after his collaborator Rudy (Wilkinson) dies suddenly. Henry and Rudy have had one big success together entitled "Marty the Beaver," and now Henry's editor forces a new illustrator, Lucy Reilly (Moore), on him to complete a "Marty" follow-up. Not easily accommodating change, Henry hates her, which isn't a surprise since he hates nearly everything. But wait, this is a romantic comedy, so of course his tune changes. Complications ensue in the forms of Rudy's ghost and Lucy's ex-lover, as well as her kooky mother. Worth a whirl if you can't get enough of the rom-com formula. **111m/C; DVD.** Billy Crudup; Mandy Moore; Tom Wilkinson; Bob Balaban; Dianne Wiest; Bobby Cannavale; Christine Taylor; Peter Bogdanovich; Martin Freeman; *D:* Justin Theroux; *W:* David Bromberg; *C:* Stephen Kazmierski; *M:* Ed Shearmur.

Dee Snider's Strangeland **WOOF!** *Strangeland* **1998 (R)** Former Twisted Sister singer Dee Snider proves that he can fail at movie-making worse than he can fail as a musician. He wrote, produced and starred in this dud that proves it's possible to be stupid, disgusting and boring at the same time. Snider plays Captain Howdy, an internet chat room sicko who lures young girls into a dungeon and tortures them by involuntarily piercing them and trying to act in front of them. Gage plays the dim detective trying to find the hair-sculpting madman. Only proves that Snider with a movie camera is more dangerous than the internet. **90m/C; VHS, DVD.** Dee Snider; Kevin Gage; Brett Harrelson; Elizabeth Pena; Robert Englund; Amy Smart; Linda Cardellini; *D:* John Pieplow; *W:* Dee Snider; *C:* Goran Paviceric; *M:* Anton Sanko.

The Deep **1977 (PG)** An innocent couple get involved in an underwater search for a shipwreck, and they quickly find themselves in over their heads. Gorgeous photography manages to keep this slow mover afloat. Famous for Bisset's wet T-shirt scene. Based on the novel by Peter Benchley. **123m/C; VHS, DVD, Blu-Ray.** Nick Nolte; Jacqueline Bisset; Robert Shaw; Louis Gossett, Jr.; Eli Wallach; *D:* Peter Yates; *W:* Peter Benchley; Tracy Keenan Wynn; *C:* Christopher Challis; *M:* John Barry.

Deep Blue **1/2 2003 (G)** British documentary from the creators of the BBC TV series "The Blue Planet" about (what else) ocean life, which was shot in some 250 locations worldwide. Killer whales, gray whales, dolphins, sea lions, sharks, penguins, and polar bears as well as sea horses, jellyfish, and a variety of other strange deep sea dwellers are shown going about their daily struggle to survive. All accompanied by some stunning cinematography and a lush score. **90m/C; DVD.** *GB GE* **Nar:** Michael Gambon; *D:* Alastair Fothergill; *W:* Alastair Fothergill; Andy Byatt; Tim Ecott; *C:* Doug Allan; Peter Scoones; *M:* George Fenton.

Deep Blue Sea **1/2 1999 (R)** It's no longer safe to go back in the water. Marine biologist Susan McAlester (Burrows) is obsessed with finding a cure for Alzheimer's and has genetically enhanced the brains of a group of test sharks at a floating research facility off the Baja coast. Oh, and she didn't bother to tell anyone else in her group about these smarter-than-the-average sharks. But they soon learn, when the research facility suffers several accidents, begins to flood, and the sharks get loose—and looking for snacks. It's not a bomb but it's also nothing that you haven't seen before. And the fake sharks look, well, fake (and hokey). **105m/C; VHS, DVD, Blu-Ray.** Saffron Burrows; Samuel L. Jackson; Thomas Jane; LL Cool J; Jacqueline McKenzie; Michael Rapaport; Stellan Skarsgard; Aida Turturro; *D:* Renny Harlin; *W:* Duncan Kennedy; Donna Powers; Wayne Powers; *C:* Stephen F. Windon; *M:* Trevor Rabin.

The Deep Blue Sea **1/2 2012 (R)** A bit too stuffy, slow, and cold for its own good, director/writer Davies' drama, based on the 1952 play by Terence Rattigan, works due to the notable skills of its talented leads. Hester Collyer (Weisz) is a married woman who has an affair with emotionally unstable pilot Freddie Page (Hiddleston), tearing her marriage and life apart. Weisz smartly plays Hester as a woman who seems to know that being with Freddie can only lead to tragedy but is powerless to stop it nonetheless. Hiddleston proves his continually rising star status to be no fluke. **98m/C; DVD, Blu-Ray.** *US GB* Rachel Weisz; Simon Russell Beale; Tom Hiddleston; Harry Hadden-Paton; Ann Mitchell; Karl Johnson; *D:* Terence Davies; *W:* Terence Davies; *C:* Florian Hoffmeister; *M:* Samuel Barber.

Deep Core **2000 (PG-13)** A rupture deep in the Earth's core causes a chain of natural disasters and could destroy the planet unless scientist Brian Goodman (Sheffer) can find a way to stop the geological threat. **90m/C; VHS, DVD.** Craig Sheffer; James Russo; Terry Farrell; James Lew; Wil Wheaton; Bruce McGill; *D:* Rodney McDonald; *W:* Martin Lazarus; *C:* Richard Clabaugh. **VIDEO**

Deep Cover **1/2 1988 (R)** A man dares to go beyond the walls of a mysterious English manor in order to expose the secrets that lie within the manor. **81m/C; VHS, DVD.** Tom Conti; Donald Pleasence; Denholm Elliott; Kika Markham; Phoebe Nicholls; *D:* Richard Loncraine.

Deep Cover **1/2 1992 (R)** Fishburne plays Russell Stevens Jr., a straight-arrow cop who goes undercover to infiltrate a Latin American cocaine cartel. While undercover, he becomes partners with drug dealer David Jason (Goldblum), and undergoes an inner transformation until he realizes he is betraying his cause. Confusing and commercial, yet marked with a moral rage. **107m/C; VHS, DVD.** Laurence Fishburne; Jeff Goldblum; Victoria Dillard; Charles Martin Smith; Sydney Lassick; Clarence Williams, III; Gregory Sierra; Roger Guenveur Smith; Cory Curtis; Glynn Turman; Def Jef; *D:* Bill Duke; *W:* Michael Tolkin; Henry Bean; *C:* Bojan Bazelli; *M:* Michel Colombier.

Deep Crimson *Profundo Carmesi* **1996** In 1949 Mexico, overweight nurse and willful romantic Coral (Orozco), impulsively answers a lonely hearts ad placed by Nicolas (Gimenez Cacho), who turns out to be a seedy con man. Coral, however, is certain she's found her true love and is obsessive in her devotion. So much so that she decides to help him with his swindling of vulnerable widows. But Coral's uncontrolled jealousy leads to murder. Based on the same true crime story that inspired the 1969 film, "The Honeymoon Killers." Spanish with subtitles. **109m/C; VHS, DVD.** *MX SP* Regina Orozco; Daniel Gimenez Cacho; Marisa Paredes; *D:* Arturo Ripstein; *W:* Paz Alicia Garciadiego; *C:* Guillermo Granillo; *M:* David Mansfield.

Deep Dark Canyon **1/2 2012 (R)** Nate Towne shoots at what he thinks is a wounded buck, but instead accidentally kills the local mayor. His teenage brother Skylar claims responsibility, thinking he'll only be tried as a minor, but the Cavanaugh clan insist on him being treated as an adult (there's bad blood between the families). Nate breaks his brother out of jail and they head into the woods, pursued by a drunken, gun-toting posse. The dumb decisions pile up but at least the pic moves swiftly along. **94m/C; DVD.** Spencer Treat Clark; Nick Eversman; Ted Levine; Martin Starr; Michael Bowen; Abraham Benrubi; *D:* Abe Levy; Silver Tree; *W:* Abe Levy; Silver Tree; *C:* Dan Stoloff; *M:* James Weston. **VIDEO**

The Deep End **2001 (R)** Moms are used to cleaning up their kids' messes and Margaret Hall (Swinton) is no different, even if her situation is. Margaret lives with her three kids and cranky father-in-law in a quiet Lake Tahoe community. Her naval husband is away, which means when Margaret learns that teenaged son Beau (Tucker) is gay and involved with sleazy older bar owner, Darby (Lucas), she has no one to turn to. Things get tricky when Darby turns up dead on the beach and mom thinks son did the deed. She gets rid of the body but is soon being blackmailed by slick stranger Alek (Visnjic). Swinton is amazing as the woman who has no limits when it comes to maternal care. Based on Elizabeth Sanxay Holding's 1947 novel "The Blank Wall," which was previously filmed by Max Ophuls in 1949 as "The Reckless Moment." **99m/C; VHS, DVD, Blu-Ray.** Tilda Swinton; Goran Visnjic; Jonathan Tucker; Raymond J. Barry; Josh(ua) Lucas; Peter Donat; Tamara Hope; Jordan Dorrance; *D:* Scott McGehee; David Siegel; *W:* Scott McGehee; David Siegel; *C:* Giles Nuttgens; *M:* Peter Nashel. Sundance '01: Cinematog. (Nuttgens).

The Deep End of the Ocean **1998 (PG-13)** Beth (Pfeiffer) and husband Pat (Williams) live the ideal life in the suburbs, with a nice home and three beautiful kids. All of that is shattered when three-year-old Ben is abducted while Beth is distracted at a hotel. Shows the tortuous road of depression that Beth travels, and the effect it has on her family. Suddenly, nine years later Ben shows up at her doorstep, now named Sam, and offers to cut the lawn. Beth and detective Candy (Goldberg) determine that he is the lost boy, and painful choices must be made by all. Glosses over the story behind the child's abduction and wraps everything up a bit too easily. **105m/C; VHS, DVD, Blu-Ray.** Michelle Pfeiffer; Treat Williams; John Kapelos; Jonathan Jackson; Ryan Merriman; Whoopi Goldberg; Michael McGrady; Brenda Strong; Alexa Vega; Tony Musante; *D:* Ulu Grosbard; *W:* Stephen Schiff; *C:* Stephen Goldblatt; *M:* Elmer Bernstein.

Deep Evil **1/2 2004 (R)** An alien microbe lands in Siberia in the 1950s, and over five decades later scientists finally succeed in cloning it. The world loses contact with them after receiving a distress call, and the military is sent in to get wasted like the cannon fodder they are in most sci-fi monster movies. **93m/C; DVD, Streaming.** *CA US* Lorenzo Lamas; Ona Grauer; Adam Harrington; Jim Thorburn; Will Sanderson; *D:* Pat Williams; *W:* Kevin Gendreau; Keith Shaw; *C:* David Pelletier; *M:* Peter Allen; Michael Lloyd. **VIDEO**

Deep Impact **1/2 1998 (PG-13)** Poor Morgan Freeman. He gets a chance to play the President of the United States only to have his term shortened by a dastardly comet the size of the Grand Canyon. Although his presidency would have been more interesting, the destruction's the star of this show, as well as the touchy-feely interaction of various two-dimensional characters. There's the astronauts (led by Duvall) sent into space to nuke the thing; ordinary teenager Leo (Wood) who initially discovered the rock; and career-conscious news anchor (Leoni), who first breaks the story. The all-star cast is underused, but lend the film a sense of gravity by their presence. The remaining stick figure characters evoke more yawns than tears. Good thing the comet comes along to, ironically, inject a little life into the flick. The special effects are the best in recent film history, and worth the long, laborious wait. **120m/C; VHS, DVD, Blu-Ray.** Morgan Freeman; Robert Duvall; Tea Leoni; Elijah Wood; Vanessa Redgrave; Maximilian Schell; James Cromwell; Blair Underwood; Ron Eldard; Jon Favreau; Leelee Sobieski; Mary McCormack; Dougray Scott; Alexander Baluyev; Charles Martin Smith; Richard Schiff; Gary Werntz; Bruce Weitz; Betsy Brantley; O'Neal Compton; Rya Kihlstedt; Denise Crosby; Laura Innes; *D:* Mimi Leder; *W:* Michael Tolkin; Bruce Joel Rubin; *C:* Dietrich Lohmann; *M:* James Horner.

Deep in My Heart **1/2 1954** A musical biography of the life and times of composer Sigmund Romberg, with guest appearances by many MGM stars. **132m/C; DVD, Blu-Ray.** Jose Ferrer; Merle Oberon; Paul Henreid; Walter Pidgeon; Helen Traubel; Rosemary Clooney; Jane Powell; Howard Keel; Cyd Charisse; Gene Kelly; Ann Miller; *D:* Stanley Donen; *C:* George J. Folsey.

Deep in the Heart *Handgun* **1983 (R)** When a young teacher is raped at gunpoint on a second date, she takes the law into her own hands. Just-off-the-target film tries to take a stand against the proliferation of guns in the U.S. Thought-provoking all the same. **99m/C; VHS, DVD.** *GB* Karen Young; Clayton Day; Ben Jones; Suzie Humphreys; *D:* Tony Garnett; *W:* Tony Garnett.

Deep in the Heart (of Texas) **1998** Two British documentary filmmakers, Robert (Cranham) and his wife Kate (Root), take an assignment for British TV to interview Texans. They choose the capital of Austin and the eccentric locals provide the requisite color but the couple are undergoing their own personal crisis that keeps interfering with their work. **90m/C; VHS, DVD.** Kenneth Cranham; Amanda Root; *D:* Stephen Purvis; *W:* Tom Huckabee; Stephen Purvis; Jesse Sublett; *C:* Thomas Flores Alcala; *M:* Joe Ellen Doering; George Doering.

Deep Murder **2019** Doug (O'Connell) is a lead character in a softcore pornography film, ready to have sex with his brother's attractive wife. Before he can do the deed, he is stabbed to death. Though his jealous brother (McDonald) is an immediate suspect, others emerge as more people--all stock softcore characters who do not realize they are in a film--are killed in the same fashion. The comedy has an original premise with characters who question their reality along with mocking the cliches of softcore porn and slasher films. **95m/C; DVD.** Jessica Parker Kennedy; Jerry O'Connell; Christopher McDonald; Katie (Kathryn) Aselton; Stephanie Drake; ***D:*** Nick Corirossi; ***W:*** Quinn Beswick; Joshua Margolin; Benjamin Smolen; Nikolai Von Keller; ***C:*** Daniella Nowitz; ***M:*** Zachary Dawes; Nick Sena.

Deep Red 🦴🦴 **1994 (R)** When a young girl has an encounter with an extra-terrestrial spacecraft her blood chemistry is mysteriously altered. Now the proteins her body manufactures can lead to immortality and ruthless scientist Newmeyer wants to take advantage of the fact—any way he can. **85m/C; VHS, DVD.** Michael Biehn; Joanna Pacula; John de Lancie; ***D:*** Craig R. Baxley; ***W:*** D. Brent Mote.

Deep Red: Hatchet Murders 🦴🦴 ½ *The Hatchet Murders; Profundo Rosso; Dripping Deep Red; The Sabre Tooth Tiger; Deep Red* **1975** A stylish but gruesome rock music-driven tale of a composer who reads a book on the occult which happens to relate to the sadistic, sangfroid murder of his neighbor. When he visits the book's author, he discovers that she has been horribly murdered as well. **100m/C; VHS, DVD, Blu-Ray.** *IT* David Hemmings; Daria Nicolodi; Gabriele Lavia; Macha Meril; Eros Pagni; Guiliana Calandra; Erykah Badu; Clara Calamai; Nicoletta Elmi; Glauco Mauri; ***D:*** Dario Argento; ***W:*** Dario Argento; Bernardino Zapponi; ***C:*** Luigi Kuveiller; ***M:*** Giorgio Gaslini.

Deep Rising 🦴🦴 ½ **1998 (R)** Huge sea serpents cause massive destruction to the cruise ship Argonautica and put major dinks in the plans of mercenaries, led by Finnegan (Williams), who board the ship for greedy motives. Sticks to a reliable action-horror formula with the good sense to not take its characters or slimy creatures too seriously. Sea critters have inventive ways of disposing of extraneous cast members, resulting in gore aplenty. Slacker humor provided by Finnegan's sidekick Pantucci (Kevin J. O'Connor) injects the film with a certain goofiness. Typical B-movie fare that leans more toward guilty pleasure than quality entertainment. **106m/C; VHS, DVD, Blu-Ray.** Treat Williams; Famke Janssen; Anthony Heald; Kevin J. O'Connor; Wes Studi; Derrick O'Connor; Jason Flemyng; Djimon Hounsou; ***D:*** Stephen Sommers; ***W:*** Stephen Sommers; ***C:*** Howard Atherton; ***M:*** Jerry Goldsmith.

Deep Shock 🦴 **2003 (R)** Gigantic, intelligent electric eels decide to melt the polar ice caps and flood the world's surface because, gosh darn it, they just don't like people. How they know about mankind is odd considering the amount of humans living in the Arctic is negligible. **93m/C; DVD, Streaming.** *GE US* David Keith; Simmone MacKinnon; Mark Sheppard; Sean Whalen; Armando Valdes; ***D:*** Phillip J. Roth; ***W:*** Phillip J. Roth; Brian Mammett; Jeff Rank; ***C:*** Todd Barron; ***M:*** Richard McHugh. **CABLE**

Deep Six 🦴🦴 ½ **1958** A WWII drama that examines the conflict between pacifism and loyalty. A staunch Quaker is called to active duty as a lieutenant in the U.S. Navy, where his beliefs put him into disfavor with shipmates. **110m/C; VHS, DVD.** Alan Ladd; William Bendix; James Whitmore; Keenan Wynn; Efrem Zimbalist, Jr.; Joey Bishop; ***D:*** Rudolph Mate.

Deep Trouble 🦴 ½ **2001** It's strictly amateur hour in this hip-hip urban drama. New York drug kingpin Perry (Stovall) decides that the world of organized crime simply isn't enough, and decides to overtake the business of Star (Scarborough), an entertainment manager who represents up-and-coming actress Diana (Horsford), as well as several stand-up comics. Star and Diana decide that they aren't going to be pushed around by this bully, so they take a stand and the "trouble" begins. Filled with bad acting and amateurish special effects (several characters get shot in the head, which is represented by a simple trickle of blood). The film is very poorly paced, having more scenes of pointless dialogue than action. **102m/C; DVD.** Count Stovall; Janel C. Scarborough; Alyah Horsford; ***D:*** Juney Smith; ***W:*** Juney Smith.

Deep Valley 🦴🦴 **1947** Awkward Libby Saul (Lupino) has been raised on an isolated farm in Deep Valley by her bitter parents (Bainter, Hull). Lonely--despite the devotion of her dog--Libby is thrilled when a chain gang from San Quentin shows up nearby to build a coastal road in Big Sur. She watches the convicts, especially hothead Barry (Clark) who manages to escape. Libby hides him on the family's property but her first romance is fraught with danger. Filmed on location. **104m/B; DVD.** Ida Lupino; Dane Clark; Fay Bainter; Henry Hull; Wayne Morris; William Robertson; ***D:*** Jean Negulesco; ***W:*** Salka Viertel; ***C:*** Ted D. McCord; ***M:*** Max Steiner.

Deep Water 🦴🦴🦴 **2006 (PG)** In 1968 the Sunday Times offered a reward to anyone who could circle the globe in a yacht non-stop by themselves. It focuses on the winner (Knox-Johnston), a man who turned back at the last moment (Moitessier), but especially on Donald Crowhurst. One of the world's unluckiest men, Donald leveraged everything to compete, and if he failed would be broke and homeless. Somewhere along the way his boat was found, but Donald wasn't. Considered one of the better documentaries of the day. **93m/B; DVD.** *GB* Jean Badin; Donald (Don) Kerr; Clare Crowhurst; Donald Crowhurst; Simon Crowhurst; Santiago Franchessie; Ted Hynds; Robin Knox-Johnston; Ron Winspear; ***V:*** Simon Russell Beale; Tilda Swinton; ***D:*** Louise Osmond; Jerry Rothwell; ***C:*** Nina Kellgren; ***M:*** Harry Escott; Molly Nyman.

Deep Waters 🦴 ½ **1948** Maine lobsterman Hod (Andrews) is persuaded by his social worker fiance Ann (Peters) to mentor troubled orphan, Danny (Stockwell). There's a crisis since Danny wants to follow in Hod's seafaring footsteps and Ann is afraid of the dangers involved. **85m/B; DVD.** Dana Andrews; Jean Peters; Dean Stockwell; Cesar Romero; Anne Revere; Ed Begley, Sr.; ***D:*** Henry King; ***W:*** Richard Murphy; ***C:*** Joseph LaShelle; ***M:*** Cyril Mockridge.

Deep Winter 🦴 ½ **2008 (PG-13)** Good snow action and scenery, lame plot. Rebellious downhill racer Tyler Crowe (Lively) reunites with equally risk-taking snowboard buddy Mark Rider (Lutz), whose sister Elisa (List) has a thing for Ty. The guys decide to head to Alaska on a sporting adventure where they'll attempt the most daring snow descent ever captured on film. Things go wrong. **96m/C; DVD.** Eric Lively; Kellan Lutz; Peyton List; Michael Madsen; Robert Carradine; Luke Goss; ***D:*** Mikey Hilb; ***W:*** John Protass; ***C:*** Patrick Reddish; ***M:*** Gerald Brunskill. **VIDEO**

Deeply 🦴🦴 ½ **1999** Fiona McKay (Watson) takes her teenaged daughter Claire (Dunst) to her childhood home on an island off the coast of Nova Scotia. Claire's been traumatized by the sudden death of her boyfriend and is susceptible to the stories told by elderly neighbor, Claire (Redgrave), who has some dark secrets. **102m/C; VHS, DVD.** *CA* Alberta Watson; Lynn Redgrave; Kirsten Dunst; Julia Brendler; Brent Carver; ***D:*** Sheri Elwood; ***W:*** Sheri Elwood; ***M:*** Micki Meuser.

Deepstar Six 🦴 ½ **1989 (R)** When futuristic scientists try to set up an undersea research and missile lab, a group of subterranean monsters get in the way. **97m/C; VHS, DVD.** Taurean Blacque; Nancy Everhard; Greg Evigan; Miguel Ferrer; Matt McCoy; Nia Peeples; Cindy Pickett; Marius Weyers; Thom Bray; Elya Baskin; ***D:*** Sean S. Cunningham; ***W:*** Lewis Abernathy; Geof Miller; ***C:*** Mac Ahlberg; ***M:*** Harry Manfredini.

Deepwater 🦴🦴 **2005 (R)** Neo-noir. Young Nat (Black) is just out of rehab and drifting around when he rescues Finch (Coyote) from a road accident and is rewarded by a job in the man's rundown motel. Finch has a lot of shady local interests and his wife Iris (Maestro) is a hot young tease. Nat's not the most reliable narrator so the plot confusion deepens, leading to an unexpected twist. Adapted from the Matthew F. Jones novel. **93m/C; DVD.** Lucas Black; Peter Coyote; Mia Maestro; Lesley Ann Warren; Michael Ironside; Kristen Bell; Ben Cardinal; Xander Berkeley; ***D:*** David S. Marfield; ***W:*** David S. Marfield; ***C:*** Scott Kevan; ***M:*** Charlie Clouser.

Deepwater Horizon 🦴🦴 **2016 (PG-13)** Based on the true story of the oil rig Deepwater Horizon that exploded in 2010, pumping thousands of gallons of oil into the Gulf of Mexico and killing innocent people in the process. Director Berg delivers another technically proficient drama/thriller, but lacks the heart and soul needed to make it anything more. The characters are introduced but we don't really get to know them before we witness them trying to survive. Berg's buddy Mark Wahlberg stars as Mike Williams, one of the leaders on board. **107m/C; DVD, Blu-Ray.** Mark Wahlberg; Kurt Russell; John Malkovich; Gina Rodriguez; Dylan O'Brien; Kate Hudson; ***D:*** Peter Berg; ***W:*** Matthew Michael Carnahan; Matthew Sand; ***C:*** Enrique Chediak; ***M:*** Steve Jablonsky.

The Deer Hunter 🦴🦴🦴🦴 **1978 (R)** A powerful and vivid portrait of Middle America with three steel-working friends who leave home to face the Vietnam War. Controversial, brutal sequences in Vietnam are among the most wrenching ever filmed; the rhythms and rituals of home are just as purely captured. Neither pro- nor anti-war, but rather the perfect evocation of how totally and forever altered these people are by the war. Emotionally shattering; not to be missed. **183m/C; VHS, DVD, Blu-Ray, HD-DVD.** Robert De Niro; Christopher Walken; Meryl Streep; John Savage; George Dzundza; John Cazale; Chuck Aspegren; Rutanya Alda; Shirley Stoler; Amy Wright; Mady Kaplan; Mary Ann Haenel; Richard Kuss; Pierre Segui; Joe Grifasi; Christopher Colombi, Jr.; Joe Strnad; Paul D'Amato; ***D:*** Michael Cimino; ***W:*** Michael Cimino; Deric Washburn; Louis Garfinkle; ***C:*** Vilmos Zsigmond; ***M:*** John Williams; Stanley Myers. Oscars '78: Director (Cimino), Film, Film Editing, Sound, Support. Actor (Walken); AFI '98: Top 100; Directors Guild '78: Director (Cimino); Golden Globes '79: Director (Cimino); L.A. Film Critics '78: Director (Cimino); Natl. Film Reg. '96; N.Y. Film Critics '78: Film, Support. Actor (Walken); Natl. Soc. Film Critics '78: Support. Actress (Streep).

Def by Temptation 🦴🦴 **1990 (R)** A potent horror fantasy about a young black theology student who travels to New York in search of an old friend. There he meets an evil woman who is determined to seduce him and force him to give in to temptation. Great soundtrack. **95m/C; VHS, DVD, Blu-Ray.** James Bond, III; Kadeem Hardison; Bill Nunn; Samuel L. Jackson; Minnie Gentry; Rony Clanton; Cynthia Bond; John Canada Terrell; ***D:*** James Bond, III; ***W:*** James Bond, III; ***C:*** Ernest R. Dickerson; ***M:*** Paul Lawrence.

Def-Con 4 🦴 ½ **1985 (R)** Three marooned space travelers return to a holocaust-shaken Earth to try to start again, but some heavy-duty slimeballs are in charge and they don't want to give it up. Good special effects bolster a weak script. **85m/C; VHS, DVD.** Maury Chaykin; Kate Lynch; Tim Choate; ***D:*** Paul Donovan.

Def Jam's How to Be a Player 🦴 *How to Be a Player* **1997 (R)** Dray (Bellamy) thinks that monogamy is a wood used to build furniture. Although he has steady girlfriend Lisa (Voorhies), he also has several other ladies in waiting. He is, in fact, a player. He even teaches others to play. What he needs, however, is a screenplay. His sister Jenny (Desselle), who has been hurt in love, cracks the numerical code to his organizer, and invites all of Dray's harem to one party. The result of this booty intervention is Dray's abandonment of his promiscuous ways. The stand-up comedy roots of much of the cast translate into clunky performances, and the direction is pretty played out, too. **93m/C; VHS, DVD.** Bill Bellamy; Natalie Desselle; Mari Morrow; Jermaine "Huggy" Hopkins; A.J. (Anthony) Johnson; Max Julien; Beverly Johnson; Gilbert Gottfried; Bernie Mac; Elise Neal; Amber Smith; Lark Voorhies; ***D:*** Lionel C. Martin; ***W:*** Mark Brown; Demetria Johnson; ***M:*** Darren Floyd.

The Defector 🦴🦴 **1966** Cold War spy thriller with a fragile Clift starring in his last role as American scientist James Bower. While visiting East Germany, Bower is contacted by CIA agent Adam (McDowell) to help a defecting Russian scientist smuggle out some microfilm. The plan is discovered by Russian agent Heinzman (Kruger) who then tries to get Bower to defect to the East. **99m/C; DVD.** *FR GE* Montgomery Clift; Hardy Kruger; Roddy McDowall; Macha Meril; David Opatoshu; Hannes Messemer; ***D:*** Raoul Levy; ***W:*** Raoul Levy; Robert Guenette; Peter Francke; Lewis Gannet; ***C:*** Raoul Coutard; ***M:*** Serge Gainsbourg.

The Defender 🦴 ½ **2004 (R)** Lundgren makes his directorial debut while also starring as Lance Rockford, a government agent hell-bent on taking out terrorists. He does his best in the overly convoluted plot that follows, but most viewers will be easily distracted by Jerry Springer acting as the President of the United States. Yes THAT Jerry Springer. Nothing screams 'the decline of western civilization' (or the script for that matter) like Jerry. **91m/C; DVD.** Dolph Lundgren; Jerry Springer; Thomas Lockyer; Shakara Ledard; Caroline Lee-Johnson; Gerald Kyd; Ian Porter; Howard Antony; Geoffrey Burton; Iddo Goldberg; James Chalke; ***D:*** Dolph Lundgren; ***W:*** Douglas W. Miller; ***C:*** Maxime Alexandre; ***M:*** Adam Norden.

Defending Our Kids: The Julie Posey Story 🦴 ½ **2003** Maybe if Posey weren't presented as so self-righteous (and without acknowledging the efforts of others) this would be a more effective true story covering a serious threat. Colorado homemaker Julie Posey (Potts) is outraged when teenaged daughter Kristyn (Solo) is approached in an online chat room by a guy who turns out to be a pedophile. So she teams up with police investigator Mike Harris (O'Keefe) to pose as a lonely teen to catch other online sexual predators. **90m/C; DVD.** Annie Potts; Michael O'Keefe; Ksenia Solo; Carl Marotte; Karen Glave; Bill MacDonald; ***D:*** Joanna Kerns; ***W:*** Eric Tuchman; ***C:*** Eric Cayla; ***M:*** Normand Corbeil. **CABLE**

Defending Your Life 🦴🦴🦴 **1991 (PG)** Brooks' cock-eyed way of looking at the world travels to the afterlife in this uneven comedy/romance. In Judgment City, where everyone goes after death, past lives are examined and judged. If you were a good enough person you get to stay in heaven (where you wear funny robes and eat all you want without getting fat). If not, it's back to earth for another go-round. Brooks plays an L.A. advertising executive who crashes his new BMW and finds himself defending his life. When he meets and falls in love with Streep, his interest in staying in heaven multiplies. Occasionally charming, seldom out-right hilarious. **112m/C; VHS, DVD.** Albert Brooks; Meryl Streep; Rip Torn; Lee Grant; Buck Henry; George D. Wallace; Lillian Lehman; Peter Schuck; Susan Walters; ***D:*** Albert Brooks; ***W:*** Albert Brooks; ***C:*** Allen Daviau; ***M:*** Michael Gore.

Defendor 🦴🦴 **2009 (R)** Delusional Arthur Poppington (Harrelson) is a social misfit who dresses up in a homemade costume as a wannabe crime fighter. He's constantly crossing paths with crooked cop Dooney (Koteas) while coming to the 'rescue' of druggie hooker Kat (Dennings). No wonder Defendor gets a court-appointed shrink (Oh) when his violent antics go too far. **101m/C; DVD, Blu-Ray, On Demand.** *CA* Woody Harrelson; Elias Koteas; Michael Kelly; Kat Dennings; Sandra Oh; Lisa Ray; Charlotte Sullivan; Clark Johnson; Kristin Booth; ***D:*** Peter Stebbings; ***W:*** Peter Stebbings; ***C:*** David (Robert) A. Greene; ***M:*** John Rowley.

Defense of the Realm 🦴🦴🦴 ½ **1985 (PG)** A British politician is accused of selling secrets to the KGB through his mistress and only a pair of dedicated newspapermen believe he is innocent. In the course of finding the answers they discover a national cover-up conspiracy. An acclaimed, taut thriller. **96m/C; VHS, DVD.** *GB* Gabriel Byrne; Greta Scacchi; Denholm Elliott; Ian Bannen; Bill Paterson; Fulton Mackay; Robbie Coltrane; ***D:*** Dr. David Drury; ***C:*** Roger Deakins. British Acad. '85: Support. Actor (Elliott).

The Defense Rests 🦴🦴 **1934** Successful defense lawyer Matthew Mitchell (Holt) advises his women clients to use their feminine charms in court to sway the judge and jury. These questionable tactics outrage his assistant Joan (Arthur), but rather than blow the whistle, she aspires to reform him. **70m/B; DVD.** Jack Holt; Jean Arthur; Nat Pendleton; Arthur Hohl; Raymond Walburn; Harold Huber; ***D:*** Lambert Hillyer; ***W:*** Jo Swerling; ***C:*** Joseph August.

Defenseless 🦴🦴 **1991 (R)** Hershey tries hard in an unplayable part as a giddy attorney who finds herself trapped in a love-affair/legal case that turns murderous. Good cast and interesting twists contend with a sexist sub-text, which proves a woman can't "have it all." **106m/C; VHS, DVD.** Barbara Hershey; Sam Shepard; Mary Beth Hurt; J.T. Walsh; Sheree North; ***D:*** Martin Campbell; ***W:*** James Cresson; ***M:*** Trevor Jones.

Defiance 🦴🦴 **1979 (PG)** A former merchant seaman moves into a tenement in a run-down area of New York City. When a local street gang begins terrorizing the neighborhood, he decides to take a stand. Familiar plotline handled well in this thoughtful film. **101m/C; VHS, DVD.** Jan-Michael Vincent; Art Carney; Theresa Saldana; Danny Aiello; Lenny Montana; ***D:*** John Flynn; ***W:*** Thomas Michael Donnelly; ***M:*** Basil Poledouris; John Beal.

Defiance 🦴🦴 **1/2 2008 (R)** Based on the true story of the Bielski brothers, Jews who led a resistance movement against the Nazis in Belarus. Tuvia (Craig) is the stoic planner; Zus (Schreiber), the hothead who joins Russian partisans so he can fight more; and naive, young Asael (Bell) who has to grow up in a hurry. In 1941, they establish an unlikely community of refugees deep in the forest while using guerilla tactics to survive. Zwick alternates (not too successfully) between action and sentimentality (the brothers all find wives among the new community) but much will still seem like standard fare seen in countless wartime flicks. Based on the non-fiction book "Defiance: The Bielski Partisans" by Nechama Tec. **136m/C; Blu-Ray, On Demand.** Daniel Craig; Liev Schreiber; Jamie Bell; Mia Wasikowska; Alexa Davalos; Jodhi May; Mark Feuerstein; Tomas Arana; Allan Corduner; Iben Hjejle; ***D:*** Edward Zwick; ***W:*** Edward Zwick; Clayton Frohman; ***C:*** Eduardo Serra; ***M:*** James Newton Howard.

The Defiant Ones 🦴🦴🦴 **1/2 1958** Thought-provoking story about racism revolves around two escaped prisoners (one black, one white) from a chain gang in the rural South. Their societal conditioning to hate each other dissolves as they face constant peril together. Critically acclaimed. **97m/B; VHS, DVD.** Tony Curtis; Sidney Poitier; Theodore Bikel; Lon Chaney, Jr.; Charles McGraw; Cara Williams; ***D:*** Stanley Kramer; ***W:*** Nedrick Young; Harold Jacob Smith; ***C:*** Sam Leavitt; ***M:*** Steve Dorff. Oscars '58: B&W Cinematog., Story & Screenplay; British Acad. '58: Actor (Poitier); Golden Globes '59: Film--Drama; N.Y. Film Critics '58: Director (Kramer), Film, Screenplay.

The Defilers 🦴 **1965 (R)** Disturbing, low-budget J.D. movie in which two thugs imprison a young girl in a basement and force her to be their love slave. **69m/B; VHS, DVD.** Byron Mabe; Jerome Eden; Mai Jansson; ***D:*** David Friedman.

Definitely, Maybe 🦴🦴🦴 **2008 (PG-13)** Almost divorced dad Will Hayes (Reynolds), at daughter Maya's (Breslin) request, recounts the great loves that led him to marry her mother in the first place. As a young, idealistic 1992 Clinton campaign worker, Will has a long distance relationship with college girlfriend Emily (Banks), but soon becomes interested in both journalist Summer (Weisz) and free-spirit campaign worker April (Fisher, in a standout performance). Both Will's love life and career have their ups and downs as he tries to figure out what he wants in his life, learning some tough and often hilarious lessons on the way, and of course, the flick keeps you guessing as to which woman is actually Mom. Bittersweet, smart, above-average romantic comedy with excellent performances from its leads. **111m/C; DVD, Blu-Ray.** *GB US* Ryan Reynolds; Abigail Breslin; Isla Fisher; Elizabeth Banks; Rachel Weisz; Derek Luke; Kevin Kline; Nestor Serrano; Annie Parisse; Liane Balaban; Kevin Corrigan; Adam Ferrara; ***D:*** Adam Brooks; ***W:*** Adam Brooks; ***C:*** Florian Ballhaus; ***M:*** Clint Mansell.

Defying Gravity 🦴🦴 **1999** Frat boy John Griffiths (Chilson) is hiding a secret from his fellow brothers—he's gay and even has a boyfriend, Pete (Handfield), who's sick of John's lying. Pete is gay-bashed and John agonizes over going to the cops with information if it means his off-campus activities could get out. Good intentions but director/writer Keitel's inexperience (this is his first film) shows in a slow pace and amateurishness. **101m/C; VHS, DVD.** Daniel Chilson; Niklaus Lange; Don Handfield; Linna Carter; Seabass Diamond; Lesley Tesh; ***D:*** John Keitel; ***W:*** John Keitel; ***C:*** Thomas M. (Tom) Harting; ***M:*** Tim Westergren.

Degree of Guilt 🦴🦴 **1/2 1995** Good miniseries adaptation of Richard Lloyd Patterson's novels "Eyes of a Child" and "Degree of Guilt." Lawyer Chris Paget (Elliott) makes the mistake of falling for associate Teresa Perlita (Zuniga), who's going through a bad divorce from Richie (Ventresca), a loser who wants custody of their daughter and a lot of money from Teresa. Meanwhile, he's taking on the defense of murder suspect Mary Carelli (Lawrence), who's also Chris's ex-lover and the mother of his son. However, this turns out not to be the only murder investigation going when Richie winds up dead and Chris becomes the prime suspect. **180m/C; VHS, DVD.** David James Elliott; Daphne Zuniga; Sharon Lawrence; Nigel Bennett; Don Francks; Patricia Kalember; ***D:*** Mike Robe; ***W:*** Cynthia Whitcomb; ***C:*** Kees Van Oostrum; ***M:*** Craig Safan. **TV**

Deja Vu 🦴 **1984 (R)** A lame romantic thriller about the tragic deaths of two lovers and their supposed reincarnation 50 years later. **95m/C; VHS, DVD, Blu-Ray.** *GB* Jaclyn Smith; Nigel Terry; Claire Bloom; Shelley Winters; ***D:*** Anthony Richmond; ***W:*** Ezra D. Rappaport; ***M:*** Pino Donaggio.

Deja Vu 🦴🦴 **1/2 1998 (PG-13)** After Dana (Foyt) has an encounter with a mysterious woman in Israel, she is led on a roundabout way to England's White Cliffs of Dover. There she meets Sean (Dillane), and they quickly fall in love, since they have so much in common, such as being married to other people. This proves to be no problem, for destiny, coincidence and director/screenwriter Jaglom conspire to have the two couples share a house for the weekend. Unfortunately, it's hard to detect the true love, since the two leads have as much chemistry as remedial science class. Vanessa Redgrave and her mother Rachel Kempson appear together for the first time as the sister and mother of the host, played by '60s pop singer Neil Harrison. **115m/C; VHS, Streaming.** Victoria Foyt; Stephen (Dillon) Dillane; Vanessa Redgrave; Glynis Barber; Michael Brandon; Vernon Dobtcheff; Noel Harrison; Rachel Kempson; Anna Massey; ***D:*** Henry Jaglom; ***W:*** Victoria Foyt; Henry Jaglom; ***C:*** Hanania Baer; ***M:*** Gaili Schoen.

Deja Vu 🦴🦴 **1/2 2006 (PG-13)** In their third outing, Scott and Washington tackle action and wormholes and bring pic to as logical a conclusion as can be expected. ATF agent Doug Carlin (Washington) is called to New Orleans when a ferry carrying U.S. sailors is blown up. Carlin discovers victim Claire (Patton) had actually died beforehand and must have some connection to the bomber. Carlin gets pulled in by FBI agent Pryzwarra (Kilmer), who tells him about a high-tech project that re-creates images from days earlier, so they can see Claire prior to the tragedy. Since Claire is a babe, Doug would naturally like to save her, and thanks to this time window, he now has a chance of getting to the bomber first. Scott has always known how to move things along and he sets a brisk pace throughout. **126m/C; DVD, Blu-Ray, HD-DVD.** Denzel Washington; Val Kilmer; Paula Patton; Bruce Greenwood; Adam Goldberg; James (Jim) Caviezel; Elden (Ratliff) Henson; Erika Alexander; ***D:*** Tony Scott; ***W:*** Terry Rossio; Bill Marsilii; ***C:*** Paul Cameron; ***M:*** Harry Gregson-Williams.

Delgo 🦴 **2008 (PG)** Computer animated sci-fi feature set in ancient times pits the winged Nohrin race against the kinetically-powered Lockni. The reign of Nohrin's king (Gossett Jr.) is threatened by his sinister sister Sedessa (the late Bancroft, in her final role) thus triggering a war that gets in the way of true love between Lockni teen Delgo (Prinze Jr.) and Nohrin princess Kyla (Love Hewitt). Little surprise that Kyla is kidnapped, thanks to Sedessa, and Delgo and his annoying pal Filo (Kattan) must save the day, along with Nohrin general Bogardus (Kilmer). Total rip-off of stories from "Star Wars" to "Romeo and Juliet" is only spared a "woof" 'cuz it's pretty to look at. **89m/C; Blu-Ray, On Demand.** ***V:*** Freddie Prinze, Jr.; Chris Kattan; Anne Bancroft; Val Kilmer; Jennifer Love Hewitt; Kelly Ripa; Eric Idle; Michael Clarke Duncan; Louis Gossett, Jr.; Malcolm McDowell; Burt Reynolds; ***Nar:*** Sally Kellerman; ***D:*** Marc Adler; Jason Maurer; ***W:*** Patrick Cowan; Carl Dream; Jennifer A. Jones; ***C:*** Herb Kossover; ***M:*** Geoff Zanelli.

Delhi Safari 🦴 **1/2 2012 (PG)** Animated tale about a group of animals traveling to Delhi to speak to the human government about why they're allowing a land devleloper to destroy their forest home. **96m/C; DVD, Blu-Ray.** *IN* ***V:*** Vanessa Williams; Tara Strong; Tom Kenny; Brad Garrett; Carlos Alazraqui; ***D:*** Nikhil Advani; ***W:*** Nikhil Advani; Girish Dhamija; Suresh Nair; ***M:*** Shankar Mahadevan; Loy Mendonsa; Ehsaan Noorani. **VIDEO**

The Deli 🦴🦴 **1997** Johnny Amico (Starr) runs a New York deli, has a bad gambling habit and a big debt to mobster Tommy Tomatoes (Vincent), an outspoken Mama (Malina), and a colorful clientele. Not much happens, the budget is small, but the actors charm. **98m/C; VHS, DVD.** Mike Starr; Judith Malina; Matt Keeslar; Frank Vincent; Ice-T; Heather Matarazzo; Iman; Jerry Stiller; Joseph (Joe) D'Onofrio; ***D:*** John A. Gallagher; ***W:*** John A. Gallagher; John Dorrian; ***C:*** Robert Lechterman; ***M:*** Ernie Mannix.

Deliberate Intent 🦴🦴 **1/2 2001** Well-done fact-based drama follows the case of a triple murder-for-hire and the First Amendment issues the case raised. When Lawrence Horn (McDaniel) hires a man (Johnson) to kill his family, it's discovered that said killer used a book called "Hot Man: A Technical Manual for Independent Contractors" to plan the crime. Lawyer Siegel (Rifkin) brings in First Amendment expert Rod Smolla (Hutton) to sue the publisher for abetting the murder. **120m/C; VHS, DVD.** Timothy Hutton; Ron Rifkin; James McDaniel; Clark Johnson; Penny Johnson; Cliff DeYoung; Kenneth Welsh; ***D:*** Andy Wolk; ***C:*** Ron Garcia. **CABLE**

The Deliberate Stranger 🦴🦴🦴 **1986** Harmon is engrossing as charismatic serial killer Ted Bundy, sentenced to death for several Florida murders and suspected in the killings of a least 25 women in several states. After eluding police for five years Bundy was finally arrested in Florida in 1979. His case became a cause celebre on capital punishment as it dragged on for nine years. Bundy was finally executed in 1989. Based on the book "Bundy: The Deliberate Stranger" by Richard W. Larsen. **188m/C; VHS, DVD.** Mark Harmon; M. Emmet Walsh; Frederic Forrest; John Ashton; George Grizzard; Ben Masters; Glynnis O'Connor; Bonnie Bartlett; Billy Green Bush; Lawrence Pressman; ***D:*** Marvin J. Chomsky. **TV**

Delicacy 🦴🦴 *La Delicatesse* **2012 (PG-13)** Nathalie (Toutou) is devastated when her husband Francois (Marmai) is killed in a car accident and throws herself into her work to escape from her grief. She also tries to fend off the unwanted advances of her boss Charles (Todeschini). Instead, the lovely woman sets her sights on dorky, rumpled co-worker Markus (Damiens), much to the surprise of her judgmental friends. Markus seems to agree with them and he resists her romantic overtures out of fear of eventual rejection. Pleasant enough debut feature by director brothers David and Stephane Foenkinos. In French with subtitles. **108m/C; DVD, Blu-Ray.** *FR* Audrey Tautou; Francois Damiens; Bruno Todeschini; Josephine DeMeaux; Melanie Bernier; Pio Marmai; ***D:*** David Foenkinos; Stephane Foenkinos; ***W:*** David Foenkinos; ***C:*** Remy Chevrin.

The Delicate Delinquent 🦴🦴 **1/2 1956** Lewis's first movie without Dean Martin finds him in the role of delinquent who manages to become a policeman with just the right amount of slapstick. **101m/B; VHS, DVD.** Jerry Lewis; Darren McGavin; Martha Hyer; Robert Ivers; Horace McMahon; ***D:*** Don McGuire; ***W:*** Don McGuire.

Delicatessen 🦴🦴🦴 **1992 (R)** Set in 21st-century Paris, this hilarious debut from directors Jeunet and Caro focuses on the lives of the oddball tenants of an apartment building over a butcher shop. Although there is a famine, the butcher shop is always stocked with fresh meat—made from the building's tenants. Part comedy, part horror, part romance, this film merges a cacophony of sights and sounds with intriguing results. Watch for the scene involving a symphony of creaking bed springs, a squeaky bicycle pump, a cello, and clicking knitting needles. In French with English subtitles. **95m/C; VHS, DVD, Blu-Ray.** *FR* Marie-Laure Dougnac; Dominique Pinon; Karin Viard; Jean-Claude Dreyfus; Ticky Holgado; Anne Marie Pisani; Edith Ker; Patrick Paroux; Jean-Luc Caron; ***D:*** Jean-Pierre Jeunet; Marc Caro; ***W:*** Gilles Adrien; Jean-Pierre Jeunet; Marc Caro; ***C:*** Darius Khondji; ***M:*** Carlos D'Alessi. Cesar '92: Art Dir./Set Dec., Writing.

The Delightful Forest 🦴 *Kuai Huo Lin* **1972** A swordmaster kills his adulterous sister-in-law and her lover and is sent to prison. He's aided in escaping a humiliating new prisoner punishment by a sympathetic guard, who asks a favor in return. The guard's restaurant, The Delightful Forest, is being taken over by a local criminal and he wants some expert help to get it back. Mandarin with subtitles or dubbed. **92m/C; DVD.** *CH* Lung Ti; Ching Tien; Mu Chu; Feng Yu; ***D:*** Cheh Chang; Hsueh Li Pao; ***W:*** Cheh Chang; Shu Mei Chin; Kuang Ni; ***C:*** Ting-pang Juan.

Delightfully Dangerous 🦴🦴 **1945** Often Deadly Dull. A farfetched musical rooted in yesteryear about mismatched sisters, one a 15-year-old farm girl, the other a New York burlesque dancer, in competition on Broadway. **92m/B; VHS, DVD.** Jane Powell; Ralph Bellamy; Constance Moore; Arthur Treacher; Louise Beavers; ***D:*** Arthur Lubin.

Delinquent Daughters 🦴 **1/2 1944** Slow-paced drama about a high school girl who commits suicide and the cop and reporter who try to find out why so darn many kids are getting into trouble. **71m/B; VHS, DVD.** June Carlson; Fifi d'Orsay; Teala Loring; ***D:*** Al(bert) Herman.

Delinquent School Girls WOOF! *Bad Girls* **1984 (R)** Three escapees from an asylum get more than they bargained for when they visit a Female Correctional Institute to fulfill their sexual fantasies. Buys into just about every conceivable stereotype. **89m/C; VHS, DVD.** Michael Pataki; Bob Minos; Stephen Stucker; ***D:*** Gregory Corarito.

Delirious 🦴 **1/2 1991 (PG)** A writer for a TV soap opera wakes from a bash on the head to find himself inside the story where murder and mayhem are brewing. Can he write himself back to safety, and find romance along the way? Somehow Candy just isn't believeable as a romantic lead and the film has few laughs. **96m/C; VHS, DVD, Blu-Ray.** John Candy; Mariel Hemingway; Emma Samms; Raymond Burr; David Rasche; Dylan Baker; Charles Rocket; Jerry Orbach; Renee Taylor; Robert Wagner; ***D:*** Tom Mankiewicz; ***W:*** Lawrence J. Cohen; ***M:*** Cliff Eidelman.

Delirious 🦴🦴 **1/2 2006** Smalltime New York paparazzo Les Galantine (the perfectly cast Buscemi) doesn't like to admit to being lonely but when homeless wannabe actor Toby (Pitt) starts hanging around, Les offers him odd jobs and a place to crash. Toby may just prove to be Les's money shot when the handsome young man catches the eye of pop phenom K'Harma (Lohman) but Toby is smarter and more ambitious than he first appears, meaning Les may be left scrambling in the crowd once again. **107m/C; DVD.** Steve Buscemi; Michael Pitt; Gina Gershon; Callie (Calliope) Thorne; Kevin Corrigan; K'Harma Leeds; Richard Short; ***D:*** Tom DiCillo; ***W:*** Tom DiCillo; ***C:*** Frank DeMarco; ***M:*** Anton Sanko.

Deliver Us from Eva 🦴🦴 **1/2 2003 (R)** Eva (Union) is the overbearing, self-righteous eldest of the four Dandridge sisters. After their parents' untimely death, Eva took on the role of the surrogate mother and since then has become an overpowering influence in their lives. Her sisters' significant others, tired of their lives being dictated by Eva, decide to hire Ray (LL Cool J), a noted ladies man, to woo her out of their lives. The attraction turns real though, and complications arise. Plot is predictable, (it's yet another updating of Shakespeare's "Taming of the Shrew") but you don't mind due to great chemistry between the two solid leads. **105m/C; VHS, DVD, Blu-Ray.** Gabrielle Union; LL Cool J; Duane Martin; Essence Atkins; Robine Lee; Meagan Good; Mel Jackson; Dartanyan Edmonds; Kym E. Whitley; Royale Watkins; ***D:*** Gary Hardwick; ***W:*** Gary Hardwick; B.E. Brauner; ***C:*** Alexander Grusynski; ***M:*** Marcus Miller.

Deliver Us From Evil 🦴🦴 **1973** Made for TV movie shows that greed is a killer. A skyjacker parachutes into a remote mountain range with $600,000 in cash and ends up dead when he crosses paths with a group of buddies on a weekend camping trip. The guys divide up the loot and then have to hike out before a blizzard—or their own paranoia—overcomes them. **74m/C; DVD.** Jan-Michael Vincent; Jack Weston; George Kennedy; Bradford Dillman; Charles Aidman; Jim Davis; Allen Pinson; ***D:*** Boris Sagal; ***W:*** Jack Sowards; ***C:*** Bill Butler; ***M:*** Andrew Belling. **TV**

Deliver Us From Evil 🦴 **2014 (R)** Another piece of nonsense that uses religious iconography to draw scares from an audience that should be exhausted by this kind of ineffective and unmemorable horror movie string-pulling. "Based on a true story," as they all are, Bana stars as New York cop Ralph Sarchie, a man caught up in a nightmare involving exorcism and the supernatural. The potential for a great film about a man dealing with his own questions about religion is there, but this is just a pale attempt at jump scares and weak screenwriting. **118m/C; DVD, Blu-Ray.** Eric Bana; Edgar Ramirez; Olivia Munn; Joel McHale; Dorian Missick; Chris Coy; Sean Harris; ***D:*** Scott Derrickson; ***W:*** Scott Derrickson; Paul Harris Boardman; ***C:*** Scott Kevan; ***M:*** Christopher Young.

Deliverance 🦴🦴🦴🦴 **1972 (R)** Terrifying exploration of the primal nature of man and his alienation from nature, based on the novel by James Dickey, which he adapted for the film (he also makes an appearance as a sheriff). Four urban professionals, hoping to get away from it all for the weekend, canoe down a southern river, encounter crazed backwoodsmen, and end up battling for survival. Excellent performances all around, especially by Voight. Debuts for Beatty and Cox. Watch for O'Neill as a sheriff, and director Boorman's son Charley as Voight's son. "Dueling Banjos" scene and tune are memorable as is scene where the backwoods boys promise to make the fellows squeal like pigs. **109m/C; VHS, DVD, Blu-Ray, HD-DVD.** Jon Voight; Burt Reynolds; Ronny Cox; Ned Beatty; James Dickey; Bill McKinney; Ed O'Neill; Charley Boorman; ***D:*** John Boorman; ***W:*** James Dickey; ***C:*** Vilmos Zsigmond; ***M:*** Eric Weissburg. Natl. Film Reg. '08.

Delivered 🦴🦴 *Death by Pizza* **1998 (R)** Pizza deliveryman Will Sherman (Strickland) is the unfortunate witness to a murder by serial killer Reed (Eldard). When Reed realizes Will saw him, he goes after him but the cops have come to the conclusion that it's Will who's the killer—so he has to evade the cops and Reed as well. It's all played for laughs. **90m/C; VHS, DVD.** David Strickland; Ron Eldard; Leslie Stefanson; Scott Bairstow; Nicky Katt; Jillian Armenante; Bob Morrisey; Mark Berry; ***D:*** Guy Ferland; ***W:*** Andrew Liotta; Lawrence Trilling; ***C:*** Shane Kelly; ***M:*** Nicholas Pike.

The Delivery 🦴🦴 **1999 (R)** Euro-thriller finds buddies Guy (Douglas) and Alfred (van Huet) so desperate for money that they agree to do a job for a crime boss. Seems he needs them to deliver a large shipment of Ecstasy from Barcelona to Amsterdam. Added into the mix is the prerequisite tough babe—in this case, Loulou (Meriel). Drugs, chases, sex, and violence. **100m/C; VHS, DVD.** *NL BE* Fedja Van Huet; Freddy Douglas; Auriele Meriel; Rik Launspach; Esmee De La Bretoniere; Jonathan Harvey; Hidde Maas; Christopher Simon; ***D:*** Roel Reine; ***W:*** David Hilton; ***C:*** Jan van den Nieuwenhuyzen.

Delivery Man 🦴 **2013 (PG-13)** Vaughn continues his steep downward trajectory to oblivion with yet another grating comedy in which his man-child has to learn to grow up. This time he appears in a remake of the 2011 French-Canadian flick, "Starbuck," about a gentleman who learns that, due to a mix-up at the sperm bank, he is the father of 533 children, some of whom now want to meet their bio dad. As David, Vaughn hems and haws his way through the awkward set-up until finally getting to a more notable degree of dramatic range than usual, but not in time to save this unfunny mess. **105m/C; DVD, Blu-Ray.** Vince Vaughn; Chris Pratt; Cobie Smulders; Bobby Moynihan; Simon Delaney; ***D:*** Ken Scott; ***W:*** Ken Scott; ***C:*** Eric Alan Edwards; ***M:*** Jon Brion.

Delos Adventure 🦴 **1986 (R)** A geological expedition in South America stumbles upon covert Russian activities and must battle to survive in this overly violent actioner. **98m/C; VHS, DVD.** Roger Kern; Jenny Neumann; Kevin Brophy; ***D:*** Joseph Purcell.

The Delphi Bureau: The Merchant of Death Assignment 🦴 ½ **1972** ABC pilot TV movie for the short-lived spy comedy series. Glenn Garth Gregory is an operative for a clandestine organization that reports only to the president. His unlikely handler is matron Sybil Van Loween and Gregory's assignment is to discover who's stealing surplus weaponry, including Army jets. **78m/C; DVD.** Laurence Luckinbill; Celeste Holm; Dean Jagger; Cameron Mitchell; Bradford Dillman; Bob Crane; ***D:*** Paul Wendkos; ***W:*** Sam Rolfe; ***C:*** Ben Colman; ***M:*** Harper MacKay. **TV**

The Delta 🦴🦴 **1997** White, middleclass Memphis teenager Lincoln Bloom (Gray) is leading a double life. He parties with his girlfriend Monica (Huss) and macho buddies but also sneaks off to cruise the city's gay pick-up spots. Which is where he meets the older John (Chan), an Amerasian immigrant from Vietnam, whose unknown father was a black soldier. The two have a brief romantic idyll but while the openly gay John is desperate for love, Lincoln is still uncertain about his sexual identity and the disparity between their lives. Feature debut for both Sachs and his two lead actors. **85m/C; VHS, DVD.** Shayne Gray; Thang Chan; Rachel Zan Huss; Ricky Little; ***D:*** Ira Sachs; ***W:*** Ira Sachs; ***C:*** Benjamin P. Speth; ***M:*** Michael Rohatyn.

Delta Farce 🦴 **2007 (PG-13)** Watching a Larry movie is like dressing squirrels in little ballet outfits. It might seem like a good idea when you're drunk, but you aren't certain you'd like your friends and neighbors to see you doing it, and you'll probably feel bad about yourself when you're done. Three idiotic weekend warriors fall asleep in a cargo plane bound for Iraq. Due to weather problems, the pilot has to dump the cargo (and them) over Mexico, which does not happen to be between the US and Iraq on any map currently in print. They immediately begin to try to 'spread freedom and democracy' by helping a village in trouble, and can't even tell the difference between Mexicans and Iraqis. Ineptly done and poorly funded, at least it does its best to insult anyone who isn't white, male, straight, drunk, and stupid. **89m/C; DVD, Blu-Ray.** Larry the Cable Guy; DJ Qualls; Marisol Nichols; Danny Trejo; Bill Engvall; Keith David; Glenn Morshower; Christina Moore; Lisa Lampanelli; Ed O'Ross; ***D:*** C.B. Harding; ***W:*** Bear Aderhold; Thomas F.X. Sullivan; ***C:*** Tom Priestley; ***M:*** James Levine.

Delta Force 🦴🦴 **1986 (R)** Based on the true hijacking of a TWA plane in June 1985. Arab terrorists take over an airliner; the Delta Force, led by Lee Marvin and featuring Norris as its best fighter, rescue the passengers in ways that cater directly to our nationalistic revenge fantasies. Average thriller, exciting and tense at times, with fine work from Marvin, Norris, and Forster. **125m/C; VHS, DVD, Blu-Ray.** Lee Marvin; Chuck Norris; Shelley Winters; Martin Balsam; George Kennedy; Hanna Schygulla; Susan Strasberg; Bo Svenson; Joey Bishop; Lainie Kazan; Robert Forster; Robert Vaughn; Kim Delaney; ***D:*** Menahem Golan; ***W:*** James Bruner; ***C:*** David Gurfinkel; ***M:*** Alan Silvestri.

Delta Force 2: Operation Stranglehold 🦴 ½ *Delta Force 2: The Colombian Connection* **1990 (R)** Delta Force is back with martial artist and military technician Norris at the helm. Action-packed and tense. **110m/C; VHS, DVD, Blu-Ray.** John P. Ryan; Chuck Norris; Billy Drago; Richard Jaeckel; Paul Perri; ***D:*** Aaron Norris; ***W:*** Lee Reynolds; ***C:*** Joao Fernandes; ***M:*** Frederic Talgorn.

Delta Force 3: The Killing Game 🦴 ½ *Young Commandos* **1991 (R)** A terrorist mastermind plants an atomic bomb in an American city, and the President has only one choice...call in the Delta Force. The leading men in this lackluster thriller are the sons of some of Hollywood's biggest stars. **97m/C; VHS, DVD.** Nick Cassavetes; Eric Douglas; Mike Norris; Matthew Penn; John P. Ryan; Sandy Ward; ***D:*** Sam Firstenberg; ***W:*** Boaz Davidson.

Delta Force Commando 🦴 ½ **1987 (R)** Two U.S. Fighter pilots fight against terrorism in the deadly Nicaraguan jungle. **90m/C; VHS, DVD.** *IT* Fred Williamson; Bo Svenson; ***D:*** Frank (Pierluigi Ciriaci) Valenti.

Delta Force One—The Lost Patrol 🦴 *D.F.1: The Lost Patrol* **1999 (R)** Fans of the original Norris and Marvin version will need to avoid this 'sequel' exploiting its popularity. It has the usual plot of army commandoes going after terrorists who have kidnapped a nuclear missile and are threatening to launch it from a cave that has no roof for the missile to go through. And with the obligatory oblivious guards left to watch it. **120m/C; DVD.** Gary Daniels; Mike Norris; Bentley Mitchum; John Rhys-Davies; Uri Gavriel; Ze'ev Revach; Michelle Kapeta; Orr Malka; Sasson Gabai; Jonathan Cherchi; Jacob Gyir Cohen; Galia Soudri; Jack Messinger; Revital Shachar; Hezi Saddik; ***D:*** Joseph Zito; ***W:*** Clay McBride; ***C:*** Gideon Porath.

Delta Heat 🦴🦴 **1992 (R)** A new designer drug hits L.A. and detective Mike Bishop (Edwards) follows his partner to the drug's source in Louisiana. When Bishop arrives he discovers his partner has been tortured and murdered in order to keep the drug lord's foes in line. Bishop must then save himself and find justice in the steamy streets of New Orleans. Routine lone guy vs. bad guys actioner. **91m/C; VHS, DVD.** Anthony Edwards; Lance Henriksen; Betsy Russell; Linda Dona; Rod Masterson; John McConnell; Clyde Jones; ***D:*** Michael Fischa.

Delta of Venus 🦴 ½ **1995 (R)** Paris, 1940—beautiful young American Elena (England), an aspiring author, falls for handsome Lawrence (Mandylor), a writer of dirty books. But she finds out Lawrence isn't faithful and winds up supporting herself as a nude model and writing her own erotic tales. Lots of sex scenes and an equal amount of pretensions. Based on the erotic novel "Delta of Venus" by Anais Nin. Prague substitutes for Paris as the film location. Also availble unrated; the theatrical version came out as NC-17. **100m/C; VHS, DVD.** Audie England; Costas Mandylor; Erick Da Silva; Raven Snow; ***D:*** Zalman King; ***W:*** Patricia Louisianna Knop; Elisa Rothstein; ***C:*** Eagle Egilsson; ***M:*** George S. Clinton.

The Deluge 🦴🦴 *Potop* **1973** Romance woven around the Polish-Swedish war in the 17th century. Adapted from the 1886 novel by Nobel prize-winning author Henryk Sienkiewicz, and filmed largely on location in authentic castles of the era. Polish with subtitles. **185m/C; VHS, DVD.** *PL* Daniel Olbrychski; Malgorzata Braunek; Wladyslaw Hancza; Leszek Herdegen; Andrzej Lapicki; ***D:*** Jerzy Hoffman; ***C:*** Jerzy Wojcik; ***M:*** Kazimierz Serocki.

Delusions of Grandeur 🦴🦴 ½ *La Folle des Grandeurs* **1976** A French comedy of court intrigue set in 17th-century Spain. In French with English subtitles. Based loosely on Victor Hugo's "Ruy Blas." **85m/C; VHS, DVD.** *FR* Yves Montand; Louis de Funes; Alice Sapritch; Karin Schubert; Gabriele Tinti; ***D:*** Gerard Oury.

Dementia 🦴🦴 ½ **1998** Wild-eyed sexual thriller owes a bit to "Diabolique." Recovering from a breakdown, wealthy Kathrine (Bursel) becomes friendly with her outpatient nurse Luisa (Sanchez). Then Luisa's smarmy ex-husband Sonny (Schulze) shows up and things get twisty. Production values are not top drawer and the cast is not well known, but director Keith keeps things moving nicely. **85m/C; DVD.** Marisol Padilla Sanchez; Patricia Bursiel; Matt Schulze; Azura Skye; Matthew Sullivan; Jesus Nebot; Susan Davis; ***D:*** Woody Keith; ***W:*** Woody Keith; R.G. Fry; ***C:*** David Trulli; ***M:*** Karl Preusser.

Dementia 13 🦴🦴 ½ *The Haunted and the Hunted* **1963** This eerie thriller, set in a creepy castle, is an early Coppola film about the members of an Irish family who are being offed by an axe murderer one by one. **75m/B; VHS, DVD, Blu-Ray.** William Campbell; Luana Anders; Bart Patton; Patrick Magee; Barbara Dowling; Ethne Dunn; Mary Mitchell; Karl Schanzer; ***D:*** Francis Ford Coppola; ***W:*** Francis Ford Coppola; ***C:*** Charles Hannawalt; ***M:*** Ronald Stein.

Demetrius and the Gladiators 🦴🦴 ½ **1954** A sequel to "The Robe," wherein the holy-robe-carrying slave is enlisted as one of Caligula's gladiators and mixes with the trampy empress Messalina. **101m/C; VHS, DVD.** Victor Mature; Susan Hayward; Michael Rennie; Debra Paget; Anne Bancroft; Jay Robinson; Barry Jones; Richard Egan; William Marshall; Ernest Borgnine; ***D:*** Delmer Daves; ***W:*** Philip Dunne; ***C:*** Milton Krasner.

The Demolisher 🦴🦴 **2015** Bruce (Ry Barrett) is an angry repairman turned vigilante, seeking revenge on the gang who assaulted his girlfriend. At least at first. Bruce's stability quickly begins to unravel, and before long it's clear he's far more of a danger to people than the local gangs. While inspired by early 70's and 80's vigilante thrillers, it's more arthouse than grindhouse, so it may not appeal entirely to fans of the films that inspired it. **86m/C; DVD, Blu-Ray, Streaming.** *CA* Ryan Barrett; Tianna Nori; Jessica Vano; Duncan McLellan; Gerrit Sepers; ***D:*** Gabriel Carrer; ***W:*** Ryan Barrett; Gabriel Carrer; Andrew Bussey; Martin Buzora; Duane Frey; Angus McLellan; ***C:*** Martin Buzora; ***M:*** Glen Nicholls. **VIDEO**

Demolition 🦴🦴 **2015 (R)** Heavy-handed metaphors and self-important filmmaking sink this collaboration between Jake Gyllenhaal and Canadian director Jean-Marc Vallee. Gyllenhaal plays Davis, a very successful investment banker whose world is shattered when his wife dies in a car accident in the opening scene. Unable to express emotion in a traditional way, Davis starts dismantling his life, literally, including demolishing his house. As his father-in-law (Cooper) begs him to keep it together, he begins a relationship with a customer service representative (Watts) and her son (Judah Lewis). It's one of those movies that thinks it's a lot smarter and edgier than it is, despite Gyllenhaal's solid work. **100m/C; DVD, Blu-Ray.** Jake Gyllenhaal; Naomi Watts; Chris Cooper; Judah Lewis; C.J. Wilson; ***D:*** Jean-Marc Vallee; ***W:*** Bryan Sipe; ***C:*** Yves Bélanger.

Demolition High 🦴🦴 ½ **1995 (R)** Standard actioner finds New York kid Lenny (Haim) having problems adjusting to his new California high school, where he's labeled a troublemaker. But real trouble comes along when a group of terrorists, fleeing police after a robbery, take over the school and hold the teachers and students as hostages. Fortunately, Lenny is able to lead a secret counterattact. **85m/C; VHS, Streaming.** Corey Haim; Alan Thicke; Jeff Kober; Dick Van Patten; ***D:*** Jim Wynorski; ***W:*** Steve Jankowski; ***C:*** Zoran Hochstatter; ***M:*** Kevin Kiner.

Demolition Man 🦴🦴 **1993 (R)** No-brain sci-fier rests on the action skills of Stallone and Snipes. Psychovillain Snipes (sporting a Dennis Rodman 'do) is pursued by equally violent cop Stallone in the late 1990s. Then they're cryogenically frozen, defrosted in 2032, and back to their old tricks. One problem. This is not a fun future: virtual reality sex is the only kind allowed and puritan ethics and political correctness are enforced to the max. Cop and bad guy get to show this highly orderly society some really violent times. Implausible plot and minimal acting, but lots of action and violence for fans. **115m/C; VHS, DVD, Blu-Ray.** Sylvester Stallone; Wesley Snipes; Sandra Bullock; Nigel Hawthorne; Benjamin Bratt; Bob Gunton; Glenn Shadix; Denis Leary; Jack Black; Steve Kahan; Grand L. Bush; Bill Cobbs; Dan Cortese; Rob Schneider; Jesse Ventura; ***D:*** Marco Brambilla; ***W:*** Daniel Waters; Robert Reneau; Peter M. Lenkov; ***C:*** Alex Thomson; ***M:*** Elliot Goldenthal.

The Demolitionist 🦴🦴 **1995 (R)** Tough undercover cop Alyssa Lloyd (Eggert) is killed by crimelord Mad Dog Burne (Grieco) and then resurrected by scientist Jack Crowley (Abbott) as a hard-hitting futuristic superheroine who's out to save Metro City from evil. **100m/C; VHS, DVD.** Nicole Eggert; Richard Grieco; Bruce Abbott; Susan Tyrrell; Peter Jason; Sarah Douglas; Andras Jones; Heather Langenkamp; David Anthony Marshall; Jack Nance; Tom Savini; ***D:*** Robert Kurtzman; ***W:*** Brian DiMuccio; Dino Vindeni; ***C:*** Marcus Hahn; ***M:*** Shawn Patterson.

The Demon 🦴 ½ **1981 (R)** A small town may be doomed to extinction, courtesy of a monster's thirst for the blood of its inhabitants. **94m/C; VHS, DVD.** *SA* Cameron Mitchell; Jennifer Holmes; ***D:*** Percival Rubens; ***W:*** Percival Rubens; ***C:*** Vincent Cox.

Demon 2016 (R) Polish director Marcin Wrona takes the classic possession tale and merges it with the story of a young man's wedding. In this clever horror flick, Piotr (Itay Tiran) becomes possessed by the Jewish legend of the Dybbuk. Wrona captures the essence of a man basically having a nervous breakdown during his wedding with a wonderful combination of black comedy and striking horror. One of the most visually outstanding horror films in years, from the stormy night on which Piotr unearths something supernatural to the beautifully designed wedding scenes. **94m/C; DVD.** Itay Tiran; Agnieszka Zulewska; Andrzej Grabowski; Tomasz Schuchardt; Katarzyna Herman; ***D:*** Marcin Wrona; ***W:*** Marcin Wrona; Pawel Maslona; ***C:*** Pawel Flis; ***M:*** Marcin Macuk; Krzysztof Penderecki.

Demon Barber of Fleet Street ½ *Sweeney Todd: The Demon Barber of Fleet Street* **1936** Loosely based on an actual event, this film inspired the 1978 smash play "Sweeney Todd." Slaughter stars as a mad barber who doesn't just cut his client's hair. He happens to have a deal cooked up with the baker to provide him with some nice 'juicy' filling for his meat pies. Manages to be creepy and funny at the same time. **68m/B; VHS, DVD, Blu-Ray.** *GB* Tod Slaughter; Eve Lister; Bruce Seton; ***D:*** George King.

A Demon in My View ½ **1992 (R)** In a role similar to his infamous Norman Bates in "Psycho," Perkins stars as a man who hides a terrible secret—he is a former serial killer. When a fellow tenant in his apartment house accidentally destroys his doll, Perkins' tenuous sanity is shaken and he begins killing again. A smart thriller. Perkins last big-screen role. **98m/C; VHS, Streaming.** Anthony Perkins; Sophie Ward; Stratford Johns; ***D:*** Petra Haffter; ***W:*** Petra Haffter.

The Demon Lover **WOOF!** *Devil Master; Master of Evil* **1977 (R)** Leader of a satanic cult calls forth the devil when he doesn't get his way. Poorly acted and badly produced. Features comic book artists Val "Howard the Duck" Mayerick and Gunnar "Leatherface" Hansen. **87m/C; VHS, DVD.** Christmas Robbins; Val Mayerick; Gunnar Hansen; Tom Hutton; David Howard; ***D:*** Donald G. Jackson; Jerry Younkins; ***W:*** Donald G. Jackson; Jerry Younkins.

Demon Lust **2001** "The Sopranos" meet "Dracula" in this ultra low-budget New Jersey independent production. Nick (Teller) and Tony (Vincent) owe $5,000 to a mobster who has sent a thug (Savini) to collect. After some allegedly comic bits, the two guys find themselves hooked up with Amanda (Stevens), a beautiful babe who's really a monster. Most of the lead roles are well acted. **?m/CDVD.** Edward Lee Vincent; Zander Teller; Brinke Stevens; Tom Savini; ***D:*** David A. Goldberg; ***W:*** Coven Balfour; ***C:*** Joseph Robert Jobe; ***M:*** Coven Balfour.

Demon of Paradise **WOOF!** **1987 (R)** Dynamite fishing off the coast of Hawaii unearths an ancient, man-eating lizard-man. Unveven, unexciting horror attempt. **84m/C; VHS, DVD.** Kathryn Witt; William (Bill) Steis; Leslie Huntly; Laura Banks; Frederick Bailey; ***D:*** Cirio H. Santiago; ***W:*** Frederick Bailey; ***C:*** Ricardo Remias.

Demon Rage ½ *Satan's Mistress; Fury of the Succubus; Dark Eyes* **1982 (R)** Neglected housewife drifts under the spell of a phantom lover. **98m/C; VHS, DVD.** Britt Ekland; Lana Wood; Kabir Bedi; Don Galloway; John Carradine; Sherry Scott; ***D:*** James Polakof.

Demon Seed **1977 (R)** When a scientist (Weaver) and his wife (Christie) separate so he can work on "Proteus," a somewhat biological supercomputer, the terminal within his computer-controlled home allows Proteus to infiltrate, taking over the house and his wife. Proteus' intent? To procreate. Bizarre and taut; based on a Dean Koontz novel. **97m/C; VHS, DVD, Blu-Ray.** Julie Christie; Fritz Weaver; Gerrit Graham; Berry Kroeger; Ron Hays; Lisa Lu; Larry J. Blake; ***V:*** Robert Vaughn; ***D:*** Donald Cammell; ***W:*** Robert Jaffe; Roger O. Hirson; ***C:*** Bill Butler.

Demonia **WOOF!** **1990** Archaeologists digging in Sicily uncover a sealed convent where five nuns were crucified in the 15th century. This discovery unleashes an ancient evil and bizarre murders begin to take place. Unfortunately, that's about it as far as the plot goes. Even by Fulci's standards, "Demonia" is slow and pondering, with many scenes taking place twice, once in reality and then again in a dream (nightmare?). Fulci's trademark gore is scant and the special effects are laughable. Even die-hard Fulci fans will be disappointed. **90m/C; DVD.** *IT* Brett Halsey; Meg Register; Carla Cassola; Al Cliver; Lucio Fulci; ***D:*** Lucio Fulci; ***W:*** Lucio Fulci; Piero Regnoli; ***C:*** Luis Ciccarese.

Demonic Toys ½ **1990 (R)** The possessed play-things attack a bunch of unfortunates in a warehouse, and pumped-up lady cop Scoggins deserves an award for keeping a straight face. Skimpily scripted gore from the horror assembly-line at Full Moon Productions. Far more entertaining are the multiple behind-the-scenes featurettes on the tape. **86m/C; VHS, DVD, Blu-Ray.** Tracy Scoggins; Bentley Mitchum; Michael Russo; Jeff Weston; Daniel Cerny; PeteR Schrum; Richard Speight, Jr.; ***D:*** Peter Manoogian.

Demonlover **2002** Big business meets the high-stakes game of high tech Internet pornography and results in a confusing, unnecessarily violent thriller. Nielsen plays Diane, a corporate spy acting as an assistant to Henri-Pierre Volf (Malartre), the head of multinational conglomerate Volf-Group. VolfGroup threatens to take over TokyoAnime, producers of revolutionary, animated 3-D smut, which sparks rival companies Mangatronics and Demonlover to get nasty. Nasty pretty much sums up just about all the characters and the rest of the action throughout, led by the particularly immoral Diane. Characters are totally devoid of sympathy while the plot begins to totally unravel halfway through. **120m/C; VHS, DVD.** *FR* Connie Nielsen; Charles Berling; Chloë Sevigny; Gina Gershon; Dominique Reymond; Jean-Baptiste Malartre; ***D:*** Olivier Assayas; ***W:*** Olivier Assayas; ***C:*** Denis Lenoir; ***M:*** Sonic Youth.

Demonoid, Messenger of Death *Macabra* **1981 (R)** Discovery of an ancient temple of Satan worship drastically changes the lives of a young couple when the husband becomes possessed by the Demonoid, which initially takes on the form of a severed hand. Poor script needs hand, producing a number of unintentionally laughable moments. **85m/C; VHS, DVD, Blu-Ray.** Samantha Eggar; Stuart Whitman; Roy Cameron Jenson; ***D:*** Alfredo Zacharias.

Demons ½ *Demoni* **1986 (R)** A horror film in a Berlin theatre is so involving that its viewers become the demons they are seeing. The new monsters turn on the other audience members. Virtually plotless, very explicit. Rock soundtrack by Accept, Go West, Motley Crue, and others. Revered in some circles, blasted in others. Followed by "Demons 2." **89m/C; VHS, DVD, Blu-Ray.** *IT* Urbano Barberini; Natasha Hovey; Paolo Cozza; Karl Zinny; Fiore Argento; Fabiola Toledo; Nicoletta Elmi; Michele (Michael) Soavi; ***D:*** Lamberto Bava; ***W:*** Lamberto Bava; Dario Argento; Franco Ferrini; Dardano Sacchetti; ***C:*** Gianlorenzo Battaglia; ***M:*** Claudio Simonetti.

The Demons ½ *Les Demons* **2019** Ten-year-old Felix (Tremblay-Grenier) sees much to fear in the world. He is scared that his parents, Claire (Bussieres) and Marc (Lucas), will break up. Felix is also terrified because of stories, told by his older brother Francois (Schneider), of bad things happening to neighborhood kids. Yet his siblings, including Emmanuelle (Mottet), adore him and try to reassure him when he fears he has AIDS. After locking Alexandre (Poirer) into a swimming pool locker, Felix experiences unexpected dangers at the pool and among people there. Thoughtful probes the consequences of adult paranoia on children. French with subtitles. **118m/C; DVD.** Edouard Tremblay-Grenier; Pier-Luc Funk; Vassili Schneider; Sarah Mottet; Laurent Lucas; ***D:*** Philippe Lesage; ***W:*** Philippe Lesage; ***C:*** Nicholas Canniccioni.

Demons 2 ½ **1987 (R)** Inferior sequel to "Demons." The son of horror-meister Mario Bava, Lamberto collaborated with Italian auteur Argento (who co-wrote and produced) to create an improbable sequel (storywise) which seems to have been edited by some kind of crazed cutting room slasher with equally hackneyed dubbing. Residents of a chi-chi high rise watching a documentary about the events of "Demons--a sort of high-tech play-within-a-play ploy—when a demon emerges from the TV, spreads his creepy cooties, and causes the tenants to sprout fangs and claws and nasty tempers. Lots of blood drips from ceilings, plumbing fixtures, and various body parts. **88m/C; VHS, DVD, Blu-Ray.** *IT* David Edwin Knight; Nancy Brill; Coralina Cataldi-Tassoni; Bobby Rhodes; Asia Argento; Virginia Bryant; ***D:*** Lamberto Bava; ***W:*** Dario Argento; Lamberto Bava; ***C:*** Gianlorenzo Battaglia; ***M:*** Simon Boswell.

Demons from Her Past ½ **2007** Despite the lurid cover art, this Lifetime effort is not a horror movie (although it is rather horrible). At 18, Allison was wrongly convicted of vehicular homicide and sent to prison. Upon her release, she moved to Paris and made a new life for herself, but years later her grandmother's funeral brings Allison home. Knowing she was framed, Allison is determined to get revenge on the men responsible, but they have no intention of letting her reveal the truth. **93m/C; DVD.** Alexandra Paul; Cynthia Gibb; Michael Woods; Rob Stewart; John Ralston; Kevin Jubinville; Sophie Gendron; ***D:*** Douglas Jackson; ***W:*** Christine Conradt; ***C:*** Bert Tougas; ***M:*** Steve Gurevitch. **CABLE**

Demons of Ludlow **1975** Demons attend a small town's bicentennial celebration intent on raising a little hell of their own. **83m/C; VHS, DVD.** Paul von Hauser; Stephanie Cushna; James Robinson; Carol Perry; ***D:*** Steven Kuether.

Demons of the Mind *Blood Evil; Blood Will Have Blood* **1972 (R)** A sordid psychological horror film about a baron in 19th century Austria who imprisons his children, fearing that mental illness is a family trait. **85m/C; VHS, DVD, Blu-Ray.** *GB* Michael Hordern; Patrick Magee; Yvonne Mitchell; Robert Hardy; Gillian Hills; Virginia Wetherell; Shane Briant; Paul Jones; Thomas Heathcote; Kenneth J. Warren; ***D:*** Peter Sykes; ***W:*** Christopher Wicking; ***C:*** Arthur Grant.

Demonstone *Heartstone* **1989 (R)** A TV reporter becomes possessed by a Filipino demon and carries out an ancient curse against the family of a corrupt government official. **90m/C; VHS, DVD.** R. Lee Ermey; Jan-Michael Vincent; Nancy Everhard; ***D:*** Andrew Prowse.

Demoted **2011 (R)** Tedious and vulgar workplace comedy where everyone is so unlikeable they should all be fired. Successful tire salesmen Rodney (Vartan) and Mike (Astin) get away with bullying schlub Ken (Cross) because they're buds with boss Bob (Klein). Bob suddenly dies and it's Ken who gets the top dog spot. Instead of firing his tormentors, he demotes them down the corporate ladder to secretaries to teach them a lesson about humiliation. **94m/C; DVD, Blu-Ray.** Michael Vartan; Sean Astin; David Cross; Robert Klein; Ron White; ***D:*** James B. Rogers; ***W:*** Dan Callahan; ***C:*** David Insley; ***M:*** David Kitay. **VIDEO**

Dempsey **1983** In this film, based on Jack Dempsey's autobiography, Williams plays the role of the famed world heavyweight champ. His rise through the boxing ranks as well as his personal life are chronicled. A bit slow-moving considering the pounding fists and other action. **110m/C; VHS, DVD.** Treat Williams; Sam Waterston; Sally Kellerman; Victoria Tennant; Peter Mark Richman; Jesse Vint; Bonnie Bartlett; James Noble; ***D:*** Gus Trikonis; ***M:*** Billy Goldenberg. **TV**

Den of Thieves ½ **2018 (R)** An experienced gang of bank robbers sets its sights on the millions of dollars' worth of bills tagged to be destroyed at L.A.'s Federal Reserve. On the other side of the law is an elite squad of the Sheriff's department that thinks it can out-macho the bad guys. Personal lives intersect, and there's a good amount of action and twisty turns. Butler does well enough but the story never quite lives up to classic heist flicks, particularly *Heat* -- clearly the inspiration for this one. **140m/C; DVD, Blu-Ray.** Gerard Butler; Pablo Schreiber; O'Shea Jackson, Jr.; 50 Cent; Meadow Williams; ***D:*** Christian Gudegast; ***W:*** Christian Gudegast; ***C:*** Terry Stacey; ***M:*** Cliff Martinez.

Denial ½ **2016 (PG-13)** Based on Deborah E. Lipstadt's book "History on Trial: My Day in Court with a Holocaust Denier," Mick Jackson's awards bait drama tells an interesting story in an incredibly uninteresting way. Weisz plays Lipstadt, who accused David Irving (Spall) of being a Holocaust denier. Irving then sued her for libel, and under the British system it is the accused's duty to prove otherwise. So, essentially, Lipstadt had to prove the Holocaust happened to prove Irving denied it. Everyone here is very good, but it's a flat, TV-movie presentation of a fascinating story. **110m/C; DVD, Blu-Ray.** Rachel Weisz; Tom Wilkinson; Timothy Spall; Andrew Scott; Jack Lowden; ***D:*** Mick Jackson; ***W:*** David Hare; ***C:*** Haris Zambarloukos; ***M:*** Howard Shore.

Dennis the Menace ½ **1993 (PG)** Straight from the Hughes kiddie farm comes Kevin McAllister—oops!?Dennis Mitchell (newcomer Gamble), curious, crafty, and blond five-year-old. He dreams and schemes, but everything he does manages to be a threat to the physical and mental well being of hot-head neighbor Mr. Wilson (Matthau, perfectly cast as the grump). Lloyd is very nasty as protagonist Switchblade Sam; Plowright, Thompson, and Stanton round out the cast as Mrs. Wilson and the Mitchell parents, respectively. Sure to please young kids, but parents may be less enthralled with this adaptation of the popular '50s comic strip and subsequent TV series. **96m/C; VHS, DVD.** Walter Matthau; Mason Gamble; Joan Plowright; Christopher Lloyd; Lea Thompson; Robert Stanton; Billie Bird; Paul Winfield; Amy Sakasitz; Kellen Hathaway; Arnold Stang; ***D:*** Nick Castle; ***W:*** John Hughes; ***C:*** Thomas Ackerman; ***M:*** Jerry Goldsmith.

A Dennis the Menace Christmas **2007** In yet another variation of "A Christmas Carol," cutie neighborhood nuisance Dennis Mitchell (Cotton) tries to help grouchy Mr. Wilson (Wagner) learn the true meaning of Christmas. **?m/CDVD.** Robert Wagner; Louise Fletcher; George Newbern; Jack Noseworthy; Maxwell Perry Cotton; Kim Schraner; ***D:*** Ron Oliver; ***W:*** Kathleen Laccinole; ***C:*** C. Kim Miles; ***M:*** Peter Allen. **VIDEO**

Dennis the Menace Strikes Again ½ **1998 (G)** Direct-to-video sequel finds hyperactive Dennis (Cooper) trying to save curmudgeonly Mr. Wilson (Rickles) from a pair of con men. **75m/C; VHS, DVD.** Justin Cooper; Don Rickles; George Kennedy; Betty White; Brian Doyle-Murray; Carrot Top; ***D:*** Charles Kanganis; ***W:*** Tim McCanlies; ***C:*** Christopher Faloona; ***M:*** Graeme Revell. **VIDEO**

The Dentist ½ **1996 (R)** After seeing this movie, you may never want to sit in that dental chair again. When his marriage falls apart, L.A. dental specialist Dr. Alan Feinstone (Bernsen) takes to pill popping and psychotic behavior, including demonic drilling and particularly bloody oral surgery. **93m/C; VHS, DVD.** Corbin Bernsen; Ken Foree; Linda Hoffman; Michael Stadvec; ***D:*** Brian Yuzna; ***W:*** Charles Finch; Stuart Gordon; Dennis Paoli; ***C:*** Levie Isaacks; ***M:*** Alan Howarth.

The Dentist 2: Brace Yourself **1998 (R)** Allan Feinstone (Bernsen) has escaped from the asylum to which he was sent in the first film. He's settled in a rural community and set up another practice. This is one guy who doesn't claim to be painless. **99m/C; VHS, DVD.** Corbin Bernsen; Jillian McWhirter; Linda Hoffman; ***D:*** Brian Yuzna; ***W:*** Brian Yuzna; ***C:*** Jurgen Baum; ***M:*** Alan Howarth. **VIDEO**

Dentist In the Chair ½ **1960** Dumb Brit comedy about dental students David (Monkhouse) and Brian (Stevens) who inadvertantly get involved with smalltime crook Sam Field (Connor) who gives them a load of expensive dental equipment. But they have to get rid of the goods before they're accused of theft. **87m/B; VHS, DVD.** *GB* Bob Monkhouse; Ronnie Stevens; Kenneth Connor; Peggy Cummins; Eric Barker; Stuart Saunders; ***D:*** Don Chaffey; ***W:*** Bob Monkhouse; Val Guest; ***C:*** Reg Wyer; ***M:*** Kenneth V. Jones.

Denver and the Rio Grande ½ **1952** In the 1870s, two rival railroad crews are working to be the first to carve a route through the Colorado Rockies. The Denver and Rio Grande group are the good guys while the Canyon City and San Juan boys are unscrupulous saboteurs. The criminal acts may be routine but director Haskin keeps the action rolling along. **90m/C; DVD, Blu-Ray.** Edmond O'Brien; J. Carrol Naish; Dean Jagger; Sterling Hayden; Lyle Bettger; Kasey Rogers; Zasu Pitts; Paul Fix; ***D:*** Byron Haskin; ***W:*** Frank Gruber; ***C:*** Ray Rennahan; ***M:*** Paul Sawtell.

The Departed 🦴🦴🦴½ **2006 (R)** Scorsese goes back to the mob (Boston Irish this time) for a complicated and violent tale of identity and betrayal based on the Hong Kong flick "Infernal Affairs." Colin (a strong Damon) is a state police officer who's actually a mole for crazy kingpin Frank Costello (Nicholson, nuttier than ever) while jittery Billy (an equally strong DiCaprio) is the cop who's infiltrated Costello's gang at the behest of his tough bosses Queenan (Sheen) and Dignam (Wahlberg). Both younger men are involved—in different ways—with femme shrink Madolyn (Farmiga). Tension builds, insults and bullets fly, and the truth will out—with some unexpected consequences. Scorsese's at his best (if in familiar territory). **150m/C; DVD, Blu-Ray, HD-DVD.** Leonardo DiCaprio; Matt Damon; Jack Nicholson; Mark Wahlberg; Martin Sheen; Ray Winstone; Vera Farmiga; Anthony Anderson; Alec Baldwin; James Badge Dale; Mark Rolston; Kevin Corrigan; James Dale; Kristen Dalton; ***D:*** Martin Scorsese; ***W:*** William Monahan; ***C:*** Michael Ballhaus; ***M:*** Howard Shore. Oscars '06: Adapt. Screenplay, Director (Scorsese), Film, Film Editing; Directors Guild '06: Director (Scorsese); Golden Globes '07: Director (Scorsese); Writers Guild '06: Adapt. Screenplay.

The Departure 2017 87m/C; DVD, Streaming. ***D:*** Lana Wilson; ***W:*** Lana Wilson; David Teague; ***C:*** Emily Topper; ***M:*** Nathan Michel.

The Departure 🦴½ **2020** Nate (Gunderson) and Jessica (Chappell) are ready for the next stage of their relationship—moving in together. The day after they make serious plans, Nate's boss gives him a six-month-long assignment in New York City, far from his Los Angeles home. Fearful that his girlfriend will cheat on him, he asks his best friend John (Lauer), who is awkwardly dating the indifferent Amber (Lemmon), to seduce her and see what happens. The outcome fundamentally changes the trio's relationship with each other. Sometimes difficult to watch, it also features a number of poorly shot and lit scenes. **70m/C; DVD.** Jon Briddell; Kendall Chappell; Grant Gunderson; Austin Lauer; Olivia Lemmon; ***D:*** Merland Hoxha; ***W:*** Merland Hoxha; ***C:*** Ludovica Isidori; Wey Wang.

Departures 🦴🦴 *Okuribito* **2008** Cellist Daigo Kobayashi (Motoki) is crushed when his Tokyo orchestra breaks up and he is jobless. Diago and his wife Mika (Hirosue) return to his hometown so they can start over and he responds to a job ad thinking it's for a travel agency. Only in this case 'preparing for departures' is a niche market for morticians which means ritually preparing bodies for cremation and working with grieving families. Although shocked at first, Daigo finds he has a natural affinity for the job, much to his wife's dismay. It gets a little sappy and it's too long but Motoki has an eccentric charm. Japanese with subtitles. **130m/C; Blu-Ray.** *JP* Masahiro Motoki; Ryoko Hirosue; Tsutomu Yamazaki; ***D:*** Yojiro Takita; ***W:*** Kundo Koyama; ***C:*** Takashi Hamada; ***M:*** Joe Hisaishi. Oscars '08: Foreign Film.

Depraved 🦴½ **1998** Opella and Dan spice up their sex lives by acting out their fantasies. But they start to go too far for Dan and he has a fight with his fiance, who storms out. Only the next morning Dan discovers Opella's dead body. Naturally, instead of calling the cops, Dan calls his brother, and they decide to dispose of the body and come up with an alibi. Can you spell trouble? **90m/C; VHS, DVD.** Seidy Lopez; Antonio Garcia Guzman; Mario Lopez; Barbara Niven; ***D:*** Rogelio Lobato. **VIDEO**

Depth Charge 🦴 **2008** A familiar submarine actioner that borrows from other, better movies. Renegade Commander Krieg (Roberts) and his henchmen take over a nuclear sub and make ransom demands to U.S. President Taylor (Bostwick). The sub's doctor, Ellers (Gedrick), has remained aboard as has a young crewman (Warren Jr.) and they try to avoid getting killed while coming up with a heroic plan to save the day. **85m/C; DVD.** Jason Gedrick; Eric Roberts; Barry Bostwick; Bridget Ann White; Chris Warren, Jr.; Corbin Bernsen; ***D:*** Terrence O'Hara; ***W:*** Dennis A. Pratt; ***C:*** Dane Peterson; ***M:*** Stephen Graziano. **VIDEO**

Deputy Marshal 🦴½ **1950** Hall trails a pair of bankrobbers, fights off landgrabbers, and finds romance as well. **75m/B; VHS, DVD.** Jon Hall; Frances Langford; Dick Foran; ***D:*** William Berke; ***W:*** William Berke.

Derailed 🦴🦴 **2002 (R)** Spy Jacques Kristoff (Van Damme) has never told his family what he does for a living, which is a problem when they decide to surprise him on one of his "business trips." It's really bad timing since they're on the same Munich-bound train as thief Galina (Harring) who is carrying vials of mutated smallpox, which is wanted by international criminal Mason Cole (Arana), who hijacks the train. Low-budget but lots of action. **89m/C; VHS, DVD.** Jean-Claude Van Damme; Laura Elena Harring; Tomas Arana; Susan Gibney; Jessica Bowman; Lucy Jenner; ***D:*** Bob Misiorowski; ***W:*** Adam Gierasch; Jace Anderson; ***C:*** Ross W. Clarkson; ***M:*** Serge Colbert. **VIDEO**

Derailed 🦴½ **2005 (R)** Disappointing thriller has Owen as Charles Schine, unhappily married, in the midst of a midlife crisis, and more than willing to be enthralled by the charms of equally unhappy Lucinda (Aniston). However, while in their seedy hotel room, the couple is attacked by psycho-thief Laroche (Cassel), who then threatens to reveal their affair unless they pay him off. Since Owen can't convincingly play a wimp (though he tries), you wait for him to mop the floor with this sleazy Frenchman. First English-language feature for Swedish director Hafstrom; adapted from the James Siegel novel. **110m/C; DVD, HD-DVD.** Clive Owen; Jennifer Aniston; Vincent Cassel; Melissa George; Giancarlo Esposito; David Morrissey; Georgina Chapman; Denis O'Hare; Tom Conti; Addison Timlin; Xzibit; RZA; ***D:*** Mikael Hafstrom; ***W:*** Stuart Beattie.

Deranged 🦴🦴🦴 **1974 (R)** Of the numerous movies based on the cannibalistic exploits of Ed Gein ("Psycho," "The Texas Chainsaw Massacre," etc.), this is the most accurate. A dead-on performance by Blossom and a twisted sense of humor help move things along nicely. The two directors, Gillen and Ormsby, previously worked together on the classic "Children Shouldn't Play with Dead Things." An added attraction is the early special effect work of gore wizard Tom Savini. **82m/C; VHS, DVD, Blu-Ray.** *CA* Roberts Blossom; Cosette Lee; Robert Warner; Marcia Diamond; Brian Sneagle; Leslie (Les) Carlson; Marion Waldman; Micki Moore; Pat Orr; Robert McHeady; ***D:*** Jeff Gillen; Alan Ormsby; ***W:*** Jeff Gillen; Alan Ormsby; ***C:*** Jack McGowan; ***M:*** Carl Zittrer.

Deranged 🦴½ **1987 (R)** A mentally unstable, pregnant woman is attacked in her apartment after her husband leaves town. She spends the rest of the movie engaged in psychotic encounters, real and imagined. Technically not bad, but extremely violent and grim. Not to be confused with 1974 movie of the same name. **85m/C; VHS, DVD.** Jane Hamilton; Paul Siederman; Jennifer Delora; James Gillis; Jill Cumer; Gary Goldman; ***D:*** Chuck Vincent.

Deranged 🦴🦴½ *Anacardium* **2001** Ultra talky thriller dealing with the conversations between renter and landlord. Soon talk of revenge and a husband out for blood creep into play. Sounds ridiculous? Somehow pulled off through decent acting and a tight script. Awarded best picture at the New York Independent Film Festival. **125m/C; DVD.** Frank John Hughes; Richard Ruccolo; Sean Masterson; Bob Rumnock; Laura Cayouette; ***D:*** Scott Thomas; ***W:*** Scott Thomas; ***C:*** Carl F. Bartels; ***M:*** Lars Anderson. **VIDEO**

Derby 🦴🦴🦴 **1971 (R)** The documentary story of the rise to fame of roller-derby stars on the big rink. **91m/C; VHS, DVD.** Charlie O'Connell; Lydia Gray; Janet Earp; Ann Colvello; Mike Snell; ***D:*** Robert Kaylor.

Derby Day 🦴🦴 *Four Against Fate* **1952** Three stories set during the famous Derby Day horse race. Lady Helen Forbes (Neagle) and David Scott (Wilding) commiserate after learning that their spouses died in the same plane crash. Housemaid Michele (Clouthier) wins a fan magazine contest and is escorted to the races by indifferent film star Gerald Berkeley (Graves). Adulterous lovers Betty (Withers) and Tommy (McCallum) are collecting their winnings when they are arrested. **84m/B; DVD.** *GB* Anna Neagle; Michael Wilding; Googie Withers; John McCallum; Suzanne Cloutier; Peter Graves; ***D:*** Herbert Wilcox; ***W:*** Alan Melville; Monckton Hoffe; John Baines; ***C:*** Mutz Greenbaum.

The Derby Stallion 🦴🦴½ **2005** No, it's not a good movie but it's got horses and Efron is as cute as heck, so you think tweener girls will care? Teenager Patrick (Efron) discovers his calling when he befriends alcoholic Houston Jones (Cobbs), who offers to train him to ride in the statewide steeplechase race. But Patrick's father (Moses), a former big leaguer, is pressuring him to stick with baseball. **98m/C; DVD.** Zac Efron; Bill Cobbs; William R. Moses; Colton James; Tonja Walker; Michael Nardini; Sarah Blackman; Crystal Hunt; Rob Pinkston; ***D:*** Craig Clyde; ***W:*** Kimberly Gough; ***C:*** John Gunselman; ***M:*** Billy Preston. **VIDEO**

Derrida 🦴🦴½ **2002** This provocative biographical documentary looks at influential French intellectual Jacques Derrida. In addition to looking at the life of the so-called "father of deconstruction," the film focuses on his critical thinking pursuits and how they impacted consideration of the nature of texts, their language, and their meaning. Also considered is his visionary influence on literature analysis, linguistics, philosophy, and law, as well as his later writings on topics such as justice. **84m/C; DVD, Streaming, Download.** Jacques Derrida; ***D:*** Kirby Dick; Amy Ziering; ***C:*** Kirsten Johnson; ***M:*** Ryuichi Sakamoto.

Dersu Uzala 🦴🦴🦴½ **1975** An acclaimed, photographically breathtaking film about a Russian surveyor in Siberia who befriends a crusty, resourceful Mongolian. They begin to teach each other about their respective worlds. Produced in Russia; one of Kurosawa's stranger films. **140m/C; VHS, DVD.** *JP RU* Yuri Solomin; Maxim Munzuk; ***D:*** Akira Kurosawa; ***W:*** Akira Kurosawa; Yuri Naginbin; ***C:*** Asakazu Nakai; Yuri Gantman; Fyodor Dobronravov; ***M:*** Isaak Shvarts. Oscars '75: Foreign Film.

The Descendants 🦴🦴🦴½ **2011 (R)** This complex dramedy finds the Oscar-winning writer/director back in prime form, using the changing physical landscape of Hawaii as a metaphor for the changing emotional landscape of its lead character, Matt King (Clooney). At the film's open, Matt's wife has been in a horrible boating accident, leaving her on life support and fading fast. King realizes he doesn't have the skill set to care for his daughters and his emotions become more conflicted when he learns his spouse was having an affair. Insightful, funny, and truly moving, Payne once again finds what is relatable and human in extreme circumstances. **115m/C; DVD, Blu-Ray.** George Clooney; Beau Bridges; Robert Forster; Matthew Lillard; Shailene Woodley; Amara Miller; Patricia Hastie; Nick Krause; Judy Greer; ***D:*** Alexander Payne; ***W:*** Alexander Payne; Nat Faxon; Jim Rash; ***C:*** Phedon Papamichael. Oscars '11: Adapt. Screenplay; Golden Globes '12: Actor--Drama (Clooney), Film--Drama; Ind. Spirit '12: Screenplay, Support. Actress (Woodley); Writers Guild '11: Adapt. Screenplay.

Descending Angel 🦴🦴🦴 **1990 (R)** The premise is familiar: a swastika-friendly collaborator is forced out of the closet. But the cast and scripting make this cable there's-a-Nazi-in the-woodwork suspenser better than average, despite its flawed finale. Scott plays a well-respected Romanian refugee—active in the community, in the church, and in Romanian-American activities—whose daughter's fiance (Roberts) suspects him of Nazi collusion. **96m/C; VHS, DVD.** George C. Scott; Diane Lane; Eric Roberts; Mark Margolis; Vyto Ruginis; Amy Aquino; Richard Jenkins; Jan Rubes; ***D:*** George C. Scott; Jeremy Paul Kagan; ***W:*** George C. Scott. **CABLE**

The Descent 🦴🦴½ **2005 (R)** Six adventure-junkie galpals go spelunking in Appalachia and find their vacation ruined by a pack of creepy humanoids who are none too happy to have guests in their cave. So much for the trip serving to distract poor Sarah (MacDonald) from her grief over the deaths of her family. Smart, nerve-jangling terror ensues as the friends battle personal demons and each other while fending off the slimy subterranean creatures. The effects aren't always very special, but horror fans will still dig both the gory splatter and the mental tension. Original ending shown in the film's U.K. version was slightly changed for its U.S. release. **99m/C; DVD, Blu-Ray.** *GB* Shauna Macdonald; Natalie Mendoza; Alex Reid; Nora-Jane Noone; Saskia Mulder; Oliver Milburn; MyAnna Buring; Molly Kayll; ***D:*** Neil Marshall; ***W:*** Neil Marshall; ***C:*** Sam McCurdy; ***M:*** David Julyan.

Descent 🦴 **2005 (PG)** The government discovers the oil drilling they've been doing under the Earth's crust is about to kill millions via earthquakes and volcanic eruptions. They hope to push the crust back up before nuclear detonations whilst arguing about whether or not to tell the public. **96m/C; DVD.** *CA* Luke Perry; Natalie Brown; Michael Dorn; Rick Roberts; Ward Marie; ***D:*** Terry Cunningham; ***W:*** Michael Konyves; ***C:*** Thom Best; ***M:*** Sean Murray. **CABLE**

Descent 🦴½ **2007 (NC-17)** Feminist empowerment or just revenge fantasy exploitation? College grad school student Maya (Dawson) is brutally raped by date Jared (Faust) in an attack that she doesn't report and that leaves her a basket case. She seems to get back some equilibrium by hitting the clubs and getting interested in dominating DJ Adrian (Patrick), which also appears to get Maya focused on planning revenge on Jared. Dawson's worth watching but the film is only so-so. Also available in an R-rated version. **104m/C; DVD.** Rosario Dawson; Chad Faust; Marcus Patrick; ***D:*** Talia Lugacy; ***W:*** Talia Lugacy; Brian Priest; ***C:*** Christopher La Vasseur; Jonathan Furmanski; ***M:*** Alex Moulton.

The Descent 2 🦴🦴 **2009 (R)** Picks up two days after the first horror flick left off. Emergency workers search around the Appalachian cave system where six female spelunkers went underground. Sarah—the only survivor—emerges covered in blood and with amnesia. Sheriff Vaines, deputy Rios, and three rescue workers make Sarah go back inside to find her missing friends only to be confronted by the same hungry crawlers who attacked before. A few twists and a lot of gore. **94m/C; DVD.** Shauna Macdonald; Gavan O'Herlihy; Kristin Cummings; Douglas Hodge; Josh Dallas; Anna Skellern; ***D:*** Jon Harris; ***W:*** J. Blakeson; James McCarthy; ***C:*** Sam McCurdy; ***M:*** David Julyan. **VIDEO**

Desert Bloom 🦴🦴🦴 **1986 (PG)** On the eve of a nearby nuclear bomb test, a beleaguered alcoholic veteran and his family struggle through tensions brought on by a promiscuous visiting aunt and the chaotic, rapidly changing world. Gish shines as the teenage daughter through whose eyes the story unfolds. From a story by Corr and Linda Ramy. **103m/C; VHS, DVD.** Jon Voight; JoBeth Williams; Ellen Barkin; Annabeth Gish; Allen Garfield; Jay Underwood; ***D:*** Eugene Corr; ***W:*** Eugene Corr; ***C:*** Reynaldo Villalobos; ***M:*** Brad Fiedel.

Desert Blue 🦴🦴 **1998 (R)** Baxter, California is a tiny (pop. 87) desert town whose one claim to fame is a towering re-creation of an ice cream cone that has drawn the attention of pop culture prof Lance (Heard). Lance has come to Baxter with his snooty teen TV star daughter, Skye (Hudson), and the duo are trapped in town when it's quarantined by a toxic spill. Skye eventually connects to the town's disaffected teens, including Blue (Sexton), Pete (Affleck), and Ely (Ricci). **87m/C; VHS, DVD.** Brendan Sexton, III; Kate Hudson; John Heard; Christina Ricci; Casey Affleck; Sara Gilbert; Ethan Suplee; Lucinda Jenney; ***D:*** Morgan J. Freeman; ***W:*** Morgan J. Freeman; ***C:*** Enrique Chediak; ***M:*** Vytas Nagisetty.

Desert Commandos 🦴🦴 **1967** When the Allies appear to be winning WWII, the Nazis devise a plan to eliminate all of the opposing forces' leaders at once. **96m/C; VHS, DVD.** *IT GE FR* Ken Clark; Horst Frank; Jeanne Valerie; Carlo Hinterman; Gianni Rizzo; ***D:*** Umberto Lenzi; ***W:*** Umberto Lenzi.

The Desert Fox *Rommel—Desert Fox* **1951** Big-budgeted portrait of German Army Field Marshal Rommel, played by Mason, focuses on the soldier's defeat in Africa during WWII and his subsequent, disillusioned return to Hitler's Germany. Mason played Rommel again in 1953's "Desert Rats." **87m/B; VHS, DVD.** James Mason; Cedric Hardwicke; Jessica Tandy; Luther Adler; ***D:*** Henry Hathaway.

Desert Guns ½ **1936** Lawman Kirk Allenby (Tearle) is hired to bring in rancher Bob Enright who's suspected of being a cattle thief. After wounding Enright, Allenby agrees to impersonate him to save Enright's sister Roberta (Morris) from being forced to marry villain Jeff Bagley (Gould). There's something freaky about Roberta then falling for Allenby, who's her brother's lookalike. Tearle retired after this low-budget western. **70m/B; DVD.** Conway Tearle; Margaret Morris; William (Bill) Gould; Charles French; Budd Buster; ***D:*** Charles (Hutchison) Hutchinson; ***W:*** Jacques Jaccard; ***C:*** J. Henry Kruse.

Desert Hearts **1986 (R)** An upstanding professional woman travels to Reno, Nevada in 1959 to obtain a quick divorce, and slowly becomes involved in a lesbian relationship with a free-spirited casino waitress. **93m/C; VHS, DVD, Blu-Ray.** Helen Shaver; Audra Lindley; Patricia Charbonneau; Andra Akers; Dean Butler; Jeffrey Tambor; Denise Crosby; Gwen Welles; ***D:*** Donna Deitch; ***W:*** Natalie Cooper; ***C:*** Robert Elswit.

Desert Heat *Inferno; Coyote Moon* **1999 (R)** Loner Eddie Lomax (Van Damme) is left for dead at an abandoned highway stop in the Mojave Desert after a gang steals his motorcycle. An unexpected rescue by an old friend leaves Eddie with one thought—revenge. **95m/C; VHS, DVD.** Jean-Claude Van Damme; Noriyuki "Pat" Morita; Danny Trejo; Gabrielle Fitzpatrick; Larry Drake; Vincent Schiavelli; ***D:*** Danny Mulroon; ***W:*** Tom O'Rourke; ***C:*** Ross A. Maehl; ***M:*** Bill Conti. **VIDEO**

Desert Migration **2016** An insightful feature-length documentary on HIV positive men in Palm Springs, California. Before the introduction of protease inhibitors, many HIV positive men believed their lifespans would be short. While the drugs saved their lives and gave them unexpected years and quality of life, many such men had build lives living with HIV. A number moved to Palm Springs in search of a healing desert oasis. Though the people that live there are tolerant and sunshine warming, they still must heal physically and emotionally—a process explored in this film. **80m/C; DVD, Streaming, Download.** ***D:*** Daniel F. Cardone; ***W:*** Daniel F. Cardone; ***C:*** Austin Ahlborg; ***M:*** Gil Talmi.

The Desert of the Tartars *Le Desert des Tartares; Il Deserto dei Tartari* **1976 (PG)** Story of a young soldier who dreams of war and discovers that the real battle for him is with time. **140m/C; VHS, DVD.** *FR IT IA* Vittorio Gassman; Giuliano Gemma; Helmut Griem; Philippe Noiret; Jacques Perrin; Fernando Rey; Jean-Louis Trintignant; Max von Sydow; ***D:*** Valerio Zurlini; ***W:*** Jean-Louis Bertucelli; Andre G. Brunelin; ***C:*** Luciano Tovoli; ***M:*** Ennio Morricone.

The Desert Rats **1953** A crusty British captain (Burton) takes charge of an Australian division during WWII. Thinking they are inferior to his own British troops, he is stiff and uncaring to the Aussies until a kind-hearted drunk and the courage of the division win him over. Crack direction from Wise and Newton's performance (as the wag) simply steal the movie. Mason reprises his role as Germany Army Field Marshal Rommel from "The Desert Fox." **88m/B; VHS, DVD.** Richard Burton; Robert Newton; Robert Douglas; Torin Thatcher; Chips Rafferty; Charles "Bud" Tingwell; James Mason; ***D:*** Robert Wise.

Desert Saints **2001 (R)** Hit man Banks (Sutherland) picks up hitchhiker Bennie (Walters) and impulsively decides to use her assistance in his next job. But Bennie turns out to be an FBI agent assigned to hunt Banks down—or maybe she isn't. **88m/C; VHS, DVD.** Kiefer Sutherland; Melora Walters; Rachel Ticotin; Jamey Sheridan; Leslie Stefanson; William Sage; ***D:*** Richard Greenberg; ***W:*** Richard Greenberg; Wally Nichols; ***C:*** John Newby; ***M:*** Richard (Rick) Marvin.

The Desert Song **1943** This musical is given an updated wartime story from the original operetta. Paul Hudson is the piano player at a nightclub in Morocco. He's also secretly working with the locals to stop the Nazis using them as forced labor to build a railroad across North Africa. Previously filmed in 1929 and remade in 1953. **90m/C; DVD.** Dennis Morgan; Irene Manning; Bruce Cabot; Victor Francen; Lynne Overman; Gene Lockhart; ***D:*** Robert Florey; ***W:*** Robert Buckner; ***C:*** Bert Glennon.

The Desert Song ½ **1953** MacRae secretly leads a band of do-gooders against the evil forces of a dastardly sheik. Grayson is the general's daughter who falls in love with our disguised hero. Third filmed version of the Sigmund Romberg operetta creaks along with the talents of MacRae and Grayson rising about the hackneyed plot. **96m/C; DVD.** Gordon MacRae; Kathryn Grayson; Raymond Massey; Steve Cochran; Dick Wesson; Allyn Ann McLerie; Ray Collins; William Conrad; ***D:*** H. Bruce Humberstone; ***W:*** Roland Kibbee; ***C:*** Robert Burks; ***M:*** Max Steiner.

Desert Thunder **1999 (R)** Lee Miller (Baldwin) is a retired Air Force pilot who rejoins the action when he's called to lead a commando mission to defeat an Iraqi terrorist threat. Low-budget still boasts some good explosions and aerial scenes. **88m/C; VHS, DVD.** Daniel Baldwin; Richard Tyson; Richard Portnow; Stacy Haiduk; ***D:*** Jim Wynorski; ***W:*** Lenny Juliano. **VIDEO**

Desert Winds **1995** Weird little fantastical romance finds Jackie (Graham), who lives near the New Mexican desert, regularly communing with nature on a rocky plateau. Lonely Jackie once heard the voice of Eugene (Nickles), who lives 500 miles away in Arizona, thanks to a rare phenomenon known as a wind tunnel, but it takes seven years before she hears his voice again. **97m/C; VHS, DVD.** Heather Graham; Michael A. (M.A.) Nickles; Grace Zabriskie; Jack Kehler; Adam Ant; ***D:*** Michael A. (M.A.) Nickles; ***W:*** Michael A. (M.A.) Nickles; ***C:*** Denis Maloney; ***M:*** James McVay.

Deserter *Simon: An English Legionnaire* **2002** Idealistic Englishman Simon Murray (Fox) joins the French Foreign Legion after a broken romance. His fellow recruits have much darker pasts yet they bond over their brutal training regime. French President DeGaulle grants Algeria its independence, leaving the Legionnaires divided between those who support the decision and those who side with the nationalists as the situation gets more violent. Set in 1960; adapted from Murray's memoirs. **95m/C; DVD, Blu-Ray.** *UK* Paul Fox; Tom (Thomas) Hardy; Yorick Van Wageningen; Aitor Merino; Javier Alcina; Felicite de Jeu; Christian Mulot; ***D:*** Martin Huberty; ***W:*** Axel Aylwen; William Akers; ***C:*** Dino Parks; ***M:*** Debbie Wiseman. **VIDEO**

The Deserters ½ **1983** Sergeant Hawley, a Vietnam-era hawk, hunts deserters and draft-dodgers in Canada. There, he confronts issues of war and peace head-on. **110m/C; VHS, DVD.** *CA* Alan Scarfe; Dermot Hennelly; Jon Bryden; Barbara March; ***D:*** Jack Darcus; ***W:*** Jack Darcus; ***C:*** Tony Westman; ***M:*** Michael Conway Baker.

Desierto **2016 (R)** Like so many do every day, Moises (Bernal) is trying to cross from Mexico to the United States in search of a better life. Sam (Morgan) is exhausted by the flow of illegal immigrants headed north across his land and decides to take justice into his own hands. He starts by shooting from a sniper perch most of Moises' traveling companions, leaving the bulk of Jonas Cuaron's drama as a cat-and-mouse game between the Mexican and the angry American. Sadly, the opportunity for cultural commentary feels lost in a pretty standard thriller template. **94m/C; DVD, Blu-Ray.** Gael Garcia Bernal; Jeffrey Dean Morgan; Alondra Hidalgo; Diego Catano; Marco Perez; ***D:*** Jonas Cuaron; ***W:*** Jonas Cuaron; Mateo Garcia; ***C:*** Damian Garcia; ***M:*** Woodkid.

Design for Living ½ **1933** Director Lubitsch only kept the title and basic theme of Noel Coward's play and had Ben Hecht rewrite all the dialogue to conform to Hays Office standards, but the pic still has a suggestive charm. Americans Thomas (March) and George (Cooper) are living in Paris when they meet another American, commercial artist Gilda (Hopkins) who's working for an advertising firm run by stuffy Max (Horton). Both men desire her but since Gilda can't make up her mind, they form a platonic trio until the men's emerging jealousy have her taking the easy way out by marrying Max, who quickly bores her. **91m/B; DVD, Blu-Ray.** Miriam Hopkins; Fredric March; Gary Cooper; Edward Everett Horton; Franklin Pangborn; Isabel Jewell; Jane Darwell; ***D:*** Ernst Lubitsch; ***W:*** Ben Hecht; ***C:*** Victor Milner; ***M:*** John Leipold.

Design for Scandal ½ **1941** Furious newspaper owner Judson Blair (Arnold) gives reporter Jeff Sherman (Pidgeon) an assignment to smear the name of Judge Cornelia Porter (Russell) after a court decision has Blair paying some serious alimony. Blair wants Porter disbarred but Sherman falls in love instead. Cornelia finds out about the plot and hauls both men into court. **82m/B; DVD.** Walter Pidgeon; Rosalind Russell; Edward Arnold; Barbara Jo Allen; Lee Bowman; Jean Rogers; Donald Meek; Guy Kibbee; Mary Beth Hughes; ***D:*** Norman Taurog; ***W:*** Lionel Houser; ***C:*** William H. Daniels; Leonard Smith; ***M:*** Franz Waxman.

The Designated Mourner ½ **1997 (R)** Adapted from the play by Wallace Shawn, this pointy-headed inaction movie laments the passing of the class of people who "appreciate the poetry of John Donne" and other forms of high art. It's probably the same class that would like this movie. Set in an unnamed politically repressive country that resembles a large table, Nichols plays the eponymous mourner Jack, a journalist who once ran with a literary crowd but betrayed their ideals for survival. Richardson plays his wife Judy, the daughter of final talking head Howard (de Keyser), who is a humanist poet who doesn't like people. If you need a lecture on culture written by a man who was in "Mom and Dad Save the World" and played the geeky social studies teacher in "Clueless," then this is your movie. To quote Shawn: "Inconceivable!" **94m/C; VHS, DVD.** *GB* Mike Nichols; Miranda Richardson; David de Keyser; ***D:*** David Hare; ***W:*** Wallace Shawn; ***C:*** Oliver Stapleton; ***M:*** Richard Hartley.

Designing Woman **1957** Bacall and Peck star in this mismatched tale of romance. She's a chic high-fashion designer, he's a rumpled sports writer. The fun begins when they try to adjust to married life together. Neither likes the other's friends or lifestyle. Things get even crazier when Bacall has to work with her ex-lover Helmore on a fashion show and Peck's former love Gray shows up as well. And as if that weren't enough, Peck is being hunted by the mob because of a boxing story he's written. It's a fun, quick, witty tale that is all entertainment and no message. Bacall's performance is of note because Bogart was dying of cancer at the time. **118m/C; VHS, DVD, Blu-Ray.** Gregory Peck; Lauren Bacall; Dolores Gray; Sam Levene; Tom Helmore; Mickey Shaughnessy; Jesse White; Chuck Connors; Edward Platt; Alvy Moore; Jack Cole; ***D:*** Vincente Minnelli; ***W:*** George Wells; ***C:*** John Alton; ***M:*** Andre Previn. Oscars '57: Story & Screenplay.

Desire **1993 (R)** A free-spirited woman finds herself attracted to a local fisherman. Hardly her intellectual equal but then what she really wants is his body. **108m/C; VHS, DVD.** Greta Scacchi; Vincent D'Onofrio; ***D:*** Andrew Birkin.

Desire and Hell at Sunset Motel ½ **1992 (PG-13)** Low-budget thriller takes place at the Sunset Motel in 1950s Anaheim. Fenn is the bombshell wife of a toy salesman who's in town for a sales meeting, while she just wants to visit Disneyland. She's soon fooling around with another guy and her husband hires a psychotic criminal to spy on her as her new lover plots to kill hubby. Very confusing plot isn't worth figuring out. Film's only redeeming quality is the imaginative and creative work used in the visuals. Castle's directorial debut. **90m/C; VHS, DVD.** Sherilyn Fenn; Whip Hubley; David Hewlett; David Johansen; Paul Bartel; Kenneth Tobey; ***D:*** Alien Castle; ***W:*** Alien Castle; ***C:*** Jamie Thompson.

Desire Me **1947** Plodding romantic drama with confusing flashbacks and Greer and Mitchum miscast as a Breton couple in a fishing village. Marise Aubert is told by former POW Jean that her husband Paul was killed trying to escape from their German camp. Jean wants Marise for himself as well as Paul's successful business and hides the fact that Paul is still alive until the man himself turns up. Marise is guilt-stricken that she has feelings for both men and takes to visit a shrink while Paul is more pro-active about his rival. MGM was forced to release the film without a director's name when George Cukor and Mervyn Leroy (among others) refused credit. **91m/B; DVD.** Greer Garson; Robert Mitchum; Richard Hart; Cecil Humphreys; George Zucco; Morris Ankrum; ***W:*** Zoë Akins; Marguerite Roberts; ***C:*** Joseph Ruttenberg; ***M:*** Herbert Stothart.

Desire Under the Elms ½ **1958** Ives, the patriarch of an 1840s New England farming family, takes a young wife (Loren) who promptly has an affair with her stepson. Loren's American film debut. Based on the play by Eugene O'Neill. **114m/B; VHS, DVD.** Sophia Loren; Anthony Perkins; Burl Ives; Frank Overton; ***D:*** Delbert Mann; ***C:*** Daniel F. Fapp; ***M:*** Elmer Bernstein.

Desiree ½ **1954** A romanticized historical epic about Napoleon and his 17-year-old mistress, Desiree. Based on the novel by Annemarie Selinko. Slightly better than average historical fiction piece. **110m/C; Blu-Ray.** Marlon Brando; Jean Simmons; Merle Oberon; Michael Rennie; Cameron Mitchell; Elizabeth Sellars; Cathleen Nesbitt; Charlotte Austin; ***D:*** Henry Koster; ***W:*** Daniel Taradash; ***C:*** Milton Krasner; ***M:*** Alex North.

Desk Set *His Other Woman* **1957** One of the later and less dynamic Tracy/Hepburn comedies, about an efficiency expert who installs a giant computer in an effort to update a TV network's female-run reference department. Still, the duo sparkle as they bicker, battle, and give in to love. Based on William Marchant's play. **103m/C; VHS, DVD, Blu-Ray.** Spencer Tracy; Katharine Hepburn; Joan Blondell; Gig Young; Dina Merrill; Neva Patterson; Harry Ellerbe; Nicholas Joy; Diane Jergens; Merry Anders; ***D:*** Walter Lang; ***W:*** Phoebe Ephron; Henry Ephron; ***C:*** Leon Shamroy; ***M:*** Cyril Mockridge.

Desolation Angels **1995** Nick Adams (Rodrick) returns to New York after a month spent unhappily visiting his mother and discovers his girlfriend Mary (Thomas) has been raped by his best friend Sid (Bassett). At least that's how Nick interprets the situation after an unwilling Mary admits they had sex. Nick goes after Sid, gets beaten up, hires a couple of thugs who botch a retaliation, and just gets increasingly enraged over his inability to settle the situation. The focus is on Nick and Rodrick is more than up to the director McCann's demands. **90m/C; VHS, DVD.** Michael Rodrick; Peter Bassett; Jennifer Thomas; ***D:*** Tim McCann; ***W:*** Tim McCann; ***C:*** Matt Howe.

Despair *Eine Reise ins Licht* **1978** A chilling and comic study of a victimized chocolate factory owner's descent into madness, set against the backdrop of the Nazi rise to power in the 1930s. Adapted from the Nabokov novel by Tom Stoppard. **120m/C; VHS, DVD, Blu-Ray.** *GE* Dirk Bogarde; Andrea Ferreol; Volker Spengler; Klaus Lowitsch; ***D:*** Rainer Werner Fassbinder; ***W:*** Tom Stoppard; ***C:*** Michael Ballhaus; ***M:*** Peer Raben.

Desperado *El Mariachi 2* **1995 (R)** Rodriguez's nameless guitar player-turned-gunman returns—this time in the persona of heartthrob Banderas. The director also has a studio budget to play with (a sizable increase over the $7000 for "El Mariachi"), so the action's on a bigger, more violent scale (you'll quickly lose count of flying bodies and bullets) as El Mariachi tracks infamous drug lord Bucho (de Almeida). Gringo Buscemi provides assistance, beautiful bookstore owner Carolina (Hayek) offers solace, and Tarantino meets his well-deserved cameo demise. You'll also find original Mariachi, Gallardo, in a cameo role as a musician/gunslinger amigo of the hero. Filmed in Mexico. **103m/C; VHS, DVD, Blu-Ray.** Antonio Banderas; Salma Hayek; Joaquim de Almeida; Steve Buscemi; Richard "Cheech" Marin; Carlos Gomez; ***Cam-***

eo(s): Quentin Tarantino; Carlos Gallardo; ***D:*** Robert Rodriguez; ***W:*** Robert Rodriguez; ***C:*** Guillermo Navarro; ***M:*** Los Lobos.

The Desperadoes 🦴🦴 1/2 **1943** Cheyenne Rogers (Ford) is a gunman trying to go straight. So he heads into the town of Red Valley, Utah, to see old pal-turned-sheriff Steve Upton (Scott). Unfortunately for Cheyenne, this is just after the town's bank has been robbed in a crooked scheme set up by a couple of sharpies (Hall, Buchanan) and he is framed for the crime. Now it's up to Cheyenne, Steve, and a couple of wild west gals (Trevor, Keyes) to prove his innocence. Set in 1863; adapted from a story by Max Brand. Columbia's first Technicolor film. **86m/C; DVD.** Glenn Ford; Randolph Scott; Claire Trevor; Evelyn Keyes; Edgar Buchanan; Porter Hall; Guinn "Big Boy" Williams; Raymond Walburn; ***D:*** Charles Vidor; ***W:*** Robert Carson; ***C:*** George Meehan, Jr.; ***M:*** John Leipold.

The Desperados 🦴 1/2 *Apache Vengeance; Five Savage Men* **1970** When a young woman is raped by outlaws robbing her stagecoach, a bevy of western heroes band together to avenge her. **86m/C; VHS, DVD.** Keenan Wynn; Henry Silva; Michele Carey; John Anderson; Joe Turkel; ***D:*** Ron Joy; ***W:*** Richard Bakalyan; ***M:*** Rupert Holmes.

Desperate 🦴🦴 1/2 **1947** An honest truck driver witnesses a mob crime and must escape with his wife in this minor film noir. Eventually, the law is on his tail, too. **73m/B; VHS, DVD.** Steve Brodie; Audrey Long; Raymond Burr; Jason Robards, Sr.; Douglas Fowley; William Challee; Ilka Gruning; Nan Leslie; ***D:*** Anthony Mann.

Desperate Cargo 🦴 1/2 **1941** Two showgirls stranded in a Latin American town manage to get aboard a clipper ship with hoodlums who are trying to steal the vessel's cargo. **69m/B; VHS, DVD.** Ralph Byrd; Carol Hughes; Jack Mulhall; ***D:*** William Beaudine; ***W:*** Morgan Cox; John T. Coyle; ***C:*** Jack Greenhalgh.

Desperate Characters 🦴🦴🦴 **1971 (R)** A slice-of-city-life story about a middle-class couple living in a once-fashionable section of Brooklyn, New York, who watch their neighborhood disintegrate around them. Their marriage on remote control, the two find their lives a series of small disappointments, routine work, uncertain friendships, and pervasive violence. Excellent performances, especially by MacLaine as the harried wife, but the film's depressing nature made it a complete boxoffice flop. **87m/C; VHS, DVD.** Shirley MacLaine; Kenneth Mars; Gerald S. O'Loughlin; Sada Thompson; Michael Higgins; Rose Gregorio; Jack Somack; Chris Gampel; Mary Alan Hokanson; Patrick McVey; Carol Kane; ***D:*** Frank D. Gilroy; ***W:*** Frank D. Gilroy.

Desperate Crimes 🦴🦴 *Mafia Docks* **1993** Two rival mobs battle over the prostitution and drug trade. When an innocent woman is murdered her brother looks for revenge with the help of a beautiful prostitute. **92m/C; VHS, DVD.** Traci Lords; Denise Crosby; Franco (Columbo) Columbu; Van Quattro; Rena Niehaus; Nicoletta Boris; Elizabeth Kaitan; Randi Ingerman; ***D:*** Andreas Marfori; ***W:*** Andreas Marfori; ***C:*** Marco Isoli.

Desperate Hours 🦴🦴🦴 **1955** A tough, gritty thriller about three escaped convicts taking over a suburban home and holding the family hostage. Plenty of suspense and fine acting. Based on the novel and play by Joseph Hayes. **112m/B; VHS, DVD.** Humphrey Bogart; Fredric March; Martha Scott; Arthur Kennedy; Gig Young; Dewey Martin; Mary Murphy; Robert Middleton; Richard Eyer; Ray Collins; Beverly Garland; ***D:*** William Wyler; ***C:*** Lee Garmes. Natl. Bd. of Review '55: Director (Wyler).

Desperate Hours 🦴🦴 **1990 (R)** An escaped prisoner holes up in a suburban couple's home, waiting for his lawyer/accomplice to take him to Mexico. Tensions heighten between the separated couple and the increasingly nerve-wracked criminals. Terrific, if not downright horrifying, performance by Rourke in an overall tepid remake of the 1955 thriller. **105m/C; VHS, DVD, Blu-Ray.** Mickey Rourke; Anthony Hopkins; Mimi Rogers; Kelly Lynch; Lindsay Crouse; Elias Koteas; David Morse; Shawnee Smith; Danny Gerard; Matt McGrath; ***D:*** Michael Cimino; ***W:*** Mark Rosenthal; Larry Konner; Joseph Hayes; ***C:*** Doug Milsome; ***M:*** David Mansfield.

Desperate Journey 🦴🦴 1/2 **1942** Flynn and Reagan are two of five Allied fighters shot down over Nazi occupied Poland. They go through various tight squeezes such as stealing Goering's car in Berlin, and eliminating a few Nazis at a chemical factory to get back to the safety of England. All the while they are hunted by Massey as Nazi Major Otto Baumester, who of course bumbles and fumbles the whole affair. Strictly propaganda intended to keep up morale on the homefront. Flynn was not pleased about having Reagan as his co-star, seeing as he was usually paired with female leads. **108m/B; VHS, DVD.** Errol Flynn; Ronald Reagan; Raymond Massey; Nancy Coleman; Alan Hale; Arthur Kennedy; Helmut Dantine; ***D:*** Raoul Walsh; ***M:*** Max Steiner.

Desperate Lives 🦴🦴 **1982** High school siblings come into contact with drugs and join their guidance counselor in the war against dope. Average made for TV fare. **100m/C; VHS, DVD.** Diana Scarwid; Doug McKeon; Helen Hunt; William Windom; Art Hindle; Tom Atkins; Sam Bottoms; Diane Ladd; Dr. Joyce Brothers; ***D:*** Robert Lewis; ***M:*** Bruce Broughton. **TV**

Desperate Living 🦴🦴 1/2 **1977** Typical John Waters trash. A mental patient (Stole) is released and becomes paranoid that her family may be out to kill her. After aiding in the murder of her husband (the hefty maid, Hill, suffocates him by sitting on him), Stole and Hill escape to Mortville, a town populated by outcasts such as transsexuals, murderers, and the woefully disfigured. **90m/C; VHS, DVD.** Mink Stole; Jean Hill; Edith Massey; Liz Renay; Mary Vivian Pearce; Cookie Mueller; Susan Lowe; Ed Peranio; Pat Moran; George Stover; Turkey Joe; Channing Wilroy; ***D:*** John Waters; ***W:*** John Waters; ***C:*** Thomas Loizeaux.

Desperate Measures 🦴 1/2 **1998 (R)** Police officer Frank Connor (Garcia) desperately searches for a bone marrow donor for his dying son. Turns out the perfect match is vicious murderer and prison inmate Pete McCabe (Keaton). McCabe seizes the opportunity to unleash an elaborate and violent prison escape in a San Francisco hospital. Keaton, as a poor man's Hannibal Lecter, offers this movie's only entertainment. If not for the dying child to propel its already ludicrious story along, it would be a great source for slapstick comedy. Film was held back for several months before its final release and you'll find out why the studio wanted to hide this one. **100m/C; VHS, DVD.** Andy Garcia; Michael Keaton; Marcia Gay Harden; Brian Cox; Efrain Figueroa; Joseph Cross; Richard Riehle; ***D:*** Barbet Schroeder; ***W:*** Henry Bean; Neal Jimenez; David Klass; ***C:*** Luciano Tovoli; ***M:*** Trevor Jones.

The Desperate Mission 🦴🦴🦴 **1969** Joaquin Murietta (Montelban) is a Mexican nobleman acting as a Robin Hood for those oppressed by corrupt authorities in gold-rushed 1840s California, along with his outlaw sidekick Three-Fingered Jack. Action scenes are well staged and direction is tight making for a greatly satisfying western. **96m/C; VHS, DVD.** Ricardo Montalban; Slim Pickens; Roosevelt "Rosie" Grier; Earl Holliman; ***D:*** Earl Bellamy; ***W:*** Rick Collins; Jack Guss. **TV**

Desperate Search 🦴🦴 **1952** Bush pilot Vince Heldon (Keel) flies over a mountainous Canadian wilderness searching for the crashed airliner that had his two kids as passengers. He's joined by ex-wife Nora (Medina), which puts a strain on his current marriage to Julie (Greer). Youngsters Don (Aakers) and Janet (Lowell) get to practice their survival skills. **71m/B; DVD.** Howard Keel; Patricia Medina; Jane Greer; Lee Aaker; Linda Lowell; Keenan Wynn; ***D:*** Joseph H. Lewis; ***W:*** Walter Doniger; ***C:*** Harold Lipstein.

The Desperate Trail 🦴🦴 1/2 **1994 (R)** Prostitute, convicted of killing an abusive client, manages to escape from the marshal who's escorting her to her hanging. She teams up with a con man in a plot to rob a bank while the marshal enlists a posse to track her down. Strong performances augmented by blazing guns, hobbled by weak writing. **93m/C; VHS, DVD.** Sam Elliott; Linda Fiorentino; Craig Sheffer; Frank Whaley; ***D:*** P.J. Pesce; ***W:*** P.J. Pesce; Tom Abrams; ***C:*** Michael Bonvillain; ***M:*** Stephen Endelman. **CABLE**

Desperately Seeking Susan 🦴🦴 **1985 (PG-13)** Roberta (Arquette) is a bored New Jersey housewife who gets her kicks reading the personals. When she becomes obsessed with a relationship between two lovers who arrange their meetings through the columns, Roberta decides to find out for herself who they are. But after an accident, Roberta loses her memory and thinks she is Susan, the free-spirited woman in the personals. Unfortunately, Susan (Madonna) is in a lot of trouble with all sorts of unsavory folk and our innocent housewife finds herself caught in the middle. Terrific characters, with special appeal generated by Arquette and Madonna. Quinn winningly plays Roberta's bewildered romantic interest, Dez. **104m/C; VHS, DVD, Blu-Ray.** Rosanna Arquette; Madonna; Aidan Quinn; Mark Blum; Robert Joy; Laurie Metcalf; Steven Wright; John Turturro; Will Patton; Richard Hell; Annie Golden; Ann Magnuson; Richard Edson; ***D:*** Susan Seidelman; ***W:*** Leora Barish; ***C:*** Edward Lachman; ***M:*** Thomas Newman. British Acad. '85: Support. Actress (Arquette); Natl. Bd. of Review '85: Support. Actress (Arquette).

Despicable Me 🦴🦴 1/2 **2010 (PG)** Evil Gru (voiced by Carrell) is planning to steal the moon to prove that he's still the top villain around. But a rivalry with a new evil genius and a chance meeting with adorable orphans Margo, Edith, and Agnes, who think Gru should become their new dad, complicates his scheme. Between the minions and the orphans, there's plenty of cute to go around, but it could have done with a bit more laugh-out-loud funny. Some great visual and dialogue gags provide adults in the audience with semi-consistent chuckles. **95m/C; Blu-Ray.** ***V:*** Steve Carell; Jason Segel; Miranda Cosgrove; Russell Brand; Elsie Fisher; Dana Gaier; Will Arnett; Danny McBride; Julie Andrews; Jemaine Clement; Kristen Wiig; Jack McBrayer; Mindy Kaling; Ken Jeong; Chris Renaud; Pierre Coffin; ***D:*** Chris Renaud; Pierre Coffin; ***W:*** Ken Daurio; Cinco Paul; ***M:*** Hans Zimmer.

Despicable Me 2 🦴🦴 1/2 **2013 (PG)** The Minions are back! And so are Gru (Carell) and his girls Margo (Cosgrove), Edith (Gaier), and Agnes (Fisher). Gru has replaced his evil lifestyle with that of family man, but he is forced by the Anti-Villain League into another job. Enter agent Lucy (Wiig) who seems like such a match for Gru...could romance be far behind? But first, Gru must find the bad guys who are responsible for making little purple demons out everyone's beloved Minions and threatening the planet. It's not rocket science folks--a minimal storyline to be sure, but why be weighed down by such details when you're having such a great time? **98m/C; DVD, Blu-Ray.** ***V:*** Steve Carell; Kristen Wiig; Miranda Cosgrove; Elsie Fisher; Dana Gaier; Russell Brand; Benjamin Bratt; Moises Arias; Steve Coogan; Ken Jeong; ***D:*** Chris Renaud; Pierre Coffin; ***W:*** Cinco Paul; Ken Daurio; ***M:*** Heitor Pereira; Pharrell Williams.

Despicable Me 3 🦴🦴 **2017 (PG)** The third installment of a franchise that's not breaking any new ground. Former villain Gru (Carrell) gets fired from the Anti-Villain League, and is tempted to return to his old ways by his newfound twin brother Dru (also voiced by Carrell), a shinier, more successful bad guy. They plan one last heist: steal the world's largest diamond from 1980s child star Balthazar Bratt (Parker). The laughs are there, but mostly for young fans. **90m/C; DVD, Blu-Ray.** ***V:*** Steve Carell; Kristen Wiig; Trey Parker; Miranda Cosgrove; Dana Gaier; ***D:*** Kyle Balda; Pierre Coffin; ***W:*** Cinco Paul; Ken Daurio; ***M:*** Pharrell Williams.

Despiser 🦴 **2003 (R)** After having the worst day of his life, Gordon (Mark Redfield) ends up in a war in Purgatory after dying in a car accident. On one side you have God's chosen, and on the other a ticked off alien trapped in the human afterlife who desperately wants escape. **105m/C; DVD.** Mark Redfield; Doug Brown; Gage Sheridan; Frank Smith; Michael Weitz; ***D:*** Philip Cook; ***C:*** Philip Cook. **VIDEO**

Destination Gobi 🦴🦴 **1953** Unusual WWII adventure. In 1944, a Navy weather team is monitoring conditions at a remote outpost in the Gobi desert and relaying info to fighting units. When they're attacked by a Japanese air raid and their commanding officer is killed, Chief Petty Officer Sam McHale (Widmark) and his men need to make a long and dangerous trek to safety. Providing some reluctant aid are a group of horse-riding Mongol nomads. **89m/C; DVD.** Richard Widmark; Ross Bagdasarian; Earl Holliman; Darryl Hickman; Martin Milner; Max (Casey Adams) Showalter; Don Taylor; ***D:*** Robert Wise; ***W:*** Everett Freeman; ***C:*** Charles G. Clarke; ***M:*** Sol Kaplan.

Destination: Infestation 🦴 *Swarm* **2007** Lame disaster flick that doesn't even follow through on its cliches. CDC etymologist Dr. Carrie Ross is aboard a flight from Colombia when another passenger dies and suddenly has swarms of mutated poisonous ants crawling out of his body. The ants are causing havoc with the plane's electric systems as well and Carrie, along with air marshal Ethan Hart, must keep things going until the plane can land at a disused Air Force base. **90m/C; DVD.** Jessalyn Gilsig; Antonio Sabato, Jr.; Serge House; Emily Tennant; Ryan McDonell; Ivan Cermak; Lisa Marie Caruk; ***D:*** George Mendeluk; ***W:*** Mary Weinstein; ***C:*** Michael Balfry; ***M:*** Peter Allen; Vincent Mai. **CABLE**

Destination Inner Space 🦴 1/2 **1966** Scientists working in an underwater lab discover an alien object at the bottom of the ocean. While exploring, they also find a smaller pod and bring it back to the lab. Big mistake since the pod starts growing and transforms into an alien creature that goes on the attack. **83m/C; DVD.** Scott Brady; Sheree North; Gary Merrill; Mike Road; John Howard; Wende Wagner; ***D:*** Francis D. Lyon; ***W:*** Arthur C. Pierce; ***C:*** Brick Marquard; ***M:*** Paul Dunlap.

Destination Mars 🦴 1/2 **2006** Faux 50s sci-fi movie written as a sequel to "Plan 9 from Outer Space." Mars unleashes a race of super women who intend to conquer our world. Currently only available as a special feature on the "Monarch of the Moon" DVD. **80m/B; DVD.** Suzette Andrea; Bryan Bodine; Dan Brinkle; Jeff Corral; ***D:*** Richard Lowry; ***W:*** Tor Reyel Lowry; ***C:*** T. Henry Amitai; ***M:*** Richard Lowry. **VIDEO**

Destination Moon 🦴🦴 1/2 **1950** Story of man's first lunar voyage contains Chesley Bonstell's astronomical artwork and a famous Woody Woodpecker cartoon. Includes previews of coming attractions from classic science fiction films. **91m/C; VHS, DVD.** Warner Anderson; Tom Powers; Dick Wesson; Erin O'Brien-Moore; ***D:*** Irving Pichel; ***W:*** Alford "Rip" Van Ronkel; Robert Heinlein; James O'Hanlon; ***C:*** Lionel Lindon; ***M:*** Leith Stevens.

Destination Moonbase Alpha 🦴🦴 *Space: 1999—Destination Moonbase Alpha* **1975** In the 21st century, an explosion has destroyed half the moon, causing it to break away from the Earth's orbit. The moon is cast far away, but the 311 people manning Alpha, a research station on the moon, must continue their search for other life forms in outer space. A thankless task. Pilot for the TV series "Space: 1999." **93m/C; VHS, DVD.** *GB* Martin Landau; Barbara Bain; Barry Morse; Nick (Nicholas) Tate; ***D:*** Tom Clegg; ***W:*** Terence Feely; ***M:*** Derek Wadsworth. **TV**

Destination Murder 🦴 1/2 **1950** Low-budget noir-thriller with a convoluted plot that's filled with holes. Smalltime hood Jackie Wales murders Laura Mansfield's father, apparently on the orders of nightclub owner Armitage. Laura gets a job as a cigarette girl in the club to get evidence but discovers more is going on and unwisely gets involved with manager Stretch Norton. **72m/B; DVD.** Hurd Hatfield; Albert Dekker; Stanley Clements; Joyce MacKenzie; Myrna Dell; James Flavin; Franklyn Farnum; John Dehner; ***D:*** Edward L. Cahn; ***W:*** Don Martin; ***C:*** Jackson Rose; ***M:*** Irving Gertz.

Destination: Outer Space 🦴🦴 **2010** In this spoof of the golden age of sci-fi movies, the pilot for Earth's first faster-than-light ship gets lost somewhere in space and ends up dealing with crazed robots, puppet monsters, aliens, and pirates while trying to find his way back. **94m/C; DVD, Blu-Ray, Streaming.** Josh Craig; Catherine Hansen; M. Scott Taulman; Stephanie Mihm; Michael G. Kaiser; ***V:*** Christopher R. Mihm; ***D:*** Christopher R. Mihm; ***W:*** Josh Craig; Christopher R. Mihm; ***C:*** Christopher R. Mihm. **VIDEO**

Destination Saturn *Buck Rogers* **1939** Buck Rogers awakens from suspended animation in the 25th century. **90m/B; VHS, DVD.** Buster Crabbe; Constance Moore; ***D:*** Ford Beebe.

Destination Tokyo **1943** A weathered WWII submarine actioner, dealing with the search-and-destroy mission of a U.S. sub sent into Tokyo harbor. Available in a colorized version. **135m/B; VHS, DVD; Open Captioned.** Cary Grant; John Garfield; Alan Hale; Dane Clark; John Ridgely; Warner Anderson; William Prince; Robert Hutton; Tom Tully; Peter Whitney; Faye Emerson; John Forsythe; ***D:*** Delmer Daves.

Destination Vegas **1995 (R)** Attorney Sommerfield is on the lam, driving across the Mojave trying to elude hitmen sent to prevent her testimony in a murder trial. She hooks up with drifter Duhamel, who just happens to be an ex-getaway driver, and it's put the pedal to the metal time. Low-budget familiar story with some saving humor. **78m/C; VHS, DVD.** Jennifer Sommerfield; Claude Duhamel; Stephen Polk; Richard Lynch; ***D:*** Paul Wynne; ***W:*** Paul Wynne; ***C:*** William H. Molina; ***M:*** Peter Tomashek. **VIDEO**

Destination Wedding **2018 (R)** While waiting for a small plane to take them to a destination wedding in California wine country, Lindsay (Ryder) meets Frank (Reeves). The pair bicker from the beginning, when Lindsay accuses Frank of cutting her off at the gate. At same time, they have common ground because neither want to be at the wedding, which is between Lindsay's ex-boyfriend and Frank's half-brother, and both have jobs that involve judging. They spend the wedding annoying each other and providing hilarious commentary on the other guests. This romantic comedy focuses on such talk and successfully showcases the charming chemistry between the co-stars. **90m/C; DVD.** Keanu Reeves; Winona Ryder; Dj Dallenbach; Greg Lucey; Ted Dubost; ***D:*** Victor Levin; ***W:*** Victor Levin; ***C:*** Giorgio Scali; ***M:*** William Ross.

Destiny *Der Mude Tod* **1921** Fritz Lang's silent fantasy is a version of the myth of Orpheus. Death takes a young man on the eve of his wedding, but agrees to return him if his fiancee can save three lives. In terms of style, it's really closer to Dreyer's "Vampyr" than to Lang's own "M." **99m/B; Silent; VHS, DVD, Blu-Ray.** *GE* Lil Dagover; Rudolf Klein-Rogge; Bernhard Goetzke; Walther Jansson; Eduard von Winterstein; Paul Biensfieldt; ***D:*** Fritz Lang; ***W:*** Thea von Harbou; ***C:*** Fritz Arno Wagner; Erich Nitzschmann; Hermann Saalfrank.

Destiny *Al-Massir* **1997** Averroes (el-Cherif) is a 12th century Arab humanist philosopher living in Andalusia, Spain. When one of his disciples is burned at the stake for heresy, the man's son Youssef (Rahouma), following his father's wishes, travels to Andalusia to study with Averroes. Youssef finds that the ruling Caliph (Memida) supports Averroes but a fundamentalist Muslim cult hopes to overthrow the Caliph and destroy Averroes and his students. Arabic with subtitles. **135m/C; VHS, DVD.** *EG* Nour (el-Sherif) el-Cherif; Fares Rahouma; Mahmoud Hemeida; Khaled el-Nabaoui; Laila Eloui; ***D:*** Youssef Chahine; ***W:*** Youssef Chahine; Khaled Youssef.

Destroy All Monsters ½ *Kaiju Soshingeki; All Monsters Attack; Operation Monsterland* **1968 (G)** When alien babes take control of Godzilla and his monstrous colleagues, it looks like all is lost for Earth. Adding insult to injury, Ghidra is sent in to take care of the loose ends. Can the planet possibly survive this madness? Classic Toho monster slugfest also features Mothra, Rodan, Son of Godzilla, Angila, Varan, Baragon, Spigas and others. **88m/C; VHS, DVD, Blu-Ray.** *JP* Akira Kubo; Jun Tazaki; Yoshio Tsuchiya; Kyoko Ai; Yukiko Kobayashi; Kenji Sahara; Andrew Hughes; Yoshifumi Tajima; Nadao Kirino; Susumu Kurobe; Hisaya Ito; ***D:*** Inoshiro Honda; ***W:*** Inoshiro Honda; Takeshi Kimura; ***C:*** Taiichi Kankura; ***M:*** Akira Ifukube.

Destroy All Planets *Gamera Tai Viras; Gamera Tai Uchukaiju Bairasu; Gamera vs. Viras; Gamera vs. Outer Space Monster Viras* **1968** Aliens whose spaceships turn into giant flying squids are attacking Earth. It's up to Gammera, the flying, fire-breathing turtle to save the day. **75m/C; VHS, DVD, Blu-Ray.** *JP* Peter Williams; Kojiro Hongo; Toru Takatsuka; ***D:*** Noriaki Yuasa.

Destroyer **1943** Trials and tribulations aboard a WWII destroyer result in tensions, but when the time comes for action, the men get the job done. **99m/B; VHS, DVD.** Edward G. Robinson; Glenn Ford; Marguerite Chapman; Edgar Buchanan; Leo Gorcey; Regis Toomey; Edward Brophy; Larry Parks; ***D:*** William A. Seiter.

Destroyer ½ **2018 (R)** Kidman transforms herself into hardened and bleak Erin Bell, a former undercover detective haunted by a sting that went horribly awry. When the gang's leader resurfaces, she's coldly determined to find him and finally exorcise the demons from that chapter of her life. Kidman is excellent, if approaching the line of over-acting, but it's the director Kusama who really shines in this L.A. noir. **123m/C; DVD, Blu-Ray.** Nicole Kidman; Toby Kebbell; Tatiana Maslany; Sebastian Stan; Scoot McNairy; ***D:*** Karyn Kusama; ***W:*** Phil Hay; Matt Manfredi; ***C:*** Julie Kirkwood; ***M:*** Theodore Shapiro.

The Destructors *The Marseille Contract* **1974 (PG)** An American narcotics enforcement officer in Paris seeks the help of a hitman in order to catch a druglord. **89m/C; VHS, DVD.** *GB* Anthony Quinn; Michael Caine; James Mason; Maureen Kerwin; Alexandra Stewart; ***D:*** Robert Parrish; ***W:*** Judd Bernard.

Destry Rides Again *Justice Rides Again* **1939** An uncontrollably lawless western town is whipped into shape by a peaceful, unarmed sheriff. A vintage Hollywood potpourri with Dietrich's finest post-Sternberg moment; standing on the bar singing "See What the Boys in the Back Room Will Have." The second of three versions of this Max Brand story. First was released in 1932; the third in 1954. **94m/B; VHS, DVD, Blu-Ray.** James Stewart; Marlene Dietrich; Brian Donlevy; Charles Winninger; Mischa Auer; Irene Hervey; Una Merkel; Billy Gilbert; Jack Carson; Samuel S. Hinds; Allen Jenkins; ***D:*** George Marshall; ***W:*** Gertrude Purcell; Felix Jackson; Henry Myers; ***C:*** Hal Mohr; ***M:*** Frank Skinner. Natl. Film Reg. '96.

Detachment ½ **2012** In his first commercial release since 1998's "American History X," mercurial director Kaye takes a gritty look at inner-city high school education. Henry (Brody) is a substitute teacher who masks the turmoil of his personal life with a cool facade in front of his students—preferring to stay disconnected. While he hasn't lost all of his idealism, almost all of his burned-out colleagues have, forcing him to step up. Excellent cast (Caan, Harden, Hendricks) and performances lift this troubling school drama slightly above average. **97m/C; DVD.** Adrien Brody; Christina Hendricks; James Caan; Marcia Gay Harden; Lucy Liu; Blythe Danner; Tim Blake Nelson; ***D:*** Tony Kaye; ***W:*** Carl Lund; ***C:*** Tony Kaye; ***M:*** The Newton Brothers.

The Details ½ **2011 (R)** Self-absorbed Dr. Jeff Lang's (Maguire) marriage to Nealy (Banks) is self-destructing into a series of vicious arguments that are only one bitter aspect in the life of a louse in writer/director Estes' suburban comedy. The seemingly likeable Jeff starts an affair with family friend Rebecca (Washington) and gets involved with his crazy neighbor Lila (Linney) when he decides to get rid of the raccoons tearing up his new lawn. **96m/C; DVD, Blu-Ray.** Tobey Maguire; Elizabeth Banks; Laura Linney; Ray Liotta; Kerry Washington; Dennis Haysbert; ***Nar:*** Christopher Curry; ***D:*** Jacob Aaron Estes; ***W:*** Jacob Aaron Estes; ***C:*** Sharone Meir; ***M:*** tomandandy.

The Detective **1968** A New York detective investigating the mutilation murder of a homosexual finds political and police department corruption. Fine, gritty performances prevail in this suspense thriller. Based on the novel by Roderick Thorpe. **114m/C; VHS, DVD, Blu-Ray.** Frank Sinatra; Lee Remick; Ralph Meeker; Jacqueline Bisset; William Windom; Robert Duvall; Tony Musante; Jack Klugman; Al Freeman, Jr.; Horace McMahon; Lloyd Bochner; Pat Henry; Patrick McVey; "Sugar Ray" Robinson; Renee Taylor; Tom Atkins; George Plimpton; ***D:*** Gordon Douglas; ***W:*** Abby Mann; ***C:*** Joseph Biroc; ***M:*** Jerry Goldsmith.

Detective **1985** Style over substance as Godard has various characters/suspects investigating a murder committed in a Paris hotel two years previously. However, Godard seems more interested in the look than the plot. French with subtitles. **95m/C; VHS, DVD, Blu-Ray.** *FR* Nathalie Baye; Claude Brasseur; Jean-Pierre Leaud; Johnny Hallyday; Laurent Terzieff; Alain Cuny; ***D:*** Jean-Luc Godard; ***W:*** Philippe Setbon; Alain Sarde; ***C:*** Bruno Nuytten.

Detective Bureau 2-3: Go to Hell Bastards! ½ *Tantei jimusho 23: Kutabare akuto-domo* **1963** When maverick director Seijun Suzuki was handed an assignment for a standard crime drama potboiler, he instead transformed it into this raucous, subversive dark comedy set to a jazz score. Tajima (Shishido) is a detective who also works as a scandal publisher hired by the police to infiltrate a gang of drug smugglers. Obviously he's gonna get caught eventually (they always do in undercover films), but you probably aren't expecting the jazz musical number set in a night club when he does. Odd considering the film isn't a musical. **88m/C; DVD, Blu-Ray.** *JP* Joe Shishido; ***D:*** Seijun Suzuki; ***W:*** Haruhiko Oyabu; Gan Yamazaki; ***C:*** Shigeyoshi Mine; ***M:*** Harumi Ibe.

Detective Sadie & Son *Sadie & Son* **1984** An elderly detective and her young son crack a case. **96m/C; VHS, Streaming.** Debbie Reynolds; Sam Wanamaker; Brian McNamara; ***D:*** John Llewellyn Moxey. **TV**

Detective School Dropouts *Dumb Dicks* **1985 (PG)** Since they couldn't pass detective school, are they smart enough to outwit a kidnapper? Find out and get a few laughs at the same time. **92m/C; VHS, DVD.** Lorin Dreyfuss; David Landsberg; Christian de Sica; George Eastman; ***D:*** Filippo Ottoni.

Detective Story ½ **1951** Intense drama about a New York City police precinct with a wide array of characters led by a disillusioned and bitter detective (Douglas). Excellent casting is the strong point, as the film can be a bit dated. Based on Sydney Kingsley's Broadway play. **103m/B; DVD.** Kirk Douglas; Eleanor Parker; Lee Grant; Horace McMahon; William Bendix; Craig Hill; Cathy O'Donnell; Bert Freed; George Macready; Joseph Wiseman; Gladys George; Frank Faylen; Warner Anderson; Gerald Mohr; ***D:*** William Wyler; ***W:*** Philip Yordan; Robert Wyler; ***C:*** Lee Garmes. Cannes '52: Actress (Grant).

Detention ½ **2003 (R)** Lundgren is history teacher and ex-Special Forces soldier Decker, in charge of detention for a group of juvenile delinquents. The school is shut down by a group of drug dealers so they can use it to finish a heroin theft. Decker and the students must fight the bad guys in the usual hail of gunfire and explosions to regain control of the school. Cartoonish action flick isn't helped by the wooden presence of "The Dolphinator." **84m/C; DVD.** *CA* Dolph Lundgren; Alex Karzis; Sidney J. Furie; John Sheppard; Corey Sevier; Dov Tiefenbach; Chris Collins; Mpho Koaho; Larry Day; Danielle Hampton; Kata Dobo; ***C:*** Curtis Petersen; ***M:*** Amin Bhatia. **VIDEO**

Detention ½ **2011 (R)** Heavy on in-references, music video director Kahn tackles the meta-horror sub-genre with mixed results. Hutcherson and Cook collaborate on the tale of a high school serial killer named Cinderhella. Thinking the best way to stop the bloodshed is to corral potential killers, the principal puts a group of the most-likely suspects in all-day detention. Sometimes smart but more often highfaluting and over-done--it just doesn't make the grade. **93m/C; DVD, Blu-Ray.** Shanley Caswell; Josh Hutcherson; Aaron David Johnson; Spencer Locke; Dane Cook; Jan Anderson; Parker Bagley; Will Wallace; ***D:*** Joseph Kahn; ***W:*** Joseph Kahn; Mark Palermo; ***C:*** Christopher Probst; ***M:*** Bryan Kei Mantia; Melissa Reese.

Deterrence **2000 (R)** Stagy one-room thriller set during the presidential campaign of 2008. Veep Walter Emerson (Pollak) became prez when the incumbant died—now he's campaigning for re-election. He's at a Colorado primary when a blizzard forces Emerson and his aides (as well as a TV crew) to take shelter in a small town diner. The diner's cable TV hookup reports an international crisis—Iraq forces have invaded Kuwait and slaughtered American peacekeepers. So Emerson decides the thing to do is nuke Baghdad. Lots of pontificating. **101m/C; DVD.** Kevin Pollak; Timothy Hutton; Sheryl Lee Ralph; Sean Astin; Badja (Medu) Djola; Clotilde Courau; ***D:*** Rod Lurie; ***W:*** Rod Lurie; ***C:*** Frank Perl; ***M:*** Lawrence Nash Groupe.

Detonator *Alistair MacLean's Death Train; Death Train* **1993 (R)** A renegade Russian general has stolen a nuclear bomb and is transporting it from Germany to Iraq via a hijacked train commandeered by his hired band of mercenaries. Stewart is the U.N. troubleshooter delegated to stop the plot, aided by a commando team featuring Brosnan and Paul. Based on the novel "Death Train" by Alistair MacLean. **98m/C; VHS, DVD.** Pierce Brosnan; Patrick Stewart; Ted Levine; Alexandra Paul; Christopher Lee; ***D:*** David S. Jackson; ***W:*** David S. Jackson. **CABLE**

The Detonator ½ **2006 (R)** Yet another ho-hum actioner from Snipes. Homeland Security agent Sonni Griffith is involved in an arms deal that goes bad. After leaving too many dead bodies behind, Sonni is given a chance to redeem himself by escorting witness Nadia (Colloca) to New York. Except the arms dealer just happens to be after Nadia and some traitor in the CIA is providing him with intel. **96m/C; DVD.** Wesley Snipes; Silvia Colloca; Michael Brandon; Matthew Leitch; William Hope; ***D:*** Po-Chih Leung; ***W:*** Martin Wheeler; ***C:*** Richard Greatrex; ***M:*** Barry Taylor. **VIDEO**

Detonator 2: Night Watch ½ *Alistair MacLean's Night Watch; Night Watch* **1995 (R)** Brosnan and Paul return as operatives for the secret United Nations Anti-Crime Organization (UNACO). Mike Graham and Sabrina Carver are teamed by their boss Nick Caldwell (Devane) when it's discovered that Rembrandt's "Night Watch" has been replaced by a forgery. This takes our intrepid duo to Hong Kong, a shady computer expert/art collector (Shannon), and a suspicious satellite about to be launched by North Korea. Based on a story by Alistair MacLean. **99m/C; VHS, DVD.** Pierce Brosnan; Alexandra Paul; William Devane; Michael J. Shannon; Lim Kay Siu; Irene Ng; ***D:*** David S. Jackson; ***W:*** David S. Jackson; ***M:*** John Scott. **CABLE**

Detour **1946** Considered to be the creme de la creme of "B" movies, a largely unacknowledged but cult-followed noir downer. Well-designed, stylish, and compelling, if a bit contrived and sometimes annoyingly shrill. Shot in only six days with six indoor sets. Down-on-his-luck pianist Neal hitches cross-country to rejoin his fiancee. His first wrong turn involves the accidental death of the man who picked him up, then he's en route to Destiny with a capital "D" when he picks up fatal femme Savage, as vicious a vixen as ever ruined a good man. Told in flashback, it's also been called the most despairing of all "B"-pictures. As noir as they get. **67m/B; VHS, DVD, Blu-Ray.** Tom Neal; Ann Savage; Claudia Drake; Edmund MacDonald; Tim Ryan; Esther Howard; Don Brodie; Pat Gleason; ***D:*** Edgar G. Ulmer; ***W:*** Martin Goldsmith; ***C:*** Benjamin (Ben H.) Kline; ***M:*** Leo Erdody. Natl. Film Reg. '92.

Detour ½ **2017 (R)** This pseudo noir with a sci-fi twist has some good ideas, but they're buried in some pretty awful filmmaking. Harper (Sheridan) is a nice young man convinced this his stepfather Vincent (Moyer) is responsible for the fact that his mother is in a coma. He's drowning his sorrows one night in a glass of whiskey when a local tough guy named Johnny Ray (Cohen) agrees to take care of the problem and kill Vincent. From here, the film splits a la "Sliding Doors" and we see what happens if he agrees and if he doesn't. It's a good idea, poorly made. **97m/C; DVD, Blu-Ray, Streaming.** *SA UK* Tye Sheridan; Bel Powley; Emory Cohen; Jared Abrahamson; ***Cameo(s):*** Stephen Moyer; ***D:*** Christopher Smith; ***W:*** Christopher Smith; ***C:*** Christopher Ross; ***M:*** Pablo Clements; James Griffith.

Detour to Terror 🦴 **1980** Terrible TV movie with Simpson as heroic tour bus driver Lee Hayes. His Vegas-bound bus is hijacked by a trio of would-be kidnappers after an heiress. They force the bus to detour into the desert, then discover their heiress isn't on board. There's a valuable stamp subplot that goes nowhere as well. **100m/C; DVD.** O.J. Simpson; Anne Francis; Lorenzo Lamas; Arte Johnson; Randall Carver; Richard (Rick) Hill; Kathryn Holcomb; Gerald S. O'Loughlin; Tom Rosales; ***D:*** Michael O'Herlihy; ***W:*** Sydney Glass; Mark Rodgers; ***C:*** John M. Nickolaus, Jr.; ***M:*** Morton Stevens. **TV**

Detroit 🦴🦴🦴 **2017 (R)** The murder of three black men in a motel ignites the charge for one of America's most explosive periods of civil unrest. Bigelow's dramatization of Detroit's 1967 riots is heavy on body count, giving a sense of the scope of the violence, but short on emotional connection to the characters. Still, it provides an overview of the "what," and primes us to ask the "why" about the volatile relationship between racism and law enforcement that's as pertinent today as it was back then. **143m/C; DVD, Blu-Ray.** John Boyega; Will Poulter; Algee Smith; Jason Mitchell; John Krasinski; ***D:*** Kathryn Bigelow; ***W:*** Mark Boal; ***C:*** Barry Ackroyd; ***M:*** James Newton Howard.

Detroit 9000 🦴 ½ *Detroit Heat* **1973 (R)** A pair of Detroit policemen investigate a robbery that occurred at a black congressman's fundraising banquet. **106m/C; VHS, DVD.** Alex Rocco; Scatman Crothers; Hari Rhodes; Lonette McKee; Herbert Jefferson, Jr.; Robert Phillips; ***D:*** Arthur Marks; ***W:*** Orville H. Hampton; ***C:*** Harry J. May; ***M:*** Luchi De Jesus.

Detroit Rock City 🦴 **1999 (R)** It's 1978, and a group of dim Kiss fans will do anything to get into a sold-out Detroit concert. And non-Kiss fans should do anything to get out of watching this movie. Manages to be tasteless and humorless even when it's not obviously annoying. Co-producer Gene Simmons and the boys only perform the title song, so Kiss fans will be left searching their neighborhood for an Old Folks Kabuki Theater for a fix of the elderly in makeup. Director Rifkin re-created the 1978 Kiss Love Gun Show with the band performing in that haven of heavy metal: Hamilton, Ontario? **95m/C; VHS, DVD, Blu-Ray.** Edward Furlong; Sam Huntington; Giuseppe Andrews; Lin Shaye; James DeBello; Natasha Lyonne; Gene Simmons; Paul Stanley; Ace Frehley; Peter Criss; ***D:*** Adam Rifkin; ***W:*** Carl DuPre; ***C:*** John R. Leonetti; ***M:*** J. Peter Robinson.

Deuce Bigalow: European Gigolo WOOF! 2005 (R) Deuce returns to clear the name of his former pimp when he's accused of murder in Amsterdam. Crass, which is not unexpected, with some almost entertaining bits (but not nearly enough). **75m/C; DVD, UMD.** Rob Schneider; Eddie Griffin; Jeroen Krabbe; Til Schweiger; Hanna Verboom; Dana Min Goodman; Miranda Raison; Douglas Sills; Charles Keating; Carlos Ponce; Oded Fehr; Adam Sandler; Norm MacDonald; Fred Armisen; ***D:*** Mike Bigelow; ***W:*** Rob Schneider; David Garrett; Jason Ward; ***C:*** Marc Felperlaan; ***M:*** James L. Venable. Golden Raspberries '05: Worst Actor (Schneider).

Deuce Bigalow: Male Gigolo 🦴🦴 **1999 (R)** Schneider tries to enter the lowbrow leading man territory now occupied by Adam Sandler (who exec produced) as Deuce Bigelow, a hapless tropical fish caretaker turned hapless gigolo. When Deuce is asked to nurse a stereotypically ethnic gigolo's fish to health, he proceeds to practically destroy his house and subsequently take over his "business" to pay for the repairs. With the help of pimp T.J. (Griffin), Deuce finds a clientele and the secret that the women want compassion, not sex. The gags (mostly of the tasteless, toilet humor variety) are very hit and miss, but they should play well to the intended audience of adolescent boys. **86m/C; VHS, DVD.** Rob Schneider; William Forsythe; Eddie Griffin; Oded Fehr; Gail O'Grady; Richard Riehle; Jacqueline Obradors; ***D:*** Mike Mitchell; ***W:*** Rob Schneider; Harris Goldberg; ***C:*** Peter Lyons Collister; ***M:*** Teddy Castellucci.

Deuces Wild 🦴 ½ **2002 (R)** Cliche piles upon cliche in this story of Brooklyn street gangs in the late '50s. The Deuces, led by Leon (Dorff) and his hot-headed younger brother Bobby (Renfro), and their rivals the Vipers, go to war over turf when Vipers leader Marco (Redus) is released from prison. Drug-dealing Marco was responsible for the heroin death of their older brother Sal, and the brothers want to keep their streets clean, which also puts them in conflict with local mobster Fritzy (Dillon) and his thugs. There's even a star-crossed romance since Bobby loves Vipers girl Annie (Balk). Director Kalvert did better with teens and drugs and violence in "The Basketball Diaries." **97m/C; VHS, DVD.** Stephen Dorff; Brad Renfro; Norman Reedus; Fairuza Balk; Max Perlich; Matt Dillon; Drea De Matteo; Frankie Muniz; Vincent Pastore; Balthazar Getty; James Franco; Louis Lombardi; Deborah Harry; Johnny Knoxville; Paul Sampson; ***D:*** Scott Kalvert; ***W:*** Paul Kimatian; Christopher Gambale; ***C:*** John A. Alonzo; ***M:*** Stewart Copeland.

Deutschland im Jahre Null 🦴🦴🦴 ½ **1947** The acclaimed, unsettling vision of post-war Germany as seen through the eyes of a disturbed boy who eventually kills himself. Lyrical and grim, in German with subtitles. **75m/B; VHS, DVD.** *GE* Franz Gruber; ***D:*** Roberto Rossellini.

Devdas 🦴🦴🦴 **1955** Third of at least six film versions of the novel by Saratchandra Chatterjee. Devdas (Dilip Kumar) and Parvati (Suchitra Sen) are childhood sweethearts, but his father disapproves and sends him to Calcutta. While he is away Parvati is arranged to marry a much older man. When Devdas learns of this upon returning he is crushed, and drowns his sorrows in alcohol, while the beautiful dancer who serves him tries to make him realize she is in love with him. **161m/C; DVD.** *IN* Dilip Kumar; Vyjayanthimala; Motilal; Suchrita Sen; Nasir Hussain; Iftekhar; Shivraj; Mohan Choti; ***D:*** Bimal Roy; ***W:*** Rajinder Singh Bedi; Saratchandra Chatterjee; Nabendu Ghosh; ***C:*** Kamal Bose; ***M:*** Sachin Dev Burman.

Devdas 🦴🦴🦴 **2002 (R)** Devdas (Sharukh Khan) is considered a slacker by his father, and sent to London to be educated (and to keep him away from his childhood sweetheart). Returning he asks to marry her, and his father rejects the idea, chiding him for trying to marry a woman of lower caste. Devdas retreats into a life of alcoholism and womanizing to forget the woman he loves, and to prevent himself from falling for another woman who has entered his life. **181m/C; DVD.** *IN* Madhuri Dixit; Aishwarya Rai; Jackie Shroff; Kiron Kher; Sharulh Khan; Tiku Talsania; Dina Pathak; Smita Jaykar; Viyajendra Ghatge; Milind Gunaji; Ananya Khare; Manoj Joshi; Ava Mukherjee; Vijay Crishna; Muni Jha; Sunil Rege; Jaya Bhattacharya; Apara Mehta; Kapil Soni; Radhika Singh; ***D:*** Sanjay Leela Bhansali; ***W:*** Sanjay Leela Bhansali; Saratchandra Chatterjee; Prakash Kapadia; ***C:*** Binod Pradhan; ***M:*** Ismail Darbar; Monty Sharma.

Devi 🦴🦴🦴 ½ *The Goddess* **1960** A minor film in the Ray canon, it is, nonetheless, a strange and compelling tale of religious superstition. An Indian farmer becomes convinced that his beautiful daughter-in-law is the reincarnation of the goddess Kali. The girl is then pressured into accepting a worship that eventually drives her mad. In Bengali with English subtitles. **93m/B; VHS, DVD.** *IN* Chhabi Biswas; Sharmila Tagore; Soumitra Chatterjee; ***D:*** Satyajit Ray; ***W:*** Satyajit Ray; ***C:*** Subrata Mitra; ***M:*** Ali Akbar Khan.

Devices and Desires 🦴🦴🦴 *P.D. James: Devices & Desires* **1991** Typically complicated mystery adapted from the novel by P.D. James. Scotland Yard Commander Adam Dalgliesh (Marsden) is on holiday on the east coast of England where, of course, there's blackmail, murder, suicide, and trouble at a nearby nuclear power station for him to contend with. Made for TV; on six cassettes. **312m/C; VHS, DVD.** *GB* Roy Marsden; Susannah York; Gemma Jones; James Faulkner; Tony Haygarth; Tom Georgeson; Tom Chadbon; Nicola Cowper; Suzan Crowley; Robert Hines; Harry Burton; Helena Michell; ***D:*** John Davies; ***W:*** Thomas Ellice. **TV**

Devil 🦴🦴 **2010 (PG-13)** Efficient, unpretentious B-movie type horror. A man leaps off a building in Philadelphia, leaving a suicide note mentioning the devil. Then five people enter an elevator in the same building that promptly gets stuck. They start to panic when they realize that every time the lights flicker, something bad happens. A religious security guard and a troubled cop try to help. **80m/C; Blu-Ray.** Chris Messina; Geoffrey Arend; Logan Marshall-Green; Bojana Novakovic; Jenny O'Hara; Bokeem Woodbine; Jacob Vargas; Caroline Dhavernas; Matt Craven; ***D:*** John Erick Dowdle; ***W:*** Brian Nelson; ***C:*** Tak Fujimoto; ***M:*** Fernando Velazquez.

The Devil and Daniel Johnston 🦴🦴🦴 **2005 (PG-13)** Having lived in relative cult obscurity in the 1980s, singer/songwriter Daniel Johnston morphed into a quasi-celebrity in the early 1990s after Nirvana's Kurt Cobain wore a T-shirt promoting him. Director Feuerzeig's lively documentary follows Johnston from his teenage years—with material that Johnston captured himself on audio and videotape—to his rise to sort-of fame with some of his music being recorded by well-known acts such as Tom Waits and Pearl Jam. However, his life has been riddled with trouble caused by his manic depression. Tends to look mostly at the bright side of his talents and ignores those who contend that he is perhaps overrated. **110m/C; DVD, Blu-Ray.** ***D:*** Jeff Feuerzeig; ***W:*** Jeff Feuerzeig; ***C:*** Fortunato Procopio; ***M:*** Daniel Johnston.

The Devil & Daniel Webster 🦴🦴🦴 ½ *All That Money Can Buy; Here Is a Man; A Certain Mr. Scratch* **1941** In 1840s New Hampshire, a young farmer, who sells his soul to the devil, is saved from a trip to Hell when Daniel Webster steps in to defend him. This classic fantasy is visually striking and contains wonderful performances. Adapted from the story by Stephen Vincent Benet who based it on Goethe's Faust. **106m/B; VHS, DVD.** James Craig; Edward Arnold; Walter Huston; Simone Simon; Gene Lockhart; Jane Darwell; Anne Shirley; John Qualen; H.B. Warner; ***D:*** William Dieterle; ***M:*** Bernard Herrmann. Oscars '41: Orig. Dramatic Score.

Devil & Leroy Basset 🦴 **1973 (PG)** Keema Gregwolf kills a deputy, breaks from jail with the Basset brothers, hijacks a church bus, kidnaps a family, and gets into other troublesome situations while on a posse-eluding cross-country adventure. **85m/C; VHS, DVD.** Cody Bearpaw; John Goff; George "Buck" Flower; ***D:*** Robert E. Pearson; ***M:*** Les Baxter.

The Devil & Max Devlin 🦴 ½ **1981 (PG)** Good cast wanders aimlessly in Disney family fantasy. The recently deceased Max Devlin strikes a bargain with the devil. He will be restored to life if he can convince three mortals to sell their souls. **95m/C; VHS, DVD.** Elliott Gould; Bill Cosby; Susan Anspach; Adam Rich; Julie Budd; Sonny Shroyer; Helene Winston; ***D:*** Steven Hilliard Stern; ***W:*** Jimmy Sangster; ***C:*** Howard Schwartz; ***M:*** Marvin Hamlisch; Buddy (Norman Dale) Baker.

The Devil & Miss Jones 🦴🦴🦴 ½ **1941** Engaging romantic comedy finds a big business boss posing as an ordinary salesclerk to weed out union organizers. He doesn't expect to encounter the wicked management or his beautiful co-worker, however. **90m/B; DVD, Blu-Ray.** Jean Arthur; Robert Cummings; Charles Coburn; Edmund Gwenn; Spring Byington; William Demarest; S.Z. Sakall; ***D:*** Sam Wood; ***W:*** Norman Krasna; ***C:*** Harry Stradling, Sr.

The Devil and the Deep 🦴 ½ **1932** British submarine commander Sturm (Laughton), who's stationed on the North African coast, is insanely jealous of his bored wife Diana (Bankhead). When she's rescued from a mob by Lt. Sempter (Cooper), the two spend the night together and Sturm discovers her infidelity. Finally cracking, Sturm traps Diana aboard the sub with his crew before sinking the vessel but Diana isn't about to die. Laughton's Hollywood debut piles on the ham and cheese although his performance was praised at the time. **72m/B; DVD.** Charles Laughton; Tallulah Bankhead; Gary Cooper; Cary Grant; Paul Porcasi; Henry Kolker; Juliette Compton; Arthur Hoyt; ***D:*** Marion Gering; ***W:*** Benn W. Levy; ***C:*** Charles B(ryant) Lang, Jr.

The Devil at 4 O'Clock 🦴🦴 ½ **1961** An alcoholic missionary and three convicts work to save a colony of leper children from a South Seas volcano. Quality cast barely compensates for mediocre script. **126m/B; VHS, DVD.** Spencer Tracy; Frank Sinatra; Kerwin Mathews; Jean-Pierre Aumont; ***D:*** Mervyn LeRoy; ***C:*** Joseph Biroc; ***M:*** George Duning.

The Devil Bat 🦴🦴 *Killer Bats* **1941** Madman Lugosi trains a swarm of monstrous blood-sucking bats to attack whenever they smell perfume. Followed by the sequel "Devil Bat's Daughter." DVD release is paired with the Lugosi vehicle "Scared to Death" (1946). **67m/B; VHS, DVD, Blu-Ray.** Bela Lugosi; Dave O'Brien; Suzanne Kaaren; Yolande Donlan; ***D:*** Jean Yarbrough; ***W:*** John Thomas "Jack" Neville; ***C:*** Arthur Martinelli.

The Devil Bat's Daughter 🦴 ½ **1946** A young woman, hoping to avoid becoming insane like her batty father, consults a psychiatrist when she starts to have violent nightmares. Unsuccessful sequel to "The Devil Bat." **66m/B; VHS, DVD.** Rosemary La Planche; Michael Hale; John James; Molly Lamont; ***D:*** Frank Wisbar; ***W:*** Griffin Jay; ***C:*** James S. Brown, Jr.

The Devil Came on Horseback 🦴🦴🦴 **2007** Documentary showcasing the photographs and testimony of former U.S. Marine Captain Brian Steidle, who witnessed in person the genocide of Darfur. **85m/C; DVD.** ***D:*** Ricki Stern; Annie Sundberg; ***W:*** Ricki Stern; Annie Sundberg.

Devil Dog: The Hound of Hell 🦴 **1978** A family has trouble with man's best friend when they adopt a dog that is the son of the "Hound of Hell." **95m/C; VHS, DVD.** Richard Crenna; Yvette Mimieux; Kim Richards; Victor Jory; Ike Eisenmann; Lou Frizzell; Ken Kercheval; R.G. Armstrong; Martine Beswick; ***D:*** Curtis Harrington; ***W:*** Elinor Karpf; Stephen Karpf; ***C:*** Gerald Perry Finnerman; ***M:*** Artie Kane. **TV**

Devil Doll 🦴🦴🦴 *The Witch of Timbuctoo* **1936** Paris banker Paul Lavond (Barrymore) is framed for robbery and murder by former associates and sent to Devil's Island prison where he hooks up with a scientist who's researching a method for reducing humans to mere inches. Levond engineers an escape from the island and returns to Paris were he sets about exacting his revenge on his betrayers. **80m/B; VHS, DVD.** Lionel Barrymore; Maureen O'Sullivan; Frank Lawton; Rafaela (Rafael, Raphaella) Ottiano; Robert Greig; Lucy Beaumont; ***D:*** Tod Browning; ***W:*** Garrett Fort; Erich von Stroheim; Guy Endore; Abraham Merritt; ***C:*** Leonard Smith; ***M:*** Franz Waxman.

Devil Doll 🦴🦴 **1964** Ventriloquist's dummy, which contains the soul of a former performer, eyes a beautiful victim in the crowd. Newspaper guy senses trouble. Cut above the usual talking, stalking dummy story. **80m/B; VHS, DVD.** *GB* Bryant Holiday; William Sylvester; Yvonne Romain; Sandra Dorne; Karel Stepanek; Francis De Wolff; ***D:*** Lindsay Shonteff; ***W:*** Lance Z. Hargreaves; George Barclay; ***C:*** Gerald Gibbs.

Devil Girl from Mars 🦴 ½ **1954** Sexy female from Mars and her very large robot arrive at a small Scottish inn to announce that a Martian feminist revolution has occurred. The distaff aliens then undertake a search of healthy Earth males for breeding purposes. Believe it or not, the humans don't want to go and therein lies the rub. A somewhat enjoyable space farce. **76m/B; VHS, DVD, Blu-Ray.** *GB* Hugh McDermott; Hazel Court; Patricia Laffan; Peter Reynolds; Adrienne Corri; Joseph Tomelty; Sophie Stewart; John Laurie; Anthony Richmond; ***D:*** David MacDonald; ***W:*** John C. Mather; James Eastwood; ***C:*** Jack Cox; ***M:*** Edwin Astley.

The Devil Horse 🦴 ½ **1926** Army scout Dave Carson's (Canutt) family was killed during an Indian attack when he was a boy and his colt Rex was taken and abused. Rex escaped and became the rogue stallion of the title as both man and horse still want revenge just as the local tribe attacks the fort. **68m/B; Silent; DVD.** Yakima Canutt; Roy Clements; Gladys McConnell; Robert F. (Bob) Kortman; ***D:*** Fred W. Jackman; ***W:*** Hal Roach; ***C:*** Floyd Jackman; George Stevens.

Devil Horse 🦴🦴 **1932** A boy's devotion to a wild horse marked for destruction as a killer leads him into trouble. A serial in 12 chapters of 13 minutes each. **156m/B; VHS, DVD.** Frankie Darro; Harry Carey, Sr.; Noah Beery, Sr.; *D:* Otto Brower; Richard Talmadge.

Devil Hunter 1/2 *Sexo canibal; The Gruesome Shock of the Devil; Mandingo Manhunter; The Man Hunter* **2008** A poor googly-eyed super cannibal with breathing problems has to deal with his home being invaded by brainless, tasty white women. Or a group of innocent girls on vacation is being stalked by a savage flesh eating monster. It's your call. Either way, the plot is secondary to Franco's fascination with certain female attributes. **89m/C; DVD.** Al Cliver; Gisela Hahn; Werner Pochath; Antonio Mayans; Antonio de Cabo; Burt Altman; Melo Costa; Ursula Buchfellner; *D:* Jess (Jesus) Franco; *W:* Jess (Jesus) Franco; Julian Esteban; *C:* Juan Soler; *M:* Jess (Jesus) Franco. **VIDEO**

Devil in a Blue Dress **1995 (R)** Down-on-his-luck Easy Rawlins (Washington) is an out of work aircraft worker in 1948 LA. He's hired to find mystery woman Daphne (Beals) by a shady businessman (Sizemore). What he finds are the usual noir staples: government corruption backed by thugs who want him to mind his own business. Easy and Daphne's torrid romance featured in the Walter Mosley novel is missing but the racism and violence are intact. Realism and accuracy in period detail enhance solid performance by Washington, though the deliberate, literary pace is at times lulling. Cheadle takes over whenever he shows up as Mouse, Rawlins' loyal friend and muscle. **102m/C; VHS, DVD, Blu-Ray.** Denzel Washington; Jennifer Beals; Don Cheadle; Tom Sizemore; Maury Chaykin; Terry Kinney; Mel Winkler; Albert Hall; Renee Humphrey; Lisa Nicole Carson; John Roselius; Beau Starr; Nick(y) Corello; *D:* Carl Franklin; *W:* Carl Franklin; *C:* Tak Fujimoto; *M:* Elmer Bernstein. L.A. Film Critics '95: Support. Actor (Cheadle); Natl. Soc. Film Critics '95: Cinematog., Support. Actor (Cheadle).

Devil in the Flesh *Le Diable au Corps* **1946** Acclaimed drama about a French soldier's wife having a passionate affair with a high school student while her husband is away fighting in WWI. From the novel by Raymond Radiguet. Dubbed. Updated and remade in 1987. **112m/B; VHS, DVD.** *FR* Gerard Philipe; Micheline Presle; Denise Grey; *D:* Claude Autant-Lara; *W:* Jean Aurenche; Pierre Bost; *C:* Michel Kelber; *M:* Rene Cloerec.

Devil in the Flesh *Il Diavolo in Corpo* **1987 (R)** A angst-ridden, semi-pretentious Italian drama about an obsessive older woman carrying on an affair with a schoolboy, despite her terrorist boyfriend and the objections of the lad's psychiatrist father, who had treated her. Famous for a graphic sex scene, available in the unrated version. Updated remake of the 1946 French film. Italian with subtitles. **110m/C; VHS, DVD.** *IT* Maruschka Detmers; Federico Pitzalis; Riccardo De Torrebruna; *D:* Marco Bellocchio; *W:* Marco Bellocchio; Ennio de Concini; Enrico Palandri; *C:* Giuseppe Lanci; *M:* Carlo Crivelli.

Devil in the Flesh 1/2 *Dearly Devoted* **1998 (R)** Troubled Debbie Strand (McGowan) has a crush on teacher Peter Rinaldi (McArthur) and no one is going to stop her getting what (or who) she wants. She tries blackmailing him when he doesn't respond and Peter learns Debbie has a very deadly past. **92m/C; VHS, DVD.** Rose McGowan; Alex McArthur; Sherrie Rose; Phil Morris; Robert Silver; *D:* Steve Cohen. **VIDEO**

Devil in the Flesh 2 1/2 *Teacher's Pet* **2000 (R)** In this sequel to the '98 flick, disturbed Debbie (O'Keefe) escapes from the looney bin and causes the accidental death of the college coed who offers her a ride, so she assumes her identity. Passing herself off as wealthy Sydney Hollings, Debbie becomes infatuated with her writing prof Sam (Garcia), who's flattered by the attention. Except that anyone who gets in Debbie's way is permanently disposed of. Sly humor and O'Keefe is remarkably appealing considering she plays a psychopath. **90m/C; VHS, DVD.** Jodi Lyn O'Keefe; Katherine Kendall; Jsu Garcia; Jeanette Brox; Bill Gratton; Todd McKee; Christiana Frank; Todd Robert Anderson; *D:* Marcus Spiegel; *W:* Richard Brandes; *C:* M. David Mullen. **VIDEO**

The Devil Incarnate 1/2 *Copiii: The 1st Entry* **2013** Classic horror-thriller about a terrifying evil lurking in unexpected places. Just after Trevor (Luzzi) and Holly (Carli) Davidson are married, they visit a tarot reader who informs them that Holly is pregnant. The tarot reader is proven correct, but Holly soon does not seem like herself. Though she and Trevor are happy, Holly begins to act in odd, even violent, ways. The couple soon believes that something evil may be inside her. Trevor's quest for answers leads to the conclusion that Holly may be a victim of demon's long-dormant ancient bloodthirsty scourge. **93m/C; DVD, Blu-Ray, Streaming, Download.** Graci Carli; Rod Luzzi; Emily Rogers; Cindy Hogan; Barbara Van Fleet; *D:* L. Gustavo Cooper; *W:* L. Gustavo Cooper; Jon Bosworth; *C:* Ryan Patrick Dean; *M:* Andrew Avitabile; Brian Jerin. **VIDEO**

The Devil Inside **2012 (R)** Low-budget, tedious, and familiar exorcism shtick complete with faux-documentary footage. In 1989, possessed Maria Rossi is arrested and convicted of the murders of three exorcists and is locked in an Italian hospital for the criminally insane. In 2009, her daughter Isabella visits and believes Maria is indeed demonically possessed. She heads to the Vatican School of Exorcism for a crash course and becomes involved with a couple of rogue priests in unauthorized exorcisms in an effort to help her mother. **83m/C; DVD, Blu-Ray.** Suzan Crowley; Simon Quaterman; Evan Helmuth; Fernanda Andrade; Brian Johnson; Ionut Grama; Bonnie Morgan; *D:* William Brent Bell; *W:* William Brent Bell; Matthew Peterman; *C:* Gonzalo Amat; *M:* Brett Detar; Ben Romans.

The Devil Is a Sissy 1/2 **1936** The 1930s three biggest juvenile stars are together in this melodrama. Upper-class English lad Claude (Bartholomew) is happy to live with his father for six months per his parents' divorce agreement. His wealthy mother doesn't feel the same since struggling dad lives in a New York slum area and Claude must attend public school. Claude has to prove himself to tough juvies Buck (Cooper) and Gig (Rooney) and everyone gets into lots of trouble before learning the lesson that crime doesn't pay. **91m/B; DVD.** Freddie Bartholomew; Jackie Cooper; Mickey Rooney; Ian Hunter; Katherine Alexander; Peggy Conklin; Gene Lockhart; Jonathan Hale; *D:* W.S. Van Dyke; *W:* Richard Schayer; John Lee Mahin; *C:* Harold Rosson; George Schneiderman; *M:* Herbert Stothart.

The Devil Is a Woman **1935** Dietrich vamps as money-hungry beauty Concha Perez, who soon has best friends and fellow military officers Pasqual (Atwill) and Antonio (Romero) dueling for her dubious affections. Turns out the man she desires may not be the man she truly needs. Flashbacks show how Concha seductively destroyed Pasquel some years earlier and how his jealousy lingered on. Based on the novel "The Woman and the Puppet" by Pierre Louys. After protests by the Spanish government over the depiction of the Spanish military, Paramount agreed to supress the film and few prints survived. **79m/B; DVD, Blu-Ray.** Marlene Dietrich; Lionel Atwill; Cesar Romero; Edward Everett Horton; Alison Skipworth; *D:* Josef von Sternberg; *W:* John Dos Passos; S.K. Winston; *C:* Josef von Sternberg; Lucien Ballard.

The Devil Makes Three **1952** In 1947 American pilot Jeff Eliot (Kelly) returns to Munich to find the family who saved his life during the war. The only survivor is Wilhelmina (Angweli), who's not an innocent young girl any longer. She involves the smitten Jeff in a gold smuggling operation that has ties to a Nazi group who wants to relaunch the Third Reich. Filmed on location, including Hitler's mountaintop aerie at Berchtesgaden. **90m/B; DVD.** Gene Kelly; Pier Angeli; Richard Rober; Richard Egan; Claus Clausen; *D:* Andrew Marton; *W:* Jerry Davis; *C:* Vaclav Vich; *M:* Rudolph Kopp.

Devil Monster **1946** A world-weary traveler searches for a girl's fiance in the South Pacific, and is attacked by a large manta. **65m/B; VHS, DVD.** Barry Norton; Blanche Mehaffey; *D:* S. Edwin Graham.

Devil of the Desert Against the Son of Hercules 1/2 **1962** The grandson of Zeus ventures into the wasteland to take on a feisty foe. **93m/C; VHS, DVD.** *IT* Kirk Morris; Michele Girardon; *D:* Riccardo Freda.

The Devil on Horseback 1/2 **1936** Hollywood star Diane (Damita) takes a press junket to a Latin American country where bandit Pancho (Campo) is her biggest fan. What starts as a kidnapping publicity stunt turns into the real thing when Pancho whisks Diane away to his hacienda in an attempt to woo her. Damita retired after this cowboy musical to marry Errol Flynn and neither choice turned out for the best. **71m/B; DVD.** Lili Damita; Fred Keating; Del Campo; Jean Chatburn; Tiffany Thayer; *D:* Crane Wilbur; *W:* Crane Wilbur; *C:* Mack Stengler.

The Devil on Wheels **1947** Inspired by his dad's reckless driving, a teenager becomes a hot rodder and causes a family tragedy. A rusty melodrama that can't be described as high-performance. **67m/B; VHS, DVD.** James B. Cardwell; Noreen Nash; Darryl Hickman; Jan Ford; Damian O'Flynn; Lenita Love; *D:* Crane Wilbur; *W:* Crane Wilbur.

The Devil, Probably *Le Diable, Probablement* **1977** Ennui among Parisian youth, lost in their polluted, consumer society. Charles (Monnier) spins deeper into depression, despite the efforts of his friends, and finally makes a bargain with a junkie to shoot him in Pere Lachaise cemetery. French with subtitles. **95m/C; DVD.** *FR* Antoine Monnier; Tina Irissari; Henri De Maublanc; *D:* Robert Bresson; *W:* Robert Bresson; *C:* Pasqualino De Santis; *M:* Philippe Sarde.

The Devil Rides Out 1/2 *The Devil's Bride* **1968** Considered by many to be Hammer's finest achievement, though several other of the studio's films rate serious consideration. This one's a solid witchcraft tale written by Richard Matheson. In 1925, the Duc de Richleau (Lee), a "good" warlock, and the evil Mocata battle each other over De Richleau's friend Simon (Mower). Some of the effects are a little dated now, but director Terence Fisher builds suspense through a stately pace. Production values are highlighted by the usual excellent sets and a fleet of vintage cars. Lee's performance is one of his strongest in a conventionally heroic role. **95m/C; DVD, Blu-Ray.** *GB* Christopher Lee; Charles Gray; Nike Arrighi; Leon Greene; Patrick Mower; Gwen Ffrangcon Davies; Sarah Lawson; Paul Eddington; *D:* Terence Fisher; *W:* Richard Matheson; *C:* Arthur Grant; *M:* James Bernard.

The Devil-Ship Pirates **1964** Hammer-produced swashbuckler stars Lee as Captain Robeles, a ruthless pirate fighting for Spain during the 1588 Armada. When his ship, the Diablo, is damaged, Robles docks it in a small English coastal village for repairs. The village is so isolated that most believe Robles when he says that Spain has defeated England and they are the new rulers. But not quite everyone is willing to accept the pirate's tale. **89m/C; DVD.** *GB* Christopher Lee; John Cairney; Barry Warren; Andrew Keir; Duncan Lamont; Michael Ripper; Ernest Clark; Suzan Farmer; Philip Latham; Natasha Pyne; *D:* Don Sharp; *W:* Jimmy Sangster; *C:* Michael Reed; *M:* Gary Hughes.

Devil Times Five 1/2 *People Toys; The Horrible House on the Hill* **1974 (R)** To take revenge for being incarcerated in a mental hospital, five children methodically murder the adults who befriend them. **87m/C; VHS, DVD, Blu-Ray.** Gene Evans; Sorrell Booke; Shelley Morrison; *D:* Sean McGregor.

The Devil Wears Prada 1/2 **2006 (PG-13)** This predictable plot (small town girl with big city dreams) gets an extra half-bone for Streep's sleek boss-from-hell. That would be Miranda Priestly, high priestess editor of the Manhattan fashion mag where wide-eyed Andy (Hathaway) is hired as a second assistant. A walking fashion faux pas, Andy slowly loses her ideals (and frumpy appearance) to the beguilement of power and designer trends. Can she be saved? Hathaway struggles to hold her own (she has the least showy role) against both Streep and the scene-stealing Tucci. Based on the chick lit book by Lauren Weisberger. **106m/C; DVD, Blu-Ray.** Anne Hathaway; Meryl Streep; Adrian Grenier; Simon Baker; Stanley Tucci; Emily Blunt; Tracie Thoms; David Marshall Grant; James Naughton; Daniel Sunjata; Rebecca Mader; Rich Sommer; *D:* David Frankel; *W:* Aline Brosh McKenna; *C:* Florian Ballhaus; *M:* Theodore Shapiro. Golden Globes '07: Actress--Mus./Comedy (Streep).

Devil Wears White **1986 (R)** A student's vacation is disrupted when he becomes involved in a war with an insane arms dealer who wants to take over a Latin American Republic. **92m/C; VHS, DVD.** Robert Livesy; Jane Higginson; Guy Ecker; Anthony Cordova; *D:* Steven A. Hull.

The Devil You Know 1/2 **2005** Micro-budgeted neo-noir only came to life in 2013 after Jennifer Lawrence, who had a tiny role in flashback scenes, became a star. Not worth the wait, it's a dull, cliched affair about a reclusive former movie star and her frustrated daughter, who's trying to break into showbiz. Zoe resents her ma, even more so after Kathryn decides to make a comeback, which is before the star gets a blackmailer's letter. **72m/C; Streaming.** Lena Olin; Rosamund Pike; Dean Winters; Molly Price; Jennifer Lawrence; *D:* James Oakey; *W:* Alex Michaelides; *C:* Kenny Brown; *M:* Mark Sayfritz.

The Devils *The Devils of Loudun* **1971 (R)** In 1631 France, a priest is accused of commerce with the devil and sexual misconduct with nuns. Since he is also a political threat, the accusation is used to denounce and eventually execute him. Based on Aldous Huxley's "The Devils of Loudun," the movie features masturbating nuns and other excesses—shocking scenes typical of film director Russell. Supposedly this was Russell's attempt to wake the public to their desensitization of modern horrors of war. Controversial and flamboyant. **109m/C; VHS, DVD.** *GB* Vanessa Redgrave; Oliver Reed; Dudley Sutton; Max Adrian; Gemma Jones; Murray Melvin; Michael Gothard; Georgina Hale; Christopher Logue; Andrew Faulds; *D:* Ken Russell; *W:* Ken Russell; *C:* David Watkin; *M:* Peter Maxwell Davies. Natl. Bd. of Review '71: Director (Russell).

The Devil's Advocate 1/2 **1997 (R)** Forget the actors, this film belongs to cinematographer Bartkowiak and production designer Bruno Rubeo, who offer a lush, rich look that's very enticing. And it's all about enticement—young Florida lawyer Kevin Lomax (Reeves) is seduced by the power and money of a position at an influential New York law firm run by the mysterious John Milton (Pacino). But soon Kevin's beautiful wife Mary Ann (Theron) is having a breakdown, his religious mother (Ivey) is prophesizing doom, and Kevin learns the boss is Satan—literally. Reeves is earnest, Pacino relishes his showy role, and the visual effects provide some much needed jolts. Based on the novel by Andrew Neiderman. **144m/C; VHS, DVD, Blu-Ray.** Al Pacino; Keanu Reeves; Charlize Theron; Judith Ivey; Craig T. Nelson; Jeffrey Jones; Connie Nielsen; Ruben Santiago-Hudson; Debra Monk; Tamara Tunie; Vyto Ruginis; Laura Harrington; Pamela Gray; Heather Matarazzo; Delroy Lindo; Gloria Lynne Henry; Chris Bauer; *D:* Taylor Hackford; *W:* Tony Gilroy; Jonathan Lemkin; *C:* Andrzej Bartkowiak; *M:* James Newton Howard.

Devil's Angels **1967** A motorcycle gang clashes with a small-town sheriff. Cheap 'n' sleazy fare. **84m/C; VHS, DVD.** John Cassavetes; Beverly Adams; Mimsy Farmer; Salli Sachse; Nai Bonet; Leo Gordon; *D:* Daniel Haller; *W:* Charles B. Griffith.

The Devil's Arithmetic 1/2 **1999** Modern teen Hannah Stern (Dunst) is indifferent to her Jewish faith and reluctant to attend her Aunt Eva's (Fletcher) Passover seder. After getting drunk, she passes out and is mysteriously transported to Poland in 1941, where she and her cousin Rivkah (Murphy) are imprisoned in a concentration camp and Hannah gets a first-hand look at faith and oppression. Pic doesn't play down the Nazi horrors and may not be suitable for the very young. Adapted from Jane Yolen's novel. **101m/C; VHS, DVD.** Kirsten Dunst; Brittany Murphy; Louise Fletcher; Paul Freeman; Mimi Rogers; *D:* Donna Deitch; *W:* Robert J. Avrech; *C:* Jacek Laskus; *M:* Frederic Talgorn. **CABLE**

The Devil's Backbone *El Espinazo del Diablo* **2001 (R)** In the final days of the Spanish Civil War, staff and children at a remote orphanage run by loyalists Casares (Luppi) and Carmen (Paredes) prepare for an uncertain fate. Carlos (Tielve) is a new arrival who quickly learns that there are many secrets, including the (possible) ghost of schoolboy Santi. Sinister janitor Jacinto (Noriega) also thinks there's gold hidden somewhere and is determined to find it. Uneasy combination of history and the supernatural. Spanish with subtitles. **106m/C; VHS, DVD, Blu-Ray.** *SP MX* Marisa Paredes; Federico Luppi; Eduardo Noriega; Fernando Tielve; Inigo Garces; Irene Visedo; Berta Ojea; ***D:*** Guillermo del Toro; ***W:*** Guillermo del Toro; Antonio Trashorros; David Munoz; ***C:*** Guillermo Navarro; ***M:*** Javier Navarrete.

The Devil's Brigade **1968** "Dirty Dozen" style film with Holden as the leader of special commando brigade consisting of the usual misfits and oddballs. The team is trained to take on the Nazis in Scandanavia but has their assignment cancelled. Instead, they take them on in the Italian Alps, making for some perilous adventures. Non-acting notables include former football great Hornung and former boxing champ Gene Fullmer. **130m/C; VHS, DVD, Blu-Ray.** William Holden; Cliff Robertson; Vince Edwards; Andrew Prine; Claude Akins; Michael Rennie; Dana Andrews; Gretchen Wyler; Carroll O'Connor; Richard Jaeckel; Jack Watson; Paul Hornung; Jeremy Slate; Don Megowan; Patric Knowles; James Craig; Richard Dawson; Tom Stern; Luke Askew; Harry Carey, Jr.; Tom Troupe; Norman Alden; David Pritchard; Wilhelm von Homburg; ***D:*** Andrew V. McLaglen; ***W:*** William Roberts; ***C:*** William Clothier; ***M:*** Alex North.

The Devil's Brother *Fra Diavolo; Bogus Bandits; The Virtuous Tramps* **1933** In one of their lesser efforts, Laurel and Hardy star as bumbling bandits in this comic operetta based on the 1830 opera by Daniel F. Auber. **88m/B; VHS, DVD.** Stan Laurel; Oliver Hardy; Dennis King; Thelma Todd; James Finlayson; Lucille Browne; ***D:*** Charles R. Rogers; Hal Roach.

The Devil's Candy ½ **2017** The intersection of art and insanity is captured well in Sean Byrne's festival horror hit. Jesse Hellman (Embry) is a struggling painter living with his wife (Appleby) and daughter in a remote country home. Jesse starts to hear voices that inspire his paintings, which take a much darker turn to images of demons and other horrors. At the same time, a clearly demented man (Vince) who has to play electric guitar loudly to drown out the voices in his head, moves toward Jesse's home with murderous intent. This is a moody, intense genre pic that horror fans should seek out. **79m/C; DVD, Blu-Ray.** Ethan (Randall) Embry; Shiri Appleby; Pruitt Taylor Vince; Kiara Glasco; Tony Amendola; ***D:*** Sean Byrne; ***W:*** Sean Byrne; ***C:*** Simon Chapman; ***M:*** Mads Heldtberg; Michael Yezerski; Jonathan McHugh.

The Devil's Daughter *La Setta; The Sect* **1991 (R)** Satan, in a desperate bid to take over the planet, orders his minions to flood the earth with horrific evil. Only one woman can prevent the HellMaster from succeeding, and she may be too late! **112m/C; VHS, DVD, Blu-Ray.** *IT* Kelly Curtis; Herbert Lom; Maria Angela Giordano; Michel Hans Adatte; Carla Cassola; Angelika Maria Boeck; Tomas Arana; ***D:*** Michele (Michael) Soavi; ***W:*** Dario Argento; ***M:*** Pino Donaggio.

Devil's Den ½ **2006** Cheapie ghoul horror/comedy. Quinn and Nick are heading towards the U.S. border from Mexico with their drug stash when they happen upon the titular club. Being your normal horny dudes, they're happy to find a bevy of beautiful strippers, who are not what they seem. Now the doofs have to stay alive until dawn with the help of a gorgeous assassin and a demon-wasting samurai. **84m/C; DVD.** Devon Sawa; Steven Schub; Kelly Hu; Ken Foree; Karen Maxwell; Ken Ohara; Dawn Olivieri; ***D:*** Jeff Burr; ***W:*** Mitch Gould; ***C:*** Viorel Sergovici, Jr.; ***M:*** Jon Lee. **VIDEO**

The Devil's Dominoes ½ **2007** A car crash kills the driver of one of the vehicles and leads to an attempted cover-up. The buddies who survived the accident find diamonds in the other car and learn the victim was the son of a Chicago mobster. Now the guys have the mob, local law enforcement, and each other to worry about. **93m/C; DVD.** Vincent Pastore; Daniel Baldwin; Tom Bateman; Crag Degel; Christopher Mur; ***D:*** Scott Prestin; ***W:*** John Pizzo; ***C:*** Marc Menet. **VIDEO**

The Devil's Doorway **1950** Revisionist western from Mann that's pro-Native American. Behind the heavy makeup, Taylor takes on the unlikely role of Shoshone Indian Lance Poole. The former Union soldier and Civil War hero returns home to Wyoming and learns crooked lawyer Verne Coolan (Calhern) is using the government to turn over his tribe's traditional lands to sheepherders. A range war ensues and Lance turns renegade to protect his people. **84m/B; DVD.** Robert Taylor; Louis Calhern; Paula Raymond; Marshall Thompson; James Mitchell; Edgar Buchanan; ***D:*** Anthony Mann; ***W:*** Guy Trosper; ***C:*** John Alton; ***M:*** Daniele Amfitheatrof.

The Devil's Double **2011 (R)** Loosely based on the true story of Latif Yahia, an Iraqi Army officer who's called to Baghdad by his former classmate, Uday Hussein. Uday tells Latif that he's chosen him to be his body double at public appearances and Latif isn't given the option to refuse. Director Tamahori intercuts news footage with depictions of predatory, drug-crazed, uncontrollable Uday's extreme behavior while Latif struggles to survive being his current best friend and decoy. Cooper's charismatic as Latif, Uday, and Latif-impersonating-Uday, but the constant sadism and violence are both sensationalized and numbing. **109m/C; DVD, Blu-Ray.** *BE* Dominic Cooper; Ludivine Sagnier; Mimoun Oaissa; Raad Rawi; Philip Quast; Khalid Laith; Jamie Harding; ***D:*** Lee Tamahori; ***W:*** Michael Thomas; ***C:*** Sam McCurdy; ***M:*** Christian Henson.

Devil's Due **2014 (R)** This Rosemary's Baby redux centers on Zach (Gilford) and Samantha (Miller), a newly married couple who become the targets of a Satanic cult who impregnates poor Samantha with demon seed. (Get it? "Due," like a due date for a child.) The result is a by-the-numbers, copycat of a mess that wouldn't even work straight-to-video, much less warrant the cost of a ticket in a movie theater. **89m/C; DVD, Blu-Ray.** Zach Gilford; Allison Miller; Sam Anderson; Roger Payano; ***D:*** Matt Bettinelli-Olpin; Tyler Gillett; ***W:*** Lindsay Devlin; ***C:*** Justin Martinez.

The Devil's Hand *Devil's Doll; The Naked Goddess; Live to Love* **1961** When Alda finds a doll that represents his ideal woman in a curio shop, the shop's owner (Hamilton, aka Commissioner Gordon), tells him the dream girl who modeled for the doll lives nearby. Trouble is, she's part of a voodoo cult, and guess who's head voodooman. Big trouble for Alda; big snooze for you. **71m/B; VHS, DVD, Blu-Ray.** Linda Christian; Robert Alda; Neil Hamilton; Ariadne Welter; ***D:*** William Hole, Jr.

The Devil's in the Details **2013 (R)** Suffering after serving a tour of duty, soldier Thomas Conrad (Mathews) is referred for therapy to Dr. Robert Michaels (Liotta). Thomas' hopes for normalcy are threatened--along with his family's safety--by a drug cartel's thug (Rivera). It helps that Dr. Michaels used to be a Navy SEAL.The actors give it a good go, but otherwise it's a so-so attempt at an overdone subject. **100m/C; DVD, Blu-Ray, Streaming.** Ray Liotta; Emilio Rivera; Joel Mathews; Raymond J. Barry; Noel Gugliemi; ***D:*** Waymon Boone; ***W:*** Waymon Boone; ***C:*** Kevin McMahon; ***M:*** Danny Cocke. **VIDEO**

Devil's Island *Djoflaeyjan* **1996** An abandoned military base is being used to house poor families outside Reykjavik in the '50s. The trash-filled landscape offers little to those who live there, including four generations of one eccentric no-hope family. The usual family dysfunction is all played for exaggerated caricature. Icelandic with subtitles. **103m/C; VHS, DVD.** *IC* Gisli Halldorsson; Baltasar Kormakur; Sveinn Geirsson; Sigurveig Jonsdottir; ***D:*** Fridrik Thor Fridriksson; ***W:*** Einar Karason; ***C:*** Ari Kristinsson; ***M:*** Hilmar Orn Hilmarsson.

Devil's Knight **2003 (R)** Brothers Hector (Serna) and Ruben (Solano) Rivera are expert "low-rider" designers who end up murdered. Their sister Delia (Alvarez) leaves the Army to find their killers. With the help of a Vietman vet mechanic (Kove), she sets out to take her own brand of revenge, which consists of wearing bikinis and rubbing against pimped-out cars at custom shows. So-so actioner is fueled by the lovingly-shot Alvarez, and the even-more-lovingly-shot custom street machines. **97m/C; VHS, DVD.** Elizabeth Alvarez; Jose Solano; Alexander Romanov; Martin Kove; Pepe Serna; Jaime Gomez; Garry Marshall; ***D:*** Quan Phillips; ***W:*** Quan Phillips; ***C:*** Robert Hayes. **VIDEO**

Devil's Knot **2014** Rather staid retelling by Egoyan of a true crime and an infamous miscarriage of justice. In 1993, three young boys are found murdered in West Memphis, Arkansas. In a rush to find the killers, the police quickly arrest three misfit teens who are supposedly into devil worship. Pam Hobbs (Witherspoon), the mother of one victim, is desperate to believe the killers have been found, but local investigator Ron Lax (Firth) doesn't believe the evidence adds up. Events end with the 1994 trials in a dramatization of a case about the 'West Memphis Three' that is the subject of several documentaries. **114m/C; DVD, Blu-Ray.** Colin Firth; Reese Witherspoon; Alessandro Nivola; Elias Koteas; Amy Ryan; Mireille Enos; Kevin Durand; Bruce Greenwood; Stephen Moyer; James Hamrick; ***D:*** Atom Egoyan; ***W:*** Paul Harris Boardman; Scott Derrickson; ***C:*** Paul Sarossy; ***M:*** Mychael Danna.

The Devil's Mercy ½ **2007** The Winters family—Beth (Valente), Matt (Cram), and young son Calvin (Everett)?have just moved into their renovated apartment in an old Connecticut house. Their downstairs neighbor Tyler Grant (Rea) is friendly and he has a niece, Kayla (Lochner), willing to hang out with Calvin. But the boy doesn't like his new abode, complaining to Beth that there are monsters in the house. And he's right. **90m/C; DVD.** Stephen Rea; Hannah Lochner; Michael Cram; Deborah Valente; Dylan Everett; ***D:*** Melanie Orr; ***W:*** James A. McLean; ***M:*** Ryan Latham. **VIDEO**

The Devil's Nightmare ½ *Succubus; The Devil Walks at Midnight* **1971 (R)** A woman leads seven tourists (representing the seven deadly sins) on a tour of a medieval European castle. There they experience demonic tortures. Lots of creepy moments. Euro-horror/sex star Blanc is fantastic in this otherwise mediocre production. **88m/C; VHS, DVD, Blu-Ray.** *BE IT* Erika Blanc; Jean Servais; Daniel Emilfork; Lucien Raimbourg; Jacques Monseau; Colette Emmanuelle; Ivana Novak; Shirley Corrigan; Frederique Hender; ***D:*** Jean Brismee; ***W:*** Patrice Rhomm; Vertunnio De Angelis; Charles Lecocq; ***C:*** Andre Goeffers; ***M:*** Alessandro Alessandroni.

Devils on the Doorstep *Guizi Laile* **2000** Chinese film needs some sharp editing before this black comedy about a tiny village's survival during WWII could be anything more than frustrating. Local peasant Ma Dasan is surprised when the Chinese Army dump two prisoners in their remote village—a Japanese POW and his Chinese interpreter. When no one comes for the prisoners after six months, the fearful villagers decide they should be executed and Ma is sent to hire an assassin. When this doesn't work out, the villagers try to return them to nearby Japanese troops. This idea isn't any better and by now the movie's exhausted a viewer's patience. Japanese and Mandarin with subtitles. **162m/B; VHS, DVD.** *CH* Jiang Wen; Kagawa Teruyuki; Jiang Hongbo; Chen Qiang; Sawada Kenya; Yuan Ding; ***D:*** Jiang Wen; ***W:*** Jiang Wen; ***C:*** Gu Changwei. Cannes '00: Grand Jury Prize.

The Devil's Own **1996 (R)** Irish-American New York cop Tom O'Meara (Ford) and wife Sheila (Colin) take charming Irish emigre Rory Devaney (Pitt) into their home and make him part of the family. But Rory, AKA Frankie McGuire, turns out to be an IRA terrorist who has hustled out of trouble in Belfast and now has a bloody purpose for coming to America. When Tom discovers just what it is, he tries to stop Rory before he destroys any more lives—including his own. More a low-key character study than a slam-bang actioner, with Pitt cooly charismatic as the troubled gunman while Ford does his usual professional work as a good cop caught up in a bad situation. **110m/C; VHS, DVD, Blu-Ray.** Harrison Ford; Brad Pitt; Margaret Colin; Ruben Blades; Treat Williams; George Hearn; Natascha (Natasha) McElhone; Mitchell Ryan; Simon Jones; Paul Ronan; ***D:*** Alan J. Pakula; ***W:*** Kevin Jarre; David Aaron Cohen; Vincent Patrick; ***C:*** Gordon Willis; ***M:*** James Horner.

The Devil's Partner ½ **1958** Yet another uninspired devil yarn in which an old-timer trades in his senior citizenship by dying and coming back in the form of his younger self. Young again, he takes a new wife and indulges in multiple ritual sacrifices. Noteworthy only by virtue of the cast's later TV notoriety—Buchanan and Foulger would later appear on "Petticoat Junction," Nelson played Dr. Rossi on "Peyton Place," and Crane beached a role on "Hawaiian Eye." **75m/B; VHS, DVD.** Ed Nelson; Jean Allison; Edgar Buchanan; Richard Crane; Spencer Carlisle; Byron Foulger; Claire Carleton; ***D:*** Charles R. Rondeau.

Devil's Party **1938** A tenement boy's reunion party turns into a night of horror when one of the guests is killed. As a result, the childhood friends band together to uncover the murderer's identity. **65m/B; VHS, DVD.** Victor McLaglen; Paul Kelly; William Gargan; Samuel S. Hinds; Scotty Beckett; ***D:*** Ray McCarey.

Devil's Pass *The Dyatlov Pass Incident* **2013 (R)** Tedious horror/thriller with an over-used plot. Five American college students are using a grant to head to a remote area of Russia's Ural Mountains to find the truth behind a mystery. In 1959, nine experienced Russian hikers are found dead under mysterious circumstances. The Americans are trying to retrace the journey, but found footage shows that wasn't a good idea. **100m/C; DVD.** Holly Goss; Gemma Atkinson; Luke Albright; Matthew Stokoe; Ryan Hawley; ***D:*** Renny Harlin; ***W:*** Vikram Weet; ***C:*** Denis Alarkon-Ramires. **VIDEO**

The Devil's Playground **1976** Sexual tension rises in a Catholic seminary, distracting the boys from their theological studies. The attentions of the priests only further their sexual confusion. **107m/C; VHS, DVD.** *AU* Arthur Dignam; Nick (Nicholas) Tate; Simon Burke; Charles Frawley; Jonathan Hardy; Gerry Dugan; Thomas Keneally; ***D:*** Fred Schepisi; ***W:*** Fred Schepisi; ***C:*** Ian Baker; ***M:*** Bruce Smeaton. Australian Film Inst. '76: Actor (Burke), Actor (Tate), Cinematog., Director (Schepisi), Film, Screenplay.

Devil's Pond *Heaven's Pond* **2003 (R)** Spoiled rich girl Julianne (Reid) impulsively marries her boyfriend Mitch (Pardue) in order to get away from her controlling family. They honeymoon in an isolated cabin, with no communication to the outside world, and Julianne soon discovers that her new hubby has no intention of ever letting her go. This is one newlywed who wasn't expecting the "till death do us part" to come so soon. You'll have to like the pretty lead actors since it's their adventure. **92m/C; VHS, DVD.** Tara Reid; Kip Pardue; Meredith Baxter; Dan Gunther; ***D:*** Joel Viertel; ***W:*** Alek Friedman; Mora Stephens; ***C:*** Matthew Jensen; ***M:*** Brad Caleb Kane. **VIDEO**

The Devil's Possessed ½ **1974** A Middle Ages despot tortures and maims the peasants in his region until they rise up and enact an unspeakable revenge. **90m/C; VHS, DVD, Blu-Ray.** *AR SP* Paul Naschy; ***D:*** Leon Klimovsky.

The Devil's Prey **2001 (R)** Partyers attending a rave discover it's a front for satanic cult leader Minister Seth (Bergin) to obtain the young flesh he needs for his blood sacrifies. But Susan (Jones) is willing to fight for her life against the masked cult members. Fast-paced horror. **91m/C; VHS, DVD.** Patrick Bergin; Ashley Jones; Charlie O'Connell; Bryan Kirkwood; Tim Thomerson; ***D:*** Bradford May. **VIDEO**

Devil's Rain ½ **1975 (PG)** The rituals and practices of devil worship, possession, and satanism are gruesomely related. Interesting cast. **85m/C; VHS, DVD, Blu-Ray.** Ernest Borgnine; Ida Lupino; William Shatner; Eddie Albert; Keenan Wynn; Tom Skerritt; Joan Prather; Claudio Brook; John Travolta; Anton La Vey; ***D:*** Robert Fuest; ***W:*** James Ashton; Gabe Essoe; Gerald Hopman; ***C:*** Alex Phillips, Jr.; ***M:*** Al De Lory.

The Devil's Rejects **WOOF!** **2005 (R)** Tortuous recycling by director Zombie of his senseless "House of 1000 Corpses" tribute-driven horror movie, featuring the psychotic Firefly clan, which was enough of a cult hit for this pointless follow-up that also honors (or insults?) other serial killer and zombie flicks as well. Only Satan would order a third installment. **101m/C; DVD, Blu-Ray, UMD.** *US GE* William Forsythe; Sid Haig; Sheri Moon Zombie; Bill Moseley; Tyler Mane; Leslie Easterbrook; Matthew McGrory; Ken Foree; Michael Berryman; Danny Trejo; Rosario Dawson; Deborah Van Valkenburgh; Geoffrey Lewis; Priscilla Barnes; Kate Norby; Dave Sheridan; Lew Temple; Elizabeth Daily; Dallas Page; Tom Towler; P.J. Soles; Chris Ellis; Mary Woronov; Daniel Roebuck; Duane Whitaker; Steve Railsback; Brian Posehn; ***D:*** Rob Zombie; ***W:*** Rob Zombie; ***C:*** Phil Parmet; ***M:*** Rob Zombie; Tyler Bates.

The Devil's Sleep 🦴 **1951** When a crusading woman sets out to break up a teen narcotics ring, the threatened thugs attempt to draw her daughter into their sleazy affairs, thus assuring the mother's silence. **81m/B; VHS, DVD.** Lita Grey Chaplin; Timothy Farrell; John Mitchum; William Thomason; Tracy Lynn; ***D:*** W. Merle Connell.

Devil's Son-in-Law WOOF! 1977 (R) A black stand-up comic makes a deal with a devil. **95m/C; VHS, DVD.** Rudy Ray Moore; ***D:*** Cliff Roquemore.

The Devil's Teardrop 🦴 ½ **2010** Predictable Lifetime thriller based on a novel by Jeffery Deaver. FBI Special Agent Margaret Lukas calls on retired agent and forensic document specialist Parker Kincaid to analyze a note from a gunman who's already killed seven people in DC's Union Station. The note promises similar attacks every 24 hours unless a 20 million dollar ransom is paid but Parker isn't certain the gunman is the brains behind the crime. **88m/C; DVD.** Natasha Henstridge; Tom Everett Scott; Rena Sofer; Gabriel Hogan; Jonathan Higgins; Rachel Marcus; John MacDonald; Jake Goodman; ***D:*** Norma Bailey; ***W:*** Ron Hutchinson; ***C:*** John Dyer; ***M:*** Gary Koftinoff. **CABLE**

The Devil's Tomb 🦴🦴 **2009 (R)** Familiar but well-paced action-horror. War vet Mack (Gooding Jr.) leads his team of mercenaries into the desert on a rescue mission to free a scientist trapped in an underground lab. The squad soon learns that the lab was deliberately sealed to contain an ancient evil that shows them their dreams, desires, and nightmares and makes them all violent and stuff. **90m/C; DVD.** Cuba Gooding, Jr.; Ron Perlman; Valerie Cruz; Taryn Manning; Henry Rollins; Jason London; Bill Moseley; Zack (Zach) Ward; Franky G.; Stephanie Jacobsen; Ray Winstone; ***D:*** Jason Connery; ***W:*** Keith Kjornes; ***C:*** Tom Calloway; ***M:*** Bill Brown. **VIDEO**

Devil's Wanton 🦴🦴 ½ *Fangelse; Prison* **1949** A young girl tries to forget an unhappy relationship by beginning a new romance with an equally frustrated beau. Gloomy, but hopeful. **80m/B; VHS, DVD.** *SW* Doris Svedlund; Eva Henning; Hasse (Hans) Ekman; ***D:*** Ingmar Bergman; ***W:*** Ingmar Bergman.

Devil's Wedding Night WOOF! *El Returno de la Drequessa Dracula; The Return of the Duchess Dracula; Full Moon of the Virgins* **1973 (R)** An archaeologist and his twin brother fight over a ring that lures virgins into Count Dracula's Transylvanian castle. Vampire queen Bay seduces the dimwit twins and strips at every chance she gets. **85m/C; VHS, DVD, Blu-Ray.** Mark Damon; Rosalba Neri; Frances Davis; ***D:*** Luigi (Paolo Solvay) Batzella.

Devon's Ghost: Legend of the Bloody Boy 🦴 **2005 (R)** Slasher flick. As a boy, Devon was nearly murdered by his parents. Now he's back (and not as a ghost) to continue his revenge against any young couple he sees. Which means all those horny teens had better watch out. **86m/C; DVD.** Matt Moore; John Yong Bosch; Karan Ashely; Reza Bahador; Jonathan Cruz; Kristy Vaughan; ***D:*** John Yong Bosch; Koichi Sakamoto; ***W:*** Karan Ashely; Ron Day; Tim Grace; ***C:*** John Rhode; Sam Lazoya; ***M:*** Cody Westheimer. **VIDEO**

Devonsville Terror 🦴🦴 **1983 (R)** Strange things begin to happen when a new school teacher arrives in Devonsville, a town that has a history of torture, murder, and witchcraft. The hysterical townspeople react by beginning a 20th-century witchhunt. **97m/C; VHS, DVD.** Suzanna Love; Donald Pleasence; Deanna Haas; Mary Walden; Robert Walker, Jr.; Paul Willson; ***D:*** Ulli Lommel; ***W:*** Ulli Lommel; ***C:*** Ulli Lommel; ***M:*** Ray Colcord.

Devotion 🦴🦴 ½ **1946** Highly romanticized and inaccurate melodrama about the literary and personal dreams of Emily (Lupino) and Charlotte (de Havilland) Bronte; Anne (Coleman) is mostly ignored. They both have literary aspirations as well as a romantic rivalry for boring curate Arthur Nicholls (Henreid) while trying to help their drunken artist brother Branwell (Kennedy). There are various travels, deaths and, finally, the publication of "Jane Eyre" and "Wuthering Heights." **106m/B; DVD.** Ida Lupino; Olivia de Havilland; Nancy Coleman; Paul Henreid; Arthur Kennedy; Sydney Greenstreet; Montagu Love; Ethel Griffies; Victor Francen; Dame May Whitty; ***D:*** Curtis Bernhardt; ***W:*** Keith Winter; ***C:*** Ernest Haller; ***M:*** Erich Wolfgang Korngold.

Devotion 🦴🦴 **1995 (R)** Lesbian comic Sheila (Derbyshire) is offered her own sitcom by now-married former lover Lynn (Girling), who admits there's still a spark. Should Sheila rekindle the flame or stay true to free-spirited lover Julie (Twa)? Cutesy at first but takes a welcome dramatic turn as the characters explore their true feelings. **124m/C; VHS, DVD.** Jan Derbyshire; Cindy Girling; Kate Twa; ***D:*** Mindy Kaplan.

Devour 🦴 **2005 (R)** Jake (Ackles) and friends play a deadly Internet game called "The Pathway" that assigns its members bizarre tasks that initially seem harmless, but soon turn violent. Fascinating premise, but too many intertwined plots and themes involving uninteresting characters leave viewers confused and bored. **90m/C; DVD.** Shannyn Sossamon; Dominique Swain; William Sadler; Martin Cummins; Jensen Ackles; Teach; Rob Stewart; ***D:*** David Winkler; ***W:*** Adam Gross; Seth Gross; ***C:*** Brian Pearson; ***M:*** Joseph LoDuca. **CABLE**

Devoured 🦴🦴 **2014** A slow-moving horror exploration of one woman's experience with evil forces. To help pay for her ill son's operation, Mexican immigrant Lourdes (Milans) works as a cleaning woman at night in an old restaurant in New York City. When her son becomes more sick, dark forces in the restaurant begin to attack Lourdes and kill people around her. As Lourdes does all she can to get back to her child, she worries about retaining her sanity and losing both her body and soul. **89m/C; DVD, Blu-Ray, Streaming, Download.** Marta Milans; Kara Jackson; Bruno Gunn; Tyler Hollinger; Salvatore Rendino; ***D:*** Greg Oliver; ***W:*** Marc Landau; ***C:*** Lyle Vincent; ***M:*** Carly Paradis.

Dheepan 🦴🦴 ½ **2016 (R)** This surprising Palme D'Or winner in 2015 is an effective immigrant drama for its first two acts that becomes a less-interesting action movie in its final third. The title refers to its protagonist (Antonythasan), a Sri Lankan immigrant in France after the Civil War in his country forces him to become a refugee. To do so, he's forced into a fake family, complete with a wife he's never met and a daughter. Then Dheepan becomes a film about how people can never leave conflict behind when its protagonist has to deal with drug dealers in a housing project. **115m/C; DVD, Blu-Ray.** Jesuthasan Antonythasan; Kalieaswari Srinivasan; Claudine Vinasithamby; Vincent Rottiers; Marc Zinga; ***D:*** Jacques Audiard; ***W:*** Jacques Audiard; Thomas Bidegain; Noe Debre; ***C:*** Eponine Momenceau; ***M:*** Nicolas Jaar.

D.I. 🦴🦴 **1957** A tough drill sergeant is faced with an unbreakable rebellious recruit, threatening his record and his platoon's status. Webb's film features performances by actual soldiers. **106m/B; VHS, DVD.** Jack Webb; Don Dubbins; Jackie Loughery; Lin McCarthy; Virginia Gregg; ***D:*** Jack Webb.

Diablo 🦴🦴 **2016 (R)** A western with classic themes and a romantic center. After his wife is kidnapped while he sleeps, Jackson (Eastwood) goes on a quest to find his beloved Alexsandra (Belle). The Civil War veteran learns she has been taken by Mexican bandits. As Jackson searches for her, he learns that there are more killers and no clear definition of who is good and who is bad. Jackson goes to the ends of the earth to find his wife, with his quest culminating in a final, decisive gunfight. **90m/C; DVD, Blu-Ray, Streaming, Download.** Scott Eastwood; Walton Goggins; Camilla Belle; Adam Beach; Samuel Marty; ***D:*** Lawrence Roeck; ***W:*** Lawrence Roeck; Carlos De Los Rios; ***C:*** Dean Cundey; ***M:*** Kirpatrick Thomas; Tim Williams.

The Diabolical Dr. Z 🦴🦴 *Miss Muerte; Dans les Griffes du Maniaque* **1965** When dad dies of cardiac arrest after the medical council won't let him make the world a kinder gentler place with his personality-altering technique, his dutiful daughter—convinced the council brought on dad's demise—is out to change some personalities in a big way. **86m/B; VHS, DVD, Blu-Ray.** *SP FR* Mabel Karr; Fernando Montes; Estella Blain; Antonio J. Escribano; Howard Vernon; Jess (Jesus) Franco; Jose Maria Prada; Guy Mairesse; ***D:*** Jess (Jesus) Franco; ***W:*** Jess (Jesus) Franco; Jean-Claude Carriere; ***C:*** Alejandro Ulloa; ***M:*** Jess (Jesus) Franco.

Diabolically Yours 🦴🦴 ½ *Diaboliquement Votre* **1967** A French thriller about an amnesiac who struggles to discover his lost identity. Tensions mount when his pretty spouse and friends begin to wonder if it's all a game. Dubbed. **94m/C; VHS, DVD, Blu-Ray.** *FR* Alain Delon; Senta Berger; ***D:*** Julien Duvivier.

Diabolique 🦴🦴🦴 ½ *Les Diabolique* **1955** Sadistic boarding school master Michel (Meurisse) has a wealthy, neurotic wife, Christina (Clouzet, the director's wife), and a cold-blooded mistress, Nicole (Signoret), who conspire to poison and then drown him in the school's swimming pool. But after the plot is carried out, Christina becomes convinced that Michel is still alive. Plot twists and double-crosses abound. Based on the novel "Celle Qui N'Etait Pas" by Pierre Boileau and Thomas Narcejac. French with subtitles. Remade for TV in 1974 as "Reflections of Murder." **107m/B; VHS, DVD, Blu-Ray.** *FR* Simone Signoret; Vera Clouzot; Paul Meurisse; Charles Vanel; Michel Serrault; Georges Chamarat; Robert Dalban; Therese Dorny; Camille Guerini; ***D:*** Henri-Georges Clouzot; ***W:*** Henri-Georges Clouzot; Frederic Grendel; Jerome Geronimi; Rene Masson; ***C:*** Armand Thirard; ***M:*** Georges Van Parys. N.Y. Film Critics '55: Foreign Film.

Diabolique 🦴 ½ **1996 (R)** Remake of the 1955 French noir classic, updated for '90s sensibilities, finds timid teacher Mia (Adjani) married to overbearing school head Guy (Palminteri), who's having an affair with fellow teacher Nicole (Stone). The two women, who loathe Guy equally, plot to kill him. But when a P.I. (Bates) investigates, it seems possible that Guy isn't dead after all. If you're having trouble accessorizing with leopard skin, watch Stone. Otherwise, watch the far superior original. The usually publicity hungry Stone refused to have anything to do with this picture after its release due to a spat with director Chechik. **105m/C; VHS, DVD.** Sharon Stone; Isabelle Adjani; Chazz Palminteri; Kathy Bates; Spalding Gray; Shirley Knight; Adam Hann-Byrd; Allen Garfield; ***D:*** Jeremiah S. Chechik; ***W:*** Don Roos; ***C:*** Peter James; ***M:*** Randy Edelman.

Diagnosis: Death 🦴 ½ **2009 (R)** Bland horror comedy from New Zealand that eventually tips more towards gore. Cancer-stricken Andre decides to take part in a 48-hour clinical drug trial. Fellow patient Juliet is convinced the hospital is actually a converted insane asylum that's haunted but maybe their hallucinations are just the result of the drugs—or maybe not. **83m/C; DVD.** *NZ* Rayborn Kan; Jessica Grace Smith; Suze Tye; Bret McKenzie; Jemaine Clement; Rhys Darby; ***D:*** Jason Stutter; ***W:*** Rayborn Kan; Jason Stutter; ***C:*** Phil Burchell; ***M:*** David Donaldson; Steve Roche; Janet Roddick.

Dial "M" for Murder 🦴🦴🦴 **1954** Unfaithful playboy Tony's (Milland) cash is all thanks to his marriage to heiress Margot (Kelly) and he fears losing her to writer Mark (Cummings). So Tony devises an elaborate plan to murder his wife for her money, but when she accidentally stabs the killer-to-be, with scissors no less, it's Tony who comes under the suspicious eye of Chief Inspector Hubbard (Williams). Filmed in 3-D. Based on the play by Frederick Knotts. Loosely remade in 1998 as "A Perfect Murder" starring Michael Douglas and Gwenyth Paltrow. **123m/C; VHS, DVD, Blu-Ray.** Ray Milland; Grace Kelly; Robert Cummings; John Williams; Anthony Dawson; ***D:*** Alfred Hitchcock; ***W:*** Frederick Knott; ***C:*** Robert Burks; ***M:*** Dimitri Tiomkin.

Dial 1119 🦴🦴 *The Violent Hour* **1950** Thompson makes for a bland sociopath in this grim MGM suspenser whose title refers to an emergency police phone number. Gunther escapes from a mental hospital determined to kill police shrink Dr. Faron (Levene), who had him committed. He stops by a bar and, after the bartender (Conrad) recognizes Gunther from a TV broadcast, he takes the bar patrons hostage while the cops try to negotiate. Flick uses television newscasts to effectively further the action. **74m/B; DVD.** Marshall Thompson; Sam Levene; Virginia Field; Andrea King; William Conrad; Leon Ames; Keefe Brasselle; Richard Rober; ***D:*** Gerald Mayer; ***W:*** John Monks, Jr.; ***C:*** Paul Vogel; ***M:*** Andre Previn.

Diamond Dogs 🦴 **2007 (R)** Stupid title, cardboard plot, disposable characters, but with enough action to be mildly diverting. Mercenary Xander Ronson (Lundgren) is stuck in Mongolia trying to pay off his debts when art collector Chambers (Shriver) offers him a job obtaining an invaluable jeweled tapestry housed in a remote Buddhist temple. But a group of Russian treasure hunters are also after the prize. **94m/C; DVD.** Dolph Lundgren; William Shiver; Yu Nan; Xue Zuren; Raicho Vasilev; ***D:*** Shimon Dotan; ***W:*** Leopold St-Pierre; ***C:*** Xiaobing Rao; ***M:*** Larry Cohen. **VIDEO**

Diamond Girl 🦴 ½ **1998** Claire (Collins) works for vineyard owner Denny (Otto) but he doesn't realize she's in love with him. His brother Regan (Cake) does and offers to make Denny jealous by pretending that Claire is his new girlfriend. Of course their romantic plan doesn't work as expected. From the Harlequin Romance Series; adapted from the Diana Palmer novel. **91m/C; DVD.** *CA* Jonathan Cake; Kevin Otto; Dyan Cannon; Denise Virieux; Joely Collins; Royston Stoffels; ***D:*** Timothy Bond; ***W:*** Charles Lazar; ***C:*** Buster Reynolds; ***M:*** Tim McCauley. **TV**

Diamond Head 🦴🦴 ½ **1962** A Hawaiian landowner brings destruction and misery to his family via his stubbornness. Based on the Peter Gilman novel. **107m/C; VHS, DVD.** Charlton Heston; Yvette Mimieux; George Chakiris; France Nuyen; James Darren; ***D:*** Guy Green; ***C:*** Sam Leavitt; ***M:*** John Williams.

Diamond Men 🦴🦴🦴 **2001** Slice of life Americana that's a showcase for actor Forster. Eddie Miller (Forster), a guy in his fifties, is a longtime diamond salesman who travels to jewelry stores throughout Pennsylvania. After having a heart attack, his company wants Eddie to retire—after he trains brash Bobby Walker (Wahlberg) to take over his route. Bobby's an eager loudmouth who bullies while Eddie knows how to finesse his clientele. Still he wants to learn and to befriend Eddie but the story turns out to more than a reluctant old dog teaching a pup some tricks to get along. **100m/C; VHS, DVD.** Robert Forster; Donnie Wahlberg; Bess Armstrong; Jasmine Guy; George Coe; ***D:*** Daniel M. Cohen; ***W:*** Daniel M. Cohen; ***C:*** John Huneck; ***M:*** Garrett Parks.

The Diamond of Jeru 🦴🦴 ½ **2001** Helen (Jefferson) and John (Carradine) travel to Borneo in search of adventure (and diamonds) in an effort to put some spice back into their marriage. Too bad Helen is very attracted to their guide, Mike (Zane). John gets jealous and decides he and the missus should head out on their own while Mike pursues them through the jungle in an effort to rescue them from certain doom. Based on the story "Off the Mangrove Coast" by Louis L'Amour. **89m/C; VHS, DVD.** Billy Zane; Keith Carradine; Paris Jefferson; Jackson Raine; Khoa Do; ***D:*** Ian Barry; Dick Lowry; ***W:*** Beau L'Amour; ***C:*** Stephen F. Windon; ***M:*** Christopher Tyng. **VIDEO**

Diamond Run 🦴 ½ **1990 (R)** A streetwise American expatriate frantically searches for his girlfriend after unwittingly involving her in an assassination plot. **89m/C; VHS, DVD.** William Bell Sullivan; Ava Lazar; Ayu Azhari; David Thornton; Peter Fox; ***D:*** Robert Chappell.

Diamond Run 🦴🦴 **1996 (R)** Convoluted heist movie. J. Sloan (Lynch) leads a special forces unit that's gone over to the dark side. Sloan's planned a big diamond heist but loses the gems to thief Megan Marlow (Ljoka), who in turn is being sought by NYPD detective Jack Gates (Valentine). Gates gets to Megan first, only to have them both be stalked by Sloan's henchman, Walker (Gleek). And it seems Megan has another secret that could prove explosive. **98m/C; VHS, DVD.** Richard Lynch; Linda Ljoka; Michael J. Valentine; Fred Gleek; Peter Harrington; ***D:*** David Giancola; ***W:*** Marty Poole; Derrick J. Costa; ***C:*** John McAleer. **VIDEO**

Diamondbacks 🦴 1/2 **1999** Militia group, led by O'Keefe, takes over a remote NASA station in order to reprogram a government weapons satellite for evil. And it's up to engineer Lottimer to stop them. Lots of action in a no-brainer adventure. **90m/C; VHS, DVD.** Miles O'Keeffe; Chris Mitchum; Timothy Bottoms; Eb Lottimer; ***D:*** Bernard Salzman. **VIDEO**

Diamonds 🦴🦴 **1972 (PG)** A tense film in which the Israel Diamond Exchange is looted by a motley array of criminal heisters. Shaw plays a dual role as twin brothers. **108m/C; VHS, DVD.** *IS* Robert Shaw; Richard Roundtree; Barbara Hershey; Shelley Winters; ***D:*** Menahem Golan.

Diamonds 🦴🦴 1/2 **1999 (PG-13)** Douglas lends both dignity and humor to his first screen role since recovering from a stroke. Harry Agrensky (Douglas) is a one-time boxing champ (recovering from a stroke) who wants to live as independently as possible. He claims to have a fortune in diamonds, given to him by a mobster, hidden away in Reno and bullies his estranged son, Lance (Aykroyd), and his grandson Michael (Allred) to go on a road trip and retrieve them. There are various adventures and bonding moments and Douglas is re-united with Bacall (as a Nevada madam), with whom he worked in 1950's "Young Man with a Horn." **90m/C; VHS, DVD.** Kirk Douglas; Dan Aykroyd; Corbin Allred; Lauren Bacall; Kurt Fuller; Jenny McCarthy; John Landis; Mariah O'Brien; ***D:*** John Mallory Asher; ***W:*** Allan Aaron Katz; ***C:*** Paul Elliott; ***M:*** Joel Goldsmith.

Diamonds Are Forever 🦴🦴🦴 1/2 **1971 (PG)** 007 once again battles his nemesis Blofeld, this time in Las Vegas. Bond must prevent the implementation of a plot to destroy Washington through the use of a space-orbiting laser. Fabulous stunts include Bond's wild drive through the streets of Vegas in a '71 Mach 1. Connery returned to play Bond in this film after being offered the then record-setting salary of $1 million. **120m/C; VHS, DVD, Blu-Ray.** *GB* Sean Connery; Jill St. John; Charles Gray; Bruce Cabot; Jimmy Dean; Lana Wood; Bruce Glover; Putter Smith; Norman Burton; Joseph Furst; Bernard Lee; Desmond Llewelyn; Laurence Naismith; Leonard Barr; Lois Maxwell; Margaret Lacey; Joe Robinson; Donna Garrat; Trina Parks; ***D:*** Guy Hamilton; ***W:*** Tom Mankiewicz; ***C:*** Ted Moore; ***M:*** John Barry.

Diamond's Edge 🦴🦴 *Just Ask for Diamond* **1988 (PG)** An adolescent private eye and his juvenescent brother snoop into the affairs of the Fat Man, and find out that the opera ain't over until they find out what's in the Fat Man's mysterious box of bon-bons. A genre-parodying kid mystery, written by Horowitz, based on his novel, "The Falcon's Malteser." **83m/C; VHS, DVD.** Susannah York; Peter Eyre; Patricia Hodge; Nickolas Grace; ***D:*** Stephen Bayly; ***W:*** Anthony Horowitz; ***M:*** Trevor Jones.

Diana 🦴 **2013 (PG-13)** Princess Diana of Wales was arguably one of history's most iconic and beloved figures. Released 16 years after her death, director Hirschbiegel's biopic plods along in telling the last two years of Diana's life as she maintains a hush-hush love affair with Pakistani heart surgeon Hasnat Khan (Andrews). Dubbed as her true love in real life, the feeling doesn't translate on the screen in the mistakenly cast Andrews. Watts excels at mimicking the princess but can't overcome the low-grade material she's given. It doesn't do her acting skills justice and, more importantly, it falls incredibly short of doing Diana justice. **107m/C; DVD, Blu-Ray.** *UK* Naomi Watts; Naveen Andrews; Douglas Hodge; Juliet Stevenson; Geraldine James; Charles Edwards; ***D:*** Oliver Hirschbiegel; ***W:*** Stephen Jeffreys; ***C:*** Rainer Klausmann; ***M:*** Keefus Ciancia; David Holmes.

Diana: Her True Story 🦴🦴 1/2 **1993** Britain's royals are held up to scandalous review in this made for tv adaptaion of Andrew Morton's sympathetic bio of the Princess of Wales. Taking Diana from her lonely childhood to her "fairytale" nuptials and subsequent disillusionment with being a royal, including her bulimia and half-hearted suicide attempts. Charles is portrayed as an arrogant, emotional cold fish, only interested in farming and continuing his liaison with Camilla Parker-Bowles. Handsome production with appropriate inpersonations by the cast. **180m/C; VHS, DVD.** Serena Scott Thomas; David Threlfall; Elizabeth Garvie; Jemma Redgrave; Tracy Hardwick; Anne Stallybrass; Jeffrey Harmer; Donald Douglas; ***D:*** Kevin Connor; ***W:*** Stephen Zito. **TV**

Diane 🦴🦴 **1955** Overstuffed medieval drama featuring Turner as Diane de Poitier, the mistress of a 16th century French King. Moore plays the king in his Hollywood debut. Gorgeous sets and costumes couldn't boost this film at the boxoffice, which had disappointing figures in spite of the expense bestowed upon it. Based on the novel "Diane de Poitier" by John Erskine. **110m/C; DVD.** Lana Turner; Pedro Armendariz, Sr.; Roger Moore; Marisa Pavan; Cedric Hardwicke; Torin Thatcher; Taina Elg; John Lupton; Henry Daniell; Sean McClory; Michael Ansara; ***D:*** David Miller; ***W:*** Christopher Isherwood; ***M:*** Miklos Rozsa.

Diane 🦴🦴 1/2 **2018** In a small, close-knit Massachusetts town, Diane (Place) helps many of her neighbors and friends as they struggle through life issues like illness. While she brings casseroles to those in need, she has her own struggles, including her resentful cousin (O'Connell) and a drug abusing, unhappy son Brian (Lacy), who refuses to go back to rehab. Through it all, Diane's complex feelings about her past and present emerge in unexpected ways. Inspired by both his own family and the character actors in his cast, writer/director Jones has constructed a meaningful, moving debut film that features a nuanced performance by Place. **95m/C; DVD.** Mary Kay Place; Jake Lacy; Estelle Parsons; Andrea Martin; Deirdre O'Connell; ***D:*** Kent Jones; ***W:*** Kent Jones; ***C:*** Wyatt Garfield; ***M:*** Jeremiah Bornfield.

Diary of a Chambermaid 🦴🦴🦴 **1946** A chambermaid wants to marry a rich man and finds herself the object of desire of a poor servant willing to commit murder for her. Excellent comic drama, but very stylized in direction and set design. Produced during Renoir's years in Hollywood. Adapted from a story by Octave Mirbeau, later turned into a play. Remade in 1964 by Luis Bumel. **86m/B; DVD, Blu-Ray.** Paulette Goddard; Burgess Meredith; Hurd Hatfield; Francis Lederer; Judith Anderson; Florence Bates; Almira Sessions; Reginald Owen; ***D:*** Jean Renoir; ***W:*** Burgess Meredith; ***C:*** Lucien N. Andriot.

Diary of a Chambermaid 🦴🦴🦴 1/2 *Le Journal d'une Femme de Chambre; Il Diario di una Cameriera* **1964** Vintage Bunuelian social satire about a young girl taking a servant's job in a provincial French family, and easing into an atmosphere of sexual hypocrisy and decadence. In French with English subtitles. Remake of the 1946 Jean Renoir film. **97m/C; VHS, DVD.** *FR* Jeanne Moreau; Michel Piccoli; Georges Geret; Francoise Lugagne; Daniel Ivernel; ***D:*** Luis Bunuel; ***W:*** Luis Bunuel; Jean-Claude Carriere; ***C:*** Roger Fellous.

Diary of a Chambermaid 🦴🦴 1/2 *Journal d'une femme de chambre* **2016** Few actresses can do the blend of scheming and seductive quite as memorably as Lea Seydoux, who shines here as Celestine, the new chambermaid of the Lanlaires, a wealthy family in a French province in the early 1900s. From the minute she meets them, Celestine becomes a major part of the Lanlaire estate, even if she's mostly just an object of lust for Mr. Lanlaire and someone to look down on from Mrs. Lanlaire. Octave Mirbeau's 1900 novel has been adapted several times, particularly because of the way it captures class issues at the turn of the century. **96m/C; DVD, Blu-Ray.** Lea Seydoux; Vincent Lindon; Clotilde Mollet; Herve Pierre; Melodie Valemberg; ***D:*** Benoit Jacquot; ***W:*** Benoit Jacquot; Helene Zimmer; ***C:*** Romain Winding; ***M:*** Bruno Coulais.

Diary of a Country Priest 🦴🦴🦴 1/2 *Le Journal d'un Cure de Campagne* **1950** With "Balthazar" and "Mouchette," this is one of Bresson's greatest, subtlest films, treating the story of an alienated, unrewarded young priest with his characteristic austerity and Catholic humanism. In French and English subtitles. **120m/B; VHS, DVD.** *FR* Claude Layou; Jean Riveyre; Nicole Ladmiral; Nicole Maurey; Antonine Balpetre; ***D:*** Robert Bresson; ***W:*** Robert Bresson; ***C:*** Leonce-Henri Burel; ***M:*** Jean Jacques Grunenwald.

Diary of a Hitman 🦴🦴 1/2 **1991 (R)** A hitman is hired to knock off the wife and child of a commodities broker who claims his wife is a drug addict and the infant is a crack baby and not his. The hired killer wants out of the business, but needs to pull off one more job for a down payment on his apartment. Beset by doubts, he breaks conduct by conversing with the victim and discovers the broker lied. Based on the play "Insider's Price" by Pressman. **90m/C; VHS, Streaming.** Forest Whitaker; James Belushi; Sherilyn Fenn; Sharon Stone; Seymour Cassel; Lewis Smith; Lois Chiles; John Bedford-Lloyd; ***D:*** Roy London; ***W:*** Kenneth Pressman; ***M:*** Michel Colombier.

Diary of a Lost Girl 🦴🦴🦴 1/2 *Das tagebuch einer verlorenen* **1929** The second Louise Brooks/G.W. Pabst collaboration (after "Pandora's Box") in which a frail but mesmerizing German girl plummets into a life of hopeless degradation. Dark and gloomy, the film chronicles the difficulties she faces, from rape to an unwanted pregnancy and prostitution. Based on the popular book by Margarete Boehme. Silent. Made after flapper Brooks left Hollywood to pursue greater opportunities and more challenging roles under Pabst's guidance. **116m/B; Silent; VHS, DVD, Blu-Ray.** *GE* Louise Brooks; Fritz Rasp; Josef Rovensky; Sybille Schmitz; ***D:*** G.W. Pabst; ***W:*** Rudolf Leonhardt; ***C:*** Sepp Allgeier; Fritz Arno Wagner; ***M:*** Timothy Brock.

Diary of a Mad Black Woman 🦴🦴 **2005 (PG-13)** The critics spoke and the intended audience ignored every disparaging comment to make this soap opera a success. After an 18-year marriage, Helen (beautiful Elise) gets tossed out of her Atlanta mansion by nasty hubby Charles (Harris) for his longtime mistress, Brenda (Marcos). Weepy Helen flees to the home of her feisty grandmamma Madea (Perry in outrageous drag) and then learns to get her own back. She even finds a blue-collar prince in handsome, loving Orlando (Moore). Yep, it's a life-affirming, over-the-top fairytale with faith as the cornerstone. Perry plays two other roles as well as adapting the script from his play. **116m/C; VHS, DVD.** Kimberly Elise; Steve Harris; Shemar Moore; Tamara Taylor; Cicely Tyson; Lisa Marcos; Tiffany Evans; Tyler Perry; ***D:*** Darren Grant; ***W:*** Tyler Perry; ***C:*** David Claessen; ***M:*** Tyler Perry; Elvin D. Ross.

Diary of a Madman 🦴🦴 **1963** Price is once again possessed by an evil force in this gothic thriller. Fairly average Price vehicle, based on Guy de Maupassant's story. **96m/C; VHS, DVD.** Vincent Price; Nancy Kovack; Chris Warfield; Ian Wolfe; Nelson Olmstead; Elaine Devry; Stephen Roberts; ***D:*** Reginald LeBorg; ***W:*** Robert E. Kent; ***C:*** Ellis W. Carter.

Diary of a Rebel 🦴 *El Che Guevara* **1968** A fictional account of the rise of Cuban rebel leader Che Guevara. **89m/C; VHS, DVD, Streaming.** *IT* John Ireland; Francisco Rabal; Howard Ross; Andrea Checchi; Giacomo "Jack" Rossi-Stuart; Jose Torres; Susanna Martinkova; ***D:*** Paolo Heusch; ***W:*** Adriano Bolzoni; ***C:*** Luciano Trasatti; ***M:*** Nico Fidenco.

Diary of a Serial Killer 🦴🦴 *Rough Draft* **1997 (R)** Down-on-his-luck journalist Nelson Keece (Busey) witnesses a murder and then is invited by the killer, Stefan (Vosloo), to conduct an exclusive interview. Stefan keeps killing and Nelson keeps writing, but the cops begin to think that Keece is the killer. Then Stefan decides to target Keece's girlfriend Juliette (Campbell) as his next victim. **92m/C; VHS, DVD.** Gary Busey; Arnold Vosloo; Michael Madsen; Julia Campbell; ***D:*** Alan Jacobs; ***W:*** Jennifer Badham-Stewart; ***C:*** Keith L. Smith; ***M:*** Stephen (Steve) Edwards. **VIDEO**

Diary of a Suicide 🦴 1/2 *Le Journal d'un Suicide* **1973** Dull drama with way too many flashbacks. A cruise ship tour guide becomes infatuated with the group's enigmatic interpreter who insists he woo her with stories. One of these is a complicated tale about a group of terrorists who blow up a politician, intending to also kill themselves. Only one of the terrorists survives and is sent to prison for life where she is guarded by a very strange jailer. French with subtitles. **82m/C; DVD.** *FR* Delphine Seyrig; Marie-France Pisier; Sacha (Sascha) Pitoeff; Sami Frey; ***D:*** Stanislav Stanojevic; ***W:*** Stanislav Stanojevic; ***C:*** Jen-Jacques Flon.

The Diary of a Teenage Girl 🦴🦴🦴 **2015 (R)** Marielle Heller's adaptation of Phoebe Gloeckner's novel is daring enough to suggest that teen sexuality is not something that should be demonized or moralized. The result is a refreshing dramedy in which breakout actress Powley plays Minnie, a teenager living with her mom (Wiig) in the '70s. Mom's boyfriend Monroe (Skarsgard) notices that Minnie has become an adult, things get, well, complicated. This Sundance breakout is often a bit too sly and sarcastic for its own good, but it's more often insightful about the way young women respond to sexuality, especially in the pre-AIDS era of the '70s. **102m/C; DVD, Blu-Ray.** Bel Powley; Kristen Wiig; Alexander Skarsgård; Christopher Meloni; Abby Wait; ***D:*** Marielle Heller; ***W:*** Marielle Heller; ***C:*** Brandon Trost; ***M:*** Nate Heller. Ind. Spirit '16: First Feature.

Diary of a Wimpy Kid 🦴🦴 **2010 (PG)** Live-action translation of Jeff Kinney's charming illustrated novel chronicling the day-to-day misadventures of wisecracking student Greg Heffley (Gordon) and his best friend Rowley (Capron) as they navigate their first year of middle school. Neither have much interest in girls until the sharp-witted, beat-poet-reading Angie (Moretz) develops a liking for the boys. And things get a little strained when Greg thinks he might be too good to hang with Rowley. The young performers are by no means wimps, never dumbing down the source material so beloved by so many a tweener. But bringing those stick figures to life proved just as tough as Greg's life. **94m/C; Blu-Ray.** Chloë Grace Moretz; Steve Zahn; Rachael Harris; Zachary Gordon; Devon Bostick; ***D:*** Thor Freudenthal; ***W:*** Jeff Filgo; Jackie Filgo; Jeff Judah; Gabe Sachs; ***C:*** Jack N. Green; ***M:*** Julia Michels.

Diary of a Wimpy Kid 2: Rodrick Rules 🦴🦴 1/2 **2011 (PG)** It's more public humiliation for often-thoughtless (but still likeable) seventh-grader Greg Heffley (Gordon) as he must deal with his bullying older brother Rodrick (Bostick) who likes nothing better than to prank his sibling. His well-meaning, but naturally clueless parents, try to force the boys to spend more time together. This results in a mild house party when the adults are away, but Greg can't stand the guilt and tells all, resulting in Rodrick being banned from competing in the school talent show. The second book in Jeff Kinney's series. **96m/C; Blu-Ray, On Demand.** Zachary Gordon; Devon Bostick; Rachael Harris; Peyton List; Steve Kahn; Owen Best; Robert Capron; Grayson Russell; Laine MacNeil; ***D:*** David Bowers; ***W:*** Jeff Judah; Gabe Sachs; ***C:*** Jack N. Green; ***M:*** Edward Shearmur.

Diary of a Wimpy Kid: Dog Days 🦴🦴 **2012 (PG)** Based on the fourth book in Jeff Kinney's series. Pre-teen Greg Heffley's (Gordon) terrible summer vacation begins when his buddy Rowley (Capron) invites him to the country club and Greg inevitably gets thrown out. Problem is he told his folks that he was working there. Things can only get worse. Some of it is clearly implausible--how did youngster Greg supposedly get a job without his parents' consent? But most of it is innocent fun that isn't totally insufferable for the grown-ups. **99m/C; DVD, Blu-Ray.** Zachary Gordon; Robert Capron; Devon Bostick; Steve Zahn; Rachael Harris; Peyton List; Laine MacNeil; ***D:*** David Bowers; ***W:*** Gabe Sachs; ***C:*** Anthony B. Richmond; ***M:*** Edward Shearmur.

Diary of a Wimpy Kid: The Long Haul 🦴 **2017 (PG)** The fourth installment of the franchise features a whole new cast and a road trip grafted onto the "Greg (Drucker) wants to be famous" plot. Grandma's turning 90, so the brood spends two days heading to her celebration. This precipitates an escalating sequence of gross-out gags and mean-spirited family trip setpieces. While the cast is talented, they are given either one-dimensional or deeply unlikeable characters to play. Silverstone and

Scott deserve better than to play the joyless, stock-character parents. Young, undiscriminating fans of the franchise might enjoy this installment, but they're the only ones. **91m/C; DVD, Blu-Ray.** Jason Drucker; Alicia Silverstone; Tom Everett Scott; Charlie Wright; Owen Asztalos; ***D:*** David Bowers; ***W:*** David Bowers; Jeff Kinney; ***C:*** Anthony B. Richmond; ***M:*** Ed Shearmur.

The Diary of Anne Frank 1/2 **1959** In June 1945, a liberated Jewish refugee returns to the hidden third floor of an Amsterdam factory where he finds the diary kept by his youngest daughter, Anne. The document recounts their years in hiding from the Nazis. Based on the actual diary of 13-year-old Anne Frank, killed in a death camp during WWII. **150m/B; VHS, DVD.** Millie Perkins; Joseph Schildkraut; Shelley Winters; Richard Beymer; Gusti Huber; Ed Wynn; Lou Jacobi; Diane Baker; ***D:*** George Stevens; ***C:*** William Mellor. Oscars '59: Art Dir./Set Dec., B&W, B&W Cinematog., Support. Actress (Winters).

The Diary of Anne Frank 1/2 **2008** Moggach's faithful script uses passages from Frank's diary to tell the story of a once-ordinary Jewish teenager (Kendricks in an engaging, nuanced performance) who is forced into tragic and extraordinary circumstances because of anti-Semitism and the Nazis. Originally shown as a five-part BBC miniseries; also available as a 100-minute feature film. **150m/C; DVD.** *GB* Ellie Kendrick; Iain Glen; Tamsin Greig; Kate Ashfield; Geoff Breton; Lesley Sharp; Ron Cook; Roger Frost; Tim Dantay; Mariah Gale; Felicity Jones; Nicholas Farrell; ***D:*** Jon Jones; ***W:*** Deborah Moggach; ***C:*** Ian Moss; ***M:*** Charlie Mole. **TV**

The Diary of Ellen Rimbauer **2003 (R)** Prequel to Stephen King's "Rose Red," shows how the marriage of innocent Ellen (Brenner) to the unfaithful and twisted John Rimbauer (Brand) eventually found her possessed by the forces surrounding their haunted Seattle mansion. Diary passages highlight a series of deadly encounters on the estate. **88m/C; VHS, DVD.** Lisa Brenner; Steven Brand; Kate Burton; Tsidii Leloka; Brad Greenquist; Tsai Chin; ***D:*** Craig R. Baxley; ***W:*** Ridley Pearson; ***C:*** Joao Fernandes; ***M:*** Gary Chang. **TV**

Diary of the Dead *George A. Romero's Diary of the Dead* **2007 (R)** Nearly 40 years after Romero's ultra-low-budget "Night of the Living Dead," he's taking another stab at the genre with his fifth zombie flick. This modern incarnation starts with some college kids shooting a horror movie in the woods when their filming is interrupted by radio reports of zombies afoot. Camera rolling, the plucky students and their professor abandon the shoot to head for safer ground, but director Jason instead gets footage of his pals succumbing to zombification. Not too much new here, but the familiarity, nostalgia and gooey gore will make some die-hards happy. Pay attention to the spoofs of the original. **95m/C; DVD, Blu-Ray.** Joshua Close; Joe Dinicol; Philip Riccio; Michelle Morgan; Shawn Roberts; Amy Lalonde; Scott Wentworth; ***D:*** George A. Romero; ***W:*** George A. Romero; ***C:*** Adam Swica; ***M:*** Norman Orenstein.

Dick **1999 (PG-13)** If you think Hollywood is done making fun of Nixon, then you don't know "Dick." Satire puts forth the theory that two dizzy teenage girls (Dunst and Williams) caused the downfall of Richard Nixon (Hedaya). They bump into all the major Watergate players, including Liddy (Shearer), Haldemann (Foley) and Dean (Breuer). The girls are blissfully blind to Tricky Dick's indiscretions, and one of them even develops a hilarious crush on him. When they overhear him abusing the presidential pup, however, they turn on him. Flouting the Constitution is one thing, but being mean to dogs is clearly icky behavior. They decide to become the famed Deep Throat for bickering reporters Woodward (Ferrell) and Bernstein (McCulloch). Rent this with "All the President's Men" and "Nixon," because this is the movie that Oliver Stone would've made if he had a sense of humor instead of flashbacks. **95m/C; VHS, DVD, Blu-Ray.** Kirsten Dunst; Michelle Williams; Dan Hedaya; Will Ferrell; Dave Foley; Harry Shearer; Jim Breuer; Bruce McCulloch; Devon Gummersall; Ted McGinley; Ryan Reynolds; Saul Rubinek; Teri Garr; G.D. Spradlin; Ana Gasteyer; ***D:*** Andrew Fleming; ***W:*** Andrew Fleming; Sheryl Longin; ***C:*** Alexander Grusynski; ***M:*** John Debney.

Dick Barton, Special Agent **1948** Dick Barton is called in when a mad scientist threatens to attack London with germ-carrying bombs. The first film production for Hammer Studios, later to be known for its horror classics. **70m/B; VHS, DVD.** *GB* Don Stannard; Geoffrey Ford; Jack Shaw; ***D:*** Alfred Goulding.

Dick Tracy **1937** Serial, based on the comic-strip character, in 15 chapters. Tracy tries to find his kidnapped brother as he faces the fiend "Spider." The first chapter is 30 minutes and each additional chapter is 20 minutes. **290m/B; VHS, DVD.** Ralph Byrd; Smiley Burnette; Irving Pichel; Jehnifer Jones; ***D:*** John English; Alan James; Ray Taylor.

Dick Tracy 1/2 **1990 (PG)** Beatty wears the caps of producer, director, and star, performing admirably on all fronts. One minor complaint: his Tracy is somewhat flat in comparison to the outstanding performances and makeup of the unique villains, especially Pacino. Stylistically superior, shot in only seven colors, the timeless sets capture the essence rather than the reality of the city, successfully bringing the comic strip to life. Madonna is fine as the seductive Breathless Mahoney, belting out Stephen Sondheim like she was born to do it. People expecting the gothic technology of "Batman" may be disappointed, but moviegoers searching for a memory made real will be thrilled. **105m/C; VHS, DVD, Blu-Ray.** Warren Beatty; Madonna; Charlie Korsmo; Glenne Headly; Al Pacino; Dustin Hoffman; James Caan; Mandy Patinkin; Paul Sorvino; Charles Durning; Dick Van Dyke; R.G. Armstrong; Catherine O'Hara; Estelle Parsons; Seymour Cassel; Michael J. Pollard; William Forsythe; Kathy Bates; James Tolkan; ***D:*** Warren Beatty; ***W:*** Jim Cash; Jack Epps, Jr.; ***C:*** Vittorio Storaro; ***M:*** Danny Elfman; Stephen Sondheim. Oscars '90: Art Dir./Set Dec., Makeup, Song ("Sooner or Later").

Dick Tracy Meets Gruesome *Dick Tracy's Amazing Adventure; Dick Tracy Meets Karloff* **1947** Gruesome and his partner in crime, Melody, stage a bank robbery using the secret formula of Dr. A. Tomic. Tracy has to solve the case before word gets out and people rush to withdraw their savings, destroying civilization as we know it. **66m/B; VHS, DVD.** Boris Karloff; Ralph Byrd; Lyle Latell; Anne Gwynne; Edward Ashley; June Clayworth; Tony Barrett; Skelton Knaggs; ***D:*** John Rawlins; ***W:*** Eric Taylor; Robertson White; ***C:*** Frank Redman; ***M:*** Paul Sawtell.

Dick Tracy Returns **1938** 15-chapter serial. Public Enemy Paw Stark and his gang set out on a wave of crime that brings them face to face with dapper Dick. **100m/B; VHS, DVD.** Ralph Byrd; Charles Middleton; ***D:*** William Witney.

Dick Tracy vs. Crime Inc. **1941** Dick Tracy encounters many difficulties when he tries to track down a criminal who can make himself invisible. A serial in 15 chapters. **100m/B; VHS, DVD.** Ralph Byrd; Ralph Morgan; Michael Owen; ***D:*** William Witney; ***W:*** John English.

Dickie Roberts: Former Child Star **2003 (PG-13)** Spade plays the impish title character, a valet parking attendant who wishes to revive his former child-star sitcom fame. Without much help from his despondent agent (a dead-on Lovitz), Dickie scores a meeting with Rob Reiner (as himself!) who's casting the lead in his new movie. When Dickie loses the role due to a lack of real character, he hires a family to relive his lost youth and help him get a real life. Pic is at its crackling best when Spade is his usual, smarmy self, but suffers when trying for earnestness. Amusing cameos by the likes of Leif Garrett, Danny Bonaduce, and Corey Feldman, and the final credits include a fun and rousing anthem sung by a gaggle of former child stars. **99m/C; VHS, DVD.** David Spade; Mary McCormack; Craig Bierko; Jon Lovitz; Alyssa Milano; Doris Roberts; Jenna Boyd; Scott Tessa; Edie McClurg; ***Cameo(s):*** Rob Reiner; Leif Garrett; Brendan Fraser; ***D:*** Sam Weisman; ***W:*** David Spade; Fred Wolf; ***C:*** Thomas Ackerman; ***M:*** Christophe Beck; Waddy Wachtel.

The Dictator 1/2 **2012 (R)** The talented Cohen plays it safe with his latest venture, mocking the bloated egos of powerful men and the brutal governments they run. During a trip to NYC, North African dictator Admiral General Haffaz Aladeen's rule is threatened by his uncle (the legendary Kingsley) while Zoey (Faris)--a health food nut--tries to change his ways. Some of Cohen's satire is sharp but too much of it is familiar and the character wears out his welcome fairly quickly, even in a film that runs less than 90 minutes. And the movie lurches about like a series of strung-together sketches. **83m/C; DVD, Blu-Ray, Streaming.** Sacha Baron Cohen; Sayed Badreya; Ben Kingsley; Megan Fox; Anna Faris; ***D:*** Larry Charles; ***W:*** Sacha Baron Cohen; Alec Berg; David Mandel; Jeff Schaffer; ***C:*** Lawrence Sher; ***M:*** Erran Baron Cohen.

Did You Hear About the Morgans? **2009 (PG-13)** Successful New York couple Meryl (Parker) and Paul (Grant) Morgan are in the midst of their unraveling marriage when they witness a murder and become the targets of a hitman. Placed into the Witness Protection Program, the Morgans trade upscale Manhattan for a tiny Wyoming town, and all-too-familiar, brutally unfunny "fish out of water" hijinks ensue. Grant and Parker display little of their individual charm in their phoned-in performances as the obnoxious Paul and grating Meryl. A cliche-ridden comedy filled with predictable jokes about how darn dumb city folk are when you take them to the heartland. The less you hear about the Morgans, the better. **103m/C; Blu-Ray, On Demand.** Hugh Grant; Sarah Jessica Parker; Sam Elliott; Mary Steenburgen; Elisabeth Moss; Michael Kelly; Seth Gilliam; Vincenzo Amato; Natalia Klimas; Jesse Liebman; ***D:*** Marc Lawrence; ***W:*** Marc Lawrence; ***C:*** Florian Ballhaus; ***M:*** Theodore Shapiro.

Die Another Day 1/2 **2002 (PG-13)** The 20th film in the James Bond series carries a lot of "in" jokes referring to previous films, including the bikini and knife belt worn by NSA agent Jinx (shades of Ursula Andress in "Dr. No"). Of course, the beautiful Berry is well worth comtemplating, which is a good thing since this Bond is fairly tiresome with its convoluted plot and over-the-top action. It starts off well and Brosnan is comfortable in the role (even with the silly double entendres) but the main villain (Stephens) is another meglomaniac with designs on taking over the world (wrapped around some political cant) and the second half of the film is one chase scene after another. Yawn. **130m/C; VHS, DVD, Blu-Ray.** Pierce Brosnan; Halle Berry; Toby Stephens; Dame Judi Dench; John Cleese; Rosamund Pike; Rick Yune; Michael Madsen; Will Yun Lee; Kenneth Tsang; Samantha Bond; Colin Salmon; Emilio Echeverria; Michael Gorevoy; Lawrence Makoare; Madonna; ***D:*** Lee Tamahori; ***W:*** Neal Purvis; Robert Wade; ***C:*** David Tattersall; ***M:*** David Arnold. Golden Raspberries '02: Worst Support. Actress (Madonna).

Die! Die! My Darling! 1/2 *Fanatic* **1965** A young widow visits her mad ex-mother-in-law in a remote English village, and is imprisoned by the mourning woman as revenge for her son's death. Bankhead's last role. Based on Anne Blaisdell's novel. **97m/C; VHS, DVD, Blu-Ray.** *GB* Tallulah Bankhead; Stefanie Powers; Peter Vaughan; Maurice Kaufmann; Donald Sutherland; Gwendolyn Watts; Yootha Joyce; Winifred Dennis; ***D:*** Silvio Narizzano; ***W:*** Richard Matheson; ***C:*** Arthur Ibbetson; ***M:*** Wilfred Josephs.

Die Hard **1988 (R)** It's Christmas Eve and NYC cop John McClane (Willis) has arrived in L.A. to spend the holiday with his estranged wife Holly (Bedelia) and their kids. Unfortunately, Holly is one of the hostages being held by a band of ruthless high-stakes terrorists in the Century City high-rise headquarters of a Japanese corporation. Soon it's the loner cop against the intruders, who are led by Eurotrash villain Hans Gruber (a marvelous performance by Rickman). A high-voltage action thriller that's just as unbelievable as it sounds, but you'll love it anyway. Based on the novel "Nothing Lasts Forever" by Roderick Thorp. **114m/C; VHS, DVD, Blu-Ray, UMD.** Bruce Willis; Bonnie Bedelia; Alan Rickman; Alexander Godunov; Paul Gleason; William Atherton; Reginald VelJohnson; Hart Bochner; James Shigeta; Mary Ellen Trainor; De'voreaux White; Robert Davi; Ric(k) Ducommun; Clarence Gilyard, Jr.; Grand L. Bush; Al Leong; Wilhelm von Homburg; ***D:*** John McTiernan; ***W:*** Jeb Stuart; Steven E. de Souza; ***C:*** Jan De Bont; ***M:*** Michael Kamen. Natl. Film Reg. '17.

Die Hard 2: Die Harder **1990 (R)** Fast, well-done sequel brings another impossible situation before the wise-cracking, tough-cookie cop. Our hero tangles with a group of terrorists at an airport under siege, while his wife remains in a plane circling above as its fuel dwindles. Obviously a repeat of the plot and action of the first "Die Hard," with references to the former in the script. While the bad guys lack the fiendishness of their predecessors, this installment features energetic and finely acted performances. Fairly gory, especially the icicle-in-the-eyeball scene. Adapted from the novel "58 Minutes" by Walter Wager and characters created by Roderick Thorp. **124m/C; VHS, DVD, Blu-Ray, UMD.** Bruce Willis; William Atherton; Franco Nero; Bonnie Bedelia; John Amos; Reginald VelJohnson; Dennis Franz; Art Evans; Fred Dalton Thompson; William Sadler; Sheila McCarthy; Robert Patrick; John Leguizamo; Robert Costanzo; Tom Verica; Don Harvey; Tony Ganios; Vondie Curtis-Hall; Colm Meaney; ***D:*** Renny Harlin; ***W:*** Doug Richardson; Steven E. de Souza; ***C:*** Oliver Wood; ***M:*** Michael Kamen.

Die Hard: With a Vengeance 1/2 *Die Hard 3* **1995 (R)** Third time is not a charm in the "Die Hard" series. McClane (Willis) is back home in the Big Apple and having another bad day. More Eurotrash terrorists, led by the brilliant and vengeful Simon (Irons), are out to blow things up, snag some gold, and make life miserable for McClane and his reluctant partner, Zeus Carver (Jackson). The claustrophobic settings of the first two outings have been replaced by the exhausting expanse of New York City, to good effect, but frenetic action scenes and good chemistry between Willis and Jackson don't quite compensate for a lackluster script and more cartoony feel. Jackson brings a fresh perspective and vitality. **131m/C; VHS, DVD, Blu-Ray.** Bruce Willis; Samuel L. Jackson; Jeremy Irons; Graham Greene; Colleen Camp; Larry Bryggman; Tony Peck; Nick Wyman; Sam (Leslie) Phillips; ***D:*** John McTiernan; ***W:*** Jonathan Hensleigh; ***C:*** Peter Menzies, Jr.; ***M:*** Michael Kamen.

Die Laughing **WOOF! 1980 (PG)** A cab driver unwittingly becomes involved in murder, intrigue, and the kidnapping of a monkey that has memorized a scientific formula that can destroy the world. Writer/actor Benson might consider renaming it "Die from Embarassment." **108m/C; DVD, Streaming.** Robby Benson; Charles Durning; Bud Cort; Elsa Lanchester; Peter Coyote; ***D:*** Jeff Werner; ***W:*** Robby Benson; Scott Parker; ***C:*** David Myers; ***M:*** Craig Safan.

Die Mommie Die! 1/2 **2003 (R)** Angela Arden (co-writer Busch, in drag) is a fading diva trapped in a loveless marriage. Her husband, Sol Hussman (Hall), a movie producer, refuses to give her a divorce. Like all good dysfunctional families, battle lines are drawn between dad, supported by daughter Edith (Lyonne) and Angela, supported by son Lance (Sands). Add in bisexual gigolo Tony Parker (Priestly) and fanatically religious maid Bootsie Carp (Conroy) plus some bawdy humor, and you've got the workings of a campy cult classic. Definitely one for John Waters fans. **90m/C; VHS, DVD.** Charles Busch; Natasha Lyonne; Jason Priestley; Frances Conroy; Philip Baker Hall; Stark Sands; Victor Raider-Wexler; Nora Dunn; ***D:*** Mark Rucker; ***W:*** Charles Busch; ***C:*** Kelly Evans; ***M:*** Dennis McCarthy.

Die, Monster, Die! *Monster of Terror* **1965** A reclusive scientist experiments with a radioactive meteorite and gains bizarre powers. Karloff is great in this adaptation of H.P. Lovecraft's "The Color Out of Space." **80m/C; VHS, DVD, Blu-Ray.** *GB* Boris Karloff; Nick Adams; Suzan Farmer; Patrick Magee; Freda Jackson; Terence de Marney; Leslie Dwyer; Paul Farrell; ***D:*** Daniel Haller; ***W:*** Jerry Sohl; ***C:*** Paul Beeson; ***M:*** Don Banks.

Die Screaming, Marianne *Die, Beautiful Marianne* **1973** A girl is on the run from her father, a crooked judge, who wants to kill her before her 21st birthday, when she will inherit evidence that will put him away for life. **81m/C; VHS, DVD, Blu-Ray.** *GB* Michael Rennie; Susan George; Karin Dor; Leo Genn; ***D:*** Pete Walker; ***W:*** Murray Smith; ***C:*** Norman G. Langley; ***M:*** Cyril Ornadel.

Die Sister, Die! **1974** Thriller about a gothic mansion with an eerie secret in the basement features a battle between a senile, reclusive sister and her disturbed, tormenting brother. **88m/C; VHS, DVD.** Jack Ging; Edith Atwater; Antoinette Bower; Kent Smith; Robert Emhardt; ***D:*** Randall Hood.

Die Watching **½ 1993 (R)** Sleazy erotic thriller about a video director (Atkins) who not only likes to film some hot Hollywood babes but may also like to kill them as well. His latest discovery just could be the next victim. **92m/C; VHS, DVD.** Christopher Atkins; Vali Ashton; Tim Thomerson; Carlos Palomino; Mike Jacobs, Jr.; ***D:*** Charles Davis; ***W:*** Kenneth J. Hall; ***C:*** Howard Wexler; ***M:*** Scott Roewe.

Diego Maradona **2019** A documentary look at soccer superstar Diego Armando Mardona. Born into a poor family in Argentina, the uneducated Maradona began supporting his family when he was a teenager. Supremely gifted, Maradona not only played well himself but also inspired his teammates to play at their best. He became instantly famous and wealthy playing for Naples and honored his country in World Cup play, but struggled to find his identity and weathered intense criticism from soccer fans. The multifaceted film includes impressive footage of Maradona at his best on the pitch as well as insightful interviews and perspectives, including the star's own. **130m/C; DVD.** Diego Armando Maradona; ***D:*** Asif Kapadia; ***M:*** Antonio Pinto. **VIDEO**

Different for Girls **1996 (R)** Boyish motorcycle dispatch rider Paul Prentice (Graves) nearly gets run over by a London taxi whose passenger Kim Foyle (Mackintosh) seems strangely familiar. Then Paul discovers Kim used to be his boyhood school chum Karl. After a shaky start, the duo discover a genuine attraction but when they get into an argument that leads to a police call and Paul gets thrown in jail, Kim's first instincts are to retreat to her sister's (Reeves) family and back into her quiet life. Director Spence refrains from camping up the situation and some fine performances, especially from the engaging Graves, make this quirky film well worth a watch. **101m/C; VHS, DVD.** *GB* Rupert Graves; Steven Mackintosh; Miriam Margolyes; Saskia Reeves; Neil Dudgeon; Charlotte Coleman; ***D:*** Richard Spence; ***W:*** Tony Marchant; ***C:*** Sean Van Hales; ***M:*** Stephen Warbeck. Montreal World Film Fest. '95: Film.

A Different Loyalty **2004 (R)** Gleaned from the true story of an American journalist, Sally (Stone), finds love with British government agent Leo (Everett) while in Beirut during the Cold War. They marry, but their happily ever after is interrupted when Leo goes missing. A desperate search takes her to the Soviet Union where his disturbing secret life endangers them both. **96m/C; VHS, DVD.** Sharon Stone; Rupert Everett; Julian Wadham; Michael Cochrane; Anne Lambton; Jim Piddock; Richard McMillan; Mimi Kuzyk; Emily Van Camp; Tamara Hope; Damir Andrei; John Bourgeois; Sonja Smits; Edward Hibbert; Joss Ackland; Jack Galloway; Matthew Scurfield; Ron Lea; Mark Rendall; ***D:*** Marek Kanievska; ***C:*** Jean Lepine; ***M:*** Normand Corbeil. **VIDEO**

Different Story **½ 1978 (PG)** Romance develops when a lesbian real estate agent offers a homosexual chauffeur a job with her firm. Resorts to stereotypes when the characters decide to marry. **107m/C; VHS, DVD.** Perry King; Meg Foster; Valerie Curtin; Peter Donat; Richard Bull; ***D:*** Paul Aaron.

DIG! **2004 (R)** Seven year documentary chronicle of two indie-rock bands, charting rise of one and downfall of the other. The Dandy Warhols, led by Courtney Taylor, seem to be blessed by the angels as they meteorically rise in the world of alterna-pop. Anton Newcombe and band, Brian Jonestown Massacre, who are great mentors to Taylor's own band, seem to have no one but Newcombe to blame for their lack of success. Belligerent and out-of-control, Newcombe amazingly crafts brilliant album after album, but scares bandmates, record companies and friends away. Truly sad up-close look at the difficulties of remaining uncompromising in the ruthless music business. **110m/C; DVD.** ***D:*** Ondi Timoner; ***W:*** Ondi Timoner; ***C:*** Ondi Timoner; Vasco Lucas Nunes; David Timoner; ***M:*** David Brownlow.

Diggers **½ 2006 (R)** Four 30-something buddies face life-changing decisions in this modest slice-of-life drama. In 1976, Long Islanders Hunt (Rudd), Jack (Eldard), Cons (Hamilton), and Lozo (Marino) continue their families' tradition as clam diggers, but their livelihood is threatened by a corporate fishery that's buying up prime water rights. Hunt's dad has just died so maybe he should finally move on but he's worried when lothario Jack starts sniffing around his divorced sister, Gina (Tierney). Meanwhile, Cons supplements his earnings dealing pot (although smoking most of it), and Lozo's large and increasing family strains his marriage and his temper. Charming and poignant despite its well-worn premise of breaking out of small-town working-class life. **90m/C; DVD.** Paul Rudd; Ron Eldard; Josh Hamilton; Ken Marino; Lauren Ambrose; Maura Tierney; Sarah Paulson; ***D:*** Katherine Dieckmann; ***C:*** Michael McDonough; ***M:*** David Mansfield.

Digging for Fire **½ 2015 (R)** Chicago filmmaker Swanberg spreads his wings and his focus with this L.A.-set film about a couple who get physically and emotionally further apart over the course of a weekend. While housesitting, Tim (Johnson) finds a bone and a gun in the backyard, convincing himself that he's uncovered a mystery. As his wife Lee (DeWitt) heads out for some time alone, Tim invites some buddies over to help investigate. Swanberg, shooting on film for the first time, crafts believable, genuine characters, and fills his ensemble with great actors like Sam Rockwell and Brie Larson. Not as deep as it could be, but fun. **85m/C; DVD.** Orlando Bloom; Anna Kendrick; Steve Berg; Mike Birbiglia; Sam Elliott; ***D:*** Joe Swanberg; ***W:*** Joe Swanberg; Jake Johnson; ***C:*** Ben Richardson; ***M:*** Dan Romer.

Digging to China **½ 1998 (PG)** Directorial debut of Hutton is the sentimental story of a sweet friendship between misfits—precocious 10-year-old Harriet (Wood) and mentally handicapped 30-year-old Ricky (Bacon). Harriet's alcoholic mom (Moriarty) runs a motel in rural New Hampshire (film is set in the mid-'60s) with Harriet's slutty older sister Gwen (Masterson). Ricky winds up at the motel with his dying mother Leah (Seldes), who was taking him to an institution when her car breaks down. Harriet thinks Ricky is a terrific playmate but after some shocking news, the young girl and her new friend decide to run away—causing a lot of trouble. **98m/C; VHS, DVD.** Evan Rachel Wood; Kevin Bacon; Mary Stuart Masterson; Cathy Moriarty; Marian Seldes; ***D:*** Timothy Hutton; ***W:*** Karen Janszen; ***C:*** Jorgen Persson; ***M:*** Cynthia Millar.

Digging Up the Marrow **½ 2014** Monster mockumentary from schlock horror veteran, Adam Green, investigating the reality of supernatural creatures. William Dekker (Wise), a mysterious loner with a video camera, sets out into the California woods determined to capture something otherworldly. Instead, he mostly captures himself talking to camera, endlessly pondering the importance of his nature trip, allowing Green to insert his own commentary on the state of horror flicks. Tepid and altogether overly introspective, relying simply on a few jump scares to satisfy the genre fans. Too much marrow, not enough bones. **98m/C; DVD, Blu-Ray.**

Diggstown **½** *Midnight Sting* **1992 (R)** Lightweight, good-natured sports comedy about a boxing scam. Con man Gabriel Caine (Woods), fresh out of prison, heads for Diggstown and the unregulated boxing matches arranged by town boss, John Gillon (Dern). The bet is that Caine's one boxer can beat any 10 boxers, chosen by Gillon, in a 24-hour period. So Caine decides to hook up with an old friend, former prizefighter "Honey" Roy Palmer (Gosset Jr.), to run the scam of his life. Dern is sufficiently nasty and Woods his usual nervy self but it's Gossett Jr. who manages to hold everything together as the aging boxer. Based on the novel "The Diggstown Ringers" by Leonard Wise. **97m/C; VHS, DVD, Blu-Ray.** James Woods; Louis Gossett, Jr.; Bruce Dern; Oliver Platt; Heather Graham; Randall "Tex" Cobb; Thomas Wilson Brown; Duane Davis; Willie Green; George D. Wallace; Wilhelm von Homburg; James (Jim) Caviezel; Marshall Bell; ***D:*** Michael Ritchie; ***W:*** Steven McKay; ***M:*** James Newton Howard.

Digital Man **½ 1994 (R)** High-tech military super-soldier prototype has his programming sabotaged and a team of human and robotic commmandoes must prevent him from starting WWIII. **95m/C; VHS, Streaming.** Ken Olandt; Adam Baldwin; Ed Lauter; Matthias Hues; Kristen Dalton; Paul Gleason; ***D:*** Phillip J. Roth; ***W:*** Phillip J. Roth; Ronald Schmidt.

Dilemma **½ 1997** On Death Row, Rudy Salazar (Trejo) volunteers to be a bone-marrow donor to a sick child. LAPD detective Quin (Howell) realizes that it's a set-up for an escape and he's right. Then the cops have to catch Salazar again, but they can't kill him without sacrificing the kid. **87m/C; DVD.** C. Thomas Howell; Danny Trejo; Sofia Shinas; ***D:*** Eric Larsen; ***W:*** Ira Israel; Chuck Conaway; ***C:*** Mark Melville; ***M:*** Albritton McClain.

The Dilemma **½ 2011 (PG-13)** Howard jumps on the bro-mance bandwagon, directing what feels like a screwball comedy but dissolves into a mean-spirited mess. Confirmed bachelor Ronny (Vaughn) thinks the world of best friend Nick's (James) marriage to Geneva (Ryder). Just as the buddies and auto design business partners are about to land a major deal, Ronny spots Geneva making out with another man. Thus begins Ronny's dilemma: keep the business dream alive without telling Nick, or ruin Nick's marriage and life as he knows it? Nothing particularly funny about the situation and, oddly, Ryder is the only one with heart and soul. **111m/C; Blu-Ray, On Demand.** Vince Vaughn; Kevin James; Winona Ryder; Jennifer Connelly; Channing Tatum; Queen Latifah; Chelcie Ross; ***D:*** Ron Howard; ***W:*** Allan Loeb; ***C:*** Salvatore Totino; ***M:*** Hans Zimmer; Lorne Balfe.

Dilili in Paris **½** *Dilili a Paris* **2018 (PG)** Feisty girl Dilili (Carballo) is a member of the indigenous Kanak culture in New Caledonia. After sneaking on a boat headed to France, the curious Dilili makes a new friend, Orel (Kesser), after she arrives. The pair take a journey in Paris where they meet feminist icons and try to solve the mystery of the Male Masters cult, which kidnaps and holds women and girls captive. The sketchy English-language translation and dubbing of the French animated film distracts from its intriguing heroine, as does the underused Belle Epoque-era icons. **94m/C; DVD.** Prunelle Charles-Ambron; Enzo Ratsito; Natalie Dessay; Bruno Paviot; Jeremy Lopez; ***D:*** Michel Ocelot; ***W:*** Michel Ocelot; ***M:*** Gabriel Yared.

Dillinger **1945** John Dillinger's notorious career, from street punk to public enemy number one, receives a thrilling fast-paced treatment. Tierney turns in a fine performance in this interesting account of the criminal life. **70m/C; VHS, DVD.** Lawrence Tierney; Edmund Lowe; Anne Jeffreys; Elisha Cook, Jr.; ***D:*** Max Nosseck; ***W:*** Philip Yordan.

Dillinger **½ 1973 (R)** The most colorful period of criminality in America is brought to life in this story of bank-robber John Dillinger, "Baby Face" Nelson, and the notorious "Lady in Red." **106m/C; VHS, DVD, Blu-Ray.** Warren Oates; Michelle Phillips; Richard Dreyfuss; Cloris Leachman; Ben Johnson; Harry Dean Stanton; ***D:*** John Milius; ***W:*** John Milius; ***C:*** Jules Brenner; ***M:*** Barry DeVorzon.

Dillinger and Capone **½ 1995 (R)** Supposedly the FBI has killed the wrong Dillinger and the gangster (Sheen) decides to make a new life. But his old friend Al Capone (Abraham), newly released from prison, is holding Dillinger's wife (Hicks) and son hostage as insurance that first he'll retrieve $15 million from a mob-owned Chicago bank. **95m/C; VHS, DVD.** Martin Sheen; F. Murray Abraham; Catherine Hicks; Stephen Davies; Don Stroud; Clint Howard; Joe Estevez; ***D:*** Jon Purdy; ***W:*** Michael B. Druxman; ***C:*** John Aronson; ***M:*** David Wurst; Eric Wurst.

Dillinger Is Dead **½** *Dillinger e Morto* **1969** Uneven combo of reality and fantasy is a trippy curiosity. Industrial designer Glauco unexpectedly finds a gun while cooking dinner and uses it to kill his wife then dreams about escaping to Tahiti. Or maybe he does. And maybe the .45 that Glauco finds belonged to American gangster John Dillinger but it doesn't seem to matter. Italian with subtitles. **90m/C; DVD.** *IT* Michel Piccoli; Anita Pallenberg; Annie Girardot; ***D:*** Marco Ferreri; ***W:*** Marco Ferreri; Sergio Bazzini; ***C:*** Mario Vulpiani; ***M:*** Teo Usuelli.

Dim Sum: A Little Bit of Heart **1985 (PG)** The second independent film from the director of "Chan Is Missing." A Chinese-American mother and daughter living in San Francisco's Chinatown confront the conflict between traditional Eastern ways and modern American life. Gentle, fragile picture made with humor and care. In English and Chinese with subtitles. **88m/C; VHS, DVD.** Laureen Chew; Kim Chew; Victor Wong; Ida F.O. Chong; Cora Miao; John Nishio; Joan Chen; ***D:*** Wayne Wang; ***W:*** Terrel Seltzer; ***M:*** Todd Boekelheide.

Dim Sum Funeral **½ 2008 (R)** Uneasy and unsuccessful mix of sentimentality and comedy. Four estranged Chinese-American siblings are reunited in Seattle when their busybody mother dies since she wanted a traditional seven-day Chinese funeral. Secrets (none of them particularly shocking or surprising) are revealed. **95m/C; DVD.** Julia Nickson-Soul; Russell Wong; Francoise Yip; Steph Song; Bai Ling; Talia Shire; Kelly Hu; Lisa Lu; ***D:*** Anna Chi; ***W:*** Donald Martin; ***C:*** Michael Balfry; ***M:*** Scott Starrett.

Diminished Capacity **2008** Recently fired Chicago political columnist Cooper (Broderick) is urged to return home to rural Illinois to convince his uncle Rollie (Alda) to check into a nursing home. Cooper and Rollie bond through a shared ailment: both suffer memory loss, Cooper from an old bar fight and Rollie from Alzheimer's. The gathered family soon discovers that one of Rollie's old baseball cards is worth a fortune and could bring him out of debt. So Cooper, an old flame (Madsen), and her son take a trip into the city in hopes of cashing it in at a sports card convention, where they haggle with dealers and fall into silly hijinks. Unfortunately, a tame script brings only light laughter and doesn't say much about anything. **92m/C; On Demand.** Matthew Broderick; Alan Alda; Virginia Madsen; Louis CK; Jimmy Bennett; Dylan Baker; Bobby Cannavale; Jim True-Frost; Jeff(rey) Perry; Lois Smith; ***D:*** Terry Kinney; ***W:*** Sherwood Kinney; ***C:*** Vanja Cernjul; ***M:*** Robert Berger; Griffin Richardson.

Dimples **½ 1936 (PG)** When Shirley's pickpocket grandfather is caught red-handed, she steps in, takes the blame, and somehow ends up in show business. Reissued version is rated. Also available colorized. **78m/B; VHS, DVD.** Shirley Temple; John Carradine; Frank Morgan; Helen Westley; Berton Churchill; Robert Kent; Delma Byron; ***D:*** William A. Seiter; ***W:*** Nat Perrin; Arthur Sheekman; ***C:*** Bert Glennon; ***M:*** Louis Silvers.

Dina **2017** A character-driven documentary that feels like a romantic comedy-drama. The film follows couple Dina Buno and her fiance Scott Levin as they move into together ahead of their wedding day. The previously married Dina is developmentally disabled and has other issues like anxiety, while Scott has Asperger's and has never lived apart from his parents. Through their honest conversations about sex, budgeting, and their different needs, the film reveals their kindness, openness, and affection for each other while dealing with sometimes difficult issues. The directors' care for their subjects gives this film heart. **103m/C; DVD.** ***D:*** Antonio Santini; Daniel Sickles; ***C:*** Adam Uhl.

Diner **½ 1982 (R)** A group of old high school friends meet at "their" Baltimore diner to find that more has changed than the menu. A bittersweet look at the experiences of a group of Baltimore twentysomethings, circa 1959, who find adulthood hard to face. Particularly notable was Levinson's casting of "unknowns" who have since become household names. Features many humorous moments and fine performances. **110m/C; VHS, DVD, Blu-Ray.** Steve Guttenberg; Daniel Stern; Mickey Rourke; Kevin Bacon; Ellen Barkin; Timothy Daly; Paul Reiser; Michael Tucker; Jessica James; Kathryn Dowling; Colette Blonigan; ***D:*** Barry Levinson; ***W:*** Barry Levinson; ***C:*** Peter Sova; ***M:*** Bruce Brody; Ivan Kral. Natl. Soc. Film Critics '82: Support. Actor (Rourke).

Dingo **½ 1990** In Davis' only film appearance he's, what else, a famous jazz trumpeter. Paris-based Billy Cross (Davis) and his combo are on tour in 1969 and momentarily stuck at a remote Australian airstrip. They give an impromptu concert heard by John "Dingo" Anderson (Friels), who instantly decides that music is the life for him. Over the years Dingo keeps in touch with his idol as he works outback bars and secretly saves to go to Paris and check out the scene—even if it means sacrificing his wife and family. **108m/C; VHS, DVD.** *FR AU* Colin Friels; Miles Davis; Helen Buday; Bernadette LaFont; ***D:*** Rolf de Heer; ***W:*** Marc Rosenberg; ***C:*** Denis Lenoir; ***M:*** Miles Davis; Michel Legrand.

The Dinner 2017 (R) At a fancy restaurant, Paul Lohman (Coogan) and his wife Claire (Linney) meet Paul's politician brother Stan (Gere) and his wife Katelyn (Hall) to discuss their sons. The cousins were caught on tape committing a crime, and their parents are discussing how to manage the situation so their sons avoid jail and Stan's ascending political star continues to rise. An overwrought drama about human interaction that features a stellar cast but lacks a cohesive look and plot to showcase their solid work. **120m/C; DVD.** Michael Chernus; Taylor Rae Almonte; Steve Coogan; Charlie Plummer; Seamus Davey-Fitzpatrick; ***D:*** Oren Moverman; ***W:*** Oren Moverman; ***C:*** Bobby Bukowski.

Dinner and Driving 1/2 1997 Twentysomething writer Jason (a charming Slotnick) looks like a nebbish but must have something else going for him because he's caught between two babes. One is longtime girlfriend Laura (Devicq), who has pressured the reluctant Jason into a marriage proposal. The other is Grace (Bako), a hottie who was Jason's college sweetie and suddenly makes a reappearance in his life. Jason, who doesn't know if he can commit to one woman for life, seeks advice from his equally clueless friends and realizes that relationships aren't easy. **89m/C; VHS, DVD.** Joey Slotnick; Paula DeVicq; Brigitte Bako; Sam Robards; Molly Shannon; Greg Grunberg; ***D:*** Lawrence Trilling; ***W:*** Lawrence Trilling; Steven Wolfson; ***C:*** Geary McLeod; ***M:*** Peter Himmelman.

Dinner at Eight 1933 Social-climbing Mrs. Jordan (Burke) and her husband Oliver (Lionel Barrymore) throw a dinner party for various members of the New York elite. During the course of the evening, all of the guests reveal too much. Special performances all around, especially John Barrymore in a parody of his drunken career, Dressler as a grande dame sliding down the social ladder, and Harlow as a gold-digging hussy. Superb comedic direction by Cukor. Adapted from the play by Edna Ferber and George Kaufman. **110m/C; VHS, DVD.** John Barrymore; Lionel Barrymore; Wallace Beery; Madge Evans; Jean Harlow; Billie Burke; Marie Dressler; Phillips Holmes; Jean Hersholt; Lee Tracy; Edmund Lowe; Karen Morley; May Robson; ***D:*** George Cukor; ***W:*** Herman J. Mankiewicz; Frances Marion; Donald Ogden Stewart; ***C:*** William H. Daniels; ***M:*** William Axt.

Dinner at Eight 1989 A social-climbing romance novelist throws an elegant dinner party. TV remake of the 1933 film does not compare well. **100m/C; DVD.** Lauren Bacall; Charles Durning; Ellen Greene; Harry Hamlin; John Mahoney; Marsha Mason; Tim Kazurinsky; ***D:*** Ron Lagomarsino; ***W:*** Tom Griffin; ***C:*** Ron Vargas; ***M:*** Jonathan Sheffer. **TV**

Dinner at the Ritz 1/2 1937 Daughter of a murdered Parisian banker vows to find his killer with help from her fiance. **78m/B; VHS, DVD.** *GB* David Niven; Annabella; Paul Lukas; Patricia Medina; ***D:*** Harold Schuster.

Dinner for Schmucks 1/2 2010 (PG-13) Corporate-ladder climbing financial exec Tim (Rudd) is invited by his boss (Greenwood) to an annual dinner where guests bring the biggest loser they can find. Tim is hesitant and his longtime girlfriend Julie (Szostak) despises the whole thing but then Tim encounters amateur mouse taxidermist Barry (an appealing Carell), who agrees to go, unaware of the party's true purpose. But before that, Barry's good intentions inadvertently wreak (hilarious) havoc on Tim's life. Rudd's straight man plays well with Carell's innocent fool with invigorating performances from Galifianakis as a self-appointed mind-controller and Clement as an absurdly pompous sex-crazed artist. Friendlier remake of the 1998 French film "The Dinner Game." **113m/C; Blu-Ray.** Steve Carell; Paul Rudd; Lucy Punch; Bruce Greenwood; Zach Galifianakis; Ron Livingston; Jemaine Clement; Stephanie Szostak; Rick Overton; ***D:*** Jay Roach; ***W:*** Michael Handelman; ***C:*** Jim Denault; ***M:*** Theodore Shapiro.

The Dinner Game *Le Diner de Cons* 1998 (PG-13) Smug publisher Pierre (Lhermitte) dines weekly with equally smug friends, their entertainment being to see who can bring the biggest fool as a dinner guest. This nasty joke gets the turnabout it deserves when Pierre intends to bring bumbling Francois (Villeret) to the party, only to have the man proceed to wreck Pierre's life before they even get there—all while Francois maintains his own sweet dignity. French with subtitles. **82m/C; VHS, DVD, Blu-Ray.** *FR* Thierry Lhermitte; Jacques Villeret; Alexandra Vandernoot; Catherine Frot; Francis Huster; Daniel Prevost; ***D:*** Francis Veber; ***W:*** Francis Veber; ***C:*** Luciano Tovoli; ***M:*** Vladimir Cosma. Cesar '99: Actor (Villeret), Support. Actor (Prevost), Writing.

The Dinner Party 2020 Playwright Jeffery (Mayhall) goes to a dinner party with wife Haley (Hart) in hopes of getting funding from the wealthy people there. The gathering is hosted by charming Sabastian (Wilson), and includes chef Carmine (Sage), novelist Agatha (McCuin), uncouth Vincent (Doleac), and tarot card reader Sadie (Williams). As the evening progresses, Jeffrey and Haley realize that this party isn't what it seems to be and their lives are in jeopardy. Nothing terribly original but it gleefully serves up the horror flick violence. The Hound suggests you skip going back for seconds! **116m/C; DVD.** Jeremy London; Bill Sage; Alli Hart; Lindsay Anne Williams; Sherri Eakin; ***D:*** Miles Doleac; ***W:*** Miles Doleac; ***C:*** Michael Williams; ***M:*** Clifton Hyde.

Dinner Rush 2000 (R) Louis, owner of a trendy Manhattan restaurant and operator of a bookmaking enterprise, must deal with various problems and people from both of his occupations in one hectic night. His son, Udo has transformed the restaurant from a simple Italian place with his pursuit of nouvelle cuisine fame, two mob guys are trying to muscle him out of the bookie business (having already killed his partner), a snooty gallery owner is hassling his staff, his sous-chef is piling up gambling debts, and a powerful food critic just walked in the door. Although pic is overstuffed, Giraldi's deft direction, and excellent performances (especially Aiello's) make for a satisfying treat. Successful restauranteur Giraldi filmed in one of his own eateries. **98m/C; VHS, DVD.** Danny Aiello; Edoardo Ballerini; Vivian Wu; Mike McGlone; Kirk Acevedo; Sandra Bernhard; Summer Phoenix; Polly Draper; Mark Margolis; John Corbett; Alex Corrado; ***D:*** Bob Giraldi; ***W:*** Brian Kalata; Rick Shaughnessy; ***C:*** Tim Ives; ***M:*** Alexander Lasarenko.

Dinner with Friends 1/2 2001 The main course is a look at the meaning of love, marriage, and friendship, with a heaping side of mid-life angst. Happily married couple Gabe (Quaid) and Karen (MacDowell) deal with the fallout of the breakup of their friends' marriage. Beth (Collette) shows up at their door after husband Tom (Kinnear) leaves her for another woman. When Gabe and Karen try to help (read: offer their advice), they're met with a less than enthusiastic response. **95m/C; VHS, DVD.** Dennis Quaid; Andie MacDowell; Greg Kinnear; Toni Collette; ***D:*** Norman Jewison; ***W:*** Donald Margulies. **CABLE**

Dino 1/2 1957 Social worker joins a young woman in helping a 17-year-old delinquent re-enter society. **96m/B; VHS, DVD.** Sal Mineo; Brian Keith; Susan Kohner; ***D:*** Thomas Carr.

Dinocroc 2004 (R) Scientists discover the remains of a prehistoric ancestor to the modern crocodile, and a geneticist uses its DNA to make a prototype monster because, apparently, man-eating monsters are in demand. Said prototype escapes and immediately devours everyone in sight except the makers of this film (who probably deserved it the most). Executive produced by Roger Corman. **90m/C; DVD.** Costas Mandylor; Charles Napier; Bruce Weitz; Matthew Borlenghi; Jane Longenecker; ***D:*** Kevin ONeill; ***W:*** Dan Acre; Frances Doel; John Huckert; ***C:*** Yoram Astrakhan; ***M:*** Damon Ebner. **VIDEO**

Dinocroc Vs. Supergator 1/2 2010 Producer Roger Corman 'presents' this mutant monster fest from the Syfy Channel. Unscrupulous mogul Jason Drake (Carradine) funds a genetics lab experimenting with a growth serum. He insists the scientists test it on a crocodile and an alligator. Naturally, the supersized critters escape the lab and begin chomping down on any likely food source (including the scientists). So Drake hires a Louisiana gator hunter (Hillis) to go after those bad boys. **87m/C; DVD, Blu-Ray.** David Carradine; Rib Hillis; Corey Landis; John Callahan; Amy Rasimas; Delia Sheppard; Lisa Clapperton; ***D:*** Jim Wynorski; ***W:*** Jim Wynorski; Mike MacLean; ***C:*** Samuel Brownfield; ***M:*** Al Kaplan; Jon Kaplan. **CABLE**

Dinosaur 1/2 2000 (PG) Young iguanodon Aladar is separated from his parents and raised by lemurs on an isolated island. Aladar must discover his heritage just as a meteor crash threatens to destroy his world. Raises the bar on animated adventures by having the impossibly realistic critters superimposed onto actual jungle footage. Pic represents the next step in animation evolution, but the amazing visuals are somewhat undercut by the script, which has a pieced-together feel at times. May be too scary for the wee ones since everything does look so lifelike. **82m/C; VHS, DVD, Blu-Ray.** ***V:*** Julianna Margulies; Alfre Woodard; D.B. Sweeney; Ossie Davis; Della Reese; Max Casella; Samuel E. Wright; Joan Plowright; Hayden Panettiere; Peter Siragusa; ***D:*** Ralph Zondag; Eric Leighton; ***W:*** John Harrison; Robert Nelson Jacobs; ***M:*** James Newton Howard.

Dinosaur Valley Girls 1/2 1996 Hollywood action hero Tony Markham comes into posession of a magic stone that hurls him backwards through time into a prehistoric world. That just happens to be populated by fierce, beautiful babes in animal-print bikinis. A PG version is also available. **94m/C; VHS, DVD.** Karen Black; William D. Russell; Ron Jeffries; Jeff Rector; Griffin (Griffen) Drew; Ed Fury; ***D:*** Don Glut; ***W:*** Don Glut.

Dinosaurus! 1960 Large sadistic dinosaurs appear in the modern world. They eat, burn, and pillage their way through this film. Also includes a romance between a Neanderthal and a modern-age woman. **85m/C; VHS, DVD, Blu-Ray.** Ward Ramsey; Kristina Hanson; Paul Lukather; Fred Engelberg; ***D:*** Irvin S. Yeaworth, Jr.; ***W:*** Dan E. Weisburd; Jean Yeaworth; ***C:*** Stanley Cortez; ***M:*** Ronald Stein.

Dinoshark 2010 Syfy Channel creature feature produced by Roger Corman (who has a cameo). Global warming releases an ancient creature from a glacier and it makes it way to Puerto Vallarta, Mexico. It promptly starts chowing down on the tourists and locals who want to make certain dinoshark gets extinct for real. **90m/C; DVD, Blu-Ray.** Eric Balfour; Iva Hasperger; Chirstina Nicole; Aaron Diaz; Humberto Busto; Roger Corman; ***D:*** Kevin O'Neill; ***W:*** Frances Doel; Guy Prevost; ***C:*** Eduardo Flores Torres; ***M:*** Cynthia Brown. **CABLE**

Dinotopia 1/2 2002 TV miniseries based on two books by author/illustrator James Gurney about a fantasy island paradise where humans and talking dinos coexist peacefully. Teenaged half-brothers Karl (Leitso) and David (Miller) survive a plane crash and wind up on Dinotopia where they are befriended by young princess Marion (Carr). But the island has problems—rogue carnivorous dinosaurs and sinister human Cyrus Crabb (Thewlis) as well as some magical sunstones that are losing their power. Fanciful storytelling with some fun special effects. **285m/C; VHS, DVD, Blu-Ray.** Tyron Leitso; Wentworth Miller; Katie Carr; David Thewlis; Jim Carter; Alice Krige; Colin Salmon; Hannah Yelland; Stuart Wilson; Anna McGuire; ***V:*** Lee Evans; ***D:*** Marco Brambilla; ***W:*** Simon Moore; ***C:*** Tony Pierce-Roberts; ***M:*** Trevor Jones. **TV**

The Diplomat *False Witness* 2008 Never push a man with nothing left to lose. British diplomat Ian Porter (Scott) is arrested by Scotland Yard on suspicion of helping Russian mobsters smuggle drugs and nuclear materials. He's actually working for MI-6 to prevent such things from happening but various doublecrosses have Porter and his ex-wife Pippa (Forlani) getting sent into witness protection in Australia. And then the story gets more complicated and dangerous. **188m/C; DVD.** *AU* Dougray Scott; Rachael Blake; Claire Forlani; Richard Roxburgh; Jeremy Lindsay Taylor; Stephen Curry; Shane Briant; Don Hany; Elan Zavelsky; ***D:*** Peter Andrikidis; ***W:*** Ronan Glennane; Nell Greenwood; ***C:*** Mark Wareham; ***M:*** Burkhard Dallwitz. **TV**

Diplomatic Courier 1952 Cold-war espionage saga has secret agent Power attempting to re-steal sensitive documents from the hands of Soviet agents. Involved and exciting thriller. Michael Ansara, Charles Bronson and Lee Marvin made brief appearances. **97m/B; VHS, DVD.** Tyrone Power; Patricia Neal; Stephen McNally; Hildegarde Knef; Karl Malden; ***D:*** Henry Hathaway; ***C:*** Lucien Ballard.

Diplomatic Siege *Enemy of My Enemy* 1999 (R) The U.S. Embassy is taken over by Serbian terrorists who demand that foreign forces clear out of Bosnia or they'll kill their hostages. But General Buck Swain (Berenger) decides to get rid of the Serbs instead. And just to keep things interesting, CIA ops Steve Parker (Weller) and Erica Long (Hannah) are in the embassy basement trying to defuse a bomb. **94m/C; VHS, DVD.** Tom Berenger; Daryl Hannah; Peter Weller; ***D:*** Gustavo Graef-Marino; ***W:*** Robert Boris; Kevin Bernhardt; Sam Bernard; Mark Amin; ***C:*** Steven Wacks; ***M:*** Terry Plumeri. **VIDEO**

Direct Contact 1/2 2009 (R) Typical action fare from Lundgren. Former Special Forces operative Mike Riggins is being held in a Russian prison. He's offered his freedom if he will find missing American Ana (May) but when he does so, he learns it's all a double-cross and now he needs to save Ana from the men who want her dead. **90m/C; DVD, Blu-Ray.** Dolph Lundgren; Michael Paré; Bashar Rahal; James Chalke; Gina May; ***D:*** Dan Lerner; ***W:*** Les Weldon; ***C:*** Ross W. Clarkson; ***M:*** Stephen (Steve) Edwards. **VIDEO**

Direct Hit 1/2 1993 (R) A CIA assassin discovers retiring is not an option. John Hatch (Forsythe) decides he wants out, particularly when his next kill, Savannah (Champa), turns out to be an innocent pawn. So Hatch turns protector and decides to best the agency at its own deadly game. **91m/C; VHS, DVD.** William Forsythe; Richard Norton; Jo Champa; John Aprea; Juliet Landau; George Segal; ***D:*** Joseph Merhi; ***W:*** Jacobsen Hart.

Dirt Bike Kid 1/2 1986 (PG) A precocious brat is stuck with a used motorbike that has a mind of its own. Shenanigans follow in utterly predictable fashion as he battles bankers and bikers with his bad bike. **91m/C; VHS, DVD, Blu-Ray.** Peter Billingsley; Anne Bloom; Stuart Pankin; Patrick Collins; Sage Parker; Chad Sheets; ***D:*** Hoite C. Caston; ***W:*** Lewis Colick; David Brandes.

Dirt Boy 1/2 2001 Ex-heroin addict Matty Matthews (Hedman) has decided to leave New York and take forensic courses in a creepy Cape Cod community where the local celeb is Attwater Bridges (Walsh), the writer of a non-fiction account of a serial killer called "Dirt Boy." But after talking to one near-victim, Matty has his own suspicions about what really happened. **90m/C; VHS, DVD.** Jacob Lee Hedman; Arthur J. Walsh; Luca Bercovici; Michelle Guthrie; ***D:*** Gerald L. Frasco; ***W:*** Gerald L. Frasco; ***C:*** Jeffrey Greeley; ***M:*** Robert Robertson.

Dirty 2005 (R) Paired on LAPD's anti-gang division with immoral cop Salim Adel (Gooding Jr. in an atypical bad-guy role), former street-thug-turned-good-guy Armando Sancho (Collins Jr.) agonizes over whether to turn Salim over to Internal Affairs for his fatal shooting of an innocent citizen until their commanding officers step in. More than subtle hint of the real-life 1990s Rampart scandal. **97m/C; DVD.** Cuba Gooding, Jr.; Clifton (Gonzalez) Collins, Jr.; Cole Hauser; Nelust Wyclef Jean; Wood Harris; Robert LaSardo; Lobo Sebastian; Khleo Thomas; Ramirez; Aimee Garcia; ***D:*** Chris Fisher; ***W:*** Chris Fisher; Gill Reavill; Eric Saks; ***C:*** Eliot Rockett; Dani Minnick; ***M:*** Peter Lopez.

Dirty 30 2016 (PG-13) A comedy about one woman's life-changing thirtieth birthday party. Kate (Hart), Evie (Helbig), and

Charlie (Hart) have been friends forever. However, as Kate nears 30, she is unhappy in her career and spends most evenings alone or on miserable dates. Though Evie is married, she has difficult in-laws and tries to find a charitable cause to support. Charlie has a strong relationship with her dream woman but cannot pull her business and her life together. When Kate agrees to allow Evie and Charlie to throw a birthday party for her, the planned low-key gathering soon becomes a wild bash with characters from their past and present. **86m/C; DVD, Streaming, Download.** Mamrie Hart; Grace Helbig; Hannah Hart; Adam Lustick; Anna Akana; ***D:*** Andrew Bush; ***W:*** Mamrie Hart; Molly Prather; ***C:*** Tom Banks; ***M:*** Ross Flournoy.

Dirty Dancing ♪♪♪ **1987 (PG-13)** An innocent 17-year-old (Grey) is vacationing with her parents in the Catskills in 1963. Bored with the program at the hotel, she finds the real fun at the staff dances. Falling for the sexy dance instructor (Swayze), she discovers love, sex, and rock and roll dancing. An old story, with little to save it, but Grey and Swayze are appealing, the dance sequences fun, and the music great. Swayze, classically trained in ballet, also performs one of the sound-track songs. **97m/C; VHS, DVD, Blu-Ray.** Patrick Swayze; Jennifer Grey; Cynthia Rhodes; Jerry Orbach; Jack Weston; Jane Brucker; Kelly Bishop; Lonny Price; Charles "Honi" Coles; Bruce 'Cousin Brucie' Morrow; ***D:*** Emile Ardolino; ***W:*** Eleanor Bergstein; ***C:*** Jeffrey Jur; ***M:*** John Morris. Oscars '87: Song ("(I've Had) the Time of My Life"); Golden Globes '88: Song ("(I've Had) the Time of My Life"); Ind. Spirit '88: First Feature.

Dirty Dancing: Havana Nights ♪♪ **2004 (PG-13)** Folks, it's not a sequel, it's not a prequel—it's a "re-imagining." This time around the dirty dancers are in Cuba (although filmed in Puerto Rico) and the year is 1958 on the eve of the Communist Revolution. Young Katey's (Garai) dad transplants the family and, bored, she meets Javier (Luna), the poor yet sexy busboy, and...well...really you know the rest. It's great eye candy and the couple is very appealing but they lack that certain something that Swayze (who makes a cameo) and Grey exuded. **86m/C; VHS, DVD, Blu-Ray.** Diego Luna; Romola Garai; Sela Ward; John Slattery; Jonathan Jackson; January Jones; Mika Boorem; Rene Lavan; Patrick Swayze; Mya; ***D:*** Guy Ferland; ***W:*** Boaz Yakin; Peter Sagal; Victoria Arch; ***C:*** Anthony B. Richmond; ***M:*** Hector Pereira.

Dirty Deeds ♪♪♪ **2002 (R)** In the late 1960s, Barry Ryan (Brown) is a Sydney crime boss who rules the slot machine trade. Having the local police chief (Neill) in his pocket is a help and Barry's Vietnam vet nephew Darcy (Worthington) is just joining the business, but Barry does have some personal trouble with his tough wife Sharon (Collette) and young mistress Margaret (Morassi). Then, a couple of Chicago wiseguys show up: down-to-earth Tony (Goodman) and his hot-headed colleague Sal (Williamson) have been instructed to muscle in on Barry's turf, but Barry is not about to let these interlopers interfere with his business. A bold combination of charm, comedy, and violence. **110m/C; VHS, DVD.** *AU* Bryan Brown; Toni Collette; John Goodman; Sam Neill; Sam Worthington; Felix Williamson; Andrew S. Gilbert; Kestie Morassi; ***D:*** David Caesar; ***W:*** David Caesar; ***C:*** Geoffrey Hall; ***M:*** Paul Healy.

The Dirty Dozen ♪♪♪ **1967 (PG)** A tough Army major is assigned to train and command 12 hardened convicts offered absolution if they participate in a suicidal mission into Nazi Germany in 1944. Well-made movie is a standout in its genre. Rough and gruff Marvin is good as the group leader. Three made-for-TV sequels followed in the '80s. **149m/C; VHS, DVD, Blu-Ray, HD-DVD.** Lee Marvin; Ernest Borgnine; Charles Bronson; Jim Brown; George Kennedy; John Cassavetes; Clint Walker; Donald Sutherland; Telly Savalas; Robert Ryan; Ralph Meeker; Richard Jaeckel; Trini Lopez; Robert Webber; Stuart Cooper; Robert Phillips; Al Mancini; ***D:*** Robert Aldrich; ***W:*** Nunnally Johnson; Lukas Heller; ***C:*** Edward (Ted) Scaife; ***M:*** Frank DeVol. Oscars '67: Sound FX Editing.

The Dirty Dozen: The Deadly Mission ♪♪ **1/2 1987** A second made-for-TV sequel to the '67 movie finds Borgnine ordering another suicide mission. Savalas (killed in the original, he's playing a new character) must pick 12 convicted army prisoners for an assault on a Nazi-held French monastery. Their mission is to rescue six scientists who are working on a deadly new nerve gas. Followed by "The Dirty Dozen: The Fatal Mission." **96m/C; VHS, DVD, Blu-Ray.** Ernest Borgnine; Telly Savalas; Vince Edwards; Gary (Rand) Graham; James Van Patten; Vincent Van Patten; Bo Svenson; ***D:*** Lee H. Katzin.

The Dirty Dozen: The Fatal Mission ♪♪ **1/2 1988** This third TV sequel has Borgnine learning of a plan to bring a group of high-ranking Nazis to Instanbul via the Orient Express. Naturally, he assigns Savalas the task of getting his motley gang together to thwart the Nazi schemes. To add intrigue, a female has joined the ranks of the Dirty Dozen and a spy may also have infiltrated the group. **91m/C; VHS, DVD, Blu-Ray.** Ernest Borgnine; Telly Savalas; Hunt Block; Jeff Conaway; Erik Estrada; Ray "Boom Boom" Mancini; Heather Thomas; Alex Cord; ***D:*** Lee H. Katzin.

The Dirty Dozen: The Next Mission ♪ **1/2 1985** Disappointing TV sequel to the 1967 hit, with Marvin reprising his role as the leader of the motley pack. In this installment, the rag-tag toughs are sent on yet another suicide mission inside Nazi Germany, this time to thwart an assassination attempt of Hitler. Followed by two more sequels. **97m/C; VHS, DVD, Streaming.** Lee Marvin; Ernest Borgnine; Richard Jaeckel; Ken Wahl; Larry Wilcox; Sonny Landham; Ricco Ross; ***D:*** Andrew V. McLaglen. **TV**

Dirty Games ♪ **1/2 1989** Nicola Kendra is part of a team sent to Africa to inspect a nuclear waste site. Once there, the scientists discover terrorists are plotting to blow up the nuclear complex unless Nicola and her new allies can prevent it. **97m/C; VHS, DVD.** Jan-Michael Vincent; Valentina Vargas; Ronald France; Michael McGovern; ***D:*** Gray Hofmeyr.

Dirty Girl ♪ **1/2 2010 (R)** Earnest, sometimes smug, teen drama (set in 1987) finds unruly blond Danielle (Temple), known as the high school slut, grudgingly befriending closeted, pudgy Clarke (Dozier) who shares an equally dysfunctional family background. Danielle's dad took off long ago and with her trailer park mom Sue-Ann (Jovovich) about to marry stern Mormon Ray (Macy), Danielle and Clarke decide to hit the road out of Oklahoma to look for him. **106m/C; DVD.** Juno Temple; Jeremy Dozier; Milla Jovovich; William H. Macy; Mary Steenburgen; Dwight Yoakam; Nicholas D'Agosto; Tim McGraw; ***D:*** Abe Sylvia; ***W:*** Abe Sylvia; ***C:*** Steve Gainer.

The Dirty Girls ♪ **1/2 1964** Typical Metzger sexcapades featuring two stories about prostitute Garance, who works in Paris, and Monique, who plies her trade in Munich. **82m/B; VHS, DVD.** Reine Rohan; Denise Roland; Marlene Sherter; Peter Parten; Lionel Bernier; ***D:*** Radley Metzger; ***W:*** Peter Fernandez.

Dirty Grandpa ♪ **2016 (R)** Efron plays the uptight young guy about to get married while De Niro slums as his horny grandfather who you just know is going to teach him a thing or two about really living as they head to Fort Lauderdale for spring break. The paper-thin plot is merely a way to cram in as many dirty jokes and bits about men behaving badly that writer John Phillips can get into his horrendous screenplay. There are bad comedies and then there are movies so embarrassing that everyone cast in them should consider firing their agents. This is the latter. **102m/C; DVD, Blu-Ray.** Robert De Niro; Zac Efron; Zoey Deutch; Aubrey Plaza; Jason Mantzoukas; Julianne Hough; ***D:*** Dan Mazer; ***W:*** John Phillips; ***C:*** Eric Alan Edwards; ***M:*** Michael Andrews.

Dirty Harry ♪♪♪ **1/2 1971 (R)** Rock-hard cop Harry Callahan attempts to track down a psychopathic rooftop killer before a kidnapped girl dies. Harry abuses the murderer's civil rights, however, forcing the police to return the criminal to the streets, where he hijacks a school bus and Harry is called on once again. The only answer to stop this vicious killer seems to be death in cold blood, and Harry is just the man to do it. Taut, suspenseful direction by Siegel, who thoroughly understands Eastwood's on-screen character. Features Callahan's famous "Do you feel lucky?" line, the precursor to his "Go ahead, make my day." **103m/C; VHS, DVD, Blu-Ray.** Clint Eastwood; Harry Guardino; John Larch; Andrew (Andy) Robinson; Reni Santoni; John Vernon; Albert "Poppy" Popwell; Craig G. Kelly; John Mitchum; Josef Sommer; Mae Mercer; Woodrow Parfrey; Angela Paton; Debralee Scott; Max Gail; ***D:*** Donald Siegel; ***W:*** Dean Riesner; Harry Julian Fink; Rita M. Fink; ***C:*** Bruce Surtees; ***M:*** Lalo Schifrin. Natl. Film Reg. '12.

Dirty Laundry ♪ **1/2 2007 (PG-13)** Preachy family comedy about acceptance with an either over-the-top or winning performance by Devine, depending on viewer perception. New York writer Sheldon (Dunbar) returns to his Georgia roots after a call from his mama (Devine). She introduces him to his 10-year-old son (a shocker for Sheldon), who's the product of a one-night stand, and does her best to not see that her boy is gay, even after his boyfriend (Costello) shows up. **100m/C; DVD.** Rockmond Dunbar; Loretta Devine; Jenifer Lewis; Joey Costello; Aaron Grady Shaw; Terri J. Vaughn; Maurice Jamal; ***D:*** Maurice Jamal; ***W:*** Maurice Jamal; ***C:*** Rory King; Liz Rubin.

Dirty Lies ♪♪ **2016** An action crime drama centered on an overworked, totally betrayed personal assistant/intern. Josh (Young) spends too many thankless hours working for a wealthy man. After he is entrusted with a million dollar necklace that his employer will be giving his wife for her birthday, Josh stashes at the home he shares with several roommates. When the necklace goes missing, Josh must figure out which of his roommates betrayed him and manage the criminals who want to steal the necklace. **94m/C; DVD, Streaming, Download.** Mark L. Young; Scout Taylor-Compton; Tania Raymonde; Beau Knapp; Lili Simmons; ***D:*** Jamie Marshall; ***W:*** Jamie Marshall; Matthew L. Schaffer; ***C:*** Laura Merians. **VIDEO**

Dirty Little Billy ♪♪ **1972 (R)** Quirky revisionist western determined to shed the Billy the Kid myths for the reality of the times (and myths of its own). Teenager Billy (Pollard) is deemed useless by his stepfather so he spends his time in the local saloon taking outlaw lessons from gambler Goldie (Evans) and whore Berle (Purcell) until he finds his violent destiny. **100m/C; DVD.** Michael J. Pollard; Richard Evans; Lee Purcell; Charles Aidman; Dran Hamilton; Willard Sage; Gary Busey; Mills Watson; ***D:*** Stan Dragoti; ***W:*** Stan Dragoti; Charles Moss; ***C:*** Ralph Woolsey; ***M:*** Sascha Burland.

Dirty Love **WOOF! 2005 (R)** Jenny McCarthy was funny once upon a time. Now, not so much. Rebecca (McCarthy) finds out her idiot boyfriend (Webster) is cheating on her, so she attempts to get back at him by sleeping with a constant stream of nerds, each more nerdy than the last. Her sidekicks Michelle (Electra) and Carrie (Heskin) are trashy, ineffectual, and stupid. In fact, everyone's stupid. An embarrassing film with little to recommend. **95m/C; DVD.** Jenny McCarthy; Carmen Electra; Eddie Kaye Thomas; Victor Webster; Kam Heskin; Lochlyn Munro; Kathy Griffin; Jessica Collins; ***D:*** John Mallory Asher; ***W:*** Jenny McCarthy; ***C:*** Eric Wycoff. Golden Raspberries '05: Worst Actress (McCarthy), Worst Director (Asher), Worst Picture, Worst Screenplay.

Dirty Mary Crazy Larry ♪♪♪ **1974 (PG)** A racecar driver, his mechanic, and a sexy girl hightail it from the law after pulling off a heist. Great action, great fun, and an infamous surprise ending. **93m/C; VHS, DVD, Blu-Ray.** Peter Fonda; Susan George; Adam Roarke; Vic Morrow; Roddy McDowall; Craig G. Kelly; ***D:*** John Hough; ***W:*** Leigh Chapman.

Dirty Mind of Young Sally **WOOF! 1972 (R)** Sally's erotic radio program broadcasts from a mobile studio, which must stay one step ahead of the police. **84m/C; VHS, DVD.** Sharon Kelly; George "Buck" Flower; Norman Fields; ***D:*** Bethel Buckalew.

Dirty Pictures ♪♪ **2000 (R)** Dull telepic on controversial subject that features real-life interviews, which only serve to cut the story's momentum. Dennis Barrie (Woods) is the director of the Cincinnati Contemporary Arts Center who decides to book an exhibition of Robert Mapplethorpe photographs in 1990. He gets indicted on obscenity charges and decides on a court fight based on First Amendment rights though it costs him personally. **104m/C; VHS, DVD.** James Woods; Diana Scarwid; Craig T. Nelson; Leon Pownall; David Huband; Judah Katz; R.D. Reid; Matt North; ***D:*** Frank Pierson; ***W:*** Ilene Chaiken; ***C:*** Hiro Narita; ***M:*** Mark Snow. **CABLE**

Dirty Pretty Things ♪♪♪ **1/2 2003 (R)** Frears revisits the theme of the plight of illegal immigrants living in London with typically moving results. Okwe (Ejiofor), a doctor who was forced to flee his native Nigeria, is now scraping by as a hotel clerk and cabbie in London, where he befriends his Turkish co-worker Senay (Tautou), a chambermaid who later is forced into sweatshop labor and a compromising relationship with her new boss. Already living in fear of being caught by immigration agents, Okwe discovers an illegal organ-selling ring at the hotel. Engagingly illuminates the mysterious and tense underworld inhabited by illegals and those who seek to exploit them in this surprisingly effective thriller. Ejiofor delivers the goods in a darkly subtle turn while Tautou delightfully broadens her range. **107m/C; VHS, DVD, Blu-Ray.** *GB* Chiwetel Ejiofor; Audrey Tautou; Sergi Lopez; Sophie Okonedo; Zlatko Buric; Benedict Wong; ***D:*** Stephen Frears; ***W:*** Steven Knight; ***C:*** Chris Menges; ***M:*** Nathan Larson.

Dirty Rotten Scoundrels ♪♪♪ **1988 (PG)** A remake of the 1964 "Bedtime Story," in which two confidence tricksters on the Riviera endeavor to rip off a suddenly rich American woman, and each other. Caine and Martin are terrific, Martin has some of his best physical comedy ever, and Headly is charming as the prey who's always one step ahead of them. Fine direction from Oz, the man who brought us the voice of Yoda in "The Empire Strikes Back." **112m/C; VHS, DVD, Blu-Ray.** Steve Martin; Michael Caine; Glenne Headly; Anton Rodgers; Barbara Harris; Dana Ivey; ***D:*** Frank Oz; ***W:*** Dale Launer; Stanley Shapiro; Paul Henning; ***C:*** Michael Ballhaus; ***M:*** Miles Goodman.

A Dirty Shame ♪♪ **2004 (NC-17)** Outrageously tasteless fare has Waters back in familiar Baltimore territory with angry and repressed Sylvia Stickles (Ullman), who runs a convenience store with unfulfilled hubby Vaughn (Isaak). Their daughter Caprice (Blair) is locked in her room so she can't continue her career as a topless dancer. Sylvia suffers a concussion in a car crash and goes nympho'joining a cult of sex addicts led by local sexual healer Ray-Ray (Knoxville). Suddenly, their quiet blue-collar neighborhood is under siege from fetish freaks! It's all low-rent and tawdry exaggeration with a flimsy plot. It doesn't quite work, but then Waters has never let slick technique interfere with his fun. **89m/C; DVD.** Tracey Ullman; Johnny Knoxville; Selma Blair; Chris Isaak; Suzanne Shepherd; Mink Stole; Patty (Patricia Campbell) Hearst; Jackie Hoffman; ***Cameo(s):*** Ricki Lake; David Hasselhoff; ***D:*** John Waters; ***W:*** John Waters; ***C:*** Steve Gainer; ***M:*** George S. Clinton.

Dirty Tricks ♪♪ **2000** Based on the novel by Michael Dibdin. Struggling Oxford language tutor Edward is both charming and a manipulative liar. A dinner invitation leads to an affair, marriage, death, and money—but does that mean murder as well? Determined police inspector Moss certainly thinks Edward has done something suspicious. **146m/C; DVD.** *GB* Martin Clunes; James Bolam; Julie Graham; George Potts; Neil Dudgeon; Lindsay Duncan; Matt Bardock; Anna Popplewell; ***D:*** Paul Seed; ***W:*** Nigel Williams; ***C:*** John Kenway; ***M:*** Jim Parker. **TV**

Dirty Wars ♪♪ **2013** Director and investigative reporter Scahill goes deep into the hidden world of covert wars conducted by America, including battles in Afghanistan, Yemen, and Somalia. The film effectively blurs the line between documentary and narrative filmmaking as Scahill's approach is very hands-on, leading to a production that's far from a detached examination. In illuminating unreported conflicts and interviewing men who hold unimaginable power on the international scene, Scahill does the kind of investigative journalism that's too often missing from TV and newspaper reporting, adding another interesting chapter to the saga of modern warfare. **90m/C; DVD.** ***D:*** Rick Rowley; ***W:*** David Riker; Jeremy Scahill; ***C:*** Rick Rowley; ***M:*** David Harrington.

Dirty Work 1/2 **1997 (PG-13)** You'll notice that star and ex-Saturday Night Live newsguy MacDonald isn't even trying to act, he's just doing his deadpan wise guy routine with a different name. His delivery and attitude, however, are about the only funny things in this tale of Mitch (MacDonald) and Sam (Lange), two losers who can't keep a job but have a talent for petty revenge. When Sam's father (Warden) has a heart attack, the boys decide to open a business specializing in dirty deeds done dirt cheap to pay for a heart transplant. Although the premise is good, the tricks are mostly of the junior high variety and don't seem quite dirty enough. Several unbilled cameos, including Adam Sandler, John Goodman and the late Chris Farley. **81m/C; VHS, DVD.** Norm MacDonald; Artie Lange; Chevy Chase; Don Rickles; Jack Warden; Traylor Howard; Christopher McDonald; Chris Farley; Gary Coleman; Ken Norton; John Goodman; Adam Sandler; Fred Wolf; ***D:*** Bob Saget; ***W:*** Fred Wolf; ***C:*** Arthur Albert; ***M:*** Richard Gibbs.

Disappearance 1/2 **2002 (PG-13)** The vacationing Henley family stumble across the ghost town of Weaver, New Mexico, decide to stop long enough to take some photos, and get stranded. Turns out that something is inhabiting the town and it probably isn't human. Ending's a let-down. **91m/C; VHS, DVD.** Harry Hamlin; Susan Dey; Jeremy Lelliott; ***D:*** Walter Klenhard; ***W:*** Walter Klenhard; ***C:*** David Connell; ***M:*** Shirley Walker. **CABLE**

The Disappearance of Alice Creed **2009 (R)** The debut feature of Blakeson is an efficient Brit crime drama with a cast of three and a claustrophobic setting. Ex-cons, paranoid Vic (Marsan) and his resentful subordinate Danny (Comptson), kidnap Alice (Arterton) to get a multimillion Euro ransom from her wealthy father. There's secret connections and multiple betrayals that complicate things and Alice turns out to be a lot tougher than she looks. **100m/C; Blu-Ray.** *GB* Gemma Arterton; Martin Compston; Eddie Marsan; ***D:*** J. Blakeson; ***W:*** J. Blakeson; ***C:*** Philipp Blaubach; ***M:*** Marc Canham.

The Disappearance of Eleanor Rigby 1/2 **2014 (R)** Technically three films, "Him," "Her" and "Them," this unique project tells the story of Connor Ludlow (McAvoy) and Eleanor Rigby (Chastain), an unhappily married couple living in New York. The "Him" version of the film tells the story from his angle, "Her" from hers, while "Them" blends the two standalone films into one experience. Whatever form the film is seen in, it's a remarkable achievement, carried by its leads. The "Them" version is the strongest and breaking them apart feels more like a clever-but-unnecessary experiment. **123m/C; DVD, Blu-Ray.** Jessica Chastain; James McAvoy; William Hurt; Isabelle Huppert; Ciaran Hinds; Jess Weixler; Viola Davis; Bill Hader; ***D:*** Ned Benson; ***W:*** Ned Benson; ***C:*** Christopher Blauvelt; ***M:*** Son Lux.

The Disappearance of Garcia Lorca 1/2 *Death in Granada; Lorca* **1996 (R)** In 1954, Spanish-born journalist Ricardo Fernandez (Morales) returns to Granada to look into the death of his idol, poet/playwright Gabriel Garcia Lorca (Garcia). Ricardo's family fled Spain for Puerto Rico in 1936, at the start of the Spanish Civil War, when anti-fascist Lorca was executed. Ricardo wants to find out just who Lorca's killers were but Franco's Spain is a country eager to bury its past. Based on two books by Ian Gibson. **114m/C; VHS, Streaming.** *SP* Esai Morales; Andy Garcia; Edward James Olmos; Jeroen Krabbe; Miguel Ferrer; Giancarlo Giannini; Marcela Wallerstein; Jose Coronado; ***D:*** Marcos Zurinaga; ***W:*** Marcos Zurinaga; Neil Cohen; Juan Antonio Ramos; ***C:*** Juan Ruiz-Anchia; ***M:*** Mark McKenzie.

The Disappearance of Vonnie **1994** CBS TV true crime story, set in 1981. Shady Ron Rickman claims his troubled wife Vonnie has left him and their daughter. Her sister Corrine is certain something much worse has happened and presses the cops to investigate. Ron is eventually arrested and tried for murder, though there's no body. **91m/C; DVD.** Joe Penny; Ann Jillian; Graham Beckel; Robert Wisden; Alicia Witt; Kim Zimmer; ***D:*** Graeme Campbell; ***W:*** Ellen Weston; ***C:*** Richard Leiterman; ***M:*** Richard Bellis. **TV**

Disappearances **2006 (PG-13)** Quebec Bill (Kristofferson) and his teenaged son Wild Bill (McDermott) travel into the Canadian backwoods to run bootleg whiskey in 1932 so they can save the family's Vermont farm. Elements of magical realism throw off the simpler family adventure plot. Based on the novel by Howard Frank Mosher. **103m/C; DVD.** Kris Kristofferson; Lothaire Bluteau; Luis Guzman; William Sanderson; Charlie McDermott; Gary Farmer; Genevieve Bujold; ***D:*** Jay Craven; ***W:*** Jay Craven; ***C:*** Wolfgang Held; ***M:*** Judy Hyman; Jeff Claus. **VIDEO**

The Disappeared **2008** Teenager Matthew suffers a breakdown and is institutionalized after his eight-year-old brother Tom goes missing while Matthew was partying. He blames himself and so does his violence-prone dad Jack (Wise), who's got his own secrets. When Matthew returns to their south London housing estate, he begins hearing Tom's voice asking for help and thinks he's going crazy again. But Matthew will do anything to find out what happened to his brother. **95m/C; DVD.** *GB* Harry Treadaway; Greg Wise; Tom Felton; Alex Jennings; Niki Amuka-Bird; Lewis Lemperuer Palmer; Ros Leeming; Finlay Robertson; ***D:*** Johnny Kevorkian; ***W:*** Johnny Kevorkian; Neil Murphy; ***C:*** Diego Rodriguez; ***M:*** Ilan Eshkeri.

Disappearing Acts 1/2 **2000 (R)** Zora Banks (Lathan) is a college-educated music teacher with dreams of becoming a singer. She meets high school dropout Franklin (Snipes), who's doing construction work and wants to become a contractor. Neither wants a relationship but opposites still attract and they get involved. But not without trouble. Based on the 1989 novel by Terry McMillan. **115m/C; VHS, DVD.** Sanaa Lathan; Wesley Snipes; Regina Hall; Clark Johnson; John Amos; CCH Pounder; Aunjanue Ellis; Lisa Arrindell Anderson; Kamaal Fareed; Michael Imperioli; ***D:*** Gina Prince-Bythewood; ***W:*** Lisa Jones; ***C:*** Tami Reiker. **CABLE**

Disappearing in America 1/2 **2008** Irishman Sean gets mixed up in an IRA bombing that makes him a fugitive. He's smuggled into San Francisco with a new identity but one of his smugglers decides to exploit Sean's vulnerable position by forcing him to help with his drug deals or he'll expose him. **84m/C; DVD.** Richard Eden; David Polcyn; Anna-Marie Wayne; Devin DiGonno; ***D:*** Erik Rodgers; ***W:*** David Polcyn; Erik Rodgers; ***C:*** Erik Rodgers; ***M:*** Chris Fudurich. **VIDEO**

The Disappointments Room **WOOF! 2016 (R)** This is yet another bland haunted house movie that basically went straight to DVD and should be avoided at all costs. How the reasonably talented D.J. Caruso got sucked into directing this is the real mystery. Dana (Beckinsale) and David (Raido) are looking for a fresh start after the death of their infant daughter. They move to a new home and, well, frightening things start happening. They learn that the house had a mysterious locked room where deplorable things happened. The realtor probably didn't include that in the listing. Based on a true story. **92m/C; DVD.** Kate Beckinsale; Mel Raido; Lucas Till; Duncan Joiner; Gerald McRaney; ***D:*** D.J. Caruso; ***W:*** D.J. Caruso; Wentworth Miller; ***C:*** Rogier Stoffers; ***M:*** Brian Tyler.

The Disaster Artist **2017 (R)** The true story of enigmatic actor Tommy Wiseau (J. Franco) and the creation of "The Room." After befriending Wiseau in an acting class, Greg Sestero (D. Franco) moves with Wiseau to Los Angeles. Though Greg lands acting auditions and a girlfriend Amber (Brie), Tommy decides to get noticed by making his own film. Seemingly self-financed, Tommy writes and directs "The Room" but shows a knack for awkward yet hilarious moments of filmmaking. Greg has a role in "The Room," which early audiences see as a comedy rather than the serious film it aspires to be. Full of heart but lacking in depth. **104m/C; DVD, Blu-Ray.** Dave Franco; James Franco; Seth Rogen; Ari Graynor; Alison Brie; ***D:*** James Franco; ***W:*** Scott Neustadter; Michael H. Weber; ***C:*** Brandon Trost; ***M:*** Dave Porter. Golden Globes '18: Actor--Mus./Comedy (Franco).

Disaster Movie **WOOF! 2008 (PG-13)** Aptly titled flick with barely a premise, let alone a plot, to set it up. There's something about a guy trying to rescue his girlfriend from a library. Devolves into a vile stew of tired pop-culture references, scatological "humor," and an unrelenting stream of send-ups that are as unfunny as they are uninspired. Writers/directors Friedberg and Selzer insist on wringing out every drop of stupidity from their movie-spoof franchise. Thankfully they're running out of genres. **90m/C; Blu-Ray, On Demand.** Matt Lanter; Tad Hilgenbrink; Carmen Electra; Vanessa Minnillo; Gary 'G-Thang' Johnson; Nicole Parker; Crista Flanagan; Kim Kardashian; Ike Barinholtz; ***D:*** Jason Friedberg; Aaron Seltzer; ***W:*** Jason Friedberg; Aaron Seltzer; ***C:*** Shawn Maurer; ***M:*** Christopher Lennertz.

Disaster Zone: Volcano in New York **2006** A secret geo-thermal experiment by crazy scientist Levering (Ironside) triggers volcanic activity beneath New York City. Tunnel construction worker Matt (Mandylor) and his geologist ex-wife Susan (Paul) are part of an unlikely team that want to use the tunnels to draw the lava flow away from the city. **92m/C; DVD.** Costas Mandylor; Alexandra Paul; Michael Ironside; Pascale Hutton; Kaj-Erik Eriksen; Matthew Bennett; ***D:*** Robert Lee; ***W:*** Sarah Watson; ***C:*** Adam Sliwinski; ***M:*** Michael Richard Plowman. **CABLE**

Disciple of Death **1972 (R)** Raven plays "The Stranger," a ghoul who sacrifices virgins to the Devil. **82m/C; VHS, DVD.** *GB* Mike Raven; Ronald Lacey; Stephen Bradley; Virginia Wetherell; ***D:*** Tom Parkinson.

Disclosure **1994 (R)** Likable, responsible executive and family man (Douglas) finds himself sexually harassed by his ex-lover turned dragon-lady boss (Moore). But when he rejects her lusty come-on, she points the finger at him. One-dimensional characters and hollow material turn sexual harassment into a trivial issue. High-tech saga of corporate politics, while flashy, is nothing we haven't seen before. Douglas just can't pass up these "Regular Joe meets beautiful, horny babe, bad things happen" roles, can he? Based on the Michael Crichton novel. **129m/C; VHS, DVD, Blu-Ray.** Michael Douglas; Demi Moore; Donald Sutherland; Caroline Goodall; Dylan Baker; Dennis Miller; Rosemary Forsyth; Roma Maffia; ***D:*** Barry Levinson; ***W:*** Paul Attanasio; ***C:*** Tony Pierce-Roberts; ***M:*** Ennio Morricone. Blockbuster '95: Drama Actress, T. (Moore); Blockbuster '96: Drama Actress, V. (Moore).

Disco and Atomic War 1/2 *Disko ja tuumasoda* **2014** This award-winning documentary offers a witty take on Estonia's liberation from the grips of the Soviet Union in the mid-1980s. Noting that until this this period, Soviet authority controlled nearly every part of life for Estonians including culture. No Western culture had reached the country, including rock music and non-propaganda television. All that changed when a large new television antenna was built just across the border in Finland, and Estonians could illegally view shows like "Dallas" and hear disco music. This event inspired a regime change which changed the course of Estonian history. **80m/C; DVD, Streaming, Download.** ***D:*** Jaak Kilmi; ***W:*** Jaak Kilmi; Kiur Aarma; ***C:*** Manfred Vainokivi; ***M:*** Ardo Ran Varres.

Disco Pigs 1/2 **2001** Pig (Murphy) and Runt (Cassidy) were born minutes apart in the same Dublin hospital and have grown up in adjoining houses. They share a telepathic bond as well as their own language and no one can separate them—until their first kiss when they turn 17. But Pig will stop at nothing to keep their bond. Adapted by Walsh from his play. **94m/C; VHS, DVD.** *IR* Cillian Murphy; Elaine Cassidy; Geraldine O'Rawe; Eleanor Methven; Brian F. O'Byrne; ***D:*** Kristen Sheridan; ***W:*** Enda Walsh; ***C:*** Igor Jadue-Lillo; ***M:*** Gavin Friday; Maurice Seezer.

The Discovery **2017** Thomas Harbor (Redford) has made arguably the most important discovery in the history of man by proving the existence of an afterlife. Almost immediately, millions of people start committing suicide, now certain that something else awaits. Into this new world, Harbor's son Will (Segel) travels to visit his father, who is now working on an even-more remarkable experiment: proving exactly what's next. On his way there, he meets a girl (Mara), and Charlie McDowell's drama gets distracted by a love story that never quite works. There are interesting ideas here that feel underdeveloped and the chemistry between the two leads simply doesn't exist. **102m/C; Streaming.** Robert Redford; Rooney Mara; Jason Segel; Mary Steenburgen; Jesse Plemons; ***D:*** Charlie McDowell; ***W:*** Charlie McDowell; Justin Lader; ***C:*** Sturla Brandth Grovlen; ***M:*** Danny Bensi; Saunder Jurriaans. **VIDEO**

The Discreet Charm of the Bourgeoisie *Le Charme Discret de la Bourgeoisie* **1972 (R)** Bunuel in top form, satirizing modern society. These six characters are forever sitting down to dinner, yet they never eat. Dreams and reality, actual or contrived, prevent their feast. **100m/C; VHS, DVD.** *FR* Fernando Rey; Delphine Seyrig; Jean-Pierre Cassel; Bulle Ogier; Michel Piccoli; Stephane Audran; Luis Bunuel; Milena Vukotic; ***D:*** Luis Bunuel; ***W:*** Luis Bunuel; Jean-Claude Carriere; ***C:*** Edmond Richard. Oscars '72: Foreign Film; British Acad. '73: Actress (Seyrig), Screenplay; Natl. Soc. Film Critics '72: Director (Bunuel), Film.

Discretion Assured 1/2 **1993 (R)** Successful businessman Trevor McCabe (York) finds himself in a romantic quandry with three women, leading to his involvement in embezzlement and murder. **97m/C; VHS, DVD.** Michael York; Jennifer O'Neill; Dee Wallace; Elizabeth (Ward) Gracen; ***D:*** Odorico Mendes.

The Disenchanted 1/2 *La Desenchantee* **1990** Seventeen-year-old Beth (Godreche) is having a rough time growing up. She's forced to look after her bedridden mother and younger brother and their survival depends on the generosity of her mother's ex-lover, who's now taking a more personal interest in the beautiful teenager. Meanwhile, Beth's arrogant boyfriend decides Beth should prove her love for him by sleeping with the ugliest man she can find. French with subtitles. **78m/C; VHS, DVD, Blu-Ray.** *FR* Judith Godreche; Ivan Desny; Therese Liotard; Malcolm Conrath; Marcel Bozonnet; ***D:*** Benoit Jacquot; ***W:*** Benoit Jacquot; ***C:*** Caroline Champetier; ***M:*** Jorge Arriagada.

Disengagement **2007** Israeli Uli (Levo) travels to France where his adoptive father has just died. He reconnects with his sister Ana (Binoche), who learns that her abandoned daughter Dana (Ivgy) is living in an Israeli settlement in Gaza and is about to be evicted because of the political situation with the Palestinians. Ana insists on going back to Israel with Uli in an effort to reunite with Dana and suffers cultural shock after meeting the fervent settlers. English, French, Hebrew, and Arabic with subtitles. **116m/C; DVD.** *FR IS* Juliette Binoche; Liron Levo; Dana Ivgy; Jeanne Moreau; Hiam Abbass; Barbara Hendricks; Tomer Russo; ***D:*** Amos Gitai; ***W:*** Amos Gitai; Marie-Jose Sanselme; ***C:*** Christian Berger; ***M:*** Simon Stockhausen.

Disgrace **2008 (R)** Contemptuous, arrogant, predatory, and racist Cape Town university academic David Lurie (Malkovich) finally pays the price for his ill-advised affair with a student when he's dismissed from his position. David then decides to visit his daughter Lucy (Haines) at her Eastern Cape farm, eventually getting a job at the local animal shelter (where he euthanizes a number of stray dogs). David and Lucy are attacked by three black youths, leaving them with physical and emotional injuries, but Lucy refuses to involve the police in a personal post-apartheid attempt at reconciliation. Adaptation of the 1999 J.M. Coetzee novel; filmed on location in South Africa. **119m/C; DVD.** *AU* John Malkovich; Eriq Ebouaney; Jessica Haines; Antoinette Engel; ***D:*** Steve Jacobs; ***W:*** Anna Maria Monticelli; ***C:*** Steve Arnold; ***M:*** Antony Partos; Greame Koehne.

The Dish **2000 (PG-13)** Tells the true story of a NASA official (Neill) and his group of local Aussie technicians as they manned the satellite dish responsible for bringing to TV sets around the world man's first footsteps on the moon in 1969. Originally only a backup plan, the Australian dish was called into action when the receiver in California became useless after a change in Apollo 11's flight path. Treats the central, spectacular event itself with dignity and appropriate awe, but also squeezes humor and emotion out of all that leads up to it. **104m/C; VHS, DVD.** *AU* Sam Neill; Patrick Warburton; Tom Long; Kevin Harrington; Bille Brown; John McMartin; Tayler Kane; Eliza Szonert; Carl Snell; ***D:*** Rob Sitch; ***W:*** Rob Sitch; Santo Cilauro; Tom Gleisner; Jane Kennedy; ***C:*** Graeme Wood; ***M:*** Edmund Choi.

The Dish & the Spoon 1/2 **2011 (R)** Frustrating drama with a too-hysterical performance from Gerwig. Rose discovers her husband is an adulterer and rushes out of the house in her pajamas, jumps in her car, and takes off. Her emotional meltdown extends to picking up a down-on-his-luck young Brit (known only as Boy) who has his own romantic woes. They eventually end up at her parent's beach house, but Rose can't control her odd and increasingly violent actions. **92m/C; DVD.** Greta Gerwig; Olly Alexander; ***D:*** Alison Bagnall; ***W:*** Alison Bagnall; Andrew Lewis; ***C:*** Mark Schwartzband; ***M:*** Dean Wareham.

Dish Dogs 1/2 **1998 (R)** Morgan (Astin) and Jason (Lillard) are a couple of bachelor best friends who cruise SoCal in their old Chevy looking for the best surfing and work as dishwashers to make ends meets. But the slacker duo are beset by love (Ward, Elizabeth) and cracks surface in their buddyhood. **96m/C; VHS, DVD.** Matthew Lillard; Sean Astin; Shannon Elizabeth; Maitland Ward; Brian Dennehy; Richard Moll; ***D:*** Bob (Robert) Kubilos; ***W:*** Ashley Scott Meyers; Nathan Ives; ***C:*** Mark Vicente; ***M:*** Herman Beeftink.

Dishdogz **2005 (PG-13)** Kevin (Allman) is tired of working hard to make a buck until he becomes part of the kitchen crew at an extreme sports summer camp. To win the affections of Cassidy (Duff), Kevin teams up with his fellow workers, who call themselves the Dishdogz, to take part in a camp competition to see who's the best skateboarder. Kevin also has to contend with his tough boss Tony (Perry), who just happens to know some old school tricks he might be willing to pass on. **90m/C; DVD.** Marshall Allman; Luke Perry; Haylie Duff; Timothy Lee DePriest; ***D:*** Mikey Hilb; ***W:*** Steven Sessions; ***C:*** Christopher Gosch. **VIDEO**

Dishonored 1/2 **1931** Dated spy drama has Dietrich playing secret agent X-27 in WWI and masquerading on the side as a peasant girl. Although not one of the more famous Dietrich-Sternberg productions, its camp plot and Dietrich's lavish performance make it worth watching. Based on the infamous spy Mata Hari, who was shot by the French in 1917 for espionage. **91m/B; DVD, Blu-Ray.** Marlene Dietrich; Victor McLaglen; Lew Cody; Gustav von Seyffertitz; Warner Oland; Barry Norton; Davison Clark; Wilfred Lucas; ***D:*** Josef von Sternberg; ***W:*** Josef von Sternberg; Daniel N. Rubin; ***C:*** Lee Garmes.

Dishonored Lady 1/2 **1947** After her ex-boyfriend is murdered, a female art director finds that she's the number one suspect. When put on trial for the dastardly deed, she takes the fifth in this mediocre melodrama. **85m/B; VHS, DVD.** Hedy Lamarr; Dennis O'Keefe; William Lundigan; John Loder; ***D:*** Robert Stevenson.

Disney's Teacher's Pet *Teacher's Pet: The Movie* **2004 (PG)** Disney strikes again with this zany Pinocchio story about a blue dog who wants to become a real boy like his owner Leonard (Fleming). Wanna-be Spot (Lane) dresses as a boy (named Scott) and follows Leonard to school until he discovers his chance: a mad scientist named Ivan Krank (Grammar) who claims to be able to change animals into people. Unfortunately, no one considers Spot's "dog years," which cause him to end up not a boy but a middle-aged man. Creative script and visual style, excellent performances by Lane and Grammar, and loads of wit and charm make this an above-average cartoon that appeals to children and parents alike. Based on the ABC cartoon. **73m/C; VHS, DVD.** ***V:*** Nathan Lane; Kelsey Grammer; David Ogden Stiers; Jerry Stiller; Shaun Fleming; Debra Jo Rupp; Paul (Pee-wee Herman) Reubens; Megan Mullally; Rob Paulsen; Wallace Shawn; Estelle Harris; Jay Thomas; Genie Francis; Anthony Geary; Pamela Segall; Lauren Tom; Ken Swofford; Mae Whitman; Rosalyn Landor; ***D:*** Timothy Bjorklund; ***W:*** Bill Steinkellner; Cheri(e) Steinkellner; ***M:*** Stephen James Taylor.

Disney's The Kid **2000 (PG)** Cynical 40-year-old Willis comes face-to-face with his 8-year-old self (Breslin), who wants to know how he grew up to become such a jerk. It's Disney, so there are Important Lessons to be learned, and dramatic changes in behavior to be witnessed, but Breslin, Willis, and Tomlin as his assistant, make the schmaltz bearable with excellent performances. Wells' sophisticated, funny script helps smooth out Turteltaub's heavy-handed direction. **104m/C; VHS, DVD.** Bruce Willis; Emily Mortimer; Jean Smart; Spencer Breslin; Chi McBride; Lily Tomlin; Dana Ivey; Daniel von Bargen; Nick (Nicholas) Chinlund; ***D:*** Jon Turteltaub; ***W:*** Audrey Wells; ***C:*** Peter Menzies, Jr.; ***M:*** Jerry Goldsmith.

Disobedience 1/2 **2017 (R)** A moving, intimate melodrama based on the novel by Naomi Alderman. When rabbi Rav Krushka (Lesser) dies suddenly during a sermon to his Orthodox Jewish congregation in London, his daughter Ronit (Weisz), a New York-based photographer who left years ago, returns for the funeral. There, the now secular Ronit learns at the funeral that her father's former protégé Dovid (Nivola) and her childhood friend - and love interest - Esti (McAdams) are now married. As she interacts with the couple, the complexity and power of their relationships become clear. The film effectively explores the strictures on women in society, and features a subtle performance by Weisz. **114m/C; DVD, Blu-Ray.** Rachel Weisz; Rachel McAdams; Anton Lesser; Alessandro Nivola; Allan Corduner; ***D:*** Sebastián Lelio; ***W:*** Sebastián Lelio; Rebecca Lenkiewicz; ***C:*** Danny Cohen; ***M:*** Matthew Herbert.

Disorder 1/2 **2006 (R)** David Randall was accused of a double murder and sent to a mental hospital where he was diagnosed as a paranoid schizophrenic. Now released, David heads back to his hometown to prove his innocence but soon thinks that the same masked killer is now after his friend Melissa. His shrink and the sheriff think David has gone off his meds and may be dangerous. **103m/C; DVD.** Darren Kendrick; Lauren Seikaly; Thomas Ruderstaller; Alan Samulski; Sean Eager; ***D:*** Jack Thomas Smith; ***W:*** Jack Thomas Smith; ***C:*** Jonathan Belinski; ***M:*** Joel Goodman. **VIDEO**

Disorder 1/2 *Maryland* **2016** Vincent (Schoenaerts) is a French Special Forces soldier dealing with PTSD as he heads into private security as a bodyguard for a wealthy Lebanese businessman. Drawn to his gorgeous wife Jessie (Kruger), he's convinced that something bad is about to happen. With incredible sound design, writer/director Winocour puts us in Vincent's head, uncertain if the threat on the horizon is imaginary or real. The two leads are fantastic but it basically descends into a routine home invasion flick. **98m/C; DVD.** Matthias Schoenaerts; Diane Kruger; Paul Hamy; Victor Pontecorvo; Zaïd Errougui-Demonsant; ***D:*** Alice Winocour; ***W:*** Alice Winocour; ***C:*** Georges Lechaptois; ***M:*** Mike Levy.

Disorderlies **1987 (PG)** Members of the popular rap group the Fat Boys cavort as incompetent hospital orderlies assigned to care for a cranky millionaire. Fat jokes abound. **86m/C; DVD.** Mark Morales; Darren Robinson; Damon Wimbley; Anthony Geary; Tony Plana; Ralph Bellamy; ***D:*** Michael A. Schultz; ***W:*** Mark Feldberg; Mitchell Klebanoff; ***C:*** Rolf Kestermann; ***M:*** Anne Dudley.

Disorderly Orderly 1/2 **1964** When Jerry Lewis gets hired as a hospital orderly, nothing stands upright long with him around. Vintage slapstick Lewis running amuck in a nursing home. **90m/C; VHS, DVD.** Jerry Lewis; Glenda Farrell; Everett Sloane; Kathleen Freeman; Susan Oliver; ***D:*** Frank Tashlin.

Disorganized Crime **1989 (R)** On the lam from the law, Bernsen attempts to organize a group of his ex-con buddies to pull off the perfect heist. Before the boys can organize, however, the cops are hot on Bernsen's trail, and he must vacate the meeting place. Good cast attempts to lift this movie beyond script. **101m/C; VHS, DVD, Blu-Ray.** Lou Diamond Phillips; Fred Gwynne; Corbin Bernsen; Ruben Blades; Hoyt Axton; Ed O'Neill; Daniel Roebuck; William Russ; ***D:*** Jim Kouf; ***W:*** Jim Kouf; ***C:*** Ron Garcia; ***M:*** Hoyt Axton; David Newman.

Disraeli **1979** Flamboyant, irreverant, a dandy, and a womanizer, Benjamin Disraeli (McShane) was also England's first Jewish Prime Minister and one of its greatest. This British miniseries examines the controversial figure and the Victorian era his life and career spanned. **208m/C; VHS, DVD.** *GB* Ian McShane; Mary Peach; Mark Dignam; Leigh Lawson; Rosemary Leach; Anton Rodgers; Margaret Whiting; ***D:*** Claude Whatham; ***W:*** David Butler.

Distant Drums **1951** A small band of adventurers tries to stop the Seminole War in the Florida Everglades. **101m/C; VHS, DVD, Blu-Ray.** Gary Cooper; Mari Aldon; Robert Barrat; Richard Webb; Ray Teal; Arthur Hunnicutt; ***D:*** Raoul Walsh; ***M:*** Max Steiner.

Distant Thunder **1988 (R)** A scarred Vietnam vet, who has become a recluse, and his estranged son reunite in the Washington State wilderness, causing him to reflect on his isolation. Strong premise and cast watered down by weak script. **114m/C; VHS, DVD.** *CA* John Lithgow; Ralph Macchio; Kerrie Keane; Janet Margolin; Rick Rosenthal; ***D:*** Rick Rosenberg; ***C:*** Ralf Bode; ***M:*** Maurice Jarre.

A Distant Trumpet 1/2 **1964** Sixties teen crush Donahue is miscast in the last western directed by Raoul Walsh, who appears to have been just going through the motions. In 1883, West Point Army grad Matthew Hazard is sent to Arizona's desolate Fort Delivery, which is soon beset by attacking Apaches. The Red Rocks/Painted Desert locations are worth a look. **117m/C; DVD.** Troy Donahue; Suzanne Pleshette; Diane McBain; James Gregory; William Reynolds; Claude Akins; ***D:*** Raoul Walsh; ***W:*** John Twist; Richard Fielder; Albert Beich; ***C:*** William Clothier; ***M:*** Max Steiner.

Distant Voices, Still Lives **1988** A profoundly executed, disturbing film chronicling a British middle-class family through the maturation of the three children, under the dark shadow of their abusive, malevolent father. An evocative, heartbreaking portrait of British life from WWII on, and of the rhythms of dysfunctional families. A film festival favorite. **87m/C; VHS, Blu-Ray, Streaming.** *GB* Freda Dowie; Pete Postlethwaite; Angela Walsh; Dean Williams; Lorraine Ashbourne; ***D:*** Terence Davies; ***W:*** Terence Davies; ***C:*** Patrick Duval. L.A. Film Critics '89: Foreign Film.

The Distinguished Gentleman **1992 (R)** A small-time con man (Murphy) manages to scam his way into a political career and winds up in Congress. The other characters serve mostly as foils for Murphy's comedic talent. Viewers will laugh despite the story's predictablity. **122m/C; VHS, DVD.** Eddie Murphy; Lane Smith; Sheryl Lee Ralph; Joe Don Baker; Victoria Rowell; Grant Shaud; Kevin McCarthy; Charles S. Dutton; James Garner; Gary Frank; ***D:*** Jonathan Lynn; ***W:*** Marty Kaplan; ***C:*** Gabriel Beristain; ***M:*** Randy Edelman.

Distorted **2018 (R)** A psychological thriller centered on a gadget-laden condominium seemingly with a deadly agenda. With her long-suffering husband Russel (Fletcher), artist Lauren (Ricci) moves into a secure condo complex. Their new home features many electronic devices intended to make their lives easier. Lauren soon believes that the gadgets are targeting her, but her concerns are dismissed by her husband and others who live in the complex, in part because of her bipolar disorder. Undeterred, she consults with an investigative journalist (Cuscack) who is researching brainwashing experiments. Though Ricci gives a convincing performance as the terrified woman, the underwhelming story does not justify her paranoia. **86m/C; Streaming.** *CA* Christina Ricci; John Cusack; Brendan Fletcher; Nicole Anthony; Vicellous Shannon; ***D:*** Rob W. King; ***W:*** Arne Olsen; ***C:*** Mark Dobrescu.

District B13 *Banlieue 13* **2004 (R)** Fast-paced and suspenseful actioner set in 2010 outside Paris. Things are so bad that the authorities have walled off the drug-ridden district and left it to crime boss Taha. Local Leito takes a stand by flushing a shipment of Taha's dope and then runs for his life and into undercover cop Damien, who learns that a massive bomb is now in Taha's possession. French with subtitles. **85m/C; DVD, Blu-Ray.** *FR* David Belle; Cyril Raffaelli; Larbi (Bibi) Naceri; Dany Verissimo; ***D:*** Pierre Morel; ***W:*** Luc Besson; Larbi (Bibi) Naceri; ***C:*** Manuel Teran.

District 9 **2009 (R)** Based on director Blomkamp's 2005 short film "Alive in Joburg" this is memorable, speculative sci fi that finds alien refugees unwillingly trapped above Johannesburg when their spacecraft breaks down. A fearful government confines the insectoid-looking creatures, derisively called 'prawns,' to an increasingly filthy shantytown. After 20 years, corporate bureaucrat Wilkus van der Merwe (Copley) is charged with moving the aliens to the even-more remote District 10. Blithely going about his job, Wilkus finds his own life changing when he encounters alien goo that begins to alter his DNA, changing him not only physically but morally as he becomes 'alien' himself—and very valuable to the powers-that-be. **111m/C; DVD, Blu-Ray.** *NZ* David James; Sharlto Copley; Mandla Gaduka; Vanessa Haywood; ***V:*** Jason Cope; ***D:*** Neill Blomkamp; ***W:*** Neill Blomkamp; Terri Tatchell; ***C:*** Trent Opaloch; ***M:*** Clinton Shorter.

District 13: Ultimatum *Banlieue 13: Ultimatum* **2009 (R)** This sequel to "District B13" has local criminal Leito (Belle) re-teaming with law enforcement buddy Damien (Raffaelli) to save the locked-down, crime-ridden sector of Paris known as District 13 once again. This time, corrupt cops led by Gassman (Duval) are trying to raze the lawless suburb and get rich off of the real estate rights. The plot is just a framework to hang the well-choreographed action sequences that utilize the acrobatic technique known as parkour, which star Belle helped originate. Fun for stunt fans, but not too deep. French with subtitles. **101m/C; Blu-Ray, On Demand.** *FR* Cyril Raffaelli; David Belle; Daniel Duval; Philippe Torreton; Elodie Yung; ***D:*** Patrick Alessandrin; ***W:*** Luc Besson; ***C:*** Jean-Francois Hensgens; ***M:*** Alexandre Mahout.

Disturbance 1/2 **1989** The two personas of a young schizophrenic get him entangled in a mysterious string of murders. **81m/C; VHS, DVD.** Timothy Greeson; Lisa Geoffreion; ***D:*** Cliff Guest.

Disturbia 1/2 **2007 (PG-13)** Unacknowledged updated teen version of "Rear Window." Troubled Kale (LaBeouf) is placed on house arrest with an electronic ankle monitor after a school incident. His fed-up mom (Moss) cuts off his videogame/cable access, so Kale begins spying on the locals with his handy binoculars. At first he's mostly interested in hottie girl next door, Ashley (Roemer), but then Kale becomes suspicious of neighbor Mr. Turner (Morse) and whether he could actually be the serial killer from local news reports. Kale recruits Ashley and pal Ronnie (Yoo) to be his legs even though they question his accusations. Morse is effectively creepy in what amounts to the Raymond Burr role and LeBeouf makes the most of Kale's foolishness and smart-aleck wit. **105m/C; DVD, Blu-Ray, HD-DVD.** Shia LaBeouf; David Morse; Carrie-Anne Moss; Jose Pablo Cantillo; Sarah Roemer; Aaron Yoo; ***D:*** D.J. Caruso; ***W:*** Christopher Landon; Carl Ellsworth; ***C:*** Rogier Stoffers; ***M:*** Geoff Zanelli.

Disturbing Behavior 1/2 **1998 (R)** Gavin (Stahl) welcomes new kid in town Steve (Marsden) by pointing out the social castes at Cradle Bay High School. The Uber-group is the goody-goody Blue Ribbons, an excessively straitlaced and perky group of athletes and cheerleaders. Along with fellow outcasts Rachel (Holmes) and U.V. (Donella), they joke about a possible conspiracy, but when Gavin shows up with a crewcut and an inordinate love of pep rallies and bake sales, his friends know something is up. They discover that parents have allowed the school shrink (Greenwood) to use drugs to tinker with the brains of the Blue Ribbons. They also discover that the Stepford Teens' vanilla lives are topped with sprinkles of homicidal fury. Director Nutter creates just the right creepy and paranoid mood in his feature debut. **84m/C; VHS, DVD, Blu-Ray.** James Marsden; Nick Stahl; Katie Holmes; Bruce Greenwood; William Sadler; Chad E. Donella; Ethan (Randall) Embry; Steve Railsback; ***D:*** David Nutter; *W:* Scott Rosenberg; *C:* John Bartley; *M:* Mark Snow. MTV Movie Awards '99: Breakthrough Perf. (Holmes).

Diva 1/2 **1982 (R)** While at a concert given by his favorite star, a young French courier secretly tapes a soprano who has refused to record. The film follows the young man through Paris as he flees from two Japanese recording pirates, and a couple of crooked undercover police who are trying to cover-up for the chief who not only has a mistress, but runs a prostitution ring. Brilliant and dazzling photography compliment the eclectic soundtrack. **123m/C; VHS, DVD.** *FR* Frederic Andrei; Roland Bertin; Richard Bohringer; Gerard Darmon; Jacques Fabbri; Wilhelmenia Wiggins Fernandez; Dominique Pinon; *D:* Jean-Jacques Beineix; *W:* Jean-Jacques Beineix; *C:* Philippe Rousselot; *M:* Vladimir Cosma. Cesar '82: Cinematog., Score, Sound; Natl. Soc. Film Critics '82: Cinematog.

Dive Bomber **1941** Exciting aviation film that focuses on medical problems related to flying. Flynn stars as an aviator-doctor who conducts experiments to eliminate pilot-blackout. MacMurray, Toomey, and Heydt perform well as three flyboys stationed in Hawaii. Great flying sequences filmed at San Diego's naval base with extra scenes shot at Pensacola. Warner Bros. released this film just months before the Japanese attacked Pearl Harbor. Based on the story "Beyond the Blue Sky" by Frank Wead. **130m/B; DVD.** Errol Flynn; Fred MacMurray; Ralph Bellamy; Alexis Smith; Regis Toomey; Robert Armstrong; Allen Jenkins; Craig Stevens; Herbert Anderson; Louis Jean Heydt; Dennie Moore; *D:* Michael Curtiz; *W:* Robert Buckner; Frank Wead; *C:* Winton C. Hoch; Bert Glennon; *M:* Max Steiner.

The Dive from Clausen's Pier 1/2 **2005** Carrie (Trachtenberg) has already realized her feelings for fiance Mike (Estes) have changed when he is left paralyzed in a diving accident. This doesn't stop her from suddenly moving to Manhattan to make a new life and find a new guy (Maher). But Carrie just as suddenly questions where she really belongs. Anyone who's read the Ann Packer novel is likely to be disappointed at the changes and Trachtenberg seems too young for her lead role. **90m/C; DVD.** Michelle Trachtenberg; Sean Maher; Will Estes; Kristin Fairlie; Dylan Taylor; Janet Land; Diana Reis; *D:* Harry Winer; *W:* John Wierick; *C:* David (Robert) A. Greene; *M:* Bruce Broughton. **CABLE**

Divergent **2014 (PG-13)** The first film based on Veronica Roth's young adult trilogy. In a postwar, future Chicago, people are divided into five factions based on their personalities. For her own survival, teenager Tris Prior (Woodley) keeps secret that she is a Divergent, a combination of three traits. She chooses the warrior Dauntless faction and undergoes brutal initiation training with hunky instructor Four (James). Then Tris learns that there's a societal power grab planned by Erudite leader Jeanine Mathews (Winslet). Lots of narrative is needed to set up the sequels so only the leads make any impact, but director Burger makes sure the action keeps you interested. **143m/C; DVD, Blu-Ray.** Shailene Woodley; Theo James; Kate Winslet; Jai Courtney; Ansel Elgort; Miles Teller; Zoë Kravitz; Ben Lloyd-Hughes; Tony Goldwyn; Ashley Judd; Maggie Q; Ray Stevenson; Mekhi Phifer; *D:* Neil Burger; *W:* Evan Daugherty; Vanessa Taylor; *C:* Alwin Kuchler; *M:* Junkie XL.

Divided Heaven *Der Geteilte Himmel* **1964** East German drama. In 1961, Rita returns to her childhood village to recover from a breakdown. She remembers her romance with chemist Manfred and how they dealt so differently with Communist worker ideology, which has the disillusioned Manfred leaving for West Berlin. He thinks Rita will follow but she remains behind even as the Berlin Wall goes up. German with subtitles; based on the novel by Wolf, who also wrote the screenplay. **109m/B; DVD.** *GE* Renate Blume; Eberhard Esche; Hans Hardt-Hardtloff; Hilmar Thate; *D:* Konrad Wolf; *W:* Christa Wolf; *C:* Werner Bergmann; *M:* Hans-Dieter Hosalla.

Divided We Fall 1/2 *Musime si Pomahat* **2000 (PG-13)** In 1943, the inhabitants of an unnamed Czechoslovakian town are existing under the Nazi occupation. Josef (Polivka) recognizes his former employer David (Kassai), a Jew who has escaped the camps. Josef and his wife Marie (Siskova) agree to hide David in their home although they are under the scrutiny of Nazi collaborator Horst (Dusek), who keeps making passes at Marie. Although they are childless, Marie claims to be pregnant to get Horst to leave her alone. Which leads Josef to ask a delicate favor of David so they can make good on Marie's lie. Czech with subtitles. **123m/C; VHS, DVD.** *CZ* Boleslav Polivka; Anna Siskova; Csongor Kassai; Jaroslav Dusek; Jiri Pecha; Simona Stasova; Martin Huba; Vladimir Marek; Jiri Kodet; Richard Tesarik; *D:* Jan Hrebejk; *W:* Petr Jarchovsky; *C:* Jan Malir; *M:* Ales Brezina.

Divided We Stand **2000 (R)** Naive college coed Lisa joins the Black Student Coalition and soon accuses fellow member Robey of rape. However, BSC member and law student Jarrod, who knows what really happened, is hesitant to get involved. **81m/C; VHS, DVD.** Andrea Lisa; Crayton Robey; J.R. Jarrod; *D:* J.R. Jarrod; *W:* J.R. Jarrod; *C:* John Crawford; *M:* Charles D. Jackson; Sherwood Seward; Derek Seward.

Divine Intervention 1/2 **2007** Church- and romance-centered comedy-drama about change. When the very traditional Reverend Matthews (Avery) has a stroke and is unable to lead his fundamentalist Baptist church, a young minister with more nontraditional, hip preaching method is brought in as a temporary replacement. Reverend Robert Gibbs (Jonathan) soon wins over the reluctant congregation and attendance starts to increase. Reverend Gibbs also finds himself helping Divine (Lewis), a young teacher who lost her faith after her mother's death. Gibbs soon learns that she is Matthews' daughter, and the recovering minister does not approve of the relationship. The plot thickens when it becomes clear that Matthews may not be able to return, and the insecure Deacon Wells (Alonso) tries to ensure Gibbs does not permanently gain a place in the church or in Divine's life. **85m/C; DVD.** James Avery; Wesley Jonathan; Jazzmin Lewis; Laz Alonso; Carl Gilliard; *D:* Van Elder; *W:* Van Elder; *C:* Jonathan Hall.

The Divine Lady 1/2 **1929** Lavish historical/romantic drama. Lower-class Emma Hart (Griffith) falls for the charms of aristocrat Charles Greville (Keith) but when he becomes embarrassed by her, Charles readily passes her off to his enamored uncle William Hamilton (Warner), the British ambassador to Naples. Hamilton marries Emma and she becomes instrumental in getting the ships of British fleet commander Nelson (Varconi), who is battling Napoleon, resupplied. Nelson and Emma fall in love, but their adulterous relationship causes a scandal when they return to England. The E. Barrington novel was remade as 1941's "That Hamilton Woman." **105m/B; Silent; DVD.** Corinne Griffith; Victor Varconi; H.B. Warner; Ian Keith; Marie Dressler; Montagu Love; Dorothy (Dorothy G. Cummings) Cumming; Michael Vavitch; Helen Jerome Eddy; *D:* Frank Lloyd; *W:* Forrest Halsey; *C:* John Sietz. Oscars '29: Director (Lloyd).

Divine Secrets of the Ya-Ya Sisterhood **2002 (PG-13)** Southern dramedy with a group of girlfriends (Smith, Flanagan, Knight) who stage an intervention to help about-to-be-married, New York-based playwright Sidda Lee (Bullock) discover the truth about her eccentric, alcoholic Southern mama Vivi (Burstyn). Flashbacks ensue as we see the women as children in the 1930s when they formed their secret Ya-Ya society and then later to Vivi as a young women (played somewhat hysterically by Judd). The most fun bits, however, are those with the slightly cracked Southern belles now in their 70s. Female bonding, estrogen-fest gives short shrift to the men in these ladies' lives (shocking!). First time director Khouri lets these kooky dames (and the plot) run a little too wild. Based on the novels "Divine Secrets of the Ya-Ya Sisterhood" and "Little Altars Everywhere" by Rebecca Wells. **116m/C; VHS, DVD.** Ashley Judd; Sandra Bullock; Ellen Burstyn; Maggie Smith; James Garner; Fionnula Flanagan; Shirley Knight; Cherry Jones; Angus MacFadyen; Jacqueline McKenzie; Katy Selverstone; Kiersten Warren; Gina McKee; Matthew Settle; David Rasche; Frederick Koehler; Leslie Silva; Ron Dortoh; David Lee Smith; *D:* Callie Khouri; *W:* Callie Khouri; Mark Andrus; *C:* John Bailey; *M:* T-Bone Burnett.

The Diving Bell and the Butterfly 1/2 *Le Scaphandre et le Papillon* **2007 (PG-13)** The true story of French "Elle" magazine editor Jean-Dominique Bauby, who suffered a stroke that left him completely paralyzed but for his left eyelid. The film chronicles the process by which Bauby dictated his memoir by blinking that left eye as an assistant spoke the alphabet, signifying each individual letter with every blink. As if Bauby's story isn't tragic enough, he died just two days after his book was published in France. An emotionally wrenching, at times difficult to watch, poetic and richly-cinematic journey ripe with colorful and sensual images from Bauby's past life and his fully-functioning inner world as imagined by director Schnable. In French with subtitles and named after Bauby's biography. **112m/C; DVD.** *FR* Mathieu Amalric; Emmanuelle Seigner; Marie Josee Croze; Patrick Chesnais; Max von Sydow; Anne Consigny; Isaach de Bankole; Niels Arestrup; *D:* Julian Schnabel; *W:* Ronald Harwood; *C:* Janusz Kaminski. British Acad. '07: Adapt. Screenplay; Golden Globes '08: Director (Schnabel), Foreign Film; Ind. Spirit '08: Cinematog., Director (Schnabel).

Division 19 1/2 **2019** In 2039, personal anonymity does not exist and prisons have been turned into popular sources of entertainment by prison boss Neilsen (Doody). Millions of viewers tune into the pay-per-view experience and get to make life choices for prisoners, including violent fights, all day every day. One of the stars among the prisoners is handsome celebrity con Hardin Jones (Draven). After an off-the-grid group that includes Hardin's brother breaks Hardin out of prison, he finds a very different life. This dystopian science fiction film has a timely plot but too many subplots crowd the main story. **93m/C; DVD.** Alison Doody; Lotte Verbeek; Linus Roache; Clarke Peters; L. Scott Caldwell; *D:* S.A. Halewood; *W:* S.A. Halewood; *C:* Ben Moulden; *M:* Sebastian Fayle; David O'Dowda.

Divorce American Style 1/2 **1967** Dated but still amusing look at love, marriage, and the big D. Richard (Van Dyke) and Barbara (Reynolds) Harmon find their longtime marriage in a tailspin as they spend all their time arguing. They split but find single life and the dating game have their own pitfalls. **103m/C; VHS, DVD.** Dick Van Dyke; Debbie Reynolds; Jason Robards, Jr.; Jean Simmons; Van Johnson; Lee Grant; Joe Flynn; Shelley Berman; Martin Gabel; Tom Bosley; Dick Gautier; Eileen Brennan; *D:* Bud Yorkin; *W:* Norman Lear; *C:* Conrad L. Hall; *M:* Dave Grusin.

Divorce His, Divorce Hers **1972** The first half of this drama shows the crumbling of a marriage through the husband's eyes. The second half offers the wife's perspective. **144m/C; VHS, DVD.** Richard Burton; Elizabeth Taylor; *D:* Waris Hussein. **TV**

The Divorce of Lady X 1/2 **1938** A spoiled British debutante, in the guise of "Lady X," makes a woman-hating divorce lawyer eat his words through romance and marriage. Based on the play by Gilbert Wakefield. **92m/C; VHS, DVD.** *GB* Merle Oberon; Laurence Olivier; Ralph Richardson; Binnie Barnes; *D:* Tim Whelan; *C:* Harry Stradling, Sr.; *M:* Miklos Rozsa.

Divorce Wars: A Love Story **1982** Self-absorbed, high-powered Seattle divorce attorney Jack Sturgess (Selleck) has neglected his wife and kids for his successful practice. Now he gets to see what it's like from the other side of the table when fed-up wife Vickey (Curtin) files her own divorce petition and things turn petty. **96m/C; DVD.** Tom Selleck; Jane Curtin; Mimi Rogers; Viveca Lindfors; Candice Azzara; Charles Haid; Maggie Cooper; Joe Regalbuto; Joan Bennett; *D:* Donald Wrye; *W:* Donald Wrye; Linda Elstad; *C:* Tak Fujimoto; *M:* Paul Chihara. **TV**

Divorce—Italian Style 1/2 *Divorzio All'Italiana* **1962** A middle-aged baron bored with his wife begins directing his amorous attentions to a teenage cousin. Since divorce in Italy is impossible, the only way out of his marriage is murder—and the baron finds a little-known law that excuses a man from murdering his wife if she is having an affair (since he would merely be defending his honor). A hilarious comedy with a twist ending. Available in Italian with English subtitles or dubbed in English. **104m/B; VHS, DVD.** *IT* Marcello Mastroianni; Daniela Rocca; Leopoldo Trieste; Stefania Sandrelli; *D:* Pietro Germi; *W:* Pietro Germi; Ennio de Concini; Alfredo Giannetti; *C:* Carlo Di Palma; Leonida Barboni; *M:* Carlo Rustichelli. Oscars '62: Story & Screenplay; British Acad. '63: Actor (Mastroianni); Golden Globes '63: Actor--Mus./Comedy (Mastroianni), Foreign Film.

The Divorcee 1/2 **1930** Early Leonard film (he'd later direct "The Great Ziegfield" and "Pride and Prejudice") casts Shearer as a woman out to beat her husband at philandering. Married to a journalist, she cavorts with her husband's best friend and a discarded old flame as only a pre-production code gal could. Shearer—who Lillian Hellman described as having "a face unclouded by thought"--grabbed an Oscar. Based on the novel "Ex-Wife" by Ursula Parrott. **83m/B; VHS, DVD.** Norma Shearer; Chester Morris; Conrad Nagel; Robert Montgomery; Mary Doran; Tyler Brooke; George Irving; Helen Johnson; *D:* Robert Z. Leonard. Oscars '30: Actress (Shearer).

Dixiana 1/2 **1930** A Southern millionaire falls for a circus performer shortly before the start of the Civil War. Part color. **99m/B; VHS, DVD.** Bebe Daniels; Bert Wheeler; Robert Woolsey; Dorothy Lamour; Bill Robinson; *D:* Luther Reed; *M:* Max Steiner.

Dixie: Changing Habits **1985** A New Orleans madam and a Mother Superior go head to head in this amusing TV movie. In the end all benefit as the nuns discover business sense and pay off a debt, while the former bordello owner cleans up her act. Above-average scripting and directing for the medium. **100m/C; VHS, DVD.** Suzanne Pleshette; Cloris Leachman; Kenneth McMillan; John Considine; Geraldine Fitzgerald; Judith Ivey; *D:* George Englund. **TV**

Dixie Dynamite **1976 (PG)** The two daughters of a Georgia moonshiner set out to avenge the murder of their father. The music is performed by Duane Eddy and Dorsey Burnette. **88m/C; VHS, DVD.** Warren Oates; Christopher George; Jane Anne Johnstone; Kathy McHaley; R.G. Armstrong; Wes Bishop; *D:* Lee Frost; *W:* Lee Frost.

Dixie Jamboree **1944** Low-budget musical has gangster on the lam using an unusual method to escape from St. Louis—the last Mississippi Showboat. **69m/B; VHS, DVD.** Guy Kibbee; Frances Langford; Louise Beavers; Charles Butterworth; *D:* Christy Cabanne.

Dixie Lanes **1988** A relentlessly nostalgic comedy set in a small town at the end of WWII. A woman, troubled by her nephew's restless antics, puts him to work. Unfortunately she adds to his plight, as her business involves the Black Market. **92m/C; VHS, DVD.** Hoyt Axton; Karen Black; Art Hindle; John Vernon; Ruth Buzzi; Tina Louise; Pamela Springsteen; Nina Foch; *D:* Don Cato.

Django 1/2 **1968 (PG)** Django is a stranger who arrives in a Mexican-border town (dragging a coffin behind him) to settle a dispute between a small band of Americans and Mexicans. **90m/C; VHS, DVD, Blu-Ray.** Franco Nero; Loredana Nusciak; Angel Alvarez; Jose Bodalo; Eduardo Fajardo; Simon Arriaga; Ivan Scratuglia; *D:* Sergio Corbucci; *W:* Sergio Corbucci; Bruno Corbucci; Jose Maesso; Piero Vivarelli; Franco (Fred Gardner) Rossetti; *C:* Enzo Barboni; *M:* Luis Bacalov.

Django and Sartana; It's the End 1/2 *Django and Sartana are Coming...It's the End; Arrivano Django e Sartana...è la fine; Django and Sartana's Showdown in the West; Django and Sartana...Showdown in the West; Final Conflict...Django Against Sartana; Sartana If Your Left Arm Offends, Cut It Off* **1970** Django and Sartana are both classic spaghetti western characters from several films, and this is one of the few in which they crossover. Despite what some alternate titles may suggest the two actually team up to fight a gang of kidnappers. Currently only available as part of the 'Westerns Unchained' collection. **90m/C; Blu-Ray.** *IT* Jack Betts; Franco Borelli; Gordon Mitchell; Simonetta Vitelli; Krista Nell; ***D:*** Demofilo Fidani; Diego Spataro; ***W:*** Demofilo Fidani; Mila Vitelli Valenza; ***C:*** Joe D'Amato; ***M:*** Coriolano Gori. **VIDEO**

Django: Last Killer 🦴 1/2 *The Last Killer; L'ultimo killer; Django the Last Gunfighter; Django the Last Killer* **1967** In yet another of many spaghetti westerns that added Django to the title, a rancher who saves the life of a famous killer is taught to defend himself from an evil local rancher intent on stealing all land in the area. Currently only available as part of the 'Westerns Unchained' collecion. **88m/C; Blu-Ray.** *IT* George Eastman; Dragomir Bojanic; Dana Ghia; Daniele Vargas; Mirko Ellis; ***D:*** Giuseppe Vari; ***W:*** Augusto Caminito; ***C:*** Angelo Filippini; ***M:*** Roberto Pregadio. **VIDEO**

Django Shoots First 🦴 1/2 *Django Spara per Primo* **1974** Spaghetti western with usual amount of action and plot twists. **96m/C; VHS, DVD, Blu-Ray.** *IT* Glen Saxson; Evelyn Stewart; Alberto Lupo; ***D:*** Alberto De Martino; ***W:*** Alberto De Martino.

Django Strikes Again 🦴🦴 *Django 2: Il Grande Ritorno* **1987** Django (Nero) has abandoned his former life of violence in favor of the peaceful life of a monk. That is, until his daughter is kidnapped. Then he manages to find that old coffin and go after the dastardly dogs. **96m/C; VHS, DVD.** *SP* Franco Nero; Donald Pleasence; Rodrigo Obregon; Christopher Connelly; William Berger; ***D:*** Nello Rossati; ***W:*** Nello Rossati; ***M:*** Gianfranco Plenizio.

Django Unchained 🦴🦴🦴 **2012 (R)** Tarantino's gonzo version of a spaghetti western is set in the south two years before the beginning of the Civil War. Bounty hunter King Schultz (Waltz) gives slave Django (Foxx) his freedom and the two team up to get Django's wife Broomhilda (Washington) away from evil plantation owner Calvin Candie (DiCaprio). Over-the-top violent, historically inaccurate, and probably a tad overlong, but Tarantino revels in the genre. The dialogue, if you can get past the somewhat excessive use of the n-word, is a treat. The cast seems to relish the free reign Tarantino obviously gave them. **165m/C; DVD, Blu-Ray.** Jamie Foxx; Leonardo DiCaprio; Christoph Waltz; Kerry Washington; Samuel L. Jackson; James Remar; Don Johnson; Dennis Christopher; Walton Goggins; David Steen; Laura Cayouette; Ato Essandoh; Franco Nero; James Russo; Tom Wopat; Don Stroud; Bruce Dern; M.C. Gainey; Cooper Huckabee; Michael Parks; Jonah Hill; Dana Michelle Gourrier; Miriam F. Glover; Nichole Galicia; Russ Tamblyn; Amber Tamblyn; Quentin Tarantino; ***D:*** Quentin Tarantino; ***W:*** Quentin Tarantino; ***C:*** Robert Richardson. Oscars '12: Actor--Supporting (Waltz), Orig. Screenplay; British Acad. '12: Actor--Supporting (Waltz), Orig. Screenplay; Golden Globes '13: Actor--Supporting (Waltz), Screenplay.

DNA 🦴 1/2 **1997 (R)** Idealistic doctor Ash Mattley (Dacascos) mistakenly reveals his radical DNA theories to creepy scientist Wessinger (Prochnow), who uses the knowledge in mutant experiments. One mutant, an insect-like creature with super powers, lurks in the rain forest, waiting for prey, while Mattley sets out to destroy it. **94m/C; VHS, DVD.** Mark Dacascos; Jurgen Prochnow; Robin McKee; ***D:*** William Mesa; ***W:*** Nick Davis; ***C:*** Gerry Lively; ***M:*** Christopher L. Stone.

The Do-Deca-Pentathlon 🦴🦴 1/2 **2012 (R)** Indie director darlings Jay & Mark Duplass return to a more low budget feel with this comedy of brotherly competition taken to extremes. Two brothers compete in their own series of unusual events during a family reunion but the actual competition is merely background for familial dramedy of the type that these talented writer/directors do so well. The Duplass brothers manage to find the gentle warmth beneath the outward battle that often exists underneath sibling rivalry. **76m/C; DVD, Blu-Ray.** Mark Kelly; Steve Zissis; Jennifer LaFleur; Julie Vorus; ***D:*** Mark Duplass; Jay Duplass; ***W:*** Mark Duplass; Jay Duplass; ***C:*** Jas Shelton; ***M:*** Julian Wass.

Do I Love You? 🦴 1/2 **2002** Biking through the streets of London in search of answers to the mysteries of life and love is 30-something lesbian Marina (writer/director Gornick) who is sent adrift after a difficult split with girlfriend Romy (Cassidy). Overly chatty and rambling, much like her trek. **73m/C; DVD.** Sarah Patterson; Lisa Gornick; Raquel Cassidy; Harri Alexander; ***D:*** Lisa Gornick; ***W:*** Lisa Gornick. **VIDEO**

Do Not Disturb 🦴 1/2 **1965** Filmed on the studio backlot, though the story is set in England and Paris, this so-so romantic comedy finds Janet Harper (Day) relocating to England with exec hubby Mike (Taylor). He promptly leaves her to settle in alone while dallying with his secretary, so Janet decides to invent her own admirer. But a real suitor, Paul (Fantoni), does show up and sweeps Janet off to Paris, thus making Mike insanely jealous. **102m/C; DVD.** Doris Day; Rod Taylor; Sergio Fantoni; Hermione Baddeley; Reginald Gardiner; ***D:*** Ralph Levy; ***W:*** Richard L. Breen; ***C:*** Leon Shamroy; ***M:*** Lionel Newman.

Do or Die 🦴 1/2 **1991 (R)** Former "Playboy" centerfolds Speir and Vasquez team up as a couple of federal agent babes who take on international crime boss Morita. But the crimelord is ready for our scantily clad heroines with a sick game of revenge—and the stakes are their very lives! **97m/C; VHS, DVD, Blu-Ray.** Erik Estrada; Dona Speir; Roberta Vasquez; Noriyuki "Pat" Morita; Bruce Penhall; Carolyn Liu; Stephanie Schick; ***D:*** Andy Sidaris; ***W:*** Andy Sidaris.

Do or Die 🦴🦴 1/2 **2001** When her young son is diagnosed with leukemia, Dr. Samantha Sheppard (Ashfield) is forced to admit to her husband (Speer) that he is not the boy's biological father. That would be a convicted criminal (Long) who escapes from jail just as Samantha arrives in Australia to seek his help. Desperate, Samantha tries to track her ex-lover down before the cops can find him. Originally an Australian miniseries that has been edited to a fast-moving pace. **90m/C; DVD.** *AU* Kate Ashfield; Tom Long; Hugo Speer; William McInnes; Martin Sacks; ***D:*** Rowan Woods; ***W:*** Christopher Lee; ***C:*** Martin McGrath; ***M:*** Edmund Butt. **TV**

Do or Die 🦴 **2003** Die, please die. A rapid aging disease affects more than half the world's population and only one drug is available to slow the process. The drug is controlled by a single manufacturer and its head will stop at nothing to continue his company's monopoly. That includes threatening pregnant Ruth, who may have been given the key to a cure. A Sci-Fi Channel original. **89m/C; DVD.** Shawn Doyle; Polly Shannon; Nigel Bennett; Alan Van Sprang; Guylaine St. Onge; Anthony Lemke; ***D:*** David S. Jackson; ***W:*** David S. Jackson; ***C:*** Rudolf Blahacek; ***M:*** Frederic Talgorn. **CABLE**

Do the Right Thing 🦴🦴🦴 1/2 **1989 (R)** An uncompromising, brutal comedy about the racial tensions surrounding a white-owned pizzeria in the Bed-Stuy section of Brooklyn on the hottest day of the summer, and the violence that eventually erupts. Ambivalent and, for the most part, hilarious; Lee's coming-of-age. **120m/C; VHS, DVD, Blu-Ray.** Spike Lee; Danny Aiello; Richard Edson; Ruby Dee; Ossie Davis; Giancarlo Esposito; Bill Nunn; John Turturro; John Savage; Rosie Perez; Frankie Faison; ***D:*** Spike Lee; ***W:*** Spike Lee; ***C:*** Ernest R. Dickerson; ***M:*** Bill Lee. L.A. Film Critics '89: Director (Lee), Film, Support. Actor (Aiello); Natl. Film Reg. '99; N.Y. Film Critics '89: Cinematog.

Do You Believe? 🦴 1/2 **2015 (PG-13)** Faith-based drama that explores the wide-ranging effects of a preacher's sermon on his flock, but the message isn't subtle. After meeting a street preacher (Lindo), Pastor Matt (McGinley) tells his parishioners to put their faith into action. This call to change impacts the lives of many including a couple suffering from the loss of their child, an man struggling from PTSD, a pregnant teenager, and a homeless man. Though the film has an impressively staged car accident scene, its production values are more TV movie than feature film, which also detracts from the filmmakers' Christian message. **120m/C; DVD.** Delroy Lindo; Ted McGinley; Sean Astin; Cybill Shepherd; Mira Sorvino; ***D:*** Jon Gunn; ***W:*** Chuck Konzelman; Cary Solomon; ***C:*** Brian Shanley; ***M:*** Will Musser.

Do You Love Me? 🦴🦴 1/2 **1946** In this Fox musical comedy, beautiful O'Hara starts off as frumpy music college dean Katherine Hilliard, who meets handsome band leader Barry Clayton (James) on a train to New York. He tries to convince her about the value of the swing sound but she's uncertain. A visit to a sympathetic friend and a makeover has Katherine reconsidering, especially after meeting band crooner Jimmy (Haymes). Katherine would like to get the fuddy-duddy college board convinced as well. **91m/C; DVD.** Maureen O'Hara; Harry James; Dick Haymes; Reginald Gardiner; Richard Gaines; Stanley Prager; ***D:*** Gregory Ratoff; ***W:*** Robert Ellis; Helen Logan; ***C:*** Edward Cronjager; ***M:*** David Buttolph.

D.O.A. 🦴🦴🦴 1/2 **1949** A man is given a lethal, slow-acting poison. As his time runs out, he frantically seeks to learn who is responsible and why he was targeted for death. Dark film noir remade in 1969 as "Color Me Dead" and in 1988 with Dennis Quaid and Meg Ryan. Also available colorized. **83m/B; VHS, DVD.** Edmond O'Brien; Pamela Britton; Luther Adler; Neville Brand; Beverly Garland; Lynne Baggett; William Ching; Henry Hart; Laurette Luez; Virginia Lee; Jess Kirkpatrick; Cay Forrester; Michael Ross; ***D:*** Rudolph Mate; ***W:*** Russell Rouse; Clarence Greene; ***C:*** Ernest Laszlo; ***M:*** Dimitri Tiomkin. Natl. Film Reg. '04.

D.O.A. 🦴🦴 1/2 **1988 (R)** Well-done remake of the 1949 thriller with Quaid portraying a college professor who is poisoned and has only 24 hours to identify his killer. His search for the suspect is further complicated by the fact that he is being sought by the police on phony charges of murder. Directed by the same people who brought "Max Headroom" to TV screens. **98m/C; VHS, DVD, Blu-Ray.** Dennis Quaid; Meg Ryan; Charlotte Rampling; Daniel Stern; Jane Kaczmarek; Christopher Neame; Jay Patterson; ***D:*** Rocky Morton; Annabel Jankel; ***W:*** Charles Edward Pogue; ***M:*** Chaz Jankel.

DOA: Dead or Alive 🦴🦴 **2006 (PG-13)** Female-centric martial arts actioner, based on a videogame, follows five woman fighters battling to the death on an island. Okay, not the most original concept in the world, but as a straightforward action-and-chicks, "turn-off-the-brain" time waster, you could do a lot worse. Hey, at least Uwe Boll didn't direct it. Corey Yuen, who knows a thing or two about staging martial arts action, did. And it does look like everyone's having a good time. **87m/C; DVD.** *GB GE US* Devon Aoki; Sarah Carter; Natassia Malthe; Jaime Pressly; Eric Roberts; Steve Howey; Matthew Marsden; Collin Chou; Holly Valance; Kane (Takeshi) Kosugi; Kevin Nash; Brian White; Robin Shou; Derek Boyer; Silvio Simac; ***D:*** Corey Yuen; ***W:*** J.F. Lawton; Adam Gross; Seth Gross; ***C:*** Chi Ying Chan; Kwok-Man Keung.

The Doberman Gang 🦴🦴 **1972 (PG)** Clever thieves train a gang of Dobermans in the fine art of bank robbery. Sequelled by "The Daring Dobermans." **85m/C; VHS, DVD.** Byron Mabe; Hal Reed; Julie Parrish; Simmy Bow; JoJo D'Amore; ***D:*** Byron Ross Chudnow; ***W:*** Frank Ray Perilli.

Doc Hollywood 🦴🦴 1/2 **1991 (PG-13)** A hotshot young physician on his way to a lucrative California practice gets stranded in a small Southern town. Will the wacky woodsy inhabitants persuade the city doctor to stay? There aren't many surprises in this fish-out-of-water comedy, but the cast injects it with considerable charm. Adapted from Neil B. Shulman's book "What?...Dead Again?" **104m/C; VHS, DVD, Blu-Ray.** Michael J. Fox; Julie Warner; Woody Harrelson; Barnard Hughes; David Ogden Stiers; Frances Sternhagen; Bridget Fonda; George Hamilton; Roberts Blossom; Helen Martin; Macon McCalman; Barry Sobel; ***D:*** Michael Caton-Jones; ***W:*** Daniel Pyne; Jeffrey Price; Peter S. Seaman; ***C:*** Michael Chapman; ***M:*** Carter Burwell.

Doc Savage 🦴🦴 1/2 **1975 (PG)** Doc and "The Amazing Five" fight a murderous villain who plans to take over the world. Based on the novels of Kenneth Robeson. **100m/C; VHS, DVD, Blu-Ray, Streaming.** Ron Ely; Pamela Hensley; Paul Gleason; Paul Wexler; William Lucking; ***D:*** Michael Anderson, Sr.; ***W:*** George Pal; Joe Morhaim; ***C:*** Fred W. Koenekamp.

Doc West 🦴🦴 **2009 (PG)** Family friendly spaghetti western. Gunslinging gambler Minnesota West (Hill) is not happy when his poker winnings are stolen and tracks the thieves to the next town. Sheriff Basehart (Sorvino) is worried about West's vendetta and throws him in jail for his own protection but then asks him to help out the townsfolk who are being harassed by the local cattle baron. Followed by "Triggerman." **97m/C; DVD.** *IT* Terence Hill; Paul Sorvino; Boots Southerland; Alessio Di Clemente; Maria Petruolo; Clare Carey; Benjamin Petry; Ornella Muti; ***D:*** Terence Hill; Giulio Base; ***W:*** Luca Biglione; Marcello Olivieri; ***C:*** Massimiliano Trevis; ***M:*** Maurizio De Angelis.

Docks of New Orleans 🦴 **1948** Winters makes his 2nd appearance as Charlie Chan, who just happens to be in New Orleans when the owner of LaFontanne Chemical Company gets suspicious over a chemical shipment. It involves a stolen secret formula and murder. The 40th film in the series is actually a remake of 1938's "Mr. Wong, Detective." **67m/B; DVD.** Roland Winters; Victor Sen Yung; Mantan Moreland; Boyd Irwin; Virginia Dale; John Gallaudet; ***D:*** Derwin Abrahams; ***W:*** Scott Darling; ***C:*** William Sickner.

The Doctor 🦴🦴 1/2 **1991 (PG-13)** A hotshot doctor develops throat cancer and gets treated at his own hospital, an ordeal that teaches him a respect and compassion for patients that he formerly lacked. Potential melodrama is saved by fine acting and strong direction. Based on the autobiographical book "A Taste of My Own Medicine" by Dr. Edward Rosenbaum. **125m/C; VHS, DVD, Blu-Ray.** William Hurt; Elizabeth Perkins; Christine Lahti; Mandy Patinkin; Wendy Crewson; Charlie Korsmo; Adam Arkin; Bill Macy; ***D:*** Randa Haines; ***W:*** Robert Caswell; ***C:*** John Seale; ***M:*** Michael Convertino.

Dr. Akagi 🦴🦴 *Kanzo Sensei* **1998** In 1945, the dedicated Dr. Akagi (Emoto) is more worried about a hepatitis epidemic in his seaside village that the Japanese wartime defeat. He becomes obsessed with finding a cure and assembles a ragtag group of compatriots to assist him, including a teenaged prostitute and an escaped Dutch prisoner of war. Based on the novel "Dr. Liver" by Ango Sakaguchi. Japanese with subtitles. **128m/C; VHS, DVD.** *JP* Akira (Tsukamoto) Emoto; Jacques Gamblin; Kumiko Aso; Masanori Sera; Jyuro Kara; Keiko Matsuzaka; ***D:*** Shohei Imamura; ***W:*** Shohei Imamura; Daisuke Tengan; ***C:*** Shigeru Komatsubara; ***M:*** Yosuke Yamashita.

Dr. Alien 🦴 **1988 (R)** Alien poses as beautiful scientist and turns a college freshman into a sex-addicted satyr. Likewise, the cast turns this flick into a dog. **90m/C; VHS, DVD.** Billy Jacoby; Olivia Barash; Stuart Fratkin; Troy Donahue; Arlene Golonka; Judy Landers; ***D:*** David DeCoteau.

The Doctor and the Devils 🦴🦴 1/2 **1985 (R)** Based on an old screenplay by Dylan Thomas, this is a semi-Gothic tale about two criminals who supply a physician with corpses to study, either digging them up or killing them fresh. **93m/C; VHS, DVD, Blu-Ray; Open Captioned.** *GB* Timothy Dalton; Julian Sands; Jonathan Pryce; Twiggy; Stephen Rea; Beryl Reid; Sian Phillips; Patrick Stewart; Phyllis Logan; T.P. McKenna; ***D:*** Freddie Francis; ***W:*** Ronald Harwood; ***M:*** John Morris.

The Doctor and the Girl 🦴🦴 1/2 **1949** Family/medical soap opera. The doctor is newly-graduated Michael Corday (Ford), who begins his internship at Bellevue by following his surgeon father's (Coburn) advice to be impersonal with his patients. This lack of sympathy quickly falls away when Michael treats working-class Evelyn (Leigh)--she would be the girl. Michael is inspired to become a physician in the slums and both actions cause a family estrangement until there's a tragedy. **98m/B; DVD.** Glenn Ford; Charles Coburn; Janet Leigh; Gloria De Haven; Bruce Bennett; Nancy Davis; Warner Anderson; ***D:*** Curtis Bernhardt; ***W:*** Theodore Reeves; ***C:*** Robert Planck.

Doctor at Large 🦴🦴 1/2 **1957** A fledgling doctor seeks to become a surgeon at a hospital for the rich. Humorous antics follow. The third of the "Doctor" series. **98m/C; VHS, DVD, Streaming.** *GB* Dirk Bogarde; Muriel Pavlow; James Robertson Justice; Shirley Eaton; Donald Sinden; Anne Heywood; ***D:*** Ralph Thomas.

Doctor at Sea 🦴🦴 1/2 **1956** To escape a troublesome romantic entanglement and the stresses of his career, a London physician signs on a cargo boat as a ship's doctor and becomes involved with French bombshell Bardot. The second of the "Doctor" series. **93m/C; VHS, DVD, Streaming.** *GB* James Robertson Justice; Dirk Bogarde; Brigitte Bardot; ***D:*** Ralph Thomas; ***W:*** Jack Davies.

Dr. Bell and Mr. Doyle: The Dark Beginnings of Sherlock Holmes 1/2 *Murder Rooms: The Dark Origins of Sherlock Holmes* **2000** In 1878, Arthur Conan Doyle (Laing) is a medical student at Edinburgh University. He is mentored by the gurff and brilliant, if unconventional, Dr. Joseph Bell (Richardson), who is a pioneer in the field of forensic science. Arthur is soon assisting Dr. Bell, who is helping the local police investigate the brutal murders of several young women. The case may also take a personal turn for Arthur when it appears his classmate and friend Elspeth (Wells) is a target. Well-done if sometimes gruesome; based in part on the letters and writings of Bell. **116m/C; VHS, DVD.** *GB* Robin Laing; Ian Richardson; Charles Dance; Dolly Wells; Sean McGinley; Alec Newman; ***D:*** Paul Seed; ***W:*** David Pirie; ***C:*** John Kenway; ***M:*** Jim Parker. **TV**

Dr. Black, Mr. Hyde *Dr. Black and Mr. White; The Watts Monster* **1976 (R)** Not-so-horrifying tale of a black Jekyll who metamorphoses into a white monster with the help of the special potion. Unintended laughs lessen suspense. **88m/C; VHS, DVD.** Rosalind Cash; Stu Gilliam; Bernie Casey; Marie O'Henry; ***D:*** William Crain.

Doctor Blood's Coffin 1/2 **1962** The aptly named doctor performs hideous experiments on the unsuspecting denizens of a lonely village. Good cast in this effective chiller. **92m/C; VHS, DVD, Blu-Ray.** *GB* Kieron Moore; Hazel Court; Ian Hunter; ***D:*** Sidney J. Furie.

Doctor Bull 1/2 **1933** Rogers is awshucks charming in the title role. George Bull is an opinionated small-town doctor who's subjected to much gossip, especially over his romance with widow Janet (Allen). When the town's water supply is contaminated and many fall ill, Bull diagnoses typhoid. Herbert Banning (Churchill), Janet's brother, tries to blame the good doctor since he's the town's health officer, but Janet defends him. **77m/B; DVD.** Will Rogers; Marion (Marian) Nixon; Berton Churchill; Louise Dresser; Vera Allen; Howard Lally; Andy Devine; ***D:*** John Ford; ***W:*** Paul Green; ***C:*** George Schneiderman; ***M:*** Samuel Kaylin.

Doctor Butcher M.D. **WOOF!** *Queen of the Cannibals; Zombie Holocaust; The Island of the Last Zombies* **1980 (R)** Mad doctor's deranged dream of creating "perfect people" by taking parts of one person and interchanging them with another backfires as his monstrosities develop strange side effects. The M.D., by the way, stands for "Medical Deviate." Dubbed. **81m/C; VHS, DVD, Blu-Ray.** *IT* Ian McCulloch; Alexandra Cole; Peter O'Neal; Donald O'Brien; Sherry Buchanan; Walter Patriarca; ***D:*** Frank Martin; Mariano Laurenti; ***W:*** Fabrizio de Angelis; Romano Scandariato; ***M:*** Nico Fidenco; Walter Sear.

Doctor Chance *Docteur Chance* **1997** Frustrated Angstel (Hestnes) decides it's time to make a big change in his life. He heads to a nightclub and buys the favors (with counterfeit cash) of dancer Ancetta (Elvire) but events get out of hand. Soon the duo are heading out of the city with a car trunk full of weapons and adventure on their minds. French with subtitles. **97m/C; VHS, DVD.** *FR* Pedro Hestnes; Elvire; Marisa Paredes; Stephane Ferrara; Joe Strummer; Feodor Atkine; ***D:*** F.J. Ossang; ***W:*** F.J. Ossang; ***C:*** Remy Chevrin.

Dr. Cyclops 1/2 **1940** The famous early Technicolor fantasia about a mad scientist miniaturizing a group of explorers who happen upon his jungle lab. Landmark F/X and a slow-moving story. **76m/C; VHS, DVD.** Albert Dekker; Janice Logan; Victor Kilian; Thomas Coley; Charles Halton; Frank Yaconelli; Paul Fix; Frank Reicher; ***D:*** Ernest B. Schoedsack; ***W:*** Tom Kilpatrick; ***C:*** Winton C. Hoch; Henry Sharp; ***M:*** Gerard Carbonara; Albert Hay Malotte; Ernst Toch.

Dr. Death, Seeker of Souls **1973 (R)** Evil doctor discovers a process for transmigrating his soul into the bodies of people he murdered 1000 years ago. Now he seeks to revive his wife. Final role for 77-year-old "Stooge" Moe Howard. **93m/C; VHS, DVD, Blu-Ray.** John Considine; Barry Coe; Cheryl Miller; Stewart Moss; Leon Askin; Jo Morrow; Florence Marly; Sivi Aberg; Athena Lorde; Moe Howard; ***D:*** Eddie Saeta.

Doctor Detroit **1983 (R)** Aykroyd is funny in thin film, portraying a meek college professor who gets involved with prostitutes and the mob, under the alias "Dr. Detroit." Aykroyd later married actress Donna Dixon, whom he worked with on this film. Features music by Devo, James Brown, and Pattie Brooks. **91m/C; VHS, DVD, Blu-Ray.** Dan Aykroyd; Howard Hesseman; Donna Dixon; T.K. Carter; Lynn Whitfield; Lydia Lei; Fran Drescher; Kate Murtagh; George Furth; Andrew Duggan; James Brown; Glenne Headly; ***D:*** Michael Pressman; ***W:*** Carl Gottlieb; Robert Boris; ***M:*** Lalo Schifrin.

Doctor Dolittle **1967** An adventure about a 19th century English doctor who dreams of teaching animals to speak to him. Realistic premise suffers from poor script. Based on Hugh Lofting's acclaimed stories. **151m/C; VHS, DVD, Blu-Ray.** Rex Harrison; Samantha Eggar; Anthony Newley; Richard Attenborough; Geoffrey Holder; Peter Bull; ***D:*** Richard Fleischer; ***W:*** Leslie Bricusse; ***C:*** Robert L. Surtees; ***M:*** Leslie Bricusse. Oscars '67: Song ("Talk to the Animals"), Visual FX; Golden Globes '68: Support. Actor (Attenborough).

Dr. Dolittle 1/2 **1998 (PG-13)** Loose non-musical adaption of the 1967 movie has Eddie Murphy playing straight man to a group of furry friends voiced by the likes of Chris Rock, Garry Shandling and Albert Brooks. He is reduced to reacting lamely, and is upstaged throughout by the wisecracking critters created by Jim Henson's Creature Shop. Fellow humans Dr. Weller (Platt) and Calloway (Boyle) are shallow villains created to prop up a shaky plot involving the corporate takeover of Dolittle's vet clinic. May contain a bit too much bathroom humor for some family tastes. No animals were harmed during the making of this movie, but there was probably cruel and unusual treatment of the interns involving pooper-scoopers. **85m/C; VHS, DVD.** Eddie Murphy; Oliver Platt; Peter Boyle; Jeffrey Tambor; Ossie Davis; Richard Schiff; Kyla Pratt; Raven; Steven Gilborn; ***V:*** Albert Brooks; Chris Rock; John Leguizamo; Garry Shandling; Julie Kavner; Norm MacDonald; Reni Santoni; Paul (Pee-wee Herman) Reubens; Gilbert Gottfried; ***D:*** Betty Thomas; ***W:*** Nat Mauldin; Larry Levin; ***C:*** Russell Boyd; ***M:*** Richard Gibbs.

Dr. Dolittle 2 **2001 (PG)** The good doctor (Murphy) returns, along with his furry talking friends, who persuade him to save their forest from human developers. The vet must also find a mate for an endangered Pacific Western bear, but the only candidate is Archie (Zahn), a circus performer who has to be taught how to survive in the wilderness. Gastrointestinal and other bodily functions dominate the humor, and a subplot involving Dolittle's moody teenage daughter (Raven-Symone) nearly undoes the charm, but it's passable entertainment. Add half a bone if you're under 12 years old for this flatulence-obsessed outing. **87m/C; VHS, DVD.** Eddie Murphy; Jeffrey Jones; Kevin Pollak; Raven; Kyla Pratt; Kristen Wilson; Zane R. (Lil' Zane) Copeland, Jr.; Andy Richter; ***V:*** Norm MacDonald; Lisa Kudrow; Steve Zahn; Mike Epps; Michael Rapaport; Jacob Vargas; Isaac Hayes; Andy Dick; Joey Lauren Adams; Richard Sarafian; ***D:*** Steve Carr; ***W:*** Larry Levin; ***C:*** Daryn Okada; ***M:*** David Newman.

Dr. Dolittle 3 1/2 **2006 (PG)** Maya Dolittle (Pratt) can also talk to the animals, which doesn't make being a teenager any easier. When she gets into trouble, mom sends Maya to a Colorado dude ranch, where she tries to make some friends while yakking with the local barnyard critters. Since the ranch is in financial trouble, it's up to Maya and the animals to win big at the local rodeo and save the day. Harmless and silly cash-in on the Eddie Murphy features. **95m/C; DVD.** Kyla Pratt; Kristen Wilson; John Amos; Walker Howard; Luciana Carro; Tommy Snider; James Kirk; ***D:*** Rich Thorne; ***W:*** Nina Colman; ***C:*** Eric Goldstein; ***M:*** Christopher Lennertz. **VIDEO**

Dr. Dolittle 4: Tail to the Chief **2008 (PG)** Dog whisperer? In her latest adventure, Maya Dolittle (Pratt) is asked by the president to come to the White House and tame the rambunctious First Dog. **90m/C; DVD.** Kyla Pratt; Peter Coyote; Malcolm Stewart; Christine Chatelain; Niall Matter; ***D:*** Craig Shapiro; ***W:*** Kathleen Laccinole; Matthew Lieberman; ***C:*** Ron Stannett; ***M:*** Don MacDonald. **VIDEO**

Dr. Dolittle: Million Dollar Mutts 1/2 **2009 (PG)** The fifth in the Dolittle series. Maya Dolittle (Pratt) heads off to San Francisco to study veterinary medicine but her rescue of a cat brings her to the attention of heiress/reality star Tiffany (Moss) and her neurotic pooch Princess. Maya heads to Hollywood to dog whisper to Princess and soon is offered a tacky show of her own by Tiffany's agent (Beverley). It sounds like a good opportunity but Maya soon learns some rude truths about showbiz. **87m/C; DVD.** Kyla Pratt; Tegan Moss; Brandon Jay McLaren; Jason Bryden; ***V:*** Norm McDonald; ***D:*** Alex Zamm; ***W:*** Alex Zamm; Daniel Altiere; Steven Altiere; ***C:*** Albert J. Dunk; ***M:*** Chris Hajian. **VIDEO**

Dr. Ehrlich's Magic Bullet 1/2 **1940** Quite provocative for its time considering the subject matter is the cure for syphilis. Berlin research scientist Paul Ehrlich's (Robinson) experiments have him battling the medical establishment and underfunding as he develops the theory of poison immunity and a synthetic antimicrobial drug to cure diphtheria and syphilis. It takes him 606 tests before his 'magic bullet' works. A good Warner bio with a particularly compelling performance by Robinson. **103m/B; DVD.** Edward G. Robinson; Ruth Gordon; Otto Kruger; Albert Bassermann; Donald Crisp; Maria Ouspenskaya; Montagu Love; Sig Rumann; Donald Meek; ***D:*** Donald Crisp; William Dieterle; John Huston; ***W:*** Ruth Gordon; Norman Burnside; Heinz Herald; John Huston; ***C:*** James Wong Howe; ***M:*** Max Steiner.

Doctor Faustus 1/2 **1968** A stilted, stagy, but well-meaning adaptation of the Christopher Marlowe classic about Faust, who sold his soul to the devil for youth and the love of Helen of Troy. **93m/C; VHS, DVD.** Richard Burton; Andreas Teuber; Elizabeth Taylor; Ian Marter; ***D:*** Richard Burton; Nevill Coghill.

Dr. Frankenstein's Castle of Freaks **1974 (PG)** Dr. Frankenstein and his dwarf assistant reanimate a few Neanderthals that are terrorizing a nearby Rumanian village. **90m/C; VHS, DVD.** *IT* Rossano Brazzi; Michael Dunn; Edmund Purdom; Christiane Royce; Simonetta Vitelli; ***D:*** Robert Oliver; ***W:*** William Rose; Mark Smith; Robert Spano; ***C:*** Mario Mancini.

Dr. Giggles **1992 (R)** Drake plays the psycho-genius Dr. Giggles, an escaped mental patient who sets out to avenge the death of his psycho-genius father (dementia runs in the family). He returns to his family home to procure the necessary medical instruments, most notably a hypodermic needle, and starts killing people—on screen with the tools and in the audience with remarkably stupid one-liners. Opening scenes are especially mired in gore. **96m/C; VHS, DVD, Blu-Ray.** Larry Drake; Holly Marie Combs; Glenn Quinn; Keith Diamond; Cliff DeYoung; ***D:*** Manny Coto; ***W:*** Manny Coto; Graeme Whifler; ***C:*** Rob Draper; ***M:*** Brian May.

Dr. Gillespie's Criminal Case **1943** Homicidal maniac Roy Todwell returns, breaking out of prison and still wanting to kill Dr. Gillespie, who has encouraged his former girlfriend Marcia to marry another man. Gillespie's new assistants, Red and Lee, have their own cases, and then Blair General's children's ward is beset by an epidemic. Third in the series; followed by "Three Men in White." **89m/B; DVD.** Lionel Barrymore; Van Johnson; Keye Luke; Donna Reed; Michael Duane; William Lundigan; Margaret O'Brien; John Craven; Alma Kruger; Nat Pendleton; ***D:*** Willis Goldbeck; ***W:*** Harry Ruskin; Lawrence Bachmann; Martin Berkeley; ***C:*** Norbert Brodine; ***M:*** Daniele Amfitheatrof.

Dr. Gillespie's New Assistant **1942** Overworked Dr. Gillespie is urged to choose a new assistant. Three likely candidates must correctly diagnose a difficult case and whoever's right gets the job. The patient is newly married Clair, who's suffering complete memory loss, but there's something suspicious about her problem. Second in series; followed by "Dr. Gillespie's Criminal Case." **87m/B; DVD.** Lionel Barrymore; Van Johnson; Keye Luke; Richard Quine; Susan Peters; Stephen McNally; Alma Kruger; Nat Pendleton; ***D:*** Willis Goldbeck; ***W:*** Willis Goldbeck; Harry Ruskin; Lawrence Bachmann; ***C:*** George J. Folsey; ***M:*** Daniele Amfitheatrof.

Dr. Goldfoot and the Bikini Machine **1966** A mad scientist employs gorgeous female robots to seduce the wealthy and powerful, thereby allowing him to take over the world. Title song by the Supremes. **90m/C; VHS, DVD, Blu-Ray.** Vincent Price; Frankie Avalon; Dwayne Hickman; Annette Funicello; Susan Hart; Kay Elkhardt; Fred Clark; Deanna Lund; Deborah Walley; ***D:*** Norman Taurog; ***M:*** Les Baxter.

Dr. Hackenstein 1/2 **1988 (R)** A doctor tries to revive his wife by "borrowing" parts from unexpected (and unsuspecting) guests. **88m/C; VHS, DVD.** David Muir; Stacey Travis; Catherine Davis Cox; Dyanne DiRosario; Anne Ramsey; Logan Ramsey; ***D:*** Richard Clark.

Doctor in Clover 1/2 **1966** The series was running out of steam by this sixth effort that has the usual sight gags and innuendos. After Dr. Gaston Grimsdyke (Phillips) loses his job at a women's prison, he enrolls in a refresher course taught by his mentor Sir Lancelot Spratt (Robertson-Justice). Spratt is determined that Gaston will stop chasing nurses long enough to become a decent physician but that may be an impossible task. **97m/C; DVD.** *GB* Leslie Phillips; James Robertson-Justice; Shirley Anne Field; John Fraser; Joan Sims; Fenella Fielding; Jeremy Lloyd; ***D:*** Ralph Thomas; ***W:*** Jack Davies; ***C:*** Ernest Steward; ***M:*** John Scott.

Doctor in Distress 1/2 **1963** Aging chief surgeon falls in love for the first time. His assistant tries to further the romance as well as his own love life. Comedic fourth in the six-film "Doctor" series. **102m/C; VHS, DVD.** *GB* Dirk Bogarde; James Robertson Justice; Leo McKern; Samantha Eggar; ***D:*** Ralph Thomas.

Doctor in Love **1960** The fourth in the series, but the first without former lead Dirk Bogarde. This time the story focuses primarily on Dr. Richard Hare (Craig) and his romance with Dr. Nicola Barrington (Maskell). Meanwhile, his friend Dr. Tony Burke (Phillips) continues to sow his wild oats, which is how some strippers come to be involved. **93m/C; DVD.** *GB* Michael Craig; Leslie Phillips; Virginia Maskell; Carole Lesley; Nicholas Phipps; Reginald Beckwith; Liz Fraser; Irene Handl; Moira Redmond; James Robertson-Justice; Joan Simms; ***D:*** Ralph Thomas; ***W:*** Nicholas Phipps; ***C:*** Ernest Steward; ***M:*** Bruce Montgomery.

Doctor in the House 1/2 **1953** Four medical student/roommates seek only to examine lovely women and make lots of cash. In the process, they are also tempted by the evils of drink, but rally to make their grades. A riotous British comedy with marvelous performances all around. Led to six sequels and a TV series. **92m/C; VHS, DVD.** *GB* Dirk Bogarde; Muriel Pavlow; Kenneth More; Donald Sinden; Kay Kendall; James Robertson Justice; Donald Houston; Geoffrey Keen; George Coulouris; Shirley Eaton; Joan Hickson; Richard Wattis; ***D:*** Ralph Thomas. British Acad. '54: Actor (More).

Dr. Jekyll and Ms. Hyde 1/2 **1995 (PG-13)** Chemist Richard Jacks (Daly) stumbles across the secret formula of great-grandad Dr. Jekyll and, after trying to improve the potion, he finds himself transformed into wicked woman Helen Hyde (Young). Cheap cross-gender gags abound. **89m/C; VHS, DVD.** Timothy Daly; Sean Young; Lysette Anthony; Stephen Tobolowsky; Harvey Fierstein; Polly Bergen; Stephen Shellen; ***D:*** David F. Price; ***W:*** William Davies; William Osborne; Tim John; Oliver Butcher; ***C:*** Tom Priestley; ***M:*** Mark McKenzie.

Dr. Jekyll and Mr. Hyde **1920** The first American film version of Robert Louis Stevenson's horror tale about a doctor's experiments that lead to his developing good and evil sides to his personality. Silent. Kino Video's edition also contains the rarely seen 1911 version of the film, as well as scenes from a different 1920 version. **96m/B; Silent; VHS, DVD, Blu-Ray.** John Barrymore; Martha Mansfield; Brandon Hurst; Charles Lane; J. Malcolm Dunn; Nita Naldi; Louis Wolheim; ***D:*** John S. Robertson; ***W:*** Clara Beranger; ***C:*** Karl Struss; Roy F. Overbaugh.

Dr. Jekyll and Mr. Hyde 𝒿𝒿𝒿 **1932** The hallucinatory, feverish classic version of the Robert Louis Stevenson story, in which the good doctor becomes addicted to the formula that turns him into a sadistic beast. Upright Dr. Jekyll (March) has a genteel fiance, Muriel (Hobart), while twisted alter-ego Hyde delights in torturing barmaid Ivy (Hopkins)?the bond between violence and sexuality in these scenes is highly charged. Possibly Mamoulian's and March's best work, and a masterpiece of subversive, pseudo-Freudian creepiness. Eighteen minutes from the original version, lost until recently, have been restored, including the infamous whipping scene. **96m/B; VHS, DVD; Open Captioned.** Fredric March; Miriam Hopkins; Halliwell Hobbes; Rose Hobart; Holmes Herbert; Edgar Norton; ***D:*** Rouben Mamoulian; ***W:*** Samuel Hoffenstein; Percy Heath; ***C:*** Karl Struss. Oscars '32: Actor (March); Venice Film Fest. '31: Actor (March).

Dr. Jekyll and Mr. Hyde 𝒿𝒿𝒿 **1941** Strangely cast adaptation of the Robert Louis Stevenson story about a doctor's experiment on himself to separate good and evil. **113m/B; VHS, DVD.** Spencer Tracy; Ingrid Bergman; Lana Turner; Donald Crisp; Ian Hunter; Barton MacLane; Sara Allgood; Billy Bevan; ***D:*** Victor Fleming; ***W:*** John Lee Mahin; ***C:*** Joseph Ruttenberg; ***M:*** Franz Waxman.

Dr. Jekyll and Mr. Hyde 𝒿𝒿 ½ *The Strange Case of Dr. Jekyll and Mr. Hyde* **1968** Yet another production of Robert Louis Stevenson's classic story of a split-personality. **90m/C; VHS, DVD.** Jack Palance; Denholm Elliott; Tessie O'Shea; Oscar Homolka; Torin Thatcher; ***D:*** Charles Jarrott. **TV**

Dr. Jekyll and Mr. Hyde 𝒿𝒿 **1973** Dr. Jekyll discovers a potion that turns him into the sinister Mr. Hyde. Based on the classic story by Robert Louis Stevenson. **90m/C; VHS, DVD.** Kirk Douglas; Michael Redgrave; Susan George; Donald Pleasence; ***D:*** David Winters.

Dr. Jekyll & Mr. Hyde 𝒿𝒿 **1999 (R)** Henry Jekyll (Baldwin) is a successful surgeon who is traveling to Hong Kong on his honeymoon. But shortly after his arrival, both he and his bride are killed in an explosion during a gang war. Henry is resurrected by Chinese healer Dr. Chau, although the potion he must take alters him physically and mentally. Henry only seeks revenge but he learns that his arrival was predestined and his fate is to become the legendary fighter known as the White Dragon. Obviously has little or nothing to do with the Robert Louis Stevenson story. **96m/C; VHS, DVD.** *CA AU* Adam Baldwin; Steve Bastoni; Chang Tseng; Jason Chong; Richard Chong; Kira Clavel; Karen Cliche; ***D:*** Colin Budds; ***W:*** Peter M. Lenkov; ***C:*** Mark Wareham; ***M:*** Garry McDonald. **VIDEO**

Dr. Jekyll and Mr. Hyde 𝒿 ½ **2008** Set in Boston, this erratic modern update of the Robert Louis Stevenson story finds respected doctor Henry Jekyll (Scott) conducting experiments on himself with a serum made from a rare flower he believes is able to separate the soul into dark and light. The dark part would be his serial-killing alter Edward Hyde. When an appalled Jekyll realizes what he's done, he turns himself into the cops and hires lawyer Claire Wheaton (Bridges) to represent him at his sensational trial. But her defense could prove misguided if not deadly. **80m/C; DVD.** Dougray Scott; Krista Bridges; Tom Skerritt; Ellen David; Cas Anvar; Danette Mackay; ***D:*** Paolo Barzman; ***W:*** Paul B. Margolis; ***C:*** Pierre Jodoin. **TV**

Dr. Jekyll and Sister Hyde 𝒿𝒿 ½ **1971 (R)** A tongue-in-cheek variation on the split-personality theme, which has the good doctor transforming himself into a sultry, knife-wielding woman who kills prostitutes. **94m/C; VHS, DVD.** *GB* Ralph Bates; Martine Beswick; Gerald Sim; ***D:*** Roy Ward Baker; ***W:*** Brian Clemens; ***C:*** Norman Warwick; ***M:*** Philip Martell; David Whitaker.

Dr. Jekyll and the Wolfman 𝒿 *Dr. Jekyll y el Hombre Lobo; Dr. Jekyll vs. the Werewolf* **1971 (R)** Naschy's sixth stint as El Hombre Lobo. This time he visits a mysterious doctor in search of a cure but ends up turning into Mr. Hyde, a man who likes to torture women. **85m/C; VHS, DVD.** *SP* Paul Naschy; Shirley Corrigan; Jack Taylor; Barta Barry; Luis Induni; Mirta Miller; ***D:*** Leon Klimovsky; ***W:*** Paul Naschy; ***C:*** Francisco Fraile.

Dr. Jekyll's Dungeon of Death 𝒿 **1982 (R)** Dr. Jekyll and his lobotomized sister, Hilda, scour the streets of San Francisco looking for human blood to recreate his great-grandfather's secret serum. **90m/C; VHS, DVD, Streaming.** James Mathers; Dawn Carver Kelly; John Kearney; Jake Pearson; ***D:*** James Wood.

Dr. Kildare Goes Home 𝒿𝒿 **1940** Kildare's completed his internship at Blair General and gets a staff position working with Dr. Gillespie. But first he goes home to help out his overworked father and gets the idea to have the community start a clinic, staffed by some unemployed city doctors he knows. But Kildare runs into opposition when his plan includes a weekly payment (of a dime!) for medical coverage. Fifth in the MGM series. **78m/B; DVD.** Lew Ayres; Lionel Barrymore; Samuel S. Hinds; Emma Dunn; Laraine Day; Gene Lockhart; ***D:*** Harold Bucquet; ***W:*** Willis Goldbeck; Harry Ruskin; ***C:*** Harold Rosson; ***M:*** David Snell.

Dr. Kildare's Crisis 𝒿𝒿 **1940** Nurse Mary Lamont is excited that her brother Doug is visiting. However, fiancé Kildare is worried about the man's odd behavior and believes he has a serious illness. His diagnosis turns out to be wrong and it's up to Dr. Gillespie to correct his protégé. Sixth in the MGM series. **73m/B; DVD.** Lew Ayres; Lionel Barrymore; Laraine Day; Robert Young; Nat Pendleton; ***D:*** Harold Bucquet; ***W:*** Willis Goldbeck; Harry Ruskin; ***C:*** John Seitz; ***M:*** David Snell.

Dr. Kildare's Strange Case 𝒿𝒿 **1940** In order to help a fellow doctor, Kildare administers a daring treatment to a man suffering from a mental disorder of a dangerous nature. The fourth film in the MGM series. **76m/B; DVD.** Lew Ayres; Lionel Barrymore; Laraine Day; Shepperd Strudwick; John Eldredge; Nat Pendleton; ***D:*** Harold Bucquet; ***W:*** Harry Ruskin; Willis Goldbeck; ***C:*** John Seitz; ***M:*** David Snell.

Dr. Kildare's Victory 𝒿𝒿 ½ **1942** A jurisdictional dispute between Blair General and Emerson Hospital causes Dr. Don Winslow (Sterling) to get fired because he sent seriously injured Cookie Charles (Ayars) to Blair General to be saved by Kildare. Kildare then uses the socialite's influence to shame the hospital bureaucracy into getting Winthrop reinstated at Emerson. The ninth and last in the "Kildare" series though MGM went on to make several films with Barrymore in his Dr. Gillespie role. **92m/B; DVD.** Lew Ayres; Lionel Barrymore; Robert Sterling; Ann Ayars; Jean Rogers; ***D:*** W.S. Van Dyke; ***W:*** Willis Goldbeck; Harry Ruskin; ***C:*** William H. Daniels; ***M:*** Lennie Hayton.

Dr. Kildare's Wedding Day 𝒿𝒿 **1941** Because Day wanted to leave the series, there's no happily-ever-after for Kildare and his longtime fiancé. Mary is killed in a traffic accident before their wedding and Kildare is grief-stricken. To get him interested in medicine again, Dr. Gillespie has him assist on a case involving a renowned conductor who's going deaf. Eighth in the MGM series. **82m/B; DVD.** Lew Ayres; Lionel Barrymore; Laraine Day; Nils Asther; Red Skelton; ***D:*** Harold Bucquet; ***W:*** Harry Ruskin; Willis Goldbeck; ***C:*** George J. Folsey; ***M:*** Bronislau Kaper.

Dr. Mabuse, The Gambler 𝒿𝒿𝒿 ½ *Doktor Mabuse der Spieler; Dr. Mabuse, Parts 1 & 2* **1922** The massive, two-part crime melodrama, introducing the raving mastermind/extortionist/villain to the world. The film follows Dr. Mabuse (Klein-Rogge) through his life of crime until he finally goes mad. Highly influential and inventive. Lang meant this to be a criticism of morally bankrupt post-WWI Germany. Lang also directed "The Crimes of Dr. Mabuse" (1932) and "The Thousand Eyes of Dr. Mabuse" (1960). **242m/B; Silent; VHS, DVD, Blu-Ray.** *GE* Rudolf Klein-Rogge; Aud Egede Nissen; Alfred Abel; Gertrude Welcker; Lil Dagover; Paul Richter; Bernhard Goetzke; ***D:*** Fritz Lang; ***W:*** Fritz Lang; Thea von Harbou; ***C:*** Carl Hoffmann.

Dr. Mabuse vs. Scotland Yard 𝒿𝒿 ½ **1964** A sequel to the Fritz Lang classics, this film features the arch-criminal attempting to take over the world with a mind-controlling camera. **90m/B; VHS, DVD.** *GE* Sabine Bethmann; Peter Van Eyck; ***D:*** Paul May.

Doctor Mordrid: Master of the Unknown 𝒿𝒿 **1990 (R)** Two immensely powerful sorcerers from the 4th dimension cross over into present time with two very different missions—one wants to destroy the Earth, one wants to save it. **102m/C; VHS, DVD.** Jeffrey Combs; Yvette Nipar; Jay Acovone; Brian Thompson; ***D:*** Albert Band; Charles Band; ***M:*** Richard Band.

Dr. No 𝒿𝒿𝒿 **1962 (PG)** The world is introduced to British secret agent 007, James Bond, when it is discovered that mad scientist Dr. No (Wiseman) is sabotaging rocket launchings from his hideout in Jamaica. The first 007 film is far less glitzy than any of its successors but boasts the sexiest "Bond girl" of them all in Andress as Honey Ryder who walks out of the surf in a white bikini, and promptly made stars of her and Connery. **111m/C; VHS, DVD, Blu-Ray.** *GB* Sean Connery; Ursula Andress; Joseph Wiseman; Jack Lord; Zena Marshall; Eunice Gayson; Margaret LeWars; John Kitzmiller; Lois Maxwell; Bernard Lee; Anthony Dawson; ***D:*** Terence Young; ***W:*** Johanna Harwood; Richard Maibaum; Berkely Mather; ***C:*** Ted Moore; ***M:*** John Barry.

Dr. Orloff and the Invisible Man 𝒿 ½ *Orloff Against the Invisible Man* **1972** In this horror film, Dr. Orloff creates an invisible ape-monster that escapes and goes on a rampage. **91m/C; VHS, DVD.** *FR SP* Howard Vernon; Brigitte Carva; Fernando (Fernand) Sancho; ***D:*** Pierre Chevalier; ***W:*** Pierre Chevalier.

Dr. Orloff's Monster WOOF! **1964** As if "The Awful Dr. Orloff" wasn't awful enough, the doctor is back, this time eliminating his enemies with his trusty killer robot. Awful awful. **88m/B; VHS, DVD, Blu-Ray.** *SP* Jose Rubio; Agnes Spaak; ***D:*** Jess (Jesus) Franco; ***C:*** Alfonso Nieva.

Dr. Otto & the Riddle of the Gloom Beam 𝒿 ½ **1986 (PG)** Ernest is in your face again. Fresh from the TV commercials featuring "Ernest" comes Varney playing a villain out to wreck the global economy. He also plays all the other characters, too. Way bizarre, "Know whut I mean?" **92m/C; VHS, DVD.** Jim Varney; ***D:*** John R. Cherry, III.

Doctor Phibes Rises Again 𝒿𝒿 ½ **1972 (PG)** The despicable doctor contines his quest to revive his beloved wife. Fun, superior sequel to "The Abominable Dr. Phibes." **89m/C; VHS, DVD, Blu-Ray.** *GB* Vincent Price; Robert Quarry; Peter Cushing; Beryl Reid; Hugh Griffith; Terry-Thomas; Valli Kemp; Peter Jeffrey; Fiona Lewis; Caroline Munro; ***D:*** Robert Fuest; ***W:*** Robert Fuest; Robert Blees; ***C:*** Alex Thomson; ***M:*** John Gale.

Dr. Seuss' Horton Hears a Who! 𝒿𝒿𝒿 *Horton Hears a Who!* **2008 (G)** Big-screen CG-animated adaptation of the Dr. Seuss classic. Toning down his shtick considerably, Jim Carrey voices Horton, an enlightened elephant who discovers an entire planet on a speck of dust. Within this planet is the harmonious city of Who-ville, threatened to be crushed by imagination-hating tyranny. Its mayor (Carell), unaccustomed to dealing with crisis, turns to Horton to save it. A timeless, allegorical story that works for kids and adults alike. Its only fault is in trying to stretch a 10-minute bedtime story into an hour and a half, which leads to obvious interference with the original voice of Dr. Seuss. **88m/C; Blu-Ray, On Demand.** ***V:*** Jim Carrey; Steve Carell; Carol Burnett; Will Arnett; Seth Rogen; Isla Fisher; Jonah Hill; Dan Fogler; Amy Poehler; Jaime Pressly; Josh Flitter; Jesse McCartney; Debi Derryberry; Laraine Newman; Joey King; ***Nar:*** Charles Osgood; ***D:*** Steve Martino; Jimmy Hayward; ***W:*** Cinco Paul; Ken Daurio; ***M:*** John Powell.

Dr. Seuss' How the Grinch Stole Christmas 𝒿𝒿 ½ *How the Grinch Stole Christmas; The Grinch* **2000 (PG)** If you've seen the cartoon, then you know it was padded. Just think of the stuff that Ron Howard added!/A new plot line here, an embellishment there, all Carreyed by a big star in green skin and hair./Crass Whos are shown doing frantic Yule shopping, and decoration-envy keeps each neighbor hopping./This anti-shop message is curiously told, considering the junk that this film clearly sold./ Cindy Lou Who loses her Christmas-time zest, and starts to research the town's Yuletide pest./In a flashback it's shown why the Grinch is so mean, and a love interest is added from when he's a teen./He's elected Cheermeister of the holiday season; but again leaves bitter, and with good Grinchy reason./Mayor May Who, his rival for Martha May's hand, repeats an insult about too-active glands./The stage is now set for his Grinchy attacks, assisted by his trusty reindeer/dog Max./Though he gave back Christmas for all the Whos' sakes, the Grinch got away with huge boxoffice takes./Young tots may think that this Grinch is too scary, but big kids will like the antics of Carrey./Fair holiday flick, even though the plot thins. Narrated by Sir Anthony Hopkins. **102m/C; VHS, DVD, Blu-Ray, HD-DVD.** Jim Carrey; Jeffrey Tambor; Christine Baranski; Taylor Momsen; Molly Shannon; Josh Ryan Evans; Clint Howard; Bill Irwin; Sloane Momsen; ***Nar:*** Anthony Hopkins; ***D:*** Ron Howard; ***W:*** Jeffrey Price; Peter S. Seaman; ***C:*** Don Peterman; ***M:*** James Horner.

Dr. Seuss' The Cat in the Hat 𝒿 ½ *The Cat in the Hat* **2003 (PG)** Another mega-star comedian goes deep under makeup cover to bring a beloved Dr. Seuss character to life. This time it's Myers, who dons the cat garb to bring some mischief to a bored brother and sister on a rainy afternoon. Conrad (Breslin) is an authority-defying slob, while Sally (Fanning) is an uptight over-achieving control freak. They rightfully distrust their neighbor Quinn (Baldwin) who has matrimonial designs on their mom (Preston), an overworked real estate agent. First-time helmer Welch reveals his art-director roots in the fully-realized Seussian sets, and in the failure to bring any joy or emotion to the proceedings. The screenwriters must also share the blame, as well, as they go to extremes to flesh out the book, only to drain the translation of charm. You'd be hard-pressed to recognize much that you or your kids love from the book. **82m/C; VHS, DVD.** Mike Myers; Dakota Fanning; Spencer Breslin; Kelly Preston; Alec Baldwin; Amy Hill; Sean P. Hayes; ***V:*** Sean P. Hayes; ***D:*** Bo Welch; ***W:*** Alec Berg; David Mandel; Jeff Schaffer; ***C:*** Emmanuel Lubezki; ***M:*** David Newman.

Dr. Seuss' The Lorax 𝒿𝒿 ½ *The Lorax* **2012 (PG)** Uninspired adaptation of the eco-friendly 1971 Dr. Seuss book. Young Ted (Efron) tries to help his girl Audrey (Swift) achieve her dream of seeing a real tree in the fabricated wasteland of Thneedville. With no real trees, people are forced to buy fresh air from cruel tycoon O'Hare (Riggle). Ted encounters the Once-ler (Helms), who is responsible for the disappearance of all the wildlife after greedily harvesting the technicolor Truffula trees for his own profit. He relates the story of the Lorax (DeVito), who vainly tried to stop him. Ted and the Lorax team up to battle O'Hare and return Thneedville to its former glory. The CGI and characters are kid-friendly but the spirit of Seuss gets lost. **94m/C; DVD, Blu-Ray.** ***V:*** Danny DeVito; Zac Efron; Taylor Swift; Ed Helms; Rob Riggle; Betty White; Willow Smith; ***D:*** Chris Renaud; Kyle Balda; ***W:*** Cinco Paul; Ken Daurio; ***M:*** John Powell.

Doctor Sleep 𝒿𝒿𝒿 **2019 (R)** Dan (McGregor) was traumatized by his childhood experiences related to his "shining" powers and uses drugs and alcohol to mask his pain. Seeking a better life, he moves to New Hampshire, joins AA, and uses his powers to help others at his hospice job. Dan's newfound peace is challenged by the True Knot, a group of immortal creatures. Its members feed off the essence they steal from children who shine, including powerful Abra (Curran), who is connected to Dan. Partly a sequel to Stanley Kubrick's 1980 adaptation of the classic Stephen King horror novel, the film successfully blends Kubrick's vision with King's source material. **151m/C; DVD, Blu-Ray.** Rebecca Ferguson; Ewan McGregor; Kyliegh Curran; Clifford Curtis; Zahn McClarnon; ***D:*** Mike Flanagan; ***W:*** Mike Flanagan; *C:* Michael Fimognari; *M:* The Newton Brothers.

Doctor Strange 2016 (PG-13) This is not your typical Marvel hero movie. On a quest to heal himself after a reckless car accident ends his career as a neurosurgeon, the egotistical Dr. Stephen Strange (Cumberbatch) encounters the Ancient One (Swinton) and reinvents himself as a powerful sorcerer. And of course he must use his newfound abilities to save the world! It's a wild and a – dare the Hound say it? – strange action-packed ride. But no one can handle that any better than Cumberbatch, whose talents in the action/humor department are on full display. And he couldn't have a better romantic interest/colleague to banter with than the sparkly McAdams. **115m/C; DVD, Blu-Ray.** Benedict Cumberbatch; Chiwetel Ejiofor; Rachel McAdams; Benedict Wong; Mads Mikkelsen; Tilda Swinton; *D:* Scott Derrickson; *W:* Scott Derrickson; Jon Spaihts; C. Robert Cargill; *C:* Ben Davis; *M:* Michael Giacchino.

Dr. Strangelove, or: How I Learned to Stop Worrying and Love the Bomb 1964 Sellers plays a tour-de-force triple role in Kubrick's classic black anti-war comedy. When a crazed general (Hayden) initiates a nuclear attack on the Soviets, the U.S. President (Sellers) deals with the consequences, "aided" by a hawkish general (Scott) and a wheelchair-bound advisor with an obvious Nazi past. Famous for Pickens' wild ride on the bomb, Hayden's character's "purity of essence" philosophy, Scott's gumchewing militarist, a soft-drink vending machine dispute, and countless other scenes. Based on the novel "Red Alert" by Peter George. **93m/B; VHS, DVD, Blu-Ray.** *GB* Peter Sellers; George C. Scott; Sterling Hayden; Keenan Wynn; Slim Pickens; James Earl Jones; Peter Bull; Tracy Reed; Shane Rimmer; Glenn Beck; Gordon Tanner; Frank Berry; Jack Creley; *D:* Stanley Kubrick; *W:* Stanley Kubrick; Terry Southern; Peter George; *C:* Gilbert Taylor; *M:* Laurie Johnson. AFI '98: Top 100; British Acad. '64: Film; Natl. Film Reg. '89; N.Y. Film Critics '64: Director (Kubrick).

Dr. Syn 1937 The story of a seemingly respectable vicar of Dymchurch who is really a former pirate. The last film of George Arliss. **90m/B; VHS, DVD.** *GB* George Arliss; Margaret Lockwood; John Loder; *D:* Roy William Neill.

Dr. Syn, Alias the Scarecrow 1/2 1964 (G) A mild-mannered minister is, in reality, a smuggler and pirate avenging King George III's injustices upon the English people. Originally broadcast in three parts on the Disney TV show. **129m/C; VHS, DVD.** Patrick McGoohan; George Cole; Tony Britton; Michael Hordern; Geoffrey Keen; Kay Cole; *D:* James Neilson. **TV**

Dr. T & the Women 2000 (R) Gere stars as Dr. Sullivan Travis, a charming and sensitive gynecologist to the affluent women of Dallas, Texas. Yet despite his respect for and adoration of the women in his life, Dr. T, as he is known, cannot truly fathom their complexity. And none are more baffling to him than those closest to him—his wife (Fawcett), who is slowly descending into mental illness, and his daughters (Hudson and Reid). Director Altman has set his sights on ordinary human weaknesses and shortcomings here, staying away from the social commentary and cynicism of some of his earlier films, and often hits his target with a sweet and humorous note. Gere's charm and mannerisms fit the doctor to a "T," while Dern, Hunt, and Long put in good performances as well. Screenwriter Ann Rapp also collaborated with Altman on his previous film, "Cookie's Fortune." **122m/C; VHS, DVD.** Richard Gere; Farrah Fawcett; Kate Hudson; Helen Hunt; Lee Grant; Liv Tyler; Shelley Long; Laura Dern; Tara Reid; Andy Richter; Matt Malloy; Robert Hays; Janine Turner; *D:* Robert Altman; *W:* Anne Rapp; *C:* Jan Kiesser; *M:* Lyle Lovett.

Doctor Takes a Wife 1940 A fast, fun screwball comedy wherein two ill-matched career people are forced via a publicity mix-up to fake being married. **89m/B; VHS, DVD.** Ray Milland; Loretta Young; Reginald Gardiner; Gail Patrick; Edmund Gwenn; George Metaxa; Charles Halton; *D:* Alexander Hall; *W:* George Seaton.

Dr. Tarr's Torture Dungeon WOOF! *Dr. Jekyll's Dungeon of Darkness; Mansion of Madness* 1975 (R) A mysterious man is sent to the forest to investigate the bizarre behavior of Dr. Tarr who runs a torture asylum. **90m/C; VHS, DVD.** *MX* Claudio Brook; Ellen Sherman; Robert Dumont; *D:* Juan Lopez Moctezuma; *W:* Carlos Illescas.

Doctor Who 1/2 1996 The late British sci-fi series, which ended in 1989, has been resurrected in this TV movie. The TARDIS is forced down in 1999 San Francisco and renegade Time Lord The Master's sluglike remains escape from the Doctor (McCoy) and into a temporary host body (Roberts). Meanwhile, the Doctor's been hospitalized and a botched operation by Dr. Grace Holloway (Ashbrook) leaves him clinically dead—until he manages to regenerate once again (as McGann). With Grace's help, the Doctor tries to stop his enemy from destroying the world on New Year's Eve in a plot that will also give the Master the Doctor's body as his new home. Production design and special effects are lavish (particularly in relation to the cheesiness of the series). **95m/C; VHS, DVD.** *GB CA* Paul McGann; Eric Roberts; Daphne Ashbrook; Yee Jee Tso; Sylvester McCoy; *D:* Geoffrey Sax; *W:* Matthew Jacobs; *C:* Glen MacPherson; *M:* John Debney. **TV**

Doctor X 1/2 1932 An armless mad scientist uses a formula for "synthetic flesh" to grow temporary limbs and commit murder. A classic, rarely seen horror oldie, famous for its very early use of two-color Technicolor. **77m/C; VHS, DVD.** Lionel Atwill; Fay Wray; Lee Tracy; Preston Foster; Arthur Edmund Carewe; Leila Bennett; Mae Busch; *D:* Michael Curtiz; *W:* Earl Baldwin; Robert Tasker; *C:* Ray Rennahan; Richard Towers.

Doctor Zhivago 1965 (PG-13) Sweeping adaptation of the Nobel Prize-winning Boris Pasternak novel. An innocent Russian poet-intellectual is caught in the furor and chaos of the Bolshevik Revolution. Essentially a poignant love story filmed as a historical epic. Panoramic film popularized the song "Lara's Theme." Overlong, with often disappointing performances, but gorgeous scenery. Lean was more successful in "Lawrence of Arabia," where there was less need for ensemble acting. **197m/C; VHS, DVD.** Omar Sharif; Julie Christie; Geraldine Chaplin; Rod Steiger; Alec Guinness; Klaus Kinski; Ralph Richardson; Rita Tushingham; Siobhan McKenna; Tom Courtenay; Bernard Kay; Gerard Tichy; Noel Willman; Geoffrey Keen; Adrienne Corri; Jack MacGowran; Mark Eden; Erik Chitty; Peter Madden; Jose Maria Caffarell; Jeffrey Rockland; Wolf Frees; Lucy Westmore; *D:* David Lean; *W:* Robert Bolt; *C:* Frederick A. (Freddie) Young; *M:* Maurice Jarre. Oscars '65: Adapt. Screenplay, Art Dir./Set Dec., Color, Color Cinematog., Costume Des. (C), Orig. Score; AFI '98: Top 100; Golden Globes '66: Actor--Drama (Sharif), Director (Lean), Film--Drama, Score, Screenplay; Natl. Bd. of Review '65: Actress (Christie).

Doctor Zhivago 1/2 2003 Miniseries version of the Pasternak novel focuses more on the story's romantic difficulties and slightly less on the politics of the Russian revolution. Noble doctor/poet Yury Zhivago (Matheson) marries his childhood sweetheart and cousin, Tonya (Lara), but falls madly in love with beautiful Lara (Knightley). As if this affair weren't dramatic enough, Lara is the obsession of the powerful Kormarovsky (Neill), who is determined to keep her as his possession and who is much more capable of bending with the changing political winds than the idealistic Yury. And if the ending seems different, you're right, it was changed for this re-telling. **214m/C; VHS, DVD.** *GB* Hans Matheson; Keira Knightley; Sam Neill; Kris Marshall; Daniele Liotti; Celia Imrie; Bill Paterson; Alexandra Maria Lara; Maryam D'Abo; *D:* Giacomo Campiotti; *W:* Andrew Davies; *C:* Blasco Giurato; *M:* Ludovico Einaudi. **TV**

The Doctor's Dilemma 1958 Though George Bernard Shaw's 1903 play focuses on the dilemma, the Asquith film is more about the marriage between dying, philandering artist Louis Dubedat and his loving wife. She begs the doctor to use a new treatment, which is in limited supply, on her husband, but the pontificating doctor and his colleagues argue about saving it for a more-worthy patient. **99m/C; DVD.** *UK* Leslie Caron; Dirk Bogarde; John Robinson; Robert Morley; Alastair Sim; Felix Aylmer; *D:* Anthony Asquith; *W:* Anatole de Grunwald; *C:* Robert Krasker; *M:* Joseph Kosma.

Doctors' Wives 1/2 1970 (R) An adaptation of the Frank Slaughter potboiler about a large city hospital's doctors, nurses, and their respective spouses, with plenty of affairs, medical traumas, and betrayals. **102m/C; VHS, DVD.** Dyan Cannon; Richard Crenna; Gene Hackman; Carroll O'Connor; Rachel Roberts; Janice Rule; Diana Sands; Ralph Bellamy; John Colicos; *D:* George Schaefer; *W:* Daniel Taradash; *C:* Charles B(ryant) Lang, Jr.; *M:* Elmer Bernstein.

Dodes 'ka-den 1/2 *Clickety Clack* 1970 In this departure from his samurai-genre films, Kurosawa depicts a throng of fringe-dwelling Tokyo slum inhabitants in a semi-surreal manner. Fascinating presentation and content. **140m/C; VHS, DVD.** *JP* Yoshitaka Zushi; Junzaburo Ban; Kiyoko Tange; *D:* Akira Kurosawa; *W:* Akira Kurosawa; Shinobu Hashimoto; Hideo Oguni; *C:* Takao Saito; Yasumichi Fukuzawa; *M:* Toru Takemitsu.

Dodge City 1939 Flynn stars as Wade Hutton, a roving cattleman who becomes the sheriff of Dodge City. His job: to run a ruthless outlaw and his gang out of town. De Havilland serves as Flynn's love interest, as she did in many previous films. A broad and colorful shoot-em-up! **104m/C; VHS, DVD, Blu-Ray.** Errol Flynn; Olivia de Havilland; Bruce Cabot; Ann Sheridan; Alan Hale; Frank McHugh; Victor Jory; Henry Travers; Charles Halton; *D:* Michael Curtiz; *M:* Max Steiner.

Dodgeball: A True Underdog Story 2004 (PG-13) Likable, easygoing schmoe (Vaughn) runs a gym for underachievers in direct competition with big box fitness fascist (Stiller) across the street. Stiller finds a way to expose Vaughn's financial failings to put him out of business. Vaughn enlists aid of his misfit patrons to win the pot of a professional dodgeball tournament—but they must beat Stiller's elite team first. Slobs vs. snobs comedy in the "Caddyshack/Meatballs" tradition, with plenty of crotch-crunching and boob humor. Don't miss Torn's crusty coach, who hurls wrenches as training. Nothing too original, but should please the frat crowd. Cameos by William Shatner, Lance Armstrong, David Hasselhoff, and Chuck Norris. **96m/C; DVD, Blu-Ray, UMD.** Ben Stiller; Vince Vaughn; Christine Taylor; Justin Long; Jason Bateman; Gary Cole; Missi Pyle; Stephen (Steve) Root; William Shatner; Rip Torn; Hank Azaria; Chris(topher) Williams; Alan Tudyk; David Hasselhoff; ***Cameo(s):*** Chuck Norris; Lance Armstrong; *D:* Rawson Marshall Thurber; *W:* Rawson Marshall Thurber; *C:* Jerzy Zielinski; Theodore Shapiro.

Dodson's Journey 1/2 2001 Worried about the impact their impending divorce will have on 10-year-old Maggie (Morton), dad James (Elliott) decides to take his daughter on a bonding fly-fishing trip. Adapted from Dodson's book "Faithful Travelers." **120m/C; VHS, DVD.** David James Elliott; Alicia Morton; Ellen Burstyn; Brenda James; Tantoo Cardinal; Nanci Chambers; *D:* Gregg Champion; *W:* John Pielmeier; *C:* Attila Szalay; *M:* Joseph Conlan. **TV**

Dodsworth 1/2 1936 The lives of a self-made American tycoon and his wife are drastically changed when they take a tour of Europe. The success of their marriage seems questionable as they re-evaluate their lives. Huston excels as does the rest of the cast in this film, based upon the Sinclair Lewis novel. **101m/B; VHS, DVD, Blu-Ray.** Walter Huston; David Niven; Paul Lukas; John Payne; Mary Astor; Ruth Chatterton; Maria Ouspenskaya; Charles Halton; *D:* William Wyler; *W:* Sidney Howard; *C:* Rudolph Mate; *M:* Alfred Newman. Natl. Film Reg. '90; N.Y. Film Critics '36: Actor (Huston).

The Doe Boy 2001 A hemophiliac half-Cherokee youth tries to live up to his father's expectations, free himself from an over-protective mother, and forge an identify for himself. He also has to overcome the stigma of accidently killing a female deer instead of a buck during his first hunting trip (giving him his nickname and the movie its title). Redroad's directorial debut doesn't break much new ground, but deals with the themes in a satisfying way. Fine cast helps things along nicely. **83m/C; VHS, DVD.** James Duval; Kevin Anderson; Andrew J. Ferchland; Jeri Arredondo; Jim Metzler; Gordon Tootoosis; Robert C. Anthony; *D:* Randy Redroad; *W:* Randy Redroad; *C:* Laszlo Kadar; *M:* Adam Dorn.

The Dog 2014 There have been plenty of great documentaries about unforgettable personalities. Add to that list this exploration of the fascinating life of John Wojtowicz, the man who chose to rob a Brooklyn bank on a hot summer day, and saw his life story become art in the timeless Sidney Lumet film "Dog Day Afternoon." Wojtowicz infamously robbed the bank in his bumbling way to pay for the sex change operation of his male lover. He is an unapologetic icon for NYC, a man who saw something he wanted and tried to take it. He makes for a fascinating interview subject. **100m/C; DVD, Blu-Ray.** *D:* Allison Berg; Frank Keraudren; *C:* Amanda Micheli.

Dog Bite Dog 2006 Violent, if routine, Hong Kong action pic. A Cambodian hit man (Chen) is up against a cop (Lee) with anger issues. Chinese, Thai, and Cambodian with subtitles. **108m/C; DVD.** *CH JP* Edison Chen; Sam Lee; Suet Lam; Weiying Pei; Siu-fai Cheung; *D:* Pou-soi Cheang; *W:* Matt Chow; Kam-yuen Szeto; *C:* Yuen Man Fung; *M:* Ben Cheung.

Dog Day 1/2 *Canicule* 1983 An American traitor, who is on the lam from the government, and his cronies, takes refuge on a small farm. A surprise awaits him when the farmers come up with an unusual plan to bargain for his life. **101m/C; VHS, DVD, Blu-Ray.** *FR* Lee Marvin; Miou-Miou; Victor Lanoux; *D:* Yves Boisset.

Dog Day Afternoon 1/2 1975 (R) Based on a true story, this taut, yet fantastic thriller centers on a bi-sexual and his slow-witted buddy who rob a bank to obtain money to fund a sex change operation for the ring-leader's lover. Pacino is breathtaking in his role as the frustrated robber, caught in a trap of his own devising. Very controversial for its language and subject matter when released, it nevertheless became a huge success. Director Lumet keeps up the pace, fills the screen with pathos without gross sentiment. **124m/C; VHS, DVD, Blu-Ray, HD-DVD.** Al Pacino; John Cazale; Charles Durning; James Broderick; Chris Sarandon; Carol Kane; Lance Henriksen; Dick Anthony Williams; Dominic Chianese; *D:* Sidney Lumet; *W:* Frank Pierson; *C:* Victor Kemper. Oscars '75: Orig. Screenplay; British Acad. '75: Actor (Pacino); Natl. Bd. of Review '75: Support. Actor (Durning); Natl. Film Reg. '09; Writers Guild '75: Orig. Screenplay.

Dog Days 2018 (PG) In contemporary Los Angeles, dog lovers find their lives intertwined over one summer. Elizabeth (Dobrev) deals with her romantic breakup by projecting onto her dog Sam, whom she takes to expensive dog therapist Danielle (Notaro). Meanwhile, loner widower Walter (Jones) becomes distraught when his pug Mabel goes missing and goes looking for her with helpful pizza delivery driver Tyler (Wolfhard). Mabel is found by Grace (Longoria) and Kurt (Corddry), and the dog helps to bond them with their adopted daughter Amela (Caro). This ensemble comedy has an infectious spirit of cheer and generosity in its story and realistic attitude towards dogs. **113m/C; DVD.** Nina Dobrev; Vanessa Anne Hudgens; Finn Wolfhard; Eva Longoria; Thomas Lennon; *D:* Ken Marino; *W:* Elissa Matsueda; Erica Oyama; *C:* Frank Barrera; *M:* Matt Novack; Craig Wedren.

Dog Eat Dog *Einer Frisst den Anderen; La Morte Vestita di Dollar* 1964 Centering on a heist scheme by Mitchell, this one has nothing to offer except Mansfield's attributes. **86m/B; VHS, DVD.** Cameron Mitchell; Jayne Mansfield; Isa Miranda; *D:* Ray Nazarro.

Dog Eat Dog 2016 Paul Schrader returns to the other side of the tracks directing this intermittently entertaining crime thriller that has pieces that work but never quite mesh. Three lifetime criminals: Troy (Cage), Diesel (Cook), and Mad Dog (Dafoe) plan one last job to set themselves up for life, and they actually pull it off. But it's the aftermath—the insecurity and the anxiety of being caught—that tears them apart. Cage is surprisingly low-key here, offset by an over-the-top turn from Dafoe. It's a decent rental, but forgettable. **93m/C; DVD, Blu-Ray.** Nicolas Cage; Willem Dafoe; Christopher Matthew Cook; Omar J. Dorsey; Louisa Krause; *D:* Paul Schrader; *W:* Matthew Wilder; *C:* Alexander Dynan; *M:* Deantoni Parks.

Dog Gone 🦴🦴 1/2 *Diamond Dog Caper* **2008 (PG)** Fast-paced family comedy. Twelve-year-old Owen rescues a golden retriever from three bumbling thieves and, after reading about a diamond heist, realizes that the jewels are stashed with the dog (you really don't want to know where). Owen goes to the cops but they don't believe his story, so he and the dog he's named Diamond plan to bring the bad guys down themselves. **108m/C; DVD.** Luke Benward; French Stewart; Kevin Farley; Garrett Morris; Kelly Perrine; Brittany Curran; *D:* Mark Stouffer; *W:* Mark Stouffer; Denis Johnson; *C:* Tom Camarda; *M:* Andrew Gross. **VIDEO**

Dog Gone Love 🦴 1/2 **2003 (R)** While doing some research at the local vet office, struggling author Steven meets foxy assistant Rebecca who thinks he's gay. So he figures faking it would be fun until—oh my!?he falls for her. Plot is all bark and no bite. **89m/C; VHS, DVD.** Lindsay Sloane; Richard Kind; Christopher Coppola; Brian Poth; Tom McGowan; Jordan Ladd; Chris Elwood; Marissa Hall; James Warwick; Alexander Chaplin; Marina Black; John Cantwell; Carmen Mormino; Alexandra Boyd; Jenni Pulos; Paul Korver; Steve Susskind; Mikyla; Brian O'Hare; Laura Pinner; Brian T. Lynch; *D:* Rob Lundsgaard; *W:* Rob Lundsgaard; *C:* Kristian Bernier; *M:* William V. Malpede. **VIDEO**

The Dog Lover 🦴🦴 *The Wrong Side of Right* **2016 (PG)** A drama about the activities of an animal rights activist. A member of the United Animal Protection Agency, Sara Gold (Paige) supports the group's agenda of conducting animal rescues and asking legislators to improve animal welfare laws. As part of the group's activities, Sara is chose for an important assignment infiltrating a puppy mill. Posing as a college intern, Sara is charged with bringing down the puppy mill's owner Daniel Holloway (Remar). **101m/C; DVD, Streaming, Download.** Allison Paige; James Remar; Lea Thompson; Jayson Blair; Sherry Stringfield; *D:* Alex Ranarivelo; *C:* Reuben Steinberg; *M:* Jamie Christopherson.

A Dog Named Christmas 🦴🦴 1/2 **2009** Sentimental Christmas mush gets you all the time in this 237th presentation from the Hallmark Hall of Fame. Kansas farmer George McCray (Greenwood) has always been adamant that his family will not get a dog (flashbacks explain why). However, when his 20-year-old mentally-challenged son Todd (Fisher) hears about an adopt-a-dog program for the holidays sponsored by the local animal shelter, Todd and mom Mary Ann (Edmond) manage to persuade George to give in. Yellow Lab Christmas is, of course, an exceptionally appealing choice and you won't be surprised by how things turn out. Adapted from the novel by Greg Kincaid. **100m/C; DVD.** Bruce Greenwood; Noel Fisher; Ken Pogue; Sonja Bennett; Linda Emond; Carrie Ruscheinsky; *D:* Peter Werner; *W:* Jenny Wingfield; *C:* Eric Van Haren Noman; *M:* Jeff Beal. **TV**

A Dog of Flanders 🦴🦴 1/2 **1959** A young Dutch boy and his grandfather find a severely beaten dog and restore it to health. **96m/C; VHS, DVD.** David Ladd; Donald Crisp; Theodore Bikel; Max Croiset; Monique Ahrens; *D:* James B. Clark.

A Dog of Flanders 🦴🦴 **1999 (PG)** Fifth screen version of Marie Louise de la Ramee's 1872 children's story is put to sleep by slow pacing and murky settings. Orphan Nello (Kissner) and his grandfather Jehan (Warden) find an abused dog and nurse it back to health. The boy and his dog team up to support the household as Jehan's health begins to fade. Nello is noticed sketching in the town square by artist Michel (Voight), who then befriends and encourages the boy. As his artistic gifts flower, he attempts to win his childhood sweetheart Aloise (Monet) over the protests of her father. The rather depressing climax of the original story is replaced by a brighter ending in an attempt to make the movie more child-friendly, but the uneven acting and accents won't even fool the kiddies. **100m/C; VHS, DVD.** Jack Warden; Jon Voight; Jeremy James Kissner; Jesse James; Cheryl Ladd; Bruce McGill; Steven Hartley; Dirk Lavrysen; Andrew Bicknell; Antje De Boeck; *D:* Kevin Brodie; *W:* Robert Singer; Kevin Brodie; *C:* Walther Vanden Ende; *M:* Richard Friedman.

Dog Park 🦴🦴 **1998 (R)** Andy (Wilson) and Lorna (Henstridge) have only their doggy companions to keep them warm after their respective lovers take a hike. At least until they find each other while walking their pups. Not that the course of true love (or even dating) will run smoothly. Pleasant enough romantic comedy but Henstridge seems out of her element. **91m/C; VHS, DVD.** *CA* Luke Wilson; Natasha Henstridge; Janeane Garofalo; Bruce McCulloch; Kathleen Robertson; Kristen Lehman; Mark McKinney; Gordon Currie; Amie Carey; Harland Williams; *D:* Bruce McCulloch; *W:* Bruce McCulloch; *C:* David Makin; *M:* Craig Northey. Genie '99: Support. Actor (McKinney).

Dog Pound Shuffle 🦴🦴🦴 *Dogpound Shuffle* **1975 (PG)** Two drifters form a new song-and-dance act in order to raise the funds necessary to win their dog's freedom from the pound. Charming Canadian production. **98m/C; VHS, DVD.** *CA* Ron Moody; David Soul; *D:* Jeffrey Bloom; *W:* Jeffrey Bloom.

The Dog Problem 🦴🦴 1/2 **2006 (R)** Solo (Ribisi) is at a personal and professional crossroads after squandering the rewards of his success on drugs, women, and therapy. At his last session with Dr. Noumand (Cheadle), the good psychiatrist suggests he get a pet to help overcome his loneliness. Upon doing so, his new pooch is soon chomped by a formidable hound in the care of a spunky stripper (Collins). This leads to a most unusual relationship plagued with canine complications. Holds your interest, develops nicely, with just the right touch of comedic urban disdain. **89m/C; DVD.** Giovanni Ribisi; Don Cheadle; Lynn Collins; Kevin Corrigan; Mena Suvari; Scott Caan; Joanna Krupa; *D:* Scott Caan; *W:* Scott Caan; *C:* Phil Parmet; *M:* Mark Mothersbaugh.

Dog Soldiers 🦴🦴 **2001 (R)** Military werewolf flick finds a British army squad on manuevers in the Scottish highlands. When they find their Special Ops war-game foes half-eaten except for leader Ryan, they're set upon by the creatures. The survivors are rescued by a passing female zoologist and taken to a cabin to hold up for the night. Pic becomes an "Assault on Precinct 13"-type siege as the creatures try to get to the soldiers, some of whom have taken on distinctly canine tendences. Hit-and-miss black humor, paired with too-British banter and low-tech effects make this one a bit hard to swallow for most. **104m/C; VHS, DVD, Blu-Ray.** *GB LU* Sean Pertwee; Kevin McKidd; Liam Cunningham; Thomas Lockyer; Emma Cleasby; *D:* Neil Marshall; *W:* Neil Marshall; *M:* Mark Thomas.

Dog Star Man 🦴🦴🦴 **1964** The silent epic by the dean of experimental American film depicts man's spiritual and physical conflicts through Brakhage's characteristically freeform collage techniques. **78m/C; Silent; VHS, DVD.** *D:* Stan Brakhage. Natl. Film Reg. '92.

The Dog Who Saved Christmas 🦴🦴 1/2 **2009 (PG)** Former K-9 police dog Zeus is the newest member of the Bannister family. Left behind to guard the house when the Bannisters go away for the holiday, Zeus seizes his chance to act heroically when the usual comically-inept burglars try to rob the home. **90m/C; DVD.** Dean Cain; Gary Valentine; Elisa Donovan; Mindy Sterling; Sierra McCormick; Charlie Stewart; Joey Diaz; Joe Torry; *V:* Mario Lopez; *D:* Michael Feifer; *W:* Michael Ciminiera; Richard Gnolfo; *C:* Hank Baumert, Jr.; *M:* Andres Boulton. **VIDEO**

The Dog Who Saved Christmas Vacation 🦴🦴 1/2 **2010 (PG)** In this sequel to the 2009 ABC Family's "The Dog Who Saved Christmas," Zeus and the Bannister family travel to a Rocky Mountain resort for what they hope will be a relaxing holiday. Unfortunately, Belinda's obnoxious brother Randy and his family are at the same resort along with their new dog, poodle Bella. Then the same two inept burglars, Ted and Stewey, show up since Bella was mistakenly given a collar made of real diamonds. **89m/C; DVD.** Dean Cain; Gary Valentine; Elisa Donovan; Casper Van Dien; Joey Diaz; Catherine Oxenberg; Mindy Sterling; *V:* Mario Lopez; Paris Hilton; *D:* Michael Feifer; *W:* Richard Gnolfo; Michael Ciminiera; Peter Sullivan; *C:* Jeffrey D. Smith; *M:* Andres Boulton; Chad Rehmann. **CABLE**

The Dog Who Saved Easter 🦴 1/2 **2015 (PG)** Fifth film in the series sticks to its family-friendly premise. As the Bannisters take off for an Easter vacation, dog Zeus is left at Alice's newly-established animal daycare. Only her rival Cressida hires some familiar and inept bad guys to try to sabotage the business. It's Zeus and his new friends to the rescue! **87m/C; DVD.** Dean Cain; Patrick Muldoon; Beverley Mitchell; Catherine Hicks; Elisa Donovan; *V:* Mario Lopez; *D:* Sean Robert Olson; *W:* Sean Robert Olson; *C:* Joseph Setele; *M:* Jason Brandt. **VIDEO**

The Dog Who Saved Halloween 🦴🦴 1/2 **2011 (PG)** The Bannisters move into a new house just before Halloween and George and Zeus decide to investigate their seemingly creepy neighbor. There are silly consequences that involve the two bumbling burglars from the first two pics. The scary factor is mostly for fun but there is an excessive number of poop and fart jokes. **88m/C; DVD.** Gary Valentine; Elisa Donovan; Dean Cain; Joey Diaz; Lance Henriksen; Kayley Stallings; Brennan Bailey; Mindy Sterling; *V:* Joseph Lawrence; Mayim Bialik; *D:* Peter Sullivan; *W:* Peter Sullivan; *C:* George Reasner; *M:* Chad Rehmann. **VIDEO**

The Dog Who Saved Summer 🦴🦴 **2015 (PG)** Family comedy about a dog who must save the day by undermining obedience school. Zeus (Lopez) is a former police K-9 who is now a member of the Bannister family. After Zeus destroys a party in the family home on accident, he is sent to obedience school where he must deal with a hard-nosed instructor (Kove) and his Marine K-9 Apollo. Zeus must outsmart the instructor and Apollo to win a big tournament and break out of school to stop a trio of diamond thieves from committing their big jewelry heist. **89m/C; DVD, Streaming, Download.** Mario Lopez; Dean Cain; Gary Valentine; Elisa Donovan; Patrick Muldoon; *D:* Sean Robert Olson; *W:* Michael Ciminera; Richard Gnolfo; Peter Sullivan; *C:* Joseph Setele; *M:* Jason Brandt. **VIDEO**

The Dog Who Saved the Holidays 🦴🦴 **2012 (PG)** The Bannisters are visiting Aunt Barbara and rival pooches Zeus and puppy Eve must team up to prevent a burglary of the family home by incompetent thieves Ted and Stewey just before Christmas. Pleasant enough holiday fare. **87m/C; DVD.** Dean Cain; Joey Diaz; Shelley Long; Gary Valentine; Elisa Donovan; Jack Scalia; *V:* Joseph Lawrence; Peyton List; *D:* Michael Feifer; *W:* Michael Ciminera; Richard Gnolfo; *C:* Roberto Schein; *M:* Chad Rehmann; Andres Boulton. **VIDEO**

The Dog Who Stopped the War 🦴🦴 **1984 (G)** A Canadian children's film about a dog who puts a halt to an escalating snowball fight between rival gangs. **90m/C; VHS, DVD.** *CA* Cedric Jourde; Marie-Pierre D'Amour; Julien Elie; Minh Vu Duc; *D:* Andre Melancon; *W:* Roger Cantin; Danyele Patenaude; *C:* Francois Protat; *M:* Germain Gauthier.

A Dog Year 🦴 1/2 **2009** Best watched for the pleasures of Jeff Bridges' acting, since his character and the too-familiar sentimental story (based on Jon Katz's 2002 memoir) leave something to be desired. Grumpy Jon, who's separated from his wife, suffering writer's block, and staying at a remote farm, takes in an abused border collie to join his two Labradors and learns some life lessons while trying to train it. **82m/C; DVD.** Jeff Bridges; Lauren Ambrose; Lois Smith; Domhnall Gleeson; Elizabeth Marvel; *V:* Karen Allen; *D:* George LaVoo; *W:* George LaVoo; *C:* Frederick Elmes; *M:* Joseph Vitarelli. **CABLE**

The Dogfather 🦴🦴 **2010 (PG)** Silly, generally unobjectionable kids fare. Was there ever a dog breed more suitable to be a mobster's pet than a bulldog? Sonny is a mafia don's best friend until he accidentally swallows his master's valuable ring. Wisely going on the lam, Sonny is adopted by the suburban Franks family and they won't allow anything to happen to their new pet after the boss sends a couple of inept henchmen to get his ring back. **88m/C; DVD.** Chris Parnell; William Cuddy; Marie Ward; Gerry Mendicino; Dax Ravina; Tony Nappo; Rachel Marcus; *D:* Richard Boddington; *W:* Michael Hamilton-Wright; Russel Scalise; *C:* Denis Maloney; *M:* Ryan Latham. **VIDEO**

Dogfight 🦴🦴🦴 **1991 (R)** It's 1963 and a baby-faced Marine and his buddies are spending their last night in San Francisco before leaving the U.S. for a tour of duty in Vietnam. They agree to throw a "dogfight," a competition to see who can bring the ugliest date to a party. Birdlace (Phoenix) chooses Taylor, a shy, average-looking waitress who dreams of becoming a folk singer and realizes too late that she doesn't deserve the treatment he's about to subject her to. This quiet film didn't see a wide release, but is worth renting due to an above average script which is held up by the splendid performances of Phoenix and Taylor. **94m/C; DVD.** River Phoenix; Lili Taylor; Richard Panebianco; Anthony Clark; Mitchell Whitfield; Elizabeth Daily; Holly Near; Brendan Fraser; Margaret "Peg" Phillips; *D:* Nancy Savoca; *W:* Bob Comfort; *C:* Bobby Bukowski; *M:* Mason Daring.

Dogma 🦴🦴 1/2 **1999 (R)** Smith packs a lot into his brave, controversial comedy on Catholicism and, as a Catholic himself, illustrates that he has some issues about his religion. He vents with a film that's both devilishly funny and agonizingly boring. A great cast does his dirty work, including Affleck and Damon as two cast out angels with a plan to re-enter heaven. Rock plays an angry apostle, Hayek is a muse turned stripper, and Rickman is the voice of God informing an abortion worker (Fiorentino) that she's to stop the angels. Rounding out the motley crew is Carlin as a cardinal. The first half is loaded with on-target jokes, but laughs are hard to find in the second hour, which falls victim to excessive religious yakety-schmakety. Smith's a talented screenwriter, unfortunately this time out, it's his directing that's really a sin. **125m/C; VHS, DVD.** Ben Affleck; Matt Damon; Linda Fiorentino; Chris Rock; Salma Hayek; Jason Lee; George Carlin; Alan Rickman; Jason Mewes; Janeane Garofalo; Kevin Smith; Alanis Morissette; Bud Cort; Jeff Anderson; Guinevere Turner; *D:* Kevin Smith; *W:* Kevin Smith; *C:* Robert Yeoman; *M:* Howard Shore.

A Dog's Breakfast 🦴🦴 1/2 **2007** Black comedy at its funniest. Patrick hates his younger sister Marilyn's fiance Ryan so much that he decides to murder him. Title is British slang for making a mess of things, although there is a dog (named Mars) and what he eats is important (and gross). **88m/C; DVD.** David Hewlett; Paul McGillion; Rachel Luttrell; Christopher Judge; Kate Hewlett; *D:* David Hewlett; *W:* David Hewlett; *C:* James Alfred Menard; *M:* Tim Williams. **VIDEO**

Dogs in Space 🦴🦴 **1987** A low-budget Australian film about a clique of aimless Melbourne rock kids in 1978, caught somewhere between post-hippiedom and punk, free love and heroin addiction. Acclaimed. Includes music by Hutchence, Brian Eno, Iggy Pop, and others. **109m/C; VHS, DVD.** *AU* Michael Hutchence; Saskia Post; Nique Needles; Tony Helou; Deanna Bond; *D:* Richard Lowenstein; *W:* Richard Lowenstein.

A Dog's Journey 🦴🦴 1/2 **2019 (PG)** Farmers Ethan (Quaid) and Hannah (Helgenberger) help their alcoholic widowed daughter-in-law Gloria (Gilpin) raise their baby granddaughter CJ (Ryder, then Prescott). The farmers' dog, a Great Pyreneese Bernese Mountain named Bailey (Gad), keeps an eye on CJ and promises Ethan that he will always be there for CJ. Though Gloria and CJ leave the farm and Bailey dies, he returns in the body of other dogs over the years and reunites with CJ at key moments in her life. Based on novels by W. Bruce Cameron, the family film sweetly delves into the unique relationship between humans and dogs while unapologetically pulling at heart-strings. **108m/C; DVD, Blu-Ray.** Josh Gad; Dennis Quaid; Kathryn Prescott; Marg Helgenberger; Betty Gilpin; *D:* Gail Mancuso; *W:* W. Bruce Cameron; Maya Forbes; Cathryn Michon; M. Wallace Wolodarsky; *C:* Rogier Stoffers; *M:* Mark Isham.

The Dogs of War 🦴🦴 ½ **1981 (R)** A graphic depiction of a group of professional mercenaries, driven by nothing but their quest for wealth and power, hired to overthrow the dictator of a new West African nation. Has some weak moments which break up the continuity of the movie. Based on the novel by Frederick Forsyth. **102m/C; VHS, DVD, Blu-Ray.** *GB* Christopher Walken; Tom Berenger; Colin Blakely; Paul Freeman; Hugh Millais; Victoria Tennant; JoBeth Williams; ***D:*** John Irvin; ***W:*** Gary De Vore; ***C:*** Jack Cardiff; ***M:*** Geoffrey Burgon.

A Dog's Purpose 🦴 ½ **2017 (PG)** A well-intentioned family drama that nonetheless feels a little creepy as it explains its title. The trick is a simple one as a great dog, voiced by Josh Gad, is reincarnated as other great dogs over the course of several lifetimes, and with several owners. So the film becomes an episodic series of stories of great dogs, but they're really the same dog! So, your dog doesn't die, it just moves on to the next plane of being a great dog. That's a nice thought but doesn't change that it's a film built around dying dogs. **100m/C; DVD, Blu-Ray, Streaming.** Dennis Quaid; Peggy Lipton; K.J. Apa; Britt Robertson; ***V:*** Josh Gad; ***D:*** Lasse Hallstrom; ***W:*** W. Bruce Cameron; Cathryn Michon; Audrey Wells; Maya Forbes; Wally Wolodarsky; ***C:*** Terry Stacey; ***M:*** Rachel Portman.

Dogs: The Rise and Fall of an All-Girl Bookie Joint 🦴🦴 **1996** On the surface, this is a story about some twenty-something women who are bad at relationships and can't pay the rent. To solve one of their problems they turn their apartment into a bookie joint. However, underneath there is the story of the girl who has just lost her mother and needs money to pay for her funeral. The thread that weaves it all together is the drive to survive and rise above what life has given you, or sometimes what you give yourself. This is an indie, low-budget film and the acting and lighting reflect its limitations, but overall it is a good story with competent acting. **88m/C; DVD.** Pam Columbus; Pamela Gray; Eve Annenberg; Toby Huss; Leo Marks; Amedo D'Adamo; ***D:*** Eve Annenberg; ***W:*** Eve Annenberg; ***C:*** Wolfgang Held.

A Dog's Way Home 🦴🦴 **2019 (PG)** After her mother is taken away, stray puppy Bella (voiced by Howard) is raised by a cat before being adopted by two med students. Though Lucas (Hauer-King), Olivia (Shipp), and Lucas's mother Terri (Judd) love Bella, local laws against pit bulls compel them to find her a temporary home in New Mexico. To get back to her humans in suburban Denver, Bella makes a long, dangerous road trip with the help of humans and a baby cougar. Heartfelt and moving, it also explores usually untouched themes such as the unfair treatment of dogs labeled -- sometimes incorrectly -- as pit bulls. **97m/C; DVD, Blu-Ray.** *CH US* Ashley Judd; Jonah Hauer-King; Edward James Olmos; Alexandra Shipp; Chris Bauer; ***D:*** Charles Martin Smith; ***W:*** W. Bruce Cameron; Cathryn Michon; ***C:*** Peter Menzies, Jr.; ***M:*** Mychael Danna.

Dogtooth 🦴 ½ *Kynodontas* **2009** Completely absurdist family drama/black comedy from Greece. Three teenaged siblings have been raised in isolation in a walled-in family compound by their nutso controlling parents. With a completely skewered view of the outside world (they even have an alternate vocabulary), it's no wonder that the situation turns violent when their one outside contact shakes things up sexually. Pic gets more than a little repetitious (and graphic). Greek with subtitles. **94m/C; DVD, Blu-Ray.** *GR* Christos Stergioglou; Michele Valley; Christos Passalis; Aggeliki Papoulia; Mary Tsoni; Anna Kalaitzidou; ***D:*** Yorgos Lanthimos; ***W:*** Yorgos Lanthimos; Efthymis Filippou; ***C:*** Thimios Bakatakis.

Dogtown 🦴🦴 **1997** Former beauty queen/cheerleader Dorothy Sternen feels trapped in her small town of Cuba, Missouri. Her longtime boyfriend Ezra Good is a bitter ex-athlete stuck in a dull job who sometimes gets violent. Then high school classmate Philip returns to town. Although he's a struggling actor, Philip is treated like a celebrity, and Dorothy starts giving him the eye. Tensions arise as they all realize how dissatisfied each of them are. **99m/C; VHS, DVD.** Mary Stuart Masterson; Trevor St. John; Jon Favreau; Rory Cochrane; Karen Black; Natasha Gregson Wagner; Maureen McCormick; Harold Russell; John Livingston; Shawnee Smith; ***D:*** George Hickenlooper; ***W:*** George Hickenlooper; ***C:*** Kramer Morgenthau; ***M:*** Steve Stevens.

Dogville 🦴🦴 ½ **2003 (R)** Another "love it or hate it" offering from director von Trier brings us yet another troubled woman, Grace (Kidman), who is on the run from mobsters and picks Dogville (a made-up U.S. locale) to hide out, even offering up free labor to the townsfolk in return for their silence. But things go south for her as she is persecuted and eventually they do an about-face and consider ratting her out for a hefty reward...though she's savvy enough to fight back. Set during the Depression and filmed on a minimalist set similar to the Thorton Wilder classic "Our Town," though the two stories are complete contradictions The Danish von Trier may be perceived as hateful toward the American way of life, whereas many will find his latest effort to be a memorably appalling, thought-provoking tale with Kidman flourishing in the challenging lead role. **178m/C; DVD.** *DK NL SW FR NO FI GE IT* Nicole Kidman; Lauren Bacall; Paul Bettany; Philip Baker Hall; Blair Brown; James Caan; Patricia Clarkson; Jeremy Davies; Ben Gazzara; Siobhan Fallon Hogan; Zeljko Ivanek; Udo Kier; Harriet Andersson; Jean-Marc Barr; Thom Hoffman; Bill Raymond; Chloë Sevigny; Stellan Skarsgard; ***Nar:*** John Hurt; ***D:*** Lars von Trier; ***W:*** Lars von Trier; ***C:*** Anthony Dod Mantle.

Dogville Shorts 🦴🦴 ½ **1930** Two-disc compilation containing nine specialty shorts from 1930-31 of the "All-Barkie" Dogville Comedies. These featured various dog breeds spoofing human behavior (with human voiceovers) and the era's popular movie themes, including prison escapes, war heroics, jungle adventures, detective stories, romance, and musicals. **142m/B; DVD.** ***D:*** Zion Myers; Jules White.

Dogwatch 🦴🦴 **1997 (R)** San Francisco police detective Charlie Falon (Elliott) tries to avenge his partner's murder but kills the wrong man. Then he learns dirty cops are behind the crime. Thriller takes the easy road by solving everything with violence. **100m/C; VHS, DVD.** Sam Elliott; Esai Morales; Paul Sorvino; Dan Lauria; Richard Gilliland; Jessica Steen; Mimi (Meyer) Craven; ***D:*** John Langley, Ph.D; ***W:*** Martin Zurla; ***C:*** Robert Yeoman; ***M:*** Lennie Niehaus. **CABLE**

Doin' Time 🦴 **1985 (R)** At the John Dillinger Memorial Penitentiary, the inmates take over the prison under the supervision of warden "Mongo." Silliness prevails. **80m/C; VHS, Streaming.** Jeff Altman; Dey Young; Richard Mulligan; John Vernon; Colleen Camp; Melanie Chartoff; Graham Jarvis; Pat McCormick; Eddie Velez; Jimmie Walker; Judy Landers; Nicholas Worth; Mike Mazurki; Muhammad Ali; Melinda Fee; Francesca "Kitten" Natividad; Ron Palillo; ***D:*** George Mendeluk; ***W:*** George Mendeluk; Dee Caruso; Ron Zwang; Franelle Silver; ***M:*** Charles Fox.

Doing Time 🦴🦴 ½ *Kimusho No Naka* **2002** After spending several years in prison, Kazuichi Hanawa managed to turn his experiences into a successful comic, and then get it made into film. Every aspect of life in a Japanese prison is micromanaged and carefully controlled until the prisoners lose all sense of identity and individuality. Fans of prison films will want to see it for the stark and surprising differences in the American and Japanese prison systems, and fans of unconventional films may also wish to give it a go. **93m/C; DVD.** *JP* Tsutomu Yamazaki; ***D:*** Yoichi Sai; ***W:*** Yoshihiro Nakamura; Yoichi Sai; Wui Sin Chong; Kazuichi Hanawa.

Doing Time for Patsy Cline 🦴🦴 ½ **1997** Yearning to make it big in faraway Nashville, Ralph (Day) forsakes his parents' down-under farm with guitar in hand. Hitchhiking with punk Boyd (Roxburgh) and pretty Patsy (Otto)?who claims country crooner Patsy Cline as her namesake—he finds out free rides don't usually end well (not in the movies anyhow) as the cops bust them on drug charges. Patsy flees, leaving the boys in the pen, though there's not much suspense to their fate as director Kennedy's story repeatedly jumps back and forth in time between locales. **95m/C; DVD.** Richard Roxburgh; Miranda Otto; Matt(hew) Day; Tony Barry; Kiri Paramore; Laurence Coy; ***D:*** Chris Kennedy; ***W:*** Chris Kennedy; ***C:*** Andrew Lesnie; ***M:*** Peter Best.

Doing Time on Maple Drive 🦴🦴 ½ **1992** College boy Matt (McNamara) brings his fiancee Alison (Loughlin) home to meet his seemingly tranquil but secretly dysfunctional family. Dad (Sikking), a retired military man, and Mom (Besch) expect their children to be perfect but elder brother Tim (Carrey) is a not-so-secret alcoholic, neurotic daughter Karen's (Brook) marriage is in trouble, and Matt himself is hiding a big secret that threatens the harmonious family facade. Made for TV. **90m/C; VHS, DVD.** William McNamara; James B. Sikking; Bibi Besch; Jim Carrey; Lori Loughlin; Jayne Brook; David Byron; ***D:*** Ken Olin; ***W:*** James Duff; ***C:*** Bing Sokolsky; ***M:*** Laura Karpman. **TV**

Doktor Faustus 🦴🦴 *Thomas Mann's Doktor Faustus* **1982** A composer sells his soul in return for a lifetime of creativity. Satan's condition is that Leverhuehn has no close human contacts but he violates the agreement with tragic consequences. Adapted from the Thomas Mann novel and updated to the 1930s and 40s as Germany descends into the coming war madness that mirrors Leverhuehn's own. German with subtitles. **137m/C; DVD.** *GE* Jon Finch; Hanns Zischler; Andre Heller; Marie Breillat; ***D:*** Franz Seitz; ***W:*** Franz Seitz; ***C:*** Rudolf Blahacek; ***M:*** Rolf Wilhelm.

Dolan's Cadillac 🦴 ½ **2009 (R)** Elizabeth Robinson (Vaugier) witnesses Vegas mobster Jimmy Dolan (Slater) committing multiple murders and burying the bodies in the desert. She and her schoolteacher husband Tom (Bentley) are under federal protection until she can testify but Elizabeth gets murdered and Dolan goes free. Tom goes nuts and hallucinates that his dead wife is telling him to get revenge. But his plan is kinda stupid and so is the movie and it gets its extra half-bone because Vaugier is just so hot. Based on Stephen's King 1993 short story. **88m/C; DVD, Blu-Ray.** Christian Slater; Wes Bentley; Emmanuelle Vaugier; Greg Bryk; Al Sapienza; Aidan Devine; ***D:*** Jeff Beesley; ***W:*** Richard Dooling; ***C:*** Gerald Packer; ***M:*** James Mark Stewart. **VIDEO**

Dolemite 🦴 ½ **1975 (R)** An ex-con attempts to settle the score with some of his former inmates. He forms a band of kung-fu savvy ladies. Strange combination of action and comedy. **88m/C; VHS, DVD, Blu-Ray.** Rudy Ray Moore; Jerry Jones; D'Urville Martin; Lady Reeds; ***D:*** D'Urville Martin; ***W:*** Jerry Jones; ***C:*** Nicholas Josef von Sternberg; ***M:*** Arthur Wright.

Dolemite 2: Human Tornado 🦴 ½ *The Human Tornado* **1976 (R)** Nobody ever said Moore was for everybody's taste. But, hey, when blaxploitation movies were the rage, Rudy the standup comic was out there rapping through a series of trashy movies that, when viewed today, have survived the test of time. This one's just as vile, violent, and sexist as the day it was released. When Rudy is surprised in bed with a white sheriff's wife, he flees and meets up with a madam and a house of kung-fu-skilled girls who are embroiled in a fight with a local mobster. **98m/C; VHS, DVD, Blu-Ray.** Rudy Ray Moore; Lady Reeds; Ernie Hudson; Howard Jackson; Herb Graham; Jerry Jones; Jimmy Lynch; ***D:*** Cliff Roquemore; ***W:*** Jerry Jones; ***C:*** Fred Conde; Bob Wilson; ***M:*** Arthur Wright.

Dolemite Is My Name 🦴🦴🦴 ½ **2019 (R)** Rudy Ray Moore (Murphy) has strived for success as an entertainer but is working in a record store when he stumbles on a way to achieve his goal. Inspired by a local wino's (Jones) stories, Moore creates a colorful character called Dolemite, records a successful comedy album, and tours as a comedian. After a night at the movies, Moore is inspired to bring Dolemite to the screen despite his lack of knowledge of the cinematic process. Based on a true story, the enthralling biopic celebrates Moore and his accomplishments while marking a spirited return by Murphy to his profane comedic origins. **118m/C; DVD.** Eddie Murphy; Keegan Michael Key; Mike Epps; Craig Robinson; Tituss Burgess; ***D:*** Craig Brewer; ***W:*** Scott Alexander; Larry Karaszweski; ***C:*** Eric Steelberg; ***M:*** Scott Bomar.

Dolittle 🦴🦴 **2020 (PG)** In mourning after the death of his wife, the depressed Dr. John Dolittle (Downey) spends his days talking to his animal friends. His retreat from the world is interrupted by two visitors. Tommy (Collett) brings him a wounded squirrel to care for, while Lady Rose (Laniado) needs his help to care for an ailing Queen Victoria (Buckley). Concluding that the monarch is being poisoned, Dolittle takes an ocean journey to the only place where the cure, Eden Tree blossoms, can be found: a remote island. A soulless adaptation of the popular children's books, it's messy and hard to follow, especially when the animals speak. **101m/C; DVD.** Robert Downey, Jr.; Antonio Banderas; Michael Sheen; Jim Broadbent; Jessie Buckley; ***D:*** Stephen Gaghan; ***W:*** Stephen Gaghan; Dan Gregor; Doug Mand; ***C:*** Guillermo Navarro; ***M:*** Danny Elfman.

Doll Face 🦴🦴 ½ *Come Back to Me* **1946** Story of a stripper who wants to go legit and make it on Broadway. Film was adapted from the play "The Naked Genius" by tease queen Gypsy Rose Lee. **80m/B; VHS, DVD.** Vivian Blaine; Dennis O'Keefe; Perry Como; Carmen Miranda; Reed Hadley; ***D:*** Lewis Seiler.

The Doll Squad 🦴 *Hustler Squad* **1973 (PG)** Three voluptuous special agents fight an ex-CIA agent out to rule the world. **93m/C; VHS, DVD, Blu-Ray.** Michael Ansara; Francine York; Anthony Eisley; John N. Carter; Rafael Campos; William Bagdad; Lisa Todd; Lillian Garrett; Herb Robbins; Tura Satana; ***D:*** Ted V. Mikels; ***W:*** Ted V. Mikels; Jack Pichesin; Pam Eddy; ***C:*** Anthony Salinas; ***M:*** Nicholas Carras.

Dollar for the Dead 🦴🦴 **1998** In this spaghetti western-inspired TNT cable movie, a gunslinging loner (Estevez) partners up with a former Confederate soldier (Forsyte) to go after a secret cache of gold. Only it's not much of a secret as they make their way to a border town with ex-Union soldiers and Mexican federales also after the loot. **94m/C; DVD.** Emilio Estevez; William Forsythe; Joaquim de Almeida; Ed Lauter; Howie Long; Jonathan Banks; ***D:*** Gene Quintano; ***W:*** Gene Quintano; ***C:*** Giovanni Fiore Coltellacci; ***M:*** George S. Clinton. **CABLE**

Dollars 🦴🦴🦴 *The Heist* **1971 (R)** A bank employee and his dizzy call-girl assistant plan to steal the German facility's assets while installing its new security system. Lighthearted fun. **119m/C; VHS, DVD.** Warren Beatty; Goldie Hawn; Gert Frobe; Scott Brady; Robert Webber; ***D:*** Richard Brooks; ***W:*** Richard Brooks; ***M:*** Quincy Jones.

Dollman 🦴 ½ **1990 (R)** An ultra-tough cop from an Earth-like planet (even swear words are the same) crashes in the South Bronx—and on this world he's only 13 inches tall. The filmmakers squander a great premise and cast with bloody shootouts and a sequel-ready non-ending. **86m/C; VHS, DVD, Blu-Ray.** Tim Thomerson; Jackie Earle Haley; Kamala Lopez; Humberto Ortiz; Nicholas Guest; Michael Halsey; Eugene Robert Glazer; Judd Omen; Frank Collison; Vincent Klyn; ***D:*** Albert Pyun.

Dollman vs Demonic Toys 🦴🦴 **1993 (R)** Let's combine elements from three separate films and make one disgusting sequel: "Dollman," the 13-inch cop from the planet Arturus; his new girlfriend, Dollchick, who was shrunk to a diminutive 10 inches in "Bad Channels"; and tough cop Judith Grey, who's once again battling those loathsome playthings from "Demonic Toys." If you feel the need for a plot—Dollchick is kidnapped by Baby Doll and needs to be rescued. **84m/C; VHS, DVD, Blu-Ray.** Tim Thomerson; Tracy Scoggins; Melissa Behr; Phil Brock; Phil Fondacaro; ***D:*** Charles Band; ***W:*** Craig Hamann; ***M:*** Richard Band.

Dolls 🦴🦴 ½ **1987 (R)** A group of people is stranded during a storm in an old, creepy mansion. As the night wears on, they are attacked by hundreds of antique dolls. Tongue-in-cheek. **77m/C; VHS, DVD, Blu-Ray.** Ian Patrick Williams; Carolyn Purdy-Gordon; Carrie Lorraine; Stephen Lee; Guy Rolfe; Bunty Bailey; Cassie Stuart; Hilary Mason; ***D:*** Stuart Gordon; ***W:*** Ed Naha; ***M:*** Richard Band.

Dolls 🦴🦴🦴 **2002** Lyrical Japanese film intertwines three character studies into a wistful movie about devotion and lost love. A man literally ties himself to the girl he loves after realizing his weaknesses drove her to attempt suicide. A gang lord remembers the promise given to a girlfriend 30 years earlier. Thirty years later he returns to the park where they met, finding her still waiting. The final chapter fumbles the connection a bit, focusing on a famous pop star becoming disfigured in an auto accident. She flees the public eye, only to let one devoted fan into her life. Lush photography and landscapes are pure dazzling eye candy, but the emotionally syrupy excess may turn off some audiences. **113m/C; DVD.** Tatsuya Mihashi; Chieko Matsubara; Miho Kanno; Hidetoshi Nishijima; Kyoko Fukada; Sebastian Blenkov; ***D:*** Takeshi "Beat" Kitano; ***W:*** Takeshi "Beat" Kitano; ***C:*** Katsumi Yanagijima; ***M:*** Joe Hisaishi.

A Doll's House 🦴🦴 1/2 **1973 (G)** Fonda plays Nora, a subjugated 19th-century housewife who breaks free to establish herself as an individual. Based on Henrik Ibsen's classic play; some controversy regarding Fonda's interpretation of her role. **98m/C; DVD.** Jane Fonda; Edward Fox; Trevor Howard; David Warner; Delphine Seyrig; ***D:*** Joseph Losey; ***W:*** Christopher Hampton; ***M:*** John Barry.

A Doll's House 🦴🦴🦴 **1973 (G)** A Canadian production of the Henrik Ibsen play about a Norwegian woman's search for independence. **96m/C; VHS, DVD.** *CA* Claire Bloom; Anthony Hopkins; Ralph Richardson; Denholm Elliott; Anna Massey; Edith Evans; ***D:*** Patrick Garland.

Dolly Dearest 🦴 1/2 **1992 (R)** Strange things start happening after an American family takes over a run-down Mexican doll factory. They create a new doll called "Dolly Dearest" with deadly results. In the same tradition as the "Chucky" series. **94m/C; VHS, DVD, Blu-Ray.** Rip Torn; Sam Bottoms; Denise Crosby; ***D:*** Maria Lease.

Dolly Parton's Coat of Many Colors 🦴🦴 *Coat of Many Colors* **2015 (G)** Autobiographical tale of a young Dolly Parton and her family as they struggle to overcome poverty and personal misfortune in rural Tennessee. While well done, it will come across as a bit hokey to modern audiences, unless they're quite religious. **170m/C; DVD, Blu-Ray, Streaming.** Alyvia Alyn Lind; Jennifer Nettles; Rick Schroder; Gerald McRaney; Stella Parton; ***D:*** Stephen Herek; ***W:*** Pamela K. Long; ***C:*** Brian J. Reynolds; ***M:*** Velton Ray Bunch; Mark Leggett. **TV**

The Dolly Sisters 🦴🦴 1/2 **1946** Competent musical about sisters Jenny (Grable) and Rosie (Haver), who become turn-of-the-century vaudeville stars and also find romance. Good songs, extravagent costuming, fine support work, and the charms of the two leading actresses provide simple enjoyment. **114m/C; DVD.** Betty Grable; June Haver; John Payne; Frank Latimore; S.Z. Sakall; Reginald Gardiner; Gene Sheldon; Sig Rumann; ***D:*** Irving Cummings; ***W:*** Marian Spitzer; John Larkin; ***C:*** Ernest Palmer.

Dolores Claiborne 🦴🦴🦴 **1994 (R)** Stephen King gets the Hollywood treatment again (the check cleared, King approved), with better results than previous outings (remember "Needful Things"?). Successful but neurotic New York journalist Selena (Leigh) confronts her troubled past when coarse, hard-talking mom Dolores (Bates) is accused of murdering her wealthy employer (Parfitt). Plummer is vengeful detective John Mackey who, like everyone else on the fictitious Maine island, believes Dolores murdered her husband 15 years before. Top-notch performances by Bates and Leigh highlight this sometimes manipulative tale. Straithairn is wonderfully despicable as the stereotypically abusive husband and father. **132m/C; VHS, DVD, Blu-Ray.** Kathy Bates; Jennifer Jason Leigh; Christopher Plummer; Judy Parfitt; David Strathairn; John C. Reilly; ***D:*** Taylor Hackford; ***W:*** Tony Gilroy; ***C:*** Gabriel Beristain; ***M:*** Danny Elfman.

Dolphin Tale 🦴🦴 1/2 **2011 (PG)** Grumps and cynics need not attempt this sweet, inspirational (and based on a true story) family flick, filmed primarily in Clearwater, Florida. A young female dolphin loses her tail in a crab trap. Rescued and cared for at the financially strapped Clearwater Marine Hospital, newly-named Winter doesn't have much of a chance until her protectors try to help by creating a prosthetic tail so she can swim. Among them are widowed marine scientist Clay (Connick Jr.) and his cute daughter Hazel (Zuehlsdorff), single mom Lorraine (Judd) and her disengaged son Sawyer (Gamble), and somewhat eccentric prosthetics expert Dr. McCarthy (Freeman) who works at the VA hospital. **113m/C; DVD, Blu-Ray.** Harry Connick, Jr.; Ashley Judd; Morgan Freeman; Nathan Gamble; Kris Kristofferson; Cozi Zuehlsdorff; Austin Stowell; ***D:*** Charles Martin Smith; ***W:*** Karen Janszen; ***C:*** Karl Walter Lindenlaub; ***M:*** Mark Isham.

Dolphin Tale 2 🦴 1/2 **2014 (PG)** Who doesn't love a dolphin? Those who saved Winter, the dolphin rescued in the first film, are forced to get back together to help her again after her surrogate mother passes. Everyone needs a companion, even dolphins. There's nothing particularly wrong with this slight bit of family entertainment--not annoying enough to be memorable, but not interesting enough either. **107m/C; DVD, Blu-Ray.** Nathan Gamble; Cozi Zuehlsdorff; Harry Connick, Jr.; Ashley Judd; Morgan Freeman; Kris Kristofferson; ***D:*** Charles Martin Smith; ***W:*** Charles Martin Smith; ***C:*** Daryn Okada; ***M:*** Rachel Portman.

Dom Hemingway 🦴🦴 1/2 **2013 (R)** Law is staggering as the title character, a larger-than-life safecracker with no internal stopping point when it comes to his profane, ridiculous behavior. It's a one-man show, for sure, but it's beyond entertaining. Dom sets off with buddy Dickie (Grant) to claim a debt he feels owed by protecting his boss Mr. Fontaine (Bichir). After he nearly dies, Dom attempts to re-connect with his estranged daughter (Clarke). A bit too in-your-face for some viewers, Law is so remarkably charismatic that most viewers won't mind the aggressive nature of his character. **93m/C; DVD, Blu-Ray.** *UK* Jude Law; Richard E. Grant; Demian Bechir; Emilia Clarke; Kerry Condon; ***D:*** Richard Shepard; ***W:*** Richard Shepard; ***C:*** Giles Nuttgens; ***M:*** Rolfe Kent.

Domain 🦴🦴 **2009** Seventeen-year-old Pierre (Sultan) is infatuated with his alcoholic 40-something mathematician aunt, Nadia (Dalle). She treats him like an adult, taking him to dance clubs when he spends weekends with her. But instead of a playmate, Pierre becomes a caretaker as the volatile Nadia becomes more self-destructive. Increasingly preoccupied with his own life, and his coming out, Pierre begins to draw away. French with subtitles. **110m/C; DVD, Blu-Ray.** *FR* Beatrice Dalle; Isaie Sultan; Manuel Marmier; Tatiana Vialle; Alain Libolt; Sylvia Rohrer; Raphael Bouvet; ***D:*** Patric Chiha; ***W:*** Patric Chiha; ***C:*** Pascal Poucet.

Domain 🦴🦴 **2018** After a flu pandemic, people live in solitary pods with a lifetime supply of food and a generator to operate needed technology. To stay connected with others, they are organized into groups of seven and use video chat to communicate. One group has become rather sick of each other, but the members, especially Phoenix (Lower) and Denver (Merriman), grow closer as they watch their friends go insane or be abducted by mysterious creatures. The limited budget science fiction mystery makes the best of a story built on talking head on screens but it is clever and offers an interesting perspective on living life online. **97m/C; DVD.** Britt Lower; Ryan Merriman; William Gregory Lee; Sonja Sohn; Cedric Sanders; ***D:*** Nathaniel Atcheson; ***W:*** Nathaniel Atcheson; ***C:*** Benjamin Kantor; ***M:*** Jonathan Snipes.

Domestic Disturbance 🦴🦴 **2001 (PG-13)** Lame entry in the "evil stepparent" genre features Travolta as Frank, a hard-working boat builder who shares custody of his son Danny (O'Leary) with ex-wife Susan (Polo). Danny starts acting out by getting in trouble and lying after Susan gets involved with suave local businessman Rick (Vaughn). Although Danny is clued into Rick's dark side from the start, it takes the appearance of Ray (Buscemi), a sleazy hood from Rick's shady past, to awaken Frank's suspicion. When Danny hides in Rick's van and witnesses Ray's murder, nobody believes him except his dad. The stage is set for the "good dad" versus "bad dad" showdown, which is handled as clumsily and unbelievably as possible. Most of the performances seem listless, with the exception of Vaughn as the oily villain and O'Leary as the terrorized kid. **89m/C; VHS, DVD.** John Travolta; Vince Vaughn; Teri Polo; Matt O'Leary; Ruben Santiago-Hudson; Susan Floyd; Steve Buscemi; Angelica Torn; ***D:*** Harold Becker; ***W:*** Lewis Colick; ***C:*** Michael Seresin; ***M:*** Mark Mancina.

Dominick & Eugene 🦴🦴🦴 **1988 (PG-13)** Dominick is a little slow, but he makes a fair living as a garbageman—good enough to put his brother through medical school. Both men struggle with the other's faults and weaknesses, as they learn the meaning of family and friendship. Well-acted, especially by Hulce, never melodramatic or weak. **96m/C; VHS, DVD.** Ray Liotta; Tom Hulce; Jamie Lee Curtis; Todd Graff; Bill Cobbs; David Strathairn; ***D:*** Robert M. Young; ***W:*** Alvin Sargent; Corey Blechman; ***C:*** Curtis Clark; ***M:*** Trevor Jones.

Dominion: Prequel to the Exorcist 🦴🦴 1/2 **2005 (R)** Paul Schrader's dark and intensely serious horror movie about demon-possession gone wrong. Released less because of the interest in another "Exorcist" spin-off, but more in hopes of cashing in on the curiosity to see such an unusual studio maneuver. This "prequel" disappointed the Morgan Creek execs, who then decided to re-shoot the entire movie with a new director and a few new actors. That movie became "Exorcist: The Beginning." With nothing to lose, the studio plunked in some CGI and released their original investment under this slightly different title. It's better than their reshoot, and makes for a fascinating experiment when paired up scene-for-scene with "The Beginning." **116m/C; DVD, Blu-Ray.** Stellan Skarsgard; Gabriel Mann; Clara Bellar; Andrew French; Israel Adurama; Eddie Osei; Antoine Kamerling; Julian Wadham; Ilario Bisi-Pedro; ***D:*** Paul Schrader; ***W:*** William Wisher; Caleb Carr; ***C:*** Vittorio Storaro; ***M:*** Trevor Rabin; Angelo Badalamenti; Dog Fashion Disco.

Dominique 🦴🦴 *Dominique is Dead* **1979 (PG)** A woman is driven to suicide by her greedy husband; now someone is trying to drive him mad. A.K.A. "Dominique" and "Avenging Spirit." **95m/C; VHS, DVD, Blu-Ray.** Cliff Robertson; Jean Simmons; Jenny Agutter; Simon Ward; Ron Moody; ***D:*** Michael Anderson, Sr.

Domino 🦴🦴 1/2 **2005 (R)** Scott, who proved that he could hang with the Tarantino crowd in "True Romance," uses every trick in his cinematic arsenal to bring to life the "sort of" true story of model-turned-bounty-hunter Domino Harvey (Knightley). Domino joins the crew of a bail-bondsman, looking for passion and thrills, and finds herself in the center of screenwriter Richard Kelly's perfect storm of bombastic sex, gunplay, criminal conspiracies, and reality TV. The plot tends to drag and the supporting cast overwhelms Knightley a bit, but you've got to love a movie that brings together Christopher Walken, Mickey Rourke, and 90210's Ian Ziering, with every camera shot that Tarantino and Oliver Stone were too chicken to use themselves. **128m/C; DVD, Blu-Ray.** Keira Knightley; Mickey Rourke; Edgar Ramirez; Delroy Lindo; Mo'Nique; Lucy Liu; Christopher Walken; Mena Suvari; Macy Gray; Jacqueline Bisset; Dabney Coleman; Brian Austin Green; Ian Ziering; Stanley Kamel; Peter Jacobson; T.K. Carter; Kel O'Neill; Shondrella Avery; Lew Temple; Tom Waits; Rizwan Abbasi; ***D:*** Tony Scott; ***W:*** Richard Kelly; Steve Barancik; ***C:*** Dan(iel) Mindel; ***M:*** Harry Gregson-Williams.

Domino 🦴 1/2 **2019 (R)** While responding to a domestic disturbance call, Danish cop Christian (Coster-Waldau) and his partner Lars (Malling) stumble into a more complex crime scene. The man they believe is the perpetrator kills Lars and escapes. Christian learns the escaped man is Libyan Ezra Tarzi (Ebouaney), who sees ISIS leader Salah Al Din (Azaay) to avenge his father's murder. After leaving the crime scene, Ezra was taken by CIA agents and forced to continue pursuing Al Din. As Christian pursues Ezra, Ezra tries to stop Al Din's suicide attack. Overall the thriller is a bit unbelievable, though some actors, including Ebouaney, shine. **88m/C; DVD, Blu-Ray.** Nikolaj Coster-Waldau; Carice van Houten; Guy Pearce; Ella-June Henrard; Soren Malling; ***D:*** Brian De Palma; ***W:*** Petter Skavlan; ***C:*** Jose Luis Alcaine; ***M:*** Pino Donaggio.

The Domino Principle 🦴 1/2 *The Domino Killings* **1977 (R)** It's got nothing to do with pizza. Viet vet Hackman is a doltish convict sprung from the joint by a government organization to do some dirty work: working as a political assassin. Heavy-handed direction and lack of suspense make it less than it should be. **97m/C; VHS, DVD, Blu-Ray.** Gene Hackman; Candice Bergen; Richard Widmark; Mickey Rooney; Edward Albert; Eli Wallach; ***D:*** Stanley Kramer; ***C:*** Fred W. Koenekamp; ***M:*** Billy Goldenberg.

Don Giovanni 🦴🦴 **1979** Losey's filmed version with the Paris Opera of the 1787 Mozart work. Philandering nobleman Don Giovanni attempts to seduce Donna Anna but her father is killed instead. Anna and her fiance Don Ottavio want revenge but it's the ghost of Anna's father who will bring about justice. Italian with subtitles. **176m/C; DVD, Blu-Ray.** *FR IT* Ruggero Raimondi; Edda Moser; Kenneth Riegel; John Macurdy; Kiri Te Kanawa; ***D:*** Joseph Losey; ***W:*** Joseph Losey; ***C:*** Gerry Fisher.

The Don Is Dead 🦴 1/2 *Beautiful But Deadly* **1973 (R)** A violent Mafia saga wherein a love triangle interferes with Family business, resulting in gang wars. **96m/C; VHS, DVD.** Anthony Quinn; Frederic Forrest; Robert Forster; Al Lettieri; Ina Balin; Angel Tompkins; Charles Cioffi; ***D:*** Richard Fleischer; ***W:*** Michael Butler; ***M:*** Jerry Goldsmith.

Don Jon 🦴🦴 *Don Jon's Addiction* **2013 (R)** Multi-talented star Gordon-Levitt takes a seat in the writer/director's chair for this surprisingly sitcomish comedy about how men and women can have their visions of love and romance altered by the movies they watch, especially the pornographic ones. The title character (Gordon-Levitt) has long-balanced a hearty addiction to porn with an active real sex life at the same time but a new woman in his life named Barbara (Johansson) catches him in the act and forces him to choose. Too much of JGL's film is a bit absurd, so that by the time that Moore (as Esther) tries to ground it in something real in the final act, it's too late. **90m/C; DVD, Blu-Ray.** Joseph Gordon-Levitt; Scarlett Johansson; Julianne Moore; Tony Danza; Glenne Headly; ***D:*** Joseph Gordon-Levitt; ***W:*** Joseph Gordon-Levitt; ***C:*** Thomas Kloss; ***M:*** Nathan Johnson.

Don Juan 🦴🦴🦴 1/2 **1926** Barrymore stars as the swashbuckling Italian duke with Spanish blood who seduces a castleful of women in the 1500s before falling in love with innocent Astor. Many exciting action sequences, including classic sword fights in which Barrymore eschewed a stunt double. Great attention is also paid to the detail of the costumes and settings of the Spanish-Moor period. Noted for employing fledgling movie sound effects and as the first film with a synchronized musical score from the Vitaphone Company, which, ironically, were responsible for eclipsing the movie's reputation. Watch for Loy as an Asian vamp and Oland as a pre-Charlie Chan Cesare Borgia. **90m/B; Silent; VHS, DVD.** John Barrymore; Mary Astor; Willard Louis; Estelle Taylor; Helene Costello; Myrna Loy; June Marlowe; Warner Oland; Montagu Love; Hedda Hopper; Gustav von Seyffertitz; ***D:*** Alan Crosland; ***W:*** Bess Meredyth; ***C:*** Byron Haskin; ***M:*** William Axt.

Don Juan DeMarco 🦴🦴 1/2 **1994 (PG-13)** Burned-out clinical psychiatrist Dr. Jack Meckler (Brando) is romantically inspired by a cape-wearing, suicidal man-child from Queens (Depp), who thinks he's legendary lover Don Juan. Delusional Depp recounts, in a convincing Castilian accent, thousands of conquests as the sympathetic shrink decides it's time to bring some spice to his own ho-hum life and marriage (to Dunaway). Depp turns in a sincere, engaging performance that avoids the huge potential for melodrama and compensates for inconsistent pacing. Brando and Dunaway make a charmingly quirky couple. Watch for slain Tejano queen Selena in a musical interlude. **92m/C; VHS, DVD, Blu-Ray.** Marlon Brando; Johnny Depp; Faye Dunaway; Geraldine Pailhas; Rachel Ticotin; Bob (Robert) Dishy; Talisa Soto; ***D:*** Jeremy Leven; ***W:*** Jeremy Leven; ***C:*** Ralf Bode; ***M:*** Michael Kamen.

Don Juan (Or If Don Juan Were a Woman) 🦴 *Don Juan 73; Ms. Don Juan; Si Don Juan Etait une Femme* **1973** Offers unintentional amusement with Bardot in the title role. Jeanne specializes in humiliation and seduction of, among others, her cousin the priest, a poltician, and a businessman. French with subtitles. **94m/C; VHS, DVD.** *FR* Brigitte Bardot; Jane Birkin; Matthieu Carriere; Robert Hossein; Maurice Ronet; Michele Sand; *D:* Roger Vadim; *W:* Jean Cau; *C:* Henri Decae.

Don Juan Quilligan 1/2 **1945** Mediocre comedy about a bigamist has some silly plot machinations. New York river barge skipper Patrick Quilligan (Bendix) has one wife at each end of his route. Marjorie (Blondell) is a hotsie-totsie gal and Lucy (Treen) is a sweet homebody. Patrick's first mate MacDenny (Slvers) tries to get him out of his dilemma but the skipper gets arrested for murder instead! **75m/B; DVD.** William Bendix; Joan Blondell; Mary Treen; Phil Silvers; Anne Revere; John Russell; Veda Ann Borg; *D:* Frank Tuttle; *W:* Arthur Kober; Frank Gabrielson; *C:* Norbert Brodine; *M:* David Raskin.

Don King: Only in America 1/2 **1997 (R)** Rhames reigns in this bio of flamboyant, notorious boxing promoter Don King. King starts off as a Cleveland numbers runner at ease with violence, which eventually sends him to a four-year prison term for manslaughter. Released in 1971, King uses his friendship with R&B singer Lloyd Price (Curtis-Hall) to meet Muhammed Ali (McCrary), leading to his set-up of the 1974 Ali-Foreman fight in Zaire. From there it's just more self-promotion. **112m/C; VHS, DVD.** Ving Rhames; Vondie Curtis-Hall; Jeremy Piven; Darius McCrary; Keith David; Bernie Mac; Loretta Devine; Lou Rawls; Ron Leibman; Gabriel Casseus; *D:* John Herzfeld; *W:* Kario Salem; *C:* Bill Butler; *M:* Anthony Marinelli. **CABLE**

Don McKay **2009 (R)** In this contemporary sunlit film noir, high school janitor Don (Church) goes back to his hometown after hearing from ex-girlfriend Sonny (Shue) who says she wants to see him before she dies. She turn out to be a lying, wannabe femme fatale who wears lots of negligees. There's also more scheming, money is involved, and there's eventually a corpse. It's both deadpan and over-the-top but Church seems too smart to play such a taken-for-a-ride schlub. **87m/C; Blu-Ray, On Demand.** Thomas Haden Church; Elisabeth Shue; Melissa Leo; M. Emmet Walsh; Keith David; Pruitt Taylor Vince; James Rebhorn; *D:* Jake Goldberger; *W:* Jake Goldberger; *C:* Phil Parmet; *M:* Steven Bramson.

Don Peyote *Aardvaark* **2014** An unemployed stoner begins having apocalyptic dreams and embarks upon a quest to film a documentary about conspiracy theories involving the end of the world. Filled with a variety of celebrity cameos, if you're into that. **98m/C; DVD, Streaming.** Jay Baruchel; Josh Duhamel; Dan Fogler; Kelly Hutchinson; Wallace Shawn; *D:* Dan Fogler; Michael Canzoniero; *W:* Dan Fogler; Michael Canzoniero; *C:* John Inwood; *M:* Ben Lovett.

Don Q., Son of Zorro **1925** Zorro's son takes up his father's fight against evil and injustice. Silent sequel to the 1920 classic. **111m/B; Silent; VHS, DVD.** Douglas Fairbanks, Sr.; Mary Astor; Donald Crisp; *D:* Donald Crisp; *W:* Jack Cunningham; *C:* Henry Sharp.

Don Quixote *Chaliapin: Adventures of Don Quixote* **1935** Miguel de Cervantes' tale of the romantic who would rather be a knight in shining armor than shining armor at night. Chaliapin stars as the knight-errant on his nightly errands, tilting at windmills and charging flocks of sheep. Certain scenes were adapted to fit the pre-WWII atmosphere, as it was filmed during the same time that the Nazis were burning books. **73m/B; VHS, DVD.** Feodor Chaliapin, Sr.; George Robey; Sidney (Sydney) Fox; Miles Mander; Oscar Asche; Emily Fitzroy; Wally Patch; *D:* G.W. Pabst; *W:* Paul Morand; Alexandre Arnoux; *M:* Jacques Ibert.

Don Quixote 1/2 *Don Kikhot* **1957** The lauded, visually ravishing adaptation of the Cervantes classic, with a formal integrity inherited from Eisenstein and Dovshenko. In Russian with English subtitles. **110m/B; VHS, DVD.** *SP RU* Nikolai Cherkassov; Yuri Tolubeyev; *D:* Grigori Kozintsev; *W:* Yevgeni Schwarz; *C:* Appolinari Dudko; Andrei Moskvin; *M:* Kara Karayev.

Don Quixote 1/2 *Orson Welles' Don Quixote* **1992** Welles started filming in 1955 but eventually abandoned the project; it was finished seven years after his death by onetime assistant Jess Franco. A patchwork mess of drawings and stills are used to fill-in the gaps of the Miguel de Cervantes novel with Quixote and his servant Sancho Panza setting off across a modern-day Spain. A rather useless addition to the Welles oeuvre; dubbed. **115m/B; DVD.** *SP* Akim Tamiroff; Orson Welles; Francisco Reiguera; *D:* Orson Welles; *W:* Orson Welles; *M:* Daniel White.

Don Verdean 1/2 **2015 (PG-13)** The title character, played by the great Rockwell, claims to be a "Biblical Archaeologist," but, of course, he's just a con man. A famous Evangelical pastor (McBride) bankrolls Verdean on some major projects and Don's lies get out of control fast. If the subject matter sounds like something with which the directors of "Napoleon Dynamite" could have some fun and even provide some satirical commentary, you're right. Sadly, they don't do that. There are about three laughs in this alleged comedy and none of the characters have anything interesting to say. It's stunningly boring, especially given the quirky comedy of its creators. **95m/C; DVD, Blu-Ray.** Sam Rockwell; Amy Ryan; Will Forte; Danny McBride; Jemaine Clement; *D:* Jared Hess; *W:* Jared Hess; Jerusha Hess; *C:* Mattias Troelstrup; *M:* Ilan Eshkeri.

Don Winslow of the Coast Guard **1943** Serial in 13 episodes features comic-strip character Winslow as he strives to keep the waters of America safe for democracy. **234m/B; VHS, DVD.** Don Terry; Elyse Knox; *D:* Ford Beebe; Ray Taylor.

Don Winslow of the Navy **1943** Thirteen episodes centered around the evil Scorpion, who plots to attack the Pacific Coast, but is thwarted by comic-strip hero Winslow. **234m/B; VHS, DVD.** Don Terry; Walter Sande; Anne Nagel; *D:* Ford Beebe; Ray Taylor.

Dona Flor and Her Two Husbands *Dona Flor e Seus Dois Maridos* **1978** Dona Flor (Braga) is widowed when her philandering husband Vadhino (Wilker) finally expires from drink, gambling, and ladies. She remarries, but her new husband Teodoro (Mendonca) is so boring and proper that she begins fantasizing spouse number one's return. But is he only in her imagination? Based on the novel by Jorge Amado. Portuguese with subtitles. Remade as "Kiss Me Goodbye." **106m/C; VHS, DVD.** *BR* Sonia Braga; Jose Wilker; Mauro Mendonca; *D:* Bruno Barreto; *W:* Bruno Barreto; *C:* Murilo Salles; *M:* Chico Buarque.

Dona Herlinda & Her Son *Dona Herlinda y Su Hijo* **1986** A Mexican sex comedy about a mother who manipulates her bisexual son's two lovers (one male, one female), until all four fit together into a seamless unit. In Spanish with English subtitles. Slow, but amusing. **90m/C; VHS, DVD.** *MX* Guadalupe Del Toro; Arturo Meza; Marco Antonio Trevino; Leticia Lupersio; *D:* Jaime Humberto Hermosillo; *W:* Jaime Humberto Hermosillo; *C:* Miguel Ehrenberg.

Donald Cried **2016 85m/C; DVD, Streaming.** Kris Avedisian; Jesse Wakeman; Louisa Krause; Ted Arcidi; *D:* Kris Avedisian; *W:* Kris Avedisian; Jesse Wakeman; Kyle Espeleta; *C:* Sam Fleischner.

Dondi **1961** American GIs are celebrating Christmas in WWII Italy when very young orphan Dondi (Kory) attaches himself to reluctant Dealey (Janssen). He then stows away on their troopship but gets lost in New York and has various adventures in Macy's department store. But Dondi wants to reunite with Dealey, longing for a real home and family. Ham-fisted direction by Zugsmith adds to the unbelievable treacle although the film is often fondly remembered by those who saw it as kids upon its release. Based on the Gus Edson and Irwin Hasen comic strip. **100m/B; DVD.** David Janssen; Patti Page; Arnold Stang; Robert Strauss; Gale Gordon; Mickey Shaughnessy; Walter Winchell; David Kory; *D:* Albert Zugsmith; *W:* Albert Zugsmith; Gus Edson; *C:* Carl Guthrie; *M:* Tommy Morgan.

Donkey Punch **2008 (R)** Three English chicks on vacation in Spain allow themselves to be picked up by a quartet of Brit boys who are crewing on a yacht. During drug-fueled, videotaped sexcapades, one of the girls is accidentally killed by the title deviant act and the guys, fearing police involvement, decide to dump the body overboard. This leads to more violence and gore. **89m/C; Blu-Ray, On Demand.** *GB* Tom Burke; Julian Morris; Robert Boulter; Sian Brecklin; Nichola Burley; Jay Taylor; Jaime Winstone; *D:* Olly Blackburn; *W:* David Bloom; Olly Blackburn; *C:* Nanu Segal; *M:* Francoise-Eudes Chanfrault.

Donkey Skin *Peau d'Ane* **1970** A charming, all-star version of the Charles Perrault fairy tale about a king searching for a suitable wife in a magical realm after his queen dies. In his quest for the most beautiful spouse, he learns that his daughter is that woman. She prefers Prince Charming, however. French with subtitles. **89m/C; VHS, DVD, Blu-Ray.** *FR* Catherine Deneuve; Jean Marais; Delphine Seyrig; Jacques Perrin; *D:* Jacques Demy; *W:* Jacques Demy; *C:* Ghislan Cloquet; *M:* Michel Legrand.

Donna on Demand 1/2 **2009** A one-time successful actor, Ben Corbin decided to give up his celebrity life to make independent films—that all fail. Twenty years later, Ben meets popular internet blonde Donna and sees a chance for a comeback. **93m/C; DVD.** Corbin Bernsen; Adrienne Frantz; Susan Ruttan; Jeanne Cooper; Dan Lauria; *D:* Corbin Bernsen; *W:* Corbin Bernsen; *C:* Eric Gustavo Petersen; *M:* Stephen Greaves. **VIDEO**

The Donner Party 1/2 **2009 (R)** A very polite retelling of the infamous story of survival by cannibalism. In 1846, a wagon train bound for California makes the mistake of taking a supposed shortcut through the Donner Pass in the Sierra Nevada Mountains and gets trapped in an early snowstorm. Lost, frozen, and starving, the survivors need to make a decision on how far they will go to stay alive. **95m/C; DVD.** Crispin Glover; Clayne Crawford; Mark Boone, Jr.; Christian Kane; Michele Santopietro; Cary Wayne Moore; Catherine Black; Alison Haislip; *D:* T.J. Martin; *W:* T.J. Martin; *C:* Seamus Tierney; *M:* Eimear Noone. **VIDEO**

Donnie Brasco **1996 (R)** Excellent look at the unglamourous working end of the mob and an undercover operation. In the late '70s, FBI agent Joe Pistone (Depp) infiltrates the New York Bonanno crime family, under the alias of Donnie Brasco, where he's mentored by aging low-level hood Lefty (Pacino). As Joe/Donnie gets deeper into the wiseguy life, Lefty takes a fatherly pride in his protege and the agent also becomes ensnared by his new identity—to the possible detriment of both feds and family. Terrific lead performances. Based on a true story and adapted from the book by Pistone and Richard Woodley. **126m/C; VHS, DVD, Blu-Ray.** Johnny Depp; Al Pacino; Anne Heche; Michael Madsen; Bruno Kirby; James Russo; Zeljko Ivanek; Gerry Becker; Zach Grenier; Robert Miano; *D:* Mike Newell; *W:* Paul Attanasio; *C:* Peter Sova; *M:* Patrick Doyle. Natl. Bd. of Review '97: Support. Actress (Heche).

Donnie Darko **2001 (R)** Stylish, exciting debut by writer/director Kelly that, like "Mulholland Drive," leaves much unexplained as dark doings occur in an idyllic suburb, circa 1988. Aptly named Darko family is full of complex characters, including the gifted but schizophrenic Donnie, a teenager able to see the future with the aid of a life-size, doomsday-spewing rabbit named Frank. Donnie's psychiatrist (Ross) discovers he's sleepwalking on Frank's orders, which actually saves his life when a jet engine falls from a plane, landing squarely in the teen's bedroom. Even more mysteriously, no plane has reported a missing engine, which turns out to be just one of the many eerie events that may be real or imagined. McDonnell and Osborne are both fine as Donnie's upper-middle class Republican parents. Like "Harvey" on anti-psychotic meds, this challenging and complex film is worth the effort. **113m/C; VHS, DVD, Blu-Ray, UMD.** Jake Gyllenhaal; Jena Malone; Drew Barrymore; Mary McDonnell; James Duval; Maggie Gyllenhaal; Holmes Osborne; Katharine Ross; Patrick Swayze; Noah Wyle; Arthur Taxier; Stuart Stone; *D:* Richard Kelly; *W:* Richard Kelly; *C:* Steven Poster; *M:* Michael Andrews.

Donnybrook **2018 (R)** To solve his financial problems, former Marine Jarhead Earl (Bell) wants to enter the Donnybrook bareknuckle fighting contest and win $100k. However, Earl needs $1k to enter, so robs a pawnshop to get the fee. When Sheriff Donny Whalen (Dale) comes in response to the cashier's call, the sheriff asks him to not press charges because he has bigger problems in the form of the violent drug dealer Chainsaw Angus (Grillo). As Earl makes his way to the contest, he must protect his son Moses (Washburn). Based on the novel by Frank Bill, the plot is thin and the characters shallow. **101m/C; DVD, Blu-Ray.** Jamie Bell; Frank Grillo; Margaret Qualley; James Badge Dale; Kevin Crowley; *D:* Tim Sutton; *W:* Tim Sutton; *C:* David Ungaro; *M:* Phil Mossman.

Donovan's Brain **1953** Dedicated scientist Dr. Cory (Ayres) has succeeded in keeping a dismembered monkey's brain alive and gets his chance to experiment on a human when the victim of a plane crash is brought to his lab. Over the objections of his wife Janice (Davis) and assistant Frank (Evans), Cory keeps the brain alive in a tank. Too bad for him, since the organ belongs to a ruthless, vicious businessman (the titular Donovan) who begins to influence Cory in horrible ways. Based on the novel by Curt Siodmak, and also filmed as "The Lady and the Monster" (1944), "Vengeance" (1963), and "The Brain" (1965). **85m/B; VHS, DVD, Blu-Ray.** Lew Ayres; Gene Evans; Nancy Davis; Steve Brodie; *D:* Felix Feist; *W:* Felix Feist; Hugh Brooke; *C:* Joseph Biroc; *M:* Eddie Dunstedter.

Donovan's Echo 1/2 **2011 (PG-13)** A dyslexic nuclear physicist who abandoned his career after the death of his family experiences deja vu when he notices many similarities between his awful past and current events. He is quickly forced to confront the unsettling prospect that either reality is about to repeat itself, or he's beginning to lose his mind. **91m/C; DVD.** *CA* Bruce Greenwood; Danny Glover; Natasha Calis; Ian Tracey; Sonja Bennett; *D:* Jim Cliffe; *W:* Jim Cliffe; Melodie Krieger; *C:* Robert Aschmann; *M:* Terry Frewer. **VIDEO**

Donovan's Reef **1963** Two WWII buddies meet every year on a Pacific atoll to engage in a perpetual bar-brawl, until a stuck-up Bostonian maiden appears to find her dad, a man who has fathered a brood of lovable half-casts. A rollicking, good-natured film from Ford. **109m/C; VHS, DVD.** John Wayne; Lee Marvin; Jack Warden; Elizabeth Allen; Dorothy Lamour; Mike Mazurki; Cesar Romero; *D:* John Ford; *W:* James Edward Grant; Frank Nugent; *C:* William Clothier; *M:* Cyril Mockridge.

Don's Party **1976** A rather dark comedy focusing on Australian Yuppie-types who decide to watch the election results on TV as a group. A lot more goes on at this party, however, than talk of the returns. Sexual themes surface. Cast members turn fine performances, aided by top-notch script and direction. **90m/C; VHS, DVD.** *AU* Pat Bishop; Graham Kennedy; Candy (Candida) Raymond; Veronica Lang; John Hargreaves; Ray Barrett; Claire Binney; Graeme Blundell; Jeanie Drynan; *D:* Bruce Beresford; *W:* David Williamson; *C:* Donald McAlpine; *M:* Leos Janacek. Australian Film Inst. '77: Actress (Bishop).

Don't Answer the Phone *The Hollywood Strangler* **1980 (R)** Deeply troubled photographer stalks and attacks the patients of a beautiful psychologist talk-show hostess. **94m/C; VHS, DVD, Blu-Ray.** James Westmoreland; Flo Gerrish; Ben Frank; *D:* Robert Hammer; *W:* Robert Hammer; Michael Castle; *C:* James L. Carter; *M:* Byron Allred.

Don't Be a Menace to South Central While Drinking Your Juice in the Hood **1995 (R)** Parody of "life in the hood" movies pokes fun at the attitudes and characters that are quickly becoming cliches in the genre. Shawn Wayans plays G-next-door Ashtray, sent by his mother to discover "what it is to be a man" from his father in South Central L.A. He hooks up with his homey Loc Dog (Marlon Wayans), a gun-crazed beer-swilling gangsta who packs a nuclear warhead. As the title implies, almost every major black film in recent memory is given the Wayans' drive-by treatment, with a majority of the plot lifted from "Boyz N the Hood." Fans of the TV series "In Living Color" will love this twisted look at ghetto life, but others may be offended. **88m/C; VHS, DVD, Blu-Ray.** Shawn Wayans; Marlon Wayans; Tracey Cherelle Jones; Chris Spencer; Suli McCullough; Darrell Heath; Helen Martin; Isaiah Barnes; Lahmard Tate; ***Cameo(s):*** Keenen Ivory Wayans; ***D:*** Paris Barclay; ***W:*** Shawn Wayans; Marlon Wayans; Phil Beauman; ***C:*** Russ Brandt; ***M:*** John Barnes.

Don't Be Afraid of the Dark ☙☙ 1/2 **1973** A young couple move into their dream house only to find that demonic little critters are residing in their basement and they want more than shelter. Made for TV with creepy scenes and eerie makeup for the monsters. **74m/C; VHS, DVD, Blu-Ray.** Kim Darby; Jim Hutton; Barbara Anderson; William Demarest; Pedro Armendariz, Jr.; Felix Silla; Patty Maloney; Tamara DeTreaux; ***D:*** John Newland; ***W:*** Giovanni Bergamini; ***C:*** Andrew Jackson; ***M:*** Billy Goldenberg. **TV**

Don't Be Afraid of the Dark ☙☙ 1/2 **2011 (R)** Producer/co-writer Del Toro creates a love letter to the 1973 made-for-TV movie that inspired him to get into filmmaking while adding another brave child heroine to his filmography. Sally (Madison)?now a 9-year-old unlike the original—unknowingly unleashes a basement of evil creatures after moving into a 19th-century Rhode Island mansion with her preoccupied father (Pearce) and his live-in girlfriend Kim (Holmes). With elements of classic Gothic storytelling—the evil stepmother, the haunted house, ancient creatures, even Tooth Fairy mythology—and an impressive young Madison, rookie director Nixey sets a spooky scene but in the end it's a run-of-the-mill scary story. **99m/C; DVD, Blu-Ray.** Bailee Madison; Guy Pearce; Katie Holmes; Jack Thompson; Alan Dale; ***D:*** Troy Nixey; ***W:*** Guillermo del Toro; Matthew Robbins; ***C:*** Oliver Stapleton; ***M:*** Marco Beltrami; Buck Sanders.

Don't Bother to Knock ☙☙ 1/2 **1952** As a mentally unstable hotel babysitter, Monroe meets a pilot (Widmark) and has a brief rendezvous with him. When the little girl she is babysitting interrupts, Monroe is furious, and later tries to murder the girl. This is one of Monroe's best dramatic roles. Bancroft's film debut as the Widmark's girlfriend. **76m/B; VHS, DVD, Blu-Ray.** Richard Widmark; Marilyn Monroe; Anne Bancroft; Elisha Cook, Jr.; Jim Backus; Lurene Tuttle; Jeanne Cagney; Donna Corcoran; ***D:*** Roy Ward Baker; ***W:*** Daniel Taradash; ***C:*** Lucien Ballard; ***M:*** Lionel Newman.

Don't Breathe ☙☙☙ **2016 (R)** Director Alvarez plays with conflicted morality in his story of three young criminals in Detroit who break into the wrong home in the quiet heart of the city. Hearing that a blind man (Lang) has a safe filled with cash from a wrongful death settlement, three young thieves decide to make him their last hit. Almost immediately things go very wrong, and they stumble upon the truth in the blind man's basement. The midsection of Alvarez's film is claustrophobic and tense, driven by great performances from Lang and Jane Levy. It gets a little silly but it's well-made silliness. **88m/C; DVD, Blu-Ray.** Stephen Lang; Jane Levy; Dylan Minnette; Daniel Zovatto; Emma Bercovici; ***D:*** Fede Alvarez; ***W:*** Fede Alvarez; Rodo Sayagues; ***C:*** Pedro Luque; ***M:*** Roque Baños.

Don't Come Knocking ☙☙ **2005 (R)** Aging movie star Howard Spence (Shepard) is better known for his life of drugs, booze, and babes. Fed-up with his latest cowboy flick, he literally rides off the set, leaving chaos behind him. Spence heads to Nevada to visit his mother (Saint), whom he hasn't seen in 30 years. She blithely informs him that an ex-flame of his had once come calling with the news of her pregnancy, and Spence tracks down barkeep Doreen (Lange) and their bitter son, Earl (Mann). Seems Spence was more fertile than he knew when he's later accosted by Sky (Polley), who claims to be his daughter. Spence wants another chance but he's pretty much a jerk so it's hard to take any interest. The desert vistas (Utah, Montana) are beautiful, though. **110m/C; DVD.** Sam Shepard; Jessica Lange; Sarah Polley; Gabriel Mann; Tim Roth; Fairuza Balk; Eva Marie Saint; James Gammon; George Kennedy; Marley Shelton; Rodney A. Grant; Tim Matheson; Julia Sweeney; Kurt Fuller; James Roday; ***D:*** Wim Wenders; ***W:*** Sam Shepard; Wim Wenders; ***C:*** Franz Lustig; ***M:*** T-Bone Burnett.

Don't Cry Now ☙ 1/2 **2007** When Bonnie (Hope) gets a phohe call from her husband Ross's (Bancroft) drunken ex Joan (Arden) about being in danger, she dismisses it until Joan is found murdered. Joan's death means that Bonnie's surly stepchildren Lauren (Maxwell) and Sam (Liboiron) come to live with them. Meanwhile, the cops investigate and Bonnie's criminal brother Nick (Priestley) suddenly shows up to complicate matters further. Adapted from the Joy Fielding novel. **90m/C; DVD.** Leslie Hope; Cameron Bancroft; Brooklynn Proulx; Landon Liboiron; Julia Maxwell; Jason Priestley; Hannes Haenicke; Terry David Mulligan; Jann Arden; Jim Byrnes; ***D:*** Jason Priestley; ***W:*** Dave Schultz; ***C:*** Craig Wrobleski; ***M:*** Bruce Leitl. **CABLE**

Don't Do It ☙☙ 1/2 **1994 (PG-13)** Three 20-something couples, attempting to find love, all wind up in the same cafe and try to tell the truth about how they feel and whom they desire. **90m/C; VHS, DVD.** James Marshall; James LeGros; Sheryl Lee; Esai Morales; Alexis Arquette; Balthazar Getty; Sarah Trigger; Heather Graham; ***D:*** Eugene Hess; ***W:*** Eugene Hess; ***C:*** Ian Fox.

Don't Drink the Water ☙☙ 1/2 **1969 (G)** Based on Woody Allen's hit play, this film places an average Newark, New Jersey, family behind the Iron Curtain, where their vacation photo-taking gets them accused of spying. **100m/C; VHS, DVD, Blu-Ray.** Jackie Gleason; Estelle Parsons; Joan Delaney; Ted Bessell; Michael Constantine; ***D:*** Howard Morris.

Don't Fence Me In ☙☙ **1945** Evans is a magazine photographer who heads west to do a story on a legendary character named Wildcat Kelly, who's supposedly dead. She meets rancher Rogers and sidekick Hayes and, of course, discovers that Rogers is the man she's looking for. **71m/B; VHS, Streaming.** Roy Rogers; Dale Evans; George "Gabby" Hayes; Robert "Bob" Livingston; ***D:*** John English; ***W:*** Dorrell McGowan; Stuart E. McGowan; ***C:*** William Bradford.

Don't Gamble with Strangers ☙ 1/2 **1946** Mike Sarno and gambling rival Fay Benton team up, posing as brother and sister, to take over a casino. When Mike dumps Fay for heiress Ruth and her dough, the doublecross leads to murder. **67m/B; DVD.** Kane Richmond; Bernadene Hayes; Gloria Warren; Philip Van Zandt; Charles Trowbridge; ***D:*** William Beaudine; ***W:*** Harvey Gates; ***C:*** William Sickner.

Don't Go in the House ☙ **1980 (R)** Long-dormant psychosis is brought to life by the death of a young man's mother. **90m/C; VHS, DVD, Blu-Ray.** Dan Grimaldi; Robert Osth; Ruth Dardick; ***D:*** Joseph Ellison; ***W:*** Joseph Ellison; Ellen Hammill; ***C:*** Oliver Wood; ***M:*** Richard Einhorn.

Don't Go in the Woods WOOF! **1981 (R)** Routine exercise in "don't do that" terror genre (includes warnings about going into houses, answering phones, looking into basements, opening windows, etc.). This time, four young campers are stalked by a crazed killer armed with prerequisite ax. **88m/C; VHS, DVD, Blu-Ray.** Angie Brown; James Hayden; Mary Gail Artz; Jack McClelland; ***D:*** James Bryan.

Don't Go in the Woods ☙ **2010** Tepid horror-in-the-woods that offers nothing but genre cliches, including the emo music. Nick gets his bandmates to give up their drugs, booze, and cellphones when they go on a camping trip to write songs. Things go wrong when their girlfriends show up and everyone starts partying before some mysterious killer gets the blood flowing (late in the flick). D'Onofrio's directorial debut. **83m/C; DVD.** Matt Sbeglia; Jorgen Jorgensen; Soomin Lee; Casey Smith; Nick Thorp; ***D:*** Vincent D'Onofrio; ***W:*** Joe Vinciguerra; Sam Bisbee; ***C:*** Michael J. Latino; ***M:*** Sam Bisbee. **VIDEO**

Don't Go Near the Water ☙☙ **1957** Somewhat amusing comedy about the happenings at a Naval installation on a South Pacific tropical paradise. Clark outshines the others in his role as a frustrated officer. Based on the novel by William Brinkley. **107m/C; VHS, DVD.** Glenn Ford; Gia Scala; Earl Holliman; Anne Francis; Keenan Wynn; Fred Clark; Eva Gabor; Russ Tamblyn; ***D:*** Charles Walters; ***W:*** Dorothy Kingsley; George Wells.

Don't Hang Up ☙☙ **2017 (R)** A horror film that explores issues like social media and bullying. Best friends Sam (Sulkin) and Brady (Clayton) have become viral sensations for their videos of their drunken prank phone calls. As they become more famous, they increase the number and intensity of pranks they pull until a mysterious caller turns the tables on them on a dark and stormy night. The caller begins to terrorize the teens and their loved ones in a way that goes beyond teaching them a lesson. Though generally fun and full of atmosphere, it's also a bit shallow. **83m/C; DVD.** Gregg Sulkin; Garrett Clayton; Bella Dayne; Sienna Guillory; Edward Killingback; ***D:*** Damien Mace; Alexis Wajsbrot; ***W:*** Joe Johnson; ***C:*** Nat Hill; ***M:*** Aleksi Aubry-Carlson.

Don't Kill It ☙☙ **2017** A gory yet entertaining horror genre film. In the small Mississippi town of Chickory Creek, a demon is causing the death of numerous residents by possessing the person who killed its previous host. After local police call in the FBI on the case, Agent Evelyn Pierce (Klebe), who spent her childhood there, takes the case. She teams up with demon hunter Jebediah Woodley (Lundgren), who has a history with this particular demon. The pair try to find a way to stop it without killing. Though the film never rises above a fun B movie, Lundgren's performance shows some comic chops. **83m/C; DVD.** Dolph Lundgren; Kristina Klebe; Aaron McPherson; Michael Aaron Milligan; Elissa Dowling; ***D:*** Mike Mendez; ***W:*** Dan Berk; Robert Olsen; ***C:*** Jan-Michael Losada; ***M:*** Juliette Beavan; Sean Beavan.

Don't Knock Twice ☙☙ **2017 (R)** A supernatural horror centered on a maternal monster. Jess (Sackhoff) neglected her daughter Chloe (Boynton) because of a substance abuse problem, and Chloe spent her childhood in foster care. By the time Chloe is a teen, Jess has gotten her life together, become a sculptor, and married wealthy lawyer Ben (Botet). After Chloe encounters a ghost in a rumored haunted house, she reconnects with her mother, who thinks of her daughter as a possession, and Chloe believes she is being personally haunted. Their new relationship becomes strained for natural and supernatural reasons. The disjointed, underdeveloped story undermines Sackhoff's strong performance. **93m/C; DVD.** Katee Sackhoff; Lucy Boynton; Richard Mylan; Nick Moran; Pascale Wilson; ***D:*** Caradog W. James; ***W:*** Mark Huckerby; Nick Ostler; ***C:*** Adam Frisch; ***M:*** James Edward Barker; Steve Moore.

Don't Leave Home ☙ 1/2 **2018** When American artist Melanie Thomas (Hollyman) becomes enraptured by an Irish urban legend, she creates a show based on the story. In the tale, an 8-year-old girl had a religious experience in front of a Virgin Mary statue that inspired a priest to paint a picture of the event. The girl later vanished from the painting and the real world at the same time. When Melanie has a chance to meet the painter priest, she travels to Ireland. Though touching on interesting ideas about faith and art, the story and acting inevitably fall short. **86m/C; DVD.** Anna Margaret Hollyman; Mark Lawrence; Karrie Cox; Helena Bereen; David McSavage; ***D:*** Michael Tully; ***W:*** Michael Tully; ***C:*** Wyatt Garfield; ***M:*** Michael Montes.

Don't Let Go ☙☙ **2019 (R)** Los Angeles cop Jack Radcliff (Oyelowo) has a strong relationship with his teenage niece Ashley (Reid). After receiving a distressing call from Ashley, Jack finds her and her parents murdered. Though the police believe it was a murder-suicide, Jack is unsure especially after he receives a call from Ashley. Coming to terms with the supernatural, Jack realizes that is Ashley calling him from another timeline, set two weeks before the murder. Together, they try to learn who was responsible for the deaths. The premise has promise but it fizzles out by not exploring the most interesting "what if" scenarios. **103m/C; DVD, Blu-Ray.** Storm Reid; Alfred Molina; Mykelti Williamson; David Oyelowo; Brian Tyree Henry; ***D:*** Jacob Aaron Estes; ***W:*** Jacob Aaron Estes; ***C:*** Sharone Meir; ***M:*** Ethan Gold.

Don't Let Me Die on a Sunday ☙☙ 1/2 *J'Aimerais pas Crever un Dimache* **1998** Bizarre, disturbing wallow in Parisian depravity begins in a morgue. That's where attendant Ben (Barr) meets Teresa (Bouchez). The details of that first encounter will not be recounted, but the two begin a downward spiral into joyless sex, angst, alienation, and despair. Not for the fainthearted. French with subtitles. **86m/C; VHS, DVD.** *FR* Elodie Bouchez; Jean-Marc Barr; Martin Petitguyot; Patrick Catalifo; Gerard Loussine; Jeanne Casilas; Florence Darel; ***D:*** Didier Le Pecheur; ***W:*** Didier Le Pecheur; ***C:*** Denis Rouden; ***M:*** Philippe Cohen-Solal.

Don't Look Back ☙☙ *Bob Dylan: Don't Look Back* **1967** Pennebaker's cinema verite documentary on Bob Dylan's 1965 concert tour in England as he begins shifting from acoustic folkie to electric rock 'n' roller. There's little onstage footage, but Pennebaker follows the confident Dylan into cars, hotel rooms, on interviews, and backstage. Features Dylan's then-girlfriend Joan Baez, his manager Albert Grossman, and musicians Donovan and Alan Price among others. **96m/C; DVD, Blu-Ray.** Bob Dylan; Joan Baez; Albert Grossman; Donovan; Alan Price; ***D:*** D.A. Pennebaker; ***C:*** D.A. Pennebaker; Howard Alk; Jones Alk. Natl. Film Reg. '98.

Don't Look Back ☙☙☙ **1996 (R)** Musician and heroin addict Jesse Parish (Stoltz) stumbles across a suitcase full of cash after witnessing a drug deal gone bad. He heads back to family and friends in Texas so he can kick his habit, but is marked for death by the dealers who want their money back. Strong script and performances. **91m/C; VHS, DVD.** Eric Stoltz; John Corbett; Josh Hamilton; Annabeth Gish; Dwight Yoakam; Amanda Plummer; ***D:*** Geoff Murphy; ***W:*** Billy Bob Thornton; Tom Epperson. **CABLE**

Don't Look Down ☙ 1/2 *Wes Craven Presents: Don't Look Down* **1998** TV reporte Carla (Ward) begins suffering from acrophobia after the falling death of her sister. She joins and extreme therapy group run by radical shrink Dr. Sadowski (Kinney) to overcome her fears. But it doesn't help when her fellow therapy mates beginning dying in fatal falls. **90m/C; VHS, DVD.** Megan Ward; Billy Burke; Terry Kinney; Angela Moore; William McDonald; Kate Robbins; Tara Spencer-Nairn; ***D:*** Larry Shaw; ***W:*** Gregory Goodell; ***C:*** David Geddes; ***M:*** J. Peter Robinson. **TV**

Don't Look in the Attic WOOF! **1981** A couple finds a haunted house with cows in the attic. **90m/C; VHS, DVD.** Beba Loncar; Jean-Pierre Aumont; ***D:*** Carl Ausino.

Don't Look in the Basement ☙ 1/2 *The Forgotten* **1973 (R)** Things get out of hand at an isolated asylum and a pretty young nurse is caught in the middle. Straight-jacketed by a low budget. **95m/C; VHS, DVD, Blu-Ray.** Rosie Holotik; Anne MacAdams; William (Bill) McGhee; Rhea MacAdams; Gene Ross; Betty Chandler; Camilla Carr; Robert Dracup; Jessie Kirby; Hugh Feagin; Harryete Warren; Jessie Lee Fulton; Michael Harvey; ***D:*** S.F. Brownrigg; ***W:*** Tim Pope; Tom Pope; ***M:*** Robert Farrar.

Don't Look Now ☙☙☙ **1973 (R)** A psychological creepfest with a chilling climax, based on the novel by Daphne Du Maurier. John (Sutherland) and Laura (Christie) Baxter travel to a dank, off-season Venice in an attempt to put the drowning death of their young daughter behind them. But while working on a church restoration, John begins to have psychic visions which are encouraged by a pair of strange sisters (Matania, Mason). There's a steamy love scene between Sutherland and Christie that became the object of much gossip. **110m/C; VHS, DVD.** *GB IT* Donald Sutherland; Julie Christie; Hilary Mason; Clelia Matania; Massimo Serato; Leopoldo Trieste; Adelina Porrio; ***D:*** Nicolas Roeg; ***W:*** Chris Bryant; Allan Scott; ***C:*** Anthony B. Richmond; ***M:*** Pino Donaggio.

Don't Look Up ☙ 1/2 **2008 (R)** Director Marcus Reed wants to remake an unfinished 1928 silent film about a gypsy curse where the director, Bela Olt, disappeared. He and his crew are working in the same Romanian village when his own set seems to be plagued by a malevolent force. Chan's remake of Hideo Nakata's 1996 film "Joyurei" is predictable horror. **98m/C; DVD, Blu-Ray.** Reshad Strik; Lothaire Bluteau; Kevin Corrigan; Carmen Chaplin; Henry Thomas; Eli Roth; Rachael Murphy; ***D:*** Fruit Chan; ***W:*** Brian Cox; ***C:*** Hang-Seng Poon; ***M:*** Tony Humecke. **VIDEO**

Don't Lose Your Head ☙☙ *Carry On, Don't Lose Your Head* **1966** In the 13th series entry, two English fops, Sir Rodney

Ffing (James) and Lord Darcy Pue (Dale), are horrified to hear about the French Revolution and decide to come to the rescue of their fellow aristocrats. So Sir Rodney disguises himself (badly) as the adventurous Black Fingernail (think a low-rent Scarlet Pimpernel) to tweak those Citizen Frenchies. **90m/C; DVD.** *GB* Sidney James; Jim Dale; Kenneth Williams; Charles Hawtrey; Peter Butterworth; Dany Robin; Peter Gilmore; Joan Sims; ***D:*** Gerald Thomas; ***W:*** Talbot Rothwell; ***C:*** Alan Hume; ***M:*** Eric Rogers.

Don't Make Waves 1967 Silly sixties sex comedy. New Yorker Carlo (Curtis) is vacationing in California when he meets Laura (Cardinale), who takes him home after accidentally destroying his car and clothes. She's the mistress of wealthy Rod Prescott (Webber) and Carlo decides he likes the SoCal life so much that he blackmails Rod into giving him a job. He also tries to keep his hands off Laura by getting involved with skydiving beach babe Malibu (Tate). **100m/C; DVD.** Tony Curtis; Claudia Cardinale; Sharon Tate; Robert Webber; Joanna Barnes; Mort Sahl; Edgar Bergen; ***D:*** Alexander MacKendrick; ***W:*** Ira Wallach; George Kirgo; Maurice Richlin; ***C:*** Philip H. Lathrop; ***M:*** Vic Mizzy.

Don't Mess with My Sister! 1/2 **1985** A married, New York junkyard worker falls in love with a belly dancer he meets at a party. The affair leads to murder and subsequently, revenge. An interesting, offbeat film from the director of "I Spit on Your Grave." **90m/C; VHS, DVD.** Joe Perce; Jeannine Lemay; Jack Gurci; Peter Sapienza; Laura Lanfranchi; ***D:*** Mier Zarchi.

Don't Open the Door! WOOF! 1974 (PG) A young woman is terrorized by a killer located inside her house. **90m/C; VHS, DVD, Blu-Ray.** Susan Bracken; Gene Ross; Jim Harrell; ***D:*** S.F. Brownrigg.

Don't Open Till Christmas WOOF! 1984 A weirdo murders various Santa Clauses in assorted gory ways. Best to take this one back to the department store. **86m/C; VHS, DVD.** *GB* Edmund Purdom; Caroline Munro; Alan Lake; Belinda Mayne; Gerry Sundquist; Mark Jones; ***D:*** Edmund Purdom.

Don't Raise the Bridge, Lower the River 1968 (G) After his wife leaves him, an American with crazy, get-rich-quick schemes turns his wife's ancestral English home into a Chinese discotheque. Domestic farce that comes and goes; if mad for Lewis, rent "The Nutty Professor." **99m/C; VHS, DVD.** Jerry Lewis; Terry-Thomas; Jacqueline Pearce; Bernard Cribbins; Patricia Routledge; ***D:*** Jerry Paris.

Don't Say a Word 1/2 **2001 (R)** Douglas plays the stable family man pushed to the brink once again in this chilly kidnaping thriller. Dr. Nathan Conrad (Douglas) is a psychiatrist whose idyllic life is shattered when his eight-year-old daughter Jessie (Bartusiak) is kidnaped by a gang of thieves. They threaten to kill his little girl unless he can retrieve a six-digit number locked in the brain of Nathan's new patient Elisabeth (Murphy), a raving lunatic who slashed an orderly to death. Meanwhile, the bad guys have rigged surveillance equipment in his apartment and are menacing his wife Aggie (Janssen), as cop Esposito stumbles across the plot, inadvertently threatening Nathan's efforts. All the plot threads are conveniently tied up in a standard final showdown scene. **112m/C; VHS, DVD.** Michael Douglas; Sean Bean; Brittany Murphy; Skye McCole Bartusiak; Famke Janssen; Guy Torry; Jennifer Esposito; Shawn Doyle; Victor Argo; Oliver Platt; Conrad Goode; Paul Schulze; Lance Reddick; ***D:*** Gary Fleder; ***W:*** Patrick Smith Kelly; Anthony Peckham; ***C:*** Amir M. Mokri; ***M:*** Mark Isham.

Don't Tell *La Bestia nel Cuore; The Beast in the Heart* **2005** An inexplicable Oscar nominee, this confusing melodrama concerns a brother and sister and family secrets coming to light. Voiceover actress Sabina (Mezzogiorno) lives in Rome with her actor boyfriend, Franco (Boni). After dubbing a rape scene, Sabina begins having nightmares about a scared child and decides to visit her brother, Daniele (Lo Cascio), who lives in Virginia. She pressures him to tell what he knows. Side stories involving Franco's work on a soap opera and a couple of Sabrina's friends finding (and losing) romance dissipate the tension. Attractive cast. Italian with subtitles. **120m/C; DVD.** *IT* Giovanna Mezzogiorno; Stefania Rocca; Angela Finocchiaro; Alessio Boni; Luigi Lo Cascio; Valerio Binasco; Lewis Lemperuer Palmer; Jeke-Omer Boyayanlar; Lucy Akhurst; Guiseppe Battiston; Francesca Inaudi; ***D:*** Cristina Comencini; ***W:*** Francesca Marciano; Cristina Comencini; Giulia Calenda; ***C:*** Fabio Cianchetti; ***M:*** Franco Piersanti.

Don't Tell **2005** Lame family drama has three siblings (Eastwood, Root, Wlcek) reuniting in their dreary, small hometown after their hard-drinking farmer dad dies. This is a dysfunctional bunch with family secrets that don't inspire sympathy or involvement. **88m/C; DVD.** Alison Eastwood; Bonnie Root; James Wlcek; ***D:*** Isaac H. Eaton; ***W:*** Julie Anne Koehnen; ***C:*** Mike King; ***M:*** Larry Brown.

Don't Tell Her It's Me *The Boyfriend School* **1990 (PG-13)** Guttenberg is determined to win the heart of an attractive writer. With the assistance of his sister, he works to become a dream man. Clever premise, promising cast, lame comedy. From the novel by Sarah Bird. **101m/C; DVD.** Steve Guttenberg; Jami Gertz; Shelley Long; Kevin Scannell; Kyle MacLachlan; Madchén Amick; ***D:*** Malcolm Mowbray; ***W:*** Sarah Bird; ***C:*** Reed Smoot; ***M:*** Michael Gore.

Don't Tell Mom the Babysitter's Dead 1/2 **1991 (PG-13)** Their mother traveling abroad, the title situation leaves a houseful of teenagers with the whole summer to themselves. Eldest daughter Applegate cons her way into the high-powered business world while the metalhead son parties hardy. Many tepid comic situations, not adding up to very much. **105m/C; VHS, DVD.** Christina Applegate; Keith Coogan; Joanna Cassidy; John Getz; Josh Charles; Concetta Tomei; Eda Reiss Merin; David Duchovny; ***D:*** Stephen Herek; ***W:*** Neil Landau; Tara Ison; ***C:*** Tim Suhrstedt; ***M:*** David Newman.

Don't Think Twice 1/2 **2016 (R)** Birbiglia's touching and hysterical comedy tackles the art of improv in a way not really seen in film before, while also serving as an interesting commentary on how fame can divide groups of friends. That's essentially what happens in a New York City improv troupe after two members get a big break on television. How does one achieve fame in the world of comedy? How do their friends respond after they do? Key and Jacobs lead a fantastic ensemble that truly understands the art of making people laugh and how it can take true drama to be truly funny. **92m/C; DVD, Blu-Ray.** Keegan Michael Key; Gillian Jacobs; Mike Birbiglia; Kate Micucci; Chris Gethard; Tami Sagher; ***D:*** Mike Birbiglia; ***W:*** Mike Birbiglia; ***C:*** Joe Anderson; ***M:*** Roger Neill.

Don't Torture a Duckling *Non Si Sevizia un Paperino* **1972** Newspaperman Andrea Martelli (Milian) investigates the deaths of several young boys in the Sicily village where his father was born. The suspicious villagers take their revenge on a couple of outcast locals but Martelli teams up with seductive Patrizia (Bouchet) to uncover the real killer. Creepy rather a gorefest, although Fulci recycled one of the more violent scenes for his later film, "The Psychic." **102m/C; VHS, DVD, Blu-Ray.** *IT* Tomas Milian; Barbara Bouchet; Irene Papas; Florinda Bolkan; Marc Porel; ***D:*** Lucio Fulci; ***W:*** Roberto Gianviti; Lucio Fulci; Robert Gianviti; ***C:*** Sergio d'Offizi; ***M:*** Riz Ortolani.

Don't Worry, He Won't Get Far on Foot 1/2 **2018 (R)** On the rocky path to sobriety after a life-changing accident, John Callahan (Phoenix) discovers the healing power of art, willing his injured hands into drawing hilarious, often controversial, cartoons, bringing him a new lease on life. The narrative's a bit choppy, but sharp acting by Phoenix and Hill, who plays his sponsor, deliver pathos and dark humor. Based on Callahan's autobiography. **113m/C; Blu-Ray, Streaming.** Joaquin Rafael (Leaf) Phoenix; Jonah Hill; Rooney Mara; Jack Black; Carrie Brownstein; ***D:*** Gus Van Sant; ***W:*** Gus Van Sant; Jack Gibson; William Andrew Eatman; ***C:*** Christopher Blauvelt; ***M:*** Danny Elfman.

Don't Worry, We'll Think of a Title **1966** Too bad they couldn't think of a funny script as well instead of this predictable groaner of a spy spoof. Diner cook Charlie Yuckapuck and his waitress friends Annie and Magda get fired for incompetence. Fortunately, Magda has just inherited a bookstore and they begin working there, only Charlie is mistaken by foreign agents for a defecting cosmonaut they want to retrieve. **84m/B; DVD.** Morey Amsterdam; Rose Marie; January Jones; Richard Deacon; Jack Heller; ***D:*** Harmon Jones; ***W:*** Morey Amsterdam; George Schenck; William Marks; ***C:*** Brick Marquard; ***M:*** Richard LaSalle.

Doogal *The Magic Roundabout* **2005 (G)** Animated kiddie adventure. Doogal the dog frees evil sorcerer Zeebad (Stewart) by mistake, and now the canine and his gang—a sassy cow (Goldberg), geeky snail (Macy), hippy bunny (Fallon), kind-hearted magician (McKellen), and a little girl (Minogue)?must keep the imp from making the world a big ball of ice. Compared with the inventive and beloved British TV show from the 1960s, the disappointment of this outing overpowers all the big-name celebrity voices involved. **80m/C; DVD.** ***V:*** Tom Baker; Jim Broadbent; Joanna Lumley; Ian McKellen; Kylie Minogue; Bill Nighy; Ray Winstone; Lee Evans; Robbie Williams; ***D:*** Frank Passingham; Dave Borthwick; Jean Duval; ***W:*** Paul Bassett Davies; Stephane Sanoussi; Raoff Sanoussi; ***C:*** Tad Safran; ***M:*** Mark Thomas.

Doom **2005 (R)** It's the live-action version of the videogame. If that's your thing, you'll enjoy the flick because everyone involved knows it's a game and they get to play Space Marines (led by the Rock and Urban) and use big guns to blow away flesh-eating mutants. Hey, what could be more fun? Anything else comes to mind. **104m/C; DVD, Blu-Ray.** Karl Urban; Rosamund Pike; DeObia Oparei; Ben Daniels; Raz Adoti; Richard Brake; Dexter Fletcher; Al Weaver; Brian Steele; Dwayne "The Rock" Johnson; Yao Chin; ***D:*** Andrzej Bartkowiak; ***W:*** David Callaham; Wesley Strick; ***C:*** Tony Pierce-Roberts; ***M:*** Clint Mansell.

Doom Asylum WOOF! 1988 (R) Several sex kittens wander into a deserted sanatorium and meet up with the grisly beast wielding autopsy instruments. The people involved with this spoof should have been (more) committed. **77m/C; VHS, DVD, Blu-Ray.** Patty Mullen; Ruth (Coreen) Collins; Kristin Davis; William Hay; Kenny L. Price; Harrison White; Dawn Alvan; Michael Rogen; ***D:*** Richard Friedman.

The Doom Generation **1995 (R)** Alienated trio on the road trip to hell (doubling as L.A.). Beautiful 17-year-old druggie Amy Blue (McGowan), her sweetly dim boyfriend Jordan White (Duval), and hot-tempered stud/drifter Xavier Red (Schaech) flee after Red kills a store clerk. They're basically from nowhere, going nowhere, and finding sex and (lots of gruesomely depicted) violence along the way. The subtitle, "A Heterosexual Movie by Gregg Araki," may be technically accurate but the homoerotic subtext is very clear. Terrific performances. Second film in Araki's teen trilogy, following "Totally F***ked Up," and preceding "Nowhere." An unrated version is also available. **84m/C; VHS, DVD.** Rose McGowan; James Duval; Johnathon Schaech; Parker Posey; Lauren Tewes; Christopher Knight; Margaret Cho; Skinny Puppy; Heidi Fleiss; ***D:*** Gregg Araki; ***W:*** Gregg Araki; ***C:*** Jim Fealy; ***M:*** Don Gallo.

Doomed to Die **1940** Cargo of stolen bonds leads to a tong war and the murder of a shipping millionaire. Part of Mr. Wong series. Worth a look if only for Karloff's performance. **67m/B; VHS, DVD.** Boris Karloff; Marjorie Reynolds; Grant Withers; ***D:*** William Nigh.

Doomsday **2008 (R)** In 2035 the Reaper Virus has left Scotland a barren wasteland, quarantined from the rest of the world. But when satellite images reveal that life may still exist, a team of soldiers led by Eden Sinclair (Mitra) return in hopes of curing the survivors, instead discovering an underground civilization of psycho bikers and gutter punks. It's hard to tell if director Marshall has assembled a tribute, spoof, or rip-off of earlier doomsday flicks, because while this one doesn't make a lot of sense, it's still cheesy, over-the-top good fun. **109m/C; DVD, Blu-Ray.** Rhona Mitra; Malcolm McDowell; Bob Hoskins; Adrian Lester; Alexander Siddig; David O'Hara; MyAnna Buring; Craig Conway; ***D:*** Neil Marshall; ***W:*** Neil Marshall; ***C:*** Sam McCurdy; ***M:*** Tyler Bates.

Doomsday Gun 1/2 **1994** Fact-based thriller about arms manufacturer Gerald Bull (Langella), who dreams of building the world's biggest gun—a behemoth with a range of 1000 miles. Only problem is Bull's willingness to sell the weapon to the highest bidder, who happens to be Saddam Hussein. This doesn't sit well with Israeli Mossad agent Yossi (Arkin). **110m/C; VHS, DVD.** Frank Langella; Alan Arkin; Kevin Spacey; Tony Goldwyn; James Fox; Michael Kitchen; Francesca Annis; Marianne (Cuau) Denicourt; ***D:*** Robert M. Young; ***W:*** Lionel Chetwynd; Walter Bernstein; ***C:*** Ian Wilson. **CABLE**

Doomsday Prophecy WOOF! 2011 (PG-13) The only thing doomed is this Syfy Channel disaster flick. Crazy author Rupert Crane's (Walker) predictions about worldwide disasters are coming true. He dies before he can explain to book editor Eric Foz (Buckley) and archeologist Brooke Calvin (Staite) but he leaves them a video and a magical rod that gives Eric glimpses of the future. Uh, yeah, as if it's supposed to make sense. **92m/C; DVD, Blu-Ray.** A.J. Buckley; Jewel Staite; Alan Dale; Bruce Ramsay; Gordon Tootoosis; Matthew (Matt) Walker; ***D:*** Jason Bourque; ***W:*** Jason Bourque; Shawn Linden; ***C:*** C. Kim Miles; ***M:*** Michael Neilson. **CABLE**

Doomsdayer 1/2 **2000 (R)** Okay, see how familiar this sounds. Jack Logan (Lara) works for a covert agency. His assignment is to prevent a new explosive from falling into terrorists' hands. This Doomsdayer device is currently held by a ruthless billionaire weapons dealer (Kier) and his equally nasty wife (Nielsen), who have their own island. Logan and his team run into trouble before they save the day. Now you won't have to actually watch the video. **93m/C; VHS, DVD.** Joe Lara; Udo Kier; Brigitte Nielsen; Sandra Gomez; January Isaac; T.J. Storm; Paige Rowland; Ravil Isyanov; ***D:*** Michael J. Sarna; ***W:*** Bob Couttie; ***C:*** David Rakoczy. **VIDEO**

Doomwatch 1/2 **1972** A scientist discovers a chemical company is dumping poison into local waters, deforming the inhabitants of an isolated island when they eat the catch of the day. Unsurprising. **89m/C; VHS, DVD, Blu-Ray.** *GB* Ian Bannen; Judy Geeson; John Paul; Simon Oates; George Sanders; ***D:*** Peter Sasdy; ***W:*** Clive Exton; ***C:*** Ken Talbot.

The Door in the Floor 1/2 **2004 (R)** This compelling feature gets an extra half-bone for Jeff Bridges' standout performance. He's dissolute but celebrated children's author/illustrator Ted Cole (the title refers to one of his books), who is spending the summer of 1958 in a Hamptons beach house with his inconsolable wife Marion (Basinger) and their precocious four-year-old daughter, Ruth (Fanning). Marion has not recovered from the car crash that killed the couple's two teenaged sons. Ted decides on a trial separation, which means he can continue an affair with wealthy Evelyn (Rogers), and he hires 16-year-old Eddie (Foster) to keep an eye on Marion. Eddie does more than that when he develops an obsession for the lonely woman who begins a sexual relationship with him. Adapted from the first section of John Irving's 1998 novel "A Widow of One Year." **111m/C; DVD.** Jeff Bridges; Kim Basinger; Jon Foster; Mimi Rogers; Elle Fanning; Bijou Philips; Louis Arcella; ***D:*** Tod Harrison Williams; ***W:*** Tod Harrison Williams; ***C:*** Terry Stacey; ***M:*** Marcelo Zarvos.

Door to Door Maniac 1/2 *Five Minutes to Live* **1961** Criminals hold a bank president's wife hostage, unaware that the husband was looking to get rid of her in favor of another woman. Cash's screen debut. Aside from the strange cast ensemble, not particularly worth seeing. **80m/B; VHS, DVD.** Johnny Cash; Ron Howard; Vic Tayback; Donald Woods; Cay Forrester; Pamela Mason; ***D:*** Bill Karn.

Door with the Seven Locks 1/2 **1962** Bizarre Edgar Wallace story of man who leaves seven keys to a treasure vault in his will. Remake of "Chamber of Horrors." **96m/C; VHS, DVD.** *GE* Eddi Arent; Heinz Drache; Klaus Kinski; Ady Berber; ***D:*** Alfred Vohrer.

The Doorbell Rang: A Nero Wolfe Mystery ✓✓ 1/2 **2001** Detective Nero Wolfe (Chaykin) and his investigator Archie Goodwin (Hutton) get involved in the case of an eccentric woman who comes to Wolfe with a tale of FBI harassment that leads to murder. Based on the mystery by Rex Stout. **100m/C; VHS, DVD.** Timothy Hutton; Maury Chaykin; Saul Rubinek; Debra Monk; Colin Fox; ***W:*** Timothy Hutton; Michael Jaffe. **CABLE**

The Doors ✓✓ 1/2 **1991 (R)** Stone approached Jim Morrison with an early incarnation of this docudrama, but it's hard to believe even the Lizard King could play himself with any more convincing abandon than Kilmer, in a great performance. Trouble is, the story—one of drugs, abuse, and abject self-indulgence—grows tiresome, and the audience, with the exception of die-hard fans, may lose sight of any sympathy they might have had. Ryan is forgettable as Morrison's hippie-chick wife, MacLachlan sports a funny wig and dabbles on the keyboards as Ray Manszarek, and Quinlan is atypically cast as a sado-masochistic journalist paramour. Based on "Riders on the Storm" by John Densmore. **138m/C; VHS, DVD, Blu-Ray, UMD.** Val Kilmer; Meg Ryan; Kevin Dillon; Kyle MacLachlan; Frank Whaley; Michael Madsen; Kathleen Quinlan; Crispin Glover; Josh Evans; John Densmore; William Jordan; Mimi Rogers; Paul Williams; Bill Graham; Billy Vera; William Kunstler; Wes Studi; Costas Mandylor; Billy Idol; Michael Wincott; Dennis Burkley; Kelly Hu; ***D:*** Oliver Stone; ***W:*** Oliver Stone; Ralph Thomas; Randy Johnson; Randall Johnson; ***C:*** Robert Richardson.

The Doorway ✓ 1/2 **2000 (R)** Four college students are fixing up a house that they discover is built over a doorway to hell—and they've just opened it up. So they ask the local expert on the paranormal (Scheider, whose role is very limited) for help. **91m/C; VHS, DVD.** Roy Scheider; Lauren Woodland; Suzanne Bridgham; Teresa De Priest; Christian Harmony; Don Maloney; ***D:*** Michael B. Druxman; ***W:*** Michael B. Druxman; ***C:*** Yoram Astrakhan. **VIDEO**

Doorway to Hell ✓✓ **1930** Generally unsentimental and brutal crime drama. Chicago racketeer Louie Ricarno (Ayres) wants to retire to Florida with his bride Doris (Mathews) but fate has other plans. Louie leaves his criminal organization in the hands of his mob lieutenant Steve Mileaway (an outstanding Cagney), who has trouble doing the job. Underling Rocco (Madison) forces Louie to come back. **78m/B; DVD.** Lew Ayres; James Cagney; Dorothy Mathews; Charles (Judel, Judells) Judels; Noel Madison; Robert Elliott; Leon Janney; ***D:*** Archie Mayo; ***W:*** George Rosener; ***C:*** Barney McGill.

Dopamine ✓✓ 1/2 **2003 (R)** Rand (Livingston), a partner in a dot-com startup, develops an interactive, AI-type computer character. When they decide to test it in a classroom, Rand falls for the teacher, Sarah (Lloyd). Rand tries to sort out his feelings, and intellectual insticts, as he ponders whether love is emotional or chemical. Perhaps he's over-thinking a bit. **79m/C; DVD.** John Livingston; Sabrina Lloyd; Bruno Campos; Reuben Grundy; Kathleen Antonia; Nicole Wilder; ***D:*** Mark Decena; ***W:*** Mark Decena; Timothy Breitbach; ***C:*** Robert Humphreys; ***M:*** Eric Holland.

Dope ✓✓✓ **2015 (R)** Taking cues from John Hughes' reign as the king of honest, goofy, heartfelt '80s teen comedies, this surprise indie hit proves that the drugs and violence of the hood isn't always the biggest problem. Three friends in Inglewood, Malcolm (Moore), Diggy (Clemons), and Jib (Revolori), are just as concerned with hiding their love for white culture as they are running from gangs. A high-speed tour de force through a madcapped LA, taking Malcolm's nerd posse to wild parties and drops them into a zany drug deal gone bad, all while they try to keep their grades up. Wisely avoids cliches, but at times throws too much at the screen, forcing the audience to be just as confused as its Ferris Bueller wanna-be antihero. **115m/C; DVD, Blu-Ray, Streaming.** Shameik Moore; Kiersey Clemons; Zoë Kravitz; Rakim Meyers; Tony Revolori; ***D:*** Rick Famuyiwa; ***W:*** Rick Famuyiwa; ***C:*** Rachel Morrison; ***M:*** Germaine Franco.

Dope Case Pending ✓ **2000** Extremely low-budget urban action picture revolves around Devon King (Prime Time), who's got a bright future in athletics ahead of him until the cops are called to a party at his house and he's arrested for drug possession. It's a downward spiral from there on. Everything about the film is substandard. Semi-professional writing, acting, and directing. **91m/C; DVD.** Prime Time; Thinline; Kid Frost; Coolio; Sean Levert; Tony Dorian; ***D:*** Patrick McKnight; Jeff Williams; ***W:*** Patrick McKnight; ***C:*** Steve Van Dyne; ***M:*** Prime Time.

Doppelganger: The Evil Within ✓✓ *Doppleganger* **1990 (R)** Holly Gooding (Barrymore) seems like such a nice girl—until the police suspect her of the brutal murder of her mother. Her new friend Patrick (Newbern) begins to see another side to the vulnerable Holly—a seductress capable of doing anything to get what she wants. **105m/C; VHS, DVD.** Drew Barrymore; George Newbern; Dennis Christopher; Sally Kellerman; Leslie Hope; ***D:*** Avi Nesher; ***W:*** Avi Nesher.

Dora and the Lost City of Gold ✓✓ 1/2 **2019 (PG)** After spending her childhood in the Peruvian forest with her zoologist mother (Longoria) and archaeologist father (Pena), perky Dora (Moner) is quite curious but has not interacted with her peers. This situation changes when her parents send her to Los Angeles to attend high school with her cousin Diego (Wahlberg) while they search for a lost city of gold. As Dora tries to fit in, she, Diego, and their friends regularly return to South America to have adventures. Based on the popular Nickelodeon series, the film remains true to the show's characters and conventions while adding humor and that widen its charm. **102m/C; DVD, Blu-Ray.** Isabela Moner; Jeffrey Wahlberg; Eva Longoria; Michael Peña; Madeleine Madden; ***D:*** James Bobin; ***W:*** Matthew Robinson; Nicholas Stoller; ***C:*** Javier Aguirresarobe; ***M:*** John Debney; Germaine Franco.

Dorfman in Love ✓✓ 1/2 **2011 (PG-13)** Cheerful, formulaic rom com. Single accountant Deb Dorfman (Rue) is the family caretaker for her morose, widowed dad (Gould) while working for her sleazy brother, Daniel (Chase). Having a hopeless crush on journalist Jay (Urb), she's eager to help when he' out of town but cat-sitting at his new L.A. loft. Soon Deb is undergoing a makeover and gaining some confidence after befriending artist neighbor Cookie (Sleiman), which could turn into something more. **92m/C; DVD.** Sara Rue; Elliott Gould; Haaz Sleiman; Johann Urb; Jonathan Chase; ***D:*** Brad Leong; ***W:*** Wendy Kout; ***C:*** Rachel Morrison; ***M:*** David Reynolds.

Dorian Gray ✓ 1/2 *The Secret of Dorian Gray; Il Dio Chiamato a Dorian; Das Bildness des Dorian Gray; The Evils of Dorian Gray* **1970 (R)** Modern-day version of the famous tale by Oscar Wilde about an ageless young man whose portrait reflects the ravages of time and a life of debauchery. More sex, less acting with Berger in lead. Not nearly as good as the original version, "The Picture of Dorian Gray." **92m/C; VHS, DVD, Blu-Ray.** *GE IT* Richard Todd; Helmut Berger; Herbert Lom; Marie Liljedahl; Margaret Lee; Maria Rohm; Beryl Cunningham; Isa Miranda; Eleanora Rossi-Drago; Renato Romano; ***D:*** Massimo Dallamano; ***W:*** Massimo Dallamano; Marcello Costa; ***C:*** Otello Spila.

Dorian Gray ✓ 1/2 **2009 (R)** Overblown and bloody version of Oscar Wilde's only novel which finds handsome young Dorian (Barnes) mentored by London libertine Lord Henry Wooton (Firth). Unwilling to grow old and ugly, Dorian sells his soul to retain his vitality while his portrait, hidden away in the attic, grows increasingly hideous with every cruelty and debauchery. **112m/C; DVD.** *GB* Ben Barnes; Colin Firth; Ben Chaplin; Rebecca Hall; Rachel Hurd-Wood; Douglas Henshall; Fiona Shaw; Maryam D'Abo; Emilia Fox; ***D:*** Oliver Parker; ***W:*** Toby Finlay; ***C:*** Roger Pratt; ***M:*** Charlie Mole.

Dorm That Dripped Blood **WOOF!** **1982 (R)** Five college students volunteer to close the dorm during their Christmas vacation. A series of grisly and barbaric incidents eliminates the youngsters one by one. As the terror mounts, the remaining students slowly realize that they are up against a terrifyingly real psychopathic killer. Merry Christmas. **84m/C; VHS, DVD, Blu-Ray.** Laura Lopinski; Stephen Sachs; Pamela Holland; ***D:*** Stephen Carpenter; Jeffrey Obrow; ***W:*** Stephen Carpenter.

Dororo ✓✓ **2007** Based on the classic manga by Osamu Tezuka (of "Astro Boy" fame), a madman exchanges the body parts of his infant son for power. Born little more than a stump with a head, his mother spirits the boy away and he is raised by a doctor who creates artificial limbs and body parts. Growing up he learns sword-fighting to kill the demons that possess his body parts, and reclaim his own. **139m/C; DVD.** *JP* Kou Shibasaki; Satoshi Tsumabaki; ***D:*** Akihiko Shiota; ***W:*** Akihiko Shiota; Osamu Tezuka; Masa Nakamura.

Dose of Reality ✓ 1/2 **2012** Bar manager Tony and bartender Matt are closing up when they find bloodied and unconscious Rose in the bathroom. When she comes to, Rose claims not to remember what happened but is quick to blame one or both of the men as her attackers. The three then play some mind games that finally come down to a twist ending. **92m/C; DVD.** Rick Ravenello; Fairuza Balk; Ryan Merriman; ***D:*** Christopher Glatis; ***W:*** Christopher Glatis; ***C:*** Seo Mutarevic; ***M:*** Gingger Shankar. **VIDEO**

Dot the I ✓✓ **2003 (R)** Carmen (Verbeke) is about to marry boring stiff Barnaby (D'Arcy) when she meets sexy, dashing filmmaker Kit (Garcia Bernal) at her bachelorette party and begins an adulterous love affair with him. Surprisingly enough, bad things come of this love triangle, including Barnaby's angry jealousy and Kit's inability to separate his personal life from his work. Add in some additional plot twists that turn the last part of the movie from romantic drama into unpredictable noir, and what you get is a fluffy, hollow movie with little sense of direction. **92m/C; DVD.** *US SP GB* Gael Garcia Bernal; Natalia Verbeke; James D'Arcy; Tom (Thomas) Hardy; Charlie Cox; ***D:*** Matthew Parkhill; ***W:*** Matthew Parkhill; ***C:*** Affonso Beato; ***M:*** Javier Navarrete.

Dot.Kill ✓ 1/2 **2005 (R)** Getting a cyber-thrill by broadcasting his victims' deaths via his website, a savage murderer is pursued by gruff, drug-addicted cop Charlie Daines (Assante) who gets put on the case and, as his bad luck would have it, ends up on the psycho's to-do list. Not much of a whodunit. **90m/C; VHS, DVD.** Armand Assante; Sonny Marinelli; Raffaello Degruttola; Clare Holman; Frank Nasso; ***D:*** John Irvin; ***W:*** Andrew Charas; Robert Malkani; ***C:*** Damian Bromley. **VIDEO**

The Double ✓ **2011 (PG-13)** Retired CIA operative Paul Shepherdson (Gere) returns to the force when the assumed-dead Soviet assassin Cassius he supposedly caught resurfaces, suspected of killing a U.S. senator. Partnered with hotshot new FBI agent Ben Geary (a miscast Grace), the duo works to search for the killer. A major plot twist is revealed early on to the audience (and even in trailers) that takes away a great deal of any suspense that may have existed. Lots of throwaway action and even Gere looks bored. **98m/C; DVD, Blu-Ray.** Richard Gere; Topher Grace; Martin Sheen; Stephen Moyer; Odette Yustman Annable; Stana Katic; Christopher Marquette; Tamer Hassan; ***D:*** Michael Brandt; ***W:*** Michael Brandt; Derek Haas; ***C:*** Jeffrey L. Kimball; ***M:*** John Debney.

The Double ✓✓✓ **2013 (R)** Eisenberg rocks as Simon James, a low-level, modest worker in a cubicle existence whose life is shaken up when he runs into his new co-worker, James Simon (also Eisenberg). The more gregarious, outgoing, obnoxious James essentially drives Simon crazy, connecting with his unrequited crush (Wasikowska), impressing his boss (Shawn), and taking credit for his work. Working from the Fyodor Dostoyevsky novel, writer/director Richard Ayoade creates a highly-stylized horror-comedy that pivots around Eisenberg's ability to meld two halves of the same personality in a truly great performance. Actually, make that two performances. A fun and original approach to a familiar tale. **93m/C; DVD, Blu-Ray.** *UK* Jesse Eisenberg; Mia Wasikowska; Wallace Shawn; Phyllis Somerville; ***D:*** Richard Ayoade; ***W:*** Richard Ayoade; Avi Korine; ***C:*** Erik Alexander Wilson; ***M:*** Andrew Hewitt.

Double Agent 73 ✓ **1980 (R)** The title refers to star Chesty Morgan's amazing bust size. Here, she's a secret agent who has a camera/bomb implanted in her oh, never mind. The result is more curiosity than exploitation. Director Doris Wishman doesn't care about the plot and neither should you. **73m/C; DVD, Blu-Ray.** Chesty Morgan; Frank Silvano; Saul Meth; Jill Harris; Louis Burdi; Peter Petrillo; Cooper Kent; ***D:*** Doris Wishman; ***W:*** Doris Wishman; Judy J. Kushner; ***C:*** Yuri Haviv.

Double Agents ✓ *La Nuit Des Espions; Night Encounter* **1959** Two double agents are sent on a rendezvous to exchange vital government secrets. Dubbed in English. **81m/B; VHS, DVD, Streaming.** *FR* Marina Vlady; Michel Etcheverry; Roger Crouzet; Robert Hossein; Robert Le Beal; Clement Harari; ***D:*** Robert Hossein; ***W:*** Robert Hossein; ***C:*** Jacques Robin; ***M:*** Andre Gosselain.

Double Bang ✓✓ **2001 (R)** Honest cop Billy Benson decides to take the law into his own hands when his ex-partner is killed by a smalltime mobster. Standard actioner. **104m/C; VHS, DVD.** William Baldwin; Adam Baldwin; Jon Seda; Elizabeth Mitchell; Richard Portnow; John Capodice; Sofia Milos; ***D:*** Heywood Gould; ***W:*** Heywood Gould; ***C:*** David Rush Morrison. **VIDEO**

Double Cross ✓ 1/2 **2006** Takes the basic plot of "Strangers on a Train" and downsizes it for TV. Kathy (Butler) and Sheryl (Soltis) spend a drunken afternoon complaining about their husbands Dean (DeVry) and James (Boxleitner) and making a pact that they could get away with murder if each killed the other's spouse. Unfortunately one of the women was serious about their deadly deal. **90m/C; DVD.** Yancy Butler; Laura Soltis; Barbara Niven; Bruce Boxleitner; William DeVry; Lucia Walters; Doug Abrahams; ***D:*** George Erschbamer; ***W:*** George Erschbamer; Jeff Barmash; ***C:*** C. Kim Miles; ***M:*** John Sereda. **CABLE**

Double Crossbones ✓✓ 1/2 **1951** Rubbery comedian O'Connor becomes an unlikely scourge of the high seas. Meek Charleston shop assistant Dave is accused of piracy after stumbling onto the governor's (Emery) nefarious schemes. Stowing away on a brigantine, Dave goes through a series of adventures and winds up a notorious pirate captain who's determined to rescue beautiful Lady Sylvia (Carter), the governor's ward, from an arranged marriage. **75m/C; DVD.** Donald O'Connor; Helena Carter; John Emery; Will Geer; Stanley Logan; Hayden Rorke; Kathryn Givney; ***D:*** Charles T. Barton; ***W:*** Oscar Brodney; ***C:*** Maury Gertsman; ***M:*** Frank Skinner.

Double Double Toil and Trouble ✓✓ 1/2 **1994** The twins come to the financial rescue of their family when Dad's business gets into trouble and their home is threatened. But first they need to get a magic moonstone from their wicked Aunt Agatha (Leachman) and rescue kind Aunt Sophia, all before midnight on Halloween. Made for TV. **93m/C; VHS, DVD.** Ashley (Fuller) Olsen; Mary-Kate Olsen; Cloris Leachman; Meshach Taylor; ***D:*** Jeff Franklin; ***W:*** Jeff Franklin. **TV**

Double Down ✓ 1/2 *Zigs* **2001 (R)** Five buddies, for whom gambling is a career, owe a lot of moolah to the local L.A. bookies. Naturally, they decide that one last bet will get them out of debt and on their way to their dream of owning a sports bar. Low-budget feature with lots of hanging around. **93m/C; VHS, DVD.** Peter Dobson; Jason Priestley; Orien Richman; Kane Picoy; Richard Portnow; Luca Palanca; Alicia Coppola; Alexandra Powers; David Proval; ***D:*** Mars Callahan; ***W:*** Mars Callahan; ***C:*** Christopher Pearson. **VIDEO**

Double Dragon ✓✓ 1/2 **1994 (PG-13)** Generally harmless brain candy, based on the videogame, finds orphaned brothers Jimmy (Dacascos) and Billy (Wolf) living in the rubble of post earthquake L.A., circa 2007. They have half of a mystical dragon amulet and obsessed mogul Koga Shuko (Patrick), who possesses the other half, after them. Seems he needs the entire amulet in order to control its vast power. Non-stop action should keep the kiddies amused. **96m/C; VHS, DVD, Blu-Ray.** Scott Wolf; Mark Dacascos; Robert Patrick; Alyssa Milano; Kristina Malandro Wagner; Julia Nickson-Soul; ***D:*** Jim Yukich; ***W:*** Michael Davis; Peter Gould; ***C:*** Gary B. Kibbe; ***M:*** Jay Ferguson.

Double Dynamite ✓ 1/2 *It's Only Money* **1951** A bank teller is at a loss when his racetrack winnings are confused with the cash lifted from his bank during a robbery. Forgettable, forgotten shambles. Originally filmed in 1948. **80m/B; VHS, DVD.** Frank Sinatra; Jane Russell; Groucho Marx; Don McGuire; Howard Freeman; Harry Hayden; Nestor Paiva; Lou Nova; Joe Devlin; ***D:*** Irving Cummings; ***W:*** Melville Shavelson.

Double Exposure **1982 (R)** A young photographer's violent nightmares become the next day's headlines. Unsurprising vision. **95m/C; VHS, DVD, Blu-Ray.** Michael Callan; James Stacy; Joanna Pettet; Cleavon Little; Pamela Hensley; Seymour Cassel; David Young; Misty Rowe; Don Potter; ***D:*** William B. Hillman.

Double Face 1/2 **1970** A wealthy industrialist kills his lesbian wife with a car bomb, but she seems to haunt him through pornographic films. **84m/C; VHS, DVD, Blu-Ray, Streaming.** *IT GE* Klaus Kinski; Annabella Incontrera; Christiane Kruger; Gunther Stoll; Syd Chaplin; ***D:*** Riccardo Freda; ***W:*** Riccardo Freda; Paul Hengge; ***C:*** Gabor Pogany; ***M:*** Nora Orlandi.

Double Happiness **1994 (PG-13)** Slice of life comedy-drama finds 20-something Chinese-Canadian Jade Li (Oh) struggling to balance her would-be acting career and new world romance with her family's traditional values. Jade wants to please her old world father (Chang) so she endures his arranged dates and puts on a pleasant demeanor for family friends. But Jade must decide who she wants to be when she gets involved with non-Asian college student Mark (Rennie). Fine performances and assured direction from Shum in her feature film debut. **87m/C; VHS, DVD.** *CA* Sandra Oh; Stephen Chang; Alannah Ong; Frances You; Johnny Mah; Callum Keith Rennie; ***D:*** Mina Shum; ***W:*** Mina Shum; ***C:*** Peter Wunstorf. Genie '94: Actress (Oh), Film Editing.

Double Harness 1/2 **1933** Naughty and unapologetic situations in a pre-Code romance. Joan (Harding) loves wealthy John Fletcher (Powell) but he prefers to play the field. So she arranges a compromising situation so he will be forced to marry her. John soon wants a divorce but Joan persuades him to wait and proves she's more than a gold-digger by helping him when his business runs into trouble. **70m/B; DVD.** Ann Harding; William Powell; Henry Stephenson; Lillian Bond; George Meeker; Lucille Browne; Reginald Owen; ***D:*** John Cromwell; ***W:*** Jane Murdin; ***C:*** J. Roy Hunt.

The Double Hour 1/2 *La Doppia Ora* **2009** Lonely Slovenian immigrant Sonia (Rappoport) -- a maid at a first-rate Turin hotel -- tries speed-dating and sparks fly with former cop Guido (Timi). They soon fall in love and embark on a seemingly carefree romantic journey in the country. But when the pair is held at gunpoint during a robbery, their relationship starts to collapse as Sonia's mysterious past re-emerges. With a compelling love story at its center, this suspenseful crime thriller turns the couple's world upside down and makes viewers question reality right along with Sonia. Italian with subtitles. **95m/C; DVD, Blu-Ray.** *IT* Antonia Truppo; Gaetano Bruno; Fausto Russo Alesi; Michele di Mauro; Lucia Poli; Kseniya Rappoport; Filippo Timi; ***D:*** Giuseppe Capotondi; ***W:*** Alessandro Fabbri; Ludovica Rampoldi; Stefano Sardo; ***C:*** Tat Radcliffe; ***M:*** Pasquale Catalano.

Double Identity 1/2 *Fake Identity* **2010 (R)** Routine thriller. American Nicholas Pinter (Kilmer) is working for Doctors Beyond Borders in Eastern Europe when the Russian mob mistake him for a diamond-smuggling spy. After escaping a hit, Pinter is rescued by the British Secret Service and then gets involved with apparent double agent Katrine (Miko). **97m/C; DVD.** Val Kilmer; Izabella Miko; Valentine Pelka; Zahary Baharov; Hristo Naumov Shopov; Kenneth Hughes; ***D:*** Dennis Dimster-Denk; ***W:*** Dennis Dimster-Denk; Ziva Dimbort; ***C:*** Lorenzo Senatore; ***M:*** Bill Wandel. **VIDEO**

Double Impact 1/2 **1991 (R)** Van Damme plays twins re-united in Hong Kong to avenge their parents' murder by local bad guys, but this lunkhead kick-em-up doesn't even take advantage of that gimmick; the basic story would have been exactly the same with just one Jean-Claude. Lots of profane dialogue and some gratuitous nudity for the kiddies. **107m/C; VHS, DVD, Blu-Ray.** Jean-Claude Van Damme; Cory (Corinna) Everson; Geoffrey Lewis; ***D:*** Sheldon Lettich; ***W:*** Jean-Claude Van Damme; Sheldon Lettich; ***C:*** Richard H. Kline; ***M:*** Arthur Kempel.

Double Indemnity **1944** The classic seedy story of insurance agent Walter Neff (MacMurray), who's seduced by deadly blonde Phyllis Dietrichson (Stanwyck) into killing her husband (Powers) so they can collect together from his company. But the husband's "accident" invites suspicions from claims adjustor Keyes (Robinson) and Walter and Phyllis begin to turn on each other. Terrific, influential film noir, the best of its kind. Based on the James M. Cain novel. **107m/B; VHS, DVD, Blu-Ray.** Fred MacMurray; Barbara Stanwyck; Edward G. Robinson; Tom Powers; Porter Hall; Jean Heather; Byron Barr; Fortunio Bonanova; ***D:*** Billy Wilder; ***W:*** Raymond Chandler; Billy Wilder; ***C:*** John Seitz; ***M:*** Miklos Rozsa. AFI '98: Top 100; Natl. Film Reg. '92.

Double Jeopardy 1/2 **1999 (R)** This film really doesn't make much sense. But it certainly struck a nerve, as well as box-office gold, as an entertaining thriller, probably because it doesn't give you much time to catch your breathe or think about plot holes. Libby (Judd) does time for murdering hubby Nick (Greenwood) after she's set up by the sleaze. Once she's released, she decides since she can't be tried for the same crime twice (this is actually faulty logic), she might as well get rid of the lowlife for real. Wisecracking parole officer Travis Lehman (Jones) winds up getting deeply involved ferreting out the truth of the messy situation. **105m/C; VHS, DVD.** Ashley Judd; Tommy Lee Jones; Bruce Greenwood; Annabeth Gish; Roma Maffia; Jay Brazeau; Gillian Barber; Davenia McFadden; Spencer Treat Clark; ***D:*** Bruce Beresford; ***W:*** David Weisberg; Douglas S. Cook; ***C:*** Peter James; ***M:*** Normand Corbeil.

A Double Life **1947** Colman plays a Shakespearean actor in trouble when the characters he plays begin to seep into his personal life and take over. Things begin to look really bad when he is cast in the role of the cursed Othello. Colman won an Oscar for this difficult role, and the moody musical score garnered another for Rosza. **107m/B; DVD, Blu-Ray.** Ronald Colman; Shelley Winters; Signe Hasso; Edmond O'Brien; Ray Collins; Millard Mitchell; ***D:*** George Cukor; ***W:*** Ruth Gordon; Garson Kanin; ***C:*** Milton Krasner; ***M:*** Miklos Rozsa. Oscars '47: Actor (Colman), Orig. Dramatic Score; Golden Globes '48: Actor--Drama (Colman).

The Double Life of Eleanor Kendall 1/2 **2008** Recently divorced Nellie's (Parilla) life is thrown into further turmoil when her identity is stolen. She travels to Montreal to track down the thief and winds up befriending the desperate Eleanor (Decary), who's on the run from her ruthless ex-husband. **90m/C; DVD.** Lana Parilla; Benedicte Decary; James Thomas; Paul Hopkins; Kathleen McAuliffe; Martin Thibaudeau; Emmanuel Charest; ***D:*** Richard Roy; ***W:*** Samantha Silva; ***C:*** Daniel Villeneuve; ***M:*** James Gelfand. **CABLE**

The Double Life of Veronique *La Double Vie de Veronique* **1991 (R)** They say everyone has a twin, but this is ridiculous. Two women—Polish Veronika and French Veronique—are born on the same day in different countries, share a singing talent, a cardiac ailment, and, although the two never meet, a strange awareness of each other. Jacob is unforgettable as the two women, and director Krzysztof creates some spellbinding scenes but the viewer has to be willing to forgo plot for atmosphere. **96m/C; VHS, DVD, Blu-Ray.** *FR PL* Irene Jacob; Philippe Volter; Sandrine Dumas; Aleksander Bardini; Louis Ducreux; Claude Duneton; Halina Gryglaszewska; Kalina Jedrusik; ***D:*** Krzysztof Kieslowski; ***W:*** Krzysztof Kieslowski; Krzysztof Piesiewicz; ***C:*** Slawomir Idziak; ***M:*** Zbigniew Preisner. Cannes '91: Actress (Jacob); Natl. Soc. Film Critics '91: Foreign Film.

The Double Man **1967** Downbeat spy drama. CIA agent Dan Slate (Brynner) goes to the Austrian Alps to investigate the suspicious death of his son. He falls into a trap, thanks to beauty Gina (Ekland), which involves him with Soviet agents and an identity problem. **105m/C; DVD.** *GB* Yul Brynner; Britt Ekland; Clive Revill; Anton Diffring; Moira Lister; Lloyd Nolan; George Mikell; ***D:*** Franklin J. Schaffner; ***W:*** Al Hayes; Frank Tarloff; ***C:*** Denys Coop; ***M:*** Ernie Freeman.

The Double McGuffin **1979 (PG)** A plot of international intrigue is uncovered by teenagers—a la the Hardy Boys—when a prime minister and her security guard pay a visit to a small Virginia community. They're not believed, though. Action-packed from the makers of Benji. Dogs do not figure prominently here. **100m/C; VHS, DVD.** Ernest Borgnine; George Kennedy; Elke Sommer; Ed "Too Tall" Jones; Lisa Whelchel; Vincent Spano; ***V:*** Orson Welles; ***D:*** Joe Camp; ***M:*** Euel Box.

Double or Nothing 1/2 **1937** Lighthearted musical comedy. An eccentric millionaire believes people are basically honest. In his will, he instructs his lawyer to drop four money-filled wallets on the streets to see if they'll be returned. The honest folk get $5000 and a chance to inherit the rest of the Clark fortune if they double their money (legally) in a month, otherwise it goes to a group of greedy relatives. The four (Crosby, Raye, Devine, Frawley) decide to pool their efforts and Der Bingle takes a shot at opening a nightclub while withstanding a series of dirty tricks. **90m/B; DVD.** Bing Crosby; Martha Raye; Andy Devine; William Frawley; Mary Carlisle; Samuel S. Hinds; Fay Holden; William Henry; ***D:*** Theodore Reed; ***W:*** Erwin Gelsey; John Moffitt; Charles Lederer; Duke Atteberry; ***C:*** Karl Struss; ***M:*** Boris Morros.

Double Parked 1/2 **2000** Meter maid Rita (Thorne) is divorced from an alcoholic abuser and finally has a steady job. Which she needs to support her teenaged son Matt (Read) who suffers from cystic fibrosis and bad judgement since his best friend is a delinquent (Fleiss). Rita's been taken care of business while putting her personal needs on hold but that's about to change. Fine performances. **98m/C; VHS, DVD.** Callie (Calliope) Thorne; Rufus Read; Noah Fleiss; William Sage; Anthony De Sando; Eileen Galindro; Michelle Hurd; P.J. Brown; ***D:*** Stephen Kinsella; ***W:*** Stephen Kinsella; Paul Solberg; ***C:*** Jim Denault; ***M:*** Craig Hazen; David Wolfert.

Double Platinum 1/2 **1999 (PG)** Baby diva Brandy squares off against mega-diva Ross—the mommy who abandoned her for a fabulous career. Eighteen years later Brandy decides to pursue a singing career herself and meets Ross—not knowing about their relationship. But when she finds out, there are a lot of abandonment issues to deal with and this teen is determined to get even by besting mommy dearest at her own game. You go, girl! **91m/C; VHS, DVD.** Diana Ross; Brandy Norwood; Harvey Fierstein; Roger Rees; Brian Stokes Mitchell; Christine Ebersole; Tony Payne; ***D:*** Robert Allan Ackerman; ***W:*** Nina Shengold; Katie Ford; Renee Longstreet. **TV**

Double Play 1/2 *Prisoner of Zenda Inc.* **1996 (PG)** Updated version of "The Prince and the Pauper" finds teenaged computer genius Rudy (Jackson) inheriting his dad's successful computer company. But his evil Uncle Mike (Shatner), who's not the boy's guardian, wants the company for himself and hires some thugs to kidnap the kid and force him to sign over control of the business. But Rudy just happens to have a double—a high school baseball star who's in town for the championship game—and confusion rules when he takes his place. Jackson's brother, Richard Lee Jackson, plays his cousin in the movie. **101m/C; VHS, DVD.** Jonathan Jackson; William Shatner; Richard Lee Jackson; Jay Brazeau; ***D:*** Stefan Scaini; ***W:*** Richard Clark; ***C:*** Maris Jansons; ***M:*** John Welsman.

Double Suicide *Shinju Ten No Amijima* **1969** From a play by Monzarmon Chikamatsu, a tragic drama about a poor salesman in 18th century Japan who falls in love with a geisha and ruins his family and himself trying to requite the hopeless passion. Stylish with Iwashita turning in a wonderful dual performance. In Japanese with subtitles. **105m/B; VHS, DVD.** *JP* Kichiemon Nakamura; Shima Iwashita; Yusuke Takita; Hosei Komatsu; ***D:*** Masahiro Shinoda; ***W:*** Masahiro Shinoda; Toru Takemitsu; Taeko Tomioka; ***C:*** Toichiro Narushima; ***M:*** Toru Takemitsu.

Double Take **2001 (PG-13)** Businessman Daryl Chase (Jones) is framed as a money-launderer for a drug cartel and assumes the identity of street hustler Freddy (Griffin) in order to clear his name. Fans of "Mad TV" and "Malcolm and Eddie" (Jones and Griffin's TV ventures, respectively) will probably be sorely disappointed with this action-comedy attempt. While the two stars trade zingers and dodge gunfire, you're left to wonder why you didn't rent "Midnight Run," or even "Beverly Hills Cop 3." **88m/C; VHS, DVD.** Orlando Jones; Eddie Griffin; Gary Grubbs; Daniel Roebuck; Sterling Macer; Garcelle Beauvais; Edward Herrmann; Benny Nieves; Shawn Elliott; Brent Briscoe; Carlos Carrasco; ***D:*** George Gallo; ***W:*** George Gallo; ***C:*** Theo van de Sande; ***M:*** Graeme Revell.

Double Team **1997 (R)** Counter-terrorist expert Jack Quinn (Van Damme) teams with weapons specialist Yaz (Rodman, in his film debut) to take down international terrorist Stavros (Roarke). After Jack kills Stavros's son, he is sent to a high-security superspy retirement village. When his wife and newborn son are kidnapped, Jack escapes, with Yaz's help, to finish the job and try to save his family. Van Damme teams with his third famous Hong Kong action director, Tsui Hark (the other two are John Woo and Ringo Lam) to create yet another disappointment. He's slightly more charismatic than usual (not saying much), but Rodman easily steals the flick as he gets most of the good lines, and delivers them with relish. **93m/C; VHS, DVD, Blu-Ray.** Jean-Claude Van Damme; Dennis Rodman; Mickey Rourke; Natacha Lindinger; Paul Freeman; Valeria Cavalli; Jay Benedict; Bruno Bilotta; ***D:*** Tsui Hark; ***W:*** Paul Mones; Don Jakoby; ***C:*** Peter Pau; ***M:*** Gary Chang. Golden Raspberries '97: Worst New Star (Rodman), Worst Support. Actor (Rodman).

Double Trouble **1967** When rock star Presley falls in love with an English heiress, he winds up involved in an attempted murder. The king belts out "Long Legged Girl" while evading cops, criminals, and crying women. A B-side. Based on a story by Marc Brandell. **92m/C; VHS, DVD.** Elvis Presley; Annette Day; John Williams; Yvonne Romain; Michael Murphy; Chips Rafferty; Helene Winston; ***D:*** Norman Taurog; ***W:*** Jo Heims.

Double Trouble **1991 (R)** Twin brothers—one a cop, one a jewel thief—team up to crack the case of an international jewel smuggling ring headed by a wealthy and politically well-connected businessman and his righthand man. **87m/C; VHS, Streaming.** David Paul; Peter Paul; James Doohan; Roddy McDowall; Steve Kanaly; A.J. (Anthony) Johnson; David Carradine; ***D:*** John Paragon.

Double Vision *Shuang Tong* **2002 (R)** FBI agent Kevin Richter (Morse) pairs up with troubled Taiwanese Foreign Affairs Officer and former detective Huang Huo-tu (Leung Ka Fai) to hunt for a serial killer who uses random methods that don't seem scientifically possible. But the victims do have one thing in common—a black fungus found in their brain that appears to cause deadly hallucinations. As Huang digs further he discovers the crimes mimic ritualized murders committed by an ancient mystic cult. English and Chinese with subtitles. **110m/C; VHS, DVD.** *CH* Tony Leung Ka-Fai; David Morse; Rene Liu; Brett Climo; Leon Dai; ***D:*** Kuo-fu Chen; ***W:*** Kuo-fu Chen; Chao-Bin Ju; ***C:*** Arthur Wong Ngok Tai; ***M:*** Sin-yun Lee.

Double Wedding **1937** Madcap comedy starring Powell as a wacky painter who doesn't believe in working and Loy as a workaholic dress designer. Loy has chosen a fiance for her younger sister, Irene, to marry, but Irene has plans of her own. When Irene and her beau meet bohemian Powell, the fun really begins. Script suffers slightly from too much slapstick and not enough wit, although the stars (in their seventh outing as a duo) play it well. Based on the play "Great Love" by Ferenc Molnar. **86m/B; VHS, DVD.** William Powell; Myrna Loy; Florence Rice; John Beal; Jessie Ralph; Edgar Kennedy; Sidney Toler; Mary Gordon; ***D:*** Richard Thorpe; ***W:*** Jo Swerling.

Double Wedding 1/2 **2010** Lifetime Channel romantic comedy has lots of personality courtesy of the Mowry twins. The identical Warren twins, pastry chef Danielle and lawyer Deanna, are both nicknamed "D" and that turns into major confusion for handsome Tate Kelley, who unwittingly dates them both. When the sisters realize what's happening it brings back all their old relationship fears, although Deanna should take a long look at her legal aide Jaz who's pining away. **89m/C; DVD.** Tamera Mowry; Tia Mowry; Chad Connell; O.T. Fagbenle; Sandra Caldwell; ***D:*** Craig Pryce; ***W:*** Jennifer Maisel; ***C:*** John Berrie; ***M:*** Lawrence Shragge. **CABLE**

Double Whammy **2001 (R)** DiCillo's attempt at Tarantino crimedy doesn't quite work out. Leary is Ray Pluto, a cop with a trick back with lousy timing and a past that haunts him. When his back gives out during a restaurant shooting, he's put on desk duty and sent to sexy chiropractor Hurley, who eventually heals his love life as well as his vertebrae. Weak subplots include his building super's attempted murder by his daughter, and a screenwriting duo who also, coincidentally, want to be the next Tarantino. Occasionally inspired, but DiCIllo can't make the comedy and romance fit with the sometimes brutal violence. **93m/C; VHS, DVD.** Denis Leary; Elizabeth Hurley; Steve Buscemi; Luis Guzman; Victor Argo; Chris Noth; Donald Adeosun Faison; Maurice Smith; ***D:*** Tom DiCillo; ***W:*** Tom DiCillo; ***C:*** Robert Yeoman; ***M:*** Jim Farmer.

Doubt **2008 (PG-13)** Shanley adapts and directs his own Pulitzer Prize-winning play. Set in 1964 in a Bronx Catholic high school, young teacher Sister James (Adams) approaches stern principal Sister Aloysius (Streep) regarding possible improper behavior of a sexual nature by the seemingly benevolent Father Flynn towards the sole black student, 12-year-old Donald (Foster II). As a detractor of his liberal views, Sister Aloysius finally realizes an opportunity to target and entrap her supervisor, but even with her fervent determination the question of doubt constantly lurks in the shadows. Streep is forboding while Hoffman holds the secret close, though trumping them all is Davis in the role of the boy's mother with her meaty scene confronting Streep. **104m/C; Blu-Ray, On Demand.** Meryl Streep; Philip Seymour Hoffman; Amy Adams; Viola Davis; Lloyd Clay Brown; Joseph Foster; Alice Drummond; Carrie Preston; John A. Costelloe; Audrie Neenan; ***D:*** John Patrick Shanley; ***W:*** John Patrick Shanley; ***C:*** Roger Deakins; ***M:*** Howard Shore. Screen Actors Guild '08: Actress (Streep).

Doubting Thomas **1/2 1935** Rogers' last film, which was in theatres when he was killed in a plane crash. Silly story of a husband and his doubts about his wife and her amateur-acting career. The show goes on in spite of his doubts, her forgotten lines, and wardrobe goofs. Remake of 1922's silent film "The Torch Bearers." **78m/B; VHS, DVD.** Will Rogers; Billie Burke; Alison Skipworth; Sterling Holloway; ***D:*** David Butler.

Douchebag **1/2 2010** Estranged brothers Sam (Dickler) and Tom (James) reunite at the suggestion of Sam's fiance, Steph (Moreau), who wants Tom to be at their Los Angeles wedding. Although the hatred is kept cool, it's obvious these guys don't have much in common. Without a date to the big day, Sam and Steph urge Tom to track down his long-lost fifth grade crush online. And so the road trip from L.A. to Palm Springs begins. A dry and snarky comedy that's not afraid to get ugly at times. The misleading title, pointing its finger at brother Sam, suggests a nasty and shocking tone, instead of this honest comedy of redemption. An underdog favorite at Sundance, with very funny and real performances from a cast of newcomers. **71m/C; DVD.** Andrew Dickler; Ben York James; Marguerite Moreau; Amy Ferguson; Nicole Vicius; ***D:*** Drake Doremus; ***W:*** Andrew Dickler; Drake Doremus; Lindsay Stidham; Jonathan Schwartz; ***C:*** Scott Uhlfedler; Chris Robertson; ***M:*** Jason Torbert; Casey Immoor.

Doughboys **1/2** *Forward March* **1930** Keaton's second talkie is a so-so comedy about a rich man who mistakenly enlists in the Army during WWI. He manages to bumble his way through basic training and win the heart of a pretty girl. There are a few bright moments, particularly a musical number between Keaton and "Ukulele Ike" Edwards. **80m/B; VHS, DVD.** Buster Keaton; Cliff Edwards; Edward Brophy; Sally Eilers; Victor Potel; Arnold Korff; Frank Mayo; ***D:*** Edward Sedgwick.

Doughboys **2008 (PG-13)** Italian-American brothers Frank (Iacono) and Lou (Lombardi) inherit the Bronx family bakery that's a neighborhood institution. Frank's the responsible one but Lou is the baking whiz. He also has a gambling addiction and owes a lot of money to a local mobster, which Frank, who has plans of his own, knows nothing about. **80m/C; DVD.** Louis Lombardi; Andrew Keegan; James Madio; Vincent Pastore; Mike Starr; Gaetano Iacono; ***D:*** Louis Lombardi; ***W:*** Louis Lombardi; Evan Jacobs; ***C:*** Stephen Franciosa, Jr.; ***M:*** Peter Cascone. **VIDEO**

Doug's 1st Movie **1999 (G)** Feature-length version of the children's animated series assumes sequels according to the title, but has problem stretching the storyline over an hour. However, kids who like the series will enjoy the adventures of 12-year-old Doug Funnie and his pal Skeeter as they try to hide the lake monster Herman Melville (so named because he tries to eat a copy of "Moby Dick") from the clutches of polluting bad guy Mr. Bluff. He also has to impress Patti before the big Valentine's Day Dance. Not overly preachy, but the animation will not impress children used to the glossy Disney style. **77m/C; VHS, DVD.** ***V:*** Thomas McHugh; Fred Newman; Chris Phillips; Constance Shulman; Frank Welker; Alice Playten; Doris Belack; Doug Preis; Guy Hadley; Eddie Korbich; ***D:*** Maurice Joyce; ***W:*** Ken Scarborough; ***M:*** Mark Watters.

The Dove **1/2 1974 (PG-13)** The true story of a 16-year-old's adventures as he sails around the world in a 23-foot sloop. The trip took him five years and along the way he falls in love with a girl who follows him to exotic locales. Photography and scenery are magnificent. **105m/C; VHS, Streaming.** Joseph Bottoms; Deborah Raffin; Dabney Coleman; Peter Gwynne; ***D:*** Charles Jarrott; ***W:*** Peter S. Beagle; ***C:*** Sven Nykvist.

Down a Dark Hall **2018 (PG-13)** Teenaged Kit (Robb) is sent away to Blackwood Manor, a boarding school hiding creepy corridors and paranormal secrets. Stylistic and strange, this Gothic horror flick hits all the right supernatural buttons for younger-than-adult fans of the genre, who aren't as picky about overacting (Thurman), lame CGI, and predictable tropes. Based on Louis Duncan's novel, which was optioned as a motion picture by Twilight-author Stephenie Meyer. **96m/C; DVD, Blu-Ray.** AnnaSophia Robb; Uma Thurman; Isabelle Fuhrman; Victoria Moroles; Noah Silver; ***D:*** Rodrigo Cortés; ***W:*** Michael Goldbach; Chris Sparling; ***C:*** Jarin Blaschke; ***M:*** Victor Reyes.

Down Among the Z Men **1952** Enlisted man helps a girl save an atomic formula from spies. Funny in spots but weighed down by musical numbers from a female entourage. From the pre-Monty Python comedy troupe "The Goons." **71m/B; VHS, DVD.** *GB* Peter Sellers; Spike Milligan; Harry Secombe; Michael Bentine; Carole Carr; ***D:*** Maclean Rogers.

Down and Derby **1/2 2005 (PG)** In this family comedy a group of overzealous fathers turn the local Boy Scout Pinewood Derby competition into a desperate rivalry to build the winning miniature car. The vehicles are supposed to be built by the 7- to 10-year-olds the competition is intended for but the dads offer much more than advice, with Phil Davis particularly determined to finally win over neighbor Ace Montana. **90m/C; DVD.** Greg Germann; Lauren Holly; Adam Hicks; Perry Anzilotti; Noriyuki "Pat" Morita; Marc Raymond; Hunter Tylo; Eric Jacobs; Ross Brockley; ***D:*** Eric Hendershot; ***W:*** Eric Hendershot; ***C:*** T.C. Christensen; Gordon C. Lonsdale; ***M:*** Chuck E. Myers. **VIDEO**

Down and Out in Beverly Hills **1/2 1986 (R)** A modern retelling of Jean Renoir's classic "Boudu Saved from Drowning" with some nice star turns. Neurotic and wealthy Beverly Hills married Dave (Dreyfuss) and Barbara (Midler) find their lives turned upside down when they prevent suicidal bum Jerry Baskin (Nolte) from drowning in their pool. Jerry takes over the household—bedding Barbara, her daughter Jenny (Nelson), and their sultry maid Carmen (Pena)?offering encouragement to a frustrated Dave and his son Max (Richards)?and even solving family dog Matisse's identity crisis. Naturally, Jerry learns there's more to life than being a bum. **103m/C; VHS, DVD.** Nick Nolte; Bette Midler; Richard Dreyfuss; Little Richard; Tracy Nelson; Elizabeth Pena; Evan Richards; Valerie Curtin; Barry Primus; Dorothy Tristan; Alexis Arquette; ***D:*** Paul Mazursky; ***W:*** Paul Mazursky; Leon Capetanos; ***C:*** Donald McAlpine; ***M:*** Andy Summers.

Down Argentine Way **1940** A lovely young woman falls in love with a suave Argentinian horse breeder. First-rate Fox musical made a star of Grable and was Miranda's first American film. **90m/C; VHS, DVD.** Don Ameche; Betty Grable; Carmen Miranda; Charlotte Greenwood; J. Carrol Naish; Henry Stephenson; Leonid Kinskey; Kay Aldridge; Chris-Pin (Ethier Crispin Martini) Martin; Charles (Judel, Judells) Judels; ***D:*** Irving Cummings; ***W:*** Rian James; Ralph Spence; Karl Tunberg; ***C:*** Leon Shamroy; Ray Rennahan; ***M:*** Mack Gordon. Natl. Film Reg. '14.

Down by Law **1986 (R)** In Jarmusch's follow-up to his successful "Stranger than Paradise," he introduces us to three men: a pimp, an out-of-work disc jockey, and an Italian tourist. When the three break out of prison, they wander through the Louisiana swampland with some regrets about their new-found freedom. Slow-moving at times, beautifully shot throughout. Poignant and hilarious, the film is true to Jarmusch form: some will love the film's offbeat flair, and others will find it bothersome. **107m/B; VHS, DVD, Blu-Ray.** John Lurie; Tom Waits; Roberto Benigni; Ellen Barkin; Billie Neal; Rockets Redglare; Vernel Bagneris; Nicoletta Braschi; ***D:*** Jim Jarmusch; ***W:*** Jim Jarmusch; ***C:*** Robby Muller; ***M:*** John Lurie; Tom Waits.

Down in the Delta **1998 (PG-13)** Chicago matriarch Rosa Lynn (Alice) tries to prevent her jobless, single-mom daughter Loretta (Woodard) from succumbing to drugs, alcohol, and the other destructive forces that are a part of her rough neighborhood. She sends her Loretta and her two grandchildren (including an autistic boy) to her brother's home in the Mississippi delta, hoping that they'll reconnect to their roots. Though reluctant at first, Loretta finds herself slowly changing her ways as she works in Uncle Earl's restaurant; she is moved by his love of family, particularly his Alzheimer-ridden wife (Rolle). Poet-novelist Maya Angelou's first outing as a director skillfully demonstrates the importance of connecting to one's heritage. Woodard shines energetically as the strung-out mom and Freeman is nearly perfect as the elegant and tender Uncle Earl. **111m/C; VHS, DVD.** Alfre Woodard; Al Freeman, Jr.; Mary Alice; Wesley Snipes; Esther Rolle; Loretta Devine; Anne-Marie Johnson; Mpho Koaho; Kulani Hassen; Richard Blackburn; ***D:*** Maya Angelou; ***W:*** Myron Goble; ***C:*** William Wages; ***M:*** Stanley Clarke. **CABLE**

Down in the Valley **2005 (R)** Wannabe cowboy hero Harlan (Edwards) befriends rebellious, aimless teen Tobe (Wood) and her shy younger brother Lonnie (Culkin). They're the children of tough San Fernando Valley sheriff Wade (Morse), who immediately distrusts this soft-spoken, tale-spinning stranger. And with good reason, since Harlan is delusional at best and dangerous at his worst. No matter the talent, flick stretches credibility—particularly in its last act. **114m/C; DVD.** Edward Norton; Evan Rachel Wood; David Morse; Rory Culkin; John Diehl; Kat Dennings; Hunter Parrish; Bruce Dern; Muse Watson; Geoffrey Lewis; Aviva; Aaron Fors; Heather Ashleigh; ***D:*** David Jacobson; ***W:*** David Jacobson; ***C:*** Enrique Chediak.

Down Mexico Way **1941** Two cowboys come to the aid of a Mexican town whose residents have been hoodwinked by a phony movie company. Very exciting chase on horseback, motorcycle, and in automobiles. **78m/B; VHS, DVD.** Gene Autry; Smiley Burnette; Fay McKenzie; Duncan Renaldo; ***D:*** Joseph Santley.

Down Periscope **1/2 1996 (PG-13)** Tom Dodge (Grammer) dreams of commanding a nuclear sub, but gets stuck with an out-of-mothballs, rusting WWII vintage tub with the usual goof-off crew. In order for Dodge to get his dream assignment, he and his losers must beat the nuclear subs of generic mean authority figure Admiral Graham (Dern), in a war game. Predictable comedy is kept afloat by amusing cast, especially Schneider as the weaselly Executive Officer Pascal. Many jokes revolve around Dodge's tattoo, which is on a body part that is normally private first-class. Denied cooperation from the U.S. Navy, the shipyard scenes were filmed on three barges tied together in the San Francisco Bay area, with empty discarded frigates and destroyers belonging to the U.S. Department of Transportation playing the fleet. **92m/C; VHS, DVD.** Kelsey Grammer; Lauren Holly; Bruce Dern; Rob Schneider; Rip Torn; Harry Dean Stanton; William H. Macy; Ken H. Campbell; Toby Huss; Duane Martin; Jonathan Penner; Bradford Tatum; Harland Williams; ***D:*** David S. Ward; ***W:*** Hugh Wilson; Andrew Kurtzman; Eliot Wald; ***C:*** Victor Hammer; ***M:*** Randy Edelman.

Down Terrace **1/2 2010 (R)** Acquitted on drug dealing charges, father and son ringleaders of a two-bit family crime syndicate, Bill (Robert Hill) and Karl (Robin Hill), are determined to track down the snitch responsible for putting them in the slammer. They get increasingly paranoid as they sit around their apartment, questioning each other, while Karl tries to cope with a child on the way. A darkly comic skew on suburban life in the U.K.'s town of Brighton, looking more like a documentary than a crime flick. Directorial debut for Wheatley, co-written by star Robin Hill, who plays opposite his real-life father, further blurring the lines between real and surreal. **93m/C; Blu-Ray, On Demand.** Robert Hill; Robin Hill; Julia Deakin; David Schaal; Tony Way; Kerry Peacock; Michael Smiley; Mark Kempner; ***D:*** Ben Wheatley; ***W:*** Robin Hill; Ben Wheatley; ***C:*** Laurie Rose; ***M:*** Jim Williams.

Down the Drain **1989 (R)** A broad-as-a-city-block farce about an unscrupulous criminal lawyer and his assortment of crazy clients. A fine first half but someone pulls the plug in the middle of the bath. **90m/C; VHS, Streaming.** Andrew Stevens; John Matuszak; Teri Copley; Joseph Campanella; Don Stroud; Stella Stevens; Jerry Mathers; Benny "The Jet" Urquidez; ***D:*** Robert C. Hughes.

Down the Shore **1/2 2011 (R)** A dull, dreary drama despite the performances of Gandolfini and Janssen. Bailey operates run-down carnival rides on the boardwalk of a small New Jersey shore town. A Frenchman named Jacques suddenly shows up with the ashes of Bailey's sister, a lot of money, and the deed to Susan's half of the family home. This outsider is the one who has a clear look at the rut of Bailey's life--stuck in a nowhere job and still pining for childhood sweetheart, Mary. Bailey is sure Jacques has some angle that he needs to figure out. **93m/C; DVD, Blu-Ray.** James Gandolfini; Eduardo Costa; Famke Janssen; Joe Pope; John Magaro; ***D:*** Harold Guskin; ***W:*** Sandra Jennings; ***C:*** Richard Rutkowski; ***M:*** Andrea Morricone. **VIDEO**

Down Three Dark Streets **1/2 1954** Crime drama filmed in a documentary style. FBI agent Zach Stewart (Tobey) is murdered and fellow agent John Ripley (Crawford) takes over his last three active cases hoping one will lead to Stewart's killer. They include a bank robbery, an interstate auto theft ring, and an extortionist targeting Kate Martel (Roman). **86m/B; DVD, Blu-Ray.** Broderick Crawford; Ruth Roman; Kenneth Tobey; Martha Hyer; Marisa Pavan; Gene Reynolds; Claude Akins; Max (Casey Adams) Showalter; ***D:*** Arnold Laven; ***W:*** Bernard C. Schoenfeld; Mildred Gordon; Gordon Gordon; ***C:*** Joseph Biroc; ***M:*** Paul Sawtell.

Down to Earth **1947** A lackluster musical and boxoffice flop with an impressive cast. Hayworth is the Greek goddess of dance sent to Earth on a mission to straighten out Broadway producer Parks and his play that ridicules the Greek gods. Anita Ellis dubs the singing of Hayworth. A parody of "Here Comes Mr. Jordan," remade in 1980 as "Xanadu." **101m/C; VHS, DVD.** Rita Hayworth; Larry Parks; Marc Platt; Roland Culver; James Gleason; Edward Everett Horton; Adele Jergens; George Macready; William Frawley; James Burke; Fred F. Sears; Lynn Merrick; Myron Healey; ***D:*** Alexander Hall; ***W:*** Edwin Blum; ***M:*** George Duning.

Down to Earth **2001 (PG-13)** Rock is called to heaven before his time by angel Levy but the only body available to send him back in is that of a 60-ish white businessman. Rock's presence and comic sensibility saves what could've been a lame time-waster but he's the only reason to see it and if you don't like Rock, don't bother. Remake of "Heaven Can Wait," which was a remake of "Here Comes Mr. Jordan." **87m/C; VHS, DVD.** Chris Rock; Regina King; Chazz Palminteri; Eugene Levy; Frankie Faison; Mark Addy; Greg Germann; Jennifer Coolidge; ***D:*** Chris Weitz; Paul Weitz; ***W:*** Chris Rock; Lance Crouther; Ali LeRoi; Louis CK; ***C:*** Richard Crudo; ***M:*** Jamshield Sharifi.

Down to the Bone 🦴🦴 1/2 **2004** Sad tale of everyday addiction, portraying the issue with a bleakness that allows for authenticity that few films accomplish. Irene (Farmiga), a mother of two saddled with financial difficulties, begins using cocaine to get through her days working as a cashier in a suburban mega-store. But as time passes, her dependence, lies, and the personal tolls all mount. Eventually she seeks help at a rehab center and meets a nurse, Bob (Dillon), who is also a recovering user. The two become friends as they try to support each other's recovery. **105m/C; DVD.** Vera Farmiga; Hugh Dillon; Clint Jordan; Caridad "La Bruja" De La Luz; Jasper Moon Daniels; Taylor Foxhall; ***D:*** Debra Granik; ***W:*** Richard Lieske; Debra Granik; ***C:*** Michael McDonough; ***M:*** Jackie O Motherfucker. L.A. Film Critics '05: Actress (Farmiga).

Down to the Sea in Ships 🦴🦴 1/2 *The Last Adventurers* **1922** Bow made her movie debut in this drama about the whalers of 19th-century Massachusetts. Highlighted by exciting action scenes of an actual whale hunt. Silent with music score and original tinted footage. **83m/B; Silent; VHS, DVD.** Marguerite Courtot; Raymond (Ray) McKee; Clara Bow; ***D:*** Elmer Clifton; ***W:*** John L.E. Pell; ***C:*** Alexander Penrod.

Down to You 🦴🦴 1/2 **2000 (PG-13)** Light romantic comedy has appealing leads and a predictable plot (and references to about a gazillion similar movies). Aspiring chef Al (Prinze Jr.) and artist Imogen (Stiles) are immediately smitten when they meet at the campus dive. The relationship develops at headlong speed but then they both realize neither of them is ready for a lifelong commitment. So, do they just split or try being friends or slow things down or what? **92m/C; VHS, DVD.** Freddie Prinze, Jr.; Julia Stiles; Selma Blair; Shawn Hatosy; Zak Orth; Rosario Dawson; Henry Winkler; Ashton Kutcher; Lucie Arnaz; ***D:*** Kris Isacsson; ***W:*** Kris Isacsson; ***C:*** Robert Yeoman; ***M:*** Edmund Choi.

Down Under 🦴 **1986** Two gold-hungry beach boys go to Australia looking for riches, and document their adventures on film. Essentially a crudely shot, tongue-in-cheek travelogue narrated by Patrick Macnee. **90m/C; VHS, DVD.** Don Atkinson; Donn Dunlop; ***Nar:*** Patrick Macnee; ***W:*** Robert H. Jamieson; ***M:*** David Gibney.

Down With Love 🦴🦴 1/2 **2003 (PG-13)** This uneven but amusing homage/satire to the Rock Hudson/Doris Day sex comedies of the early '60s gets the look and feel right, but loses something in the attitude by superimposing modern sensibilities and perspective over the whole thing. Proto-feminist author Barbara Novak (Zellweger) writes a book proclaiming that women should claim their equality in the workplace by acting like men when it comes to sex. This puts a crimp in the style of Babe magnet/cad Catcher Block (McGregor), a magazine writer who conspires to expose her as an old-fashioned girl at heart. McGregor and Zellweger do a good job channelling Hudson and Day, and the production design and costumes perfectly capture the movie version of 1962 Manhattan that never existed in real life. Pierce is perfect in the old Tony Randall role. **94m/C; VHS, DVD.** Renée Zellweger; Ewan McGregor; David Hyde Pierce; Sarah Paulson; Tony Randall; Jack Plotnick; Rachel Dratch; John Aylward; Jeri Ryan; Melissa George; Florence Stanley; Laura Kightlinger; ***D:*** Peyton Reed; ***W:*** Dennis Drake; Eve Ahlert; ***C:*** Jeff Cronenweth; ***M:*** Marc Shaiman.

Downfall 🦴🦴🦴 1/2 *Der Untergang* **2004 (R)** Controversial German film explores the last days of Hitler (Ganz) and his cronies in the bunker before the fall of Berlin in 1945. Overlong but engrossing look at the mundane, very human face of evil. Ganz is amazing in the role of a lifetime, virtually becoming the most hated man in history. All the smaller roles, Hitler's secretary Traudl Junge (Lara) for instance, are wonderfully fleshed out by an incredibly talented cast. **155m/C; DVD, Blu-Ray.** *GE* Bruno Ganz; Agustin Lara; Corinna Harfouch; Ulrich Matthes; Heino Ferch; Christian Berkel; Matthias Habich; Thomas Kretschmann; Ulrich Noethen; Goetz Otto; Juliane Koehler; Donevan Gunia; ***D:*** Oliver Hirschbiegel; ***W:*** Bernd Eichinger; ***C:*** Rainer Klausmann; ***M:*** Stephan Zacharias.

Downhill 🦴🦴 **2020 (R)** While on a family ski trip at an Austrian resort, Pete (Ferrell) and Billie (Dreyfus) are eating lunch with their young sons on an elevated patio when an avalanche hits them. While Billie protects her sons, Pete moves away from the table with his cell phone, then returns to his meal as if nothing happened. Billie's feelings of betrayal color the rest of the trip and shift her perspective on her marriage as Pete repeatedly displays his selfishness in unexpected ways. The American remake of the European dark comedy features high profile talent but the film relies on cheap laughs without edginess. **86m/C; DVD, Blu-Ray.** Julia Louis-Dreyfus; Will Ferrell; Miranda Otto; Zoe Chao; Zach Woods; ***D:*** Nat Faxon; Jim Rash; ***W:*** Nat Faxon; Jim Rash; Jesse Armstrong; ***C:*** Danny Cohen; ***M:*** Volker Bertelmann.

Downhill Racer 🦴🦴 1/2 **1969 (PG)** An undisciplined American skier locks ski-tips with his coach and his new-found love while on his way to becoming an Olympic superstar. Character study on film. Beautiful ski and mountain photography keep it from sliding downhill. **102m/C; VHS, DVD, Blu-Ray.** Robert Redford; Camilla Sparv; Gene Hackman; Dabney Coleman; ***D:*** Michael Ritchie.

Downhill Willie 🦴 1/2 **1996 (PG)** Willie (Coogan) isn't the brightest guy around—except on skies. Now he wants to enter the Kamikaze Run, which takes place on an extreme race course, and win the half-million top prize as well as the prettiest snow bunny (Keanan) on the slopes. **90m/C; VHS, DVD.** Keith Coogan; Staci Keanan; Lochlyn Munro; Estelle Harris; Fred Stoller; Lee Reherman; ***D:*** David Mitchell; ***W:*** Stephanie Cedar; ***C:*** David Pelletier; ***M:*** Norman Orenstein.

Downloading Nancy 🦴 1/2 **2008** Deeply disturbing drama about a suicidal incest 'survivor' with a death wish. Nancy (Bello) was sexually abused as a child by her uncle and her rage and despair have remained despite therapy. Married to Albert (Sewell), an emotionally cold businessman, Nancy self-mutilates, eventually getting into the s/m scene via online chatrooms. It's here Nancy contacts Louis (Patric) who vows to honor her desire for death despite his attraction to her after they finally meet in person. Bello's performance is fearless but to no particular end since Nancy's only aim is to die, which isn't necessarily compelling to watch. **102m/C; On Demand.** Maria Bello; Jason Patric; Rufus Sewell; Amy Brenneman; Michael Nyqvist; ***D:*** Johan Renck; ***W:*** Pamela Cuming; Lee H. Ross; ***C:*** Christopher Doyle; ***M:*** Krister Linder.

Downsizing 🦴🦴 **2017 (R)** A science fiction-tinged comedy-drama that explores a near future in which people can shrink themselves to five inches tall to save the world and increase their personal wealth. After hearing about the benefits of going small, occupational therapist Paul (Damon) and his wife Audrey (Wiig) decide to shrink. Though she backs out at the last minute, Paul goes through with the procedure and moves to a downsized community, Leisureland. Through cleaning lady Ngoc Lan Tran (Chau), he learns about the dark side of Leisureland and she enlists him to help the needy. A deeply flawed flick that does not live up to its intriguing premise. **135m/C; DVD, Blu-Ray.** Matt Damon; Christoph Waltz; Hong Chau; Kristen Wiig; Rolf Lassgard; ***D:*** Alexander Payne; ***W:*** Alexander Payne; Jim Taylor; ***C:*** Phedon Papamichael; ***M:*** Rolfe Kent.

Downstairs 🦴🦴 **1932** A story by Gilbert is worked into a melodrama as he stars as Karl, the chauffeur to Baron von Burgen. The cad is soon borrowing money from cook Sophie while trying to seduce maid Anna, the bride of butler Albert. He then blackmails the Baroness over an indiscretion and generally causes havoc until his schemes backfire. Still, since this is a Pre-Code film, Karl just goes on to charm a new employer without any real consequences. **77m/B; DVD.** John Gilbert; Virginia Bruce; Paul Lukas; Reginald Owen; Olga Baclanova; Bodil Rosing; Hedda Hopper; ***D:*** Monta Bell; ***W:*** Lenore Coffee; Melville Baker; ***C:*** Harold Rosson.

Downton Abbey 🦴🦴🦴 **2019 (PG)** In 1920s Britain, the aristocratic Crawley family has evolved with the times to keep their estate financially solvent and productive. When they are informed that they will be hosting a visit by the British monarch, the family and their staff, including recently retired butler Carson (Carter), come together to prepare for the honor. Though constructed so that non-viewers of the popular television drama could easily follow, it serves as a glorious series wrap-up. **122m/C; DVD, Blu-Ray.** Michelle Dockery; Maggie Smith; Matthew Goode; Tuppence Middleton; Imelda Staunton; ***D:*** Michael Engler; ***W:*** Julian Fellowes; ***C:*** Ben Smithard; ***M:*** John Lunn.

Downtown 🦴 1/2 **1989 (R)** Urban comedy about a naive white suburban cop who gets demoted to the roughest precinct in Philadelphia, and gains a streetwise black partner. Runs a routine beat. **96m/C; VHS, DVD.** Anthony Edwards; Forest Whitaker; Joe Pantoliano; Penelope Ann Miller; ***D:*** Richard Benjamin; ***M:*** Alan Silvestri.

Dracula 🦴🦴🦴 **1931** Lugosi, in his most famous role, plays a vampire who terrorizes the countryside in his search for human blood. From Bram Stoker's novel. Although short of a masterpiece due to slow second half, deservedly rated a film classic. What would Halloween be like without this movie? Sequelled by "Dracula's Daughter." The 1999 re-release was re-scored by Philip Glass and performed by the Kronos Quartet. **75m/B; VHS, DVD, Blu-Ray.** Bela Lugosi; David Manners; Dwight Frye; Helen Chandler; Edward Van Sloan; Frances Dade; Herbert Bunston; ***D:*** Tod Browning; ***W:*** Garrett Fort; ***C:*** Karl Freund. Natl. Film Reg. '00.

Dracula Spanish Version 🦴🦴 1/2 **1931** Filmed at the same time as the Bela Lugosi version of "Dracula," using the same sets and the same scripts, only in Spanish. Thought to be more visually appealing and more terrifying than the English-language counterpart. The only thing it's missing is a presence like Lugosi. Based on the novel by Bram Stoker. **104m/B; VHS, DVD, Blu-Ray.** Carlos Villarias; Lupita Tovar; Eduardo Arozamena; Pablo Alvarez Rubio; Barry Norton; Carmen Guerrero; ***D:*** George Melford; ***W:*** Garrett Fort. Natl. Film Reg. '15.

Dracula 🦴🦴 1/2 *Bram Stoker's Dracula* **1973** Count on squinty-eyed Palance to shine as the Transylvanian vampire who must quench his thirst for human blood. Adaptation of the Bram Stoker novel that really flies. **105m/C; VHS, DVD, Blu-Ray.** Jack Palance; Simon Ward; Fiona Lewis; Nigel Davenport; Pamela Brown; Penelope Horner; Murray Brown; Virginia Wetherell; Sarah Douglas; Barbara Lindley; ***D:*** Dan Curtis; ***W:*** Richard Matheson; ***C:*** Oswald Morris; ***M:*** Wojciech Kilar. **TV**

Dracula 🦴🦴 1/2 **1979 (R)** Langella recreates his Broadway role as the count who needs human blood for nourishment. Notable for its portrayal of Dracula as a romantic and tragic figure in history. Overlooked since the vampire spoof "Love at First Bite" came out at the same time. **109m/C; VHS, DVD, Blu-Ray.** Frank Langella; Laurence Olivier; Kate Nelligan; Donald Pleasence; Janine Duvitsky; Trevor Eve; Tony Haygarth; ***D:*** John Badham; ***W:*** W.D. Richter; ***C:*** Gilbert Taylor; ***M:*** John Williams.

Dracula 🦴 **2006** Nonsensical adaptation of the Dracula story that uses little of Stoker's tale (and much ridiculous invention). Lord Holmwood (Stevens) discovers he has syphilis, which endangers his marriage to Lucy (Myles). Apparently inviting the fanged one (Warren)?who seems to now be a member of a sinister blood cult—to England will offer a potential cure. **90m/C; DVD.** Marc Warren; Dan Stevens; Sophia Myles; David Suchet; Tom Burke; Stephanie Leonidas; Rafe Spall; ***D:*** Bill Eagles; ***W:*** Stewart Harcourt; ***M:*** Dominik Scherrer. **TV**

Dracula 2: Ascension 🦴 1/2 *Wes Craven Presents Dracula 2: Ascension* **2003 (R)** Wheelchair-bound medical scientist Lowell (Sheffer) and his students decide to use the blood from Dracula's burned corpse (from the first film, which is now in the local New Orleans morgue) to find a cure for Lowell's paralysis. But it's always a mistake to resurrect a vampire. Lame sequel to the "Dracula 2000" film has a cliffhanger ending to be resolved in "Dracula 3: Legacy." **85m/C; VHS, DVD, Blu-Ray.** Jason Scott Lee; Jason London; Craig Sheffer; Diane Neal; Stephen Billington; Roy Scheider; Rutger Hauer; ***D:*** Patrick Lussier; ***W:*** Patrick Lussier; Joel Soisson; ***C:*** Doug Milsome; ***M:*** Kevin Kliesch. **VIDEO**

Dracula 3: Legacy 🦴🦴 **2005 (R)** Badass Father Uffizi (Lee) is back, accompanied by sidekick Luke (London), and they travel to Transylvania to hunt Dracula (Hauer) at his castle and get rid of him once and for all. Lots of action and a healthy helping of cheese. If you've seen the first two installments, you know what to expect. **90m/C; DVD.** Jason Scott Lee; Jason London; Rutger Hauer; Roy Scheider; Diane Neal; Alexandra Wescourt; ***D:*** Patrick Lussier; ***W:*** Patrick Lussier; Joel Soisson; ***C:*** Doug Milsome; ***M:*** Kevin Kliesch; Cieri Torjussen. **VIDEO**

Dracula A.D. 1972 🦴🦴 *Dracula Today* **1972** Lee returned to England for his sixth (and by most accounts, worst) go-round as Dracula for Hammer Films, where the creative juices seemed to be drying up. The decision was made to turn Dracula loose in the modern world. The movie actually opens in 1872 with a scene that is one of the highlights of the entire production—an action scene that features Dracula battling his nemesis Van Helsing (Cushing) atop a speeding stagecoach. When the coach is wrecked, Dracula is impaled on a wheel spoke and dies. From that point, the scene immediately jumps ahead one century. A Satanist named Johnny Alucard and a group of naive hippie teenagers revive the long-dead vampire in an abandoned church building in England. The teens and Dracula are opposed by Van Helsing's grandson (Cushing again) and his granddaughter Jessica (Beacham). Hammer's unwillingness to pay Lee to speak more than a few lines, together with a sterile plot that had Dracula essentially paralyzed by the modern world, forced the teenagers to carry the story. It appears that the idea for *Dracula A.D. 1972* came from the Count Yorga movies, which had some success in placing an Old World vampire in modern Los Angeles. However, the Yorga movies were only moderately successful and this Hammer copy did not even do that well. *Dracula A.D. 1972* was the sequel to *The Scars of Dracula* (1971) and was followed by *The Satanic Rites of Dracula* (1973). **95m/C; VHS, DVD, Blu-Ray.** *GB* Christopher Lee; Peter Cushing; Christopher Neame; Stephanie Beacham; Michael Coles; Caroline Munro; Marsha A. Hunt; Philip Miller; Janet Key; William Ellis; ***D:*** Alan Gibson; ***W:*** Don Houghton; ***C:*** Dick Bush; ***M:*** Michael Vickers.

Dracula Blows His Cool 🦴 **1982 (R)** Three voluptuous models and their photographer restore an ancient castle and open a disco in it. The vampire lurking about the castle welcomes the party with his fangs. **91m/C; VHS, DVD.** John Garco; Betty Verges; ***D:*** Carlo Ombra; ***W:*** Carlo Ombra.

Dracula: Dead and Loving It WOOF! **1995 (PG-13)** King of the spoofs Nielsen takes on the title role as the ever-loving, if clumsy, Count who still enjoys necking—particularly with luscious damsels in distress, Lucy (Anthony) and Mina (Yasbeck). And he's still got his bug-eating minion Renfield (MacNichol) and egomaniacal vampire-hunter Van Helsing (Brooks) around. As usual, Brooks throws everything possible on the screen, hoping some schtick will stick (not very much does). **90m/C; VHS, DVD.** Leslie Nielsen; Mel Brooks; Peter MacNichol; Lysette Anthony; Amy Yasbeck; Steven Weber; Harvey Korman; Anne Bancroft; Darla Haun; Megan Cavanagh; Mark Blankfield; Clive Revill; ***D:*** Mel Brooks; ***W:*** Mel Brooks; Rudy DeLuca; Steve Haberman; ***C:*** Michael D. O'Shea; ***M:*** Hummie Mann.

Dracula Has Risen from the Grave 🦴🦴 1/2 **1968 (G)** Lee's Dracula is foiled by the local priest before he can drain the blood from innocent villagers. Effectively gory. One of the Hammer series of Dracula films followed by "Taste the Blood of

Dracula." **92m/C; VHS, DVD, Blu-Ray.** *GB* Christopher Lee; Rupert Davies; Veronica Carlson; Barbara Ewing; Barry Andrews; Michael Ripper; Ewan Hooper; Marion Mathie; ***D:*** Freddie Francis; ***W:*** John (Anthony Hinds) Elder; ***C:*** Arthur Grant; ***M:*** James Bernard.

Dracula, Prince of Darkness *The Bloody Scream of Dracula; Disciple of Dracula; Revenge of Dracula* **1966** Sequel to 1958's "Horror of Dracula" finds the Count (Lee) extending his hospitality at Castle Dracula to four unwary tourists, one of whom is immediately killed for his blood. Then Dracula takes the dead man's wife (Shelley) and turns her into a vampire and the gruesome twosome go after the remaining couple. Standard Hammer horror. **90m/C; VHS, DVD, Blu-Ray.** *GB* Christopher Lee; Barbara Shelley; Andrew Keir; Francis Matthews; Suzan Farmer; Charles "Bud" Tingwell; Thorley Walters; Philip Latham; ***D:*** Terence Fisher; ***W:*** John Sansom; John (Anthony Hinds) Elder; ***C:*** Michael Reed; ***M:*** James Bernard.

Dracula Rising 1/2 **1993 (R)** A modern-day art historian (Travis) turns out to have been a witch, burned at the stake, in a past life. She was also the blood-drinking Count's lost love. Now Dracula's a monk and when he sees this reincarnated beauty is he going to be able to keep his hands—er, fangs—off her? **85m/C; VHS, DVD.** Christopher Atkins; Stacey Travis; Doug Wert; Zahari Vatahov; ***D:*** Fred Gallo.

Dracula: The Dark Prince 1/2 *Dark Prince: The True Story of Dracula* **2001 (R)** Costume bio on the life of Vlad the Impalder AKA Vlad Dracula (Martin). In the 15th century, Vlad and his brother are captured by the Turkish sultan who rules over their native Romania. During their captivity, the boys' father (the country's regent) is killed and when Vlad returns home years later he seeks to expel the Turks and rule himself. But his dreams of a unified country are undermined by tragedy and his own brutality. **89m/C; DVD.** Rudolf Martin; Jane March; Peter Weller; Roger Daltrey; Michael Sutton; Christopher Brand; ***D:*** Joe Chappelle; ***W:*** Thomas Baum; ***C:*** Dermott Downs; ***M:*** Frankie Blue. **CABLE**

Dracula 2000 *Wes Craven Presents: Dracula 2000* **2000 (R)** Dracula finds his way to New Orleans to terrorize the modern world in this adaptation of the classic vampire tale that borrows freewheelingly from many supernatural legends. Butler plays Dracula well enough, but doesn't add anything memorable to a character that's been done, redone, and overdone so many times, while Plummer struggles to make the most of a bad situation. Horror fans will no doubt enjoy the gore, but the overall clumsiness is hard to take by anyone's standards. Presented by Wes Craven, but directed by Patrick Lussier, Craven's editor on many films, including the "Scream" trilogy. **98m/C; VHS, DVD, Blu-Ray.** Jonny Lee Miller; Justine Waddell; Gerard Butler; Colleen (Ann) Fitzpatrick; Jennifer Esposito; Danny Masterson; Jeri Ryan; Lochlyn Munro; Sean Patrick Thomas; Omar Epps; Christopher Plummer; ***D:*** Patrick Lussier; ***W:*** Joel Soisson; ***C:*** Peter Pay; ***M:*** Marco Beltrami.

Dracula Untold 1/2 **2014 (PG-13)** Transylvanian prince and family man Vlad (Evans) is an honored war hero not to be threatened. Still, a Turkish Sultan (Cooper) demands Vlad release a thousand of his boys for induction into the Sultan's army. Big mistake. Vlad seeks the wisdom of a cave monster who grants him the power of an eternal Hellraiser, with a thirst for blood. Stealing from every other Dracula entry along the way, this cheap reboot injects the usual CGI bat swarms, flashy cutting, and slo-mo battlefield sword clanking to little effect. Muddled in B-movie cliches, there's no bite to this sludgy vampire saga. **92m/C; DVD, Blu-Ray.** Luke Evans; Dominic Cooper; Sarah Gadon; Charles Dance; Art Parkinson; ***D:*** Gary Shore; ***W:*** Matt Sazama; Burk Sharpless; ***C:*** John Schwartzman; ***M:*** Ramin Djawadi.

Dracula vs. Frankenstein *Assignment: Terror* **1969** An alien reanimates Earth's most infamous monsters in a bid to take over the planet. Rennie's last role. **91m/C; VHS, DVD, Blu-Ray.** *IT GE SP* Michael Rennie; Paul Naschy; Karin Dor; Patty (Patti) Shepard; Craig Hill; ***D:*** Hugo Fregonese; Tulio Demicheli; ***W:*** Paul Naschy.

Dracula vs. Frankenstein WOOF! *Blood of Frankenstein; They're Coming to Get You; Dracula Contra Frankenstein; The Revenge of Dracula; Satan's Bloody Freaks* **1971 (PG)** The Count makes a deal with a shady doctor to keep him in blood. Vampire spoof that's very bad but fun. Last film for both Chaney and Naish. Features a cameo by genre maven Forrest J. Ackerman. **90m/C; VHS, DVD, Blu-Ray.** *SP* J. Carrol Naish; Lon Chaney, Jr.; Regina Carrol; Russ Tamblyn; Jim Davis; Anthony Eisley; Zandor Vorkov; John Bloom; Angelo Rossitto; Forrest J Ackerman; ***D:*** Al Adamson; ***W:*** William Pugsley; Sam M. Sherman; ***C:*** Paul Glickman; Gary Graver; ***M:*** William Lava.

Dracula's Daughter **1936** Count Dracula's daughter, Countess Marya Zaleska, heads to London supposedly to find the cure to a mysterious illness. Instead she finds she has a taste for human blood, especially female blood. She also finds a man, falls in love, and tries to keep him by casting a spell on him. A good script and cast keep this sequel to Bela Lugosi's "Dracula" entertaining. **71m/B; VHS, DVD, Blu-Ray.** Gloria Holden; Otto Kruger; Marguerite Churchill; Irving Pichel; Edward Van Sloan; Nan Grey; Hedda Hopper; ***D:*** Lambert Hillyer; ***W:*** Garrett Fort; ***C:*** George Robinson.

Dracula's Great Love WOOF! *Gran Amore del Conde Dracula; Count Dracula's Great Love; Dracula's Virgin Lovers; Vampire Playgirls* **1972 (R)** Four travellers end up in Dracula's castle for the night, where the horny Count takes a liking to one of the women. Left out in the sun too long. **96m/C; VHS, DVD, Blu-Ray.** *SP* Paul Naschy; Charo Soriano; Haydee Politoff; Rossana Yanni; Ingrid Garbo; Mirta Miller; ***D:*** Javier Aguirre; ***W:*** Paul Naschy; Javier Aguirre.

Dracula's Last Rites WOOF! *Last Rites* **1979 (R)** Blood-curdling tale of a sheriff and a mortician in a small town who are up to no good. Technically inept: film equipment can be spotted throughout. Don't stick your neck out for this one. **86m/C; VHS, DVD.** Patricia Lee Hammond; Gerald Fielding; Victor Jorge; ***D:*** Domonic Paris.

Dracula's Widow **1988 (R)** Countess Dracula, missing her hubby and desperately in need of a substitute, picks innocent Raymond as her victim. His girlfriend and a cynical cop fight to save his soul from the Countess' damnation. Directed by the nephew of Frances Ford Coppola. **85m/C; VHS, Streaming.** Sylvia Kristel; Josef Sommer; Lenny Von Dohlen; George Stover; ***D:*** Christopher Coppola.

Draft Day 1/2 **2014 (PG-13)** Director Reitman's sports rom-com is just a depressing waste of time for both NFL nuts and those who don't know a quarterback from a cornerback in equal measures. In full shaggy dog mode, Costner plays Sonny Weaver Jr., General Manager of the Cleveland Browns and a man going through a rough patch leading up to the most crucial draft day of his career. His beloved Browns coach and father recently passed. His girlfriend (Garner) is pregnant. And he just traded away his future for the number one pick. It's not romantic, the sports writing isn't realistic, and a talented cast is wasted. The Hound throws the penalty flag! **109m/C; DVD, Blu-Ray.** Kevin Costner; Jennifer Garner; Ellen Burstyn; Denis Leary; Frank Langella; Terry Crews; Chadwick Boseman; ***D:*** Ivan Reitman; ***W:*** Scott Rothman; Rajiv Joseph; ***C:*** Eric Steelberg; ***M:*** John Debney.

Drag Me to Hell **2009 (PG-13)** Raimi returns to his lower-budget over-the-top horror roots. In order to impress her boss, L.A. loan officer Christine Brown (Lohman) refuses to allow Mrs. Ganush (Raver) a loan extension on her home. Big mistake since the elderly gypsy places a curse on Christine that involves an evil spirit that starts destroying her life and in three days—well, you can see what'll happen from the title. Lots of gross-out moments, delivered in Raimi's tongue-in-cheek schlock style with Lohman being a particularly good sport considering what her character goes through (mud, bugs, and projectile vomiting included). **99m/C; Blu-Ray, On Demand.** Alison Lohman; Justin Long; Lorna Raver; David Paymer; Dileep Rao; Adriana Barraza; Chelcie Ross; Reggie Lee; ***D:*** Sam Raimi; ***W:*** Sam Raimi; Ivan Raimi; ***C:*** Peter Deming; ***M:*** Christopher Young.

The Drag-Net 1/2 **1936** The playboy son of a prominent attorney is given a job in the district attorney's office in an effort to make him more responsible. He still likes to hang out with showgirls at nightclubs but this time he's also investigating murder and organized crime. **90m/B; DVD.** Rod La Rocque; Marion (Marian) Nixon; Betty Compson; Ed Le-Saint; Jack Adair; John Dilson; Joseph Girard; Edward (Ed Kean, Keene) Keane; ***D:*** Vin Moore; ***W:*** James Mulhauser; ***C:*** Edward Kull.

Dragged Across Concrete 1/2 **2018 (R)** When 60ish cop Brett Ridgeman (Gibson) is videotaped acting brutal and racist during a drug bust, he is suspended from the force. Brett decides he is no longer going to play by the rules and makes plans to rob a money exchange so he can retire and move his family to a safer neighborhood. At the same time, young African American Henry Johns (Kittles) has recently been released from prison and plans on committing a crime to support his family. The well-crafted and well-acted ultraviolent flick explores dark themes but its slow pacing make the long run time feel drawn out. **158m/C; DVD, Blu-Ray.** *CA US* Mel Gibson; Vince Vaughn; Tory Kittles; Michael Jai White; Thomas Kretschmann; ***D:*** S. Craig Zahler; ***W:*** S. Craig Zahler; ***C:*** Benji Bakshi; ***M:*** S. Craig Zahler; Jeff Herriott; The O'Jays.

Dragnet 1/2 **1954** Sgt. Joe Friday and Officer Frank Smith try to solve a mob slaying but have a rough time. Alexander plays the sidekick in "Dragnet" pre-Morgan days. Just the facts: feature version of the TV show that's suspenseful and well-acted. **88m/C; VHS, DVD, Streaming.** Jack Webb; Ben Alexander; Richard Boone; Ann (Robin) Robinson; ***D:*** Jack Webb.

Dragnet **1987 (PG-13)** Semi-parody of the vintage '60s TV cop show. Sgt. Joe Friday's straitlaced nephew (Aykroyd) and his sloppy partner Pep (Hanks) take on a crooked reverend (Plummer) and a pagan organization called, well, P.A.G.A.N. Neither Aykroyd nor Hanks can save this big-budget but lackluster spoof that's full of holes, although they both have their moments. **106m/C; VHS, DVD, Blu-Ray.** Dan Aykroyd; Tom Hanks; Christopher Plummer; Harry (Henry) Morgan; Elizabeth Ashley; Dabney Coleman; Alexandra Paul; Kathleen Freeman; Jack O'Halloran; ***D:*** Tom Mankiewicz; ***W:*** Dan Aykroyd; Tom Mankiewicz; Alan Zweibel; ***C:*** Matthew F. Leonetti; ***M:*** Ira Newborn.

Dragon Blade 1/2 *Tian jiang xiong shi* **2015 (R)** A Han Dynasty-set historical action epic centered on a fight for the Silk Road. Seeking Roman control of the Silk Road, Tiberius (Brody), the corrupt Roman leader, leads a massive army to stake his empire's claim. However, a number of his soldiers defect, led by General Lucius (Cusack), and form their own elite Legion. Teaming up with Chinese warrior Huo An (Chan) and his army, the Lucius and the rebellious Romans do all they can do defeat Tiberius. English and Mandarin with subtitles. **127m/C; DVD, Blu-Ray, Streaming, Download.** Jackie Chan; John Cusack; Adrien Brody; Si Won Choi; Peng Lin; ***D:*** Daniel Lee; ***W:*** Daniel Lee; ***M:*** Henry Lai.

Dragon Eyes 1/2 **2012 (R)** Van Damme has little screen time as the mentor to Cung Le's martial arts lone hero. Hong leaves behind his teacher when he gets out of the joint and lands in St. Jude, which is overwhelmed by drugs and vilolence. He pits two rival gangs against each other but trying to clean up the 'hood brings him to the attention of the corrupt police chief (Weller). **90m/C; DVD, Blu-Ray.** Cung Le; Peter Weller; Jean-Claude Van Damme; Edrick Browne; ***D:*** John Hyams; ***W:*** Tim Tori; ***C:*** Stephen Schlueter; ***M:*** Michael Krassner. **VIDEO**

Dragon Lord **1982** Young kung-fu hero (Chan) defends his village against greedy outlaws. Comic interludes tend to slow the action. **90m/C; VHS, DVD.** Jackie Chan.

Dragon Seed 1/2 **1944** The lives of the residents of a small Chinese village are turned upside down when the Japanese invade it. Based on the Pearl S. Buck novel. Lengthy and occasionally tedious, though generally well-made with heart-felt attempts to create Oriental characters, without having Asians in the cast. **145m/B; VHS, DVD.** Katharine Hepburn; Walter Huston; Agnes Moorehead; Akim Tamiroff; Hurd Hatfield; J. Carrol Naish; Henry Travers; Turhan Bey; Aline MacMahon; ***D:*** Jack Conway.

Dragon Storm 1/2 **2004 (PG-13)** In this Sci-Fi Channel original production, medieval men must fight to free the planet from an other-worldly infestation of fearsome, foul, flying, fire-breathing alien dragons. And they didn't even call first! **92m/C; VHS, DVD, On Demand.** Tony Amendola; Angel Boris; Maxwell Caulfield; Jeff Rank; Iskra Angelova; Maxim Gentchev; Ivaylo Geraskov; John Hansson; Woon Young Park; Tyrone Pinkham; John Rhys-Davies; Richard Wharton; ***D:*** Stephen Furst; ***W:*** Patrick Phillips. **CABLE**

Dragon: The Bruce Lee Story **1993 (PG-13)** Entertaining, inspiring account of the life of Chinese-American martial-arts legend Bruce Lee. Jason Scott Lee (no relation) is great as the talented artist, exuding his joy of life and gentle spirit, before his mysterious brain disorder death at the age of 32. Ironically, this release coincided with son Brandon's accidental death on a movie set. The martial arts sequences in "Dragon" are extraordinary, but there's also romance as Lee meets and marries his wife (Holly, who acquits herself well). Based on the book "Bruce Lee: The Man Only I Knew" by his widow, Linda Lee Caldwell. **121m/C; VHS, DVD, Blu-Ray.** Jason Scott Lee; Lauren Holly; Robert Wagner; Michael Learned; Nancy Kwan; Kay Tong Lim; Sterling Macer; Ric Young; Sven-Ole Thorsen; ***D:*** Rob Cohen; ***W:*** Edward Khmara; John Raffo; Rob Cohen; ***C:*** David Eggby; ***M:*** Randy Edelman.

Dragon Tiger Gate *Lung fu moon; Long hu men* **2007** Based on the popular manga "Dragon and Tiger Heroes", this is the story of the Dragon Tiger Gate martial arts school founded by the father of Dragon (Donnie Yen) and Tiger (Nicholas Tse). Separated as children, Dragon grows up to be the bodyguard of a vicious drug dealer. Tiger becomes a local hero, and eventually gets into a scrap with a gang run by Dragon's boss. While trying to redeem his brother, he ends up in possession of a magical artifact his gang wants back, and he must rely on he help of his brother and a newcomer to the city named Turbo (Shawn Yue) to stay alive. Over the top CGI martial arts and spurious dubbing ensues. **94m/C; DVD, Blu-Ray.** *CH* Donnie Yen; Nicholas Tse; Shawn Yue; Jie Dong; Xiao Ran Li; Wah Yuen; Kuan Tai Chen; Vincent Sze; Tommy Yuen; Sam Chan Yu-Sum; Alan Lam; Nick Lam; Yu Xing; Hua Yan; Yu Kan; ***D:*** Wilson (Wai-Shun) Yip; ***W:*** Yuk Long Wong; Edmond Wong; ***C:*** Chiu-lam Ko; ***M:*** Kenji Kawai.

Dragon Wars 1/2 *D-War; Dragon Wars: D-War* **2007 (PG-13)** Originally announced in 2002 but not released until five years later, this pic wracked up a massive budget that made it the most expensive Korean film ever made. Unfortunately it's far from the best. Apparently every 500 years a girl is born who can change an Imoogi (giant snake) into a celestial dragon. An evil Imoogi (Buraki) has attempted to kidnap her in the past, and attempts to do so again in the modern day. Thankfully she has some college kid to protect her from the evil 300-foot-long snake and his enormous army of monsters. Worth seeing for the monster attack scenes, but don't try following the plot. **90m/C; DVD, Blu-Ray, UMD.** *NK* Jason Behr; Amanda Brooks; Robert Forster; Craig Robinson; Aimee Garcia; Chris Mulkey; John Ales; Elizabeth Pena; Billy Gardell; Cody Arens; Craig Anton; Hyun Jin Park; Hyojin Ban; Ji-hwan Min; Jongman Lee; Kyuho Moon; Cheyenne Alexis Dean; Roberta Farkas; Ethan Grant; Kerry Liu; Richard Steen; ***D:*** Hyung Rae Shim; ***W:*** Hyung Rae Shim; ***C:*** Hubert Taczanowski; ***M:*** Steve Jablonsky.

Dragon Wasps **2012** Goofy cheese-fest from the SyFy Channel involving the U.S. military fighting giant, fire-breathing wasps and voodoo-worshiping drug runners in Belize. Sure to please fans of similar bad movies riddled with scientific inaccuracies. **84m/C; DVD, Streaming.** Corin "Corky" Nemec; Dominika Juillet; Nikollette Noel; Benjamin Easterday; Gildon Roland; *D:* Joe Knee; *W:* Mark Atkins; Rafael Jordan; *C:* Mikey Jechort; *M:* Chris(topher) Cano. **CABLE**

Dragonard ½ *Master of Dragonard Hill* **1988 (R)** Slaves on a West Indies island rebel against their cruel masters. **93m/C; VHS, Streaming.** Eartha Kitt; Oliver Reed; Annabel Schofield; Patrick Warburton; *D:* Gerard Kikoine; *W:* R.J. Marx.

Dragonball: Evolution **2009 (PG)** Based on the popular Japanese manga created by Akira Toriyama, whose work spawned best selling graphic novels, video games, and a phenomenally successful television series. The live-action adventure centers on a team of warriors, each of whom possesses special abilities. Teenager Goku (Chatwin) must find Master Roshi (Chow) and gather all seven dragonballs before evil Lord Piccolo (Marsters) does so that he can prevent him from taking over the world. Unfortunately pic relies on martial arts action and uneven, unimpressive CGI. Only saved by a few entertaining fight scenes, which basically relegate it to a not-so-good video game. A complete waste of Hong Kong legend Chow Yun Fat's talent with horrible dialogue and enough cliches to choke a dragon. **84m/C; Blu-Ray, On Demand.** Justin Chatwin; James Marsters; Chow Yun-Fat; Emmy Rossum; Ernie Hudson; Randall Duk Kim; Texas Battle; *D:* James Wong; *W:* James Wong; *C:* Robert McLachlan; *M:* Brian Tyler.

Dragonfly ½ **2002 (PG-13)** I see dead performances. Cheesy, self-gratifying supernatural snorer has Costner as Chicago's dour ER doctor Joe Darrow, righteously widowed when his doctor wife bites the dust tending to the poor in Venezuela, while pregnant, no less. Unable to accept her death, Darrow is convinced she's trying to contact him from Beyond as he receives a series of cryptic messages, some from the children in his wife's pediatric oncology ward. Darrow's talking parrot provides some of the sillier scenes in this slow-paced, must-miss melodrama. Bates as the neighbor manages to liven up her scenes, anyway. Director Shadyac ("Patch Adams") certainly didn't want his lead here displaying any of his other doctor's kid-loving antics, and glum and glummer Costner is a dutiful downer as he pumps the kids in the ward for info about his dead wife. **103m/C; VHS, DVD, Blu-Ray.** Kevin Costner; Joe Morton; Susanna Thompson; Ron Rifkin; Linda Hunt; Kathy Bates; Jay Thomas; Matt Craven; Robert Bailey, Jr.; Lisa Banes; Jacob Smith; *D:* Tom Shadyac; *W:* David Seltzer; Brandon Camp; Mike Thompson; *C:* Dean Semler; *M:* John Debney.

Dragonfly Squadron **1954** Korean war drama about pilots and their romantic problems. Never gets off the ground. **82m/C; DVD, Blu-Ray.** John Hodiak; Barbara Britton; Bruce Bennett; Jess Barker; Gerald Mohr; Chuck Connors; *D:* Lesley Selander; *W:* John C. Champion; *C:* Harry Neumann; *M:* Paul Dunlap.

Dragonheart ½ **1996 (PG-13)** Okay, get past the fact that Connery's Scottish burr is coming out of the teeth-filled mouth of an 18 ft. tall, 43 ft. long dragon and you'll be well on your way to enjoying this 10th-century fantasy. Knightly Bowen (Quaid) is the one-time mentor of evil-hearted King Einon (Thewlis) and it's up to him, Draco the dragon, feisty Kara (Meyer), and some fearful peasants to band together and free themselves from the king's tyranny. There's some slow spots but Bowen and Draco make for an amusing pairing and the dragon does seem, well, real. Work on Draco took more than a year of Industrial Light & Magic's expertise. **103m/C; DVD, Blu-Ray.** Dennis Quaid; David Thewlis; Pete Postlethwaite; Dina Meyer; Julie Christie; Jason Isaacs; Brian Thompson; Wolf Christian; Terry O'Neill; *V:* Sean Connery; John Gielgud; *D:* Rob Cohen; *W:* Charles Edward Pogue; *C:* David Eggby; *M:* Randy Edelman.

Dragonheart 3: The Sorcerer's Curse ½ **2015 (PG-13)** Young squire Gareth tracks a fallen comet, after hearing it might contain gold ore that could pay for his knighthood. Instead, he finds Drago, a dragon being pursued by a sorcerer. **97m/C; DVD, Blu-Ray.** Julian Morris; Tamzin Merchant; Jake Curran; Jassa Ahluwalia; *V:* Ben Kingsley; *D:* Colin Teague; *W:* Matthew Feitshans; *C:* David Luther; *M:* Mark McKenzie. **VIDEO**

Dragonheart: A New Beginning **2000 (PG)** Geoff (Masteron) is a monastery stableboy who wants to become a knight. Then he discovers Friar Peter (Woodnutt) has secretly been raising a young dragon called Drake (voiced by Benson). When the evil Lord Osric (Van Gorkum) learns of the beast's existence, he wants to claim its powers for himself. But Geoff, who's aided by two mysterious warriors from the east, is determined to save both Drake and the kingdom. **85m/C; DVD, Blu-Ray.** Christopher K. Masterson; Henry O; Harry Van Gorkum; John Woodnutt; Rona Figueroa; Ken Shorter; *V:* Robby Benson; *D:* Doug Lefler; *W:* Shari Goodhartz; *C:* Buzz Feitshans, IV. **VIDEO**

Dragonquest ½ **2009 (PG-13)** Evil warlord Krill (Thompson) summons up a flying, fire-breathing beastie to help him conquer the world. Would-be hero Arkadi (Bonjour) is taken under the wing of knight Maxim (Singer) and must complete a series of quests to get the jewels for a sacred amulet that will give him the power to summon his own dragon and defeat Krill. **90m/C; DVD.** Marc Singer; Brian Thompson; Daniel Bonjour; Jason Connery; Jennifer Dorogi; Russell Reynolds; Richard Lund; *D:* Mark Atkins; *W:* Brian Brinkman; Micho Rutare; *C:* Mark Atkins; *M:* Chris Ridenhour; Sanya Mateyas. **VIDEO**

Dragons Forever ½ *Dragon Forever* **1988** A big time lawyer is persuaded to work against a chemical plant who wants to take over a site used by local fisherman. Complications arise when he falls for the beautiful cousin of the fishery's owner. A comic king-fu battle between Chan, Hung, and Biao is the rousing finale. In Cantonese with English subtitles. **88m/C; VHS, DVD.** *CH* Jackie Chan; Yuen Biao; Sammo Hung; Pauline Yeung; Yuen Wah; *D:* Sammo Hung; Corey Yuen; *W:* Roy Szeto; Gordon Chan.

Dragonslayer **1981 (PG)** A sorcerer's apprentice suddenly finds himself the only person who can save the kingdom from a horrible, fire-breathing dragon. Extreme violence but wonderful special effects, smart writing, and a funny performance by Richardson. **110m/C; VHS, DVD.** Peter MacNichol; Caitlin Clarke; Ralph Richardson; John Hallam; Albert Salmi; Chloe Salaman; *D:* Matthew Robbins; *W:* Matthew Robbins; Hal Barwood; *M:* Alex North.

Dragonwyck **1946** In the 1840s, wealthy Nicholas Van Ryn (Price) is living on an estate called Dragonwyck in the Hudson Valley. He's unhappily married and blames wife Abigail (Revere) for not giving him a son and heir. When his beautiful distant cousin Miranda (Tierney) comes to be a companion to his daughters, it isn't long before Nicholas is a widower. Naive Miranda eventually becomes his bride but things don't work out very well for her either until local doctor Turner (Langan) becomes suspicious. Mankiewicz's directorial debut; adapted from the Anya Seton novel. **103m/B; DVD, Blu-Ray.** Vincent Price; Gene Tierney; Walter Huston; Glenn Langan; Anne Revere; Spring Byington; Harry (Henry) Morgan; *D:* Joseph L. Mankiewicz; *W:* Joseph L. Mankiewicz; *C:* Arthur C. Miller; *M:* Alfred Newman.

Dragstrip Girl **1957** An 18-year-old girl comes of age while burning rubber at the dragstrip—the world of boys, hot rods, and horsepower. A definite "B" movie that may seem dated. **70m/B; VHS, DVD.** Fay Spain; Steven Terrell; John Ashley; Frank Gorshin; Paul Blaisdell; *D:* Edward L. Cahn.

Dragstrip Girl ½ **1994** Remake of the 1957 "B" movie; a part of Showtime's Rebel Highway series. Latino Johnny (Dacasos) works as a valet during the day and goes drag racing at night. He's got big plans that may be derailed by rich white girl Laura (Wagner) who likes taking a walk on the wild side. **82m/C; VHS, DVD.** Mark Dacascos; Natasha Gregson Wagner; Raymond Cruz; Traci Lords; *D:* Mary Lambert; *W:* Jerome Gary; *C:* Sandi Sissel. **CABLE**

The Draughtsman's Contract **1982 (R)** A beguiling mystery begins when a wealthy woman hires an artist to make drawings of her home. Their contract is quite unusual, as is their relationship. Everything is going along at an even pace until murder is suspected, and things spiral down to darker levels. A simple story turned into a bizarre puzzle. Intense enough for any thriller fan. **103m/C; VHS, DVD.** *GB* Anthony (Corlan) Higgins; Janet Suzman; Anne Louise Lambert; Hugh Fraser; *D:* Peter Greenaway; *W:* Peter Greenaway; *C:* Sacha Vierny; *M:* Michael Nyman.

Draw on Sweet Night ½ **2015** This period drama from director Tony Britten is a follow-up to his "Peace and Conflict," created in collaboration with vocal group I Fagiolini. In this film, the life and music of Elizabethan madrigalist/composer John Wilbye is the focus. Wilbye spent the whole of his career in the service of Sir Thomas and Lady Elizabeth Kytson at their Suffolk home, Hengrave Hall. The film considers the whole of his life and career, including his two books of published madrigals, the gifts showered on him by Lady Elizabeth, his actions after her death in 1628, and his relationship to the notorious Lady Arabella Stewart. **86m/C; DVD.** Mark Arends; Doon Mackichan; Sophia Di Martino; Christian McKay; Ania Sowinski; *D:* Tony Britten; *W:* Tony Britten; *C:* Phil Wood. **VIDEO**

Dread **2009 (R)** Writer/director DiBlasi adapts a short story of horrormeister Clive Barker for this nihilistic nightmare. Introverted film student Stephen (Rathbone) is pressured by philosophy student Quaid (Evans) to do a thesis film about fear. The guys team up with editor Cheryl (Steen) but neither Stephen nor Cheryl realize that a traumatic incident from his childhood has pushed the obsessed Quaid past the point of control. **108m/C; DVD.** *UK US* Jackson Rathbone; Shaun Evans; Hanne Steen; Laura Donnelly; Jonathan Readwin; Vivian Gray; Carl McCrystal; *D:* Anthony DiBlasi; *W:* Anthony DiBlasi; *C:* Sam McCurdy; *M:* Theo Green. **VIDEO**

Dream a Little Dream **1989 (PG-13)** Strange teen transformation drama about an old man and his wife trying mystically to regain their youth. When they collide bikes with the teenagers down the street, their minds are exchanged and the older couple with the now young minds are transported to a permanent dream-like state. Same old switcheroo made bearable by cast. **114m/C; VHS, DVD.** Corey Feldman; Corey Haim; Meredith Salenger; Jason Robards, Jr.; Piper Laurie; Harry Dean Stanton; Victoria Jackson; Alex Rocco; William McNamara; *D:* Marc Rocco; *W:* Marc Rocco.

Dream a Little Dream 2 ½ **1994 (PG-13)** Friends Dinger Holefield (Haim) and Bobby Keller (Feldman) receive a mysterious package containing two pairs of sunglasses, which they discover have magic powers. The wearer of one pair is driven to do the bidding of the wearer of the second pair of specs—whether for good or evil. Naturally, there are evildoers who want the glasses as well. **91m/C; VHS, DVD.** Corey Haim; Corey Feldman; Stacie Randall; Michael Nicolosi; *D:* James (Momel) Lemmo; *W:* David Weissman; Susan Forman.

Dream Boy ½ **2008 (R)** Wispy, tremulously romantic adaptation of the Jim Grimsley novel. Shy and sensitive Nathan (Bender), the new boy at his backwater Louisiana high school, has a lot of nasty family secrets he tries to hide, especially from farm boy neighbor Roy (Roeg) with whom he falls in love. **90m/C; DVD.** Stephen Bender; Max Roeg; Thomas Jay Ryan; Diana Scarwid; Randy Wayne; Owen Beckman; Rickie Lee Jones; *D:* James Bolton; *W:* James Bolton; *C:* Sarah Levy; *M:* Richard Buckner.

The Dream Catcher ½ *The Dreamcatcher* **1999** With his girlfriend pregnant, Freddy (Compte) hits the road to look for his uncle, who might be able to give him some cash. With no car, he takes to hitchhiking and riding trains, and along the way befriends a klepto. When Freddy finds out his dad is out of prison. Quirky characters and a thoughtful script help this pleasing road flick along. **93m/C; VHS, DVD.** Maurice Compte; Paddy Connor; Jeanne Heaton; Joseph Arthur; Larry John Meyers; *D:* Edward A. Radtke; *W:* Edward A. Radtke; M.S. Nieson; *C:* Terry Stacey; *M:* Georgiana Gomez.

Dream Chasers **1982 (PG)** A bankrupt old codger and an 11-year-old boy stricken with cancer run away together during the Great Depression. **97m/C; VHS, DVD.** Harold Gould; Justin Dana; Wesley Bishop; Carolyn Carradine; *D:* Arthur Dubs; David E. Jackson; *W:* Wesley Bishop; *C:* Milas C. Hinshaw; *M:* William Loose.

Dream for an Insomniac ½ **1996 (R)** Irritating characters put the kibbosh on this attempt at twentysomething romantic comedy. Whiny would-be actress Frankie (Skye) works at her Uncle Leo's (Cassel) cafe and hangs out with assorted, equally whiny friends. Frankie seems more interested in finding the "perfect" boyfriend than a career anyway and her interest is sparked by new guy David (a sweet Astin). Lots of overacting. Debut for writer/director DeBartolo. **108m/C; VHS, DVD.** Ione Skye; MacKenzie Astin; Jennifer Aniston; Seymour Cassel; Michael Landes; Robert Kelker-Kelly; *D:* Tiffanie DeBartolo; *W:* Tiffanie DeBartolo; *C:* Guillermo Navarro; *M:* John Laraio.

Dream House ½ **2011 (PG-13)** Convoluted genre fare that wastes its cast on the absurd and is a decided letdown for director Sheridan. Aspiring writer Will Atenton (Craig) relocates his wife Libby (Weisz) and their two young daughters to a New England town. They discover their new home was the scene of the murders of a mother and her children, with the husband landing in a mental hospital. Will starts investigating, but the neighbors are strange and the house appears to be haunted. **92m/C; DVD, Blu-Ray.** Daniel Craig; Rachel Weisz; Naomi Watts; Marton Csokas; Elias Koteas; Jane Alexander; *D:* Jim Sheridan; *W:* David Loucka; *C:* Caleb Deschanel; *M:* John Debney.

Dream Lover **1985 (R)** Terrifying nightmares after an assault lead McNichol to dream therapy. Treatment causes her tortured unconscious desires to take over her waking behavior, and she becomes a violent schizophrenic. Slow, heavy, and not very thrilling. **105m/C; VHS, DVD.** Kristy McNichol; Ben Masters; Paul Shenar; Justin Deas; Joseph Culp; Gayle Hunnicutt; John McMartin; *D:* Alan J. Pakula; *W:* Jon Boorstin; *C:* Sven Nykvist.

Dream Lover **1993 (R)** Divorced architect Ray (Spader) meets and marries Lena (Amick), beautiful and seemingly perfect, who nonetheless warns him that she's just your average mixed-up gal. Suspense is supposed to come into play as Ray suspects Lena's been lying to him about her past. Visually appealing (considerably helped by the attractive leads) but good looks don't make up for the lack of substance and the minimal number of surprises expected in a thriller. Directorial debut of Kazan. Also available in an unrated version. **103m/C; VHS, DVD.** James Spader; Madchen Amick; Frederic Lehne; Bess Armstrong; Larry Miller; Kathleen York; Blair Tefkin; Scott Coffey; William Shockley; Clyde Kusatsu; *D:* Nicholas Kazan; *W:* Nicholas Kazan; *C:* Jean-Yves Escoffier; *M:* Christopher Young.

Dream Lovers ½ *Meng zhong ren* **1986** Supernatural love story moves back and forth from contemporary Hong Kong to the mysterious Qin dynasty. When an orchestra conductor and the daughter of a noted architect meet at an exhibit featuring the famed terracotta army, an affair from the past is resurrected. In Cantonese with English subtitles. **95m/C; VHS, DVD.** *CH* Chow Yun-Fat; Brigitte Lin; Cher Yeung; *D:* Tony Au; *W:* Yau Da Ah-Pin; Manfred Wong; *C:* Bill Wong.

Dream Man ½ **1994 (R)** Kris Anderson (Kensit) is a Seattle cop with the clairvoyant ability to see crimes as they're committed. But that doesn't stop her from getting involved with the handsome murder suspect (McCarthy) she's supposed to be investigating. **94m/C; VHS, Streaming.** Patsy Kensit; Andrew McCarthy; Bruce Greenwood; *D:* Rene Bonniere; *W:* Michael Alexander Miller; *M:* Graeme Coleman.

Dream No Evil ½ **1970** A mentally disturbed woman is forced to commit bizarre murders to protect her warped fantasy world. **93m/C; VHS, DVD.** Edmond O'Brien; Brooke Mills; Marc Lawrence; Arthur Franz; *D:* John Hayes; *W:* John Hayes; *C:* Paul Hipp; *M:* Jaime Mendoza-Nava.

A Dream of Kings **1969 (R)** Quinn is exceptional in this Petrakis story of an immigrant working to get his dying son home to Greece. Last film appearance for Stevens before committing suicide at age 36. **107m/C; VHS, DVD.** Anthony Quinn; Irene Papas; Inger Stevens; Sam Levene; Val Avery; *D:* Daniel Mann; *M:* Alex North.

Dream Street ♪♪ **1921** A weak morality tale of London's lower classes. Two brothers, both in love with the same dancing girl, woo her in their own way, while a Chinese gambler plans to take her by force. Silent with music score. Based on Thomas Burke's "Limehouse Nights." **138m/B; Silent; VHS, DVD.** Tyrone Power, Sr.; Carol Dempster; Ralph Graves; Charles Emmet Mack; *D:* D.W. Griffith.

The Dream Team ♪♪ ½ **1989 (PG-13)** On their way to a ball game, four patients from a mental hospital find themselves lost in New York City after their doctor is knocked out by murderers. Some fine moments from a cast of dependable comics. Watch for numerous nods to "One Flew Over the Cuckoo's Nest," another Lloyd feature. Keaton fans won't want to miss this one. **113m/C; VHS, DVD, Blu-Ray.** Michael Keaton; Christopher Lloyd; Peter Boyle; Stephen Furst; Lorraine Bracco; Milo O'Shea; Dennis Boutsikaris; Philip Bosco; James Remar; Cynthia Belliveau; *D:* Howard Zieff; *W:* Jon Connolly; David Loucka; *M:* David McHugh.

D.R.E.A.M. Team ♪♪ **1999 (R)** Garrison (Sheen) heads a secret United Nations agency that has uncovered terrorist activities in Puerto Rico involving a bomb laced with anthrax. He turns to CIA agent Zack (Kaake) to form a team of agents to stop the madness. Their cover just happens to be as models working on a fashion shoot, which means Zack gets to choose three babes to kick butt. **81m/C; VHS, DVD.** Jeff Kaake; Angie Everhart; Traci Lords; Traci Bingham; Martin Sheen; Roger Moore; Ian McShane; James Remar; *D:* Dean Hamilton; *W:* Michael Snyder; *M:* Matthias Weber. **TV**

Dream to Believe ♪♪ **1985** Slice of the life of your typical high school coed—mom's dying, stepdad's from hell, sports injury hurts, and, oh yeah, championship gymnastic competitions loom. Designed to make you feel oh-so-good in that MTV kind of way. Reeves is most excellent as the girl's blushing beau. **96m/C; VHS, DVD.** Rita Tushingham; Keanu Reeves; Olivia D'Abo; Jessica Steen; *D:* Paul Lynch.

Dream West ♪♪ ½ **1986** CBS TV miniseries stars Chamberlain as adventurer, explorer, and politician John Charles Fremont. After forging the Oregon trail, Fremont became the governor of California and fought for the Union during the Civil War, among other frontier exploits. Adapted from David Nevin's historical novel. **337m/C; DVD.** Richard Chamberlain; F. Murray Abraham; Gayle Hunnicutt; Alice Krige; Ben Johnson; Jerry Orbach; G.D. Spradlin; Rip Torn; Fritz Weaver; Anthony Zerbe; Claude Akins; *D:* Dick Lowry; *W:* Evan Hunter; *C:* Robert M. "Bob" Baldwin, Jr.; *M:* Fred Karlin. **TV**

Dream Wife ♪♪ **1953** A battle of the sexes comedy that doesn't seem quite so funny anymore. State department official Priscilla Effington (Kerr) is not willing to give up her career to marry Clemson Reade (Grant). A miffed Clem decides to make a formal marriage proposal to Princess Tarji (St. John), the daughter of the Khan (Franz) of oil-rich Bukistan where Clem previously worked. Effie is sent to Bukistan to solve an oil crisis and decides to inform Tarji about that whole female equality thing and suddenly Clem's perfect fiancee is thinking for herself. **99m/B; DVD.** Cary Grant; Deborah Kerr; Walter Pidgeon; Betta St. John; Eduard Franz; Buddy Baer; Les Tremayne; Bruce Bennett; Richard Anderson; *D:* Sidney Sheldon; *W:* Sidney Sheldon; Herbert Baker; Alfred Lewis Levitt; *C:* Milton Krasner; *M:* Conrad Salinger.

Dream with the Fishes ♪♪ ½ **1997 (R)** Suicidal voyeur Terry (Arquette) is about to jump from a bridge when terminally ill thief Nick (Adams) strikes a strange deal with him. In exchange for funding a few of Nick's fantasies, he will kill Terry in a less messy way. After various strange escapades (including an unplanned robbery and nude bowling), the pair arrive in Nick's hometown, where he attempts to resolve old issues with an ex-girlfriend and his abusive father. As Nick's health fades, Terry reexamines his wish to die. As the story develops, the cliches of both the buddy and road movie genres fall away, letting you actually care about both of these guys. In an homage to the independent spirit of movies of the early 70s, the film stock copies their grainy look, gradually dissolving over the course of the movie to a clearer look. Debut for director Finn Taylor. **97m/C; VHS, DVD.** David Arquette; Brad Hunt; Kathryn Erbe; Cathy Moriarty; Allyce Beasley; Patrick McGaw; J.E. Freeman; *D:* Finn Taylor; *W:* Finn Taylor; *C:* Barry Stone; *M:* Tito Larriva.

Dreamcatcher ♪ ½ **2003 (R)** Four childhood buddies with telepathic abilities bestowed on them by a mentally retarded boy they protected meet in the Maine woods for an annual hunting trip just in time for a body-snatching alien jamboree. Of course, the military is there, too, waiting for the chance to eliminate the aliens by toasting the town, literally. Convoluted story doesn't seem like an adaptation of King's novel, it's more like an adaptation of all of 'em, from "It" to "Stand By Me." With some "The Thing" and "Outbreak" thrown in for good measure. None of it works, unless you like bloody scenes of alien rectal excavation. **134m/C; VHS, DVD, Blu-Ray.** Morgan Freeman; Thomas Jane; Jason Lee; Damian Lewis; Timothy Olyphant; Tom Sizemore; Donnie Wahlberg; Michael O'Neill; Rosemary Dunsmore; Mike Holekamp; Reece Thompson; Giacomo Baessato; Joel Palmer; Andrew Robb; *D:* Lawrence Kasdan; *W:* Lawrence Kasdan; William Goldman; *C:* John Seale; *M:* James Newton Howard.

Dreamchild ♪♪♪ **1985 (PG)** A poignant story of the autumn years of Alice Hargreaves, the model for Lewis Carroll's "Alice in Wonderland." Film follows her on a visit to New York in the 1930s, with fantasy sequences including Wonderland characters created by Jim Henson's Creature Shop invoking the obsessive Reverend Dodgson (a.k.a. Carroll). **94m/C; VHS, DVD.** *GB* Coral Browne; Ian Holm; Peter Gallagher; Jane Asher; Nicola Cowper; Amelia Shankley; Caris Corfman; Shane Rimmer; James Wilby; *D:* Gavin Millar; *W:* Dennis Potter; *C:* Billy Williams; *M:* Max Harris; Stanley Myers.

Dreamer: Inspired by a True Story ♪♪ ½ **2005 (PG)** Family-friendly heart-warmer about a girl and her race horse. Ben Crane (Russell) has a failing Kentucky horse farm, so he's working as a trainer for stable owner Palmer (Morse). The stable's most promising filly Sonador ("Dreamer") breaks a leg during a race and is supposed to be put down, but Ben's plucky daughter Cale (Fanning) insists the horse is a keeper. So Ben quits his job, takes the filly as severance pay, and decides to not only nurse the horse back to health, but get her racing again. Well-matched cast with some especially good moments between Russell and Fanning. **98m/C; DVD.** Kurt Russell; Dakota Fanning; Kris Kristofferson; Elisabeth Shue; Luis Guzman; Freddy Rodriguez; David Morse; Oded Fehr; Ken Howard; Holmes Osborne; *D:* John Gatins; *W:* John Gatins; *C:* Fred Murphy; *M:* John Debney.

The Dreamers ♪♪ **2003 (NC-17)** A carnal odyssey among a trio of cinephiles set against the political background of the 1968 Paris student riots. Matthew (Pitt), an impressionable American student, meets flirtatious Isabelle (Green) and her twin brother Theo (Garrel) at a protest march. He soon joins the siblings at their apartment even though he's uncomfortable at their closeness. Matthew's inhibitions dissolve as he begins a sexual relationship with Isabelle while there's increasing friction with the volatile Theo. Eventually, Matthew begins to question the insularity of the twins' privileged world. Bertolucci's a meticulous craftsman but here it's in the service of a sometimes overwrought romanticism. Screenwriter Adair adapted from his novel "The Holy Innocents." Some subtitled French. **115m/B; VHS, DVD.** Louis Garrel; Michael Pitt; Robin Renucci; Eva Green; Anna Chancellor; Mike Colter; Lucia Rijker; Florian Cadiou; *D:* Bernardo Bertolucci; *W:* Gilbert Adair; *C:* Fabio Cianchetti.

Dreamgirls ♪♪♪ **2006 (PG-13)** The stage musical was coyly set in Chicago; Condon starts his movie off in 1962 Detroit, where three young black women—Effie (Hudson), Deena (Knowles), and Lorell (Rose)?are singing in a talent contest. Sharp wannabe manager Curtis Taylor Jr. (Foxx) takes them on as backup singers to soul shouter James Early (Murphy) and then sees the girl trio's potential to move into pop stardom, as long as the out-of-place Effie, who's a little too black, is replaced. Follows the up-and-down showbiz cliches with lots of intensity even if the music can't compare to the real Motown sound of the 60s and 70s. (Come on—as if the shades of Diana Ross and the Supremes aren't all over the plot.) Anyway, Hudson can belt out her big number, "And I Am Telling You I'm Not Going," with real heartache, and, man, Murphy just scorches the stage. **130m/C; DVD, Blu-Ray, HD-DVD.** Jamie Foxx; Eddie Murphy; Beyonce Knowles; Anika Noni Rose; Jennifer Hudson; Danny Glover; Sharon Leal; Keith D. Robinson; Loretta Devine; *D:* Bill Condon; *W:* Bill Condon; *C:* Tobias Schliessler; *M:* Henry Krieger. Oscars '06: Sound, Support. Actress (Hudson); British Acad. '06: Support. Actress (Hudson); Golden Globes '07: Film--Mus./Comedy, Support. Actor (Murphy), Support. Actress (Hudson); Screen Actors Guild '06: Support. Actor (Murphy), Support. Actress (Hudson).

The Dreaming ♪ ½ **1988** A curse is spawned when whalers attack a group of Australian aborigines, and later unleashed by archaeologists and a young woman who violates her tribe's taboos. Hallucinations and bizarre dreams soon plague the doctor who tried to save her, You havet o wonder if they mention the possibility of infectious tribal curses as a professional hazard in medical school. **87m/C; DVD.** *AU* Arthur Dignam; Penny Cook; Gary Sweet; Laurence Clifford; Kristina Nehm; *D:* Mario Andreacchio; *W:* Mario Andreacchio; Rob George; Stephanie McCarthy; *C:* David Foreman; *M:* Frank Strangio.

Dreaming About You ♪♪ ½ *Anoche Sone Contigo* **1992** Teeangers Toto (Altomaro) and Quique (Mora) are spending their summer break biking around the neighborhood, dreaming about girls, and spying on Chabelita (Aguirre), Quique's family's pretty maid. But Toto will soon be doing more than dreaming when his attractive and experienced cousin Azucena (Perdigon) comes for a visit. Spanish with subtitles. **90m/C; VHS, DVD.** *MX* Martin Altomaro; Moises Ivan Mora; Leticia Perdigon; Patricia Aguirre; *D:* Marisa Sistach; *W:* Jose Buil; *C:* Alex Phillips, Jr.; *M:* Alberto Delgado.

Dreaming of Joseph Lees ♪♪ **1999 (R)** Eva (Morton) has long had fantasies about her worldly older cousin Joseph Lees (Graves), but he's retreated from society after a terrible accident and lives in Italy. Meanwhile, lonely Eva is stuck in boring rural England in 1958. So she's willing to respond to the romantic gestures of working-class Harry Flyte (Ross) and, shockingly, decides to move in with him. Then Eva re-meets Joseph at a family wedding and, perversely, her desire for him only increases, which leads Harry to desperate measures. Strained symbolism pushes the plot but the accomplished performances take up the slack. **92m/C; VHS, Streaming.** *GB* Rupert Graves; Samantha Morton; Lee Ross; Miriam Margolyes; Frank Finlay; Nicholas Woodeson; Holly Aird; *D:* Eric Styles; *W:* Catherine Linstrum; *C:* Jimmy Dibling; *M:* Zbigniew Preisner.

Dreaming Out Loud ♪♪ **1940** Screen debut of popular radio team Lum 'n Abner. The boys get involved in several capers to bring progress to their small Arkansas town. Rural wisecracks make for pleasant outing. First in film series for the duo. **65m/B; VHS, DVD.** Frances Langford; Phil Harris; Clara Blandick; Robert Wilcox; Chester Lauck; Norris Goff; Frank Craven; Bobs Watson; Irving Bacon; *D:* Harold Young.

Dreamland ♪♪♪ **2006 (PG-13)** Well-told (and cast) coming-of-age story. The title refers to the name of the New Mexico trailer park where 18-year-old Audrey (Bruckner) lives with her agoraphobic, hard-drinking, widowed dad Henry (Corbett). Because she's a natural caregiver, Audrey has put her college plans on hold and works at the local mini-mart while also looking out for her best friend Calista (Garner), whose beauty pageant dreams are hindered by her MS. When Mookie (Long) and his family move into the neighborhood, Audrey sets him and Calista up on a date even though she likes the guy herself—and discovers the feeling is mutual. **90m/C; DVD.** Agnes Bruckner; Kelli Garner; Justin Long; John Corbett; Gina Gershon; Chris Mulkey; Brian Klugman; *D:* Jason Matzner; *W:* Tom Willett; *C:* Jonathan Sela; *M:* Anthony Marinelli.

The Dreamlife of Angels ♪♪♪ *La Vie Revee des Anges* **1998** Deceptively simple debut from director Zouca follows the friendship of two opportunistic working class French women, Marie (Regnier) and Isa (Bouchez). Tensions between the two arise when Marie becomes involved with brutal nightclub owner Chriss (Cohn). Zouca had his female leads live together during filming to create the realistic bickering scenes. French with subtitles. **113m/C; VHS, DVD.** *FR* Elodie Bouchez; Natacha Regnier; Gregoire Colin; Jo Prestia; Patrick Mercado; *D:* Erick Zonca; *W:* Erick Zonca; Roger Bohbot; *C:* Agnes Godard; *M:* Yann Tiersen. Cesar '99: Actress (Bouchez), Film.

Dreams and Shadows ♪ ½ **2010** Teenaged Billy has a dead-end job and goes home to care for his bitter, alcoholic paraplegic father John. He's only happy escaping into a dream world where he's a brave, sword-wielding warrior. Billy decides to take his heroics into the real world by getting revenge on the man who crippled his dad but he doesn't know the whole story. **94m/C; DVD.** Shawn Caulin-Young; James Russo; Natalie Garcia Fryman; Londale Theus; Julie Clark; *D:* Tamarat Makonnen; *W:* Tamarat Makonnen; *C:* Grisha Alasadi; *M:* Jeffrey Michael. **VIDEO**

Dreams Lost, Dreams Found ♪ ½ **1987** A young widow journeys from the U.S. to Scotland in search of her heritage. The third "Harlequin Romance Movie." **102m/C; VHS, Streaming.** Kathleen Quinlan; Betsy Brantley; Charles Gray; *D:* Willi Patterson. **CABLE**

Dreams With Sharp Teeth ♪♪♪ *Harlan Ellison: Dreams With Sharp Teeth* **2007** Documentarian Nelson had his hands full depicting such a larger-than-life character as writer Harlan Ellison. Ellison's immense body of work includes more than 2000 published stories as well as episodes for "The Outer Limits" and "Star Trek," but is nearly eclipsed by his own story. Described by friends as "a cranky old Jew" or "a skin graft on a leper" (in the case of good friend Robin Williams), Ellison no doubt has made a few enemies during his journey from runty Cleveland kid bullied by anti-semites to the self-made success, welcoming of any verbal joust, be it with a publishing executive or the driver in the next car. At its best, pic provides a view of the creative world of one of the most renowned popular writers of our time. **96m/C; On Demand.** *D:* Erik Nelson; *C:* Wes Dorman; *M:* Richard Thompson.

Dreamscape ♪♪ ½ **1984 (PG-13)** When a doctor teaches a young psychic how to enter into other people's dreams in order to end their nightmares, somebody else wants to use this psychic for evil purposes. The special effects are far more convincing than the one man-saves-the-country-with-his-psychic-powers plot. **99m/C; VHS, DVD, Blu-Ray, UMD.** Dennis Quaid; Max von Sydow; Christopher Plummer; Eddie Albert; Kate Capshaw; David Patrick Kelly; George Wendt; Jana Taylor; *D:* Joseph Ruben; *W:* Chuck Russell; *C:* Brian Tufano; *M:* Maurice Jarre.

Dredd ♪♪♪ **2012 (R)** Nearly two decades later, Hollywood has atoned for its crimes against a beloved comic character in 1995's awful "Judge Dredd" starring Sylvester Stallone. Paring down the style and removing the tongue-in-cheek nonsense of the first movie in favor of non-stop action, the new Dredd (Urban) is a lean, mean, fighting machine. Trapped inside an enormous future housing project with judge-in-training Cassandra (Thirlby), Dredd must combat an arsenal assembled by the powerful drug lord "Ma-ma" (Headey). Effectively using 3D technology while deftly blending dark humor and stylized special effects, the new Dredd serves as judge, jury, and executioner on the original. **95m/C; DVD, Blu-Ray.** Karl Urban; Olivia Thirlby; Lena Headey; Wood Harris; Langley Kirkwood; *D:* Pete Travis; *W:* Alex Garland; *C:* Anthony Dod Mantle; *M:* Paul Leonard-Morgan.

Dresden ♪♪ ½ **2006** In 1945, German nurse Anna Mauth (Woll) discovers an injured British pilot, Robert Newman (Light), hiding in the hospital's cellar. She first helps him believing he's a German deserter, but even after discovering that Robert's an enemy combatant, Anna can't bring herself to betray him since they've fallen in love. But time is not on their side as the Allied bombing of the city of Dresden is about to begin. Made for German TV; English and German with subtitles. **180m/C; DVD.** *GE* Heiner Lauterbach; Kai Wiesinger; Felicitas Woll; John Light; Benjamin Sadler; Katharina Meinecke; Marie Baumer; ***D:*** Roland Suso Richter; ***W:*** Stefan Kolditz; ***C:*** Holly Fink; ***M:*** Harald Kloser; Thomas Wanker. **TV**

The Dress **1996** The title character turns out to be a very malevolent object indeed, in this Dutch absurdist comedy. The bright blue dress with the striking leaf design first causes havoc for the fabric designer, who's nearly fired, while the garment manufacturers get into a fight over the pattern. The dress goes from wearer to wearer, causing havoc for them all, until it is finally destroyed. Dutch with subtitles. **103m/C; VHS, DVD.** *NL* Henri Garcin; Ariane Schluter; Alex Van Warmerdam; ***D:*** Alex Van Warmerdam; ***W:*** Alex Van Warmerdam; ***C:*** Marc Felperlaan; ***M:*** Vincent van Warmerdam.

The Dress Code *Bruno* **1999 (PG-13)** Eight-year-old Bruno is the kind of meek kid who gets picked on by schoolyard bullies and is a disappointment to his dad. So his grandma comes up with a plan to toughen the kid up. **108m/C; VHS, DVD.** Alex D. Linz; Gary Sinise; Jennifer Tilly; Kathy Bates; Joey Lauren Adams; Shirley MacLaine; Brett Butler; Gwen Verdon; Stacey Halprin; Kiami Davael; ***D:*** Shirley MacLaine; ***W:*** David Ciminello; ***C:*** Jan Kiesser; ***M:*** Chris Boardman.

Dress Gray **1986** Fine, exciting adaptation of the Lucian K. Truscott IV novel about a coverup at an Eastern military academy. Baldwin is cadet Slaight, an upperclassman who finds more secrets than he can handle when a younger cadet (Cassidy), with whom he had an adversarial relationship, is murdered. He's torn between investigating the death or keeping quiet--for the sake of his career if not his life. **192m/C; DVD.** Alec Baldwin; Hal Holbrook; Eddie Albert; Lloyd Bridges; Susan Hess; Timothy Van Patten; Patrick Cassidy; Alexis Smith; James B. Sikking; Lane Smith; ***D:*** Glenn Jordan; ***W:*** Gore Vidal; ***C:*** Gayne Rescher; ***M:*** Billy Goldenberg. **TV**

Dress Parade 1/2 **1927** A familiar plot even during the silent era. In order to win the heart of military commander's daughter Janet (Love), brash amateur boxer Vic (Boyd) enters West Point. He promptly alienates his classmates and the girl he loves because of his cocky behavior and must redeem himself in some heroic manner. **73m/B; Silent; DVD.** William Boyd; Bessie Love; Clarence Gledart; Hugh Allan; Walter Yennyson; Maurice Ryan; Louis Natheaux; ***D:*** Donald Crisp; ***W:*** Douglas Z. Doty; ***C:*** J. Peverell Marley.

Dress to Kill 1/2 *Crossing* **2007** Silly mob story finds Daniel (Spence) making a deathbed promise to his gangster grandpa to take the family business legit while others just want to take over the business, including Uncle Bunny (Peterson). Hooker Davina (Buble) is pressured by Bunny to get some dirt on Danny, which turns out to be some blackmail-worthy photos of Danny wearing women's clothes. **110m/C; DVD.** *CA* Sebastian Spence; Crystal Buble; Alan C. Peterson; Fred Ewanuick; ***D:*** Roger Evan Larry; ***W:*** Sandra Tomc; ***C:*** Kamal Derkaoui; ***M:*** Frank Decarlo.

Dressed for Death 1/2 *Straight on Till Morning; Til Dawn Do Us Part* **1974 (R)** A tale of true love gone bad as a woman is chased and murdered in her castle by the psychopath she loves. **121m/C; VHS, DVD, Blu-Ray.** *GB* Rita Tushingham; Shane Briant; Tom Bell; Annie Ross; Katya Wyeth; James Bolam; Claire Kelly; ***D:*** Peter Collinson.

Dressed to Kill 1/2 **1946** Sherlock Holmes finds that a series of music boxes holds the key to plates stolen from the Bank of England. The plot's a bit thin, but Rathbone/Bruce, in their final Holmes adventure, are always a delight. **72m/B; VHS, DVD.** Basil Rathbone; Nigel Bruce; Patricia Morison; Edmund Breon; Tom Dillon; ***D:*** Roy William Neill; ***W:*** Frank Gruber; Leonard Lee; ***C:*** Maury Gertsman; ***M:*** Hans J. Salter.

Dressed to Kill 1/2 **1980 (R)** Contemporary thriller merges bombastic DePalma with a tense Hitchcockian flare. Sexually unsatisfied Kate (Dickinson) is counseled by her sympathetic shrink Dr. Elliott (Caine) and ends up in bed with a man who catches her eye in a museum. Then Kate's found brutally murdered by prostitute Liz (Allen). Kate's son Peter (Gordon) teams up with Liz to track and lure the killer into their trap. Suspenseful and fast paced. Dickinson's museum scene is wonderfully photographed and edited. DePalma was repeatedly criticized for using a stand-in during the Dickinson shower scene; he titled his next film "Body Double" as a rebuttal. **105m/C; VHS, DVD, Blu-Ray.** Angie Dickinson; Michael Caine; Nancy Allen; Keith Gordon; Dennis Franz; David Margulies; Brandon Maggart; ***D:*** Brian De Palma; ***W:*** Brian De Palma; ***C:*** Ralf Bode; ***M:*** Pino Donaggio.

The Dresser 1/2 **1983 (PG)** Film adaptation of Harwood's play (he also wrote the screen version) about an aging English actor/manager (Finney), his dresser (Courtenay), and their theatre company touring England during WWII. Marvelous showbiz tale is lovingly told, superbly acted. **119m/C; VHS, DVD.** Albert Finney; Tom Courtenay; Edward Fox; Michael Gough; Zena Walker; Eileen Atkins; Cathryn Harrison; ***D:*** Peter Yates; ***W:*** Ronald Harwood; ***M:*** James Horner. Golden Globes '84: Actor--Drama (Courtenay).

The Dresser **2015** A World War II-era drama centered on an aging actor in a touring company. Sir (Hopkins) and his wife Her Ladyship (Watson) have been bringing Shakespeare to the British provinces with their company. Sir becomes so ill that he must be hospitalized, but discharges himself. Though his wife wants him to cancel an upcoming production of King Lear, Sir's dresser Norman (McKellen) believes the show must go on. Norman essentially forces Sir to perform one last time, as their relationship parallels a central one in the play. **105m/C; DVD, Blu-Ray, Streaming, Download.** Emily Watson; Ian McKellen; Sarah Lancashire; Anthony Hopkins; Vanessa Kirby; ***D:*** Richard Eyre; ***W:*** Richard Eyre; ***C:*** Ben Smithard; ***M:*** Stephen Warbeck. **VIDEO**

The Dressmaker 1/2 **2016 (R)** Jocelyn Moorhouse's adaptation of the hit Rosalie Ham book was a massive success in its home country of Australia but a tough sell worldwide. This is a defiantly strange movie—part revenge thriller, part comedy, part drama, part wacky. Winslet stars in the title role, a haute couture dressmaker who returns to her small Australian town in the mid-'50s, seeking revenge. This stylish femme fatale quickly transforms the small town with her stylish designs and her girl power righteousness. Winslet is typically fantastic but the movie gets messy. Davis plays her mother and Hemsworth a love interest. **119m/C; DVD, Blu-Ray.** Kate Winslet; Liam Hemsworth; Hugo Weaving; Sarah Snook; Judy Davis; ***D:*** Jocelyn Moorhouse; ***W:*** Jocelyn Moorhouse; ***C:*** Donald McAlpine; ***M:*** David Hirschfelder.

Drew Peterson: Untouchable **2012** Lifetime true crime story of 30-year Illinois police vet Drew Peterson (Lowe) whose fourth wife Stacy (Cuoco) disappeared in 2007. This questionable circumstance leads to reopening an investigation into the death of Peterson's third wife, Kathleen (Buono), which was originally ruled an accident. All-around unpleasant and Lowe is unbelievable as the egotistical media hungry creep. Based on the book "Fatal Vows" by Joseph Hosey. **120m/C; DVD.** Rob Lowe; Kaley Cuoco; Cara Buono; Catherine Dent; William Mapother; Teddy Sears; ***D:*** Mikael Salomon; ***W:*** Teena Booth; ***C:*** Zoran Popovic; ***M:*** Tree Adams. **VIDEO**

Drew: The Man Behind the Poster 1/2 **2013** This feature-length biographical documentary focuses on the life, career, and influence of poster and commercial artist Drew Struzan. Known primarily for his work creating posters for Indiana Jones, Harry Potter, Back to the Future, and Star Wars movies, Struzan's career also included designing album cover art. The documentary includes interviews with such Hollywood luminaries as George Lucas, Harrison Ford, and Steven Spielberg. **97m/C; DVD, Streaming, Download.** ***D:*** Erik Sharkey; ***W:*** Erik Sharkey; Greg Boas; Charles Ricciardi; Jeff Yorkes; ***C:*** Greg Boas; Thomas Mumme; ***M:*** Ryan Shore.

Drift **2000** Angsty relationship drama concerns Ryan (Lee) who's working in an L.A. coffee shop as he tries to become a screenwriter. He's living with Joel (Dayne) but that situation becomes tenuous when Ryan meets young college student Leo (Roessler) and begins to wonder what would happen if he left Joel to pursue this new relationship. Three talky scenarios are offered. **86m/C; DVD.** *CA* R. T. Lee; Greyson Dayne; Jonathon Roessler; ***D:*** Quentin Lee; ***W:*** Quentin Lee; ***C:*** Quentin Lee; ***M:*** Steven Panoto.

The Drifter 1/2 **1988 (R)** It's psychos, psychos everywhere as a beautiful young woman learns to regret a one-night stand. A good, low-budget version of "Fatal Attraction." Director Brand plays the cop. **90m/C; VHS, DVD.** Kim Delaney; Timothy Bottoms; Miles O'Keeffe; Al Shannon; Thomas Wagner; Larry Brand; ***D:*** Larry Brand; ***W:*** Larry Brand; ***C:*** David Sperling; ***M:*** Rick Conrad.

Drifter **WOOF!** **2009 (R)** Yet another in Feifer's line of serial killer flicks. Drifter Henry Lee Lucas confesses to more than 300 murders between 1975 and his arrest in 1983 but then tries recanting while in prison. Sabato Jr. just doesn't seem creepy/sleazy enough for the loser role. **81m/C; DVD.** Antonio Sabato, Jr.; Kostas Sommer; Kelly Curran; John Diehl; Caia Coley; ***D:*** Michael Feifer; ***W:*** Michael Feifer; Wood Dickinson; ***C:*** Hank Baumert, Jr.; ***M:*** Andres Boulton. **VIDEO**

Drifting Weeds 1/2 *Floating Weeds; The Duckweed Story; Ukigusa* **1959** A remake by Ozu of his 1934 silent film about a troupe of traveling actors whose leader visits his illegitimate son and his lover after years of separation. Classic Ozu. In Japanese with English subtitles. **128m/B; VHS, DVD.** *JP* Ganjiro Nakamura; Machiko Kyo; Haruko Sugimura; Ayako Wakao; ***D:*** Yasujiro Ozu.

The Driftless Area **2016 (R)** A crime drama about fate, based on a novel by Tom Drury. After the death of his parents, optimistic bartender Pierre Hunter (Yelchin) goes back to his small hometown. There, he meets and falls in love with the cryptic Stella (Deschanel). In the process, Pierre becomes entangled in a game of cat and mouse with a criminal over a bag full of cash and a mystery with life changing implications for all of them. **95m/C; DVD, Streaming, Download.** Anton Yelchin; Zooey Deschanel; John Hawkes; Alia Shawkat; Frank Langella; ***D:*** Zachary Sluser; ***W:*** Zachary Sluser; Tom Drury; ***C:*** Daniel Voldheim; ***M:*** Danny Bensi; Saunder Jurriaans. **VIDEO**

Driftwood **1997 (R)** The plot is plebian and the acting uninspired. Lonely sculptor Sarah lives in a remote area along the Northern Ireland coast. She discovers an injured man washed ashore and takes him home to recover. He has amnesia and is willing to believe Sarah when she says they are on an island with limited outside contact. Sarah becomes obsessed with her visitor who eventually gets restless, but she's not about to let him leave. **100m/C; DVD.** *IR* Anne Brochet; James Spader; Barry McGovern; Anna Massey; Aiden Grennell; ***D:*** Ronan O'Leary; ***W:*** Ronan O'Leary; ***C:*** Billy Williams; ***M:*** John Cameron.

Drillbit Taylor **2008 (PG-13)** Three freshman dweebs find high-school life a nightmare, especially when two ruthless bullies are out for blood. Pooling together pocket change and savings, they hire Drillbit Taylor (Wilson), a panhander posing as a freelance body guard with plans to quietly steal from their nice suburban homes. Taylor's scheme is thwarted when he discovers a genuine sympathy for the boys, as well as a budding romance with a teacher (Mann). Wilson is typically sweet and likable, but he's lost in a bland script. **102m/C; DVD, Blu-Ray.** Owen Wilson; Leslie Mann; Troy Gentile; David Dorfman; Alex Frost; Josh Peck; Nate Hartley; ***D:*** Steven Brill; ***W:*** Seth Rogen; Kristofor Brown; ***C:*** Fred Murphy; ***M:*** Christophe Beck.

Driller Killer **WOOF!** **1979 (R)** Frustrated artist goes insane and begins to kill off Manhattan residents with a carpenter's drill. Likewise, the plot is full of holes. Director Ferrara starred in his own film under the name Jimmy Laine. **94m/C; VHS, DVD, Blu-Ray.** Abel Ferrara; Carolyn Marz; Bob DeFrank; Peter Yellen; Baybi Day; Harry Schultz; ***D:*** Abel Ferrara; ***W:*** Nicholas St. John; ***C:*** Ken Kelsch; ***M:*** Joe Delia.

Drinking Buddies 1/2 **2013 (R)** Free spirits, Kate (Wilde) and Luke (Johnson), both work at a Chicago microbrewery and are heavily into supporting the company product and friendly flirting. It might be more except Luke has a longtime girlfriend, Jill (Kendricks), he's avoiding proposing to, and Kate is dating wealthy, older Chris (Livingston). There's a lot of sexual tension between them and when both couples share a weekend at a cabin, too much of their favorite brew turns it into a situation. Familiar, but a move up for mumblecore auteur Swanberg from micro-indie productions. **91m/C; Blu-Ray, Streaming.** Olivia Wilde; Jake Johnson; Anna Kendrick; Ron Livingston; ***D:*** Joe Swanberg; ***W:*** Joe Swanberg; ***C:*** Ben Richardson.

Drive **1996 (R)** A technologically enhanced man (Dacascos), running from biotech corporate hitmen, offers a down-on-his-luck stranger (Hardison) $5 million to drive him from San Francisco to L.A. And he won't take no for an answer. **99m/C; VHS, DVD.** Mark Dacascos; Kadeem Hardison; Brittany Murphy; John Pyper-Ferguson; Tracey Walter; James Shigeta; Masaya Kato; ***D:*** Steve Wang.

Drive 1/2 **2011 (R)** A daringly stylish piece of modern noir, Refn's film plays both like twisted fairy tale and as an ode to the underbelly of Los Angeles. An unnamed stunt driver (Gosling) moonlights as a getaway man and becomes involved in a very dangerous situation when he works to protect the lovely woman (Mulligan) who lives down the hall. The driver only works in two gears, waiting or moving, and Gosling gives him just the right strong, silent edge to become one of the more instantly-iconic characters of the year. And what starts as standard fare gives way to extreme, stylized violence. **100m/C; DVD, Blu-Ray.** Ryan Gosling; Carey Mulligan; Bryan Cranston; Ron Perlman; Christina Hendricks; Albert Brooks; Oscar Isaac; Kaden Leos; ***D:*** Nicolas Winding Refn; ***W:*** Hossein Amini; ***C:*** Newton Thomas (Tom) Sigel; ***M:*** Cliff Martinez.

Drive a Crooked Road **1954** A subdued Rooney stars as lonely mechanic and amateur race driver Eddie, who's properly bamboozled by leggy babe Barbara (Foster) into being the getaway driver in a bank heist. Of course her gangster boyfriend Steve (McCarthy) plans to off the patsy when the job is done but Barbara isn't such a heartless dame after all. A noir with a sunny California setting and attractive scenery--not all of it coming from Foster in a bathing suit on the beach. **83m/B; DVD.** Mickey Rooney; Dianne Foster; Kevin McCarthy; Jack Kelly; Harry Landers; Jerry Paris; Paul Picerni; ***D:*** Richard Quine; ***W:*** Richard Quine; Blake Edwards; ***C:*** Charles Lawton, Jr.

Drive Angry 1/2 **2011 (R)** Silly Charles Bronson revenge flick throwback but with $50 million to splurge on car crashes, explosions, and heaping piles of 3D CGI. Milton (Cage) targets the cult members who killed his daughter and now want to sacrifice his infant granddaughter at the next full moon. Sexy diner waitress Piper (Heard) snags her ex-boyfriend's black 1971 Challenger to join him and the two blood-thirsty mavericks tear up the asphalt in hot pursuit. Luckily, a heavy dose of irony and tongue-in-cheek grindhouse flair keep the roadtrip truckin' but it wears thin. Oddly, Cage's signature maniacal shtick feels toned down compared to the other crazies. **104m/C; Blu-Ray, On Demand.** Nicolas Cage; Amber Heard; William Fichtner; Katy Mixon; Pruitt Taylor Vince; David Morse; Billy Burke; ***W:*** Todd Farmer; ***C:*** Brian Pearson; ***M:*** Michael Wandmacher.

Drive By 1/2 **2001 (R)** Ceasar (Acosta), the young brother of the leader of the neighborhood gang, hates the drugs and murder on the streets, but the pull of gang life is strong. He is tipped off about a set-up of his brother, and must choose between his future and his family. Not quite expertly filmed and acted, but the artistry is secondary to the message. The film's emotion and sincerity come through in the credible script (from obvious life experience). The non-professional actors and location shooting add to the realism. **98m/C; DVD.** Mario Acosta; Felipe Camacho; Alberto Viruena; Raul Salinas; Vincente Zuniga C; ***D:*** Juan J. Frausto; ***W:*** Vincente Zuniga C; Juan J. Frausto; ***C:*** Gennadi Balitski; ***M:*** Christopher Morford. **VIDEO**

Drive Hard 🦴 1/2 **2014** For no particular reason, a couple of Americans wind up in trouble in Australia in this flat action-crime comedy. Former race car driver Peter Roberts (Jane) is eking out a living as a driving instructor when Simon Keller (Cusack) turns up for a lesson. Simon then kidnaps Peter and forces him to be his getaway driver for a bank heist that has lots of angry bad guys (and the cops) after them. **92m/C; DVD, Blu-Ray.** *CA* Thomas Jane; John Cusack; Zoe Ventoura; Christopher Morris; Yesse Spence; ***D:*** Brian Trenchard-Smith; ***W:*** Brian Trenchard-Smith; ***C:*** Tony O'Loughlan; ***M:*** Bryce Jacobs.

Drive-In **WOOF!** **1976 (PG)** A low-budget bomb showing a night in the life of teenage yahoos at a Texas drive-in. **96m/C; VHS, DVD.** Lisa Lemole; Glenn Morshower; Gary Cavagnaro; ***D:*** Rod Amateau.

Drive-In Massacre **WOOF!** **1974 (R)** Two police detectives investigate a bizarre series of slasher murders at the local drive-in. Honk the horn at this one. **78m/C; VHS, DVD, Blu-Ray.** Jake Barnes; Adam Lawrence; Austin Johnson; Douglas Gudbye; Valdesta; ***D:*** Stu Segall; ***W:*** George "Buck" Flower; John Goff.

Drive Me Crazy 🦴🦴 **1999 (PG-13)** Nicole (Hart) and Chase (Grenier) have grown up next door to each other and attend the same high school, but that's all they think they have in common. Pep rallying Nicole yearns to date BMOC Brad (Carpenter), but he's only interested in a rival cheerleader. Slacker-type Chase just wants to hang out at the coffeehouse with his animal activist girlfriend Dulcie (Larter), but he gets dumped hard. They conspire to win their dream dates to the prom by pretending to be a couple in order to provoke jealousy. As the two grow closer, they inevitably fall in love. Unfortunately, they don't do it in a very entertaining or amusing manner. Slow paced, unfunny and trite is no way to go through life, son. Based on the novel "How I Created My Perfect Prom Date" by Todd Strasser. **91m/C; VHS, DVD.** Melissa Joan Hart; Adrian Grenier; Stephen Collins; Faye Grant; Susan May Pratt; Kris Park; Mark Webber; Ali Larter; Mark Metcalf; William Converse-Roberts; Gabriel Carpenter; ***D:*** John Schultz; ***W:*** Rob Thomas; ***C:*** Kees Van Oostrum; ***M:*** Greg Kendall.

Driven 🦴🦴 **2001 (PG-13)** Hotshot rookie racer Jimmy Bly (Pardue) is slipping in the rankings thanks to pressure from his promoter brother (Leonard) and his ongoing affair with Sophia (Warren), the girlfriend of top rival Beau (Schweiger). Owner Henry (Reynolds) brings in former hotshot Joe Tanto (Stallone) to straighten the kid out, but Joe has his own demons, including a horrific, nearlydeadly crash, an ex married to his arch-rival (De la Fuente), and a hovering female reporter (Edwards). There's a lot going on, what with all the CGI-created car crashes, the bed-hopping, and the tempers flaring, but it's all over the road, so as not to tax anyone's attention span. It doesn't get anywhere, but at least it gets there fast. **117m/C; VHS, DVD, Blu-Ray.** Sylvester Stallone; Burt Reynolds; Kip Pardue; Til Schweiger; Gina Gershon; Robert Sean Leonard; Stacy Edwards; Estella Warren; Christian de la Fuente; Brent Briscoe; ***D:*** Renny Harlin; ***W:*** Sylvester Stallone; ***C:*** Mauro Fiore; ***M:*** BT (Brian Transeau).

The Driver 🦴 1/2 **1978 (PG)** A police detective will stop at nothing to catch "The Driver," a man who has the reputation of driving the fastest getaway car around. Chase scenes win out over plot. **131m/C; VHS, DVD, Blu-Ray.** Ryan O'Neal; Bruce Dern; Isabelle Adjani; Ronee Blakley; Matt Clark; ***D:*** Walter Hill; ***W:*** Walter Hill.

Driver's Seat **WOOF!** ***Psychotic; Identikit*** **1973 (R)** Extremely bizarre film with a cult following that was adapted from the novel by Muriel Spark. Liz stars as a deranged woman trying to keep a rendezvous with her strange lover in Rome. In the meantime she wears tacky clothes and delivers stupid lines. **101m/C; VHS, DVD.** *IT* Elizabeth Taylor; Ian Bannen; Mona Washbourne; Andy Warhol; Guido Mannari; Maxence Mailfort; ***D:*** Giuseppe Patroni-Griffi; ***W:*** Giuseppe Patroni-Griffi; Raffaele La Capria; ***M:*** Franco Mannino.

Driveways 🦴🦴🦴 **2019** In a small New York town at the beginning of summer, sensitive Cody (Jaye) helps his mother Kathy (Chau) clean out his late aunt's home so it can be sold. As his mother cleans and learns about her hoarder sister's life, he makes a friend with the lonely old man who lives next door, Del (Dennehy). As their friendship develops, Del tells him little stories about his life, to which Cody listens with awareness. Their conversations ease loneliness they both feel. An understated and moving drama on connection and empathy with outstanding performances by the leads. **83m/C; DVD, Blu-Ray.** Hong Chau; Lucas Jaye; Brian Dennehy; Christine Ebersole; Jeter Rivera; ***D:*** Andrew Ahn; ***W:*** Hannah Bos; Paul Thureen; ***C:*** Ki Jin Kim; ***M:*** Jay Wadley. **VIDEO**

Driving Lessons 🦴🦴 1/2 **2006 (PG-13)** Red-headed Grint gets to step out from just being Harry Potter's sidekick in this cozy generational comedy. Ben is a shy teen who's usually dragged into helping steely mom Laura (Linney) with her Christian charity work, even agreeing to her suggestion of a summer job. He ends up with the alcoholic and somewhat delusional Evie (Walters), an over-the-hill actress who convinces Ben to drive her to Edinburgh, a trip that turns out to be quite eventful. It's a case of dueling divas for the carcass of one bewildered boy—predictable, but it's still a laugh. **98m/C; DVD.** *GB* Julie Walters; Rupert Grint; Laura Linney; Nicholas Farrell; Jim Norton; Tamsin Egerton; Michaelle Duncan; ***D:*** Jeremy Brock; ***W:*** Jeremy Brock; ***C:*** David Katznelson; ***M:*** John Renbourn; Clive Carroll.

Driving Miss Daisy 🦴🦴🦴 1/2 **1989 (PG)** Tender and sincere portrayal of a 25-year friendship between an aging Jewish woman and the black chauffeur forced upon her by her son. Humorous and thought-provoking, skillfully acted and directed, it subtly explores the effects of prejudice in the South. The development of Aykroyd as a top-notch character actor is further evidenced here. Part of the fun is watching the changes in fashion and auto design. Adapted from the play by Alfred Uhry. **99m/C; VHS, DVD, Blu-Ray.** Jessica Tandy; Morgan Freeman; Dan Aykroyd; Esther Rolle; Patti LuPone; ***D:*** Bruce Beresford; ***W:*** Alfred Uhry; ***C:*** Peter James; ***M:*** Hans Zimmer. Oscars '89: Actress (Tandy), Adapt. Screenplay, Film, Makeup; British Acad. '90: Actress (Tandy); Golden Globes '90: Actor--Mus./Comedy (Freeman), Actress--Mus./Comedy (Tandy), Film--Mus./Comedy; Natl. Bd. of Review '89: Actor (Freeman); Writers Guild '89: Adapt. Screenplay.

Drone 🦴🦴 **2017** Ordinary suburban dad Neil (Bean), a CIA subcontractor, bombs villages in the middle east from the comfort of his office chair. Only when a Pakistani (Sabongui) shows up with a briefcase of revenge does it sink in that he might actually be killing more than just bad guys. Intended to be a thinker about the effects of war, but doesn't hit the target. **91m/C; DVD, Blu-Ray.** Sean Bean; Patrick Sabongui; Mary McCormack; Maxwell Haynes; Joel David Moore; ***D:*** Jason Bourque; ***W:*** Jason Bourque; Paul A. Birkett; ***C:*** Graham Talbot; Nelson Talbot; ***M:*** Michael Neilson.

The Drone Virus 🦴 1/2 **2004** A father suspects a conspiracy at a local hospital when his cancer stricken daughter dies during a routine MRI. **96m/C; DVD, Streaming.** Billy Wirth; Maeve Quinlan; Philip Boyd; Michael Ensign; David Jean Thomas; ***D:*** Damon O'Steen; ***W:*** Damon O'Steen; Gerald Clarke; ***C:*** Florian Stadler; ***M:*** Kostas Christides. **VIDEO**

The Drop **2006** Naive college student Carter (Bondies) accepts suspiciously big bucks to drive a sports car from San Francisco to L.A. While waiting in a parking garage for the pickup, Carter gets curious about a briefcase in the trunk and makes the mistake of opening it. Supposed to be spooky; instead, the whole thing is silly and nonsensical. **?m/CDVD.** John Savage; Sean Young; Michael P. Bondies; ***D:*** Kevin Lewis; ***W:*** Kevin Lewis; ***C:*** Chris Wilson. **VIDEO**

The Drop 🦴🦴🦴 **2014 (R)** Crime writer Dennis Lehane returns with a star-studded ensemble piece about a Brooklyn bartender (Hardy) who gets caught up with the criminal element when he realizes that the bar he works at is a "drop" bar, a place where criminals launder money. It's really standard, implausible material that's greatly elevated by an A-list cast also including Rapace and the final performance of Gandolfini. This makes it easier to forgive its tired storyline. Don't go looking for the reinvention of the wheel, but it's a solid genre pic. **106m/C; DVD, Blu-Ray.** Tom (Thomas) Hardy; James Gandolfini; Noomi Rapace; Matthias Schoenaerts; Michael Aronov; ***D:*** Michael R. Roskam; ***W:*** Dennis Lehane; ***C:*** Nicolas Karakatsanis; ***M:*** Marco Beltrami.

Drop Dead Fred **WOOF!** **1991 (PG-13)** As a little girl, Lizzie Cronin had a manic, imaginary friend named Fred, who protected her from her domineering mother. When her husband dumps her 20 years later, Fred returns to "help" as only he can. Although the cast is fine, incompetent writing and direction make this a truly dismal affair. Plus, gutter humor and mean-spirited pranks throw the whole "heart-warming" premise out the window. Filmed in Minneapolis. **103m/C; VHS, DVD.** Phoebe Cates; Rik Mayall; Tim Matheson; Marsha Mason; Carrie Fisher; Daniel Gerroll; Ron Eldard; ***D:*** Ate De Jong; ***W:*** Carlos Davis; Anthony Fingleton; ***M:*** Randy Edelman.

Drop Dead Gorgeous 🦴🦴 1/2 ***Dairy Queens*** **1999 (PG-13)** Oh, the ambitions of stage moms and their daughters in this mockumentary of small-town Minnesota beauty pageants. Satire takes the lowest road whenever possible, because that's where the laughs happen to be. Naive Amber (Dunst) has a trailer-trash babe, Annette (Barkin), for a mom, while rival rich bitch, Becky (Richards), is stuck with the horror that is Gladys (Alley). And someone is taking the contest way too seriously, since other contestants are dropping like flies. Piles it on a little thick sometimes, but overall it works. Watch for Richards' cringe-inducing talent show dance number. **97m/C; VHS, DVD.** Denise Richards; Kirsten Dunst; Kirstie Alley; Ellen Barkin; Allison Janney; Sam McMurray; Mindy Sterling; Amy Adams; Tara Redepenning; Sara Stewart; Shannon Nelson; Matt Malloy; Michael McShane; Brooke Bushman; Will Sasso; Brittany Murphy; Mo Gaffney; Nora Dunn; Amanda Detmer; ***Cameo(s):*** Adam West; ***D:*** Michael Patrick Jann; ***W:*** Lona Williams; ***C:*** Michael Spiller; ***M:*** Mark Mothersbaugh.

Drop Dead Gorgeous 🦴 **2010 (R)** Lame black comedy finds fashion model Cynthia unexpectedly dropping dead at a photo shoot. With a deadline and major money involved, her manager decides to save the campaign by using Cynthia as a designer corpse. **90m/C; DVD.** Jeremy London; Steven Berkoff; Natasha Alam; Ivy Levan; Joshua Cox; Nicholas Irons; Kristen Berman; ***D:*** Phillip Alderton; ***W:*** Phillip Alderton; ***C:*** Zoran Hochstatter; ***M:*** Rajan Kamahl. **VIDEO**

Drop Dead Sexy 🦴🦴 1/2 **2005 (R)** The ick factor seems high but it's more comic/thriller than disturbing. Frank (Lee) and Eddie (Glover) are a couple of smalltime Texas losers: Frank works for a used car dealer, Eddie is a gravedigger, and both moonlight for thug Spider (Vince) to whom they owe money. After seeing the obit of Crystal (Keller), the beautiful blonde wife of the richest man (Berkeley) in town, Frank learns she's been buried with an expensive necklace. He convinces Eddie to dig up the body, only to find the necklace missing. They also can't immediately rebury the corpse. So Eddie takes the body home for safekeeping while Frank tries to come up with another plan. **83m/C; DVD.** Jason Lee; Crispin Glover; Pruitt Taylor Vince; Xander Berkeley; Melissa Keller; Brad Dourif; Lin Shaye; ***D:*** Michael Philip; ***W:*** Michael Philip; ***C:*** Thomas Callaway; ***M:*** Deborah Lurie.

DROP Squad 🦴🦴 **1994 (R)** Not quite on target social satire revolving around buppie Burford Jackson Jr. (La Salle), a token minority ad exec who's job is to push questionable products, using gross stereotypes, to the black community. His family's appalled and Buford becomes a prime target of D.R.O.P. (Deprogramming and Restoration of Pride), a vigilante organization that kidnaps erring black brethren and leads them back to their cultural heritage. Frequently intense performances but the script raises some serious issues on which it doesn't deliver. Based on the short story "The Deprogrammer" by David Taylor. **88m/C; VHS, DVD.** Eriq La Salle; Vondie Curtis-Hall; Ving Rhames; Kasi Lemmons; Vanessa Williams; Nicole Powell; Afemo Omilami; Spike Lee; ***D:*** David C(lark) Johnson; ***W:*** David C(lark) Johnson; Butch Robinson; David Taylor; ***C:*** Ken Kelsch; ***M:*** Michael Bearden.

Drop Zone 🦴🦴 1/2 **1994 (R)** Routine action-thriller finds U.S. marshal Pete Nessip (Snipes) and his brother Terry (Warner) assigned to protect drug cartel snitch Earl Leedy (Jeter). The plane they're on is skyjacked by criminal Moncrief (Busey) who parachutes off with Leedy, Terry's killed, and while Pete's on suspension he decides to go undercover into the world of sky-driving with the aid of ex-con cutie Jessie (Butler). Plot holes are big enough to pilot a plane through but the stunts are good and Snipes is never less than professional. **101m/C; VHS, DVD.** Wesley Snipes; Gary Busey; Yancy Butler; Michael Jeter; Corin "Corky" Nemec; Kyle Secor; Luca Bercovici; Malcolm Jamal Warner; Rex Linn; Grace Zabriskie; Sam Hennings; Claire Stansfield; Mickey Jones; Andy Romano; ***D:*** John Badham; ***W:*** John Bishop; Peter Barsocchini; ***C:*** Roy Wagner; ***M:*** Hans Zimmer.

Drowning by Numbers 🦴🦴🦴 1/2 **1987 (R)** Three generations of women, each named Cissie Colpitts, solve their marital problems by drowning their husbands and making deals with a bizarre coroner. Further strange visions from director Greenaway, complemented by stunning cinematography courtesy of Sacha Vierny. A treat for those who appreciate Greenaway's uniquely curious cinematic statements. **121m/C; VHS, DVD.** *GB* Bernard Hill; Joan Plowright; Juliet Stevenson; Joely Richardson; ***D:*** Peter Greenaway; ***W:*** Peter Greenaway; ***C:*** Sacha Vierny; ***M:*** Michael Nyman.

Drowning Mona 🦴🦴 **2000 (PG-13)** Strident comedy about the low-IQ denizens of small town Verplanck, New York, where everybody still drives a Yugo (the town was a test market). Nasty Mona Dearly (Midler) drives her car into the Hudson River and drowns. It turns out to be murder and Chief Wyatt Rash (DeVito) must investigate. He's not lacking in suspects since Mona was the most hated woman in the community. Everyone in the cast looks like they're enjoying themselves which may be more than the viewer will say. **95m/C; VHS, DVD.** Danny DeVito; Bette Midler; Jamie Lee Curtis; Casey Affleck; Neve Campbell; William Fichtner; Peter Dobson; Marcus Thomas; Kathleen Wilhoite; Tracey Walter; Paul Ben-Victor; Paul Schulze; Mark Pellegrino; ***D:*** Nick Gomez; ***W:*** Peter Steinfeld; ***C:*** Bruce Douglas Johnson; ***M:*** Michael Tavera.

Drowning on Dry Land 🦴🦴 **2000 (R)** After being fired, Hershey decides to take a cross-country trip—by taxi—to find herself in the desert. Naturally, bonding goes on. **90m/C; VHS, DVD.** Barbara Hershey; Naveen Andrews; Carol Lynley; John Doe; Stephen Polk; ***D:*** Carl Colpaert; ***W:*** Julie Jacobs; Sheila Nayar; ***C:*** Dean Lent; ***M:*** Richard Horowitz. **VIDEO**

The Drowning Pool 🦴🦴 **1975 (PG)** Newman returns as detective Lew Harper (after 1966's "Harper") to solve a blackmail case. Uneventful script and stodgy direction, but excellent character work from all the cast members keep this watchable. Title is taken from a trap set for Newman, from which he must escape using most of his female companion's clothing. Adapted from Ross MacDonald's novel about detective Lew Archer. **109m/C; VHS, DVD, Blu-Ray.** Paul Newman; Joanne Woodward; Anthony (Tony) Franciosa; Murray Hamilton; Melanie Griffith; Richard Jaeckel; ***D:*** Stuart Rosenberg; ***W:*** Tracy Keenan Wynn; Walter Hill; ***C:*** Gordon Willis; ***M:*** Charles Fox.

Drug War 🦴🦴🦴 ***Du Zhan*** **2013 (R)** Hong Kong's action wizard Johnnie To brings his sharp bite to mainland China with a story just as smart and complex as his criminal masterminds. After busting a huge drug operation in the big city, a group of Chinese cops led by Captain Zhang (Honglei) push the ringleader (Koo) into going undercover and bringing down the organization from the inside. Never predictable and always speeding towards another chase scene, To's never been better. **107m/C; DVD, Blu-Ray, Download.** *CH* Louis Koo; Ka-tung Lam; Honglei Sun; Yi Huang;

Suet Lam; *D:* Johnnie To; *W:* Ryker Chan; Ka-Fai Wai; Nai-Hoi Yau; Xi Yu; *C:* Siu-keung Cheng; *M:* Xavier Jamaux.

Drug Wars: The Camarena Story ♪♪♪ **1990 (PG-13)** Enrique "Kiki" Camerena (Bauer) is an undercover DEA agent working in Mexico in 1985 His discovery of a major drug operation leads to a top drug kingpin. When his cover is blown, Kiki is kidnapped, tortured, and murdered and the cover-up highlights corruption in the government itself. Based on the book "Desperados" by Elaine Shannon. **130m/C; VHS, DVD.** Steven Bauer; Elizabeth Pena; Miguel Ferrer; Benicio Del Toro; Treat Williams; Craig T. Nelson; Guy Boyd; Tony Plana; Tomas Milian; Raymond J. Barry; Everett McGill; Eddie Velez; Rosalind Chao; *D:* Brian Gibson; *W:* Rose Schacht; Ann Powell; Christopher Canaan; Mel Frohman; *C:* Sandi Sissel; *M:* Charles Bernstein. **TV**

Drugstore Cowboy ♪♪♪ 1/2 **1989 (R)** A gritty, uncompromising depiction of a pack of early 1970s drugstore-robbing junkies as they travel around looking to score. Brushes with the law and tragedy encourage them to examine other life-styles, but the trap seems impossible to leave. A perfectly crafted piece that reflects the "me generation" era, though it tends to glamorize addiction. Dillon's best work to date. Based on a novel by prison inmate James Fogle. **100m/C; VHS, DVD.** Matt Dillon; Kelly Lynch; James Remar; James LeGros; Heather Graham; William S. Burroughs; Beah Richards; Grace Zabriskie; Max Perlich; *D:* Gus Van Sant; *W:* Gus Van Sant; Daniel Yost; *C:* Robert Yeoman; *M:* Elliot Goldenthal. Ind. Spirit '90: Actor (Dillon), Cinematog., Screenplay, Support. Actor (Perlich); L.A. Film Critics '89: Screenplay; N.Y. Film Critics '89: Screenplay; Natl. Soc. Film Critics '89: Director (Van Sant), Film, Screenplay.

Druids ♪♪ 1/2 *Vercingetorix* **2001 (R)** Gallic chieftain Vercingetorix (Lambert) must rally his people when they are threatened by Roman army commander Julius Caesar (Brandauer) in 60 B.C. The action is well-done even if the story drags occassionally. **115m/C; VHS, DVD.** Christopher Lambert; Klaus Maria Brandauer; Max von Sydow; Ines Sastre; Stefan Ivanov; Barnard Pierre Donnadieu; *D:* Jacques Dorfmann; *W:* Jacques Dorfmann; Rospo Pallenberg; Norman Spinrad; *M:* Pierre Charvet. **VIDEO**

Drum WOOF! **1976 (R)** This steamy sequel to "Mandingo" deals with the sordid interracial sexual shenanigans at a Southern plantation. Bad taste at its best. **101m/C; VHS, Blu-Ray, Streaming.** Ken Norton; Warren Oates; Pam Grier; Yaphet Kotto; Fiona Lewis; Isela Vega; Cheryl "Rainbeaux" Smith; *D:* Steve Carver; *C:* Lucien Ballard.

Drum Beat ♪♪ **1954** An unarmed Indian fighter sets out to negotiate a peace treaty with a renegade Indian leader. Bronson is especially believable as chief. Based on historical incident. **111m/C; VHS, DVD.** Alan Ladd; Charles Bronson; Marisa Pavan; Robert Keith; Rodolfo Acosta; Warner Anderson; Elisha Cook, Jr.; Anthony Caruso; *D:* Delmer Daves.

Drumline ♪♪♪ **2002 (PG-13)** Devon Miles, (Cannon), a hip-hop drummer from Harlem, receives a full music scholarship to the fictitious Atlanta A&T University. Although his hotdogging antics brought him recognition at home, they aren't appreciated by bandleader Dr. Lee, who's philosophy is "one band, one sound." The university president is aching for more showmanship during halftime and supports Devon's hot-shot performing. This, along with Devon's wisecracking attitude, grates on section-leader and rival Sean, (Roberts). Stone does well dealing with ethnic issues without falling into character cliches and stereotypes, but with so many issues explored, some ideas go undeveloped. Good story is helped along by the flair and power of the marching band scenes. **118m/C; VHS, DVD, Blu-Ray.** Nick Cannon; Zoe Saldana; Orlando Jones; Leonard Roberts; GQ; Jason Weaver; Earl C. Poitier; Candace Carey; Afemo Omilami; Shay Rountree; Miguel A. Gaetan; J. Anthony Brown; *D:* Charles Stone, III; *W:* Shawn Schepps; Tina Gordon Chism; *C:* Shane Hurlbut; *M:* John Powell.

Drums ♪♪ 1/2 *The Drum* **1938** A native prince helps to save the British army in India from being annihilated by a tyrant. Rich melodrama with interesting characterizations and locale. **96m/B; VHS, DVD.** *GB* Sabu; Raymond Massey; Valerie Hobson; Roger Livesey; David Tree; *D:* Zoltan Korda.

Drums Across the River ♪ 1/2 **1954** A Colorado mining town is going to go bust unless miners can make a deal with the local Ute tribe to mine gold on tribal land. Corrupt mine boss Walker (Bettger) just wants to cause trouble and Gary Brannon (Murphy) and his dad Sam (Brennan) become pawns to break the government treaty with the Cheyenne so the cavalry can be sent in. **78m/C; DVD.** Audie Murphy; Walter Brennan; Lyle Bettger; Lisa Gaye; Hugh O'Brian; Jay Silverheels; Regis Toomey; Morris Ankrum; Mara Corday; Emile Meyer; *D:* Nathan "Jerry" Juran; *W:* John K. Butler; Lawrence Roman; *C:* Harold Lipstein.

Drums Along the Mohawk ♪♪♪ 1/2 **1939** Grand, action-filled saga about pre-Revolutionary America, detailing the trials of a colonial newlywed couple as their village in Mohawk Valley is besieged by Indians. Based on the Walter Edmonds novel, and vintage Ford. **104m/C; VHS, DVD, Blu-Ray.** Henry Fonda; Claudette Colbert; Edna May Oliver; Eddie Collins; John Carradine; Dorris Bowdon; Arthur Shields; Ward Bond; Jessie Ralph; Robert Lowery; *D:* John Ford; *C:* Ray Rennahan.

Drums in the Deep South ♪♪ **1951** A rivalry turns ugly as two former West Point roommates wind up on opposite sides when the Civil War breaks out. Historical drama hampered by familiar premise. **87m/C; VHS, DVD.** James Craig; Guy Madison; Craig Stevens; Barbara Payton; Barton MacLane; *D:* William Cameron Menzies; *W:* Philip Yordan.

Drums of Africa ♪ **1963** Low-budget travelogue uses stock African footage to tell a dull story about three do-gooders on safari in 1897 who get involved in doing away with the slave trade in East Africa. Avalon still finds time to sing. **91m/C; DVD.** Frankie Avalon; Mariette Hartley; Lloyd Bochner; Torin Thatcher; Hari Rhodes; *D:* James B. Clark; *W:* Robin Estridge; *C:* Paul Vogel; *M:* Johnny Mandel.

Drums of Fu Manchu ♪♪♪ **1940** Fu Manchu searches for the scepter of Genghis Khan, an artifact that would give him domination over the East. Brandon smoothly evil as the Devil Doctor. Originally a serial in 15 chapters. **150m/B; VHS, DVD.** Henry (Kleinbach) Brandon; Robert Kellard; George Cleveland; Dwight Frye; Gloria Franklin; Tom Chatterton; Philip Ahn; *D:* William Witney; John English; *W:* Barney A. Sarecky; Frank (Franklyn) Adreon; Norman S. Hall; Morgan Cox; *C:* William Nobles; *M:* Cy Feuer.

Drums of Jeopardy ♪ *Mark of Terror* **1931** A father wanders through czarist Russia and the U.S. to seek revenge on his daughter's killer. Cheap copy of "Dr. Fu Manchu." **65m/B; VHS, DVD.** Warner Oland; June Collyer; Lloyd Hughes; George Fawcett; Mischa Auer; *D:* George B. Seitz.

Drums O'Voodoo WOOF! *She Devil* **1934** A voodoo princess fights to eliminate the town bad guy in this all-black feature that is greatly hampered by shoddy production values. **70m/B; VHS, DVD.** Laura Bowman; J. Augustus Smith; Edna Barr; *D:* Arthur Hoerl.

Drunk Parents ♪ 1/2 **2019 (PG-13)** After Frank (Baldwin) and Nancy (Hayek) Teagarten drop their daughter off for her first year of college, the somewhat wealthy couple realizes the extent of their financial troubles when possessions begin to get repossessed. Struggling to pay their daughter's tuition, the couple hosts a yard sale and engages in heavy drinking which only makes the situation worse. As they try to hide their decreasing net worth, they begin a series of money-making schemes, including renting out a friend's mansion and selling his possessions. Though the comedy has a stellar cast, it's just not one of those "funny drunks." **97m/C; DVD.** Alec Baldwin; Salma Hayek; Jim Gaffigan; Joe Manganiello; Treat Williams; *D:* Fred Wolf; *W:* Fred Wolf; Peter Gaulke; *C:* Timothy A. Burton; *M:* Andrew Feltenstein; John Nau.

Drunken Angel ♪♪♪ *Yoidore tenshi* **1948** Alcoholic doctor gets mixed up with local gangster. Kurosawa's first major film aided by strong performances. With English subtitles. **108m/B; VHS, DVD.** *JP* Toshiro Mifune; Takashi Shimura; Choko Iida; *D:* Akira Kurosawa; *W:* Keinosuke Uegusa; *C:* Takeo Ito; *M:* Fumio Hayasaka.

Drunks ♪♪ **1996 (R)** Ensemble story set in a church basement in Manhattan where a diverse group of people go to their Alcoholics Anonymous meetings. Recovering alcoholic Jim (Lewis) has gone on a bender after his wife's death; Rachel's (Wiest) an overworked doctor with drug and alcohol dependencies; alcoholic Becky's (Dunaway) a divorcee with problem kids; Brenda's (Hamilton) an ex-heroin addict who's HIV positive; Joseph's (Rollins) still haunted by his son's death, which he caused while driving drunk. There's more and everyone gets their chance at the spotlight. Adapted from Lennon's play "Blackout." **88m/C; VHS, DVD.** Richard Lewis; Faye Dunaway; Dianne Wiest; Lisa Gay Hamilton; Howard E. Rollins, Jr.; Parker Posey; Spalding Gray; Amanda Plummer; Calista Flockhart; George Martin; Anna Thomson; *D:* Peter Cohn; *W:* Gary Lennon; *C:* Peter Hawkins; *M:* Joe Delia.

Dry Cleaning ♪♪ *Nettoyage a Sec* **1997** Marrieds Nicole (Miou-Miou) and Jean-Marie (Berling) Kunstler are sharing a midlife crisis. The hard-working owners of a dry cleaning establishment are bored by their routine and decide to visit a racy nightclub where the featured performers are a brother/sister drag act. And before the Kunstlers know quite how it happened, they are both involved with handsome Loic (Merhar), whose sister has suddenly broken up their performing partnership. So Loic is now both working for and living with the Kunstlers and the erotic waters are getting very murky indeed. French with subtitles. **97m/C; VHS, DVD.** *FR* Miou-Miou; Charles Berling; Stanislas Merhar; Mathilde Seigner; *D:* Anne Fontaine; *W:* Anne Fontaine; Gilles Taurand; *C:* Caroline Champetier.

The Dry Land ♪♪ **2010 (R)** Small scale sentimental indie tackling post-war trauma in a small Texas town. Iraq war vet James (O'Nan) returns to his family and their hardscrabble existence in El Paso, taking up a job at the local slaughterhouse. Not surprisingly, he struggles with life and his wife (Ferrera) and best buddy (Ritter) don't know how to help. James jets, picking up war-worn buddy Raymond (Valderrama) along the way, hoping the roadtrip will trigger some pleasant memories. Things go from serious to silly when they visit a friend in the VA hospital, sending the story into fuzzy territory. **92m/C; Blu-Ray.** America Ferrera; Wilmer Valderrama; Jason Ritter; June Raphael; Diego Klatenhoff; Benito Martinez; Ryan O'Nan; Evan Jones; *D:* Ryan Piers Williams; *W:* Ryan Piers Williams; *C:* Gavin Kelly; *M:* Dean Parks.

A Dry White Season ♪♪♪ **1989 (R)** A white Afrikaner living resignedly with apartheid confronts the system when his black gardener, an old friend, is persecuted and murdered. A well-meaning expose that, like many others, focuses on white people. **105m/C; VHS, DVD, Blu-Ray.** Donald Sutherland; Marlon Brando; Susan Sarandon; Zakes Mokae; Janet Suzman; Jurgen Prochnow; Winston Ntshona; Susannah Harker; Thoko Ntshinga; Rowan Elmes; *D:* Euzhan Palcy; *W:* Colin Welland; Euzhan Palcy; *M:* Dave Grusin.

Du Barry Was a Lady ♪♪ 1/2 **1943** Skelton is a washroom attendant who daydreams that he is King Louis XV of France. Dorsey's band gets to dress in period wigs and costumes. **112m/C; VHS, DVD.** Lucille Ball; Gene Kelly; Red Skelton; Virginia O'Brien; Zero Mostel; Dick Haymes; Rags Ragland; Donald Meek; George Givot; Louise Beavers; *D:* Roy Del Ruth; *W:* Irving Brecher; *C:* Karl Freund.

Duane Hopwood ♪♪♪ **2005 (R)** Duane (Schwimmer), a casino pit boss, is a loving husband and father, with a steadfast unwillingness to deal with his alcoholism. It's a sad but familiar story in which Duane watches as his wife (Garofalo) and daughters drift away, he loses his job as a result of a costly mistake, and his life becomes increasingly defined by his drinking schedule, his drinking friends, and his drinking spots. While Duane's alcoholism is never fully resolved, his life is viewed from an entirely human, even sympathetic point of view. Cast somewhat against type, Schwimmer brings a visceral heartache to his portrayal. **83m/C; DVD.** David Schwimmer; Janeane Garofalo; Judah Friedlander; Susan Lynch; Dick Cavett; Steven R. Schirippa; John Krasinski; Lenny Venito; *D:* Matt Mulhern; *W:* Matt Mulhern; *C:* Mauricio Rubinstein; *M:* Michael Rohatyn.

The Duchess ♪♪♪ **2008 (PG-13)** Based on the tempestuous life and times of Georgiana, the Duchess of Devonshire, who was married off by her mother at age 16 to endure a scarring relationship with a husband who demanded obedience and used her for breeding much the way he did his beloved dogs. She grew to become one of Britain's most outspoken liberals and groundbreaking feminists, supporting the American and French revolutions and speaking publicly on politics. Impeccably detailed from the costumes to the sets to Knightly's powerhouse performance, crafted from cold, hard realism rather than some whimsical Jane Austin novel. Despite the historical accuracies, however, it sticks close to genre standards with scenes of endless debate broken up with the usual bed-hopping. **110m/C; Blu-Ray, On Demand.** Keira Knightley; Ralph Fiennes; Dominic Cooper; Hayley Atwell; Charlotte Rampling; Simon McBurney; Aidan McArdle; Georgia King; *D:* Saul Dibb; *W:* Saul Dibb; Jeffrey Hatcher; Anders Thomas Jensen; *C:* Gyula Pados; *M:* Rachel Portman. Oscars '08: Costume Des.; British Acad. '08: Costume Des.

The Duchess and the Dirtwater Fox ♪ 1/2 **1976 (PG)** Period western strung together with many failed attempts at humor, all about a music-hall hooker who meets a bumbling card shark on the make. **105m/C; VHS, DVD.** George Segal; Goldie Hawn; Conrad Janis; Thayer David; *D:* Melvin Frank; *W:* Barry Sandler; *C:* Joseph Biroc; *M:* Charles Fox.

The Duchess of Buffalo ♪♪ **1926** American dancer Marian (Talmadge) is performing in pre-Revolutionary Russia and falls in love with handsome Army officer Vladimir (Carminati). Unfortunately, Marian also draws the lecherous attentions of married Grand Duke Gregory (Martindel), which causes a scandal and a case of mistaken identity in this generally lighthearted farce. **75m/B; Silent; DVD.** Constance Talmadge; Tullio Carminati; Edward Martindel; Madam Rose (Dion) Dione; Chester Conklin; *D:* Sidney Franklin; *W:* Hans Kraly; *C:* Oliver Marsh.

The Duchess of Duke Street ♪♪♪ **1978** Cockney Rosa Lewis (Jones), a clockmaker's daughter born in 1869, goes into service with the ambition to become the best cook in London. She learns from a society household's French chef, where she was a kitchen maid, and eventually won success by an unexpected opportunity to cook for Edward, the Prince of Wales. A marriage-of-convenience and a mysterious legacy allows Rosa to buy the rundown Bentinck Hotel (actually the Cavendish) and cater fashionable dinners. By unceasing hard work, Rosa turns her establishment into an exclusive and discreet haunt for aristocrats, the wealthy, and various celebrities. British series on seven cassettes. **880m/C; VHS, DVD.** *GB* Gemma Jones; Christopher Cazenove; John Welsh; George Pravda; June Brown; Victoria Plucknett; Richard Vernon; Doreen Mantle; Elizabeth Bennett; Donald Burton; John Cater; Holly DeJong; John Rapley; *D:* Cyril Coke; Gerry Mill; Simon Langton; Bill Bain; Raymond Menmuir; *W:* Julian Bond; Julia Jones; Rosemary Anne Sisson; Maggie Wadey; Jeremy Paul; Jack Rosenthal; Bill Craig; John Hawkesworth. **TV**

The Duchess of Idaho ♪♪ 1/2 **1950** Williams tries to help her roommate patch up a romance gone bad, but ends up falling in love herself. MGM guest stars liven up an otherwise routine production. **98m/C; VHS, DVD.** Esther Williams; Van Johnson; John Lund; Paula Raymond; Amanda Blake; Eleanor Powell; Lena Horne; *D:* Robert Z. Leonard.

The Duchess of Langeais ♪♪♪ *Ne Touchez pas la Hache; Don't Touch the Axe* **2007** Set in 1820s Paris during the Restoration. The Duchess of Langeais, Antoinette (Balibar), is pursued by general Armand de Montriveau (Guillaume Depardieu—Gerard's son) who falls for her at first sight. She's a smart socialite, schooled in the ways of high living—he's a handsome Napoleonic war hero with stories of bravery. Although married, she's flattered by his attentions and engages him in a skillful game of cat and mouse. Montriveau eventually is angered by her game and attempts to exact his revenge, which finally piques Antoinette's interest—except now it may be too late. The politics of the period are palpable as the social constraints of the would-be lovers stand sentinel to their unrequited love. Gorgeous settings and painful formalities heighten the cruel irony of the ill-fated lovers, and it's oh-so-enticing to watch. **137m/C; DVD.** *FR IT* Jeanne Balibar; Guillaume Depardieu; Bulle Ogier; Michel Piccoli; Barbet Schroeder; ***D:*** Jacques Rivette; ***W:*** Jacques Rivette; Pascal Bonitzer; Christian Laurent; ***C:*** William Lubtchansky; ***M:*** Pierre Allio.

Duck 🦴 ½ **2005 (PG-13)** Ducks just don't have a lot of personality (unless they're the cartoon kind) so the story of a man and his feathered friend starts at a disadvantage. Aged Arthur (Hall) is homeless in L.A. without family or friends when an orphaned duck starts waddling after him. Arthur decides that he and Joe will head towards the ocean (shouldn't he just find a nice pond?) and as they meander along, they run into the usual assortment of oddballs. **98m/C; DVD.** Philip Baker Hall; French Stewart; Bill Cobs; Bill Brochtrup; ***D:*** Nicole Bettauer; ***W:*** Nicole Bettauer; ***C:*** Ann Etheridge; ***M:*** Alan Ari Lazar.

Duck Season 🦴🦴🦴 *Temporada de patos* **2004 (R)** Left alone one afternoon in a Mexico City apartment, two young teenaged boys settle in with video games. A neighbor girl joins them, wanting to use their oven, followed by the pizza guy (who the boys refuse payment for supposedly being seconds late but who won't leave until he gets his money). This sets the stage for some genuinely warm exchanges among the quartet as they chatter about life and act goofy in the way only aimless youths can. Of course the marijuana-spiked brownies the girl cooks up adds to their careless mood. **90m/B; DVD.** Enrique Arreola; Diego Catano; Daniel Miranda; Danny Perea; ***D:*** Fernando Eimbcke; ***W:*** Fernando Eimbcke; Paula Markovitch; ***C:*** Alexis Zabe; ***M:*** Alejandro Rosso.

Duck Soup 🦴🦴🦴🦴 **1933** The Marx Brothers satiric masterpiece (which failed at the box office). Groucho becomes the dictator of Freedonia, and hires Chico and Harpo as spies. Jam-packed with the classic anarchic and irreverent Marx shtick; watch for the mirror scene. Zeppo plays a love-sick tenor, in this, his last film with the brothers. **70m/B; VHS, DVD, Blu-Ray.** Groucho Marx; Chico Marx; Harpo Marx; Zeppo Marx; Louis Calhern; Margaret Dumont; Edgar Kennedy; Raquel Torres; Leonid Kinskey; Charles Middleton; ***D:*** Leo McCarey; ***W:*** Harry Ruby; Nat Perrin; Bert Kalmar; Arthur Sheekman; ***C:*** Henry Sharp; ***M:*** Harry Ruby; Bert Kalmar. AFI '98: Top 100; Natl. Film Reg. '90.

DuckTales the Movie: Treasure of the Lost Lamp 🦴🦴 ½ **1990 (G)** Uncle Scrooge and company embark on a lost-ark quest, ala Harrison Ford, for misplaced treasure (a lamp that can make the sky rain ice cream). Based on the daily Disney cartoon of the same name, it's more like an extended-version Saturday morning sugar smacks'n'milk 'toon. See it with someone young. **74m/C; VHS, DVD, Streaming.** ***V:*** Alan Young; Christopher Lloyd; Rip Taylor; June Foray; Chuck McCann; Richard Libertini; Russi Taylor; Joan Gerber; Terence McGovern; ***D:*** Bob Hathcock; ***W:*** Alan Burnett; ***M:*** David Newman.

The Dude Bandit 🦴🦴 **1933** An unscrupulous money-lender tries to gain control of a ranch but Gibson comes to the rescue. Gibson actually plays three roles: the rancher's best friend, an aw-shucks cowpoke disguise in order to find out what's going on, and the title character used to bedevil the crooks. **68m/B; VHS, DVD.** Hoot Gibson; Gloria Shea; Hooper Atchley; Skeeter Bill Robbins; Horace Carpenter; Neal Hart; Lafe (Lafayette) McKee; Gordon DeMain; ***D:*** George Melford; ***W:*** Jack Natteford; ***C:*** Tom Galligan; Harry Neumann.

The Dude Goes West 🦴🦴 ½ **1948** East Coast gunsmith Daniel (Albert) plans a move to Arsenic City, Arizona figuring he can make a fortune in the wild west. The only good thing to happen to the tenderfoot on the trail is meeting Liza (Storm), who's got a map to her murdered father's gold mine. Naturally, she needs a little help. **86m/B; DVD.** Eddie Albert; Gale Storm; James Gleason; Binnie Barnes; Gilbert Roland; Barton MacLane; ***D:*** Kurt Neumann; ***W:*** Mary Loos; Richard Sale; ***C:*** Karl Struss; ***M:*** Dimitri Tiomkin.

Dude, Where's My Car? 🦴🦴 **2000 (PG-13)** Slow-witted roommates Jesse and Chester wake one morning to a bizarre, seemingly unexplainable situation. To make matters worse, they appear to have trashed their girlfriends' home the night before and, of course, their car is missing. Dude. Too hung over to remember how this all came to be, the two boys set out to piece things together and, in the process, involve themselves with angry transsexuals, ostriches, and extraterrestrials. Follows the grand tradition of stoned and/or goofball duos like Cheech and Chong, Bill and Ted, and Wayne and Garth, but just can't reach their level. **83m/C; VHS, DVD, UMD.** Ashton Kutcher; Seann William Scott; Jennifer Garner; Marla Sokoloff; Kristy Swanson; David Herman; Charlie O'Connell; Hal Sparks; ***D:*** Danny Leiner; ***W:*** Philip Stark; ***C:*** Robert M. Stevens; ***M:*** David Kitay.

Dudley Do-Right 🦴🦴 ½ **1999 (PG)** Lightning didn't strike twice for Fraser, who successfully starred as Jay Ward's 60s cartoon character "George of the Jungle" and then decided to tackle Ward's brainless-but-noble Canadian Mountie, Dudley. The big goof is still protecting Semi-Happy Valley from the dastardly Snidely Whiplash (Molina), who manages to take over the town and rename it Whiplash City. Snidely is also twirling his mustache in the direction of Dudley's sweetie, fair maiden Nell Fenwick (Parker), which the right-minded Mountie won't allow. Unfortunately, the film only manages a few chuckles. **75m/C; VHS, DVD, Blu-Ray.** Brendan Fraser; Sarah Jessica Parker; Alfred Molina; Robert Prosky; Eric Idle; Alex Rocco; Jack Kehler; Louis Mustillo; Regis Philbin; Kathie Lee Gifford; ***Nar:*** Corey Burton; ***D:*** Hugh Wilson; ***W:*** Hugh Wilson; ***C:*** Donald E. Thorin; ***M:*** Steve Dorff.

Due Date 🦴 ½ **2010 (R)** Peter Highmant (Downey) is flying home to L.A. where his wife (Monaghan) is in labor and finds himself seated next to aspiring actor Ethan Tremlay (Galifianakis). When Ethan innocently comments about bombs and terrorists, the two find themselves tossed from the flight and on the no-fly list with no apparent option but to drive cross-country together, launching them into an updated "Planes, Trains and Automobiles." Pair an uptight suit with a simple-minded dingbat in a car for thousands of miles and you get a fun trip with absurd slapstick action, lowbrow humor, and outrageous car crashes. **100m/C; Blu-Ray.** Robert Downey, Jr.; Zach Galifianakis; Michelle Monaghan; Jamie Foxx; RZA; Juliette Lewis; Danny McBride; ***D:*** Todd Phillips; ***W:*** Todd Phillips; Alan R. Cohen; Adam Freedland; Adam Sztykiel; ***C:*** Lawrence Sher; ***M:*** Christophe Beck.

Due East 🦴🦴 ½ **2002 (PG-13)** Sixteen-year-old Mary Faith (Bryant) is about to be named class valedictorian when she reveals she's pregnant. The small southern town of Due East is scandalized, especially when she refuses to name the father and intends to have the baby. But Mary Faith's predicament yields some unexpected blessings with new friendships and romance. Based on the young adult novels "Due East" and "How I Got Him Back" by Valerie Sayers. **104m/C; VHS, DVD.** Clara Bryant; Robert Forster; Cybill Shepherd; Kate Capshaw; Erich Anderson; Katharine Isabelle; James Kirk; ***D:*** Helen Shaver; ***W:*** Tricia Brock. **CABLE**

Duel 🦴🦴🦴 **1971 (PG)** Spielberg's first notable film, a truly scary made-for-TV exercise in paranoia. A docile traveling salesman is repeatedly attacked and threatened by a huge, malevolent tractor-trailer on an open desert highway. Released theatrically in Europe. **90m/C; VHS, DVD, Blu-Ray.** Dennis Weaver; Lucille Benson; Eddie Firestone; Cary Loftin; Jacqueline Scott; Lou Frizzell; Gene Dynarski; ***D:*** Steven Spielberg; ***W:*** Richard Matheson; ***C:*** Jack Marta; ***M:*** Billy Goldenberg. **TV**

The Duel 🦴🦴 ½ **2016 (R)** This western centers on the small town of Helena, Texas, which harbors dark secrets. Texas Ranger David Kingston (Hemsworth) is sent undercover to Helena to investigate a series of missing persons and murders. His investigation includes the town's charismatic preacher Abraham (Harrelson). David's investigation becomes unexpectedly personal and he is challenged to solve the case before he loses everything to Helena. **110m/C; DVD, Blu-Ray, Streaming, Download.** Woody Harrelson; Liam Hemsworth; Alice Braga; Emory Cohen; Felicity Price; ***D:*** Kieran Darcy-Smith; ***W:*** Matt Cook; ***C:*** Jules O'Loughlin; ***M:*** Craig Eastman.

Duel at Diablo 🦴🦴🦴 **1966** An exceptionally violent film that deals with racism in the Old West. Good casting; western fans will enjoy the action. **103m/C; VHS, DVD, Blu-Ray.** James Garner; Sidney Poitier; Bibi Andersson; Dennis Weaver; Bill Travers; ***D:*** Ralph Nelson.

Duel at Silver Creek 🦴🦴 ½ **1952** A group of claim jumpers murder anyone who gets in their way, including the family of the Silver Kid (Murphy), who's deputized by Sheriff Lightning (McNally) to help him get the varmints. **76m/B; VHS, DVD.** Audie Murphy; Faith Domergue; Stephen McNally; Susan Cabot; Gerald Mohr; Eugene Iglesias; Kyle James; Lee Marvin; ***D:*** Donald Siegel; ***W:*** Gerald Drayson Adams; ***C:*** Irving Glassberg; ***M:*** Hans J. Salter.

Duel in the Sun 🦴🦴🦴 **1946** A lavish, lusty David O. Selznick production of a minor western novel about a vivacious half-breed Indian girl, living on a powerful dynastic ranch, who incites two brothers to conflict. Selznick's last effort at outdoing his epic success with "Gone With the Wind." **130m/C; VHS, DVD, Blu-Ray.** Gregory Peck; Jennifer Jones; Joseph Cotten; Lionel Barrymore; Lillian Gish; Butterfly McQueen; Harry Carey, Sr.; Walter Huston; Charles Bickford; Herbert Marshall; ***D:*** King Vidor; ***W:*** Oliver H.P. Garrett; David O. Selznick; ***C:*** Ray Rennahan; ***M:*** Dimitri Tiomkin.

Duel of Champions 🦴 *Orazi e Curiazi* **1961** It's ancient Rome, and the prodigal gladiator has come home. Now the family must have a duel to decide who will rule. **90m/C; VHS, DVD.** *IT SP* Alan Ladd; Francesca Bett; ***D:*** Ferdinando Baldi.

Duel of Fists 🦴 **1971** When the owner of a boxing institute dies, he instructs his son in his will to go searching for his long-lost brother in Thailand. All he can go on is an old photograph and the knowledge that his brother is a Thai boxer. **111m/C; VHS, DVD.** *CH* David Chiang; Chen Hsing; Ti Lung; Tang Ti; ***D:*** Chen Chang; ***W:*** Kuang Ni.

Duel of Hearts 🦴🦴 **1992** Beautiful Caroline falls in love with wealthy Lord Vane Brecon, who unfortunately is accused of murder. When Caroline tries to help him clear his name she discovers he's hiding a number of secrets. Based on the romance novel "Duel of Love" by Barbara Cartland. Nothing too inspiring here, although regency romance fans will appreciate the attention to detail. **95m/C; DVD.** *UK* Alison Doody; Michael York; Geraldine Chaplin; Benedict Taylor; Billie Whitelaw; Virginia McKenna; Richard Johnson; Jeremy Kemp; Beryl Reid; Suzanna Hamilton; Jolyon Baker; Julie Kate; ***D:*** John Hough; ***W:*** Terence Feely; ***C:*** Terry Cole; ***M:*** Laurie Johnson. **CABLE**

The Duel of the Century 🦴 *Liu Xiao Feng Zhi Jue Zhan Quian Hou* **1981** Two champion swordsmen engage in a duel to the death and an investigation is launched into the cause of the dispute, since they weren't enemies. Mandarin with subtitles or dubbed. **94m/C; DVD.** *CH* Tony Liu; Jason Pai Piao; Hua Yueh; Helen Poon; ***D:*** Yuen Chor; ***W:*** Yu Chin; ***C:*** Chieh Huang; ***M:*** Eddie Wang.

Duel to the Death 🦴🦴 **1982** A legendary battle is held every ten years between the best Japanese and Chinese martial arts experts to determine who's tops. During the Ming Dynasty, as the next duel approaches, the candidates are caught in a war between Shaolin monks and ninjas. Chinese with subtitles. **90m/C; VHS, DVD.** *CH* Damian Lau; Borman Chu; Flora Cheung; ***D:*** Siu-Tung Ching.

The Duelist 🦴🦴 ½ *Duelyant* **2016 (R)** Ambitious Russian period drama set in St. Petersburg in 1860, shrewd Yakovlev (Fyodorov) acts as a replacement for nobleman in duels for money. His partner, Baron Staroe (Wuttke) arranges Yakovlev's assignments in this illegal business. Count Beklemishev (Mashkov) has secretly masterminded Yakovlev's career from the shadows through the baron. As Yakovlev's story unfolds, it becomes clear that he has secrets in his past and a complicated history with Beklemishev. Featuring ornate storytelling and well-crafted visuals, the film offers a complicated yet appealing plot reminiscent of a nineteenth century novel. Russian, German, and Ukrainian with subtitles. **109m/C; DVD.** Pyotr Fyodorov; Vladimir Mashkov; Yuliya Khlynina; Yuri Kolokolnikov; Aleksandr Mizev; ***D:*** Aleksey Mizgirev; ***C:*** Maksim Osadchiy-Korytkovskiy; ***M:*** Igor Vdovin.

The Duellists 🦴🦴🦴 **1977 (PG)** A beautifully photographed picture about the long-running feud between two French officers during the Napoleonic wars. Based on "The Duel" by Joseph Conrad. **101m/C; VHS, DVD, Blu-Ray.** *GB* Keith Carradine; Harvey Keitel; Albert Finney; Edward Fox; Tom Conti; Christina Raines; Diana Quick; William Morgan Sheppard; ***D:*** Ridley Scott.

Duets 🦴🦴 **2000 (R)** Bruce Paltrow misuses the talents of his fine ensemble cast (including daughter Gwyneth) in this off-key comedy-melodrama about karaoke culture. The three subplots each center on a pair of misfits en route to a karaoke contest in Omaha. Ricky (Lewis) is a karaoke hustler who meets his daughter Liv (Paltrow) for the first time after the death of her mother in Las Vegas. Suzi (Bello) is a steely waitress who bullies and beguiles mild cab driver Billy (Speedman) into taking her halfway across the country with the promise of sex. Todd's (Giamatti) a freaked-out businessman fleeing his family and Reggie's (Braugher) a deep-thinking escaped convict with a killer voice. Flashes of feeling and humor offset some of the hokiness of the characters, but not enough to save the movie. **112m/C; VHS, DVD, Blu-Ray.** Gwyneth Paltrow; Maria Bello; Scott Speedman; Andre Braugher; Paul Giamatti; Huey Lewis; Marian Seldes; Kiersten Warren; Angie Phillips; Angie Dickinson; ***D:*** Bruce Paltrow; ***W:*** John Byrum; ***C:*** Paul Sarossy; ***M:*** David Newman.

The DUFF 🦴🦴 ½ **2015 (PG-13)** This ugly duckling comedy shouldn't work but does through the sheer charisma of its talented leading lady, Mae Whitman, miscast as the titular character (Designated Ugly Fat Friend). The film posits that every group of female friends has a DUFF, the girl who they're nice to in theory but doesn't really roll with the most popular young ladies at school. Bianca (Whitman) is startled to learn that she's the DUFF in her school clique and does everything she can to try to change her social status. The script is smarter than a lot of modern teen comedies and Whitman is truly charismatic. **101m/C; DVD, Blu-Ray.** Mae Whitman; Robbie Amell; Bella Thorne; Skyler Samuels; Bianca Santos; Nick Eversman; Ken Jeong; Allison Janney; ***D:*** Ari Sandel; ***W:*** Josh A. Cagan; ***C:*** David Hennings; ***M:*** Dominic Lewis.

Duffy 🦴 ½ **1968** Predictable caper comedy that's too groovy for its own good. Retired thief Duffy (Coburn) is living in Tangiers when he's approached by half-brothers Stephane (Fox) and Antony (Alderton) who want Duffy to steal two million in banknotes from their loathed tycoon dad Charles (Mason). Sexy chick Segolene (York) is an added enticement for Duffy to take the job. **101m/C; DVD.** James Coburn; James Mason; Susannah York; James Fox; John Alderton; Guy Deghy; ***D:*** Robert Parrish; ***W:*** Donald Cammell; Harry Joe Brown, Jr.; ***C:*** Otto Heller; ***M:*** Ernie Freeman.

Duffy of San Quentin 🦴 ½ **1954** Highminded and dull drama based on the memoirs of Clinton T. Duffy, who spent 12 years as the warden at San Quentin. The reform-minded Duffy reaches out to the hardcases, including Edwrad 'Romeo' Harper, who wants a chance to revenge himself on crooked prosecutor John Winant, who sent him away and who's now in the joint himself. **78m/B; DVD.** Paul Kelly; Louis Hayward; George Macready; Joanne Dru; Maureen O'Sullivan; ***D:*** Walter Doniger; ***W:*** Walter Doniger; ***C:*** John Alton; ***M:*** Paul Dunlap.

The Duke 🦴🦴 ½ **1999 (G)** Talk about the dog who has everything! Hubert is the faithful bloodhound companion to the Duke of Dingwall (Neville). When the Duke dies, Hubert inherits everything—even the title! Trusted butler Clive (Doohan) and his niece

Charlotte (Draper) are there to make certain Hubert is safe from the plots of the late Duke's sniveling nephew, Cecil (Muirhead), who wants the estate for himself and even tries to arrange a doggie wedding to get the riches. **88m/C; VHS, DVD.** *CA* James Doohan; John Neville; Courtnee Draper; Oliver Muirhead; Sophie Heyman; Judy Geeson; ***D:*** Philip Spink; ***W:*** Craig Detweiler; Anne Vince; Robert Vince; ***C:*** Mike Southon; ***M:*** Brahm Wenger. **VIDEO**

Duke 🦴🦴 1/2 **2012** Hallmark Channel tear-jerker based on true events. Marine Terry Pulaski returns home from Afghanistan with physical wounds and PTSD. He eventually abandons his family for life on the streets with his dog, Duke. Duke becomes seriously ill but Terry doesn't have money for his care and tells the vet to put him down. The vet isn't ready to give up on the dog and Terry discovers that his daughter Alice hasn't given up on finding him. **87m/C; DVD.** Steven Weber; Sarah Smyth; Allison Hossack; Martin Cummins; Kendall Cross; ***D:*** Mark Jean; ***W:*** Michael J. Murray; ***C:*** Adam Sliwinski; ***M:*** Michael Richard Plowman. **CABLE**

The Duke Is Tops 🦴🦴 1/2 **1938** In Horne's earliest existing film appearance, she's off to attempt the "big-time," while her boyfriend joins a traveling medicine show. **80m/C; VHS, DVD.** Ralph Cooper; Lena Horne; Lawrence Criner; Monte Hawley; Edward Thompson; ***D:*** William Nolte; ***W:*** Phil Dunham; ***C:*** Robert E. Cline; J. Henry Kruse; ***M:*** Harvey Brooks; Ben Ellison.

The Duke of Burgundy 🦴🦴🦴 **2014** Visually striking with a fascinating story, writer/director Strickland's drama could casually be described as a lesbian BDSM expose, but that's not really the heart of what makes this memorable. It's not tawdry in its depiction of a romance that depends on roles of master and servant to stay exciting. Rather, the drama is filmed like a dream, focusing on insect imagery (butterflies coming out cocoons for example) to convey a mood of foreboding dread. At its core, it's about a master who no longer wants to be one and how sexuality can be as complex as a butterfly's wings. **104m/C; DVD.** *UK* Sidse Babett Knudsen; Chiara D'Anna; ***D:*** Peter Strickland; ***W:*** Peter Strickland; ***C:*** Nicholas D. Knowland; ***M:*** Cat's Eyes.

Duke of the Derby 🦴🦴 *Le Gentleman d'Epsom* **1962** A scheming racehorse handicapper bets over his head and ruins his higher-than-means lifestyle. In French with English subtitles. **83m/C; VHS, DVD.** *FR* Jean Gabin; Madeleine Robinson; Frank Villard; Jean (Lefevre) Lefebvre; Jacques Marin; ***D:*** Gilles Grangier; ***W:*** Gilles Grangier; ***C:*** Louis Page; ***M:*** Michel Legrand.

The Dukes 🦴🦴 **2007 (PG-13)** Actor Davi makes his directorial debut in a crime comedy about a golden oldie do-wop group who had a few minor hits in the 1950s. Now occasionally working the nostalgia circuit, George (Palminteri) wants to persuade his fellow Dukes to buy their own nightclub so they can be headliners. But since no one has the money, George's idea is to rob a dental clinic of the gold that's used for dental fillings. **96m/C; DVD.** Robert Davi; Chazz Palminteri; Peter Bogdanovich; Frank D'Amico; Elya Baskin; Miriam Margolyes; Melora Hardin; Bruce Weitz; Joseph Campanella; ***D:*** Robert Davi; ***W:*** Robert Davi; James Andronica; ***C:*** Michael Goi; ***M:*** Nicolas Tenbroek; Butch Barbella; Morris I. Diamond.

The Dukes of Hazzard 🦴🦴 1/2 **2005 (PG-13)** Yee-haw! The '70s TV show jumps (literally!) onto the big screen. Good ole Georgia boys, moonshinin' cousins Bo (Scott) and Luke (Knoxville) Duke try to keep their Hazzard County family farm from corrupt county commissioner Boss Hogg (Reynolds), with the help of Uncle Jessie (Nelson), Daisy (Simpson), and Cooter (Koechner). But then, you knew that, because that was the plot of every episode. This version is a little less lighthearted, but it is funny (thanks to script doctoring by the Broken Lizard troupe), and doesn't take itself as seriously as the show. What it does take seriously are the car chases and stunts, which show off the General Lee, the Dukes' beloved 1969 Dodge Charger, to great effect. If you were a fan then, especially of the General, you'll be pleased. If not, you're probably wondering why they bothered at all. **105m/C; DVD, Blu-Ray, UMD, HD-DVD.** Johnny Knoxville; Seann William Scott; Burt Reynolds; Willie Nelson; M.C. Gainey; Michael Weston; Lynda Carter; David Koechner; Jessica Simpson; Jack Polick; Steve Lemme; Michael Roof; Nikki Griffin; Alice Greczyn; James Roday; Kevin Heffernan; Joe Don Baker; Jacqui Maxwell; ***D:*** Jay Chandrasekhar; ***W:*** Jay Chandrasekhar; Jonathan Davis; ***C:*** Lawrence Sher; ***M:*** Nathan Barr.

The Dukes of Hazzard: The Beginning 🦴 1/2 **2006** All-in-good-fun, raunchy DTV comedy that's something of a prequel to the family-oriented TV series. Cousins Bo and Luke are sent to live with their Uncle Jesse to keep them out of trouble. Only Jesse is a moonshiner having problems with Boss Hogg, who is demanding a big cut of Jesse's illegal earnings. Jesse has Luke and Bo running 'shine throughout the county while minimally-clad cousin Daisy helps out as well. **95m/C; DVD.** Jonathan Bennett; Randy Wayne; Willie Nelson; April Scott; Christopher Macdonald; Harland Williams; Joel David Moore; Sherilyn Fenn; ***D:*** Robert Berlinger; ***W:*** Shane Morris; ***C:*** Roy H. Wagner; ***M:*** John DeFaria. **VIDEO**

Duma 🦴🦴🦴 **2005 (PG)** Family friendly pic with a kid, a cat, and a beautiful setting. Xan (Michaletos) lives on a South African farm and adopts an orphaned cheetah cub he names Duma. When his father (Scott) dies, and Xan and his mom (Davis) must move to the city, Xan is determined to release Duma into the wild himself. Not a very bright idea, especially when he gets lost in the desert—only to be found by the shifty Ripkuna (Walker). Based on fact; adapted from the book "How It Was With Dooms" by Xan and Carol Hopcraft. And no, you can't have a pet cheetah, no matter how cute they are. **100m/C; DVD.** Eamonn Walker; Campbell Scott; Hope Davis; Alexander Michaletos; ***D:*** Carroll Ballard; ***W:*** Karen Janszen; ***C:*** Werner Maritz.

Dumb & Dumber 🦴🦴 1/2 **1994 (PG-13)** Moronic limo driver Lloyd Christmas (Carrey) and equally dense dog groomer Harry Dunne (Daniels) travel (in the hilarious "sheep dog" van) from Rhode Island to Colorado'at one point going east!?to return a briefcase full of cash to a beautiful socialite (Holly). Engaging in all sorts of gross-out bathroom, bodily function, and slapstick humor, this one will definitely not appeal to the stuffy critic or arthouse snob. It will provide plenty of laughs, however embarrassingly rendered, for everyone else. Daniels proves a convincing dimwit sidekick, while Carrey mugs shamelessly. Occasional "Seinfeld" writer Farrelly makes his directorial debut. **110m/C; VHS, DVD, Blu-Ray, UMD.** Jim Carrey; Jeff Daniels; Lauren Holly; Teri Garr; Karen Duffy; Mike Starr; Charles Rocket; Victoria Rowell; Felton Perry; Harland Williams; Rob Moran; Cam Neely; Lin Shaye; Fred Stoller; ***D:*** Peter Farrelly; ***W:*** Bennett Yellin; Bobby Farrelly; Peter Farrelly; ***C:*** Mark Irwin; ***M:*** Todd Rundgren. MTV Movie Awards '95: Comedic Perf. (Carrey), Kiss (Jim Carrey/Lauren Holly); Blockbuster '96: Comedy Actor, V. (Carrey).

Dumb and Dumber To 🦴🦴 **2014 (PG-13)** Funnier than it had any right to be and yet still about a decade too late, this works simply because Carrey and Daniels give it their absolute all. It's certainly not because the Farrelly brothers have any new jokes to tell or filmmaking skills to show off. They catch up with Harry and Lloyd 20 years after their first adventure, and send the pair on another road trip, this time in an effort to find Harry's newly discovered daughter. Even though it's been two decades, the comedic sequel trap of just telling the same joke louder and with more gross-out humor sinks much of the film. **109m/C; DVD, Blu-Ray.** Jim Carrey; Jeff Daniels; Rachel Melvin; Steve Tom; Laurie Holden; Rob Riggle; Kathleen Turner; ***D:*** Bobby Farrelly; Peter Farrelly; ***W:*** Bobby Farrelly; Peter Farrelly; Sean Anders; Mike Cerrone; John Morris; Bennett Yellin; ***C:*** Matthew F. Leonetti; ***M:*** Empire of the Sun.

Dumb and Dumberer: When Harry Met Lloyd 🦴 **2003 (PG-13)** The title is probably the most inspired part of this flick. Harry (Richardson) and Lloyd (Olsen) meet in high school and are immediately recruited to attend a "special needs" class set up by the corrupt principal (Levy) to steal grant money. The school paper's star reporter (Nichols) investigates the scam, setting up possible romance. Richardson and Olsen do a commendable job impersonating Daniels and Carrey, but the charm of the original has been replaced by a double dose of poo and retard jokes, done with less subtlety and class (!) than the Farrelly outing. Stick with the original. **82m/C; VHS, DVD.** Derek Richardson; Eric Christian Olsen; Eugene Levy; Luis Guzman; Cheri Oteri; Rachel Nichols; Elden (Ratliff) Henson; William Lee Scott; Mimi Rogers; Shia LaBeouf; Lin Shaye; Teal Redmann; Josh Braaten; Michelle Krusiec; Julia Duffy; ***D:*** Troy Miller; ***W:*** Troy Miller; Robert Brener; ***C:*** Anthony B. Richmond; ***M:*** Eban Schletter.

Dumbo 🦴🦴 **2019 (PG)** World War I veteran Holt Farrier (Farrell) returned home wounded in body and spirit but must take care of his motherless children, Milly (Parker) and Joe (Hobbins). Formerly a trick horseman, his circus has fallen on hard times. Taking a job with the circus's elephants, his life changes after elephant Mrs. Jumbo gives birth to an unusual looking baby, Dumbo. Milly and Joe learn that the shunned Dumbo can fly, which has an unexpected effect on his life and those around him. This live action remake of the classic Disney animated feature has moving moments but falls short of the classic story. **112m/C; DVD, Blu-Ray.** Colin Farrell; Michael Keaton; Danny DeVito; Eva Green; Alan Arkin; ***D:*** Tim Burton; ***W:*** Ehren Kruger; ***C:*** Ben Davis; ***M:*** Danny Elfman.

Dummy 🦴🦴 **1979** TV movie based on a true crime story. Ghetto teen Donald Lang is taken into custody for allegedly murdering a hooker. But Donald is a deaf-mute who can't read, write, or understand sign language so even his deaf attorney Lowell Meyers doesn't know how to communicate with him. And if Donald can't communicate, how can he aide in his defense? Tidyman adapted from his book. **98m/C; DVD.** LeVar Burton; Paul Sorvino; Brian Dennehy; James D. O'Reilly; Rose Gregorio; Gregg Henry; Steven Williams; Helen Martin; ***D:*** Frank Perry; ***W:*** Ernest Tidyman; ***C:*** Gayne Rescher; ***M:*** Gil Askey. **TV**

Dummy 🦴🦴 **2002 (R)** Sappy farce/latent coming-of-ager about a man and his dummy. Shy outsider Steven (Brody), nearly 30 and still living at home with his parents, embarks on his dream career in ventriloquism. His wooden buddy, along with high-school friend Fanny (Jovovich), give Steven the confidence to woo his pretty unemployment counselor Lorena (Farmiga). Ranges from genuinely sweet to annoyingly cloying. Despite a decent turn from Oscar-winner Brody, who did all his own ventriloquism, lovable schmuck routine wears thin rather quickly. Supports are uniformly strong. **90m/C; VHS, DVD.** Adrien Brody; Milla Jovovich; Illeana Douglas; Vera Farmiga; Jessica Walter; Ron Leibman; Jared Harris; ***D:*** Greg Pritkin; ***W:*** Greg Pritkin; ***C:*** Horacio Marquinez; ***M:*** Paul Wallfisch.

Dune 🦴🦴 **1984 (PG-13)** Lynch's sci-fi opus based on the Frank Herbert novel boasting great set design, muddled scripting, and a good cast. The story: controlling the spice drug of Arrakis permits control of the universe in the year 10991. Paul, the heir of the Atreides family, leads the Freemen in a revolt against the evil Harkhonens who have violently seized control of Arrakis, also known as Dune, the desert planet. That's as clear as it ever gets. **137m/C; VHS, DVD, Blu-Ray, HD-DVD.** Kyle MacLachlan; Francesca Annis; Jose Ferrer; Sting; Max von Sydow; Jurgen Prochnow; Linda Hunt; Freddie Jones; Dean Stockwell; Virginia Madsen; Brad Dourif; Kenneth McMillan; Silvana Mangano; Jack Nance; Sian Phillips; Paul Smith; Richard Jordan; Everett McGill; Sean Young; Patrick Stewart; ***D:*** David Lynch; ***W:*** David Lynch; ***C:*** Freddie Francis; ***M:*** Brian Eno.

Dune 🦴🦴 1/2 *Frank Herbert's Dune* **2000** Frank Herbert's 1965 sci-fi classic was previously made into a disappointing 1984 film by David Lynch. This miniseries more successfully combines visuals with character, although the complicated plot is still somewhat overwhelming. Duke Leto (Hurt) of the House of Atreides has been appointed by the Emperor to harvest and export Spice—the most prized commodity on the desert planet of Arrakis (or Dune). But a rival faction, led by Baron Harkonnen (McNeice), causes trouble for Atreides and his heir, Paul (Newman), who must look to Dune's native inhabitants for support. **270m/C; VHS, DVD, Blu-Ray.** Alec Newman; William Hurt; Saskia Reeves; Ian McNeice; P. H. Moriarty; Julie Cox; Matt Keeslar; Giancarlo Giannini; Barbara Kodetova; Robert Russell; Miljen Kreka Kljakovic; ***D:*** John Harrison; ***W:*** John Harrison; ***C:*** Vittorio Storaro; Harry B. Miller, III; ***M:*** Graeme Revell. **CABLE**

Dungeon of Harrow 🦴 **1964** Unbelievably cheap tale of shipwrecked comrades who encounter a maniacal family on an otherwise deserted island. Not your stranded-on-a-desert-island fantasy come true. Filmed in San Antonio; a harrowing bore. **74m/B; VHS, DVD.** Russ Harvey; Helen Hogan; Bill McNulty; Pat Boyette; ***D:*** Pat Boyette.

Dungeonmaster 🦴 1/2 *Ragewar* **1983 (PG-13)** A warlord forces a computer wiz to participate in a bizarre "Dungeons and Dragons" styled game in order to save a girl held captive. Consists of seven segments, each by a different director. Save yourself the trouble. **80m/C; VHS, Blu-Ray, Streaming.** Jeffrey Byron; Richard Moll; Leslie Wing; Danny Dick; ***D:*** John Carl Buechler; Charles Band; Dave Allen; Stephen Ford; Peter Manoogian; Ted Nicolaou; Rosemarie Turko; ***W:*** Allen Actor; ***M:*** Richard Band.

Dungeons and Dragons 🦴 1/2 **2000 (PG-13)** Based (probably very loosely) on the role-playing game of the same name, "D & D" tells the story of the land of Izmer, whose reformer ruler, Empress Savina (Birch), wants to empower the lowly commoners and put them on equal footing with the ruling Mages. An elitist Mage, Profion (Irons, in an obvious pay-the-bills role) wants to overthrow her. Luckily, she's aided by young hero Ridley (Whalin) and his sidekick Snails (Wayans). It's hard to decide what's more ridiculous: plot, dialogue, settings, effects, costumes, or the idea that anyone would pay to see this mess. The mere title is enough to turn off anyone who never played the game as a kid, and the target audience will probably nit-pick it to death with "that's not like in the game"-type complaints. **107m/C; VHS, DVD.** Justin Whalin; Marlon Wayans; Jeremy Irons; Thora Birch; Zoe McLellan; Kristen Wilson; Lee Arenberg; Bruce Payne; Richard O'Brien; Tom Baker; Robert Miano; ***D:*** Courtney Solomon; ***W:*** Topper Lilien; Carroll Cartwright; ***C:*** Doug Milsome; ***M:*** Justin Caine Burnett.

Dunkirk 🦴🦴🦴 1/2 **2017 (PG-13)** The thrilling true tale of the rescue of 400,000 Allied troops from the shores of Dunkirk, France, in 1940. Writer/director Nolan delivers us into the heart of the war itself, and true to his form, the narrative is non-linear--the beach scenes take place during the week before evacuation, the boat rescue begins the day before, and the air battle transpires during the final hour. Don't look for backstories, character development, or even much dialogue; there's no time for that (and you won't miss it) in this spellbinding, heroic call to action by soldiers and civilians. **106m/C; DVD, Blu-Ray.** Fionn Whitehead; Tom Glynn-Carney; Jack Lowden; Harry Styles; Aneurin Barnard; ***D:*** Christopher Nolan; ***W:*** Christopher Nolan; ***C:*** Hoyte Van Hoytema; ***M:*** Hans Zimmer. Oscars '17: Film Editing, Sound; British Acad. '17: Sound.

Dunston Checks In 🦴🦴 1/2 **1995 (PG)** This just in: Hollywood thinks monkeys are funny. But, as far as "stupid people learn important life lessons from a monkey who wears clothes" movies go, this one's not bad. Robert Grant (Alexander) is the manager of a five-star hotel. His Leona Helmsley-esque boss (Dunaway) is convinced that aristocratic guest Lord Rutledge (Everett) is a travel guide critic who is there to bestow an elusive sixth star on the hotel. Actually he's a jewel thief, and Dunston the orangutan is his accomplice. When Dunston flees from his abusive owner, he's adopted by Grant's two children. Together, Dunston and the kids are left to straighten out the whole mess. **88m/C; VHS, DVD.** Jason Alexander; Faye Dunaway; Eric Lloyd; Rupert Everett; Graham Sack; Paul (Pee-wee Herman) Reubens; Glenn Shadix; Nathan Davis; Jennifer Bassey; ***D:*** Ken Kwapis; ***W:*** Bruce Graham; John Hopkins; ***C:*** Peter Lyons Collister; ***M:*** Miles Goodman.

The Dunwich Horror 🦴🦴 **1970** Young warlock acquires a banned book of evil spells, starts trouble on the astral plane. Stockwell hammy. Loosely based on H. P.

Lovecraft story. **90m/C; VHS, DVD, Blu-Ray.** Sandra Dee; Dean Stockwell; Lloyd Bochner; Ed Begley, Sr.; Sam Jaffe; Joanna Moore; Talia Shire; Barboura Morris; Beach Dickerson; Michael Fox; Donna Baccala; ***D:*** Daniel Haller; ***W:*** Curtis Hanson; Henry Rosenbaum; Ronald Silkosky; ***C:*** Richard C. Glouner; ***M:*** Les Baxter.

Duplex 🦴🦴 **2003 (PG-13)** New York yuppies try to bump off a sweet old lady for her rent-controlled apartment in Brooklyn. Alex (Stiller) and Nancy (Barrymore), however, didn't start out as would-be assassins in the name of real estate. After moving into a picture-perfect duplex downstairs from Mrs. Connell, they discover that, although very old and in poor health, she still manages a host of irksome behaviors. With her health not declining nearly fast enough, the senior-crazed couple are driven to desperate measures. Stiller is top-notch and Barrymore a worthy co-star despite a far-fetched plot that revenge comedy specialist/director DeVito ultimately doesn't sell. **88m/C; VHS, DVD.** Drew Barrymore; Ben Stiller; Eileen Essell; Harvey Fierstein; Justin Theroux; Robert Wisdom; Amber Valletta; James Remar; Maya Rudolph; Swoosie Kurtz; Wallace Shawn; Michelle Krusiec; ***D:*** Danny DeVito; ***W:*** Larry Doyle; ***C:*** Anastas Michos; ***M:*** David Newman.

Duplicity 🦴🦴 **½ 2009 (PG-13)** CIA officer Claire Stenwick (Roberts) and MI6 agent Ray Koval (Owen) have left the world of government intelligence to cash in on the highly profitable cold war raging between two rival multinational corporations. Their mission? Secure the formula for a product that will bring a fortune to the company that patents it first. Pic is a strange but surprisingly effective combination of romantic comedy and crime caper. From the two leads to the lavish hotel suites throughout Europe, everything looks exquisite. While it keeps the viewer guessing who is conning who, it begins to boarder on the absurd with one contrived, implausible double-cross after another. A worthy effort from writer/director Gilroy but not on the level of his excellent "Michael Clayton." **125m/C; Blu-Ray, On Demand.** Julia Roberts; Clive Owen; Tom Wilkinson; Paul Giamatti; Carrie Preston; Thomas (Tom) McCarthy; Denis O'Hare; Kathleen Chalfant; Wayne Duvall; Rick Worthy; Oleg Stefan; ***D:*** Tony Golroy; ***W:*** Tony Golroy; ***C:*** Robert Elswit; ***M:*** James Newton Howard.

Dust 🦴 **½ 2001 (R)** Skewered Euro-western set primarily in a war-torn Macedonia (where it was filmed) at the turn of the 20th century. It begins awkwardly in a present-day New York apartment where the aged Angela (Murphy) holds would-be burglar Edge (Lester) at gunpoint so he will listen to the story of her father and uncle. Gunfighter brothers Luke (Wenham) and Elijah (Fiennes) both fall for prostitute Lilith (Brochet), but it's Elijah who marries her. An embittered Luke eventually winds up in Macedonia, where revolutionary gangs battle the occupying Turks. Luke lends his gun, finds a girl (Kujaca), and then Elijah shows up. The old-west tale is visually stunning (and bloody) but the New York story is intrusive and sentimental. **124m/C; VHS, DVD.** *GB GE IT MA* Joseph Fiennes; David Wenham; Adrian Lester; Rosemary Murphy; Anne Brochet; Nikolina Kujaca; ***D:*** Milcho Manchevski; ***W:*** Milcho Manchevski; ***C:*** Barry Ackroyd; ***M:*** Kiril Dzajkovski.

Dust Be My Destiny 🦴🦴 **1939** Cynical drifter Joe Bell (Garfield) winds up on a prison work farm after a vagrancy charge. He falls for the pretty stepdaughter (Lane) of drunken foreman Garrett (Ridges), who doesn't like what's happening. After a fight, Joe and Mabel go on the lam when Garrett's sudden death leads to a murder charge hanging over Joe's head. **87m/B; DVD.** John Garfield; Priscilla Lane; Alan Hale; Billy Halop; Bobby Jordan; Frank McHugh; Stanley Ridges; ***D:*** Lewis Seiler; ***W:*** Robert Rossen; ***C:*** James Wong Howe; ***M:*** Max Steiner.

Dust Devil 🦴🦴 **1993 (R)** Three travelers find themselves in Namibia's vast desert: a policeman, a woman on the run, and her abusive husband. They all have the misfortune of meeting up with a supernatural being known as the "Dust Devil," who kills humans in order to steal their souls and increase his other worldly powers. **87m/C; VHS, DVD.** *GB* Robert John Burke; Chelsea Field; Zakes Mokae; Rufus Swart; John Matshikiza; William Hootkins; Marianne Saegebrecht; ***D:*** Richard Stanley; ***W:*** Richard Stanley; ***C:*** Steven Chivers; ***M:*** Simon Boswell.

Dust of Life 🦴🦴 *Poussieres de vie* **1995** Set in Vietnam after the fall of Saigon and the withdrawal of American forces in 1975, the film is based on a true story about life under the Communist regime. Internal conflict continues as the former North Vietnam is convinced that those living in what was South Vietnam were corrupted and need to go to re-education camps. Among them are orphaned street boys collected by Northern soldiers. A few boys plot a risky escape from the repressive experience at the Phu Van camp. French and Vietnamese with subtitles. **85m/C; DVD, Streaming.** Daniel Guyant; Gilles Chitlaphone; Jehan Pages; Eric Nguyen; Leon Outtrabady; ***D:*** Rachid Bouchareb; ***W:*** Rachid Bouchareb; Bernard Gesbert; ***C:*** Youcef Sahraoui; ***M:*** Safy Boutella. **VIDEO**

Dust to Glory 🦴🦴🦴 **2005 (PG)** Son of "The Endless Summer" creator Bruce Brown, Dana Brown brings his father's sense of kineticism to the races in this high-octane documentary. The Baja 1000 is the world's more dangerous and notorious race, open to dirt bikes, souped-up VW bugs, 4x4s, and just about anything else. Its dusty trails and Mexican highways are captured in all their white-knuckled madness through the use of 50 different cameras, edited seamlessly. However, once a few of the race's more eccentric characters are introduced along the way, things slow down considerably. It takes a few jump starts to get going now and then, but overall it's a whopping 97-minute condensed version of this 16 hour trek. Racing legends Robby Gordon, Mario Andretti, and Jimmy Vasser join in the fun. **97m/C; DVD.** ***D:*** Dana Brown; ***W:*** Dana Brown; ***C:*** Kevin Ward; ***M:*** Nathan Furst.

Dusty and Sweets Mcgee 🦴 **1971** Some weird leftover hippie tale about the dangers of drug addiction with a 'cast' of real-life, essentially nameless heroin addicts whose delusions about their lives are striking. It's not a documentary, although first-time film director Mutrux started off interviewing the addicts before filming. **87m/C; DVD.** ***D:*** Floyd Mutrux; ***W:*** Floyd Mutrux; ***C:*** William A. Fraker; ***M:*** Ricky Nelson.

Dutch 🦴 **½ 1991 (PG-13)** Working class boob attempts to pick up his girlfriend's son from boarding school. Their trip together gives them an unexpected chance to connect, if they don't kill each other first. Silly premise from the Hughes factory has little innovation and uses type-casting instead of acting. **107m/C; VHS, DVD.** Ed O'Neill; Ethan (Randall) Embry; JoBeth Williams; Elizabeth Daily; ***D:*** Peter Faiman; ***W:*** John Hughes.

Dutch Girls WOOF! 1987 Muddled mayhem as a horny high school field hockey team travels through Holland, cavorts about, and discovers the meaning of life. **83m/C; VHS, DVD.** *GB* Bill Paterson; Colin Firth; Timothy Spall; ***D:*** Giles Foster.

The Dybbuk 🦴🦴🦴 **½** *Der Dibuk* **1937** A man's bride is possessed by a restless spirit. Set in the Polish-Jewish community before WWI and based on the play by Sholom Anski. Considered a classic for its portrayal of Jewish religious and cultural mores. In Yiddish with English subtitles. **123m/B; VHS, DVD.** *PL* Abraham Morewski; Isaac Samberg; Moshe Lipman; Lili Liliana; Dina Halpern; Leon Liebgold; ***D:*** Michal Waszynski; ***W:*** S.A. Kacyzna; Marek Arenstein; ***C:*** Albert Wywerka; ***M:*** Krzysztof Komeda.

The Dying Gaul 🦴🦴🦴 **2005 (R)** Elaine (Clarkson) is one twisted sister—although she has reason to act on her ugly impulses and feelings of betrayal. A former screenwriter, Elaine is the wife of powerful movie exec Jeffrey (Scott), who wants to buy the script of fledgling writer Robert (Sarsgaard). With one large caveat: Robert must change his tragic, autobiographical gay love story into a standard straight tearjerker. Robert caves and winds is seduced by the predatory Jeffrey as well. Elaine goes online under an assumed identity and learns about the affair. Elaine's revenge is outrageous and not too believable. The actors make it somewhat plausible. Lucas adapted his 1998 play for his directorial debut. **105m/C; DVD.** Peter Sarsgaard; Campbell Scott; Patricia Clarkson; ***D:*** Craig Lucas; ***W:*** Craig Lucas; ***C:*** Bobby Bukowski; ***M:*** Steve Reich.

Dying of the Light 🦴 **2014 (R)** Evan Lake (Cage) is a veteran CIA agent ordered to retire after health issues start to decimate his field effectiveness. Lake is forced into one last mission when his protégé, Milton Schultz (Yelchin) uncovers evidence that his nemesis is still alive. Lake and Schultz are forced into action. Viewers are forced to sleep. **94m/C; DVD, Blu-Ray.** Nicolas Cage; Anton Yelchin; Alexander Karim; Irene Jacob; ***D:*** Paul Schrader; ***W:*** Paul Schrader; ***C:*** Gabriel Kosuth; ***M:*** Frederik Wiedmann.

Dying Room Only 🦴🦴 **½ 1973** Travelling through the desert, a woman's husband suddenly disappears after they stop at a secluded roadside diner. A real spooker. **74m/C; VHS, DVD.** Cloris Leachman; Ross Martin; Ned Beatty; Louise Latham; Dana Elcar; Dabney Coleman; ***D:*** Philip Leacock; ***W:*** Richard Matheson; ***M:*** Charles Fox. **TV**

Dying to Get Rich 🦴🦴 *Susan's Plan* **1998 (R)** Slow pacing stunts the humor but doesn't manage to destroy it. Divorced Susan (Kinski) wants her lover, Sam (Zane), to knock off her ex-husband (Paul) so she can collect his life insurance policy. He hires the job out to a couple of losers (Schneider, Biehn), who fail. So the lovers hire a crazy biker (Aykroyd) to finish the job. **90m/C; VHS, DVD.** Nastassja Kinski; Billy Zane; Dan Aykroyd; Rob Schneider; Lara Flynn Boyle; Adrian Paul; Michael Biehn; Carl Ballantine; Thomas Haden Church; Bill Duke; Sheree North; ***D:*** John Landis; ***W:*** John Landis; ***C:*** Ken Kelsch; ***M:*** Peter Bernstein.

Dying Young 🦴 **½ 1991 (R)** Muted romance has a wealthy leukemia victim hire a spirited, unschooled beauty as his nurse. They fall in love, but the film is either too timid or too unimaginative to mine emotions denoted by the title. Nobody dies, in fact, a grim ending (faithful to the Marti Leimbach novel on which this was based) got scrapped after testing poorly with audiences. The actors try their best, photography is lovely, and Kenny G's mellow music fills the soundtrack, but this is basically overmelodramatic drivel. Scott is the late Dewhurst's son. **111m/C; VHS, DVD, Blu-Ray.** Julia Roberts; Campbell Scott; Vincent D'Onofrio; Colleen Dewhurst; Ellen Burstyn; David Selby; ***D:*** Joel Schumacher; ***W:*** Richard Friedenberg; ***C:*** Juan Ruiz-Anchia.

Dylan Dog: Dead of Night 🦴 **½ 2011 (PG-13)** Scattered action-horror-comedy adaptation of Tiziano Sclavi's Italian comic book series. PI Dylan Dog (Routh) and his motor-mouth assistant Marcus (Huntington) work in a retro-noirish New Orleans with its human populace supplemented by vampires, werewolves, and zombies. A murder breaks a truce between the paranormals and humans because someone is after an artifact that's able to control the non-humans. The plot is schlock, Routh is bland in the title role, and the monsters aren't very exciting. **107m/C; Blu-Ray.** Brandon Routh; Sam Huntington; Peter Stormare; Taye Diggs; Kurt Angel; Anita Briem; ***D:*** Kevin Monroe; ***W:*** Thomas Dean Donnelly; Joshua Oppenheimer; ***C:*** Geoffrey Hall; ***M:*** Klaus Badelt.

Dynamite 🦴 **1949** Romance explodes as two young demolitions experts vie for the same girl. Stand back. **68m/B; VHS, DVD.** William Gargan; Virginia Welles; Richard Crane; Irving Bacon; ***D:*** William H. Pine.

The Dynamite Brothers 🦴 **1974 (R)** Two tough guys, one a Hong Kong immigrant with martial arts skills, the other a brother from the streets of the ghetto, team up to rid Los Angeles of a Chinese crimelord. **90m/C; VHS, DVD.** James Hong; Aldo Ray; Alan Tang; Timothy Brown; Carolyn Ann Speed; Don Oliver; ***D:*** Al Adamson; ***M:*** Charles Earland.

Dynamite Chicken 🦴🦴 **1970 (R)** Melange of skits, songs, and hippie satire is dated. Includes performances by Joan Baez, Lenny Bruce, B.B. King, and others. **75m/C; VHS, DVD.** Joan Baez; Richard Pryor; Jimi Hendrix; ***D:*** Ernest Pintoff.

The Dynamiter 🦴 **½ 2011** Low-key, southern-fried family drama. At the start of a Mississippi summer, 14-year-old Robbie is left to take care of his 8-year-old half-brother Fess and his dementia-stricken grandma since his feckless mother has abandoned them once again. His deadbeat older brother Lucas is slithering his way back into their lives and the teenager isn't too young to realize he needs to make some hard choices about choosing his own destiny. **73m/C; DVD.** William Ruffin; John Alex Nunnery; Patrick Rutherford; Joice Baldwin; Ciara McMillan; Sara Fortner; ***D:*** Matthew Gordon; ***W:*** Brad Ingelsby; ***C:*** Jeffrey Waldron; ***M:*** Casey Immoor.

Dynasty 🦴🦴 **1976** Pulitzer Prize-winning author James Michener creates the usual sweeping saga of a family torn by jealousy, deception, and rivalry in love and business as husband, wife, and brother-in-law seek their fortune in the Ohio frontier of the 1820s. **90m/C; VHS, DVD.** Sarah Miles; Harris Yulin; Stacy Keach; Harrison Ford; Amy Irving; Granville Van Dusen; Charles Weldon; Gerrit Graham; ***D:*** Lee Philips; ***W:*** Sidney Carroll; ***C:*** William Cronjager; ***M:*** Gil Melle.

Dynasty of Fear 🦴 **½** *Fear in the Night; Honeymoon of Fear* **1972 (PG)** Matters get rather sticky at a British boys' school when the headmaster's wife seduces her husband's assistant. Together they conspire to murder her husband and share his fortune. **93m/C; VHS, DVD, Blu-Ray.** *GB* Peter Cushing; Joan Collins; Ralph Bates; Judy Geeson; James Cossins; John Bown; Brian Grellis; Gillian Lind; ***D:*** Jimmy Sangster; ***W:*** Jimmy Sangster; Michael Syson; ***C:*** Arthur Grant.

Each Dawn I Die 🦴🦴 **½ 1939** Cagney stars as a reporter who is a fervent critic of the political system. Framed for murder and imprisoned, he is subsequently befriended by fellow inmate Raft, a gangster. Once hardened by prison life, Cagney shuns his friend and becomes wary of the system. Despite its farfetched second half and mediocre script, the film makes interesting viewing thanks to a stellar performance from Cagney. **92m/B; VHS, DVD.** James Cagney; George Raft; George Bancroft; Jane Bryan; Maxie "Slapsie" Rosenbloom; Alan Baxter; Thurston Hall; Stanley Ridges; Victor Jory; ***D:*** William Keighley; ***W:*** Norman Reilly Raine; ***C:*** Arthur Edeson; ***M:*** Max Steiner.

The Eagle 🦴🦴🦴 **1925** In this tale of a young Cossack "Robin Hood," Valentino assumes the persona of the Eagle to avenge his father's murder. The romantic rogue encounters trouble when he falls for the beautiful Banky much to the chagrin of the scorned Czarina Dresser. Fine performances from Valentino and Dresser. Silent, based on a Alexander Pushkin story. Released on video with a new score by Davis. **77m/B; Silent; VHS, DVD, Blu-Ray.** Rudolph Valentino; Vilma Banky; Louise Dresser; George Nichols, Jr.; James A. Marcus; ***D:*** Clarence Brown; ***C:*** George Barnes; ***M:*** Carl Davis.

The Eagle 🦴🦴 **½ 2011 (PG-13)** Set in 140 AD, young centurion Marcus Aquila (Tatum) and his slave Esca (Bell) attempt to solve the long-unexplained disappearance of the entire Ninth Legion in Caledonia. Marcus seeks to mend his commander father's reputation and recover the legion's gold eagle emblem by confronting savage tribes and exploring uncharted highlands. A ho-hum adventure saga that sets out to be a true historical drama gets bogged down in obligatory sword fights, though steers clear of CGI overload. Tatum sufficiently fakes through the emotional stuff and director MacDonald thankfully avoids unnecessary romantic traps. Adapted from Rosemary Sutcliff's 1954 novel "The Eagle of the Ninth." **114m/C; Blu-Ray, On Demand.** Channing Tatum; Jamie Bell; Donald Sutherland; Mark Strong; Denis O'Hare; Douglas Henshall; ***D:*** Kevin MacDonald; ***W:*** Jeremy Brock; ***C:*** Anthony Dod Mantle; ***M:*** Atli Orvarsson.

The Eagle and the Hawk 🦴🦴🦴 **1933** Americans Jerry Young (March), Henry Crocker (Grant), and Mike Richards (Oakie) volunteer for flying duty with the British Army in 1918. Jerry is a heroic pilot but becomes depressed by the horrors of war, while gung ho Henry, who's serving as his observer/gunner, also becomes his rival. On leave, Jerry briefly finds solace with a society babe (Lombard) only to discover on his return that Henry's cockiness has gotten their buddy Mike killed. He denounces the war but Henry manages to ensure Jerry's status as a hero despite his actions. **73m/B; VHS, DVD.** Fredric March; Cary Grant; Jack Oakie; Carole Lombard; Guy Standing; Forrester Harvey; Kenneth Howell; Leyland Hodgson; ***D:*** Stuart Walker; ***W:*** Seton I. Miller; Bogart Rogers; ***C:*** Harry Fischbeck.

Eagle Eye **2008 (PG-13)** Slacker Jerry's (LaBeouf) twin brother has died under suspicious circumstances and single mom Rachel's (Monaghan) child is missing. The two strangers are thrown together when they get mysterious calls on their cell phones from an unknown woman who forces them into one death-defying situation after another, ultimately to frame them as terrorists planning a political assassination. FBI agent Morgan (Thornton) is on their trail but doesn't believe the pair are truly assassins. Too loud and too slick, it borrows unapologetically from better political thrillers while attempting to deliver serious messages about civil liberties, surveillance and technology in a post 9/11 America. **117m/C; DVD, Blu-Ray.** Shia LaBeouf; Michelle Monaghan; Billy Bob Thornton; Rosario Dawson; Michael Chiklis; Cameron Boyce; Bill Smitrovich; Anthony Mackie; Marc Singer; Nick Searcy; Lynn Cohen; Anthony Azizi; ***D:*** D.J. Caruso; ***W:*** Hillary Seitz; Dan McDermott; John Glenn; Travis Adam Wright; ***C:*** Dariusz Wolski; ***M:*** Brian Tyler.

The Eagle Has Landed **1977 (PG)** Duvall, portraying a Nazi colonel in this WWII spy film, commissions Sutherland's Irish, English-hating character to aid him in his mission to kill Prime Minister Winston Churchill. Adapted from the bestselling novel by Jack Higgins. A restored version is available at 134 minutes. **123m/C; VHS, DVD, Blu-Ray.** Michael Caine; Donald Sutherland; Robert Duvall; Larry Hagman; Jenny Agutter; Donald Pleasence; Treat Williams; Anthony Quayle; ***D:*** John Sturges; ***W:*** Tom Mankiewicz; ***C:*** Anthony B. Richmond; ***M:*** Lalo Schifrin.

The Eagle Huntress **2016 (G)** This inspirational documentary tells the true story of Aisholpan, a 13-year-old girl from Mongolia who wants to be the first eagle hunter in her country. Of course, there's no movie if she's not successful in overcoming the gender roles that have been in place for centuries in Mongolia, but it's difficult to deny the moving power of her story. It's also encouraging to see her father train her to rise to the top of what has been a historically male pursuit, proving yet again that people are capable even of that which society has told them they are not. **87m/C; DVD, Blu-Ray.** Daisy Ridley; Aisholpan Nurgaiv; Rys Nurgaiv; ***D:*** Otto Bell; ***C:*** Simon Niblett; ***M:*** Jeff Peters.

Eagle vs. Shark 1/2 **2007 (R)** Lily (Horseley) and Jarrod (Clement) are small-town mall employees united by a decided lack of social skills who meet at a costume party dedicated to dressing as their favorite animals. Lily's sweet, Jarrod's completely unlikable, and something resembling clingy love ensues as the two bounce from awkward situation to awkward situation. Tries to be simultaneously edgy and charming but ultimately just makes jokes at the expense of its protagonists. **94m/C; DVD.** *NZ* Brian Sergent; Craig Hall; Joel Tobeck; Jemaine Clement; Loren Horsley; Rachel House; ***D:*** Taika Waititi; ***W:*** Taika Waititi; ***C:*** Adam Clark; ***M:*** Phoenix Foundation.

Eagles Attack at Dawn 1/2 *The Big Escape; From Hell to Victory; Hostages in the Gulf* **1970 (PG)** After escaping from an Arab prison, an Israeli soldier vows to return with a small commando force to kill the sadistic warden. **96m/C; VHS, DVD.** *IS* Rick Jason; Peter Brown; Joseph Shiloah; Yehuda Barkan; Yehoram Gaon; ***D:*** Menahem Golan; ***W:*** Menahem Golan; ***C:*** Ya'ackov Kallach; ***M:*** Dov Seltzer.

Eagles Over London 1/2 *La Battaglia d'Inghilterra* **1969** Italian-produced war action that's supposed to represent the Battle of Britain. German saboteurs kill a squad of British troops, steal their ID tags, and infiltrate England. Their intention is to blow up coastal radar installations so that the Luftwaffe can bomb London. Captain Paul Stevens discovers what's happening and tries to find the bad guys. **110m/C; DVD.** *IT* Frederick Stafford; Francisco Rabal; Van Johnson; Luigi Pistilli; Ida Galli; Renzo Palmer; ***D:*** Enzo G. Castellari; ***W:*** Enzo G. Castellari; Tito Carpi; Vincenzo Flamini; ***C:*** Alejandro Ulloa; ***M:*** Francesco De Masi.

Eagle's Shadow **1984** After a poor orphan boy rescues an aged beggar, the grateful old man tutors the lad in Snake-Fist techniques. **101m/C; VHS, DVD.** Jackie Chan; Juan Jan Lee; Simon Yuen; Roy Horan; ***D:*** Yuen Woo Ping.

Eagle's Wing 1/2 **1979** John Briley, screenwriter of the award-winning epic "Gandhi," attempts to weave the threads of allegory smoothly in this white man vs. red man Western from England. The mediocre story finds Native American Waterston dueling white trapper Sheen in a quest to capture an elusive, exotic white stallion. **111m/C; VHS, DVD, Blu-Ray.** *GB* Martin Sheen; Sam Waterston; Harvey Keitel; Stephane Audran; Caroline Langrishe; ***D:*** Anthony Harvey; ***W:*** John Briley; ***C:*** Billy Williams.

The Earl of Chicago 1/2 **1940** Downbeat drama with Montgomery starring as a violent Chicago gangster. Orphaned Robert 'Silky' Kilmount learns he's actually British aristocracy when he inherits a title and estate. He's a fish-out-of-water in England even as butler Munsey (Gwenn) tries to teach him some proper manners. Kilmount's got bigger problems since he trusts his manager 'Doc' Ramsey (Arnold) even though he was responsible for Ramsey spending years in the joint. All Ramsey really wants is revenge. **87m/B; DVD.** Robert Montgomery; Edward Arnold; Reginald Owen; Edmund Gwenn; E.E. Clive; Halliwell Hobbes; ***D:*** Richard Thorpe; ***W:*** Lesser Samuels; ***C:*** Ray June.

The Early Bird 1/2 **1925** Union! Union! (And love.) Milkman Jimmy Burke (Hines) attends a costume party and falls for wealthy Jean Blair (Holmquist), who's the president of the Milk Trust. Her manager, George Fairchild (Standing), is crooked and when Jimmy finds out about his schemes he organizes the independent milkmen to defy the company. **79m/B; Silent; DVD.** Johnny Hines; Wyndham Standing; Maude Turner Gordon; Edmund Breese; Sigrid Holmquist; Flora Finch; John ("Jack") De Lacey; Bradley Barker; ***W:*** Argyle Campbell; Victor Grandin; ***C:*** Charles Hines; Charles E. Gilson; John Geisel; Neil Sullivan.

Early Frost 1/2 **1984** Near suspenseful whodunit centering around a simple divorce investigation that leads to the discovery of a corpse. **95m/C; VHS, DVD.** Diana McLean; Jon Blake; Janet Kingsbury; David Franklin; ***D:*** Terry O'Connor.

An Early Frost 1/2 **1985** Highly praised, surprisingly intelligent drama following the anguish of a successful lawyer who tells his closed-minded family that he is gay and dying of AIDS. Sensitive performance by Quinn in one of the first TV films to focus on the devastating effects of HIV. Rowlands adeptly displays her acting talents as the despairing mother. **97m/C; VHS, DVD.** Aidan Quinn; Gena Rowlands; Ben Gazzara; John Glover; D.W. Moffett; Sylvia Sidney; ***D:*** John Erman. **TV**

Early Man **2018 (PG)** A stop-motion animated comedy by the creator of "Wallace and Gromit." Dim yet kind caveman Dug (Redmayne) is part of a prehistoric tribe living in a peaceful valley. Their way of life is threatened by the invasion of a nearby Bronze Age society who want the valley's bronze deposits. Dug is captured and taken to the society's town, where he sees a soccer game for the first time. He challenges the local team to a match for possession of the valley but must first train his tribe in the game. Though full of sports and prehistoric cliches, the film includes much detailed, appealing humor. **89m/C; DVD, Blu-Ray.** Tom Hiddleston; Eddie Redmayne; Maisie Williams; Timothy Spall; Richard Ayoade; ***D:*** Nick Park; ***W:*** Mark Burton; James Higginson; ***C:*** Dave Alex Riddett; ***M:*** Harry Gregson-Williams; Tom Howe.

Early Summer *Bakushu* **1951** A classic from renowned Japanese director Ozu, this film chronicles family tensions in post-WWII Japan caused by newly independent women rebelling against the social conventions they are expected to fulfill. Perhaps the best example of this director's work. Winner of Japan's Film of the Year Award. In Japanese with English subtitles. **150m/B; VHS, DVD.** *JP* Ichiro Sugai; Chishu Ryu; Setsuko Hara; Chikage Awashima; Chieko Higashiyama; Haruko Sugimura; Kuniko Miyake; Kan Nihon-yanagi; Shuji Sano; Toyoko Takahashi; Seiji Miyaguchi; ***D:*** Yasujiro Ozu.

The Earrings of Madame De. . . *Diamond Earrings; Madame De...* **1954** A simple story about a society woman who sells a pair of diamond earrings that her husband gave her, then lies about it. Transformed by Ophuls into his most opulent, overwrought masterpiece, the film displays a triumph of form over content. In French with English subtitles. **105m/C; VHS, DVD, Blu-Ray.** *FR* Charles Boyer; Danielle Darrieux; Vittorio De Sica; Lea di Lea; Jean Debucourt; ***D:*** Max Ophuls; ***W:*** Max Ophuls; Marcel Archard; Annette Wademant; ***C:*** Christian Matras; ***M:*** Oscar Straus; Georges Van Parys.

Earth *Zemlya; Soul* **1930** Classic Russian silent film with English subtitles. Problems begin in a Ukrainian village when a collective farm landowner resists handing over his land. Outstanding camera work. Kino release runs 70 minutes. **101m/B; Silent; VHS, DVD.** *RU* Semyon Svashenko; Nikolai Nademsky; Stephan Shkurat; Yelena Maximova; Yulia Solntseva; ***D:*** Alexander Dovzhenko; ***W:*** Alexander Dovzhenko; ***C:*** Daniil Demutsky.

Earth **1998** The second of Mehta's projected trilogy (after 1997's "Fire"), "Earth" follows the events surrounding the partitioning of India in 1947, forcing neighbors to take sides in a ferocious religious conflict. The story is seen through the eyes of eight-year-old Lenny (Sthna), the daughter of a wealthy Parsi family in Lahore who are trying to remain neutral. But Lenny is cared for by her lovely Hindu nanny, Shanta (Das), whose Muslim suitors are deeply affected by the violence. Based on the novel "Cracking India" by Bapsi Sidhwa. Hindi, Urdu, Parsi, and Punjabi with subtitles. **101m/C; VHS, DVD.** *CA* Aamir Khan; Nandita Das; Rahul Khanna; Maia Sethna; ***D:*** Deepa Mehta; ***W:*** Deepa Mehta; ***C:*** Giles Nuttgens; ***M:*** A.R. Rahman.

Earth 1/2 *Disneynature: Earth* **2007 (G)** Feature-length version of the BBC/Discovery TV series "Planet Earth," which was originally released theatrically in Europe and Japan. The first theatrical release from DisneyNature, it follows the migration of a trio of animal families: polar bears, elephants, and humpback whales using cutting-edge photographic technology, which allowed filming from great distances so as not to disturb the subjects. Fothergill and Linfield worked for five years on the project, including 250 days of aerial photography, at some 200 locations in 64 countries. **90m/C; DVD, Blu-Ray.** *GB GE* ***Nar:*** James Earl Jones; ***D:*** Alastair Fothergill; Mark Linfield; ***W:*** Alastair Fothergill; Mark Linfield; Leslie Megahey; ***M:*** George Fenton.

Earth Girls Are Easy 1/2 **1989 (PG)** Valley girl Valerie is having a bad week: first she catches her fiancee with another woman, then she breaks a nail, then furry aliens land in her swimming pool. What more could go wrong? When the aliens are temporarily stranded, she decides to make amends by giving them a head-to-toe makeover. Devoid of their excessive hairiness, the handsome trio of fun-loving extraterrestrials set out to experience the Southern California lifestyle. Sometimes hilarious sci-fi/musical, featuring bouncy shtick and a gleeful dismantling of modern culture. **100m/C; VHS, DVD.** *GB* Geena Davis; Jeff Goldblum; Charles Rocket; Julie Brown; Jim Carrey; Damon Wayans; Michael McKean; Angelyne; Larry Linville; Rick Overton; Diane Stilwell; Terrance McNally; Stacey Travis; ***D:*** Julien Temple; ***W:*** Julie Brown; Terrance McNally; Charlie Coffey; ***C:*** Oliver Stapleton; ***M:*** Nile Rodgers.

Earth II 1/2 **1971** A space station set up for scientific research and as an example of worldwide peaceful cooperation is threatened when the Chinese launch a nuclear satellite. Astronauts David Seville (Lockwood) and Jim Capa (Hylands) debate the best course of action after failing to disarm the satellite as the Chinese decide to activate their weapon as payback for the station's interference. **94m/C; DVD.** Gary Lockwood; Scott Hylands; Hari Rhodes; Anthony (Tony) Franciosa; Mariette Hartley; Edward Bell; Inga Swenson; Lew Ayres; ***D:*** Tom Gries; ***W:*** Allan Balter; William Read Woodfield; ***C:*** Michel Hugo; ***M:*** Lalo Schrifrin. **TV**

Earth: One Amazing Day **2017 (G)** A beautifully shot sequel to the nature documentary Earth shows the wonders of the natural world. Structured from early morning to late night, the film follows various animals throughout their day and allows viewers to marvel at the intimate details. Stories are told, including the suspenseful escape a newly hatched iguana must make from a group of ravenous snakes and a zebra foal trying to cross a raging river. Comedy comes from such moments as a bear scratching its back on a tree. Though some footage is recycled from other documentaries, the stunning photography and dry narration by Robert Redford make it memorable. **95m/C; DVD.** Robert Redford; Jackie Chan; ***D:*** Richard Dale; Lixin Fan; Peter Webber; ***W:*** Richard Dale; Frank Cottrell Boyce; Geling Yan; ***M:*** Alex Heffes.

Earth to Echo 1/2 **2014 (PG)** There have been a number of Steven Spielberg-inspired films in the last four decades and a number of found footage films in the last two decades. It was time for the two to meet. And so we have this found footage "E.T." rip-off about three kids who find an alien in their neighborhood and try to get the little guy home again. There are echoes of inspiration (pun intended) but the filmmaking here is generic at best. The shaky cam is overdone, the acting is bland and the storytelling is deeply unoriginal. Watch "Super 8" instead. **91m/C; DVD, Blu-Ray.** Brian "Astro" Bradley; Teo Halm; Reese Hartwig; Ella Wahlestedt; Jason Gray-Stanford; ***D:*** Dave Green; ***W:*** Henry Gayden; ***C:*** Maxime Alexandre; ***M:*** Joseph Trapanese.

Earth vs. the Flying Saucers 1/2 *Invasion of the Flying Saucers* **1956** Extraterrestrials land on Earth and issue an ultimatum to humans concerning their constant use of bombs and missiles. Peace is threatened when the military disregards the extraterrestrials' simple warning. Superb special effects by Ray Harryhausen. **83m/B; VHS, DVD.** Hugh Marlowe; Joan Taylor; Donald Curtis; Morris Ankrum; ***D:*** Fred F. Sears; ***W:*** George Worthing Yates; Bernard Gordon; ***C:*** Fred H. Jackman, Jr.; ***M:*** Mischa Bakaleinikoff.

Earth vs. the Spider *The Spider* **1958** Man-eating giant mutant (teenage ninja?) tarantula makes life miserable for a small town in general and high school partyers in particular. Silly old drive-in fare is agony for many, camp treasure for a precious few. **72m/B; VHS, DVD.** Edward Kemmer; June Kenney; Gene Persson; Gene Roth; Hal Torey; Mickey Finn; ***D:*** Bert I. Gordon; ***W:*** Laszlo Gorog; George Worthing Yates; ***C:*** Jack Marta.

Earth vs. the Spider **2001 (R)** Shares the title of the 1958 drive-in feature but not much else. Nerdy comic book fanatic Quentin (Gummersall) works as a security guard at a biotech research lab. After his partner is killed during a break-in, Quentin injects himself with a drug made from a mutated lab spider in the hopes of becoming an avenging superhero. Soon Quentin begins to mutate and no one is safe! **90m/C; VHS, DVD.** Devon Gummersall; Dan Aykroyd; Amelia Heinle; Christopher Cousins; John Cho; Theresa Russell; Mario Roccuzzo; ***D:*** Scott Ziehl; ***W:*** Cary Solomon; Chuck Konzelman; Max Enscoe; Annie de Young; ***C:*** Thomas Callaway; ***M:*** Charles Bernstein. **CABLE**

Earthly Possessions 1/2 **1999 (R)** Sarandon can't really pass for a drab housewife but she does her best in this adaptation of Anne Tyler's novel. Charlotte Emory (Sarandon) is the very sheltered wife of a smalltown minister (Sanders), who longs for a break from her tedious routine. She gets her chance when she's unexpectedly taken hostage by would-be bankrobber, Jake Simms Jr. (Dorff), who suffers from impulse control problems and continual bad luck. Both their fortunes change when Jake forces Charlotte on the road with him (he wants to see his pregnant girlfriend) and an increasingly close bond forms between the two strangers as they try to stay out of police custody. **120m/C; VHS, DVD.** Susan Sarandon; Stephen Dorff; Jay O. Sanders; Elisabeth Moss; Margo Martindale; ***D:*** James Lapine; ***W:*** Steven Rogers; ***C:*** David Franco; ***M:*** Stephen Endelman. **CABLE**

Earthquake **1974 (PG)** Less-than-mediocre drama centers on a major earthquake in Los Angeles and its effect on the lives of an engineer, his spoiled wife, his mistress, his father-in-law, and a suspended policeman. Filmed in much-hyped Sensurround—a technique intended to shake up the theatre a bit, but which will have no effect on your TV set. Good special effects, but not enough to compensate for lackluster script. **123m/C; VHS, DVD, Blu-Ray.** Charlton Heston; Ava Gardner; George Kennedy; Lorne Greene; Genevieve Bujold; Richard Roundtree; Marjoe Gortner; Barry Sullivan; Victoria Principal; Lloyd Nolan; Walter Matthau; Scott Hylands; ***D:*** Mark Robson; ***W:*** Mario Puzo; ***C:*** Philip H. Lathrop; ***M:*** John Williams. Oscars '74: Sound, Visual FX.

Earthquake Bird 🦴🦴 1/2 **2019 (R)** In 1989 Tokyo, a naïve American (Keough) comes between an English translator (Vikander) and her photographer boyfriend, and then disappears. Although beautifully shot, this would-be thriller lacks the psychosexual tension of Susanna Jones's debut novel, delivering a predictable, earth hiccup rather than anything truly ground shaking. **107m/C; DVD, Streaming.** Alicia Vikander; Riley Keough; Naoki Kobayashi; Jack Huston; Kiki Sukezane; ***D:*** Wash Westmoreland; ***W:*** Wash Westmoreland; ***C:*** Chung-hoon Chung; ***M:*** Atticus Ross; Leopold Ross; Claudia Sarne.

Earthquake in Chile 🦴 1/2 *Erdbeben in Chili* **1974** Jeronimo is hired to tutor heiress Josefa and they fall in love. But their forbidden romance is discovered and she's shipped off to a convent; things get worse when it's discovered she's pregnant. Jeronimo tries to rescue her and gets thrown in jail but a fateful earthquake intervenes. German with subtitles; made for German television. **86m/C; DVD.** *GE* Victor Alcazar; Fernando Villena; Julia Pena; Juan Amigo; ***D:*** Helma Sanders-Brahms; ***W:*** Helma Sanders-Brahms; ***C:*** Dietrich Lohmann. **TV**

Earth's Final Hours 🦴 1/2 **2012 (PG-13)** A typical Syfy Channel disaster pic as dense matter from a white hole hits Earth, which could stop the planet's rotation and spell doom. So the feds and the scientists are investigating and a supposedly crazy scientist has a plan for survival if anyone would just listen to him. **91m/C; DVD, Blu-Ray.** Robert Knepper; Julia Benson; Cameron Bright; Bruce Davison; Michael Kropsa; Roark Critchlow; Julia Maxwell; ***D:*** David (W.D.) Hogan; ***W:*** Robert Westcott; ***C:*** Anthony C. Metchie; ***M:*** Michael Neilson. **CABLE**

Earthstorm 🦴 1/2 **2006** Cheesy low-budget B-pic from the Sci-Fi Channel. An asteroid hits the moon, resulting in changes to the ocean's tides that cause massive storms. With the moon now unstable and threatening to break apart, a crew of scientists, plus a demolitions expert, head into space to see if they can prevent further destruction. **89m/C; DVD.** Stephen Baldwin; Dirk Benedict; John Ralston; Jason Blicker; Anna Silk; Amy Price-Francis; Matt Gordon; Conrad Coates; ***D:*** Terry Cunningham; ***W:*** Michael Kenyves; ***C:*** John Tarver. **CABLE**

Easier With Practice 🦴 1/2 **2010** Phone sex. Yep, misfit writer Davy (Geraghty) is a pathetic soul on a disastrous book tour with his mean-spirited younger brother Sean (O'Neill). One night, Davy answers their motel room phone and dirty-talking Nicole (Aselton) is on the line—first titillating Davy with her sexual verbiage and then enticing him with her personal interest as their conversations continue. Since Nicole refuses to personally meet Davy, he finally has to decide if a fantasy is actually enough. **100m/C; DVD.** Brian Geraghty; Katie (Kathryn) Aselton; Marguerite Moreau; Kel O'Neil; Jeanette Brox; Jenna Gavigan; ***D:*** Kyle Patrick Alvarez; ***W:*** Kyle Patrick Alvarez; ***C:*** David Rush Morrison.

The Easiest Way 🦴🦴 1/2 **1931** The way turns out to be not-so-easy for beautiful, poverty-stricken salesclerk Laura (Bennett) who gets a new job modeling for Willard Brockton's (Menjou) agency. Soon she's the suave Brockton's mistress and sending dough to her poor and disapproving family. Laura falls in love with Argentine tycoon Jack (Montgomery), who must suddenly return home to Buenos Aires. When he comes back, he's dismayed to find that Laura has continued her arrangement with Brockton. Includes two markedly different endings. **73m/B; DVD.** Constance Bennett; Adolphe Menjou; Robert Montgomery; Anita Page; J. Farrell MacDonald; Clara Blandick; Marjorie Rambeau; Clark Gable; ***D:*** Jack Conway; ***W:*** Edith Ellis; ***C:*** John Mescall.

The East 🦴🦴 **2013 (PG-13)** Director/writer Batmanglij reunites with Marling, the co-writer/star of "The Sound of My Voice" for this similar but less successful examination of a group of eco-terrorists and the woman who starts off trying to take them down from within but becomes emotionally involved with their cause. Sarah (Marling), an employee for a firm that helps stop groups who try to sabotage businesses, goes undercover with The East, headed by charismatic Benji (Skarsgard) and confident Izzy (Page). Of course, Sarah falls for Benji and the film loses its opportunity for commentary in favor of soap opera melodrama. **116m/C; DVD, Blu-Ray.** Brit Marling; Alexander Skarsgård; Ellen Page; Shiloh Fernandez; Toby Kebbell; Julia Ormond; Patricia Clarkson; ***D:*** Zal Batmanglij; ***W:*** Brit Marling; Zal Batmanglij; ***C:*** Roman Vasyanov; ***M:*** Harry Gregson-Williams.

East Is East 🦴🦴🦴 **1999 (R)** Culture clash comedy is set in 1971 in the northern working-class community of Salford, England. Pakistani immigrant George Khan (Puri) is the would-be stern patriarch to a brood of six sons and one daughter. While he wants to raise his kids traditionally, they're rebelling. Especially in the marriage department: despite his own long marriage to the English Ella (Bassett), George tries to arrange marriages to fellow Pakistanis for his two eldest sons, with disastrous results. Story is swift-paced, definitely not p.c., and is told in amusingly broad strokes. Based on Khan-Din's play. **96m/C; VHS, DVD.** *GB* Om Puri; Linda Bassett; Archie Panjabi; Chris Bisson; Jimi Mistry; Ian Aspinall; Jordan Routledge; Raji James; ***D:*** Damien O'Donnell; ***W:*** Ayub Khan-Din; ***C:*** Brian Tufano; ***M:*** Deborah Mollison. British Acad. '99: Film.

East L.A. Warriors 🦴 1/2 **1989** A mobster, Hilton-Jacobs, manipulates Los Angeles gangs in this non-stop action adventure. **90m/C; VHS, DVD.** Tony Bravo; Lawrence-Hilton Jacobs; Kamar De Los Reyes; William (Bill) Smith; ***D:*** Addison Randall.

East Meets West 🦴🦴 **1936** Arliss steals the movie as the crafty Sultan of Rungay, who plays the British and the Japanese off against each other since they both want to use his country's harbor. Meanwhile, the Sultan's son Nazim is having an affair with the unhappy wife of a British aristocrat, which could cause problems. **74m/B; DVD.** *GB* George Arliss; Lucie Mannheim; Norma Varden; Godfrey Tearle; Ballard Berkeley; Romney Brent; ***D:*** Herbert Mason; ***W:*** Maude Howell; ***C:*** Bernard Knowles.

East of Borneo 🦴 1/2 **1931** Tropical adventure involving a "lost" physician whose worried wife sets out to find him in the jungle. She locates her love only to discover he has a prestigious new job tending to royalty and didn't want to be found. **76m/B; VHS, DVD.** Charles Bickford; Rose Hobart; Georges Renavent; ***D:*** George Melford.

East of Eden 🦴🦴🦴🦴 **1954** Steinbeck's contemporary retelling of the biblical Cain and Abel story receives superior treatment from Kazan and his excellent cast. Dean, in his first starring role, gives a reading of a young man's search for love and acceptance that defines adolescent pain. Though filmed in the 1950s, this story still rivets today's viewers with its emotional message. **115m/C; VHS, DVD, Blu-Ray.** James Dean; Julie Harris; Richard (Dick) Davalos; Raymond Massey; Jo Van Fleet; Burl Ives; Albert Dekker; ***D:*** Elia Kazan; ***W:*** Paul Osborn; ***M:*** Leonard Rosenman. Oscars '55: Support. Actress (Van Fleet); Golden Globes '56: Film--Drama; Natl. Film Reg. '16.

East of Eden 🦴🦴 1/2 **1980** Remade into a TV mini series, this Steinbeck classic tells the tale of two brothers who vie for their father's affection and the woman who comes between them. Seymour is notable as the self-serving mother who abandons her babies to lead a disreputable life. Rife with biblical symbolism and allusions. **375m/C; VHS, DVD.** Jane Seymour; Bruce Boxleitner; Warren Oates; Lloyd Bridges; Anne Baxter; Timothy Bottoms; Soon-Teck Oh; Karen Allen; Hart Bochner; Sam Bottoms; Howard Duff; Richard Masur; Wendell Burton; Nicholas Pryor; Grace Zabriskie; M. Emmet Walsh; Matthew "Stymie" Beard; ***D:*** Harvey Hart. **TV**

East of Fifth Avenue 🦴 **1933** The lives of a group of New York boardinghouse residents are shown. A pregnant showgirl discovers her lover is married although his wife has fallen for another man; an elderly couple want to move to London despite health issues; missing money causes problems for all the residents. **75m/B; DVD.** Dorothy Tree; Wallace Ford; Mary Carlisle; Walter Connolly; Louise Carter; Walter Byron; ***D:*** Albert Rogell; ***W:*** Jo Swerling; ***C:*** Benjamin (Ben H.) Kline.

East of Kilimanjaro 🦴🦴 *The Big Search* **1957** A freelance photographer and a doctor search frantically to find the carrier of a fatal disease near the slopes of the majestic Mt. Kilimanjaro. Routine killer virus flick filmed in Africa. **75m/C; VHS, DVD.** Marshall Thompson; Gaby Andre; Fausto Tozzi; ***D:*** Arnold Belgard.

East of Sudan 🦴🦴 **1964** The British outpost of Barash is overrun by Mahdi forces leading experienced Army private Baker (Quayle) and his new officer Murchison (Fowlds) to rescue a governess (Sims) and her charge (Agutter). They take a boat on a treacherous journey down the Nile, hoping to find a safe refuge in Khartoum. **85m/C; DVD.** *UK* Anthony Quayle; Derek Fowlds; Sylvia Syms; Jenny Agutter; Johnny Sekka; ***D:*** Nathan "Jerry" Juran; ***W:*** Jud Kinberg; ***C:*** Wilkie Cooper; ***M:*** Laurie Johnson.

East of the River 🦴 1/2 **1940** Melodramatic family drama. Joe Lorenzo (Garfield) is an ex-con who comes back to the Lower East Side tenement where he grew up with his shady girlfriend Laurie (Marshall). He reconnects with his beloved Italian mama (Rambeau) and his good guy adopted brother Nick (Lundigan), but Joe is soon in trouble again and takes off, leaving Laurie behind. The dame soon decides she likes the straight and narrow and she and Nick become engaged, which causes a jealous Joe to reappear despite him getting on the wrong side of some mobsters. **73m/B; DVD.** John Garfield; William Lundigan; Brenda Marshall; Marjorie Rambeau; Moroni Olsen; George Tobias; ***D:*** Alfred E. Green; ***W:*** Fred Niblo, Jr.; ***C:*** Sidney Hickox; ***M:*** Adolph Deutsch.

East Palace, West Palace 🦴🦴 *Behind the Forbidden City; Donggong, Xigong* **1996** Bold and controversial examination of a shadow world in Chinese society. A-Lan (Han) is a young homosexual, cruising the park outside the Forbidden Palace in Beijing. He's detained in a roundup by a cop, Xiao Shi (Jun), who takes him to the park's police station for interrogation. A-Lan is unashamed of his lifestyle and the cop presses him to tell his life story. It soon becomes clear that the Xiao Shi, though outwardedly homophobic, is actually sexually intrigued by A-Lan's presence as the duo mentally and verbally dance around the charged situation. Chinese with subtitles. **95m/C; VHS, DVD.** *CH* Si Han; Hu Jun; ***D:*** Zhang Yuan; ***W:*** Zhang Yuan; Wang Xiaobo; ***C:*** Zheng Jian; ***M:*** Xiang Min.

East Side of Heaven 🦴🦴 **1939** Denny (Crosby) is hired by drunken Cyrus Barrett Jr. (Kent) to deliver a singing telegram to his crusty father (Smith), who is threatening to take custody of his baby grandson. Mona (Hervey), Junior's wife, is an old friend of Denny's and leaves her son with him to sort out her troubled marriage. Denny's interference costs him his job and his chance to marry longtime girlfriend Mary (Blondell). Meanwhile, gossip columnist Claudius De Wolfe (Cowan) discovers that Denny is actually a long-lost relation of Barrett Sr. **88m/B; DVD.** Joan Blondell; Mischa Auer; Irene Hervey; Bing Crosby; Sir C. Aubrey Smith; Robert Kent; Jerome Cowan; ***D:*** David Butler; ***W:*** William Conselman; ***C:*** George Robinson; ***M:*** Johnny Burke.

East Side Story 🦴 1/2 **2007** Handsome Diego's (Alvarado) life is in upheaval: he feels obligated to keep working in his grandma's (De Bari) Mexican restaurant rather than pursue his own dreams; his closeted boyfriend (Beron) just broke up with him; he's been outed by his desperate Aunt Blanca (Jimenez); and his East L.A. neighborhood is being gentrified. The last may not be so bad since Anglo Wesley (Callahan) moves in across the street—along with his jealous, patronizing boyfriend Jonathan (Schneider). Still, Diego may find more than one dream coming true. Some over-the-top performances mar what is frequently a sweet story. **88m/C; DVD.** David Beron; Rene Alvarado; Steve Callahan; Cory Alan Schneider; Irene De Bari; Gladise Jimenez; ***D:*** Carlos Portugal; ***W:*** Carlos Portugal; Charo Toledo; ***C:*** Neil De la Pena; ***M:*** Steven Cahill.

East Side Sushi 🦴🦴🦴 **2015 (PG)** In this drama, a woman overcomes naysayers to achieve her goals. Juana (Torres) uses her talents at fruit-vending cart where she slice and dices everything with speed and precision. To gain more job security and benefits, she finds a job at a Japanese restaurant where she learns how to make sushi. Juana soon applies her culinary talents to create fusion of Mexican and sushi, and decides to become a sushi chef on her own. Though she is told that she is not of the correct race or gender to become a sushi chef, Juana fights to achieve her goals despite the obstacles blocking her path. **100m/C; DVD, Streaming, Download.** Diana Elizabeth Torres; Yutaka Takeuchi; Rodrigo Duarte Clark; Kaya Jade Aguirre; Roji Oyama; ***D:*** Anthony Lucero; ***W:*** Anthony Lucero; ***C:*** Martin Rosenberg; ***M:*** Alex Mandel.

East Side, West Side 🦴🦴 **1949** Stanwyck and Mason try hard to make this simple-minded soaper work, with mixed results. A wealthy couple experiences marital woes, aggravated by a ambitious young woman and a soft-hearted man suffering from unrequited love. Based on the popular novel by Marcia Davenport. **110m/B; VHS, DVD.** Barbara Stanwyck; James Mason; Ava Gardner; Van Heflin; Gale Sondergaard; William Frawley; Nancy Davis; ***D:*** Mervyn LeRoy; ***C:*** Charles Rosher; ***M:*** Miklos Rozsa.

East-West 🦴🦴 *Est-Ouest* **1999 (PG-13)** In 1946, Stalin offered amnesty to any Russians who left the country after the 1917 revolution. But he executed or imprisoned many of the homesick expatriates and others found their gray motherland hard to bear (and impossible to leave). Russian doctor Alexei Golovin (Menshikov) bows to circumstances while his marriage to French wife Marie (Bonnaire) becomes increasingly strained. Marie befriends a champion swimmer, Sasha (Bodrov), with the hopes that they can both escape but things don't go as planned. Old-fashioned storytelling hampers the drama and the story (which leaps ahead months and years) becomes confused. French and Russian with subtitles. **125m/C; VHS, DVD.** *FR* Sandrine Bonnaire; Oleg Menshikov; Sergei Bodrov, Jr.; Catherine Deneuve; Tatiana Dogileva; ***D:*** Regis Wargnier; ***W:*** Regis Wargnier; Sergei Bodrov; Rustam Ibragimbekov; Louis Gardel; ***C:*** Laurent Dailland; ***M:*** Patrick Doyle.

Easter Parade 🦴🦴🦴 1/2 **1948** Big musical star Don Hewes (Astaire) splits with his partner Nadine (Miller) claiming that he could mold any girl to replace her in the act. He tries and finally succeeds with clumsy chorus girl Hannah Brown (Garland) after much difficulty. Astaire and Garland in peak form, aided by a classic Irving Berlin score. **103m/C; VHS, DVD, Blu-Ray.** Fred Astaire; Judy Garland; Peter Lawford; Ann Miller; Jules Munshin; Joi Lansing; ***D:*** Charles Walters; ***W:*** Sidney Sheldon; Frances Goodrich; Albert Hackett; ***C:*** Harry Stradling, Sr.; ***M:*** Irving Berlin. Oscars '48: Scoring/Musical.

Eastern Condors 🦴🦴 **1987** At the end of the Vietnam War, a band of Chinese convicts are recruited by the U.S. Army (and promised their freedom) if they can destroy an ammunition dump before the Viet Cong can make use of it. Considered a Hong Kong version of "The Dirty Dozen," with the requisite level of high energy and blood. Dubbed or Chinese with English subtitles. **94m/C; VHS, DVD.** *CH* Sammo Hung; Joyce Godenzi; Yuen Biao; Haing S. Ngor; ***D:*** Sammo Hung.

Eastern Promises 🦴🦴🦴 1/2 **2007 (R)** Midwife Anna (Watts) delivers a baby in a London hospital as the baby's mother, Tatiana, a teen prostitute from Russia, dies in Anna's arms. Haunted by the young girl's demise as well as her own demons, Anna's attempts to track down Tatiana's identity lead her to a Russian mafia gang led by Semyon (Mueller-Stahl). Seymon's son Kirill (Cassel) and bodyguard/driver Nikolai (a marvelous

Mortenson) dole out a fierce brand of brutality, brought to full-tilt in a bloody bathhouse scene. Director Cronenberg's vision is unflinching, messy, and raw in all the right places in this complicated but resonating morality tale. **95m/C; DVD, Blu-Ray, HD-DVD.** *GB CA* Viggo Mortensen; Naomi Watts; Vincent Cassel; Armin Mueller-Stahl; Sinead Cusack; Jerzy Skolimowski; Donald (Don) Sumpter; Mina E. Mina; ***D:*** David Cronenberg; ***W:*** Steven Knight; ***C:*** Peter Suschitzky; ***M:*** Howard Shore.

Eastside **1999** After being released from prison, Antonio Lopez pays a visit to his successful lawyer brother and learns that he's a mouthpiece for the mob. So Antonio gets an in with East L.A. kingpin De La Rosa as a strongarm guy. Only when he's asked to intimidate the owner of an inner-city youth center, Antonio's latent conscience begins to bother him. Of course, if he betrays De La Rosa, he's dead. **94m/C; VHS, DVD.** Mario Lopez; Efrain Figueroa; Mark Espinoza; Elizabeth Bogush; Gulshan Grover; Richard Lynch; Carlos Gallardo; ***D:*** Lorena David; ***W:*** Eric P. Sherman; ***C:*** Lisa Wiegand; ***M:*** Armando Avila. **VIDEO**

Easy A **2010 (PG-13)** Stone gives a dazzling performance as exasperated, overlooked smart teen Olive (Stone), who tells a lie about losing her virginity that happens to be overheard by ultra-conservative Marianne (Bynes) who self-righteously gossips the story all over school. Olive then decides to embrace her notoriety and help other misfits improve their social standing. Nathaniel Hawthorne's "A Scarlet Letter" figures prominently. Refreshing alternative to the usual teen fare. **92m/C; Blu-Ray, On Demand.** Emma Stone; Penn Badgley; Cam Gigandet; Amanda Bynes; Patricia Clarkson; Stanley Tucci; Malcolm McDowell; Lisa Kudrow; Thomas Haden Church; Fred Armisen; Stacey Travis; Alyson Michalka; Dan Byrd; ***D:*** Will Gluck; ***W:*** Bert V. Royal; ***C:*** Michael Grady; ***M:*** Brad Segal.

Easy Come, Easy Go **1967 (PG)** Elvis, as a Navy frogman, gets excited when he accidentally discovers what he believes is a vast sunken treasure. Music is his only solace when he finds his treasure to be worthless copper coins. **96m/C; VHS, DVD.** Elvis Presley; Dodie Marshall; Pat Priest; Elsa Lanchester; Frank McHugh; Pat Harrington, Jr.; Sonny Tufts; ***D:*** John Rich.

Easy Kill 1/2 **1989** A man takes the law into his own hands to exact revenge on drug lords. **100m/C; VHS, DVD.** Jane Badler; Cameron Mitchell; Frank Stallone; ***D:*** Josh Spencer.

Easy Living **1937** Exasperated Wall Street millionaire J.B. Ball (Arnold) throws his spoiled wife's (Nash) fur coat out their apartment window and it just happens to land on poor-but-hardworking secretary Mary Smith (Arthur). Ball insists Mary keep the coat and even buys her a matching hat. Soon, rumors are flying that Mary is the millionaire's tootsie. She meets cute with John (Milland), who turns out to be Ball's son and, after the usual misunderstandings, the twosome realize that they're meant for each other. **91m/B; VHS, DVD, Blu-Ray.** Jean Arthur; Edward Arnold; Ray Milland; Franklin Pangborn; Mary Nash; William Demerest; ***D:*** Mitchell Leisen; ***W:*** Preston Sturges; ***C:*** Ted Tetzlaff; ***M:*** Boris Morros.

Easy Living 1/2 **1949** Compromised melodrama about an over-the-hill football player who must cope with his failing marriage and looming retirement. Based on an Irwin Shaw story. **77m/B; VHS, DVD.** Victor Mature; Lucille Ball; Jack Paar; Lizabeth Scott; Sonny Tufts; Lloyd Nolan; Paul Stewart; ***D:*** Jacques Tourneur.

Easy Money **1983 (R)** A basic slob has the chance to inherit $10 million if he can give up his loves: smoking, drinking, and gambling among others. Dangerfield is surprisingly restrained in this harmless, though not altogether unpleasing comedy. **95m/C; VHS, DVD, Blu-Ray.** Rodney Dangerfield; Joe Pesci; Geraldine Fitzgerald; Jennifer Jason Leigh; Tom Ewell; Candice Azzara; Taylor Negron; ***D:*** James Signorelli; ***W:*** Rodney Dangerfield; Dennis Blair.

Easy Money *Snabba Cash* **2010 (R)** Business student JW (Kinnaman) enters high society through lies and turns to crime to keep up his numerous facades. He gets mixed up with a fugitive named Jorge (Varela), who is being hunted by a Serbian Mafia enforcer named Mrado (Mrsic). Director Espinosa takes what could have been a cut-rate thriller and turns it into something stylish. His men-behaving-badly do so for very well-defined and relatable reasons, making their descent into action-packed mayhem easier to identify with and enjoy. Swedish, Serbian, Spanish, and Arabic with subtitles. **124m/C; DVD.** *SW* Joel Kinnaman; Matias Varela; Dragomir Mrsic; Lisa Henni; Mahmut Suvakci; ***D:*** Daniel Espinosa; ***W:*** Maria Karlsson; Hassan Loo Sattarvandi; Fredrik Wikstrom; ***C:*** Aril Wretblad; ***M:*** Jon Ekstrand.

Easy Money: Hard to Kill *Snabba Cash II* **2012** Former Stockholm money launderer/drug dealer JW (Kinnaman) has been productive during his time in prison, even befriending wheelchair-bound Serbian thug Mrado (Mrsic). But during an authorized leave, JW discovers he's been betrayed in his plans to go legit and he and Mrado (who's escaped) reluctantly get back into the criminal life. This also brings them back into contact with players from the first film. Kinnaman is charismatic, but this sequel is a standard placeholder, leading into the last film in the trilogy. Swedish with subtitles. **99m/C; DVD, Blu-Ray.** *SW* Joel Kinnaman; Dragomir Mrsic; Dejan Cukic; Matias Varela; Fares Fares; Joel Spira; Madeleine Martin; ***D:*** Babak Najafi; ***W:*** Maria Karlsson; ***C:*** Aril Wretblad; ***M:*** Jon Ekstrand.

Easy Rider 1/2 **1969 (R)** Slim-budget, generation-defining movie. Two young men in late 1960s undertake a motorcycle trek throughout the Southwest in search of the real essence of America. Along the way they encounter hippies, rednecks, prostitutes, drugs, Nicholson, and tragedy. One of the highest-grossing pictures of the decade, undoubtedly an influence on two generations of "youth-oriented dramas," which all tried unsuccessfully to duplicate the original accomplishment. Psychedelic scenes and a great role for Nicholson are added bonuses. Look for the graveyard dancing scene in New Orleans. Features one of the best '60s rock scores around, including "Mean Streets" and "The Wanderers." **94m/C; VHS, DVD, Blu-Ray.** Peter Fonda; Dennis Hopper; Jack Nicholson; Karen Black; Toni Basil; Robert Walker, Jr.; Luana Anders; Luke Askew; Warren Finnerty; Mac Mashorian; Antonio Mendoza; Sabrina Scharf; Phil Spector; ***D:*** Dennis Hopper; ***W:*** Peter Fonda; Dennis Hopper; Terry Southern; ***C:*** Laszlo Kovacs. AFI '98: Top 100; Natl. Film Reg. '98; N.Y. Film Critics '69: Support. Actor (Nicholson); Natl. Soc. Film Critics '69: Support. Actor (Nicholson).

Easy to Love 1/2 **1953** Williams is in love with her boss, but he pays her no attention until a handsome singer vies for her affections. Set at Florida's Cypress Gardens, this aquatic musical features spectacular water ballet productions choreographed by Busby Berkeley, and the title song penned by Cole Porter. **96m/C; VHS, DVD.** Esther Williams; Van Johnson; Tony Martin; John Bromfield; King Donovan; Carroll Baker; ***D:*** Charles Walters; ***W:*** William Roberts.

Easy to Wed 1/2 **1946** Mild MGM musical remake of 1936's "Libeled Lady." Wealthy J.B. Allenbury (Kellaway) is suing for big bucks after an unflattering write-up of his daughter Connie's (Williams) lifestyle (she's accused of being a playgirl who likes married men). So newspaper editor Warren Haggerty (Wynn) sends suave reporter Bill (Johnson) to pretend to be married and prove the accusations true while Haggerty's fiancee Gladys (Ball) gets caught in the middle of the farce. Williams is winning but Ball steals the picture. **109m/C; DVD.** Esther Williams; Van Johnson; Keenan Wynn; Lucille Ball; Cecil Kellaway; Ben Blue; June Lockhart; Grant Mitchell; Paul Harvey; Jonathan Hale; James Flavin; ***D:*** Edward Buzzell; ***W:*** Dorothy Kingsley; ***C:*** Harry Strandling, Jr.; ***M:*** Johnny Green.

Easy Virtue 1/2 **1927** Hitchcock directs this adaptation of a Noel Coward play as a social melodrama. Larita is an unhappily married socialite with a lover. When her husband discovers her infidelity they divorce and she is marked as a woman of loose morals. Her reputation is not enhanced by her marriage to a younger man whose family diapproves. **79m/B; Silent; VHS, DVD.** *GB* Isabel Jeans; Ian Hunter; Franklin Dyall; Eric Bransby Williams; Robin Irvine; Violet Farebrother; ***D:*** Alfred Hitchcock.

Easy Virtue 1/2 **2008 (PG-13)** In the mid-1920s, upper-class John Whittaker (Barnes) meets glamorous race car-driving Larita (Biel) in Monte Carlo and they impulsively marry. John then takes the all-too-modern American home to his all-too-hide-bound aristocratic family, only to meet with swift disapproval by John's snappish, snobbish mother (Scott Thomas) who is determined to break up their union so her son can take a more suitable wife. John settles into the role of country squire (boring), although Larita realizes that the times have definitely changed. Director Elliot's production is lavish and Biel almost manages to hold her own (she looks lovely) against the pinched hauteur of Scott Thomas. Based on the 1924 play by Noel Coward. **96m/C; Blu-Ray, On Demand.** *GB US* Jessica Biel; Ben Barnes; Colin Firth; Kimberly Nixon; Kris Marshall; Pip Torrens; Charlotte Riley; Kristin Scott Thomas; Katherine Parkinson; ***D:*** Stephan Elliot; ***W:*** Stephan Elliot; Sheridan Jobbins; ***C:*** Martin Kenzie; ***M:*** Marius De Vries.

Easy Wheels 1/2 **1989** Like most decent biker movies, "Wheels" is propelled by bad taste and a healthy dose of existentialist nihilism. But there's an unusual plot twist in this parody. A biker named She-Wolf and her gang kidnap female babies and let wolves rear the children. Their elaborate plan is to create a race of super women who will subdue the troublesome male population. But can this "noble" plan succeed? **94m/C; VHS, DVD.** Paul LeMat; Eileen Davidson; Marjorie Bransfield; Jon Menick; Mark Holton; Karen Russell; Jami Richards; Roberta Vasquez; Barry Livingston; George Plimpton; ***D:*** David O'Malley; ***W:*** Ivan Raimi; Celia Abrams; David O'Malley; ***M:*** John Ross.

Eat a Bowl of Tea **1989 (PG-13)** Endearing light drama-comedy concerning a multi-generational Chinese family. They must learn to deal with the problems of life in America and in particular, marriage, when Chinese women are finally allowed to immigrate with their husbands to the United States following WWII. Adaptation of Louis Chu's story, directed by the man who brought us "Dim Sum." A PBS "American Playhouse" presentation. **102m/C; VHS, DVD.** Cora Miao; Russell Wong; Lau Siu Ming; Eric Tsiang Chi Wai; Victor Wong; Jessica Harper; Lee Sau Kee; ***D:*** Wayne Wang; ***W:*** Judith Rascoe; ***C:*** Amir M. Mokri; ***M:*** Mark Adler.

Eat Drink Man Woman 1/2 **1994 (R)** In Taipei, widowed master chef serves weekly feast of elaborate food and familial guilt to his three grown daughters, all of whom still live at home. They spend their time sorting out professional and romantic difficulties, searching for independence, and fulfilling traditional family obligations. Each character has a lot going on, but no one's story gets lost in the mix. Lee uses irony to great effect, introducing us to the culinary artist who has lost his sense of taste and has a daughter who works at a Wendy's. Food preparation scenes (more than 100 recipes are served up) illustrate a careful attention to detail (and are guaranteed to make you hungry). Lee's follow-up to "The Wedding Banquet" is a finely observed, comic tale of generational drift, the richness of tradition, and the power of love to redeem or improve. In Chinese with subtitles or dubbed. **123m/C; VHS, DVD, Blu-Ray.** *TW* Sihung Lung; Kuei-Mei Yang; Yu-Wen Wang; Chien-Lien Wu; Sylvia Chang; Winston Chao; Ah-Leh Gua; Lester Chen; ***D:*** Ang Lee; ***W:*** Ang Lee; James Schamus; Hui-Ling Wang; ***C:*** Jong Lin; ***M:*** Mader. Natl. Bd. of Review '94: Foreign Film.

Eat My Dust **1976 (PG)** Teenage son of a California sheriff steals the best stock cars from a race track to take the town's heartthrob for a joy ride. Subsequently he leads the town on a wild car chase. Brainless but fast-paced. **89m/C; VHS, DVD.** Ron Howard; Christopher Norris; Warren Kemmerling; Dave Madden; Robert Broyles; Jessica Potter; Don Brodie; Evelyn Russell; Clint Howard; Paul Bartel; Rance Howard; Corbin Bernsen; ***D:*** Charles B. Griffith; ***W:*** Charles B. Griffith; ***C:*** Eric Saarinen; ***M:*** David Grisman.

Eat, Pray, Love **2010 (PG-13)** Repetitious adaptation of Elizabeth Gilbert's 2006 memoir "Eat, Pray, Love: One Woman's Search for Everything Across Italy, India and Indonesia." Writer Gilbert (Roberts) decides her current life isn't what she wants so, following her divorce, she travels on a journey of self-discovery, including a protracted time in Italy for pleasure; India for meditation—where Jenkins steals every scene; and Indonesia for both the spiritual and an unexpected love affair with Felipe (Bardem, whose screen time seems brief). Roberts is fine but Gilbert's guilt gets annoying and the flashbacks are also distracting and unnecessary. **140m/C; Blu-Ray, On Demand.** Julia Roberts; Javier Bardem; Richard Jenkins; Viola Davis; Billy Crudup; James Franco; Michael O'Malley; Hadi Subiyanto; Tuva Novotny; Luca Argentero; Giuseppe Gandini; Sophie Thompson; Rushita Singh; Christine Hakim; Arlene Tur; ***D:*** Ryan Murphy; ***W:*** Ryan Murphy; Jennifer Salt; ***C:*** Robert Richardson; ***M:*** Dario Marianelli.

Eat That Question: Frank Zappa in His Own Words **2016 (R)** A feature-length documentary look at the life, work, and influence of eccentric musician Frank Zappa. Featuring a number of interviews with Zappa and those he influenced, the film includes revealing archival footage that shows the development of iconoclastic attitude and distinctive sound. Topics covered include his outspoken efforts to address the political forces trying to censor him and his insatiable quest to find new artistic challenges. **93m/C; DVD, Streaming, Download.** ***D:*** Thorsten Schutte.

Eat the Rich **1987 (R)** A British farce about a group of terrorists who take over the popular London restaurant, Bastard's. Led by a former, disgruntled transvestite employee, they turn diners into menu offerings. Music by Motorhead. **89m/C; VHS, DVD.** *GB* Nosher Powell; Lanah Pellay; Fiona Richmond; Ronald Allen; Sandra Dorne; Paul McCartney; Linda McCartney; Bill Wyman; Koo Stark; Miranda Richardson; Angie Bowie; Sandie Shaw; ***D:*** Peter Richardson; ***W:*** Peter Richardson; ***C:*** Witold Stok.

Eat Your Heart Out 1/2 **1996 (R)** Routine romantic comedy about talented but struggling young chef Daniel (Oliver) who gets his shot at success with his own TV cooking show. He doesn't realize his best gal pal (Seagall) loves him, while Daniel becomes intrigued by his sexy agent (San Giacomo). **96m/C; VHS, DVD.** Christian Oliver; Laura San Giacomo; Pamela Segall; Linda Hunt; ***D:*** Felix Adlon; ***W:*** Felix Adlon; ***C:*** Judy Irola; ***M:*** Alex Wurman.

Eaten Alive *Death Trap; Starlight Slaughter; Legend of the Bayou; Horror Hotel Massacre* **1976 (R)** A Southerner takes an unsuspecting group of tourists into a crocodile death trap. Director Tobe Hooper's follow-up to "The Texas Chainsaw Massacre." Englund is more recognizable with razor fingernails as Freddy Krueger of the "Nightmare on Elm Street" films. **96m/C; VHS, DVD.** Neville Brand; Mel Ferrer; Carolyn Jones; Marilyn Burns; Stuart Whitman; Robert Englund; William Finley; Roberta Collins; Kyle Richards; Janus Blythe; ***D:*** Tobe Hooper; ***W:*** Marti Rustam; Alvin L. Fast; Kim Henkel; ***C:*** Robert Caramico; ***M:*** Wayne Bell.

Eaters 1/2 **2015 (R)** A road trip goes very bad in this horror film set in the summer of 1976. When five friends decide to go on the road trip of a lifetime through the desert in a Mustang, the last thing they think they will find is problems. However, when they take a break at a rest stop, one of the five—Jill (Risinger)—goes missing. As the friends search for her, they must confront a biker gang with deadly intentions and survive being stalked in an abandoned town. **90m/C; DVD, Streaming, Download.** Tristan Parrish Moore; Hannah Risinger; Jonathan Haltiwanger; Marcelle Bowman; Robert Dean; ***D:*** Johnny Tabor; ***W:*** Johnny Tabor; ***C:*** Ryan Valdez. **VIDEO**

Eating 1/2 **1990 (R)** Set in Southern California, women gather to celebrate birthdays for three of their friends who are turning 30, 40 and 50. As the party commences, women from two generations discuss their attitudes towards food and men...and discover hilarious parallels. **110m/C; VHS, DVD.** Nelly Alard; Frances Bergen; Mary Crosby; Lisa Richards; Gwen Welles; Daphna Kastner; Elizabeth Kemp; Marlena Giovi; Marina Gregory; Toni Basil; ***D:*** Henry Jaglom; ***W:*** Henry Jaglom; ***C:*** Hanania Baer.

Eating Out 2: Sloppy Seconds ½ **2006** Goofy low-budget gay comedy. Kyle (Verraros) has been dumped by Marc (Chukerman) so he's on the prowl. He's drawn to hunky-but-dumb art class model Troy (Dapper), who says he's straight. Since Kyle and his gal pals Gwen (Brooke) and Tiffani (Kochan) have their doubts, Kyle claims he's a member of a "going straight" group and decides to take Troy to a meeting and see what happens. **85m/C; DVD.** Mink Stole; Jim Verraros; Marco Dapper; Emily Brooke; Rebekah Kochan; Brett Chukerman; ***D:*** Phillip J. Bartell; ***W:*** Phillip J. Bartell; Q. Allan Brocka; ***C:*** Lisa Wiegand; ***M:*** Cary Berger; Boris Worister.

Eating Out 3: All You Can Eat **WOOF! 2009** Pandering and inept gay sex comedy. Fag hag Tiffani befriends shy new boy Casey and tries to match him up with hunky Zack using a phony social networking profile. **80m/C; DVD.** Daniel Skelton; Rebekah Kochan; Chris Salvatore; Leslie Jordan; Mink Stole; Michael E.R. Walker; ***D:*** Glenn Gaylord; ***W:*** Phillip J. Bartell; ***C:*** Tom Camarda. **VIDEO**

Eating Out 4: Drama Camp ½ **2011** In this flamboyantly raunchy gay comedy, a group of hunks decide to get some summer action at Dickie's Drama Camp. Dickie insists on his campers maintaining some self-restraint but that's impossible. Zack and Casey are in a relationship slump so Zack isn't resisting his attraction to Benji while fellow thespian Beau is crushing on Casey; straight director Jason is uncomfortable about his interest in transgendered Lily; and cougar Aunt Helen is after boy toy Andy. **90m/C; DVD.** Chris Salvatore; Daniel Skelton; Aaron Milo; Ronnie Kroell; Drew Droege; Garikayi Mutambirwa; Harmony Santana; Mink Stole; Joel Rush; ***D:*** Q. Allan Brocka; ***W:*** Q. Allan Brocka; Phillip J. Bartell; ***C:*** Amanda Treyz; ***M:*** Meiro Stamm.

Eating Out: The Open Weekend ½ **2011** The fifth pic in the franchise offers more male eye candy along with the usual sexual situations. Zack and new boyfriend Benji are spending the weekend at a gay resort in Palm Springs, with Benji persuading Zack that some sexual freedom is okay. Casey runs into ex-boyfriend Zack and is quick to proclaim his friend Peter is his new beau. Of course Benji and Peter want to be 'open' together, which changes the situation for the others. **80m/C; DVD, Blu-Ray.** Chris Salvatore; Daniel Skelton; Aaron Milo; Michael A. Vera; ***D:*** Q. Allan Brocka; ***W:*** Q. Allan Brocka; Phillip J. Bartell; ***C:*** Amanda Treyz; ***M:*** Meiro Stamm. **VIDEO**

Eating Raoul ½ **1982 (R)** The Blands are a happily married couple who share many interests: good food and wine, entrepreneurial dreams, and an aversion to sex. The problem is, they're flat broke. So, when the tasty swinger from upstairs makes a pass at Mary and Paul accidentally kills him, they discover he's got loads of money; Raoul takes a cut in the deal by disposing of—or rather recycling—the body. This may just be the way to finance that restaurant they've been wanting to open. Wonderful, offbeat, hilariously dark comedy. **83m/C; VHS, DVD, Blu-Ray.** Mary Woronov; Paul Bartel; Robert Beltran; Buck Henry; Ed Begley, Jr.; Edie McClurg; John Paragon; Hamilton Camp; Billy Curtis; Susan Saiger; Richard Paul; Don Steele; Mark Woods; ***D:*** Paul Bartel; ***W:*** Richard Blackburn; Paul Bartel; ***C:*** Gary Thieltges; ***M:*** Arlon Ober.

Eban and Charley ½ **2001** Draggy romance about a couple of misfits—one of whom is underage. 29-year-old Eban (Fellows) returns to his parents' home in a coastal Oregon community after leaving his job as a soccer coach. He's hanging around town when he meets the 15-year-old Charley (Andrade), who's been sent to live with his resentful divorced father after Charley's mother dies. Eventually, the relationship becomes physical (there are no depictions of sex) and they're headed for trouble. **88m/C; VHS, DVD.** Brent Fellows; Giovanni Andrade; Nolan V. Chard; Ron Upton; Pam Munter; ***D:*** James Bolton; ***W:*** James Bolton; ***C:*** Judy Irola; ***M:*** Stephin Merritt.

The Ebb-Tide ½ **1997** Capt. Chisholm (Coltrane) is bothered by a scandalous past, so he doesn't ask a lot of questions about transporting a secret cargo to Australia. A storm strands Chisholm and two sailors on an uncharted island that's inhabited by the malevolent Ellstrom (Terry) and has Chisholm in a battle of good versus evil. Based on a novel by Robert Louis Stevenson. **104m/C; VHS, DVD.** Robbie Coltrane; Nigel Terry; Steven Mackintosh; ***D:*** Nicholas Renton; ***W:*** Simon Donald. **CABLE**

Ebony Tower ½ **1986** Based on the John Fowles novel about a crusty old artist who lives in a French chateau with two young female companions. They are visited by a handsome young man, thereby initiating sexual tension and recognizably Fowlesian plot puzzles. Features some partial nudity. Currently only available as part of a collection. **80m/C; DVD.** *GB* Laurence Olivier; Roger Rees; Greta Scacchi; Toyah Willcox; ***D:*** Robert Knights; ***M:*** Richard Rodney Bennett. **TV**

Eccentricities of a Blonde-Haired Girl *Singularidades de uma Rapariga Loura* **2010** An adaptation of a short story by Portuguese author Eca de Queiroz, made by 101-year-old filmmaker Manoel de Oliveira. Riding a train to Algarve, an upset Macario (Trepa) relates his romantic problems to his sympathetic female seatmate. He tells her about his deep interest in a young blond woman he watches from his apartment window. Having moved to Lisban to work as an accountant and broker, Macario moves heaven and earth to win the heart of the mysterious woman, overcoming all challenges. Yet when he achieves his goal and gains Luisa's (Wallenstein) love, he learns that the woman lacks the kind of character he hoped she'd have. Portuguese with subtitles. **64m/C; DVD.** Ricardo Trepa; Catarina Wallenstein; Diogo Doria; Julia Buisel; Leonor Silveira; ***D:*** Manoel de Oliveira; ***W:*** Manoel de Oliveira; ***C:*** Sabine Lancelin.

ECCO ½ **2019 (R)** For years, Michael (Walker) has worked as an assassin for a secret organization and disposes of his targets with ease. At least twice, Michael has tried to have a normal life with a partner, one of whom becomes pregnant with his child. Though he paid a price to be free of the hitman life, he was forced back in. Michael must look to his past to save himself and his loved ones. A repetitive and unmoving thriller that takes itself too seriously...though it is pretty to look at. **123m/C; DVD.** Lathrop Walker; Tabitha Bastien; Helena Grace Donald; Michael Winters; Vincent Cardinale; ***D:*** Benny Medina; ***W:*** Benny Medina; ***C:*** Duncan Cole; ***M:*** Chris Morphitis.

Echelon Conspiracy ½ *The Gift* **2009 (PG-13)** Computer security analyst Max Peterson receives a series of text messages on his new cell phone promising gambling tips that make him rich. The situation turns out to be too good to be true since there's an international conspiracy involving government agencies collecting surveillance material that has Max running for his life. **105m/C; DVD.** Shane West; Edward Burns; Ving Rhames; Martin Sheen; Sergey Gubanov; ***D:*** Greg Marcks; ***W:*** Kevin Elders; Michael Nitsberg; ***C:*** Lorenzo Senatore; ***M:*** Joseph Gutowski; Bobby Tahouri. **VIDEO**

The Echo ½ **2008 (R)** Somewhat effective but slow-moving ghostly horror. Parolee Bobby (Bradford) moves into his dead mother's apartment and soon hears violent disturbances from the next-door neighbors. Only that apartment is empty because the family is dead. If Bobby wants any peace, he has to put the spirits to rest. Laranas remakes his own 2004 Filipino film "Sigaw." **96m/C; DVD, Blu-Ray.** Jesse Bradford; Amelia Warner; Carlos Leon; Iza Calzado; Kevin Durand; Pruitt Taylor Vince; Louise Linton; Jaime Bloch; ***D:*** Yam Lazaram; ***W:*** Eric Brent; Shintaro Shimosawa; ***C:*** Matthew Irving; ***M:*** tomandandy.

Echo in the Canyon ½ **2018 (PG-13)** A documentary look at the mid-1960s music scene that formed in Laurel Canyon. Inspired by acts such as the Beatles, the Laurel Canyon musicians, including The Byrds and The Mamas & The Papas, influenced each other as they experimented with the length and complexity of songs. Through interviews with key players, including Brian Wilson, and members of Crosby, Stills & Nash, the sources of their sound are explored as well as their influence on later generations of musicians. Though the documentary covers familiar themes and ideas, it shows how considering elements such as folk and rock in a new way can result in a revolution. **82m/C; DVD.** Jakob Dylan; ***D:*** Andrew Slater; ***W:*** Andrew Slater; Eric Barrett; ***C:*** Vance Burberry; Pat Darrin; Kyle Kibbe; Brett Turnbull; Garry Waller; Mark Williams.

Echo Murders ½ **1945** A Sexton Blake mystery wherein he investigates a mine owner's mysterious death, opening up a veritable can of murdering, power-hungry worms. **75m/B; VHS, DVD.** David Farrar; Dennis Price; Julien Mitchell; Ferdinand "Ferdy" Mayne; Pamela Stirling; ***D:*** John Harlow; ***W:*** John Harlow; ***C:*** James Wilson; ***M:*** Percival Mackey.

Echo of Murder *Who Killed Atlanta's Children?* **2000** Docudrama focuses on the 29 child murders in Atlanta, which took place in the late '70s and early '80s, from the point of view of investigative journalists Hines and Belushi. Their theory is that convicted killer Wayne Williams is the scapegoat for a police conspiracy and the killings were perpetrated by the Ku Klux Klan. But they seem to spend most of their time yelling at each other so the story's emotional impact is lost. **105m/C; VHS, DVD.** James Belushi; Gregory Hines; ***D:*** Charles Robert Carner; ***W:*** Charles Robert Carner; ***C:*** Michael Goi; ***M:*** James Verboort. **CABLE**

Echo Park ½ **1986 (R)** An unsung sleeper comedy about three roommates living in Los Angeles' Echo Park: a body builder, a single-mother waitress, and an itinerant songwriter. Charts their struggles as they aim for careers in showbiz. Offbeat ensemble effort. **93m/C; VHS, DVD.** *AU* Tom Hulce; Susan Dey; Michael Bowen; Richard "Cheech" Marin; Christopher Walker; Shirley Jo Finney; Cassandra Peterson; Yana Nirvana; Timothy Carey; ***D:*** Robert Dornhelm; ***W:*** Michael Ventura; ***C:*** Karl Kofler; ***M:*** David Rickets.

Echoes *Living Nightmare* **1983 (R)** A young painter's life slowly comes apart as he is tormented by nightmares that his stillborn twin brother is attempting to murder him. **90m/C; VHS, DVD.** Gale Sondergaard; Mercedes McCambridge; Richard Alfieri; Ruth Roman; John Spencer; Nathalie Nell; ***D:*** Arthur Allan Seidelman; ***W:*** Richard Alfieri; Richard J. Anthony; ***C:*** Hanania Baer.

Echoes ½ **1988** Shopkeeper's daughter Clare O'Brien (Garahy) and doctor's son David Power (Hines) both want to escape from their 1950s Irish seaside town. They meet again at university in Dublin where their friendship turns to romance but their return home comes complete with family troubles and differing dreams. Based on the novel by Maeve Binchy. **208m/C; VHS, DVD.** *GB* Siobhan Garahy; Robert Hines; Geraldine James; Stephen Holland; Alison Doody; Dermot Crowley; ***W:*** Donald Churchill; Barbara Rennie. **TV**

Echoes ½ **2015** A dramatic thriller-horror about the impact horrifying visions have on the life of one young writer. While continuing to have horrible visions while suffering from sleep paralysis, writer Anna Parker (French) and her boyfriend travel to an isolate desert house to find some peace. Instead, Anna's visions grow stronger and she believes she might be having a mental breakdown. In the process, however, she learns that her visions might be related to a life-threatening secret. **93m/C; DVD, Blu-Ray, Streaming, Download.** Kate French; Steven Brand; Steve Hanks; Billy Wirth; Caroline Whitney Smith; ***D:*** Nils Timm; ***W:*** Nils Timm; ***C:*** Robert Toth; ***M:*** Dre Nitze. **VIDEO**

The Eclipse ½ *L'eclisse* **1962** The last of Antonioni's trilogy (after "L'Avventura" and "La Notte"), wherein another fashionable and alienated Italian woman passes from one lover to another searching unsuccessfully for truth and love. Highly acclaimed. In Italian with subtitles. **123m/B; VHS, DVD, Blu-Ray.** *IT* Monica Vitti; Alain Delon; Francisco Rabal; Louis Seigner; ***D:*** Michelangelo Antonioni; ***W:*** Michelangelo Antonioni; Tonino Guerra; Elio Bartolini; Ottiero Ottieri; ***C:*** Gianni Di Venanzo; ***M:*** Giovanni Fusco.

The Eclipse **2009 (R)** Cobh, Ireland is having its annual literary festival and widowed dad Michael (Hinds) has volunteered to drive around authors Lena (Hjejle), who writes ghost stories, and Nicholas (Quinn), who writes macho tales ala Hemingway. Michael's having ghostly visions and nightmares that include his bitter, ailing father-in-law Malachy (Norton) and beautiful Lena tries to help Michael figure out what his dreams mean. She's also trying to avoid egotistical drunken Nicholas with whom she shared a brief fling, but the lives of all three will dangerously collide. Adaptation of co-screenwriter Billy Roche's short story from "Tales from Rainwater Pond." **88m/C; Blu-Ray, On Demand.** *IR* Ciaran Hinds; Aidan Quinn; Iben Hjejle; Jim Norton; Eanna Hardwicke; Hannah Lynch; ***D:*** Conor McPherson; ***W:*** Conor McPherson; Billy Roche; ***C:*** Ivan McCullough; ***M:*** Fionnuala Ni Chiosain.

Ecstasy ½ *Extase; Ekstase; Symphony of Love* **1933** A romantic, erotic story about a young woman married to an older man, who takes a lover. Features Lamarr, then Hedy Kiesler, before her discovery in Hollywood. Film subsequently gained notoriety for Lamarr's nude scenes. In Czech with English subtitles. **90m/B; VHS, DVD.** *CZ* Hedy Lamarr; Jaromir Rogoz; Aribert Mog; ***D:*** Gustav Machaty; ***W:*** Gustav Machaty.

Ed **WOOF! 1996 (PG)** A must see for all fans of flatulent animatronic chimpanzees who play third base. Everyone else should stay away. LeBlanc (who should've been tipped off when they couldn't even get a real chimp to appear) plays Coop, a phenom pitcher stuck on a losing team in the minor leagues. After Ed the chimpanzee is bequeathed to the team by the late Mickey Mantle, (forgive them Mick, they know not what they do) he starts playing the hot corner like Brooks Robinson. Surprise! Ed becomes a national sensation, the team goes on a winning streak and sets up the showdown game climax. Most of the humor is derived from Ed tearing things up and passing gas, while LeBlanc yells in pop-eyed exasperation. Cameo from Tommy Lasorda playing a fat major league manager. **94m/C; VHS, DVD.** Matt LeBlanc; Jayne Brook; Bill Cobbs; Jack Warden; Doren Fein; Patrick Kerr; Charlie Schlatter; Carl Anthony Payne, II; Curt Kaplan; Zack (Zach) Ward; Mike McGlone; James (Jim) Caviezel; Valente Rodriguez; ***D:*** Bill Couturie; ***W:*** David Mickey Evans; ***C:*** Alan Caso; ***M:*** Stephen Endelman.

Ed and His Dead Mother **1993 (PG-13)** Ed's just an average guy who happens to really love his mother. So much so that when she dies Ed tries to bring her back from the dead—and succeeds. Only death has made a few changes in Mom's personality. Now she's a bug-eating, chainsaw-wielding fiend. Just what's a good son supposed to do? **93m/C; VHS, DVD.** Ned Beatty; Steve Buscemi; John Glover; Miriam Margolyes; Sam Jenkins; ***D:*** Jonathan Wacks; ***W:*** Chuck Hughes.

Ed Gein **2001** Considering the subject matter, this is a mild account of murdering, grave-robbing, dismembering psycho/cannibal Ed Gein (Railsback) and the Wisconsin farm community who just can't believe what their neighbor has been up to. **88m/C; VHS, DVD.** Steve Railsback; Carrie Snodgress; Pat Skipper; Sally Champlin; ***D:*** Chuck Parello; ***W:*** Stephen Johnston; ***C:*** Vanja Cernjul; ***M:*** Robert F. McNaughton.

Ed McBain's 87th Precinct: Heatwave *Heatwave* **1997** Isola is in the midst of a heatwave and in the grip of a serial rapist who's targeting previous victims. Detective Eileen Burke (Eleniak) goes undercover but becomes a victim herself, making the case extremely personal for boyfriend Bert Kling (Johansson) and the other detectives. TV movie based on the crime novel by Ed McBain. **90m/C; DVD.** Erika Eleniak; Paul Johansson; Michael Gross; Dale Midkiff; Paul Ben-Victor; Andrea Ferrell; Ron Kuhlman; ***D:*** Douglas Barr; ***W:*** Larry Cohen; ***C:*** Malcolm Cross; ***M:*** Patrick Williams. **TV**

Ed McBain's 87th Precinct: Lightning ½ *Lightning* **1995** Dull adaptation of McBain's 1984 novel. A young woman's death turns into a hunt for a serial killer when more bodies turn up and the victims are all collegiate runners. The 87th precinct detectives have to set aside personal issues to catch the killer. **89m/C; DVD.** Randy Quiad; Alex McArthur; Ving Rhames; Alan

Blumenfeld; Ron Perkins; Steve Flynn; Deanne Bray; Tracy Middendorf; Eddie Jones; *D:* Bruce Paltrow; *W:* Mike Krohn; Daniel Levine; *C:* Kenneth Zunder; *M:* Peter Bernstein. **CABLE**

Ed Wood 🦴🦴🦴 1/2 **1994 (R)** Leave it to Burton to bring to the screen the story of a director many consider to be the worst of all time (he's at least in the top three) and who now occupies a lofty position as a cult icon. In this hilarious and touching tribute to a Hollywood maverick with grade-Z vision, detailed homage is paid to Wood's single-mindedness and optimism in the face of repeated failure and lack of financing, even down to the black and white photography. Depp is convincing (and engaging) as Ed Wood, Jr., the cross-dressing, angora-sweater-wearing, low-budget auteur of such notoriously "bad" cult films as "Glen or Glenda" and "Plan 9 From Outer Space." Depp is supported by terrific portrayals of the motley Wood crew, led by Landau's morphine-addicted, down-on-his-luck Bela Lugosi. Burton focuses on Wood's relationship with Lugosi, whose career is over by the time Wood befriends him. Based on Rudolph Grey's book, "Nightmare of Ecstasy: The Life and Art of Edward D. Wood Jr." **127m/B; VHS, DVD, Blu-Ray.** Johnny Depp; Sarah Jessica Parker; Martin Landau; Bill Murray; Jim Myers; Patricia Arquette; Jeffrey Jones; Lisa Marie; Vincent D'Onofrio; Ned Bellamy; Conrad Brooks; Rance Howard; Juliet Landau; G.D. Spradlin; Mike Starr; George "The Animal" Steele; Gregory Walcott; Max Casella; *D:* Tim Burton; *W:* Scott M. Alexander; Larry Karaszewski; *C:* Stefan Czapsky; *M:* Howard Shore. Oscars '94: Makeup, Support. Actor (Landau); Golden Globes '95: Support. Actor (Landau); L.A. Film Critics '94: Cinematog., Score, Support. Actor (Landau); N.Y. Film Critics '94: Cinematog., Support. Actor (Landau); Natl. Soc. Film Critics '94: Cinematog., Support. Actor (Landau); Screen Actors Guild '94: Support. Actor (Landau).

Eddie 🦴🦴 **1996 (PG-13)** Basketball nut Edwina (Goldberg) wins a chance to be honorary coach of her beloved Knicks in a free throw contest. When some of her courtside advice works, and the other fans seem to respond to her, the publicity-seeking maverick owner (Langella) gives her the job full-time. Predictable comedy with the usual "new team member leads underdogs to contention" characters won't suprise, or particularly thrill, anyone. Goldberg's lively performance somewhat redeems standard script but reduces everyone around her, including an All-Star roster of NBA players, to window dressing. Basically the hoops version of "Little Big League." **100m/C; VHS, DVD.** Whoopi Goldberg; Frank Langella; Dennis Farina; Richard Jenkins; Lisa Ann Walter; John Benjamin Hickey; John Salley; *D:* Steve Rash; *W:* Jon Connolly; David Loucka; Eric Champnella; Keith Mitchell; Steve Zacharias; Jeff Buhai; *C:* Victor Kemper; *M:* Stanley Clarke.

Eddie and the Cruisers 🦴🦴 **1983 (PG)** In the early 1960s, rockers Eddie and the Cruisers score with one hit album. Amid their success, lead singer Pare dies mysteriously in a car accident. Years later, a reporter decides to write a feature on the defunct group, prompting a former band member to begin a search for missing tapes of the Cruisers' unreleased second album. Questions posed at the end of the movie are answered in the sequel. Enjoyable soundtrack by John Cafferty and the Beaver Brown Band. **90m/C; VHS, DVD, Blu-Ray.** Tom Berenger; Michael Paré; Ellen Barkin; Joe Pantoliano; Matthew Laurance; Helen Schneider; David Wilson; Michael "Tunes" Antunes; Joe Cates; John Stockwell; Barry Sand; Vebe Borge; Howard Johnson; Robin Karfo; Rufus Harley; Bruce Brown; Louis D'Esposito; Michael Toland; Bob Garrett; Joanne Collins; *D:* Martin Davidson; *W:* Martin Davidson; Arlene Davidson; *C:* Fred Murphy; *M:* John Cafferty.

Eddie and the Cruisers 2: Eddie Lives! 🦴 1/2 **1989 (PG-13)** A sequel to the minor cult favorite, in which a rock star believed to be dead emerges under a new name in Montreal to lead a new band. The Beaver Brown Band again provides the music. **106m/C; VHS, DVD, Blu-Ray; Open Captioned.** *CA* Michael Paré; Marina Orsini; Matthew Laurance; Bernie Coulson; Anthony Sherwood; *Cameo(s):* Larry King; Bo Diddley; Martha Quinn; Merrill Shindler; *D:* Jean-Claude Lord; *W:* Charles Zev Cohen; *C:* Rene Verzier; *M:* Leon Aronson.

The Eddie Cantor Story 🦴🦴 1/2 **1953** Standard Warner Bros. showbiz bio. Eddie Cantor (Brasselle) goes from his Lower East Side boyhood to singing waiter, Ziegfeld Follies star, radio pioneer, and humanitarian. The music includes such popular Cantor tunes as "Makin' Whoopie," "If You Knew Susie," "Ma, He's Making Eyes at Me," and "Ida, Sweet as Apple Cider." Cantor himself dubbed Brasselle on the soundtrack and has a cameo along with his wife Ida. **116m/C; DVD.** Keefe Brasselle; Marilyn Erskine; Aline MacMahon; Arthur Franz; William Forrest; Alex Gerry; Greta Granstedt; Gerald Mohr; Marie Windsor; Will Rogers, Jr.; Jackie Barnett; *D:* Alfred E. Green; *W:* Sidney Skolsky; Ted Sherdeman; Jerome Weidman; *C:* Edwin DuPar; *M:* Ray Heindorf.

Eddie Macon's Run 🦴🦴 **1983 (PG)** Based on a true story; Eddie Macon has been unjustly jailed in Texas and plans an escape to run to Mexico. He is followed by a tough cop who is determined to catch the fugitive. Film debut of Goodman. **95m/C; VHS, DVD, Blu-Ray, Streaming.** Kirk Douglas; John Schneider; Lee Purcell; John Goodman; Leah Ayres; *D:* Jeff Kanew; *M:* Wendy Blackstone.

Eddie Presley 🦴🦴 1/2 **1992** Eddie Presley is an Elvis impersonator at the lowest rung of the entertainment industry ladder. He's a true believer whose act is a heartfelt homage. He lives in his van and has a crappy security guard job, and has a tenuous hold on his dignity. When he gets a gig at a seedy hotel, he has a meltdown on stage and gives a performance the audience will never forget. Well-crafted, bittersweet showbiz drama is packed fine performances. Based on writer/star Whitaker's play. **106m/C; DVD, On Demand.** Duane Whitaker; Stacie Randall; Lawrence Tierney; Roscoe Lee Browne; Theodore (Ted) Raimi; Joe Estevez; Tom Everett; Clu Gulager; John Lazar; Francesca "Kitten" Natividad; Ian Ogilvy; Willard Pugh; Daniel Roebuck; Tim Thomerson; Patrick Thomas; *Cameo(s):* Quentin Tarantino; Bruce Campbell; *D:* Jeff Burr; *W:* Duane Whitaker; *C:* Thomas Callaway; *M:* Jim Manzie.

Eddie the Eagle 🦴🦴 *Eddie the Eagle: Alles ist Möglich* **2016 (PG-13)** Feel-good movies about athletes who overcome incredible odds are a relatively predictable subgenre of their very own. Sometimes they break out ("Rudy"), but more often they're disposable comfort food cinema. This telling of the story of Michael "Eddie" Edwards" is the latter. Eddie was a pint-sized Brit who somehow convinced himself that he could be an Olympian ski-jumper, and made it all the way to the 1988 Calgary Winter Olympics. Egerton is a bit exaggerated as Eddie but Jackman is charismatic as his coach. You know exactly what you're getting here—no more, no less. **106m/C; DVD, Blu-Ray, Streaming.** *GE UK US* Taron Egerton; Hugh Jackman; Jo Hartley; Keith Allen; Edvin Endresen; *D:* Dexter Fletcher; *W:* Sean Macaulay; Simon Kelton; *C:* George Richmond; *M:* Matthew Margeson.

Eddie the Sleepwalking Cannibal 🦴🦴 **2012** Has-been artist Lars (Lindhardt), struggling to find inspiration, takes a teaching job in rural Canada for a change of pace. There he finds a roommate and muse in Eddie (Smith), a mute, sleepwalking giant whose nighttime walks end in murder, mayhem, and gruesome eating habits. Lars, initially horrified, discovers that his inspiration returns as Eddie's body count grows. Film aspires to be part horror-comedy, part satire of the pressures of the art world, but lacks the execution to succeed at either. An inspired premise that ultimately settles for being a slightly above-average B-movie. **90m/C; DVD, Blu-Ray.** *CA DK* Thure Lindhardt; Dylan Smith; Georgina Reilly; Stephen McHattie; Alain Goulem; *D:* Boris Rodriguez; *W:* Boris Rodriguez; *C:* Philippe Kress; *M:* David G. Burns.

The Eddy Duchin Story 🦴🦴 **1956** Glossy tearjerker that profiles the tragic life of Eddy Duchin, the famous pianist/bandleader of the 30s and 40s. Features almost 30 songs, including classics by Cole Porter, George and Ira Gershwin, Hammerstein, Chopin, and several others. **123m/C; VHS, DVD, Blu-Ray.** Tyrone Power; Kim Novak; Victoria Shaw; James Whitmore; Rex Thompson; *D:* George Sidney; *W:* Samuel A. Taylor; *C:* Harry Stradling, Sr.; *M:* George Duning.

Eden 🦴🦴 **1993** Eden is a luxury resort designed to cater to personal fantasies and filled with numerous intrigues. Part-owner Eve Sinclair faces a number of professional and personal complications, including the tragic death of her husband, a brother-in-law who's interested in more than business, and an old friend with uncertain motives. Lots of sex in beautiful settings. **107m/C; VHS, DVD.** Barbara Alyn Woods; Jack Armstrong; Steve Chase; Darcy Demoss; Jeff Griggs; *D:* Victor Lobl; *W:* Stephen Black; Henry Stern. **CABLE**

Eden 🦴🦴 **1998 (R)** Frustrated, Multiple Sclerosis-afflicted housewife Helen (Going) deals with the physical and emotional limitations of her life with dreams of astral projection. Husband Bill (Walsh) is a prep school teacher who doesn't want her to work even though she reaches one of his problem students (Flanery) more effectively than he can. First-time director Goldberg won a Sundance competition for his screenplay, but can't quite deliver on its promise. A tight budget and too many unanswered questions keep this one on the intriguing but ultimately disappointing level. **106m/C; VHS, DVD.** Joanna Going; Dylan Walsh; Sean Patrick Flanery; *D:* Howard Goldberg; *W:* Howard Goldberg; *C:* Hubert Taczanowski; *M:* Brad Fiedel.

Eden 🦴🦴 1/2 **2014 (R)** Recapping the narrative of Mia Hanson-Love's latest drama is to miss its purpose. It's not a plot-driven film, but one designed to replicate the hazy days of music-obsessed youth, a time in which the culture with which one surrounds himself is more important than what he actually does. Based loosely on real music, with a number of DJs actually playing themselves, including Daft Punk, Eden follows Paul (de Givry), a teenager who dives deep into the music scene in Paris in the early '90s. Paul forms a DJ collective with his friends and the movie follows their interactions for the next two decades. **130m/C; DVD, Streaming.** *FR* Felix de Givry; Pauline Etienne; Vincent Macaigne; Hugo Conzelmann; Roman Kolinka; *D:* Mia Hansen-Love; *W:* Mia Hansen-Love; Sven Hansen-Love; *C:* Denis Lenoir.

The Eden Formula 🦴 *Tyrannosaurus Wrecks* **2006** When a scientist creates a formula that will allow him to reproduce any genetic organism he gets raided by an old rival who accidentally sets loose the sock puppet dinosaur he has lying about caged as proof of his success. **92m/C; DVD.** Jeff Fahey; Dee Wallace; Tony Todd; Alexandra Ford; Stephen Wastell; *D:* John Carl Buechler; *W:* John Carl Buechler; *C:* James M. LeGoy; *M:* Andy Garfield. **VIDEO**

The Edge 🦴🦴 1/2 *Bookworm* **1997 (R)** Wealthy Charles Morse (Hopkins) isn't too pleased that fashion photog Bob Greene (Baldwin) takes such an interest in his lovely fashion model wife (Macpherson) and feels the two are out to kill him. Despite his conspiracy theory, Morse and Greene end up depending on each other for survival when their plane crashes in the Alaskan wilderness. To compound their problems, they must do battle with a stalking killer bear. Mamet screenplay dices things up a bit with cutting dialogue which leads to the mind games Mamet is so famous for. Hopkins and Baldwin give understated, intact performances, with an intensity shared only by Bart the Bear, in this small comtemporary parable on the meaning of life. The splendid Alaskan scenery is actually breathtaking aerial and ground footage in Canada. **120m/C; VHS, DVD.** Anthony Hopkins; Alec Baldwin; Elle Macpherson; Harold Perrineau, Jr.; L.Q. Jones; *D:* Lee Tamahori; *W:* David Mamet; *C:* Donald McAlpine; *M:* Jerry Goldsmith.

The Edge 🦴🦴 *Krai* **2010** In 1945, wounded war hero and train engineer Ignat is posted to a nearly-forgotten Siberian labor camp where the prisoners do some logging and basically run their own community. Train tracks stop at a damaged bridge leading to an island once used as a logging camp by Russians and Germans before their countries' non-aggression pact fell apart. When he learns a locomotive was abandoned on the island, Ignat is determined to restore the bridge and the locomotive so he can have his own train to drive. Naturally, there are some unexpected complications. Russian and German with subtitles. **123m/C; DVD.** *RU* Vladimir Mashkov; Yulia Peresild; Anjorka Strechel; Alexsei Gorbanov; *D:* Alexey Uchitel; *W:* Alexander Gonorosvsky; *C:* Yuri Klimenko; *M:* David Holmes.

Edge of Darkness 🦴🦴🦴 1/2 **1943** Compelling war-drama about the underground movement in Norway during Nazi takeover of WWII. Flynn plays a Norwegian fisherman who leads the local underground movement and Sheridan is his loyal fiancee. Although several problems occurred throughout filming, this picture earned high marks for its superb performances and excellent camera work. Based on the novel by William Woods. **120m/B; VHS, DVD.** Errol Flynn; Ann Sheridan; Walter Huston; Nancy Coleman; Helmut Dantine; Judith Anderson; Ruth Gordon; John Beal; *D:* Lewis Milestone; *W:* Robert Rossen.

Edge of Darkness 🦴🦴 **1986** Miniseries mystery involves a police detective who investigates his daughter's murder and uncovers a web of espionage and intrigue. **307m/C; VHS, DVD.** *GB* Bob Peck; Joe Don Baker; Jack Woodson; John Woodvine; Joanne Whalley; *D:* Martin Campbell; *M:* Eric Clapton; Michael Kamen. **TV**

Edge of Darkness 🦴🦴 **2010 (PG-13)** Widowed cop Thomas Craven's (Gibson) only child—activist daughter Emma—is gunned down in front of his home and it's assumed Thomas was actually the target. When he investigates, Thomas discovers more than he expected: a tangled web of corporate and political cover-ups and conspiracies. Based on the British miniseries, the movie is overpacked with more information than two hours can contain, and fails to put all the pieces of the puzzle together. Strong supporting roles, especially from Winstone, but Gibson crowds everyone else off the screen with a one-dimensional boiling rage as the movie devolves into a self-important "Death Wish." **126m/C; Blu-Ray.** Mel Gibson; Ray Winstone; Danny Huston; Shawn Roberts; Denis O'Hare; Bojana Novakovic; *D:* Martin Campbell; *W:* William Monahan; Andrew Bovell; *C:* Phil Meheux; *M:* Howard Shore.

The Edge of Democracy 🦴🦴 1/2 **2019** Brazilian documentarian Costa explores how she came of age at the same time as democracy in her country. She cast her first presidential vote for union leader Lula da Silva, who became president in 2002. Though Costa describes his many achievements, she also notes that corruption destroyed the party he founded from the inside. Da Silva's successor, Dilma Rousseff, enforced anticorruption laws, but became caught up in a scandal of her own and was forced out in an impeachment coup. Costa expertly weaves the personal with broader political and national themes, offering insights and perspective on democracy's meaning in the face of facism. **121m/C; DVD.** *D:* Petra Costa; *W:* Petra Costa; *C:* Joao Atala; *M:* Vitor Araujo; Rodrigo Leao; Gilberto Monte; Lucas Santtana. **VIDEO**

Edge of Eternity 🦴🦴 **1959** Modern western with a so-so script but some good action thanks to director Siegel and a beautiful location in the Grand Canyon. Former miner Eli is murdered after discovering gold is being stolen from the closed mine owned by the Kendon family. Deputy sheriff Les Martin (Wilde) investigates and goes after the killer who's taken his girlfriend Janice Kendon (Shaw) hostage. The finale takes place aboard a tram car dangling over the canyon. **79m/C; DVD, Blu-Ray.** Cornel Wilde; Mickey Shaughnessy; Victoria Shaw; Rian Garrick; Edgar Buchanan; Jack Elam; *D:* Donald Siegel; *W:* Richard Collins; *C:* Burnett Guffey; *M:* Daniele Amfitheatrof.

The Edge of Heaven 🦴🦴🦴 *Auf der Anderen Seite; On the Other Side* **2007** Intertwining story focusing on six very different characters bouncing into each other across countries. Yeter, a devout Muslim and working prostitute, is taken in as a roommate by a lonely john named Ali, but soon is forced into sex slavery. Her daily torture eases after meeting Ali's son Nejat, a German-speaking professor. Unexpectedly, Yeter dies and Nejat takes it upon himself to travel to Turkey in search of Yeter's lost daughter. An excellent cast holds it all together, while director Akin smoothly transitions from story to story. **122m/C; On Demand.** *GE TU* Hanna Schygulla; Baki Davrak; Tuncel Kurtiz; Nursel Kose; Nurgul Yesilcay; Patrycia Ziolkowska; ***D:*** Fatih Akin; ***W:*** Fatih Akin; ***C:*** Rainer Klausmann; ***M:*** Shantel.

Edge of Honor 1/2 **1991 (R)** Young Eagle Scouts camping in the Pacific Northwest discover a woodland weapons cache and wage guerilla war against killer lumberjacks out to silence them. A boneheaded, politically correct action bloodbath; you don't have to like the logging industry to disapprove of the broad slurs against its men shown here. **92m/C; VHS, DVD.** Corey Feldman; Meredith Salenger; Scott Reeves; Ken Jenkins; Christopher Neame; Don Swayze; ***D:*** Michael Spence; ***W:*** David O'Malley.

The Edge of Love 1/2 **2008** Despite the cast (and only Rhys is believable), Maybury's downbeat drama suffers from unlikeable characters and an overwrought plot. Welsh poet Dylan Thomas (Rhys), who's a drunken lout, is doing war work in London in 1940. He reconnects with ex-girlfriend Vera Phillips (Knightley) who then befriends Dylan's hard-drinking Irish wife Caitlin (Miller). Vera marries English soldier William Killick (Murphy) but sets up house with the Thomases when he's sent overseas. Much bad behavior, jealousy, and resentment ensues, leading to violence when a shell-shocked William returns. **110m/C; Blu-Ray, On Demand.** *GB* Matthew Rhys; Keira Knightley; Sienna Miller; Cillian Murphy; ***D:*** John Maybury; ***W:*** Sharman MacDonald; ***C:*** Jonathan Freeman; ***M:*** Angelo Badalamenti.

Edge of Madness 1/2 *A Wilderness Station* **2002 (R)** In 1850, naive Annie (Dhavernas) agrees to an arranged marriage with Manitoba homesteader Simon (Fehr). But although Annie befriends Simon's younger brother George (Sevier), her husband turns out to be angry and abusive. So she kills him after he attacks her. At least that's what she tells constable Mullen (Johansson) when the half-frozen and terrified Annie stumbles into town from her wilderness home. But when Mullen investigates, he finds only more questions. **99m/C; VHS, DVD.** *CA* Caroline Dhavernas; Brendan Fehr; Paul Johansson; Corey Sevier; Tantoo Cardinal; Peter Wingfield; Currie Graham; Jonas Chernick; ***D:*** Anne Wheeler; ***W:*** Anne Wheeler; Charles Kristian Pitts.

Edge of Sanity 1/2 **1989 (R)** An overdone Jekyll-Hyde reprise, with cocaine serving as the villainous substance. Dr. Jekyll (Perkins) is working in his lab, testing cocaine for use as an anaesthetic, when a lab monkey knocks a liquid into the coke and the fumes cause the doc to turn into Jack Hyde, a prototype for Jack the Ripper. Perkins knows the schizoid territory and the production values are good but this is not for the easily queazy. Available in a 90 minute, unrated version. **85m/C; VHS, DVD, Blu-Ray.** *GB* Anthony Perkins; Glynis Barber; David Lodge; Sarah Maur-Thorp; Ben Cole; Lisa Davis; Jill Melford; ***D:*** Gerard Kikoine; ***W:*** J.P. Felix; Ron Raley; ***C:*** Tony Spratling; ***M:*** Frederic Talgorn.

Edge of Seventeen 1/2 **1999** Perceptive gay coming of age tale set in 1984 Ohio. Naive 16-year-old Eric (Stafford) is eager to explore his burgeoning sexuality with the help of college man, Rod (Gabrych). Unfortunately for Eric, Rod's the love 'em and leave 'em type. Disillusioned, Eric tries to remake himself in Brit-pop, New Wave fashion (think Boy George and Duran Duran), while turning to best friend Maggie (Holmes), without realizing the depths of her feelings for him. Eric's coming out tellingly provides confusion not just for himself but for everyone around him. **100m/C; VHS, DVD, Blu-Ray.** Chris Stafford; Tina Holmes; Andersen Gabrych; Stephanie McVay; Lea DeLaria; John Eby; ***D:*** David Moreton; ***W:*** Todd Stephens; ***C:*** Gina DeGirolamo; ***M:*** Tom Bailey.

The Edge of Seventeen **2016 (R)** Steinfeld gives a star-making performance as Nadine Franklin in this clever, funny, smart ode to John Hughes coming-of-age comedies, although arguably better than most of those. The structure of this comedy is a flashback one as Nadine relays events to her supportive history teacher Mr. Bruner (Harrelson). The actual plot here isn't as important as the tone and reliance on characters that you come to identify with and like. Steinfeld carries the film, nailing its comic timing and grounding it emotionally. She may have been a child star (Oscar nominee for True Grit) but this is the movie that should make her huge. **104m/C; DVD, Blu-Ray.** Hailee Steinfeld; Haley Lu Richardson; Blake Jenner; Kyra Sedgwick; Woody Harrelson; ***D:*** Kelly Fremon Craig; ***W:*** Kelly Fremon Craig; ***C:*** Doug Emmett; ***M:*** Atli Orvarsson.

Edge of the City 1/2 **1957** Axel North (Cassavetes) left his family, who blamed him for his brother's death, and now has gone AWOL from the Army. He gets a job working on the New York docks and becomes friendly with Tommy (Poitier), who stoically puts up with his racist boss Malik (Warden) until the man goads him into a fight. Tommy is killed and Alex stays quiet to the cops before confronting Malik on his own. Based on the play "A Man Is Ten Feet Tall" by Robert Alan Aurthur. Directorial debut of Ritt. **85m/B; DVD.** John Cassavetes; Sidney Poitier; Jack Warden; Kathleen Maguire; Ruby Dee; Robert F. Simon; Ruth White; ***D:*** Martin Ritt; ***W:*** Robert Alan Aurthur; ***C:*** Joseph Brun; ***M:*** Leonard Rosenman.

Edge of the World **1937** Moody, stark British drama of a mini-society in its death throes, expertly photographed on a six-square-mile island in the Shetlands. A dwindling fishing community of fewer than 100 souls agonize over whether to migrate to the mainland; meanwhile the romance of a local girl with an off-islander takes a tragic course. Choral effects were provided by the Glasgow Orpheus Choir. **80m/B; VHS, DVD.** *GB* Finlay Currie; Niall MacGinnis; Grant Sutherland; John Laurie; Michael Powell; ***D:*** Michael Powell; ***W:*** Michael Powell.

Edge of Tomorrow *Live Die Repeat: Edge of Tomorrow* **2014 (PG-13)** Sharing an amazing amount of creative DNA with video games like Halo and Gears of War, Liman's sci-fi blockbuster is one of the rare pieces of Hollywood escapism that completely delivers on that which it promises. Cruise plays Cage, a man thrown into a waking nightmare when he's forced to the frontline of the battle against an alien race that has been kicking human ass. Case is almost instantly killed but he returns to the start of that day a la "Groundhog Day," and is forced to try again. Joining forces with the fantastic Blunt as the force's best soldier, Cage could be the answer for human survival. **113m/C; DVD, Blu-Ray.** Tom Cruise; Emily Blunt; Brendan Gleeson; Bill Paxton; Noah Taylor; ***D:*** Doug Liman; ***W:*** Christopher McQuarrie; Jez Butterworth; John-Henry Butterworth; ***C:*** Dion Beebe; ***M:*** Christophe Beck.

Edge of Winter **2016 (R)** Elliot Baker (Kinnaman) is spending time with his kids while their mother is away with her new husband. He really wants to bond with the boys as he's feeling increasingly distant, but his plans go haywire when a snowstorm locks them in a deserted cabin. Feeling that the events of the trip will cause him to lose custody, Elliot panics and his boys come to realize that their father may be the biggest threat to their safety. Kinnaman is solid but this thriller isn't quite effective at producing thrills. **89m/C; DVD.** Joel Kinnaman; Tom Holland; Percy Hynes White; Rachelle Lefevre; Shaun Benson; ***D:*** Rob Connolly; ***W:*** Rob Connolly; Kyle Mann; ***C:*** Norm Li; ***M:*** Brooke Blair; Will Blair.

Edges of the Lord **2001 (R)** Jewish Romek (Osment) is taken out of Krakow at his parents' behest to save him from the Nazi camps. A farmer agrees to pass the blond, blue-eyed boy off as a distant relative who has come to stay and the parish priest (Dafoe) quietly coaches the child in Catholic catechism so he can 'pass' in the suspicious community. The horrors and deprivations of war are generally seen through the eyes of the local children. **95m/C; DVD.** Haley Joel Osment; Willem Dafoe; Liam Hess; Richard Banel; ***D:*** Yurek Bogayevicz; ***W:*** Yurek Bogayevicz; ***C:*** Pawel Edelman; ***M:*** Jan A.P. Kaczmarek.

Edie 1/2 **2019** Once a free spirit who enjoyed camping with her father, 83-year-old Edie (Hancock) spent most of her adulthood married to a controlling man who limited her life. Three years after her husband's death, Edie's daughter moves her into an assisted living facility where she is miserable. One day, she decides to go to Scotland to climb a mountain. Hiring a guide, Jonny (Guthrie), whom she runs into at the Scottish train station, Edie challenges herself, and Jonny, to grow in unexpected ways as she pursues her goal. An average drama that's uplifted by Hancock's illuminating performance and beautiful backdrop. **102m/C; DVD.** Sheila Hancock; Kevin Guthrie; Paul Brannigan; Amy Manson; Wendy Morgan; ***D:*** Simon Hunter; ***W:*** Elizabeth O'Halloran; ***C:*** August Jakobsson; ***M:*** Debbie Wiseman.

Edie & Pen 1/2 **1995 (PG-13)** Tilly seems to be making a career of playing the ditz who's smarter than she seems as she shows here as Edie, who meets Pen (Channing) in Reno where both are looking for quickie divorces. They hit a bar to celebrate and hook up with soft-hearted Harry (Glenn), who's been dumped by his wife. Some drunken life discussions follow and then Edie finds out that her fiance is Pen's cold-hearted, newly ex hubby (Wilson). Slight script, charming performances. **97m/C; VHS, DVD.** Jennifer Tilly; Stockard Channing; Scott Glenn; Stuart Wilson; ***Cameo(s):*** Beverly D'Angelo; Louise Fletcher; Joanna Gleason; Michael McKean; Martin Mull; Michael O'Keefe; Chris Sarandon; Randy Travis; Jean Smart; Victoria Tennant; ***D:*** Matthew Irmas; ***W:*** Victoria Tennant; ***C:*** Alicia Weber; ***M:*** Shawn Colvin.

Edie in Ciao! Manhattan *Ciao! Manhattan* **1972 (R)** Real-life story of Edie Sedgwick, Warhol superstar and international fashion model, whose life in the fast lane led to ruin. **84m/C; VHS, DVD.** Edie Sedgwick; Baby Jane Holzer; Roger Vadim; Paul America; Viva; Isabel Jewell; Pat Hartley; ***D:*** David Weisman; John Palmer; ***W:*** David Weisman; John Palmer; ***C:*** John Palmer; Kjell Rostand; ***M:*** Gino Piserchio.

Edison Force 1/2 *Edison* **2005 (R)** Pollack (Timberlake) is a junior reporter at a lowly community paper in suburban Edison when he stumbles across information on a police unit whose results at cleaning up crime (at any cost) have left them above the law they purportedly serve. When Pollack asks too many questions, bad things happen. Self-important and heavy-handed. **97m/C; DVD.** Morgan Freeman; Kevin Spacey; Justin Timberlake; LL Cool J; Dylan McDermott; Cary Elwes; Piper Perabo; Roselyn Sanchez; ***D:*** David J. Burke; ***W:*** David J. Burke; ***C:*** Francis Kenny.

VIDEO

Edison the Man 1/2 **1940** Story of Tommy Edison's early years of experimentation in the basement. The young genious eventually invents light bulbs, motion pictures, and a sound recording device. Well played by Tracy. **108m/C; VHS, DVD.** Spencer Tracy; Rita Johnson; Lynne Overman; Charles Coburn; Gene Lockhart; Henry Travers; Felix Bressart; ***D:*** Clarence Brown.

Edmond **2005 (R)** Dissatisfied with his middle-aged, middle-management life, Edmond (Macy) reacts to a psychic's dismal prophecy by leaving his wife and turning his regretful existence upside down with a homicidal night on the town. Following the dubious advice of a sleazeball barfly (Mantegna), Edmond, in a nutshell, gets kicked out of a strip club, kills a would-be mugger, beds then kills a waitress half his age (Stiles), and ends up the plaything of his burly, black cellmate (Woodbine). Sound unpleasant? It is. Macy's usual, utterly convincing portrayal earns pic a half bone. Based on a 1982 play by David Mamet, which ran off-Broadway. Rent it with "Bad Lieutenant" for a night that'll destroy your faith in humanity. **76m/C; DVD.** William H. Macy; Joe Mantegna; Jeffrey Combs; Denise Richards; Rebecca Pidgeon; Julia Stiles; Mena Suvari; Bai Ling; Dulé Hill; Dylan Walsh; Russell Hornsby; Debi Mazar; Lionel Mark Smith; Bokeem Woodbine; Jack Wallace; George Wendt; Frances Bay; ***D:*** Stuart Gordon; ***W:*** David Mamet; ***C:*** Denis Maloney; ***M:*** Bobby Johnston.

EDtv 1/2 **1999 (PG-13)** Ed (McConaughey) is a scruffy redneck video clerk who agrees to have his life broadcast 24/7 for a reality show produced by DeGeneres. Of course the show becomes a hit, and an entire nation watches breathlessly as Ed steals his brother's girlfriend Shari (Elfman), restocks shelves, and goes to the bathroom with the door open. His family life immediately turns melodramatic, with Ed learning "shocking secrets" about his mom (Kirkland), dad (Landau), and brother (Harrelson). Compared to the "The Truman Show," thanks to their back-to-back release in theatres, but director (and TV child star survivor) Ron Howard's version lacks the biting satire. **122m/C; VHS, DVD, Blu-Ray.** Matthew McConaughey; Jenna Elfman; Woody Harrelson; Ellen DeGeneres; Sally Kirkland; Martin Landau; Elizabeth Hurley; Rob Reiner; Dennis Hopper; Adam Goldberg; Viveka Davis; Clint Howard; Larry "Flash" Jenkins; Donny Most; Rick Overton; RuPaul Charles; Gedde Watanabe; Harry Shearer; Jennifer Elise Cox; ***D:*** Ron Howard; ***W:*** Lowell Ganz; Babaloo Mandel; ***C:*** John Schwartzman; ***M:*** Randy Edelman.

Educating Rita 1/2 **1983 (PG)** Walters and Caine team beautifully in this adaptation of the successful Willy Russell play which finds Rita, an uneducated hairdresser, determined to improve her knowledge of literature. In so doing, she enlists the aid of tutor Frank: a disillusioned alcoholic, adeptly played by Caine. Together, the two find inspiration in one another's differences and experiences. Ultimately, the teacher receives a lesson in how to again appreciate his work and the classics as he observes his pupil's unique approach to her studies. Some deem this a "Pygmalion" for the '80s. **110m/C; VHS, DVD.** *GB* Michael Caine; Julie Walters; Michael Williams; Maureen Lipman; ***D:*** Lewis Gilbert; ***W:*** Willy Russell. British Acad. '83: Actor (Caine), Actress (Walters), Film; Golden Globes '84: Actor--Mus./Comedy (Caine), Actress--Mus./Comedy (Walters).

An Education **2009 (PG-13)** Mulligan is bewitching as 16-year-old Jenny in a coming-into-womanhood story. Bored, bright and inexperienced, Jenny can't wait to throw off her sheltered suburban upbringing and the restraints of her strict girls' school in a drab 1961 London. Desperate to be thought a sophisticate, she's ripe for the plucking after she meets smooth-talking thirtysomething David (Sarsgaard), who starts taking her out on the town. But Jenny isn't quite the naif he thinks she is. Adapted from a memoir by journalist Lynn Barber. **100m/C; Blu-Ray, On Demand.** *GB* Carey Mulligan; Peter Sarsgaard; Dominic Cooper; Rosamund Pike; Alfred Molina; Olivia Williams; Emma Thompson; Cara Seymour; Matthew Beard; Sally Hawkins; ***D:*** Lone Scherfig; ***W:*** Nick Hornby; ***C:*** John de Borman; ***M:*** Paul Englishby. British Acad. '09: Actress (Mulligan); Ind. Spirit '10: Foreign Film.

The Education of Little Tree **1997 (PG)** Child's eye view of a large scale epic on par with modern classics like "The Secret Garden." In 1935, poor, orphaned, and part Native American Little Tree (Ashton) is sent to live with his grandfather (Cromwell) and Native American grandmother (Cardinal) in the Smokey Mountains of Tennessee. There he learns "The Way" of his Cherokee ancestors and how to make moonshine from his Scottish/Irish grandfather. A nosy, Bible-thumping Aunt tips off authorities and soon Little Tree is shipped off to an evil state institution to cure him of his inappropriate Indian ways. There, the old-fashioned discipline runs fierce and abusive. Adapted from a children's book by Forrest Carter. Cardinal and Cromwell carve out memorable performances alongside first-rate newcomer Joseph Ashton. **112m/C; VHS, DVD.** James Cromwell; Tantoo Cardinal; Joseph Ashton; Graham Greene; Lisa Bronwyn Moore; ***D:*** Richard Friedenberg; ***W:*** Richard Friedenberg; ***C:*** Anastas Michos; ***M:*** Mark Isham.

The Education of Sonny Carson 1/2 **1974 (R)** Chilling look at the tribulations of a black youth living in a Brooklyn ghetto amid drugs, prostitution, crime, and other forms of vice. Based on Sonny Carson's autobiography. Still pertinent some 20 years after its theatrical release. **104m/C; VHS, DVD.** Rony Clanton; Don Gordon; Paul Benjamin; ***D:*** Michael Campus.

The Edukators *Die Fetten Jahre sind vorbei* **2004 (R)** In Berlin, three twenty-something political idealists, dogmatic and naive, commit various property pranks on the bourgeoisie. Roomies Jan (Bruehl) and Peter (Erceg) and Peter's girlfriend Julie (Jentsche) (who likes Jan, too) happily vandalize until ineptly graduating to kidnapping when businessman Hardenberg (Klaussner) comes home early and interrupts them. Clueless, the trio decide to hide out with their captive (who turns out to be a former 60s radical) at a mountain cabin. Much generational talk and romantic tension ensues. German with subtitles. **126m/C; DVD.** *GE AT* Daniel Brühl; Julia Jentsch; Stipe Erceg; Burghart Klaussner; ***D:*** Hans Weingartner; ***W:*** Hans Weingartner; Katharina Held; ***C:*** Matthias Schellenberg; Daniela Knapp; ***M:*** Andreas Wodraschke.

Edvard Munch **1974** Biographical portrait of the Norwegian Expressionist painter and his tormented life in the stuffy society of 19th-century Oslo. Concentrates mainly on his early years, including the deaths of his mother and younger sister, his brother's suicide, Munch's affair with a married woman, and his struggle to maintain his sanity. Based on Munch's memoirs. In German and Norwegian with English subtitles. **167m/C; VHS, DVD.** *NO* Geir Westby; Gro Fraas; Eli Ryg; ***D:*** Peter Watkins; ***W:*** Peter Watkins; ***C:*** Odd Geir Saether.

Edward and Mrs. Simpson **1980** Dramatic reconstruction of the years leading to the abdication of King Edward VIII, who forfeited the British throne in 1936 so that he could marry American divorcee Wallis Simpson. Originally aired on PBS. **270m/C; VHS, DVD.** Edward Fox; Cynthia Harris; ***D:*** Waris Hussein. **TV**

Edward, My Son **1949** Tracy isn't quite ruthless enough in this adaptation of the British play by Noel Langley and Robert Morley (who played the role onstage). Arnold Boult will do anything for his only son Edward (who's never seen onscreen), including arson for the insurance money, ruining his business partner, and turning his wife Evelyn (Kerr) into an embittered drunk. Meanwhile, Edward grows up overindulged and irresponsible. **113m/B; DVD.** Spencer Tracy; Deborah Kerr; Ian Hunter; James Donald; Mervyn Johns; Walter Fitzgerald; Colin Gordon; Harriette Johns; Leueen MacGrath; ***D:*** George Cukor; ***W:*** Donald Ogden Stewart; ***C:*** Frederick A. (Freddie) Young; ***M:*** John Wooldridge.

Edward Scissorhands **1990 (PG-13)** Depp's a young man created by loony scientist Price, who dies before he can attach hands to his boy-creature. Then the boy is rescued from his lonely existence outside of suburbia by an ingratiating Avon lady. With scissors in place of hands, he has more trouble fitting into suburbia than would most new kids on the block, and he struggles with being different and lonely in a cardboard-cutout world. Visually captivating fairy tale full of splash and color, however predictable the Hollywood-prefab denouement. **100m/C; VHS, DVD, Blu-Ray.** Johnny Depp; Winona Ryder; Dianne Wiest; Vincent Price; Anthony Michael Hall; Alan Arkin; Kathy Baker; Conchata Ferrell; Caroline Aaron; Dick Anthony Williams; Robert Oliveri; John Davidson; ***D:*** Tim Burton; ***W:*** Tim Burton; Caroline Thompson; ***C:*** Stefan Czapsky; ***M:*** Danny Elfman.

Edward II 1/2 **1992 (R)** Jarman's controversial adaptation of Christopher Marlowe's play "The Troublesome Reign of Edward II" portrays the weak-willed monarch as neglecting his kingdom for love. Unfortunately, it's not for his queen but for his commoner male lover. His neglect of both queen and country lead to a swift and brutal downfall. Jarman's use of contemporary anachronisms, stream of conscienceness approach, and heavy symbolism may leave more than one viewer wondering what's going on. **91m/C; VHS, DVD, Blu-Ray.** *GB* Steven Waddington; Kevin Collins; Andrew Tiernan; John Lynch; Dudley Sutton; Tilda Swinton; Jerome Flynn; Jody Graber; Nigel Terry; Annie Lennox; ***D:*** Derek Jarman; ***W:*** Derek Jarman; ***M:*** Simon Fisher Turner. Venice Film Fest. '92: Actress (Swinton).

Edward the King 1/2 **1975** British miniseries follows the long life of Prince Edward, who waited some 60 years for his overbearing mother, Queen Victoria, to die so he could ascend the throne. Bertie scandalized with his affairs and carousing but, nevertheless, proved his worth as king-in-waiting. On six cassettes. **708m/C; VHS, DVD.** *GB* Timothy West; Annette Crosbie; John Gielgud; Francesca Annis; Robert Hardy; ***D:*** John Gorrie; ***C:*** Tony Imi. **TV**

Edwin 1/2 **1984** Sir Fennimore Truscott (Guinness) is a retired High Court Judge who suspects that his neighbor once had an affair with Truscott's wife. These long-fermenting fears assert themself as Truscott presents his case (to the audience) and even suspects the paternity of his son, Edwin. When Edwin comes for a visit, Truscott's obsessions are forced into the open. **78m/C; VHS, DVD.** *GB* Alec Guinness; Paul Rogers; Renee Asherson; ***D:*** Rodney Bennett; ***W:*** John Mortimer. **TV**

Eegah! WOOF! 1962 Another Arch Hall-directed (under the Nicholas Merriwether pseud.) epic in which an anachronistic Neanderthal falls in love in '60s California. Reputed to be one of the worst films of all time. **93m/C; VHS, DVD, Blu-Ray.** Marilyn Manning; Richard Kiel; Arch Hall, Jr.; William Waters; Carolyn Brandt; William Lloyd; Ray Dennis Steckler; ***D:*** Arch (Archie) Hall, Sr.; ***W:*** Bob Wehling; ***C:*** Vilis Lapenieks; ***M:*** Arch Hall, Jr.

The Eel *Unagi* **1996** Yamashita (Yakusho) has just been paroled after spending eight years in prison for killing his adulterous wife in a jealous rage. While there, he found and cared for an eel, which became his only confidante, and which accompanies him to his new life as a barber in a small town outside Tokyo. The newcomer is soon befriended by the locals but Yamashita's life changes most when he saves the suicidal Keiko (Shimizu) from drowning. She comes to work in his shop and would obviously like a more intimate relationship but some secrets in her past and some strange incidents in the town may jepordize Yamashita's hopes for a normal life. Based on the novel "Glimmering in the Dark" by Akira Yoshimura. Japanese with subtitles. **117m/C; VHS, DVD.** *JP* Koji Yakusho; Misa Shimizu; Mitsuko Baisho; Shou Aikawa; Fujio Tsuneta; Akira (Tsukamoto) Emoto; Etsuko Ichihara; Tomorowo Taguchi; Ken Kobayashi; Sabu Kawahara; ***D:*** Shohei Imamura; ***W:*** Shohei Imamura; Motofumi Tomikawa; Daisuke Tengan; ***C:*** Shigeru Komatsubara; ***M:*** Shinichiro Ikebe. Cannes '97: Film.

Effi Briest 1/2 *Fontane Effi Briest* **1974** A 19th-century tragedy well-played by Schygulla and empowered with Fassbinder's directorial skills. Effi (Schygulla) is a 17 year-old beauty, unhappily married to a much older man. She drifts into a brief affair, which is not discovered for several years. When her husband does discover her past infidelity, the Prussian legal code permits him a chilling revenge. Based on a popular 19th-century novel by Theodor Fontane. In German with English subtitles. **135m/B; VHS, DVD.** *GE* Hanna Schygulla; Wolfgang Schenck; Lilo Pempeit; Ulli Lommel; ***D:*** Rainer Werner Fassbinder; ***W:*** Rainer Werner Fassbinder; ***C:*** Jurgen Jurges; Dietrich Lohmann.

The Efficiency Expert 1/2 *Spotswood* **1992 (PG)** Lighthearted Australian comedy about a dingy moccasin factory where a rigid efficiency consultant is invited to save the eccentric family-run company from bankruptcy. Predictable ending contains a nevertheless timely message about the importance of the bottom line. **97m/C; VHS, DVD.** *AU* Anthony Hopkins; Ben Mendelsohn; Alwyn Kurts; Bruno Lawrence; Angela Punch McGregor; Russell Crowe; Rebecca Rigg; Toni Collette; ***D:*** Mark Joffe; ***W:*** Andrew Knight; Max Dann; ***M:*** Ricky Fataar.

Effie Gray **2015 (PG-13)** Lush to a fault, this Victorian period piece feels like it's trapped inside its own ornate borders. Real-life 19th century celebutaunt Effie Gray (Fanning), a young woman stuck in a sexless marriage with art critic John Ruskin (Wise), has a wandering eye for her husband's protege, Millais (Sturridge). Although the love triangle triggered a huge scandal in its day, this lightweight treatment keeps most of the steamy drama under wraps. Painfully slow, and lacking any type of passion, screenwriter and supporting actress Thompson, hogged the only zest for her portrayal of a noblewoman offering advice to the young Effie. Much like a beautiful painting, you look at it and move on. **108m/C; DVD.** Dakota Fanning; Emma Thompson; Tom Sturridge; Claudia Cardinale; Julie Walters; ***D:*** Richard Laxton; ***W:*** Emma Thompson; ***C:*** Andrew Dunn; ***M:*** Paul Cantelon.

Egg and I **1947** Based on the true-life adventures of best-selling humorist Betty MacDonald. A young urban bride agrees to help her new husband realize his life-long dream of owning a chicken farm. A dilapidated house, temperamental stove, and suicidal chickens test the bride's perseverance, as do the zany antics of her country-bumpkin neighbors, Ma and Pa Kettle, who make their screen debut. Plenty of old-fashioned laughs. **104m/B; VHS, DVD, Blu-Ray.** Claudette Colbert; Fred MacMurray; Marjorie Main; Percy Kilbride; Louise Allbritton; Richard Long; Billy House; Donald MacBride; ***D:*** Chester Erskine; ***C:*** Milton Krasner.

The Egyptian 1/2 **1954** Based on the sword-and-sandal novel by Mika Waltari, this is a ponderous big-budget epic about a young Egyptian Sinuhe (Purdom) in Akhnaton's epoch who becomes physician to the Pharaoh, dealing with the rise and fall of his pharoah's fortunes, as well as his own. **140m/C; VHS, DVD, Blu-Ray.** Edmund Purdom; Victor Mature; Peter Ustinov; Bella Darvi; Gene Tierney; Henry Daniell; Jean Simmons; Michael Wilding; Judith Evelyn; John Carradine; Carl Benton Reid; Angela (Clark) Clarke; Tommy Rettig; Michael Ansara; Leo Gordon; Bruno VeSota; ***D:*** Michael Curtiz; ***W:*** Philip Dunne; Casey Robinson; ***C:*** Leon Shamroy.

An Egyptian Story *Hadduta Misriya* **1982** An Egyptian film director (Dine) goes to London for open-heart surgery and as he hovers between life and death, he remembers his past. Scenes from Chahine's other films highlight the director's reminiscences. Part 2 of the Alexandria trilogy, preceded by "Alexandria...Why?" and followed by "Alexandria Again and Forever." Arabic with subtitles. **127m/C; VHS, DVD.** *EG* Mohiel Dine; Nour (el-Sherif) el-Cherif; Oussama Nadir; Magda El Khatib; ***D:*** Youssef Chahine; ***W:*** Youssef Chahine; ***C:*** Mohsen Nasr; ***M:*** Gamal Salama.

Eichmann **2007** The banality of evil is shown once again in this true story. After the Mossad capture Nazi Adolf Eichmann in Argentina in 1960, he's taken to Israel to be tried as a war criminal. It's up to police Captain Avner Less to interrogate Eichmann and build a case against him. The SS officer maintains he was just following Hitler's orders as he set up concentration camps to put the 'Final Solution' into operation. **100m/C; DVD.** Troy Garity; Franka Potente; Stephen Fry; Thomas Kretschmann; Stephen Greif; Delaine Yates; Tereza Srbova; Judit Viktor; ***D:*** Robert Young; ***W:*** Snoo Wilson; ***C:*** Michael Connor; ***M:*** Richard Harvey.

The Eiger Sanction **1975 (R)** An art teacher returns to the CII (a fictionalized version of the CIA) as an exterminator hired to assassinate the killers of an American agent. In the process, he finds himself climbing the Eiger. Beautiful Swiss Alps scenery fails to totally compensate for several dreary lapses. Based on the novel by Trevanian. **125m/C; VHS, DVD, Blu-Ray.** Clint Eastwood; George Kennedy; Vonetta McGee; Jack Cassidy; Thayer David; ***D:*** Clint Eastwood; ***W:*** Hal Dresner; Warren B. Murphy; Rod Whitaker; ***C:*** Frank Stanley; ***M:*** John Williams.

8 1/2 *Otto e mezzo; Federico Fellini's 8 1/2* **1963** The acclaimed Fellini self-portrait of a revered Italian film director struggling with a fated film project wanders through his intermixed life, childhood memories, and hallucinatory fantasies. Subtitled in English. **135m/B; VHS, DVD, Blu-Ray.** *IT* Marcello Mastroianni; Claudia Cardinale; Anouk Aimee; Sandra Milo; Barbara Steele; Rossella Falk; Eddra Gale; Mark Herron; Madeleine LeBeau; Caterina Boratto; ***D:*** Federico Fellini; ***W:*** Tullio Pinelli; Ennio Flaiano; Brunello Rondi; Federico Fellini; ***C:*** Gianni Di Venanzo; ***M:*** Nino Rota. Oscars '63: Costume Des. (B&W), Foreign Film; N.Y. Film Critics '63: Foreign Film.

8 1/2 Women 1/2 **1999 (R)** A typically baffling presentation from Greenaway concerns wealthy Swiss businessman Philip Emmenthal (Standing), who is grief-stricken over the recent death of his wife. His son, Storey (Delamere), comes to Geneva to console his father. After seeing Fellini's "8 1/2" they suddenly decide to assemble their own harem of decidedly offbeat females and pursue sexual fantasies. Remarkably unappealing and dull. **122m/C; VHS, DVD.** *GB* John Standing; Vivian Wu; Annie Shizuka Inoh; Matthew Delamere; Toni Collette; Amanda Plummer; Manna Fujiwara; Barbara Sarafian; Polly Walker; Karina Mano; Natacha Amal; ***D:*** Peter Greenaway; ***W:*** Peter Greenaway; ***C:*** Sacha Vierny.

Eight Below 1/2 **2006 (PG)** Disney goes to the dogs with appropriately tail-wagging results. Jerry (Walker), a guide at the U.S. National Science Research Base in Antarctica, is deeply devoted to his eight beautiful sled dogs. Ambitious scientist McClaren (Greenwood) gets them involved in a risky mission that results in evacuation for the humans—but not the dogs—due to early winter storms. While the dogs scavenge to survive, Jerry tries to organize a rescue trip to save his best friends. Shot in Canada, Norway, and Greenland. **120m/C; DVD, Blu-Ray.** Paul Walker; Bruce Greenwood; Jason Biggs; Gerard Plunkett; Connor Christopher Levins; August Schellenberg; Wendy Crewson; Moon Bloodgood; Belinda Metz; ***D:*** Frank Marshall; ***W:*** Dave DiGilio; ***C:*** Don Burgess; ***M:*** Mark Isham.

Eight Days a Week 1/2 **1997 (R)** Shy, nerdy high-schooler Peter (Schaefer) is obsessed with Erica (Russell), the popular babe who lives across the street. Peter decides a sit-in on her front lawn and constant protestations about his devotion is the way to get her attention. Title comes from the Beatles tune and is the cleverest thing in the movie. **92m/C; VHS, DVD.** Joshua Schaefer; Keri Russell; R.D. Robb; Mark L. Taylor; Catherine Hicks; ***D:*** Michael Davis; ***W:*** Michael Davis; ***C:*** James Lawrence Spencer; ***M:*** Kevin Bassinson.

Eight Days to Live 1/2 **2006** Based on a true story. Nineteen-year-old Joe tells his parents he's going to a party and won't be home until Monday. He falls asleep while driving and goes off the road and down a steep embankment. When Joe's friend calls to say he never made it there, his worried mom Teresa calls the cops but Joe hasn't been gone long enough to be considered missing and she begins her own search. **90m/C; DVD.** Kelly Rowan; Dustin Milligan; Shawn Doyle; Tegan Moss; Ryan McDonell; Katharine Isabelle; Kimberly Warnat; Michael Eklund; ***D:*** Norma Bailey; ***W:*** Greg Spottiswood; ***C:*** Paul Sarossy; ***M:*** Robert Carli. **CABLE**

8 Diagram Pole Fighter *Wu Lang ba gua gun; Invincible Pole Fighter; Ng Leung bat gwa gwun; Magnificent Pole Fighters; Eight Diagram Cudgel Fighter* **1984** The Yangs are a well respected family of martial artists in the service of the government. Betrayed by a corrupt official, they are nearly wiped out or captured by the Mongols. Of the two who return, one is mad, and the other becomes a monk in his sorrow. When he learns that the same Mongols who slaughtered his brothers have kidnapped his sister he leaves the temple for revenge. Originally meant as a vehicle for Fu Sheng, it was retooled to present Chia Hui Liu (aka Gordon Liu) as the protagonist when Fu died during filming. **90m/C; DVD.** *CH* Chia Hui Liu; Sheng Fu; Lily Li; Kara Hui; Ching-Ching Yeung; Lung Wei Wang; ***D:*** Chia-Liang Lu; ***W:*** Chia-Liang Lu; Kuang Ni; ***C:*** An-sung Tsao; ***M:*** Chin Yung Shing; Chen-hou Su.

8 Heads in a Duffel Bag **1996 (R)** Mob bag man Tommy (Pesci, in a real stretch) loses his heads, the evidence of a successful hit, to med student Charlie Pritchett (Comeau), who's headed for a Mexican vacation with his fiance's (Swanson) uptight family. Desperate, Tommy "persuades" Charlie's roommates (Spade and Louiso) to help him find some replacement noggins. Excellent premise is almost done in by a timid script that relies a little too much on slapstick. Schulman's uneven directorial debut does little to mask the problem. Newcomer Comeau tries for a "Bachelor Party" era Tom Hanks thing, but doesn't quite get there. Pesci and Spade save flick from disaster, and get most of the good lines, pitted in a generational "battle of the smart-asses," but neither one strays from their previous screen personas. Louiso hilariously makes the most of his role as the naive roommate. **95m/C; VHS, DVD, Blu-Ray.** Joe Pesci; David Spade; Andy Comeau; Kristy Swanson; George Hamilton; Dyan Cannon; Todd Louiso; Frank Roman; Anthony Mangano; Joe Basile; Ernestine Mercer; Howard George; ***D:*** Tom Schulman; ***W:*** Tom Schulman; ***C:*** Adam Holender; ***M:*** Andrew Gross.

800 Bullets 1/2 *800 Balas* **2002** Director Iglesia pays tribute to the films of Sergio Leone in this Spanish dramatic comedy. Fourteen-year-old Carlos (Castro) runs away from his uptight widowed mother, Laura (Maura), in search of his paternal grandfather. He finds his grandfather Julian (Gracia) living in Almeria, a region in Spain that doubled for the American West in countless spaghetti westerns. Julian, a former stuntman, is now an alcoholic employee of a theme park cobbled together from the abandoned sets of old cowboy movies. Julian and his fellow stuntmen welcome Carlos into their band of Lost Boys, that is, until Laura shows up, threatening to close the party down. Iglesia has great fun orchestrating complex comedic set pieces, but has trouble balancing the dramatic tone in the last act. **123m/C; DVD.** Sancho Gracia; Carmen Maura; Eusebio Poncela; Terele Pavez; Angel de Andres Lopez; Luis Castro; *D:* Alex de la Iglesia; *W:* Alex de la Iglesia; *C:* Flavio Martinez Labiano; *M:* Roque Baños.

800 Leagues Down the Amazon 🦴 1/2 **1993 (PG-13)** A 19th-century journey down the Amazon on a raft with a planter, his daughter, and various complications. Based on a novel by Jules Verne. **100m/C; VHS, DVD.** Daphne Zuniga; Barry Bostwick; Adam Baldwin; Tom Verica; E.E. Bell; *D:* Luis Llosa; *W:* Laura Schiff; Jackson Barr; *C:* Pili Flores-Guerra; *M:* Jorge Tafur.

Eight Iron Men 🦴🦴 **1952** Character-driven low-budget quickie. A WWII infantry squad is holed up in a bombed-out house in Italy. One of the squad, Pvt. Small, is pinned down in a foxhole by enemy fire and when their orders come through to move out, tough Sgt. Mooney has to make a decision about whether to leave him behind. Brown adapted his own 1945 play "A Sound of Hunting." **81m/B; DVD.** Lee Marvin; Richard Kiley; Bonar Colleano; Arthur Franz; Nick Dennis; James J. Griffith; Dickie Moore; George Cooper; *D:* Edward Dmytryk; *W:* Harry Brown; *C:* J. Roy Hunt; *M:* Leith Stevens.

Eight Legged Freaks 🦴🦴 1/2 **2002 (PG-13)** Attack of the B-Movie Redos! Boy (Arquette) meets girl (Wuhrer) and battle giant mutant spiders in this updated 1950s sci-fi horror/comedy. Prosperity, Arizona is the unlikely site of a toxic waste mishap near a spider farm, spawning SUV-sized creepy crawlies. Slow-witted but sweet local boy Arquette joins forces with foxy sheriff Wuhrer and a posse of locals to rid the town of the huge spideys. Scary, campy, self-parodying fun. Director Elkayem gives props to the '50s horror cult classic, "Them!" which plays in the background of one scene. **99m/C; VHS, DVD.** David Arquette; Kari Wuhrer; Scott Terra; Scarlett Johansson; Doug E. Doug; Riley Smith; Leon Rippy; Rick Overton; Eileen Ryan; Tom Noonan; *D:* Ellory Elkayem; *W:* Jesse Alexander; Ellory Elkayem; *C:* John Bartley; *M:* John Ottman.

Eight Men Out 🦴🦴🦴🦴 **1988 (PG)** Taken from Eliot Asinof's book, a moving, full-blooded account of the infamous 1919 "Black Sox" scandal, in which members of the Chicago White Sox teamed to throw the World Series for $80,000. A dirge of lost innocence, this is among Sayles' best films. Provides an interesting look at the "conspiracy" that ended "Shoeless" Joe Jackson's major-league career. The actual baseball scenes are first-rate, and Straithairn, Sweeney, and Cusack give exceptional performances. Sayles makes an appearance as Ring Lardner. Enjoyable viewing for even the non-sports fan. **121m/C; VHS, DVD, Blu-Ray.** John Cusack; D.B. Sweeney; Perry Lang; Jace Alexander; Bill Irwin; Clifton James; Michael Rooker; Michael Lerner; Christopher Lloyd; Studs Terkel; David Strathairn; Charlie Sheen; Kevin Tighe; John Mahoney; John Sayles; Gordon Clapp; Richard Edson; James Read; Don Harvey; John Anderson; Maggie Renzi; Michael Mantell; Nancy Travis; Michael Laskin; Barbara Garrick; Wendy Makkena; *D:* John Sayles; *W:* John Sayles; *C:* Robert Richardson; *M:* Mason Daring.

8 Mile 🦴🦴🦴 **2002 (R)** Although claiming to be fiction, director Hanson's thinly veiled bio of star Eminem's escape from the streets of Detroit will please more than the rapper's fans. Rabbit (Eminem) is a joyless autoworker living in the trailer park with his loose mother (Basinger) and little sister Lily (Greenfield). The only time that Rabbit has a chance to shine is at the rap battles organized by pal Future (Phifer), who sees talent in his friend. Also recognizing greatness (and a possible ticket out of the 'hood) is aspiring model Alex (Murphy), who quickly consummates a calculating relationship with Rabbit. The climactic rap battle allows Eminem to showcase the talent that made this "Rocky"-esque vehicle possible, although it wisely ends with Rabbit on the cusp of success and not at the pinnacle. Shot on location in Detroit. **118m/C; VHS, DVD, Blu-Ray, UMD.** Eminem; Kim Basinger; Brittany Murphy; Mekhi Phifer; Evan Jones; Eugene Byrd; Omar Benson Miller; De'Angelo Wilson; Taryn Manning; Michael Shannon; Anthony Mackie; Chloe Greenfield; Paul Bates; Craig Chandler; *D:* Curtis Hanson; *W:* Scott Silver; *C:* Rodrigo Prieto; *M:* Eminem. Oscars '02: Song ("Lose Yourself").

Eight Miles High 🦴 1/2 *Das Wilde Leben* **2007** Flashy, trashy autobiopic of frequently undressed German model/sixties icon Uschi Obermaier (Avelon), from her provincial childhood to her time at a radical Berlin commune and other adventures. Then there's her sexual exploits with Mick Jagger and Keith Richards (among other rockers) before Uschi runs off to explore the Third World with adventurer Deiter Bockhorn. Unless you're enamored of the era, you'll wonder what the fuss is about, though end credits showcase photos of the real Obermaier. English and German with subtitles. **114m/C; DVD.** *GE* Natalia Avelon; David Scheller; Alexander Scheer; Friederike Kempter; Victor Noven; *D:* Achim Bornhak; *W:* Olaf Kraemer; *C:* Benjamin Dernbecker; *M:* Alexander Hacke.

8mm 🦴🦴 1/2 **1998 (R)** Surveillance expert Tom Welles (Cage) leads a normal family life until he's hired by widow Mrs. Christian (Carter). She wants him to find out the identity of a young girl apparently slashed to death in a porno film found in her late husband's safe. He descends into the underbelly of the pornography industry, guided by sleazeballs with names like Max California (Phoenix) and Dino Velvet (Stormare), and is both disgusted and fascinated by what he sees and learns. After he ferrets out the villain, he is forced into a showdown in order to save his family. Scripted by "Seven" writer Andrew Kevin Walker, but lacks some of the psychological punch of his previous effort. **123m/C; VHS, DVD, Blu-Ray.** Nicolas Cage; Joaquin Rafael (Leaf) Phoenix; James Gandolfini; Peter Stormare; Anthony Heald; Catherine Keener; Chris Bauer; Myra Carter; Amy Morton; *D:* Joel Schumacher; *W:* Andrew Kevin Walker; *C:* Robert Elswit; *M:* Mychael Danna.

8mm 2 WOOF! **2005 (R)** Lots of female nudity can't make up for a trite story filled with dumb, unpleasant characters in this name only sequel. Engaged Tish and David are living in Budapest and exploring their sexual fantasies. This includes a weekend away where they are filmed having a threesome and then blackmailed over the sex tape. Tish's diplomat dad refuses to pay which leads the couple into the city's criminal underworld and a ridiculous twist. **106m/C; DVD.** Johnathon Schaech; Lori Heuring; Bruce Davison; Julie Benz; Valentine Pelka; *D:* J.S. Cardone; *W:* Robert Sullivan; *C:* Darko Suvak; *M:* Timothy S. (Tim) Jones. **VIDEO**

Eight on the Lam 🦴 **1967 (PG)** Unfunny comedy features widower Henry Dimsdale (Hope) taking off with his kids and family maid Golda (Diller) when he's accused of embezzling bank funds. Jasper Lynch (Winters) is on their trail until Henry can prove who the real culprit is. **103m/C; VHS, DVD.** Bob Hope; Phyllis Diller; Jonathan Winters; Jill St. John; Shirley Eaton; *D:* George Marshall; *W:* Albert Lewin; Arthur Marx; Bob Fisher; Burt Styler; *C:* Alan Stensvold; *M:* George Romanis.

8.5 Hours 🦴🦴 **2008** Four Dublin software engineers realize their economic bubble is about to burst over the course of one working day. Rachel, Eoin, Tony, and Frank try to deal with their financial and personal problems as they struggle to get the most out of the company before its collapse. **107m/C; DVD.** *IR* Lynette Callaghan; Victor Burke; Jonathan Byrne; Art Kearns; Geraldine Plunkett; Tom O'Sullivan; Clodagh Reid; *D:* Brian Lally; *W:* Brian Lally; *C:* Arthur Mulhern; *M:* Karim Elmahmoudi.

8 Seconds 🦴🦴 1/2 *The Lane Frost Story* **1994 (PG-13)** Love, not sports, dominates the true-life story of rodeo star Lane Frost (Perry), a world champion bull rider killed in the ring at the age of 25 in 1990. A decent guy, he finds quick success on the rodeo circuit, marries (to Geary), and finds his career getting in the way of their happiness. Bull-riding sequences are genuinely stomach churning, the performances low-key. Title refers to the amount of time a rider must stay aboard his animal. **104m/C; VHS, DVD.** Luke Perry; Cynthia Geary; Stephen Baldwin; James Rebhorn; Carrie Snodgress; Red Mitchell; Ronnie Clair Edwards; *D:* John G. Avildsen; *W:* Monte Merrick; *C:* Victor Hammer; *M:* Bill Conti.

Eight Witnesses 🦴🦴 **1954** Suspense thriller about a man being murdered in front of eight blind witnesses. **67m/B; VHS, DVD.** *GB* Peggy Ann Garner; Dennis Price; *D:* Lawrence Huntington; *W:* Halsted Welles.

8 Women 🦴🦴🦴 *8 femmes* **2002 (R)** Wacky musical murder mystery starring eight of France's top actresses. Grand dame Gaby (Deneuve) and her daughters, Suzon (Ledoyen) and Catherine (Sagnier), share a remote estate with her husband Marcel (Lamure), her mother Mamy (Darrieux), spinster sister Augustine (Huppert), loyal housemaid Mme. Chanel (Richard), and pouty chambermaid Louise (Beart). Louise discovers Marcel stabbed to death—the phone doesn't work, the car won't start, and there's a blizzard. To make matters more interesting, Marcel's estranged sister Pierrette (Ardant) literally comes in from the cold. Now, the eight women are trapped together. Is one of them a killer? Secrets and accusations spill out in song, like a Technicolor '50s musical melodrama. It may not make sense but with this cast, plot will be the last thing on your mind. Based on the play by Robert Thomas; French with subtitles. **103m/C; VHS, DVD.** *FR* Catherine Deneuve; Isabelle Huppert; Emmanuelle Beart; Fanny Ardant; Virginie Ledoyen; Danielle Darrieux; Ludivine Sagnier; Firmine Richard; Dominique Lamure; *D:* Francois Ozon; *W:* Francois Ozon; Marina de Van; *C:* Jeanne Lapoirie; *M:* Krishna Levy.

Eighteen 🦴🦴 **2004** After leaving his dysfunctional family, Pip (Anthony) is living on the streets where his father (Houde) finds him when Pip turns 18. Dad hands his son a tape that his grandfather (McKellen) recorded about his own experiences at 18, which happened while he was a soldier during WWII. The flashbacks are the best part and, despite the "Pip" name, the story has nothing to do with Charles Dickens or "Great Expectations." **101m/C; DVD.** *CA* Paul Anthony; Brendan Fletcher; Carly Pope; Serge Houde; Clarence Sponagle; Thea Gill; *D:* Richard Bell; *W:* Richard Bell; *C:* Kevin Van Niekerk; *M:* Bramwell Tovey.

18 Again! 🦴🦴 1/2 **1988 (PG)** After a bump on the head, an 81-year-old man and his 18-year-old grandson mentally switch places, giving each a new look at his life. Lightweight romp with Burns in especially good form, but not good enough to justify redoing this tired theme. **100m/C; VHS, DVD.** George Burns; Charlie Schlatter; Anita Morris; Jennifer Runyon; Tony Roberts; Red Buttons; Miriam Flynn; George DiCenzo; Pauly Shore; Anthony Starke; *D:* Paul Flaherty; *W:* Jonathan Prince; Josh Goldstein; *C:* Stephen M. Katz; *M:* Billy Goldenberg.

18 Fingers of Death 🦴 1/2 **2005 (PG-13)** Kung fu spoof about an actor, Buford Lee (Lew), who has starred in 803 low-budget action movies. When the producers cancel the film that he believes will make him a superstar, Lee really goes into fighting mode. **87m/C; DVD.** James Lew; Noriyuki "Pat" Morita; Robin Shou; Lorenzo Lamas; Maurice Patton; Bokeem Woodbine; Don "The Dragon" Wilson; Lisa Arturo; Roark Critchlow; *D:* James Lew; *W:* James Lew; *C:* Jan Michalik; *M:* Eddie Griffin; Aaron Bolden. **VIDEO**

The Eighteenth Angel 🦴🦴 **1997 (R)** The unexpected death of his wife (Crewson) finds Hugh Stanton (McDonald) clinging to his 15-year-old daughter Lucy (Cook), who has fallen into a deep depression. Then a mysterious modeling agent "discovers" Lucy, claiming she has the face of an angel, and offers Lucy a trip to Italy. Unexplainable things happen during their stay and when Hugh investigates it seems that good and evil are in a battle for Lucy's soul. **90m/C; VHS, DVD.** Christopher McDonald; Rachael Leigh Cook; Maximilian Schell; Stanley Tucci; Wendy Crewson; Ted Rusoff; *D:* William Bindley; *W:* David Seltzer; *C:* Thomas Ackerman.

Eighth Grade 🦴🦴🦴 **2018 (R)** Like it or not, you'll probably feel the pain of Kayla Day, an awkward, quiet 13-year-old enduring her last week of middle school. Deftly portrayed by Elsie Fisher, Kayla is comfortable and confident on her online video channel, but agonizes over the impending social and emotional landmine that is high school. Writer/director Burnham delivers a raw, honest, oftentimes uncomfortable portrayal of those early teen years, warts and all, but balances the misery with moments of utter happiness. **94m/C; DVD, Blu-Ray.** Elsie Fisher; Josh Hamilton; Emily Robinson; Jake Ryan; Daniel Zolghadri; *D:* Bo Burnham; *W:* Bo Burnham; *C:* Andrew Wehde; *M:* Anna Meredith. Ind. Spirit '19: First Screenplay; Writers Guild '18: Orig. Screenplay.

8213: Gacy House 🦴 **2010** Yet another tired found-footage movie involving the theme of ghost hunters. This particularly foolish group decides to visit the abandoned house of serial killer John Gacy in an attempt to summon his ghost and ask him pertinent questions. **90m/C; DVD, Streaming.** James Lewis; Matthew Temple; Michael Gaglio; Brett A. Newton; Diana Terranova; Sylvia Panacione; Rachel Riley; *D:* Anthony Fankhauser; *W:* Anthony Fankhauser; *C:* Matt Hoefler. **VIDEO**

84 Charing Cross Road 🦴🦴🦴 **1986 (PG)** A lonely woman in New York and a book-seller in London begin corresponding for business reasons. Over a 20-year period, their relationship grows into a friendship, and then a romance, though they communicate only by mail. Based on a true story and adapted from the book by Helene Hanff. **100m/C; VHS, DVD, Blu-Ray.** Anne Bancroft; Anthony Hopkins; Dame Judi Dench; Jean De Baer; Maurice Denham; Eleanor David; Mercedes Ruehl; Daniel Gerroll; Hugh Whitemore; *D:* David Hugh Jones; *C:* Brian West; *M:* George Fenton. British Acad. '87: Actress (Bancroft).

88 🦴 **2015** Gwen finds herself at a diner with a gun and no idea how she got there although she remembers her lover was murdered and she wants revenge. Is Gwen a victim or killer? The answer isn't very exciting although Isabelle does well by her good girl/bad girl personas. **88m/C; DVD, Blu-Ray.** Katharine Isabelle; Christopher Lloyd; Michael Ironside; Kyle Schmid; Jesse McCartney; Tim Doiron; April Mullen; *D:* April Mullen; *W:* Tim Doiron; *C:* Brooks Reynolds. **VIDEO**

88 Minutes 🦴 1/2 **2008 (R)** Predictable thriller sat on the shelves developing mold before Sony studios finally released it, and it's easy to see why. Jack Gramm (Pacino'either indifferent or ranting) is an allegedly hotshot forensic shrink whose testimony put away serial killer Jon Forster (McDonough). Forster is on death row when similar crimes are committed. Gramm gets the fisheye from FBI agent Parks (Forsythe) over the latest murder and then receives a call saying he's got 88 minutes to live. There's no sense of urgency and a viewer can easily discern who's sticking it to Jack, making suspense an afterthought. **108m/C; DVD, Blu-Ray.** *US GE* Al Pacino; Alicia Witt; Leelee Sobieski; Amy Brenneman; Neal McDonough; William Forsythe; Deborah Kara Unger; Ben(jamin) McKenzie; Stephen Moyer; *D:* Jon Avnet; *W:* Gary Scott Thompson; *C:* Denis Lenoir; *M:* Ed Shearmur.

Eisenstein in Guanajuato 🦴🦴 **2015** A Peter Greenaway biopic of Soviet filmmaker Sergei Eisenstein's experience shooting a film in Mexico. Widely respected as a director, Eisenstein (Back) is struggling in 1931 after experiencing rejection in Hollywood. Though being pressured by Soviet authorities to return to his native country, Eisenstein travels to Mexico to shoot a new film, Que Viva Mexico, funded by Americans who sympathize with Communism. During the production, Eisenstein has brushes with sex and death which impact his film, career, and life. **105m/C; DVD.** Elmer Back; Luis Alberti; Jose Montini; Cristina Velasco Lozano; Rasmus Slatis; *D:* Peter Greenaway; *W:* Peter Greenaway; *C:* Reinier van Brummelen. **VIDEO**

El Amor Brujo 🦴🦴🦴 *Love, the Magician* **1986** An adaptation of the work of Miguel de Falla, in which flamenco dancers enact the story of a tragic romance. **100m/C; VHS, DVD.** Antonio Gades; Cristina Hoyos; Laura Del Sol; *D:* Carlos Saura.

El Bola 🦴🦴 *Pellet* **2000** A graphic portrayal of child abuse. 12-year-old Pablo (Ballesta) is nicknamed "Bola" or "Pellet" because he carries a small wooden ball as a good luck charm. Which he needs since his embittered father Mariano (Maron) regularly beats him. Pablo is quick to make friends with new kid in school, Alfredo (Galan), who eventually tells his own father, Jose (Gimenez), about the bruises he's seen on Pablo's body. Jose wants to get involved but it's not as simple as it seems. Spanish with subtitles. **88m/C; DVD.** *SP* Juan Jose Ballesta; Pablo Galan; Alberto Gimenez; Manuel Maron; Nieve De Medina; Ana Wagener; Gloria Munoz; ***D:*** Achero Manas; ***W:*** Achero Manas; ***C:*** Juan Carlos Gomez; ***M:*** Eduardo Arbide.

El Bruto 1/2 *The Brute* **1952** A mid-Mexican-period Bunuel drama, about a brainless thug who is used as a bullying pawn in a struggle between a brutal landlord and discontented tenants. In Spanish with English titles. **83m/B; VHS, DVD, Blu-Ray.** *MX* Pedro Armendariz, Sr.; Katy Jurado; Andres Soler; Rosita (Rosa) Arenas; ***D:*** Luis Bunuel.

El Bulli: Cooking in Progress 1/2 **2011** This feature-length documentary offers a behind-the-scenes look at the work of acclaimed Spanish chef Ferran Adria at his restaurant El Bulli. Focusing on the six months of the year that the restaurant is closed, the film explores the time Adria and his culinary team spend preparing the menu for the next season. Much of the documentary centers on Adria's innovative cooking and approaching the culinary sciences as art. Catalan and French with subtitles. **108m/C; DVD, Blu-Ray, Streaming, Download.** ***D:*** Gereon Wetzel; ***C:*** Josef Mayerhofer; ***M:*** Stephan Diethelm.

El Camino 1/2 **2008** Minimalist road movie about self-discovery. When Matthew dies it bonds three strangers together on a road trip to scatter his ashes in Mexico. Elliot and Matthew were in foster care together; Lilly was his ex-girlfriend; and Gary, a current friend, felt Matthew was the anchor in his troubled life. The trip from North Carolina isn't very eventful, there are no big emotional revelations, and no romantic triangle develops. Cinematographer Neumann offers magnificent landscapes to make up for the lack of action. **86m/C; DVD.** Leo Fitzpatrick; Christopher Denham; Elisabeth Moss; Wes Studi; Amy Hargreaves; Richard Gallagher; ***D:*** Erik S. Weigel; ***W:*** Erik S. Weigel; Salvatore Interlandi; ***C:*** Till Neumann; ***M:*** Adam Balazs.

El Cantante **2006 (R)** Fiery passion is evident in this ode to a likely little-known artist who may be responsible for bringing salsa to the states. Puerto Rican-born Hector Lavoe—musician, singer, and addict—died of AIDS in 1993 at 46 after firing up the salsa scene in the U.S. The film showcases Lavoe and wife Puchi (Lopez) as they navigate the world of music, drugs, sex, and family. The music throbs but the story bobs, and we can't help but scratch our heads at the pair and their thorny relationship (he shares their bed with myriad others—of both sexes). It's the music that steals the show in this thumping, grinding tribute to a shooting star. **116m/C; DVD.** John Ortiz; Marc Anthony; Jennifer Lopez; Manny Perez; Vincent Laresca; Federico Castelluccio; Nelson Vasquez; ***D:*** Leon Ichaso; ***W:*** Leon Ichaso; David Darmstaedter; Todd Anthony Bello; ***C:*** Claudio Chea; ***M:*** Andres Levin.

El Carro 1/2 *The Car* **2004** Winning Colombian comedy about the Velez family and the arrival of its latest member, a cherry red Chevy. Narrated by the youngest daughter, Paola, recounting the drastic social and moral transformations brought on by this new car—a vehicle both for transportation and for plot development. Divided into quirky little episodes all revolving around the new wheels. Consistently funny. **93m/C; DVD, On Demand.** Cesar Badillo; Luly Bossa; Zaira Valenzuela; Diego Cadavid; Andrea Gomez; ***D:*** Luis Orjuela; ***W:*** Dago Garcia; ***C:*** J.C. Vasquez; ***M:*** Jymmi Pulido.

El Cid **1961** Charts the life of Rodrigo Diaz de Bivar, known as El Cid, who was the legendary 11th-century Christian hero who freed Spain from Moorish invaders. Noted for its insanely lavish budget, this epic tale is true to its setting and features elaborate battle scenes. **184m/C; VHS, DVD.** Charlton Heston; Sophia Loren; Raf Vallone; Hurd Hatfield; Genevieve Page; ***D:*** Anthony Mann; ***W:*** Philip Yordan; ***C:*** Robert Krasker; ***M:*** Miklos Rozsa.

El Cochecito *The Wheelchair* **1960** Great Spanish actor Isbert stars as the head of a large family whose closest friends are all joined together in a kind of fraternity defined by the fact that they each use a wheelchair. He feels excluded because he does not have or need one, so he goes to great lengths to gain acceptance in this "brotherhood." In Spanish with English subtitles. **90m/B; VHS, DVD.** *SP* Jose Isbert; Maria Luisa Ponte; Pedro Porcel; Antonio Gavilan; ***D:*** Marco Ferreri; ***W:*** Marco Ferreri; Rafael Azcona; ***C:*** Juan Julio Baena; ***M:*** Miguel Asins Arbo.

El Condor 1/2 **1970 (R)** Two drifters search for gold buried in a Mexican fort. **102m/C; VHS, DVD.** *SP* Jim Brown; Lee Van Cleef; Patrick O'Neal; Marianna Hill; Iron Eyes Cody; Elisha Cook, Jr.; ***D:*** John Guillermin; ***W:*** Larry Cohen; Steven W. Carabatsos; ***M:*** Maurice Jarre.

El Crimen Perfecto 1/2 *Ferpect Crime; Crimen Ferpecto; El Crimen Ferpecto* **2004** The "perfect crime"? Seemingly not, but this dark comedy delivers. Womanizing department store salesman Rafael (Toledo) finds himself in a predicament. A dressing room scuffle leaves his arch-nemesis and men's department manager (Varela) dead, and Rafael takes it upon himself to dispose of the body. But unattractive Lourdes (Cervera), a sales assistant in love with Rafael, saw it all and even helps him, only to later blackmail him into marriage. Now Rafael must find a way to loosen Lourdes' clutches. In Spanish with English subtitles. **105m/C; DVD.** *SP IT* ***D:*** Alex de la Iglesia; ***W:*** Alex de la Iglesia; Jorge Guerricaechevarria; ***C:*** Jose L. Moreno; ***M:*** Roque Baños.

El Diablo 1/2 **1990 (PG-13)** A young man finds the West more wild than he expected. He finds "help" in the shape of Gossett as he tries to free a young girl who's being held by the notorious El Diablo. Better than average. **107m/C; VHS, DVD.** Louis Gossett, Jr.; Anthony Edwards; John Glover; Robert Beltran; M.C. Gainey; Miguel (Michael) Sandoval; Sarah Trigger; Joe Pantoliano; ***D:*** Peter Markle; ***W:*** John Carpenter; Bill (William) Phillips; ***C:*** Ron Garcia; ***M:*** William Olvis. **CABLE**

El Dorado **1967** A gunfighter rides into the frontier town of El Dorado to aid a reckless cattle baron in his war with farmers over land rights. Once in town, the hired gun meets up with an old friend—the sheriff—who also happens to be the town drunkard. Switching allegiances, the gunslinger helps the lawman sober up and defend the farmers. This Hawks western displays a number of similarities to the director's earlier "Rio Bravo" (1959), staring Wayne, Dean Martin, and Ricky Nelson—who charms viewers as the young sidekick "Colorado" much like Caan does as "Mississippi" in El Dorado. **126m/C; VHS, DVD, Blu-Ray.** John Wayne; Robert Mitchum; James Caan; Charlene Holt; Ed Asner; Arthur Hunnicutt; Christopher George; R.G. Armstrong; Jim Davis; Paul Fix; Johnny Crawford; Michele Carey; ***D:*** Howard Hawks.

El Gringo **2012 (R)** Repetitive but watchable action flick. A nameless DEA agent (Adkins) fakes his own death, escapes to Mexico with $2 million in drug money, and lands in some small, dusty town. Things get complicated when he runs into the local cartel, the town's corrupt sheriff, and his former boss (Slater) who's tracked him down. **102m/C; DVD, Blu-Ray.** Scott Adkins; Christian Slater; Yvette Yates; Erando Gonzalez; Israel Islas; ***D:*** Eduardo Rodriguez; ***W:*** Jonathan Stokes; ***C:*** Yaron Levy; ***M:*** Luis Ascanio. **VIDEO**

El Mariachi **1993 (R)** Extremely low-budget but clever mixture of humor and violence in a tale of mistaken identity set in a small Mexican border town. Unemployed singer/musician Gallardo wanders into a small town and is mistaken for a hitman who carries his weapons in a guitar case. Eventually, the real hitman also shows up. 24-year-old director Rodriguez makes his feature film debut with this $7000 feature, originally intended only for the Spanish-language market. Film festival awards and critical attention brought the work to wider release. Spanish with subtitles or dubbed. **81m/C; VHS, DVD.** *MX* Carlos Gallardo; Consuelo Gomez; Peter Marquardt; Jaime de Hoyos; Reinol Martinez; Ramiro Gomez; ***D:*** Robert Rodriguez; ***W:*** Carlos Gallardo; Robert Rodriguez; ***C:*** Robert Rodriguez; ***M:*** Eric Guthrie. Ind. Spirit '94: First Feature; Natl. Film Reg. '11; Sundance '93: Aud. Award.

El Matador **2003** Wanting to escape the doldrums of his pizza delivery job, young Mexican-American Johnny dreams of emulating his father by becoming a matador. But much absurdity ensues after a not-so-friendly loan shark captures the "family jewels"?bronzed bull testicles—and he must fight to regain the prized family heirloom. **74m/C; VHS, DVD, Blu-Ray, On Demand.** Robert Wolfskill; Martin Klebba; Gabriel Iglesias; Emilio Rivera; ***D:*** Joey Medina; ***W:*** Joey Medina; ***C:*** Tom Hobbs. **VIDEO**

El Norte **1983 (R)** Gripping account of a Guatemalan brother and sister, persecuted in their homeland, who make an arduous journey north ("El Norte") to America. Their difficult saga continues as they struggle against overwhelming odds in an attempt to realize their dreams. Passionate, sobering, and powerful. In English and Spanish with English subtitles. Produced in association with the "American Playhouse" series for PBS. Produced by Anna Thomas who also co-wrote the story with Nava. **139m/C; VHS, DVD, Blu-Ray.** *SP* David Villalpando; Zaide Silvia Gutierrez; Ernesto Cruz; Eracio Zepeda; Stella Quan; Alicia del Lugo; Lupe Ontiveros; ***D:*** Gregory Nava; ***W:*** Anna Thomas; Gregory Nava. Natl. Film Reg. '95.

El Padrino 1/2 *El Padrino: The Latin Godfather* **2004 (R)** The life and times of an up-and-coming drug dealer in Los Angeles who's trying to be like his father, a notorious crime lord. Alas for the lead actor (who also directs), he spends the entire film overshadowed by an over-the-top Tilly as a young prostitute/insane killer. **127m/C; DVD.** Damian Chapa; Sal Lopez; Emilio Rivera; Jennifer Tilly; Faye Dunaway; Ismael Carlo; Joanna Pacula; Robert Wagner; Gary Busey; Stacy Keach; Brad Dourif; Ralph (Ralf) Moeller; Melora Hardin; Kathleen Quinlan; Ricco Chapa; Henry Pittman; Tommy (Tiny) Lister; ***D:*** Damian Chapa; ***W:*** Damian Chapa; Troy Barker; Carlton Holder; Aaron Pugliese; ***C:*** Pierre Chemaly; ***M:*** Gerard K. Marino.

El Paso 1/2 **1949** Frontier lawyer (and ex-soldier) Clayton Fletcher (Payne) reunites with former flame Susan Jeffers (Russell) but discovers her father, Judge Jeffers (Hull), has become a drunk and is under the thumb of crooked and land-grabbing town boss Donner (Hayden). In order to save the town, Fletcher has to take the law into his own hands. **91m/B; DVD, Blu-Ray.** John Payne; Gail Russell; Sterling Hayden; George "Gabby" Hayes; Henry Hull; Dick Foran; ***D:*** Lewis R. Foster; ***W:*** Lewis R. Foster; ***C:*** Ellis W. Carter; ***M:*** Darrell Calker.

El Topo 1/2 *The Gopher; The Mole* **1971** Bizarre western finds Jodorowsky as a man out to avenge his wife's death, then trapped into more and more violent action. Eventually, he tries to save his own soul with a Christ-like resurrection. Difficult to follow, with poor production values and heavy handed allegorical plotline. Initial release created a large cult viewership, but it looks worse as time progresses. **123m/C; VHS, Blu-Ray.** *MX* Alejandro Jodorowsky; Brontis Jodorowsky; Alfonso Arau; Mara Lorenzio; David Silva; Paula Romo; Jose Luis Fernandez; Robert John; Jacqueline Luis; ***D:*** Alejandro Jodorowsky; ***W:*** Alejandro Jodorowsky; ***C:*** Rafael Corkidi; ***M:*** Alejandro Jodorowsky; Nacho Mendez.

Elaine Stritch: Shoot Me **2014** The legendary Tony and Emmy winner is profiled in this excellent biographical documentary that chronicles her successes on stage and screen while also serving as a heartbreaking reminder of the impact of age. Elaine Stritch is still performing regularly, seemingly unable to retire, but she's increasingly having difficulty remembering the lyrics to the songs she performs and the film captures more than one trip to the hospital. Through it all, Stritch's captivating presence adds poignancy to the closing chapters of a life very well-lived. One of the most important stage performers in Broadway history gets the documentary a star as bright as hers deserves. **80m/C; DVD.** Elaine Stritch; ***D:*** Chiemi Karasawa; ***C:*** Shane Sigler; Joshua Z Weinstein; Rod Lamborn; ***M:*** Kristopher Bowers.

The Elder Son 1/2 **2006 (R)** L.A. car thief Bo (West) needs a place to hide out after a job goes wrong. So Bo manages to convince Russian immigrant musician Max (Serbedzija) that he's his long-lost son. Then the situation gets more complicated when Bo falls for his hottie "sister" Lolita (Sobieski). **84m/C; DVD.** Shane West; Leelee Sobieski; Rade Serbedzija; Eric Balfour; Regina Hall; Ed Begley, Jr.; ***D:*** Marius Balchunas; ***W:*** Marius Balchunas; Scott Sturgeon; ***C:*** Andrew Huebscher; ***M:*** Yagmur Kaplan. **VIDEO**

Ele, My Friend 1/2 **1993** The British Raj still rules India in the 1920s, when 10-year-old Charles comes across a herd of wild elephants living in the jungle. Charles befriends a baby elephant he names Ele but what can he do when hunters also discover the animals? Filmed on location in south India. **104m/C; VHS, DVD.** Jacob Paul Guzman; Gazan Khan; R.S. Shivaji; Amjad Khan; Prabhu; ***D:*** Dharan Mandrayar; ***W:*** Dharan Mandrayar; ***M:*** Barry Phillips.

Eleanor & Franklin 1/2 **1976** An exceptional dramatization of the personal lives of President Franklin D. Roosevelt and his wife Eleanor. Based on Joseph Lash's book, this Emmy award-winning film features stunning performances by Alexander and Herrmann in the title roles. **208m/C; VHS, DVD.** Jane Alexander; Edward Herrmann; Ed Flanders; Rosemary Murphy; MacKenzie Phillips; Pamela Franklin; Anna Lee; Linda Purl; Linda Kelsey; Lindsay Crouse; ***D:*** Daniel Petrie; ***M:*** John Barry. **TV**

Eleanor: First Lady of the World 1/2 **1982 (G)** Stapleton plays the former first lady after her husband's death as she goes on to work at the United Nations and emerges as even more of an influential public figure. **96m/C; VHS, DVD.** Jean Stapleton; E.G. Marshall; Coral Browne; Joyce Van Patten; Gail Strickland; Kenneth Kimmins; ***D:*** John Erman; ***M:*** John Addison. **TV**

Election **1999 (R)** Payne uses a high school student council election to skewer the American political system in general and the election process in particular. Smart comedy has wildly ambitious Tracy (Witherspoon) running for council president unopposed until dedicated but flawed civics teacher Mr. McAllister (Broderick) decides she must be stopped. He recruits likeable but dim jock Paul (Klein) to run against her. Then Paul's lesbian (and anarchic) sister Tammy (Campbell) joins the race. As in Payne's previous effort, "Citizen Ruth," no side of the political spectrum is spared. Everyone's foibles and hypocrisy are shown, to great effect. Witherspoon gives an energized performance, while Broderick is excellent as the respected, conflicted mentor with a touch of Bueller in him. **105m/C; VHS, DVD, Blu-Ray.** Matthew Broderick; Reese Witherspoon; Chris Klein; Jessica Campbell; Mark Harelik; Molly Hagan; Colleen Camp; Frankie Ingrassia; Matt Malloy; Holmes Osborne; Phil Reeves; Delaney Driscoll; Jeanine Jackson; ***D:*** Alexander Payne; ***W:*** Alexander Payne; Jim Taylor; ***C:*** James Glennon; ***M:*** Rolfe Kent. Ind. Spirit '00: Director (Payne), Film, Screenplay; N.Y. Film Critics '99: Screenplay; Natl. Soc. Film Critics '99: Actress (Witherspoon); Writers Guild '99: Adapt. Screenplay.

Electra Glide in Blue **1973 (R)** An Arizona motorcycle cop uses his head in a world that's coming apart at the seams. Good action scenes; lots of violence. **113m/C; VHS, DVD, Blu-Ray.** Robert (Bobby) Blake; Billy Green Bush; Mitchell Ryan; Jeannine Riley; Elisha Cook, Jr.; Royal Dano; ***D:*** James W. Guercio; ***W:*** Robert Boris; ***C:*** Conrad L. Hall.

Electra, My Love 1/2 *Szerelmem, Elektra* **1974** Acclaimed Hungarian filmmaker Miklos Jancso offers an updated, epic take on the Greek myth of Electra. Set on a desolate region of the Hungarian plains, the Electra's story is told as a drama—if not a choreographed musical—with elaborate visuals and revealing cinematography underscoring the plot. Jansco also uses Electra's story to create a metaphor under communist rule. Hungarian with subtitles. **70m/C; DVD.** Mari Torocsik; Gyorgy Cserhalmi; Jozsef Madaras; Tamas Zoltan Cseh; Gabi Jobba; ***D:*** Miklos

Jancso; **W:** Gyula Hernadi; **C:** Janos Kende; **M:** Tamas Zoltan Cseh.

Electra Woman & Dyna Girl **2016** A comedy re-boot of the classic Sid and Marty Krofft TV series featuring two YouTube stars. Electra Woman/Lori (Helbig) and Dyna Girl/Judy (Hart) form a crime-fighting duo. Seeking new challenges, the pair moves from a small town in Ohio to Los Angeles. There, the pair must find a way to be true to themselves and manage the darker side of the city of angels. **81m/C; DVD, Streaming, Download.** Hannah Hart; Grace Helbig; Christopher Coutts; Trevor Lerner; Matreya Fedor; **D:** Chris Marrs Piliero; **C:** Brendan Uegama; **M:** Chris Ridenhour. **VIDEO**

The Electric Horseman ½ **1979 (PG)** Journalist Fonda sets out to discover the reason behind the kidnapping of a prized horse by an ex-rodeo star. The alcoholic cowboy has taken the horse to return it to its native environment, away from the clutches of corporate greed. As Fonda investigates the story she falls in love with rebel Redford. Excellent Las Vegas and remote western settings. **120m/C; VHS, DVD, Blu-Ray.** Robert Redford; Jane Fonda; John Saxon; Willie Nelson; Valerie Perrine; Wilford Brimley; Nicolas Coster; James B. Sikking; **D:** Sydney Pollack; **W:** Robert Garland; **C:** Owen Roizman; **M:** Dave Grusin.

The Electronic Monster *Escapement; The Electric Monster* **1957** Insurance claims investigator Cameron looks into the death of a Hollywood starlet and discovers an exclusive therapy center dedicated to hypnotism. At the facility, people vacation for weeks in morgue-like body drawers, while evil Dr. Illing uses an electronic device to control the sleeper's dreams and actions. Eerie. Intriguingly, it is one of the first films to explore the possibilities of brainwashing and mind control. **72m/B; VHS, DVD.** *GB* Rod Cameron; Mary Murphy; Meredith Edwards; Peter Illing; **D:** Montgomery Tully.

Elegy ½ **2008 (R)** With a penchant for pursuing his much younger female graduate students, literature professor and serial seducer David Kepesh (Kingsley) is taken off-guard by his strong feelings for his latest, and particularly alluring conquest, Consuela (Cruz). Despite her hopes to the contrary, David is seemingly incapable of changing his bachelor ways, including his continued bedding of former student Carolyn (Clarkson). His life is further complicated by a strained relationship with his adult son. Hopper has an unusually understated role as David's ill-advised advice-giver. Based on the 2001 novel "The Dying Animal" by Philip Roth. **108m/C; On Demand.** Ben Kingsley; Penelope Cruz; Dennis Hopper; Patricia Clarkson; Peter Sarsgaard; Deborah Harry; Sonja Bennett; Chelah Horsdal; **D:** Isabel Coixet; **W:** Nicholas Meyer; **C:** Jean-Claude Larrieu.

Elektra **2005 (PG-13)** When we last saw her in the movie "Daredevil," Elektra had died, but thanks to the magical healing power of her mentor Stick (Stamp) she's alive and kicking. Regrettably, she came back only to be in yet another wretched film. Elektra is an assassin-for-hire. Her next assignment is to kill 13-year-old Abby (Prout) and Abby's father (Visnjic) who are the target of a powerful faction called The Hand...which (dramatic music here) is a powerful secret society. Through heavy-handed flashbacks of her own childhood, Elektra instantly bonds with the girl and decides to protect them instead. **97m/C; DVD, Blu-Ray.** Jennifer Garner; Terence Stamp; Goran Visnjic; Cary-Hiroyuki Tagawa; Kirsten Prout; Will Yun Lee; **D:** Rob Bowman; **W:** Zak Penn; Stuart Zicherman; Raven Metzner; **C:** Bill Roe; **M:** Christophe Beck.

Elektra Luxx ½ **2010 (R)** Equally soap opera-ish series of interconnected scenes follows Gutierrez's 2009 flick "Women in Trouble." Pregnant Elektra (Gugino) has retired from her porn star career and is now trying to make it teaching sex courses to L.A. housewives. There's some intrigue surrounding unrecorded songs left by her deceased rocker boyfriend, a porn blogger's obsessed with Elektra, and other situations involving her porn-making friends. Elektra is also given advice and comfort by the Virgin Mary (cameo by Julianne Moore). **100m/C; DVD, Blu-Ray.** Carla Gugino; Timothy Olyphant; Joseph Gordon-Levitt; Adrianne Palicki; Emmanuelle Chriqui; Malin Akerman; Marley Shelton; Kathleen Quinlan; Justin Kirk; Vincent Kartheiser; **Cameo(s):** Julianne Moore; **D:** Sebastian Gutierrez; **W:** Sebastian Gutierrez; **C:** Cale Finot; **M:** Robyn Hitchcock. **VIDEO**

The Element of Crime ½ *Forbrydelsens Element* **1984** In a monochromatic, post-holocaust future, a detective tracks down a serial killer of young girls. Made in Denmark, this minor festival favorite features an impressive directional debut and awaits cult status. Filmed in Sepiatone. **104m/C; VHS, DVD.** *DK* Michael Elphick; Esmond Knight; Jerold Wells; Me Me Lai; Astrid Henning-Jensen; Preben Leerdorff-Rye; Gotha Andersen; **D:** Lars von Trier; **W:** Lars von Trier; Niels Vorsel; **C:** Tom Elling; **M:** Bo Holten.

Element of Doubt ½ **1996** Beth Murray's (McKee) family have always been suspicious of her ambitious husband, Richard (Havers). Although Beth desperately wants children, Richard has persuaded her to wait until after he's closed some mysterious business deal. Suddenly, Richard promises Beth a home in the country and the family she desires. Then, Beth discovers her husband has been in close contact with his ex-wife. So, is Beth merely suffering from hysterics or is Richard actually contemplating murder? **90m/C; VHS, DVD.** *GB* Nigel Havers; Gina McKee; Polly Adams; Judy Parfitt; Sarah Berger; Michael Jayston; Dennis (Denis) Lill; Robert Reynolds; **D:** Christopher Morahan; **C:** Brian Tufano; **M:** Stephen Warbeck. **TV**

Elena **2011** Dowbeat family drama. Dowdy, middle-aged Elena married up when the former nurse wed her wealthy, older patient Vladimir. They live comfortably in their Moscow apartment but Vladimir refuses to come to the financial aid of Elena's freeloading son Sergey and his family. After Vladimir has a heart attack, Elena manages a reconciliation between her husband and his estranged daughter, Katerina. But it backfires when Vladimir decides to leave the bulk of his money to Katerina, which leaves Elena feeling betrayed and plotting a different outcome. Russian with subtitles. **109m/C; DVD, Blu-Ray.** *RU* Nadezhda Vasilievna Markina; Andrey Smirnov; Aleksey Rozen; Elena Lyadova; Evgeniya Konushkina; **D:** Andrey Zvyagintsev; **W:** Andrey Zvyagintsev; Oleg Negin; **C:** Mikhail Krichman; **M:** Philip Glass.

Elena and Her Men *Paris Does Strange Things; Elena et les Hommes* **1956** The romantic entanglements and intrigues of a poor Polish princess are explored in this enjoyable French film. Beautiful cinematography by Claude Renoir. In French with subtitles. **98m/C; VHS, DVD.** *FR* Ingrid Bergman; Jean Marais; Mel Ferrer; Jean Richard; Magali Noel; Pierre Bertin; Juliette Greco; **D:** Jean Renoir; **C:** Claude Renoir.

Elena Undone ½ **2010** Elena is not-so-happily married to pastor Barry, whose church is anti-gay. This doesn't matter much until sometime-photog Elena works on a project with lesbian self-help writer Peyton. The women go from flirtation to full-blown affair, which is also when the pic turns awkward and meandering. **111m/C; DVD.** Necar Zedegan; Traci Dinwiddie; Gary Weeks; **D:** Nicole Conn; **W:** Nicole Conn; **C:** Tal Lazar; **M:** Mark Chait. **VIDEO**

Elephant **2003 (R)** Made for HBO film depicting a day in the life at a typical American high school that ends in tragedy. Film lazily follows a number of the banal goings-on of various students before wandering to a shocking climax involving the violence of a Columbine-type massacre by two young social outcasts. The motivation of killers Alex and Eric (Frost and Deulen) isn't explored but merely offered up as fact, save a few shots of the boys watching a documentary about Hitler and sharing a brief kiss. Mainly utilizing non-actors and a largely improvised script, Van Sant genuinely imparts the reality of high school life in modern day America without trying to explain it but creates a sense of detachment from the characters and subject matter along the way. **81m/C; VHS, DVD.** Alex Frost; Eric Deulen; John Robinson; Elias McConnell; Nathan Tyson; Carrie Finklea; Kristen Hicks; Jordan Taylor; Nicole George; Brittany Mountain; Timothy Bottoms; Matt Malloy; **D:** Gus Van Sant; **W:** Gus Van Sant; **C:** Harris Savides. Cannes '03: Director (Van Sant), Film. **CABLE**

Elephant Boy **1937** An Indian boy helps government conservationists locate a herd of elephants in the jungle. Sabu's first film. Available in digitally remastered stereo. **80m/B; VHS, DVD.** *GB* Sabu; Walter Hudd; W.E. Holloway; **D:** Robert Flaherty; Zoltan Korda. Venice Film Fest. '37: Director (Flaherty).

An Elephant Called Slowly ½ **1969 (G)** In a sequel of sorts to the 1966 hit "Born Free," McKenna and Travers star as an English couple who trek to Africa to meet game warden George Adamson (here playing himself). Once in Africa, they are introduced to a menagerie of animals, such as lions and hippos. Along the way, the meet Pole Pole (Swahili for "Slowly"), a baby elephant who adopts McKenna and Travers and attempts to travel with them. The first 20 minutes are rather slow, but the last 70 are very watchable with gorgeous cinematography and astounding nature shots. **91m/C; VHS, DVD.** *GB* Virginia McKenna; Bill Travers; George Adamson; Joab Collins; Vinay Inambar; Ali Twaha; **D:** James Hill; **W:** Bill Travers; James Hill; **C:** Simon Trevor; **M:** Howard Blake; Bert Kaempfert.

The Elephant King ½ **2006 (R)** Jake Hunt (Robert) is staying put in Thailand after being accused of fraud. His introverted younger brother Oliver (Ellington) is sent by their parents to bring Jake back to the U.S. but Oliver succumbs to Jake's expat lifestyle of drinking and bar girls instead. A baby elephant figures into the plot too. **90m/C; DVD.** Ellen Burstyn; Josef Sommer; Jonno Robert; Tate Ellington; Florence Faivre; **D:** Seth Grossman; **C:** Diego Quemada Diaz; **M:** Adam Balazs.

The Elephant Man **1980 (PG)** A biography of John Merrick, a severely deformed man who, with the help of a sympathetic doctor, moved from freak shows into posh London society. Lynch's first mainstream film, shot in black and white, it presents a startlingly vivid picture of the hypocrisies evident in the social mores of the Victorian era. Moving performance from Hurt in title role. **125m/B; VHS, DVD.** Anthony Hopkins; John Hurt; Anne Bancroft; John Gielgud; Wendy Hiller; Freddie Jones; Kenny Baker; Michael Elphick; **D:** David Lynch; **W:** Eric Bergren; Christopher DeVore; David Lynch; **C:** Freddie Francis; **M:** John Morris; Samuel Barber. British Acad. '80: Actor (Hurt), Film; Cesar '82: Foreign Film.

Elephant Stampede ½ **1951** Two poachers arrive in the village and want Bomba to lead them to a hidden cache of ivory. He's a bit busy since pretty Lola (Martell) is teaching him to read, but Bomba still calls on his elephant friends to exact the proper, if grisly, revenge. The 6th film in the Mongoram series. **70m/B; DVD.** John(ny) Sheffield; John Kellogg; Myron Healey; Donna Martell; Edith Evanson; Leonard Mudie; **D:** Ford Beebe; **W:** Ford Beebe; **C:** William Sickner.

Elephant Walk ½ **1954** Sri Lanka's balmy jungles provide the backdrop for a torrid love triangle in this post-prime Dieterle effort. Taylor, ignored by her wealthy drunkard hubby, finds solace in the arms of her spouse's sexy right-hand man. As if keeping the affair secret weren't a big enough task, she also braves a cholera epidemic and a pack of vengeful elephants who take an unscheduled tour of her humble home. Lethargic lead performances make this more of a sleep walk, but Sofaer and Biberman's supporting roles are worth the price of rental. Taylor replaced Vivian Leigh early in the filming after she fell ill, but footage of Leigh in faraway shots is included. **103m/C; DVD.** Elizabeth Taylor; Dana Andrews; Peter Finch; Abraham Sofaer; Abner Biberman; **D:** William Dieterle; **W:** John Lee Mahin; **C:** Loyal Griggs; **M:** Franz Waxman.

Elephant White **2011 (R)** Ridiculous action-thriller with little discernable plot (and what's there is predictable and dumb) and action sequences that Thai director Pinkaew has done before. Mercenary Curtie Church (Hounsou) is hired by a vengeful father to take down the sex-trafficking ring that murdered his daughter only to be caught between two rival Bangkok gangs and a lot of lies. **90m/C; DVD, Blu-Ray.** Djimon Hounsou; Kevin Bacon; Jirantanin Pitakporntrakul; **D:** Prachya Pinkaew; **W:** Kevin Bernhardt; **C:** Wade Muller; **M:** Robert Folk. **VIDEO**

11-11-11 **2011 (R)** Another supernatural tale spun around numerology and signs of the apocalypse, this dull affair offers nothing new to its overdone genre and is even less memorable than usually seen in similar films. On 11-11-11 at 11:11, the 11th gate of Heaven will open. American author Joseph Crone (Gibbs) travels to Barcelona after the death of his wife and child, which has haunted him and made him spiritually unsound. There he begins to see numerous indications that the number 11 should be heeded, even as no one believes him. Silly instead of scary, Bousman's horror film was barely released theatrically. **95m/C; DVD, Blu-Ray.** Timothy Gibbs; Michael Landes; Denis Rafter; Wendy Glenn; Salome Jimenez; **D:** Darren Lynn Bousman; **W:** Darren Lynn Bousman; **C:** Joseph White; **M:** Joseph Bishara.

11:14 **2003 (R)** Rcounts the half hour of events prior to a tragedy at 11:14 pm from five character perspectives. First time effort by Marcks is laudable—smart writing, well shot, wonderfully cast. Characters could have been given more dimension, but the overall effect is acceptable. **85m/C; DVD.** Henry Thomas; Blake Heron; Barbara Hershey; Clark Gregg; Hilary Swank; Shawn Hatosy; Colin Hanks; Ben Foster; Patrick Swayze; Rachael Leigh Cook; Stark Sands; Rick Gomez; Jason Segel; **D:** Greg Marcks; **W:** Greg Marcks; **C:** Shane Hurlbut; **M:** Clint Mansell. **VIDEO**

11 Harrowhouse *Anything for Love; Fast Fortune* **1974 (PG)** The Consolidated Selling System at 11 Harrowhouse, London, controls much of the world's diamond trade. Four adventurous thieves plot a daring heist relying on a very clever cockroach. A rather successful stab at spoofing detailed "heist" films. **95m/C; VHS, DVD.** *GB* Charles Grodin; Candice Bergen; James Mason; Trevor Howard; John Gielgud; **D:** Aram Avakian; **W:** Jeffrey Bloom.

Eleven Men and a Girl *Maybe It's Love* **1930** Sports comedy finds Nan Sheffield (Bennett), the daughter of the Upton College president, trying to recruit 11 football heroes to play on the school's perennial losing team so her father can keep his job. She vamps the dazzled jocks while unlikely football player Speed Hanson (Brown) worries he'll lose his place on the team. **72m/B; DVD.** Joan Bennett; Joe E. Brown; James Hall; George Irving; Howard Jones; Laura Lee; Sumner Getchell; **D:** William A. Wellman; **W:** Joseph Jackson; **C:** Robert B. Kurrle.

The 11th Hour ½ **2007 (PG)** Global warming is certainly "the" hot topic, and this film doesn't present anything we haven't heard before, plus throws around enough stats and figures to make your head spin. Leonardo DiCaprio multitasks as narrator, actor, and co-writer; he even helped produce. It's grim, but provides some real solutions. Make no mistake—this is a documentary, not intended to entertain, but to inspire outrage and action. **95m/C; DVD.** **Nar:** Leonardo DiCaprio; **D:** Leila Conners Petersen; Nadia Conners; **W:** Leonardo DiCaprio; Leila Conners Petersen; Nadia Conners; **C:** Peter Youngblood Hills; Andrew Roland; Brian Knappenberger; **M:** Jean Pascal Beintus; Eric Avery.

The Eleventh Hour **2008** Low-budget action flick emphasizes action. After a raid goes bad, Navy SEAL Michael Adams spends three years being tortured in a North Korean prison before he's released. Suffering from PTSD, Michael is estranged from his hot wife Rachel, who winds up as a pawn in an assassination plot orchestrated by renegade North Korean general Kun. Kun has a bomb implanted in Rachel's head that will explode in 12 hours unless Michael assassinates U.S. Senator Mason Chambers, Michael's former commanding officer. **93m/C; DVD.** K. Danor Gerald; Matthew Reese; Jennifer Klekas; Scott Chun; **M:** Adam Abram. **VIDEO**

The 11th Hour **WOOF!** *I Am Here* **2014** Maria (Basinger) can't have children. In fact, she's had a series of increasingly violent miscarriages that have led her to the point that her doctors advise her to stop trying. But she refuses to give up. In fact, she's literally haunted by a spirit who calls her mother and tells her that she needs to find her. There's no way that's going to end well. Maria gets it in her head that many child prostitutes are in a position where they need to sell their baby, and Maria's shopping. She heads into a seedy underworld, driven by a maternal need. **97m/C; Streaming.** *DK GE* Kim Basinger; Jordan Prentice; Sebastian Schipper; Peter Stormare; ***D:*** Anders Morgenthaler; ***W:*** Anders Morgenthaler; ***C:*** Sturla Brandth Grovlen; ***M:*** Johann Johannsson. **VIDEO**

The Eleventh Victim ½ **2012** In this Lifetime crime thriller, an allegedly smart woman makes some really stupid decisions. After Atlanta ADA Hailey Dean is attacked in court by convicted serial killer Clinton Cruise, she quits, moves to New York, and becomes a therapist. When her patients are murdered and the M.O. is the same as the imprisoned Cruise's, Hailey goes back to Atlanta for answers. Based on the novel by Nancy Grace. **96m/C; Streaming.** Jennie Garth; Colin Cunningham; Ron Artest; Jason Schombing; ***D:*** Mike Rohl; ***W:*** John Fasano; ***C:*** C. Kim Miles; ***M:*** Michael Richard Plowman. **CABLE**

Elf **2003 (PG)** As a baby, Buddy (Ferrell) had snuck into Santa's bag and found himself transported to the North Pole. The elves adopted the human and raised him as an elf. When he learns of his human origins (the enormous size difference didn't tip him off?), he goes to New York to search for his real father. Daddy turns out to be a Walter Hobbs (Caan), a highly insensitive children's book publisher who needs a good dose of Christmas cheer. While it's all straight-ahead Christmas movie formula, Ferrell's unabashed innocence and delight in everything helps pull it off. It also helps that he looks so darn funny in yellow tights. Director Favreau makes a cameo as a doctor. **95m/C; VHS, DVD, Blu-Ray, UMD.** Will Ferrell; James Caan; Bob Newhart; Ed Asner; Mary Steenburgen; Zooey Deschanel; Faizon Love; Daniel Tay; Peter Dinklage; Amy Sedaris; Michael Lerner; Andy Richter; Jon Favreau; ***D:*** Jon Favreau; ***W:*** David Berenbaum; ***C:*** Greg Gardiner; ***M:*** John Debney.

Eli **2019 (R)** Because 11-year-old Eli (Shotwell) has a severely compromised immune system, he must wear an astronaut's suit nearly all the time. Seeking a cure, his desperate parents take him to a private medical facility operated by Dr. Horn (Taylor) in a weird old house. Convincing them that only she can cure Eli, she begins a series of painful yet odd medical procedures. As Eli is treated, he feels there is a force in the home trying to tell himself something. Though the horror film's story has potential, it's mostly confusing. **98m/C; DVD.** Charlie Shotwell; Kelly Reilly; Maximillian Martini; Lili Taylor; Sadie Sink; ***D:*** Ciaran Foy; ***W:*** David Chirchirillo; Ian Goldberg; Richard Naing; ***C:*** Jeff Cutter; ***M:*** Bear McCreary.

Eliminators **2016 (R)** An action flick about one man's effort to save his daughter from the men who are targeting him. Thomas (Adkins) is a former U.S. federal agent living in London as part of a witness protection program. When his home is invaded by mistake and several people are murdered, the criminal element who have been searching for him now know exactly where to find him. As an assassin is sent to kill him, Thomas goes on the run with his daughter to find her a safe place before those who want him dead finally catch up to him. **94m/C; DVD, Blu-Ray, Streaming, Download.** Scott Adkins; Stu Bennett; Daniel Caltagirone; James Cosmo; Mem Ferda; ***D:*** James Nunn; ***W:*** Nathan Brookes; Bobby Lee Darby; ***C:*** Luke Bryant; ***M:*** Claude Foisy. **VIDEO**

Elizabeth **1998 (R)** And you thought modern day politics were dirty! Indian director Kapur takes a look at the turbulent life of Queen Elizabeth I of England (a brilliant Blanchett) from her uncertain days as a beseiged Protestant Princess to her ascension to the throne and the machinations surrounding her early reign. Elizabeth indeed proves to be her father's daughter as she must keep her head (literally) while dealing with religion, war, assassination, and the vexing question of a political marriage. Rush is notable as spidery spymaster Walsingham and Eccleston's hissably evil as the arrogant Catholic Duke of Norfolk. Wonderful shadowy cinematography by Adefarasin adds to the atmosphere but it does help to know some history in order to keep the plots and plotters straight. **124m/C; VHS, DVD, Blu-Ray, HD-DVD.** *GB* Cate Blanchett; Geoffrey Rush; Joseph Fiennes; Christopher Eccleston; Richard Attenborough; Fanny Ardant; Vincent Cassel; Daniel Craig; Kathy Burke; James Frain; Edward Hardwicke; Eric Cantona; John Gielgud; Emily Mortimer; ***D:*** Shekhar Kapur; ***W:*** Michael Hirst; ***C:*** Remi Adefarasin; ***M:*** David Hirschfelder. Oscars '98: Makeup; British Acad. '98: Actress (Blanchett), Cinematog., Film, Score; Golden Globes '99: Actress--Drama (Blanchett); Natl. Bd. of Review '98: Director (Kapur); Broadcast Film Critics '98: Actress (Blanchett).

Elizabeth R **1972** Jackson is outstanding in the title role of this TV drama focusing on the life of Elizabeth I, from 17 to 70. Constantly besieged by court intrigue and political machinations, the Virgin Queen managed to restore England to glory and power amidst private and public turmoil. Six 90-minute cassettes. **540m/C; VHS, DVD.** *GB* Glenda Jackson; Rosalie Crutchley; Robin Ellis; Robert Hardy; Peter Jeffrey; Stephen Murray; Vivian Pickles; Sarah Frampton; Ronald Hines; ***D:*** Claude Whatham; Herbert Wise; Roderick Graham; Richard Martin; Donald Whatham; ***W:*** Hugh Whitemore; John Hale; Julian Mitchell; John Prebble; Ian Rodger; Rosemary Anne Sisson.

Elizabeth I **2005** Mirren gives an outstanding performance as the imperious British monarch. In 1579, Elizabeth is being pressured to marry, but not her lover and confidante, the Earl of Leicester (Irons). Matters are complicated by the rebellion of her cousin, Mary Queen of Scots (Flynn), and war with Spain. On his deathbed, Leicester bequeaths his relationship to his handsome and arrogant stepson, the Earl of Essex (Dancy). Flattered and flustered, Elizabeth gradually realizes that the callow Essex is a threat to her throne. **220m/C; DVD.** Dame Helen Mirren; Jeremy Irons; Hugh Dancy; Ian McDiarmid; Patrick Malahide; Barbara Flynn; Toby Jones; ***D:*** Tom Hooper; ***W:*** Nigel Williams; ***C:*** Larry Smith; ***M:*** Robert (Rob) Lane. **CABLE**

Elizabeth: The Golden Age ½ **2007 (PG-13)** Kapur's 1998 film dealt with Elizabeth's early reign. She's now been in power 27 years and is still doing an intricate political dance to keep her head and her Protestant throne against the Catholic opposition, who want Mary, Queen of Scots (Morton) ruling in her place. Then there's pesky Philip II of Spain (Molla) and his armada threatening her shores. Blanchett returns in the titular role as does Rush as spymaster Walsingham. Owen's cast as a swashbuckling Sir Walter Raleigh (very Errol Flynn), whom Elizabeth uses as a distraction. Lavish pomp and circumstance, but a disappointingly routine costumer. **114m/C; DVD, Blu-Ray.** *GB* Cate Blanchett; Geoffrey Rush; Clive Owen; Abbie Cornish; Rhys Ifans; Jordi Molla; Samantha Morton; Tom Hollander; David Threlfall; Eddie Redmayne; John Shrapnel; Antony Carrick; ***D:*** Shekhar Kapur; ***W:*** Michael Hirst; William Nicholason; ***C:*** Remi Adefarasin; ***M:*** Craig Armstrong. Oscars '07: Costume Des.

Elizabethtown **2005 (PG-13)** Over-stuffed romantic comedy from Crowe begins with the career meltdown of Drew Baylor (Bloom with a so-so American accent). Before Drew can wallow in suicidal depression, his manic mother Hollie (Sarandon) and sister Heather (Greer) inform Drew that dad died while visiting his hometown of Elizabethtown, Kentucky and Drew must deal with the funeral arrangements. This leads to his meeting cute but psychotically perky flight attendant Claire (Dunst), who decides she must console Drew at all costs. Drew discovers things about himself and his family that you may not care about at all, and takes a road trip—accompanied, as per usual in Crowe's movies, by copious amounts of music. **120m/C; DVD.** Orlando Bloom; Kirsten Dunst; Susan Sarandon; Judy Greer; Jessica Biel; Alec Baldwin; Paul Schneider; Loudon Wainwright, III; Bruce McGill; Paula Deem; Gailard Sartain; Dan Biggers; ***D:*** Cameron Crowe; ***W:*** Cameron Crowe; ***C:*** John Toll; ***M:*** Nancy Wilson.

Eliza's Horoscope ½ **1970** A frail Canadian woman uses astrology in her search for love in Montreal, and experiences bizarre and surreal events. An acclaimed Canadian film. **120m/C; VHS, DVD.** *CA* Tommy Lee Jones; Elizabeth Moorman; ***D:*** Gordon Sheppard.

Ella Enchanted **2004 (PG)** Enchanting modern Cinderella story is a fresh and funny mix of fantasy, romance, and pop culture. Hathaway appealingly plays the title's Ella of Frell, cursed by her fairy godmother Lucinda (Fox) with the spell of obedience, which forces the budding teen to obey every command she is given. She hooks up with the ogres, elves, and giants and begins a crusade for their equal rights. Her quest leads her to the total hottie Prince Charmont (Dancy) who is the intended victim of a coup planned by the throne-seeking Prince Edgar. Updated fairy tale sports top-notch special effects, a cool 70s soundtrack, and fun modern anachronisms. Based on the novel by Gail Carson Levine. **101m/C; DVD, Blu-Ray.** Anne Hathaway; Hugh Dancy; Cary Elwes; Vivica A. Fox; Joanna Lumley; Minnie Driver; Patrick Bergin; Parminder K. Nagra; Jimi Mistry; Heidi Klum; ***V:*** Steve Coogan; ***Nar:*** Eric Idle; ***D:*** Tommy O'Haver; ***W:*** Laurie Craig; Karen McCullah Lutz; Kirsten Smith; Jennifer Heath; Michele J. Wolff; ***C:*** John de Borman; ***M:*** Shaun Davey.

Elle **2016 (R)** After successful video game executive Michèle Leblanc (Huppert) is violated in her own home, she embarks upon a cat-and-mouse game to catch her rapist. Verhoeven's film is a complex, fascinating dissection of gender roles, particularly in how they relate to power (at work, in relationships, between parent and child, etc.), with a searing performance from Huppert at its center. It's a tough film to describe, but know that Huppert pulls off something amazing here, carrying us stridently through a complex, challenging film. She's awardworthy. **130m/C; DVD, Blu-Ray.** Isabelle Huppert; Laurent Lafitte; Anne Consigny; Charles Berling; Virginie Efira; ***D:*** Paul Verhoeven; ***W:*** David Birke; ***C:*** Stephane Fontaine; ***M:*** Anne Dudley. Golden Globes '17: Actress--Drama (Huppert), Foreign Film; Ind. Spirit '17: Actress (Huppert).

Ellen Foster ½ **1997 (PG-13)** Coming-of-age TV drama concerns 10-year-old Ellen (Malone), who lives with her abusive, drunken dad (Levine) and her gentle mom (O'Connor). After mom dies, Ellen is shuffled between uncaring relatives, including a nasty grandma, Leonora (Harris), while trying to draw strength from the few friends and teachers who do care about her. Based on the book by Kaye Gibbons. **97m/C; VHS, DVD.** Jena Malone; Julie Harris; Ted Levine; Glynnis O'Connor; Debra Monk; Barbara Garrick; Kate Burton; Zeljko Ivanek; Lynne Moody; Bill Nunn; Amanda Peet; Allison Jones; Timothy Olyphant; ***D:*** John Erman; ***W:*** Maria Nation; William Hanley; ***C:*** Brian West; ***M:*** John Morris. **TV**

Elles **2011 (NC-17)** Pretentious sexual drama somewhat redeemed by Binoche's performance. Anne (Binoche) is a harried wife and mother who's also a magazine journalist working on a story about college students earning their tuition through prostitution. She interviews Charlotte (Demoustier) and Alicja (Kulig) who are frank and nonchalant about the services they perform, some of them shown in detail, which gives the film its rating. French and Polish with subtitles. **96m/C; DVD, Blu-Ray, Streaming.** *FR PL GE* Juliette Binoche; Anais Demoustier; Joanna Kulig; Louis-Do de Lencquesaing; Ali Marhyar; ***D:*** Malgorzata (Malgoska) Szumowska; ***W:*** Malgorzata (Malgoska) Szumowska; Tine Byrckel; ***C:*** Michal Englert; ***M:*** Pawel Mykietyn.

Ellie ½ **1984 (R)** A murderous widow's stepdaughter tries to save her father from being added to the woman's extensive list of dearly departed husbands. **90m/C; VHS, DVD.** Shelley Winters; Sheila Kennedy; Pat Paulsen; George Gobel; Edward Albert; ***D:*** Peter Wittman.

Ellie Parker **2005** Ellie (Watts) is the typical struggling actress in L.A., frantically driving from audition to audition, transforming her clothes and personality in an instant to please a series of dismissive casting directors. While Ellie wrestles with her integrity and the absurdity of Hollywood, her friends and manager (Chevy Chase, in an odd cameo role) try and fail to re-inspire her love of acting. Coffey uses 16-millimeter film to emphasize Ellie's disconsolate search for something authentic. A low-budget verite production, but Watts' performance is spot-on. **95m/C; DVD.** Naomi Watts; Rebecca Rigg; Chevy Chase; Mark Pelligrino; Blair Mastbaum; Scott Coffey; ***Cameo(s):*** Keanu Reeves; ***D:*** Scott Coffey; ***W:*** Scott Coffey; ***C:*** Blair Mastbaum; Scott Coffey; ***M:*** B.C. Smith.

Elling ½ **2001 (R)** Witty, gentle comedy has two Noregian misfits, recently released from a mental institution, living together in a government-subsidized Oslo flat in order to learn how to live in the outside world. Elling, who had to be dragged from his mother's home when she died, is extremely agoraphobic, fastidious, and socially inept. His roomie Kjell Bjarne is a hulking man with no sense of personal hygiene and an overdeveloped sexual imagination. Their friendship helps them to slowly and amusingly adapt to, and enter, the world. This allows Kjell to befriend, and become romantic with, their pregnant upstairs neighbor, while Elling writes poetry (and slips it into saurkraut packages at the market), finally attends a reading, and meets fellow poet Alfons. Sentimental without being cloying. **89m/C; VHS, DVD.** *NO* Per Christian Ellefsen; Sven Nordin; Marit Pia Jacobsen; Jorgen Langhelle; Per Christensen; ***D:*** Petter Naess; ***W:*** Axel Hellstenius; ***C:*** Svein Krovel; ***M:*** Lars Lillo Stenberg.

Elmer Gantry ½ **1960** The classic multi-Oscar-winning adaptation of the Sinclair Lewis novel written to expose and denounce the flamboyant, small-town evangelists spreading through America at the time. In the film, Lancaster is the amoral Southern preacher who exacts wealth and power from his congregation, and takes a nun as a mistress. Jones stars as his ex-girlfriend who resorts to a life of prostitution. **146m/C; VHS, DVD, Blu-Ray.** Burt Lancaster; Shirley Jones; Jean Simmons; Dean Jagger; Arthur Kennedy; Patti Page; Edward Andrews; John McIntire; Hugh Marlowe; Rex Ingram; Wendell Holmes; ***D:*** Richard Brooks; ***W:*** Richard Brooks; ***C:*** John Alton; ***M:*** Andre Previn. Oscars '60: Actor (Lancaster), Adapt. Screenplay, Support. Actress (Jones); Golden Globes '61: Actor--Drama (Lancaster); Natl. Bd. of Review '60: Support. Actress (Jones); N.Y. Film Critics '60: Actor (Lancaster).

Elmer the Great ½ **1933** Baseball comedy based on a play by Ring Lardner and George M. Cohan. Small town slugger Elmer Kane (Brown) doesn't want to sign with the Chicago Cubs if it means leaving his gal Nellie (Ellis) behind. So Nellie rejects Elmer for the sake of his career and he gets the team to the World Series. But Elmer has inadvertently gotten into debt with some gamblers who now want him to throw the pennant race. **73m/B; DVD.** Joe E. Brown; Patricia Ellis; Frank McHugh; Preston Foster; Claire Dodd; Russell Hopton; J. Carrol Naish; Sterling Holloway; ***D:*** Mervyn LeRoy; ***W:*** Tom Geraghty; ***C:*** Arthur L. Todd.

Elmore Leonard's Gold Coast ½ *Gold Coast* **1997 (R)** Miami mobster Frank DiCilia (Bradford) is dead and his widow Karen (Helgenberger) is not happy. Yes, she's inherited $15 mil but Frank's will also stipulates that she has to remain faithful to him forever. Too bad Karen and smalltime con man Maguire (Caruso) are instantly attracted to one another. And too bad Frank's also left behind loathsome hit man Roland (Kober) to enforce the edict (although if Karen wants him, Roland's willing to be flexible). Based on the novel by Elmore Leonard. **109m/C; VHS, Streaming.** David Caruso; Marg Helgenberger; Jeff Kober; Barry Primus; Richard Bradford; Wanda De Jesus; ***D:*** Peter Weller; ***W:*** Harley Peyton; ***C:*** Jacek Laskus; ***M:*** Peter Harris. **CABLE**

Eloise at the Plaza ½ **2003** Hyperactive adaptation of the first of Kay Thompsn's books about six-year-old enfant terrible Eloise (Vassilieva), who lives with her mother at the Plaza Hotel in New York. Mom is away in Paris, so it's up to Nanny (Andrews) to try to reign in her charge's exuberant behavior and frequently disastrous schemes. This time Eloise is determined to attend the prestigious Debutante's Ball that is being held at the Plaza, despite her age (and the lack of an invitation). **90m/C; VHS, DVD.** Sofia Vassilieva; Julie Andrews; Jeffrey Tambor; Kenneth Welsh; Debra Monk; Jonas Chernick; Christine Baranski; ***D:*** Kevin Lima; ***W:*** Janet Brownell; ***C:*** James Chressanthis; ***M:*** Bruce Broughton. **TV**

Elopement 1/2 **1951** Mild-mannered comedy. Industrial designer Howard (Webb) wants his daughter Jake (Francis) to join his firm after college. Instead, she suddenly elopes with psychology professor Matt (Lundigan). Both Howard and Matt's dad Tom (Bickford) are outraged and track down their errant offspring who are already having second thoughts about their impulsiveness. **82m/B; DVD.** Clifton Webb; Anne Francis; William Lundigan; Charles Bickford; Evelyn Varden; Margalo Gillmore; Tommy Rettig; Reginald Gardiner; ***D:*** Henry Koster; ***W:*** Bess Boyle; ***C:*** Joseph LaShelle; ***M:*** Cyril Mockridge.

Elsa & Fred **2014 (PG-13)** After his wife dies, Fred (Plummer) unwillingly moves into a New Orleans apartment, pushed by his over-solicitous daughter (Harden). He wants to be left alone to age ungracefully but his vivacious neighbor Elsa (MacLaine), whose favorite movie is "La Dolce Vita," has other ideas. Cliched comedy-drama goes for shameless emotional string-pulling although the leads can't be blamed. **97m/C; DVD, Blu-Ray.** Christopher Plummer; Shirley MacLaine; Marcia Gay Harden; Chris Noth; Erika Alexander; Scott Bakula; James Brolin; Wendell Pierce; George Segal; ***D:*** Michael Radford; ***W:*** Michael Radford; Anna Pavignano; ***C:*** Michael McDonough; ***M:*** Luis Bacalov.

Elsewhere 1/2 **2009 (R)** A young teen girl decides to meet men online in a desperate quest to escape her dull home town, and apparently only one friend cares enough to tell her it's a bad idea or look for her when she inevitably ends up missing. **106m/C; DVD, Blu-Ray.** Anna Kendrick; Paul Wesley; Tania Raymonde; Chuck Carter; Olivia Dawn York; ***D:*** Nathan Hope; ***W:*** Nathan Hope; ***C:*** Mike Karasick; ***M:*** Bernie Larsen. **VIDEO**

The Elusive Corporal 1/2 *Le Caporal Epingle* **1962** Set in a P.O.W. camp on the day France surrendered to Germany, this is the story of the French and Germans, complete with memories of a France that is no more. **108m/B; VHS, DVD.** Jean-Pierre Cassel; Claude Brasseur; O.E. Hasse; Claude Rich; ***D:*** Jean Renoir.

Elvira Madigan **1967 (PG)** Chronicles the true 19th-century Swedish romance between teenaged Elvira (Degermark), a beautiful circus tight-rope walker, and young Army officer Sixten Sparre (Berggren) who leaves his wife and children to be with her. Exceptional direction and photography and a notable use of classical music by Mozart and Vivaldi. Swedish with subtitles. **90m/C; VHS, DVD.** *SW* Pia Degermark; Thommy Berggren; Lennart Malmer; Nina Widerberg; Cleo Jensen; ***D:*** Bo Widerberg; ***W:*** Bo Widerberg; Johan Lindstroem Saxon; ***C:*** Jorgen Persson; ***M:*** Ulf Bjorlin. Cannes '67: Actress (Degermark).

Elvira, Mistress of the Dark **1988 (PG-13)** A manic comedy based on Peterson's infamous B-movie horror-hostess character. The mega-busted terror-queen inherits a house in a conservative Massachusetts town and causes double-entendre chaos when she attempts to sell it. **96m/C; VHS, DVD, Blu-Ray.** Cassandra Peterson; Jeff Conaway; Susan Kellerman; Edie McClurg; Daniel Greene; William Morgan Sheppard; Kurt Fuller; Pat Crawford Brown; William Duell; William Cort; John Paragon; ***D:*** James Signorelli; ***W:*** Cassandra Peterson; John Paragon; Sam Egan; ***C:*** Hanania Baer; ***M:*** James Campbell.

Elvira's Haunted Hills 1/2 **2002 (PG-13)** That bodacious vamp returns as Elvira (Peterson) and her French maid Zou Zou (Smith) are stranded in Carpathia in 1851. They manage to find shelter at the Transylavania castle of the twitchy Vladimir Hellsubus (O'Brien) where all sorts of high camp happenings occur. **89m/C; VHS, DVD.** Cassandra Peterson; Richard O'Brien; Mary Jo Smith; Mary Scheer; Scott Atkinson; ***D:*** Sam Irvin; ***W:*** Cassandra Peterson; John Paragon; ***C:*** Viorel Segovia; ***M:*** Eric Allaman.

Elvis and Annabelle **2007 (PG-13)** If you like quirky then this indie is worth viewing. Reluctant Texas beauty queen Annabelle (Lively) actually drops dead during a pageant. Mortician Elvis (Minghella), who's taken over the family funeral home business, impulsively kisses the beauty on his table, and she revives. Annabelle's revival is big news but she gets tired of being exploited and her notoriety puts a crimp in her would-be romance with Elvis. **103m/C; DVD.** Max Minghella; Blake Lively; Joe Mantegna; Mary Steenburgen; Keith Carradine; Brent Smiga; ***D:*** Will Geiger; ***W:*** Will Geiger; ***C:*** Conrad W. Hall; ***M:*** Blake Neely.

Elvis & Nixon 1/2 **2016 (R)** The oddity of real life trumps anything that filmmaking could bring to it, but two of our best actors do everything they can to make this dramedy entertaining anyway. Shannon plays Elvis Presley and Spacey steps into the large shoes of President Richard Nixon on the occasion of the taking of one of the most notorious photographs in the history of the form. In December of 1970, Elvis decided he wanted to meet the President. It was that simple. The story behind the photo that was taken that day is fun and clever, even if it's a little shallow. **86m/C; DVD, Blu-Ray.** Michael Shannon; Kevin Spacey; Alex Pettyfer; Johnny Knoxville; Colin Hanks; ***D:*** Liza Johnson; ***W:*** Joey Sagal; Hanala Sagal; Cary Elwes; ***C:*** Terry Stacey; ***M:*** Ed Shearmur.

Elvis Has Left the Building 1/2 **2004 (PG-13)** Once upon a time Elvis gave Harmony Jones (Basinger) a ride in his pink Caddy, making her feel so indebted to the King that, years later, the cosmetics saleswoman thinks he's using her from beyond the grave when she begins unintentionally offing his impersonators. While on the lam from the law, Harmony teams up with Miles (Corbett), a down-and-out New York advertising executive who has his own issues with the King. Offbeat yet not amusing. **90m/C; VHS, DVD.** Kim Basinger; John Corbett; Annie Potts; Sean Astin; Denise Richards; Mike Starr; Phill Lewis; Philip Charles MacKenzie; Billy Ray Cyrus; Richard Kind; David Leisure; Tom Hanks; Joel Zwick; Angie Dickinson; Noriyuki "Pat" Morita; ***D:*** Joel Zwick; ***W:*** Adam-Michael Garber; Mitchell Ganem; ***C:*** Paul Elliott; ***M:*** David Kitay. **VIDEO**

Elvis in Hollywood **1993** A tribute highlighting Presley's first four films, "Love Me Tender," "Loving You," "Jailhouse Rock," and "King Creole," completed prior to his reporting for active duty in the army. Features his 1956 screen test at Paramount Studios; photos from the movie sets; interviews with co-stars, directors, writers, business associates, songwriters, and friends; and home movies as well as out-take footage from "Jailhouse Rock." **65m/C; VHS, DVD.** ***D:*** Frank Martin.

Elvis: The Movie 1/2 **1979** Biography of the legendary singer, from his high school days to his Las Vegas comeback. Russell gives a convincing performance and lip syncs effectively to the voice of the King (provided by country singer Ronnie McDowell). Also available in 150-minute version. **117m/C; VHS, DVD.** Kurt Russell; Season Hubley; Shelley Winters; Ed Begley, Jr.; Dennis Christopher; Pat Hingle; Bing (Neil) Russell; Joe Mantegna; ***D:*** John Carpenter. **TV**

Elysium 1/2 **2013 (R)** Director/writer Blomkamp suffers a sophomore slump, following up his Best Picture-nominated "District 9" with this messy story that's too similar to its predecessor and not as inventive. In the future, the wealthy migrated to Elysium, a community circling Earth, leaving the working class on an Earth increasingly depleted of resources and without basic care. Average worker Max (Damon) is sucked into a plan to assault Elysium and its Secretary (Foster) after a workplace accident leaves him in dire need of treatment, which is only available to those who live above. Adequate sci-fi but the big-name leads deserved better. **109m/C; DVD, Blu-Ray.** Matt Damon; Jodie Foster; Sharlto Copley; William Fichtner; Alice Braga; Diego Luna; Wagner Moura; ***D:*** Neill Blomkamp; ***W:*** Neill Blomkamp; ***C:*** Trent Opaloch; ***M:*** Ryan Amon.

The Embalmer *L'Imbalsamatore* **2003** Peppino (Mahieux) is a dwarfish middle-aged taxidermist (the Embalmer of the title) who attaches himself to handsome but dumb Valerio (Manzillo). Peppino hires Valerio, gives him a place to live, and uses hookers to put the two men in bed together at the same time. When Valerio meets Deborah, a beautiful drifter, on a business trip, the result is a tug-of-war for Valerio's attention. Mahieux is brilliant as the creepy Peppino, who supplements his income with shady underworld deals. Manzillo does an adequate job as the blank, naive Valerio, who can't decide between barracuda Deborah and a relationship he doesn't entirely understand with Peppino. Director Garrone fills every moment with lurking dread and foreboding, adding distinctive visual flourishes and gritty details. **104m/C; DVD.** *IT* Ernesto Mahieux; Valerio Foglia Manzillo; Elisabetta Rocchetti; Pietro Biondi; David Ryall; Bernardino Terracciano; Marcella Granito; ***D:*** Matteo Garrone; ***W:*** Matteo Garrone; Ugo Chiti; Massimo Gaudioso; ***C:*** Marco Onorato; ***M:*** Banda Osiris.

Embassy *Target: Embassy* **1972** In this mediocre espionage thriller, von Sydow is a Soviet defector under asylum at the U.S. embassy in Beirut. Colonel Connors, a Russian spy, penetrates embassy security and wounds von Sydow. He is caught, escapes, is captured, escapes, and is caught again. Great cast, but script is often too wordy and contrived. **90m/C; VHS, DVD.** *GB* Richard Roundtree; Chuck Connors; Max von Sydow; Ray Milland; Broderick Crawford; Marie-Jose Nat; ***D:*** Gordon Hessler.

Embrace of the Serpent 1/2 *El abrazo de la serpiente* **2015** The first Colombian film ever nominated for the Oscar for Best Foreign Language Film, this psychedelic epic uniquely captures a formative chapter in history. The film tells two stories—one in 1909 and one in 1940—both featuring Karamakate, the last survivor of his Amazonian tribe. Karamakate travels the Amazon with two scientists, a German and an American, in search of the yakruna, a rare plant sacred to his people. Inspired by the diaries of the two scientists, the film feels like sci-fi at times, taking viewers to a part of the world likely to feel completely alien to their own. Spanish, Portuguese, German, Catalan, and Latin with subtitles. **125m/B; DVD, Blu-Ray.** *AR CO VZ* Nilbio Torres; Jan Bijvoet; Antonio Bolivar; Brionne Davis; Yauenku Migue; ***D:*** Ciro Guerra; ***W:*** Ciro Guerra; Jacques Toulemonde Vidal; ***C:*** David Gallego; ***M:*** Nascuy Linares.

Embrace of the Vampire **1995 (R)** Innocent young Charlotte (Milano) must make a choice between her college boyfriend Chris (Pruett) and a new nighttime lover (Kemp) with some decidedly different habits. Seems Charlotte looks exactly like a love lost hundreds of years ago and he's not going to take no for an answer. Also available in an unrated version. **92m/C; VHS, DVD, Blu-Ray.** Alyssa Milano; Martin Kemp; Harrison Pruett; Charlotte Lewis; Jordan Ladd; Rachel True; Jennifer Tilly; ***D:*** Anne Goursaud; ***W:*** Halle Eaton; Nicole Coady; Rick Bitzelberger; ***C:*** Suki Medencevic; ***M:*** Joseph Williams. **VIDEO**

Embryo *Created to Kill* **1976 (PG)** An average sci-fi drama about a scientist who uses raw genetic material to artificially produce a beautiful woman, with ghastly results. **108m/C; VHS, DVD.** Rock Hudson; Barbara Carrera; Diane Ladd; Roddy McDowall; Ann Schedeen; John Elerick; Dr. Joyce Brothers; ***D:*** Ralph Nelson; ***W:*** Anita Doohan; Jack W. Thomas; ***C:*** Fred W. Koenekamp; ***M:*** Gil Melle.

The Emerald Forest **1985 (R)** Bill (Boothe) moves his family to Brazil where he has a job as an engineer working on a dam project. His young son Tommy wanders into the rainforest and is taken in by a primitive tribe of Amazons. Bill searches 10 years for him, finally discovering a happily adjusted teenager named Tomme (Boorman, the director's son), who may not want to return to so-called civilization. An engrossing look at tribal life in the vanishing jungle. Beautifully photographed and based upon a true story. **113m/C; VHS, DVD, Blu-Ray.** Powers Boothe; Meg Foster; Charley Boorman; Dira Paes; Rui Polonah; ***D:*** John Boorman; ***W:*** Rospo Pallenberg; ***C:*** Philippe Rousselot.

Emerald Jungle 1/2 *Eaten Alive by Cannibals; Eaten Alive; Mangiati Vivi dai Cannibali* **1980** While searching for his missing sister in the jungle, Agren encounters cannibal tribes and a colony of brainwashed cult followers. This Italian feature was cut for its U.S. release. **92m/C; VHS, DVD, Blu-Ray.** *IT* Robert Kerman; Janet Agren; Mel Ferrer; Luciano Martino; Mino Loy; Ivan Rassimov; Paola Senatore; Me Me Lai; Maria Fiammi Maglione; Franco Fantasia; ***D:*** Umberto Lenzi; ***W:*** Umberto Lenzi; ***C:*** Frederico Zanni.

Emil and the Detectives 1/2 *Emil Und Die Detektive* **1964** A German ten-year-old is robbed of his grandmother's money by gangsters, and subsequently enlists the help of pre-adolescent detectives to retrieve it. Good Disney dramatization of the Erich Kastner children's novel. Remake of the 1931 German film starring Rolf Wenkhaus. **99m/C; VHS, DVD, Streaming.** Bryan Russell; Walter Slezak; Roger Mobley; ***D:*** Peter Tewkesbury; ***W:*** A.J. Carothers.

Emile 1/2 **2003 (R)** McKellen shines in this story of a man confronting the demons of his past. Emile, a respected British scientist and professor, travels to Canada to receive an honorary degree and visit his niece Nadia (Unger). Although Emile acts like the perfect uncle, in reality he deserted Nadia in an orphanage when her parents died and has never been a part of her life. Reconnecting with his past leads into a series of oddly-shot flashbacks to Emile's youth and his painful relationships with his brothers, and in the end Emile must come to terms with his own painful past as well as his selfish treatment of Nadia. Despite Bessai's efforts to break up the narrative, the story is routine and predictable, with McKellen's performance the most distinctive part of the film. **96m/C; VHS, DVD.** *CA GB* Ian McKellen; Deborah Kara Unger; Tygh Runyan; Ian Tracey; Chris William Martin; Janet Wright; ***D:*** Carl Bessai; ***W:*** Carl Bessai; ***C:*** Carl Bessai; ***M:*** Vincent Mai.

Emily Bronte's Wuthering Heights 1/2 *Wuthering Heights* **1992 (PG)** Miscast version of the tragic tale of doomed lovers Cathy (Binoche) and Heathcliff (Fiennes). While Fiennes may seem too refined for the role, he manages to be both brooding and brutal. However, the beautiful Binoche can't successfully supress her French accent enough to pass for a heedless Yorkshire lass. Good supporting cast, with O'Connor posing as writer/narrator Bronte. **107m/C; VHS, DVD.** *GB* Ralph Fiennes; Juliette Binoche; Janet McTeer; Sophie Ward; Simon Shepherd; Jeremy Northam; Jason Riddington; Jonathan Firth; Paul Geoffrey; Sinead O'Connor; ***D:*** Peter Kosminsky; ***W:*** Anne Devlin; ***C:*** Mike Southon; ***M:*** Ryuichi Sakamoto.

Emma 1/2 **1932** Not the Jane Austen heroine. This Emma (Dressler) is hired as housekeeper/nanny to widow Frederick Smith's (Hersholt) children, spending 20 years looking after them until Smith proposes marriage while Emma takes a vacation in Niagara Falls. He dies shortly thereafter, leaving Emma his money, and three of the children she's looked after suddenly turn on her, accusing her of murdering their father for the inheritance. A trial ensues. **71m/B; DVD.** Marie Dressler; Jean Hersholt; Richard Cromwell; Myrna Loy; Kathryn Crawford; George Meeker; Purnell Pratt; John Miljan; ***D:*** Clarence Brown; ***W:*** Zelda Sears; Leonard Praskins; ***C:*** Oliver Marsh.

Emma 1/2 **1972** BBC TV version of the Jane Austen saga with young Emma trying her matchmaking skills on all her friends and neighbors—with disastrous results. Mr. Knightly tries to provide both a voice of reason and romance, if only Emma could realize it. **257m/C; VHS, DVD.** *GB* Doran Goodwin; Vivienne Moore; John Carson; Donald Eccles; Debbie Bowen; ***D:*** John Glenister.

Emma **1996 (PG)** Jane Austen's 1816 novel about wealthy, 21-year-old Emma Woodhouse (Paltrow) who makes it her goal to "fix" the lives of all her friends, while ignoring her own problems (the modern adaptation was "Clueless"). Emma focuses much of her attention on Harriet Smith (Collete), a simple young woman who Emma believes is in need of the perfect mate. Meanwhile, Emma neglects to notice the attractive, and exasperated, Mr. Knightley (Northam). McGrath's screenplay makes Emma and Knightley more likable than in the book, but otherwise stays true. After the success of "Sense and Sensibility," Austen's name is making it in the movies in the footsteps of the likes of John Grisham. **120m/C; VHS, DVD.** Gwyneth Paltrow; Jeremy Northam; Greta Scacchi; Toni Collette; Alan Gumming; Juliet Stevenson; Polly Walker; Ewan McGregor; James Cosmo; Sophie Thompson; Phyllida Law; ***D:*** Douglas McGrath; ***W:*** Douglas McGrath; ***C:*** Ian Wilson; ***M:*** Rachel Portman. Oscars '96: Orig. Score.

Emma *Jane Austen's Emma* **1997** British TV adaptation of the Jane Austen novel featuring young, matchmaking Emma

(Beckinsale) wrecking havoc amongst her friends and neighbors with her would-be romantic alliances. Screenplay is truer to the book, with slightly less likable personalities than the 1996 big-screen version. Excellent cast, and beautiful locations and costumes make this one worth seeing. A&E Network offered "Emma" after the overwhelming success of their miniseries "Pride and Prejudice," also adapted from Austen. **107m/C; VHS, DVD.** *GB* Kate Beckinsale; Mark Strong; Samantha Bond; Prunella Scales; Bernard Hepton; Raymond Coulthard; Dominic Rowan; James Hazeldine; Samantha Morton; Lucy Robinson; Olivia Williams; ***D:*** Diarmuid Lawrence; ***W:*** Andrew Davis.

Emma 🦴🦴 ½ **2009** Cast wins out in this charmingly sunlit BBC adaptation of the Austen novel with Garai bright and well-meaning (if self-absorbed) in the title role. Wealthy Emma Woodhouse believes she has a future as a matchmaker but her efforts nearly cause a social disaster for new (and poor) friend Harriet Smith (Dylan) when Emma discourages a marriage proposal from someone she deems unsuitable. No wonder acerbic neighbor Mr. Knightley (Miller) finds Emma both exasperating and amusing. Of course neither can admit to a romantic attraction to each other. **240m/C; DVD.** *GB* Romola Garai; Jonny Lee Miller; Louise Dylan; Rupert Evans; Laura Pyper; Blake Ritson; Jodhi May; Michael Gambon; Christina Cole; Robert Bathurst; ***D:*** Jim O'Hanlon; ***W:*** Sandy Welch; ***C:*** Adam Suschitzky; ***M:*** Samuel Sim. **TV**

Emma 🦴🦴 ½ **2020 (PG) 124m/C; DVD, Blu-Ray.** Anya Taylor-Joy; Bill Nighy; Johnny Flynn; Mia Goth; Miranda Hart; ***D:*** Autumn de Wilde; ***W:*** Eleanor Catton; ***C:*** Christopher Blauvelt; ***M:*** David Schweitzer; Isobel Waller-Bridge.

Emmanuelle 🦴🦴 ½ **1974** Filmed in Bangkok, a young, beautiful woman is introduced by her husband to an uninhibited world of sensuality. Above-average soft-core skin film, made with sophistication and style. Kristel maintains a vulnerability and awareness, never becoming a mannequin. **92m/C; VHS, DVD.** *FR* Sylvia Kristel; Alain Cuny; Marika Green; Daniel Sarky; ***D:*** Just Jaeckin; ***W:*** Jean-Louis Richard; ***C:*** Richard Suzuki; ***M:*** Pierre Bachelet.

Emmanuelle 4 🦴 **1984 (R)** Emmanuelle flees a bad relationship and undergoes plastic surgery to mask her identity. Ultimately, she becomes a beautiful young model in the form of a different actress, of course. **95m/C; VHS, DVD.** *FR* Sylvia Kristel; Mia Nygren; Patrick Bauchau; ***D:*** Francis Giacobetti.

Emmanuelle 5 🦴 ½ **1987 (R)** This time around sexy Emmanuelle flees aboard a convenient yacht when she's chased by adoring fans at the Cannes Film Festival. But she winds up being forced to join an Arab sheik's harem of slaves. A good example of a series that should have quit while it was ahead. **78m/C; VHS, DVD.** *FR* Monique Gabrielle; Charles Foster; ***D:*** Steve Barnett; Walerian Borowczyk; ***M:*** Pierre Bachelet.

Emmanuelle 6 🦴 **1988 (R)** The saga of the sexy beauty continues. This time Emmanuelle and a group of models head for the paradise of an Amazon jungle where they promptly become the prized captives of a drug lord. **80m/C; VHS, DVD.** *FR* Natalie Uher; Jean-Rene Gossart; Thomas Obermuller; Gustavo Rodriguez; ***D:*** Jean Rollin; Bruno Zincone; ***C:*** Serge Godet; ***M:*** Olivier Day.

Emmanuelle in the Country 🦴 *L'Infermiera di Campagna; Country Nurse* **1978** Emmanuelle becomes a nurse in an attempt to bring comfort and other pleasures to those in need. **90m/C; VHS, DVD.** *IT* Laura Gemser; Gabriele Tinti; Aldo Sambrell; ***D:*** Mario Bianchi; ***W:*** Luigi Petrini; ***C:*** Umberto Galeassi; ***M:*** Ubaldo Continiello.

Emmanuelle on Taboo Island 🦴 ½ *La Spiaggia del Desiderio; A Beach Called Desire* **1976 (R)** Marooned young man discovers a beautiful woman on his island. This delights him. **95m/C; VHS, DVD.** *IT* Laura Gemser; Paul(o) Giusti; Arthur Kennedy; ***D:*** Enzo D'Ambrosio; ***W:*** Enzo D'Ambrosio; ***C:*** Riccardo (Pallton) Pallottini; ***M:*** Marcello Giombini.

Emmanuelle, the Joys of a Woman 🦴 *Emmanuelle l'Antivierge; Emmanuelle's 7th Heaven; Emmanuelle 2* **1976** The amorous exploits of a sensuous, liberated couple take them and their erotic companions to exotic Hong Kong, Bangkok, and Bali. **92m/C; VHS, DVD, Blu-Ray.** *FR* Sylvia Kristel; Umberto Orsini; Catherine Rivet; Frederic Lagache; Laura Gemser; Henri Czarniak; Tom Clark; Caroline Laurence; ***D:*** Francis Giacobetti; ***W:*** Francis Giacobetti; Jean-Marc Vasseur; ***C:*** Robert Fraisse; ***M:*** Pierre Bachelet; Francis Lai.

Emmanuelle, the Queen 🦴 *Black Emmanuelle; Mavri Emmanouella* **1979** Seeking revenge, Emmanuelle plots the murder of her sadistic husband. The lecherous assassin she hires tries to blackmail her, and she challenges him at his own game of deadly seduction. **90m/C; VHS, DVD.** *GR* Laura Gemser; Gabriele Tinti; Livia Russo; Vagelis Vartan; Pantelis Agelopou; ***D:*** Ilias Milonakos; ***W:*** Ilias Milonakos; ***C:*** Vassilis Christomoglou; ***M:*** Giovanni Ullu.

Emmanuelle's Daughter 🦴 **1979** A Greek-made thriller in which a vapidly sensuous heroine cavorts amid episodes of murder, blackmail, and rape. **91m/C; DVD.** *GR* Laura Gemser; Gabriele Tinti; Livia Russa; Vagelis Vartan; Nadia Neri; ***D:*** Ilias Mylonakos; ***W:*** Ilias Mylonakos; ***C:*** Vassilis Christomoglou; ***M:*** Giovanni Ullu.

Emma's Chance 🦴🦴 **2016 (PG)** A family drama about a horse and a girl both finding their second chance in each other. After getting into legal trouble with mean-girl friends, Emma (Grammer) is sentenced to community service. Serving at a horse rescue, Emma finds new purpose by learning to ride and bonding with a show horse that has been abused and will not let anyone but Emma ride him. As she grows as a person and finds a new purpose for his life, Emma forms a plan to save the ranch where the horse rescue is housed. **93m/C; DVD, Streaming, Download.** Greer Grammer; Joseph Lawrence; Missi Pyle; Jennifer Taylor; Christina Robinson; ***D:*** Anna Elizabeth James; ***W:*** Anna Elizabeth James; ***C:*** Alex Jacobs; ***M:*** Gareth Coker. **VIDEO**

Emma's Wish 🦴🦴 **1998** Somewhat maudlin family drama, originally shown on CBS. Emma makes a wish on her 75th birthday to reunite with her estranged daughter Joy. The next morning Emma wakes up looking like she's 40 and sets out to see Joy, persisting until Joy agrees to hire her as a nanny. Emma finds out Joy's marriage is in trouble and tries to set things right. However, she has to complete her mission in a month before she turns geriatric again. **90m/C; DVD.** Joanna Kerns; Harley Jane Kozak; William R. Moses; Della Reese; Seymour Cassel; Courtland Mead; Jeanne Allen; ***D:*** Mike Robe; ***W:*** Cynthia Whitcomb; ***C:*** Edward Pei; ***M:*** Laura Karpman. **TV**

The Emoji Movie 🦴 **2017 (PG)** Sinking to a new low in opportunism {dollar sign}, Hollywood churns out a feature-length commercial for apps. And a terribly unfunny one, at that. Gene, who lives inside a smartphone, is embarrassed {blushed face} that he can make multiple expressions, so he sets out on a journey to be like his peers, only to discover that his uniqueness is good {thumbs up}. It's a clichéd lesson that's delivered with no charm, wit, or humor. Unfortunately, it was a box office success. {red angry face} **86m/C; DVD, Blu-Ray.** ***V:*** T.J. Miller; James Corden; Anna Faris; Maya Rudolph; Steven Wright; ***D:*** Tony Leondis; ***W:*** Tony Leondis; Eric Siegel; Mike White; ***M:*** Patrick Doyle. Golden Raspberries '17: Worst Director (Leondis), Worst Picture, Worst Screenplay.

Emperor 🦴🦴 ½ **2012 (PG-13)** Set in the immediate aftermath of WWII as American General MacArthur (Jones) and his team debate the fate of captured war criminal Emperor Hirohito (Kataoka). The proceeding are occasionally put on hold as the story flashes back to happier times, including a star-crossed romance between young brigadier general Bonner Feller (Fox) and the Japanese woman he loves even as their countries are at war. The fictionalized interruptions to otherwise somewhat true events injects the lifeless rhetoric with a much needed human element. Solid performances, despite some clichéd Hollywood moments, and a keen eye for detail keep it from falling too far into melodramatic mush. **98m/C; DVD, Blu-Ray.** Tommy Lee Jones; Matthew Fox; Eriko Hatsune; Takataro Kataoka; Kaori Momoi; Toshiyuki Nishida; Masayoshi Haneda; Colin Moy; ***D:*** Peter Webber; ***W:*** Vera Blasi; David Klass; ***C:*** Stuart Dryburgh; ***M:*** Alex Heffes.

The Emperor and the Assassin 🦴🦴 **1999 (R)** Sumptuous historical drama (and a complicated storyline) concerns a united China's first emperor. Set in 320 B.C., China is a collection of seven rival kingdoms with Ying Zheng, the King of Qin (Xuejian) obsessed with uniting the country and then dividing it into provinces for proper ruling (with himself as supreme head). Naturally, this means war. Also involved is his lover, Lady Zhao (Li), who plans a fake assassination attempt to aid Zheng. But the assassin she chooses, Jing Ke (Fengyi), is trying to reform and things don't go exactly according to plan. Remember—power corrupts. Mandarin with subtitles. **161m/C; VHS, DVD.** *CH* Xuejian Li; Gong Li; Fengyi Zhang; Zhiwen Wang; Sun Zhou; Chen Kaige; ***D:*** Chen Kaige; ***W:*** Chen Kaige; Wang Peigong; ***C:*** Fei Zhao; ***M:*** Jiping Zhao.

Emperor Jones 🦴🦴 ½ **1933** Loosely based on Eugene O'Neill's play, film portrays the rise and fall of a railroad porter whose exploits take him from a life sentence on a chain gang to emperor of Haiti. Robeson re-creates his stage role in his first screen appearance. **72m/B; VHS, DVD.** Paul Robeson; Dudley Digges; Frank Wilson; Fredi Washington; Ruby Elzy; ***D:*** Dudley Murphy. Natl. Film Reg. '99.

Emperor of the Bronx 🦴 **1989** A look at crime, sleaze, violence, and the actions of bad guys in the inner-city. **90m/C; VHS, DVD.** William (Bill) Smith; Alex D'Andrea; Adrian Drake; Anthony Gioia; ***D:*** Joseph Merhi; ***W:*** Joseph Merhi; Sean Dash; ***C:*** Richard Pepin.

Emperor of the North Pole 🦴🦴🦴 *Emperor of the North* **1973 (PG)** Violent and well-done tale of hobos riding the rails during the Depression has Marvin as A#1, a legendary hobo who can get on any train, and his protege Cigaret (Carradine), trying to catch a ride on the train of sadistic conductor Shack (Borgnine), who's been known to kill to keep the hobos away. Tense and gritty, with the usual tight direction of Aldrich, beautiful cinematography, and a gripping screenplay. Borgnine is exceptional among a very strong cast. **118m/C; VHS, DVD.** Lee Marvin; Ernest Borgnine; Keith Carradine; Charles Tyner; Malcolm Atterbury; Simon Oakland; Harry Caesar; Hal Baylor; Matt Clark; Elisha Cook, Jr.; Liam Dunn; Robert Foulk; Ray Guth; Sid Haig; Vic Tayback; ***D:*** Robert Aldrich; ***W:*** Christopher Knopf; ***C:*** Joseph Biroc; ***M:*** Frank DeVol.

Emperor Waltz 🦴🦴 ½ **1948** Typical Hollywood musical finds phonograph salesman Crosby travelling to Vienna, hoping to sell his goods to the Austrian royal family of Emperor Franz Joseph. He meets up with the Emperor's snobby niece (Fontaine) and attempts to charm her into an audience with her royal uncle. Naturally the two fall in love and everything ends in a happy fade-out. **106m/C; VHS, DVD.** Bing Crosby; Joan Fontaine; Roland Culver; Richard Haydn; Lucile Watson; Sig Rumann; Harold Vermilyea; ***D:*** Billy Wilder; ***W:*** Billy Wilder; Charles Brackett; ***C:*** George Barnes; ***M:*** Victor Young.

The Emperor's Candlesticks 🦴🦴 **1937** Convoluted pic complete with spies, kidnapping, mistaken identity, masked balls, European travel, and romance. In pre-WWI Europe, Polish patriots kidnap the Romanov Grand Duke Peter. However, their ransom demand gets mixed-up with secret correspondence by Austro-Hungarian agent Baron Wolensky and Czarist spy Countess Muranova that's been hidden in a pair of candlesticks, which get stolen. Adapted from a Baroness Orczy novel. **92m/B; DVD.** William Powell; Luise Rainer; Robert Young; Maureen O'Sullivan; Frank Morgan; Henry Stephenson; Douglass Dumbrille; ***D:*** George Fitzmaurice; ***W:*** Harold Goldman; Monckton Hoffe; ***C:*** Harold Rosson; ***M:*** Franz Waxman.

The Emperor's Club 🦴🦴 *The Palace Thief* **2002 (PG-13)** "A man's character is his fate." This statement is eminently displayed through events both past and present of a prep school teacher (Kline) and one of his more challenging students (Hirsch). Ethics are questioned, schools of thought examined and hearts changed in this "Dead Poet Society" type drama. Hoffman's development of Ethan Canin's book "The Palace Thief" is unfortunately accomplished through manipulation and fake sincerity. **109m/C; VHS, DVD.** Kevin Kline; Emile Hirsch; Embeth Davidtz; Rob Morrow; Paul Dano; Edward Herrmann; Harris Yulin; Roger Rees; Jesse Eisenberg; Rishi Mehta; Joel Gretsch; Steven Culp; Patrick Dempsey; Rahul Khanna; ***D:*** Michael Hoffman; ***W:*** Neil Tolkin; ***C:*** Lajos Koltai; ***M:*** James Newton Howard.

The Emperor's New Clothes 🦴🦴 ½ **2001 (PG)** Historical comedy about Napoleon Bonaparte (Holm). Confined to the island of St. Helena by the British, the former emperor and his advisers plot to regain power in France by recruiting a look-alike named Eugene (Holm again) to trade places while the real Napoleon heads to Paris and restakes his claim to power. The first part of the plan works fine; the second part doesn't. Eugene likes playing the exiled ruler too much to reveal himself as an imposter and Napoleon turns out to enjoy his more simple life, especially with comely widow Pumpkin (Hjejle) proffering her charms. Loosely based on the French novel "The Death of Napoleon" by Simon Leys. **107m/C; VHS, DVD.** *GB* Ian Holm; Iben Hjejle; Tim (McInnerny) McInnery; Tom Watson; Nigel Terry; Hugh Bonneville; Murray Melvin; Eddie Marsan; Clive Russell; ***D:*** Alan Taylor; ***W:*** Kevin Molony; Herbie Wave; ***C:*** Alessio Gelsini Torresi; ***M:*** Rachel Portman.

The Emperor's New Groove 🦴🦴🦴 **2000 (G)** Animated fantasy about self-centered young emperor Kusco (Spade) who gets turned into a llama by sorceress Yzma (Kitt) and must team up with peasant Pacha (Goodman) to get his throne back. Refreshingly devoid of "important lessons" and sappy pop tunes, the only mission here is to provide laughs, and that it does. Like the great Warner Bros. cartoons of old, sarcastic and sophisticated humor abounds (Spade really helps out here), and the sidekicks get plenty of face (and hero) time, not to mention some of the best lines, including Warburton as Yzma's distracted and clumsy right-hand villain, Kronk. **79m/C; VHS, DVD, Blu-Ray.** ***V:*** David Spade; John Goodman; Eartha Kitt; Patrick Warburton; Wendie Malick; Patti Deutsch; John Fiedler; Kellyann Kelso; Eli Russell Linnetz; ***D:*** Mark Dindal; ***W:*** Dave Reynolds; ***M:*** John Debney. Broadcast Film Critics '00: Song ("My Funny Friend and Me").

The Emperor's Shadow 🦴🦴 *Qin Song* **1996** Saga of two boyhood friends in China around 220 BC. Gao Jianli (You) is a famous musician and the childhood friend of powerful Emperor Ying Sheng (Wen). Jianli basically wants to be left alone to work on his music but the Emperor demands he stick around and compose a stirring imperial anthem. Add into the mix Yueyang (Qing), the Emperor's daughter who has the hots for the musician (and vice versa) although she's betrothed to another, and tragedy is bound to be the result. Mandarin with subtitles. **123m/C; VHS, DVD.** *CH* Ge You; Jiang Wen; Xu Qing; ***D:*** Xiaowen Zhou; ***W:*** Wei Lu; ***C:*** Lu Gengxin; ***M:*** Jiping Zhao.

Empire 🦴🦴 ½ **2002 (R)** Leguizamo is Victor Rosa, a slick South Bronx drug entrepreneur hustling to keep his patch of heroin turf. Through narration, Victor walks us through his seedy world and his decision to leave it. His opportunity arises when he meets Wall Street couple Trish (Richards) and Jack (Sarsgaard). Jack cuts him in on an investment deal that helps launder his money, but Victor soon finds out that even a player can get played. Reyes's gangster flick aspires to the heights of "Scarface" and "The Godfather," but sinks in a quagmire of cliches and obvious plot devices. Excellent cast includes Rosellini as an over-the-top drug queenpin as well as rappers Fat Joe and Treach. **195m/C; VHS, DVD, Blu-Ray, On Demand.** John Leguizamo; Peter Sarsgaard; Denise Richards; Delilah Cotto; Vincent Laresca; Isabella Rossellini; Sonia Braga; Nestor Serrano; Fat Joe; Treach; ***D:*** Franc Reyes; ***W:*** Franc Reyes; ***C:*** Kramer Morgenthau; ***M:*** Ruben Blades.

Empire Falls 🦴🦴 ½ **2005** Passive Miles Roby (Harris), manager of the Empire Grill, has been unable to sever ties with either his economically depressed Maine mill town or his demanding family, including ne'er-do-well father Max (Newman), ex-wife Janice (Hunt), teen daughter Tick (Panabaker), and brother David (Quinn). Also in the picture is the town's manipulative matriarch (Woodward) and secrets involving Miles' dead mother (Wright Penn) and another man (Hoffman). HBO miniseries based on the Pulitzer Prize-winning book by Richard Russo is sometimes slow going but the cast is worth the effort. **240m/C; DVD.** Ed Harris; Paul Newman; Joanne Woodward; Helen Hunt; Aidan Quinn; Robin Wright; Philip Seymour Hoffman; Danielle Panabaker; Dennis Farina; William Fichtner; Estelle Parsons; Theresa Russell; Jeffrey DeMunn; Lou Taylor Pucci; Kate Burton; Josh(ua) Lucas; ***D:*** Fred Schepisi; ***W:*** Richard Russo; ***C:*** Ian Baker; ***M:*** Paul Grabowsky. **CABLE**

Empire of Assassins WOOF! **2011** A warlord destroys all the major martial arts schools but spares the lives of two young brothers, who are raised separately. Zhang has been honing his skills to get revenge and then discovers his opponent wll be his brother, Wang. The fighting action is familiar and the dubbing is atrocious. Originally filmed as part of a Chinese TV series. **93m/C; DVD.** *CH* Yuan Li; Tse Mo; Kar-yan Leung; ***D:*** Xiao Dou; ***W:*** Qi Liu; ***C:*** Yongwei Zhang. **TV**

The Empire of Passion 🦴🦴🦴 *In the Realm of Passion* **1976** A peasant woman and her low-life lover kill the woman's husband, but find the future they planned with each other is not to be. The husband's ghost returns to haunt them, and destroy the passionate bond which led to the murder. Oshima's follow-up to "In the Realm of the Senses." In Japanese with English subtitles. **110m/C; VHS, DVD.** *JP* Nagisa Oshima; Kazuko Yoshiyuki; Tatsuya Fuji; Takahiro Tamura; Takuzo Kawatani; ***D:*** Nagisa Oshima. Cannes '78: Director (Oshima).

Empire of the Ants 🦴 1/2 **1977 (PG)** A group of enormous, nuclear, unfriendly ants stalk a real estate dealer and prospective buyers of undeveloped oceanfront property. Story originated by master science-fiction storyteller H. G. Wells. **90m/C; VHS, DVD, Blu-Ray.** Joan Collins; Robert Lansing; John David Carson; Albert Salmi; Jacqueline Scott; Robert Pine; ***D:*** Bert I. Gordon; ***W:*** Bert I. Gordon; ***C:*** Reginald Morris.

Empire of the Sun 🦴🦴🦴 **1987 (PG)** Spielberg's mature, extraordinarily vivid return to real storytelling, from the best-selling J.G. Ballard novel. Yearns to be a great film, but occasional flat spots keep it slightly out of contention. Young, wealthy British Jim (Bale) lives in Shanghai, but is thrust into a life of poverty and discomfort when China is invaded by Japan at the onset of WWII and he's separated from his family and interred in a prison camp. A mysterious, breathtaking work, in which Spielberg's heightened juvenile romanticism has a real, heartbreaking context. Two other 1987 releases explore the WWII memories of young boys: "Au Revoir Les Enfants" and "Hope and Glory." **153m/C; VHS, DVD, Blu-Ray.** Christian Bale; John Malkovich; Miranda Richardson; Nigel Havers; Joe Pantoliano; Leslie Phillips; Rupert Frazer; Ben Stiller; Robert Stephens; Burt Kwouk; Masato Ibu; Emily Richard; David Neidorf; Ralph Seymour; Emma Piper; Peter Gale; Zhai Nai She; Guts Ishimatsu; J.G. Ballard; ***D:*** Steven Spielberg; ***W:*** Tom Stoppard; Menno Meyjes; ***C:*** Allen Daviau; ***M:*** John Williams. Natl. Bd. of Review '87: Director (Spielberg).

Empire of the Wolves 🦴 1/2 *L'Empire des Loups* **2005 (R)** Confusing police thriller. Anna Heymes (Jover) experiences terrifying dreams and memory loss. Later she learns that her face has been completely altered by plastic surgery. Meanwhile, young police detective Nerteaux (Quivrin) and his shady older partner Schiffer (Reno) are investigating the brutal murders of three women who were all illegal Turkish workers and they think the Turkish mafia has something to do with the crimes. Eventually, the link between Anna and the dead women will become apparent. French with subtitles. **128m/C; DVD.** *FR* Arly Jover; Jean Reno; Jocelyn Quivrin; Vernon Dobtcheff; Laura Morante; Philippe Bas; David Kammenos; ***D:*** Chris Nahon; ***W:*** Chris Nahon; Jean-Christophe Grange; ***C:*** Michel Abramowicz.

Empire Records 🦴🦴 **1995 (PG-13)** Well, the soundtrack's good and that's about all this frantic movie has going for it (besides a photogenic cast). Joe's (LaPaglia) the manager of an independent record store about to be taken over by a faceless conglomerate unless he and his young-and-crisis-prone staff can come up with the cash to buy the place within 24 hours. **91m/C; VHS, DVD, Blu-Ray.** Anthony LaPaglia; Rory Cochrane; Liv Tyler; Renée Zellweger; Johnny Whitworth; Robin Tunney; Ethan (Randall) Embry; Maxwell Caulfield; Debi Mazar; ***D:*** Allan Moyle; ***W:*** Carol Heikkinen; ***C:*** Walt Lloyd; ***M:*** Mitchell Leib.

The Empire Strikes Back 🦴🦴🦴🦴 *Star Wars: Episode 5—The Empire Strikes Back* **1980 (PG)** Second film in the epic "Star Wars" trilogy finds young Luke Skywalker and the Rebel Alliance plotting new strategies as they prepare to battle the evil Darth Vader and the forces of the Dark Side. Luke learns the ways of a Jedi knight from master Yoda, while Han and Leia find time for romance and a few adventures of their own. Introduces the charismatic Lando Calrissian and a mind-blowing secret from Vadar. Offers the same superb special effects and hearty plot as set by 1977's excellent "Star Wars." Followed by "Return of the Jedi" in 1983. **124m/C; VHS, DVD, Blu-Ray.** Mark Hamill; Carrie Fisher; Harrison Ford; Billy Dee Williams; Alec Guinness; David Prowse; Kenny Baker; Frank Oz; Anthony Daniels; Peter Mayhew; Clive Revill; Julian Glover; John Ratzenberger; Jeremy Bulloch; ***V:*** James Earl Jones; ***D:*** Irvin Kershner; ***W:*** Leigh Brackett; Lawrence Kasdan; ***C:*** Peter Suschitzky; ***M:*** John Williams. Oscars '80: Sound, Visual FX; Natl. Film Reg. '10.

Employee of the Month 🦴 1/2 **2006 (PG-13)** Amy (the ever-clueless Simpson) is the hot new employee at mega-store Super Club and rumor has it that she has a serious fetish for the employee of the month. This sparks a battle for the title between slacker Zack (weirdly appealing Cook) and 17-time consecutive winner Vince (Shepard). Dopey comedy is only rescued from complete mediocrity by some sharp jabs at consumerism. **103m/C; DVD, Blu-Ray.** Dane Cook; Jessica Simpson; Dax Shepard; Andy Dick; Tim Bagley; Danny Woodburn; Efren Ramirez; Harland Williams; Sean M. Whalen; Brian George; ***D:*** Greg Coolidge; ***W:*** Greg Coolidge; Dan Calame; Chris Conroy; ***C:*** Anthony B. Richmond; ***M:*** John Swihart.

Employees' Entrance 🦴🦴🦴 **1933** William stars as a ruthless department store manager in this story about commerce and compromise during the Depression. Young gives an excellent performance as the wife of one of his employees. Outrageous, and racy, this pre-Code film was expertly directed by veteran craftsman Del Ruth. Based on a play by David Boehm. **74m/B; DVD.** Warren William; Loretta Young; Wallace Ford; Alice White; Allen Jenkins; ***D:*** Roy Del Ruth; ***W:*** Robert Presnell, Sr.; ***C:*** Barney McGill; ***M:*** Bernhard Kaun. Natl. Film Reg. '19.

An Empress and the Warriors 🦴🦴 *Kong saan mei yan; Jiang shan mei ren; The Kingdom and the Beauty* **2008 (R)** Set during a fictional war between two kingdoms during China's warring states period, Muyong Xuehu (Yeng) is the leader of the Yan kingdoms armies. At least until the Emperor is murdered by his nephew in a blatant power grab. Muyong then takes over and appoints the Emperor's daughter Yan Fei'er (Chen) his second, only to nearly lose her to the usurper as well. She finds love with her rescuer but faces an important decision in order to protect her kingdom. Very pretty, but you've seen it all before. **99m/C; DVD, Blu-Ray.** *HK CH* Donnie Yen; Leon Lai; Xiaodong Guo; Zhenghai Kou; Weihua Liu; Shan Zhang; Chen Zhi Hui; Bo Zhou; Kelly Chen; ***D:*** Siu-Tung Ching; ***W:*** James Yuen; Tan Cheung; Tin Chun; ***C:*** Zhang Liu; Ze Xie; Xiaoding Zhao; ***M:*** Mark Lui. **VIDEO**

The Empty Acre WOOF! **2007** The idyllic world of Beth and Jacob Nance is shattered when their infant son is missing. Might it have something to do with the creepy acre of land on their property, where nothing grows and cattle die? And of course more people get abducted into the blackness that starts to rise from it. That's about as exciting and edge of your seat as it gets folks. Seriously suspense challenged. Not even eerie. **90m/C; DVD.** Jennifer Plas; John Wilson; Robert Paisley; Ari Pavel; Sally Bremenkamp; Ric Averill; ***D:*** Patrick Rea; ***W:*** Patrick Rea; ***C:*** Jeremy Osbern; ***M:*** Don James.

The Empty Mirror 🦴🦴 **1999 (PG-13)** Boring fictionalized account of Hitler's (Rodway) final hours, hidden away in his bunker, as he realizes his Third Reich dreams have come to nothing. He does a lot of ranting but what is more interesting are the clips from Leni Riefenstahl's "Triumph of the Will" that are screened behind him. **108m/C; VHS, DVD.** Norman Rodway; Joel Grey; Camilla Soeberg; Glenn Shadix; Peter Michael Goetz; Doug McKeon; ***D:*** Barry J. Hershey; ***W:*** Barry J. Hershey; R. Buckingham; ***C:*** Frederick Elmes; ***M:*** John (Gianni) Frizzell.

Empty Saddles 🦴 1/2 **1936** One of the empty comeback attempts for exotic silent star Brooks was this routine oater from Jones. Buck Devlin successful turns a deserted property into a dude ranch with the help of Swap Boone and his daughter Boots. Devlin tries to liven things up by restaging an old feud between the sheepmen and cattle ranchers but someone takes it seriously. **67m/B; DVD.** Buck Jones; Louise Brooks; Harvey Clark; Charles Middleton; Frank Campeau; Gertrude Astor; Claire Rochelle; Lloyd Ingraham; ***D:*** Lesley Selander; ***W:*** Frances Guihan; ***C:*** Herbert Kirkpatrick; Allen Q. Thompson.

Enchanted 🦴🦴 **2007 (PG)** Princess Giselle (Adams) idly sings in wait for "true love's kiss" to rescue her. Vain Prince Edward (Marsden) hears her love song and falls fast, but meddling Queen Narissa (Sarandon) thinks they'll steal her queendom away so she banishes the princess to New York by tossing her down a wishing well (the film turns from animated to real once they hit the city). Divorce lawyer Robert (Dempsey) and his daughter rescue Giselle from the streets of Manhattan, where she promptly makes herself a new dress from his curtains and calls on her animal friends to clean the apartment. Edward has followed and is combing the streets gallantly searching for Giselle; meanwhile, Robert is falling for the princess. It would be a generally happy and fun little film if it ended about there, but no'the queen has more mayhem to unleash. Some painfully slow and cliche moments, but Adams, Marsden, and Dempsey keep up the charm. **107m/C; Blu-Ray, On Demand.** Amy Adams; Patrick Dempsey; James Marsden; Timothy Spall; Idina Menzel; Susan Sarandon; Rachel Covey; ***Nar:*** Julie Andrews; ***D:*** Kevin Lima; ***W:*** Bill Kelly; ***C:*** Don Burgess; ***M:*** Alan Menken.

Enchanted April 🦴🦴 1/2 **1992 (PG)** Lotte (Lawrence) and Rose (Richardson), tired of their overbearing husbands, rent a villa in Portofino, Italy, for a month with two other very different women—Lady Caroline (Walker), a beautiful but bored socialite, and crusty old Mrs. Fisher (Plowright), who has an impeccable literary pedigree. The effects of the charming villa, with plenty of wisteria and sunshine, do wonders for the women. A charming and romantic period piece. Based on the 1922 novel by Elizabeth von Arnim. **93m/C; VHS, DVD.** *GB* Miranda Richardson; Joan Plowright; Josie Lawrence; Polly Walker; Alfred Molina; Jim Broadbent; Michael Kitchen; Adriana Fachetti; ***D:*** Mike Newell; ***W:*** Peter Barnes; ***C:*** Rex Maidment; ***M:*** Richard Rodney Bennett. Golden Globes '93: Actress--Mus./Comedy (Richardson), Support. Actress (Plowright).

The Enchanted Cottage 🦴🦴 1/2 **1945** Represents Hollywood's "love conquers all" fantasy hokum, as a disfigured war vet and a homely girl retreat from the horrors of the world into a secluded cottage, where they both regain youth and beauty. A four-tissue heart-tugger. Adopted from the Arthur Pinero play. **91m/B; VHS, DVD.** Dorothy McGuire; Robert Young; Herbert Marshall; Mildred Natwick; Spring Byington; Hillary Brooke; Richard Gaines; Robert Clarke; ***D:*** John Cromwell.

The Enchanted Forest 🦴🦴 1/2 **1945** An elderly man teaches a boy about life and the beauty of nature when the boy gets lost in a forest. **78m/C; VHS, DVD.** *AR* Harry Davenport; Edmund Lowe; Brenda Joyce; ***D:*** Lew Landers.

Enchanted Island 🦴 1/2 **1958** Sailor stops on an island to find provisions and ends up falling in love with a cannibal princess. Thinly based upon Herman Melville's "Typee." **94m/C; VHS, DVD.** Jane Powell; Dana Andrews; Arthur Shields; ***D:*** Allan Dwan.

Enchantment 🦴🦴 **1948** Roland Dane falls in love with his adopted sister Lark but his sister Selina's jealousy and his own military career, which takes him to India, thwart their love. Many years later, Roland is living alone in the London family home when his granddaughter Grizel asks for his romantic advice before her own beau goes off to war. **102m/B; DVD.** David Niven; Teresa Wright; Jayne Meadows; Evelyn Keyes; Farley Granger; Philip Friend; Shepperd Strudwick; Leo G. Carroll; ***D:*** Irving Reis; ***W:*** John Patrick; ***C:*** Gregg Toland; ***M:*** Hugo Friedhofer.

Encino Man 🦴🦴 *California Man* **1992 (PG)** Two, like, totally uncool Valley dudes dig up a 10,000-year-old caveman in the backyard. After giving him a makeover and teaching him the necessities like the four basic food groups (Milk Duds in the dairy group, Sweet Tarts in the fruit group), they use the gnarly caveman as their ticket to popularity and dates to the prom. Juvenile humor appealing to teens; strictly brain candy. **88m/C; VHS, DVD.** Pauly Shore; Brendan Fraser; Sean Astin; Megan Ward; Robin Tunney; Ric(k) Ducommun; Mariette Hartley; Richard Masur; Michael DeLuise; Rose McGowan; Jack Noseworthy; Erik Avari; ***D:*** Les Mayfield; ***W:*** Shawn Schepps; ***C:*** Robert Brinkmann. Golden Raspberries '92: Worst New Star (Shore).

Encore 🦴🦴🦴 **1952** The third W. Somerset Maugham omnibus (following "Quartet" and "Trio") which includes: "Winter Cruise," "The Ant and the Grasshopper," and "Gigolo and Gigolette." **85m/B; VHS, Streaming.** *GB* Nigel Patrick; Kay Walsh; Roland Culver; John Laurie; Glynis Johns; Ronald Squire; Noel Purcell; Peter Graves; ***D:*** Pat Jackson; Anthony Pelissier; Harold French; ***W:*** Eric Ambler.

Encounter at Raven's Gate 🦴 1/2 **1988 (R)** Punk rockers and extraterrestrials meet amid hard rock and gallons of gore. **85m/C; VHS, Streaming.** Eddie Cleary; Steven Vidler; ***D:*** Rolf de Heer.

An Encounter with the Messiah 🦴🦴 **2015** A drama based on three stories from the New Testament in the Bible, set in modern day. In the story of the woman with the issue of blood, Maria (Green) has suffered from an incurable blood disorder for 12 years and lost everything she had. She has kept her faith and it leads to her life being changed forever. The stories of Barabbas (Dorsey) and blind Bartimeaus (Keopfinger) are told as well, as the two men with difficult lives find their lives transformed because of their faith. **124m/C; DVD, Streaming, Download.** Yavette Green; Kibwe Dorsey; David Koepfinger; Aaron Quick Nelson; Jorge Diaz; ***D:*** Deon Gibson; ***W:*** Deon Gibson. **VIDEO**

Encounter with the Unknown 🦴🦴 1/2 **1975** Relates three fully documented supernatural events including a death prophesy and a ghost. **90m/C; VHS, DVD, Blu-Ray.** Rosie Holotik; Gene Ross; ***Nar:*** Rod Serling; ***D:*** Harry Z. Thomason.

Encounters at the End of the World 🦴🦴🦴🦴 **2007** McMurdo Station, headquarters of the National Science Foundation and the base for U.S. research at the South Pole, sits at the bottom of the Earth and is populated by about 1,000 scientists, loners, dreamers, and outcasts for a brief five-month period each year—the only time the Pole is remotely hospitable to research. Director Herzog doesn't lead, but lets McMurdo's unique residents tell their own stories about the stark and dramatic landscape that draws them to leave the rest of the world behind. Herzog gives us stunning images of the otherworldly, subzero terrain, including underwater cathedrals and glacial mountains. Although scientific evidence being gathered at McMurdo points to global warming, Herzog isn't filming to smack you over the head with it; rather, he's exploring the explorers. Absolutely unmissable. **99m/C; Blu-Ray, On Demand.** ***Nar:*** Werner Herzog; ***D:*** Werner Herzog; ***W:*** Werner Herzog; ***C:*** Peter Zeitlinger; ***M:*** Henry Kaiser; David Lindley.

Encrypt 🦴 **2003** By 2068, the Earth's atmosphere is ravaged and survivors fight for every scrap. Mercenary Garth (Show) is promised medicine and food if he and his men will recover what they are told is priceless art from an abandoned estate. Of course they've been lied to and they discover a very dangerous automated defense system is set to kill any intruder. But a hologram named Diana (Wu) may be the key to everyone's survival. A Sci-Fi Channel original. **90m/C; DVD.** Grant Show; Vivian Wu; Steve Bacic; Hannah Lochner; Matthew G. Taylor; ***D:*** Oscar Luis Costo; ***W:*** Richard Taylor; Robinson Young; ***C:*** Michael Galbraith; ***M:*** Misha Segal. **CABLE**

The End **1978 (R)** Reynolds plays a young man who discovers he is terminally ill. He decides not to prolong his suffering and attempts various tried-and-true methods for committing suicide, receiving riotous but incompetent help from the crazed DeLuise. **100m/C; VHS, DVD, Blu-Ray.** Burt Reynolds; Sally Field; Dom DeLuise; Carl Reiner; Joanne Woodward; Robby Benson; Kristy McNichol; Norman Fell; Pat O'Brien; Myrna Loy; David Steinberg; ***D:*** Burt Reynolds; ***W:*** Jerry Belson; ***C:*** Bobby Byrne; ***M:*** Paul Williams.

End Game **1/2 2006 (R)** Secret Service agent Alex Thomas (Gooding Jr.) fails to prevent a presidential assassination. He's pulled out of his alcoholic funk by reporter Kate Crawford (Harmon) and the more the two dig, the more dangerous their situation becomes. Well-done conspiracy thriller. **93m/C; DVD.** Cuba Gooding, Jr.; Angie Harmon; Peter Greene; James Woods; Anne Archer; Burt Reynolds; David Selby; Jack Scalia; ***D:*** Andy Cheng; ***W:*** Andy Cheng; J.C. Pollock; ***C:*** Chuck Cohen; ***M:*** Kenneth Burgomaster. **VIDEO**

End Game **WOOF! 2009 (R)** Pro wrestler Angle tries that acting thing (unsuccessfully) in a crappy sex and serial killer pic. Psycho killer Brad Mayfield targets stripper Carol who develops a relationship with one of the detectives assigned to the case. **93m/C; DVD.** Kurt Angle; Eric Wright; Jenna Morasca; Sam Nicotero; Clayton Hill; ***D:*** Bruce Koehler; ***W:*** James "Jim" McCartney; ***C:*** Bruce Koehler; ***M:*** Jon Denney. **VIDEO**

End of a Gun **1/2 2016 (R)** A Steven Seagal action crime thriller in which he finds his life being threatened after he helps someone else. Former DEA agent Decker (Seagal) now works as a security guard in a mall. When Decker saves a beautiful woman in danger, he goes on the run with her and two million dollars in drug money. As a result, Decker finds himself targeted by a crazy, major drug dealer and his enforcer, and must do all he can to survive. **87m/C; DVD, Blu-Ray, Streaming, Download.** Steven Seagal; Florin Piersic, Jr.; Jade Ewen; Jacob Grodnik; Jonathan Rosenthal; ***D:*** Keoni Waxman; ***W:*** Keoni Waxman; Chuck Hustmyre; ***C:*** Nathan Wilson; ***M:*** Michael Richard Plowman.

End of Days **1999 (R)** Alcoholic ex-cop Jericho Cane (Schwarzenegger) becomes a reluctant savior, who must battle a literal Satan (Byrne) who has the opportunity to rule both Heaven and Hell if he can make young Christine (Tunney) his bride before the millenial midnight. There's lots of action, Arnold looks great (post heart surgery), and Byrne is a very sexy devil but there's also an excessive amount of gore and silly mumbo-jumbo to suffer through. **123m/C; VHS, DVD, Blu-Ray, HD-DVD.** Arnold Schwarzenegger; Gabriel Byrne; Robin Tunney; Kevin Pollak; CCH Pounder; Rod Steiger; Derrick O'Connor; Miriam Margolyes; Udo Kier; ***D:*** Peter Hyams; ***W:*** Andrew Marlowe; ***C:*** Peter Hyams; ***M:*** John Debney.

The End of Innocence **1990 (R)** In her attempts to please everyone in her life, a woman experiences a nervous breakdown. Released two years after Schaeffer's murder. **102m/C; VHS, DVD.** Dyan Cannon; John Heard; George Coe; Lola Mason; Rebecca Schaeffer; Stephen Meadows; Billie Bird; Michael Madsen; Madge Sinclair; Renee Taylor; Viveka Davis; ***D:*** Dyan Cannon; ***W:*** Dyan Cannon; ***M:*** Michael Convertino.

The End of St. Petersburg **1/2 1927** A Russian peasant becomes a scab during a workers' strike in 1914. He is then forced to enlist in the army prior to the 1917 October Revolution. Fascinating, although propagandistic film commissioned by the then-new Soviet government. Silent. **75m/B; Silent; VHS, DVD, Blu-Ray.** Ivan Chuvelov; ***D:*** Vsevolod Pudovkin.

End of the Affair **1955** In WWII London, Sarah (Kerr), the wife of a British civil servant (Cushing), falls in love with her neighbor Maurice (Johnson). The two make plans for their future together, but suddenly and mysteriously, Sarah brings the affair to an end. **105m/B; DVD.** *GB* Deborah Kerr; Van Johnson; John Mills; Peter Cushing; ***D:*** Edward Dmytryk; ***W:*** Lenore Coffee; ***C:*** Wilkie Cooper; ***M:*** Benjamin Frankel.

The End of the Affair **1999 (R)** During the Blitz of WWII, married Londoner Sarah Miles (Moore) suddenly breaks off her affair with writer Maurice Bendrix (Fiennes). An unexpected meeting with her husband, Henry (Rea), leads Bendrix to believe Sarah is having a new affair and he hires a detective (Hart) to follow her. Instead, Bendrix discovers her reasons for breaking off with him and her spiritual reawakening. Compellingly adult drama about love, faith, and moral dilemmas that is based on the 1955 novel by Graham Greene. **101m/C; VHS, DVD.** *GB* Ralph Fiennes; Julianne Moore; Stephen Rea; Ian Hart; Sam Bould; Jason Isaacs; ***D:*** Neil Jordan; ***W:*** Neil Jordan; ***C:*** Roger Pratt; ***M:*** Michael Nyman. British Acad. '99: Adapt. Screenplay.

End of the Century: The Story of the Ramones **2003** Documents the underground music scene in New York (and abroad) during the late 1970s and chronicles the music, addictions, lineup changes, and pressures of life on the road, as well as just about every petty squabble the Ramones ever had. **110m/C; DVD.** ***D:*** Michael Gramaglia; Jim Fields; ***C:*** Jim Fields.

End of the Line **1/2 1988 (PG)** Two old-time railroad workers steal a locomotive for a cross-country jaunt to protest the closing of the local railroad company. Produced by Steenburgen. **103m/C; VHS, DVD.** Wilford Brimley; Levon Helm; Mary Steenburgen; Kevin Bacon; Holly Hunter; Barbara Barrie; Bob Balaban; Howard Morris; Bruce McGill; Clint Howard; Trey Wilson; Rita Jenrette; ***D:*** Jay Russell; ***W:*** John Wohlbruck; ***M:*** Andy Summers.

End of the Road **1/2 1970 (X)** Keach is a troubled college professor whose bizarre treatment by his psychologist (Jones) produces tragic results. He eventually enters into an affair with the wife of a co-worker. Fascinating, if uneven script adapted from John Barth's story. Rated X upon release for adult story and nudity. **110m/C; VHS, DVD.** Stacy Keach; James Earl Jones; James Coco; Harris Yulin; Dorothy Tristan; ***D:*** Aram Avakian; ***W:*** Terry Southern; ***C:*** Gordon Willis.

End of the Spear **2006 (PG-13)** Based on the true events of a 1956 missionary trip during which five Americans were speared to death by the very Ecuadorian tribesmen they were seeking to convert. Unfortunately, studio production values coat the jungle and its visitors with a big bottle of syrup. To its credit, it at least tries to develop the tribesmen into something more than savages. Anyone looking for something more than an overt martyrs' tale will be disappointed. **112m/C; DVD.** Chad Allen; Chase Ellison; Louie Leonardo; Sara Kathryn Bakker; Cara Stoner; Jack Guzman; Christina Souza; ***D:*** Jim Hanon; ***W:*** Bart Gavigan; Jim Hanon; Bill Ewing; ***C:*** Robert A. Driskell, Jr.; ***M:*** Ronald Owen.

The End of the Tour **2015 (R)** Director Ponsoldt examines the intersection of celebrity and ability in this story of five days spent between Rolling Stone journalist David Lipsky (Eisenberg) and the hottest writer of the '90s, David Foster Wallace (Segel). After Wallace's suicide over a decade later, Lipsky remembers the interview time he spent with the author. The film is less a story of this specific writer than intellectualism in general, and how ashamed people can be just to embrace their intelligence. Segel is phenomenal, capturing the heart of a man too smart not to be known but too shy to be famous. **106m/C; DVD, Blu-Ray, Streaming.** Anna Chlumsky; Jesse Eisenberg; Jason Segel; Mamie Gummer; Joan Cusack; ***D:*** James Ponsoldt; ***W:*** Donald Margulies; ***C:*** Jakob Ihre; ***M:*** Danny Elfman.

End of the World **WOOF! 1976 (PG)** A coffee machine explodes, sending a man through a window and into a neon sign, where he is electrocuted. A priest witnesses this and retreats to a convent where he meets his alien double and heads for more trouble with outer space invaders. Interesting premise. **88m/C; VHS, DVD.** Christopher Lee; Sue Lyon; Lew Ayres; MacDonald Carey; Dean Jagger; Kirk Scott; ***D:*** John Hayes; ***M:*** Andrew Belling.

End of the World **2013 (PG-13)** The title tells all in this goofy Syfy Channel homage to disaster/apocalyptic films, which video store owners/buddies reference when some kind of space debris threatens good old Earth again. Naturally, the trio, a crazy sci-fi writer they spring from a mental institution, and a nuclear missile are needed to save the planet. **85m/C; DVD.** Greg Grunberg; Neil Grayston; Amitai Marmorstein; Caroline Cave; Brad Dourif; Mark Hildreth; ***D:*** Steven R. Monroe; ***W:*** Jason Bourque; David Ray; ***C:*** Anthony C. Metchie. **CABLE**

The End of Violence **1997 (R)** Slick, manipulative action-movie producer Mike Max (Pullman) evolves from his Hollywood roots to tranquility as a gardener after his own life is touched by the violence so pervasive in his pictures. There's a sinister government agent (Benzali) and a reclusive surveillance expert (Byrne) and Max gets kidnapped, only the kidnappers mysteriously wind up dead, and then he disappears. And, no, the plot doesn't really make much sense and all the characters are paranoid anyway. But it does give you something to try to figure out. Director Wenders drastically re-edited his movie after its lukewarm work-in-progress appearance at the 1997 Cannes Film Festival. **122m/C; VHS, DVD, Blu-Ray.** *FR* Bill Pullman; Gabriel Byrne; Andie MacDowell; Daniel Benzali; Traci Lind; Rosalind Chao; Loren Dean; Nicole Ari Parker; Enrique Castillo; K. Todd Freeman; John Diehl; Pruitt Taylor Vince; Peter Horton; Udo Kier; Marshall Bell; Frederic Forrest; Henry Silva; Samuel Fuller; ***D:*** Wim Wenders; ***W:*** Nicholas Klein; ***C:*** Pascal Rabaud; ***M:*** Ry Cooder.

End of Watch **2012 (R)** Just as the cop buddy movie genre seemed tired, writer/director Ayer delivers with this striking and even harrowing day in the life of a pair of young Los Angeles police officers stuck in a nightmare. Using handheld cameras and the plentiful talents and appeal of stars Gyllenhaal and Pena, Ayer tells the story of two cops who stumble upon a secret that could get them killed. The story doesn't necessarily have much new to say about being a cop in South Central but it has an effective you-are-there feeling. **109m/C; DVD, Blu-Ray.** Jake Gyllenhaal; Michael Peña; Anna Kendrick; America Ferrera; Frank Grillo; Cody Horn; ***D:*** David Ayer; ***W:*** David Ayer; ***C:*** Roman Vasyanov; ***M:*** David Sardy.

Endangered Species **1/2 1982 (R)** Offbeat thriller with sci-fi leanings about a retired New York cop on vacation in America's West who is drawn into a female sheriff's investigation of a mysterious series of cattle killings. Could it be UFOs? Based on a true story. **97m/C; VHS, DVD.** Robert Urich; JoBeth Williams; Paul Dooley; Hoyt Axton; Peter Coyote; Harry Carey, Jr.; Dan Hedaya; John Considine; ***D:*** Alan Rudolph; ***W:*** Alan Rudolph; John Binder.

Endangered Species **2002 (R)** A spree of bizarre health spa murders and missing victims stumps police detective Sullivan (Roberts). Of course the culprit is an up-to-no-good alien who just wants human skin to make an out-of-this-world fashion statement. Luckily there's a rival alien who arrives to aide the confused copper. **90m/C; VHS, DVD.** Eric Roberts; Arnold Vosloo; John Rhys-Davies; Tony LoBianco; Al Sapienza; James W. Quinn; Sarah Kaite Coughlan; Miranda Coughlan; Sophie Bielders; Alisa Hensley; Monika Verbutaite; Evgenija Zakarevieiute; ***D:*** Kevin S. Tenney; ***W:*** Kevin S. Tenney; ***C:*** Chris Manley; ***M:*** Harry Manfredini. **VIDEO**

Ender's Game **2013 (PG-13)** The first book in Orson Scott Card's five-novel series has been finally adapted for the big screen but the result is yet another modern sci-fi film that focuses on special effects rather than its characters. Set in the future, the title refers to Ender Wiggin (Butterfield), the latest recruit in a war with an alien race and the human race's only hope for survival. Like a sci-fi Harry Potter, Wiggin goes from a wide-eyed recruit to the chosen one under the guidance of a gruff commander played by Ford. The cast is solid, but in the end the book's army of fans deserved a better product. **114m/C; DVD, Blu-Ray.** Asa Butterfield; Harrison Ford; Hailee Steinfeld; Abigail Breslin; Ben Kingsley; Viola Davis; ***D:*** Gavin Hood; ***W:*** Gavin Hood; ***C:*** Donald McAlpine; ***M:*** Steve Jablonsky.

Endgame **2001** Tom (Newman) is a troubled rent boy beholden to sadistic London gangster George Norris (McGann), who uses him in blackmail schemes. Norris is also involved in drug distribution with crooked cop Dunstan (Benfield). When Tom accidentally kills Norris during a fight, he goes to married neighbors Max (Johnson) and Nikki (Barry) for help in escaping Dunston's wrath. Only Nikki has a personal fascination for Tom that comes out when she agrees to hide him. Moody and sometimes brutal. **113m/C; VHS, DVD.** *GB* Daniel Newman; Mark McGann; John Benfield; Toni Barry; Corey Johnson; ***D:*** Gary Wicks; ***W:*** Gary Wicks; ***C:*** David Bennett; ***M:*** Adrian Thomas.

Endgame **1/2 2009** Sharply-told docudrama about the secret talks that bring about the end of apartheid in South Africa. In 1985, the segregationist government of President P.W. Botha is about to collapse and Nelson Mandela is in the final days of his prison term. But money is really the ruler as Michael Young (Miller), the chairman of a British mining company, initiates dialogues between white Afrikaner leaders and the African National Congress. Young arranges a series of discussions at an English estate between ANC leader Thabo Mbeki (Ejifor) and Afrikaner professor Willie Esterhuyse (Hurt). Meanwhile, Barnard himself is privately negotiating with Mandela (Peters). Based on the book "The Fall of Apartheid" by Robert Harvey. **109m/C; DVD.** *GB* William Hurt; Chiwetel Ejiofor; Jonny Lee Miller; Mark Strong; Clarke Peters; John Kani; Derek Jacobi; Timothy West; Robert John Burke; Keith David; ***D:*** Billy Kent; ***W:*** Adam Wierzbianski; ***C:*** Ramsay Nickell; ***M:*** Bruno Coon.

Endings, Beginnings **2020** After breaking up with her boyfriend and quitting her professional job, 30-something Daphne (Woodley) is lost. She lives in her sister's pool house and takes stock of her life while working shifts at a thrift shop. Her plan to avoid alcohol and men falls away when she meets two men at a party. They happen to be best friends and fulfill different needs for her. Frank (Stan) is her lover, while Jack (Dornan) challenges her intellectually. Daphne has feelings for both but lies to them about what is going on. The excellent cast can't keep this uneven romantic drama from getting lost somewhere in the middle. **110m/C; DVD.** Shailene Woodley; Jamie Dornan; Sebastian Stan; Matthew Gray Gubler; Lindsay Sloane; ***D:*** Drake Doremus; ***W:*** Drake Doremus; Jardine Libaire; ***C:*** Marianne Bakke; ***M:*** Philip Ekstrom.

The Endless **1/2 2017** Justin (Benson) rescued his younger brother Aaron (Moorhead) from the cult they were raised in and they now live normal lives, Aaron sees a message from a cult member which makes him miss his former home. Though Justin warns him against going even for closure, he accompanies him there. Unexplained images and events occur that seem to bend reality, truth, and time. Cult members such as de facto leader Tim (Temple) also show the cult's powerful grip. Though low budget, it's a well-told, complex story, strong performances, and intelligent direction. **111m/C; DVD, Blu-Ray.** Justin Benson; Aaron Moorhead; Callie Hernandez; Emily Montague; Lew Temple; ***D:*** Justin Benson; ***W:*** Justin Benson; ***C:*** Aaron Moorhead; Jimmy Lavalley; ***M:*** Jimmy LaValle.

Endless Love **1981 (R)** Although only 17, David and Jade are in love. Her parents think they are too serious and demand that the two spend time apart. David attempts to win her parents' affection and approval, goes mad in the process, and commits a foolish act (he burns the house down) that threatens their love forever. Based on the novel by Scott Spencer. Of interest only to those with time on their hands or smitten by a love so bad that this movie will seem grand in comparison. Features Cruise's first film appearance. **115m/C; VHS, Blu-Ray, Streaming.** Brooke Shields; Martin Hewitt; Don Murray; Shirley Knight; Beatrice Straight; Richard Kiley; Tom Cruise; James

Spader; Robert Moore; Jami Gertz; *D:* Franco Zeffirelli; *W:* Judith Rascoe; *C:* David Watkin.

Endless Love 𝄞 1/2 **2014 (PG-13)** Tepid rehashing of the gonzo 1981 Zefferelli teen love story, about the good girl falling for the bad boy. When daddy's angel, Jade (Wilde), dives head-first into a summer romance with David (Pettyfer), a heartthrob with a record, her overprotective father, Hugh (Greenwood) is willing to go to mad lengths to put an end to the relationship. A thin melodrama that doesn't realize the boyfriend vs. girlfriend's dad story isn't nearly as good as the girlfriend's dad vs. boyfriend's dad battle, with Robert Patrick turning in the best performance as David's strong, but troubled, old man. **104m/C; DVD, Blu-Ray.** Alex Pettyfer; Gabriella Wilde; Bruce Greenwood; Joely Richardson; Robert Patrick; Rhys Wakefield; *D:* Shana Feste; *W:* Shana Feste; Joshua Safran; *C:* Andrew Dunn; *M:* Christophe Beck.

Endless Night 𝄞𝄞 *Agatha Christie's Endless Night* **1971** An adaptation of an Agatha Christie tale. Focuses on a young chauffeur who wants to build a dream house, and his chance meeting with an American heiress. **95m/C; VHS, DVD, Blu-Ray.** *GB* Hayley Mills; Hywel Bennett; Britt Ekland; George Sanders; Per Oscarsson; Peter Bowles; *D:* Sidney Gilliat; *W:* Sidney Gilliat; *C:* Harry Waxman; *M:* Bernard Herrmann.

The Endless Summer 𝄞𝄞𝄞 **1966** Classic surfing documentary about the freedom and sense of adventure that surfing symbolizes. Director Brown follows two young surfers around the world in search of the perfect wave. (They finally find it at a then-unknown break off Cape Saint Francis in South America.) Besides the excellent surfing photography, Big Kahuna Brown provides the amusing tongue-in-cheek narrative. Considered by many to be the best surf movie ever. **90m/C; VHS, DVD, UMD.** Mike Hynson; Robert August; *Nar:* Bruce Brown; *D:* Bruce Brown; *W:* Bruce Brown. Natl. Film Reg. '02.

The Endless Summer 2 𝄞𝄞𝄞 *Bruce Brown's The Endless Summer 2; Bruce Brown's The Endless Summer Revisited* **1994 (PG)** You don't have to personally hang ten to get stoked about this long-awaited sequel that once again follows two surfer dudes in their quest for the perfect wave. This time out pro surfers O'Connell and Weaver circle the globe seeking adventure and the world's best waves. Traces the evolution of surfing from the lazy, golden days of the '60s to the worldwide phenomenon it is today, complete with its own pro tour circuit. Breathtaking scenery and spectacular surfing sequences highlight this look at a unique subculture. Thirty years later and it's still a great ride, though the travelogue wears thin and the sub-culture's now fairly well exploited. **107m/C; VHS, DVD.** Robert "Wingnut" Weaver; Pat O'Connell; Robert August; *Nar:* Bruce Brown; *D:* Bruce Brown; *W:* Bruce Brown; Dana Brown.

Endure 𝄞 1/2 **2010 (R)** Florida detective Emory Lloyd (Nelson) is called in when a photo of a young woman tied to a tree in a swamp is found at the scene of a car accident. The driver is dead and Emory and his cocky partner Zeth Arnold (Sawa) try to piece together the clues to find the woman. But they aren't the only ones looking. **90m/C; DVD.** Judd Nelson; Devon Sawa; Tom Arnold; Joey Lauren Adams; Clare Kramer; Brett Rice; Stuart Stone; *D:* Joe O'Brien; *W:* Joe O'Brien; *C:* Stephen Campbell; *M:* Adam Davidson. **VIDEO**

Enduring Love 𝄞𝄞 **2004 (R)** Brit psychodrama, based on Ian McEwan's 1997 novel, is triggered by a bizarre accident. A runaway hot air balloon disturbs the country picnic of science prof Joe Rose (Craig) and his girlfriend Claire (Morton). Several men, including Joe, try to rescue the boy trapped inside the balloon's basket and one would-be rescuer is killed. Joe doesn't know how to react and his conflict is echoed by loner/misfit Jed (Ifans), also on the scene. In fact, Jed is convinced that he and Joe now share a profound connection. His increasingly chilling persistence leads to the breakdown of Joe and Claire's relationship and Joe's own fury. Film heads down a predictable path and the characters become cliches but Craig and Ifans manage to overcome those limitations. **98m/C; DVD.** Daniel Craig; Rhys Ifans; Samantha Morton; Joe Dunton; Susan Lynch; Helen McCrory; Andrew Lincoln; Corin Redgrave; *D:* Roger Michell; *W:* Joe Penhall; *C:* Haris Zambarloukos; *M:* Jeremy Sams.

Enemies, a Love Story 𝄞𝄞𝄞 1/2 **1989 (R)** A wonderfully resonant, subtle tragedy based on the novel by Isaac Bashevis Singer. A post-Holocaust Jew, living in Coney Island, can't choose between three women—his current wife (who hid him during the war), his tempestuous lover, and his reappearing pre-war wife he presumed dead. A hilarious, confident tale told with grace and patience. **119m/C; VHS, DVD, Blu-Ray.** Ron Silver; Lena Olin; Anjelica Huston; Margaret Sophie Stein; Paul Mazursky; Alan King; Judith Malina; Rita Karin; Phil Leeds; Elya Baskin; Marie-Adele Lemieux; *D:* Paul Mazursky; *W:* Paul Mazursky; *C:* Fred Murphy; *M:* Maurice Jarre. N.Y. Film Critics '89: Director (Mazursky), Support. Actress (Olin); Natl. Soc. Film Critics '89: Support. Actress (Huston).

Enemies Among Us 𝄞 **2010 (R)** The first enemy is the dumb script, the second is the cast's generally over-the-top performances, and the third is the deceptive prominence of Billy Zane in the credits since he's maybe onscreen for a total of five minutes. Anyway, the plot revolves around corrupt Louisiana Governor Chip Majors (DuMont) who strangles a hooker who's really an assassin (don't ask) and whose crime is witnessed by one corrupt cop (Roberts) and one conflicted cop (Hood) and whether they'll participate in a cover-up. Givens plays a violent CIA agent by the way. **89m/C; DVD.** Griffin Hood; Eric Roberts; James DuMont; Robin Givens; Steven Bauer; Billy Zane; *D:* Dan Garcia; *W:* Dan Garcia; *C:* Mark Rutledge; *M:* Travis Long. **VIDEO**

Enemies Closer 𝄞 1/2 **2014 (R)** Tolerable actioner with Van Damme in a rare villainous role. A small plane crash on the U.S./Canada border leads troubled U.S. park ranger Henry (Scott) to a heroin shipment that drug dealer Xander wants back by any means necessary. **84m/C; DVD, Blu-Ray.** Jean-Claude Van Damme; Tom Everett Scott; Orlando Jones; Linzey Cocker; *D:* Peter Hyams; *W:* James Bromberg; Eric Bromberg; *C:* Peter Hyams; *M:* Tony Morales. **VIDEO**

Enemies of Laughter 𝄞𝄞 1/2 **2000** Aspiring playwright and TV sitcom writer Paul is dejected as his first big stage venture totally tanks—and he can't seem to find true love either despite a steady string of prospects. But as fate would have it his buddy makes a successful documentary about Paul's romantic woes that attracts the attention of a gorgeous producer who rattles him with her desire to revive his failed play. **91m/C; VHS, DVD.** David Paymer; Judge Reinhold; Rosalind Chao; Bea Arthur; Peter Falk; Vanessa Angel; Kathy Griffin; Marilu Henner; Kristina Fulton; Daphne Zuniga; Shera Danese; Leila Kenzle; Glen Merzer; *D:* Joey Travolta; *W:* Glen Merzer; *C:* Kristian Bernier; *M:* Barry Coffing. **VIDEO**

The Enemy 𝄞𝄞 1/2 **2001 (R)** Mike Ashton (Perry) lives in Canada with his retired chemist father (Buchholz) who has been keeping secrets from his son. But they don't stay hidden when the bad guys come looking for dad and his work on bio-weapons making. A kidnapping attempt and a murder bring in the authorities, including Penny (d'Abo) who has a past with Mike and isn't adverse to fanning some flames. Story gets too convoluted for its own good but the pace is fast. **98m/C; VHS, DVD.** Luke Perry; Olivia D'Abo; Roger Moore; Horst Buchholz; Tom Conti; Hendrick Haese; *D:* Tom Kinninmont; Charlie Watson; *W:* John Penney; *C:* Mike Garfath; *M:* Gast Waltzing.

Enemy 𝄞𝄞 **2013 (R)** In this moody, confounding thriller, mild-mannered university prof Adam Bell (Gyllenhaal) notices a minor actor in a film with an uncanny resemblance to him. He tracks down Anthony St. Claire (also Gyllenhaal) and finds his doppelganger is very much the opposite in personality, having all the charisma that bland Adam lacks. After Anthony insinuates himself into Adam's life, chaos ensues. Maybe it's real or maybe it's some psycho-sexual fantasy but director Villeneuve certainly isn't telling. Loose adaptation of "The Double" by Jose Saramago. **90m/C; DVD, Blu-Ray.** *CA SP* Jake Gyllenhaal; Melanie Laurent; Sarah Gadon; Isabella Rossellini; *D:* Denis Villeneuve; *W:* Javier Gullon; *C:* Nicolas Bolduc; *M:* Danny Bensi; Saunder Jurriaans.

Enemy at the Gates 𝄞𝄞 **2000 (R)** World War II saga set during the siege of Stalingrad in 1942 as Russian sniper Zaitsev (Law) tracks his equal in German sniper Konig (Harris). Law is also involved in a romantic triangle with a female Russian soldier (Weisz) and smarmy commissar Danilov (Fiennes). Only the sniper story is based on actual events and real people, from William Craig's historical account. Otherwise, the story as put on screen leaves out a lot, namely any real exploration of either the German or the Russian social and political stances of the time. We're left with good-looking men shooting it out in front of dramatic scenery, and a World War II lacking historical commentary. **131m/C; VHS, DVD, Blu-Ray.** *GE GB IR US* Jude Law; Ed Harris; Joseph Fiennes; Rachel Weisz; Bob Hoskins; Gabriel Marshall-Thomson; Eva Mattes; Ron Perlman; Matthias Habich; *D:* Jean-Jacques Annaud; *W:* Jean-Jacques Annaud; Alain Godard; *C:* Robert Fraisse; *M:* James Horner.

Enemy Below 𝄞𝄞𝄞 **1957** Suspenseful WWII sea epic, in which an American destroyer and a German U-Boat chase one another and square off in the South Atlantic. **98m/C; VHS, DVD, Blu-Ray.** Robert Mitchum; Curt Jurgens; David Hedison; Theodore Bikel; Doug McClure; Russell Collins; *D:* Dick Powell.

Enemy Gold 𝄞 1/2 **1993 (R)** A crime czar and a beautiful killer without a conscience go after federal agents who have stumbled across a cache of Confederate gold. Basically, a babes-with-guns blowout. **92m/C; VHS, DVD, Blu-Ray.** Bruce Penhall; Rodrigo Obregon; Mark Barriere; Suzi Simpson; Tai Collins; Julie Strain; *D:* Drew Sidaris; *W:* Wess Rahn; Christian Sidaris.

Enemy Mine 𝄞𝄞 **1985 (PG-13)** A space fantasy in which two pilots from warring planets, one an Earthling, the other an asexual reptilian Drac, crash land on a barren planet and are forced to work together to survive. **108m/C; VHS, DVD, Blu-Ray.** Dennis Quaid; Louis Gossett, Jr.; Brion James; Richard Marcus; Lance Kerwin; Carolyn McCormick; *D:* Wolfgang Petersen; *W:* Edward Khmara; *C:* Tony Imi; *M:* Maurice Jarre.

An Enemy of the People 𝄞 **1977** Heavy-handed adaptation of the Henrik Ibsen play (which is no comedy to begin with). McQueen took a chance getting away from his action roles to portray a noble 19th-century doctor but it doesn't work. Thomas (McQueen) learns the local tannery is contaminating the water in the hot springs that brings tourists into the town. His brother, the mayor (Durning), warns him to keep quiet but Thomas can't and ends up the town pariah. **106m/C; DVD.** Steve McQueen; Charles Durning; Bibi Andersson; Eric Christmas; Michael Cristofer; Richard Dysart; *D:* George Schaefer; *W:* Alexander Jacobs; *C:* Paul Lohmann; *M:* Leonard Rosenman.

Enemy of the State 𝄞𝄞 1/2 **1998 (R)** Paranoia-thriller shows what the nerds would do if they really wanted revenge. After a friend slips him a videocassette without his knowledge, lawyer Robert Dean (Smith) is targeted by a surveillance-and-gizmo-happy government agency headed by the sinister Reynolds (Voight). They hound Dean relentlessly, cutting him off from everything he holds dear by ruining his career and marriage, forcing him underground. Just when he has no place left to turn, he is aided by Brill (Hackman), a remorseful ex-agent who helped create the cyber-surveillance monster. From this point, our two heroes bicker, buddy-film fashion, and things blow up until the inevitable shootout crescendo. Smith's good guy vibe sustains interest in tale of technology run amok. **132m/C; VHS, DVD, Blu-Ray.** Will Smith; Gene Hackman; Jon Voight; Jason Lee; Regina King; Gabriel Byrne; Barry Pepper; Scott Caan; Loren Dean; Jake Busey; Lisa Bonet; Stuart Wilson; Tom Sizemore; James LeGros; Ian Hurt; Dan E. Butler; Jamie Kennedy; Rebeca Silva; Jason Robards, Jr.; Bobby Boriello; Anna Gunn; Seth Green; Philip Baker Hall; Lillo Brancato; John Capodice; Jack Black; Bodhi (Pine) Elfman; *D:* Tony Scott; *W:* David Marconi; *C:* Dan(iel) Mindel; *M:* Trevor Rabin; Harry Gregson-Williams.

Enemy of Women 𝄞 1/2 *The Private Life of Paul Joseph Goebbels* **1944** Chronicles the life and loves of Nazi propagandist Dr. Joseph Goebbels. **90m/B; VHS, DVD.** Claudia Drake; Paul Andor; Donald Woods; H.B. Warner; Sigrid Gurie; Ralph Morgan; Gloria Stuart; Charles Halton; *D:* Alfred Zeisler; *W:* Alfred Zeisler.

The Enemy Within 𝄞𝄞 1/2 **1994** Cable TV remake of the 1964 political thriller "Seven Days in May." Set in the late 1990s, President William Foster's (Waterston) approval rating is at an all-time low and his heavy defense cuts have certain government officials plotting a coup. Hero of the tale is Joint Chief of Staffs officer, Col. Mac Casey (Whitaker), whose military career is warring with his sense of ethics. The updating is fairly clunky; for true suspense stick with the original. **86m/C; VHS, DVD.** Forest Whitaker; Sam Waterston; Josef Sommer; Jason Robards, Jr.; Dana Delany; George Dzundza; *D:* Jonathan Darby; *W:* Darryl Ponicsan; Ronald Bass; *C:* Kees Van Oostrum. **CABLE**

The Enforcer 𝄞𝄞 1/2 *Murder, Inc.* **1951** A district attorney goes after an organized gang of killers in this film noir treatment of the real-life "Murder, Inc." case. **87m/B; DVD, Blu-Ray.** Humphrey Bogart; Zero Mostel; Ted de Corsia; Everett Sloane; Roy Roberts; Michael (Lawrence) Tolan; King Donovan; Bob Steele; Adelaide Klein; Don Beddoe; Tito Vuolo; John Kellogg; *D:* Bretaigne Windust; Raoul Walsh; *W:* Martin Rackin; *C:* Robert Burks; *M:* David Buttolph.

The Enforcer 𝄞𝄞 1/2 **1976 (R)** Dirty Harry takes on a female partner and a vicious terrorist group that is threatening the city of San Francisco. See how many "punks" feel lucky enough to test the hand of the tough cop. **96m/C; VHS, DVD, Blu-Ray.** Clint Eastwood; Tyne Daly; Harry Guardino; Bradford Dillman; John Mitchum; Albert "Poppy" Popwell; Will MacMillan; John Crawford; Jocelyn Jones; DeVeren Bookwalter; Dick Durock; Joe Spano; *D:* James Fargo; *W:* Stirling Silliphant; Stuart Hagmann; *C:* Charles W. Short; *M:* Jerry Fielding.

The English Patient 𝄞𝄞𝄞𝄞 **1996 (R)** Filled with flashbacks and moral ambiguities, this adult romance is a complicated WWII saga that finds fragile French-Canadian nurse Hana (Binoche) caring for Almasy (Fiennes), an enigmatic, dying burn patient, in an abandoned monastery in Tuscany. Hana's joined by thief-turned-spy Caravaggio (Dafoe), who has a private score to settle with Almasy, and two British bomb disposal experts, Kip (Andrews), a Sikh who falls in love with Hana, and Sgt. Hardy (Whately). Almasy spends his days recalling his illicit love affair with Katharine Clifton (Scott Thomas), the wife of fellow cartographer, Geoffrey (Firth), as they map the North African desert. Exquisitely photographed in a golden glow by Seale with wonderful performances by the entire cast. Based on the novel by Michael Ondaatje. **162m/C; VHS, DVD.** Ralph Fiennes; Kristin Scott Thomas; Juliette Binoche; Willem Dafoe; Naveen Andrews; Colin Firth; Julian Wadham; Jurgen Prochnow; Kevin Whately; Clive Merrison; Nino Castelnuovo; *D:* Anthony Minghella; *W:* Anthony Minghella; *C:* John Seale; *M:* Gabriel Yared. Oscars '96: Art Dir./Set Dec., Cinematog., Costume Des., Director (Minghella), Film, Film Editing, Orig. Dramatic Score, Sound, Support. Actress (Binoche); British Acad. '96: Adapt. Screenplay, Cinematog., Film, Score, Support. Actress (Binoche); Directors Guild '96: Director (Minghella); Golden Globes '97: Film--Drama, Score; L.A. Film Critics '96: Cinematog.; Natl. Bd. of Review '96: Support. Actress (Binoche), Support. Actress (Scott Thomas); Broadcast Film Critics '96: Director (Minghella), Screenplay.

The English Teacher 𝄞𝄞 **2013 (R)** Comedy-drama provides some squirmy humiliations for Moore, who still gives a sensitive turn as unmarried, 40-something Linda Sinclair. Linda's an overly-romantic high school English teach in Pennsylvania who's delighted when former student Jason (Angarano) returns. He has an unproduced play she reads and then passes to the school's flamboyant drama teacher, Carl (Lane), who intends to stage it. Linda lets her emotional impulses get the better of her to sad effect but the ending is a dismaying betrayal of what's gone before. **93m/C; DVD, Blu-Ray, Streaming.** Julianne Moore; Michael Angarano;

Nathan Lane; Lily Collins; Greg Kinnear; Norbert Lee Butz; Jessica Hecht; *Nar:* Fiona Shaw; *D:* Craig Zisk; *W:* Dan Chariton; Stacy Chariton; *C:* Vanja Cernjul; *M:* Rob Simonsen.

An Englishman in New York 🦴🦴 1/2 **2009** Made-for-British TV with Hurt reprising his role as gay raconteur Quentin Crisp from 1975's "The Naked Civil Servant." Crisp moves to New York in 1981 at the age of 72, works on a one-man stage show, and writes for a gay magazine. However, after the aged contrarian quips that AIDS is a 'fad,' many in the gay community turn on him (especially after he refuses to apologize) despite his quiet support for various AIDS charities. Crisp still carried on and died in 1999 in England while preparing for a tour. **74m/C; DVD.** *GB* John Hurt; Swoosie Kurtz; Denis O'Hare; Jonathan Tucker; Cynthia Nixon; *D:* Richard Laxton; *W:* Brian Fillis; *C:* Yaron Orbach; *M:* Paul Englishby. **TV**

The Englishman Who Went up a Hill But Came down a Mountain 🦴🦴🦴 **1995 (PG)** Charming if slight tale of town pride based on writer/director Monger's family stories. In 1917 two English cartographers—pompous George (McNeice) and naive Reginald (Grant)?travel into Wales to measure the height of Ffynnon Garw (a running gag has the surveyors struggling with the Welsh language). To the proud locals it is the first mountain in Wales, and without that designation they might as well redraw the maps and be part of England—God forbid. But in order to be designated a mountain Ffynnon Garw must be 1000 feet high, and she measures only 984. Grant stammers boyishly as the Englishman who is not only captivated by the village, but by spirited local lass Betty (Fitzgerald, with whom he starred in "Sirens"). Meaney slyly shines as innkeeper Morgan the Goat, leading the townful of color characters. Wales is shown to great advantage by cinematographer Layton. **96m/C; VHS, DVD.** *GB* Hugh Grant; Tara Fitzgerald; Colm Meaney; Ian McNeice; Ian Hart; Kenneth Griffith; *D:* Christopher Monger; *W:* Christopher Monger; *C:* Vernon Layton; *M:* Stephen Endelman.

Enid Is Sleeping 🦴🦴 *Over Her Dead Body* **1990 (R)** Well-done comedy noir in the now-popular there's-a-corpse-in-the-closet subgenre. A woman in a mythical New Mexican town tries to hide the body of her sister Enid, who she's accidentally killed. Enid, it turns out, wasn't thrilled to discover her sister sleeping with her police-officer husband. Phillips and Perkins restored the film to its original state after it was ruthlessly gutted by the studio. **105m/C; VHS, DVD.** Elizabeth Perkins; Judge Reinhold; Rhea Perlman; *D:* Maurice Phillips; *W:* Maurice Phillips; *C:* Affonso Beato.

Enigma 🦴🦴 **1982 (PG)** Trapped behind the Iron Curtain, a double agent tries to find the key to five pending murders by locating a Russian coded microprocessor holding information that would unravel the assassination scheme. **101m/C; VHS, DVD, Blu-Ray.** *FR GB* Martin Sheen; Brigitte Fossey; Sam Neill; Derek Jacobi; Frank Finlay; Michael (Michel) Lonsdale; Warren Clarke; *D:* Jeannot Szwarc; *W:* John Briley.

Enigma 🦴🦴 1/2 **2001 (R)** Tom Jericho (Scott) is a British codebreaker working at Bletchley Park during WWII. He has a breakdown after a romantic breakup with colleague Claire (Burrows), who's mysteriously dispeared. Could she have been working for the Germans? Tom is determined to find out, aided by Claire's roommate Hester (Winslet). Meanwhile, intelligence operative Wigram (Northam) is keeping an eye on them both, thinking they know more than they appear to. Excessive subplots make for some confusion but the story's still compelling. Based on a novel by Robert Harris. **117m/C; VHS, DVD.** *GB* Dougray Scott; Kate Winslet; Saffron Burrows; Jeremy Northam; Nikolaj Waldau; Tom Hollander; Corin Redgrave; Robert Pugh; Matthew Macfadyen; Donald (Don) Sumpter; *D:* Michael Apted; *W:* Tom Stoppard; *C:* Seamus McGarvey; *M:* John Barry.

Enigma Secret 🦴🦴 **1979** Three Polish mathematicians use their noggins to break the Nazi secret code machine during WWII. Based on a true story; in Polish with English subtitles. **158m/C; VHS, DVD.** *PL* Tadeusz Borowski; Piotr Fronczewski; Piotr Garlicki; *D:* Rom Wionczek; *W:* Rom Wionczek; *C:* Jacek Zygadio; *M:* Henryk Kuzniak; Jerzy Maksymiuk.

Enough 🦴🦴 **2002 (PG-13)** Revenge fantasy that's been compared to both "Sleeping with the Enemy" (Julia Roberts) and "Double Jeopardy" (Ashley Judd). Working-class waitress Slim (Lopez) marries wealthy contractor Mitch (Campbell) and for a while everything appears perfect. But Mitch turns out to be an abusive, cheating, control freak who forces Slim to take their daughter and run. When Mitch finds and threatens her, Slim decides to literally toughen up and give Mitch a taste of his own medicine. Okay, it's nice to see Lopez kick butt but this movie has a very nasty taste and some lame advice for battered women (who probably won't discover that their biological fathers are filthy rich and can help them out financially). **115m/C; VHS, DVD.** Jennifer Lopez; Billy Campbell; Juliette Lewis; Dan Futterman; Noah Wyle; Tessa Allen; Fred Ward; Bill Cobbs; Christopher Maher; Janet Carroll; *D:* Michael Apted; *W:* Nicholas Kazan; *C:* Rogier Stoffers; *M:* David Arnold.

Enough Said 🦴🦴🦴 1/2 **2013 (PG-13)** Louis-Dreyfus does career-best work and Gandolfini matches her with a bittersweet final performance in writer/director Holofcener's dramedy about second chances and how we often sabotage our own chances at true love. Eva' s a divorced masseuse on the verge of an empty nest. She meets two important people at a party: a potential friend named Marianne (Keener) and a potential beau named Albert (Gandolfini). As she gets closer to both, she's startled to learn that they're ex-spouses. The sitcomish conceit is overcome by the honesty of the performances. **93m/C; DVD, Blu-Ray.** Julia Louis-Dreyfus; James Gandolfini; Catherine Keener; Toni Collette; Ben Falcone; *D:* Nicole Holofcener; *W:* Nicole Holofcener; *C:* Xavier Perez Grobet; *M:* Marcelo Zarvos.

Enron: The Smartest Guys in the Room 🦴🦴🦴 1/2 **2005** Based on the book by Fortune magazine reporters Bethany McLean and Peter Elkind. Director Gibney deftly compiles vast amounts of in-house video and audio footage along with after-the-fact interviews and Congressional hearings chronicling the devastating downfall in 2001 of corporate behemoth Enron. An engaging, thorough, and coherent profile of the hustle created by chief executives Kenneth Lay, Jeffrey Skilling, and Andy Fastow and the resulting economic destruction, from the loss of 20,000 jobs and $2 million in employee pensions to the $30 billion cost of California's energy crisis. Matter-of-fact narration by Peter Coyote contrasts well with sly use of several pop music songs. **110m/C; DVD, Blu-Ray.** *D:* Alex Gibney; *W:* Alex Gibney; *C:* Maryse Albert; *M:* Matt Hauser. Ind. Spirit '06: Feature Doc.; Writers Guild '05: Documentary Screenplay.

Ensign Pulver 🦴🦴 **1964** A continuation of the further adventures of the crew of the U.S.S. Reluctant from "Mister Roberts," which was adapted from the Broadway play. **104m/C; VHS, DVD.** Walter Matthau; Robert Walker, Jr.; Larry Hagman; Jack Nicholson; Millie Perkins; James Coco; James Farentino; Burl Ives; Gerald S. O'Loughlin; Al Freeman, Jr.; *D:* Joshua Logan.

Enter the Dragon 🦴🦴🦴 *The Deadly Three* **1973 (R)** The American film that broke Bruce Lee worldwide combines Oriental conventions with 007 thrills. Spectacular fighting sequences including Karate, Judo, Tae Kwon Do, and Tai Chi Chuan are featured as Lee is recruited by the British to search for opium smugglers in Hong Kong. **98m/C; VHS, DVD, Blu-Ray, UMD, HD-DVD.** Bruce Lee; John Saxon; Jim Kelly; Ahna Capri; Shih Kien; Bob Wall; Angela (Mao Ying) Mao; Betty Chung; Jackie Chan; Tony Liu; Sammo Hung; *D:* Robert Clouse; *W:* Michael Allin; *C:* Gil Hubbs; *M:* Lalo Schifrin. Natl. Film Reg. '04.

Enter the Ninja 🦴 **1981 (R)** First and most serious of the Cannon canon of relatively well-done ninja epics (faint praise) that created original boxoffice stir for genre (mostly among adolescents needing outlet). Ninja Nero visits old friend in Philippines who's being terrorized by ruthless evil guy George. Nero dispatches numerous thugs before indulging in ninja slugfest with Kosugi. Just because they take it seriously doesn't mean you should. **99m/C; VHS, DVD, Blu-Ray, Streaming.** Franco Nero; Susan George; Sho Kosugi; Christopher George; Alex Courtney; *D:* Menahem Golan; *W:* Judd Bernard.

Enter the Void 🦴 **2009** Long and gimmick-ridden flick finds dope-smoking drug dealer Oscar dead in the Void nightclub. Which doesn't get rid of him, as his spirit floats through Tokyo in a series of overly-stylistic, graphically disturbing scenes and camera flourishes like a wannabe Kubrick "2001." **161m/C; Blu-Ray.** *FR* Paz de la Huerta; Emily Alyn Lind; Nathaniel Brown; Cyril Roy; Jesse Kuhn; Olly Alexander; Masto Tanno; Ed Spear; *D:* Gaspar Noé; *W:* Gaspar Noé; *C:* Benoît Debie.

Enter the Warriors Gate 🦴🦴 *The Warriors Gate* **2017 (PG-13)** A martial arts fantasy action-adventure in which a bullied teen travels back in time. High schooler Jack Thornton (Shelton) lacks self-confidence but finds solace playing an invincible warrior in his favorite videogame. One night after his employer gives him an antique wooden chest, he is surprised to find Su Lin (Ni) come out of the chest followed by ancient thugs. Entranced by her, Jack follows her into the chest and finds himself in ancient China. Mustering inner strength, Jack helps Zhao (Chao) to try and save her from the power hungry Arun (Bautista). Highlighted by humor, strong character development, and well-shot action sequences. **108m/C; DVD.** Mark Chao; Ni Ni; Dave Bautista; Sienna Guillory; Uriah Shelton; *D:* Matthias Hoene; *W:* Luc Besson; Robert Mark Kamen; *C:* Maxime Alexandre; *M:* Klaus Badelt.

The Entertainer 🦴🦴🦴 1/2 **1960** Splendid drama of egotistical, third-rate vaudevillian Archie Rice (Olivier), who tries vainly to gain the fame his dying father Billy (Livesey) once possessed. His blatant disregard for his alcoholic wife Phoebe (De Banzie), his superficial sons (Bates and Finney), and his loyal daughter (Plowright) brings his world crashing down around him, as Archie discovers how self-destructive his life has been. Adapted from the play by John Osborne. Remade for TV in 1975 with Jack Lemmon. **104m/B; VHS, DVD.** *GB* Laurence Olivier; Brenda de Banzie; Roger Livesey; Joan Plowright; Daniel Massey; Alan Bates; Shirley Anne Field; Albert Finney; Thora Hird; *D:* Tony Richardson; *W:* John Osborne; Nigel Kneale; *C:* Oswald Morris; *M:* John Addison.

Entertaining Angels: The Dorothy Day Story 🦴🦴 1/2 **1996 (PG-13)** Dorothy Day (Kelly) was a social activist who founded the left-wing publication The Catholic Worker and was dedicated to sheltering and feeding the poor, founding soup kitchens across America. A radical journalist and New York bohemian, Day converts to Catholicism in the '20s and is soon working with the city's poor and homeless. Episodic story works mainly on indignation and its heroine's compassion. **110m/C; VHS, DVD.** Moira Kelly; Martin Sheen; Melinda Dillon; Lenny Von Dohlen; Heather Graham; Geoffrey Blake; Boyd Kestner; Allyce Beasley; Brian Keith; *D:* Michael Ray Rhodes; *W:* John Wells; *C:* Mike Fash; *M:* Bill Conti; Ashley Irwin.

Entertainment 🦴 1/2 **2015 (R)** Alverson's latest is another aggressively annoying film, a movie that alternates beautiful cinematography of the American West with one of the least likable protagonists you'll ever meet. Said protagonist is a stand-up comedian played by Turkington, in a variation on a character he's actually played on stage in recent years. The comedian barely tells jokes, spitting out anger and tangential nonsense to audiences who look back at him with blank stares. You're likely to do the same. Alverson's drama is for a very specific audience, those interested in Turkington's schtick or those who like films that dare you to like them at all. **110m/C; DVD, Blu-Ray.** Gregg Turkington; Tye Sheridan; John C. Reilly; Mike Hickey; Kevin Guthrie; *D:* Rick Alverson; *W:* Gregg Turkington; Rick Alverson; Tim Heidecker; *C:* Lorenzo Hagerman; *M:* Robert Donne.

The Entitled 🦴 1/2 **2011 (R)** Struggling Paul Dynan kidnaps one offspring each from three wealthy men with a ransom of one million per kid. Only they're all hard-partying brats and the dads don't seem so eager to part with their dough even as Paul has problems with his plan, his two fellow kidnappers, and his hostages. **91m/C; DVD, Blu-Ray.** *CA* Kevin Zegers; Ray Liotta; Victor Garber; Stephen McHattie; Laura Vandervoort; Dustin Milligan; John Bregar; Devon Bostick; Tatiana Maslany; *D:* Aaron Woodley; *W:* William Morrissey; *C:* David (Robert) A. Greene; *M:* Robert Duncan. **VIDEO**

The Entity 🦴🦴 **1983 (R)** Supposedly based on a true story about an unseen entity that repeatedly rapes a woman. Hershey's the victim whom nobody believes. She eventually ends up at a university for talks with parapsychologist Silver. Pseudo-science to the rescue as the over-sexed creature is frozen dead in its tracks. Exploitative violence, gore, and nudity aplenty, balanced to a degree by Hershey's strong performance. **115m/C; VHS, DVD, Blu-Ray.** Barbara Hershey; Ron Silver; Alex Rocco; *D:* Sidney J. Furie; *W:* Frank De Felitta; *C:* Stephen Burum; *M:* Charles Bernstein.

Entourage 🦴🦴 1/2 **2015 (R)** A strange and unnecessary big-screen adaptation of HBO's popular Tinseltown love letter, bringing the gang back together for one last romp. Vinnie Chase (Grenier) wants to direct, and luckily his old pal Ari (Piven) is now running the studio. They turn to an eccentric Texas business tycoon (Thornton) to bankroll the project. Creator Doug Ellin has too much on his plate, and doesn't quite find the balance to give proper attention to E's (Connolly) new family, Turtle's (Ferrara) successful business, or Drama's (Dillon) new career-saving role. What is essentially just an abbreviated season 9 will likely disappoint current fans and certainly doesn't aim to make any new ones. **105m/C; DVD, Blu-Ray, Streaming.** Kevin Connolly; Adrian Grenier; Kevin Dillon; Jerry Ferrara; Jeremy Piven; Debi Mazar; *D:* Doug Ellin; *W:* Doug Ellin; Robin Weiss; *C:* Steven Fierberg.

Entrapment 🦴🦴 1/2 **1999 (PG-13)** Too tricky for its own good crime caper features insurance investigator Virginia Baker (Zeta-Jones) convincing her boss, Hector Cruz (Patton), that master thief Mac MacDougall (Connery) is behind the theft of a Rembrandt. Only when Gin catches up to Mac, she convinces him that she's also a thief and she has a very elaborate, very rich heist in mind, that needs his expertise. However, nobody involved in anything that goes on in this movie is exactly what they seem. Nice scenery (and not just that offered by the beautiful Zeta-Jones). **112m/C; VHS, DVD, Blu-Ray.** Sean Connery; Catherine Zeta-Jones; Ving Rhames; Will Patton; Maury Chaykin; *D:* Jon Amiel; *W:* Ronald Bass; William Broyles, Jr.; *C:* Phil Meheux; *M:* Christopher Young.

Entre-Nous 🦴🦴🦴 1/2 *Between Us; Coup de Foudre; At First Sight* **1983 (PG)** Two attractive, young French mothers find in each other the fulfillment their husbands cannot provide. One of the women was confined in a concentration camp during WWII; the other is a disaffected artist. In French with English subtitles. **112m/C; VHS, DVD.** *FR* Isabelle Huppert; Miou-Miou; Guy Marchand; Jean-Pierre Bacri; Patrick Bauchau; Jacqueline Doyen; *D:* Diane Kurys; *W:* Diane Kurys; Alain Le Henry; *C:* Bernard Lutic; *M:* Luis Bacalov.

Entry Level 🦴🦴 **2007** Middle-aged chef Clay Maguire's (Sweeney) restaurant goes under and Clay decides to get out of the food business and look for a different line of work. Of course Clay has no other job skills (he can't even use a computer) so that really limits his choices, but he gets encouragement from some unlikely sources. **85m/C; DVD.** D.B. Sweeney; Kurtwood Smith; Missi Pyle; Cedric Yarbrough; Taylor Negron; Steve Ryan; Lisa Ann Walter; *D:* Douglas Horn; *W:* Douglas Horn; *C:* Aasulv Austad; *M:* Brandon Roberts. **VIDEO**

Envy 🦴🦴 1/2 **2004 (PG-13)** Tim (Stiller) and Nick (Black) are buddies, neighbors, and coworkers at a sandpaper plant. Nick is a dreamer who's constantly coming up with wacky inventions that Tim reminds him are impossible or impractical. One of these ideas is Vapoorize, a spray that makes dog doo disappear. When Tim passes on a chance to get in on the deal and the spray becomes a monster success, his wife's (Weisz) scorn triggers a jealousy that sends him on a trail of petty revenge on Nick. Uneven comedy is elevated by the gleefully manic performance of Walken, as Tim's criminal inspiration, the

J-Man. Black's clueless immersion in the overly opulent lifestyle is a kick, as well. **99m/C; DVD.** Ben Stiller; Jack Black; Rachel Weisz; Amy Poehler; Christopher Walken; Hector Elias; Edward "Blue" Deckert; Ariel Gade; Sam Lerner; Lily Jackson; Connor Matheus; ***D:*** Barry Levinson; ***W:*** Steve Adams; ***C:*** Tim Maurice-Jones; ***M:*** Mark Mothersbaugh.

Epic ½ **2013 (PG)** A girl named M.K. (Seyfried) is home visiting her estranged father (Sudeikis), a scientist who believes that a colony of little people lives in the forest behind his house. Of course, he's right, a truth that M.K. learns when she's shrunken down and placed at the center of a battle between the soldiers trying to save the foliage and the creatures trying to destroy it. Too reminiscent of similar stories of colonies fighting for the sake of Mother Nature's future, this animated adventure nonetheless features gorgeous-enough visuals that the thin storytelling can sometimes be overlooked. **102m/C; DVD, Blu-Ray.** ***V:*** Amanda Seyfried; Josh Hutcherson; Colin Farrell; Beyonce Knowles; Jason Sudeikis; Christoph Waltz; Chris O'Dowd; Aziz Ansari; ***D:*** Chris Wedge; ***W:*** James V. Hart; William Joyce; ***C:*** Renato Falcao; ***M:*** Danny Elfman.

Epic Movie WOOF! 2007 (PG-13) Another cobbled together, extremely unfunny spoof of popular movies. Four orphans (Mays, Penn, Chambers, Campbell) wind up in a chocolate factory where Glover is an even more sinister candy maker than Johnny Depp's Willy Wonka. Then they escape to a parody of "Narnia" (although Coolidge makes a fairly cool ice queen) and it just goes downhill from there. Someone somewhere must still finds this stuff funny. **85m/C; DVD.** Kal Penn; Adam Campbell; Jennifer Coolidge; Faune A. Chambers; Jayma Mays; Crispin Glover; Fred Willard; Hector Jimenez; Darrell Hammond; Carmen Electra; David Carradine; ***D:*** Jason Friedberg; Aaron Selzer; ***W:*** Jason Friedberg; Aaron Selzer; ***C:*** Shawn Maurer; ***M:*** Ed Shearmur.

Epoch ½ **2000 (PG-13)** Alien monolith suddenly appears and hovers over Bhutan, seemingly causing worldwide power disruptions and earthquakes. National security adviser Lysander (O'Neal) assigns special ops Kasia Czaban (Niznik) and weapons specialist Mason Rand (Keith) to figure out just what the object is—and wants—and, if necessary, to destroy it. **97m/C; VHS, DVD.** David Keith; Stephanie Niznik; Ryan O'Neal; James Hong; Brian Thompson; Craig Wasson; Donna Magnani; Shannon Lee; ***D:*** Matt Cold; ***C:*** Ken Stipe. **CABLE**

Epoch: Evolution **2003 (R)** It's been 10 years since the alien monolith, Torus, wreaked havoc with the planet. In this passable sequel to 2000's Epoch, Rand (Keith) must now summon it as a drastic measure to prevent a catastrophic third world war. **90m/C; VHS, DVD.** David Keith; Angel Boris; Billy Dee Williams; Brian Thompson; ***D:*** Ian Watson; ***M:*** Jason Christopherson. **CABLE**

The Equalizer ½ **2014 (R)** More enjoyable for what it's not than what it is, Washington's action hit reteams him with director Fuqua. Washington plays a retired killing machine brought back into action when a young hooker he's befriended (well-played by Moretz) gets sent to the hospital by her Russian keepers. Washington's strong-and-silent type is the kind who sees action in slow motion, predicting the moves of his enemies before they happen. Fuqua takes his time in the set-up, doesn't force a relationship on Denzel and allows the piece to be less frenzied, at least until the ridiculous climax. **132m/C; DVD, Blu-Ray.** Denzel Washington; Chloë Grace Moretz; Marton Csokas; David Harbour; Vladimir Kulich; Bill Pullman; Melissa Leo; ***D:*** Antoine Fuqua; ***W:*** Richard Werk; ***C:*** Mauro Fiore; ***M:*** Harry Gregson-Williams.

The Equalizer 2 ½ **2018 (R)** Robert McCall serves an unflinching justice for the exploited and oppressed, but how far will he go when that is someone he loves? **129m/C; Blu-Ray.** Denzel Washington; Ashton Sanders; Pedro Pascal; Melissa Leo; Bill Pullman; ***D:*** Antoine Fuqua; ***W:*** Richard Wenk; ***C:*** Oliver Wood; ***M:*** Harry Gregson-Williams.

Equals **2016 (PG-13)** Doremus' sci-fi/drama is more ambitious than many modern dystopian future flicks but ultimately falls victim to the same traps. In this vision of the future, illness and emotion are eradicated. Silas (Hoult) develops something called "Switched On Syndrome," making him both an outcast and deeply attracted to his co-worker Nia (Stewart), who is also infected. When a cure is found, they have to decide whether to remain "sick" to remain in love. Stewart continues to impress post-Twilight but this is generic, uninspired stuff. **101m/C; DVD, Blu-Ray.** Nicholas Hoult; Kristen Stewart; Guy Pearce; Bel Powley; Scott Lawrence; Jacki Weaver; ***D:*** Drake Doremus; ***W:*** Drake Doremus; Nathan Parker; ***C:*** John Guleserian; ***M:*** Dustin O'Halloran; Sascha Ring.

Equilibrium WOOF! 2002 (R) It's the near future, in which society self-administers Prozium daily to thwart all emotions. The emotion cops, Grammaton Cleric, arrest sense offenders using the time-tested method of massive gun-kata battles. Agent John Preston's (Bale) position is compromised when he's attracted to Mary (Watson), a woman working with a resistance group. Poor attempt at sci-fi drama raises the question "Would the future suck less if we stopped making lousy movies about it in the present?" **106m/C; VHS, DVD, Blu-Ray.** Christian Bale; Emily Watson; Taye Diggs; Angus MacFadyen; Sean Bean; William Fichtner; Matthew Harbour; ***D:*** Kurt Wimmer; ***W:*** Kurt Wimmer; ***C:*** Dion Beebe; ***M:*** Klaus Badelt.

Equinox *The Beast* **1971 (PG)** Young archaeologists uncover horror in a state forest. The ranger, questing for a book of spells that the scientists have found, threatens them with wonderful special effects, including winged beasts, huge apes, and Satan. Though originally an amateur film, it is deemed a minor classic in its genre. **80m/C; VHS, DVD.** Edward Connell; Barbara Hewitt; Frank Bonner; Robin Christopher; Jack Woods; Fritz Leiber, Jr.; Patrick Burke; Jim Phillips; ***D:*** Jack Woods; Dennis Muren; ***W:*** Jack Woods; ***C:*** Mike Hoover; ***M:*** John Caper, Jr.

Equinox Flower **1958** Ozu's first color film tells the sensitive story of two teenage girls who make a pact to protect each other from the traditional prearranged marriages their parents have set up. Lovely film that focuses on the generation gap between young and old in the Japanese family. In Japanese with English subtitles. **118m/C; VHS, DVD.** *JP* Shin Saburi; Kinuyo Tanaka; Ineko Arima; Miyuki Kuwano; Chishu Ryu; ***D:*** Yasujiro Ozu.

Equity ½ **2016 (R)** A female version of Wall Street sounds like a fantastic idea, especially in today's world of increased demand for stories created by and about the female experience. The fact is that movies about finance are dominated by men; let's switch it up. Sadly, this one doesn't quite work beyond a few decent performances. Gunn (of TV's "Breaking Bad" fame) plays Naomi Bishop, one of the Wall Street's power players caught up in a web of corruption and sexism. Menon's direction is good but uninspired, and several of the supporting performances are distractingly bad. **100m/C; DVD, Blu-Ray.** Anna Gunn; James Purefoy; Sarah Megan Thomas; Alysia Reiner; Craig Bierko; ***D:*** Meera Menon; ***W:*** Amy Fox; ***C:*** Eric Lin; ***M:*** Samuel Jones; Alexis Marsh.

Equus ½ **1977 (R)** A psychiatrist undertakes the most challenging case of his career when he tries to figure out why a stable-boy blinded horses. Based upon the successful play by Peter Shaffer, but not well transferred to film. **138m/C; VHS, DVD, Blu-Ray.** Richard Burton; Peter Firth; Jenny Agutter; Joan Plowright; Colin Blakely; Harry Andrews; ***D:*** Sidney Lumet; ***W:*** Peter Shaffer; ***C:*** Oswald Morris; ***M:*** Richard Rodney Bennett. British Acad. '77: Support. Actress (Agutter); Golden Globes '78: Actor--Drama (Burton), Support. Actor (Firth).

Era Notte a Roma *Escape by Night; Blackout in Rome* **1960** An American, Russian, and British soldier each escape from a concentration camp in the waning days of WWII and find refuge in the home of a young woman. **145m/C; VHS, DVD.** *IT* Giovanna Ralli; Renato Salvatori; Leo Genn; Sergei Bondarchuk; Peter Baldwin; ***D:*** Roberto Rossellini; ***W:*** Roberto Rossellini; ***C:*** Carlo Carlini; ***M:*** Renzo Rossellini.

Eragon **2006 (PG)** The dragon, voiced with maternal concern by Weisz, is a lot more charismatic than its rider—the teen-aged farm boy of the title (Speleers in his film debut). A sword-and-sorcery flick, based on the first novel in a trilogy by Christopher Paolini (who was a teen himself when he wrote it), has a bad king (Malkovich) and his evil wizard (Carlyle) oppressing the little people in a mythic land—until Eragon and his dragon Saphira, aided by mentor Brom (Irons), can rally the rebels (there's always rebels). The kids will probably enjoy the adventure—even though the film is left open-ended for a sequel—but it doesn't hold much crossover appeal for adults. **104m/C; DVD, Blu-Ray.** Jeremy Irons; Sienna Guillory; Robert Carlyle; John Malkovich; Ed Speleers; Djimon Hounsou; Garrett Hedlund; Joss Stone; Alun Armstrong; Gary Lewis; Christopher Egan; Richard Rifkin; Caroline Chikezie; Andrea Fazekas; Steve Speirs; ***V:*** Rachel Weisz; ***D:*** Stefan Fangmeier; ***W:*** Peter Buchman; ***C:*** Hugh Johnson; ***M:*** Patrick Doyle.

Erased **2012 (R)** Single father and ex-CIA agent Ben Logan (Eckhart) is a security expert in Belgium. He comes to work to find all traces of his company have disappeared. With his teenage daughter Amy (Liberato), he digs into a mystery that has left his co-workers in a morgue. Meanwhile, agents from the U.S. government and European security heads are hot on his trail to complete the cover-up. A messy, convoluted plot leads the two through substandard foot chases and some clunky fist fights with unnamed villains. Eckhart does his best to save the world from corporate cover-ups, but can't save this unimaginative Euro-thriller from mediocrity. **100m/C; DVD, Blu-Ray.** Aaron Eckhart; Liana Liberato; Olga Kurylenko; Garrick Hagon; Eric Gordon; ***D:*** Philipp Stolzl; ***W:*** Arash (A.E.) Amel; ***C:*** Kolja Brandt; ***M:*** Jeff Danna.

Eraser ½ **1996 (R)** Arnold returns to familiar big-budget action territory and looks right at home. He plays elite U.S. Marshal John Kruger, who protects federal witnesses by "erasing" their previous identities. When a beautiful witness uncovers a high-level conspiracy, the two go on the run to stay alive long enough to expose the truth. Fans of the big bang Schwarzenegger of yore will not be disappointed. Rumors of production delays and budget overruns, not to mention difficulties between director Russell and producer Kopelson, brought up the spectre of "Waterworld," but the final result is more reminiscent of the success of "True Lies." **115m/C; VHS, DVD, Blu-Ray.** Arnold Schwarzenegger; Vanessa L(ynne) Williams; James Caan; James Coburn; Robert Pastorelli; Andy Romano; James Cromwell; Danny Nucci; Nick (Nicholas) Chinlund; Mark Rolston; Gerry Becker; Joe (Johnny) Viterelli; Michael (Mike) Papajohn; ***D:*** Chuck Russell; ***W:*** Tony Puryear; Walon Green; ***C:*** Adam Greenberg; ***M:*** Alan Silvestri.

Eraserhead **1978** The infamous cult classic about a numb-brained everyman wandering through what amounts to a sick, ironic parody of the modern urban landscape, innocently impregnating his girlfriend and fathering a pestilent embryonic mutant. Surreal and bizarre, the film has an inner, completely unpredictable logic all its own. Lynch's first feature-length film stars Nance, who later achieved fame in Lynch's "Twin Peaks" as Pete the Logger. **90m/B; VHS, DVD, Blu-Ray.** Jack Nance; Charlotte Stewart; Allen Joseph; Jeanne Bates; Judith Anna Roberts; Laurel Near; V. Phipps-Willson; Jack Fisk; Jean Lange; Darwin Joston; Hal Landon, Jr.; Jennifer Lynch; Gill Dennis; ***D:*** David Lynch; ***W:*** David Lynch; ***C:*** Frederick Elmes; Herbert Cardwell; ***M:*** David Lynch; Fats Waller; Peter Ivers. Natl. Film Reg. '04.

Erik, the Viking **1965** The Norse Warrior discovers not only the New World but traitorous subordinates among his crew, calling for drastic measures. **95m/C; VHS, DVD, Streaming.** *IT SP* Giuliano Gemma; Gordon Mitchell; ***D:*** Mario Caiano; ***W:*** Mario Caiano; ***C:*** Enzo Barboni; ***M:*** Carlo Franci.

Erik the Viking ½ **1989 (PG-13)** A mediocre Monty Pythonesque farce about a Viking who grows dissatisfied with his barbaric way of life and decides to set out to find the mythical Asgaard, where Norse gods dwell. Great cast of character actors is wasted. **104m/C; VHS, DVD, Blu-Ray.** *GB* Tim Robbins; Terry Jones; Mickey Rooney; John Cleese; Imogen Stubbs; Anthony Sher; Gordon John Sinclair; Freddie Jones; Eartha Kitt; Gary Cady; Neil Innes; Jim Broadbent; Andrew McLachlan; Charles McKeown; ***D:*** Terry Jones; ***W:*** Terry Jones; ***C:*** Ian Wilson; ***M:*** Neil Innes.

Erin Brockovich **2000 (R)** Erin Brockovich (Roberts) is a divorced mom desperate for a job. She bullies her way into a file clerk position at the small law office of Ed Masry (Finney) where her salty language, take-no-prisoners attitude, and scanty attire unnerve her co-workers. But that's just the appeal that Erin needs when she uncovers and investigates some shady corporate dealings that eventually lead to a multimillion dollar settlement against a public utility over contaminated water. Standout role for Roberts who's ably backed-up by the rumpled Finney. Based on a true story and yes, the real Erin is a looker who dresses every bit as provocatively as her screen counterpart. **131m/C; VHS, DVD, Blu-Ray, HD-DVD.** Julia Roberts; Albert Finney; Aaron Eckhart; Marg Helgenberger; Cherry Jones; Veanne Cox; Conchata Ferrell; Tracey Walter; Peter Coyote; ***D:*** Steven Soderbergh; ***W:*** Susannah Grant; ***C:*** Edward Lachman; ***M:*** Thomas Newman. Oscars '00: Actress (Roberts); British Acad. '00: Actress (Roberts); Golden Globes '01: Actress--Drama (Roberts); L.A. Film Critics '00: Actress (Roberts), Director (Soderbergh); Natl. Bd. of Review '00: Actress (Roberts), Director (Soderbergh); N.Y. Film Critics '00: Director (Soderbergh); Natl. Soc. Film Critics '00: Director (Soderbergh); Screen Actors Guild '00: Actress (Roberts), Support. Actor (Finney); Broadcast Film Critics '00: Actress (Roberts), Director (Soderbergh).

Ernest & Celestine ½ **2013 (PG)** A sweetly old-fashioned animated feature about the unlikely friendship between a bear and a mouse. Musician Ernest prefers to live alone in a woodland cottage than with his fellow bears in town. Orphaned mouse Celestine lives underground, where her fellow mice only come above ground to steal provisions, including the discarded bear teeth they need to survive. Celestine wishes to become an artist, not a dentist, and it's only when she meets Ernest that they both can follow their dreams. Based on the children's book series by Gabrielle Vincent. The original French-language version was redone with English-speaking actors. **80m/C; DVD, Blu-Ray.** *FR BE* ***V:*** Forest Whitaker; Mackenzie Foy; Lauren Bacall; Paul Giamatti; Megan Mullally; William H. Macy; Nick Offerman; Jeffrey Wright; ***D:*** Benjamin Renner; Vincent Patar; Stephanie Aubier; ***W:*** Daniel Pennac; ***M:*** Vincent Courtois.

Ernest Goes to Africa ½ **1997 (PG)** Ernest P. Worrel (Varney) finds himself in a heap 'o trouble when he's accused of buying some stolen diamonds and he and would-be girlfriend Renee are kidnapped and taken to Africa where a prince wants his property returned. Lots of sight gags and low humor. **90m/C; VHS, DVD.** Jim Varney; Linda Kash; Jamie Bartlett; ***D:*** John R. Cherry, III; ***W:*** John R. Cherry, III; ***C:*** James Robb.

Ernest Goes to Camp ½ **1987 (PG)** Screwball, slapstick summer camp farce starring the character Ernest P. Worrell as an inept camp counselor. When progress threatens the camp, Ernest leads the boys on a turtle-bombing, slop-shooting attack on the construction company. Followed by "Ernest Saves Christmas" and "Ernest Goes to Jail." **92m/C; VHS, DVD, Blu-Ray.** Jim Varney; Victoria Racimo; John Vernon; Iron Eyes Cody; Lyle Alzado; Gailard Sartain; Daniel Butler; Hakeem Abdul-Samad; Richard Speight, Jr.; ***D:*** John R. Cherry, III; ***W:*** John R. Cherry, III.

Ernest Goes to Jail **1990 (PG)** The infamous loon Ernest P. Worrell winds up in the jury box and the courtroom will never be the same again. Jury duty suddenly becomes hard-time in the slammer for poor Ernest when he is mistaken for a big-wig organized crime boss. Sequel to "Ernest Goes to Camp" and "Ernest Saves Christmas." **81m/C; VHS, DVD.** Jim Varney; Gailard Sartain; Randall "Tex" Cobb; Bill Byrge; Barry Scott; Charles Napier; ***D:*** John R. Cherry, III; ***W:*** Charlie Cohen; ***M:*** Bruce Arntson.

Ernest in the Army ½ **1997 (PG)** Ernest is talked into joining the Army reserves and promptly causes all sorts of trouble when he's assigned to drive various military vehicles. **85m/C; VHS, DVD.** Jim Varney; Hayley Tyson; David Muller; Ivan Lucas; Robert Foster; ***D:*** John R. Cherry, III; ***W:*** Jeffrey Pillars; ***C:*** James Robb; ***M:*** Mark Adler.

Ernest Saves Christmas 🦴 1/2 **1988 (PG)** Ernest P. Worrell is back. When Santa decides that it's time to retire, Ernest must help him recruit a has-been children's show host who is a bit reluctant. For Ernest fans only, and only the most dedicated of those. Second in the series featuring the nimble-faced Varney, the first of which was "Ernest Goes to Camp," followed by "Ernest Goes to Jail." **91m/C; VHS, DVD; Open Captioned.** Jim Varney; Douglas Seale; Oliver Clark; Noelle Parker; Billie Bird; ***D:*** John R. Cherry, III.

Ernest Scared Stupid 🦴 1/2 **1991 (PG)** Pea-brained Ernest P. Worrell returns yet again in this silly comedy. When he accidentally releases a demon from a sacred tomb a 200-year-old curse threatens to destroy his hometown, unless Ernest can come to the rescue. Would you want your town depending on Ernest's heroics? Who would have thought that the annoying Ernest P. Worrell could appear in one movie, let alone four? **93m/C; VHS, DVD.** Jim Varney; Eartha Kitt; Austin Nagler; Jonas Moscartolo; Shay Astar; ***D:*** John R. Cherry, III; ***W:*** John R. Cherry, III; ***C:*** Hanania Baer; ***M:*** Bruce Arntson.

Eros 🦴🦴 1/2 **2004 (R)** Three short films by renowned directors intended to convey their own interpretation of eroticism. Whether or not they're actually intended to be erotic is yet to be determined. Wong Kar-Wai's "The Hand" nails it. There's no nudity, no explicit sex, nothing to tell you what to feel. But it's poetic and stays with you. Steven Soderbergh's "Equilibrium" stars Robert Downey, Jr. as a patient explaining his sexually-obscure dream to psychiatrist Alan Arkin over and over and over. The doc doesn't listen much. Neither do we. Finally, director Michelangelo Antonioni closes the program with a real stinker. His Zabriskien roots place the characters in a land of causal nudity and dopey music. Trilogies need to get better with each installment, but this one rolls downhill the entire way. **104m/C; DVD.** *US FR IT LU* Gong Li; Chen "Chang Chen" Chang; Tin Fung; Zhou Jianjun; Robert Downey, Jr.; Alan Arkin; Ele Keats; Christopher Buchholz; Regina Nemni; Luisa Ranieri; ***D:*** Wong Kar-Wai; Steven Soderbergh; Michelangelo Antonioni; ***W:*** Wong Kar-Wai; Steven Soderbergh; Michelangelo Antonioni; ***C:*** Tonino Guerra; Christopher Doyle; Marco Pontecorvo; ***M:*** Peer Raben; Enrica Antonioni; Vinicio Milani; Chico O'Farrill.

Erotique 🦴🦴 **1994** Sex quartet from female filmmakers. "Let's Talk About Sex" finds struggling Latina actress Rosie (Lopez-Dawson) supporting herself by working at a phone sex agency where a caller (Cranston) wants to know about her sexual fantasies. "Taboo Parlor" finds lesbian lovers Claire (Barnes) and Julia (Soeberg) picking up boy toy Victor (Carr) and planning some s/m games. "Wonton Soup" has Australian-born Chinese Adrian (Lounibos) reuniting with his lover Ann (Man) in Hong Kong and deciding to hold her interest by practicing some ancient Chinese sexual techniques. And in "Final Call," a school teacher (Ohana) tries a sexual adventure with a stranger. **120m/C; VHS, DVD.** Kamala Lopez; Bryan Cranston; Priscilla Barnes; Camilla Soeberg; Michael Carr; Tim Lounibos; Hayley Man; Claudia Ohana; ***D:*** Lizzie Borden; Monika Treut; Clara Law; Ana Maria Magalhaes; ***W:*** Lizzie Borden; Monika Treut; Susie Bright; Eddie Ling-Ching Fong; ***C:*** Larry Banks; Elfi Mikesch; Arthur Wong Ngok Tai.

The Errand Boy 🦴🦴 1/2 **1961** Jerry Lewis' patented babbling schnook hits Hollywood in search of a job. When he lands a position as an errand boy, Hollywood may never be the same again in this prototypical comedy; a must for Lewis fans only. **92m/B; VHS, DVD.** Jerry Lewis; Brian Donlevy; Dick Wesson; Howard McNear; Felicia Atkins; Fritz Feld; Sig Rumann; Renee Taylor; Doodles Weaver; Mike Mazurki; Lorne Greene; Michael Landon; Dan Blocker; Pernell Roberts; Snub Pollard; Kathleen Freeman; ***D:*** Jerry Lewis; ***W:*** Jerry Lewis.

Escanaba in da Moonlight 🦴🦴 **2001 (PG-13)** If you're not a "Yooper" or familiar with those denizens of Michigan's Upper Penisula, Daniels's film (based on his play) will probably be lost on you. This is the kind of local humor that rarely travels well. The story is basically a tall tale—middleaged Reuben Soady (Daniels) has reached his advanced years without ever having bagged a deer on his annual hunting trip with his dad (Presnell) and brother (Albright). He is a community laughingstock but that is about to change. **90m/C; VHS, DVD.** Jeff Daniels; Harve Presnell; Joey Albright; Wayne David Parker; Randall Godwin; Kimberly Norris Guerrero; ***D:*** Jeff Daniels; ***W:*** Jeff Daniels; ***C:*** Richard Brawer.

Escape 🦴🦴 **1940** Early anti-Nazi pic that got banned in Germany by Hitler. American Mark Preysing (Taylor) travels to Germany to find his German-born mother Emmy (Nazimova), who returned to the fatherland to sell her estate. He's befriended by Countess Ruby von Treck (Shearer), the mistress of General Von Kolb (Veidt), who comes to Mark's aid when he discovers his mother is in dire straits. **104m/B; DVD.** Norma Shearer; Robert Montgomery; Conrad Veidt; Alla Nazimova; Felix Bressart; Albert Bassermann; Philip Dorn; Bonita Granville; ***D:*** Mervyn LeRoy; ***W:*** Marguerite Roberts; Arch Oboler; ***C:*** Robert Planck; ***M:*** Franz Waxman.

Escape 🦴🦴 **1990 (PG)** A fun-loving, care-free Irish officer is sent to oversee the toughest POW prison in Scotland. There, he becomes consumed with keeping the facility secure despite the intricate escape plans laid out by a group of rioters. **90m/C; VHS, DVD, Streaming.** Brian Keith; Helmut Griem; ***D:*** Lamont Johnson.

Escape 🦴 1/2 *Flukt* **2012** A young girl is taken hostage by a pack of killers when her family flees the horrors of the Black Plague by crossing a lonely mountain pass. She quickly escapes, but being alone in the wilderness with a pack of lunatics not far behind are not the best place for a young girl. **79m/C; DVD, Blu-Ray, Streaming.** *NO* Isabel Christine Andreasen; Ingrid Bolso Berdal; Kristian Espedal; Hallvard Holmen; Bjorn Moan; ***D:*** Roar Uthaug; ***W:*** Thomas Moldestad; ***C:*** John Christian Rosenlund; ***M:*** Magnus Beite. **VIDEO**

The Escape 🦴🦴 **2018** Tara (Arterton) is stuck in an unhappy marriage with a husband (Cooper) who is primarily concerned with his needs, sexual and otherwise. When the depressed Tara tells him about French medieval tapestries she saw in an art book, his dismissal of her interests prompts her to leave him and their two children for Paris to see them firsthand. Once there, she encounters a handsome man, which changes lonely Tara in unexpected ways. Former Bond Girl Arterton gives an intelligent performance in an underwhelming film. **101m/C; DVD.** Gemma Arterton; Dominic Cooper; Frances Barber; Marthe Keller; Jalil Lespert; ***D:*** Dominic Savage; ***W:*** Dominic Savage; ***C:*** Laurie Rose; ***M:*** Alexandra Harwood; Anthony John.

The Escape Artist 🦴🦴🦴 **1982 (PG)** Award-winning cinematographer Deschanel's first directorial effort is this quirky film about a teenage escape artist who sets out to uncover the identity of his father's killers. **96m/C; VHS, DVD.** Griffin O'Neal; Raul Julia; Teri Garr; Joan Hackett; Desi Arnaz, Sr.; Gabriel Dell; Huntz Hall; Jackie Coogan; Elizabeth Daily; ***D:*** Caleb Deschanel; ***W:*** Melissa Mathison; ***C:*** Stephen Burum; ***M:*** Georges Delerue.

The Escape Artist 🦴🦴🦴 **2013** Compelling BBC courtroom/crime drama. The title character is Will Burton (Tennant), an in-demand defense lawyer who specializes in getting off those who are probably guilty. But when Will's talents get psycho Liam Foyle (Kebbell), the prime suspect in a notorious murder, released, Will's own life takes a chilling turn and justice isn't going to prevail. Unless Will helps it along. **180m/C; DVD, Blu-Ray.** *UK* David Tennant; Toby Kebbell; Sophie Okonedo; Ashley Jensen; Anton Lesser; ***D:*** Brian Welsh; ***W:*** David Wolstencroft; ***C:*** David Higgs; ***M:*** Nicholas Hooper. **TV**

Escape Clause 🦴🦴 **1996 (R)** Insurance exec Richard Ramsay (McCarthy) gets a call from a hitman informing him that his wife Sarah (McNeil) has hired him to kill Richard. The hitman says if Richard will pay him, the contract's off. Instead Richard tries to figure out what's going on, with some help from police detective Ferrand (Sorvino), who discovers Richard has been treated for paranoid delusions. Fast-paced mystery with a few too many twists. **131m/C; VHS, Streaming.** Andrew McCarthy; Paul Sorvino; Kate McNeil; Peter Donaldson; Kenneth Welsh; Connie Britton; Stan(ford) Egi; John Evans; ***D:*** Brian Trenchard-Smith; ***W:*** Danilo Bach; ***M:*** Ken Thorne; Richard (Rick) Marvin. **VIDEO**

Escape from Alcatraz 🦴🦴🦴 **1979 (PG)** A fascinating account of the one and only successful escape from the maximum security prison at Alcatraz in 1962. The three men were never heard from again. **112m/C; VHS, DVD, Blu-Ray.** Clint Eastwood; Patrick McGoohan; Roberts Blossom; Fred Ward; Jack Thibeau; Paul Benjamin; Larry Hankin; Carl Lumbly; Danny Glover; ***D:*** Donald Siegel; ***W:*** Richard Tuggle; ***C:*** Bruce Surtees; ***M:*** Jerry Fielding.

Escape from Death Row 🦴 *Dio, Sei Proprio un Padrenterno!* **1973 (R)** Convicted criminal mastermind, sentenced to die, devises a brilliant and daring plan of escape on the eve of his execution. **85m/C; VHS, DVD.** *IT* Lee Van Cleef; Jean Rochefort; Tony LoBianco; Edwige Fenech; Fausto Tozzi; Mario Erpichini; Jess Hahn; ***D:*** Michele Lupo; ***W:*** Nicola Badalucco; Sergio Donati; Luciano Vincenzoni; ***C:*** Joe D'Amato; Aldo Tonti; ***M:*** Riz Ortolani.

Escape from Fort Bravo 🦴🦴 1/2 **1953** A Civil War era western set in an Arizona stockade. Holden is the hard-bitten Union cavalry officer who ruthlessly guards his Confederate prisoners, who are led by Forsythe. Parker is a southern spy whose job is to break the rebels out of jail by seducing Holden from his duty, which she does. When Holden discovers what's happened, he recaptures his prisoners only to be beset by hostile Mescalero Indians while trying to get everyone back to the fort. It's an old story but well-executed with lots of action. **98m/C; VHS, DVD.** William Holden; Eleanor Parker; John Forsythe; William Demarest; William Campbell; Polly Bergen; Richard Anderson; Carl Benton Reid; John Lupton; Howard McNear; Alex Montoya; Forrest Lewis; Fred Graham; William "Billy" Newell; ***D:*** John Sturges; ***W:*** Frank Fenton; ***C:*** Robert L. Surtees.

Escape from Hell **WOOF!** *Hellfire on Ice, Part 2: Escape from Hell; Femmine Infernali* **1979** Two scantily clad women escape from a jungle prison and are pursued by their sadistic warden. **93m/C; VHS, DVD.** *IT SP* Anthony Steffen; Ajita Wilson; ***D:*** Edward (Edoardo Mulargia) Muller.

Escape from L.A. 🦴🦴 1/2 *John Carpenter's Escape from L.A.* **1996 (R)** Well, Snake Plissken is back (Russell once again) and so's Carpenter, who did the original "Escape from New York" saga, and technology's advanced a lot in 15 years, so sit back and enjoy the action. In 2013, L.A.'s been turned into a gang-infested island, thanks to a 9.6 earthquake, where Snake is forced to find a doomsday weapon in just 10 hours. Seems he's been injected with a virus that will kill him unless he can complete his job and escape to get the antidote. Naturally, there's lots of bad guys who'll try to stop him. Russell not only reprises his old role but found Snake's original leathers, which still fit, and wore the outfit in some scenes of the sequel. **101m/C; VHS, DVD, Blu-Ray.** Kurt Russell; Georges Corraface; Stacy Keach; Peter Fonda; Steve Buscemi; Pam Grier; Valeria Golino; Cliff Robertson; Michelle Forbes; Bruce Campbell; A.J. (Allison Joy) Langer; ***D:*** John Carpenter; ***W:*** Kurt Russell; John Carpenter; Debra Hill; ***C:*** Gary B. Kibbe; ***M:*** John Carpenter; Shirley Walker.

Escape from New York 🦴🦴 1/2 **1981 (R)** The ultimate urban nightmare: a ruined, future Manhattan is an anarchic prison for America's worst felons. When convicts hold the President hostage, a disgraced war hero unwillingly attempts an impossible rescue mission. Cynical but largely unexceptional sci-fi action, putting a good cast through tight-lipped peril. **99m/C; VHS, DVD, Blu-Ray, UMD.** Kurt Russell; Lee Van Cleef; Ernest Borgnine; Donald Pleasence; Isaac Hayes; Adrienne Barbeau; Harry Dean Stanton; Season Hubley; Tom Atkins; Charles Cyphers; George "Buck" Flower; ***V:*** Jamie Lee Curtis; ***D:*** John Carpenter; ***W:*** John Carpenter; Nick Castle; ***C:*** Dean Cundey; ***M:*** John Carpenter.

Escape from Planet Earth 🦴 *The Doomsday Machine* **1967** A spaceship is damaged deep in space and only a few of the crew can make it back to Earth. But who will decide who lives or dies? (Unfortunately, the Earth has been totally destroyed so who cares anyway.) Lousy special effects. **91m/B; VHS, DVD.** Grant Williams; Bobby Van; Ruta Lee; Henry Wilcoxon; Mala Powers; Casey Kasem; Mike Farrell; Harry Hope; ***D:*** Lee Sholem.

Escape From Planet Earth 🦴 **2013 (PG)** A star-studded voice ensemble can't save this loud, annoying 3D animated flick. Astronaut Scorch Supernova (Fraser) answers the SOS from a notoriously dangerous planet and falls right into the trap of the evil Shanker (Shatner). This leaves Scorch's pint-sized brother Gary (Corddry) to save his brother and the fate of the universe. Less entertaining or visually interesting than most Nick Jr. shows, this might work for the youngest viewers but their older siblings will know they've seen it before and done better. **89m/C; DVD, Blu-Ray.** ***V:*** Brendan Fraser; Rob Corddry; Sarah Jessica Parker; Jessica Alba; Jane Lynch; Ricky Gervais; Jonathan Morgan Heit; Sofia Vergara; William Shatner; ***D:*** Callan Brunker; ***W:*** Callan Brunker; Bob Barlen; ***C:*** Matthew A. Ward; ***M:*** Aaron Zigman.

Escape from Pretoria 🦴🦴 1/2 **2020 (PG-13)** This jailbreak flick tells the true story of Tim Jenkin and Stephen Lee, two white South African men imprisoned in 1978 by the African National Congress for their "terrorist" opposition to apartheid. Based on the book by Jenkin himself, it's a race-against-time thriller as the prisoners craft wooden keys to unlock the 10 steel doors imprisoning them. A shaggy-bearded Radcliffe solidly conveys his character's white-knuckled desperation and determination. **106m/C; DVD, Blu-Ray.** Daniel Radcliffe; Daniel Webber; Ian Hart; Mark Leonard Winter; Nathan Page; ***D:*** Francis Annan; ***W:*** Francis Annan; L.H. Adams; ***C:*** Geoffrey Hall; ***M:*** David Hirschfelder.

Escape from Sobibor 🦴🦴🦴 **1987 (PG-13)** Nail-biting, true account of the largest successful escape from a Nazi prison camp, adapted from Richard Rashke's book. Made for TV. **120m/C; VHS, DVD.** Alan Arkin; Joanna Pacula; Rutger Hauer; Hartmut Becker; Jack Shepherd; ***D:*** Jack Gold; ***M:*** Georges Delerue. **TV**

Escape from the Planet of the Apes 🦴🦴🦴 **1971 (G)** Reprising their roles as intelligent, English-speaking apes, McDowall and Hunter flee their world before it's destroyed, and travel back in time to present-day America. In L.A. they become the subjects of a relentless search by the fearful population, much like humans Charlton Heston and James Franciscus were targeted for experimentation and destruction in simian society in the earlier "Planet of the Apes" and "Beneath the Planet of the Apes." Sequelled by "Conquest of..." and a TV series. **98m/C; VHS, DVD, Blu-Ray.** Roddy McDowall; Kim Hunter; Sal Mineo; Ricardo Montalban; William Windom; Bradford Dillman; Natalie Trundy; Eric Braeden; Jason Evers; Harry Lauter; John Randolph; M. Emmet Walsh; ***D:*** Don Taylor; ***W:*** Paul Dehn; ***C:*** Joseph Biroc; ***M:*** Jerry Goldsmith.

Escape From Tomorrow 🦴 1/2 **2013** Surreal fantasy horror from debuting writer/director Moore was secretly filmed at Florida's Disney World. Schlub dad Jim doesn't tell his wife and kids that he's suddenly been fired so it won't ruin the last day of their vacation at the Magic Kingdom. Maybe it's preying on his mind anyway since Jim begins experiencing disturbing (sometimes disgusting) situations amidst his own increasingly creepy behavior. Although the Mouse House is usually very protective (i.e. litigious) of their brand, maybe they figured this B&W indie parody was too cult to bother about. **91m/B; Blu-Ray, On Demand.** Roy Abramsohn; Elena Schuber; Katelynn Rodriguez; Jack Dalton; Danielle Safady; Annet Mahendru; ***D:*** Randy Moore; ***W:*** Randy Moore; ***C:*** Lucas Lee Graham; ***M:*** Abel Koreniowski.

Escape from Wildcat Canyon 🦴 1/2 **1999** Grandfather Weaver and his young grandson must fight for survival after their small plane crashes in the mountains. **96m/C; VHS, DVD.** Dennis Weaver; Michael Caloz; Peter Keleghan; Frank Schorpion; Vlasta Vrana; ***D:*** Marc Voizard. **CABLE**

Escape From Zahrain 🦴 1/2 **1962** Typical action-adventure pic set in a fictional Middle East country. Rebel leader Sharif is fighting government corruption when his cohorts spring him from police custody. They steal an ambulance and take off across the desert to escape the soldiers bent on capturing them. **92m/C; DVD, Blu-Ray.** Yul Brynner; Sal Mineo; Jack Warden; Madlyn Rhue; Anthony Caruso; Jay Novello; James Mason; ***D:*** Ronald Neame; ***W:*** Robin Estridge; ***C:*** Ellsworth Fredericks; ***M:*** Lyn Murray.

Escape: Human Cargo 🦴🦴🦴 *Human Cargo* **1998** Suspenseful and fact-based drama set in 1977. Texan John McDonald (Williams) thinks he's scored big when he gets a contract to build housing in Dhahran, Saudi Arabia. Despite government warnings, McDonald decides to travel there himself to oversee the deal. But his partners prove deceitful and when McDonald tries to enforce the contract, he's the one that winds up in prison. He's eventually released, but with his passport confiscated, the only way for McDonald to get out of the Middle East is to try smuggling himself home as cargo. Based on the book "Flight from Dhahran" by John McDonald and Clyde Burleson. **110m/C; VHS, DVD.** Treat Williams; Stephen Lang; Sasson Gabai; ***D:*** Simon Wincer; ***W:*** William Mickelberry; Dan Vining; ***C:*** David Burr; ***M:*** Eric Colvin. **CABLE**

Escape Me Never 🦴 1/2 **1947** Flynn plays a struggling composer in this sappy period piece about poverty-stricken artists in Italy at the turn of the century. Flynn falls for his brother's wealthy fiancee (Parker), although he is married to the faithful Lupino. Atypical role for Flynn and definitely not one of his best. Based on the novel "The Fool of the Family," by Margaret Kennedy and the play "Escape Me Never" by Kennedy. **101m/B; DVD.** Errol Flynn; Ida Lupino; Eleanor Parker; Gig Young; Reginald Denny; Isobel Elsom; ***D:*** Peter Godfrey; ***W:*** Thames (Thomas) Williamson; ***C:*** Sol Polito; ***M:*** Erich Wolfgang Korngold.

Escape Plan 🦴🦴 **2013 (R)** Ray Breslin (Stallone) is a structural engineer who makes a living teaching prison wardens about the weaknesses in their own design. He can get out of high-security buildings designed to keep people in. Well, not all of them. When Ray is drugged, kidnapped, and thrown in the most high-level, secret prison in the world, he'll need the help of a fellow inmate (Schwarzenegger) to break out of the death trap. This action flick is designed as a throwback to films made far more often in the '80s (with these two stars) and sometimes works as a nostalgic kick but not often enough. **115m/C; DVD, Blu-Ray.** Sylvester Stallone; Arnold Schwarzenegger; Jim Caviezel; Amy Ryan; Sam Neill; Vincent D'Onofrio; Vinnie Jones; ***D:*** Mikael Hafstrom; ***W:*** Miles Chapman; Jason Keller; ***C:*** Brendan Galvin; ***M:*** Alex Heffes.

Escape Plan 2: Hades 🦴 *Escape Plan II* **2018 (R)** The sequel to the 2013 action film Escape Plan. Security expert Ray Benson (Stallone) advises prisons on how to prevent inmates from escaping. He draws on these skills when Shu (Xiaoming), a member of his team, and Shu's cousin Yusheng (Tang) are kidnapped and tossed into a high security facility. The warden, The Zookeeper (Welliver), wants the patent for Yusheng's new satellite system. To rescue the men, Ray brings together his team, including Hush (Jackson), Luke (Metcalfe), Abigail (King), and Trent (Bautista). Falls short of the first installment, lacking its wit and humor as well as quality of action sequences and visual style. **96m/C; DVD, Blu-Ray, Streaming.** *CH US* Sylvester Stallone; Dave Bautista; Xiaoming Wang; Jaime King; Jesse Metcalfe; ***D:*** Steven C. Miller; Vincent Tabaillon; ***W:*** Miles Chapman; ***M:*** Brandon Cox; The Newton Brothers. **VIDEO**

Escape Room 🦴🦴 **2019 (PG-13)** After receiving a mysterious invitation, six strangers take part in an escape room to win a $10,000 prize. Each person has their own secret or struggle, including shy yet gifted math student Zoey (Russell) and Iraq war vet Amanda (Woll). Gathering in a deserted office building, the deadly nature of the game reveals itself when a waiting room turns into a place where the players can be burned alive. Each room in the interconnected puzzle has a unique way for the players to struggle to survive. Obviously influenced by the Saw films, this film has memorable moments but its characters and plot are unremarkable. **100m/C; DVD, Blu-Ray.** *US SA* Taylor Russell; Logan Miller; Jay Ellis; Tyler Labine; Deborah Ann Woll; ***D:*** Adam Robitel; ***W:*** Bragi F. Schut; Maria Melnik; ***C:*** Marc Spicer; ***M:*** John Carey.

Escape to Athena 🦴🦴 1/2 **1979 (PG)** A motley group is stuck in a German P.O.W. camp on a Greek island during WWII. **102m/C; DVD, Streaming.** *UK* Roger Moore; Telly Savalas; David Niven; Claudia Cardinale; Richard Roundtree; Stefanie Powers; Sonny Bono; Elliott Gould; William Holden; ***D:*** George P. Cosmatos; ***W:*** Edward Anhalt; ***C:*** Gilbert Taylor; ***M:*** Lalo Schifrin.

Escape to Burma 🦴 1/2 **1955** A man on the run for a murder he did not commit finds refuge and romance in an isolated jungle home. **86m/C; VHS, DVD.** Barbara Stanwyck; Robert Ryan; Reginald Denny; ***D:*** Allan Dwan.

Escape to Witch Mountain 🦴🦴🦴 **1975 (G)** Two young orphans with supernatural powers find themselves on the run from a greedy millionaire who wants to exploit their amazing gift. Adapted from a novel by Alexander Key. **97m/C; VHS, DVD.** Kim Richards; Ike Eisenmann; Eddie Albert; Ray Milland; Donald Pleasence; Tony Giorgio; Walter Barnes; Denver Pyle; Reta Shaw; ***D:*** John Hough.

Escape 2000 **WOOF!** *Turkey Shoot* **1981 (R)** In a future society where individuality is considered a crime, those who refuse to conform are punished by being hunted down in a jungle. Gross, twisted takeoff of Richard Connell's "The Most Dangerous Game." **80m/C; VHS, DVD.** *AU* Steve Railsback; Olivia Hussey; Michael Craig; ***D:*** Brian Trenchard-Smith; ***W:*** George Schenck; ***M:*** Brian May.

Escape under Pressure 🦴🦴 1/2 *The Cruel Deep; Under Pressure* **2000 (R)** Cheapie version of "Die Hard" holds interest thanks to lots of action. Engineer John Spencer (Lowe) and wife Chloe (Miller) are aboard a Greek ferry that get hijacked by lowlifes who are after a priceless ancient statue of Artemis. They manage to protect the statue but have to save themselves as well from the killers. **90m/C; VHS, DVD.** Rob Lowe; Larisa Miller; Craig Wasson; Harry Van Gorkum; Stanley Kamel; ***D:*** Jean Pellerin; ***W:*** James Christopher; ***C:*** Richard Clabaugh. **CABLE**

Escape Velocity 🦴🦴 **1999 (R)** Scientists Cal (Bergin), Billie (Crewson) and their daughter Ronnie (Beaudoin) are on a deep space project when they discover a seemingly abandoned space ship. They find one crewman, Nash (Outerbridge), in suspended animation and make the mistake of bringing him out of his deep sleep. Of course, he turns out to be a psychotic. **100m/C; VHS, DVD.** Patrick Bergin; Wendy Crewson; Peter Outerbridge; Michelle Beaudoin; ***D:*** Lloyd A. Simandl; ***M:*** Peter Allen. **VIDEO**

The Escapist 🦴🦴 **2008** Frank Perry is a lifer in a London prison who receives word that his only daughter is critically ill after an overdose. He decides to escape and enlists the help of some younger inmates in his plan. Then Frank gets distracted by the arrival of his new cellmate James Lacey, who draws the unwelcome attention of sadistic drug addict Tony, whose inmate brother Rizza runs the prison, and Frank's plans are put into jeopardy. **102m/C; DVD.** *GB IR* Brian Cox; Dominic Cooper; Steven Mackintosh; Damian Lewis; Joseph Fiennes; Liam Cunningham; Seu Jorge; ***D:*** Rupert Wyatt; ***W:*** Rupert Wyatt; Daniel Hardy; ***C:*** Philipp Blaubach; ***M:*** Benjamin Wallfisch.

Escobar: Paradise Lost 🦴🦴 *Paradise Lost; Escobar: Paraiso Perdido* **2015 (R)** Andrea di Stefano's debut thriller is a confidently made film that's also surprisingly disappointing due to its bizarre choice of focus. Benicio Del Toro as the legendary drug kingpin Pablo Escobar should be a slam dunk but di Stefano turns him Escobar into a supporting character, telling his story from the perspective of a naïve Canadian transplant (Hutcherson), who happens to fall in love with Pablo's niece. Del Toro is riveting in the few scenes he's in, but he casts such a long shadow over the rest of the film that you'll feel the loss when he's not on screen. **120m/C; DVD, Blu-Ray, Streaming.** *BE FR PM SP* Benicio Del Toro; Josh Hutcherson; Claudia Traisac; Brady Corbet; Carlos Bardem; Ana Girardot; ***D:*** Andrea Di Stefano; ***W:*** Andrea Di Stefano; Francesca Marciano; ***C:*** Luis David Sansans; ***M:*** Max Richter.

ESL: English as a Second Language 🦴🦴 1/2 **2005 (R)** Bad title, good movie. Bolivar (Becker) is an illegal Mexican immigrant who comes to L.A. looking for work and winds up with a job as a stripper because the money is good and he has a pregnant wife back home. Bolivar's struggles are contrasted with those of privileged party girl Lola (Camastra), who has to do community service after a DUI conviction. She signs up to teach an ESL class where Bolivar is a student and, for all their differences in wealth and class, they have similar problems with identity, responsibility, and what makes the American Dream. English and Spanish with subtitles. **105m/C; DVD.** Kuno Becker; Danielle Camastra; Maria Conchita Alonso; John Michael Higgins; Sal Lopez; Efrain Figueroa; Harold Gould; Treva Etienne; ***D:*** Youssef Delara; ***W:*** Youssef Delara; ***C:*** Ben Kufrin; ***M:*** Gary Chang.

Esmeralda Comes by Night 🦴🦴 1/2 *De Noche Vienes, Esmeralda* **1998 (R)** Fluff Mexican comedy about a very nuturing nurse named Esmeralda (Rojo) who just loves men so much that she's married to five of them—at the same time. When she decides to take a sixth spouse, that's one man too many for one of her jealous hubbies and he formally accuses her of polyandry. She gets arrested and must explain herself to a grim inspector (Obregon), who will naturally fall under her considerable spell. Based on a story by Elena Poniatowska. Spanish with subtitles. **107m/C; VHS, DVD.** *MX* Maria Rojo; Claudio Obregon; Roberto Cobo; Ernesto Laguardia; Humberto Pineda; Pedro Armendariz, Jr.; Alberto Estrella; ***D:*** Jaime Humberto Hermosillo; ***W:*** Jaime Humberto Hermosillo; ***C:*** Xavier Perez Grobet; ***M:*** Omar Guzman.

Espionage in Tangiers 🦴 1/2 *Marc Mato, Agent S.077* **1965** Bond rip-off with Davila as super-spy Mike Murphy, who's assigned to find a ray gun stolen from a lab. From there it's all gadgets, cars, villains, and babes (who get slapped around when they don't cooperate). Attractive settings in Nice and Tangiers; dubbed. Available as a Drive-In Double Feature with "Assassination in Rome." **92m/C; DVD.** *IT SP* Luis Davila; Perla Cristal; Jose Greci; Ana Castor; Alfonso Rojas; ***D:*** Gregg Tallas; ***W:*** Gregg Tallas; ***C:*** Alvaro Mancori.

Essex Boys 🦴🦴 **1999 (R)** British gangster movie inspired by the true-crime 1995 murders of three criminals. Ambitious young Billy (Creed-Miles) is hired to chauffeur violent Jason Locke (Bean), who's just out of prison. Jason partnered with John Dyke (Wilkinson) in the drug trade but times have changed and double-crosses are the new name of the game. Billy gets sucked in and betrayed, but beware, because the female (Kingston) does turn out to be deadlier than the male. **102m/C; VHS, DVD.** *GB* Charlie Creed-Miles; Sean Bean; Tom Wilkinson; Alex Kingston; Larry Lamb; Terence Rigby; Billy Murray; Amelia Lowdell; ***D:*** Terry Winsor; ***W:*** Terry Winsor; Jeff Pope; ***C:*** John Daly; ***M:*** Colin Towns.

Estate of Insanity 🦴 *The Black Torrent* **1964** An English lord and his second wife become involved in a web of death when a maniac stalks their ancient estate. **90m/C; VHS, DVD.** *GB* John Turner; Heather Sears; Ann Lynn; ***D:*** Robert Hartford-Davis; ***W:*** Derek Ford; Donald Ford; ***C:*** Peter Newbrook; ***M:*** Robert Richards.

Esther 🦴🦴 1/2 **1998** Biblical story of a young Jewish girl named Esther who is sought as the bride of Ahasuerus, the King of Persia. She persuades him to stop the slaughter of her people. **91m/C; VHS, DVD.** Louise Lombard; Thomas Kretschmann; F. Murray Abraham; Jurgen Prochnow; Ornella Muti; ***D:*** Raffaele Mertes. **CABLE**

Esther and the King 🦴 1/2 **1960** Biblical costumer with Egan as Persian king and Collins as the Judean maiden he wants in place of the murdered queen. Long, rambling, and torturous. **109m/C; DVD.** *IT* Joan Collins; Richard Egan; Denis O'Dea; Sergio Fantoni; ***D:*** Raoul Walsh; ***W:*** Raoul Walsh; Michael Elkins; ***C:*** Mario Bava; ***M:*** Angelo Francesco Lavagnino.

Esther Kahn 🦴🦴 **2000 (PG)** Esther (Phoenix) is growing up in the poor East End of London at the end of the 19th century—the daughter of a Jewish tailor. When Esther attends a Yiddish stage play, she decides that she must become an actress and approaches a local theatre for work. She is later taken under the wing of older actor Nathan (Holm), who advises her to take a lover for emotional experience. Esther gets involved with drama critic, Philip Haygard (Desplechin), is betrayed, but achieves a more-desired stage triumph. Adapted from a short story by Arthur Symons. **145m/C; VHS, DVD.** *FR GB* Summer Phoenix; Ian Holm; Emmanuelle Devos; Fabrice Desplechin; Frances Barber; Laszlo Szabo; ***D:*** Arnaud Desplechin; ***W:*** Arnaud Desplechin; Emmanuel Bourdieu; ***C:*** Eric Gautier; ***M:*** Howard Shore.

Esther Waters 🦴 1/2 *Sin of Esther Waters* **1948** Bleak late-Victorian era drama with a dreary ending. Esther goes into service as a maid for a wealthy family and is promptly seduced by caddish footman William Latch. Pregnant and forced into a workhouse, Esther makes her way to London and a series of menial jobs to support herself and her baby. Several years later, William has made a successful career as a racetrack bookie and finds Esther to make an honest woman of her, but troubles follow. **108m/B; DVD.** *UK* Kathleen Ryan; Dirk Bogarde; Cyril Cusack; Fay Compton; Ivor Barnard; ***D:*** Ian Dalrymple; Peter Proud; ***W:*** William Rose; ***C:*** C.M. Pennington-Richards; ***M:*** Gordon Jacob.

E.T.: The Extra-Terrestrial 🦴🦴🦴🦴 **1982 (PG)** Spielberg's famous fantasy, one of the most popular films in history, portrays a limpid-eyed alien stranded on earth and his special bonding relationship with a young boy. A modern fairy tale providing warmth, humor and sheer wonder. Held the first place spot as the highest grossing movie of all time for years until a new Spielberg hit replaced it?"Jurassic Park." Debra Winger contributed to the voice of E.T. **115m/C; VHS, DVD, Blu-Ray.** Henry Thomas; Dee Wallace; Drew Barrymore; Robert MacNaughton; Peter Coyote; C. Thomas Howell; Sean Frye; K.C. Martel; Erika Eleniak; ***V:*** Debra Winger; ***D:*** Steven Spielberg; ***W:*** Melissa Mathison; ***C:*** Allen Daviau; ***M:*** John Williams. Oscars '82: Orig. Score, Visual FX; AFI '98: Top 100; Golden Globes '83: Film--Drama, Score; L.A. Film Critics '82: Director (Spielberg), Film; Natl. Film Reg. '94; Natl. Soc. Film Critics '82: Director (Spielberg); Writers Guild '82: Orig. Screenplay.

The Eternal 🦴🦴 *The Eternal Kiss of the Mummy* **1999 (R)** Nora (Elliott) plays a young wife and mother who's tormented by blinding headaches and dizziness. Along with her husband and young son, she decides to return to her childhood home in Ireland to visit her ailing grandmother. But her symptoms worsen the closer she gets to her ancestral home, and Elliott discovers that her creepy uncle (Walken) has retrieved the body of a witch who died hundreds of years before. Only she's not quite dead. **95m/C; VHS, DVD.** Alison Elliott; Jared Harris; Christopher Walken; Lois Smith; Karl Geary; ***D:*** Michael Almereyda; ***W:*** Michael Almereyda; ***C:*** Jim Denault; ***M:*** Simon Fisher Turner.

Eternal 🦴 **2004 (R)** Remarkably dull erotic vampire thriller (which only hints at kink). Detective Raymond Pope (Pla) is searching for his missing wife, which leads him to the Montreal estate of wealthy Elizabeth Kane (Neron) and her maid, Irina (Sanchez). Seems Elizabeth is actually 16th-century Countess Elizabeth Bathory, who kills and then bathes in the blood of young women to maintain her own beauty and immortality. Eventually, the obsessed Pope follows Elizabeth to a masked ball in Venice in order to stop the bloodletting. **107m/C; DVD.** *CA* Conrad Pla; Caroline Neron; Victoria Sanchez; Liane Balaban; Sarah Manninen; Ilona Elkin; Nick Baillie; ***D:*** Wilhelm Liebenberg; Frederico Sanchez; ***W:*** Wilhelm Liebenberg; Frederico Sanchez; ***C:*** Jamie Thompson.

Eternal Evil 🦴 **1987 (R)** A bored TV director is taught how to have out-of-body experiences by his devil-worshipping girlfriend. He eventually realizes that when he leaves his body, it runs around killing people.

85m/C; VHS, DVD. Karen Black; Winston Rekert; Lois Maxwell; ***D:*** George Mihalka; ***W:*** Robert Geoffrion; ***C:*** Paul Van der Linden.

Eternal Sunshine of the Spotless Mind 1/2 **2004 (R)** Unhappy couple uses latest technology to vacuum their minds clean of all memories of each other in this black comedy. Carrey plays it mostly straight as Joel, a lovesick sap who undergoes the memory-erasing procedure when he finds out his strident girlfriend Clementine (Winslet) had similar treatment to wipe him out of her trendy blue-streaked head. Joel begins to have second thoughts, however. Clever story penned by Kaufman in his second venture with director Gondry. Leads earn their stellar salaries here, along with excellent supports, including Wood, Ruffalo, Wilkinson, and Dunst. **108m/C; DVD, Blu-Ray, HD-DVD.** Jim Carrey; Kate Winslet; Elijah Wood; Mark Ruffalo; Thomas Jay Ryan; Jane Adams; David Cross; Kirsten Dunst; Tom Wilkinson; Ellen Pompeo; Paulie (Litowsky) Litt; ***D:*** Michel Gondry; ***W:*** Michel Gondry; Charlie Kaufman; ***C:*** Ellen Kuras; ***M:*** Jon Brion. Oscars '04: Orig. Screenplay; British Acad. '04: Film Editing, Orig. Screenplay; Writers Guild '04: Orig. Screenplay.

Eternally Yours 1/2 **1939** A witty magician's career threatens to break up his marriage. **95m/B; VHS, DVD.** David Niven; Loretta Young; Hugh Herbert; Broderick Crawford; Sir C. Aubrey Smith; Billie Burke; Eve Arden; Zasu Pitts; ***D:*** Tay Garnett.

Eternity and a Day *Mia Eoniotita Ke Mia Mera* **1997** Seriously ill writer Alexander (Ganz) is putting his affairs in order and revisiting his past, particularly moments with his beloved late wife, Anna (Renauld). But the present isn't finished with Alexander yet. He rescues a young boy (Skevis), an illegal immigrant from Albania, who says he was taken from his grandmother. Alexander decides to take the boy home and the two set out on the journey that will surely be Alexander's last. Greek with subtitles. **134m/C; VHS, DVD.** *GR FR* Bruno Ganz; Isabelle Renauld; Achileas Skevis; Fabrizio Bentivoglio; ***D:*** Theo Angelopoulos; ***W:*** Theo Angelopoulos; ***C:*** Yorgos Arvanitis; Andreas Sinanos; ***M:*** Eleni Karaindrou. Cannes '98: Film.

Ethan Frome 1/2 **1992 (PG)** Neeson stars as the lonely, poverty-stricken 19th-century New England farmer who has long and faithfully cared for his bitter, invalid wife. When his wife's distant young cousin comes to take over as housekeeper they both succumb to their forbidden passion with tragic results. The performers carry the burden of the film's sluggish pacing, where the bleak setting of Massachusetts in winter tends to overwhelm the events. Based on the novel by Edith Wharton. **107m/C; VHS, DVD, Blu-Ray.** Liam Neeson; Patricia Arquette; Joan Allen; Tate Donovan; Katharine Houghton; Stephen Mendillo; ***D:*** John Madden; ***W:*** Richard Nelson; ***C:*** Bobby Bukowski.

The Etruscan Smile 1/2 *Rory's Way* **2019 (R)** Rory MacNeil (Cox), an ornery and terminally ill Scotsman, seeks medical treatment in San Francisco. Living with his estranged son (Feild), Rory falls in love with his infant grandson, and is determined to change his ways to become a better grandfather than he was a father. The actors, especially the veteran pro Cox, are all pulling their weight, but the screenplay offers few surprises in this fish-out-of-water heartstring tugger. Based on the novel by Jose Luis Sampedro. **107m/C; DVD.** Brian Cox; Rosanna Arquette; J.J. Feild; Thora Birch; Peter Coyote; ***D:*** Oded Binnun; Mihal Brezis; ***W:*** Michael McGowan; Michal Lali Kagan; Sarah Bellwood; ***C:*** Javier Aguirresarobe; ***M:*** Haim Frank Ilfman.

Eulogy 1/2 **2004 (R)** Unworkable ensemble black comedy that wastes its good cast. The dysfunctional Collins family is forced back together to bury their toxic family patriarch (Torn). Accommodating granddaughter Kate (Deschanel) is expected to deliver the eulogy but neither her brooding father (Azaria) nor his crude brother (Romano) or their neurotic sisters (Winger, Preston) have anything good to say. No wonder all the bickering is driving Grandma Charlotte (Laurie) to multiple suicide attempts. And yes, the contrivances extend to a not-unexpected surprise at the reading of the will. **91m/C; VHS, DVD.** Hank Azaria; Jesse Bradford; Zooey Deschanel; Glenne Headly; Famke Janssen; Piper Laurie; Kelly Preston; Ray Romano; Rip Torn; Debra Winger; Curtis Garcia; Keith Garcia; Rene Auberjonois; ***D:*** Michael Clancy; ***W:*** Michael Clancy; ***C:*** Michael Chapman; ***M:*** Richard (Rick) Marvin.

Euphoria **2019 (R)** When Emilie (Green) reaches the late stages of cancer, she meets up with her artist sister Ines (Vikander) for the first time in many years. Unbeknownst to Ines, the pair are traveling to a peaceful estate in the beautiful countryside where clients chose to spend their final days before their deaths. As the pair spend time together, they discuss their problems and their past, including trauma involving their mother and their strained relationship with each other, as well as Emilie's inevitable demise. The meaningful themes and impressive actresses can't overcome an otherwise poor effort. **98m/C; DVD.** Alicia Vikander; Eva Green; Charles Dance; Charlotte Rampling; Adrian Lester; ***D:*** Lisa Langseth; ***W:*** Lisa Langseth; ***C:*** Rob Hardy; ***M:*** Lisa Holmqvist.

Eureka! 1/2 **1981 (R)** A bizarre, wildly symbolic slab of Roegian artifice that deals with the dream-spliced life of a rich, bored gold tycoon who becomes tortured over his daughter's marriage and his own useless wealth. Eventually he is bothered by the Mafia and led to the courtroom by business competitors. From the book by Paul Mayersberg. **130m/C; VHS, DVD, Blu-Ray.** *GB* Gene Hackman; Theresa Russell; Joe Pesci; Rutger Hauer; Mickey Rourke; Ed Lauter; Jane Lapotaire; ***D:*** Nicolas Roeg.

Europa, Europa 1/2 *Hitlerjunge Salomon* **1991 (R)** The incredible, harrowing and borderline-absurdist true story of Solomon Perel, a young Jew who escaped the Holocaust by passing for German at an elite, Nazi-run academy. Such a sharp evocation of the era that the modern German establishment wouldn't submit it for the Academy Awards. In German and Russian with English subtitles. **115m/C; VHS, DVD, Blu-Ray.** *GE* Marco Hofschneider; Klaus Abramowsky; Michele Gleizer; Rene Hofschneider; Nathalie Schmidt; Delphine Forest; Julie Delpy; ***D:*** Agnieszka Holland; ***W:*** Agnieszka Holland; ***C:*** Jacek Petrycki; Jacek Zaleski; ***M:*** Zbigniew Preisner. Golden Globes '92: Foreign Film; Natl. Bd. of Review '91: Foreign Film; N.Y. Film Critics '91: Foreign Film.

Europa Report **2013 (PG-13)** Due to the discovery of potential ice on Europa, there is reason to suspect there may be life of some kind on Jupiter's moon. Director Cordero and writer Gelatt imagine what a manned mission there might discover along the way, staging the piece as a found-footage film, incorporating footage from the cameras on the fictional Europa with a faux documentary being made about the fantastic voyage. The low-budget sci-fi film focuses on two things often lost in the wave of CGI special effects--the human characters and actual science (they consulted with NASA). **90m/C; DVD, Blu-Ray.** Sharlto Copley; Christian Camargo; Anamaria Marinca; Michael Nyqvist; Daniel Wu; Embeth Davidtz; Karolina Wydra; Isiah Whitlock, Jr.; Dan Fogler; ***D:*** Sebastian Cordero; ***W:*** Philip Gelatt; ***C:*** Enrique Chediak; ***M:*** Bear McCreary.

The Europeans **1979** Fine adaptation of Henry James's satiric novel. British brother and sister visit their staid American cousins in 19th-century New England in an effort to improve their prospects through fortuitous marriages. **90m/C; VHS, DVD, Blu-Ray.** Lee Remick; Lisa Eichhorn; Robin Ellis; Wesley Addy; Tim Woodward; ***D:*** James Ivory; ***W:*** Ruth Prawer Jhabvala.

Eurotrip **2004 (R)** Straight-arrow Scotty, freshly dumped by his girlfriend, realizes his German pen-pal is not a man coming on to him over the internet but an insanely hot girl. What's a boy to do? Why, jet off to Europe with three friends to meet her, of course! Scott and Cooper (Pitts) get cheap tickets to England and plan to meet up with twins Jamie (Wester) and Jenny (Trachtenberg). At that point, the plot goes out the window as the movie descends into an endless string of insulting, laugh-free jokes about mimes, soccer hooligans, hookers, gay train passengers, and the Vatican. Recommended if you think bottom-of-the-barrel gags based on European stereotypes make a movie. Everyone else should avoid this Trip. **89m/C; DVD, Blu-Ray.** Scott Mechlowicz; Jacob Pitts; Michelle Trachtenberg; Travis Wester; Jessica Boehrs; Fred Armisen; Lucy Lawless; Vinnie Jones; Kristin Kreuk; Jeffrey Tambor; Matt Damon; Diedrich Bader; J.P. Manoux; Rade Serbedzija; Steve Hytner; Patrick Malahide; Joanna Lumley; ***D:*** Jeff Schaffer; ***W:*** Jeff Schaffer; Alec Berg; David Mandel; ***C:*** David Eggby; ***M:*** James L. Venable.

Eva 1/2 *Eva the Devil's Woman* **1962** Writer Tyvian (Baker) becomes obsessed with prostitute Eva (Moreau), spends all his money on her, leaves his fiancee Francesca (Lisi) for her, but all she does is taunt and abandon him. He marries Francesca but leaves his bride (who kills herself) for Eva, who discards him again, leaving Tyvian broke and betrayed. Based on the novel "Eve" by James Hadley Chase. **103m/B; VHS, DVD.** *FR IT* Jeanne Moreau; Stanley Baker; Virna Lisi; James Villiers; Giorgio Albertazzi; Riccardo Garrone; ***D:*** Joseph Losey; ***W:*** Hugo Butler; Evan Jones; ***C:*** Gianni Di Venanzo; ***M:*** Michel Legrand.

Eva **2009** Poor soap opera romance set in Romania. Eva falls in love with the mysterious Tudor, who comes and goes throughout the years from the 1930s through WWII. Eva has other romances and then must deal with a postwar country in disarray before she finally figures out Tudor's secrets. **106m/C; DVD.** Amy Beth Hayes; Vincent Regan; Patrick Bergin; Dustin Milligan; ***D:*** Adrian Popovici; ***W:*** Adrian Popovici; ***C:*** Mihail Sarbusca; ***M:*** Vlady Cnejerici.

Evan Almighty **2007 (PG)** Holy spinoff! Former TV anchor-turned-politician Evan (Carell) is about to give up his values and ruin the environment when God (Freeman, reprising his "Bruce Almighty" role) orders him to build an ark. Wife Joan (Graham) and his sons are doubtful, but eventually get on the boat. Smarmy blend of animal-based potty humor and tepid life-lessons about taking care of the environment and being nice fails to take advantage of Carell's talents. **95m/C; DVD, Blu-Ray.** Steve Carell; Morgan Freeman; Lauren Graham; John Goodman; John Michael Higgins; Wanda Sykes; Jimmy Bennett; Johnny (John W.) Simmons; Jonah Hill; Ed Helms; Rachael Harris; Molly Shannon; Graham Phillips; ***D:*** Tom Shadyac; ***W:*** Steve Oedekerk; Josh Stolberg; Bob Florsheim; ***C:*** Ian Baker; ***M:*** John Debney.

Evangeline 1/2 **1929** Based on the Henry Wadsworth Longfellow poem about the struggles of Evangeline and the tragedy of lost love. Evangeline lives in an Acadian (with ties to France) village in Nova Scotia and is engaged to Gabriel. But when France and England declare war, the village sides with France and the men are forcibly deported to Louisiana. But Evangeline is determined to be reunited with her love. **90m/B; Silent; VHS, DVD.** Dolores Del Rio; Roland Drew; Alec B. Francis; George F. Marion, Sr.; Donald Reed; ***D:*** Edwin Carewe; ***W:*** Finis Fox; ***C:*** Robert B. Kurrle; ***M:*** Hugo Riesenfeld; Philip Carli.

Eve of Destruction **WOOF! 1990 (R)** Hell knows no fury like a cutting-edge android-girl on the warpath. Modeled after her creator, Dr. Eve Simmons, Eve VII has android-babe good looks and a raging nuclear capability. Wouldn't you know, something goes haywire during her trial run, and debutante Eve turns into a PMS nightmare machine, blasting all the good Doctor's previous beaux. That's where military agent Hines comes in, though you wonder why. Dutch actress Soutendijk plays dual Eves in her first American film. **101m/C; VHS, DVD, Blu-Ray.** Gregory Hines; Renee Soutendijk; Kurt Fuller; Ross Malinger; Eugene Robert Glazer; John M. Jackson; Loren Haynes; Michael Greene; ***D:*** Duncan Gibbins; ***W:*** Duncan Gibbins; Yale Udoff; ***C:*** Alan Hume.

Eve of Destruction **2013** Average doomsday miiniseries from Reelz Channel. Scientists Karl Dameron and Sarah Reed are working on a dark matter porject to harness the energy as an eco-friendly solution to global problems. Karl then has doubts about the project's safety and an eco-terrorist group doesn't want it done at all. It all means that Earth is in danger of annihilation once again. **200m/C; DVD, Blu-Ray.** Steven Weber; Christina Cox; Treat Williams; Jessica McLeod; Aleks Paunovic; Colin Lawrence; ***D:*** Robert Lieberman; ***W:*** Richard Beattie; ***C:*** David Pelletier; ***M:*** Shawn Pierce. **CABLE**

Evel Knievel **1972 (PG)** The life of motorcycle stuntman Evel Knievel is depicted in this movie, as portrayed by George Hamilton. Stunts will be appreciated by Evel Knievel fans. **90m/C; VHS, DVD.** George Hamilton; Bert Freed; Rod Cameron; Sue Lyon; ***D:*** Marvin J. Chomsky; ***W:*** John Milius; ***C:*** David M. Walsh; ***M:*** Patrick Williams.

Evelyn **2002 (PG)** Lovable but ale-soaked Desmond Doyle (Brosnan) is abandoned by his wife in 1953. At that time it was believed that a man couldn't care for his children alone, so the children are placed in a church orphanage. A barmaid (Margulies) takes pity on him and convinces him to sober up and seek legal counsel to regain custody. Beresford's straightforward classic style thankfully only alludes to the punishment the children faced rather than exploiting it, choosing instead to focus on the true story of the case against the Family Act of 1941. Faithful retelling brings pertinent items to light, with notable character development. It's refreshing to see Brosnan as an average bloke vs. his 007 persona, and Vavasseu, as the nine-year old Evelyn is one to watch. **94m/C; VHS, DVD, Blu-Ray.** *IR GB* Pierce Brosnan; Aidan Quinn; Julianna Margulies; Sophie Vavasseur; Stephen Rea; Alan Bates; John Lynch; Andrea Irvine; Karen Ardiff; Niall Beagan; Hugh MacDonagh; ***D:*** Bruce Beresford; ***W:*** Paul Pender; ***C:*** Andre Fleuren; ***M:*** Stephen Endelman.

Evelyn Prentice 1/2 **1934** Powell and Loy again team up as a married couple (after their "The Thin Man" success) but this time things aren't so rosy. He is an attorney with a wandering eye who has an affair with Russell (in her film debut). Loy finds out and turns for sympathy to Stephens but then she decides to stay with her husband after all. Only she's written some steamy letters to Stephens and he tries blackmailing her—and winds up dead. Dramatic courtroom scene straightens things out. Adapted from the novel by W.E. Woodward. Film was remade as "Stronger Than Desire" in 1939. **78m/B; VHS, DVD.** Myrna Loy; William Powell; Harvey Stephens; Isabel Jewell; Una Merkel; Rosalind Russell; Henry Wadsworth; Edward Brophy; Cora Sue Collins; Jessie Ralph; Sam Flint; Pat O'Malley; ***D:*** William K. Howard; ***W:*** Lenore Coffee.

Even Cowgirls Get the Blues 1/2 **1994 (R)** '70s counterculture loses its ill-defined charm in a meandering adaptation of cult author Tom Robbins' 1976 novel. An interesting failure, but likely to alienate both Van Sant and Robbins fans. Sissy Hackshaw (Thurman) possesses enormous thumbs which she hopes will make her the greatest hitchhiker in the world. But first they take her to a NYC modeling career for The Countess (Hurt in a high camp performance), who sends her to the Rubber Rose ranch, recently liberated by female cowhands, who are happy to welcome her. Theatrical release was delayed numerous times as Van Sant recut but it doesn't matter—the only successful feature is the soundtrack. **106m/C; VHS, DVD.** Uma Thurman; John Hurt; Rain Phoenix; Lorraine Bracco; Noriyuki "Pat" Morita; Angie Dickinson; Keanu Reeves; ***Cameo(s):*** Sean Young; Crispin Glover; Roseanne; Ed Begley, Jr.; ***D:*** Gus Van Sant; ***W:*** Gus Van Sant; ***C:*** Eric Alan Edwards; John J. Campbell; ***M:*** k.d. lang; Ben Mink.

Even Money 1/2 **2006 (R)** Dull ensemble drama despite some over-the-top performances. Basinger, DeVito, and Whitaker are gambling addicts who lie, cheat, and steal for another chance at that big score, despite having family and bookie problems. **108m/C; DVD, Blu-Ray.** Danny DeVito; Kim Basinger; Forest Whitaker; Tim Roth; Kelsey Grammer; Jay Mohr; Ray Liotta; Nick Cannon; Carla Gugino; Grant Sullivan; ***D:*** Mark Rydell; ***W:*** Robert Tannen; ***C:*** Robbie Greenberg; ***M:*** Dave Grusin.

Even the Rain *Tambien la lluvia* **2010** Bollain's fifth feature is a political morality tale about capitalism that occasionally descends into the preachy. Penny-pinching film producer Costa (Tosar), director Sebastian (Garcia Bernal) and their cast and crew come to Bolivia to make a revisionist film about Christopher Columbus' exploitation of the natives and the Taino chief who lead a rebellion against the Spanish. The film bleeds into reality as rabble-rouser Daniel (Aduviri) gets hired for a lead role at the same time he's protesting the government's privatization of the water supply, which is ruinous for the poverty-stricken locals. Spanish with subtitles. **103m/C; Blu-Ray, On Demand.** *SP FR MX* Gael Garcia Bernal; Luis Tosar; Karra Elejalde; Raul Arevalo; Juan Carlos Aduviri; Carlos Santos; ***D:*** Iciar Bollain; ***W:*** Paul Laverty; ***C:*** Alex Catalan; ***M:*** Alberto Iglesias.

Evening 🦴 ½ **2007 (PG-13)** Ann (Redgrave, chewing scenery) is on her deathbed, and she flashes back to a time when her younger self (Danes) experienced love and loss and possibly caused the death of a friend's brother. Meanwhile, her grown daughters (Collette and Richardson) struggle with their own issues while tending to their dying mother. Adapted by Minot from her novel, the film fails to escape its leaden dialogue, miscast actors, and unlikable, stereotypical characters. **117m/C; DVD, Blu-Ray.** Vanessa Redgrave; Natasha Richardson; Toni Collette; Meryl Streep; Claire Danes; Patrick Wilson; Hugh Dancy; Ebon Moss-Bachrach; Mamie Gummer; Eileen Atkins; Glenn Close; Barry Bostwick; ***D:*** Lajos Koltai; ***W:*** Susan Minot; Michael Cunningham; ***C:*** Gyula Pados; ***M:*** Jan A.P. Kaczmarek.

The Evening Star 🦴🦴 ½ **1996 (PG-13)** Sequel to 1983's "Terms of Endearment" starts in 1988 and finds the overbearing Aurora (MacLaine) now wreacking havoc on the lives of her three grown grandchildren (and vice versa). And Aurora's lovelife is as active as ever—old beau Hector Scott (Moffat) is hanging around, young psychiatrist Jerry Bruckner (Paxton) becomes her lover, and former astronaut flame Garrett Breedlove (Nicholson) also makes a brief appearance to cock an eyebrow at the shenanigans. Last screen role for Johnson as neighbor Arthur Cotten. Based on the novel by Larry McMurtry. Bring a hankie for the tears. **128m/C; DVD.** Shirley MacLaine; Juliette Lewis; George Newbern; MacKenzie Astin; Bill Paxton; Miranda Richardson; Marion Ross; Ben Johnson; Donald Moffat; Scott Wolf; China Kantner; Jack Nicholson; ***D:*** Robert Harling; ***W:*** Robert Harling; ***C:*** Don Burgess; ***M:*** William Ross.

The Event 🦴 ½ **2003 (R)** Unbalanced effort begins with AIDS-stricken Matt dying at his so-called farewell party, arousing the suspicions of Assistant D.A. Nick (Posey). As Matt's suffering is recounted in flashbacks, Nick has a hard time pursuing the case after recently witnessing her father's painful death. **112m/C; VHS, DVD.** *CA* Parker Posey; Don McKellar; Sarah Polley; Jane Leeves; Brent Carver; Olympia Dukakis; Joanna Adler; Rejean Cournoyer; Christina Zorich; Dick Latessa; Cynthia (Cyndy, Cindy) Preston; Gianna Marciante; Jaclyn Markowitz; Glen Michael Grant; Ruth Moore; Chaz Thorne; ***D:*** Thom Fitzgerald; ***W:*** Thom Fitzgerald; Steven Hillyer; Tim Marback; ***C:*** Thomas M. (Tom) Harting; ***M:*** Christophe Beck. **VIDEO**

Event Horizon 🦴🦴 ½ **1997 (R)** Cross between "Alien" and "The Shining" has Fishburne heading an ensemble cast out to rescue a prototype spaceship that's been missing for seven years. Their own ship is sabatoged by their own demons and certain extraterrestial ones, too, that cause much mayhem on their once peaceful mission. **97m/C; VHS, DVD, Blu-Ray.** Laurence Fishburne; Sam Neill; Kathleen Quinlan; Joely Richardson; Richard T. Jones; Jack Noseworthy; Sean Pertwee; Jason Isaacs; ***D:*** Paul W.S. Anderson; ***W:*** Philip Eisner; ***C:*** Adrian Biddle; ***M:*** Michael Kamen.

Ever After: A Cinderella Story 🦴🦴🦴 **1998 (PG-13)** The adorable Barrymore takes on Cinderella, renamed Danielle and very capable, in this not-quite-a-fairytale version set in 16th-century France. Huston's the peeved stepmom, Rodmilla, who reduces Danielle to the role of servant in her own home after her beloved father (Krabbe) dies. Danielle still falls for handsome Prince Henry (Scott), only she's not above trying to change the arrogant snob's opinions and tweak him about his privileged upbringing. Artist/genius Leonardo da Vinci (Godfrey) serves as the prince's confidante and there's still a lovely masked ball and a shoe to be lost (and found). **122m/C; VHS, DVD, Blu-Ray.** Drew Barrymore; Anjelica Huston; Dougray Scott; Patrick Godfrey; Megan Dodds; Melanie Lynskey; Timothy West; Judy Parfitt; Jeroen Krabbe; ***Cameo(s):*** Jeanne Moreau; ***D:*** Andy Tennant; ***W:*** Andy Tennant; Susannah Grant; Rick Parks; ***C:*** Andrew Dunn; ***M:*** George Fenton.

Everest 🦴🦴 **2007 (PG-13)** Made-for-Canadian-TV miniseries based on the true story of the 1982 Canadian expedition to reach the top of Mount Everest. After John (Priestley) loses his life during a solo attempt, his friends decide to commemorate his effort by trying again, only to run into bad weather, injuries, and other problems. Shatner has a small role as a journalist documenting the climb. **137m/C; DVD.** *CA* Eric Johnson; John Pyper-Ferguson; Zachary Bennett; Ted Atherton; Leslie Hope; William Shatner; Jason Priestley; Tom Rooney; ***D:*** Graeme Campbell; ***W:*** Keith Ross Leckie; ***C:*** Derick Underschultz; ***M:*** Christopher Dedrick. **TV**

Everest 🦴🦴 **2015 (PG-13)** The climbing expedition that began its final ascent up Mount Everest on May 10, 1996 has become a famous one, chronicled in John Krakauer's "Into Thin Air" and now this well-cast (Gyllenhaal, Brolin, Clarke, and Hawkes) but ineffective CGI-heavy blockbuster. On that day, a group of climbers were beset upon by a violent storm, which has been deftly captured in the film, but no one asks the interesting questions about the people on this mountain—most notably, why they were there in the first place. The result is essentially a disaster pic, recreating the fury of Mother Nature in interesting ways, but obscuring the humanity. **94m/C; DVD, Blu-Ray.** Robin Wright; Keira Knightley; Clive Standen; Jake Gyllenhaal; Josh Brolin; ***D:*** Baltasar Kormakur; ***W:*** Simon Beaufoy; William Nicholson; ***C:*** Salvatore Totino; ***M:*** Dario Marianelli.

Evergreen 🦴🦴 **2004 (PG-13)** Troubled mother Kate (Seymour) and daughter Henri (Land) move to a new community in hope of a fresh start. Henri resents her family's dire position and sets out to create a better niche with her newfound boyfriend's affluent but screwed up family. Dreary independent coming-of-age film is helped by good performances, especially from Land, but offers few surprises. **85m/C; DVD, Streaming.** Cara Seymour; Mary Kay Place; Noah Fleiss; Gary Farmer; Bruce Davison; Addie Land; ***D:*** Enid Zentelis; ***W:*** Enid Zentelis; ***C:*** Matthew Clark; ***M:*** John Sirratt; Patrick Sansone.

An Evergreen Christmas 🦴🦴 ½ **2014 (PG)** A family Christmas drama about difficult choices and finding your true path in life. After her father dies unexpectedly, Evie Lee (Closshey) travels from Los Angeles to her small home town in Tennessee. Though she is pursuing a music career in LA, Evie must deal with major issues at home because she is the executor of her father's estate. Her family owned a once-successful Christmas tree farm but now owes a large inheritance tax. Now, Evie must choose between her music career and her family's legacy. **98m/C; DVD, Streaming, Download.** Charleene N. Closshey; Robert Loggia; Naomi Judd; Booboo Stewart; Jake Sandvig; ***D:*** Jeremy Culver; ***W:*** Jeremy Culver; Morgen Culver; ***C:*** Jeff Osborne; ***M:*** Charleene N. Closshey; Derek Wieland.

Everlasting Moments 🦴🦴 ½ *Maria Larssons Eviga Ogonblick* **2008** Set in Sweden in 1907 and covering some 10 years, Troell's drama concerns downtrodden Maria Larsson's (Heiskanen) awakening to life's possibilities. Dockworker husband Sigfrid (Persbrandt) is an abusive womanizing drunk who doesn't support their large family. Needing money, Maria decides to pawn a camera but photographer Sebastian (Christensen) instead persuades Maria to take pictures herself. A natural talent, Maria begins making money and becomes more estranged from her husband as the years pass. Swedish with subtitles. **131m/C; Blu-Ray.** *SW* Maria Heiskanen; Mikael Persbrandt; Jesper Christensen; Ghita Norby; Amanda Ooms; Callin Ohrvall; Emil Jensen; Claire Wikholm; ***D:*** Jan Troell; ***W:*** Jan Troell; Niklas Radstrom; Agneta Ulfster Troell; ***C:*** Jan Troell; Mischa Gavrjusjov; ***M:*** Matti Bye.

An Everlasting Piece 🦴🦴 ½ **2000 (R)** Director Levinson moves from working-class Baltimore to working-class Belfast in the 1980s in this goofball comedy. Best pals and fellow barbers Colm (McEvoy) and George (O'Byrne) don't let their different religions come between them. In fact, they decide it will be an advantage when they take on a new toupee business (called The Piece People)?Colm can sell to the Catholics and George will handle the Protestants. But it turns out they have a rival firm, Toupee or Not Toupee, and then Colm winds up with a substantial order from the IRA. He's willing to separate politics for business but is anyone else? **103m/C; VHS, DVD.** Barry McEvoy; Brian F. O'Byrne; Anna Friel; Billy Connolly; Pauline McLynn; Laurence Kinlan; Ruth McCabe; ***D:*** Barry Levinson; ***W:*** Barry McEvoy; ***C:*** Seamus Deasy; ***M:*** Hans Zimmer.

The Everlasting Secret Family 🦴🦴 **1988** Politics and family life make strange bedfellows. A top political figure joins a secret homosexual organization in his search for power. **93m/C; VHS, DVD.** *AU* Arthur Dignam; Mark Lee; Dennis Miller; Heather Mitchell; ***D:*** Michael Thornhill.

Everly 🦴🦴 **2014 (R)** Hayek returns to her action movie roots in this outdated update of girl power action films like "Kill Bill." She plays the title character, a prostitute working for a criminal overlord, who is attached in her apartment by the underlings of her awful boss. Of course, they underestimate their target. After torturing her, she escapes and systematically takes them down one by one. Hayek brings her all to a movie that doesn't really deserve it. Director Lynch just doesn't have the style or flair of Robert Rodriguez or Quentin Tarantino. See it for Hayek, but lower your expectations. **91m/C; DVD, Blu-Ray.** Salma Hayek; Hiroyuki Watanabe; Laura Cepeda; ***D:*** Joe Lynch; ***W:*** Yale Hannon; ***C:*** Steve Gainer; ***M:*** Bear McCreary.

Every Day 🦴🦴 **2010 (R)** Ned writes for a TV show his demanding boss Garrett says needs to be more edgy, which means late-nights with sexy co-worker Robin. Already suffering from a midlife crisis, this puts a further strain on Ned's marriage to frazzled wife Jeannie, who's caring for her depressed, dying father Ernie, and his relationship with his sons, including teenager Jonah who's just come out. **93m/C; DVD.** Liev Schreiber; Helen Hunt; Brian Dennehy; Eddie Izzard; Carla Gugino; Ezra Miller; Skyler Forgang; David Harbour; ***D:*** Richard Levine; ***W:*** Richard Levine; ***C:*** Nancy Schreiber; ***M:*** Jeanine Tesori.

Every Day 🦴🦴 **2018 (PG-13)** An adaptation of the David Levithan's young adult best-selling novel about an unconventional romance. High school student Rhiannon (Rice) has a handsome boyfriend Justin (Smith) who does not treat her well. One day, Justin acts completely different: kind, attentive, and caring. Rhiannon learns that Justin's body was inhabited by a spirit who goes by "A" and moves from body to body every 24 hours. A feels an emotional connection to Rhiannon, and the pair falls in love as A moves among teens near Rhiannon. The ending might leave something to be desired, still the message about the importance of appreciating people for who they truly are rings true. **97m/C; DVD.** Angourie Rice; Justice Smith; Jeni Ross; Lucas Jade Zumann; Katie Douglas; ***D:*** Michael Sucsy; ***W:*** Jesse Andrews; ***C:*** Rogier Stoffers; ***M:*** Elliott Wheeler.

Every Day's a Holiday 🦴🦴 ½ **1938** In the 1890s, West stars as confidence woman Peaches O'Day, who sells the Brooklyn Bridge and is run out of New York City. But she comes back, in disguise as a French singer, to expose some crooked cops. The Hays office again came down heavily on Mae's suggestive behavior, which left her with little to rely on. West's last film for Paramount. **79m/B; DVD.** Mae West; Edmund Lowe; Charles Butterworth; Charles Winninger; Walter Catlett; Lloyd Nolan; Herman Bing; ***D:*** Edward Sutherland; ***W:*** Mae West.

Every Girl Should Be Married 🦴🦴 ½ **1948** A shopgirl sets her sights on an eligible bachelor doctor. **84m/B; VHS, DVD.** Cary Grant; Betsy Drake; Diana Lynn; Franchot Tone; ***D:*** Don Hartman.

Every Girl Should Have One 🦴 ½ **1978** A rambunctious comedy about a chase following a million-dollar diamond theft. **90m/C; VHS, DVD.** Zsa Zsa Gabor; Robert Alda; Alice Faye; Sandra Vacey; John Lazar; ***D:*** Robert Hyatt; ***W:*** Robert Hyatt; ***C:*** Michael Jones; ***M:*** Johnny Pate.

Every Little Step 🦴🦴 ½ **2008 (PG-13)** Directors Stern and Del Deo track the audition process of Bob Avian's 2006 Broadway revival of creator-choreographer Michael Bennett's 1975's "A Chorus Line," which mirrors the musical's storyline. Included are reel-to-reel tapes of Bennett's 1974 workshop interviews, current interviews with some performers involved in the original production, casting calls, and selection of the final cast. **96m/C; DVD.** Donna McKechnie; Charlotte d'Amboise; Jacques D'Amboise; Marvin Hamlisch; Baayork Lee; ***D:*** James D. Stern; Adam Del Deo; ***M:*** Marvin Hamlisch; Jane Antonia Cornish.

Every Man for Himself 🦴🦴🦴🦴 *Slow Motion; Sauve qui peut; Sauve qui peut la vie* **1979** One of the funniest, most beautiful, and most deeply disturbing films of Godard's career. Set in the cold, symbolic neutrality of Switzerland, the three loosely intertwined plot threads tell of lovers who manipulate and control each other with varying degrees of passion and disgust, and for very different reasons. (A businessman's precisely choreographed "scene" with a prostitute is one of the more appalling and brilliant depictions of joyless, power-centered sexuality in cinema history.) Often hard to follow and maddeningly fragmented, it is also so rich that you may just have your priorities realigned. **87m/C; DVD, Blu-Ray.** *FR* Roland Amstutz; Nathalie Baye; Jacques Dutronc; Isabelle Huppert; ***D:*** Jean-Luc Godard; ***W:*** Jean-Luc Godard; Jean-Claude Carriere; Anne-Marie Mieville; ***C:*** Renato Berta; William Lubtchansky; Barnard Menoud; ***M:*** Gabriel Yared.

Every Man for Himself & God Against All 🦴🦴🦴🦴 *The Mystery of Kaspar Hauser; Jeder fur Sich und Gott gegen Alle; The Enigma of Kaspar Hauser* **1975** Kaspar Hauser is a young man who mysteriously appears in the town square of Nuremberg, early in the 19th century. He cannot speak or stand upright and is found to have been kept in a dungeon for the first 18 years of his life. He becomes an attraction in society with his alternate vision of the world and attempts to reconcile with reality. A lovely, though demanding film which is based on a true story. In German with English subtitles. **110m/C; VHS, DVD.** *GE* Bruno S; Brigitte Mira; Walter Ladengast; Hans Musaus; Willy Semmelrogge; Michael Kroecher; Henry van Lyck; ***D:*** Werner Herzog; ***W:*** Werner Herzog; ***C:*** Jorge Schmidt-Reitwein; ***M:*** Orlando Di Lasso.

Every Second Counts 🦴🦴 ½ **2008** Entertaining Hallmark Channel family flick. Teen Brooke Preston (Apanowicz) is a champion in the rodeo sport of penning, trained by her dad Joe (Collins), a former champion himself. Brooke's dedication is partly to earn money because her family has hit hard times and the financial pressure may mean giving up her college dreams in favor of continuing on the rodeo circuit. **88m/C; DVD.** Stephen Collins; Barbara Williams; Eric Keenleyside; Brett Dier; Magda Apanowicz; ***D:*** John Bradshaw; ***W:*** Kevin Commins; Robert Vaughn; Arthur Martin, Jr.; Barbara Kymlicka; ***C:*** Paul Mitchnick; ***M:*** Stacey Hersh. **CABLE**

Every Secret Thing 🦴 ½ **2015 (R)** Documentary director Berg stumbles with her first narrative film, a cliché-laden thriller about a missing girl. Banks is miscast as Detective Nancy Porter, the investigator on a missing child case with striking similarities to one she solved earlier in her career involving two young girls who killed a baby. The two girls (Fanning and Macdonald) are now out of jail and Porter worries that at least one of them may have done something horrible again. Lethargically paced, the urgency of the kidnapping case gets lost amid the domestic drama. **93m/C; DVD.** Diane Lane; Elizabeth Banks; Dakota Fanning; Danielle MacDonald; Nate Parker; ***D:*** Amy Berg; ***W:*** Nicole Holofcener; ***C:*** Ron Hardy; ***M:*** Robin Coudert.

Every Thing Will Be Fine 🦴 ½ **2015** The once-so-great Wenders reaches his career nadir with this stunted, bizarre, and shockingly boring drama about the line between art and tragedy. Tomas (a half-asleep Franco) is a writer who is driving on a snowy night when a kid sleds into the road. Tomas hits him, changing both his life and that of the boy's mother's (Gainsbourg). As the boy's mother lingers in grief, Tomas comes out the other side, turning that painful night into a literary career. Wenders can't figure out the right tone for such a depressing story and Franco is simply awful. **118m/C; Blu-Ray, Download.** Rachel McAdams; James Franco; Peter Stormare; Charlotte Gainsbourg; Marie Josee Croze; ***D:*** Wim Wenders; ***W:*** Bjorn Olaf Johannessen; ***C:*** Benoît Debie; ***M:*** Alexandre Desplat.

Every Time We Say Goodbye 1/2 **1986 (PG-13)** In 1942, Jerusalem, an American flyboy falls in love with a young Sephardic Jewish girl, whose family resists the match. **97m/C; VHS, DVD.** Tom Hanks; Christina Marsillach; Benedict Taylor; Anat Atzmon; Gila Almagor; ***D:*** Moshe Mizrahi; ***W:*** Moshe Mizrahi; Leah Appet; ***M:*** Philippe Sarde.

Every Which Way But Loose **1978 (R)** Fairly pointless Eastwood foray featuring Clint as a beer-guzzling, country-music loving truck driver earning a living as a barroom brawler. He and his orangutan travel to Colorado in pursuit of the woman he loves. Behind him are a motorcycle gang and an L.A. cop. All have been victims of his fists. Sequel is "Any Which Way You Can." **119m/C; VHS, DVD, Blu-Ray.** Clint Eastwood; Sondra Locke; Geoffrey Lewis; Beverly D'Angelo; Ruth Gordon; Walter Barnes; ***D:*** James Fargo; ***W:*** Jeremy Joe Kronsberg; ***C:*** Rexford Metz; ***M:*** Steve Dorff.

Every Woman Knows a Secret **1999** Twenty-something Rob (Bettany) is blamed for the death of divorced, fortyish Jess's (Redmond) son in a drunk driving crash. Oddly drawn together by grief and guilt, the two begin an affair that reveals more secrets. **95m/C; DVD.** *GB* Paul Bettany; Siobhan Redmond; ***D:*** Paul Seed; ***W:*** William Humble; ***C:*** Ian Punter; ***M:*** Nigel Hess. **TV**

Everybody Knows *Todos lo saben* **2018 (R)** Laura (Cruz) returns to her homeland of Spain with her two daughters to attend her sister's wedding, but after one daughter is kidnapped, suspicions and secrets abound among family members. This isn't a Hollywood action-thriller, however. It's slow-paced and a bit dull, despite fine acting (particularly by real-life husband and wife Bardem and Cruz) that was somewhat handicapped by the material. **132m/C; DVD, Blu-Ray.** Penelope Cruz; Javier Bardem; Ricardo Darin; Bárbara Lennie; Inma Cuesta; ***D:*** Asghar Farhadi; ***W:*** Asghar Farhadi; ***C:*** Jose Luis Alcaine; ***M:*** Javier Limon.

Everybody Loves Somebody *Todos queremos a alguien* **2017 (PG-13)** Superb dialogue, an appealing cast, and bilingual novelty conspire to turn "something old" into "something new." Cynical L.A. gynecologist Clara enlists a co-worker to pose as her boyfriend at a family wedding in Mexico, but the event gets complicated when her ex-boyfriend shows up to rekindle their romance. It's a formula that's been "something borrowed" from dozens, nay hundreds, of rom-coms, yet its clever delivery will delight, not make you "something blue." **100m/C; DVD.** Karla Souza; Jose Maria Yazpik; Ben O'Toole; Alejandro Camacho; Patricia Bernal; ***D:*** Catalina Aguilar Mastretta; ***W:*** Catalina Aguilar Mastretta; ***C:*** Jon Aguirresarobe; ***M:*** Victor Hernandez Stumpfhauser.

Everybody Says I'm Fine! 1/2 **2006** A horrible accident during his childhood that left Xen (Engineer) an orphan also gave him the power as an adult to hear people's thoughts as he cuts hair for a living. While he uses his gift for the greater good by helping customers with problems in their lives, he's otherwise lonely and unhappy. He becomes intrigued by the beautiful Nikita (Purie) but is baffled when her thoughts are silent; his interest in her might be a dire mistake. **103m/C; DVD.** *IN* Rehaan Engineer; Koel Purie; Rahul Bose; Pooja Bhatt; Anahita Oberoi; ***D:*** Rahul Bose; ***W:*** Rahul Bose. **VIDEO**

Everybody Sing **1938** A down-on-their-luck theatrical family, including Garland (who is kicked out of boarding school for singing Mendelssohn with a swing beat) decides to put on a show in hopes of making a comeback. Dumb plot and boring songs make this one for die-hard Garland fans only. **80m/B; DVD.** Allan Jones; Fanny Brice; Judy Garland; Reginald Owen; Billie Burke; Reginald Gardiner; Lynne Carver; Monty Woolley; ***D:*** Edwin L. Marin; ***W:*** Florence Ryerson; Edgar Allan Woolf; ***C:*** Joseph Ruttenberg.

Everybody Wants Some!! 1/2 **2016 (R)** Richard Linklater's spiritual successor to his timeless "Dazed and Confused" jumps forward a decade, capturing youthful camaraderie in the '80s among a group of male friends. In terms of plot, that's really it. Again, Linklater tells a loose, character-driven story that's more interested in evoking the energy of youth at a certain time in America than specifics. Again, he employs almost all unknown actors, including Blake Jenner, Juston Street, Ryan Guzman, and Tyler Hoechlin. **117m/C; DVD, Blu-Ray.** Blake Jenner; Juston Street; Ryan Guzman; Tyler Hoechlin; Wyatt Russell; ***D:*** Richard Linklater; ***W:*** Richard Linklater; ***C:*** Shane F. Kelly.

Everybody Wants to Be Italian **2008 (R)** Jay Bianski (Jablonski), a fish market worker in Boston's North End, is having cold feet about asking his girlfriend Isabella (Petroro) to marry him. Fed up with Jay's indecisiveness, his coworkers invite Marisa (Vincent), a sexy veterinarian who shows up at the market looking for a cat, out to the local Italian-American club for drinks, hoping to spark something new for Jay. She's Hispanic, Jay think she's Italian. Jay's Polish, she thinks he's Italian. In a case of "mistaken ethnicity," the two anxiously prime themselves for the dos-and-don'ts when dating an Italian. Harmless and charmless, coming off like a cheap retread of "My Big Fat Greek Wedding." **105m/C; On Demand.** Jay Jablonski; Cerina Vincent; Marisa Petroro; John Kapelos; John Enos; Richard Libertini; Dan Cortese; Penny Marshall; ***D:*** Jason Todd Ipson; ***W:*** Jason Todd Ipson; ***C:*** Michael Fimognari; ***M:*** Michael Cohen.

Everybody Wins **1990 (R)** A mystery-romance about a befuddled private eye trying to solve a murder and getting caught up with the bizarre prostitute who hired him. Arthur Miller based this screenplay on his stage drama "Some Kind of Love Story." Confused and, given its pedigree, disappointing mystery. **110m/C; VHS, DVD.** Nick Nolte; Debra Winger; Will Patton; Jack Warden; Kathleen Wilhoite; Frank Converse; Frank Military; Judith Ivey; ***D:*** Karel Reisz; ***W:*** Arthur Miller; ***C:*** Ian Baker.

Everybody's All American *When I Fall in Love* **1988 (R)** Shallow, sentimental melodrama about a college football star and his cheerleader wife whose lives, subsequent to their youthful glories, is a string of disappointments and tragedies. Decently acted and based on Frank Deford's novel. **127m/C; VHS, DVD.** Jessica Lange; Dennis Quaid; Timothy Hutton; John Goodman; Carl Lumbly; Ray Baker; Savannah Smith; ***D:*** Taylor Hackford; ***M:*** James Newton Howard.

Everybody's Dancin' 1/2 **1950** A ballroom proprietor's business is marred by random killings in her establishment as the bands play on. **66m/B; VHS, DVD.** Spade Cooley; Dick Lane; Hal Derwin; Roddy McDowall; ***D:*** Will Jason.

Everybody's Famous! 1/2 *Iedereen Beroemd!* **2000 (R)** Factory worker Jean (De Pauw) is convinced that his teenaged daughter Marva (Van der Gucht) has the talent to become a famous singer, though she suffers from stage fright and seems hopeless. Devoted dad goes to the extreme of kidnapping Debbie (Reuten), a Belgian pop star burned out by her successful career. Jean's demand is that Debbie's lowlife manager (Loew) make Marva a star. Meanwhile, Debbie falls for her young co-kidnapper Willy (De Smedt). It's all played for laughs as it skewers the idea of media madness and fame at any price but there's a warped sweetness at the core as well. Dutch, Flemish, and French with subtitles. **99m/C; VHS, DVD.** *BE* Josse De Pauw; Eva Van der Gucht; Werner De Smedt; Thekla Reuten; Victor Low; Gert Portael; ***D:*** Dominique Deruddere; ***W:*** Dominique Deruddere; ***C:*** Willy Stassen; ***M:*** Raymond van het Groenewoud.

Everybody's Fine 1/2 **2009 (PG-13)** Nobody's even close to fine in this unappealing family dramedy. After none of his grown children show up at a planned family gathering, widower Frank (De Niro) decides to go on a road trip to catch up with them. What follows is a series of visits to children he realizes he barely knows as he discovers that none of them are leading the lives they've led him to believe. Unfortunately, that's all there is to offer, as De Niro deadpans his way through a mediocre story that no amount of charm from his co-leads Barrymore, Rockwell, or Beckinsale can save. A remake of Giuseppe Tornatore's 1990 film of the same name ("Stanno Tutti Bene," in Italian). **99m/C; Blu-Ray.** Robert De Niro; Drew Barrymore; Kate Beckinsale; Sam Rockwell; Katherine Moenning; James Frain; ***D:*** Kirk Jones; ***W:*** Kirk Jones; ***C:*** Henry Braham; ***M:*** Dario Marianelli.

Everyday 1/2 **2012** Dreary family drama made for British TV that Winterbottom filmed over a five year period. Ian's in prison and his wife Karen struggles to raise their four kids and make the long trek to visit her husband. The kids act out, Karen's lonely, and Ian gets a glimmer of what he's missing as the kids grow up and change during his time in the slammer. **91m/C; On Demand.** *UK* John Simm; Shirley Henderson; Valerie Lilley; Darren Tighe; ***D:*** Michael Winterbottom; ***W:*** Michael Winterbottom; Laurence Coriat; ***M:*** Michael Nyman. **TV**

Everyday Black Man 1/2 **2010 (R)** Moses has put his violent past long behind him to run a small neighborhood grocery store that's now in financial trouble. So he's willing to accept a loan from newcomer Malik who's making all the right noises about establishing himself and benefitting the community. Only Malik and the offer turn out to be too good to be true. **105m/C; DVD.** Henry Brown; Omari Hardwick; Tessa Thompson; Corey Jackson; Mo McRae; Marjorie Sears; ***D:*** Carmen Madden; ***W:*** Carmen Madden; ***C:*** Philip Briggs; ***M:*** Dwayne P. Wiggins.

Everyman's War 1/2 **2009** Low-budget war drama filmed in Oregon. It's based on the true story of the 94th Infantry, which was ordered to hold off the 11th Panzer tank division in Nenning, Germany in January, 1945 during the Battle of the Bulge. The unit is led by Staff Sgt. Don Smith, whose letter to gal-back-home Dorine becomes a sentimental symbol of what the soldiers are fighting for. The writer and director are the sons of the real-life Don Smith. **104m/C; DVD.** Cole Carson; Lauren Blair; Michael J. Prosser; Sean McGrath; Eric Martin Reid; Brian Julian; ***D:*** Thad T. Smith; ***W:*** Craig D. Smith; ***C:*** Joel Stirnkorb; ***M:*** Chad Rehmann.

Everyone Else 1/2 *Alle Anderen* **2009** An intelligent, realistic comedy-drama about the truth in relationships in a film by Maren Ade. When Chris (Eidinger) and Gitti (Minichmayr) take a trip to Sardinia, the young couple seems in love. Soon, however, games and teasing reveal unspoken fears and desires. Tensions between them grow deeper after they meet an other couple that seems happier and more successful than them. German with subtitles. **119m/C; DVD, Streaming, Download.** Lars Eidinger; Birgit Minichmayr; Hans-Jochen Wagner; Nicole Marischka; Mira Partecke; ***D:*** Maren Ade; ***W:*** Maren Ade; ***C:*** Bernhard Keller.

Everyone Says I Love You **1996 (R)** Woody sings! Granted, he doesn't sing very well, but who else could twist a story of love among the neurotic rich with lavish production numbers from the golden age of movie musicals? The excellent cast (who weren't told that they were in a musical until after they signed) prove that as singers, they're pretty good actors. The plot centers around the wandering love lives of Steffi (Hawn), her husband Bob (Alda), her ex-husband Joe (Allen) and their assorted children; especially the preppy Skylar (Barrymore) and her fiance Holden (Norton). Some of the musical productions are shaky (Allen's duet with Julia Roberts is straight out of Tin Ear Alley), but the feeling behind them is genuine; Besides, where else are you going to hear Groucho's "Hooray for Captain Spaulding" sung in French or a chorus of pregnant women sing "Makin' Whoopee"? **105m/C; VHS, DVD.** Woody Allen; Alan Alda; Drew Barrymore; Goldie Hawn; Gaby Hoffman; Edward Norton; Natalie Portman; Julia Roberts; Tim Roth; Natasha Lyonne; Lukas Haas; David Ogden Stiers; ***D:*** Woody Allen; ***W:*** Woody Allen; ***C:*** Carlo Di Palma; ***M:*** Dick Hyman. L.A. Film Critics '96: Support. Actor (Norton); Natl. Bd. of Review '96: Support. Actor (Norton).

Everyone's Hero **2006 (G)** Reeve completed pre-production on this lackluster animated feature before his death, which is why he's sharing directorial credit (pic is also dedicated to both Christopher and Dana Reeve). During the 1932 World Series between the Yankees and the Chicago Cubs, Babe Ruth's lucky bat, Darlin' (Goldberg), is stolen. Pint-sized baseball fan Yankee Irving (Austin) hops the rails, accompanied by wisecracking baseball Screwie (Reiner), to find the bat, stolen by unhygienic Cubs pitcher Lefty (Macy), and get it to the Bambino in time to win the big game. Anachronistic adventure might distract the younger kiddies (the fart and booger jokes will probably help). **88m/C; DVD, Blu-Ray.** ***V:*** Jake T. Austin; Rob Reiner; Whoopi Goldberg; William H. Macy; Stanley Irving; Raven; Robert Wagner; Forest Whitaker; Brian Dennehy; Robin Williams; Joe Torre; Dana Reeve; ***D:*** Christopher Reeve; Daniel St. Pierre; Colin Brady; ***W:*** Robert Kurtz; Jeff Hand; ***C:*** Andy Wang; Jan Carlee; ***M:*** John Debney.

Everything, Everything **2017 (PG-13)** Adaptation of the YA novel by Nicola Yoon has spunky teen Maddy (Stenberg) stuck in her house by a severe immune deficiency disorder. Her only human contact is with her very protective mother, her nurse, and her nurse's daughter, until brooding bad boy Olly (Robinson) moves in next door. They immediately start a text-fueled romance and she decides it's time to experience the outside world, health risks be damned. Mawkish dialogue, ridiculous departures from common sense or reality, and a jarring plot twist sabotage the excellent chemistry and fine performances of the leads. While the plot elements fail, the depiction of first love is everything, everything. **96m/C; DVD, Blu-Ray.** Amandla Stenberg; Nick Robinson; Anika Noni Rose; Ana de la Reguera; Taylor Hickson; ***D:*** Stella Meghie; ***W:*** J. Mills Goodloe; ***C:*** Igor Jadue-Lillo; ***M:*** Ludwig Göransson.

Everything for Sale *Wszysiko na Sprzedaz* **1968** An unacknowledged tribute to actor Zbigniew Cybulski, an actor who starred in several films for Wajda and who died in the same manner as the actor in this behind-the-scenes look at moviemaking. The lives of the director and actors are disrupted when their leading man, who lead a complicated offscreen life, is killed during filming. Polish with subtitles. **94m/C; DVD.** *PL* Andrzej Lapicki; Daniel Olbrychski; Beata Tyszkiewicz; Elzbieta Czyzewska; ***D:*** Andrzej Wajda; ***W:*** Andrzej Wajda; ***C:*** Witold Sobocinski; ***M:*** Andrzej Korzynski.

Everything I Have is Yours **1952** The Gowers were better dancers than actors as they proved in their leading roles in this below-average MGM musical. The married Hubbards split up their Broadway act when Pamela retires to stay home and care for their baby. Chuck's wandering eye soon falls on new costar Sybil. **91m/C; DVD.** Marge Champion; Gower Champion; Monica Lewis; Dennis O'Keefe; Dean Miller; Eduard Franz; ***D:*** Robert Z. Leonard; ***W:*** George Wells; ***C:*** William V. Skall.

Everything is Illuminated **2005 (PG-13)** Based on a novel by Jonathon Safran Foer, the film follows the journey of Jonathon (Wood), a fastidious New Yorker attempting to locate the Ukrainian woman he feels saved his grandfather from the Nazis. After traveling to the Ukraine, Jonathon employs Alex (Hutz), who narrates the film, and his grandfather (Leskin) as tour guides. The two specialize in taking "rich Jewish people" on trips to find ancestral homes and relatives. The beauty of the film is in finding its way from the humorous early scenes to the solemn conclusion. **104m/C; DVD.** Elijah Wood; Eugene Hutz; Boris Leskin; Laryssa Lauret; ***D:*** Liev Schreiber; ***W:*** Liev Schreiber; ***C:*** Matthew Libatique; ***M:*** Paul Cantloni.

Everything Must Go 1/2 **2010 (R)** Nick (Ferrell), a salesman and recovering alcoholic, relapses and spirals into complete failure. He gets fired from his job, and his frustrated wife kicks him—and all of his stuff—out of the house and onto the front yard. To make a new beginning, Nick holds a yard sale that becomes his key to recovery. Ferrell shows range as a dramatic actor, though the script gets a tad predictable and isn't as interesting as its star. Adapted and directed by Rush, based on the Raymond Carver short story "Why Don't You Dance?". **97m/C; Blu-Ray, On Demand.** Will Ferrell; Christopher Jordan Wallace; Rebecca Hall; Michael Peña; Laura Dern; Rosalie Michaels; Stephen (Steve) Root; ***D:*** Dan Rush; ***W:*** Dan Rush; ***C:*** Michael Barrett; ***M:*** David Torn.

Everything Put Together 🦴🦴 ½ **2000** Suburban housewife Angie (Mitchell) is pregnant as are her best friends Judith (Burns) and Barbie (Mullally). But Angie seems overly anxious and her worst fears are realized when her seemingly healthy son dies in the hospital from SIDS. Although husband Russ (Louis) tries to be as understanding and caring as possible, Anglie sinks into severe depression, especially when her friends, in their discomfort, begin to withdraw from her. **85m/C; VHS, DVD.** Radha Mitchell; Megan Mullally; Justin Louis; Catherine Lloyd Burns; Alan Ruck; Matt Malloy; Michele Hicks; ***D:*** Marc Forster; ***W:*** Catherine Lloyd Burns; Adam Forgash; ***C:*** Roberto Schaefer; ***M:*** Thomas Koppel.

Everything Relative 🦴🦴 ½ **1996** Seven college buddies reunite and spend a weekend in the country together in this lesbian twist on "The Big Chill." A bris held by partners Katie and Sarah for their new baby brings the mostly single fortysomething women together, and bring out the unfulfilled desires and regrets of the six lesbians and one straight woman. Standouts include Weber as the stunt woman mourning the loss of a lover to a car accident 15 years prior, as well as the relationship between Josie (McLaughlin) and Maria (Negron), the woman who left her to get married and have children, and is now divorced and losing her children in the custody battle. Low budget ($100,000) indie debut of writer/director Pollack is right on the mark emotionally and manages to keep the characters and their stories engaging, but loses something with neatly pat solutions to the intricate problems facing these women. **110m/C; VHS, DVD.** Stacey Nelkin; Ellen McLaughlin; Olivia Negron; Monica Bell; Andrea Weber; Gabriella Messina; Carol Schneider; ***D:*** Sharon Pollack; ***W:*** Sharon Pollack; ***C:*** Rachel Othmer; ***M:*** Frank London.

Everything Strange and New 🦴 ½ **2009** Semi-experimental, non-narrative indie is Bradshaw's feature film debut. Wayne works as an Oakland construction worker to support his family but is vaguely frustrated with his life and the conventionality of work, marriage, house, and kids in increasingly hard times. Actually, Wayne is much more articulate and perceptive in the voiceover monologues Bradshaw uses as Wayne contemplates his world but the film plays like bits of a life and not a whole, which may be the point. **84m/C; Blu-Ray.** Jerry McDaniel; Beth Lisick; Rigo Chacon, Jr.; Luis Saguar; ***D:*** Frazer Bradshaw; ***W:*** Frazer Bradshaw; ***C:*** Frazer Bradshaw; ***M:*** Dan Plonsey; Kent Sparling.

Everything You Always Wanted to Know about Sex (But Were Afraid to Ask) 🦴🦴🦴 **1972 (R)** Satiric comical sketches about sex includes a timid sperm cell, an oversexed court jester, a sheep folly, and a giant disembodied breast. Quite entertaining in its own jolly way. Based on the book by Dr. David Reuben. **88m/C; VHS, DVD, Blu-Ray.** Woody Allen; John Carradine; Lou Jacobi; Louise Lasser; Anthony Quayle; Geoffrey Holder; Lynn Redgrave; Tony Randall; Burt Reynolds; Gene Wilder; Robert Walden; Jay Robinson; ***D:*** Woody Allen; ***W:*** Woody Allen; ***C:*** David M. Walsh; ***M:*** Mundell Lowe.

Everything You Want 🦴 **2005** Bookstore clerk/art student Abby seems to have a happy life, including a perfect boyfriend in Sy. Only problem is Sy isn't real, he's the imaginary friend Abby's had since childhood. Then Abby actually falls for the flesh-and-blood Quinn and has to make a decision. Seriously, a 20-something chick who still hangs out with her imaginary playmate sounds like a looney. **92m/C; DVD.** Shiri Appleby; Nick Zano; Orlando Seale; Alexandra Holden; Will Friedle; Edie McClurg; ***D:*** Ryan Little; ***W:*** Steven A. Lee; ***C:*** Geno Salvatori; ***M:*** J Bateman. **CABLE**

Everything's Ducky WOOF! **1961** There's an alcoholic talking duck that can't swim and a couple of idiot sailors stationed at a rocket site who must look after the duck since it's memorized a secret rocket-guidance system. Not even the kiddies will fall for this idiocy. **80m/B; DVD.** Mickey Rooney; Buddy Hackett; Jackie Cooper; Richard Deacon; Roland Winters; Joanie Sommers; Walker Edmiston; Elizabeth MacRae; ***D:*** Don Taylor; ***W:*** Benedict Freedman; John Fenton Murray; ***C:*** Carl Guthrie; ***M:*** Bernard Green.

Everything's Gone Green 🦴🦴 ½ **2006 (R)** Happy-go-lucky slacker Ryan (Costanzo) loses his job and girlfriend in one worst-day-of-his-life swoop. New employment at a lottery magazine draws him into a money laundering scheme that produces loot, ladies, and lots of opportunity for moral growth. Cleverly and hilariously weaves recurrent "green" references into each outlandish circumstance (dare you to tally them). Not a waste to watch but does lack that secret box-office hit ingredient. **95m/C; DVD.** *CA* Paulo Costanzo; Steph Song; J.R. Bourne; Aidan Devine; Susan Hogan; Tom Butler; Gordon Michael Woolvett; Katharine Isabelle; ***D:*** Paul Fox; ***W:*** Douglas Coupland; ***C:*** David Frazee.

Eve's Bayou 🦴🦴🦴 ½ **1997 (R)** Eve (newcomer Smollett) comes from the upper-middle class Batiste family that seems all too perfect on the outside, but secrets and lies slowly surface when she mistakenly catches her doctor father Louis (Jackson) doing more than a routine check-up with a female patient. With her innocence shattered by the discovery, Eve's torment soon affects her emotionally strained mother Roz (Whitfield) and adolescent tease older sister Cisely (Good). Set in Louisiana 1962, and told in flashback, film presents a mesmerizing and complex story with haunting visuals. Ghostly appearance from Carroll adds a touch of voodoo and heightens the melodramatic intensity. Jackson is solid as the charming, yet flawed womanizer and Whitfield his equal as the suspecting wife. Impressive, multi-layered directorial debut from Lemmons didn't draw much attention during theatrical run, but has gained a following since. **109m/C; VHS, DVD.** Samuel L. Jackson; Lynn Whitfield; Debbi (Deborah) Morgan; Diahann Carroll; Jurnee Smollett; Meagan Good; Vondie Curtis-Hall; Lisa Nicole Carson; Jake Smollett; Ethel Ayler; ***Nar:*** Tamara Tunie; ***D:*** Kasi Lemmons; ***W:*** Kasi Lemmons; ***C:*** Amy Vincent; ***M:*** Terence Blanchard. Ind. Spirit '98: First Feature, Support. Actress (Morgan); Natl. Film Reg. '18.

Evidence of Blood 🦴🦴 ½ **1997 (PG-13)** Crime writer investigates a 40-year-old murder in a small town that would rather keep its secrets to itself. Based on the book by Thomas H. Cook. **109m/C; VHS, Streaming.** David Strathairn; Mary McDonnell; ***D:*** Andrew Mondshein; ***W:*** Dalene Young; ***C:*** Philip Linzey; ***M:*** Mason Daring.

The Evil 🦴🦴 **1978 (R)** A psychologist must destroy an evil force that is killing off the members of his research team residing at an old mansion. **80m/C; VHS, DVD, Blu-Ray.** Richard Crenna; Joanna Pettet; Andrew Prine; Victor Buono; Cassie Yates; George O'Hanlon, Jr.; Lynne Moody; Mary Louise Weller; Milton Selzer; ***D:*** Gus Trikonis; ***W:*** Donald G. Thompson; ***C:*** Mario DiLeo.

Evil 🦴🦴🦴 *Ondskan* **2003** Wanting her son to escape his stepdad's beatings, Erik's (Wilson) mom scrapes up the funds to send him to a supposedly classy boarding school. Unfortunately it's ruled by upperclassmen who like to keep the pecking order alive by tormenting younger students. But Erik's violent past—including his expulsion from his last school as a gang leader—makes him a poor target for their abuse, and despite his desire to please his mom he must fight to protect himself and the other victims. Based on Swede Jan Guillou's 1981 autobiographical novel "Ondskan." **113m/C; DVD.** *SW* Marie Richardson; Andreas Wilson; Henrik Lundstrom; Gustaf Skarsgard; Linda Zilliacus; Johan Rabeus; Kjell Bergqvist; Magnus Roosman; ***D:*** Mikael Hafstrom; ***W:*** Mikael Hafstrom; Hans Gunnarsson; ***C:*** Peter Mokrosinski; ***M:*** Francis Shaw.

Evil Alien Conquerors 🦴 **2002 (PG-13)** Extremely lame sci-fi comedy. Inept evil aliens My-ik and Du-ug, armed only with swords, are sent to Earth to behead the planet's entire population or suffer the wrath of giant Croker. With a two-day time limit they've got problems, especially since the dopey duo get distracted by alcohol, Earth women, and cows. **89m/C; DVD.** Diedrich Bader; Chris Parnell; Tori Spelling; Elden (Ratliff) Henson; Beth Grant; Taylor Labine; Missy Yager; ***D:*** Chris Matheson; ***W:*** Chris Matheson; ***C:*** Russell Lyster; ***M:*** David E. Russo.

Evil Behind You 🦴 **2006 (PG-13)** Two young couples are kidnapped by muslim terrorists and subjected to medical experiments that either have them seeing demons or hallucinating like mad. **90m/C; DVD, Streaming.** Hilary Kennedy; Manuel Velazquez; D.C. Lee; Gwedolynn Murphy; Jim Garrity; ***D:*** Jim Carroll; Jason Kerr; ***W:*** Jim Carroll; ***C:*** Bo Hopper; Russell McLaughlin; ***M:*** Chris George. **VIDEO**

Evil Brain from Outer Space 🦴 **1965** Starman must once again rescue the Earth from evil aliens, this time an evil space brain with disease spreading minions. **90m/B; DVD, Streaming.** *JP* Ken Utsui; ***D:*** Koreyoshi Akasaka; Teruo Ishii; Akira Mitsuwa; ***W:*** Ichiro Miyagawa; ***C:*** Takashi Watanabe; ***M:*** Michiaki Watanabe. **TV**

Evil Clutch 🦴 ½ **1989 (R)** A young couple vacationing in the Alps encounter several creepy locals when they find themselves in the midst of a haunted forest. The cinematography is extremely amateurish in this Italian gorefest and the English dubbing is atrocious. However, the special makeup effects are outstanding and the musical score adds a touch of class to this otherwise inept horror film. **88m/C; VHS, DVD.** *IT* Coralina Cataldi-Tassoni; Diego Riba; Elena Cantarone; Luciano Crovato; Stefano Molinari; ***D:*** Andreas Marfori; ***W:*** Andreas Marfori; ***C:*** Marco Isoli.

Evil Dead 🦴🦴 ½ **2013 (R)** The gore meter is turned up to eleven in director/writer Alvarez's long-anticipated remake of the independent horror movie that made stars of Sam Raimi and Bruce Campbell. Mia (an effective Levy) holes herself up in a cabin in the woods to kick her drug addiction along with her brother and three very unlucky friends. After one of her mates reads from the "Book of the Dead," evil forces possess Mia and the carnage ensues. Alvarez's a whiz at staging horrific action scenes but slashes the tension and dread that could've made it so much more. A fun yet forgettable thrill ride. **90m/C; DVD, Blu-Ray.** Jane Levy; Shiloh Fernandez; Lou Taylor Pucci; Jessica Lucas; Elizabeth Blackmore; ***D:*** Fede Alvarez; ***W:*** Fede Alvarez; Rodo Sayagues; ***C:*** Aaron Morton; ***M:*** Roque Baños.

Evil Dead 🦴🦴 ½ **1983 (NC-17)** Five college students, vacationing in the Tennessee mountains, take refuge in an abandoned cabin. They find a tape and a Book of the Dead, which unwittingly lets them resurrect demons, which transform the students into evil monsters until only Ash (Campbell) remains to fight the evil. Exuberantly gory low-budgeter followed by two sequels. **85m/C; VHS, DVD, Blu-Ray, UMD.** Bruce Campbell; Ellen Sandweiss; Betsy Baker; Hal Delrich; Sarah York; Theodore (Ted) Raimi; Sam Raimi; Scott Spiegel; ***D:*** Sam Raimi; ***W:*** Sam Raimi; ***C:*** Tim Philo; ***M:*** Joseph LoDuca.

Evil Dead 2: Dead by Dawn 🦴🦴 ½ **1987 (R)** A gory, tongue-in-cheek sequel/remake of the original festival of gag and gore, in which an ancient book of magic invokes a crowd of flesh-snacking, joke-tossing ghouls. Followed by yet a third bloodfest. **84m/C; VHS, DVD, Blu-Ray, UMD.** Bruce Campbell; Sarah Berry; Dan Hicks; Kassie Wesley; Theodore (Ted) Raimi; Denise Bixler; Richard Domeier; Scott Spiegel; Josh Becker; Lou Hancock; ***Cameo(s):*** Sam Raimi; ***D:*** Sam Raimi; ***W:*** Sam Raimi; Scott Spiegel; ***C:*** Peter Deming; ***M:*** Joseph LoDuca.

Evil Dead Trap 🦴🦴🦴 ½ **1988** Nami (Miyuki Ono), a Japanese late-night TV show host, is sent a tape that appears to show a brutal murder. Her cheap boss refuses to do anything, but she and her female crew decide to follow up on the tape and find the location where it was made. What follows in an abandoned factory owes much to Argento with even more visceral sex and violence. Director Ikeda's camera is almost never still. The script combines supernatural elements with a realistic setting and believable characters. **90m/C; VHS, DVD.** *JP* Miyuki Ono; Fumi Katsuragi; Hitomi Kobayashi; Eriko Nakagawa; ***D:*** Toshiharu Ikeda; ***W:*** Takashi Ishii.

Evil Dead Trap 2: Hideki 🦴 ½ *Shiryo No Wana 2: Hideki* **1991** A shy theater film projectionist is haunted by a child (who may be from the first film), a quirky female reporter, and her equally quirky married boyfriend. They all have several things in common. They're all involved in a story about a recent series of serial killings, they all have serious emotional issues, and they're creepy. This sequel in name only is hard to watch, as the protagonists are clearly unsympathetic walking train wrecks. **102m/C; DVD.** Shiro Sano; Shoko Nakajima; Jaimie Alexander; ***D:*** Izo Hashimoto.

Evil Ed 🦴 ½ **1996 (R)** Formerly mild-mannered film editor Ed (Ruebeck) becomes obsessed with the horror series he's working on, goes off the deep end, and begins a series of killings that mimic the ones from the films. Lots of splatter. **90m/C; VHS, DVD, Blu-Ray.** *SW* Johan Ruebeck; Olof Rhodin; Pete Lofbergh; ***D:*** Anders Jakobsson; ***W:*** Anders Jakobsson; ***C:*** Anders Jakobsson; ***M:*** Goran Lundstrom.

Evil Eyes 🦴 ½ **2004 (R)** Hard-up screenwriter Jeff Stenn (Baldwin) is happy to accept a producer's (Kier) offer to pen a horror flick about a guy who went psycho and offed his family with an axe. But Jeff starts suffering from violent hallucinations and is soon living out his character's nightmare. Familiar plot moves briskly but if you really need see a crazy guy with an axe, watch "The Shining." **80m/C; DVD.** Adam Baldwin; Udo Kier; Mark Sheppard; Jennifer Gates; Kristin Lorenz; ***D:*** Mark Atkins; ***W:*** Naomi L. Selfman; ***C:*** Mark Atkins. **VIDEO**

Evil Judgment 🦴 ½ **1985** A young girl investigates a series of murders and finds the culprit is a psychopathic judge. **93m/C; VHS, DVD.** Pamela Collyer; Jack Langedijk; Nanette Workman; ***D:*** Claude Castravelli.

Evil Laugh WOOF! **1986 (R)** Medical students and their girlfriends party at an abandoned orphanage, until a serial killer decides to join them. **90m/C; VHS, DVD.** Tony Griffin; Kim McKamy; Jody Gibson; Dominick Brascia; ***D:*** Dominick Brascia.

Evil Lives 🦴🦴 ½ *Soulmates* **1992** Now here's a horror premise you don't run into every day. Horror novelist Richard Wayborn (Rodgers) leaves a trail of dead women during his lecture tours. Seems he's really 700-years-old and his long-dead wife can temporarily resurrect herself using the nubile forms of other women. Now, Wayborn has chosen a new babe but so far she's managing to elude his deadly charms. **90m/C; VHS, DVD.** Tristan Rogers; Arabella Holzbog; Tyrone Power, Jr.; Sonia Curtis; Griffin O'Neal; Melissa Moore; Wendy Barry; Paul Bartel; Dawn Wells; ***D:*** Thunder Levin.

The Evil Mind 🦴🦴 ½ *The Clairvoyant* **1934** A fraudulent mind reader predicts many disasters that start coming true. **80m/B; VHS, DVD.** *GB* Claude Rains; Fay Wray; Jane Baxter; Felix Aylmer; ***D:*** Maurice Elvey; ***W:*** Charles Bennett.

The Evil of Frankenstein 🦴🦴 **1964** The third of the Hammer Frankenstein films, with the mad doctor once again finding his creature preserved in ice and thawing him out. Preceded by "The Revenge of Frankenstein" and followed by "Frankenstein Created Woman." **84m/C; VHS, DVD, Blu-Ray.** *GB* Peter Cushing; Duncan Lamont; Peter Woodthorpe; Sandor Eles; Kiwi Kingston; Katy Wild; ***D:*** Freddie Francis; ***W:*** John (Anthony Hinds) Elder; ***C:*** John Wilcox; ***M:*** Don Banks.

Evil Remains 🦴 *Trespassing* **2004 (R)** A lot of yakking and not much slashing. Five college students travel to an isolated Louisiana plantation to investigate a local legend. A teen killed his parents and an evil aura has built up around the house, which is reinvigorated by the presence of fresh meat. The three males are brothers and the two females are a lesbian couple if it makes any difference. **88m/C; DVD.** Daniel Gillies; Jeff Bryan Davis; Clayne Crawford; Estella Warren; Ashley Scott; Jeff Galpin; Maryam D'Abo; Will Rokos; ***D:*** James Merendino; ***W:*** James Merendino; ***C:*** Tom Calloway; ***M:*** Elmo Weber.

Evil Roy Slade 🦴🦴🦴 **1971** Goofy family comedy (a failed TV pilot) that's a parody of every western cliche imaginable. Roy (Astin) is the meanest gunslinger in the west (he was raised by vultures) who's trying to turn over a new leaf after he falls for a pretty schoolteacher. He's aided by a shrink, who wants Roy to give up his weapons fetish, but singing glamour boy lawman Bing Bell (Shawn) has a score to settle with Roy. **97m/C; VHS, DVD.** John Astin; Dick Shawn; Mickey Rooney; Pam(ela) Austin; Henry Gibson; Edie Adams; Milton Berle; Dom DeLuise; Noriyuki "Pat" Morita; Penny Marshall; John Ritter; ***Cameo(s):*** Jerry Paris; ***Nar:*** Pat Buttram; ***D:*** Jerry Paris; ***W:*** Garry Marshall; Jerry Belson; ***C:*** Sam Leavitt. **TV**

Evil Spawn 🦴 *Deadly Sting; Alive by Night; Alien Within* **1987** A fading movie queen takes an experimental drug to restore her youthful beauty, but it only turns her into a giant silverfish. Releases under several alternate titles, and with varying running times. **70m/C; VHS, DVD.** Bobbie Bresee; John Carradine; Drew Godderis; John Terrance; Dawn Wildsmith; Jerry Fox; Pamela Gilbert; Forrest J Ackerman; ***D:*** Kenneth J. Hall; ***W:*** Kenneth J. Hall; ***C:*** Christopher Condon.

Evil Spirits 🦴 ½ **1991 (R)** Boarding-house tenants are murdered while the crazy landlady cashes their social security checks. This seedy horror cheapie doesn't take itself seriously, and like-minded genre buffs may enjoy the cult-film cast. **95m/C; VHS, DVD.** Karen Black; Arte Johnson; Virginia Mayo; Michael Berryman; Martine Beswick; Bert Remsen; Yvette Vickers; Robert Quarry; Mikel Angel; Debra Lamb; ***D:*** Gary Graver; ***W:*** Mikel Angel.

The Evil That Men Do 🦴🦴 **1984 (R)** A hitman comes out of retirement to break up a Central American government's political torture ring and, in the process, brings a friend's killer to justice. Based on the novel by R. Lance Hill. **90m/C; VHS, DVD.** Charles Bronson; Theresa Saldana; Joseph Maher; Jose Ferrer; Rene Enriquez; John Glover; Raymond St. Jacques; Antoinette Bower; Enrique Lucero; Jorge Luke; ***D:*** J. Lee Thompson; ***W:*** John Crowther; ***C:*** Xavier Cruz; ***M:*** Ken Thorne.

Evil Toons 🦴 ½ **1990 (R)** A quartet of lovely coeds on a cleaning job venture into a deserted mansion. There they accidentally release a vulgar, lustful, animated demon who proceeds to cause their clothes to fall off. Can the girls escape the haunted mansion with their sanity, virtue and wardrobes intact? **86m/C; VHS, DVD.** David Carradine; Dick Miller; Monique Gabrielle; Suzanne Ager; Stacy Nix; Madison Stone; Don Dowe; Arte Johnson; Michelle (McClellan) Bauer; ***D:*** Fred Olen Ray.

Evil under the Sun 🦴🦴 **1982 (PG)** An opulent beach resort is the setting as Hercule Poirot attempts to unravel a murder mystery. Based on the Agatha Christie novel. **112m/C; VHS, DVD.** *GB* Peter Ustinov; Jane Birkin; Maggie Smith; Colin Blakely; Roddy McDowall; Diana Rigg; Sylvia Miles; James Mason; Nicholas Clay; ***D:*** Guy Hamilton; ***W:*** Anthony Shaffer; ***C:*** Christopher Challis; ***M:*** Cole Porter.

The Evil Within WOOF! *Baby Blood* **1989 (R)** Parasitic beast, with an unquenchable thirst for blood, slithers from the center of the earth into the convenient womb of a young woman. She takes to murdering everyone within reach while preparing to give birth. As disgusting as it sounds. **88m/C; VHS, DVD, Blu-Ray.** Emmanuelle Escourrou; Jean-Francois Guillotte; ***D:*** Alain Robak; ***W:*** Alain Robak; Serge Cukier.

Evils of the Night 🦴 **1985** Teenage campers are abducted by sex-crazed alien vampires. Bloody naked mayhem follows. **85m/C; VHS, DVD, Blu-Ray.** John Carradine; Julie Newmar; Tina Louise; Neville Brand; Aldo Ray; Karrie Emerson; Bridget Holloman; ***D:*** Marti Rustam; ***W:*** Marti Rustam; Phillip D. Connors.

Evilspeak WOOF! **1982 (R)** Bumbling misfit enrolled at a military school is mistreated by the other cadets. With the help of his computer, he retaliates with satanic power. Bits, bytes, and gore. **89m/C; VHS, DVD, Blu-Ray.** Clint Howard; Don Stark; Lou Gravance; Lauren Lester; R.G. Armstrong; Joe Cortese; Claude Earl Jones; Haywood Nelson; Lenny Montana; ***D:*** Eric Weston.

Evita 🦴🦴 ½ **1996 (PG)** Webber/Rice rock opera about the life and death of Eva Peron finally comes to the big screen with all its extravaganza intact. Madonna's in the title role (in fine voice, lavishly costumed but unflatteringly lit) about an ambitious poor girl willing to do anything to make her mark—in this version by sleeping her way up the ladder of power to Argentine strongman Juan Peron (Pryce as wax dummy). Evita becomes a would-be champion of the people, even as the government ruthlessly suppresses their freedoms. The surprisingly strong-voiced Banderas (perhaps his emphatic enunciation is to make his English as clear as possible) is everyman narrator Che (changed from the stage version's revolutionary Che Guevera). The highlight is still Madonna's balcony scene, singing "Don't Cry for Me, Argentina," but some of the other songs are drowned by loud orchestration. Director Parker has a cameo as a frustrated film director trying to work with Evita. **133m/C; VHS, DVD, Blu-Ray.** Madonna; Antonio Banderas; Jonathan Pryce; Jimmy Nail; Victoria Sus; Julian Littman; Olga Merediz; Laura Pallas; Julia Worsley; ***Cameo(s):*** Alan Parker; ***D:*** Alan Parker; ***W:*** Oliver Stone; Alan Parker; ***C:*** Darius Khondji; ***M:*** Andrew Lloyd Webber; ***M:*** Tim Rice. Oscars '96: Song ("You Must Love Me"); Golden Globes '97: Actress--Mus./Comedy (Madonna), Film--Mus./Comedy, Song ("You Must Love Me").

Evolution 🦴 ½ **2001 (PG-13)** A meteor containing microscopic organisms crashes in the New Mexico desert and they begin evolving at an enormous rate. A misfit team consisting of community college prof Duchovny, government scientist Moore, wannabe fireman Scott, and kooky geologist Jones try to prevent the spores (which evolve into a number of crazy critters) from taking over the planet. It's supposed to be sci-fi comedy, but the effectively scary monsters eliminate whatever comedic elements the writers and Reitman forgot to kill. **101m/C; VHS, DVD.** David Duchovny; Julianne Moore; Orlando Jones; Seann William Scott; Ted Levine; Ethan Suplee; Michael Ray Bower; Katharine Towne; Dan Aykroyd; Richard Moll; Gregory Itzin; Ty Burrell; ***D:*** Ivan Reitman; ***W:*** David Diamond; David Weissman; Don Jakoby; ***C:*** Michael Chapman; ***M:*** John Powell.

Evolution 🦴🦴 ½ **2016** Ten-year-old Nicolas seems like a normal boy in a beautiful, peaceful, seaside village. Except there's something odd about this village. There are no men. There are women and boys, but no men. What will happen to Nicolas when he grows up? This is the mystery at the core of this dreamlike hybrid of horror stories and coming-of-age narratives that's often mesmerizing. The dread that comes with growing up is given palpable resonance in this unique foreign film. It can sometimes be a bit too strange for its own good, but it's certainly never boring or forgettable. **81m/C; DVD, Blu-Ray.** Max Brebant; Roxane Duran; Julie-Marie Parmentier; Mathieu Goldfeld; Nissim Renard; ***D:*** Lucile Hadzihalilovic; ***W:*** Lucile Hadzihalilovic; Alante Kavaite; ***C:*** Manuel Dacosse; ***M:*** Jesus Diaz; Zacarias De la Riva.

Evolver 🦴 ½ **1994 (R)** Teenager Kyle Baxter (Randall) wins a robot patterned after a video arcade game but the robot has a secret military weapon's program built into its brain, causing it to evolve into a killing machine. **90m/C; VHS, DVD.** Ethan (Randall) Embry; John de Lancie; Cassidy Rae; Cindy Pickett; Paul Dooley; ***V:*** William H. Macy; ***D:*** Mark Rosman; ***W:*** Mark Rosman; ***C:*** Jacques Haitkin.

The Ewok Adventure 🦴🦴 ½ **1984 (G)** Those adorable, friendly and funny characters from "Return of the Jedi" make the jump from film to TV in a new adventure from George Lucas. In this installment, the Ewoks save a miraculous child from harm with the help of a young human. This fun-filled adventure has Lucas's thumbprint all over it and great special effects. Followed by "Ewoks: The Battle for Endor." **96m/C; VHS, DVD.** Warwick Davis; Eric Walker; Aubree Miller; Fionnula Flanagan; ***Nar:*** Burl Ives; ***D:*** John Korty; ***M:*** Elmer Bernstein; Peter Bernstein. **TV**

The Ewoks: Battle for Endor 🦴🦴 ½ **1985** TV movie based on the furry creatures from "Return of the Jedi," detailing their battle against an evil queen to retain their forest home. Preceded by "The Ewok Adventure." **98m/C; VHS, DVD.** Wilford Brimley; Warwick Davis; Aubree Miller; Sian Phillips; Paul Gleason; Eric Walker; Carel Struycken; Niki Botelho; ***D:*** Jim Wheat; Ken Wheat; ***M:*** Peter Bernstein. **TV**

The Ex 🦴🦴 *Fast Track* **2007 (PG-13)** Tom (Braff) loses his job after his wife (Peet) quits hers to raise their first child. To save the family, he moves them from New York to Ohio to accept an advertising job with his father-in-law. Then he discovers that his new boss is a wheelchair-bound paraplegic who had a one night stand with his wife in high school, and has been obsessing over her ever since. Plays like a mean sitcom, but without the laughs that would normally accompany black comedies. Although it might make you squirm like one. **90m/C; DVD.** Zach Braff; Amanda Peet; Jason Bateman; Charles Grodin; Mia Farrow; Donal Logue; Lucian Maisel; Amy Poehler; Fred Armisen; Bob Stephenson; Josh Charles; Paul Rudd; Amy Adams; Romany Malco; ***D:*** Jesse Peretz; ***W:*** Michael Handelman; Paul Guion; ***C:*** Tom Richmond; ***M:*** Ed Shearmur.

Ex Machina 🦴🦴🦴 **2015 (R)** Alex Garland has a thing or two to say about the intersection of humanity and technology in his latest sci-fi drama. The great Gleeson stars as Caleb, the lucky winner of a week's internship with legendary technology pioneer Nathan (Isaac). Caleb arrives at Nathan's remote complex, and is quickly introduced to Ava (Vikander), a remarkable A.I. creation. Caleb is asked to perform "The Turing Test" on her to determine her level of consciousness. Is she real? Is Caleb? And what's Nathan's greater purpose? Fascinating and engaging throughout. **108m/C; DVD, Blu-Ray.** Domhnall Gleeson; Corey Johnson; Oscar Isaac; Alicia Vikander; Sonya Mizuno; ***D:*** Alex Garland; ***W:*** Alex Garland; ***C:*** Rob Hardy; ***M:*** Geoff Barrow; Ben Salisbury. Oscars '15: Visual FX; Ind. Spirit '16: First Feature (Garland).

Ex-Mrs. Bradford 🦴🦴🦴 **1936** Amateur sleuth Dr. Bradford teams up with his ex-wife to solve a series of murders at the race track. Sophisticated comedy-mystery; witty dialogue. **80m/B; VHS, DVD.** William Powell; Jean Arthur; James Gleason; Eric Blore; Robert Armstrong; ***D:*** Stephen Roberts.

Exam 🦴🦴 **2009** British psycho-thriller finds eight anonymous applicants vying for the same job at a major corporation. Confined to an exam room with a time limit and a series of rules, they are supposed to answer a single question but the paper placed before each of them is blank. At first they cooperate to figure out the question but it soon appears there's some sort of corporate mind game involved and their momentary unity dissolves. **101m/C; DVD.** *GB* Luke Mably; Jimi Mistry; Chukwudi Iwuji; John Lloyd Fillingham; Pollyanna McIntosh; Nathalie Cox; Adar Beck; Gemma Chan; Colin Salmon; ***D:*** Stuart Hazeldine; ***W:*** Stuart Hazeldine; ***C:*** Tim Wooster; ***M:*** Stephen Barton.

Examined Life: Philosophy in the Streets 🦴🦴 ½ **2009** This powerful documentary takes philosophy out of academia and into real life to make concepts more relevant to everyday life. Filmmaker Astra Taylor has several of the most influential thinkers discuss their thoughts in this context. The ethics of consumption are considered by Pete Singer in boutiques located in New York City's Fifth Avenue, while environmental philosophy is pondered by Slavoj Zizek in a garbage dump. Individualism, cultural, and other philosophical topics are similarly discussed, with the goal of being thought provoking. **87m/C; DVD, Streaming, Download.** ***D:*** Astra Taylor; ***W:*** Astra Taylor; ***C:*** John M. Tran.

Excalibur 🦴🦴🦴 ½ **1981 (R)** A sweeping, visionary retelling of the life of King Arthur, from his conception, to the sword in the stone, to the search for the Holy Grail and the final battle with Mordred. An imperfect, sensationalized version, but still the best yet filmed. **140m/C; VHS, DVD, HD-DVD.** Nigel Terry; Nicol Williamson; Nicholas Clay; Dame Helen Mirren; Cherie Lunghi; Paul Geoffrey; Gabriel Byrne; Liam Neeson; Patrick Stewart; Charley Boorman; Corin Redgrave; Robert Addie; Keith Buckley; Niall O'Brien; ***D:*** John Boorman; ***W:*** John Boorman; Rospo Pallenberg; ***C:*** Alex Thomson; ***M:*** Trevor Jones.

Excellent Cadavers 🦴🦴 ½ **1999 (R)** Giovanni Falcone (Palminteri) was an incorruptible Italian prosecutor who took on the Mafia in Sicily in the 1980s. By the end of the decade, and with the help of informer Tommaso Buscetta (Abraham), Falcone had 300 convictions and sealed his own grim fate. Title refers to the corpses of public officials who challenged the mobsters. Based on the book by Alexander Stille. **86m/C; VHS, DVD.** Chazz Palminteri; F. Murray Abraham; Anna Galiena; Bruno Bilotta; ***D:*** Ricky Tognazzi; ***W:*** Peter Pruce; ***M:*** Joseph Vitarelli. **CABLE**

The Exception 🦴🦴 ½ *The Kaiser's Last Kiss* **2017 (R)** Sexy, espionage thriller set in World War II's Holland. As Nazis prepare to occupy the Netherlands, a German soldier (Courtney) is sent ahead to ensure that the secluded mansion of Kaiser Wilhelm II (Plummer) is safeguarded against spies. Once there, he falls for a beautiful maid (James), who confides that she's secretly Jewish. Is their love the exception to his duty, or is she a spy who will betray him at the eleventh hour? Alongside the lovely period setting and the magnetic performances of Plummer and James is an element of ridiculousness, albeit enjoyable ridiculousness. **107m/C; DVD.** Lily James; Jai Courtney; Janet McTeer; Christopher Plummer; Eddie Marsan; ***D:*** David Leveaux; ***W:*** Simon Burke; ***C:*** Roman Osin; ***M:*** Ilan Eshkeri.

Excess Baggage 🦴 ½ **1996 (PG-13)** Attention-seeking rich girl Emily (Silverstone) fakes her own kidnapping to get back at dear old dad, involving car thief Vincent Roche (del Toro) in the crime. Things get out of control when her creepy "Uncle" Ray (Walken), who's an ex-CIA assassin, is hired by Emily's father to get her back. Silverstone's character is alternately whiny and pouting, you'll wonder why dad would want her back and why Vincent hangs on at all. First picture in Silverstone's pricey production deal with Columbia went through the rumor mill (for supposed clashes between Silverstone and director Brambilla) and was originally scheduled for release in the fall of '96. **101m/C; VHS, DVD, Blu-Ray.** Alicia Silverstone; Benicio Del Toro; Christopher Walken; Harry Connick, Jr.; Jack Thompson; Nicholas Turturro; Michael Bowen; Leland Orser; Robert Wisden; Sally Kirkland; ***D:*** Marco Brambilla; ***W:*** Mikhaila Max Adams; Dick Clement; Ian La Frenais; ***C:*** Jean-Yves Escoffier; ***M:*** John Lurie.

Excessive Force 🦴 ½ **1993 (R)** Routine actioner lives up to its title by offering lots of violence, but little else. Gang leader Young seeks revenge on the cops who he believes ruined a $3 million drug deal. Loner cop Griffith is the only one to survive the grudge killings and goes after Young himself. Talented cast underachieves. Limited theatrical release sent this one almost straight to video. **87m/C; VHS, DVD.** Thomas Ian Griffith; Lance Henriksen; James Earl Jones; Charlotte Lewis; Tony Todd; Burt Young; W. Earl Brown; ***D:*** Jon Hess; ***W:*** Thomas Ian Griffith; ***C:*** Donald M. Morgan; ***M:*** Charles Bernstein.

Excessive Force 2: Force on Force 🦴 ½ **1995 (R)** Special agent Harly Cordell (Randall) volunteers to hunt down an assassination squad that is turning L.A. into murder central. Seems her former lover Francis Lydell (Gauthier) is head killer and Harly's got a score to settle. Lots of action and nifty weapons. **88m/C; VHS, DVD.** Stacie Randall; Dan Gauthier; Jay Patterson; John Mese; ***D:*** Jonathan Winfrey; ***W:*** Mark Sevi; ***C:*** Russ Brandt; ***M:*** Kevin Kiner.

Excision 🦴🦴 **2012** Maliciously weird, in-your-face comedy/horror. Delusional and proud high school misfit Pauline (McCord) is seeking her controlling mother's (Lords) approval with her desire for a medical career and curing her sister's (Winter) cystic fibrosis. Pauline's obsession with human flesh and surgery goes to extremes--as seen in her violent sexual fantasies. **81m/C; DVD, Blu-Ray.** AnnaLynne McCord; Traci Lords; Ariel Winter; Roger Bart; Jeremy Sumpter; Malcolm McDowell; Ray Wise; Marlee Matlin; John Waters; ***D:*** Richard A. Bates, Jr.; ***W:*** Richard A. Bates, Jr.; ***C:*** Itay Gross; ***M:*** Steve Damstra, II; Mads Heldtberg. **VIDEO**

Exclusive Story 🦴🦴 **1936** Ripped-from-the-headlines MGM programmer loosely based on the career of New York DA Thomas E. Dewey. Crime reporter Timothy Higgins (Erwin) is approached by Ann Devlin (Evans) after her dad's business is threatened by a mobster. While Higgins is snooping around, special prosecutor Dick Barton (Tone) joins in to put the crooks behind bars It all ends with a steamship disaster reflecting the real life 1934 Morro Castle fire. **73m/B; DVD.** Franchot Tone; Stuart Erwin; Madge Evans; Joseph Calleia; Robert Barrat; Louise Henry; J. Farrell MacDonald; J. Carrol Naish; ***D:*** George B. Seitz; ***W:*** Michael Fessier; ***C:*** Lester White; ***M:*** Edward Ward.

Excuse Me for Living 🦴 1/2 **2012** Superficial, unconvincing rom com with familiar faces if you watch daytime TV soaps. After a suicide attempt, druggie Dan is remanded into the care of Dr. Bernstein at his upstate New York rehab clinic. Dan can't resist sneaking out to party with his friend Bruce until he meets Laura who (of course) turns out to be Bernstein's daughter. Lead Pelphrey is endearing despite the weak material. **105m/C; DVD.** Tom Pelphrey; Melissa Archer; Robert Vaughn; David A. Gregory; Jerry Stiller; Christopher Lloyd; ***D:*** Ric Klass; ***W:*** Ric Klass; ***C:*** Chase Bowman; ***M:*** Robert Miller. **VIDEO**

Excuse My Dust 🦴🦴 1/2 **1951** This lighthearted MGM musical is set in the 1890s. Loony inventor Joe Belden (Skelton) is fascinated by the horseless carriage to the rage of livery stable owner Harvey Bullitt (Demarest), the father of Joe's gal Liz (Forrest). Joe is determined to prove his worth against rival Cyrus Random Jr. (Carey) by entering a cross-country auto race. **82m/C; DVD.** Red Skelton; Sally Forrest; William Demarest; MacDonald Carey; Jane Darwell; Monica Lewis; Lillian Bronson; Paul Harvey; ***D:*** Roy Rowland; ***W:*** George Wells; ***C:*** Alfred Gilks; Arthur Schwartz.

Execution 🦴 1/2 **1968** Clips (Mimmo Palmara) is a bounty hunter after his former partner for betraying him and leaving him for dead. Currently only available as part of the 'Westerns Unchained' collection. **100m/C; Blu-Ray.** *IT* John Richardson; Rita Klein; Franco Giornelli; Piero Vida; ***D:*** Domenico Paolella; ***W:*** Domenico Paolella; Fernando Franchi; Giancarlo Zagni; ***C:*** Mimmo Palmara; Aldo Scavarda; ***M:*** Coriolano Gori. **VIDEO**

The Execution 🦴 1/2 **1985** Five female friends who discover that the Nazi doctor who brutalized them in a concentration camp during WWII is now living a normal life in California. Together they plot his undoing. **92m/C; VHS, DVD.** Loretta Swit; Valerie Harper; Sandy Dennis; Jessica Walter; Rip Torn; Barbara Barrie; Robert Hooks; Michael Lerner; ***D:*** Paul Wendkos; ***M:*** Georges Delerue.

Execution of Raymond Graham 🦴🦴 1/2 **1985** The lawyers and family of Raymond Graham struggle to keep him from being executed for murder. Based on a true story. **104m/C; VHS, DVD.** Morgan Freeman; Jeff Fahey; Kate Reid; Laurie Metcalf; Josef Sommer; ***D:*** Daniel Petrie. **TV**

The Executioner 🦴🦴 **1970 (PG)** A thriller wherein a British spy must prove that his former colleague is a double agent. Elements of backstabbing, betrayal, and espionage abound. **107m/C; VHS, DVD.** *GB* Judy Geeson; Oscar Homolka; Charles Gray; Nigel Patrick; George Peppard; Joan Collins; Keith Michell; ***D:*** Sam Wanamaker.

Executioner of Venice 🦴 **1963** Marauding pirates with time on hands swarm in from the Adriatic Sea and attempt to rob the Venetians blind. The Doge and his godson come to the rescue. **90m/C; VHS, DVD.** Guy Madison; Lex Barker; Alessandra Panaro; ***D:*** Louis Capauno.

The Executioner, Part 2: Frozen Scream 🦴 **1984 (R)** Brutal feud rocks the Mafia, and a crime kingpin's passionate son seeks revenge on his father's slayers. Not a sequel to any other films bearing similar titles. Strange thing is, no "Executioner, Part I" was ever made. Pretty laughable. **150m/C; VHS, Streaming.** Chris Mitchum; Aldo Ray; Antoine John Mottet; Renee Harmon; ***D:*** James Bryant.

The Executioners 🦴 1/2 **1993** When a nuclear explosion contaminates most of the city's drinking water, the remainder falls under the harsh control of the Black Knight. Now, it's up to the Heroic Trio to defeat their nemesis. Chinese with subtitles. **100m/C; VHS, DVD.** *CH* Anita (Yim-Fong) Mui; Michelle Yeoh; Maggie Cheung; ***D:*** Ching Siu Tung; ***W:*** Susan Chan; ***C:*** Hang-Seng Poon; ***M:*** Cacine Wong.

The Executioner's Song 🦴🦴 1/2 **1982** European version of the TV movie based on Norman Mailer's Pulitzer Prize-winner, recounting the life and death of convicted murderer Gary Gilmore. Features adult-minded footage not seen in the U.S. version. **157m/C; VHS, DVD, Blu-Ray.** Tommy Lee Jones; Rosanna Arquette; Eli Wallach; Christine Lahti; Jenny Wright; Jordan Clark; Steven Keats; ***D:*** Lawrence Schiller.

Executive Action 🦴🦴 1/2 **1973 (PG)** Political thriller providing a different look at the events leading to the assassination of JFK. In this speculation, a millionaire pays a professional spy to organize a secret conspiracy to kill President Kennedy. Ryan's final film. Adapted by Dalton Trumbo from Mark Lane's "Rush to Judgement." **91m/C; VHS, DVD.** Burt Lancaster; Robert Ryan; Will Geer; Gilbert Green; John Anderson; ***D:*** David Miller; ***C:*** Robert Steadman; ***M:*** Randy Edelman.

Executive Decision 🦴🦴 **1996 (R)** Those wacky terrorists are at it again. You would think that after getting their butts kicked in almost every action picture since 1980 that they would learn. But here they are, hijacking a 747, cutting off communications, and affixing a nerve gas bomb to the plane. This time a group of high tech commandos, led by Russell and (briefly) Seagal, must sneak onto the plane and generally mess up the bad guys' plans. Brave stewardess Berry helps tango with the central casting mad dog terrorists. The title refers to the President's decision on whether or not to blow the plane up in order to avert disaster. Or maybe "Die Hard: Ad Nauseum" wasn't available. **132m/C; VHS, DVD, Blu-Ray.** Kurt Russell; Halle Berry; Oliver Platt; John Leguizamo; Steven Seagal; Joe Morton; David Suchet; B.D. Wong; Len Cariou; Whip Hubley; J.T. Walsh; Mary Ellen Trainor; ***D:*** Stuart Baird; ***W:*** Jim Thomas; John Thomas; ***C:*** Alex Thomson; ***M:*** Jerry Goldsmith.

Executive Koala 🦴🦴🦴 *Koara Kacho* **2006** In director Minoru Kawasaki's latest parody, a six-foot tall talking koala bear happens to be an executive at a pickle manufacturer and suffers blackouts. Unfortunately for him during one of these blackouts his ex suffers a bad case of death, and he looks to be the main suspect. Others soon follow, and it's a race for the poor Koala and his animal friends to prove his innocence. **86m/C; DVD.** *JP* Lee Ho; Eiichi Kikuchi; Arthur Kuroda; Hironobu Nomura; ***D:*** Minoru Kawasaki; ***W:*** Minoru Kawasaki; Masakazu Migita; ***C:*** Yasatako Nagano.

Executive Power 🦴🦴 **1998 (R)** The President has a secret and his people will do anything to prevent a scandal. Secret Service agent Nick (Scheffer) realizes this when a staffer who knows turns up dead. Above average thriller. **115m/C; VHS, DVD.** Craig Sheffer; Andrea Roth; Joanna Cassidy; John Heard; William Atherton; Denise Crosby; John Capodice; ***D:*** David Corley; ***W:*** David Corley. **VIDEO**

Executive Suite 🦴🦴🦴 **1954** One of the first dog-eat-dog dramas about high finance and big business. The plot centers on the question of a replacement for the freshly buried owner of a gigantic furniture company. **104m/B; DVD.** William Holden; June Allyson; Barbara Stanwyck; Fredric March; Walter Pidgeon; Louis Calhern; Shelley Winters; Paul Douglas; Nina Foch; Dean Jagger; ***D:*** Robert Wise; ***W:*** Ernest Lehman; ***C:*** George J. Folsey.

Executive Target 🦴🦴 **1997 (R)** Stunt-car driver Nick James (Madsen) is grabbed by a gang of mercenaries who want him as their getaway man when they attempt to kidnap the president (Scheider) and overthrow the U.S. government. He agrees because the gang have also taken his wife as a hostage. Lots of action sequences show where the money went. **96m/C; VHS, DVD.** Michael Madsen; Keith David; Angie Everhart; Roy Scheider; Dayton Callie; Kathy Christopherson; ***D:*** Joseph Merhi; ***W:*** Dayton Callie; ***C:*** Ken Blakey. **VIDEO**

Exile Express 🦴 1/2 **1939** Russian emigre Nadine (Sten) is aboard a train carrying refugees to New York where they'll be deported. She's in trouble because the research chemist she worked for has been murdered and foreign agents are after the missing piece of a formula for poison gas. Nadine is helped out by journalist Steve (Marshal) as they have to outrun bad guy spies and government officials. There's a lot of inappropriate comedy thrown into the thriller mix. **70m/B; DVD.** Anna Sten; Alan Marshal; Jerome Cowan; Jed Prouty; Walter Catlett; Harry Davenport; ***D:*** Otis Garrett; ***W:*** Edwin Justus Mayer; ***C:*** John Mescall; ***M:*** George Parrish.

Exiled 🦴🦴 **2006 (R)** High-octane Hong Kong actioner. In 1998, Macau's gangsters are settling old scores and divvying up their loot before the Portuguese island is turned over to communist China. Wo (Nick Cheung) has just returned from exile but Boss Fay (Yam), whom he tried to kill, still wants revenge and sends Blaze (Wong Chau-Sang) and Fat (Lam) to do the deed. But when gangsters Tai (Ng) and Cat (Roy Cheung) show up, it's to prevent Wo's death. Turns out, all five men once belonged to the same gang and they agree to first hijack a gold shipment before finishing other business. Cantonese with subtitles or dubbed. **109m/C; DVD.** *CH* Nick Cheung; Roy Cheung; Frances Ng; Suet Lam; Anthony Wong Chau-Sang; Ka-tung Lam; Simon Yam; Josie Ho; Richie Jen; ***D:*** Johnny To; ***W:*** Kam-yeun Szeto; Tin-Shing Yip; ***C:*** Sui-keung Cheung; ***M:*** Guy Zerafa.

Exiled to Shanghai 🦴🦴 1/2 **1937** A couple of newsreel men invent a television device that revolutionizes the business. **65m/B; VHS, DVD.** Wallace Ford; June Travis; Dean Jagger; William "Billy" Bakewell; Arthur Lake; Jonathan Hale; William Harrigan; Sarah Padden; ***D:*** Nick Grinde.

The Exiles 🦴🦴 **1961** A slice-of-bygone-life drama, set in L.A., that briefly made the festival circuit and then disappeared until its 2008 restoration by the UCLA Film and Television Archive. Mackenzie, then a USC film student, turned his attention to the now-razed downtown neighborhood of Bunker Hill, an area peopled by immigrants and marginally employed Native Americans: He follows one fairly typical evening with several characters who spend their time worrying, drinking, and raising a little hell. **72m/B; DVD.** Yvonne Williams; Homer Nish; Tommy Reynolds; ***D:*** Kent Mackenzie; ***W:*** Kent Mackenzie; ***C:*** Erik Daarstad; Robert Kaufman; John Morrill; ***M:*** Anthony Hilder; Robert Hafner; Eddie Sunrise. Natl. Film Reg. '09.

eXistenZ 🦴🦴 1/2 **1999 (R)** Typically scary and weird Cronenberg production finds security guard Law saving the life of computer-game designer Leigh. They both get sucked into one of her alternate-reality creations and are pursued by assassins. In this future world, game players are literally hooked up to their computer with an umbilical-like cord plugged directly into their spines—no doubt the fantasy of teenage boys everywhere. Surreal visuals and excellent performances won't help the viewer keep track of what's going on, but for Cronenberg linear plotting is rarely the point. **97m/C; VHS, DVD, Blu-Ray.** *CA* Jennifer Jason Leigh; Jude Law; Ian Holm; Willem Dafoe; Sarah Polley; Christopher Eccleston; Don McKellar; Callum Keith Rennie; ***D:*** David Cronenberg; ***W:*** David Cronenberg; ***C:*** Peter Suschitzky; ***M:*** Howard Shore. Genie '99: Film Editing.

Exit Plan 🦴🦴 *Selvmords Turisten* **2020** Though dully insurance investigator Max Isakson (Coster-Waldau) has a lovely girlfriend (Novotny), he has a brain tumor and is considering how much longer he wants to live. Still working, he is looking into a case involving Hotel Aurora, a so-called suicide resort where people go to end their lives. When Max checks in to the hotel to do his investigation, he becomes trapped and questions his sanity and the nature of reality. Though not entirely disinteresting, it can't escape being heavy-handed and predictable. **90m/C; DVD.** Nikolaj Coster-Waldau; Kate Ashfield; Tuva Novotny; Robert Aramayo; Jan Bijvoet; ***D:*** Jonas Alexander Arnby; ***W:*** Rasmus Birch; ***C:*** Niels Thastum; ***M:*** Mikkel Hess.

Exit Smiling 🦴🦴 1/2 **1926** Wannabe actress Violet (Lillie in her film debut) joins a third-rate traveling troupe as their wardrobe mistress hoping for a chance to get onstage. During a railroad stop, Violet meets Jimmy Marsh (Pickford), a fugitive who's been falsely accused of embezzlement. Violet persuades him to disguise himself as their new male lead and, having fallen in unrequited love, works to clear his name. **77m/B; Silent; DVD.** Beatrice Lillie; Jack Pickford; Doris Lloyd; Louise Lorraine; DeWitt Jennings; Harry C. (Henry) Myers; Franklin Pangborn; Tenen Holtz; ***D:*** Sam Taylor; ***W:*** Sam Taylor; Tim Whelan; ***C:*** Andre Barlatier.

Exit Speed 🦴 1/2 **2008 (R)** On Christmas Eve, ten strangers board a bus traveling across Texas. They accidentally collide with a meth-addict biker and his equally drug-crazed buds who force the bus off the road. The passengers take refuge in an abandoned junkyard where they improvise weapons to repel attacks by the murderous gang. **93m/C; DVD, Blu-Ray.** Fred Ward; Desmond Harrington; Lea Thompson; Julie Mond; Gregory Jbara; David Rees Snell; ***W:*** Scott Ziehl; Michael Stokes; ***C:*** Thomas Callaway; ***M:*** Doug Besterman. **VIDEO**

Exit Through the Gift Shop 🦴🦴 **2010 (R)** An unexpectedly comic art documentary from British artist/prankster Bansky that turns on its original filmmaker Thierry Guetta. Guetta is a compulsive videographer (especially of his own life) while Bansky has protected his own anonymity (and uses voice and face distortions in the film) while achieving success and notoriety. Brought together by their interest in street art, Guetta filmed various artists but didn't know what to do with the material as became abundantly clear when he teamed with Bansky and later attempted to establish his own celebrity guerilla identity in L.A. The look at other street artists and their work may be of the most interest. **87m/C; Blu-Ray, On Demand.** *GB* ***Nar:*** Rhys Ifans; ***D:*** Banksy; ***C:*** Thierry Guetta; ***M:*** Geoff Barrow. Ind. Spirit '11: Feature Doc.

Exit to Eden 🦴 1/2 **1994 (R)** Anne Rampling's (AKA Anne Rice) novel focused on fulfilling S&M sexual fantasies, but director Marshall goes for laughs with a buddy cops-out-of-water sitcom subplot, as undercover cops Aykroyd and O'Donnell track a suspected jewel thief to the fantasy resort of Eden, run by dominatrix Delany. (What was the pitch for this one? Think "Another Stakeout" meets "Tie Me Up, Tie Me Down." It'll be great. Really.) Neither plot works, resulting in a kinky movie with no kink, and a comedy with few laughs. O'Donnell holds up her end, providing what few yuks there are. Everyone else, especially Aykroyd and Delany, seem to be sleepwalking. Lucky for them. **113m/C; VHS, DVD.** Dana Delany; Paul Mercurio; Dan Aykroyd; Rosie O'Donnell; Hector Elizondo; Stuart Wilson; Iman; Sandi Korn; Laura Elena Harring; ***D:*** Garry Marshall; ***W:*** Deborah Amelon; Bob Brunner; ***M:*** Patrick Doyle. Golden Raspberries '94: Worst Support. Actress (O'Donnell).

Exit Wounds 🦴🦴 **2001 (R)** Unpredictable, unorthodox Detroit police detective Orin Boyd (Seagal, of course) gets sent to the baddest part of town after successfully, but unconventionally, breaking up a plot to kill the Vice President. There, along with his rambunctious new partner (Washington), he uncovers corrupt cops and a drug-running scheme involving the notorious crime lord Walker (DMX). Lots of martial arts sequences and loads of gunfire from, presumably, really bad shots. Romance also blossoms between Mr. Loose Canon and a precinct commander played by Hennessy. Typical Seagal flick, sure to be enjoyed by fans. Others should be wary. **98m/C; VHS, DVD, Blu-Ray.** Steven Seagal; DMX; Isaiah Washington, IV; Anthony Anderson; Michael Jai White; Bill Duke; Jill(ian) Hennessey; Tom Arnold; Bruce McGill; David Vadim; Eva Mendes; ***D:*** Andrzej Bartkowiak; ***W:*** Ed Horowitz; Richard D'Ovidio; ***C:*** Glen MacPherson; ***M:*** Jeff Rona; Damon Blackman.

Exodus 🦴🦴🦴 **1960** Chronicles the post-WWII partition of Palestine into a homeland for Jews; the anguish of refugees from Nazi concentration camps held on ships in the Mediterranean; the struggle of the tiny nation with forces dividing it from within and destroying it from the outside; and the heroic men and women who saw a job to be done and did it. Based on the novel by Leon Uris; filmed in Cyprus and Israel. Preminger battled the Israeli government, the studio, and the novel's author to complete this epic. Cost more than $4 million, a phenomenal amount at the time. **208m/C; VHS, DVD, Blu-Ray.** Paul Newman; Eva Marie Saint; Lee J. Cobb; Sal Mineo; Ralph Richardson; Hugh Griffith; Gregory Ratoff; Felix Aylmer; Peter Lawford; Jill Haworth; John Derek; David Opatoshu; Marius Goring; Alexandra Stewart; Michael Wager; Martin Benson; Paul Stevens; George Maharis; ***D:*** Otto Preminger; ***W:*** Dalton Trumbo; ***M:*** Ernest Gold. Oscars '60: Orig. Dramatic Score; Golden Globes '61: Support. Actor (Mineo).

Exodus: Gods and Kings 🦴 1/2 **2014 (PG-13)** Bale plays Moses, who learns via prophecy that he will be the leader of his people, not the petulant son of Seti I (Turturro), Ramesses II (Edgerton). When Seti dies and power is handed down the bloodline, Moses is exiled. After years communicating with a God who is envisioned as a pre-teen child, Moses leads his people back to the promised land. Writer/director Scott creates a plodding, dull overly CGI-ed piece of nonsense that wastes a talented cast, mega-budget, and beloved source material on something shockingly forgettable. **150m/C; DVD, Blu-Ray.** Christian Bale; Joel Edgerton; Sigourney Weaver; John Turturro; Ben Kingsley; Ben Mendelsohn; Maria Valverde; Aaron Paul; Isaac Andrews; Hiam Abbass; Golshifteh Farahani; ***D:*** Ridley Scott; ***W:*** Bill Collage; Jeffrey Caine; Steven Zaillian; Adam Cooper; ***C:*** Dariusz Wolski; ***M:*** Alberto Iglesias.

Exorcism 🦴 1/2 *Exorcismo* **1974** A satanic cult in a small English village commits a series of gruesome crimes that have the authorities baffled. **90m/C; VHS, DVD, Blu-Ray.** *SP* Paul Naschy; Maria Perschy; Maria Kosti; Grace Mills; Jorge Torras; Marta Avile; ***D:*** Juan Bosch; ***W:*** Paul Naschy; Juan Bosch; ***C:*** Francisco Sanchez.

The Exorcism of Emily Rose 🦴🦴🦴 **2005 (PG-13)** Nineteen year old student Emily Rose (Carpenter) died during an exorcism performed by Father Richard Moore (Wilkinson), who is being tried for negligent homicide. Attorney Erin Bruner (Linney) hopes her defense of the priest will propel her career to the next level. This courtroom drama is interwoven with horror as the freakish circumstances of Emily's death are recounted from the stand. Somewhat predictable, but well worth the viewing for fans of the genre. **114m/C; DVD, UMD.** Laura Linney; Tom Wilkinson; Campbell Scott; Jennifer Carpenter; Colm Feore; Joshua Close; Kenneth Welsh; Duncan Fraser; J.R. Bourne; Mary Beth Hurt; Henry Czerny; Shohreh Aghdashloo; ***D:*** Scott Derrickson; ***W:*** Scott Derrickson; Paul Harris Boardman; ***C:*** Tom Stern; ***M:*** Christopher Young.

The Exorcist 🦴🦴🦴 1/2 **1973 (R)** Truly terrifying story of a young girl who is possessed by a malevolent spirit. Brilliantly directed by Friedkin, with underlying themes of the workings and nature of fate. Impeccable casting and unforgettable, thought-provoking performances. A rare film that remains startling and engrossing with every viewing, it spawned countless imitations and changed the way horror films were made. Based on the bestseller by Blatty, who also wrote the screenplay. Not for the squeamish. When first released, the film created mass hysteria in theatres, with people fainting and paramedics on the scene. **120m/C; VHS, DVD, Blu-Ray.** Ellen Burstyn; Linda Blair; Jason Miller; Max von Sydow; Jack MacGowran; Lee J. Cobb; Kitty Winn; Barton Heyman; Peter Masterson; ***V:*** Mercedes McCambridge; ***D:*** William Friedkin; ***W:*** William Peter Blatty; ***C:*** Owen Roizman; Billy Williams; ***M:*** Jack Nitzsche. Oscars '73: Adapt. Screenplay, Sound; Golden Globes '74: Director (Friedkin), Film--Drama, Screenplay, Support. Actress (Blair); Natl. Film Reg. '10.

The Exorcist 2: The Heretic 🦴🦴 **1977 (R)** Unnecessary sequel to the 1973 hit "The Exorcist" which featured extensive recutting by Boorman. After four years, Blair is still under psychiatric care, suffering from the effects of being possessed by the devil. Meanwhile, a priest investigates the first exorcist's work as he tries to help the head-spinning lass. Decent special effects. **118m/C; VHS, DVD, Blu-Ray.** Richard Burton; Linda Blair; Louise Fletcher; Kitty Winn; James Earl Jones; Ned Beatty; Max von Sydow; Paul Henreid; ***D:*** John Boorman; ***W:*** William Goodhart; ***C:*** William A. Fraker; ***M:*** Ennio Morricone.

Exorcist 3: Legion 🦴🦴 **1990 (R)** Apparently subscribing to the two wrongs make a right school of sequels, this time novelist Blatty is the director. The result is slightly better than the first sequel, but still a far cry from the original. Fifteen years later, Detective Kinderman (Scott) is faced with a series of really gross murders bearing the mark of a serial killer who was flambeed in the electric chair on the same night as the exorcism of the pea-soup expectorating devil of the original. With the aid of priests Flanders and Dourif, the detective stalks the transmigratory terror—without the help of Linda Blair, who was at the time spoofing "The Exorcist" in "Repossessed." **105m/C; VHS, DVD, Blu-Ray.** George C. Scott; Ed Flanders; Jason Miller; Nicol Williamson; Scott Wilson; Brad Dourif; Nancy Fish; George DiCenzo; Viveca Lindfors; Patrick Ewing; Fabio; ***D:*** William Peter Blatty; ***W:*** William Peter Blatty; ***C:*** Gerry Fisher; ***M:*** Barry DeVorzon.

Exorcist: The Beginning 🦴 1/2 **2004 (R)** Once upon a time, Paul Schrader was set to make a prequel to the 1973 horror classic "The Exorcist." He shot his film, which was rejected by the producer as insufficiently scary. So Renny Harlin was hired to basically re-shoot (and re-cast) the entire movie. This backstory has got to be more interesting than what finally showed up on screen. In 1949, Merrin (holdover Skarsgard) has temporarily rejected the priesthood and is working as an archeologist. He agrees to travel to Kenya and bring back an artifact unearthed at a mysteriously preserved Byzantine church. Scary, possibly supernatural, things begin to happen—a child even becomes possessed! Would that any of the cheap theatrics could, more than momentarily, hold a viewer's interest. Schrader's version is also expected to be released on DVD. **114m/C; DVD, Blu-Ray.** Stellan Skarsgard; James D'Arcy; Izabela Scorupco; Remy Sweeney; Julian Wadham; Andrew French; Ben Cross; David Bradley; ***D:*** Renny Harlin; ***W:*** William Wisher; Caleb Carr; Alexi Hawley; ***C:*** Vittorio Storaro; ***M:*** Trevor Rabin.

Exotic House of Wax 🦴 1/2 *Erotic House of Wax* **1997** Young woman inherits her uncle's bizarre wax museum upon his death and discovers that the museum's inhabitants have this habit of coming to life and acting out their sexual fantasies. **90m/C; VHS, DVD.** Jacqueline Lovell; Josie Hunter; ***D:*** Cybil (Sybil) Richards.

Exotica 🦴🦴🦴 **1994 (R)** Daunting look at eroticism, secrecy, and despair. Christina (Kirshner) is at the center of some complicated relationships. She dresses as a schoolgirl while working at the Exotica strip club in Toronto, where her former lover Eric (Koteas) is the creepily suggestive DJ. Christina's also the obsession of seemingly mild-mannered tax man Francis (Greenwood), who has turned her table dancing into a strange private ritual. Lest this seem to make sense be assured that director Egoyan has much, much more going on—not all of it clear and most of it disturbing. **104m/C; VHS, DVD.** *CA* Mia Kirshner; Elias Koteas; Bruce Greenwood; Don McKellar; Victor Garber; Arsinee Khanjian; Sarah Polley; Calvin Green; David Hemblen; ***D:*** Atom Egoyan; ***W:*** Atom Egoyan; ***C:*** Paul Sarossy; ***M:*** Mychael Danna. Genie '94: Art Dir./Set Dec., Cinematog., Costume Des., Director (Egoyan), Film, Orig. Screenplay, Score, Support. Actor (McKellar); Toronto-City '94: Canadian Feature Film.

Expect No Mercy 🦴 **1995 (R)** Government agent must rescue a fellow agent being held in a virtual reality center that trains assassins to commit murder. **91m/C; VHS, DVD.** Billy Blanks; Jalal Merhi; Wolf Larson; Laurie Holden; Real Andrews; ***D:*** Zale Dalen; ***W:*** J. Stephen Maunder; ***C:*** Curtis Petersen; ***M:*** Varouje.

Expecting a Miracle 🦴🦴 1/2 **2009** Hallmark Channel original. Pete and Donna's marriage is in trouble when the fertility treatments Donna undergoes are unsuccessful and she doesn't want to adopt. Pete's boss offers them a getaway at his Mexican vacation home but they take a wrong turn and then their SUV breaks down in the desert. They manage to walk into a small town that's preparing for a local festival and a chance encounter with a priest and a handicapped young boy has Pete and Donna wondering if fate (and faith) has shown them a new path to follow. **89m/C; DVD.** Jason Priestley; Teri Polo; Cheech Marin; Shalim Ortiz; Ed Lauter; Barry Livingston; Kevin Hernandez; Rebeka Montoya; ***D:*** Steve Gomer; ***W:*** Donald Davenport; ***C:*** Maximo Munzi; ***M:*** Kevin Kiner. **CABLE**

The Expendables 🦴 1/2 **2010 (R)** Triple-threat Stallone (cast, co-writer, and director) leads a group of mercenaries on a mission to overthrow a South American dictator in this old-school action-adventure flick. Stallone went for a cast combo of veterans and more recent action stars but it plays like a throwback to his own halcyon macho days. It's mindless fun (if you don't expect too much) with a high body count and fists, guns, knives, and lots of things blowing up real good. Rourke steals his scenes as a retired mercenary turned tattoo artist. **103m/C; Blu-Ray, On Demand.** Sylvester Stallone; Terry Crews; Randy Couture; Eric Roberts; Dolph Lundgren; Jet Li; Jason Statham; Mickey Rourke; Steve Austin; Bruce Willis; Arnold Schwarzenegger; Charisma Carpenter; Nick Searcy; David Zayas; Gary Daniels; Giselle Itie; ***D:*** Sylvester Stallone; ***W:*** Sylvester Stallone; David Callaham; ***C:*** Jeffrey L. Kimball; ***M:*** Brian Tyler.

The Expendables 2 🦴🦴 1/2 **2012 (R)** With larger roles for Willis and Schwarzenegger and a bigger budget, it's easy to say that this follow-up to Stallone's comeback hit is just the "more" version of the last flick. Another mission goes wrong (of course) that ends in the death of one of the group, and it sends them on a quest for revenge. The amped-up aspect of this story makes for some B-movie thrills even if none of this can be taken seriously. And when the team behind the sequel sets aside action for things like character and dialogue, the concept seems flatter than ever. **103m/C; DVD, Blu-Ray; Closed Captioned.** Sylvester Stallone; Jason Statham; Jet Li; Dolph Lundgren; Randy Couture; Terry Crews; Liam Hemsworth; Bruce Willis; Yu Nan; Charisma Carpenter; Jean-Claude Van Damme; Arnold Schwarzenegger; Chuck Norris; ***D:*** Simon West; ***W:*** Sylvester Stallone; ***C:*** Shelly Johnson; ***M:*** Brian Tyler.

The Expendables 3 🦴 1/2 **2014 (PG-13)** The natural law of diminishing returns in sequels is amplified by an action film that's overcrowded and reduced in entertainment value by taking a violent world and conforming it to a PG-13 rating. The unimportant plot centers on the title gang, once again headed by Sly, who also co-wrote, facing off with a ruthless arms dealer named Conrad Stonebanks (Gibson), who has set out to destroy The Expendables. Sly and company go with the "More is More" operating theory of action sequels, flooding the film with cameos and nostalgic co-stars, but nothing fun enough to stand on its own. **126m/C; DVD, Blu-Ray.** Sylvester Stallone; Jason Statham; Wesley Snipes; Mel Gibson; Terry Crews; Dolph Lundgren; Randy Couture; Harrison Ford; Kellan Lutz; Kelsey Grammer; Arnold Schwarzenegger; Antonio Banderas; Jet Li; ***D:*** Patrick Hughes; ***W:*** Sylvester Stallone; Creighton Rothenberger; Katrin Benedikt; ***C:*** Peter Menzies, Jr.; ***M:*** Brian Tyler. Golden Raspberries '14: Worst Support. Actor (Grammer).

The Experiment 🦴🦴 **2001 (R)** A prestigious medical institute recruits 20 men to spend two weeks in a controlled prison environment for a psychology experiment. Eight are chosen as guards and the remaining 12 are prisoners. The guards, led by sadist Berus (von Dohnanyi), soon begin abusing their power and their prisoners while the prisoners, led by Tarek (Bleibtreu), challenge their authority and the scientists simply lose control of their experiment. Based on the novel "Black Box" by Giordano. German with subtitles. **119m/C; VHS, DVD.** *GE* Moritz Bleibtreu; Christian Berkel; Justus von Dohnanyi; Oliver Stokowski; Wotan Wilke Mohring; Nicki von Tempelhoff; Timo Dierkes; Antoine Munot, Jr.; Edgar Selge; Andrea Sawatzki; Philip Hochmair; ***D:*** Oliver Hirschbiegel; ***W:*** Don Bohlinger; Mario Giordano; Christoph Darnstadt; ***C:*** Rainer Klausmann; ***M:*** Alexander von Bubenheim.

Experiment 🦴 1/2 **2005 (R)** Low-budget sci fi (filmed in Prague). Morgan (Hopkins) and Anna (French) both wake up in different parts of the same city with no idea who or where they are or what happened to them. But someone is watching them very closely and it turns out the unfortunate duo are the subjects of a mind control experiment. **95m/C; DVD.** John Hopkins; David Grant; Georgina French; Nick Simons; ***D:*** Dan Turner; ***W:*** John Harrison; Dan Turner; ***C:*** Gareth Pritchard; ***M:*** John Rand. **VIDEO**

The Experiment 🦴 **2010 (R)** Nonsensical and tiresome drama based on the 1971 Stanford Prison Experiment. Twenty-four male subjects are hired to participate in a two-week behavioral project. One group is assigned to be guards and the other is prisoners. The guards are not supposed to use force but as everyone goes deeper into their roles, control is lost. **96m/C; DVD.** Adrien Brody; Forest Whitaker; Cam Gigandet; Clifton Collins, Jr.; Travis Fimmel; David Banner; Ethan Cohn; Fisher Stevens; Maggie Grace; ***D:*** Paul Scheuring; ***W:*** Paul Scheuring; ***C:*** Amelia Vincent; ***M:*** Graeme Revell. **VIDEO**

Experiment in Terror 🦴🦴🦴 **1962** A psychopath kidnaps a girl in order to blackmail her sister, a bank teller, into embezzling $100,000. **123m/B; DVD, Blu-Ray.** Lee Remick; Glenn Ford; Stefanie Powers; Ross Martin; ***D:*** Blake Edwards; ***W:*** Gordon Gordon; Mildred Gordon; ***C:*** Philip H. Lathrop; ***M:*** Henry Mancini.

Experiment Perilous 🦴🦴🦴 **1945** A psychologist and a recently widowed woman band together to find her husband's murderer. An atmospheric vintage mystery. **91m/B; VHS, DVD.** Hedy Lamarr; Paul Lukas; George Brent; Albert Dekker; ***D:*** Jacques Tourneur.

Experimenter 🦴🦴 1/2 **2015 (PG-13)** Michael Almereyda captures a unique life with his own unique style, employing fourth-wall breaks and even rear-screen projection to tell the story of Stanley Milgram, one of the most influential psychologists of all time. In 1961, Milgram (Peter Sarsgaard) began a series of behavioral experiments in which one subject was named the "Teacher" and asked to shock a man known as the "Learner" when he answered questions incorrectly. The "Learner" wasn't actually being shocked, but the disturbing truth was how much those in the role of "Teacher" were willing to follow orders. This is a nice, tight, educational drama with excellent performances throughout. **98m/C; DVD, Blu-Ray, Streaming.** Taryn Manning; Winona Ryder; Anton Yelchin; Kellan Lutz; Peter Sarsgaard; John Leguizamo; ***D:*** Michael Almereyda; ***W:*** Michael Almereyda; ***C:*** Ryan Samul; ***M:*** Bryan Senti.

Expert Weapon 🦴 1/2 **1993** It's a low-budget, male version of "La Femme Nikita" with an imprisoned cop killer recruited as an assassin by a secret government org (are there any other kind in these flicks). He even falls in love and then wants out. Fat chance. **90m/C; VHS, DVD.** Ian Jacklin; Sam Jones; Mel Novak; Judy Landers; Joe Estevez; ***D:*** Steven Austin.

Expired 🦴🦴 **2007** Convincingly played but still disturbing debut drama from Miniucchi. SoCal setting finds kind, vulnerable meter maid Claire hooking up with her polar opposite—abusive, if occasionally charming, loner Jay. (Must be something to do with the Christmas timeframe.) Lacking confidence, Claire doesn't protest Jay's erratic behavior until the catalyst of her mother's death finally opens Claire's eyes. **107m/C; DVD.** Samantha Morton; Jason Patric; Teri Garr; Illeana Douglas; ***D:*** Cecilia Miniucchi; ***W:*** Cecilia Miniucchi; ***C:*** Zoran Popovic; ***M:*** Jeffrey Coulter.

Explicit Ills 🦴🦴 **2008 (R)** Ensemble drama chronicles the lives of various residents of a tough North Philly neighborhood and their struggles with poverty, drugs, and health care. Webber's directorial debut. **87m/C; DVD.** Paul Dano; Rosario Dawson; Naomie Harris; Lou Taylor Pucci; Tariq Trotter; Francisco Burgos; Frankie Shaw; ***D:*** Mark Webber; ***W:*** Mark Webber; ***C:*** Patrice Lucien Crochet; ***M:*** Khari Mateen.

The Exploding Girl 🦴🦴 **2009** Contemplative, mostly uneventful drama that works precisely because writer/director Gray takes his time. Ivy is home from college and living back in her mom's New York apartment. Her best friend Al is also staying with them and the two hang out while Ivy tries to stay connected to her distant boyfriend and deal with her epilepsy and fears of having a seizure. **80m/C; DVD.** Zoe Kazan; Mark Rendall; Maryann Urbano; Hunter Canning; ***D:*** Bradley Rust Gray; ***W:*** Bradley Rust Gray; ***C:*** Eric Lin.

Exploding Sun WOOF! 2013 Warning: May cause your head to explode. However, this Reelz Channel doomsday flick is so mind-numbingly stupid it can't even be enjoyed as a bad movie. A military scientist must persuade a renegade theorist to help when a ginormous solar flare threatens Earth. **120m/C; DVD, Blu-Ray.** David James Elliot; Natalie Brown; Anthony Lemke; Alex Weiner; ***D:*** Michael Robison; ***W:*** Jeff Schechter; ***C:*** Michel St. Martin; ***M:*** James Gelfand. **CABLE**

Explorers 1/2 1985 (PG) Intelligent family fare involving three young boys who use a contraption from their makeshift laboratory to travel to outer space. From the director of "Gremlins," displaying Dante's characteristic surreal wit and sense of irony. **107m/C; DVD.** Ethan Hawke; River Phoenix; Jason Presson; Amanda Peterson; Mary Kay Place; Dick Miller; Robert Picardo; Dana Ivey; Meshach Taylor; Brooke Bundy; ***D:*** Joe Dante; ***W:*** Eric Luke; ***M:*** Jerry Goldsmith.

The Explosive Generation 1/2 1961 Low-budget youth flick, based on a true story, has a freedom of speech/social conscience plot. Idealistic California high school teacher Peter Gifford (Shatner) gets suspended by his prudish school board when he dares to discuss sex with his senior life class and some parents find out. The students stage a protest. **89m/B; DVD.** William Shatner; Lee Kinsolving; Patty McCormack; Suzi Carnell; Billy Gray; Virginia Field; Arch Johnson; Jocelyn Brando; Edward Platt; Steve (Stephen) Dunne; Phillip Terry; ***D:*** Buzz Kulik; ***W:*** Joseph Landon; ***C:*** Floyd Crosby; ***M:*** Hal Borne.

Expose WOOF! 1997 Congressman's daughter Tiffany gets mistaken for a call girl and propositioned by one of dad's colleagues. When the geezer pays her off to keep quiet, Tiff decides extortion is a viable career option. **78m/C; VHS, DVD.** Tracy Tutor; Kevin E. West; Daneen Boone; Libby George; ***D:*** B.A. Rudnick.

Exposed 1/2 2003 (R) Bob Smith (Donovan) hosts a TV tabloid show that is digging for dirt on three popular female TV personalities who are all up for a big award: Martha Stewart-like Susan Andrews (Strong), Brit wit Jade Blake (Carides), and morning show host Laura Silvera (Cavazos). Lame satire. **95m/C; On Demand.** Tate Donovan; Brenda Strong; Gia Carides; Lumi Cavazos; David Rasche; Missi Pyle; Tom Irwin; Coolio; Jane Lynch; ***D:*** Misti Barnes; ***W:*** Misti Barnes; ***M:*** Mark Lewis.

Exposed 2016 (R) A dramatic exploration of the unexpected truths uncovered by a police detective after the death of his partner. When Joey Culen (Hoch), the partner of police detective Scott Galban (Reeves) dies in a shocking manner, Scott begins to look into his passing. The recently widowed Scott struggles with the weight of both losses, and the investigation helps him cope. The more he digs, however, the more unexpected truths he learns. First, there disturbing evidence related to police corruption, but at the heart of the mystery is a woman and a secret dangerous to all involved. **102m/C; DVD, Blu-Ray, Streaming, Download.** Keanu Reeves; Danny Hoch; Ana de Armas; Mira Sorvino; Christopher McDonald; ***D:*** Declan Dale; ***W:*** Gee Malik Linton; ***C:*** Trevor Forrest; ***M:*** Carlos Jose Alvarez.

The Express 1/2 2008 (PG) Raised in a poverty-stricken Pennsylvania coal-mining town, Ernie Davis (Brown) is determined to play football for Syracuse University coach Ben Schwartzwalder (Quaid), who is equally determined to win a national championship with the running back who will become the first African-American to win the Heisman Trophy. Set in the 1960s, pic does a decent if not original job of telling the predictable story of overcoming obstacles to achieve greatness, but liberal doses of cliche and melodrama detract from excellent performances. Davis died of leukemia at 23 before ever playing in the pros. **129m/C; Blu-Ray, On Demand.** Rob Brown; Dennis Quaid; Clancy Brown; Charles S. Dutton; Darrin Dewitt Henson; Nelsan Ellis; Omar Benson Miller; Geoff Stults; Frank Grillo; ***D:*** Gary Fleder; ***W:*** Charles Leavitt; ***C:*** Kramer Morgenthau; ***M:*** Mark Isham.

Expresso Bongo 1/2 1959 Soho singer/bongo player (Richards) is "discovered" by seedy talent agent Johnny Jackson (Harvey) who manages the young man into a teen idol with a 50-50 contract. But women come between the duo and Johnny finds himself without a star. **111m/B; VHS, DVD.** *GB* Laurence Harvey; Sylvia Syms; Yolande Donlan; Cliff Richard; ***D:*** Val Guest; ***W:*** Wolf Mankowitz; ***C:*** John Wilcox.

Extasis *Ecstasy* **1996** Petty thieves Rober (Bardem), Max (Guzman), and Ona (Berrocal) hatch a plan to rob celebrated theater director Daniel Peligro (Luppi). He's Max's biological father but has never met his son, and the trio decide there would be less emotional trouble if Rober poses as Max. Rober is surprised when Daniel actually welcomes him and he begins to enjoy his new lifestyle, but his partners are getting impatient. Spanish with subtitles. **92m/C; DVD.** *SP* Javier Bardem; Federico Luppi; Daniel Guzman; Leire Berrocal; Silvia Munt; ***D:*** Mariano Barroso; ***W:*** Mariano Barroso; Joaquin Oristrell; ***C:*** Flavio Martinez Labiano; ***M:*** Bingen Mendizabal.

The Exterminating Angel 1/2 *El Angel exterminador* **1962** A fierce, funny surreal nightmare, wherein dinner guests find they cannot, for any definable reason, leave the dining room; full of dream imagery and characteristically scatological satire. One of Bunuel's best, in Spanish with English subtitles. **95m/B; VHS, DVD, Blu-Ray.** *MX SP* Silvia Pinal; Enrique Rambal; Jacqueline Andere; Jose Baviera; Augusto Benedico; Luis Beristain; Claudio Brook; Cesar del Campo; Lucy Gallardo; Enrique Garcia Alvarez; Tito Junco; Ofelia Montesco; Bertha Moss; Pancho Cordova; ***D:*** Luis Bunuel; ***W:*** Luis Bunuel; Luis Alcoriza; ***C:*** Gabriel Figueroa; ***M:*** Raul Lavista.

Exterminator 1980 (R) Vietnam veteran hunts down the gang that assaulted his friend and becomes the target of the police, the CIA and the underworld in this bloody banal tale of murder and intrigue. Followed by creatively titled "Exterminator II." **101m/C; VHS, DVD, Blu-Ray, UMD.** Christopher George; Samantha Eggar; Robert Ginty; Steve James; Tony DiBenedetto; Dick Boccelli; Patrick Farrelly; Michele Harrell; Stan Getz; Roger Grimsby; ***D:*** James Glickenhaus; ***W:*** James Glickenhaus; ***C:*** Robert M. "Bob" Baldwin, Jr.; ***M:*** Joe Renzetti.

ExTerminators 1/2 2009 (R) The theme in this minor comedy is that most men are scum and deserve what they get. Alex, Stella, and Nikki meet in the same anger management class to deal with their relationship issues. Stella owns a pest control business that goes from eliminating bugs to eliminating various despicable men after they accidentally kill a friend's abusive spouse. **92m/C; DVD.** Heather Graham; Jennifer Coolidge; Amber Heard; Matthew Settle; Joey Lauren Adams; Sam Lloyd; Drena De Niro; ***D:*** John Inwood; ***W:*** Suzanne Weinert; ***C:*** Robert Baumgartner; ***M:*** Chris Hajian. **VIDEO**

The External *Michael Almereyda's The Mummy; Trance* **1999 (R)** Alcoholic Nora (Elliott) keeps experiencing strange trances that have nothing to do with her drinking. So, Nora, her husband (Harris) and their young son travel to Ireland to visit Nora's freaky uncle (Walken) in hopes of some kind of explanation. Yep, it all has something to do with a 2,000-year-old druid he's keeping in the basement of the family castle. No, it doesn't make much sense. **95m/C; VHS, DVD.** Alison Elliott; Jared Harris; Christopher Walken; Karl Geary; ***D:*** Michael Almereyda.

Extra Girl 1923 A silent melodrama/farce about a farm girl, brilliantly played by Normand, who travels to Hollywood to be a star. Once in the glamour capital, she gets used and abused for her trouble. **87m/B; Silent; VHS, DVD.** Mabel Normand; Ralph Graves; Vernon Dent; ***D:*** F. Richard Jones; ***W:*** Mack Sennett.

The Extra Man 2010 (R) Eccentric, aggravating, impecunious New Yorker Henry Harrison (Kline) becomes a mentor to his young and happily-eccentric new boarder Louis Ives (Dano). Henry is a self-proclaimed aristocrat who serves as an escort to wealthy older women (hence the title) while Louis is obsessed with literature and cross-dressing. There are a couple of subplots that don't matter much since it's the interactions between Kline and Dano that hold the viewers' attention. Adaptation of Jonathan Ames' 1998 novel. **108m/C; Blu-Ray, On Demand.** Kevin Kline; Paul Dano; John C. Reilly; Katie Holmes; Marian Seldes; Celia Weston; Patti D'Arbanville; Dan Hedaya; Lynn Cohen; John Pankow; ***D:*** Robert Pulcini; Shari Springer Berman; ***W:*** Robert Pulcini; Shari Springer Berman; Jonathan Ames; ***C:*** Terry Stacey; ***M:*** Klaus Badelt.

Extra Ordinary 1/2 2020 (R) Small town driving instructor Rose (Higgins) inherited psychic abilities from her famous spiritualist father Vincent (Cooper) but has ignored them for much of her life. This situation changes when she teaches attractive widower Martin Martin (Ward) how to drive. Martin and his teenage daughter Emma (Coleman) have tired of the attempted interventions by deceased wife/mother Bonnie.The situation grows more dire when musician Christian Winter (Forte) makes a deal with the devil that includes sacrificing Emma. The first feature by Ahern and Loughman, the quirky supernatural film is continually funny and its humor subtly effective. **93m/C; DVD.** Maeve Higgins; Barry Ward; Will Forte; Claudia O'Doherty; Jamie Beamish; ***D:*** Mike Ahern; Enda Loughman; ***W:*** Mike Ahern; Enda Loughman; ***C:*** James Mather; ***M:*** George Brennan.

Extract 2009 (R) Sketchy and fitfully amusing comedy finds mild-mannered Joel (Bateman), the owner of a flavor-extract factory, besieged at work and at home. An assembly-line accident lawsuit is trouble since Joel was about to sell the company while newly-hired hottie Cindy (Kunis) turns out to be a con woman whom Joel stills lusts after. Meanwhile, to appease his conscience, Joel tries to have himbo Brad (Mulligan) seduce Joel's frigid wife Suzie (Wiig). Doesn't really hold together but may follow Judge's other work-related flick "Office Space" into belated cultdom. **91m/C; Blu-Ray.** Jason Bateman; Mila Kunis; Kristen Wiig; Dustin Milligan; Ben Affleck; Clifton (Gonzalez) Collins, Jr.; J.K. Simmons; David Koechner; Gene Simmons; ***D:*** Mike Judge; ***W:*** Mike Judge; ***C:*** Tim Suhrstedt; ***M:*** George C. Clinton.

Extraction 2015 (R) A action-thriller centering on terrorism, the CIA, and a son going to extraordinary lengths to save his father. Leonard Turner (Willis) is a retired CIA field operative who does small jobs. Leonard is kidnapped by a terrorist group while ensuring an important piece of hardware dubbed the Condor has arrived in New Jersey. Leonard's son Harry (Lutz) is a government analyst who longs to follow in his father's footsteps in field service. After his father's kidnapping, Harry takes matters into his own hands. Drawing on his combat training, Harry does all he can to find his father and ensure the terrorists cannot complete their plans. **96m/C; DVD, Blu-Ray, Streaming, Download.** Bruce Willis; Kellan Lutz; Gina Carano; D.B. Sweeney; Joshua Mikel; ***D:*** Steven C. Miller; ***W:*** Max Adams; Umair Aleem; ***C:*** Brandon Cox; ***M:*** Ryan Dodson.

Extraction 1/2 2020 (R) When Ovi (Jaiswal), the teen son of an imprisoned Mumbai gangster (Tripathi), is kidnapped by his father's rival Amir (Painyuli), it puts Saju (Hooda), Ovi's protector, in danger. Because his father's money is frozen, the ransom cannot be paid. However, his syndicate intercedes by hiring mercenary Tyler Rake (Hemsworth) to rescue Ovi. An unflappable Aussie, Rake comes to the mission with his own issues, including alcohol abuse, a death wish, and a need for money. Based on a graphic novel, the drama has excellent editing that ramps up the violent action sequences but Rake is an action movie cliché despite Hemsworth's charismatic performance. **116m/C; DVD.** Chris Hemsworth; Rudhraksh Jaiswal; Shivam Vichare; Randeep Hooda; Pankaj Tripathi; ***D:*** Sam Hargrave; ***W:*** Joe Russo; ***C:*** Newton Thomas (Tom) Sigel; ***M:*** Alex Belcher; Henry Jackman. **VIDEO**

Extramarital 1998 (R) Magazine editor Fahey assigns reporter Lords to investigate a woman whose affair with a mystery man turns deadly. **90m/C; VHS, DVD.** Jeff Fahey; Traci Lords; Brian Bloom; Maria Isabel Diaz; ***D:*** Yael Russcol. **VIDEO**

Extraordinary Measures 1/2 2010 (PG) John Crowley (Fraser) seems to have the perfect life with wife Aileen and their children until the two youngest are diagnosed with a fatal genetic disorder. John teams up with unconventional doctor Robert Stonehill (Ford) and they start a bio-tech company focused on developing a new drug to save his children. Only Ford distinguishes himself as the rest of the high profile cast struggles with the weak material they've been given in this predictable, run-of-the-mill tearjerker. The first production from CBS Films has the look and feel of a made-for-TV-movie. Based on a true story. **105m/C; Blu-Ray, On Demand.** Harrison Ford; Brendan Fraser; Keri Russell; Dee Wallace; Jared Harris; Patrick Bauchau; Courtney B. Vance; Alan Ruck; Sam Hall; Meredith Droeger; Diego Velazquez; ***D:*** Tom Vaughan; ***W:*** Robert Nelson Jacobs; ***C:*** Andrew Dunn; ***M:*** Andrea Guerra.

Extraordinary Rendition 2007 Low-budget and short run time work against this sketchy story that does have some powerful scenes. Zaafir Ahmadi (Berdouni), a British citizen of Moroccan descent, has made some inflammatory statements during his college lectures on terrorism and democracy. This gets him drugged and kidnapped off a London street, taken to an unnamed Mideastern country, and tortured by Maro (Serkis), who accuses Ahmadi of funding terrorists. Flashbacks and flash-forwards show his life before and after his release as the broken man tries to pick up the pieces of his life. **77m/C; DVD.** *GB* Omar Berdouni; Andy Serkis; Ania Sowinski; ***D:*** Jim Threapleton; ***W:*** Jim Threapleton; ***C:*** Duncan Telford; ***M:*** James Edward Barker.

Extraterrestrial 2014 A sci fi-horror hybrid involving aliens and the trip to a cabin gone bad. After her parents' divorce, April (Allen) is struggling but goes with her boyfriend (Stroma) and a group of his friends to a cabin in the woods where she spent many childhood summers. The trip takes an unexpected turn when a fireball comes from the sky and explodes in the woods. When the group finds the crash site, they discover a damaged ship from another planet and footprints of aliens walking away the site. The friends soon find themselves being attacked by these visitors and fighting to stay alive. **101m/C; DVD, Blu-Ray, Streaming, Download.** Brittany Allen; Freddie Stroma; Melanie Papalia; Jesse Moss; Gil Bellows; ***D:*** Colin Minihan; ***W:*** Colin Minihan; Stuart Ortiz; ***C:*** Samy Inayeh; ***M:*** Blitz/Berlin.

The Extreme Adventures of Super Dave 1/2 1998 (PG) Cable TV character Super Dave Osborne (Einstein) comes to the big screen as Super Dave comes out of retirement for one last megastunt. He and protege Van Wormer plot a death-defying leap to raise money for neighbor Carides who has an ill son (Lindner). **91m/C; VHS, DVD.** Bob Einstein; Gia Carides; Carl Michael Lindner; Steve Van Wormer; Dan Hedaya; ***D:*** Peter Macdonald; ***W:*** Lorne Cameron; Don Lake; ***C:*** Bernd Heinl; ***M:*** Andrew Gross.

Extreme Dating 2004 (R) Four young ad execs head to a ski resort to continue their concept of extreme dating, which has so far been a disaster. The latest scheme is equally stupid: Troy (Keegan) and his crush Amy (DiScala) will get kidnapped, Troy will save the day, and Amy will be forever grateful and in love. Only the ex-cons hired by their pals Daniel (Sawa) and Lindsay (Detmer) decide to change the plan. No hilarity ensues, just embarrassment. **96m/C; DVD.** Devon Sawa; Amanda Detmer; Andrew Keegan; Jamie-Lynn Sigler; Ian Virgo; Meat Loaf Aday; Lee Tergesen; John DiMaggio; ***D:*** Lorena David; ***W:*** Jeff Schectman; ***C:*** Sonja Rom; ***M:*** Scott Gilman. **VIDEO**

Extreme Honor 2001 (R) This is an action movie with little action until the finale and a too-familiar storyline. Brascoe (Anderson) is forced out of the Navy SEALS when he's framed by his partner (Gruner). Now he needs a lot of cash in order to pay for his son's cancer treatments. So Brascoe teams up with some crooks (Madsen, Bush) to rip off a billionaire (Ironside). **95m/C; VHS, DVD.** Dan Anderson; Michael Ironside; Michael Madsen; Olivier Gruner; Grand L. Bush; Martin Kove; Antonio Fargas; Edward Albert; Charles Napier; Odile Corso; ***D:*** Steven Rush; ***W:*** Steven Rush; ***C:*** Ken Blakey; ***M:*** David Powell; Geoff Levin. **VIDEO**

Extreme Justice 1/2 1993 (R) A violent expose of the Special Investigations Section of the Los Angeles Police Department, an elite, undercover squad which specialized in catching violent repeat offenders. But their tactics left something to be desired. They were accused of stalking their prey until they committed a crime and then dealing with the criminal by shooting them in the act. Lots of gunplay. Originally a theatrical film that was pulled for release in the wake of the Rodney King verdict. **96m/C; VHS, DVD.** Lou Diamond Phillips; Scott Glenn; Yaphet Kotto; Ed Lauter; Chelsea Field; Stephen (Steve) Root; ***D:*** Mark L. Lester; ***W:*** Robert Boris; ***C:*** Mark Irwin; ***M:*** David Michael Frank.

Extreme Limits **2001 (R)** CIA agent Williams heads to Alaska to find a plane that has crashed in the mountains. As well as helping the survivors, he must find a mystery bomb that's also being sought by terrorists. Typical action fare. Wynorski directed under the pseudonym Jay Andrews. **105m/C; VHS, DVD.** Treat Williams; Hannes Jaenicke; John Beck; Susan Blakely; Gary Hudson; Julie St. Claire; ***D:*** Jim Wynorski; ***C:*** Andrea V. Rossotto. **VIDEO**

Extreme Measures 1/2 **1996 (R)** Dr. Grant, Action Guy! Cast against type, Grant takes on action-suspense in this urbane medical thriller, and it works. Plot is pretty standard for the genre—doctor Luthan (Grant) suspects foul play when homeless people are turning up with mysterious symptoms before expiring in his ward. Seeking to expose what he believes is a medical conspiracy, his "darn meddling" gets him in all kinds of trouble. Enter Dr. Lawrence Myrick (Hackman), a genius neurologist who reeks of suspicion. Luthan must get by him to uncover the dangerous human experimentation that's been going on. Producer and real-life love Hurley may have had something to do with the fact that Grant pulls off a mostly convincing turn, where his normally comic persona is used to humanize an otherwise cardboard hero. Adapted from a book by Michael Palmer. **118m/C; VHS, DVD.** Hugh Grant; Gene Hackman; Sarah Jessica Parker; David Cronenberg; Bill Nunn; Debra Monk; John Toles-Bey; Paul Guilfoyle; Andre De Shields; Shaun Austin-Olsen; Peter Appel; J.K. Simmons; ***D:*** Michael Apted; ***W:*** Tony Gilroy; ***C:*** John Bailey; ***M:*** Danny Elfman.

Extreme Movie **2008 (R)** Raunchy sketch comedy about teen sex includes geek Mike after his dream girl; Fred wanting to hook up with a sex chatroom babe; Chuck's once-innocent girlfriend getting into kink; and a sex puppet called Blue Ballsy. **75m/C; DVD.** Ryan Pinkston; Michael Cera; Frankie Muniz; Jamie Kennedy; Christina DeRosa; Cherilyn Wilson; Rob Pinkston; ***D:*** Adam Jay Epstein; Andrew Jacobson; ***W:*** Adam Jay Epstein; Andrew Jacobson; ***C:*** Eric Haase; ***M:*** Jim Latham. **VIDEO**

Extreme Ops 1/2 **2002 (PG-13)** Shameless attempt to cash in on the popularity of extreme sports does a faceplant in every area but stunt work. The plot revolves around the antics of a group of snowboarders and skiers as they film a commercial for director Ian (Sewell). In their exploration of a half-finished resort, boarders Silo (Absolom) and Kittie (Pallaske) accidentally film a supposedly dead Serbian war criminal (Lowitsch). The intrepid crew must then evade the villain's armed henchmen while still finding time to poke fun at frosty downhill skier Chloe (Wilson-Sampras). No reason to be stoked about this one. **93m/C; VHS, DVD.** *GB GE* Devon Sawa; Bridgette Wilson-Sampras; Rupert Graves; Rufus Sewell; Heino Ferch; Liliana Komorowska; Klaus Lowitsch; Jean-Pierre Castaldi; Joe Absolom; Jana Pallaske; David Scheller; ***D:*** Christian Duguay; ***W:*** Michael Zaidan; ***C:*** Hannes Hubach; ***M:*** Normand Corbeil; Stanislas Syrewicz.

Extreme Prejudice **1987 (R)** A redneck Texas Ranger fights a powerful drug kingpin along the U.S.-Mexican border. Once best friends, they now fight for justice and the heart of the woman they both love. **104m/C; VHS, DVD.** Nick Nolte; Powers Boothe; Maria Conchita Alonso; Michael Ironside; Rip Torn; Clancy Brown; Matt Mulhern; William Forsythe; Tommy (Tiny) Lister; Larry B. Scott; ***D:*** Walter Hill; ***W:*** Deric Washburn; ***M:*** Jerry Goldsmith.

Extreme Private Eros: Love Song 1974 1/2 *Gokushiteki erosu: Renka* **1974** A landmark Japanese documentary from the mid-1970s, intimately focusing on a complex woman and created by filmmaker Kazuo Hara. At the center of the film is a maverick in Japanese society. Takeda Miyuki is a feminist and bisexual who was once Hara's lover and with whom she has a son. When she informs him that she is going Okinawa with their son, Hara visits several times and documents the people in her life. Hara continues to follow her when she returns to Tokyo, pregnant by an African-American soldier, and when she joins a women's commune. The film unexpectedly reveals the emotions of the filmmaker as much as the focus of his film. **98m/C; DVD.** ***D:*** Kazuo Hara; ***C:*** Kazuo Hara. **VIDEO**

Extremedays 1/2 **2001 (PG)** Four buddies take an aimless road California trip after graduating from college, indulging in their love of extreme sports such as surfing, skateboarding, dirt bike racing, and snowboarding. But when one of the guys learns of his grandfather's death, they decide to make the trip into a pilgrimage to pay their respects. For the most part it's silly fluff. **93m/C; VHS, DVD.** Dante Basco; Ryan Browning; A.J. Buckley; Derek Hamilton; Cassidy Rae; ***D:*** Eric Hannah. **VIDEO**

Extremely Dangerous 1/2 **1999** Convoluted thriller that originated as a four-part British miniseries. Neil Byrne (Bean) was a British intelligence agent working deep undercover after infiltrating a group of gangsters. But his life is blown apart when Neil is convicted of the brutal murders of his wife and daughter. Naturally, he's innocent and when he makes his escape from prison transport, he heads back to find the true killers and get his revenge while being pursued by mobsters, police, and the agency he worked for. Some of the violence is very nasty. **200m/C; VHS, DVD.** *GB* Sean Bean; Juliet Aubrey; Ralph Brown; Anthony Booth; Ron Donachie; Sean Gallagher; ***D:*** Sallie Aprahamian; ***C:*** Peter Middleton; ***M:*** Rupert Gregson-Williams. **TV**

Extremely Loud and Incredibly Close 1/2 **2011 (PG-13)** Follows the journey of distressed 11-year-old Oskar Schell (Horn) seeking emotional stability after the death of his father (Hanks) in the World Trade Center on 9/11. Since he may be suffering from Asperger syndrome, Oskar's mom (Bullock) struggles to relate to him, whereas it came more naturally for his dad. When Oskar finds a key trapped in a vase in his father's closet, he uses it to explore New York's five boroughs to determine its meaning. An unfortunately overwrought and exploitive adaptation of Jonathan Safran Foer's acclaimed novel as it plays upon one of the worst American tragedies as well as the grief associated with losing a parent. **129m/C; DVD, Blu-Ray.** Thomas Horn; Sandra Bullock; Tom Hanks; Zoe Caldwell; Max von Sydow; John Goodman; Jeffrey Wright; Viola Davis; ***D:*** Stephen Daldry; ***W:*** Eric Roth; ***C:*** Chris Menges; ***M:*** Alexandre Desplat.

Extremely Wicked, Shockingly Evil and Vile 1/2 **2019 (R)** During the 1970s, while parts of the U.S. were terrorized by a vicious rapist and murderer, single mother Elizabeth Kloepfer (Collins) unwittingly falls in love with the perpetrator. Told largely from Kloepfer's perspective, this biopic doesn't show the gruesome crimes themselves (described in the title, a direct quote from Judge Cowart's sentencing), but rather focuses on her relationship with Bundy and the courtroom trial that transfixed the nation. Efron skillfully exudes the charm, moviestar good looks, and sociopathy of the killer. Real-life clips are shown during the closing credits. Based on the book *The Phantom Prince: My Life with Ted Bundy*, by Elizabeth Kendall. **110m/C; Streaming.** Zac Efron; Lily Collins; Kaya Scodelario; Jeffrey Donovan; John Malkovich; ***D:*** Joe Berlinger; ***W:*** Michael Werwie; ***C:*** Brandon Trost; ***M:*** Marco Beltrami; Dennis Smith.

Extremities **1986 (R)** An adaptation of the topical William Mastrosimone play about an intended rape victim who turns on her attacker, captures him, and plots to kill him. Violent and exploitive. **83m/C; VHS, DVD, Blu-Ray.** Farrah Fawcett; Diana Scarwid; James Russo; Alfre Woodard; ***D:*** Robert M. Young; ***W:*** William Mastrosimone; ***C:*** Curtis Clark; ***M:*** J.A.C. Redford.

Eye *Dead Innocent* **1996 (R)** When attorney Suzanne St. Laurent's (Bujold) daughter is kidnapped, only mom can outwit the video-obsessed culprit before her child is killed. **90m/C; VHS, DVD.** *CA* Genevieve Bujold; Graham Greene; Jonathan Scarfe; Emily Hampshire; Nancy Beatty; Susan Glover; ***D:*** Sara Botsford; ***W:*** Mort Pattigo; Dolores Payne; ***C:*** Rodney Gibbons; ***M:*** David Findlay.

The Eye *Jian Gui* **2002 (R)** Stylish Asian ghost story follows the blind-since-childhood Mun (Lee), who receives a corneal transplant that restores her sight. Some adjustment is expected, but Mun sees shadowy figures lurking about that no one else sees, accident scenes miles from where they occurred, and, yes, dead people. Mun goes to a shrink, Dr. Wah (Chou), who doesn't think his patient is crazy. Instead, the doctor investigates the cornea donor—and is not reassured to discover the young woman committed suicide. Cantonese, Mandarin, and Thai with subtitles. **98m/C; VHS, DVD.** *CH* Sin-Je (Angelica) Lee; Lawrence Chou; Chutcha Rujinanon; Candy Lo; ***D:*** Oxide Pang; Danny Pang; ***W:*** Oxide Pang; Danny Pang; Jojo Hui; ***C:*** Decha Seementa.

The Eye 1/2 **2008 (PG-13)** Sydney Wells (Alba) is a concert violinist who has been blind since a childhood firecracker accident. As an adult, she undergoes a corneal transplant and promptly begins seeing ghouls, fire, premonitions of death, and eventually the image of the cornea donor (Romero), who it seems is trying to communicate something important through her eyes. Naturally her doctor and everyone else around her assume she is merely struggling with her transition to the sighted world; boy, are they wrong. Another ho-hum Hollywood re-make of a popular Asian formula horror film, but Alba fans will appreciate the tight, lingering shots of her lovely face and her obligatory shower scene. **97m/C; DVD, Blu-Ray.** Jessica Alba; Alessandro Nivola; Parker Posey; Rade Serbedzija; Rachel Ticotin; Chloë Grace Moretz; Fernanda Romero; Obba Babatunde; Danny Mora; ***D:*** David Moreau; Xavier Palud; ***W:*** Sebastian Gutierrez; ***C:*** Jeffrey Jur; ***M:*** Marco Beltrami.

The Eye 2 *Gin Gwai 2; Khon hen phi 2* **2004 (R)** Joey Cheng (Shu Qi) is feeling a little depressed and moody, and she should be. She's broken up with a married man, failed at committing suicide, and learned she's pregnant with his baby—and now she can see ghosts when near children or pregnant women. Some of them even defend her, and one even beats down a would-be rapist. Unfortunately her ghostly defender is also a rabid stalker, and Joey soon comes to believe it's only waiting around for her to give birth. **98m/C; DVD.** *CH TH* Qi Shu; Eugenia Yuan; Jesdaporn Pholdee; ***D:*** Oxide Pang Chun; Danny Pang; ***W:*** Lawrence Cheng; Jojo Hui; ***C:*** Decha Srimantra; ***M:*** Payont Permsith.

The Eye 3 1/2 *Gin Gwai 3; The Eye 10; Gin Gwai 10* **2005** Four teens are on vacation in Thailand when a local friend introduces them to a book that highlights ten ways to see ghosts or contact the dead. They give it a try, but once they start seeing ghosts it seems they can't shut it off. And then they start disappearing. Each of the "3 Eye" films done by the Pang brothers is different; this one is a comedy as well as a horror flick, but the mix doesn't work very well. **86m/C; DVD.** *CH TH* Isabella Leong; Ray Macdonald; Bo-lin Chen; Yu Gu; Kate Yeung; ***D:*** Oxide Pang Chun; Danny Pang; ***W:*** Oxide Pang Chun; Danny Pang; Mark Wu; ***C:*** Decha Srimantra; ***M:*** Payont Permsith.

The Eye Creatures **1965** Alien creatures in the form of eyeballs are fought off by a teenager and his girlfriend. A low-budget, gory, science fiction feature. **80m/B; VHS, DVD.** John Ashley; Cynthia Hull; Warren Hammack; Chet Davis; Bill Peck; ***D:*** Larry Buchanan.

An Eye for an Eye **1981 (R)** A story of pursuit and revenge with Norris as an undercover cop pitted against San Francisco's underworld and high society. **106m/C; VHS, DVD, Blu-Ray.** Chuck Norris; Christopher Lee; Richard Roundtree; Matt Clark; Mako; Maggie Cooper; ***D:*** Steve Carver; ***W:*** James Bruner; ***C:*** Roger Shearman; ***M:*** William Goldstein.

An Eye for an Eye **1995 (R)** A made-for-TV script that ended up on the feature film pile (and we do mean pile). Manipulative story has Karen McCann (Field) listening on the phone as her daughter is raped and killed by a scuzzball drifter (Sutherland). He's caught, but released on a technicality, driving Mom to join a vigilante group and plot revenge. Not a great career move for the director or surprisingly distinguished cast, who are given nothing but cardboard characters and push-button emotional cliches to work with. Shamelessly plays on middle class fears of crime and doubts about the judicial system. Based on the novel by Erika Holzer. **102m/C; VHS, DVD.** Sally Field; Ed Harris; Kiefer Sutherland; Beverly D'Angelo; Joe Mantegna; Keith David; ***D:*** John Schlesinger; ***W:*** Amanda Silver; Rick Jaffa; ***C:*** Amir M. Mokri; ***M:*** James Newton Howard.

Eye in the Sky **2015 (R)** Modern warfare is deftly analyzed in Gavin Hood's drama. Colonel Katherine Powell (Mirren) is the head of a UK-based operation designed to stop terrorism in Kenya. She is a modern military leader in that she leads not from the ground but a drone center, at which people make life-and-death decisions from halfway around the world. As a drone pilot (Paul) is preparing to initiate a kill order, a girl wanders into the kill zone, leading everyone to argue over how much collateral damage we're willing to accept to maintain order. Mirren is great, and it's Alan Rickman's last role. **102m/C; DVD, Blu-Ray.** *UK* Dame Helen Mirren; Aaron Paul; Alan Rickman; Barkhad Abdi; Jeremy Northam; ***D:*** Gavin Hood; ***W:*** Guy Hibbert; Mark Kilian; ***C:*** Haris Zambarloukos; ***M:*** Paul Hepker.

Eye of God **1997 (R)** Darkly dramatic story of lonely small-town waitress Ainsley (Plimpton), who marries newly released, born-again ex-con Jack (Anderson) with whom she has been corresponding. Movie kicks off when veteran sheriff (Holbrook) questions a shaken up youth, Tommy (Stahl), who is mysteriously covered in blood but rendered mute by his experience. First-time director Nelson's spare narrative seeks to explore deep issues like faith and violence in the Bible Belt locale. Performances are universally powerful, especially Plimpton's lovable dim-bulb and Anderson's maniacal Jack, giving credence to the clever but sometimes overly flashy cinematic style. **88m/C; VHS, DVD.** Martha Plimpton; Kevin Anderson; Hal Holbrook; Nick Stahl; Richard Jenkins; Margo Martindale; Maggie Moore; Mary Kay Place; ***D:*** Tim Blake Nelson; ***W:*** Tim Blake Nelson; ***C:*** Russell Fine; ***M:*** David Van Tiegham.

Eye of the Beast **2007** Scientist Dan Leland (Van Der Beek) comes to the small Canadian fishing town of Fells Island, where several deaths have been reported off the coast. Locals blame a sea monster but fishery officer Katrina Tomas (Castillo) says it's a giant squid. Since the sea beastie is ruining the fishing industry, the locals organize to get the tentacled troublemaker. Because this creature feature is low-budget, you don't get much in the way of visuals (a tentacle here, a giant eye there) so the fright quotient is minimal. **90m/C; DVD.** James Van Der Beek; Ryan Black; Alexandra Castillo; Brian Roach; Larissa Tobacco; Arne MacPherson; ***D:*** Gary Yates; ***W:*** Mark Mullin; ***C:*** Michael Marshall; ***M:*** Jonathan Goldsmith. **TV**

Eye of the Beholder **1999 (R)** Disengaged surveillence expert, known only as "The Eye" (McGregor), works for British intelligence out of their embassy in Washington. His latest assignment is to keep track of blackmailing Joanna (Judd), who turns out to be a psychotic serial killer of many identities. This must provide some strange turn-on, since instead of calling the cops, he proceeds to track her cross-country, protecting her from capture. Judd's an attractive femme fatale but the picture makes little sense and soon falls into the jaw-dropping, I-don't-believe-what-I'm-seeing category. Based on the novel by Marc Behm. **101m/C; VHS, DVD.** Ewan McGregor; Ashley Judd; Patrick Bergin; k.d. lang; Jason Priestley; Genevieve Bujold; ***D:*** Stephan Elliott; ***W:*** Stephan Elliott; ***C:*** Guy Dufaux; ***M:*** Marius De Vries.

Eye of the Demon **1987** A couple moves to a small town in Massachusetts and discovers that the area had once been a haven for witchcraft. To their horror, they soon find that old habits die hard, and the spellcasting continues in a nearby graveyard. **92m/C; VHS, DVD.** Tim Matheson; Pamela

Sue Martin; Woody Harrelson; Barbara Billingsley; Susan Ruttan; *D:* Carl Schenkel. **CABLE**

Eye of the Devil ♪♪ *13* **1967** Marquis Philippe de Montfaucon travels to his isolated French vineyard after drought destroys his crop for the third straight year. He asks wife Catherine to stay home but she gets suspicious and follows him only to be horrified that the locals still practice pagan rituals, including a human sacrifice to ensure future prosperity that Philippe has agreed to be part of. **89m/B; DVD.** *GB* David Niven; Deborah Kerr; Emlyn Williams; David Hemmings; Sharon Tate; Donald Pleasence; Flora Robson; John Le Mesurier; *D:* J. Lee Thompson; *W:* Robin Estridge; Dennis Murphy; *C:* Erwin Hillier; *M:* Gary McFarland.

Eye of the Dolphin ♪♪ ½ **2006 (PG)** Come on, who doesn't love a dolphin? After her mother's death, troubled teen Alyssa (Schroeder) is sent to live with her previously unknown father Hawk (Dunbar), who runs a dolphin research facility in the Bahamas. Alyssa discovers she has a natural ability to communicate with the dolphins and when the facility is threatened with closure, she and a wild dolphin pal come to the rescue. Good family fare. **100m/C; DVD.** Carly Schroeder; Adrian Dunbar; Katharine Ross; Christine Adams; Jane Lynch; George Harris; *D:* Michael D. Sellers; *W:* Michael D. Sellers; Wendell Morris; *C:* Guy Livneh; *M:* Alan Derian. **VIDEO**

Eye of the Eagle ♪ ½ **1987 (R)** A special task force is given a dangerous assignment during the Vietnam war. **84m/C; VHS, DVD.** Brett (Baxter) Clark; Ed Crick; Robert Patrick; William (Bill) Steis; Cec Verrell; *D:* Cirio H. Santiago.

Eye of the Eagle 2 ♪ **1989 (R)** When his platoon is betrayed and killed in Vietnam, a surviving soldier joins with a beautiful girl and seeks revenge. **79m/C; VHS, DVD.** Todd Field; Andy Wood; Ken Jacobson; Ronald Lawrence; *D:* Carl Franklin.

Eye of the Eagle 3 ♪ ½ **1991 (R)** Filipino-made Vietnam-War shoot-em-up, rack-em-up, shoot-em-up again, with U.S. forces pinned down against seemingly overwhelming odds. Violent. **90m/C; VHS, DVD.** Steve Kanaly; Ken Wright; Peter Gill Nelson; Carl Franklin; *D:* Cirio H. Santiago; *W:* Carl Franklin.

Eye of the Killer ♪♪ ½ **1999 (R)** Mickey Hayden is a drunken detective who is forced to re-open the serial killer case that led to his present wretched state. But this time Mickey finds himself having psychic visions when he touches the victims' belongings that put him into the mind of the killer. Now he's tracking a serial killer that may tie into a ten-year-old case. **100m/C; VHS, DVD.** Kiefer Sutherland; Henry Czerny; Polly Walker; Gary Hudson; *D:* Paul Marcus; *W:* Jeffrey D. Miller; *C:* Brian Pearson; *M:* Michael Hoenig.

Eye of the Needle ♪♪ ½ **1981 (R)** Based on Ken Follett's novel about a German spy posing as a shipwrecked sailor on a deserted English island during WWII. Lonely, sad, yet capable of terrible violence, he is stranded on an isolated island while en route to report to his Nazi commander. He becomes involved with an English woman living on the island, and begins to contemplate his role in the war. **112m/C; VHS, DVD, Blu-Ray.** Donald Sutherland; Kate Nelligan; Ian Bannen; Christopher Cazenove; Philip Brown; Stephen MacKenna; Faith Brook; Colin Rix; Alex McCrindle; John Bennett; Sam Kydd; Rik Mayall; Bill Fraser; *D:* Richard Marquand; *W:* Stanley Mann; *C:* Alan Hume; *M:* Miklos Rozsa.

Eye of the Storm ♪♪ ½ **1991 (R)** At the highway gas station/motel/diner where they live, two young brothers witness their parent's murder. Their younger brother is blinded in the same incident. Ten years later both brothers are still there and the tragedy may have turned one of them psychotic. When the abusive Gladstone and his young and sexy wife are stranded at the gas station it brings out the worst in everyone, with a violent climax during an equally violent thunderstorm. **98m/C; VHS, DVD.** Craig Sheffer; Bradley Gregg; Lara Flynn Boyle; Dennis Hopper; Leon Rippy; Wilhelm von Homburg; *D:* Yuri Zeltser.

Eye of the Storm ♪ ½ *The Farmhouse* **1998 (R)** What's the elegant Danner during in this horror mishmash? (Maybe it worked better as a stage play.) College student Jenny (Kendall) is in rural Kansas during research on a typical American family. That turns out not to be the Millers—the farming family Jenny is forced to shelter with because of a tornado. Seems mom Irma (Danner) went whacko and killed daughter Sally and the event was covered up by her husband and adult son. Now, Irma's delusions mistake Jenny for Sally and the local sheriff is also snooping into Sally's disappearance. Adapted by co-scripter Watson from his play "The Farmhouse." **100m/C; VHS, DVD.** Katherine Kendall; Blythe Danner; Leo Burmester; Guy Ale; Kurt Deutsch; Keith Reddin; *D:* Marcus Spiegel; *W:* Marcus Spiegel; Randy Watson; *C:* Horacio Marquinez; *M:* Anton Sanko.

Eye of the Stranger ♪ ½ **1993 (R)** Suspenser about a nameless stranger who sets out to solve the mystery of a small western town and its corrupt mayor. **96m/C; VHS, DVD.** David Heavener; Sally Kirkland; Martin Landau; Don Swayze; Stella Stevens; John Pleshette; Joe Estevez; Thomas F. Duffy; *D:* David Heavener; *W:* David Heavener; *M:* Robert Garrett.

Eye of the Tiger ♪♪ **1986 (R)** A righteous ex-con battles a crazed, crack-dealing motorcycle gang that terrorized and murdered his wife, and is moving on to infest his town. **90m/C; VHS, DVD.** Gary Busey; Yaphet Kotto; Seymour Cassel; Bert Remsen; William (Bill) Smith; Judith Barsi; *D:* Richard Sarafian; *W:* Michael Thomas Montgomery; *C:* Peter Lyons Collister; *M:* Don Preston.

Eye See You ♪♪ *D-Tox* **2001 (R)** Substandard cop vs. serial killer yarn has FBI man Jake Malloy (Stallone) tracking a serial killer who likes to remove his victims' eyes with a drill. When his girlfriend becomes the maniac's latest victim, Sly goes on the sauce and ends up in a Wyoming detox center for cops. Shortly after he arrives, the patients start dying in apparent suicides and Malloy suspects his old nemesis might be on the premises. The plot wavers between illogical and laughable, while everybody involved overacts in an apparent attempt to figure out what the heck's going on. **95m/C; VHS, DVD, Blu-Ray.** Sylvester Stallone; Tom Berenger; Charles S. Dutton; Sean Patrick Flanery; Christopher Fulford; Dina Meyer; Robert Patrick; Robert Prosky; Courtney B. Vance; Polly Walker; Jeffrey Wright; Kris Kristofferson; Stephen Lang; Rance Howard; *D:* Jim Gillespie; *W:* Ron L. Brinkerhoff; *C:* Dean Semler; *M:* John Powell.

Eye Witness ♪♪ ½ *Your Witness* **1949** An American attorney goes abroad to free a friend from the British legal system. A book of poems becomes the necessary device in deducing the whereabouts of the witness testifying to his friend's alibi. **104m/B; VHS, DVD.** *GB* Robert Montgomery; Felix Aylmer; Leslie Banks; Michael Ripper; Patricia Wayne; *D:* Robert Montgomery; *M:* Malcolm Arnold.

Eye Witness ♪♪ *Sudden Terror* **1970 (PG)** The murder of an African dignitary is witnessed by a young boy who has trouble convincing his parents and the police about the incident. Suspenseful but less than original. Shot on location in Malta. **95m/C; VHS, DVD, Blu-Ray.** *GB* Mark Lester; Lionel Jeffries; Susan George; Tony Bonner; *D:* John Hough; *W:* Bryan Forbes; *C:* David Holmes.

Eyeborgs ♪♪ **2009 (R)** Ambitious sci fi indie with cool title robots. A major terrorist attack has the U.S. government instituting a surveillance program linking one countrywide network system through mobile robotic cameras. But a Homeland Security agent is suspicious that a series of murders are the result of someone manipulating the eyeborgs and it's leading up to a presidential assassination. **102m/C; DVD.** Adrian Paul; Luke Eberl; Megan Blake; Danny Trejo; *D:* Richard Clabaugh; *W:* Richard Clabaugh; Fran Clabaugh; *C:* Kenneth Wilson; *M:* Mark Brisbane; Guy-Roger Duvert. **VIDEO**

Eyes Behind the Stars ♪ *Occhi Dalle Stelle* **1972** A news photographer accidentally gets a few pictures of invading aliens, but nobody takes him seriously, particularly the government. **95m/C; VHS, DVD.** *IT* Martin Balsam; Robert Hoffman; Nathalie Delon; Sherry Buchanan; *D:* Mario Gariazzo.

Eyes in the Night ♪ ½ **1942** Wartime B-crime/mystery. Norma (Harding) calls on her friend, blind PI Duncan MacLain (Arnold)--and his guide dog Friday--to help her with her teen stepdaughter Barbara (Reed), who's involved with Norma's self-absorbed ex-lover Paul (Emery). Paul gets murdered and Babs sees Norma with the body, convincing her that her hated stepmommy did the deed. Just to complicate things, there's also a Nazi plot involving Norma's scientist husband, Stephen (Denny). **80m/B; DVD.** Edward Arnold; Ann Harding; Donna Reed; Reginald Denny; Allen Jenkins; John Emery; *D:* Fred Zinnemann; *W:* Guy Trosper; Howard Emmett Rogers; *C:* Robert Planck; Charles Lawton, Jr.

Eyes of a Stranger WOOF! **1981 (R)** Terrifying maniac stalks his female prey by watching their every move. Tewes is cast as a journalist, the stronger of the two sisters in this exploitative slasher. **85m/C; VHS, DVD.** Lauren Tewes; John Disanti; Jennifer Jason Leigh; *D:* Ken Wiederhorn; *W:* Eric L. Bloom; *M:* Richard Einhorn.

Eyes of an Angel ♪♪ ½ **1991 (PG-13)** A widower (Travolta), who's heavily involved in gambling, is forced to go on the run with his young daughter (Raab) when a deal goes sour. She must abandon the family dog, who manages to follow them from Chicago to California anyway. Talk about loyalty! **91m/C; VHS, DVD.** John Travolta; Ellie Raab; Jeffrey DeMunn; *D:* Robert Harmon.

The Eyes of Charles Sand ♪ ½ **1974** Unsold ABC TV pilot paranormal thriller. With the death of his uncle, businessman Charles Sand inherits the family legacy of second sight. Adjusting to his new psychic abilities, Sand agrees to help troubled Emily Parkhurst, who claims her brother's been murdered. Emily's older sister Katharine tries to reassure Sand that her sister's just crazy. **74m/C; DVD.** Peter Haskell; Joan Bennett; Barbara Rush; Sharon Farrell; Bradford Dillman; Adam West; *D:* Reza Badiyi; *W:* Henry Farrell; Stanford Whitmore; *C:* Ben Colman. **TV**

Eyes of Laura Mars ♪♪ ½ **1978 (R)** A photographer exhibits strange powers—she can foresee a murder before it happens through her snapshots. In time she realizes that the person responsible for a series of killings is tracking her. Title song performed by Barbra Streisand. **104m/C; VHS, DVD, Blu-Ray.** Faye Dunaway; Tommy Lee Jones; Brad Dourif; Rene Auberjonois; Raul Julia; Darlanne Fluegel; Michael Tucker; *D:* Irvin Kershner; *W:* John Carpenter; David Zelag Goodman; *C:* Victor Kemper.

The Eyes of My Mother ♪♪ **2016 (R)** Pesce's horror debut offers a striking, disturbing look into the formation of and solitary life of a sociopathic killer. Francisca (Magalhaes) lives with her parents on a farm far from civilization. One day, a lunatic stops by and kills her mother before being stopped by her father. A young Francisca keeps the injured killer in the barn, cutting out his eyes and tongue. And Pesce's film gets weirder. Influenced more by David Lynch than modern horror directors, this movie is certainly not for everyone, but you also haven't really seen much like it before. **76m/B; DVD, Blu-Ray.** Kika Magalhaes; Diana Agostini; Olivia Bond; Will Brill; Paul Nazak; *D:* Nicolas Pesce; *W:* Nicolas Pesce; *C:* Zach Kuperstein; *M:* Ariel Loh.

The Eyes of Tammy Faye ♪♪ ½ **2000 (PG-13)** Documentary examines the eventful life of a not-particularly interesting woman, Tammy Faye Bakker Messner. She was most famous for being married to televangelist Jim Bakker when their PTL ministry went belly up. Since much of the story is told through static interviews and TV news footage, the image is nothing special. Neither is the sound, though the choice of RuPaul Charles as narrator is inspired. The film was a hit on the festival circuit, and is recommended to that audience. **79m/C; DVD.** Tammy Faye Bakker; Jim Bakker; *Nar:* RuPaul Charles; *D:* Fenton Bailey; Randy Barbato.

The Eyes of Youth ♪♪ **1919** A young woman searches her soul for answers: to marry or not to marry is the question. A little foresight, in the form of a glimpse into the hypothetical future, helps her make the right choice. Very early Valentino fare in which the sheik plays a cad. **78m/B; Silent; VHS, DVD.** Clara Kimball Young; Edmund Lowe; Rudolph Valentino; *D:* Albert Parker; *W:* Albert Parker; *C:* Arthur Edeson.

Eyes Wide Open ♪♪ **2009** Responsible married father Aaron is part of Jerusalem's ultra-Orthodox Jewish community and runs the family butcher shop. When young student Ezri needs a job and a place to stay, Aaron quickly comes to his aid, believing his more-than-friendly feelings can be controlled. They can't, especially since they're reciprocated by the reckless Ezri. Hebrew and Yiddish with subtitles. **90m/C; DVD.** *IS FR GE* Zohar Strauss; Ran Danker; Tinkerbell; *D:* Haim Tabakman; *W:* Merav Doster; *C:* Axel Schneppat; *M:* Nathaniel Mechaly.

Eyes Wide Shut ♪♪ **1999 (R)** Kubrick's psychosexual drama (two years in the making), and last film, turned out to be visually interesting (because everything was done on soundstages) but less than compelling. Society doc William Harford (Cruise) and wife Alice (Kidman) seem to have it all, until a stoned Alice confesses to having lustful thoughts for others besides her hubby. Bill can't admit to the same (he's kind of a chilly guy), but this revelation sends him reeling out into the Manhattan night looking for adventure. He ends his evening observing, but not joining in, an aristocratic, anonymous orgy before heading home, presumably a wiser man. Kidman's role basically fades out after her bravura confessional and Cruise seems more like an interested bystander than a man whose known world has crumbled. Based on Arthur Schnitzler's 1926 novel "Traumnovelle." **159m/C; VHS, DVD, Blu-Ray, HD-DVD.** Tom Cruise; Nicole Kidman; Sydney Pollack; Marie Richardson; Vinessa Shaw; Todd Field; Rade Serbedzija; Leelee Sobieski; Alan Cumming; Thomas Gibson; Sky Dumont; Fay Masterson; Treva Etienne; *D:* Stanley Kubrick; *W:* Stanley Kubrick; *C:* Larry Smith; *M:* Jocelyn Pook.

Eyewitness ♪♪ **1956** Efficient Brit crime drama. As she's leaving a movie theater, Lucy witnesses a robbery in progress. She runs into the street, is knocked down by a bus, and taken to the hospital. Ruthless Wade decides Lucy must be silenced before she can identify them but his scared partner Barney doesn't want to go along. **83m/B; DVD.** *UK* Donald Sinden; Muriel Pavlow; Nigel Stock; Ada Reeve; *D:* Muriel Box; *W:* Janet Green; *C:* Reginald Wyer; *M:* Bruce Montgomery.

Eyewitness ♪♪ ½ *The Janitor* **1981 (R)** When a murder occurs in the office building of a star-struck janitor, he fabricates a tale in order to initiate a relationship with the TV reporter covering the story. Unfortunately the killers think he's telling the truth, which plunges the janitor and reporter into a dangerous and complicated position, pursued by both police and foreign agents. Somewhat contrived, but Hurt and Weaver are always interesting. Woods turns in a wonderful performance as Hurt's somewhat-psychotic best friend. **102m/C; VHS, DVD.** William Hurt; Sigourney Weaver; Christopher Plummer; James Woods; Kenneth McMillan; Pamela Reed; Irene Worth; Steven Hill; Morgan Freeman; *D:* Peter Yates; *W:* Steve Tesich.

F6 Twister ♪ *Christmas Twister* **2012** ION Television holiday disaster flick. A small Texas town is hit by an unusual Christmastime tornado and weather guy Ethan Walker realizes more are coming. His reporter wife Addison wants to get a warning out but her station manager doesn't want to be a bah-humbug so it's up to the Walkers to go on a rescue mission. **90m/C; DVD.** Casper Van Dien; Victoria Pratt; Richard Burgi; Haley Lu Richardson; Steven Williams; *D:* Peter Sullivan; *W:* Peter Sullivan; *C:* Roberto Schein; *M:* Marc Jovani. **TV**

F/X ♪♪♪ **1986 (R)** Rollie Tyler (Brown) is a New York-based special effects expert who is contracted by government agent Lipton (DeYoung) to fake an assassination in order to protect mob informer DeFranco (Orbach). After completing the assignment, Rollie learns that he's become involved in a real crime and is forced to reach into his bag of F/X tricks to survive, aided by tough cop Leo McCarthy (Dennehy), who's trying to figure out just what's going on. Twists and turns abound in this fast-paced story that was the sleeper hit of the year. Followed by a sequel. **109m/C; VHS, DVD, Blu-Ray.** Bryan Brown; Cliff DeYoung; Diane Venora; Brian Dennehy;

Jerry Orbach; Mason Adams; Joe Grifasi; Martha Gehman; Angela Bassett; *D:* Robert Mandel; *W:* Robert T. Megginson; Gregory Fleeman; *C:* Miroslav Ondricek; *M:* Bill Conti.

F/X 2: The Deadly Art of Illusion ✗✗ **1991 (PG-13)** Weak follow-up finds the special-effects specialist set to pull off just one more illusion for the police. Once again, corrupt cops use him as a chump for their scheme, an over-complicated business involving a stolen Vatican treasure. **107m/C; VHS, DVD, Blu-Ray.** Bryan Brown; Brian Dennehy; Rachel Ticotin; Philip Bosco; Joanna Gleason; *D:* Richard Franklin; *W:* Bill Condon; *C:* Victor Kemper; *M:* Lalo Schifrin; Michael Boddicker.

Fabiola ✗✗✗ **1948** The first of the big Italian spectacle movies, this one opened the door for a flood of low-budget imitators. Fabiola, the daughter of a Roman senator, becomes a Christian when her father's Christian servants are accused of murdering him. In the meantime, the Emperor Constantine speeds toward Rome to convert it to Christian status. You can bet plenty of Christians will lose their heads, be thrown to the lions and generally burn at the stake before he does. **96m/C; VHS, DVD.** *IT* Michel Simon; Henri Vidal; Michele Morgan; Gino Cervi; *D:* Alessandro Blasetti.

Fabled ✗ 1/2 **2002 (R)** Is it all in his head? And do you care? Paranoid Joseph Fable (Askew) believes his ex-girlfriend Liz (Winnick) is in cahoots with his shrink and that his co-workers have stolen his dog. His friend Alex (Nash) thinks Joe should stop mixing booze and his meds. **84m/C; DVD.** Desmond Askew; Katheryn Winnick; Michael Panes; J. Richey Nash; *D:* Ari Kirschenbaun; *W:* Ari Kirschenbaun; *C:* Yaron Orbach; *M:* Jack Lingo.

The Fabulous Baker Boys ✗✗✗ **1989 (R)** Two brothers have been performing a tired act as nightclub pianists for 15 years. When they hire a sultry vocalist to revitalize the routine, she inadvertently triggers long-suppressed hostility between the "boys." The story may be a bit uneven, but fine performances by the three leading actors, the steamy atmosphere, and Pfeiffer's classic rendition of "Makin' Whoopee," are worth the price of the rental. **116m/C; VHS, DVD, Blu-Ray; Open Captioned.** Michelle Pfeiffer; Jeff Bridges; Beau Bridges; Ellie Raab; Jennifer Tilly; *D:* Steve Kloves; *W:* Steve Kloves; *C:* Michael Ballhaus; *M:* Dave Grusin. Golden Globes '90: Actress--Drama (Pfeiffer); L.A. Film Critics '89: Actress (Pfeiffer), Cinematog.; Natl. Bd. of Review '89: Actress (Pfeiffer); N.Y. Film Critics '89: Actress (Pfeiffer); Natl. Soc. Film Critics '89: Actress (Pfeiffer), Cinematog., Support. Actor (Bridges).

The Fabulous Dorseys ✗✗ **1947** The musical lives of big band leaders Tommy and Jimmy Dorsey are portrayed in this less than fabulous biography that's strong on song but weak on plot. Guest stars include Art Tatum, Charlie Barnet, Ziggy Elman, Bob Eberly and Helen O'Connell. Highlights are the tunes. **91m/B; DVD.** Tommy Dorsey; Jimmy Dorsey; Janet Blair; Paul Whiteman; Sara Allgood; Arthur Shields; *D:* Alfred E. Green.

Face ✗✗ **1997 (R)** A violent Brit-take on "Reservoir Dogs" has a group of East End armed robbers realizing someone in their gang has betrayed them after a heist goes wrong. Chief among the crooks are Ray (Carlyle) and his partner Dave (Winstone), plus three rookies and the unexpected involvement of a crooked cop. Lots of energy but not much that's new. **107m/C; VHS, DVD.** *GB* Robert Carlyle; Steven Waddington; Ray Winstone; Philip Davis; Damon Albarn; Peter Vaughan; Lena Headey; Andrew Tiernan; *D:* Antonia Bird; *W:* Ronan Bennett; *C:* Fred Tammes; *M:* Andy Roberts.

The Face at the Window ✗✗ **1939** Melodramatic crime story of a pair of ne'er-do-well brothers who terrorize Paris to conceal their bank robberies. **65m/B; VHS, DVD.** Tod Slaughter; Marjorie Taylor; John Warwick; Robert Adair; Harry Terry; *D:* George King.

A Face in the Crowd ✗✗✗ 1/2 **1957** Journalist (Neal) discovers a down-home philosopher (Griffith) and puts him on her TV show. His aw-shucks personality soon wins him a large following and increasing influence—even political clout. Off the air he reveals his true nature to be insulting, vengeful, and power-hungry—all of which Neal decides to expose. Marks Griffith's spectacular film debut as a thoroughly despicable character and debut of Remick as the pretty cheerleader in whom he takes an interest. Schulburg wrote the screenplay from his short story "The Arkansas Traveler." He and director Kazan collaborated equally well in "On the Waterfront." **126m/B; VHS, DVD, Blu-Ray.** Andy Griffith; Patricia Neal; Lee Remick; Walter Matthau; Anthony (Tony) Franciosa; *D:* Elia Kazan; *W:* Budd Schulberg; *C:* Harry Stradling, Sr. Natl. Film Reg. '08.

A Face in the Fog ✗✗ **1936** Two newspaper reporters set out to solve a number of murders that have plagued the cast of a play. Also interested is the playwright. Good low-budget thriller. **66m/B; VHS, DVD.** June Collyer; Lloyd Hughes; Lawrence Gray; Al "Fuzzy" St. John; Jack Mulhall; Jack Cowell; John Elliott; Sam Flint; Forrest Taylor; Edward Cassidy; *D:* Robert F. "Bob" Hill.

The Face of an Angel ✗ 1/2 **2014** Talented director Winterbottom is one of those auteurs who might work too often as he produces more of these inert, bland dramas that one of his skill level should on a regular basis. This true crime story loosely tells the narrative of Amanda Knox, an American student who was studying in Italy when she was accused of murder. The resulting case captivated the world. Instead of telling Amanda's story, Winterbottom fictionalizes it and tells it from the perspective of a journalist and a filmmaker. It's misguided, and, worst of all, just plain dull. Bad TV movie writing and performances from people who should know better. **100m/C; DVD, Blu-Ray, Streaming.** *IT SP UK US* Daniel Brühl; Kate Beckinsale; Valerio Mastandrea; Cara Delevingne; Ava Acres; *D:* Michael Winterbottom; *W:* Paul Viragh; Harry Escott; *C:* Hubert Taczanowski.

Face of Another ✗✗ *Tanin no kao; I Have a Stranger's Face; Stranger's Face* **1966** A severely burned man gets a second chance when a plastic surgeon makes a mask to hide the disfigurement. Unfortunately this face leads him to alienation, rape, infidelity, and murder. In Japanese with English subtitles. **124m/B; VHS, DVD.** *JP* Tatsuya Nakadai; Machiko Kyo; Minoru Chiaki; Robert Dunham; Kyoko Kishida; Beverly (Bibari) Maeda; Eiji Okada; Koreya Senda; *D:* Hiroshi Teshigahara; *W:* Kobe Abe; *C:* Hiroshi Segawa; *M:* Toru Takemitsu.

Face of Fire ✗ 1/2 **1959** Uneven psychological drama adapted from the Stephen Crane short story, "The Monster." Well-liked handyman Monk Johnson is horribly disfigured by a fire at the home of Dr. Ned Trescott. Though he rescued the doctor's young son, instead of being a hero, Monk finds himself shunned by the increasingly belligerent townsfolk, who make the Trescott family (who are caring for Monk) pariahs as well. **80m/B; DVD.** James Whitmore; Cameron Mitchell; Royal Dano; Bettye Ackerman; Richard Erdman; Lois Maxwell; *D:* Albert Band; *W:* Albert Band; Louis Garfinkle; *M:* Erik Nordgren.

The Face of Fu Manchu ✗✗ **1965** Lee's first appearance as the crimelord from the Sax Rohmer novels. Fu Manchu discovers a potion that can easily kill thousands and plans to use it in his quest for world domination. Scotland Yard's Nayland Smith (Green) is once again after the fiend in Edwardian London. Followed by 1966's "The Brides of Fu Manchu." **96m/C; DVD.** *UK* Christopher Lee; Nigel Green; Joachim Fuchsberger; Karin Dor; James Robertson Justice; Tsai Chin; Howard Marion-Crawford; *D:* Don Sharp; *W:* Harry Alan Towers; *C:* Ernest Steward; *M:* Christopher Whelen.

The Face of Love ✗✗ 1/2 **2013 (PG-13)** After five years mourning the death of her beloved husband Garrett, lonely L.A. widow Nikki (Bening) meets his apparent double in artist Tom (Harris). Stunned, embarrassed by her feelings, yet determined, Nikki nurtures their growing romance while hiding photos as well as family and friends from Tom so nothing can interfere with her self-deluding obsession. The leads make this middle-aged love story work well enough. **92m/C; DVD.** Annette Bening; Ed Harris; Jess Weixler; Robin Williams; Amy Brenneman; *D:* Arie Posin; *W:* Arie Posin; Matthew McDuffie; *C:* Antonio Riestra; *M:* Marcelo Zarvos.

Face of Terror ✗ **2004 (R)** Four writers only managed to come up with every action cliche imaginable. LAPD officer Nick Harper lands in Barcelona after his aspiring model sister goes missing. Sympathetic Ana, who works at a modeling agency, helps Nick out as he learns sis became involved with a sleazy photographer involved in the drug trade and a terrorist who uses women for deadly purposes. **100m/C; DVD.** Rick Schroder; Eric Balfour; Paulina Galvez; Dean Haglund; Abel Folk; Kadeem Hardison; *D:* Bryan Goeres; *W:* Brent Huff; Titus Llangort; Robert Tiffe; Douglas Walton; *C:* Jacques Haitkin; *M:* Sean Murray. **VIDEO**

Face/Off ✗✗✗ 1/2 **1997 (R)** Woo returns to his blood-soaked, violence-as-poetry-in-motion roots with the story of a Fed who assumes the identity of the presumed-dead terrorist who killed his son. When the master criminal wakes up, he "steals" the cop's identity. Travolta's back for another wild ride, eating up the scenery when he takes on the bad-guy role. Cage, fresh from action hits in "The Rock" and "Con Air" gets to study the nature of good and evil (another Woo specialty) while he learns the nuances of the "leap across the room with two pistols blazing" move. Woo's Hong Kong efforts have always explored the blurry line between the good guys and the bad guys, and with Cage and Travolta, he has the perfect actors to display his findings. Woo cultists will welcome the return to the old style, while those only familiar with his stateside work will understand what all the fuss was about. **140m/C; VHS, DVD, Blu-Ray, HD-DVD.** John Travolta; Nicolas Cage; Joan Allen; Alessandro Nivola; Gina Gershon; Nick Cassavetes; Dominique Swain; Harve Presnell; Margaret Cho; CCH Pounder; Colm Feore; John Carroll Lynch; Matt Ross; *D:* John Woo; *W:* Mike Werb; Michael Colleary; *C:* Oliver Wood; *M:* John Powell. MTV Movie Awards '98: Action Seq., On-Screen Duo (John Travolta/Nicolas Cage).

Face the Evil ✗ 1/2 **1997 (R)** TV star Sharon (Tweed) gets taken hostage in an art gallery where she's filming by a gang of thieves. But that's not the real problem—seems their leader, Dangler (Henriksen), wants to retrieve a shipment of nerve gas that's been hidden in some art work. **92m/C; VHS, DVD.** Shannon Tweed; Lance Henriksen; Bruce Payne; Jayne Heitmeyer; *D:* Paul Lynch; *W:* Richard Beattie; *C:* Barry Gravelle; *M:* Paul Zaza. **VIDEO**

Face the Music ✗✗ 1/2 **2000 (PG-13)** After being dumped by their record label, a band decides to have lead singer Dan (Christopher) fake his death for the publicity. But when a hot reporter (Lyons) arrives to cover the story, Dan finds it increasingly difficult to keep quiet. **85m/C; DVD.** Tyler Christopher; Elena Lyons; Patrick Malone; Ted McGinley; Sharon Leal; Gloria Leroy; Jill Ritchie; Harry Van Gorkum; *D:* Jeffrey Howard; *W:* Beth Hollander-Harris; *C:* David Trulli; *M:* Philip W. Gough. **VIDEO**

Face to Face ✗✗✗ *Ansikte mot Ansikte* **1976** Bergman's harrowing tale of a mental breakdown. Ullmann has a bravura role as a psychiatrist deciding to vacation at her grandparent's house in the country. Once there she begins to experience depression and hallucinations tied to her past with both her mother and grandmother. Her deeply repressed feelings eventually lead to a suicide attempt, which brings some much needed help. Originally a four-hour series made for Swedish TV; subtitled. **136m/C; VHS, DVD.** *SW* Liv Ullmann; Erland Josephson; Gunnar Bjornstrand; Aino Taube-Henrikson; Sven Lindberg; Kari Sylway; Sif Ruud; *D:* Ingmar Bergman; *W:* Ingmar Bergman; *C:* Sven Nykvist. Golden Globes '77: Foreign Film; L.A. Film Critics '76: Actress (Ullmann), Foreign Film; Natl. Bd. of Review '76: Actress (Ullmann); N.Y. Film Critics '76: Actress (Ullmann). **TV**

Faceless ✗✗ *Les Predateurs de la Nuit* **1988** Franco gorefest has model Barbara disappear after going to a plastic surgery clinic run by the crazed Dr. Flamand. Her father sends a P.I. to find her, and he finds much more, as beautiful women are being killed for their skin and other needed accessories for the doctor's sister, who was disfigured in an acid-throwing incident. Bigger budget and better production values than Franco usually uses provides quality scares and squirms for fans of his work. Others may not be as enamored. **98m/C; DVD.** *SP FR* Helmut Berger; Brigitte Lahaie; Chris Mitchum; Telly Savalas; Stephane Audran; Anton Diffring; Caroline Munro; Howard Vernon; *D:* Jess (Jesus) Franco; *W:* Fred (Rene Chateau) Castle; Pierre Ripert; Jean Mazarin; Michele Lebrun; *C:* Roger Fellous; *M:* Romano Musumarra.

Faces ✗✗✗ 1/2 **1968 (R)** Cassavettes' first independent film to find mainstream success portrays the breakup of the 14-year marriage of middle-aged Richard (Marley) and Maria (Carlin) Forst. Both seek at least momentary comfort with others—Richard with prostitute Jeannie (Rowlands) and Maria with aging hippie Chet (Cassel). The director's usual improvisational and documentary style can either be viewed as compelling or tedious but the performances are first-rate. **129m/B; VHS, DVD, Blu-Ray.** John Marley; Lynn Carlin; Gena Rowlands; Seymour Cassel; Val Avery; Dorothy Gulliver; Joanne Moore Jordan; Fred Draper; Darlene Conley; *D:* John Cassavetes; *W:* John Cassavetes; *C:* Al Ruban; *M:* Jack Ackerman. Natl. Film Reg. '11; Natl. Soc. Film Critics '68: Screenplay, Support. Actor (Cassel).

Faces in the Crowd ✗ 1/2 **2011 (R)** Forgettable thriller despite the heroine's unusual condition. After escaping a serial killer, Anna (Jovovich) awakens from a coma with face blindness. She can't recognize faces and facial features change randomly (which is confusing for the viewer as well). This means the killer could be right in front of her and Anna wouldn't know it, so Detective Kerrest (McMahon) is sticking close by. **102m/C; DVD, Blu-Ray.** Milla Jovovich; Julian McMahon; Michael Shanks; Sarah Wayne Callies; Valentina Vargas; Marianne Faithfull; *D:* Julien Magnat; *W:* Julien Magnat; *C:* Rene Ohashi; *M:* John McCartney. **VIDEO**

Faces Places *Visages villages* **2017 (PG) 89m/C; DVD, Blu-Ray, Streaming.** *FR* *D:* JR; Agnes Varda; *W:* JR; Agnes Varda; *C:* Roberto De Angelis; Claire Duguet; Julia Fabry; Nicolas Guicheteau; Romain Le Bonniec; Raphael Minnesota; Valentin Vignet; *M:* Matthieu Chedid. Ind. Spirit '18: Feature Doc.

Facing the Enemy ✗✗ **2000 (R)** Harlan Moss (Caulfield) believes in revenge and he blames Detective Griff McCleary (Ashby) for the death of his wife (Preston). So his idea is to seduce McCleary's estranged wife (Paul)?and then kill her. The surprise ending isn't very and it's a familiar ride but if you're in the mood for a cop thriller, this one will pass the time. **98m/C; VHS, DVD.** Linden Ashby; Maxwell Caulfield; Alexandra Paul; Cynthia (Cyndy, Cindy) Preston; Max Gail; Bruce Weitz; Melanie Wilson; *D:* Rob Malenfant; *W:* Martin Kitrosser; *C:* Steve Adcock; *M:* Richard Bowers. **VIDEO**

Facing Windows ✗✗ 1/2 *La Finestra di Fronte* **2003 (R)** Unhappy Giovanna (Mezzogiorno) is a working wife and mother with an oblivious husband, Filippo (Nigro), and a dull job in a chicken factory. Her only sliver of excitement is her handsome neighbor, Lorenzo (Bova), whom she ogles from her kitchen window (as he watches back). Things change when Filippo brings home a confused elderly gentleman who thinks his name is Davide (Girotti). Giovanna reluctantly allows the stranger to stay the night after spotting a concentration camp number tattooed on his arm. In a round about way, this leads to Giovanna getting involved with Lorenzo, learning about Davide's lost love, and even satisfying her secret dream of becoming a pastry chef. Poignant if undemanding slice of life drama. Girotti's last role; Italian with subtitles. **106m/C; DVD.** *IT GB PT TU* Giovanna Mezzogiorno; Massimo Girotti; Raoul Bova; Filippo Nigro; Serra Yilmaz; Massimo Poggio; Ivan Bacchi; *D:* Ferzan Ozpetek; *W:* Ferzan Ozpetek; Gianni Romoli; *C:* Gianfilippo Corticelli; *M:* Andrea Guerra.

The Factory ✗ **2010 (R)** A more-than-familiar plot, some tired acting, and a stupid ending doom this crime drama. Buffalo, NY cops Mike Fletcher and Kelsey Walker have spend three years tracking an apparent serial killer targeting prostitutes although no bodies have never been found. Then Gary is shown in his lair with his not-dead victims and his reason for taking them. But he changes his M.O. to kidnap Mike's teenaged daughter, which means the cop is going to break the law to get her back. **108m/C; DVD.** John Cusack; Jennifer Carpenter; Dallas Roberts; Mae Whitman; *D:* Morgan O'Neill; *W:* Morgan O'Neill; Paul Leyden; *C:* Kramer Morgenthau; *M:* Mark Isham. **VIDEO**

Factory Girl 🦴 1/2 **2006 (R)** The brief life of Warhol wild child Edie Sedgwick (Miller) is retold in a conventional biopic. Blonde, beautiful, and from a wealthy-but-troubled family, Sedgwick trades in art school for the sixties New York scene and her chance as Warhol's (Pearce) latest muse. But Edie falls into a drug-fueled trap and bad romantic choices, including a seductive musician (Christensen). While Miller certainly looks the part, there's nothing substantial or particularly interesting about her performance or the flick. **90m/C; DVD.** Sienna Miller; Guy Pearce; Hayden Christensen; Jimmy Fallon; Mena Suvari; Shawn Hatosy; Illeana Douglas; James Naughton; Beth Grant; Jack Houston; *D:* George Hickenlooper; *W:* Captain Mauzner; *C:* Michael Grady; *M:* Ed Shearmur.

Factotum 🦴🦴🦴 **2006 (R)** Adaptation of Charles Bukowski's 1975 book of the same name is a bleak, darkly funny examination of ideals and ambivalence. Bukoswki's booze-soaked alter-ego Hank Chinaski (Dillon) lives by the slacker code with his series of changeable jobs and changeable women while he tends to his mediocre writing. Girlfriends Jan (Taylor) and Laura (Tomei) are excellent as Hank's enablers, but it's Dillon who brings style and swagger to a "man of many jobs" (a definition of the movie's title) who eschews soul-sucking opportunity and success in favor of being true to his distasteful, deep self. **94m/C; DVD.** *US GE NO* Matt Dillon; Lili Taylor; Marisa Tomei; Fisher Stevens; Didier Flamand; Adrienne Shelly; Karen Young; Tom Lyons; *D:* Bent Hamer; *W:* Bent Hamer; Jim Stark; *C:* John Christian Rosenlund; *M:* Kristin Asbjornsen.

The Facts of Life 🦴🦴 1/2 **1960** Risque bedroom comedy finds Larry Gilbert (Hope) and Kitty Weaver (Ball) running off from boredom in suburbia and their respective spouses (Hussey and DeFore) to have a little interlude together. **103m/B; DVD, Blu-Ray.** Bob Hope; Lucille Ball; Ruth Hussey; Don DeFore; Louis Nye; Philip Ober; *D:* Melvin Frank; *W:* Melvin Frank; Norman Panama; *C:* Charles B(ryant) Lang, Jr.; *M:* Leigh Harline. Oscars '60: Costume Des. (B&W).

The Faculty 🦴🦴 1/2 **1998 (R)** Nerd (Wood), beauty queen (Brewster), jock (Hatosy), new girl (Harris), rebel (Hartnett), and lovelorn girl (DuVall) come up against the greatest challenge of their lives. No, not the SATs. Parasitic aliens have nested in their high school and replaced the rumpled, frumpy staff with pleasure-seeking sexpots out for excitment. It's "The Breakfast Club" against "Them" in a battle royale! More style, less substance dictates the union between indie director Rodriguez and screenwriter Williamson. As expected, the dialogue is hip, the fashions are crisp, and kids are spunky, but pic never explains the aliens' visit. The multi-generational cast is enjoyable enough and the scares (however recycled they may be) are effective if you like icky scenes of alien projectiles sprouting from a human orifice or two. **102m/C; VHS, DVD, Blu-Ray.** Elijah Wood; Robert Patrick; Bebe Neuwirth; Salma Hayek; Jon Stewart; Piper Laurie; Famke Janssen; Christopher McDonald; Jordana Brewster; Clea DuVall; Laura Harris; Josh Hartnett; Usher Raymond; Shawn Hatosy; Jon Abrahams; Daniel von Bargen; Danny Masterson; *D:* Robert Rodriguez; *W:* Kevin Williamson; *C:* Enrique Chediak; *M:* Marco Beltrami.

Fade to Black WOOF! **1980 (R)** Young man obsessed with movies loses his grip on reality and adopts the personalities of cinematic characters (Hopalong Cassidy and Dracula among them) to seek revenge on people who have wronged him. Thoroughly unpleasant, highlighted by clips from old flicks. **100m/C; VHS, DVD.** Dennis Christopher; Tim Thomerson; Linda Kerridge; Mickey Rourke; Melinda Fee; Gwynne Gilford; Norman Burton; Morgan Paull; James Luisi; John Steadman; Marcie Barkin; Eve Brent; *D:* Vernon Zimmerman; *W:* Vernon Zimmerman; *C:* Alex Phillips, Jr.; *M:* Craig Safan.

Fade to Black 🦴🦴🦴 **2004 (R)** Jay-Z's brilliant goodbye letter to the public eye. What's touted as the final concert of his career is magnificently captured in an exploding Madison Square Gardens in November of 2003, along with studio time during the making of "The Black Album." Jay-Z waxes ill-osophic about the methods to his badness, gets a haircut, and scowls as his posse bumrush his ColecoVision, dropping furious rhymes everywhere he turns. The entire affair is a little too long, but the energy carries well. **109m/C; DVD.** *D:* Michael John Warren; *C:* Scott Lochmus; Theron Smith; Paul Bozymowski; Luke McCoubrey.

Fading Gigolo 🦴🦴 **2013 (R)** Director/writer Turturro continues his unique career with this dramedy about struggling florist Fioravante (also Turturro), who is talked into a second career as a gigolo by friend Murray (Allen), who becomes his pimp. Yes, you read that right. This fertile ground for comedy takes a surprising turn when Turturro focuses on a young Jewish woman (the great Vanessa Paradis) who goes to his gigolo character not for traditional sex but just basic human connection. The drama works but the slapstick comedy with Vergara and Stone simply does not. And Allen's schtick undermines Turturro's attempts at serious commentary on a modern role for the world's oldest profession. **98m/C; DVD, Blu-Ray.** John Turturro; Woody Allen; Vanessa Paradis; Liev Schreiber; Sharon Stone; Sofia Vergara; Tonya Pinkins; *D:* John Turturro; *W:* John Turturro; *C:* Marco Pontecorvo; *M:* Abraham Laboriel; Bill Maxwell.

Fading of the Cries 🦴 **2010 (R)** Inept genre mash-up. Teenaged Sarah finds a necklace belonging to her uncle and releases Mathias, a malevolent entity. She's hunted by demonic forces and aided by Jacob, some goth-looking dude with a sword and an attitude. **93m/C; DVD.** Hallee Hirsch; Jordan Matthews; Brad Dourif; Thomas Ian Nicholas; Elaine Hendrix; Julia Whelan; *D:* Brian Metcalf; *W:* Brian Metcalf; *C:* Brad Rushing; *M:* Nathaniel Levisay. **VIDEO**

Fahrenheit 451 🦴🦴🦴 **1966** Chilling adaptation of the Ray Bradbury novel about a totalitarian futuristic society that has banned all reading material and the firemen whose job it is to keep the fires at 451 degrees: the temperature at which paper burns. Werner is Montag, a fireman who begins to question the rightness of his actions when he meets the book-loving teacher Clarisse (Christie)--who also plays the dual role of Werner's TV-absorbed wife, Linda. Truffaut's first color and English-language film. **112m/C; VHS, DVD, Blu-Ray.** *FR GB* Oskar Werner; Julie Christie; Cyril Cusack; Anton Diffring; Alex Scott; Anna Palk; Ann Bell; Mark Lester; Tom Watson; *D:* Francois Truffaut; *W:* Francois Truffaut; Helen Scott; Jean-Louis Richard; David Rudkin; *C:* Nicolas Roeg; *M:* Bernard Herrmann.

Fahrenheit 11/9 🦴🦴 1/2 **2018 (R)** Michael Moore's latest documentary explores the broken state of America in 2018 as a bipartisan blame-fest, issuing culpability on both Democrats and Republicans. It looks beyond the Oval Office to examine gun violence and the Flint water crisis, but this lack of focus may be the film's downfall. Moore is obviously injecting heartfelt emotions into this passion project, which is intended to be a political and social call to action rather than a balm for a nation's ravaged nerves. You're not going to feel better after watching it, and that's probably the point. **128m/C; DVD, Blu-Ray.** Michael Moore; Donald J. Trump; Hillary Rodham Clinton; George W. Bush; Barack Obama; *D:* Michael Moore; *W:* Michael Moore; *C:* Luke Geissbuhler; Jayme Roy. Golden Raspberries '18: Worst Actor (Trump).

Fahrenheit 9/11 🦴🦴🦴 **2004 (R)** Michael Moore's indictment of the Bush administration's handling of the Iraq War begins with the 2000 election and follows Bush up to and through the 9/11 attacks, pointing out lost opportunities to stop Bin Laden's plot. Continues through the War on Terrorism and the Iraq War. Party affiliation will determine viewer opinion, but Moore's poisoned pen letter of a documentary is effective and bracing. This is pure propaganda, but of the strongest kind. Moore uses every weapon in his arsenal to attack Bush and his cronies, with outtakes and bloopers by Ashcroft, Rumsfeld, and Bush especially juicy. Sobering, horrific footage of ongoing carnage in Iraq—the stuff they don't show on the nightly news—balances out some of the more outlandish buffoonery and lampooning. Viciously funny and gut-wrenchingly heartbreaking. **110m/C; DVD.** Britney Spears; George W. Bush; Donald Rumsfeld; Condoleeza Rice; *D:* Michael Moore; *W:* Michael Moore; *C:* Mike Desjarlais; *M:* Bob Golden. Golden Raspberries '04: Worst Actor (Bush), Worst Support. Actor (Rumsfeld), Worst Support. Actress (Spears).

Fail-Safe 🦴🦴🦴 1/2 **1964** A nail-biting nuclear age nightmare, in which American planes have been erroneously sent to bomb the USSR, with no way to recall them. An all-star cast impels this bitterly serious thriller, the straight-faced flipside of "Dr. Strangelove." **111m/B; VHS, DVD, Blu-Ray.** Henry Fonda; Dan O'Herlihy; Walter Matthau; Larry Hagman; Fritz Weaver; Dom DeLuise; *D:* Sidney Lumet; *W:* Walter Bernstein; *C:* Gerald Hirschfeld.

Fail Safe 🦴🦴 **2000** Claustrophobic remake of the 1964 Cold War thriller shown originally as a live CBS TV broadcast. Thanks to a computer glitch, a nuclear strike is launched against the USSR and the president and the military must find a way to recall the bombers or deal with the consequences. **86m/B; DVD.** George Clooney; Richard Dreyfuss; Noah Wyle; Brian Dennehy; Sam Elliott; Don Cheadle; Harvey Keitel; Hank Azaria; James Cronwell; John Diehl; Norman Lloyd; *D:* Stephen Frears; *W:* Walter Bernstein; *C:* John Alonzo. **TV**

Failure to Launch 🦴🦴 **2006 (PG-13)** Finally, a movie that lives up to its title. Tripp (McConaughey) is a 35-year-old slacker still living with his parents (Bradshaw and Bates). They want him out, so they hire a woman, Paula (Parker), who specializes at getting grown men to move out of their parents' homes. Along the way characters are bitten by a chipmunk, a lizard, a dolphin, even a mockingbird. Both Parker and McConaughey play their usual smiling, glowing selves. Since this is a romantic comedy, they eventually fall in love. Guess Paula's not used to these freeloaders being buff and charming. **97m/C; DVD, Blu-Ray, HD-DVD.** Matthew McConaughey; Sarah Jessica Parker; Zooey Deschanel; Justin Bartha; Bradley Cooper; Terry Bradshaw; Kathy Bates; Katheryn Winnick; Tyrell Jackson Williams; Patton Oswalt; Stephen Tobolowsky; Peter Jacobson; Kate McGregor-Stewart; *D:* Tom Dey; *W:* Tom J. Astle; Matt Ember; *M:* Rolfe Kent.

Fair Game WOOF! **1986** In the Australian outback, three loathesome excuses for human beings come across a beautiful woman alone on a remote farm. Naturally, they try to do despicable things but she fights back. **83m/C; VHS, DVD.** *AU* Cassandra Delaney; Peter Ford; David Sandford; Gary Who; *D:* Mario Andreacchio; *W:* Rob George; *C:* Andrew Lesnie; *M:* Ashley Irwin.

Fair Game WOOF! *Mamba Snakes* **1989 (R)** A psychotic but imaginative ex-boyfriend locks his former girlfriend in her apartment with a lethal giant Mamba snake. Understandably uninterested in its serpentine attention, the young woman must trespass against the Hollywood code and keep her wits in the face of danger. Guaranteed not to charm you. **81m/C; VHS, DVD.** *IT* Gregg Henry; Trudie Styler; Bill Moseley; *D:* Mario Orfini; *W:* Mario Orfini; Linda Ravera; *C:* Dante Spinotti; *M:* Giorgio Moroder.

Fair Game 🦴🦴 1/2 **1995 (R)** Miami police detective Max (Baldwin) defies orders so he can protect family attorney Kate (Crawford, in her big-screen debut) from high-tech assassins. Nice work if you can get it. Generic action plot provides Crawford and first-time director Sipes with relatively safe proving ground. Cindy wears the "Die Hard" dirty white tank top look fetchingly enough (and showers when the action slackens), while Baldwin is no slouch in the babe department (male division) either. Based on Paula Gosling's 1978 novel "Fair Game," which was previously filmed as 1986's "Cobra." **91m/C; VHS, DVD.** William Baldwin; Cindy Crawford; Steven Berkoff; Miguel (Michael) Sandoval; Christopher McDonald; Johann Carlo; Salma Hayek; John Bedford Lloyd; Jenette Goldstein; *D:* Andrew Sipes; *W:* Charlie Fletcher; *C:* Richard Bowen; *M:* Mark Mancina.

Fair Game 🦴🦴🦴 **2010 (PG-13)** Based on the controversial disclosure of Valerie Plame's (Watts) identity as a covert CIA operative by a Washington, D.C. journalist. Plame was outed after her diplomat husband, Joseph Wilson (Penn), wrote a 2003 New York Times op-ed criticism of the Bush administration's involvement in perpetuating questionable information about weapons of mass destruction in Iraq. Highly subjective but compelling portrayal of modern politics that inspires as much controversy as the events it portrays. Tone is inconsistent at times but the excellent performances of Watts and Penn manage to overcome. **106m/C; Blu-Ray, On Demand.** Naomi Watts; Sean Penn; Noah Emmerich; Ty Burrell; Bruce McGill; Sam Shepard; David Andrews; Brooke Smith; David Denman; Khaled Nabawy; Kristoffer Ryan Winters; Geoffrey Cantor; *D:* Doug Liman; *W:* Jez Butterworth; John Henry Butterworth; *M:* John Powell.

Fairfield Road 🦴🦴 **2010** Hallmark Channel drama that's part romance and part politics. Noah McManus (Metcalfe) loses his high-powered political job and his cheating fiance on the same day. Needing to get out of Boston, Noah heads to the Cape Cod town of Harpswell and begins to appreciate small-town life after meeting bookstore owner Hailey (Lisinska). He gets involved in a political battle that pits the locals against a greedy developer. **84m/C; DVD.** Jesse Metcalfe; Natalie Lisinska; Derek McGrath; Chick Reid; Brandon Firla; *D:* David Weaver; *W:* Tracy Rosen; *C:* Boris Mojsovski; *M:* Ian Thomas. **CABLE**

Fairy Tales 🦴🦴 *Fairytales* **1976 (R)** A ribald musical fantasy follows the equally risque "Cinderella." In order to save the kingdom, the prince must produce an heir. The problem is that only the girl in the painting of "Princess Beauty" can "interest" the prince and she must be found. Good-natured smut. **83m/C; VHS, DVD, Blu-Ray.** Don Sparks; Prof. Irwin Corey; Brenda Fogarty; Sy Richardson; Nai Bonet; Martha Reeves; *D:* Harry (Hurwitz) Tampa.

FairyTale: A True Story 🦴🦴 1/2 *Illumination* **1997 (PG)** Discovery of hope and fantasy in bleak reality when two girls in 1917 war-torn England claim to have photographed fairies in their garden. Skeptical debunker Harry Houdini (Keitel) and spiritual believer Sir Arthur Conan Doyle (O'Toole) show up to investigate the photos of cousins Elsie (Hoath) and Frances (Earl). The issues of science and spiritualism are profusely debated between the two men, getting a little in the way of the girls and their story. Tries to appeal to both adults and children, which may leave both feeling a bit unsatisfied. Perky pixies flitting about throughout picture, courtesy of special f/x wizard Tim Webber, are bound to delight even hardened audience skeptics. Don't blink for Mel Gibson's cameo as Frances' father. This same true story, known as the Cottingley Fairies, is also part of the plotline in the surreal British film "Photographing Fairies." **99m/C; VHS, DVD.** Harvey Keitel; Peter O'Toole; Florence Hoath; Elizabeth Earl; Paul McGann; Phoebe Nicholls; Bill Nighy; Bob Peck; Tim (McInnerny) McInnery; ***Cameo(s):*** Mel Gibson; *D:* Charles Sturridge; *W:* Ernie Contreras; *C:* Michael Coulter; *M:* Zbigniew Preisner.

Faith 🦴🦴 **1994** Nick Simon (Hannah) is a widowed tabloid journalist who falls in love with Holly (Harker), daughter of politician Peter Moreton (Gambon). Nick gets an unexpected scoop when Holly tells him about her father's affair and now must choose between using the information or protecting his girlfriend's dad even as Peter struggles to save his career. **206m/C; DVD.** *GB* John Hannah; Michael Gambon; Susannah Harker; John Strickland; *W:* Simon Burke; *C:* Peter Fearon. **TV**

Faithful 🦴🦴 1/2 **1995 (R)** Black comedy about depressed, rich housewife Margaret (Cher) who is rudely interrupted by Tony the hitman (Palminteri) while trying to commit suicide on her 20th wedding anniversary. Unfaithful hubby Jack (O'Neal), who has put the contract out on Margaret, is conveniently away on business. As Margaret sits tied to a chair and Tony waits for a call to confirm the hit, the two connect and decide to turn the tables. Director Mazursky succeeds in bringing Palminteri's three-character play to the screen, even if it does suffer at times from too much stage talk and not enough action. First film for Cher since 1990's "Mermaids" and the first for O'Neal since 1989's "Chances

Are." Big rift between Mazursky and the film's producers over final cut led him to threaten to pull his name from the credits. Mazursky cameos as the hitman's therapist. **91m/C; VHS, DVD.** Cher; Ryan O'Neal; Chazz Palminteri; ***Cameo(s):*** Paul Mazursky; ***D:*** Paul Mazursky; ***W:*** Chazz Palminteri; ***C:*** Fred Murphy.

Faithless 1/2 **1932** In this romantic melodrama, careless socialite Carol Morgan (Bankhead) doesn't control her spendthrift ways despite the Depression and soon finds herself broke. She tries to reunite with former fiance Bill Wade (Montgomery) but he's lost his job and is struggling as well. There are money troubles galore when they finally reconcile. **77m/B; DVD.** Tallulah Bankhead; Robert Montgomery; Hugh Herbert; Maurice Murphy; Anna Appel; ***D:*** Harry Beaumont; ***W:*** Carey Wilson; ***C:*** Oliver Marsh.

Faithless 1/2 *Trolosa* **2000 (R)** Ullman again directs a Bergman screenplay about raw emotions and the pain of broken relationships. Evidently semi-autobiographical (it's set on Bergman's island home of Faro), an aging filmmaker (Josephson) in a spare office contemplates his newest screenplay when he's visited by an actress. This visitation is wholly in his mind, however, as Marianne (Endre) aids "Bergman" in writing about a painful affair in his past. Married to Markus (Hanzon), Marianne falls into an affair with close family friend David, who turns out to be the filmmaker in his younger days. The affair wreaks havoc on all three, while Marianne and David's daughter becomes a pawn. While the older filmmaker is thoughtful and even wistful, Bergman shows his younger, more reckless self little sympathy, while Ullman captures the director's languorous style. In Swedish with subtitles. **142m/C; VHS, DVD.** *SW* Lena Endre; Erland Josephson; Thomas Hanzon; Krister Henriksson; Philip Zanden; Marie Richardson; Michelle Gylemo; Juni Dahr; Therese Brunnander; ***D:*** Liv Ullmann; ***W:*** Ingmar Bergman; ***C:*** Jorgen Persson.

Fake 1/2 **2010** Struggling artist Daniel Jakor turns out to be very successful at painting forgeries and Boston gallery owner Tay Murphy uses Daniel's work to pay his debt to mobster Seamus White. The situation goes bad when the FBI is brought in by Daniel's ex-girlfriend, who works at Sotheby's and recognizes his handiwork. Daniel's dead unless he can figure a way out. **102m/C; DVD.** Gabriel Mann; Robert Loggia; Jill Flint; Fisher Stevens; David Thorton; Blanche Baker; ***D:*** Gregory Friedle; ***W:*** Gregory Friedle; ***C:*** Matthew Boyd; ***M:*** Jay Vincent. **VIDEO**

Fake Out *Nevada Heat* **1982** Nightclub singer is caught between the mob and the police who want her to testify against her gangland lover. Typical vanity outing for Zadora. **89m/C; VHS, DVD.** Pia Zadora; Telly Savalas; Desi Arnaz, Jr.; ***D:*** Matt Cimber.

Fakers **2004** A London con man (Rhys) orchestrates an art heist to pay back a $50,000 debt. With the help of an artist buddy (Chambers), who came to possess a lost sketch by an Italian master, they hope to produce five copies and sell them to various London galleries in one single morning, and then blow town before anyone is the wiser. Chirpy crime caper with a lackluster plot. **85m/C; DVD.** *GB* Matthew Rhys; Kate Ashfield; Art Malik; Tony Haygarth; Tom Chambers; ***D:*** Richard Janes; ***W:*** Paul Gerstenberger; ***C:*** Balasz Bolygo; ***M:*** Kevin Sargent.

Falco 1/2 **2008** Biopic of Austrian pop singer Johann Holzel, AKA Falco, who had several campy hits in the 1980s. Falls into price-of-fame cliches as Falco becomes addicted to booze and cocaine and his marriage and career fall apart. The singer was killed in a car crash in 1998. German with subtitles. **109m/C; DVD.** *GE* Manuel Rubey; Patricia Aulitzky; Christian Tramitz; Martin Loos; Nicholas Ofczarek; Susi Stach; ***D:*** Thomas Roth; ***W:*** Thomas Roth; ***C:*** Jo Molitoris; ***M:*** Lothar Scherpe.

The Falcon and the Co-Eds 1/2 **1943** The Falcon (Conway) is called in to investigate the murder of a professor at the all-girls' Bluecliff school, meaning he's surrounded by a bevy of beauties and more dead bodies. The seventh in the series. **67m/B; DVD.** Tom Conway; Jean Brooks; Amelita Ward; Rita (Paula) Corday; Isabel Jewell; George Givot; Cliff Clark; Edward (Ed) Gargan; ***D:*** William Clemens; ***W:*** Ardel Wray; Gerald Geraghty; ***C:*** J. Roy Hunt.

The Falcon and the Snowman **1985 (R)** True story of Daulton Lee and Christopher Boyce, two childhood friends who, almost accidentally, sell American intelligence secrets to the KGB in 1977. Hutton and Penn are excellent, creating a relationship we care about and strong characterizations. **110m/C; VHS, DVD, Blu-Ray.** Sean Penn; Timothy Hutton; Lori Singer; Pat Hingle; Dorian Harewood; Richard Dysart; David Suchet; Jennifer Runyon; Priscilla Pointer; Nicholas Pryor; Joyce Van Patten; Mady Kaplan; Michael Ironside; ***D:*** John Schlesinger; ***W:*** Steven Zaillian; ***C:*** Allen Daviau; ***M:*** Lyle Mays; Pat Metheny.

The Falcon in Danger 1/2 **1943** Two industrialists and a lot of dough disappear mid-flight from a small passenger plane, which then crashes. Tom (Conway) is asked to investigate by the men's daughters who have each received ransom demands. The Falcon is once again engaged, this time to Texan Bonnie Caldwell (Ward), who doesn't want him to get involved until the gals' plight softens her up. The sixth in the series. **69m/B; DVD.** Tom Conway; Jean Brooks; Elaine Shepard; Amelita Ward; Cliff Clark; Edward (Ed) Gargan; Eddie Dunn; ***D:*** William Clemens; ***W:*** Craig Rice; Fred Niblo, Jr.; ***C:*** Frank Redman.

The Falcon in Mexico 1/2 **1944** When paintings from a supposedly dead artist turn up for sale in New York City, the Falcon and the artist's daughter wind up journeying to Mexico to solve the mystery. Part of "The Falcon" series. **70m/B; DVD.** Tom Conway; Mona Maris; Nestor Paiva; Martha Vickers; ***D:*** William Berke; ***W:*** George Worthing Yates; Gerald Geraghty; ***C:*** Frank Redman.

The Falcon Strikes Back 1/2 **1943** The fifth film in the series has George Sanders' brother Tom Conway flying solo after co-starring in 1942's "The Falcon's Brother." In an elaborate set-up, Tom is wrongly accused of murder and stealing war bonds. The fugitive makes his way to a mountain resort that turns out to be the lair of the real criminals. **63m/B; DVD.** Tom Conway; Jane Randolph; Harriet Hilliard Nelson; Edgar Kennedy; Cliff Edwards; Rita (Paula) Corday; Cliff Clark; Edward (Ed) Gargan; ***D:*** Edward Dmytryk; ***W:*** Gerald Geraghty; Edward Dein; ***C:*** Jack MacKenzie; ***M:*** Roy Webb.

The Falcon Takes Over 1/2 **1942** Escaped con Moose Malloy (Bond) is trying to track down his missing ex-girlfriend Velma in New York. The Falcon (Sanders) becomes interested in the case and investigates alongside reporter Ann Riordan (Bari), uncovering a gambling operation. Currently only available as part of 'The Falcon Mystery Movie Collection'. **65m/B; VHS, DVD.** George Sanders; Lynn Bari; Ward Bond; James Gleason; Allen Jenkins; Helen Gilbert; Edward (Ed) Gargan; Anne Revere; ***D:*** Irving Reis; ***W:*** Lynn Root; Frank Felton; ***C:*** George Robinson.

Fall **1997** Brainy supermodel falls for literary cabbie in this portrait of life in the Big Apple. Within minutes of a chance encounter in a cab, married fare Sarah Easton (DeCadenet) is whiling the hours that her gorgeous, rich, doting husband is away, listening to romantic hack Michael's poetry and writhing seductively while feasting on carry-out like it's "9 1/2 Weeks." Schaeffer places himself opposite yet another gorgeous model and egotistically pens his character as a supersensitive writer (who does this guy think he is, Woody Allen?) faced with overwhelming acclaim after his first novel, who decides to chuck it all and drive a cab. Although nicely acted and not bad to look at, the main characters and both their dilemmas are just a little hard to relate to. **92m/C; VHS, DVD.** Eric Schaeffer; Amanda DeCadenet; Francie Swift; Lisa Vidal; Rudolf Martin; ***D:*** Eric Schaeffer; ***W:*** Eric Schaeffer; ***C:*** Joe DeSalvo; ***M:*** Amanda Kravat.

The Fall **1998 (R)** Or should that be "The Patsy"? American novelist Sheffer, who's living in Budapest, gets chosen as the savior of femme de Fourgerolles, who is being stalked by Prochnow. Or so she says—and she wants Sheffer to kill her tormenter. **90m/C; VHS, DVD.** Craig Sheffer; Jurgen Prochnow; Helene de Fougerolles; ***D:*** Andrew Piddington. **VIDEO**

The Fall **2006 (R)** The R-rating seems silly (although it's not for the kiddies) in this visually striking and dramatically absurd creation from Tarsem, which took four years to film. In an L.A. hospital, circa 1915, a five-year-old Romanian migrant worker named Alexandria (Untaru) is convalescing after a fall. Movie stuntman Roy (Pace) is in the same hospital also after an accident—but he is paralyzed. Bored, Alexandria is happy to have her new friend tell her stories that change with her imagination and limited grasp of English (Indians to her are the eastern kind with elephants and palaces). However, a despondent Roy (whose girlfriend has dumped him) has an ulterior motive for befriending Alexandria. Based on the 1981 Bulgarian movie "Yo Ho Ho." **117m/C; DVD, Blu-Ray.** *US GB IN* Lee Pace; Justine Waddell; Leo Bill; Catinca Untaru; Marcus Wesley; Daniel Caltagirone; ***D:*** Tarsem Singh; ***W:*** Dan Gilroy; Tarsem Singh; Nico Soultanakis; ***C:*** Colin Watkinson; ***M:*** Krishna Levy.

Fall Down Dead **2007 (R)** Derivative slasher. Christie survives a Christmas Eve attack by a serial killer by escaping into a nearby office building. Unfortunately, the city is hit by a blackout precisely when Christie and several others are trapped in the building with the killer starting his hunt. **93m/C; DVD.** Dominique Swain; Udo Kier; David Carradine; Mehmet Gunsur; R. Keith Harris; Monica Dean; Burgess Jenkins; Jennifer (Jenny) Alden; Austin James; ***D:*** Jon Keeyes; ***W:*** Roy Sallows; ***C:*** Richard Clabaugh; ***M:*** Pinar Toprak. **VIDEO**

Fall Guy *Kamata Koshin-Kyoku* **1982** Ginshiro Kuraoka (Kazama) is a megalomaniac actor whose once-hot career is on the skids. He's planned a spectacular fight scene for his latest picture in order to one-up his acting rival, but it's so dangerous that no stuntman will take the job. Until desperate and loyal bit player Yasu (Hirata) comes along. Ginshiro has already foisted his pregnant mistress Konatsu (Matsuzaka) off on his lackey and to provide for his new bride (whom he has always loved), Yasu is ready to tackle the dangerous stunt. It's a comedy. Japanese with subtitles. **108m/C; DVD.** *JP* Keiko Matsuzaka; Sonny Chiba; Morio Kazama; Mitsuru Hirata; Chika Takami; Keizo Kanie; ***D:*** Kinji Fukasaku; ***W:*** Kouhei Tsuka; ***C:*** Kiyoshi Kitasaka; ***M:*** Masato Kai.

The Fall of the American Empire 1/2 *La chute de l'empire americain* **2019 (R)** After car thieves Jacmel (Abellard) and Chenier (St-Eloy) organize a heist for the mob that goes wrong, courier Pierre-Paul (Landry) steals and launders some of the stolen money. Other groups, including the West End Gang and law enforcement, want to get the money back. To avoid capture and ensure his survival, Pierre-Paul puts together his own group to invest the money in fake charities and off-shore bank accounts. The third and weakest entry of filmmaker Arcand's trilogy, the story is bogged down by the conscious exploration of issues of global finance, dull characters, and the use of difficult Socratic dialogue. French with American subtitles. **128m/C; DVD.** Maxim Roy; Maripier Morin; Eric Bruneau; Juliette Gosselin; Vincent Leclerc; ***D:*** Denys Arcand; ***W:*** Denys Arcand; ***C:*** Van Royko; ***M:*** Louis Dufort; Mathieu Lussier.

The Fall of the House of Usher **1949** Lord Roderick Usher is haunted by his sister's ghost in this poor adaptation of the Poe classic. **70m/B; VHS, DVD.** *GB* Kay Tendeter; Gwen Watford; Irving Steen; Lucy Pavey; ***D:*** Ivan Barnett.

The Fall of the House of Usher *House of Usher* **1960** The moody Roger Corman/Vincent Price interpretation, the first of their eight Poe adaptations, depicting the collapse of the famous estate due to madness and revenge. Terrific sets and solid direction as well as Price's inimitable presence. **85m/C; VHS, DVD, Blu-Ray.** Vincent Price; Myrna Fahey; Mark Damon; Harry Ellerbe; Bill Borzage; Nadajan; ***D:*** Roger Corman; ***W:*** Richard Matheson; ***C:*** Floyd Crosby; ***M:*** Les Baxter. Natl. Film Reg. '05.

The Fall of the House of Usher 1/2 **1980 (PG)** Another version of Edgar Allan Poe's classic tale of a family doomed to destruction. Stray to the Roger Corman/Vincent Price version to see how it should have been done. **101m/C; VHS, DVD.** Martin Landau; Robert Hays; Charlene Tilton; Ray Walston; ***D:*** James L. Conway.

The Fall of the Roman Empire **1964** An all-star, big budget extravaganza set in ancient Rome praised for its action sequences. The licentious son of Marcus Aurelius arranges for his father's murder and takes over as emperor while Barbarians gather at the gate. Great sets, fine acting, and thundering battle scenes. **187m/C; VHS, DVD.** Sophia Loren; Alec Guinness; James Mason; Stephen Boyd; Christopher Plummer; John Ireland; Anthony Quayle; Eric Porter; Mel Ferrer; Omar Sharif; ***D:*** Anthony Mann; ***W:*** Philip Yordan; ***C:*** Robert Krasker. Golden Globes '65: Score.

Fall Time *Falltime* **1994 (R)** Crime drama set in small-town Minnesota, circa 1957. Three high schoolers set in motion a prank that turns bad when they pull up in front of the local bank. David (Arquette), Joe (Blechman), and Tim (London) intend to stage a mock robbery—but a real robbery is going down and the teens wind up the terrified hostages of creepy criminals Florence (Rourke) and Leon (Baldwin). Promising premise derailed by narrative inadequacies. **88m/C; VHS, DVD.** Mickey Rourke; Stephen Baldwin; Jason London; David Arquette; Jonah Blechman; Sheryl Lee; ***D:*** Paul Warner; ***W:*** Steve Alden; Paul Skemp; ***C:*** Mark J. Gordon; ***M:*** Hummie Mann.

Fallen **1997 (R)** Take a police-story suspense thriller, add the occult and a big dose of the supernatural, stir in a heaping helping of philosophy, a dash of a wrong-man subplot, shake vigorously, and out pours the bitter "Fallen." After the execution of serial killer Edgar Reese (Koteas), crack cop Hobbes (Washington) is soon chasing down copycat killings springing up everywhere. The real culprit is not Reese, but a fallen angel who inhabits body after body, creating new killers with each new host. Washington manages to hold his own as the pic gets messy and overly complicated. Goodman's character provides needed earthbound common sense when the banter gets a bit too lofty, debating things like the meaning of life, existence of God, and other issues that don't belong here. Hoblit's second feature tries to take on way too much in its already lengthy span. With a mish-mash of conflicting film styles and dicey dialogue, film manages to land on the careers of an otherwise talented cast and crew. **124m/C; VHS, DVD, Blu-Ray.** Denzel Washington; Donald Sutherland; John Goodman; Elias Koteas; Embeth Davidtz; James Gandolfini; Robert Joy; Gabriel Casseus; ***D:*** Gregory Hoblit; ***W:*** Nicholas Kazan; ***C:*** Newton Thomas (Tom) Sigel; ***M:*** Tan Dun.

The Fallen **2005** Set in the beautiful Italian countryside during the latter stage of World War II, follows the daily struggles of German, Italian, and American soldiers in October 1944 as Italian rebels battle with Italian and German troops forcing common villagers to choose between fascism and communism. The Allies head north to attack Germany's "Gothic Line." Intimate look at the common soldier's life filmed on a modest budget (under $1 million) unusual to modern war films. **105m/C; DVD.** Fabio Sartor; Sergio Leone; John McVay; Thomas Pohn; Ruben Pla; Dirk Schmidt; ***D:*** Ari Taub; ***W:*** Caio Ribeiro; Nick Day; ***C:*** Claudia Amber; Ian Dudley; ***M:*** Sergei Dreznin.

Fallen **2017 (PG-13)** Young lovers bond at a reform school in a film based on the YA novel by Lauren Kate. After allegedly murdering a male peer, troubled teen Lucinda (Timlin) attends a spooky reform school. Lucinda becomes attracted to the moody Cam (Gilbertson) and the unfriendly yet buff Daniel (Irvine). Choosing Daniel, she learns he is a fallen angel, as are all the school's outcasts. Though a type of religious extremism there makes Daniel deny his true feelings, a near tragedy changes his mind. Unoriginal YA fare with subpar special effects. **91m/C; DVD.** Hermione Corfield; Lola Kirke; Addison Timlin; Joely Richardson; Jeremy Irvine; ***D:*** Scott Hicks; ***W:*** Michael Arlen Ross; Kathryn Price; Nichole Millard; ***C:*** Alar Kivilo; ***M:*** Mark Isham.

Fallen Angel **1945** Broke Eric Stanton (Andrews) drifts into a small town diner and the sights of sexy waitress Stella

(Darnell), who bluntly tells him she only likes guys with dough. Eric seduces rich, lonely June Mills (Faye), marries her, and figures on a comfortable divorce settlement. But Eric's plans are derailed by murder--with him as the prime suspect. Preminger focuses on the chemistry between sexpot Darnell and an intense Andrews, leaving Faye to languish in the thankless good woman role. **98m/B; DVD.** Dana Andrews; Linda Darnell; Alice Faye; Charles Bickford; Bruce Cabot; Percy Kilbride; Anne Revere; John Carradine; ***D:*** Otto Preminger; ***W:*** Harry Kleiner; ***C:*** Joseph LaShelle; ***M:*** David Raskin.

Fallen Angel 🦴 ½ *Revenge* **1999 (R)** Mystery woman seduces and murders her victims and a police detective tries to undercover the link between the crimes. **90m/C; VHS, DVD.** Alexandra Paul; Vlasta Vrana; Anthony Michael Hall; Michelle Johnson; ***D:*** Marc S. Grenier; ***W:*** Neil Goldberg; ***C:*** Georges Archambault; ***M:*** Milan Kymlicka. **VIDEO**

Fallen Angel 🦴🦴 ½ **2003** Sentimental story about making peace with your past and your family. Successful L.A. lawyer Terry McQuinn (Sinise) returns to Maine when his father dies. A caretaker for wealthy summer home people, the senior McQuinn and Terry were long estranged. Katherine Wentworth (Richardson) also has parental issues—her father abandoned the family after a tragic car accident and her wealthy mother is a much-remarried cold fish. Terry remembers Katherine from a childhood tragedy and they are gradually drawn together for a second chance at love and family. Snyder adapted from his novel. **110m/C; DVD.** Gary Sinise; Joely Richardson; Gordon Pinsent; Jordy Benattar; ***D:*** Michael Switzer; ***W:*** Don Snyder; ***C:*** William Wages; ***M:*** Ernest Troost. **TV**

Fallen Angels 🦴🦴 *Duoluo Tianshi* **1995** The visuals dazzle but the disjointed narrative proves a challenge in what Kar-Wai originally intended to be a third story for his film "Chungking Express." Contract killer Wong Chi-Ming (Lai) has been getting his assignments from a nameless female agent (Reis) who's fallen for him. Wong wants to retire, which upsets her. Then there's mute ex-con He Zhiwo (Kaneshiro) who gets involved with a strange young woman named Cherry (Young) who still loves her ex-boyfriend, and everybody crosses paths but there's really no connection and nothing makes much sense anyway. **97m/C; VHS, DVD, Blu-Ray.** *CH* Leon Lai; Michelle Reis; Takeshi Kaneshiro; Charlie Young; Karen Mok; ***D:*** Wong Kar-Wai; ***W:*** Wong Kar-Wai; ***C:*** Christopher Doyle; ***M:*** Frankie Chan.

The Fallen Idol 🦴🦴🦴 *The Lost Illusion* **1949** A young boy wrongly believes that a servant he admires is guilty of murdering his wife. Unwittingly, the child influences the police investigation of the crime so that the servant becomes the prime suspect. Richardson as the accused and Henrey as the boy are notable. Screenplay adapted by Greene from his short story, "The Basement Room." **92m/B; VHS, DVD.** *GB* Ralph Richardson; Bobby Henrey; Michele Morgan; Sonia Dresdel; Jack Hawkins; Bernard Lee; Denis O'Dea; Dora Bryan; Walter Fitzgerald; Karel Stepanek; Geoffrey Keen; James Hayter; Dandy Nichols; George Woodbridge; John Ruddock; Joan Young; Gerard Heinz; ***D:*** Carol Reed; ***W:*** Graham Greene; Lesley Storm; William Templeton; ***C:*** Georges Perinal. British Acad. '48: Film; Natl. Bd. of Review '49: Actor (Richardson); N.Y. Film Critics '49: Director (Reed).

The Fallen Ones 🦴 **2005** In Biblical time the Nephilim were the sons of Angels and human women wiped out by the flood. Ammon (Navid Neghaban) saves his giant son by mummifying him, intending to resurrect him hundreds of years later in a plot to rule the world. **89m/C; DVD, Blu-Ray, Streaming.** Caspar Van Dien; Kristen Miller; Geoffrey Lewis; Navid Negahban; Scott Whyte; ***D:*** Kevin VanHook; ***W:*** Kevin VanHook; ***C:*** Matt Steinauer; ***M:*** Kevin Kaska; William Richter. **TV**

The Fallen Sparrow 🦴🦴🦴 **1943** Garfield is superb as a half-mad veteran of the Spanish Civil War. Captured and brutalized, he never revealed the whereabouts of a valuable possession. His return to the U.S. continues his torture as Nazi agent Slezak uses the woman Garfield loves to set a trap and finish the job. Solid performances and good plot are highlights. **94m/B; VHS, DVD.** John Garfield; Maureen O'Hara; Walter Slezak; Patricia Morison; Martha O'Driscoll; Bruce Edwards; John Miljan; John Banner; Hugh Beaumont; ***D:*** Richard Wallace.

Falling 🦴🦴 *Fallen* **2006** Intimate character study of five women who reunite at the funeral of their former teacher. Together they crash a wedding, kick up their heels at a nightclub, and share secrets that liberate them. As things are brought to a close, one is left feeling empty and unfulfilled, much like the lives of our five friends. German with subtitles. **88m/C; DVD.** *AT* Birgit Minichmayr; Ursula Strauss; Kathrin Resatarits; Nina Proll; Gabriela Hegedus; ***D:*** Barbara Albert; ***W:*** Barbara Albert; ***C:*** Bernhard Keller.

Falling Angels 🦴🦴 **2003** Domineering Jim Field has driven his wife Mary into alcoholism and depression, leaving their three teenaged daughters to make their own way in 1960s Saskatchewan. Eldest daughter Norma has no self-confidence and is burdened by the suspicious death of their infant brother; middle daughter Lou becomes rebellious; and youngest daughter Sandy gets involved with a married man with some kinky ideas. Adaptation of the Barbara Gowdy novel. **109m/C; DVD.** *CA* Callum Keith Rennie; Miranda Richardson; Monte Gagne; Katharine Isabelle; Kristin Adams; Mark McKinney; Kett Turton; ***D:*** Scott Smith; ***W:*** Scott Smith; Esta Spalding; ***C:*** Gregory Middleton; ***M:*** Ken Whiteley.

Falling Down 🦴🦴 **1993 (R)** Douglas is "D-FENS" (taken from his license plate), a normally law-abiding white-collar geek who snaps while stuck in a traffic jam on a hot day in LA. Like Charles Bronson in "Death Wish," he decides to take matters into his own hands. Unlike Bronson, he is not avenging an attack by a specific criminal, but raging against whomever gets in his way. Duvall is a detective on his last day before retirement, Hershey has the thankless role of Douglas' ex. Essentially a revenge fantasy that was vilified by some for catering to the baser emotions. **112m/C; VHS, DVD.** Michael Douglas; Robert Duvall; Barbara Hershey; Rachel Ticotin; Tuesday Weld; Frederic Forrest; Lois Smith; D.W. Moffett; Dedee Pfeiffer; Vondie Curtis-Hall; Michael Paul Chan; Raymond J. Barry; Jack Kehoe; John Diehl; ***D:*** Joel Schumacher; ***W:*** Ebbe Roe Smith; ***C:*** Andrzej Bartkowiak; ***M:*** James Newton Howard.

Falling Fire 🦴🦴 ½ *The Cusp* **1997 (R)** Good visual effects highlight this cable sci-fier that combines terrorists and asteroids. Daryl Boden (Pare) has the task of getting his spacecraft to steer an asteroid into earth orbit for the purpose of mining its resources. But an eco-terrorist group, led by Lopez (Vidosa), want to force the asteroid to crash into the planet, thus "cleansing" it of man. Oh, there's a terrorist aboard Boden's craft to help things along, while his ex-wife Marilyn (von Palleske) fights the eco-villians back on earth. **84m/C; VHS, DVD.** *CA* Michael Paré; Heidi von Palleske; Christian Vidosa; Zehra Leverman; ***D:*** Daniel D'or; ***W:*** Daniel D'or; ***C:*** Jonathan Freeman; ***M:*** Donald Quan. **CABLE**

Falling for a Dancer 🦴🦴 ½ **1998** When young Elizabeth Sullivan (Dermot-Walsh) gets pregnant after a brief affair, there's not much she can do since she lives in Ireland during the 1930s. She's forced by her family into marriage with a drunken widower and resigns herself to loneliness until love is found again. Purcell adapted from her own novel. **200m/C; VHS, DVD.** *GB* Elisabeth Dermot-Walsh; Dermot Crowley; Liam Cunningham; Rory Murray; Brian McGrath; Maureen O'Brien; Colin Farrell; ***D:*** Richard Standeven; ***W:*** Deirdre Purcell; ***C:*** Kevin Rowley; ***M:*** Stephen McKeon. **TV**

Falling for Grace 🦴 ½ *East Broadway* **2006 (PG-13)** Lee would have had a much more interesting film if she had chosen the immigrant parents/first-generation American children story rather than the lame mistaken identity romance. Ambitious Chinese-American investment banker Grace Tang (Lee) is mistaken for a Hong Kong heiress. This allows her to be swept up by Manhattan's elite and into the arms of the city's most eligible WASP bachelor (Harold, with whom Lee has no romantic chemistry). **98m/C; DVD.** Gale Harold; Ken Leung; Roger Rees; Christine Baranski; Elizabeth Sung; Clem Cheung; Fay Ann Lee; Stephanie March; Margaret Cho; Lewis Black; ***D:*** Fay Ann Lee; ***W:*** Fay Ann Lee; Karen Rousso; ***C:*** Luke Geissbuhler; Toshiaki Ozawa; ***M:*** Andrew Hollander.

Falling from Grace 🦴🦴 ½ **1992 (PG-13)** Bud Parks (Mellencamp) is a successful country singer who, accompanied by his wife and daughter, returns to his small Indiana hometown to celebrate his grandfather's 80th birthday. He's tired of both his career and his marriage and finds himself taking up once again with an old girlfriend (Lenz), who is not only married to Bud's brother but is also having an affair with his father. Bud believes he's better off staying in his old hometown but the problems caused by his return may change his mind. Surprisingly sedate, although literate, family drama with good ensemble performances. Actor-director debut for Mellencamp. **100m/C; VHS, DVD.** John Cougar Mellencamp; Mariel Hemingway; Kay Lenz; Claude Akins; Dub Taylor; Brent Huff; Deirdre O'Connell; Larry Crane; ***D:*** John Cougar Mellencamp; ***W:*** Larry McMurtry.

Falling in Love 🦴🦴 ½ **1984 (PG-13)** Two married New Yorkers unexpectedly fall in love after a coincidental meeting at the Rizzoli Book Store. Weak but gracefully performed reworking of "Brief Encounter," where no one seems to ever complete a sentence. An unfortunate re-teaming for Streep and De Niro after their wonderful work in "The Deer Hunter." **106m/C; DVD.** Robert De Niro; Meryl Streep; Harvey Keitel; Dianne Wiest; George Martin; Jane Kaczmarek; David Clennon; ***D:*** Ulu Grosbard; ***W:*** Michael Cristofer; ***C:*** Peter Suschitzky; ***M:*** Dave Grusin.

Falling in Love Again 🦴 ½ *In Love* **1980 (PG)** Romantic comedy about middle-aged dreamer Gould and realistic wife York. They travel from Los Angeles to their hometown of New York for his high school reunion, where Gould is suddenly attacked by nostalgia vibes for his youth, seen in countless flashbacks, and prominently featuring Pfeiffer, notable in her film debut. Like watching a home movie about people you don't care about. **103m/C; VHS, DVD.** Elliott Gould; Susannah York; Michelle Pfeiffer; ***D:*** Steven Paul; ***W:*** Ted Allan; ***C:*** Michael Mileham; ***M:*** Michel Legrand.

Falling Up 🦴🦴 **2008** Predictable romantic comedy that at least has a decent cast to get past some of the cliches. Flatbush boy Henry O'Shea (Cross) is a newly-hired Manhattan doorman who breaks the first rule of the job: he falls for Scarlett (Roemer), the daughter of one of the building's wealthiest tenants. After getting fired, Henry decides pursuing a romance with the uptown girl is worth the aggravation (fortunately Scarlett likes him too). **98m/C; DVD.** Joseph Cross; Sarah Roemer; Joe Pantoliano; Mimi Rogers; Jim Piddock; Rachael Leigh Cook; Snoop Dogg; Annette O'Toole; Frankie Shaw; Gordon Clapp; Peter Jason; Sam Page; ***D:*** David M. Rosenthal; ***W:*** David M. Rosenthal; Joseph Matthew Smith; ***C:*** Joseph Gallagher; ***M:*** Mark Mothersbaugh.

Fallout 🦴🦴 ½ **2001** It is horribly ironic that filmmaker Palumbo chose to film the introduction to his independent feature on top of one of the World Trade Center towers. His film concerns the interplay among four high-rise office workers who flee a disaster of uncertain origin and find themselves trapped in a basement fallout shelter. His story really has nothing to do with the 9/11/01 atrocities. It's a well-made character study that attempts to work with some serious ideas within the limitations of a modest budget. It's mostly successful, too, and certainly doesn't need any extra baggage. Parallels to reality are difficult to ignore, however. **88m/C; DVD.** Claire Beckman; Mark Deakins; Keith Randolph Smith; David Wasson; ***D:*** Robert Palumbo; ***W:*** Robert Palumbo; Mark Gallini; ***C:*** Wolfgang Held; ***M:*** Frank Ferrucci.

The Falls: Covenant of Grace 🦴🦴 **2016** The third part of the Falls trilogy completes the love story of Chris (Farmer) and RJ (Ferrucci). The former Mormon missionaries have now been in love for seven years but still struggle to make their relationship work while managing conflicts with their church and their families. The pair begin a quest to ensure they can be together forever, a journey which takes them to top leaders in the Mormon church. **119m/C; DVD, Blu-Ray, Streaming, Download.** Nick Ferrucci; Benjamin Farmer; Curtis Edward Jackson; Bruce Jennings; Harold Phillips; ***D:*** Jon Garcia; ***W:*** Jon Garcia; Rodney Moore; ***C:*** Seth Whelden; ***M:*** Jon Garcia. **VIDEO**

The Falls: Testament of Love 🦴🦴 **2013** The second installment of The Falls trilogy, a romantic drama about two gay Mormon missionaries. Five years after RJ (Ferrucci) and Chris (Farmer) met and fell in love while serving as missionaries together, their lives have gone in different directions. When a mutual friend dies, the pair is reunited. They soon discover they still have feelings for each other, and must face difficult decisions if they are going to make their reunion more permanent. **123m/C; DVD, Blu-Ray, Streaming, Download.** Nick Ferrucci; Benjamin Farmer; Hannah Barefoot; Bruce Jennings; Thomas Stroppel; ***D:*** Jon Garcia; ***W:*** Jon Garcia; ***C:*** Christopher Stephens. **VIDEO**

False Arrest 🦴🦴 ½ **1992** A woman is falsely accused of killing her husband's business partner and winds up in prison where she continues to fight to prove her innocence. Mills does well in this less-than-glamorous role. Based on a true story. **102m/C; VHS, DVD.** Donna Mills; Steven Bauer; James Handy; Lane Smith; Lewis Van Bergen; Dennis Christopher; Robert Wagner; ***D:*** Bill W.L. Norton. **TV**

False Faces 🦴 ½ **1932** A ruthless, money-hungry quack is hounded by the law and the victims of his unscrupulous plastic surgery. **80m/B; VHS, DVD.** Lowell Sherman; Peggy Shannon; Lila Lee; Joyce Compton; Berton Churchill; David Landau; Eddie Anderson; Ken Maynard; Veda Ann Borg; ***D:*** Lowell Sherman.

False Pretenses 🦴 ½ **2004** Con man Michael (Bick) gets Randal Ackers (Lemke) to put all his assets into his investment scheme and when Randal loses everything he commits suicide. Now Texas housewife Diane (Wilson) is not only widowed but broke and she wants revenge. Michael really isn't so smart when a couple of cosmetic adjustments and a false name make Diane apparently unrecognizable but you don't really expect reality from a Lifetime flick. **90m/C; DVD.** Peta Wilson; Stewart Bick; Anthony Lemke; Conrad Pla; Melanie Nicholls-King; ***D:*** Jason Hreno; ***W:*** Tom Swale; ***C:*** Daniel Vincelette; ***M:*** James Gelfand. **CABLE**

False Prophets **2006** Waitress Maggie (Heuring) is pregnant and wants an abortion until a fundamentalist group talks her into adoption because they believe there's something miraculous about the baby. Except Maggie gets suspicious and runs away and winds up at a rural gas station with a spiritually-minded attendant named Manny (Lyons), who helps her give birth in a field. There's supposed to be some meaning to all this. **?m/CDVD.** Lori Heuring; Patrick Bergin; Clayne Crawford; Tucker Smallwood; Antonio David Lyons; ***C:*** David Gossard; ***M:*** Brian Arbuckle. **VIDEO**

Fame 🦴🦴🦴 **1980 (R)** Follows eight talented teenagers from their freshmen year through graduation from New York's High School of Performing Arts. Insightful and absorbing, director Parker allows the kids to mature on screen, revealing the pressures of constantly trying to prove themselves. A faultless parallel is drawn between these "special" kids and the pressures felt by high schoolers everywhere. Great dance and music sequences. Basis for a TV series. **133m/C; DVD.** Irene Cara; Barry Miller; Paul McCrane; Anne Meara; Joanna Merlin; Richard Belzer; Maureen Teefy; Albert Hague; ***D:*** Alan Parker; ***M:*** Michael Gore. Oscars '80: Orig. Score, Song ("Fame"); Golden Globes '81: Song ("Fame").

Fame 🦴 ½ **2009 (PG)** Unnecessary update of the 1980 musical (and subsequent TV series) about an ambitious group of students at New York's prestigious High School for the Performing Arts. The teens soon learn that getting into the program is only their first challenge. The actors are then required to play out a script riddled with stuffy cliches aimed at a hip teen audience that's way too smart for this type of outdated, soapy mush. The original R-rated account of the pain behind achieving dreams is now a watered-down, PG-rated knock-off of "High School

Musical." **107m/C; Blu-Ray.** Paul Iacono; Kay Panabaker; Debbie Allen; Charles S. Dutton; Kristy Flores; Kelsey Grammer; Megan Mullally; Bebe Neuwirth; Tim Jo; Walter Perez; Naturi Naughton; Collins Pennie; Asher Book; Kherington Payne; Paul McGill; ***D:*** Kevin Tancharoen; ***W:*** Allison Burnett; Christopher Gore; ***C:*** Scott Kevan; ***M:*** Mark Isham.

Familia 🦴🦴 **2005** Divorced Michele has a gambling problem and when she loses her job, she and rebellious teen daughter Marguerite impose on her childhood friend Janine for a place to stay. Uptight Janine lives a seemingly perfect life in suburban Montreal but the cracks are showing since her husband is a chronic adulterer and she is having trouble with her own two children. Janine's demure daughter Gabrielle easily bonds with Marguerite while Michele is soon betraying Janine's hospitality. English and French with subtitles. **102m/C; DVD.** *CA* Sylvie Moreau; Macha Grenon; Juliette Gosselin; Mylene St-Sauveur; Paul Savoie; Vincent Graton; ***D:*** Louise Archambault; ***W:*** Louise Archambault; ***C:*** Andre Turpin; ***M:*** Ramachandra Bocar.

Familiar Strangers 🦴🦴 ½ **2008 (PG-13)** Brian Worthington left home to get away from dad Frank, who can't understand any of his kids and prefers his pets. Brian finally returns for Thanksgiving and finds little has changed: mom Dottie is still trying to hold the family together; aimless 20-something Kenny still lives at home; and Erin has moved back in, with daughter Maddy, after a messy divorce. Brian does reconnect with family friend Allison but the shocker is when he gets pressured to dispose of the family member Frank loves the best—dog Argus. **86m/C; DVD.** Shawn Hatosy; Tom Bower; Ann Dowd; DJ Qualls; Cameron Richardson; Georgia Mae Lively; Nikki Reed; ***D:*** Zackary Adler; ***W:*** John Bell; ***C:*** H. Michael Otano; ***M:*** Dawn Landes; Steve Salett.

The Family 🦴 ½ *Violent City* **1970** As a New Orleans hit-man who resists joining the mob, Bronson initiates an all-out war on the syndicate and its boss, played by Savalas. A poorly dubbed Italian action film. **94m/C; VHS, DVD.** *IT* Charles Bronson; Jill Ireland; Telly Savalas; George Savalas; Michel Constantin; Umberto Orsini; ***D:*** Sergio Sollima; ***W:*** Sergio Sollima; ***C:*** Aldo Tonti; ***M:*** Ennio Morricone.

The Family 🦴 **2013 (R)** Besson's first live-action film in years proves that he either should have stayed in animation or followed through on the hints that he would soon retire. Tragically unfunny, lazy, and boring, Besson plays with Italian stereotypes in his action-comedy about a patriarch named Giovanni Manzoni (De Niro, resting on all of his acting crutches) who enters witness protection with his troublesome family. Pfeiffer offers little as the matriarch and Jones looks like he literally falls asleep at one point from being as bored as you will be watching this excuse for a movie. **111m/C; DVD, Blu-Ray.** *US FR* Robert De Niro; Michelle Pfeiffer; Dianna Agron; John DiLeo; Tommy Lee Jones; ***D:*** Luc Besson; ***W:*** Luc Besson; Michael Caleo; ***C:*** Thierry Arbogast; ***M:*** Evgueni Galperine; Sacha Galperine.

A Family Affair 🦴🦴 ½ **1937** The first in the Andy Hardy series focuses on Judge Hardy whose opposition to the construction of an alleged civic project could cost him his re-election. He also has to deal with family troubles: married daughter Joan has separated from her husband and becomes the target of a political smear campaign and younger daughter Marian is upset about boyfriend Wayne's job prospects. Only Andy has it easy when he discovers that childhood pal Polly Benedict, whom he must take to a dance, has grown up just swell. **70m/B; DVD.** Lionel Barrymore; Mickey Rooney; Julie Haydon; Cecilia Parker; Spring Byington; Eric Linden; Charley Grapewin; Sara Haden; Margaret Marquis; Allen Vincent; ***D:*** George B. Seitz; ***W:*** Kay Van Riper; ***C:*** Lester White; ***M:*** David Snell.

A Family Affair 🦴🦴 ½ **2001** Rachel (Lesnick), a Jewish lesbian New Yorker, has been brutally dumped by her manipulative girlfriend Reggie (Greene). She flees to San Diego for the succor of her PFLAG mom (Golonka), who's more than happy to help her daughter find Ms. Right. And that seems to be blonde and perky WASP, Christine (Shaffer). Insecurity leads to romance leads to love—and the sudden re-appearance of Reggie. **107m/C; VHS, DVD.** Helen Lesnick; Arlene Golonka; Erica Shaffer; Michele Greene; Suzanne Westenhoefer; Michael Moerman; Barbara Stuart; ***D:*** Helen Lesnick; ***W:*** Helen Lesnick; ***C:*** Jim Orr; ***M:*** Danny De La Isla; Kelly Neill; Robert Westlind.

Family Business 🦴🦴 ½ **1989 (R)** A bright Ivy Leaguer, impressed by the exploits and vitality of his criminal grandfather, recruits him and his ex-con dad to pull off a high-tech robbery, which goes awry. Caper film, with its interest in family relationships and being true to one's nature. Casting Connery, Hoffman, and Broderick as the three leaves a big believability problem in the family department. **114m/C; VHS, DVD.** Sean Connery; Dustin Hoffman; Matthew Broderick; Rosanna Desoto; Janet Carroll; Victoria Jackson; Bill McCutcheon; Deborah Rush; Marilyn Cooper; Salem Ludwig; Rex Everhart; James Tolkan; Tony DiBenedetto; Wendell Pierce; John Capodice; Luis Guzman; ***D:*** Sidney Lumet; ***W:*** Vincent Patrick; ***C:*** Andrzej Bartkowiak; ***M:*** Cy Coleman.

Family Enforcer 🦴 *Death Collector* **1976 (R)** A small-time hoodlum is bent on becoming the best enforcer in an underworld society. **82m/C; VHS, DVD.** Joe Cortese; Lou Criscuola; Joe Pesci; Anne Johns; Keith Davis; ***D:*** Ralph De Vito; ***W:*** Ralph De Vito; ***C:*** Bob Bailin.

The Family Fang 🦴 ½ **2016 (R)** Annie (Kidman) and Baxter Fang (Bateman, who also directs) had a unique childhood, the centerpiece of "pranks" or bits of public performance art orchestrated by their parents (Butler Harner & Hahn in flashbacks, Walken & Plunkett in present day). When the Fangs appear to have died, Annie and Baxter get back together and question exactly what's going on. This is one of those smug, callous, nauseating family comedies that doesn't get either family or comedy. You won't buy a minute of it, and the only joy comes from Walken's performance as the latest bad movie dad. **105m/C; DVD, Blu-Ray.** Nicole Kidman; Jason Bateman; Christopher Walken; Maryann Plunkett; Marin Ireland; ***D:*** Jason Bateman; ***W:*** David Lindsay-Abaire; ***C:*** Ken Seng; ***M:*** Carter Burwell.

The Family Game 🦴🦴🦴 *Kazoku gaimu; Kazoku Game* **1983** An obsessive satire about a poor, belligerent college student hired by a wealthy contemporary Japanese family to tutor their spoiled teenage son. Provides an all-out cultural assault on the Japanese bourgeoisie. From an original story by Yohei Honma. In Japanese with English subtitles. **107m/C; VHS, DVD.** *JP* Yusaku Matsuda; Juzo Itami; Saori Yuki; Ichirota Miyagawa; Junichi Tsujita; ***D:*** Yoshimitsu Morita; ***W:*** Yoshimitsu Morita; ***C:*** Yonezo Maeda.

The Family Holiday 🦴🦴 **2007** Con man Donald "Doc" Holiday (Coulier) must become the perfect family man (complete with kids and dog) before he can inherit his uncle's estate. He finds a couple of cute, mouthy orphans who have run away so they won't be separated in foster care and hires a nanny who doesn't realize it's all a scam. Except, of course, since it's also a holiday-set film, everything will turn out for the best. **94m/C; DVD.** Dave Coulier; Christina Pickles; Craig Clyde; Alexa Fischer; Terisa Greenan; ***C:*** Paul Mayne; ***M:*** Justin Melland. **CABLE**

Family Honeymoon 🦴 ½ **1949** Widow Katie (Colbert) marries Grant (MacMurray) and they are forced to take her three bratty, disapproving kids on their Grand Canyon honeymoon. Unfortunately, Grant's ex-flame Minna (Johnson) is staying at the same hotel, Katie gets jealous, the kids misbehave, Grant gets fed up, and the couple return home separately. Can this marriage be saved? **90m/B; DVD.** Claudette Colbert; Fred MacMurray; Rita Johnson; Gigi Perreau; Jimmy Hunt; Peter Miles; Lillian Bronson; Hattie McDaniel; Paul Harvey; ***D:*** Claude Binyon; ***W:*** Dane Lussier; ***C:*** William H. Daniels; ***M:*** Frank Skinner.

Family in Hiding 🦴 ½ **2006** Makes the folks in the Witness Protection Program look mighty incompetent. After single mom Carol Peterson (Strong) witnesses the murder of a D.A., she learns that her testimony will implicate a crime boss so she and her two children are shuttled into WITSEC. It seems everyone is ill-prepared so Carol has no job and they're living in a dump. And there's a bunch of crooked feds on the bad guy's payroll and they can easily track Carol down. **90m/C; DVD.** Brenda Strong; Elyse Levesque; Brett Dier; Hrothgar Mathews; Jerry Wasserman; Gary Hetherington; Raoul Ganeev; ***D:*** Timothy Bond. **CABLE**

The Family Jewels 🦴🦴 **1965** A spoiled child-heiress has to choose among her six uncles to decide which should be her new father. If you like Jerry Lewis, you can't miss this! In addition to playing all six uncles, Lewis plays the chauffeur, as well as serving as producer, director, and coauthor of the script. **100m/C; DVD.** Jerry Lewis; Donna Butterworth; Sebastian Cabot; Robert Strauss; ***D:*** Jerry Lewis; ***W:*** Jerry Lewis; Bill Richmond; ***C:*** W. Wallace Kelley; ***M:*** Pete King.

Family Man 🦴🦴 **2000 (PG-13)** With the help of a guardian angel/taxi driver (Cheadle), money-loving investment banker Jack Campbell (Cage) gets to see how life could have been if he'd married college sweetie Leoni, had kids, and was living in New Jersey and working as a tire salesman. Lost in this new world of responsibility and funnel cakes, Jack can't help but pine for his old life. But, in the end, will he choose ambition and "freedom" over love? Darker and not as tidy as "It's a Wonderful Life," its obvious inspiration, "Family Man" seeks to teach Jack a lesson we see coming miles off. **125m/C; VHS, DVD, Blu-Ray.** Nicolas Cage; Tea Leoni; Don Cheadle; Amber Valletta; Jeremy Piven; Saul Rubinek; Josef Sommer; Harve Presnell; Mary Beth Hurt; Kate Walsh; ***D:*** Brett Ratner; ***W:*** David Diamond; David Weissman; ***C:*** Dante Spinotti; ***M:*** Danny Elfman.

Family of Cops 🦴🦴 ½ **1995 (PG-13)** Trouble comes calling on Inspector Paul Fein's (Bronson) close-knit Milwaukee family when his party girl daughter Jackie (Featherstone) comes home to visit. She's soon accused of murdering a wealthy businessman she picked up in a drunken stupor and her cop family gets deeply involved in the investigation. Made for TV. **90m/C; VHS, DVD.** Charles Bronson; Daniel Baldwin; Angela Featherstone; Sebastian Spence; Lesley-Anne Down; Barbara Williams; Simon MacCorkindale; ***D:*** Ted Kotcheff; ***W:*** Joel Blasberg. **TV**

Family of Cops 2: Breach of Faith 🦴🦴 ½ *Breach of Faith: A Family of Cops 2* **1997 (PG-13)** The investigation of a priest's murder makes Inspector Paul Fein (Bronson) and his cop family the target of Russian mobsters. TV movie once again filmed in Toronto, which substitutes for Milwaukee. **90m/C; VHS, DVD.** Charles Bronson; Joe Penny; Diane Ladd; Sebastian Spence; Angela Featherstone; Barbara Williams; Andrew Jackson; Matt Birman; Kim Weeks; David Hemblen; Mimi Kuzyk; Real Andrews; ***D:*** David Greene; ***W:*** Joel Blasberg; ***C:*** Ronald Orieux; ***M:*** Peter Manning Robinson. **TV**

Family of Cops 3 🦴🦴 ½ **1998 (PG-13)** Police inspector Paul Fein (Bronson) decides to run for chief while detective son Ben (Penny) investigates the murder of a banker. There's also a corruption problem and time for a little romance. **90m/C; VHS, DVD.** Charles Bronson; Joe Penny; Kim Weeks; Sebastian Spence; Barbara Williams; Torri Higginson; Nicole de Boer; ***D:*** Sheldon Larry; ***W:*** Noah Jubelirer; ***C:*** Bert Dunk. **TV**

A Family of Spies 🦴🦴 ½ **1990** Based on the true story of Navy petty officer John A. Walker Jr. (Boothe) who began selling secrets to the Soviets in 1967 to cover mounting debts and a lavish lifestyle. Eventually Walker drags his Naval son Michael (Lowery) into his schemes until the FBI becomes involved. **174m/C; DVD.** Powers Boothe; Lesley Ann Warren; Andrew Lowery; Lili Taylor; Graham Beckel; John M. Jackson; Gordon Clapp; Jeroen Krabbe; ***D:*** Stephen Gyllenhaal; ***W:*** Richard DeLong Adams; ***C:*** Doug Milsome; ***M:*** Paul Chihara. **TV**

Family of Strangers 🦴 ½ **1993** Melodramatic made-for-TV fare. Before having brain surgery, Julie Lawson (Gilbert) needs her medical history and learns for the first time that she was adopted as a baby. This sends her on a quest to find her biological parents, but when Julie finds her birth mother Beth (Duke), she learns the disquieting reasons she was given up. **94m/C; DVD.** Melissa Gilbert; Patty Duke; William Shatner; Gordon Clapp; Martha Gibson; Chuck Shamata; Eric McCormick; ***D:*** Sheldon Larry; ***W:*** Anna Sandor; William Gough; ***C:*** Ronald Orieux; ***M:*** Peter Manning Robinson. **TV**

Family Pictures 🦴🦴🦴 **1993** A photographer remembers growing up in the '50s with her autistic brother, the mother who lavished her attention on him almost to the exclusion of her five other children, and the father who blamed his wife for their son's deficiencies. Interesting portrait of an American family, which eventually cracks under pressure and splits up. Adapted from the novel by Sue Miller (no relation to screenwriter Jennifer). **240m/C; VHS, DVD.** Anjelica Huston; Sam Neill; Kyra Sedgwick; Dermot Mulroney; Gemma Barry; Tara Strong; Torri Higginson; Jamie Harrold; ***D:*** Philip Saville; ***W:*** Jennifer Miller.

The Family Plan 🦴🦴 ½ **2005 (PG)** Charlie Mackenzie (Spelling) wants to keep her executive job, but new boss Ed Walcott (Germann) insists on family values and mistakenly believes Charlie is married. When she is forced to invite Ed and his wife (Vernon) to dinner, Charlie borrows a house and child (Breslin) from a friend and hires actor Buck (Bridges) to play her husband. Their ruse works for the evening, but Charlie is horrified to learn that the Walcotts are planning to rent the house next door. Should she keep lying or will the truth set Charlie free (or just make her unemployed)? **85m/C; DVD.** Tori Spelling; Greg Germann; Jordan Bridges; Kate Vernon; Abigail Breslin; Jon Polito; Kali Rocha; Christopher Cass; ***D:*** David S. Cass, Sr.; ***W:*** Richard Gitelson; ***C:*** James W. Wrenn; ***M:*** David Kitay. **CABLE**

Family Plot 🦴🦴 ½ **1976 (PG)** Alfred Hitchcock's last film focuses on the search for a missing heir which is undertaken by a phony psychic and her private-eye boyfriend, with all becoming involved in a diamond theft. Campy, lightweight mystery that stales with time and doesn't fit well into Hitchcock's genre. **120m/C; VHS, DVD, Blu-Ray.** Karen Black; Bruce Dern; Barbara Harris; William Devane; Ed Lauter; Katherine Helmond; Cathleen Nesbitt; Warren Kemmerling; Edith Atwater; William Prince; Nicholas Colasanto; Alfred Hitchcock; ***D:*** Alfred Hitchcock; ***W:*** Ernest Lehman; ***C:*** Leonard J. South; ***M:*** John Williams.

Family Reunion 🦴 ½ **1979** The Andrews family is on vacation and visiting the ghost town of Sutterville. Grandpa Henry didn't want to stop and for good reason—it seems the town was once in the grip of a satanic cult. Forty years before, when Tom Andrews was a child, he was the designated satanic sacrifice and was rescued by Henry, who adopted him. Now Tom's real father has willed the family back to Sutterville to complete the ritual. **88m/C; VHS, DVD.** Mel Novak; John Andes; A.J. Woods; Kaylin Cool; Pam Phillips; Mark McTague; ***D:*** Michael Hawes; ***W:*** Michael Hawes; ***C:*** Jack Anderson.

Family Reunion 🦴🦴 **1981** Retired New England schoolteacher Elizabeth Winfield (Davis) heads out on a cross-country trip in order to reconcile with some long-estranged family members. But back home, her unscrupulous nephew wants to sell off some family property to a real estate developer, thus ruining the Winfield's annual reunion. The story, which plays like a TV pilot movie, culminates at the Founders' Day celebration. **180m/C; DVD.** Bette Davis; J. Ashley Hyman; David Huddleston; Roberts Blossom; Roy Dotrice; David Rounds; Paul Hecht; Paul Rudd; John Shea; Kathryn Walker; ***D:*** Fielder Cook; ***W:*** Allan Sloane; ***C:*** Jack Priestley. **TV**

The Family Secret 🦴🦴 **1924** Working-class Garry (Earle) secretly marries wealthy sweetheart Margaret (Hulette) although she continues to live in her father's (Currier) house. When she gives birth to a daughter, her disapproving dad kicks her out and raises the child himself. One night, Garry sneaks in to visit his daughter and is arrested as a burglar and sent to prison. Now it's up to young Peggy (Montgomery) to set things right. **70m/B; Silent; DVD.** Baby Peggy (Montgomery); Edward Earle; Gladys Hulette; Frank Currier; Lucy Beaumont; Martin Turner; Martha Mattox; Cesare Gravina; Elizabeth Mackey; ***D:*** William A. Seiter; ***W:*** Lois Zellner; ***C:*** John Stumar.

The Family Secret 🦴 ½ **1951** Law student David Clark (Derek) accidentally kills his drunken friend in self-defense, but instead of telling the cops, he confesses to his lawyer dad, Howard (Cobb). After some family turmoil, Howard agrres to keep quiet and, instead, defends the innocent man (Bissell) who's been accused of the crime, but the situation goes from bad to worse. As does the movie, with Derek overly-emoting while Cobb stands strong. **85m/B; DVD.** Lee J. Cobb; John Derek; Erin O'Brien-Moore; Whit Bissell; Jody Lawrance; ***D:*** Henry Levin; ***W:*** Francis Cockrell; Andrew Solt; ***C:*** Burnett Guffey; ***M:*** George Duning.

The Family Stone **2005 (PG-13)** Parker plays against her "Sex in the City" role. She's still a New Yorker here, but an uptight one—who's dragged to boyfriend Everett's (Mulroney) family home for the holidays. Mix of characters (gay, deaf, African American, tomboy girl) hits all those let's-not-overlook-anyone buttons. Unfortunately, the likeable ones are rare. No one likes Meredith and they're not shy about it. Another attempt at screwball holiday comedy with a decent cast that delivers on low expectations. **102m/C; DVD.** Claire Danes; Diane Keaton; Rachel McAdams; Dermot Mulroney; Craig T. Nelson; Sarah Jessica Parker; Luke Wilson; Ty(rone) Giordano; Brian White; Elizabeth Reaser; Paul Schneider; ***D:*** Thomas Bezucha; ***W:*** Thomas Bezucha; ***C:*** Jonathan Brown; ***M:*** Michael Giacchino.

A Family Thanksgiving **2010** Hallmark Channel holiday flick. Hard-driving single corporate lawyer Claudia (Zuniga) is determined to make partner and doesn't have time for family obligations, including Thanksgiving at her married sister Jen's (Holden). That is until Claudia encounters the mysterious Gina (Dunaway), who drops Claudia into an alternate reality where she's married with kids. The idea is to show Claudia that she can balance work with a personal life but it comes off as cliched (and a little sexist). **90m/C; DVD.** Daphne Zuniga; Faye Dunaway; Dan Payne; Gina Holden; Kennedi Clements; Nicolai Guistra; ***D:*** Neill Fearnley; ***W:*** Emily Baer; ***C:*** Michael Balfry; ***M:*** Peter Allen. **CABLE**

The Family That Preys *Tyler Perry's The Family That Preys* **2008 (PG-13)** Lifelong pals and business partners Alice (Woodward) and Charlotte (Bates) clash when Alice's married son William (Hauser) sparks up an affair with Charlotte's daughter Andrea (Lathan), emptying the family closets of all its skeletons. Meanwhile, Andrea's dense husband Chris (Dunbar) continues to ask William for start-up money for a construction business, while Andrea's sister Pam (Henson) and her husband Ben (Perry) can only stand back and watch. Despite criticism, Perry's cheap, melodramatic soap opera formula shows no sign of improving or appealing to any sense of artistry. Notable for the first Perry movie to treat a white character as more than a "white character." **111m/C; DVD, Blu-Ray, On Demand.** Alfre Woodard; Kathy Bates; Sanaa Lathan; Cole Hauser; Rockmond Dunbar; KaDee Strickland; Taraji P. Henson; Robin Givens; Tyler Perry; Sebastian Siegel; ***C:*** Toyomichi Kurita; ***M:*** Aaron Zigman.

A Family Thing **1996 (PG-13)** Racial issues are addressed in this character-driven story of two brothers. Southerner Earl Pilcher (Duvall) learns his biological mother was black and that she died during his birth. In a letter written by the recently deceased woman who raised him, Earl discovers he also has a half brother, Ray (Jones), who is black and living in Chicago. He drives to Chicago, and seeks out Ray, who to Earl's surprise knows about him already, and is not exactly thrilled about the family ties, either. As the two brothers, expertly played by Duvall and Jones, slowly find common ground, Hall steals the show as the irascible Aunt T. **109m/C; VHS, DVD.** Robert Duvall; James Earl Jones; Irma P. Hall; Michael Beach; Grace Zabriskie; Regina Taylor; Mary Jackson; Paula Marshall; Jim Harrell; ***D:*** Richard Pearce; ***W:*** Billy Bob Thornton; Tom Epperson; ***C:*** Fred Murphy.

The Family Tree **2010** A misfire of a black comedy with an undeveloped plot and characters. The unhappily dysfunctional Burnett family gets a jolt when nasty, adulterous mom Bunnie suffers a blow to the head, gets temporary amnesia about her current character, and reverts to being a nice newlywed to her confused hubby Jack. This personality change also affects her two unhappy children and a few other subplots. **90m/C; DVD, Blu-Ray.** Hope Davis; Dermot Mulroney; Britt Robertson; Max Thieriot; Chi McBride; Evan Ross; Christina Hendricks; Keith Carradine; Jane Seymour; ***D:*** Vivi Friedman; ***W:*** Mark Lisson; ***C:*** Joplin Wu; ***M:*** Stacey Hersh. **VIDEO**

Family Viewing **1987** Surrealistic depiction of a family—obsessed with television and video'whose existence is a textbook model of home sweet dysfunctional home. An early, experimental film from Canada's Egoyan, it won considerable praise for its social commentary. **92m/C; VHS, DVD.** *CA* David Hemblen; Adian Tierney; Gabrielle Rose; Arsinee Khanjian; ***D:*** Atom Egoyan; ***W:*** Atom Egoyan; ***C:*** Robert MacDonald; Peter Mettler; ***M:*** Mychael Danna. Toronto-City '87: Canadian Feature Film.

Family Weekend **1/2 2013 (R)** Self-consciously quirky family/teen comedy. Sixteen-year-old Emily is so furious that her parents, type-A mom Samantha and benign dad Duncan, missed her major jump-rope competition that she pays back their apparent neglect by drugging them, tying them to chairs, and holding them hostage. Since her brother Jackson is filming the unlikely intervention and posting it online, the standoff becomes a media sensation. **106m/C; DVD.** Olesya Rulin; Kristin Chenoweth; Matthew Modine; Eddie Hassell; Joey King; Robbie Tucker; Shirley Jones; ***D:*** Benjamin Epps; ***W:*** Matt K. Turner; ***C:*** Christopher Norr; ***M:*** Mateo Messina.

The Fan **1/2 1949** Preminger's misfire is a bowdlerized version of Oscar Wilde's "Lady Windermere's Fan." Judgmental Lady Margaret Windermere (Crain) doesn't understand why her husband, Lord Arthur (Greene), is giving money to scandalous Mrs. Erlynne (Carroll). Rather than listen to an explanation, she runs off with scheming Lord Darlington (Sanders). The fan in question is a birthday present from Arthur to Margaret. **79m/B; DVD.** Jeanne Crain; Richard Greene; Madeleine Carroll; George Sanders; Martita Hunt; ***D:*** Otto Preminger; ***W:*** Dorothy Parker; Walter Reisch; ***C:*** Joseph LaShelle; ***M:*** Daniele Amfitheatrof.

The Fan **1981 (R)** A Broadway star is threatened and her immediate circle cut down when a lovestruck fan feels he has been rejected by his idol. The stellar cast makes this bloody and familiar tale seem better than it is. **95m/C; VHS, DVD, Blu-Ray.** Lauren Bacall; Maureen Stapleton; James Garner; Hector Elizondo; Michael Biehn; Griffin Dunne; ***D:*** Edward Bianchi; ***W:*** Priscilla Chapman; ***C:*** Dick Bush; ***M:*** Pino Donaggio.

The Fan **1/2 1996 (R)** Obsessed baseball fan Gil Renard (De Niro, who owns the copyright on playing deranged) stalks favorite player Bobby Rayburn (Snipes) who just signed a big contract with the hometown team. When Rayburn goes into a slump, Renard figures he can help his idol—by any means necessary. As an added bonus, Gil's a knife salesman. De Niro does the psycho thing with his usual aplomb, while Snipes successfully returns to the diamond. Scott keeps the familiar storyline from becoming tedious. Based on the book by Peter Abrahams. **117m/C; VHS, DVD, Blu-Ray.** Robert De Niro; Wesley Snipes; Ellen Barkin; John Leguizamo; Benicio Del Toro; Patti D'Arbanville; Jack Black; Chris Mulkey; Brandon Hammond; Charles Hallahan; Dan E. Butler; Michael Jace; Frank Medrano; M.C. Gainey; Eric Bruskotter; Kim Robillard; ***D:*** Tony Scott; ***W:*** Phoef Sutton; ***C:*** Dariusz Wolski; ***M:*** Hans Zimmer.

Fanatic **WOOF!** *The Last Horror Film* **1982 (R)** Beautiful queen of horror films is followed to the Cannes Film Festival by her number one fan who, unbeknownst to her, is slowly murdering members of her entourage in a deluded and vain attempt to capture her attentions. Title refers to lack of plans for a sequel. **87m/C; VHS, DVD, Blu-Ray.** Caroline Munro; Joe Spinell; Judd Hamilton; Devin Goldenberg; David Winters; ***D:*** David Winters; ***W:*** Judd Hamilton; David Winters; Tom Klassen; ***C:*** Thomas Denove; ***M:*** Jesse Frederick.

The Fanatic **1/2 2019 (R)** Autistic horror movie fan Moose (Travolta) often quotes his favorite films and has spent years building his personal memorabilia collection. When Moose tries to get the autograph of one of his favorite actors, Dunbar (Sawa), at a local poster shop signing, Hunter is mean to him, then pushes Moose when he shows up at his house with a fan letter. Moose been targeted by bullies before, and the situation escalates into violence. Shallow and dull, it lacks not only logic but is also tone deaf in its depiction of people, especially those who are on the spectrum. **88m/C; DVD.** John Travolta; Devon Sawa; Ana Golja; Jacob Grodnik; James Paxton; ***D:*** Fred Durst; ***W:*** Fred Durst; Dave Bekerman; ***C:*** Conrad W. Hall; ***M:*** John Swihart; Gary Hickeson; Blvck Ceiling. Golden Raspberries '19: Worst Actor (Travolta).

Fanboys **1/2 2009 (PG-13)** Four Star Wars fanatics who've strayed since high school reunite over the news that their buddy Linus has cancer. Set in 1999, a few months before the release of "Star Wars: Episode 1 - The Phantom Menace," the posse decides that Linus needs to see this movie before things take a turn for the worse. They set out on a road trip to Skywalker Ranch with the intention of stealing an unreleased copy from George Lucas himself. Along the way they pick up hot comic book fanchick Zoe (Bell), run into William Shatner, and fall in love again with Carrie Fisher. Unfortunately, a great cast can't save an uninspired script that takes its dopey concept too seriously. Weinstein's insistence on removing the cancer subplot stalled post-production for almost two years. **90m/C; Blu-Ray, On Demand.** Sam Huntington; Christopher Marquette; Dan Fogler; Jay Baruchel; Kristen Bell; Craig Robinson; ***D:*** Kyle Newman; ***W:*** Adam F. Goldberg; Ernest Cline; ***C:*** Lukas Ettlin; ***M:*** Mark Mothersbaugh.

Fancy Pants **1/2 1950** Remake of "Ruggles of Red Gap" features Hope, a British actor posing as a butler. Also featuring Ball, an amusing contrast. Fine performances all around. **92m/C; VHS, DVD.** Bob Hope; Lucille Ball; Bruce Cabot; Jack Kirkwood; Lea Penman; Eric Blore; John Alexander; Norma Varden; ***D:*** George Marshall; ***C:*** Charles B(ryant) Lang, Jr.

Fandango **1/2 1985 (PG)** Five college friends take a wild weekend drive across the Texas Badlands for one last fling before graduation and the prospect of military service. Expanded by Reynolds with assistance from Steven Spielberg, from his student film. Provides a look at college and life during the Vietnam crisis. **91m/C; VHS, DVD.** Judd Nelson; Kevin Costner; Sam Robards; Chuck Bush; Brian Cesak; Elizabeth Daily; Suzy Amis; Glenne Headly; Pepe Serna; Marvin J. McIntyre; ***D:*** Kevin Reynolds; ***W:*** Kevin Reynolds; ***M:*** Alan Silvestri.

Fanfan la Tulipe *Fanfan the Tulip; Fearless Little Soldier* **1951** Fanfan (Philipe) escapes an unwanted marriage by joining the army of Louis XV (Herrand), after being promised an illustrious career and a royal marriage. And after many heroics, it all comes true. Amusing satire of swashbucklers and historical romance movies. French with subtitles. **98m/B; VHS, DVD.** *FR* Gerard Philipe; Gina Lollobrigida; Marcel Herrand; Sylvia Pelayo; Genevieve Page; Noel Roquevert; ***D:*** Christian-Jaque; ***W:*** Rene Wheeler; Jean Fallet; Christian-Jaque; ***C:*** Christian Matras; ***M:*** Georges Van Parys; Maurice Thiriet. Cannes '52: Director (Christian-Jaque).

Fangs of the Living Dead **1/2** *Malenka, the Vampire; La Nipote del Vampiro; The Niece of the Vampire; The Vampire's Niece* **1968** When a young woman inherits a castle, her uncle, who happens to be a vampire, tries to persuade her to remain among the undead. **80m/C; VHS, DVD, Blu-Ray.** *SP IT* Anita Ekberg; Rossana Yanni; Diana Lorys; Fernando Bilbao; Paul Muller; Julian Ugarte; Andriana Ambesi; ***D:*** Armando de Ossorio; ***W:*** Armando de Ossorio.

Fangs of the Wild *Follow the Hunter* **1954** When a young boy witnesses a murder at his father's hunting lodge, no one but the killer believes him. When the killer decides to get rid of the boy, Buck the Wonder Dog gets involved. **72m/B; VHS, DVD.** Charles Chaplin, Jr.; Onslow Stevens; Margia Dean; Freddy Ridgeway; Phil Tead; Robert Stevenson; ***D:*** William Claxton.

Fanny **1932** Second part of Marcel Pagnol's trilogy depicting the lives of the people of Provence, France. The poignant tale of Fanny, a young woman who marries an older man when Marius, her young lover, leaves her pregnant when he goes to sea. Remade several times but the original holds its own very well. "Marius" was first in the trilogy; "Cesar" was third. **128m/B; VHS, DVD, Blu-Ray.** *FR* Raimu; Charpin; Orane Demazis; Pierre Fresnay; Alida Rouffe; ***D:*** Marc Allegret; ***W:*** Marcel Pagnol; ***M:*** Vincent Scotto.

Fanny **1961** Young girl falls in love with an adventurous sailor, and finds herself pregnant after he returns to the sea. With the help of the sailor's parents, she finds, marries, and eventually grows to love a much older man, who in turn cares for her and adores her son as if he were his own. When the sailor returns, all involved must confront their pasts and define their futures. Beautifully made, with fine performances and a plot which defies age or nationality. Part of the "A Night at the Movies" series, this tape simulates a 1961 movie evening, with a Tweety Pie cartoon, a newsreel and coming attractions for "Splendor in the Grass" and "The Roman Spring of Mrs. Stone." **148m/C; VHS, DVD, Blu-Ray.** *FR* Leslie Caron; Maurice Chevalier; Charles Boyer; Horst Buchholz; Lionel Jeffries; ***D:*** Joshua Logan; ***W:*** Julius J. Epstein; ***C:*** Jack Cardiff.

Fanny and Alexander *Fanny Och Alexander* **1983 (R)** The culmination of Bergman's career, this autobiographical film is set in a rural Swedish town in 1907. It tells the story of one year in the lives of the Ekdahl family, as seen by the young children, Fanny and Alexander. Magic and religion, love and death, reconciliation and estrangement are skillfully captured in this carefully detailed, lovingly photographed film. In Swedish with English subtitles or dubbed. **197m/C; VHS, DVD, Blu-Ray.** *SW* Pernilla Allwin; Bertil Guve; Gunn Wallgren; Allan Edwall; Ewa Froling; Erland Josephson; Harriet Andersson; Jarl Kulle; Jan Malmsjo; ***D:*** Ingmar Bergman; ***W:*** Ingmar Bergman; ***C:*** Sven Nykvist; ***M:*** Daniel Bell. Oscars '83: Art Dir./Set Dec., Cinematog., Costume Des., Foreign Film; Cesar '84: Foreign Film; Golden Globes '84: Foreign Film; L.A. Film Critics '83: Cinematog., Foreign Film; N.Y. Film Critics '83: Director (Bergman), Foreign Film.

Fanny Hill **1983 (R)** A softcore adaptation of the racy Victorian classic. **80m/C; VHS, DVD.** *GB* Lisa Raines; Shelley Winters; Wilfrid Hyde-White; Oliver Reed; Alfred Marks; ***D:*** Gerry O'Hara; ***W:*** Stephen Chesley; ***C:*** Tony Spratling; ***M:*** Paul Hoffert.

Fanny Hill **1/2 2007** John Cleland's bawdy 18th-century novel is turned into an entertainingly smutty romp. Orphaned country girl Fanny Hill (Night) heads to London to make her fortune and winds up in the brothel of Mrs. Brown (Steadman). She falls in love and runs away with client Charles Standing (Robertson), but they are parted by his family and Fanny must use her considerable skills to make her own way while penning her scandalous memoirs. **117m/C; DVD.** *GB* Alex Robertson; Alison Steadman; Hugo Speer; Philip Jackson; Samantha Bond; Rebecca Night; Emma Stansfield; ***D:*** James Hawes; ***W:*** Andrew Davies; ***C:*** James Aspinall; ***M:*** Rohan Stevenson. **TV**

Fantasia **1940** Disney's most personal animation feature first bombed at the boxoffice and irked purists who couldn't take the plotless, experimental mix of classical music and cartoons. It became a cult movie, embraced by more liberal generations of moviegoers. Reissue of the original version, painstakingly restored, ceased because of a planned remake. **116m/C; DVD, Blu-Ray.** ***V:*** Walt Disney; ***Nar:*** Deems Taylor; ***D:*** Ben Sharpsteen; James Nelson Algar; Samuel Armstrong; Ford Beebe; Jim Handley; T. Hee; Wilfred Jackson; Hamilton Luske; Bill Roberts; Paul Satterfield; ***W:*** Lee Blair; Phil Dike; Otto Englander; Carl Fallberg; Campbell Grant; Albert Heath; Graham Heid; Arthur Heinemann; Bianca Majolie; William Martin; John McLeish; Sylvia Moberly-Holland; Perce Pearce; Bill Peet; Edward Penner; Joseph Sabo; Webb Smith; Leo Thiele; Norman Wright; ***M:*** Leopold Stokowski. AFI '98: Top 100; Natl. Film Reg. '90.

Fantasia 2000 **1/2 2000 (G)** Lightweight continuation of Disney's 1940 film hangs on to Mickey Mouse's popular "The Sorcerer's Apprentice" and adds seven new animated sequences of varying charm with celebrity introductions. Probably the most fun sequence is that of the yo-yo-ing flamingo set to Saint-Saens' "Carnvial of the Animals." Music is conducted by James Levine and performed by the Chicago Symphony Orchestra. Originally released in the IMAX format. **75m/C; DVD, Blu-Ray.** ***D:*** Hendel Butoy; Eric Goldberg; James Nelson Algar; Gaetan Brizzi; Paul Brizzi; Pixote Hunt; Francis Glebas.

Fantasies WOOF! *And Once Upon a Love* **1973 (R)** Teenage lovers Derek and Hooten return to their Greek island home and decide to improve their village by turning it into a tourist haven. First collaboration of the Dereks is a loser, lacking plot, direction, and decent acting. Bo shows no talent but the obvious one and is actually credited as Kathleen Collins. **81m/C; VHS, DVD.** Bo Derek; Peter Hooten; Anna Alexiades; ***D:*** John Derek.

Fantastic Beasts and Where to Find Them 🦴🦴 1/2 **2016 (PG-13)** This prequel franchise to the Harry Potter juggernaut is a surprisingly enjoyable fantasy family flick. Redmayne plays Newt Scamander, a wizard from England visiting New York in the '20s. The United States is cracking down on wizardry and Newt finds himself in the middle of an international controversy when his briefcase of magical creatures is stolen. (His adventures will be read by Harry Potter at Hogwarts many years later.) Potter director David Yates visually ties the film into the series while also giving it a personality of its own. A great cast helps. It doesn't quite have the Potter magic yet but it could get there. **133m/C; DVD, Blu-Ray.** Eddie Redmayne; Katherine Waterston; Alison Sudol; Dan Fogler; Colin Farrell; ***D:*** David Yates; ***W:*** J. K. Rowling; ***C:*** Philippe Rousselot; ***M:*** James Newton Howard. Oscars '16: Costume Des.; British Acad. '16: Production Design.

Fantastic Beasts: The Crimes of Grindelwald 🦴 1/2 **2018 (PG-13)** The second installment of the five-part*Fantastic Beasts* series feels more like a place holder than a fully fledged film. Dark wizard Gellert Grindelwald (Depp) escapes custody to amass pure-blood followers to rule over muggles, so Albus Dumbledore (Law) enlists his former student Newt Scamander (Redmayne) to stop him. Lacking much of the, ahem, magic of J.K. Rowling's wizarding world, this one is heavy on exposition and light on fantastic beasts, working too hard to tie-in with the Harry Potter realm. **134m/C; DVD, Blu-Ray, Streaming.** *UK US* Johnny Depp; Ezra Miller; Zoë Kravitz; Katherine Waterston; Eddie Redmayne; Jude Law; ***D:*** David Yates; ***W:*** J. K. Rowling; ***C:*** Philippe Rousselot; ***M:*** James Newton Howard.

A Fantastic Fear of Everything 🦴🦴 **2014 (R)** A fantastic Pegg performance is wasted in this inert, dull comedy that has a great premise and game leading man but goes nowhere except from boring to ludicrous. Jack is a children's author who has allowed research on a book about Victorian serial killers to make him a paranoid mess. He can't even go to his laundry room because of his fear of everything. When a potential big break comes his way, he's forced to face the things that go bump in the night and the film about him goes off the rails, trying to switch gears and getting nowhere. **100m/C; On Demand.** *UK* Simon Pegg; Clare Higgins; Paul Freeman; Alan Drake; Amara Karan; ***D:*** Crispian Mills; ***W:*** Crispian Mills; ***C:*** Simon Chaudoir; ***M:*** Michael Price.

Fantastic Four 🦴 **2005 (PG-13)** Or, more like the "So-So Four." The Stan Lee/Jack Kirby Marvel Comic foursome, who made their print debut in 1961, finally get on the big screen, though beyond introducing them and showing off their newly-acquired superpowers from exposure to outer-space radiation, they don't have much to do. Lee cameos as mailman Willy Lumpkin. **105m/C; DVD, Blu-Ray, UMD.** *US GE* Ioan Gruffudd; Jessica Alba; Michael Chiklis; Chris Evans; Julian McMahon; Kerry Washington; Stan Lee; Laurie Holden; ***D:*** Tim Story; ***W:*** Mark Frost; Michael France; Simon Kinberg; ***C:*** Oliver Wood; ***M:*** John Ottman.

Fantastic Four 🦴 **2015 (PG-13)** Consider this strike three for Invisible Girl. Made almost entirely so Fox could hold on to the rights of the characters and keep them from the Marvel Cinematic Universe, this dull action-adventure won't work for watchers of any age. For some inexplicable reason, the producers went back to the origin story concept yet again for Reed Richards (Teller), Sue Storm (Mara), Johnny Storm (Jordan) and The Thing (Bell). So, an hour of the film is set-up for a 20-minute action sequence. It's all CGI nonsense with no soul or heart to speak of. **100m/C; DVD, Blu-Ray.** Miles Teller; Michael B. Jordan; Kate Mara; Jamie Bell; Toby Kebbell; ***D:*** Josh Trank; ***W:*** Josh Trank; Jeremy Slater; Simon Kinberg; ***C:*** Matthew Jensen; ***M:*** Marco Beltrami. Golden Raspberries '15: Worst Director (Trank), Worst Picture, Worst Remake/Sequel.

Fantastic Four: Rise of the Silver Surfer 🦴 1/2 **2007 (PG)** They weren't fantastic the first time and this sequel is almost as dull. Mr. Fantastic (Gruffudd) keeps getting distracted while trying to marry invisible sweetie Sue (Alba). But he's got good reason, with intergalactic traveler Silver Surfer deciding to visit our little planet. Seems dead planets follow in the visitor's wake and the mild foursome doesn't want that happening to Earth. At least the 3-D animation for the Surfer deserves a look-see. **92m/C; DVD, Blu-Ray.** Ioan Gruffudd; Jessica Alba; Chris Evans; Michael Chiklis; Julian McMahon; Doug Jones; Andre Braugher; Kerry Washington; Gonzalo Menendez; ***V:*** Laurence Fishburne; ***D:*** Tim Story; ***W:*** Don Payne; Mark Frost; ***C:*** Larry Blanford; ***M:*** John Ottman.

Fantastic Mr. Fox 🦴🦴🦴 **2009 (PG)** Animated adaptation of Roald Dahl's classic children's book by director Anderson, who puts his quirky dark humor to good use in telling the sardonic story of a clever fox forced to outwit the farmers after him and his family for stealing their chickens and cider. Great visual appeal with the use of stop-motion photography and miniature puppets instead of drawings. All-star cast delivers the goods with Anderson regulars, Murray and Schwartzman, plus Clooney, Streep, Blanchett, Gambon, Dafoe, and Wilson. And even though it has moments of trying a little too hard, all in all, as one of the characters might say, it's a "cussing" good time. **87m/C; Blu-Ray.** ***V:*** George Clooney; Meryl Streep; Bill Murray; Willem Dafoe; Jason Schwartzman; Michael Gambon; Helen McCrory; Brian Cox; Adrien Brody; Owen Wilson; Wes Anderson; Karen Duffy; ***D:*** Wes Anderson; ***W:*** Wes Anderson; Noah Baumbach; ***C:*** Tristan Oliver; ***M:*** Alexandre Desplat.

The Fantastic Night 🦴🦴🦴 *La Nuit Fantastique* **1942** Considering that this film was made in France during the Nazi occupation, it is a remarkably clear work. It's a fantasy about Denis (Gravey), who is visited by a beautiful woman (Presle) as he sleeps and then follows her through a series of adventures. According to the box copy, the star was working with the Resistance while he was making the film. French with subtitles. **90m/B; VHS, DVD.** *FR* Fernand Gravey; Micheline Presle; Marcel Levesque; Christiane Nere; ***D:*** Marcel L'Herbier; ***W:*** Louis Chavance; Marcel L'Herbier; ***C:*** Pierre Montazel; ***M:*** Maurice Thiriet.

Fantastic Planet 🦴🦴🦴 *La Planete Sauvage; Planet of Incredible Creatures; The Savage Planet* **1973 (PG)** A critically acclaimed French, animated, sci-fi epic based on the drawings of Roland Topor. A race of small humanoids are enslaved and exploited by a race of giants on a savage planet, until one of the small creatures manages to unite his people and fight for equality. **72m/C; VHS, DVD, Blu-Ray.** *FR* ***V:*** Barry Bostwick; ***D:*** Rene Laloux; Roland Topor; ***W:*** Rene Laloux; Roland Topor; Steve Hayes; ***C:*** Boris Baromykin; Lubomir Rejthar; ***M:*** Alain Goraguer.

Fantastic Voyage 🦴🦴🦴 *Microscopia; Strange Journey* **1966** An important scientist, rescued from behind the Iron Curtain, is so severely wounded by enemy agents that traditional surgery is impossible. After being shrunk to microscopic size, a medical team journeys inside his body where they find themselves threatened by the patient's natural defenses. Great action, award-winning special effects. **100m/C; VHS, DVD, Blu-Ray.** Stephen Boyd; Edmond O'Brien; Raquel Welch; Arthur Kennedy; Donald Pleasence; Arthur O'Connell; William Redfield; James Brolin; Barry Coe; Brendan Fitzgerald; Shelby Grant; Ken Scott; ***D:*** Richard Fleischer; ***W:*** Harry Kleiner; ***C:*** Ernest Laszlo; ***M:*** Leonard Rosenman. Oscars '66: Art Dir./Set Dec., Color, Visual FX.

A Fantastic Woman 🦴🦴 1/2 *Una Mujer Fantastica* **2018 (R)** An insightful drama centered on a transgender woman. Orlando (Reyes), a divorced, 57-year-old man, is involved with the far younger Marina (Vega), a transgender bar singer. After Orlando suffers an aneurysm, he is gravely injured falling down the stairs and dies on the operating table. After his death, the grieving Marina is treated shamefully by the hospital staff, police, and Orlando's family despite her genuine relationship with him. Barred from the funeral, she must find her own way to process her loss. Full of empathy for the transgender experience, the film features a stunning soundtrack and a remarkable performance by Vega. Spanish with subtitles. **100m/C; DVD, Blu-Ray.** Daniela Vega; Francisco Reyes; Luis Gnecco; Aline Kuppenheim; Nicolas Saavedra; ***D:*** Sebastián Lelio; ***W:*** Sebastián Lelio; Gonzalo Maza; ***C:*** Benjamin Echazarreta; ***M:*** Matthew Herbert. Oscars '17: Foreign Film; Ind. Spirit '18: Foreign Film.

The Fantasticks 🦴🦴 1/2 **1995 (PG)** The stage's longest-running musical gets the big-screen treatment with a story about two fathers (Grey and Hughes) who decide to matchmake for their children Matt (McIntyre) and Luisa (Kelly). They hire the members of a traveling carnival (called the Fantasticks) to kidnap Luisa, so that Matt can play the hero and rescue her. The plan seems to work but the course of true love never runs that smoothly. Adapted by Jones and Schmidt from their play. **86m/C; VHS, DVD, Blu-Ray.** Joel Grey; Barnard Hughes; Jean Louisa Kelly; Joe McIntyre; Jonathan Morris; ***D:*** Michael Ritchie; ***W:*** Tom Jones; Harvey Schmidt; ***C:*** Fred Murphy; ***M:*** Harvey Schmidt.

Fantasy Island 🦴 **1976** Three people fly ("De plane, boss!") to an island paradise and get to live out their fantasies for a price. Pilot for the TV series. **100m/C; VHS, DVD.** Ricardo Montalban; Bill Bixby; Sandra Dee; Peter Lawford; Carol Lynley; Hugh O'Brian; Eleanor Parker; Dick Sargent; Victoria Principal; ***D:*** Richard Lang. **TV**

Fantasy Island 🦴🦴 **2020 (PG-13)** When a plane full of contest winners arrives at a mysterious island resort, their host, Mr. Roarke (Pena) tells them they each can live out their greatest personal fantasy but must see it through to its conclusion. Brothers JD (Hansen) and Brax (Yang) want to live the high life, while former police officer Patrick (Stowell) wants to be a soldier. Melanie (Hale) wants revenge on a bully, while Gwen (Q) wants to accept the marriage proposal she turned down. Nothing goes as planned. An unentertaining horror take on the classic television series. **110m/C; DVD, Blu-Ray.** Michael Peña; Maggie Q; Lucy Kate Hale; Austin Stowell; Jimmy O. Yang; ***D:*** Jeff Wadlow; ***W:*** Jeff Wadlow; Jillian Jacobs; Christopher Roach; ***C:*** Toby Oliver; ***M:*** Bear McCreary.

Fantasy Mission Force 🦴 **1984** In this indescribably silly action comedy, Japanese troops capture an international group of generals (some in Civil War-era uniforms). An invasion of Canada is underway. Jackie is part of a group trying to rescue them. UN troops wear kilts; others wear armor. **90m/C; VHS, DVD, Blu-Ray.** *CH* Jackie Chan; Brigitte Lin; Adam Cheng; Jimmy Wang Yu; ***D:*** Yen Ping Chu.

Far and Away 🦴🦴 1/2 **1992 (PG-13)** Meandering old-fashioned epic about immigrants, romance, and settling the American West. In the 1890s, Joseph Donelly (Cruise) is forced to flee his Irish homeland after threatening the life of his landlord, and emigrates to America in the company of the landlord's daughter, feisty Shannon Christie (Kidman). Particularly brutal scenes of Cruise earning his living as a bare-knuckled boxer contrast with the expansiveness of the land rush ending. Slow, spotty, and a little too slick for its own good, though real-life couple Cruise and Kidman are an attractive pair. Filmed in 70-mm Panavision on location in Ireland and Montana. **140m/C; VHS, DVD, Blu-Ray.** Tom Cruise; Nicole Kidman; Thomas Gibson; Robert Prosky; Barbara Babcock; Colm Meaney; Eileen Pollock; Michelle Johnson; Cyril Cusack; Clint Howard; Rance Howard; ***D:*** Ron Howard; ***W:*** Bob Dolman; ***C:*** Mikael Salomon; ***M:*** John Williams.

Far Country 🦴🦴🦴 **1955** Cattlemen must battle the elements and frontier lawlessness in this classic. Stewart leads his herd to the Yukon in hopes of large profits, but ends up having to kidnap it back from the crooked sheriff and avenging the deaths of his friends. Entertaining and the Yukon setting takes it out of the usual Western arena. **97m/C; VHS, DVD, Blu-Ray.** James Stewart; Ruth Roman; Walter Brennan; Harry (Henry) Morgan; Corinne Calvet; Jay C. Flippen; John McIntire; ***D:*** Anthony Mann; ***C:*** William H. Daniels; ***M:*** Henry Mancini.

Far Cry WOOF! 2008 (R) A far cry from barely being considered a movie since director Boll doesn't seem to be making much of an effort in this videogame adaptation and the actors look bored or bewildered. Reporter Valerie (Vaugier) hires ex-special operative Jack Carver (Schweiger) to check out multiple mysterious deaths on a Pacific Northwest island. Seems crazy Dr. Krieger (Kier) has been experimenting with the creation of genetically-enhanced super soldiers and has them kill mercenaries to test their abilities. **95m/C; DVD.** Til Schweiger; Udo Kier; Emmanuelle Vaugier; Ralph (Ralf) Moeller; Chris Coppola; Don S. Davis; Michael Paré; Craig Fairbrass; Jay Brazeau; ***D:*** Uwe Boll; ***W:*** Michael Roesch; Peter Scheerer; Masaji Takei; ***C:*** Mathias Neumann; ***M:*** Jessica de Rooij. **VIDEO**

Far from Heaven 🦴🦴🦴 1/2 **2002 (PG-13)** Perfect '50s homemaker, mother, and wife Cathy (Moore) faces her husband Frank's (Quaid) emerging homosexual desires, which culminate in her witnessing him in an intimate kiss with another man at the office. When Cathy seeks comfort from her black gardener (Haysbert), scandal and hatred spread and wrenching truths are found. Melodramatic (in the Douglas Sirk tradition) tale of social/racial taboos and a woman's sacrifice is intriguing. Moore's performance is Oscar caliber (she got a nomination), Quaid's fearless, and Lachman's retro-chic visuals also exhibit stunning craftsmanship, while Bernstien's lush score sets the proper mood. **107m/C; VHS, DVD, Blu-Ray.** Julianne Moore; Dennis Quaid; Dennis Haysbert; Patricia Clarkson; James Rebhorn; Celia Weston; Viola Davis; ***D:*** Todd Haynes; ***W:*** Todd Haynes; ***C:*** Edward Lachman; ***M:*** Elmer Bernstein. Ind. Spirit '03: Actress (Moore), Cinematog., Director (Haynes), Film, Support. Actor (Quaid); L.A. Film Critics '02: Actress (Moore), Cinematog., Score; Natl. Bd. of Review '02: Actress (Moore); N.Y. Film Critics '02: Cinematog., Director (Haynes), Film, Support. Actor (Quaid), Support. Actress (Clarkson); Natl. Soc. Film Critics '02: Cinematog., Support. Actress (Clarkson).

Far from Home 🦴🦴 **1989 (R)** Drew Barrymore is the seductive teen being scoped by a psychotic killer while on vacation with her father. Lots of over-the-top performances by the familiar cast. **86m/C; VHS, DVD.** Matt Frewer; Drew Barrymore; Richard Masur; Karen Austin; Susan Tyrrell; Anthony Rapp; Jennifer Tilly; Andras Jones; Dick Miller; ***D:*** Meiert Avis; ***C:*** Paul Elliott; ***M:*** Jonathan Elias.

Far from Home: The Adventures of Yellow Dog 🦴🦴 **1994 (PG)** Stalwart lad Angus (Bradford) and his faithful pooch Yellow (Dakotah) battle the elements, wild animals and fatigue as they try to get back home after being shipwrecked on a remote island in British Columbia. Good thing Dad (Davidson) gave them all those cool survival tips before they left, or else they never would've known that you can eat bugs. (Okay, the dog probably knew that already.) Mom (Rogers) does her bit by making sure the search mission stays focused. You usually can't go wrong with a kid and his dog lost in the wilderness, but this one is really short—on time and drama. Nice scenery, though. **81m/C; VHS, DVD.** Jesse Bradford; Bruce Davison; Mimi Rogers; Tom Bower; ***D:*** Phillip Borsos; ***W:*** Phillip Borsos.

Far from the Madding Crowd 🦴🦴🦴 **1967 (PG)** A lavish, long adaptation of Thomas Hardy's 19th-century classic about the beautiful Bathsheba (Christie) and the three very different men who love her. Her first love is handsome and wayward soldier Sgt. Troy (Stamp), her second the local noble lord William Boldwood (Finch), and her third the ever-loving and long-patient farmer Gabriel Oaks (Bates). Christie is well cast as the much-desired beauty. Gorgeous cinematography by Nicolas Roeg. Remade for British TV in 1997. **165m/C; VHS, DVD, Blu-Ray.** *GB* Julie Christie; Terence Stamp; Peter Finch; Alan Bates; Prunella Ransome; ***D:*** John Schlesinger; ***W:*** Frederic Raphael; ***C:*** Nicolas Roeg; ***M:*** Richard Rodney Bennett. Natl. Bd. of Review '67: Actor (Finch).

Far from the Madding Crowd **1997** TV version of the Thomas Hardy novel (filmed for the big screen in 1967) that follows the adventures of young Bathsheba (Baeza), who's the object of desire for three very different men in 19th-century rural England. Independent-minded Bathsheba Everdene inherits a farm and insists on managing it herself. She's aided by steadfast head man Gabriel Oak (Parker), who loves her but doesn't feel he can offer her anything; wealthy older neighbor William Boldwood (Terry), whose love for Bathesheba becomes an obsession; and rakish Sgt. Frank Troy (Firth), who captivates Bathsheba but proves to be a scoundrel. **200m/C; VHS, DVD.** *GB* Paloma Baeza; Nigel Terry; Nathaniel Parker; Jonathan Firth; ***D:*** Nicholas Renton; ***W:*** Philomena McDonagh. **TV**

Far from the Madding Crowd **2015 (PG-13)** Thomas Hardy's timeless novel gets another adaptation that lacks the socio-cultural depth of the landmark book, despite (another) really solid performance from Mulligan. The Oscar nominee stars as Bathsheba Everdene, the rare headstrong woman in Victorian England, who is confronted with three very different suitors—a sheep farmer (Schoenaerts), a reckless soldier (Sturridge), and the safe choice of a prosperous older bachelor (Sheen). Performances and production values are strong but inevitably it often feels like an empty chamber piece—pretty people in pretty places with nothing to say. **119m/C; DVD, Blu-Ray.** Carey Mulligan; Matthias Schoenaerts; Tom Sturridge; Juno Temple; Bradley Hall; ***D:*** Thomas Vinterberg; ***W:*** David Nicholls; ***C:*** Charlotte Bruus Christensen; ***M:*** Craig Armstrong.

The Far Horizons **1955** Meriwether Lewis (MacMurray) and William Clark (Heston) lead an expedition to survey the territory after the Louisiana Purchase. Along the way they gain the assistance of Sacajawea, played by blue-eyed Donna Reed. Vintage Hollywood at its "best" takes a historical premise and turns it into comical love-triangle that comes full circle—in the White House, no less. Check your knowledge of history at the door, but enjoy the beautiful scenery and some unintentional giggles. **107m/C; DVD.** Fred MacMurray; Charlton Heston; Donna Reed; Barbara Hale; William Demarest; Herbert (Hayes) Heyes; Lester Matthews; Alan Reed; Larry Pennell; ***D:*** Rudolph Mate; ***W:*** Winston Miller; Edmund H. North; ***C:*** Daniel F. Fapp; ***M:*** Hans J. Salter.

Far North **1/2 1988 (PG-13)** Quirky comedy about a woman who returns to her rural family homestead after her father is seriously injured by a horse, and tries to deal with her eccentric family's travails. Fine cast never reaches its potential. Shepard's directing debut. **96m/C; VHS, DVD.** Jessica Lange; Charles Durning; Tess Harper; Donald Moffat; Ann Wedgeworth; Patricia Arquette; Nina Draxton; ***D:*** Sam Shepard; ***W:*** Sam Shepard; ***C:*** Robbie Greenberg.

Far North **1/2 2007 (R)** Nomadic Saiva (Yeoh) is constantly struggling to survive in the Arctic tundra. A shaman predicted she was cursed to bring harm to anyone she gets close to (flashbacks prove that point), so Saiva avoids people except for Anja (Krusiec), an orphan she's raised from infancy. One day Saiva finds a dying man (Bean) and impulsively decides to care for him, which invariably brings trouble. **89m/C; DVD.** *GB* Michelle Yeoh; Michelle Krusiec; Sean Bean; ***D:*** Asif Kapadia; ***W:*** Asif Kapadia; Tim Miller; ***C:*** Roman Osin; ***M:*** Dario Marianelli.

A Far Off Place **1993 (PG-13)** Adolescent boy, adolescent girl, adolescent bushperson, and mature dog set out across the African desert to escape elephant poachers who want to kill them. The boy and girl find romance in the sand, bushperson finds water by listening, and dog gets very nice walk. Strong performances by the youthful leads lend charm to this Disney/Amblin flick, particularly Bok as the bushperson. Unusually violent film for studios involved (animals and people bite sand), though care is taken to edit actual blood shed on screen. Filmed in Zimbabwe and Namibia and based on the books "A Story Like the Wind" and "A Far Off Place" by Laurens van der Post. **107m/C; VHS, DVD.** Reese Witherspoon; Ethan (Randall) Embry; Sarel Bok; Jack Thompson; Maximilian Schell; Robert John Burke; Patricia Kalember; Daniel Gerroll; Miles Anderson; ***D:*** Mikael Salomon; ***W:*** Robert Caswell; Jonathan Hensleigh; Sally Robinson; ***C:*** Juan Ruiz-Anchia; ***M:*** James Horner.

Far Out Isn't Enough: The Tomi Ungerer **1/2 2013** This insightful feature-length biographical documentary explores the life, art, and influence of Tomi Ungerer. This French children's book author and illustrator has created subversive art for seven decades. In addition to including a retrospective of his personal complexities and contradictions, the documentary features original animation created from Ungerer's artistic works. **98m/C; DVD.** ***D:*** Bradley Bernstein; ***W:*** Bradley Bernstein; ***C:*** Paul Birman; Jimmy O'donnell.

Far Out Man **WOOF!** *Soul Man 2* **1989 (R)** An unalterable middle-aged hippie is sent by his worried family and his psychiatrist on a cross-country journey to rediscover himself. The script makes no sense and has very few laughs. **81m/C; VHS, DVD.** Thomas Chong; Rae Dawn Chong; C. Thomas Howell; Shelby Chong; Martin Mull; Paris Chong; Paul Bartel; Judd Nelson; Michael Winslow; Richard "Cheech" Marin; ***D:*** Thomas Chong; ***W:*** Thomas Chong.

The Far Pavilions **1/2** *Blade of Steel* **1984** A British officer falls in love with an Indian princess during the second Afghan War. Cross is appropriately noble and stiff-upper-lipped but Irving is miscast as his ethnic love. This lavish production was based on the romantic bestseller by M.M. Kaye. **108m/C; VHS, DVD.** *GB* Ben Cross; Amy Irving; Omar Sharif; Benedict Taylor; Rossano Brazzi; Christopher Lee; John Gielgud; Rupert Everett; ***D:*** Peter Duffell; ***C:*** Jack Cardiff; ***M:*** Carl Davis. **CABLE**

The Far Side of Jericho **1/2 2006 (R)** In the 1880s, the widows of three executed outlaw brothers are forced to flee their homes and are pursued by a posse determined to find their husbands' buried ill-gotten gains. Routine oater. **99m/C; DVD.** Patrick Bergin; James Gammon; Lawrence Pressman; C. Thomas Howell; Suzanne Andrews; Judith Burnett; Lissa Negrin; John Diehl; Jason Connery; ***D:*** Tim Hunter; ***W:*** Rob Sullivan; James Crumley; ***C:*** Patrick Cady; ***M:*** Mark Adler. **VIDEO**

Far Side of the Moon *La Face Cachee de la Lune* **2003** Lepage directed, wrote (an adaptation of his play), and stars as Quebec brothers Philippe and Andre. Philippe is a failed doctoral student obsessed with space, while gay younger brother Andre is a vacuous TV weatherman. They are brought into each other's orbit by the death of their mother, although Philippe has apparently never quite reached adulthood anyway. Alienation—rather than aliens—rule. French with subtitles. **105m/C; DVD.** *CA* Robert Lepage; Anne-Marie Cadieux; Celine Bonnier; Marco Poulin; ***D:*** Robert Lepage; ***W:*** Robert Lepage; ***C:*** Ronald Plante; ***M:*** Benoit Jutras. **VIDEO**

Faraway, So Close! *In Weiter Ferne, So Nah!* **1993 (PG-13)** Wenders' erratic follow-up to his magnificent "Wings of Desire." Cassiel (Sander), the angel left behind when Damiel (Ganz) chose to become human, once again surveys Berlin, noticing the changes (not necessarily for the better). Angelic companion Raphaela (Kinski) watches events passively, including an old man's (Ruhamnn) reflections on life and the philosophical musings of Emit Flesti (Dafoe, Time Itself, get it?), even as Cassiel impulsively chooses humanity over his heavenly world. Falk makes a return appearance to little effect. Overlong and under-developed. **146m/C; VHS, DVD.** *GE* Otto Sander; Peter Falk; Horst Buchholz; Nastassja Kinski; Heinz Ruhmann; Bruno Ganz; Solveig Dommartin; Ruediger Vogler; Willem Dafoe; Lou Reed; ***D:*** Wim Wenders; ***W:*** Ulrich Zieger; Richard Reitinger; Wim Wenders; ***C:*** Jurgen Jurges; ***M:*** Laurent Petitgand; David Darling. Cannes '93: Grand Jury Prize.

Farewell *L'Affaire Farewell* **2009** Combo spy/political thriller based on a true story. In 1981, innocuous French engineer Pierre Froment (Canet) is working in Moscow. He's encouraged to meet with disenchanted KGB Colonel Sergei Gregoriev (Kusturica), who wants to leak info to the west in an effort to end the cold war. Because the intelligence services are riddled with double agents, Pierre is considered a safe contact who's unnoticed by any agency and he and Sergei become friends. However, shifting politics between the French and U.S. governments (and the CIA) cause trouble. English, Russian, and French with subtitles. **118m/C; DVD, Blu-Ray.** *FR* Guillaume Canet; Emir Kusturica; Alexandra Maria Lara; Evgeniy Kharlanov; Dina Korzun; Ingeborga Dapkounaite; Willem Dafoe; Fred Ward; Philippe Magnan; David Soul; ***D:*** Christian Carion; ***W:*** Christian Carion; Eric Raynaud; ***C:*** Walther van den Ende; ***M:*** Clint Mansell.

The Farewell **2019 (PG)** When writer Billi (Awkwafina) and her parents (Ma and Lin) learn that her beloved paternal grandmother is dying of cancer, they make plans to travel to China for the hasty marriage of her cousin. Billi is shocked that her family will hide the truth from her grandmother (Shuzhen), and her family hesitates to include her in the proceedings for fear she will reveal it. Based on filmmaker Wang's experiences, the comedy-drama is deeply moving and features memorable performances by the leads. **98m/C; DVD, Blu-Ray.** Nora Lum; Tzi Ma; Diana Lin; Jim Liu; Gil Perez-Abraham; Shuzhen Zhao; ***D:*** Lulu Wang; ***W:*** Lulu Wang; ***C:*** Anna Franquesa Solano; ***M:*** Alex Weston. Golden Globes '20: Actress--Mus./Comedy (Lum); Ind. Spirit '20: Actress--Supporting (Zhao), Film.

Farewell My Concubine *Bawang Bie Ji* **1993 (R)** Exotic film covers 50 years of sexual, social, and political Chinese history wrapped around the story of two male Peking Opera stars. Deposited as boys at the Opera's training school Douzi and Shitou become fast friends in their hermetically sealed world, but their friendship is tested during the chaos of Communism and the cultural revolution. Sumptuous and well-acted, but the sheer length and emotional detachment prove to be drawbacks. Adapted from a novel by Lee, who based the work on a 2000-year-old Chinese opera about an imperial concubine. Filmed on location in Beijing. In Mandarin Chinese with subtitles. **157m/C; VHS, DVD.** *CH* Leslie Cheung; Fengyi Zhang; Gong Li; Lu Qi; Da(nniel) Ying; Ge You; Fei Yang; Ma Mingwei; ***D:*** Chen Kaige; ***W:*** Lilian Lee; Lu Wei; ***C:*** Gu Changwei; ***M:*** Jiping Zhao. British Acad. '93: Foreign Film; Cannes '93: Film; Golden Globes '94: Foreign Film; L.A. Film Critics '93: Foreign Film; Natl. Bd. of Review '93: Foreign Film; N.Y. Film Critics '93: Foreign Film, Support. Actress (Li).

Farewell, My Lovely **1975 (R)** A remake of the 1944 Raymond Chandler mystery, "Murder, My Sweet," featuring private eye Phillip Marlowe hunting for an ex-convict's lost sweetheart in 1941 Los Angeles. Perhaps the most accurate of Chandler adaptations, but far from the best, this film offers a nicely detailed production. Mitchum is a bit too world-weary as the seen-it-all detective. **95m/C; VHS, DVD, Blu-Ray.** *GB* Robert Mitchum; Charlotte Rampling; Sylvia Miles; John Ireland; Anthony Zerbe; Jack O'Halloran; Harry Dean Stanton; Sylvester Stallone; Cheryl "Rainbeaux" Smith; ***D:*** Dick Richards; ***W:*** David Zelag Goodman; ***C:*** John A. Alonzo; ***M:*** David Shire.

Farewell, My Queen *Les Adieux a la Reine* **2012 (R)** French director Jacquot re-imagines the oft-told story of Marie Antoinette (Kruger) as a lesbian love affair as one of Antoinette's ladies-in-waiting (Seydoux) gets closer and closer to the woman who sparked a social revolution and influences her romantic and political decisions. With lavish period details and gorgeous costumes, Jacquot's film looks stunning even if it does come off a bit hollow at times. Best viewed as a film exercise in beautiful people in beautiful costumes in beautiful places more than as a social commentary or historical document. Based on the 2004 novel by Chantal Thomas. **100m/C; DVD, Blu-Ray.** *FR SP* Diane Kruger; Lea Seydoux; Noemie Lvovsky; Virginie Ledoyen; Xavier Beauvois; Michel Robin; ***D:*** Benoit Jacquot; ***W:*** Benoit Jacquot; Gilles Taurand; ***C:*** Romain Winding; ***M:*** Bruno Coulais.

A Farewell to Arms **1932** The original film version of Ernest Hemingway's novel about the tragic love affair between an American ambulance driver and an English nurse during the Italian campaign of WWI. The novelist disavowed the ambiguous ending, but the public loved the film. Fine performances and cinematography. **85m/B; VHS, DVD, Blu-Ray.** Helen Hayes; Gary Cooper; Adolphe Menjou; Mary (Phillips) Philips; Jack La Rue; Blanche Frederici; ***D:*** Frank Borzage; ***W:*** Oliver H.P. Garrett; Benjamin Glazer; ***C:*** Charles B(ryant) Lang, Jr. Oscars '33: Cinematog., Sound.

A Farewell to Arms **1/2 1957** Third version of the Hemingway novel, set during WWI, was designed as a vehicle for faded star Jones, wife of producer David O. Selznick. But she was too old for the part of the innocent young nurse who gets pregnant by ambulance driver Hudson (equally unconvincing). Selznick's interference with the script didn't help either (he actually wrote a letter of apology to Hemingway). The overblown production was a boxoffice bomb. **152m/C; DVD, Blu-Ray.** Jennifer Jones; Rock Hudson; Alberto Sordi; Mercedes McCambridge; Oscar Homolka; Elaine Stritch; Kurt Kasznar; Vittorio De Sica; ***D:*** Charles Vidor; ***W:*** Ben Hecht; ***C:*** Piero Portalupi; Oswald Morris; ***M:*** Mario Nascimbene.

Farewell to the King **1/2 1989 (PG-13)** During WWII, a ship-wrecked American deserter becomes the chief of a tribe of Borneo headhunters until his jungle kingdom is caught between the forces of the U.S. and Japanese. With the help of a British officer he helps them defend themselves when the Japanese invade. An old-fashioned war epic with a beautiful location and solid if uninspired-performances by the leads. Based on Pierre Schoendoerffer's novel "L'Adieu Au Roi." **114m/C; VHS, DVD.** Nick Nolte; Nigel Havers; Marius Weyers; Frank McRae; Marilyn Tokuda; Elan Oberon; William Wise; James Fox; Aki Aleong; ***D:*** John Milius; ***W:*** John Milius; ***C:*** Dean Semler; ***M:*** Basil Poledouris.

Fargo **1996 (R)** Another malicious, extra-dark comedy from the Coen brothers. Car salesman Jerry Lundegaard (Macy) hires a couple of losers to kidnap his wife so he can swindle the ransom money out of his father-in-law. Naturally, the scheme begins to unravel and the very pregnant police chief Marge Gunderson (McDormand) treks through the frozen tundra of Minnesota to put the pieces of the puzzle together. McDormand's performance as the chatty competent chief is first rate. Needling the flat-accented Midwesterners of their youth, the Coens have also returned to their filmmaking roots after the disappointing big-budget "Hudsucker Proxy." Because Minneapolis was having its warmest, driest winter in 100 years, the Coens were forced to shoot most of the exteriors in wintery North Dakota. **97m/C; VHS, DVD, Blu-Ray.** William H. Macy; Frances McDormand; Steve Buscemi; Peter Stormare; Harve Presnell; Steve Reevis; John Carroll Lynch; Kristin Rudrud; Steve Park; Jose Feliciano; ***D:*** Joel Coen; ***W:*** Ethan Coen; Joel Coen; ***C:*** Roger Deakins; ***M:*** Carter Burwell. Oscars '96: Actress (McDormand), Orig. Screenplay; AFI '98: Top 100; Australian Film Inst. '96: Foreign Film; British Acad. '96: Director (Coen); Cannes '96: Director (Coen); Ind. Spirit '97: Actor (Macy), Actress (McDormand), Cinematog., Director (Coen), Film, Screenplay; Natl. Bd. of Review '96: Actress (McDormand), Director (Coen); Natl. Film Reg. '06; N.Y. Film Critics '96: Film; Screen Actors Guild '96: Actress (McDormand); Writers Guild '96: Orig. Screenplay; Broadcast Film Critics '96: Actress (McDormand), Film.

Farinelli *Farinelli the Castrato; Farinelli Il Castrato* **1994 (R)** A movie to make men cringe. Floridly depicts the complex professional and personal ties of 18th-century opera composer Riccardo Broschi (Lo Verso) and his younger brother Carlo (Dionisi), a celebrated castrato singer under the stage name "Farinelli." In part, because of an early church prohibition against women singing in public, boys were castrated before puberty to preserve their pure soprano voices while vocal power and agility grew as they became men. Castrati were the rock stars of their day and Farinelli lived a flamboyant life before retiring to the Spanish court of Philip V. The castrato voice heard in the movie is an electronic mixture of countertenor Derek Lee Ragin and soprano Ewa Mallas Godlewska. French and Italian with subtitles. **110m/C; VHS, DVD.** *FR IT BE* Stefano Dionisi; Enrico Lo Verso; Jeroen Krabbe; Elsa Zylberstein; Caroline Cellier; Omero Antonutti; Jacques Boudet; ***D:*** Gerard Corbiau; ***W:*** Gerard Corbiau; Andree Corbiau; Marcel Beaulieu; ***C:*** Walther Vanden Ende; ***M:*** Christopher Rousset. Cesar '95: Art Dir./Set Dec., Sound; Golden Globes '95: Foreign Film.

The Farmer Takes a Wife 1/2 **1935** Henry Fonda's first film, recreating his stage role, as a mid-19th century farmer at odds with the Erie canal builders and struggling to court the woman he loves. Remade as a musical in 1953. **91m/B; DVD.** Janet Gaynor; Henry Fonda; Charles Bickford; Slim Summerville; Jane Withers; ***D:*** Victor Fleming; ***W:*** Edwin J. Burke; ***C:*** Ernest Palmer.

The Farmer's Other Daughter *Farm Girl* **1965** A rural comedy about Farmer Brown whose lovely daughter is eyed by all the farmhands. He also has to contend with dastardly Mr. Barksnapper who wants to take his farm away from him until one of his daughter's beaus comes to the rescue. **84m/C; VHS, DVD.** Ernest Ashworth; Judy Pennebaker; Bill Michael; ***D:*** John Patrick Hayes.

The Farmer's Wife 1/2 **1928** Silent British comedy about a recently widowed farmer searching for a new wife. Meanwhile, his lovely housekeeper would be the perfect candidate. Based on Eden Philpott's play. **97m/B; Silent; VHS, DVD, Blu-Ray.** *GB* Jameson Thomas; Lillian Hall-Davis; Gordon Harker; ***D:*** Alfred Hitchcock; ***W:*** Alfred Hitchcock; ***C:*** Jack Cox.

Farmhouse **WOOF! 2008 (R)** Icky torture porn that features a dead child and tries to tie up its plot holes with some supernatural hogwash. After Chad and Scarlet's baby dies, they decide to start over in a new city. They get into a car accident and are offered shelter at the farmhouse of crazy Samael and his wife Lilith (those names should be a warning). These are not folks you want to be under the same roof with. **95m/C; DVD.** Jamie Anne Allman; William Lee Scott; Steven Weber; Kelly Hu; ***W:*** Daniel P. Coughlin; Jason Hice; ***C:*** Tim Hudson; ***M:*** Mark Petrie. **VIDEO**

Farming 1/2 **2019 (R)** In 1970s England, Nigerian parents Femi (Akinnuoye-Agbaje) and Tolu (Nnaji) pay a white working class woman, Ingrid (Beckinsale), to foster their infant son Enitan. As Enitan (Amissah) grows up with other black children cared for by Ingrid, he struggles under her racist threats. As a teen, still friendless Eni (Idris) is targeted by a white skinhead gang but soon becomes the leader's pet to prove that he can be as racist as them and be part of their group. Based on filmmaker Akkinuoye-Agbaje's experiences as a teenager in 1980s England, the dark film is unflinching in its exploration of issues of race and self-perception. **107m/C; DVD.** Kate Beckinsale; Adewale Akinnuoye-Agbaje; Gugu Mbatha-Raw; Tom Canton; Damson Idris; ***D:*** Adewale Akinnuoye-Agbaje; ***W:*** Adewale Akinnuoye-Agbaje; ***C:*** Kit Fraser; ***M:*** Ilan Eshkeri; Nick Angel.

Fascination **WOOF! 2004 (R)** Bisset's beauty at 60 is the only fascinating thing in this mess of a thriller. Dad (Naughton) dies in a mysterious swimming accident, son (Garcia) thinks foul play, Mom remarries quickly, son sleeps with new stepsister (Evans). The plot twists and surprise revelations stretch things beyond the point of believability, the dialogue is terrible, and the performances lack any spark. It all adds up to a shallow, painful movie that will either induce groans or laughs. **102m/C; DVD.** Jacqueline Bisset; Adam Garcia; Alice Evans; James Naughton; Stuart Wilson; ***D:*** Klaus Menzel; ***W:*** Klaus Menzel; ***C:*** Reinhart Pesche; ***M:*** John Du Prez.

Fashions of 1934 *Fashions* **1934** A typical, lightweight '30s musical with impressive choreography by Busby Berkeley. Powell plays a disreputable clothing designer who goes to Paris to steal the latest fashion designs and winds up costuming a musical and falls in love. **78m/B; VHS, DVD.** Bette Davis; William Powell; Frank McHugh; Hugh Herbert; Reginald Owen; Busby Berkeley; ***D:*** William Dieterle.

Fast and Furious 1/2 **1939** A third set of actors take on the roles of the sleuthing Sloanes (after "Fast and Loose") to clear a friend who's accused of bumping off a beauty pageant promoter. While on vacation, Joel not only looks for clues but at the bathing beauties as a contest judge, much to his wife Garda's dismay. **73m/B; DVD.** Franchot Tone; Ann Sothern; Allyn Joslyn; Ruth Hussey; Lee Bowman; John Miljan; ***D:*** Busby Berkeley; ***W:*** Harry Kurnitz; ***C:*** Ray June; ***M:*** Daniele Amfitheatrof.

Fast & Furious **2009 (PG-13)** The fourth installment in the series really is a prequel for *Tokyo Drift* and puts the original cast and characters back together in L.A. Dom (Diesel) and Brian (Walker) end their feud to combine forces against a common enemy and agree to help the feds bring down a heroin importer. Diesel will definitely draw his fans in, but in the end there's not much else but a bunch of sweet cars, flashy driving, fiery crashes, and all other manner of things blowing up real good. **107m/C; Blu-Ray, On Demand.** Vin Diesel; Paul Walker; Michelle Rodriguez; Jordana Brewster; Laz Alonso; ***D:*** Justin Lin; ***W:*** Chris Morgan; ***C:*** Amir M. Mokri; ***M:*** Brian Tyler.

Fast & Furious 6 **2013 (PG-13)** Building on the cartoonish, over-the-top approach to action that made Fast Five a smash hit, director Lin one-ups his own insanity by creating new forms of vehicular chaos. Dom (Diesel) and his team are called back into action after the thought-dead Letty (Rodriguez) surfaces as a member of a deadly European team of criminals out to buy a weapon that could start WWIII. Incredibly well-choreographed action scenes, both behind the wheel and in hand-to-hand combat scenes, disguise a story that's even more ridiculous than before but also escapist fun. Sit through the credits to see the cameo that leads into F&F 7. **130m/C; DVD, Blu-Ray.** Vin Diesel; Paul Walker; Michelle Rodriguez; Luke Evans; Jordana Brewster; Dwayne "The Rock" Johnson; Tyrese Gibson; Sung Kang; Gal Gadot; Chris Bridges; Elsa Pataky; Gina Carano; ***D:*** Justin Lin; ***W:*** Chris Morgan; ***C:*** Stephen F. Windon; ***M:*** Lucas Vidal.

Fast & Furious Presents: Hobbs & Shaw 1/2 **2019 (PG-13)** Though Luke Hobbs (Johnson) and Deckard Shaw (Statham) have previously been reluctant allies, they team up again when the world is threatened. Brixton (Elba), a superhuman agent of a covert military-tech group, is trying to obtain the Snowflake virus, which could quickly wipe out the planet, but MI6 agent Hattie (Kirby), Shaw's sister, gets her hands on it first and injects herself with it. The duo must save her and everyone else. The spin-off of the popular Fast & Furious franchise successfully puts the chemistry of Statham and Johnson at center. Though fun, the inane plot does not have enough energy for a feature-length film. **137m/C; DVD, Blu-Ray.** Dwayne "The Rock" Johnson; Jason Statham; Idris Elba; Vanessa Kirby; Dame Helen Mirren; ***D:*** David Leitch; ***W:*** Chris Morgan; Drew Pearce; ***C:*** Jonathan Sela; ***M:*** Tyler Bates.

Fast and Loose 1/2 **1939** The Sloanes return (played by different actors) after "Fast Company" to figure out who would kill for a stolen Shakespeare manuscript. Since Joel was trying to buy the work for a third party, he's a suspect too. Followed by "Fast and Furious." **80m/B; DVD.** Robert Montgomery; Rosalind Russell; Ralph Morgan; Reginald Owen; Etienne Girardot; ***D:*** Edwin L. Marin; ***W:*** Harry Kurnitz; ***C:*** George J. Folsey.

The Fast and the Furious **1954** On the lam after being falsely charged with murder, Ireland picks up a fast car and a loose woman (or is it a loose car and a fast woman?) and makes a run for the border by entering the Pebble Beach race. **73m/B; VHS, DVD.** John Ireland; Dorothy Malone; Bruce Carlisle; Iris Adrian; Jean Howell; ***D:*** John Ireland; Edwards Sampson; ***W:*** Jean Howell; Jerome Odlum; ***C:*** Floyd Crosby; ***M:*** Alexander Gerens.

The Fast and the Furious 1/2 **2001 (PG-13)** Rookie L.A. cop Brian (Walker) goes undercover to infiltrate a street gang that adapts sports cars for illicit street racing and other, even less legal, uses. But first he has to earn the respect and trust of their leader, Dominic (Diesel), and the love of Dom's sister Mia (Brewster). Dominic is the head of a tight-knit "family" of quirky thieves hopped up on car exhaust and adrenaline, very much in the B-movie tradition of "Gone in 60 Seconds" (the original), "Eat My Dust," and "Grand Theft Auto." And hey, let's face it, kids. That's all this is, a summer B-movie where reality, plot, and dialogue have no place. Diesel does impress (again) in the patriarch-philosopher-thief role. **101m/C; VHS, DVD, Blu-Ray, UMD, HD-DVD.** Vin Diesel; Paul Walker; Jordana Brewster; Michelle Rodriguez; Rick Yune; Ted Levine; Ja Rule; Thom Barry; Chad Lindberg; Johnny Strong; Matt Schulze; Vyto Ruginis; ***D:*** Rob Cohen; ***W:*** Gary Scott Thompson; Erik Bergquist; David Ayer; ***C:*** Ericson Core; ***M:*** BT (Brian Transeau).

The Fast and the Furious: Tokyo Drift 1/2 **2006 (PG-13)** In the third installment, the franchise heads to Japan (just like the Bad News Bears!) with new anti-hero Sean (Black), a bad-attitude teenager sent to live with his estranged military dad. Sean soon finds himself involved in the illegal neon world of drift racing and rebel/gangster types out to teach this gaijin some hard lessons. Pic delivers on its fast-cars-fast-races premise. **105m/C; DVD, Blu-Ray, HD-DVD.** Lucas Black; Bow Wow; Sung Kang; Jason J. Tobin; Zachery Ty Bryan; Leonardo Nam; Brian Tee; Nathalie Kelley; Brian Goodman; Sonny Chiba; Nikki Griffin; Lynda Boyd; Keiko Kitagawa; Vincent Laresca; Vin Diesel; ***D:*** Justin Lin; ***W:*** Chris Morgan; ***C:*** Stephen F. Windon; ***M:*** Brian Tyler.

Fast Break 1/2 **1979 (PG)** New York deli clerk who is a compulsive basketball fan talks his way into a college coaching job. He takes a team of street players with him, with predictable results on and off the court. Kaplan's screen debut. **107m/C; VHS, Streaming.** Gabe Kaplan; Harold Sylvester; Randee Heller; ***D:*** Jack Smight; ***M:*** David Shire.

Fast, Cheap & Out of Control 1/2 **1997 (PG)** Director Morris' use of odd camera angles, unusual editing, and dark humor increases with each outing but always seems to enhance interest in the subject matter rather than detract from it. While his previous films have focused on just one subject, this one features four: a wild-animal trainer, a topiary gardener, a scientist who creates robotic insects, and a man who studies mole rats. Through inter-cutting and the overlapping of the subjects (at times audio from one is played over the visuals of another), Morris gives the impression that they are all linked together. Old movie footage is used to add an unreal quality, and the score by Caleb Sampson of the Alloy Orchestra hypnotically completes the surrealism. This is the story of four obsessed men, but none as obsessed as director Morris himself, with his need to show that truth is stranger than fiction. **82m/C; VHS, DVD.** ***D:*** Errol Morris; ***C:*** Robert Richardson; ***M:*** Caleb Sampson. Natl. Bd. of Review '97: Feature Doc.; N.Y. Film Critics '97: Feature Doc.; Natl. Soc. Film Critics '97: Feature Doc.

Fast Color 1/2 **2018 (PG-13)** As Ruth (Mbatha-Raw) travels through the parched American West in the near future, she is pursued by the government because she has secrets as well as a power in that her major seizures cause earthquakes. An addict in recovery, Ruth is trying to get back to the home of her mother Bo (Toussaint) and her daughter Lila (Sidney), whom Bo has been raising. Bo and Lila have their own unique powers. When they reunite, it takes time to connect but soon larger supernatural events come into play. The powerful film is a meaningful exploration of power and creativity of women. **100m/C; DVD, Blu-Ray.** Gugu Mbatha-Raw; David Strathairn; Lorraine Toussaint; Christopher Denham; Saniyya Sidney; ***D:*** Julia Hart; ***W:*** Julia Hart; Jordan Horowitz; ***C:*** Michael Fimognari; ***M:*** Rob Simonsen.

Fast Company 1/2 **1938** Rare book dealers Joel and Garda Sloane practice their sleuthing to find out who killed bibliophile Otto Brockler. Joel finds stolen, lost, and bogus rare books and collects the insurance company rewards. But given Otto's questionable business ethics, there are lots of suspects Followed by "Fast and Loose" and "Fast and Furious" (both 1939). **75m/B; DVD.** Melvyn Douglas; Florence Rice; Claire Dodd; Shepperd Strudwick; Louis Calhern; George Zucco; ***D:*** Edward Buzzell; ***W:*** Harry Kurnitz; ***C:*** Clyde De Vinna; ***M:*** William Axt.

Fast Company **1978** The life story of champion race car driver Lonnie Johnson including women, money, and the drag racing sponsors. **90m/C; VHS, DVD, Blu-Ray.** William (Bill) Smith; John Saxon; Claudia Jennings; Nicholas (Nick) Campbell; Don Francks; ***D:*** David Cronenberg; ***W:*** David Cronenberg.

Fast Five 1/2 **2011 (PG-13)** Rousing sequel in the successful "The Fast and the Furious" franchise. Ex-cop Brian O'Connor (Walker), ex-con Dominic Toretto (Diesel), and Dom's sister Mia (Brewster) team up with an elite group of racers in Rio de Janeiro for one last job. Dangerous complications arise with a brutal drug lord out for their blood and ruthless U.S. agent Luke Hobbs (Johnson) hot on their trail. With charismatic performances from the cast, especially Johnson, it's chock-full of engrossing action that proves the series is still thriving. **130m/C; Blu-Ray, On Demand.** Paul Walker; Vin Diesel; Jordana Brewster; Dwayne "The Rock" Johnson; Chris Bridges; Tyrese Gibson; Joaquim Almeida; Matt Schulze; Sung Kang; Gal Gadot; ***D:*** Justin Lin; ***W:*** Chris Morgan; ***C:*** Stephen F. Windon; ***M:*** Brian Tyler.

Fast Food **1989** A super-cheap, strangulated attempt at low comedy, wherein an entrepreneurial hamburger peddler invents a secret aphrodisiac sauce. Look for former porn-star Traci Lords. **90m/C; VHS, DVD.** Clark Brandon; Tracy Griffith; Randal Patrick; Traci Lords; Kevin McCarthy; Michael J. Pollard; Jim Varney; ***D:*** Michael A. Simpson; ***W:*** Clark Brandon.

Fast Food Nation **2006 (R)** Director Richard Linklater's attempt to show the public that fast food is both figuratively and literally crappy suffers from some slow pacing and wandering plotlines, but its point is effectively super-sized. After Don (Kinnear), an executive at fictional restaurant chain Mickey's, discovers that some cows may have dropped a chalupa in the meat patties, he starts an investigation that crosses ethnic and class barriers. The story then weaves the lives of illegal immigrants (Moreno, Valderrama), cattle ranchers (Kristofferson, Willis) and suburbanites (Arquette, Hawke, Johnson) together to show why most burger shack value meals should be called the "number two." Linklater wrote the screenplay with Eric Schlosser, whose eponymous nonfiction book provided inspiration. Salad, anyone? **114m/C; DVD.** *GB US* Patricia Arquette; Paul Dano; Luis Guzman; Ethan Hawke; Bobby Canavale; Greg Kinnear; Ashley Johnson; Kris Kristofferson; Avril Lavigne; Esai Morales; Catalina Sandino Moreno; Wilmer Valderrama; Bruce Willis; ***D:*** Richard Linklater; ***W:*** Richard Linklater; Eric Schlosser; ***C:*** Lee Daniel; ***M:*** Dean Martinez.

Fast Forward 1/2 **1984 (PG)** A group of eight teenagers from Ohio learn how to deal with success and failure when they enter a national dance contest in New York City. A break-dancing variation on the old show business chestnut. **110m/C; VHS, DVD.** John Scott Clough; Don Franklin; Tracy Silver; Cindy McGee; ***D:*** Sidney Poitier; ***W:*** Richard Wesley; ***M:*** Tom Bahler.

Fast Girl 1/2 **2007 (PG)** After her dad is killed in a racing accident, Alex (Monroe) wants to prove she can win in the male-dominated sport. But her Uncle Bill (Brown), who runs the local speedway, refuses to allow her to compete, and then a romance with driver Darryl (Guarini) messes with Alex's concentration. **85m/C; DVD.** Mircea Monroe; Justin Guarini; Dwier Brown; Caroline Rhea; James DuMont; Cameron Gordon; ***D:*** Daniel Zirilli; ***W:*** Luke Ricci; D. Glase Lomond; ***C:*** Jason Dittmer; ***M:*** Nicholas O'Toole. **VIDEO**

Fast Lane 1/2 **2008 (R)** Tough babes in leather with guns. L.A. is having a problem with two competing car theft rings so Lt. Baynes (Bauer) sends cop Baby Martinez (Lizette) undercover into the all-girl group, which is run by Mama (Brown). Trouble ensues with Mama's violent rival, Knight (Parker), who has some problems with his own crew that reflect back on Baby. **100m/C; DVD.** Melina Lizette; Kenyetta Lethridge; Steven

Bauer; Sevier Crespo; Olivia Brown; Anthony Ray Parker; Elika Crespo; Sara Sanderson; *D:* David Betances; *W:* David Betances; *C:* Jeff Carolan; *M:* Johnny Wilson. **VIDEO**

Fast Life 1/2 **1932** Haines plays his usual wisecracking, shady character as a former sailor turned inventor. Sandy comes up with a new speedboat motor that has a chance to win a big boat race and save the floundering company of his gal Shirley's (Evans) father (Thomson). Filmed around Catalina. **89m/B; DVD.** William Haines; Madge Evans; Kenneth Thomson; Cliff Edwards; Conrad Nagel; A.S. Byron; *D:* Harry A. Pollard; *W:* Ralph Spence; Byron Morgan; *C:* Harold Wenstrom.

The Fast Runner *Atanarjuat, the Fast Runner* **2001 (R)** The first Inuktikut language feature film is a remarkably compelling drama based on an ancient Inuit legend and set in the north Baffin region of the Candian Arctic. Atanarjuat (Ungalaaq) is in love with Atuat (Ivalu), who is already promised to the jealous Oki (Arnatsiaq) who decides to kill his rival. Atanarjuat manages to escape by running (naked) across the ice, outlasting his pursuers until he finds a safe refuge. Then he decides to go back to his community and settle the score. **172m/C; VHS, DVD.** *CA* Pakkak Innuksuk; Natar Ungalaaq; Peter Henry Arnatsiaq; Sylvia Ivalu; Lucy Tulugarjuk; *D:* Zacharias Kunuk; *W:* Paul Apak Angilirq; *C:* Norman Cohn; *M:* Chris Crilly. Cannes '01: First Feature; Genie '01: Director (Kunuk), Film, Film Editing, Score, Screenplay.

Fast Sofa **2001 (R)** Lowlife, small-time L.A. drug dealer Rick (Busey) has a one-nighter with porn actress Ginger (Tilly) and decides to follow her to Palm Springs. Too bad her jealous (and violent) movie-producer husband (Roberts) is also about to show up. Based on the book by Bruce Craven. **95m/C; VHS, DVD.** Jake Busey; Jennifer Tilly; Eric Roberts; Adam Goldberg; Crispin Glover; Natasha Lyonne; Bijou Phillips; *D:* Salome Breziner; *W:* Salome Breziner; Peter Chase; Bruce Craven; *C:* Dean Lent; *M:* William V. Malpede.

Fast Times at Ridgemont High **1982 (R)** Teens at a Southern California high school revel in sex, drugs, and rock 'n' roll. A full complement of student types meet at the Mall—that great suburban microcosm percolating with angst-ridden teen trials—to contemplate losing their virginity, plot skipping homeroom, and move inexorably closer to the end of their adolescence. The talented young cast became household names: Sean Penn is most excellent as the California surfer dude who antagonizes teacher, Walston, aka "Aloha Mr. Hand." Based on the best-selling book by Cameron Crowe, it's one of the best of this genre. **91m/C; VHS, DVD, Blu-Ray.** Sean Penn; Jennifer Jason Leigh; Judge Reinhold; Robert Romanus; Brian Backer; Phoebe Cates; Ray Walston; Scott Thomson; Vincent Schiavelli; Amanda Wyss; Forest Whitaker; Kelli Maroney; Eric Stoltz; Pamela Springsteen; James Russo; Martin Brest; Anthony Edwards; Nicolas Cage; *D:* Amy Heckerling; *W:* Cameron Crowe; *C:* Matthew F. Leonetti. Natl. Film Reg. '05.

Fast Walking **1982 (R)** A prison guard is offered $50,000 to help a militant black leader escape from jail, the same man his cousin has contracted to kill. **116m/C; VHS, DVD.** James Woods; Kay Lenz; M. Emmet Walsh; Robert Hooks; Tim McIntire; Timothy Carey; Susan Tyrrell; *D:* James B. Harris.

Fast Workers 1/2 **1933** Since one-time silent star Gilbert had trouble with his MGM contract, he got stuck in a lot of cheapie productions, including this working-class romantic drama. Steelworker buddies Gunner (Gilbert) and Bucker (Armstrong) look out for each other in the dame department. Streetwise grifter Mary (Clarke) comes between the two men and this time it's serious. **68m/B; DVD.** John Gilbert; Robert Armstrong; Mae Clarke; Muriel Kirkland; Sterling Holloway; *D:* Tod Browning; *W:* Laurence Stallings; *C:* J. Peverell Marley.

Faster 1/2 **2010 (R)** Fresh from a 10-year prison stint for a robbery gone bad that led to his brother's murder, Driver (Johnson) is itching for revenge. With big guns, a score to settle, a 1970 Chevelle and list of guys that done him wrong, Driver hot-rods around town ticking names of his checklist via a bullet to the head. Chasing him down are Cop (Thornton), a nearly-retired junkie police officer, and Killer (Jackson-Cohen), an admiring hitman. It's a muscle movie, loaded with straight-up action and American-made muscle cars. **98m/C; Blu-Ray, On Demand.** Dwayne "The Rock" Johnson; Billy Bob Thornton; Oliver Jackson-Cohen; Carla Gugino; Maggie Grace; Moon Bloodgood; Tom Berenger; Jennifer Carpenter; Adewale Akinnuoye-Agbaje; Xander Berkeley; Courtney Gains; Lester "Rasta" Speight; Mike Epps; *D:* George Tillman, Jr.; *W:* Joe Gayton; Tony Gayton; *C:* Michael Grady; *M:* Clint Mansell.

Faster, Pussycat! Kill! Kill! *The Leather Girls; Pussycat* **1965** It doesn't get any better than this! Three sexy go-go dancers get their after-work kicks by hot-rodding in the California desert. They soon find themselves enveloped in murder, kidnapping, lust and robbery after a particular race gets out of hand. Easily the most watchable, fun and funny production to spring from the mind of Russ Meyer. Those who haven't seen this cannot truly be called "cool." **83m/B; VHS, DVD, Blu-Ray.** Tura Satana; Haji; Lori Williams; Susan Bernard; Stuart Lancaster; Paul Trinka; Dennis Busch; Ray Barlow; Mickey Foxx; *D:* Russ Meyer; *W:* Jack Moran; Russ Meyer; *C:* Walter Schenk; *M:* Paul Sawtell; Bert Shefter; The Bostweeds.

Fastest Guitar Alive 1/2 **1968** Debut of the legendary Orbison is strictly for inveterate fans only. Rebel operative/crooner during the Civil War, whose rhythm is good but timing is bad, steals a Union gold supply, but the war ends before he makes it back to the land of Dixie. Seems that makes him a common thief. **88m/C; VHS, DVD.** Roy Orbison; Sammy Jackson; Margaret Pierce; Joan Freeman; *D:* Michael D. Moore; *M:* Fred Karger.

Fastest Gun Alive **1956** Suspenseful western with ex-gunfighter Ford challenged to a showdown by Crawford. **89m/C; VHS, DVD.** Glenn Ford; Jeanne Crain; Broderick Crawford; Russ Tamblyn; Allyn Joslyn; Leif Erickson; John Dehner; Noah Beery, Jr.; J.M. Kerrigan; Rhys Williams; *D:* Russell Rouse; *W:* Russell Rouse; Frank D. Gilroy; *C:* George J. Folsey; *M:* Andre Previn.

Fat Albert 1/2 **2004 (PG)** Clunky live-action version of Bill Cosby's standup routines and the animated series "Fat Albert and the Cosby Kids." Depressed South Philly teen Doris (Pratt) is watching TV Land reruns of the show when a magic portal opens up allowing Fat Albert (an agreeable Thompson) and his gang to pop into her living room. F.A. feels obliged to offer advice to help Doris gain some self-esteem and even develops a crush on Doris' popular foster sister, Lauri (Ramirez). Meanwhile, the '70s-era tooners react to the real world of the 21st century in expected fish-out-of-water ways. Hey, hey, hey is more why, why, why? **93m/C; VHS, DVD.** Kenan Thompson; Kyla Pratt; Marques Houston; Dania Ramirez; Omari (Omarion) Grandberry; Shedrack Anderson, III; Jermaine Williams; Keith D. Robinson; Alphonso McAuley; Aaron A. Frazier; J. Mack Slaughter, Jr.; *Cameo(s):* Bill Cosby; *D:* Joel Zwick; *W:* Charles Kipps; *C:* Paul Elliott; *M:* Richard Gibbs.

Fat City 1/2 **1972 (PG)** One of Huston's later triumphs, a seedy, street-level drama based on the Leonard Gardner novel about an aging alcoholic boxer trying to make a comeback and his young worshipful protege. Highly acclaimed. Tyrrell earned an Oscar nomination as the boxer's world-weary lover. **93m/C; VHS, DVD.** Stacy Keach; Jeff Bridges; Susan Tyrrell; Candy Clark; Nicholas Colasanto; *D:* John Huston; *C:* Conrad L. Hall; *M:* Marvin Hamlisch.

Fat Kid Rules the World 1/2 **2012 (R)** Slow-moving teen comedy. Overweight Seattle misfit high schooler Troy is saved from his suicide attempt by drug-addled school dropout Marcus. Then Marcus decides to recruit Troy as the drummer for his punk rock duo and even though Troy knows it's probably a scam, he goes along. Adapted from K.L. Going's young adult novel. **99m/C; DVD.** Jacob Wysocki; Matt O'Leary; Lili Simmons; Dylan Arnold; Billy Campbell; *D:* Matthew Lillard; *W:* Peter Speakman; Michael M.B. Galvin; *C:* Noah Rosenthal; *M:* Mike McCready.

Fat Man and Little Boy 1/2 **1989 (PG-13)** A lavish, semi-fictional account of the creation of the first atomic bomb, and the tensions between J. Robert Oppenheimer and his military employer, Gen. Leslie Groves. Overlong but interesting. Cusack, whose character never existed, is especially worthwhile as an idealistic scientist. **127m/C; VHS, DVD.** Paul Newman; Dwight Schultz; Bonnie Bedelia; John Cusack; Laura Dern; John C. McGinley; Natasha Richardson; Ron Frazier; *D:* Roland Joffé; *W:* Bruce Robinson; Tony Garnett; Roland Joffé; *M:* Ennio Morricone.

Fat, Sick & Nearly Dead 1/2 **2011 (PG)** This insightful feature-length documentary follows Joe Cross on his personal quest to regain his health. More than 100 lbs. overweight and ill with an autoimmune disorder, he did not believe he would live a full life nor gain any long-term benefits from conventional medicines. He commits to spending 60 days only drinking fresh fruits and vegetables, and spending 60 days on the road while talking to more than 500 Americans about related issues. Joe finds others sharing his issues and inspires another man with similar problems to join him on self-carved path to wellness. **97m/C; DVD, Streaming, Download.** Joe Cross; *D:* Joe Cross; Kurt Engfehr; *W:* Joe Cross; Kurt Engfehr; *C:* Richard Lopez; Daniel Marracino; *M:* M.E. Manning.

The Fat Spy WOOF! **1966** Campy beach movie parody has a gaggle of treasure hunting teens, a tycoon's daughter, her boyfriend, his twin brother, and the twin's girlfriend descending on an island off the Florida coast looking for the Fountain of Youth. Flick tries hard, with plenty of (awful) "rock" music by The Wild Ones, Jayne Mansfield, and Phyllis Diller among the participants wildly mugging for laughs. None of it works, as parody or straight comedy. Unless you're a fan of ultabad quickie exploitation, don't bother. **75m/C; VHS, DVD.** Phyllis Diller; Jack E. Leonard; Brian Donlevy; Jayne Mansfield; Joseph Brun; Joel Hirschhorn; Al Kasha; *D:* Joseph Cates; *W:* Matthew Andrews.

Fatal Attraction **1987 (R)** When a very married New York lawyer is seduced by a beautiful blonde associate, the one-night stand leads to terror as she continues to pursue the relationship. She begins to threaten his family and home with possessive, violent acts. An expertly made, manipulative thriller; one of the most hotly discussed films of the 1980s. A successful change of role for Close as the sexy, scorned, and deadly other woman. Also available in a special "director's series" edition, featuring Lyne's original, controversial ending. **120m/C; VHS, DVD, Blu-Ray.** Michael Douglas; Glenn Close; Anne Archer; Stuart Pankin; Ellen Hamilton-Latzen; Ellen Foley; Fred Gwynne; Meg Mundy; J.J. Johnston; *D:* Adrian Lyne; *W:* James Dearden; *C:* Howard Atherton; *M:* Maurice Jarre.

Fatal Beauty 1/2 **1987 (R)** A female undercover cop in Los Angeles tracks down a drug dealer selling cocaine (from which the title is taken). Elliott is the mob bodyguard who helps her out. Violent and sensational, the film tries to capitalize on the success of "Beverly Hills Cop" and fails miserably. Goldberg is wasted in this effort and the picture tiptoes around the interracial romance aspects that are implied. **104m/C; VHS, DVD, Blu-Ray.** Whoopi Goldberg; Sam Elliott; Ruben Blades; Harris Yulin; Richard "Cheech" Marin; Brad Dourif; *D:* Tom Holland; *W:* Hilary Henkin; Dean Riesner; *C:* David M. Walsh; *M:* Harold Faltermeyer.

Fatal Call 1/2 **2012** Thriller with a cliched plot. Mitch moves to the city, starts a romance with Amy, and then gets accused of murder. He goes on the run to clear his name before the law catches him but how does his girlfriend fit into the frame? **90m/C; DVD.** Jason London; Danielle Harris; Kevin Sorbo; Lochlyn Munro; *D:* Jack Snyder; *W:* Jack Snyder; *C:* Chris Benson; *M:* Tony Esterly. **VIDEO**

Fatal Charm **1992 (R)** There's a serial killer at work in a small town. So far six women have been raped and murdered. But cute-teen Valerie can't believe it when the townspeople accuse that sweet guy Adam, especially since he's the one boy Valerie is so very attracted to. **90m/C; DVD.** Christopher Atkins; Amanda Peterson; Mary Frann; James Remar; Andrew (Andy) Robinson; Peggy Lipton; *D:* Alan Smithee; *W:* Nicholas Niciphor.

Fatal Contact: Bird Flu in America **2006** Oh no! Another really terrible disaster flick! Avian flu has mutated and is now transmittable from human to human, which causes widespread panic. Poor scientist Iris Varnack (Richardson) is trying to come up with a vaccine or something but gosh darn, it's just so hard with all those people running around screaming and dying! **83m/C; DVD.** Joely Richardson; Scott Cohen; Stacy Keach; Justina Machado; Ann Cusack; David Ramsey; *D:* Richard Pearce; *W:* Ron McGee; *C:* Ivan Strasburg; *M:* Mark Adler. **TV**

Fatal Deception: Mrs. Lee Harvey Oswald **1993** NBC TV movie released for the 30th anniversary of the JFK assassination. Told in flashbacks, it covers decades (not always convincingly) in the life of Soviet-born Marina, the wife of Lee Harvey Oswald, from their courtship to their move to Dallas and what happened to Marina and the Oswald children after that fateful November day. In attempting to cope with the aftermath, Marina comes to believe various conspiracy theorists that her husband did not act alone. **91m/C; DVD.** Helena Bonham Carter; Frank Whaley; Robert Picardo; Bill (William) Bolender; *D:* Robert Dornhelm; *W:* Steve Bello; *C:* Yuri Neyman; *M:* Harald Kloser. **TV**

Fatal Desire **2005** Divorced and lonely ex-cop Joe (Roberts) is working as a pit boss in Atlantic City. He tries online dating and hooks up with younger Tanya (Heche) who flies in from Pittsburgh to start their torrid affair. Eventually Tanya turns out to be a manipulator who uses Joe as her patsy. Based on a true story. **90m/C; DVD.** Eric Roberts; Anne Heche; Mark A. Owen; Kathleen York; James Edward Campbell; *D:* Ralph Hemecker; *W:* Ray Wright; *C:* Anghel Decca; *M:* Joel Goldsmith. **CABLE**

Fatal Error 1/2 *Outsider in Amsterdam; The Outsider; Grijpstra and de Gier* **1983** Dutch police thriller about the investigation of a cop killing. Based on the mystery series by Janwillem van de Wetering. Dubbed. **85m/C; VHS, DVD, Streaming.** *NL* Rutger Hauer; Rijk de Gooyer; Willeke Van Ammelrooy; Donald M. Jones; *D:* Wim Verstappen; *M:* Ennio Morricone.

Fatal Error 1/2 **1999** Digicron, the world's largest media company, is about to connect all the televisions and computers worldwide. But Dr. Nick Baldwin (Sabato Jr.) and Army medical researcher Samantha Carter (Turner) discover that people are dying from an untraceable virus. So is the virus linked to Digicron. Well, what do you think? Adapted from the novel "Reaper" by Ben Mezrich. **91m/C; VHS, DVD.** Antonio Sabato, Jr.; Janine Turner; Robert Wagner; Malcolm Stewart; *D:* Armand Mastroianni; *W:* Rockne S. O'Bannon; *C:* David Geddes; *M:* Ron Ramin. **CABLE**

Fatal Honeymoon 1/2 **2012** Clunky true crime, woman-in-peril Lifetime flick. In 2003, Tina Watson dies under questionable circumstances while scuba diving with her newlywed hubby Gabe on their Australian honeymoon. And Australian detective Campbell and Tina's father Tommy aren't buying Gabe's 'it was an accident' story. **90m/C; Streaming.** Harvey Keitel; Billy Miller; Amber Clayton; Gary Sweet; *D:* Nadia Tass; *W:* Teena Booth; Mac Gudgeon; *C:* David Parker; *M:* Robert Kral. **CABLE**

The Fatal Hour 1/2 **1940** Karloff is enlisted to aid police in solving the murder of a detective. As Karloff is rounding up suspects, three more murders take place. Feeble. **68m/B; VHS, DVD.** Boris Karloff; Marjorie Reynolds; Grant Withers; Charles Trowbridge; John Hamilton; Frank Puglia; Jason Robards, Sr.; *D:* William Nigh; *W:* Scott Darling; George Waggner; *C:* Harry Neumann.

The Fatal Image 1/2 **1990** A mother and daughter on vacation in Paris inadvertantly videotape an international mob hit, making them the target of ruthless assassins. Filmed on location in Paris. **96m/C; VHS, DVD.** Michele Lee; Justine Bateman; Francois Dunoyer; Jean-Pierre Cassel; Sonia Petrovna; *D:* Thomas J. Wright; *C:* Jean-Yves Le Mener. **TV**

Fatal Instinct 1/2 **1992 (R)** A tough-guy cop trying to solve a murder instead finds himself a victim of sexual obsession in this erotic thriller. Also available in an unrated version. Not to be confused with (but doesn't everything sound familiar) "Basic Instinct."

93m/C; VHS, DVD, Streaming. Michael Madsen; Laura Johnson; Antony (Tony) Hamilton; ***D:*** John Dirlam.

Fatal Instinct **1993 (PG-13)** Spoof on erotic thrillers such as "Fatal Attraction" and "Basic Instinct." Suave Assante plays a guy with dual careers—he's both cop and attorney, defending the criminals he's arrested. Young plays a lovelorn psycho who's lost her panties. Plot is worth mentioning only in passing, since the point is to mercilessly skewer the entire film noir tradition. The gags occasionally hit deep-chuckle level, though for every good joke there's at least three that misfire. Clemons of "E Street Band" fame wanders around with sax for background music purposes, typical of the acute self-consciousness of the film. **90m/C; VHS, DVD.** Armand Assante; Sean Young; Sherilyn Fenn; Kate Nelligan; Christopher McDonald; James Remar; Tony Randall; ***Cameo(s):*** Clarence Clemons; Doc Severinsen; ***D:*** Carl Reiner; ***W:*** David O'Malley; ***M:*** Richard Gibbs.

Fatal Justice **1993** Mars is a topnotch assassin who's been in the business too long and knows too much so the agency he works for decides to kill him off. They send young and beautiful professional Diana to do the job but will she be able to when she discovers Mars is actually her father? **90m/C; VHS, DVD.** Joe Estevez; Suzanne Ager; Richard Folmer; Tom Bertino; ***D:*** Gerald Cain; ***W:*** Bret McCormick; ***C:*** Gerald Cain; ***M:*** Jeff Walton.

Fatal Mission **1989 (R)** A Vietnam soldier captures a female Chinese guerilla and uses her as his hostage and guide through the jungle. **84m/C; VHS, DVD.** Peter Fonda; Mako; Tia Carrere; Ted Markland; Jim Mitchum; ***D:*** George Rowe; ***C:*** Phil Parmet.

Fatal Passion *Dark Red* **1994** Two sisters escape from the city after an accidental murder but run straight into the middle of a sacrifical backwoods cult. **90m/C; VHS, DVD.** Lisa Hayland; Joe Pilato; ***D:*** Hugh Parks; ***C:*** Greg Patterson.

Fatal Secrets 1/2 *Balancing the Books* **2009 (R)** Successful, divorced Julia is urged by her two best friends to start dating again but they don't know she's been secretly seeing Scott. He turns out to fall into the psycho category and is soon threatening her, so Julia turns to Rebecca and Sharlene for help. **88m/C; DVD.** Dina Meyer; Vincent Spano; Lea Thompson; Lela Rochon; Ed Begley, Jr.; Ernie Hudson; Tess Harper; ***D:*** Meir Sharony; ***W:*** Marie Burton; ***C:*** James Mathers; ***M:*** Ben Sharony. **VIDEO**

Fatal Trust **2006** After her husband dies, Kate (Johnson) and her young son return to the rural commuity of Ridgewood. She gets a job working for local physician Dr. Mark Lucas (Haydn-Jones) but is warned by elderly Harry Goodman (Fontaine) that Lucas is not what he seems. It turns out the doctor has a bigger god complex than most and that's dangerous. Made for Lifetime. **96m/C; DVD.** Amy Jo Johnson; David Haydn-Jones; Frank Fontaine; Paul Popowich; Carol Alt; Lorne Bass; ***D:*** Philippe Gagnon; ***W:*** Andrew Hilton; ***C:*** Pierre Jodoin; ***M:*** Martin Roy; Vincent Rehel. **CABLE**

Fate Is the Hunter 1/2 **1964** A plane crash kills 53 people and investigators place the blame on pilot Jack Savage (Taylor) and his alleged drinking. Sam McBane (Ford), the director of airline flight ops, doesn't believe his wartime buddy would do anything to endanger his passengers so he enlists the sole survivor, stewardess Martha Webster (Pleshette), to re-create the event. A series of flashbacks show Savage's behavior up to the crash. Adaptation of the Ernest K. Gann novel. **106m/B; DVD, Blu-Ray.** Glenn Ford; Suzanne Pleshette; Rod Taylor; Wally Cox; Mark Stevens; Nancy Kwan; Nehemiah Persoff; Max (Casey Adams) Showalter; Mary Wickes; ***Cameo(s):*** Jane Russell; ***D:*** Ralph Nelson; ***W:*** Harold Medford; ***C:*** Milton Krasner; ***M:*** Jerry Goldsmith.

The Fate of the Furious 1/2 **2017 (PG-13)** The eighth installment of the franchise finds Dom (Diesel) forced into a life of crime and betrayal of his friends by a mysterious new villain, Cipher (Theron), who has something big on him. She's into world domination, or at least showing the people who currently dominate the world what power is all about. The old gang gets back together to try to save the world and bring Dom back into the fold. With this franchise, you pretty much know what to expect: lots of car porn, flying vehicles and insults, and quirky cameos. The latest chapter delivers on all fronts (Helen Mirren!), and seems to bring the crew into "international men of mystery" status. **136m/C; DVD, Blu-Ray.** Vin Diesel; Dwayne "The Rock" Johnson; Jason Statham; Michelle Rodriguez; Tyrese Gibson; ***D:*** F. Gary Gray; ***W:*** Chris Morgan; ***C:*** Stephen F. Windon; ***M:*** Brian Tyler.

Fateless 1/2 *Sorstalansag* **2005** Gyuri is a 14-year-old Hungarian Jewish boy subjected to the horrors of three different concentration camps, surviving only to find isolation in the world around him. An emphasis on the dehumanization of the Jews as they were corralled into these camps gives a unique look and tone from that of other Holocaust pictures. Muddy and miserable perspective is nonetheless visually beautiful. Adapted from a novel by Nobel Prize-winning author Imre Kertesz. **114m/C; DVD.** *HU GE GB* Marcell Nagy; Daniel Craig; Aron Dimeny; Andras M. Kecskes; Jozsef Gyabronka; Endre Harkanyi; Janos Ban; Judit Schell; ***D:*** Lajos Koltai; ***W:*** Imre Kertesz; ***C:*** Gyula Pados; ***M:*** Ennio Morricone.

Father *Apa* **1967** After WWII, a Hungarian youth makes up stories about his dead father's heroism that enhance his own position. Eventually he becomes obsessed with the facts surrounding his father's death at the hands of the enemy and, learning the truth, lays the past to rest. In Hungarian with English subtitles. **85m/B; VHS, DVD.** *HU* Andras Balint; Miklos Gabor; ***D:*** Istvan Szabo; ***W:*** Istvan Szabo.

Father and Scout 1/2 **1994 (PG)** Would-be Eagle Scout Michael (Bonsall) has a problem when he takes his city-bred, whiny, basically incompetent, dad Spenser (Saget) on a camping trip. Made for TV. **92m/C; VHS, DVD.** Bob Saget; Brian Bonsall; Heidi Swedberg; Stuart Pankin; David Graf; Troy Evans; ***D:*** Richard Michaels; ***M:*** David Kitay. **TV**

Father and Son 1/2 *Otets I Syn* **2003** Intense look at a father-son relationship. The father (Shetini), a widower, and son (Neimyshev) have lived a largely hermetic life, creating a relationship that more closely resembles partners than of father and son (and not in the business sense either). As each face new choices, however, they are forced to realize that they may have to let go of their dependence on each other. Second chapter of Alexander Sokurov's trilogy on family relationships, the first being "Mother and Son". **83m/C; DVD.** *GE* Andrei Shetinin; Alexei Neimyshev; Alexander Rasbash; ***D:*** Alexander Sokurov; ***W:*** Sergei Potepalov; ***C:*** Alexander Burov; ***M:*** Andrei Sigle.

The Father Clements Story 1/2 **1987** The true story of a black priest in Chicago who battled the Roman Catholic hierarchy in order to adopt a troubled teenager. **100m/C; VHS, Streaming.** Louis Gossett, Jr.; Malcolm Jamal Warner; Carroll O'Connor; Leon Robinson; Rosetta LeNoire; Ron McClarty; ***D:*** Edwin Sherin. **TV**

Father Figures **2017 (R)** A comedy about adult twin brothers on a quest to learn who their father really is. Fraternal twins Peter (Helms) and Kyle (Wilson) have long believed that their biological father is dead. When their mother Helen (Close) marries Gene (Shearer), she tells them that their father is football star Terry Bradshaw. When that proves untrue, the brothers attempt to learn who their mother could have conceived them with while part of the swinging '70s scene at New York City's famed Studio 54. Unfocused, insincere, and full of lazy humor and superficial performances. **113m/C; DVD, Blu-Ray.** Robert Jon Mello; Ed Helms; Retta; Zachary Haven; Mary Grill; ***D:*** Lawrence Sher; ***W:*** Justin Malen; ***C:*** John Lindley; ***M:*** Rob Simonsen.

Father Goose 1/2 **1964** During WWII, a liquor-loving plane-spotter stationed on a remote Pacific isle finds himself stuck with a group of French refugee schoolgirls and their teacher. Some predictable gags, romance, and heroism fill out the running time pleasantly. Scriptwriters Stone and Tarloff, who were competitors, not collaborators on the project, shared an Oscar. **116m/C; VHS, DVD, Blu-Ray.** Cary Grant; Leslie Caron; Trevor Howard; ***D:*** Ralph Nelson; ***W:*** Peter Stone; Frank Tarloff; ***C:*** Charles B(ryant) Lang, Jr.; ***M:*** Cy Coleman. Oscars '64: Story & Screenplay.

Father Hood **1993 (PG-13)** Family drama has Swayze playing a small-time criminal whose daughter tracks him down after leaving the foster-care shelter where she and her brother are being abused. The family takes to the road, running from both the police and a journalist (Berry) who wants to expose the corrupt foster-care system. The children are obnoxious, Swayze is miscast, and the entire film is a misfire. **94m/C; VHS, DVD, Blu-Ray.** Patrick Swayze; Halle Berry; Sabrina Lloyd; Brian Bonsall; Diane Ladd; Michael Ironside; Bob Gunton; ***D:*** Darrell Roodt; ***W:*** Scott Spencer.

Father Is a Bachelor 1/2 **1950** Sentimental family flick with some musical numbers (Holden's singing voice is dubbed). When his medicine show job comes to an abrupt end, drifter Johnny (Holden) resumes his aimless passion for fishing until five orphans decide to adopt him and make Johnny into a responsible man. They figure he needs a wife to accomplish this and choose small town beauty Prudence (Gray) as his intended. **83m/B; DVD.** William Holden; Coleen Gray; Mary Jane Saunders; Charles Winninger; Lloyd Corrigan; Stuart Erwin; Sig Rumann; Gary Gray; Billy Gray; Clinton Sundberg; ***D:*** Abby Berlin; Norman Foster; ***W:*** James Grant; Aleen Leslie; ***C:*** Burnett Guffey; ***M:*** Arthur Morton.

Father of Invention 1/2 **2011 (PG-13)** Awkward, wannabe comedy has infomercial guru Robert Axle (Spacey) taking a hard fall for a gadget promotion gone wrong. He gets out of prison minus his money and family and tries to make amends to his daughter Claire (Belle), whom workaholic Robert neglected, as well as rebuild his questionable career. **93m/C; DVD, Blu-Ray.** Kevin Spacey; Camilla Belle; Heather Graham; Johnny Knoxville; John Stamos; Virginia Madsen; Michael Rosenbaum; ***D:*** Trent Cooper; ***W:*** Trent Cooper; Jonathan D. Krane; ***C:*** Steve Yedlin; ***M:*** Nick Urata.

Father of Lies 1/2 **2007** Bishop Calvin Jacobs (Powell) has a drinking problem and a church that's deep in debt and he's willing to go to some unscrupulous means to save his ministry. He learns that not trusting in the Lord is his biggest mistake. **102m/C; DVD.** Clifton Powell; Vivica A. Fox; DMX; Clyde Jones; Veronica Berry; Lucius Basten; ***D:*** Phenomenon; ***W:*** Anthony Faia; Evan Scott.

Father of My Children *Le Pere de Mes Enfants* **2009** Workaholic Paris film producer Gregoire Canvel is showing increasing strain as his business collapses. He hides these developments from his frustrated wife Sylvia and his three neglected daughters. He commits suicide and as Sylvia copes with the family's grief she also tries to maintain the company as Gregoire's legacy. French with subtitles. **110m/C; DVD.** *FR* Louis-Do de Lencquesaing; Alice De Lencquesaing; Alice Gautier; Manelle Driss; Chiara Caselli; Eric Elmosnino; Sandrine Dumas; Dominique Frot; ***D:*** Mia Hansen-Love; ***W:*** Mia Hansen-Love; ***C:*** Pascal Auffray.

Father of the Bride 1/2 **1950** A classic, quietly hilarious comedy about the tribulations of a father preparing for his only daughter's wedding. Tracy is suitably overwhelmed as loving father Stanley Banks and Taylor radiant as the bride, Kay. A warm vision of American family life, accompanied by the 1940 MGM short "Wedding Bills." Followed by "Father's Little Dividend" (1951) and later a TV series. Remade in 1991. **106m/C; VHS, DVD, Blu-Ray.** Spencer Tracy; Elizabeth Taylor; Joan Bennett; Billie Burke; Leo G. Carroll; Russ Tamblyn; Don Taylor; Moroni Olsen; ***D:*** Vincente Minnelli; ***W:*** Frances Goodrich; Albert Hackett; ***C:*** John Alton.

Father of the Bride 1/2 **1991 (PG)** Remake of the 1950 comedy classic portrays one of the most overextravagant weddings in recent film history, but falls short of the original. Predictable plot and characters don't hide any surprises, but nothing detracts from the purpose of the film: to be a nice, charming movie. Martin is fine as the reluctant dad but Keaton is little more than window dressing as the bride's mom; Short is annoying as a pretentious wedding coordinator. Williams pulls off a nice film debut—and was almost immediately cast in a TV ad as a young-bride-to-be calling her dad long distance to tell him she's engaged. Adapted from a novel by Edward Streeter. **105m/C; VHS, DVD, Blu-Ray.** Steve Martin; Diane Keaton; Kimberly Williams; Kieran Culkin; George Newbern; Martin Short; B.D. Wong; Peter Michael Goetz; Kate McGregor-Stewart; Martha Gehman; Eugene Levy; ***D:*** Charles Shyer; ***W:*** Charles Shyer; Nancy Meyers; ***C:*** John Lindley; ***M:*** Alan Silvestri.

Father of the Bride Part 2 1/2 **1995 (PG)** Sweetly sentimental update of the 1951 film "Father's Little Dividend" finds George Banks (Martin) once again thrown for a loop—first by his beloved daughter Annie's (Williams) pregnancy and then by wife Nina's (the radiant Keaton) announcement that they are about to become parents themselves. George doesn't deal very well with either situation but, aided by fey party planner Franck (Short), he manages to get through the predictable chaos. Martin's physical expressiveness and sly charm are a big plus. **106m/C; VHS, DVD, Blu-Ray.** Steve Martin; Diane Keaton; Kimberly Williams; Martin Short; George Newbern; Kieran Culkin; Peter Michael Goetz; Kate McGregor-Stewart; Eugene Levy; B.D. Wong; Jane Adams; ***D:*** Charles Shyer; ***W:*** Nancy Meyers; Charles Shyer; ***C:*** William A. Fraker; ***M:*** Alan Silvestri.

Fathers and Daughters 1/2 **2016 (R)** A moving exploration of the connections of family and the impacts of unexpected events told in two parts that occur 25 years apart from two perspectives. After Pulitzer Prize-winning author Jake Davis (Crowe) is involved in a car accident that kills his wife, he is left with a brain injury and has a mental breakdown. His in-laws try to gain custody of his daughter, who inspires him to write his book Fathers and Daughters. As an adult, Katie (Seyfried) is a social worker left with personal issues related to her emotionally traumatic childhood. She struggles to become connected to others as she tries to find love herself. **116m/C; DVD, Streaming, Download.** Russell Crowe; Amanda Seyfried; Aaron Paul; Diane Kruger; Quvenzhane Wallis; ***D:*** Gabriele Muccino; ***W:*** Brad Desch; ***C:*** Shane Hurlbut; ***M:*** Paolo Buonvino.

A Father's Choice 1/2 *Cowboy Dad* **2000** After witnessing their mother's shooting death in L.A., young Chris and Kelly are sent to live in the country with their estranged rodeo-loving dad Mac. With the help of a counselor, the broken family begins to mend until their mother's sister Gayle becomes determined to gain custody of her nieces. Forget the murder subplot because the killer is never identified. **88m/C; DVD.** Peter Strauss; Mary McDonnell; Yvonne Zima; Michelle Trachtenberg; Susan Hogan; Roger R. Cross; Eddie Velez; ***D:*** Christopher Cain; ***W:*** Richard Leder; ***C:*** William Wages; ***M:*** Steve Dorff. **TV**

Father's Day 1/2 **1996 (PG-13)** The comedy team of Williams and Crystal makes its feature film debut in this affable take on fatherhood. Freelance writer Putley (Williams) unites with attorney Lawrence (Crystal) to help their mutual ex-girlfriend Kinski search for her runaway son (she's led each man to believe he's the boy's father). Their quest leads to some inevitable sticky situations, but the erratic, adolescent Williams is wonderfully balanced by the calm, upstanding Crystal. Who needs a son when you have to deal with Williams? Together, they're fun to watch and almost make you forget the contrived plot. Almost. Remake of the 1984 French film "Les Comperes." **98m/C; VHS, DVD.** Robin Williams; Billy Crystal; Nastassja Kinski; Julia Louis-Dreyfus; Charlie Hofheimer; Bruce Greenwood; Jared Harris; Patti D'Arbanville; Charles Rocket; Dennis Burkley; Louis Lombardi; ***D:*** Ivan Reitman; ***W:*** Lowell Ganz; Babaloo Mandel; ***C:*** Stephen Burum; ***M:*** James Newton Howard.

Father's Day 1/2 **2012** Troma is back with another over-the-top gore extravaganza about a serial killer who rapes and kills fathers and the one-eyed vigilante (Brooks), young Priest (Kennedy), and gay prostitute (Sweeney) who literally follow him to Hell seeking vengeance. Extremely unrated, including scenes of ludicrously detailed violence, this grindhouse experiment eventually finds its groove and develops into a kind of loony oddity. Not all of the humor/gore works, but it's certainly as effective as similar higher profile affairs like "Hobo With a Shotgun" and "Machete." **99m/C; DVD, Blu-Ray.** Adam Brooks; Mathew Kennedy; Conor Sweeney; Amy Groening; Garrett Hnatiuk; *D:* Adam Brooks; Mathew Kennedy; Conor Sweeney; Jeremy Gillespie; Steven Kostanski; *W:* Adam Brooks; Mathew Kennedy; Conor Sweeney; Jeremy Gillespie; Steven Kostanski; *C:* Astron-6; *M:* Jeremy Gillespie; Paul Joyce.

Father's Little Dividend 🦴🦴🦴 **1951** Tracy expects a little peace and quiet now that he's successfully married off Taylor in this charming sequel to "Father of the Bride." However, he's quickly disillusioned by the news he'll soon be a grandfather—a prospect that causes nothing but dismay. Reunited the stars, director, writers, and producer from the successfull first film. **82m/B; VHS, DVD.** Spencer Tracy; Joan Bennett; Elizabeth Taylor; Don Taylor; Billie Burke; Russ Tamblyn; Moroni Olsen; *D:* Vincente Minnelli; *W:* Frances Goodrich; Albert Hackett; *C:* John Alton; *M:* Albert Sendrey.

A Father's Revenge 🦴🦴 ½ **1988 (R)** Dennehy is the only reason to bother with this average hostage drama. He's the father of a stewardess who's one of a group being held by terrorists. They're scheduled to die in 72 hours unless Dennehy can find a way to rescue them. **93m/C; VHS, DVD.** Brian Dennehy; Joanna Cassidy; Ron Silver; *D:* John Herzfeld; *M:* Klaus Doldinger. **TV**

Fathom 🦴🦴 ½ **1967** Welch and her bikini fill out the title role as Fathom Harvill, a parachutist who is hired to find a nuclear triggering device that has been lost in the Mediterranean. She eventually hooks up with spy guy Peter Merriweather (Franciosa) and gets involved in a case involving priceless jewelry stolen from China. Spy spoof is oh so '60s. Based on the novel by Larry Forrester. **104m/C; VHS, DVD.** *GB* Raquel Welch; Anthony (Tony) Franciosa; Ronald Fraser; Clive Revill; Richard Briers; Tom Adams; *D:* Leslie Martinson; *W:* Lorenzo Semple, Jr.; *C:* Douglas Slocombe; *M:* John Dankworth.

Fatso 🦴 ½ **1980 (PG)** After the shocking death of his obese cousin, an obsessive overeater struggles to overcome his neurosis with the aid of his sister and a self-help group called "Chubby Checkers." Bancroft's first work as both writer and director. **93m/C; VHS, DVD, Blu-Ray.** Dom DeLuise; Anne Bancroft; Ron Carey; Candice Azzara; *D:* Anne Bancroft; *W:* Anne Bancroft.

Fatwa 🦴🦴 **2006** Junior senator Maggie Davidson (Holly) lets her ambitions get the better of her when she takes a hard-line stance on Islamic terrorism. She attracts the notice of a D.C. sleeper cell that may decide to use a dirty bomb on the National Mall to make a point. **91m/C; DVD.** Lauren Holly; Rachel Miner; John Doman; Lacey Chabert; Angus MacFadyen; Mykelti Williamson; Ryan Sands; *D:* John Carter; *W:* Scott Schafer; *C:* Brian Gurley. **VIDEO**

The Fault In Our Stars 🦴🦴 ½ **2014 (PG-13)** Unabashedly sentimental, emotional, and intense in a way that's not just designed to pull heartstrings but rip them out of your chest, this adaptation of the hit John Green book is a bit superficial but works thanks to a yet-another great performance from Woodley in a film that doesn't really deserve it. Woodley plays Hazel Grace Lancaster, a young woman dying of cancer. Hazel meets Augustus (a slightly miscast Elgort), who shows her that it's not too late for her to find love and happiness. There's nothing overtly wrong with a melodrama every now and then but Woodley is the only one who really finds the truth in Green's book. **125m/C; DVD, Blu-Ray.** Shailene Woodley; Ansel Elgort; Laura Dern; Sam Trammell; Willem Dafoe; Nat Wolff; Mike Birbiglia; Lotte Verbeek; *D:* Josh Boone; *W:* Scott Neustadter; Michael H. Weber; *C:* Ben Richardson; *M:* Mike Mogis; Nate Walcott.

Faults 🦴🦴 ½ **2015** Flawed but effective comedy-drama about cult expert who meets his match when he takes a lucrative deprogramming job. Dr. Ansel Roth (Orser) is a down-on-his-luck cult expert who is broke, in debt, and uncaring about his profession. Life looks up when he meets a couple desperate to rescue their daughter Claire (Winstead) from a cult called Faults. Roth gets Claire off the street and begins the deprogramming process. The dance between Roth and Claire proves them to be formidable opponents. Otherwise the plot fails when focusing on Ansel's debt to his manager and the absurd actions taken to collect it. **89m/C; DVD.** Leland Orser; Mary Elizabeth Winstead; Chris Ellis; Jon(athan) Gries; Lance Reddick; *D:* Riley Stearns; *W:* Riley Stearns; *C:* Michael Ragen; *M:* Heather McIntosh.

Faust 🦴🦴🦴 ½ *Faust-Eine deutsche Volkssage* **1926** The classic German silent based upon the legend of Faust, who sells his soul to the devil in exchange for youth. Based on Goethe's poem, and directed by Murnau as a classic example of Germanic expressionism. Remade as "All That Money Can Buy" in 1941. **117m/B; Silent; VHS, DVD.** *GE* Emil Jannings; Warner Fuetterer; Gosta Ekman; Camilla Horn; *D:* F.W. Murnau; *W:* Hans Kyser; *C:* Carl Hoffmann; *M:* Timothy Brock; Werner R. Heymann.

Faust: Love of the Damned 🦴🦴 **2000 (R)** Very gory, visually impressive horror flick finds artist John Jaspers (Frost) selling his soul to Lucifer minion "M" (Divoff) in exchange for revenge on his wife's killers. Eventually, he gets sent to hell but returns as avenger Faust (in a red rubber suit). There's also a good guy detective (Combs) and a troubled shrink named Jade (Brook) involved in the action. Based on the comic book by Tim Vigil and David Quinn. An unrated version is also available. **96m/C; VHS, DVD.** Mark Frost; Andrew Divoff; Jeffrey Combs; Isabel Brook; *D:* Brian Yuzna; *W:* David Quinn; *C:* Jacques Haitkin; *M:* Xavier Capellas.

The Favor 🦴🦴 ½ **1992 (R)** Lighthearted romance rife with comic confusion, vivid fantasies, secrets, and the all-important favor. Kathy (Kozak) seeks to relieve the boredom of her marriage through best friend Emily's (McGovern) tryst with Kathy's old beau, Tom. Or so she thinks, until Em spills all the juicy details. In a change of pace, the males take a back seat to the women. Good comic performances from Kozak and McGovern and witty dialogue help overcome the plot's sheer silliness. Damian Elwes (actor Cary's brother) provided Pitt's paintings. Theatrical release was delayed three years due to financial crisis at Orion Pictures. **97m/C; VHS, DVD, Blu-Ray.** Harley Jane Kozak; Elizabeth McGovern; Bill Pullman; Brad Pitt; Ken Wahl; Larry Miller; Holland Taylor; *D:* Donald Petrie; *W:* Josann McGibbon; Sara Parriott; *C:* Tim Suhrstedt; *M:* Thomas Newman.

The Favor, the Watch, & the Very Big Fish 🦴🦴 **1992 (R)** Set in a fairytale version of Paris. Hoskins is a photographer of religious subjects searching for a man to pose as Jesus. He discovers his subject in the hirsute Goldblum, a mad bar pianist who actually thinks he's the savior. Richardson plays the object of Hoskin's shy affections, an actress who does dubbing work by providing the moaning and groaning for porno flicks. Messy attempt at screwball-comedy with some brief humorous moments. **89m/C; VHS, Streaming.** *GB FR* Bob Hoskins; Jeff Goldblum; Natasha Richardson; Michel Blanc; Jacques Villeret; Angela Pleasence; Jean-Pierre Cassel; Bruce Altman; Jack Arnold; *D:* Ben Lewin; *W:* Ben Lewin; *C:* Bernard Zitzermann; *M:* Vladimir Cosma.

The Favourite 🦴🦴🦴 **2018 (R)** In this darkly funny romp with royalty, a frail and moderately unhinged Queen Anne (Colman) relies on her companion Lady Sarah (Weisz) to tend to her personal needs and secretly govern England. When a new servant (Stone) arrives and slyly ingratiates herself with the queen, she and Lady Sarah duke it out, aristocratically speaking, to determine who will be crowned the queen's favorite. A stiff period-piece this is not -- the three leads are so delightfully devilish and the humor so anachronistic that corsets are not recommended while viewing. **119m/C; DVD, Blu-Ray.** Olivia Colman; Emma Stone; Rachel Weisz; Nicholas Hoult; Joe Alwyn; *D:* Yorgos Lanthimos; *W:* Deborah Davis; Tony McNamara; *C:* Robbie Ryan. Oscars '18: Actress (Colman); British Acad. '18: Actress (Colman), Actress--Supporting (Weisz), Costume Des., Makeup, Orig. Screenplay, Production Design; Golden Globes '19: Actress--Mus./Comedy (Colman).

Fay Grim 🦴🦴 **2006 (R)** Hartley's sequel to 1998's "Henry Fool" follows the misbegotten adventures of Henry's estranged wife Fay (Posey). Henry's been on the lam for years, but CIA op Fulbright (Goldblum) suddenly turns up and informs Fay that A) Henry's dead; B) Henry was in the CIA; C) his notebook memoirs are actually coded secrets; and D) Fay needs to retrieve them from Paris. So Fay agrees, heads off to Europe, and discovers much chicanery, eventually winding up among terrorists in Istanbul. Posey's game but the elaborate, international thriller spoof of a plot is hard to swallow (or follow). **118m/C; DVD.** *US GE* Parker Posey; Jeff Goldblum; James Urbaniak; Liam Aiken; Saffron Burrows; Elina Lowensohn; Leo Fitzpatrick; Chuck Montgomery; Thomas Jay Ryan; *D:* Hal Hartley; *W:* Hal Hartley; *C:* Sarah Crawley Cabiya.

FBI Code 98 🦴 ½ **1963** FBI Inspector Leroy Gifford investigates whether a bomb discovered in a suitcase is a case of sabotage or attempted murder. Shot as a TV pilot it was released to theaters instead. **104m/B; DVD.** Phil Carey; Jack Kelly; Ray Danton; Andrew Duggan; William Reynolds; Peggy McCay; Jack Cassidy; *D:* Leslie Martinson; *W:* Stanley Niss; *C:* Robert Hoffman; *M:* Max Steiner.

FBI Girl 🦴🦴 **1952** An FBI clerk is used as bait to trap a murderer and break up a gang. Burr, pre-Perry Mason, plays a bad guy. **74m/B; VHS, DVD.** Cesar Romero; George Brent; Audrey Totter; Raymond Burr; Tom Drake; *D:* William Berke.

FBI: Negotiator 🦴 ½ **2005** FBI agent Laura Martin must negotiate with desperate mom Elizabeth Moss who has taken over a hospital. Elizabeth's teen daughter Annie, who happens to be friend of Laura's daughter Taylor, has cancer and Elizabeth is determined that Annie become part of an experimental drug program that is only being handled by a lottery system. **90m/C; DVD.** Elisabeth Rohm; Chandra West; Taylor Anne Reid; Britt Mckillip; Malcolm Stewart; Jerry Wasserman; Matthew (Matt) Walker; *D:* Nicholas (Nick) Kendall; *W:* Joseph Nasser; *C:* Danny Nowak. **CABLE**

The FBI Story 🦴🦴🦴 **1959** Mr. Stewart goes to Washington in this anatomy of the Federal Bureau of Investigation. If you're a fan of the gangster genre (LeRoy earlier directed "Little Caesar"), and not especially persnickity about fidelity to the facts, this actioner offers a pseudo-factual (read fictional) glimpse—based on actual cases from the 1920s through the 1950s—into the life of a fictitious agent-family man. **149m/C; VHS, DVD.** James Stewart; Vera Miles; Nick Adams; Murray Hamilton; Larry Pennell; Diane Jergens; Jean Willes; Joyce Taylor; Ann Doran; Parley Baer; Victor Millan; *D:* Mervyn LeRoy; *W:* Richard L. Breen; John Twist; *C:* Joseph Biroc; *M:* Max Steiner.

Fear 🦴 *Honor Betrayed* **1988 (R)** A vacationing family is plagued by a murderous Vietnam vet and other psychotic cons. **96m/C; VHS, DVD.** Frank Stallone; Cliff DeYoung; Kay Lenz; Robert Factor; Edward (Eddie) Bunker; *D:* Robert A. Ferretti.

Fear 🦴🦴 ½ **1990 (R)** A young psychic (Sheedy) delves into the minds of serial killers and writes novels about her experiences. But what happens when the next killer is also a psychic and decides to play mind-games with her? Above-average suspense sustains this cable thriller. **98m/C; VHS, DVD.** Ally Sheedy; Lauren Hutton; Michael O'Keefe; Stan Shaw; Dina Merrill; John Agar; Marta DuBois; *D:* Rockne S. O'Bannon; *M:* Henry Mancini. **CABLE**

The Fear 🦴 ½ **1994 (R)** Student psychologist (Bowz) takes a group to a remote cabin to explore their fears as part of his research project. Then, they begin to die horribly and gradually figure out that the cabin's wooden mascot, Morty (Weiss), is coming to life and doing them in. **98m/C; VHS, DVD.** Eddie Bowz; Darin Heames; Anna Karin; Leland Hayward; Monique Mannen; Heather Medway; Antonio Todd; Erick Weiss; Vince Edwards; Ann Turkel; Wes Craven; *D:* Vincent Robert; *W:* Ron Ford; *C:* Bernd Heinl; *M:* Robert O. Ragland.

Fear 🦴 ½ *No Fear* **1996 (R)** Wahlberg is a parents' worst nightmare: the violent, obsessed boyfriend of a 16-year-old girl (Witherspoon) as "Fatal Attraction" goes to the prom. Some cleverness, but ultimately follows a familiar, cliched path littered with one-dimensional characters and predictable plot twists. Gory, unconvincing climax kills any credibility that was left. The one standout is Petersen as the girl's protective father. **96m/C; VHS, DVD, Blu-Ray.** Reese Witherspoon; Mark Wahlberg; William L. Petersen; Amy Brenneman; Alyssa Milano; Tracy Fraim; Christopher Gray; Todd Caldecott; *D:* James Foley; *W:* Christopher Crowe; *C:* Thomas Kloss; *M:* Carter Burwell. MTV Movie Awards '97: Song ("Machinehead").

Fear and Loathing in Las Vegas 🦴🦴 **1998 (R)** Hunter S. Thompson's 1971 cult memoir arrives on the big screen about 20 years too late to have any meaning or much entertainment value. Director Gilliam, never one to shy away from weirdness, overdoes everything in trying to capture the wretched excess of the book. Thompson's screen alter-ego Duke (Depp) packs his Caddy with illicit drugs and his equally wasted lawyer (Del Toro), and heads for his next writing assignment—to cover a drug enforcement conference in Vegas. Depp does a great job of impersonating the completely wasted and unlikable Thompson, while Del Toro passes out and pukes a lot in the sidekick role. It's most definitely a one-of-a-kind trip, but not one that most people will be willing to take. **119m/C; VHS, DVD, Blu-Ray, HD-DVD.** Johnny Depp; Benicio Del Toro; Christina Ricci; Gary Busey; Craig Bierko; Ellen Barkin; Cameron Diaz; Flea; Mark Harmon; Katherine Helmond; Michael Jeter; Penn Jillette; Lyle Lovett; Tobey Maguire; Harry Dean Stanton; Tim Thomerson; *D:* Terry Gilliam; *W:* Terry Gilliam; Alex Cox; Tony Grisoni; Tod Davies; *C:* Nicola Pecorini.

The Fear Chamber **WOOF!** *Torture Zone; Chamber of Fear; La Camara del Terror; Torture Chamber* **1968** Hardly a Karloff vehicle. Boris shot the footage for this and three other Mexican "horror" films in LA, an unfortunate swan song to his career, though he was fortunate to be quickly written out of this story. The near plot concerns a mutant rock that thrives on human fear. Doctor Karloff and his assistants make sure the rock is rolling in sacrificial victims (women, of course). A prodigious devaluation of the "B"-grade horror flick, it's so bad it's just bad. **88m/C; VHS, DVD.** *MX* Boris Karloff; Yerye Beirut; Julissa; Carlos East; Sandra Chavez; Eva Muller; Pamela Rosas; Santanon; Isela Vega; *D:* Juan Ibanez; Jack Hill; *W:* Jack Hill; Luis Enrique Vergara; *C:* Austin McKinney; Raul Dominguez.

Fear City 🦴 ½ **1985 (R)** Two partners who own a talent agency are after the psychopath who is killing off their prized strippers with the aid of a local cop. Sleazy look at Manhattan low life. **93m/C; VHS, DVD, Blu-Ray.** Billy Dee Williams; Tom Berenger; Jack Scalia; Melanie Griffith; Rae Dawn Chong; Joe Santos; Maria Conchita Alonso; Rossano Brazzi; *D:* Abel Ferrara; *W:* Nicholas St. John; *C:* James (Momel) Lemmo; *M:* Dick Halligan.

The Fear: Halloween Night 🦴🦴 *Fear 2; Fear: Resurrection* **1999 (R)** Mike Hawthorne, the son of a psycho killer, has been plagued by blackouts. According to a friend, a Halloween eve ritual where a group of friends all face their worst fears could help Mike get rid of the fear of his father that continues to haunt him. Only when Mike awakens from another blackout, it's to discover a murdered friend. Palmer played another serial killer's mom (Jason) in "Friday the 13th." **87m/C; VHS, DVD.** Gordon Currie; Stacy Grant; Brendan Beiser; Betsy Palmer; Emmanuelle Vaugier; Rachel Hayward; Larry Pennell; Phillip Rhys; Myc Agnew; Kelly Benson; *D:* Chris Angel; *W:* Kevin Richards. **VIDEO**

Fear in the Night 🦴🦴🦴 **1947** Suspenseful tale of a murder committed by a man under hypnosis. Fearing his nightmares are real Kelley talks his detective friend into investigating his "crime," which leads them to a mansion, a mirrored room, and a plot that takes some clever and unexpected twists. Remade in 1956 as "Nightmare." **72m/B; VHS, DVD.** Paul Kelly; DeForest Kelley; Ann Doran; Kay Scott; Robert Emmett Keane; *D:* Maxwell Shane; *W:* Maxwell Shane; *C:* Jack Greenhalgh; *M:* Rudolph (Rudy) Schrager.

Fear No Evil 🦴🦴 **1980 (R)** A teenager who is the human embodiment of the demon Lucifer commits acts of demonic murder and destruction. His powers are challenged by an 18-year-old girl, who is the embodiment of the archangel Gabriel. First feature from La Loggia is better than it sounds. **90m/C; VHS, DVD.** Stefan Arngrim; Kathleen Rowe McAllen; Elizabeth Hoffman; ***D:*** Frank Laloggia; ***W:*** Frank Laloggia.

The Fear of 13 🦴🦴🦴 **2015** A feature-length documentary thriller about a convicted murder who is demanding his own execution. For two decades, Nick has been on death row yet not been executed. The documentary follows his efforts to petition the court to force the execution to take place. However, as Nick tells his story, inconsistencies and untruths emerge. As the story twists and turns, information is revealed that makes Nick's story seem more like fiction than fact. **96m/C; DVD.** ***D:*** David Sington; ***C:*** Clive North; ***M:*** Philip Sheppard.

Fear of a Black Hat 🦴🦴 **1994 (R)** Think "Spinal Tap" as gangsta rap and you've the plot of this good-natured imitator. The dim-witted Ice Cold (Cundieff), Tone-Def (Lawrence), and Tasty-Taste (Scott), the trio known as NWH (Niggaz With Hats), are touring in support of their album and trying to convince filmmaker Nina Blackburn (Lemmons) of their street cred. Like Tap's metal-heads, the more they explain themselves, the less sense they make. **87m/C; VHS, DVD.** Larry B. Scott; Mark Christopher Lawrence; Kasi Lemmons; Rusty Cundieff; Lamont Johnson; Howie Gold; Faizon Love; Deezer D; Barry (Shabaka) Henley; Penny Johnson; Eric Laneuville; ***D:*** Rusty Cundieff; ***W:*** Rusty Cundieff; ***C:*** John L. (Ndiaga) Demps, Jr.

Fear of Fear 🦴🦴 *Angst vor der Angst* **1975** Middleclass housewife Margot (Carstensen) begins experiencing intense fear after having her second child but her husband and family dismiss her concerns. So she turns to drugs and alcohol for relief, which only makes her situation worse. German with subtitles. **88m/C; VHS, DVD.** *GE* Margit Carstensen; Brigitte Mira; Irm Hermann; Ulrich Faulhaber; Armin Meier; Adrian Hoven; ***D:*** Rainer Werner Fassbinder; ***W:*** Rainer Werner Fassbinder; ***C:*** Jurgen Jurges; ***M:*** Peer Raben.

Fear of the Dark 🦴🦴 **2002 (PG-13)** Brian doesn't sleep at night because he knows something in the dark is after him. His brother Dale thinks he's just trying to get attention, until the two are home alone when a storm knocks out the power. Creepy and atmospheric, but anyone over the age of 15 will be disappointed by the lack of gore or any over-the-top scares. **86m/C; VHS, DVD.** *CA* Jesse James; Kevin Zegers; Linda Purl; Charles Powell; Rachel (Racheal) Skarsten; ***D:*** K.C. Bascombe; ***W:*** K.C. Bascombe; John Sullivan; ***C:*** Marc Charlebois; ***M:*** Sari Dijani. **VIDEO**

Fear Runs Silent 🦴🦴 **1999 (R)** High school class heads to the woods for an overnight campout. They get stranded. Can you guess what happens? Yes, someone or something tries to kill them! Busy production tries to make up for lack of storyline freshness. **90m/C; VHS, DVD.** Stacy Keach; Billy Dee Williams; Dan Lauria; Bobby Jacoby; Suzanne Davis; Ethan Erickson; Elizabeth Low; ***D:*** Serge Rodnunsky; ***W:*** Serge Rodnunsky; ***C:*** Pierre Chemaly. **VIDEO**

Fear Strikes Out 🦴🦴🦴 **1957** Perkins plays Jimmy Piersall, star outfielder for the Boston Red Sox, and Malden, his demanding father, in the true story of the baseball star's battle for sanity. One of Perkins' best screen performances. **100m/B; VHS, DVD.** Anthony Perkins; Karl Malden; Norma Moore; Adam Williams; Perry Wilson; ***D:*** Robert Mulligan; ***W:*** Raphael David Blau; ***M:*** Elmer Bernstein.

Fear X 🦴🦴🦴 **2003 (PG-13)** Grim, intense thriller stars Turturro as Harry, a security guard at a Wisconsin shopping mall obsessed with finding the truth about his wife's murder. His pursuit takes him across the Midwest into Montana and directly into the path of respected cop Peter (Remar) and his wife, Kate (Unger). Minimal in dialogue and feel, the movie depends on Turturro to hold it together and he does so impressively, portraying Harry as a man so disturbed by grief that the chase becomes more important than finding the truth. Swedish director Refn's American debut. **91m/C; DVD.** John Turturro; Deborah Kara Unger; William Allen Young; James Remar; Stephen McIntyre; Eugene M. Davis; Mark Houghton; Jacqueline Ramel; ***D:*** Nicolas Winding Refn; ***W:*** Nicolas Winding Refn; Hubert Selby, Jr.; ***C:*** Larry Smith; ***M:*** Brian Eno; J. Peter Schwalm.

Feardotcom 🦴 *fear dot com* **2002 (R)** Cyber-thriller features a killer virus on the loose in Manhattan. All the victims shared one thing—48 hours before they logged onto the same web site, which features a live feed of sicko Alistair (Rea) torturing and murdering women. Detective Mike Reilly (Dorff) and Health Department investigator Terry Huston (McElhone) investigate. The visuals are actually interesting; too bad everything else about the movie is awful. **101m/C; VHS, DVD.** *US GB GE LU* Stephen Dorff; Natascha (Natasha) McElhone; Stephen Rea; Jeffrey Combs; Udo Kier; Nigel Terry; Michael Sarrazin; Amelia Curtis; ***D:*** William Malone; ***W:*** Josephine Coyle; ***C:*** Christian Sebaldt; ***M:*** Nicholas Pike.

Fearless 🦴 **1977** An Italian detective has found a Viennese banker's daughter, but continues to pursue the unanswered questions of the case, embroiling himself in a web of intrigue and plotting. **89m/C; VHS, DVD.** *IT* Joan Collins; Maurizio Merli; Franz Antel; ***D:*** Stelvio Massi; ***W:*** Stelvio Massi; ***C:*** Riccardo (Pallton) Pallottini; ***M:*** Stelvio Cipriani.

Fearless 🦴🦴🦴 **1993 (R)** Two plane crash survivors reach out to each other as they try and cope with everday life. Bridges is riveting as the transformed Max, and Perez compelling as the sorrowful Carla. Hulce provides dead-on amusement as a casualty lawyer who knows he's slime but can't help himself. Opening sequences of smoke in the corn fields are haunting as are flashbacks of the crash itself. Weir provides an engrossing look at facing death, both psychological and spiritual, but the ending is something of a letdown in its sappiness. Based on the novel by Yglesias. **122m/C; VHS, DVD, Blu-Ray.** Jeff Bridges; Isabella Rossellini; Rosie Perez; Tom Hulce; John Turturro; Benicio Del Toro; Deirdre O'Connell; John de Lancie; ***D:*** Peter Weir; ***W:*** Rafael Yglesias; ***C:*** Allen Daviau; ***M:*** Maurice Jarre. L.A. Film Critics '93: Support. Actress (Perez).

Fearless Fagan 🦴🦴 ½ **1952** Carnival clown Floyd Hilston is drafted and reports to the Army base with Fearless Fagan, the tame lion he's raised since Fagan was a cub. Floyd needs to convince Sgt. Kellwin to give him a chance to find Fagan a proper new home. Based on a true story from an article published in "Life" magazine. **79m/B; DVD.** Carleton Carpenter; Keenan Wynn; Janet Leigh; Richard Anderson; ***D:*** Stanley Donen; ***W:*** Frederick Hazlitt Brennan; Charles Lederer; ***C:*** Harold Lipstein; ***M:*** Rudolph Kopp.

Fearless Tiger 🦴 ½ **1994 (R)** Martial arts action flick includes the usual combination of fierce swordplay, hand-to-hand show-downs, and the intrigue of exotic locations. **88m/C; VHS, DVD.** *CA* Bolo Yeung; Monica Schnarre; Jamie Farr; Jalal Merhi; ***D:*** Ron Hulme; ***W:*** Ron Hulme; ***M:*** Varouje.

The Fearless Vampire Killers 🦴🦴🦴 *Pardon Me, Your Teeth Are in My Neck; Dance of the Vampires* **1967** Underrated, off-off-beat, and deliberately campy spoof of vampire films in which Tate is kidnapped by some fangy villains. Vampire trackers MacGowran and Polanski pursue the villains to the haunted castle and attempt the rescue. Only vampire movie with a Jewish bloodsucker ("Boy, have you got the wrong vampire," he proclaims to a maiden thrusting a crucifix at him). Inside the castle, Polanski is chased by the count's gay vampire son. Highlight is the vampire ball with a wonderful mirror scene. Many other amusing moments. **98m/C; VHS, DVD, Blu-Ray.** *GB* Jack MacGowran; Roman Polanski; Alfie Bass; Jessie Robins; Sharon Tate; Ferdinand "Ferdy" Mayne; Iain Quarrier; Terry Downes; Fiona Lewis; Ronald Lacey; ***D:*** Roman Polanski; ***W:*** Roman Polanski; Gerard Brach; ***C:*** Douglas Slocombe; ***M:*** Krzysztof Komeda.

The Fearmakers 🦴 ½ **1958** Low-budget red scare conspiracy thriller. Alan Easton (Andrews) is a Korean War vet who was brainwashed as a POW. He returns to his public relations firm in D.C. only to discover his partner has been murdered. He also figures out that the firm is now run by communists who are trying to fix opinion polls and manipulate elections but, with his past, who'll believe him? **84m/B; DVD.** Dana Andrews; Marilee Earle; Dick Foran; Mel Torme; Veda Ann Borg; Kelly Thordsen; Roy Gordon; ***D:*** Jacques Tourneur; ***W:*** Elliot West; Chris Appley; ***C:*** Sam Leavitt; ***M:*** Irving Gertz.

Feast 🦴 ½ **2006 (R)** The third (and last) of Bravo's "Project Greenlight" series finds strangers hanging out in a dive desert bar when Hero (Dane) barges in with a shotgun and a thing's decapitated head. Hero quickly bites it but his wife, Heroine (Rawat), takes over and warns everyone that they are about to be attacked by carnivorous creatures and must work together to survive. Familiar horror story although fast-paced and mildly amusing. Also available unrated. **85m/C; DVD, Blu-Ray, HD-DVD.** Navi Rawat; Balthazar Getty; Henry Rollins; Krista Allen; Clu Gulager; Judah Friedlander; Duane Whitaker; Eric Dane; Jenny Wade; Diane Goldner; ***D:*** John Gulager; ***W:*** Marcus Dunstan; Patrick Melton; ***C:*** Thomas Callaway; ***M:*** Stephen (Steve) Edwards.

Feast 2: Sloppy Seconds **2008** The original was a plotless gorefest involving monsters assaulting a bar in the middle of nowhere in the dead of night. The sequel is a plotless gorefest involving monsters assaulting a small western town in the middle of nowhere in broad daylight. Despite the sequel's bold change of pace, it's really just more of the same. If only it revealed why biker chicks favor middle-of-nowhere western locales. **?m/CDVD.** Jenny Wade; Clu Gulager; Carl Anthony Payne, II; Hanna Putnam; Diane Goldner; Chelsea Richards; Tom Gulager; Martin Klebba; Juan Garcia; Melissa Reed; Katie Supple Callais; Kent Jude Bernard; ***D:*** John Gulager; ***W:*** Patrick Melton; Marcus Dunstan; ***C:*** Kevin Atkinson; ***M:*** Stephen (Steve) Edwards. **VIDEO**

Feast of July 🦴🦴 **1995 (R)** Victorian-era drama, adapted from an H. E. Bates novel, has young Bella (Davidtz) pregnant and abandoned by super-cad Arch (Wise) whom she sets out to find. After a miscarriage, she is taken in by the Wainwright family where she becomes the object of the affections of the three grown sons. Predictably, she falls for and weds the troubled loafer, Con (Chaplin). Naturally (this being Victorian England) tragedy results. Well-crafted, a given considering the producers, but ultimately a familiar telling of an average story. Feature film debut for director Menaul, after an award-winning career in British TV. **116m/C; VHS, DVD, Blu-Ray.** Embeth Davidtz; Ben Chaplin; Tom Bell; Gemma Jones; James Purefoy; Kenneth Anderson; Greg Wise; ***D:*** Christopher Menaul; ***W:*** Christopher Neame; ***C:*** Peter Sova; ***M:*** Zbigniew Preisner.

Feast of Love 🦴 ½ **2007 (R)** University professor Harry (Freeman) dispenses wisdom at his friend Bradley's (Kinnear) coffee shop. And Bradley sure needs it: his wife Kathryn (Blair) has left him for another woman, and his new girlfriend Diana (Mitchell) is still sleeping with her married lover. Meanwhile, Harry also contemplates the love affair between Bradley's teenage employees Chloe (Davalos) and Oscar (Hemingway). As the narrator of these stories of love and loss, Harry doesn't seem to have any problems at all. Hmm. A strange movie that tries to be profound but is largely weightless. **102m/C; DVD.** Morgan Freeman; Greg Kinnear; Jane Alexander; Radha Mitchell; Billy Burke; Selma Blair; Alexa Davalos; Toby Hemingway; Fred Ward; Stana Katic; ***D:*** Robert Benton; ***W:*** Allison Burnett; ***C:*** Kramer Morgenthau; ***M:*** Stephen Trask.

Fed Up 🦴🦴🦴 **2014** Like the crash after the sugar high, this eye-popping documentary sheds light on America's obesity epidemic brought on mostly by a monopolization of corporate food suppliers. Often with a soundtrack similar to that of a horror flick, the voice of Katie Couric warns about the relationship between junk food and diabetes, accompanied with frightening statistics and flashy graphics. At times bordering on a conspiracy rant, at times approaching made-for-TV fluff. But it clicks into place once they follow four obese kids. It's tough to hear a 200-pound 12-year-old sadly explain, "My doctor has said I'm a statistic." **92m/C; DVD, Blu-Ray.** ***Nar:*** Katie Couric; ***D:*** Stephanie Soechtig; ***W:*** Stephanie Soechtig; Mark Monroe; ***C:*** Scott Sinkler; ***M:*** Michael Brook.

Federal Hill 🦴🦴 **1994 (R)** Familiar plot and characters are still well-handled by cast and first time writer/director Corrente. Federal Hill is a working-class, Little Italy section of Providence, Rhode Island. Five buddies, mostly losers, hang out together at a weekly card game. Nicky's (De Sando) a small-time dealer who meets his uptown Brown University sweetie, Wendy (Langdon), when he sells her cocaine. His friends try to warn him, especially short-fused burglar Ralphie (Turturro). And, of course, things go very wrong for practically everyone. The video is available colorized or in the director's version in B&W. **100m/B; VHS, DVD.** Anthony De Sando; Nicholas Turturro; Libby Langdon; Michael Raynor; Jason Andrews; Frank Vincent; Robert Turano; Michael Corrente; ***D:*** Michael Corrente; ***W:*** Michael Corrente; ***C:*** Richard Crudo; ***M:*** Bob Held; David Bravo.

Federal Protection 🦴 ½ **2002 (R)** Chicago mobster Frank Carbone (Assante) decides to go into the witness protection program after barely surviving a hit. But his suburban neighborhood heats up when next-door neighbor Leigh (Featherstone) finds out her husband is cheating on her with her own sister (Meyer) and she turns to Frank for comfort. Meanwhile, Frank is finding life a little too quiet and decides to stir things up by contacting his former partners. Slickly made genre piece if you don't mind watching a familiar story. **94m/C; VHS, DVD.** Armand Assante; Angela Featherstone; Dina Meyer; David Lipper; Maxim Roy; Tony Calabretta; ***D:*** Anthony Hickox; ***W:*** Craig Smith.

Fedora 🦴 ½ **1978** Campy showbiz melodrama. The retired film diva of the title commits suicide and, while attending her funeral, failed indie producer Barry Detweiler recalls how he recently travelled to her Greek villa to try and persuade the actress to make a comeback in his film. Her entourage continually thwarted him and Barry uncovers a secret that easy to discern. Based on the Thomas Tryon novel "Crowned Heads." **110m/C; DVD, Blu-Ray.** *GE* William Holden; Hildegarde Knef; Marthe Keller; Jose Ferrer; Frances Sternhagen; Gottfried John; ***D:*** Billy Wilder; ***W:*** Billy Wilder; I.A.L. Diamond; ***C:*** Gerry Fisher; ***M:*** Miklos Rozsa.

Feds 🦴 ½ **1988 (PG-13)** Two women enter the FBI Academy and take on the system's inherent sexism with feebly comic results. **82m/C; VHS, DVD.** Rebecca De Mornay; Mary Gross; Ken Marshall; Fred Dalton Thompson; Larry Cedar; James Luisi; Raymond Singer; ***D:*** Dan Goldberg; ***W:*** Dan Goldberg; Len Blum; ***M:*** Randy Edelman.

Feed WOOF! **2005** Yuck. A police officer investigates a fetish website where a dominant feeder controls submissive gainers. Only he goes too far and they are force-fed to death. Will definitely put you off your dinner. **105m/C; DVD.** *AU* Jack Thompson; Alex O'Loughlin; Patrick Thompson; Rose Ashton; Gabby Millgate; ***D:*** Brett Leonard; ***W:*** Kieran Galvin; ***C:*** Steve Aronold; ***M:*** Gregg Leonard. **VIDEO**

Feed the Fish 🦴🦴 **2009** Quirky small town rom com filmed in Door County, Wisconsin. Children's writer Joe Peterson (Partridge) is suffering from writer's block so his friend JP (Chernus) convinces him to leave L.A. and travel with him to his hometown of Sturgeon Bay, WI. JP wants to continue his family's Christmas tradition of participating in the Polar Bear Plunge into Lake Michigan. Once there, Joe falls for beautiful waitress Sif Anderson (Aselton), but has to deal with her overprotective sheriff father (Shalhoub) and her fisherman granddad (Corbin). **92m/C; DVD.** Ross Partridge; Tony Shalhoub; Katie (Kathryn) Aselton; Barry Corbin; Michael Chernus; Vanessa Branch; ***D:*** Michael Matzdorff; ***W:*** Michael Matzdorff; ***C:*** Steven Parker; ***M:*** T.D. Lind.

Feedback 🦴🦴 **2020** Provocative disc jockey Jarvis Dolan (Marsan) is at work in his studio when masked invaders break in and hold him at gunpoint. They demand that he reads a text on air in which he confesses that he and his former partner Andrew (Anderson) violently sexually assaulted someone at a resort. The question lingers about the truthfulness of their accusation as Jarvis is well known for his left-leaning rants and the invaders may be linked to right wing trolls who want to ruin Jarvis. The riveting suspense thriller is timely and tense but its story is at times muddled. **97m/C; DVD.** Eddie Marsan; Paul Anderson; Ivana Baquero; Richard Brake;

Oliver Coopersmith; *D:* Pedro C. Alonso; *W:* Pedro C. Alonso; Alberto Marini; *C:* Angel Iguacel; *M:* Sergio Moure.

Feeders WOOF! 1996 Ya gotta love a low-budget film with the tagline "Earth was just an appetizer!" Okay, so maybe "love" isn't exactly what you'll be thinking. Anyway, Derek and Bennett are heading to the east coast for a vacation when they have a deadly UFO encounter with some flesh-eating aliens, who think earthlings are the perfect snack food. **80m/C; VHS, DVD.** Jon McBride; John Polonia; Sebastian Barran; Melissa Torpy; Maria Russo; Todd Carpent; Gary LeBlanc; *D:* Jon McBride; John Polonia; Mark Alan Polonia; *W:* Jon McBride; Mark Alan Polonia; *C:* Arthur Daniels.

Feel My Pulse 🦴🦴 **1928** Silent comedy about a rich fanatic who leaves everything in his will to his young niece on the stipulation that she lead a germ-free life; when she reaches 21, she moves into the sanitarium she's inherited, not knowing it has become a base for prohibition-era rum runners. **86m/B; Silent; VHS, DVD.** Bebe Daniels; Richard Arlen; William Powell; *D:* Gregory La Cava.

Feel the Beat 🦴🦴 **2020** Dancer April (Carson) is Broadway hopeful until a failed audition and related public humiliation leads her to return home to Wisconsin. Taking a job teaching a local ballet studio where she was once a student, she revives her dance career by taking part in a youth dance composition with her students, including Kari (Jewett) and Sarah (Hauge). April's selfish personality and difficult teaching style damages her efforts and scares her students. It's the usual underdog story, but the enthusiastic performances from the young ensemble cast make the comedy-drama watchable. **109m/C; DVD.** Sofia Carson; Pamela MacDonald; Sonia Laplante; Brandon Kyle Goodman; Rex Lee; *D:* Elissa Down; *W:* Michael Armbruster; Shawn Ku; *C:* Amir M. Mokri; *M:* Michael Yezerski.

Feel the Noise 🦴 **1/2 2007 (PG-13)** Familiar scenario plays out to the sultry beat of reggaeton. When Harlem rapper Rob (Grandberry) tangles with a local gangster, his mom ships him off to Puerto Rico to live with his estranged dad (Esposito) and his family. Stepbrother Javi (Rasuk) introduces Rob to the local scene and music as well as sexy sweet dancer C.C. (Henao). She pushes Rob's musical ambitions, which eventually leads everyone back to New York. The soundtrack will probably do better than the movie. **86m/C; DVD.** Omari (Omarion) Grandberry; Victor Rasuk; James McCaffrey; Giancarlo Esposito; Zulay Henao; Kellita Smith; Melonie Diaz; *D:* Alejandro Chomski; *W:* Albert Leon; *C:* Zoran Popiv; *M:* Andres Levin.

Feeling Minnesota 🦴 **1996 (R)** A truly stupid movie about truly stupid, mostly nasty people. Petty criminal Jjaks (Reeves) shows up at sleazy older brother Sam's (D'Onofrio) wedding and promptly falls for beautiful-but-unhappy bride Freddie (Diaz), who's being forced into the marriage by local crime boss Red (Lindo). Manipulative Freddie easily convinces Jjaks to run away to Vegas with her but Sam isn't willing to let his bride go so easily. The only character who comes off with any dignity is the diner waitress played by Love. A very lame first effort from Baigelman. Title's from a Soundgarden song about "looking California and feeling Minnesota." **96m/C; VHS, DVD.** Keanu Reeves; Cameron Diaz; Vincent D'Onofrio; Delroy Lindo; Dan Aykroyd; Courtney Love; Tuesday Weld; Levon Helm; *D:* Steven Baigelman; *W:* Steven Baigelman; *C:* Walt Lloyd.

Feet First 🦴🦴 **1/2 1930** A shoe salesman puts on "upper crust" airs as he begins a shipboard romance with a girl who thinks he's wealthy. Lloyd's second sound film shows him grappling with technique and has scenes that recall highlights of his silent hits. **85m/B; VHS, DVD.** Harold Lloyd; Barbara Kent; Robert McWade; *D:* Clyde Bruckman.

Felicia's Journey 🦴🦴🦴 **1999 (PG-13)** Joseph Ambrose Hilditch (Hoskins) is a mild-mannered, fastidious, middle-aged Brit whose mother problems have turned him into a serial killer. He's a catering manager who watches tapes of his flamboyant late mother Gala's (Khanjian) cooking show, where young Hilditch was an embarassed foil. Into his structured world stumbles pregnant Irish teen, Felicia (Cassidy), who's trying to find the father of her baby. Hilditch begins to take a warped interest in Felicia, who may be naive but who isn't dumb. Cold and elegant adaptation of William Trevor's novel. **111m/C; VHS, DVD.** *CA GB* Bob Hoskins; Elaine Cassidy; Arsinee Khanjian; Peter McDonald; Gerard McSorley; Brid Brennan; Claire Benedict; *D:* Atom Egoyan; *W:* Atom Egoyan; *C:* Paul Sarossy; *M:* Mychael Danna. Genie '99: Actor (Hoskins), Adapt. Screenplay, Cinematog., Score.

Felicidades 🦴🦴 *Merry Christmas* **2000** A not exactly joyous story set on Christmas Eve but probably much more realistic about the expectations that the holiday brings to people. A random group of men and women randomly cross paths during the evening—a doctor eager to seduce a beautiful woman, a father doing some last-minute shopping, a man in a wheelcar, a writer—all looking for some connection that they're not finding. Bittersweet rather than bitter but also frustrating because you learn so little about the characters. Spanish with subtitles. **100m/C; VHS, DVD.** *AR* Gaston Pauls; Silke Klein; Luis Machin; Pablo Cedron; Carlos Bellaso; Marcello Mazzarello; *D:* Lucho Bender; *W:* Pablo Cedron; Lucho Bender; Emilio Bender; *C:* Daniel Sotelo; *M:* Andres Goldstein; Daniel Tarrals.

Fellini: I'm a Born Liar 🦴🦴 *Fellini: Je suis un grand menteur; Federico Fellini: Sono un gran bugiardo; Fellini: Sono un gran bugiardo* **2003** Documentary includes an interview with the filmmaker Frederico Fellini, as well as with those who worked with him, most notably Donald Sutherland and Roberto Benigni. Director Pettigrew uses Fellini's interview as the foundation of the film, but focuses on Fellini the enigma rather than his work or his life. Clips from Fellini's films are used frequently but not labeled; nor are the numerous interviews with the people who have been part of the filmmaker's career. You get a sense of his style, but very little information about his life or his films. For dedicated Fellini fans only—everyone else should just start with his movies. **89m/C; VHS, DVD.** *GE* Federico Fellini; Donald Sutherland; Terence Stamp; Giuseppe Rotunno; Roberto Benigni; *D:* Damian Pettigrew; *W:* Damian Pettigrew; Olivier Gal; *C:* Paco Wiser.

Fellini Satyricon 🦴🦴🦴 *Satyricon* **1969 (R)** Fellini's famous, garish, indulgent pastiche vision of ancient Rome, based on the novel "Satyricon" by Petronius, follows the adventures of two young men through the decadences of Nero's reign. Actually an exposition on the excesses of the 1960s, with the actors having little to do other than look good and react to any number of sexual situations. Crammed with excesses of every variety. In Italian with English subtitles. **129m/C; VHS, DVD, Blu-Ray.** *IT FR* Martin Potter; Capucine; Hiram Keller; Salvo Randone; Max Born; Alain Cuny; *D:* Federico Fellini; *W:* Federico Fellini; Bernardino Zapponi; *C:* Giuseppe Rotunno; *M:* Nino Rota.

Fellini's Roma 🦴🦴 **1/2** *Roma* **1972 (R)** Fellini reviews his youth in this stream-of-consciousness homage to Rome and Italy. Best left for fervent Fellini fans. **128m/C; VHS, DVD, Blu-Ray.** *FR IT* Peter Gonzales; Britta Barnes; Pia de Doses; Fiona Florence; Marne Maitland; Renato Giovannoli; ***Cameo(s):*** Gore Vidal; Anna Magnani; Marcello Mastroianni; *V:* Federico Fellini; *D:* Federico Fellini; *W:* Federico Fellini; *C:* Giuseppe Rotunno; *M:* Nino Rota.

Felon 🦴🦴 **2008 (R)** Prison pic avoids preaching and exploitation. Wade Porter (Dorff) takes a swing at a burglar with a baseball bat, the intruder ends up dead, and Wade ends up in the joint for manslaughter. In the highly polarized prison atmosphere, Wade is forced to find allies, especially since the only way lead guard Jackson (Perrineau) keeps order is through violence. Wade's cellmate is lifer John Smith (Kilmer), who gives him a crash course in survival, and Wade's dehumanization begins. Filmed on location at a New Mexico correction facility. **104m/C; DVD.** Stephen Dorff; Harold Perrineau, Jr.; Val Kilmer; Sam Shepard; Nick (Nicholas) Chinlund; Johnny Lewis; Marisol Nichols; Anne Archer; *D:* Ric Roman Waugh; *W:* Ric Roman Waugh; *C:* Dana Gonzales; *M:* Gerhard Daum.

Felony 🦴 **1/2 1995 (R)** Police seek revenge when 12 cops are murdered. Turns out the culprit is a rogue CIA agent, whose spree was captured on video by a tabloid-show cameraman. **90m/C; VHS, DVD.** Lance Henriksen; Leo Rossi; Joe Don Baker; Charles Napier; Ashley Laurence; Cory (Corinna) Everson; *D:* David A. Prior; *W:* David A. Prior; *M:* Jan A.P. Kaczmarek.

Felony 🦴🦴 **1/2 2013** Three police detectives find themselves at odds when a horrific accident puts them on opposing sides. A successful drug bust leads to Mal celebrating too hard and causing a hit-and-run when he strikes a young bicyclist, who's then hospitalized in a coma. Veteran detective Carl helps Mal cover up the facts, but rookie Jim's persistent questions--and Mal's increasingly guilty conscience-- make for a moral quagmire. **116m/C; DVD, Blu-Ray, Streaming.** *AU* Jai Courtney; Joel Edgerton; Tom Wilkinson; Melissa George; Sarah Roberts; *D:* Matthew Saville; *W:* Joel Edgerton; *C:* Mark Wareham; *M:* Bryony Marks.

Felt 🦴🦴 **2015** Inspired by the real life experiences and art Amy Everson, this feminist thriller explores a woman's means of coping with all that has happened in her life. As she lives her daily life, Amy (Everson) can barely handle the effects of past sexual traumas and the nature of a male-dominated society. To cope, she creates alter egos—complete with elaborate, sometimes grotesque costumes—to give her a sense of power. Amy's world is profoundly changed when she starts a relationship with a nice new guy (Audley). Though she can be vulnerable, her alter egos emerge threatening to create havoc and seek vengeance. **80m/C; DVD.** Amy Everson; Kentucker Audley; Ryan Creighton; Brendan Miller; Tony Ruiz; *D:* Jason Banker; *W:* Amy Everson; Jason Banker; *C:* Jason Banker.

The Female Brain 🦴🦴 **2018** A romantic comedy based on a 2007 nonfiction bestseller by Louann Brizendine. Neurologist Julia Brizendine (Cummings) studies the effects of stimuli on male and female brain chemistry. Because of her work, Julia refuses to be involved a relationship, until she meets Kevin (Kebbell) who comes into her lab to serve as a test subject. The film also explores the relationships of three couples who have served as Julia's subjects, including a probasketball player (Griffin) and advertising executive (Strong) who find their marriage strained when he is injured. Comedian Cummings' filmmaking debut is uneven but has memorable moments. **98m/C; DVD, Blu-Ray.** Whitney Cummings; Toby Kebbell; Sofia Vergara; Beanie Feldstein; James Marsden; *D:* Whitney Cummings; *W:* Whitney Cummings; Neal Brennan; Louann Brizendine; *C:* Bradford Lipson; *M:* Jeff Cardoni.

Female On the Beach 🦴 **1/2 1955** There's more scenery chewing than acting in this woman-in-peril pic. Wealthy widow Lynn Markham (Crawford) rents a beach house where the previous female tenant died in a mysterious fall. The icy dame is melted by local gigolo Drummond Hall (Chandler) and Lynn marries the hunk despite her misgivings, putting her own life in danger. **97m/B; DVD, Blu-Ray.** Joan Crawford; Jeff Chandler; Jan Sterling; Cecil Kellaway; Natalie Schafer; Charles Drake; *D:* Joseph Pevney; *W:* Richard Alan Simmons; Robert Hill; *C:* Charles B(ryant) Lang, Jr.

Female Perversions 🦴🦴 **1996 (R)** Psycho-sexual story of Los Angeles attorney Eve Stephens (Swinton), who, because of bizarre dreams and fantasies, leads a dual life. Successful Eve is being considered for appointment as a judge, but her enormous insecurity and neuroses only increase, landing her in kinky relationships with both sexes. During an unlikely reunion with her sister, Madelyn (Madigan), a kleptomaniac with a Ph.D., Eve is forced to spend time with Madelyn's motley roommates—her landlady and the landlady's odd daughter and sister. This semi-reunion brings about some self-realization on the part of both sisters about their dysfunctional behavior. Filled with detailed symbolism, powerful imagery, and dream sequences. Rife with Freudian psychology, movie is based on Louise J. Kaplan's feminist study on female behavior and sexuality, "Female Perversions: The Temptations of Emma Bovary." Extremely glossy visuals and rich production design brings life to this rather heavy story. **110m/C; VHS, DVD.** Tilda Swinton; Amy Madigan; Karen Sillas; Laila Robins; Clancy Brown; Frances Fisher; Paulina Porizkova; Lisa Jane Persky; Dale Shuger; *D:* Susan Streitfeld; *W:* Susan Streitfeld; Julie Hebert; *C:* Teresa Medina; *M:* Debbie Wiseman.

Female Trouble 🦴🦴 **1/2 1974 (R)** Divine leads a troublesome existence in this $25,000 picture. She turns to a life of crime and decadence, seeking to live out her philosophy: "Crime is beauty." Look closely at the Divine rape scene where she plays both rapist and victim. Climax of her deviant ways comes with her unusual night club act, for which the law shows no mercy. Trashy, campy; for die-hard Waters fans. **95m/C; VHS, DVD, Blu-Ray.** Divine; David Lochary; Mary Vivian Pearce; Mink Stole; Edith Massey; Cookie Mueller; Susan Walsh; Michael Potter; Ed Peranio; Paul Swift; George Figgs; Susan Lowe; Channing Wilroy; Pat Moran; Elizabeth Coffey; George Stover; *D:* John Waters; *W:* John Waters; *C:* John Waters.

Female Vampire 🦴 *Erotikill; The Loves of Irina; Les Avaleuses; The Bare Breasted Contessa* **1973** Franco's dreamy, sanguine, produced-on-a-dime tale of a vampiress. She cruises the Riviera, seducing and nibbling on a variety of men and women. Not for most tastes. **95m/C; VHS, DVD, Blu-Ray.** *FR SP GE* Lina Romay; Monica Swin; Jack Taylor; Alice Arno; *D:* Jess (Jesus) Franco; *C:* Jess (Jesus) Franco; *M:* Daniel White.

Femalien 🦴 **1996 (R)** Advanced alien beings, composed of pure light energy, travel to earth to assume corporal form so they can once again experience sexual pleasure. **90m/C; VHS, DVD.** Vanessa Taylor; Jacqueline Lovell; Matt Schue; *D:* Cybil (Sybil) Richards; David DeCoteau; *W:* Cybil (Sybil) Richards; David DeCoteau. **VIDEO**

Femalien 2 🦴 **1/2 1998** Sofcore sequel offers more of the same, with slightly more wit and the semblance of story between the canoodling. Two more aliens come to Earth looking for their colleague Kara. Much sexy shenanigans and madcap things ensue, in typical exploitation fashion. **93m/C; DVD.** Vanessa Taylor; Debra Summers; Bethany Lorraine; Josh Edwards; Summer Leeds; Damian Wells; *D:* Cybil (Sybil) Richards; David DeCoteau; *W:* Cybil (Sybil) Richards; David DeCoteau; *C:* Gary Graver; *M:* Wayne Scott Joness. **VIDEO**

Femme Fatale 🦴🦴 **1/2 2002 (R)** DePalma's latest exercise in leering style over substance works because he does stunning, sparkling visuals so well, and because he uses Rebecca Romijn-Stamos to show them off. She's Laure, a sleek jewel thief who, when we first see her, is seducing the diamond-encrusted bra off a supermodel at Cannes. Convoluted heist-doublecross-mistaken-identity plot keeps the surprises coming often enough that you don't have much time to consider their plausibility as Laure goes from thief to grieving widow to ambassador's wife and back, while toying with paparazzo Banderas. **112m/C; VHS, DVD.** *FR* Rebecca Romijn; Antonio Banderas; Peter Coyote; Gregg Henry; Eriq Ebouaney; Edouard Montoute; Rie Rasmussen; Thierry Fremont; *D:* Brian De Palma; *W:* Brian De Palma; *C:* Thierry Arbogast; *M:* Ryuichi Sakamoto.

The Fence 🦴🦴 **1/2 1994** Interesting presentation of standard bad boy grows up, attempts to go straight. Terry Griff (Wirth) has been bounced from juvenile detention to prison since he was 15. On the streets for the first time in 14 years, Terry wants to lead a clean life with potential girlfriend Jackie (Gimpel). But when Terry gets on the wrong side of his dishonest parole officer, the harsh world of the streets pulls him back. Bleak urban drama with sincere performances. **90m/C; VHS, DVD.** Billy Wirth; Erica Gimpel; Marc Alaimo; Paul Benjamin; Lorenzo Clemons; *D:* Peter Pistor; *W:* Peter Fedorenko; *C:* John Newby; *M:* Jeff Beal.

The Fencer 🦴🦴🦴 *Miekkailija* **2015** Partly based on the life of Estonian fencer Endel Nelis, Endel is a fencer who returns to his homeland to evade the Russian secret police who seek him because of dubious past actions. There, he trains children in fencing, but when his past finds him, he must chose between being in danger and abandoning his students. **93m/C; DVD.** Mart Avandi; Liisa Koppel; Lembit Ulfsak; Kirill Karo; Kai Nordberg;

D: Klaus Haro; *W:* Anna Heinamaa; *C:* Tuomo Hutri; *M:* Gert Wilden, Jr.

Fences 🦴🦴🦴 **2016 (PG-13)** Denzel Washington directs and stars in this adaptation of August Wilson's award-winning play, wisely casting his co-star Viola Davis in arguably the most essential role (both won Tonys in 2010 for their performances). Davis plays Rose, wife to Washington's Troy, and father to Cory (Adepo). Set in Pittsburgh in the 1950s, Troy is a belligerent, selfish man, who butts heads with his son after the boy seeks an athletic scholarship. Troy is full of stories, but is also a defiantly selfish man, and Washington captures him perfectly, although Davis steals the movie. **139m/C; DVD, Blu-Ray.** Denzel Washington; Viola Davis; Stephen Henderson; Jovan Adepo; Russell Hornsby; *D:* Denzel Washington; *W:* August Wilson; *C:* Charlotte Bruus Christensen; *M:* Marcelo Zarvos. Oscars '16: Actress--Supporting (Davis); British Acad. '16: Actress--Supporting (Davis); Golden Globes '17: Actress--Supporting (Davis); Screen Actors Guild '16: Actor (Washington), Actress (Davis).

Fender Bender 🦴🦴 **2016** In a somewhat unbelievable premise, a serial killer travels America, rear ending other drivers to get their insurance information to track them down and off them later while dressed in a leather gimp suit. Sadly, this time around his plans for a quick and easy kill are spoiled by his target holding a house party, but he manages to muddle though with dogged persistence. **87m/C; DVD, Blu-Ray, Streaming.** Makenzie Vega; Cassidy Freeman; Bill Sage; Dre Davis; Kelsey Montoya; *D:* Mark Pavia; *W:* Mark Pavia; *C:* Tyler Lee Cushing.

Fer-De-Lance 🦴 **1/2** *Operation Serpent* **1974** A stricken submarine is trapped at the bottom of the sea, with a nest of deadly snakes crawling through the ship. **120m/C; VHS, DVD.** David Janssen; Hope Lange; Ivan Dixon; Jason Evers; *D:* Russ Mayberry. **TV**

Ferdinand 🦴🦴 **1/2 2017 (PG)** Animated feature about a nonconformist bull, based on a popular children's book. Since childhood, Ferdinand (Cena) wasn't interested in bullfighting but instead enjoys flowers and being a little girl's pet. After growing to full size, massive Ferdinand is forced to train to fight in the ring. When he learns that bulls who fight lose their lives, he wants to avoid the ring more than ever. This position is tested when he is selected to fight respected matador El Primero (Silvestre). Fun and thoughtful with clever moments, an interesting cast, and an unexpected questioning of male gender expectations. **108m/C; DVD, Blu-Ray.** John Cena; Bobby Cannavale; Raul Esparza; Jack Gore; Jet Jurgensmeyer; *D:* Carlos Saldanha; *W:* Robert L. Baird; Tim Federle; Brad Copeland; *C:* Renato Falcao; *M:* John Powell.

Ferngully: The Last Rain Forest 🦴🦴 **1/2 1992 (G)** Animated eco-musical follows the adventures of independent-minded flying sprite Crysta, who lives in a rain forest beset by pollution. She discovers the outside world and becomes smitten with the human Zak, who is helping to cut down the forest. Crysta decides to reduce him to her size and show him the error of his ways. She's aided by fellow sprite, Pips, and a crazy bat (Batty Koda with a voice provided by the lively Williams). So-so script with politically pristine environmental message may grow tiresome for both adults and children, though decent animation and brilliant coloring enlivens the tale. **80m/C; VHS, DVD, Blu-Ray.** *V:* Samantha Mathis; Christian Slater; Robin Williams; Tim Curry; Jonathan Ward; Grace Zabriskie; Richard "Cheech" Marin; Thomas Chong; Tone Loc; Jim Cox; *D:* Bill Kroyer; *W:* Jim Cox; *M:* Alan Silvestri.

Ferocious Female Freedom Fighters 🦴 **1988** A typical foreign-made action flick with female wrestlers is spoofed by the L.A. Connection comedy troupe which did the totally ridiculous dubbed dialog. **90m/C; VHS, DVD.** Eva Arnaz; Barry Prima; Leyli Sagita; Wieke Widowati; Ruth Pelupessi; Aminah Cendrakasih; *D:* Yopi Burnama; *W:* Deddy Armand; Charles Kaufman; Joey Gaynor; *C:* Asmawi; *M:* Gatot Sudarto.

Ferocious Planet 🦴 **2011** Part of the Syfy Channel's "Maneater" series. Scientists trying to get more government funding show off their project, which is supposed to allow glimpses into alternate universes. The device malfunctions and actually transports those present into a universe populated by large creatures that want to eat the strangers. **88m/C; DVD.** Joe Flanigan; Catherine Walker; Dagmar Doring; Yare Michael Jegbefume; Chris Newman; John Rhys-Davies; Robert Soohan; *D:* Billy O'Brien; *W:* Douglas Davis; *C:* Peter J. Robertson; *M:* Ray Harman. **CABLE**

Ferris Bueller's Day Off 🦴🦴🦴 **1986 (PG-13)** It's almost graduation and if Ferris can get away with just one more sick day—it had better be a good one. He sweet talks his best friend into borrowing his dad's antique Ferrari and sneaks his girlfriend out of school to spend a day in Chicago. Their escapades lead to fun, adventure, and almost getting caught. Broderick is charismatic as the notorious Bueller with Grey amusing as his tattletale sister doing everything she can to see him get caught. Early Sheen appearance as a juvenile delinquent who pesters Grey. Led to TV series. One of Hughes' more solid efforts. **103m/C; VHS, DVD, Blu-Ray.** Matthew Broderick; Mia Sara; Alan Ruck; Jeffrey Jones; Jennifer Grey; Cindy Pickett; Edie McClurg; Charlie Sheen; Del Close; Virginia Capers; Max Perlich; Louie Anderson; Richard Edson; Lyman Ward; Kristy Swanson; Larry "Flash" Jenkins; Ben Stein; *D:* John Hughes; *W:* John Hughes; *C:* Tak Fujimoto; *M:* Ira Newborn. Natl. Film Reg. '14.

Ferry to Hong Kong 🦴 **1/2 1959** World-weary, heavy drinking traveler comes aboard the "Fat Annie," a ship skippered by the pompous Captain Hart. The two men clash, until an act of heroism brings them together. Embarrassingly hammy performance by Welles as the ferry skipper. **103m/C; VHS, DVD.** Curt Jurgens; Orson Welles; Sylvia Syms; *D:* Lewis Gilbert.

Fertile Ground 🦴 **1/2 2010 (R)** All-too-obvious haunted house horror. After a miscarriage, grieving Nate (Harold) and Emily (Hailey) Weaver relocate to his secluded ancestral home in upstate New York. Soon Emily is pregnant again, and terrified after seeing bloody ghosts of previous inhabitants, while Nate's personality undergoes a radical change to the dark side. **95m/C; DVD.** Leisha Hailey; Gale Harold; Chelcie Ross; Jonelle Kennedy; Jami Bassman; *D:* Adam Gierasch; *W:* Adam Gierasch; Jace Anderson; *C:* Yaron Levy; *M:* Joseph Conlan. **VIDEO**

Festival at Cannes 🦴🦴 **1/2 2002 (PG-13)** That would be the Cannes Film Festival where everyone is hustling in one way or another. American actress Alice (Scacchi) is looking for financing for her first directorial effort and offers the lead to aging actress Millie Marquand (Aimee). But Millie has been offered major moolah to play a mother role in a big studio pic by desperate producer Rick Yorkin (Silver). Then there's Millie's flagrantly unfaithful director/husband Viktor (Schell), wheeler-dealer Kaz (Norman), and Blue (Gabrielle), a starlet promoting an indie pic that's an unexpected hit, as well as numerous other associates, assistants, and hangers-on. **99m/C; VHS, DVD.** Greta Scacchi; Anouk Aimee; Ron Silver; Zack Norman; Jenny Gabrielle; Maximilian Schell; Kim Kolarich; Rachel Bailit; Alex Craig Mann; Peter Bogdanovich; Camilla Campanale; *D:* Henry Jaglom; *W:* Henry Jaglom; *C:* Hanania Baer; *M:* Gaili Schoen.

Festival Express 🦴🦴🦴🦴 **2003 (R)** In 1970, rock promoters Ken Walker and Thor Eaton orchestrated a lollapalooza featuring Janis Joplin, the Grateful Dead, the Band, the Flying Burrito Bros., Delany & Bonnie, Ian & Sylvia, Buddy Guy and Sha Na Na. For five days the musicians traveled by private train across Canada, playing concerts, socializing, trading riffs, and partying. A film crew recorded the event, but in the chaos following the tour the footage was lost for decades, only to later be restored by the producer's son. The electrifying sequences of Janis Joplin capture her at the height of a self-consuming talent months prior to her death. A must-see for fans of the bands, the era, and its music. **90m/C; DVD, Blu-Ray.** *CA D:* Bob Smeaton; *C:* Bob Fiore; Peter Biziou.

Feu Mathias Pascal 🦴🦴 **1/2** *The Living Dead Man* **1926 (PG)** A disillusioned young man restarts his life after striking it rich and being declared falsely dead. To his dismay, he quickly finds his new life is no better than his old one. **170m/B; Silent; Blu-Ray.** *FR* Ivan Mozzhukhin; Lois Moran; Michel Simon; Pierre Batcheff; Marcelle Pradot; *D:* Marcel L'Herbier; *W:* Marcel L'Herbier; *C:* Jimmy Berliet; Fedote Bourgassof; Paul Guichard; Rene Guichard; Jean Letort; Nikolas Roudakoff; *M:* J. E. Szyfer. **VIDEO**

Feudin', Fussin', and A-Fightin' 🦴🦴 **1/2 1948** Cornpone slapstick comedy highlighted by the musical accomplishments of O'Connor. Quick-moving traveling salesman Wilbur McMurty is passing through the tiny western town of Rim Rock when the inhabitants force him to represent them in the annual footrace (which they always lose) with their rival community Big Bend. **78m/B; DVD.** Donald O'Connor; Marjorie Main; Penny Edwards; Percy Kilbride; Joe Besser; Harry Shannon; Fred Kohler, Jr.; *D:* George Sherman; *W:* D.D. Beauchamp; *C:* Irving Glassberg; *M:* Leith Stevens.

Fever 🦴🦴 **1991 (R)** An ex-con and a high-powered lawyer join forces to rescue the woman both of them love from a vicious killer. Available in Spanish. **99m/C; VHS, DVD.** Armand Assante; Sam Neill; Marcia Gay Harden; Joe Spano; John Dennis Johnston; Mark Boone, Jr.; Jon(athan) Gries; Gordon Clapp; Gregg Henry; John Capodice; Rainbow Harvest; John David (J.D.) Cullum; *D:* Larry Elikann; *W:* Larry Brothers; *C:* Bojan Bazelli; *M:* Michel Colombier. **CABLE**

Fever 🦴🦴 **1999 (R)** Twentysomething Nick Parker (Thomas) is a struggling artist living in a Brooklyn tenement and fighting a losing battle to keep both his physical health and his sanity. Neither are helped when his landlord's murder leads to a police investigation; a suspicious new tenant moves into the apartment above Nick's; and Nick realizes that he's been sleepwalking. Since the film is told from his fractured point-of-view, the viewer can never be sure just what's real. **90m/C; VHS, DVD.** Henry Thomas; David O'Hara; Bill Duke; Teri Hatcher; Sandor Tecsy; Irma St. Paule; Marisol Padilla Sanchez; *D:* Alex Winter; *W:* Alex Winter; *C:* Joe DeSalvo; *M:* Joe Delia.

The Fever 🦴🦴 **2004** Works because of Redgrave's outstanding performance, although the idea teeters (if not topples) into pretension. A nameless privileged woman decides to shake up her life by traveling to a nameless country that's in the midst of a civil war. Falling ill, she has hallucinations, seeing images of violence and revolutionaries (including Jolie) who condemn her indifference and discuss oppression. Based on the play by Wallace Shawn. **83m/C; DVD.** Vanessa Redgrave; Angelina Jolie; Geraldine James; Joely Richardson; Rade Serbedzija; Michael Moore; *D:* Carlo Gabriel Nero; *W:* Wallace Shawn; *C:* Mark Moriarty; *M:* Claudio Capponi. **CABLE**

A Fever In the Blood 🦴🦴 **1961** A principled judge (Zimbalist Jr.), an ambitious district attorney (Kelly), and a dishonest senator (Ameche) are all interested in an upcoming gubernatorial nomination. But a society murder and the subsequent scandal and trial bring backroom machinations into the courtroom. **117m/B; DVD.** Efrem Zimbalist, Jr.; Jack Kelly; Don Ameche; Angie Dickinson; Ray Danton; Carroll O'Connor; Herbert Marshall; *D:* Vincent Sherman; *W:* Roy Huggins; *C:* J. Peverell Marley; *M:* Ernest Gold.

Fever Mounts at El Pao 🦴🦴 **1/2** *Los Ambiciosos* **1959** A minor effort from director Bunuel about the regime of a dictator in an imaginary South American country. In Spanish with English subtitles. **97m/B; DVD.** *MX* Gerard Philipe; Jean Servais; *D:* Luis Bunuel; *W:* Luis Bunuel; *C:* Gabriel Figueroa; *M:* Paul Misraki.

Fever Pitch 🦴🦴 **1/2 1996 (R)** Mildly amusing sports/romance based on Nick Hornby's 1992 sports memoir and set in late '80s London. English teacher/school coach Paul Ashworth (Firth) is an obsessed fan of the Arsenal football (soccer) club. Although completely oppposite in temperament, Paul begins a romance with fellow teacher, Sarah (Gemmell), who's only mildly interested in sports. When Sarah gets pregnant, they drift apart as Sarah begins more and more to resent Paul's perpetual adolescent behavior. Finally, it all comes down to Arsenal's championship match and how they both react. **103m/C; VHS, DVD, Blu-Ray.** *GB* Colin Firth; Ruth Gemmell; Neil Pearson; Mark Strong; Holly Aird; Ken Stott; Stephen Rea; Lorraine Ashbourne; *D:* David Evans; *W:* Nick Hornby; *C:* Chris Seager; *M:* Neil MacColl; Boo Hewerdine.

Fever Pitch 🦴🦴 **1/2 2005 (PG-13)** Math teacher Ben meets unlucky-in-love career woman Lindsey. Looking for a change from the usual (successful) guys she dates, she agrees to go out with him, and a relationship ensues. Then the other spike drops. He's an obsessive Red Sox fan and must choose between his love for Lindsey and the Sox. Standard romantic comedy is raised a level by coinciding with the Red Sox' historic 2004 comeback against the Yankees and subsequent World Series victory. Adapted from Nick Hornby's novel about an obsessive soccer fan. A solid outing, but the brothers Farrelly show signs of losing a little zip off their fastball. **98m/C; DVD.** Jimmy Fallon; Drew Barrymore; KaDee Strickland; Ione Skye; Willie Garson; James B. Sikking; JoBeth Williams; Jack Kehler; Lenny Clarke; Siobhan Fallon Hogan; Marissa Jaret Winokur; Evan Helmuth; Scott Severance; Zen Gesner; *D:* Peter Farrelly; Bobby Farrelly; *W:* Lowell Ganz; Babaloo Mandel; *C:* Matthew F. Leonetti; *M:* Craig Armstrong.

A Few Best Men 🦴🦴 **2011** A wedding comedy centered on a clash of cultures. During a vacation, David (Samuel) and Mia (Brent) meet and fall in love. Within a week, David asks her to marry him. The wedding is planned for a few days later. When David returns to England to get his three best friends to return with him to Australia, the Brits and the Aussies experience both chaos and the unforgettable during the wedding. **97m/C; DVD, Blu-Ray, Streaming, Download.** Laura Brent; Xavier Samuel; Kris Marshall; Kevin Bishop; Tim Draxl; *D:* Stephan Elliot; *W:* Dean Craig; *C:* Stephen F. Windon; *M:* Guy Gross. **VIDEO**

A Few Days in September 🦴 **1/2** *Quelques Jours en Septembre* **2006** Confusing spy thriller. CIA agent Elliott (Nolte) disappears ten days before 9/11 after contacting French agent Irene (Binoche). Elliott makes Irene responsible for his two children, half-siblings Orlando (Forestier) and David (Riley). But setting up a meeting proves difficult as they follow his trail from Paris to Venice, pursued by an over-the-top assassin (Turturro), in an effort to discover what Elliott's learned that's so dangerous. English, French, and Arabic with subtitles. **112m/C; DVD.** *FR IT* Juliette Binoche; Nick Nolte; John Turturro; Sara Forestier; Tom Riley; Mathieu Demy; Said Amadia; *D:* Santiago Amigorena; *W:* Santiago Amigorena; *C:* Christophe Beaucarne; *M:* Laurent Martin.

A Few Good Men 🦴🦴🦴 **1/2 1992 (R)** Strong performances by (and incredible verbal fireworks between) Cruise and Nicholson carry this story of a peacetime military coverup. Cruise is smart aleck Navy lawyer Dan Kaffee, sleepwalking through his comfortable career in DC. He's ready to write off two soldiers pinned for the murder of their cohort until he interviews their commanding officer, Nicholson. Cruise smells a rat, but Nicholson practically dares him to prove it. Moore is another military lawyer assigned to the case, though her function seems to be holding Kaffee's hand. Based on the play by Sorkin, who also wrote the screenplay. **138m/C; VHS, DVD, Blu-Ray.** Tom Cruise; Jack Nicholson; Demi Moore; Kevin Bacon; Kevin Pollak; Kiefer Sutherland; James Marshall; J.T. Walsh; Christopher Guest; J.A. Preston; Matt Craven; Wolfgang Bodison; Xander Berkeley; Cuba Gooding, Jr.; Noah Wyle; *D:* Rob Reiner; *W:* Aaron Sorkin; *C:* Robert Richardson; *M:* Marc Shaiman. MTV Movie Awards '93: Film; Natl. Bd. of Review '92: Support. Actor (Nicholson).

Few Options 🦴🦴 **2011** Frank Connors is released from prison after more than 20 years for drug smuggling. All he wants is to go straight but he finds life as an ex-con isn't easy. His old partners get him an allegedly legit job but Frank's former boss has a new crime planned and is determined Frank will be involved. **90m/C; DVD.** Kenny Johnson; Brad Dourif; Erin Daniels; David Marciano; Christian Stokes; Rainn Wilson; Michael Sheen; *D:* George A. Pappy, Jr.; *W:* George A. Pappy, Jr.; *C:* Peter Hawkins; *M:* Victoria Kelly. **VIDEO**

ffolkes 🦴🦴 *Assault Force; North Sea Hijack* **1980 (PG)** Rufus Excalibur Ffolkes is an eccentric underwater expert who is called upon to stop a madman (Perkins, indulging himself) from blowing up an oil rig in the North Sea. Entertaining farce with Moore playing the opposite of his usual suave James Bond character. **99m/C; VHS, DVD, Blu-Ray.** Roger Moore; James Mason; Anthony Perkins; David Hedison; Michael Parks; *D:* Andrew V. McLaglen.

The Fiance 1996 (R) Faith (Anthony) suspects husband Richard (Cassidy) of being unfaithful and confides her suspicions to the friendly Walter (Moses). Only the unbalanced guy then becomes unhealthily involved in Faith's life. **94m/C; VHS, DVD.** William R. Moses; Lysette Anthony; Patrick Cassidy; Alina Thompson; Wanda Acuna; Gordon Thomson; *D:* Martin Kitrosser; *W:* Greg Walker; Frank Rehwaldt; *C:* M. David Mullen; *M:* Richard Bowers. **VIDEO**

Fiances *The Engagement; I Fidanzati; Ermanno Olmi's I Fadanzati* **1963** Young man from Milan takes a welding job in Sicily that will separate him from his fiancee for 18 months. He thinks the separation will be good for them but loneliness and the strange environment makes him long for her. Nonprofessional leads provide strength. Italian with subtitles. **84m/B; VHS, DVD.** *IT* Carlo Carbrini; Anna Canzi; *D:* Ermanno Olmi; *W:* Ermanno Olmi; *C:* Lamberto Caimi; *M:* Gianni Ferrio.

Fiddler on the Roof 1/2 **1971 (G)** Based on the long-running Broadway musical. The poignant story of Tevye, a poor Jewish milkman at the turn of the century in a small Ukrainian village, and his five dowryless daughters, his lame horse, his wife, and his companionable relationship with God. Topol, an Israeli who played the role in London, is charming, if not quite as wonderful as Zero Mostel, the Broadway star. Finely detailed set decoration and choreography, strong performances from the entire cast create a sense of intimacy in spite of near epic proportions of the production. Play was based on the Yiddish stories of Tevye the Dairyman, written by Sholem Aleichem. **184m/C; VHS, DVD, Blu-Ray.** Topol; Norma Crane; Leonard Frey; Molly Picon; Paul Mann; Rosalind Harris; Michele Marsh; Neva Small; Paul Michael Glaser; Ray Lovelock; *D:* Norman Jewison; *W:* Joseph Stein; *C:* Oswald Morris; *M:* John Williams. Oscars '71: Cinematog., Orig. Song Score and/or Adapt., Sound; Golden Globes '72: Actor--Mus./Comedy (Topol), Film--Mus./Comedy.

Fidel 2002 Excellent bio of Fidel Castro's rise to power in Cuba loses a little steam in its later moments but keeps interest with a strong performance by Martin in the title role. The politics are also kept simple; Castro is an idealistic lawyer who fights for the underdog as a rebel leader after his country's military takeover by Batista (Plana). But once he himself takes power, Castro blurs the lines into a dictatorship of his own. Based on the books "Guerilla Prince" by Georgie Anne Geyer and "Fidel Castro" by Robert E. Quirk. **140m/C; VHS, DVD.** Victor Huggo Martin; Gael Garcia Bernal; Patricia Velasquez; Maurice Compte; Tony Plana; Guillermo Diaz; Margarita d'Francisco; Enrique Arce; *D:* David Attwood; *W:* Stephen Tolkin; *C:* Checco Varese; *M:* John Altman. **CABLE**

Fidelio: Alice's Odyssey 1/2 *Fidelio: Alice's Journey; Fidelio, l'odyssee d'Alice* **2014** An award-winning dramatic study of a young woman working in a male-dominated world and facing romantic challenges. Thirty-year-old Alice (Labed) works as an engineer on freighters, and takes an assignment on the Fidelio. Leaving behind her fiance Felix (Lie) on land, Alice soon learns that the ship's captain is Gael (Poupaud). Once in love and romantically involved with Gael, she must manage her feelings for him while working aboard the ship. French, Romanian, Tagalog, and Norwegian with subtitles. **97m/C; DVD.** Ariane Labed; Melvil Poupaud; Anders Danielsen Lie; Pascal Tagnati; Jean-Louis Coulloc'h; *D:* Lucie Borleteau; *W:* Lucie Borleteau; Clara Bourreau; *C:* Simon Beaufils; *M:* Thomas De Pourquery.

Fido 2006 (R) Amusing—if mild—zom-com. In the near-future (although it looks like the 1950s), a radioactive cloud has turned the dead into zombies. But a shady corporation has domesticated some zombies (thanks to electronic collars), and turned them into household help. When Timmy's (Ray) family finally acquires one, the lonely kid names his loyal zombie Fido (Connolly) and makes him his best friend. Despite Fido's unwavering desire to eat the neighbors (hey, that old lady was mean!). **91m/C; DVD.** *CA* Billy Connolly; Carrie-Anne Moss; Dylan Baker; Henry Czerny; Tim Blake Nelson; K'Sun Ray; Sonja Bennett; *D:* Andrew Currie; *W:* Andrew Currie; Robert Chomiak; Dennis Heaton; *C:* Jan Kiesser; *M:* Don MacDonald.

The Field 1/2 **1990 (PG-13)** After an absence from the big screen, intense and nearly over the top Harris won acclaim as an iron-willed peasant fighting to retain a patch of Irish land he's tended all his life, now offered for sale to a wealthy American. His uncompromising stand divides the community in this glowing adaptation of John B. Keane's classic play, an allegory of Ireland's internal conflicts. **113m/C; VHS, DVD.** *GB* Richard Harris; Tom Berenger; John Hurt; Sean Bean; Brenda Fricker; Frances Tomelty; John Cowley; Sean McGinley; Jenny Conroy; *D:* Jim Sheridan; *W:* Jim Sheridan; *C:* Jack Conroy; *M:* Elmer Bernstein.

A Field in England **2014** Director Wheatley continues to defy expectations, delivering another film that pushes genre boundaries. It's England in 1648 and a group of deserters are fleeing a battle. They are captured by two men who force them to look for a hidden treasure in a field of mushrooms, which the gentlemen eat and basically trip on. The rest of the movie consists of fighting, paranoia, and unpredictable visuals as these men get lost in a field in England. **90m/C; Blu-Ray, On Demand.** *UK* Michael Smiley; Reece Shearsmith; Ryan Pope; Peter Ferdinando; Richard Glover; *D:* Ben Wheatley; *W:* Amy Jump; *C:* Laurie Rose; *M:* Jim Williams.

Field of Dreams 1/2 **1989 (PG)** Uplifting mythic fantasy based on W.P. Kinsella's novel "Shoeless Joe." Iowa corn farmer Ray Kinsella (Costner) heeds a mysterious voice that instructs "If you build it, he will come" and cuts a baseball diamond in his corn field. Soon the ball field is inhabited by the spirit of Joe Jackson (Liotta) and others who were disgraced in the notorious 1919 "Black Sox" baseball scandal. Jones is Terence Mann, a character based on reclusive author J.D. Salinger, is reluctantly pulled into the mystery. It's all about chasing a dream, maintaining innocence, finding redemption, reconciling the child with the adult, and celebrating the mythic lure of baseball. Costner and Madigan (as wife Anni) are strong, believable characters. **106m/C; VHS, DVD, Blu-Ray, HD-DVD.** Kevin Costner; Amy Madigan; James Earl Jones; Burt Lancaster; Ray Liotta; Timothy Busfield; Frank Whaley; Gaby Hoffman; Dwier Brown; *D:* Phil Alden Robinson; *W:* Phil Alden Robinson; *C:* John Lindley; *M:* James Horner. Natl. Film Reg. '17.

Field of Lost Shoes 1/2 **2014 (PG-13)** A historical drama based on true events during the American Civil War. Though cadets at the Virginia Military Institute are kept from the Civil War for much of the conflict, the fighting nears them by 1864. The desperate Confederacy calls on the cadets to march into battle with its army and help defend the Shenandoah Valley. As a result, the cadets participate in what is known as the Battle of New Market. For the cadets, they must face issues such as why they are fighting and the true nature of honor. **96m/C; DVD, Streaming, Download.** Luke Benward; Jason Isaacs; Keith David; Lauren Holly; Nolan Gould; *D:* Sean McNamara; *W:* Thomas Farrell; David M. Kennedy; *C:* Brad Shield; *M:* Frederik Wiedmann.

Field of Vision 1/2 **2011** NBC TV family drama. Foster kid Corey is a new high school student and new guy on the football team. After being ruthlessly bullied, talented Corey quits, which sets up a dilemma for quarterback Tyler. The bullies are his friends and if he tells the coach, they'll be booted off the team. There's also a magical camera used by Tyler's younger sister Lucy that reveals information on the characters. Supposedly inspirational but teeters from reality to fantasy for no good reason. **90m/C; DVD.** Tony Oiler; Joe Adler; Faith Ford; Alyssa Shafer; Philip Casnoff; L. Warren Young; Dave Davenport; *D:* Gregg Champion; *W:* Wesley Bishop; *C:* William Wages; *M:* Joseph Conlan. **TV**

Fielder's Choice 1/2 **2005** There are no surprises in this Hallmark Channel family drama. After his sister is killed in a car accident, Philip Fielder has temporary custody of his autistic, 8-year-old nephew Zach. Career-driven Philip doesn't believe he can cope with his new responsibility and tries to find an alternative living arrangement for the boy. Of course, he comes to realize what's truly important is family. **85m/C; DVD.** Chad Lowe; Kesun Loder; Marin Hinkle; George Segal; Bodhi (Pine) Elfman; Ellen Greene; *D:* Kevin Connor; *W:* Dan Roberts; *C:* James W. Wrenn; *M:* Andrew Rose. **CABLE**

The Fields 1/2 **2011** In 1973, young Steven (Ormond) is sent to stay with his grandparents on their Pennsylvania farm. The kid's imagination starts running wild after hearing about the Manson family and being told to stay out of the cornfields. Of course, Steven goes into the cornfields and finds the dead body of a young woman--maybe one of the hippies passing through the area. Actually, not much really happens in this mishmash of scenes that promises more than it delivers. **100m/C; DVD, Blu-Ray.** Joshua Ormond; Cloris Leachman; Bev Appleton; Tara Reid; Brian Anthony Wilson; *D:* Tom Mattera; David Mazzoni; *W:* Harrison Smith; *C:* Daniel Watchulonis; *M:* John Avarese.

The Fiend **1971 (R)** A religious cultist, already unbalanced, grabs a knife and starts hacking away Jack-the-Ripper style. **87m/C; VHS, DVD.** *GB* Ann Todd; Patrick Magee; Tony Beckley; Madeline Hinde; Suzanna Leigh; Percy Herbert; *D:* Robert Hartford-Davis.

Fiend **WOOF! 1983** Glowing supernatural thing flits around graveyard before animating dead guy who needs to kill in order to go on living. Murderous dead guy becomes a small-town music teacher feeding parasitically on his students to satisfy his supernatural hunger. His neighbor suspects some discord. Low-budget time waster. **93m/C; VHS, DVD, Blu-Ray.** Don Leifert; Richard Nelson; Elaine White; George Stover; *D:* Donald M. Dohler.

The Fiend Who Walked the West 1/2 **1958** Brutal western has incarcerated bankrobber Dan letting slip the location of his loot to fellow inmate Griffin, who unfortunately turns out to be psychotic and due for release. When Dan's family is endangered, lawmen release him for a showdown with Griffin. Tense remake of "Kiss of Death" provides effective atmosphere and graphic violence in an Old West setting. **101m/B; DVD.** Hugh O'Brian; Robert Evans; Dolores Michaels; Linda Cristal; Stephen McNally; Ron Ely; Edward Andrews; Ken Scott; Emile Meyer; Gregory Morton; *D:* Gordon Douglas; *W:* Philip Yordan; *C:* Joe MacDonald; *M:* Les Baxter.

Fiend without a Face **1958** An isolated air base in Canada is the site for a scientist using atomic power in an experiment to make a person's thoughts materialize. Only his thoughts are evil and reveal themselves as flying brains with spinal cords that suck human brains right out of the skull. Tons of fun for '50s SF fans and anyone who appreciates the sheer silliness of it all. **77m/B; VHS, DVD.** Marshall Thompson; Kim Parker; Terence (Terry) Kilburn; Michael Balfour; Gil Winfield; Shane Cordell; Kynaston Reeves; *D:* Arthur Crabtree; *W:* Herbert J. Leder; *C:* Lionel Banes; *M:* Buxton Orr.

The Fiendish Plot of Dr. Fu Manchu **WOOF! 1980 (PG)** A sad farewell from Sellers, who in his last film portrays Dr. Fu in his desperate quest for the necessary ingredients for his secret life-preserving formula. Sellers portrays both Dr. Fu and the Scotland Yard detective on his trail, but it's not enough to save this picture, flawed by poor script and lack of direction. **100m/C; VHS, DVD, Streaming.** *GB* Peter Sellers; David Tomlinson; Sid Caesar; Dame Helen Mirren; Simon Williams; Steve Franken; Stratford Johns; John Le Mesurier; John Sharp; Clement Harari; *D:* Piers Haggard; *W:* Rudy Dochtermann; Jim Moloney; *C:* Jean Tournier; *M:* Marc Wilkinson.

Fierce Creatures **1996 (PG-13)** This not-really-a-sequel features the same cast as "A Fish Called Wanda" and was jokingly known as "Death Fish II" until a more appropriate title was thought of. A failing London zoo gets a new lease on life, and officious new manager Rollo Lee (Cleese) by stocking only man-eating predators. This plan has kindly, insect house manager Bugsy (Palin) tongue-tied at the thought of destroying the zoo's cuddly current occupants. Kline is again in fine form with his dastardly dual role of zoo's Aussie owner Rod McCain and his idiot son, Vince. Curtis displays her obvious talents as Willa Weston, Vince's more sympathetic partner. Despite inspired moments, flick's not as tightly told or as wickedly funny as "Fish," (an admittedly tough act to follow). A family-friendlier attitude has effectively declawed this "Creature." Many scenes were reshot after unfavorable advance screenings, necessitating a new director and the recall of the actors from far and wide. **93m/C; VHS, DVD, Blu-Ray.** John Cleese; Jamie Lee Curtis; Kevin Kline; Michael Palin; Ronnie Corbett; Robert Lindsay; Carey Lowell; Bille Brown; Derek Griffiths; Cynthia Cleese; *D:* Robert M. Young; Fred Schepisi; *W:* John Cleese; Iain Johnstone; *C:* Adrian Biddle; Ian Baker; *M:* Jerry Goldsmith.

Fierce People **2005 (R)** In 1980, fifteen-year-old Finn (Yelchin) is supposed to summer in South America with his wayward anthropologist father. Instead, train-wreck addict/masseuse mom (Lane), who's trying her luck at sobriety, plucks him from their New York City existence to spend the season at the New Jersey country estate of superloaded and super-eccentric Osborne (Sutherland), where the idle rich pursue their own brand of summer fun. Finn falls for the billionaire's granddaughter (Stewart), and a twisted coming-of-age story unfolds amid the darkness. Be warned: a brutal rape sequence is totally jarring, and the already thin plot never recovers. Teen drug use, bizarre twists, and outrageous characters send the entire mess over the top. **135m/C; DVD.** Diane Lane; Donald Sutherland; Anton Yelchin; Chris Evans; Kristen Stewart; Elizabeth Perkins; Christopher Shyer; Blu Mankuma; *D:* Griffin Dunne; *W:* Dirk Wittenborn; *C:* William Rexer; *M:* Nick Laird-Clowes.

15 Amore **1998** Dorothy's husband is off fighting in WWII while she struggles with the family farm and three young kids in rural Australia. But soon she gets the help of two Italian POWs, Alfredo and Joseph, who settle right in. Then, Dorothy takes in German Jewish refugees Frau Gutman and her daughter Rachel. While Dorothy and Alfredo have an unacknowledged love for each other, Joseph and Rachel engage in a secret romance. Secret until Rachel's disapproving mother finds out. A last-minute bombshell accusation needlessly skewers everything that's gone before. Title refers to a tennis score, one of the local pasttimes. **92m/C; VHS, DVD.** *AU* Lisa Hensley; Steve Bastoni; Domenic Galati; Tara Jakszewicz; Gertraud Ingeborg; *D:* Maurice Murphy; *W:* Maurice Murphy; *C:* John Brock; *M:* Carlo Giacco.

15 Minutes 1/2 **2001 (R)** New York cop and publicity hound De Niro teams up with arson investigator Burns to hunt down a couple of violent criminals who are videotaping their crimes for celebrity purposes. Is writer/director Herzfeld exploring our culture's fascination with violence, nihilism, and fame, or just using images of those ideas to sell tickets? Most likely it's the latter, but either way, Warhol would probably approve. Grammer tries his hand at playing the sleazy, Jerry Springerish shock-TV host, and mostly pulls it off. **120m/C; VHS, DVD, Blu-Ray.** Robert De Niro; Edward Burns; Kelsey Grammer; Avery Brooks; Melina Kanakaredes; Vera Farmiga; Karel Roden; Oleg Taktarov; John DiResta; James Handy; Darius McCrary; Charlize Theron; Kim Cattrall; David Alan Grier; *D:* John Herzfeld; *W:* John Herzfeld; *C:* Jean-Yves Escoffier; *M:* Anthony Marinelli; J. Peter Robinson.

15 Minutes of War 1/2 *L'intervention* **2019** In 1976 Djibouti, the last French colony in Africa, American school teacher Jane Andersen (Kurylenko) has bonded with her young charges. When a school bus carrying some of them is hijacked by terrorists demanding France's permanent withdrawal from the region, France sends elite special forces led by Andre Gerval (Lenoir) to help. Andre organizes a rescue effort using his small team and Jane, who ran on the bus to be with her students. Based on a true story, the well-crafted film captures the fear and violence that comes with a rescue but is bogged down by its political point of view. French with subtitles. **98m/C; DVD.** Alban Lenoir; Olga Kurylenko; Sebastien Lalanne; David Murgia; Ben Cura; *D:* Fred Grivois; *W:* Fred Grivois; *C:* Julien Meurice; *M:* Fabien Kourtzer; Mike Kourtzer.

The 15:17 to Paris 🦴 1/2 **2018 (PG-13)** Three real-life heroes play themselves in Eastwood's tribute to a thwarted act of terror aboard a Paris-bound train on August 21, 2015. His decision to cast non-actors in the lead roles is a questionable one, doing little more than giving the film an interesting side note. Perhaps he was satisfied with what nugget of interest he could garner, because their childhood backstories, jaunts through Europe, and heavy-handed musings on the Purpose of Life are just the parts to sit through until the climax aboard the train. **94m/C; DVD, Blu-Ray.** Alek Skarlatos; Anthony Sadler; Spencer Stone; Ray Corasani; Judy Greer; *D:* Clint Eastwood; *W:* Dorothy Blyskal; *C:* Tom Stern; *M:* Christian Jacob.

Fifth Avenue Girl 🦴 1/2 **1939** An unhappy millionaire brings home a poor young woman to pose as his mistress to make his family realize how they've neglected him. As this below-par social comedy drones toward its romantic conclusion, the rich folks see the error of their ways and love conquers all. **83m/B; VHS, DVD.** Ginger Rogers; Walter Connolly; Tim Holt; James Ellison; Franklin Pangborn; *D:* Gregory La Cava.

The Fifth Commandment 🦴🦴 **2008 (R)** Hitman Max Templeton raises Chance when the boy is left orphaned by Chinese killer Z. Chance follows Max's profession but when he reneges on his latest job, Z takes it on instead, giving Chance his shot at revenge. **90m/C; DVD.** Rick Yune; Bokeem Woodbine; Dania Ramirez; Roger Yuan; Keith David; *D:* Jesse Johnson; *W:* Rick Yune; *C:* Robert Hayes; *M:* Paul Haslinger. **VIDEO**

Fifth Day of Peace 🦴🦴 **1972 (PG)** In the aftermath of the WWI armistice, two German soldiers are tried and executed for desertion by their commander, even though the Allies forbade German military trials. An interesting plot that is marred by too obvious plot twists. Based on a true story. **95m/C; VHS, DVD.** *IT* Richard Johnson; Franco Nero; Larry Aubrey; Helmuth Schneider; *D:* Guiliano Montaldo.

The Fifth Element 🦴🦴 1/2 **1997 (PG-13)** Besson's view of the future is colorful, loud and fashionable. Dressed in costumes by Jean Paul Gaultier, Willis is a New York City cab driver turned unwilling hero who must save earth from destruction at the hands of evil arms dealer Zorg (Oldman). He takes time to romance orange-haired nymph Jovovich, who holds the key to all the madness going on. Oldman is over-the-top as the icy villain, more of a bad gag than a bad guy. Jumbled story fortunately takes a backseat to weird aliens and stunning visuals which makes this an eye-catching (albeit confusing) sci-fi trip. **125m/C; VHS, DVD, Blu-Ray, UMD.** Bruce Willis; Gary Oldman; Ian Holm; Milla Jovovich; Luke Perry; Lee Evans; Chris Tucker; Brion James; Tommy (Tiny) Lister; John Neville; John Bluthal; Maiwenn Le Besco; Mathieu Kassovitz; *D:* Luc Besson; *W:* Luc Besson; *C:* Thierry Arbogast; *M:* Éric Serra. British Acad. '97: Visual FX; Cesar '98: Art Dir./Set Dec., Cinematog., Director (Besson).

The Fifth Estate 🦴🦴 **2013 (R)** Cumberbatch gives his charming all to this biopic of the controversial Julian Assange, founder of Wikileaks, a company that reveals hidden documents and government secrets worldwide. While Assange's story starts simply enough, as a businessman trying to form a company and correct perceived wrongs in the power structure, the film becomes something of a thriller when powerful people feel crossed by him. The biggest problem with this often-dull film (computer hacking = boring) is that Assange's story is still being written. Not to mention he wasn't too pleased about the honesty behind this "biography." **128m/C; DVD, Blu-Ray.** Benedict Cumberbatch; Daniel Brühl; David Thewlis; Peter Capaldi; Alicia Vikander; *D:* Bill Condon; *W:* Josh Singer; *C:* Tobias Schliessler; *M:* Carter Burwell.

The Fifth Horseman Is Fear 🦴🦴 **1964** In Nazi-occupied Prague, Dr. Braun is forbidden from practicing medicine because he is a Jew. Instead, he catalogs confiscated property in a warehouse. But when a wounded resistance fighter is secretly brought to Braun for treatment, he journeys throughout the chaotic city trying to find morphine for his patient, whom he is hiding in his apartment building. But he fears his scared neighbors may become informers. Czech with subtitles. **100m/B; DVD.** *CZ* Jiri Adamira; Miroslav Machacek; Josef Vinklar; Jiri Virtala; *D:* Zbynek Brynych; *W:* Zbynek Brynych; *C:* Jan Kalis.

The Fifth Musketeer 🦴🦴 *Behind the Iron Mask* **1979 (PG)** A campy adaptation of Dumas's "The Man in the Iron Mask," wherein a monarch's evil twin impersonates him while imprisoning the true king. A good cast and rich production shot in Austria make for a fairly entertaining swashbuckler. **90m/C; DVD.** *GB* Beau Bridges; Sylvia Kristel; Ursula Andress; Cornel Wilde; Ian McShane; Alan Hale, Jr.; Helmut Dantine; Olivia de Havilland; Jose Ferrer; Rex Harrison; *D:* Ken Annakin; *W:* David Ambrose; *C:* Jack Cardiff.

The 5th Quarter 🦴 1/2 **2010 (PG)** Well-meaning but oh-so-cliched sports/family drama. In 2006, 16-year-old high school football player Luke Abbate (Guy) suffers irreparable brain damage in a car accident and soon dies. As his family grieves, older brother Jon (Merriman) tries to keep it together and works on his pigskin prowess at Wake Forest, encouraged by his teammates who dedicated their season to Luke and begin winning. **98m/C; DVD.** Ryan Merriman; Aidan Quinn; Andie MacDowell; Stefan Guy; Michael Harding; Jillian Batherson; Josh Smith; Anessa Ramsey; *D:* Rick Bieber; *W:* Rick Bieber; *C:* Craig Haagensen; *M:* Andy Mendelson.

The 5th Wave 🦴 **2016 (PG-13)** Sixteen-year-old Cassie Sullivan (Moretz) is trying to survive in a world destroyed after an alien invasion, removing all technology from it. Oh, yeah, another post-apocalyptic flick about a teenager who can save the world. The non-stop assault of Young Adult book-to-screen adaptations in the wake of Harry Potter, Twilight, Divergent, and The Hunger Games continues unabated, and continues to produce some absolute garbage. There's absolutely no reason to care about what happens at all, despite the best efforts of the talented Moretz. Even the effects are subpar. **112m/C; DVD, Blu-Ray.** Chloë Grace Moretz; Gabriela Lopez; Nick Robinson; Ron Livingston; Maggie Siff; Zackary Arthur; *D:* J. Blakeson; *W:* Susannah Grant; Akiva Goldsman; Jeff Pinkner; *C:* Enrique Chediak; *M:* Henry Jackman.

Fifty Dead Men Walking 🦴🦴 **2008** It's 1988 in Belfast with British soldiers in the streets and the IRA waging war. Petty hustler and criminal Martin McGartland (Sturgess) drifts into becoming an informant for intelligence agent Fergus (Kingsley). Then his friend Frankie (MacNeill) gets kneecapped and Martin wrangles his way into the IRA itself. Title refers to the 50 men Martin reputedly saved from IRA execution. Exceptional performances from Sturgess and Kingsley in a somewhat convoluted story. **118m/C; DVD.** *GB CA* Jim Sturgess; Ben Kingsley; Kevin Zegers; Nathalie Press; Rose McGowan; Conor MacNeill; *D:* Keri Skogland; *W:* Keri Skogland; *C:* Jonathan Freeman; *M:* Ben Mink.

50/50 🦴🦴🦴 1/2 **2011 (R)** An average twenty-something guy, Adam (an impressive Gordon-Levitt), is diagnosed with a rare form of spinal cancer and given a 50/50 shot at surviving. Trying to go on with his life, he turns to his best friend Kyle (Rogen) and a young shrink (Kendrick) for support while his girlfriend (Howard) drops the ball. In the very-small subgenre of "cancer comedy," this is a subtle, moving effort by director Levine and writer Reiser, who composed this from some of his own experiences (the cancer, and his relationship with real-life friend Rogen). An incredible ensemble performs ably in a tightrope-walking act between comedy and gloom. **99m/C; DVD, Blu-Ray.** Joseph Gordon-Levitt; Seth Rogen; Anna Kendrick; Bryce Dallas Howard; Anjelica Houston; *D:* Jonathan Levine; *W:* Will Reiser; *C:* Terry Stacey; *M:* Michael Giacchino. Ind. Spirit '12: First Screenplay.

50 First Dates 🦴🦴 1/2 **2004 (PG-13)** Barrymore is the sweet girl with no short-term memory and Sandler is the love-struck island veterinarian who tries to woo her...over and over again. Sweetly charming at times, as Sandler tones down his more outrageous behavior for a decent romantic comedy. Clark does a fine job as Barrymore's slightly over-protective but loving father. Astin goes 180 degrees from anything resembling a hobbit as the pumped-up brother. **96m/C; DVD, Blu-Ray, UMD.** Adam Sandler; Drew Barrymore; Rob Schneider; Sean Astin; Blake Clark; Dan Aykroyd; Amy Hill; Allen Covert; Maya Rudolph; Missi Pyle; Lusia Strus; Pomaika'i Brown; *D:* Peter Segal; *W:* George Wing; *C:* Jack N. Green; *M:* Teddy Castellucci.

Fifty Shades Darker 🦴 1/2 **2017 (R)** This loathsome franchise based on the books by E.L. James gets a second chapter that's somehow even more foolish than the original. Anastasia Steele (Johnson) is now the girlfriend of the kinky Christian Grey (a bland Dornan). Anastasia suspects that she doesn't know everything she should about her boy toy when she meets one of Christian's former submissives (Heathcote). She also meets Christian's former dominant, played by a too-good-for-this Basinger. Even Gay Harden gets sucked into this silliness, which is just flat and boring when it should be sexy and intriguing. **118m/C; DVD, Blu-Ray.** Dakota Johnson; Jamie Dornan; Eric Johnson; Eloise Mumford; Bella Heathcote; Kim Basinger; *D:* James Foley; *W:* Niall Leonard; *C:* John Schwartzman; *M:* Danny Elfman. Golden Raspberries '17: Worst Remake/Sequel, Worst Support. Actress (Basinger).

Fifty Shades Freed 🦴 1/2 **2018 (R)** The trilogy climaxes, giving us the final installment of unintentionally hilarious dialogue, wooden acting by Dornan, and could-be-steamy sex scenes tamed down for an R rating. Anastasia (Johnson) still submits to Christian's penchant for bondage, but now she's doing it as Mrs. Grey, thank you very much. An old nemesis (another Johnson) returns to foil their matrimonial bliss through brute force, and Ana and Christian take turns pouting over perceived betrayals by each other. The sweet release felt like an eternity in coming, but we're finally freed. **105m/C; DVD, Blu-Ray.** Dakota Johnson; Jamie Dornan; Eric Johnson; Eloise Mumford; Rita Ora; Marcia Gay Harden; *D:* James Foley; *W:* Niall Leonard; *C:* John Schwartzman; *M:* Danny Elfman. Golden Raspberries '18: Worst Screenplay.

Fifty Shades of Black 🦴 **2016 (R)** In theory, this is a comedy send-up of "Fifty Shades of Grey" with Wayans in the Christian role, but that's just the starting point for another film a la "Scary Movie" or "A Haunted House," flicks that try to skewer as many current movies as possible under one running time. Of course, most of these movies are horrible, and this is no exception. Making a reference to another movie is not the same thing as actually writing a joke about it, and these lazy Wayans flicks simply exaggerate behavior we've already laughed at. **92m/C; DVD, Blu-Ray.** Marlon Wayans; Kali Hawk; Fred Willard; Mike Epps; Affion Crockett; Jane Seymour; *D:* Michael Tiddes; *W:* Marlon Wayans; Rick Alvarez; *C:* David Ortkiese; *M:* Jim Dooley.

Fifty Shades of Grey 🦴🦴 **2015 (R)** E.L. James' massive hit book becomes a totally mediocre drama that reveals more of the source material's flaws than anything else. It's a dull story spiced up with sexual perversity, and that kind of thing works better on the tawdry page than on the big screen. Lit student Anastasia Steele (Johnson) goes to interview the powerful Christian Grey (Dornan). The two form a sexual relationship, which gets kinkier as Grey's BDSM proclivities are revealed. The book proposed a commentary on the war of the sexes while the film is just another '80s-style sex drama without the true heat or characters that work. **125m/C; DVD, Blu-Ray.** Dakota Johnson; Jamie Dornan; Jennifer Ehle; Marcia Gay Harden; Luke Grimes; Eloise Mumford; Victor Rasuk; Rita Ora; Dylan Neal; *D:* Sam Taylor-Johnson; *W:* Kelly Marcel; *C:* Seamus McGarvey; *M:* Danny Elfman. Golden Raspberries '15: Worst Actor (Dornan), Worst Actress (Johnson), Worst Picture, Worst Screenplay.

50 to 1 🦴 1/2 **2014 (PG-13)** Based on the true story of some misfit cowboys in New Mexico whose undersized racehorse--Mine That Bird--becomes an unlikely qualifier for the 2009 Kentucky Derby. Story's more about the friendship between trainer and owner than racing and it's heavy on the clichés. **111m/C; DVD.** Skeet Ulrich; Christian Kane; William Devane; Madelyn Deutch; *D:* Jim Wilson; *W:* Jim Wilson; Faith Conroy; *C:* Tim Suhrstedt; *M:* William Ross.

51 Birch Street 🦴🦴🦴 **2005** A moving, personal documentary by filmmaker Doug Block that explores the idea of the disconnect of knowledge between children and their parents. For the whole of his life until his mother's sudden death, he thought his parents had a solid marriage for 54 years. Three months after her demise, Block's father marries a woman who had once served as his secretary. These events prompted Block to look into his family history and the information he learned showed his family's story was more disquieting than he ever expected. **90m/C; DVD, Streaming, Download.** Doug Block; *D:* Doug Block; *W:* Doug Block; *C:* Doug Block; *M:* H. Scott Salinas.

52 Pick-Up 🦴🦴 1/2 **1986 (R)** After a fling, a wealthy industrialist is blackmailed by a trio of repulsive criminals and determines to save himself. First he becomes deeply caught in their web of murder. Based on an Elmore Leonard novel with lots of gruesome violence and good performances. **111m/C; VHS, DVD, Blu-Ray.** Roy Scheider; Ann-Margret; Vanity; John Glover; Doug McClure; Clarence Williams, III; Kelly Preston; Robert Trebor; Lonny (Lonnie) Chapman; *D:* John Frankenheimer; *W:* John Steppling; Elmore Leonard; *M:* Gary Chang.

54 🦴 1/2 **1998 (R)** The days of '70s disco, drugs, and hedonism rear their heads in this look back at New York's infamous Studio 54. Myers takes the drama route as druggie club co-owner Steve Rubell, while Phillippe starts off as innocent New Jersey boy Shane O'Shea, who gets a job as a bartender and is soon taking the low road to debauchery. Others hitting the dance floor include pouty soap star Julie (Campbell), coat-check girl/would-be disco diva Anita (Hayek), and her busboy hubby Greg (Meyer). But Shane is a dunce and his story a bore, while the effective Myers takes a decided backseat storywise. Film went through a lot of last-minute re-editing but it didn't seem to help. **92m/C; VHS, DVD, Blu-Ray.** Mike Myers; Ryan Phillippe; Breckin Meyer; Salma Hayek; Neve Campbell; Sela Ward; Sherry Stringfield; Ellen A. Dow; Heather Matarazzo; Skipp (Robert L.) Sudduth; Cindy Crawford; ***Cameo(s):*** Lauren Hutton; Michael York; *D:* Mark Christopher; *W:* Mark Christopher; *C:* Alexander Grusynski.

55 Days at Peking 🦴🦴🦴 **1963** A costume epic depicting the Chinese Boxer Rebellion and the fate of military Britishers caught in the midst of the chaos. Standard fare superbly handled by director Ray and an all-star cast. **150m/C; VHS, DVD.** Charlton Heston; Ava Gardner; David Niven; John Ireland; Flora Robson; Paul Lukas; Jacques Sernas; *D:* Nicholas Ray; *W:* Philip Yordan; *C:* Jack Hildyard.

A Fig Leaf for Eve 🦴 *Desirable Lady* **1944** Silly and dull feature finds exotic dancer Eve incensed when she learns her publicist/boyfriend is behind a morals complaint that gets her arrested. That's just the beginning of her troubles when a shyster lawyer convinces the dame to pose as a long-missing heiress in a plot that turns deadly. **68m/B; DVD.** Jan Wiley; Philip Warren; Eddie Dunn; Emmett Vogan; Janet Scott; Betty Blythe; Edward (Ed Kean, Keene) Keane; *D:* Don Brodie; *W:* Elizabeth Hayter; *C:* Marcel Le Picard.

Fight Club 🦴🦴🦴 1/2 **1999 (R)** Young, male, repressed rage comes in the form of Norton's disillusioned yuppie, emotionally numbed by chronic insomnia, who meets the answer to all his pent-up frustrations in malcontent Pitt. Tyler's his name and anarchy's his game as the duo eventually establish fight clubs where the participants beat each other up and stage massive acts of terrorism to undermine the allure of consumerism. Bonham Carter plays a kinky, death-obsessed woman both men fancy. Fincher heads for the dark side again and puts a middle finger on the pulse of several hot topics without missing a beat or skirting the issues. Film's dark humor and stylistic vision of young male malaise is made even more biting by newcomer Uhl's faithful adaptation of Chuck Palahniuk's debut novel. Performances by all three leads are equal to the powerful subject matter. **139m/C; VHS, DVD,**

Blu-Ray, UMD. Brad Pitt; Edward Norton; Helena Bonham Carter; Meat Loaf Aday; Jared Leto; Eion Bailey; *D:* David Fincher; *W:* Jim Uhls; *C:* Jeff Cronenweth; *M:* Howard Shore.

Fight for Your Life 🦴 *Getting Even; Held Hostage; Staying Alive* **1977 (R)** Three escaped convicts—a white bigot, an Asian, and a Chicano take a black minister's family hostage. After suffering all manner of vicious torture, the family exacts an equally brutal revenge. Shades of "The Desperate Hours" and "Extremities," but with much more graphic violence and a racial twist. **89m/C; VHS, DVD.** *CA* William Sanderson; Robert Judd; Lela Small; Reggie Rock Bythewood; *D:* Robert A. Endelson; *W:* Straw Weisman; *C:* Lloyd Freidus; *M:* Jeff Slevin.

Fight to the Finish 🦴 1/2 **2016 (PG-13)** An amateur fighter faces many challenges inside and outside the cage. BIlly (Olney) is a young adult son of a boxing champion—and an aspiring fighter himself—who finds himself protecting a neighbor by fighting her abusive former boyfriend. Because of the former boyfriend's criminal past and present, Billy finds his personal live at risk. Billy ultimately finishes this fight in the ring, with a championship at stake. **94m/C; DVD, Streaming, Download.** Dillon Olney; Shane Warren Jones; Jennifer Hale; Caleb Smith; Evan Hannemann; *D:* Warren Sheppard; *W:* Warren Sheppard; *C:* Adam Sherer; *M:* David Gonzalez. **VIDEO**

The Fight Within 🦴🦴 **2016 (PG-13)** A sports action drama centered on a young MMA fighter. For years, Logan Chandler (Davis) has found his identity in MMA and left his difficult past behind. Looking for more, he has left the sport. Falling in love with Emma (Symington), he also has found new meaning in his faith. However, Hayden Dressler (Leddo) complicates Logan's life by forcing him back into MMA. Logan must find a way to be true to himself and all he now holds as important to him. **94m/C; DVD, Streaming, Download.** John Major Davis; Lelia Symington; Matt Leddo; Mike H. Taylor; Wesley Williams; *D:* Michael William Gordon; *W:* Jim Davis; *C:* DJ Dittenhoefer; *M:* Will Musser.

The Fighter 🦴🦴🦴 *The First Time* **1952** A Mexican patriot, involved in a struggle to overthrow a dictator, falls for a co-revolutionist. Flashbacks show the destruction of his family and village, and his pugilistic expertise, which he uses to fight for a huge purse to help the cause. Adapted from Jack London's "The Mexican." **78m/B; VHS, DVD.** Richard Conte; Vanessa Brown; Lee J. Cobb; Frank Silvera; Roberta Haynes; Hugh Sanders; Claire Carleton; Martin Garralaga; *D:* Herbert Kline; *W:* Herbert Kline; Aben Kandel; *C:* Floyd Crosby; James Wong Howe; *M:* Vincente Gomez.

The Fighter 🦴🦴🦴 **2010 (R)** Boxing biopic, based on the life of welterweight 'Irish' Micky Ward (Wahlberg) and his dysfunctional half-brother, trainer, and full blown crackhead Dickie (Bale). Surrounded by an imbalanced mother and seven disgruntled sisters, Micky finds solace in bartender Charlene (Adams), who wants him to think outside the mean streets of Lowell, Massachusetts. But it's Dickie that takes center stage here, with Bale turning in a visceral performance as the former boxer, still basking in the clouded glory of a bout 15 years prior against champ Sugar Ray Leonard. However, what effectively begins as 'Raging Bull,' takes a dive in round seven with 'Rocky'-like training montages and underdog cliches. Should have been a KO, instead it ends up a TKO. **115m/C; Blu-Ray.** Mark Wahlberg; Christian Bale; Amy Adams; Melissa Leo; Jack McGee; Bianca Hunter; Erica McDermott; Sean Patrick Doherty; Salvatore Santone; Jackson Nicoll; Sue Costello; Melissa McMeekin; *D:* David O. Russell; *W:* David O. Russell; Scott Silver; Eric Johnson; Paul Tamasy; *C:* Hoyte Van Hoytema; *M:* Michael Brook. Oscars '10: Support. Actor (Bale), Support. Actress (Leo); Golden Globes '11: Support. Actor (Bale), Support. Actress (Leo); Screen Actors Guild '10: Support. Actor (Bale), Support. Actress (Leo).

Fighter Squadron 🦴🦴 **1948** Okay airborne WWII action-drama. Major Ed Hardin (O'Brien) leads a small squadron of U.S. pilots from an airbase in the English countryside against the Luftwaffe in 1943. Rock Hudson makes his uncredited film debut in a one-line role. **96m/C; DVD.** Edmond O'Brien; Robert Stack; John Rodney; Tom D'Andrea; Henry Hull; Shepperd Strudwick; James Holden; Walter Reed; *D:* Raoul Walsh; *W:* Seton I. Miller; Martin Rackin; *C:* Sidney Hickox; Wilfred M. Cline; *M:* Max Steiner.

Fighting 🦴🦴 1/2 **2009 (PG-13)** You can anticipate all the sports cliches within minutes, but for some reason it still has appeal. Alabama-born Shawn MacArthur (Tatum) hustles various jobs on the New York streets while going nowhere fast. Until he meets equally hustling fight coach Harvey Boarden (Howard), who introduces him to the world of underground bare-knuckles fighting. Shawn discovers he's a winner at something that may get him killed as the payday for the matches increases against better competitors. There's also some romance between Shawn and single mom/waitress Zulay (Henao) who falls for the lug despite her better judgment. **105m/C; Blu-Ray, On Demand.** Channing Tatum; Terrence Howard; Luis Guzman; Brian White; Zulay Henao; Roger Guenveur Smith; *D:* Dito Montiel; *W:* Dito Montiel; Robert Munic; *C:* Stefan Czapsky; *M:* Dave Wittman; Jonathan Elias.

Fighting Back 🦴🦴 *Death Vengeance* **1982 (R)** Reactionary tale of an angry resident in a crime-ridden Philadelphia neighborhood who organizes a patrol of armed civilian vigilantes. The police attempt to head off a racial confrontation in this effective drama graced with some fine performances. **96m/C; VHS, Streaming.** Tom Skerritt; Patti LuPone; Michael Sarrazin; Yaphet Kotto; *D:* Lewis Teague; *W:* David Zelag Goodman; *C:* Franco Di Giacomo.

Fighting Caravans 🦴🦴 *Blazing Arrows* **1931** In this early big-budget western, based on a story by Zane Grey, a wagon train sets out west from Missouri. Cooper emerges as the hero after warding off an Indian attack that takes the lives of the original leaders. **80m/B; VHS, DVD.** Gary Cooper; Ernest Torrence; Tully Marshall; Fred Kohler, Sr.; Lili Damita; *D:* Otto Brower; David Burton.

The Fighting Eagle 🦴🦴 **1927** Etienne Girard (La Rocque), a young officer in Napoleon's army, saves a beautiful diplomatic courier (Haver) from the duplicitous Talleyrand (de Grasse) and uncovers a plot to overthrow the Emperor. Based on the comic "Brigadier Gerard" stories by Sir Arthur Conan Doyle. **71m/B; Silent; DVD.** Rod La Rocque; Phyllis Haver; Sam De Grasse; Max Barwyn; Julia Faye; Clarence Burton; Sally Rand; *D:* Donald Crisp; *W:* Douglas Z. Doty; *C:* J. Peverell Marley.

Fighting Elegy 🦴🦴 *Kenka Ereji* **1966** A high school boy longs for an unattainable girl and channels all those teenaged hormones into brawling with street gangs. Then he has an encounter with an ultra-right wing militarist that changes his life and sets him on the path to fascism. Japanese with subtitles. **86m/B; VHS, DVD.** *JP* Hideki Takahashi; Yusuke Kawazu; Jinko Asano; Mitsuo Kataoka; *D:* Seijun Suzuki.

Fighting Fists of Shanghai Joe 🦴 **1965** Fearsome fighting man from the Far East engages a vile American land baron in a battle of honor. **94m/C; VHS, DVD.** Klaus Kinski; Gordon Mitchell; Carla Romanelli; Claudio Undari; Chen Lee; *D:* Mario Caiano.

The Fighting Kentuckian 🦴🦴 1/2 **1949** Homeward bound from the Battle of New Orleans in 1814, a Kentucky rifleman lingers in a French settlement in Alabama. His romance with the daughter of a French general is blocked by the father until the American saves the community from an assault by land grabbers. Hardy as a frontiersman is well worth the view. An action-packed, well-photographed hit. **100m/B; DVD, Blu-Ray.** John Wayne; Oliver Hardy; Vera Hruba Ralston; Marie Windsor; Philip Dorn; John Howard; Hugo Haas; Grant Withers; *D:* George Waggner.

The Fighting Lawman 🦴 1/2 **1953** Brisk stock western. Deputy Marshal Jim Burke goes after four bank robbers only to learn that the sister of one of the men intends to get to the stashed stolen money first. **71m/B; DVD.** Wayne Morris; Virginia Grey; John Kellogg; Harry Lauter; John Pickard; Rick Vallin; Myron Healy; *D:* Thomas Carr; *W:* Daniel Ullman; *C:* Gilbert Warrenton; *M:* Raoul Kraushaar.

Fighting Mad 🦴🦴 1/2 **1976 (R)** A peaceful land owner is driven to violence when he discovers that the business men who want his property are planning to murder two of his family members in order to get it. The local sheriff's apathy forces the man to take the law into his own hands. Unlike other Fonda films of the time which consist of chaotic violence and car crashes, this story is a well performed character study. **90m/C; VHS, DVD.** Peter Fonda; Lynn Lowry; John Doucette; Phil Carey; Scott Glenn; Kathleen Miller; *D:* Jonathan Demme; *W:* Jonathan Demme.

Fighting Mad 🦴 1/2 *Fierce* **1977 (R)** Soldiers leave their buddy for dead in wartime Vietnam. He is alive, but captured by Japanese soldiers who believe they are still fighting in WWII. **96m/C; VHS, DVD.** James Iglehart; Jayne Kennedy; Leon Isaac Kennedy; *D:* Cirio H. Santiago.

A Fighting Man 🦴🦴 **2014 (R)** Unscrupulous boxing promoter Fast Eddie is pushing up-and-coming King Solomon so he arranges a fight with aging Sailor O'Conor, an ex-boxer with an unbeaten streak. Sailor accepts because he needs the dough for his dying mom and King has a pregnant wife to support. Also in the mix is Dianne, who did five years in prison for a crime that's slowly revealed. She's looking for redemption and forgiveness as is more than one character in this somewhat convoluted drama. **88m/C; DVD.** Dominic Purcell; Izaak Smith; Adam Beach; Famke Janssen; Sheila McCarthy; James Caan; Michael Ironside; Louis Gossett, Jr.; Kim Coates; *D:* Damian Lee; *W:* Damian Lee; *C:* Bobby Shore; *M:* Jonathan Goldsmith. **VIDEO**

Fighting Marines 🦴 1/2 **1936** U.S. Marines are trying to establish an air base on Halfway Island in the Pacific, but are thwarted by the "Tiger Shark," a modern-day pirate. First appeared as a serial. **69m/B; VHS, DVD.** Jason Robards, Sr.; Grant Withers; Ann Rutherford; Pat O'Malley; *D:* Joseph Kane; B. Reeves Eason; *W:* Barney A. Sarecky.

The Fighting Prince of Donegal 🦴🦴 1/2 **1966** An Irish prince battles the invading British in 16th Century Ireland. Escaping their clutches, he leads his clan in rescuing his mother and his beloved in this Disney swashbuckler. Based on the novel "Red Hugh, Prince of Donegal" by Robert T. Reilly. **110m/C; VHS, DVD, Streaming.** Peter McEnery; Susan Hampshire; Tom Adams; Gordon Jackson; Andrew Keir; *D:* Michael O'Herlihy; *M:* George Bruns.

The Fighting Rats of Tobruk 🦴🦴 *The Rats of Tobruk* **1944** Australian film about the Egyptian campaign against Rommel in World War II attempts to take a slightly documentary approach to the subject. It's notable mostly for providing an early role for Peter Finch. **71m/B; VHS, DVD.** *AU* Grant Taylor; Peter Finch; Chips Rafferty; Pauline Garrick; *D:* Charles Chauvel; *C:* George Heath.

Fighting Seabees 🦴🦴 1/2 **1944** As a hot-tempered construction foreman who battles Navy regulations as well as the Japanese, Wayne emerges as a larger-than-life hero in this action-packed saga of the Pacific theater of WWII. Extremely popular patriotic drama depicts the founding of the Seabees, the naval construction corps, amidst the action and the would-be romance with a woman reporter. Also available colorized. **100m/B; DVD, Blu-Ray.** John Wayne; Susan Hayward; Dennis O'Keefe; William Frawley; Grant Withers; Tom London; Wally Wales; Paul Fix; William Forrest; J.M. Kerrigan; Leonid Kinskey; Duncan Renaldo; Addison Richards; Ben Welden; Crane Whitley; Charles Trowbridge; *D:* Edward Ludwig; *W:* Borden Chase; Aeneas MacKenzie; *C:* William Bradford; *M:* Walter Scharf; Roy Webb.

The Fighting 69th 🦴🦴🦴 **1940** Cornball but entertaining WWI drama with lots of action. Cagney is a Brooklyn street tough who joins the all-Irish 69th New York regiment but could care less about its famed military history. He promptly defies his superiors and barely scrapes through his training. Sent to France, the swaggering Cagney turns coward when confronted by the horrors of war but eventually redeems himself. O'Brien is the famed regimental chaplain Father Duffy, while Brent is commander "Wild Bill" Donovan, who would later found the OSS in WWII. Lots of heart-tugging emotion backed with a fine supporting cast. **90m/B; DVD.** James Cagney; Pat O'Brien; George Brent; Jeffrey Lynn; Alan Hale; Frank McHugh; Dennis Morgan; William Lundigan; Dick Foran; Guinn "Big Boy" Williams; George Reeves; John Litel; *D:* William Keighley; *W:* Fred Niblo; Norman Reilly Raine; Dean Franklin; *C:* Gaetano Antonio "Tony" Gaudio; *M:* Adolph Deutsch.

The Fighting Sullivans 🦴🦴🦴 1/2 *The Sullivans* **1942** The true story of five brothers killed on the Battleship Juneau at Guadalcanal during WWII. The tale tells of the fury felt by the siblings after Pearl Harbor, their enlistment to fight for their country, and their tragic fate in the heat of battle. Truly a stirring tribute to all lives lost in combat. **110m/B; VHS, DVD.** Anne Baxter; Thomas Mitchell; Selena Royle; Eddie Ryan; Trudy Marshall; James B. Cardwell; Roy Roberts; Ward Bond; Mary McCarty; Bobby Driscoll; Addison Richards; Selmer Jackson; Mae Marsh; Harry Strang; Barbara Brown; George Offerman, Jr.; John Campbell; John Alvin; Patrick Curtis; Nancy June Robinson; Marvin Davis; *D:* Lloyd Bacon; *W:* Edward Doherty; Mary C. McCall; Jules Schermer; *C:* Lucien N. Andriot; *M:* Cyril Mockridge; Alfred Newman.

The Fighting Temptations 🦴🦴 **2003 (PG-13)** New York adman Darrin marries a witch and hilarity ensues. Oh wait, that's something else. Okay, Darrin (Gooding, Jr.) is an adman in New York. . .for about 15 minutes. Before long he's unemployed and heading to his small Georgia hometown in order to collect an inheritance. Only there's a catch—he must return a gospel choir to its former greatness in order to collect. Waferthin plot is merely filler connecting the great gospel and R&B music that is the real star of this show. Beyonce Knowles is the love interest and mainstay of the choir, but she's only one of the prominent musical talents who help to raise this flick above the mundane. Shirley Caesar, Melba Moore, The O'Jays, Faith Evans, Eddie LeVert, and Montel Jordan are among the luminaries. **123m/C; VHS, DVD.** Cuba Gooding, Jr.; Beyonce Knowles; Mike Epps; LaTanya Richardson Jackson; Steve Harvey; Melba Moore; *D:* Jonathan Lynn; *W:* Elizabeth Hunter; Saladin Patterson; *C:* Affonso Beato; *M:* Jimmy Jam; Terry Lewis; James "Big Jim" Wright.

Fighting the Odds: The Marilyn Gambrell Story 🦴🦴 1/2 **2005** Inspirational true story finds former parole officer Marilyn Gambrell (Gertz) beginning a high school program to help teens who have a parent in prison regain control of their lives. However, the administration at the pilot school insists that every senior must graduate or the program will not continue. **90m/C; DVD.** Jami Gertz; Ernie Hudson; Eugene Clark; Stacy Meadows; Sicily Sewell; Zak Santiago; Trent Cameron; Edwin Hodge; *D:* Andy Wolk; *W:* Peter Wolk; *C:* John Berrie; *M:* Bruce Leitl. **CABLE**

Fighting with Anger 🦴 **2007** Hitwoman Ray (Fleming) is looking for answers to her past and doesn't realize that mentor Will (Nelson) is keeping things from her. These secrets prove problematic when her next assignment, which involves illegal antiques and the Korean government, goes bad and leaves Ray with a new enemy. Poorly acted with a laughably executed plot. **90m/C; DVD.** Willie Nelson; Kelli Fleming; Jonathan Boatwright; Trant Batey; *D:* Sam Um; *W:* Sam Um; Lauran James; *C:* Phil Curry; *M:* Rick DeJonge. **VIDEO**

Fighting with Kit Carson 🦴🦴 **1933** Famous guide and Indian fighter lead bands of settlers westward. Action-packed. Twelve chapters. **230m/B; VHS, DVD.** Johnny Mack Brown; Noah Beery, Sr.; Noah Beery, Jr.; Betsy King Ross; *D:* Armand Schaefer; Colbert Clark.

Fighting with My Family 🦴🦴 1/2 **2019 (PG-13)** In a working class British town, Ricky (Frost) and his wife Julie (Headey) run a wrestling gym and small wrestling league. They have encouraged the wrestling pursuits of their children Saraya (Pugh) and Zac (Lowden) since childhood, and the pair have become the stars of their league. The tight-knit clan faces challenges when the siblings audition for the WWE, and only Saraya is chosen for development. As she trains, Saraya must overcome limits to move forward while Zac faces his own set of problems. Based on a true story, the feel-good film features inspiring performances that reflect the difficulties of pursuing one's dreams. **108m/C; DVD, Blu-Ray.** *US UK* Dwayne "The Rock" Johnson; Nick Frost; Lena Headey; Florence Pugh; Jack Lowden; ***D:*** Stephen Merchant; ***W:*** Stephen Merchant; ***C:*** Remi Adefarasin; ***M:*** Vik Sharma.

The File of the Golden Goose 🦴 1/2 **1969** Treasury agent Peter Novak (Brynner) heads to London to team up with Scotland Yard detective Arthur Thompson (Woodward) to infiltrate the Golden Goose counterfeiting ring. They get close to minion Harrison (Gray) who wants to betray his fellow crooks and go into business for himself. But Novak suspects there's about to be a doublecross. **106m/C; DVD, Blu-Ray.** Yul Brynner; Edward Woodward; Charles Gray; John Barrie; Adrienne Corri; Graham Crowden; Walter Gotell; Anthony Jacobs; James B. Gordon; ***D:*** Sam Wanamaker; ***W:*** John C. Higgins; ***C:*** Ken Hodges; ***M:*** Harry Robinson.

The File on Thelma Jordon 🦴🦴🦴 **1950** Oh so bad Thelma (Stanwyck) takes an evening saunter into the D.A.'s office where she finds a somewhat drunken Cleve Marshall (Corey). She complains about recent burglary attempts at her wealthy aunt's home and, as they head to a bar, he complains about his troubled marriage. Before long, the duo gets involved in adultery and Thelma's aunt is dead. Thelma stands accused of murder and through various manipulations brings about the obsessed Cleve's ruin--and her own--in this underrated, quality noir from director Siodmak. **100m/C; DVD, Blu-Ray.** Barbara Stanwyck; Wendell Corey; Paul Kelly; Richard Rober; Joan Tetzel; ***D:*** Robert Siodmak; ***W:*** Ketti Frings; ***C:*** George Barnes; ***M:*** Victor Young.

Fill the Void 🦴🦴 1/2 *Lemale et ha'halal* **2012** In her accomplished first feature, writer-director Burshstein showcases the insular Orthodox Hassidic community in Tel Aviv that she is part of. The family of Rabbi Aharon is plunged into tragedy during the Purim holiday when elder daughter Esther dies giving birth. This postpones the arranged marriage of teenage daughter Shira while everyone deals with their grief. Since widower Yochay is left with an infant, he's encouraged to find a new wife and his mother-in-law suggests that he marry Shira. Pressure increases but the decision is ultimately Shira's. Hebrew with subtitles. **90m/C; DVD.** *IS* Hadas Yaron; Yiftach Klein; Irit Sheleg; Chaim Sharir; ***D:*** Rama Burshtein; ***W:*** Rama Burshtein; ***C:*** Asaf Sudry; ***M:*** Yitzhak Azulay.

Filly Brown 🦴 1/2 **2012 (R)** In this unflinching look at the compromises facing those seeking a record deal, street poet Maria Jose "Majo" Tonorio (Rodriguez) realizes that she can use her talents as a hip hop artist to help her family. A meeting with a talented DJ leads to cutting her first demo with the help of a hustler who wants to capitalize on her looks more than her words. After attracting the attention of a major label and its demanding executive, Majo must chose between signing the deal and compromising herself to help her family or staying true to her friends and herself. **99m/C; DVD, Blu-Ray.** Gina Rodriguez; Khoolaid Rios; Jenni Rivera; Lou Diamond Phillips; Lala Romero; Jorge Diaz; Edward James Olmos; ***D:*** Youssef Delara; Michael D. Olmos; ***W:*** Youssef Delara; ***C:*** Ben Kufrin; ***M:*** Reza Safinia.

The Film Critic 🦴🦴 1/2 **2015** Victor Tellez is a bitter, misanthropic film critic. Like so many in the profession, he has seen so many falsities and clichés in romantic comedies that they have only made him more responsive to schmaltz and sentimentality in real life. Along with his fellow critics, he mopes through the world, wondering why everyone else embraces the clichés of meet-cutes and life-changing relationships that they see in cinema. And then his myopic worldview is shattered by love. Of course. And he realizes the tropes of romantic movies are that way because sometimes they really happen. It's a little slight, but smart. **98m/C; DVD.** Rafael Spregelburd; Dolores Fonzi; Ignacio Rogers; Telma Crisanti; Ana Katz; ***D:*** Hernan Guerschuny; ***W:*** Hernan Guerschuny; ***C:*** Marcelo Lavintman.

Film Geek 🦴🦴 1/2 **2006** Pitiful Scotty (Malkasian) loses his video store job because of the pain and suffering he's caused coworkers and customers (and viewers) alike with his endless chit-chat about the cinema and his lame zero-visitor movie website. The forlorn film fanatic gets really bummed out until his life takes an undue fairytale-ending twist thanks in part to a cool movie-loving chick he's preoccupied with. **78m/C; DVD.** Melik Malkasian; Tyler Gannon; Matt Morris; ***D:*** James Westby; ***C:*** Jason Hughes; ***M:*** Jason Wells.

Film Socialisme 🦴🦴 **2010** Jean-Luc Goddard's experimental three-section film, with its combo of live-action (including camera phone) and archive footage, first takes place aboard a Mediterranean cruise ships as it stops in ports in Egypt, Hellas, Odessa, Naples, and Barcelona. The numerous passengers, who play themselves or characters, debate European socio-political themes but even the English subtitles aren't accurate, deliberately truncating or abstracting what's actually said. (A version has also been released in French with fully-translated English subtitles.) Then there's a completely different second section where the owners of a rural gas station are having a family crisis and the children want to vote on who's in charge. Two women journalists, a llama and a donkey are also involved. Finally, the closing reels include a montage juxtaposing a tourist's visit to the Odessa Steps with the scene from Eisenstein's "Battleship Potemkin." It will most likely be of interest to those who like the 'art' in arthouse and Godard completists. **102m/C; DVD, Blu-Ray.** *SI* ***D:*** Jean-Luc Godard; ***W:*** Jean-Luc Godard; ***C:*** Jean-Luc Godard; Jean-Paul Battaggia; Francois Aragno; Paul Grivas.

Film Stars Don't Die in Liverpool 🦴🦴 1/2 **2017 (R)** Romantic drama based on the life of actress Gloria Grahame (Bening). Though Gloria was once a femme fatale in '50s noirs, her career went downhill over subsequent decades. By the late 1970s, the oft-married star is single and primarily performing stage roles in England. There, she begins a relationship with much younger actor, Peter Turner (Bell). After the pair becomes estranged a few years later, Gloria collapses before going on stage to perform and insists that Peter take her to his working-class family home in Liverpool to recuperate. Though the leads are passionate, the story lacks context to care about Gloria. **105m/C; DVD.** Jamie Bell; Annette Bening; Julie Walters; Vanessa Redgrave; Stephen Graham; ***D:*** Paul McGuigan; ***W:*** Matt Greenhalgh; ***C:*** Urszula Pontikos; ***M:*** J. Ralph.

A Film Unfinished 🦴🦴 1/2 **2010** In May 1942, a Nazi film unit shot material in Warsaw's Jewish ghetto for use in a propaganda film that went unfinished. Discovered by East German archivists after the war, it was used by scholars as a record of ghetto life. Then another reel of film was found in 1998—unedited outtakes that showed scenes had been staged amidst the often grim street footage. Israeli director Hersonski offers a critical analysis of the material with readings of journal material and interviews with five survivors who viewed the original footage. English, Hebrew, German, Polish, and Yiddish with subtitles. **88m/C; DVD.** *GE IS* ***Nar:*** Rona Kenan; ***D:*** Yael Heronski; ***C:*** Itai Neeman; ***M:*** Ishai Adar.

Filth 🦴🦴 1/2 **2008** A gently satiric look at the real-life morality crusade of staid British teacher and housewife Mary Whitehouse (Walters). It might be the swinging '60s in London, but Mary and her genteel circle are appalled by the sex and vulgarities that are turning up on the telly. Mary's crusade eventually gains a momentum that even lecherous, haughty BBC head, Sir Hugh Greene (Bonneville), can't ignore forever. Unfortunately, the deeper Mary gets into her clean-up campaign, the more self-righteous she becomes. **90m/C; DVD.** *GB* Julie Walters; Hugh Bonneville; Alun Armstrong; Ron Cook; Georgie Glen; Timothy Davies; ***D:*** Andy de Emmony; ***W:*** Amanda Coe; ***C:*** David Odd; ***M:*** Norwell & Green. **TV**

Filth 🦴🦴 1/2 **2013 (R)** Misogynistic, perverse, and in love with all things intoxicating, Edinburgh detective Bruce Robertson (McAvoy) is assigned to investigate the murder of a Japanese student, but is easily distracted. Quickly, the case takes a back seat to Robertson's quest for more booze, more drugs, more sex, and more dirty phone calls to his best friend's unsuspecting wife. Slowly, the demons from his past emerge, fleshing out a clear portrait of his sickness. Much like director Baird's unapologetic take on Irvine Welsh's filthy, daring novel, McAvoy's full-blown take on hedonism is just as courageous and unapologetic, blurring the lines between actor and raging madman. **97m/C; DVD, Blu-Ray.** *UK* James McAvoy; Imogen Poots; Jamie Bell; Eddie Marsan; Shirley Henderson; Shauna Macdonald; ***D:*** Jon S. Baird; ***W:*** Jon S. Baird; ***C:*** Matthew Jensen; ***M:*** Clint Mansell.

The Filth and the Fury 🦴🦴 1/2 **1999 (R)** British punk anarchists The Sex Pistols get their documentary due. Combines new and old footage and interviews of the (surviving) band members (Sid Vicious died of a heroin overdose). Director Temple previously covered the group in 1980's "The Great Rock 'n' Roll Swindle," which was told from the viewpoint of their former manager, Malcolm McLaren. **105m/C; VHS, DVD.** *GB* John (Johnny Rotten) Lydon; Paul Cook; Steve Jones; Malcolm McLaren; Sid Vicious; Glen Matlock; Nancy Spungen; ***D:*** Julien Temple; ***M:*** John (Johnny Rotten) Lydon.

Filth and Wisdom 🦴🦴 **2008** Pop queen, author, actress, and now director Madonna helms this uneven comedy focusing on three flatmates struggling to make a name for themselves in modern day London. Ukrainian-born singer-songwriter A.K. (Gogol Bordello frontman Eugene Hutz) pays the bills as a male dominatrix, dancer Holly (Weston) turns to stripping once ballet stops paying the bills, and pharmacist Juliette (McClure), trying to fund a nursing trip to Africa, has to put up with her married boss's leering stares. Unfairly ravaged by international critics once the Material Girl compared her aspirations to that of Godard and Fellini, but still aimless and amateurish. **80m/C; DVD.** *GB* Eugene Hutz; Richard E. Grant; Stephen Graham; Holly Weston; Vicky McLure; Inder Manocha; Elliot Levey; Francesca Kingdon; ***D:*** Madonna; ***W:*** Madonna; Dan Cadan; ***C:*** Tim Maurice-Jones.

Final 🦴🦴 1/2 **2001 (R)** Bill (Leary) wakes up confused in a Connecticut psychiatric hospital after an apparent suicide attempt. He's assigned to Ann (Davis), a young staff therapist who tries to help Bill sort out his memories from his delusions, which include the fear that he's to be executed by lethal injection and must escape. The story takes on some strange twists, including patients' rights and conspiracy theories. **111m/C; VHS, DVD.** Denis Leary; Hope Davis; J.C. MacKenzie; Jim Gaffigan; ***D:*** Campbell Scott; ***W:*** Bruce McIntosh; ***C:*** Dan Gillham; ***M:*** Guy Davis.

The Final 🦴 1/2 **2010 (R)** Teen horror flick that ventures into talky torture porn. Outcast Dane has inherited some rural property and fakes a costume party invite to the popular students at Hohn High School. What he and a group of fellow misfits are planning is a single night vendetta against the teens who made their lives miserable. **92m/C; DVD.** Marc Donato; Jascha Washington; Travis Tedford; Whitney Hoy; Justin Arnold; Mark Nutter; ***D:*** Joey Stewart; ***W:*** Jason Kabolati; ***C:*** Dave McFarland; ***M:*** Damon Criswell. **VIDEO**

Final Analysis 🦴🦴 1/2 **1992 (R)** Glossy thriller starring Gere as a San Francisco psychiatrist who falls for the glamorous sister of one of his patients. Basinger plays the femme fatale and Thurman is Gere's sexually neurotic patient. Although heavily influenced by "Vertigo," this film never comes close to attaining the depth of Hitchock's cinematic masterpiece. Roberts gives the most gripping performance in this slick suspense movie as Basinger's sleazy gangster husband. **125m/C; VHS, DVD.** Richard Gere; Kim Basinger; Uma Thurman; Eric Roberts; Paul Guilfoyle; Keith David; Robert Harper; Jolyon Baker; Harris Yulin; Agustin Rodriguez; ***D:*** Phil Joanou; ***W:*** Wesley Strick; Robert Berger; ***C:*** Jordan Cronenweth; ***M:*** George Fenton.

Final Approach 🦴🦴 *Junior Pilot* **2004** Hijackers take control of a plane full of elementary students and, to make things worse, the pilot collapses. Luckily 10-year-old Ricky (Garrett)?who has mastered computer flight simulation games—is put in charge of landing the plane. He and his friends must keep the terrorists at bay. Family-oriented though perhaps a little scary for the younger set. **92m/C; DVD.** Jordan Garrett; Larry Miller; Eric Roberts; Mark Dacascos; Angela Watson; David Rasche; Tim Thomerson; Steve Hynter; ***D:*** James Becket; ***W:*** James Becket; ***C:*** Denis Maloney; ***M:*** Peter Tomashek. **VIDEO**

Final Approach 🦴🦴 **2008** FBI agent Jack Bender (Cain) is part of a raid on a white supremacist compound. Sometime later, he just happens to be aboard a flight that's hijacked by members of the group, lead by the ruthless Gilliad (Hall), who want their leader released from prison. Jack quietly enlists some of the other passengers to assist him in overpowering the bad guys but there's not much new about this hostage-crisis-in-the-sky saga. **130m/C; DVD.** Dean Cain; Anthony Michael Hall; Ernie Hudson; Sunny Mabrey; Lea Thompson; Barry Livingston; Tracey Gold; Richard Roundtree; Scott Paulin; Christopher Cousins; William Forsythe; ***D:*** Armand Mastroianni; ***W:*** Adam Armus; Kay Foster; ***C:*** Dane Peterson; ***M:*** Kevin Kiner. **CABLE**

Final Assignment 🦴 *The Moscow Chronicle* **1980** A Canadian TV reporter agrees to smuggle a dissident Soviet scientist's ill granddaughter out of Russia for treatment along with a videotape documenting tragic experiments on children with steroids. She manages to evade the KGB while carrying on with a Russian press officer, and enlists the support of a Jewish fur trader. Location shooting in Canada instead of Russia is just one pitfall of this production. **101m/C; VHS, DVD.** *CA* Genevieve Bujold; Michael York; Burgess Meredith; Colleen Dewhurst; ***D:*** Paul Almond.

Final Combination 🦴 1/2 **1993** Boxer Welton (Stretch) lures two girls to his hotel room where he rapes and beat them to death. Trying to catch the psycho is hard-bitten, hard-drinking L.A. cop Matt Dickson (Madsen), who figures out he's after a serial killer using the names of famous boxers as aliases. Also involved is supposed journalist Catherine Briggs (Bonet), who offers info to Dickson but has her own agenda. Ordinary thriller with sillier-than-usual dialogue. **92m/C; VHS, Streaming.** Michael Madsen; Lisa Bonet; Gary Stretch; Tim Russ; Damian Chapa; Carmen Argenziano; Susan Byun; ***D:*** Nigel Dick; ***W:*** Larry Golin; ***M:*** Rolfe Kent.

Final Comedown 🦴 **1972 (R)** A black revolutionary attempts to get white radicals behind his war against racism. He fails and starts a racial bloodbath. **84m/C; VHS, DVD.** Billy Dee Williams; D'Urville Martin; Celia Kaye; Raymond St. Jacques; Pamela Jones; R.G. Armstrong; ***D:*** Oscar Williams.

The Final Conflict 🦴 1/2 *Omen 3: The Final Conflict* **1981 (R)** Unwelcomed third installment in the "Omen" series, concerning Satan's son Damien. Now 32, and the head of an international conglomerate, he is poised for world domination but fears another savior is born. Several monks and many babies meet gruesome deaths before he gets his comeuppance. The last theatrical release; the next entry was made for TV. **108m/C; VHS, DVD, Blu-Ray.** Sam Neill; Lisa Harrow; Barnaby Holm; Rossano Brazzi; Don Gordon; Mason Adams; Robert Arden; Marc Boyle; Tommy Duggan; Richard Oldfield; Arwen Holm; ***D:*** Graham Baker; ***W:*** Andrew Birkin; ***C:*** Phil Meheux; Robert Paynter; ***M:*** Jerry Goldsmith.

The Final Countdown 🦴🦴🦴 **1980 (PG)** A U.S. nuclear-powered aircraft carrier, caught in a time warp, is transported back to 1941, just hours before the bombing of Pearl Harbor. The commanders face the ultimate decision—leave history intact or stop the incident and thus avoid WWII. Excellent photography and a surprise ending. **92m/C; VHS, DVD, Blu-Ray.** Kirk Douglas; Martin Sheen; Katharine Ross; James Farentino; Charles Durning; ***D:*** Don Taylor; ***W:*** Thomas Hunter; David Ambrose.

Final Cut 🦴 1/2 **1988** While filming in a secluded swampland, a crew stumbles on a local sheriff's crooked scheme and one by one, the crew members disappear. **92m/C; VHS, DVD.** Carla De Lane; T.J. Kennedy; Joe

Rainer; Brett Rice; Jordan Williams; ***D:*** Larry G. Brown.

The Final Cut 1995 Follows "House of Cards" and "To Play the King" in portraying the political adventures of Francis Urquardt (Richardson), Prime Minister. At 65, Urquardt has two goals: he wants to beat Margaret Thatcher's 11-year reign and he wants to establish a secret retirement fund (the plot involves Cyprus and could—finally—leads to Urquardt's downfall). Author Michael Dobbs objected to the adaptation and insisted his name be removed from the script. On two cassettes. **200m/C; VHS, DVD.** *GB* Ian Richardson; Diane Fletcher; Paul Freeman; Isla Blair; Nick Brimble; Erika Hoffman; Nickolas Grace; Julian Fellowes; ***D:*** Mike Vardy; ***W:*** Andrew Davies; ***C:*** Ian Punter; ***M:*** Jim Parker.

Final Cut **1998 (R)** A self-indulgent, apparently largely improvised mess. Jude (Law) has died and after his friends pay their respects at his funeral, his wife Sadie (Frost) insists they view the home video he'd been working on for the past two years. It turns out Jude must have been quite the voyeur—hidden cameras recorded his pals at their worst behavior, all of which is now revealed to the uncomfortable ensemble. **93m/C; VHS, DVD.** *GB* Jude Law; Sadie Frost; Ray Winstone; Ray Burdis; Dominic Anciano; Perry Benson; John Beckett; ***D:*** Ray Burdis; Dominic Anciano; ***W:*** Ray Burdis; Dominic Anciano; ***C:*** John Ward; ***M:*** John Beckett.

The Final Cut ½ **2004 (PG-13)** After "One Hour Photo" Williams plays another guy involved in images, this time in a subdued sci-fi thriller. In the near-future, newborns are implanted with a chip that records their entire life—good, bad, and in-between. Alan Hakman (Williams) is a cutter who splices the appropriate footage of the deceased together as a funeral memorial. Then Hakman is asked to create a memorial of the recently-deceased chipmaker, a guy with some shady dealings that put Hakman in danger. Caviezel plays an anti-chip activist who wants an expose and Sorvino is Williams' ex-girlfriend who didn't care for his video obsession. The premise has certainly been done before and in much more enthralling movies. **104m/C; DVD.** *CA GE* Robin Williams; Mira Sorvino; James (Jim) Caviezel; Mimi Kuzyk; Brendan Fletcher; Vincent Gale; Thom Bishops; Casey Dubois; Liam Ranger; ***D:*** Omar Naim; ***W:*** Omar Naim; ***C:*** Tak Fujimoto; ***M:*** Brian Tyler.

Final Days of Planet Earth **2006** Scientists discover a conspiracy when they realize the San Francisco government are carnivorous space bugs who want to use humans as cattle. **170m/C; DVD, Blu-Ray.** *CA US* Daryl Hannah; Campbell Scott; Gil Bellows; Suleka Mathew; Serge Houde; ***D:*** Robert Lieberman; ***W:*** Christian Ford; Roger Soffer; Bill Thumm; ***C:*** Thomas Burstyn; ***M:*** Jeff Rona. **CABLE**

Final Destination **2000 (R)** Teenager Alex (Sawa) predicts that a plane filled with classmates will explode. It does but he and some others manage to make it off the plane beforehand. Things get interesting (and a little philosophical) when the survivors start dying. Seems Death feels cheated and is getting even. Typical body count slasher genre gets a twist from the machinations of fate...or whatever. Filmmakers paid tribute to some of their favorite horror stars and directors with the characters' surnames. **97m/C; VHS, DVD, Blu-Ray.** Devon Sawa; Ali Larter; Kristen Cloke; Daniel Roebuck; Roger Guenveur Smith; Chad E. Donella; Seann William Scott; Tony Todd; Kerr Smith; Amanda Detmer; ***D:*** James Wong; ***W:*** Glen Morgan; James Wong; Jeffrey Reddick; ***C:*** Robert McLachlan; ***M:*** Shirley Walker.

Final Destination 2 **2003 (R)** Sequel has the same premise as the original. Kimberly (Cook) has a horrifying vision of a traffic accident as she heads onto the highway. She blocks the ramp with her SUV, thus saving the lives of the drivers behind her. However, Death doesn't like to be cheated and the drivers start to die in bizarre accidents. Less philosophical than the first one, it ups the ante on the gore factor. Death also has a tendency to lay elaborate, convoluted plans to bring the intended victims to their gruesome deaths (kinda like Bond villains). The accidents can be so improbable that it borders on being tiresome, but if you accept the premise on a certain level you can enjoy it as a guilty pleasure. Larter returns as the sole survivor from the first movie and Tony Todd has a cameo as a morgue attendant. **100m/C; VHS, DVD, Blu-Ray.** Ali Larter; A.J. Cook; Michael Landes; Terrence "T.C." Carson; Lynda Boyd; Jonathan Cherry; Keegan Connor Tracy; Sarah Carter; Tony Todd; Justina Machado; David Paetkau; James Kirk; ***D:*** David R. Ellis; ***W:*** J. Mackye Gruber; Eric Bress; ***C:*** Gary Capo; ***M:*** Shirley Walker.

Final Destination 3 **2006 (R)** Death stalks a whole new batch of interchangeable teenagers who survive a huge rollercoaster crash thanks to the premonition of Wendy (Winstead). You weren't really expecting anything different, were you? Demises come in really gross, over-the-top, more-gore-the-better ways as the Grim Reaper makes like a deranged Wile E. Coyote. **92m/C; DVD, Blu-Ray.** Mary Elizabeth Winstead; Ryan Merriman; Kris Lemche; Texas Battle; Jesse Moss; Crystal Lowe; Chelan Simmons; Alexz Johnson; Gina Holden; Sam Easton; Amanda Crew; ***V:*** Tony Todd; ***D:*** James Wong; ***W:*** James Wong; Glen Morgan; ***C:*** Robert McLachlan; ***M:*** Shirley Walker.

The Final Destination *Final Destination 4; Final Destination: Death Trip 3D* **2009 (R)** It's probably not the end, although the cliched plot and characters couldn't be thinner and the actors couldn't be prettier or more wooden. While at the racetrack, Nick (Campo) has a horrible premonition of cars crashing, the stands collapsing, and his friends dying. He persuades them to leave just in time, which makes Death very unhappy, and soon the survivors are getting killed off in very gruesome ways, including decapitation, impalement, and mutilation. The killings get boring and the 3D effects generally just highlight blood and organs spewing at the audience. **75m/C; Blu-Ray, On Demand.** Nick Zano; Krista Allen; Bobby Campo; Shantel VanSanten; Haley Webb; Mykelti Williamson; Justin Welborn; ***D:*** David R. Ellis; ***W:*** Eric Bress; ***C:*** Glen MacPherson; ***M:*** Brian Tyler.

Final Destination 5 **2011 (R)** More tongue-in-bloody-cheek humor than the last lifeless installment in this unending franchise. And it works for its first few reels, especially during a bridge collapse that fully employs 3D in more interesting ways than any horror film to date, but typical genre traps abound. A few better actors (including the return of horror staple Todd) are added to the mix but it's impossible to care about the paper-thin characters who must eventually succumb to the death-driven chaos. **92m/C; Blu-Ray.** Emma Bell; Nicholas D'Agosto; P.J. Byrne; Ellen Wroe; Tony Todd; Courtney B. Vance; Miles Fisher; Arlen Escarpeta; David Koechner; Jacqueline MacInnes-Wood; ***D:*** Steven Quale; ***W:*** Eric Heisserer; ***C:*** Brian Pearson; ***M:*** Brian Tyler.

Final Draft ½ **2007** Once-successful screenwriter Paul Twist (Van der Beek) has been on a downhill slide since his divorce and has a bad case of writer's block. Twist decides to isolate himself in his apartment to work on his new screenplay, which involves characters and situations from his past, including a childhood incident about a circus clown dying in a fire. Too bad Paul starts losing sight of the boundaries between fiction and reality. **92m/C; DVD.** James Van Der Beek; Tara Spencer-Nairn; Darryn Luci; Jeff Roop; ***D:*** Jonathan Dueck; ***W:*** Darryn Luci; ***C:*** Mick Reynolds; ***M:*** Ryan Latham. **VIDEO**

Final Encounter *For the Cause* **2000 (R)** Confusing sci-fier based on the Warhammer videogame. A 100-year-old war between two technologically advanced colonies may finally be decided by a weapon of mass destruction. Sutherland (Whalen) is told by Gen. Murran (Cain) to lead a unit into enemy territory and stop the devastation. They're aided by witches who can turn computer programs into physical monsters but they also have to deal with a traitor. **98m/C; DVD, Blu-Ray.** Dean Cain; Justin Whalin; Thomas Ian Griffith; Jodi Bianca Wise; Michelle Krusiec; ***D:*** David Douglas; Tim Douglas; ***W:*** David Douglas; Christopher Salazar; ***C:*** Adolfo Bartoli; ***M:*** Kevin Memley. **VIDEO**

Final Engagement ½ **2007** Jacqueline is being used as a pawn by her Miami criminal dad Jimmy Bombay. In order to join with an international drug cartel, Jimmy's arranged a marriage between his daughter and the drug lord's son. Jacqueline turns to a priest for guidance, but he may not be exactly what he seems either. **96m/C; DVD.** Peter Greene; Arlene Tur; Greg Schroeder; Mike Maria; John Trapani; Ted Bell; ***D:*** Ari Vovak; ***C:*** Ari Vovak; ***M:*** Mel Lewis. **VIDEO**

Final Exam WOOF! **1981 (R)** Psychotic killer stalks college students during exam week. This one's too boring to be scary. You root for the psycho to off everyone just to have the movie over. **90m/C; VHS, DVD, Blu-Ray.** Cecile Bagdadi; Joel Rice; ***D:*** Jimmy Huston.

Final Fantasy: The Spirits Within ½ **2001 (PG-13)** Photorealistic computer-generated animation may be the highlight of this fantasy adventure, which is based on the videogame series. In the year 2065, life on Earth is threatened by aliens who steal energy from all living things on the planet. A team of scientists, led by Aki Ross (Ming-Na) and Dr. Sid (Sutherland) are at odds with the military, in the form of General Hein (Woods) over how to deal with the creatures. Plot, dialogue, and characterization, the movie's obvious weaknesses, definitely take a back seat to the visuals. The human characters, while not completely lifelike, are the closest anyone's come so far. Where the techology shines is in the landscapes and non-human creatures, which are all striking. **104m/C; VHS, DVD, Blu-Ray, UMD.** ***V:*** Ming Na; Alec Baldwin; Steve Buscemi; Peri Gilpin; Ving Rhames; Donald Sutherland; James Woods; Keith David; Jean Simmons; Matt McKenzie; ***D:*** Hironobu Sakaguchi; ***W:*** Al Reinert; Jeff Vintar; ***M:*** Elliot Goldenthal.

The Final Girls ½ **2015 (PG-13)** Todd Strauss-Schulson's horror-comedy is the kind of self-referential meta commentary that we saw a lot of in the years post Scream, but it works on its own modern terms. Max Cartwright (Taissa Farmiga) lost her mother Amanda (Malin Akerman) years earlier, but she has the films of this once-famous scream queen to keep her company. One night, at a showing of one of mom's biggest hits, something impossible happens when Max and her friends are transported "into the movie," waking up in an '80s slasher pic. A bit of mother-daughter reconciliation happens as the gang tries to survive the night. Often clever and well-cast. **91m/C; DVD, Blu-Ray, Streaming.** Taissa Farmiga; Malin Akerman; Alexander Ludwig; Nina Dobrev; Alia Shawkat; ***D:*** Todd Strauss-Schulson; ***W:*** M. A. Fortin; Joshua John Miller; Gregory Jenkins; ***C:*** Elie Smolkin; ***M:*** Gregory James Jenkins.

The Final Goal ½ **1994 (R)** Evil businessman (and ex-soccer star) Paulo Ramirez (Estrada) meddles with his country's current soccer star, who's playing in the Global Cup of Soccer. He wants the player to throw the game and thinks death threats will accomplish his goal. **85m/C; VHS, DVD, On Demand.** Erik Estrada; Steven Nijjar; Dean Butler; ***D:*** Jon Cassar.

The Final Hit **2002 (R)** Washed-up Hollywood producer Sonny Wexler (Reynolds) prefers to reminisce about his past success than raise the money to option a hot script and get back in the game. Maybe he should stick with his memories, since Sonny hooks up with a shady businessman who expects a guaranteed return on his investment—or else. **90m/C; VHS, DVD.** Burt Reynolds; Lauren Holly; Benjamin Bratt; Sean Astin; ***D:*** Burt Reynolds.

Final Impact ½ **1991 (R)** Nick Taylor seeks vengeance on reigning kickboxing champ Jake Gerard through his prodigy, Danny Davis. Will sweet revenge for the wicked beating, suffered at the hands of Gerard years earlier, be his? **99m/C; VHS, DVD.** Lorenzo Lamas; Kathleen Kinmont; Mimi Lesseos; Kathrin Lautner; Jeff Langton; Mike Worth; ***D:*** Joseph Merhi; Stephen Smoke; ***M:*** John Gonzalez.

Final Justice **1984 (R)** A small-town Texan sheriff wages a war against crime and corruption that carries him to Italy and the haunts of Mafia hitmen. **90m/C; VHS, DVD.** Joe Don Baker; Rossano Brazzi; Patrizia Pellegrino; Venantino Venantini; ***D:*** Greydon Clark; ***W:*** Greydon Clark; ***C:*** Nicholas Josef von Sternberg; ***M:*** David Bell.

Final Justice **1994 (R)** Icky revenge drama has bad guys Red (Huff) and Bobby (Marotta) hiding out in a woodsy cabin that's owned by lawyer Alan Massard (Brolin) and his wife Amy (Fitzgerald). Unfortunately for them, the Massards have chosen to invite some friends and hang out at the cabin for the weekend, where the bad guys do nasty things before Alan manages to kill Bobby and trap Red. Then there's a stupid debate on just what to do with Red and more violence. **92m/C; VHS, DVD.** James Brolin; Annie Fitzgerald; Brent Huff; Rick Marotta; Beau Billingslea; ***D:*** Brent Huff; ***W:*** Brent Huff.

Final Justice ½ **1998** Teacher Gwen (O'Toole) is outraged when a sleazy attorney (McKean) gets her murdered gay brother's killer acquitted. So she kidnaps him for some rough justice of her own but then winds up on trial herself. **120m/C; VHS, DVD.** Annette O'Toole; Michael McKean; CCH Pounder; Brian Wimmer; ***D:*** Tommy Lee Wallace; ***W:*** Babs Greyhosky; ***M:*** Brian Tyler. **CABLE**

The Final Master ½ *Shi Fu* **2016** A powerful animated film about a young girl's life in Afghanistan under the Taliban, based on Deborah Ellis's young adult novel. Eleven-year-old Parvana (Chaudry) lives in Kabul with her family. Because women are forbidden to leave their homes unaccompanied, Parvana can only go to the marketplace with her former teacher father (Badshah). After he is imprisoned, the family, which includes a sickly mother, older sister, and baby brother, struggles. To help them, Parvana cuts her hair to pass as a boy, an act that does not stave off reality forever. **109m/C; DVD.** Fan Liao; Jia Song; Wenli Jiang; Shijie Jin; Yang Song; ***D:*** Haofeng Xu; ***W:*** Haofeng Xu; ***C:*** Tianlin Wang; ***M:*** Wei An.

Final Mission **1993 (R)** Virtual reality becomes a weapon in a military conspiracy when pilots start dying. Air Force jets are supposed to be unstoppable thanks to the new technology and a general is only too willing to blame the deaths on pilot error but one fly boy is out to find the truth. **91m/C; VHS, Streaming.** Billy Wirth; Corbin Bernsen; Elizabeth (Ward) Gracen; Steve Railsback.

Final Move **2006 (R)** After using his psychic powers to help the LAPD solve a chess-related serial-killer case, former detective Dan Marlowe (Schulze) becomes obsessed by thoughts that he might have put an innocent man to death. A rash of similar slayings seems to confirm his worst fears, causing him to rejoin the force to crack the case. Produces a serious case of deja vu for the onslaught of rehashed plot twists. **90m/C; DVD.** Matt Schulze; Lochlyn Munro; Amanda Detmer; Daniel Baldwin; David Carradine; ***D:*** Joey Travolta; ***W:*** Richard Preston, Jr; David Shoshan. **VIDEO**

The Final Patient ½ **2005** When an elderly doctor lifts a tractor off a boy, two curious medical students come to regret asking him how he came by his impossible physical prowess. **100m/C; DVD, Blu-Ray.** Matthew Borish; Guy Boyd; Jason Scott Campbell; Bill Cobbs; Desmond Confoy; ***D:*** Jerry Mainardi; ***W:*** Jerry Mainardi; Michael J. Mainardi; ***C:*** Joe Vandergast; ***M:*** Ron Burns. **VIDEO**

Final Payback WOOF! **1999** A cast of faded TV stars long since past their prime time (Richard Grieco of "21 Jump Street," Corbin Bernsen of "L.A. Law," Martin Kove of "Cagney and Lacey," Priscilla Barnes of "Three's Company") collect their paychecks for this ineptly directed thriller that leaves no direct-to-video cliche unturned. Grieco stars as an ex-cop who finds himself "pushed over the fence" after he is framed for the murder of the police chief's wife. Gee, you think the police chief himself (B-movie vet John Saxon) may be involved in the conspiracy? No nudity and only one car explosion. Why bother? **102m/C; VHS, DVD, UMD.** Richard Grieco; Corbin Bernsen; Martin Kove; Priscilla Barnes; John Saxon; ***D:*** Art Camacho.

Final Portrait ½ **2017 (R)** Drama about artist Alberto Giacometti (Rush) and author James Lord (Hammer), based on Lord's memoir. In 1964 Paris, Alberto asks Lord to sit for a portrait for one day. One day stretches out over three weeks. Through this period, James shows his understanding of Alberto's artistic language while the artist is plagued by self-doubt and re-starts several times. As Alberto struggles, James also learns much from the artist's circle, including his assistant/brother Diego (Shalhoub) and his dutiful wife Annette (Testud). Visually lovely and thematically insightful, director/screenwriter Tucci has created an interesting chamber piece. **90m/C; DVD, Blu-Ray, Streaming.** *UK* Geoffrey Rush; Armie Hammer; Clemence Poesy; Tony Shalhoub; Sylvie Testud; ***D:*** Stanley Tucci; ***W:*** Stanley Tucci; ***C:*** Danny Cohen; ***M:*** Evan Lurie.

The Final Programme 1/2 *The Last Days of Man on Earth* **1973** In this futuristic story, a man must rescue his sister—and the world—from their brother, who holds a microfilmed plan for global domination. Meanwhile, he must shield himself from the advances of a bisexual .computer programmer who wants to make him father to a new, all-purpose human being. Based on the Michael Moorcock "Jerry Cornelius" stories, the film has gained a cult following. **85m/C; VHS, DVD, Blu-Ray.** *GB* Hugh Griffith; Harry Andrews; Jon Finch; Jenny Runacre; Sterling Hayden; Patrick Magee; Sarah Douglas; ***D:*** Robert Fuest; ***W:*** Robert Fuest; ***C:*** Norman Warwick; ***M:*** Gerry Mulligan; Paul Beaver; Bernard Krause.

The Final Project WOOF! 2016 The film industry may have finally found the bottom of the well when it comes to found footage horror films with this deeply incompetent movie about a group of students investigating a haunted house for a school project that would earn them an 'F' in class. Six dumb kids who don't know how to hold a film camera at the right level go a supposedly (in real life) haunted plantation to play ghost hunters. Director Taylor Ri'chard makes too many mistakes to count, almost creating a checklist of bad found footage tropes. Other disasters in the genre look better because this movie exists. **82m/C; DVD.** Benjamin Anderson; Amber Erwin; Teal Haddock; Arin Jones; Leonardo Santaiti; ***D:*** Taylor Ri'chard; ***W:*** Taylor Ri'chard; Zachary Davis.

Final Score 2018 (R) Career military man Michael Knox (Bautista) feels guilt after his British best friend is killed in combat under his watch. Because of his death, Michael regularly travels to England to care for the man's widow, bartender Rachel (Gaskell), and daughter Danni (Peake). When Michael takes Danni to a professional soccer match, it is the target of Russian terrorists led by Arkady (Stevenson). Their goal is to gain custody of a rogue Russian agent (Brosnan) by any means necessary, including blowing up the whole stadium. Though the film is a Die Hard clone, Bautista's balance of brutal action and genuine warmth make it worthwhile. **104m/C; DVD, Blu-Ray.** Dave Bautista; Lara Peake; Martyn Ford; Pierce Brosnan; Ray Stevenson; ***D:*** Scott Mann; ***W:*** Jonathan Frank; David T. Lynch; Keith Lynch; ***C:*** Emil Topuzov; ***M:*** James Edward Barker; Tim Despic.

The Final Season 2007 (PG) A tiny city in Iowa revels in the success of the local high school baseball team, with its multiple state championships. But administrators are plotting to merge the school with a neighboring high school, putting both coaches and players in jeopardy. Brand new head coach Kent Stock (Astin) wants the team to end their legendary run on a high note. No surprises here—there's a romance, a troubled transfer student who straightens up, a legendary final game. Yet another based-on-a-true-story sports drama that makes up for its flaws with a whole lotta heart. **114m/C; On Demand.** Sean Astin; Powers Boothe; Rachael Leigh Cook; James Gammon; Larry Miller; Marshall Bell; Tom Arnold; Michael Angarano; Angela Paton; ***D:*** David Mickey Evans; ***W:*** Art D'Alessandro; James Grayford; ***C:*** Daniel Styoloff; ***M:*** Nathan Wang.

Final Shot: The Hank Gathers Story 1/2 **1992** Inspirational story of Gathers, who rose from the ghetto to become one of America's top college basketball stars at Loyola Marymount, until tragedy strikes during a game. **92m/C; VHS, DVD.** Victor Love; Duane Davis; Nell Carter; George Kennedy; ***D:*** Charles Braverman; ***W:*** Fred Johnson; ***C:*** Stephen Blake; ***M:*** Stanley Clarke.

The Final Storm WOOF! 2009 (R) Maybe director Boll isn't entirely to blame since he didn't write the script for this apocalyptic whatsit. The Gradys are a farm family who notice after a seven-day storm that the animals and birds have disappeared as have their neighbors. Then stranger Silas (Perry) stumbles onto their doorstep yammering about the end of days. Husband Tom (Bacic) is really suspicious, but he's more concerned that Silas is some homicidal maniac who keeps leering at his wife Gillian (Holly). The apocalypse plot is briefly resurrected but it doesn't matter. **85m/C; DVD.** *CA* Cole Heppell; Steve Bacic; Lauren Holly; Luke Perry; Blu Mankuma; ***D:*** Uwe Boll; ***W:*** Blu Mankuma; Tim McGregor; ***C:*** Mathias Neumann; ***M:*** Hal Beckett. **VIDEO**

The Final Terror *Campsite Massacre; Bump in the Night; The Forest Primeval* **1983 (R)** Group of young campers is stalked by a mad killer in a desolate, backwoods area. Better-than-average stalked-teens entry is notable for the presence of some soon-to-be stars. **90m/C; VHS, DVD, Blu-Ray.** John Friedrich; Rachel Ward; Adrian Zmed; Daryl Hannah; Joe Pantoliano; Ernest Harden, Jr.; Mark Metcalf; Lewis Smith; Cindy Harrel; Akosua Busia; ***D:*** Andrew Davis.

Final Verdict 1/2 **1991** A trial lawyer defends a man he knows is guilty, throwing his life and his family into turmoil. **93m/C; DVD.** Treat Williams; Glenn Ford; Amy Wright; Olivia Burnette; Ashley Crow; Raphael Sbarge; Lance Kerwin; Fionnula Flanagan; ***D:*** Jack Fisk; ***W:*** Lawrence Roman; ***C:*** Paul Elliott. **CABLE**

Final Voyage 1999 (R) Hijackers, led by Ice-T, take over the cruise ship Britannica and their robbery of the ship's vault leads to a threat to sink the boat as well. Bodyguard Walsh manages to escape and wages a one-man war against the bad guys throughout the ship. It's better than "Speed 2." Wynorski directed under the pseudonym Jay Andrews. **95m/C; VHS, DVD.** Ice-T; Dylan Walsh; Erika Eleniak; Claudia Christian; Ric(k) Ducommun; ***D:*** Jim Wynorski; ***W:*** Jim Wynorski; J. Everitt Morley; ***C:*** Ken Blakey; ***M:*** David Wurst; Eric Wurst. **VIDEO**

The Finances of the Grand Duke *Die Finanzen des Grossherzogs* **1924** Rare Murnau comedy. The Grand Duke of Abacco (Liedtke) is in desperate need of money to save his bankrupt duchy. He proposes to Olga (Christians), the Grand Duchess of Russia, but some revolutionaries wish to thwart his plans until the Duke's adventurous friend, Philip (Abel), intervenes. **77m/B; Silent; Blu-Ray, On Demand.** *GE* Harry Liedtke; Alfred Abel; Mady Christians; Walter Rilla; Adolphe Engers; Julius Falkenstein; ***D:*** F.W. Murnau; ***W:*** Thea von Harbou; ***C:*** Karl Freund; Franz Planer.

Find Me Guilty 2006 (R) Amusingly cutting mockery of courtroom ritual from master Lumet that's based on a true story. From 1986-88, 20 members of the New Jersey-based Lucchese crime family were prosecuted by the feds; all had attorneys except for low-level goombah Giacomo "Jackie Dee" DiNorscio (Diesel), who represented himself. Jackie wisecracks throughout the trial, garnering unexpected sympathy while causing agita in both the presiding judge (Silver) and mob boss Nick Calabrese (Rocco). Performances are excellent; note Sciorra's cameo as Jackie's bitter ex-wife. **125m/C; DVD, Blu-Ray.** Vin Diesel; Peter Dinklage; Linus Roache; Ron Silver; Alex Rocco; Annabella Sciorra; Richard Portnow; Robert Stanton; Raul Esparza; Domenick Lombardozzi; Paul Borghese; Jerry Adler; Marcia Jean Kurtz; ***D:*** Sidney Lumet; ***W:*** Sidney Lumet; T.J. Mancini; Robert J. McCrea; ***C:*** Ron Fortunato; ***M:*** Richard Glasser.

Finder's Fee 2001 (R) A basic psycho-thriller set primarily in a New York apartment. Tepper (Palladino) finds a wallet in the street and contacts the owner, Avery Phillips (Jones). Later, Tepper also discovers a lottery ticket worth $6 mil inside the wallet and spills the news to his poker buddy, Fishman (Lillard), who can't keep the news from the other guys—Quigley (Reynolds) and Bolan (Mihok). Then, Avery shows up and sits in on the game, suposedly unaware of his potential good fortune. Now, does Tepper keep the ticket? And will his buddies also keep quiet? **99m/C; VHS, DVD.** Erik Palladino; James Earl Jones; Matthew Lillard; Ryan Reynolds; Dash Mihok; Carly Pope; Robert Forster; Frances Bay; ***D:*** Jeff Probst; ***W:*** Jeff Probst; ***C:*** Francis Kenny; ***M:*** B.C. Smith.

Finding a Family 2010 A Hallmark Channel movie. At 10, Alex becomes a ward of the court when his single mom Ileana is deemed an unfit parent after a serious car accident. As he grows older, Alex's constant dream is to go to Harvard. He's an excellent student, but Alex needs to stay in a school district that will offer him the most opportunities. The foster care system threatens to move him again making Alex decide to find his own family. Based on a true story. **88m/C; DVD.** Jared Abrahamson; Kim Delaney; Paul McGillion; Sarah Jane Redmond; Colin MacKechnie; ***D:*** Mark Jean; ***W:*** Pamela Wallace; ***C:*** David Pelletier; ***M:*** Michael Richard Plowman. **CABLE**

Finding Altamira 1/2 *Altamira* **2016** A historical drama based on the real life events of the man who discovered Altamira's caves in the 19th century. During an expedition in 1879, Marcelino (Banderas), a Spanish archaeologist, and his daughter Maria (Allen) make an unexpected discovery when they find paintings of bison on the walls of a hidden cave. Dubbed the caves of Altamira, they draw a wide swath of people who want to see the seemingly impossible paintings. When Marcelino realizes that the art must be at least 10,000 years old, he sets off a firestorm of controversy that includes the Catholic church, scientists, and his own family. When his discovery is repressed, Marcelino must fight to ensure the truth is heard. **97m/C; DVD, Streaming, Download.** Antonio Banderas; Allegra Allen; Clement Sibony; Rupert Everett; Nicholas Farrell; ***D:*** Hugh Hudson; ***W:*** Olivia Hetreed; Jose Luis Lopez-Linares; ***C:*** Jose Luis Alcaine; ***M:*** Mark Knopfler; Evelyn Glennie.

Finding Amanda 1/2 **2008 (R)** TV writer Taylor (Broderick) is a not-so-recovering alcohol, drug, and gambling addict with a failing marriage and career. In an effort to redeem himself (so he says), he heads off to Vegas to find his 20-year-old niece Amanda (Snow), an overly-perky hooker, and get her to clean up her life. Veers from pathos to comedy (and back again) with about as much control as the characters have. **96m/C; DVD.** Matthew Broderick; Brittany Snow; Maura Tierney; Peter Facinelli; Steve Coogan; ***D:*** Peter Tolan; ***W:*** Peter Tolan; ***C:*** Tom Houghton; ***M:*** Christopher Tyng.

Finding Bliss 2009 (R) Film school grad Jody (Sobieski) can't find work until she takes an editing job at a porn studio. Then she decides to use the studio's soundstage after hours to film her own flick with some of the adult movie stars willing to moonlight in a legit enterprise though they don't understand the pretensions of her script. Jody's a little too easy to shock but there's a quirky cuteness to Davis' indie. **96m/C; DVD.** Leelee Sobieski; Jamie Kennedy; Denise Richards; Matthew Davis; Kristen Johnston; Mircea Monroe; P.J. Byrne; Garry Marshall; ***D:*** Julie Davis; ***W:*** Julie Davis; ***C:*** Peter N. Green; ***M:*** John Swihart.

Finding Buck McHenry 1/2 **2000** When 11-year-old Jason (Schiffman) gets cut from Little League, he decides to form his own team. He persuades school custodian Buck McHenry (Davis) to coach but the man's knowledge about the game leads Jason to suspect that Buck is a Negro League legend who's long dropped out of sight and he decides to uncover the truth. **88m/C; VHS, DVD.** Ossie Davis; Ruby Dee; Ernie Banks; Michael Schiffman; Duane McLaughlin; Karl Pruner; Megan Bower; Catherine Blythe; ***D:*** Charles Burnett; ***W:*** Alfred Slote; ***C:*** John L. (Ndiaga) Demps, Jr.; ***M:*** Stephen James Taylor. **CABLE**

Finding Dory 2016 (PG) It took 13 years for this follow-up to one of the biggest animated films of all time, but it was more than worth the wait. DeGeneres returns as the lovable Dory, a blue tang fish with severe problems retaining memories for more than a few seconds. One of the few memories that has stuck with the sweet heroine is the day she got separated from her parents. Of course, she reunites with Marlin and Nemo, heading out on a journey to find her family that takes her to the Marine Life Institute and a whole new cast of characters. It's familiar to "Finding Nemo" but extraordinarily so. **97m/C; DVD, Blu-Ray.** Ellen DeGeneres; Albert Brooks; Ed O'Neill; Kaitlin Olson; Hayden Rolence; ***D:*** Andrew Stanton; Angus MacLane; ***W:*** Andrew Stanton; Victoria Strouse; ***C:*** Jeremy Lasky; ***M:*** Thomas Newman.

Finding Forrester 2000 (PG-13) Underprivileged kid (Brown) from the Bronx, who has smarts and basketball skills, wins a scholarship to an Upper East Side prep school where he's befriended by wealthy classmate Paquin and eccentric writer Connery. Predictable, cloying script almost undermines excellent performances by Connery and newcomer Brown. The only good thing about the screenplay is their dialogue together. **133m/C; VHS, DVD, Blu-Ray.** Anna Paquin; Sean Connery; Rob Brown; F. Murray Abraham; Busta Rhymes; April Grace; Michael Nouri; Zane R. (Lil' Zane) Copeland, Jr.; ***D:*** Gus Van Sant; ***W:*** Mike Rich; ***C:*** Harris Savides; ***M:*** Hal Willner.

Finding Graceland 1/2 **1998 (PG-13)** Down-on-his-luck Byron (Schaech) is driving his 1959 Cadillac convertible through New Mexico when he stops for a hitchhiker and Elvis impersonator (Keitel), who's on his way to Memphis. Except this Elvis believes he's the real thing and he's heading for his Graceland home. Odd things seem to happen to Byron as long as Elvis is around. Not the least being his finding Marilyn Monroe impersonator, Ashley (Fonda). **97m/C; VHS, DVD.** Johnathon Schaech; Harvey Keitel; Bridget Fonda; Gretchen Mol; ***D:*** David Winkler; ***W:*** Jason Horwitch; ***C:*** Elliot Davis; ***M:*** Stephen Endelman.

Finding Home 2003 (PG-13) Workaholic exec Amanda (Brenner) inherits her grandmother Esther's (Fletcher) B&B, located on a remote island off the Maine coast. When Amanda travels there to decide if she should sell the property, she begins having flashbacks of some terrible childhood event that she has repressed. But maybe things are better left forgotten. Conventional family melodrama in a picturesque setting. **124m/C; DVD.** Lisa Brenner; Genevieve Bujold; Louise Fletcher; Johnny Messner; Justin Henry; Jason Miller; Misha Collins; ***D:*** Lawrence Foldes; ***W:*** Lawrence Foldes; Grafton S. Harper; ***C:*** Jeffrey Seckendorf; ***M:*** Joseph Conlan. **VIDEO**

Finding Mr. Wright 1/2 **2011** Fitfully funny and uneven gay rom com. Ambitious, workaholic talent manager Clark Townsend (Montgomery) is forced to attend a wilderness therapy weekend to save his scandal-prone client Eddy's (Kochan) career. Focused on Eddy's issues, Clark's the only one not to realize that her cute life coach Pearce Wright (Moretti) is interested in him. **101m/C; Streaming.** Matthew Montgomery; David Moretti; Rebekah Kochan; Jason Stuart; ***D:*** Nancy Criss; ***W:*** Jake Helgren; ***C:*** Damon Britain; ***M:*** Matthew Janszen.

Finding Nemo 2003 (G) Despite the dead mom beginning, this is not from the Disney animation studio. It's Pixar (of "Toy Story" fame). Little clown fish Nemo (Gould) was born with an undersized fin and is the sole survivor of a barracuda attack. This makes nervous dad Marlin (Brooks) overprotective. When curious Nemo is scooped up by a scuba diver for life in a fish tank, it's dad to the rescue! He's aided by chipper blue tang Dory (DeGeneres), who unfortunately suffers from short-term memory loss, a sea turtle (director Stanton), and other denizens of both sea and air (including a helpful pelican), while Nemo is making new friends (and escape plans) with his tank mates. Since water is considered the hardest thing to animate, the undersea sequences are particularly breathtaking. There's the usual humor to keep adults interested as well as sweetness amidst the comedy. **101m/C; VHS, DVD, Blu-Ray.** ***V:*** Albert Brooks; Ellen DeGeneres; Willem Dafoe; Alexander Gould; Barry Humphries; Andrew Stanton; Brad Garrett; Allison Janney; Austin Pendleton; Stephen (Steve) Root; Vicki Lewis; Joe Ranft; Geoffrey Rush; Eric Bana; Bruce Spence; Elizabeth Perkins; Erik Per Sullivan; John Ratzenberger; Bill Hunter; LuLu Ebeling; Erica Beck; Bob Peterson; ***D:*** Andrew Stanton; ***W:*** Andrew Stanton; Bob Peterson; Dave Reynolds; ***C:*** Sharon Calahan; Jeremy Lasky; ***M:*** Thomas Newman. Oscars '03: Animated Film.

Finding Neverland 2004 (PG) Genteel drama takes the usual biographical license and makes sometimes-obvious conclusions between the life and work of author J.M. Barrie (an equally genteel Depp). A celebrated writer in Edwardian London, Barrie is looking for inspiration when he meets recent widow Sylvia Llewelyn Davies (Winslet) and her four young sons: Peter (Highmore), Jack (Prospero), George (Roud), and Michael (Spill). The childless Barrie, detached from his own marriage, becomes increasingly involved with their lives, leading them in games and telling stories that revitalize his own creative juices, which result in the successful 1904 theatrical opening of his new work, "Peter Pan." Though Barrie maintains a courtly, platonic friendship with Sylvia, his actions alarm his wife, Mary (Mitchell), and Sylvia's formidable mother, Emma (Christie). A three-hanky affair, beautifully photographed by Schaefer, and adapted from the play "The Man Who Was Peter Pan" by Allan Knee. **108m/C; DVD, Blu-Ray.** Johnny Depp; Kate Winslet; Julie Christie; Radha Mitchell; Dustin Hoffman; Kelly Macdonald; Ian Hart; Eileen Essell; Freddie Highmore; Joe Prospero; Nick Roud; Luke Spill; ***D:*** Marc Forster; ***W:*** David Magee; ***C:*** Roberto Schaefer; ***M:*** Jan A.P. Kaczmarek. Oscars '04: Orig. Score.

Finding Normal 🦴🦴 1/2 **2013** Sweet, basic rom com with a low-key Christian focus. Dr. Lisa Leland is driving from L.A. to the Hamptons for her wedding when she gets pulled over in the small town of Normal, North Carolina. Because of a number of outstanding tickets (and the usual movie delay clichés), Lisa must do three days of community service in lieu of jail time. Then she's introduced to local bachelor Lucas. **80m/C; DVD.** Candace Cameron Bure; Trevor St. John; Lou Beatty, Jr.; Jim Elliott; ***D:*** Brian Herzlinger; ***W:*** Chuck Konzelman; Cary Solomon; ***C:*** Akis Konstantakopoulos; ***M:*** Will Musser. **VIDEO**

Finding North 🦴🦴 **1997** Predictable dramedy about the friendship between a straight woman and gay man. Talkative, bored bank clerk Rhonda (Makkena) meets suicidal yuppie, Travis (Hickey), who's just lost his lover to AIDS, and decides to help him regain his emotional balance. Even if this means following him from New York to the small Texas town where Travis' late lover grew up. **95m/C; VHS, DVD.** Wendy Makkena; John Benjamin Hickey; Angela Pietropinto; Freddie Roman; Molly McClure; ***V:*** Jonathan Walker; ***D:*** Tanya Wexler; ***W:*** Kim Powers; ***C:*** Michael Barrett.

Finding Rin Tin Tin 🦴🦴 **2007 (PG)** How a star is discovered. Corporal Lee Duncan (Jensen) finds a German shepherd puppy in France and uses his expertise as a POW dog handler to train Rin Tin Tin to aid his WWI platoon. When the war is over, Lee decides to take his photogenic find to Hollywood and see if they can get in the movies, and the dog becomes a star. **90m/C; DVD.** Ben Cross; William Hope; Todd Jensen; Tyler Jensen; ***D:*** Dan Lerner; ***W:*** David Rolland; Jim Tierney; ***C:*** Emil Topuzov; ***M:*** Stephen (Steve) Edwards.

Finding Steve McQueen 🦴🦴 **2019 (R)** In 1980, Harry Barber (Fimmel) admits to girlfriend Molly Murphy (Taylor) that he has been on the run for eight years after helping rob a bank. He was the getaway driver when friends broke into the United California Bank in Laguna Nagel and stole $9 million. They targeted dirty money donated to Richard Nixon's re-election campaign. Though the heist did not go as planned, those involved became folk heroes, including the Steve McQueen-admiring Barber, as they were pursued by FBI agents Howard Lambert (Whitaker) and Sharon Price (Rabe). The light comedic, sometimes eccentric, take on real events adds to the film's broad appeal. **90m/C; DVD, Blu-Ray.** Travis Fimmel; Rachael Taylor; William Fichtner; Forest Whitaker; Lily Rabe; ***D:*** Mark Steven Johnson; ***W:*** Ken Hixon; Keith Sharon; ***C:*** Jose David Montero; ***M:*** Victor Reyes.

Finding Vivian Maier 🦴🦴 1/2 **2014** Maloof directs this complex documentary about a woman who basically lived in deep, private seclusion but may have been one of the best photographers of the 20th century. Maloof happened upon negatives while researching a book on Chicago's history and developed them leading to the discovery of Vivian Maier's remarkable talent. Who was this woman, a nanny who never shared her art with the world? That last question makes the movie sometimes feel like an invasion of privacy but the photos are breathtaking. And once Maloof released them to the world, tracking the history of their creator was inevitable. **83m/C; DVD.** ***D:*** John Maloof; Charlie Siskel; ***W:*** John Maloof; Charlie Siskel; ***C:*** John Maloof; ***M:*** J. Ralph.

Finding Your Feet 🦴🦴 1/2 **2018 (PG-13)** A British comedy that explores the process of achieving personal redemption. During a retirement party for her husband of 35 years, Mike (Sessions), snobby Lady Sandra (Staunton) discovers him having sex with her best friend Pamela (Lawrence). After learning that the pair have been having an affair for five years, Sandra moves in with her free-spirited sister Bif (Imrie) in her cluttered apartment. Sandra gets a chance at redemption when she agrees to join her sister's community dance class. There, Sandra is forced to dance with handyman Charlie (Spall) and finds an unexpected connection. A talented cast makes the most of the predictable story. **111m/C; DVD.** Joanna Lumley; Celia Imrie; Timothy Spall; Imelda Staunton; Phoebe Nicholls; ***D:*** Richard Loncraine; ***W:*** Megan Leonard; Nick Moorcroft; ***C:*** John Pardue; ***M:*** Michael J. McEvoy.

Fine Dead Girls 🦴🦴 *Fine Mrtve Djevojke* **2002** Lesbian couple Iva and Marija try to keep their relationship a secret when they move to a new apartment in Zagreb. But what seems to be a safe haven turns out to be filled with creepy, sometimes violent neighbors and Olga, their nosy, bigoted landlady. Olga begins a witch-hunt against the new tenants that leads to rape, kidnapping, and murder, which writer/director Matanic uses as a microcosm for the upheavals of Croatian society at the time. Croatian with subtitles. **77m/C; DVD.** *CR* Olga Pakalovic; Jadranka Djokic; Nina Violic; Kresimir Mikic; Inge Apelt; Ivica Vidovic; ***D:*** Dalibor Matanic; ***W:*** Dalibor Matanic; ***C:*** Branko Linta; ***M:*** Jura Ferina.

A Fine Madness 🦴🦴🦴 **1966** A near-classic comedy about a lusty, rebellious poet thrashing against the pressures of the modern world, and fending off a bevy of lobotomy-happy psychiatrists. Shot on location in New York City, based on Elliot Baker's novel. **104m/C; VHS, DVD.** Sean Connery; Joanne Woodward; Jean Seberg; Patrick O'Neal; Colleen Dewhurst; Clive Revill; John Fiedler; Werner Peters; Kay Medford; Jackie Coogan; Zohra Lampert; Sorrell Booke; Sue Ane Langdon; Bibi Osterwald; Gerald S. O'Loughlin; Richard S. Castellano; ***D:*** Irvin Kershner; ***W:*** Elliott Baker; ***C:*** Ted D. McCord; ***M:*** John Addison.

Fine Manners 🦴🦴 **1926** While on a New Year's Eve toot, millionaire Brian meets chorus girl Orchid. Worried that she'll be rejected by his Park Avenue crowd, Brian asks his aunt to teach Ochid how to behave like a lady. Only Brian discvoers he'd rather Orchid behave like herself. **70m/B; Silent; DVD.** Gloria Swanson; Eugene O'Brien; Helen Dunbar; Roland Drew; ***D:*** Richard Rosson; ***W:*** J. Clarkson Miller; ***C:*** George Webber.

A Fine Mess 🦴 1/2 **1986 (PG)** Two buffoons cash in when one overhears a plan to dope a racehorse, but they are soon fleeing the plotters' slapstick pursuit. The plot is further complicated by the romantic interest of a gangster's wife. The TV popularity of the two stars did not translate to the big screen; perhaps it's Edwards's fault. **100m/C; VHS, DVD.** Ted Danson; Howie Mandel; Richard Mulligan; Stuart Margolin; Maria Conchita Alonso; Paul Sorvino; ***D:*** Blake Edwards; ***W:*** Blake Edwards; ***C:*** Harry Stradling, Jr.; ***M:*** Henry Mancini.

A Fine Romance 🦴🦴 **1992 (PG-13)** An improbable romance set in Paris features Andrews and Mastroianni as abandoned spouses falling in love. Andrews is the prim English Pamela who has been abandoned by her docter husband. Mastroianni is the irrepresible Cesareo, whose wife has just happened to run off with the aforementioned doctor. They meet to plan how to get their spouses back and wind up with opposites attracting. Not much story and the charm is spread thin. Based on the play "Tchin, Tchin" by Francois Billetdoux. **83m/C; VHS, DVD.** Julie Andrews; Marcello Mastroianni; Ian Fitzgibbon; Jean-Pierre Castaldi; Jean-Jacques Dulon; Maria Machado; Jean-Michel Cannone; Catherine Jarrett; Gene Saks; ***W:*** Ronald Harwood; ***M:*** Pino Donaggio.

The Finest Hour 🦴 1/2 **1991 (R)** Two Navy buddies have a falling out when they both fall for the same woman. But they must put aside their differences when their next mission sends them to Iraq to deal with the deadly threat of biological warfare. **105m/C; VHS, DVD.** Rob Lowe; Gale Hansen; Tracy Griffith; Eb Lottimer; ***D:*** Shimon Dotan; ***W:*** Shimon Dotan.

The Finest Hours 🦴🦴 1/2 **2016 (PG-13)** There is room in this movie world for old-fashioned thriller-dramas like Gillespie's true story about a daring Coast Guard rescue off the coast of New England in 1952. Bernie (Pine) has fallen in love with Miriam (Grainger) but he has to take one last mission before marriage and rescue an oil tanker broken in half off the Chatham coast. He goes to save the ship with a crew ably filled out by Kyle Gallner, John Magaro and Ben Foster. Casey Affleck also co-stars in this nice nautical adventure that will appeal to fans of "The Perfect Storm." **117m/C; DVD, Blu-Ray.** Chris Pine; Casey Affleck; Ben Foster; Eric Bana; Holliday Grainger; ***D:*** Craig Gillespie; ***W:*** Scott Silver; Paul Tamasy; Eric Johnson; ***C:*** Javier Aguirresarobe; ***M:*** Carter Burwell.

Fingers 🦴🦴🦴 **1978 (R)** Keitel is Johnny Fingers, a mobster's son, reluctantly working as a mob debt-collector, all the while dreaming of his ambitions to be a concert pianist. The divisions between his dreams and reality cause him to crack. Toback's first film generates psychological tension and excellent performances. **89m/C; VHS, DVD.** Harvey Keitel; Tisa Farrow; Jim Brown; James Toback; Danny Aiello; Tanya Roberts; Marian Seldes; Michael V. Gazzo; Lenny Montana; ***D:*** James Toback; ***W:*** James Toback; ***C:*** Michael Chapman; ***M:*** George Barrie.

Finian's Rainbow 🦴🦴🦴 **1968 (G)** A leprechaun comes to America to steal back a pot of gold taken by an Irishman and his daughter in this fanciful musical comedy based on a 1947 Broadway hit. Both the sprite and the girl find romance; the sharecropping locals are saved by the cash; a bigot learns the error of his ways; and Finian (Astaire) dances off to new adventures. The fine production and talented cast are not used to their best advantage by the director who proved much better suited for "The Godfather." Entertaining, nonetheless. **141m/C; VHS, DVD, Blu-Ray.** Fred Astaire; Petula Clark; Tommy Steele; Keenan Wynn; Al Freeman, Jr.; Don Francks; Susan Hancock; Dolph Sweet; ***D:*** Francis Ford Coppola.

Finish Line 🦴 1/2 **2008** Chachi's a bad guy—is nothing sacred? Mitch Camponella (Page) needs a new car to compete in the pro stock car racing circuit. So he agrees to become a bodyguard to Jessie (Cole), the flirty daughter of shady importer Frank Chase (Baio). Chase is smuggling bomb-making materials into the U.S. and naive Mitch is forced to work undercover for the FBI, which makes every situation more dangerous. **86m/C; DVD.** Sam Page; Scott Baio; Dan Lauria; Ian Reed Kesler; John Enos; Taylor Cole; Timilee Romolini; ***D:*** Gerry Lively; ***W:*** Ron McGee; ***C:*** Maximo Munzi; ***M:*** Paul D'Amour. **TV**

Finishing School 🦴 1/2 **1933** Girls' school roommates Rogers and Dee experience heartaches and loves lost while enduring disinterested parents and snobbish peers. Boxoffice bomb when released, despite a strong cast. **73m/B; VHS, DVD.** Ginger Rogers; Frances Dee; George Nicholls, Jr.; Beulah Bondi; Bruce Cabot; Billie Burke; John Halliday; Sara Haden; Jack Norton; Joan Barclay; Jane Darwell; John David Horsley; ***D:*** George Nicholls, Jr.; ***M:*** Max Steiner.

Finn on the Fly 🦴🦴 **2009 (PG)** Silly kiddie fare. Shy 13-year-old Ben (Knight) is in a new town at a new junior high and his only friend is his Frisbee-loving border collie Finn. Finn gets into the house of next-door scientist neighbor Dr. Madsen (Gasteyer) and laps up an experimental potion that turns him human. Ben tries to get Finn to act human, while Finn makes Ben find his own new pack of friends. But Finn is in danger once Madsen realizes what's happened. **101m/C; DVD.** *CA* Matthew Knight; Ryan Belleville; Ana Gasteyer; Brandon Firla; David Milchard; Wendy Anderson; Juan Chioran; ***D:*** Mark Jean; ***W:*** Mark Jean; Teza Lawrence; Michael Souther; Kellie Ann Benz; ***C:*** Thom Best; ***M:*** Jeff Danna. **VIDEO**

Fiona 🦴 1/2 **1998** Fiona was abandoned as a baby, raised in an abusive foster home, and is now a crack-smoking hooker on the streets of New York. After casually killing three cops, she hides out in a crackhouse where she hooks up with Anita—who naturally turns out to be Fiona's long-lost mama. Film is a blend of fiction and documentary footage of real prostitutes and drug houses. **85m/C; VHS, DVD.** Anna Thomson; Mike Hodge; Anna Grace; Felicia Maguire; ***D:*** Amos Kollek; ***W:*** Amos Kollek; ***C:*** Ed Talavera; ***M:*** Alison Gordy.

Fiorile 🦴🦴🦴 *Wild Flower* **1993 (PG-13)** Covers several generations of a Tuscan clan living under a family curse which dates back to Napoleon's invasion of Italy. At that time Jean, a handsome French lieutenant, falls in love with Tuscan peasant girl Elisabetta, nicknamed Fiorile. When Jean is executed for a theft committed by her brother, the pregnant Fiorile vows revenge. Throughout sucessive generations, haunted by the past, the family's personal bad luck persists. Several of the actors play their character's ancestors, lending continuity. Attractive cast does well with the Taviani brothers' visual style and romantic narrative. In Italian with English subtitles. **118m/C; VHS, DVD.** *IT* Michael Vartan; Galatea Ranzi; Claudio Bigagli; Lino Capolicchio; Constanze Engelbrecht; Athina Cenci; Giovanni Guidelli; Chiara Caselli; ***D:*** Paolo Taviani; Vittorio Taviani; ***W:*** Paolo Taviani; Vittorio Taviani; Sandro Petraglia; ***C:*** Giuseppe Lanci; ***M:*** Nicola Piovani.

Fire 🦴 1/2 **1977** A fire started by an escaped convict rages through Oregon timberland in this suspenseful Irwin Allen disaster drama. **98m/C; VHS, DVD.** Ernest Borgnine; Vera Miles; Patty Duke; Alex Cord; Donna Mills; ***D:*** Earl Bellamy. **TV**

Fire 🦴🦴 1/2 **1996** Follows the relationship of two sisters-in-law in New Delhi—both stuck in frustrating, loveless marriages—while examining the harsh patriarchal culture of India. Radha (Azmi) is married to Ashok (Kharbanda), a video store clerk who has taken a vow of celibacy under the teachings of a scruffy swami. Sita (Das) is married to Ashok's brother Jatin (Jaaferi), who is openly having an affair with a Chinese Canadian woman. As her frustration grows, the younger Sita acts on her attraction to her sister-in-law and the two begin a lesbian affair, which is taboo in the strict Hindu culture. Dialogue is in "Hinglish," or English with occasional Hindi phrases thrown in. The attitudes portrayed must exist, because the film was banned in India. **104m/C; VHS, DVD.** *CA* Shabana Azmi; Nandita Das; Kulbashan Kharbanda; Jaaved Jaaferi; Ranjit (Chaudry) Chowdhry; Kushal Rekhi; ***D:*** Deepa Mehta; ***W:*** Deepa Mehta; ***C:*** Giles Nuttgens; ***M:*** A.R. Rahman.

Fire and Ice 🦴🦴 1/2 **1983 (PG)** An animated adventure film that culminates in a tense battle between good and evil, surrounded by the mystical elements of the ancient past. Designed by Frank Frazetta. **81m/C; VHS, DVD.** Randy Norton; Cynthia Leake; ***V:*** Susan Tyrrell; William Ostrander; ***D:*** Ralph Bakshi; ***W:*** Ralph Bakshi; Willy Bogner; Gerry Conway.

Fire and Ice 🦴 **1987 (PG)** A tale of love on the slopes. Two skiers realize that their feelings for each other are perhaps even stronger than their feelings about skiing. You won't care though, except for some fine ski footage. **83m/C; VHS, DVD.** Suzy Chaffee; John Eaves; ***Nar:*** John Denver; ***D:*** Willy Bogner; ***W:*** George Schlatter; ***M:*** Harold Faltermeyer.

Fire & Ice: The Dragon Chronicles 🦴 1/2 **2008 (PG-13)** Typically low-budget fantasy cheese from the Sci-Fi Channel. Irritating Princess Luisa searches for a warrior who can slay the fire dragon decimating her father's kingdom. She finds disgruntled Gabriel, the son of a legendary dragonslayer, and they summon an ice dragon to do battle but that may prove to be a mistake. **85m/C; DVD.** Tom Wisdom; John Rhys-Davies; Arnold Vosloo; Oana Pellea; Amy Akcers; Razvan Vesilescu; Ovidiu Niculescu; ***D:*** Pitof; ***W:*** Michael Konyves; Angela Mancuso; ***C:*** Emmanuel (Manu) Kadosh; ***M:*** Frankie Blue. **CABLE**

Fire at Sea 🦴🦴🦴 *Fuocoammare* **2016** Writer/director Rosi's documentary is the first non-fiction film to win the Golden Bear in the

66 years of the Berlin Film Festival, a win likely helped by the immigrant and refugee issues currently going on worldwide. Rosi shot his film on the Sicilian island of Lampedusa during the European migrant crisis, focusing on a 12-year-old boy from a local fishing family and a doctor who assists in treatment of the people arriving on Italian shores every day. The harrowing danger of crossing the Mediterranean hasn't really been captured on film like this before, making for a documentary that feels urgent and terrifying. **114m/C; DVD, Blu-Ray.** Samuele Pucillo; Pietro Bartolo; Maria Costa; Giuseppe Fragapane; Francesco Paterna; ***D:*** Gianfranco Rosi; ***W:*** Gianfranco Rosi; ***C:*** Gianfranco Rosi.

Fire Birds *Wings of the Apache* **1990 (PG-13)** Army attack helicopters and the people who fly them are used in the war on drugs in South America. Failed to match the exciting flight sequences, the romantic interest, or the boxoffice of "Top Gun." **85m/C; VHS, DVD, Blu-Ray.** Nicolas Cage; Tommy Lee Jones; Sean Young; Bryan Kestner; Dale Dye; Mary Ellen Trainor; J.A. Preston; Peter Onorati; ***D:*** David Green; ***W:*** Dale Dye; Nick Thiel; Paul F. Edwards; ***M:*** David Newman.

Fire Down Below ½ **1957** Hayworth is the been-around-the-block beauty who persuades Mitchum and Lemmon, two small-time smugglers, to take her to a safe haven, no questions asked. Both men fall for her obvious charms, causing them to have a falling out until a life or death situation puts their friendship to the test. An unoriginal melodrama indifferently acted by everyone but Lemmon. Good location work in Trinidad and Tobago. **116m/C; VHS, DVD.** *GB* Robert Mitchum; Jack Lemmon; Rita Hayworth; Herbert Lom; Anthony Newley; ***D:*** Robert Parrish; ***W:*** Irwin Shaw; ***C:*** Desmond Dickinson; ***M:*** Arthur Benjamin; Douglas Gamley.

Fire Down Below **1997 (R)** Seagal comes armed with his trademark ponytail, martial arts expertise, big leather jackets, and environment-friendly message to the Appalachians in this hoedown showdown. As undercover (yeah, he blends right in) EPA agent Jack Taggart, Seagal must stop evil industrialist Hanner (Kristofferson) from dumping toxic waste. Of course, the company town sends the usual band of thugs (thoughtfully attacking one at a time) to make him go away. He finds allies in the local outcasts (Helgenberger and Stanton) en route to the final confrontation. Not Seagal's worst, but that's not saying much. Even the usually impressive fight scenes become tedious after a while. At least he didn't try to direct this one. Originally conceived as a Bruce Willis project at Columbia. **105m/C; VHS, DVD.** Steven Seagal; Marg Helgenberger; Kris Kristofferson; Harry Dean Stanton; Stephen Lang; Levon Helm; Brad Hunt; Richard Masur; Ed Bruce; Randy Travis; Mark Collie; Alex Harvey; ***D:*** Felix Alcala; ***W:*** Jeb Stuart; ***C:*** Tom Houghton; ***M:*** Nick Glennie-Smith.

Fire From Below **WOOF!** **2009 (PG-13)** No one really expects a Syfy Channel flick to be scientifically accurate but this one is so off-the-wall dumb as to be unwatchable. Miners unearth a vein of lithium which, when exposed to water, turns into a fireball that threatens a small town. Seismologist Jake (Sorbo) tries to stop the disaster while the lithium apparently has a mind of its own and goes on some weird fiery rampage. **89m/C; DVD, Blu-Ray.** Kevin Sorbo; Maeghan Albach; Alex Cord; Glenn Morshower; Alex Meneses; ***D:*** Andrew Stevens; Jim Wynorski; ***W:*** Andrew Stevens; Jim Wynorski; ***C:*** Ken Blakey; ***M:*** David Wurst; Eric Wurst. **CABLE**

Fire in the Sky **1993 (PG-13)** Mysterious disappearance of Sweeney sparks a criminal investigation, until he returns, claiming he was abducted by aliens. Though everybody doubts his story, viewers won't, since the alleged aliens have already made an appearance, shifting the focus to Sweeney as he tries to convince skeptics that his trauma is genuine. Perhaps this mirrors what director Lieberman went through while trying to convince backers the film should be made. He could have benefitted by understanding the difference between what he was telling viewers and what he was showing them. Captivating special effects are one of the few bright spots. Based on a story that might be true. **98m/C; DVD.** D.B. Sweeney; Robert Patrick; Craig Sheffer; Peter Berg; James Garner; Henry Thomas; ***D:*** Robert Lieberman; ***W:*** Tracy Torme; ***C:*** Bill Pope; ***M:*** Mark Isham.

Fire Maidens from Outer Space *Fire Maidens of Outer Space* **1956** Fire maidens prove to be true to the space opera code that dictates that all alien women be in desperate need of male company. Astronauts on an expedition to Jupiter's 13th moon discover the lost civilization of Atlantis, which, as luck would have it, is inhabited by women only. Possibly an idea before its time, it might've been better had it been made in the '60s, when space-exploitation came into its own. **80m/B; VHS, DVD, Blu-Ray.** *GB* Anthony Dexter; Susan Shaw; Paul Carpenter; Harry Fowler; Jacqueline Curtiss; Sydney Tafler; Maya Koumani; Jan Holden; Kim Parker; Rodney Diak; Owen Berry; ***D:*** Cy Roth; ***W:*** Cy Roth; ***C:*** Ian Struthers.

Fire Monsters Against the Son of Hercules *Maciste Contro i Mostri* **1962** The son of the muscular one does battle with a hydra-headed monster in this average sword and sandal adventure. **82m/C; VHS, DVD.** *IT* Reg Lewis; Margaret Lee; ***D:*** Guido Malatesta; ***W:*** Guido Malatesta; Arpad De Riso; ***C:*** Guiseppe La Torre; ***M:*** Guido Robuschi; Gian Stellari.

The Fire Next Time ½ **1993** In the year 2017, the United States is being ravaged by an ecological holocaust caused by a deadly combination of pollution and global warming. Nelson, Bedelia, and their children are forced from their Louisiana home by a natural disaster and decide to head for better times in Canada. Their travels aren't easy. **195m/C; VHS, DVD.** Craig T. Nelson; Bonnie Bedelia; Jurgen Prochnow; Richard Farnsworth; Justin Whalin; Charles Haid; Sal Lopez; Shawn Toovey; Ashley Jones; ***Cameo(s):*** Odetta; ***D:*** Tom McLoughlin; ***W:*** James Henerson. **TV**

Fire on the Amazon ½ **1993 (R)** Really dumb "save-the-environment" movie with Bullock the rainforest activist and Sheffer the photojournalist. The duo hook up to investigate the assassination of an environmentalist. The big woo-hoo is Bullock's brief nude sex scene with Sheffer. **81m/C; VHS, DVD, Blu-Ray.** Sandra Bullock; Craig Sheffer; Judith Chapman; Juan Fernandez; ***D:*** Luis Llosa; ***W:*** Catherine Cyran; Jane Gray; ***C:*** Pili Flores-Guerra; ***M:*** Roy J. Ravio.

Fire Over England **1937** Young naval officer volunteers to spy at the Spanish court to learn the plans for the invasion of his native England and to identify the traitors among the English nobility. He arouses the romantic interest of his queen, Elizabeth I, one of her ladies, and a Spanish noblewoman who helps with his missions, and later leads the fleet to victory over the huge Spanish Armada. The first on-screen pairing of Olivier and Leigh is just one of the many virtues of this entertaining drama. **81m/B; DVD, Blu-Ray.** *UK* Flora Robson; Raymond Massey; Laurence Olivier; Vivien Leigh; Leslie Banks; James Mason; ***D:*** William K. Howard; ***W:*** Clemence Dane; Sergei Nolbandov; ***C:*** James Wong Howe; ***M:*** Richard Addinsell.

Fire Serpent **WOOF!** **2007 (R)** Another laughably bad cheapie from the Sci-Fi Channel. Solar flares cast off living flames that occasionally make it to Earth, not only starting fires but possessing people. A firefighter (Brendon) is drawn into a government conspiracy involving flame hunter Dutch Fallon (Mantooth), an arson investigator (Holt), and a Fed (Beltran). **89m/C; DVD.** Nicholas Brendon; Randolph Mantooth; Sandrine Holt; Robert Beltran; ***D:*** John Terlesky; ***W:*** Judith Reeves-Stevens; Garfield Reeves-Stevens; ***C:*** Patrick Mcgowan; ***M:*** Chuck Cirino. **CABLE**

Fire with Fire **1986 (PG-13)** A boy at a juvenile detention center and a Catholic school girl fall in love. However, they find themselves on the run from the law when he escapes to be with her. Sheffer and Madsen are appealing in this otherwise unspectacular film. **103m/C; VHS, DVD, Blu-Ray.** Craig Sheffer; Virginia Madsen; Jon Polito; Kate Reid; Jean Smart; D.B. Sweeney; ***D:*** Duncan Gibbins; ***W:*** Bill (William) Phillips; Paul Boorstin; Sharon Boorstin; ***M:*** Howard Shore.

Fire With Fire ½ **2012 (R)** Miscast, mediocre actioner. Fireman Jeremy Coleman (Duhamel) is threatened by David Hagan (D'Onofrio), a Neo-Nazi he's testifying against in a murder trial. Jeremy goes into Witness Protection but his new identity is compromised and he comes out of hiding when Hagan's goons threaten his family and friends. **97m/C; DVD, Blu-Ray.** Josh Duhamel; Rosario Dawson; Bruce Willis; Vincent D'Onofrio; Vinnie Jones; Julian McMahon; Arie Verveen; ***D:*** David Barrett; ***W:*** Tom O'Connor; ***C:*** Christopher Probst; ***M:*** Trevor Morris. **VIDEO**

The Fire Within *Le Feu Follet; Fuoco Fatuo* **1964** Ronet plays an alcoholic writer recently released from a sanitorium after a breakdown. Believing his life will only continue its downward spiral, he pays a final visit to friends and calmly plots his suicide. Malle clearly and pitilessly describes a man beyond despair. Based on a novel by Pierre Drieu La Rochelle, which itself fictionalized the suicide of writer Jacques Rigaut. In French with English subtitles. **104m/B; VHS, DVD.** *FR* Maurice Ronet; Lena Skerla; Yvonne Clech; Hubert Deschamps; Jean-Paul Moulinot; Bernard Noel; Jeanne Moreau; Alexandra Stewart; Henri Serre; ***D:*** Louis Malle; ***W:*** Louis Malle; ***C:*** Ghislan Cloquet.

Fireback ½ **1978** A Vietnam vet's wife is kidnapped by the mob, causing him to take up arms and spill blood yet again. **90m/C; VHS, DVD.** Bruce Baron; Richard Harrison; ***D:*** Teddy Page; ***M:*** Patrick Wales.

The Fireball ½ **1950** At 30, Rooney was a little old to be playing a runaway orphan but the action of the roller derby craze moves this predictable story along. Johnny hightails it out of Father O'Hara's orphanage and meets Mary, who gets him a spot on the team. He becomes a crowd favorite, gets a swelled head, and then gets smacked down by polio. **84m/B; DVD.** Mickey Rooney; Pat O'Brien; Beverly Tyler; Marilyn Monroe; Ralph Dumke; Milburn Stone; Sam Flint; ***D:*** Tay Garnett; ***W:*** Tay Garnett; Horace McCoy; ***C:*** Lester White; ***M:*** Victor Young.

Fireball **2009 (PG-13)** Washed-up pro football linebacker Tyler 'The Fuse' Draven lands in prison after a public 'roid rage meltdown. Draven suddenly discovers he has pyrokinetic abilities and sets the prison on fire. When the fire mixes with all those designer chemicals in his body, it seems that Draven himself is now fireproof so the paranoid psycho decides to get revenge on everyone he believes wronged him. Seems like this would be exciting in a cheap way but instead it's boring. **94m/C; DVD.** Aleks Paunovic; Lexa Doig; Ian Somerhalder; Colin Cunningham; ***D:*** Kristopher Tabori; ***W:*** Kraig Wenman; ***C:*** Adam Sliwinski. **CABLE**

Fireball 500 ½ **1966** Your basic low-budget teen flick from AIP finds Frankie and Fabian as rival stock car drivers in South Carolina. Newcomer Frankie makes a play for Annette, who's already Fabian's girl. But then Frankie switches cars to romance wealthy raceway owner Parrish. Bootleggers try to trick Frankie into illegal doings during a cross-country race, but he wises up and helps the Feds close the moonshiners down. He also croons a few tunes and the action is a little more adventurous than in the "Beach Party" series. **92m/C; DVD.** Frankie Avalon; Annette Funicello; Fabian; Julie Parrish; Chill Wills; Harvey Lembeck; ***D:*** William Asher; ***W:*** William Asher; Leo Townsend; ***C:*** Floyd Crosby; ***M:*** Les Baxter.

Firecracker **1981** Female martial arts expert retaliates against the crooks who murdered her sister. **83m/C; VHS, DVD.** Jillian Kesner; Darby Hinton; ***D:*** Cirio H. Santiago.

Firecreek ½ **1968** Fonda and his thugs terrorize a small town protected by part-time sheriff Stewart. Beautiful photography and competent cast, but meandering and long. **104m/C; VHS, DVD.** Henry Fonda; James Stewart; Inger Stevens; Gary Lockwood; Dean Jagger; Ed Begley, Sr.; Jay C. Flippen; Jack Elam; Barbara Luna; ***D:*** Vincent McEveety; ***C:*** William Clothier.

Fired Up! ½ **2009 (PG-13)** Really? We're supposed to believe the two lead guys are high schoolers? 'Cause they look old enough to be teachers not students. So suspend all sense of reality and relax into a typically silly teen sex comedy. Football players Shawn (D'Agosto) and Nick (Olsen) decide they can bag more babes going to summer cheerleading camp than sweating over a pigskin. Considering the PG-13 rating, these two really get around with some minor complications, including a nasty rival cheer squad. **89m/C; Blu-Ray, UMD, On Demand.** Nicholas D'Agosto; Eric Christian Olsen; Sarah Roemer; Molly Sims; Danneel Harris; AnnaLynne McCord; Philip Baker Hall; John Michael Higgins; Juliette Goglia; David Walton; Adhir Kalyan; ***D:*** Will Gluck; ***W:*** Freedom Jones; ***C:*** Thomas Ackerman; ***M:*** Richard Gibbs.

Firefall *Freefall* **1994** Wildlife photog Katy Mazur (Gidley) has a brief affair with sportsman Grant Orion (Roberts) while on assignment in Africa. When they meet again, Orion tells Katy he's actually an Interpol agent who's assigned to protect her—although she has no idea why. Katy's fiance (Fahey) thinks this is strange. **95m/C; VHS, DVD.** Pamela Gidley; Eric Roberts; Jeff Fahey; ***D:*** John Irvin.

Firefight ½ **2003 (R)** Armored car driver Jonas (Bacic) is desperate to save his family's restaurant from bankruptcy so, aided by chopper pilot George (Mancuso), he robs his own vehicle and uses a forest fire as cover. But that's not Jonas's only problem—bad guy Wolf (Baldwin) learns about the crime and he's determined to get the cash for himself. **94m/C; DVD.** Steve Bacic; Nick Mancuso; Stephen Baldwin; Sonya Salomaa; ***D:*** Paul Ziller; ***W:*** Paul Ziller; Elizabeth Sanchez; ***C:*** Kamal Derkaoui; ***M:*** Ken Williams. **VIDEO**

Firefighter **1986** CBS TV movie based on a true story. Cindy Fralick wants to become the first female firefighter in the 60-year history of Los Angeles County. No woman has been able to pass the physical skills test and there's lots of opposition to Cindy's quest. **100m/C; DVD.** Nancy McKeon; Vincent Irizarry; Barry Corbin; Guy Boyd; Whip Hubley; ***W:*** Kathryn Montgomery; ***C:*** Frank Watts; ***M:*** Dana Kaproff. **TV**

Fireflies in the Garden ½ **2008 (R)** Dysfunctional family drama that, despite a star-studded cast, can't overcome its basic clumsy storytelling, which erratically varies between the past and the present. Lisa (Roberts) is married to domineering university prof Charles (Dafoe), who is abusive to their son Michael (Reynolds) although he gains a friend in Lisa's teen sister Jane (Watson) who joins the family. Twenty years later, successful novelist Michael has returned home to celebrate his mother's belated college graduation but there's tragedy instead. The title refers to a Robert Frost poem. **89m/C; DVD.** Julia Roberts; Ryan Reynolds; Willem Dafoe; Emily Watson; Carrie-Anne Moss; Ioan Gruffudd; Shannon Lucio; George Newbern; Hayden Panettiere; Cayden Boyd; ***D:*** Dennis Lee; ***W:*** Dennis Lee; ***C:*** Daniel (Danny) Moder.

The Firefly ½ **1937** Although slow-paced and long, this adaptation of the 1912 Rudolf Friml operetta was one of MacDonald's most popular films. Co-star Jones gets to sing the best song in the film, "Donkey Serenade," while MacDonald sings most of the others. **140m/B; VHS, DVD.** Jeanette MacDonald; Allan Jones; Warren William; Billy Gilbert; Henry Daniell; Douglass Dumbrille; George Zucco; ***D:*** Robert Z. Leonard.

Firefox ½ **1982 (PG)** A retired pilot sneaks into the Soviet Union for the Pentagon to steal a top-secret, ultra-sophisticated warplane and fly it out of the country. Best for the low-altitude flight and aerial battle sequences, but too slow on character and much too slow getting started. **136m/C; VHS, DVD, Blu-Ray.** Clint Eastwood; Freddie Jones; David Huffman; Warren Clarke; Ronald Lacey; Kenneth Colley; Nigel Hawthorne; Kai Wulff; ***D:*** Clint Eastwood; ***C:*** Bruce Surtees; ***M:*** Maurice Jarre.

Firehead ½ **1990 (R)** A pyrokinetic Soviet defector begins using his powers to destroy American munitions in the name of peace. When a clandestine pro-war organization hears of this, they attempt to capture the man and use him for their own evil purposes. **88m/C; VHS, DVD.** Christopher Plummer; Chris Lemmon; Martin Landau; Gretchen Becker; Brett Porter; ***D:*** Peter Yuval.

Firehouse **1972** Tempers ignite in a lily-white firehouse when a black rookie replaces an expired veteran. March—of "Paper Lion" renown—directed this made-for-TV emergency clone, which ran ever-so-briefly as an adventure series on TV in 1974 (with a largely different cast). **73m/C; VHS, DVD.** Richard Roundtree; Vince Edwards; Andrew Duggan; Richard Jaeckel; Sheila Frazier; Val Avery; Paul LeMat; Michael Lerner; ***D:*** Alex March; ***M:*** Tom Scott. **TV**

Firehouse 🦴 **1987 (R)** In the style of "Police Academy," three beautiful and sex-starved fire-fighting recruits klutz up an urban firehouse. A softcore frolic. **91m/C; VHS, DVD.** Barrett Hopkins; Shannon Murphy; Violet Brown; John Anderson; Julia Roberts; ***D:*** J. Christian Ingvordsen; ***W:*** J. Christian Ingvordsen; Steven Kaman; Rick Marx; ***C:*** Steven Kaman; ***M:*** Michael Montes.

Firehouse Dog 🦴🦴 **2007 (PG)** Movie dog Rexxx, aka Dewey, is lost during an airplane stunt and winds up in the reluctant care of sullen 12-year-old Shane Fahey (Hutcherson). Shane and his dad, Connor (Greenwood), are going through a rough time as Connor has taken charge of an embattled inner-city fire station called Dogpatch. But the kid soon realizes that Dewey is no ordinary mutt and his furry pal becomes both a rescue dog and the perfect PR tool. There's lots of bonding and hey, it's a dog movie! What could be better? Okay there are a few things better than this particular dog movie. Like a trip to the vet. **111m/C; DVD.** Josh Hutcherson; Bruce Greenwood; Dash Mihok; Steven Culp; Bill Nunn; Bree Turner; Mayte Garcia; ***D:*** Todd Holland; ***W:*** Mike Werb; Michael Colleary; Claire-Dee Lim; ***C:*** Victor Hammer; ***M:*** Jeff Cardoni.

Firelight 🦴🦴 ½ **1997 (R)** Governess Elisabeth (Marceau) needs to pay off her father's debts and makes a deal with married British aristocrat Charles Godwin (Dillane) to give him a child since his own wife is comatose from a riding accident. She gives her baby daughter up but, seven years later, is still so haunted by her memories that she decides to seek them out. So Elisabeth gets hired as her own spoiled daughter's governess. Charles is at least momentarily outraged but soon they can't keep their sexual desires quiescent any longer. Set in 1838. **104m/C; VHS, DVD, Streaming.** Sophie Marceau; Stephen (Dillon) Dillane; Joss Ackland; Kevin Anderson; Lia Williams; Dominique Belcourt; ***D:*** William Nicholson; ***W:*** William Nicholson; ***C:*** Nic Morris; ***M:*** Christopher Gunning.

Firelight 🦴🦴 **2012** In this typically inspirational Hallmark Hall of Fame drama, hard-luck Caroline (Kilcher) winds up in a correctional center after being involved in a robbery with her sleazy boyfriend. With no self-esteem, Caroline first connects with the bad girls in the cell block, but counselor Dwayne Johnson (Gooding Jr.) gets Caroline the opportunity to join the volunteer firefighting force and make something of herself. **90m/C; DVD; Closed Captioned.** Cuba Gooding, Jr.; Q'orianka Kilcher; DeWanda Wise; Rebecca Rivera; Sianoa Smit-McPhee; Bruce McKinnon; ***D:*** Darnell Martin; ***W:*** Ligiah Villalobos; ***C:*** Frank Prinzi; ***M:*** Paul Cantelon. **TV**

The Firemen's Ball 🦴🦴🦴 *Hori, ma panenko* **1968** A critically acclaimed comedy about a small-town ball held for a retiring fire chief. Plans go amusingly awry as beauty contestants refuse to show themselves, raffle prizes and other items—including the gift for the guest of honor—are stolen, and the firemen are unable to prevent an old man's house from burning down. Forman's second film is sometimes interpreted as political allegory; Czech with subtitles. **73m/C; VHS, DVD.** *CZ* Vaclav Stockel; Josef Svet; ***D:*** Milos Forman; ***W:*** Milos Forman; Ivan Passer; Jaroslav Papousek; Vaclav Sasek; ***C:*** Miroslav Ondricek; ***M:*** Karel Mares.

Firepower 🦴 ½ **1979 (R)** Loren blames her chemist husband's death on a rich industrialist and hires hitman Coburn to take care of the matter. Less than compelling. **104m/C; DVD, Blu-Ray.** Sophia Loren; James Coburn; O.J. Simpson; Christopher F. Bean; Dominic Chianese; ***D:*** Michael Winner; ***W:*** Michael Winner; ***M:*** Gato Barbieri.

Firepower 🦴 ½ **1993 (R)** Two cops chase "The Swordsman" into a federally sanctioned area of legalized gambling, prostitution and crime (Las Vegas?), risking life and limb in the treacherous "Caged Ring of Death." **95m/C; VHS, DVD.** Chad McQueen; Gary Daniels; Jim Hellwig; Joseph Ruskin; George Murdock; ***D:*** Richard Pepin; ***W:*** Michael January; ***C:*** Ken Blakey.

Fireproof 🦴🦴 **2008 (PG)** Firefighter Caleb (Cameron) has let his obsession with work get in the way of his marriage to neglected spouse Catherine (Bethea) and they have separated. Caleb's dad (Malcom) urges him to attempt a reconciliation by trying a Christian-based 40-day marriage program but it won't be easy. Commendable and sincere effort that gets a little heavy-handed in its last act. **122m/C; Blu-Ray, On Demand.** Kirk Cameron; Erin Bethea; Harris Malcom; Ken Bevel; Phyllis Malcom; James McLeod; ***D:*** Alex Kendrick; ***W:*** Alex Kendrick; Stephen Kendrick; ***C:*** Bob Scott; ***M:*** Mark Willard.

Fires on the Plain 🦴🦴🦴 *Nobi* **1959** A grueling Japanese antiwar film about an unhinged private in the Philippines during WWII who roams the war-torn countryside encountering all manner of horror and devastation. In Japanese with English subtitles. **105m/B; VHS, DVD.** *JP* Eiji Funakoshi; Osamu Takizawa; Mickey Custis; Asao Sano; Kyu Sazanka; Yoshihiro Hamaguchi; Hikaru Hoshi; Yasushi Sugita; Masaya Tsukida; Mantaro Ushio; ***D:*** Kon Ichikawa; ***W:*** Natto Wada; ***C:*** Setsuo Kobayashi; ***M:*** Yashushi Akutagawa.

Fires Within 🦴🦴 **1991 (R)** A curiously flat romance with political overtones. After eight years as a political prisoner in Cuba, Nestor (Smits) is released and goes to Miami to be reunited with his wife and daughter. Once there he finds his wife has fallen in love with another man. Now Nestor must choose between his politics and the chance to win back his family. Secondary plotlines fizzle out and a talented cast is largely wasted. Scacchi is beautiful but hardly believable as the Cuban wife. **90m/C; VHS, DVD.** Jimmy Smits; Greta Scacchi; Vincent D'Onofrio; ***D:*** Gillian Armstrong; ***W:*** Cynthia Cidre; ***C:*** David Gribble; ***M:*** Maurice Jarre.

Firestarter 🦴🦴 **1984 (R)** A C.I.A.-like organization is after a little girl who has the ability to set anything on fire in this filmed adaptation of Stephen King's bestseller. Good special effects help a silly plot. **115m/C; VHS, DVD, Blu-Ray.** David Keith; Drew Barrymore; Freddie Jones; Martin Sheen; George C. Scott; Heather Locklear; Louise Fletcher; Moses Gunn; Art Carney; Antonio Fargas; Drew Snyder; ***D:*** Mark L. Lester; ***W:*** Stanley Mann; ***C:*** Giuseppe Ruzzolini; ***M:*** Tangerine Dream.

Firestarter 2: Rekindled 🦴🦴 **2002** Original sequel to the 1984 film, based on the Stephen King novel. A now-adult Charlie (Moreau) is researching the project that sparked her fire-starting powers, without realizing that her former mentor (McDowell) wants to eliminate all survivors of the Lot 6 project. Meanwhile, insurance agent Vincent Sforza (Nucci) is looking for Charlie and a mysterious scientist (Hopper) is also involved. **168m/C; VHS, DVD.** Marguerite Moreau; Malcolm McDowell; Danny Nucci; Dennis Hopper; Skye McCole Bartusiak; John Dennis Johnston; Darnell Williams; Deborah Van Valkenburgh; ***D:*** Robert Iscove; ***W:*** Philip Eisner; ***C:*** David Boyd. **CABLE**

Firestorm 🦴 ½ **1997 (R)** Ex-NFL tough guy Long plays Jesse Graves, a parachuting firefighter with a really square head in his first starring role. Jesse, along with "smoke jumping" mentor Wynt (Glenn), must drop into a raging Wyoming forest fire in order to save a group of trapped firemen. Except they aren't really firemen, they're convicts in disguise who have escaped through a hole in the plot. Ringleader Shaye (Forsythe) had his lawyer set the fire so that he could use the volunteer murderer/fire fighter release program to escape and find the $37 million he has hidden. Happens all the time. The smoky chain gang also stumble across beautiful bird-watcher Jennifer (Amis) and take her hostage. Jesse must foil the bad guys, save the girl and douse the fire; all the while lugging around his humongous chin and speaking in monotone. Fire effects were enhanced by computer generated graphics. **89m/C; VHS, DVD.** Howie Long; Scott Glenn; William Forsythe; Suzy Amis; Christianne Hirt; Garwin Sanford; Sebastian Spence; Michael Greyeyes; Benjamin Ratner; Barry Pepper; Vladimir Kulich; Tom McBeath; ***D:*** Dean Semler; ***W:*** Chris Soth; ***C:*** Stephen F. Windon; ***M:*** J. Peter Robinson.

Firetrap 🦴🦴 ½ **2001 (R)** Combo heist/disaster flick is routine material. Thief Jack (Cain) is hired to steal a computer chip from a L.A. high-rise corporate headquarters but is double-crossed by a crooked company insider (Tyson) who sets fire to the building, trapping Jack and the other occupants. **99m/C; VHS, DVD.** Dean Cain; Richard Tyson; Lori Petty; Mel Harris; James Storm; Vanessa Angel; John O'Hurley; Elena Sahagun; Steven Williams; ***D:*** Harris Done; ***W:*** Richard Preston, Jr.; Diane Fine; ***C:*** Mark W. Gray; ***M:*** Sean Murray. **VIDEO**

Firewalker 🦴 **1986 (PG)** An "Indiana Jones" clone about three mercenaries endeavoring to capture a fortune in hidden gold. Paper-mache sets and a villain with an eye patch that consistently changes eyes are just some of the gaffes that make this one of the worst edited movies in history. **106m/C; VHS, DVD, Blu-Ray.** Chuck Norris; Louis Gossett, Jr.; Melody Anderson; ***D:*** J. Lee Thompson; ***W:*** Norman Aladjem; ***M:*** Gary Chang.

Firewall 🦴🦴 **2006 (PG-13)** The 60-something Ford does the heroic family man thing again. Here he plays Jack Stanfield, a security specialist at a Seattle bank, whose family is held hostage by psycho thief Bill Cox (Bettany) and his gang. Cox needs Jack to circumvent his own security system so that $100 million can be transferred to an offshore account. Jack, of course, decides to thwart their nefarious plan and save his family. Ford is his usual stalwart self, but the movie is a paint-by-numbers disappointment that brings nothing new to the well-worn genre **120m/C; DVD, Blu-Ray, HD-DVD.** Harrison Ford; Paul Bettany; Virginia Madsen; Mary Lynn Rajskub; Robert Patrick; Robert Forster; Alan Arkin; Carly Schroeder; Jimmy Bennett; Vince Vieluf; Kett Turton; Vincent Gale; Nikolaj Coster-Waldau; ***D:*** Richard Loncraine; ***W:*** Joe Forte; ***C:*** Marco Pontecorvo; ***M:*** Alexandre Desplat.

Fireworks 🦴🦴 *Hana-Bi* **1997** Idiosyncratic mixture of drama, comedy, violence, and sentiment. Nishi (Kitano) is a tough detective whose wife, Miyuki (Kishimoto), is dying from leukemia. He's visiting her in the hospital when his partner Horibe (Osugi) is gunned down and paralyzed. Deciding to get justice on his own terms, Nishi quits the force and decides to settle his debts with the yakuza by robbing a bank (which also funds a last trip with his wife). Kitano (who uses his acting alias of Beat Takeshi) is the strong, silent, violent type and a very visual director. Those are Kitano's own paintings in the scenes where Horibe takes up art as his new hobby. Japanese with subtitles. **103m/C; VHS, DVD, Blu-Ray.** *JP* Takeshi "Beat" Kitano; Kayoko Kishimoto; Ren Osugi; Susumu Terajima; Tetsu Watanabe; ***D:*** Takeshi "Beat" Kitano; ***W:*** Takeshi "Beat" Kitano; ***C:*** Hideo Yamamoto; ***M:*** Joe Hisaishi.

The Firing Line 🦴🦴 **1991** The Central American government hires a mercenary rebel-buster to squash insurgents. Everything's great until he finds out he agrees with the rebel cause, and he trains them to fight the government. Below average renegade-with-a-hidden-heart warpic. **93m/C; VHS, DVD.** Reb Brown; Shannon Tweed; Michael Monty; Kathlena Marie; Melvin Davidson; Carl Terry; Andy Jacobson; ***D:*** John Gale; ***W:*** John Gale; Sonny Sanders; ***C:*** Carl Sommers; ***M:*** Martia Manuel.

The Firm 🦴🦴🦴 **1993 (R)** Top-flight cast promises a good time—the script based on the top-selling 1991 novel by John Grisham nearly guarantees it. Ambitious, idealistic Ivy League law school grad Cruise accepts a great offer from a small but wealthy Memphis law firm. As with anything that seems too good to be true, he discovers too late that nothing in life is free. Good performances by nearly everyone involved makes up for predictability. Sorvino has an uncredited cameo as a mob boss. Book fans beware: the script is fairly faithful until the end. The movie rights were snapped up before the book was published. Placed third in the 1993 race for top boxoffice gross. **154m/C; VHS, DVD, Blu-Ray.** Tom Cruise; Jeanne Tripplehorn; Gene Hackman; Hal Holbrook; Terry Kinney; Wilford Brimley; Ed Harris; Holly Hunter; David Strathairn; Gary Busey; Steven Hill; Tobin Bell; Barbara Garrick; Jerry Hardin; Karina Lombard; John Beal; Paul Sorvino; Joe (Johnny) Viterelli; ***D:*** Sydney Pollack; ***W:*** Robert Towne; David Rayfiel; ***C:*** John Seale; ***M:*** Dave Grusin.

First a Girl 🦴🦴 ½ **1935** Delivery girl Elizabeth (Matthews) is dropping off costumes at the local theatre, which is where she meets a female impersonator with throat trouble. He gets Elizabeth to take his place on stage and she becomes famous overnight. So she keeps up the charade until a princess (Lee) and her boyfriend (Jones) become suspicious and decide to uncover the truth. If the plot sounds familiar, it's because the film was remade as "Victor/Victoria" (1982). **93m/B; VHS, DVD.** *GB* Jessie Matthews; Sonnie Hale; Anna Lee; Griffith Jones; Alfred Drayton; Martita Hunt; ***D:*** Victor Saville; ***W:*** Marjorie Gaffney; ***C:*** Glen MacWilliams.

The First Auto 🦴🦴 **1927** In 1895, successful Hank Armstrong (Simpson) owns the town's livery stable and is also a prize-winning race horse owner. His son Bob (Mack) is enamored of the new horseless carriage, which appalls Hank. Over the years, the automobile takes over, Hank's business goes bust, and he is forced to sell his beloved horses. Becoming bitter, Hank sabotages an automobile, not realizing that Bob will be driving it in an exhibition race. Ironically, Mack was killed in a car accident during filming and he is notably absent in later scenes. **78m/B; Silent; DVD.** Russell Simpson; Charles Emmet Mack; Frank Campeau; Patsy Ruth Miller; William Demarest; Douglas Gerrard; ***D:*** Roy Del Ruth; ***W:*** Darryl F. Zanuck; ***C:*** David Abel.

First Blood 🦴🦴 **1982 (R)** Stallone is a former Green Beret survivor of Vietnam whose nightmares of wartime horrors are triggered by a wrongful arrest in a small town. He escapes into the mountains of the Northwest and leads his pursuers to all manner of bloody ends. Finally, the Army is summoned to crush him. Extremely violent and frequently confused, fueled on the revenge fantasy and not much concerned with the rules of plot realism. Screen debut of Caruso. Based on David Morrell's novel. A boxoffice hit that launched the "Rambo" series. Followed by "Rambo: First Blood, Part 2." **96m/C; VHS, DVD, Blu-Ray, UMD.** Sylvester Stallone; Richard Crenna; Brian Dennehy; Jack Starrett; David Caruso; ***D:*** Ted Kotcheff; ***W:*** Sylvester Stallone; ***C:*** Andrew Laszlo; ***M:*** Jerry Goldsmith.

First Cow 🦴🦴🦴 **2020 (PG-13)** A slow-paced exploration of ingenuity and friendship in the Oregon Territory during the 1820s. A cook (Magaro), part of a group of fur trappers, befriends a Chinese refugee (Lee), and the two scheme to steal milk from the settlement's only cow to bake and sell cakes to the trappers, eager for a taste of something different. Jonathan Raymond wrote the screenplay, which is loosely based on his 2004 debut novel "The Half-Life." **122m/C; DVD.** John Magaro; Orion Lee; Rene Auberjonois; Toby Jones; Ewen Bremner; ***D:*** Kelly Reichardt; ***W:*** Kelly Reichardt; Jonathan Raymond; ***C:*** Christopher Blauvelt; ***M:*** William Tyler.

First Daughter 🦴 ½ **2004 (PG)** Ever hear of a flick called "Chasing Liberty" about a president's daughter who wants to escape from her duties and just have a little fun? Well, let's just play follow the government leader. Samantha Mackenzie (Holmes) chafes under the restrictions of being presidential dad's (Keaton) proper only offspring. So she heads to college in California where she tries to ditch her security detail to party with diva roommate Mia (Amerie), getting into some mild hijinks that cause mom Melanie (Colin) to lay down the law (it's an election year), even as Sam gets flirty with faculty adviser James (Blucas). Everyone seems to be sleepwalking (even director Whitaker) as if it's too much effort to pump some hot air into this snoozefest. **104m/C; VHS, DVD.** Katie Holmes; Marc Blucas; Margaret Colin; Michael Keaton; Amerie; Lela Rochon Fuqua; ***Nar:*** Forest Whitaker; ***D:*** Forest Whitaker; ***W:*** Jessica Bendinger; Kate Kondell; ***C:*** Toyomichi Kurita; ***M:*** Michael Kamen; Blake Neely; Damon Elliot.

The First Deadly Sin 🦴 ½ **1980 (R)** Police lieutenant Sinatra tracks down a homicidal killer in spite of wife Dunaway's illness and his impending retirement. Read Lawrence Sanders' bestselling novel; it's a lot more exciting than this. **112m/C; DVD.** Frank Sinatra; Faye Dunaway; David Dukes; Brenda Vaccaro; James Whitmore; ***D:*** Brian G. Hutton; ***W:*** Mann Rubin; ***C:*** Jack Priestley; ***M:*** Gordon Jenkins.

First Degree 🦴 1/2 **1995 (R)** N.Y.C. homicide detective Rick Mallory (Lowe) goes up against the mob while investigating the murder of a rich man and falling for the widow. **98m/C; VHS, DVD.** *CA* Rob Lowe; Leslie Hope; Tom McCamus; Nadia Capone; Brett Halsey; ***D:*** Jeff Woolnough; ***W:*** Ron Base; ***C:*** Glen MacPherson. **CABLE**

First Degree 🦴🦴 *Charades; Felons* **1998 (R)** Quinn (Wilder) and wife Lara (Kates) invite some friends and co-workers to their house for a barbecue. But there's more than hamburgers about to be grilled. Seems widow Jude (Black) is convinced that her husband Paul's killer is attending the festivities. And she soon has everyone turning on each other. **80m/C; VHS, DVD.** Erika Eleniak; C. Thomas Howell; Jack Scalia; James Wilder; James Russo; Karen Black; Kimberley Kates; James Andronica; ***D:*** Stephen Eckelberry; ***W:*** S.P. Somtow; ***C:*** Susan Emerson. **VIDEO**

First Descent 🦴🦴 **2005 (PG-13)** Documentary attempts to chronicle the history as well as the current state of free-ride snowboarding. Nick Perata, Shawn Farmer, Terji Haakonsen, Shaun White and Hannah Teter ride virgin powder throughout Alaska's spectacular Chugach Mountains. The narration darts around a bit but the obvious enthusiasm more than makes up. **110m/C; DVD, UMD.** ***D:*** Kevin Harrison; ***W:*** Kevin Harrison; Kemp Curley; ***C:*** Scott Duncan; ***M:*** Mark Mothersbaugh.

First Do No Harm 🦴🦴 1/2 **1997 (PG-13)** Well-intentioned but routine TV movie depicts the crisis of the farming Reimuller family when the youngest child, four-year-old Robbie (Adkins), is diagnosed with epilepsy. Their health insurance won't cover Robbie's drug treatment and the bank is about to foreclose on the farm so dad Dave (Ward) takes up truck driving while mom Lori (Streep) tries to hold things together. Dismayed at Robbie's doctors, Lori also pursues an unorthodox treatment for Robbie that involves diet therapy rather than drugs. Director Abraham's own son has his epilepsy controlled by this alternative method. **94m/C; VHS, DVD.** Meryl Streep; Fred Ward; Seth Adkins; Allison Janney; Michael Yarmush; ***D:*** Jim Abrahams; ***W:*** Ann Beckett; ***C:*** Pierre Letarte. **TV**

First Dog 🦴🦴 1/2 **2010** Cute dog, cute kid. First dog Teddy mistakenly gets left behind at an out-of-town ceremony and decides to have an adventure. Teddy's found by foster child Danny Milbright, who figures out who Teddy belongs to and then decides to personally return the President's dog to his White House home, which means a road trip for them both. **90m/C; DVD.** Jean-Paul Howard; Eric Roberts; Eliza Roberts; Tommy (Tiny) Lister; Priscilla Barnes; Paula DeVicq; ***D:*** Bryan Michael Stoller; ***W:*** Bryan Michael Stoller; ***C:*** Bruce Alan Greene; ***M:*** Harry Hansen. **VIDEO**

First Family 🦴 1/2 **1980 (R)** Flat satire of life in the White House. The humor is weak and silly at best, despite the excellent comedy cast. Henry's first directorial effort. **100m/C; DVD, Streaming.** Bob Newhart; Madeline Kahn; Gilda Radner; Richard Benjamin; ***D:*** Buck Henry; ***W:*** Buck Henry; ***C:*** Fred W. Koenekamp; ***M:*** Ralph Burns.

First Kid 🦴🦴 **1996 (PG)** Formulaic "Home Alone Guarding Tess" does have its moments, but if you're over 14, probably not enough of them. Latest in a bevy of films to be inaugurated into the white hot "White House" genre-of-the-moment. Innocuous family comedy casts Sinbad as Sam Simms, an offbeat Secret Service agent who is given the menial job of guarding Prez's bratty son Luke (Pierce). Simms sees that Luke is merely a misunderstood misfit like himself, and helps the lad have more fun than a Presidential son is allowed. Flick's clean, inoffensive humor makes it hard to dislike. Watch for cameo from Sonny Bono. **101m/C; VHS, DVD.** Sinbad; Brock Pierce; James Naughton; Blake Boyd; Timothy Busfield; Art LaFleur; Robert Guillaume; Lisa Eichhorn; Zachery Ty Bryan; Bill Cobbs; ***D:*** David Mickey Evans; ***W:*** Tim Kelleher; ***C:*** Anthony B. Richmond; ***M:*** Richard Gibbs.

First Kill 🦴 **2017 (R)** To rescue his young son, Will (Christensen) must track down money from a failed bank robbery, but a police chief (Willis) keeps interfering. The twists and turns aren't surprising enough to keep you from noticing the atrocious acting; even the cinematography and musical score are amateurish. Should've gone straight to video. **97m/C; DVD.** Bruce Willis; Hayden Christensen; Ty Shelton; Megan Leonard; Gethin Anthony; ***D:*** Steven C. Miller; ***W:*** Nick Gordon; ***C:*** Brandon Cox; ***M:*** Ryan Franks; Scott Nickoley.

First Knight 🦴 1/2 **1995 (PG-13)** King Arthur/Camelot legend comes to life again, but isn't worth the time it takes to watch. Wandering swordsman Lancelot (Gere) saves beautiful Guinevere (Ormond), soon to be Arthur's (Connery) queen, from evil renegade knight Malagant. They yearn, they gaze, they kiss—you gag. Written like a Harlequin romance, the dialogue (especially when uttered by Gere) is unintentionally funny, and the plot will cause much eye-rolling. Connery's regal (he knows his costume epics) and Ormond's lovely, but Gere is badly miscast. He offers a contemporary take on the flawed hero complete with American accent, an amazing feat in the 13th century. Big-scale battles, betrayals, passion, even Disneyland-like Camelot sets—the pieces for a tremendous epic are all here, it just doesn't work. **134m/C; VHS, DVD.** Sean Connery; Richard Gere; Julia Ormond; Ben Cross; John Gielgud; Liam Cunningham; Christopher Villiers; Valentine Pelka; ***D:*** Jerry Zucker; ***W:*** William Nicholson; ***C:*** Adam Greenberg; ***M:*** Jerry Goldsmith.

First Lady 🦴 1/2 **2020 (PG)** During her husband's (King) first term as president, Kathryn Morales (Stafford) has been an excellent first lady. As she looks forward to continuing her initiatives during his second term, her husband's sudden death puts an end that to that goal. However, when widower vice president Taylor Brooks (Dane), takes over the presidency then runs for the presidency himself, Kathryn supports him by running for first lady. After she becomes the first elected first lady, she finds that the position and her perspective on life undergo significant changes. A jumbled and forgettable political fantasy/romantic comedy. **101m/C; DVD.** Nancy Stafford; Corbin Bernsen; Stacey Dash; Benjamin Dane; Melissa Temme; ***D:*** Nina May; ***W:*** Nina May; ***C:*** Steven Shulgach; ***M:*** Andrei Shulgach.

First, Last and Deposit 🦴🦴 1/2 **2000** Christine and her daughter 13-year-old Tessa end up living in their car when Christine is unable to cover the rent on her cashier's salary after her boyfriend moves them to Santa Barbara, loses his job, and splits. Tessa tries to get along with her new classmates by lying about her home life as the bonds between mother and daughter begin to strain under the pressure of their situation. First-time director Hyoguchi's use of digital video helps convey the desparation and immediacy of the family's plight, as well as giving a sense of gritty realism. Mostly inexperienced cast does a fine job. **92m/C; VHS, DVD.** Sara Wilcox; Jessica White; Don Margolin; Alanna Learned; Robin Alcorn; Katie Hatcher; Jason Hallows; ***D:*** Peter Hyoguchi; ***W:*** Peter Hyoguchi; Duffy Hecht.

First Light 🦴🦴 **2010** BBC docudrama. Geoffrey Wellum is only 18 when he becomes the youngest Spitfire pilot during the Battle of Britain in 1940. The toll of his combat experiences leads to a mental breakdown that haunts him 70 years later. Based on Wellum's memoirs and he serves as narrator. **79m/C; DVD.** *GB* Sam Heughan; Ben Aldridge; Jordan Bernarde; Alex Robertson; Paul Kynman; ***Nar:*** Geoffrey Wellum; ***D:*** Matthew Whiteman; ***W:*** Matthew Whiteman; Caleb Ranson; ***C:*** Mark Wolf; ***M:*** Gabriel Currington. **TV**

First Love 🦴🦴 1/2 **1939** Best known for Durbin's first screen kiss, this lightweight romance finds orphaned Connie Harding moving to New York to live with her wealthy Uncle James Clinton (Pallette) and his family. Connie meets handsome rich boy Ted Drake (Stack's screen debut) but her snobby debutante cousin Barbara (Parrish) already has Ted in her sights. Barbara tries to prevent Connie from going to the Drakes fancy dance but, in Cinderella fashion, the Clinton family servants help her become the belle of the ball. Durbin also does some singing. **85m/B; VHS, DVD.** Deanna Durbin; Robert Stack; Eugene Pallette; Helen Parrish; Leatrice Joy; June Storey; Frank Jenks; Kathleen Howard; Charles Coleman; Mary Treen; ***D:*** Henry Koster; ***W:*** Bruce Manning; Lionel Houser; ***C:*** Joseph Valentine; ***M:*** Frank Skinner.

First Love 🦴🦴 1/2 **1970 (R)** A 16-year-old lad falls in love with a slightly older woman only to have his feelings rejected and to discover that she's his father's mistress. Actor Schell's directorial debut. **90m/C; VHS, DVD.** *GE SI* John Moulder-Brown; Dominique Sanda; Maximilian Schell; Valentina Cortese; ***D:*** Maximilian Schell; ***C:*** Sven Nykvist.

First Love and Other Pains / One of Them 🦴🦴 1/2 **1999** Two gay shorts explore first love. In "First Love" (50 minutes), Hong Kong college student Mark begins an English lit course with a stern British professor, Hugh Graham. Depressed by creative burnout, Hugh is flattered by Mark's attentions and they have a one-nighter—at least in Hugh's mind because Mark is looking for a longer-lasting romance. Cantonese and English with subtitles. In "One of Them" (47 minutes), two gay teens in the 60s strike up a friendship that makes their small, boring town almost bearable. **97m/C; VHS, DVD.** Edward Strode; Alex Wong; Ciaran Pennington; Cameron J. Watt; ***D:*** Simon Chung; Stewart Main; ***W:*** Simon Chung; Peter Wells; ***C:*** Ping Hung Wong; Stewart Main.

First Man 🦴🦴 1/2 **2018 (PG-13)** A look at the life of the astronaut, Neil Armstrong, and the legendary space mission that led him to become the first man to walk on the Moon on July 20, 1969. **141m/C; DVD, Blu-Ray, Streaming.** *US JP* Ryan Gosling; Claire Foy; Jason Clarke; Kyle Chandler; Corey Stoll; ***D:*** Damien Chazelle; ***W:*** Josh Singer; ***C:*** Linus Sandgren; ***M:*** Justin Hurwitz. Oscars '18: Visual FX; Golden Globes '19: Orig. Score.

First Man into Space 🦴🦴 *Satellite of Blood* **1959** An astronaut returns to Earth covered with strange space dust and with an organism feeding inside him (shades of "Alien"). The alien needs human blood to survive and starts killing in order to get it. **78m/B; VHS, DVD.** Marshall Thompson; Marla Landi; Bill Edwards; ***D:*** Robert Day; ***W:*** John C. Cooper; Lance Z. Hargreaves; ***C:*** Geoffrey Faithfull; ***M:*** Buxton Orr.

First Men in the Moon 🦴🦴 **1964** A fun, special effects-laden adaptation of the H. G. Wells novel about an Edwardian civilian spacecraft visiting the moon and the creature found there. Visual effects by Ray Harryhausen. Finch makes a brief appearance. **103m/C; VHS, DVD, Blu-Ray.** *GB* Martha Hyer; Edward Judd; Lionel Jeffries; Erik Chitty; Peter Finch; ***D:*** Nathan "Jerry" Juran; ***W:*** Nigel Kneale; Jan Read; ***C:*** Wilkie Cooper; ***M:*** Laurie Johnson.

First Monday in October 🦴🦴 1/2 **1981 (R)** Clayburgh, as the first woman appointed to the Supreme Court, finds a friendly rival in colleague Matthau, a crusty but benign liberal judge. Though based on a Broadway hit, it ended up seeming to foreshadow the real-life appointment of Sandra Day O'Connor, which occurred at about the time the film was released. The title refers to the date the court begins its sessions. **99m/C; DVD.** Walter Matthau; Jill Clayburgh; Barnard Hughes; James Stephens; Jan Sterling; Joshua Bryant; Noble Willingham; ***D:*** Ronald Neame; ***C:*** Fred W. Koenekamp; ***M:*** Ian Fraser.

First Name: Carmen 🦴🦴🦴 *Prenom: Carmen* **1983** Carmen, although posing as an aspiring filmmaker, really is a bank robber and terrorist. She is also such a femme fatale that during a bank robbery one of the guards decides to run away with her. Godard cast himself as Carmen's uncle. Amusing late Godard. French with subtitles. **95m/C; VHS, DVD, Blu-Ray.** *FR* Maruschka Detmers; Jacques Bonnaffe; Jean-Luc Godard; Myriem Roussel; Christophe Odent; ***D:*** Jean-Luc Godard; ***W:*** Anne-Marie Mieville; ***C:*** Raoul Coutard.

The First 9 1/2 Weeks WOOF! 1998 (R) Prequel to "9 1/2 Weeks" finds investor Matt Wade trying to close the biggest deal of his career with eccentric New Orleans businessman Francois Dubois. But Dubois' wife starts raising Wade's temperature even more than steamy New Orleans. **99m/C; VHS, DVD.** Paul Mercurio; Clara Bellar; Malcolm McDowell; Frederic Forrest; Dennis Burkley; James Black; Anna Jacyszyn; William Keane; Richard Durden; ***D:*** Alexander Wright; ***W:*** Alexander Wright; ***C:*** John Tarver; ***M:*** Norman Orenstein.

The First Nudie Musical 🦴🦴 **1975 (R)** A producer tries to save his studio by staging a 1930s style musical, but with a naked cast and risque lyrics. Has attained semi-cult/trash status. **93m/C; VHS, DVD.** Cindy Williams; Stephen Nathan; Diana Canova; Bruce Kimmel; Alan Abelew; Alexandra Morgan; Frank Doubleday; Kathleen Hietala; Leslie Ackerman; Ron Howard; ***D:*** Bruce Kimmel; Mark Haggard; ***W:*** Bruce Kimmel; ***C:*** Douglas Knapp; ***M:*** Bruce Kimmel.

The First Olympics: Athens 1896 🦴🦴 1/2 **1984** Recounts the organization and drama surrounding the first modern-day Olympic games when the inexperienced American team shocked the games with their success. **260m/C; VHS, DVD.** Louis Jourdan; Angela Lansbury; David Ogden Stiers; Virginia McKenna; Jason Connery; Alex Hyde-White; Honor Blackman; Bill Travers; ***D:*** Alvin Rakoff; ***M:*** Bruce Broughton. **TV**

First Position 🦴🦴 1/2 **2011** Documentary follows six young ballet students from all over the world as they prepare for the Youth America Grand Prix. **90m/C; VHS, DVD, Streaming.** ***D:*** Bess Kargman; ***C:*** Nick Higgins; ***M:*** Chris Hajian.

The First Power 🦴 1/2 **1989** A detective and psychic join forces to track down a serial killer who, after being executed, uses his satanic powers to kill again. **90m/C; VHS, DVD, Blu-Ray.** Lou Diamond Phillips; Tracy Griffith; Jeff Kober; Mykelti Williamson; Elizabeth Arlen; ***D:*** Robert Resnikoff; ***W:*** Robert Resnikoff; ***C:*** Theo van de Sande; ***M:*** Stewart Copeland.

The First Purge 🦴 **2018 (R)** As the title suggests, this is a prequel about the nation's first formal 12-hour period of carte blanche lawlessness and the events that led to this socio-psychological experiment. What could have been another by-the-numbers yet enjoyable installment in the violent franchise is instead a racist, politically divisive piece of propaganda. And that's no fun for anyone. **98m/C; DVD, Blu-Ray.** Y'lan Noel; Lex Scott Davis; Joivan Wade; Marisa Tomei; Luna Lauren Valez; ***D:*** Gerard McMurray; ***W:*** James DeMonaco; ***C:*** Anastas Michos; ***M:*** Kevin Lax.

First Reformed 🦴🦴 1/2 **2017 (R)** Alcoholic Protestant minister Ernst Toller (Hawke) is undergoing an intense crisis. Previously a happily married military chaplain, his personal life left fell apart after his son was killed fighting in Iraq. Toller's current church has few active members, and he often drinks alone. Toller's situation grows more complicated when pregnant Mary (Seyfriend) asks that he counsel her husband, Michael (Ettinger), a troubled environmentalist who may be suicidal. Though well told and acted, the art house style might limit mainstream appeal. **113m/C; Blu-Ray, Streaming.** Ethan Hawke; Amanda Seyfried; Cedric the Entertainer; Michael Gaston; Van Hansis; ***D:*** Paul Schrader; ***W:*** Paul Schrader; ***C:*** Alexander Dynan; ***M:*** Brian Williams. Ind. Spirit '19: Actor (Hawke).

The First Saturday in May 🦴🦴 1/2 **2008 (PG-13)** That would be the Saturday that the Kentucky Derby is run. The Hennegan brothers are the sons of a thoroughbred trainer and their documentary follows six demographically disparate trainers as they try to qualify their horses for the big 2006 race. There's lots of off-track human and equine drama and that Derby was the one that featured the ill-fated Barbaro. **100m/C; On Demand.** ***D:*** Brad Hennegan; John Hennegan; ***W:*** Brad Hennegan; John Hennegan; ***C:*** Brad Hennegan; John Hennegan; ***M:*** Mark Krewatch; Ryan Brothers.

First Snow 🦴🦴 **2007 (R)** Sleazy traveling salesman Jimmy (Pearce) impulsively gets his fortune told by Vacaro (Simmons), who suffers a seizure and abruptly ends their session. After his other predictions come true, Jimmy returns and insists that the psychic tell him the rest—which is of Jimmy's death by the first snowfall. Jimmy starts to unravel as his past mistakes catch up to him, but maybe his impending doom is a self-fulfilling prophecy. Pearce (angular and spooked) is made for paranoid types, although the flick ultimately underachieves. **102m/C; DVD.** Guy Pearce; Piper Perabo; William Fichtner; J.K. Simmons; Shea Whigham; Rick Gonzales; ***D:*** Mark Fergus; ***W:*** Mark Fergus; Hawk Ostby; ***C:*** Eric Alan Edwards; ***M:*** Cliff Martinez.

First Spaceship on Venus *Der Schweigende Stern; Milczaca Gwiazda* **1960** Eight scientists from various countries set out for Venus and find the remains of a civilization far in advance of Earth's that perished because of nuclear weapons. A sometimes compelling anti-nuclear sci-fi effort made with German and Polish backing. Originally released at 130 minutes. **78m/C; VHS, DVD.** *GE PL* Yoko Tani; Oldrich Lukes; Ignacy Machowski; Julius Ongewe; Michal Postnikow; Kurt Rackelmann; Gunther Simon; Tang-Hua-Ta; Lucyna Winnicka; ***D:*** Kurt Maetzig; ***C:*** Joachim Hasler.

First Strike **1985** The United States and the USSR engage in nuclear submarine warfare when the Soviets hijack a U.S. sub and aims its weapons at Arab oil fields. **90m/C; VHS, DVD, Streaming.** Stuart Whitman; Persis Khambatta; ***D:*** Allan Kuskowski; ***W:*** Allan Kuskowski; ***C:*** Glenn Roland.

First Sunday **2008 (PG-13)** Durell (Ice Cube) and LeeJohn (Morgan) are buddies who both find themselves in need of some large money in a big hurry in order to escape tight spots. Naturally, they hatch a plan to rob the local Baltimore neighborhood church since, hey, who else has that kind of cash? Just one problem: someone has already unloaded the safe, and a handful of church officials are on hand to witness the whole caper. Undaunted, the two pals take the whole lot hostage, setting up a few lame attempts at humor as the characters find themselves stuck together. The overly sweet choirmaster (Williams) proves to be a high point in a mostly predictable and ridiculous movie. See this one if you have the entire N.W.A catalogue on your iPod. **98m/C; DVD, Blu-Ray.** Ice Cube; Katt Micah Williams; Tracy Morgan; Loretta Devine; Michael Beach; Chi McBride; Keith David; Regina Hall; Malinda Williams; ***D:*** David E. Talbert; ***W:*** David E. Talbert; ***C:*** Alan Caso; ***M:*** Stanley Clarke.

The First Texan **1/2** **1956** Mediocre bio of Sam Houston (McCrea) from young lawyer to the Battle of San Jacinto to gain Texas independence from Mexico to his presidency of the Republic of Texas. **82m/C; DVD.** Joel McCrea; Felicia Farr; Jeff Morrow; James Griffin; David Silva; Carl Benton Reid; Wallace Ford; William Hopper; Dayton Lummis; ***D:*** Byron Haskin; Daniel Ullman; ***W:*** Daniel Ullman; ***C:*** Byron Haskin; Wilfred M. Cline; ***M:*** Roy Webb.

First They Killed My Father **1/2** **2017** An emotionally charged war film told from the perspective of a child, based on a memoir by Loung Ung (Srey Moch). As the Khmer Rouge take over Cambodia near the end of the Vietnam War, young Loung and her middle-class family leave the capital city and do whatever it takes to survive. Shedding beloved possessions as their situation grows more dire, Loung and her family find themselves in a re-education agricultural camp where they both work and starve. Khmer with subtitles. **156m/C; DVD.** Sareum Srey Moch; Phoeung Kompheak; Sveng Socheata; Mun Kimhak; Heng Dara; ***D:*** Angelina Jolie; ***W:*** Angelina Jolie; Loung Ung; ***C:*** Anthony Dod Mantle; ***M:*** Marco Beltrami.

The First Time **1/2** **1952** Dated domestic comedy that looks at the first year of bringing up baby for new parents Joe (Cummings) and Betsey (Hale). He needs to make more money and takes a hated job as a salesman for his dad's company. She is frazzled by the strict, prevailing ideas of infant care while her hubby still expects a hot meal (and a hot wife) when he gets home. Something's gotta give. **89m/B; DVD.** Robert Cummings; Barbara Hale; Bill Goodwin; Jeff Donnell; ***D:*** Frank Tashlin; ***W:*** Hugo Butler; ***C:*** Ernest Laszlo; ***M:*** Frederick "Friedrich" Hollander.

The First Time **1/2** *You Don't Need Pajamas at Rosie's; The Beginners Three; The Beginners; They Don't Wear Pajamas at Rosie's; Doin' It* **1969 (R)** It's pre-Porky's zaniness as a vacationing youth understandably wants to spend his "first time" with Bisset. Other than her presence, this film has little to offer. **90m/C; VHS, DVD.** Jacqueline Bisset; Wes Stern; Rick Kelman; Wink Roberts; ***D:*** James Neilson.

The First Time **2012 (PG-13)** L.A. high schooler Dave longs for Jane, who only wants to be friends, while Aubrey is sorta dating Ronny although they don't have much in common. Dave and Aubrey meet cute and proceed from there in a predictable teen romance fashion. **95m/C; DVD.** Dylan O'Brien; Britt Robertson; Victoria Justice; James Frecheville; Joshua Malina; Christine Taylor; ***D:*** Jonathan Kasdan; ***W:*** Jonathan Kasdan; ***C:*** Rhet W. Bear; ***M:*** Alec Puro.

First Time Felon **1/2** **1997 (R)** Based on the true story of a young Chicago drug dealer Greg Yance (Epps), who's convicted as a first-time offender and sent to a prison boot camp to straighten up. But the real challenge is when he's released and returns to his old neighborhood, with its old temptations, and tries to find an honest job. **106m/C; VHS, DVD.** Omar Epps; William Forsythe; Rachel Ticotin; Delroy Lindo; ***D:*** Charles S. Dutton; ***W:*** Daniel Therriault. **CABLE**

First to Fight **1967** Marine Jack Connell (Everett) wins the Congressional Medal of Honor after defending his position against the Japanese on Guadalcanal. Sent stateside, he falls in love and marries Peggy (Devin) and is assigned to train recruits. However, Jack decides he must return to action, only to fear he's lost his nerve during a front-line battle. Film takes its title from the Marines' Hymn. **101m/C; DVD.** Chad Everett; Dean Jagger; Gene Hackman; Marilyn Devin; Bobby Troup; Claude Akins; James Best; ***D:*** Christian Nyby; ***W:*** Gene L. Coon; ***C:*** Harold E. Wellman; ***M:*** Fred Steiner.

The First to Go **1997 (PG-13)** Impulsive Adam is the first of his crowd to get engaged. His friends don't approve of his decision and decide to take him on vacation to get him to change his mind. Only his fiancee decides to come along too and she has plans of her own. **91m/C; VHS, DVD.** Zach Galligan; Laurel Holloman; Mark Harmon; Corin "Corky" Nemec; Steve Parlavecchio; Jennifer Jostyn; Lisanne Falk; ***D:*** John Jacobs.

First Turn On **1983 (R)** Not to be confused with "The Thomas Edison Story," this sex-comedy follows the adventures of several young campers who decide to die happy when an avalanche leaves them trapped in a cave. A longer unrated version is available. **88m/C; VHS, DVD.** Georgia Harrell; Michael Sanville; Googy Gress; Jenny Johnson; Heide Basset; Vincent D'Onofrio; Sheila Kennedy; ***D:*** Michael Herz; Lloyd Kaufman; ***W:*** Georgia Harrell; Michael Herz; Lloyd Kaufman; Stuart Strutin; ***C:*** Lloyd Kaufman.

The First $20 Million is Always the Hardest **2002 (PG-13)** Dismal "comedy" about the late dot-com economy is itself late by at least a year. Not that timeliness would've helped this muddled, desperate-for-laughs mess. Marketing whiz Andy (Garcia) leaves his corporate gig to "do something important." He joins a hot tech firm run by digital guru Francis (Colantoni) who immediately resents him and assigns him to the hopeless project of trying to create a $99 PC. He assembles a quirky team of misfits for the project and geek jokes ensue. Only Dawson, as Andy's love interest, escapes with any dignity. Based on the Po Bronson novel. **105m/C; VHS, DVD.** Adam Garcia; Rosario Dawson; Jake Busey; Enrico Colantoni; Ethan Suplee; Gregory Jbara; Dan E. Butler; Linda Hart; Anjul Nigam; ***D:*** Mick Jackson; ***W:*** Jon Favreau; Gary Tieche; ***C:*** Ron Garcia; ***M:*** Marco Beltrami.

The First Wives Club **1/2** **1996 (PG)** As the first Mrs. Trump, who makes a most appropriate cameo, so wisely puts it, "Don't get mad, get everything." But to the three rich, middle-aged friends who are dumped by their husbands so the guys can marry younger "trophy" wives, there's just nothing like revenge. Comedy begins in 1969 with the young and idealistic Annie (Keaton), Brenda (Midler), Elise (Hawn) and Cynthia graduating college, then moves to the present with the wronged Cynthia (Channing) ledge-diving from her swanky Manhattan apartment because her husband left her. The remaining mistreated trio goes into action, using their exes' own money, businesses, power, and various mistresses against them. This film's appeal and success had Hollywood tongues wagging, predicting the dawn of new roles for older actresses. Based on the book by Olivia Goldsmith. **104m/C; VHS, DVD.** Goldie Hawn; Diane Keaton; Bette Midler; Sarah Jessica Parker; Heather Locklear; Marcia Gay Harden; Elizabeth Berkley; Victor Garber; Dan Hedaya; Stephen Collins; Maggie Smith; Stockard Channing; Bronson Pinchot; Jennifer (Jennie) Dundas Lowe; Eileen Heckart; Philip Bosco; Rob Reiner; James Naughton; Dina Spybey; Timothy Olyphant; J.K. Simmons; Debra Monk; Edward Hibbert; Stephen Mendillo; ***D:*** Hugh Wilson; ***W:*** Robert Harling; ***C:*** Donald E. Thorin; ***M:*** Marc Shaiman.

A Fish Called Wanda **1988 (R)** Absurd, high-speed farce about four criminals trying to retrieve $20 million they've stolen from a safety deposit box—and each other. Meanwhile, barrister Archie Leech (Cleese) falls in love with the female thief, Wanda (Curtis). Some sick, but tastelessly funny, humor involves Palin's problem with stuttering and some very dead doggies. Written by Monty Python alum Cleese and director Crichton, who understand that silence is sometimes funnier than speech, and that timing is everything. Wickedly funny. **98m/C; VHS, DVD, Blu-Ray.** John Cleese; Kevin Kline; Jamie Lee Curtis; Michael Palin; Tom Georgeson; Maria Aitken; Patricia Hayes; Geoffrey Palmer; Andrew MacLachlan; ***D:*** Charles Crichton; ***W:*** John Cleese; Charles Crichton; ***C:*** Alan Hume; ***M:*** John Du Prez. Oscars '88: Support. Actor (Kline); British Acad. '88: Actor (Cleese), Support. Actor (Palin).

Fish Hawk **1/2** **1979 (G)** When an alcoholic Indian, Fish Hawk, meets a young boy in the forest, they strike up a friendship and he attempts to clean up his act. Attempts to be heartwarming. **95m/C; VHS, DVD.** *CA* Will Sampson; Charlie (Charles) Fields; ***D:*** Donald Shebib.

Fish in a Barrel **2001 (R)** Familiar heist gone wrong flick is supposed to be played for laughs but doesn't have any. Four petty thieves are suprised to find themselves with four million in uncut diamonds and then wind up with two more partners to split the loot—a hitwoman and a dirty cop. **85m/C; VHS, DVD.** Jeremy Renner; Arly Jover; Kent Dalian; Stephen Ingle; Rene Rigal; David Kelsey; ***D:*** Kent Dalian; ***W:*** Kent Dalian; ***C:*** Lisa Wiegand; ***M:*** Matt Sorum; Lanny Cordola.

A Fish in the Bathtub **1999 (PG-13)** Sam and Molly have been married 40 years and their relationship has become one of constant bickering and mutual one-upmanship. Sam's latest stunt is putting a live carp in the guest bathroom tub. However, when he humiliates Molly in front of their friends, she leaves him, moves in with their son Joel, and starts dating Lou. Sam thinks things will blow over but daughter Ruth isn't so sure. **96m/C; DVD.** Jerry Stiller; Anne Meara; Mark Ruffalo; Jane Adams; Bob (Robert) Dishy; Missy Yager; Paul Benedict; Doris Roberts; Phyllis Newman; ***D:*** Joan Micklin Silver; ***W:*** John Silverstein; David Chudnovsky; Raphael D. Silver; ***C:*** Daniel Shulman; ***M:*** John Hill.

Fish Tank **2009** Raw and grim depiction of the life of a sexually awakening teen girl in lower-class London. Sullen 15-year-old Mia (Jarvis) has been kicked out of school and is trapped in a rough housing project with her boozy mum Joanne (Wareing) and her hostile sister Tyler (Griffiths). Alienated from her peers, Mia's only escape is breaking into an abandoned apartment where she practices hip-hop dance routines. Everything changes when Joanne brings home hunky boyfriend Connor (Fassbender), who may have designs on Mia as well. Jarvis, who carries the film with her performance, was a non-professional actress discovered by director Arnold while loudly fighting with her boyfriend in a train station. **123m/C; Blu-Ray.** *GB* Michael Fassbender; Harry Treadaway; Katie Jarvis; Kierston Wareing; Rebecca Griffiths; Sydney Mary Nash; Jason Maza; ***D:*** Andrea Arnold; ***W:*** Andrea Arnold; ***C:*** Robbie Ryan.

The Fish that Saved Pittsburgh **1979 (PG)** A floundering basketball team hires an astrologer to try and change their luck. She makes sure all the team members' signs are compatible with their star's Pisces sign (the fish). Produced a disco soundtrack with several Motown groups who also performed in the movie. **104m/C; VHS, DVD.** Jonathan Winters; Stockard Channing; Flip Wilson; Julius Erving; Margaret Avery; Meadowlark Lemon; Nicholas Pryor; James Bond, III; Kareem Abdul-Jabbar; Jack Kehoe; Debbie Allen; ***D:*** Gilbert Moses; ***M:*** Thom Bell.

Fish Without a Bicycle *Girls Will Be Girls* **2003 (R)** Too many dating cliches floating around in lead actress/writer Mattison's story of a woman who dumps her dutiful and handsome beau Danny (Rowe) to pursue her dreams of acting—and other men, including the self-absorbed director Michael (Callen). She also hooks up with her caring, studly co-star Ben (Green). Her lesbian best friend Vicki also has a thing for her. **95m/C; DVD, On Demand.** Brian Austin Green; Jenna Mattison; Jennifer Blanc; Brad Rowe; Bryan Callen; ***D:*** Brian Austin Green; ***W:*** Jenna Mattison. **VIDEO**

The Fisher King **1991 (R)** In derelict-infested Manhattan a down-and-out radio deejay meets a crazed vagabond (Williams) obsessed with medieval history and in search of the Holy Grail. At first the whimsical mix of Arthurian myth and modern urban hell seems amazingly wrongheaded. In retrospect it still does. But while this picture runs it weaves a spell that pulls you in, especially in its quiet moments. Your reaction to the silly ending depends entirely on how well you're bamboozled by a script that equates madness with enlightment and the homeless with holy fools. Filmed on the streets of New York, with many street people playing themselves. **138m/C; VHS, DVD, Blu-Ray.** Robin Williams; Jeff Bridges; Amanda Plummer; Mercedes Ruehl; Michael Jeter; Harry Shearer; John de Lancie; Kathy Najimy; David Hyde Pierce; ***D:*** Terry Gilliam; ***W:*** Richard LaGravenese; ***C:*** Roger Pratt; ***M:*** George Fenton. Oscars '91: Support. Actress (Ruehl); Golden Globes '92: Actor--Mus./Comedy (Williams), Support. Actress (Ruehl); L.A. Film Critics '91: Actress (Ruehl).

Fisherman's Friends **2019** When music executive Danny (Mays) takes a trip to rural Cornwall on a boys weekend, his friends prank him into signing a local a cappella group, Fisherman's Friends, they hear singing one evening. After he learns about the joke, Danny remains moved by their music and invested in their success. At the same time, Danny begins to fall in love with single mother Alwyn (Middleton), a daughter of one of the singers. Taking the signing seriously, Danny takes action to bring Fisherman's Friends and their music to the world. Based on a true story, it's heartfelt and entertaining. **112m/C; DVD.** Tuppence Middleton; James Purefoy; Daniel Mays; Christian Brassington; David Hayman; ***D:*** Chris Foggin; ***W:*** Piers Ashworth; Megan Leonard; Nick Moorcroft; ***C:*** Simon Tindall; ***M:*** Rupert Christie. **VIDEO**

Fisherman's Wharf **1/2** **1939** Breen stars as an orphan adopted by a San Francisco fisherman who runs away when his aunt and bratty cousin come to live with them. **72m/B; VHS, DVD.** Bobby Breen; Leo Carrillo; Henry Armetta; Lee Patrick; Rosina Galli; Leon Belasco; ***D:*** Bernard Vorhaus.

Fishing Without Nets **1/2** **2014** A young Somalian husband and father named Abdi is forced into a criminal enterprise when his society gives him no other hope for freedom in this variation of "A Hijacking" and "Captain Phillips." Sadly, this version is remarkably thin in terms of realism, casting Abdi as the only "good pirate" and surrounding him with villainous caricatures instead of accepting the idea that everyone in this tumultuous part of the world may not be so morally black and white. Some striking visual images can't make up for what the story lacks. **109m/C; DVD.** *US SM KY* Abdikani Muktar; Eric Godon; Reda Kateb; Abdi Siad; ***D:*** Cutter Hodierne; ***W:*** Cutter Hodierne; John Hibey; David Burkman; ***C:*** Alex Disenhof; ***M:*** Patrick Taylor; Kevin Hilliard.

Fishtales **1/2** **2007 (PG)** Family fluff. Widowed history professor Thomas Bradley (Zane) is desperate to continue his studies on ancient Greek love spells. He's given one last chance to make an academic breakthrough before losing his research grant, so

Thomas and his 12-year-old daughter Serena (Sawa) travel to the Greek island of Spetses. Serena tries playing matchmaker after meeting Neried (Brook), who turns out to be a mermaid. The Bradleys must then come to her rescue when she's menaced by a local fisherman (David) who wants Neried's jewel-encrusted tail. That's not the only problem: if the mermaid falls in love with a mortal, she gives up her immortality (and presumably the tail). **87m/C; DVD.** Billy Zane; Kelly Brook; Amber Sawa; Alki David; ***D:*** Alki David; ***W:*** Melissa Painter; Alki David; ***C:*** Aggelos Viskadourakis. **VIDEO**

Fist 🦴 *Black Fist; The Black Streetfighter; Homeboy* **1976 (R)** Street fighter battles his way through the urban jungle seeking personal freedom and revenge. **84m/C; VHS, DVD.** Richard Lawson; Annazette Chase; Dabney Coleman; Philip Michael Thomas; ***D:*** Timothy Galfas; Richard Kaye; ***W:*** Tim Kelly; ***M:*** Ed Townsend.

F.I.S.T. 🦴🦴 **1/2 1978 (R)** A young truck driver turns union organizer for idealistic reasons, but finds himself teaming with gangsters to boost his cause. His rise to the top of the union comes at the cost of his integrity, as Stallone does a character resembling Jimmy Hoffa. **145m/C; VHS, DVD, Blu-Ray.** Sylvester Stallone; Rod Steiger; Peter Boyle; David Huffman; Melinda Dillon; Tony LoBianco; Kevin Conway; Peter Donat; Cassie Yates; Brian Dennehy; ***D:*** Norman Jewison; ***W:*** Sylvester Stallone; ***M:*** Bill Conti.

Fist Fight 🦴 **1/2 2017 (R)** Charlie Day and Ice Cube bring all the charisma and comic timing they can to a comedy that doesn't really know what to do with them. The pair stars as two teachers who butt heads repeatedly, leading to a promised fight after school. Tracy Morgan, Jillian Bell, Christina Hendricks, and Kumail Nanjiani co-star in this sporadically entertaining comedy that just never quite develops the rhythm it needs to not feel like an extended sitcom. **91m/C; DVD, Blu-Ray.** Ice Cube; Charlie Day; Tracy Morgan; Jillian Bell; Christina Hendricks; Kumail Nanjiani; Chris Cornwell; ***D:*** Richie Keen; ***W:*** Van Robichaux; Evan Susser; ***C:*** Eric Alan Edwards; ***M:*** Dominic Lewis.

Fist of Fear, Touch of Death 🦴 *Fist of Fear; The Dragon and the Cobra* **1980 (R)** Madison Square Garden is the scene for a high stakes martial arts face-off. Standard kung-fu film highlighted by short clips of the late Bruce Lee. **81m/C; VHS, DVD, Blu-Ray.** Fred Williamson; Ron Van Clief; Adolph Caesar; Aaron Banks; Bill Louie; ***D:*** Matthew Mallinson; ***W:*** Ron Harvey; ***C:*** John Hazard; ***M:*** Keith Mansfield.

Fist of Honor 🦴 **1992 (R)** A young boxer seeks to avenge his fiance's death, a beautiful girl squares off against a bad-cop, and two mobster leaders try to take control of the same city. When a member of one family breaks a truce and begins killing rival family members, the violence escalates and old scores will be settled. **90m/C; VHS, DVD.** Sam Jones; Joey House; Harry Guardino; Nicholas Worth; Frank Sivero; Abe Vigoda; Bubba Smith; ***D:*** Richard Pepin; ***W:*** Charles Kanganis.

Fist of Legend 🦴🦴 **1994 (R)** Chen Zuen (Li) is a martial arts practitioner studying abroad during WWII, who returns to his homeland to avenge his teacher's death at the hands of the invading Japanese. Homage to Bruce Lee's 1972 "Fists of Fury" AKA "Chinese Connection." Cantonese with subtitles or dubbed. **92m/C; VHS, DVD.** *CH* Jet Li; Yasuka Kurata; ***D:*** Woo-ping Yuen; Gordon Chan; ***M:*** Joseph Koo.

Fist of the North Star 🦴🦴 **1995 (R)** Legendary warrior Kenshiro (Daniels) returns from the grave to avenge the death of his father (McDowell) and restore his North Star clan. He must battle evil Lord Shin (Mandylor) and his henchmen in a post-apocalyptic future. Based on the Japanese comic book series, which is also available in anime form. **90m/C; VHS, DVD.** Gary Daniels; Costas Mandylor; Christopher Penn; Julie Brown; Malcolm McDowell; Melvin Van Peebles; Isako Washio; ***D:*** Tony Randel; ***W:*** Tony Randel; ***C:*** Jacques Haitkin; ***M:*** Christopher L. Stone.

A Fistful of Dollars 🦴🦴🦴 **1964 (R)** The epitome of the "spaghetti western" pits Eastwood as "the man with no name" against two families who are feuding over land. A remake of Kurosawa's "Yojimbo," and followed by Leone's "For a Few Dollars More," and "The Good, The Bad, and The Ugly." **101m/C; VHS, DVD, Blu-Ray.** *IT* Clint Eastwood; Gian Marie Volonte; Marianne Koch; ***D:*** Sergio Leone; ***W:*** Sergio Leone; Victor Andres Catena; Duccio Tessari; G. Schock; ***C:*** Massimo Dallamano; Federico G. Larraya; ***M:*** Ennio Morricone.

A Fistful of Dynamite 🦴🦴🦴 *Duck, You Sucker; Giu la Testa* **1972 (PG)** A spaghetti western, with Leone's trademark humor and a striking score by Morricone. An Irish demolitions expert and a Mexican peasant team up to rob a bank during a revolution in Mexico. **138m/C; VHS, DVD, Blu-Ray.** *IT* James Coburn; Rod Steiger; Romolo Valli; ***D:*** Sergio Leone; ***M:*** Ennio Morricone.

Fistful of Lead 🦴🦴 **1970** Hilton is Sartana, this film's version of Clint Eastwood's "Man with No Name" in a blatant rip-off of "Fistful of Dollars." Of the many copycats that came in the wake of Leone's classic, this is one of the better efforts, which considering the field is damning with faint praise. **92m/C; VHS, DVD.** *IT* George Hilton; Charles Southwood; Pierro Lulli; Erika Blanc; ***D:*** Giuliano Carnimeo; ***W:*** Tito Carpi; ***C:*** Stelvio Massi; ***M:*** Francesco De Masi.

Fists of Fury 🦴🦴🦴 *The Big Boss; Tang Shan da Xiong* **1973 (R)** Bruce Lee stars in this violent but charming Kung Fu action adventure in which he must break a solemn vow to avoid fighting in order to avenge the murder of his teacher by drug smugglers. **102m/C; VHS, DVD, Blu-Ray.** Bruce Lee; Maria Yi; ***D:*** Lo Wei; ***W:*** Bruce Lee; Lo Wei; ***C:*** Chen Ching Chu; ***M:*** Fu-ling Wang.

Fit for a King 🦴🦴 **1937** A reporter becomes a princess' knight in shining armor when he foils an assassination plot in this screwball romance. **73m/B; VHS, DVD.** Joe E. Brown; Leo Carrillo; Helen Mack; Paul Kelly; Harry Davenport; ***D:*** Edward Sedgwick; ***C:*** Paul Vogel.

Fit to Kill 🦴 **1/2 1993 (R)** Once again special agents Donna Hamilton and Nicole Justine (former Playboy centerfolds Speir and Vasquez) reteam for an adventure that matches them with an old enemy, double agents, diamonds, and revenge. Filmed on location in Hawaii. **94m/C; VHS, DVD, Blu-Ray.** Dona Speir; Roberta Vasquez; R.J. (Geoffrey) Moore; Bruce Penhall; Julie Strain; Rodrigo Obregon; Cynthia Brimhall; Tony Peck; ***D:*** Andy Sidaris; ***W:*** Andy Sidaris.

The Fits 🦴🦴 **1/2 2016** Eleven-year-old Toni (Hightower) spends her days working out with her brother at a local youth group facility in Cincinnati, but she's drawn to the young women, just a bit older than her, who mesmerizingly dance in a team down the hall. Toni seems eager to fit in, copying the routines of the girls and dreaming of joining the dance troupe. Then the girls at this facility start having, well, fits. They're something like epileptic seizures—terrifying and unexplained. Anna Rose Holmer's stunning debut captures the mystery of adolescence while also announcing a new voice in visual storytelling. **72m/C; DVD, Blu-Ray.** Royalty Hightower; Alexis Neblett; Makyla Burnam; Da'Sean Minor; Lauren Gibson; ***D:*** Anna Rose Holmer; ***W:*** Anna Rose Holmer; ***C:*** Paul Yee; ***M:*** Danny Bensi; Saunder Jurriaans.

Fitzcarraldo 🦴🦴🦴🦴 **1982 (PG)** Although he failed to build a railroad across South America, Fitzcarraldo is determined to build an opera house in the middle of the Amazon jungles and have Enrico Caruso sing there. Based on a true story of a charismatic Irishman's impossible quest at the turn of the century. Of note: No special effects were used in this movie—everything you see actually occurred during filming, including hauling a large boat over a mountain. **157m/C; VHS, DVD, Blu-Ray.** *GE* Klaus Kinski; Claudia Cardinale; Jose Lewgoy; Miguel Angel Fuentes; Paul Hittscher; ***D:*** Werner Herzog; ***W:*** Werner Herzog; ***C:*** Thomas Mauch; ***M:*** Popul Vuh. Cannes '82: Director (Herzog).

The Fitzgerald Family Christmas 🦴🦴 **1/2 2012 (PG-13)** Long-absent dad Jim Fitzgerald (Lauter) is dying and wants to reunite with his family for his last Christmas. His still bitter ex-wife, Rosie (Gillette), is opposed and his numerous children are divided about the holiday, especially since they have their own issues to deal with. Burns is in familiar New York territory and the dysfunctional family clichés abound, but he keeps the sentimentality low and the likeability factor high. **97m/C; DVD, Blu-Ray.** Edward Burns; Ed Lauter; Anita Gillette; Connie Britton; Mike McGlone; Kerry Bishe; Marsha Dietlein; Heather Burns; Caitlin FitzGerald; Tom Guiry; ***D:*** Edward Burns; ***W:*** Edward Burns; ***C:*** William Rexer; ***M:*** P.T. Walkley.

Fitzwilly 🦴🦴 **1967** Aimless comedy with some decent slapstick from Van Dyke in the title role. Claude Fitzwilliam is the loyal butler to aged philanthropist Victoria Woodworth (Evans). Her servants have kept the fact that she's nearly broke by pulling off various scams but Miss Woodworth's new secretary Juliet (Feldon) may be their downfall. Their final scheme comes on Christmas Eve at Gimbel's department store. **102m/C; DVD.** Dick Van Dyke; Barbara Feldon; Edith Evans; John McGiver; Norman Fell; Cecil Kellaway; Anne Seymour; ***D:*** Delbert Mann; ***W:*** Isobel Lennart; ***C:*** Joseph Biroc; ***M:*** John Williams.

Five 🦴🦴 **1951** A curiosity as an early (and low-budget) example of survivors after a nuclear holocaust plot. Pregnant Roseanne (Douglas), naturalist Michael (Phipps), black doorman Charles (Lampkin), elderly bank clerk Barnstaple (Lee), and cynical intellectual Eric (Anderson) find shelter together in a California house (designed by Frank Lloyd Wright) and have to decide what happens next. **93m/B; DVD.** William Phipps; Susan Douglas; James Anderson; Charles Lampkin; Earl Lee; ***D:*** Arch Oboler; ***W:*** Arch Oboler; ***C:*** Louis Clyde Stoumen; Sid Lubow; ***M:*** Henry Russell.

The Five 🦴 **1/2 2010** Five kids find themselves trapped in their favorite mythological book series as a backdrop for exploring serious family issues like death and divorce. **90m/C; DVD.** Madisen Beaty; Emily Cho; Ry Feder Pruett; Ben Larned; Allison Larned; ***D:*** Dave Yasuda; ***W:*** J. Reuben Appelman; ***C:*** David Klein; ***M:*** Jeffrey Rice. **VIDEO**

Five 🦴🦴🦴 **2011** Lifetime anthology of five short films made for Breast Cancer Awareness month that subtly makes the point that cancer doesn't discriminate based on race, creed, politics, economics, or any other societal divide. The character tying the stories together is Pearl (Tripplehorn), the compassionate oncologist who appears in all the vignettes, whose own mother died from the disease. **87m/C; DVD.** Jeanne Tripplehorn; Ginnifer Goodwin; Josh Holloway; Patricia Clarkson; Tony Shalhoub; Lyndsy Fonseca; Taylor Kinney; Rosario Dawson; Bob Newhart; ***D:*** Demi Moore; Jennifer Aniston; Penelope Spheeris; Alicia Keys; Patty Jenkins; ***W:*** Stephen Godchaux; Wendy West; Howard J. Morris; Jill Gordon; Deirdre O'Connor; ***C:*** Tami Reiker; Eric Alan Edwards; Christopher Popp; Jim Orr; Guy Livneh; ***M:*** Lorne Balfe. **CABLE**

5 Against the House 🦴🦴 **1955** College buddies, who are going to school on the G.I. Bill after serving in Korea, plan to rob a Reno casino just to prove they can and then give the money back. However, Brick (Keith) is mentally unstable after his war experiences and deeply in debt so he doesn't want to return the loot. Al (Madison) goes along out of loyalty but then his babe girlfriend Kay (Novak) gets pulled into the scheme. **84m/B; DVD, Blu-Ray.** Guy Madison; Kim Novak; Brian Keith; Alvy Moore; Kerwin Mathews; William Conrad; ***D:*** Phil Karlson; ***W:*** Stirling Silliphant; William Bowers; John Barnwell; ***C:*** Lester White; ***M:*** George Duning.

Five and Ten 🦴🦴 **1931** John Rarick moves his family from the Midwest to the Big Apple so he can expand his five-and-dime empire and introduce his new money into society. Daughter Jennifer gets laughed at by Muriel, the fiancé of playboy Berry Rhodes, who still makes a play for the new girl. Meanwhile, her brother Avery becomes a depressed drunk, realizing the family is falling apart thanks to their workaholic dad. Based on the Fanny Hurst novel. **88m/B; DVD.** Marion Davies; Leslie Howard; Richard Bennett; Douglass Montgomery; Mary Duncan; Irene Rich; ***D:*** Robert Z. Leonard; ***W:*** A.P. Younger; Edith Fitzgerald; ***C:*** George Barnes.

5 Broken Cameras 🦴🦴 **2011** Emad Burnat is a Palestinian farmer from the village of Bilin, which had its olive groves and other agricultural land taken to build an Israeli housing development beginning in 2005. The residents protested, which lead to protests that Burnat filmed (hence the title as the clashes with the Israeli military and settlers became violent). Burnat worked with Israeli filmmaker Davidi to edit hundreds of hours of film into this powerful, though sometimes emotionally manipulative, documentary. Arabic and Hebrew with subtitles. **94m/C; DVD.** *PA IS* ***Nar:*** Emad Burnat; ***D:*** Emad Burnat; Guy Davidi; ***C:*** Emad Burnat.

Five Came Back 🦴🦴🦴 **2017** A documentary exploring World War II filmmakers. During this conflict, five high-profile Hollywood filmmakers--John Ford, William Wyler, John Huston, Frank Capra, and George Stevens--traveled to the front lines to record combat and its aftermath as well as the wider impacts of war. The men put themselves at risk to film such important events as D-Day. Though early efforts were used to encourage the purchase of war bonds, their films became more complex in content and artistic value over time. With archival footage and the insights of five leading contemporary directors, the documentary effectively shows how the World War II filmmakers changed the world. **180m/C; DVD.** Francis Ford Coppola; Guillermo del Toro; Paul Greengrass; Lawrence Kasdan; Steven Spielberg; ***D:*** Laurent Bouzereau; ***W:*** Mark Harris; ***C:*** Sean Kirby; ***M:*** Jeremy Turner. **VIDEO**

Five Card Stud 🦴 **1/2 1968 (PG)** Five members of a lynching party are being killed one by one, and a professional gambler, who tried to prevent the lynching, attempts to ensnare the killer with the aid of a preacher with a gun. The poor script was based on a novel by Ray Gaulden. **103m/C; VHS, DVD.** Robert Mitchum; Dean Martin; Inger Stevens; Roddy McDowall; Yaphet Kotto; John Anderson; Katherine Justice; ***D:*** Henry Hathaway; ***W:*** Marguerite Roberts; ***C:*** Daniel F. Fapp; ***M:*** Maurice Jarre.

Five Corners 🦴🦴🦴 **1988 (R)** A quixotic, dramatic comedy about the inhabitants of the 5 Corners section of the Bronx in 1964, centering around a girl being wooed by a psychotic rapist, her crippled boyfriend, and the hero-turned-racial-pacifist who cannot rescue her out of principle. **92m/C; VHS, DVD.** Jodie Foster; John Turturro; Todd Graff; Tim Robbins; Elizabeth Berridge; Rose Gregorio; Gregory Rozakis; Rodney Harvey; John Seitz; ***D:*** Tony Bill; ***W:*** John Patrick Shanley; ***C:*** Fred Murphy; ***M:*** James Newton Howard. Ind. Spirit '89: Actress (Foster).

Five Days 🦴🦴 **1/2 2007** Leanne (Tremarco) and her two children disappear from their car while at a rest stop—all of which is captured by CCTV cameras. The children are later found but the police investigation becomes a major news story and the action unfolds on days 1, 3, 28, 33, and 79. As the story proceeds, it becomes clear that nothing (and no one) is quite as it seems, even when the missing persons case turns into a murder inquiry. **300m/C; DVD.** *GB* David Oyelowo; Hugh Bonneville; Janet McTeer; Penelope Wilton; Patrick Malahide; Edward Woodward; Sarah Smart; Christine Tremarco; Philip Davis; Rory Kinnear; Niki Amuka-Bird; ***D:*** Simon Curtis; Otto Bathurst; ***W:*** Gwyneth Hughes; ***C:*** Florian Hoffmeister; ***M:*** Magnus Fiennes. **TV**

5 Days of War 🦴 **1/2 2011 (R)** War drama set in 2008 during the troubles between Russia and Georgia. Combat correspondent Thomas Anders (Friend) and his cameraman Sebastian Gantz (Coyle) run into general media indifference while covering the dangerous situation, including documenting atrocities committed by mercenaries against civilians. Director Harlin's combo of action, politics, and character study doesn't mesh easily. English, Russian, and Georgian with subtitles. **153m/C; DVD, Blu-Ray.** Rupert Friend; Richard Coyle; Emmanuelle Chriqui; Andy Garcia; Val Kilmer; Heather Graham; ***D:*** Renny Harlin; ***W:*** Mikko Alanne; ***C:*** Checco Varese; ***M:*** Trevor Rabin.

Five Days One Summer 🦴🦴 **1982 (PG)** Set in 1932, the story of a haunting and obsessive love affair between a married Scottish doctor and a young woman who happens to be his niece. While on vacation in the Swiss Alps, the doctor must vie for her love with their handsome young mountain climbing guide. Based on a story by Kay Boyle. **108m/C; VHS, Streaming.** Sean Connery; Betsy Brantley; Lambert Wilson; ***D:*** Fred Zinnemann; ***W:*** Michael Austin; ***M:*** Elmer Bernstein.

Five Deadly Venoms 🦴🦴🦴 *Wu du; Five Venoms; Ng duk* **1978** While this film stopped just short of bombing in its native China it has become a huge cult success in the Western world, influencing films, video games, and even rap music. The Master of the hated Poison Clan is dying, and he asks his final student to hunt down the other remaining five and destroy them if they have become corrupt. The catch being that Yan Tieh (Sheng) hasn't trained nearly as far in his abilities so he needs to convince at least one of the other students to help him, assuming he can find them. **102m/C; DVD, Blu-Ray.** *HK* Sheng Chiang; Philip Kwok; Feng Lu; Pai Wei; Chien Sun; Meng Lo; Feng Ku; Lung Wei Wang; ***D:*** Cheh Chang; ***W:*** Cheh Chang; Kuang Ni; ***C:*** Hui-chi Tsao; Kung Mo To; ***M:*** Yung-Yu Chen.

$5 a Day 🦴🦴 **2008** Smoothly-done father-son road trip comedy. Aging Atlantic City con man Nat (Walken) is getting by on five bucks a day, lots of freebies, and his own agenda. That includes pressing estranged son Flynn (Nivola) into taking the wheel of a customized pink PT cruiser and heading out on a cross-country road trip. They make a stop in Amarillo, Texas so Nat can visit Flynn's former babysitter and successful swindler Dolores (Stone), who knows some family secrets that Flynn doesn't (yet). **90m/C; DVD.** Christopher Walken; Alessandro Nivola; Sharon Stone; Peter Coyote; Amanda Peet; ***D:*** Nigel Cole; ***W:*** Neal Dobrofsky; Tippi Dobrofsky; ***C:*** Peter Donahue; ***M:*** Alex Wurman.

Five Dolls for an August Moon 🦴🦴 *5 Dolls for an August Moon; 5 bambole per la luna d'agosto; Island of Terror* **1970** A group of investment speculators try to talk scientist Gerry Farrell (Berger) into selling them the rights to a new formula, while at a wild weekend retreat on an isolated island. As the competitors try to cheat one another with secret bids, Farrell seems disinterested, and tempers rise with the stakes. The wives and girlfriends along for the fun and games feel the tension as their men stray, or try to get them to use sex to close a deal. But once the murders begin, the possibility of anyone trusting anyone is left far behind. Allegedly a professional assignment given Bava with just two days' notice, the film is a fair murder mystery in which even this director's visual tricks can't sustain interest. The cast of connivers is interchangeable and hard to keep straight, and in some cases more easily identifiable by their now-hideous 1970 fashions than their faces. **78m/C; DVD, Blu-Ray.** *IT* William Berger; Edwige Fenech; Ira Furstenberg; Howard Ross; Helena Ronee; Teodoro Corra; Ely Galleani; Edith Meloni; Mauro Bosco; Maurice Poli; ***D:*** Mario Bava; ***W:*** Mario di Nardo; Mario di Nardo; ***C:*** Mario Bava; Antonio Rinaldi; ***M:*** Pierro Umiliani. **VIDEO**

Five Easy Pieces 🦴🦴🦴🦴 **1970 (R)** Nicholson's superb acting brings to life this character study of a talented musician who has given up a promising career and now works on the oil rigs. After a few years he returns home to attempt one last communication with his dying father and perhaps, reconcile himself with his fear of failure and desire for greatness. Black, Anspach, and Bush create especially memorable characters. Nicholson ordering toast via a chicken salad sandwich is a classic. **98m/C; VHS, DVD, Blu-Ray.** Jack Nicholson; Karen Black; Susan Anspach; Lois Smith; Billy Green Bush; Fannie Flagg; Ralph Waite; Sally Struthers; Helena Kallianiotes; Richard Stahl; Lorna Thayer; ***D:*** Bob Rafelson; ***W:*** Adrien (Carole Eastman) Joyce; Bob Rafelson; ***C:*** Laszlo Kovacs. Golden Globes '71: Support. Actress (Black); Natl. Bd. of Review '70: Support. Actress (Black); Natl. Film Reg. '00; N.Y. Film Critics '70: Director (Rafelson), Film, Support. Actress (Black); Natl. Soc. Film Critics '70: Support. Actress (Smith).

Five Element Ninjas 🦴🦴 *Rhen zhe wu di; Chinese Super Ninjas; Yan je mo dik; Super Ninjas* **1982** Two Kung-Fu schools are having a tournament to determine who is best, but when the Masters are to compete the Master of one school sends a Japanese Samurai to fight in his place. The Samurai is soundly defeated and before committing seppuku promises that the Ninjas of the 5 Elements will take revenge upon the school. Sure enough weird ninjas in theme costumes begin killing everyone in sight. Made as one of the last efforts director Chang Cheh did for the Shaw Brothers, it is entertaining for its sheer oddity. **104m/C; DVD, Blu-Ray.** *CH* Meng Lo; Wai-Man Chan; Tien-chi Cheng; Tien Hsiang Lung; Chen Hei Psi; Wang Lieh; Ke Chu; ***D:*** Cheh Chang; ***W:*** Cheh Chang; Kuang Ni; ***C:*** Wen Yun Huang; ***M:*** Chin Yung Shing; Chun Hao So.

Five Feet Apart 🦴🦴 ½ **2019 (PG-13)** When teen cystic fibrosis (CF) patient Stella (Richardson) checks into the hospital because of an infection, she feels at home with the familiar staff, routine, and self-soothing activities. Her perspective is changed when she meets fellow teen CF patient Will (Sprouse), who is receiving an experimental drug. Though Stella is hopeful and does all she can to be prepared for a lung transplant, he is more cynical in part because an infection will make him ineligible for one. The film deftly explores the intersection of CF and teen romance, with moving performances by both leads, and greater questions of living in an uncertain world. **116m/C; DVD, Blu-Ray.** Haley Lu Richardson; Cole Sprouse; Moises Arias; Kimberly Hebert Gregory; Parminder K. Nagra; ***D:*** Justin Baldoni; ***W:*** Mikki Daughtry; Tobias Iaconis; ***C:*** Frank G. DeMarco; ***M:*** Brian Tyler; Breton Vivian.

Five Finger Exercise 🦴 ½ **1962** An unfortunately dull adaptation of Peter Shaffer's 1958 play that was transferred to a California setting, thus losing its necessary English postwar tensions. Louise and Stanley Harrington are the overbearing parents of two high-strung teenagers. They make their family situation worse by hiring German refugee Walter as a live-in tutor and then succeed in making him miserable as well. Title refers to a piano study for beginners. **109m/B; DVD.** Rosalind Russell; Jack Hawkins; Richard Beymer; Annette Gorman; Maximilian Schell; Lana Wood; ***D:*** Daniel Mann; ***W:*** Albert Hackett; Frances Goodrich; ***C:*** Harry Stradling, Sr.; ***M:*** Jerome Moross.

Five Fingers 🦴🦴🦴 ½ *Operation Cicero* **1952** Under the alias "Cicero," Albanian valet Mason joins the espionage ring, selling highly confidential British war papers to the Germans during WWII. True story with odd real-life ending—unconvinced of document authenticity, the Nazis never acted on the information, even when they had the time and date of the European invasion! Fast-paced and absorbing. Adapted from the book "Operation Cicero" by L.C. Moyzisch. **108m/B; VHS, DVD, Streaming.** James Mason; Danielle Darrieux; Michael Rennie; Walter Hampden; Oskar Karlweis; Herbert Berghof; John Wengraf; Michael Pate; Ivan Triesault; Hannelore Axman; David Wolfe; Nestor Paiva; Richard Loo; Keith McConnell; ***Nar:*** John Sutton; ***D:*** Joseph L. Mankiewicz; ***W:*** Michael Wilson; ***M:*** Bernard Herrmann. Golden Globes '53: Screenplay.

Five Fingers 🦴🦴 **2006 (R)** Idealistic Dutch pianist Martijn (Phillippe) travels to his girlfriend's home country of Morocco in order to start a food program for children. He and his guide Gavin (Meaney) are promptly kidnapped and wake up in a warehouse where Gavin is killed. Then Ahmat (Fishburne) begins to question Martijn, believing he's actually a CIA operative. When Ahmat doesn't think the pianist is telling the truth, he begins cutting off Martijn's fingers. Martijn starts changing his story, but is he lying or not? **89m/C; DVD.** Laurence Fishburne; Ryan Phillippe; Gina Torres; Colm Meaney; Said Taghmaoui; Touriya Haoud; ***D:*** Laurence Malkin; ***W:*** Laurence Malkin; Chad Thumann; ***C:*** Alexander Grusynski; ***M:*** Vernon Reid; Noah Arguss.

5 Flights Up 🦴🦴 **2015 (PG-13)** Alex Carver (Freeman) has lived in a run-down apartment in Brooklyn with his schoolteacher wife Ruth (Keaton) for four decades. Given how much their neighborhood has changed over the years, they decide to put their apartment on the market just to see what they might get. Meanwhile, a potential terrorist attack in NYC raises tension as Alex and Ruth realize that they may be at another turning point in their long lives together. It's a gentle, sweet film—and Freeman and Keaton are rarely bad—but it feels a bit too slight and inconsequential. **92m/C; DVD, Blu-Ray.** Morgan Freeman; Diane Keaton; Carrie Preston; Cynthia Nixon; Miriam Shor; ***D:*** Richard Loncraine; ***W:*** Charlie Peters; ***C:*** Jonathan Freeman; ***M:*** David Newman.

Five for Hell 🦴 **1967** The army picks five of its meanest men for a suicide mission during WWII. They must go behind German lines and find the plans for the enemy offensive. Parolini used the pseudonym Frank Kramer. **88m/C; VHS, DVD.** *IT* Klaus Kinski; Gianni "John" Garko; Aldo Canti; Margaret Lee; ***D:*** Gianfranco Parolini.

Five Golden Dragons 🦴 **1967** A typical action film about an American running afoul of ruthless gold trafficking in Hong Kong. Even this stellar cast can't help the script. **92m/C; VHS, Blu-Ray, Streaming.** *GB* Robert Cummings; Christopher Lee; Brian Donlevy; Klaus Kinski; George Raft; Dan Duryea; Margaret Lee; ***D:*** Jeremy Summers.

Five Graves to Cairo 🦴🦴🦴 **1943** Tense WWII thriller finds British soldier John Bramble (Tone) stranded in a small desert town after the defeat of the British garrison by General Rommel's (Von Stroheim) Afrika Korps. Arab hotel owner Farid (Tamiroff) agrees to let Bramble assume the identity of a dead hotel waiter, much to the dismay of French maid Moush (Baxter), whose only interest is in getting her brother out of a German POW camp. The real waiter turns out to have been a secret Nazi spy, fortunately known to Rommel only by name, so Bramble attempts to learn where the German supply depots have been hidden (the "five graves" of the title-)?that is, unless Moush decides to betray him to win her brother's release. Based on the play "Hotel Imperial" by Lajos Biro. **97m/B; DVD.** Franchot Tone; Anne Baxter; Erich von Stroheim; Akim Tamiroff; Peter Van Eyck; Fortunio Bonanova; Miles Mander; Konstantin Shayne; Leslie Denison; Ian Keith; Frederick Giermann; Fred Nurney; ***D:*** Billy Wilder; ***W:*** Billy Wilder; Charles Brackett; ***C:*** John Seitz; ***M:*** Miklos Rozsa.

Five Guns to Tombstone 🦴 ½ **1960** Routine oater. Outlaw Matt Wade (Karnes) escapes prison, he frames his retired gunslinger brother Billy (Brown) into helping him in a bank heist. When Billy kills Matt in self-defense, he goes back to the townsfolk to try to clear his name but the only way to prove his innocence is returning to the remaining gang and bringing them to justice. **71m/B; DVD.** James Brown; Robert Karnes; John Wilder; Walter Coy; Jeff DeBenning; ***D:*** Edward L. Cahn; ***W:*** Jack DeWitt; Richard Schayer; ***C:*** Maury Gertsman; ***M:*** Paul Sawtell; Bert Shefter.

The Five Heartbeats 🦴🦴🦴 **1991 (R)** Well told story of five black singers in the 1960s, their successes and failures as a group and as individuals. Although every horror story of the music business is included, the story remains fresh and the acting excellent. Music is fine, but secondary to the people. Well written characters with few cliches. Skillfully directed by Townsend (of "Hollywood Shuffle") who did research by talking to the Dells. Less than memorable showing at the boxoffice but fun and entertaining. **122m/C; VHS, DVD, Blu-Ray.** Robert Townsend; Tressa Thomas; Michael Wright; Harry J. Lennix; Diahann Carroll; Leon; Hawthorne James; Chuck Patterson; Roy Fegan; Tico Wells; John Canada Terrell; Harold Nicholas; Paul Benjamin; Norma Donaldson; Eugene Robert Glazer; Lamont Johnson; ***D:*** Robert Townsend; ***W:*** Robert Townsend; Keenen Ivory Wayans; ***C:*** Bill Dill; ***M:*** Stanley Clarke.

(500) Days of Summer 🦴🦴 ½ **2009 (PG-13)** Downbeat romantic comedy. Sweet-natured Tom (Gordon-Levitt) works for an L.A. greeting card company and is instantly smitten by new hire, the elusive Summer (Deschanel), although he's too shy to make the first move. He believes in true and lasting love, she does not and their romantic travails are indicated in a nonlinear 500 days. Told from the baffled male point-of-view, not just Tom's but his buddies Paul (Gubler) and McKenzie (Arend), so Summer is a generally enigmatic fantasy woman/object rather than a person who speaks for herself. **95m/C; Blu-Ray, On Demand.** Joseph Gordon-Levitt; Zooey Deschanel; Geoffrey Arend; Chloë Grace Moretz; Matthew Gray Gubler; Clark Gregg; Rachel Boston; ***D:*** Marc Webb; ***W:*** Scott Neustadter; Michael H. Weber; ***C:*** Eric Steelberg; ***M:*** Mychael Danna; Rob Simonsen. Ind. Spirit '10: Screenplay.

500 MPH Storm 🦴 *Hypercane* **2013** Scientists working on creating a renewable energy source accidentally set off a chain of hurricanes and tornadoes which they fear will somehow merge to become a malevolent super hurricane. **90m/C; DVD, Blu-Ray, Streaming.** Caspar Van Dien; Michael Beach; Sarah Lieving; Bryan Head; Keith Meriweather; ***D:*** Daniel Lusko; ***W:*** Hank Woon, Jr.; ***C:*** Richard J. Vialet; ***M:*** Chris Ridenhour. **VIDEO**

The Five Man Army 🦴 ½ *Un Esercito di 5 Uomini* **1969** During the Mexican Revolution, five mercenaries are hired to go after a train carrying a gold shipment meant for the army. Flies under the spaghetti western banner although it's not really a western and it was filmed in Mexico. It's also long on action and short on sense. **105m/C; DVD.** *IT* Peter Graves; Bud Spencer; Nino Castelnuovo; Tetsuro Tanba; James Daly; Claudio Gora; ***D:*** Don Taylor; ***W:*** Dario Argento; Marc Richards; ***C:*** Enzo Barboni; ***M:*** Ennio Morricone.

Five Minutes of Heaven 🦴🦴 ½ **2009** Director Hirschbiegel's tense thriller begins in 1975 during The Troubles in Northern Ireland as 17-year-old Alistair Little (Davison) tries to earn his stripes via an anti-Catholic assassination, initially unaware that the victim's 11-year-old brother Joe Griffen (O'Neill) witnesses the slaying. Based on fact, the story steps ahead three decades to the fabricated scenario of Griffen (Nesbitt) and Little's (Neeson) planned face-to-face meeting prompted by a TV reality program looking more for ratings than amends. After serving 12 years, Little now thrives in the field of conflict resolution, and hopes to reconcile, whereas behind Griffen's seemingly normal life masks a broken man seeking revenge, dubbed his "five minutes in heaven." Told in three parts, screenwriter Hibbert plays out this "what if" scenario with guidance from the real Alistair and Griffen. **89m/C; Blu-Ray.** *GB IR* Liam Neeson; James Nesbitt; Mark David; Kevin O'Neill; Anamaria Marinca; Richard Dormer; ***D:*** Oliver Hirschbiegel; ***W:*** Guy Hibbert; ***C:*** Ruairi O'Brien; ***M:*** David Holmes; Leo Abrahams.

Five Minutes to Love 🦴 *The Rotten Apple; It Only Take Five Minutes* **1963** McClanahan (one of TV's "Golden Girls") plays a young, sleazy hussy named "Poochie, the girl from the shack." This exploitation schlocker appears to be McClanahan's first film. **85m/B; VHS, DVD.** Rue McClanahan; Paul Leder; King Moody; ***D:*** John Hayes.

Five Nights in Maine 🦴🦴 **2016** Sherwin (Oyelowo) loses his wife in a car accident, sending him into a grief spiral dominated by alcoholism. To try and pull himself out of the tailspin, he contacts his estranged mother-in-law Lucinda (Wiest), who is herself dealing with the grief of losing a child while also facing a terminal cancer diagnosis. Yes, there's a lot of melodrama here, and debut writer/director Maris Curran can't quite make the grief contest feel genuine but she lucks out by having Oyelowo and Wiest in her cast. It warrants a look but can't avoid the soap opera. **82m/C; DVD, Blu-Ray.** David Oyelowo; Dianne Wiest; Rosie Perez; Hani Furstenberg; Teyonah Parris; ***D:*** Maris Curran; ***W:*** Maris Curran; ***C:*** Sofian El Fani.

The Five Pennies 🦴🦴 ½ **1959** Sentimental biography starring Kaye as famed jazzman Red Nichols features performances by legendary musicians Bob Crosby, Bobby Troup, Ray Anthony and Louis Armstrong. This movie marked Weld's film debut. **117m/C; DVD.** Danny Kaye; Louis Armstrong; Barbara Bel Geddes; Tuesday Weld; Harry Guardino; ***D:*** Melville Shavelson; ***W:*** Melville Shavelson; Jack Rose; ***C:*** Daniel F. Fapp.

The Five Senses 🦴🦴🦴 **1999** Follows the trials of five urbanites, each of whom is linked to a missing child, as well as being linked to one of the five senses. Massage therapist Ruth (Rose) is losing her sense of touch; cake baker Rona (Parker) has an impaired sense of taste; housecleaner Robert (MacIvor) believes his acute sense of smell will lead to love; optholmologist Richard (Volter) is losing his hearing; and teenager Rachel (Litz) is drawn into spying games (sight) with a voyeur. Suprisingly accessible given the complex construct, each story is not only well-acted but frequently warm and witty. **105m/C; VHS, DVD.** *CA* Mary-Louise Parker; Philippe Volter; Gabrielle Rose; Daniel MacIvor; Molly Parker; Pascale Bussieres; Marco Leonardi; Brendan Fletcher; Nadia Litz; ***D:*** Jeremy Podeswa; ***W:*** Jeremy Podeswa; ***C:*** Gregory Middleton; ***M:*** Alex Pauk; Alexina Louie. Genie '99: Director (Podeswa); Toronto-City '99: Canadian Feature Film.

5 Star Day 1/2 **2010** Gimmicky concept turns into an overly-quirky dramedy. Jake Gibson's birthday horoscope promises him a '5-star day.' Instead it's a disaster. For his college ethics class project, Jake decides to track down other people born on the same day within minutes of him and at the same Chicago hospital. He finds three who all had terrible birthdays as well and lessons are learned. **97m/C; DVD, Blu-Ray.** Cam Gigandet; Jena Malone; Brooklyn Sudano; Max Hartman; Will Yun Lee; Nick (Nicholas) Chinlund; ***D:*** Danny Buday; ***W:*** Danny Buday; ***C:*** Jason Oldak; ***M:*** Ryan Beveridge. **VIDEO**

Five Star Final 1/2 **1931** Tabloid newspaper editor Joseph Randall (Robinson) is pressured by his publisher (Apfel) to come up with a sensational story to increase readership and revenue. Randall assigns slimy reporter Isopod (Karloff) to do a follow-up to a 20-year-old murder and the subsequent expose leads to multiple tragedies that finally reawaken Randall's conscience. Title refers to the last newspaper edition of the day. Some of the acting seems stilted but Karloff is repulsively watchable and Robinson gets a bravura speech. Based on the play by former tabloid newspaper editor Louis Weitzenkom. **89m/B; DVD.** Edward G. Robinson; Boris Karloff; Marian Marsh; Anthony Bushnell; Frances Starr; Ona Munson; Oscar Apfel; Aline MacMahon; George E. Stone; ***D:*** Mervyn LeRoy; ***W:*** Robert Lord; Byron Morgan; ***C:*** Sol Polito.

The 5000 Fingers of Dr. T **1953 (G)** In Dr. Seuss' only non-animated movie, a boy tries to evade piano lessons and runs right into the castle of the evil Dr. Terwilliger, where hundreds of boys are held captive for piano lessons. Worse yet, they're forced to wear silly beanies with "happy fingers" waving on top. Luckily, the trusted family plumber is on hand to save the day through means of an atomic bomb. Wonderful satire, horrible music, mesmerizing Seussian sets. The skating brothers (who are joined at their beards) are a treat. **88m/C; VHS, DVD, Blu-Ray.** Peter Lind Hayes; Mary Healy; Tommy Rettig; Hans Conried; Noel Cravat; ***D:*** Roy Rowland; ***W:*** Theodore "Dr. Seuss" Geisel; Allan Scott; ***C:*** Franz Planer; ***M:*** Frederick "Friedrich" Hollander; Hans J. Salter.

5 Time Champion **2011** Coming of age indie finds small town Texas nerd tween Julius (Akin) researching the asexual reproduction of worms for his prep school science project. Human relationships are much more confusing as Julius tries to deal with his own sexual feelings--and those of his girlfriend, Shiley (Coet). His role models are equally conflicted: his dad Harold (Longstreet) allegedly left because he's gay; his mom Danielle (Wheeler-Nicholson) is caught between two suitors; and his grandma Fran (Buckley) is upset that his grandpa Alwyn (Pirl) is spending a lot of time with his old flame, Betty (Erickson). **85m/C; DVD.** Ryan Akin; Dana Wheeler-Nicholson; Jon(athan) Gries; Betty Buckley; Don Pirl; Justin Arnold; Noell Coet; Juli Erickson; Robert Longstreet; ***D:*** Berndt Mader; ***W:*** Berndt Mader; ***C:*** Jimmy Lee Phelan; ***M:*** Graham Reynolds. **VIDEO**

5x2 1/2 *Cinq fois deux; Five Times Two* **2004 (R)** The unhappy marriage of Marion (Bruni-Tedeschi) and Gilles (Freiss) is chronicled backwards in five scenes (with two characters, hence the title), beginning with their divorce and ending with their first meeting and includes a dinner party, childbirth, and their wedding night. The couple is basically a disaster from the beginning of their relationship and you won't be terribly sympathetic (or surprised) about what happens. French with subtitles. **90m/C; DVD.** *FR* Valeria Bruni-Tedeschi; Stephane Freiss; Geraldine Pailhas; Francoise Fabian; Michael (Michel) Lonsdale; Antoine Chappey; ***D:*** Francois Ozon; ***W:*** Francois Ozon; Emmanuele Bernheim; ***C:*** Yorick Le Saux; ***M:*** Philippe Rombi.

5 to 7 1/2 **2015 (R)** If you're a fan of modest romantic comedies, you could do worse than this tale of star-crossed lovers who can only meet between the hours of 5 and 7. Could you fall in love in only two hours a day? Brian (Yelchin) falls for a beautiful French woman (Marlohe), but she's married, so can only escape her unhappy union two hours a day. Clichéd dialogue and a script that's way too proud of its concept (writer/director Levin mistakes whimsical for deep) sink the cast's notable efforts, which also includes Frank Langella, Glenn Close, and Olivia Thirlby. **95m/C; DVD.** Olivia Thirlby; Berenice Marlohe; Anton Yelchin; Glenn Close; Eric Stoltz; ***D:*** Victor Levin; ***W:*** Victor Levin; ***C:*** Arnaud Potier; ***M:*** Danny Bensi; Saunder Jurriaans.

Five Weeks in a Balloon **1962 (PG)** This adaptation of the Jules Verne novel follows the often-comic exploits of a 19th-century British expedition that encounters many adventures on a balloon trek across Africa. Pleasant fluff with a good cast. **101m/C; VHS, DVD.** Fabian; Peter Lorre; Red Buttons; Cedric Hardwicke; Barbara Eden; ***D:*** Irwin Allen; ***W:*** Charles Bennett; Irwin Allen; ***C:*** Winton C. Hoch.

The Five-Year Engagement 1/2 **2012 (R)** Segel and Blunt have surprisingly strong chemistry in the latest Apatow-produced comedy about relationships and identity crises. Segel plays Tom, a sous chef, who falls for lovely psychologist Violet (Blunt). The San Francisco-based couple gets engaged a year after they start dating but a series of unique situations conspire to delay the actual wedding. Can the bride and groom stay together long enough to walk down the aisle? Like most Apatow films, the comedy wears out its welcome with a bloated running time, but it's still smart, swift, and well-delivered. **124m/C; DVD, Blu-Ray, Streaming.** Jason Segel; Emily Blunt; Chris Pratt; Alison Brie; Mimi Kennedy; David Paymer; Jim Piddock; Rhys Ifans; ***D:*** Nicholas Stoller; ***W:*** Jason Segel; Nicholas Stoller; ***C:*** Javier Aguirresarobe; ***M:*** Michael Andrews.

Fix **2008 (R)** Diverting and heedless feature debut from Ruspoli. Bella (Wilde) is not enthusiastic about helping her filmmaking partner Milo (Ruspoli) get his scamster/junkie brother Leo (Andrews) into a drug rehab program so he won't wind up in prison. It doesn't help that unconcerned Leo runs around L.A. getting the money for the program by suspicious means, including picking up both medical marijuana and his girlfriend Carmen (Echikunwoke). **93m/C; DVD.** Shawn Andrews; Olivia Wilde; Dedee Pfeiffer; Douglas Spain; Megalyn Echikunwoke; Jakob Von Eichel; Tao Ruspoli; ***D:*** Tao Ruspoli; ***W:*** Tao Ruspoli; Jeremy C. Fels; ***C:*** Chris Gallo; Tao Ruspoli.

Fixed Bayonets! 1/2 **1951** Fuller's second Korean War epic is just as gritty as his first ("Steel Helment"), and it stood in direct contrast to the sappy and/or nostalgic WWII pictures of the time. A unit covering the retreat of a division from an icy mountainous terrain sees its commanding officers killed off until Corporal Menno (Baseheart) remains to lead the men. Menno, hesitant to kill, learns whether he can do what needs to be done for the survival of his men. One of Fuller's best films, and that's saying a lot. **92m/B; DVD, Blu-Ray.** Richard Basehart; Gene Evans; Michael O'Shea; Richard Hylton; Craig Hill; Skip Homeier; Richard Monahan; James Dean; John Doucette; ***D:*** Samuel Fuller; ***W:*** Samuel Fuller; ***C:*** Lucien Ballard; ***M:*** Roy Webb.

The Fixer 1/2 **1997** Jack Killoran (Voight) is a corrupt Chicago lawyer who can get anything done for a price. But after he's temporarily paralyzed in an accident, Jack has a crisis of conscience and decides he'd like to go legit. However, his bosses decide he knows too much to let him go. **105m/C; VHS, DVD.** Jon Voight; Brenda Bakke; J.J. Johnston; Miguel (Michael) Sandoval; Karl Pruner; Brent Jennings; Jack Wallace; ***D:*** Charles Robert Carner; ***W:*** Charles Robert Carner; ***C:*** Michael Goi; ***M:*** Lennie Niehaus. **CABLE**

Flags of Our Fathers 1/2 **2006 (R)** Director Eastwood tells the dark and ultimately sad story behind Joe Rosenthal's iconic 1945 photograph, the flag-raising by six soldiers at Iwo Jima, in his most ambitious outing to date. The government decides to whisk the three survivors home and use them on a nationwide war bonds drive, although only marine Rene Gagnon (Bradford) takes to the hoopla. Navy corpsman "Doc" Bradley (Phillippe) is haunted by the deaths and those left behind while alcoholic Pima Indian Ira Hayes (Beach) would rather fight than be subjected to the casual prejudice he constantly experiences. Successfully avoids the cliches and Hollywood conventions injected into most war stories, leaving room for surprise and genuine emotion. "Letters from Iwo Jima," also released in 2006, is Eastwood's companion film, told from the Japanese point of view. **131m/C; DVD, Blu-Ray, HD-DVD.** Ryan Phillippe; Jesse Bradford; Adam Beach; Barry Pepper; John Benjamin Hickey; John Slattery; Jamie Bell; Paul Walker; Robert Patrick; Neal McDonough; Thomas (Tom) McCarthy; Melanie Lynskey; Joseph Cross; Judith Ivey; Chris Bauer; Harve Presnell; George Grizzard; Len Cariou; ***D:*** Clint Eastwood; ***W:*** William Broyles, Jr.; Paul Haggis; ***C:*** Tom Stern; ***M:*** Clint Eastwood.

Flakes 1/2 **2007** Slacker comedy set in New Orleans. Hippie geezer Willie (Lloyd) owns the titular restaurant that serves only breakfast cereal. It's managed by would-be rocker Neal (Stanford), whose arty girlfriend Pussy Katz (Deschanel) is frustrated by his lack of ambition. So she's delighted when yuppie Stuart (O'Donnell) opens a slick competitor across the street. An outraged Neal engages in a series of dirty tricks to deal with the upstart but Pussy goes to work for Stuart, hoping that if Neal is left jobless he'll finally take his music career seriously. Very fitfully amusing, though Deschanel is an oddball charmer. **81m/C; DVD.** Aaron Stanford; Zooey Deschanel; Christopher Lloyd; Keir O'Donnell; Frank Wood; Ryan Donowho; ***D:*** Michael Lehmann; ***W:*** Karey Kirkpatrick; Chris Poche; ***C:*** Nancy Schreiber; ***M:*** Jason Derlatka; Jon Ehrlich.

Flambards 1/2 **1978** In the early 1900s, teenaged orphan Christine is sent to live with her tyrannical Uncle Russell and his two sons on their crumbling English estate, Flambards. Bitter rivalries and jealousies abound between arrogant, tradition-bound Mark and younger brother William, who's obsessed with the new-fangled airplane. Quarrels intensify as both young men fall in love with Christine and WWI begins, leading to sacrifice and tragedy. Based on the trilogy by K.M. Peyton. **676m/C; VHS, DVD.** *GB* Christine McKenna; Stephen Grives; Alan Parnaby; Edward Judd; Sebastian Abineri; Peter Settelen; Carol Leader; Frank Mills; ***D:*** Lawrence Gordon-Clark; Peter Duffell. **TV**

The Flame & the Arrow **1950** Dardo the Arrow, a Robin Hood-like outlaw in medieval Italy, leads his band of mountain fighters against a mercenary warlord who has seduced his wife and kidnapped his son. Spectacular acrobatics, with Lancaster performing his own stunts, add interest to the usual swashbuckling. **88m/C; VHS, DVD.** Burt Lancaster; Virginia Mayo; Aline MacMahon; Nick Cravat; Robert Douglas; Frank Allenby; ***D:*** Jacques Tourneur; ***M:*** Max Steiner.

Flame in the Streets **1961** Working class Jacko Palmer (Mills) is a liberal trade unionist leader who averts a strike at a London factory by backing new shop steward, West Indian Gabriel Gomez. That doesn't mean he and his wife Nell (de Banzie) are happy when their daughter Kathie (Syms) becomes engaged to Jamaican teacher Peter Lincoln (Sekka). Racial tensions increase on the streets with Teddy Boys planning to attack West Indian immigrants at the traditional Guy Fawkes Night bonfire. **93m/C; DVD.** *GB* John Mills; Sylvia Syms; Brenda de Banzie; Johnny Sekka; Earl Cameron; Ann Lynn; ***D:*** Roy Ward Baker; ***W:*** Ted Willis; ***C:*** Christopher Challis; ***M:*** Philip Green.

The Flame of New Orleans **1941** Dietrich is naturally the flame in question as Claire, Countess of New Orleans. She becomes engaged to Girard (Young) but then is attracted to sailor Robert (Cabot) and strings both men along while she tries to decide what to do. Claire's temporary solution is a harebrained plan involving her posing as a lookalike cousin, just come to town. French director Clair's first U.S. film was critically panned upon its release. **79m/B; DVD, Blu-Ray.** Marlene Dietrich; Bruce Cabot; Roland Young; Mischa Auer; Andy Devine; Frank Jenks; Franklin Pangborn; Laura Hope Crews; ***D:*** Rene Clair; ***W:*** Norman Krasna; ***C:*** Rudolph Mate; ***M:*** Frank Skinner.

Flame of the Barbary Coast 1/2 **1945** A rancher from Montana vies with a gambling czar for a beautiful dance hall queen and control of the Barbary Coast district of San Francisco. The great earthquake of 1906 provides the plot with a climax. Also available colorized. **91m/B; DVD, Blu-Ray.** John Wayne; Ann Dvorak; Joseph Schildkraut; William Frawley; ***D:*** Joseph Kane.

Flame of the Islands **1955** De Carlo plays a smoldering, passionate chanteuse who struggles with love and gangsters for possession of a Bahamian casino in this tropical heat wave. **92m/C; VHS, Streaming.** Yvonne De Carlo; Howard Duff; Zachary Scott; James Arness; Kurt Kasznar; Barbara O'Neil; ***D:*** Edward Ludwig.

Flame of the West 1/2 **1945** Former lawman John Poole (Brown) has become a doctor and wants to live a peaceful life. Sheriff Tom Nightlander (Dumbrille) is shot and Poole decides he must strap on his guns and go after the criminals to make the town safe again. **71m/B; DVD.** Johnny Mack Brown; Raymond Hatton; Joan Woodbury; Douglass Dumbrille; Harry Woods; Ray Bennett; Lynne Carver; ***D:*** Lambert Hillyer; ***W:*** Adele Buffington; ***C:*** Harry Neumann.

Flame Over India *Northwest Frontier* **1959** When Moslems lay siege to a British fortress in India, Governess Wyatt (Bacall) and Captain Scott (More) save the Maharaja's son and escape by commandeering a train. Along the way they find treason, adventure and love. **130m/C; VHS, DVD, Blu-Ray.** *GB* Kenneth More; Lauren Bacall; Herbert Lom; Wilfrid Hyde-White; I.S. Johar; Ursula Jeans; Ian Hunter; Eugene Deckers; Jack (Gwyllam) Gwillim; Govind Raja Ross; Frank Olegario; ***D:*** J. Lee Thompson; ***C:*** Geoffrey Unsworth.

The Flame Trees of Thika **1981** In 1913, a British family travels to East Africa to start a coffee plantation. Seen through the eyes of the young daughter, her childhood consists of the local Masai and Kikuyu tribes, the eccentric and sometimes unhappy English neighbors, and the wild animals that roam the plains. Based on the memoirs of writer Elspeth Huxley. Four cassettes; shown on PBS "Masterpiece Theatre." **366m/C; VHS, DVD.** *GB* Hayley Mills; Holly Aird; David Robb; Ben Cross; ***D:*** Roy Ward Baker; ***W:*** John Hawkesworth; ***C:*** Ian Wilson; ***M:*** Alan Blaikley.

Flaming Frontiers **1938** A frontier scout matches wits against gold mine thieves. In 15 episodes. **300m/B; VHS, DVD.** Johnny Mack Brown; Eleanor Hanson; Ralph Bowman; ***D:*** Ray Taylor.

Flaming Star **1960** In 1870s Texas, a family with a white father and an Indian mother is caught in the midst of an Indian uprising. The mixed-blood youth, excellently played by Presley, must choose a side with tragic results for all. A stirring, well-written drama of frontier prejudice and one of Presley's best films. **101m/C; DVD, Blu-Ray.** Elvis Presley; Dolores Del Rio; Barbara Eden; Steve Forrest; John McIntire; Richard Jaeckel; L.Q. Jones; Douglas Dick; Rodolfo Acosta; Ford Rainey; Karl Swenson; ***D:*** Donald Siegel; ***W:*** Nunnally Johnson; Clair Huffaker; ***C:*** Charles G. Clarke; ***M:*** Cyril Mockridge.

The Flaming Teen-Age **1956** Schlocky pseudo-documentary demonstrating the evils of drugs and alcohol. Exploitative, and the teenagers look really old. Cheaply made, and it shows. **67m/B; VHS, DVD.** Noel Reyburn; Ethel Barrett; Jerry Frank; Shirley Holmes; ***D:*** Irvin S. Yeaworth, Jr; Charles Edwards.

The Flamingo Kid **1984 (PG-13)** Brooklyn teen Jeffrey Willis (Dillon) gets a summer job at a fancy beach club on Long Island. His plumber father, Arthur (Elizondo), remembers how to dream but is also aware of how rough the world is on dreamers. Suddenly making lots of money at a mostly easy job, the kid's attracted to the high style of local sports car dealer Phil Brody

(Crenna), and finds his father's solid life a bore. By the end of the summer, he's learned the true value of both men, and the kind of man he wants to be. Excellent performances all around, nice ensemble acting among the young men who play Dillon's buddies. Great sound track. Film debut of Jones, who seems a little old for her part as a California college sophomore. **100m/C; VHS, DVD, Blu-Ray.** Matt Dillon; Hector Elizondo; Molly McCarthy; Martha Gehman; Richard Crenna; Jessica Walter; Carole (Raphaelle) Davis; Janet Jones; Fisher Stevens; Bronson Pinchot; ***D:*** Garry Marshall; ***W:*** Garry Marshall; Neil Marshall; ***C:*** James A. Contner; ***M:*** Curt Sobel.

Flamingo Road **1949** A scandalously entertaining melodrama in which Crawford portrays a carnival dancer who intrigues Scott and Brian in a small Southern town where the carnival stops. Crawford shines in a role that demands her to be both tough and sensitive in a corrupt world full of political backstabbing and sleazy characters. Remade as a TV movie and television soap-opera series in 1980. **94m/B; VHS, DVD.** Joan Crawford; Zachary Scott; David Brian; Sydney Greenstreet; Gertrude Michael; Gladys George; Virginia Huston; Fred Clark; Alice White; ***D:*** Michael Curtiz; ***W:*** Edmund H. North; Robert Wilder; ***M:*** Max Steiner.

Flanders **2006** Dumont's work (with nonprofessionals) is an acquired, frequently polarizing taste, and in this case, numbingly boring. Andre (Boidin) is a brute of a farmer who boffs local trollop Barbe (Leroux). He gets drafted and goes off to fight some nameless war in the desert. One of his fellow soldiers is Blondel (Cretel), who also knew Barbe in the biblical sense. She's back home having an abortion and going temporarily nuts while the soldiers pay the price for brutal acts against the local militia. French with subtitles. **91m/C; DVD.** *FR* Samuel Boidin; Adelaide Leroux; Henri Cretel; ***D:*** Bruno Dumont; ***W:*** Bruno Dumont; ***C:*** Yves Cape.

Flannel Pajamas **2006 (R)** Raw but talky look at the nearly-three year relationship between two New Yorkers from their first date to their final breakup. Jewish Stuart (Kirk) and Catholic Nicole (Nicholson) date, marry, and try to settle into domestic life while family dilemmas (Nicole's mother is an anti-Semite, among other problems) and personal and professional disappointments take their toll. Equal opportunity nudity by both leads. **124m/C; DVD.** Julianne Nicholson; Justin Kirk; Rebecca Schull; Jamie Harrold; Tom Bower; Stephanie March; Chelsea Altman; ***D:*** Jeff Lipsky; ***W:*** Jeff Lipsky; ***C:*** Martina Radwan; ***M:*** Paul Hsu.

Flap **1970** Remarkably ludicrous comedy adapted by Huffaker from his novel "Nobody Loves a Drunken Indian." Quinn was cast in a variety of ethnic roles during his long career and here he's an alcoholic Native American living on a reservation. Suddenly developing a social conscience (or maybe just drunk out of his gourd), Flapping Eagle goes to ridiculous lengths to bring attention to government lies and Indian rights. **107m/C; DVD.** Anthony Quinn; Claude Akins; Shelley Winters; Tony Bill; Victor Jory; Victor French; Don Collier; ***D:*** Carol Reed; ***W:*** Clair Huffaker; ***C:*** Fred W. Koenekamp; ***M:*** Marvin Hamlisch.

The Flash **1990** When police scientist Barry Allen is accidentally doused by chemicals and then struck by lightening the combination makes him into a new superhero. His super quickness help his quest in fighting crime in Central City where he's aided by fellow scientist Tina McGee (the only other person to know his secret). In this adventure, the Flash seeks out the violent and mesmerizing leader of a biker gang who caused the death of Barry's brother. Based on the DC comic book character, this is the pilot episode for the short-lived TV series. The look is dark and stylized and not played for camp. **94m/C; VHS, DVD.** John Wesley Shipp; Amanda Pays; Michael Nader; ***M:*** Danny Elfman. **TV**

Flash **1998** Fourteen-year-old Connor's (Black) best friend is a horse named Flash. When his family hits hard times, Connor's dad (Kerwin) joins the merchant marines, his grandmother (Burstyn) goes to work in a factory, and Connor is forced to sell Flash. The teen takes a job in the new owner's stables and when he sees how badly the animal is treated, Connor steals Flash and sets off to meet his father's ship in New York. **90m/C; VHS, DVD.** Lucas Black; Ellen Burstyn; Brian Kerwin; Shawn Toovey; Tom Nowicki; Dan Biggers; ***D:*** Simon Wincer. **TV**

Flash Gordon **1980 (PG)** Camp version of the adventures of Flash Gordon in outer space. This time, Flash and Dale Arden are forced by Dr. Zarkov to accompany him on a mission to far-off Mongo, where Ming the Merciless is threatening the destruction of Earth. Music by Queen. **111m/C; VHS, DVD, Blu-Ray.** Sam Jones; Melody Anderson; Topol; Max von Sydow; Ornella Muti; Timothy Dalton; Brian Blessed; ***D:*** Mike Hodges; ***W:*** Lorenzo Semple, Jr.; ***C:*** Gilbert Taylor; ***M:*** Howard Blake.

Flash Gordon Conquers the Universe *Purple Death from Outer Space* **1940** Ravaging plague strikes the earth and Flash Gordon undertakes to stop it. A serial in 12 chapters. **240m/B; VHS, DVD.** Buster Crabbe; Carol Hughes; Charles Middleton; Frank Shannon; Anne Gwynne; John Hamilton; Herbert Rawlinson; Tom Chatterton; ***D:*** Ford Beebe; Ray Taylor; ***W:*** George Plympton; Basil Dickey; Barry Shipman; ***C:*** Jerome Ash; William Sickner.

Flash Gordon: Mars Attacks the World *The Deadly Rays from Mars; Flash Gordon's Trip to Mars* **1939** The earth is plagued by the evil Ming, but Flash Gordon steps in. From the serial. **97m/B; VHS, DVD.** Buster Crabbe; Jean Rogers; Charles Middleton; ***D:*** Robert F. "Bob" Hill; Ford Beebe.

Flash Gordon: Rocketship 1/2 *Spaceship to the Unknown; Perils from Planet Mongo; Space Soldiers; Atomic Rocketship* **1940** Re-edited from the original Flash Gordon serial in which Flash and company must prevent the planet Mongo from colliding with Earth. Good character acting and good clean fun. **82m/B; VHS, DVD.** Buster Crabbe; Jean Rogers; Frank Shannon; Charles Middleton; Priscilla Lawson; Jack Lipson; ***D:*** Frederick Stephani.

Flash of Genius **1/2 2008 (PG-13)** In 1967 Detroit, engineering professor Robert Kearns patented an idea for intermittent windshield wipers—ones that aren't just set at on or off. He pitched the idea, without giving away the mechanics, to Ford, who stole the idea and didn't pay up. Two decades later, Kearns sued and won, with automakers coming to a settlement without admitting to any wrongdoing. Kearns, played affectionately by Kinnear, struggles to perfect his invention, testing the patience of his business partner (Mulroney) and his lawyer (Alda), while trying to squeeze in time for his loved ones. In the end, the audience is left to decide whether all those maddening years that resulted in ruined friendships and family strife were worth the payoff. **120m/C; On Demand.** Greg Kinnear; Lauren Graham; Dermot Mulroney; Daniel Roebuck; Jake Abel; Tim Kelleher; Alan Alda; Bill Smitrovich; ***D:*** Marc Abraham; ***W:*** Philip Railsback; ***C:*** Dante Spinotti; ***M:*** Aaron Zigman.

A Flash of Green **1985** A crooked politician is helping a construction firm exploit valuable waterfront property. He enlists the influence of a hesitant local journalist, who then falls for the woman leading the homeowner's conservation drive against the development plan. Made for American Playhouse and produced by costar Jordon. Based on the work of John D. MacDonald. **122m/C; VHS, Streaming.** Ed Harris; Blair Brown; Richard Jordan; George Coe; ***D:*** Victor Nunez; ***W:*** Victor Nunez; ***M:*** Charles Engstrom.

Flash Point 1/2 *Dou fo sin; Flashpoint; City with No Mercy; Dao huo xian; Po jun* **2007** Detective Sergeant Ma Jun (Donnie Yen) is a cop who always gets his man, no matter how much collateral damage is done in the process. His lifelong nemeses are three Vietnamese brothers who are rising stars in organized crime, and he assigns a cop named Wilson (Louis Koo) to infiltrate their gang. Although Wilson violently disagrees with Jun, he does as ordered, and gets caught. **87m/C; DVD, Blu-Ray.** *CH CH* Donnie Yen; Louis Koo; Collin Chou; Bingbing Fan; Kent Cheng; Ben Lam; Ray Lui; Yu Xing; Qing Xu; Lan Law; Irene Wang; Austin Wai; Wai Ai; Chi Wai Wong; Aaron Leung; ***D:*** Wilson (Wai-Shun) Yip; ***W:*** Kam-yeun Szeto; Lik-Kei Tang; ***C:*** Man Po Cheung; ***M:*** Kwong Wing Chan.

Flashback **1989 (R)** FBI agent Sutherland's assignment sounds easy: escort aging 1960s radical Hopper to prison. But Hopper is cunning and decides not to go without a fight. He uses his brain to outwit the young Sutherland and to turn him against himself. Good moments between the two leads and with Kane, as a woman who never left the '60s behind. **108m/C; VHS, DVD.** Dennis Hopper; Kiefer Sutherland; Carol Kane; Cliff DeYoung; Paul Dooley; Michael McKean; Richard Masur; ***D:*** Franco Amurri; ***M:*** Barry Goldberg.

Flashbacks of a Fool **1/2 2008 (R)** Washed-up British movie star Joe Scot (Craig) is living in L.A. and spending more time with drugs and sex than his career. News of the sudden death of his best childhood mate leads Joe to a drunken night, a suicide attempt, and an extended flashback to his teenaged years in 1970s Britain and an ultimately tragic affair with a married woman. Not terribly compelling or coherent despite the cast. **113m/C; DVD.** *GB* Daniel Craig; Harry Eden; Jodhi May; Felicity Jones; Max Deacon; Claire Forlani; Olivia Williams; Eve; Helen McCrory; Mark Strong; Keeley Hawes; James D'Arcy; ***D:*** Baillie Walsh; ***W:*** Baillie Walsh; ***C:*** John Mathieson.

Flashdance **1983 (R)** 18-year-old Alex (Beals) wants to dance. She works all day as a welder, has a hot affair going with her boss Nick (Nouri), dances at a local bar at night, and hopes someday to get enough courage to audition for a spot at the School of Ballet. Glossy music video redeemed somewhat by exciting choreography with Marine Jahan doing the dancing for Beals. Oscar-winning title song sung by Irene Cara. Inspired the torn-sweatshirt trend in fashion of the period. **95m/C; VHS, DVD, Blu-Ray.** Jennifer Beals; Michael Nouri; Belinda Bauer; Lilia Skala; Cynthia Rhodes; Sunny Johnson; Lee Ving; Kyle T. Heffner; Ron Karabatsos; Robert Wuhl; Elizabeth Sagal; ***D:*** Adrian Lyne; ***W:*** Joe Eszterhas; ***C:*** Don Peterman; ***M:*** Giorgio Moroder. Oscars '83: Song ("Flashdance. . .What a Feeling"); Golden Globes '84: Score, Song ("Flashdance. . .What a Feeling").

Flashfire **1/2 1994 (R)** The torching of an apartment building and the murder of a cop seem unrelated until troubled detective Jack Flinder (Zane) becomes involved. Soon, he and murder witness Lisa (Minter) are on the run from the arsonists and crooked police. **88m/C; VHS, DVD.** Billy Zane; Kristin Minter; Louis Gossett, Jr.; ***D:*** Elliot Silverstein; ***W:*** John Warren; Dan York; ***C:*** Albert J. Dunk; ***M:*** Sylvester Levay.

Flashpoint **1984 (R)** A pair of Texas border patrolmen discover an abandoned jeep that contains a fortune in cash, apparently from the 1960s. As they try to figure out how it got there, they become prey to those who want to keep the secret. With this cast, flick ought to be better. **95m/C; VHS, DVD.** Treat Williams; Kris Kristofferson; Tess Harper; Rip Torn; Miguel Ferrer; Roberts Blossom; Terry Alexander; ***D:*** William (Bill) Tannen; ***W:*** Michael Butler.

The Flat **2012** Writer/director Arnon Goldfinger was cleaning out his grandmother's home in Tel Aviv when he came across correspondence between his Jewish relatives and some Germans who would go on to be major figures in the Nazi party. Not only were his family's ties much closer to the Holocaust than he ever knew but his ancestors resumed their friendship with their German friends who participated in the Third Reich. This documentary expertly examines how people deal with tragedy and betrayal on a massive scale by burying it deep in the past. Some of the structure is a bit too flat (pardon the pun) but the story is remarkable. **97m/C; DVD.** *IS GE* Arnon Goldfinger; ***D:*** Arnon Goldfinger; ***W:*** Arnon Goldfinger; ***C:*** Talia Galon; Philippe Bellaiche; ***M:*** Yoni Rechter.

Flat Top **1/2 1952** The training of Navy fighter pilots aboard "flat top" aircraft carriers during WWII provides the drama here. A strict commander is appreciated only after the war when the pilots realize his role in their survival. The film makes good use of actual combat footage; fast-paced and effective. **85m/C; DVD, Blu-Ray.** Sterling Hayden; Richard Carlson; Keith Larsen; John Bromfield; William Phipps; William Schallert; ***D:*** Lesley Selander; ***W:*** Steve Fisher; ***C:*** Harry Neumann; ***M:*** Marlin Skiles.

Flatland **2002** Two rivals have been fighting each other in an alternate dimension for 4,000 years or so. They reincarnate in modern-day Hong Kong and stage the Apocalypse. Originally a mini-series in China, the U.S. version suffers from being condensed into movie form. **84m/C; DVD.** *CH* Dennis Hopper; Phillip Rhys; Francoise Yip; Bumper Robinson; ***D:*** Richard Franklin; Ian Gilmour; Vic Sarin; Joseph L. Scanlan; Brendan Maher; ***W:*** Steve Feke; Steven Whitney; ***C:*** Mark Wareham; ***M:*** Fletcher Beasley; Velton Ray Bunch; Eric Hester; J. Peter Robinson.

Flatliners **1990 (R)** A group of medical students begin after-hours experimentation with death and out-of-body experiences. Some standard horror film images but Roberts and Sutherland create an energy that makes it worth watching. **111m/C; VHS, DVD, Blu-Ray.** Kiefer Sutherland; Julia Roberts; William Baldwin; Oliver Platt; Kevin Bacon; Kimberly Scott; Joshua Rudoy; Aeryk Egan; ***D:*** Joel Schumacher; ***W:*** Peter Filardi; ***C:*** Jan De Bont; ***M:*** James Newton Howard.

Flatliners **1/2 2017 (PG-13)** An essentially failed remake of the 1990 dramatic medical horror-thriller. Carrying guilt about her role in her younger sister's death years earlier, Dr. Courtney Holmes (Page) convinces four of her fellow medical students to help her die with drugs that stop her heart and come back to life with a defibrillator. While "dead," she has unexpected glimpses of the world around her. As three others undergo the treatment, they all experience increasingly distressing visions and creepy events. **110m/C; DVD, Blu-Ray.** Ellen Page; Diego Luna; Nina Dobrev; James Norton; Kiersey Clemons; ***D:*** Niels Arden Oplev; ***W:*** Ben Ripley; ***C:*** Eric Kress; ***M:*** Nathan Barr.

Flawless **1999 (R)** Former New York City cop and resident tough guy Walt Koontz (De Niro) lives across the hall from nosily outrageous drag queen Rusty (Hoffman). The odd couple have a mutual animosity that's put to the test when Walt suffers a stroke and it's recommended that he take singing lessons to help him recover his ability to speak. So he makes an offer to Rusty who needs the cash. Soon they're not only tolerating each other but bonding as well. There are distracting subplots about hidden drug money and a drag queen beauty contest that take the focus off of what could have worked as a two-character study about an unlikely friendship. **111m/C; VHS, DVD, Blu-Ray.** Robert De Niro; Philip Seymour Hoffman; Barry Miller; Chris Bauer; Skipp (Robert L.) Sudduth; Wanda De Jesus; Daphne Rubin-Vega; Rory Cochrane; ***D:*** Joel Schumacher; ***W:*** Joel Schumacher; ***C:*** Declan Quinn; ***M:*** Bruce Roberts.

Flawless **2007 (PG-13)** A soon-to-retire janitor (Caine) of the London Diamond Corporation convinces the company's only female executive (Moore) to help him make off with the merchandise—a scheme she easily agrees to after years of sexist, lying bosses stepping on her head to climb higher on the ladder. Set in 1960's London, told in flashback by an elderly, heavily made-up Moore. Slow pace and cheesy ending keep the drama and suspense in mediocrity. **108m/C; DVD.** *LU GB US* Demi Moore; Michael Caine; Joss Ackland; Lambert Wilson; ***D:*** Michael Radford; ***W:*** Edward A. Anderson; ***C:*** Richard Greatrex; ***M:*** Stephen Warbeck.

Fled **1996 (R)** Charles Piper (Fishburne) and Luke Dodge (Baldwin) are combative prison escapees who need to find a stash of cash and a computer disk that could save them from both the Cuban mob and the cops. Bombshell Cora (Hayek) decides to help the duo and tries to get steamy with Piper. Lots of chases, lots of violence, not much sense. The climactic battle (the film was shot around Atlanta) takes place in a sightseeing gondola at Georgia's Stone Mountain. **98m/C; VHS, DVD, Blu-Ray.** Laurence Fishburne; Stephen Baldwin; Salma Hayek; Will Patton; Robert John Burke; ***D:*** Kevin Hooks; ***W:*** Preston A. Whitmore, II; ***C:*** Matthew F. Leonetti; ***M:*** Graeme Revell.

The Flemish Farm **1943** Fact-based WWII story about a Belgian commando who returns to his Nazi-occupied homeland to retrieve his regiment's flag, which he and a friend buried before their escape. **82m/B; DVD.** *UK* Clive Brook; Clifford Evans; Jane Baxter; Philip Friend; Mary Jerrold; ***D:*** Jeffrey Dell; ***W:*** Jeffrey Dell; Jill Craigie; ***C:*** Eric Cross; ***M:*** Ralph Vaughan Williams.

Flesh **1932** Pre-Hays Code melodrama. Sultry ex-con Laura (Morley) takes advantage of nice guy Polikai (Beery), a German waiter who becomes a wrestling champ. She persuades him to help bail out her abusive lover Nicky (Cortez) but when Laura tells Nicky she's pregnant, she again turns to Polikai for help. Though Nicky isn't done causing trouble. **95m/B; DVD.** Wallace Beery; Karen Morley; Ricardo Cortez; Jean Hersholt; John Miljan; ***D:*** John Ford; ***W:*** Moss Hart; Leonard Praskins; Edgar Allan Woolf; ***C:*** Arthur Edeson.

Flesh *Andy Warhol's Flesh* **1968** An Andy Warhol-produced seedy urban farce about a bisexual street hustler who meets a variety of drug-addicted, deformed, and sexually deviant people. Dallesandro fans will enjoy his extensive exposure (literally). **90m/C; VHS, DVD.** Joe Dallesandro; Geraldine Smith; Patti D'Arbanville; Candy Darling; Jackie Curtis; Geri Miller; Barry Brown; ***D:*** Paul Morrissey; ***W:*** Paul Morrissey; ***C:*** Paul Morrissey.

Flesh and Blood **1922** An unjustly convicted lawyer is released from prison to find out his wife has died. He vows revenge on those who falsely imprisoned him and assumes the disguise of a crippled beggar to begin his plot. Silent with musical score. **75m/B; Silent; VHS, DVD.** Lon Chaney, Sr.; ***D:*** Irving Cummings.

Flesh and Blood ½ *The Rose and the Sword* **1985 (R)** A rowdy group of 16th Century hellions makes off with a princess who is already spoken for and pillage and plunder their way to revenge. Hauer leads the motley group through sword fights, raids, and the like. Dutch director Verhoeven's first English language film. Not for children; with rape scenes, nudity, and graphic sex. **126m/C; VHS, DVD, Blu-Ray.** Rutger Hauer; Jennifer Jason Leigh; Tom Burlinson; Susan Tyrrell; Jack Thompson; Ronald Lacey; Brion James; Bruno Kirby; ***D:*** Paul Verhoeven; ***W:*** Paul Verhoeven; Gerard Soeteman; ***C:*** Jan De Bont; ***M:*** Basil Poledouris.

Flesh and Blood Show *Asylum of the Insane* **1973 (R)** Rehearsal turns into an execution ritual for a group of actors at a mysterious seaside theatre. Truth in titling: features blood, gore, and some sex. Shot in part in 3-D. **93m/C; VHS, DVD, Blu-Ray.** *GB* Robin Askwith; Candace Glendenning; Tristan Rogers; Ray Brooks; Jenny Hanley; Luan Peters; Patrick Barr; Judy Matheson; Penny Meredith; ***D:*** Pete Walker; ***W:*** Alfred Shaughnessy; ***C:*** Peter Jessop.

Flesh and Bone **1993 (R)** Quaid is exact as a vending machine distributor with a desolate rural Texas circuit, haunted by the memory of a decades-old murder committed by his father (Caan) during a botched farmhouse robbery. Alcoholic Ryan (Quaid's real-life wife) emerges from a bad marriage and helps Quaid rebuild his life, never suspecting that they may have met before. Challenging but successful role for Ryan, better known for her girlish, romantic-comedy appeal. Paltrow's unforgettable as a heartless casket robber and Caan's partner/girlfriend. Director Kloves extracts moments of earthy beauty from the bleak, humble West Texas setting. **127m/C; VHS, DVD.** Dennis Quaid; Meg Ryan; James Caan; Gwyneth Paltrow; Scott Wilson; Christopher Rydell; ***D:*** Steve Kloves; ***W:*** Steve Kloves; ***M:*** Thomas Newman.

The Flesh and the Devil ½ **1927** Classic Garbo at her seductive best as a woman who causes a feud between two friends. Gilbert is an Austrian officer, falls for the married Garbo and winds up killing her husband in a duel. Banished to the African Corps he asks his best friend (Hanson) to look after his lady love. But Hanson takes his job too seriously, falling for the lady himself. Great silent movie with surprise ending to match. The first Gilbert and Garbo pairing. **112m/B; Silent; VHS, DVD.** John Gilbert; Greta Garbo; Lars Hanson; Barbara Kent; George Fawcett; Eugenie Besserer; ***D:*** Clarence Brown; ***C:*** William H. Daniels. Natl. Film Reg. '06.

The Flesh and the Fiends ½ *Mania; Fiendish Ghouls; Psycho Killers* **1960** Fine adaptation of the Burke and Hare grave robbing legend. Cushing is the doctor who needs corpses and Pleasence and Rose provide them by any means. Highly atmospheric representation of dismal, 19th century Edinburgh. Very graphic for its time. **87m/B; VHS, DVD, Blu-Ray.** *GB* Peter Cushing; June Laverick; Donald Pleasence; George Rose; Dermot Walsh; Renee Houston; Billie Whitelaw; John Cairney; Michael Balfour; ***D:*** John Gilling; ***W:*** John Gilling; Leon Griffiths; ***C:*** Monty Berman; ***M:*** Stanley Black.

Flesh and the Spur ½ **1957** A cowboy tracks the killer of his brother. Future Mannix Mike Connors (nicknamed 'Touch' at the time) joins the search. Unedifying western with oddball touches, notably a theme song by Chipmunks creator Ross Bagdasarian. **78m/C; VHS, DVD.** John Agar; Marla English; Mike Connors; Raymond Hatton; Maria Monay; Joyce Meadows; Kenne Duncan; ***D:*** Edward L. Cahn.

The Flesh Eaters ½ **1964** A claustrophobic low-budget thriller about a film queen and her secretary who crash-land on an island inhabited by your basic mad scientist. His latest experiment is with tiny flesh-eating sea creatures. Shock ending. **87m/C; VHS, DVD.** Martin Kosleck; Rita Morley; Byron Sanders; Barbara Wilkin; Ray Tudor; ***D:*** Jack Curtis; ***W:*** Arnold Drake; ***C:*** Carson Davidson.

Flesh Eaters from Outer Space **2005** Smalltown America turns to a psychic and some burned-out metalheads to save them when flesh eating aliens practically begin raining from the sky. **90m/C; DVD.** Warren Disbrow, Sr.; Stephen Mezo; Kathy Monks; ***D:*** Warren F. Disbrow; ***W:*** Warren F. Disbrow. **VIDEO**

Flesh Eating Mothers **1989** Housewives are transformed into cannibals after a mystery virus hits their town. Their kids must stop the moms from eating any more people. **90m/C; VHS, DVD, Blu-Ray.** Robert Lee Oliver; Donatella Hecht; Valorie Hubbard; Neal Rosen; Terry Hayes; ***D:*** James Aviles Martin.

Flesh Feast **WOOF!** **1969 (R)** Classically horrendous anti-Nazi bosh, in which a mad female plastic surgeon (Lake) rejuvenates Hitler and then tortures him to death with maggots to avenge her mother's suffering. Lake's last film, and the sorriest sign-off any actress ever had. **72m/C; VHS, DVD.** Veronica Lake; Phil Philbin; Heather Hughes; Martha Mischon; Yanka (Doris Keating) Mann; Dianne Wilhite; Chris Martell; ***D:*** Brad F. Ginter.

Flesh Gordon **1972** Soft-core spoof of the "Flash Gordon" series. Flesh takes it upon himself to save Earth from the evil Wang's sex ray; Wang, of course, being the leader of the planet Porno. Lackluster special effects and below par story dull an already ridiculous movie. Look for cameo by real-life porn starlet Candy Samples. The restored (90-minute) version also includes the theatrical trailer; a 72-minute R-rated version is also available. **90m/C; VHS, DVD, Blu-Ray.** Jason Williams; Suzanne Fields; Joseph Hudgins; John Hoyt; Howard Zieff; Michael Benveniste; ***Cameo(s):*** Candy Samples; ***V:*** Craig T. Nelson; ***D:*** Michael Benveniste; Howard Ziehm; ***W:*** Michael Benveniste; ***C:*** Howard Ziehm; ***M:*** Ralph Ferraro.

Flesh Gordon 2: Flesh Gordon Meets the Cosmic Cheerleaders **1990** Emperor Wang (Hunt) threatens the Universe with his powerful Impotence ray. Flesh (Murdocco), along with Dale (Kelly) and Dr. Flexi Jerkoff (Travis), do battle with a belt of farting asteroids and other weirdos. Director Ziehm delivers this one on a shoestring of under $1 million, even improving technically on the original. The sex scenes are, however, more watered down in an apparent attempt to gain a wider audience. Scatological jokes are the basis for much of the humor. **98m/C; VHS, DVD.** *CA* Vince Murdocco; Tony Travis; William Dennis Hunt; Robyn Kelly; Morgan Fox; Melissa Mounds; ***D:*** Howard Ziehm; ***W:*** Howard Ziehm; ***C:*** Danny Nowak.

Flesh Wounds **2010 (R)** Cheesy sci fi action with a rip-off plot. Scientists conducting a secret weapons experiment at a remote Army facility go missing and a covert ops team is given 24 hours to find them. Lt. Tyler (Sorbo) soon discovers the scientists have been slaughtered by a cyborg-like super-soldier that's run amok. **80m/C; DVD.** Kevin Sorbo; Heather Marie Marsden; Bokeem Woodbine; John Edward Lee; Kirk Kepper; ***D:*** Dan Garcia; ***W:*** Gabriel Saint; ***C:*** John Lands. **VIDEO**

Fleshburn **1984 (R)** An Indian Vietnam War veteran escapes from a mental institution to get revenge on the four psychiatrists who committed him. **91m/C; VHS, DVD.** Steve Kanaly; Karen Carlson; Sonny Landham; Macon McCalman; ***D:*** George Gage; ***W:*** George Gage; Beth Gage; Brian Garfield; ***M:*** Arthur Kempel.

Fletch **1985 (PG)** Somewhat charming comedy. When newspaper journalist Fletch goes undercover to get the scoop on the local drug scene, a wealthy young businessman enlists his help in dying. Something's rotten in Denmark when the man's doctor knows nothing of the illness and Fletch comes closer to the drug scene than he realizes. Throughout the entire film, Chevy Chase assumes a multitude of flippant comic characters to discover the truth. Based on Gregory McDonald's novel. **98m/C; VHS, DVD, Blu-Ray.** Chevy Chase; Tim Matheson; Joe Don Baker; Dana Wheeler-Nicholson; M. Emmet Walsh; Kenneth Mars; Geena Davis; Richard Libertini; George Wendt; Kareem Abdul-Jabbar; Alison La Placa; George Wyner; Tony Longo; James Avery; William Sanderson; Beau Starr; Ralph Seymour; Larry "Flash" Jenkins; ***D:*** Michael Ritchie; ***W:*** Andrew Bergman; ***C:*** Fred Schuler; ***M:*** Harold Faltermeyer.

Fletch Lives **1989 (PG)** In this sequel to "Fletch," Chase is back again as the super-reporter. When Fletch learns of his inheritance of a Southern estate he is eager to claim it. During his down-home trip he becomes involved in a murder and must use his disguise skills to solve it before he becomes the next victim. Based on the novels of Gregory MacDonald. **95m/C; VHS, DVD, Blu-Ray.** Chevy Chase; Hal Holbrook; Julianne Phillips; Richard Libertini; R. Lee Ermey; Cleavon Little; Randall "Tex" Cobb; Richard Belzer; Geoffrey Lewis; Patricia Kalember; Phil Hartman; George Wyner; ***D:*** Michael Ritchie; ***W:*** Leon Capetanos; ***M:*** Harold Faltermeyer.

Flexing with Monty **2010** So what happens to your film when your lead actor suddenly dies (as Goddard did in 2003)? Well, Albo (who also had financial problems) apparently carried on in some fashion to finally get a release. Bigoted, narcissist bodybuilder Monty (Goddard) lives to indulge his gym rat obsession and to torment his emotionally fragile younger brother Bertin (Davis). Their delicately-balanced lives are upended by the arrival of Catholic nun Lilith (Kirkland), who's fundraising for a very strange charity. **90m/C; DVD.** Trevor Goddard; Rudi Davis; Sally Kirkland; ***D:*** John Albo; ***W:*** John Albo; ***C:*** Thomas Denove; ***M:*** Miriam Cutler. **VIDEO**

Flick ½ **2007** Nonsensical British horror-comedy. Drowned 1950s teddy-boy Johnny (O'Conor) is resurrected as a zombie when his car and body are found after the harbor is dredged. He wants revenge on those who done him wrong although he doesn't seem to realize that 40 years have passed. Memphis cop McKenzie (Dunaway), who's on an exchange program in Britain, helps out the locals. Title refers to the flick knife Johnny likes to use. **95m/C; DVD.** *GB* Hugh O'Conor; Faye Dunaway; Michelle Ryan; Mark Benton; Liz Smith; Julia Foster; Terence Rigby; Hayley Angel Wardle; ***D:*** David Howard; ***W:*** David Howard; ***C:*** Chris Seager; ***M:*** Richard Hawley.

Flicka ½ **2006 (PG)** A girl and her horse. Katy McLaughlin (Lohman) is happy to return to her family's struggling Wyoming ranch after having blown her year at boarding school. She would much rather help her traditionalist father, Rob (McGraw), breed quarter horses, although dad is leaning on her older brother Howard (Kwanten). Mom Nell (Bello) plays peacemaker. The situation worsens when Katy corrals and decides to tame the wild black stallion of the title. But when dad sells Flicka to the rodeo, Katy is determined to get the horse back. C-W singing star McGraw is a natural while the twentysomething Lohman can still easily pass for a big-hearted, hard-headed teen. **94m/C; DVD, Blu-Ray.** Alison Lohman; Tim McGraw; Maria Bello; Ryan Kwanten; Dallas Roberts; Nick Searcy; Jeffrey Nordling; Danny Pino; ***D:*** Michael Mayer; ***W:*** Mark Rosenthal; Larry Konner; ***C:*** J.(James) Michael Muro; ***M:*** Aaron Zigman.

Flicka: Country Pride ½ **2012 (G)** Toby (Black) and his wild horse Flicka come to Cherry Creek to manage the boarding stable of recent widow Lindy (Hartman Black). Lindy's teenage daughter Kelly (Rohl) bonds with Flicka and hopes she can train the horse for an upcoming competition. Kelly has a rival in her ex-friend Stephanie (Williams) since they fell out over their interest in the same boy. **92m/C; DVD, Blu-Ray.** Clint Black; Lisa Hartman Black; Kacey Rohl; Siobhan Williams; Max Lloyd-Jones; Teryl Rothery; ***D:*** Michael Damian; ***W:*** Jennifer Robinson; ***C:*** Ron Stannett; ***M:*** Mark Thomas. **VIDEO**

Flickering Lights ½ *Blikende Lygter* **2001** Trokild (Pilmark) is deeply in debt to gangster Eskimo (Andersson). He and pals Peter (Thomsen), Arne (Mikkelsen), and Stefan (Kaas) are surprised to discover the briefcase they've been forced to steal contains a lot of money. They decide to keep the cash and are heading for Spain when their getaway truck breaks down in the woods. The foursome finds refuge in an abandoned inn and Torkild, who's tired of the criminal life, decides to use the money to buy the inn and open it back up so they can all start new lives. Of course, Eskimo may have other ideas when he finds them. An uncertain mixture of dark humor and sentimentality. Danish with subtitles. **109m/C; VHS, DVD.** *DK* Soren Pilmark; Ulrich Thomsen; Mads Mikkelsen; Nikolaj Lie Kaas; Peter Andersson; Sofie Gråbøl; Iben Hjejle; Frits Helmuth; ***D:*** Anders Thomas Jensen; ***W:*** Anders Thomas Jensen; ***C:*** Eric Kress; ***M:*** Bent Fabricius-Bjerre; Jeppe Kaas.

Flickers ½ **1980** Uncouth, ambitious Cockney Arnie Cole (Hoskins), wants to go from bioscope exhibitor to owner of his own silent-film production company. But he needs money—and upper middle-class Maud (de la Tour) needs a husband since she's pregnant and being a single mum won't do. The oddball duo make a business arrangement that turns into something more, all the while surrounded by the eccentrics and egotists who are involved with Arnie's new venture. Hoskins and de la Tour are an amusing visual mismatch (she's a stork and he's a fireplug) and a delight as sparring partners. 6 episodes. **307m/C; DVD.** *GB* Bob Hoskins; Frances de la Tour; Peggy Wood; Dickie Arnold; Valerie Holliman; Fraser Cains; Granville Saxon; Jim Hooper; Joanna Foster; ***D:*** Cyril Coke; ***W:*** Roy Clarke. **TV**

Flight **2012 (R)** One of the best performances of Washington's career anchors this stunning adult drama about responsibility and addiction. Whip Whitaker is a pilot tragically addicted to booze and cocaine. After a disastrous plane crash in which he performs a near-miracle by saving 96 out of 102 lives, a toxicology test reveals his weaknesses and his own life crashes to the ground. Director Zemeckis and Washington work together to tell the complex story of a man who may be both a lifesaver and an irredeemable jerk. **138m/C; DVD, Blu-Ray.** Denzel Washington; Don Cheadle; Kelly Reilly; John Goodman; Bruce Greenwood; Brian Geraghty; Tamara Tunie; Gabrielle Union; ***D:*** Robert Zemeckis; ***W:*** John Gatins; ***C:*** Don Burgess; ***M:*** Alan Silvestri.

Flight Angels ½ **1940** Tacky and dated romantic drama about stewardesses and the pilots they want to marry. Hotshot Chick (Morgan) is grounded for failing eyesight and becomes an instructor at stew school. He hears the Army is going to test the experimental aircraft he helped design, and he wants to be the pilot on the test flight. Somewhere along the way, philandering Chick does marry his ditzy girlfriend Mary (Bruce). **73m/B; DVD.** Dennis Morgan; Ralph Bellamy; Virginia Bruce; Jane Wyman; Wayne Morris; John Litel; ***D:*** Lewis Seiler; ***W:*** Maurice Leo; ***C:*** L. William O'Connell; ***M:*** Heinz Roemheld.

Flight Command **1940** Over-confident Pensacola air cadet Alan Drake (Taylor) gets off on the wrong wing when he begins training with the elite Navy Hell Cats fighter squadron in San Diego. There are further misunderstandings until Drake volunteers to test some new equipment that has already killed one pilot. Taylor himself joined the Navy Air Corps during WWII. **115m/B; DVD.** Robert Taylor; Ruth Hussey; Walter Pidgeon; Paul Kelly; Shepperd Strudwick; Nat Pendleton; Red Skelton; *D:* Frank Borzage; *W:* Wells Root; Harvey Haislip; *C:* Harold Rosson; *M:* Franz Waxman.

Flight From Ashiya 1/2 **1964** A trio of Air Force pilots are sent to rescue survivors from a sinking Japanese cargo ship during a storm. Each pilot has a flashback story that has repercussions for their current mission. Shot on location in Japan. **102m/C; DVD.** Yul Brynner; George Chakiris; Richard Widmark; Suzy Parker; Shirley Knight; Daniele Gaubert; *D:* Michael Anderson, Sr.; *W:* Waldo Salt; Elliott Arnold; *C:* Burnett Guffey; Joe MacDonald; *M:* Frank Cordell.

Flight from Glory 1/2 **1937** A group of pilots fly supplies over the Andes from their isolated base camp to even more isolated mines. Morris is their leader who watches as, one by one, the men are killed on their dangerous flights. To make a bad situtation worse, Heflin arrives as a new recruit—along with his pretty wife. **66m/B; VHS, DVD.** Chester Morris; Onslow Stevens; Van Heflin; Whitney Bourne; *D:* Lew Landers.

Flight of Black Angel 1/2 **1991 (R)** Wacked-out F-16 pilot fancies himself an angel of death, and, after annihilating a number of trainees, sets out to make Las Vegas a nuked-out ghost town. Squadron commander Strauss, however, is not pleased with his pilot's initiative. Made-for-cable script runs out of gas and heads into a nosedive. **102m/C; VHS, DVD.** Peter Strauss; William O'Leary; James O'Sullivan; Michael Keys Hall; *D:* Jonathan Mostow; *W:* John Brancato. **CABLE**

Flight of Dragons 1/2 **1982** Animated tale takes place between the Age of Magic and the Age of Science, in a century when dragons ruled the skies. **98m/C; VHS, DVD, Blu-Ray.** *V:* John Ritter; Victor Buono; James Earl Jones; Donald E. Messick; Larry Storch; *D:* Arthur Rankin, Jr; Jules Bass.

Flight of the Doves **1971 (G)** Greedy Hawk Dove (Moody) is determined to claim a family inheritance even though it means eliminating two young relatives: Finn (Wild) and his little sister Derval (Raye). The kids run away from Liverpool to find safety with their grandmother (McGuire) who lives somewhere in Ireland. Hawk uses a number of disguises while on their trail (the best part of this family flick), which is based on the Walter Macken novel. **105m/C; DVD.** *GB* Jack Wild; Helen Raye; Ron Moody; Dorothy McGuire; Stanley Holloway; William Rushton; *D:* Ralph Nelson; *W:* Frank Gabrielson; *C:* Harry Waxman; *M:* Roy Budd.

Flight of the Grey Wolf 1/2 **1976** A tame, innocent wolf is mistaken for a killer and must run for his life with the help of his boy-owner. **82m/C; VHS, DVD.** Bill Williams; Barbara Hale; Jeff East; *D:* Frank Zuniga; *W:* Calvin Clements, Jr.

Flight of the Innocent 1/2 **1993 (R)** The innocent 10-year-old Vito comes from a family who make their living as kidnappers. He is the only witness (and the only survivor) when his family is massacred by a rival gang. Vito flees the carnage and sets off to find his cousin who lives in Rome. But his journey truly ends when he is taken in by a wealthy industrialist family whose own son has been kidnapped. Directorial debut of Carlei who tends to rely on striking visuals rather than his characters. In Italian with English subtitles. **105m/C; VHS, DVD.** *IT* Manuel Colao; Francesca Neri; Jacques Perrin; Frederico Pacifici; Sal Borgese; *D:* Carlo Carlei; *W:* Carlo Carlei; Gualtiero Rosella.

Flight of the Intruder 1/2 **1990 (PG-13)** Vietnam naval pilots aboard an aircraft carrier don't like the way the war is being handled, so they go rogue and decide to go on a mission to bomb an enemy air base in Hanoi. Loads of male bonding. **115m/C; VHS, DVD.** Danny Glover; Willem Dafoe; Brad Johnson; Rosanna Arquette; Tom Sizemore; Ving Rhames; David Schwimmer; *D:* John Milius; *W:* Robert Dillon; *C:* Fred W. Koenekamp; *M:* Basil Poledouris.

Flight of the Living Dead: Outbreak on a Plane *Plane Dead* **2007** Campy, fast-paced gore. A scientist brings a corpse infected with a genetically engineered virus aboard a flight from L.A. to Paris. The zombie escapes from the cargo hold and infects the passengers, who really have nowhere to run. **93m/C; DVD.** Kevin J. O'Connor; Derek Webster; Raymond J. Barry; Dale Midkiff; David Chisum; Kristen Kerr; Erik Avari; Richard Tyson; *D:* Scott Thomas; *W:* Scott Thomas; Mark Onspaugh; *C:* Mark Eberle; *M:* Nathan Wang. **VIDEO**

Flight of the Navigator 1/2 **1986 (PG)** A boy boards an alien spacecraft and embarks on a series of time-travel adventures with a crew of wisecracking extraterrestrial creatures. When he returns home eight years later, a NASA investigation ensues. Paul Reubens, better known as Pee-wee Herman, provides the voice of the robot. **90m/C; VHS, DVD.** Joey Cramer; Veronica Cartwright; Cliff DeYoung; Sarah Jessica Parker; Matt Adler; Howard Hesseman; *V:* Paul (Pee-wee Herman) Reubens; *D:* Randal Kleiser; *W:* Michael Burton; Matt MacManus; *M:* Alan Silvestri.

The Flight of the Phoenix **1965** A group of men stranded in the Arabian desert after a plane crash attempt to rebuild their plane in order to escape before succumbing to the elements. Big budget, all-star survival drama based on the novel by Elleston Trevor. **147m/C; VHS, DVD.** James Stewart; Richard Attenborough; Peter Finch; Hardy Kruger; Dan Duryea; George Kennedy; Ernest Borgnine; Ian Bannen; *D:* Robert Aldrich; *C:* Joseph Biroc.

Flight of the Phoenix 1/2 **2004 (PG-13)** Old-fashioned remake of Robert Aldrich's 1965 film makes use of both Lukas Heller's original screenplay and the Elleston Trevor novel. Frank Towns (Quaid) is the tough, cynical pilot of a rusty C-119 cargo plane who has just picked up a disparate group of oil rig workers, including lone woman Kelly (Otto), from the Mongolian desert. They crash during a sandstorm and their survival comes to depend on arrogant oddball Elliott (Ribisi). Claiming to be an aircraft designer, Elliott announces he can make a new plane from the crash pieces, if the reluctant Towns will cede him authority. Tensions grow, supplies dwindle, and desert nomads wait like vultures to prey on the weakening survivors. Remake has CGI advantages but less-compelling characters. **112m/C; VHS, DVD, Blu-Ray.** Dennis Quaid; Miranda Otto; Giovanni Ribisi; Tyrese Gibson; Hugh Laurie; Tony Curran; Kirk "Sticky Fingaz" Jones; Jacob Vargas; Scott Michael Campbell; Kevork Malikyan; *D:* John Moore; *W:* Scott Frank; Edward Burns; *C:* Brendan Galvin; *M:* Marco Beltrami.

Flight of the Red Balloon *Le Voyage du Ballon Rouge* **2008** Hou's homage to Albert Lamorisse's 1956 film "The Red Balloon" does have a red balloon, a little boy, and Paris, but Simon (Iteanu) doesn't wander the streets accompanied by the balloon so much as he wanders with his new nanny Song (Fang), a Taiwanese film student who serves as Hou's calm observer. Simon's single mom is frazzled bleach-blonde Suzanne (Binoche), who doesn't seem to be coping with her son, her career, or her emotions very well. Not much actually happens so the film can be something of a slog but it looks beautiful. French with subtitles. **113m/C; On Demand.** *FR TW* Juliette Binoche; Hippolyte Girardot; Simon Iteanu; Song Fang; Louise Margolin; Anna Sigalevitch; *D:* Hou Hsiao-hsien; *W:* Hou Hsiao-hsien; Francois Margolin; *C:* Mark Ping Bin Lee; *M:* Constance Lee.

Flight 7500 **2016 (PG-13)** A supernatural thriller centered on a trans-Pacific flight. After a Tokyo-bound plane leaves Los Angeles, the passengers experience a severe weather event that causes the plane to experience turbulence. When they pass the system, they slowly realize that something is wrong. First, one passenger gets sick. Then, more strange events occur. The passengers soon realize a supernatural force is aboard, wonder what it is, and must consider the possibility that they will never make it to Japan. **97m/C; DVD, Streaming, Download.** Ryan Kwanten; Amy Smart; Leslie Bibb; Jamie Chung; Scout Taylor-Compton; *D:* Takashi Shimizu; *W:* Craig Rosenberg; *C:* David Tattersall; *M:* Tyler Bates. **VIDEO**

Flight to Mars **1952** An expedition crash lands on the red planet and discovers an advanced underground society that wants to invade earth using the U.S. spacecraft. Includes previews of coming attractions from classic science fiction films. First movie of this genre to be shot in color. **72m/C; VHS, DVD.** Cameron Mitchell; Marguerite Chapman; Arthur Franz; Virginia Huston; *D:* Lesley Selander; *W:* Arthur Strawn; *C:* Harry Neumann; *M:* Marlin Skiles.

Flight to Nowhere WOOF! **1946** An FBI agent tracks down a stolen map of atomic bomb source material with the help of a charter pilot and a dizzy blonde. Muddled plot and no discernable acting. **74m/B; VHS, DVD.** Alan Curtis; Evelyn Ankers; Jack Holt; *D:* William Rowland.

Flightplan 1/2 **2005 (PG-13)** Kyle Pratt (Foster) and her daughter Julia (Lawston) are on the flight from Berlin to New York to bury Kyle's husband who, she's told, died after falling (or jumping?) from their apartment roof. She happens to be a propulsion engineer who knows planes inside and out. Kyle wakes from a nap to find Julia simply gone. Worse, the crew and even the passengers don't recall Julia being there, as flight and boarding lists seem to confirm that she wasn't. Tense, psychological and... implausible, but Foster makes it work. Not for the claustrophobic—most of the film's 90 minutes is spent inside the plane. **93m/C; DVD, Blu-Ray.** Jodie Foster; Peter Sarsgaard; Erika Christensen; Sean Bean; Kate Beahan; Greta Scacchi; Judith Scott; Michael Irby; Brent Sexton; Marlene Lawston; Haley Ramm; Stephanie Faracy; *D:* Robert Schwentke; *W:* Billy Ray; Peter A. Dowling; *M:* James Horner.

Flim-Flam Man *One Born Every Minute* **1967** A con man teams up with an army deserter to teach him the fine art of flim-flamming as they travel through small southern towns. Love may lead the young man back to the straight and narrow, but not his reprobate mentor. Scott is wonderful; and the slapstick episodes move at a good pace. **104m/C; VHS, DVD.** George C. Scott; Michael Sarrazin; Slim Pickens; Sue Lyon; Jack Albertson; Harry (Henry) Morgan; *D:* Irvin Kershner; *C:* Charles B(ryant) Lang, Jr.; *M:* Jerry Goldsmith.

Fling *Lie to Me* **2008 (R)** Samantha and Mason seem like the perfect couple and talk a good game about having an open relationship. Then they attend the wedding of Sam's sister and Sam sees her ex James, who's still smitten. Meanwhile, Mason does some serious canoodling with his best pal Luke's teenaged sister Olivia. When they reveal their peccadilloes to each other, the reactions are unexpected. **98m/C; DVD.** Courtney Ford; Steve Sandvoss; Brandon Routh; Nick Wechsler; Shoshana Bush; Ellen Hollman; *D:* John Stewart Muller; *W:* John Stewart Muller; Laura Boersma; *C:* Frederick Schroeder; *M:* Nick Urata.

The Flintstones 1/2 **1994 (PG)** Preceded by massive hype, popular '60s cartoon comes to life thanks to a huge budget and creative sets and props. Seems that Fred's (Goodman) being set up by evil corporate types Cliff Vandercave (MacLachlan) and Miss Rosetta Stone (Berry) to take the fall for their embezzling scheme. Soon he gives up dining at RocDonald's for Cavern on the Green and cans best buddy Barney (Moranis). Forget the lame plot (32 writers took a shot at it) and sit back and enjoy the spectacle. Goodman's an amazingly true-to-type Fred, O'Donnell has Betty's giggle down pat, and Perkins looks a lot like Wilma. Wilma's original voice, VanderPyl, has a cameo as Mrs. Feldspar; listen for Korman's voice as the Dictabird. Add half a bone if you're under 12. **92m/C; VHS, DVD, Blu-Ray.** John Goodman; Rick Moranis; Elizabeth Perkins; Rosie O'Donnell; Elizabeth Taylor; Kyle MacLachlan; Halle Berry; Jonathan Winters; Richard Moll; Irwin Keyes; Dann Florek; *Cameo(s):* Laraine Newman; Jean Vander Pyl; Jay Leno; *V:* Harvey Korman; *D:* Brian Levant; *W:* Tom S. Parker; Jim Jennewein; Steven E. de Souza; *C:* Dean Cundey; *M:* David Newman. Golden Raspberries '94: Worst Screenplay, Worst Support. Actress (O'Donnell).

The Flintstones in Viva Rock Vegas **2000 (PG)** In a prequel to the 1994 film, a young Fred (Addy) and his best pal Barney (Baldwin) take their girlfriends Wilma (Johnson) and Betty (Krakowski) on a would-be romantic weekend to Rock Vegas. There's a whole lot going on, as runaway society girl Wilma is being wooed by playboy Chip Rockefeller (Gibson), Chip's trying to bankrupt and frame Fred, and the Great Gazoo (Cumming) is on hand to observe earthly mating habits. Everything is appropriately cartoonish, including the story and the acting. Unfortunately, the only ones who'll be entertained are the ones who are too young to remember the original series (or the original movie for that matter). **90m/C; VHS, DVD, Blu-Ray.** Mark Addy; Kristen Johnston; Stephen Baldwin; Jane Krakowski; Thomas Gibson; Joan Collins; Alan Cumming; Harvey Korman; Alex Meneses; *D:* Brian Levant; *W:* Harry Elfont; Deborah Kaplan; Jim Cash; Jack Epps, Jr.; *C:* Jamie Anderson; *M:* David Newman.

Flipped **2010 (PG)** Awkward coming of age teen romance (set in 1960s suburbia) about a junior high first romance. Tomboyish Juli (Carroll) lives across the street from all-American Bryce (McAuliffe). Her family is close and blue-collar; his is judgmental and middle-class. Juli has a longstanding crush that Bryce doesn't really understand and isn't quite ready to reciprocate and she begins to change her mind about his potential merit. Adaptation of Wendelin Van Draanen's 2001 young-adult novel. **90m/C; Blu-Ray.** Madeline Carroll; Rebecca De Mornay; Anthony Edwards; John Mahoney; Aidan Quinn; Penelope Ann Miller; Kevin Weisman; Callan McAuliffe; *D:* Rob Reiner; *W:* Rob Reiner; Andrew Scheinman; *C:* Thomas Del Ruth; *M:* Marc Shaiman.

Flipper **1963** A fisherman's son befriends an injured dolphin, is persuaded to return him to the wild, and earns the animal's gratitude. Prime kids' fare, as its sequels and TV series attest. **87m/C; VHS, DVD.** Chuck Connors; Luke Halpin; Kathleen Maguire; Connie Scott; *D:* James B. Clark.

Flipper **1996 (PG)** They still call him Flipper! Flipper, who in some scenes is played by a robot dolphin, reappears in a feature film for the first time since 1966. Sullen 14-year-old city boy Sandy Ricks (Wood) must spend the summer with crusty bachelor uncle Porter (Hogan), who would rather fish than look after his troublesome nephew. The duo witness the heartless killing of Flipper's family and are adopted by him. In addition to causing their seafood bill to skyrocket, the dolphin helps them uncover an illegal toxic waste dumper, who happens to be the same guy who made Flipper's mama sleep with the fishes. Updated along with the story is the soundtrack, which features a version of the famous theme song by Matthew Sweet. **97m/C; VHS, DVD.** Elijah Wood; Paul Hogan; Chelsea Field; Isaac Hayes; Jonathan Banks; Luke Halpin; *D:* Alan Shapiro; *W:* Alan Shapiro; *C:* Bill Butler; *M:* Joel McNeely.

Flipper's New Adventure *Flipper and the Pirates* **1964** Believing they are to be separated, Flipper and Sandy travel to a remote island. Little do they know, a British family is being held for ransom on the island they have chosen. It's up to the duo to save the day. An enjoyable, nicely done family adventure. **103m/C; VHS, DVD.** Luke Halpin; Pamela Franklin; Tom Helmore; Francesca Annis; Brian Kelly; Joe Higgins; Ricou Browning; *D:* Leon Benson.

Flirtation Walk 1/2 **1934** West point musical that has cadet Powell falling in love with the general's daughter (Keeler), who is already engaged to lieutenant Eldredge. Some fairly good numbers, including "Mr. and Mrs. Is The Name," and "Flirtation Walk." In an attempt to change her image, Keeler hardly dances at all, which is too bad for the viewer. Based on a story by Lou Edelman and Delmer Daves. **98m/B; VHS, DVD.** Dick Powell; Ruby Keeler; Pat O'Brien; Ross Alexander; *D:* Frank Borzage; *W:* Delmer Daves.

Flirting **1989 (R)** Set in an Australian boarding school in 1965, a charming story following the misadventures of the adolescent Danny Embling, who has the misfortune to be both bright and sensitive, putting him seriously at odds with his masculine peers. He finds love with an outcast at the neighboring girls boarding school, the daughter of a diplomat from Uganda. Kidman has a supporting role as a snobbish older boarding school girl, not quite as bad as she seems. Tender and amusing. The second of director Duigan's coming-of-age trilogy, preceded by "The Year My Voice Broke" (the third film isn't yet completed). **100m/C; VHS, DVD.** *AU* Noah Taylor; Thandie Newton; Nicole Kidman; Bartholomew Rose; Felix Nobis; Josh Picker; Kiri Paramore; Marc Gray; Joshua Marshall; David Wieland; Craig Black; Leslie Hill; ***D:*** John Duigan; ***W:*** John Duigan. Australian Film Inst. '90: Film.

Flirting With Danger **1935** Three buddies, who are explosive experts, head to South America for a job and unwittingly get involved in a political revolution (played for laughs). A fireworks mishap creates more mayhem for the boys. **69m/C; DVD.** William Cagney; Robert Armstrong; Edgar Kennedy; Maria Alba; Marion Burns; Wilhelm Von Brincken; Ernest Hilliard; Gino Corrado; ***D:*** Vin Moore; ***W:*** Albert DeMond; Norman S. Hall; ***C:*** Archie Stout.

Flirting with Disaster **1995 (R)** Mel Coplin (Stiller) is your average neurotic New York entomologist searching for his birth parents so he can finally name his four-month-old child and make love to his wife. Tagging along on his bumpy ride are his wife Nancy (Arquette), a beautiful quirky adoption agency shrink (Leoni), and a pair of bisexual FBI agents. The excellent cast also features Moore as Mel's bra-baring adoptive mother, Segal as his weirdly paranoid adoptive father, and Alda and Tomlin as hilarious send-ups of ex-hippie mentality. As events spin madly out of control, every type of relationship is satirized, and every character is left in their underwear. This is director Russell's first big-budget movie, and is as close to a vintage screwball comedy as you'll see in the '90s. **92m/C; VHS, DVD.** Ben Stiller; Patricia Arquette; Tea Leoni; Alan Alda; Mary Tyler Moore; George Segal; Lily Tomlin; Josh Brolin; Richard Jenkins; Celia Weston; Glenn Fitzgerald; Beth Ostrosky; Cynthia Lamontagne; David Patrick Kelly; John Ford Noonan; Charlet Oberly; ***D:*** David O. Russell; ***W:*** David O. Russell; ***C:*** Eric Alan Edwards; ***M:*** Stephen Endelman.

Flirting with Forty ½ **2009** Sunny romantic fantasy from Lifetime is an adaptation of the Jane Porter novel. Recently divorced mom and successful businesswoman Jackie (Locklear) is feeling blue about turning forty. Her pal Kristine (Williams) talks her into a restorative Hawaiian vacation where Jackie promptly has a romance with her twenty-something surf instructor, free-spirit Kyle (Buckley). But when it turns out to be more than a fling, her kids, ex, and jealous friends make a big deal out of the situation. **87m/C; DVD.** Heather Locklear; Vanessa Williams; Cameron Bancroft; Robert Buckley; Sam Duke; Anne Hawthorne; ***D:*** Mikael Salomon; ***W:*** Julia Dahl; ***C:*** Jon Joffin; ***M:*** Jeff Beal. **CABLE**

Float ½ **2008** Ray Fulton (Itzin) is the 55-year-old owner of a popular ice cream parlor. After a bewildering separation from his wife, Ray moves in with manager Gevorg (Titizian) and former employee Ramon (Asuncion) to try to figure things out. Ray's daughter Emily (Cohan) arrives to help and impresses the womanizing Gevorg while Ramon contemplates a marriage of convenience to Gevorg's beautiful Armenian cousin Susannah (Saraci) who wants a green card. **95m/C; DVD.** Gregory Itzin; Hrach Titizian; Lauren Cohan; Alma Saraci; Cristine Rose; Ken Davitian; Anais Thomassian; Ashley Peldon; Johnny Asuncion; ***D:*** Johnny Asuncion; ***W:*** Johnny Asuncion; ***C:*** Matt Egan; ***M:*** Mary Kouyoumdjian; Jay McMeekan. **VIDEO**

Floating **1997** Van (Reedus) is a moody 20-year-old ex-high school swimming champ who's basically treading water. He looks after his drunken paraplegic father (Lyman) in their run-down cottage and drifts into home burglaries with two equally loser friends. It's Van's idea to stash their ill-gotten gains in the basement of his former family home—of course the empty dwelling immediately gets a new owner—and Van winds up befriending the family's son, Doug (Lowe), who's not only a swimming champ but has Dad problems as well. This male bonding leads to some (predictable) attitude changes but the sincerity of the cast goes a long way in overcoming the cliches. **91m/C; VHS, DVD.** Norman Reedus; Chad Lowe; Will Lyman; Jonathan Quint; Josh Marchette; Sybil Temchen; ***D:*** William Roth; ***W:*** William Roth; ***C:*** Wolfgang Held; ***M:*** David Mansfield.

The Flock **2007 (R)** Burned-out federal agent Erroll Babbage (Gere) is training his replacement, Allison Laurie (Danes), while investigating a missing girl he thinks is the victim of a paroled sex offender. First English-language pic for Hong Kong director Lau, best-known for "Infernal Affairs," but the reshoots were done by Niels Mueller. Having another director take over is not considered a good sign. Sleazy and confusing, but features some good work by Gere and Danes. **91m/C; DVD.** Richard Gere; Claire Danes; KaDee Strickland; Matt Schulze; Russell Sams; Avril Lavigne; Ray Wise; French Stewart; Kristina Sisco; ***D:*** Wai Keung (Andrew) Lau; ***W:*** Hans Bauer; Craig Mitchell; ***C:*** Enrique Chediak; ***M:*** Guy Farley.

Flood! **1976** Irwin Allen's first made-for-TV disaster film. A dam bursts and devastates a small town, so a helicopter pilot must save the day. Good cast is swept along in a current of disaster-genre cliches. **98m/C; VHS, DVD.** Robert Culp; Martin Milner; Barbara Hershey; Richard Basehart; Carol Lynley; Roddy McDowall; Cameron Mitchell; Teresa Wright; Francine York; ***D:*** Earl Bellamy. **TV**

Flood ½ **2007** Typical disaster flick. A storm of hurricane proportions devastates Scotland and moves along the coast on its way to London. Authorities are convinced the city is safely protected by the Thames Barrier but discredited scientist Leonard Morrison (Courtenay) thinks otherwise and turns to his estranged son Rob (Carlyle), an engineer, for help. In turn, Rob gets his ex-wife Sam (Gilsig), the operations director for the barrier project, to listen but it still isn't enough to prevent water, water everywhere. **188m/C; DVD.** *GB CA* Robert Carlyle; Jessalyn Gilsig; Tom Courtenay; Joanne Whalley; David Suchet; Nigel Planer; Martin Ball; ***D:*** Tony Mitchell; ***W:*** Justin Bodle; Matthew Cope; ***C:*** Pierre Jodoin; ***M:*** Debbie Wiseman. **TV**

Flood: A River's Rampage ½ **1997 (PG-13)** Community struggles to rebuild after a devastating flood. **92m/C; VHS, DVD.** Richard Thomas; Kate Vernon; Jan Rubes; ***D:*** Bruce Pittman. **TV**

Flooding ½ **1997** Clever homage to Alfred Hitchcock on a budget. Joyce Calloway (Gibson) has become agoraphobic after the unsolved murder of her husband and has spent the past six months in her house. She is working with a new doctor (who comes to the house, of course) to get over her fear of the outside world, and she better hurry, because her parents are selling the house in an effort to get her to go outside. After a fling, a man comes to her back door, falls inside, and dies after uttering a name she doesn't recognize. The tension mounts as it becomes clear that her subconscious mind is holding out on her and that someone wants her dead or at least out of the way. The why of the story is the weak link in the film; it is the journey to the answer that is absorbing. This is not a perfect film, but it is worth watching for fans of suspense. **86m/C; DVD.** Brenna Gibson; Lauren Bailey; Kary Cawley; ***D:*** Todd Portugal; ***W:*** Todd Portugal.

Florence Foster Jenkins ½ **2016 (PG-13)** The title character, played delightfully by Streep, was a New York City heiress who had one dream—to play Carnegie Hall. When an injury in her youth derailed her work to get there as a pianist, she decided she would get there as a singer. Small problem was that she couldn't sing. Frears' period comedy is incredibly likeable, strengthened by enjoyable supporting performances from Helberg and Grant. It all feels a little sitcom-y at times but the cast makes it into something more. Streep's Jenkins is certainly another memorable character in her legendary filmography. **111m/C; DVD, Blu-Ray.** Meryl Streep; Hugh Grant; Simon Helberg; Rebecca Ferguson; Nina Arianda; Stanley Townsend; ***D:*** Stephen Frears; ***W:*** Nicholas Martin; ***C:*** Danny Cohen; ***M:*** Alexandre Desplat. British Acad. '16: Makeup.

Florence Nightingale ½ **1985** Respectable bio of Florence Nightingale (Smith), a privileged Victorian who rejects marriage for the chance to become a nurse. Appalled by reports of Army hospital care for British soldiers during the Crimean War, Florence and 40 volunteer nurses travel to Turkey in 1854 only to face hostility and rejection by the military and medical establishments. Florence forges ahead—making nursing a respectable profession and improving patient care despite her own doubts. The beautiful Smith may seem an odd casting choice and her English accent wobbles but she's as determined as her character to succeed. **140m/C; DVD.** Jaclyn Smith; Timothy Dalton; Jeremy Brett; Claire Bloom; Peter McEnery; Brian Cox; Jeremy Child; Stephan Chase; ***D:*** Daryl Duke; ***W:*** Ivan Moffett; ***C:*** Jack Hildyard; ***M:*** Stanley Myers. **TV**

Florence Nightingale ½ **2008** BBC co-production, along with Faith & Values Media, that focuses on Florence Nightingale's (Fraser) spiritual calling, leading her to reject her privileged life to become a nurse. Despite medical and military objections, Florence improves conditions for soldiers during the Crimean War and then continues pushing for reforms using her wealth and political connections. There are a number of music-hall interludes that are supposed to help tell the story but they're odd interruptions. **130m/C; DVD.** *GB* Laura Fraser; Michael Pennington; Barbara Marten; Sean McKenzie; Wendy Patterson; ***D:*** Norman Shore; ***C:*** Mike J. Fox; ***M:*** Jeremy Soule. **TV**

The Florentine **1998 (R)** A decaying steel town is home to a bar called The Florentine, its owner Whitey (Madsen), and the usual drinking denizens. But with profits sinking, Whitey may lose his livelihood. And then there's his sister Molly's (Madsen) problems. Her wedding to Frankie (Perry) is in jeopardy because of a con man (Belushi) and her ex-fiance, Teddy (Sizemore), who's back in town. **104m/C; VHS, DVD.** Michael Madsen; Virginia Madsen; Luke Perry; Tom Sizemore; James Belushi; Christopher Penn; Mary Stuart Masterson; ***D:*** Nick Stagliano. **VIDEO**

The Florida Project **2017 (R)** A poignant drama that follows 6-year-old Moonee through a summer of adventure and misadventure in and around the Magic Castle, a garish, ramshackle motel located in the underbellied shadow of Disney World. Her mom Halley, like the other long-term inhabitants, is desperate and angry, and Moonee and her young playmates embody both the ignorance of youth and the worldliness of the impoverished. Dafoe gives a warm, authentic performance as the motel manager trying to plug his own dam while protecting and advising the flailing residents. **115m/C; DVD, Blu-Ray.** Willem Dafoe; Brooklynn Prince; Bria Vinaite; Christopher Rivera; Aiden Malik; ***D:*** Sean Baker; ***W:*** Sean Baker; Chris Bergoch; ***C:*** Alexis Zabe; ***M:*** Lorne Balfe.

Floundering ½ **1994 (R)** Misguided satire uses the 1992 L.A. riots as a backdrop to tell the saga of unemployed James Boyz (LeGros), whose life is a walking disaster. He owes the IRS, his unemployment compensation has run out, his brother (Hawke) has fled from a drug rehab clinic, and he finds his girlfriend (Zane) in bed with another man. John drags himself among the city's downtrodden as he fantasizes about life. Drag pretty much sums up the film despite good performances by LeGros and Hawke. **97m/C; VHS, DVD.** James LeGros; Ethan Hawke; Steve Buscemi; John Cusack; Lisa Zane; Sy Richardson; Jeremy Piven; Billy Bob Thornton; ***D:*** Peter McCarthy; ***W:*** Peter McCarthy; ***C:*** Denis Maloney; ***M:*** Pray for Rain.

Flourish **2006 (PG-13)** Desperate for cash, Gaby (Morrison) agrees to babysit precocious 16-year-old Lucy (Meester), who soon disappears from the house. Now Gaby spends an increasingly wild night, running into lots of very strange people, trying to find Lucy before her parents get home. **95m/C; DVD.** Jennifer (Jenny) Morrison; Leighton Meester; Jesse Spencer; Connie Ray; Daniel Roebuck; Olivia Burnette; ***D:*** Kevin Palys; ***W:*** Kevin Palys; ***C:*** Maximilian Gutierrez; ***M:*** Luigi Pittorino; Melinda Doring.

Flower ½ **2018 (R)** To earn money and help bail her absentee father out of jail, Erica (Deutch) organizes a blackmail scheme that involves performing sex acts on a local police officer. While keeping that scheme going, she helps her soon-to-be stepbrother. Luke (Morgan) is an overweight, shy, recovering drug addict who tells Erica that he was molested by local hot guy Will (Scott) as a child. To get payback for Luke, Erica launches a blackmail scheme on Will. The indie comedy-drama's obliviousness to the suffering of its characters makes it difficult to watch. **90m/C; DVD.** Zoey Deutch; Kathryn Hahn; Adam Scott; Dylan Gelula; Eric Edelstein; ***D:*** Max Winkler; ***W:*** Max Winkler; Alex McAulay; Matt Spicer; ***C:*** Carolina Costa; ***M:*** Joseph Stephens.

Flower & Snake *Hana to hebi* **2004** Originally a series of fetish novels by Dan Oniroku, there have been as many as 10 different versions of this film made, this one by Takashi Ishii (best known in Japan for his horror and erotica films). An internationally famous tango dancer is sold by her estranged husband to a local Yakuza to whom he owes a great deal of money. Despite excellent cinematography and themes of sexual and social liberation, most viewers will only remember the many bondage scenes. **115m/C; DVD.** *JP* Aya Sugimoto; Renji Ishibashi; Kenichi Endo; Misaki Mori; Yoshiyuki Yamaguchi; Shun Nakayama; Shigeo Kobayashi; Naoki Matsuda; Tomoo Yageta; Miyako Kawahara; Mr. Buddhaman; Tomezo Tsunokake; Daisuke Iijima; Go Arisue; Susumu Terajima; Hironobu Nomura; ***D:*** Takashi Ishii; ***W:*** Takashi Ishii; Oniroku Dan; ***C:*** Takashi Komatsu; Kazuto Sato; Hiro'o Yanagida; ***M:*** Goro Yasukawa.

Flower & Snake 2 *Hana to hebi 2: Pari/Shizuko* **2005** Still together with her husband after the events of the first film, Shizuko (Aya Sugimoto) finds that her increasingly aging husband can't always perform, but likes watching her in erotic situations. He hires a painter to bring their fantasies to life and she becomes the object of desire to a parade of rich lechers. Still as pretty as the first film, still has a bit of a message, all of which will still be lost in all the nakedness. **113m/C; DVD.** *JP* Aya Sugimoto; Kenichi Endo; Fujiko; Mieko Arai; Toru Shinagawa; Joe Shishido; ***D:*** Takashi Ishii; ***W:*** Takashi Ishii; Oniroku Dan; ***C:*** Takashi Komatsu; Hiro'o Yanagida; ***M:*** Goro Yasukawa.

Flower & Snake '74 ½ *Hana to hebi; Flowers and Snakes* **1974** With actual porn putting a dent in their money in the mid-80s, Pink Film producers Nikkatsu began a series of nostalgic remakes of S&M films with this one based on the novels by Dan Oniroku. A young boy kills an American soldier for consorting with his mother, and grows up impotent unless he can tie up and whip his girlfriends. When the president of the company he works for asks the man to abduct his wife and educate her sexually, she doesn't exactly receive the education he is thinking of. **90m/C; DVD.** *JP* Naomi Tani; Nagatoshi Sakamoto; ***D:*** Masaura Konuma; ***W:*** Oniroku Dan; Yozo Tanaka; ***C:*** Shohei Ando; ***M:*** Richiro Manabe.

Flower Drum Song **1961** The Rodgers and Hammerstein musical played better on Broadway than in this overblown adaptation of life in San Francisco's Chinatown. Umeki plays the young girl who arrives from Hong Kong for an arranged marriage. Her intended (Soo) is a fast-living nightclub owner already enjoying the love of singer Kwan. Meanwhile Umeki falls for the handsome Shigeta. Naturally, everything comes together in a happy ending. **133m/C; VHS, DVD.** Nancy Kwan; Jack Soo; James Shigeta; Miyoshi Umeki; Juanita Hall; ***D:*** Henry Koster; ***C:*** Russell Metty; ***M:*** Richard Rodgers. Natl. Film Reg. '08.

The Flower of My Secret *La Flor de My Secreto* **1995 (R)** Emotional yet restrained story about middle-aged Leo (Paredes), whose longtime marriage is fast ending (and it's not her idea). Leo writes hugely popular romance novels under a pseudonym but her current work is so bleak it's unpublishable. So, Leo gets a job at a newspaper where editor Angel (Echanove) immediately falls for her, and indeed, lives up to his name as her guardian. Willfully myopic about her own life, Leo undergoes further trials until she slowly realizes the mess she's in and becomes willing to change. Surprisingly subdued given Almodovar's usual flamboyance but it's a welcome change of pace. Spanish with subtitles. **107m/C; VHS, DVD.** *SP FR* Marisa Paredes; Juan Echanove; Imanol Arias; Carmen Elias; Rossy de Palma; Chus

(Maria Jesus) Lampreave; Joaquin Cortes; Manuela Vargas; ***D:*** Pedro Almodóvar; ***W:*** Pedro Almodóvar; ***C:*** Affonso Beato; ***M:*** Alberto Iglesias.

Flowers for Algernon 1/2 **2000** Previously filmed as the 1968 feature "Charly," this TV adaptation of Daniel Keyes' novel unfortunately descends into mawkish sentimentality. Mentally handicapped bakery worker Charlie Gordon (Modine) is chosen to be part of an experimental surgery to enhance intelligence. The method was previously tested on a mouse called Algernon with apparent success. It works on Charlie as well (to an overwhelming extent) but he's able to figure out that the effect is only temporary when Algernon has problems and learns he'll soon regress to his former mental state. **120m/C; DVD.** Matthew Modine; Kelli Williams; Ron Rifkin; Bonnie Bedelia; Richard Chevolleau; ***D:*** Jeff Bleckner; ***W:*** John Pielmeier; ***C:*** Mike Fash; ***M:*** Mark Adler. **TV**

Flowers in the Attic 1/2 **1987 (PG-13)** Based on the V.C. Andrews bestseller, a would-be thriller about four young siblings locked for years in their family's old mansion by their grandmother with their mother's selfish acquiescence. A chicken-hearted, clumsy flop that skimps on the novel's trashier themes. **93m/C; VHS, DVD, Blu-Ray.** Victoria Tennant; Kristy Swanson; Louise Fletcher; Jeb Stuart Adams; ***D:*** Jeffrey Bloom; ***W:*** Jeffrey Bloom; ***C:*** Gil Hubbs; ***M:*** Christopher Young.

Flowers in the Attic 1/2 **2014** Bland Lifetime adaptation of V.C. Andrews' 1979 lurid novel is marginally better than its 1987 big screen predecessor. In the 1950s, recent widow Corinne moves back into her wealthy parents' home with her four children. Grandma Foxworth is a cruel, religious nut and, because of their disapproval of the marriage, the children are forced to live in isolation in the attic. As time passes, teens Cathy and Christopher (discreetly) act on their sexual urges while their mother essentially pretends they don't exist. Followed by "Petals on the Wind." **90m/C; DVD.** Kiernan Shipka; Mason Dye; Heather Graham; Ellen Burstyn; Dylan Bruce; Ava Telek; Maxwell Kovach; Beau Daniels; ***D:*** Deborah Chow; ***W:*** Kayla Alpert; ***C:*** Miroslaw Baszak; ***M:*** Mario Grigorov. **CABLE**

The Flowers of St. Francis *Francesco, giullare di Dio; Francis, God's Jester* **1950** Rossellini's presentation of St. Francis and his friars' attainment of spiritual harmony. In Italian with English subtitles. This is the British release version, 10-15 minutes longer than the U.S. version. **75m/B; VHS, DVD.** *IT* Aldo Fabrizi; Bro. Nazario Gerardi; Arabella Lemaitre; ***D:*** Roberto Rossellini; ***W:*** Federico Fellini; Roberto Rossellini; Fr. Antonio Lisandrini; Fr. Felix Morlion; ***C:*** Otello Martelli; ***M:*** Enrico Buondonno; Renzo Rossellini.

Flowers of Shanghai *Haishang Hua* **1998** Slow costume drama/soap opera set in the brothels of late 19th-century Shanghai. In this self-contained world, the elegant "flower girls" depend on their ability to hold onto wealthy clients and Crimson (Hada) seems to be losing her charms. Her longtime patron, Wang (Leung Chui Wai), is also seeing Jasmin (Wei). Meanwhile, among the other ladies, Emerald (Reis) is working to buy her freedom and Jade (Hsuan) is refusing other clients because she believes Zhu (Chang) will marry her. Based on the novel "Biographies of Flowers of Shanghai" by Han Ziyun. Mandarin with subtitles. **125m/C; VHS, DVD.** *JP TW* Tony Leung Chiu-Wai; Michiko Hada; Hsiao-hui Wei; Jack Kao; Michelle Reis; Annie Shizuka Inoh; Fang Hsuan; Simon Chang; ***D:*** Hou Hsiao-hsien; ***W:*** Tien-wen Chu; ***C:*** Mark Ping Bin Lee; ***M:*** Yoshihiro Yanno.

The Flowers of War *Jin Ling Shi San Chai* **2011** Yimou Zhang's visually impressive, if melodramatic, historical drama about the brutal 1937 Japanese invasion of Nanking, China. Drunken American mortician John Miller (Bale) is trapped in a Catholic church along with a group of convent schoolgirls and prostitutes. When Japanese soldiers invade their church sanctuary, pillaging and threatening sexual assault, Miller tries to help by posing as a priest to get his new flock to safety outside the city. English, Japanese, and Mandarin with subtitles. **141m/C; DVD, Blu-Ray.** *CH* Christian Bale; Shigeo Kobayashi; Ni Ni; Tianyuan Huang; Xinyi Zhang; Kefan Cao; Atsuro Watabe; ***D:*** Yimou Zhang; ***W:*** Heng Liu; ***C:*** Xiaoding Zhao; ***M:*** Quigang Chan.

Flowing Gold 1/2 **1940** John Alexander's (Garfield) on the lam after killing a man in self defense. Using the name Johnny Blake, he gets a job as an oil field roughneck after befriending foreman Hap O'Connor (O'Brien). Hard case Linda Chalmers (Farmer) and her dad (Walburn) have staked everything on one last oil lease, but with the deadline looming can the men hit a gusher before the gal comes between the two men or the law catches up with Johnny? **81m/B; DVD.** John Garfield; Pat O'Brien; Frances Farmer; Raymond Walburn; Granville Bates; Cliff Edwards; ***D:*** Alfred E. Green; ***W:*** Kenneth Gamet; ***C:*** Sidney Hickox; ***M:*** Adolph Deutsch.

Flu Birds WOOF! *Flu Bird Horror* **2008 (R)** Even the box art is misleading in this Sci-Fi Channel dreck. A group of juvenile delinquents are at some kind of wilderness boot camp (or something) and become prey to giant mutant birds infected by a killer virus. A local doc and a park ranger try to help. **95m/C; DVD.** Clare Carey; Lance Guest; Sarah Butler; Brent Lydic; Bill Posley; ***D:*** Leigh Scott; ***W:*** Brian J. Smith; Tony Daniel; ***C:*** Gabriel Kosuth; ***M:*** Alan Howarth. **CABLE**

Flubber **1997 (PG)** Bland remake of Disney's "The Absent-Minded Professor" with Williams as the befuddled, yet brilliant Prof. Brainard. Putting his wedding on the back Bunsen burner, much to the dismay of his fiancee Sara Jean (Harden), Brainard invents a bouncy, flying green slime named "flubber." As the substance becomes the cure-all for romantic turmoil and fledging school basketball teams, it also attracts the attention of a corrupt businessman and his moronic henchmen. Due to the dull subplots, kids and adults will be disappointed that the main attraction (the cute green goo) doesn't have much screen time. Williams, oddly enough, seems comfortable playing second banana to a substance that could describe his comedic skills. **93m/C; VHS, DVD.** Robin Williams; Marcia Gay Harden; Christopher McDonald; Raymond J. Barry; Clancy Brown; Ted Levine; Wil Wheaton; Edie McClurg; ***D:*** Les Mayfield; ***W:*** John Hughes; ***C:*** Dean Cundey; ***M:*** Danny Elfman.

The Fluffer **2001** Naive aspiring filmmaker Sean (Cunio) has his romantic illusions destroyed and is rather rudely forced to grow up. Gay Sean gets a job with a Hollywood porn production company and falls for one of the company's stars—the immature and self-destructive gay-for-pay Mikey (Gurney) whose nom-de-porn is Johnny Rebel. Mikey's on a downward slide despite Sean's admiration and the love of his stripper girlfriend Julie (Day) and if the two aren't careful, Mikey will take them with him. Title refers to one of the personal services Sean is expected to offer Mikey. **94m/C; VHS, DVD.** Michael Cunio; Scott Gurney; Rozanne Day; Richard Riehle; Taylor Negron; Tim Bagley; Adina Porter; Deborah Harry; ***D:*** Richard Glatzer; Wash West; ***W:*** Wash West; ***C:*** Mark Putnam.

The Fluffy Movie: Unity Through Laughter 1/2 **2014 (PG-13)** A glorified cable-quality stand-up comedy special diving into the stories of comedian Gabriel "Fluffy" Iglesias, trying his best to get real, while making every single person know he's just kidding. He talks of growing up poor LA, but glosses over the tragedies with a smile and maybe a bad impression of an Indian person. Entertaining as he may be, this unnecessary theatrical release is best served as background clatter while preparing dinner. Living up to his name in more ways than one, this heavyweight comic belongs with the lightweights. Pure fluff. **101m/C; DVD, Blu-Ray.** Gabriel "Fluffy" Iglesias; ***D:*** Manny Rodriguez; ***C:*** Larry Blanford.

Fluke **1995 (PG)** "Ghost" meets "Oh, Heavenly Dog" as Tom (Modine) dies in a suspicious car accident and is reincarnated as a dog who remembers his past life. He returns to his former family (Travis and Pomeranc) to protect them from his former business partner (Stoltz), battling such puppy perils as cosmetic testing labs and dogcatchers along the way. While there's plenty of squishy sentimentality to go around, some of the scenes involving animal abuse may be a little much for the target audience of pre-teen kids. Jackson and Stoltz trade "Pulp Fiction" for pup fiction, but this dog won't hunt. Based on the novel by James Herbert. **96m/C; VHS, DVD.** Matthew Modine; Nancy Travis; Eric Stoltz; Max Pomeranc; Ron Perlman; Jon Polito; Bill Cobbs; Frederico Pacifici; Collin Wilcox-Paxton; ***V:*** Samuel L. Jackson; ***D:*** Carlo Carlei; ***W:*** James Carrington; Carlo Carlei; ***C:*** Raffaele Mertes; ***M:*** Carlo Siliotto.

Flushed Away **2006 (PG)** The Aardman studio ventures from its usual clay figure stop-motion look into computer animation but the inventiveness remains. Roddy (Jackman) is a posh London pet mouse who is unceremoniously flushed down the loo by baddie sewer rat Sid (Richie). Roddy discovers a raucous underground community that is threatened by evil gangster The Toad (McKellen) and his French cousin Le Frog (Reno). Fortunately, the pampered Roddy is taken in by tough working-class rat Rita (Winslet) as they try to save the day. The harmonizing singing slugs are an added highlight. **84m/C; DVD, Blu-Ray.** *US GB* ***V:*** Hugh Jackman; Kate Winslet; Ian McKellen; Jean Reno; Bill Nighy; Andy Serkis; Kathy Burke; David Suchet; Shane Richie; Miriam Margolyes; Rachel Rawlinson; ***D:*** David Bowers; Sam Fell; ***W:*** Dick Clement; Ian La Frenais; Chris Lloyd; Joe Keenan; William Davies; ***M:*** Harry Gregson-Williams.

The Fly **1958** The historic, chillingly original '50s sci-fi tale about a hapless scientist experimenting with teleportation who accidentally gets anatomically confused with a housefly. Campy required viewing; two sequels followed, and a 1986 remake which itself has spawned one sequel. **94m/C; VHS, DVD, Blu-Ray.** David Hedison; Patricia Owens; Vincent Price; Herbert Marshall; Kathleen Freeman; Betty Lou Gerson; Charles Herbert; ***D:*** Kurt Neumann; ***W:*** James Clavell; ***C:*** Karl Struss; ***M:*** Paul Sawtell.

The Fly **1986 (R)** A sensitive, humanistic remake of the 1958 horror film about a scientist whose flesh is genetically intermixed with a housefly via his experimental transportation device. A thoughtful, shocking horror film, with fine performances from Goldblum and Davis and a brutally emotional conclusion. Followed by "The Fly II" in 1989. **96m/C; VHS, DVD, Blu-Ray.** Jeff Goldblum; Geena Davis; John Getz; Joy Boushel; Cosette Lee; ***D:*** David Cronenberg; ***W:*** David Cronenberg; Charles Edward Pogue; ***C:*** Mark Irwin; ***M:*** Howard Shore. Oscars '86: Makeup.

The Fly 2 1/2 **1989 (R)** Inferior sequel to Cronenberg's opus, in which the offspring of Seth Brundle achieves full genius maturity in three years, falls in love, and discovers the evil truth behind his father's teleportation device and the corporate auspices that backed it. **105m/C; VHS, DVD; Open Captioned.** Eric Stoltz; Daphne Zuniga; Lee Richardson; John Getz; Harley Cross; ***D:*** Chris Walas; ***W:*** Mick Garris; Jim Wheat; Ken Wheat; Frank Darabont; ***C:*** Robin Vidgeon; ***M:*** Christopher Young.

Fly Away Home *Father Goose; Flying Wild* **1996 (PG)** Does for geese what "Babe" did for pigs. Young Amy (Paquin) withdraws when she loses her mother in a car crash and is forced to live with her estranged father, Thomas (Daniels), a scruffy sculptor/inventor, in rural Ontario. Still dealing with her own mother's death, Amy suddenly becomes a mother herself to a tiny gaggle of goslings when she happens upon a nest of uprooted eggs. Extraordinary technical achievements make up for some unnecessary melodrama in the second half as the geese head South, led by Amy, in a glider built by her father. Touching but unsentimental, mostly well scripted and acted, and extraordinarily shot. Based on the true story of inventor Bill Lishman, who led domesticated geese on a winter migration from Toronto, Canada to North Carolina, leading the formation in his motor-powered glider. **107m/C; VHS, DVD.** Jeff Daniels; Anna Paquin; Dana Delany; Terry Kinney; Jeremy Ratchford; ***D:*** Carroll Ballard; ***W:*** Robert Rodat; Vince McKewin; ***C:*** Caleb Deschanel; ***M:*** Mark Isham.

Fly by Night **1993 (PG-13)** Mismatched New York rappers Rich and I join forces to make it big as hard-core gangstas. When they're propelled to the top of the charts, forces both personal and professional work to tear them apart. **93m/C; DVD.** Jeffrey D. Sams; Ron Brice; Daryl (Chill) Mitchell; Todd Graff; Leo Burmester; Soulfood Jed; Larry (Lawrence) Gilliard, Jr.; Omar Carter; Maura Tierney; Yul Vazquez; M.C. Lyte; Christopher-Michael Gerrard; Ebony Jo-Ann; ***D:*** Steve Gomer; ***W:*** Todd Graff; ***C:*** Larry Banks; ***M:*** Kris Parker; Sidney Mills; Dwayne Sumal. Sundance '93: Filmmakers Trophy.

Fly Me to the Moon 1/2 **2008 (G)** A literal "fly on the wall" perspective of 1969's historic Apollo 11 launch to the moon, as experienced by three young stowaway houseflies aboard the shuttle. Its crude computer animation is saved only by its innovative 3-D tricks, carefully planned out by director Stassen, fresh off his duties on "Wild Safari 3-D." Nevertheless, preschool jokes, not-so-clever "2001" references, and an awkward script that mixes kiddy fun with sterile technical information about the mission ultimately bring about its failure to launch. **84m/C; On Demand.** Philip Daniel Bolden; Christopher Lloyd; ***V:*** Trevor Gagnon; Kelly Ripa; David Gore; Nicolette Sheridan; Tim Curry; Edwin E. Aldrin, Jr.; Lorraine Nicholson; ***D:*** Ben Stassen; ***W:*** Domonic Paris; ***M:*** Ramin Djawadi.

Flyboys 1/2 **2006 (PG-13)** Old-fashioned war flick based on the exploits of the Lafayette Escadrille—young Americans who volunteered for the French military during WWI, before the U.S. entered the war. Formulaic script has the new recruits, who had a life expectancy as biplane pilots of six weeks, training under the paternal eye of Capt. Thenault (Reno). Besides the heroics, there's a corny romance between laconic Texan Rawlings (Franco) and local beauty Lucienne (Decker). Extensive CGI is combined with actual footage for the dynamic air sequences. **139m/C; DVD, Blu-Ray.** James Franco; Martin Henderson; Jean Reno; Philip Winchester; David Ellison; Jennifer Decker; Tyler Labine; Abdul Salis; Christien Anholt; ***D:*** Tony Bill; ***W:*** Blake T. Evans; David S. Ward; Phil Sears; ***C:*** Henry Braham; ***M:*** Trevor Rabin.

Flying Blind 1/2 **1941** Foreign agents are thwarted in their attempt to steal a vital air defense secret. Unconvincing espionage plot cobbled into a story about a Los Angeles-Las Vegas puddle jumper. **69m/B; VHS, DVD.** Richard Arlen; Jean Parker; Marie Wilson; Nils Asther; Roger Pryor; Eddie Quillan; Grady Sutton; Dick Purcell; ***D:*** Frank McDonald; ***W:*** Richard Murphy; Maxwell Shane; ***C:*** Fred H. Jackman, Jr.; ***M:*** Dimitri Tiomkin.

Flying By 1/2 **2009 (PG-13)** Real estate developer George Barron (Cyrus) goes to his 25-year high school reunion, san wife Pamela (Locklear), and discovers his old band has reunited. After sitting in, he agrees to rehearse with the guys and gets the old music bug back, especially when they have a successful gig at the local bar. Pamela gets worried when George's midlife crisis starts interfering with their marriage and his work, especially when he contemplates touring with the band. **90m/C; DVD.** Billy Ray Cyrus; Heather Locklear; Patricia Neal; Olesya Rulin; ***D:*** Jim Amatulli; ***W:*** Jim Amatulli; ***C:*** Chris Chomyn; ***M:*** Geoff Levin. **VIDEO**

The Flying Deuces *Flying Aces* **1939** Ollie's broken heart lands Laurel and Hardy in the Foreign Legion. The comic pair escape a firing squad only to suffer more indignities. A musical interlude with a Laurel soft shoe while Hardy sings "Shine On, Harvest Moon" is one of the film's highlights. **65m/B; VHS, DVD, Blu-Ray.** Stan Laurel; Oliver Hardy; Jean Parker; Reginald Gardiner; James Finlayson; ***D:*** Edward Sutherland; ***W:*** Ralph Spence; Charles R. Rogers; Harry Langdon; Alfred Schiller; ***C:*** Elmer Dyer; Art Lloyd; ***M:*** Leo Shuken; John Leipold.

Flying Down to Rio 1/2 **1933** The first Astaire-Rogers musical, although they are relegated to supporting status behind Del Rio and Raymond. Still, it was enough to make them stars and a team that epitomizes the height of American musical films. The slim story revolves around singer Del Rio's two suitors and receives a splendid, art deco production. Showgirls dancing on plane wings in flight provide another memorable moment. **89m/B; VHS, DVD.** Fred Astaire; Ginger Rogers; Dolores Del Rio; Eric Blore; Gene Raymond; Franklin Pangborn; ***D:*** Thornton Freeland; ***M:*** Vincent Youmans; Max Steiner.

The Flying Fleet 1929 Annapolis grads, who call themselves the 'Flying Six,' vow to fulfill their dreams and apply for extended and dangerous training to become naval pilots. But the camaraderie is strained between buddies Tommy (Navarro) and Steve (Graves) when they both fall in love with Anita (Page). The exciting aviation sequences were shot by Charles A. Marshall and there's footage of the Navy's first aircraft carrier, the USS Langley. The film was originally released as a silent and then re-released after some synchronized music and sound effects were added. **87m/B; Silent; DVD.** Ramon Novarro; Ralph Graves; Anita Page; Eddie Nugent; Carroll Nye; Gardner James; Sumner Getchell; ***D:*** George W. Hill; ***W:*** Richard Schayer; ***C:*** Ira Morgan; ***M:*** William Axt.

The Flying Fool 1929 Ace pilot Bill returns from the war to find his younger brother has fallen for a singer. When Bill meets the lady, he also notices her charms and the two brothers have a duel in the skies to see who'll get the girl. **75m/B; VHS, DVD.** William Boyd; Marie Prevost; Russell Gleason; ***D:*** Tay Garnett; ***W:*** James Gleason.

Flying High 1931 MGM musical comedy, based on the 1930 Broadway production, with choreography by Busby Berkeley. Lahr reprises his stage role (in his first film lead) as Rusty, a goofy inventor/pilot, who inadvertently breaks the record for high-altitude flying in an experimental aerocopter. Greenwood steals the film as gawky spinster Pansy who is determined to get the flummoxed Rusty to marry her, even coming to his airborne rescue. Note the Prohibition booze scene when Rusty undergoes a physical exam. **79m/B; DVD.** Bert Lahr; Charlotte Greenwood; Pat O'Brien; Kathryn Crawford; Charles Winninger; Hedda Hopper; Guy Kibbee; ***D:*** Charles Riesner; ***W:*** Charles Riesner; Robert Hopkins; A.P. Younger; ***C:*** Merritt B. Gerstad.

Flying Leathernecks 1951 Tough squadron leader Wayne fights with his fellow officer Ryan in Guadalcanal when their leadership styles clash. But when the real fighting begins all is forgotten as Wayne leads his men into victorious battle, winning the admiration and devotion of his fliers. Memorable WWII film deals with war in human terms. **102m/C; VHS, DVD.** John Wayne; Robert Ryan; Janis Carter; Don Taylor; James Bell; James Dobson; Jay C. Flippen; Gordon Gebert; William Harrigan; Brett King; Adam Williams; Carleton Young; Dick Wessel; Gail Davis; Harlan Warde; Michael (Steve Flagg) St. Angel; Maurice Jara; John Mallory; Britt Nelson; Lynn Stalmaster; ***D:*** Nicholas Ray; ***W:*** Kenneth Gamet; James Edward Grant; ***C:*** William E. Snyder; ***M:*** Roy Webb.

The Flying Saucer 1/2 1950 U.S. and Russian scientists clash over their search for a huge flying saucer that is hidden under a glacier. The first movie to deal with flying saucers. The cassette includes animated opening and closing sequences plus previews of coming attractions. **71m/B; VHS, DVD.** Mikel Conrad; Pat Garrison; Hanz von Teuffen; ***D:*** Mikel Conrad; ***W:*** Mikel Conrad; Howard Irving Young; ***C:*** Philip Tannura; ***M:*** Darrell Calker.

The Flying Scotsman 1/2 2006 (PG-13) Based on the story of Graeme Obree, a Scottish amateur cyclist who broke several world speed records using a bike of his own design made from, among other things, parts from a washing machine. "Scotsman" highlights his nightmarish problems of self doubt and depression. Despite the litany of cliches, it's well enough done, and there are good moments, though some will find it a definite downer. **96m/C; DVD.** *GB* Johnny Miller; Sean Brown; Julie Austin; Billy Boyd; Laura Fraser; Brian Cox; Ron Donachie; Morven Christie; Steven Berkoff; Philip Wright; Adrian Smith; Joseph Carney; Niall Macgregor; Christopher Anderson; Moray Hunter; Niall Greig Fulton; Daniel Andre Pageon; Gudrun Mangel; Muzaffer Cakar; ***D:*** Douglas Mackinnon; ***W:*** John Brown; Declan Hughes; Simon Rose; ***C:*** Gavin Finney; ***M:*** Martin Phipps.

Flying Tigers 1/2 1942 Salutes the All-American Volunteer Group which flew for China under General Claire Chennault against the Japanese before the U.S. entered WWII. A squadron leader and a brash new recruit both vie for the affections of a pretty nurse in-between their flying missions. Romance and a few comic touches take a back seat to graphic scenes of aerial battles and dramatization of heroic sacrifice in this rousing war film. **101m/B; VHS, DVD, Blu-Ray.** John Wayne; Paul Kelly; John Carroll; Anna Lee; Mae Clarke; Gordon Jones; ***D:*** David Miller.

Flynn 1/2 *My Forgotten Man* 1996 Details the adventurous early years of Tasmania-born Errol Flynn (Pearce) before he became the swashbuckling hero of Hollywood films. His sexual exploits get him kicked out of school and he makes his way as gigolo, thief, liar, and alleged spy. **96m/C; VHS, DVD.** *AU* Guy Pearce; Claudia Karvan; Steven Berkoff; ***D:*** Frank Howson; ***W:*** Frank Howson; ***C:*** John Wheeler; ***M:*** Anthony Marinelli.

Flypaper 1997 (R) Parking-lot bigshot Marvin (Loggia) and his business associate Jack (Brolly) help out junkie Natalie (Frost), who is being pressured by low-rent hood Bobby Ray (Sheffer). There's actually three separate but connected stories revolving around a big score and the various lowlifes who want to get their hands on it one California afternoon. **111m/C; VHS, DVD.** Robert Loggia; Sadie Frost; Craig Sheffer; Shane Brolly; Lucy Liu; James Wilder; Illeana Douglas; Talisa Soto; John C. McGinley; ***D:*** Klaus Hoch; ***W:*** Klaus Hoch; ***C:*** Jurgen Baum; ***M:*** Peter Manning Robinson.

Flypaper 1/2 2011 Two gangs of bank robbers (one slick, one stupid) are trying to rob the same bank at the same time, causing complications in this occasionally amusing heist comedy. While the robbers argue, the bank hostages are figuring a way out, including teller Kaitlin (Judd) and customer Tripp (Dempsey). **87m/C; DVD, Blu-Ray.** Patrick Dempsey; Ashley Judd; Tim Blake Nelson; Pruitt Taylor Vince; Mekhi Phifer; John Ventimiglia; Jeffrey Tambor; ***D:*** Rob Minkoff; ***W:*** Jon Lucas; Scott Moore; ***C:*** Steven Poster; ***M:*** John Swihart.

FM *Citizen's Band* 1978 (PG-13) The disc jockeys at an L.A. radio station rebel in the name of rock'n'roll. Despite the promising cast and setting (Mull makes his movie debut as a memorable space case), this is just disjointed and surprisingly unhip; one producer took his name off it due to creative difficulties. The decent soundtrack includes concert footage of Jimmy Buffet and Linda Ronstadt. **104m/C; VHS, DVD, Blu-Ray.** Eileen Brennan; Alex Karras; Cleavon Little; Martin Mull; Cassie Yates; Linda Ronstadt; Jimmy Buffett; ***D:*** John A. Alonzo; ***W:*** Ezra Sacks; ***C:*** David Myers.

Focus 1/2 2001 (PG-13) Based on a 1945 novel by playwright Arthur Miller, this exploration of anti-Semitism and bigotry features Macy as Larry Newman, a nebbish personnel worker who lives with his invalid mother. After 20 years on the job, he is demoted after he gets glasses because they make him look "too Jewish" to his bosses. After quitting his job in protest, he is interviewed for a new job by Gertrude (Dern), a woman that he had turned away from his firm because she may or may not have been a Jew. A whirlwind romance ensues, and the two are soon married as their neighborhood is becoming a battleground of ethnic tension. Strong-arm tactics are used on local newsstand owner Finkelstein (Paymer), and he warns the Newmans about collective hate. Macy gives a great performance, but the material is a bit blunt and preachy. **106m/C; VHS, DVD.** William H. Macy; Laura Dern; David Paymer; Meat Loaf Aday; Michael Copeman; Kenneth Welsh; Kay Hawtrey; Joseph Ziegler; Arlene Meadows; ***D:*** Neil Slavin; ***W:*** Kendrew Lascelles; ***C:*** Juan Ruiz-Anchia; ***M:*** Mark Adler.

Focus 2015 (R) Smith proves for the first time in a while why he was a movie star in the first place with a charismatic leading man performance, ably supported by future star Robbie. Smith plays Nicky Spurgeon, a seasoned con man who crosses paths with gorgeous rookie Jess Barrett (Robbie). When she tries to pull a seduction con on Nicky, he calls her bluff and the two form a partnership, going to New Orleans for the biggest con of both of their lives. Of course, Glenn Ficarra and John Requa's film works on crosses and double crosses of the eye-rolling variety but the blinding star power of the leads carries the movie. **104m/C; DVD.** Will Smith; Margot Robbie; Rodrigo Santoro; Gerald McRaney; B.D. Wong; Adrian Martinez; Robert Taylor; ***D:*** Glenn Ficarra; John Requa; ***W:*** Glenn Ficarra; John Requa; ***C:*** Xavier Perez Grobet; ***M:*** Nick Urata.

The Fog 1978 (R) John Carpenter's blustery follow-up to his success with "Halloween." An evil fog containing murderous, vengeful ghosts envelops a sleepy seaside town and subjects the residents to terror and mayhem. **91m/C; VHS, DVD, Blu-Ray.** Hal Holbrook; Adrienne Barbeau; Jamie Lee Curtis; Janet Leigh; John Houseman; Tom Atkins; ***D:*** John Carpenter; ***W:*** John Carpenter; Debra Hill; ***C:*** Dean Cundey; ***M:*** John Carpenter.

The Fog 1/2 2005 (PG-13) Remake of the 1980s film of the same name, this foggy feature is updated by utterly ludicrous special effects. It does, however, stay true to the original film's roots, where a misty fog overtakes the sleepy (and fictional) town of Antonio Bay, bringing in the ghosts of some seafarers murdered 100 years ago. Of course, the ghosts are ticked off and they exact revenge on the poor townsfolk. The original was at least scarier, and even better-acted, which isn't saying a whole lot. **100m/C; VHS, DVD, UMD.** Tom Welling; Maggie Grace; Selma Blair; DeRay Davis; Kenneth Welsh; Sara Botsford; Rade Serbedzija; Adrian Hough; ***D:*** Rupert Wainwright; ***W:*** Cooper Layne; ***C:*** Nathan Hope; ***M:*** Graeme Revell.

Fog Island 1/2 1945 Murder and terror lurk after a greedy inventor, who was framed for fraud by his business partner, is released from prison. He plots revenge by inviting his foes to his island home. **72m/B; VHS, DVD, Blu-Ray.** George Zucco; Lionel Atwill; Terry Morse; Jerome Cowan; Veda Ann Borg; ***D:*** Terry Morse; ***W:*** Pierre Gendron; ***C:*** Ira Morgan.

The Fog of War: Eleven Lessons from the Life of Robert S. McNamara 1/2 2003 (PG-13) Oscar winner for Best Documentary not only gave prolific documentarian Morris his first Academy Award, but also presents a startlingly honest and three-dimensional portrayal of one of the major architects of twentieth-century American history, Robert McNamara. A former president of the Ford Automotive Company and the Secretary of Defense for both Kennedy and Johnson, McNamara speaks frankly about his role in the Bay of Pigs and the Vietnam War, alternating between offering fascinating insights and arguing with his off-screen interviewer. He'll make you love him one moment and cringe the next. A must-see for history buffs. **106m/C; DVD.** ***D:*** Errol Morris; ***C:*** Peter Donahue; Robert Chappell; ***M:*** Philip Glass. Oscars '03: Feature Doc.; Ind. Spirit '04: Feature Doc.; L.A. Film Critics '03: Feature Doc.; Natl. Bd. of Review '03: Feature Doc.; Natl. Film Reg. '19.

Fog Over Frisco 1934 Made while Davis was still playing supporting parts, she has a pivotal but small role in this fast-paced crime melodrama. Arlene (Davis) is a volatile, bored San Francisco society dame who gets involved with mobsters who launder the bonds she has her fiance Spencer (Talbot) steal from her despised stepfather's (Bradford) bank. In contrast, her stepsister Val (Lindsay) is the good girl who tries to uphold the family name and is outraged over articles about Arlene written by newshound Tony Sterling (Woods). Arlene gets into big trouble and it's up to Val and Tony to investigate. **68m/B; DVD.** Bette Davis; Margaret Lindsay; Donald Woods; Lyle Talbot; Arthur Byron; Hugh Herbert; Douglass Dumbrille; Robert Barrat; Irving Pichel; ***D:*** William Dieterle; ***W:*** Eugene Solow; Robert N. Lee; ***C:*** Gaetano Antonio "Tony" Gaudio.

Folies Bergere de Paris 1/2 *The Man From the Folies Bergere* 1935 Nightclub entertainer Eugene Charlier (Chevalier) often impersonates his lookalike—wealthy Baron Fernand Cassini—in his Folies Bergere act. This comes in handy when Eugene is hired to poses as Cassini, who needs to secretly be out of town for an important meeting and still be seen at an important social function. Confusion ensues for both Eugene's girlfriend Mimi (Sothern) and Cassini's wife Genevieve (Oberon). Filmed simultaneously in a French-language version (complete with topless showgirls). **83m/B; DVD.** Maurice Chevalier; Merle Oberon; Ann Sothern; Walter Byron; Lumsden Hare; Eric Blore; Robert Greig; ***D:*** Roy Del Ruth; ***W:*** Hal Long; Bess Meredyth; ***C:*** J. Peverell Marley; Barney McGill; ***M:*** Alfred Newman.

Folks! 1992 (PG-13) Selleck is a Chicago stockbroker whose wife and kids have left him, the FBI is after him, and, worst of all, his parents have moved in with him. His parents don't want to be a burden, so Selleck decides that the best way to solve his financial woes is to help his parents commit suicide so he can collect on their insurance policies. Tasteless comedy that makes fun of aging and Alzheimer's Disease. Selleck is too sweet and cuddly for his role, but Ameche is good as the senile father, and Ebersole is great as Selleck's unpleasant sister. **109m/C; VHS, DVD.** Tom Selleck; Don Ameche; Anne Jackson; Christine Ebersole; Wendy Crewson; Robert Pastorelli; Michael Murphy; Kevin Timothy Chevalia; Margaret Murphy; ***D:*** Ted Kotcheff; ***M:*** Michel Colombier.

Follies Girl 1943 There's folly in expecting that this wartime tuner would hold up today. An army private romances a dress designer and a musical show somehow results. Currently only sold as part of a collection. **74m/B; VHS, DVD.** Wendy Barrie; Doris Nolan; Gordon Oliver; Anne Barrett; Arthur Pierson; ***D:*** William Rowland.

Follow Me 1969 (G) Round-the-world odyssey of three moon doggies searching for adventure—and the perfect wave. Spectacular surfing scenes are complemented by songs performed by Dino, Desi, and Billy. **90m/C; VHS, DVD.** Claude Codgen; Mary Lou McGinnis; Bob Purvey; ***D:*** Gene McCabe.

Follow Me, Boys! 1966 A Disney film about a simple man who decides to put down roots and enjoy the quiet life, after one year too many on the road with a ramshackle jazz band. That life is soon interrupted when he volunteers to lead a high-spirited boy scout troop. **120m/C; VHS, DVD.** Fred MacMurray; Vera Miles; Lillian Gish; Charlie Ruggles; Elliott Reid; Kurt Russell; Luana Patten; Ken Murray; ***D:*** Norman Tokar; ***W:*** Louis Pelletier; ***M:*** George Bruns.

Follow That Camel 1/2 *Carry On Follow That Camel* 1967 Foreign Legion sergeant who invents acts of heroism finally gets a chance to really help out a friend in need. Part of the "Carry On" series. **95m/C; VHS, Streaming.** *GB* Phil Silvers; Kenneth Williams; Anita Harris; Jim Dale; ***D:*** Gerald Thomas.

Follow That Car 1980 (PG) Three southern kids become FBI agents and begin a thigh-slappin', rip-snortin' down-home escapade. **96m/C; VHS, DVD.** Dirk Benedict; Tanya Tucker; Teri Nunn; ***D:*** Daniel Haller.

Follow That Dream 1961 (G) Elvis plays a musical hillbilly whose family is trying to homestead on government land along the sunny Florida coast. Based on Richard C. Powell's novel "Pioneer Go Home." The songs—the only reason to see this movie—include "Angel," "What a Wonderful Life," and the title track. **111m/C; VHS, DVD, Blu-Ray.** Elvis Presley; Arthur O'Connell; Anne Helm; Simon Oakland; Jack Kruschen; Joanna Moore; Howard McNear; ***D:*** Gordon Douglas; ***W:*** Charles Lederer; ***C:*** Leo Tover; ***M:*** Hans J. Salter.

Follow the Boys 1/2 1963 Rather dull romantic fluff that's a sequel to 1960's "Where the Boys Are." Bonnie, Toni, Liz, and Michele dash around Europe in an effort to keep track of their Navy boyfriends and spouses who are serving aboard the USS Independence. **95m/C; DVD.** Connie Francis; Paula Prentiss; Dany Robin; Janis Paige; Russ Tamblyn; Roger Perry; Ron Randell; Richard Long; ***D:*** Richard Thorpe; ***W:*** David Osborn; David Chantler; ***C:*** Edward (Ted) Scaife; ***M:*** Alexander Courage; Ronald Goodwin.

Follow the Fleet 1936 A song-and-dance man joins the Navy and meets two sisters in need of help in this Rogers/Astaire bon-bon featuring a classic Berlin score. Look for Betty Grable, Lucille Ball, and Tony Martin in minor roles. Hilliard went on to be best known as the wife of Ozzie Nelson in TV's "The Adventures of Ozzie and Harriet." **110m/B; VHS, DVD.** Fred Astaire; Ginger Rogers; Randolph Scott; Harriet Hilliard Nelson; Betty

Grable; Lucille Ball; **D:** Mark Sandrich; **M:** Irving Berlin; Max Steiner.

Follow the River ✓✓ 1/2 **1995 (PG)** It's 1775 and Mary Ingles (Lee) is living with her husband and family on a frontier farm in the Blue Ridge Mountains. The community is raided by the Shawnee, lead by Wildcat (Schweig), who take Mary and several other settlers miles away to their home camp. Once there, Mary befriends another captive, the older Gretl (Burstyn), proves her courage to the smitten Wildcat, and plots to escape and find her way home. Based on the 1981 novel by James Alexander Thom; filmed in North Carolina. **93m/C; VHS, DVD.** Sheryl Lee; Eric Schweig; Ellen Burstyn; Tim Guinee; Renee O'Connor; **D:** Martin Davidson.

Follow the Stars Home ✓✓ 1/2 **2001** Dianne (Williams) falls for charming fisherman Mark McCune (Close), they get married, and she's soon pregnant. But when Dianne learns that their baby daughter will be born will severe disabilities, Mark can't cope and leaves her. Flash forward six years, with Dianne making a life for herself and Julia—aided by her mother (Brown) and Mark's steadfast pediatrician brother, David (Scott), who obviously loves her. Then an accident brings Mark back into their lives, but will Dianne make a different choice this time? Based on the novel by Luanne Rice. A Hallmark Hall of Fame production that's a predictable tearjerker. **97m/C; VHS, DVD.** Kimberly Williams; Campbell Scott; Eric Close; Blair Brown; Alexa Vega; Roxanne Hart; **D:** Dick Lowry; **W:** Sally Robinson. **TV**

Follow Your Heart ✓✓ **1936** Met opera star Marion Talley's only film has her typecast as a talented singer in an eccentric musical family. Too familiar with career hardships, her ex-star mother doesn't want her daughter following in her footsteps but Marian is equally determined to make her own choices. There are various 'let's put on a show' moments to highlight the talents of the performers. **79m/B; DVD.** Marion Talley; Michael Bartlett; Nigel Bruce; Henrietta Crosman; Vivienne Osborne; Luis Alberni; Walter Catlett; **D:** Aubrey Scotto; **W:** Lester Cole; Samuel Ornitz; Nathanael West; **C:** Alan Jones; John Mescall; **M:** Hugo Riesenfeld.

Following ✓✓ **1999 (R)** Nolan's feature debut is an odd little neo-noir about a young man named Bill (Theobald) who likes to follow strangers. He picks the wrong guy in burglar Cobb (Haw) who has his own voyeuristic tastes. Cobb turns the tables on Bill and decides to become his mentor in crime. And sticking with the noir tradition, there's a mysterious blonde femme (Russell) whose relationship to the men is gradually revealed. As in his 2001 film "Memento," Nolan plays twister with the chronology, which means more than one viewing may be necessary to figure things out. **71m/B; VHS, DVD, Blu-Ray.** Jeremy Theobald; Alex Haw; Lucy Russell; John Nolan; **D:** Christopher Nolan; **W:** Christopher Nolan; **C:** Christopher Nolan; **M:** David Julyan.

Following Her Heart ✓✓ **1994** Middle-aged Swedish housewife Lena (Ann-Margaret) was long-held back in her unhappy marriage. Now that she's a widow, Lena decides to finally follow her dream of becoming a country singer by leaving Sweden and joining a bus tour heading for Nashville. **100m/C; DVD.** Ann-Margret; George Segal; Brenda Vaccaro; Kirk Baltz; Scott Marlowe; Greg Mullavey; **D:** Lee Grant; **W:** Merry M. Helm; **C:** Doug Milsome; **M:** Mark Snow. **TV**

A Fond Kiss ✓✓ **2004 (R)** A modern-day Scottish "Romeo & Juliet," with star-crossed mediocrity between a Pakistani DJ and a Catholic music teacher. The culture-clash throws both families into panic (you know the story). Another notch in a series of socially-adept films from director Ken Loach and writer Paul Laverty. This time around they bring a little less humor and a little more drama, albeit stilted, which, along with weak performances and nearly unintelligible accents may turn off a majority of Western audiences. **104m/C; VHS, DVD.** Eva Birthistle; Atta Yaqub; Ahmad Riaz; Shabana Bakhsh; Shamshad Akhtar; Ghizala Avan; Pasha Bocarie; Gerard Kelly; **D:** Ken Loach; **C:** Barry Ackroyd; **M:** George Fenton.

Food, Inc. ✓ 1/2 **2008 (PG)** Despite the rating, this muckraking expose on the food industry isn't something for younger children to see and will probably be of limited interest to most adults. It covers familiar territory—basically stating that almost everything we buy and eat is bad for us because the food industry is a big agri-business with big government subsidies and is more interested in volume and profit than in consumer health. Nor does it reasonably address the fact that most consumers are unable to find or afford so-called organic food easily or cheaply and it makes fast food a convenient villain (which we have seen before). **94m/C; Blu-Ray, On Demand.** **D:** Robert Kenner; **C:** Richard Pearce; **M:** Mark Adler.

Food of Love ✓✓ **2002** Melodramatic gay romance set in the world of classical music. 18-year-old piano student Paul Porterfield (Bishop) is hired as a page turner for a concert given by his idol, middle-aged pianist Richard Kennington (Rhys). While traveling in Barcelona with his clinging mother Pamela (Stevenson), Paul re-meets Richard and they have a fling, which means more to Paul than to Richard whose longtime lover is his manager Joseph (Corduner). At school in New York, Paul happens to meet Joseph (lots of coincidences here) and Pamela finally realizes her son is gay. Based on the novel "The Page Turner" by David Leavitt. Spanish director Pons's English-language debut feels abrupt and Paul is an unsympathetic character. **112m/C; VHS, DVD.** *SP GE* Kevin Bishop; Paul Rhys; Juliet Stevenson; Allan Corduner; Geraldine McEwan; **D:** Ventura Pons; **W:** Ventura Pons; **C:** Mario Montero; **M:** Carles Cases.

Food of the Gods WOOF! **1976 (PG)** On a secluded island giant rats, chickens, and other creatures crave human flesh, blood, bones, etc. This cheap, updated version of the H. G. Wells novel suffers from lousy performances and a lack of imagination. **88m/C; VHS, DVD, Blu-Ray.** Marjoe Gortner; Pamela Franklin; Ralph Meeker; Ida Lupino; Jon Cypher; **D:** Bert I. Gordon.

Food of the Gods: Part 2 WOOF! *Gnaw: Food of the Gods 2* **1988 (R)** The killer beasts and animals of the first film (and of H.G. Wells' classic novel) strike again; gigantic rats maim young girls. Easily as bad as the original. **93m/C; VHS, DVD.** Paul Coufos; Lisa Schrage; **D:** Damian Lee; **W:** E. Kim Brewster.

A Fool and His Money ✓✓ 1/2 **1988 (R)** Adman Morris Codman (Penner) decides to market a shady new religion based on greed but, naturally, finds the true road. Bullock is skeptical girlfriend Debby. **84m/C; VHS, DVD.** Jonathan Penner; Sandra Bullock; Gerald Orange; George Plimpton; **D:** Daniel Adams; **W:** Daniel Adams.

Fool for Love ✓✓ **1986 (R)** Explores the mysterious relationship between a modern-day drifter and his long-time lover, who may or may not be his half-sister, as they confront each other in a seedy New Mexico motel. Adapted by Shepard from his play. **108m/C; VHS, DVD.** Sam Shepard; Kim Basinger; Randy Quaid; Harry Dean Stanton; **D:** Robert Altman; **W:** Sam Shepard; **M:** George Burt.

A Fool There Was ✓✓ 1/2 **1914** The rocket that blasted Theda Bara to stardom and launched the vamp film genre. One of the few extant Bara films, it tells the now familiar story of a good man whom crumbles from the heights of moral rectitude thanks to the inescapable influence of an unredeemable vamp. Bette Davis described Bara as "divinely, hysterically, insanely malevolent." Much heavy emoting; subtitled (notoriously) "Kiss Me, My Fool!" Based on Rudyard Kipling's "The Vampire." **70m/B; Silent; VHS, DVD.** Theda Bara; Edward Jose; Runa Hodges; Clifford Bruce; Mabel Frenyear; Victor Benoit; **D:** Frank Powell; **W:** Roy L. McCardell; **C:** George Schneiderman. Natl. Film Reg. '15.

Foolish WOOF! **1999 (R)** Foolish? You bet it is. Eddie Griffin stars as the title character, a struggling comic who rips off old Eddie Murphy routines to a hip-hop beat. He butts heads with his brother Fifty Dollah, played by rapper/sports agent/bad actor Master P, who also wrote and executive produced this clunker. The boom mike falls into the picture so often that you expect Master P to grab it and bust a rhyme at any given moment. Strictly for sucka MCs. **96m/C; VHS, DVD.** Eddie Griffin; Master P; Frank Sivero; Amy Petersen; Jonathan Banks; Andrew Silverstein; Marla Gibbs; Daphne Lynn Duplaix; Sven-Ole Thorsen; Bill Nunn; Bill Duke; **D:** Dave Meyers; **W:** Master P; **C:** Steve Gainer; **M:** Wendy Melvoin; Lisa Coleman.

Foolish Wives ✓✓✓ 1/2 **1922** A remake of Von Stroheim's classic depicting the confused milieu of post-war Europe as reflected through the actions of a bogus count and his seductive, corrupt ways. Comes as close as possible to the original film. **107m/B; Silent; VHS, DVD, Blu-Ray.** Erich von Stroheim; Mae Busch; Maud(e) (Ford) George; Cesare Gravina; Harrison Ford; **D:** Erich von Stroheim; **W:** Erich von Stroheim; **C:** William H. Daniels; **M:** Sigmund Romberg. Natl. Film Reg. '08.

Fools ✓ **1970 (PG)** Two lonely people—he an aging horror film actor and she a young woman estranged from her husband—start a warm romance when they meet in San Francisco. The husband reacts violently. Good cast seems lost. **93m/C; VHS, DVD.** Jason Robards, Jr.; Katharine Ross; Scott Hylands; **D:** Tom Gries.

Fool's Gold ✓ 1/2 **2008 (PG-13)** Lame attempt at a romantic adventure. Feckless, newly-divorced treasure hunter Finn is certain he's found a new clue to the whereabouts of a sunken ship filled with gold and jewels but his ex-wife Tess, who's unwillingly involved, is used to things not working out. But Finn's luck better be changing since he's got a lot of debts to repay, including to his not-so-former backer, hip-hop mogul Big Bunny, who's not as cuddly as his name suggests. **112m/C; DVD, Blu-Ray.** Matthew McConaughey; Kate Hudson; Donald Sutherland; Alexis Dziena; Ewen Bremner; Ray Winstone; Kevin Hart; Malcolm Jamal Warner; Brian Hooks; David Roberts; **D:** Andy Tennant; **W:** Andy Tennant; John Claflin; Daniel Zelman; **C:** Don Burgess; **M:** George Fenton.

Fool's Gold: The Story of the Brink's-Mat Robbery ✓✓ 1/2 **1992** True story focuses on a robbery that nets the thieves a windfall—and the problems that follow. In November of 1983, Mickey McAvoy (Bean) has set up a heist to rob the high-security warehouse of Brink's-Mat at Heathrow airport. The thieves are after gold bullion but what they find in the vaults are 6,800 gold bars, worth roughly eight times more than their intended haul. The police are quickly on to various members of the gang, but just what happened to all that loot? (Most of the bars have never been recovered; the police believe some were smelted down, but many may be buried. McAvoy was sentenced in 1984 to 25 years in prison.) **93m/C; VHS, DVD.** *GB* Sean Bean; Larry Lamb; Trevor Byfield; George Jackos; Brian Croucher; David Cardy; Jeremy Child; Rob Spendlove; **D:** Terry Winsor; **W:** Terry Winsor; Jeff Pope; **C:** Dick Pope; **M:** William Woolf. **TV**

Fools Rush In ✓✓ **1997 (PG-13)** Uptight eastern yuppie Alex Whitman (Perry) meets cute in Vegas with beautiful Latina casino worker Isabel Fuentes (Hayek) and the duo spend the night together. Three months later, Isabel shows up at Alex's New York door to announce her pregnancy and say she's keeping the baby. Movie cliches collide with movie stereotypes when they decide to marry but find the relationship suffers over their vast ethnic and cultural differences. At least the leads are attractive. Perry's real-life dad plays his character's father. **110m/C; VHS, DVD.** Matthew Perry; Salma Hayek; Jon Tenney; Carlos Gomez; Tomas Milian; John Bennett Perry; Jill Clayburgh; Stanley DeSantis; Anne Betancourt; **D:** Andy Tennant; **W:** Katherine Reback; **C:** Robbie Greenberg; **M:** Alan Silvestri.

The Foot Fist Way ✓✓ **2008 (R)** Cringe-worthy, slapdash, and super-cheap comedy about self-deluded Fred Simmons (McBride) who teaches tae kwon do (the title is an English translation) at a strip mall dojo where he belittles and sexually harasses his inexplicably devoted students. A bonehead, Fred's wannabe macho behavior is undermined when his bimbo wife Suzie (Bostic) cheats and then leaves him, causing Fred to fall apart. Besides his domestic woes, Fred is obsessed with meeting his idol, Chuck 'The Truck' Wallace (Best), which naturally turns into a disaster. Under the radar for most audiences, it's a big hit among comedians. **85m/C; DVD.** Danny McBride; Mary Jane Bostic; Ben Best; Spencer Moreno; Carlos Lopez, IV; Jody Hill; **D:** Jody Hill; **W:** Danny McBride; Ben Best; Jody Hill; **C:** Brian Mandle; **M:** Pyramid.

Footlight Parade ✓✓✓ **1933** Broadway producer Cagney is out of work. Sound films have scared off his backers until his idea for staging live musical numbers before the cinema features lures them back. Lots of authentic backstage action precedes three spectacular Busby Berkeley-choreographed numbers that climax the film, including the giant water ballet featuring more than 100 performers. **104m/B; DVD, Blu-Ray.** James Cagney; Joan Blondell; Dick Powell; Ruby Keeler; Guy Kibbee; Ruth Donnelly; **D:** Lloyd Bacon; **C:** George Barnes. Natl. Film Reg. '92.

Footloose ✓✓ 1/2 **1984 (PG)** When a city boy moves to a small Midwestern town, he discovers some disappointing news: rock music and dancing have been forbidden by the local government. Determined to bring some '80s-style life into the town, he sets about changing the rules and eventually enlists the help of the daughter of the man responsible for the law. Rousing music, talented young cast, and plenty of trouble make this an entertaining musical-drama. **107m/C; VHS, DVD, Blu-Ray.** Kevin Bacon; Lori Singer; Christopher Penn; John Lithgow; Dianne Wiest; John Laughlin; Sarah Jessica Parker; **D:** Herbert Ross; **M:** Miles Goodman.

Footloose ✓✓ **2011 (PG-13)** This remake of the Bacon-y 1984 teen flick is remarkably faithful to the original. Boston teen Ren (Wormald) challenges an antiquated dancing ban after moving to a small southern town and falling in love with the preacher's daughter Ariel (Hough). Can he convince Reverend Moore (Quaid) that dancing doesn't make you the devil's hand puppet? Can he teach rhythm-impaired pal Willard (Teller) how to shake it? If you don't know the answers, then you've never danced away your rage and anger in a choreographed warehouse scene. Lovers of the '80s version will be happy to know that four songs and large blocks of dialogue from the original are used in this update. **113m/C; DVD, Blu-Ray.** Kenny Wormald; Julianne Hough; Dennis Quaid; Andie MacDowell; Miles Teller; Patrick Flueger; Ray McKinnon; **D:** Craig Brewer; **W:** Craig Brewer; Dean Pitchford; **C:** Amy Vincent; **M:** Deborah Lurie.

Footnote ✓✓ *Down the Hill; Hearat Shulayim* **2011 (PG)** Despite the PG rating, this Israeli drama about fathers, sons, and back-stabbing academia is intended for adults. Grumpy Professor Eliezer Shkolnik has spent his life in relative obscurity comparing texts of the Talmud and publishing little. His pompous son Uriel, who also teaches at Hebrew University, publishes constantly on broader Talmudic culture, receiving many awards and basking in the attention. The father-son rivalry reaches a crescendo when the winners of a particularly coveted award are announced. Hebrew with subtitles. **103m/C; DVD, Blu-Ray.** *IS* Shlomo Bar-Aba; Lior Ashkenazi; Alma Zack; Aliza Rosen; Daniel Marcovich; Micah Lewensohn; Yuval Scharf; **D:** Joseph Cedar; **W:** Joseph Cedar; **C:** Yaron Scharf; **M:** Amit Poznansky.

Footsteps ✓✓ *Expose* **1998 (R)** Reporter Jason Davis (Chapa) gets a tip that makes him an eyewitness to a judge's murder. Separated from wife Nancy (Alonso), Jason gets involved with photographer Amber (Lombard), who is also connected to D.A. Steve Carlen (Schanley). When Jason turns up evidence that links Amber and Carlen to the murdered judge and he begins to receive threatening messages, Jason can trust only himself to catch the killer. **93m/C; VHS, DVD.** Damian Chapa; Karina Lombard; Tom Schanley; Maria Conchita Alonso; Steven Schub; Sandra Bernhard; Tippi Hedren; **D:** Daphna Edwards; **W:** Daphna Edwards; **C:** David J. Miller; **M:** Alex Wurman. **VIDEO**

Footsteps ✓✓ **2003** Suspense novelist Daisy Lowendahl (Bergen) is still recovering from a nervous breakdown when she decides to face her fear of being alone by spending time at her isolated Long Island beach house. But she's soon disturbed by over-zealous fan Spencer (Hall) and detective Eddie Bruno (Brown) who says Daisy's husband (Murphy) wants him to keep an eye on her. But Daisy just can't shake this feeling that something's wrong. **95m/C; DVD.** Candice Bergen; Bug Hall; Bryan Brown; Michael Murphy; ***D:*** John Badham; ***W:*** Shelley Evans; ***C:*** Ron Stannett; ***M:*** Christopher Franke. **TV**

Footsteps in the Dark ♪♪ 1/2 **1941** Fairly amusing comedy-mystery with investment counselor Flynn doubling as detective. Based on the play "Blondie White" by Ladislaus Fodor, Bernard Merivale, and Jeffrey Dell. **96m/B; VHS, DVD.** Errol Flynn; Brenda Marshall; Ralph Bellamy; Alan Hale; Lee Patrick; Allen Jenkins; Lucile Watson; William Frawley; Roscoe Karns; Grant Mitchell; Maris Wrixon; Noel Madison; Jack La Rue; Turhan Bey; ***D:*** Lloyd Bacon; Hugh MacMullen; ***W:*** Lester Cole; John Wexley.

Footsteps in the Fog ♪♪ 1/2 **1955** Victorian-era melodrama/thriller. London maid Lily Watkins (Simmons) knows Stephen Lowry (Granger) has murdered his wealthy ailing wife. She turns this knowledge to her advantage but takes her scheming too far since Stephen decides to get away from Lily's blackmail by violent means. **90m/C; DVD, Blu-Ray.** *GB* Stewart Granger; Jean Simmons; Bill Travers; Finlay Currie; Ronald Squire; Belinda Lee; William Hartnell; ***D:*** Arthur Lubin; ***W:*** Lenore Coffee; Dorothy Davenport Reid; Arthur Pierson; ***C:*** Christopher Challis; ***M:*** Benjamin Frankel.

For a Few Dollars More ♪♪ 1/2 **1965 (PG)** The Man With No Name returns as a bounty hunter who teams up with a gunslinger/rival to track down the sadistic leader of a gang of bandits. Violent. Sequel to "A Fistful of Dollars" (1964) and followed by "The Good, The Bad, and The Ugly." **127m/C; VHS, DVD, Blu-Ray.** *IT* Clint Eastwood; Lee Van Cleef; Klaus Kinski; Gian Marie Volonte; ***D:*** Sergio Leone; ***W:*** Sergio Leone; Luciano Vincenzoni; ***C:*** Massimo Dallamano; ***M:*** Ennio Morricone.

For a Good Time, Call... ♪♪ 1/2 **2012 (R)** A raunchy, female-centric comedy about two roommates who were once enemies but form a unique friendship as workers at a phone sex company. Funny and sweet, director Travis' film has a heartfelt approach to a potentially gross-out concept that works for the most part. It still amounts to little more than an extended high-quality sitcom but the engaging cast, including a great turn by lead Graynor, and a clever script make for a call that connects with the funny bone more often than not. **86m/C; DVD, Blu-Ray.** Lauren Anne Miller; Ari Graynor; Justin Long; James Wolk; Mark Webber; Don McManus; Mimi Rogers; Nia Vardalos; ***D:*** Jamie Travis; ***W:*** Lauren Anne Miller; Katie Anne Naylon; ***C:*** James Laxton; ***M:*** John Swihart.

For a Lost Soldier ♪♪ *Voor een Verloren Soldaat* **1993** Middle-aged Dutch choreorapher Jeroen (Krabbe), working on a piece about the Allied liberation, recalls his relationship with a Canadian soldier more than 40 years before. During WWII, the 13-year-old Jeroen (Smit) is sent from Amsterdam to live in the country with a foster family. With the first twinges of puberty and sexuality he longs for a special friend, whom he finds in Walt (Kelley), a young gay Canadian soldier who is part of the Allied liberation forces. Very provocative subject, delicately handled, without any implication of child abuse. In English and Dutch with subtitles. **92m/C; VHS, DVD.** *NL* Marten Smit; Andrew Kelley; Jeroen Krabbe; Feark Smink; Elsje de Wijn; Derk-Jan Kroon; ***D:*** Roeland Kerbosch; ***W:*** Roeland Kerbosch; ***C:*** Nils Post; ***M:*** Joop Stokkermans.

For Better or Worse ♪♪ **1995 (PG-13)** Pathetic loser Michael Makeshift (Alexander, also making his directorial debut) falls in love with his new sister-in-law Valerie (Davidovich) even as he gets entangled in his brother Reggie's (Woods) business scams. **95m/C; VHS, Streaming.** Jason Alexander; Lolita Davidovich; James Woods; Joe Mantegna; Jay Mohr; Bea Arthur; Robert Costanzo; John Amos; Eda Reiss Merin; ***Cameo(s):*** Rob Reiner; Rip Torn; ***D:*** Jason Alexander; ***W:*** Jeff Nathanson; ***C:*** Wayne Keenan; ***M:*** Miles Goodman. **CABLE**

For Colored Girls ♪♪ **2010 (R)** Perry's divisive narrative version of Ntozake Shange's Obie Award-winning 1975 play "For Colored Girls Who Have Considered Suicide/When the Rainbow Is Enuf." Each woman represents a character in a collection of poems depicting black women in society. Perry connects them through the same Harlem apartment building as they suffer through various emotional and physical abuses as well as understanding and empowerment. **134m/C; DVD.** Janet Jackson; Loretta Devine; Kimberly Elise; Thandie Newton; Anika Noni Rose; Tessa Thompson; Kerry Washington; Whoopi Goldberg; Phylicia Rashad; Macy Gray; Michael Ealy; Omari Hardwick; ***D:*** Tyler Perry; ***W:*** Tyler Perry; Frederique Gruyer; ***C:*** Alexander Grusynski; ***M:*** Aaron Zigman.

For Ever Mozart ♪♪ **1996** Godard's film puzzle makes references to literature, music, and cinema itself without making any particular sense. Veteran film director Vicky Vitalis (Messica) agrees to help his daughter Camille (Assas) stage a comedic play by Alfred de Musset in Sarajevo, in order to cheer up its war-tired residents. This doesn't go well, but the director has already abandoned the project to return to his latest film idea, which also turns out to be a disaster. French with subtitles. **85m/C; VHS, DVD, Blu-Ray.** *FR SI* Vicky Messica; Madeleine Assas; Frederic Pierrot; Ghalia Lacroix; ***D:*** Jean-Luc Godard; ***W:*** Jean-Luc Godard; ***C:*** Christophe Pollock.

For Greater Glory ♪ 1/2 **2012 (R)** Well-intentioned but overlong and plodding drama about the 1926-29 civil war in Mexico that pitted the government and its forced secular policies against opposition rebels known as the Cristeros. They are led by former military hero Enrique Gorotieta Velarde (Garcia) whose own religious journey leads him from agnosticism to Catholicism. Wright's directorial debut has too many speeches, too much jumping between characters, and a few battles to liven up the repetitious proceedings. English and Spanish with subtitles. **145m/C; DVD, Blu-Ray; Closed Captioned.** Andy Garcia; Oscar Isaac; Ruben Blades; Peter O'Toole; Bruce Greenwood; Eva Longoria; Nestor Carbonell; Bruce McGill; ***D:*** Dean Wright; ***W:*** Michael Love; ***C:*** Eduardo Martinez Solares; ***M:*** James Horner.

For Heaven's Sake ♪ 1/2 **1950** Odd, dated comedy. The Boltons are a New York theatrical couple more interested in their careers than babies, which upsets angel Charles (Webb) who needs to get a couple of heavenly souls born. He comes to Earth, posing as a wealthy Texan, with the intention of persuading them to expand their family. Only Charles gets a little too interested in enjoying some earthly delights. **87m/B; DVD.** Clifton Webb; Joan Bennett; Robert Cummings; Edmund Gwenn; Joan Blondell; Tommy Rettig; Gigi Perreau; ***D:*** George Seaton; ***W:*** George Seaton; ***C:*** Lloyd Ahern; ***M:*** Alfred Newman.

For Hire ♪♪ 1/2 **1998** Suffering from cancer and with a pregnant wife, Chicago cabbie Mitch Lawrence (Lowe) is desperate for money. So, he agrees to kill an associate of famous writer Louis Webber (Mantegna) for $50,000. When the job is done, Mitch learns just why he was chosen to do the deed. **96m/C; VHS, DVD.** Rob Lowe; Joe Mantegna; Dominic Philie; Bronwen Black; ***D:*** Jean Pellerin; ***M:*** Alan Reeves.

For Keeps ♪ 1/2 **1988 (PG-13)** Two high school sweethearts on the verge of graduating get married after the girl becomes pregnant, and suffer all the trials of teenage parenthood. Tends toward the unrealistic and trite. **98m/C; VHS, DVD.** Molly Ringwald; Randall Batinkoff; Kenneth Mars; ***D:*** John G. Avildsen; ***W:*** Tim Kazurinsky; Denise DeClue; ***M:*** Bill Conti.

For Love of Ivy ♪♪ **1968 (PG)** Poitier is a trucking executive who has a gambling operation on the side. Ivy is the Black maid of a rich white family who is about to leave her job to look for romance. The two are brought together but the road to true love doesn't run smooth. Based on a story by Poitier. **102m/C; VHS, DVD, Blu-Ray.** Sidney Poitier; Abbey Lincoln; Beau Bridges; Carroll O'Connor; Nan Martin; ***D:*** Daniel Mann; ***M:*** Quincy Jones.

For Love of the Game ♪♪ 1/2 **1999 (PG-13)** The baseball glove has long been gold for Costner. In his third baseball outing, he moderately scores as veteran Detroit Tigers pitcher Billy Chapel, facing a crossroad in his professional and personal life. In 1-2-3 manner, he learns that the team he's played on for 20 years has been sold, the new owners want to trade him, and his longtime girlfriend, Jane (Preston), is dumping him prior to an important game with the Yankees. Magically, he's this close to pitching a perfect game, as the last five years of his life flash before him. Sudsy, predictable romance overshadows the game action, but harder-edged Raimi, with his own love for the game, injects some striking visual flair. Based on the novel by Michael Shaara. **137m/C; VHS, DVD, HD-DVD.** Kevin Costner; Kelly Preston; John C. Reilly; Jena Malone; Brian Cox; J.K. Simmons; Bill E. Rogers; Vin Scully; Carmine D. Giovinazzo; Hugh Ross; Michael (Mike) Papajohn; Steve Lyons; ***D:*** Sam Raimi; ***W:*** Dana Stevens; ***C:*** John Bailey; ***M:*** Basil Poledouris.

For Love or Country: The Arturo Sandoval Story ♪♪ 1/2 **2000 (PG-13)** Biopic of Cuban trumpeter Arturo Sandoval (Garcia) who stays in Cuba for the sake of wife Marianela (Maestro) and their children, all the while chafing under his artistic restrictions. Finally, his wife agrees to defect and during a tour in Athens, Sandoval asks for political asylum. Both Garcia and Maestro have a believable chemistry but also look for Dutton's portrayal of Dizzy Gillespie, who hired Sandoval for his U.N. Orchestra, allowing the musician to travel abroad. **120m/C; VHS, DVD.** Andy Garcia; Mia Maestro; Charles S. Dutton; David Paymer; Gloria Estefan; Tomas Milian; Freddy Rodriguez; Jose Zuniga; Steven Bauer; Fionnula Flanagan; Michael O'Hagan; ***D:*** Joseph Sargent; ***W:*** Timothy J. Sexton; ***C:*** Donald M. Morgan; ***M:*** Arturo Sandoval. **CABLE**

For Love or Money ♪♪ **1963** A super-rich hotel owner wants her lawyer to find her three beautiful daughters. However, she doesn't trust him enough not to meddle in the search. Lavish production and a good cast can't overcome the mediocrity of the script and direction. **108m/C; DVD.** Kirk Douglas; Mitzi Gaynor; Thelma Ritter; William Bendix; Julie Newmar; Gig Young; Leslie Parrish; William Windom; Dick Sargent; ***D:*** Michael Gordon.

For Love or Money ♪♪ 1/2 **1993 (PG)** Struggling hotel concierge with a heart of gold finds himself doing little "favors" for a slimy entrepreneur who holds the key to his dreams—the cash to open an elegant hotel of his own. Romantic comedy is reminiscent of the classic screwball comedies of the '30s and '40s, but lacks the trademark tight writing and impeccable timing. Fox is appealing and likable as the wheeling and dealing concierge, a role undermined by a mediocre script offering too few laughs. **89m/C; VHS, DVD.** Michael J. Fox; Gabrielle Anwar; Isaac Mizrahi; Anthony (Corlan) Higgins; Michael Tucker; Bobby Short; Dan Hedaya; Bob Balaban; Udo Kier; Patrick Breen; Paula Laurence; ***D:*** Barry Sonnenfeld; ***W:*** Mark Rosenthal; Larry Konner; ***M:*** Bruce Broughton.

For Love or Money ♪♪ *The Revenger: An Unromantic Comedy* **2019** Since they were kids, Mark (Kazinsky) has had a crush on Connie (Barks). Though they have become engaged as adults, he learns that she is only interested because he is expected to come into money that she plans to share with her true love Johnny (Speleers). With help of best friend Tim (Way) and Connie's ex-friend Kendra (Hurd-Wood), Mark decides to get revenge on Connie. The British comedy lives up to its black, cynical billing as an "unromantic comedy" though the material and acting are relatively run-of-the-mill. **95m/C; DVD, Blu-Ray.** Robert Kazinsky; Samantha Barks; Rachel Hurd-Wood; Ed Speleers; Tony Way; ***D:*** Mark Murphy; ***W:*** Mark Murphy; ***C:*** Joan Bordera; ***M:*** Simone Vallecorsa.

For Me and My Gal ♪♪ 1/2 **1942** In his film debut, Kelly plays an opportunistic song-and-dance man who lures a young vaudevillian (Garland) away from her current partners. WWI interrupts both their career and romance, but you can count on them being reunited. Loaded with vintage tunes. **104m/B; VHS, DVD.** Gene Kelly; Judy Garland; George Murphy; Martha Eggerth; Ben Blue; Richard Quine; Keenan Wynn; Stephen McNally; ***D:*** Busby Berkeley; ***M:*** George Bassman.

For No Good Reason ♪♪ 1/2 **2013 (R)** If you don't know the name Ralph Steadman, you probably know what the deep recesses of his mind look like. Steadman is the famed illustrator, best known for his wild, "gonzo" drawings that accompanied the works of Hunter S. Thompson, most notably Thompson's magnum opus "Fear and Loathing in Las Vegas." And this good-natured documentary attempts to give the artist his pop culture due. Steadman's life story is definitely interesting, but the segments where movie star and Thompson's old pal Depp visits the illustrator dominate the film far more than they should. **89m/C; DVD, Blu-Ray.** Ralph Steadman; Johnny Depp; Hunter S. Thompson; ***D:*** Charlie Paul; ***C:*** Charlie Paul; ***M:*** Sacha Skarbek; Ed Harcourt.

For One More Day ♪ 1/2 *Oprah Winfrey Presents: Mitch Albom's For One More Day* **2007** As the sap rises. Chick Benetto (Imperioli) is a washed-up baseball player turned alcoholic who's made such a mess of his life that he's suicidal. Suddenly, Chick's dead mom Posey (Burstyn) shows up and leads Chick on a trip down memory lane to show him that he can still turn his life around. A weepie family drama adapted from Albom's novel. **92m/C; DVD.** Michael Imperioli; Ellen Burstyn; Samantha Mathis; Alice Drummond; Vadim Imperioli; Scott Cohen; Emily Wickersham; ***D:*** Lloyd Kramer; ***W:*** Mitch Albom; ***C:*** Tami Reiker; ***M:*** Lennie Niehaus. **TV**

For One Night ♪♪ 1/2 **2006** Based on a true story. African-American teenager Brianna (Raven-Symone) decides to protest her hometown's tradition of two racially separate senior proms after her suggestion that the proms finally be combined brings out the community's simmering prejudices. She's aided by New Orleans-based reporter Desiree Howard (Tyler) who grew up in the town and went through the same situation. **90m/C; DVD.** Raven; Aisha Tyler; Jason Lewis; Sam Jones, III; Gary Grubbs; Harold Sylvester; William Ragsdale; ***D:*** Ernest R. Dickerson; ***W:*** Denitria Harris-Lawrence; ***C:*** Phil Oetiker; ***M:*** Patrice Rushen. **CABLE**

For Pete's Sake ♪♪ *July Pork Bellies* **1974 (PG)** Topsy-turvy comedy about a woman whose efforts to get together enough money to put her husband through school involve her with loan sharks, a madame, and even cattle rustling in NYC. Not one of Streisand's best. **90m/C; VHS, DVD.** Barbra Streisand; Michael Sarrazin; Estelle Parsons; William Redfield; Molly Picon; ***D:*** Peter Yates; ***W:*** Stanley Shapiro; Maurice Richlin; ***C:*** Laszlo Kovacs; ***M:*** Artie Butler.

For Real ♪♪ 1/2 **2002 (PG-13)** Mac (Reid) is a wealthy, workaholic middle-aged black record promotor, living in the suburbs of Richmond, Virigina, and looked after by his housekeeper Hardy (Lepart). When Hardy's inner-city, 18-year-old niece CeCe (Curry) gets into serious trouble, Hardy and Mac ask for leniency from the judge and Mac is expected to keep CeCe on the straight and narrow. But there's a generation clash since CeCe thinks Mac is a sellout and Mac thinks CeCe is a punk with a fatalistic attitude. But CeCe's opportunities may be threatened by her own insecurities and her narrow notions of what being "real" mean, while Mac has to learn to loosen up. **95m/C; VHS, DVD.** Tim Reid; Tamara Curry; Kweli Leapart; Eugene Long; Susan Fales-Hill; ***D:*** Tim Reid; ***W:*** Tim Reid; Shirley Pierce. **VIDEO**

For Richer, for Poorer ♪ 1/2 *Father, Son and the Mistress* **1992 (PG)** A very rich, successful businessman notices his son is happy just to sit back and let dad earn all the dough while he waits for his share. In order to teach his son a lesson, Dad decides to give all his money away. But the plan backfires when both realize that earning a second fortune may not be as easy as they assumed. Below average cable fare. **90m/C; VHS, DVD.** Jack Lemmon; Talia Shire; Joanna Gleason; Jonathan Silverman; Madeline Kahn; George Wyner; ***D:*** Jay Sandrich; ***W:*** Stan Daniels. **CABLE**

For Richer or Poorer ♪ **1997 (PG-13)** Definitely poorer. Don't pity the Amish because they can't defend themselves against movies like this—envy them because they don't have to see it. Shallow New York real-estate hustler Brad (Allen) is supposed to be divorcing socialite wife Caroline (Alley). Their inept accountant (Knight), however, has cooked the books, causing them to head for the Pennsylvania hills. They hide out with a community of Amish people, rediscovering their love along with a bunch of manure jokes. Proves once again the inherent unfunniness of butter churns and barn raisings. **122m/C; VHS, DVD, Blu-Ray.** Tim Allen; Kirstie Alley; Wayne Knight; Larry Miller; Jay O. Sanders; Michael Lerner; Miguel A. Nunez, Jr.; Megan Cavanagh; John Pyper-Ferguson; June Claman; Katie Moore; ***D:*** Bryan Spicer; ***W:*** Jana Howington; Steve Lukanic; ***C:*** Buzz Feitshans, IV; ***M:*** Randy Edelman.

For Roseanna 🦴🦴 1/2 *Roseanna's Grave* **1996 (PG-13)** Romantic comedy (despite the subject matter) about Marcello (Reno), the owner of a trattoria in an Italian village and his ailing wife Cecilia (Ruehl), whose dream is to be buried next to their daughter in one of the three remaining plots in their ancient local cemetery. Marcello goes to great lengths to ensure the health of the town's more at-risk citizens to save his wife's spot. Pleasant enough comedy boasts a fine job by an excellent cast, and the Italian scenery is beautiful. Overlooked at the time of its theatrical release, but worth a look for the sentimentally inclined. **99m/C; VHS, DVD.** Jean Reno; Mercedes Ruehl; Polly Walker; Mark Frankel; Trevor Peacock; Fay Ripley; Giuseppe Cederna; Luigi Diberti; Renato Scarpa; George Rossi; Roberto Della Casa; Romano Ghini; ***D:*** Paul Weiland; ***W:*** Saul Turteltaub; ***C:*** Henry Braham; ***M:*** Trevor Jones.

For Sale 🦴🦴 *A Vendre* **1998** After France (Kiberlain) leaves her groom-to-be at the altar, he hires private detective Luigi (Castellito) to track her down and bring her back. Luigi discovers France has left a string of lovers in her wake and that she has been charging them for her favors. The more he learns, the more obsessed he becomes with a woman he has yet to meet in the flesh. French with subtitles. **116m/C; VHS, DVD.** *FR* Sandrine Kiberlain; Sergio Castellitto; Jean-Francois Stevenin; Chiara Mastroianni; Aurore Clement; Samuel Le Bihan; ***D:*** Laetitia Masson; ***W:*** Laetitia Masson; ***C:*** Antoine Hebale; ***M:*** Siegfried.

For Sale By Owner 🦴 1/2 *13Teen* **2005 (R)** Slow-paced, low-budget indie thriller. Emeryville, Texas has been targeted by a serial killer who carves the number 13 into the victim's chest. One stormy night, Sera (who's home alone) allows both real estate agent Andrew and home security tech John into the house though she's expecting neither man. Then, Sera starts getting paranoid about being trapped with a killer. **90m/C; DVD.** Amanda Brown; John Lansch; Marc Hustvedt; ***D:*** Pritesh Chheda; ***W:*** Pritesh Chheda; ***C:*** J.P Lips; ***M:*** Ari Koinuma.

For Sale by Owner 🦴 1/2 **2009 (PG-13)** Preservation architect Will Custis (Cooper) undertakes the restoration of a colonial-era house near Chesapeake Bay and may finally discover the fate of British colonists who vanished from a nearby settlement. Of course finding this out may be a big mistake. **94m/C; DVD.** Scott Cooper; Rachel Nichols; Skeet Ulrich; Kris Kristofferson; Tom Skerritt; Joanna Cassidy; Frankie Faison; ***D:*** Robert Wilson; ***W:*** Scott Cooper; ***C:*** Bill Roe; ***M:*** Joseph Conlan. **VIDEO**

For Sama 🦴🦴🦴 **2019** A documentary look at the conflict in Syria through the eyes of rebel Waad al-Kateab. In 2012, as protests increased against the dictatorship of Bashar al-Assad as part of the Arab Spring uprising, al-Kateab was a business student at Aleppo University. She began documenting events with her cellphone. As the situation grew more complex and violent, al-Kateab stayed in Syria to fight her country while continuing to film what occurred around her. An intimate, unflinching take on events co-directed by al-Kateab and Edward Watts, it serves as a scrapbook of everyday tragedies and a confessional journal created for al-Kateab's infant daughter Sama. Arabic with subtitles. **100m/C; DVD.** Waad Al-Khateab; ***D:*** Waad Al-Khateab; Edward Watts; ***C:*** Waad Al-Khateab; ***M:*** Nainita Desai. British Acad. '19: Feature Doc.

For the Boys 🦴🦴 **1991 (R)** Midler stars as Dixie Leonard, a gutsy singer-comedian who hooks up with Eddie Sparks (Caan) to become one of America's favorite USO singing, dancing, and comedy teams. The movie spans 50 years and three wars—including Korea and Vietnam—and raises such issues as the blacklist and the role of politics in showbiz. Glitzy Hollywood entertainment falters despite Midler's strong performance. **120m/C; VHS, DVD, Blu-Ray.** Bette Midler; James Caan; George Segal; Patrick O'Neal; Christopher Rydell; Arye Gross; Norman Fell; Rosemary Murphy; Dori Brenner; Bud Yorkin; Jack Sheldon; Melissa Manchester; Brandon Call; Arliss Howard; ***D:*** Mark Rydell; ***W:*** Marshall Brickman; Neal Jimenez; Lindy Laub; ***C:*** Stephen Goldblatt; ***M:*** Dave Grusin. Golden Globes '92: Actress--Mus./Comedy (Midler).

For the Love of Benji 🦴🦴 **1977 (G)** In this second "Benji" film, the adorable little dog accompanies his human family on a Greek vacation. He is kidnapped to be used as a messenger for a secret code, but escapes, to have a series of comic adventures in this entertaining family fare. **85m/C; VHS, DVD, Blu-Ray.** Benji; Patsy Garrett; Cynthia Smith; Allen Finzat; Ed Nelson; ***D:*** Joe Camp; ***W:*** Joe Camp; ***C:*** Don Reddy; ***M:*** Euel Box.

For the Love of Grace 🦴🦴 **2008** Hallmark Channel romance. How-to author Grace is engaged to constantly traveling businessman Cliff. After Grace is rescued from a fire by widowed firefighter Steve Lockwood, she decides to take some chances with her life and uses the excuse of writing a firehouse cookbook to stay close to Steve. **90m/C; DVD.** Chandra West; Mark Consuelos; Kevin Jubinville; Corbin Bernsen; Ennis Esmer; Cara Pifko; ***D:*** Craig Pryce; ***W:*** Ramona Berckert; Paul Ruehl; ***C:*** Gerald Packer. **CABLE**

For the Love of It 🦴 1/2 **1980** TV stars galore try to hold together this farce about car chases in California, stolen secret documents, and (of course) true love. Outstandingly mediocre. **100m/C; VHS, Streaming.** Deborah Raffin; Jeff Conaway; Tom Bosley; Norman Fell; Don Rickles; Henry Gibson; Noriyuki "Pat" Morita; William (Bill) Christopher; Lawrence-Hilton Jacobs; Adrian Zmed; Barbi Benton; Adam West; ***D:*** Hal Kanter. **TV**

For the Love of Mary 🦴🦴 1/2 **1948** Durbin retired after this fluff romantic comedy (with some musical numbers) in which she played White House switchboard operator Mary Peppertree. Mary has three potential suitors and juggling her romances causes job-related problems. Includes a second ending and song, which runs an additional eight minutes. **91m/B; VHS, DVD.** Deanna Durbin; Edmond O'Brien; Don Taylor; Jeffrey Lynn; Harry Davenport; Ray Collins; Hugo Haas; ***D:*** Fred de Cordova; ***W:*** Oscar Brodney; ***C:*** William H. Daniels.

For the Moment 🦴🦴 1/2 **1994 (PG-13)** Aussie aviator Lachlan (Crowe) has joined the British Commonwealth Training Plan in 1942, a crash course for fighter pilots that drew men from several countries to bases across Canada. Stationed with best buddy Johnny (Outerbridge) in Manitoba, Lachlan falls for the married Lill (Hirt), sister of Johnny's honey Kate (McMillan), whose husband is away fighting. The emotional stakes are high for all concerned since they know the fliers will soon be sent off to combat. Old-fashioned (and sometimes slow-moving) romance with excellent performances and some gorgeous scenery. **120m/C; VHS, DVD.** *CA* Russell Crowe; Christianne Hirt; Peter Outerbridge; Sara McMillan; Wanda Cannon; Scott Kraft; ***D:*** Aaron Kim Johnston; ***W:*** Aaron Kim Johnston; ***C:*** Ian Elkin; ***M:*** Victor Davies.

For Whom the Bell Tolls 🦴🦴🦴 1/2 **1943** Hemingway novel, gorgeously translated to the big screen, features a star-crossed romantic tale of derring-do. American schoolteacher Robert Jordan (Cooper) decides to join the Spanish Civil War and fight the fascists. He's ordered to rendezvous with peasant guerillas, to aid in blowing up a bridge, and in the rebel camp Jordan meets the beautiful Maria (Bergman). Lots of heroics (and some romance under the stars). Both leads were personally selected by the author. Originally released at 170 minutes. **130m/C; VHS, DVD, Blu-Ray.** Gary Cooper; Ingrid Bergman; Akim Tamiroff; Katina Paxinou; Arturo de Cordova; Vladimir Sokoloff; Mikhail Rasumny; Fortunio Bonanova; Victor Varconi; Joseph Calleia; Alexander Granach; Yakima Canutt; George Coulouris; Yvonne De Carlo; Martin Garralaga; Soledad Jiminez; Duncan Renaldo; Tito Renaldo; Pedro de Cordoba; Frank Puglia; John (Jack) Mylong; Eric Feldary; Lilo Yarson; Leo Bugakov; Antonio Molina; ***D:*** Sam Wood; ***W:*** Dudley Nichols; ***C:*** Ray Rennahan; ***M:*** Victor Young. Oscars '43: Support. Actress (Paxinou).

For You I Die 🦴🦴 **1947** Young convict Johnny Coulter (Langton) is forced to take part in a prison break by inmate Matt Gruber (Harvey). Gruber tells Johnny to hide out at a secluded tourist camp and contact Gruber's gal Hope (Novak). Johnny does, but discovers Hope wants nothing more to do with the gangster. Johnny and Hope fall for each other but they're expecting Gruber to show and the law is still hunting for the fugitives. **75m/B; DVD.** Paul Langton; Cathy Downs; Don Harvey; Marian Kerby; Mischa Auer; Rory Mallinson; ***D:*** John Reinhardt; ***W:*** Robert Presnell, Sr.; ***C:*** William Clothier; ***M:*** Paul Sawtell.

For Your Consideration 🦴🦴 1/2 **2006 (PG-13)** Writing team Guest and Levy drop their patented "mockumentary" format, but not their sly satire in this send-up of Hollywood's awards season. Marilyn Hack (O'Hara) is a fading actress stuck in a bad low-budget movie until an Internet rumor deems her performance Oscar-worthy. As the buzz grows, she and her co-stars (Shearer, Posey) begin campaigning for nominations and the studio head (Gervais) becomes interested. Levy and Guest get the most out of their ensemble cast (including themselves), especially O'Hara. Fred Willard and Jane Lynch are a highlight as clueless entertainment show hosts. **86m/C; DVD.** Catherine O'Hara; Harry Shearer; Parker Posey; John Michael Higgins; Christopher Moynihan; Jennifer Coolidge; Fred Willard; Jane Lynch; Ricky Gervais; Bob Balaban; Michael McKean; Ed Begley, Jr.; Jim Piddock; Rachael Harris; Eugene Levy; Carrie Aizley; Christopher Guest; ***D:*** Christopher Guest; ***W:*** Eugene Levy; Christopher Guest; ***C:*** Roberto Schaefer; ***M:*** C.J. Vanston.

For Your Eyes Only 🦴🦴🦴 **1981 (PG)** In this James Bond adventure, 007 must keep the Soviets from getting hold of a valuable instrument aboard a sunken British spy ship. Sheds the gadgetry of its more recent predecessors in the series in favor of some spectacular stunt work and the usual beautiful girl and exotic locale. Glen's first outing as director, though he handled second units on previous Bond films. Sheena Easton sang the hit title tune. **136m/C; VHS, DVD, Blu-Ray.** *GB* Roger Moore; Carole Bouquet; Topol; Lynn-Holly Johnson; Julian Glover; Cassandra Harris; Jill Bennett; Michael Gothard; John Wyman; Jack Hedley; Lois Maxwell; Desmond Llewelyn; Geoffrey Keen; Walter Gotell; Charles Dance; ***D:*** John Glen; ***W:*** Michael G. Wilson; ***C:*** Alan Hume; ***M:*** Bill Conti.

Forbidden 🦴 1/2 **1932** Weepie, drawn-out melodrama even Stanwyck can't save. Lulu (Stanwyck) has an affair with ambitious district attorney Bob Grover (Menjou) who eventually reveals he's married. Lulu tries kicking him to the curb but she's pregnant and, later, Bob adopts their daughter. Lulu has gone to work for scandal-mongering newspaper editor Al Holland (Bellamy) and marries him while Bob gets elected governor. When Al learns of Lulu and Bob's romantic past, he's ready to expose everything in print. It's never a good idea to threaten any Stanwyck character. **87m/B; DVD.** Barbara Stanwyck; Adolphe Menjou; Ralph Bellamy; Dorothy Peterson; ***D:*** Frank Capra; ***W:*** Jo Swerling; ***C:*** Joseph Walker.

The Forbidden City 🦴🦴 **1918** San San is a young Chinese maiden who has the misfortune to fall in love with a Western diplomat. After he is sent away on business San San keeps secret the fact she has born her lover a child but her actions are unforgiven by her father, a deposed mandarin. **72m/B; Silent; VHS, DVD.** Norma Talmadge; Thomas Meighan; ***D:*** Sidney Franklin.

The Forbidden Dance **WOOF!** **1990 (PG-13)** The first of several quickies released in 1990 applying hackneyed plots to the short-lived Lambada dance craze. The nonsensible plot has a Brazilian princess coming to the U.S. in order to stop further destruction of the rain forest. Instead, she winds up falling for a guy, teaching him to Lambada, and going on TV for a dance contest. Features an appearance by Kid Creole and the Coconuts. **90m/C; VHS, DVD.** Laura Elena Harring; Jeff James; Sid Haig; Richard Lynch; ***D:*** Greydon Clark.

Forbidden Games 🦴🦴🦴🦴 *Les Jeux Interdits* **1952** Famous anti-war drama about two French children play-acting the dramas of war amid the carnage of WWII. Young refugee Fossey sees her parents and dog killed. She meets a slightly older boy whose family takes the girl in. The children decide to bury the animals they have seen killed in the same way that people are buried—even stealing crosses from the cemetery to use over the animal graves. Eventually they are discovered and Fossey is again separated from her newfound home. Acclaimed; available in both dubbed and English-subtitled versions. **90m/B; VHS, DVD.** *FR* Brigitte Fossey; Georges Poujouly; Amedee; Louis Herbert; Suzanne Courtal; Jacques Marin; Laurence Badie; Andre Wasley; Louis Sainteve; ***D:*** Rene Clement; ***W:*** Rene Clement; Jean Aurenche; Pierre Bost; Francois Boyer; ***C:*** Robert Juillard; ***M:*** Narciso Yepes. Oscars '52: Foreign Film; British Acad. '53: Film; N.Y. Film Critics '52: Foreign Film; Venice Film Fest. '52: Film.

Forbidden Games 🦴 **1995 (R)** When a modeling agency head is murdered, the investigator finds there are more than enough suspects to go around. **89m/C; VHS, DVD.** Jeff Griggs; Gail Harris; Amy Weber; Lesli Kay; Jefferson Wagner; ***D:*** Edward Holzman; ***W:*** Edward Holzman; ***C:*** Harris Done; ***M:*** K. Alexander (Alex) Wilkinson.

The Forbidden Kingdom 🦴🦴 1/2 **2008 (PG-13)** Introduce the kiddies to kung fu action-lite in this mild adventure (that could easily be a PG). Boston teen Jason (Angarano) is magically transported back to ancient China thanks to a golden staff that must be returned to its imprisoned owner, the Monkey King (Li). He's helped by drunken fighter Lu Yan (Chan), orphaned babe Golden Sparrow (Yifei), and a guy known as the Silent Monk (Li again). They're opposed by the Jade Warload (Chou), white-haired witch Ni Chang (Bing Bing Li), and various evil minions. Plays it safe but it's also (surprisingly) the first pairing between martial art stars Chan and Li, so that's a treat. **105m/C; DVD, Blu-Ray.** Michael Angarano; Jackie Chan; Jet Li; Collin Chou; Li Bingbing; Liu Yifei; Morgan Benoit; ***D:*** Rob Minkoff; ***W:*** John Fusco; ***C:*** Peter Pau; ***M:*** David Buckley.

Forbidden Love 🦴 **1982** A man in his early 20s falls in love with a woman twice his age, much to the chagrin of her daughters. **96m/C; VHS, Streaming.** Andrew Stevens; Yvette Mimieux; Dana Elcar; Lisa Lucas; Jerry Houser; Randi Brooks; Lynn Carlin; Hildy Brooks; John Considine; ***D:*** Steven Hilliard Stern; ***M:*** Hagood Hardy. **TV**

Forbidden Planet 🦴🦴🦴 1/2 **1956** In A.D. 2200, a space cruiser visits the planet Altair-4 to uncover the fate of a previous mission of space colonists. They are greeted by Robby the Robot and discover the only survivors of the Earth colony which has been preyed upon by a terrible space monster. A classic science-fiction version of the Shakespearean classic "The Tempest." **98m/C; VHS, DVD, HD-DVD.** Walter Pidgeon; Anne Francis; Leslie Nielsen; Warren Stevens; Jack Kelly; Richard Anderson; Earl Holliman; George D. Wallace; Robert Dix; Frankie Darro; ***V:*** Marvin Miller; ***Nar:*** Les Tremayne; ***D:*** Fred M. Wilcox; ***W:*** Cyril Hume; ***C:*** George J. Folsey; ***M:*** Bebe Barron; Louis Barron. Natl. Film Reg. '13.

The Forbidden Quest 🦴🦴 **1993** In 1941, a journalist (Ward) tracks down the only survivor of the Hollandia's 1905 expedition to Antarctica, ship's carpenter Sullivan (O'Conor), to find out about the tragic journey. Director Delpeut mixes archival footage of actual turn-of-the-century voyages to reveal the Hollandia's murderous secrets. **75m/C; VHS, DVD.** *NL* Joseph O'Conor; Roy Ward; ***D:*** Peter Delpeut; ***W:*** Peter Delpeut.

Forbidden Relations 🦴🦴 *Visszaesok* **1983 (R)** Based on a true story, this sensual, beautifully shot drama centers on an incestuous couple who insist on defying convention. Though Juli (Monori) and Gyorgy (Szekely) are half-brother and half-sister, they fall in love and become intimately involved. After Juli becomes pregnant, Gyorgy is put in jail because of their relationship. Despite the arrest and related publicity, the couple remains committed to each other. Hungarian with subtitles. **92m/C; DVD.** Lili Monori; Miklos B. Szekely; Mari Torocsik; Gyorgy Banffy; Jozsef Horvath; ***D:*** Zsolt Kezdi-Kovacs; ***W:*** Zsolt Kezdi-Kovacs; ***C:*** Janos Kende.

Forbidden Sins 🦴🦴 **1999 (R)** Defense attorney Maureen Doherty (Tweed) is hired to defend an arrogant multi-millionaire accused of murdering a stripper during kinky sex games. Maureen's search for the truth soon takes her into forbidden territory, in opposition to her ex-husband, the detective assigned to the case. **87m/C; VHS, DVD.** Shannon Tweed; Corbin Timbrook; ***D:*** Robert Angelo; ***W:*** Daryl Haney; Hel Styverson; ***C:*** Michael Goi; ***M:*** Herman Beeftink. **VIDEO**

The Forbidden Street *Britannia Mews; The Affairs of Adelaide* **1949** Victorian lady Adelaide Culver (O'Hara) leaves respectability behind when she marries alcoholic art teacher Henry Lambert (Andrews) and moves to the London slums. Henry dies in an accidental fall, and Adelaide meets his lookalike Gilbert Lauderdale (Andrews again), who helps her out of a crisis. They hope they can make a new life together (and it involves a marionette theatre). **91m/B; DVD.** *UK* Maureen O'Hara; Dana Andrews; Sybil Thorndike; A.E. Matthews; Fay Compton; Wilfrid Hyde-White; ***D:*** Jean Negulesco; ***W:*** Ring Lardner, Jr.; ***C:*** Georges Perinal; ***M:*** Malcolm Arnold.

Forbidden Sun **1989 (R)** An Olympic gymnastics coach and her dozen beautiful students go to Crete to train. When one of them is brutally raped, vengeance is meted out by the girls. **88m/C; VHS, DVD.** Lauren Hutton; Cliff DeYoung; Renee Estevez; ***D:*** Zelda Barron.

Forbidden Trail **1/2 1932** Crooked politico Cash Karger plans to take over the local ranches through nefarious means. He's opposed by easygoing cowhand Tom Devlin. Tom's fallen for newspaper editor Mary Middleton, who's being forced to do Karger's bidding. With Tom interfering, Karger decides to frame him for murder. **68m/B; DVD.** Buck Jones; Barbara Weeks; Wallis (Clarke) Clark; Mary Carr; George Cooper; Albert J. Smith; Frank Rice; Frank LaRue; ***D:*** Lambert Hillyer; ***W:*** Milton Krims; ***C:*** L. William O'Connell.

Forbidden Valley **1/2 1938** Ring Hazzard (Beery) has been raised in a remote New Mexico canyon by his father (Hinds), who years earlier fled a bogus murder charge. Ring meets rancher's daughter, Wilda Lanning (Robinson), when he has to save her from stampeding horses, but his father is killed by a wild bronco so he and Wilda begin to drive a herd of mustangs into town to sell them and begin a life together. Their plan is interrupted by rattle snake bites and a rival, Matt Rogan (Kohler), who attempts to steal Ring's herd. **68m/B; DVD.** Noah Beery, Jr.; Frances Robinson; Fred Kohler, Sr.; Alonzo Price; Samuel S. Hinds; ***D:*** Wyndham Gittens; ***W:*** Stuart Hardy; ***C:*** Elwood "Woody" Bredell.

Forbidden World **WOOF!** *Mutant* **1982 (R)** Lives of a genetic research team become threatened by the very life form they helped to create: a man-eating organism capable of changing its genetic structure as it grows and matures. Corman-produced quickie follow-up to "Galaxy of Terror" is a graphically violent rip-off of "Alien." **82m/C; VHS, DVD, Blu-Ray.** Jesse Vint; Dawn Dunlap; June Chadwick; Linden Chiles; Scott Paulin; Michael Bowen; ***D:*** Allan Holzman; ***W:*** Jim Wynorski; R.J. Robertson; Tim Curnen; ***C:*** Tim Suhrstedt; ***M:*** Susan Justin.

Forbidden Zone **1/2 1980 (R)** A sixth dimension kingdom is ruled by the midget, King Fausto, and inhabited by dancing frogs, bikini-clad footsies, robot boxers, and degraded beings of all kinds. Original music by Oingo Boingo, and directed by founding member Elfman. **75m/B; VHS, DVD, Blu-Ray.** Herve Villechaize; Susan Tyrrell; Viva; Marie-Pascale Elfman; Joe Spinell; Richard Elfman; Danny Elfman; ***D:*** Richard Elfman; ***W:*** Richard Elfman; Matthew Bright; ***C:*** Gregory Sandor; ***M:*** Danny Elfman.

Forbidden Zone: Alien Abduction **1996 (R)** Three babes sharing a sauna also share sexual confidences and discover they've each had an encounter with the same unusual man. Then one of the girls figures out they've had an alien encounter of the very close kind. **90m/C; VHS, DVD.** Darcy Demoss; Pia Reyes; Dumitri Bogmaz; Carmen Lacatus; Alina Chivulescu; Florin Chiriac; Meredyth Holmes; ***D:*** Lucian S. Diamonde; ***W:*** Vernon Lumley; ***C:*** Adolfo Bartoli; ***M:*** Reg Powell.

Force: Five **1981 (R)** Mercenary gathers a group of like-minded action groupies together to rescue the daughter of a powerful man from a religious cult. All action and no brains. **95m/C; VHS, DVD, Blu-Ray.** Joe Lewis; Pam Huntington; Master Bong Soo Han; ***D:*** Robert Clouse; ***W:*** Robert Clouse; ***M:*** William Goldstein.

Force Majeure *Turist* **2014 (R)** A brilliant drama unfolds in a gorgeous ski resort in the French Alps in this internationally acclaimed pic with edges of black comedy scattered throughout. While at lunch on a ski vacation with their two children Tomas (Kuhnke) and Ebba (Kongsli), a controlled avalanche appears to get out of control and threatens to overtake the family on the terrace on which they're eating. Dad gets up and runs, leaving his wife and kids behind. Mom struggles to get over it. A fantastic dissection of how easily family dynamics can be altered forever in the blink of an eye. Swedish with subtitles. **120m/C; DVD, Blu-Ray.** *SW* Johannes Kuhnke; Lisa Loven Kongsli; Vincent Wettergren; Clara Wettergren; ***D:*** Ruben Ostlund; ***W:*** Ruben Ostlund; ***C:*** Frederik Wenzel; ***M:*** Ola Flottum.

Force of Arms **1/2 1951** Romantic war drama. In 1943, Sgt. Joe Peterson (Holden) is on R&R in Naples when he meets and falls in love with WAC Eleanor MacKay (Olson). Returning to duty, Joe fears his new romance had him hesitating during battle, causing lives to be lost. Plagued by guilt, Joe volunteers for the front lines and is listed as MIA but Eleanor is sure Joe is still alive. Holden and Olson previously starred together in 1950's "Sunset Boulevard." **99m/B; DVD.** William Holden; Nancy Olson; Frank Lovejoy; Gene Evans; Dick Wesson; Paul Picerni; ***D:*** Michael Curtiz; ***W:*** Orin Jannings; ***C:*** Ted D. McCord; ***M:*** Max Steiner.

Force of Evil **1949** A cynical attorney who works for a mob boss and for Wall Street tries to save his brother from the gangster's takeover of the numbers operation. The honorable, though criminal, brother refuses the help of the amoral lawyer, and he is finally forced to confront his conscience. Garfield's sizzling performance and the atmospheric photography have made this a film noir classic. **82m/B; VHS, DVD, Blu-Ray.** John Garfield; Thomas Gomez; Marie Windsor; Sheldon Leonard; Roy Roberts; ***D:*** Abraham Polonsky; ***W:*** Abraham Polonsky; ***C:*** George Barnes. Natl. Film Reg. '94.

Force of Execution **2013 (R)** Seagal stars as a bad guy with a code of honor as an old-school mobster beset by trouble in Albuquerque. He's got a rival that's just out of prison and wants control of the city, trouble with a Mexican cartel, an injured former protégé to look after, and something is going on at the diner he owns as well. **99m/C; DVD, Blu-Ray.** Steven Seagal; Ving Rhames; Danny Trejo; Bren Foster; Jenny Gabrielle; ***D:*** Keoni Waxman; ***W:*** Richard Beattie; ***C:*** Nathan Wilson; ***M:*** Michael Richard Plowman. **VIDEO**

Force of Impulse **1960** J.D. schlocker featuring an impressive cast involved with everything from hot rods to robbery to parental problems. **84m/B; VHS, DVD.** J. Carrol Naish; Robert Alda; Tony Anthony; Christina Crawford; Jody McCrea; Lionel Hampton; ***D:*** Saul Swimmer; ***W:*** Richard Bernstein; Francis Swann; ***C:*** Clifford Poland; ***M:*** Joseph Liebman.

Force of One **1979 (PG)** A team of undercover narcotics agents is being eliminated mysteriously, and karate expert Norris saves the day in this sequel to "Good Guys Wear Black." **91m/C; VHS, DVD, UMD.** Chuck Norris; Bill Wallace; Jennifer O'Neill; Clu Gulager; ***D:*** Paul Aaron.

Force 10 from Navarone **1978 (PG)** So-so sequel to Alistair MacLean's "The Guns of Navarone," follows a group of saboteurs whose aim is to blow up a bridge vital to the Nazi's in Yugoslavia. Keep an eye out for Ford, Nero, and Bach. Lots of double-crosses and action sequences, but doesn't quite hang together. **118m/C; VHS, DVD, Blu-Ray.** Robert Shaw; Harrison Ford; Barbara Bach; Edward Fox; Carl Weathers; Richard Kiel; Franco Nero; ***D:*** Guy Hamilton; ***W:*** Robin Chapman; ***C:*** Christopher Challis; ***M:*** Ronald Goodwin.

Forced to Fight **1/2 2011** Retired fighter Shane (Daniels) must return to the world of illegal bloodsports to save his brother from an enraged crime boss (Weller). The results might not be in his favor. **100m/C; DVD, Blu-Ray, Streaming.** *CA* Gary Daniels; Peter Weller; Alexandra Weaver; Arkie Reece; Corbin Thomas; ***D:*** Jonas Quastel; ***W:*** Jonas Quastel; Andrew Bronstein; Patrick Dussault; ***C:*** Radu Lopotaru; ***M:*** Kenton Gilchrist. **VIDEO**

Forced to Kill **1/2 1993 (R)** A repo man is on his way to deliver a Jaguar when he's captured by a bizarre family and forced to fight in an illegal bare-fist tournament run by the local lunatic sheriff. Professional stuntman Eubanks has his work cut out for him in this actioner. **91m/C; VHS, DVD.** Corey Michael Eubanks; Michael Ironside; Rance Howard; Don Swayze; Clint Howard; Brian Avery; Kari Whitman; Mickey Jones; Carl Ciarfalio; Cynthia J. Blessington; Alan Gelfant; ***D:*** Russell Solberg; ***W:*** Corey Michael Eubanks; ***M:*** Martin D. Bolin.

Forced Vengeance **1982 (R)** Vietnam vet pits himself against the underworld in Hong Kong. With Norris in the lead, you can take it for granted there will be plenty of martial arts action. **103m/C; VHS, DVD.** Chuck Norris; Mary Louise Weller; ***D:*** James Fargo; ***M:*** William Goldstein.

Forces of Nature **1999 (PG-13)** Lightweight romantic screwball comedy has straight-laced nice guy Ben (Affleck) trying to get to Savannah in time for his wedding with Tierney. When his plane skids off the runway, he's paired up with free spirit Sarah (Bullock) on an obstacle-filled trip down south. Some fine moments and unusually well done characterization are undone by inconsistency and a lack of chemistry. Enjoyment of the conclusion depends on your opinion of romantic comedy conventions. **104m/C; VHS, DVD.** Sandra Bullock; Ben Affleck; Maura Tierney; Steve Zahn; Blythe Danner; Ronny Cox; Michael Fairman; Janet Carroll; Richard Schiff; Meredith Scott Lynn; George D. Wallace; John Doe; Steve Hytner; David Strickland; Jack Kehler; ***D:*** Bronwen Hughes; ***W:*** Marc Lawrence; ***C:*** Elliot Davis; ***M:*** John Powell.

Ford: The Man & the Machine **1/2 1987** Episodic biography of ruthless auto magnate Henry Ford I from the building of his empire to his personal tragedies. The cast lacks spark and Robertson (Ford) is positively gloomy. The only one appearing to have any fun is Thomas (Ford's mistress). Based on the biography by Robert Lacey. **200m/C; VHS, DVD.** Cliff Robertson; Hope Lange; Heather Thomas; Michael Ironside; Chris Wiggins; R.H. Thomson; ***D:*** Allan Eastman; ***C:*** Thomas Burstyn.

Ford v Ferrari **1/2 2019 (PG-13)** After race car driver Carroll Shelby (Damon) is forced to retire, he turns to car sales and design. He also manages other racers, including hotheaded yet talented Ken Miles (Bale). Shelby is given an unexpected opportunity to manage drivers in Ford cars in the 24-hour long Le Mans race after the Ford team, led by Henry Ford II (Betts), tries and fails to buy Italian manufacturer Ferrari. Based on a true story, the action drama tells its engrossing story in a retro fashion that captures the spirit of the early 1960s while still appealing to modern audiences with its sense of fun. **152m/C; DVD, Blu-Ray.** Matt Damon; Christian Bale; Jon Bernthal; Caitriona Balfe; Josh(ua) Lucas; ***D:*** James Mangold; ***W:*** James Mangold; Jez Butterworth; John-Henry Butterworth; Jason Keller; ***C:*** Phedon Papamichael; ***M:*** Marco Beltrami; Buck Sanders. Oscars '19: Film Editing, Sound FX Editing; British Acad. '19: Film Editing.

Foreign Body **1/2 1986 (PG-13)** An Indian (played by "Passage to India" star, Banerjee) visiting London pretends to be a doctor and finds women flocking to him. Excellent overlooked British comedy. Based on the novel by Roderick Mann. **108m/C; DVD.** *UK* Victor Banerjee; Warren Mitchell; Trevor Howard; Geraldine McEwan; Amanda Donohoe; Denis Quilley; Eve Ferret; Anna Massey; ***D:*** Ronald Neame; ***W:*** Celine La Freniere; ***M:*** Ken Howard.

Foreign Correspondent **1940** A classic Hitchcock tale of espionage and derring-do. A reporter is sent to Europe during WWII to cover a pacifist conference in London, where he becomes romantically involved with the daughter of the group's founder and befriends an elderly diplomat. When the diplomat is kidnapped, the reporter uncovers a Nazi spy-ring headed by his future father-in-law. **120m/B; DVD, Blu-Ray.** Joel McCrea; Laraine Day; Herbert Marshall; George Sanders; Robert Benchley; Albert Bassermann; Edmund Gwenn; Eduardo Ciannelli; Harry Davenport; Martin Kosleck; Charles Halton; ***D:*** Alfred Hitchcock; ***W:*** Robert Benchley; Charles Bennett; Joan Harrison; James Hilton; ***M:*** Alfred Newman.

Foreign Exchange **1/2 2008 (R)** Teen sex comedy about four high schoolers determined to take the easiest classes possible in their senior year so they can devote their time to hosting the school's sexy exchange students. As usual, their plans get derailed and humiliations follow. **85m/C; DVD.** Ryan Pinkston; Vanessa Lengies; Jennifer Coolidge; Curtis Armstrong; Clint Howard; Miles Thompson; Tania Raymonde; Ashley Edner; Randy Wayne; Daniel Booko; ***D:*** Danny Roth; ***W:*** Danny Roth. **VIDEO**

A Foreign Field **1/2 1993** Comedy/drama focuses on several WW2 veterans returning to the Normandy beaches in honor of the 50th anniversary of the invasion. Blustery British Cyril (McKern) and equally demanding Yank Waldo (Randolph) also must deal with their 50-year rivalry over their wartime love, the cheerfully vulgar Angelique (Moreau). Veteran performers get the chance to show their stuff but film descends into pathos. **90m/C; VHS, DVD.** *GB* Leo McKern; John Randolph; Jeanne Moreau; Lauren Bacall; Alec Guinness; Edward Herrmann; Geraldine Chaplin; ***D:*** Charles Sturridge; ***W:*** Roy Clarke; ***M:*** Geoffrey Burgon.

Foreign Land *Terra Estrangeira* **1995** Twenty-one-year-old Paco is an impoverished student living in Sao Paulo who naively agrees to take a suitcase to Lisbon for shady businessman Igor (Melo) and give it to his compatriot, Miguel (Borges). But Paco discovers Miguel has been murdered—leading him to the dead man's girlfriend, unhappy Brazilian exile, Alex (Torres). The two bond while seeking to avoid the newly arrived Igor and Miguel's other treacherous associates. Portuguese with subtitles. **100m/B; VHS, DVD.** *BR PT* Alexandre Borges; Tcheky Karyo; Fernanda Torres; Laura Cardoso; Joao Lagarto; Luis Mello; Fernando Pinto; ***D:*** Walter Salles; ***W:*** Walter Salles; Marcos Bernstein; Daniela Thomas; ***C:*** Walter Carvalho; ***M:*** Jose Miguel Wisnik.

Foreign Student **1/2 1994 (R)** In 1956 Philippe (Hofschneider) is a French exchange student at a tradition-bound Virginia college. At a professor's home he meets part-time housekeeper April (Givens), who wants to practice her schoolbook French (among other things). They begin a romance but, since April is black, there's trouble. Hofschneider is charming though Givens appears too glamorous and self-aware. Dutton and Battle are notable in their small roles as blues musicians Howlin' Wolf and Sonny Boy Williamson. Directorial debut for Sereny. Based on the novel "The Foreign Student" by Philippe Labro. **96m/C; VHS, Streaming.** Marco Hofschneider; Robin Givens; Jack Coleman; Edward Herrmann; Rick Johnson; Charlotte Ross; Charles S. Dutton; Hinton Battle; ***D:*** Eva Sereny; ***W:*** Menno Meyjes; ***C:*** Franco Di Giacomo; ***M:*** Jean-Claude Petit.

The Foreigner **1978** Secret agent who comes to New York City to meet his contact becomes entrapped in a series of mysterious events revolving around the underground club scene. **90m/B; VHS, DVD.** Eric Mitchell; Patti Astor; Deborah Harry; ***D:*** Amos Poe; ***W:*** Amos Poe.

The Foreigner **2003 (R)** Ludicrous would-be actioner stars immovable hulk Seagal as a former spy turned mercenary. His latest job is to carry the black box recorder from a downed plane from France to Germany but the sinister Van Arken (Van Gorkum) has other ideas. **96m/C; VHS, DVD.** Steven Seagal; Harry Van Gorkum; Sherman Augustus; Anna-Louise Plowman; ***D:*** Michael Oblowitz; ***W:*** Darren O. Campbell; ***C:*** Michael Slovis; ***M:*** David Wurst; Eric Wurst. **VIDEO**

The Foreigner **1/2 2017 (R)** Based on Stephen Leather's novel *The Chinaman*, this action-thriller contains the twists and turns requisite of the terror-political genre, and showcases a surprisingly adept dramatic performance by action-hero Chan. After his last remaining family member, a teenage daughter, is killed by a bomb in London's Chinatown, ordinary businessman (Chan) targets an Irish government official (Brosnan) whom he suspects of knowing more than he admits about the terrorists responsible. Chan's stuntwork is still breathtaking, all the more so because it bursts unexpectedly from the shell of a quiet, grieving father. **113m/C; DVD, Blu-Ray.** Jackie Chan; Pierce Brosnan; Ray Fearon; Rory Fleck-Byrne; Stephen Hogan; ***D:*** Martin Campbell; ***W:*** David Marconi; ***C:*** David Tattersall; ***M:*** Cliff Martinez; Jason Markey.

Foreplay WOOF! *The President's Women* **1975** Inane trilogy of comedy segments involving characters with White House connections. Stories are introduced by former President Mostel discussing his downfall in a TV interview. Lame rather than risque, wasting talents of all involved. Each segment was scripted and directed by a different team. **100m/C; VHS, DVD.** Pat Paulsen; Jerry Orbach; Estelle Parsons; Zero Mostel; ***D:*** Bruce Malmuth; John G. Avildsen; ***C:*** Ralf Bode.

Foresaken 1/2 **2016 (R)** A moody western centering on a tense father-son relationship. After leaving behind his career as a gunslinger, John Henry Clayton (K. Sutherland) goes back to hometown of Fowler, Wyoming. His goal is to re-establish a relationship with his estranged father. Reverend Clayton (D. Sutherland) is a pastor in the town and does not approve of his son's life of violence. When John Henry returns, Fowler is full of tension and violence ahead of the railroad reaching the town. To stop the criminal gang attacking ranchers who do not want to sell their land and save the town, John Henry must return to his gunslinging ways and risk further alienating his father. **90m/C; DVD, Blu-Ray, Streaming, Download.** Kiefer Sutherland; Donald Sutherland; Brian Cox; Michael Wincott; Aaron Poole; ***D:*** Jon Cassar; ***W:*** Brad Mirman; ***C:*** Rene Ohashi; ***M:*** Jonathan Goldsmith.

The Forest 1/2 **2016 (PG-13)** Zada's senseless horror-thriller is set in a real place called the Aokigahara Forest, in Japan, where many people have reportedly committed suicide. Using this real tragedy to create a dated ghost story movie, Dormer stars as an American woman who travels there after her sister was last seen going into the forest. Dormer is perfectly fine but the script here is horrendous, and Zada's story falls flat. A documentary about the forest would have been scarier. **93m/C; DVD, Blu-Ray.** Natalie Dormer; Eoin Macken; Stephanie Vogt; Noriko Sakura; Taylor Kinney; ***D:*** Jason Zada; ***W:*** Nick Antosca; Sarah Cornwell; Ben Ketai; ***C:*** Mattias Troelstrup; ***M:*** Bear McCreary.

Forest Warrior **1995 (PG)** Children fight to save the local forests of Tanglewood Mountain from greedy developer Kiser with the help of ghostly mountain man John McKenna (Norris), who was murdered in the same woods a century before. Mild adventure with good ecology theme. **98m/C; VHS, DVD, Blu-Ray, Streaming.** Chuck Norris; Terry Kiser; Max Gail; Roscoe Lee Browne; William Sanderson; ***D:*** Aaron Norris; ***W:*** Ron Swanson; ***C:*** Joao Fernandes.

Forever Amber 1/2 **1947** Seventeenth century rags to riches story features Darnell as the poverty stricken girl who uses sex to gain wealth and status. She makes it to the bed of King Charles II, only to lose the one man she ever really loved (Wilde). The censorship of the 1940s hindered the film's erotic potential. Adapted from the best-selling novel by Kathleen Winsor. **140m/C; DVD, Blu-Ray.** Linda Darnell; Cornel Wilde; Richard Greene; George Sanders; Richard Haydn; Jessica Tandy; Anne Revere; John Russell; Leo G. Carroll; Robert Coote; Margaret Wycherly; Alma Kruger; Edmund Breon; Alan Napier; ***D:*** Otto Preminger; ***W:*** Philip Dunne; Ring Lardner, Jr.; ***C:*** Leon Shamroy; ***M:*** David Raksin.

Forever and a Day **1943** Tremendous salute to British history centers around a London manor originally built by an English admiral during the Napoleonic era and the exploits of succeeding generations. The house even manages to survive the blitz of WWII showing English courage during wartime. Once-in-a-lifetime casting and directing. **104m/B; VHS, DVD.** Brian Aherne; Robert Cummings; Ida Lupino; Charles Laughton; Herbert Marshall; Ray Milland; Anna Neagle; Merle Oberon; Claude Rains; Victor McLaglen; Buster Keaton; Jessie Matthews; Roland Young; Sir C. Aubrey Smith; Edward Everett Horton; Elsa Lanchester; Edmund Gwenn; ***D:*** Rene Clair; Edmund Goulding; Cedric Hardwicke; Frank Lloyd; Victor Saville; Robert Stevenson; Herbert Wilcox; Kent Smith; ***W:*** Charles Bennett; Michael Hogan; Peter Godfrey; Christopher Isherwood; Gene Lockhart; Donald Ogden Stewart; ***C:*** Robert De Grasse; Lee Garmes; Russell Metty; Nicholas Musuraca; ***M:*** Anthony Collins.

Forever Darling **1956** Mixed effort from the reliable comedy duo sees Desi playing a dedicated chemist who neglects his wife while pursuing the next great pesticide. Lucy calls on her guardian angel (Mason) to help her rekindle her marriage. He advises her to go with Desi when he tests his new bug killer, and a series of hilarious, woodsy calamities occur. Lucy and Desi are always fun to watch, but '60s TV sitcom fans will enjoy the fact that Mrs. Howell (Schaefer) and Jane Hathaway (Kulp) appear in the same picture. **91m/C; VHS, DVD.** Lucille Ball; Desi Arnaz, Sr.; James Mason; Louis Calhern; John Emery; John Hoyt; Natalie Schafer; Nancy Kulp; ***D:*** Alexander Hall.

Forever Emmanuelle *Laure* **1975 (R)** Sensual young woman finds love and the ultimate erotic experience in the wilds of the South Pacific in this sequel to the porn-with-production-values "Emmanuelle." **89m/C; VHS, DVD.** *IT FR* Annie Belle; Emmanuelle Arsan; Al Cliver; ***D:*** Emmanuelle Arsan; Ovidio G. Assonitis; ***W:*** Emmanuelle Arsan; ***C:*** Roberto D'Ettorre Piazzoli; ***M:*** Franco Micalizzi.

Forever Evil **1987** The vacationing denizens of a secluded cabin are almost killed off by the cult followers of a mythic god. **107m/C; VHS, DVD.** Red Mitchell; Tracey Huffman; Charles Trotter; Howard Jacobsen; Kent Johnson; ***D:*** Roger Evans; ***W:*** Freeman Williams; ***C:*** Horacio Fernandez; ***M:*** Marianne Pendino.

Forever Female **1953** Bright comedy about show business, egos, and love. Holden is a young playwright whose first play is accepted by stage producer Douglas on the condition that the lead role, featuring a 19-year-old heroine, be rewritten for his ex-wife Rogers. She's an aging leading lady smitten by Holden's charms—as is the ingenue Crowley, who would be perfect for the role as written. Complications and manipulations abound as the play makes its way to production. Adaptation of the Sir James Barrie play "Rosalind." **93m/B; DVD, Blu-Ray.** Ginger Rogers; William Holden; Paul Douglas; Pat(ricia) Crowley; James Gleason; Jesse White; George Reeves; Marjorie Rambeau; King Donovan; Vic Perrin; Marion Ross; ***D:*** Irving Rapper; ***W:*** Julius J. Epstein; Philip G. Epstein.

Forever Love 1/2 **1998** Lizzie Brooks (McEntire) is a wife and mother who has just awakened from a 20-year coma. Her daughter Emma (Stephens) is a grownup, her husband Peter (Matheson) is a stranger, and she discovers her best friend Gail (Armstrong) has taken her place in both her home and Peter's heart. Now Lizzie seeks to find her own place in a totally new world. Based on a true story. **120m/C; VHS, DVD.** Reba McEntire; Tim Matheson; Bess Armstrong; Heather Stephens; Richard Biggs; Scott Foley; ***D:*** Michael Switzer; ***W:*** Joyce Heft Brotman. **TV**

Forever, Lulu *Crazy Streets* **1987 (R)** A down-on-her-luck novelist winds up involved with the mob and a gangster's girlfriend. Completely laughless comedy with amateurish direction. **86m/C; VHS, DVD.** Hanna Schygulla; Deborah Harry; Alec Baldwin; Annie Golden; Paul Gleason; Dr. Ruth Westheimer; ***D:*** Amos Kollek.

Forever Mine **1999 (R)** In 1973, cabana boy Alan (Fiennes) meets Ella (Mol), the seductive young wife of politico Mark (Liotta) at the Miami Beach resort where he works. It's lust at first sight but ends badly when Mark discovers the affair. But in 1987, Alan re-enters both their lives with a new identity, a new occupation, and a desire for revenge. Noir wannabe whose story doesn't always hold together (but is at least titillating for the sex scenes). **117m/C; VHS, DVD.** Joseph Fiennes; Ray Liotta; Gretchen Mol; Vincent Laresca; ***D:*** Paul Schrader; ***W:*** Paul Schrader; ***C:*** John Bailey; ***M:*** Angelo Badalamenti.

Forever My Girl 1/2 **2018 (PG)** Liam Page (Roe) jilts his fiancée Josie (Rothe) at the altar, and goes on to become a country music superstar. Eight years later, at the height of his success, he visits his Louisiana hometown and discovers that his would-be wife has a 7-year-old daughter, so he forges a relationship with his offspring while reigniting one with Josie. A faithful adaptation of Heidi McLaughlin's bestselling novel in which the people and setting are attractive, the dialogue is trite, and bad behavior has no lasting consequences. **108m/C; DVD.** Alex Roe; Jessica Rothe; Abby Ryder Fortson; Travis Tritt; Peter Cambor; ***D:*** Bethany Ashton Wolf; ***W:*** Bethany Ashton Wolf; ***C:*** Duane Manwiller; ***M:*** Brett Boyett.

Forever Strong **2008 (PG-13)** High-strung rugby star Rick Penning (Faris) gets nailed with a DUI, and the way out of trouble puts him on a rival team, where he clashes with the hard-nosed coach. Then a shot at the national championship puts Rick's loyalty and character to the test. Tired bad-boy jock redemption story does itself in with sap and schmaltz. Based on an all-too-familiar but true story of sports glory that finds freshness only because it doesn't involve football, baseball, basketball, or hockey. **112m/C; On Demand.** Sean Faris; Gary Cole; Julie Warner; Neal McDonough; Penn Badgley; Sean Astin; Arielle Kebbel; Nathan West; Larry Bagby; ***D:*** Ryan Little; ***W:*** David Pliler; ***C:*** T.C. Christensen; ***M:*** J Bateman.

Forever Together 1/2 *Can't Be Heaven* **2000 (PG)** The perils of young, first love are sweetly explored as fatherless seventh-grader Danny (Burke) thinks he's falling in love with best friend, Julie (Tractenberg). His widowed mom (Ticotin) is having her own romantic troubles, so Danny turns for advice to a friendly jazz musician (Macchio). **88m/C; VHS, DVD.** Michelle Trachtenberg; Rachel Ticotin; Ralph Macchio; Bryan Burke; Matt McCoy; Diane Ladd; Garry Marshall; ***D:*** Richard Friedman. **VIDEO**

Forever Young **1985** A young boy immerses himself in Catholicism. Admiring a priest, he is unaware that the priest's friend is involved with his mother. Tangled, but delicate handling of the coming-of-age story. **85m/C; VHS, DVD, Streaming.** *GB* James Aubrey; Nicholas Gecks; Alec McCowen; ***D:*** Dr. David Drury; ***W:*** Ray Connolly. **TV**

Forever Young 1/2 **1992 (PG)** When test pilot Gibson's girlfriend is hit by a car and goes into a coma, he volunteers to be cryogenically frozen for one year. Oops!?he's left frozen for 50 years, until he is accidentally thawed out by a couple of kids. Predictable, designed to be a tear jerker, though it serves mostly as a star vehicle for Gibson who bumbles with '90s technology, finds his true love, and escapes from government heavies, adorable as ever. Through all the schmaltz, the relationship Gibson develops with the young Wood turns out to be the most authentic and endearing love in the film. **102m/C; VHS, DVD.** Mel Gibson; Jamie Lee Curtis; Elijah Wood; Isabel Glasser; George Wendt; Joe Morton; Nicolas Surovy; David Marshall Grant; Art LaFleur; John David (J.D.) Cullum; ***D:*** Steve Miner; ***W:*** J.J. (Jeffrey) Abrams; ***C:*** Russell Boyd; ***M:*** Jerry Goldsmith.

Forfeit 1/2 **2007 (R)** A teenaged Frank skedaddled out of L.A. after killing his abusive father, leaving girlfriend Karen behind. Years later, Frank returns, gets a job at an armored car company, and wants to reconnect with Karen. Only problem is Frank is a whacko who believes a TV evangelist is giving him signs about what to do. In this case, it's plan a heist, fake his death, and put the blame on poor, bewildered Karen. **84m/C; DVD.** Billy Burke; Sherry Stringfield; Gregory Itzin; Wayne Knight; Kirk Baltz; ***D:*** Andrew Shea; ***W:*** John Rafter Lee; ***C:*** Roberto Blasini; ***M:*** Andrew Gross. **VIDEO**

The Forger 1/2 **2015 (R)** Another flat drama from the king of the genre, John Travolta. He stars as the world's best art forger, who cuts a deal with a crime syndicate for an early release from prison. He has to pull off the art heist of the century—stealing a painting by Claude Monet and replacing it with a forgery of his own creation that mimics the original with such precision that no one will notice. Easy, right? He asks his dad (Plummer) and son (Sheridan) to help, and, of course, family issues and past resentments come to the surface. **92m/C; DVD.** John Travolta; Christopher Plummer; Tye Sheridan; Abigail Spencer; Anson Mount; ***D:*** Philip Martin; ***W:*** Richard D'Ovidio; ***C:*** John Bailey.

Forget About It **2006 (PG-13)** In a trailer park outside Phoenix, retired war vets Sam (Reynolds), Carl (Loggia), and Eddie (Durning) genially vie for the attention of sexy neighbor Christine (Welch) while enjoying their golden years. Then wiseguy Angelo Nitti (Paloma) is relocated as part of the Witness Protection Program without admitting that he's stolen four million bucks from his cohorts. When the trio find the cash and begin to live it up, they also find themselves pursued by the mob and the feds. **85m/C; DVD.** Burt Reynolds; Raquel Welch; Robert Loggia; Charles Durning; Richard Grieco; Tim Thomerson; Phyllis Diller; Joanna Pacula; Michael Paloma; ***D:*** B.J. Davis; ***W:*** Julia Davis; ***C:*** Mark Trengove.

Forget Me Not **2009 (R)** Lame and predictable teen horror. On graduation weekend, small town class president Sandy Channing's (Schroeder) friends begin disappearing. It leads back to a childhood tragedy and a young woman in a coma, whose spirit suddenly wants revenge. **102m/C; DVD.** Carly Schroeder; Cody Linley; Chloe Bridges; Brie Gabrielle; Jillian Murray; Micah Alberti; Brittany Renee Finamore; ***D:*** Tyler Oliver; ***W:*** Tyler Oliver; ***C:*** Jamieson Stern; ***M:*** Elia Cmiral. **VIDEO**

Forget Me Not **2010** Lonely opposites find an unlikely attraction in this 24-hour indie romance. Suicidal musician Will Fletcher heads home after a bar gig only to be called back by barmaid Eve since he's left his guitar behind. This allows Will to rescue Eve from an obnoxious drunk and they unexpectedly bond, deciding to walk the London streets, confiding personal stories and realizing an attraction that still may not save Will. **93m/C; DVD.** *GB* Tobias Menzies; Genevieve O'Reilly; Gemma Jones; ***D:*** Alexander Holt; Lance Roehrig; ***W:*** Mark Underwood; ***C:*** Shane Daly; ***M:*** Michael J. McEvoy.

Forget Paris 1/2 **1995 (PG-13)** Pro basketball referee Mickey (Crystal) and airline executive Ellen (Winger) meet in Paris, fall in love and get married. But once the honeymoon is over, the marital bliss unravels due to conflicting work schedules and the lack of romantic scenery. This look at yuppie love and courtship finds Crystal in pre-"City Slickers 2" form, launching three-point one-liners and "When Harry Met Sally" sentiment. Bland direction and an obligation to be cute intensify the "been-there-seen-that" feeling. Winger's presence may hint of miscasting, but she has one of the films funniest scenes involving a stray pet and a pigeon. **101m/C; VHS, DVD.** Billy Crystal; Debra Winger; Joe Mantegna; Cynthia Stevenson; Richard Masur; Julie Kavner; William Hickey; Cathy Moriarty; John Spencer; ***D:*** Billy Crystal; ***W:*** Billy Crystal; Lowell Ganz; Babaloo Mandel; ***C:*** Don Burgess; ***M:*** Marc Shaiman.

Forgetting Sarah Marshall **2008 (R)** Apatow produced this raunchy arrested male development comedy that stars (and was written by) second-banana Segel. Slacker couch potato Peter is an underachieving L.A. composer of TV music who's devastated when he's dumped by ambitious starlet hottie girlfriend Sarah (Bell). The woebegone Peter eventually decides to vacation at a Hawaiian resort but—ta-da!?finds Sarah and her new beau, self-absorbed Brit rocker Aldous Snow (Brand), are also guests. Despite frequent humiliations, Peter sticks it out, supported by brunette beauty Rachael (Kunis) and various odd hotel encounters. Segel is game since he gets naked (twice) and does a lot of crying and moping, but you're more likely to say "get over it already" than be amused. **112m/C; DVD, Blu-Ray.** Jason Segel; Kristen Bell; Mila Kunis; Bill Hader; Russell Brand; Jonah Hill; Paul Rudd; William Baldwin; Jason Bateman; Maria Thayer; Steve Landesberg; Jack McBrayer; Liz Cackowski; Gedde Watanabe; ***D:*** Nicholas Stoller; ***W:*** Jason Segel; ***C:*** Russ T. Alsobrook; ***M:*** Lyle Workman.

Forgive and Forget **1999** Macho London construction worker David (Shepherd) can't admit to himself or anyone else that he's gay, including his best mate since childhood, Theo (Simon). But when Theo decides to move in with his girlfriend Hannah (Fraser), David schemes to break them up. He also decides to publicly declare his love by appearing with Theo on a TV talk show, with unforgetable consequences. **96m/C; VHS, DVD.** *GB* Steve John Shepherd; John Simm; Laura Fraser; Maurice Roeves; Ger Ryan; Meera Syal; ***D:*** Aisling Walsh; ***W:*** Mark Burt; ***C:*** Kevin Rowley; ***M:*** Hal Lindes.

The Forgiven **2018 (R)** Inspired by a true, post-Apartheid story, Archbishop Desmond Tutu (Whitaker) meets with a white prisoner (Bana) seeking clemency--without remorse--for his brutal crimes. Despite powerful performances from the two leads, its over-explanations and sluggish pace keep this film from realizing its good intentions. **115m/C; DVD, Blu-Ray.** Forest Whitaker; Eric Bana; Jeff Gum; Morné Visser; Thandi Makhubele; ***D:*** Roland Joffé; ***W:*** Roland Joffé; Michael Ashton; ***C:*** William Wages; ***M:*** Zethu Mashika.

Forgiveness **2015 (R)** A church-based drama centered on a pastor trying to do the right thing but losing himself in the process. Pastor Joseph Jenkins (Jones) is beloved by the members of his 100 year old church. Yet he faces challenges while serving his flock and trying to keep his church afloat. In doing so, he makes several poor decisions that make him pay an unexpected price. **90m/C; DVD, Streaming, Download.** Richard T. Jones; Robinne Lee; Maya Gilbert; Inny Clemons; Kelly Pendygraft; ***D:*** Hakim Khalfani; ***W:*** Hakim Khalfani; ***C:*** Keith L. Smith; ***M:*** Jason Solowsky. **VIDEO**

The Forgotten **2004 (PG-13)** Convoluted conspiracy-minded sci-fi thriller. Telly (Moore) is still acutely grieving over her young son's death in a plane crash 14 months before. Despite the help of hubby Jim (Edwards) and shrink Jack Munce (Sinise), Telly can't let go of the pain until the mementos of her son's life disappear. Now Jim claims they never had a child. Ash (West), the father of a daughter killed on the same flight, can't remember his child and thinks Telly is nuts. But Telly knows she's not—someone is erasing the evidence of their kids' existence and she's going to find out who and why (even if it means getting chased by those nasty men in black). **89m/C; VHS, DVD.** Julianne Moore; Dominic West; Gary Sinise; Alfre Woodard; Robert Wisdom; Jessica Hecht; Anthony Edwards; Linus Roache; ***D:*** Joseph Ruben; ***W:*** Gerald Di Pego; ***C:*** Anastas Michos; ***M:*** James Horner; Paul Kelly.

Forgotten City *The Vivero Letter* **1998 (R)** James Wheeler is out to uncover a city from the Mayan civilization but he faces a rival expedition, an unhappy native tribe, and mysterious disappearances and deaths that point to someone—or something—wanting the city and its treasures to remain undisturbed. Based on the novel "The Vivero Letter" by Desmond Bagley. Filmed on location in Costa Rica. **96m/C; VHS, DVD.** Robert Patrick; Fred Ward; Chiara Caselli; ***D:*** H. Gordon Boos; ***W:*** Denne Bart Petitclerc; Arthur Sellers; ***C:*** Fabrizio Lucci. **VIDEO**

Forgotten Silver **1996** Jackson's mockumentary finds the director and co-director Botes "discovering" the lost films of Colin McKenzie, a pioneering New Zeland filmmaker of the early 1900s. These include McKenzie's epic film "Salome" which the duo decide to restore. The entire escapade is a fiction, including the silent film footage that's shown. The tape also includes the short film "Signing Off" about the final show for a radio DJ and the special request he has trouble fulfilling. **70m/C; VHS, DVD.** *NZ* Sam Neill; Leonard Maltin; Harvey Weinstein; John O'Shea; Hannah McKenzie; Lindsay Shelton; Johnny Morris; Marguerite Hurst; Costa Botes; ***Nar:*** Jeffrey Thomas; ***D:*** Peter Jackson; Costa Botes; Robert Sarkies; ***W:*** Peter Jackson; Costa Botes; ***C:*** Alun Bollinger.

Formosa Betrayed **2009 (R)** Heavy-handed political thriller. In 1983, FBI agent Jack Kelly is sent to Taipei, Taiwan to bring the killers of Taiwanese-American professor Henry Wen back to the U.S. to face trial. He's partnered with self-serving American diplomat Susan Kane, Taiwanese official Kuo, and political activist Ming, but is caught between government cover-ups, shady deals, and various betrayals. **108m/C; DVD.** James Van Der Beek; Wendy Crewson; Tzi Ma; Will Tiao; John Heard; Leslie Hope; Chelcie Ross; Kenneth Tsang; Joseph Forunda; ***D:*** Adam Kane; ***W:*** Charles (Charlie) Stratton; ***C:*** Irek Hartowicz; ***M:*** Jeff Danna.

The Formula **1/2 1980 (R)** Convoluted story about a secret formula for synthetic fuel that meanders it's way from the end of WWII to the present. A U.S. soldier waylays, and then joins forces with, a German general entrusted with the formula. Years later, after the American is murdered, his friend, a hard-nosed L.A. cop, starts investigating, meeting up with spies and a reclusive oil billionaire. Scott and Brando have one good confrontation scene but the rest of the movie is just hot air. From the novel by Steve Shagan. **117m/C; VHS, DVD.** Marlon Brando; George C. Scott; Marthe Keller; G.D. Spradlin; Beatrice Straight; John Gielgud; Richard Lynch; ***D:*** John G. Avildsen; ***M:*** Bill Conti.

Formula 51 *The 51st State* **2001 (R)** Good cast is wasted in this ridiculous plot revolving around drugs and crime lords. Elmo (Jackson) is a pharmacology grad student who loses his ability to work in the field due to a marijuana bust. He ends up toiling for drug kingpin Lizard (Meat Loaf) and invents a drug that is allegedly more powerful than crack, heroin or ecstasy. After he arranges an unpleasant surprise for Lizard, he flees to Liverpool in an attempt to sell his formula to English criminal Durant (Tomlinson). Aside from the asinine and convoluted storyline, Jackson is inexplicably forced to parade around in a kilt for most of the film. Just say no. **92m/C; VHS, DVD.** *GB CA* Samuel L. Jackson; Robert Carlyle; Emily Mortimer; Meat Loaf Aday; Sean Pertwee; Ricky Tomlinson; Rhys Ifans; ***D:*** Ronny Yu; David Wu; ***W:*** Stel Pavlou; ***C:*** Hang-Seng Poon.

Formula 17 *Shi qi sui de tian kong* **2004** Classic romantic comedy—that is if you live in director DJ Chen's world set in an apparent hetero-free Taipei. This is a boy meets boy tale about young, attractive, sexually innocent country boy Tien's (Tang) move to the big city in search of love. Soon after arriving he runs into an old friend from home, Yu (Chin), who is a gay club bartender. Naturally he's swept into a hilarious circle of new friends including flamer CC (JI) and fitness trainer Alan (Yang). Tien meets a hot one-night-stand artist named Bai (Duncan) who deflowers Tien but can't deliver the relationship Tien expects. High energy sinopop soundtrack and attractive cast carries this light-hearted film. **93m/C; DVD.** Tony Yang; Duncan; King Chin; Dada Ji; Jimmy Yang; Jason Chang; ***D:*** D.J. Chen; ***W:*** Rady Fu; ***C:*** Chen Huei-Sheng; ***M:*** George Chen; Hung Tze-Li.

Forrest Gump **1/2 1994 (PG-13)** Grandly ambitious and slightly flawed, amounting to a wonderful bit of movie magic. As the intelligence-impaired Gump with a heart of gold and more than enough character and dignity, Hanks supplies another career highlight. Field contributes a nice turn as his dedicated mama (they were last together in "Punchline"), while Sinise is particularly effective as a handicapped Vietnam veteran with a bad attitude. Incredible special effects put Gump in the middle of historic events over a four decade period, but the real story is the life-affirming, non-judgmental power of Gump to transform the lives of those around him. From the novel by Winston Groom. **142m/C; VHS, DVD, Blu-Ray.** Tom Hanks; Robin Wright; Sally Field; Gary Sinise; Mykelti Williamson; Haley Joel Osment; Michael Conner Humphreys; Hanna Hall; Sonny Shroyer; Siobhan Fallon Hogan; Peter Dobson; Michael Jace; Geoffrey Blake; Mary Ellen Trainor; David Brisbin; ***D:*** Robert Zemeckis; ***W:*** Eric Roth; ***C:*** Don Burgess; ***M:*** Alan Silvestri. Oscars '94: Actor (Hanks), Adapt. Screenplay, Director (Zemeckis), Film, Film Editing, Visual FX; AFI '98: Top 100; Directors Guild '94: Director (Zemeckis); Golden Globes '95: Actor--Drama (Hanks), Director (Zemeckis), Film--Drama; Natl. Bd. of Review '94: Actor (Hanks), Film, Support. Actor (Sinise); Natl. Film Reg. '11; Screen Actors Guild '94: Actor (Hanks); Writers Guild '94: Adapt. Screenplay; Blockbuster '95: Drama Actor, T. (Hanks), Movie, T.; Blockbuster '96: Drama Actor, V. (Hanks).

The Forsaken **2001 (R)** Vampire films need a little smarts to go with their gore but this film has only the latter. It was apparently gutted by the studio prior to release so maybe there was a story at some point. Sean (Smith) is driving from L.A. to Miami when he picks up hitchhiker Nick (Fehr) and the disoriented Megan (Miko). Both turn out to be infected by a blood disease thanks to a vampire's bite. They have to kill the sire if they don't want to become bloodsuckers themselves and then Megan bites Sean, so now it's personal. The vamp in question is suave Kit (Schaech), who has the usual band of trashy minions. The whole movie is trashy but not in a fun way. **90m/C; VHS, DVD.** Kerr Smith; Izabella Miko; Johnathon Schaech; Brendan Fehr; Simon Rex; Carrie Snodgress; Phina Oruche; ***D:*** J.S. Cardone; ***W:*** J.S. Cardone; ***C:*** Steven Bernstein; ***M:*** Johnny Lee Schell; Timothy S. (Tim) Jones.

Forsaken **2015 (R)** John Henry Clayton (Kiefer Sutherland) returns home in this decent Western to find a local gang terrorizing the small town in which he was raised, making the hoped-for reunion with his father (Donald Sutherland) difficult. It also doesn't help that the once-violent John Henry has put his guns away for a peaceful life. Does he have one more shoot-out in him to save home and family? Seeing the two Sutherland legends work together has an intrinsic charm that elevates the film in ways that it wouldn't have without the casting. Sadly, that only goes so far, and this is pretty familiar, predictable stuff. **90m/C; DVD, Blu-Ray, Streaming.** *CM FR US* Demi Moore; Kiefer Sutherland; Donald Sutherland; Brian Cox; Michael Wincott; ***D:*** Jon Cassar; ***W:*** Brad Mirman; ***C:*** Rene Ohashi; ***M:*** Jonathan Goldsmith.

Forsaking All Others **1/2 1935** Screwball comedy featuring several MGM superstars. Friends since childhood, Gable has been in love with Crawford for 20 years, but she never realizes it and plans to marry Montgomery. Crawford is very funny in this delightful story of a wacky romantic triangle. **84m/B; VHS, DVD.** Joan Crawford; Clark Gable; Robert Montgomery; Charles Butterworth; Billie Burke; Rosalind Russell; Frances Drake; ***D:*** W.S. Van Dyke; ***W:*** Joseph L. Mankiewicz; ***C:*** George J. Folsey.

Fort Apache **1/2 1948** The first of director Ford's celebrated cavalry trilogy, in which fanatical Lt. Col. Owen Thursday (a decidely unsympathetic Fonda) leads his reluctant men to an eventual slaughter when he battles Apache chief Cochise (Inclan), recalling George Custer at Little Big Horn. Wayne is his seasoned second-in-command Kirby Yorke, who's unable to prevent what occurs. In residence: Ford hallmarks of spectacular landscapes and stirring action, as well as many vignettes of life at a remote outpost. Don't forget to catch "She Wore a Yellow Ribbon" and "Rio Grande," the next films in the series. **125m/B; VHS, DVD, Blu-Ray.** Henry Fonda; John Wayne; Shirley Temple; John Agar; Pedro Armendariz, Sr.; Victor McLaglen; Ward Bond; Anna Lee; Guy Kibbee; Miguel Inclan; Mae Marsh; ***D:*** John Ford; ***W:*** Frank Nugent; ***C:*** Archie Stout; ***M:*** Richard Hageman.

Fort Apache, the Bronx **1981 (R)** A police drama set in the beleaguered South Bronx of NYC, based on the real-life experiences of two former New York cops who served there. Newman is a decent cop who goes against every kind of criminal and crazy and against his superiors in trying to bring law and justice to a downtrodden community. **123m/C; VHS, DVD.** Paul Newman; Ed Asner; Ken Wahl; Danny Aiello; Rachel Ticotin; Pam Grier; Kathleen Beller; ***D:*** Daniel Petrie; ***W:*** Heywood Gould; ***C:*** John Alcott; ***M:*** Jonathan Tunick.

Fort Bowie **1/2 1958** B-movie military western with some good action sequences. Ambitious Major Wharton (Douglas) has a cavalry detachment kill a band of Apaches who only wanted to surrender. This leads to problems for Fort Bowie's commander, Col. James Garrett (Taylor), who also has trouble with his bored wife Alison (Harrison). She falsely accuses Capt. Thompson (Johnson) of making improper advances leading Garrett to send Thompson out to convince Apache leader Victorio (Chance) to return to the reservation but he has other ideas. **80m/B; DVD.** Ben Johnson; Kent Taylor; Jan Harrison; Larry Chance; J. Ian Douglas; Maureen Hingert; Peter Mamakos; ***D:*** Howard Koch; ***W:*** Maurice Tombragel; ***C:*** Carl Guthrie; ***M:*** Les Baxter.

Fort Defiance **1/2 1951** Melodramatic revenge western. Ben Selby (Johnson) was a member of the Union Army's volunteer Arizona unit and the only survivor of a battle that killed his brother. He blames Johnny Tallon (Clark), who deserted rather than deliver a message for reinforcements, so he heads to Fort Defiance to get his revenge. The situation is complicated by Johnny's family, bad guy saloon owner Dave Parker (Woods), and an attack by a band of Navahos. **81m/C; DVD.** Dane Clark; Ben Johnson; Peter Graves; George Cleveland; Dennis Moore; Craig Woods; Iron Eyes Cody; Tracey Roberts; Ralph Sanford; Bryan "Slim" Hightower; ***D:*** John Rawlins; ***W:*** Louis Lantz; ***C:*** Stanley Cortez; ***M:*** Paul Sawtell.

Fort Dobbs **1958** Wrongly accused killer Gar (Walker) eludes a posse and rescues farm woman Celia Gray and her son from marauding Comanches, taking them to Fort Dobbs. Trouble follows since Celia mistakenly believes that Gar has killed her husband and the soldiers at the fort are preparing for an Indian attack. Since Gar's a heroic sorta guy, he devises a plan of defense that involves gun runner Clett's stash of repeating rifles. **93m/B; DVD.** Clint Walker; Virginia Mayo; Brian Keith; Richard Eyer; Russ Conway; Michael Dante; ***D:*** Gordon Douglas; ***W:*** Burt Kennedy; George W. George; ***C:*** William Clothier; ***M:*** Max Steiner.

Fort Massacre **1/2 1958** CinemaScope military western. Embittered Sgt. Vinson (McCrea) must take over the cavalry regiment when their lieutenant is killed in an Apache attack. He leads the survivors through Apache-held territory as the quickest way to Fort Crane. The soldiers suspect he's crazy and only wants revenge for the murder of his family without caring how many of them will die as well. **90m/C; DVD, Blu-Ray.** Joel McCrea; Forrest Tucker; John Russell; George Neise; Robert Osterloh; Denver Pyle; Anthony Caruso; Susan Cabot; Francis McDonald; ***D:*** Joseph M. Newman; ***W:*** Martin Goldsmith; ***C:*** Carl Guthrie; ***M:*** Marlin Skiles.

Fort McCoy **2011 (R)** Low-budget, sentimental homefront family drama based on a true story. In the summer of 1944, German-American Frank Stirn does his bit for the war by moving his family to the Wisconsin military base where he works as an Army barber. His wife and young sister-in-law also working on the base, which serves as a POW camp for German and Japanese prisoners, causing unexpected complications in their lives. **100m/C; DVD.** Eric Stoltz; Kate Connor; Lyndsy Fonseca; Andy Hirsch; Seymour Cassel; Camryn Manheim; Brendan Fehr; ***D:*** Kate Connor; Michael Worth; ***W:*** Kate Connor; ***C:*** Neil Lisk; ***M:*** Dana Niu.

Fort Osage **1951** Scout Tom Clay (Cameron) is hired to lead a wagon train through Indian territory but encounters hostile tribes because Arthur Pickett (Ankrum) and his partner George Keane (Kennedy) have violated a treaty. **72m/C; DVD.** Rod Cameron; Jane Nigh; Morris Ankrum; Douglas Kennedy; John Ridgely; I. Stanford Jolley; ***D:*** Lesley Selander; ***W:*** Daniel Ullman; ***C:*** Harry Neumann; ***M:*** Marlin Skiles.

Fort Saganne **1984** Charles Saganne (Depardieu), a soldier from a peasant background, is posted to the French Sahara, where he becomes a natural leader. He gains fame and fortune, marries, and then WWI begins. Good, if cliched, adventure saga. Based on the novel by Louis Gardel. French with subtitles. **180m/C; VHS, DVD.** *FR* Gerard Depardieu; Catherine Deneuve; Philippe Noiret; Sophie Marceau; Michel Duchaussoy; ***D:*** Alain Corneau; ***W:*** Alain Corneau; Louis Gardel; ***M:*** Philippe Sarde.

Fort Tilden **1/2 2014 (R)** Two clueless hipsters shun their responsibilities for a beach party, and their awkward journey there becomes a metaphor for how directionless and meaningless their lives are. Were it not for the sharp humor, it would be difficult to empathize with the narcissistic leads whose emotional callowness is front and center. Also, cat lovers should probably avoid as one of the plot points will send you into deep depression. **97m/C; DVD, Blu-Ray, Streaming.** Bridey Elliott; Claire McNulty; Neil Casey;

Griffin Newman; Peter Vack; *D:* Sarah-Violet Bliss; Charles Rogers; *W:* Sarah-Violet Bliss; Charles Rogers; Brian Lannin; *C:* Brian Lannin; *M:* Alexander Moro.

Fort Vengeance ½ **1953** Card cheat Carey Ross (Larsen) and his brother Dick (Craig) escape into Canada after a gunfight. Good guy Dick joins the newly-formed North West Mounted Police while Carey murders a trapper for his goods and blames a Blackfoot Chief's son. Dick has to bring his brother to justice before an Indian uprising. **75m/C; DVD.** James Craig; Keith Larsen; Rita Moreno; Reginald Denny; Morris Ankrum; Paul Marion; Michael Granger; *D:* Lesley Selander; *W:* Daniel Ullman; *C:* Harry Neumann; *M:* Paul Dunlap.

Fort Yuma ½ **1955** Planning revenge for the murder of his father, an Apache chief, Mangas and his band of renegades decide to attack Lt. Keegan's supply column and steal federal uniforms to disguise themselves to enter the fort. Keegan fears betrayal from his native guide and then has to survive to warn the soldiers. **79m/C; DVD.** Peter Graves; Abel Fernandez; John Hudson; Joan Taylor; Joan Vohs; Addison Richards; James O'Hara; *D:* Lesley Selander; *W:* Danny Arnold; *C:* Gordon Avil; *M:* Paul Dunlap.

Fort Yuma Gold ½ *For a Few Extra Dollars; Per Pochi Dollari Ancora; Die Now, Pay Later* **1966** Former Confederate Gary Diamond has become a scout at the end of the war. He's leading some Union soldiers to Fort Yuma to help prevent Confederate fanatic Sanders from attacking. But unbeknownst to Diamond what Sanders is really after is the gold that's hidden in the fort. Dubbed spaghetti western. **105m/C; DVD, Blu-Ray.** *IT* Giuliano Gemma; Dan Vadis; Jacques Sernas; Nello Pazzafini; Sophie Daumier; Jose Calvo; Angel Del Pozo; *D:* Giorgio Ferroni; *W:* Massimilano Capriccioli; *C:* Rafael Pacheco; *M:* Gianni Ferrio.

Fortress **1985 (R)** A teacher and her class are kidnapped from their one-room schoolhouse in the Australian outback. They must use their ingenuity and wits to save their lives in this violent suspense drama. **90m/C; VHS, DVD.** *AU* Rachel Ward; Sean Garlick; Rebecca Rigg; *D:* Arch Nicholson; *M:* Danny Beckerman. **CABLE**

Fortress **1993 (R)** How come the future is never a place you'd want to be? Thanks to overpopulation a woman is only allowed one pregnancy. When John and Karen Brennick are caught trying to have a second child they are shipped to the Fortress, an underground prison in the middle of the desert. Discipline is enforced with numerous sadistic toys, including the intestinator, so-called because it's implanted in the stomach of each prisoner and infractions result in excruciating laser-activated pain. Lambert does well with his action hero but it's character actor Smith as the warden, a techno-human with some sick fantasies, who has the real fun in this horrific depiction of the future. **91m/C; VHS, DVD.** Christopher Lambert; Kurtwood Smith; Loryn Locklin; Lincoln Kilpatrick; *D:* Stuart Gordon; *W:* Steve Feinberg; Troy Neighbors; Terry Curtis Fox; *C:* David Eggby.

Fortress 2: Re-Entry **1999 (R)** John Brennick (Lambert) and his wife and son have escaped from a maximum security prison known as The Fortress. But Brennick is re-captured and his new prison is in orbit, 26,000 miles from Earth. Brennick wants to escape but there's mucho surveillance to overcome (including a camera placed inside his body) and the problem of returning to Earth. **92m/C; VHS, DVD.** Christopher Lambert; Pam Grier; Patrick Malahide; Nick Brimble; *D:* Geoff Murphy; *W:* Steve Feinberg; Troy Neighbors. **VIDEO**

Fortress of Amerikka ½ **1989** In the not-too-distant future, mercenaries get their hands on a secret weapon that could allow them to take over the USA. **97m/C; VHS, DVD.** Gene Le Brock; Kellee Bradley; *D:* Eric Louzil; *W:* Eric Louzil; *C:* Ron Chapman; *M:* Dave Ouimet.

The Fortune Cookie *Meet Whiplash Willie* **1966** After receiving a minor injury during a football game, a TV cameraman is convinced by his seedy lawyer brother-in-law to exaggerate his injury and start an expensive lawsuit. A classic, biting comedy by Wilder. First of several Lemmon-Matthau comedies. **125m/B; VHS, DVD, Blu-Ray.** Jack Lemmon; Walter Matthau; Ron Rich; Cliff Osmond; Judi West; Lurene Tuttle; *D:* Billy Wilder; *W:* Billy Wilder; I.A.L. Diamond; *C:* Joseph LaShelle; *M:* Andre Previn. Oscars '66: Support. Actor (Matthau).

Fortunes **2005 (R)** Three thirty-something buddies are having early midlife crises in this surprisingly appealing comedy-drama. After a bar night, two of the guys impulsively stop at a fortune teller. Married Phil (Hale) is told his young son is in danger and he becomes neurotically overprotective, while Lewis (Urbaniak) becomes a weird recluse after suddenly quitting his stressful job. This leaves cocky James (McGlone) to help out his boys while dealing with a career setback when he fails to get an expected promotion. **91m/C; DVD.** James Urbaniak; Mike McGlone; Tony Hale; Diana Henry; *D:* Parker Cross; *W:* Matt Salzberg; *M:* Tobin Sprout.

Fortunes of War **1987** British professor Guy Pringle arrives with his bride, Harriet, to take up a teaching post in the Balkans in 1939. The idealistic Guy soon becomes enmeshed in anti-fascist politics and involved with the local members of the British embassy. When threatened by war they travel to Athens and then Cairo, where Guy's increasing involvement in the political situation, and his neglect of Harriet, causes a crisis in their marriage. Slow-moving drama with some self-centered characters is redeemed by the acting skills of those involved. Based on the autobiographical novels of Olivia Manning. Originally shown on "Masterpiece Theater" on PBS. **160m/C; VHS, DVD.** *GB* Kenneth Branagh; Emma Thompson; Rupert Graves; Ronald Pickup; Robert Stephens; Charles Kay; James Villiers; Harry Burton; Ciaran Madden; Diana Hardcastle; Greg Hicks; Alan Bennett; Jeremy Brudenell; Jeremy Sinden; *D:* James Cellan Jones; *W:* Alan Plater.

Fortunes of War **1994 (R)** Peter Kernan (Salinger) is a burned-out relief worker in Thailand. Desperate for money, he agrees to smuggle a rare medicine across the Cambodian border to a rural war lord. Travelling with refugee Khoy Thoun (Ngor) and French Red Cross worker, Johanna (Jenkins), Peter begins to realize his need to do the right thing, even if the cost is high. Filmed on location in Manila. **107m/C; VHS, DVD.** Matt Salinger; Michael Ironside; Haing S. Ngor; Sam Jenkins; Martin Sheen; Michael Nouri; *D:* Thierry Notz; *W:* Mark Lee.

Forty Carats ½ **1973 (PG)** Ullmann plays the just-turned 40 divorcee who has a brief fling with the half-her-age Albert while on vacation in Greece. She figures she'll never see him again but, back in New York, he turns up on the arm of her beautiful daughter (Raffin). Except he's still interested in mom. The rest of the movie is spent trying to convince Ullmann that love can conquer all. Ullmann's very attractive but not well-suited for the part; Raffins's screen debut. Based on the Broadway hit. **110m/C; VHS, DVD.** Liv Ullmann; Edward Albert; Gene Kelly; Binnie Barnes; Deborah Raffin; Nancy Walker; *D:* Milton Katselas; *W:* Jay Presson Allen; *C:* Charles B(ryant) Lang, Jr.

40 Days and 40 Nights ½ **2002 (R)** Abstinence comedy has womanizer Matt (Hartnett) suffering from a brutal romantic break-up, so for Lent he vows to go cold turkey in the sack. His always-supportive friends and co-workers rush to place odds on when Matt's self-control will eventually crumble, even posting his progress on the Internet. With babes aplenty seemingly everywhere, Matt's vow is really tested when, of course, he meets the girl of his dreams (Sossamon). Director Lehmann deftly directs the crew of likeable characters, keeping things light and moving along. Memorable funny scenes includes a dinner with Matt's dad describing sex with a hip replacement, and any with Bagel Guy (Maronna). **94m/C; VHS, DVD, Blu-Ray.** Josh Hartnett; Shannyn Sossamon; Maggie Gyllenhaal; Vinessa Shaw; Paulo Costanzo; Glenn Fitzgerald; Emmanuelle Vaugier; Michael Maronna; Mary Gross; Stanley Anderson; Adam Trese; Barry Newman; Griffin Dunne; Monet Mazur; Dylan Neal; Chris Gauthier; *D:* Michael Lehmann; *W:* Rob Perez; *C:* Elliot Davis; *M:* Rolfe Kent.

40 Days and Nights **2012** A tectonic event causes the sea to rise and the military constructs an 'ark' containing the DNA of all living things. **90m/C; DVD, Blu-Ray, Streaming.** Alex Carter; Monica Keena; Christianna Carmine; Mitch Lerner; Emily Sandifer; *D:* Peter Geiger; *W:* H. Perry Horton; *C:* Ulf Soderqvist; *M:* Chris Ridenhour. **VIDEO**

48 Angels ½ **2006 (PG-13)** Nine-year-old Seamus (newcomer Flynn) is terminally ill. Inspired by the story of Saint Columcille, he sets off in a rowboat to find God and ask for a miracle. When Seamus meets wounded Darry (Brolly) and teenaged runaway James (Travers), the unlikely trio decides to stay together and help each other. Touching but not maudlin story; beautiful Irish scenery. **90m/C; DVD.** *IR* Shane Brolly; John Travers; Darragh Kelly; Ciaran Flynn; *D:* Marion Comer; *W:* Marion Comer; *M:* Patrick Duffner.

44 Minutes: The North Hollywood Shootout ½ **2003 (R)** In 1997, two heavily-armed, media-junkie bank robbers (Bryniarski, Taktarov) hold the ill-prepared LAPD at bay for 44 minutes when their heist goes wrong. Told from the point-of-view of various officers, detectives, and SWAT team members called to the scene. **120m/C; VHS, DVD.** Michael Madsen; Ron Livingston; Mario Van Peebles; Andrew Bryniarski; Oleg Taktarov; Ray Baker; Douglas Spain; Alex Meneses; Dale Dye; J.E. Freeman; *D:* Yves Simoneau; *W:* Tim Metcalfe; *C:* David Franco; *M:* George S. Clinton. **CABLE**

Forty Guns ½ **1957** Typically over-the-top Fuller production filled with melodrama, violence, and lots of sexual innuendo. The Bonnel brothers—Griff (Sullivan), Wes (Barry), and Chico (Dix)?are lawmen out to arrest Brockie (Ericson), the nasty younger brother of tough, whip-cracking Jessica Drummond (Stanwyck). Jessica basically owns and runs everything and everyone around her with the help of her hired guns. Griff falls for this western wildcat, making his job more difficult. A climatic shootout helps the movie live up to its title. **79m/B; DVD, Blu-Ray.** Barbara Stanwyck; Barry Sullivan; Gene Barry; Robert Dix; John Ericson; Dean Jagger; Eve Brent; *D:* Samuel Fuller; *W:* Samuel Fuller; *C:* Joseph Biroc; *M:* Harry Sukman.

40 Guns to Apache Pass **1967** Heroic cavalry captain Coburn (Murphy) singlehandedly saves the day after shifty Army corporal Bodine (Tobey) helps traders and some mutinous soldiers sell guns to the Apaches. **95m/C; DVD.** Audie Murphy; Kenneth Tobey; Michael Keep; Robert Brubaker; Michael Burns; Michael Blodgett; Laraine Stephens; *D:* William Witney; *W:* Mary Willingham; Willard Willingham; *C:* Jacques "Jack" Marquette; *M:* Richard LaSalle.

40 Love *Terre battue* **2015** A low-key family sports drama about a father and son trying to achieve their dreams. When Jerome (Gourmet) loses his job as a senior executive at a large chain store, he wants to start his own business. This dream brings him into conflict with his wife. At the same time, their 11-year-old son Ugo (Merienne) is a promising tennis player and hopes that his talents take him to training at Roland-Garros. Though father and son do not fully understand each other, they remain emotionally close. As Jerome and his wife grow further apart, both father and son come to understand success comes at a price. French with subtitles. **95m/C; DVD.** Olivier Gourmet; Valeria Bruni-Tedeschi; Charles Merienne; Vimala Pons; Jean-Yves Berteloot; *D:* Stephane Demoustier; *W:* Stephane Demoustier; *C:* Julien Poupard. **VIDEO**

Forty Naughty Girls **1937** The 6th and last of the RKO series that degenerated from wit to stupidity. Hildegarde Withers (Pitts) and Inspector Piper (Gleason) are enjoying a night out at a Broadway musical until the show's press agent is murdered backstage and then the playwright is also killed. The two carry on their investigation while the show goes on. **63m/B; DVD.** Zasu Pitts; James Gleason; Marjorie Lord; George Shelley; Joan Woodbury; Alan Edwards; *D:* Edward F. (Eddie) Cline; *W:* John Grey; *C:* Russell Metty.

The Forty-Ninth Parallel *The Invaders* **1941** Six Nazi servicemen, seeking to reach neutral American land, are trapped and their U-boat sunk by Royal Canadian Air Force bombers, forcing them into Canada on foot, where they run into an array of stalwart patriots. Dated wartime propaganda made prior to the U.S. entering the war; riddled with entertaining star turns. **90m/B; VHS, DVD.** *GB* Laurence Olivier; Leslie Howard; Eric Portman; Raymond Massey; Glynis Johns; Finlay Currie; Anton Walbrook; *D:* Michael Powell; *W:* Emeric Pressburger; Rodney Ackland. Oscars '42: Story.

40 Pounds of Trouble ½ **1962** Lake Tahoe casino/hotel manager Steve McCluskey (Curtis) likes to avoid complications in his life. But first he's charmed by his boss' niece Chris (Pleshette), the hotel's new headliner, and then he becomes a surrogate father to five-year-old Penny (Wilcox), abandoned by her debt-ridden dad. So what does Steve decide to do? Why take them to Disneyland, of course! Director Jewison's feature film debut. **106m/C; VHS, DVD.** Tony Curtis; Suzanne Pleshette; Claire Wilcox; Phil Silvers; Larry Storch; Howard Morris; Stubby Kaye; Edward Andrews; Mary Murphy; Kevin McCarthy; Sharon Farrell; *D:* Norman Jewison; *W:* Marion Hargrove; *M:* Mort Lindsey.

47 Meters Down **2017 (PG-13)** Two vacationing sisters get up close and personal with undersea critters from inside a shark cage, but when it breaks loose from its tether and sinks, they go from being tourists to potential snacks in their quest for the water's surface. Nothing genre-breaking here, but the murk hides enough surprises to give the viewer some genuine fright-jumps. **89m/C; DVD, Blu-Ray.** Claire Holt; Mandy Moore; Chris Johnson; Yani Gellman; Matthew Modine; *D:* Johannes Roberts; *W:* Johannes Roberts; Ernest Riera; *C:* Mark Silk; *M:* tomandandy.

47 Meters Down: Uncaged **2019 (PG-13)** After moving to Mexico with her undersea explorer father Grant (Corbett), his new wife (Long), and her daughter Sasha (Foxx), Mia (Nelisse) struggles to fit in at her new school. When Grant tries to bring Sasha and Mia together by arranging for an excursion, Sasha's friends, Alexa (Tju) and Nicole (Stallone), turn up with a better idea and take Mia along. Exploring a recently discovered submerged Mayan city, the teens become trapped with a shark. Though a sequel, the story is not connected to the original, which was an unexpected sleeper hit. But the formula still works swimmingly enough. **89m/C; DVD, Blu-Ray.** Sophie Nelisse; Corinne Foxx; Brianne Tju; Sistine Stallone; Brec Bassinger; *D:* Johannes Roberts; *W:* Johannes Roberts; Ernest Riera; *C:* Mark Silk; *M:* tomandandy.

Forty Shades of Blue ½ **2005** Character study set in Memphis in which music industry legend Alan James (Torn), his much younger Russian live-in, Laura (Korzun), and adult son from a previous marriage, Michael (Burrows) are brought together when Alan is given a prestigious music industry award. The film unwinds painfully slowly as each character's flawed motivations and dark compromises are examined. Use of local music is a high point in this Sundance award winner. **107m/C; DVD.** Rip Torn; Dina Korzun; Darren E. Burrows; Paprika Steen; Red West; Jenny O'Hara; *D:* Ira Sachs; *W:* Ira Sachs; *M:* Michael Rohatyn; Dickon Hinchliffe.

Forty Thousand Horsemen ½ **1941** The story of the ANZACS of Australia, created to fight Germany in the Middle East during WWII. This Australian war drama is full of cavalry charges, brave young lads, and "Waltzing Matilda." **86m/B; VHS, DVD.** *AU* Chips Rafferty; Grant Taylor; Betty Bryant; Pat Twohill; *D:* Charles Chauvel; *W:* Elsa Chauvel; *C:* George Heath; *M:* Lindley Evans.

The 40 Year Old Virgin **2005 (R)** Forty year old Andy (Carell) is a virgin, obsessed with pre-teen pursuits like video games, action heroes and collectibles. His work buddies find out his terrible secret and take on the task of initiating Andy into the world of adulthood and sex. Yes, it's raunchy and sophomoric, but the underlying sweetness and the well-done slapstick humor are worth it. Along with "Wedding Crashers," helped bring back the successful R-rated comedy. **116m/C; DVD, Blu-Ray, HD-DVD.** Steve Carell; Catherine Keener; Paul Rudd; Romany Malco; Elizabeth Banks; Leslie Mann; Jane

Lynch; Seth Rogen; Kat Dennings; David Koechner; Loudon Wainwright, III; ***D:*** Judd Apatow; ***W:*** Steve Carell; Judd Apatow; ***C:*** Jack N. Green; ***M:*** Lyle Workman. L.A. Film Critics '05: Actress (Keener).

42 **2013 (PG-13)** A sentimental but nonetheless powerful portrayal of the struggles Jackie Robinson (Boseman) endured in breaking the color barrier in Major League Baseball in 1947 with the Brooklyn Dodgers. Boseman's charismatic performance guides the emotionally manipulative tale (director/writer Helgeland never met a slo-mo shot he didn't like), as does Ford's forceful rendition of Dodgers bullheaded general manager and president who signs Jackie and Beharie as his elegantly strong-willed wife Rachel. Somewhat glosses over the issues at hand in favor of melodrama but Helgeland drives home the importance of Robinson's story to a wider audience than it would have otherwise. **128m/C; DVD, Blu-Ray.** Chadwick Boseman; Harrison Ford; Nicole Beharie; Christopher Meloni; Ryan Merriman; Lucas Black; Hamish Linklater; T.R. Knight; John C. McGinley; ***D:*** Brian Helgeland; ***W:*** Brian Helgeland; ***C:*** Don Burgess; ***M:*** Mark Isham.

42nd Street **1933** A Broadway musical producer faces numerous problems in his efforts to reach a successful opening night. Choreography by Busby Berkeley. A colorized version of the film is also available. **89m/B; VHS, DVD, Blu-Ray.** Warner Baxter; Ruby Keeler; Bebe Daniels; George Brent; Dick Powell; Guy Kibbee; Ginger Rogers; Una Merkel; Busby Berkeley; Ned Sparks; George E. Stone; ***D:*** Lloyd Bacon; ***W:*** Rian James; James Seymour; ***C:*** Sol Polito; ***M:*** Harry Warren; Al Dubin. Natl. Film Reg. '98.

44 Inch Chest **2009 (R)** Good cast overcomes a so-so script (filled with unrelentingly crude dialogue) and direction. Liz (Whalley) tells husband Colin (Winstone) she's leaving him for her lover and he goes nuts, vowing retribution. He and four pals--all shady, violent criminal types--kidnap said lover (a French waiter) and lock him in a closet in an empty flat until an increasingly maudlin and drunken Colin decides exactly what he wants to do. **95m/C; DVD.** ***US UK AU*** Ray Winstone; Ian McShane; John Hurt; Tom Wilkinson; Stephen (Dillon) Dillane; Joanne Whalley; Melvil Poupaud; ***D:*** Malcolm Venville; ***W:*** Louis Mellis; David Scinto; ***C:*** Daniel Landin; ***M:*** Angelo Badalamenti.

.45 **2006 (R)** New York bad girl Kat (Jovovich) hates being controlled by her violent, gun-selling boyfriend Big Al (Macfayden). She starts making her own deals and is willing to go to any lengths to break free, with the help of the hopelessly-devoted Riley (Dorff) and her lesbian friend Vic (Strange). Good tough role for Jovovich in a woman's revenge flick. **97m/C; DVD.** Milla Jovovich; Stephen Dorff; Angus MacFadyen; Aisha Tyler; Sarah Strange; Vincent Laresca; ***D:*** Gary Lennon; ***W:*** Gary Lennon; ***C:*** Teodoro Maniaci; ***M:*** John Robert Wood. **VIDEO**

45 Years **2015 (R)** Haigh's adaptation of David Constantine's short story is a devastating examination of regret and the complications that arise when one considers alternate paths their lives could have taken. Geoff (Courtenay) and Kate (Rampling) are planning their 45th wedding anniversary when he receives a letter that the body of his old flame, who disappeared 50 years, has been found. It sends both halves of the couple reeling into memory and consideration of a life unlived. Courtenay is great and Haigh's subtle direction is understated, but the film belongs to Rampling, who does the best work of her career. **95m/C; DVD, Blu-Ray.** Charlotte Rampling; Tom Courtenay; Geraldine James; Dolly Wells; David Sibley; ***D:*** Andrew Haigh; ***W:*** Andrew Haigh; ***C:*** Lol Crawley.

47 Ronin **2013 (PG-13)** Hundreds of millions of dollars were wasted on this flat, generic, box-office failure that could maybe only please hardcore fans of its star or the genre. Kai (Reeves) is a half-Japanese and half-British samurai in 18th-century Japan, who is forced into action with his fellow Ronin to avenge the murder of their master. Reeves is a flat lead and the action of the film is bizarrely weighed down with CGI and expensive visuals instead of simply offering well-choreographed fight scenes. It doesn't work as drama and may disappoint even more as a martial arts' escape. **118m/C; DVD, Blu-Ray.** Keanu Reeves; Hiroyuki (Henry) Sanada; Ko Shibasaki; Tadanobu Asano; ***D:*** Carl Rinsch; ***W:*** Chris Morgan; Hossein Amini; ***C:*** John Mathieson; ***M:*** Ilan Eshkieri.

47 Ronin, Part 1 *The Loyal 47 Ronin; 47 Samurai* **1942** Turn of the 18th-century epic chronicling the samurai legend. The warriors of Lord Asano set out to avenge their leader, tricked into committing a forced seppuku, or hara-kiri. The photography is generously laden with views of 18th century gardens as well as panoramic vistas. This is the largest and most popular film of the Kabuki version of the story by Seika Mayama. In Japanese with English subtitles. **111m/C; VHS, DVD.** ***JP*** Yoshisaburo Arashi; Utaemon Ichikawa; Chojuro Kawarazaki; Kunitaro Kawarazaki; Mantoyo Mimasu; Micko Takamine; ***D:*** Kenji Mizoguchi; ***W:*** Yoshikata Yoda; Kenichiro Hara; ***C:*** Kohei Sugiyama; ***M:*** Shiro Fukai.

47 Ronin, Part 2 **1942** Second half of the film in which the famous Japanese folklore tale of Lord Asano and his warriors is told. The film follows Asano's samurai as they commit themselves to avenging their leader in 1703. In Japanese with English subtitles. **108m/C; VHS, DVD.** ***JP*** Yoshisaburo Arashi; Utaemon Ichikawa; Chojuro Kawarazaki; Kunitaro Kawarazaki; Mantoyo Mimasu; ***D:*** Kenji Mizoguchi; ***W:*** Kenichiro Hara; Yoshikata Yoda; ***C:*** Kohei Sugiyama; ***M:*** Shiro Fukai.

48 Hrs. **1982 (R)** An experienced San Francisco cop (Nolte) springs a convict (Murphy) from jail for 48 hours to find a vicious murdering escaped con. Murphy's film debut is great and Nolte is perfect as his gruff foil. **97m/C; VHS, DVD, Blu-Ray.** Nick Nolte; Eddie Murphy; James Remar; Annette O'Toole; David Patrick Kelly; Sonny Landham; Brion James; Denise Crosby; Ned Dowd; ***D:*** Walter Hill; ***W:*** Walter Hill; Larry Gross; Steven E. de Souza; Roger Spottiswoode; ***M:*** James Horner.

Foster **1/2 2018** A documentary look at the complexities of foster care, focusing on the Los Angeles County Department of Children and Family Services. Through interviews with social workers, children in foster care, caretakers, and others, the film highlights the experiences of those involved in the foster care system. Each story offers a different perspective on foster care, underscored by devastating statistics and traumatized youth. At the same time, the experiences of social workers like Jessica Chandler and foster teen Denyshin display an unexpected resilience and spirit. In its making, Oppenheimer and Harris wanted to dispel biases related to foster care and generally succeed. **113m/C; DVD.** ***D:*** Mark Jonathan Harris; ***W:*** Mark Jonathan Harris; ***C:*** Nick Higgins; ***M:*** Gary Lionelli. **VIDEO**

The Foul King **1/2** *Banchikwang* **2000** Dae-Ho (Song Kang-ho) is bullied by his boss and father, so to deal with his frustration he decides to train as a professional wrestler known as the villainous Foul King. After accidentally winning his first match, he is challenged to a tag-team match by the sport's reigning champion, who needs an easy win to bolster his own career. Purists should note the only available version in the U.S. is dubbed in Chinese, and subtitled in English. Foreign editions are required to view it in its original language. **112m/C; DVD.** ***NK*** Kang-ho Song; Jin-Young Yang; Su-ro Kim; ***D:*** Ji-woon Kim; ***W:*** Ji-woon Kim.

Foul Play **1978 (PG)** Hawn is a librarian who picks up a hitchhiker which leads to nothing but trouble. She becomes involved with San Francisco detective Chase in an effort to expose a plot to kill the Pope during his visit to the city. Also involved is Moore as an English orchestra conductor with some kinky sexual leanings. Chase is charming (no mugging here) and Hawn both bubbly and brave. A big winner at the boxoffice; features Barry Manilow's hit tune "Ready to Take a Chance Again." **116m/C; VHS, DVD.** Goldie Hawn; Chevy Chase; Dudley Moore; Burgess Meredith; Billy Barty; Rachel Roberts; Eugene Roche; Brian Dennehy; Chuck McCann; Bruce Solomon; Marc Lawrence; Don Calfa; Marilyn Sokol; Frances Bay; ***D:*** Colin Higgins; ***W:*** Colin Higgins; ***C:*** David M. Walsh; ***M:*** Charles Fox.

The Founder **2017 (PG-13)** John Lee Hancock directs the fantastic story of how one man in the heart of the Midwest created one of the most important businesses in the history of the world. Keaton's fantastic performance drives the film as Ray Kroc, the salesman stunned at how quickly two brothers (Nick Offerman & John Carroll Lynch) could make hamburgers at a little eatery called McDonald's in San Bernardino, California. Kroc essentially steals their business, making a fortune in the heartland of the country, and making some enemies along the way. It's a relatively straightforward drama, but it's a well-made one. You'll want a Big Mac. **115m/C; DVD, Blu-Ray.** Michael Keaton; Nick Offerman; John Carroll Lynch; Linda Cardellini; B.J. Novak; Laura Dern; ***D:*** John Lee Hancock; ***W:*** Robert Siegel; ***C:*** John Schwartzman; ***M:*** Carter Burwell.

The Fountain **2006 (PG-13)** Given the pic's long and troubled production history, maybe Aronofsky getting anything onscreen is a miracle. Of course this fantastical odyssey may be considered as a new "2001" and best seen by an audience in the same trippy condition. Anyway, Jackman and Weisz tackle three time periods and three characters but not in a linear fashion. In the 16th-century, Spanish conquistador Tomas is dispatched by Queen Isabel to find the Tree of Life worshipped by the Mayans. In the present, Tommy is a medical researcher who is trying to cure his dying wife, Izzi, who's writing a novel called "The Fountain." And in the 26th century, Tom is floating in a space bubble towards a nebula and Izzi shows up in his dreams. Or something. Feel free to interpret as you wish or just call it hooey and forget it. **95m/C; DVD, Blu-Ray, HD-DVD.** Hugh Jackman; Rachel Weisz; Ellen Burstyn; Clifford Curtis; Mark Margolis; ***D:*** Darren Aronofsky; ***W:*** Darren Aronofsky; ***C:*** Matthew Libatique; ***M:*** Clint Mansell.

The Fountainhead **1949** Cooper is an idealistic, uncompromising architect who refuses to change his designs. When he finds out his plans for a public housing project have been radically altered he blows up the building and winds up in court defending his actions. Neal is the sub-plot love interest. Based on the novel by Ayn Rand. **113m/C; VHS, DVD.** Gary Cooper; Patricia Neal; Raymond Massey; Ray Collins; Henry Hull; Robert Douglas; Kent Smith; Moroni Olsen; Ann Doran; ***D:*** King Vidor; ***C:*** Robert Burks; ***M:*** Max Steiner.

The Four *Si da ming bu* **2012** In a combination of Chinese wuxia films and American style superhero films, a group of four superhumans finds itself competing with the feudal Chinese version of the police in their efforts to bring in a necromancer who is creating counterfeit cash. **118m/C; DVD, Blu-Ray, Streaming.** ***CH*** Chao Deng; Yifei Liu; Ronald Cheng; Colin Chou; Anthony Wong; ***D:*** Gordon Chan; Janet Chun; ***W:*** Gordon Chan; Frankie Tam; Maria Wong; ***C:*** Yiu-fai Lai; ***M:*** Henry Lai. **VIDEO**

Four **2012** Brief, low-budget, atmospheric, and emotional drama adapted from Christopher Shinn's play. On the evening of July 4th, cocky biracial jock Dexter persuades brainy African-American Abigayle to see fireworks with him. Abi is supposed to be caring for her bedridden mother while her college professor father Joe is on a business trip. Little does she know that the closeted Joe is meeting with an Internet hookup, who turns out to be June, an underage white teenager grappling with his sexuality. Nothing's explicit but director/writer Sanchez effectively depicts the queasy discomfort of the sexual tension between both would-be couples. **75m/C; DVD.** Wendell Pierce; Emory Cohen; E.J. Bonilla; Aja Naomi King; ***D:*** Joshua Sanchez; ***W:*** Joshua Sanchez; ***C:*** Gregg Conde; ***M:*** Bryan Senti.

Four and a Half Women **1/2** *Chocolate for Breakfast* **2005** Cute comedy about four roommates dealing with the day-to-day shuffle of being young, female, and running wild around the Big Apple. Things get complicated when one of the girls becomes pregnant after a one-night-stand and decides to keep the baby. **125m/C; VHS, DVD.** Isabel Gillies; Marin Hinkle; Callie (Calliope) Thorne; Michael Showalter; Josh Hamilton; ***D:*** Emily Baer; ***W:*** Emily Baer; ***C:*** Joaquin Boca-Asay; ***M:*** Jason Frederick.

Four Bags Full **1/2 1956** A bitter comedy about two smugglers during WWII who try to get a slaughtered pig to the black market under the Nazis' noses. In French with English subtitles. **82m/C; VHS, DVD.** ***FR*** Jean Gabin; Louis de Funes; Andre Bourvil; Jeanette Batti; ***D:*** Claude Autant-Lara.

Four Boxes **2009 (R)** Estate hunters Trevor, Amber, and Rob are at a dilapidated house where they discover a note by the computer for fourboxes.tv. It's a live cam website with a creepy protagonist named Havoc who sleeps in a cage and builds bombs. Is he just crazy or dangerous as well? The dialogue and plot twists are particularly artificial and annoying. **84m/C; DVD.** Justin Kirk; Sam Rosen; Terryn Westbrook; ***D:*** Wyatt McDill; ***W:*** Wyatt McDill; ***C:*** Brain Lundy; ***M:*** Ken Brahmstedt. **VIDEO**

Four Boys and a Gun **1957** Four juvenile delinquents get into more trouble than they bargained for when Ollie (Sutton) tries a holdup with pals Johnny (Franciscus), Eddie (Green), and Stanley (Hinnant). A cop gets killed, the quartet is caught, and the District Attorney (Hulett) offers a deal: if they say who the shooter was, three will get lighter sentences but the triggerman gets the chair. **74m/B; DVD.** Frank Sutton; Larry Green; James Franciscus; William Hinnant; Otto Hulett; Robert Dryden; ***D:*** William Berke; ***W:*** Leo Townsend; Philip Yordan; ***C:*** J. Burgi Contner; ***M:*** Albert Glasser.

Four Brothers **1/2 2005 (R)** Urban remake of "The Sons of Katie Elder." Ma Mercer (Flanagan) is gunned down in a Detroit market hold-up, which brings her four adopted sons, two white and two black, to reunite and avenge her not-so-accidental death, leading to an elaborate conspiracy implicating the upper echelons of Motor City politics. For all its action scenes, violence and verbal ugliness, the final result is disappointing. **109m/C; DVD, Blu-Ray, UMD, HD-DVD.** Mark Wahlberg; Andre Benjamin; Tyrese Gibson; Garrett Hedlund; Josh Charles; Chiwetel Ejiofor; Fionnula Flanagan; Terrence Howard; Sofia Vergara; Taraji P. Henson; Barry (Shabaka) Henley; Kenneth Welsh; ***D:*** John Singleton; ***W:*** David Elliot; Paul Lovett; ***C:*** Peter Menzies, Jr.

Four Christmases **2008 (PG-13)** When Kate (Witherspoon) and Brad's (Vaughn) holiday vacation plans are ruined by weather, they no longer have an excuse not to visit each of their divorced parents on Christmas. Brad can't wait for the day of parents, steps, sibs, and other relations to be over with, while Kate discovers she enjoys all the familial hoopla. Flick is awkward and uneven as first half leans on slapstick humor for a few cheap laughs while second half devolves into contrived schmaltz. And there's no zip between the mismatched leads, as her honed, straight cuteness doesn't mesh with his loose, off-the-cuff goofiness. Might be the worst film starring five Oscar-winners ever. **88m/C; Blu-Ray, On Demand.** Reese Witherspoon; Vince Vaughn; Robert Duvall; Kristin Chenoweth; Jon Favreau; Dwight Yoakam; Tim McGraw; Sissy Spacek; Jon Voight; Mary Steenburgen; Katy Mixon; Colleen Camp; ***D:*** Seth Gordon; ***W:*** Jon Lucas; Scott Moore; Matt R. Allen; Caleb Wilson; ***C:*** Jeffrey L. Kimball; ***M:*** Alex Wurman.

Four Corners of Suburbia **1/2** **2005** Dull, talky drama (it's based on Puccini's play) about several New Englanders who spend an uncomfortable weekend hashing out their lives at a beach house. Walt Samson (Blackthorne) and wife Rachel (Amick) are expecting to discuss their shaky marriage when Walt's troubled artist friend Benjamin (Newman) shows up as well as friends from Rachel's past. **104m/C; DVD.** Madchen Amick; Paul Blackthorne; Alec Newman; Katie Carr; Alice Evans; Brad Rowe; ***D:*** Elizabeth Puccini; ***W:*** Elizabeth Puccini; ***C:*** Antoine Vivas Denisov; ***M:*** Nikos Kypourgos.

Four Daughters **1938** Classic, three-hankie outing in which four talented daughters of music professor Rains fall in love and marry. Garfield shines, in a role tailor-made for him, as the world-weary suitor driven to extremes in the name of love. Great performances from all. Based on the novel "Sister Act" by Fannie Hurst. **90m/B; VHS, DVD.** Claude Rains; John Garfield; May Robson; Priscilla Lane; Lola Lane; Rosemary Lane; Gale Page; Dick Foran; Jeffrey Lynn; Frank McHugh;

D: Michael Curtiz; *W:* Lenore Coffee; Julius J. Epstein; *C:* Ernest Haller; *M:* Max Steiner.

Four Days in July **1985** Two couples from Belfast, one Catholic and one Protestant, find they have something in common when they meet in the maternity ward as both couples become first-time parents. Script and dialog were mainly improvised, which provides both dull stretches and the film's charm. **99m/C; VHS, DVD.** *GB* Des McAleer; Brid Brennan; Charles Lawson; Paula Hamilton; Shane Connaughton; Eileen Pollock; Stephen Rea; *D:* Mike Leigh. **TV**

Four Days in September **1997 (R)** Based on the true story of Charles Burke Elbrick (Arkin), the American ambassador to Brazil who, in 1969, was kidnapped by four idealistic students, part of a Marxist revolutionary group protesting their government's military dictatorship. Their leader, Fernando Gabeira (Cardoso), wants the release of political prisoners and gives the government four days to meet his terms. Adapted from the book "What's Up, Comrade?" by Gabeira. **105m/C; VHS, DVD.** *BR* Alan Arkin; Pedro Cardoso; Marco Ricca; Fernanda Torres; *D:* Bruno Barreto; *W:* Leopoldo Serran; *C:* Felix Monti; *M:* Stewart Copeland.

Four Deuces **1/2 1975** Gang war is underway between the Chico Hamilton mob and Vic Morano and the Four Deuces during the Depression. Comedy and action combine with elements of strong language, strong sex, and strong violence. **87m/C; VHS, DVD.** Jack Palance; Carol Lynley; Warren Berlinger; Adam Roarke; *D:* William H. Bushnell, Jr.

Four Dogs Playing Poker **1/2 2000 (R)** Four friends plan an art heist and then lose the prize, which gets them into trouble with the gangster who's expecting the goods. So they come up with another scheme that involves collecting on one of the group's life insurance policies (to pay off the gangster-)?which means one of them will have to die. Sketchy thriller. **98m/C; VHS, DVD.** Olivia Williams; Balthazar Getty; Stacy Edwards; Daniel London; Tim Curry; Forest Whitaker; George Lazenby; John Taylor; *D:* Paul Rachman; *W:* Thomas Durham; William Quist; *C:* Claudio Rocha; *M:* Brian Tyler; Scott Hackwith.

Four Dollars of Revenge **1/2** *Cuatro Dolares de Venganza; Four Dollars for Vengeance* **1966** Typical spaghetti western. Wounded after an ambush, Lt. Roy Dexter (Woods) is charged with the theft of the gold shipment he was supposed to deliver. Then he's given a long sentence at hard labor and all he wants is revenge. Spanish with subtitles or dubbed. **88m/C; DVD.** *IT SP* Robert Woods; Dana Ghia; Angelo Infanti; Antonio Casas; Jose Martin; Gerard Tichy; *W:* Jaime Jesus Balcazar; Bruno Corbucci; Aldo Grimaldi; Giovanni Grimaldi; *C:* Victor Monreal; *M:* Angelo Francesco Lavagnino.

Four Faces West **1/2** *They Passed This Way* **1948** McCrea is an honest rancher who nevertheless robs the local bank in order to save his father's ranch from foreclosure. His humanity in helping a diphtheria-ridden family leads to his capture, but the sheriff promises a light sentence, since he is not a typical bad guy. Fine performances strengthen this low-key western. **90m/B; VHS, DVD, Blu-Ray.** Joel McCrea; Frances Dee; Charles Bickford; *D:* Alfred E. Green.

Four Fast Guns **1959** Gunfighter Tom Sabin (Craig) travels to Purgatory in the guise of helping the townspeople wrest control away from wheelchair-bound town boss Hoag (Richards). Hoag doesn't want any interference so he hires three outlaws, believing one of them will be able to kill Sabin. The showdown winds up involving Sabin and his outlaw brother Johnny Naco (Halsey). **72m/B; DVD.** James Craig; Paul Richards; Brett Halsey; Martha Vickers; Edgar Buchanan; Richard Martin; John Swift; Blu Wright; *D:* William Hole, Jr.; *W:* James Edmiston; Dallas Gaultois; *C:* John M. Nickolaus, Jr.

The Four Feathers **1939** A grand adventure from a story by A.E.W. Mason. After resigning from the British Army a young man is branded a coward and given four white feathers as symbols by three of his friends and his lady love. Determined to prove them wrong he joins the Sudan campaign of 1898 and rescues each of the men from certain death. They then take back their feathers as does his girl upon learning of his true courage. Excellent performances by Smith and Richardson. **99m/C; VHS, DVD.** *GB* John Clements; Ralph Richardson; Sir C. Aubrey Smith; June Duprez; Donald Gray; Jack Allen; Allan Jeayes; Frederick Culley; Hal Walters; Henry Oscar; John Laurie; Clive Baxter; Robert Rendel; Derek Elphinstone; Norman Pierce; Amid Taftazani; Archibald Batty; Hay Petrie; Alexander Knox; *D:* Zoltan Korda; *W:* R.C. Sherriff; Lajos Biro; Arthur Wimperis; *C:* Osmond H. Borradaile; Georges Perinal; Jack Cardiff; *M:* Miklos Rozsa.

The Four Feathers **1978** Determined to return the symbols of cowardice, four feathers, to his friends and fiancee, a man courageously saves his friends' lives during the British Sudan campaign and regains the love of his lady, in this fifth remake of the story. **95m/C; VHS, DVD.** Beau Bridges; Jane Seymour; Simon Ward; Harry Andrews; Richard Johnson; Robert Powell; *D:* Don Sharp. **TV**

The Four Feathers **2002 (PG-13)** Featherweight remake has Ledger as Harry, a British officer in the late 1800's in love and engaged to marry hottie Ethne (Hudson, sporting an unfortunate English accent). Best friend and fellow officer Jack (Bentley) also fancies English muffin Ethne, unbeknownst to Harry. When Harry resigns from service with battle in the Sudan looming, he's labeled a coward and given four white feathers as a sign of his cowardice. Ditched and dissed, a suitably shamed Harry, determined to prove his courage, disguises himself as an African native (Riiight) and heads to the Sudan. Seem dated and implausible, but action scenes are well done. Based on A.E.W. Mason's 1902 novel. **130m/C; VHS, DVD.** Heath Ledger; Wes Bentley; Kate Hudson; Djimon Hounsou; Michael Sheen; Kris Marshall; Rupert Penry-Jones; Tim Pigott-Smith; Alex Jennings; *D:* Shekhar Kapur; *W:* Michael Schiffer; Hossein Amini; *C:* Robert Richardson; *M:* James Horner.

Four Flies on Grey Velvet *Quattro Moschi di Velluto Grigio* **1972** Convoluted pulp thriller from Argento. Roberto Tobias (Brandon) accidentally kills a stalker, an act witnessed by a mask-wearing figure. He's then plagued by nightmares of decapitation and starts getting blackmail threats as his relationship with high-strung wife Nina (Farmer) is increasingly strained. The body count rises but the answers lie closer to home than Roberto thinks. **102m/C; DVD, Blu-Ray.** *IT* Michael Brandon; Mimsy Farmer; Jean-Pierre Marielle; Francine Racette; Bud Spencer; Marissa Fabbri; Oreste Lionello; *D:* Dario Argento; *W:* Dario Argento; *C:* Franco Di Giacomo; *M:* Ennio Morricone.

Four for Texas **1963** Perhaps Aldrich's later success with "The Dirty Dozen" can be attributed, in part, to this exercise in how not to make a comic western; poorly made, over long, and far too dependant on the feminine charisma of Ekberg and Andress. Slow-moving Sinatra-Martin vehicle tells the tale of con men in the Old West who battle bandits and bad bankers for a stash of loot. **124m/C; VHS, DVD.** Frank Sinatra; Dean Martin; Anita Ekberg; Ursula Andress; Charles Bronson; Victor Buono; Jack Elam; Arthur Godfrey; Moe Howard; Larry Fine; Joe DeRita; *D:* Robert Aldrich; *W:* Robert Aldrich; Teddi Sherman; W.R. Burnett; *C:* Ernest Laszlo; *M:* Nelson Riddle.

4:44 Last Day on Earth **2011 (R)** Ferrara's aimless yawner about the end of the world. At 4:44 a.m. the world will end because of ozone depletion. Artists Cisco (Dafoe) and Skye (Leigh) spend their remaining time together in their New York apartment indulging in sex and other distractions, including saying goodbye to family and friends. **85m/C; DVD, Blu-Ray.** Willem Dafoe; Sharyn Leigh; Natasha Lyonne; Paul Hipp; Anita Pallenberg; *D:* Abel Ferrara; *W:* Abel Ferrara; *C:* Ken Kelsch.

Four Friends *Georgia's Friends* **1981 (R)** The magical good and bad dream of the 1960s is remembered in this story of four friends. A young woman and the three men in love with her first come together in high school and then separate, learning from college, war and drug abuse, and each other in this ambitious movie from Steve Tesich, the writer of "Breaking Away." Good performances by all. **114m/C; VHS, DVD.** James Leo Herlihy; Craig Wasson; Jodi Thelen; Michael Huddleston; Jim Metzler; Reed Birney; *D:* Arthur Penn; *W:* Steve Tesich; *C:* Ghislan Cloquet.

Four Frightened People **1934** Indulgent DeMille jungle adventure filmed in Hawaii. Four passengers steal a lifeboat when bubonic plague breaks out on their coastal steamer ship. They land on a remote Malaysian island, find themselves beset by hostile natives and various deadly wildlife, and must use their newfound survival skills to their advantage. **79m/B; DVD.** Claudette Colbert; Herbert Marshall; William Gargan; Mary Boland; Leo Carrillo; *D:* Cecil B. DeMille; *W:* Lenore Coffee; Bartlett Cormack; *C:* Karl Struss.

The Four Horsemen of the Apocalypse **1/2 1921** Silent classic and star maker for Valentino concerning an Argentine family torn apart by the outbreak of WWI. Valentino is a painter who moves from his native Argentina to France and is persuaded to enlist by a recruiter who invokes the image of the Biblical riders. His excellence as a soldier, however, proves to be his undoing. The 1962 remake can't hold a candle to original, adapted from a novel by Vicente Blasco-Ibanez. **110m/B; Silent; VHS, DVD.** Rudolph Valentino; Alice Terry; Pomeroy Cannon; Josef Swickard; Alan Hale; Mabel van Buren; Nigel de Brulier; Bowditch Turner; Wallace Beery; Bridgetta Clark; Virginia Warwick; Stuart Holmes; John St. Polis; Mark Fenton; Derek Ghent; *D:* Rex Ingram; *W:* June Mathis; *C:* John Seitz; *M:* Louis F. Gottschalk. Natl. Film Reg. '95.

The Four Horsemen of the Apocalypse **1/2 1962** The members of a German family find themselves fighting on opposite sides during WWII. This remake of the vintage Valentino silent failed at the boxoffice, with complaints about its length, disjointed script, and uninspired performances. The title refers to the horrors of conquest, pestilence, war, and death. Adapted from the book by Vincente Blasco-Ibanez. **153m/C; VHS, DVD.** Glenn Ford; Charles Boyer; Lee J. Cobb; Paul Henreid; Yvette Mimieux; Ingrid Thulin; Paul Lukas; Karl-Heinz Boehm; Kathryn Givney; Marcel Hillaire; George Dolenz; Nestor Paiva; *D:* Vincente Minnelli; *W:* John Gay; *C:* Milton Krasner; *M:* Andre Previn.

The 400 Blows *Les Quartre Cents Coups* **1959** The classic, groundbreaking semi-autobiography that initiated Truffaut's career and catapulted him to international acclaim, about the trials and rebellions of 12-year-old French schoolboy, Antoine Doinel (Leaud). One of the greatest and most influential of films, and the first of Truffaut's career-long Doinel series. French with subtitles. **97m/B; VHS, DVD, Blu-Ray.** *FR* Jean-Pierre Leaud; Claire Maurier; Albert Remy; Guy Decomble; Georges Flament; Patrick Auffay; Francois Truffaut; Jeanne Moreau; Jean-Claude Brialy; Jacques Demy; Robert Beauvais; *D:* Francois Truffaut; *W:* Francois Truffaut; Marcel Moussey; *C:* Henri Decae; *M:* Jean Constantin. Cannes '59: Director (Truffaut); N.Y. Film Critics '59: Foreign Film.

Four in a Jeep **1/2 1951** In Vienna in 1945, soldiers from different countries are serving as an international military police force. They clash as a result of political demands and their love for the same woman. Shot on location in Austria. **83m/B; VHS, DVD.** Ralph Meeker; Viveca Lindfors; Joseph Yadin; Michael Medwin; *D:* Leopold Lindtberg.

Four in the Morning **1/2 1965** Bleak, dated drama in which two British couples are unexpectedly tied together by a drowning. A lonely wife resents being left at home with their baby while her husband goes drinking with his mate and a young man and his girlfriend go down to the Thames and steal a motor boat to take a joyride. **90m/B; DVD.** *UK* Dame Judi Dench; Norman Rodway; Ann Lynn; Brian Phelan; Joe Melia; *D:* Anthony Simmons; *W:* Anthony Simmons; *C:* Larry Pizer; *M:* John Barry.

Four Jills in a Jeep **1/2 1944** Francis, Landis, Raye, and Mayfair all play themselves in this Fox musical comedy that has Francis organizing a USO tour (as they'd actually done in 1943) for the boys overseas. Landis married an airman she met (and wrote about it) so their romance is chronicled as well. Many other Fox players offer support, including Alice Faye, Betty Grable, Carmen Miranda, George Jessel, and Jimmy Dorsey and his band. **89m/B; DVD.** Kay Francis; Carole Landis; Martha Raye; John Harvey; Phil Silvers; Dick Haymes; Mitzi Mayfair; *D:* William A. Seiter; *W:* Helen Logan; Snag Werris; Robert Ellis; *C:* J. Peverell Marley.

Four Last Songs **1/2 2006** Lounge pianist Larry (Tucci) is trying for musical acclaim by holding a tribute concert to a late classical composer, who was a native of his Mediterranean resort town. However, life keeps getting in his way. There's his long-lost daughter, neurotic lovers and friends, and eccentric neighbors ruining his big chance. Lots of over-acting. **110m/C; DVD.** *GB SP* Stanley Tucci; Rhys Ifans; Hugh Bonneville; Jena Malone; Jessica Stevenson; Marisa Paredes; Emmanuelle Seigner; Karl Johnson; Virgile Bramly; *D:* Francesca Joseph; *W:* Francesca Joseph; *C:* Javier Salmones; *M:* Dan (Daniel) Jones.

A Four Letter Word **1/2 2007** Breezy and colorful gay rom com. Gym bunny Luke and his social activist friend Zeke work in a Chelsea sex shop. Zeke chastises his friend for his sexual shallowness until Luke falls for less flamboyant Stephen. Luke even contemplates monogamy (horrors!) but doesn't realize just how many secrets Stephen is hiding. **82m/C; DVD.** Charlie David; Jesse Archer; Cory Grant; Virginia Bryan; Steven Goldsmith; J.R. Rolley; *D:* Casper Andreas; *W:* Jesse Archer; Casper Andreas; *C:* Jon Fordham; *M:* Scott Starrett.

Four Lions **1/2 2010 (R)** Satire about some British-Muslim would-be jihadists who don't know how to get the job done. Dumb, violent, and possibly crazy, the five are aimless, incompetent would-be bombers who spend much of their time bickering among themselves and succumbing to peer pressure. The black comedy is funny and horrifying at the same time. **97m/C; DVD.** *GB* Rizwan Ahmed; Kayvan Novak; Adeel Akhtar; Nigel Lindsay; Arsher Ali; Preeya Kalidas; *D:* Christopher Morris; *W:* Jesse Armstrong; Christopher Morris; Sam Bain; *C:* Lol Crawley.

Four Lovers **1/2** *Happy Few* **2010** Shallow romantic drama about two married couples who become friends and swap sexual partners. The arrangement is casual and seemingly without much conflict, although a little jealousy creeps in, and doesn't damage either marriage. The actors don't have any issues with nudity but it isn't nearly as sexually enticing as you might imagine. English and French with subtitles. **105m/C; DVD.** *FR* Marina Fois; Elodie Bouchez; Roschdy Zem; Nicolas Duvauchelle; *D:* Anthony Cordier; *W:* Anthony Cordier; Julie Peyr; *C:* Nicolas Gaurin; *M:* Frederic Verrieres.

Four Men and a Prayer **1938** The four Leigh brothers (Greene, Sanders, Niven, Henry) seek the truth behind their colonel father's (Smith) dismissal from military service in India and his alleged suicide, which they believe was murder. Stiff upper lips prevail as the siblings travel from India to Argentina to Egypt and back home to England to restore the family honor. **85m/B; DVD.** Richard Greene; George Sanders; David Niven; William Henry; Sir C. Aubrey Smith; Loretta Young; Alan Hale, Jr.; John Carradine; Reginald Denny; J. Edward Bromberg; Berton Churchill; Barry Fitzgerald; *D:* John Ford; *W:* Sonya Levien; Richard Sherman; Walter Ferris; *C:* Ernest Palmer.

The Four Minute Mile **1988** Four athletes become determined to break the record of running the mile in under four minutes. **186m/C; DVD.** *UK* Richard Huw; Nique Needles; John Philbin; Lewis Fitz-Gerald; Michael York; *D:* Jim (James) Goddard; *W:* David Williamson; *C:* Ian Warburton. **TV**

4 Months, 3 Weeks and 2 Days **1/2** *4 Luni, 3 Saptamani si 2 Zile* **2007** Stunning, intense thriller about two college roommates who seek an illegal abortion for one of them in the hellish totalitarian state of 1987 Romania. To do so they must enter the Romanian underworld and find someone to do the procedure while dealing with low-lifes who threaten them with violence, blackmail, and humiliation every step of the way. A tightly crafted noir that uses the challenging issue of abortion as a backdrop rather than a centerpiece, instead focusing on the struggles of the two women in the face of a dangerous world they aren't meant to see. **113m/C; DVD, Blu-Ray.** *RO* Laura Vasiliu; Anamaria Marinca; Alex Potocean; Vlad Ivanov; ***D:*** Cristian Mungiu; ***W:*** Cristian Mungiu; ***C:*** Oleg Mutu.

Four More Years *Fyra Ar Till* **2010** Amusing political/sex comedy from Sweden. An upset deprives career politician David Holst (Kjellman) of his rise to prime minister, and he goes into a depression despite his wife Fia's (Magnusson) already plotting their next strategy. He reluctantly returns to the fray and gets to know gay colleague Martin (Ericson) better than expected since they begin an affair. Despite their being in opposition political parties, things get serious both personally and professionally. Swedish with subtitles. **90m/C; DVD.** *SW* Bjorn Kjellman; Eric Ericson; Tova Magnusson-Norling; Andre Wickstrom; Sten Ljunggren; ***D:*** Tova Magnusson-Norling; ***W:*** Wilhelm Behrman; ***C:*** Trolle Davidson; Victor Davidson; ***M:*** Mauro Scocco.

Four Mothers **1941** Last-gasp sequel to 1939's "Four Wives" puts the Lemp family through an emotional grinder before a contrived happy ending. The Lemp sisters are all married with families of their own and dad Adam has been boasting about son-in-law Ben's Florida real estate development. The Lemps invest as do all their friends and neighbors--just in time for a hurricane to destroy the property. Adam feels it's his responsibility to cover everyone's losses, which will bankrupt him. **85m/B; DVD.** Priscilla Lane; Rosemary Lane; Lola Lane; Gale Page; Claude Rains; May Robson; Jeffrey Lynn; Frank McHugh; Dick Foran; Eddie Albert; ***D:*** William Keighley; ***W:*** Stephen Morehiouse Avery; ***C:*** Charles Rosher; ***M:*** Heinz Roemheld.

The Four Musketeers *The Revenge of Milady* **1975 (PG)** A fun-loving continuation of "The Three Musketeers," reportedly filmed simultaneously. Lavish swashbuckler jaunts between France, England, and Italy, in following the adventures of D'Artagnan and his cohorts. Pictures give an amusing depiction of Lester-interpreted 17th-century Europe, with fine performances especially by Dunaway as an evil countess seeking revenge on our heroes and Welch as the scatterbrained object of York's affections. Followed, in 1989, by "The Return of the Musketeers." **108m/C; VHS, DVD.** Michael York; Oliver Reed; Richard Chamberlain; Frank Finlay; Raquel Welch; Christopher Lee; Faye Dunaway; Jean-Pierre Cassel; Geraldine Chaplin; Simon Ward; Charlton Heston; Roy Kinnear; Nicole Calfan; ***D:*** Richard Lester; ***W:*** George MacDonald Fraser; ***C:*** David Watkin; ***M:*** Lalo Schifrin.

The 4 Musketeers ½ *D'Artagnan et les Trois Mousquietaires; D'Artagnan and the Three Musketeers* **2005 (R)** Yet another (remarkably dull and silly) version of the Dumas swashbuckler, only this time the evil Milady de Winter (Beart) has made a pact with the devil for some supernatural powers. The musketeers still use their swords a lot and battle the corrupt Cardinal Richelieu (Karyo) as well. Made for French TV; dubbed into English. **190m/C; DVD.** *FR* Emmanuelle Beart; Tcheky Karyo; Vincent Elbaz; Gregori Derangere; Heino Ferch; Stefania Rocca; Tristan Ulloa; Gregory Gadebois; Diana Amft; ***D:*** Pierre Aknine; ***W:*** Pierre Aknine; ***C:*** Allen Smith; ***M:*** Matt Dunkley. **TV**

Four of Hearts **2013** A romantic drama about a couple trying to reconnect and make their marriage stronger via an unexpected path. Though April (Ellis) and Derrick (Henson) seem to be happily married, they struggle to feel connected through the busyness of life and work. After months-long dry spell, they want to find their passion again. To do so, they share a night with more free-thinking friends, Matt (Olds) and Christy (Krusiec). Though the encounter leaves April and Derrick questioning much about themselves and their relationship, they decide to seek a path that allows them to fully reconnect as a married couple. **99m/C; DVD, Streaming, Download.** Charles Divins; Nadine Ellis; Darrin Dewitt Henson; Jenn Korbee; Michelle Krusiec; ***D:*** Eric Haywood; ***W:*** Eric Haywood; ***C:*** Finnian Riley; ***M:*** Olivier Roulon. **VIDEO**

Four Rode Out **1969** A Mexican outlaw is pursued by his girlfriend, one-time partner, and the law. Brutal, inferior western. **99m/C; VHS, DVD.** Pernell Roberts; Sue Lyon; Leslie Nielsen; Julian Mateos; ***D:*** John Peyser.

Four Rooms **1995 (R)** Four stories by four hot indie filmers set in the same L.A. hotel on New Year's Eve are tied together by bellboy Roth, stumbling around in a Jerry/Carrey-like stupor. Leading off is Anders's roomful of witches trying to resurrect spirit of '50s stripper DeCadenet. After this disappointing start is Rockwell's bland look at infidelity, with wife Beals tied and gagged by her husband (Proval) over an alleged fling with Roth. Bandaras heads the best seg as a mobster who leaves his demonic children in Roth's hands. Tarantino is the anchor man with his take on Hitchcock, dealing with a macabre bet involving the removal of body parts. Altogether disjointed and uninspired. **98m/C; VHS, DVD.** Tim Roth; Antonio Banderas; Jennifer Beals; Paul Calderon; Sammi Davis; Valeria Golino; Madonna; Ione Skye; Marisa Tomei; Tamlyn Tomita; Bruce Willis; David Proval; Lili Taylor; Alicia Witt; Amanda DeCadenet; Danny Verduzco; Lana McKissack; Quentin Tarantino; ***Cameo(s):*** Salma Hayek; ***D:*** Quentin Tarantino; Alexandre Rockwell; Robert Rodriguez; Allison Anders; ***W:*** Quentin Tarantino; Alexandre Rockwell; Robert Rodriguez; Allison Anders; ***C:*** Phil Parmet; Guillermo Navarro; Andrzej Sekula; Rodrigo Garcia; ***M:*** Combustible Edison; Esquivel. Golden Raspberries '95: Worst Support. Actress (Madonna).

The Four Seasons ½ **1981 (PG)** Three upper-middle-class New York couples share their vacations together, as well as their friendship, their frustrations and their jealousies. Alda's first outing as a film director is pleasant and easy on the eyes. **108m/C; VHS, DVD.** Alan Alda; Carol Burnett; Sandy Dennis; Len Cariou; Jack Weston; Rita Moreno; Bess Armstrong; ***D:*** Alan Alda; ***W:*** Alan Alda.

Four Sheets to the Wind **2007 (R)** Seminole-Cree Cufe Smallhill discovers that his ill father has committed suicide. When his older sister Miri comes home for the funeral, she persuades Cufe that he needs a break from their small hometown and should come and stay with her in Tulsa. Miri is a party-hard gal and Cufe finds more sympathy from her neighbor Francie and a chance to decide what's next in his life. **81m/C; DVD.** Cody Lightning; Jeri Arredondo; Christian Kane; Tamara Podemski; Laura Bailey; ***D:*** Sterlin Harjo; ***W:*** Sterlin Harjo; ***C:*** Frederick Schroeder; ***M:*** Jeff Johnson.

Four Sided Triangle **1953** Two mad scientists find their friendship threatened when they discover that they are both in love with the same woman. So they do what anyone would do in this situation—they invent a machine and duplicate her. **81m/B; VHS, DVD.** *GB* James Hayter; Barbara Payton; Stephen Murray; John Van Eyssen; Percy Marmont; ***D:*** Terence Fisher; ***W:*** Terence Fisher; Paul Tabori; ***C:*** Reg Wyer; ***M:*** Malcolm Arnold.

4 Single Fathers ½ **2009** Four Italian-born men, now living in New York, are or were married to American women with whom they have children. Dentist Jacopo is separated from Ilana and sleeps around; architect Dom is separated from Julia but is desperate to reconcile; real estate agent Ennio is shocked when his wife Sarah asks for a divorce; and cop George and wife Maria are in an abusive marriage. The four men meet in a bar and start offering each other advice but their stories aren't terribly interesting. **98m/C; DVD.** Alessandro Gassman; Francesco Quinn; Lenny Venito; Joe Urla; Sarah Rafferty; Mary Testa; Colleen Dunn; Margot White; Will Chase; Jennifer Esposito; ***D:*** Paolo Monico; ***W:*** Liz Tuccillo; ***C:*** Andres E. Sanchez; ***M:*** Paolo Buonvino.

Four Skulls of Jonathan Drake ½ **1959** Jivaro Indians living in the Amazon jungle placed a curse on the Drake family of traders. It's still in place 200 years later as Jonathan discovers when he goes to his brother Kenneth's funeral and the man's head is missing. Jonathan fears he'll be the next victim of a witch doctor who likes to shrink heads. Some creepy scenes and the Amazonian servant has his lips sewn shut. **70m/B; DVD, Blu-Ray.** Eduard Franz; Valerie French; Henry Daniell; Grant Richards; Paul Wexler; Paul Cavanagh; ***D:*** Edward L. Cahn; ***W:*** Orville H. Hampton; ***C:*** Maury Gertsman; ***M:*** Paul Dunlap.

Four Sons **1928** Mother Bernle lives with her four sons in Burgendorf, Bavaria. Joseph has a job offer in America and his mother gives him money to help him immigrate. The other three boys enlist in WWI and when America enters the war, Joseph enlists on the other side. After the war is over, and after much hardship and sorrow, Mother Bernle goes through Ellis Island herself. **100m/B; Silent; DVD.** Margaret Mann; James Hall; George Meeker; June Collyer; Charles Morton; Ralph Bushman; Earle Foxe; Albert Gran; ***D:*** John Ford; ***W:*** Philip Klein; ***C:*** George Schneiderman.

Four Sons **1940** Update of the 1928 silent pic. The four Czech Bern brothers are bitterly divided during WWII after Hitler marches into their homeland. Chris (Ameche) joins the resistance; Karl (Curtis) becomes a fervent Nazi; Fritz (Ernest) is conscripted into the German army and is sent to Poland; and Joseph (Lowery) emigrates to America to become an artist. Meanwhile, Mama Bern (Leontovich) frets about her sons. **88m/B; DVD.** Don Ameche; Alan Curtis; George Ernest; Robert Lowery; Eugenie Leontovich; Mary Beth Hughes; ***D:*** Archie Mayo; ***W:*** John Howard Lawson; ***C:*** Leon Shamroy; ***M:*** David Buttolph.

4.3.2.1 **2010** Mildly interesting Brit crime drama, divided into four segments, about four young women coincidentally involved in a diamond heist in London. Shannon unwittingly comes into possession of blood diamonds making the rounds of criminals; there's rich girl Cassandra's secret romance and New York weekend; lesbian Kerry's, whose half-brother Manuel is mixed-up with the crime along with his friend Tee; and supermarket worker Joanne, whose boss is Tee. **117m/C; DVD, Blu-Ray.** *UK* Ophelia Lovibond; Tamsin Egerton; Shanika Warren-Markland; Emma Roberts; Michelle Ryan; Gregg Chillin; Noel Clarke; ***D:*** Noel Clarke; ***W:*** Noel Clarke; ***C:*** Franco Pezzino; ***M:*** Adam Lewis; Barnaby Robson. **VIDEO**

Four Times That Night *Quante Volte...Quella Notte* **1969 (R)** Though he's known for his work in horror, Mario Bava also made one sex comedy and it's not a bad little movie, though its appeal is mostly nostalgia. Technically, it's a "Rashomon" story with the events of one night told from different points of view. What happens when Gianni (Halsey) takes the lovely Tina (Giordano) to his bachelor pad? Is it date rape or does she seduce him? The film is still grand stuff for '60s fans. The shagadelic apartment must be seen to be believed. **83m/C; DVD, Blu-Ray.** *IT* Brett Halsey; Daniela Giordano; Pascale Petit; Brigitte Skay; ***D:*** Mario Bava; ***M:*** Lallo Gori.

Four Warriors ½ **2015 (PG-13)** A low-budget adventure fantasy drama about four men's efforts to save a village. Having seen it all while participating in the Crusades, four men agree to take on a new mission. In a village devastated by battle, all the men and children have been taken by a depraved predator—leaving all the women behind. Through sorcery and battles, the Crusaders work to find the abductees, bring them home, and fight the evil involved. **95m/C; DVD, Blu-Ray, Streaming, Download.** Christopher Dane; Hadrian Howard; Fergal Philips; Glenn Speers; Alex Childs; ***D:*** Phil Hawkins; ***W:*** Christopher Dane; ***C:*** David Meadows; ***M:*** Richard Bodgers. **VIDEO**

Four Weddings and a Funeral **1994 (R)** Refreshing, intelligent adult comedy brimming with stiff upper-lip wit and sophistication. Thirtyish Brit bachelor Charles (Grant) spends his time attending the weddings of his friends, but manages to avoid taking the plunge himself. Then he falls for American Carrie (MacDowell), who's about to wed another. Great beginning offers loads of laughs as the first two weddings unfold, then becomes decidedly bittersweet. While Grant makes this a star turn as the romantic bumbler, MacDowell charms without seeming particularly needed. Supporting characters are superb, especially Coleman as the "flirty" Scarlett and Atkinson as a new minister. Surprising boxoffice hit found a broad audience. **118m/C; VHS, DVD, Blu-Ray.** *GB* Hugh Grant; Andie MacDowell; Simon Callow; Kristin Scott Thomas; James Fleet; John Hannah; Charlotte Coleman; David Bower; Corin Redgrave; Rowan Atkinson; Rosalie Crutchley; Jeremy Kemp; Sophie Thompson; Kenneth Griffith; David Haig; ***D:*** Mike Newell; ***W:*** Richard Curtis; ***C:*** Michael Coulter; ***M:*** Richard Rodney Bennett. Australian Film Inst. '94: Foreign Film; British Acad. '94: Actor (Grant), Director (Newell), Film, Support. Actress (Scott Thomas); Golden Globes '95: Actor--Mus./Comedy (Grant); Writers Guild '94: Orig. Screenplay.

Four Wives ½ **1939** Sequel to 1938's "Four Daughters." Thea and Emma Lemp have married, Kay has her eye on a doctor, and even widowed Ann is being wooed by former beau Felix. Just when Ann is about to accept Felix's proposal, she realizes she's pregnant by her late husband, Mickey. Garfield, whose character died in the first film, has a cameo in a flashback scene. Followed by 1941's "Four Mothers." **99m/B; DVD.** Priscilla Lane; Rosemary Lane; Lola Lane; Gale Page; Claude Rains; May Robson; Frank McHugh; Dick Foran; Jeffrey Lynn; Eddie Albert; Henry O'Neill; ***Cameo(s):*** John Garfield; ***D:*** Michael Curtiz; ***W:*** Julius J. Epstein; Philip G. Epstein; ***C:*** Sol Polito; ***M:*** Max Steiner.

The 4D Man ½ **1959** A physicist makes two fateful discoveries while working on a special project that gets out of control, leaving him able to pass through matter and see around corners. He also finds that his touch brings instant death. Cheap but effective sci-fier. Young Duke has a small part. **85m/C; VHS, DVD, Blu-Ray.** Robert Lansing; Lee Meriwether; James Congdon; Guy Raymond; Robert Strauss; Patty Duke; ***D:*** Irvin S. Yeaworth, Jr.; ***W:*** Theodore Simonson; Cy Chermack; ***C:*** Theodore J. Pahle; ***M:*** Ralph Carmichael.

Four's a Crowd ½ **1938** Rather complicated screwball comedy with some unexpected romantic complications. With her newspaper about to fold, reporter Jean Christy (Russell) persuades publisher Patterson Buckley (Knowles) to rehire former editor Robert Lansford (Flynn), who's now doing public relations. Ambitious Lansford wants to get tightwad millionaire John Dillingwell (Connolly) as a client and change his image using the media so he agrees, especially after meeting Dillingwell's daughter Lorri (de Havilland). Jean says Lorri is her romantic rival for Patterson, but later Lansford decides he's in love with Lorri and Dillingwell doesn't approve in either case. **91m/B; DVD.** Errol Flynn; Olivia de Havilland; Rosalind Russell; Patric Knowles; Walter Connolly; Hugh Herbert; Melville Cooper; Franklin Pangborn; Margaret Hamilton; ***D:*** Michael Curtiz; ***W:*** Sid Herzig; Casey Robinson; ***C:*** Ernest Haller; ***M:*** Heinz Roemheld; Ray Heindorf.

The Foursome ½ **2006 (PG-13)** Four buddies reunite at their twentieth college reunion, discussing work, money, wives, and sex. Still competitive, the guys indulge in a golf game that results in some personal and awkward revelations. Harmless enough but leans toward boring and dumb. **80m/C; DVD.** Kevin Dillon; Siri Baruc; Chris Gauthier; Paul Jarrett; John Shaw; ***D:*** William Dear; ***W:*** Jackson Davies; ***M:*** Chris Ainscough. **VIDEO**

14 Blades ½ *Jin yi wei* **2014 (R)** This period piece set during the Ming Dynasty in the royal court is a dramatic thriller. From childhood, Qinglong (Yen) has been trained in a secret form of combat. As an adult, he gained a reputation as a legendary royal guard and serves the emperor. When the Imperial Court falls into the hands of traitor Jia (Kar-Ying), Qinglong must overcome betrayals and evade former allies who were hunting him. Becoming the most wanted man in the country, he seeks out and rallies loyalists to restore the emperor to the throne. Mandarin with subtitles. **114m/C; DVD, Blu-Ray, Streaming, Download.** Donnie Yen; Wei Zhao; Chun Wu; Sammo Hung; Kate Tsui; ***D:*** Daniel Lee; ***W:*** Daniel Lee; Kwong Man Wai; Tin Shu Mak; Ho Leung Lau; ***C:*** Tony Cheung; ***M:*** Henry Lai.

1408 ½ **2007 (PG-13)** Professional skeptic Mike Enslin (Cusack) specializes in debunking haunted houses and other paranormal spots in his bestselling books. His next target is room 1408 at Manhattan's

Dolphin Hotel, despite the warnings of manager Gerald Olin (Jackson) that it's just plain evil. The room preys on an occupant's deepest, darkest fears and since Mike is grieving the death of his young daughter Katie (Anthony), should he be surprised when she shows up? Creepiness builds effectively. Adapted from a Stephen King short story. **94m/C; DVD, Blu-Ray.** John Cusack; Samuel L. Jackson; Mary McCormack; Jasmine Jessica Anthony; ***D:*** Mikael Hafstrom; ***W:*** Matt Greenberg; Scott M. Alexander; Larry Karaszewski; ***C:*** Benoit Delhomme; ***M:*** Gabriel Yared.

1492: Conquest of Paradise 🦴🦴 1/2 **1992 (PG-13)** Large-scale Hollywood production striving for political correctness is a drawn-out account of Columbus's (Depardieu) discovery and subsequent exploitation of the "New World." Skillful directing by Ridley Scott and impressive scenery add interest, yet don't make up for a script which chronicles events but tends towards trite dialogue and characterization. Available in both pan-and-scan and letterbox formats. **142m/C; VHS, DVD, Blu-Ray.** Gerard Depardieu; Sigourney Weaver; Armand Assante; Frank Langella; Loren Dean; Angela Molina; Fernando Rey; Michael Wincott; Steven Waddington; Tcheky Karyo; Kario Salem; ***D:*** Ridley Scott; ***W:*** Roselyne Bosch; ***M:*** Vangelis.

The Fourth Angel 🦴🦴 **2001 (R)** London-based journalist Jack Elgin (Irons) is on holiday with his family when their plane is hijacked by terrorists. Jack's wife and two daughters are among the dead. He's naturally outraged after learning the hijackers have been released and decides to hunt the criminals himself, which draws the attention of CIA agents Bernard (Whitaker) and Davidson (Priestley). A not unfamiliar revenge thriller. Based on the novel "Angel" by Robin Hunter. **95m/C; VHS, DVD.** Jeremy Irons; Forest Whitaker; Jason Priestley; Charlotte Rampling; Lois Maxwell; Timothy West; Ian McNeice; ***D:*** John Irvin; ***W:*** Allan Scott; ***C:*** Mike Molloy; ***M:*** Paul Zaza.

The 4th Dimension 🦴 1/2 **2006** Child genius turned OCD loner, Jack Emitni's (Morabito) fascinated with Einstein's unsolved Unified Field Theory. Yeah, we don't know what that is either, which is probably a good thing since it seems to drive Jack nuts. He also regards sleeping as the fourth dimension, allowing him to travel between his memories or something like that. The directors don't have anything so mundane as a linear, clear plot. Mostly filmed in B&W with some scenes in color. **82m/B; DVD.** Louis Morabito; Karen Peakes; Miles Williams; Kate LaRoss; Suzanne Inman; ***D:*** Tom Mattera; Dave Mazzoni; ***W:*** Tom Mattera; Dave Mazzoni; ***C:*** Daniel Watchulonis; ***M:*** John Avarese.

The 4th Floor 🦴🦴 **1999 (R)** Lewis, who's engaged to older and successful TV weatherman Hurt, inherits a rent-controlled apartment and is then terrorized by her neighbor, who may be working for someone else. Twist ending leaves viewer with more questions than answers. **90m/C; VHS, DVD.** Juliette Lewis; William Hurt; Austin Pendleton; Shelley Duvall; Artie Lange; Tobin Bell; ***D:*** Josh Klausner; ***W:*** Josh Klausner; ***C:*** Michael Slovis; ***M:*** Brian Tyler.

The Fourth Kind 🦴 **2009 (PG-13)** Dopey alien abduction pic with fake documentary footage that's allegedly based on actual psychological case studies. Nome, Alaska shrink Dr. Tyler (Jovovich) uses hypnosis on her patients who have a tendency to levitate or go insane. And the good doc isn't too reliable either since her husband was murdered and she hears weird voices and has hallucinations of white owls (as do her patients). Not campy enough to fall into the 'so-bad-it's-good' category, it's just boring. **98m/C; DVD, Blu-Ray.** Milla Jovovich; Corey Johnson; Enzo Cilenti; Alisha Seaton; Elias Koteas; Will Patton; Hakeem Kae-Kazim; Mia McKenna-Bruce; ***D:*** Olatunde Osunsanmi; ***W:*** Olatunde Osunsanmi; ***C:*** Lorenzo Senatore; ***M:*** Atli Orvarsson.

The 4th Man 🦴🦴🦴 1/2 *Die Vierde Man* **1979** Steeped in saturated colors and jet black comedy, with an atmospheric score, Verhoeven's nouveau noir mystery enjoyed considerable art-house success but was not released in the US until 1984. The story is decidedly non-linear, the look stylish and symbolic. Krabbe is an alcoholic bisexual Catholic writer who inadvertently becomes the hypotenuse of a love triangle involving Herman, a young man he encounters at a railway station, and his lover Christine, who owns the Sphinx beauty parlor and whose three husbands died, shall we say, mysteriously. In Dutch with English subtitles. **102m/C; VHS, DVD.** *NL* Jeroen Krabbe; Renee Soutendijk; Thom Hoffman; Jon (John) DeVries; Geert De Jong; ***D:*** Paul Verhoeven; ***W:*** Gerard Soeteman; ***C:*** Jan De Bont; ***M:*** Loek Dikker. L.A. Film Critics '84: Foreign Film.

The Fourth Protocol 🦴🦴🦴 **1987 (R)** Well-made thriller based on the Frederick Forsyth bestseller about a British secret agent trying to stop a young KGB agent from destroying NATO and putting the world in nuclear jeopardy. Brosnan, as the totally dedicated Russkie, gives his best performance to date while Caine, as usual, is totally believable as he goes about the business of tracking down the bad guys. **119m/C; VHS, Streaming.** *GB* Michael Caine; Pierce Brosnan; Ned Beatty; Joanna Cassidy; Julian Glover; Ray McAnally; Michael Gough; Ian Richardson; Betsy Brantley; Matt Frewer; Peter Cartwright; David Conville; ***D:*** John MacKenzie; ***W:*** Frederick Forsyth; Richard Burridge; George Axelrod; ***C:*** Phil Meheux; ***M:*** Lalo Schifrin; Francis Shaw.

The 4th Tenor 🦴🦴 1/2 **2002 (PG-13)** Well, Rodney doesn't get much respect in this movie either—at least not at first. Italian restaurateur Lupo (Dangerfield) has fallen for one of his operatic singing waitresses (Gurwitch) but she doesn't return his interest. So he decides he has to learn to sing himself to impress her and flies to Italy for professional coaching, only to be taken in by a couple of con men. **97m/C; VHS, DVD.** Rodney Dangerfield; Robert Davi; Annabelle Gurwitch; Anita De Simone; Charles Fleischer; Richard Libertini; Vincent Schiavelli; ***D:*** Harry Basil; ***W:*** Rodney Dangerfield; Harry Basil; ***C:*** Ken Blakey; ***M:*** Christopher Lennertz. **VIDEO**

The Fourth War 🦴🦴 **1990 (R)** Scheider and Prochnow are American and Russian colonels, respectively, assigned to guard the West German-Czechoslovakian border against each other. With the end of the cold war looming, these two frustrated warriors begin to taunt each other with sallies into the other's territory, threatening to touch off a major superpower conflict. **109m/C; VHS, DVD, Blu-Ray.** Roy Scheider; Jurgen Prochnow; Tim Reid; Lara Harris; Harry Dean Stanton; Dale Dye; ***D:*** John Frankenheimer; ***M:*** Bill Conti.

Fourth Wise Man 🦴🦴 **1985** A Biblical Easter story about a rich physician searching for Christ in Persia. **72m/C; VHS, DVD.** Martin Sheen; Lance Kerwin; Alan Arkin; Harold Gould; Eileen Brennan; Ralph Bellamy; Adam Arkin; Richard Libertini; ***D:*** Michael Ray Rhodes; ***W:*** Tom Fontana; ***C:*** Jon Kranhouse; ***M:*** Bruce Langhorne.

Fox and His Friends 🦴🦴🦴 1/2 *Faustrecht der Freiheit; Fist Right of Freedom* **1975** Fassbinder's breakthrough tragi-drama, about a lowly gay carnival barker who wins the lottery, thus attracting a devious, exploiting lover, who takes him for everything he has. In German with English subtitles. **123m/C; VHS, DVD, Blu-Ray.** *GE* Rainer Werner Fassbinder; Peter Chatel; Karl-Heinz Boehm; Adrian Hoven; Harry Baer; Ulla Jacobsson; Kurt Raab; ***D:*** Rainer Werner Fassbinder; ***C:*** Michael Ballhaus.

The Fox and the Hound 🦴🦴🦴 **1981 (G)** Sweet story of the friendship shared by a fox and hound. Young and naive, the animals become friends and swear their allegiance to one another when they are separated for a season. Upon return, the hound has become his master's best hunting dog and warns his friend the fox to stay clear of their hunting grounds, for the master is determined to catch the docile fox. Saddened, the fox retreats but soon finds himself boldly standing his ground against a bear that attacks the hound, and the hound inevitably protects the fox from the mean-spirited hunter. Very good animation, but not in the same class as other Disney favorites like "Beauty and the Beast." **83m/C; VHS, DVD, Blu-Ray.** ***V:*** Mickey Rooney; Kurt Russell; Pearl Bailey; Jack Albertson; Sandy Duncan; Jeannette Nolan; Pat Buttram; John Fiedler; John McIntire; Richard Bakalyan; Paul Winchell; Keith Coogan; Corey Feldman; ***D:*** Art Stevens; Ted Berman; Richard Rich; ***W:*** Art Stevens; Peter Young; Steve Hulett; Earl Kress; Vance Gerry; Laury Clemmons; Dave Michener; Burny Mattinson; ***M:*** Buddy (Norman Dale) Baker.

The Fox and the Hound 2 🦴🦴 **2006 (G)** Fox Tod and hound dog Copper are still buddies but their friendship is tested when Copper's head is turned by a group of hound dog howlers. **69m/C; DVD, Blu-Ray.** ***V:*** Reba McEntire; Jeff Foxworthy; Patrick Swayze; Rob Paulsen; ***D:*** Jim Kammerud; ***W:*** Rich Burns; Roger S.H. Schulman; ***M:*** Joel McNeely. **VIDEO**

Foxcatcher 🦴🦴🦴 **2014 (R)** Director Miller continues his dissection of Americana with this fascinating true story about bizarre John Du Pont (an unrecognizable Carell), a man who started an Olympic Games-worthy wrestling training facility on his massive estate (from which the film takes its title) and who ended up a murderer. Tatum and Ruffalo co-star as the wrestler brothers brought into this web of insecurity and insanity. Arguably a cold portrayal, it's also powerful as it peels back the curtain on a world of privilege that can lead to tragedy. Tatum and Ruffalo do career-best work. **130m/C; DVD, Blu-Ray.** Steve Carell; Mark Ruffalo; Channing Tatum; Sienna Miller; Vanessa Redgrave; ***D:*** Bennett Miller; ***W:*** Dan Futterman; E. Max Frye; ***C:*** Greig Fraser; ***M:*** Rob Simonsen.

Foxes 🦴🦴 **1980 (R)** Four young California girls grow up with little supervision from parents still trying to grow up themselves. They rely on each other in a world where they have to make adult choices, yet are not considered grown-up. They look for no more than a good time and no tragic mistakes. **106m/C; VHS, DVD, Blu-Ray.** Jodie Foster; Cherie Currie; Marilyn Kagan; Scott Baio; Sally Kellerman; Randy Quaid; Laura Dern; ***D:*** Adrian Lyne; ***W:*** Gerald Ayres.

The Foxes of Harrow 🦴 1/2 **1947** Adapted from Frank Yerby's historical potboiler. In the early 19th century, Irish gambler Stephen Fox (Harrison) heads to New Orleans to make his fortune. He wins a plantation in a card game, marries southern belle Lilli (O'Hara), and learns that both are too strong-willed to make life easy on themselves. Stephen leaves to try his gambling luck while Lilli runs the plantation and deals with the slaves. **117m/B; DVD.** Rex Harrison; Maureen O'Hara; Victor McLaglen; Richard Haydn; Gene Lockhart; Vanessa Brown; Patricia Medina; ***D:*** John M. Stahl; ***W:*** Wanda Tuchock; ***C:*** Joseph LaShelle; ***M:*** David Buttolph.

Foxfire 🦴🦴🦴 **1987 (PG)** In the role that won her Tony and Emmy awards, Tandy stars as Annie Nations, a woman who has lived her entire life in the Blue Ridge Mountains. Widowed, all she has left are the memories of her beloved husband, with whom she regularly communes. Her son tries to convince her to move, and it becomes a clash of the wills as Annie tries to decide whether to stay in her past or change her future. **118m/C; VHS, DVD.** Jessica Tandy; Hume Cronyn; John Denver; Gary Grubbs; Harriet Hall; ***D:*** Jud Taylor; ***C:*** Thomas Burstyn. **TV**

Foxfire 🦴🦴 **1996 (R)** Not much more than "The Craft" without the hocus-pocus. Lusty Legs Sadovsky (Jolie) is a liberated drifter who empowers a quartet of abused teens to take action against their molester, who happens to be their biology teacher. Based on the book by Joyce Carol Oates originally written in the 1950s, modern adaptation suffers from time warp, most notably when the girls expose their teacher's behavior to their principal and he promptly suspends them without further ado. After some bonding and tattooing in an abandoned house, flick descends into the more masculine and mundane territory of car chases, kidnapping and gunplay. Filmmakers rather timidly back off of leather-clad Legs' obvious lesbianism and her relationship with the adoring Maddy (Burress). Decent acting by most would've benefitted from a more cohesive screenplay. **102m/C; VHS, DVD.** Angelina Jolie; John Diehl; Jenny Lewis; Cathy Moriarty; Richard Beymer; Hedy Burress; Jenny Shimizu; Sarah Rosenberg; Peter Facinelli; ***D:*** Annette Haywood-Carter; ***W:*** Elizabeth White; ***C:*** Newton Thomas (Tom) Sigel; ***M:*** Michel Colombier.

Foxfire Light 🦴 **1982 (PG)** A young woman vacationing in the Ozarks is drawn into a romance with a cowboy. But her mother's social ambitions and her own indecesion may tear them apart. **102m/C; VHS, Streaming.** Tippi Hedren; Lara Parker; Leslie Nielsen; Barry Van Dyke; ***D:*** Allen Baron; ***C:*** Thomas Ackerman.

Foxtrot 🦴🦴 1/2 **2018 (R)** A powerful dramatic look at chance and grief, divided into three parts. When Dafna Feldmann (Adler) and her husband Michael (Ashkenazi) learn that their son Jonathan (Shiray) has died in the line of duty, they both have deeply felt reactions. Shifting to Jonathan, his dull experiences at a remote military outpost are explored. His only task is to check the papers of the few vehicles that pass through his checkpoint. The stark reality of grief re-emerges in the film's third part. With memorable imagery and a complex construction, the film is wrenching in its exploration of loss. Hebrew with subtitles. **114m/C; DVD.** Lior Ashkenazi; Sarah Adler; Yonathan Shiray; Shira Haas; Danny Isserles; ***D:*** Samuel Maoz; ***W:*** Samuel Maoz; ***C:*** Giora Bejach; ***M:*** Ophir Leibovitch; Amit Poznansky.

Foxy Brown 🦴 **1974 (R)** A bitter woman poses as a prostitute to avenge the mob-backed deaths of her drug dealer brother and undercover cop boyfriend. Extremely violent black exploitation flick. **92m/C; VHS, DVD, Blu-Ray.** Pam Grier; Terry Carter; Antonio Fargas; Kathryn Loder; Peter Brown; Sid Haig; Juanita Brown; Tony Giorgio; ***D:*** Jack Hill; ***W:*** Jack Hill; ***C:*** Brick Marquard; ***M:*** Willie Hutch.

The FP WOOF! **2012 (R)** If you're in the mood for a so-bad-it's-good satire, then this wannabe cult piece of ridiculousness might be for you. In a dystopian near-future, outlandishly clad gangs fight for a grimy patch of turf called Frazier Park (or "The FP"). Instead of shooting it out, however, these foul-mouthed "Mad Max" refugees settle scores playing a cheesy dance videogame called Beat-Beat Revelation. JTRO (Trost) is the noble warrior who must overcome the nasty L Dubba E (Valmassy) to avenge his brother's death and save his trampy girlfriend and his town. **82m/C; DVD, Blu-Ray.** Jason Trost; Lee Valmassy; Art Hsu; Caitlyn Folley; Nick Principe; Brandon Barrera; ***D:*** Jason Trost; Brandon Trost; ***W:*** Jason Trost; Brandon Trost; ***C:*** Brandon Trost; ***M:*** George Holdcroft.

F.P. 1 🦴🦴 *F.P. 1 Doesn't Answer* **1933** An artifical island (Floating Platform 1) in the Atlantic is threatened by treason. This slow-moving 1930s technothriller is the English-language version of the German "F.P. 1 Antwortet Nicht" ("F.P. 1 Doesn't Answer"). Both were directed at the same time by Hartl, using different casts. **74m/B; VHS, DVD, Streaming.** *GE* Leslie Fenton; Conrad Veidt; Jill Esmond; ***D:*** Karl Hartl.

F.P. 1 Doesn't Answer 🦴🦴 *F.P. 1 Antwortet Nicht* **1933** A mid-Atlantic refueling station (Floating Platform 1) is threatened by treason and a pilot sets out to put things right. Features pre-Hollywood vintage Lorre; Albers was Germany's number one boxoffice draw at the time. In German. **74m/B; VHS, DVD.** *GE* Hans Albers; Sybille Schmitz; Paul Hartmann; Peter Lorre; Hermann Speelmanns; ***D:*** Karl Hartl.

Fracture 🦴🦴 1/2 **2007 (R)** Old Turk vs. young Turk as Hopkins and Gosling play mind games. Arrogant Ted Crawford (Hopkins) shoots his adulterous trophy wife Jennifer (Davitz). Prosecutor Willy Beachum (Gosling) is leaving for a cushy private job when he gets the case, which proceeds to fall apart. Since Ted is taunting him, Willy can't let things go, no matter what it costs. Hopkins plays his part with sadistic relish (yes, Hannibal Lecter will come to mind), while Gosling handles an emotional roller-coaster from cockiness to vulnerability to determination. **112m/C; DVD.** Anthony Hopkins; Ryan Gosling; David Strathairn; Rosamund Pike; Embeth Davidtz; Billy Burke; Clifford Curtis; Fiona Shaw; Bob Gunton; Xander Berkeley; Josh Stamberg; Zoe Kazan; ***D:*** Gregory Hoblit; ***W:*** Daniel Pyne; Glen Gers; ***C:*** Kramer Morgenthau; ***M:*** Mychael Danna; Jeff Danna.

Fractured 🦴🦴 **2019** While on a road trip, Ray Monroe (Worthington) and wife Joanne (Rabe) experience a tragedy. During a gas station stop, daughter Peri (Capri) walks over to a construction site and falls down backward onto a concrete floor after being startled by a stray dog. Though Ray tries to save her, he also falls. At the hospital, the family experiences issues with the healthcare being provided before Ray questions his sanity when his family goes missing. A promising premise becomes disjointed with a less-than-creepy atmosphere needed for the story being told. **99m/C; DVD.** Sam Worthington; Lily Rabe; Lucy Capri; Adjoa Andoh; Stephen Tobolowsky; ***D:*** Brad Anderson; ***W:*** Alan B. McElroy; ***C:*** Bjorn Charpentier; ***M:*** Anton Sanko. **VIDEO**

Fragile 🦴 **2005 (PG-13)** Dreary, monotonous horror set on the Isle of Wight where Mercy Falls Children's Hospital is about to close its doors after a century. A newly-hired replacement nurse, pill-popping American Amy (Flockhart), soon is literally haunted by resident child ghost Charlotte who is determined not to be left alone. **95m/C; DVD.** *SP* Calista Flockhart; Richard Roxburgh; Elena Anaya; Gemma Jones; Yasmin Murphy; Colin McFarlane; Susie Taryling; ***D:*** Jaume Balaguero; ***W:*** Jaume Balaguero; Jordi Galceran; ***C:*** Xavi Gimenez; ***M:*** Roque Bands.

Fragment of Fear 🦴🦴 **1970** After visiting his Aunt Lucy (Robson) in Italy, ex-junkie turned successful author Tim Brett (Hemmings) decides to return and investigate her murder when the local police prove ineffective. It seems Lucy wasn't the kindly old lady everyone thought (there's blackmail involved) but when Tim becomes increasingly paranoid it leads to a breakdown. **94m/C; DVD.** *GB* David Hemmings; Gayle Hunnicutt; Flora Robson; Wilfrid Hyde-White; Arthur Lowe; Daniel Massey; Roland Culver; Adolfo Celi; Mona Washbourne; ***D:*** Richard Sarafian; ***W:*** Paul Dehn; ***C:*** Oswald Morris; ***M:*** Johnny Harris.

Fragments 🦴 1/2 *Winged Creatures* **2008 (R)** Another ensemble drama that follows characters dealing with the aftermath of a tragedy. A gunman randomly opens fire in an L.A. diner, killing several people. The survivors cope (or don't) in various fashion: a waitress begins neglecting her young son; a teen turns to religion after her father is killed; a doctor who felt powerless begins poisoning his wife so he can save her; and a driving instructor, who was shot, decides to try his newfound luck at the casinos. **96m/C; DVD.** Dakota Fanning; Kate Beckinsale; Embeth Davidtz; Soren Fulton; Tim Guinee; Forest Whitaker; Jeanne Tripplehorn; Robin Weigert; Guy Pearce; Jackie Earle Haley; Jennifer Hudson; Beth Grant; Josh Hutcherson; Hayley McFarland; Kevin Cooney; Walton Goggins; Troy Garity; Brooke Mackenzie; ***D:*** Rowan Woods; ***C:*** Eric Alan Edwards; ***M:*** Marcelo Zarvos.

Frailty 🦴🦴🦴 **2002 (R)** Impressive directorial debut by Paxton has him as Dad, a seemingly normal West Texas widower. One day, however, he tells his boys that their family has been chosen by God to destroy demons who are disguised as normal people. This sounds okay by impressionable nine year old Adam (Sumpter), but older Fenton (O'Leary) seems skeptical. Told mostly in flashback, from the point of view of now-grown, haunted Fenton (McConaughey), the story keeps the gore mostly offscreen, while focusing on such lofty ideas as the wages of religious fanaticism, the trust between parents and their kids, and toll of insanity. Screenwriting debut for Hanley. Paxton acquits himself well on both sides of the camera, but it's O'Leary who shines. McConaughey turns in his best performance to date. **100m/C; VHS, DVD.** Bill Paxton; Matthew McConaughey; Powers Boothe; Luke Askew; Matt O'Leary; Jeremy Sumpter; Derk Cheetwood; Missy (Melissa) Crider; Alan Davidson; Cynthia Ettinger; Vincent Chase; Levi Kreis; ***D:*** Bill Paxton; ***W:*** Brent Hanley; ***C:*** Bill Butler; ***M:*** Brian Tyler.

Framed 🦴 1/2 **1930** Rose Manning wants revenge after her racketeer father is killed by detective Butch McArthur. While hostessing at a nightclub, Rose and customer Jimmy fall for each other, and Rose learns he's the hated McArthur's son. **65m/B; DVD.** Evelyn Brent; William Holden; Regis Toomey; Ralf Harolde; ***D:*** George Archainbaud; ***W:*** Wallace Smith; ***C:*** Leo Tover.

Framed 🦴🦴 **1947** Unemployed boozer Mike (Ford) gets bailed out of jail by waitress Paula (Carter), who needs a patsy for an embezzlement scheme she and her banker boyfriend Stephen Price (Sullvan) have concocted. Only this icy dame doesn't like to share and is planning a doublecross. **82m/B; DVD.** Glenn Ford; Janis Carter; Barry Sullivan; Edgar Buchanan; Karen Morley; ***D:*** Richard Wallace; ***W:*** Ben Maddow; ***C:*** Burnett Guffey; ***M:*** Marlin Skiles.

Framed 🦴🦴 **1975 (R)** A nightclub owner is framed for murder, which understandably irks him. He's determined to get paroled and then seek revenge on the crooked cops responsible for his incarceration. This action melodrama features the writer, director and star of "Walking Tall." **106m/C; VHS, DVD, Blu-Ray.** Joe Don Baker; Gabriel Dell; Brock Peters; Conny Van Dyke; John Marley; ***D:*** Phil Karlson; ***W:*** Mort Briskin.

Framed 🦴🦴 **1990** An art forger gets tripped up by a beautiful con artist. However, when they meet again he is willingly drawn into her latest swindle. **87m/C; VHS, DVD.** Jeff Goldblum; Kristin Scott Thomas; Todd Graff; ***D:*** Dean Parisot.

Framed 🦴🦴🦴 **1993** British miniseries about a mediocre cop and a master criminal. Sgt. Larry Jackson (Morrissey) is on vacation in Spain when he spots the supposedly dead master thief/murderer Eddie Myers (Dalton). Once back in London, Larry's assigned the dubious task of guarding Eddie and finding out the names of his associates. Only the sophisticated Eddie starts to dangle temptation in front of the younger man until Larry begins to waver in his duty. Intricate plotting, with Dalton particular fine as the suave, immoral crook. LaPlante also wrote the very successful "Prime Suspect" police dramas for TV. **115m/C; VHS, DVD.** *GB* Timothy Dalton; David Morrissey; Timothy West; Annabelle Apsion; Penelope Cruz; Rowena King; Francis Johnson; Glyn Grimstead; Wayne Foskett; Trevor Cooper; ***D:*** Geoffrey Sax; ***W:*** Lynda La Plante; ***M:*** Nick Bicat. **TV**

Framed 🦴🦴 1/2 **2010** When London's National Gallery floods, curator Quentin Lester finds a safe place to store the priceless masterpieces in an abandoned slate mine in Manod, North Wales. Completely out of his element in the small community, the urbane Lester befriends 10-year-old Dylan Hughes, whose family is in dire financial straits. So Dylan concocts a plan that involves an art heist. Frank Cottrell Boyce adapted his children's novel. **82m/C; DVD.** *GB* Trevor Eve; Sam Davies; Mari Ann Bull; Eve Myles; Robert Pugh; Nicola Reynolds; Mark Lewis Jones; Margaret John; Gwenyth Petty; ***D:*** Andy de Emmony; ***W:*** Frank Cottrell Boyce; ***C:*** David Odd; ***M:*** Nick Green; Tristin Norwell. **TV**

Framed for Murder 🦴 1/2 **2007** Predictable woman-in-jeopardy movie from Lifetime. June (Donovan) argues with her philandering husband, hits him with a heavy object, and splits. The cops find him dead and June goes to the slammer for eight years. When released, June is still declaring her innocence, but proving who really dunnit could be perilous for her health. **94m/C; DVD.** Elisa Donovan; Susan Walters; Perry King; Kevin Jubinville; Claire Brosseau; Jonathan Higgins; Sophie Gendron; ***D:*** Douglas Jackson; ***W:*** Christine Conradt; Richard Dana Smith; ***C:*** Bert Tougas; ***M:*** Steve Gurevitch. **CABLE**

Frances 🦴🦴🦴 **1982** The tragic story of Frances Farmer, the beautiful and talented screen actress of the '30s and early '40s, who was driven to a mental breakdown by bad luck, drug and alcohol abuse, a neurotic, domineering mother, despicable mental health care, and her own stubbornness. After being in and out of mental hospitals, she is finally reduced to a shadow by a lobotomy. Not nearly as bleak as it sounds, this film works because Lange understands this character from the inside out, and never lets her become melodramatic or weak. **134m/C; VHS, DVD.** Jessica Lange; Kim Stanley; Sam Shepard; Jeffrey DeMunn; Gerald S. O'Loughlin; Chris Pennock; John Randolph; Lane Smith; ***D:*** Graeme Clifford; ***W:*** Christopher DeVore; Nicholas Kazan; Eric Bergren; ***C:*** Laszlo Kovacs; ***M:*** John Barry.

Frances Ha 🦴🦴🦴 **2013 (R)** The remarkable charm of Gerwig carries Baumbach's latest dramedy, filmed in lush B&W, about a woman who might not have it all together (or even some of it) but she greets the world with a smile. Frances doesn't really have a place to live, serves as an apprentice for a dance company even though she doesn't really know how to dance, and has a best friend (Sumner) who she doesn't really talk to. While most people would disappear into depression, Frances plunges into new adventures. Baumbach's typical misanthropy is tempered by the incredibly likable natural persona of his star. **86m/B; DVD, Blu-Ray.** Greta Gerwig; Mickey Sumner; Michael Esper; Adam Driver; ***D:*** Noah Baumbach; ***W:*** Greta Gerwig; Noah Baumbach; ***C:*** Sam Levy.

Francesco 🦴🦴 **1993 (PG-13)** Set in 13th-century Italy and depicting the life of St. Francis of Assisi. Follows the pleasure-loving son of a wealthy merchant through his religious awakening, and the founding of the Franciscan order of monks. Rourke, in a definite change-of-pace role, is actually believable, while Bonham Carter offers fine support as a devoted disciple. **119m/C; VHS, DVD.** Mickey Rourke; Helena Bonham Carter; Paolo Bonacelli; Andrea Ferreol; Hanns Zischler; Peter Berling; ***D:*** Liliana Cavani; ***W:*** Liliana Cavani; ***C:*** Giuseppe Lanci; Ennio Guarnieri; ***M:*** Vangelis.

Francis Covers the Big Town 🦴🦴 1/2 **1953** The fourth in the series finds Peter Stirling (O'Connor) trying to become an ace reporter with a New York newspaper. Thanks to Francis he gets some big scoops but then runs afoul of the mob and is accused of murder. And it's up to his smarter pal to come to the rescue. **86m/B; DVD.** Donald O'Connor; Yvette Dugay; Gene Lockhart; Nancy Guild; Larry Gates; Gale Gordon; ***V:*** Chill Wills; ***D:*** Arthur Lubin; ***W:*** Oscar Brodney; ***C:*** Carl Guthrie; ***M:*** Joseph Gershenson.

Francis Goes to the Races 🦴🦴 1/2 **1951** The second in the talking-mule series finds O'Connor and Francis taking up residence on Kellaway's failing horse ranch. When mobsters seize control of the property to pay off a debt, Francis decides to check with the horses at the Santa Anita race track and find a sure winner to bet on. **88m/B; DVD.** Donald O'Connor; Piper Laurie; Cecil Kellaway; Jesse White; Barry Kelley; Hayden Rorke; Vaughn Taylor; Larry Keating; ***V:*** Chill Wills; ***D:*** Arthur Lubin; ***W:*** Oscar Brodney; ***M:*** Frank Skinner.

Francis Goes to West Point 🦴🦴 1/2 **1952** Peter (O'Connor) and Francis get into West Point where the unfortunate freshman winds up last in his class. But thanks to Francis, Peter makes it past school hazing, grades, and other campus hijicks. Look for Leonard Nimoy in the bit role of a football player. Third in the series. **81m/B; DVD.** Donald O'Connor; Lori Nelson; William Reynolds; Gregg (Hunter) Palmer; Alice Kelley; Les Tremayne; David Janssen; Paul Burke; ***V:*** Chill Wills; ***D:*** Arthur Lubin; ***W:*** Oscar Brodney; ***C:*** Carl Guthrie; ***M:*** Joseph Gershenson.

Francis in the Haunted House 🦴 1/2 **1956** The sixth and last entry in the series finds star Donald O'Connor, director Arthur Lubin, and even Chill Wills (the voice of Francis) all abandoning the sinking series. So, its left to Rooney (as hapless David Prescott) to get himself into trouble (trapped in a haunted house with thieves) and for Francis to get him out. Ho-hum. **80m/B; DVD.** Mickey Rooney; Virginia Welles; James Flavin; Paul Cavanagh; David Janssen; Richard Deacon; ***V:*** Paul Frees; ***D:*** Charles Lamont; ***W:*** Herbert Margolis; William Raynor; ***C:*** George Robinson; ***M:*** Joseph Gershenson.

Francis in the Navy 🦴🦴 **1955** The precocious talking mule, Francis, is drafted, and his buddy, played by O'Connor, comes to the rescue. The loquacious beast proves he has the superior grey matter however, and ends up doing all the thinking. Look for Clint Eastwood in his second minor role. **80m/B; DVD.** Donald O'Connor; Martha Hyer; Jim Backus; Paul Burke; David Janssen; Clint Eastwood; Martin Milner; ***D:*** Arthur Lubin.

Francis Joins the WACs 🦴🦴 1/2 **1954** The fifth entry in the series finds O'Connor working as a bank clerk when he is mistakenly drafted back into the military—and sent to a WAC base. Francis tries to keep him out of trouble with the ladies. Wills, the voice of Francis, also turns up as a general. **94m/B; DVD.** Donald O'Connor; Julie Adams; Chill Wills; Mamie Van Doren; Lynn Bari; Zasu Pitts; Joan Shawlee; Mara Corday; Allison Hayes; ***V:*** Chill Wills; ***D:*** Arthur Lubin.

Francis the Talking Mule 🦴🦴🦴 *Francis* **1949** The first of the silly but funny series about, what else, a talking mule. Peter Stirling (O'Connor) is the dim-bulb G.I. who hooks up with Francis while fighting in Burma. Francis helps Peter become a war hero but of course everyone thinks he's crazy when Peter insists the mule can talk. The joke is that Francis is smarter than any of the humans. O'Connor starred in six of the films, with Mickey Rooney taking over the final adventure. Director Lubin went on to create the TV series "Mr. Ed," about a talking horse. Watch for Tony Curtis in a small role. **91m/B; DVD.** Donald O'Connor; Patricia Medina; Zasu Pitts; Ray Collins; John McIntire; Eduard Franz; Howland Chamberlain; Frank Faylen; Tony Curtis; ***V:*** Chill Wills; ***D:*** Arthur Lubin; ***M:*** Frank Skinner.

Frank 🦴🦴 **2007 (PG)** When Jennifer York (Watros) inherits her family's vacation home on the beach, she and her uptight hubby Colin (Gries) take protesting teen daughter Anna (Robertson) and young son Patrick (Dierks) there for the summer. The kids find a large, slobbery, injured stray dog and plead until reluctant Colin agrees to let them care for Frank with the proviso that he's put up for adoption before they go home. Right, like that's really going to happen. **90m/C; DVD.** Jon(athan) Gries; Cynthia Watros; Brittany Robertson; Ashton Dierks; Brian Burnett; ***D:*** Douglas Cheney; ***W:*** Robin Bradford; ***C:*** Paul Mayne; ***M:*** Massimiliano Frani. **VIDEO**

Frank 🦴🦴🦴 **2014 (R)** Where do insanity and creativity intersect? It's a common theme of fiction and life, brought to new focus in director Abrahamson's clever dramedy about a mysterious and talented lead singer of an indie rock band. The title character, played with exceptional physicality by Fassbender, wears a paper mache head at all times, even in the shower. Jon (Gleeson) becomes the newest member of Frank's band, and tries to take them into a spotlight of fame for which they may not be socially prepared. Smart, funny, and insightful, this is a defiant and unique piece of work, much like its leading man. **95m/C; DVD, Blu-Ray.** *IR* Michael Fassbender; Domhnall Gleeson; Maggie Gyllenhaal; Scoot McNairy; Carla Azar; Francois Civil; ***D:*** Lenny Abrahamson; ***W:*** Jon Ronson; Peter Straughan; ***C:*** James Mather; ***M:*** Stephen Rennicks.

Frank and Jesse 🦴🦴 1/2 **1994 (R)** Another revisionist western finds outlaw Jesse James (Lowe) brooding about his violent existence while brother Frank (Paxton) keeps the gang together and they all try to avoid capture by a vengeful Alan Pinkerton (Atherton) and his detective agency. **106m/C; VHS, DVD, Blu-Ray.** Rob Lowe; Bill Paxton; Randy Travis; William Atherton; Alexis Arquette; ***D:*** Robert Boris; ***W:*** Robert Boris; ***C:*** Walt Lloyd; ***M:*** Mark McKenzie.

Frank & Lola 🦴🦴 **2016** Low-key noir produces low-key results in this indie oddity with a great cast but a mediocre script. Frank (Shannon) is a Las Vegas chef, and Lola (Poots) the femme fatale for whom he falls. After Lola cheats on Frank, he becomes obsessed with her past relationships, including one she claims was abusive. He decides to do something to correct a perceived wrong, but is she just using him? Shannon and Poots are perfect for the world of noir but Matthew Ross' script is flat and his direction is flatter. Noir needs more style than this to work. **88m/C; DVD, Blu-Ray.** Michael Shannon; Imogen Poots; Justin Long; Rosanna Arquette; Michael Nyqvist; ***D:*** Matthew Ross; ***W:*** Matthew Ross; ***C:*** Eric Koretz; ***M:*** Danny Bensi; Saunder Jurriaans.

Frank McKlusky, C.I. 🦴🦴 **2002 (PG-13)** Frank McKlusky (Sheridan) is a klutzy but dedicated insurance claims investigator with an over-protective mama (Parton) who worries that her sonny boy will end up in a coma like his daredevil dad (Quaid). But Frank learns it can't always be safety first when he and his gay partner Jimmy (Farley) investigate a couple of slimy lawyers (Pollak, Morgan). **83m/C; VHS, DVD, Blu-Ray.** Dave Sheridan; Dolly Parton; Randy Quaid; Kevin Farley; Kevin Pollak; Tracy Morgan; Orson Bean;

Joan Laurer; Andy Richter; ***D:*** Arlene Sanford; ***W:*** Mark Perez; ***C:*** Tim Suhrstedt; ***M:*** Randy Edelman. **VIDEO**

Frankenfish **2004 (R)** Hungry, jumbo-sized mutant fish feast on any humans they can get their fins on in the Louisiana Bayou whether they're on land or water. **84m/C; VHS, DVD.** Tory Kittles; K.D. Aubert; China Chow; Tomas Arana; Richard Edson; Muse Watson; Raoul Trujillo; Matthew Rauch; Donna Biscoe; Mark Boone, Jr.; Reggie Lee; Noelle Evans; Eugene Collier; Sean Patterson; ***D:*** Mark Dippe; ***W:*** Simon Barrett; Scott Clevenger; ***C:*** Eliot Rockett; ***M:*** Ryan Beveridge. **VIDEO**

Frankenhooker 1/2 **1990 (R)** Jeffrey Franken is a nice guy; he didn't mean to mow his fiancee down on the front lawn. But sometimes bad things just happen to good people. Luckily Jeff thought to save her head and decides to pair it up with the body of some sexy streetwalkers. Voila! You have Frankenhooker: the girlfriend with (someone else's) heart of gold. The posters say it best, "A Terrifying Tale of Sluts and Bolts." **90m/C; VHS, DVD, Blu-Ray.** James Lorinz; Patty Mullen; Charlotte J. Helmkamp; Louise Lasser; Shirley Stoler; Joseph Gonzalez; Beverly Bonner; John Zacherle; ***D:*** Frank Henenlotter; ***W:*** Frank Henenlotter; Robert Martin; ***C:*** Robert M. "Bob" Baldwin, Jr.; ***M:*** Joe Renzetti.

Frankenstein **1931** The definitive expressionistic Gothic horror classic that set the mold. Adapted from the Mary Shelley novel about Dr. Henry Frankenstein (Clive), the scientist who creates a terrifying, yet strangely sympathetic monster aided by his hunchbacked assistant, Fritz (Frye). Great performance by Karloff as the creation, which made him a monster star (in part, thanks to Jack Pierce's makeup). Several powerful scenes, excised from the original version, have been restored, including that of young Maria (Marilyn Harris), who is spotted by the monster innocently picking flowers by a pond. The first in the Universal series. **71m/B; VHS, DVD, Blu-Ray.** Boris Karloff; Colin Clive; Mae Clarke; John Boles; Dwight Frye; Edward Van Sloan; Frederick Kerr; Lionel Belmore; Arletta Duncan; ***D:*** James Whale; ***W:*** Garrett Fort; John Lloyd Balderston; Robert Florey; Francis Edwards Faragoh; ***C:*** Arthur Edeson; ***M:*** David Broekman. AFI '98: Top 100; Natl. Film Reg. '91.

Frankenstein 1/2 **1973** A brilliant scientist plays God, unleashing a living monster from the remains of the dead. A TV movie version of the legendary horror story. Good atmosphere provided by producer Dan "Dark Shadows" Curtis. **130m/C; VHS, DVD.** Robert Foxworth; Bo Svenson; Willie Aames; Susan Strasberg; ***D:*** Glenn Jordan.

Frankenstein 1/2 **1993** Yet another remake of Mary Shelley's 1818 novel. Bergin stars as Dr. Victor Frankenstein, fanatically believing in the power of science to solve all mankind's ills. This leads him to prove his theories on the "secret of life" with his creation of the monster (Quaid), which Frankenstein finds he cannot ultimately control. Slow-moving story but while the monster isn't really terrifying, he's vengeful and intelligent enough to be a good enemy. **117m/C; DVD.** Patrick Bergin; Randy Quaid; John Mills; Lambert Wilson; Fiona Gillies; Jacinta Mulcahy; Timothy Stark; ***D:*** David Wickes; ***W:*** David Wickes. **CABLE**

Frankenstein 1970 1/2 **1958** Victor (Karloff), the horribly scarred grandson of the late Baron von Frankenstein, wants to continue granddad's experiments but lacks the cash to do so. He agrees to rent his castle to a TV crew, giving him the money to buy an atomic reactor (it was the 1950s after all) to bring his monster to life. The title is apparently meaningless and Karloff enjoys hamming up the horror but it's a minor pleasure at best. **83m/C; DVD, Blu-Ray.** Boris Karloff; Tommy Duggan; Jana Lund; Donald (Don "Red") Barry; Charlotte Austin; Irwin Berke; ***D:*** Howard W. Koch; ***W:*** Richard H. Landau; George Worthing Yates; ***C:*** Carl Guthrie.

Frankenstein and the Monster from Hell **1974 (R)** A young doctor is discovered conducting experiments with human bodies and thrown into a mental asylum run by none other than Dr. Frankenstein himself. They continue their gruesome work together, creating a monster who develops a taste for human flesh. This really lame film was the last of the Hammer Frankenstein series. **93m/C; DVD.** *UK* Peter Cushing; Shane Briant; Madeleine Smith; David Prowse; John Stratton; Bernard Lee; Patrick Troughton; Sydney Bromley; ***D:*** Terence Fisher; ***W:*** John (Anthony Hinds) Elder; ***C:*** Brian Probyn; ***M:*** James Bernard.

Frankenstein Conquers the World 1/2 *Furankenshutain tai chitai kaiju Baragon; Frankenstein Meets the Giant Devil Fish; Frankenstein vs. Baragon; Frankenstein vs. the Subterranean Monster; Furankensuten to Baragon; Frankenstein vs. the Giant Devil Fish* **1964** During WWII the heart of Frankenstein's monster is taken from Europe by the Nazis and sent to Japan, where it is irradiated by the blast at Hiroshima. Years later a disfigured young boy is caught eating local animals, and at a local hospital it's discovered that he is becoming immune to radiation. He begins growing, and as the doctors and scientists study him, they come to believe he has eaten Frankenstein's heart. He escapes and is blamed for massive destruction, which is actually caused by the newly awakened gigantic reptile monster Baragon. Hounded by the military, the new Frankenstein's monster and Baragon eventually clash. It spawned a sequel, "War of the Gargantuas," but all references to this film were removed from the American version for some reason. **94m/C; DVD.** *JP* Tadao Takashima; Nick Adams; Kumi Mizuno; Yoshio Tsuchiya; Keiko Sawai; Haruo Nakajima; Koji Furuhata; Peter Mann; Kenichiro Kawaji; ***D:*** Ishio Honda; ***W:*** Takeshi Kimura; Jerry Sohl; Reuben Bercovitch; ***C:*** Hajime Koizumi; ***M:*** Akira Ifukube.

Frankenstein Created Woman *Frankenstein Made Woman* **1966** In Hammer's fourth take on the Frankenstein story, traditional lab scenes are replaced with less expensive "soul" translocations, though the filmmakers retain an ongoing fascination with decapitations. Oddly, the story has a warmth that's often lacking in the genre, and it's aimed at a younger audience, reflecting the changes that were going on when it was made. **86m/C; DVD, Blu-Ray.** Peter Cushing; Susan Denberg; Thorley Walters; Robert Morris; Duncan Lamont; Peter Blythe; Alan MacNaughton; Peter Madden; Barry Warren; Derek Fowlds; ***D:*** Terence Fisher; ***W:*** John (Anthony Hinds) Elder; ***C:*** Arthur Grant.

Frankenstein '80 **WOOF!** *Mosaic* **1979** Guy named Frankenstein pieces together a monster who goes on a killing spree. Bottom of the barrel Italian production with funky music and lots of gore. **88m/C; VHS, DVD.** *IT GE* John Richardson; Gordon Mitchell; Leila Parker; Dada Galloti; Marisa Travers; Xiro Papas; Renato Romano; ***D:*** Mario Mancini; ***W:*** Mario Mancini; Ferdinando De Leone; ***C:*** Emilio Varriano.

Frankenstein Island **WOOF!** **1981 (PG)** Four balloonists get pulled down in a storm and end up on a mysterious island. They are greeted by one Sheila Frankenstein and encounter monsters, amazons, and other obstacles. Completely inept; Carradine "appears" in a visionary sequence wearing his pajamas. **97m/C; VHS, DVD.** Cameron Mitchell; Andrew Duggan; John Carradine; ***D:*** Jerry Warren.

Frankenstein Meets the Space Monster **WOOF!** *Mars Invades Puerto Rico; Frankenstein Meets the Spacemen; Duel of the Space Monsters* **1965** A classic grade-Z epic about a space robot gone berserk among Puerto Rican disco dancers. **80m/B; VHS, DVD.** James Karen; Nancy Marshall; Marilyn Hanold; David Kerman; Robert Reilly; Lou (Cutel) Cutell; ***D:*** Robert Gaffney; ***W:*** George Garret; ***C:*** Saul Midwall.

Frankenstein Meets the Wolfman **1942** The two famous Universal monsters meet and battle it out in this typical grade-B entry, the fifth from the series. The Werewolf wants Dr. Frankenstein to cure him, but only his monster (played by Lugosi) remains. **73m/C; VHS, DVD, Blu-Ray.** Lon Chaney, Jr.; Bela Lugosi; Patric Knowles; Lionel Atwill; Maria Ouspenskaya; Ilona Massey; Dwight Frye; ***D:*** Roy William Neill; ***W:*** Curt Siodmak; ***C:*** George Robinson.

Frankenstein Must Be Destroyed 1/2 **1969** Evil Dr. Frankenstein (Cushing) gets interested in brain transplants but discovers the expert, Dr. Pravda, he hoped to work with has gone mad and is in an asylum. He forces a young medical couple to help him free Pravda but the man is accidentally killed. Nevertheless, Frankenstein transplants Pravda's brain into the body of an asylum inmate that Frankenstein has murdered. These things never work out as intended. Followed by "The Horror of Frankenstein." **97m/C; VHS, DVD, Blu-Ray.** *GB* Peter Cushing; Veronica Carlson; Freddie Jones; Maxine Audley; Simon Ward; Thorley Walters; George Pravda; Colette O'Neil; ***D:*** Terence Fisher; ***W:*** Bert Batt; ***C:*** Arthur Grant.

Frankenstein Reborn 1/2 **1998 (PG)** Thirteen-year-old Anna Frankenstein is impressed with her eccentric scientist uncle, Victor, but things get a little spooky when she meets his latest creation. Yes, Uncle Vic is still working on creating a man from stitched together parts of dead bodies and this time his creature has a human soul. DeCoteau used the pseudonym Julian Breen. **70m/C; VHS, DVD.** Jaason Simmons; Ben Gould; Haven Burton; Ethan Wilde; ***D:*** David DeCoteau. **VIDEO**

The Frankenstein Syndrome 1/2 **2010** In this variation of the familiar Mary Shelley story, unorthodox researcher Elizabeth Barnes joins a secret project with other scientists who are conducting stem-cell experiments. Elizabeth develops a serum that can regenerate dead tissue and eventually it's tested on murdered security guard David with disastrous results. **90m/C; DVD.** Tiffany Shepis; Scott Leet; Patti Tindall; Louis Mandylor; Ed Lauter; Jonathan Northover; Zena Otsuka; Kristina Wayborn; ***D:*** Sean Tretta; ***W:*** Sean Tretta; ***C:*** Eve Cohen. **VIDEO**

The Frankenstein Theory **2013** Yet another entry in the numerous examples of found footage horror films that have interesting premises but fail on the follow through. The premise of this one is a documentary crew setting off for the Arctic circle to prove that Mary Shelley's story 'Frankenstein' was nonfiction. **87m/C; DVD, Streaming.** Kris Lemche; Joe Egender; Timothy V. Murphy; Eric Zuckerman; ***D:*** Adam Weiner; ***W:*** Adam Weiner; Vlady Pildysh; ***C:*** Luke Geissbuhler; ***M:*** James T. Sale. **VIDEO**

Frankenstein Unbound *Roger Corman's Frankenstein Unbound* **1990 (R)** Corman returns after nearly 20 years with a better than ever B movie. Hurt plays Dr. Joseph Buchanan, a nuclear physicist time traveler who accidentally goes back to 1816 and runs into Lord Byron (Patric), Percy (Hutchence) and Mary (Fonda) Shelley and their neighbor Baron Frankenstein (Julia) and his monster (Brimble). But Frankenstein is not done experimenting just yet. Great acting, fun special effects, intelligent and subtle message, with a little sex to keep things going. **86m/C; VHS, DVD.** John Hurt; Raul Julia; Bridget Fonda; Jason Patric; Michael Hutchence; Catherine Rabett; Nick Brimble; Catherine Corman; Mickey Knox; ***V:*** Terri Treas; ***D:*** Roger Corman; ***W:*** Roger Corman; F.X. Feeney; ***C:*** Michael Scott; Armando Nannuzzi; ***M:*** Carl Davis.

Frankenstein's Daughter *She Monster of the Night* **1958** Demented descendant of Dr. Frankenstein sets a den of gruesome monsters loose, including the corpse of a teenaged girl he revitalizes, as he continues the mad experiments of his forefathers. **85m/B; VHS, DVD.** John Ashley; Sandra Knight; Donald Murphy; Felix Locher; Sally Todd; Harry Wilson; ***D:*** Richard Cunha; ***C:*** Meredith Nicholson; ***M:*** Nicholas Carras.

Frankenstein's Great Aunt Tillie **WOOF!** **1983** An excrutiatingly bad send up of the Frankenstein saga with the good doctor about to be evicted from his estate because of back taxes. Gabor appears for a few seconds in a flashback. **99m/C; VHS, DVD.** Donald Pleasence; Yvonne Furneaux; Aldo Ray; June Wilkinson; Zsa Zsa Gabor; ***D:*** Myron G. Gold; ***W:*** Myron G. Gold.

Frankenweenie **2012 (PG)** Returning to the short film that first got him attention in 1984, writer/director Burton lovingly transforms his early work into a bizarre black and white stop-motion animated feature. Science-crazed kid Victor Frankenstein (voiced by Tahan), suffers childhood loss when his beloved dog Sparky meets an untimely death. After an electrical experiment involving a reanimated frog in his science class, Victor returns to the pet cemetery where Sparky was laid to rest to bring his best friend back to life. As expected, this macabre, but harmless, effort works for kids and grown-ups alike, filled with weirdo characters and wacky eye candy. **87m/B; DVD, Blu-Ray.** ***V:*** Charlie Tahan; Martin Short; Catherine O'Hara; Winona Ryder; Martin Landau; Robert Capron; Conchata Ferrell; Christopher Lee; ***D:*** Tim Burton; ***W:*** John August; ***C:*** Peter Sorg; ***M:*** Danny Elfman.

Frankie **2019 (PG-13)** In the mountain resort town of Sintra, Portugal, family and friends of witty famous French actress Frankie (Huppert) have gathered for a vacation retreat. Over the course of a single day, the group, which includes husband Jimmy (Gleeson), daughter Sylvia (Robinson), son-in-law Ian (Bakare), and troubled son Paul (Renier), talk and reminisce on life and experiences, and tie up loose ends in relationships. At the same time, they discuss the cancer that has returned in Frankie's body and the amount of time she has left. The empathetic, moving drama features an exquisite setting and actors who shine. **98m/C; DVD, Blu-Ray.** Isabelle Huppert; Sennia Nanua; Ariyon Bakare; Vinette Robinson; Jeremie Renier; ***D:*** Ira Sachs; ***W:*** Ira Sachs; Mauricio Zacharias; ***C:*** Rui Poças; ***M:*** Dickon Hinchliffe.

Frankie and Alice 1/2 **2010 (R)** Unfortunately melodramatic cliche about mental illness, based on a true story, with Berry looking incredibly attractive despite the personal drama and allegedly grimy atmosphere. A teenage trauma has black woman Frankie (Berry), who works as a stripper in 1970s L.A., suffering from multiple personalities, including a white, racist southern belle and a young child. One too many violent episodes lands her in a mental hospital, where she comes under the care of noble Dr. Oswald (Skarsgard). In this case too many screenwriters fractured the film as completely as Frankie's multiple personalities have fractured her life. **100m/C; DVD, Blu-Ray.** *CA* Halle Berry; Stellan Skarsgard; Phylicia Rashad; Chandra Wilson; Adrian Holmes; Brian Markinson; Christine Schild; Emily Tennant; James Kirk; Vanessa Morgan; Matt Frewer; Joanne Baron; ***D:*** Geoffrey Sax; ***W:*** Cheryl Edwards; Marko King; Mary King; Jonathan Watters; Joe Schrapnel; Anna Waterhouse; ***C:*** Newton Thomas (Tom) Sigel; ***M:*** Andrew Lockington.

Frankie and Johnny 1/2 **1965** Elvis is a riverboat gambler/singer with lousy luck until Kovack changes the odds. This upsets his girlfriend Douglas who shoots him (but not fatally). Elvis wears period costumes, but this is otherwise similar to his contemporary films. **88m/C; VHS, DVD, Blu-Ray.** Elvis Presley; Donna Douglas; Harry (Henry) Morgan; Audrey Christie; Anthony Eisley; Sue Ane Langdon; Robert Strauss; Nancy Kovack; ***D:*** Fred de Cordova; ***W:*** Alex Gottlieb; ***C:*** Jacques "Jack" Marquette; ***M:*** Fred Karger.

Frankie and Johnny **1991 (R)** Ex-con gets a job as a short-order cook and falls for a world-weary waitress. She doesn't believe in romance, but finally gives into his pleas for a chance and finds out he may not be such a bad guy after all. Nothing can make Pfeiffer dowdy enough for this role, but she and Pacino are charming together. In a change of pace role, Nelligan has fun as a fellow waitress who loves men. Based on the play "Frankie and Johnny in the Clair de Lune" by McNally who also wrote the screenplay. **117m/C; VHS, DVD.** Al Pacino; Michelle Pfeiffer; Hector Elizondo; Nathan Lane; Kate Nelligan; Jane Morris; Greg Lewis; Al Fann; K. Callan; Phil Leeds; Tracy Reiner; Dey Young; ***D:*** Garry Marshall; ***W:*** Terrance McNally; ***C:*** Dante Spinotti; ***M:*** Marvin Hamlisch. British Acad. '91: Support. Actress (Nelligan); Natl. Bd. of Review '91: Support. Actress (Nelligan).

Franklyn **2008 (R)** Visually interesting (feature film-debuting director McMorrow has a background in music vids and commercials) flick time-shifts uneasily between contemporary London and a totalitarian future city. In the future, masked Jonathan Preest (Phillippe) is sent to assassinate a man who killed an abducted girl while in the present, artist Emilia (Green) is in the hospital after a suicide attempt. Various characters circle each others' lives and it's really not worth the effort to figure out how things are supposed to tie together. **98m/C; DVD.** *GB* Eva Green; Ryan Phillippe; Sam Riley; Bernard Hill; James Faulkner; Art Malik; Susannah York; Richard Coyle; Stephen Walters; ***D:*** Gerald McMorrow; ***W:*** Gerald McMorrow; ***C:*** Benjamin Davis; ***M:*** Joby Talbot.

Frantic *Elevator to the Gallows; Ascenseur pour L'Echafaud* **1958** From Louis Malle comes one of the first French New Wave film noir dramas. A man kills his boss with the connivance of the employer's wife, his lover, and makes it look like suicide. Meanwhile, teenagers have used his car and gun in the murder of a tourist couple and he is indicted for that crime. Their perfectly planned murder begins to unravel into a panic-stricken nightmare. A suspenseful and captivating drama. Director Malle's first feature film. Musical score by jazz legend Miles Davis. **92m/B; VHS, DVD, Blu-Ray.** *FR* Maurice Ronet; Jeanne Moreau; Georges Poujouly; ***D:*** Louis Malle; ***C:*** Henri Decae; ***M:*** Miles Davis.

Frantic **1988 (R)** While in Paris, an American surgeon's wife is kidnapped when she inadvertantly picks up the wrong suitcase. Her kidnappers want their hidden tresure returned, which forces the husband into the criminal underground and into unexpected heroism when he seeks to rescue her. Contrived ending weakens on the whole, but Polanski is still master of the dark film thriller. **120m/C; VHS, DVD.** Harrison Ford; Betty Buckley; John Mahoney; Emmanuelle Seigner; Jimmie Ray Weeks; Yorgo Voyagis; David Huddleston; Gerard Klein; ***D:*** Roman Polanski; ***W:*** Roman Polanski; Gerard Brach; ***C:*** Witold Sobocinski; ***M:*** Ennio Morricone.

Frantz **2017 (PG-13)** A haunting, thoughtful look at loss, guilt, and the desire for happiness, set in the aftermath of World War I. Anna, a young German woman whose fiancé, Frantz, died in battle, discovers a mysterious Frenchman repeatedly visiting his grave. Their shared bond overcomes the community's post-war distrust of Adrien, and romance blossoms, but wartime secrets don't remain hidden. Shot in black/white with occasional scenes in color, and employing both French and German, this film is an accidental remake of 1932's *Broken Lullaby* (both movies are adaptations of the French play of the same name, a fact that was initially unknown to writer/director Ozon). **113m/B; DVD.** Pierre Niney; Paula Beer; Ernst Stötzner; Marie Gruber; Johann von Bülow; ***D:*** Francois Ozon; ***W:*** Francois Ozon; ***C:*** Pascal Marti; ***M:*** Philippe Rombi.

Frasier the Sensuous Lion *Frasier the Lovable Lion* **1973 (PG)** A zoology professor is able to converse with Frasier, a lion known for his sexual stamina and whose potency is coveted by a billionaire (shadow of monkey glands rejuvenation therapy). A fairly typical, if slightly risque, talking critter film. **97m/C; VHS, DVD.** Michael Callan; Katherine Justice; Frank De Kova; Malachi Throne; Victor Jory; Peter Lorre, Jr.; Marc Lawrence; ***D:*** Pat Shields.

Frat Party **2009 (R)** Typical raunchy and dumb campus sex comedy. Duffy is going to marry wine heiress Adriana right after college graduation. But his last major frat party is the night before the wedding and Adriana's unhappy father will stop at nothing to prevent Duffy from showing up for the ceremony. **85m/C; DVD.** Randy Wayne; Caroline D'Amore; Jareb Dauplaise; Lauren C. Mayhew; ***D:*** Robert Bennettt; ***W:*** Robert Bennettt; ***C:*** William Garcia. **VIDEO**

The Fraternity *The Circle* **2001 (R)** Despite the title, these aren't frat boys but a group of elite boarding school students who call themselves "The Circle" and run Runice Academy until headmaster Williams discovers their involvement in a cheating scandal and one of them is expelled. When the alleged informant winds up dead, another (Dunne) in the group decides he has to come clean about the group's other activities. **100m/C; VHS, DVD, On Demand.** Treat Williams; Robin Dunne; Gordon Currie; ***D:*** Sidney J. Furie. **VIDEO**

Fraternity Massacre at Hell Island ½ **2007** Campy gay horror. The pledges of Zeta Alpha Rio are supposed to be spending fraternity Hell night at an abandoned river park island. However, they don't expect to be murdered by a homophobic killer clown and it's up to pledge Jack (Farrell) to save his brothers. **80m/C; DVD.** Tyler Farrell; Billie Worley; Corie Ventura; Kaleo Quenzer; Scott Fletcher; Michael Gravois; Jon Devin; Tosh Newman; ***D:*** Mark Goshorn Jones; ***W:*** Mark Goshorn Jones; ***C:*** Ryan Parker. **VIDEO**

Fraternity Vacation **1985 (R)** Two college fraternity men show a nerd the greatest time of his life while he's on vacation in Palm Springs. **95m/C; VHS, DVD, Blu-Ray.** Stephen Geoffreys; Sheree J. Wilson; Cameron Dye; Leigh McCloskey; Tim Robbins; Matt McCoy; Amanda Bearse; John Vernon; Nita Talbot; Barbara Crampton; Kathleen Kinmont; Max Wright; Julie Payne; Franklin Ajaye; Charles Rocket; Britt Ekland; ***D:*** James Frawley; ***W:*** Lindsay Harrison; ***C:*** Dr. Paul Ryan; ***M:*** Brad Fiedel.

Fraulein ½ **1958** Wartime romance shot on location in Germany. Towards the end of WWII, young German Erika (Wynter) helps hide escaped American POW McClain (Ferrer). They meet again in a postwar divided Berlin after Erika runs into trouble with lecherous Russian colonel Bucaron (Bikel). They fall in love and McClain wants to take Erika back to the States but she's been mistakenly registered as a prostitute and can't get the correct papers to leave. **95m/C; DVD.** Dana Wynter; Mel Ferrer; Theodore Bikel; Helmut Dantine; Margaret (Maggie) Hayes; Herbert Berghof; ***D:*** Henry Koster; ***W:*** Leo Townsend; ***C:*** Leo Tover; ***M:*** Daniele Amfitheatrof.

Frayed **2007 (R)** Really? It took five writers to come up with this slasher dreck? Small-town sheriff Pat Baker's worst nightmare comes true when his deranged son Kurt escapes from a psych hospital where he was incarcerated for the murder of his mother when he was only eight. Kurt (wearing a clown mask) runs into the woods and the sheriff is horrified when he figures out that daughter Sara is camping in the same area with some friends. As Kurt becomes even more unhinged, he goes on a killing spree. **111m/C; DVD.** Tony Doupe; Kellee Bradley; Alena Dashiell; Aaron Blakely; Don Brady; Tasha Smith-Floe; ***D:*** Norb Caoili; Rob Portman; ***W:*** Norb Caoili; Rob Portman; Kurt Svennungsen; Dana Svennungsen; Dino Moore; ***C:*** Karel Bauer; ***M:*** Norb Caoili. **VIDEO**

Freak Show **2018** Adolescent Billy Bloom (Lawther), who is gay and enjoys subverting conventional masculinity, is raised by his supportive mother Mauvine (Midler) until she has to go into rehab. Moving into his father William's (Pine) mansion, Billy is rejected by him and most of the students at his new high school. After Billy becomes the unlikely friend of art-loving football star Flip (Nelson), he challenges Bible-quoting evangelical Christian Lynette (Breslin) for the title of homecoming queen. The directing debut of Styler is well-intentioned and Lawther's performance has appeal, but the film is superficial. **91m/C; DVD.** Alex Lawther; AnnaSophia Robb; Abigail Breslin; Laverne Cox; Bette Midler; ***D:*** Trudie Styler; ***W:*** Patrick J. Clifton; Beth Rigazio; ***C:*** Dante Spinotti; ***M:*** Jeffrey Coulter; Dan Romer.

Freaked *Hideous Mutant Freekz* **1993 (PG-13)** Bizarre little black comedy throws everything at the screen, hoping some of the gross-out humor will prove amusing (and some does). Greedy TV star Ricky Coogin (Winter) agrees to be the spokesman for E.E.S. Corporation, which markets a toxic green slime fertilizer to the third world. He's sent to South America to promote the product and is captured by the mad scientist proprietor (Quaid) of a mysterious sideshow, who douses him with the fertilizer. Before you know it he's an oozing half-man, half-beast, perfect to join other freaks as the latest attraction. Lots of yucky makeup. Reeves has an uncredited cameo as the Dog Boy. **80m/C; VHS, DVD, Blu-Ray.** Alex Winter; Randy Quaid; Megan Ward; Michael Stoyanov; Brooke Shields; William Sadler; Derek McGrath; Alex Zuckerman; Karyn Malchus; Mr. T; Morgan Fairchild; ***Cameo(s):*** Keanu Reeves; Tom Stern; Tim Burns; ***V:*** Bobcat Goldthwait; ***D:*** Alex Winter; Tom Stern; ***W:*** Alex Winter; Tom Stern; Tim Burns; ***C:*** Jamie Thompson; Jene Omens; ***M:*** Kevin Kiner.

The Freakmaker *Mutations; The Mutation* **1973 (R)** Mad professor attempts to breed plants with humans in his lab and has the usual bizarre results. Experiments that fail go to Dunn, a dwarf who runs a freak show. Shamelessly includes real freaks as if plot was not strange enough. **90m/C; VHS, DVD, Blu-Ray.** *GB* Donald Pleasence; Tom Baker; Brad Harris; Julie Ege; Michael Dunn; Jill Haworth; Olga Anthony; Lisa Collings; Scott Antony; ***D:*** Jack Cardiff; ***W:*** Edward Andrew (Santos Alcocer) Mann; Robert D. Weinbach; ***C:*** Paul Beeson; ***M:*** Basil Kirchin.

Freakonomics ½ **2010 (PG-13)** Big screen adaptation of the surprise 2005 bestseller by economist Stephen D. Levitt and journalist Stephen J. Dubner. Told in four parts, with each made by a different A-list documentary filmmaker. Like the book these true stories filter out human behavior and pop psychology theories through statistics and economics. As with most anthologies, the results are inconsistent, with the best entry coming from Gibney, "Taxi to the Dark Side," on the deep-seated corruption in Japan's sumo wrestling business. The others are: Spurlock's "Super Size Me" on the importance of having a good name; "Why We Fight" on the lowered crime rates post-Roe vs. Wade; and "Jesus Camp" on an experimental Chicago program paying children for good grades. Ultimately, this idea would've worked better as television series. **86m/C; Blu-Ray, On Demand.** ***Nar:*** Melvin Van Peebles; ***D:*** Seth Gordon; Morgan Spurlock; Alex Gibney; Eugene Jarecki; Rachel Grady; Heidi Ewing; ***W:*** Seth Gordon; Morgan Spurlock; Alex Gibney; Eugene Jarecki; Jeremy Chilnick; Peter Bull; ***C:*** Bradford Whitaker; Daniel Marracino; Darren Lew; Junji Aoki; Ferne Pearlstein; Tony Hardmon; Rob Vanalkemade; ***M:*** Jon Spurney; Peter Nashel; Pete Miser; Paul Brill.

Freaks ½ *Nature's Mistakes; Forbidden Love; The Monster Show* **1932** The infamous, controversial, cult-horror classic about a band of circus freaks that exact revenge upon a beautiful aerialist and her strongman lover after enduring humiliation and exploitation. Based on Ted Robbins story "Spurs." It was meant to out-horror "Frankenstein" but was so successful that it was repeatedly banned. Browning's film may be a shocker but it is never intended to be exploitative since the "Freaks" are the only compassionate, loyal, and loving people around. **66m/B; VHS, DVD.** Wallace Ford; Olga Baclanova; Leila Hyams; Roscoe Ates; Harry Earles; Henry Victor; Daisy Earles; Madam Rose (Dion) Dione; Daisy Hilton; Violet Hilton; ***D:*** Tod Browning; ***W:*** Al Boasberg; Willis Goldbeck; Leon Gordon; Edgar Allan Woolf; ***C:*** Merritt B. Gerstad. Natl. Film Reg. '94.

Freaks of Nature ½ **2015 (R)** A comedic horror/science fiction about one unusual town facing an alien invasion. The small down of Dilford is the peaceful home to humans, vampires, and zombies. There are no issues until an alien apocalypse comes to Dilford. After the aliens arrive, the social balance in Dilford is torn apart, and humans, vampires, and zombies begin to attack each other. All three are trying to evade the aliens. Three teenagers—one from each major group in Dilford—begin to work together to rid Dilford of the aliens and bring back the normal ways of life in Dilford. **92m/C; DVD, Blu-Ray, Download.** Nicholas Braun; Mackenzie Davis; Josh Fadem; Denis Leary; Ed Westwick; ***D:*** Robbie Pickering; ***W:*** Oren Uziel; ***C:*** Uta Briesewitz; ***M:*** Fil Eisler.

Freakshow **1995 (R)** Two teens wander into the sideshow at a local carnival and meet the Freakmaster (Hansen), whose grisly exhibits have equally grisly stories to tell. Campy horror with routine special effects. **102m/C; VHS, DVD.** Gunnar Hansen; Veronica Carlson; Brian D. Kelly; Shannon Michelle Parsons; ***D:*** William Cooke; Paul Talbot.

Freakshow **2007** Thieves hiding out as security workers in a circus sideshow make the mistake of crossing the freaks. Slutty Lucy discovers aging owner Lon has a lot of dough and convinces her partners she can seduce and marry the guy and then inherit after they kill him. Turns out it's a really bad plan—especially for Lucy. **85m/C; DVD.** Rebekah Kochan; Chris(topher) Adamson; Dane Rosselli; Mckenna Geu; Mighty Mike Murga; ***D:*** Drew Tyler Bell; ***W:*** Keith Leopard; ***C:*** Mark Atkins. **VIDEO**

Freaky Deaky **2012 (R)** Yet another Elmore Leonard adaptation turns into near-sludge. In 1974, boozing Detroit detective Chris Mankowski has just tranferred into sex crimes when Greta Wyatt claims that she was raped by wealthy eccentric Woody Ricks. As Chris investigates, a couple of revenge-minded bombers and Woody's ex-Black Panther bodyguard Donnell Lewis are thrown into the mix but it never makes much sense. **90m/C; DVD.** Billy Burke; Crispin Glover; Sabrina Gadeki; Michael Jai White; Christian Slater; Breanne Racano; Andy Dick; ***D:*** Charles Matthau; ***W:*** Charles Matthau; ***C:*** John J. Connor; ***M:*** Joseph LoDuca. **VIDEO**

Freaky Faron ½ **2006** At 11, Faron is institutionalized after shooting a local weatherman and claiming that aliens made her do it. Released after five years of rehabilitation, Faron wants to lead a quiet life but something strange is going on in her hometown and Faron is the only one who can save its residents. Maybe she wasn't crazy after all. **94m/C; DVD.** Courtney Halverson; Catharine Scott; Lydia Milner; Carly Hayes; Jerib Kaiser; Sewell Whitney; ***D:*** John (William) Ross; ***W:*** John (William) Ross; ***C:*** Kelly Richard; ***M:*** Ryan Adison Amen. **VIDEO**

Freaky Friday ½ **1976 (G)** A housewife and her teenage daughter inadvertently switch bodies and each then tries to carry on the other's normal routine. Mary Rodgers' popular book is brought to the screen with great charm in this above average Disney film. **95m/C; VHS, DVD, Blu-Ray.** Barbara Harris; Jodie Foster; Patsy Kelly; John Astin; Dick Van Patten; Ruth Buzzi; Kaye Ballard; Charlene Tilton; James Van Patten; ***D:*** Gary Nelson; ***W:*** Mary Rodgers.

Freaky Friday **2003 (PG)** Worthy remake of the 1976 Disney original breathes some life into the body-switch genre. Curtis plays Tess, a widowed psychiatrist and mom to rebellious 15-year-old Anna (Lohan). Anna's upset that her mom is about to remarry. Following a fight over said wedding at a Chinese restaurant, mom and daughter are hexed by a cursed fortune cookie and wake up the next day in each other's bodies. After the initial shock wears off, the talented leads seem right at home in the other's role, resulting in more laughs than you'd expect from a Disney remake. Curtis is especially fun to watch, successfully tapping into her inner teen and kicking out the jams in Anna's garage band. Light comedy deftly blends with morality in fun family comedy. **93m/C; VHS, DVD, Blu-Ray.** Jamie Lee Curtis; Lindsay Lohan; Mark Harmon; Harold Gould; Chad Michael Murray; Ryan Malgarini; Stephen Tobolowsky; Christina Vidal; Rosalind Chao; Willie Garson; Dina Spybey; ***D:*** Mark S. Waters; ***W:*** Leslie Dixon; Heather Hach; ***C:*** Oliver Wood; ***M:*** Rolfe Kent.

Fred Claus **2007 (PG)** Vaughn attempts to bring his familiar shtick to pre-teens and fails miserably in this story about Santa's repo man brother, who's looking to make a quick buck in order to start a restaurant. Santa (Giamatti) offers Fred (Vaughn) money if he comes back to the North Pole to help with the Christmas rush, and something that fails to resemble hilarity ensues. The laughs are few, and the considerable talents of Vaughn, Giamatti, and fellow cast members Spacey, Weisz, and Bates are frittered, as the pic seems to rely exclusively on Vaughn's trademark big mouth and cliched family-movie sap. **115m/C; Blu-Ray, On Demand.** Vince Vaughn; Paul Giamatti; Miranda Richardson; Rachel Weisz; John Michael Higgins; Kathy Bates; Trevor Peacock; Chris Bridges; Elizabeth Banks; Jeremy Swift; Elizabeth Berrington; Kevin Spacey; ***D:*** David Dobkin; ***W:*** Dan Fogelman; ***C:*** Remi Adefarasin; ***M:*** Christophe Beck.

Fred: The Movie **2010** The YouTube phenomenon gets a feature-length adventure from Nickelodeon. Dorky teenage babbler Fred Figglehorn wants to duet (yes, we mean sing) with dream girl Judy but has constant problems even finding her as rival Kevin and Fred's own idiocy puts obstacles in his way. **83m/C; DVD.** Lucas Cruikshank; Pixie Lott; Jake Weary; Jennette McCurdy; Siobhan Fallon Hogan; John Cena; ***D:*** Clay Weiner; ***W:*** David A. Goodman; ***C:*** Scott Henriksen; ***M:*** Roddy Bottum. **CABLE**

Freddy Got Fingered **WOOF!** **2001 (R)** Green, making his feature directorial debut, is our hero, Gord, a dedicated slacker who refuses to get a job and move out of his father's (Torn) house. Green the director loves Green the "actor," almost as much as he loves human and animal bodily fluids—all of them. What he does to horses and elephants will poison forever your fond memories of trips to the zoo. He also enjoys oral sex, performed by a wheelchair-bound girlfriend, of course. Then, just to appeal to the family-values crowd, he falsely accuses his overbearing father of sexually abusing his younger brother. Taken in small doses, Green's act can induce "I can't believe I'm laughing at this"-type chuckles, but an hour and a half could cause permanent brain damage. Look what its apparently done to him! To say "Freddy" wallows in the gutter is to besmirch the gutter's good name. **88m/C; VHS, DVD.** Tom Green; Rip Torn; Harland Williams; Eddie Kaye Thomas; Julie Hagerty; Anthony Michael Hall; Marisa Coughlan; ***D:*** Tom Green; ***W:*** Tom Green; Derek Harvie; ***C:*** Mark Irwin; ***M:*** Mike Simpson. Golden Raspberries '01: Worst Actor (Green), Worst Director (Green), Worst Picture, Worst Screenplay.

Freddy vs. Jason ⚊⚊ 1/2 **2003 (R)** Highly anticipated cinematic showdown between Freddy Krueger and Jason Vorhees begins with the clever premise that Freddy is dying of neglect. The children of Elm Street have forgotten about him, so Freddy is ceasing to exist. Freddy gets it into his head to inject a little horror into the real world and summons Jason from whatever hell he's been languishing in and sets him loose. The only problem is that Jason is taking center stage, which displeases Freddy. Ronny Yu's frenetic direction sets a suitable pace, but after the setup, it all settles into standard "slasher film" mode until the climactic battle. Forgettable cast of victims adequately plays off of Robert Englund's scene-devouring Freddy. **97m/C; VHS, DVD, Blu-Ray, UMD.** Robert Englund; Ken Kirzinger; Monica Keena; Jason Ritter; Kelly Rowland; Katharine Isabelle; Brendan Fletcher; Tom Butler; Lochlyn Munro; James Callahan; ***D:*** Ronny Yu; ***W:*** Damian Shannon; Mark Swift; ***C:*** Fred Murphy; ***M:*** Graeme Revell.

Freddy's Dead: The Final Nightmare ⚊⚊ *A Nightmare on Elm Street 6: Freddy's Dead* **1991 (R)** Freddy's daughter journeys to Springwood, Ohio, to put a stop to her father's evil ways. Will she be able to destroy this maniac, or is a new reign of terror just beginning? The sixth film in the "Nightmare" series; followed by "Wes Craven's New Nightmare." **96m/C; DVD, Blu-Ray.** Robert Englund; Lisa Zane; Shon Greenblatt; Lezlie (Dean) Deane; Ricky Dean Logan; Breckin Majer; Yaphet Kotto; Elinor Donahue; Roseanne; Johnny Depp; Alice Cooper; Tom Arnold; ***D:*** Rachel Talalay; ***W:*** Michael De Luca; ***C:*** Declan Quinn.

Frederick Forsyth's Icon ⚊⚊ 1/2 **2005 (PG-13)** Based on bestseller Frederick Forsyth's book Icon. Jason Monk (Swayze), an ex-CIA agent, comes out of retirement to save an entire country from the brink of ruin. Russian presidential candidate Igor Komarov (Bergin) promises his people a new Russia, but his plan is based on a secret "Black Manifesto" that lays a foundation for dictatorship and military rule, among other evils. Monk's also charged with seeking out Anatoli Grishin (Cross), an evil KGB officer whom Monk has a personal vendetta against. Forsyth fans may be disappointed by the many deviations from the book; breathtaking Russian scenery and some thrilling suspense may make up for it. **180m/C; DVD.** Patrick Swayze; Patrick Bergin; Michael York; Ben Cross; Annika Peterson; Jeff Fahey; Joss Ackland; ***D:*** Charles Martin Smith; ***W:*** Adam Armus; Nora Kay Foster; ***C:*** David Cannell; ***M:*** Daniel Licht. **CABLE**

Free and Easy ⚊⚊ 1/2 *Easy Go* **1930** Keaton plays the incompetent manager of a beauty contest winner (Page) from Gopher City, Kansas. Page and her overbearing mother, accompanied by Keaton, go to Hollywood to make the girl a star. They gate-crash the MGM studio where all cause havoc and it turns out Keaton is the one who lands in front of the cameras (Page has to settle for romancing Montgomery). Provides a behind-the-scenes look at the MGM studio, with a number of MGM stars making cameo appearances. **92m/B; VHS, DVD.** Buster Keaton; Anita Page; Robert Montgomery; Trixie Friganza; Fred Niblo; ***Cameo(s):*** Cecil B. DeMille; Jackie Coogan; Lionel Barrymore; William Haines; ***D:*** Edward Sedgwick.

Free Birds ⚊ **2013 (PG)** Modern animation doesn't get more generic, cheap, and boring than this nonsensical, unfunny rip-off of superior works. Wilson voices a turkey named Reggie, the lucky one pardoned by the President before Thanksgiving and told he'll be given a second chance at life. Before you can be surprised this is a plot for a movie, the story gets much weirder as Reggie is kidnapped and put in a time machine in an effort to stop turkeys from even being on the holiday menu in the first place. The voice work is lazy but it's the bad writing that really sinks this to sub-TV level animated fare. **91m/C; DVD, Blu-Ray.** ***V:*** Owen Wilson; Woody Harrelson; Amy Poehler; George Takei; Colm Meaney; ***D:*** Jimmy Hayward; ***W:*** Jimmy Hayward; Scott Mosier; ***M:*** Dominic Lewis.

Free Enterprise ⚊⚊ 1/2 **1998 (R)** Funny and inventive semi-autobiographical tale of a couple of aspiring filmmakers facing 30 without a clue about becoming adults. Schlock screenwriter Robert (Weigel) and best bud, film editor Mark (McCormack), filter their existence through sci fi and '70s TV shows. The two are completely geeked by a chance meeting with their "Star Trek" idol William Shatner (who slyly pokes fun at his own persona), who offers them enouragement. The duo actually make some attempts at that grown-up thing by the clever finale. **114m/C; VHS, DVD.** Rafer Weigel; Eric McCormack; William Shatner; Audie England; Patrick Van Horn; Jonathan Slavin; Phil LaMarr; Deborah Van Valkenburgh; ***D:*** Robert Meyer Burnett; ***W:*** Robert Meyer Burnett; Mark Altman; ***C:*** Charles L. Barbee; ***M:*** Scott Spock.

Free Fall ⚊⚊ **2014 (R)** Learning corporate secrets has potentially deadly consequences for one woman in this crime action-thriller. After a top executive at Gault Capital seemingly commits suicide by jumping off the company's skyscraper headquarters, his loyal protege Jane Porter (Butler) finds evidence that his death was a crime. To permanently silence Jane, the company calls in its crisis manager Frank (Sweeney). He decides to trap Jane in an elevator between floors on a holiday weekend when the building should be empty. Frank does not count on Jane's tenacity as she works to survive the drop to the bottom floor. **90m/C; DVD, Blu-Ray, Streaming, Download.** Sarah Butler; D.B. Sweeney; Malcolm McDowell; Ian Gomez; Adam Tomei; ***D:*** Malek Akkad; ***W:*** Dwayne Alexander Smith; ***C:*** Jonathan Hall; ***M:*** Timothy Andrew Edwards. **VIDEO**

Free Fire ⚊⚊ 1/2 **2017 (R)** A wildly fun action comedy-drama about a deal gone bad. In a warehouse in Boston in 1978, Irish Republican Army members meet a weapons dealer and his associates to purchase firearms. Despite the presence of two intermediaries, Justine (Larson) and Ord (Hammer), to ensure the transaction is satisfactory for all involved, nothing goes according to plan, hidden shooters open fire, and it becomes every person for himself or herself. Who will get out alive? The actors truly seem to be enjoying playing their characters. **91m/C; DVD.** Enzo Cilenti; Sam Riley; Michael Smiley; Brie Larson; Cillian Murphy; Armie Hammer; ***D:*** Ben Wheatley; ***W:*** Ben Wheatley; Amy Jump; ***C:*** Laurie Rose; ***M:*** Geoff Barrow; Ben Salisbury.

Free Men ⚊⚊ 1/2 *Les hommes libres* **2012** Respectable tale of the WWII French Resistance has an appealing modern twist: Muslims rescuing Jews from the Nazis. After getting arrested for black market dealing, Younes (a convincing Rahim) is forced to spy on a mosque for the Vichy police. After being exposed to underground leader Ben (Lonsdale) and becoming friends with Jewish singer Salim (Shalaby), Younes becomes drawn into the resistance. Many of the characters, including Ben and Salim, are based on actual resistance members. In French with English subtitles. **99m/C; DVD, Blu-Ray.** *FR* Tahar Rahim; Mahmoud Shalaby; Christopher Buchholz; Michael (Michel) Lonsdale; Lubna Azabal; Farid Larbi; ***D:*** Ismael Ferroukhi; ***W:*** Ismael Ferroukhi; Alain-Michel Blanc; ***C:*** Jerome Almeras; ***M:*** Armand Amar.

Free Money ⚊⚊ **1999 (R)** Kinda dumb buddy comedy finds Bud (Sheen) and Larry (Church) stuck in North Dakota and forced to marry the twin daughters of local prison warden The Swede (Brando, overacting as usual). The two losers decide the best way to get away from their father-in-law's watchful eye is to rob a train loaded with cash. **94m/C; VHS, DVD.** Charlie Sheen; Marlon Brando; Donald Sutherland; Thomas Haden Church; Mira Sorvino; David Arquette; ***D:*** Yves Simoneau; ***W:*** Tony Peck; Joseph Brutsman; ***C:*** David Franco.

Free of Eden ⚊⚊ 1/2 **1998** Successful New York businessman Poitier reluctantly agrees to mentor a troubled inner-city teenaged girl (played by Poitier's daughter). **97m/C; VHS, DVD.** Sidney Poitier; Sydney Tamiia Poitier; Phylicia Rashad; Robert Hooks; ***D:*** Leon Ichaso; ***W:*** Delle Chatman; Yule Caise; ***C:*** Claudio Chea; ***M:*** Terence Blanchard. **CABLE**

Free Ride ⚊⚊ **2013** Betz's semiautobiographical story (set in the 1970s) is carried by Paquin as struggling single mom Christina, who escapes an abusive boyfriend by packing up her two daughters and heading to Florida. Her friend Sandy (de Matteo) gets Christina involved with a large-scale pot importer and soon she's got a nice life for if family thanks to the drug trade. Until the party's over. **86m/C; DVD.** Anna Paquin; Drea De Matteo; Cam Gigandet; Liana Liberato; Ava Acres; Lloyd Owen; ***D:*** Shana Betz; ***W:*** Shana Betz; ***C:*** Quyen Tran; ***M:*** Jeff Russo.

Free Samples ⚊⚊ 1/2 **2012 (R)** This indie comedy-drama explores a day in the life of a law school dropout trying to figure out her reason for being. After leaving Stanford Law School, Jillian (Weixler) moved to Los Angeles and now bides her time working in food truck. While giving out free ice cream samples one very odd day in which she is extremely hung over, she meets a number of interesting people including her hookup from the previous night Tex (Eisenberg), her ex-fiance, and Wally (Ritter), a friend with his own ice cream dream. The experience makes her consider what she wants to do with her life moving forward. **80m/C; DVD, Streaming, Download.** Jess Weixler; Jesse Eisenberg; Halley Feiffer; Jason Ritter; Jeff Sloniker; ***D:*** Jay Gammill; ***W:*** Jim Beggarly; ***C:*** Reed Morano; ***M:*** Eric Elbogen.

Free Solo ⚊⚊⚊ **2018 (PG-13)** A breathtaking documentary about celebrated climber Alex Honnold, who climbs cliffs without any climbing equipment. The film explores his background, which includes a somewhat unusual childhood. His life changed forever when he discovered climbing. Though he became famous for his free solo climbs, he lives in a van for many years, channels most of the money he makes into a nonprofit, and is managing his first romantic relationship. Seeking a new challenge, Alex wants to conquer the El Capitan formation in Yosemite. This film documents his attempts to free solo climb El Capitan, emphasizing the suspense and danger involved. **100m/C; DVD.** Jimmy Chin; ***D:*** Jimmy Chin; Elizabeth Chai Vasarhelyi; ***C:*** Jimmy Chin; Matt Clegg; Clair Popkin; Mikey Schaefer; ***M:*** Marco Beltrami. Oscars '18: Feature Doc.; British Acad. '18: Feature Doc.

A Free Soul ⚊⚊ 1/2 **1931** Tippling litigator Barrymore helps low-life mobster Gable beat a murder rap, only to discover the hood has stolen his daughter's heart. Bargaining with his ditzy daughter, he vows to eschew the bottle if she'll stay away from good-for-nothing Gable. Directed by Brown, best known for his work with Garbo, and based on the memoirs of Adela Rogers St. John. The final courtroom scene—a cloak-and-gavel classic—cinched Barrymore's Oscar. Remade with Liz Taylor as "The Girl Who Had Everything" (although, ironically, the earlier version is the racier of the two). **94m/B; VHS, DVD.** Norma Shearer; Leslie Howard; Lionel Barrymore; Clark Gable; James Gleason; Lucy Beaumont; ***D:*** Clarence Brown; ***C:*** William H. Daniels. Oscars '31: Actor (Barrymore).

Free State of Jones ⚊⚊ **2016 (R)** McConaughey plays Newton Knight in Gary Ross' well-intentioned and historically-dense Civil War film. During the war, Knight led a rebellion in Mississippi against the Confederacy, forming his own community, the Free State of Jones. The community was made up of fellow men who disagreed with the South's position in the war, including small farmers and local slaves. Unfortunately it fails to find the right storytelling hook to make this tale an interesting one for modern audiences. There's a story to be told about standing up against tyranny, but it escapes Ross. **139m/C; DVD, Blu-Ray.** Matthew McConaughey; Gugu Mbatha-Raw; Mahershala Ali; Keri Russell; Christopher Berry; ***D:*** Gary Ross; ***W:*** Gary Ross; ***C:*** Benoit Delhomme; ***M:*** Nicholas Britell.

Free Style ⚊ 1/2 **2009 (PG)** Generic inspirational family/sports film that will probably appeal most to Bleu's fans. Hard-working Cale Bryant (Bleu) is forced to put his college plans on hold to help support his family—struggling single mom Jeanette (Parker) and cutie younger sis Bailey (Pettis). He's also determined to beat the odds and win a spot on the Grand National motocross racing team without sacrificing his family and friends while also making goo-goo eyes at bright hottie Alex (Echeverria). Both Bleu and Echeverria are appealing and can use the film as an eventual stepping stone to more complicated fare. **97m/C; On Demand.** *US CA* Sandra Echeverria; Corbin Bleu; Penelope Ann Miller; Madison Pettis; David Reivers; Tegan Moss; Jesse Moss; Jeff Nicholson; ***D:*** William Dear; ***W:*** Joshua Leibner; Jeff Nicholson; ***M:*** Stephen Endelman.

Free to Run ⚊⚊ 1/2 **2016** An insightful feature-length documentary on the transformation of running to a sport of the masses. In the mid-twentieth century, running was seen as something that was essentially limited to elite male athletes and only done on a track. During the 1960s, changes in society such as the women's liberation movement and a broader sense of personal freedom helped change attitudes towards running. As running moved into the streets, famous runners like Steve Prefontaine, Fred Lebow, and Kathrine Switzer also changed perceptions of the sport and made it something that anyone could do. **90m/C; DVD, Streaming, Download.** ***D:*** Pierre Morath; ***C:*** Thomas Queille.

Free, White, and 21 ⚊⚊ **1962** A black motel owner is accused of raping a white civil rights worker. Produced in a "pseudo-documentary" form which sometimes drags. **104m/B; VHS, DVD.** Frederick O'Neal; Annalena Lund; George Edgely; John Hicks; Hugh Crenshaw; George Russell; ***D:*** Larry Buchanan.

Free Willy ⚊⚊ 1/2 **1993 (PG)** Sentimental story about a 12-year-old runaway (Richter) who befriends a whale. Should appeal to children for its heartwarming story and delightful sea acrobatics. An electronically operated stand-in whale was used for far-off shots; a domesticated performing whale named Keiko for the close-ups. Director Wincer was known to grumble about the temperamental Keiko during shooting. Suggested viewing for students of animal behavior. Proof that family films can make money, "Free Willy" placed tenth for total boxoffice receipts in 1993. **112m/C; VHS, DVD, Blu-Ray.** Jason James Richter; Lori Petty; Jayne Atkinson; August Schellenberg; Michael Madsen; ***D:*** Simon Wincer; ***W:*** Keith A. Walker; Corey Blechman; ***C:*** Robbie Greenberg; ***M:*** Basil Poledouris. MTV Movie Awards '94: Song ("Will You Be There").

Free Willy 2: The Adventure Home ⚊⚊ 1/2 **1995 (PG)** While camping in the Pacific Northwest, Jesse is reunited with his orca-pal Willy, who has found a new home along with his whale siblings. But an offshore oil spill separates Willy from his family and threatens their lives, so his human friends must once again come to the rescue. All the principal characters are back, except for Willy (real name Keiko), who is recuperating from a skin virus in Mexico. Animatronics and Gump-like digital effects were used to replicate the real Willy. **98m/C; VHS, DVD.** Jason James Richter; Michael Madsen; Jayne Atkinson; August Schellenberg; Jon Tenney; Elizabeth Pena; ***D:*** Dwight Little; ***W:*** Corey Blechman; John Mattson; ***C:*** Laszlo Kovacs; ***M:*** Basil Poledouris.

Free Willy 3: The Rescue ⚊⚊ 1/2 **1997 (PG)** Isn't this poor whale ever going to be left in peace? This time around an illegal whaling operation threatens Willie and his orca pod. But 17-year-old Jesse (Richter), who has a summer job as a whale tracker on a research vessel, is determined to rescue his friend, aided by 10-year-old Max (Berry), who's horrified to discover his commercial fisherman father (Kilpatrick) is one of the whalers. **86m/C; VHS, DVD.** Jason James Richter; Vincent Berry; August Schellenberg; Annie Corley; Patrick Kilpatrick; ***D:*** Sam Pillsbury;

W: John Mattson; *C:* Tobias Schliessler; *M:* Cliff Eidelman.

Free Willy: Escape from Pirate's Cove 🦴🦴 ½ **2010 (PG)** After her father is in a serious accident, Kira (Irwin) is sent from Australia to stay with her grandfather Gus (Bridges) in South Africa. Gus owns a rundown amusement park and grumpy Kira is having issues until an ailing orca shows up in a nearby lagoon. Soon gramps is exploiting the whale for tourist dollars while Kira wants to help Willy return to his pod. Bindi, daughter of the late Steve Irwin, makes her feature film debut in this family friendly franchise entry. **101m/C; DVD.** Beau Bridges; Kevin Otto; Bindi Irwin; Stephen Jennings; *D:* Will Geiger; *W:* Will Geiger; *C:* Robert Malpage; *M:* Enis Rotthoff. **VIDEO**

Free Zone 🦴🦴 ½ **2005** Three women with ethnic ties to the Middle East converge in Jordan and become traveling companions for dissimilar reasons. An American with Israeli roots, Rebecca (Portman) kicks things off with a 10-minute crying jag in a cab by the Wailing Wall, though her sorrow appears connected not to religion but to her break-up with her fiance after he makes an appalling admission to her. The cab driver is Hanna (a spirited Laslo), an Israeli woman who has endured the regional turmoil but needs to collect cash that an associate of her husband owes to her. Woman number three, Leila (Abbass), is a Palestinian who works at Hanna's husband's office, who informs Hanna that the associate has vanished, causing the women to embark on a road trip to the Free Zone to look for him—and the cash. While an interesting trip, the political lessons stall out along the way. **94m/C; DVD.** *BE FR IS SP* Natalie Portman; Uri Klauzner; Carmen Maura; Hiam Abbass; Hana Laszlo; Makram Khoury; Aki Avni; *D:* Amos Gitai; *W:* Amos Gitai; Marie-Jose Sanselme; *C:* Laurent Brunet.

The Freebie 🦴🦴 **2010 (R)** Mostly improvised rom com set in L.A.'s Silverlake neighborhood. Darren (Shepard) and Annie (Aselton) have hit a lull in their seven-year marriage with their sex lives more cuddly than passionate. So they decide to spice things up by each taking a night off to go out and fool around with a stranger. Naturally this isn't a smart idea but whether it's also a marriage breaker is questionable. Efficiently personal and thoughtful directorial debut for Aselton. **78m/C; On Demand.** Dax Shepard; Ken Kennedy; Sean Nelson; Bellamy Young; Katie (Kathryn) Aselton; Leonora Gershman; Marguerite Phillips; Scott Pitts; *D:* Katie (Kathryn) Aselton; *W:* Katie (Kathryn) Aselton; *C:* Benjamin Kasulke; *M:* Julian Wass.

Freebie & the Bean 🦴 ½ **1974 (R)** Two San Francisco cops nearly ruin the city in their pursuit of a numbers-running mobster. Top-flight car chases and low-level, bigoted humor combine. Watch for Valerie Harper's appearance as Arkin's wife. Followed by a flash-in-the-pan TV series. **113m/C; VHS, DVD, Blu-Ray.** Alan Arkin; James Caan; Loretta Swit; Valerie Harper; Jack Kruschen; Mike Kellin; *D:* Richard Rush.

Freedom 🦴 ½ **2014 (R)** This flat, faith-based historical drama is so dull that it could be used to put insomniac children to sleep. Samuel (Gooding, Jr.) is a slave in 1856 who has escaped his plantation in Richmond, Virginia. A notorious slave hunter named Plimpton (Sadler) hunts him across the country. As if this narrative wasn't boring or poorly handled enough, director Peter Cousens doubles down with flashbacks to the journey of Samuel's grandfather from Africa over a 100 years earlier. Samuel's ancestor plays a role in the safety of the ship on which he's being transported and inspires generations to come. You'll only be inspired to sleep. **98m/C; DVD, Streaming.** Cuba Gooding, Jr.; William Sadler; Sharon Leal; Diane Salinger; *D:* Peter Cousens; *W:* Timothy A. Chey; *C:* Dean Cundey; *M:* James Lavino. **VIDEO**

Freedom Road 🦴🦴 **1979** Drama about a Reconstruction Era ex-slave, portrayed by heavyweight champion Ali, who is elected to the U.S. Senate and subsequently killed while trying to obtain total freedom for his race. Based on a novel by Howard Fast. **186m/C; VHS, DVD.** Ron O'Neal; Edward Herrmann; John McLiam; Ernest Dixon; Alfre Woodard; Kris Kristofferson; Muhammad Ali; *D:* Jan Kadar. **TV**

Freedom Song 🦴🦴🦴 **2000** In Mississippi in 1961, Will Walker (Glover) is a black man both angry and afraid. Civil rights, freedom rights and increasing racial violence make for tense times for the Walker family as teenaged Owen (Shannon) is drawn to organizer Daniel Wall (Curtis-Hall). Complex, conflicted people and situations make for a fine drama. **150m/C; VHS, DVD.** Danny Glover; Vondie Curtis-Hall; Vicellous Shannon; Loretta Devine; Glynn Turman; Stan Shaw; Michael Jai White; Rae'ven (Alyia Larrymore) Kelly; John Beasley; Jason Weaver; Marcello Thedford; David Strathairn; *D:* Phil Alden Robinson; *W:* Phil Alden Robinson; Stanley Weiser; *M:* James Horner. **CABLE**

Freedom Strike 🦴 ½ **1998 (R)** Navy pilots Stone and MacDonald are sent on a covert mission to sabotage an Iraqui nuclear reactor before terrorists can use it. **93m/C; VHS, DVD.** Michael Dudikoff; Tone Loc; Felicity Waterman; *D:* Jerry P. Jacobs. **VIDEO**

Freedom Summer 🦴 **2014** Veteran documentarian Nelson turns his lens on the civil rights movement of the summer of 1964, a time where the world's attention turned to the marches for freedom in the southern United States. Mississippi remained one of the country's most violently segregated areas, and Robert Moses of the Student Nonviolent Coordinating Committee battled it with manpower, bringing people there to encourage voter registration and educate locals on the importance of equal rights. Nelson's film contains interesting interviews but lacks truly new insight into an oft-told chapter of American history. **113m/C; DVD.** *D:* Stanley Nelson; *W:* Stanley Nelson; *C:* Antonio Rossi; *M:* Tom Phillips.

Freedom Writers 🦴🦴 ½ **2007 (PG-13)** Oh so earnest (yet affecting) dedicated teacher true story set in 1994. White-bread newbie Erin Gruwell (Swank) is unprepared for teaching freshman English to an ethnically diverse, underprivileged class at a Long Beach high school. In order to get their attention, Erin, inspired by "The Diary of Anne Frank," gives her students journals to write about their own lives in their own raw vernacular. A collection of entries is eventually published as "The Freedom Writers Diary," which continues to cause classroom/parental clashes for its eye-opening depictions of teen experience. Swank, complete with gleaming smile and pearls, is filled with can-do spirit while Dempsey is wasted as her neglected hubby. **123m/C; DVD, Blu-Ray, HD-DVD.** Hilary Swank; Patrick Dempsey; Scott Glenn; Imelda Staunton; John Benjamin Hickey; Pat Carroll; April Lee Hernandez; Deance Wyatt; Mario; Vanetta Smith; *D:* Richard LaGravenese; *W:* Richard LaGravenese; *C:* Jim Denault; *M:* Mark Isham.

Freedomland 🦴🦴 ½ **2006 (R)** White girl (Moore) from "the right side of the tracks" walks into a medical center in the projects with the story of a carjacking/kidnapping of her son. Black detective Lorenzo (Jackson) must find out the truth and prevent a riot as the cops, one of whom (Eldard) is her brother, lock down the neighborhood. Tension is effectively built as Lorenzo works the case while trying to balance his allegiances to his instincts, his neighborhood, and his job. Jackson's presence is vital to keeping the movie from spinning out of control into preachy "good-for-you" territory. Still gets a bit heavy, and more than a little depressing. **113m/C; DVD, Blu-Ray.** Samuel L. Jackson; Julianne Moore; Edie Falco; Ron Eldard; William Forsythe; Aunjanue Ellis; Anthony Mackie; LaTanya Richardson Jackson; Clarke Peters; *D:* Joe Roth; *W:* Richard Price; *C:* Anastas Michos; *M:* James Newton Howard.

Freeheld 🦴 ½ **2015 (PG-13)** As a highly recognized New Jersey police officer, Laurel Hester (Moore) kept her homosexuality secret because she feared her fellow cops wouldn't respond well to it. A terminal cancer diagnosis outs her, as the only way her partner Stacie (Page) could keep their home was with Laurel's pension, as the partners of heterosexual cops would. The city first refused the request, but Laurel's story became a rallying cry for equal rights and a foundation for gay marriage. Based on a true story, Sollett's film sadly chooses politics and melodrama instead of the human story. **103m/C; DVD, Blu-Ray.** Julianne Moore; Ellen Page; Steve Carell; Michael Shannon; Josh Charles; Luke Grimes; *D:* Peter Sollett; *W:* Ron Nyswaner; *C:* Maryse Alberti; *M:* Hans Zimmer; Johnny Marr.

Freejack 🦴🦴 ½ **1992 (R)** Futuristic thriller set in the year 2009, where pollution, the hole in the ozone layer, and the financial gap between the social classes have grown to such horrific proportions that the rich must pillage the past to find young bodies to replace their own. Estevez is a young race car driver whose sudden death makes him an ideal candidate for this bizarre type of surgery. Once transported to the future, he becomes a "Freejack" who must run for his life. Good cast including Jagger and Hopkins brings this one up slightly. Adapted from the novel "Immortality Inc." by Robert Sheckley. **110m/C; DVD, Blu-Ray.** Emilio Estevez; Mick Jagger; Rene Russo; Anthony Hopkins; Jonathan Banks; David Johansen; Amanda Plummer; Grand L. Bush; Frankie Faison; Esai Morales; John Shea; *D:* Geoff Murphy; *W:* Dan Gilroy; Steven Pressfield; Ronald Shusett; *C:* Amir M. Mokri; *M:* Michael Boddicker; Trevor Jones.

Freelancers 🦴 **2012 (R)** Did De Niro do this mess of a dirty cop flick for the money? New NYPD cop Malo (Jackson) is mentored by his slain dad's old partner, Joe Sarcone (De Niro) on how to be a dirty cop. Malo also wants to learn the truth abouth his dad's death. **96m/C; DVD, Blu-Ray; Closed Captioned.** 50 Cent; Robert De Niro; Forest Whitaker; Ryan O'Neal; Malcolm Goodwin; Matt Gerald; *D:* Jesse Torrero; *W:* L. Philippe Casseus; *C:* Igor Martinovic. **VIDEO**

Freerunner 🦴 **2010 (R)** Ryan and his fellow extreme sports competitors are forced into running through the city in a bored billionaires' contest. They've been fitted with explosive collars and the winner will get a big payout if he can stick to the course and survive. (The others just go boom.) **90m/C; DVD, Blu-Ray.** Sean Faris; Danny Dyer; Rebecca Da Costa; Seymour Cassel; Tamer Hassan; *D:* Lawrence Silverstein; *W:* Raimund Huber; *C:* Claudio Chea; *M:* Peter DiStefano. **VIDEO**

Freeway 🦴🦴 ½ **1988 (R)** A nurse attempts to find the obsessive killer who shot her husband. The murderer phones a radio psychiatrist from his car, using Biblical quotes, while cruising for new victims. Okay thriller, based on the L.A. freeway shootings. **91m/C; VHS, DVD, Blu-Ray.** Darlanne Fluegel; James Russo; Billy Drago; Richard Belzer; Michael Callan; Steve Franken; Kenneth Tobey; Clint Howard; *D:* Francis Delia; *W:* Larry Ketron; Darrell Fetty; Francis Delia; *M:* Joe Delia.

Freeway 🦴 ½ **1995 (R)** Grubby modern retelling of "Little Red Riding Hood" finds surly 16-year-old Vanessa (Witherspoon) escaping from her parole officer to avoid foster care when the cops arrest her mom and stepdad. She takes the family car and heads off to grandma's but car trouble on the freeway leads to a ride from the big bad wolf—Bob Wolverton (Sutherland)?a serial killer preying on young women. Lots of lurid unpleasantness. **102m/C; VHS, DVD.** Reese Witherspoon; Kiefer Sutherland; Brooke Shields; Wolfgang Bodison; Dan Hedaya; Amanda Plummer; Bokeem Woodbine; Brittany Murphy; Michael T. Weiss; Guillermo Diaz; Susan Barnes; Alanna Ubach; Conchata Ferrell; Tara Subkoff; Sydney Lassick; *D:* Matthew Bright; *W:* Matthew Bright; *C:* John Thomas; *M:* Danny Elfman.

Freeway 2: Confessions of a Trickbaby 🦴 **1999 (R)** The 1995 film was a violent modern update of "Little Red Riding Hood" and the sequel is a twisted fairytale "Hansel and Gretel." Crystal (Lyonne) escapes from juvenile prison with cell buddy Cyclona (Celedonio) and heads to Tijuana where she hopes psychic Sister Gomez (Gallo) can cure her of her compulsion to murder. The body count rises a lot on their journey. As grubby and unappealing as its predecessor. **90m/C; VHS, DVD, Blu-Ray.** Natasha Lyonne; Maria Celedonio; Vincent Gallo; David Alan Grier; Michael T. Weiss; John Landis; Max Perlich; *D:* Matthew Bright; *W:* Matthew Bright; *C:* Joel Ransom; *M:* Kennard Ramsey. **VIDEO**

Freeze Frame 🦴🦴 **2004 (R)** Sean Vail (Evans) was accused of multiple murders but released on a technicality. Ten years later, Sean's paranoia is in full bloom and he obsessively videotapes every moment of his life so he will have an alibi if it's ever needed, which happens when a new victim is discovered. But Sean can't account for his whereabouts because the tapes of those specific hours are mysteriously missing. Brit Evans is best known for his comedy so this psycho-thriller is a real departure. Strong visually, the flick falls apart at the end. **90m/C; DVD.** *IR GB* Lee Evans; Sean McGinley; Rachael Stirling; Ian McNeice; Colin Salmon; Rachel O'Riordan; *D:* John Simpson; *W:* John Simpson; *C:* Mark Garret; *M:* Debbie Wiseman.

Freezer 🦴 ½ **2014 (R)** After ordinary guy Robert (McDermott) is thrown into, you guessed it, a walk-in freezer by the Russian mob, he must figure out not only why he's there, but how to escape before his body seizes up. However, things may not be as they seem, as Robert pulls information from one of his female captors (Snigir), and deftly maneuvers out of zip-tie handcuffs. McDermott does his best frost-bitten impression and, with the help of icy make-up, pulls off the gag. A practical and sometimes cold-blooded action-thriller that makes the most out of its very limited location. **91m/C; DVD, Blu-Ray.** Dylan McDermott; Peter Facinelli; Yuliya Snigir; Andrey Ivchenko; Pascal Petardi; Milan Malisic; *D:* Mikael Salomon; *W:* Tom Doganoglu; Shane Weisfeld; *C:* John Dyer; *M:* David C. Williams.

Freezer Burn: The Invasion of Laxdale 🦴🦴 **2008 (R)** Laxdale is a Canadian farming community where crop circles have been popping up in the cornfields and the temperature is unnaturally high. An odd oil company exec (Glover) is trying to buy the local grain silo but bitter former hockey player Bill Swanson (Green) refuses to sell. Then Bill stumbles across a dead alien wearing an oil company uniform and tries to warn the townspeople about what's really going on. **90m/C; DVD.** *CA* Tom Green; Crispin Glover; Sarain Boylan; Scott Hylands; Paul J. Spence; David Brown; *D:* Grant Harvey; *W:* Grant Harvey; *C:* John Spooner; *M:* Michael Shields.

The French Atlantic Affair 🦴🦴 **1979** ABC TV miniseries. The SS Festivale leaves New York harbor for France with cult leader Craig Dunleavy (Savalas) and members of his flock among the passengers. They seize control of the luxury liner and Dunleavy demands millions in gold as a ransom. He issues dire threats but, since he intends to kill everyone anyway, some of the passengers and crew intend to foil his plans. Based on the Ernest Lehman novel. **294m/C; DVD.** Telly Savalas; Chad Everett; Louis Jourdan; Shelley Winters; John Rubinstein; Michelle Phillips; Jose Ferrer; Jean-Pierre Aumont; *D:* Douglas Heyes; *W:* Douglas Heyes; *C:* Ralph Woolsey; *M:* John Addison. **TV**

French Can-Can 🦴🦴🦴 *Only the French Can!* **1955** Dramatically sparse but visually stunning depiction of the can-can's revival in Parisian nightclubs. Gabin plays the theatre impressario who discovers laundress Arnoul and decides to turn her into the dancing star of his new revue at the Moulin Rouge. In French with English subtitles. **93m/C; VHS, DVD.** *FR* Jean Gabin; Francoise Arnoul; Maria Felix; Jean-Roger Caussimon; Edith Piaf; Patachou; *D:* Jean Renoir.

The French Connection 🦴🦴🦴 ½ **1971 (R)** Popeye Doyle (Hackman) and his partner Buddy Russo (Scheider) are a couple of hard-nosed NYC narcotics detectives who stumble onto what turns out to be one of the biggest narcotics rings of all time, involving French mastermind Alain Charnier (Rey). Cat-and-mouse thriller will keep you on the edge of your seat; contains one of the most exciting chase scenes ever filmed. Hackman's portrayal of Doyle is exact and the teamwork with Scheider special. Based on a true story from the book by Robin Moore. Followed in 1975 by "French Connection 2." **102m/C; VHS, DVD, Blu-Ray.** Gene Hackman; Roy Scheider; Fernando Rey; Tony LoBianco; Eddie Egan; Sonny Grosso; Marcel Bozzuffi; *D:* William Friedkin; *W:* Ernest Tidyman; *C:* Owen Roizman; *M:* Don Ellis. Oscars '71: Actor (Hackman), Adapt. Screenplay, Director (Friedkin), Film, Film Editing; AFI '98: Top 100; British Acad. '72: Actor (Hackman); Directors Guild '71: Director (Friedkin); Golden Globes '72: Actor--Drama (Hackman), Director (Friedkin), Film--Drama; Natl. Bd. of Review '71: Actor (Hackman); Natl. Film Reg.

'05; N.Y. Film Critics '71: Actor (Hackman); Writers Guild '71: Adapt. Screenplay.

French Connection 2 1975 (R) New York policeman "Popeye" Doyle goes to Marseilles to crack a heroin ring headed by his arch nemesis, Frog One, whom he failed to stop in the United States. Dour, super-gritty sequel to the 1971 blockbuster, and featuring one of Hackman's most uncompromising performances. **118m/C; VHS, DVD, Blu-Ray.** Gene Hackman; Fernando Rey; Bernard Fresson; *D:* John Frankenheimer; *W:* Robert Dillon; *C:* Claude Renoir; *M:* Don Ellis.

French Film ½ 2008 Smug British journalist Jed is interviewing pretentious French film director Thierry, who offers his views on British insecurities about love. Jed and longtime girlfriend Cheryl have only inertia keeping them together until Jed's friend Marcus leaves his girlfriend Sophie and Jed decides to make a move on her. **88m/C; DVD.** *GB* Hugh Bonneville; Eric Cantona; Victoria Hamilton; Anne-Marie Duff; Douglas Henshall; *D:* Jackie Oudney; *W:* Aschlin Ditta; *C:* Sean Van Hales; *M:* Stephen Warbeck.

French Fried Vacation *Les Bronzes* **1979** Zany antics erupt when a group of unattached and consenting adults vacation in Africa. French with English subtitles. **90m/C; VHS, DVD.** *FR* Josiane Balasko; Michel Blanc; Mariann (Marie-Anne) Chazel; Thierry Lhermitte; Gerard Jugnot; Dominque Lavanant; Christian Clavier; *D:* Patrice Leconte.

A French Gigolo *Cliente* **2008** Working-class Marco (Caravaca) secretly moonlights as an escort to help get his wife Fanny's (Carre) hairdressing business going. Middle-aged TV personality Judith (Baye) is recently divorced and living with her sister (Balasko), so she decides to try an online service to have a fling. When Judith and Marco get together it's more than a one-night stand, and more than sexual as they become emotionally involved as well. French with subtitles. **104m/C; DVD.** *FR* Nathalie Baye; Eric Caravaca; Isabelle Carre; Catherine Hiegel; George Aguilar; Marilou Berry; Josiane Balasko; *D:* Josiane Balasko; *W:* Josiane Balasko; Franck Lee Joseph; *C:* Robert Alazraki; *M:* DJ Kore.

French Kiss ½ **1995 (PG-13)** Ultra cute Kate (Ryan) has a fear of flying but she's more afraid of losing her fiance (Hutton) to a newly met French babe. She jets off to Paris and on the way meets a dashing, but disheveled, French rogue (Kline). What happens next is predictable, but amusing just the same. Plot drags a bit in the middle, but the scenery and banter between Ryan and Kline are a pleasant enough diversion. Kline is at his charming best, while Ryan is typically perky. Watch for Spielvogel's stereotypically rude French hotel concierge. He's a hoot. **111m/C; VHS, DVD, Blu-Ray.** Meg Ryan; Kevin Kline; Timothy Hutton; Jean Reno; Francois Cluzet; Renee Humphrey; Michael Riley; Susan Anbeh; Laurent Spielvogel; *D:* Lawrence Kasdan; *W:* Adam Brooks; *C:* Owen Roizman; *M:* James Newton Howard.

The French Lieutenant's Woman ½ **1981 (R)** Romantic love and tragedy in the form of two parallel stories, that of an 19th-century woman who keeps her mysterious past from the scientist who loves her, and the lead actor and actress in the film of the same story managing an illicit affair on the set. Extraordinary performances and beautifully shot. Based on the John Fowles novel. **124m/C; VHS, DVD, Blu-Ray.** Meryl Streep; Jeremy Irons; Leo McKern; Lynsey Baxter; *D:* Karel Reisz; *W:* Harold Pinter; *C:* Freddie Francis; *M:* Carl Davis. British Acad. '81: Actress (Streep); Golden Globes '82: Actress--Drama (Streep); L.A. Film Critics '81: Actress (Streep).

The French Minister *Quai d'Orsay* **2013** Political satire. Pompous yet dynamic career diplomat (and France's foreign minister) Alexandre Taillard de Vorms (Lhermitte) gives his harried staff fits with his vague pronouncements. Recent grad student Arthur Vlaminck (Personnaz) is hired as a speech writer without any guidance as to what he should to be writing, although Taillard is supposed to deliver a major speech at the U.N. Based on Abel Lanzac's graphic novels. French with subtitles. **113m/C; DVD.** *FR* Thierry Lhermitte; Raphael Personnaz; Niels Arestrup; Julie Gayet; Anais Demoustier; Thomas Chabrol; *D:* Bertrand Tavernier; *W:* Bertrand Tavernier; Antonin Baudry; Christophe Blain; *C:* Jerome Almeras; *M:* Philippe Sarde.

French Postcards **1979 (PG)** Three American students study all aspects of French culture when they spend their junior year of college at the Institute of French Studies in Paris. By the same writers who penned "American Graffiti" a few years earlier. **95m/C; VHS, DVD, Blu-Ray.** Miles Chapin; Blanche Baker; Valerie Quennessen; Debra Winger; Mandy Patinkin; Marie-France Pisier; *D:* Willard Huyck; *W:* Gloria Katz; Willard Huyck.

French Quarter ½ **1978 (R)** A dual story about a young girl in the modern-day French Quarter of New Orleans who is also the reincarnation of a turn-of-the-century prostitute. Everyone gets to play two roles but this film is more curiosity than anything else. **101m/C; VHS, DVD.** Bruce Davison; Virginia Mayo; Lindsay Bloom; Alisha Fontaine; Lance LeGault; Anne Michelle; *D:* Dennis Kane.

French Silk ½ **1994 (PG-13)** Homicide detective (Horsley) falls for a lingerie designer (Lucci) who's a murder suspect. Filmed on location in New Orleans. Made for TV production with additional footage. "R" rating is for nudity (not Lucci's). Based on the novel by Sandra Brown. **90m/C; VHS, DVD.** Susan Lucci; Lee Horsley; Shari Belafonte; R. Lee Ermey; Sarah Marshall; Bobby Hosea; Jim Metzler; Joe Warfield; Paul Rosenberg; *D:* Noel Nosseck. **TV**

The French Touch ½ **1954** Fernandel stars in this French farce about a shepherd who decides to open his own clip joint as a hairdresser and finds himself a hit among the Parisiennes. Fair to middling comedy. **84m/B; VHS, DVD, Streaming.** *FR* Fernandel; Renee Devillers; Georges Chamarat; *D:* Jean Boyer.

French Twist ½ *Bushwhacked; Gazon Maudit* **1995 (R)** Romantic comedy about housewife Loli (Abril), tiredly coping with her realtor/husband Laurent (Chabat) and their two sons. Then Loli meets appealing stranger Marijo (Balasko), a very matter-of-fact lesbian, and when she discovers her hubby is a chronic philanderer, Loli gets revenge by inviting Marijo to move in with them. Laurent realizes he loves his wife but she's having too much fun and there's finally an interesting showdown between Laurent and Marijo over Loli. The French title, which translates literally to "Cursed Lawn," is an old slang term for lesbian. French with subtitles. **100m/C; VHS, DVD.** *FR* Victoria Abril; Alain Chabat; Josiane Balasko; Ticky Holgado; *D:* Josiane Balasko; *W:* Josiane Balasko; Telsche Boorman; *C:* Gerard de Battista; *M:* Manuel Malou. Cesar '96: Writing.

The French Woman **1979 (R)** Softcore story of blackmail, murder, and sex involving French cabinet ministers mixing passion and politics. From the director of "Emmanuelle." **97m/C; VHS, DVD.** Francoise Fabian; Klaus Kinski; *D:* Just Jaeckin; *M:* Serge Gainsbourg.

Frenchman's Creek ½ **1944** Adventure set in the 17th century features English noblewoman Lady Dona (Fontaine) fleeing her spineless husband Harry St. Columb (Forbes) and his lecherous friend, Lord Rockingham (Rathbone). She finds a Frenchman's ship anchored in a creek off her country estate and becomes dazzled by its dashing pirate captain (de Cordova). Unfortunately, the pirate is also a spy (since the Frenchies and the Brits are fighting as usual) and Rockingham discovers their secrets. When the Frenchman is captured, Lady Dona risks all to rescue him. Based on the novel by Daphne du Maurier and remade for British TV in 1998. **112m/C; DVD.** Joan Fontaine; Arturo de Cordova; Basil Rathbone; Ralph Forbes; Nigel Bruce; Cecil Kellaway; Moyna MacGill; *D:* Mitchell Leisen; *W:* Talbot Jennings; *C:* George Barnes; *M:* Victor Young. **TV**

Frenchman's Creek ½ **1998** Lady Dona St. Columb (Fitzgerald) is bored both with London society and her husband, Sir Harry (Fleet), so she and her children head for her family's estate on the Cornish coast. There, Dona discovers dashing French privateer, Jean Aubrey (Delon), is using a nearby cove to anchor his ship while he spies on the English. Dona and the pirate get very, very close and she decides to help him outwit the authorities. But soon Dona must choose between passion and duty. **120m/C; VHS, DVD.** *GB* Tara Fitzgerald; Anthony Delon; Tim Dutton; James Fleet; Danny (Daniel) Webb; Jeremy Child; *D:* Ferdinand Fairfax; *W:* Patrick Harbinson; *C:* Chris Seager. **TV**

Frenchman's Farm ½ **1987 (R)** A young woman witnesses a killing at a deserted farmhouse. When she tells the police, they tell her that the murder happened 40 years before. Average thriller that probably won't keep you on the edge of your seat. **90m/C; VHS, DVD.** *AU* Tracey Tanish; David Reyne; John Meillon; Norman Kaye; Tui Bow; *D:* Ron Way.

Frenemy *Little Fish, Strange Pond* **2009 (R)** Mr. Jack and Sweet Stephen drift aimlessly through L.A., boring everyone stupid with their equally aimless philosophical discussions. Mr. Jack is actually a hitman and Sweet Stephen is the personification of his conscience. Uh, yeah. Another bait-and-switch cover art scam since the prominently featured Galifianakis' part is little better than a cameo. **80m/C; DVD.** Matthew Modine; Callum Blue; Paul Adelstein; Liza Weil; Adam Baldwin; Don McManus; Zach Galifianakis; *D:* Gregory Brown; *W:* Robert Dean Klein; *C:* Gavin Kelly; *M:* Paul Rabjohns. **VIDEO**

Frenzy ½ *Latin Quarter* **1946** A sculptor, pushed over the brink of sanity when he discovers that his wife is having an affair, turns to his art for solace. . .and seals his wife's corpse in a statue. Creepy. **75m/B; VHS, DVD.** *GB* Derrick DeMarney; Frederick Valk; Joan Greenwood; Joan Seton; Valentine Dyall; Martin Miller; *D:* Vernon Sewell; *W:* Vernon Sewell.

Frenzy **1972 (R)** The only film in which Hitchcock was allowed to totally vent the violence and perverse sexuality of his distinctive vision, in a story about a strangler stalking London women in the late '60s. Finch plays the convicted killer-only he's innocent and must escape prison to find the real killer. McGowen is wonderful as the put-upon police inspector. A bit dated, but still ferociously hostile and cunningly executed. **116m/C; VHS, DVD, Blu-Ray.** *GB* Jon Finch; Barry Foster; Barbara Leigh-Hunt; Anna Massey; Alec McCowen; Vivien Merchant; Billie Whitelaw; Jean Marsh; Bernard Cribbins; Michael Bates; Rita Webb; Jimmy Gardner; Clive Swift; Madge Ryan; George Tovey; Noel Johnson; *D:* Alfred Hitchcock; *W:* Anthony Shaffer; *C:* Gilbert Taylor; *M:* Ronald Goodwin.

Frequency ½ **2000 (PG-13)** In 1999, New York cop John (Caviezel) finds he can communicate with his dead father (Quaid) in 1969 through dad's old ham radio. Since his father was a fireman who died in a warehouse fire almost exactly 30 years ago, John decides to tell him how not to get killed. This leads to changes in the present (messing with the past always does), including the murder of John's mother by a serial killer. Father and son must solve and prevent the killings in the past and the present using their respective skills and, amazingly, John's knowledge of the 1969 World Series. It's all very convoluted and ridiculous (especially the ending), but the underlying sentiment, and the fine work of Caviezel and Quaid make it easy to suspend disbelief and go along for the ride. **117m/C; VHS, DVD, Blu-Ray.** Dennis Quaid; James (Jim) Caviezel; Elizabeth Mitchell; Andre Braugher; Shawn Doyle; Noah Emmerich; Jordan Bridges; Melissa Errico; Daniel Henson; *D:* Gregory Hoblit; *W:* Toby Emmerich; *C:* Alar Kivilo; *M:* Michael Kamen.

Fresh ½ **1994 (R)** Intelligent 12-year-old boy runs heroin in the morning and sells crack after school in a tough Brooklyn neighborhood. Enterprising young man draws life lessons from chess-hustler father Jackson and heroin-dealing mentor Esposito, so he looks for a way out of the dead-end business. First time director Yakin plays it straight, foregoing the usual Hollywood-style rap and automatic weapons approach to convey the message that circumstances can kill innocence just as effectively as a bullet. Startling but subdued atmosphere allows the plot and characters to become more complicated than first suspected. Excellent performance by newcomer Nelson as the kid. **114m/C; VHS, DVD, Blu-Ray.** *FR* Samuel L. Jackson; Giancarlo Esposito; Sean Nelson; N'Bushe Wright; Ron Brice; Jean LaMarre; Luis Lantigua; Yul Vazquez; Cheryl Freeman; *D:* Boaz Yakin; *W:* Boaz Yakin; *C:* Adam Holender. Ind. Spirit '95: Debut Perf. (Nelson); Sundance '94: Filmmakers Trophy, Special Jury Prize.

Fresh Cut Grass ½ **2004** Debut for writer/director Coppola is an overly earnest story about college grad and wannabe writer Zac (Wilke). After his father's death, Zac's biding his time cutting lawns while deciding what to do next. He finds romance with the exotically named Eastern Star (Hansz), who helps him on the path to adulthood. **101m/C; DVD.** Katy Hansz; James McCaffrey; Bobby Cannavale; Dylan Bruno; David Wilke; Alicia Coppola; *D:* Matthew Coppola; *W:* Matthew Coppola; *C:* Tom Agnello.

Fresh Dressed ½ **2015** An insightful documentary history of hip-hop and urban fashion and its impact on wider cultural. Focusing especially on the link between music and fashion, the documentary explores how originality, the desire for freedom of expression, and the aspirational want for a better life influenced the development of this fashion. In addition to explaining how this look made it from the streets to shopping malls to high fashion, the rise of designers influenced by this culture, most notably Tommy Hilfiger, is considered as well. **90m/C; DVD, Download.** *D:* Sacha Jenkins; *W:* Sacha Jenkins; *C:* David Vollrath; *M:* Tyler Strickland.

Fresh Horses **1988 (PG-13)** A wrong-side-of-the-tracks Depression-era romance. McCarthy is the engaged college boy who falls for backwoods girl Ringwald, who turns out to have a destructive secret. **92m/C; VHS, DVD.** Molly Ringwald; Andrew McCarthy; Patti D'Arbanville; Ben Stiller; Viggo Mortensen; *D:* David Anspaugh; *M:* David Foster.

The Freshman **1925** Country boy Lloyd goes to college and, after many comic tribulations, saves the day with the winning touchdown at the big game and wins the girl of his dreams. This was one of the comedian's most popular films. **75m/B; Silent; VHS, DVD, Blu-Ray.** Harold Lloyd; Jobyna Ralston; Brooks Benedict; James Anderson; Hazel Keener; *D:* Fred Newmeyer; Sam Taylor; *W:* Sam Taylor. Natl. Film Reg. '90.

The Freshman ½ **1990 (PG)** Brando, in an incredible parody of his Don Corleone character, makes this work. Broderick is a college student in need of fast cash, and innocent enough to believe that any work is honest. A good supporting cast and a twisty plot keep things interesting. Sometimes heavy handed with its sight gags, but Broderick and Brando push the movie to hilarious conclusion. Don't miss Bert Parks's musical extravaganza. **102m/C; VHS, DVD.** Marlon Brando; Matthew Broderick; Maximilian Schell; Penelope Ann Miller; Bruno Kirby; Frank Whaley; Jon Polito; Paul Benedict; Richard Gant; B.D. Wong; Bert Parks; *D:* Andrew Bergman; *W:* Andrew Bergman; *C:* William A. Fraker; *M:* David Newman.

Freshman Orientation ½ *Home of Phobia* **2004 (R)** Would-be campus comedy that also seems to be trying (and failing) to teach a lesson on personal responsibility and identity. College freshman Clay (Huntington) is sure he's going to bag a lot of girls but he's a social zero on campus. Freshman Amanda (Doubleday) is a sorority pledge whose initiation includes picking up a certain type of campus outcast and taking him to a sorority party where humiliation is on the agenda. Amanda's supposed to bring a gay guy and mistakenly picks Clay, who goes along for the chance to be with a pretty girl. He gets lessons in gay behavior from outgoing bartender Rodney (Goodman) but eventually the ruse is exposed. Debut film for Shiraki. **91m/C; DVD.** Sam Huntington; Kaitlin Doubleday; John Goodman; Heather Matarazzo; Marla Sokoloff; Mike Erwin; Judy Tylor; Bryce Johnson; *D:* Ryan Shivaki; *W:* Ryan Shivaki; *C:* Amelia Vincent; *M:* tomandandy.

Frida ½ **1984** The life of controversial Mexican painter Frido Kahlo is told via deathbed flashbacks using the artist's paintings to set the scenes. In Spanish with English subtitles. **108m/C; VHS, DVD.** *SP* Ofelia Medina; Juan Jose Gurrola; Max Kerlow; *D:* Paul Leduc.

Frida 1/2 **2002 (R)** Biography of nonconformist Mexican artist Frida Kahlo (Hayek) from her teen years to her death at the age of 44. The story relies heavily on her stormy marriage and continued relationship with famed muralist Diego Rivera (Molina). Director Julie Taymor also surrealistically brings to life several of Kahlo's paintings, although her glamorization of the famously uni-browed and mustachioed painter drew fire from ardent fans. Based on the book by Hayden Herrera. **120m/C; VHS, DVD, Blu-Ray.** Salma Hayek; Alfred Molina; Ashley Judd; Geoffrey Rush; Antonio Banderas; Roger Rees; Edward Norton; Valeria Golino; Mia Maestro; Saffron Burrows; Patricia Reyes Spindola; Margarita Sanz; Diego Luna; *D:* Julie Taymor; *W:* Gregory Nava; Anna Thomas; Clancy Sigeland; Diane Lake; *C:* Rodrigo Prieto; *M:* Elliot Goldenthal. Oscars '02: Makeup, Orig. Score; British Acad. '02: Makeup; Golden Globes '03: Score.

Friday 1/2 **1995 (R)** It's "Boyz N' the Hood" meets "Good Times." Ice Cube wrote and stars as Craig in this humorous look into life in the 'hood. Craig's just lost his job and spends his time sitting on the porch with his pot smoking sidekick Smokey (Tucker), with the two getting mixed up in a variety of crazy antics involving their kooky neighbors. The laughs come at the expense of overworn cliches and sterotypical characters, but there's originality in the movie's energy and boldness (i.e. the local dope dealer is also the neighborhood ice cream man). To some, this "Friday" could be something to look forward to. **91m/C; VHS, DVD, UMD.** Ice Cube; Chris Tucker; Bernie Mac; John Witherspoon; Regina King; Nia Long; Tommy (Tiny) Lister; Anna Maria Horsford; LaWanda Page; *D:* F. Gary Gray; *W:* Ice Cube; DJ Pooh; *C:* Gerry Lively; *M:* Frank Fitzpatrick.

Friday After Next 1/2 **2002 (R)** Third installment of the series shows Christmas in the 'hood, as heroes Craig (Ice Cube) and Day-Day (Epps) are forced to take jobs as mall security guards after a ghetto Santa (Smiley) steals their presents and rent money. The usual brand of lowbrow humor is shoveled out in heaping piles and most of the regulars return, including John Witherspoon as Craig's chronically flatulent father. **85m/C; VHS, DVD.** Ice Cube; Mike Epps; John Witherspoon; Don "DC" Curry; Anna Maria Horsford; Clifton Powell; Terry Crews; BeBe Drake; Sommore; Starletta DuPois; K.D. Aubert; Katt Micah Williams; Rickey Smiley; Joel McKinnon Miller; Reggie Gaskins; *D:* Marcus Raboy; *W:* Ice Cube; *C:* Glen MacPherson; *M:* John Murphy.

Friday Foster 1/2 **1975 (R)** A beautiful, young photographer investigates an assassination attempt and uncovers a conspiracy against black politicians. Based on the Chicago Tribune comic strip. **90m/C; VHS, DVD, Blu-Ray.** Pam Grier; Yaphet Kotto; Thalmus Rasulala; Carl Weathers; Godfrey Cambridge; *D:* Arthur Marks; *W:* Orville H. Hampton; *C:* Harry J. May; *M:* Luchi De Jesus.

Friday Night *Vendredi Soir* **2002** Laure (Lemercier) is packing up her Paris apartment one wintery evening prior to moving in with her lover. She's a little uncertain about the upcoming changes as she heads out to dinner with friends. There's a public transport strike and a massive traffic jam, so Laure takes to watching the stranded commuters, one of whom is burly and calm Jean (Lindon). It's bitterly cold and Laure decides to offer Jean a ride. Laure also decides to cancel her plans and make new ones (the one-night stand kind) with Jean. Based on the novel by Emmanuele Bernheim. French with subtitles. **90m/C; DVD.** *FR* Valerie Lemercier; Vincent Lindon; *D:* Claire Denis; *W:* Claire Denis; Emmanuele Bernheim; *C:* Agnes Godard; *M:* Dickon Hinchliffe.

Friday Night Lights **2004 (PG-13)** Excellent tale about West Texas's love for high school football. Based on the 1990 nonfiction H.G. Bissinger account of the 1988 season of the Odessa-Permian Panthers team, the film showcases the be-all, end-all small town fervor for the game and the all-consuming impact that it has on its teenaged players. Among those are arrogant star running back James "Boobie" Miles (Luke), shy and insecure quarterback Mike Winchell (Black), and troubled tailback Don Billingsley (Hedlund), who's abused by his alcoholic dad (country singer McGraw, making a notable debut). Thornton gives a fine performance as Coach Gaines, a reserved man who knows his job is on the line. **117m/C; VHS, DVD, Blu-Ray, UMD, HD-DVD.** Billy Bob Thornton; Derek Luke; Jay Hernandez; Lucas Black; Garrett Hedlund; Connie Britton; Lee Jackson; Lee Thompson Young; Tim McGraw; Grover Coulson; Amber Heard; *D:* Peter Berg; *W:* Peter Berg; David Aaron Cohen; *C:* Tobias Schliessler; *M:* Brian Reitzell; David Torn.

Friday the 13th **2009 (R)** The guys who brought you the remake of "Texas Chainsaw Massacre" no doubt want to reignite another franchise with this slasher re-do about a group of teens who encounter hockey-masked Jason Voorhees (Mears) at the boarded-up Camp Crystal Lake. Sadly, Jason barely had time to decompose after the last of the tired franchise's bombs before being dug up and trotted out to slaughter his way to the bank. The gritty, low-rent camp that was key to the first few has been replaced with high-tech, high-gloss production and a menace that takes itself too seriously. Even the standard gratuitous sex, violence and gore is overdone—a hack job for sure. **99m/C; Blu-Ray.** Jared Padalecki; Danielle Panabaker; Amanda Righetti; Travis Van Winkle; Derek Mears; Aaron Yoo; Willa Ford; Nana Visitor; *D:* Marcus Nispel; *W:* Mark Swift; Damian Shannon; *C:* Daniel Pearl; *M:* Steve Jablonsky.

Friday the Thirteenth **1933** At one minute before midnight on Friday the 13th, a London bus crashes into a shop, killing two. Flashbacks then cover the previous 24 hours in the lives of the six people on the bus and who exactly died isn't revealed until the end. **89m/B; DVD.** *UK* Jessie Matthews; Sonnie Hale; Cyril Smith; Muriel Aked; Richard Hulton; Max Miller; *D:* Victor Saville; *W:* Emlyn Williams; *C:* Charles Van Enger.

Friday the 13th **1980 (R)** Notable as among the first in a very long series of slasher flicks, with effects by Tom Savini. A New Jersey camp reopens after it's been closed for 20 years after a history of "accidental" deaths. And the horror begins again. Six would-be counselors arrive to get the place ready. Each is progressively murdered: knifed, speared, and axed. Followed by numerous, equally gory sequels. **95m/C; VHS, DVD, Blu-Ray.** Betsy Palmer; Adrienne King; Harry Crosby; Laurie Bartram; Mark Nelson; Kevin Bacon; Jeannine Taylor; Robbi Morgan; Peter Brouwer; Walt Gorney; *D:* Sean S. Cunningham; *W:* Victor Miller; *C:* Barry Abrams; *M:* Harry Manfredini.

Friday the 13th, Part 2 WOOF! 1981 (R) New group of teen camp counselors are gruesomely executed by the still undead Jason. Equally as graphic as the first installment; followed by several more gorefests. **87m/C; VHS, DVD, Blu-Ray.** Amy Steel; John Furey; Adrienne King; Betsy Palmer; Kirsten Baker; Stu Charno; Warrington Gillette; Walt Gorney; Marta Kober; Bill Randolph; Jack Marks; *D:* Steve Miner; *W:* Ron Kurz; *C:* Peter Stein; *M:* Harry Manfredini.

Friday the 13th, Part 3 WOOF! 1982 (R) Yet another group of naive counselors at Camp Crystal Lake fall victim to the maniacal Jason. The 3-D effects actually helped lessen the gory effects, but this is still awful. Followed by more disgusting sequels. **96m/C; VHS, DVD, Blu-Ray.** Dana Kimmell; Paul Kratka; Richard Brooker; Catherine Parks; Dr. Jeffrey Rogers; Tracie Savage; Larry Zerner; *D:* Steve Miner; *W:* Martin Kitrosser; Carol Watson; *C:* Gerald Feil.

Friday the 13th, Part 4: The Final Chapter WOOF! 1984 (R) Jason escapes from the morgue to once again slaughter and annihilate teenagers at a lakeside cottage. Preceded by three earlier "Friday the 13th" films, equally as graphic. The title's also a lie since there's several more sequels to look forward to. **90m/C; VHS, DVD, Blu-Ray.** Erich Anderson; Judie Aronson; Kimberly Beck; Peter Barton; Tom Everett; Corey Feldman; Crispin Glover; Richard Brooker; *D:* Joseph Zito; *W:* Barney Cohen; *C:* Joao Fernandes.

Friday the 13th, Part 5: A New Beginning WOOF! 1985 (R) The hapless and anonymous residents of a secluded halfway house are the designated victims here. The sequels, and the sameness, never stop. See Part 6... **92m/C; VHS, DVD, Blu-Ray.** John Shepherd; Melanie Kinnaman; Shavar Ross; Richard Young; Juliette Cummins; Corey Feldman; Carol Lacatell; Vernon Washington; *D:* Danny Steinmann; *W:* Danny Steinmann; David M. Cohen; Martin Kitrosser; *C:* Stephen Posey.

Friday the 13th, Part 6: Jason Lives WOOF! 1986 (R) One of the few youths not butchered by Jason digs him up and discovers he's not (and never will be) dead. Carnage ensues. . .and the sequels continue. **87m/C; VHS, DVD, Blu-Ray.** Thom Mathews; Jennifer Cooke; David Kagen; Kerry Noonan; Renee Jones; Tom Fridley; C.J. Graham; Darcy Demoss; *D:* Tom McLoughlin; *W:* Tom McLoughlin; *C:* Jon Kranhouse; *M:* Harry Manfredini.

Friday the 13th, Part 7: The New Blood WOOF! 1988 (R) A young camper with telekinetic powers accidentally unchains Jason from his underwater lair with the now-familiar results. There's still another bloody sequel to go. **90m/C; VHS, DVD, Blu-Ray.** Lar Park-Lincoln; Kevin Blair Spirtas; Susan Blu; Terry Kiser; Kane Hodder; Elizabeth Kaitan; John Otrin; Heidi Kozak; *D:* John Carl Buechler; *W:* Daryl Haney; *C:* Paul Elliott.

Friday the 13th, Part 8: Jason Takes Manhattan **1989 (R)** Yet another sequel, with the hockey-masked walking slaughterhouse transported to New York. Most of the previous action in the movie takes place on a cruise ship. This one is less gruesome than others in the series. Followed by "Jason Goes to Hell: The Final Friday." **96m/C; VHS, DVD, Blu-Ray.** Jensen (Jennifer) Daggett; Scott Reeves; Peter Mark Richman; Barbara Bingham; Kane Hodder; Martin Cummins; Sharlene Martin; Vincent Craig Dupree; Kelly Hu; *D:* Rob Hedden; *W:* Rob Hedden; *C:* Bryan England.

Fried Green Tomatoes **1991 (PG-13)** Two stories about four women, love, friendship, Southern charm, and eccentricity are untidily held together by wonderful performances. Unhappy, middle-aged Evelyn (Bates), meets the talkative 83-year-old Ninny Threadgoode (Tandy). Ninny reminisces about her Depression-era life in the town of Whistle Stop, Alabama and the two women, Idgie (Masterson) and Ruth (Parker), who ran the local cafe. Back-and-forth narrative as it tracks multiple storylines is occasionally confusing, though strong character development holds interest. Surprising box office hit adapted by Fannie Flagg from her novel "Fried Green Tomatoes at the Whistle Stop Cafe." **130m/C; VHS, DVD, Blu-Ray.** Kathy Bates; Jessica Tandy; Mary Stuart Masterson; Mary-Louise Parker; Cicely Tyson; Chris O'Donnell; Stan Shaw; Gailard Sartain; Timothy Scott; Gary Basaraba; Lois Smith; Grace Zabriskie; *D:* Jon Avnet; *W:* Fannie Flagg; Carol Sobieski; *C:* Geoffrey Simpson; *M:* Thomas Newman.

Friend of the Family 1/2 *Elke* **1995** While backpacking across the U.S., Elke (O'Brien) is invited to stay in Malibu with the Stillman family—husband Jeff, wife Linda, and their 20-something children, Josh and Montana. Naturally, the sexy Elke becomes very involved with the family. **98m/C; VHS, DVD.** Shauna O'Brien; C.T. Miller; Lisa Boyle; Griffin (Griffen) Drew; *D:* Edward Holzman; *W:* Edward Holzman; April Moskowitz; *C:* Kim Haun; *M:* Richard Bronskill.

Friend of the Family 2 **1996 (R)** Disturbed young woman decides to get revenge on the man who used and abandoned her by becoming his family's nanny. Also available in an unrated version. Ray used the pseudonym Nicholas Medina. **90m/C; VHS, DVD.** Shauna O'Brien; Paul Michael Robinson; Jenna Bodnar; Jeff Rector; *D:* Fred Olen Ray; *W:* Henry Krinkle; *C:* Gary Graver.

Friend Request **2016 (R)** A cyber-horror film with more unintentional laughs than successful scares. In a fit of charity, über-popular Laura (Debnam-Carey) accepts the friend request of lonely Marina (Ahler). But when Laura becomes creeped out by Marina's, well, creepiness, she unfriends her, and bad things begin to happen: her real life friends die and (horror!) her online friend-count plummets. It's a nifty lesson for the kids -- don't be nice to people in lower social strata. **92m/C; DVD, Blu-Ray.** Alycia Debnam-Carey; William Moseley; Connor Paolo; Brit Morgan; Brooke Markham; *D:* Simon Verhoeven; *W:* Simon Verhoeven; Matthew Ballen; Philip Koch; *C:* Joe Heim; *M:* Gary Go; Martin Todsharow.

Friendly Fire **1979** Based on a true story of an American family in 1970 whose soldier son is killed by "friendly fire" in Vietnam, and their efforts to uncover the circumstances of the tragedy. Touching and powerful, with an excellent dramatic performance by Burnett. **146m/C; DVD, Streaming.** Carol Burnett; Ned Beatty; Sam Waterston; Timothy Hutton; *D:* David Greene; *W:* Fay Kanin; *C:* Harry J. May; *M:* Leonard Rosenman. **TV**

Friendly Persuasion *Except for Me and Thee* **1956** Earnest, solidly acted tale about a peaceful Quaker family struggling to remain true to its ideals in spite of the Civil War which touches their farm life in southern Indiana. Cooper and McGuire are excellent as the parents with Perkins fine as the son worried he's using his religion to hide his cowardice. Based on a novel by Jessamyn West. **140m/C; VHS, DVD.** Gary Cooper; Dorothy McGuire; Anthony Perkins; Marjorie Main; Charles Halton; *D:* William Wyler; *W:* Michael Wilson; *C:* Ellsworth Fredericks; *M:* Dimitri Tiomkin. Cannes '57: Film.

Friends **1971 (R)** Ho-hum drama about an orphaned French girl and an unloved English boy who meet, become friends, and decide to run away together, setting up house in a deserted beach cottage. They even have a baby before they're discovered. Provides no insight into the teenagers dilemmas. Followed by "Paul and Michelle." **101m/C; VHS, Streaming.** *GB* Sean Bury; Anicee Alvina; Pascale Roberts; Sady Rebbot; Ronald Lewis; *D:* Lewis Gilbert; *M:* Sir Elton John.

Friends & Crocodiles **2005** Flashy real estate mogul Paul Reynolds (Lewis) is living a hedonistic lifestyle in 1980s London. He hires practical Lizzie Thomas (May) as his secretary but she's disturbed by his reckless, sometimes criminal, behavior and soon quits. Over a 20-year period, Paul's fortunes unravel while life is kinder to Lizzie, and the two maintain a sometimes strained friendship. **105m/C; DVD.** *GB* Damian Lewis; Jodhi May; Robert Lindsay; Patrick Malahide; Eddie Marsan; Allan Corduner; Chris Larkin; *D:* Stephen Poliakoff; *W:* Stephen Poliakoff; *C:* Barry Ackroyd; *M:* Adrian Johnston. **TV**

Friends and Family 1/2 **2001** Very broad comedy tries to shoehorn in a few too many subplots but it's slickly-done and harmless. Danny (Gartin) and Stephen (Lauren) are enforcers for New York mobster Victor Patrizzi (Lo Bianco), who has no problem with the fact that they are gay. Nor do Stephen's parents, who decide to make a surprise visit to the city to celebrate Mr. Torcelli's (Pellegrino) birthday. But what Stephen's parents don't know is what the two actually do for a living—the guys have been passing themselves off as caterers. With Patrizzi's assistance, they arrange a celebration that unexpectedly turns into an inept hostage situation. **87m/C; VHS, DVD.** Greg Lauren; Christopher Gartin; Tony LoBianco; Rebecca Creskoff; Brian Lane Green; Meshach Taylor; Edward Hibbert; Beth Fowler; Frank Pellegrino; Tovah Feldshuh; Anna Maria Alberghetti; Frank Minucci; Patrick Collins; *D:* Kristen Coury; *W:* Joseph Triebwasser; *C:* John Leuba; *M:* Kurt Hoffman.

Friends & Lovers 1/2 **1999** Nonsensical and mediocre would-be romantic comedy about wealthy widower, Richard (Rasche), who invites his estranged son, Ian (Newbern), and his son's L.A. friends to spend Christmas with him at his Park City chalet. Everyone has some kind of sexual agenda except for Richard, who just wants to come to terms with Ian. **104m/C; VHS, DVD, On Demand.** David Rasche; George Newbern; Stephen Baldwin; Danny Nucci; Robert Downey, Jr.; Leon; Alison Eastwood; Suzanne Cryer; Neill Barry; Claudia Schiffer; *D:* George Haas; *W:* George Haas; *C:* Carlos Montaner; *M:* Emilio Kauderer.

Friends Forever **1986** Conformity, sexuality, and friendship are explored in this coming-of-age drama. Kristian is a shy, conformist 16-year-old, starting off at a new school. He finds himself drawn to two different young men who equally dominate his class. Henrik's androgynous sexual charm is equaled by his independence while the moody Patrick is the leader of a band of troublemakers. Kristian gains in self-confidence by their friendship but is tested when he learns Patrick is gay. **95m/C; VHS, DVD.** *DK* Claus Bender Mortensen; Thomas Elholm; Christine Skou; ***D:*** Stefan Christian Henszelman; ***C:*** Marcel Berga; ***M:*** Kim Sagild.

Friends With Benefits 🦴🦴 1/2 **2011 (R)** New York headhunter Jamie (Kunis) gets L.A.-based art director Dylan (Timberlake) to move to the Big Apple. Since they're immediately attracted to one another, but commitment-phobic, they decide to keep things strictly physical while becoming friends. Naturally their emotions get in the way. The leads are likeable and actually have chemistry and this rom com doesn't go squish, thanks to a lot of brisk banter. If the plot sounds familiar it's because it's the same premise as the less-appealing 2011 release "No Strings Attached." **109m/C; DVD, Blu-Ray.** Mila Kunis; Justin Timberlake; Patricia Clarkson; Jenna Elfman; Bryan Greenberg; Richard Jenkins; Woody Harrelson; Rashida Jones; Nolan Gould; Andy Samberg; ***D:*** Will Gluck; ***W:*** Will Gluck; Keith Merryman; David A. Newman; ***C:*** Michael Grady.

Friends with Kids 🦴🦴 1/2 **2012 (R)** Platonic best friends Jason (Scott) and Julie (Westfeldt) notice that their married friends have become unrecognizable after having babies. Formerly hot-blooded Ben (Hamm) and Missy (Wiig) constantly carp at each other, and cosmopolitan Alex (O'Dowd) and Leslie (Rudolph) have exiled themselves to the sticks. They decide that the best course of action is to have a baby with each other and split custody so that they can maintain their romantic freedom. After dipping their toes in a chilly dating pool, the two begin to question their plan. **100m/C; DVD, Blu-Ray.** Jennifer Westfeldt; Adam Scott; Jon Hamm; Kristen Wiig; Maya Rudolph; Chris O'Dowd; Megan Fox; Edward Burns; ***D:*** Jennifer Westfeldt; ***W:*** Jennifer Westfeldt; ***C:*** William Rexer; ***M:*** Marcelo Zarvos.

Friends with Money 🦴🦴 1/2 **2006 (R)** L.A.-set story about the friendship between three wealthy, married, middle-aged women and their slightly younger, unmarried, and decidedly not-rich pal. That's Olivia (Aniston), who has quit her teaching job in a fit of ennui to become a maid. Her friend Franny (Cusack) is a generous stay-at-home mom with a great marriage to Matt (Germann), while Jane (McDormand) is a continuously furious fashion designer whose metrosexual Brit hubby Aaron (McBurney) is suspected of being gay. Screenwriting partners Christine (Keener) and David (Isaacs) discover they don't even like each other as their marriage fractures. The women talk and support one another (and the actresses are great fleshing out some thin characters) but not much happens. **88m/C; DVD.** Jennifer Aniston; Joan Cusack; Catherine Keener; Frances McDormand; Jason Isaacs; Scott Caan; Simon McBurney; Greg Germann; Ty Burrell; Bob Stephenson; ***D:*** Nicole Holofcener; ***W:*** Nicole Holofcener; ***C:*** Terry Stacey; ***M:*** Craig Richey; Rickie Lee Jones. Ind. Spirit '07: Support. Actress (McDormand).

Friendship, Secrets and Lies 🦴🦴 **1979** TV movie features numerous familiar actresses. The skeleton of a newborn baby is discovered when an old college building is torn down. Forensics determines the bones are 20-years-old and the building then housed a sorority. Now, there are seven possible moms among the former sorority sisters to be investigated. Adapted from the Babs H. Deal novel "The Walls Came Tumbling Down." **97m/C; DVD.** Loretta Swit; Cathryn Damon; Shelley Fabares; Sondra Locke; Tina Louise; Paula Prentiss; Stella Stevens; ***D:*** Marlene Laird; Ann Zane Shanks; ***W:*** Joanna Crawford; ***C:*** Michael D. Margulies; ***M:*** Angela Morley. **TV**

Fright 🦴 *Spell of the Hypnotist* **1956** A woman—convinced that she died in 1889 as part of a suicide pact with Prince Rudolph of Austria—seeks help from a psychiatrist who promptly falls in love with her (didn't Freud say it was supposed to be the other way around?). **68m/B; VHS, DVD.** Nancy Malone; Eric Fleming; Frank Marth; Humphrey Davis; Ned Glass; Norman Burton; ***D:*** W. Lee Wilder.

Fright 🦴🦴 *Night Legs* **1971** A baby-sitter is menaced by a mental hospital escapee. He turns out to be the father of the boy she is watching. Tense but violent thriller. **87m/C; VHS, DVD, Blu-Ray.** *GB* Susan George; Honor Blackman; Ian Bannen; John Gregson; George Cole; Dennis Waterman; Tara Collinson; Maurice Kaufmann; Michael Brennan; Roger Lloyd-Pack; ***D:*** Peter Collinson; ***W:*** Tudor Gates; ***C:*** Ian Wilson; ***M:*** Harry Robinson.

Fright Flick 🦴🦴 **2010** Gory genre spoof of showbiz horror. A movie crew is stuck in a small town filming the second sequel to a lousy, low-budget horror pic. Then they start getting killed off in various cliched ways featured in the script and the killings are videotaped. **93m/C; DVD, Blu-Ray.** Chad Allen; Richard Curtin; Todd Jenkins; Adam Kitchen; Tyler Brockington; Valerie Nelson; Daphne Khoury; Tom Zembrod; Natali Jones; ***D:*** Israel Luna; ***W:*** Israel Luna; ***C:*** Christopher Simpson. **VIDEO**

Fright Night 🦴🦴 1/2 **1985 (R)** It's Dracula-versus-the-teens time when Charley suspects that his new neighbor descends from Count Vlad's line. He calls in the host of "Fright Night," the local, late-night, horror-flick series, to help de-ghoul the neighborhood. But they have a problem when the vampire discovers their plans (and nobody believes them anyway). Sarandon is properly seductive as the bloodsucker. **106m/C; VHS, DVD, Blu-Ray.** William Ragsdale; Chris Sarandon; Amanda Bearse; Roddy McDowall; Stephen Geoffreys; Jonathan Stark; Dorothy Fielding; Art Evans; ***D:*** Tom Holland; ***W:*** Tom Holland; ***C:*** Jan Kiesser; ***M:*** Brad Fiedel.

Fright Night 🦴🦴 1/2 **2011 (R)** A rare horror comedy that is actually both scary and funny, director Gillespie's loyal remake of the 1985 cult hit is anchored ably by Farrell as the vampire, innocently known as Jerry, new neighbor to the unlucky Charlie Brewster (Yelchin). Can the sometimes-gawky kid save his girlfriend (Poots) and mother (Collette) from the suave bloodsucker? Rowdy fun at times, forgoing the mopey brooding that has dominated the vampire genre in recent years, and even pokes fun at Stephanie Meyer's "Twilight" series. Perhaps the least necessary use of 3D in the history of the trend. **106m/C; Blu-Ray.** Anton Yelchin; Colin Farrell; Toni Collette; Christopher Mintz-Plasse; Imogen Poots; David Tennant; Dave Franco; ***D:*** Craig Gillespie; ***W:*** Marti Noxon; ***C:*** Javier Aguirresarobe; ***M:*** Ramin Djawadi.

Fright Night 2 🦴🦴 **1988 (R)** The sequel to the 1985 release "Fright Night," in which the harassed guy from the original film learns slowly that the vampire's sister and her entourage have come to roost around his college. Not quite as good as the original but the special effects are worth a look. **108m/C; VHS, DVD.** Roddy McDowall; William Ragsdale; Traci Lind; Julie Carmen; Jon(athan) Gries; Russ Clark; Brian Thompson; ***D:*** Tommy Lee Wallace; ***W:*** Tommy Lee Wallace; Tim Metcalfe; Miguel Tejada-Flores; ***C:*** Mark Irwin; ***M:*** Brad Fiedel.

Fright Night 2: New Blood 🦴 1/2 **2013 (R)** Not a sequel to the 2011 remake but a somewhat decent direct-to-video timewaster that uses some of the same characters. High school students are on a study exchange progam in Romania. Charley Brewster discovers hot professor Gerri Dandridge is actually a cold-blooded vampire who's after his virginal ex-girlfriend, Amy. He finally convinces his pal, 'Evil' Ed, he's not crazy and, fortunately, vampire-hunting reality host Peter Vincent is in Romania filming his TV show and can help out. **100m/C; DVD, Blu-Ray.** Jaime Murray; Will Payne; Chris Waller; Sacha Parkinson; Sean Power; ***D:*** Eduardo Rodriguez; ***W:*** Matt Venne; ***C:*** Yaron Levy; ***M:*** Luis Ascanio. **VIDEO**

The Frightened City 🦴🦴 1/2 **1961** Waldo Zhernikov (Lom) decides to unite all six of London's crime syndicates into one conglomerate that would control the city. But when he gets power-mad, rival gangster Harry Foulcher (Marks) breaks away and forms his own organization. Naturally, there's a war between the factions. Paddy Damion (Connery in an early role), one of Waldo's gunsels, is sent to get rid of Foulcher. **91m/B; VHS, DVD.** *GB* Herbert Lom; John Gregson; Sean Connery; Alfred Marks; Yvonne Romain; Kenneth Griffith; Olive McFarland; Frederick Piper; John Stone; David Davies; Tom Bowman; Robert Cawdron; Norrie Paramor; ***D:*** John Lemont; ***W:*** Leigh Vance; ***C:*** Desmond Dickinson; ***M:*** Norrie Paramor.

The Frightened Man 🦴🦴 **1952** Julius Roselli (Walsh) is kicked out of Oxford after a drunken brawl, which disappoints his junk dealer father (Victor). Soon Julius gets involved with a gang of jewel thieves who use his father as their fence. Neither father nor son knows of the other's involvement, which figures in when the old man tips off the police about an upcoming robbery after being cut out of the deal. **69m/B; DVD.** *GB* Dermot Walsh; Charles Victor; Barbara Murray; John Blythe; Michael Ward; Thora Hird; John Horsley; ***D:*** John Gilling; ***W:*** John Gilling; ***C:*** Monty Berman; ***M:*** John Lanchbery.

The Frightened Woman 🦴🦴 **1971** Wealthy Sayer (Leroy) likes to get his sexual kicks by playing master and slave in his villa outside Rome. When his usual hired call girl isn't available, he decides to lure a lovely journalist (Lassander) into his domination games. Dubbed into English. **90m/C; VHS, DVD.** *IT* Phillippe LeRoy; Dagmar Lassander; ***D:*** Piero Schivazappa; ***W:*** Piero Schivazappa; ***M:*** Stelvio Cipriani.

The Frighteners 🦴🦴 1/2 **1996 (R)** Con man Frank Bannister (Fox) has a unique scam—he works with a group of ghosts who haunt a home until Frank comes along to drive them out, for the right price. But the small town of Fairwater is plagued by a serial killer's evil spirit and Frank and his spiritual cronies face the challenge of getting rid of the ghost before the police decide to get rid of Frank. Interesting horror-comedy takes a lot of twists and turns to get where its going, but the payoff in gore and humor is worth it for fans of the genre. New Zealand helmer Jackson makes his American directorial debut. **106m/C; VHS, DVD, Blu-Ray, HD-DVD.** Michael J. Fox; Trini Alvarado; Peter Dobson; Dee Wallace; John Astin; Jeffrey Combs; Troy Evans; Chi McBride; Jake Busey; R. Lee Ermey; Jim Fyfe; ***D:*** Peter Jackson; ***W:*** Peter Jackson; Fran Walsh; ***C:*** Alun Bollinger; John Blick; ***M:*** Danny Elfman.

Frightmare 🦴🦴 1/2 *Frightmare 2* **1974 (R)** A seemingly quiet British couple do indulge in one strange habit—they're cannibals. Released on video as "Frightmare 2" to avoid confusion with the 1981 film. **86m/C; VHS, DVD, Blu-Ray.** *GB* Deborah Fairfax; Kim Butcher; Rupert Davies; Sheila Keith; ***D:*** Pete Walker; ***W:*** David McGillivray; ***C:*** Peter Jessop; ***M:*** Stanley Myers.

Frightmare 🦴 **1981 (R)** Great horror star dies, but he refuses to give up his need for adoration and revenge. **84m/C; VHS, DVD, Blu-Ray.** Ferdinand "Ferdy" Mayne; Luca Bercovici; Nita Talbot; Peter Kastner; ***D:*** Norman Thaddeus Vane.

Frisco Jenny 🦴🦴 **1932** Pregnant Jenny (Chatterton) loses both her father and lover during the 1906 San Francisco earthquake. Without a home, she eventually gives up her illegitimate son to a wealthy couple and becomes a successful bordello madam on the Barbary Coast. Son Dan (Cook) grows up to be a crusading district attorney, but a criminal cohort (Calhern) of Jenny's wants him dead. Her actions save Dan but lead to her own downfall. **70m/B; DVD.** Ruth Chatterton; Donald Cook; Louis Calhern; James Murray; Hallam Cooley; Harold Huber; Helen Jerome Eddy; Berton Churchill; ***D:*** William A. Wellman; ***W:*** Wilson Mizner; Robert Lord; ***C:*** Sidney Hickox.

Frisco Kid 🦴🦴 **1935** Bat Morgan (Cagney) goes from a nearly-shanghaied sailor to a Barbary Coast power broker in 1850s San Francisco. He opens a gambling den/saloon and almost gets lynched when some law-abiding citizens, fed up with the area's lawlessness, turn vigilante. Good thing Bat's got crusading newspaper owner Jean Barrat (Lindsay) to plead his case. **77m/B; DVD.** James Cagney; Margaret Lindsay; Ricardo Cortez; Lili Damita; Donald Woods; Barton MacLane; George E. Stone; Joe Sawyer; Fred Kohler, Sr.; ***D:*** Lloyd Bacon; ***W:*** Seton I. Miller; Warren Duff; ***C:*** Sol Polito.

The Frisco Kid 🦴🦴 *No Knife* **1979 (R)** An innocent orthodox rabbi (Wilder) from Poland is sent to the wilds of San Francisco during the 1850s gold rush to lead a new congregation. He lands in Philadelphia, joins a wagon train and is promptly robbed and abandoned. He eventually meets up with a not-too-bright robber (Ford) who finds himself unexpectedly befriending the man and undergoing numerous tribulations in order to get them both safely to their destination. This isn't a laugh riot and some scenes fall distinctly flat but Wilder is sweetness personified and lends the movie its charm. **119m/C; VHS, DVD.** Gene Wilder; Harrison Ford; Ramon Bieri; Val Bisoglio; George DiCenzo; Penny Peyser; William (Bill) Smith; ***D:*** Robert Aldrich; ***W:*** Michael Elias; ***C:*** Robert B. Hauser.

Frisk 🦴🦴 **1995** Disturbing depictions of sex/murder fantasies come courtesy of letters written by Dennis (Gunther), a part of the L.A. S&M scene, to his former boyfriend, Julian (Laplante). Just exactly how far Dennis has gone with some of his like-minded sexual partners is the question. Has he become the killer he claims to be? Adapted from Dennis Cooper's 1991 novel. **87m/C; VHS, DVD.** Michael Gunther; Jaie Laplante; Craig Chester; Parker Posey; James Lyons; Alexis Arquette; Raoul O'Connell; Michael Stock; ***D:*** Todd Verow; ***W:*** Todd Verow; Jim Dwyer; George LaVoo; ***C:*** Greg Watkins.

Fritz the Cat 🦴🦴🦴 **1972** Ralph Bakshi's animated tale for adults about a cat's adventures as he gets into group sex, college radicalism, and other hazards of life in the '60s. Loosely based on the underground comics character by Robert Crumb. Originally X-rated. **77m/C; VHS, DVD.** ***V:*** Skip Hinnant; Rosetta LeNoire; John McCurry; ***D:*** Ralph Bakshi; ***W:*** Ralph Bakshi; ***C:*** Ted C. Bemiller; Gene Borghi; ***M:*** Ed Bogas; Ray Shanklin.

Frogs 🦴🦴 1/2 **1972 (PG)** An environmental photographer working on a small island in Florida interrupts the birthday celebration of a patriarch. He and the folks at the party soon realize that various amphibians animals in the surrounding area are going berserk and attacking humans. One of the first environmentally motivated animal-vengeance films, and one of the best to come out of the '70s. **91m/C; VHS, DVD, Blu-Ray.** Ray Milland; Sam Elliott; Joan Van Ark; Adam Roarke; Judy Pace; Lynn Borden; Mae Mercer; David Gilliam; George Skaff; Holly Irving; ***D:*** George McCowan; ***W:*** Robert Blees; Robert Hutchison; ***C:*** Mario Tosi; ***M:*** Les Baxter.

Frogs for Snakes 🦴🦴 **1998 (R)** Self-conscious black comedy about New York loan shark Al Santana (Coltrane) who also spends his time as a wanna-be East Village theatrical impressario. And how everybody who works for Al as a collector is even more desperate to be an actor, including his struggling ex-wife Eva (Hershey). And how all the characters suddenly break into monologues from their favorite movies. And how none of this makes much sense and the actors have really done better work elsewhere. **98m/C; VHS, DVD.** Barbara Hershey; Robbie Coltrane; Harry Hamlin; Ian Hart; John Leguizamo; Lisa Marie; Debi Mazar; David Deblinger; Ron Perlman; Clarence Williams, III; Justin Theroux; Nick (Nicholas) Chinlund; Mike Starr; Taylor Mead; ***D:*** Amos Poe; ***W:*** Amos Poe; ***C:*** Enrique Chediak.

Frolics on Ice 🦴🦴 *Everything's on Ice* **1939** Pleasant musical-comedy about a family man saving to buy the barber shop at which he works. Irene Dare is featured in several ice skating production numbers. **65m/B; VHS, DVD.** Roscoe Karns; Lynne Roberts; Irene Dare; Edgar Kennedy; Eric Linden; George Meeker; Bobby Watson; Mary Currier; ***D:*** Erle C. Kenton; ***W:*** Sherman Lowe; Adrian Landis; ***C:*** Russell Metty.

From a Far Country: Pope John Paul II 🦴🦴 **1981** TV biography of Polish Pope John Paul II begins in 1926 as Karol Wojtila celebrates Christmas with his father and continues through the important highlights of his life. **120m/C; VHS, DVD.** *PL GB* Sam Neill; Christopher Cazenove; Warren Clarke; Kathleen Byron; Maurice Denham; Lisa Harrow; ***Nar:*** Michael Jayston; ***D:*** Krzysztof Zanussi; ***W:*** Krzysztof Zanussi; ***C:*** Slawomir Idziak; ***M:*** Wojciech Kilar. **TV**

From Above 🦴 1/2 *Chasing Shakespeare* **2013 (PG)** Edward Ward recalls his life with dying wife Venus whom he met when she tried out for a Shakespeare play in high school. She is a Native American--a member of the Lightning Clan--and he is African-American. Their love is electric in more ways than one and they must overcome cultural differences to make a life together. Sincere, but the behind-the-camera inexperience shows. **116m/C; DVD.** Danny Glover; Tantoo Cardinal; Chelsea Ricketts; Mike Wade; Graham Greene; Clarence Gilyard, Jr.; *D:* Norry Niven; *W:* James Bird; *C:* Norry Niven; *M:* Eric Kaye. **VIDEO**

From Beginning to End ☙☙ *Do Comeco ao Fim* **2009** Francisco and his five-years-younger half-brother Thomas are raised in comfort in Rio by their doting parents. The boys' closeness raises some concerns, eventually with good reason since the young men become lovers. Swimming champ Thomas is chosen to train for the Olympics and it means moving to Russia with the Brazilian team and a separation neither man knows if he can bear. Portuguese with subtitles. **96m/C; DVD.** *BR* Joao Gabriel Vasconcellos; Rafael Cardoso; Lucas Cotrin; Gabriel Kaufmann; Julia Lemmertz; Jean Pierre Noher; Fabio Assuncao; *D:* Aluisio Abranches; *W:* Aluisio Abranches; *C:* Ueli Steiger; *M:* Andre Abujamra.

From Beyond ☙☙☙ **1986 (R)** A gruesome, tongue-in-cheek adaptation of the ghoulish H.P. Lovecraft story. Scientists discover another dimension through experiments with the pineal gland. From the makers of "Re-Animator," and just as funny. **90m/C; DVD, Blu-Ray.** Jeffrey Combs; Barbara Crampton; Ted (Theodore) Sorel; Ken Foree; Carolyn Purdy-Gordon; Bunny Summers; Bruce McGuire; *D:* Stuart Gordon; *W:* Dennis Paoli; Brian Yuzna; *C:* Mac Ahlberg; *M:* Richard Band.

From Beyond the Grave ☙☙ *Creatures* **1973 (PG)** This horror compendium revolves around a mysterious antique shop whose customers experience various supernatural phenomena, especially when they try to cheat the shop's equally mysterious owner. **98m/C; VHS, DVD, Blu-Ray.** *GB* Peter Cushing; David Warner; Ian Bannen; Donald Pleasence; Margaret Leighton; Lesley-Anne Down; Diana Dors; Ian Ogilvy; *D:* Kevin Connor.

From Dusk Till Dawn ☙☙ ½ **1995 (R)** Escaped cons Seth and Richie Gecko (Clooney and Tarantino) pick up an ex-preacher (Keitel) and his two kids (Lewis and Liu) as hostages en route to their Mexican rendezvous spot, a raunchy biker joint run (unbenownst to them) by vampires. Feels like two movies in one, as Rodriguez's and Tarantino's styles don't necessarily mesh as much as they coexist. The first half features Tarantino's gift for snappy dialogue and somewhat sympathetic scumbags while the barroom finale shows off Rodriguez's mastery of the go-for-broke action set piece. Clooney proves the jump from TV to movies can be made successfully. Penned by Tarantino in 1990 during his video store days, he used the fee to get "Reservoir Dogs" off the ground. **108m/C; VHS, DVD, Blu-Ray, UMD.** George Clooney; Quentin Tarantino; Harvey Keitel; Juliette Lewis; Ernest Liu; Fred Williamson; Richard "Cheech" Marin; Salma Hayek; Michael Parks; Tom Savini; Kelly Preston; John Saxon; Danny Trejo; Tia Texada; *D:* Robert Rodriguez; *W:* Quentin Tarantino; *C:* Guillermo Navarro; *M:* Graeme Revell. MTV Movie Awards '96: Breakthrough Perf. (Clooney).

From Dusk Till Dawn 2: Texas Blood Money ☙☙ *Texas, Blood Money* **1998 (R)** Buck (Patrick) and his partner-in-crime Luther (Whitaker) decide to get a few bad men together and knock over a bank in Mexico. However, the group unwittingly come into contact with the vampire denizens of the Titty Twister bar and soon join the ranks of the undead. Except for Buck, who's somehow managed to avoid having the bite put on him—for now. Direct-to-video sequel is set two weeks after the first film's carnage. **88m/C; VHS, DVD, Blu-Ray.** Robert Patrick; Bo Hopkins; Muse Watson; Duane Whitaker; Raymond Cruz; Tiffani(-Amber) Thiessen; Brett Harrelson; Danny Trejo; Bruce Campbell; *D:* Scott Spiegel; *W:* Duane Whitaker; Scott Spiegel; *C:* Philip Lee; *M:* Joseph Williams. **VIDEO**

From Dusk Till Dawn 3: The Hangman's Daughter ☙☙ **1999 (R)** This is actually a prequel to the "From Dusk Till Dawn" mayhem. In 1914, a group of refugees wind up in an isolated Mexican saloon, "La Tetilla del Diablo," that's the home of Santanico Pandemonium, the Queen of the Vampires (Braga). Oh, and the hangman's daughter is lovely Esmeralda (Celi), who doesn't know that Santanico is her mom. **94m/C; VHS, DVD, Blu-Ray.** Michael Parks; Sonia Braga; Marco Leonardi; Rebecca Gayheart; Temuera Morrison; Lenny Y. Loftin; Danny Trejo; Ara Celi; *D:* P.J. Pesce. **VIDEO**

From Hell ☙☙☙ **2001 (R)** The Hughes brothers take on the legend of Jack the Ripper in this grisly period thriller. Inspector Abberline (Depp) is the fictional opium-addled detective charged with finding the notorious killer of London's ladies of the night in 1888. With the help of his police sidekick Godley (Coltrane) and the cockney hooker-with-a-heart-of-gold Mary (Graham), Abberline pries into the medical community, the royal family and other less respectable areas in his search for the Ripper. Beautiful visuals and taut suspense raise this effort a notch above other adaptions of the material. Based on a graphic novel (a.k.a. fancy-schmancy comic book) by Alan Moore and Eddie Campbell. **121m/C; VHS, DVD, Blu-Ray.** Johnny Depp; Heather Graham; Ian Holm; Robbie Coltrane; Ian Richardson; Jason Flemyng; Katrin Cartlidge; Terence Harvey; Susan Lynch; Lesley Sharp; Annabelle Apsion; *D:* Albert Hughes; Allen Hughes; *W:* Terry Hayes; Rafael Yglesias; *C:* Peter Deming; *M:* Trevor Jones.

From Hell It Came WOOF! **1957** And to hell it should return for complete mind-numbing stupidity. Scientists studying residue left from an atomic bomb blast on a South Sea island are befriended by chief's son Kimo who gets killed by witch doctor Tano for breaking tribal law. Kimo curses said doctor and comes back as a tree stump spirit/monster (because a tree grew on the grave) and lumbers around getting revenge. **71m/B; DVD, Blu-Ray.** Gregg (Hunter) Palmer.

From Hell to Victory ☙☙ **1979 (PG)** Group of friends of different nationalities vow to meet each year in Paris on the same date but WWII interrupts their lives and friendships. Director Lenzi used the alias Hank Milestone. Good battle scenes but nothing special. **100m/C; VHS, DVD.** *SP FR* George Peppard; George Hamilton; Horst Buchholz; Jean-Pierre Cassel; Capucine; Sam Wanamaker; Anny (Annie Legras) Duperey; Ray Lovelock; *D:* Umberto Lenzi.

From Here to Eternity ☙☙☙☙ **1953** Complex, hard-hitting look at the on and off-duty life of soldiers at the Army base in Honolulu in the days before the Pearl Harbor attack. There's sensitive Pvt. Prewitt (Clift), his always in trouble best friend Maggio (Sinatra), and their good-guy top sergeant (Lancaster) who just happens to be having a torrid affair with the commander's wife (Kerr). Prewitt, meanwhile, is introduced to a club "hostess" (Reed) who is a lot more vulnerable than she's willing to admit. A movie filled with great performances. Still has the best waves-on-the-beach love scene in filmdom. Based on the novel by James Jones, which was toned down by the censors. **118m/B; VHS, DVD.** Burt Lancaster; Montgomery Clift; Frank Sinatra; Deborah Kerr; Donna Reed; Ernest Borgnine; Philip Ober; Jack Warden; Mickey Shaughnessy; George Reeves; Claude Akins; Harry Bellaver; John Dennis; Tim Ryan; John Bryant; John Cason; Doug(las) Henderson; Robert Karnes; Robert J. Wilke; Carleton Young; Merle Travis; Arthur Keegan; Barbara Morrison; Tyler McVey; *D:* Fred Zinnemann; *W:* Daniel Taradash; *C:* Burnett Guffey; *M:* George Duning. Oscars '53: B&W Cinematog., Director (Zinnemann), Film, Film Editing, Screenplay, Sound, Support. Actor (Sinatra), Support. Actress (Reed); AFI '98: Top 100; Directors Guild '53: Director (Zinnemann); Golden Globes '54: Support. Actor (Sinatra); Natl. Film Reg. '02; N.Y. Film Critics '53: Actor (Lancaster), Director (Zinnemann), Film.

From Hollywood to Deadwood ☙☙ **1989 (R)** A beautiful starlet is kidnapped and the private eye searching for her discovers blackmail and danger. **90m/C; VHS, Streaming.** Scott Paulin; Jim Haynie; Barbara Schock; *D:* Rex Pickett; *W:* Rex Pickett; *C:* Peter Deming.

From Justin to Kelly WOOF! **2003 (PG)** Justin Guarini and Kelly Clarkson hurry to cash in on their "American Idol" success with another remake of "Where the Boys Are." Justin and Kelly chase romance between ludicrous dance numbers. In the pantheon of bad pop star flicks, this ranks well south of Elvis's worst fare, and even manages to sneak under the Unholy Trinity of Vanilla Ice-Mariah-Britny. **90m/C; VHS, DVD.** Justin Guarini; Kelly Clarkson; Katherine Bailess; Anika Noni Rose; Greg Siff; Brian Dietzen; *D:* Robert Iscove; *W:* Kim Fuller; *C:* Francis Kenny; *M:* Michael Wandmacher.

From Mao to Mozart: Isaac Stern in China ☙☙☙ **1980** An outstanding and enjoyable film record of the great violinist's ground-breaking visit to Communist China. The scenes in which Stern instructs young Chinese musicians are poignant and moving. One of the world's finest musicians confirms that his is a universal language. Acclaimed. **84m/C; VHS, DVD.** Isaac Stern; David Golub; *Nar:* Tan Shuzhen; *D:* Murray Lerner. Oscars '80: Feature Doc.

From Mexico With Love ☙☙ ½ **2009 (PG-13)** Effective and affecting boxing drama. Illegal migrant worker Hector (Becker) makes more money as a successful backroom boxer. This gets him into trouble with racist Big Al (Lang), who controls the town and whose son Robert (Nesic) is supposed to be the local great white hope. Big Al tries to get rid of the competition, which eventually leads to a grudge match. **98m/C; DVD.** Kuno Becker; Bruce McGill; Alex Nesic; Stephen Lang; Danay Garcia; Steven Bauer; *D:* Jimmy Nickerson; Nicholas Siapkaris; *W:* Glen Hartford; *C:* Rick Lamb; *M:* John (Gianni) Frizzell. **VIDEO**

From Noon Till Three ☙☙ ½ **1976 (PG)** A change of pace role for Bronson as a two-bit gunfighter in a spoof of western legends. Bronson has a brief romance with Ireland who, believing him dead, fictionalizes their relationship in a series of books and builds the mediocre Dorsey into a western hero. When he turns up alive no one, including Ireland, believes that he is the real Dorsey and he's gradually driven crazy. Good script, weak direction but Bronson is likeable. **99m/C; VHS, Blu-Ray, Streaming.** Charles Bronson; Jill Ireland; Douglas Fowley; Stan Haze; Damon Douglas; *D:* Frank D. Gilroy; *W:* Frank D. Gilroy; *C:* Lucien Ballard; *M:* Elmer Bernstein.

From Other Worlds ☙ ½ **2004** Dull sci-fi comedy. Depressed Brooklyn housewife Joanne believes she has been abducted by aliens and decides to meet with a group of fellow abductees, who include Abraham. They bond and begin to look for clues, meeting an alien who gives them advice on saving Earth from destruction. **88m/C; DVD.** Cara Buono; Isaach de Bankole; David Lansbury; Joel de la Fuente; Robert Peters; Melissa Leo; *D:* Barry Strugatz; *W:* Barry Strugatz; *C:* Morris Flam; *M:* Pierre Foldes.

From Paris With Love ☙☙ **2010 (R)** James (Rhys Meyers) is a desk jockey at the American embassy in Paris who longs to be a CIA field agent. He gets his chance when he is called to spring loose-cannon operative Charlie (Travolta) from French customs agents. The two then team up to foil plots by Chinese drug smugglers and Pakistani bombers. The confused plot is merely an excuse for Travolta to chew up the scenery and spray bullets and catchphrases at various stuntmen. The action is chaotic and the humor isn't very funny in this lame attempt at a buddy flick/thriller. Acceptable for those who just want to see gunplay and explosions, but those who prefer a sensible plot may want to send this one packing. **92m/C; Blu-Ray, On Demand.** John Travolta; Jonathan Rhys Meyers; Richard Durden; Amber Rose Revah; Kasia Smutniak; Yin Bing; *D:* Pierre Morel; *W:* Adi Hasak; *C:* Michel Abramowicz; *M:* David Buckley.

From Prada to Nada ☙ ½ **2011 (PG-13)** Contemporary take on Jane Austen's "Sense and Sensibility." This time, two Latina sisters from Beverly Hills (Belle and Vega) are forced to move to East L.A. to live with their estranged Aunt Aurelia (Barraza) after the death of their father. Naturally, they suffer severe culture shock when they are deprived of their privileged lifestyles. Predictable and racially stereotypical, albeit touching at times, as the leads are actually likeable. **107m/C; Blu-Ray.** Camilla Belle; Alexa Vega; Adriana Barraza; Wilmer Valderrama; Nicholas D'Agosto; *D:* Angel Gracia; *W:* Fina Torres; Luis Alfaro; Craig Fernandez; *C:* Hector Ortega; *M:* Heitor Pereira.

From Russia with Love ☙☙☙ ½ **1963 (PG)** Bond is back and on the loose in exotic Istanbul looking for a super-secret coding machine. He's involved with a beautiful Russian spy and has the SPECTRE organization after him, including villainess Rosa Klebb (she of the killer shoe). Lots of exciting escapes but not an overreliance on the gadgetry of the later films. The second Bond feature, thought by many to be the best. **125m/C; VHS, DVD, Blu-Ray.** *GB* Sean Connery; Daniela Bianchi; Pedro Armendariz, Sr.; Lotte Lenya; Robert Shaw; Eunice Gayson; Walter Gotell; Lois Maxwell; Bernard Lee; Desmond Llewelyn; Nadja Regin; Alizia Gur; Martine Beswick; Leila; *D:* Terence Young; *W:* Johanna Harwood; Richard Maibaum; *C:* Ted Moore; *M:* John Barry.

From the Dead of Night ☙☙☙ **1989** A spooky chiller about a near-death experience. Fashion designer Wagner narrowly escapes death but gets close enough to the other side that six of the dead feel cheated that she didn't join them. They decide to rectify the mistake and Wagner is pursued by the shadowy figures. Based on the novel "Walkers" by Gary Bradner. **192m/C; VHS, DVD.** Lindsay Wagner; Bruce Boxleitner; Diahann Carroll; Robert Prosky; Robin Thomas; Merritt Butrick; Joanne Linville; *D:* Paul Wendkos. **TV**

From the Earth to the Moon ☙☙☙ **1998** Executive producer Tom Hanks shows off his fascination with the space program in this 12-part series covering the Apollo space program through the 1960s and '70s. Covers behind-the-scenes at NASA, the heroics of the astronauts and their missions, and the families that are left behind to wait and worry. On six cassettes. **720m/C; VHS, DVD.** David Andrews; Bryan Cranston; Timothy Daly; Al Franken; Tony Goldwyn; Chris Isaak; Cary Elwes; Brett Cullen; Robert John Burke; Peter Scolari; Nick Searcy; Lane Smith; Dan Lauria; Mark Rolston; Mason Adams; Ronny Cox; Dakin Matthews; Kevin Pollak; Ben Marley; Joe Spano; Daniel Hugh-Kelly; Stephen (Steve) Root; Dann Florek; John Slattery; Ted Levine; Ann Cusack; Jo Anderson; James Rebhorn; Mark Harmon; Rita Wilson; Tom Amandes; John Aylward; Dylan Baker; Adam Baldwin; Reed Birney; Betsy Brantley; Bart Braverman; David Brisbin; Jimmy Buffett; Dan E. Butler; David Clennon; Gary Cole; Matt Craven; Wendy Crewson; Blythe Danner; Dave Foley; Jack Gilpin; John Michael Higgins; Peter Horton; Clint Howard; Zeljko Ivanek; Tcheky Karyo; John Carroll Lynch; Ann Magnuson; Joshua Malina; Andrew Masset; DeLane Matthews; Paul McCrane; Doug McKeon; Jay Mohr; Kieran Mulroney; Holmes Osborne; Conor O'Farrell; Elizabeth Perkins; Ethan Phillips; Andrew Rubin; Alan Ruck; Diana Scarwid; Grant Shaud; Cynthia Stevenson; Tom Verica; Gareth Williams; JoBeth Williams; Max Wright; Steve Zahn; *D:* Tom Hanks; David Frankel; Lili Fini Zanuck; Graham Yost; Frank Marshall; Jon Turteltaub; Gary Fleder; David Carson; Sally Field; Jonathan Mostow; *W:* Tom Hanks; Graham Yost; Stephen Katz; Remi Aubuchon; Al Reinert; Andy Wolk; Jeffrey Alladin Fiskin; Karen Janszen; Jonathan Marc Feldman; *C:* Gale Tattersall; *M:* Michael Kamen; Mark Mancina. **CABLE**

From the Edge of the City ☙☙ **1998** Sasha (Papadopoulos) is a teenaged emigre from Russia, who's working the Athens streets as a hustler. His older (and ruthless) mentor Giorgos (Papoulidis) is a pimp and offers Sasha the chance to move up by temporarily turning over the management of one of his girls—fellow emigre, Natasha (Tzimou). But Sasha, who isn't nearly as hardened as some of his friends, struggles not to become emotionally involved with the girl, to disastrous effect. Greek with subtitles. **94m/C; VHS, DVD.** *GR* Stathis Papadopoulos; Dimitris Papoulidis; Theadora Tzimou; Costas Cotsianidis; *D:* Constantine Giannaris; *W:* Constantine Giannaris; *C:* George Argiroilipoulos; *M:* Akis Daoutis.

From the Hip ☙☙ **1986 (PG)** A young lawyer (Nelson) gets the chance of a lifetime when his office assigns a murder case to him.

The only problem is that he suspects his client is very guilty indeed and must discover the truth without breaking his code of ethics. Nelson's courtroom theatrics are a bit out of hand, as he flares his nostrils at every opportunity. The movie is encumbered by a weak script and plot as well as a mid-story switch from comedy to drama. **111m/C; VHS, DVD.** Judd Nelson; Elizabeth Perkins; John Hurt; Ray Walston; ***D:*** Bob (Benjamin) Clark; ***W:*** Bob (Benjamin) Clark; David Kelly; ***C:*** Dante Spinotti; ***M:*** Paul Zaza.

From the Journals of Jean Seberg 🦴🦴 **1995** An imaginary look at the life of the ill-fated actress, who began her career as a 17-year-old, miscast in Otto Preminger's "Saint Joan," achieved fame in Godard's "Breathless," and became a suicide at age 40 in 1979. Seberg (Hurt) dispassionately narrates her life story as she views film clips, from small-town Iowa teenager to would-be star, through abusive relationships, drugs and drinking, political activisim, and FBI harassment. **97m/C; DVD.** Mary Beth Hurt; ***D:*** Mark Rappaport; ***W:*** Mark Rappaport; ***C:*** Mark Daniels.

From the Life of the Marionettes 🦴🦴🦴 **1980 (R)** A repressed man in a crumbling marriage rapes and kills a young prostitute. Another look at the powers behind individual motivations from Bergman, who uses black and white and color to relate details of the incident. **104m/C; VHS, DVD, Blu-Ray.** *SW* Robert Atzorn; Christine Buchegger; Martin Benrath; Rita Russek; Lola Muethel; Walter Schmidinger; Heinz Bennent; ***D:*** Ingmar Bergman; ***W:*** Ingmar Bergman; ***C:*** Sven Nykvist.

From the Manger to the Cross 🦴🦴 **1912** This version of the Passion play was the first film to be done on location in Palestine. Re-enacts the Nativity, the flight into Egypt, and the crucifixion. Color-tinted. **71m/B; Silent; VHS, DVD.** R. Henderson-Bland; Alice Hollister; Gene Gauthier; ***D:*** Sidney Olcott; ***W:*** Gene Gauthier; Sidney Olcott. Natl. Film Reg. '98.

From the Mixed-Up Files of Mrs. Basil E. Frankweiler 🦴🦴 ½ **1995 (PG)** Runaway siblings (Barnwell and Lee) secretly hide out in a New York art museum. They get caught up in trying to determine the authenticity of a sculpture (could it be the work of Michelangelo?) and turn to the statue's last owner, elusive art patron Mrs. Basil E. Frankweiler (Bacall). Based on the Newbery Award-winning novel by E.L. Konigsburg. Made for TV. **92m/C; VHS, DVD.** Lauren Bacall; Jean Marie Barnwell; Jesse Lee; ***D:*** Marcus Cole. **TV**

From the Terrace 🦴🦴 ½ **1960** Newman is a wealthy Pennsylvania boy who goes to New York and marries into even more money and social position when he weds Woodward. He gets a job with her family's investment company and neglects his wife for business. She turns to another man and when he goes home for a visit he also finds a new romance which leads to some emotional soul searching. The explicitness of O'Hara's very long novel was diluted by the censors and Newman's performance is a stilted disappointment. Loy, as Newman's alcoholic mother, earned the best reviews. **144m/C; VHS, DVD, Blu-Ray.** Paul Newman; Joanne Woodward; Myrna Loy; Ina Balin; Felix Aylmer; Leon Ames; George Grizzard; Patrick O'Neal; Barbara Eden; Mae Marsh; ***D:*** Mark Robson; ***W:*** Ernest Lehman; ***C:*** Leo Tover; ***M:*** Elmer Bernstein.

The Front 🦴🦴🦴 **1976 (PG)** Woody is the bookmaker who becomes a "front" for blacklisted writers during the communist witch hunts of the 1950s in this satire comedy. The scriptwriter and several of the performers suffered blacklisting themselves during the Cold War. Based more or less on a true story. **95m/C; VHS, DVD, Blu-Ray.** Woody Allen; Zero Mostel; Herschel Bernardi; Michael Murphy; Danny Aiello; Andrea Marcovicci; ***D:*** Martin Ritt; ***W:*** Walter Bernstein; ***C:*** Michael Chapman; ***M:*** Dave Grusin.

The Front Line 🦴🦴 **2006** Joe (Ebouaney), a political refugee from the Congo, is working as a bank security guard in Dublin. Psycho Eddie (Frain) and his gang kidnap Joe's family, using them as leverage to make Joe their inside man for their heist. Only Joe isn't the innocent he seems and when things go wrong, he utilizes an underground network of fellow African immigrants to track the gang down, including crime boss Erasmus (Kae-Kazim), another Congolese native. **90m/C; DVD.** *GB IR* Eriq Ebouaney; James Frain; Gerard McSorley; Ian McElhinney; Hakeem Kae-Kazim; Fatou N'Diaye; Bryan Eli Sebunya; ***D:*** David Gleeson; ***W:*** David Gleeson; ***C:*** Volker Tittel; ***M:*** Patrick Cassidy.

The Front Page 🦴🦴🦴 ½ **1931** The original screen version of the Hecht-MacArthur play about the shenanigans of a battling newspaper reporter and his editor in Chicago. O'Brien's film debut here is one of several hilarious performances in this breathless pursuit of an exclusive with an escaped death row inmate. **101m/B; VHS, DVD, Blu-Ray.** Adolphe Menjou; Pat O'Brien; Edward Everett Horton; Mae Clarke; Walter Catlett; ***D:*** Lewis Milestone; ***C:*** Hal Mohr. Natl. Film Reg. '10.

The Front Page 🦴🦴 ½ **1974 (PG)** A remake of the Hecht-MacArthur play about the managing editor of a 1920s Chicago newspaper who finds out his ace reporter wants to quit the business and get married. But first an escaped convicted killer offers the reporter an exclusive interview. **105m/C; VHS, DVD, Blu-Ray.** Jack Lemmon; Walter Matthau; Carol Burnett; Austin Pendleton; Vincent Gardenia; Charles Durning; Susan Sarandon; ***D:*** Billy Wilder; ***W:*** Billy Wilder; I.A.L. Diamond; ***C:*** Jordan Cronenweth; ***M:*** Billy May.

Front Page Woman 🦴🦴 ½ **1935** Battle of the sexes comedy features rival newshounds Ellen Garfield (Davis) and Curt Devlin (Brent) who are also in love. Devlin refuses to admit that women are just as good at getting a story and Ellen won't marry him until he does. So they make a marital wager when an apartment fire leads to an arson and murder investigation over who can find the killer first. **83m/B; DVD.** Bette Davis; George Brent; Roscoe Karns; Wini Shaw; Gordon Westcott; Joseph Crehan; ***D:*** Michael Curtiz; ***W:*** Roy Chanslor; Laird Doyle; Lillie Hayward; ***C:*** Tony Gaudio; ***M:*** Heinz Roemheld.

The Front Runner 🦴🦴 **2018 (R)** Hugh Jackman delivers a powerful performance as Senator Gary Hart, whose 1988 presidential campaign implodes after the press unearths evidence of an extramarital affair. Farmiga as his wife and Simmons as his campaign manager are equally good in their roles, but the story itself doesn't thrill, whether that's because it's already well-known or because 30 years later we're no longer regarding the sour politics-media relationship as entertainment. **113m/C; DVD, Blu-Ray.** Hugh Jackman; Vera Farmiga; J.K. Simmons; Mark O'Brien; Molly Ephraim; ***D:*** Jason Reitman; ***W:*** Jason Reitman; Matt Bai; Jay Carson; ***C:*** Eric Steelberg; ***M:*** Rob Simonsen.

The Frontier 🦴🦴 **2016** An American crime drama filtered through neo-noir style and filmed in the California desert. When Laine (Donahue), a female drifter on the run from the law, stops at the Frontier, a seedy motel in the desert, she finds more than just a place to spend the night. The motel is run by the mysterious Luanne (Lynch), who offers Laine a job. Taking the post, Laine soon learns that the motel houses a violent gang of thieves. With nothing to lose, Laine devises a plan to escape with the gang's stolen cash and start her own new life. **88m/C; DVD, Blu-Ray, Streaming, Download.** Jocelin Donahue; Kelly Lynch; Jim Beaver; Izabella Miko; Jamie Harris; ***D:*** Oren Shai; ***W:*** Oren Shai; Webb Wilcoxen; ***C:*** Jay Keitel; ***M:*** Ali Helnwein.

Frontier Marshal 🦴🦴 ½ **1939** Remake of the 1934 film is a romanticized version of the gunfight at the OK Corral. Wyatt Earp (Scott) is sworn in as marshal of the lawless mining town of Tombstone. He's aided in his pursuit of justice by gambling gunslinger Doc Halliday (Romero), whose girlfriend from back east, nurse Sarah Allen (Kelly), shows up in town. Doc rejects her and Earp starts courting Sarah instead. A death in the group sets up the shootout. **71m/B; DVD.** Randolph Scott; Cesar Romero; Nancy Kelly; Binnie Barnes; Joe Sawyer; John Carradine; Charles Stevens; ***D:*** Allan Dwan; ***W:*** Sam Hellman; ***C:*** Charles G. Clarke.

Frontier of Dawn 🦴 ½ *La Frontiere de L'aube* **2008** An unhappy love triangle with some silly supernatural elements. Photographer Francois (Garrel, son of the director) is hired to shoot actress Carole (Smet) who, despite her recent marriage, is all too eager to begin an affair. Shallow Francois is willing to oblige though Carole is soon shown to be sexy-but-crazy. French with subtitles. **106m/B; DVD.** *FR* Louis Garrel; Laura Smet; Clementine Poidatz; Emmanuel Broche; Olivier Massart; Eric Rulliat; ***D:*** Philippe Garrel; ***W:*** Philippe Garrel; Arlette Langmann; Marc Cholodenko; ***C:*** William Luctchansky; ***M:*** Jean-Claude Vannier.

Frontier Uprising 🦴 ½ **1961** Stunning cinematography makes up for weak narrative in this otherwise routine oater. Davis stars as a frontier scout battling hordes of Mexicans and Indians while trying to gain control of California for the U.S. Based on the short story "Kit Carson" by George Bruce. **68m/B; VHS, DVD.** Jim Davis; Nancy Hadley; Ken Mayer; Nestor Paiva; Don O'Kelly; ***D:*** Edward L. Cahn; ***W:*** Owen Harris.

The Frontiersmen 🦴🦴 **1938** Things plod along at the little red schoolhouse until Hoppy and the guys have to take off after some rustlers. Features the members of the St. Brendan Boys Choir as the schoolboys. Unusual for its lack of gunplay until near the end. **71m/B; VHS, DVD.** William Boyd; George "Gabby" Hayes; Russell Hayden; Evelyn Venable; Clara Kimball Young; Charles Hughes; Dick(ie) Jones; Roy Barcroft; Emily Fitzroy; ***D:*** Lesley Selander.

Frost/Nixon 🦴🦴🦴 ½ **2008 (R)** Engrossing dramatization of the 1977 interviews between British journalist David Frost (Sheen) and former president Richard Nixon (Langella), about three years after Nixon's resignation due to the Watergate scandal. Follows Frost as he struggles to earn credibility within journalistic circles and has to front $600,000 of his own funds to entice Nixon. Figuring he can easily handle Frost, a beleaguered Nixon hopes to redeem himself to the nation, but his underestimation leads to a surprising admission. Adapted by Peter Morgan from his highly acclaimed 2006 play of the same name; the lead actors reprise their stage roles and a stellar Langella lives up to the Tony he received. Director Howard filmed at actual locations such as Nixon's San Clemente, California, home as well as Frost's hotel suite. **122m/C; Blu-Ray, On Demand.** Michael Sheen; Frank Langella; Sam Rockwell; Kevin Bacon; Rebecca Hall; Matthew Macfadyen; Oliver Platt; Toby Jones; Pat McCormick; Jenn Gotzon; ***D:*** Ron Howard; ***W:*** Peter Morgan; ***C:*** Salvatore Totino; ***M:*** Hans Zimmer.

Frostbiter: Wrath of the Wendigo 🦴 **1994 (R)** Disappointing Troma entry takes itself a bit too seriously. It wants to be an "Evil Dead on Ice" (we even see a movie poster for same in the flick); the plot involves hunters trapped in the frozen woods of Northern Michigan by the evil spirit "Wendigo." It's short on original horror and the laff-factor is not up to usual Troma standards (although the killer chili was a nice touch). The only saving grace is the quirky soundtrack, including said chili's theme song by Randall and Allan Lynch, "March of the Undead" by the 3-D Invisibles, and "I'm a Hellbilly" by Elvis Hitler. Based on the comic book character of the same name. **90m/C; VHS, DVD.** Ron Asheton; Lori Baker; Patrick Butler; Devlin Burton; ***D:*** Tom Chaney; ***W:*** Tom Chaney; ***C:*** Tom Chaney.

Frozen 🦴 ½ **2010 (R)** Dim college-aged snowboarders Joe (Ashmore), Dan (Zegers) and Parker (Bell) become trapped on a ski lift as a blizzard approaches. Since they're apparently the only people their age without cell phones, the trio must overcome the perils of frostbite, ravenous wildlife, poor decision-making and even worse dialogue. At turns tedious and gory. All this movie proves is that while you can suspend three people in the air indefinitely, you can't suspend the audience's disbelief that long. In a touch of irony, Ashmore played the character of Iceman in the "X-Men" series. **94m/C; Blu-Ray, On Demand.** Kevin Zegers; Shawn Ashmore; Emma Bell; Rileah Vanderbilt; Adam Johnson; Ed Ackerman; Chris York; ***D:*** Adam Green; ***W:*** Adam Green; ***C:*** Will Barratt; ***M:*** Andy Garfield.

The Frozen 🦴 ½ **2012 (PG-13)** Being alone in the woods become a quest for survival in this thriller. On a cold winter's day, Mike (Mitchell) and Emma (Morgan) go on a camping trip in a mountainous area. During a snowmobile ride deep into the forest, the pair crash and get stranded at their camp. After Mike suddenly disappears, Emma is totally alone and finds that a mysterious man (Segan) has been tracking them through the forest. Between the elements and the hunter, Emma must take drastic action to make it through this experience. **95m/C; DVD, Streaming, Download.** Brit Morgan; Seth David Mitchell; Noah Segan; Sedona James; ***D:*** Andrew Hyatt; ***W:*** Andrew Hyatt; ***C:*** Maximilian Gutierrez; ***M:*** James Grundler.

Frozen 🦴🦴🦴 ½ **2013 (PG)** A beautiful piece of animation from Disney, built around gorgeous original music and a heart-lifting message for young girls trying to find visions of themselves outside of princesses and fairy tales. After royal heir Elsa nearly kills her sister Anna with a magical power to freeze the air around her, the two are separated for most of their young lives. Anna grows up strong and confident; Elsa grows up afraid and insecure. When an incident sends Elsa off into an ice castle in the mountains, Anna chases after her. Naturally, she has the help of some sidekicks, including the naïve, talkative snowman, Olaf. **108m/C; DVD, Blu-Ray.** ***V:*** Kristen Bell; Idina Menzel; Jonathan Groff; Josh Gad; Santino Fontana; ***D:*** Chris Buck; Jennifer Lee; ***W:*** Jennifer Lee; ***M:*** Christophe Beck. Oscars '13: Animated Film, Song ("Let It Go"); British Acad. '13: Animated Film; Golden Globes '14: Animated Film.

Frozen Alive 🦴 **1964** A scientist experiments with suspended animation but, wouldn't you know, someone murders his wife while he's on ice. Apparently being frozen stiff does not an alibi make, and he becomes the prime suspect. Much unanimated suspense. **80m/B; VHS, DVD.** *GB GE* Mark Stevens; Marianne Koch; Delphi Lawrence; Joachim Hansen; Walter Rilla; Wolfgang Lukschy; ***D:*** Bernard Knowles.

The Frozen Dead **WOOF! 1966** Low-budget, boring Brit horror where a telepathic head defeats the mad scientist. Fugitive Nazi doctor Rupert Norberg (Andrews) has been hiding out in an English castle with lots of cryogenically frozen Nazis in the dungeon. He's supposed to reanimate the corpses so the Third Reich can rise again but the brains don't function. That's where the telpathic head comes into the plot--not that you'll care. **95m/C; DVD.** *UK* Dana Andrews; Anna Palk; Philip Gilbert; Karel Stepanek; Kathleen Breck; ***D:*** Herbert J. Leder; ***W:*** Herbert J. Leder; ***C:*** Davis Boulton; ***M:*** Don Banks.

The Frozen Ground 🦴 ½ **2013 (R)** Increasingly B-movie-reliant Cusack and Cage star as serial killer Robert Hansen and the Alaska State Trooper who caught him, respectively, in this cut-rate, barely-released thriller. Writer/director Walker mistakenly focuses too heavily on Cindy Paulson (a horrendously miscast Hudgens), the stripper who escapes and eventually leads the authorities back to the man who seemed like a normal community member but was actually a torturer and killer. Cusack and Cage aren't as lazy as some of their other recent ventures but the film doesn't thrill, largely because the time spent in the stripper's life feels exploitive. **105m/C; DVD, Blu-Ray.** Nicolas Cage; John Cusack; Vanessa Anne Hudgens; Dean Norris; Radha Mitchell; Kevin Dunn; Katherine LaNasa; 50 Cent; ***D:*** Scott Walker; ***W:*** Scott Walker; ***C:*** Patrick Murguia; ***M:*** Lorne Balfe.

Frozen in Fear 🦴🦴 *The Flying Dutchman* **2000** Variation on the 1933 film "The Mystery of the Wax Museum" and the Vincent Price 1953 remake "House of Wax." Admiring art dealer Oxenberg tracks reclusive painter Roberts down to his remote cabin in Montana. Turns out the artist uses real female bodies for his work—killing young women, arranging them in provocative poses, and then encasing them in ice. Will Oxenberg become part of his next tableau? **91m/C; VHS, DVD.** Eric Roberts; Catherine Oxenberg; Rod Steiger; Scott Plank; Barry Sigismondi; Joan Benedict; Douglas Sebern; ***D:*** Robin P. Murray. **VIDEO**

Frozen River 🦴🦴🦴🦴 **2008 (R)** Unsentimental and honest independent film set in a shabby trailer park on the U.S.-Quebec border, following the desperate attempts of two single mothers to break free of their economic struggles. Ray Eddy (Leo), mother of two and part-time employee at the local dollar store, is left scrambling to pay the bills after her husband disappears on a gambling spree. Lila Littlejohn (Upham), now living alone after her mother-in-law snatched up her one-year-old, discovers the keys to Ray's husband's abandoned car and drives off. Ray follows Lila and soon the two women hatch a scheme to smuggle illegal aliens across the border. First-time director Courtney Hunt never drags the material into cheap thriller mode, instead trusting Leo and Upham to carry the story through their incredible chemistry. Winner of the Grand Jury Prize at Sundance 2008. **97m/C; Blu-Ray, On Demand.** Melissa Leo; Charlie McDermott; Michael O'Keefe; Mark Boone, Jr.; Misty Upham; James Reilly; Jay Klaitz; John Canoe; ***D:*** Courtney Hunt; ***W:*** Courtney Hunt; ***C:*** Reed Dawson Morano; ***M:*** Peter Golub; Shahzad Ali Ismaily. Ind. Spirit '09: Actress (Leo).

Frozen II 🦴🦴🦴 **2019 (PG)** Queen Elsa (Menzel) and her sister Anna (Bell) are happily living in their castle, when Elsa hears voices calling to her from the enchanted forest. Though a fairy tale their father told them as children makes her afraid, Elsa decides she wants to investigate. Traveling with Anna, their cheerful snowman friend Olaf (Gad), and Anna's love Kristoff (Groff), the group enters the forest and faces outfall from earlier choices made by their family. An entertaining sequel to the popular animated feature mostly succeeds in capturing what made the first film beloved, such as great songs and beautiful scenery. **103m/C; DVD, Blu-Ray.** Kristen Bell; Idina Menzel; Josh Gad; Jonathan Groff; Sterling K. Brown; ***D:*** Chris Buck; Jennifer Lee; ***W:*** Jennifer Lee; ***M:*** Christophe Beck.

Fruitvale Station 🦴🦴 **1/2 2013 (R)** Jordan shines in the true story of Oscar Grant, an unarmed man shot on a platform of the San Francisco BART train on New Year's Eve. Writer/director Coogler's Sundance Award-winning film then flashes back to detail the 24 hours before Grant's murder with supporting work from Spencer as Grant's mother. Coogler and Jordan do an excellent job of turning a man who became a headline back into a real human being, but the film feels too manipulative and too tidy in its presentation when the truth of this story is much more jagged, dirty, and less clichéd. **90m/C; DVD, Blu-Ray.** Michael B. Jordan; Melonie Diaz; Octavia Spencer; Kevin Durand; Chad Michael Murray; ***D:*** Ryan Coogler; ***W:*** Ryan Coogler; ***C:*** Rachel Morrison; ***M:*** Ludwig Göransson. Ind. Spirit '14: First Feature.

Fudoh: The New Generation 🦴🦴 **1/2** *Gokudo sengokushi: Fudo* **1996** Riki Fudoh (Tanihara) is a high school kid whose father is a Yakuza. Dear old dad murders Riki's brother to save himself when he angers his bosses, and Riki decides the old man and his cronies have to go. Aiding him in his quest are his crack team of assassins composed of a giant teenage boy, two 10 year old kids, a few teenage schoolgirl strippers, and the occasional hermaphrodite. This ultra-violent film led to infamous Japanese director Takashi Miike receiving international attention. **100m/C; DVD.** *JP* Shosuke Tanihara; Kenji Takano; Marie Jino; Tamaki Kenmochi; Toru Menigishi; Miho Nomoto; Riki Takeuchi; Takeshi Caesar; ***D:*** Takashi Miike; ***W:*** Hitoshi Tanimura; Toshiyuki Morioka; ***C:*** Hideo Yamamoto; ***M:*** Chu Ishikawa.

Fuel 🦴🦴🦴 **2008** Eleven years in the making, director and narrator Tickell spiritedly expounds upon the merits of biofuels over the oil industry, as supported by such celebrities as Sheryl Crow, Woody Harrelson, and Willie Nelson, as well as more credible folks actually working in the field with footage taken from his "Veggie Van" travels—a van using vegetable oil as fuel. Despite his predisposition against big oil after growing up in an industrial-polluted section of Louisiana, Tickell uses his background to share what he's learned for a fair debate, though no opposing viewpoint is put forth. Tweaked after his 2008 festival showing, the alternative fuel focus was switched from ethanol due to concerns about its use and environmental hazards. But the bigger question of the effects of energy dependence on mankind and the planet still loom. **112m/C; Blu-Ray, On Demand.** Joshua Tickell; ***D:*** Joshua Tickell; ***W:*** Johnny O'Hara; ***C:*** Jim Mulryan; ***M:*** Ryan Demaree; Edgar Rothermich.

The Fugitive 🦴🦴🦴🦴 **1948** Fonda is a priest devoted to God and the peasants under his care when he finds himself on the run after religion is outlawed in this nameless South-of-the-border dictatorship. Despite the danger of capture, he continues to minister to his flock. His eventual martyrdom unites the villagers in prayer. Considered Fonda's best performance; Ford's favorite film. Shot on location in Mexico. Excellent supporting performances. Based on the Graham Greene novel "The Power and the Glory" although considerably cleaned up for the big screen—Greene's priest had lost virtually all of his faith and moral code. Here the priest is a genuine Ford hero. A gem. **99m/B; VHS, DVD.** Henry Fonda; Dolores Del Rio; Pedro Armendariz, Sr.; J. Carrol Naish; Leo Carrillo; Ward Bond; Robert Armstrong; John Qualen; ***D:*** John Ford; ***W:*** Dudley Nichols.

The Fugitive 🦴🦴🦴 **1/2 1993 (PG-13)** Exciting big-screen version of the '60s TV series with the same basic storyline: Dr. Richard Kimble's (Ford) wife (Ward) is murdered and he's convicted, so he escapes and goes on the lam to find the real killer, the mysterious one-armed man. Dogged marshal Sam Gerard (Jones) is determined to retrieve his man. Lots of mystery and action, particularly a spectacular train/bus crash sequence, keeps the tension high. Due to illness, Richard Jordan was replaced by Krabbe after production had begun. Alec Baldwin was originally slated to star as Kimble, but backed out and Ford was cast. Sound familiar? Ford also replaced Baldwin as Jack Ryan in "Patriot Games." **127m/C; VHS, DVD, Blu-Ray, HD-DVD.** Harrison Ford; Tommy Lee Jones; Jeroen Krabbe; Julianne Moore; Sela Ward; Joe Pantoliano; Andreas Katsulas; Daniel Roebuck; ***D:*** Andrew Davis; ***W:*** David N. Twohy; Jeb Stuart; ***C:*** Michael Chapman; ***M:*** James Newton Howard. Oscars '93: Support. Actor (Jones); Golden Globes '94: Support. Actor (Jones); L.A. Film Critics '93: Support. Actor (Jones); MTV Movie Awards '94: Action Seq., On-Screen Duo (Harrison Ford/Tommy Lee Jones); Blockbuster '95: Action Actor, V. (Ford).

Fugitive Among Us 🦴🦴 **1992** Dedicated cop is determined to return an escaped rapist to a life behind bars and he's aided by a victim who would really rather forget the whole thing. Made for TV. **97m/C; VHS, DVD.** Peter Strauss; Eric Roberts; Elizabeth Pena; Lauren Holly. **TV**

Fugitive at 17 🦴🦴 **1/2 2012** Lifetime teen thriller. Teenage computer hacker Holly goes to a college party with best friend Blake. Both girls are roofied, but Blake dies of a drug overdose and Holly gets accused of murder. This puts her on the run from the Philly cops as she tries to prove her innocence. Familiar but fast-paced and Holly's a savvy heroine. **88m/C; DVD.** Marie Avgeropoulos; Christina Cox; Danny Blanco Hall; Casper Van Dien; Frank Schorpion; Daniel Rindress-Kay; Rosemary Dunsmore; ***D:*** Jim Donovan; ***W:*** Douglas Howell; David DeCrane; ***C:*** Bill St. John; ***M:*** Richard Bowers. **CABLE**

Fugitive Champion 🦴🦴 **1999** Gangsters bust motor-cross champion Jake McKnight (Mayer) out of a chain-gang so that he can search for his kidnapped daughter, a participant in an internet sex site. The silly plot is a framework upon which to hang some inventive lively chase scenes. Standard action for a video premiere with a generic title. **94m/C; DVD.** Chip (Christopher) Mayer; Charlene Blaine; Thomas Burr; Carlos Cervantes; ***D:*** Max Kleven; ***W:*** Steven Baio; Jack Burkhead, Jr.; ***C:*** Jason C. Poteet; ***M:*** Ennio di Berardo. **VIDEO**

The Fugitive Kind 🦴🦴 **1/2 1960** A young drifter walks into a sleepy Mississippi town and attracts the attention of three of its women with tragic results. Based upon the Tennessee Williams' play "Orpheus Descending." good performances but the writing never hangs well-enough together for coherence. **122m/B; VHS, DVD, Blu-Ray.** Marlon Brando; Anna Magnani; Joanne Woodward; Victor Jory; R.G. Armstrong; Maureen Stapleton; ***D:*** Sidney Lumet; ***C:*** Boris Kaufman.

Fugitive Mind 🦴 **1/2 1999 (PG-13)** Robert Dean (Dudikoff) is suffering from severe memory loss. As he begins to piece together his past, Dean discovers his mind has been programmed to carry out bizarre crimes. So now what does he do? **94m/C; VHS, DVD.** Michael Dudikoff; Heather Langenkamp; Michele Greene; David Hedison; Ian Ogilvy; ***D:*** Fred Olen Ray; ***W:*** Sean McGinley; Tripp Reed; ***C:*** Theo Angell; ***M:*** David Wurst; Eric Wurst. **VIDEO**

Fugitive Rage 🦴🦴 **1996 (R)** Tara McCormick (Schumacher) winds up behind bars when she shoots the mobster who was acquitted for murdering her sister. She teams up with her cellmate Josie (O'Brien) to fight back against the mob who's put a bounty on her head and a covert government agency also out to use her. Prerequisite prison shower sequences, tough babes, and lots of action. **90m/C; VHS, DVD.** Wendy Schumacher; Shauna O'Brien; Jay Richardson; ***D:*** Fred Olen Ray.

Fugitive Road 🦴🦴 **1934** The great von Stroheim stars as a crusty but soft-hearted border guard who arbitrarily detains people at the crossing. **69m/B; VHS, DVD.** Erich von Stroheim; Wera Engels; Leslie Fenton; Harry Holman; ***D:*** Frank Strayer.

Fugly! 🦴 **1/2 2014** Uneven film in which Leguizamo plays a Latino comic who doesn't blossom until he moves out of his brother's shadow and into a local college. The standup performances and cartoons are the highlights of an otherwise disjointed rom-com. **90m/C; DVD, Blu-Ray, Streaming.** John Leguizamo; Radha Mitchell; Rosie Perez; Griffin Dunne; Ally Sheedy; ***D:*** Alfredo de Villa; ***W:*** John Leguizamo; Kathy Demarco; ***C:*** Nancy Schreiber; ***M:*** Michael A. Levine. **VIDEO**

Full Clip 🦴 *Blood Money* **2006 (R)** Joshua Pope (Rhymes) returns home to collect his inheritance after his father is killed, only to find the town under the iron grip of a corrupt sheriff. In a cliche move, he calls in some old buddies to gun the crooked lawmen down. **95m/C; DVD.** Busta Rhymes; Xzibit; Bubba Smith; Mark Boone, Jr.; ***D:*** Mink; ***W:*** Kantz; ***C:*** M. Dietrick Schumacher; ***M:*** Don MacBain.

Full Contact 🦴🦴 *Xia dao Gao Fei* **1992** Nightclub bouncer Jeff helps his friend Sam escape from a loan shark. But Sam has doublecrossed him and now thinks that Jeff is dead in an arranged explosion. But Jeff's survived and plans to seek a suitable revenge. Cantonese with subtitles. **99m/C; VHS, DVD.** *CH* Chow Yun-Fat; Anthony Wong; Simon Yam; Bonnie Fu; Franklin Chin; Ann Bridgewater; Chan Chi Leung; ***D:*** Ringo Lam; ***W:*** Yin Nam; ***M:*** Teddy Robin Kwan.

Full Contact 🦴🦴 **1993 (R)** Farmhand Luke Powers heads for the decadence of Los Angeles to find his older brother. When three thugs make the mistake of trying to rob him, Luke shows off his martial arts skills. When Luke finds out his brother has been murdered by gamblers involved in an illegal back alley kickboxing circuit, he vows to get revenge. **97m/C; VHS, DVD.** Jerry Trimble; Howard Jackson; Alvin Prouder; Gerry Blanck; Denise Buick; ***D:*** Rick Jacobson; ***W:*** Beverly Gray.

Full Count 🦴🦴 *Lenexa, 1 Mile* **2006 (R)** Sports figure in, but this is more a story about friendship despite the curves in the plot. Five high school buddies are spending their last summer in their Kansas hometown before separating to go to college. They play a money game of basketball against the local cops and celebrate their win by getting drunk and driving. When disgruntled cop Russ pulls the boys over, he gets even by taking the money back and threatening them with arrest. They retaliate and things go downhill until there's another showdown between the boys (who have joined a softball league) and Russ' team. (And no, there's no showing of the "big game".) **90m/C; DVD.** Austin Nichols; Paul Wesley; Jason Ritter; Chris Klein; Josh Stewart; Timothy Ryan Hensel; Michael Rooker; William Baldwin; Michael Beach; ***D:*** Jason Wiles; ***W:*** Jason Wiles; Shem Bitterman; ***C:*** David Boyd; ***M:*** Gary Clark, Jr.

Full Disclosure 🦴🦴 **1/2 2000 (R)** Veteran journalist McWhirter (Ward) gets an incredible opportunity when a group of radicals he sent to prison ask him to protect a Palestinian operative (Ticotin) involved in the murder of a pro-Israeli media mogul. But neither an FBI agent (Plummer) nor an assassin (Miller) want McWhirter in the way and he'll have to decide just how badly he wants this story. **137m/C; VHS, DVD.** Fred Ward; Christopher Plummer; Penelope Ann Miller; Rachel Ticotin; Virginia Madsen; Kim Coates; Nicholas (Nick) Campbell; Dan Lauria; Roberta Maxwell; ***D:*** John Bradshaw; ***W:*** Tony Johnston; ***C:*** Barry Stone; ***M:*** Claude Desjardins; Eric N. Robertson. **VIDEO**

Full Eclipse 🦴🦴 **1993 (R)** Max Dire (Van Peebles) is seduced by the fetching Casey (Kensit) into joining a fierce elite group of underground cops whose mission is to wipe out crime. However, Max soon learns that the secret of their power is a serum which turns them into werewolves. Max is now faced with a decision: join forces with them, or expose them. Either way, blood will flow. Interesting special effects. Unrated version also available. **97m/C; VHS, DVD.** Mario Van Peebles; Patsy Kensit; Bruce Payne; Anthony John (Tony) Denison; ***D:*** Anthony Hickox; ***W:*** Richard Christian Matheson; ***C:*** Sandi Sissel.

Full Exposure: The Sex Tape Scandals 🦴 **1/2 1989 (R)** Sleazy drama about a murdered call girl who was blackmailing her clients with sex videos. A cop and his inexperienced female partner are assigned to catch the killer. **95m/C; VHS, DVD.** Jennifer O'Neill; Lisa Hartman Black; Vanessa L(ynne) Williams; Anthony John (Tony) Denison; Peter Jurasik; ***D:*** Noel Nosseck; ***W:*** Stephen Zito; ***M:*** Dana Kaproff. **TV**

Full Frontal 🦴 **1/2 2002 (R)** Despite its suggestive title, Soderbergh's film is arty, meandering, and uninvolving. Shot mostly on digital video in 18 days, the director's unofficial sequel to "sex, lies and videotape" tracks the loosely related lives and loves of various Los Angeles movie business types working on a film called "Rendezvous" over a 24-hour period. Katt, hilarious as a self-involved stage actor playing Hitler; Keener, as the somewhat demented Lee; and masseuse McCormack are the real standouts. However, improv-feel performances are good all around, with canny insider humor. The film's ambiguous presentation, including voice-overs, plays within movies, and movies-within-movies-within movies (whew!), undermine its intention to reveal the whole Hollywood circus that is really best kept under wraps. **101m/C; VHS, DVD, Blu-Ray.** David Duchovny; Nicky Katt; Catherine Keener; Mary McCormack; David Hyde Pierce; Julia Roberts; Blair Underwood; Enrico Colantoni; Dina Spybey; ***D:*** Steven Soderbergh; ***W:*** Coleman Hough; ***C:*** Steven Soderbergh.

Full Metal Jacket 🦴🦴🦴 **1/2 1987 (R)** A three-act Vietnam War epic, about a single Everyman impetuously passing through basic training then working in the field as a Marine Corps photojournalist and fighting at the onset of the Tet offensive. First half of the film is the most realistic bootcamp sequence ever done. Unfocused but powerful. Based on the novel by Hasford, who also coscripted. **116m/C; VHS, DVD, Blu-Ray, HD-DVD.** Matthew Modine; R. Lee Ermey; Vincent D'Onofrio; Adam Baldwin; Dorian Harewood; Arliss Howard; Kevyn Major Howard; Ed O'Ross; John Terry; Jon Stafford; Marcus D'Amico; Kieron Jecchinis; Bruce Boa; Kirk Taylor; Tim Colceri; Ian Tyler; Gary Landon Mills; Sal Lopez; Ngoc Le; Peter Edmund; Tan Hung Francione; Leanne Hong; Costas Dino Chimona; ***D:*** Stanley Kubrick; ***W:*** Stanley Kubrick; Michael Herr; Gustav Hasford; ***C:*** Doug Milsome; ***M:*** Abigail Mead.

The Full Monty 🦴🦴🦴 **1996 (R)** A group of laid off Yorkshire mill workers come up with a unique way to earn some money in this amusing Britcom. When exuberant Gaz (Carlyle) notices the local women lining up to see the Chippendale dancers, he persuades his mates to launch a striptease act themselves. But these guys are hardly cover boy material—they're variously overweight, middle-aged, depressed, and shy. Nevertheless, they turn out to be an unexpected success despite numerous mishaps and misunderstandings. Title refers to the fact that they strip down to their birthday suits. The film audience merely gets the moon view. **90m/C; VHS, DVD, Blu-Ray.** *GB* Robert Carlyle; Tom Wilkinson; Mark Addy; Steve Huison; William Snape; Paul Barber; Hugo Speer; Lesley Sharp; Emily Woof; Deirdre Costello; ***D:*** Peter Cattaneo; ***W:*** Simon Beaufoy; ***C:*** John de Borman; ***M:*** Anne Dudley. Oscars '97: Orig. Mus./Comedy Score; British Acad. '97: Actor (Carlyle), Film, Support. Actor (Wilkinson); Screen Actors Guild '97: Cast.

Full Moon in Blue Water ✌✌ 1/2 **1988 (R)** His wife's been dead a year, he owes back taxes on his bar, his father has Alzheimer's, and his only form of entertainment is watching old home movies of his wife. Floyd has problems. Enter Louise, a lonely spinster who feels that it is her personal duty to change his life. If she doesn't do it, the bizarre things that happen after her arrival will. **96m/C; VHS, DVD; Open Captioned.** Gene Hackman; Teri Garr; Burgess Meredith; Elias Koteas; Kevin Cooney; David Doty; ***D:*** Peter Masterson; ***W:*** Bill Bozzone; ***C:*** Fred Murphy; ***M:*** Phil Marshall.

Full Moon in Paris ✌✌ 1/2 *Les Nuits de la Pleine* **1984 (R)** A young woman in Paris moves out on her architect lover in order to experience freedom. Through a couple of random relationships, she soon finds that what she hoped for is not what she really wanted. The fourth of Rohmer's Comedies and Proverbs series. French with subtitles. **101m/C; VHS, DVD, Blu-Ray.** *FR* Pascale Ogier; Tcheky Karyo; Fabrice Luchini; ***D:*** Eric Rohmer; ***W:*** Eric Rohmer; ***C:*** Renato Berta. Venice Film Fest. '84: Actress (Ogier).

Full of It ✌ 1/2 **2007 (PG-13)** Mildly amusing teen comedy. Sam (Pinkston) is the small, geeky kid who tries to fit it at his new high school by telling a few white lies. Only by the next morning they've magically come true. But it's a definite case of "be careful what you wish for," including Sam almost losing out on the right girl (Mara) because of his typical teen boy cheerleader (Walsh) fantasy. **91m/C; DVD.** Kate Mara; Craig Kilborn; John Carroll Lynch; Cynthia Stevenson; Amanda Walsh; Derek McGrath; Teri Polo; Joshua Close; Ryan Pinkston; ***Cameo(s):*** Carmen Electra; ***D:*** Christian Charles; ***W:*** Jon Lucas; Scott Moore; ***C:*** Kramer Morgenthau; ***M:*** John Swihart.

Full of Life ✌✌ 1/2 **1956** Holliday stars in this domestic comedy about a non-religious young woman who had married, in a civil ceremony, into a strict, Italian-Catholic family. Although Emily is now eight months pregnant the family still wants her and husband Nick (Conte) to have a church wedding. Holliday is a winning personality and the humor is lightly handled. Fante adapts from his own novel. **91m/B; DVD.** Judy Holliday; Richard Conte; Salvatore Baccaloni; Esther Minciotti; Joe De Santis; ***D:*** Richard Quine; ***W:*** John Fante; ***C:*** Charles Lawton, Jr.; ***M:*** George Duning.

Full Out ✌✌ **2015** A biopic based on the life of gymnast Ariana Berlin (Golja). Training as a gymnast with the goal of making the 2008 U.S. Olympic team, Berlin's life takes an unexpected detour when she is involved in a serious car accident at the age of 14. Though her Olympic goals seem out of reach, Berlin begins training in hip-hop dance to aid her recovery. She is able to return to gymnastics when she is recruited to attend UCLA and competes in the NCAA championships. **90m/C; DVD, Streaming, Download.** Ana Golja; Jennifer Beals; Sarah Fisher; Asha Bromfield; Lamar Johnson; ***D:*** Sean Cisterna; ***W:*** Willem Wennekers; ***C:*** Pasha Patriki; ***M:*** Grayson Matthews. **VIDEO**

Full Ride ✌✌ **2002 (PG-13)** Typical teen romance with a sports background. High school senior Matt (Smith) is picked to play in the all-state football game but his bad attitude keeps getting him in trouble. It's clear that he doesn't care about the game until Matt meets Amy (Monroe), one of the town's hosts, who tells him he'll be missing out on the chance of a full college scholarship if he doesn't become a team player. **95m/C; DVD.** Riley Smith; Meredith Monroe; Bob Cady; Jonathan Wayne Wilson; Mario Foxbaker; ***D:*** Mark Hoeger; ***W:*** George Mills; Don Winslow; ***C:*** Andy Anderson; ***M:*** Peter Buffett. **TV**

Full Speed ✌✌ *A Toute Vitesse* **1996** Quentin (Cervo) published a semi-autobiographical novel about disenfranchised youth that's based on his friends from a Lyon housing project, including drug-dealing DJ, Jimmy (Rideau). Although he has a girlfriend, Julie (Bouchez), Quentin flirts with Algerian-born Samir (Bardadi) to learn about Samir's murdered boyfriend to use the story in his writing. Julie, meanwhile, becomes involved with the charismatic Jimmy when Quentin goes to Paris. There are several melodramatic twists in Morel's feature debut about live-for-today youth and racial tensions. French with subtitles. **84m/C; VHS, DVD.** *FR* Pascal Cervo; Stephane Rideau; Elodie Bouchez; Meziane Bardadi; ***D:*** Gael Morel; ***W:*** Gael Morel; Catherine Corsini; ***C:*** Jeanne Lapoirie.

Full Tilt Boogie ✌✌ 1/2 **1997 (R)** Director Sarah Kelly's documentary films the making of hipster crime-vampire flick "From Dusk Till Dawn" by Quentin Tarantino and Robert Rodriguez. Watching this clash of show biz egos is actually more fun than watching the movie they made. Probes the inner workings of big shots Tarantino, Clooney, Keitel, and the interns that hate to go to Taco Bell for them. Keitel, in his best "I can't believe you talked me into making this movie" tone, has a brief monologue about...well, he probably had a point when he started talking. Also shows the problems that went on during the production, including the destruction of a set by fire and the process of saving it. Included on the "From Dusk Till Dawn" special edition DVD. **110m/C; VHS, DVD.** ***D:*** Sarah Kelly; ***C:*** Chris Gallo; ***M:*** Cary Berger; Dominic Kelly.

Full Time Killer ✌✌ 1/2 *Fulltime Killer; Chunchik satsau; Chuen jik sat sau* **2001 (R)** O (Sorimachi) is the number one assassin in Hong Kong. Despondent over the murder of his housekeeper with whom he was in love, he has shut himself off from the outside world and become obsessed with her replacement. Tok (Lau) is a loud up-and-coming assassin eager to be number one, who seduces O's housekeeper to lure him out of hiding into a confrontation. **98m/C; DVD.** *CH* Andy Lau; Simon Yam; Kelly Lin; Suet Lam; Takashi Sorimachi; Cherrie Ying; Teddy Lin; ***D:*** Johnny To; ***W:*** Kai-Fai Wai; Ho-Cheung Pang; Joey O'Bryan; ***C:*** Siu-keung Cheng; ***M:*** Guy Zerafa; Alex Khaskin.

The Fuller Brush Girl ✌✌ 1/2 **1950** Lots of slapstick with Ball as a door-to-door saleswoman unexpectedly involved in a murder. She and dim-bulb boyfriend Albert are chased by cops, murderers, and smugglers in this frantic farce. Sequel to Red Skelton's (who has a cameo) 1948 film "The Fuller Brush Man." **84m/B; VHS, DVD.** Lucille Ball; Eddie Albert; Carl Benton Reid; Gale Robbins; Jeff Donnell; John Litel; Fred Graham; Lee Patrick; ***Cameo(s):*** Red Skelton; ***D:*** Lloyd Bacon; ***W:*** Frank Tashlin.

The Fuller Brush Man ✌✌ 1/2 *That Man Mr. Jones* **1948** A newly hired Fuller Brush man becomes involved in murder and romance as he tries to win the heart of his girlfriend. A slapstick delight for Skelton fans. **93m/B; VHS, Streaming.** Red Skelton; Janet Blair; Don McGuire; Adele Jergens; ***D:*** Frank Tashlin.

Fun ✌✌ **1994** Another in the thrill kill genre. 14-year-old Bonnie (Witt) and 15-year-old Hillary (Humphrey) are best friends (and possibly lovers) who have stabbed to death an old woman—seemingly for kicks and to cement their loyalty to each other. (Can you say Leopold and Loeb?) Convicted and in a reformatory, they're documenting their actions, separately (in black & white sequences), to counselor Jane (Hope) and tabloid journalist John (Moses). Bleak dysfunction adapted by Bosley from his play. **95m/C; VHS, DVD.** Alicia Witt; Renee Humphrey; Leslie Hope; William R. Moses; Ania Suli; ***D:*** Rafal Zielinski; ***W:*** James Bosley; ***C:*** Jens Sturup; ***M:*** Marc Tschantz.

Fun & Fancy Free ✌✌✌ **1947 (G)** Part-animated, part-live-action Disney feature is split into two segments: "Bongo" with Dinah Shore narrating the story of a happy-go-lucky circus bear looking for love; and "Mickey and the Beanstalk"?a "new" version of an old fairy tale. Disney's last performance as the voice of Mickey and the only film to star Mickey, Donald Duck, Jiminy Cricket and Goofy. **73m/C; VHS, DVD, Blu-Ray.** ***V:*** Walt Disney; Cliff Edwards; Billy Gilbert; Clarence Nash; Anita Gordon; ***Nar:*** Edgar Bergen; Dinah Shore; ***D:*** Jack Kinney; Hamilton Luske; William M. Morgan; ***C:*** Charles P. Boyle; ***M:*** Paul J. Smith; Oliver Wallace; Eliot Daniel.

Fun Down There **WOOF!** **1988** This smalltown boy-comes-to-the-big city is so bad, it's—bad. A naive—and unsympathetic—gay man from upstate New York moves to Greenwich Village and has fun down there (and they don't mean Australia). **110m/C; VHS, DVD.** Michael Waite; Nickolas Nagurney; Gretschen Somerville; Martin Goldin; Kevin Och; ***D:*** Roger Stigliano; ***W:*** Michael Waite; Roger Stigliano.

Fun in Acapulco ✌✌ **1963 (PG)** Former trapeze artist Elvis romances two beauties and acts as a part-time lifeguard and night club entertainer. He must conquer his fear of heights for a climactic dive from the Acapulco cliffs. Features ten musical numbers. **97m/C; VHS, DVD.** Elvis Presley; Ursula Andress; Elsa Cardenas; Paul Lukas; Alejandro Rey; Larry Domasin; Howard McNear; ***D:*** Richard Thorpe; ***C:*** Daniel F. Fapp.

Fun Size ✌ 1/2 **2012 (PG-13)** Josh Schwartz's laugh-free flick is a teen comedy whose cast is the best thing about it, particularly Levy's April, best friend to Wren (Justice), a girl stuck with watching her little brother Albert (Nicoll) on Halloween. He gets lost and she gets frantic to find the tyke before her mother finds out. **90m/C; DVD, Blu-Ray.** Victoria Justice; Jackson Nicoll; Jane Levy; Chelsea Handler; Thomas Mann; Osric Chau; Thomas A. McDonnell; Thomas Middleditch; Johnny Knoxville; ***D:*** Josh Schwartz; ***W:*** Max Werner; ***C:*** Yaron Orbach; ***M:*** Deborah Lurie.

Fun with Dick and Jane ✌✌ **1977 (PG)** An upper-middle class couple turn to armed robbery to support themselves when the husband is fired from his job. Though it has good performances, the film never develops its intended bite. **104m/C; VHS, DVD.** George Segal; Jane Fonda; Ed McMahon; ***D:*** Ted Kotcheff; ***W:*** Jerry Belson; David Giler; Mordecai Richler; ***C:*** Fred W. Koenekamp; ***M:*** Ernest Gold.

Fun With Dick and Jane ✌✌ **2005 (PG-13)** Recycled version of the 1977 film with Jane Fonda and George Segal. Dick (Carrey) has a great life with gorgeous wife Jane (Leoni), a super house and an important executive position. Then Dick's company goes bust in a big way, and his efforts to find a comparable job (or any job) go bust as well. So what do they do? Why, of course, they turn to a life of crime. None-too-subtle political message (an Enron-esque company blowup) is rendered ineffective by too much gas and not enough go. If Jim Carrey's trademark slapstick doesn't drive you nuts, you'll get a few laughs out of it. **90m/C; DVD, UMD, HD-DVD.** Jim Carrey; Tea Leoni; Alec Baldwin; Richard Jenkins; Angie Harmon; John Michael Higgins; Richard Burgi; Carlos Jacott; Aaron Michael Drozin; Gloria Garayua; ***D:*** Dean Parisot; ***W:*** Judd Apatow; Nicholas Stoller; ***C:*** Jerzy Zielinski; ***M:*** Theodore Shapiro; Randall Poster.

The Fundamentals of Caring ✌ 1/2 **2016** Ben (Rudd) is trying to fill an unimaginable hole in his heart by becoming a caretaker for handicapped young man Trevor (Craig Roberts), who pushes all of his new friend's buttons, but you just know that the two of them will change each other for the better by the third act. Burnett's adaptation of Jonathan Evison's 2012 novel means well, and contains a typically likable performance from Rudd, but it's ultimately more emotionally manipulative than believable. Throw in the runaway (Gomez) and the pregnant woman named Peaches (Ferguson) and it's hard to imagine movies this sentimental still get made. **97m/C; DVD.** Alex Huff; Paul Rudd; Donna Biscoe; Julia Denton; Jennifer Ehle; ***D:*** Rob Burnett; ***W:*** Rob Burnett; ***C:*** Giles Nuttgens; ***M:*** Ryan Miller. **VIDEO**

The Funeral ✌✌✌ 1/2 *Funeral Rites; Ososhiki* **1984** A sharp satire of the clash of modern Japanese culture with the old. The hypocrisies, rivalries and corruption in an average family are displayed at the funeral of its patriarch who also happened to own a house of ill repute. Itami's breakthrough film; Japanese with subtitles. **112m/C; VHS, DVD.** *JP* Tsutomu Yamazaki; Nobuko Miyamoto; Kin Sugai; Ichiro Zaitsu; Nekohachi Edoya; Hideji Otaki; ***D:*** Juzo Itami; ***W:*** Juzo Itami; ***C:*** Yonezo Maeda; ***M:*** Joji Yuasa.

The Funeral ✌✌✌ **1996 (R)** Ferrara fuels fantastic performances from his famous thesps in this fatalistic tale of a family of gangsters in 1930s New York. Flashbacks from the opening funeral scene show a complex and troubled family of Italian brothers (Walken, Penn, and Gallo), from their formative years through their quest for justice after youngest brother Johnny is murdered. Not just another mob movie; characters are multi-dimensional with interesting quirks and Penn, especially, sprints into his role. More subtle than "Bad Lieutenant" and less pretentious than "The Addiction," this Ferrara flick is the one to see. **96m/C; VHS, DVD.** Christopher Walken; Benicio Del Toro; Vincent Gallo; Christopher Penn; Isabella Rossellini; Annabella Sciorra; John Ventimiglia; Paul Hipp; Gretchen Mol; ***D:*** Abel Ferrara; ***W:*** Nicholas St. John; ***C:*** Ken Kelsch; ***M:*** Joe Delia.

Funeral for an Assassin ✌ 1/2 **1977 (PG)** A professional assassin seeks revenge for his imprisonment by the government of South Africa, a former client. Planning to kill all of the country's leading politicians, he masquerades as a black man, a cover which is designed to fool the apartheid establishment. **92m/C; VHS, DVD.** Vic Morrow; Peter Van Dissel; ***D:*** Ivan Hall.

Funeral Home ✌ 1/2 *2 Cries in the Night* **1982** Terrified teen spends her summer vacation at her grandmother's tourist home, a former funeral parlor. Rip-off of "Psycho." **90m/C; VHS, DVD.** *CA* Lesleh Donaldson; Kay Hawtrey; ***D:*** William Fruet.

Funeral in Berlin ✌✌✌ **1966 (R)** Second of the Caine/Harry Palmer espionage films (following up "Ipcress File"), in which the deadpan antihero British secret serviceman arranges the questionable defection of a Russian colonel (Homolka). Good look at the spy biz and postwar Berlin. Based on the novel by Len Deighton. "Billion Dollar Brain" continues the series. **102m/C; DVD, Blu-Ray.** Michael Caine; Eva Renzi; Oscar Homolka; Paul (Christian) Hubschmid; Guy Doleman; Hugh Burden; ***D:*** Guy Hamilton; ***W:*** Evan Jones; ***C:*** Otto Heller; ***M:*** Konrad Elfers.

The Funhouse ✌ 1/2 **1981 (R)** Four teenagers spend the night at a carnival funhouse, witness a murder, and become next on the list of victims. From the director of cult favorite "The Texas Chainsaw Massacre," but nothing that hasn't been seen before. **96m/C; VHS, DVD, Blu-Ray.** Elizabeth Berridge; Shawn Carson; Cooper Huckabee; Largo Woodruff; Sylvia Miles; Miles Chapin; Kevin Conway; William Finley; Wayne Doba; ***D:*** Tobe Hooper; ***W:*** Larry Block; ***C:*** Andrew Laszlo; ***M:*** John Beal.

Funkytown ✌ 1/2 **2011** An excess of story and stereotypes limit this disco drama. It's 1976 and disco rules at Montreal's trendiest club Starlight, which is run by Daniel Lefebvre but owned by his overbearing record producer father Gilles. Among its denizens are radio DJ Bastien Lavellee, host of Quebec's top TV dance program, openly gay trend columnist Jonathan Aaronson, wannabe model and singer Adriana, and dancers Tino and Tina. Behind the bright lights and loud music are drugs and sex as well as Montreal's political future with the issue of separatism and the rise of the Parti Quebecois. English and French with subtitles. **132m/C; DVD.** *CA* Patrick Huard; Paul Doucet; Raymond Bouchard; Francois Letourneau; Justin Chatwin; Sarah Mutch; Romina D'Ugo; Genevieve Brouillette; ***D:*** Daniel Roby; ***W:*** Steve Galluccio; ***C:*** Ronald Plante; ***M:*** Jean Robitaille.

Funland ✌ **1989 (PG-13)** In the world's weirdest amusement park a clown goes nuts over the new corporate owners' plans for the place and decides to seek revenge. **86m/C; VHS, DVD.** David Lander; William Windom; Bruce Mahler; Michael McManus; ***D:*** Michael A. Simpson.

Funny About Love ✌ 1/2 **1990 (PG-13)** Fairly absurd tale with dashes of inappropriate black humor about a fellow with a ticking biological clock. Nimoy sheds his Spock ears to direct a star-studded cast in this lame tale of middle-aged cartoonist Wilder who strays from wife Lahti after having problems on the conception end into the welcoming arms of fertile college co-ed Masterson in his quest to contribute to the population count. **107m/C; VHS, DVD.** Gene Wilder; Christine Lahti; Mary Stuart Masterson; Robert Prosky; Stephen Tobolowsky; Anne Jackson; Susan Ruttan; David Margulies; ***D:*** Leonard Nimoy; ***W:*** Norman Steinberg; David Frankel.

Funny Bones ✌✌✌ **1994 (R)** Struggling comedian Tommy Fawkes (Platt) bombs in Vegas big-time while his Mr. Showbiz father George (Lewis) easily overshadows him at every turn. So Tommy decides to head back to his childhood home in Blackpool, England and figure out his life. What he discovers are the Parkers, a family of British vaudevillians, and the fact that his father stole their routines and, briefly, Mrs. Parker (Caron), resulting in half-brother Jack (Evans) who has all the natural talent Tommy can only dream about. Serious, funny, and hostile with notable performances from Platt and Evans. **128m/C; VHS, DVD, Blu-Ray.** Oliver Platt; Lee Evans; Leslie Caron; Jerry Lewis; Oliver Reed; Ian McNeice; Ruta Lee; Richard Griffith; George Carl; Freddie Davies; ***D:*** Peter Chelsom; ***W:*** Peter Chelsom; Peter Flannery; ***C:*** Eduardo Berra; ***M:*** John Altman.

Funny, Dirty Little War 🦴🦴 ½ *No Hambra mas Penas ni Olvido; Funny Little Dirty War* **1983** An Argentinian farce about the petty rivalries in a small village erupting into a violent, mini-civil war. Based on the novel by Osvaldo Soriano. In Spanish with English subtitles. **80m/C; VHS, DVD.** *AR* Federico Luppi; Julio de Grazia; Miguel Angel Sola; ***D:*** Hector Olivera; ***W:*** Hector Olivera; Roberto Cassa; ***C:*** Leonardo Solis; ***M:*** Oscar Cardozo Ocampo.

Funny Face 🦴🦴🦴 **1957** Musical satire on beatniks and the fashion scene also features the May-December romance between Astaire and the ever-lovely Hepburn. He is a high-fashion photographer (based on Richard Avedon); she is a Greenwich Village bookseller fond of shapeless, drab clothing. He decides to take her to Paris and show her what modeling's all about. The elegant musical score features classic Gershwin. **103m/C; VHS, DVD, Blu-Ray.** Fred Astaire; Audrey Hepburn; Kay Thompson; Suzy Parker; ***D:*** Stanley Donen; ***M:*** Ira Gershwin.

Funny Farm 🦴🦴 **1988 (PG)** Chevy Chase as a New York sportswriter finds that life in the country is not quite what he envisioned. The comedy is uneven throughout, with the best scenes coming at the end. **101m/C; VHS, DVD.** Chevy Chase; Madolyn Smith; Joseph Maher; Jack Gilpin; Brad Sullivan; MacIntyre Dixon; ***D:*** George Roy Hill; ***W:*** Jeffrey Boam; ***C:*** Miroslav Ondricek; ***M:*** Elmer Bernstein.

Funny Games 🦴🦴 **1997** Georg (Muhe), his wife, Anna (Lothar), and young son, Georgie (Clapczynski) are vacationing at their lakeside cottage when their peace is invaded by psycho Paul (Frisch) and his sniveling partner Frank (Giering). The family is tied up and forced to play humiliating games with a couple of amoral killers. Most of the physical violence occurs off-screen but the psychological torture is relentless. German with subtitles. **103m/C; VHS, DVD, Blu-Ray.** *AT* Susanne Lothar; Ulrich Muhe; Frank Giering; Arno Frisch; Stefan Clapczynski; ***D:*** Michael Haneke; ***W:*** Michael Haneke; ***C:*** Jurgen Jurges.

Funny Games 🦴🦴🦴 **2007 (R)** Haneke's shot-by-shot remake of his 1997 German art house thriller about two preppy 20-somethings, Paul and Peter (Pitt and Corbet), who descend upon a family, first as annoying guests, then as vicious sadists out for blood. Haneke had always said this movie would work better in America as social commentary, and he's probably right. Roth and Watts turn in harrowing performances as the tortured husband and wife, with Watts also credited as producer. Deliberately shocking and manipulative, which may validate its premise, but still, a nasty little flick. **112m/C; DVD.** *IT GE FR GB US* Naomi Watts; Tim Roth; Michael Pitt; Brady Corbet; Devon Gearhart; ***D:*** Michael Haneke; ***W:*** Michael Haneke; ***C:*** Darius Khondji.

Funny Girl 🦴🦴🦴 **1968 (G)** Follows the early career of comedian Fanny Brice, her rise to stardom with the Ziegfeld Follies, and her stormy romance with gambler Nick Arnstein in a fun and funny look at back stage music hall life in the early 1900s. Streisand's film debut followed her auspicious performance of the role on Broadway. Score was augmented by several tunes sung by Brice during her performances. Excellent performances from everyone, captured beautifully by Wyler in his musical film debut. Followed by "Funny Lady." **151m/C; VHS, DVD, Blu-Ray.** Barbra Streisand; Omar Sharif; Walter Pidgeon; Kay Medford; Anne Francis; ***D:*** William Wyler; ***W:*** Isobel Lennart; ***C:*** Harry Stradling, Sr.; ***M:*** Jule Styne; Walter Scharf. Oscars '68: Actress (Streisand); Golden Globes '69: Actress--Mus./Comedy (Streisand); Natl. Film Reg. '16.

Funny Lady 🦴🦴 ½ **1975 (PG)** A continuation of "Funny Girl," recounting Fanny Brice's tumultuous marriage to showman Billy Rose in the 1930s and her lingering affection for first husband Nick Arnstein. One of the rare sequels which are just as good, or at least almost, as the original. **137m/C; VHS, DVD, Blu-Ray.** Barbra Streisand; Omar Sharif; James Caan; Roddy McDowall; Ben Vereen; Carole Wells; Larry Gates; Heidi O'Rourke; ***D:*** Herbert Ross; ***W:*** Jay Presson Allen; Arnold Schulman; ***C:*** James Wong Howe.

Funny People 🦴🦴 **2009 (R)** Apatow might think longer is better, but brevity is the soul of comedy. Endless raunchy dialogue spouted by boy-men just can't sustain the pic's length. Superstar comedian George Simmons (Sandler) learns he has a rare and probably fatal illness. George, of course, lives only for performing and has no friends because offstage he's such a jerk. Aspiring comedian Ira (Rogen) can write material but he's a lousy performer so George makes him his personal assistant. George decides to seriously go after his onetime love (Mann) who's married with children. (Let's see—agonizing over Eric Bana or Adam Sandler? Only in Apatow-land.) Momentum mostly gets lost in the third act when it goes all serious. **146m/C; Blu-Ray, On Demand.** Adam Sandler; Seth Rogen; Leslie Mann; Eric Bana; Jonah Hill; Jason Schwartzman; Aubrey Plaza; Iris Apatow; Maude Apatow; RZA; ***D:*** Judd Apatow; ***W:*** Judd Apatow; ***C:*** Janusz Kaminski; ***M:*** Michael Andrews.

A Funny Thing Happened on the Way to the Forum 🦴🦴🦴 **1966** A bawdy Broadway farce set in ancient Rome where a conniving, slave plots his way to freedom by aiding in the romantic escapades of his master's inept son. Terrific performances by Mostel and Gilford. Keaton's second-to-last film role. The Oscar-winning score includes such highlights as "Comedy Tonight," "Lovely," and "Everybody Ought to Have a Maid." **100m/C; VHS, DVD, Blu-Ray.** Zero Mostel; Phil Silvers; Jack Gilford; Buster Keaton; Michael Hordern; Michael Crawford; Annette Andre; ***D:*** Richard Lester; ***W:*** Melvin Frank; Michael Pertwee; ***C:*** Nicolas Roeg; ***M:*** Ken Thorne. Oscars '66: Adapt. Score.

Funny Valentine 🦴 **2005 (R)** Josh (Hall) is having trouble with New York's singles scene so his buddies Tim (Lord Jamar) and Sean (Martin) offer dating advice, including placing a personal ad and vetting the responses. Embittered single mom Doreen (Marron) is not one of their choices but Josh decides to follow his heart. A romantic comedy that's weak on both the romance and the comedy. There is a lot of unwarranted seminudity that is more appropriate to softcore porn. **90m/C; DVD.** Anthony Michael Hall; Marlo Marron; Ivan Martin; Larry Storch; Lord Jamar; ***D:*** Jeff Oppenheim; ***W:*** Jeff Oppenheim; ***C:*** Stephen Treadway; ***M:*** Greg Arnold. **VIDEO**

Funnyman 🦴🦴 **1994 (R)** Cartoon splatter courtesy of a demon dressed in classic British jester regalia. Rock 'n' roll mogul Young obtains Lee's creepy ancestral home in a card game but when he visits with his family, everyone but Young is killed by the Funnyman, who uses his victims own weaknesses to dispatch them. A second set of likely candidates arrive when Young's brother Devitt shows up with a motley collection of hangers-on, including psychic Black, who's the only one to realize something's seriously off. **89m/C; VHS, DVD.** *GB* Tim James; Benny Young; Matthew Devitt; Pauline Black; Ingrid Lacey; ***Cameo(s):*** Christopher Lee; ***D:*** Simon Sprackling; ***W:*** Simon Sprackling.

Fur: An Imaginary Portrait of Diane Arbus 🦴🦴 **2006 (R)** Imaginary indeed as tall, pale Kidman looks nothing like the small, dark Arbus, not to mention that Downey's character Lionel Sweeney suffers from an extreme form of hirsuteness that covers him in hair so he's reduced to acting with eyes and voice. So here's this married 1950s New York housewife who helps out husband Allan (Burrell) with his commercial photography career suddenly transforming herself into a snapper of those marginalized by society. Apparently Diane is tired of being the good girl and wants to take a walk on the wild side and fulfill her own artistic desires. It's a well-intentioned but somehow unsatisfactory effort. **120m/C; DVD.** Nicole Kidman; Robert Downey, Jr.; Ty Burrell; Harris Yulin; Jane Alexander; ***D:*** Steven Shainberg; ***W:*** Erin Cressida Wilson; ***C:*** Bill Pope; ***M:*** Carter Burwell.

The Furies 🦴🦴 ½ **1950** Huston's last film is a brooding western from director Mann with Stanwyck as the ultimate daddy's girl who wants revenge when she feels betrayed. In 1870s New Mexico, ruthless widowed rancher T.C. Jeffords (Huston) has secured a large bank loan in exchange for driving off some squatters, including a Mexican family whom daughter Vance (Stanwyck) regards as friends. Vance is furious when daddy marries scheming socialite Florence (Anderson), so she attacks her unwelcome stepmommy. There's also problems involving Vance's dowry (and who's getting the money) and Rip (Corey), a gambler-turned-banker with his own agenda when he teams up with Vance to ruin her father. **109m/B; DVD.** Walter Huston; Barbara Stanwyck; Wendell Corey; Judith Anderson; Gilbert Roland; Thomas Gomez; Beulah Bondi; Albert Dekker; Wallace Ford; John Bromfield; ***D:*** Anthony Mann; ***W:*** Charles Schnee; ***C:*** Victor Milner; ***M:*** Franz Waxman.

Furious 7 🦴🦴 ½ *Fast & Furious 7* **2015 (PG-13)** Head bro Dom (Diesel) and his crew must stop terrorist Jakarde (Hounsou) and Deckard Shaw (Statham), brother of arch enemy Owen Shaw, from stealing a deadly computer program. Silly, confusing, but always beefed up with killer car chases, director Wan keeps the tradition alive, pumping sweat and muscles into every frame. In a franchise that has never quite accepted death as the end, there's finally a sense of mortality by this seventh installment. The passing of lead actor Paul Walker halfway through filming put up certain roadblocks, but with the help of his younger brothers, and a little CGI magic, Walker's tragic death breathes humanity into an otherwise ridiculous action flick. **137m/C; DVD, Blu-Ray.** Vin Diesel; Paul Walker; Jason Statham; Michelle Rodriguez; Jordana Brewster; Tyrese Gibson; Chris Bridges; Dwayne "The Rock" Johnson; Lucas Black; ***D:*** James Wan; ***W:*** Chris Morgan; ***C:*** Marc Spicer; Stephen F. Windon; ***M:*** Brian Tyler.

Furlough 🦴🦴 **2018 (R)** Tightly wound, upstate New York prison guard Nicole (Thompson) is tasked with escorting prisoner Joan (Leo) on a 36-hour visit to her dying mother in Long Island. From the first, the trip is challenging as the bus driver is uncomfortable with the prisoner on his bus, and Nicole is attacked by her family, including her ill mother (Goldberg), for leaving. When Nicole allows Joan some experiences in New York City, she sneaks off with a man from sex addicts meeting. Despite a promising premise, the comedy is not particularly funny and fails to take advantage of Thompson and Leo's talents. **83m/C; DVD.** Melissa Leo; Tessa Thompson; Edgar Ramirez; Erik Griffin; Drena De Niro; ***D:*** Laurie Collyer; ***W:*** Barry Strugatz; ***C:*** Berenice Eveno; ***M:*** Jeff Cardoni.

Furry Vengeance **WOOF! 2010 (PG)** A pro-environmental message family comedy that hurts its cause more than it helps. A real estate developer (Fraser) moves his family to rural Oregon for his work on a new housing project, but construction threatens the local forest population. The animals—a combination of live and CGI—rise up together to sabotage the project, and make Fraser the target of two movies' worth of slapstick bee stings, skunk sprays, and kicks to the crotch. It's hard to tell if the animals are angry about their habitat, or the fact that they're in such a despicably bad movie. Lame jokes, bad performances, and very little to appeal to adults or kids, but at least the animals don't talk. **92m/C; Blu-Ray, On Demand.** Brendan Fraser; Brooke Shields; Matt Prokop; Ken Jeong; Samantha Bee; Rob Riggle; ***D:*** Roger Kumble; ***W:*** Michael Carnes; Josh Gilbert; ***C:*** Peter Lyons Collister; ***M:*** Ed Shearmur.

The Further Adventures of Tennessee Buck 🦴 **1988 (R)** Mercenary adventurer travels through tropical jungles acting as a guide to a dizzy couple. Along the way, they encounter cannibals, headhunters, and other bizarre jungle things in this lame take on "Indiana Jones." Shot on location in Sri Lanka. **90m/C; VHS, DVD.** David Keith; Kathy Shower; Brant Van Hoffman; ***D:*** David Keith; ***M:*** John Debney.

Further Adventures of the Wilderness Family, Part 2 🦴🦴 ½ *Wilderness Family, Part 2* **1977 (G)** Depicts the Robinson family who left civilization for the freedom of the Colorado wild. Predictable retread, but more good family adventure drama from the makers of "Adventures of the Wilderness Family." **104m/C; VHS, DVD.** Heather Rattray; Ham Larsen; George "Buck" Flower; Robert F. Logan; Susan Damante-Shaw; ***D:*** Frank Zuniga.

Further Up the Creek 🦴 ½ **1958** Quick follow-up to "Up the Creek" (which was also released in 1958) about the further adventures of naive naval officer Fairweather (Tomlinson) who must deliver the Aristotle to its new owners in Algerocco. He discovers his venal Bos'n (Howerd taking over from Peter Sellers) has once again made the ship out to be a cruise liner and sold tickets to passengers. **91m/B; DVD.** *GB* David Tomlinson; Frankie Howerd; Shirley Eaton; Thora Hird; Lionel Jeffries; Lionel Murton; ***D:*** Val Guest; ***W:*** Val Guest; Len Heath; John Warren; ***C:*** Len Harris; ***M:*** Stanley Black.

Fury 🦴🦴🦴 ½ **1936** Tracy gives an excellent performance as an innocent young man framed for kidnapping and then nearly murdered by a lynch mob. His plans for revenge are thwarted by his girlfriend, who fears that he will turn into the murderer he has been accused of being. Powerful anti-violence message is well-made, with strong ensemble acting. Lang's favorite of his American-made films. **96m/B; VHS, DVD.** Spencer Tracy; Sylvia Sidney; Walter Abel; Bruce Cabot; Edward Ellis; Walter Brennan; Frank Albertson; ***D:*** Fritz Lang; ***C:*** Joseph Ruttenberg. Natl. Film Reg. '95.

Fury 🦴 **1978** A man and woman meet in the Amazonian jungle and the sparks begin to fly. **75m/C; VHS, DVD.** *IT SP* Stuart Whitman; Laura Gemser; Pilar Velasquez; Francisco Algora; ***D:*** Jose Maria Froque; ***W:*** Jose Maria Froque; ***C:*** Alejandro Ulloa; ***M:*** Carlo Savina.

The Fury 🦴🦴 **1978 (R)** The head of a government institute for psychic research finds that his own son is snatched by supposed terrorists who wish to use his lethal powers. The father tries to use another a young woman with psychic power to locate him, with bloody results. A real chiller. **117m/C; VHS, DVD, Blu-Ray.** Kirk Douglas; John Cassavetes; Carrie Snodgress; Andrew Stevens; Amy Irving; Charles Durning; Carol Rossen; Rutanya Alda; William Finley; Jane Lambert; Joyce Easton; Daryl Hannah; Dennis Franz; James Belushi; ***D:*** Brian De Palma; ***W:*** John Farris; ***C:*** Richard H. Kline; ***M:*** John Williams.

Fury 🦴🦴 **2014 (R)** Director Ayer takes viewers back to World War II, this time in an effort to present the underreported story of tank warfare in the European conflict. A grizzled Pitt stars as Don 'Wardaddy' Collier, Captain of the titular tank, also manned by the religious Boyd (LaBeouf), sociopathic Grady (Bernthal), eager Trini (Pena) and newbie Norman (Lerman). The quintet moves through one of the most Nazi-run areas of Germany in an attempt to clear a path for the Allied forces, killing hundreds of bad guys along the way. It's a WWII movie for those raised on Call of Duty video games. **134m/C; DVD, Blu-Ray.** Brad Pitt; Logan Lerman; Shia LaBeouf; Michael Peña; Jon Bernthal; Jason Isaacs; Jim Parrack; Brad William Henke; Scott Eastwood; ***D:*** David Ayer; ***W:*** David Ayer; ***C:*** Roman Vasyanov; ***M:*** Steven Price.

Fury of Achilles 🦴🦴 *L'ira di Achille* **1962** Traditional Peplum film based on 'The Iliad' (a knowledge of which would be helpful when watching). It's the tenth year of the Trojan War and fighting between Achilles (Mitchell) and Agamemnon (Petri) is making the troops nervous. **116m/C; DVD.** *IT* Gordon Mitchell; Jacques Bergerac; Cristina Gaioni; Gloria Milland; Pierro Lulli; Roberto Risso; Mario Petri; Eleanora Bianchi; Emilio Spalla; Fosco Giachetti; Nando Tamberlani; Ennio Girolami; Tina Gloriani; ***D:*** Marino Girolami; ***W:*** Gino De Santis; ***C:*** Mario Fioretti; ***M:*** Carlo Savina.

The Fury of Hercules 🦴 ½ *La Furia Di Ercole; Fury of Samson* **1961** It's up to the mighty son of Zeus to free an enslaved group of people from an oppressive, evil ruler. Surely all who stand in his way will be destroyed. Another Italian muscleman film. **95m/C; VHS, DVD.** *IT* Brad Harris; Luisella Boni; Mara Berni; Carlo Tamberlani; Serge Gainsbourg; Elke Arendt; Alan Steel; ***D:*** Gianfranco Parolini.

Fury of the Congo 🦴 **1951** Smugglers are in the Congo looking for the Okongo, a horse-like creature sacred to a local tribe. The Okongo produce a powerful narcotic from their glands and the bad guys enslave the tribe so they will lead them to the herd. Jungle Jim (Weissmuller) comes to their rescue but he needs to fight a giant spider (among other battles) to do so. The 6th in the series. **69m/B; DVD.** Johnny Weissmuller; Sherry Moreland; Lyle Talbot; William Henry; Joel Friedkin; George Eldredge; Paul Marion; Blanca Vischer; ***D:*** William Berke; Richard Fantl; ***W:*** Carroll Young; ***C:*** Ira Morgan.

The Fury of the Wolfman 🦴 *La Furia del Hombre Lobo* **1970** A murdering werewolf is captured by a female scientist who tries to cure his lycanthropy with drugs and brain implants. Pretty slow going, but hang in there for the wolfman versus werewoman climax. **80m/C; VHS, DVD.** *SP* Paul Naschy; Perla Cristal; Michael Rivers; Mark Stevens; Veronica Lujan; ***D:*** Jose Maria Zabalza; ***W:*** Paul Naschy.

Fury to Freedom: The Life Story of Raul Ries 🦴🦴 **1985** A young man raised in the volatile world of abusive and alcoholic parents grows into an abusive and violent adult. One night, however, he meets something he can't beat up, and it changes his life. **78m/C; VHS, DVD.** Gil Gerard; John Quade; Tom Silardi; ***D:*** Eric Jacobson; ***W:*** Eric Jacobson; ***C:*** Don Burgess.

Fuse 🦴🦴 **2003** Two years after the civil war, the Bosnian town of Tesanj expects a visit from President Bill Clinton. The entire community is determined to present a wholesome image (turning the brothel into a cultural center) but a black marketeer, a crazy ex-police chief, and a continuing Serbian rivalry could derail the process. Bosnian and Serbian with subtitles. **105m/C; DVD.** *BH* Bogdan Diklic; Enis Beslagic; Sasa Petrovic; Izudin Bajrovic; ***D:*** Pjer Zalica; ***W:*** Pjer Zalica; ***C:*** Mirsad Herovic; ***M:*** Sasa Losic.

The Future 🦴 ½ **2011 (R)** Absurdist romantic drama is narrated by Paw Paw, a wounded stray cat taken into the L.A. lives of Sophie (writer/director July) and Jason (Linklater). The cat is the catalyst for the passive, insecure quasi-adult couple to make some radical changes to their lives and relationship as they wait the 30 days for hospitalized Paw Paw to heal. They decide to quit their nowhere jobs and find some sort of cosmic connection to their existence. In Sophie's case this means having an affair; Jason decides to talk to the moon. Viewer interest will depend on how much of the whimsy factor they can take. **91m/C; DVD, Blu-Ray.** *US GE* Miranda July; Hamish Linklater; David Warshofsky; Isabella Acres; Joe Putterlik; ***D:*** Miranda July; ***W:*** Miranda July; ***C:*** Nikolai Graevenitz; ***M:*** Jon Brion.

Future Fear 🦴 ½ **1997 (R)** Genetic scientist Dr. John Denniel (Wincott) has to find a solution for a flesh-eating virus that threatens mankind. Along with wife Anna (Ford), John tries cominbing human DNA with that of other species. But it turns out the virus was engineered by maniacal General Wallace (Keach) as a form of human cleansing—and he's not happy when he hears about a potential cure. **82m/C; VHS, DVD.** Jeff Wincott; Maria Ford; Stacy Keach; Shawn Thompson; ***D:*** Lewis Baumander; ***W:*** Lewis Baumander; ***C:*** Graeme Mears; ***M:*** Donald Quan. **VIDEO**

Future Force 🦴 **1989 (R)** In the crime-filled future cops can't maintain order. They rely on a group of civilian mercenaries to clean up the streets. **90m/C; VHS, DVD.** David Carradine; Robert Tessier; Anna Rapagna; William Zipp; ***D:*** David A. Prior; ***W:*** David A. Prior; ***C:*** Andy Parke; ***M:*** Mark Mancina.

Future Kill 🦴 **1985 (R)** Anti-nuclear activists battle fraternity brothers in this grim futuristic world. Shaky political alliances form between revenge-seeking factions on both sides. **83m/C; VHS, DVD.** Edwin Neal; Marilyn Burns; Doug Davis; ***D:*** Ronald W. Moore; ***W:*** Ronald W. Moore.

The Future of Emily 🦴🦴 *Flugel und Fesseln* **1985** Film actress Isabelle (Fossey) has essentially given over the raising of her young daughter Emily (Raymond) to her parents, who live quietly in Normandy. After finishing a film shoot in Berlin, Isabelle comes for a visit but her smitten co-star Friedrich (Treusch) unexpectedly follows, leading to a clash between Isabelle and her mother Paula (Knef) about responsibility and Emily's future. German and French with subtitles. **106m/C; DVD.** *GE* Brigitte Fossey; Hildegarde Knef; Ivan Desny; Herman Treusch; Camille Raymond; ***D:*** Helmer Sanders-Brahms; ***W:*** Helmer Sanders-Brahms; ***C:*** Sacha Vierny; ***M:*** Jurgen Knieper.

Future Shock 🦴🦴 **1993 (PG-13)** Dr. Russell Langdon is a psychiatrist who has been experimenting with virtual reality technology. Unbeknownst to three of his patients he decides to use them as guinea pigs in his work. But confronting their deepest fears only leads to new terrors. Also available in an unrated version. **93m/C; VHS, DVD.** Bill Paxton; Vivian Schilling; Brion James; Martin Kove; ***D:*** Eric Parkinson; Matt Reeves; Oley Sassone; ***W:*** Vivian Schilling.

Future World 🦴 **2018 (R)** A futuristic sci-fi film co-directed by actor/director/writer Franco. Because his mother (Liu) is dying, Prince (Whalberg) journeys to a potentially mythical place called Paradise Beach where he hopes to buy medicine to save her. Along the way, he stops in Love Town, which is run by pimp Love Lord (Dogg). There, Prince escapes with a rebellious sex android Ash (Waterhouse), who helps him on his perilous journey for the medicine. Not only does the film feel like a copycat of Mad Max films, it's pretty uninteresting despite the highly creative casting. **90m/C; DVD, Blu-Ray, Streaming.** James Franco; Suki Waterhouse; Jeffrey Wahlberg; Margarita Levieva; Snoop Dogg; ***D:*** James Franco; Bruce Thierry Cheung; ***W:*** Bruce Thierry Cheung; Jeremy Cheung; Jay Davis; ***C:*** Peter Zeitlinger; ***M:*** Toydrum.

Future Zone 🦴🦴 **1990 (R)** In an attempt to save his father from being murdered, a young man travels backwards in time. **88m/C; VHS, DVD.** David Carradine; Charles Napier; Ted Prior; ***D:*** David A. Prior.

Futurekick 🦴 ½ **1991 (R)** In the not so distant future, a kickboxer with an attitude and cyborg capabilities must use every ounce of strength in a battle against evil. **80m/C; VHS, DVD.** Don "The Dragon" Wilson; Meg Foster; Christopher Penn; Eb Lottimer; Linda Dona; Maria Ford; ***D:*** Damian Klaus; ***W:*** Damian Klaus; Catherine Cyran; ***C:*** Ken Arlidge; ***M:*** Stan Ridgway.

Futuresport 🦴🦴 ½ **1998 (R)** In 2025, Tre Ramsey (Cain) is the arrogant star of a popular violent sport that's a combo of skateboarding and basketball. Only the key game turns out to have more on the line than endorsements when terrorists take over the arena. Tre's mentor, and Futuresport creator Orbike Fixx (Snipes), suggests it's just a gigantic turf war and that matters can be settled by an arena match to the death. Caught in the middle is newscaster Alejandra (Williams), the woman Tre once loved and left behind. **89m/C; VHS, DVD.** Dean Cain; Vanessa L(ynne) Williams; Wesley Snipes; Bill Smitrovich; Francoise Yip; ***D:*** Ernest R. Dickerson; ***W:*** Robert Hewitt Wolfe. **TV**

Futureworld 🦴🦴 **1976 (PG)** In the sequel to "Westworld," two reporters junket to the new "Futureworld" theme park, where they first support a scheme to clone and control world leaders. Includes footage shot at NASA locations. **107m/C; DVD, Blu-Ray.** Peter Fonda; Blythe Danner; Arthur Hill; Yul Brynner; Stuart Margolin; ***D:*** Richard T. Heffron; ***W:*** George Schenck; ***C:*** Gene Polito; Howard Schwartz; ***M:*** Fred Karlin.

Fuzz 🦴🦴 ½ **1972 (PG)** Reynolds in the Boston cop on the track of a bomber killing policemen, punks setting winos on fire, and some amorous fellow officers. Combines fast action and some sharp-edged humor. **92m/C; VHS, DVD, Blu-Ray.** Burt Reynolds; Tom Skerritt; Yul Brynner; Raquel Welch; Jack Weston; Charles Martin Smith; Albert "Poppy" Popwell; ***D:*** Richard A. Colla; ***M:*** Dave Grusin.

G 🦴 ½ **2002 (R)** Black urban adaptation of "The Great Gatsby." Successful hip-hop mogul Summer G (Jones) uses his bling to buy a mansion in the Hamptons and throw lots of parties. G is still upset that lover Sky (Maxwell) ran off long ago to marry old-money rich Chip Hightower (Underwood). Chip's cheating on his wife so G figures it's time to get Sky back. Journalist Tre (Royo) documents the happenings. Contrived mish-mash was filmed in 2001. **96m/C; DVD.** Richard T. Jones; Chenoa Maxwell; Blair Underwood; Andrew Lauren; Laz Alonso; Andre Royo; ***D:*** Christopher Scott Cherot; ***W:*** Andrew Lauren; Charles E. Drew, Jr.; ***C:*** Horacio Marquinez; ***M:*** Bill Conti.

G-Force 🦴🦴 ½ **2009 (PG)** Silly 3-D comic adventure, basically for the preteen set, about a covert government program that trains rodents to work as operatives. Guinea pigs—squad leader Darwin (Rockwell), weapons expert Blaster (Morgan), and martial arts pro Juarez (Cruz)?are joined by computer specialist mole Spreckles (Cage) to prevent greedy billionaire Saber (Nighy) from using household appliances (that he can turn into robots) from taking over the world. References to more adult Jerry Bruckheimer-produced movies will go over the heads of the kiddie set although parents might appreciate the nod in their direction. **86m/C; Blu-Ray.** Steve Buscemi; Bill Nighy; Will Arnett; Zach Galifianakis; Kelli Garner; Tyler Patrick Jones; Piper Mackenzie Harris; ***V:*** Sam Rockwell; Tracy Morgan; Penelope Cruz; Nicolas Cage; Jon Favreau; ***D:*** Hoyt Yeatman; ***W:*** Cormac Wibberley; Marianne S. Wibberley; Tim Firth; ***C:*** Bojan Bazelli; ***M:*** Trevor Rabin.

"G" Men 🦴🦴🦴 ½ **1935** Powerful story based loosely on actual events that occurred during FBI operations in the early 1930s, with Cagney on the right side of the law, though still given to unreasonable fits of anger. Raised and educated by a well-known crime kingpin, a young man becomes an attorney. When his friend the FBI agent is killed in the line of duty, he joins the FBI to seek vengeance on the mob. But his mob history haunts him, forcing him to constantly prove to his superiors that he is not under its influence. Tense and thrilling classic. **86m/B; VHS, DVD.** James Cagney; Barton MacLane; Ann Dvorak; Margaret Lindsay; Robert Armstrong; Lloyd Nolan; William Harrigan; Regis Toomey; ***D:*** William Keighley; ***W:*** Seton I. Miller; ***C:*** Sol Polito.

G-Men vs. the Black Dragon 🦴🦴 ½ **1943** Reedited serial of "Black Dragon of Manzanar" stars Cameron as Fed who battles Asian Axis agents during WWII. Action-packed. **244m/B; VHS, DVD.** Rod Cameron; Roland Got; Constance Worth; Nino Pipitone; Noel Cravat; ***D:*** William Witney.

The G-String Horror 🦴 **2012** A film crew is making a horror film in a haunted movie palace/strip club. Predictably the resident ghosts object and begin killing people in time honored fashion. **74m/C; DVD, Streaming.** Genna Darling; Mike Gleason; Debra Lamb; Trevor O'Donnell; Natasha Talonz; ***D:*** Charles Webb; ***M:*** Kevin MacLeod. **VIDEO**

G2: Mortal Conquest 🦴🦴 **1999 (R)** In the year 2003, Steven Colin (Bernhardt) unknowingly possesses the secret of an ancient martial arts power he learned in a former incarnation. Now the foes from the ancient battle have returned and Colin must remember his past if he's to save his present. **93m/C; VHS, DVD.** Daniel Bernhardt; James Hong; ***D:*** Nick Rotundo; ***W:*** Nick Rotundo; ***M:*** Gary Koftinoff. **VIDEO**

Gabbeh 🦴🦴🦴 ½ **1996** Gabbeh is not only the name of the film's heroine (Djobat), it is also the name of the finely embroidered woolen rugs that the nomadic Ghashgai tribe is known for. Gabbeh has a simple desire—she wishes to marry a mysterious horseman but her father keeps placing obstacles in her path. She tells her story to an old married couple, who are washing their own gabbeh in a stream. The film is visually lush but a challenge for Western sensibilities with its slow pace and allegorical content. Farsi with subtitles. **75m/C; VHS, DVD.** *IA* Shaghayeh Djodat; Hossein Moharami; Rogheih Moharami; Abbas Sayah; ***D:*** Mohsen Makhmalbaf; ***W:*** Mohsen Makhmalbaf; ***C:*** Mahmoud Kalari; ***M:*** Hossein Alizadeh.

The Gabby Douglas Story 🦴🦴 ½ **2014** Inspirational but routinely told Lifetime sports bio of Gabby Douglas, the teenaged African-American gymnast who won two gold medals at the 2012 London summer Olympics. Her struggling family sacrifices so Gabby can achieve her dream, even though this means the young girl moves to live with a host family in Iowa so she can train with a winning coach (Tee). **86m/C; DVD.** Imani Hakim; Sydney Mikayla; Regina King; Brian Tee; S. Epatha Merkerson; ***D:*** Gregg Champion; ***W:*** Maria Nation; ***C:*** Gordon C. Lonsdale; ***M:*** Robert Duncan. **CABLE**

Gabriel & Me 🦴 ½ **2001** Rather unlikeable characters (and strong accents) put a crimp in this family fantasy/drama. Jimmy Spud is 11 and lives with his working-class family in Newcastle. Jimmy wants to become an angel and prays about his job aspirations while in church, resulting in a visit from the archangel Gabriel. Jimmy's dad thinks he's daft but he's got bigger problems—lung cancer—so Jimmy decides Gabriel can help him perform a miracle to save his dad. Adapted from a radio play. **84m/C; DVD.** *GB* Billy Connolly; Iain Glen; Rosie Rowell; David Bradley; Jordan Routledge; Sean Landless; Ian Cullen; ***D:*** Udayan Prasad; ***W:*** Lee Hall; ***C:*** Alan Almond; ***M:*** Stephen Warbeck.

Gabriel Over the White House 🦴🦴🦴 **1933** Part political satire, part fantasy, and completely fascinating. Huston is venal politician Judson Hammond, completely in thrall to his crooked cohorts, who manages to get elected President. While recuperating from an auto accident Hammond thinks he sees a vision of the Archangel Gabriel, who essentially tells him to change his crooked ways. From bought man Hammond changes to righteous do-gooder, much to the dismay of his criminal companions, who'll stop at nothing to get rid of the man they think has simply gone insane. Huston gives a powerful performance in this decidedly oddball film. **86m/B; VHS, DVD.** Walter Huston; Karen Morley; Arthur Byron; Franchot Tone; Dickie Moore; C. Henry Gordon; David Landau; Samuel S. Hinds; Jean Parker; ***D:*** Gregory La Cava; ***W:*** Carey Wilson.

Gabriela 🦴🦴 **1984 (R)** A sultry romance develops between a Brazilian tavern keeper and the new cook he's just hired. Derived from Jorge Amado's novel. In Portuguese with English subtitles. **102m/C; VHS, Streaming.** *BR* Sonia Braga; Marcello Mastroianni; Nelson Xavier; Antonio Cantafora; ***D:*** Bruno Barreto; ***W:*** Bruno Barreto; ***C:*** Carlo Di Palma; ***M:*** Antonio Carlos.

Gabriela 🦴🦴 ½ **2001 (R)** Student Gabriela (Lopez) takes a job at a mental health clinic where she meets social worker Mike (Gomez). She's pretty, he's handsome, there's a strong mutual attraction but Gabriela is engaged to Pat (Galligan) even though she doesn't really love him and only agreed to please her strict mother (Fernandez). So will this twosome manage to overcome their romantic obstacles and be together? Expect the expected. **93m/C; VHS, DVD.** Seidy Lopez; Jaime Gomez; Zach Galligan; Troy Winbush; Evelina Fernandez; Lupe Ontiveros; Stacy Haiduk; ***D:*** Vincent Jay Miller; ***W:*** Vincent Jay Miller; ***C:*** Adrian Rudomin; ***M:*** Craig Stuart Garfinkle.

Gabrielle 🦴🦴 ½ **2005** French superstars give this highly stylized French period piece some bite despite one set and a whole lot of arguing, crying, and talking. Wealthy publisher Jean (Gregory) is living the high life, complete with a statue-filled mansion, an army of servants and a beautiful but dissatisfied wife, Gabrielle, (Huppert) with whom he barely has a relationship. Gabrielle upsets their high-end facade when she leaves her husband a Dear John letter, only to inexplicably return just as he begins to digest its contents. The bulk of the film is spent watching, sometimes painfully, as the two dissect their phony marriage and sacrifices in the name of appearances. Based on the short story, "The Return," by Joseph Conrad. **90m/C; DVD.** *FR GE IT* Isabelle Huppert; Pascal Greggory; Chantal Neuwirth; Claudia Coli; Thierry Hancisse; Thierry Fortineau; Louise Vincent; Clement Hervieu-Leger; ***D:*** Patrice

Chereau; *W:* Patrice Chereau; Anne-Louise Trividic; *C:* Eric Gautier; *M:* Fabio Vacchi.

Gabrielle 2013 (R) Les Muses de Montreal is a choir made up of singers with special needs. One of the most outgoing and happy members is Gabrielle (Rivard) - a 22-year-old woman born with low cognitive development, but advanced musical abilities. She's fallen in love with fellow singer Martin (Landy), whose mother thinks neither of them can handle the complications of a relationship, and does her best to keep them apart. Canadian director Archambault skillfully balances the line between after school fluff and honest views on sexuality. Predictably sweet, in the best way. French with subtitles. **104m/C; DVD.** *CA* Gabrielle Marion-Rivard; Alexandre Landry; Marie Gignac; Melissa Desormeaux-Poulin; Vincent-Guillaume Otis; *D:* Louise Archambault; *W:* Louise Archambault; *C:* Matthieu Laverdiere; *M:* Francois Lafontaine.

Gainsbourg: A Heroic Life *Gainsbourg: Vie Heroique* **2010** A French phenomenon, the singer, of Russian-Jewish parentage, was haunted by his upbringing in Nazi-occupied Paris. Serge pays for art school by working as a cafe piano player and finds his way as a songwriter and performer. His appetite for women, including Brigitte Bardot and Jane Birkin, scandal, alcohol, and cigarettes lead to a constant, losing battle with his personal demons. French with subtitles. **122m/C; DVD, Blu-Ray.** *FR* Eric Elmosnino; Kacey Mottet Klein; Doug Jones; Deborah Grall; Anna Mouglalis; Laetitia Casta; Lucy Gordon; Sara Forestier; Mylene Jampanoi; Philippe Katerine; *D:* Joann Sfar; *W:* Joann Sfar; *C:* Guillaume Schiffman; *M:* Olivier Daviaud.

Galactic Gigolo WOOF! **1987 (R)** An alien broccoli (yes, the vegetable) descends to earth on vacation, and discovers he's irresistible to Connecticut women. Must be something in the water. Amateurish effort intended as science-fiction satire, but there's more sleaze than humor. **80m/C; DVD.** Carmine Capobianco; Debi Thibeault; Ruth (Coreen) Collins; Angela Nicholas; Frank Stewart; *D:* Gorman Bechard.

Galaxina 1/2 **1980 (R)** In the 31st century, a beautiful robot woman capable of human feelings is created. Stumbling parody of superspace fantasies features murdered Playmate Stratten in one of few film appearances. **95m/C; VHS, DVD, Blu-Ray.** Dorothy Stratten; Avery Schreiber; Stephen Macht; James D. Hinton; Ronald J. Knight; Lionel Mark Smith; Tad Horino; Herb Kaplowitz; Nancy McCauley; *D:* William Sachs; *W:* William Sachs; *C:* Dean Cundey.

Galaxy Invader **1985 (PG)** Chaos erupts when an alien explorer crash lands his spacecraft in a backwoods area of the United States. **79m/C; VHS, DVD.** Richard Ruxton; Faye Tilles; Don Leifert; *D:* Donald M. Dohler; *W:* Donald M. Dohler.

Galaxy of Terror 1/2 *Mindwarp: An Infinity of Terror; Planet of Horrors* **1981 (R)** Astronauts sent to rescue a stranded spaceship get killed by vicious aliens. Big first: Moran (Joanie on "Happy Days") explodes. Inferior Corman-produced "Alien" imitation still manages to shock and displays generous gore. Followed by "Forbidden World." **85m/C; VHS, DVD, Blu-Ray.** Erin Moran; Edward Albert; Ray Walston; Grace Zabriskie; Zalman King; Taaffe O'Connell; Robert Englund; Bernard Behrens; Jack Blessing; Sid Haig; *D:* Bruce (B.D.) Clark; *W:* Bruce (B.D.) Clark; Mark Siegler; *C:* Jacques Haitkin; *M:* Barry Schrader.

Galaxy Quest 1/2 **1999 (PG)** An ingratiating goof on "Star Trek" and other cheesy TV shows that draw rabid fans and typecast actors. At a sci-fi convention, the actors from the campy '70s TV space series "Galaxy Quest" are mistaken for real space traveling heroes by naive aliens who need them to aid in an intergalactic war and whisk the troupe off to a galaxy far, far away (or thereabouts). Naturally, the "crew" is ill-prepared for their latest mission. Playful acting includes Allen's vain leader Peter Nesmith, blond bosomy babe Gwen DeMarco (Weaver), and cynical Brit, Alexander Dane (Rickman). **104m/C; VHS, DVD, Blu-Ray.** Tim Allen; Sigourney Weaver; Alan Rickman; Tony Shalhoub; Sam Rockwell; Daryl (Chill) Mitchell; Robin Sachs; Enrico Colantoni; Missi Pyle; *D:* Dean Parisot; *W:* David Howard; Robert Gordon; *C:* Jerzy Zielinski; *M:* David Newman.

Gale Force 1/2 **2001 (R)** The reality TV show "Treasure Hunt" involves eight contestants, one of whom is L.A. detective Sam Garrett (Williams), competing to find 10 million buried on the remote island on which they are marooned. But Sam is suspicious of executive producer Stuart McMahon (DeYoung), who'll do anything for ratings, and show host Jack MacRae (Nozick), who has a plot to get the money for himself. Oh, and then Mother Nature decides to make things even more interesting. Lots of action, including a good storm sequence. Wynorski directs under his Jay Andrews pseudonym. **96m/C; VHS, DVD.** Treat Williams; Michael Dudikoff; Tim Thomerson; Curtis Armstrong; Cliff DeYoung; Bruce Nozick; *D:* Jim Wynorski. **VIDEO**

The Gallant Hours **1960** Biography of Admiral "Bull" Halsey (Cagney) covers five weeks, October 18 through December 1, 1942, in the WWII battle of Guadalcanal in the South Pacific. Director Montgomery forgoes battle scenes to focus on the human elements in a war and what makes a great leader. Fine performance by Cagney. **115m/B; VHS, DVD, Blu-Ray.** James Cagney; Dennis Weaver; Ward (Edward) Costello; Richard Jaeckel; Les Tremayne; Robert Burton; Raymond Bailey; Karl Swenson; Harry Landers; James T. Goto; Walter Sande; Vaughn Taylor; Leon Lontoc; Carleton Young; James Yagi; Carl Benton Reid; Selmer Jackson; Nelson Leigh; John McKee; Tyler McVey; William Schallert; John Zaremba; Richard Carlyle; Herbert Lylton; Sydney Smith; Art Gilmore; *D:* Robert Montgomery; *W:* Frank D. Gilroy; Beirne Lay, Jr.; *C:* Joe MacDonald; *M:* Roger Wagner.

Gallant Lady **1933** In this weepie melodrama, unwed mother Sally (Harding) is aided by alcoholic ex-doctor Dan (Brook) in placing her son with friends of his. Years later, she discovers that her son's (Moore) adoptive mother has died, she tries to get close to his father, Philip (Kruger), in hopes of a happy ending. **84m/B; DVD.** Ann Harding; Clive Brook; Otto Kruger; Dickie Moore; Janet Beecher; Betty Lawford; *D:* Gregory La Cava; *W:* Sam Mintz; *C:* J. Peverell Marley; *M:* Alfred Newman.

Gallant Sons 1/2 **1940** Johnny Davis (Reynolds) and his best pal Byron Newbold (Cooper) have a falling out when Johnny's gambler dad Harlan (Hunter) is sent to prison for murder. Johnny is convinced his dad is innocent and that it was thanks to sensational newspaper stories by Bryon's dad Barton (Watson) that got the conviction. Byron and Johnny's friends play sleuth to get the real killer and put on a play that mirrors their suspicions to get the person to confess. **76m/B; DVD.** Jackie Cooper; Gene Reynolds; Ian Hunter; Minor Watson; Bonita Granville; Tommy Kelly; William Tracy; Leo Gorcey; June Preisser; Gail Patrick; *D:* George B. Seitz; *W:* William R. Lipman; Marion Parsonnet; *C:* Sidney Wagner; *M:* David Snell.

Gallery of Horrors *Dr. Terror's Gallery of Horrors* **1967** Really low-budget AIP horror anthology with lots of stock footage to fill in the scenery. Carradine serves as narrator and also appears in "The Witch's Clock" about a cursed antique clock. A doctor (Chaney) brings an executed killer back from the dead in "A Spark of Life." A corpse comes back to life in "Monster Raid." And Dracula appears in "Count Alucard" and "King of the Vampires." **83m/C; DVD.** John Carradine; Lon Chaney, Jr.; Mitch Evans; Roger Gentry; Vic McGee; Karen Joy; Ron Doyle; *D:* David L. Hewitt; *W:* David Prentiss; Gary Heacock; *C:* Austin McKinney.

Gallipoli **1981 (PG)** History blends with the destiny of two friends as they become part of the legendary WWI confrontation between Australia and the German-allied Turks. A superbly filmed, gripping commentary on the wastes of war. Haunting score; excellent performances by Lee and a then-unknown Gibson. Remake of a lesser 1931 effort "Battle of Gallipoli." **111m/C; VHS, DVD.** *AU* Mel Gibson; Mark Lee; Bill Kerr; David Argue; Tim McKenzie; Robert Grubb; Graham Dow; Stan Green; Heath Harris; Harold Hopkins; Charles Yunupingu; Ronny Graham; Gerda Nicolson; *D:* Peter Weir; *W:* Peter Weir; David Williamson; *C:* Russell Boyd; *M:* Brian May. Australian Film Inst. '81: Actor (Gibson), Film.

The Galloping Ghost 1/2 **1931** A 12-chapter serial starring football great "Red" Grange about big games, gambling, and underworld gangs. Grange is ousted from football when he's accused of throwing a game and he sets out to prove his innocence. **226m/B; VHS, DVD.** Harold "Red" Grange; Dorothy Gulliver; Walter Miller; Tom Dugan; *D:* B. Reeves Eason.

The Gallows *Superstition* **2015 (R)** It's been 20 years since a horrific backstage accident killed a young man during a school play in a small town. To mark the anniversary, someone who's never seen a horror movie before decides to resurrect the same play on which the young man was working when he died. We all know how this is going to turn out. And yet the found footage style of this movie is even more aggressively annoying than anyone would expect. It's just boring, shaky-cam nonsense, the kind of which you've seen literally four dozen times before. It's not scary, not fun, and not good. **87m/C; DVD, Blu-Ray, Streaming.** Reese Mishler; Pfeifer Brown; Ryan Shoos; Cassidy Gifford; Travis Cluff; *D:* Travis Cluff; Chris Lofing; *W:* Travis Cluff; Chris Lofing; *C:* Edd Lukas; *M:* Zach Lemmon.

The Gallows Act II **2019 (R)** Teen Auna Rue (Horvath) transfers to a prestigious school and quickly becomes an important part of its drama program. Her rise in prominence, as well as in her social standing, come after she does a monologue from a cursed play, "The Gallows," which unleashes evil when performed. Auna also gains internet infamy when she read a passage from the play as part of the Charlie Challenge. Her actions change her life and those around her in unexpected ways. The low budget horror sequel is horrifying atrocious. **99m/C; DVD.** Ema Horvath; Chris Milligan; Brittany Falardeau; Pfeifer Brown; Erika Miranda; *D:* Travis Cluff; Chris Lofing; *W:* Travis Cluff; Chris Lofing; *C:* Kyle Gentz; *M:* Zach Lemmon.

Gambit 1/2 **1966** Caine's first Hollywood film casts him as a burglar who develops a "Topkapi"-style scheme to steal a valuable statue with MacLaine as the lure and Lom as the equally devious owner. Once Caine's careful plan is put into operation, however, everything begins to unravel. **109m/C; VHS, DVD.** Shirley MacLaine; Michael Caine; Herbert Lom; Roger C. Carmel; *D:* Ronald Neame; *W:* Alvin Sargent; Jack Davies; *M:* Maurice Jarre.

Gambit 1/2 **2012 (PG-13)** Uninspired sort of remake of the 1966 caper comedy written (but not directed) by the Coen brothers that unsuccessfully tries to play on broad stereotypes for laughs. Mild-mannered art dealer Harry (Firth) is tired of being abused by his philistine billionaire boss, Shabandar (Rickman), so he decides to trick him into buying a forgery of a Monet painting. The forger (Courtenay) is in place but Harry needs the help of loud-mouthed Texan PJ (Diaz) and her tenuous connection to the actual art work to sell the con. Diaz and Firth have little chemistry, which also limits their putative romantic gestures. **89m/C; DVD, Blu-Ray.** *UK* Colin Firth; Cameron Diaz; Alan Rickman; Tom Courtenay; Cloris Leachman; Stanley Tucci; Togo Igawa; Julian Rhind-Tutt; *D:* Michael Hoffman; *W:* Joel Coen; Ethan Coen; *C:* Florian Ballhaus; *M:* Rolfe Kent. **VIDEO**

The Gamble **1988 (R)** A young man (Modine) seeks to rescue his father from gambling debts by wagering himself against a lustful countess (Dunaway). When he loses the bet, however, he flees and joins up with a runaway (Beals) with the countess and her henchmen in close pursuit. **108m/C; VHS, DVD.** Matthew Modine; Jennifer Beals; Faye Dunaway; *D:* Carlo Vanzina.

The Gambler **1974 (R)** College professor Axel Freed has a gambling problem so vast that it nearly gets him killed by his bookies. He goes to Las Vegas to recoup his losses and wins big, only to blow the money on stupid sports bets that get him deeper into trouble. Excellent character study of a compulsive loser on a downward spiral. **111m/C; VHS, DVD.** James Caan; Lauren Hutton; Paul Sorvino; Burt Young; James Woods; Jacqueline Brookes; M. Emmet Walsh; *D:* Karel Reisz; *W:* James Toback; *C:* Victor Kemper; *M:* Jerry Fielding.

The Gambler **1997** In St. Petersburg in 1866, Russian writer Dostoyevsky (Gambon) is a middle-aged compulsive gambler who is currently indebted to his publisher Stellovsky (Jansen) and must now write a new novel in 27 days to pay him off. He hires poverty-stricken Anna (May) to be his secretary and the dictated novel turns out to be the story of a gambling couple who are trying to get out of hock at a German resort. The real and fictional intertwine as Anna becomes more and more protective of Dostoyevsky and is determined to help him succeed. **97m/C; VHS, DVD.** *GB NL HU* Michael Gambon; Jodhi May; Polly Walker; Dominic West; Luise Rainer; John Wood; Johan Leysen; Thom Jansen; Angeline Ball; *D:* Karoly Makk; *W:* Charles Cohen; Nick Dear; Katharine Odgen; *C:* Jules Van Den Steenhoven; *M:* Brian Lock.

The Gambler **2014 (R)** Wahlberg stars in the James Caan role in this remake of the '70s drama from Rupert Wyatt. The title character, Jim Bennett, is a literature professor with a serious gambling addiction. Now in debt thousands of dollars to multiple nefarious types (including Williams and Goodman), Bennett struggles to keep his head above water and his legs from being broken. Wyatt sketches an interesting portrait of a man who doesn't believe in the middle ground—life is win/lose proposition—and how that leads to extreme, dangerous behavior. The problem is Wahlberg's flat style doesn't work for the character. **111m/C; DVD, Blu-Ray.** Mark Wahlberg; John Goodman; Brie Larson; Jessica Lange; Michael K(enneth) Williams; Alvin Ing; *D:* Rupert Wyatt; *W:* William Monahan; *C:* Greig Fraser; *M:* Jon Brion; Theo Green.

The Gambler & the Lady 1/2 **1952** A successful London-based gambler and casino owner endeavors to climb the social ladder by having an affair with a member of the British aristocracy. He not only has to contend with his jilted nightclub singer girlfriend but also with the gangsters who would like to take over his clubs. Dull direction and a mediocre script. **72m/B; VHS, DVD.** *GB* Dane Clark; Naomi Chance; Kathleen Byron; Meredith Edwards; Eric Pohlmann; George Pastell; *D:* Patrick Jenkins; Sam Newfield; *W:* Sam Newfield; *C:* Walter J. (Jimmy W.) Harvey; *M:* Ivor Slaney.

The Gambler from Natchez 1/2 **1954** Colorful western takes place in the 1840s. Army Capt. Vance Colby (Robertson) returns home to find his gambler father dead. The police insist he cheated at a card game, but Vance knows better and is going to clear his father's name and get revenge. **88m/C; DVD.** Dale Robertson; Debra Paget; Thomas Gomez; Kevin McCarthy; Douglas Dick; John Wengraf; *D:* Henry Levin; *W:* Gerald Drayson Adams; Irving Wallace; *C:* Lloyd Ahern; *M:* Lionel Newman.

The Gambler Returns: The Luck of the Draw 1/2 **1993** You'll see lots of familiar western TV stars as Rogers returns yet again as debonair gambler Brady Hawkes. This time he's on a cross country trip to San Francisco and the biggest card game around—only some varmints are out to stop him playing that first hand. **180m/C; VHS, DVD.** Kenny Rogers; Reba McEntire; Rick Rossovich; Chuck Connors; Patrick Macnee; Linda Evans; James Drury; Mickey Rooney; Jere Burns; Clint Walker; Claude Akins; Gene Barry; Doug McClure; Hugh O'Brian; Brian Keith; Park Overall; Jack Kelly; David Carradine; Johnny Crawford; Marianne Rogers; *D:* Dick Lowry. **TV**

The Gambler, the Girl and the Gunslinger 1/2 **2009** In this Hallmark Channel western Cain steals every scene as smooth-talking 1860s gambler Shea McCall. He wins half-ownership of a ranch, much to the dismay of the other half-owner, semi-retired gunslinger B.J. Stoker (Tupper). McCall then causes a romantic kerfuffle when he flirts with Stoker's widowed neighbor Liz (Hossack). However, trouble with some would-be land grabbers turns them into reluctant allies. **90m/C; DVD.** Dean Cain; James Tupper; Allison Hossack; Michael Eklund; Keith Mackechnie; *D:* Anne Wheeler; *W:* Larry Cohen; Bob Barbash; *C:* Paul Mitchnick. **CABLE**

Gambler's Choice ✂✂ **1944** A police lieutenant and his boyhood friend find themselves on opposite sides of the law in this crime drama. Even though both men are romantically involved with the same woman, their friendship remains intact. **66m/B; VHS, DVD.** Chester Morris; Nancy Kelly; Russell Hayden; Sheldon Leonard; Lee Patrick; Lloyd Corrigan; Tom Dugan; Lyle Talbot; Charles Arnt; *D:* Frank McDonald; *W:* Maxwell Shane; Irving Reis; James Edward Grant; Howard Emmett Rogers; *C:* Fred H. Jackman, Jr.

Gambling Daughters ✂ 1/2 **1941** Diana and Lillian attend a private girls school but while snooping into Prof. Bedoin's off-campus life, they get mixed up with crooked gambler Chance Landon at his roadhouse. After losing some major money, Chance threatens the gals unless they steal jewelry from their wealthy families to pay off their debts. This brings in insurance investigator Jimmy Parker and he turns sleuth to figure out what's going on. **65m/B; DVD.** Cecilia Parker; Gale Storm; Roger Pryor; Robert Baldwin; Sig Arno; Janet Shaw; Charles Miller; *D:* Max Nosseck; *W:* Joel Kay; Arnold Phillips; *C:* Mack Stengler.

The Game ✂✂✂ **1997 (R)** Investment banker Nicholas Van Orton (Douglas) is an uptight corporate control freak. He receives a dangerous birthday present from his black-sheep younger brother Conrad (Penn). It's a subscription to Consumer Recreation Services, a real life-and-death version of a role-playing game that is designed to tap the hidden emotional and physical resources of the client. His life is overrun with an escalating series of traps and terrors, with the game reaching into every facet of his life. Excellent portrayal by Douglas as a man stuck in a Hitchcockian nightmare. **128m/C; VHS, DVD, Blu-Ray, HD-DVD.** Michael Douglas; Sean Penn; Deborah Kara Unger; Armin Mueller-Stahl; James Rebhorn; Peter Donat; Carroll Baker; Anna (Katerina) Katarina; *D:* David Fincher; *W:* John Brancato; Michael Ferris; *C:* Harris Savides; *M:* Howard Shore.

Game Change ✂✂ 1/2 **2012** Sarah Palin objected to Moore's portrayal but most viewers will probably think she's spot-on in this HBO behind-the-scenes docudrama about the game changing vice-presidential choice for John McCain's (Harris) 2008 presidential campaign. GOP strategist Steve Schmidt (Harrelson), among others, came to regret their controversial choice as the hastily-vetted and ill-prepared Palin became an object of both ridicule and sympathy in a shrill, cynical political world. Based on the campaign book by John Heilemann and Mark Halperin. **118m/C; DVD, Blu-Ray.** Julianne Moore; Woody Harrelson; Ed Harris; Peter MacNichol; Jamey Sheridan; Sarah Paulson; Ron Livingston; Bruce Altman; *D:* Jay Roach; *W:* Danny Strong; *C:* Jim Denault; *M:* Theodore Shapiro. **CABLE**

The Game Is Over ✂✂ 1/2 *La Curee* **1966 (R)** A wealthy neglected wife falls in love with her grown stepson, causing her to divorce her husband and shatter her life. A good performance by Fonda, then Vadim's wife. Modern version of Zola's "La Curee." **96m/C; VHS, DVD.** *FR* Jane Fonda; Peter McEnery; Michel Piccoli; Tina Aumont; *D:* Roger Vadim; *W:* Roger Vadim; *C:* Claude Renoir; *M:* Jean Bouchety.

Game Night ✂✂ 1/2 **2018 (R)** A surprisingly deep and definitely fun comedy about a game night gone sideways. Suburban couple Max (Bateman) and Annie (McAdams) regularly host a game night with long-time friends. When Max's estranged and seemingly more successful brother Brooks (Chandler) takes part one night, Brooks invites everyone to his own game night. Brooks hosts a murder mystery dinner party but is kidnapped in a home invasion before it can begin and everyone is told that he will be killed unless they deliver a specific Faberge egg. It becomes clear that Brooks was really kidnapped and the players must work to save him. **100m/C; DVD, Blu-Ray.** Jason Bateman; Rachel McAdams; Kyle Chandler; Sharon Horgan; Billy Magnussen; *D:* John Francis Daley; Jonathan Goldstein; *W:* Mark Perez; *C:* Barry Peterson; *M:* Cliff Martinez.

Game of Death ✂✂ *Goodbye Bruce Lee: His Last Game of Death; Bruce Lee's Game of Death* **1979 (R)** Bruce Lee's final kung fu thriller about a young martial arts movie star who gets involved with the syndicate. Lee died halfway through the filming of this movie and it was finished with out-takes and a double. **100m/C; VHS, DVD, Blu-Ray.** Bruce Lee; Dean Jagger; Kareem Abdul-Jabbar; Colleen Camp; Chuck Norris; *D:* Robert Clouse; *M:* John Barry.

Game of Death ✂ 1/2 **2010 (R)** Familiar, forgettable thriller. CIA hitman Marcus Jones (Snipes) is doublecrossed, framed for murder, and targeted by killers. Trying to clear his name leads to a cat-and-mouse situation in a Detroit hospital. **86m/C; DVD, Blu-Ray.** Wesley Snipes; Zoe Bell; Gary Daniels; Robert Davi; Quinn Duffy; *D:* Giorgio Serafini; *W:* Jim Agnew; Megan Brown; *C:* Erik Curtis; *M:* Jesse Voccia. **VIDEO**

Game of Seduction ✂ *Une Femme Fidele* **1976** A murdering, womanizing playboy pursues a married woman and gets caught up in a treacherous cat-and-mouse game. Dubbed. **81m/C; VHS, DVD.** *FR* Sylvia Kristel; Jon Finch; Nathalie Delon; *D:* Roger Vadim; *W:* Roger Vadim; Daniel Boulanger; *C:* Claude Renoir; *M:* Pierre Porte.

The Game of Their Lives ✂ **2005 (PG)** Bland account of the United States' long-shot 1950 soccer team—a hodgepodge of players haphazardly rounded up—that jolted a heavily superior English team in the first round of the World Cup in Brazil. Weak script that, while it scores on facts, gives the cast of mostly cookie-cut pretty boys very little to get fired up about. **101m/C; DVD.** Gerard Butler; Wes Bentley; Jay Rodan; Gavin Rossdale; Costas Mandylor; Louis Mandylor; Zachery Ty Bryan; Patrick Stewart; Jimmy Jean-Louis; Terry Kinney; John Rhys-Davies; Marilyn Dodds Frank; Richard Jenik; Bill Smitrovich; *D:* David Anspaugh; *W:* Angelo Pizzo; *C:* Johnny E. Jensen; *M:* William Ross.

Game of Your Life ✂✂ 1/2 **2011** NBC TV family action-drama. High school gamer Zach Taylor wins a college scholarship to the prestigious Digital Institute of Game Design. The freshman project he must complete weeds out about half the class and then Zach discovers his dad Bill is in financial trouble. An overwhelmed Zach works with would-be mentor Marcus Bentton on a side project that the teen suspects is shady business. **90m/C; DVD.** Titus Maklin, Jr.; Tom Nowicki; Lea Thompson; Thom Gossom, Jr.; Nathan Kress; *D:* John Kent Harrison; *W:* John Kent Harrison; *C:* William Wages; *M:* Lawrence Shragge. **TV**

The Game Plan ✂ 1/2 **2007 (PG)** The Rock is the only one who scores in this Disney retread. Swaggering star quarterback Joe Kingman (Johnson) suddenly finds his bachelor lifestyle cramped by the sudden arrival of Peyton (Pettis), the eight-year-old daughter he never knew he had. In a premise that only Disney could serve up, Peyton is from a previous marriage, although the idea that somehow Joe had no idea that his ex-wife had a child is not the most ridiculous aspect of the movie. This sets up an endless series of gags based on Joe not knowing how to interact with a little girl or, really, anyone outside of his agent (Sedgwick). Johnson's charm is undeniable, and Pettis is button-cute, but the rest is lukewarm family fare. **110m/C; DVD, Blu-Ray.** Dwayne "The Rock" Johnson; Kyra Sedgwick; Roselyn Sanchez; Morris Chestnut; Madison Pettis; Brian White; Paige Turco; Gordon Clapp; Hayes MacArthur; Jamal Duff; Jackie Flynn; *D:* Andy Fickman; *W:* Nichole Millard; Kathryn Price; *C:* Greg Gardiner; *M:* Nathan Wang.

Game 6 ✂✂ 1/2 **2005 (R)** It's October 25, 1986, and Nicky (Keaton) has quite the dilemma—should he attend his play's opening night or watch his beloved Bosox battle the New York Mets in the soon-to-be-legendary game six of the World Series? With his crumbling marriage (having a mistress doesn't help), distant daughter, stalled career, and a cutthroat theater critic set to make or break his new work, he feels just as wrapped in failure as his once-cursed baseball team. Keaton cleanly fields his distressed-man act but the story flubs the grounder. **87m/C; DVD.** Michael Keaton; Robert Downey, Jr.; Griffin Dunne; Catherine O'Hara; Bebe Neuwirth; Shalom Harlow; Roger Rees; Ari Graynor; Nadia Dajani; Harris Yulin; Tom Aldredge; Lillias White; Amir Ali Said; *D:* Michael Hoffman; *W:* Don DeLillo; *C:* David M. Dunlap; *M:* Yo La Tengo.

Game Time: Tackling the Past ✂✂ 1/2 **2011** In this football/family drama, Jake Walker (McPartlin) left his North Carolina hometown after high school and eventually found success as an NFL quarterback for 10 years. His career is in question because of a bum knee and he returns home for the first time in years when his high school coach dad Frank (Bridges) is hospitalized for heart surgery. Jake didn't leave on good terms and, when his contract isn't picked up, he has a chance to make amends by helping out his brother Dean (Braaten), the team's assistant coach, who must take over the so-so team and lead them to victory. **90m/C; DVD.** Ryan McPartlin; Beau Bridges; Josh Braaten; Catherine Hicks; Lisa Varga; Katie Carr; Maxwell Perry Cotton; *D:* Douglas Barr; *W:* Brian Bird; *C:* Peter Benison; *M:* Eric Allaman. **TV**

Gamebox 1.0 ✂✂ **2004 (PG-13)** Video game tester Charlie gets hooked on a new virtual-reality system that's plugged directly into a user's brain. The object is to rescue the Princess, who looks suspiciously like Charlie's dead girlfriend. The game infests Charlie's brain so the only way for him to survive is to win. The CGI's not bad considering the low budget, but the story's formulaic. **83m/C; DVD.** Danielle Fishel; Patrick Kilpatrick; Patrick Cavanaugh; Nate Richert; *D:* David Hillenbrand; Scott Hillenbrand; *W:* Patrick Casey; Worm Miller; *C:* Philip D. Schwartz. **VIDEO**

Gamer ✂✂ *Game* **2009 (R)** Performing in the online game "Slayers" is death row inmate Kable (the ever-so-macho Butler)--a controlled avatar of 17-year-old virtual game master Simon (Lerman)--who gets closer to winning his freedom with each violent and victorious battle he endures. Meanwhile, his desperate wife is an avatar forced to act out the deviant sexual desires in another game, all created by Ken Castle (Hall) who has grown filthy rich in the process. But a hacker resistance group threatens the whole operation. Lost amidst the not-unexpected hyper action of writers/directors Neveldine and Taylor is the message that technology isn't always such a good thing. **95m/C; Blu-Ray, On Demand.** Gerard Butler; Michael C. Hall; Milo Ventimiglia; Alison Lohman; Amber Valletta; Logan Lerman; Kyra Sedgwick; John Leguizamo; Terry Crews; Zoe Bell; *D:* Mark Neveldine; Brian Taylor; *W:* Mark Neveldine; Brian Taylor; *C:* Ekkehart Pollack; *M:* Robert Williamson; Geoff Zanelli.

Gamera the Brave ✂✂ 1/2 *Gamera: Chiisaki yusha-tachi; Gamera: Little Braves* **2006** The original Gamera films were targeted at youngsters, while the redone series from the 1990s were more for adults. This sequel to the newer trilogy returns to its kid-oriented roots while retaining the higher production values. A young boy raises a newly hatched turtle, which turns out to be a baby Gamera. Thank goodness, because a man-eating monster has just appeared and there's a need for another giant critter to fight him, as the world's military is apparently capable of nuking countries, but can't put down one really big salamander. **96m/C; DVD, Blu-Ray.** *JP* Kanji Tsuda; Susumu Terajima; Kaho; *D:* Ryuta Tazaki; *W:* Yukari Tatsui.

Gamera, the Invincible ✂ 1/2 *Gamera; Gammera; Daikaiju Gamera* **1966** This Japanese monster flick features the ultimate nuclear super-turtle who flies around destroying cities and causing panic. First in the series of notoriously bad films, this one is cool in black and white and has some impressive special effects. Dubbed in English. **86m/B; VHS, DVD, Blu-Ray.** *JP* Eiji Funakoshi; Harumi Kiritachi; Junichiro Yamashiko; Yoshiro Uchida; Brian Donlevy; Albert Dekker; Diane Findlay; John Baragrey; Dick O'Neill; *D:* Noriaki Yuasa; *W:* Fumi Takahashi; *C:* Nobuo Munekawa.

Gamera vs. Barugon ✂ 1/2 *Gamera Tai Barugon; Gambara vs. Barugon; The War of the Monsters* **1966** The monstrous turtle returns to Earth from his outer space prison, now equipped with his famous leg-jets. He soon wishes he had stayed airborne, however, when he is forced to do battle with 130-foot lizard Barugon and his rainbow-melting ray. Tokyo and Osaka get melted in the process. **101m/C; VHS, DVD, Blu-Ray.** *JP* Kojiro Hongo; Kyoko Enami; *D:* Shigeo Tanaka.

Gamera vs. Gaos ✂ 1/2 *The Return of the Giant Monsters; Gamera vs. Gyaos; Boyichi and the Supermonster; Gamera Tai Gaos* **1967** Now fully the good guy, Gamera slugs it out with a bat-like critter named Gaos. Suspense rules the day when Gaos tries to put out the super turtle's jets with his built-in fire extinguisher but luckily for Earth, Gamera has a few tricks of his own up his shell. **87m/C; VHS, DVD, Blu-Ray.** *JP* Kojiro Hongo; Kichijiro Ueda; Naoyuki Abe; *D:* Noriaki Yuasa.

Gamera vs. Guiron ✂ *Attack of the Monsters; Gamera Tai Guiron* **1969** Gamera risks it all to take on an evil, spear-headed monster on a distant planet. Highlight is the sexy, leotard clad aliens who want to eat the little Earth kids' brains. **88m/C; VHS, DVD, Blu-Ray.** *JP* Nobuhiro Kashima; Christopher Murphy; Miyuki Akiyama; Yuko Hamada; Eiji Funakoshi; *D:* Noriaki Yuasa.

Gamera vs. Zigra ✂ *Gamera Tai Shinkai Kaiju Jigara; Gamera vs. the Deep Sea Monster Zigra* **1971** Gamera the flying turtle chose an ecological theme for this, his final movie. It seems that the alien Zigrans have come to Earth to wrest the planet from the hands of the pollutive humans who have nearly destroyed it. The aliens kill the staunch turtle, but the love and prayers of children revive him that he may defend Earth once more. **91m/C; VHS, DVD, Blu-Ray.** *JP* Reiko Kasahara; Mikiko Tsubouchi; Koji Fujiyama; Arlene Zoellner; Gloria Zoellner; *D:* Noriaki Yuasa.

Gamers ✂ 1/2 **2006** If you're big into role-playing games you might find this mockumentary amusing, otherwise it's sorta weirdly disturbing. Five socially inept geeks—still living with their parents and working minimal effort jobs—are about to break the all-time record for the most hours spent playing "Demons, Nymphs, and Dragons." They have been playing for 23 years but the nearer they get to their goal, the more tensions arise within the group. **87m/C; DVD.** Scott Rinker; Dave Hanson; John Heard; Beverly D'Angelo; Kevin Kirkpatrick; Joe Nieves; Kevin Sherwood; *D:* Christopher Folino; *W:* Christopher Folino; *C:* Roberto Blasini; *M:* Tom Hite. **VIDEO**

Games ✂✂ 1/2 **1967** Bored married Manhattanites Paul (Caan) and Jennifer (Ross), who are looking for some kinky entertainment, get involved with amateur medium Lisa (Signoret). Suddenly what's "real," isn't and there's more than one double-cross to cope with. Lots of atmosphere but not enough suspense. **100m/C; VHS, DVD, Blu-Ray.** Simone Signoret; James Caan; Katharine Ross; Don Stroud; Kent Smith; Estelle Winwood; Marjorie Bennett; Ian Wolfe; **Cameo(s):** Florence Marly; Luana Anders; *D:* Curtis Harrington; *W:* Gene R. Kearney; *C:* William A. Fraker; *M:* Samuel Matlovsky.

Games Girls Play ✂ 1/2 *The Bunny Caper; Sex Play* **1975** The daughter of an American diplomat organizes a contest at a British boarding school to see which of her classmates can seduce important dignitaries. **90m/C; VHS, DVD.** Christina Hart; Jane Anthony; Jill Damas; Drina Pavlovic; *D:* Jack Arnold.

Games of Love and Chance ✂✂ *L'esquive* **2003** Centered around North African immigrant Krimo (Elkharraz), a closed-up teenager living in a Paris suburb whose emotional walls force girlfriend Magali (Ganito) to dump him. He quickly finds a new love interest in the extroverted Lydia (Forestier) and pushes his way into a school play to be near her. The camera provides a close view of the many effusive confrontations between the teenaged cast, all of whom are played by acting neophyte residents of the working class suburb where the film is set. Many of the themes explored are universal to the teen movie genre. This film, Kechiche's second effort, has been an award-winning hit in France. **119m/C; DVD.** *FR* Osman Elkharraz; Sara Forestier; Sabrina Ouazani; Nanou Benhamou; Aurelie Ganito; Rachid Hami; *D:* Abdellatif Kechiche; *W:* Abdellatif Kechiche; *C:* Lubomir Bakchev.

Gandhi ✂✂✂ 1/2 **1982 (PG)** The biography of Mahatma Gandhi, from the prejudice he encounters as a young attorney in South

Africa, to his role as spiritual leader to the people of India and his use of passive resistance against the country's British rulers, and his eventual assassination. Kingsley is a marvel in his Academy Award-winning role and the picture is a generally riveting epic worthy of its eight Oscars. **188m/C; VHS, DVD.** *GB* Ben Kingsley; Candice Bergen; Edward Fox; John Gielgud; John Mills; Saeed Jaffrey; Trevor Howard; Ian Charleson; Roshan Seth; Athol Fugard; Martin Sheen; Daniel Day-Lewis; Rohini Hattangadi; Ian Bannen; Geraldine James; Nigel Hawthorne; Om Puri; John Ratzenberger; ***D:*** Richard Attenborough; ***W:*** John Briley; ***C:*** Billy Williams; ***M:*** George Fenton. Oscars '82: Actor (Kingsley), Art Dir./Set Dec., Cinematog., Costume Des., Director (Attenborough), Film, Film Editing, Orig. Screenplay, Sound; British Acad. '82: Actor (Kingsley), Director (Attenborough), Film, Support. Actress (Hattangadi); Directors Guild '82: Director (Attenborough); Golden Globes '83: Actor--Drama (Kingsley), Director (Attenborough), Foreign Film, Screenplay; L.A. Film Critics '82: Actor (Kingsley); Natl. Bd. of Review '82: Actor (Kingsley); N.Y. Film Critics '82: Actor (Kingsley), Film.

Gandu 🦴🦴 **2010** An Indian indie drama about one young man's quest to become a rap star. Gandu (Basu) is angry about everything. An aspiring rapper, he talks about how much he hates life and his mother in his words. With his only friend, a rickshaw puller, Gandu tries to find his identity in a musical world where rap, porn, horror, fiction, surrealism, and the bizarre meet. However, this quest of personal discovery may come at a high price. Bengali with subtitles. **85m/B; DVD, Blu-Ray, Streaming, Download.** Anubrata Basu; Joyraj Bhattacharya; Rii; Kamalika Banerjee; Shilajit Majumdar; ***D:*** Qaushiq Mukherjee; ***W:*** Qaushiq Mukherjee; ***C:*** Qaushiq Mukherjee. **VIDEO**

Gang Boys 🦴 ½ **1997** When a young man is brutally beaten by an L.A. street gang, mom Blair does not take things lying down. She contacts her estranged, ex-cop husband Hauser and he organizes a group of local victims to fight back. This time it's the gang members who should watch out. **87m/C; VHS, DVD.** Wings Hauser; Linda Blair; Cole Hauser; Daryl Roach; Carmen Zapata; Ernest Harden, Jr.; Talbert Morton; Dave Buzzotta; ***D:*** Wings Hauser; ***W:*** Wings Hauser; Maria Dylan; ***C:*** Francis Grumman; ***M:*** Geoff Levin; Chris Many. **VIDEO**

Gang Busters 🦴🦴 **1942** Men battle crime in the city in this serial in 13 episodes based on the popular radio series of the same name. **253m/B; VHS, DVD.** Kent Taylor; Irene Hervey; Robert Armstrong; Ralph Morgan; Richard Davies; Ralf Harolde; ***D:*** Ray Taylor; Noel Mason Smith; ***W:*** Morgan Cox; Phillips Lord; Victor McLeod; George Plympton; ***C:*** John Boyle; William Sickner.

Gang Busters 🦴 ½ **1955** Prisoners plan a breakout. Slow and uninteresting adaptation of the successful radio series. Filmed in Oregon. **78m/B; VHS, DVD.** Myron Healey; Sam Edwards; Frank Gerstle; ***D:*** Bill Karn.

Gang in Blue 🦴🦴 ½ **1996 (R)** Black officer Michael Rhoades (Van Peebles) is secretly investigating a white supremacist group of cops, called the Phantoms, within the LAPD. Marine Corp vet and police rookie Keith DeBruler (Brolin) becomes Rhoades's new partner and his racial comments make him a likely initiate for the Phantoms. So can he be trusted to be Rhoades's inside man and help Michael expose the corruption within the ranks? **99m/C; VHS, DVD.** Mario Van Peebles; Josh Brolin; Melvin Van Peebles; J.T. Walsh; Cynda Williams; Stephen Lang; Sean McCann; ***D:*** Mario Van Peebles; Melvin Van Peebles; ***W:*** David Fuller; Rick Natkin; ***C:*** Rhett Morita; ***M:*** Larry Brown. **CABLE**

Gang Justice 🦴 **1994** Low-budget melodrama finds sensitive Asian student Paul (Kim) battling racists at school and his crippled alcoholic father at home. Some martial arts fight scenes but this is amateur time. **92m/C; VHS, DVD.** Joon Kim; Jonathan Gorman; Erik Estrada; Angel Dashek; ***D:*** Richard W. Park.

Gang of Roses 🦴🦴 **2003 (R)** In the old west, Rachel, Chasity, Kim, Ming Li, and Maria formed the Rose Gang. Successful bank robbers, they retired after five years but regroup when Rachel's sister is killed. **88m/C; VHS, DVD.** Monica Calhoun; Stacey Dash; LisaRaye; Marie Matiko; Kimberly (Lil' Kim) Jones; Bobby Brown; Louis Mandylor; ***C:*** Ben Kufrin; ***M:*** Michael Cohen. **VIDEO**

Gang Related 🦴 ½ **1996 (R)** Rodriguez (Shakur) and Divinci (Belushi) are a couple of scuzzball homicide cops who set up drug deals with impounded dope, then kill the customers. They keep the dope and the money, and call the murders "gang-related." Their plan unravels when they whack an undercover DEA agent posing as a dealer. They try to play a game of "pin the crime on the wino" with a derelict (Quaid) who the duo thinks is easy prey. As their scheming spins out of control, Rodriguez tries to hold things together, while Divinci rips them apart. Shakur rises above the average material as the most likable of the entirely distasteful cast of characters. **109m/C; VHS, DVD, Blu-Ray.** James Belushi; Tupac Shakur; Dennis Quaid; Lela Rochon; James Earl Jones; David Paymer; Wendy Crewson; Gary Cole; Terrence "T.C." Carson; Brad Greenquist; James Handy; Victor Love; Robert LaSardo; Gregory Scott Cummins; ***D:*** Jim Kouf; ***W:*** Jim Kouf; ***C:*** Brian Reynolds; ***M:*** Mickey Hart.

Gangland 🦴 **2000 (R)** In 2010 there's been a small nuclear disaster and a flesh-eating virus, and the survivors are essentially on their own. Jared (Mitchell) and Derek (Mandylor) are imprisoned by the local gang but they escape and hook up with fugitive Alexis (Kinmont). The trio decides payback is in order, especially when they discover that gang leader Lucifer (Klyn) is keeping the antidote to the virus all to himself. Don't get excited seeing Ice-T and Coolio on the box art because they play cops who get offed in the first scene. Talk about bait-and-switch. **93m/C; DVD.** Sasha Mitchell; Costas Mandylor; Kathleen Kinmont; Vincent Klyn; Tim Thomerson; Jennifer Gareis; Ice-T; Coolio; ***Cameo(s):*** Kristanna Loken; ***D:*** Art Camacho; ***W:*** David DeFalco; ***C:*** Andrea V. Rossotto; ***M:*** Thomas Morse. **VIDEO**

The Gang's All Here 🦴🦴 *The Girls He Left Behind* **1943** Produced smack in the middle of World War II, the film has (what else?) a war backdrop, but set to the tunes of Benny Goodman and his crew. On leave from his army post, playboy Andy Mason (Willock) falls for showgirl Edie Allen (Faye), sweeping her off her feet for an evening of romance that leaves her swooning, only to leave for duty the next morning. He returns, but with a secret. **103m/C; VHS, DVD, Blu-Ray.** Carmen Miranda; Phil Baker; Benny Goodman; Eugene Pallette; Charlotte Greenwood; Edward Everett Horton; James Ellison; Alice Faye; Dave Willock; Tony De Marco; ***D:*** Busby Berkeley; ***W:*** Nancy Wintner; George Root, Jr. Natl. Film Reg. '14.

Gangs, Inc. 🦴🦴 *Crimes, Inc.; Paper Bullets* **1941** A woman is sent to prison for a hit-and-run accident, actually the fault of a wealthy playboy. When she learns his identity she vows revenge and turns to crime to achieve her evil ends. Okay thriller suffers from plot problems. Ladd has a minor role filmed before he became a star. **72m/B; VHS, DVD.** Joan Woodbury; Jack LaRue; Linda Ware; John Archer; Vince Barnett; Alan Ladd; Gavin Gordon; Selmer Jackson; George Pembroke; ***D:*** Phil Rosen; ***W:*** Martin Mooney; ***C:*** Arthur Martinelli.

Gangs of New York 🦴🦴🦴 **2002 (R)** Scorsese's flawed but rich and powerful epic recounts the mid-19th Century struggles in New York's Five Points section between the Irish immigrant gang the Dead Rabbits and the second-generation nativist gangs led by the brutal but mesmerizing Bill the Butcher (Day-Lewis). Young Amsterdam Vallon (DeCaprio) witnesses the death of his father (Neeson), the leader of the Rabbits, in a bloody street melee and is sent away. When he returns, unrecognized, he insinuates himself into Bill's inner circle, waiting for his chance at vengeance and catching the eye of pickpocket Jenny (Diaz). This plot is set against the backdrop of the political corruption of "Boss" Tweed's New York empire and the draft riots that were tearing the city apart at the time. Scorsese's vision is realized through meticulous attention to period detail, a standout performance by Day-Lewis, and the willingness to show hero and villain alike as well-rounded characters. Uneven pacing and underuse (probably out of necessity) of excellent supporting cast are the only complaints. Loosely based on the 1928 book by Herbert Asbury. **168m/C; VHS, DVD, Blu-Ray.** Leonardo DiCaprio; Daniel Day-Lewis; Cameron Diaz; Liam Neeson; Jim Broadbent; John C. Reilly; Henry Thomas; Brendan Gleeson; Gary Lewis; Stephen Graham; Eddie Marsan; Alec McCowen; David Hemmings; Larry (Lawrence) Gilliard, Jr.; Cara Seymour; Roger Ashton-Griffiths; Cian McCormack; ***Cameo(s):*** Martin Scorsese; ***D:*** Martin Scorsese; ***W:*** Jay Cocks; Steven Zaillian; Kenneth Lonergan; ***C:*** Michael Ballhaus; ***M:*** Howard Shore. British Acad. '02: Actor (Day-Lewis); Golden Globes '03: Director (Scorsese), Song ("The Hands That Built America"); L.A. Film Critics '02: Actor (Day-Lewis); N.Y. Film Critics '02: Actor (Day-Lewis); Screen Actors Guild '02: Actor (Day-Lewis).

The Gangster 🦴🦴 ½ **1947** Sullivan plays a small-time slum-bred hood who climbs to the top of the underworld, only to lose his gang because he allows his fears to get the better of him. (There's nothing to fear except when someone knows you're afeared.) Noir crimer with an interesting psychological perspective, though a bit sluggish at times. **84m/B; VHS, DVD.** Barry Sullivan; Joan Lorring; Akim Tamiroff; Harry (Henry) Morgan; John Ireland; Fifi d'Orsay; Shelley Winters; ***D:*** Gordon Wiles.

Gangster No. 1 🦴🦴 ½ **2000 (R)** An aging London crime boss—who's only known as Gangster 55 (McDowall)?learns that his mentor Freddie Mays (Thewlis) is just out of prison after a 30-year stretch for murder. Flashback to 1968, when a young, ruthless Gangster (a ferocious Bettany) earns his place by taking on Freddie's rivals. Then Gangster becomes jealous of Freddie's girlfriend, Karen (Burrows), and learns of a plot to rub out Freddie. He plans on setting up his boss and becoming head man but never expects to have to confront his past someday. Based on the play by Louis Mellis and David Scinto. **103m/C; VHS, DVD.** *GB GE* Malcolm McDowell; Paul Bettany; David Thewlis; Saffron Burrows; Kenneth Cranham; Jamie Foreman; Eddie Marsan; Andrew Lincoln; ***D:*** Paul McGuigan; ***W:*** Johnny Ferguson; ***C:*** Peter Sova; ***M:*** John Dankworth.

Gangster Squad 🦴 ½ **2013 (R)** Set during Christmas in 1949, former Chicago boxer now LA mob up-and-comer Mickey Cohen (Penn) plans to cut his bosses out of a monopolized drugs and gambling racket. Police sergeant John O'Mara (Brolin) has full reign to hire a ragtag group of crime fighters to take out Cohen, including Sgt. Jerry Wooters (Gosling) who falls for Cohen's sultry main squeeze (Stone). Penn is capable as a cold-hearted thug, but the star-studded cast never quite gels including the zero-chemistry romantic twist. No amount of flashy editing and slo-mo gunplay can overcome this lackluster imitation of "The Untouchables." Taken from Paul Lieberman's series for the Los Angeles Times. **113m/C; DVD, Blu-Ray.** Sean Penn; Ryan Gosling; Josh Brolin; Emma Stone; Nick Nolte; Robert Patrick; Holt McCallany; Mireille Enos; Michael Peña; Giovanni Ribisi; Anthony Mackie; Wade Andrew Williams; Troy Garity; ***D:*** Ruben Fleischer; ***W:*** Will Beall; ***C:*** Dion Beebe; ***M:*** Steve Jablonsky.

Gangster World 🦴🦴 **1998 (R)** In the 21st century, Gangster World is an adult theme part that caters to fulfilling a human's most decadent fantasies—aided by cyborgs in a 1930s setting. But with a name like that, it's easy to believe that a battle for control turns the park into the most dangerous place in the universe. Lots of action and decent enough special effects. **91m/C; VHS, DVD.** Xavier DeClie; David Leisure; Gabriel Dell, Jr.; Stacey Williams; Bridget Flannery; ***D:*** David Bishop. **VIDEO**

Gangster's Boy 🦴 ½ **1938** When popular high school senior Larry Kelly's father Ted returns home, his past as a bootlegger is finally exposed and Larry is ostracized. Judge Davis, the stern father of Larry's best friends, Bill and Julie, refuses to allow his kids to have anything to do with the teen, but it's Larry who takes the blame when Bill gets into trouble. **80m/B; DVD.** Jackie Cooper; Robert Warwick; Tommy Wonder; Lucy Gilman; Selmer Jackson; Louise Lorimer; ***D:*** William Nigh; ***W:*** Robert D. (Robert Hardy) Andrews; ***C:*** Harry Neumann.

Gangway 🦴 ½ **1937** Pat Wayne (Matthews), a London newspaper reporter, is mistaken for a jewel thief and kidnapped by gangsters aboard a New York-bound ocean liner. In the meantime, the real thief is aboard posing as a Hollywood actress (Blakeney), and it's up to Scotland Yard inspector Bob Deering (Mackay) to solve the crime. Matthews was considered by many to be the English equivalent of America's Eleanor Powell. Based on an original story by Dwight Taylor. **90m/B; DVD.** *UK* Jessie Matthews; Barry Mackay; Olive Blakeney; Liane Ordeyne; Patrick Ludlow; Nat Pendleton; Noel Madison; Alastair Sim; Doris Rogers; Laurence Anderson; Bennie Dorn; ***D:*** Sonnie Hale; ***W:*** Sonnie Hale; Lesser Samuels; ***C:*** Glen MacWilliams.

Ganja and Hess 🦴 ½ *Blood Couple; Black Vampire; Double Possession; Black Out: The Moment of Terror; Black Evil* **1973 (R)** Jones plays a professor of African studies who is turned into a vampire by another vampire. He then marries the villain's ex-wife, played by Clark, a veteran of Russ Meyer films. Not much of a story but the acting is actually quite good and there are some creepy moments thanks mainly to an interesting score. **110m/C; VHS, DVD, Blu-Ray.** Duane Jones; Marlene Clark; Bill Gunn; Sam Waymon; Leonard Jackson; Candece Tarpley; Mabel King; ***D:*** Bill Gunn; ***W:*** Bill Gunn; ***C:*** James E. Hinton; ***M:*** Sam Waymon.

Ganked 🦴 **2005 (PG-13)** Ricky (Mitchell) is an undiscovered songwriter living in his parents' basement hoping to hit the big-time any day now. When he wins a contest and is offered a position in a record company he thinks he's made it. Instead, he's stuck working in their mailroom, while the company's sexy singer Kennedy Ross (Bombay) steals his song and his glory. And he won't rest until he's got his revenge. **108m/C; DVD.** Kel Mitchell; Katt Micah Williams; Antwon Tanner; Bombay; ***D:*** Kenn Michael; ***W:*** Kel Mitchell; ***C:*** Kenn Michael; ***M:*** Kel Mitchell; Kenn Michael. **VIDEO**

Gappa the Trifibian Monster 🦴 ½ *Daikyoju Gappa; Monster from a Prehistoric Planet* **1967 (PG)** Researchers visiting a tropical island find a giant egg and take it back to Tokyo with them, dismaying the egg's giant monster parents. Dubbed. **90m/C; VHS, DVD, Blu-Ray.** *JP* Tamio Kawaji; Yoko Yamamoto; Tatsuya Fuji; Koji Wada; Yuji Okada; ***D:*** Haruyasu Hoguchi; ***W:*** Ryuzo Nakanishi; ***C:*** Muneo Ueda.

Garage Days 🦴🦴 ½ **2003 (R)** Sydney, Australia garage band tries to hit it big in this goofy comedy directed by Proyas. Freddy (Gurry) just wants to make it big as the singer of a rock and roll band, but he has to cope with the quirks and problems of his bandmates: girlfriend/bassist Tanya (Miranda), guitarist with an identity crisis Joe (Stiller), and dedicated drug user/drummer Lucy (Sadrinna) who spends more time creating pharmaceutical cocktails than practicing the drums. Further complicating the mix is the attraction between Freddy and Joe's girlfriend, Kate (Stange) and the band's misguided attempt to blackmail a big-time manager (Csokas) to come see them play. Proyas fills the movie with inventive visuals and keeps the comedy level high, but with characters that alternate between appealing and one-dimensional, and a familiar plot, some may find too little substance to go with the style. **105m/C; DVD.** *AU* Maya Stange; Russell Dykstra; Andy Anderson; Marton Csokas; Kick (Christopher) Gurry; Pia Miranda; Brett Stiller; Chris Sadrinna; Tiriel Mora; ***D:*** Alex Proyas; ***W:*** Alex Proyas; Dave Warner; ***C:*** Simon Duggan; ***M:*** Antony Partos; David McCormack.

Garage Sale Mystery 🦴🦴 **2013** Hallmark Channel adaptation from the Suzi Weinert cozy mystery series. Jennifer Shannon (Loughlin) owns a consignment shop and makes the rounds of garage sales to find items she can refurbish and sell. When a string of neighborhood burglaries occur, Jennifer can't help trying to find the culprit, but it turns out to be more dangerous than she thought. **90m/C; DVD.** Lori Loughlin; Rick Ravanello; Cameron Bancroft; Sarah Strange; Andrew Dunbara; Sara Canning; ***D:*** Peter DeLuise; ***W:*** Walter Klenhard; Ronald Parker; ***M:*** Terry Frewer. **CABLE**

The Garbage Pail Kids Movie
WOOF! **1987 (PG)** The disgusting youngsters, stars of bubblegum cards, make their first and last film appearance in this live action dud. The garbage is where it should be thrown. **100m/C; VHS, DVD, Blu-Ray.** Anthony Newley; MacKenzie Astin; Katie Barberi; ***D:*** Rod Amateau; ***W:*** Rod Amateau.

Garbo Talks 🦴🦴 **1984 (PG-13)** A dying eccentric's last request is to meet the reclusive screen legend Greta Garbo. Bancroft amusingly plays the dying woman whose son goes to extreme lengths in order to fulfill his mother's last wish. **104m/C; VHS, DVD.** Anne Bancroft; Ron Silver; Carrie Fisher; Catherine Hicks; Steven Hill; Howard da Silva; Dorothy Loudon; Harvey Fierstein; Hermione Gingold; ***D:*** Sidney Lumet; ***C:*** Andrzej Bartkowiak; ***M:*** Cy Coleman.

The Garden of Allah 🦴🦴🦴 **1936** Dietrich finds hyper-romantic encounters in the Algerian desert with Boyer, but his terrible secret may doom them both. This early Technicolor production, though flawed, is an absolute must for Dietrich fans. Yuma, Arizona substituted for the exotic locale. **85m/C; VHS, DVD, Blu-Ray.** Marlene Dietrich; Charles Boyer; Basil Rathbone; Sir C. Aubrey Smith; Tilly Losch; Joseph Schildkraut; Henry (Kleinbach) Brandon; John Carradine; Alan Marshal; ***D:*** Richard Boleslawski; ***W:*** W.P. Lipscomb; Lynn Riggs; ***C:*** William Howard Greene; ***M:*** Max Steiner. Oscars '36: Color Cinematog.

The Garden of Eden 🦴🦴🦴 **1928** Milestone—whose "Two Arabian Nights" had won an Academy Award the previous year, and who went on to direct "All Quiet on the Western Front" and "Of Mice and Men"?directed this sophisticated ersatz Lubitsch sex comedy. Griffith, the so-called "Orchid Lady," is a young girl who dreams of diva-dom but falls deep into the underbelly of the seedy side of Budapest. With the aid of a fallen baroness, however, she finds her way to Monte Carlo and has her turn in the limelight. A handsome production designed by William Cameron Menzies, art director for "Gone With the Wind." **115m/B; Silent; VHS, DVD, Blu-Ray.** Corinne Griffith; Louise Dresser; Charles Ray; Lowell Sherman; ***D:*** Lewis Milestone; ***W:*** Hans Kraly; ***C:*** John Arnold.

Garden of Evil 🦴🦴 ½ **1954** On their way to the gold fields, Hooker (Cooper), Fiske (Widmark), and Daly (Mitchell) are stranded in a Mexican village. Leah (Hayward) offers the three strangers big bucks if they'll rescue her husband (Marlowe), who was injured in a gold mining accident. The mine is located in a remote mountain region and the group find themselves besieged by Apaches. Equal excitement went on behind the camera as a temperamental Hayward walked off the set whenever she didn't like Hathaway's brusque directing. **100m/C; DVD, Blu-Ray.** Gary Cooper; Susan Hayward; Richard Widmark; Cameron Mitchell; Hugh Marlowe; Victor Manuel Mendoza; Rita Moreno; ***D:*** Henry Hathaway; ***W:*** Frank Fenton; ***C:*** Milton Krasner; ***M:*** Bernard Herrmann.

The Garden of the Finzi-Continis 🦴🦴🦴🦴 *Il Giardino Del Finzi-Contini* **1971 (R)** Acclaimed film by De Sica about an aristocratic Jewish family living in Italy under increasing Fascist oppression on the eve of WWII. The garden wall symbolizes the distance between the Finzi-Continis and the Nazi reality about to engulf them. Flawless acting and well-defined direction. Based on the novel by Giorgio Bassani, who collaborated on the script but later repudiated the film. Music by De Sica's son, Manuel. In Italian with English subtitles or dubbed. **94m/C; VHS, DVD.** *IT* Dominique Sanda; Helmut Berger; Lino Capolicchio; Fabio Testi; Romolo Valli; ***D:*** Vittorio De Sica; ***W:*** Cesare Zavattini; ***C:*** Ennio Guarnieri; ***M:*** Manuel De Sica; Bill Conti. Oscars '71: Foreign Film; Berlin Intl. Film Fest. '71: Golden Berlin Bear.

Garden of the Moon 🦴🦴 **1938** Ruthless L.A. nightclub owner John Quinn (O'Brien) is forced to substitute new bandleader Don Vincente (Payne) when his headlining act is injured. They start clashing over professional and personal matters, including Quinn's secretary/press agent Toni (Lindsay). Don becomes a success and is offered a radio job, which leaves Quinn with more problems. **94m/B; DVD.** Pat O'Brien; John Payne; Margaret Lindsay; Mabel Todd; Johnnie Davis; Melville Cooper; Isabel Jeans; Penny Singleton; ***D:*** Busby Berkeley; ***W:*** Jerry Wald; Richard Macaulay; ***C:*** Gaetano Antonio "Tony" Gaudio.

Garden Party 🦴 ½ **2008** It's a too-familiar story about chasing fame (and finding humiliation) in Hollywood. Realtor Sally (Shaw) has a successful pot operation sideline that becomes the focal point for the other lost souls, including a runaway teen, a porn photographer, a would-be dancer, and a struggling musician, as they drift along and momentarily cross paths. **88m/C; DVD.** Vanessa Shaw; Patrick Fischler; Christopher Allport; Ross Patterson; Willa Holland; Alex Cendese; Erik Scott Smith; Richard Gunn; Jeff Newman; Fiona Duff; ***D:*** Jason Freeland; ***W:*** Jason Freeland; ***C:*** Robert Benavides; ***M:*** John Swihart.

Garden State 🦴🦴🦴 **2004 (R)** Zach Braff stars in his directorial debut (which he also wrote) as Andrew Largeman, Large to his friends, a struggling actor whose biggest role so far has been a retarded quarterback in a cable movie. Things aren't going well. He works at a Vietnamese restaurant, is in a perpetually medicated state, and his father just called to tell him his mother died. Large flies home to New Jersey for the first time in nine years for the funeral, leaving his medication behind. Reunited with his high school friends, who form a motley crew ranging from a gravedigger to a millionaire who invented silent Velcro, Large begins to experience life again. His awakening is further helped by the arrival of Sam (Portman), a cute, quirky free spirit. While there are some minor flaws, the stellar cast and some genuinely amusing moments are well worth a look. **109m/C; DVD, Blu-Ray.** Zach Braff; Ian Holm; Ron Leibman; Method Man; Natalie Portman; Ann Dowd; Denis O'Hare; Peter Sarsgaard; Michael Weston; Jean Smart; Jim Parsons; Jackie Hoffman; Amy Ferguson; Ato Essandoh; ***D:*** Zach Braff; ***W:*** Zach Braff; ***C:*** Lawrence Sher; ***M:*** Chad Fisher. Ind. Spirit '05: First Feature.

Gardens of Stone 🦴🦴 **1987 (R)** A zealous young cadet during the Vietnam War is assigned to the Old Guard patrol at Arlington Cemetery, and clashes with the patrol's older officers and various pacifist civilians. Falls short of the mark, although Jones turns in an excellent performance. **112m/C; VHS, DVD.** James Caan; James Earl Jones; D.B. Sweeney; Anjelica Huston; Dean Stockwell; Lonette McKee; Mary Stuart Masterson; Bill Graham; Sam Bottoms; Casey Siemaszko; Laurence Fishburne; Dick Anthony Williams; Elias Koteas; Peter Masterson; Carlin Glynn; Eric Holland; ***D:*** Francis Ford Coppola; ***W:*** Ronald Bass; ***C:*** Jordan Cronenweth; ***M:*** Carmine Coppola.

Gardens of the Night 🦴🦴 **2008 (R)** The first half of the film is the most harrowing and then it sorta peters out. Deviant child pornographer Alex (Arnold) and his sidekick Frank (Zegers) kidnap 8-year-old Leslie (Simpkins) and dump her in their lair alongside young Donnie (Smith). They eventually convince both children that their parents don't want them and the youngsters bond over their ordeal. Years later, they are homeless teens hustling the streets of San Diego until Leslie (Jacobs) enters a teen rescue program that could reunite her with her family. **110m/C; DVD.** Tom Arnold; Ryan Simpkins; Kevin Zegers; Gillian Jacobs; Jermaine Scooter Smith; Evan Ross; Jeremy Sisto; Harold Perrineau, Jr.; John Malkovich; Raynold Gideon; Cornelia Guest; Kyle Gallner; ***D:*** Damian Harris; ***W:*** Damian Harris; ***C:*** Paul Huidobro; ***M:*** Craig Richey.

Garfield: A Tail of Two Kitties 🦴🦴 ½ **2006 (PG)** Jon (Meyer), his fat (CGI-rendered) kitty (voiced again by Murray), and dumb dog Odie follow vet Liz (Hewitt) to London where Garfield eventually switches places with a spoiled look-alike named Prince (Curry) who just inherited a country estate. Except Lord Dargis (Connolly), next in line to inherit, wants to do the feline in. It's like a furry version of "The Prince and the Pauper." **80m/C; DVD, Blu-Ray.** Jennifer Love Hewitt; Breckin Meyer; Billy Connolly; Lucy Davis; Ian Abercrombie; Roger Rees; ***V:*** Bill Murray; Tim Curry; Bob Hoskins; Jane Leeves; Jane Horrocks; Sharon Osbourne; Richard E. Grant; Vinnie Jones; Rhys Ifans; Roscoe Lee Browne; ***D:*** Tim Hill; ***W:*** Joel Cohen; Alec Sokolow; ***C:*** Peter Lyons Collister; ***M:*** Christophe Beck.

Garfield: The Movie 🦴 ½ **2004 (PG)** The best thing that this escapee from the comic pages has going for it is that fat, nap-taking, lasagna-loving orange cat Garfield (a CGI-creation) is perfectly voiced by the sardonic Murray. The lazy feline dominates nice guy owner Jon (Meyer) and is appalled when life in paradise is threatened by the arrival of excitable mongrel Odie, who arrives via Garfield's sexy vet, Dr. Liz (Hewitt). Naturally, Garfield does his best to get rid of his doggy nuisance until Odie winds up in the clutches of nasty TV show host Happy Chapman (Tobolowsky), who's a decidedly unhappy guy. So it's Garfield to the rescue! Despite the daily comic strip, Garfield's long past his cultural prime, so it's a mystery how he made it to the big screen, especially in this unfunny, slapstick exercise in tedium. **80m/C; DVD, Blu-Ray.** Breckin Meyer; Jennifer Love Hewitt; Stephen Tobolowsky; Mark Christopher-Lawrence; Evan Arnolds Christopher; ***V:*** Bill Murray; Debra Messing; Brad Garrett; Alan Cumming; David Eigenberg; Nick Cannon; Jimmy Kimmel; ***D:*** Peter Hewitt; ***W:*** Joel Cohen; Alec Sokolow; ***C:*** Dean Cundey; ***M:*** Christophe Beck.

Gargoyles, The Movie: The Heroes Awaken 🦴🦴 ½ **1994 (G)** Mythical crimefighting creatures, trapped in stone by day thanks to a sorcerer's spell but released to live at night, are displaced in time from their medieval Scottish home, winding up in modern-day New York City. But they discover they still have old enemies to fight. First aired as a five-episode part of the animated TV series. **80m/C; VHS, DVD.** ***V:*** Ed Asner; Keith David; Jonathan Frakes; Marina Sirtis; Bill Fagerbakke; Salli Richardson-Whitfield; Frank Welker; Thom Adcox; Jeff Glenn Bennett; ***D:*** Saburo Hashimoto; ***W:*** Eric Luke; Michael Reaves; ***M:*** Carl Johnson.

Garm Wars: The Last Druid 🦴🦴 **2015 (PG-13)** A visually strong sci-fi thriller about a future world dominated by clone wars and the experiences of one clone soldier who finds herself having an unexpected adventure. In this world, there are three military tribes of clones who are forever at war on many battlefields including air, land, and technology. When clone Khara (St-Pierre) becomes disconnected from the battle, she falls in with an unexpected group and goes on the run. **102m/C; DVD, Blu-Ray, Streaming, Download.** Lance Henriksen; Kevin Durand; Melanie St-Pierre; Summer Howell; Dawn Ford; ***D:*** Mamoru Oshii; ***W:*** Mamoru Oshii; Geoffrey Gunn; ***C:*** Benoit Beaulieu; ***M:*** Kenji Kawai.

The Garment Jungle 🦴🦴 ½ **1957** Rather luridly told pro-union film. Korean war vet Alan Mitchell (Mathews) discovers his father Walter (Cobb), who owns a dress company, has been paying protection money to union-busting mobster Ravidge (Boone). Having joined the firm, Alan likes what union boss Tulio Renata (Loggia) has to say and tries to convince his pops, which results in two murders. So Alan looks for dirt on Ravidge to take to the D.A. after getting some personal revenge first. Director Robert Aldrich was replaced by Sherman near the end of the shoot and went uncredited. **88m/B; DVD.** Kerwin Mathews; Lee J. Cobb; Richard Boone; Robert Loggia; Gia Scala; Valerie French; Joseph Wiseman; ***D:*** Vincent Sherman; ***W:*** Harry Kleiner; ***C:*** Joseph Biroc; ***M:*** Leith Stevens.

Garrison 🦴 ½ **2007 (R)** Low-budget indie. Sgt. Daniel McManus and fellow soldier Lucas Cain search for their AWOL squad leader Nathan Cross who seems tied into a series of violent acts. Filmed on location in San Antonio, Texas and loosely inspired by the 2002 Ft. Bragg killings of four soldiers' wives. **94m/C; DVD.** James Barnes; Erik Collins; Elizabeth Ingalls; Brent Boller; Jason Cox; Kerry Valderrama; ***D:*** Kerry Valderrama; ***W:*** Kerry Valderrama; ***C:*** J. Lamar King; ***M:*** Douglas Edward.

Gas Food Lodging 🦴🦴🦴 **1992 (R)** Saga casts Adams as Nora, a weary waitress in Laramie, New Mexico, trying her best to raise two teenaged daughters on her own. The daughters, Skye and Balk, are disillusioned about love and family. Balk's special friend is Darius, an eccentric window dresser, played by Leitch, Skye's brother. Nothing works out quite as intended but multi-dimensional characters, poignant situtations, and enormous emotional appeal highlight the directorial debut of Anders. Based on the Richard Peck novel "Don't Look and It Won't Hurt." **100m/C; VHS, DVD, Blu-Ray.** Brooke Adams; Ione Skye; Fairuza Balk; James Brolin; Robert Knepper; Donovan Leitch; David Lansbury; Jacob Vargas; Chris Mulkey; Tiffany Anders; ***D:*** Allison Anders; ***W:*** Allison Anders; ***C:*** Dean Lent; ***M:*** J. Mascis; Barry Adamson. Ind. Spirit '93: Actress (Balk).

Gas House Kids 🦴 **1946** The first in a three-film spinoff of the "East Side Kids" series with a group of underprivileged East Side youths working together to help a disabled vet run a chicken ranch. Their plan to get him some dough is to get the reward money from turning in a wanted criminal. Minor even by cheaply-made series standards. **71m/B; DVD.** Rex Downing; Carl "Alfalfa" Switzer; Billy Halop; Robert Lowery; Teala Loring; Rocco Lanzo; David Reed; ***D:*** Sam Newfield; ***W:*** George Bricker; Elsie Bricker; Raymond L. Schrock; ***C:*** Jack Greenhalgh; ***M:*** Leo Erdody.

Gas Pump Girls 🦴 ½ **1979 (R)** Comedy about five lovely ladies who manage a gas station and use their feminine wiles to win the battle against a shady oil sheik. **102m/C; VHS, Blu-Ray, Streaming.** Kirsten Baker; Dennis Bowen; Huntz Hall; Steve Bond; Leslie King; Linda Lawrence; ***D:*** Joel Bender.

Gas-s-s-s! 🦴🦴 ½ *Gas-s-s-s. . . or, It May Become Necessary to Destroy the World in Order to Save It* **1970 (PG)** A gas main leak in an Alaskan defense plant kills everyone beyond 30-something and the post-apocalyptic pre-boomer survivors are left to muddle their way through the brume. Trouble is, AIP edited the heck out of the movie, much to Corman's chagrin, and the result is a truncated comedy; Corman was so displeased, in fact, he left to create New World studios. **79m/C; VHS, DVD, Blu-Ray.** Robert Corff; Elaine Giftos; Pat Patterson; George Armitage; Alex Wilson; Ben Vereen; Cindy Williams; Bud Cort; Talia Shire; ***D:*** Roger Corman; ***W:*** George Armitage; ***C:*** Ron Dexter; ***M:*** Barry Melton.

GasLand 🦴🦴 ½ **2010** New York theater director Josh Fox receives a lease offer from a natural gas company to explore drilling on family-owned land in Pennsylvania's Delaware River Basin, which is part of the Marcellus Shale field containing natural gas deposits. After refusing the deal, Fox researches the environmental impact of the hydraulic fracturing drilling ('fracking') process the companies use. The results are a nightmare of toxic chemicals and polluted watersheds that sidestep needed government regulations that are opposed by drillers. **105m/C; DVD.** ***Nar:*** Josh Fox; ***D:*** Josh Fox; ***W:*** Josh Fox; ***C:*** Josh Fox; Matthew Sanchez.

Gaslight 🦴🦴🦴 ½ *Angel Street* **1940** A forgotten British classic that fell victim to the American production of the same title and theme that was filmed only four years later. Set in late Victorian London, Wynyard is the rich innocent married to the calculating Walbrook, who slowly tries driving his bride insane in order to discover some hidden family jewels. She comes under the protection of a Scotland Yard detective (Pettingell) who suspects Walbrook has already murdered once. An outstandingly eerie psychological thriller. Based on the play "Angel Street" by Patrick Hamilton. **88m/C; VHS, DVD.** *GB* Anton Walbrook; Diana Wynyard; Frank Pettingell; Cathleen Cordell; Robert Newton; Jimmy Hanley; Minnie Rayner; Mary Hinton; Marie Wright; Jack Barty; Moyna MacGill; Darmora Ballet; ***D:*** Thorold Dickinson; ***W:*** A.R. Rawlinson; Bridget Boland; ***C:*** Bernard Knowles; ***M:*** Richard Addinsell.

Gaslight 🦴🦴🦴 ½ *The Murder in Thorton Square* **1944** Lavish remake of the 1940 film, based on the Patrick Hamilton play "Angel Street." A man tries to drive his beautiful wife insane while searching for priceless jewels. Her only clue to his evil acts is the frequent dimming of their gaslights. A suspenseful Victorian era mystery. Lansbury's film debut, as the tarty maid. **114m/B; VHS, DVD, Blu-Ray.** Charles Boyer; Ingrid Bergman; Joseph Cotten; Angela Lansbury; Terry Moore; May Whitty; Barbara Everest; Emil Rameau; Edmund Breon; Halliwell Hobbes; Tom Stevenson; ***D:*** George Cukor; ***W:*** John Van Druten; Walter Reisch; John Lloyd Balderston; ***C:*** Joseph Ruttenberg; ***M:*** Bronislau Kaper. Oscars '44: Actress (Bergman); Golden Globes '45: Actress--Drama (Bergman); Natl. Film Reg. '19.

Gasoline Alley 1/2 **1951** The first in the film series based on the Frank O. King comic strip. Corky and Hope get married and open a diner, then have to deal with financial problems. Family and friends come to their rescue. Followed by "Corky of Gasoline Alley." **76m/B; DVD.** Scotty Beckett; Susan Morrow; James Lydon; Don Beddoe; Dick Wessel; Gus Schilling; Pat Brady; ***D:*** Edward L. Bernds; ***C:*** Lester White.

The Gate **1987 (PG-13)** Kids generally like to explore and Dorff and Tripp are no exception. When a large hole is exposed in their backyard, it would be a childhood sin not to see what's in it, right? What they don't know is that this hole is actually a gateway to and from Hell. The terror they unleash includes more than just run-of-the-mill demons. Good special effects. Followed by "Gate 2." **85m/C; VHS, DVD, Blu-Ray.** Christa Denton; Stephen Dorff; Louis Tripp; Kelly Rowan; Jennifer Irwin; ***D:*** Tibor Takacs; ***W:*** Michael Nankin; ***C:*** Thomas Vamos.

Gate 2 1/2 **1992 (R)** Tripp returns in his role as Terry, a young student of demonology in this lame sequel to "The Gate." Terry and a few of his teen buddies call up a group of demons that have been confined behind a gate for billions of years. The demons are used to grant modest wishes, but the wishes end up having very evil effects. Incredibly weak plot saved only by the special monster effects, which include live action and puppetry. **90m/C; VHS, DVD, Blu-Ray.** Louis Tripp; Simon Reynolds; Pamela Segall; James Villemaire; Neil Munro; James Kidnie; Andrea Ladanyi; ***D:*** Tibor Takacs; ***W:*** Michael Nankin; ***C:*** Bryan England; ***M:*** George Blondheim.

Gate of Flesh *Nikutai No Mon* **1964** In postwar Japan, four prostitutes survive the American Occupation by sticking to their own code of conduct, including a restriction on anyone giving away their services for free. However, conduct becomes a flexible point when the women harbor a wounded black marketeer whom each comes to desire. Based on a novel by Taijiro Tamura. Japanese with subtitles. **90m/C; VHS, DVD.** *JP* Joe Shishido; Yumiko Nogawa; Kayo Matsuo; Satoko Kasai; Misako Tominaga; Tomiko Ishi; ***D:*** Seijun Suzuki.

Gate of Hell 1/2 *Jigokumen* **1954** Set in 12th-century Japan. A warlord desires a beautiful married woman and seeks to kill her husband to have her. However, he accidentally kills her instead. Filled with shame and remorse, the warlord abandons his life to seek solace as a monk. Heavily awarded and critically acclaimed; the first Japanese film to use color photography. In Japanese with English subtitles. **89m/C; DVD, Blu-Ray.** *JP* Kazuo Hasegawa; Machiko Kyo; Isao Yamagata; Koreya Senda; ***D:*** Teinosuke Kinugasa; ***W:*** Teinosuke Kinugasa; ***C:*** Kohei Sugiyama; ***M:*** Yashushi Akutagawa. Oscars '54: Costume Des. (C), Foreign Film; Cannes '54: Film.

The Gatekeepers *Shomerei Ha'saf* **2012 (PG-13)** Provocative and astonishingly frank documentary offers candid interviews with six former heads of Israel's secretive internal intelligence agency, Shin Bet, who served from 1980 to the present. They detail efforts to establish military control over Palestinians in the aftermath of 1967's Six-Day War and subsequent (untenable) control over terrorist activities and the occupation amidst the pursuit of the peace process. Hebrew with subtitles. **95m/C; DVD, Blu-Ray.** *IS* ***D:*** Dror Moreh; ***C:*** Avner Shahaf; ***M:*** Ab Ovo; Daniel Meir.

Gates of Heaven **1978** Venerated documentary about pet cemeteries, the proprietors, and the pet owners themselves. A quizzical, cold-eyed look at the third-rail side of American middle-class life. Morris' first film is shockingly gentle, yet telling, allowing the subjects to present their own stories. **85m/C; VHS, DVD, Blu-Ray.** ***D:*** Errol Morris; ***C:*** Ned Burgess.

Gates of Hell WOOF! *Paura Nella Citta Dei Morti Viventi; City of the Living Dead; The Fear; Twilight of the Dead; Fear in the City of the Living Dead* **1980** The Seven Gates of Hell have been opened and in three days the dead will rise and walk the earth. A reporter (George) and a psychic (MacColl) fight to close the portals before Salem, Massachusetts is overrun by the risen dead. A gorefest that tried to disguise itself under many other titles. **93m/C; VHS, DVD, Blu-Ray.** *IT* Christopher George; Janet Agren; Katherine (Katriona) MacColl; Robert Sampson; Carlo De Mejo; Antonella Interlenghi; Lucio Fulci; Michele (Michael) Soavi; ***D:*** Lucio Fulci; ***W:*** Dardano Sacchetti; Lucio Fulci; ***C:*** Sergio Salvati; ***M:*** Fabio Frizzi.

Gates of Hell 2: Dead Awakening **1996** Occultists performing an initiation rite reopen the portal to hell and a creature from its depths reawakens to cause the usual unholy terror. **87m/C; VHS, DVD.** Tom Campitelli; Tamara Hext; Randy Strickland; ***D:*** G.D. Marcum.

Gateway **1938** Irish immigrant Catherine is detained on Ellis Island after being accused of improper conduct on the ship by would-be Lothario McNutt, who attempted to molest her. Smitten war correspondent Dick Court (who was another passenger) comes to her aid. **75m/B; DVD.** Don Ameche; Arleen Whelan; Raymond Walburn; Gilbert Roland; Gregory Ratoff; Binnie Barnes; Lyle Talbot; ***D:*** Alfred Werker; ***W:*** Lamar Trotti; ***C:*** Edward Cronjager.

The Gathering 1/2 **1977** A dying man seeks out the wife and family he has alienated for a final Christmas gathering. James Poe authored this well-acted holiday tearjerker that won the 1977-78 Emmy for outstanding TV drama special. **94m/C; VHS, DVD.** Ed Asner; Maureen Stapleton; Lawrence Pressman; Stephanie Zimbalist; Bruce Davison; Gregory Harrison; Veronica Hamel; Gail Strickland; ***D:*** Randal Kleiser; ***M:*** John Barry. **TV**

The Gathering **2002 (R)** Backpacker Cassie (Ricci) is headed for the English village of Ashby Wake when she's hit by a car. The driver, Marion Kirkman (Fox), takes Cassie to her house to recover since she's lost her memory. Marion's husband Simon (Dillane) is researching a recently uncovered first-century church with some unusual iconography that's drawing a number of strangers to the site. Cassie begins to have premonitions about the Kirkmans and the church and her possible ties to the mystery. **92m/C; DVD.** *US GB* Christina Ricci; Ioan Gruffudd; Kerry Fox; Stephen (Dillon) Dillane; Simon Russell Beale; Robert Hardy; Peter McNamara; ***D:*** Brian Gilbert; ***W:*** Anthony Horowitz; ***C:*** Martin Fuhrer; ***M:*** Anne Dudley.

The Gathering: Part 2 **1979** Sequel in which a widow has a Christmas reunion with her family, but conflict arises when she introduces a new man in her life. Not as effective as the original, also made for TV. **98m/C; VHS, DVD.** Maureen Stapleton; Efrem Zimbalist, Jr.; Jameson Parker; Bruce Davison; Lawrence Pressman; Gail Strickland; Veronica Hamel; ***D:*** Charles S. Dubin. **TV**

The Gathering Storm **2002** Finney stars as a typically pugnacious Winston Churchill, who in the mid-1930s is in the political wilderness as he tries to warn an indifferent England about German re-armament and Hitler's rise to power. But he also has problems at home, since his beloved wife Clemmie (Redgrave) has gone off on an extended trip abroad to ease some marital strain and Winston is feeling lonely, jealous, and vulnerable. **96m/C; VHS, DVD.** Albert Finney; Vanessa Redgrave; Jim Broadbent; Linus Roache; Lena Headey; Tom Wilkinson; Derek Jacobi; Ronnie Barker; Celia Imrie; Hugh Bonneville; ***D:*** Richard Loncraine; ***W:*** Hugh Whitemore; ***C:*** Peter Hannan; ***M:*** Trevor Jones. **CABLE**

The Gatling Gun 1/2 *King Gun* **1972 (PG)** Poor tale of the Cavalry, Apache Indians, and renegades all after the title weapon. **93m/C; VHS, DVD.** Guy Stockwell; Woody Strode; Patrick Wayne; Robert Fuller; Barbara Luna; John Carradine; Pat Buttram; Phil Harris; ***D:*** Robert Gordon.

Gator **1976 (PG)** Sequel to "White Lightning" (1973) follows the adventures of Gator (Reynolds), who is recruited to gather evidence to convict a corrupt political boss who also happens to be his friend. Reynolds in his good ole' boy role with lots of chase scenes. Talk show host Michael Douglas made his film debut in the role of the governor. First film Reynolds directed. **116m/C; VHS, DVD, Blu-Ray.** Burt Reynolds; Jerry Reed; Lauren Hutton; Jack Weston; Alice Ghostley; Dub Taylor; Sonny Shroyer; Mike Douglas; ***D:*** Burt Reynolds; ***W:*** William W. Norton, Sr.; ***M:*** Charles Bernstein.

Gator King 1/2 **1970 (R)** Villainous Santos (Fargas) imports Chinese crocodiles to serve them up as dinner at his restaurant and for other nefarious purposes. Spunky journalist Maureen (Foley) and her ex-beau Ranger Ronny (Richardson) decide to investigate. It's a standard-issue micro-budget action flick with nothing really to recommend it, even to fans of the genre. **86m/C; DVD.** Antonio Fargas; Jay Richardson; Shannon K. Foley; Michael Berryman; Joe Estevez; ***D:*** Grant Austin Waldman; ***W:*** John L. Denk; ***C:*** Richard Lacy; ***M:*** Joe Pegram.

Gattaca **1997 (PG-13)** It's a future world where genetic tinkering allows parents to tweak their children's DNA before birth and a caste system of "perfect" humans exists. Vincent (Hawke) dreams of employment with the aerospace corporation Gattaca, so he assumes the identity of the genetically superior Jerome (Law). Soon Vincent is falling for icy co-worker Thurman and getting involved in a murder investigation, which could uncover his true identity. Thinking man's sci-fi (read: no spaceships or explosions) along the lines of George Lucas' "THX-1138." **112m/C; VHS, DVD, Blu-Ray.** Ethan Hawke; Uma Thurman; Jude Law; Gore Vidal; Alan Arkin; Loren Dean; Jayne Brook; Elias Koteas; Tony Shalhoub; Ernest Borgnine; ***D:*** Andrew Niccol; ***W:*** Andrew Niccol; ***C:*** Slawomir Idziak; ***M:*** Michael Nyman.

The Gaucho **1927** Fairbanks stars as the title character, an immoral swashbuckler who lusts after a virginal religious (Greear) before undergoing a change of heart (but not before dancing a red-hot tango with the less-than-virginal Velez). **96m/B; Silent; VHS, DVD.** Douglas Fairbanks, Sr.; Lupe Velez; Geraine Greear; Gustav von Seyffertitz; ***D:*** F. Richard Jones; ***W:*** Lotta Woods; ***C:*** Gaetano Antonio "Tony" Gaudio.

Gaudi Afternoon **2001** Cassandra (Davis) is a translator, working in Barcelona, who gets caught up in the volatile relationship between transsexual Frankie (Harden) and her estranged female lover Ben (Taylor), who is now involved with hippie April (Lewis). It seems that Frankie and Ben also share a daughter and a custody fight is brewing that Cassandra doesn't want to get caught up in. On the other hand, all the melodrama is making her life quite interesting. Based on a novel by Barbara Wilson. **88m/C; VHS, DVD.** *SP* Judy Davis; Marcia Gay Harden; Lili Taylor; Juliette Lewis; Maria Barranco; Christopher Bowen; Courtney Jines; ***D:*** Susan Seidelman; ***W:*** James Mhyre; ***C:*** Josep Civit; ***M:*** Bernardo Bonezzi.

The Gauntlet **1977 (R)** Clint is a broken-down cop ordered to Las Vegas to bring back a key witness for an important trial—but the witness turns out to be a beautiful prostitute being hunted by killers. Violence-packed action with some decent setpieces. **111m/C; VHS, DVD, Blu-Ray.** Clint Eastwood; Sondra Locke; Pat Hingle; Bill McKinney; ***D:*** Clint Eastwood; ***W:*** Michael Butler; ***C:*** Rexford Metz; ***M:*** Jerry Fielding.

The Gay Bed and Breakfast of Terror **2007** Camp horror cheapie populated with obnoxious characters whose murders you'll be openly rooting for. Squabbling couples arrive at the remote, ramshackle desert Sahara Salvation Inn, run by a religious nutjob, for an annual gay bash and soon are shrieking and dying. **110m/C; DVD.** Shannon Lee; Mari Marks; Michael Soldier; Georgia Jean; Robert Borzych; Hilary Schwartz; Vinny Markus; Derek Long; Denise Heller; Lisa Block-Wieser; Allie Rivenbark; Noah Naylor; ***D:*** Jaymes Thompson; ***W:*** Jaymes Thompson; ***C:*** Joel Deutsch; ***M:*** Swerve South.

The Gay Buckaroo 1/2 **1932** Don't anybody get the wrong idea. Successful horse rancher Clint Hale is in love with Mildred, the daughter of gold miner "Sporty" Bill Field, who has become a gentleman cattle rancher. Silly Mildred is taken with gambler Dave Dumont, so Clint tries to become a flashier guy (hence the title), with little success. Clint beats Dumont in a crooked card game, so then Dumont tries to frame Clint for murder. **66m/B; DVD.** Hoot Gibson; Edward Peil, Sr.; Merna Kennedy; Roy D'Arcy; Lafe (Lafayette) McKee; Charles King; ***D:*** Phil Rosen; ***W:*** Philip Graham White.

The Gay Deceivers **1969 (R)** Unmistakably grounded in the '60s, the performances of this comedy are still fresh, but the script is a little stale. Danny (Coughlin) and Elliot (Casey) are two straight guys who avoid the draft by posing as a loving couple. When an army Colonel appears to be investigating the duo, they move into a gay apartment complex to carry on their scam. Naturally, hilarity ensues. The jokes are stereotype-based and show no true skill from the writer or director. Unfortunately, the film is credited with ruining the careers of its leads. **97m/C; DVD.** Lawrence Casey; Brooke Bundy; Kevin Coughlin; ***D:*** Bruce Kessler; ***W:*** Gil Lasky; Jerome Wish; ***C:*** Richard C. Glouner; ***M:*** Stu Phillips.

The Gay Deception **1935** Prince Sandro (Lederer) wants to see how the common folk live, so he takes a job as a bellhop in a posh New York hotel. Small town secretary Mirabel (Dee) decides to blow her lottery winnings by posing as a socialite at that same hotel. Light-hearted romantic deception follows. **76m/B; DVD.** Francis Lederer; Frances Dee; Benita Hume; Alan Mowbray; Akim Tamiroff; ***D:*** William Wyler; ***W:*** Don Hartman; Stephen Morehiouse Avery; ***C:*** Joseph Valentine.

The Gay Desperado 1/2 **1936** Mexican bandit Pablo (Carrillo), who styles himself after American screen gangsters, kidnaps singing caballero Chivo (Martini) and heiress Jane (Lupino). The reason everybody is so gay is that they're always singing in this goofy musical comedy. **85m/B; VHS, DVD.** Leo Carrillo; Ida Lupino; Harold Huber; Nino Martini; Stanley Fields; Mischa Auer; ***D:*** Rouben Mamoulian; ***W:*** Wallace Smith; ***C:*** Lucien N. Andriot; ***M:*** Alfred Newman.

The Gay Divorcee *The Gay Divorce* **1934** Astaire pursues Rogers to an English seaside resort, where she mistakes him for the hired correspondent in her divorce case. Based on the musical play "The Gay Divorce" by Dwight Taylor and Cole Porter. The title was slightly changed for the movie because of protests from the Hays Office. **107m/B; VHS, DVD.** Fred Astaire; Ginger Rogers; Edward Everett Horton; Eric Blore; Alice Brady; Erik Rhodes; Betty Grable; ***D:*** Mark Sandrich; ***M:*** Max Steiner. Oscars '34: Song ("The Continental").

The Gay Dog 1/2 **1954** Working-class Northerner Jim Gay (Pickles) has all his friends betting on his greyhound Raving Beauty to win a big race. But after seeing the competition, Jim bets his money on a rival dog! **83m/B; DVD.** *GB* Wilfred Pickles; Petula Clark; John Blythe; Margaret Barton; William Russell; Megs Jenkins; ***D:*** Maurice Elvey; ***W:*** Peter Rogers; ***C:*** James Wilson.

The Gay Falcon 1/2 **1941** The first in the fast-paced RKO series finds amateur sleuth and ladies man Gay Lawrence (Sanders) promising to change his rakish ways for society fiancee Elinor (Vale). Instead, he gets involved with jewel thieves, some hard-luck society dames, and an insurance scam. **67m/B; DVD.** George Sanders; Wendy Barrie; Allen Jenkins; Nina Vale; Gladys Cooper; Edward Brophy; Arthur Shields; Turhan Bey; ***D:*** Irving Reis; ***W:*** Lynn Root; Frank Fenton; ***C:*** Nicholas Musuraca; ***M:*** Paul Sawtell.

Gay Purr-ee **1962** Delightful tale of feline romance in the City of Lights. For all ages. **85m/C; DVD.** ***V:*** Judy Garland; Robert Goulet; Red Buttons; Hermione Gingold; Mel Blanc; ***D:*** Abe Levitow; ***W:*** Chuck Jones; ***M:*** Harold Arlen.

Gayby 1/2 **2012** Charming, if occassionally predictable, indie comedy about making a family. Thirty-something Jenn hears her biological clock ticking but she wants to get pregnant the old-fashioned way. She reminds her gay best friend Matt of his promise to help her out and he consents, with awkwardness ensuing. Jenn's consumption of horny goat weed tea and subsequent impulsiveness complicates matters. **89m/C; DVD; Closed Captioned.** Jenn Harris; Matthew Wilkas; Mike Doyle; Louis Cancelmi; Jack Ferver; Jonathan Lisecki; ***D:*** Jonathan Lisecki;

W: Jonathan Lisecki; ***C:*** Clay Liford; ***M:*** Giancarlo Vulcano.

The Gazebo **1959** Wacky comedy about a TV writer who is being blackmailed by someone who has nude photos of his Broadway star wife. He decides murder is the only solution to this problem. Reynolds sings "Something Called Love." Based on a play by Alec Coppel from a story by Myra and Alec Coppel. **102m/B; VHS, DVD.** Glenn Ford; Debbie Reynolds; Carl Reiner; John McGiver; Doro Merande; Bert Freed; Martin Landau; ***D:*** George Marshall; ***W:*** George Wells.

G.B.F. **1/2 2013 (R)** In a heated race for prom queen, North Gateway High's three "queen be-atches," drama-class diva Caprice (Roquemore), chaste priss 'Shley (Bowen), and the ambitious blonde Fawcett (Pieterse), all fight to one-up each other. What's the one thing that will give them the edge? A gay best friend--the Holy Grail of trendy accessories. In a school where no one's come out, the three attempt to sniff out a homosexual, eventually vying for once-closeted Tanner (Willett). This cartoonish comedy follows in the footsteps of "Clueless" with snotty actresses snapping out non-stop off-kilter teen slang. Smart, and definitely not clueless. **92m/C; DVD, Download.** Michael J. Willett; Sasha Pieterse; Xosha Roquemore; Andrea Bowen; Paul Iacono; Megan Mullally; ***D:*** Darren Stein; ***W:*** George Northy; ***C:*** Jonathan Hall; ***M:*** Brian Kim.

G.B.H. **1991** Convoluted British political comedy-drama, set during the Margaret Thatcher era, with the title standing for 'grievous bodily harm.' Ambitious bully Michael Murray (Lindsay) is elected to his northern city council as a member of the socialist Militant Labour party. He gets into trouble when his old-school mentor calls a trade union strike but Murray's thugs neglect to shut down the special needs school run by neurotic headmaster Jim Nelson (Palin) and the newspapers pick up on this faux pas. The humiliation puts Murray and Nelson at odds until they realize they're just pawns in a larger political game. **588m/C; DVD.** *GB* Robert Lindsay; Michael Palin; Dearbhla Molloy; Lindsay Duncan; Michael Angelis; Julia St. John; Tom Georgeson; Andrew Schofield; Paul Daneman; Julie Walters; Anna Friel; John Schrapnel; Daniel Massey; ***D:*** Robert Young; ***W:*** Alan Bleasdale; ***C:*** Peter Jessop; ***M:*** Elvis Costello; Richard Harvey. **TV**

Geek Charming **1/2 2011 (G)** Disney Channel movie finds A-list teen Dylan Schoenfield helped by film geek Josh Rosen so she agrees to be the focus of his documentary on high school popularity. She decides Josh needs a makeover, but he turns out to be a true friend as is when Dylan's dumped by her jock boyfriend and her chance to be voted Blossom Queen plummets. **97m/C; DVD.** Sarah Hyland; Matt Prokop; Jordan Nichols; Vanessa Morgan; Sasha Pieterse; Jimmy Bellinger; ***D:*** Jeffrey Hornaday; ***W:*** Elizabeth Hackett; ***C:*** Robert Brinkmann; ***M:*** Nathan Wang. **CABLE**

Geek Maggot Bingo *The Freak from Suckweasel Mountain* **1983** It's too bad director Zedd waited until mid-"Bingo" to post a sign warning "Leave Now, It Isn't Going Get Any Better!" Conceived by the New York underground's don of the "Cinema of Transgression" to be an off-the-rack cult classic, this horror spoof is too long on in-jokes and short on substance to earn its number in the cult hall of fame. It does, however, boast Death as Scumbalina the vampire queen and Hell as a punk cowboy crooner (before alternative country hit the airwaves). TV horror-meister Zacherle narrates. **70m/C; VHS, DVD.** Robert Andrews; Richard Hell; Donna Death; Brenda Bergman; Tyler Smith; Bruno Zeus; John Zacherle; ***D:*** Nick Zedd; ***W:*** Nick Zedd; ***C:*** Nick Zedd.

Geek Mythology **2008** Bumbling geek Tim has no luck with women unlike his best friend Steve who has a beautiful girlfriend, Renee. Then Tim finds a magical statue that makes him a chick magnet but Renee is one of the chicks that comes under the statue's spell, which causes problems for Tim. **81m/C; DVD.** Gregg Martin; Joy Boden; Cullen Cowan; Dave Gist; Michelle Davis; Sandra Rapale; ***D:*** Phil Hwang; ***W:*** Phil Hwang; ***C:*** Marco Escobar; ***M:*** Phil Hwang. **VIDEO**

The Geisha Boy **1/2 1958** Jerry is a floundering magician who joins the USO and tours the Far East. His slapstick confrontations with the troupe leader and an officer who dreams of attending his own funeral provide hearty laughs, plus Lewis finds romance with a Japanese widow after her son claims him as a father. Pleshette's film debut, with an appearance by the Los Angeles Dodgers. **98m/C; VHS, DVD, Blu-Ray.** Jerry Lewis; Marie McDonald; Sessue Hayakawa; Barton MacLane; Suzanne Pleshette; Nobu McCarthy; ***D:*** Frank Tashlin.

Geisha Girl **1/2 1952** Forgotten sci-fi film about a mad scientist and his Japanese cohorts who develop small explosive pills that are more powerful than nuclear bombs. Their plans of world conquest are thwarted when the pills inadvertently fall into the hands of two American G.I.s. **67m/B; VHS, DVD.** Martha Hyer; Steve Forrest; Archer MacDonald; Kekao Yokoo; Teddy Nakamura; ***D:*** George Breakston; C. Ray Stahl; ***W:*** C. Ray Stahl.

Gemini **2017 (R)** A dreamy neo noir thriller on celebrity and personal autonomy set in Los Angeles. One evening, starlet Heather (Kravitz) is out with her assistant Jill (Kirke) when Heather's ex-boyfriend threatens her life. The terrified and paranoid Heather borrows Jill's gun when they return home. The next day, Jill finds her life altered and that she is now the center of attention. A thoughtful exploration of the nature of modern fame, led by Kirke's intriguing performance. **93m/C; DVD, Blu-Ray.** Lola Kirke; Zoë Kravitz; John Cho; Greta Lee; Ricki Lake; ***D:*** Aaron Katz; ***W:*** Aaron Katz; ***C:*** Andrew Reed; ***M:*** Keegan DeWitt.

Gemini Man **1/2 2019 (PG-13)** There was a time when Smith was a dependable action-film star and when one could expect that director Lee would easily deliver a surefire solid film almost every time out. Both star and director flounder here however as the film drones on wearily as a stale police-drama with little flecks of science fiction (Smith is chasing his own clone, who also happens to be a government-trained assassin) thrown in every so often to try and pump some life into an otherwise lifeless and uninteresting film. **117m/C; DVD, Blu-Ray.** *CH US* Will Smith; Mary Elizabeth Winstead; Clive Owen; Benedict Wong; Douglas Hodge; ***D:*** Ang Lee; ***W:*** David Benioff; Billy Ray; Darren Lemke; ***C:*** Dion Beebe; ***M:*** Lorne Balfe.

Gemma Bovery **2015 (R)** The luminous Gemma Arterton plays the title character, a woman who shares a name with the legendary title character of Gustave Flaubert's "Madame Bovary," and she's the only interesting one in this smug dramedy. Martin (Luchini) is a man obsessed with Flaubert's novel who befriends Gemma and her husband Charlie (Flemyng). Martin, and the viewer by extension, starts to see parallels between Gemma & Charlie's "real" life and that of Flaubert's novel. Filmmakers who use classic literature to comment on contemporary times are often well-intentioned, but also often undeniably sure of their notable abilities. **100m/C; DVD.** Fabrice Luchini; Gemma Arterton; Jason Flemyng; Isabelle Candelier; Niels Schneider; ***D:*** Anne Fontaine; ***W:*** Anne Fontaine; Pascal Bonitzer; ***C:*** Christophe Beaucarne; ***M:*** Bruno Coulais.

Gen-X Cops *Tejing Xinrenlei* **1999 (R)** Hong Kong police break a ring of smugglers, who are selling a massive shipment of explosives. But the cops then lose the goods to major criminal, Akatura (Nakamura). So a rebellious trio of young cops go undercover and discover the bad guy has very sinister plans. Cantonese with subtitles. **113m/C; VHS, DVD.** *CH* Nicholas Tse; Stephen Fung; Sam Lee; Grace Kip; Toru Nakamura; Jackie Chan; ***D:*** Benny Chan; ***W:*** Benny Chan; ***C:*** Arthur Wong Ngok Tai.

The Gene Generation **2007 (R)** Cyberpunk action. In the futuristic city of Olympia, scientists discover a human gene therapy that can stop any disease but the downside is genetic mutations. DNA hackers steal the technology for evil purposes and assassin Michelle (Ling) is hired to stop them. When Michelle's naive brother Jackie (Shen) gets pulled in, she goes hunting in a dangerous cyber-underworld. Adapted from director Teo's graphic novel. **96m/C; DVD.** Bai Ling; Parry Shen; Alec Newman; Faye Dunaway; Robert David Hall; Michael Shamus Wiles; ***D:*** Pearry Reginald Teo; ***W:*** Keith Collea; ***C:*** Anthony G. Nakonechnyi; ***M:*** Scott Glasgow; Ronan Harris. **VIDEO**

The Gene Krupa Story **1/2 1959** The story of the famous jazz drummer and his career plunge after a drug conviction. Krupa recorded the soundtrack, mimed by Mineo, who was too young for a convincing portrayal. Gavin McLeod (of "Love Boat" fame) has a small part as Mineo's dad. **101m/B; VHS, DVD.** Sal Mineo; James Darren; Susan Kohner; Susan Oliver; Anita O'Day; Red Nichols; ***D:*** Don Weis.

Genealogies of a Crime *Genealogies d'un Crime* **1997** Complex puzzle with the ever-beautiful Deneuve in dual roles. In one role, she's Solange, a criminal lawyer who agrees to defend a young man, Rene (Poupaud), who's accused of murdering his psychologist aunt Jeanne (Deneuve again, in flashback). Jeanne, who raised Rene, long suspected him of homicidal tendencies, became his shrink, and even expected to be killed by him. Solange believes Jeanne's ministrations programmed Rene to kill. As Solange investigates Rene's background, she becomes too involved with the unstable young man—leading her down the path to madness as well. French with subtitles. **114m/C; VHS, DVD.** *FR* Catherine Deneuve; Melvil Poupaud; Michel Piccoli; Andrzej Seweryn; Bernadette LaFont; Hubert Saint Macary; ***D:*** Raul Ruiz; ***W:*** Raul Ruiz; Pascal Bonitzer; ***C:*** Stefan Ivanov; ***M:*** Jorge Arriagada.

The General **1926** Keaton's masterpiece and arguably the most formally perfect and funniest of silent comedies. Concerns a plucky Confederate soldier who single-handedly retrieves a pivotal train from Northern territory. Full of eloquent man-vs-machinery images and outrageous sight gags. Remade as "The Great Locomotive Chase" in 1956 with Fess Parker. **78m/B; Silent; VHS, DVD, Blu-Ray.** Buster Keaton; Marion Mack; Glen Cavender; Jim Farley; Joe Keaton; Frederick Vroom; Charles Smith; Frank Barnes; Mike Donlin; ***D:*** Buster Keaton; Clyde Bruckman; ***W:*** Buster Keaton; Clyde Bruckman; Al Boasberg; Charles Henry Smith; ***C:*** Bert Haines; Devereaux Jennings. Natl. Film Reg. '89.

The General **1998 (R)** Biopic of maverick Dublin crime lord Martin Cahill (Gleeson), nicknamed "The General" for his planning abilities. Film is one long flashback as it begins in 1994 with Cahill's assassination. Cahill supports his family through various burglaries, making a mockery of the local cops, including Ned Kenny (Voight). But Cahill's rise from petty criminal to local mobster is noted by the IRA and when he refuses to cut them in on his profits, things turn very dicey for the cocky, ruthless Cahill. **123m/B; VHS, DVD.** *IR GB* Brendan Gleeson; Adrian Dunbar; Sean McGinley; Jon Voight; Maria Doyle Kennedy; Angeline Ball; Ciaran Fitzgerald; Eamon Owens; ***D:*** John Boorman; ***W:*** John Boorman; ***C:*** Seamus Deasy; ***M:*** Richie Buckley. Cannes '98: Director (Boorman).

The General Died at Dawn **1936** A clever, atmospheric suspense film about an American mercenary in Shanghai falling in love with a beautiful spy as he battles a fierce Chinese warlord who wants to take over the country. Playwright-to-be Odets' first screenplay; he, O'Hara and '30s gossip hound Skolsky have cameos as reporters. **93m/B; VHS, DVD, Blu-Ray.** Gary Cooper; Madeleine Carroll; Akim Tamiroff; Dudley Digges; Porter Hall; William Frawley; Philip Ahn; ***Cameo(s):*** John O'Hara; Clifford Odets; Sidney Skolsky; ***D:*** Lewis Milestone; ***W:*** Clifford Odets; ***C:*** Victor Milner.

Generale Della Rovere **1/2** *Il Generale Della-Rovere* **2009** A WWII black marketeer is forced by the Nazis to go undercover in a local prison. To find out who the resistance leaders are, he poses as a general. But when prisoners begin to look to him for guidance, he finds the line between his assumed role and real identity diminished, leading to a tragic conclusion. Acclaimed film featuring a bravura lead performance by veteran director De Sica. In Italian with English subtitles. **139m/B; DVD, Blu-Ray.** *IT* Vittorio De Sica; Otto Messmer; Sandra Milo; ***D:*** Roberto Rossellini; ***W:*** Roberto Rossellini; Sergio Amidei; Diego Fabbri; Indro Montanelli; ***C:*** Carlo Carlini; ***M:*** Renzo Rossellini.

The General's Daughter **1999 (R)** Disturbing and convoluted military thriller based on the 1992 bestseller by Nelson DeMille. Paul Brenner (Tavolta) is an Army criminal investigator whose latest case is the rape and murder of Capt. Elisabeth Campbell (Stefanson), whose father (Cromwell) is a legendary general. Elisabeth specialized in psychological warfare but she had more than a few mental problems of her own. Naturally, for the good of the service, everyone but Brenner would like a quick and tidy solution to the sleazy goings-on. Goes a little too over the top (including some performances) and you may come out wondering just who done what. **116m/C; VHS, DVD.** John Travolta; Madeleine Stowe; James Cromwell; Timothy Hutton; James Woods; Leslie Stefanson; Clarence Williams, III; Daniel von Bargen; Boyd Kestner; Mark Boone, Jr.; John Beasley; Peter Weireter; John Benjamin Hickey; Rick Dial; Brad Beyer; ***D:*** Simon West; ***W:*** William Goldman; Christopher Bertolini; ***C:*** Peter Menzies, Jr.; ***M:*** Carter Burwell.

A Generation *Pokolenie* **1954** During WWII, a young man escapes from the Warsaw Ghetto and finds his way to the Polish Resistance. He falls in love with the leader of the local group and finds the courage to fight for his freedom. Strong directorial debut from Wajda. Part 1 of his "War Trilogy," followed by "Kanal" and "Ashes and Diamonds." Scripted by Czeszko from his novel "Pokolenie." Polish with subtitles. **90m/B; VHS, DVD.** *PL* Tadeusz Lomnicki; Urszula Modrzynska; Zbigniew Cybulski; Roman Polanski; ***D:*** Andrzej Wajda; ***W:*** Bohdan Czeszko; ***C:*** Jerzy Lipman; ***M:*** Andrzej Markowski.

Generation Iron **2013 (PG-13)** Narrated by Academy Award winner Mickey Rourke, this insightful feature-length documentary provides an in-depth look at the world of competitive body building. Focusing on the Mr. Olympia competition, the film follows seven serious-minded rivals, including Phil Heath, Branch Warren, and Dennis Wolf. By showing the men in the gym and on the stage, the film shows how far they will go to achieve physical perfection and win the title. Misconceptions about competitive body building are examined as well. **107m/C; DVD, Blu-Ray, Streaming, Download.** Mickey Rourke; ***D:*** Vlad Yudin; ***W:*** Vlad Yudin; ***C:*** Guy Livneh; Colin Morvan; ***M:*** Jeff Rona.

Generation Kill **2008** Based on the book by "Rolling Stone" reporter Evan Wright that gives his first-person account of being embedded with the First Recon unit of Marines during the first 40 days of the Iraq invasion. The scene is chaotic, tense, and claustrophobic as the foul-mouthed grunts deal with bureaucratic screw-ups and contradictory orders from officers they frequently disdain as incompetent. **362m/C; DVD, Blu-Ray.** Lee Tergesen; Alexander Skarsgård; James Ransone; Jon Huertas; Stark Sands; Billy Lush; Pawel Szajda; Jonah Lotan; Wilson Bethel; ***D:*** Susanna White; Simon Cellan Jones; ***W:*** David Simon; Ed Burns; ***C:*** Ivan Strasburg. **CABLE**

Generation Um... **2013 (R)** Dreary, tedious, and aimless urban drama. Gloomy, boozy escort service driver John (Reevs) ferries young hos Violet (Novakvic) and Mia (Clemens) around New York City one evening. After stealing a videocamera, he starts taping the girls, asking them to spill secrets that are neither illuminating or interesting. **96m/C; DVD.** Keanu Reeves; Bojana Novakovic; Adelaide Clemens; Daniel Sunjata; Sarita Choudhury; ***D:*** Mark Mann; ***W:*** Mark Mann; ***C:*** Mauricio Rubinstein.

Generation War *Unsere Mutter, Unsere Vater; Our Mothers, Our Fathers* **2013** German TV miniseries follows the lives of five young adults who come of age in Nazi Germany during WWII from Berlin in 1941 to postwar life in 1945. Patriotic officer Wilhelm is sent to the eastern front along with his poetry-loving younger brother, Friedhelm while nurse Charlotte, who's in love with Wilhelm, hopes to follow him. Meanwhile, singer Greta decides how far she'll go to fulfill her ambitions while her Jewish boyfriend, Viktor, increasingly fights just to survive. German with subtitles. **279m/C; DVD, Blu-Ray.** *GE* Volker Bruch; Tom Schilling; Miriam Stein;

Katherina Schuttler; Ludwig Trepte; *D:* Philipp Kadelbach; *W:* Stefan Kolditz; *C:* David Slama; *M:* Fabian Romer. **TV**

Genesis II **1973** Failed TV pilot by Roddenberry finds scientist Dylan Hunt (Cord) taking part in a NASA suspended animation experiment that goes wrong. He is revived 150 years later to a post-WWIII Earth. A confused Hunt is cared for by sexy Lyra-a (Hartley), a member of a mutant race called the Tyranians. It seems the Tyranians are battling the Pax movement for control of what's left of the planet and Hunt gets caught in the middle. **74m/C; DVD.** Alex Cord; Mariette Hartley; Ted Cassidy; Harvey Jason; Tito Vandia; Percy Rodrigues; Lynn(e) Marta; *D:* John Llewellyn Moxey; *W:* Gene Roddenberry; *C:* Gerald Perry Finnerman; *M:* Harry Sukman. **TV**

Genevieve **1953** A 1904 Darracq roadster is the title star of this picture which spoofs "classic car" owners and their annual rally from London to Brighton. Two married couples challenge each other to a friendly race which becomes increasingly intense as they near the finish line. **86m/C; VHS, DVD, Blu-Ray.** *GB* John Gregson; Dinah Sheridan; Kenneth More; Kay Kendall; Geoffrey Keen; Reginald Beckwith; Arthur Wontner; Joyce Grenfell; Leslie Mitchell; Michael Medwin; Michael Balfour; Edie Martin; Harold Siddons; *D:* Henry Cornelius; *W:* William Rose; *C:* Christopher Challis; *M:* Larry Adler. British Acad. '53: Film; Golden Globes '55: Foreign Film.

Genghis Khan **1965** Temujin-Genghis Khan (Sharif) rises from outcast status to unite and lead the Mongols against his mentor-turned-rival Jamuga (Boyd). Ridiculously miscast Irwin Allen production filmed on location in Yugoslavia in Cinemascope and Technicolor. **125m/C; DVD, Blu-Ray.** Omar Sharif; Stephen Boyd; Francoise Dorleac; James Mason; Eli Wallach; Telly Savalas; Woody Strode; Robert Morley; Michael Hordern; *D:* Henry Levin; *W:* Beverley Cross; Clarke Reynolds; *C:* Geoffrey Unsworth; *M:* Dusan Radic.

Genghis Khan: To the Ends of the Earth and Sea *Blue Wolf: To the Ends of the Earth and Sea; Aoki Okami: Chi Hate Umi Tsukiru Made* **2007 (R)** Despite the name this attempt at a historical biography doesn't cover all of Khan's life, but focuses on his troubled youth as the man known as Temujin at the beginning of his war with China. Incredible battle scenes, though the family-based melodrama in between the fights is lacking as is the historical accuracy (for the sake of political correctness). Despite only costing $30 million, 27,000 (presumably Mongolian) extras were employed as well as 5,000 Mongolian soldiers during the four-month film shoot. **136m/C; DVD, Blu-Ray.** *JP* Takashi Sorimachi; Ken'ichi Matsuyama; Yoshihiko Hakamada; Eugene Nomura; Rei Kikukawa; Mayumi Wakamura; *D:* Shinichiro Sawai; *W:* Takehiro Nakajima; Shoichi Maruyama; *C:* Yonezo Maeda; *M:* Taro Iwashiro.

Genius **2016 (PG-13)** You may not know the name Max Perkins (Firth), but you almost certainly know those who he worked with in his formative years at Scribner, the publisher of works by Thomas Wolfe (Law), Ernest Hemingway (West), F. Scott Fitzgerald (Pearce), and many more. As with many of these dramas that are filled with real-life historical figures already considered larger than life, the filmmaking doesn't seem to do them justice. The cast is strong and production values are high, but it lacks the energy needed to make it more interesting than a "well-made period piece." **104m/C; DVD.** Nicole Kidman; Jude Law; Colin Firth; Guy Pearce; Laura Linney; *D:* Michael Grandage; *W:* John Logan; *C:* Ben Davis; *M:* Adam Cork.

Gentle Giant **1967** An orphaned bear is taken in by a boy and his family and grows to be a 750 pound giant who must be returned to the wild. "Gentle Ben" TV series was derived from this feature. **93m/C; VHS, Streaming.** Dennis Weaver; Vera Miles; Ralph Meeker; Clint Howard; Huntz Hall; *D:* James Neilson.

The Gentleman from Arizona ½ **1939** Chronic gambler Coburn will lose his ranch to back taxes unless his thoroughbred can win the Arizona Derby. Cowboy Pokey is hired on and brings along a wild mustang he has trained, which will prove useful since Coburn's rival Van Wyck is determined to win the race by cheating so he can marry Coburn's daughter Georgia. Monogram studio filmed this western in Cinecolor. **71m/C; DVD.** John "Dusty" King; J. Farrell MacDonald; Joan Barclay; Craig Reynolds; Ruth Reece; Nora Lane; *D:* Earl Haley; *W:* Jack O'Donnell; *C:* John Boyle; *M:* C. Bakaleinikoff.

Gentleman Jim ½ **1942** A colorful version of the life of old-time heavyweight boxing great Jim Corbett, transformed from a typical Warner Bros. bio-pic by director Walsh into a fun-loving, anything-for-laughs donnybrook. Climaxes with Corbett's fight for the championship against the great John L. Sullivan. One of Flynn's most riotous performances. **104m/B; DVD.** Errol Flynn; Alan Hale; Alexis Smith; Jack Carson; Ward Bond; Arthur Shields; William Frawley; *D:* Raoul Walsh.

The Gentleman Killer **1969** A man-with-no-name clears a ravaged border town of murdering bandits. **95m/C; VHS, DVD.** *IT SP* Anthony Steffen; Silvia Solar; *D:* Giorgio Stegani; *W:* Jaime Jesus Balcazar; *C:* Francis Marin; *M:* Bruno Nicolai.

Gentleman's Agreement **1947** Magazine writer Phil Green (Peck) looks for a new angle when he agrees to write a series of articles on anti-Semitism for publisher John Minify (Dekker). Phil pretends to be Jewish, and his new identity pervades his life in unexpected ways, almost destroys his relationships. Garfield has a small but powerful role as Phil's Jewish friend Dave, who has long had to deal with both overt and covert prejudice. This movie was Hollywood's first major attack on anti-Semitism. Controversial in its day, yet still timely. **118m/B; VHS, DVD, Blu-Ray.** Gregory Peck; Dorothy McGuire; John Garfield; Celeste Holm; Anne Revere; June Havoc; Albert Dekker; Jane Wyatt; Dean Stockwell; Nicholas Joy; *D:* Elia Kazan; *W:* Moss Hart; *C:* Arthur C. Miller; *M:* Alfred Newman. Oscars '47: Director (Kazan), Film, Support. Actress (Holm); Golden Globes '48: Director (Kazan), Film--Drama, Support. Actress (Holm); Natl. Film Reg. '17; N.Y. Film Critics '47: Director (Kazan), Film.

A Gentleman's Game ½ **2001 (R)** Twelve-year-old Timmy (Gamble) is a gifted young golfer who is pushed by his father to improve his game. He becomes a caddy at the local country club and manages to get tips from reluctant club pro Foster Pearce (Sinise) but learns about more than just golf. Based on the novel by Coyne, who co-scritped. **91m/C; VHS, DVD.** Mason Gamble; Gary Sinise; Philip Baker Hall; Dylan Baker; Henry Simmons; Ellen Muth; Brian Doyle-Murray; *D:* J. Mills Goodloe; *W:* J. Mills Goodloe; Tom Coyne; *C:* Conrad W. Hall; *M:* Jeff Beal.

The Gentlemen ½ **2020 (R)** Fletcher (Grant) is a cunning private detective who has gathered incriminating information about drug lords working in Britain and wrote a screenplay with this material to blackmail everyone. One night, he shows up at Raymond's (Hunnam) home to lay out all he knows about Raymond's boss, American drug lord Mickey (McConaughey), and his marijuana empire, in the form a pitch script. Mickey is ready to retire and sell his enterprise but the actions of his potential buyers impact his plans. The crime comedy-drama truly reflects a Ritchie "lads" film, and Grant's performance is well-crafted and hilarious. **103m/C; Download.** Matthew McConaughey; Charlie Hunnam; Michelle Dockery; Jeremy Strong; Colin Farrell; *D:* Guy Ritchie; *W:* Guy Ritchie; *C:* Alan Stewart; *M:* Christopher Benstead.

Gentlemen Broncos ½ **2009 (PG-13)** When misfit teenager Benjamin Purvis (Angarano) attends a fantasy writers convention, he discovers that one of his stories has been ripped off and rewritten by blocked fantasy novelist Ronald Chevalier (Clement) and is even being made into a movie by a local filmmaker. This sets off a series of slow, stuffy events as Benjamin fights for his craft. Writer-director Hess attempts to relive the offbeat charm of his debut, "Napoleon Dynamite," but it's stilted and forced with the opening credits being by far the best part. **90m/C; Blu-Ray, On Demand.** Michael Angarano; Jemaine Clement; Sam Rockwell; Mike White; Jennifer Coolidge; Hector Jimenez; Josh Pais; Halley Feiffer; *D:* Jared Hess; *W:* Mike White; Jared Hess; Jerusha Hess; *C:* Munn Powell; *M:* David Wingo.

Gentlemen Prefer Blondes **1953** Amusing satire involving two show-business girls from Little Rock trying to make it big in Paris. Seeking rich husbands or diamonds, their capers land them in police court. Monroe plays Lorelei Lee, Russell is her sidekick. Despite an occasionally slow plot, the music, comedy, and performances are great fun. Film version of a Broadway adaptation of a story by Anita Loos. Followed by (but without Monroe) "Gentlemen Marry Brunettes." **91m/C; VHS, DVD, Blu-Ray.** Marilyn Monroe; Jane Russell; Charles Coburn; Elliott Reid; Tommy Noonan; George Winslow; *D:* Howard Hawks; *W:* Charles Lederer; *C:* Harry Wild; *M:* Leo Robin; Jule Styne; Lionel Newman.

Gentlemen's Relish ½ **2001** Artist Kingdom Swann (Connolly) is dismayed to learn Edwardian London finds his paintings old-fashioned, so loyal servant Violet (Lancashire) buys him a camera so he can experiment. With the help of unscrupulous assistant Marsh (Henshall), Swann becomes a successful society photographer, progressing into "artistic" nudes. However, Marsh is selling the increasingly naughty pics to a specialist clientele without the naive Swann's knowledge. **89m/C; DVD.** *GB* Billy Connolly; Sarah Lancashire; Douglas Henshall; Katie Blake; *D:* Douglas Mackinnon; *W:* David Nobbs; *C:* Gavin Finney; *M:* Julian Nott. **TV**

Geordie ½ *Wee Geordie* **1955** A wee, if charming, comedy. As a youngster growing up in the Scottish Highlands, Geordie is puny and bullied. He takes up a body-building course and a few years later is muscled enough to be the hammer-throwing champion at the Highland Games. This makes Geordie a member of the Olympic team traveling to Melbourne, Australia, where he meets Danish shot-putter Helga, who's instantly smitten. When Geordie breaks the world record, Helga's enthusiastic reaction is misinterpreted, leaving Geordie with a lot of explaining to do back home to his heartbroken girlfriend Jean. **96m/C; DVD.** *GB* Bill Travers; Alastair Sim; Paul Young; Francis De Wolff; Norah Gorsen; Doris Goddard; Molly Urquhart; *D:* Frank Launder; *W:* Frank Launder; Sidney Gilliat; *C:* Wilkie Cooper; *M:* William Alwyn.

George! ½ **1970 (G)** A carefree bachelor takes his girlfriend and his 250-pound St. Bernard on a trip to the Swiss Alps where he proves that a dog is not always man's best friend. **87m/C; VHS, DVD.** Marshall Thompson; Jack Mullaney; Inge Schoner; *D:* Wallace C. Bennett; *W:* Wallace C. Bennett.

George A. Romero's Land of the Dead *Land of the Dead* **2005 (R)** Romero brings the walkers back for a fourth time, but with a tasty new twist—they aren't as dumb as they used to be. And worse yet, they've stumbled upon some ammo. But the upper-crust think they're now safe in their walled-in super tower until a renegade supplies runner, who's living among the poverty-plagued street people and angry because the elite won't invite him in, threatens their comfy confines. Compelling statement about societal classes embedded within usual gore. **93m/C; DVD, Blu-Ray, UMD, HD-DVD.** *FR CA US* Simon Baker; John Leguizamo; Asia Argento; Robert Joy; Dennis Hopper; Eugene Clark; Boyd Banks; Joanne Boland; Krista Bridges; Jennifer Baxter; Pedro Miguel Arce; Phil Fondacaro; Simon Pegg; *D:* George A. Romero; *W:* George A. Romero; *C:* Miroslaw Baszak; *M:* Reinhold Heil; Johnny Klimek.

George and the Dragon ½ **2004 (PG)** The CGI may not be the best in this low-budget fantasy but it's still good family fare. Heroic medieval knight George (Purefoy) returns to England after the First Crusade intending to settle down. King Edgar (Callow) offers George some land in exchange for finding his daughter, Princess Luma (Perabo), who has run away from her betrothal to bad Sir Garth (Swayze). But the Princess is having her own adventure; after finding a cave-dwelling dragon down by the lake, she unexpectedly becomes the protector of the dragon's egg. **93m/C; DVD.** James Purefoy; Piper Perabo; Patrick Swayze; Simon Callow; Jean-Pierre Castaldi; Rollo Weeks; Paul Freeman; Michael Clarke; Bill Treacher; *D:* Tom Reeve; *W:* Tom Reeve; Michael Burks; *C:* Joost van Starrenburg; *M:* Gast Waltzing.

George Balanchine's The Nutcracker ½ *The Nutcracker* **1993 (G)** Pas de deux redeux. Tchaikovsky's classic ballet about the magic of Christmas and a little girl (Cohen) who dreams on Christmas Eve that she is in an enchanted kingdom. Culkin lamely grins through his wooden performance as the Nutcracker Prince, but the talent of the Sugarplum Fairy (Kistler) and the other dancers is such that conventional camera techniques sometimes fail to keep up with their exacting moves. Adapted from the 1816 book by E.T.A. Hoffmann. **93m/C; VHS, DVD.** Macaulay Culkin; Jessica Lynn Cohen; Bart Robinson Cook; Darci Kistler; Damian Woetzel; Kyra Nichols; Wendy Whelan; Gen Horiuchi; Margaret Tracey; *Nar:* Kevin Kline; *D:* Emile Ardolino; *W:* Susan Cooper; *C:* Ralf Bode.

George Harrison: Living in the Material World ½ **2011** Martin Scorsese's extended, two-part HBO documentary of the complex life of George Harrison, made in cooperation with his widow, Olivia Harrison. Part 1 deals with Harrison's childhood, years with the Beatles, and his eventual exploration of LSD and Eastern religion and music. Part 2 begins in 1970 with the Beatles' break-up, Harrison's solo musical work and film projects, and his eventual death from cancer in 2001. Scorsese does assume a familiarity with Harrison's life and his various collaborators through interviews, photographs, home movies, and archival footage. **208m/C; DVD, Blu-Ray.** Olivia Harrison; Dhani Harrison; Paul McCartney; Ringo Starr; Patti Boyd; Eric Clapton; Tom Petty; *D:* Martin Scorsese. **CABLE**

George of the Jungle **1997 (PG)** The '60s cartoon hero goes big screen and live-action with Fraser starring as the clumsy (but very hunky) jungle hero. While on safari, socialite Ursula (Mann) falls in love with George and takes him back to San Francisco, leaving behind obnoxious fiancee Lyle (Church). But when poachers capture George's "brother" Ape (voiced by Cleese), he returns to save the day (aided by various jungle companions). Fraser is an appealing lead, and the script is sweetly funny while retaining creator Ward's smart, subversive edge. The stunts are more impressive than you'd usually expect from a cartoon adaptation. **91m/C; VHS, DVD, Blu-Ray.** Brendan Fraser; Leslie Mann; Thomas Haden Church; Holland Taylor; Richard Roundtree; Greg Cruttwell; Abraham Benrubi; John Bennett Perry; Kelly Miller; *V:* John Cleese; *Nar:* Keith Scott; *D:* Sam Weisman; *W:* Dana Olsen; Audrey Wells; *C:* Thomas Ackerman; *M:* Marc Shaiman.

The George Raft Story ½ **1961** Often in financial difficulty, actor Raft sold his life story, which became a fairly typical Hollywood bio. Raft (Danton) starts off as a dancer in a Hell's Kitchen joint but gets on the wrong side of mobster Frank Donatella (de Santis). So he departs for Hollywood and gets his (typecasting) break in "Scarface." Unable to resist the company of wiseguys, Raft's career eventually fades and he then gets involved in a Havana casino operation that ends with the Castro revolution. The film ends when Raft gets a role (parodying his tough guy image) in "Some Like It Hot." **103m/B; DVD.** Ray Danton; Jayne Mansfield; Julie London; Barrie Chase; Frank Gorshin; Barbara Nichols; Brad Dexter; Neville Brand; Joe De Santis; Herschel Bernardi; Margo Moore; *D:* Joseph M. Newman; *W:* Daniel Mainwaring; Crane Wilbur; *C:* Carl Guthrie; *M:* Jeff Alexander.

George Wallace ½ **1997** Follows 20 years (1955-1975) in the life of politician George Wallace (Sinise) from his career as a state circuit judge, his four terms as Alabama's hard-line segregationist governor, to the first years after he was paralyzed by a would-be assassin while campaigning for the presidency. Some elements are disturbingly dramatized, including Archie (Williams), the fictional black manservant who serves as Wallace's conscience. Based on the book "Wallace" by co-scripter Frady. **178m/C; VHS, DVD.** Gary Sinise; Mare Winningham; Clarence Williams, III; Joe Don Baker; Angelina Jolie; Mark Valley; Cliff DeYoung; Skipp (Robert L.) Sudduth; Mark Rolston; William Sanderson; Terry Kinney; *D:* John Frankenheimer; *W:* Marshall Frady; Paul Monash; *C:* Alan Caso; *M:* Gary Chang. **CABLE**

George Washington Slept Here **1942** Hilarious side-splitter about a couple who moves from their Manhattan apartment to an old, broken-down country home in Connecticut. It's one catastrophe after another as the couple tries to renovate their home and deal with a greedy neighbor. Based on the play by George S. Kaufman and Moss Hart. **93m/B; DVD.** Jack Benny; Ann Sheridan; Charles Coburn; Percy Kilbride; Hattie McDaniel; William Tracy; *D:* William Keighley; *W:* Everett Freeman; *C:* Ernest Haller; *M:* Adolph Deutsch.

George White's Scandals **1945** RKO musical based on White's Broadway revues has a flimsy plot to tie the many production numbers together. Performer Joan (Davis) announces she's engaged to Jack (Haley) much to the disapproval of his sister Clarabelle (Hamilton). Stage manager Tom (Terry) hires new dancer Jill (Holliday) and they fall in love. But there's obstacles to their romance too since she's hiding her identity as an English socialite so she won't embarrass her parents. **95m/B; DVD.** Joan Davis; Jack Haley; Phillip Terry; Martha Holliday; Margaret Hamilton; Jane Greer; Glenn Tryon; *D:* Felix Feist; *W:* Hugh Wedlock, Jr.; Howard Snyder; Howard J. Green; Peter Levy; *C:* Robert De Grasse.

George White's Scandals of 1935 **1935** Broadway revue producer White (playing himself) is Florida-bound when he stops in a small Georgia town and takes in a local show. Impressed by songbird Honey (Faye), he hires her to come to New York along with her beau, Eddie (Dunn), and several others. When White's new show is a success, Honey and Eddie's heads are turned and they have some trouble. **84m/B; DVD.** Alice Faye; James Dunn; Ned Sparks; Emma Dunn; Arline Judge; Cliff Edwards; Eleanor Powell; Lyda Roberti; George White; *D:* George White; *W:* Patterson McNutt; Jack Yellen; *C:* George Schneiderman.

Georgia **1995 (R)** Character study about sibling rivalry, self-destruction, and the Seattle music scene. Struggling rock singer Sadie (Leigh), who relies on booze, drugs, and men to help her make it through the night, returns to Seattle to crash with big-sister Georgia (Winningham). Settled, with loving husband and kids, the much more talented Georgia is also a popular folk icon and has the type of personal/career success angry and ambitious Sadie can only dream about. Fine performances—particularly from the chameonlike Leigh; both leads do their own singing. Screenwriter Turner is Leigh's mother. **117m/C; VHS, DVD.** Jennifer Jason Leigh; Mare Winningham; Ted Levine; Max Perlich; John Doe; John C. Reilly; Jimmy Witherspoon; Mina Badie; *D:* Ulu Grosbard; *W:* Barbara Turner; *C:* Jan Kiesser. Ind. Spirit '96: Support. Actress (Winningham); Montreal World Film Fest. '95: Actress (Leigh), Film; N.Y. Film Critics '95: Actress (Leigh).

Georgia, Georgia 1/2 **1972 (R)** Sands is a black entertainer on tour in Sweden who falls for a white photographer. Her traveling companion, who hates whites, takes drastic action to separate the lovers. Poor acting, script, and direction. Based on a book by Maya Angelou. **91m/C; VHS, DVD.** Diana Sands; Dirk Benedict; Minnie Gentry; *D:* Stig Bjorkman; *W:* Maya Angelou.

Georgia O'Keefe **2009** The relationship between artist Georgia O'Keefe (Allen) and 23-years-older photographer Alfred Stieglitz (Irons) begins with an adulterous affair in New York. Despite their marriage in 1924, O'Keefe lived the equality revolution that others merely preached though she was heartbroken and driven to a nervous breakdown when her fame increased a needy Stieglitz's insecurities and infidelities. This didn't stop O'Keefe's travels to the southwest nor her decision to live and work (minus her husband) part of the year in her beloved New Mexico. Irons gets stuck with a rather one-note characterization and the Lifetime drama does indeed belong to Allen's provocative title character. **89m/C; DVD.** Joan Allen; Jeremy Irons; Ed Begley, Jr.; Kathleen Chalfant; Linda Edmond; Henry Simmons; Tyne Daly; *D:* Bob Balaban; *W:* Michael Cristofer; *C:* Paul Elliott; *M:* Jeff Beal. **CABLE**

Georgia Rule 1/2 **2007 (R)** Generally misbegotten female family saga from director Marshall takes a decided turn into the unpleasant. Rebellious troubled teen Rachel (Lohan) finally screws up so badly that her alcoholic mom Lily (Huffman) sends her off for a summer of tough love at her own estranged mother Georgia's (Fonda) small-town home in Idaho Mormon territory. Rachel proceeds to be both outrageous and obnoxious, casually revealing that she's been molested by stepdad Arnold (Elwes), although she's such a liar no one knows what to believe. Then Lily shows up, also seeking a safe haven and adding to the family tension. Yes, this is the film where Lohan's own outrageous and obnoxious behavior drew public reprimands from the producer and others. **113m/C; DVD.** Jane Fonda; Lindsay Lohan; Felicity Huffman; Dermot Mulroney; Cary Elwes; Garrett Hedlund; Laurie Metcalf; Hector Elizondo; *D:* Garry Marshall; *W:* Mark Andrus; *C:* Karl Walter Lindenlaub; *M:* John Debney.

Georgy Girl **1966** Redgrave finely plays the overweight ugly-duckling Georgy who shares a flat with the beautiful and promiscuous Meredith (Rampling). Georgy is, however, desired by the wealthy and aging Mason and soon by Meredith's lover (Bates) who recognizes her good heart. When Meredith becomes pregnant, Georgy persuades her to let her raise the baby, leaving Georgy with the dilemma of marrying the irresponsible Bates (the baby's father) or the settled Mason. The film and title song (sung by the Seekers) were both huge hits. Based on the novel by Margaret Foster who also co-wrote the screenplay. **100m/B; VHS, DVD.** *GB* Lynn Redgrave; James Mason; Charlotte Rampling; Alan Bates; Bill Owen; Claire Kelly; Rachel Kempson; Denise Coffey; Dorothy Alison; Peggy Thorpe-Bates; Dandy Nichols; *D:* Silvio Narizzano; *W:* Margaret Forster; Peter Nichols; *C:* Ken Higgins. Golden Globes '67: Actress--Mus./Comedy (Redgrave); N.Y. Film Critics '66: Actress (Redgrave).

Geostorm 1/2 **2017 (PG-13)** After catastrophic weather events wipe out entire cities in 2019, global warming is accepted as a dangerous reality. Countries, including the United States, come together to create a satellite system to find and eliminate extreme weather systems before they can create havoc. Dubbed Dutch Boy, the system works well for several years until an act of sabotage puts life on Earth in jeopardy. Chaotic and unbelievable, it also doesn't make much use of Butler's considerable action star talents. **109m/C; Blu-Ray, Streaming.** Gerard Butler; Jim Sturgess; Abbie Cornish; Alexandra Maria Lara; Daniel Wu; *D:* Dean Devlin; *W:* Dean Devlin; Paul Guyot; *C:* Roberto Schaefer; *M:* Lorne Balfe.

Gepetto **2000** Kinda goopy Pinocchio update that focuses on toymaker dad, Geppetto (Carey). His longing for a kid of his own is granted by the Blue Fairy (Louis-Dreyfus), who makes puppet Pinocchio (Adkins) come alive. But Geppetto's parenting skills leave something to be desired and soon his new son disappears with travelling showman, Stromboli (Spiner), and gets into all kinds of trouble. Some catchy tunes. **90m/C; VHS, DVD.** Drew Carey; Seth Adkins; Julia Louis-Dreyfus; Brent Spiner; Rene Auberjonois; Usher Raymond; Ana Gasteyer; Wayne Brady; *D:* Tom (Thomas R.) Moore; *W:* David Stern; *C:* Stephen M. Katz; *M:* Stephen Schwartz. **TV**

The German Doctor 1/2 *Wakolda* **2014 (PG-13)** This tense, foreign-language Argentine thriller by directed Puenzo does an excellent job at creating a creeping sense of pervading dread in the most minimalist ways possible. In 1960 Patagonia, young Jewish girl Lilith (Bado) meets an intriguing German stranger (Alex Brendemuehl), a doctor, new to Argentina, who needs a place to stay. Lilith's family has just inherited an isolated, coastal inn, so the doctor moves in with Lilith's family and the audience grows more and more uncomfortable as the stranger's origins (which might've included opening night tickets for "Springtime for Hitler") become more and more obvious. **93m/C; DVD.** Natalia Oreiro; Alex Brendemuhl; Florencia Bado; Diego Peretti; *D:* Lucia Puenzo; *W:* Lucia Puenzo; *C:* Nicolas Puenzo; *M:* Warren Ellis.

Germany in Autumn *Deutschland im Herbst* **1978** Twelve West German filmmakers offer political statements and artistic commentary on the political situation in their country after the kidnapping and murder of industrialist Hans Martin Schleyer. In German with English subtitles. **124m/C; VHS, DVD.** *GE* *D:* Volker Schlondorff; Rainer Werner Fassbinder; Alf Brustellin; Alexander Kluge; Maximiliane Mainka; Edgar Reitz; Katja Rupe; Hans Peter Cloos; Bernhard Sinkel; Beate Mainka-Jellinghaus; Peter Schubert; Heinrich Boll; *W:* Heinrich Boll.

Germany, Pale Mother *Deutschland, Bleiche Mutter* **1980** In 1939, young, pregnant German hausfrau Lene (Mattes) sends her husband, Hans (Jacobi), to the front lines. Lene and her daughter struggle for survival through the war years until she has a bitter-sweet reunion with the embittered Hans. Director Sanders-Brahms based her story on her own mother's wartime experiences but the film suffers from the relentless parade of atrocities. German with subtitles. **123m/C; VHS, DVD.** *GE* Eva Mattes; Ernst Jacobi; *D:* Helmer Sanders-Brahms; *W:* Helmer Sanders-Brahms; *C:* Jurgen Jurges; *M:* Jurgen Knieper.

Germany Year Zero *Deutschland im Jahre Null; Germania Anno Zero* **1948** There's no happy ending in Rossellini's neorealist drama that follows 1945's "Rome Open City" and 1946's "Paisan" in his war trilogy. Twelve-year-old Edmund is living in a bombed-out and occupied Berlin following the end of the war. His father is ill and cannot work, his brother Karl-Heinz is an ex-soldier hiding out because he's afraid of being accused of war crimes, and his sister Eva is doing 'escort' work. Edmund must help the family survive any way possible and he easily falls under the sway of his treacherous former teacher, Mr. Henning, who soon has Edmund selling Nazi items on the black market. English, French, and German with subtitles. **73m/B; DVD.** *GE IT* Edmund Moeschke; Ernst Pitschau; Ingetraud Hinze; Franz-Otto Kruger; Erich Guhne; *D:* Roberto Rossellini; *W:* Roberto Rossellini; *C:* Robert Juillard; *M:* Renzo Rossellini.

Geronimo **1993** Not to be confused with the big screen version, this made-for-cable drama uses three actors to portray the legendary Apache warrior (1829-1909) at various stages of his life. The intrepid teenager who leads attacks on Mexican troops, the adult fighting the duplicitous bluecoats, and the aged man witnessing the destruction of his way of life. The true story is told from the point of view of Native American culture and historical records. Somewhat overly earnest. **120m/C; VHS, DVD.** Joseph Runningfox; Jimmy Herman; Ryan Black; Nick Ramus; Michelle St. John; Michael Greyeyes; Tailinh Forest Flower; Kimberly Norris; August Schellenberg; Geno Silva; Harrison Lowe; *D:* Roger Young; *W:* J.T. Allen; *M:* Patrick Williams. **CABLE**

Geronimo: An American Legend 1/2 **1993 (PG-13)** Well-intentioned bio-actioner about the legendary Apache leader who fought the U.S. Army over forcing Native Americans onto reservations. The division of young Army officer Gatewood (Patric) is to round up the renegades led by Geronimo (Studi), whom Gatewood naturally comes to admire. Hackman and Duvall (as a General and a scout respectively) steal any scene they're in although the leads manage to hold their own. An unknown Damon plays the narrator, Lt. Britton Davis. Too noble for its own good and somewhat plodding. Great location filming around Moab, Utah. **115m/C; VHS, DVD, Blu-Ray.** Wes Studi; Jason Patric; Robert Duvall; Gene Hackman; Matt Damon; Rodney A. Grant; Kevin Tighe; Carlos Palomino; Stephen McHattie; *D:* Walter Hill; *W:* John Milius; Larry Gross; *C:* Lloyd Ahern, II; *M:* Ry Cooder.

Gerry **2002 (R)** Even for Van Sant, this is a bizarro film with a number of obscure (and-not-so-obscure) influences. Two young men, both named Gerry (Damon, Affleck), are driving along a desert highway when they decide to get out of the car and hike along a wilderness trail. They get lost and start wandering around. They have no food or water and, after a couple of days, start to hallucinate, eventually the Affleck Gerry can't go on (but the film does). Something to make you go hmmmmmm. Or maybe, what were they thinking?! **103m/C; DVD.** Matt Damon; Casey Affleck; *D:* Gus Van Sant; *W:* Matt Damon; Casey Affleck; Gus Van Sant; *C:* Harris Savides; *M:* Arvo Part.

Gertrud 1/2 **1964** The simple story of an independent Danish woman rejecting her husband and lovers in favor of isolation. Cold, dry, minimalistic techniques make up Dreyer's final film. In Danish with subtitles. **116m/B; VHS, DVD.** *DK* Nina Pens Rode; Bendt Rothe; Ebbe Rode; Baard Owe; *D:* Carl Theodor Dreyer; *W:* Carl Theodor Dreyer; *C:* Arne Abrahamsen; Henning Bendtsen; *M:* Jorgen Jersild.

Gervaise **1956** The best of several films of Emile Zola's "L'Assommoir." A 19th-century middle-class family is destroyed by the father's plunge into alcoholism despite a mother's attempts to save them. Well acted but overwhelmingly depressing. In French with English subtitles. **89m/B; VHS, DVD.** *FR* Maria Schell; Francois Perier; Suzy Delair; Armand Mestral; *D:* Rene Clement; *M:* Georges Auric. British Acad. '56: Actor (Perier), Film; N.Y. Film Critics '57: Foreign Film; Venice Film Fest. '56: Actress (Schell).

Get a Clue! *The Westing Game* **1998 (PG)** Teenaged Turtle discovers the body of a millionaire recluse and then learns that whoever can find the murderer will be awarded $20 million. Adapted from the book "The Westing Game." **95m/C; VHS, DVD.** Ashley Peldon; Diane Ladd; Sally Kirkland; Cliff DeYoung; Ray Walston; Lewis Arquette; Billy Morrissette; Ernest Liu; Shane West; Sandy Faison; *D:* Terence H. Winkless; *W:* Dylan Kelsey Hadley; *C:* Kurt Brabbee; *M:* Parmer Fuller. **VIDEO**

Get a Clue 1/2 **2002 (G)** Pampered rich girl and school gossip columnist (Lohan) becomes an amateur detective when one of her teachers goes missing. Lohan fans will love this good-natured Disney Channel teen mystery, others probably not so much. **107m/C; DVD.** Lindsay Lohan; Bug Hall; Ian Gomez; Brenda Song; Amanda Plummer; Charles Shaughnessy; Dan Lett; Kimberly Roberts; *D:* Maggie Greenwald; *W:* Alana Sanko; *C:* Rhett Morita; *M:* David Mansfield. **CABLE**

Get a Job 1/2 **2016 (R)** A comedy about what really happens after graduation from college. Recent college grad Will (Teller) and his girlfriend Jillian (Kendrick) thought finding a job with their degree in hand would be easy. Instead, they find themselves taking a series of unusual gigs. Through it all, Will and Jillian learn that life is an unexpected adventure experienced with family, friends, and coworkers. **83m/C; DVD, Blu-Ray, Streaming.** Miles Teller; Anna Kendrick; Alison Brie; Bryan Cranston; Nicholas Braun; *D:* Dylan Kidd; *W:* Kyle Pennekamp; Scott Turpel; *C:* David Hennings; *M:* Jonathan Sadoff.

Get Carter **1971 (R)** Tough and stylish crime drama that has gained in stature since its release. Small-timer London hood Jack Carter (Caine) arrives in Newcastle determined to find out who killed his brother. After meeting local crime boss Cyril Kinnear (Osborne), Carter is told to go back home and leave things alone. But he doesn't and things (and the film) don't turn out exactly as expected. Caine shows just how ruthless he can make a character. Film debut for director Hodges. Based on the novel "Jack's Return Home" by Ted Lewis. Remade in 1972 as "Hit Man" and in 2000. **112m/C; VHS, DVD, Blu-Ray.** *GB* Michael Caine; Ian Hendry; John Osborne; Geraldine Moffatt; Glynn Edwards; Dorothy White; Petra Markham; Bryan Mosley; Britt Ekland; Tony Beckley; George Sewell; Alun Armstrong; Bernard Hepton; Terence Rigby; *D:* Mike Hodges; *W:* Mike Hodges; *C:* Wolfgang Suschitzky; *M:* Roy Budd.

Get Carter **2000 (R)** Stallone is Las Vegas tough guy Jack Carter, who goes home to Seattle for his brother's funeral and decides that his death wasn't natural. Hoping to redeem himself in the eyes of sister-in-law Gloria (Richardson) and niece Doreen (Cook), Carter searches the seedy underbelly for the killers. Or he may be searching for some decent lighting, since most of the scenes are dark even for a seedy underbelly. His injury-inducing tour of the underworld leads him to a sleazy pornographer (Roarke) and whiny billionaire (Cumming), setting the stage for a climactic showdown involving Doreen. Remake fails because Stallone's catalog of cinematic carnage waters down the feeling of nihilistic violence of the original 1971 Brit thriller. Michael Caine (who had the original title role) makes an appearance as a wily bar owner. **104m/C; DVD, Blu-Ray.** Sylvester Stallone; Michael Caine; Rachael Leigh Cook; Alan Cumming; Miranda Richardson; Mickey Rourke; John C. McGinley; Rhona Mitra; Johnny Strong; John Cassini; Garwin Sanford; Gretchen Mol; ***D:*** Stephen Kay; ***W:*** David McKenna; ***C:*** Mauro Fiore; ***M:*** Tyler Bates.

Get Christie Love! **1974** Vintage blaxploitation from the genre's halcyon days, when going undercover meant a carte blanche for skimpy outfits. Based on Dorothy Uhnak's detective novel, the eponymous policewoman goes undercover to bring a thriving drug empire to it knees. The outcome: a TV series. Graves previously appeared on TV as one of the "Laugh-In" party girls. **95m/C; VHS, DVD.** Teresa Graves; Harry Guardino; Louise Sorel; Paul Stevens; Andy Romano; Debbie Dozier; ***D:*** William A. Graham. **TV**

Get Crazy 1/2 *Flip Out* **1983** The owner of the Saturn Theatre is attempting to stage the biggest rock-and-roll concert of all time on New Year's Eve 1983, and everything is going wrong in this hilarious, off-beat film. **90m/C; VHS, DVD.** Malcolm McDowell; Allen Garfield; Daniel Stern; Gail Edwards; Ed Begley, Jr.; Lou Reed; Bill Henderson; Fabian; Bobby Sherman; Miles Chapin; Howard Kaylan; Franklin Ajaye; Mary Woronov; Paul Bartel; Jackie Joseph; Dick Miller; Lee Ving; Clint Howard; ***D:*** Allan Arkush; ***W:*** Henry Rosenbaum; Danny Opatoshu; David Taylor; ***C:*** Thomas Del Ruth; ***M:*** Michael Boddicker.

Get Hard 1/2 **2015 (R)** Ferrell and Hart are too undeniably talented for this borderline racist, homophobic nonsense about a multi-millionaire who essentially gets lessons on how to go to jail. James King (Ferrell) is sentenced for fraud and is bound for San Quentin. Knowing that pampered, privileged people like him don't do well behind bars, King reaches out to Darnell Lewis (Hart) for advice and "training" on how to survive. The comedic duo finds some laughs buried in this horrible script but they are mostly lost among the tasteless rape jokes and unrelenting cultural stereotyping. **100m/C; DVD, Blu-Ray.** Will Ferrell; Kevin Hart; Craig T. Nelson; Alison Brie; Edwina Findley Dickerson; ***D:*** Etan Cohen; ***W:*** Etan Cohen; Jay Martel; Ian Roberts; ***C:*** Tim Suhrstedt; ***M:*** Christophe Beck.

Get Him to the Greek **2010 (R)** Rambling, rude comedy. "The Greek" is L.A.'s Greek Theatre and record company intern Aaron Green (Hill) is sent to escort uncooperative British bad boy rocker Aldous Snow (Brand) from London to L.A. for his comeback performance. Aaron is nervous, naive, and more than a little willing to sample the decadent lifestyle of drink, drugs, and sex that the devilishly dissolute Snow wallows in. Judd Apatow produces so you know what to expect as far as boy-men behaving stupidly. The Snow character first appeared in director Stoller's 2008 pic "Forgetting Sarah Marshall." **109m/C; Blu-Ray.** Jonah Hill; Russell Brand; Rose Byrne; Elisabeth Moss; Sean (Puffy, Puff Daddy, P. Diddy) Combs; ***D:*** Nicholas Stoller; ***W:*** Nicholas Stoller.

Get Low **2009 (PG-13)** Compelling and confidently-told Depression-era set story follows taciturn eccentric Felix Bush (Duvall), who's been a backwoods-Tennessee hermit for 40 years. Rumors abound about his violent past and there's much talk when Felix decides to plan his own living funeral service, which reunites him with widow Mattie Darrow (Spacek) and Rev. Charlie Jackson (Cobbs). Felix intends to hear what people have to say about him, but no one is harder on Felix than himself. Effortless performances by all, including Murray as the greedy funeral director. **102m/C; Blu-Ray, On Demand.** Bill Murray; Sissy Spacek; Bill Cobbs; Robert Duvall; Lucas Black; Gerald McRaney; Scott Cooper; Lori Beth Edgeman; ***D:*** Aaron Schneider; ***W:*** Chris Provenzano; C. Gaby Mitchell; ***C:*** David Boyd; ***M:*** Jan A.P. Kaczmarek.

Get Lucky 1/2 **2013** Lucky certainly doesn't live up to his name in this stilted crime pic. Owing the wrong kind of guys a lot of money finds Lucky getting involved in a casino heist. Only no one seems to know it's owned by a gangster who's not pleased someone would rip him off and he wants revenge. **85m/C; DVD.** *UK* Luke Treadaway; Craig Fairbrass; Emily Atack; James Cosmo; Marek Oravec; T.J. Ramini; ***D:*** Sacha Bennett; ***W:*** T.J. Ramini; Walter Taylaur; ***C:*** Peter Wignall; ***M:*** Greg Hatwell.

Get On the Bus **1996 (R)** Lee looks at the personal side of the Million Man March through a fictional group of men who board a bus in south central L.A. and head for Washington, D.C. Practically ignoring the event itself, Lee and writer Bythewood focus on the the men who participated, their reasons, and their interaction with each other. Standouts in the melting pot of characters include Dutton as the attentive bus driver, a brash young actor (Braugher), a likable old man (Davis), an absentee father (Byrd) and his potentially delinquent son (Bonds), and a cop (Smith). Despite low budget (2.4 mil) and tight shooting schedule (21 days), Lee manages to drive the story home with fine dialogue and characterization that (for the most part) avoids stereotypes. **122m/C; VHS, DVD.** Andre Braugher; Ossie Davis; Charles S. Dutton; De'Aundre Bonds; Gabriel Casseus; Albert Hall; Hill Harper; Harry J. Lennix; Bernie Mac; Wendell Pierce; Roger Guenveur Smith; Isaiah Washington, IV; Steve White; Thomas Jefferson Byrd; Richard Belzer; Randy Quaid; ***D:*** Spike Lee; ***W:*** Reggie Rock Bythewood; ***C:*** Elliot Davis; ***M:*** Terence Blanchard.

Get On Up 1/2 **2014 (PG-13)** James Brown finally gets an overdue biopic treatment in director Taylor's generic musical drama carried entirely by Boseman's fearless performance as the "Hardest Working Man in Show Business." Taylor's film hits every single one of the expected beats in Brown's life, chronicling his tough upbringing in extreme poverty to being one of the most famous and influential musicians in the history of music. The complete lack of style or surprises is offset by a solid cast throughout, especially Boseman, Ellis as Bobby Byrd, and Davis as Susie Brown. Great cast, great music, but ultimately a mediocre movie. **139m/C; DVD, Blu-Ray.** Chadwick Boseman; Dan Aykroyd; Nelsan Ellis; Octavia Spencer; Jill Scott; Viola Davis; Lennie James; ***D:*** Tate Taylor; ***W:*** Jez Butterworth; John-Henry Butterworth; ***C:*** Stephen Goldblatt; ***M:*** Thomas Newman.

Get Out **2017 (R)** Jordan Peele's smash hit directorial debut is a fantastic horror thriller that uses racial tensions to produce honest scares and social insight. Black Chris Washington (Kaluuya) and his white girlfriend Rose (Williams) are going to visit her parents for the weekend. Everything seems relatively normal as Chris gets to know Dean (Whitford), Missy (Keener), and brother Jeremy (Landry Jones), but he soon suspects something is wrong in this film that plays off paranoia classics like "Rosemary's Baby" and "The Stepford Wives." It doesn't quite stick the landing but this is funny, scary, and incredibly entertaining. **104m/C; DVD, Blu-Ray.** Daniel Kaluuya; Allison Williams; Catherine Keener; Bradley Whitford; Caleb Landry Jones; ***D:*** Jordan Peele; ***W:*** Jordan Peele; ***C:*** Toby Oliver; ***M:*** Michael Abels. Oscars '17: Orig. Screenplay; Ind. Spirit '18: Director (Peele), Film; Writers Guild '17: Orig. Screenplay.

Get Out Your Handkerchiefs 1/2 *Preparez Vous Mouchoirs* **1978 (R)** Unconventional comedy about a husband desperately attempting to make his sexually frustrated wife happy. Determined to go to any lengths, he asks a Mozart-loving teacher to become her lover. She is now, however, bored by both men. Only when she meets a 13-year-old genius at the summer camp where the three adults are counselors does she come out of her funk and find her sexual happiness. Laure is a beautiful character, but Depardieu and Dewaere are wonderful as the bewildered would-be lovers. Academy Award winner for Best Foreign Film. In French with English subtitles. **109m/C; VHS, DVD, Blu-Ray.** *FR* Gerard Depardieu; Patrick Dewaere; Carole Laure; ***D:*** Bertrand Blier; ***W:*** Bertrand Blier; ***C:*** Jean Penzer; ***M:*** Georges Delerue. Oscars '78: Foreign Film; Cesar '79: Score; Natl. Soc. Film Critics '78: Film.

Get Over It! 1/2 **2001 (PG-13)** Professes to be thematically related to "A Midsummer Night's Dream," but don't let this get your hopes up. Thankfully, there's little chance of that happening, as the practice of basing teen comedies on Shakespeare plays reached the saturation point not too long ago and audiences realized that a film claiming to have been inspired by the Bard rarely met such high expectations. So it goes with this below-average kiddie comedy, which follows the sad breakup of Berke Landers (Foster), the nice but slightly dull boy, and Alison (Sagemiller), his popular former girlfriend, who soon takes up with Striker (West), the hot new boy in school. Berke's obsession with his old flame seems unrelenting until Kelly (Dunst) enters the scene. **90m/C; VHS, DVD.** Kirsten Dunst; Ben Foster; Colin Hanks; Melissa Sagemiller; Sisqo; Shane West; Martin Short; Swoosie Kurtz; Ed Begley, Jr.; Zoe Saldana; Mila Kunis; Carmen Electra; ***Cameo(s):*** Coolio; Colleen (Ann) Fitzpatrick; ***D:*** Tommy O'Haver; ***W:*** R. Lee Fleming, Jr.; ***C:*** Maryse Alberti; ***M:*** Steve Bartek.

Get Real 1/2 **1999 (R)** Gay coming of age tale about Brit suburban teen, Steven (Silverstone), deciding to come out of the closet. Steven's only confidante is fellow outsider Linda (Brittain). Then he has an unexpected encounter with popular jock John (Gorton), who's confused about his sexuality and terrified that anyone will suspect he's gay, even to the point of helping his jock buddies gay-bash Steven. Eventually, Steven decides secrecy is not worth the pain. Good performances in a somewhat self-conscious drama. Adapted from Wilde's play "What's Wrong with Angry?" **111m/C; VHS, DVD.** *GB* Ben Silverstone; Brad Gorton; Charlotte Brittain; Stacy A. Hart; Kate McEnery; Jacquetta May; David Lumsden; Louise J. Taylor; Tim Harris; ***D:*** Simon Shore; ***W:*** Patrick Wilde; ***C:*** Alan Almond; ***M:*** John Lunn.

Get Rich or Die Tryin' 1/2 **2005 (R)** Gangsta melodrama loosely based on the experiences of star/rapper 50 Cent and something of a departure for Irish director Sheridan. Thug Marcus wants easy money by selling drugs; instead he gets into some nasty turf wars and winds up in prison. He reconnects with homeboy Bama (Howard) who offers to be his manager if Marcus wants to pursue that rap career. He also gets a good woman, Charlene (Bryant), who loves and believes in him. None of this is particularly interesting, maybe because familiarity breeds, if not contempt, then indifference. **134m/C; DVD.** 50 Cent; Terrence Howard; Joy Bryant; Bill Duke; Adewale Akinnuoye-Agbaje; Omar Benson Miller; Viola Davis; Tory Kittles; Marc John Jefferies; Brian O'Hara; Sullivan Walker; Russell Hornsby; Ashley Walters; Serena Reeder; Mpho Koaho; ***D:*** Jim Sheridan; ***W:*** Terence Winter; ***C:*** Declan Quinn; ***M:*** Quincy Jones; Gavin Friday; Maurice Seezer.

Get Rita *Gun Moll; Poopsie; Oopsie Poopsie; La Puppa del Gangster* **1975** Italian prostitute sets up her gangster boyfriend for a murder she committed and she winds up as mob boss. **90m/C; VHS, DVD.** Sophia Loren; Marcello Mastroianni; ***D:*** Tom Rowe.

Get Shorty **1995 (R)** Low-level Miami loan shark and film buff Chili Palmer (Travolta) heads to Hollywood via Las Vegas, looking for a deadbeat drycleaner (Paymer) and a grade-Z movie producer (Hackman) who owes Vegas $150,000. Aided by B-movie scream-queen Russo, Palmer is pitted against a variety of shady Hollywood-types, including an egomaniacal star (DeVito) while trying to get into showbiz himself. Snappy scripting and performances finally do screen justice to an Elmore Leonard novel. DeVito, with the smaller title role, was originally cast as Chili Palmer, a role Travolta twice turned down until the ubiquitous Quentin Tarantino advised him to take it. **105m/C; VHS, DVD, Blu-Ray.** John Travolta; Gene Hackman; Danny DeVito; Rene Russo; Dennis Farina; Delroy Lindo; David Paymer; James Gandolfini; Bobby Slayton; ***Cameo(s):*** Bette Midler; Harvey Keitel; Penny Marshall; ***D:*** Barry Sonnenfeld; ***W:*** Scott Frank; ***C:*** Don Peterman; ***M:*** John Lurie. Golden Globes '96: Actor--Mus./Comedy (Travolta).

Get Smart 1/2 **2008 (PG-13)** Excellent casting brings the dusty 1960s TV comedy series back to life. Maxwell Smart (played brilliantly by Carell), the bumbling secret agent, is promoted within the CONTROL organization (like the CIA, but not as cool) and sent to Russia to take out super-villain Siegfried (Stamp). Balancing Smart's buffoonery is his new partner, the beautiful Agent 99 (Hathaway), who continually saves him from his own blunders. Not a cheap knock-off, but a slick spy spoof that could easily pass for a James Bond installment (if weren't so funny, that is). **110m/C; Blu-Ray, On Demand.** Steve Carell; Anne Hathaway; Dwayne "The Rock" Johnson; Alan Arkin; Terence Stamp; Terry Crews; David Koechner; Ken Davitian; Bill Murray; Masi Oka; Bernie Kopell; Nate Torrence; Patrick Warburton; James Caan; ***D:*** Peter Segal; ***W:*** Tom J. Astle; Matt Ember; ***C:*** Dean Semler; ***M:*** Trevor Rabin.

Get Smart, Again! 1/2 **1989** Would you believe Maxwell Smart is back again as CONTROL's most incompetent agent? How about Agent 99 as his sidekick? Hymie the robot and those no-good-niks at KAOS? Well, it's all true. This second reunion movie (following "The Nude Bomb") from the '60s TV show highlights all the wacky gadgetry, including the shoe phone, but fails to find the show's original outlandishness. **93m/C; VHS, DVD.** Don Adams; Barbara Feldon; Dick Gautier; Bernie Kopell; Kenneth Mars; Harold Gould; Roger Price; Fritz Feld; Robert Karvelas; King Moody; ***D:*** Gary Nelson. **TV**

Get the Gringo **2012 (R)** Gibson's in action mode as a sarcastic, nameless career criminal and getaway driver who heads across the Mexican border with his take only to be caught by some corrupt Mexican officers who confiscate the dough and throw him in prison. It's run like it's own city where the inmates families live with them. The gringo befriends a 10-year-old kid, whose dad was killed by Javi, the con running the joint. The kid's got prison smarts and he and the gringo make a surpisingly effective team. English and Spanish with subtitles. **95m/C; DVD, Blu-Ray.** Mel Gibson; Kevin Hernandez; Dolores Heredita; Daniel Gimenez Cacho; Peter Stormare; Bob Gunton; ***D:*** Adrian Grunberg; ***W:*** Mel Gibson; Adrian Grunberg; Stacy Perskie; ***C:*** Benoît Debie; ***M:*** Antonio Pinto. **VIDEO**

Get to Know Your Rabbit **1972** Absurdist indie satire from De Palma. Fed-up businessman Donald Beeman (Smothers) shucks his career to enroll in Mr. Delasandro's (Welles) magic school. Donald finds minor success as a tap-dancing magician (complete with rabbit) while his ex-boss Mr. Trumbull (Astin) goes off the rails. Trumbull becomes Donald's manager, eventually exploiting him by opening a fantasy camp for execs needing a corporate break, using the beleaguered Donald as a role model. **91m/C; DVD.** Tom Smothers; John Astin; Orson Welles; Suzanne Zenor; Allen Garfield; Katharine Ross; Samantha Jones; ***D:*** Brian De Palma; ***W:*** Jordan Crittenden; ***C:*** John A. Alonzo; ***M:*** Jack Elliott; Allyn Ferguson.

Get Well Soon 1/2 **2001 (R)** Disjointed romantic comedy finds midnight TV talk show host Bobby Bishop (Gallo) suffering a nervous breakdown that results in a number of scandals. Bobby takes off to see ex-girlfriend Lily (Cox) in New York but she's not happy to see him when he arrives and neither is her new boyfriend (Donovan). **95m/C; VHS, DVD.** Vincent Gallo; Courteney Cox; Jeffrey Tambor; Tate Donovan; Elina Lowensohn; Anne Meara; ***D:*** Justin McCarthy; ***W:*** Justin McCarthy; ***M:*** Vincent Gallo; Ric Markmann.

Get Yourself a College Girl 1/2 **1964** The title sounds salacious but this musical-comedy is tame fluff. Coed Terry Taylor (Mobley) attends a traditional women's college but secretly writes feminist folk songs. Her double life is discovered and she's in trouble but her fate will have to wait while she's on winter break at a Sun Valley resort. School benefactor Senator Hubert Morrison (Waterman) is also there and he's courting the youth vote, so he might come to Terry's rescue. Best seen for the musical performances of Stan Getz, the Jimmy Smith Trio, the Dave Clark Five, the Animals, and others. **86m/C; DVD.** Mary Ann Mobley; Willard Waterman; Chad Everett; Joan O'Brien; Nancy Sinatra; Chris Noel; Fabrizio Mioni; Dorothy Neumann; ***D:*** Sidney Miller; ***W:*** Robert E. Kent; ***C:*** Fred H. Jackman, Jr.; ***M:*** Fred Karger.

The Getaway **1972 (PG)** McQueen plays a thief released on a parole arranged by his wife (McGraw) only to find out a corrupt politician wants him to rob a bank. After the successful holdup, McQueen finds out his cohorts are in the politician's pocket and trying to doublecross him. McQueen and McGraw are forced into a feverish chase across Texas to the Mexican border, pursued by the politician's henchmen and the state police. Completely amoral depiction of crime and violence with McQueen taciturn as always and McGraw again showing a complete lack of acting skills. Based on a novel by Jim Thompson. McQueen and McGraw had a romance during filming and later married. Remade in 1993. **123m/C; VHS, DVD, Blu-Ray, HD-DVD.** Steve McQueen; Ali MacGraw; Ben Johnson; Sally Struthers; Al Lettieri; Slim Pickens; Jack Dodson; Dub Taylor; Bo Hopkins; ***D:*** Sam Peckinpah; ***W:*** Walter Hill; ***C:*** Lucien Ballard; ***M:*** Quincy Jones.

The Getaway ☙ 1/2 **1993 (R)** It was a bad movie in 1972 and the remake hasn't improved the situation. Doc and Carol are husband and wife crooks (played by marrieds Basinger and Baldwin). Doc gets double-crossed and winds up in a Mexican jail; Carol gets a well-connected crook (Woods) to spring her hubby—by sleeping with him and promising Doc will pull off another heist. The robbery's botched, there are double-crosses galore, and the couple go on the run. The stars are pretty but everything's predictable. An unrated version is also available. **110m/C; VHS, DVD, HD-DVD.** Alec Baldwin; Kim Basinger; James Woods; Michael Madsen; Jennifer Tilly; David Morse; ***D:*** Roger Donaldson; ***W:*** Walter Hill; Amy Holden Jones; ***C:*** Peter Menzies, Jr.; ***M:*** Mark Isham.

Getaway WOOF! 2013 (PG-13) Retired race car driver Brent Magna's (Hawke) life is turned upside down when his wife is kidnapped and her tormentor plays vehicular games with the speed demon. Brent is forced to steal a specific car, one equipped with cameras and microphones, and takes on a passenger (Gomez) who will play into his wife's kidnapper's (Voight) evil schemes. Senseless, the film doesn't work even as a B-movie thrill ride because of its incompetent production. Poorly edited, poorly written, poorly performed--well, just poor all around, really--producer Courtney Solomon's directorial effort is one from which viewers should flee. **90m/C; DVD, Blu-Ray.** Ethan Hawke; Selena Gomez; Jon Voight; Rebecca Budig; Bruce Payne; Ivailo Geraskov; ***V:*** Paul Freeman; ***D:*** Courtney Solomon; ***W:*** Sean Finegan; Gregg Maxwell Parker; ***C:*** Yaron Levy; ***M:*** Justin Caine Burnett.

Getting Away With Murder WOOF! 1996 (R) An utterly distasteful bomb that proves the Holocaust just isn't as funny as it used to be. College professor Aykroyd takes matters into his own hands when he learns that his kindly neighbor (Lemmon) is a Nazi war criminal. After finding out he may have been a wee bit hasty, he marries the coot's daughter as penance. Writer-director Miller tries to squeeze gags out of such topics as Nazi death camps and Holocaust denial. Definitely career lows for everyone involved. (What were they thinking?) One of the last films released (with no advance warning and no advance screenings) by Savoy pictures. **92m/C; VHS, DVD.** Dan Aykroyd; Lily Tomlin; Jack Lemmon; Bonnie Hunt; Brian Kerwin; ***D:*** Harvey Miller; ***W:*** Harvey Miller; ***C:*** Frank Tidy; ***M:*** John Debney.

Getting Even with Dad ☙ 1/2 **1994 (PG)** Crook Danson can't find the money he stole in his last heist. Why? because his precocious son has hidden it with the intention of blackmailing dear old dad into going straight and acting like a real father. Title is unintentionally funny in light of Mac's domineering dad Kit, who makes everybody in Hollywood want to go hide when he appears. Fairly bland family film squanders charm of Danson and Culkin, running formulaic plot into ground. Headly is likewise wasted as district attorney who prosecutes and then falls for Pops. **108m/C; VHS, DVD, Blu-Ray.** Macaulay Culkin; Ted Danson; Glenne Headly; Hector Elizondo; Saul Rubinek; Gailard Sartain; Kathleen Wilhoite; Sam McMurray; Dann Florek; ***D:*** Howard Deutch; ***W:*** Tom S. Parker; Jim Jennewein; ***C:*** Tim Suhrstedt; ***M:*** Miles Goodman.

Getting Gertie's Garter ☙☙ **1927** Engaged lawyer Ken Walrick (Ray) is embarrassed by his one-time gift to showgirl Gertie (Prevost)?an engraved jeweled garter he feels he must retrieve before his jealous fiancee Barbara (Ridgeway) finds out about his former dalliance. **70m/B; Silent; DVD.** Marie Prevost; Charles Ray; Fritzi Ridgeway; Franklin Pangborn; Sally Rand; Harry C. (Henry) Myers; ***D:*** E. Mason Hopper; ***W:*** F. McGrew Willis; ***C:*** Harold Rosson.

Getting Gertie's Garter ☙☙ 1/2 **1945** Light romantic farce that hinges on the fact the befuddled lead doesn't dare mention a lady's undergarment in public. (Yes, life was once like that.) Ken (O'Keefe) has just obtained a swell promotion and is happily married to Patty (Ryan). But in his reckless youth, he gave former flame Gertie (McDonald) a bejeweled garter as a token of his affections. Now, Gertie is about to get married to Ken's friend Ted (Sullivan) and that darn garter is wantd by the District Attorney as evidence in a robbery. Ken needs to quietly retrieve the garter before Patty, Ted, the D.A., and Ken's stuffy board of directors gets wind of the scandalous trinket. Lots of standard farce moments such as hiding in closets and shimmying down drainpipes. **72m/B; VHS, DVD.** Dennis O'Keefe; Marie McDonald; Barry Sullivan; Binnie Barnes; Sheila Ryan; J. Carrol Naish; Jerome Cowan; ***D:*** Allan Dwan; ***W:*** Allan Dwan; Karen DeWolf; ***C:*** Charles Lawton, Jr.

Getting Gotti ☙☙ 1/2 **1994 (R)** Story of the seven-year investigation and six-month trial by U.S. Attorney's Office prosecutor Diane Giacalone (Bracco) against reputed mobster "Teflon Don" John Gotti. (She lost.) **93m/C; VHS, DVD.** Lorraine Bracco; Anthony John (Tony) Denison; Kathleen Lasky; August Schellenberg; Kenneth Welsh; Ellen Burstyn; Lawrence Bayne; ***D:*** Roger Young; ***W:*** James Henerson; ***M:*** Patrick Williams. **TV**

Getting High ☙ 1/2 *5 Up 2 Down* **2006 (R)** Druggie artist Hunter gets a big advance for his New York art exhibit and buys a week's worth of coke for him and buddy Santo. But as their drug binge takes its toll, is it enough to convince them to get clean? **98m/C; DVD.** Isaach de Bankole; Kirk Acevedo; Paz de la Huerta; Mike Doyle; ***D:*** Steven Kessler; ***W:*** Steven Kessler; Steve Soto; Brady Hart; ***C:*** Till Neumann; ***M:*** John Swihart.

Getting It ☙☙ **2006** Teen sex comedy hero Silver is unlucky in love until by some twist of fate a rumor spreads about town that he has a two-foot (fill in the blank). Suddenly the ladies are lined up around the block to boyfriend young Silver. But alas, true love rules as he decides to woo back his dream girl. **97m/C; DVD.** Patrick Censoplano; Cheryl Dent; Sajen Corona; Sandra Staggs; Salvatore Crivelo; ***D:*** Nick Gaitatjis; ***W:*** Nick Gaitatjis; ***C:*** Jonathan Hale; ***M:*** Holly Amber Church. **VIDEO**

Getting It On ☙ **1983 (R)** High school student uses his new-found video equipment for voyeuristic activity. **100m/C; VHS, DVD.** Martin Yost; Heather Kennedy; Jeff Edmond; Kathy Rockmeier; Mark Alan Ferri; ***D:*** William Olsen.

Getting It Right ☙☙ 1/2 **1989 (R)** A sweet-natured British comedy about an inexperienced, shy adult male who is quite suddenly pursued by a middle-aged socialite, a pregnant, unstable rich girl, and a modest single mother. Novel and screenplay by Elizabeth Jane Howard. **101m/C; DVD.** *UK* Jesse Birdsall; Helena Bonham Carter; Lynn Redgrave; Peter Cook; John Gielgud; Jane Horrocks; Richard Huw; Shirley Anne Field; Pat Haywood; Judy Parfitt; Bryan Pringle; ***D:*** Randal Kleiser; ***W:*** Elizabeth Jane Howard; ***M:*** Colin Towns; Steve Tyrell.

The Getting of Wisdom ☙☙ 1/2 **1977** A 13-year-old girl from the Australian outback tries to establish her identity, and her individuality, within the restricting confines of a Victorian girl's boarding school. Based on the novel by Henry Handel Richardson. **100m/C; VHS, DVD, Streaming.** *AU* Susannah Fowle; Hilary Ryan; Alix Longman; Sheila Helpmann; Patricia Kennedy; Barry Humphries; John Waters; ***D:*** Bruce Beresford.

Getting Out ☙☙ 1/2 **1994** Arlie (DeMornay) is an ex-con on her way home to Georgia and what she hopes will be a reunion with the son she bore in jail. She thinks he's in a foster home but instead her mother (Burstyn) had the child adopted and if she interferes, Arlie's parole will be revoked. Arlie's trying desperately to rehabilitate herself but the system and old contacts are close to dragging her back down. TV movie adapted from Marsha Norman's 1977 play. **92m/C; VHS, DVD.** Rebecca De Mornay; Ellen Burstyn; Robert Knepper; Richard Jenkins; Carol Mitchell-Leon; Tandy Cronyn; Norman Skaggs; ***D:*** John Korty; ***W:*** Eugene Corr; Ruth Shapiro; ***M:*** Mason Daring.

Getting Played ☙☙ 1/2 **2005 (PG-13)** Three attractive women bet that any man can be seduced, but their mark knows their game and decides to play it his way. Slight story, predictable ending, attractive cast. **85m/C; DVD.** Vivica A. Fox; Carmen Electra; Stacey Dash; Bill Bellamy; Joe Torry; Dorian Gregory; Kathy Najimy; ***D:*** David Silberg; ***W:*** David Silberg; ***C:*** Francis Kenny; ***M:*** David Lawrence. **VIDEO**

Getting Straight ☙☙ **1970 (R)** A returning Vietnam soldier (Gould) goes back to his alma mater to secure a teaching degree and gets involved in the lives of his fellow students and the turbulence of the end of the '60s, including campus riots. A now-dated "youth" picture somewhat watchable for Gould's performance. **124m/C; VHS, DVD.** Elliott Gould; Candice Bergen; Jeff Corey; Cecil Kellaway; Jeannie Berlin; Harrison Ford; John Rubinstein; Robert F. Lyons; Max Julien; ***D:*** Richard Rush.

Getting Wasted ☙ 1/2 **1980 (PG)** Set in 1969 at a military academy for troublesome young men, chaos ensues when the cadets meet hippies. **98m/C; VHS, DVD.** Brian Kerwin; Stephen Furst; Cooper Huckabee; David Caruso; Stefan Arngrim; ***D:*** Paul Fritzler; ***C:*** Daniel Pearl.

Gettysburg ☙☙☙ 1/2 **1993 (PG)** Civil War buff Ted Turner (who has a cameo as a Confederate soldier) originally intended Michael Shaara's Pulitzer Prize-winning novel "The Killer Angels" to be adapted as a three-part miniseries for his "TNT" network, but the lure of the big screen prevailed, marking the first time the battle has been committed to film and the first time a film crew has been allowed to film battle scenes on the Gettysburg National Military Park battlefield. The greatest battle of the war and the bloodiest in U.S. history is realistically staged by more than 5,000 Civil War re-enactors. The all-male cast concentrates on presenting the human cost of the war, with Daniels particularly noteworthy as the scholarly Colonel Chamberlain, determined to hold Little Round Top for the Union. Last film role for Jordan, to whom the movie is co-dedicated. The full scale recreation of Pickett's Charge is believed to be the largest period scale motion-picture sequence filmed in North America since D.W. Griffith's "Birth of a Nation." **254m/C; VHS, DVD.** Jeff Daniels; Martin Sheen; Tom Berenger; Sam Elliott; Richard Jordan; Stephen Lang; Kevin Conway; C. Thomas Howell; Maxwell Caulfield; Andrew Prine; James Lancaster; Royce D. Applegate; Brian Mallon; Cooper Huckabee; Bo Brinkman; Kieran Mulroney; Patrick Gorman; William Morgan Sheppard; James Patrick Stuart; Tim Ruddy; Joseph Fuqua; Ivan Kane; Warren Burton; MacIntyre Dixon; George Lazenby; Alex Harvey; John Diehl; John Rothman; Richard Anderson; Billy Campbell; David Carpenter; Donal Logue; Dwier Brown; Mark Moses; Ken Burns; Ted Turner; ***D:*** Ronald F. Maxwell; ***W:*** Ronald F. Maxwell; ***C:*** Kees Van Oostrum; ***M:*** Randy Edelman.

The Ghastly Love of Johnny X ☙☙ **2012** A juvenile delinquent from outer space is exiled to Earth, where his girlfriend promptly leaves him after stealing a powerful artifact known as the Resurrection Suit. Meant for fans of campy 50s sci-fi and comic musicals, this film is notable for being the last movie starring actor Kevin McCarthy and the last film made on Kodak Plus-X B&W film stock. It also took the director and actors over 10 years to get it made due to the director running out of money and going on a 6 year break. That kind of dedication alone prompts a viewing. If that doesn't get you it also has Creed Bratton. Whom we suspect is secretly playing himself. **106m/B; DVD, Streaming.** Will Keenan; Creed Bratton; De Anna Joy Brooks; Reggie Bannister; Les Williams; ***D:*** Paul Bunnell; ***W:*** Paul Bunnell; Steve Bingen; Mark D. Murphy; George Wagner; ***C:*** Francisco Bulgarelli; ***M:*** Ego Plum.

The Ghastly Ones WOOF! 1968 Three couples must stay in a haunted mansion to inherit an estate, but they're soon being violently killed off. No budget and no talent. Remade as "Legacy of Blood." **81m/C; VHS, DVD.** Don Williams; Maggie Rogers; Hal Belsoe; Veronica Redburn; Hal Sherwood; ***D:*** Andy Milligan; ***W:*** Andy Milligan; Hal Sherwood; ***C:*** Andy Milligan.

Ghetto Dawg ☙ 1/2 **2002 (R)** Standard urban actioner finds Tariq (J-King) wanting to escape his job working for mobster Gresh (Winslow) after falling for Robin (Coe). But Gresh wants Tariq to help him in his illegal pit bull fights and threatens to hurt Tariq's loved ones if he won't cooperate. **89m/C; VHS, DVD.** Drena De Niro; J-King; Portia Coe; Gianna Palminteri; Lawrence Winslow; P.J. Marshall; ***D:*** Brian Averill; ***W:*** Allen Cognata; ***C:*** Shawn Kim; ***M:*** Wendell Hanes. **VIDEO**

Ghetto Dawg 2: Out of the Pits ☙ 1/2 **2005 (R)** Aimless teen Donte (Outlaw) has revenge on his mind when his brother is murdered. He joins his brother's violent crew but discovers he's not the killer type. Hooker girlfriend Brynn (Faith) comes up with a scheme to rip off crime boss Big Daddy (Torres) but there's one last thing Donte needs to do before blowing town with his squeeze and it involves dog-fighting competitions. A basic rehash of the first flick. **88m/C; VHS, DVD.** Daniel Outlaw; Janisha Faith; Lou Torres; Paris Campbell; J-Hood; Randi Pannell; ***D:*** Jeff Crook; Josh Crook; ***W:*** Christine Conradt; ***C:*** Till Newman; ***M:*** Capone. **VIDEO**

Ghidrah the Three Headed Monster ☙☙ 1/2 *Ghidorah Sandai Kaiju Chikyu Saidai No Kessan; Ghidora, the Three-Headed Monster; Ghidrah; The Greatest Battle on Earth; The Biggest Fight on Earth; Monster of Monsters* **1965** When a three-headed monster from outer-space threatens the world, humans, having nowhere else to turn, appeal to the friendly Mothra, Rodan, and Godzilla. Rock'em, sock 'em giant thrashing about as Tokyo once again gets trampled. Dependable afternoon monster fare complete with usual dubious dubbing. **85m/C; VHS, DVD, Blu-Ray.** *JP* Akiko Wakabayashi; Yosuke Natsuki; Yuriko Hoshi; Hiroshi Koizumi; Takashi Shimura; Emi Ito; Yumi Ito; Kenji Sahara; Hisaya Ito; ***D:*** Inoshiro Honda; ***W:*** Shinichi Sekizawa; ***C:*** Hajime Koizumi; ***M:*** Akira Ifukube.

The Ghost ☙ 1/2 *Lo Spettro; Lo Spettro de Dr. Hitchcock; The Spectre* **1963** A woman is driven mad by her supposedly dead husband and their evil housekeeper. Sequel to "The Horrible Dr. Hichcock." **96m/C; VHS, DVD.** *IT* Barbara Steele; Peter Baldwin; Leonard Elliott; Harriet White; Harriet Medin; Umberto Raho; ***D:*** Riccardo Freda; ***W:*** Riccardo Freda; Oreste Biancoli; ***C:*** Raffaele Masciocchi; ***M:*** Franco Mannino; Roman Vlad.

Ghost ☙☙☙ **1990 (PG-13)** Zucker, known for overboard comedies like "Airplane!" and "Ruthless People," changed tack and directed this undemanding romantic thriller, which was the surprising top grosser of 1990. Murdered investment consultant Sam Wheast (Swayze) attempts (from somewhere near the hereafter) to protect his lover, Molly (Moore), from imminent danger when he learns he was the victim of a hit gone afoul. Goldberg is medium Oda Mae Brown, who suddenly discovers that the powers she's been faking are real. A winning blend of action, special effects (from Industrial Light and Magic) and romance. **127m/C; VHS, DVD, Blu-Ray.** Patrick Swayze; Demi Moore; Whoopi Goldberg; Tony Goldwyn; Rick Aviles; Vincent Schiavelli; Gail Boggs; Armelia McQueen; Phil Leeds; Stephen (Steve) Root; ***D:*** Jerry Zucker; ***W:*** Bruce Joel Rubin; ***C:*** Adam Greenberg; ***M:*** Maurice Jarre. Oscars '90: Orig. Screenplay, Support. Actress (Goldberg); British Acad. '90: Support. Actress (Goldberg); Golden Globes '91: Support. Actress (Goldberg).

The Ghost ☙☙ 1/2 *Ryeong; Dead Friend* **2004** Ji-won (Kim Ha-neul) has some sort of accident that wipes out her memory. And it must've been a pretty bad event because all her friends are shunning her when she comes back to school. While she tries to figure out what the deal is, they all start drowning. That'll show 'em! Of course the rest of her acquaintances blame her for the troubles, and the more she remembers the more she comes to realize they may be right. **94m/C; DVD.** *NK* Yi Shin; Ha-Neul Kim; Sang-mi Nam; Bin; Hie-ju Jeon; Yun-ji Lee; ***D:*** Tae-kyeong Kim; ***W:*** Tae-kyeong Kim.

The Ghost and Mrs. Muir
1947 A charming, beautifully orchestrated fantasy about a feisty widow who, with her young daughter, buys a seaside house and refuses to be intimidated by the crabby ghost of its former sea captain owner. When the widow falls into debt, the captain dictates his sea adventures, which she adapts into a successful novel. The ghost also falls in love with the beautiful lady. Tierney is exquisite and Harrison is sharp-tongued and manly. Based on R. A. Dick's novel. **104m/B; VHS, DVD, Blu-Ray.** Gene Tierney; Rex Harrison; George Sanders; Edna Best; Anna Lee; Vanessa Brown; Robert Coote; Natalie Wood; Isobel Elsom; ***D:*** Joseph L. Mankiewicz; ***W:*** Philip Dunne; ***C:*** Charles B(ryant) Lang, Jr.; ***M:*** Bernard Herrmann.

The Ghost and Mr. Chicken 1/2 **1966** Fraidy cat Luther Heggs (Knotts) works for a small town newspaper and longs to be a hot-shot reporter. One night he thinks he sees a woman's corpse at the vacant Simmons mansion but of course there's no body when the cops come. The house is considered haunted and there is a 20-year-old murder scandal, so Luther is very reluctantly persuaded to spend the night and solve the sinister goings-on. **90m/C; VHS, DVD, Blu-Ray.** Don Knotts; Joan Staley; Dick Sargent; Liam Redmond; Skip Homeier; Reta Shaw; Lurene Tuttle; Philip Ober; ***D:*** Alan Rafkin; ***W:*** James Fritzell; ***C:*** William Margulies; ***M:*** Vic Mizzy.

The Ghost and the Darkness 1/2 **1996 (R)** Based on the true story of two man-eating lions who killed 130 people and nearly derailed the building of the East African railroad in 1896. Engineer John Patterson (Kilmer) is sent to build a bridge over the Tsavo river, but as African liaison Samuel (Kani) informs him, Tsavo prophetically means place of slaughter. The workers become convinced the lions, nicknamed "The Ghost" and "The Darkness" are actually demons and, try as he might, Patterson has little luck killing the beasts. Then, legendary big game hunter Remington (Douglas) is called in—but the lions still seem to have the advantage. Lots of crunching bones, slurping blood, and quick cut editing is used to depict the lions' attacks. **110m/C; VHS, DVD.** Val Kilmer; Michael Douglas; John Kani; Bernard Hill; Om Puri; Brian McCardie; Tom Wilkinson; Emily Mortimer; Henry Cele; ***D:*** Stephen Hopkins; ***W:*** William Goldman; ***C:*** Vilmos Zsigmond; ***M:*** Jerry Goldsmith. Oscars '96: Sound FX Editing.

The Ghost Breakers **1940** As a follow-up to the Hope/Goddard 1939 comedy thriller "The Cat and the Canary," this spooky comedy was even better. Lots of laughs and real chills as Hope and Goddard investigate a haunted mansion that she's inherited in Cuba. Effective horror scenes are expertly handled by director Marshall. Remade in 1953 as "Scared Stiff" with Dean Martin and Jerry Lewis. Based on the play by Paul Dickey and Charles Goddard. **83m/B; VHS, DVD.** Bob Hope; Paulette Goddard; Richard Carlson; Paul Lukas; Willie Best; Pedro de Cordoba; Noble Johnson; Anthony Quinn; ***D:*** George Marshall; ***W:*** Walter DeLeon; ***C:*** Charles B(ryant) Lang, Jr.

The Ghost Brigade 1/2 *The Killing Box; Grey Knight* **1993 (R)** Civil War ghost story finds a Union general (Sheen) trying to discover who's slaughtering both Confederate and Union soldiers on the battlefield. So he sends Captain Harling (Pasdar) to investigate, with the help of rebel prisoner Strayn (Bernsen) and a slave (Williams). What they find is an evil brigade of soldiers—who already happen to be dead—and are eager for new recruits. **80m/C; VHS, DVD.** Corbin Bernsen; Martin Sheen; Adrian Pasdar; Ray Wise; Cynda Williams; Roger Wilson; Billy Bob Thornton; Alexis Arquette; David Arquette; Dean Cameron; A.J. (Allison Joy) Langer; Matt LeBlanc; ***D:*** George Hickenlooper; ***W:*** Matt Greenberg; ***C:*** Kent Wakeford.

Ghost Cat 1/2 **2003 (PG)** After her mother's death, 14-year-old Natalie Merritt (Page) and her grieving father Will (Ontkean) move to her mother's hometown. There's trouble involving the house Will is supposed to buy from elderly owner Mrs. Ashboro (Knight), who dies unexpectedly, and her greedy nephew Boyd (Barnett). Then there's the ghostly presence of Mrs. Ashboro's cat, Margaret, who died the same day as her owner. Mild but appealing suspenser, made for Canadian TV, shouldn't upset the younger members of the family. **90m/C; DVD.** *CA* Ellen Page; Michael Ontkean; Shirley Knight; Tom Barnett; Lori Hallier; Shawn Roberts; Nigel Bennett; ***D:*** Don McBrearty; ***W:*** Larry Betron; Heather Conkie; ***C:*** David Perrault; ***M:*** Robert Carli. **TV**

Ghost Chase 1/2 **1988 (PG-13)** A young filmmaker desperate for funds inherits his dead relative's clock, from which issues the ghost of the deceased's butler. The ghostly retainer aids in a search for the departed's secret fortune. Neither scary nor funny. **89m/C; VHS, DVD; Open Captioned.** Jason Lively; Jill Whitlow; Tim McDaniel; Paul Gleason; Chuck "Porky" Mitchell; ***D:*** Roland Emmerich; ***W:*** Roland Emmerich; Oliver Eberle; ***C:*** Karl Walter Lindenlaub.

Ghost City **1932** Our hero must deal with a masked gang that is "haunting" a town. **60 &m/B; VHS, DVD, Streaming.** Bill Cody; Helen Foster; Ann Rutherford; John Shelton; Reginald Owen; ***D:*** Harry Fraser.

Ghost Dad **1990 (PG)** A widowed workaholic dad is prematurely killed and returns from the dead to help his children prepare for the future. Cosby walks through doors, walls, and other solid objects for the sake of comedy—only none of it is funny. **84m/C; VHS, DVD.** Bill Cosby; Denise Nicholas; Ian Bannen; Christine Ebersole; Dana Ashbrook; Arnold Stang; ***D:*** Sidney Poitier; ***W:*** S.S. Wilson; Brent Maddock; ***M:*** Henry Mancini.

Ghost Dance **1983** Sacred Indian burial ground is violated, with grim results. **93m/C; VHS, DVD.** Sherman Hemsley; Henry Ball; Julie Amato; ***D:*** Peter Bufa.

Ghost Dog: The Way of the Samurai 1/2 **1999 (R)** Jarmusch takes a Far Eastern approach to the Mob-hit man genre with "Dog," whose title character, a contract killer played excellently by Whitaker, pledges himself to small-time hood Louie in the tradition of the Samurai after Louie saves his life. When one of his hits goes wrong, Ghost Dog is targeted for elimination, which leads to many dead bodies. Like most Jarmusch offerings, this one's quirky, disjointed, and not for everyone, but Whitaker's performance, and the offbeat humor make up for a lot. **116m/C; VHS, DVD.** Forest Whitaker; Cliff Gorman; Henry Silva; John Tormey; Isaach de Bankole; Tricia Vessey; Victor Argo; Gene Ruffini; Richard Portnow; Camille Winbush; ***D:*** Jim Jarmusch; ***W:*** Jim Jarmusch; ***C:*** Robby Muller.

Ghost Fever WOOF! **1987 (PG)** Two bumbling cops try to evict the inhabitants of a haunted house and get nowhere. A bad rip-off of "Ghostbusters." Alan Smithee is a pseudonym used when a director does not want his or her name on a film—no wonder. **86m/C; VHS, Streaming.** Sherman Hemsley; Luis Avalos; ***D:*** Alan Smithee; ***W:*** Oscar Brodney.

The Ghost Goes West **1936** A brash American family buys a Scottish castle and transports the pieces to the United States along with the Scottish family ghost (Donat). Also along is the ghost's modern-day descendant (also played by Donat) who is the new castle caretaker and in love with the new owner's daughter. It turns out to be up to the ghost to get the two lovers together and find his own eternal rest. A rather lovable fantasy. Rene Clair's first English film. Available in digitally remastered stereo with original movie trailer. **90m/B; VHS, DVD.** *GB* Robert Donat; Jean Parker; Eugene Pallette; Elsa Lanchester; Ralph Bunker; Patricia Hilliard; Everley Gregg; Morton Selten; Chili Bouchier; Mark Daly; Herbert Lomas; Elliot Mason; Jack Lambert; Hay Petrie; ***D:*** Rene Clair; ***W:*** Robert Sherwood; Geoffrey Kerr; ***C:*** Harold Rosson.

Ghost Image 1/2 **2007 (PG-13)** Low-budget horror in which the acting leaves a lot to be desired. Video editor Jennifer's (Rohm) boyfriend Wade (Payne) dies in a car crash that may not have been an accident. When Jen watches video footage from a party she and Wade hosted the night before it seems her beau is trying to communicate with her from beyond the grave. But the cops think she did Wade in. **96m/C; DVD.** Elisabeth Rohm; Stacey Dash; Waylon Malloy Payne; Roma Maffia; Matthew Del Negro; David Webb; Lily Rains; ***D:*** Jack Snyder; ***W:*** Jack Snyder; James Dean Schulte; Srikant Chellappa; ***C:*** Christopher Benson; ***M:*** Jamie Christopherson. **VIDEO**

Ghost in the Invisible Bikini 1/2 **1966** Yes, it is very silly and you can understand why the seventh film in AIP's "Beach Party" series was also the last, but it's still a guilty pleasure. Greedy millionaire Hiram Stokley (Karloff) has died but because of his misdeeds he can't get into heaven. Then ghostly Cecily (Hart), whom Hiram once knew, shows up to say if he can perform a good deed within 24 hours he'll get through the pearly gates. Hiram realizes that his sinister lawyer Ripper (Rathbone) is going to kill off the benefactors of his will, so thwarting him will be his good deed. Ripper's invited the heirs (who include Kirk, Walley, and Kelly) to Hiram's creepy mansion to carry out his evil plan. **82m/C; DVD.** Boris Karloff; Susan Hart; Basil Rathbone; Tommy Kirk; Deborah Walley; Patsy Kelly; Aron Kincaid; Quinn O'Hara; Jesse White; Harvey Lembeck; Bobbi Shaw; Nancy Sinatra; Benny Dubin; ***D:*** Don Weis; ***W:*** Louis M. Heyward; ***C:*** Stanley Cortez; ***M:*** Les Baxter.

Ghost in the Machine 1/2 **1993 (R)** Serial killer dies while undergoing an X-ray scan and somehow, because of a lightning storm and a power outage, his soul manages to infiltrate the hospital's computer and go on to terrorize more victims via their home computers and appliances. (You expect this to make sense?) Outlandish, predictable flick hovers between high-tech horror and satiric comedy and wastes some pretty decent talent. Horror buffs may get a kick out of it but be forewarned: You may never view your microwave, dishwasher, or electrical outlets in quite the same way again. **104m/C; VHS, DVD.** Karen Allen; Chris Mulkey; Ted Marcoux; Jessica Walter; Ric(k) Ducommun; Wil Horneff; Nancy Fish; Brandon Adams; ***D:*** Rachel Talalay; ***W:*** William Davies; William Osborne; ***M:*** Graeme Revell.

Ghost in the Shell *Koukaku Kidoutai* **1995** Major Motoko Kusanagi of the Security Police Section 9 is on the trail of a super hacker known as the Puppet Master. His techniques are so advanced that almost nothing is known about him. The time is 2029 and many people are cybernetically enhanced which allows the Puppet Master to make almost anyone his pawn. The more the Major works on the case, the more conflicted she becomes, for all that remains of her original body is a small slice of brain. In a world where the only humanity some people have are their ghosts (or souls), where they may or may not be within the shells (or bodies) they were born with, what happens when a ghost exists where it should not? Along with the philosophical questions about the nature of humanity that are heavily interlaced within the plot, this anime features a slick science fiction story and top-quality animation. Based on the story by Masamune Shirow. A special edition is available which includes the 30-minutes documentary "The Making of Ghost in the Shell." **82m/C; VHS, DVD, Blu-Ray, UMD.** *JP* ***D:*** Mamoru Oshii; ***W:*** Kazunori Ito.

Ghost in the Shell **2017 (PG-13)** Major Motoko Kusanagi (Johansson) was once a normal young woman, but she was augmented with cybernetics after a terrorist attack killed her parents. Half-human and half-android, she is the future of the species, but she starts remembering things about her past and investigates how she has been used and manipulated. Based on a wildly influential anime film, this controversial remake ticks a few boxes for action/genre fans looking for a diversion, but it's the last thing the original movie was: forgettable. It looks pretty and ScarJo is always game for an interesting venture but this one is hollow. **107m/C; DVD, Blu-Ray.** Scarlett Johansson; Pilou Asbaek; Takeshi "Beat" Kitano; Juliette Binoche; Michael Pitt; ***D:*** Rupert Sanders; ***W:*** Jamie Moss; William Wheeler; Ehren Kruger; ***C:*** Jess Hall; ***M:*** Lorne Balfe; Clint Mansell.

Ghost Machine 1/2 **2009 (R)** A group of soldiers, scientists, and computer types are all part of a secret government project that uses a simulator to train the soldiers in real-life dangerous situations. The virtual world turns into a nightmare when the vengeful ghost of a young girl haunts the system, killing those who cross her path. **92m/C; DVD.** Sean Faris; Luke Ford; Rachael Taylor; Josh Dallas; Sam Corry; Richard Dormer; Halla Vilhjalmsdottir; ***D:*** Chris Hartwill; ***W:*** Sven Hughes; Malachi Smyth; ***C:*** George Richmond; ***M:*** Bill Grishaw. **VIDEO**

Ghost of a Chance *Eonios Ftitis* **2001** Vera is a dealer at a casino where med student Takis tries to make some cash. After becoming lovers, they rig a roulette game, take the money, and leave it with Vera's mother while they hide out at a friend's house. But their romantic dreams soon succumb to reality and when Vera returns home for her father's funeral, she's confronted by the casino boss who threatens her unless he gets his money back. Greek with subtitles. **100m/C; VHS, DVD.** *GR* Maria Solomou; Emilios Chilakis; Mae Savastopoulou; Spyros Stavrinidis; ***D:*** Vangelis Seitanidis; ***W:*** Vangelis Seitanidis; ***C:*** Alekos Yannaros; ***M:*** Fotini Baxevani; Dimitris Tsakas.

The Ghost of Dragstrip Hollow **1959** Low-budget AIP teen fodder has the members of the hotrod, drag-racing Zenith Club losing their hangout. Anastasia Abernathy (Neumann), a friend of member Lois' (Fair) family, offers the teens her old mansion if they can get rid of the resident ghost. They decide to hold a come as your favorite monster Halloween bash to celebrate and discover there's a party-crasher! **65m/B; DVD.** Jody Fair; Russ Bender; Dorothy Neumann; Elaine DuPont; Henry McCann; Martin Braddock; Leon Tyler; Kirby Smith; ***D:*** William Hole, Jr.; ***W:*** Lou Rusoff; ***C:*** Gilbert Warrenton; ***M:*** Ronald Stein.

The Ghost of Frankenstein 1/2
1942 Fourth Frankenstein film in the Universal Studios series with Chaney filling in for Karloff as the monster. Not as good as its predecessors, but the cast is enjoyable, especially Lugosi as the monster's deformed sidekick, Ygor. Based on a story by Eric Taylor. **68m/B; VHS, DVD.** Cedric Hardwicke; Lon Chaney, Jr.; Lionel Atwill; Ralph Bellamy; Bela Lugosi; Evelyn Ankers; Dwight Frye; ***D:*** Erle C. Kenton; ***W:*** Scott Darling; ***C:*** Milton Krasner; ***M:*** Charles Previn.

The Ghost of Greville Lodge
2000 Old-fashioned British haunted house story. Fifteen-year-old James Greville has been living in a children's home ever since his parents died when he was six. His great uncle has finally found him and James moves into the creepy family estate where there are secrets involving a fatal fire and ghosts. Adapted from the Nicholas Wilde novel "Down Came a Blackbird." **90m/C; DVD.** *GB* Jon Newman; George Cole; Prunella Scales; Kevin Howarth; Billy Smith; Howard Coggins; Rebecca Weeks; ***D:*** Niall Johnson; ***W:*** Niall Johnson; ***C:*** Gordon Hickie; ***M:*** Craig Johnson; Sam Parker.

Ghost of Hidden Valley 1/2 **1946** Billy (Crabbe) and Fuzzy (St. John) help out Englishman Henry Trenton (Meredith) who's just arrived to take over his family's supposedly haunted ranch. Rustler Dawson (King) has been using the abandoned property for his stolen cattle and tries to get rid of them. **56m/B; DVD.** Buster Crabbe; Al "Fuzzy" St. John; John Meredith; Charles "Blackie" King; Jimmy Aubrey; Jean Carlin; ***D:*** Sam Newfield; ***W:*** Ellen Coyle; ***C:*** Arthur Reed; ***M:*** Lee Zahler.

The Ghost of Spoon River *The Mystery of Spoon River* **2000 (R)** Chicago lawyer Emma Masters (Sinclair) heads home to defend her brother-in-law Jesse (McNamara) who's been accused of killing the local game warden. A killing that seems racially motivated and seems to tie into the town's dark past and a 1941 lynching. And despite the title, this standard thriller has really nothing to do with Edgar Lee Masters' "Spoon River Anthology." **90m/C; VHS, DVD.** Lauren Sinclair; Brian McNamara; Richard Portnow; Michael Monks; ***D:*** Scott A. Meehan. **VIDEO**

Ghost of the Needle **2003 (R)** Jacob (Avenet-Bradley) is a serial killer who likes to drug, photograph, and vacuum seal his female victims—watching as they suffocate. Except his latest victim, Aimee (Christian), is apparently getting her revenge from beyond the grave. **86m/C; DVD.** Brian Avenet-Bradley; Frank Warlick; Greg Thompson; Leigh Hill; ***D:*** Brian Avenet-Bradley; ***W:*** Brian Avenet-Bradley; ***C:*** Laurence Avenet-Bradley; ***M:*** Mark Lee Fletcher.

Ghost Rider 1/2 **2007 (PG-13)** Critic-proof nonsense based on the Marvel comic character with the flaming skull head and motorcycle. Stunt rider Johnny Blaze (Cage) makes a deal with the devil (Fonda) who, naturally, doesn't follow through as intended. So Johnny is left as hell's bounty hunter, up against devil spawn Blackheart (Bentley). Beautiful Mendes is wasted in the girl role while Cage and Bentley overact, Fonda and Elliott stay cool, and viewers wait for some superhero fire to ignite. **108m/C; DVD, Blu-Ray, UMD.** Nicolas Cage; Eva Mendes; Wes Bentley; Sam Elliott; Donal Logue; Peter Fonda; Brett Cullen; Matt Long; Raquel Alessi; ***D:*** Mark Steven Johnson; ***W:*** Mark Steven Johnson; ***C:*** Russell Boyd; ***M:*** Christopher Young.

Ghost Rider: Spirit of Vengeance *Ghost Rider 2* **2012 (PG-13)** The questionable filmmakers behind two "Crank" movies might seem the perfect fit for this similarly larger-than-life franchise, but this tepid sequel only serves as a reminder of why the first film wasn't that big of a hit. In the follow-up that no one but Cage's accountants (and the few people not yet tired of his recent over-acting) really wanted to see, Johnny Blaze (Cage) is called back into service as the Ghost Rider in an Eastern European setting to save a young boy (Riordan) from the devil (Hinds). Surprisingly boring for a film about a man with flames shooting out of his head. **95m/C; DVD, Blu-Ray.** Nicolas Cage; Fergus Riordan; Ciaran Hinds; Violante Placido; Idris Elba; Johnny Whitworth; ***D:*** Mark Neveldine; Brian Taylor; ***W:*** Scott Gimple; Seth Hoffman; ***C:*** Brandon Trost; ***M:*** David Sardy.

The Ghost Ship 1/2 **1943** A young sailor signs on as third mate on a ship, only to find out theat the captain is a sadistic martinet who doesn't mind endangering his crew to prove his authority. Better than it should have been B-picture was supposedly commissioned because the studio had an expensive leftover ship set and wanted an excuse to use it again. **69m/B; DVD.** Richard Dix; Russell Wade; Edith Barrett; Lawrence Tierney; Steve Forrest; Ben Bard; Edmund Glover; ***D:*** Mark Robson; ***W:*** Donald Henderson Clarke; ***C:*** Nicholas Musuraca; ***M:*** Roy Webb.

Ghost Ship 1/2 **1953** Young couple is tortured by ghostly apparitions when they move into an old yacht with a dubious past. Grade-B haunting featuring the murdered wife of the ship's former owner as the poltergeist. **69m/B; VHS, DVD.** *GB* Dermot Walsh; Hazel Court; Hugh Burden; John Robinson; ***D:*** Vernon Sewell.

Ghost Ship **2002 (R)** Promising premise sinks into formulaic horror-on-the-high-seas after a gruesome and startling beginning. A boat salvage crew led by Murphy (Byrne) is working in a remote area of the Bering Sea when they're led to the remains of a passenger liner that's been missing for more than 40 years. First mate Epps (Margulies) is the first crewmember to figure out that things are not as they should be, but the rest are caught in a web of greed that may have been the undoing of the ship's original passengers. **88m/C; VHS, DVD, Blu-Ray.** Julianna Margulies; Ron Eldard; Desmond Harrington; Isaiah Washington, IV; Gabriel Byrne; Alex Dimitriades; Karl Urban; Emily Browning; Francesca Rettondini; ***D:*** Steve Beck; ***W:*** John Pogue; Mark Hanlon; ***C:*** Gale Tattersall; ***M:*** John (Gianni) Frizzell.

Ghost Son 1/2 **2006** Mark (Hannah) and his American wife Stacey (Harring) live on a ranch in South Africa. When he dies in a car crash, the suicidal Stacey begins to see (and feel) his ghost. After delivering a son, Stacey is certain that her baby is possessed by Mark's spirit and is out to kill her. **97m/C; DVD.** Laura Elena Harring; John Hannah; Pete Postlethwaite; Coralina Cataldi-Tassoni; Mosa Kaiser; Mary Twala; ***D:*** Lamberto Bava; ***W:*** Lamberto Bava; Silvia Ranfagni; ***C:*** Tani Canivari; ***M:*** Paolo Vivaldi.

Ghost Story **1981 (R)** Four elderly men, members of an informal social club called the Chowder Society, share a terrible secret buried deep in their pasts—a secret that comes back to haunt them to death. Has moments where it's chilling, but unfortunately they're few. Based on the best-selling novel by Peter Straub. **110m/C; VHS, DVD, Blu-Ray.** Fred Astaire; Melvyn Douglas; Douglas Fairbanks, Jr.; John Houseman; Craig Wasson; Alice Krige; Patricia Neal; ***D:*** John Irvin; ***W:*** Lawrence D. Cohen; ***C:*** Jack Cardiff; ***M:*** Philippe Sarde.

A Ghost Story **2017 (R)** A meditative look at loss and the meaning of existence, felt not just by living survivors but also by decedents. Casey Affleck spends much of the movie beneath a white sheet with eye holes, watching from the background as his wife, played by Rooney Mara, moves through life without him. Gradually, he is swept through time and place to understand the concept of "legacy." A beautiful and poignant film. **92m/C; DVD, Blu-Ray.** Casey Affleck; Rooney Mara; McColm Cephas, Jr.; Kenneisha Thompson; Grover Coulson; ***D:*** David Lowery; ***W:*** David Lowery; ***C:*** Andrew Droz Palermo; ***M:*** Daniel Hart.

Ghost Team **2016 (PG-13)** Louis (Heder) is obsessed with the paranormal but has little focus in life. When a customer in his copy shop mentions that his barn may be haunted, Louis finally gets some purpose in life, recruiting his depressed best friend (Krumholtz), misfit nephew (Downs), a cable access TV star who claims to be a medium (Sedaris), a beautician (Diaz) who works down at the strip mall, and a security guard named Ross (Long). While humor or ghost hunting or at least something should happen next, nothing really does. It's a stunningly unfocused and boring movie. **83m/C; DVD.** Jon Heder; David Krumholtz; Justin Long; Melonie Diaz; Amy Sedaris; Paul W. Downs; ***D:*** Oliver Irving; ***W:*** Oliver Irving; Peter Warren; ***C:*** Timothy Naylor; ***M:*** Joe Hastings.

Ghost Town **1956** A stagecoach is attacked by a band of Cherokees and the passengers take refuge in a nearby ghost town. Over a sleepless night, they discover who can be counted on if there's an attack when secrets are revealed. **77m/B; DVD.** Kent Taylor; Marian Carr; John Smith; John Doucette; Joel Ashley; ***D:*** Allen Miner; ***W:*** Jameson Brewer; ***C:*** Joseph Biroc; ***M:*** Paul Dunlap.

Ghost Town **2008 (PG-13)** Dentist Bertram Pincus (Gervais), an unmarried, friendless, and overall grumpy guy, is granted the ability to hang out with ghosts after momentarily dying during a colonoscopy. A gift or a curse, he's not sure, but either way he finds it incredibly annoying. Enter Frank Herlihy (Kinnear), a man cheating on his girlfriend with his yoga instructor, who is hit by a bus. Frank desperately pleads with his new supernatural middleman to find his girlfriend Gwen (Leoni) and let her know that he's sorry. Of course, as despicable as Bertram may be, he and Gwen fall in love, to the endless frustration of helpless Frank. A light comedy, carried and saved by its performances, especially the brilliant and effortless Gervais. **102m/C; Blu-Ray, On Demand.** Ricky Gervais; Greg Kinnear; Tea Leoni; Dana Ivey; Billy Campbell; Kristen Wiig; Alan Ruck; ***D:*** David Koepp; ***W:*** David Koepp; John Kamps; ***C:*** Fred Murphy; ***M:*** Geoff Zanelli.

The Ghost Train 1/2 **1941** Badly dated mystery/thriller. Grating musical hall comedian Tommy Gander (Askey) causes a group of passengers to miss their connecting train and they are all forced to wait overnight in an eerie Cornish station. The stationmaster (Lomas) tells them that the station is haunted by a ghost train (the result of a deadly rail disaster) and that very night is the anniversary of the original tragedy. But what happens next turns out to be far less supernatural (note the film was made during wartime). **82m/B; DVD, Blu-Ray.** *GB* Arthur Askey; Richard Murdock; Kathleen Harrison; Peter Murray-Hill; Herbert Lomas; Morland Graham; Carole Lynne; Betty Jardine; Stuart Latham; ***D:*** Walter Forde; ***W:*** Val Guest; J.O.C. Orton; Marriott Edgar; ***C:*** Jack Cox.

The Ghost Walks **1934** A playwright has his new masterpiece acted out in front of an unsuspecting producer, who thinks that a real murder has taken place. But when the cast really does start disappearing, who's to blame? **69m/B; VHS, DVD, Blu-Ray.** John Miljan; June Collyer; Richard Carle; Spencer Charters; Johnny Arthur; Henry Kolker; ***D:*** Frank Strayer.

Ghost World 1/2 **2001 (R)** Zwigoff makes his feature debut with this dark comedy that contains echoes of his documentary "Crumb." Enid (Birch) and Rebecca (Johansson) are not your typical acid-tongued teenage outsiders. Instead of struggling to fit in, they wear their contempt for the empty mall culture that surrounds them like a badge of honor. On a whim, the girls answer a personal ad from Seymour, a middle-aged schmoe who collects old records. Seymour, whose personal quirks are similar to those of former Zwigoff documentary subject R. Crumb, is also baffled by modern culture and Enid is eventually drawn to him. She decides to help him in his attempt to find a woman, developing a special yet strange bond with him. Swinging from bleak to hilarious, the plot refuses to follow your standard romantic formula. That would be, like, so mainstream. Based on the underground comics of Daniel Clowes. **111m/C; VHS, DVD.** Thora Birch; Scarlett Johansson; Steve Buscemi; Brad Renfro; Illeana Douglas; Bob Balaban; Teri Garr; Stacey Travis; Dave Sheridan; Brian George; ***D:*** Terry Zwigoff; ***W:*** Daniel Clowes; Terry Zwigoff; ***C:*** Affonso Beato; ***M:*** David Kitay. Ind. Spirit '02: Support. Actor (Buscemi); N.Y. Film Critics '01: Support. Actor (Buscemi); Natl. Soc. Film Critics '01: Support. Actor (Buscemi).

Ghost Writer *Suffering Man's Charity* **2007** Cumming goes for high hysterics in this black comedy. Prissy music instructor John Vandermark (Cumming) is happy to rent a room to hunky struggling writer Sebastian (Boreanaz), who is equally happy to take advantage of John's obvious personal interest. But when John eventually realizes he's being used, bad things happen to both men. **92m/C; DVD.** Alan Cumming; David Boreanaz; Anne Heche; Karen Black; Henry Thomas; Jane Lynch; ***D:*** Alan Cumming; ***W:*** Thomas Gallagher; ***C:*** Alex Vendler; ***M:*** Paul Cantelon.

The Ghost Writer 1/2 **2010 (PG-13)** A successful British ghostwriter (McGregor), known only as The Ghost, is hired to complete the memoirs of former British prime minister Adam Lang (Brosnan). He travels to the Long Island mansion where Lang and his family are staying just when Lang is accused of turning suspected terrorists over to the CIA for torture during his tenure. The place is soon swarming with reporters and protesters and The Ghost's work may just uncover secrets no one wants revealed. Robert Harris co-scripted from his novel. **128m/C; Blu-Ray, On Demand.** Ewan McGregor; Pierce Brosnan; Kim Cattrall; Olivia Williams; Tom Wilkinson; Timothy Hutton; James Belushi; Eli Wallach; Tim Preece; Jon Bernthal; ***D:*** Roman Polanski; ***W:*** Roman Polanski; Robert Harris; ***C:*** Pawel Edelman; ***M:*** Alexandre Desplat.

Ghostboat 1/2 **2006** The British sub Scorpion goes missing (presumably sunk) in WWII and lone survivor Jack Hardy has amnesia. The sub suddenly reappears 40 years later, minus all signs of its crew. The government wants Jack (Jason), now a marine biologist, to join the crew they're sending to retrace the sub's course and figure out what happened. Of course, this is a mistake. An anti-climatic ending spoils the chills. **145m/C; DVD.** *GB* David Jason; Ian Puleston-Davies; Tony Haygarth; Julian Wadham; Crispin Bonham Carter; James Laurenson; Jonathan Cullen; ***D:*** Stuart Orme; ***W:*** Guy Burt; ***C:*** Tony Coldwell; ***M:*** Colin Towns. **TV**

Ghostbusters **1984 (PG)** After losing their scholastic funding, a group of "para-normal" investigators decide to go into business for themselves, aiding New York citizens in the removal of ghosts, goblins and other annoying spirits. Comedy-thriller about Manhattan being overrun by ghosts contains great special effects, zany characters, and some of the best laughs of the decade. Oscar nominated title song written and sung by Ray Parker Jr. Followed by a sequel. **103m/C; VHS, DVD, Blu-Ray, UMD.** Bill Murray; Dan Aykroyd; Harold Ramis; Rick Moranis; Sigourney Weaver; Annie Potts; Ernie Hudson; William Atherton; David Margulies; Steven Tash; Reginald VelJohnson; Timothy Carhart; ***D:*** Ivan Reitman; ***W:*** Dan Aykroyd; Harold Ramis; ***C:*** Laszlo Kovacs; ***M:*** Elmer Bernstein. Natl. Film Reg. '15.

Ghostbusters 1/2 **2016 (PG-13)** After much controversy, director/writer Feig's reboot of the hit '80s series with an all-female cast can be appreciated not just because it's an all-female cast. It's actually pretty funny. And pretty well-made. Abby Yates (McCarthy) and Erin Gilbert (Wiig) are physics researchers trying to prove the existence of apparitions. When ghosts begin to terrorize NYC, they're essentially called in as experts and team up with engineer Jillian Holtzmann (McKinnon) and subway worker Patty Tolan (Jones). The action/CGI work is a bit lacking but Feig's knack for ensemble comedy saves the day. **116m/C; DVD, Blu-Ray.** Melissa McCarthy; Kristen Wiig; Kate McKinnon; Leslie Jones; Chris Hemsworth; ***D:*** Paul Feig; ***W:*** Paul Feig; Katie Dippold; ***C:*** Robert Yeoman; ***M:*** Theodore Shapiro.

Ghostbusters 2 1/2 **1989 (PG)** After being sued by the city for the damages they did in the original "Ghostbusters," the boys in khaki are doing kiddie shows at birthday parties. When a river of slime that is actually the physical version of evil is discovered running beneath the city, the Ghostbusters are back in action. They must do battle with a wicked spirit in a painting or the entire world will fall pray to its ravaging whims. Murray is the highlight of this serviceable sequel, although MacNicol gives him a good run as the painting's henchman. **102m/C; VHS, DVD, Blu-Ray.** Bill Murray; Dan Aykroyd; Sigourney Weaver; Harold Ramis; Rick Moranis; Ernie Hudson; Peter MacNichol; David Margulies; Wilhelm von Homburg; Harris Yulin; Annie Potts; Ben Stein; Richard "Cheech" Marin; Brian Doyle-Murray; Janet Margolin; Mary Ellen Trainor; ***D:*** Ivan Reitman; ***W:*** Dan Aykroyd; Harold Ramis; ***C:*** Michael Chapman; ***M:*** Randy Edelman.

Ghosted 1/2 *Ai Mei* **2009** German artist Sophie (Busch) is in Taipei with an art exhibit dedicated to her late lover Ai-ling (Ke). She's approached for an interview by pushy reporter Mei-li (Hu), who seems to also want a more personal relationship to commence. Flashbacks to Sophie's previous life and Ai-ling's search for her father are more confusing than enlightening. English, Mandarin and German with subtitles. **92m/C; DVD.** *GE TW* Jack Kao; Inga Busch; Huan-ru Ke; Ting-Ting Hu; Jana Schulz; Marek Harloff; ***D:*** Monika Treut; ***W:*** Monika Treut; Astrid Stroher; ***C:*** Bernd Meiners; ***M:*** Uwe Haas.

The Ghosts in Our Machine **2013** Jo-Anne McArthur is an acclaimed animal photographer who becomes the focus of Marshall's well-intentioned but relatively unfocused documentary about how the animals of our modern world are impacted by the human technological evolution. Marshall followed McArthur for a year as the animal rights activist tracked stories across the globe. But the film's straightforward approach to its subject makes it often feel more like a well-made Discover Channel special than a film. **93m/C; DVD.** *US CA* ***D:*** Liz Marshall; ***W:*** Liz Marshall; ***C:*** Liz Marshall; Iris Ng; Nick de Pencier; John Price; ***M:*** Robert Wiseman.

Ghosts Never Sleep **2005** A screenwriter sells a script that exposes a family secret his wife doesn't know about and his mother wants to keep hidden at all costs. Dunaway keeps her drama queen mannerisms to a minimum. **?m/CDVD.** Faye Dunaway; Tony Goldwyn; Sean Young; Shea Alexander; ***D:*** Steve Freeedman; ***W:*** Steve Freeedman; Christopher Joyce; ***C:*** Jan Michalik; ***M:*** Craig Stuart Garfinkle. **VIDEO**

Ghosts of Berkeley Square 1/2 **1947** The ghosts of two retired soldiers of the early 18th century are doomed to haunt their former home, and only a visit from a reigning monarch can free them. **85m/B; VHS, DVD.** Wilfrid Hyde-White; Robert Morley; Felix Aylmer; ***D:*** Vernon Sewell.

Ghosts of Girlfriends Past 1/2 **2009 (PG-13)** Here's a plot that sounds suspiciously like something you'd expect at Christmas (Scrooge, anyone?). Celebrity photog Connor Mead (McConaughey) is a romantic jerk and his attitude threatens to ruin his brother Paul's (Meyer) wedding. Until the ghosts of jilted girlfriends make an appearance to see if Connor can change his caddish ways. Douglas is comically creepy as Connor's ghostly uncle—a womanizer who taught Connor how to be a heartless sleaze. But plucky Garner is wasted as Jenny, the woman Connor should never have let get away, mainly because she's obviously too smart to ever fall for Connor's smarm. **115m/C; Blu-Ray, On Demand.** Matthew McConaughey; Michael Douglas; Breckin Meyer; Jennifer Garner; Lacey Chabert; Robert Forster; Anne Archer; Emma Stone; Daniel Sunjata; Devin Brochu; ***D:*** Mark S. Waters; ***W:*** Jon Lucas; Scott Moore; ***C:*** Daryn Okada; ***M:*** Rolfe Kent.

Ghosts of Goldfield 🦴 **2007 (R)** Julie is doing her college thesis on ghosts and persuades some friends to travel with her to derelict Goldfield, Nevada, so she can check out Room 109 in the local hotel. That's where a man killed his wife (who was a maid) and baby and the woman's ghost is still hanging around. Then Julie learns she's got some personal ties to the crime. **90m/C; DVD, Blu-Ray.** Marne(tte) Patterson; Kellan Lutz; Roddy Piper; Scott Whyte; Mandy Amano; Richard ("Richie") Chance; Ashly Margaret Rae; ***D:*** Ed Winfield; ***W:*** Dominic Biondi; ***C:*** Roland Smith; ***M:*** Steve Yeaman. **VIDEO**

The Ghosts of Hanley House 🦴 ½ **1968** No-budget spooker with no-brain plot. Several unlucky guests spend an evening in a creepy mansion. . .sound familiar? Shot in Texas. **80m/C; VHS, DVD.** Barbara Chase; Wilkie De Martel; Elsie Baker; Cliff Scott; ***D:*** Louise Sherrill; ***W:*** Louise Sherrill; ***M:*** David C. Parsons.

Ghosts of Mississippi 🦴🦴 *Ghosts from the Past* **1996 (PG-13)** Director Reiner attempts to tell the story of civil rights leader Medgar Evers, murdered in 1963, and the three trials of Byron De la Beckwith (Woods), who was finally convicted (after two hung juries) in 1994. Unfortunately, he filters the story through the eyes of white assistant D.A. Bobby De Laughter (Baldwin) while ignoring Evers' accomplishments almost completely. Woods chews up the scenery as the wily old racist, bringing perhaps a little too much glee into a portrait of true evil. Goldberg sleepwalks through her role as Evers' widow, Myrlie; Evers' sons, Darrell and Van, play themselves; daughter Reena plays a juror while her character is played by Yolanda King, the daughter of slain civil rights leader Martin Luther King, Jr. Filmed on location in Jackson, Mississippi. **123m/C; VHS, DVD.** Alec Baldwin; Whoopi Goldberg; James Woods; Craig T. Nelson; Wayne Rogers; William H. Macy; Michael O'Keefe; Yolanda King; Susanna Thompson; Lucas Black; James Pickens, Jr.; Virginia Madsen; Bill Cobbs; Alexa Vega; Jerry Levine; Bill Smitrovich; Terry O'Quinn; Rex Linn; Richard Riehle; Bonnie Bartlett; Diane Ladd; Andy Romano; Rance Howard; Margo Martindale; ***D:*** Rob Reiner; ***W:*** Lewis Colick; ***C:*** John Seale; ***M:*** Marc Shaiman.

Ghostwarrior 🦴 *Swordkill* **1986 (R)** A 16th-century samurai warrior's ice-packed body is revived and runs amuck in the streets of modern-day Los Angeles. **86m/C; VHS, DVD, Blu-Ray.** Hiroshi Fujioka; Janet (Johnson) Julian; Andy Wood; John Calvin; ***D:*** Larry Carroll; ***W:*** Tim Curnen; ***C:*** Mac Ahlberg.

GhostWatcher 🦴 ½ **2002 (R)** A horrid ordeal makes Laura too scared to leave the house but then some evil spirits had to go and ruin that too. Things only get worse when the ghost hunter she hires turns out to be a fraud. **94m/C; VHS, DVD.** Jillian Byrnes; Marianne Hayden; Jennifer Servary; Kevin Floyd; Kevin Quinn; Ray Schueler; ***D:*** David Cross; ***W:*** David Cross; ***C:*** Dan Poole; ***M:*** David Cross; Jerry Gaskill; Doug Pinnick; Ty Tabor. **VIDEO**

The Ghoul 🦴🦴 ½ **1934** An eccentric English Egyptologist desires a sacred jewel to be buried with him and vows to come back from the grave if the gem is stolen. When that happens, he makes good on his ghostly promise. A minor horror piece with Karloff only appearing at the beginning and end of the film. This leaves the middle very dull. **73m/B; VHS, DVD, Blu-Ray.** *GB* Boris Karloff; Cedric Hardwicke; Ernest Thesiger; Dorothy Hyson; Ralph Richardson; Anthony Bushell; Kathleen Harrison; Harold Huth; D. A. Clarke-Smith; Jack Raine; ***D:*** T. Hayes Hunter; ***W:*** Roland Pertwee; John Hastings Turner; Rupert Downing; ***C:*** Gunther Krampf.

The Ghoul 🦴🦴 **1975 (R)** A defrocked clergyman has a cannibal son to contend with—especially after the drivers in a local auto race begin to disappear. Hurt is the lunatic family gardener. **88m/C; VHS, DVD.** *GB* Peter Cushing; John Hurt; Alexandra Bastedo; Don Henderson; Stewart Bevan; ***D:*** Freddie Francis.

Ghoul School 🦴 **1990 (R)** A spoof of horror films and college flicks, with lots of scantily clad women and bloody creatures in dark hallways. **90m/C; VHS, DVD.** Joe Franklin; Nancy Siriani; William Friedman; ***D:*** Timothy O'Rawe; ***W:*** Timothy O'Rawe; ***C:*** Michael Raso; ***M:*** Rodney Shields.

Ghoulies 🦴 **1984 (PG-13)** A young man gets more than he bargained for when he conjures up a batch of evil creatures when dabbling in the occult. Ridiculous but successful. Followed by three sequels. **81m/C; VHS, DVD, Blu-Ray.** Lisa Pelikan; Jack Nance; Scott Thomson; Tamara DeTreaux; Mariska Hargitay; Bobbie Bresee; ***D:*** Luca Bercovici; ***W:*** Luca Bercovici; ***C:*** Mac Ahlberg; ***M:*** Richard Band.

Ghoulies 2 🦴 **1987 (R)** Inept sequel to "Ghoulies" (1985), wherein the little demons haunt a failing carnival horror house, whose revenues begin to soar. Followed by a second sequel. **89m/C; VHS, DVD, Blu-Ray.** Damon Martin; Royal Dano; Phil Fondacaro; J. Downing; Kerry Remsen; ***D:*** Albert Band.

Ghoulies 3: Ghoulies Go to College **WOOF! 1991 (R)** Third in the series has the best special effects and the worst storyline. Not satisfied with ripping off "Gremlins," this one imposes Three Stooges personae upon a trio of demons at large on a beer- and babe-soaked campus. **94m/C; VHS, Streaming.** Kevin McCarthy; Griffin O'Neal; Evan Mackenzie; ***D:*** John Carl Buechler.

Ghoulies 4 🦴 ½ **1993 (R)** Dopey series continues with the satanic creatures roaming the streets of Los Angeles, searching for a way to return to their netherworld home. They get their chance when they meet a Satan-worshipping dominatrix out on a killing spree. **84m/C; VHS, DVD.** Barbara Alyn Woods; Peter Paul Liapis; Bobby DiCicco; ***D:*** Jim Wynorski; ***W:*** Mark Sevi.

Ghouls 🦴 **2007** Typically low-budget trash from the Sci-Fi Channel. Jennifer (Renton) accompanies her parents to her grandmother's funeral in a small town in Romania. She meets Thomas (DeBello), a spirit-hunting Druid, who tells Jen that there's ghouls haunting the local forest, preying on the townspeople, and her family has a connection to the creatures. Turns out her dad (Atherton) intends to sacrifice Jennifer, making her the new ghoul queen. **88m/C; DVD.** James DeBello; William Atherton; Erin Gray; Ion Haiduc; Kristen Renton; Dan Badarau; Lucia Maier; Constantin Florescu; ***D:*** Gary Jones; ***W:*** Brian D. Young; ***C:*** Toni Cartu; ***M:*** Alan Howarth. **VIDEO**

G.I. Blues 🦴🦴 **1960 (PG)** Three G.I.'s form a musical combo while stationed in Germany. Prowse is the nightclub singer Presley falls for. Presley's first film after his military service. **104m/C; VHS, DVD.** Elvis Presley; Juliet Prowse; Robert Ivers; Leticia Roman; Ludwig Stossel; James Douglas; Jeremy Slate; ***D:*** Norman Taurog; ***C:*** Loyal Griggs.

G.I. Executioner 🦴 *Wit's End; Dragon Lady* **1971 (R)** An adventure set in Singapore featuring a Vietnam veteran turned executioner. **86m/C; VHS, DVD.** Tom Kenna; Victoria Racimo; Angelique Pettyjohn; Janet Wood; Walter Hill; ***D:*** Joel M. Reed.

G.I. Jane 🦴🦴 ½ *In Pursuit of Honor; Navy Cross* **1997 (R)** Moore is buffed, bold and bald in this modern day fable of the first female to become a Navy SEAL. As Jordan O'Neil, Moore endures grueling training exercises and sexist remarks from male collegues that are tortuous for her, but enjoyable for those who sat through Moore's three previous films. Impressive supporting cast, including Mortensen as the vicious and misogynist master chief and Bancroft as a fiesty senator with a secret political agenda, pick things up when the story flags in the middle. The beginning holds the most interest, but the movie's length encourages improbable plot points. Scott shows he still knows how to make a movie look great, even if the writing doesn't quite measure up. **124m/C; VHS, DVD, Blu-Ray.** Demi Moore; Viggo Mortensen; Anne Bancroft; Jason Beghe; Scott Wilson; Morris Chestnut; Lucinda Jenney; James (Jim) Caviezel; ***D:*** Ridley Scott; ***W:*** David N. Twohy; Danielle Alexandra; ***C:*** Hugh Johnson; ***M:*** Trevor Jones. Golden Raspberries '97: Worst Actress (Moore).

G.I. Joe: The Rise of Cobra 🦴🦴 **2009 (PG-13)** When a flick is based on a toy—even if it's a classic one—the expectations are already low, as seen here: a basic plot, a bunch of interchangeable military-type characters, and a lot of CGI action. Cobra is an evil organization bent on world domination and there's an arms dealer and a super weapon and a bad ninja and a good ninja and the various members of the G.I. Joe squad running around Paris, but the blinding and deafening explosions and dazzling gizmos will distract from all that anyway. **117m/C; DVD, Blu-Ray.** Brendan Fraser; Channing Tatum; Joseph Gordon-Levitt; Sienna Miller; Dennis Quaid; Rachel Nichols; Ray Park; Marlon Wayans; Christopher Eccleston; Jonathan Pryce; Said Taghmaoui; Adewale Akinnuoye-Agbaje; Byung-hun Lee; Brandon Soo Hoo; ***D:*** Stephen Sommers; ***W:*** Stuart Beattie; David Elliot; Paul Lovett; ***C:*** Mitchell Amundsen; ***M:*** Alan Silvestri. Golden Raspberries '09: Worst Support. Actress (Miller).

G.I. Joe: Retaliation 🦴🦴 **2013 (PG-13)** As you might expect from a sequel to a movie based on a toy line, the silly script is the biggest problem here but the effects, action, and general macho behavior make for a passably fun--if senseless--blockbuster. The Joes are betrayed and left for dead, and the evil Cobra appears prepped to take over the world and start nuclear annihilation. Roadblock (Johnson) and his team lead an assault on the Cobra Commander and his enemy allies. It's all an excuse to make things blow up real good, which this movie mostly does, especially an action junkie's squeal-inducing mountainside ninja scene. **110m/C; DVD, Blu-Ray.** Channing Tatum; Dwayne "The Rock" Johnson; Ray Park; Bruce Willis; Elodie Yung; Adrianne Palicki; Ray Stevenson; Joseph Mazzello; Arnold Vosloo; Walton Goggins; ***D:*** Jon M. Chu; ***W:*** Rhett Reese; Paul Wernick; ***C:*** Stephen F. Windon; ***M:*** Henry Jackman.

Gia 🦴🦴 **1998 (R)** Based on the life of self-destructive supermodel/drug addict Gia Carangi (Jolie), who died from AIDS at the age of 26. Gia grew up in an abusive Philadelphia family and hid her insecurities under a tough and wanton persona. Taken under the wing of New York modeling exec Wilhelmina Cooper (Dunaway), Gia's exoticness gets her noticed but the hedonistic lifestyle of the late '70s quickly leads to her downfall. Jolie goes all out for the title role. **120m/C; VHS, DVD, Blu-Ray.** Angelina Jolie; Mercedes Ruehl; Kylie Travis; Faye Dunaway; Elizabeth Mitchell; Louis Giambalvo; John Considine; Scott Cohen; ***D:*** Michael Cristofer; ***W:*** Michael Cristofer; Jay McInerney; ***C:*** Rodrigo Garcia; ***M:*** Terence Blanchard. **CABLE**

Giallo 🦴 **2009 (R)** Badly-acted, low-budget, cliched Argento rubbish. A Turin taxi driver (a heavily-disguised Brody) tortures and kills the foreign women he picks up as fares. When Linda's (Seigner) sister Celine (Pataky) is abducted, she and Inspector Avolfi (Brody again) race to find her before Giallo (the serial killer's nickname) finishes her off. **92m/C; DVD.** *IT* Adrien Brody; Emmanuelle Seigner; Elsa Pataky; Robert Miano; Valentina Izumi; ***D:*** Dario Argento; ***W:*** Dario Argento; Jim Agnew; Sean Keller; ***C:*** Frederic Fasano; ***M:*** Marco Werba.

Giant 🦴🦴🦴 ½ **1956** Based on the Edna Ferber novel, this epic saga covers two generations of a wealthy Texas cattle baron (Hudson) who marries a strong-willed Virginia woman (Taylor) and takes her to live on his vast ranch. It explores the problems they have adjusting to life together, as well as the politics and prejudice of the time. Dean plays the resentful ranch hand (who secretly loves Taylor) who winds up striking oil and beginning a fortune to rival that of his former boss. Dean's last movie—he died in a car crash shortly before filming was completed. **201m/C; VHS, DVD, Blu-Ray.** Elizabeth Taylor; Rock Hudson; James Dean; Carroll Baker; Chill Wills; Dennis Hopper; Rod Taylor; Earl Holliman; Jane Withers; Sal Mineo; Mercedes McCambridge; ***D:*** George Stevens; ***W:*** Ivan Moffat; Fred Guiol; ***C:*** William Mellor. Oscars '56: Director (Stevens); AFI '98: Top 100; Directors Guild '56: Director (Stevens); Natl. Film Reg. '05.

The Giant Behemoth **WOOF!** *Behemoth; Behemoth, the Sea Monster* **1959** Quick science lesson: What animal is radioactive, breathes air and water, shoots electricity, is invisible to radar, can shrug off atomic bombs, but can be killed by a torpedo? Give up? Why, dinosaurs of course. This and many other fun lessons of science are yours to learn in this educational science fiction film from the 50's. A classic of the old black-and-white monster genre, this film is the second in Eugene Lourie's "giant reptiles whoop a major city" trilogy. The first ("The Beast from 20,000 Fathoms") is so similar many believe this film is a direct ripoff. Originally the monster was meant to be invisible, and when that idea was scrapped the stop motion animation effects provided by an ailing Willis O'Brien absorbed much of the budget. **90m/B; DVD, Blu-Ray.** Gene Evans; Andre Morell; John Turner; Jack MacGowran; Maurice Kaufmann; ***D:*** Eugene Lourie; Douglas Hickox; ***W:*** Eugene Lourie; Robert Abel; Alan J. Adler; Daniel James; ***C:*** Desmond Davis; Ken Hodges; ***M:*** Edwin Astley.

The Giant Claw 🦴 ½ **1957** Giant, winged (and stringed) bird attacks from outer space and scientists Morrow, Corday and Ankrum attempt to pluck it. Good bad movie; Corday was Playboy's Miss October, 1958. **76m/B; VHS, DVD.** Jeff Morrow; Mara Corday; Morris Ankrum; Louis D. Merrill; Edgar Barrier; Robert Shayne; Morgan Jones; Clark Howat; ***D:*** Fred F. Sears.

Giant from the Unknown **WOOF! 1958** Giant conquistador is revived after being struck by lightning and goes on a murderous rampage. Unbelievably bad. **80m/B; VHS, DVD.** Edward Kemmer; Buddy Baer; Bob Steele; Sally Fraser; Morris Ankrum; ***D:*** Richard Cunha; ***W:*** Ralph Brooke; Frank Hart Taussig; ***C:*** Richard Cunha; ***M:*** Albert Glasser.

The Giant Gila Monster 🦴 ½ **1959** A giant lizard has the nerve to disrupt a local record hop, foolishly bringing upon it the wrath of the local teens. Rear-projection monster isn't particularly effective, but the film provides many unintentional laughs. **74m/B; VHS, DVD.** Don Sullivan; Lisa Simone; Shug Fisher; Jerry Cortwright; Beverly Thurman; Don Flourney; Pat Simmons; ***D:*** Ray Kellogg; ***W:*** Jay Simms; ***C:*** Wilfred M. Cline; ***M:*** Jack Marshall.

Giant Little Ones 🦴🦴 ½ **2019 (R)** Attractive teen Franky (Wiggins) finds himself struggling with something about himself he does not quite understand. He finds himself less attracted to his girlfriend Priscilla (Kittle) and unhappy in her presence. After Franky and his best friend Ballas (Mann) are taunted by homophobes and gain a measure of revenge, the pair have a sexual encounter. Ballas distances himself from his feelings and Franky, and takes alienating actions that negatively affect Franky at school. At the same time, Franky finds a new connection with Ballas's sister Natasha (Hickson). This indie drama features strong performances, effective plotting, and a meaningful message of self-acceptance. **93m/C; DVD.** Darren Mann; Josh Wiggins; Maria Bello; Taylor Hickson; Kyle MacLachlan; ***D:*** Keith Behrman; ***W:*** Keith Behrman; ***C:*** Guy Godfree; ***M:*** Michael Brook.

The Giant Mechanical Man 🦴🦴 ½ **2012 (PG-13)** Quirky, low-budget romantic comedy finds unhappy outsider Janice (Fischer) meeting her unlikely soulmate in Tim (Messina), who makes a sometime living as the street performer of the title. They meet after getting jobs at the local zoo and it's their likeable bond that keeps the movie's other predictable characters and situations at bay. It's an imperfect film but one with its heart in the right place. **94m/C; DVD.** Jenna Fischer; Chris Messina; Topher Grace; Malin Akerman; Rich Sommer; Lucy Punch; Bob Odenkirk; ***D:*** Lee Kirk; ***W:*** Lee Kirk; ***C:*** Doug Emmett; ***M:*** Rich Ragsdale.

The Giant of Marathon 🦴🦴 **1960** Reeves shrugs off the role of Hercules to play Philippides, a marathoner (who uses a horse) trying to save Greece from invading Persian hordes. Lots of muscle on display, but not much talent. **90m/C; VHS, DVD.** *IT* Steve Reeves; Mylene Demongeot; Daniela

Rocca; Ivo Garrani; Alberto Lupo; Sergio Fantoni; *D:* Jacques Tourneur; *C:* Mario Bava.

The Giant of Metropolis ⚐⚐ *Il Gigante Di Metropolis* **1961** Muscle-bound hero goes shirtless to take on the evil, sadistic ruler of Atlantis (still above water) in 10,000 B.C. Ordinary Italian adventure, but includes interesting sets and bizarre torture scenes. **92m/C; VHS, DVD.** *IT* Gordon Mitchell; Roldano Lupi; Bella Cortez; Liana Orfei; *D:* Umberto Scarpelli.

The Giant Spider Invasion ⚐ **1975 (PG)** A meteorite carrying spider eggs crashes to Earth and soon the alien arachnids are growing to humongous proportions. Notoriously bad special effects, but the veteran "B" cast has a good time. **76m/C; VHS, DVD, Blu-Ray.** Steve Brodie; Barbara Hale; Leslie Parrish; Robert Easton; Alan Hale, Jr.; Dianne Lee Hart; Bill Williams; Christiane Schmidtmer; Kevin Brodie; *D:* Bill Rebane; *W:* Robert Easton; Bill Rebane; Richard L. Huff; *C:* Jack Willoughby.

Giants of Rome **WOOF!** **1963** Rome is in peril at the hands of a mysterious secret weapon that turns out to be a giant catapult. Ludicrous all around. **87m/C; VHS, DVD.** *IT* Richard Harrison; Ettore Manni; *D:* Anthony M. Dawson; *W:* Ernesto Gastaldi; Luciano Martino; *C:* Fausto Zuccoli; *M:* Carlo Rustichelli.

The Giants of Thessaly ⚐⚐ **1960** Jason and Orpheus search for the Golden Fleece, encountering and defeating monsters, wizards, and a scheming witch. **86m/C; VHS, DVD.** *IT* Roland Carey; Ziva Rodann; Massimo Girotti; Alberto Farnese; *D:* Riccardo Freda.

Gideon's Army ⚐⚐ **2013** HBO documentary follows the lives of three overworked public defenders: Mississippi-based June Hardwick and Georgia-based Travis Williams and Brandy Alexander. The three struggle to provide legal counsel when they are burdened with too many cases in underfunded, understaffed jurisdictions and the serious toll it takes both personally and professionally. **93m/C; DVD.** *D:* Dawn Porter; *C:* Chris Hilleke.

Gideon's Daughter ⚐⚐ **2005** Public relations whiz Gideon Warner (Nighy) is a professional star and a personal disaster. As he struggles to maintain some kind of relationship with estranged daughter Natasha (Blunt), Gideon finds unexpected romance with Stella (Richardson), who's grieving over the death of her young son. **144m/C; DVD.** *GB* Bill Nighy; Miranda Richardson; Emily Blunt; Robert Lindsay; *D:* Stephen Poliakoff; *W:* Stephen Poliakoff; *C:* Barry Ackroyd; *M:* Adrian Johnston. **TV**

Gideon's Day ⚐⚐ 1/2 *Gideon of Scotland Yard* **1958** Minor Ford crime comedy/drama is a day in the life of overworked Scotland Yard inspector George Gideon. His day starts off with an over-eager young police constable giving him a traffic ticket and then works its way to more serious cases, including a snitch saying an officer is on the take, murder, and robbery. Gideon can't even find peace at home when he misses his daughter's recital and brings back the wrong fish for dinner. Based on John Creasy's 1955 novel; the firstin the 'Gideon' series. **91m/C; DVD, Blu-Ray.** *UK* Jack Hawkins; Derek Bond; Cyril Cusack; Laurence Naismith; Andrew Ray; Anna Lee; Anna Massey; *D:* John Ford; *W:* T.E.B. Clarke; *C:* Frederick A. (Freddie) Young; *M:* Douglas Gamley.

Gideon's Trumpet ⚐⚐ 1/2 **1980** True story of Clarence Earl Gideon, a Florida convict whose case was decided by the Supreme Court and set the precedent that everyone is entitled to defense by a lawyer, whether or not they can pay for it. Based on the book by Anthony Lewis. **104m/C; VHS, DVD.** Henry Fonda; Jose Ferrer; John Houseman; Dean Jagger; Sam Jaffe; Fay Wray; *D:* Robert E. Collins. **TV**

Gidget ⚐⚐ **1959** A plucky, boy-crazy teenage girl (whose nickname means girl midget) discovers romance and wisdom on the beaches of Malibu when she becomes involved with a group of college-aged surfers. First in a series of Gidget/surfer films. Based on a novel by Frederick Kohner about his daughter. **95m/C; VHS, DVD, Blu-Ray.** Sandra Dee; James Darren; Cliff Robertson; Mary Laroche; Arthur O'Connell; Joby Baker; *D:* Paul Wendkos; *W:* Gabrielle Upton; *C:* Burnett Guffey.

Gidget Gets Married ⚐ 1/2 **1972** In this dated ABC TV movie, semi-mature Gidget, now a teacher, finally marries longtime boyfriend/surfer, Jeff "Moondoggie" Stevens, and they head to Florida for his new job. But Gidget soon finds life as a corporate wife in a company town boring and decides to shake things up for Jeff's controlling, eccentric boss, Otis Ramsey. **74m/C; DVD.** Monie Ellis; Michael Burns; Don Ameche; Joan Bennett; Paul Lynde; Elinor Donahue; MacDonald Carey; *D:* E.W. Swackhamer; *W:* John McGreevey; *C:* Joseph Biroc; *M:* Mike Post; Pete Carpenter. **TV**

Gidget Goes Hawaiian ⚐⚐ **1961** Gidget is off to Hawaii with her parents and is enjoying the beach (and the boys) when she is surprised by a visit from boyfriend "Moondoggie." Sequel to "Gidget" and followed by "Gidget Goes to Rome." **102m/C; VHS, DVD.** Deborah Walley; James Darren; Carl Reiner; Peggy Cass; Michael Callan; Eddie Foy, Jr.; *D:* Paul Wendkos.

Gidget Goes to Rome ⚐ 1/2 **1963** Darren returns in his third outing as boyfriend "Moondoggie" to yet another actress playing "Gidget" as the two vacation in Rome and find themselves tempted by other romances. Second sequel to "Gidget." **104m/C; VHS, DVD.** Cindy Carol; James Darren; Jeff Donnell; Cesare Danova; Peter Brooks; Jessie Royce Landis; *D:* Paul Wendkos; *M:* John Williams.

The Gift ⚐⚐ **2000 (R)** Widowed mom Blanchett uses her psychic gifts to help find the murderer of rich girl Holmes in their Georgia town. Among those involved are battered wife Swank, abuser Reeves, Holmes's fiance Kinnear and mentally slow tow-truck driver Ribisi. By-the-numbers thriller loses steam after a promising start, but is saved by the performances of a fine cast. The characters are stock Southern Gothic types, but they're given dimension by the portrayals. Raimi shows (early on) that he still knows how to startle an audience and create a creepy atmosphere. **112m/C; VHS, DVD.** Cate Blanchett; Katie Holmes; Hilary Swank; Keanu Reeves; Greg Kinnear; Giovanni Ribisi; Michael Jeter; Gary Cole; Kim Dickens; Rosemary Harris; J.K. Simmons; Chelcie Ross; John Beasley; *D:* Sam Raimi; *W:* Billy Bob Thornton; Tom Epperson; *C:* Jamie Anderson; *M:* Christopher Young.

The Gift ⚐⚐ 1/2 **2015 (R)** Edgerton's directorial debut, which he also wrote, is a confident thriller cut from the same cloth as the Roman Polanski thrillers of the '70s. Simon (Bateman) and Robyn (Hall) are trying to get their lives and marriage back together when an old friend of Simon's named Gordo (Edgerton) comes back into their lives. At first, Gordo seems like a good friend but his awkwardness is off-putting to Simon, and he holds some secrets about their shared past that eventually come out. A few of the twists don't work but this surprising word-of-mouth hit was so for a reason. It's fun. **108m/C; DVD, Blu-Ray.** Jason Bateman; Rebecca Hall; Joel Edgerton; Busy Philipps; David Denman; *D:* Joel Edgerton; *W:* Joel Edgerton; *C:* Eduard Grau; *M:* Danny Bensi; Saunder Jurriaans.

The Gift of Love ⚐ 1/2 **1990** Saccharine TV adaption of O. Henry's Christmas romance "The Gift of the Magi." **96m/C; VHS, DVD.** James Woods; Marie Osmond; Timothy Bottoms; June Lockhart; David Wayne; *D:* Don Chaffey. **TV**

Gift of the Magi ⚐⚐ **2010** Hallmark Channel modern (and excessively-padded) update of the O. Henry story. Struggling newlyweds Jim and Della Young are secretly determined to find the perfect Christmas gift for each other. A series of misunderstandings and fate show them the true meaning of love and the spirit of the season. **85m/C; DVD.** Lesa Thurman; Marla Sokoloff; Mark Webber; Tomas O'Suilleabhain; Megan Riordan; Gary Hetzler; *D:* Lisa Mulcahy; *W:* Jennifer Notas; *C:* Ciaran Tanham; *M:* Stephen McKeon. **CABLE**

Gifted ⚐⚐ 1/2 **2017 (PG-13)** Frank (Evans) is a single guy raising his niece Mary (Grace), a mathematical genius at seven years old, and he's trying to give her a normal childhood. Mary's grandmother, Evelyn, also a mathematical genius (as was the girl's mother), wants her to abandon Frank and normality to attend a specialized school. While the actors mostly succeed in giving their characters depth and dimension, the predictable, melodramatic, and in some parts ridiculous plot undercuts them. The film succeeds in the tearjerking department, but it should feel less forced and manipulative. **101m/C; DVD, Blu-Ray.** Chris Evans; McKenna Grace; Lindsay Duncan; Jenny Slate; Octavia Spencer; *D:* Marc Webb; *W:* Tom Flynn; *C:* Stuart Dryburgh; *M:* Rob Simonsen.

Gifted Hands: The Ben Carson Story ⚐⚐ 1/2 **2009** Inspirational, though conventionally told, biopic. Ben Carson (Gooding Jr.) is the head of pediatric neurosurgery at Johns Hopkins Children's Center. As he works to separate twins who are conjoined at the head, flashbacks depict how Carson, though initially a poor student, is pushed to succeed by his illiterate single mother Sonya (Elise) and overcome the racism and setbacks he encounters. **90m/C; DVD.** Cuba Gooding, Jr.; Kimberly Elise; Aunjanue Ellis; Gus Hoffman; Jaishon Fisher; *D:* Thomas Carter; *W:* John Pielmeier; *C:* John Aronson; *M:* Martin Davich. **CABLE**

Gigantic ⚐⚐ **2008 (R)** Mattress salesman Brian (Dano) wants to better himself, adopt a Chinese baby, and leave the shadow of his brothers, not necessarily in that order. Into his store and life comes Happy (Deschanel) who falls asleep on one of his products and then wreaks havoc when a relationship blooms. Overly quirky, albeit intermittently engaging, this one seems to be trying just a little too hard to be offbeat. The uniformly excellent cast helps leaven the whimsy a bit. **98m/C; On Demand.** Paul Dano; Zooey Deschanel; Ed Asner; Jane Alexander; John Goodman; Zach Galifianakis; Marthe Keller; Sean Dugan; *D:* Matt Aselton; *W:* Matt Aselton; Adam Nagata; *C:* Peter Donahue; *M:* Roddy Bottum.

Gigi ⚐⚐⚐⚐ **1958** Based on Colette's story of a young Parisian girl (Caron) trained to become a courtesan to the wealthy Gaston (Jourdan). But he finds out he prefers her to be his wife rather than his mistress. Chevalier is Gaston's roguish uncle, who casts an always admiring eye on the ladies. Gingold is Gigi's grandmother and former Chevalier flame, and Gabor amuses as Gaston's current, and vapid, mistress. One of the first MGM movies to be shot on location, this extravaganza features some of the best tributes to the French lifestyle ever filmed. Score includes memorable classics. **119m/C; VHS, DVD.** Leslie Caron; Louis Jourdan; Maurice Chevalier; Hermione Gingold; Eva Gabor; Isabel Jeans; Jacques Bergerac; *D:* Vincente Minnelli; *W:* Alan Jay Lerner; *C:* Joseph Ruttenberg; *M:* Frederick Loewe. Oscars '58: Adapt. Screenplay, Art Dir./Set Dec., Color Cinematog., Costume Des., Director (Minnelli), Film, Film Editing, Scoring/Musical, Song ("Gigi"); Directors Guild '58: Director (Minnelli); Golden Globes '59: Director (Minnelli), Film--Mus./Comedy, Support. Actress (Gingold); Natl. Film Reg. '91.

Gigli ⚐ **2003 (R)** The one where Ben met Jen. The title is pronounced "Geely" and is the last name of smalltime mobster hitman Larry (Affleck). His latest job is to kidnap and babysit a prosecutor's mentally impaired brother (Bartha in his film debut) as leverage in mob boss Starkman's (an overacting Pacino) trial, but he begins to feel sorry for his hostage. So his worried boss Louis (Venito) decides to send Ricki (Lopez), another contract killer, to keep an eye on them. Oh, and Ricki's a lesbian, which doesn't preclude Larry hitting on her. Not quite as bad as most of Madonna's oeuvre but the film's vulgar come-on of "gobble, gobble" succintly describes the movie—it's a turkey. **124m/C; VHS, DVD.** Ben Affleck; Jennifer Lopez; Justin Bartha; Christopher Walken; Al Pacino; Lainie Kazan; Missy (Melissa) Crider; Lenny Venito; *D:* Martin Brest; *W:* Martin Brest; *C:* Robert Elswit; *M:* John Powell. Golden Raspberries '03: Worst Actor (Affleck), Worst Actress (Lopez), Worst Director (Brest), Worst Picture, Worst Screenplay.

Gilda ⚐⚐⚐ 1/2 **1946** An evil South American gambling casino owner hires young American Ford as his trusted aide, unaware that Ford and his sultry wife Hayworth have engaged in a steamy affair. Hayworth does a striptease to "Put the Blame on Mame" in this prominently sexual film. This is the film that made Hayworth into a Hollywood sex goddess. **110m/B; VHS, DVD, Blu-Ray.** Rita Hayworth; Glenn Ford; George Macready; Joseph Calleia; Steven Geray; *D:* Charles Vidor; *W:* Jo Eisinger; Marion Parsonnet; *C:* Rudolph Mate. Natl. Film Reg. '13.

The Gilded Lily ⚐⚐ 1/2 **1935** The first of seven Paramount pairings for Colbert and MacMurray is a sharp screwball comedy. Newshound Peter (MacMurray) wants to be more than friends with stenographer Marilyn (Colbert) but she's interested in wealthy Englishman (and incognito Duke) Charles (Milland). An argument leads to Marilyn refusing Charles' proposal and Peter makes her an instant celebrity when he writes a story dubbing her "The No Girl." **85m/B; DVD.** Claudette Colbert; Fred MacMurray; Ray Milland; Sir C. Aubrey Smith; Donald Meek; *D:* Wesley Ruggles; *W:* Claude Binyon; *C:* Victor Milner; *M:* Arthur Johnston.

Gildersleeve on Broadway ⚐⚐ 1/2 **1943** Longtime bachelor Throckmorton Gildersleeve (Peary) has finally proposed to girlfriend Matilda (Doran) when he decides to make a trip to New York. He has two purposes: to track down niece Margie's (Landry) wandering beau Jimmy (Road) and to help out town druggist Mr. Peavey (LeGrand), which leads him into the company of lonely widow (and pharmaceutical company owner) Laura (Burke). Soon there are three women, including blonde babe Francine (Carleton), after our man. Third of four films based on the radio serial "The Great Gildersleeve." **65m/B; DVD.** Harold (Hal) Peary; Billie Burke; Claire Carleton; Ann Doran; Hobart Cavanaugh; Margaret Landry; Richard LeGrand; Freddie Mercer; Michael Road; *D:* Gordon Douglas; *W:* Robert E. Kent; *C:* Jack MacKenzie.

Gilles' Wife ⚐ 1/2 *La Femme de Gilles* **2004** In provincial 1930s France, Elisa is contented with her life as wife and mother. Suspecting her husband Gilles' infidelity during her third pregnancy, she begins to spy and learns he's stepping out with her own sister, Victorine. Will Elisa confront them or wait until their passion dies? French with subtitles. **103m/C; DVD.** *FR* Emmanuelle Devos; Clovis Cornillac; Colette Emmanuelle; Laura Smet; Chloe Verlinden; Alice Verlinden; Gil Lagay; *D:* Frederic Fonteyne; *W:* Frederic Fonteyne; Philippe Blasband; Marion Hansel; *M:* Vincent D'Hondt.

Gimme Shelter ⚐⚐ 1/2 **1970** The '60s ended as violence occurred at a December 1969 free Rolling Stones concert attended by 300,000 people in Altamont, California. This "Woodstock West" became a bitter remembrance in rock history, as Hell's Angels (hired for security) do some ultimate damage to the spectators. A provocative look at an out-of-control situation. **91m/C; VHS, DVD.** Mick Jagger; Keith Richards; Charlie Watts; Bill Wyman; Mick Taylor; Marty Balin; Grace Slick; Paul Kantner; Jerry Garcia; David Crosby; Stephen Stills; Graham Nash; Tina Turner; Ike Turner; Melvin Belli; Bill Graham; *D:* David Maysles; Albert Maysles; Charlotte Zwerin; *C:* Haskell Wexler; *M:* Rolling Stones.

Gimme Shelter ⚐ 1/2 **2014 (PG-13)** Director/writer Krauss' homeless teen drama is one of those films that means well and everyone appears to have the best of intentions but that doesn't make it any less melodramatic or poorly cast. Agnes "Apple" Bailey (Hudgens) has an addict for a mom (Dawson). She runs away from home, crashing on the couch of her estranged father (Fraser), before hitting the streets again when dad discovers she's pregnant. Eventually, she finds support and religion but the story goes through so many manipulative moments to get there; not helped by a miscast Hudgens, too forcefully trying to ditch her Disney pedigree. **100m/C; DVD, Blu-Ray.** Vanessa Anne Hudgens; Rosario Dawson; Brendan Fraser; James Earl Jones; Stephanie Szostak; Ann Dowd; *D:* Ron Krauss; *W:* Ron Krauss; *C:* Alain Marcoen; *M:* Onafur Arnalds.

Gimme the Loot ⚐⚐ **2012** In this energetic street-level first feature from writer-director Leon, Bronx taggers Malcolm and Sofia want revenge on some Queens rivals who defaced their work with Mets logos.

They take it to the Mets' home at Citi Field and tag the giant apple that signifies a home run. Malcolm figures they need $500 to bribe their way into the stadium's behind-the-scenes areas and they hustle their way to get the necessary loot. **79m/C; DVD.** Ty Hickson; Tashiana Washington; ***D:*** Adam Leon; ***W:*** Adam Leon; ***C:*** Jonathan Miller; ***M:*** Nicholas Britell.

Gin Game 🦴🦴🦴 **1984** Taped London performance of the Broadway play about an aging couple who find romance in an old age home. Two-character performance won awards; touching and insightful. **82m/C; VHS, DVD.** Jessica Tandy; Hume Cronyn; ***D:*** Mike Nichols.

Ginger 🦴 **1972** Fabulous super-sleuth Ginger faces the sordid world of prostitution, blackmail and drugs. Prequel to "The Abductors" and followed eventually by "Girls Are for Loving." **90m/C; VHS, DVD.** Cheri Caffaro; William Grannel; Calvin Culver; Cindy Barnett; Lise Mauer; Michele Norris; Linda Susoeff; ***D:*** Don Schain; ***W:*** Don Schain; ***C:*** R. Kent Evans; ***M:*** Robert G. Orpin.

Ginger and Cinnamon 🦴🦴 *Dillo con Parole Mie* **2003** Fun in the summer sun in this equally light romance set on a picturesque Greek island. Thirty-year-old Stefania (Montorsi) has broken up with longtime beau Andrea (Morelli) and ends up vacationing with 14-year-old neice, Meggy (Merlino), on Ios. Meggy's decided her vacation is the perfect opportunity to lose her viriginity and she's found the perfect guy—who turns out to be Andrea. Italian with subtitles. **105m/C; DVD.** *IT* Stefania Montorsi; Giampaolo Morelli; Martina Merlino; Alberto Cucca; ***D:*** Daniele Luchetti; ***W:*** Stefania Montorsi; Daniele Luchetti; Ivan Cotroneo; ***C:*** Paolo Carnera.

Ginger & Fred 🦴🦴🦴 **1986 (PG-13)** An acclaimed story of Fellini-esque poignancy about an aging dance team. Years before they had gained success by reverently impersonating the famous dancing duo of Astaire and Rogers. Now, after 30 years, they reunite under the gaudy lights of a high-tech TV special. Wonderful performances by the aging Mastroianni and the still sweet Masina. Italian with English subtitles. **126m/C; VHS, DVD.** *IT* Marcello Mastroianni; Giulietta Masina; Franco Fabrizi; Frederick Von Ledenberg; Martin Blau; Toto Mignone; ***D:*** Federico Fellini; ***W:*** Federico Fellini; Tonino Guerra; Tullio Pinelli; ***C:*** Tonino Delli Colli; ***M:*** Nicola Piovani.

Ginger & Rosa 🦴🦴 **1/2 2013 (PG-13)** Coming-of-age story set in 1962 London focusing on two inseparable teenage best friends, Ginger (Fanning) and Rosa (Englert), dreaming of escaping the domestic drudgery that their mothers are chained to. The Cold War is booming and the fear of the nuclear bomb weighs heavily on the minds of everyone, especially these two girls, who are awakening to ideas of pacifism, religion, gender, music, poetry, and smoking cigarettes. A fairly straight-forward telling, brimming with talk of love and war, with Fanning proving her importance as the star of new generation of actors. **90m/C; DVD, Blu-Ray.** *UK* Elle Fanning; Alice Englert; Alessandro Nivola; Christina Hendricks; Annette Bening; Timothy Spall; Oliver Platt; Jodhi May; ***D:*** Sally Potter; ***W:*** Sally Potter; ***C:*** Robbie Ryan.

Ginger in the Morning 🦴🦴 **1973** A salesman is enamored of a young hitchhiker whom he picks up on the road. This is the same year Spacek played the innocent-gone-twisted in "Badlands." **90m/C; VHS, DVD.** Sissy Spacek; Slim Pickens; Monte Markham; Susan Oliver; Mark Miller; ***D:*** Gordon Wiles.

Ginger Snaps 🦴🦴 **2001 (R)** Modern teen horror goes for quite a ride. Teenaged sisters Ginger (Isabelle) and Brigitte (Perkins) are proud misfits in their quiet Canadian community. Then they're attacked by a werewolf in the woods and Ginger starts behaving very strangely (even for her). Brigitte turns to local pot dealer Sam (Lemche) for help while Ginger just gets more and more aggressive. **107m/C; VHS, DVD, Blu-Ray.** *CA* Emily Perkins; Katharine Isabelle; Kris Lemche; Mimi Rogers; Jesse Moss; Danielle Hampton; John Bourgeois; Peter Keleghan; ***D:*** John Fawcett; ***W:*** Karen Walton; ***C:*** Thom Best; ***M:*** Michael Shields.

Ginger Snaps Back: The Beginning 🦴🦴 *Ginger Snaps 3* **2004 (R)** The trilogy snaps back from the depths of hell in this prequel that finds sisters Ginger and Brigitte time-warped to 19th century Canada and seeking shelter from the woods at an all-male trading fort that—unbeknownst to them—has been trying to fend off those pesky werewolves. **94m/C; VHS, DVD.** *CA* Katharine Isabelle; Emily Perkins; Nathaniel Arcand; J.R. Bourne; Hugh Dillon; Adrien Dorval; Brendan Fletcher; David La Haye; Tom McCamus; Matthew (Matt) Walker; ***D:*** Grant Harvey; ***W:*** Stephen Massicotte; Christina Ray; ***C:*** Michael Marshall. **VIDEO**

Ginger Snaps: Unleashed 🦴 *Ginger Snaps 2: The Sequel* **2004 (R)** In this why-did-they-bother sequel, it's Brigitte's turn to be afflicted with a case of the lycanthropy, but she keeps it at bay with wolfsbane. The whole thing goes haywire when she's taken to a rehab clinic after being mauled by another werewolf and can't take her meds. **93m/C; VHS, DVD.** *CA* Emily Perkins; Katharine Isabelle; Janet Kidder; Tatiana Maslany; Eric Johnson; Pascale Hutton; Jack Mackinnon; ***D:*** Brett Sullivan; ***W:*** Megan Martin; ***C:*** Gavin Smith; ***M:*** Kurt Swinghammer. **VIDEO**

The Gingerbread Man 🦴🦴 **1/2 1997 (R)** Lawyer Rick Macgruder (Branagh) falls for a scheming femme (Davidtz) who hires him to have her deranged, stalker father (Duvall) committed. Set in the new hot spot of filmdom, steamy Savannah, it becomes clear that nothing is clear and plot takes on noirish twists and turns of intrigue and suspense before the cigarette smoke clears. Shakespeare savant Branagh proves he can also master a Southern accent. Hannah, as Rick's mousy partner, surprises with an unusually good performance. Grisham's first original screenplay. Studio Polygram disliked Altman's original cut, replaced his editor, and recut the movie to its own specifications, angering Altman who threatened to remove his name from the film. Though not an Altman masterpiece, sly thriller doesn't fail to entice. **114m/C; VHS, DVD, Blu-Ray.** Kenneth Branagh; Embeth Davidtz; Robert Duvall; Tom Berenger; Daryl Hannah; Robert Downey, Jr.; Famke Janssen; Mae Whitman; Jesse James; Sonny Shroyer; ***D:*** Robert Altman; ***W:*** John Grisham; Al Hayes; ***C:*** Gu Changwei; ***M:*** Mark Isham.

Ginostra 🦴 **1/2 2002 (R)** Dull crime drama. FBI agent Matt Benson takes his wife and young daughter along when he's sent to Sicily to interview 11-year-old Ettore, the only survivor of a car bombing that killed his family. Ettore's mobster dad was going against omerta to testify against a fellow wiseguy with ties to New York organized crime. The title is the name of the local volcano, which erupts. **135m/C; DVD.** *FR* Harvey Keitel; Andie MacDowell; Harry Dean Stanton; Stefano Dionisi; Mattia de Martino; ***D:*** Manuel Pradal; ***W:*** Manuel Pradal; ***C:*** Maurizio Calvesi; ***M:*** Carlo Crivelli.

Girl 🦴🦴 **1/2 1998 (R)** Suburban 18-year-old Andrea Marr (Swain) is bored by her usual life and her virginity. She decides to try on the local club scene and spots musician Todd Sparrow (Flanery), becoming his groupie, and also taking up with cool chick singer Cybil (Reid) and her friends who are in a band. This try at self-discovery ultimately proves less-than-satisfying for Andrea. Lots of cliched issues are dealt with in the most cursory fashion. Based on the novel by Blake Nelson. **99m/C; VHS, DVD.** Dominique Swain; Sean Patrick Flanery; Tara Reid; Summer Phoenix; Selma Blair; Channon Roe; Portia de Rossi; Christopher K. Masterson; Rosemary Forsyth; James Karen; ***D:*** Jonathan Kahn; ***W:*** David E. Tolchinsky; ***C:*** Tami Reiker; ***M:*** Michael Tavera.

The Girl 🦴🦴 **1/2 2001** Stylish lesbian love story has a Paris artist meeting sultry nightclub singer and initiating a one-night stand which becomes a torrid affair. This upsets the club owner, who considers the singer his property. First time director (and co-writer) Zeig has confidence and an eye for subtle nuance, but occasionally wanders into pretentiousness (an occupational hazard for a first-time director). **84m/C; VHS, DVD.** Claire Keim; Agathe de la Boulaye; Sandra N'Kake; Cyril Lecomte; ***D:*** Sande Zeig; ***W:*** Monique Wittig.

The Girl 🦴🦴 **1/2 2012** Compelling HBO/BBC co-production explores the behind-the-scenes drama while Alfred Hitchcock (Jones) was filming 1963's "The Birds." The obsessed director chose another aloof-seeming blonde for his leading lady, Tippi Hedren (Miller), whom he proceeded to sexually proposition. Hedren rebuffed his advances, and Hitchcock made filming her role extremely difficult, including the (re-created) sequences where Hedren's character is attacked by the feathered furies. Adapted from Donald Spoto's book "Spellbound by Beauty." **90m/C; DVD.** Toby Jones; Sienna Miller; Imelda Staunton; Penelope Wilton; ***D:*** Julian Jarrold; ***W:*** Gwyneth Hughes; ***C:*** John Pardue; ***M:*** Philip Miller. **CABLE**

Girl 🦴🦴🦴 **2018 (R)** So young Lara (Polster) can attend an elite ballet school, her father and younger brother move with her to a big city. As she begins training, she is undergoing gender transition and taking care of her family. Though her father is supportive, Lara must catch up with the other female dancers, including how to dance en pointe. At the same time, Lara struggles with body-related issues. Inspired by the real-life experience of trans ballet dancer Nora Monsecour, the first feature by Dhont focuses on Lara's body and emotional problems instead of telling the inspiring story of her becoming who she wants to be. **105m/C; DVD.** Victor Polster; Arieh Worthalter; Katelijne Damen; Valentijn Dhaenens; Oliver Bodart; ***D:*** Lukas Dhont; ***W:*** Lukas Dhont; Angelo Tijssens; ***C:*** Frank van den Eeden; ***M:*** Valentin Hadjadj.

A Girl, 3 Guys and a Gun 🦴🦴 **2001 (R)** Best buds Neil (Leffler), Frank (Florence), and Joey (Luper) want to blow out of their smalltown by getting involved in a botched robbery that leads to an unexpected kidnapping. An indie that starts off as larky and then turns serious (and somewhat confusing). **88m/C; VHS, DVD.** Christian Leffler; Josh Holland; Tracy Zahoryin; Michael Trucco; Tava Smiley; Kenny Luper; Brent Florence; ***D:*** Brent Florence; ***W:*** Brent Florence; ***C:*** Matt Davis.

The Girl by the Lake 🦴🦴 *La Ragazza del Lago* **2007** Beautiful local girl Anna is found dead by the side of a lake near a small town in the Italian Dolomites and police inspector Sanzio (Servillo) is called in from the provincial capital. There's several possible suspects but Sanzio's investigation just brings up more questions in this troubling, compelling thriller. Italian with subtitles. **95m/C; DVD.** *IT* Toni Servillo; Fabrizio Gifuni; Valeria Golino; Nello Mascia; Marco Baliani; Fausto Maria Sciarappa; Franco Ravera; Guilia Michelini; Alessia Piovan; ***D:*** Andrea Molaioli; ***W:*** Sandro Petraglia; ***C:*** Ramiro Civita; ***M:*** Teho Teardo.

The Girl Can't Help It 🦴🦴 **1/2 1956** Satiric rock and roll musical comedy about a retired mobster who hires a hungry talent agent to promote his girlfriend, a wanna-be no-talent singer. Mansfield's first starring role. Classic performances by some of the early greats including Eddie Cochran, Gene Vincent, the Platters, Little Richard, and Fats Domino. **99m/B; VHS, DVD.** Jayne Mansfield; Tom Ewell; Edmond O'Brien; Julie London; Ray Anthony; Henry Jones; John Emery; Juanita Moore; Barry J. Gordon; Fats Domino; Abbey Lincoln; Eddie Fontaine; Little Richard; Eddie Cochran; Gene Vincent; ***D:*** Frank Tashlin; ***W:*** Frank Tashlin; Herbert Baker; ***C:*** Leon Shamroy; ***M:*** Lionel Newman.

Girl Crazy 🦴🦴 **1932** New York playboy Danny Churchill opens a dude ranch in Custerville, Arizona and persuades his friends—Slick and Kate—to join him. They arrive via a cross-country road trip with cabbie Jimmy and find Danny's place is a success. However, this upsets rival Lank Sanders who is running for sheriff so he can shut the place down. This adaptation of the 1930 George and Ira Gershwin Broadway musical put the emphasis on the Wheeler & Woolsey comedy team instead of the music. **75m/B; DVD.** Bert Wheeler; Robert Woolsey; Eddie Quillan; Kitty Kelly; Stanley Fields; Mitzie Green; Arline Judge; Dorothy Lee; ***D:*** William A. Seiter; ***W:*** Herman J. Mankiewicz; Tim Whelan; Walter DeLeon; Eddie Welch; ***C:*** J. Roy Hunt.

Girl Crazy 🦴🦴🦴 *When the Girls Meet the Boys* **1943** A wealthy young playboy is sent to an all-boy school in Arizona to get his mind off girls. Once there, he still manages to fall for a local girl who can't stand the sight of him. The eighth film pairing for Rooney and Garland. **99m/B; VHS, DVD.** Mickey Rooney; Judy Garland; Nancy Walker; June Allyson; ***D:*** Norman Taurog; ***C:*** William H. Daniels; ***M:*** Ira Gershwin.

A Girl Cut in Two 🦴🦴 **1/2** *La Fille Coupee en Deux* **2007** Innocent young TV weather girl Gabrielle (Sagnier) finds herself prey for two oversexed men in another of director Claude Chabrol's black comedies that highlights self-destructive and sexually perverse behavior. Sparks fly when the older, successful writer Charles (Berleand) is interviewed at the TV station and charms Gabrielle into becoming his Parisian plaything. The fact that he's married only seems to add fuel to the fantasy, infuriating Gabrielle's younger suitor Paul (Magimel), a spoiled playboy and heir to the family fortune. Those familiar with director Chabrol's prolific career as a sexual satirist will find more of the same, as well as his usual commentary on class struggle. **115m/C; DVD.** *FR GE* Ludivine Sagnier; Benoît Magimel; Francois Berleand; Mathilda May; Marie Bunel; Valeria Cavalli; Caroline Sihol; ***D:*** Claude Chabrol; ***W:*** Claude Chabrol; Cecile Maistre; ***C:*** Eduardo Serra; ***M:*** Matthieu Chabrol.

Girl Fight 🦴🦴 **1/2 2011** Lifetime movie inspired by a true story. Sixteen-year-old Haley posts online criticism about the popular high school seniors before she gets accepted into their clique. Her comments are discovered and they viciously beat her and post video of the attack online. Haley's parents soon see the footage and go to the authorities. **88m/C; DVD.** Jodelle Ferland; Anne Heche; James Tupper; Tess Atkins; Keely Purvis; ***D:*** Stephen Gyllenhaal; ***W:*** Benita Garvin; ***C:*** Adam Sliwinski; ***M:*** Nick Urata. **CABLE**

Girl from Calgary 🦴 **1932** A female rodeo champ ropes her boyfriends much like she ropes her cows, but not without a knock-down, drag-out fight between the two which forces our cowgirl to make the choice she seems to know is fated. Stock rodeo footage is intercut with the heroine riding an obviously mechanical bucking bronc. **66m/B; VHS, DVD.** Fifi d'Orsay; Paul Kelly; ***D:*** Philip H. (Phil, P.H.) Whitman.

Girl from Chicago 🦴🦴 **1932** In this crime melodrama a secret service agent falls in love while on assignment in Mississippi. When he's back in New York he finds a good friend of his girl's in serious trouble with the numbers racket. **69m/C; VHS, DVD.** Starr Calloway; Grace Smith; Eugene Brooks; Frank Wilson; ***D:*** Oscar Micheaux.

The Girl from Jones Beach 🦴🦴 **1/2 1949** Lighthearted rom com. Pinup artist Bob Randolph (Reagan) has a secret: the woman featured in his work is made up of 12 different models. Offered a lot of money to make a TV appearance with his model, Bob finds the perfect woman in teacher Ruth Wilson (Mayo), who wants to be admired for her brains and not just her beauty. A picture of Ruth in a bathing suit causes even more issues. **78m/B; DVD.** Ronald Reagan; Virginia Mayo; Eddie Bracken; Henry Travers; Dona Drake; ***D:*** Peter Godfrey; ***W:*** I.A.L. Diamond; ***C:*** Carl Guthrie; ***M:*** David Buttolph.

The Girl From Mexico 🦴🦴 **1/2 1939** Velez starred in eight "Mexican Spitfire" comedies for RKO and this is the first and best of the predictable lot. Sexy Carmelita is spotted by ad agency rep Dennis, who hires her for his company's new radio program in New York. Her wild antics with Dennis' shifty Uncle Matt add to the publicity and Dennis is manipulated (not so unwillingly) into proposing to the fiery entertainer. **71m/B; DVD.** Lupe Velez; Donald Woods; Leon Errol; Linda Hayes; Donald MacBride; Elisabeth Risdon; Ward Bond; Edward Raquello; ***D:*** Leslie Goodwins; ***W:*** Joseph Fields; Lionel Houser; ***C:*** Jack MacKenzie.

The Girl from Missouri 🦴🦴🦴 *One Hundred Percent Pure* **1934** Cute comedy in which Harlow tries to snag a millionaire without sacrificing her virtues. Lots of laughs and hilarious action, especially the scene where Harlow arrives at the yacht in Florida. Kelly is great as Harlow's wise-cracking girlfriend. Witty dialogue by Emerson and Loos, who also wrote "Gentleman Prefer Blondes." **75m/B; VHS, DVD.** Jean Harlow; Lionel Barrymore; Franchot Tone; Lewis Stone; Patsy Kelly; Alan Mowbray; Clara Blandick; Russell Hopton; John David Horsley; ***D:*** Jack Conway; ***W:*** Anita Loos; John Emerson.

The Girl From Monaco 🦴🦴 *La Fille de Monaco* **2008 (R)** An uneasy mix of sex farce with thrillerish tendencies. Controlled, 50-something Paris lawyer Bertrand Beauvois (Luchini) arrives in Monaco to defend 70-something widow Edith Lasalle Audran, who is accused of murdering her young Russian gigolo. Because said gigolo was reputed to have mob ties, Edith's son Louis (Cohen) hires street-smart Christophe Abadi (Zem) to bodyguard the irritated Bertrand. But it's really not about the murder and subsequent trial, it's about the sexually voracious, beautiful bimbo weather girl Audrey (Bourgoin in her film debut), who makes a successful play for Betrand who knows amour fou when it strikes him but can't resist despite Christophe's warnings (he's been one of Audrey's numerous lovers). French with subtitles. **95m/C; On Demand.** *FR* Fabrice Luchini; Roschdy Zem; Louise Bourgoin; Stephane Audran; Gilles Cohen; Jeanne Balibar; ***D:*** Anne Fontaine; ***W:*** Anne Fontaine; Benoit Graffin; Jacques Fieschi; ***C:*** Patrick Blossier; ***M:*** Philippe Rombi.

The Girl from Paris 🦴🦴🦴 *Une Hirondelle a Fait le Printemps* **2002** A Parisian internet worker leaves the city and buys a mountaintop farm from a cranky farmer. Sandrine (Seigner) gives up her high-stress city life and buys a goat farm from Adrien (Serrault), who's ready to be done with farming but resentfully agrees to stick around for 18 months to help out. Sandrine initially does big business through internet advertising, drawing visitors who buy the farm's products and sleep in the barn, but soon must confront the harsh, relentless realities of managing a farm by herself. As she does, her adversarial relationship with Adrien evolves into a friendship. Moves a bit slowly, but farm-raised Carion directs it with sincerity and precision, and creates an honest story of country life and the relationships it builds. **103m/C; DVD.** *FR* Michel Serrault; Mathilde Seigner; Jean-Paul Roussillon; Frederic Pierrot; Marc Berman; Francoise Bette; ***D:*** Christian Carion; ***W:*** Christian Carion; Eric Assous; ***C:*** Antoine Heberle; ***M:*** Philippe Rombi.

The Girl from Petrovka 🦴 ½ **1974 (PG)** A high-spirited Russian ballerina falls in love with an American newspaper correspondent. Their romance is complicated by the suspicious KGB. Bittersweet with a bleak ending. **103m/C; VHS, Streaming.** Goldie Hawn; Hal Holbrook; Anthony Hopkins; ***D:*** Robert Ellis Miller; ***W:*** Chris Bryant; Allan Scott; ***M:*** Henry Mancini.

The Girl from 10th Ave. 🦴🦴 ½ **1935** Working class Miriam Brady (Davis) takes pity on attorney and society guy Geoffrey Sherwood (Hunter) when he gets drunk after seeing his ex-girlfriend Valentine (Alexander) marry wealthier John Marland (Clive). On an impulse, Miriam marries Geoff and then tries to educate herself on how to behave in his world. However, he keeps returning to the booze and there's trouble when Valentine deserts her hubby because she wants Geoff back. Miriam decides she's not going to get him. **69m/B; DVD.** Bette Davis; Ian Hunter; Colin Clive; Katherine Alexander; Alison Skipworth; John Eldredge; Phillip Reed; Helen Jerome Eddy; ***D:*** Alfred E. Green; ***W:*** Charles Kenyon; ***C:*** James Van Trees.

The Girl Getters 🦴🦴 *The System* **1966** Tinker (Reed) and his rowdy London pals take a vacation at a seaside resort, where they proceed to pick fights, chase girls, and cause general (minor) mayhem. Tinker's busy chasing Nicola (Merrow) but surprises himself when he actually starts to fall for her. **79m/B; VHS, DVD.** *GB* Oliver Reed; Jane Merrow; David Hemmings; John Alderton; Harry Andrews; ***D:*** Michael Winner; ***W:*** Peter Draper; ***C:*** Nicolas Roeg.

Girl Happy 🦴🦴 **1965** The King's fans will find him in Fort Lauderdale, Florida this time as the leader of a rock 'n' roll group. His mission: to chaperone the daughter of a Chicago mobster who naturally falls for him. Why not? **96m/C; VHS, DVD.** Elvis Presley; Harold J. Stone; Shelley Fabares; Gary Crosby; Nita Talbot; Mary Ann Mobley; Jackie Coogan; ***D:*** Boris Sagal; ***W:*** Harvey Bullock.

The Girl He Left Behind 🦴🦴 **1956** Despite the somewhat melodramatic title, this is a military comedy. Wealthy mama's boy Andy Shaeffer (Hunter) gets dumped by girlfriend Susan (Wood) because he doesn't seem to take anything seriously. He goes into a tailspin, flunks out of college, and is then drafted. Andy makes it clear he's not cut out for the rigors of boot camp, although his drill sergeants have other ideas, and the point of the pic is to show Andy how to grow up and be a man. **103m/B; DVD.** Tab Hunter; Natalie Wood; Jim Backus; Murray Hamilton; David Janssen; James Garner; Jessie Royce Landis; Alan King; Henry Jones; ***D:*** David Butler; ***W:*** Guy Trosper; ***C:*** Ted D. McCord; ***M:*** Roy Webb.

The Girl Hunters 🦴🦴 ½ **1963** That intrepid private eye, Mike Hammer (played by his creator, Spillane), is caught up with communist spies, wicked women, and a missing secretary. Hammer is his usual judge-and-jury character but the action is fast-paced. **103m/B; DVD, Blu-Ray.** Mickey Spillane; Lloyd Nolan; Shirley Eaton; Hy Gardner; Scott Peters; Charles Farrell; ***D:*** Roy Rowland; ***W:*** Roy Rowland; Robert Fellows; ***C:*** Ken Talbot; ***M:*** Philip Green.

The Girl in a Swing 🦴 ½ **1989 (R)** An Englishman impulsively marries a beautiful German girl and both are subsequently haunted by phantoms from her past—are they caused by her psychic powers? Cliche-ridden silliness. Based on the Richard Adams novel. **119m/C; DVD.** Meg Tilly; Rupert Frazer; Elspet Gray; Lynsey Baxter; Nicholas Le Prevost; Jon Kroll; ***D:*** Gordon Hessler; ***W:*** Gordon Hessler; ***C:*** Claus Loof; ***M:*** Carl Davis.

Girl in Black 🦴🦴 *To Koritsi Me Ta Mavra* **1956** The shy daughter of a once wealthy household gets the chance to escape her genteel poverty when she falls in love with the young man boarding with her family. He is attracted to her but a shocking tragedy changes everything. In Greek with English subtitles. **100m/B; VHS, DVD.** *GR* Ellie Lambetti; Eleni Zafirou; Georges Foundas; Dimitri Horne; Stefanos Stratigos; ***D:*** Michael Cacoyannis; ***W:*** Michael Cacoyannis; ***C:*** Walter Lassally; ***M:*** Manos Hadjidakis.

Girl in Black Stockings 🦴🦴 **1957** Beautiful women are mysteriously murdered at a remote, Utah hotel. Interesting, little known thriller similar to Hitchcock's "Psycho," but pre-dating it by three years. **75m/B; VHS, DVD, Blu-Ray.** Lex Barker; Anne Bancroft; Mamie Van Doren; Ron Randell; Marie Windsor; John Dehner; John Holland; Diana Van Der Vlis; ***D:*** Howard W. Koch; ***M:*** Les Baxter.

The Girl in Blue 🦴🦴 **1974 (R)** A lawyer, ill at ease with his current romance, suddenly decides to search for a beautiful woman he saw once, and instantly fell in love with, years before. **103m/C; VHS, DVD.** *CA* Maud Adams; David Selby; Gay Rowan; William Osler; Diane Dewey; Michael Kirby; ***D:*** George Kaczender.

Girl in Gold Boots 🦴 **1969** Aspiring starlet meets up with a draft evader and a biker on her way to Hollywood where she gets a job as a go-go dancer in a sleazy club. But things don't go smoothly when a murder and a drug theft are revealed. **91m/C; VHS, DVD.** Jody Daniels; Leslie McRae; Tom Pace; Mark Herron; ***D:*** Ted V. Mikels; ***W:*** Art Names; Leighton J. Peatman; John T. Wilson; ***C:*** Robert Maxwell; ***M:*** Nicholas Carras.

Girl in His Pocket 🦴🦴 *Amour de Poche; Nude in His Pocket* **1957** Mad scientist creates a potion that turns things into three-inch statues. He uses it mostly to have trystes with his lab assistant so his fiancee won't find out. Based on "The Diminishing Draft" by Waldemar Kaempfert. **82m/C; VHS, DVD.** *FR* Jean Marais; Genevieve Page; Agnes Laurent; ***D:*** Pierre Kast; ***C:*** Ghislan Cloquet.

The Girl in Lover's Lane 🦴🦴 **1960** A drifter falls in love with a small town girl but becomes a murder suspect when she turns up dead. Interesting mainly for Elam's uncharacteristic portrayal of a village idiot. **78m/B; VHS, DVD.** Brett Halsey; Joyce Meadows; Lowell Brown; Jack Elam; ***D:*** Charles R. Rondeau.

Girl in Progress 🦴🦴 **2012 (PG-13)** Ansiedad (Ramirez), which means 'anxiety' in Spanish, is a Seattle teen who went from level-headed to rebellious. She's tired of her mom Grace's (Mendes) irresponsibility, her menial jobs that leave them struggling, and her bad taste in men, including the affair she's having with a married doctor (Modine). Since Grace doesn't have time for her, Ansiedad takes the coming of age stories she's reads and plots her own life around them. The parallels between the two stories are somewhat heavy-handed (Grace was a teen mom and hasn't grown up herself) but the leads are strong. English and Spanish with subtitles. **90m/C; DVD; Closed Captioned.** Eva Mendes; Cierra Ramirez; Matthew Modine; Patricia Arquette; Landon Liboiron; ***D:*** Patricia Riggen; ***W:*** Hiram Martinez; ***C:*** Checco Varese; ***M:*** Christopher Lennertz.

The Girl in Room 2A WOOF! **1976 (R)** A young woman is trapped in a mansion with the elderly owner and her demented son. Routine horrorfest. **90m/C; VHS, DVD.** Raf Vallone; Daniela Giordano; ***D:*** William Rose.

The Girl in the Book 🦴🦴 ½ **2015** Book-focused drama centered on the concept of being true to one's self. Alice Harvey (VanCamp) leads a complicated life. Though she is the daughter of an important literary agent, she is a writer suffering from writer's block and is unhappy in her job as a junior editor at a publisher. Her life and career are changed she must take charge of a new release of a best-selling novel that features events from her life. Alice must also engage with the author, Milan Daneker (Nyqvist) who also stirs up painful memories. Finally facing the past, Alice emerges with her own voice, sense of self, an openness to love, and new purpose as a writer. **86m/C; DVD, Streaming, Download.** Emily VanCamp; Michael Nyqvist; Ana Mulvoy-Ten; Talia Balsam; Ali Ahn; ***D:*** Marya Cohn; ***W:*** Marya Cohn; ***C:*** Trevor Forrest; ***M:*** Will Bates.

The Girl in the Cafe 🦴🦴 ½ **2005** When a tender but offbeat romance develops between Lawrence (Nighy), a mellow-and-lonely middle-aged British public official, and Gina (MacDonald), a younger New Ager, he decides to take her along on his trip to the G8 Summit in Iceland but is taken aback when she abruptly shocks the crowd with a rant about the starvation of African children. **95m/C; DVD.** Bill Nighy; Kelly Macdonald; Ken Stott; Penny Downie; Meneka Das; ***D:*** David Yates; ***W:*** Richard Curtis. **CABLE**

The Girl in the Empty Grave 🦴🦴 ½ **1977** In this NBC TV movie, Griffith stars as another small town sheriff. In the resort town of Jasper Lake, Abel Marsh isn't the only one to see Elizabeth Alden driving through town. Only problem is that Elizabeth supposedly died when her car went over a mountain road months ago. But then she comes to the funeral of her parents, who were murder victims, and Abel has questions. **105m/C; DVD.** Andy Griffith; Jonathan Banks; James Cromwell; Mitzi Hoag; Claude Earl Jones; Deborah White; George Gaynes; ***D:*** Lou Antonio; ***W:*** Lane Slate; ***C:*** Gayne Rescher; ***M:*** Mundell Lowe. **TV**

The Girl in the News 🦴🦴 ½ *The Girl in the Case* **1941** Wealthy wheelchair-bound Edward Bentley (Goldie) is poisoned by his butler Tracy (Williams), who is having an affair with Mrs. Bentley (Scott). He frames Bentley's nurse Anne Graham (Lockwood), who was acquitted of murdering another of her elderly patients. Her lawyer, Stephen Garrington (Barnes), takes the new case but wonders about Anne's innocence until the big courtroom denouement. **78m/B; DVD.** *GB* Margaret Lockwood; Barry Barnes; Emlyn Williams; Margaretta Scott; Roger Livesey; Basil Radford; Irene Handl; Felix Aylmer; Wyndham Goldie; ***D:*** Carol Reed; ***W:*** Sidney Gilliat; ***C:*** Otto Kanturek; ***M:*** Louis Levy.

The Girl in the Red Velvet Swing 🦴🦴 **1955** Rather genteel reworking of a 1906 New York society scandal. Evelyn Nesbit (Collins) is a hotsy showgirl who's being courted by famous married architect Stanford White (Milland). However, Evelyn marries wealthy-but-unstable society boy Harry Thaw (Granger). Harry is pathologically jealous of Evelyn's relationship with White and shoots him dead in public. Then he uses an insanity plea (and family money) to avoid the death penalty in the ensuing trial. Collins is catnip but her character is depicted as boringly naive. **109m/C; DVD.** Joan Collins; Ray Milland; Farley Granger; Luther Adler; Glenda Farrell; Cornelia Otis Skinner; Frances Fuller; Phillip Reed; Gale Robbins; John Hoyt; Harvey Stephens; Emile Meyer; Richard Travis; Jack Raine; Ainslie Pryor; Kay Hammond; Edith Evanson; ***D:*** Richard Fleischer; ***W:*** Walter Reisch; Charles Brackett; ***C:*** Milton Krasner; ***M:*** Leigh Harline; Edward B. Powell.

The Girl in the Sneakers 🦴🦴 *Dokhtari ba kafsh-haye-katani* **1999** A coming of age story set in Tehran in the 1990s that also functions as a satire on Iranian morals. In this time, strict laws govern the interaction between the sexes in the public. A rebellious upper middle class girl, 15-year-old Tadai (Ahangarani) is walking through a park with her male friend Aideen (Hajizadeh). The pair are in love, but their future plans are ended when a police officer arrests Aideen and accuses him of taking Tadai's virginity. Though Aideen is released, Tadai's angy family forbids her from seeing Aideen ever again. Spirited Tadaie refuses tc give in, leaves home, and searches the streets of Tehran for her love. Persian with subtitles. **110m/C; DVD.** Pegah Ahangarani; Majid Hajizadeh; Akram Mohammadi; Abdolreza Akbari; Mahmoud Jafari; ***D:*** Rasoul Sadrameli; ***W:*** Fereydoun Farhudi; Peyman Ghassemkhani; ***C:*** Dariush Ayari; ***M:*** Iraj Panahi. **VIDEO**

The Girl in the Spider's Web 🦴 ½ **2018 (R)** Sweden produced three movies based on Stieg Larsson's posthumously published *Millennium* trilogy. Hollywood remade the first one, "The Girl with the Dragon Tattoo," and then jumped to this one, which is based on David Lagercrantz's continuation of the series. No one asked for it, and it shows. Claire Foy valiantly and capably plays Lisbeth Salander, a goth hacker with a strong social conscience, who becomes embroiled in far-reaching espionage, cybercrime, and government corruption. This plot is too commercial, too James Bond, and too senselessly violent for the true Lisbeth, whose strength is a subtle, psychological complexity. **115m/C; DVD, Blu-Ray, Streaming.** *UK GE SW CA US* Claire Foy; Sverrir Gudnason; Lakeith Stanfield; Sylvia Hoeks; Stephen Merchant; ***D:*** Fede Alvarez; ***W:*** Fede Alvarez; Jay Basu; Steven Knight; ***C:*** Pedro Luque; ***M:*** Roque Baños.

The Girl in White 🦴🦴 **1952** Earnest and noble-minded bio of Emily Dunning (Allyson), the first woman to work as a doctor in a New York city hospital and to become a hospital staff surgeon. Naturally, Emily has to overcome much male prejudice to follow her ambitions. Based on Dunning's autobiography. **92m/B; DVD.** June Allyson; Arthur Kennedy; Mildred Dunnock; Gary Merrill; Jesse White; ***D:*** John Sturges; ***W:*** Irma Von Cube; Allen Vincent; Philip Stevenson; ***C:*** Paul Vogel; ***M:*** David Raksin.

Girl, Interrupted 🦴🦴 ½ **1999 (R)** Ryder stars as neurotic 18-year-old Susanna who, after making a half-hearted suicide attempt, is diagnosed with borderline personality disorder. So, in 1967, she's sent to Claymoore, a psychiatric hospital outside Boston, where she'll spend the next two years. There, Susanna meets some young woman who are truly disturbed, including compelling sociopath, Lisa (Jolie). Yes, the story's predictable but it's also touching—just don't expect the fireworks of "One Flew Over a Cuckoo's Nest." Based on the 1993 memoir by Susanna Kaysen. **127m/C; VHS, DVD.** Winona Ryder; Angelina Jolie; Vanessa Redgrave; Whoopi Goldberg; Clea DuVall; Brittany Murphy; Elisabeth Moss; Jared Leto; Jeffrey Tambor; Mary Kay Place; ***D:*** James Mangold; ***W:*** James Mangold; Anna Hamilton Phelan; Lisa Loomer; ***C:*** Jack N. Green; ***M:*** Mychael Danna. Oscars '99: Support. Actress (Jolie); Golden Globes '00: Support. Actress (Jolie); Screen Actors Guild '99: Support. Actress (Jolie); Broadcast Film Critics '99: Support. Actress (Jolie).

A Girl Like Her 🦴🦴 **2015 (PG-13)** The deconstruction of a high school bully filmed in a fake found-footage format by fictitious documentary filmmaker Amy (Weber), following bullied teen Jessica (Ainsworth) through a failed suicide attempt and her time in a coma. The camera then switches perspective to show Jessica's former best friend, turned tormenter, Avery (King), through a troubled home life with an overbearing mother. Exceptionally natural performances from both leads isn't enough to validate the forced sorrow and sadness around every corner. The best venue for this heavy duty melodrama would be at a high school assembly. **91m/C; DVD.** Jimmy Bennett; Hunter King; Lexi Ainsworth; Luke Jaden; Linda Boston; ***D:*** Amy S. Weber; ***W:*** Amy S. Weber; ***C:*** Samuel Brownfield; ***M:*** David Bateman.

A Girl Like Me: The Gwen Araujo Story 🦴🦴 **2006** As if growing up in a macho Latino culture wasn't difficult enough, Eddie Araujo (Pardo) realizes as a child that he should have been born a girl. He starts his transformation as a teenager and Eddie becomes Gwen with his single mother Sylvia's (Ruehl) support. But when Gwen's transgendered status is revealed, tragedy ensues. **90m/C; DVD.** Mercedes Ruehl; J.D. Pardo; Corey Stoll; Lupe Ontiveros; Henry Darrow; Zak Santiago; ***D:*** Agnieszka Holland; ***W:*** Shelley Evans; ***C:*** David Frazee; ***M:*** Jan A.P. Kaczmarek. **CABLE**

Girl Loves Boy 🦴 1/2 **1937** At his wealthy father's insistence, playboy Robert (Linden) marries gold-digger Sally (Hayes) instead of poor-but-true-blue love Dorothy (Parker). Then he finds out Sally never properly divorced her first husband. **77m/B; DVD.** Eric Linden; Cecilia Parker; Bernadene Hayes; Roger Imhof; Dorothy Peterson; ***D:*** Duncan Mansfield; ***W:*** Duncan Mansfield; Carroll Graham; ***C:*** Edward Snyder.

Girl Meets Boy 🦴 *Peace and Riot* **2013 (R)** In this lacklusterand all-too predictable rom com, LA singer/songwriter Crystal and novelist Scott are both struggling with writer's block. To work things out, they each book a cabin at a remote resort. Oops, it's double-booked and they'll have to share! You know where this is going, especially with a couple of nosy neighbors pushing them along. **87m/C; DVD.** Ben Savage; Anna Pheil; Richard Riehle; Janet Wood; Jake Busey; ***D:*** Damion Stephens; ***W:*** Damion Stephens; ***C:*** Allen Achterberg; ***M:*** Jonathan Price. **VIDEO**

Girl Missing 🦴🦴 **1933** Gold-digging showgirl Daisy (Shannon) marries millionaire Henry Gibson (Lyon) but then disappears on her wedding night from their hotel. The groom offers a big reward and chorus girls Kay (Farrell) and June (Brian) turn amateur sleuths so they can get the dough. **69m/B; DVD.** Ben Lyon; Glenda Farrell; Mary Brian; Peggy Shannon; Lyle Talbot; Guy Kibbee; Edward Ellis; Harold Huber; Louise Beavers; ***D:*** Robert Florey; ***W:*** Don Mullaly; Carl Erickson; Ben Markson; ***C:*** Arthur L. Todd.

Girl Most Likely 🦴🦴 **2012 (PG-13)** Wiig is too good for this sitcom material, a movie that barely got released after a dismal reception at the Toronto Film Festival. Wiig is forced into a thankless, awful lead role as a playwright who fakes a suicide attempt to get her ex back, but ends up being put in the custody of her gambling-addict mother Zelda (Bening). If it sounds like the set-up for a bad sitcom pilot, that's because it clearly is. The physical humor and unbelievable characters feel even more grating because Wiig and Bening are so much more talented than the clichéd the script that they've been given. **103m/C; DVD, Blu-Ray.** Kristen Wiig; Annette Bening; Matt Dillon; Darren Criss; Christopher Fitzgerald; Natasha Lyonne; Mickey Sumner; Bob Balaban; ***D:*** Shari Springer Berman; Robert Pulcini; ***W:*** Michelle Morgan; ***C:*** Steve Yedlin; ***M:*** Rob Simonsen.

The Girl Most Likely to. . . 🦴🦴 1/2 **1973** Frumpy coed Miriam Knight (Channing) is looking for Mr. Right but all she finds is humiliation from football players, frat boys, and sorority gals. Then Miriam gets her own back in a unique way. After a terrible car crash, plastic surgery means Miriam is now an unrecognizable babe and she avenges herself on her tormentors in lethal ways. She also gets an actual admirer in gruff detective Ralph Varone (Asner) who's investigating this spate of unusual campus "accidents." **74m/C; DVD, Blu-Ray.** Stockard Channing; Ed Asner; Jim Backus; Joe Flynn; Carl Ballantine; Chuck McCann; Larry Wilcox; Fred Grandy; Suzanne Zenor; Warren Berlinger; ***D:*** Leo Phillips; ***W:*** Joan Rivers. **TV**

The Girl Next Door 🦴🦴 1/2 **1953** Widowed comic strip writer Bill Carter (Dailey) is a single dad to 10-year-old son Joe (Gray). Then pretty nightclub star Jeannie (Haver) moves in next-door and their romance causes friction. Haver's last film before she decided to enter a convent for several months. **92m/C; DVD.** Dan Dailey; June Haver; Billy Gray; Dennis Day; Cara Williams; Natalie Schafer; ***D:*** Richard Sale; ***W:*** Isobel Lennart; ***C:*** Leon Shamroy; ***M:*** Cyril Mockridge.

The Girl Next Door 🦴🦴 **1998 (R)** Married doctor Czerny agrees to keep an eye on his neighbor's 18-year-old hot-babe daughter (Shannon) while her parents are out of town. Only he takes the good neighbor relationship too far. When the teen winds up dead, the local Sheriff (Busey) is out to discover just what happened. **100m/C; VHS, DVD.** *CA* Henry Czerny; Gary Busey; Polly Shannon; Robin Gammell; Alberta Watson; Simon MacCorkindale; ***D:*** Eric Till.

The Girl Next Door 🦴🦴 **2004 (R)** Porn goddess Danielle (Cuthbert) moves to suburbia to taunt and tease nerdy teen next door, Matt (Hirsch). The two meet cute and a "Risky Business" redo ensues: Matt hooks up with Danielle, to the delight of his two geeky friends (Marquette and Dano), who inform Matt of the illicit past Danielle is trying to leave behind. That past includes former producer Olyphant, who shows up to woo Danielle back to "the life" while schooling the studious Matt in the ways of the world. He must then juggle a trip to a Vegas porn convention and work on a speech on morality to win a scholarship to Georgetown. Though Cuthbert and Hirsch are attractive and have decent chemistry, it's Olyphant that scores with an above average comedic performance in this otherwise uninspired genre fare. **108m/C; DVD, Blu-Ray.** Elisha Cuthbert; Emile Hirsch; Timothy Olyphant; James Remar; Christopher Marquette; Paul Dano; Timothy Bottoms; Donna Bullock; Amanda Swisten; Jacob Young; Brian Kolodziej; ***D:*** Luke Greenfield; ***W:*** David T. Wagner; Brent Goldberg; Stuart Blumberg; ***C:*** Jamie Anderson; ***M:*** Paul Haslinger.

Girl of the Golden West 🦴🦴 **1938** A musical version of the David Belasco chestnut about a Canadian frontier girl loving a rogue. One of Eddy and MacDonald's lesser efforts but features Ebsen's song and dance talents. **120m/B; DVD.** Jeanette MacDonald; Nelson Eddy; Walter Pidgeon; Leo Carrillo; Buddy Ebsen; Leonard Penn; Priscilla Lawson; Bob Murphy; Olin Howlin; Cliff Edwards; Billy Bevan; ***D:*** Robert Z. Leonard.

A Girl of the Limberlost 🦴🦴🦴 **1990** A young Indiana farmgirl fights to bring her estranged parents back together, in spite of a meddling aunt and the unexplained phenomena that haunt her. Fine acting and beautiful scenery. Originally broadcast as part of PBS's "Wonderworks" family movie series, it's best appreciated by young teens. Adapted from Gene Stratton Porter's much-filmed novel. **120m/C; VHS, DVD.** Annette O'Toole; Joanna Cassidy; Heather Fairfield; ***D:*** Burt Brinckerhoff; ***W:*** Pamela Douglas; ***C:*** Gordon C. Lonsdale; ***M:*** Misha Segal. **TV**

Girl of the Night 🦴🦴 **1960** Surprisingly frank depiction of prostitution based on an academic study. New York hooker Bobbie (Francis) reveals the sordid details of her profession to shrink Dr. Mitchell (Nolan). She hopes by discovering why she became a call girl she can escape her madam (Medford) and the pimp (Kerr) she thinks she loves, gain some self-esteem, and change her life. **93m/B; DVD.** Anne Francis; Lloyd Nolan; Kay Medford; John Kerr; James Broderick; Arthur Storch; Eileen Fulton; ***D:*** Joseph Cates; ***W:*** Ted Berkman; Raphael David Blau; ***C:*** Joseph Brun; ***M:*** Sol Kaplan.

The Girl of Your Dreams 🦴🦴 1/2 *La nina de tus ojos* **1999 (R)** Macarena Granada (Cruz) headlines a troop of Spanish actors who travel from their war-torn country to Berlin in 1938 to turn an Andalusian musical into a movie. Things get grimly messy when she seeks to rescue a prisoner from a nearby concentration camp. In Spanish, with subtitles. **121m/C; VHS, DVD.** Penelope Cruz; Antonio Resines; Jorge Sanz; Rosa Maria Sarda; Santiago Segura; Loles Leon; Jesus Bonilla; Neus Asensi; Miroslav Taborsky; Karel Dobry; Johannes Silberschneider; Goetz Otto; Hanna Schygulla; Maria Barranco; Juan Luis Galiardo; Heinz Rilling; Jan Preucil; Borivoj Navratil; Martin Faltyn; Otto Sevcik; ***D:*** Fernando Trueba; ***W:*** Rafael Azcona; Miguel Angel Egea; Carlos Lopez; David Trueba; ***C:*** Javier Aguirresarobe; ***M:*** Antoine Duhamel. **VIDEO**

Girl on a Chain Gang **WOOF!** **1965** A girl on the run gets caught by police and does her time on a chain gang—an otherwise all-male chain gang. Predictable. **96m/B; VHS, DVD.** William Watson; Julie Ange; R.K. Charles; ***D:*** Jerry Gross; ***W:*** Jerry Gross.

The Girl on a Motorcycle 🦴🦴 *Naked under Leather; La Motocyclette* **1968 (R)** Singer Faithfull is a bored housewife who dons black leather and hops on her motorcycle to meet up with her lover (Delon), all the while remembering their other erotic encounters. **92m/C; VHS, DVD.** *GB* Alain Delon; Marianne Faithfull; Roger Mutton; ***D:*** Jack Cardiff; ***W:*** Gillian Freeman; Ronald Duncan; ***C:*** Jack Cardiff; ***M:*** Les Reed.

The Girl on the Bridge 🦴🦴🦴 *Le Fille sure le Pont* **1998 (R)** An unconventional romance that finds middle-aged professional knife-thrower Gabor (Auteuil) calmly engaging in conversation with suicidal Adele (Paradis), the titular character. After a young lifetime of perpetual bad luck, what could be better for Adele than to risk everything every night by becoming Gabor's new partner. The duo seem to have a telepathic communication that makes them a great success but luck has a way of changing. Great chemistry between the world-weary Auteuil and the gamine Paradis that is all the more apparent because their characters maintain a hands-off relationship. French with subtitles. **92m/B; VHS, DVD.** *FR* Daniel Auteuil; Vanessa Paradis; Demetre Georgalas; Isabelle Petit-Jacques; ***D:*** Patrice Leconte; ***W:*** Serge Frydman; ***C:*** Jean-Marie Dreujou. Cesar '00: Actor (Auteuil).

Girl On the Run 🦴 **1953** Exploitation drivel. Reporter Bill Martin is investigating a vice ring operating out of a two-bit carnival. Bill becomes the suspect in a murder and hides out at the carnival, thanks to his girlriend Janet who has nobly taken a job as a carny burlesque dancer so Bill can find the real killer. Steve McQueen makes his first (uncredited) onscreen appearance as an extra. **65m/B; DVD.** Richard Coogan; Rosemary Pettit; Harry Bannister; Edith King; Frank Albertson; ***D:*** Arthur Beckhard; ***W:*** Arthur Beckhard; ***C:*** Victor Lukens.

The Girl on the Train 🦴🦴 *La Fille du RER* **2009** Based on a 2004 media-sensational true story. Aimless early 20-something Jeanne (Dequenne) lives with her respectable widowed mother Louise (Deneuve) in the insular Parisian suburbs. After a bad breakup with her thuggish boyfriend Franck (Duvauchelle), Jeanne suddenly pretends that she was violently attacked on a train by Arab and black youths who thought she was Jewish. The assault makes international news but Jeanne is soon forced to admit that she lied. What you never find out from the enigmatic Jeanne is why she did it. In contrast, writer/director Techine also introduces the liberal Jewish Bleistein family whose lawyer patriarch Samuel (Blanc), an old acquaintance of Louise, comes to Jeanne's aid. French and Hebrew with subtitles. **105m/C; On Demand.** *FR* Emilie Dequenne; Michel Blanc; Ronit Elkabetz; Catherine Deneuve; Jeremy Quaegebeur; Mathieu Demy; Nicolas Duvauchelle; ***D:*** Andre Techine; ***W:*** Andre Techine; Odile Barski; Jean-Marie Besset; ***C:*** Julien Hirsch; ***M:*** Philippe Sarde.

The Girl On the Train 🦴 1/2 **2013 (R)** Film noir wannabe finds documentary filmmaker Danny Hart (Cusick) on a train heading to upstate New York when he encounters femme fatale passenger Lexi (Aycox). Soon, Danny is unreliably discussing events with Det. Martin (Lang), who hasn't quite determined if Danny's a victim, suspect, or both. **80m/C; DVD.** Henry Ian Cusick; Nicki Aycox; Stephen Lang; David Margulies; ***D:*** Larry Brand; ***W:*** Larry Brand; ***C:*** David Sperling; ***M:*** Alexander Janko. **VIDEO**

The Girl on the Train 🦴🦴 **2016 (R)** The talented Blunt does her best to keep this adaptation of the 2015 hit mystery novel by Paula Hawkins interesting but it suffers on two fronts. One, ridiculous plot twists go down easier in books than in films. Two, director Taylor mishandles this material, delivering a flat film in much need of personality. Blunt plays Rachel Watson, a divorced woman dealing with alcoholism who becomes obsessed with a couple she spies on from the train she takes every day. Then things get strange when Rachel blacks out and spying turns into intervening. There's enough plot to serve as a distraction, but you'll feel dirty about it. **112m/C; DVD, Blu-Ray.** Emily Blunt; Haley Bennett; Rebecca Ferguson; Justin Theroux; Luke Evans; ***D:*** Tate Taylor; ***W:*** Erin Cressida Wilson; ***C:*** Charlotte Bruus Christensen; ***M:*** Danny Elfman.

Girl Play 🦴🦴 **2004** When two lesbians meet while doing a play they begin to fall for one another despite the fact Robin (Greenspan) has a long-term partner and Lacie (Harmon) loathes commitment. Drawn from the real-life story of the lead actresses who adapted the script from their play "Real Girls." **74m/C; VHS, DVD.** Mink Stole; Dom DeLuise; Robin Greenspan; Lacie Harmon; Katherine Randolph; ***D:*** Lee Friedlander; ***W:*** Lee Friedlander; Robin Greenspan; Lacie Harmon. **VIDEO**

Girl, Positive 🦴🦴 **2007** Not-too-preachy Lifetime teen drama finds high school senior Rachel (Bowen) having unprotected sex with athlete Jason (von Detten). When Jason is killed in a car accident, it turns out he was a drug user and HIV-positive. Substitute teacher Sarah (Garth), who volunteers at an HIV clinic, has been keeping her own positive status a secret, but she steps up when Rachel can't deal with her own newly-discovered results. **88m/C; DVD.** Jennie Garth; Andrea Bowen; S. Epatha Merkerson; Nathan Anderson; Evan Gamble; Rhoda Griffis; Andrew Matthews; Erik von Detten; ***D:*** Peter Werner; ***W:*** Nancey Silvers; ***C:*** Neil Roach; ***M:*** Richard (Rick) Marvin. **CABLE**

Girl Rising 🦴🦴🦴 **2013 (PG-13)** Narrated by numerous Hollywood female A-listers, this subtle-yet-powerful documentary from director Robbins brings to life the suffering of girls in many developing regions of the world. Told in nine different segments, in most cases by each actual real-life girl reenacting the events of her life--ranging from poverty, abuse, to arranged marriage--in the location where it happened. Though the overall message is that of hope there is also no mistaking the fact that this abuse happens on a larger level, as statistics that are given throughout the film by narrator Neeson demonstrate. **101m/C; On Demand.** ***Nar:*** Anne Hathaway; Cate Blanchett; Selena Gomez; Freida Pinto; Meryl Streep; Kerry Washington; Liam Neeson; Salma Hayek; Alicia Keys; Chloë Grace Moretz; ***D:*** Richard Robbins; ***W:*** Marie Arana; Doreen Baingana; Edwige Dantical; Mona Eltahawy; Aminatta Forna; Zarghuna Kargar; Maaza Mengiste; Sooni Taraporevala; Manjushree Thapa; Loung Ung; ***C:*** Mike Ozier; Heloisa Passos; Islam Abdelsamle; Adam Beckman; David Rush Morrison; Felipe Perez-Burchard; Steven Piet; Kiran Reddy; Nicole Hirsch Whitaker; ***M:*** Lorne Balfe.

The Girl Said No 🦴 1/2 **1930** Typical Haines comedy and character. Obnoxious Tom won't take no for an answer despite Mary's (Hyams) engagement to pompous J. Marvin McAndrews (Bushman). When Tom gets fired and his father dies, he must change his selfish ways to support his family but he's still determined to woo Mary, even if it means kidnapping her from her own wedding! **90m/B; DVD.** William Haines; Leila Hyams; Francis X. Bushman; Polly Moran; Marie Dressler; Clara Blandick; William V. Mong; ***D:*** Sam Wood; ***W:*** Charles MacArthur; Sarah Y. Mason; ***C:*** Ira Morgan.

Girl Shy 🦴🦴🦴 **1924** Harold is a shy tailor's apprentice who is trying to get a collection of his romantic fantasies published. Finale features Lloyd chasing wildly after girl of his dreams. **65m/B; Silent; VHS, DVD.** Harold Lloyd; Jobyna Ralston; Richard Daniels; ***D:*** Fred Newmeyer; ***W:*** Sam Taylor.

Girl 6 🦴🦴 1/2 **1996 (R)** Aspiring actress (Randle) takes job as a phone sex operator in order to make ends meet. After finally finding stardom in the world of titillating telecommunications, she starts to take her work home. Bound to be compared, unfairly and probably unfavorably, to Lee's debut "She's Gotta Have It." Terrific performance by Randle is hampered by the lack of a strong story and too many unresolved subplots. Features the obligatory Lee cameo, while Tarantino shows up as a young hotshot director. Prince provides old and new tunes (as well as his previous moniker, apparently) to the proceedings. **107m/C; VHS, DVD.** Theresa Randle; Isaiah Washington, IV; Ron Silver; John Turturro; Naomi Campbell; Halle Berry; Madonna; Quentin Tarantino; Debi Mazar; Peter Berg; Richard Belzer; Spike Lee; Jenifer Lewis; Michael Imperioli; Kristen Wilson; Dina Pearlman; Maggie Rush; Desi Moreno; Susan Batson; ***D:*** Spike Lee; ***W:*** Suzan-Lori Parks; ***C:*** Malik Hassan Sayeed; ***M:*** Prince.

A Girl Thing 🦴🦴 **2001** In four individual stories, shrink Dr. Noonan (Channing) listens to her female patients' dreams and woes. Macpherson is a successful lawyer who finds herself attracted to Capshaw in a complicated affair. Headly and her sisters DeMornay and Janney bicker over their mother's final request—they must spend a week together in her house in order to collect their inheritance. Whitfield suspects her husband Bakula is having an affair and hires Hamilton to check things out. Manheim stars as a deeply disturbed patient who forces the doctor to re-evaluate her own life and profession. **237m/C; VHS, DVD.** Stockard Channing; Elle Macpherson; Kate Capshaw; Glenne Headly; Rebecca De Mornay; Allison Janney; Lynn Whitfield; Linda Hamilton; Camryn Manheim; Scott Bakula; Bruce Greenwood; Brent Spiner; Mia Farrow; ***D:*** Lee Rose. **CABLE**

Girl vs. Monster 🦴🦴 1/2 **2012** Halloween-themed family comedy/horror from the Disney Channel. Since she's about to turn 16, Skylar's parents think they should tell her what the family business really is--monster hunting. But before they have a chance, Skylar picks Halloween to disarm the alarm system because she's trying to sneak out to a party and inadvertently sets loose the monsters trapped in a secret chamber. Skylar and her pals quickly learn that the monsters feed on fear, but how do you find the courage to overcome that? **89m/C; Streaming.** Olivia Holt; Brendan Meyer; Kerris Dorsey; Brian Palermo; Katherine McNamara; Luke Benward; ***D:*** Stuart Gillard; ***W:*** Annie DeYoung; Ron McGee; ***C:*** Thomas Burstyn; ***M:*** Robert Duncan. **CABLE**

A Girl Walks Home Alone at Night 🦴🦴 1/2 **2014** Amirpour's directorial debut is a striking, original B&W horror film billed as cinema's first Iranian vampire western. The title is a bait-and-switch in that you need not worry about this "Girl" as she happens to be the town bloodsucker, ridding her neighborhood of ne'er-do-wells and feeding her needs. Abundantly stylish to a fault, Amirpour has amazing visuals but lacks the storytelling skills to give the story much depth. Still, this is about as original as filmmaking gets; a graphic novel come to life on the big screen and a promising debut. Persian with subtitles. **107m/B; DVD, Blu-Ray.** Sheila Vand; Arash Marandi; Marshall Manesh; Dominic Rains; ***D:*** Ana Lily Amirpour; ***W:*** Ana Lily Amirpour; ***C:*** Lyle Vincent.

The Girl Who Had Everything 🦴🦴 1/2 **1953** Good melodrama with top cast, intelligent script and smooth direction. Taylor plays the spoiled daughter of a criminal lawyer (Powell) who falls for her father's client (Lamas), a suave, underground syndicate boss. Remake of the 1931 film "A Free Soul," which starred Norma Shearer, Clark Gable, and Lionel Barrymore. Based on the novel of the same name by Adela Rogers St. John. **69m/B; VHS, DVD.** Elizabeth Taylor; Fernando Lamas; William Powell; Gig Young; James Whitmore; Robert Burton; ***D:*** Richard Thorpe; ***M:*** Andre Previn.

The Girl Who Kicked the Hornet's Nest 🦴🦴 *Luftslottet Som Sprangdes* **2010 (R)** The final installment of the Dragon Tattoo trilogy opens with anti-hero Lisbeth Salander (Rapace) hospitalized and under armed guard—accused of triple murder. In prison she learns her father survived the ax blow to the head she gave him after he double-crossed her and her half-brother while they were attempting to root out a frightening government conspiracy. Making a case for her freedom seems dire, but she's got puncture studs, a mean streak, and a wicked cool tattoo. Based on the novel by Stieg Larsson; Swedish with subtitles. **146m/C; Blu-Ray, On Demand.** *SW* Noomi Rapace; Michael Nyqvist; Annika Hallin; Per Oscarsson; Lena Endre; Peter Andersson; Jacob Ericksson; Sofia Ledarp; Anders Ahlbom; Aksel Morisse; ***D:*** Daniel Alfredson; ***W:*** Ulf Rydberg; ***C:*** Peter Mokrosinski; ***M:*** Jacob Groth.

The Girl Who Knew Too Much 🦴🦴 1/2 *La Ragazza Che Sapeva Troppo; The Evil Eye* **1963** Ten years ago in Italy a string of "alphabet murders" began on "A" and ended on "C." Now a pretty young American named Nora Davis (Roman) is visiting a family friend in Italy. When the friend dies and Nora goes for help—in the middle of the night, in the rain, wearing only a raincoat, alone, through an empty plaza—she witnesses a murder that happened ten years ago or does she? She shouldn't worry, though, because handsome young Dr. Marcello Bassi (Saxon speaking fluent Italian) wants to help her. Typically fun and frightening Bava fare with the script, cinematography and direction working much more smoothly than usual. **86m/B; DVD, Blu-Ray.** *IT* Leticia Roman; John Saxon; Valentina Cortese; Robert Buchanan; ***D:*** Mario Bava; ***W:*** Mario Bava; Ennio de Concini; Mino Guerrini; ***C:*** Mario Bava.

The Girl Who Knew Too Much **WOOF! 1969** Apparently no one knew anything when they made this embarrassing dreck. Nightclub owner Johnny Cain (West) is coerced by both the CIA and some organized crime thugs into investigating the murder of a crime boss. Some Chinese commies are behind all the trouble. **97m/C; DVD, Blu-Ray.** Adam West; Nancy Kwan; Robert Alda; Nehemiah Persoff; Buddy Greco; Chick Chandler; ***D:*** Francis D. Lyon; ***W:*** Charles A. Wallace; ***C:*** Alan Stensvold; ***M:*** Joe Greene.

The Girl Who Played With Fire 🦴🦴 *Flickan Som Lekte Med Elden* **2010 (R)** Follows "The Girl With the Dragon Tattoo" as super-hacker Lisbeth keeps an eye on magazine journalist Mikael Blomkvist and an investigation into a sex-trafficking ring between Eastern Europe and Sweden. When the two journalists who write the article are murdered, Lisbeth's fingerprints are found on the weapon, though Mikael is certain it's a frame. However, trying to see who's really behind the crimes reveals more of Lisbeth's horrific past. Adapted from the Stieg Larsson novel and followed by "The Girl Who Kicked the Hornet's Nest." Swedish with subtitles. **125m/C; Blu-Ray, On Demand.** *SW* Noomi Rapace; Michael Nyqvist; Per Oscarsson; Lena Endre; Peter Andersson; Annika Hallin; Jacob Ericksson; Sofia Ledarp; ***D:*** Daniel Alfredson; ***W:*** Jonas Frykberg; ***C:*** Peter Mokrosinski; ***M:*** Jacob Groth.

Girl with a Pearl Earring 🦴🦴🦴 1/2 **2003 (PG-13)** Based on the novel by Tracy Chevalier about the fictional relationship between the famous Dutch painter Vermeer and the servant girl who posed for his most famous work. Griet (Johansson, bearing an uncanny similarity to the actual painting) is sent to work for Vermeer after her father can no longer support the family. Vermeer (Firth) is intrigued by her intuitive sensibilities to art and soon has her helping in the studio and then posing for him. Johansson gives an exceptionally flawless performance in an intelligent and visually stunning film. **95m/C; VHS, DVD.** *GB LU* Colin Firth; Scarlett Johansson; Tom Wilkinson; Judy Parfitt; Essie Davis; Cillian Murphy; Alakina Mann; Joanna Scanlan; ***D:*** Peter Webber; ***W:*** Olivia Hetreed; ***C:*** Eduardo Serra; ***M:*** Alexandre Desplat. L.A. Film Critics '03: Cinematog.

The Girl with a Suitcase 🦴🦴 *La Ragazza con la Valgia* **1960** Young nightclub singer Aida (Cardinale) falls for rich cad Marcello (Pani) and leaves her job to follow him to his family home in Parma. He was just stringing her along and instructs his 16-year-old brother Lorenzo (Perrin) to get rid of Aida. But instead Lorenzo decides to become her protector and the unlikely duo fall in love. Italian with subtitles; the original release was 135 minutes. **111m/B; VHS, DVD.** *IT* Claudia Cardinale; Jacques Perrin; Corrado Pani; Luciana Angiolillo; Romolo Valli; Gian Marie Volonte; ***D:*** Valerio Zurlini; ***W:*** Valerio Zurlini; ***C:*** Tino Santoni; ***M:*** Mario Nascimbene.

The Girl with All the Gifts 🦴🦴 1/2 **2017 (R)** Melanie (Nanua) looks like an ordinary girl, but she has restraints on her limbs and head, and she's kept in a cell every night. It turns out that this is a vision of a future ravaged by mindless zombies, known as hungrys, and Melanie is the second generation of these freaks, now being monitored and studied by a military organization. When the bunker is overwhelmed by killing machines, Melanie heads out on a road trip with a few survivors, including her favorite teacher (Arterton), a Sergeant (Considine), and a heartless doctor (Close). This is a smart, harrowing riff on the zombie genre. **111m/C; DVD, Blu-Ray.** Gemma Arterton; Paddy Considine; Glenn Close; Sennia Nanua; Anamaria Marinca; ***D:*** Colm McCarthy; ***W:*** Mike Carey; ***C:*** Simon Dennis; ***M:*** Cristobal Tapia de Veer.

Girl with Green Eyes 🦴🦴 1/2 **1964** Kate Brady (Tushingham) is a young Catholic farm girl who comes to Dublin for work and falls in love with much older divorced writer Eugene Gaillard (Finch). She moves in with him despite her moral misgivings but both discover their differences are too great to sustain their relationship. O'Brien adapted the screenplay from her novel "The Lonely Girl." **91m/B; VHS, DVD.** *GB* Peter Finch; Rita Tushingham; Lynn Redgrave; Marie Kean; Julian Glover; T.P. McKenna; Yolande Finch; Arthur O'Sullivan; ***D:*** Desmond Davis; ***W:*** Edna O'Brien; ***C:*** Manny Wynn; ***M:*** John Addison.

The Girl With the Dragon Tattoo 🦴🦴🦴 *Man Som Hatar Kvinnor* **2009** This thriller based on the novel by Stieg Larsson was already an international critical and box-office success before landing on American shores. The eponymous tattooed girl is Lisbeth (Rapace), a goth private eye/hacker who helps reporter Mikael (Nyqvist) investigate the 40-year-old disappearance of a girl from a rich and powerful family. The girl's uncle Henrik (Taube) suspects that the person responsible is a member of his loathsome family. Rapace excels as the angry and rebellious Lisbeth, who has some secrets of her own. Some scenes may be too graphic for squeamish viewers, but they reinforce the original Swedish title: "Men Who Hate Women." In Swedish with subtitles. **152m/C; Blu-Ray, On Demand.** *SW DK GE* Michael Nyqvist; Noomi Rapace; Sven-Bertil Taube; Ingvar Hirdwall; Marika Lagercrantz; Ewa Froling; Peter Haber; ***D:*** Niels Arden Oplev; ***W:*** Rasmus Heisterberg; Nicolaj Arcel; ***C:*** Jens Fischer; Eric Kress; ***M:*** Jacob Groth. British Acad. '10: Foreign Film.

The Girl With the Dragon Tattoo 🦴🦴🦴 **2011 (R)** Thrilling, entertaining first film in the English-language version of Swedish writer Steig Larsson's "Millennium" trilogy. Disgraced investigative journalist Mikael Blomkvist (Craig) teams up with computer hacker Lisbeth Salander (Mara) to investigate a conspiracy surrounding a woman who's been missing for 40 years. Blomkvist and Salander find out that the girl's wealthy family has lots of skeletons in its collective closet, and wants 'em to stay there. Fincher uses the desolate winter settings to great effect, and keeps the sense of dread and danger at a high level throughout. Mara's fantastic as Lisbeth. **158m/C; DVD, Blu-Ray.** Daniel Craig; Rooney Mara; Stellan Skarsgard; Christopher Plummer; Robin Wright; Embeth Davidtz; Joely Richardson; Joel Kinnaman; Goran Visnjic; Steven Berkoff; Julian Sands; Geraldine James; Donald (Don) Sumpter; Ulf Friberg; Per Myrberg; David Dencik; Martin Jarvis; Yorick Van Wageningen; Tony Way; Leo Bill; Simon Reithner; Jurgen Klein; ***D:*** David Fincher; ***W:*** Steven Zaillian; ***C:*** Jeff Cronenweth; ***M:*** Trent Reznor; Atticus Ross. Oscars '11: Film Editing.

The Girl with the Hungry Eyes 🦴🦴 **1994 (R)** In 1937, top fashion model and hotel owner Louise (Fulton) kills herself over a cheating fiancee. Except Louise doesn't die, instead she becomes a vampire and, in the present-day, decides to return to her now-derelict haunts. Louise is determined to restore her hotel to its former glory and get her revenge on men in general. Filmed in Miami's South Beach. Adapted from a short story by Fritz Leiber. **84m/C; VHS, DVD.** Christina (Kristina) Fulton; Isaac Turner; Leon Herbert; Bret Carr; Susan Rhodes; ***D:*** Jon Jacobs; ***W:*** Jon Jacobs; ***M:*** Paul Inder.

Girlfight 🦴🦴🦴 **1999 (R)** Scrappy feminist coming-of-age drama is the feature debut from director Karyn Kusama. Diana (Rodriguez) is a high-school senior with a bad temper and a penchant for trouble. Her single dad, Sandro (Calderon), encourages her brother Tiny (Santiago) to work with a boxing trainer but refuses to allow his daughter to participate. Diana decides to train anyway, and her determination finds her becoming the gym's first female champ. She falls in love with fellow promising amateur Adrian (Douglas), setting the stage for an unlikely mixed gender bout between the two. The movie strains reality when it has Diana fight Adrian, but the feeling throughout is heartfelt without being overly sentimental. And at least she doesn't howl "Yo Adrian" afterwards. **90m/C; VHS, DVD.** Jamie Tirelli; Michelle Rodriguez; Santiago Douglas; Ray Santiago; Elisa Bacanegra; Paul Calderon; John Sayles; ***D:*** Karyn Kusama; ***W:*** Karyn Kusama; ***C:*** Patrick Cady; ***M:*** Theodore Shapiro. Ind. Spirit '01: Debut Perf. (Rodriguez); Sundance '00: Director (Kusama), Grand Jury Prize.

The Girlfriend Experience 🦴🦴 **2009 (R)** Soderbergh's digitally-shot, brief film indulgence into five days (set before the 2008 election) in the life of high-end Manhattan call girl Chelsea (Grey), who thinks her life is all under control. Chelsea offers her clients more than just the sexual experience, she gives them the illusion of being a 'girlfriend:' going out to dinner, inquiring after their families, listening to their chatter, and asking for financial advice (then the sex). But despite her website and apparent sophistication, there's a good deal of self-delusion as well. Grey, better-known as a porn actress, has a blank beauty that serves her well. **78m/C; Blu-Ray, On Demand.** Sasha Grey; Chris Santos; Peter Zizzo; Glenn Kenny; ***D:*** Steven Soderbergh; ***W:*** Brian Koppelman; David Levien; ***C:*** Steven Soderbergh; ***M:*** Ross Godfrey.

Girlfriends 🦴🦴🦴 **1978 (PG)** Bittersweet story of a young Jewish photographer learning to make it on her own. Directorial debut of Weill reflects her background in documentaries as the true-to-life episodes unfold. **87m/C; VHS, DVD.** Melanie Mayron; Anita Skinner; Eli Wallach; Christopher Guest; Amy Wright; Viveca Lindfors; Bob Balaban; Kathryn Walker; Kristopher Tabori; Mike Kellin; Kenneth McMillan; ***D:*** Claudia Weill; ***W:*** Vicki Polon; ***C:*** Fred Murphy. Natl. Film Reg. '19; Sundance '78: Grand Jury Prize.

Girlhood 🦴🦴🦴 *Bande de Filles* **2014** French black teenager Marieme (Touré) is in that unique period between childhood and adulthood in Céline Sciamma's phenomenal, confident coming-of-age drama. Marieme faces the stark realities of growing up poor, female, and a minority in a major city but she truly develops when she forms a bond with three other local girls. Seeing how a young woman forms her identity through the support of others is something that filmmakers have tried before but rarely with this much authenticity. And it helps that Touré is a natural screen talent. **113m/C; DVD, Blu-Ray.** *FR* Karidja Toure; Assa Sylla; Lindsay Karamoh; Marietou Toure; Idrissa Diabate; ***D:*** Céline Sciamma; ***W:*** Céline Sciamma; ***C:*** Crystel Fournier; ***M:*** Jean-Baptiste de Laubier.

Girls Against Boys 🦴 **2012 (R)** After being raped, a young woman gets revenge and goes on a subsequent twisted spiral of carnage, slaughtering men for any perceived slight, real or imaginary. Basically the same cliched revenge/torture flick masquerading as feminism you've seen repeated endlessly since at least the 70s. **93m/C; DVD, Blu-Ray, Streaming.** Danielle Panabaker; Nicole LaLiberte; Liam Aiken; Michael Stahl-David; Andrew Howard; ***D:*** Austin Chick; ***W:*** Austin Chick; ***C:*** Kathryn Westergaard; ***M:*** Nathan Larson.

Girls Are for Loving 🦴 **1973** Undercover agent Ginger faces real adventure when she battles it out with her counterpart, a seductive enemy agent. Her third adventure following "Ginger" (1970) and "The Abductors" (1971). **90m/C; VHS, DVD.** Cheri Caffaro; Timothy Brown; William Grannel; Scott Ellsworth; Robert C. Jefferson; Jocelyn Peters; Yuki Shimoda; Fred Vincent; ***D:*** Don Schain; ***W:*** Don Schain; ***M:*** Robert G. Orpin.

Girl's Best Friend 🦴🦴 1/2 **2008** Dog-hating Mary (Garofalo), who's also phobic about committing to her boyfriend, reluctantly agrees to drive her mother's troublesome Jack Russell terrier Binky cross-country to her mom's new home. This gives Mary time to readjust her attitude to both dogs and boyfriends. **90m/C; DVD.** Janeane Garofalo; Kris Holden-Ried; Nicolas Wright; ***D:*** Peter

Svatek; *W:* Muffy Marraco; *C:* Manfred Guthe; *M:* Luc St. Pierre. **CABLE**

Girls Can't Swim 🦴🦴 ½ *Les Filles Ne Savent Pas Nager* **1999** Fifteen-year-old Gwen (Le Bresco) and her best friend Lise (Alyx) always spend their summers together on the Brittany coast where Gwen lives and Lise's family rents a cottage. But when there's a family tragedy, Lise must stay home until the gloomy atmosphere has her traveling to Gwen's on her own. Gwen's parents (who have their own problems) let Lise stay but things between the friends have changed. Gwen has been flaunting her sexuality with the local boys and comes to resent Lise, who feels abandoned. Gwen's thoughtless sexual impulses finally cause the divisions between the girls to spin out of control. French with subtitles. **98m/C; VHS, DVD.** *FR* Islid Le Besco; Karen Alyx; Pascal Elso; Pascale Bussieres; Julien Cottereau; Marie Riviere; *D:* Anne-Sophie Birot; *W:* Anne-Sophie Birot; Christophe Honore; *C:* Nathalie Durand; *M:* Ernest Chausson.

Girl's Dormitory 🦴🦴 ½ **1936** French actress Simon made her American debut in this sharp romance. Dr. Stephen Dominik (Marshall), the middle-aged headmaster of a strict Swiss girls' finishing school, is secretly loved by teenaged student Marie (Simon) and attractive professor Anna (Chatterton). Marie is in despair after being threatened with expulsion for writing Stephen a steamy love letter. She's comforted by the headmaster, who now believes that he does have feelings for the chit. Power had a one-scene role as a dashing young count romancing Marie and he made such an impression on the audience that the Fox studio started giving him bigger and better roles. **65m/B; DVD.** Herbert Marshall; Ruth Chatterton; Simone Simon; Constance Collier; J. Edward Bromberg; Tyrone Power; Dixie Dunbar; *D:* Irving Cummings; *W:* Gene Markey; *C:* Merritt B. Gerstad; *M:* Arthur Lange; Charles Maxwell.

Girls! Girls! Girls! 🦴🦴 **1962 (PG)** Poor tuna boat fisherman Elvis moonlights as a nightclub singer to get his father's boat out of hock. He falls for a rich girl pretending to be poor; and after some romantic trials, there's the usual happy ending. **106m/C; VHS, DVD.** Elvis Presley; Stella Stevens; Laurel Goodwin; Jeremy Slate; Benson Fong; Robert Strauss; Ginny Tiu; Guy Lee; Beulah Quo; Frank Puglia; Nestor Paiva; Alexander Tiu; Elizabeth Tiu; Lili Valenty; *D:* Norman Taurog; *W:* Edward Anhalt; *C:* Loyal Griggs; *M:* Joseph J. Lilley.

Girls in Chains 🦴 ½ **1943** Girls in a reformatory, a teacher, a corrupt school official, and the detective trying to nail him. There's also a murder with the killer revealed at the beginning of the film. **72m/B; DVD.** Arline Judge; Roger Clark; Robin Raymond; Barbara Pepper; Dorothy Burgess; Clancy Cooper; Sid Melton; Betty Blythe; Peggy Stewart; Francis Ford; *D:* Edgar G. Ulmer; *W:* Albert Beich; *C:* Ira Morgan; *M:* Leo Erdody.

Girls in Prison 🦴🦴 **1994 (R)** Not exactly a remake of the same-titled 1956 film (although it's still set in the '50s) but it's a familiar "babes behind bars" saga. Aspiring country singer Aggie (Crider) is wrongfully convicted of murdering a record company exec and winds up in the big house. Then she learns an inmate has been contracted to kill her. Can she find the hit girl before it's too late (and find out who's framing her)? **82m/C; VHS, DVD.** Missy (Melissa) Crider; Ione Skye; Anne Heche; William Boyett; Tom Towler; Miguel (Michael) Sandoval; Jon Polito; Richmond Arquette; *D:* John McNaughton; *W:* Christa Lang; Samuel Fuller; *C:* Jean De Segonzac; *M:* Hummie Mann. **CABLE**

Girls Just Want to Have Fun 🦴 ½ **1985 (PG)** An army brat and her friends pull out all the stops and defy their parents for a chance to dance on a national TV program. **90m/C; VHS, DVD, Blu-Ray.** Sarah Jessica Parker; Helen Hunt; Ed Lauter; Holly Gagnier; Morgan Woodward; Lee Montgomery; Shannen Doherty; Biff Yeager; *D:* Alan Metter; *W:* Janice Hirsch; Amy Spies; *C:* Thomas Ackerman; *M:* Thomas Newman.

Girls Night Out 🦴 *The Scaremaker* **1983 (R)** Ex-cop must stop a killer who is murdering participants in a sorority house scavenger hunt and leaving cryptic clues on the local radio station. **96m/C; VHS, DVD.** Hal Holbrook; Rutanya Alda; Julia Montgomery; James Carroll; *D:* Robert Deubel.

Girls of the White Orchid 🦴 *Death Ride to Osaka* **1985** A naive American girl thinks she's getting a job singing in a Japanese nightclub, but it turns out to be a front for a prostitution ring run by the Japanese Yakuza. Based on real stories, though the producers concentrate on the seamy side. **96m/C; VHS, DVD.** Ann Jillian; Jennifer Jason Leigh; Thomas Jefferson Byrd; Carolyn Seymour; Mako; *D:* Jonathan Kaplan; *C:* John Lindley; *M:* Brad Fiedel. **TV**

Girls on the Road 🦴 ½ **1973 (PG)** Two girls are just out for fun cruising the California coast, but that handsome hitchhiker turns out to be a deadly mistake. **91m/C; VHS, DVD.** *CA* Kathleen (Kathy) Cody; Michael Ontkean; Dianne Hull; Ralph Waite; Rigg Kennedy; *D:* Thomas J. Schmidt.

Girls School Screamers 🦴 **1986 (R)** Six young women and a nun are assigned to spend the weekend checking the contents for sale in a scary mansion bequeathed to their school. Unfortunately, the psychotic killer inhabiting the place doesn't think that's a good idea. **85m/C; VHS, DVD.** Mollie O'Mara; Sharon Christopher; Vera Gallagher; *D:* John P. Finegan; *W:* John P. Finegan; *C:* Albert R. Jordan; *M:* John Hodian.

Girls Town 🦴🦴 **1995 (R)** Tough look at the lives of three working-class high school seniors who are shattered by the suicide of Nikki (Ellis), the fourth member of their group, who killed herself from guilt over an undisclosed rape. Single mom Patti (Taylor), ambitious Emma (Grace), and strong-willed Angela (Harris) argue, commiserate, battle their foes (Patti's abusive boyfriend, Nikki's rapist), and lean on each other as they struggle to figure out themselves and their ambiguous futures. Lots of time's spent in the girls' bathroom at school (how realistic can you get?) **90m/C; VHS, Streaming.** Lili Taylor; Anna Grace; Bruklin Harris; Aunjanue Ellis; Guillermo Diaz; John Ventimiglia; *D:* Jim McKay; *W:* Lili Taylor; Anna Grace; Bruklin Harris; Aunjanue Ellis; Denise Casano; Jim McKay; *C:* Russell Fine. Sundance '96: Filmmakers Trophy.

Girls Trip 🦴🦴🦴 **2017 (R)** Don't bemoan the missing apostrophe--in this comedy, "trip" is a verb, and these ladies are definitely verbing it up, New Orleans style. Four college pals (Hall, Queen Latifah, Pinkett Smith, and Haddish) reunite for the annual Essence Festival, where the raucous good times roll with drinking, dancing, and romancing. Character-driven laughs and an electric chemistry between the leads elevate what could have been a mindless and clichéd romp in lesser hands. **122m/C; DVD, Blu-Ray.** Regina Hall; Queen Latifah; Jada Pinkett Smith; Tiffany Haddish; Larenz Tate; *D:* Malcolm Lee; *W:* Kenya Barris; Tracy Oliver; *C:* Greg Gardiner; *M:* David Newman.

Girly 🦴 *Mumsy, Nanny, Sonny, and Girly* **1970 (R)** An English gothic about an excessively weird family that lives in a crumbling mansion and indulges in murder, mental aberration, and sexual compulsion. **101m/C; VHS, DVD, Blu-Ray, Streaming.** *GB* Michael Bryant; Ursula Howells; Pat Heywood; Howard Trevor; Vanessa Howard; Michael Ripper; *D:* Freddie Francis.

Giulia Doesn't Date at Night 🦴 ½ *Giulia Non Esce la Sera* **2009** Author Guido (Mastandrea) is bored and experiencing writer's block when he meets his daughter's swimming teacher Giulia (Golino). She turns out to be a criminal only permitted out of prison on a daily work pass (hence the title) but that only heightens Guido's interest. He attempts a new book, and various would-be scenarios come to life, but it only works when he starts writing about Giulia. Italian with subtitles. **105m/C; DVD.** *IT* Valeria Golino; Valerio Mastandrea; Sonia Bergamasco; Lidia Vitale; Chiara Nicola; Paolo Sassanelli; Jacopo Domenicucci; *D:* Giuseppe Piccioni; *W:* Giuseppe Piccioni; Federica Pontremoli; *C:* Luca Bigazzi; *M:* Baustelle.

Giuliani Time 🦴🦴 **2005** A mostly-warts documentary on Rudy Giuliani, from his early career at the Department of Justice to his controversial two terms as the mayor of New York City and his response to the disaster of 9/11, ending with his speech at the 2004 Republican National Convention. Filmmaker Keating is not a fan. **119m/C; DVD.** *D:* Kevin Keating; *C:* Kevin Keating; *M:* David Carbonara.

Give a Girl a Break 🦴🦴 ½ **1953** Three talented but unknown babes vie for the lead in a stage production headed for Broadway after the incumbent prima donna quits. After befriending one of the various men associated with the production, each starlet thinks she's a shoe-in for the part. Entertaining but undistinguished musical with appealing dance routines of Fosse and the Champions. Ira Gershwin, collaborating for the first and only time with Burton Lane, wrote the lyrics to two of the songs. **84m/C; VHS, DVD.** Marge Champion; Gower Champion; Debbie Reynolds; Helen Wood; Bob Fosse; Kurt Kasznar; Richard Anderson; William Ching; Larry Keating; Donna Martell; *D:* Stanley Donen; *M:* Andre Previn.

Give 'Em Hell, Harry! 🦴🦴🦴 **1975** James Whitmore's one-man show as Harry S. Truman filmed in performance on stage; Whitmore was nominated for a Tony. **103m/C; VHS, DVD.** James Whitmore; *D:* Steve Binder.

Give 'Em Hell Malone 🦴 ½ **2009 (R)** If there's any reason for tough PI Malone (Jane) to come across as a retro '50s figure in a contemporary world, it's unclear but so is much of the flick. Malone walks into a trap when he's hired to retrieve a briefcase that's the property of mob boss Whitmore (Harrison). Blonde bombshell Evelyn (Pataky) figures in as do three silly-named thugs hired by Whitmore when Malone refuses to turn over the goods. **96m/C; DVD, Blu-Ray.** Thomas Jane; Elsa Pataky; Ving Rhames; Chris Yen; Doug Hutchison; Gregory Harrison; Leland Orser; William Abadie; Eileen Ryan; French Stewart; *D:* Russell Mulcahy; *W:* Mark Hosack; *C:* Jonathan Hall; *M:* David Williams.

Give Me a Sailor 🦴🦴 ½ **1938** Hope and Whiting play brothers, and fellow Naval officers, who meet sisters Grable and Raye on shore leave. Naturally, there's comic romantic complications until a double wedding ends the farce. Not much of a musical score from Ralph Rainger and Leo Robin but the movie's fun. Based on a play by Anne Nichols. **71m/B; DVD.** Bob Hope; Martha Raye; Betty Grable; Jack Whiting; Clarence (C. William) Kolb; Nana Bryant; Emerson Treacy; *D:* Elliott Nugent; *W:* Frank Butler; Doris Anderson.

Give Me Liberty 🦴🦴 ½ **2019** Working as a medical transport driver, Vic (Galust) is overwhelmed by the demands of his position. He drives clients to their medical appointments and is often late. While transporting clients to a job training program for people with disabilities, he learns that transportation never showed up for a group of elderly singing mourners that includes his grandfather. Vic picks them up, too, and the situation grows chaotic due in part to the actions of a con man, Dima (Stoyanov), who is tagging along to the funeral. A bit choppy but the comedy-drama has realistic dialogue and scenarios. **110m/C; DVD.** Lauren Spencer; Chris Galust; Maxim Stoyanov; Steve Wolski; Michelle Caspar; *D:* Kirill Mikhanovsky; *W:* Kirill Mikhanovsky; Alice Austen; *C:* Wyatt Garfield.

Give Me Your Hand 🦴 **2009** Identical teenaged twin brothers alternate between fighting, rivalry, and protectiveness on a road trip across France as they head to Spain for their mother's funeral while indulging in various sexual escapades. The Carrils are so inexpressive and the plot so simplistic that all a viewer will want is for the trip to end as quickly as possible. French with subtitles. **77m/C; DVD.** *FR* Alexandre Carril; Victor Carril; Samir Harrag; Anais Demoustier; *D:* Pascal-Alex Vincent; *W:* Pascal-Alex Vincent; Martin Drouot; Olivier Nicklaus; *C:* Alexis Kavyrchine; *M:* Bernd Jestram; Ronald Lippock.

Give Me Your Heart 🦴🦴 **1936** Former socialite Belinda (Francis) has an affair with titled Englishman Robert (Knowles), who is married to invalid Rosamond (Inescourt). When Belinda gets pregnant, she is persuaded to give up the baby boy to the couple since Rosamond can't have children. Belinda flees to New York, eventually marrying lawyer James Baker (Brent) without telling him of her past. But she can't stop thinking about her child and secrets have a way of getting out. **77m/B; DVD.** Kay Francis; George Brent; Patric Knowles; Frieda Inescort; Roland Young; Henry Stephenson; Zeffie Tilbury; *D:* Archie Mayo; *W:* Casey Robinson; *C:* Sidney Hickox.

Give My Regards to Broad Street 🦴 **1984 (PG)** McCartney film made for McCartney fans. Film features many fine versions of the ex-Beatle's songs that accompany his otherwise lackluster portrayal of a rock star in search of his stolen master recordings. **109m/C; VHS, DVD.** *GB* Paul McCartney; Bryan Brown; Ringo Starr; Barbara Bach; Tracey Ullman; Ralph Richardson; Linda McCartney; *D:* Peter Webb.

Give Us the Moon 🦴 ½ **1944** Minor Brit comedy set in 1947. An eccentric group of Soho idlers decide they don't want to work for a living. They're joined by Peter Pyke, the wastrel son of an hotel magnate who quickly forces his offspring to take over the management of a hotel. Soon the other idlers are lending a hand, much to the dismay of the group's leaders. **95m/B; DVD.** *UK* Peter Graves; Margaret Lockwood; Vic Oliver; Roland Culver; Max Bacon; Jean Simmons; *D:* Val Guest; *W:* Val Guest; *C:* Phil Grindrod; *M:* Bob Busby.

The Giver 🦴🦴 **2014 (PG-13)** Lois Lowry's award-winning and beloved 1993 teen action novel is added to an overrun YA adaptation genre, and the result is predictably meh. Another vision of the future finds a world that has no pain or darkness. It's perfect. Of course, that can't last. A young man names Jonas (Thwaites) is given the key to the truth of the universe when he is named Receiver of Memories, and he learns about pain, sadness, and war from the title character (Bridges). But tearing down the façade of his perfect world proves dangerous in ways he never imagined. **97m/C; DVD, Blu-Ray.** Brenton Thwaites; Jeff Bridges; Meryl Streep; Alexander Skarsgård; Katie Holmes; Odeya Rush; Taylor Swift; *D:* Phillip Noyce; *W:* Michael Mitnick; Robert B. Weide; *C:* Ross Emery; *M:* Marco Beltrami.

Giving It Up 🦴 ½ *Casanova Falling* **1999 (R)** Bland and predictable romantic comedy. Successful New York ad exec Ralph (Feuerstein) is a sexaholic. This pleases his boss Jonathan (Coleman) since it seems to enhance Ralph's work but makes him a pariah to his female co-workers. He meets his match in sophisticated Elizabeth (Redford) and decides to change his horn dog ways for true love. Only Ralph slips when he gets a chance with supermodel Amber (Larter). It ain't pretty when Liz finds out. **90m/C; VHS, DVD.** Mark Feuerstein; Dabney Coleman; Ali Larter; Amy Redford; Callie (Calliope) Thorne; James Toback; *D:* Christopher Kublan; *W:* Christopher Kublan; *C:* Leland Krane.

The Gladiator 🦴 ½ **1986** An angry Los Angeles citizen turns vigilante against drunk drivers after his brother is one of their victims. **94m/C; VHS, DVD.** Ken Wahl; Nancy Allen; Robert Culp; Stan Shaw; Rosemary Forsyth; *D:* Abel Ferrara. **TV**

Gladiator 🦴 ½ **1992 (R)** When suburban Golden Gloves boxing champion Tommy Riley (Marshall) is forced to move to the inner city because of his father's gambling debts, he becomes involved with an evil boxing promotor who thrives on pitting different ethnic races against each other in illegal boxing matches. Eventually Riley is forced to fight his black friend Lincoln (Gooding), even though Lincoln has been warned that another blow to the head could mean his life. Although this film tries to serve some moral purpose, it falls flat on the mat. **98m/C; VHS, DVD.** Cuba Gooding, Jr.; James Marshall; Robert Loggia; Ossie Davis; Brian Dennehy; Cara Buono; John Heard; Jon Seda; Lance Slaughter; *D:* Rowdy Herrington; *W:* Lyle Kessler; Robert Mark Kamen; *C:* Tak Fujimoto; *M:* Brad Fiedel.

Gladiator 🦴🦴🦴 **2000 (R)** Emperor Marcus Aurelius (Harris) decides to name victorious general Maximus (Crowe) his heir over the ruler's own son, the decadent Commodus (Phoenix). But Commodus manages to take over the Empire anyway. Maximus is betrayed, his family killed, and he is sold as a slave, eventually learning the ways of a gladiator. Then he returns to Rome to fight before the new Emperor and get his revenge. Last role for Reed (playing owner/trainer Proximo), who died during production. Unlike the cheesy Italian muscle epics of the early '60s this is swords, sandals, and killer beasts for a new generation, with a compelling hero in Crowe. **154m/C; VHS, DVD, Blu-Ray.** Russell Crowe; Joaquin Rafael (Leaf) Phoenix; Connie Nielsen; Djimon Hounsou; Ralph (Ralf) Moeller; Derek Jacobi; Oliver Reed; Richard Harris; David Schofield; John Shrapnel; Tomas Arana; Spencer Treat Clark; Tommy Flanagan; David Hemmings; Sven-Ole Thorsen; ***D:*** Ridley Scott; ***W:*** David Franzoni; John Logan; William Nicholson; ***C:*** John Mathieson; ***M:*** Hans Zimmer. Oscars '00: Actor (Crowe), Costume Des., Film, Sound, Visual FX; British Acad. '00: Cinematog., Film; Golden Globes '01: Film--Drama, Score; Natl. Bd. of Review '00: Support. Actor (Phoenix); Broadcast Film Critics '00: Actor (Crowe), Cinematog., Film, Support. Actor (Phoenix).

Gladiator Cop: The Swordsman 2 ♂ ½ **1995 (R)** A legendary sword, believed to have magic powers, is stolen and an ex-detective winds up fighting modern-day gladiators and a man who believes himself to be a reincarnation of Alexander the Great. **92m/C; VHS, DVD.** Lorenzo Lamas; James Hong; Frank Anderson; Christopher Lee Clements; Heather Gillan; ***D:*** Nick Rotundo; ***W:*** Nick Rotundo; ***C:*** Edgar Egger; ***M:*** Guy Zerafa.

Gladiator of Rome ♂ *Il Gladiatore Di Roma* **1963** A gladiator flexes his pecs to save a young girl from death at the hands of evil rulers. **105m/C; VHS, DVD.** *IT* Gordon Scott; Wandisa Guida; Roberto Risso; Ombretta Colli; Alberto Farnese; ***D:*** Mario Costa.

The Gladiators ♂ *The Peace Game; Gladiatorerna* **1970** Televised gladiatorial bouts are designed to subdue man's violent tendencies in a futuristic society until a computer makes a fatal error. **90m/C; VHS, DVD.** Arthur Pentelow; Frederick Danner; ***D:*** Peter Watkins.

Gladiators 7 ♂ ½ **1962** Sparta must be freed from the tyrannical rule of the Romans. In lieu of samurai or cowboys, who better than the Gladiators 7 to do the deed? Plenty of sword-to-sword action and scantily clad Italian babes. **92m/C; VHS, DVD.** *SP IT* Richard Harrison; Loredana Nusciak; Livio Lorenzon; Gerard Tichy; Edoardo Toniolo; Joseph Marco; Barta Barry; ***D:*** Pedro Lazaga.

Glam ♂♂ **1997 (R)** Eccentric writer Sonny Daye (McNamara) arrives in L.A. and is promptly exploited. His cousin Franky (Frank) takes Sonny's journal to a pair of schlocky producers who are impressed by the writing. So vain and ruthless Sid Dalgren (Danza) decides to control Sonny even while his tootsie, Vanessa (Wagner), begins to fall for the oddball's sweetness. Very talky. Director Evan's mom, Ali McGraw, has a cameo. **93m/C; VHS, DVD.** William McNamara; Frank Whaley; Natasha Gregson Wagner; Tony Danza; Valerie Kaprisky; Caroline Lagerfelt; Lou (Cutel) Cutell; Robert DoQui; Jon Cryer; Donal Logue; ***Cameo(s):*** Ali MacGraw; ***D:*** Josh Evans; ***W:*** Josh Evans; ***M:*** Josh Evans.

Glass ♂♂ ½ **2019 (PG-13)** The third film in a trilogy with Unbreakable and Split finds David (Willis) acting as a superhero-like protector named the Overseer with the help of his son Joseph (Clark). One day, he rescues four young women held by DID sufferer Kevin (McAvoy) and his many personalities. The pair are captured by Dr. Ellie Staple (Paulson) and held in a psych ward with Elijah Price/Mr. Glass (Jackson). Though the doctor tries to convince the three that they do not have super powers, each man undermines her belief. The film fails to live up to its ambitious story, but McAvoy continues his powerful presence. **110m/C; DVD, Blu-Ray.** James McAvoy; Bruce Willis; Samuel L. Jackson; Anya Taylor-Joy; Sarah Paulson; ***D:*** M. Night Shyamalan; ***W:*** M. Night Shyamalan; ***C:*** Mike Gioulakis; ***M:*** West Dylan Thordson.

The Glass Bottom Boat ♂♂ ½ **1966** A bubbly but transparent Doris Day comedy, in which she falls in love with her boss at an aerospace lab. Their scheme to spend time together gets her mistaken for a spy. Made about the time they stopped making them like this anymore, it's innocuous slapstick romance with a remarkable 1960s cast, including a Robert Vaughn cameo as the Man From U.N.C.L.E. Doris sings "Que Sera, Sera" and a few other numbers. **110m/C; VHS, DVD, Blu-Ray.** Doris Day; Rod Taylor; Arthur Godfrey; Paul Lynde; Eric Fleming; Alice Pearce; Ellen Corby; John McGiver; Dom DeLuise; Dick Martin; Edward Andrews; ***Cameo(s):*** Robert Vaughn; ***D:*** Frank Tashlin; ***W:*** Everett Freeman; ***C:*** Leon Shamroy.

The Glass Castle ♂♂ ½ **2017 (PG-13)** Based on the best-selling autobiography by journalist Jeannette Wells, this adaptation offers an insightful view into her difficult, impoverished upbringing. Alcoholic father Rex (Harrelson) and oddball artist mother Rose Mary (Watts) raise Jeannette (Larson, Anderson, and Head) and her three siblings using abysmal, destructive parenting techniques, which include living as vagabonds. As an adult, Jeannette faces the dark despair of her childhood with resilience, resourcefulness, and determination to create her own life path. The talented cast performs well, but the material fails them - and Wells - by not fully capturing the memoir's complexities. **127m/C; DVD, Blu-Ray.** Brie Larson; Woody Harrelson; Naomi Watts; Ella Anderson; Chandler Head; ***D:*** Destin Daniel Cretton; ***W:*** Destin Daniel Cretton; Andrew Lanham; ***C:*** Brett Pawlak; ***M:*** Joel P. West.

Glass Chin ♂♂ ½ **2014** The fantastic character actor Corey Stoll gets a chance to shine in a lead role in this better-than-average boxing drama. Stoll plays a former welterweight champ named Bud Gordon, who is struggling with normal life outside of the ring. Like so many athletes, he has no idea what to do with the rest of his life And Gordon's lack of direction leads him down a shady path when he gets involved with the criminal underworld. Narratively, there's not much here that's new, but the film is really well-made and carried by another great performance from Stoll. **87m/C; DVD, Streaming.** Corey Stoll; Billy Crudup; Kelly Lynch; Michael Chernus; Brendan Sexton, III; Marin Ireland; ***D:*** Noah Buschel; ***W:*** Noah Buschel; ***C:*** Ryan Samul. **VIDEO**

The Glass House ♂♂♂ *Truman Capote's The Glass House* **1972** Alda stars as a middle-aged college professor, convicted on a manslaughter charge, who is sent to a maximum security prison and must learn to deal with life inside. Filmed at Utah State Prison, real-life prisoners as supporting cast add to the drama. Still has the power to chill, with Morrow particularly effective as one of the inmate leaders. Adapted from a Truman Capote story. **92m/C; VHS, DVD, Blu-Ray.** Alan Alda; Vic Morrow; Clu Gulager; Billy Dee Williams; Dean Jagger; Kristopher Tabori; ***D:*** Tom Gries; ***M:*** Billy Goldenberg. **TV**

The Glass House ♂ ½ **2001 (PG-13)** With a brittle plot you can see right through, this flick is aptly named. After their parents are killed in a car accident, 16-year-old Ruby (Sobieski) and her little brother Rhett (Morgan) are sent to live with their former neighbors Erin and Terry Glass (Lane and Skarsgaard). The Glasses live in a swanky glass mansion with all the charm of a Windex bottle. Although they lavish the kids with clothes and gadgets, Ruby begins to suspect what we already know: evil stepparents! Ruby then tries to tell all the adults in her life that the Glasses have ugly streaks, but no one believes her or even suggests a rinsing agent. Obvious plot devices and cliched techniques (including the ever-popular "tinkling danger piano music") shatter what could have been a great thriller given the cast and concept. **111m/C; VHS, DVD.** Leelee Sobieski; Stellan Skarsgard; Diane Lane; Trevor Morgan; Bruce Dern; Kathy Baker; Chris Noth; Rita Wilson; Michael O'Keefe; Vyto Ruginis; ***D:*** Daniel Sackheim; ***W:*** Wesley Strick; ***C:*** Alar Kivilo; ***M:*** Christopher Young.

Glass House: The Good Mother ♂♂ **2006 (R)** Orphaned Abby (Hinson) and her younger brother Ethan (Coleman) are adopted by a seemingly perfect couple, Eve (Harmon) and Raymond (Gretsch) Goode. Soon uptight Eve is doting exclusively on Ethan, who suddenly gets sick, and Abby is suspicious. She learns the Goodes have previously fostered several young boys who have all disappeared. She also figures out that Raymond has been covering for his wife. But Abby is determined her brother will not become their next victim. **93m/C; DVD.** Angie Harmon; Joel Gretsch; Jason London; Jordan Hinson; Bobby Coleman; ***D:*** Steve Antin; ***W:*** Brett Merryman; ***C:*** Bobby Bukowski; ***M:*** Steve Gutheinz. **VIDEO**

The Glass Key ♂♂♂ **1942** Previously filmed in 1935, this version of Dashiell Hammet's novel is a vintage mystery concerning nominally corrupt politician Madvig (Donlevy) being framed for murder, and his assistant Ed Beaumont (Ladd) sleuthing out the real culprit. One of Ladd's first starring vehicles; Lake is the mystery woman who loves him, and Bendix a particularly vicious thug. **85m/B; DVD, Blu-Ray.** Alan Ladd; Veronica Lake; Brian Donlevy; William Bendix; Bonita Granville; Richard Denning; Joseph Calleia; Moroni Olsen; Dane Clark; ***D:*** Stuart Heisler; ***W:*** Jonathan Latimer; ***C:*** Theodor Sparkuhl; ***M:*** Victor Young.

The Glass Menagerie ♂♂♂ **1987 (PG)** An aging Southern belle deals with her crippled daughter Laura, whose one great love is her collection of glass animals. The third film adaptation of the Tennessee Williams classic, which preserves the performances of the Broadway revival cast, is a solid-but-not-stellar adaptation of the play. All-star acting ensemble. **134m/C; VHS, DVD.** Joanne Woodward; Karen Allen; John Malkovich; James Naughton; ***D:*** Paul Newman; ***W:*** Tennessee Williams; ***C:*** Michael Ballhaus; ***M:*** Henry Mancini.

The Glass Mountain ♂ ½ **1949** Dull plot but opera singer Tito Gobbi's performance is worth catching. British composer Richard Wilder (Denison) is serving as a WWII airman when he's shot down over Italy's Dolemite Mountains and rescued by pretty partisan Alida (Cortese). Eventually reunited with his wife Ann (Gray) back in London, Richard tries writing an opera based on a peasant legend he'd heard, but can't do it without returning to Italy. But which woman is truly his muse? **98m/B; DVD.** *UK* Michael Denison; Valentina Cortese; Dulcie Gray; Tito Gobbi; Sebastian Shaw; ***D:*** Henry Cass; ***W:*** Henry Cass; Emery Bonnet; ***C:*** William McLeod; ***M:*** Nino Rota.

The Glass Shield ♂♂ ½ **1995 (PG-13)** Timely look at racism and corruption in the Los Angeles sheriff's department as seen through the eyes of African American rookie J.J. Johnson (Boatman). His dream of being a police officer turns to disillusionment when he slowly realizes his own department is framing a black man (Ice Cube) for a murder he did not commit. First half grabs your attention, but the momentum is lost in murky plot twists and a rushed ending. Made on a shoestring, but has an interesting cast, including the reliably slimy Ironside as (what else) one of the bad cops and an almost unrecognizable Petty, who becomes Johnson's only ally on the force. **109m/C; VHS, DVD, Blu-Ray.** Michael Boatman; Lori Petty; Michael Ironside; M. Emmet Walsh; Ice Cube; Richard Anderson; Elliott Gould; ***D:*** Charles Burnett; ***W:*** Charles Burnett; ***C:*** Elliot Davis; ***M:*** Stephen James Taylor.

The Glass Slipper ♂♂ **1955** In this version of the "Cinderella" saga, Caron plays an unglamourous girl gradually transformed into the expected beauty. Winwood is the fairy godmother who inspires the girl to find happiness, rather then simply providing it for her magically. The film is highlighted by the stunning dance numbers, choreographed by Roland Petit and featuring the Paris ballet. **93m/C; DVD.** Leslie Caron; Michael Wilding; Keenan Wynn; Estelle Winwood; Elsa Lanchester; Barry Jones; Amanda Blake; Lurene Tuttle; ***Nar:*** Walter Pidgeon; ***D:*** Charles Walters.

The Glass Trap ♂ ½ **2004 (PG-13)** It's never pretty when an experiment goes afoul, resulting in freakishly large, angry, and human-hungry ants. Naturally, this can't be good for the scientists responsible for the demons when they get stuck in a really big skyscraper with them. **90m/C; VHS, DVD.** C. Thomas Howell; Stella Stevens; Siri Baruc; Brent Huff; Chick Vennera; ***D:*** Fred Olen Ray; ***W:*** Lisa Morton; Brett Thompson. **VIDEO**

The Glass Wall ♂♂ ½ **1953** Displaced person Peter (Gassman) is about to be deported from New York for not having the proper papers so he slips past the feds to find ex-Army pilot Tom (Paris) as a witness to Peter helping the Allies in WWII. Peter not only finds a jazz-playing Tom but befriends a couple of babes—down-on-her-luck Maggie (Grahame) and burlesque dancer Tanya (Raymond) before pleading his case before the United Nations (the glass wall of the title). **78m/B; DVD.** Vittorio Gassman; Gloria Grahame; Jerry Paris; Robin Raymond; Ann (Robin) Robinson; Douglas Spencer; ***D:*** Maxwell Shane; ***W:*** Maxwell Shane; Ivan Tors; ***C:*** Joseph Biroc; ***M:*** Leith Stevens.

Gleaming the Cube ♂ ½ **1989 (PG-13)** A skateboarding teen investigates his brother's murder. Film impresses with its stunt footage only. For those with adolescent interests. **102m/C; VHS, DVD.** Christian Slater; Steven Bauer; Min Luong; Art Chudabala; Le Tuan; ***D:*** Graeme Clifford; ***W:*** Michael Tolkin; ***M:*** Jay Ferguson.

Gleason ♂♂♂ **2016 (R)** Steve Gleason was a hero in New Orleans, blocking a punt and running it in for a touchdown in the first game after Hurricane Katrina. Five years later, he was diagnosed with ALS and started recording his journey for his unborn son. Working with director Clay Tweel, the footage was assembled into an amazingly powerful documentary about the cruelty of disease and the resilience of a true hero. We also come to get to know Gleason's family, including his supportive wife Michel. Ultimately, this is a film not about dying but about living, and overcoming obstacles in whatever manner possible. **110m/C; DVD.** Steve Gleason; Michel Varisco-Gleason; Scott Fujita; Mike Gleason; Rivers Gleason; ***D:*** J. Clay Tweel; ***W:*** J. Clay Tweel; ***C:*** David Lee; Ty Minton-Small; ***M:*** Saul Simon MacWilliams; Dan Romer.

Glee: The 3D Concert Movie ♂ ½ **2011 (PG)** Follows the popular Fox television musical comedy-drama series as the high-schoolers go on tour in 2011 ("Glee Live! In Concert!"). Though it's a documentary, the actors stay in character throughout as they perform their hit cover songs to a real audience. Goes a little overboard with its message of acceptance and inclusion but Gleeks won't stop believin' in the franchise (in other words, nonfans need not bother). **100m/C; Blu-Ray.** Dianna Agron; Lea Michele; Gwyneth Paltrow; Darren Criss; Chris Colfer; Cory Monteith; ***D:*** Kevin Tancharoen; ***C:*** Glen MacPherson.

The Gleiwitz Case ♂♂ *Der Fall Gleiwitz; The Affair Gleiwitz* **1961** A reconstruction of an actual event. On August 31, 1939, six Germans living in Poland are selected for a secret mission: to take over a radio transmitter near Gleiwitz on the German-Polish border. Under the command of an SS officer, the attack will appear to come from Polish insurgents and thus justify the Nazi invasion of Poland. German with subtitles. **70m/B; DVD.** *GE* Hilmar Thate; Hannjo Hasse; Herwart Grosse; Georg Leopold; ***D:*** Gerhard Klein; ***W:*** Wolfgang Kohlhaas; Gunther Ruckev; ***C:*** Jan Curik; ***M:*** Kurt Schwaen.

Glen and Randa ♂♂ ½ **1971 (R)** Two young people experience the world after it has been destroyed by nuclear war. Early McBride, before the hired-gun success of "The Big Easy." **94m/C; VHS, DVD.** Steven Curry; Shelley Plimpton; ***D:*** Jim McBride; ***W:*** Rudy Wurlitzer; Jim McBride.

Glen or Glenda? **WOOF!** *He or She; I Changed My Sex; I Led Two Lives; The Transvestite; Glen or Glenda: The Confessions of Ed Wood* **1953** An appalling, quasi-docudrama about transvestism, interspersed with meaningless stock footage, inept dream sequences and Lugosi sitting in a chair spouting incoherent prattle at the camera. Directorial debut of Wood, who, using a pseudonym, played the lead; one of the phenomenally bad films of this century. An integral part of the famous anti-auteur's canon. **67m/B; VHS, DVD.** Edward D. Wood, Jr.; Bela Lugosi; Lyle Talbot; Timothy Farrell; Dolores Fuller; Charles Crafts; Tommy Haynes; Captain DeZita; Evelyn Wood; Shirley Speril; Conrad Brooks; Henry Bederski; William C. Thompson; Mr. Walter; Harry Thomas; George Weiss; ***D:*** Edward D. Wood, Jr.; ***W:*** Edward D. Wood, Jr.; ***C:*** William C. Thompson.

Glengarry Glen Ross ♂♂♂ **1992 (R)** Seven-character study chronicling 48 hours in the lives of some sleazy real estate men in danger of getting the ax from their hard-driving bosses. A standout cast includes Pacino as the glad-handing sales leader, Lemmon as the hustler fallen on dim prospects, and Baldwin, briefly venomous, as the company hatchet-man. Brutal and hard-edged with very strong language. Mamet scripted from his Tony-award winning Broadway play. **100m/C; VHS, DVD, Blu-Ray.** Al Pacino; Jack Lemmon; Ed Harris; Alec Baldwin; Alan Arkin; Kevin Spacey; Jonathan Pryce; Bruce Altman; Jude Ciccolella; *D:* James Foley; *W:* David Mamet; *C:* Juan Ruiz-Anchia; *M:* James Newton Howard. Natl. Bd. of Review '92: Actor (Lemmon); Venice Film Fest. '93: Actor (Lemmon).

The Glenn Miller Story 1954 **(G)** The music of the Big Band Era lives again in this warm biography of the legendary Glenn Miller, following his life from the late '20s to his untimely death in a WWII plane crash. Stewart's likably convincing and even fakes the trombone playing well. **113m/C; VHS, DVD, Blu-Ray.** James Stewart; June Allyson; Harry (Henry) Morgan; Gene Krupa; Louis Armstrong; Ben Pollack; *D:* Anthony Mann; *W:* Oscar Brodney; Valentine Davies; *C:* William H. Daniels; *M:* Henry Mancini. Oscars '54: Sound.

The Glimmer Man 1/2 **1996 (R)** When a vicious LA serial killer starts dispatching whole families, NY detective Jack Cole (Seagal) is teamed with local homicide detective Jim Campbell (Wayans). Since, however, this is a Seagal movie, things have to be a little different. Cole, for example, is an ex-CIA operative who has been convinced by a Buddhist monk to stop killing people and start wearing goofy Nehru jackets and prayer beads. Campbell is a couch potato who cries over old movies (or perhaps he was watching the dailies from this one). After Cole's ex-wife is killed, he's implicated; and then somehow the Russian Mafia and the CIA are brought into the mix. Cole uses his unique brand of non-violence to slash, chop and impale his way to justice. Predictable when it's not being unbelievable, this could have been called "Hard to Watch." **92m/C; VHS, DVD.** Steven Seagal; Keenen Ivory Wayans; Michelle Johnson; Brian Cox; Bob Gunton; Stephen Tobolowsky; Johnny Strong; Ryan Cutrona; Peter Jason; Nikki Cox; Richard Gant; Alexa Vega; *D:* John Gray; *W:* Kevin Brodbin; *C:* Rick Bota; *M:* Trevor Rabin.

A Glimpse Inside the Mind of Charles Swan III 2012 **(R)** Director/writer Coppola delivers a surreal, quasi-commentary on the real life of friend Charlie Sheen in this bizarre tale of fame and ego in a stylized vision of Los Angeles. Sheen plays Swan, a graphic designer who seems to have it all but loses his mind after a breakup with the love of his life (Winnick). The very loose plot is little more than an excuse for Coppola, Sheen, and friends like Jason Schwartzman, Bill Murray, and Patricia Arquette to play with storytelling and the cult of celebrity. Impossible to care about but never boring. **86m/C; DVD, Blu-Ray, Streaming.** Charlie Sheen; Jason Schwartzman; Bill Murray; Patricia Arquette; Katheryn Winnick; Aubrey Plaza; Mary Elizabeth Winstead; Dermot Mulroney; *D:* Roman Coppola; *W:* Roman Coppola; *C:* Nick Beal; *M:* Roger Neill.

A Glimpse of Hell 1/2 **2001 (PG-13)** Excellent depiction of the 1989 explosion aboard the USS Iowa, and the subsequent investigations by the Navy, Congress. Lt. Dan Meyer (Leonard) is put in charge of a gun turret but soon finds equipment problems, unauthorized munitions experiments, and lax training of the gunnery crew. When one of the turrets is rocked by an explosion and 47 men are killed, the Navy, and the ship's commander, Capt. Moosally (Caan), ignore the mounting physical evidence of accidental explosion to focus on a sabotage scenario involving one of the crew, Clay Hartwig (Eaves), supposedly distraught over the end of a homosexual affair with a fellow crewmember. As the investigations progress, Moosally comes to defend his men, and both he and Meyer must struggle with the question of truth vs. career. **85m/C; VHS, DVD.** Robert Sean Leonard; James Caan; Daniel Roebuck; Jamie Harrold; Cherie Devanney; Dashiell Eaves; *D:* Mikael Salomon; *W:* Charles C. Thompson, II; David Freed. **TV**

Glitch! 1/2 **1988 (R)** A throng of beautiful Hollywood hopefuls draw two youngsters unconnected with the film into posing as the film's director and producer in the hopes of conducting personal interviews on the casting couch. **88m/C; VHS, DVD.** Julia Nickson-Soul; Will Egan; Steve Donmyer; Dan Speaker; Dallas Cole; Ji-Tu Cumbuka; Dick Gautier; Ted Lange; Teri Weigel; Fernando Carzon; John Kreng; Lindsay Carr; *D:* Nico Mastorakis; *W:* Nico Mastorakis; *C:* Peter C. Jensen; *M:* Tom Marolda. **VIDEO**

Glitter WOOF! **2001 (PG-13)** Following in the footsteps of "Cool as Ice" and "Spice World," this may be the third in the pop star "why was this allowed to happen?" trilogy. Mariah Carey, showing her acting range of two emotions ("Yay!" and "Huh?"), stars as Billie Frank, a backup singer who climbs to stardom with the help from her svengali boyfriend Dice (Beesley). Together they struggle through the hard times and the wooden dialogue. Will success and the crappy plot stolen from "A Star is Born" tear them apart? You'll be wishing that wild dogs will tear them apart before the end of this mess. So bad it's nearly unintentionally funny. The key word is nearly. **104m/C; VHS, DVD, Blu-Ray.** Mariah Carey; Max Beesley; Tia Texada; Da Brat; Valarie Pettiford; Ann Magnuson; Terrence Howard; Dorian Harewood; Grant Nickalls; Eric Benet; Padma Lakshmi; Isabel Gomes; *D:* Vondie Curtis-Hall; *W:* Kate Lanier; *C:* Geoffrey Simpson; *M:* Terence Blanchard. Golden Raspberries '01: Worst Actress (Carey).

Gloomy Sunday *Ein Lied von Liebe und Tod* **2002** Story of a complex love triangle and Nazi oppression in 1930's Budapest, told in extended flashback. Jewish restaurant owner Laszlo (Krol), his waitress/lover Ilona (Marozsan) and pianist Andras (Dionisi) are all involved with one another when German salesman Hans (Ben Becker) falls for Ilona and eventually befriends the trio. Inspired by Ilona, Andras composes a hit song (the titular "Gloomy Sunday") that causes a rash of suicides. Three years later, Hans returns to Budapest as an SS colonel and is immediately torn between his dedication to the ideals of the Third Reich and his three friends. The characters are complex and well-written, and the tension is thick as they all struggle with the ethical implications of their actions as war encroaches on Budapest. Somewhat marred by stilted, melodramatic moments, but the excellent story and fine acting more than makes up for it. **114m/C; DVD.** *GE HU* Joachim Krol; Stefano Dionisi; Ben Becker; Erika Marozsan; Sebastian Koch; Laszlo I. Kish; Rolf Becker; *D:* Rolf Schuebel; *W:* Rolf Schuebel; Ruth Thoma; *C:* Edward Klosinski; *M:* Detlef Petersen; Rezso Seress.

Gloria 1/2 **1980 (PG)** She used to be a Mafia moll, now she's outrunning the Mob after taking in the son of a slain neighbor. He's got a book that they want, and they're willing to kill to get it. Trademark Cassavetes effort in which he has actors plumb their souls to discomfiting levels. **123m/C; VHS, DVD, Blu-Ray.** Gena Rowlands; John Adams; Buck Henry; Julie Carmen; *D:* John Cassavetes; *M:* Bill Conti. Venice Film Fest. '80: Film; Golden Raspberries '80: Worst Support. Actor (Adams).

Gloria **1998 (R)** Remake of the 1980 Cassavetes film, with Stone as title character, a gang moll who reluctantly becomes the guardian of a boy whose parents were killed by her low-life boyfriend Kevin (Northam). Entertainment value is derived from listening to Stone mangle her Noo Yawk accent. Stick with the original. **108m/C; VHS, DVD.** Sharon Stone; Jeremy Northam; Cathy Moriarty; George C. Scott; Mike Starr; Don Billett; Tony DiBenedetto; Bonnie Bedelia; Jean-Luke Figueroa; Barry McEvoy; Jerry Dean; Teddy Atlas; *D:* Sidney Lumet; *W:* Steve Antin; *C:* David Watkin; *M:* Howard Shore.

Gloria **2013 (R)** Engaging romantic comedy/drama with a vibrant performance by Garcia in the title role. Gloria is an outspoken, 58-year-old divorcee with a job, two adult children with lives of their own, and a desire for sexual companionship if not love. At a Santiago nightclub, she meets Rodolfo, who's getting back into dating after a recent divorce, and they quickly become lovers. Their romance is marred by Rodolfo's being at the beck-and-call of his ex-wife and daughters. Exasperated, Gloria cuts her losses, but reconsiders when Rodolfo begs for a second chance. English and Spanish with subtitles. **110m/C; DVD.** *CL* Paulina Garcia; Sergio Hernandez; Diego Fontecilla; Fabiola Zamora; Alejandro Goic; *D:* Sebastián Lelio; *W:* Sebastián Lelio; Gonzalo Maza; *C:* Benjamin Echazarreta; *M:* Lorne Balfe.

Gloria Bell 1/2 **2018 (R)** The optimistic Gloria (Moore) is a fiftysomething long-divorced woman living in L.A. and working at an insurance agency. At night, she goes to a nightclub to dance and, perhaps, meet a man. One night, she meets Arnold (Turturro), who is about the same age but newly divorced. As they spend time getting to know each other, Gloria continues to live her life, helping her friends and having regular lunches with her mother (Taylor) but cannot hide her loneliness. Both Moore and Turturro give deep, complex performances, skillfully guided by writer/director Lelio. **102m/C; DVD, Blu-Ray.** *CL US* Julianne Moore; Sean Astin; John Turturro; Alanna Ubach; Rita Wilson; *D:* Sebastián Lelio; *W:* Sebastián Lelio; *C:* Natasha Braier; *M:* Matthew Herbert.

Glorifying the American Girl **1930** Eaton's a chorus girl performing in the Ziegfeld Follies, which lends itself to numerous production numbers. The only film Ziegfeld ever produced. **96m/B; VHS, DVD, Blu-Ray.** Mary Eaton; Dan Healey; Eddie Cantor; Rudy Vallee; *D:* Millard Webb.

Glorious 39 1/2 **2009** In the summer of 1939, Anne, the adopted daughter of the traditional, political Keyes family, stumbles across some secret audio recordings. They implicate the family, headed by Sir Alexander Keyes, in the pro-appeasement movement towards Nazi Germany. Anne goes to London to confirm her suspicions and winds up betrayed and in danger. **129m/C; DVD.** *GB* Romola Garai; Bill Nighy; David Tennant; Jeremy Northam; Julie Christie; Juno Temple; Eddie Redmayne; Christopher Lee; Hugh Bonneville; Jenny Agutter; Charlie Cox; *D:* Stephen Poliakoff; *W:* Stephen Poliakoff; *C:* Danny Cohen; *M:* Adrian Johnston.

Glory 1/2 **1989 (R)** A rich, historical spectacle chronicling the 54th Massachusetts, the first black volunteer infantry unit in the Civil War. The film manages to artfully focus on both the 54th and their white commander, Robert Gould Shaw. Based on Shaw's letters, the film uses thousands of accurately costumed "living historians" (reenactors) as extras in this panoramic production. A haunting, bittersweet musical score pervades what finally becomes an anti-war statement. Stunning performances throughout, with exceptional work from Freeman and Washington. **122m/C; VHS, DVD, Blu-Ray.** Matthew Broderick; Morgan Freeman; Denzel Washington; Cary Elwes; Jihmi Kennedy; Andre Braugher; John Finn; Donovan Leitch; John David (J.D.) Cullum; Bob Gunton; Jane Alexander; Raymond St. Jacques; Cliff DeYoung; Alan North; Jay O. Sanders; Richard Riehle; Ethan Phillips; RonReaco Lee; Peter Michael Goetz; *D:* Edward Zwick; *W:* Kevin Jarre; Marshall Herskovitz; *C:* Freddie Francis; *M:* James Horner. Oscars '89: Cinematog., Sound, Support. Actor (Washington); Golden Globes '90: Support. Actor (Washington).

The Glory Boys 1/2 **1984** A secret agent is hired to protect an Israeli scientist who is marked for assassination by the PLO and IRA. **78m/C; VHS, DVD.** Rod Steiger; Anthony Perkins; Gary Brown; Aaron Harris; *D:* Michael Ferguson.

The Glory Brigade **1953** Greek-American Army Lt. Sam Prior (Mature) is chosen to lead a platoon of Greek and American troops on a combined mission during the Korean War. The Greeks are accused of cowardice during a battle, but it turns out to be cultural differences and Prior and his men learn to respect their allies in this fast-paced war drama. **81m/B; DVD.** Victor Mature; Alexander Scourby; Lee Marvin; Richard Egan; Nick Dennis; *D:* Robert D. Webb; *W:* Franklin Coen; *C:* Lucien Ballard.

Glory Daze **1996 (R)** Gen-X comedy about graduation week for five Santa Cruz college friends/housemates. There's Jack (Affleck), Mickey (DeRamus), Rob (Rockwell), Josh (Hong), and Dennis (Stewart) who basically party and kvetch about their uncertain futures, with various girlfriends, professors, and parents around to nag the boys. Not much you haven't seen before, although a number of the cast have gone on to bigger and better things. **100m/C; VHS, DVD.** Ben Affleck; Sam Rockwell; French Stewart; Vinnie DeRamus; Vien Hong; Alyssa Milano; Megan Ward; John Rhys-Davies; Elizabeth Ruscio; Spalding Gray; Mary Woronov; ***Cameo(s):*** Matthew McConaughey; Brendan Fraser; Matt Damon; Meredith Salenger; *D:* Rich Wilkes; *W:* Rich Wilkes; *C:* Christopher Taylor.

Glory Road 1/2 **2006 (PG)** Yet another inspirational, fact-based sports drama. In 1966, the Miners, an under-funded basketball team at small Texas Western, became legends by defeating the sport's Goliaths—the all-white University of Kentucky Wildcats—in the NCAA championship. Their coach, Don Haskins (Lucas), made history when he recruited seven black players and had five of them in his starting lineup. Naturally, there are problems leading up to their triumph, which are dealt with efficiently by first-time director Gartner. End credits showcase Haskins and several of the actual players reflecting on the game. **106m/C; DVD, Blu-Ray.** Josh(ua) Lucas; Derek Luke; Austin Nichols; Jon Voight; Evan Jones; Alphonso McAuley; Sam Jones, III; Emily Deschanel; Al Shearer; Schin A.S. Kerr; Mehcad Brooks; Damaine Radcliff; *D:* James Gartner; *W:* Chris Cleveland; Bettina Gilois; *C:* John Toon; Jeffrey L. Kimball; *M:* Trevor Rabin.

The Glory Stompers WOOF! **1967** Hopper prepares for his Easy Rider role as the leader of a motorcycle gang who battles with a rival leader over a woman. Very bad, atrocious dialogue, and a "love-in" scene that will be best appreciated by insomniacs. **85m/C; VHS, DVD, Streaming.** Dennis Hopper; Jody McCrea; Chris Noel; Jock Mahoney; Lindsay Crosby; Robert Tessier; Casey Kasem; *D:* Anthony M. Lanza.

Glory Years **1987** Three old friends find themselves in charge of the scholarship fund at their 20th high school reunion. Unfortunately, they decide to increase the fund by gambling in Las Vegas and lose it all on a fixed fight! **150m/C; VHS, DVD.** George Dzundza; Archie Hahn; Tim Thomerson; Tawny Kitaen; Donna Pescow; Donna Denton; *D:* Arthur Allan Seidelman.

The Glove 1/2 *The Glove: Lethal Terminator; Blood Mad* **1978 (R)** Ex-cop turned bounty hunter has his toughest assignment ever. It's his job to bring in a six-and-a-half foot, 250-pound ex-con who's been wreaking havoc with an unusual glove—it's made of leather and steel. **93m/C; VHS, DVD.** John Saxon; Roosevelt "Rosie" Grier; Joanna Cassidy; Joan Blondell; Jack Carter; Aldo Ray; *D:* Ross Hagen.

The Gnome-Mobile **1967** A lumber baron and his two grandchildren attempt to reunite a pair of forest gnomes with a lost gnome colony. Brennan has a dual role as both a human and a gnome grandfather. Wynn's last film. Based on a children's novel by Upton Sinclair. **84m/C; VHS, DVD.** Walter Brennan; Richard Deacon; Ed Wynn; Karen Dotrice; Matthew Garber; *D:* Robert Stevenson; *C:* Edward Colman; *M:* Buddy (Norman Dale) Baker.

Gnomeo & Juliet 1/2 **2011 (G)** It's Shakespeare with garden gnomes in this animated Disney take on "Romeo & Juliet" (with a happier ending we hope). Romance blooms between gnomes Gnomeo and Juliet but they are soon caught up in a feud between neighbors. Popular young British actors McAvoy and Blunt voice the two lead characters, but that doesn't stop the movie from being a one-note, predictable concept despite the nine credited writers and fine supporting cast (including Stewart as the Bard himself). Still, the animation is decent, and the story may charm younger viewers, while the adults will find the 84-minute run time excessive. Classic and original songs by Elton John, who also served as executive producer. **84m/C; Blu-Ray, On Demand.** *V:* James McAvoy; Emily Blunt; Michael Caine; Jason Statham; Maggie Smith; Patrick Stewart; Julie Walters; Ashley Jensen; Matt Lucas; Jim (Jonah) Cummings; Ozzy Osbourne; Stephen Merchant; Hulk Hogan; Dolly Parton; *D:* Kelly Asbury; *W:* Kelly Asbury; Rob Sprackling; John R. Smith; Mark Burton; Kevin Cecil; Emily Cook; Kathy Greenberg; Andy Riley; Steve Hamilton Shaw; *M:* James Newton Howard; Chris P. Bacon; Sir Elton John.

Go **1999 (R)** Episodic tale of Christmas Eve in L.A. and Vegas follows grocery clerk Ronna (Polley) as she takes over a shift for Vegas-bound co-worker Simon (Askew) and also agrees to sub as a go-between for a drug deal between two actors (Mohr and Wolf) and Simon's dealer Todd (Olyphant). Three-part narrative also shows Simon's wild ride in Vegas with his buddies and the actors' involvement with a weird cop (Fichtner). Everybody seems to be doing everything at a break-neck pace, and the fact that all the activity is dangerous or illegal makes it that much more fun. Liman does a fine job of sorting out characters and plotlines, and the performances tag this as a star maker for a few of the cast members, most notably Polley and Diggs. **103m/C; VHS, DVD.** Sarah Polley; Katie Holmes; Scott Wolf; Jay Mohr; Desmond Askew; Taye Diggs; William Fichtner; Breckin Meyer; Jane Krakowski; Timothy Olyphant; J.E. Freeman; James Duval; Nathan Bexton; Jay Paulson; Jimmy Shubert; ***D:*** Doug Liman; ***W:*** John August; ***C:*** Doug Liman.

The Go-Between ♪♪♪ 1/2 **1971 (PG)** Wonderful tale of hidden love. Young boy Guard acts as a messenger between the aristocratic Christie and her former lover Bates. But tragedy befalls them all when the lovers are discovered. The story is told as the elderly messenger (now played by Redgrave) recalls his younger days as the go-between and builds to a climax when he is once again asked to be a messenger for the lady he loved long ago. Based on a story by L.P. Hartley. **116m/C; VHS, Streaming.** *GB* Julie Christie; Alan Bates; Dominic Guard; Margaret Leighton; Michael Redgrave; Michael Gough; Edward Fox; ***D:*** Joseph Losey; ***W:*** Harold Pinter; ***C:*** Gerry Fisher; ***M:*** Michel Legrand. British Acad. '71: Screenplay, Support. Actor (Fox), Support. Actress (Leighton); Cannes '71: Film.

Go Fish ♪♪♪ **1994 (R)** Low-budget girl-meets-girl romantic comedy finds Kia (McMillan) playing matchmaker for her roommate, energetic Max (Turner), by setting her up with shy Ely (Brodie). The opposites do, eventually, attract, with their friends eager for every detail. Good-natured and candid, with a welcome lack of melodrama. **87m/B; VHS, DVD.** Guinevere Turner; V.S. Brodie; T. Wendy McMillan; Anastasia Sharp; Migdalia Melendez; ***D:*** Rose Troche; ***W:*** Guinevere Turner; Rose Troche; ***C:*** Ann T. Rossetti; ***M:*** Brendan Dolan; Jennifer Sharpe.

Go for Broke! ♪♪ 1/2 **1951** Inexperienced officer Johnson heads a special WWII attack force which is made up of Japanese Americans. Sent to fight in Europe, they prove their bravery and loyalty to all. Good, offbeat story. **92m/B; VHS, DVD.** Van Johnson; Gianna Maria Canale; Warner Anderson; Lane Nakano; George Miki; ***D:*** Robert Pirosh; ***W:*** Robert Pirosh; ***C:*** Paul Vogel; ***M:*** Alberto Colombo.

Go For It! ♪♪ **2010 (PG-13)** Unpretentious dance drama that's meant to be inspirational. Troubled Latina Carmen (Garcia) loves hip-hop dancing in Chicago's underground clubs but, to please her Mexican immigrant parents, she also works and goes to junior college. Her rich, white boyfriend Jared (Denicola) wants a commitment but Carmen's teacher Frank Martin (Bandiero) encourages her to audition for a California dance school. Carmen needs to decide if she can overcome her self-doubts and go through with following her dream. **105m/C; DVD, Blu-Ray.** Aimee Garcia; Derrick Denicola; Al Bandiero; Jossara Jinaro; Louie Alegria; Gina Rodgriguez; Andres Perez-Molina; Gustavo Mellado; Liliana Montenegro; ***D:*** Carmen Marron; ***W:*** Carmen Marron; ***C:*** Christian Sprenger; ***M:*** Ken Wood.

Go for Sisters ♪♪ **2013** Sayles does a cross-border crime drama that focuses on former best friends Fontayne (Ross) and Bernice (Hamilton). After her release from jail, Fontayne becomes part of parole officer Bernice's case load. When her estranged son, Rodney (Belcher III), goes missing, Bernice hopes that some of Fontayne's criminal contacts can be of help, but they're lead to a nearly blind, ex-detective, Freddy Suarez (Olmos), who takes them into Tijuana. There, they discover Rodney's been smuggling illegal immigrants and he's now in serious trouble. English and Spanish with subtitles. **123m/C; DVD.** Lisa Gay Hamilton; Yolonda Ross; Edward James Olmos; Harold Perrineau, Jr.; Mckinley Belcher, III; ***D:*** John Sayles; ***W:*** John Sayles; ***C:*** Kathryn Westergaard; ***M:*** Mason Daring.

Go for Zucker ♪♪ *Alles Auf Zucker!* **2005** Two estranged Jewish brothers, one living in eastern Germany, the other in the west, must clean up their act in order to receive the inheritance their recently-deceased mother left behind. As stated in the will, they must reconcile their differences and, more importantly, adhere to strict Jewish Orthodox conventions. Contrived storyline and loads of Jewish stereotypes drag this one into sitcom territory. A hit in Germany, but something is lost in translation for sure. **90m/C; DVD.** Henry Hubchen; Hannelore Elsner; Udo Samel; Sebastian Blomberg; Rolf Hoppe; Golda Tencer; Steffen Groth; Anja Franke; Elena Uhlig; ***D:*** Dani Levy; ***W:*** Dani Levy; Holgar Franke; ***C:*** Carl F. Koschnick; ***M:*** Niki Reiser.

Go Further ♪ 1/2 **2003** Documentary follows Woody Harrelson and his "Merry Hempsters" as they travel up and down the Pacific coast by bike, preaching the virtues of a Green lifestyle. Pushing its message to the converted, film is cloying and about as subtle as a jackhammer. Harrelson does, however, come across as surprisingly intelligent and well-informed. Who could have guessed? **80m/C; DVD.** *CA* Woody Harrelson; ***D:*** Ron Mann; ***C:*** Robert Fresco; ***M:*** Guido Luciani.

The Go-Getter ♪♪ **2007 (R)** Quirky indie with a certain charm. Aimless 19-year-old Mercer White (Pucci) needs to inform his long-gone half-brother Arlen (Garcia) that their mother has died. So he steals a station wagon and heads off on a road adventure. A cell phone left behind rings and it's car owner Kate (Deschanel), who for some reason that will eventually be revealed, allows Mercer to continue his journey as long as he fills her in on his progress. Which is problematic since Arlen's a louse who has left trouble wherever he's been. Eventually, Mercer hooks up with Kate in the flesh and there's a confrontation with Arlen down Mexico way. **93m/C; DVD.** Lou Taylor Pucci; Zooey Deschanel; Jena Malone; Jsu Garcia; William Lee Scott; Julio Oscar Mechoso; Nick Offerman; ***Cameo(s):*** Bill Duke; ***D:*** Martin Hynes; ***W:*** Martin Hynes; ***C:*** Byron Shah; ***M:*** M. Ward.

Go Into Your Dance ♪♪ **1935** Irresponsible Broadway star Al Howard (Jolson) is blackballed by producers so his agent sister Molly (Farrell) teams him with her dancer friend Dorothy (Keller) for a Chicago nightclub gig. When they're a success, Al wants to open his own club in New York and borrows money from gangster Duke (Maclane). Then he ignores sweet Dorothy for sultry chanteuse Luana (Morgan), who's already involved with Duke. Jolson and Keeler were married at the time they filmed this. **89m/B; DVD.** Al Jolson; Ruby Keeler; Barton MacLane; Glenda Farrell; Helen Morgan; Patsy Kelly; ***D:*** Archie Mayo; ***W:*** Earl Baldwin; ***C:*** Gaetano Antonio "Tony" Gaudio.

Go, Johnny Go! ♪♪ **1959** Rock promoter Alan Freed molds a young orphan into rock sensation "Johnny Melody." Musical performances include Ritchie Valens (his only film appearance), Eddie Cochran, Jackie Wilson. **75m/B; VHS, DVD, Streaming.** Alan Freed; Sandy Stewart; Chuck Berry; Jimmy Clanton; Eddie Cochran; Jackie Wilson; Ritchie Valens; ***D:*** Paul Landres.

Go Kill and Come Back ♪ **1968 (PG)** A bounty hunter tracks down a notoriously dangerous train robber. **95m/C; VHS, DVD.** Gilbert Roland; George Helton; Edd Byrnes; ***D:*** Enzo G. Castellari.

Go Tell It on the Mountain ♪♪ 1/2 **1984** Young black boy tries to gain the approval of his stern stepfather in this fine adaptation of James Baldwin's semiautobiographical novel. Set in the 1930s; originally a PBS "American Playhouse" presentation. **100m/C; VHS, DVD.** Paul Winfield; Olivia Cole; Ruby Dee; Alfre Woodard; James Bond, III; Rosalind Cash; Linda Hopkins; ***D:*** Stan Lathan.

Go Tell the Spartans ♪♪♪ **1978 (R)** In Vietnam, 1964, a hard-boiled major is ordered to establish a garrison at Muc Wa with a platoon of burned out Americans and Vietnamese mercenaries. Blundering but politically interesting war epic pre-dating the flood of 1980s American-Vietnam apologetics. Based on Daniel Ford's novel. **114m/C; VHS, DVD, Blu-Ray.** Burt Lancaster; Craig Wasson; David Clennon; Marc Singer; Jonathan Goldsmith; Joe Unger; Dennis Howard; Evan C. Kim; John Megna; Hilly Hicks; Dolph Sweet; Clyde Kusatsu; James Hong; ***D:*** Ted Post; ***W:*** Wendell Mayes; ***C:*** Harry Stradling, Jr.; ***M:*** Dick Halligan.

Go West ♪♪♪ **1925** After failing to find work in his home town and the bustle of New York City, a young man tries for a life as a cowboy after falling off a train near a ranch. While it seems like luck at first, he soon finds himself in shootouts and taking a thousand cattle by train to L.A. **68m/B; Silent; DVD, Blu-Ray.** Howard Truesdale; Kathleen Myers; Ray Thompson; Buster Keaton; ***D:*** Buster Keaton; ***W:*** Buster Keaton; Lex Neal; Raymond Cannon; Konrad Elfers; ***C:*** Bert Haines; Elgin Lessley. **VIDEO**

Go West ♪♪ 1/2 *Marx Brothers Go West* **1940** The brothers Marx help in the making and un-making of the Old West. Weak, late Marx Bros., but always good for a few yucks. **80m/B; VHS, DVD.** Groucho Marx; Chico Marx; Harpo Marx; John Carroll; Diana Lewis; Walter Woolf King; George Lessey; Robert Barrat; June MacCloy; ***D:*** Edward Buzzell; ***W:*** Irving Brecher; ***C:*** Leonard Smith; ***M:*** George Bassman; Roger Edens.

Go West ♪♪ **2005** Ambitious but not always successful stew of ethnic hatred, war, romance, and identity. Kenan (Drmac) is Muslim; his lover Milan (Filpovic) is a Bosnian Serb and when the ethnic conflicts break out in Sarajevo in 1992, the two decide to flee to the Netherlands. Only their train is stopped by Bosnian soldiers, so Milan disguises Kenan as a woman and says she's his wife. Forced to find refuge with Milan's father Ljubo (Serbedzija) in his Bosnian hometown, the two attempt to continue their deception. Then Milan gets drafted and barkeep Ranka (Burina) discovers Kenan's secret. Bosnian with subtitles. **97m/C; DVD.** *BS* Rade Serbedzija; Mirjana Karanovic; Tarik Filpovic; Mavio Drmac; Haris Burina; ***Cameo(s):*** Jeanne Moreau; ***D:*** Ahmed Imamovic; ***W:*** Ahmed Imamovic; Enver Puska; ***C:*** Mustafa Mustafic; ***M:*** Enes Zlatar.

Go West, Young Man ♪♪ 1/2 **1936** West is a movie star whose latest film is premiering in a small town, where she's naturally a sensation. Scott is the muscular farm boy who catches her eye and she decides to hang around in order to catch the rest of him as well. The censors again cut West's most overt sexual and satiric barbs. **80m/B; VHS, DVD.** Mae West; Randolph Scott; Warren William; Alice Brady; Elizabeth Patterson; Lyle Talbot; Isabel Jewell; ***D:*** Henry Hathaway; ***W:*** Mae West; ***C:*** Karl Struss.

Go With God Gringo ♪♪ 1/2 *Vaya con dios gringo; Good Luck Gringo* **1966** After being framed for the death of his brother, Gringo (Glenn Saxson) stages a jailbreak with the help of the other inmates before going on a series of outlaw shenanigans leading up to a confrontation with his brother's murderer. Currently only available as part of the 'Unchained Westerns' collection. **79m/C; Blu-Ray.** *IT SP* Glenn Saxson; Lucretia Love; Pedro Sanchez; Aldo Berti; Livio Lorenzon; ***D:*** Edoardo Mulargia; ***W:*** Edoardo Mulargia; Vincenzo Musolino; ***C:*** Ugo Brunelli; ***M:*** Felice Di Stefano. **VIDEO**

Goal 2: Living the Dream ♪♪ **2007 (PG-13)** Now that Santiago (Becker) has gained experience with the Newcastle United football (soccer) team, he gets transferred to superstar club Real Madrid. There he's reunited with his old friend Gavin (Nivola), who's thinking about retirement (and some guy named Beckham, who's got a cameo). But with success comes the expansion of Santiago's ego, which alienates fiancee Roz (Friel), among others. **115m/C; DVD.** *GB* Kuno Becker; Alessandro Nivola; Anna Friel; Rutger Hauer; Leonor Varela; Stephen (Dillon) Dillane; Elizabeth Pena; Miriam Colon; Sean Pertwee; Frances Barber; ***Cameo(s):*** David Beckham; ***D:*** Jaume Collet-Serra; ***W:*** Mike Jefferies; ***C:*** Flavio Martinez Labiano; ***M:*** Stephen Warbeck.

Goal! The Dream Begins ♪♪ 1/2 **2006 (PG)** Illegal Mexican immigrant Santiago Munez (Becker) dreams of making it big playing soccer. L.A. talent scout Foy (Dillane), who's got U.K. contacts, offers a tryout with Newcastle United. First, the poor Santiago has to get across the pond (grandma helps) but his adjustment is difficult until his partying superstar teammate Gavin (Nivola) gives him a boost. Hits all the inspirational sports cliches (it's a Disney release) but it's good-hearted and good-looking (and that's not just the players). First of a planned trilogy. **118m/C; DVD.** Kuno Becker; Alessandro Nivola; Marcel Iures; Stephen (Dillon) Dillane; Anna Friel; Kieran O'Brien; Sean Pertwee; Gary Lewis; Cassandra Bell; Tony Plana; Miriam Colon; Jorge Cervera; Lee Ross; Ashley Walters; Frances Barber; Kevin Knapman; ***Cameo(s):*** Kieron Dyer; David Beckham; ***D:*** Danny Cannon; ***W:*** Dick Clement; Ian La Frenais; Adrian Butchart; ***C:*** Michael Barrett; ***M:*** Graeme Revell.

Goat ♪♪ 1/2 **2016 (R)** Brad (Schnetzer) has his safety and self-image shattered when he's beaten up one night after a party. Perhaps to assuage a sense of lost masculinity, he pledges the fraternity at which his brother Brett (Jonas) is one of the power players. From here, Brad's story becomes a cautionary, nightmarish vision of the pledge process at many fraternities around the country. Brad is beaten, ridiculed, abused, and nearly killed in a series of rituals designed to instill brotherhood, but that only ends in tragedy. A dark look into a terrifying world of misplaced aggression and false ideas of masculinity. **96m/C; DVD.** Ben Schnetzer; Nick Jonas; Danny Flaherty; Virginia Gardner; ***D:*** Andrew Neel; ***W:*** Andrew Neel; David Gordon Green; Mike Roberts; ***C:*** Ethan Palmer; ***M:*** Arjan Miranda.

Goats ♪ 1/2 **2012 (R)** Minor dysfunctional family/coming of age dramedy. Fifteen-year-old Ellis lives with his narcissistic, bitter mom Wendy and her boyfriend Bennet in Arizona along with caretaker Javier who's better known as Goat Man for his pets. He offers Ellis fatherly advice and lots of pot while Ellis' own dad, Frank, lives in DC with his wife Judy. There's a shift when Ellis attends an East Coast prep school but the flick never adds up to much. Adapted by Poirier from his 2001 novel. **94m/C; DVD, Blu-Ray.** Graham Phillips; David Duchovny; Vera Farmiga; Justin Kirk; Ty Burrell; Keri Russell; Dakota Johnson; ***D:*** Christopher Neil; ***W:*** Mark Jude Poirier; ***C:*** Wyatt Troll; ***M:*** Jason Schwartzman; Woody Jackson.

Goblin WOOF! **1993** Newlywed couple regret the purchase of their new home when the devilish creature once brought to life by the previous homeowner, a witchcraft performing farmer, is raised from the depths of hell to rip to pieces anyone in its view. Any movie whose promo says "You won't believe your eyes...until he rips them from their sockets" is sure to be a crowd pleaser. Enjoy. **75m/C; VHS, DVD.** Bobby Westrick; Jenny Admire; ***D:*** Todd Sheets.

Goblin ♪ **2010** Typically terrible Syfy original movie, although the 7-foot tall goblin is at least different. In 1831, the villagers of Hollow Glen celebrate Halloween by burning their diseased crops in hopes of a good harvest the next year. That year they also decide to burn the deformed infant of the local alleged witch and the town is promptly cursed. Each year since that night, a goblin comes and seeks revenge by killing the town's newborns. And this Halloween the Perkins family has an infant son. **92m/C; DVD.** Gil Bellows; Tracy Spiridakos; Camille Sullivan; Donnelly Rhodes; Colin Cunningham; Reilly Dolman; Andrew Wheeler; ***D:*** Jeffrey Scott Lando; ***W:*** Raul Inglis; ***C:*** Thomas M. (Tom) Harting; ***M:*** Chris Nickel. **CABLE**

God Bless America ♪♪ 1/2 **2011 (R)** Frank (Murray) has had enough of America's obsession with instant fame and goes on a killing spree, starting with the spoiled brat who complains about the model of her new SUV and climbing the ladder to an American Idol-esqe grotesquerie. Murray gives a stellar performance but the role of the Bonnie to his Clyde, a girl who rides along with him and encourages his crimes, is deeply flawed and horrendous. Still, he finds some clever jokes. Writer/director Goldthwait's latest social satire starts off strong but becomes too frustrating to forgive by the final reel. **105m/C; DVD, Blu-Ray.** Joel Murray; Tara Lynne Barr; Melinda Page Hamilton; Mackenzie Brooke Smith; Maddie Hasson; ***D:*** Bobcat Goldthwait; ***W:*** Bobcat Goldthwait; ***C:*** Bradley Stonesifer; ***M:*** Matt Kollar.

God Bless the Broken Road ½ **2018 (PG)** After her husband is killed in military action in Afghanistan, Amber (Pulsipher) loses her faith. Two years later, the grieving widow is working as a waitress in a local diner, on the verge of losing her home to foreclosure, and struggling to make ends meet as she raises her young daughter Bree (Moss). While working one day, handsome bad boy NASCAR driver Cody (Walker) enters the diner and her life as he comes to town to complete required community service. Loosely based on a Rascal Flatts song, the film strains credibility, especially in the development and treatment of its plot and characters. **111m/C; DVD, Blu-Ray.** Lindsay Pulsipher; Jordin Sparks; LaDainian Tomlinson; Andrew W. Walker; Robin Givens; ***D:*** Harold Cronk; ***W:*** Harold Cronk; Jennifer Dornbush; ***C:*** Philip Roy; ***M:*** Will Musser.

God Bless the Child **1988** A young single mother loses her home and she and her seven-year-old daughter are forced to live on the streets. Harrowing TV drama providing no easy answers to the plight of the homeless. **93m/C; VHS, DVD.** Mare Winningham; Dorian Harewood; Grace Johnston; Charlaine Woodard; Obba Babatunde; L. Scott Caldwell; ***D:*** Larry Elikann; ***W:*** Dennis Nemec; ***M:*** David Shire. **TV**

God Grew Tired of Us **2006 (PG)** Continuation of 2003's "The Lost Boys of Sudan," which revisits three young Sudanese men—John Bul Dau, Panther Bior, and Daniel Abul Pach—and their adjusting to life in the U.S. as refugees. **89m/C; DVD.** John Bul Dau; Panther Bior; Daniel Abul Pach; ***D:*** Christopher Quinn; ***C:*** Paul Daley; ***M:*** Mark Nelson; Mark McAdam; Jamie Staff.

God Help the Girl **2014** Murdoch, of Belle & Sebastian fame, writes and directs this indie musical that should appeal to his target demographic but doesn't quite work outside of that twee/indie/hipster/pixie group. Eve (Browning) is in a hospital managing an emotional breakdown. She writes songs to deal with her issues, and she meets two fellow travelers on the sonic highway, James (Alexander) and Cassie (Murray). Three people heal over a summer through music. It's perfectly delightful at times but also remarkably self-conscious of that fact. **111m/C; Streaming.** *UK* Emily Browning; Olly Alexander; Hannah Murray; Pierre Boulanger; ***D:*** Stuart Murdoch; ***W:*** Stuart Murdoch; ***C:*** Giles Nuttgens.

God is My Co-Pilot **1945** Based on the book by Col. Robert Lee Scott (played by Morgan), an ace fighter pilot with Maj. Gen. Chennault's (Massey) famed Fighting Tigers squadron. After multiple engagements against the Japanese in the air over China, Scott is battling illness and nerves in 1942 when he's grounded just before a major air assault. Fairly standard hero story, told in flashbacks, although there's an emphasis on Scott's faith sustaining him, as you might guess from the title. **88m/B; VHS, DVD.** Dennis Morgan; Raymond Massey; Dane Clark; Alan Hale; Andrea King; John Ridgely; Stanley Ridges; Craig Stevens; Richard Loo; Warren Douglas; ***D:*** Robert Florey; ***W:*** Abem Finkel; Peter Milne; ***C:*** Sidney Hickox; ***M:*** Franz Waxman.

God on Trial **2008** Grim but thoughtful argument about religion (supposedly based on a true incident). Several Jewish prisoners at Auschwitz decide to hold a tribunal to prove that God broke his covenant with Israel by allowing the Holocaust to happen. A trio of judges presides over the trial but the real intent is the discussion about survival and maintaining sanity. **86m/C; DVD.** *GB* Anthony Sher; Rupert Graves; Dominic Cooper; Stellan Skarsgard; Stephen (Dillon) Dillane; Jack Shepherd; Blake Ritson; Eddie Marsan; ***D:*** Andy de Emmony; ***W:*** Frank Cottrell Boyce; ***C:*** Wojciech Szepel. **TV**

God Said "Ha!" **1999 (PG-13)** Julia Sweeney recounts a very trying year in her life in this adaptation of her one-woman Broadway show. She tells of her brother's fight with lymphoma, which caused him (as well as her parents) to move in with her, as well as her own battle with cervical cancer. Sweeney's wry observations and loving rememberances prevent melodrama from seeping in. As with most monologues-turned-movies, this one works much better in the small-screen setting. **87m/C; VHS, DVD.** Julia Sweeney; ***D:*** Julia Sweeney; ***W:*** Julia Sweeney; ***C:*** John Hora; ***M:*** Anthony Marinelli.

God Told Me To ½ *Demon* **1976 (R)** A religious New York cop is embroiled in occult mysteries while investigating a series of grisly murders. He investigates a religious cult that turns out to be composed of half-human, half-alien beings. A cult-fave Larry Cohen epic. **89m/C; VHS, DVD, Blu-Ray.** Tony LoBianco; Deborah Raffin; Sylvia Sidney; Sandy Dennis; Richard Lynch; Sam Levene; Andy Kaufman; Robert Drivas; Mike Kellin; ***D:*** Larry Cohen; ***W:*** Larry Cohen; ***C:*** Paul Glickman; ***M:*** Frank Cordell.

The Goddess **1958** Sordid story of a girl who rises to fame as a celluloid star by making her body available to anyone who can help her career. When the spotlight dims, she keeps going with drugs and alcohol to a bitter end. **105m/B; VHS, DVD, On Demand.** Kim Stanley; Lloyd Bridges; Patty Duke; Steven Hill; Joyce Van Patten; Joan Copeland; Gerald Hiken; Elizabeth Wilson; Bert Freed; Werner Klemperer; ***D:*** John Cromwell; ***W:*** Paddy Chayefsky.

The Goddess of 1967 **2000** A quest for a dream car turns into an unexpectedly strange roadtrip through the Australian desert in this film by experimental filmmaker Clara Law. A young, wealthy Japanese man (Kurokawa) desparately wants to own a Citroen DS, the type of car driven by Alain Delon in the film Le Samourai. Finding one for sale in Australia, he makes a deal with a man for it and travels from his Tokyo home to complete the sale. Arriving there, he finds the seller dead, but takes up the offer of a 17-year-old blind girl (Byrne) to go to the real owner. The pair drive through the desert for five days, through abandoned mining towns and desolate landscapes as he learns of her dark childhood and many family secrets. **118m/C; DVD.** Rikiya Kurokawa; Rose Byrne; Nicholas Hope; Elise McCredie; Tim Richards; ***D:*** Clara Law; ***W:*** Clara Law; Eddie Ling-Ching Fong; ***C:*** Dion Beebe; ***M:*** Jen Andersen. **VIDEO**

The Godfather **1972 (R)** Coppola's award-winning adaptation of Mario Puzo's novel about a fictional Mafia family in the late 1940s. Revenge, envy, and parent-child conflict mix with the rituals of Italian mob life in America. Minutely detailed, with excellent performances by Pacino, Brando, and Caan as the violence-prone Sonny. Film debut of Coppola's daughter Sofia, the infant in the baptism scene, who returns in "Godfather III." The horrific horse scene is an instant chiller. Indisputably an instant piece of American culture. Followed by two sequels. **171m/C; VHS, DVD, Blu-Ray.** Marlon Brando; Al Pacino; Robert Duvall; James Caan; Diane Keaton; John Cazale; Talia Shire; Richard Conte; Richard S. Castellano; Abe Vigoda; Alex Rocco; Sterling Hayden; John Marley; Al Lettieri; Sofia Coppola; Al Martino; Morgana King; Joe Spinell; Gianni Russo; Lenny Montana; Richard Bright; Tony Giorgio; Victor Rendina; Simonetta Stefanelli; Angelo Infanti; ***D:*** Francis Ford Coppola; ***W:*** Mario Puzo; Francis Ford Coppola; ***C:*** Gordon Willis; ***M:*** Nino Rota. Oscars '72: Actor (Brando), Adapt. Screenplay, Film; AFI '98: Top 100; Directors Guild '72: Director (Coppola); Golden Globes '73: Actor--Drama (Brando), Director (Coppola), Film--Drama, Score, Screenplay; Natl. Bd. of Review '72: Support. Actor (Pacino); Natl. Film Reg. '90; N.Y. Film Critics '72: Support. Actor (Duvall); Natl. Soc. Film Critics '72: Actor (Pacino); Writers Guild '72: Adapt. Screenplay.

The Godfather, Part 2 **1974 (R)** A continuation and retracing of the first film, interpolating the maintenance of the Corleone family by the aging Michael, and its founding by the young Vito (De Niro, in a terrific performance) 60 years before in NYC's Little Italy. Often considered the second half of one film, the two films stand as one of American film's greatest efforts, and as a 1970s high-water mark. Combined into one work for TV presentation. Followed by a sequel. **200m/C; VHS, DVD, Blu-Ray.** Al Pacino; Robert De Niro; Diane Keaton; Robert Duvall; James Caan; Danny Aiello; John Cazale; Lee Strasberg; Talia Shire; Michael V. Gazzo; Troy Donahue; Joe Spinell; Abe Vigoda; Marianna Hill; Fay Spain; G.D. Spradlin; Bruno Kirby; Harry Dean Stanton; Roger Corman; Kathleen Beller; John Aprea; Morgana King; Dominic Chianese; Frank Sivero; Gianni Russo; Peter Donat; ***D:*** Francis Ford Coppola; ***W:*** Francis Ford Coppola; Mario Puzo; ***C:*** Gordon Willis; ***M:*** Nino Rota; Carmine Coppola. Oscars '74: Adapt. Screenplay, Art Dir./Set Dec., Director (Coppola), Film, Orig. Dramatic Score, Support. Actor (De Niro); AFI '98: Top 100; Directors Guild '74: Director (Coppola); Natl. Film Reg. '93; Natl. Soc. Film Critics '74: Director (Coppola); Writers Guild '74: Adapt. Screenplay.

The Godfather, Part 3 **1990 (R)** Don Corleone (Pacino), now aging and guilt-ridden, determines to buy his salvation by investing in the Catholic Church, which he finds to be a more corrupt brotherhood than his own. Meanwhile, back on the homefront, his young daughter discovers her sexuality as she falls in love with her first cousin. Weakest entry of the trilogy is still a stunning and inevitable conclusion to the story; Pacino adds exquisite finishing touches to his time-worn character. Beautifully photographed in Italy by Gordon Willis. Video release contains the final director's cut featuring nine minutes of footage not included in the theatrical release. **170m/C; VHS, DVD, Blu-Ray.** Al Pacino; Diane Keaton; Andy Garcia; Joe Mantegna; George Hamilton; Talia Shire; Sofia Coppola; Eli Wallach; Don Novello; Bridget Fonda; John Savage; Al Martino; Raf Vallone; Franc D'Ambrosio; Donal Donnelly; Richard Bright; Helmut Berger; ***D:*** Francis Ford Coppola; ***W:*** Mario Puzo; Francis Ford Coppola; ***C:*** Gordon Willis; ***M:*** Carmine Coppola. Golden Raspberries '90: Worst New Star (Coppola), Worst Support. Actress (Coppola).

Godmoney ½ **1997 (R)** Nathan (Rodney) is a New York street kid who tries to clean up his life of drugs and crime by moving to the Los Angeles suburbs where he is recruited by Matthew (Field), a dealer who tries to get him back into his old ways. Director Doane's debut made an impression on the festival circuit, and it deserves its reputation. Despite a background in music videos, he is able to tell a coherent story about interesting characters without letting style overpower substance. **99m/C; VHS, DVD.** Rick Rodney; Bobby Field; Christi Allen; ***D:*** Darren Doane; ***W:*** Darren Doane; Sean Atkins; Sean Nelson; ***M:*** Nicholas Rivera.

Gods and Generals **2003 (PG-13)** Maxwell's ambitious second film in his "Civil War trilogy" is exquisite in its attention to period detail, and grand in its depiction of the battles it covers, but suffers when it gets to the stories of the men it portrays. A prequel to 1993's "Gettysburg," this one covers the years 1861-63, beginning with Gen. Lee (Duvall) declining command of the Union Army, through the battles of First Manassas, Fredericksburg, and Chancelorsville, and finishing with Stonewall Jackson's death and the events leading up to Gettysburg. The main problem is that the dialogue (housed in many self-important and overlong speeches) is stilted, lifeless, and humorless, which handcuffs a very talented cast. Historic personages are raised to icon status, showing none of the real-life flaws that would've made them interesting. Based on the novel by Jeffrey M. Shaara. **220m/C; VHS, DVD, Blu-Ray, HD-DVD.** Jeff Daniels; Stephen Lang; Robert Duvall; Kevin Conway; C. Thomas Howell; Patrick Gorman; Brian Mallon; Matt Letscher; William Sanderson; Mira Sorvino; Frankie Faison; Jeremy London; Kali Rocha; Bruce Boxleitner; Billy Campbell; Bo Brinkman; Mia Dillon; Stephen Spacek; Royce D. Applegate; William Morgan Sheppard; ***Cameo(s):*** Ted Turner; ***D:*** Ronald F. Maxwell; ***W:*** Ronald F. Maxwell; ***C:*** Kees Van Oostrum; ***M:*** John (Gianni) Frizzell; Randy Edelman.

Gods and Monsters ½ **1998** Although British director James Whale (McKellen) had a varied (if short) Hollywood career in the '30s and '40s, his name rested on his Universal horror films: "The Invisible Man," "Frankenstein," and "The Bride of Frankenstein." Now long-retired and suffering from ill-health, the openly gay Whale lives quietly in L.A. with his protective housekeeper, Hanna (Redgrave). Whale does enjoy the company of his new gardener—hunky, hetero ex-Marine Clayton Boone (Fraser)?but a stroke has left the director with a confusing sense of reality—returning him to his soldiering days in WWI and "Frankenstein" re-creations. Brilliant performance from McKellen, with solid support from Fraser and Redgrave. Based on the novel "Father of Frankenstein" by Christopher Bram. **105m/C; VHS, DVD, Blu-Ray.** Ian McKellen; Brendan Fraser; Lynn Redgrave; Lolita Davidovich; David Dukes; Kevin J. O'Connor; Brandon Kleyla; Jack Plotnick; Rosalind Ayres; Arthur Dignam; Jack Betts; Martin Ferrero; David Millbern; ***D:*** Bill Condon; ***W:*** Bill Condon; ***C:*** Stephen M. Katz; ***M:*** Carter Burwell. Oscars '98: Adapt. Screenplay; Golden Globes '99: Support. Actress (Redgrave); Ind. Spirit '99: Actor (McKellen), Film, Support. Actress (Redgrave); L.A. Film Critics '98: Actor (McKellen); Natl. Bd. of Review '98: Actor (McKellen), Film; Broadcast Film Critics '98: Actor (McKellen).

God's Comedy *A Comedia de Deus* **1995** Joao de Deus (Monteiro) is a lecherous ice-cream maker who indulges himself with the ice cream counter girls and some nighttime fantasies. But when he asks the daughter of the local butcher to indulge him as well, her father decides that Joao needs to be taught a lesson. Portuguese with subtitles. **163m/C; VHS, DVD.** *PT* Joao Cesar Monteiro; Claudia Teixeira; Manuela de Freitas; Raquel Ascensao; Saraiva Serrano; ***D:*** Joao Cesar Monteiro; ***W:*** Joao Cesar Monteiro; ***C:*** Mario Barroso.

God's Gift to Women ½ **1931** Broadway comedian Frank Fay stars as an unlikely Casanova in this generally predictable romantic farce. Paris ladies' man Jacques 'Toto' Duryea is juggling several romances when he falls for wealthy American Diane (LaPlante). She disapproves of his amours and tries to shake off his attentions but he's persistent. Louise Brooks has a minor role as Florine, one of Jacques' romantic conquests. **72m/B; DVD.** Frank Fay; Laura La Plante; Joan Blondell; Charles Winninger; Alan Mowbray; Louise Brooks; ***D:*** Michael Curtiz; ***W:*** Joseph Jackson; Raymond Griffith; ***C:*** Robert B. Kurrle.

God's Gun *A Bullet from God* **1975 (R)** Preacher who was once a gunfighter seeks revenge on the men who tried to kill him. Parolini used the pseudonym Frank Kramer. **93m/C; VHS, DVD.** Richard Boone; Lee Van Cleef; Jack Palance; Sybil Danning; ***D:*** Gianfranco Parolini.

God's Little Acre **1958** Delves into the unexpectedly passionate lives of Georgia farmers. One man, convinced there's buried teasure on his land, nearly brings himself and his family to ruin trying to find it. Based on the novel by Erskine Caldwell. **110m/B; VHS, DVD, Blu-Ray.** Robert Ryan; Tina Louise; Michael Landon; Buddy Hackett; Vic Morrow; Jack Lord; Aldo Ray; Fay Spain; ***D:*** Anthony Mann; ***W:*** Philip Yordan; ***C:*** Hans J. Haller; ***M:*** Elmer Bernstein.

God's Lonely Man **1996** Ernest Rackman (Wyle) is one of life's losers. He gets fired from his videostore job and suffers bouts of violence and suicidal impulses. Then he poses as a police officer in order to "rescue" teenaged prostitute Christiane (McComb) so they can begin a new life together but this also doesn't go as planned. **98m/C; VHS, DVD.** Michael Wyle; Heather McComb; Justine Bateman; Paul Dooley; Roxana Zal; Wallace (Wally) Langham; Kieran Mulroney; ***D:*** Frank Von Zerneck; ***W:*** Frank Von Zerneck; ***C:*** Dennis Smith; ***M:*** James Fearnley.

The Gods Must Be Crazy ½ **1984 (PG)** An innocent and charming film. A peaceful Bushman travels into the civilized world to return a Coke bottle "to the gods." Along the way he meets a transplanted schoolteacher, an oafishly clumsy microbiologist and a gang of fanatical terrorists. A very popular film, disarmingly crammed with slapstick and broad humor of every sort. Followed by a weak sequel. **109m/C; VHS, DVD.** *SA* N!xau; Marius Weyers; Sandra Prinsloo; Louw Verwey; Jamie Uys; Michael Thys; Nic de Jager; ***D:*** Jamie Uys; ***W:*** Jamie Uys; ***C:*** Robert M. Lewis; Buster Reynolds; ***M:*** Johnny Bishop; John Boshoff.

The Gods Must Be Crazy 2 ½ **1989 (PG)** A slapdash sequel to the original 1981 African chortler, featuring more ridiculous shenanigans in the bush. This time the bushman's children find themselves in civilization and N!xau must use his unique ingenuity to secure their safe return. **90m/C; VHS, DVD.** N!xau; Lena Farugia; Hans Strydom; Eiros Nadies; Eric Bowen; ***D:*** Jamie Uys; ***M:*** Charles Fox.

God's Not Dead 🦴 **2014 (PG)** This inept, hypocritical "faith-based" drama pretends to debate the existence of God, but it's just a ham-fisted slice of propaganda that would even cause eyes to roll in Sunday school. Good Christian college-boy Josh (Harper) takes his first philosophy class and his mustache-twirling professor Radisson (Sorbo) requires him to write a paper arguing that God is dead or else fail the class. Thus begins a banal series of debates between the pious freshman and the evil universe version of Hercules. Their debates have some decent moments, but every single non-Christian character is painted as vain and cruel, which completely torpedoes the movie's so-called message of faith and tolerance. **113m/C; DVD, Blu-Ray.** Kevin Sorbo; Shane Harper; Dean Cain; Trisha LaFache; Cory Oliver; David A.R. White; ***D:*** Harold Cronk; ***W:*** Cary Solomon; ***C:*** Brian Shanley; ***M:*** Will Musser.

God's Not Dead 2 🦴 **2016 (PG)** While one would assume that movies like this are designed for the faithful, they should actually be the most offended by such weak writing, production values, and filmmaking. In this sequel, Grace Wesley (Hart) is a history teacher who dares suggest a belief in God when a student needs emotional comfort, and gets sued for doing so. Of course, the film sides with the teacher, presenting the non-religious world as evil and inconsiderate. It's poorly-made propaganda. **120m/C; DVD, Blu-Ray.** Maria Canals-Barrera; Pat Boone; Robin Givens; Melissa Joan Hart; Brad Heller; ***D:*** Harold Cronk; ***W:*** Chuck Konzelman; Cary Solomon; ***C:*** Brian Shanley; ***M:*** Will Musser.

God's Not Dead: A Light in Darkness 🦴 1/2 **2018 (PG)** A more complex entry in the God's Not series. The university-based church of Pastor Dave (White) is under fire because of his controversial sermons. After Dave is jailed for refusing to give sermon transcripts to a judge, an act of violence at the church leads to the death of his friend Reverend Jude (Onyango). Amidst these tensions, the university expropriates the church's land. With the help of his brother (Corbett), Dave decides to fight. Though the Christian film shares a feel of political propaganda with its predecessors, it more deeply considers ideas behind concepts such as the hostility of secular society. **105m/C; DVD, Blu-Ray.** David A. R. White; John Corbett; Shane Harper; Ted McGinley; Jennifer Taylor; ***D:*** Michael Mason; ***W:*** Michael Mason; ***C:*** Brian Shanley; ***M:*** Pancho Burgos-Goizueta.

Gods of Egypt 🦴 **2016 (PG-13)** Alex Proyas' CGI-heavy blockbuster is a total disaster, unable to rise to even the low-quality levels of something like Clash of the Titans. The latest swords-and-sandals epic tells the story of Set (Butler), the God of Darkness, who has taken over Egypt and must be defeated. Of course, a young thief (Thwaites) steps forward to take on the God with the help of Horus (Coster-Waldau). Not only is this whitewashed tale remarkably boring on a plot level, it looks horrendous, as if they ran out of money to finish the visual effects. It doesn't even qualify as eye candy. **127m/C; DVD, Blu-Ray.** Brenton Thwaites; Courtney Eaton; Nikolaj Coster-Waldau; Gerard Butler; Rachael Blake; ***D:*** Alex Proyas; ***W:*** Matt Sazama; Burk Sharpless; ***C:*** Peter Menzies, Jr.; ***M:*** Marco Beltrami.

Gods of the Plague 🦴🦴🦴 *Gotter der Pest* **1969** Fassbinder goes noir—or grey with lots of sharp lighting—in this gangster-auteur tale of robbery gone awry. The requisite trappings of the crime genre (guys and dolls and cops and robbers) provide a vague backdrop (and a vague plot) for a moody story full of teutonic angst and alienation, and that certain Fassbinder feeling (which, need we say, isn't to everyone's taste). An early effort by the director, who remade the story later the same year as "The American Soldier" (Fassbinder acts in both). In German with (difficult-to-read) English subtitles. **92m/C; VHS, DVD.** ***GE*** Hanna Schygulla; Harry Bear; ***D:*** Rainer Werner Fassbinder.

God's Own Country 🦴🦴🦴 **2017** A moving drama about a struggling rural farmer in northern England whose life is changed by a Romanian immigrant who comes to work for him. The only son of a beat-down farming couple, Johnny Saxby (O'Connor) barely manages to keep his livestock going. Johnny is also gay, which adds to tensions with his family and community. When Gheorghe (Secareanu) arrives, initial hostilities are set aside as the pair find a deeper relationship and the immigrant's talents improve the lot of the farm. A beautiful filmed exploration of homophobia and the difficulties of rural life. **104m/C; DVD, Blu-Ray.** Josh O'Connor; Gemma Jones; Ian Hart; Alec Secareanu; Melanie Kilburn; ***D:*** Francis Lee; ***W:*** Francis Lee; ***C:*** Joshua James Richards; ***M:*** A Winged Victory for the Sullen.

God's Pocket 🦴🦴 **2014 (R)** One of Hoffman's final roles is in this directorial debut of "Mad Men" star Slattery, an adaptation of Pete Dexter's first novel about a working-class, tight-knit community dealing with crisis. An obnoxious kid is killed on a work site and the murder is covered up. Hoffman's world-weary Mickey happens to be married to the boy's mom, Jeanie (Hendricks), and so he's forced to deal with the funeral arrangements, courtesy of the slimy Smilin' Jack (Marsan), which requires him to call in debts owed by buddy "Bird" (Turturro). A fantastic cast is let down by a mediocre script. **88m/C; DVD, Blu-Ray.** Philip Seymour Hoffman; Richard Jenkins; Christina Hendricks; Eddie Marsan; John Turturro; Domenick Lombardozzi; Caleb Landry Jones; ***D:*** John Slattery; ***W:*** John Slattery; Alex Metcalf; ***C:*** Lance Acord; ***M:*** Nathan Larson.

Godsend 🦴🦴 **2004 (PG-13)** Playing like a dozen similar demon-child redos, pic tries for originality by combining modern technology with typical genre supernatural creepiness. Cute 8-year-old Adam Duncan is killed in a freak auto accident. Grieving parents Paul (Kinnear) and Jessie (Romijn-Stamos) have no sooner buried their adored son when they are approached by Dr. Wells (De Niro) who offers to harvest their dead son's cells for cloning and subsequent rebirth via Jessie. Naturally, the couple agree. When the Adam clone reaches his eighth birthday, however, things start to go eerily awry. Kinnear and Romijn-Stamos are convincing while De Niro has more problems with his cliched character. **102m/C; VHS, DVD.** Greg Kinnear; Rebecca Romijn; Cameron Bright; Robert De Niro; Merwin Mondesir; Deborah Odell; Jack Simons; Elle Downs; Zoie Palmer; ***D:*** Nick Hamm; ***W:*** Mark Bomback; ***C:*** Kramer Morgenthau; ***M:*** Brian Tyler.

The Godson 🦴 **1998 (PG-13)** When Guiseppe "the Guppy" Calzone becomes the head of his crime family, he realizes his son and heir will need some tutoring to become the next big boss. So he sends the kid to Mafia U. to pick up some tricks of the trade. But the head of a rival family sees this as the perfect opportunity to get rid of the Calzone clan. Really, really dumb, despite the comic cast. **100m/C; VHS, DVD.** Rodney Dangerfield; Dom DeLuise; Kevin McDonald; Fabiana Udenio; Lou Ferrigno; Barbara Crampton; ***D:*** Bob Hoge; ***W:*** Bob Hoge; ***C:*** Tom Lappin; ***M:*** Boris Elkis. **VIDEO**

Godspell 🦴🦴 1/2 **1973 (G)** Musical retelling of the story of Jesus, set in New York City. Adapted from an enjoyable Broadway play but the film version comes off as silly. Good dancing and interesting score. **103m/C; VHS, DVD, Blu-Ray.** Victor Garber; David Haskell; Jerry Sroka; Lynne Thigpen; Gilmer McCormick; ***D:*** David Greene; ***M:*** Stephen Schwartz.

Godzilla 🦴🦴 *Gojira* **1954** If you're a fan of Godzilla, you'll be interested in the original Japanese version about the radioactive monster that's destroying Tokyo, which started off the long series. Gojira is a Jurassic-era sea monster whose existence has been disturbed by recent American H-bomb testing. No wonder he's upset! Japanese with subtitles. **96m/B; DVD, Blu-Ray.** ***JP*** Takashi Shimura; Akira Takarada; Momoko Kochi; Akihiko Hirata; Fuyuki Murakami; ***D:*** Ishiro Honda; ***W:*** Takeo Murata; Ishiro Honda; ***C:*** Masao Tamai; ***M:*** Akira Ifukube.

Godzilla 🦴🦴 1/2 **1998 (PG-13)** Over-the-top remake of the 1954 cult classic has nuclear testing in France creating a giant mutant lizard to destroy all boats, piers, people, and buildings that happen to get in its way. Gone are the days of a man in a rubber suit menacing Tokyo, replaced by state-of-the-art special effects. Third rate storyline has wimpy biologist Niko Tatopoulos (Broderick) hired to track down and connect with the beast, only to realize that Godzilla has chosen the Big Apple as the birthing place for its huge brood. When various supporting characters (including Reno as a French secret agent out to destroy Godzilla) cross paths with the creature, what results looks amazingly similar to one hugely successful dinosaur movie and its sequel. Ending leaves door wide open for an inevitable sequel of its own. **138m/C; VHS, DVD, Blu-Ray, UMD.** Matthew Broderick; Jean Reno; Maria Pitillo; Hank Azaria; Kevin Dunn; Michael Lerner; Harry Shearer; Arabella Field; Vicki Lewis; Doug Savant; Malcolm Danare; ***D:*** Roland Emmerich; ***W:*** Roland Emmerich; Dean Devlin; ***C:*** Ueli Steiger; ***M:*** David Arnold. Golden Raspberries '98: Worst Remake/Sequel, Worst Support. Actress (Pitillo).

Godzilla 🦴🦴🦴 **2014 (PG-13)** Joe Brody (Cranston) and his wife (Binoche) are involved in a nuclear accident that he suspects was more than mere system failure. Years later, he watches as the title character, in hiding since World War II, returns to defeat a pair of MUTOs, his prehistoric nemeses. Eventually, only Joe's son Ford (Taylor-Johnson) can stop the super-sized carnage that spans the globe and climaxes in San Francisco. With nods to the series of films that inspired it and a keen understanding of how to create thrills, director Edwards proves to be the perfect choice to reboot the saga of everyone's favorite movie monster. **123m/C; DVD, Blu-Ray.** Aaron Taylor-Johnson; Bryan Cranston; Ken(saku) Watanabe; Sally Hawkins; David Strathairn; Elizabeth Olsen; Juliette Binoche; ***D:*** Gareth Edwards; ***W:*** Max Borenstein; ***C:*** Seamus McGarvey; ***M:*** Alexandre Desplat.

Godzilla Against Mechagodzilla 🦴🦴 *Gojira tai Mekagojira* **2002 (PG)** Realizing the current Godzilla is immune ot their weapons, the Japanese government grabs the skeleton of his predecessor and resurrects it as the cyborg Kiryu. Unfortunately their mechanical Godzilla continues destroying the city when the real Godzilla leaves, prompting some nervousness on the part of Tokyo. **88m/C; DVD, Blu-Ray, Streaming.** ***JP*** Yumiko Shaku; Shin Takumaa; Kana Onodera; Tsutomu Kitagawa; Hirofumi Ishigaki; ***D:*** Masaaki Tezuka; ***W:*** Wataru Mimura; ***C:*** Masahiro Kishimoto; ***M:*** Michiru Ohshima. **VIDEO**

Godzilla: Final Wars 🦴 1/2 *Gojira: Fainaru uôzo* **2004 (PG-13)** Massive homage to Toho's fantasy films (particularly 'Destroy All Monsters' and 'Atragon.') Aliens arrive to prevent a horde of giant monsters from wiping out humanity and warn of an impending asteroid collision. Quickly exposed as the source behind the giant monsters, they unleash them once again, and a decision is made to free Godzilla from his Antarctic prison to help fight them. **125m/C; DVD, Blu-Ray, Streaming.** ***JP*** Masahiro Matsuoka; Rei Kikukawa; Don Frye; Akira Takarada; ***D:*** Ryuhei Kitamura; ***W:*** Ryuhei Kitamura; Isao Kiriyama; Wataru Mimura; Shogo Tomiyama; ***C:*** Takumi Furuya; ***M:*** Keith Emerson; Nobuhiko Morino; Daisuke Yano. **VIDEO**

Godzilla, King of the Monsters 🦴🦴 1/2 *Gojira* **1956** An underwater prehistoric reptile emerges from the depths to terrorize Tokyo after he has been awakened by atomic testing. Burr's scenes are intercut in the American version, where he serves as a narrator telling the monster's tale in flashbacks. Ridiculously primitive special effects even in its own day. One of the first post-WWII Japanese films to break through commercially in the U.S. **80m/B; VHS, DVD, Blu-Ray.** ***JP*** Raymond Burr; Takashi Shimura; Akira Takarada; Akihiko Hirata; Momoko Kochi; Sachio Sakai; Fuyuki Murakami; Ren Yamamoto; ***D:*** Inoshiro Honda; Terry Morse; ***W:*** Inoshiro Honda; Takeo Murata; ***C:*** Masao Tamai; Guy Roe; ***M:*** Akira Ifukube.

Godzilla: King of the Monsters 🦴🦴 1/2 **2019 (PG-13)** In the sequel to 2014's Godzilla, scientists Mark (Chandler) and Emma (Farmiga) Russell have divorced after the death of their son. While Mark finds peace in nature, Emma continues to work for the Monarch Initiative to address the giant monster issue that puts life on Earth in danger. While Monarch keeps the monsters contained, ecoterrorist Jonah (Dance) believes that the monsters should be unleashed to punish humanity for harming the environment. Though the well-crafted film includes timely ideas and interesting monster fights, there are too many characters and too much explanation. **132m/C; DVD, Blu-Ray.** Kyle Chandler; Vera Farmiga; Millie Bobby Brown; Ken(saku) Watanabe; Ziyi Zhang; ***D:*** Michael Dougherty; ***W:*** Michael Dougherty; Zach Shields; ***C:*** Lawrence Sher; ***M:*** Bear McCreary.

Godzilla, Mothra, and King Ghidorah: Giant Monsters All-Out Attack 🦴🦴 1/2 *Gojira, Mosura, Kingu Gidorâ: Daikaijû sôkôgeki* **2001** Godzilla returns to Japan 50 years after his initial appearance in 1954, and an old man claims the government will not be able to stop him because he has accumulated the need for vengeance from all those who died in WWII. Instead, he recommends awakening the three mythical guardian monsters of Japan to stop him. **105m/C; DVD, Blu-Ray.** ***JP*** Chiharu Niiyama; Ryudo Uzaki; Masahiro Kobayashi; Adm. (Ret.) Mizuhi Yoshida; ***D:*** Shusuke (Shu) Kaneko; ***W:*** Shusuke (Shu) Kaneko; Masahiro Yokotani; Kei'ichi Hasegawa; ***C:*** Masahiro Kishimoto; ***M:*** Kou Otani. **VIDEO**

Godzilla on Monster Island 🦴🦴 *Godzilla vs. Gigan* **1972** Even Godzilla himself cannot hope to take on both Ghidra and Gigan alone and hope to succeed. Therefore he summons his pal Angillus for help. Together, they offer Earth its only hope of survival. Though the terror may repel you, the movie is a must for Godzilla fans; it's his first speaking part. **89m/C; VHS, DVD, Blu-Ray.** ***JP*** Hiroshi Ichikawa; Tomoko Umeda; Yuriko Hishimi; Minoru Takashima; Zan Fujita; ***D:*** Jun Fukuda.

Godzilla Raids Again 🦴🦴 *Gigantis, the Fire Monster; Godzilla's Counter Attack* **1955** Warner Bros. had a problem securing rights to Godzilla's name. Yearning for a change of pace, the King of Monsters opts to destroy Osaka instead of Tokyo, but the spiny Angorous is out to dethrone our hero. Citizens flee in terror when the battle royale begins. The first Godzilla sequel. **78m/B; VHS, DVD, Blu-Ray.** ***JP*** Hugo Grimaldi; Makayama; Minoru Chiaki; ***D:*** Motoyoshi Oda; ***W:*** Shigeaki Hidaka; ***C:*** Seichi Endo; ***M:*** Masaru Sato.

Godzilla-Tokyo S.O.S. 🦴🦴 *Gojira tai Mosura tai Mekagojira: Tokyo S.O.S.* **2003 (PG)** Taking place one year after the events of "Godzilla Against Mechagodzilla," Mothra returns to Tokyo and tells Japan to return Mechagodzilla to the sea for burial and it will defend Japan against Godzilla. Otherwise Mothra will declare war on humanity. **90m/C; DVD, Blu-Ray, Streaming.** ***JP*** Noboru Kaneko; Miho Yoshioka; Mitsuki Koga; Hiroshi Koizumi; Akira Nakao; ***D:*** Masaaki Tezuka; ***W:*** Masaaki Tezuka; Masahiro Yokotani; ***C:*** Yoshinori Sekiguchi; ***M:*** Michiru Ohshima. **VIDEO**

Godzilla 2000 🦴🦴🦴 **1999 (PG)** Any other bigger-than-life movie-house hero staring in a series of films that span almost 50 years would have to answer some serious questions about plot repetition—but not Godzilla. The familiarity is what you pay to see. If Godzilla didn't clumsily destroy Tokyo office buildings and knock commuter trains off their elevated tracks, you'd be asking for a refund, pronto. So, with the latest Japanese flick to make it to our shores—featuring the REAL Godzilla, not that sophisticated American excuse for a Godzilla from a couple of years back—all is well. Funny dubbing, rubber suits, miniature sets—perfect comfort food on a rainy afternoon. As far as the plot goes...in short, spacecraft attacks Tokyo'the radioactive dinosaur comes to the rescue. **97m/C; VHS, DVD.** ***JP*** Takehiro Murata; Shiro Sano; Hiroshi Abe; Naomi Nishida; Mayu Suzuki; ***D:*** Takao Okawara; ***W:*** Hiroshi Kashiwabara; Waturu Mimura; ***C:*** Katsuhiro Kato; ***M:*** Takayuki Hattori.

Godzilla vs. Destroyah 🦴🦴 **1995** Japan's defense forces scramble to prevent the apocalypse after it is determined Godzilla is undergoing a sort of nuclear meltdown and may take the world with him when he dies. Complicating matters are a race of Pre-Cambrian life forms unleashed by the weapon that was originally used to stop the Big G back in the 50s. **210m/C; DVD, Blu-Ray, Streaming.** *JP* Takuro Tatsumi; Yoko Ishino; Yasufumi Hayashi; Megumi Odaka; Kenpachiro Satsuma; *D:* Takao Okawara; *W:* Kazuki Ohmori; *C:* Masahiro Kishimoto; Yoshinori Sekiguchi; *M:* Akira Ifukube.

Godzilla vs. King Ghidora 🦴 1/2 **1991** Tokyo begins to panic when aliens from the 23rd century make an appearance. But these aliens supposedly come in peace—warning that Godzilla will soon reawaken and destroy Japan unless he can be destroyed first. But it turns out these beings aren't so benign and soon Godzilla is confronted by his arch-enemy—flying, three-headed King Ghidora. **89m/C; VHS, DVD, Blu-Ray.** *JP* Richard Berger; Kiwako Harada; Kent Gilbert; Shoji Kobayashi; *D:* Kazuki Omori; *W:* Kazuki Omori; *C:* Yoshinori Sekiguchi; *M:* Akira Ifukube.

Godzilla vs. Mechagodzilla II 🦴 1/2 **1993** Mechagodzilla II, a mammoth robot fueled by a nuclear reactor and sheathed in a synthetic diamond shield, is supposed to protect Japan from Godzilla. The mechanical monster has its work cut out for it now that Godzilla and Rodan have both arrived to claim the recently hatched baby Godzilla from a team of scientists. **108m/C; VHS, DVD, Blu-Ray.** *JP* Masahiro Takashima; Leo Mangetti; *D:* Takao Okawara.

Godzilla vs. Megaguirus 🦴🦴 *Gojira tai Megagirasu: Ji shometsu sakusen; Godzilla vs. Megaguirus: The G Annihilation Strategy* **2000** In an effort to stop Godzilla from attacking their nuclear power plants, Japan invents the Dimension Tide satellite to fire miniature black holes back at Earth. In testing it, they awaken a swarm of giant prehistoric insects who immediately perceive Godzilla as a threat to their territory and the fight is on. **105m/C; DVD, Blu-Ray, Streaming.** *JP* Misato Tanaka; Shosuke Tanihara; Masato Ibu; Tsutomu Kitagawa; *D:* Masaaki Tezuka; *W:* Hiroshi Kashiwabara; Wataru Mimura; *M:* Michiru Ohshima. **VIDEO**

Godzilla vs. Megalon 🦴 1/2 *Gojira tai Megaro* **1976 (G)** Godzilla's creators show their gratitude to misguided but faithful American audiences by transforming the giant monster into a good guy. This time, the world is threatened by Megalon, the giant cockroach, and Gigan, a flying metal creature, simultaneously. Fortunately, the slippery hero's robot pal Jet Jaguar is on hand to slug it out side by side with Tokyo's ultimate defender. **80m/C; VHS, DVD, Blu-Ray.** *JP* Katsuhiko Sasakai; Hiroyuki Kawase; Yutaka Hayashi; Robert Dunham; Kotaro Tomita; *D:* Jun Fukuda; *W:* Jun Fukuda; Shinichi Sekizawa; *C:* Yuzuru Aizawa; *M:* Richiro Manabe.

Godzilla vs. Monster Zero 🦴🦴 *Monster Zero; Battle of the Astros; Invasion of the Astro-Monsters; Invasion of the Astros; Invasion of Planet X; Kaiju Daisenso; The Great Monster War; War of the Monsters* **1968 (G)** Novel Godzilla adventure with the big guy and Rodan in outer space. Suspicious denizens of Planet X require the help of Godzilla and Rodan to rid themselves of the menacing Ghidra, whom they refer to as Monster Zero. Will they, in return, help Earth as promised, or is this just one big, fat double cross? **93m/C; VHS, DVD, Blu-Ray.** *JP* Akira Takarada; Nick Adams; Kumi Mizuno; Jun Tazaki; Akira Kubo; Keiko Sawai; Yoshio Tsuchiya; Noriko Sengoku; Fuyuki Murakami; *D:* Inoshiro Honda; *W:* Shinichi Sekizawa; *C:* Hajime Koizumi; *M:* Akira Ifukube.

Godzilla vs. Mothra 🦴🦴 *Godzilla vs. the Thing; Godzilla vs. the Giant Moth; Godzilla Fights the Giant Moth; Mothra vs. Godzilla; Mosura tai Gojira* **1964** Mighty Mothra is called in to save the populace from Godzilla, who is on a rampage; and he's aided by two junior Mothras who hatch in the nick of time. The hesitant moth avoids the fire-breathing behemoth until succumbing to the pleadings of the Peanut Sisters to save humanity. Hilarious special effects inspire more laughter from derision than anything else. **88m/C; VHS, DVD, Blu-Ray.** *JP* Akira Takarada; Yuriko Hoshi; Hiroshi Koizumi; Emi Ito; Yumi Ito; Yoshifumi Tajima; Kenji Sahara; Yu Fujiki; *D:* Inoshiro Honda; *W:* Shinichi Sekizawa; *C:* Hajime Koizumi; *M:* Akira Ifukube.

Godzilla vs. Mothra 🦴 1/2 *Godzilla and Mothra: The Battle for Earth; Gojira vs. Mosura* **1992** Mothra arrives to warn that the Earth (who is apparently a sentient being) has awoken the monster Battra to protect itself. Caught in between the two warring giant insects is Godzilla, who blunders ashore to do damage to inner city Japan. **100m/C; DVD, Blu-Ray, Streaming.** *JP* Tetsuya Bessho; Satomi Kobayashi; Takehiro Murata; Kenpachiro Satsuma; *D:* Takao Okawara; *W:* Kazuki Ohmori; *C:* Masahiro Kishimoto; *M:* Akira Ifukube. **VIDEO**

Godzilla vs. SpaceGodzilla 🦴 1/2 *Gojira vs. Supesugojira* **1994** In the after-events of Godzilla vs. Biollante, Mothra took DNA from both Godzilla and Biollante into space by accident, which went into a black hole. The black hole spits out Space Godzilla who immediately hones in on Earth to take on Godzilla and the United Nations latest anti-Godzilla robot. **106m/C; DVD, Blu-Ray, Streaming.** *JP* Megumi Odaka; Jun Hashizume; Akira (Tsukamoto) Emoto; Kenpachiro Satsuma; *D:* Kensho Yamashita; *W:* Kanji Kashiwa; Hiroshi Kashiwabara; *C:* Masahiro Kishimoto; *M:* Takayuki Hattori. **VIDEO**

Godzilla vs. the Cosmic Monster 🦴🦴 *Godzilla Versus the Bionic Monster; Godzilla vs. Mechagodzilla; Gojira Tai Meka-Gojira* **1974 (G)** Godzilla's worst nightmares become a reality as he is forced to take on the one foe he cannot defeat—a metal clone of himself! To make matters worse, Earth is in dire peril at the hands of cosmic apes. We all need friends, and Godzilla is never more happy to see his buddy King Seeser, who gladly lends a claw. **80m/C; VHS, DVD, Blu-Ray.** *JP* Masaki Daimon; Kazuya Aoyama; Reiko Tajima; Barbara Lynn; Akihiko Hirata; *D:* Jun Fukuda.

Godzilla vs. the Sea Monster **WOOF!** *Nankai No Kai Ketto; Ebirah, Terror of the Deep; Big Duel in the North* **1966** Godzilla makes friends with former rival Mothra (a giant moth) and together they bash on Ebirah, an enormous lobster backed by an evil cadre of (human) totalitarians. The unrepentant crusteacean turns the tables on our heroes, however, by growing a new tentacle everytime one is ripped off. Meanwhile, a frenzied batch of helpless humans are trapped on an island about to explode, if they aren't drowned first in a shower of reptilian backwash. **80m/C; VHS, DVD, Blu-Ray.** *JP* Kumi Mizuno; Chotaro Togin; Hideo Sunazuka; Akira Tekarada; *D:* Jun Fukuda; *W:* Shinichi Sekizawa; Kazuo Yamada; *C:* Masaru Sato.

Godzilla vs. the Smog Monster 🦴 *Gojira Tai Hedora; Godzilla vs. Hedora* **1972 (G)** Godzilla battles a creature borne of pollution, a 400-pound sludge blob named Hedora. Early 1970s period piece conveys interesting attitude towards pollution; it's treated as a sinister force that people are powerless to stop. Japanese teenagers marshal their dancing talents to combat the threat amid the hypnotic swirl of disco lighting. Great opening song: "Save the Earth." Dubbed in English. **87m/C; VHS, DVD, Blu-Ray.** *JP* Akira Yamauchi; Hiroyuki Kawase; Toshio Shibaki; *D:* Yoshimitu Banno.

Godzilla's Revenge 🦴 *Oru Kaiju Daishingeki* **1969** A young boy who is having problems dreams of going to Monster Island to learn from Minya, Godzilla's son. Using the lessons in real life, the boy captures some bandits and outwits a bully. Uses footage from "Godzilla vs. the Sea Monster" and "Son of Godzilla" for battle scenes. One of the silliest Godzilla movies around. **70m/C; VHS, DVD, Blu-Ray.** *JP* Kenji Sahara; Tomonori Yazaki; Machiko Naka; Sachio Sakai; Chotaro Togin; Yoshifumi Tajima; Eisei Amamoto; Ikio Sawamura; *D:* Inoshiro Honda; *W:* Shinichi Sekizawa; *C:* Sokei Tomioka; *M:* Kunio Miyauchi.

The Goebbels Experiment 🦴🦴 **2005** Documentary on Joseph Goebbels, Hitler's minister of propaganda, taken from diaries covering 1924 to 1945. Archival footage illustrates the readings. Kenneth Branagh narrates the English version; Udo Samel the German one. **107m/C; DVD.** *D:* Lutz Hachmeister; *W:* Lutz Hachmeister; Michael Kloft; *C:* Hajo Schomerus; *M:* Hubert Bittman.

GOG 🦴🦴 **1954** Scientists in a secret underground facility are being killed mysteriously and investigators who arrive quickly suspect the base's two robots and super-computer may be behind the problems. **83m/C; DVD, Blu-Ray.** Richard Egan; Constance Dowling; Herbert Marshall; John Wengraf; Philip Van Zandt; Valerie Vernon; Stephen Roberts; *D:* Herbert L. Strock; *W:* Tom Taggart; Ivan Tors; Richard G. Taylor; *C:* Lothrop Worth; *M:* Harry Sukman. **VIDEO**

Goin' Coconuts 🦴 **1978 (PG)** Donny and Marie are miscast as Donny and Marie in this smarmy story of crooks and jewels. Seems someone covets the chanteuse's necklace, and only gratuitous crooning can spare the twosome from certain swindling. Big bore on the big island. **93m/C; VHS, DVD.** Donny Osmond; Marie Osmond; Herb Edelman; Kenneth Mars; Ted Cassidy; Marc Lawrence; Harold Sakata; *D:* Howard Morris.

Goin' South 🦴🦴🦴 **1978 (PG)** An outlaw is saved from being hanged by a young woman who agrees to marry him in exchange for his help working a secret gold mine. They try to get the loot before his old gang gets wind of it. A tongue-in-cheek western that served as Nicholson's second directorial effort. Movie debuts of Steenburgen and Belushi. **109m/C; VHS, DVD.** Jack Nicholson; Mary Steenburgen; John Belushi; Christopher Lloyd; Veronica Cartwright; Richard Bradford; Danny DeVito; Luana Anders; Ed Begley, Jr.; Anne Ramsey; *D:* Jack Nicholson; *W:* Charles Shyer; *C:* Nestor Almendros; *M:* Perry Botkin.

Goin' to Town 🦴🦴 1/2 **1935** Complicated yarn with West as a woman who inherits an oil field and becomes the wealthiest woman in the state. She falls for British engineer Cavanagh and decides to become a "lady" in order to get his attention. There's a subplot about Buenos Aires and a crooked horse race, an in-name-only marriage to a high society type, and a murder before Mae finally gets her man. **71m/B; VHS, DVD.** Mae West; Paul Cavanagh; Gilbert Emery; Ivan Lebedeff; Marjorie Gateson; Tito Coral; Monroe Owsley; *D:* Alexander Hall; *W:* Mae West; *C:* Karl Struss.

Going All the Way 🦴🦴 1/2 **1997 (R)** Korean War vets Sonny Burns (Davies) and Gunner Casselman (Affleck) find themselves becoming best buds after returning to their Indianapolis hometown in 1954. Gunner's the self-confident stud, who vaguely wants to be an artist, while aspiring photographer Sonny's an anxious geek. The boys have mom troubles (Sonny's is a bible-thumper while Gunner's is a seductive flirt) and chase girls with varying success but the true bonding is strictly male. Davies is appropriately twitchy while Affleck gets to effectively use his natural charisma. Wakefield adapted from his 1970 novel. **110m/C; VHS, DVD.** Jeremy Davies; Ben Affleck; Jill Clayburgh; Lesley Ann Warren; Rose McGowan; Rachel Weisz; Amy Locane; *D:* Mark Pellington; *W:* Dan Wakefield; *C:* Bobby Bukowski.

Going Back 🦴 1/2 **1983** Four friends reunite after college to relive a memorable summer they spent together after graduating from high school. **85m/C; VHS, DVD.** Bruce Campbell; Christopher Howe; Perry Mallette; Susan W. Yamasaki; *D:* Ron Teachworth.

Going Berserk 🦴🦴 1/2 **1983 (R)** The members of SCTV's television comedy troupe are featured in this comedy which lampoons everything from religious cults to kung fu movies. Has moments of inspired lunacy, interspersed with more pedestrian fare. Includes wicked send-up of "Father Knows Best," with former cast member Donahue. **85m/C; VHS, DVD.** *CA* John Candy; Joe Flaherty; Eugene Levy; Paul Dooley; Pat Hingle; Richard Libertini; Ernie Hudson; Alley Mills; Dixie Carter; Murphy Dunne; Elinor Donahue; *D:* David Steinberg.

Going Clear: Scientology and the Prison of Belief 🦴🦴🦴 **2015** Riveting, in-depth documentary looks at the controversial Church of Scientology. Created by Alex Gibney, it is based on the popular book by Lawrence Wright. Explores Scientology's origins, its founder L. Ron Hubbard, recruiting practices, and current practices and explains many details that make the church's tactics to attract and retain followers more clear yet shocking. Much of "Going Clear" includes revealing profiles of eight former members of the Church, including filmmaker Paul Haggis. Though the documentary can feel weighted down by information, its cumulative effect is powerful. **119m/C; DVD, Blu-Ray, Download.** *D:* Alex Gibney; *W:* Alex Gibney; *C:* Samuel Painter; *M:* Will Bates. Writers Guild '16: Documentary Screenplay.

Going for Gold: The '48 Games 🦴🦴 1/2 *Bert & Dickie* **2012** BBC TV nostalgia based on the true sports story of Britain's unexpected Olympic gold medal winners Bert Bushnell (Smith) and Richard Burnell (Hoare). Bombed-out London's 1948 'austerity' games, held so closely after the end of WWII, saw the unlikely pairing of working-class Bert and upper-class Dickie who were pushed to compete together in double sculling just weeks before the actual event. **90m/C; DVD; Closed Captioned.** *UK* Matt Smith; Sam Hoare; James Frain; Geoffrey Palmer; Douglas Hodge; *D:* David Blair; *W:* William Ivory; *C:* Kieran McGuigan; *M:* Robert Lane. **TV**

Going Greek 🦴 1/2 **2001 (R)** College freshman/football star Jake (Bruno) is in school on a scholarship and must keep up his grades. That's not going to be easy when his geeky cousin Gil (James) wants to join a fraternity and won't be accepted unless Jake agrees to pledge as well. Jake finds himself loosening up with all the raucous antics of his frat brothers, but his grades begin to suffer as does his relationship with girlfriend Paige (Harris), who despises all fraternities. Gross-out gags and gratuitous nudity abound as you might expect. **90m/C; VHS, DVD.** Dylan Bruno; Laura Harris; Simon Rex; Dublin James; Corey Pearson; Oliver Hudson; Steve Monroe; *D:* Justin Zackham; *W:* Justin Zackham; *C:* Kirk Douglas; *M:* Nathan Barr. **VIDEO**

Going Hollywood 🦴🦴🦴 **1933** Amusing musical/romantic fluff about a French teacher (Davies) who falls in love with a radio crooner (Crosby in his first MGM film). He's got the movie bug and heads for Hollywood, where he becomes an overnight sensation with a sultry costar (D'Orsay). Davies follows and proceeds to get Crosby out of D'Orsay's clutches and winds up replacing her rival in the film, promptly becoming a star herself. The underrated Davies was a fine light comedienne and supplied glamour to the production as well. Kelly, in her film debut, supplied the slapstick. The last Hearst-Cosmopolitan production made with MGM. **78m/B; DVD.** Marion Davies; Bing Crosby; Fifi d'Orsay; Stuart Erwin; Patsy Kelly; Ned Sparks; *D:* Raoul Walsh; *W:* Donald Ogden Stewart; *C:* George J. Folsey.

Going Home 🦴 1/2 **1971** Family melodrama with a sleepwalk performance from Mitchum. Harry Graham murdered his wife Ann (Kirkland) in a drunken rage and in front of their six-year-old son Jimmy. He does his time, gets paroled, and winds up in a trailer park being looked after by good-hearted Jenny (Vacarro). She's also the go-between for Harry and his troubled, now-grown son (Vincent) when Jimmy comes looking for his dad. **97m/C; DVD.** Robert Mitchum; Jan-Michael Vincent; Brenda Vaccaro; Sally Kirkland; *D:* Herbert B. Leonard; *W:* Lawrence B. Marcus; *C:* Fred H. Jackman, Jr.; *M:* Bill Walker.

Going in Style 🦴🦴🦴 1/2 **1979 (PG)** Three elderly gentlemen, tired of doing nothing, decide to liven up their lives by pulling a daylight bank stick-up. They don't care about the consequences because anything is better than sitting on a park bench all day long. The real fun begins when they get away with the robbery. Great cast makes this a winner. **91m/C; VHS, DVD.** George Burns; Art Carney; Lee Strasberg; *D:* Martin Brest; *W:* Martin Brest.

Going in Style 🦴🦴 **2017 (PG-13)** Modern retelling of the 1979 geriatric heist film has Freeman, Arkin, and Caine deciding to get back at the bank that is taking the gold out of their golden years with foreclosures and pension freezes. If it wasn't for the excellence of the three leads, a nice supporting turn by Kenan Thompson, and some occasionally sweet character moments, there wouldn't be much to recommend this one. Director Braff uses, but doesn't really explore, the large issues of the ruthlessness of financial institutions and the disposability of the elderly to provide sitcom laughs and an unrealistic happy ending. **96m/C; DVD, Blu-Ray.** Morgan Freeman; Michael Caine; Alan Arkin; Ann-Margret; Joey King; *D:* Zach Braff; *W:* Theodore Melfi; *C:* Rodney Charters; *M:* Rob Simonsen.

Going My Way ♪♪♪ 1/2 **1944** A musical-comedy about a progressive young priest assigned to a downtrodden parish who works to get the parish out of debt, but clashes with his elderly curate, who's set in his ways. Followed by "The Bells of St. Mary's." Fitzgerald's Oscar-winning Supporting Actor performance was also nominated in the Best Actor category. **126m/B; VHS, DVD, Blu-Ray.** Bing Crosby; Barry Fitzgerald; Rise Stevens; Frank McHugh; Gene Lockhart; Porter Hall; ***D:*** Leo McCarey; ***W:*** Frank Butler; Frank Cavett; Leo McCarey; ***C:*** Lionel Lindon. Oscars '44: Actor (Crosby), Director (McCarey), Film, Screenplay, Song ("Swinging on a Star"), Story, Support. Actor (Fitzgerald); Golden Globes '45: Director (McCarey), Film--Drama, Support. Actor (Fitzgerald); Natl. Film Reg. '04; N.Y. Film Critics '44: Actor (Fitzgerald), Director (McCarey), Film.

Going Overboard ♪ *Babes Ahoy* **1989 (R)** Cruise ship waiter dreams of becoming a comedian and gets his big break when the ship's comic disappears. **99m/C; VHS, DVD.** Adam Sandler; Burt Young; Billy Zane; Peter Berg; ***D:*** Valerie Breiman.

Going Places ♪♪♪ *Les Valseuses; Making It* **1974 (R)** A cynical, brutal satire about two young thugs traversing the French countryside raping, looting and cavorting as they please. Moreau has a brief role as an ex-con trying to go straight. An amoral, controversial comedy that established both its director and two stars. In French with English subtitles or dubbed. **122m/C; VHS, DVD, Blu-Ray.** *FR* Gerard Depardieu; Patrick Dewaere; Miou-Miou; Isabelle Huppert; Jeanne Moreau; Brigitte Fossey; ***D:*** Bertrand Blier; ***W:*** Bertrand Blier; ***C:*** Bruno Nuytten; ***M:*** Stephane Grappelli.

Going Postal ♪♪ *Postal Worker* **1998** Psychologist Dr. Nicolas Brink (Portnow) is hired to create an early warning system to prevent the ticking timebombs of the postal world from going off. But he may be too late as paranoid postal worker Oren Starks (Garrett) becomes obsessed with fellow worker Tammy (Cavanagh), who has already survived one postal shootout. Oren gets fired for harrassment and then Tammy's boyfriend Harry (Futzgerald) gets fired as well for nearly killing another employee in a machinery mishap. So just which of these two will go postal first? A very dark and violent satire. **98m/C; VHS, DVD.** Brad Garrett; Grace Cavanaugh; Rob Roy Fitzgerald; Richard Portnow; William Long, Jr.; ***D:*** Jeffrey F. Jackson; ***W:*** Jeffrey F. Jackson; ***C:*** Mark Parry; ***M:*** Tim Bryson; Tracy Adams.

Going Postal ♪♪ *Terry Pratchett's Going Postal* **2010** TV adaptation of Prachett's 33rd "Discworld" novel has less comedy and more action and romance. Lord Vetinari gives conman Albert Spangler the opportunity to save his life by accepting a new identity and filling the long-vacant job of postmaster at Ankh-Morpork. Now called Moist von Lipwig, he discovers that rebuilding the postal system means going against the evil Reacher Gilt, who owns the telegraph system, and making amends to Adora Belle Dearheart, whose father was the victim of one of his scams. **185m/C; DVD, Blu-Ray.** *GB* Richard Coyle; Charles Dance; Claire Foy; David Suchet; Timothy West; Andrew Sachs; Tamsin Greig; Steve Pemberton; John Henshaw; ***D:*** Jon Jones; ***W:*** Bev Doyle; Richard Kurti; ***C:*** Gavin Finney; ***M:*** John Lunn. **TV**

Going Shopping ♪♪ **2005 (PG-13)** Jaglom indulges his penchant for talky, femme-centered comedies by focusing on Holly (Foyt), the deeply in debt (a man done her wrong) owner of a trendy boutique. She searches for an infusion of cash while hoping a big Mother's Day sale will draw in customers and help salvage her enterprise. Interspersed with Holly's travails is a chorus of women who offer their thoughts on what shopping means to them. **106m/C; DVD.** Victoria Foyt; Rob Morrow; Lee Grant; Mae Whitman; Bruce Davison; Cynthia Sikes; Martha Gehman; Pamela Bellwood; Juliet Landau; ***D:*** Henry Jaglom; ***W:*** Victoria Foyt; Henry Jaglom; ***C:*** Hanania Baer; ***M:*** Harriet Schock.

Going the Distance ♪♪ 1/2 **2010 (R)** Cute modern romance with cute leads and an unfortunate overabundance of self-conscious vulgar sexual humor. After an internship, journalist Erin (Barrymore) goes home to San Francisco while her music scout boyfriend Garrett (Long) remains in Manhattan. They try the bicoastal relationship thing but frustration, jealousy, bad advice, and their own ambitions could derail their love. **102m/C; Blu-Ray.** Drew Barrymore; Justin Long; Charlie Day; Jason Sudeikis; Ron Livingston; Kelli Garner; Christina Applegate; Jim Gaffigan; Rob Riggle; Matt Servitto; Natalie Morales; Leighton Meester; June Raphael; Kirsten Schaal; ***D:*** Nanette Burstein; ***W:*** Geoff LaTulippe; ***C:*** Eric Steelberg; ***M:*** Mychael Danna.

Going to America ♪♪ 1/2 *Last Supper* **2015** One man's quest for love is at the heart of this comedy-drama. Fumnanya (Griffin) claims to be an African prince and is in Los Angeles looking for the woman of his dreams. Having little luck on his own, he has his sidekick Andy (Meyers) help him find his princess so he can share a kiss with her. The result is an unexpected adventure for the pair. **90m/C; DVD, Streaming, Download.** Eddie Griffin; Josh Meyers; Najarra Townsend; Mindy Robinson; Joe Sabatino; ***D:*** Param Gill; ***W:*** Param Gill; John Buchanan; ***C:*** Rudy Harbon.

Going Under ♪ **1991 (PG)** Subsurface military satire about the U.S.S. Sub Standard, the worst nuclear vessel in the Navy. It's so poorly constructed that the brass would rather sink than inspect it—if only they could. Interesting cast sinks with script headed for dry dock. **81m/C; VHS, Streaming.** Bill Pullman; Wendy Schaal; Ned Beatty; Robert Vaughn; Bud Cort; Michael Winslow; ***D:*** Mark W. Travis; ***W:*** Randolph Davis; Darryl Zarubica; ***C:*** Victor Hammer; ***M:*** David Michael Frank.

Going Undercover ♪ **1988 (PG-13)** A bumbling private investigator is hired to protect a rich, beautiful, and spoiled young woman on her European vacation. Poor excuse for a comedy. **90m/C; VHS, DVD.** Lea Thompson; Jean Simmons; Chris Lemmon; ***D:*** James Kenelm Clarke.

Going Upriver: The Long War of John Kerry ♪♪ 1/2 **2004** Director Butler has known former senator and 2004 presidential candidate John Kerry for some 40 years and has been photographing him since 1969. This matter-of-fact documentary looks at Kerry's military service (with some archival footage shot in Vietnam) and his later role in helping establish the group Vietnam Veterans Against the War. Based on the nonfiction book "Tour of Duty" by Douglas Brinkley. **89m/C; DVD.** ***D:*** George Butler; ***W:*** Joseph Dorman; ***C:*** Sandi Sissel; ***M:*** Philip Glass.

Going Wild ♪♪ **1930** Stranded in a resort town, broke newspaperman Rollo Smith (Brown) gets mistaken for publicity-shy aviator Robert Story (Hoyt). He takes advantage of the mistake even though the aviator is expected to compete is a competition and Rollo knows nothing about flying. The sight gags of Brown trying to teach himself flying using a bed, an electric fan, and other props are worth wading through the increasingly cumbersome plot. **68m/B; DVD.** Joe E. Brown; Lawrence Gray; Walter Pidgeon; Ona Munson; Frank McHugh; Arthur Hoyt; Laura Lee; ***D:*** William A. Seiter; ***W:*** Henry McCarty; Humphrey Pearson; ***C:*** Sol Polito.

Gold ♪♪ **2016 (R)** A magnetic performance from McConaughey almost saves this bloated drama. But not quite. McConaughey plays Kenny Wells in this drama/thriller loosely based on the true story of Bre-X, a company that tried to find gold in Indonesia. In the fictional version, Wells has been a lifelong loser, who sees his big break when rumors spread of a gold deposit deep in the jungles of Borneo. Can a man's business skills translate to a trip into the wild in search of gold? This is a project from an incredibly talented team but all that glitters is not, well, you know. **120m/C; Streaming.** Matthew McConaughey; Edgar Ramirez; Bryce Dallas Howard; Macon Blair; Adam LeFevre; ***D:*** Stephen Gagham; ***W:*** Patrick Massett; John Zinman; ***C:*** Robert Elswit; ***M:*** Daniel Pemberton.

Gold Diggers in Paris ♪♪ **1938** A low budget (by musical standards) didn't deter choreographer Busby Berkeley from putting on a girlie show in back-lot Paris. Terry (Vallee) and Duke (Jenkins) own the failing Club Ballee and are quick to accept the mistaken invitation to take their dancers to the Paris International Dance Exposition. A shipboard romance ensues between singer Terry and ballet dancer Kay (Lane) but the troupe is eventually exposed as imposters before a decision is made to let them perform anyway. **100m/B; DVD.** Rudy Vallee; Hugh Herbert; Rosemary Lane; Allen Jenkins; Gloria Dickson; Mabel Todd; Melville Cooper; Fritz Feld; Curt Bois; Edward Brophy; ***D:*** Ray Enright; ***W:*** Warren Duff; Earl Baldwin; ***C:*** George Barnes; Sol Polito; ***M:*** Harry Warren.

Gold Diggers of 1933 ♪♪♪ 1/2 **1933** In this famous period musical, showgirls help a songwriter save his Busby Berkeley-choreographed show. Followed by two sequels. **96m/B; VHS, DVD.** Joan Blondell; Ruby Keeler; Aline MacMahon; Dick Powell; Guy Kibbee; Warren William; Ned Sparks; Ginger Rogers; ***D:*** Mervyn LeRoy. Natl. Film Reg. '03.

Gold Diggers of 1935 ♪♪♪ **1935** The second Gold Diggers film, having something to do with a New England resort, romance, and a charity show put on at the hotel. Plenty of Berkeleian large-scale drama, especially the bizarre, mock-tragic "Lullaby on Broadway" number, which details the last days of a Broadway baby. **95m/B; VHS, DVD.** Dick Powell; Adolphe Menjou; Gloria Stuart; Alice Brady; Frank McHugh; Glenda Farrell; Grant Mitchell; Hugh Herbert; Wini Shaw; ***D:*** Busby Berkeley; ***C:*** George Barnes. Oscars '35: Song ("Lullaby of Broadway").

Gold Diggers of 1937 ♪♪ **1936** Choreographer Busby Berkeley got an Oscar nomination for his dance direction in this glossy film with so-so musical numbers. Insurance agent Peek (Powell) is pressured into selling a million dollar policy to Broadway producer J.J. Hobart (Moore). When J.J. realizes his crooked partners (Perkins, Brown) lost the dough to put on their latest musical, he has a breakdown and Peek and his showgirl squeeze Norma (Blondell) come to the rescue. **101m/B; DVD.** Dick Powell; Joan Blondell; Victor Moore; Osgood Perkins; Charles D. Brown; Glenda Farrell; Lee Dixon; ***D:*** Lloyd Bacon; ***W:*** Warren Duff; ***C:*** Arthur Edeson; ***M:*** Harold Arlen.

Gold Diggers: The Secret of Bear Mountain ♪♪ 1/2 **1995 (PG)** Thirteen-year-old Beth (Ricci) moves to the small town of Wheaton, Washington, and forms an unlikely friendship with rebellious tomboy Jody (Chlumsky). Together, the girls set out on a treasure hunt that takes them into a dangerous trek through sea-coast mountain terrain. The grownups are dumb (and the story's fairly boring) but the two heroines have real appeal. **94m/C; VHS, DVD.** Christina Ricci; Anna Chlumsky; Polly Draper; Brian Kerwin; Diana Scarwid; David Keith; ***D:*** Kevin James Dobson; ***W:*** Barry Glasser; ***C:*** Ross Berryman; ***M:*** Joel McNeely.

Gold for the Caesars ♪ 1/2 *Oro per i Caesari* **1963** Slave Lacer (Hunter) manages the gold-mining operation of Roman proconsul Maximus (Girotti), whose mistress (Demongeot) is the woman Lacer loves. Ambitious Maximus sends Lacer off to open a new mine but things don't go smoothly. **85m/C; DVD.** *IT* Jeffrey Hunter; Massimo Girotti; Mylene Demongeot; Ron Randell; Ettore Manni; ***D:*** Sabatino Ciuffini; Andre de Toth; ***W:*** Sabatino Ciuffini; Arnold Perl; ***C:*** Raffaele Masciocchi; ***M:*** Franco Mannino.

Gold Is Where You Find It ♪ 1/2 **1938** The Technicolor photography makes up for a familiar plot. Gold mining engineer Jared Whitney is overseeing an operation that pits the local farmers, whose land is being destroyed, against the miners. He falls for farmer's daughter Serena, but her family is determined to stop the mining and Jared must choose sides. **91m/C; DVD.** George Brent; Olivia de Havilland; Tim Holt; Claude Rains; Margaret Lindsay; John Litel; Barton MacLane; ***D:*** Michael Curtiz; ***W:*** Warren Duff; Robert Buckner; ***C:*** Sol Polito; ***M:*** Max Steiner.

The Gold of Naples ♪♪♪ *L'Oro Di Napoli* **1954** A four-part omnibus film about life in Naples, filled with romance and family tragedies, by turns poignant, funny and pensive. Originally six tales; two were trimmed for U.S. release. In Italian with subtitles. **107m/B; VHS, DVD.** *IT* Vittorio De Sica; Eduardo de Filippo; Paolo Stoppa; Sophia Loren; Silvana Mangano; ***D:*** Vittorio De Sica.

Gold of the Amazon Women ♪ *Amazon Women* **1979** When two explorers set out to find gold, they stumble onto a society of man-hungry women who follow them into the urban jungle of Manhattan. There is also a European "R" rated version. **94m/C; VHS, DVD.** Bo Svenson; Anita Ekberg; Bond Gideon; Donald Pleasence; ***D:*** Mark L. Lester; ***W:*** Stanley Ralph Ross; ***C:*** David Quaid; ***M:*** Gil Melle. **TV**

Gold of the Seven Saints ♪ 1/2 **1961** Cheaply-made western adventure story has partners Jim (Walker) and Shaun (Moore) striking gold and then trying to transport it through desert and mountain territory with every crook around chasing after them for their treasure. **88m/B; DVD.** Clint Walker; Roger Moore; Gene Evans; Chill Wills; Leticia Roman; Robert Middleton; ***D:*** Gordon Douglas; ***W:*** Leonard Freeman; Leigh Brackett; ***C:*** Joseph Biroc; ***M:*** Howard Jackson.

The Gold Racket ♪ 1/2 **1937** Government agents Alan O'Connor and Bobbie Reynolds must bust up a smuggling ring at the Mexican border so Bobbie goes undercover as a nightclub singer. The gang's ringleader likes to hang out at the club but when Bobbie tries to vamp him she gets kidnapped instead. **66m/B; DVD.** Conrad Nagel; Eleanor Hunt; Fuzzy Knight; Frank Milan; William Thorne; Warner Richmond; Karl Hackett; Charles Delaney; ***D:*** Louis Gasnier; ***W:*** David S. Levy; ***C:*** Mack Stengler.

The Gold Retrievers ♪ 1/2 **2010** When his dad warns 12-year-old Josh that the family business is in trouble, it also means they'll be moving into an apartment where Josh can't keep his dog Bosco. So Josh and Bosco team up with his new friend Ana to find a legendary fortune in gold, but two petty criminals are also treasure hunting. **90m/C; DVD.** Steve Guttenberg; Curtis Armstrong; Billy Zane; Thomas Wiseman; Noah Centino; Courtney Briggs; ***D:*** James D.R. Hickox; ***W:*** Aaron Pope; ***C:*** Andrew Strahorn; ***M:*** Jeffrey Alan Jones. **VIDEO**

The Gold Rush ♪♪♪♪ **1925** Chaplin's most critically acclaimed film. The best definition of his simple approach to film form; adept maneuvering of visual pathos. The "Little Tramp" searches for gold and romance in the Klondike in the mid-1800s. Includes the dance of the rolls, pantomime sequence of eating the shoe, and Chaplin's lovely music. **85m/B; Silent; VHS, DVD, Blu-Ray.** Charlie Chaplin; Mack Swain; Tom Murray; Georgia Hale; ***D:*** Charlie Chaplin; ***W:*** Charlie Chaplin; ***C:*** Roland H. Totheroh; Jack Wilson; ***M:*** Charlie Chaplin. AFI '98: Top 100; Natl. Film Reg. '92.

Gold Rush Maisie ♪♪ 1/2 **1940** Maisie (Sothern) is stranded in Arizona and meets a farm family who has fallen on hard times. The Davis' are migrant workers and are prospecting for gold in an abandoned mining town. Local rancher Bill Anders (Bowman) doesn't want any squatters on his property but Maisie shows him the error of his ways. Third film in the MGM series. **84m/B; DVD.** Ann Sothern; Lee Bowman; Slim Summerville; Virginia Weidler; Mary Nash; John Hamilton; Scotty Beckett; Irving Bacon; ***D:*** Edwin L. Marin; ***W:*** Mary C. McCall; Elizabeth Reinhardt; ***C:*** Charles Lawton, Jr.; ***M:*** David Snell.

Gold Star ♪♪ 1/2 **2017** Twentysomething Vicki (Negri) once wanted a classical music career but now works part-time in a health club. Her world shifts when her father Carmine (Vaughn) suffers a stroke and her mother (Curtin) becomes overwhelmed caring for him. Though the self-absorbed Vicki assists with her father, she is also irritated by his current state. While dealing with her family issues, she also has a problematic relationship with her boyfriend (Rhyser) but finds more support with Chris (Heimer). The final film appearance by Vaughn is also filmmaker Negri's first effort and a moving, if unfocused, personal statement. **90m/C; DVD.** Robert Vaughn; Catherine Curtin; Victoria Negri; Jacob Heimer; Anna Garduno; ***D:*** Victoria Negri; ***W:*** Victoria Negri; ***C:*** Saro Varjabedian; ***M:*** Ben Levin.

The Golden Arrow ♪♪ **1936** Waitress Daisy is hired by a publicist to pose as the heiress to a cosmetic company. She's besieged by fortune hunters so Daisy proposes a marriage of convenience to reporter

Johnny, who wants to quit his job and write a novel. He gets tired of being her social escort and flirts with wealthy Hortense who knows Daisy is a phony. **68m/B; DVD.** Bette Davis; George Brent; Carol Hughes; Eugene Pallette; Dick Foran; Ivan Lebedeff; ***D:*** Alfred E. Green; ***W:*** Charles Kenyon; ***C:*** Arthur Edeson; ***M:*** Heinz Roemheld.

The Golden Bowl 𝄞𝄞𝄞 **1972** Wealthy widower Adam Verver (Morris) and his naive daughter, Maggie (Townsend), are utterly devoted to each other. A situtation that doesn't change with Maggie's marriage to an impoverished Italian prince (Massey). Then Maggie decides her lonely father should also remarry and who could be better than Maggie's old chum, the beautiful Charlotte (Hunnicutt). But what the Ververs don't realize is how well the Prince and Charlotte already know each other. However, a gilded crystal cup—The Golden Bowl—will bring unwelcome knowledge. Based on the novel by Henry James. **270m/C; VHS, DVD.** *GB* Barry Morse; Jill Townsend; Daniel Massey; Gayle Hunnicutt; Cyril Cusack; Kathleen Byron; ***D:*** James Cellan Jones; ***W:*** Jack Pulman. **TV**

The Golden Bowl 𝄞𝄞 **1/2 2000 (R)** Beautiful but bloodless Merchant/Ivory adaptation of Henry James' complex 1904 novel set in turn-of-the-century London. Wealthy American aesthete Adam Verver (Nolte) dotes on his only daughter, Maggie (Beckinsale), and even buys her a husband—an impoverished Italian aristocrat, Prince Amerigo (a miscast Northam), whom she loves. But, unknown to both Ververs, the prince and Maggie's best friend, the equally poor Charlotte (Thurman), had a long ago affair that gets rekindled, even though Charlotte has become the wife of Adam. A studied menage a quartre where just what anyone knows (or suspects) is never made clear. **130m/C; VHS, DVD.** *GB US FR* Nick Nolte; Uma Thurman; Kate Beckinsale; Jeremy Northam; Anjelica Huston; James Fox; Madeleine Potter; Peter Eyre; ***D:*** James Ivory; ***W:*** Ruth Prawer Jhabvala; ***C:*** Tony Pierce-Roberts; ***M:*** Richard Robbins.

Golden Boy 𝄞𝄞𝄞 **1939** Holden plays a young and gifted violinist who earns money for his musical education by working as a part-time prizefighter. Fight promoter Menjou has Stanwyck cozy up to the impressionable young man to convince him to make the fight game his prime concern. She's successful but it leads to tragedy. Holden's screen debut, with Cobb as his immigrant father and Stanwyck successfully slinky as the corrupting love interest. Classic pugilistic drama with well-staged fight scenes. Based on Clifford Odets' play with toned down finale. **99m/B; VHS, DVD.** William Holden; Adolphe Menjou; Barbara Stanwyck; Lee J. Cobb; Joseph Calleia; Sam Levene; Don Beddoe; Charles Halton; ***D:*** Rouben Mamoulian; ***W:*** Daniel Taradash; Victor Heerman; Sarah Y. Mason.

The Golden Boys 𝄞 **1/2 2008 (PG)** Surprisingly boring flick billed as a romantic comedy that's not very romantic. It's set in 1905 on Cape Cod where three grisly retired sea captains decide one of them should marry so they can be looked after properly. Widow Martha Snow answers their newspaper ad but Perez and Jeremiah try to back out of the arrangement, leaving Zebulon to woo the take-charge female. **97m/C; DVD.** David Carradine; Bruce Dern; Rip Torn; Mariel Hemingway; Charles Durning; John Savage; Angelica Torn; Julie Harris; ***D:*** Daniel Adams; ***W:*** Daniel Adams; ***C:*** Philip D. Schwartz; ***M:*** Jonathan Edwards.

The Golden Child 𝄞𝄞 **1986 (PG-13)** When a Tibetan child with magic powers is kidnapped and transported to Los Angeles, Chandler, a professional "finder of lost children" must come to the rescue. The search takes him through Chinatown in a hunt that cliches every Oriental swashbuckler ever made. Good fun. **94m/C; VHS, DVD.** Eddie Murphy; Charlotte Lewis; Charles Dance; Victor Wong; Randall "Tex" Cobb; James Hong; ***D:*** Michael Ritchie; ***W:*** Dennis Feldman; ***C:*** Donald E. Thorin; ***M:*** Michel Colombier.

A Golden Christmas 𝄞𝄞 **1/2 2009** A young boy and girl make friends over a summer and bury a time capsule together, with Michael telling his wish to his Golden Retriever pal. Years later, he's a single dad and Jessica is a widowed mom and they don't recognize each other but the dog (and some cute puppies) comes to the rescue. **89m/C; DVD, Blu-Ray.** Nicholas Brendon; Andrea Roth; Elisa Donovan; Bruce Davison; Alley Mills; ***D:*** John Murlowski; ***W:*** Jay Cipriani; ***C:*** John Murlowski; ***M:*** Lawrence Shragge. **CABLE**

A Golden Christmas 2: The Second Tail 𝄞𝄞 **1/2** *3 Holiday Tails* **2011** Florida retirees Rod and Katherine Wright are feeling restless and decide to play matchmaker for their dog-loving neighbor Lisa. Three adorable golden retriever pups play their part during an 'oops' moment when Lisa runs into her ex-boyfriend David, whom the Wrights still think is perfect for Lisa. Only David has just gotten engaged. **90m/C; DVD, Blu-Ray.** Bruce Davison; Alley Mills; Julie Gonzalo; K.C. Clyde; Kelly Stables; ***D:*** Joe Menendez; ***W:*** Jay Cipriani; ***M:*** Dave Volpe. **VIDEO**

The Golden Coach 𝄞𝄞𝄞 *Le Carrosse D'Or* **1952** Based on a play by Prosper Merimee, the tale of an 18th-century actress in Spanish South America who takes on all comers, including the local viceroy who creates a scandal by presenting her with his official coach. Rare cinematography by Claude Renoir. **101m/C; VHS, DVD.** *FR* Anna Magnani; Odoardo Spadaro; Nada Fiorelli; Dante Rino; Duncan Lamont; ***D:*** Jean Renoir; ***W:*** Jean Renoir; Ginette Doynel; Jack Kirkland; Giulio Macchi; ***C:*** Claude Renoir; Ronald Hill; ***M:*** Antonio Vivaldi.

The Golden Compass 𝄞𝄞 **2007 (PG-13)** 12-year-old Lyra (Richards) lives in a world similar to Victorian England and ruled by the church-like Magisterium, who seem dead set on controlling the minds of everyone in the world and eliminating free will. When best friend Roger (Walker) disappears, Lyra, alongside a strange assortment of allies including a talking, armored bear (McKellan) and a pilot with a Texas accent (Elliot), travels north to rescue him, despite the Magisterium and their ice-queen agent Ms. Coulter's(Kidman) best efforts to stop her. The all-star cast is exceptional, but the story may confound without the book as a roadmap. The film stirred a mild controversy because of the anti-religion themes of the book upon which it was based (the first installment of Philip Pullman's popular British fantasy trilogy), even though writer/director Weitz mostly cut those parts from the movie. **118m/C; DVD, Blu-Ray.** Nicole Kidman; Daniel Craig; Eva Green; Christopher Lee; Dakota Blue Richards; Sam Elliott; Ben Walker; Tom Courtenay; Derek Jacobi; Kathy Bates; ***V:*** Kristin Scott Thomas; Freddie Highmore; Ian McKellen; Ian McShane; ***D:*** Chris Weitz; ***W:*** Chris Weitz; ***C:*** Henry Braham; ***M:*** Alexandre Desplat. Oscars '07: Visual FX; British Acad. '07: Visual FX.

Golden Dawn 𝄞 **1930** A legendarily bad production with a very strange plot that's based on the 1927 Broadway operetta (yes, there's singing in the movie too). Dawn (Siegel) is a white woman, apparently adopted and raised by a native tribe in WWI-era Dutch East Africa. She's first shown in a German POW camp but is released when trouble arises with her tribe since Dawn has been chosen as the sacrificial bride to the tribe's god. However, Dawn is in love with rubber planter Tom Allen (King), who must rescue her. It was originally filmed in two-strip Technicolor although those prints have been lost. **81m/B; DVD.** Vivienne Siegel; Walter Woolf King; Noah Beery, Sr.; Lupino Lane; Alice Gentle; Edward Martindel; ***D:*** Ray Enright; ***W:*** Walter Anthony; ***C:*** Devereaux Jennings.

Golden Earrings 𝄞𝄞 **1/2 1947** Enjoyable, yet incredulous story about British agent Milland joining up with gypsy Dietrich for espionage work. Absurd film was so bad it became a camp classic overnight. Although Dietrich and Milland couldn't stand each other and battled constantly during production, the movie did quite well at the boxoffice. Based on a novel by Yolanda Foldes. **95m/B; VHS, DVD.** Ray Milland; Marlene Dietrich; Bruce Lester; Dennis Hoey; Quentin Reynolds; Reinhold Schunzel; Ivan Triesault; ***D:*** Mitchell Leisen; ***W:*** Abraham Polonsky; Frank Butler; Helen Deutsch; ***C:*** Daniel F. Fapp.

Golden Exits 𝄞𝄞 **1/2 2017 (R)** Relationships fissure when an attractive, 25-year-old Australian woman (Browning) spends a semester in Brooklyn. The men in two families take notice of her, the women notice the men noticing, and suspicion and doubt run amok. In true indie fashion, dialogue reigns supreme, and Perry's language is thoughtful and real, if occasionally self-indulgent. Doesn't rate among similar works by Ingmar Bergman and Woody Allen at their heights, but it can stand among their less-than-perfect offerings. **94m/C; DVD.** Emily Browning; Adam Horovitz; Mary-Louise Parker; Lily Rabe; Jason Schwartzman; ***D:*** Alex Ross Perry; ***W:*** Alex Ross Perry; ***C:*** Sean Price Williams; ***M:*** Keegan DeWitt.

The Golden Eye 𝄞 *The Mystery of the Golden Eye* **1948** In the 42nd film in the series, Charlie Chan is on vacation in Arizona when he's called upon to investigate a seemingly-played out gold mine that's suddenly profitable again. The owner fears for his life, believing something criminal is going on. **68m/B; DVD.** Roland Winters; Victor Sen Yung; Mantan Moreland; Bruce Kellogg; Wanda McKay; ***D:*** William Beaudine; ***W:*** Scott Darling; ***C:*** William Sickner.

Golden Gate 𝄞𝄞 **1993 (R)** Young Fed Dillon is thrown into the hysteria of the communist witch hunt in 1952 San Francisco. He snares Song, a Chinese labor activist, on some very dubious charges. Ten years later he finds himself getting involved with Song's daughter Marilyn (Chen), who knows nothing about her lover's involvement with her family. Then she finds out. Ever-changing moods, sometimes film noir, sometimes a love story, sometimes a nostalgic look back, are confusing. Promising storyline meanders and fades as Director Madden tries to do too much in a short time. Beware of broad stereotypes in every character. **95m/C; VHS, DVD.** Matt Dillon; Joan Chen; Bruno Kirby; Teri Polo; Tzi Ma; Stan(ford) Egi; Peter Murnik; Jack Shearer; George Giudall; ***D:*** John Madden; ***W:*** David Henry Hwang; ***C:*** Bobby Bukowski; ***M:*** Elliot Goldenthal.

Golden Girl 𝄞𝄞 **1/2 1951** Hollywood bio of popular entertainer Lotta Crabtree (spritely Gaynor). Lotta supports her gambler father and overbearing stage mother by first singing and dancing in the California gold mining camps. From there, she travels from town to town, finding time for a romance with Tom Richmond (Robertson), who's a Confederate spy. **108m/C; DVD.** Mitzi Gaynor; Dale Robertson; Dennis Day; James Barton; Una Merkel; ***D:*** Lloyd Bacon; ***W:*** Walter Bullock; Charles "Blackie" O'Neal; Gladys Lehman; ***C:*** Charles G. Clarke; ***M:*** Eliot Daniel; Lionel Newman.

Golden Gloves 𝄞 **1/2 1940** Early example of the boxing noir genre looks inside the seedy world of racketeer Naish (Taggerty), who operates small clubs featuring badly mismatched fights to give the customers the brutal knockouts they're hungry for. When a young fighter is killed in a match, Richard Denning (Crane), a regular in Naish's clubs joins newspaperman Robert Paige (Matson) in an effort to clean up the amateur matches. Naish doesn't take the threat to his racket lying down and sends out his goons with the classic cloak and dagger. **66m/B; DVD.** Richard Denning; J. Carrol Naish; Robert Paige; William Frawley; ***D:*** Edward Dmytryk; Felix Feist; ***W:*** Lewis R. Foster; Maxwell Shane; Joe Ansen; ***C:*** Henry Sharp; John L. "Jack" Russell; ***M:*** Arthur Lange.

The Golden Hawk 𝄞 **1/2 1952** Swashbuckling buccaneer Kit "The Hawk' Gerardo (Hayden) rescues pirate captain Rouge (Fleming) when her ship is besieged by soldiers of evil Governor del Toro (Sutton). Kit and Rouge are both secretive and their romance doesn't go smoothly amidst confusing plot adventures. **82m/C; DVD.** Sterling Hayden; Rhonda Fleming; John Sutton; Helena Carter; Paul Cavanagh; Michael Ansara; Raymond Hatton; ***D:*** Sidney Salkow; ***W:*** Robert E. Kent; ***M:*** William V. Skall.

The Golden Idol 𝄞 **1/2 1954** Bomba is in possession of the Golden Idol of the Watusi tribe. Evil Prince Ali sends his henchman Joe to take it from him while archeologist Karen Marsh wants to return the treaure to the tribe. 10th in the series. **71m/B; DVD.** John(ny) Sheffield; Paul Guilfoyle; Anne Kimbell; Lane Bradford; Leonard Mudie; ***D:*** Ford Beebe; ***W:*** Ford Beebe; ***C:*** Harry Neumann; ***M:*** Marlin Skiles.

Golden Needles 𝄞 **1/2** *The Chase for the Golden Needles* **1974** Goofy story, filmed in Hong Kong, about an ancient Chinese statue embedded with seven golden acupuncture needles that supposedly can restore male sexual vigor. Naturally it's sought by a number of people and mercenary Dan (Baker) is hired to track it down for his employer Felicity (Ashley). **92m/C; DVD.** Joe Don Baker; Elizabeth Ashley; Jim Kelly; Burgess Meredith; Ann Sothern; ***D:*** Robert Clouse; ***W:*** S. Lee Pogostin; ***C:*** Gil Hubbs; ***M:*** Lalo Schifrin.

The Golden Salamander 𝄞𝄞 **1951** Howard shines in otherwise lackluster adventure about archaeologist searching for ancient ruins in Tunisia who must deal with gun runners and their evil leader, while torridly romancing a beautiful Tunisian girl. Filmed on location in Tunis. Based on the novel by Victor Canning. **96m/B; VHS, Streaming.** *GB* Trevor Howard; Anouk Aimee; Herbert Lom; Miles Malleson; Walter Rilla; Jacques Sernas; Wilfrid Hyde-White; Peter Copley; Eugene Deckers; Henry Edwards; Marcel Poncin; Percy Walsh; Sybilla Binder; Kathleen Boutall; Valentine Dyall; ***D:*** Ronald Neame; ***C:*** Oswald Morris.

The Golden Seal 𝄞𝄞 **1/2 1983 (PG)** Tale of a small boy's innocence put in direct conflict, because of his love of a rare wild golden seal and her pup, with the failed dreams, pride and ordinary greed of adults. **94m/C; VHS, DVD.** Steve Railsback; Michael Beck; Penelope Milford; Torquil Campbell; ***D:*** Frank Zuniga; ***M:*** John Barry.

Golden Shoes 𝄞 **1/2 2015** A family film about the power of soccer in the life of one boy. Eight-year-old Christian Larou (Koza) loves soccer and his favorite player Cristiano Ronaldo. With a goal of becoming the best soccer player in the United States, he focuses more and more on soccer after his father is deployed to Afghanistan and his mother is hospitalized. However, playing in the youth soccer league involves dealing with bullying and deceptive adults, but is necessary for his goal of playing for the U.S. national youth team. After gaining special soccer shoes, Christian plays in a championship game where he can lead his team to victory. In the process, he can try to bring his family together and inspire many more people. **89m/C; DVD, Streaming, Download.** Christian Koza; David DeLuise; John Rhys-Davies; Vivica A. Fox; Dina Meyer; ***D:*** Lance Kawas; ***W:*** Lance Kawas; ***C:*** Bryan Greenberg; ***M:*** Gregory Prechel; Brahm Wenger. **VIDEO**

The Golden Spiders: A Nero Wolfe Mystery 𝄞 **1/2 2000** It's actually not much of a mystery but writer Rex Stout's eccentric Wolfe (Chaykin) and his idiosyncratic cast of helpers as well as the setting (Manhattan in the late '40s) make for some amusing moments. Gourmand and orchid grower Wolfe never leaves his brownstone, preferring right-hand man Archie Goodwin (Hutton) take care of the leg work. The golden spiders of the title are a pair of flashy earrings worn by a damsel in distress that leads to several hit-and-run deaths, blackmail, and fraud. **100m/C; VHS, DVD.** Maury Chaykin; Timothy Hutton; Bill Smitrovich; Saul Rubinek; Mimi Kuzyk; Beau Starr; Robert Clark; Larissa Lapchinski; Gary Reineke; Nicky Guadagni; Robert Bockstael; Trent McMullen; ***D:*** Bill Duke; ***W:*** Paul Monash; ***C:*** Mike Fash; ***M:*** Michael Small. **CABLE**

The Golden Stallion 𝄞 **1/2 1949** Trigger falls in love with a stunning mare. He sees her villainous owners abusing her and kills them. Roy takes the blame for his equine pal, but true love triumphs to save the day. **67m/B; VHS, DVD.** Roy Rogers; Dale Evans; Estelita Rodriguez; Pat Brady; Douglas Evans; Frank Fenton; ***D:*** William Witney.

Golden Swallow 𝄞𝄞𝄞 *Jin yan zi; The Girl with the Thunderbolt Kick; The Shaolin Swallow* **1968** Not to be confused with a Chinese ghost film from the 1980s with a similar name, this is technically a sequel to the film "Come Drink With Me." The Golden Swallow (Cheng Pei-pei) must investigate several murders that have her trademark calling card left at the scene, thus implicating her. She discovers a young man seeking revenge for the murder of his loved ones and eventually agrees to help him bring them to justice. Far more violent than the previous film, it also includes an unfortunate romantic triangle, as our young would-be hero and another kung fu fighter vie for Golden Swallow's affections. **104m/C; DVD.** *CH* Pei Pei Cheng; Yu Wang; Lie Lo; Hsin Yen Chao; ***D:*** Cheh Chang; ***W:*** Cheh Chang; Yun Chih Tu; ***C:*** Hsueh Li Pao; ***M:*** Fu-ling Wang.

Golden Voyage of Sinbad 1/2 **1973 (G)** In the mysterious ancient land of Lemuria, Sinbad and his crew encounter magical and mystical creatures. A statue of Nirvana comes to life and engages in a sword fight with Sinbad. He later meets up with a one-eyed centaur and a griffin. Ray Harryhausen can once again claim credit for the unusual and wonderful mythical creatures springing to life. **105m/C; VHS, DVD, Blu-Ray.** John Phillip Law; Caroline Munro; Tom Baker; Douglas Wilmer; Martin Shaw; John David Garfield; Gregoire Aslan; ***D:*** Gordon Hessler; ***W:*** Brian Clemens; ***C:*** Ted Moore; ***M:*** Miklos Rozsa.

Goldeneye **1995 (PG-13)** Bond is back, in the long-awaited (eight years) debut of Brosnan as legendary Brit agent 007. Since we're through the Cold War, Bond has to make do with the villainy of the Russian Mafia, who are planning to sabotage global financial markets utilizing the "Goldeneye" satellite weapon. There's a spectacularly impossible stunt to start things out in familiar territory and lots more noisy (if prolonged) action pieces. Brosnan (who looks great in a tux) is slyly self-aware that his character is more myth than man and Janssen does a suitably over-the-top job as bad Bond girl Xenia Onatopp. Tina Turner sings the dreary title track. **130m/C; VHS, DVD, Blu-Ray.** Pierce Brosnan; Famke Janssen; Sean Bean; Izabela Scorupco; Joe Don Baker; Robbie Coltrane; Dame Judi Dench; Tcheky Karyo; Gottfried John; Alan Cumming; Desmond Llewelyn; Michael Kitchen; Serena Gordon; Samantha Bond; Minnie Driver; ***D:*** Martin Campbell; ***W:*** Jeffrey Caine; Michael France; ***C:*** Phil Meheux; ***M:*** Éric Serra. Blockbuster '96: Action Actor, T. (Brosnan).

The Goldfinch 1/2 **2019 (R)** The life of young Theo Decker (Fegley) is forever changed when he visits a museum with his mother and a terrorist attack takes place. His mother dies, and Theo steals the painting they were viewing. After the incident, he is taken in by an upper class family and spends much time in an antique shop run by Hobie (Wright), whose partner also died in the attack, while coping with his loss. A feeble and adaptation of a Pulitzer Prize-winning novel. **149m/C; DVD, Blu-Ray.** Oakes Fegley; Ansel Elgort; Nicole Kidman; Jeffrey Wright; Luke Wilson; ***D:*** John Crowley; ***W:*** Peter Straughan; ***C:*** Roger Deakins; ***M:*** Trevor Gureckis.

Goldfinger **1964 (PG)** Ian Fleming's James Bond, Agent 007, attempts to prevent international gold smuggler Goldfinger and his pilot Pussy Galore from robbing Fort Knox. Features villainous assistant Oddjob and his deadly bowler hat. The third in the series is perhaps the most popular. Shirley Bassey sings the theme song. **117m/C; VHS, DVD, Blu-Ray.** *GB* Sean Connery; Honor Blackman; Gert Frobe; Shirley Eaton; Tania Mallet; Harold Sakata; Cec Linder; Bernard Lee; Lois Maxwell; Desmond Llewelyn; Nadja Regin; ***D:*** Guy Hamilton; ***W:*** Paul Dehn; Richard Maibaum; ***C:*** Ted Moore; ***M:*** John Barry. Oscars '64: Sound FX Editing.

Goldrush: A Real Life Alaskan Adventure 1/2 **1998** Well-bred Frances (Milano) decides to leave New York society life behind and join an expedition to Alaska (as a would-be gold miner) during the 1899 gold rush. **89m/C; VHS, DVD.** Alyssa Milano; Bruce Campbell; Stan Cahill; Tom Scholte; William Morgan Sheppard; ***D:*** John Power; ***W:*** Jacqueline Feather; David Seidler. **TV**

Goldstein 1/2 **1964** After strolling out of Lake Michigan, a mysterious old man roams around Chicago and causes a profound reaction in the people he meets. One man, a sculptor, becomes so affected that he scours the city for him while trying to make up with his pregnant ex-girlfriend, who decides to have an abortion that becomes an oddly comical experience. Unique debut film of notable director Kaufman was filmed in various locations throughout Chicago in the 1960s. **79m/B; DVD.** Lou Gilbert; Tomas Erhart; Severn Darden; Ellen Madison; Benito Carruthers; ***D:*** Philip Kaufman; Benjamin Manaster; ***W:*** Philip Kaufman; Benjamin Manaster; ***C:*** Jean-Phillippe Carson; ***M:*** Meyer Kupferman.

Goldstone 1/2 **2018 (R)** In this sequel to *Mystery Road*, Jay Swan (Pedersen) returns as a detective investigating the disappearance of female migrant workers in the Australian outback. In the small town of Goldstone, run by a deliciously wicked mayor (Weaver), he discovers that corruption and crime run rampant. A languid shoot-em-up that replaces gratuitous gore and sex with exquisite cinematography, particularly overhead shots filmed by drones. **110m/C; DVD, Blu-Ray.** Aaron Pedersen; Alex Russell; Jacki Weaver; David Wenham; David Gulpilil; ***D:*** Ivan Sen; ***W:*** Ivan Sen; ***C:*** Ivan Sen; ***M:*** Ivan Sen.

The Goldwyn Follies **1938** Lavish disjointed musical comedy about Hollywood. A movie producer chooses a naive girl to give him advice on his movies. George Gershwin died during the filming. **115m/C; VHS, DVD.** Adolphe Menjou; Vera Zorina; Al Ritz; Harry Ritz; Jimmy Ritz; Helen Jepson; Phil Baker; Bobby Clark; Ella Logan; Andrea Leeds; Edgar Bergen; ***D:*** George Marshall; ***C:*** Gregg Toland; ***M:*** George Gershwin; Ira Gershwin.

The Golem 1/2 *Der Golem, wie er in die Welt kam* **1920** A huge clay figure is given life by a rabbi in hopes of saving the Jews in the ghetto of medieval Prague. Rarely seen Wegener expressionist mythopus that heavily influenced the "Frankenstein" films of the sound era. **80m/B; Silent; VHS, DVD, Blu-Ray.** *GE* Paul Wegener; Albert Steinruck; Ernst Deutsch; Lyda Salmonava; Otto Gebuehr; Max Kronert; Loni Nest; Greta Schroder; Hans Sturm; ***D:*** Paul Wegener; Carl Boese; ***W:*** Paul Wegener; Henrik Galeen; ***C:*** Karl Freund; ***M:*** Hans Landberger.

Golem: The Petrified Garden *Golem, le jardin petrifie* **1993** This darkly humorous film offers an insightful look at the Soviet Union as it was collapsing. Daniel (xxx) is an international art dealer who must travel to the autonomous Soviet Jewish zone of Birobidzhan to claim a valuable inherited collection. Included in the collection is a large statue of Golem, and Daniel will do whatever is necessary to find and take possession of the collection. As he travels across the Soviet Union to Birobidzhan, located on the far side of Siberia, he also witnesses the aftermath of the collapse.Yiddish, Russian, French, and Hebrew with subtitles. **87m/C; DVD.** Jerome Koenig; Hanna Schygulla; Samuel Fuller; Macha Itkina; Natalia Voitulevitch-Manor; ***D:*** Amos Gitai; ***W:*** Amos Gitai; Tonino Guerra; ***C:*** Henri Alekan; Luc Drion; Eduard Timlin; ***M:*** Markus Stockhausen; Simon Stockhausen. **VIDEO**

Golf in the Kingdom **2010 (PG)** Might appeal to golfing gurus or fans of Michael Murphy's 1971 bestseller but otherwise this shoestring drama is a waste of tee time. Brash American Michael (Gamble) stops in Scotland on his way to India and gets an introduction to the game from Burningbush golf pro Shivas Irons (O'Hara). Suddenly Michael doesn't need to head to that ashram to have a life-altering experience. Filmed in Brandon, Oregon. **87m/C; DVD.** Mason Gamble; David O'Hara; Malcolm McDowell; Frances Fisher; Tony Curran; Julian Sands; Joanne Whalley; ***D:*** Susan Streitfeld; ***W:*** Susan Streitfeld; ***C:*** Arturo Smith; ***M:*** Evelyn Glennie; Ian Dean. **VIDEO**

Goliath Against the Giants 1/2 *Goliath Contro I Giganti; Goliat Contra Los Gigantes; Goliath and the Giants* **1963** Goliath takes on Bokan, who has stolen his throne. Goliath must fight Amazons, storms, and sea monsters to save the lovely Elea. Goliath conquers all. **95m/C; VHS, DVD.** *IT SP* Brad Harris; Gloria Milland; Fernando Rey; Barbara Carroll; ***D:*** Guido Malatesta.

Goliath and the Barbarians *Il Terror Dei Baraberi* **1960** Goliath and his men go after the barbarians who are terrorizing and ravaging the Northern Italian countryside during the fall of the Roman Empire. A basic Reeves muscleman epic. **86m/C; VHS, DVD.** *IT* Steve Reeves; Bruce Cabot; ***D:*** Carlo Campogalliani; ***M:*** Les Baxter.

Goliath and the Dragon **WOOF!** *La Vendetta di Ercole* **1961** Even Goliath must have doubts as he is challenged by the evil and powerful King Eurystheus. A must for fans of ridiculous movies with ridiculous monsters. **90m/C; VHS, DVD.** *IT FR* Bruce Cabot; Mark Forest; Broderick Crawford; Gaby Andre; Leonora Ruffo; ***D:*** Vittorio Cottafavi; ***W:*** Marco Piccolo; Archibald Zounds, Jr.; ***C:*** Mario Montuori; ***M:*** Les Baxter.

Goliath and the Sins of Babylon *Maciste, L'Eroe Piu Grande Del Mondo* **1964** Well-sculpted Forest plays yet another mesomorph to the rescue in this poorly dubbed spaghetti legend. Goliath must spare 24 virgins whom the evil Crisa would submit as human sacrifice. Forest—who played the mythic Maciste in a number of films—was randomly assigned the identity of Goliath, Hercules, or Samson for U.S. viewing; go figure. **80m/C; VHS, DVD.** *IT* Mark Forest; Eleanora Bianchi; Jose Greco; Giuliano Gemma; Paul Muller; ***D:*** Michele Lupo.

Gomorrah **2008** This is nothing like "The Godfather." Instead it's a dramatization of Saviano's expose of Neapolitan crime as controlled by the so-called Camorra families. Director Garrone avoids glamorizing the violence as he uses five interconnecting stories to demonstrate their insidious control in all areas of daily life. Then things actually get worse as rival factions start a turf war. It's complicated keeping track of the different characters and power struggles but it's slice-of-life realism at its best. Italian with subtitles. **137m/C; Blu-Ray.** *IT* Salvatore Abruzzese; Gianfelice Imparato; Maria Nazionale; Toni Servillo; Carmine Paternoster; Salvatore Cantalupo; Gigio Morra; Marco Macor; Ciro Petrone; ***D:*** Matteo Garrone; ***W:*** Matteo Garrone; Ugo Chiti; Massimo Gaudioso; Roberto Saviano; Maurizio Braucci; ***C:*** Marco Onorato; ***M:*** Neil Davidge; Robert Del Naja; Euan Dickinson.

Gone 1/2 **2010** Due to his past, Mike (John Brotherton) is forbidden by law to return to his home town or past associates. This works just fine for him, until he is asked to return to avenge the death of his brother. Based loosely on a true story. **81m/C; Blu-Ray.** John Brotherton; George Castan; Andrew Coney; Joey Covington; Eric Escalante; ***D:*** Matthew McLaughlin; ***W:*** Matthew McLaughlin; ***C:*** Brandon Musselman; ***M:*** Steven Mclaughlin; Mike Muvment. **VIDEO**

Gone 1/2 **2012 (PG-13)** Promising young star Seyfried continues her string of surprisingly awful career choices with a "thriller" that was purposefully left unscreened for lucky critics—and shouldn't have been allowed to screen for paying audiences either. Jill Parrish (Seyfried, very flat here) was kidnapped and held by a serial killer but the police were skeptical of her story. When her sister disappears two years later, Jill is convinced that it must be the same maniac who snatched her. Plays more like a straight-to-basic-cable movie-of-the-week, only with even more leaden acting and melodramatic dialogue. **85m/C; DVD, Blu-Ray.** Amanda Seyfried; Emily Wickersham; Wes Bentley; Daniel Sunjata; Michael Paré; Joel David Moore; Jennifer Carpenter; Sebastian Stan; ***D:*** Heitor Dhalia; ***W:*** Allison Burnett; ***C:*** Michael Grady; ***M:*** David Buckley.

Gone Are the Days 1/2 *The Man From C.O.T.T.O.N., Purlie Victorious* **1963** Shaky adaptation of the play, "Purlie Victorious." A black preacher wants to cause the ruin of a white plantation owner. Alda's screen debut. **97m/B; VHS, DVD.** Ossie Davis; Ruby Dee; Sorrell Booke; Godfrey Cambridge; Alan Alda; Beah Richards; ***D:*** Nicholas Webster; ***W:*** Ossie Davis; ***C:*** Boris Kaufman.

Gone Are the Days **1984** Government agent (Korman) is assigned to protect a family who witnessed an underworld shooting, but the family would like to get away from both the mob and the police. Disney comedy is well-acted but done in by cliches. **90m/C; VHS, DVD.** Harvey Korman; Susan Anspach; Robert Hogan; ***D:*** Gabrielle Beaumont. **CABLE**

Gone Baby Gone **2007 (R)** In working-class Dorchester (Boston), four-year-old Amanda McCready has been abducted. Cops Jack Doyle (Freeman) and Remy Bressant (Harris) are on the scene, but it's not enough for Amanda's Aunt Beatrice (Madigan). She hires private detectives Patrick Kenzie (the younger Affleck) and Angie Gennaro (Monaghan), locals with better access to neighborhood folks who may not talk to police. Mom Helene (Ryan) is tough to sympathize with—a drinker and druggie who lives in near squalor and who seems apathetic at best about her daughter's disappearance. Stellar performances, nuance, plot twists, and a distinctly un-Hollywood gritty Boston backdrop create a crime thriller that offers an uncomfortable edge of moral dilemma. The brothers Affleck and the rest of the crew put out a commendable effort, with Ben a pleasant surprise behind the camera and Casey an equally pleasant surprise in front of it. **115m/C; DVD, Blu-Ray.** Casey Affleck; Michelle Monaghan; Morgan Freeman; Ed Harris; John Ashton; Amy Ryan; Amy Madigan; Titus Welliver; Michael K(enneth) Williams; Edi Gathegi; Jill Quigg; ***D:*** Ben Affleck; ***W:*** Ben Affleck; Aaron Stockard; ***C:*** John Toll; ***M:*** Harry Gregson-Williams.

Gone, But Not Forgotten **2003** Very low-budget indie has sweet, gay small-town forest ranger Drew (Orr) saving the life of city boy Mark (Montgomery) from a not-so-accidental fall while rock climbing. Drew falls in love while caring for Mark, who has temporary amnesia from the trauma. Mark's struggling with his sexuality and has to make a life-changing decision--as does Drew. **90m/C; DVD.** Aaron Orr; Matthew Montgomery; Joel Bryant; Brenda Lasker; Ariadne Shaffer; Bryna Weiss; ***D:*** Michael D. Akers; ***W:*** Michael D. Akers; ***C:*** Jennifer Derbin; ***M:*** Shaun Cromwell. **VIDEO**

Gone Dark *The Limit* **2003 (R)** Out to score a big drug bust, undercover agent Monica (Forlani) is in too deep as she has affairs with the kingpin and his right-hand man, Denny, all while becoming addicted to heroin. When Denny ends up dead, Monica fears that an elderly neighbor, May (Bacall), might know too much and in her frenzied state she holds her captive but May's not about to succumb. Forlani and Bacall do their best to redeem director Webb's freshman effort as it labors through jerky scene cuts. **83m/C; VHS, DVD.** Claire Forlani; Lauren Bacall; Henry Czerny; Pete Postlethwaite; ***D:*** Lewin Webb; ***W:*** Matt Holland; ***C:*** Curtis Petersen; ***M:*** Norman Orenstein. **VIDEO**

Gone Fishin' **WOOF!** **1997 (PG)** Long delayed comedy (thanks to some on-set disasters and well founded doubts about quality) finds best friends and bassmasters of disaster Gus (Glover) and Joe (Pesci) thinking they're going on a peaceful fishing trip. Instead they meet two women (Arquette and Whitfield) who are on the trail of a dangerous British con artist (Brimble). Pesci and Glover have reeled in one stinky old shoe of a movie here. Granted, it's not entirely their fault, but they should've known better. There are no surprises (or laughs) as every joke and set piece is tipped way ahead of time, just so you won't miss it. Less fun than a fish hook in the eye. **94m/C; VHS, DVD, Blu-Ray.** Danny Glover; Joe Pesci; Rosanna Arquette; Lynn Whitfield; Willie Nelson; Nick Brimble; Gary Grubbs; Carol Kane; Edythe Davis; ***D:*** Christopher Cain; ***W:*** J.J. (Jeffrey) Abrams; Jill Mazurzsky Cody; ***C:*** Dean Semler; ***M:*** Randy Edelman.

Gone Girl 1/2 **2014 (R)** Director Fincher masterfully adapts Gillian Flynn's hit thriller novel. Nick (Affleck) is forced into a nightmare when he comes home to find a scene of a struggle and his wife Amy (Pike) missing. Nick instantly becomes the suspect in what everyone begins to presume is his wife's murder as evidence of foul play mounts up. But there's more to the story of Nick & Amy than meets the eye. With expert technical precision, Fincher delivers another film as tightly wound as a Swiss watch. It's wildly entertaining from first frame to last with great performances throughout. **145m/C; DVD, Blu-Ray.** Ben Affleck; Rosamund Pike; Neil Patrick Harris; Carrie Coon; Kim Dickens; Patrick Fugit; Tyler Perry; Missi Pyle; Sela Ward; David Clennon; Lisa Banes; ***D:*** David Fincher; ***W:*** Gillian Flynn; ***C:*** Jeff Cronenweth; ***M:*** Trent Reznor; Atticus Ross.

Gone in 60 Seconds 1/2 **1974** Car thief working for an insurance adjustment firm gets double-crossed by his boss and chased by the police. Forty minutes are consumed by a chase scene which destroyed more than 90 vehicles. **105m/C; VHS, DVD, Blu-Ray.** H.B. Halicki; Marion Busia; George Cole; James McIntyre; Jerry Daugirda; ***D:*** H.B. Halicki; ***W:*** H.B. Halicki; ***C:*** Jack Vacek; ***M:*** Philip Kachaturian.

Gone in 60 Seconds ☌☌ **2000 (PG-13)** Cage is an ex-car thief who must steal 50 cars in one night in order to save his ne'er-do-well brother (Ribisi) while gung-ho cop Castleback (Lindo) stays on his tail. "Rounding-up-the-old-crew" montage ensues, followed by much highway mayhem and the odd humorous one-liner. As with most Bruckheimer-produced epics, flash and stunts run roughshod over plot and character, but the target audience won't care because the cars just look so damn cool. Jolie is woefully underutilized in the girlfriend/partner-in-crime role. Remake of the 1974 film notable for its 40-minute chase scene. **117m/C; VHS, DVD, Blu-Ray, UMD.** Nicolas Cage; Angelina Jolie; Giovanni Ribisi; Robert Duvall; Scott Caan; Vinnie Jones; Will Patton; Delroy Lindo; Chi McBride; Christopher Eccleston; Timothy Olyphant; William Lee Scott; Frances Fisher; Grace Zabriskie; James Duval; TJ Cross; Arye Gross; Bodhi (Pine) Elfman; Master P; ***D:*** Dominic Sena; ***W:*** Scott Rosenberg; ***C:*** Paul Cameron; ***M:*** Trevor Rabin.

Gone with the West ☌ ½ **1972** Little Moon and Jud McGraw seek revenge upon the man who stole their cattle. **92m/C; VHS, DVD.** James Caan; Stefanie Powers; Sammy Davis, Jr.; Aldo Ray; Michael Conrad; Michael Walker, Jr.; ***D:*** Bernard Giraudeau.

Gone with the Wind ☌☌☌☌ **1939** Epic Civil War drama focuses on the life of petulant southern belle Scarlett O'Hara. Starting with her idyllic lifestyle on a sprawling plantation, the film traces her survival through the tragic history of the South during the Civil War and Reconstruction, and her tangled love affairs with Ashley Wilkes and Rhett Butler. Classic Hollywood doesn't get any better than this; one great scene after another, equally effective in intimate drama and sweeping spectacle. The train depot scene, one of the more technically adroit shots in movie history, involved hundreds of extras and dummies, and much of the MGM lot was razed to simulate the burning of Atlanta. Based on Margaret Mitchell's novel, screenwriter Howard was assisted by producer Selznick and novelist F. Scott Fitzgerald. For its 50th anniversary, a 231-minute restored version was released that included the trailer for "The Making of a Legend: GWTW." **231m/C; VHS, DVD, Blu-Ray.** Clark Gable; Vivien Leigh; Olivia de Havilland; Leslie Howard; Thomas Mitchell; Hattie McDaniel; Butterfly McQueen; Evelyn Keyes; Harry Davenport; Jane Darwell; Ona Munson; Barbara O'Neil; William "Billy" Bakewell; Rand Brooks; Ward Bond; Laura Hope Crews; Yakima Canutt; George Reeves; Marjorie Reynolds; Ann Rutherford; Victor Jory; Carroll Nye; Paul Hurst; Isabel Jewell; Cliff Edwards; Eddie Anderson; Oscar Polk; Eric Linden; Violet Kemble-Cooper; Fred Crane; Howard Hickman; Leona Roberts; Cammie King; Mary Anderson; Frank Faylen; ***D:*** Victor Fleming; ***W:*** Sidney Howard; ***C:*** Ray Rennahan; ***M:*** Max Steiner. Oscars '39: Actress (Leigh), Color Cinematog., Director (Fleming), Film, Film Editing, Screenplay, Support. Actress (McDaniel); AFI '98: Top 100; Natl. Film Reg. '89; N.Y. Film Critics '39: Actress (Leigh).

Gonin 2 ☌ ½ *Five Women* **1996** A sequel in name only. A factory owner in debt to the Yazuka is beaten, and his wife commits suicide after being raped by the gangsters because her husband can't pay his debts. He sets out on a killing spree after making himself a sword, and he wanders into a jewelry store to get his dead wife a diamond ring, only to find that five women who have just fought off several Yakuza thieves are robbing the store themselves. They escape with the ring he wanted, and he follows to get the ring back. **107m/C; DVD.** *JP* Ken Ogata; Yui Natsukawa; Shinobu Ootake; Kimiko Yo; Mai Kitajima; Yumi Nishiyama; Yumi Takigawa; ***D:*** Takashi Ishii; ***W:*** Takashi Ishii; ***C:*** Yasushi Sasakibara; ***M:*** Goro Yasukawa.

Gonzo: The Life and Work of Dr. Hunter S. Thompson ☌☌☌ **2008 (R)** Chronicles his life and career through interviews of the many famous people who knew (or at least encountered) Thompson, the "Rolling Stone" columnist known as the father of gonzo journalism (wherein the reporter involves himself in the events he's reporting on to the extent the story revolves around himself), as well as his massive use of psychedelic drugs and his stubborn hatred of authority. Wildly popular in the 1960s and 1970s, his career declined in his later years, and in 2005 he was found dead from a self-inflicted gunshot wound. **120m/C; DVD.** ***D:*** Alex Gibney; ***C:*** Maryse Alberti; ***M:*** David Schwartz. **VIDEO**

Goobers! ☌ *Mystery Monsters!* **1997 (PG)** After joining a top-rated children's show, a young boy realizes the puppet monsters aren't puppets, but living aliens on the run from an evil queen. **80m/C; DVD.** Ashley Tesoro; Tim Redwine; Sam Zeller; Daniel Hartley; Michael Dennis; Caroline Ambrose; J.W. Perra; ***D:*** Charles Band; ***W:*** Benjamin Carr; ***C:*** James Lawrence Spencer; ***M:*** Richard Kosinski. **VIDEO**

Gooby ☌ ½ **2009 (PG)** Has a good message, but that Gooby is kinda creepy. 11-year-old Willy is filled with all sorts of fears of aliens and monsters and other assorted evils. This is made worse when his family moves into a new house and he's the new kid at school. But Willy has a secret weapon—his childhood protector Gooby, a six-foot, orange, teddy-bearish talking monster that gives him courage. **99m/C; DVD.** Matthew Knight; David James Elliott; Ingrid Kavelaars; Eugene Levy; ***V:*** Robbie Coltrane; ***D:*** Wilson Coneybeare; ***W:*** Wilson Coneybeare; ***C:*** Michael Storey; ***M:*** Kevin Lau; Ronald Royer. **VIDEO**

Good ☌ ½ **2008** Passive to the point of inertia, even Mortensen can't do much with his character—German university professor John Halder who's willfully blind to Nazi atrocities in order to protect himself. A proponent of euthanasia, Halder's position is but one neat propaganda step to justify the 'final solution' as far as Hitler's chancellery is concerned. Stuck in a marriage to an unstable wife (Hille), Halder is only too willing to let himself be guided by others, including his Aryan mistress Anne (Whittaker). Isaacs gives the most energized performance as fellow teacher Maurice, a Jew whose friendship is betrayed by Halder. Adapted from the play by C.P. Taylor. **96m/C; Blu-Ray.** *GB* Viggo Mortensen; Jason Isaacs; Jodie Whitaker; Anastasia Hille; Steven Mackintosh; Mark Strong; Gemma Jones; ***D:*** Vicente Amorim; ***W:*** John Wrathall; ***C:*** Andrew Dunn; ***M:*** Simon Lacey.

Good Advice ☌☌ ½ **2001 (R)** Stockboker Ryan Turner (Sheen) loses all his money on a bad stock tip and decides to ghostwrite his ex-girlfriend's (Richards) lame newspaper advice column. Suddenly the column is hot and the newspaper's publisher (Harmon) is showing interest in more than newsprint. **93m/C; VHS, DVD.** Charlie Sheen; Denise Richards; Angie Harmon; Jon Lovitz; Rosanna Arquette; Estelle Harris; Barry Newman; ***D:*** Steve Rash; ***W:*** Robert Horn; Daniel Margosis; ***C:*** Daryn Okada; ***M:*** Teddy Castellucci.

A Good Baby ☌☌ ½ **1999** In a sparsely populated North Carolina community, loner Raymond Toker (Thomas) dicovers an abandoned newborn in the woods. He rescues the infant and attempts to find the baby's parents but no one will claim her. Toker gets more and more attached to the baby when slick traveling salesman Truman Lester (Strthairn) suddenly appears in town and the child's origins are finally revealed. Hasty ending mars an otherwise notably affecting debut for director Dieckmann. **98m/C; VHS, DVD.** Henry Thomas; David Strathairn; Cara Seymour; Danny Nelson; ***D:*** Katherine Dieckmann; ***W:*** Katherine Dieckmann; Leon Rooke; ***C:*** Jim Denault; ***M:*** David Mansfield.

Good Boy! ☌☌ **2003 (PG)** "E.T." meets "Benji" in this amiable talking dog pic with very young kiddie appeal. Twelve-year-old Owen (Aiken) is a lonely little boy who begs his parents for a pup of his own when a doggie-piloted spacecraft conveniently crashes into his neighborhood carrying the adorable Hubble, who comes from (where else?) the Dog Star. Owen adopts Hubble but quickly realizes this is no ordinary pooch. Soon Owen is speaking dog while Hubble tries to train Earthling dogs to begin taking charge or face the threat of a en-masse canine "recall" to the home planet. While visual mechanics of the animal's speech are crude, vital performances of both humans and hounds alike elevate this recycled story. **89m/C; VHS, DVD.** Liam Aiken; Molly Shannon; Kevin Nealon; Brittany Moldowan; Hunter Elliot; ***V:*** Matthew Broderick; Delta Burke; Donald Adeosun Faison; Vanessa Redgrave; Richard "Cheech" Marin; Brittany Murphy; Carl Reiner; ***D:*** John Hoffman; ***W:*** John Hoffman; ***C:*** James Glennon; ***M:*** Mark Mothersbaugh.

Good Boys ☌☌ ½ **2019 (R)** Three slightly nerdy sixth grade boys--the romance-seeking Max (Trembly), tough guy Thor (Noon), and game-loving Lucas (Williams)--have been friends their whole lives. When the trio uses Max's father's (Forte) drone to spy on teen neighbors and break it, they must scramble to replace the drone before he gets home. Otherwise, Max will miss an all-important kissing party where he hopes to have his first kiss with his crush Brixlee (Davis). Intended for adult audiences with often profane humor, the three leads have good chemistry though the story of their misadventures grows thin by the end. **95m/C; DVD, Blu-Ray.** Jacob Tremblay; Keith L. Williams; Brady Noon; Molly Gordon; Midori Francis; ***D:*** Gene Stupnitsky; ***W:*** Gene Stupnitsky; Lee Eisenberg; ***C:*** Jonathan Furmanski; ***M:*** Lyle Workman.

Good Burger ☌☌ ½ **1997 (PG)** Teen actors Kel and Kenan from Nickelodeon fame make their feature film debut in this innocent, silly romp as employees trying to prevent the takeover of their fast food restaurant by the mega burger conglomerate across the street. Similar to comedy teams of the past, Kel is the dim-witted Ed and Kenan is the schemer Dexter, always looking for a quick way out of hard labor. The pre-adolescent humor of the film is as goofy as it is charming and the energetic duo of K&K serves up an entertaining meal for the kiddies. Shaquille O'Neal makes a cameo as does funk meister George Clinton. And yes, that is Abe Vigoda by that fry machine! **95m/C; VHS, DVD.** Kenan Thompson; Kel Mitchell; Sinbad; Abe Vigoda; Dan Schneider; Shar Jackson; Jan Schweiterman; Ron Lester; ***Cameo(s):*** Shaquille O'Neal; George Clinton; ***D:*** Brian Robbins; ***W:*** Dan Schneider; Kevin Kopelow; Heath Seifert; ***C:*** Mac Ahlberg; ***M:*** Stewart Copeland.

Good-bye, Emmanuelle ☌ ½ **1977 (R)** Follows the further adventures of Emmanuelle in her quest for sexual freedom and the excitement of forbidden pleasures. The second sequel to "Emmanuelle." **92m/C; VHS, DVD, Blu-Ray.** Sylvia Kristel; Umberto Orsini; Jean-Pierre Bouvier; Charlotta Alexandra; ***D:*** Francois Leterrier; ***W:*** Emmanuelle Arsan; Francois Leterrier; ***C:*** Jean Badal; ***M:*** Serge Gainsbourg.

Good Bye, Lenin! ☌☌☌ **2003 (R)** Communism has come to an end as the Berlin Wall falls in 1989 which may be too much of a shock for Alex's (Bruhl) mom Christiane (Sass)?a staunch Socialist—who has a heart attack right before the event and slips into an eight-month coma. In an effort to protect her from the changes capitalism has brought, he comically yet believably revives the vestiges of the fallen regime and even goes so far as to stage a newscast as part of the clever ruse. Although the practicality of the scenario is stretched, Bruhl impressively delivers in this offbeat farce. In German, with English subtitles. Winner of the 2003 European Film Awards for best picture. **121m/C; DVD.** Chulpan Khamatova; Alexander Beyer; Daniel Brühl; Katrin Sass; Maria Simon; Florian Lukas; ***D:*** Wolfgang Becker; ***W:*** Wolfgang Becker; Bernd Lichtenberg; ***C:*** Martin Kukula; ***M:*** Yann Tiersen.

The Good Catholic ☌☌ ½ **2017 (PG-13)** Spicer deftly transmits the internal agony of a young, earnest priest who questions his calling after he forms a relationship with a mysterious woman seeking a late-night Confession. A thoughtful rom-dramedy that speaks of choices, passion, and faith, but that may not appeal to many outside of the church. **96m/C; DVD, Blu-Ray.** Zachary Spicer; Wrenn Schmidt; Danny Glover; John C. McGinley; Alex Miro; ***D:*** Paul Shoulberg; ***W:*** Paul Shoulberg; ***C:*** Justin Montgomery; ***M:*** Zachary Walter.

The Good Companions ☌☌ **1933** Jess (Gwenn), Elizabeth (Glynne), and Inigo (Gielgud) change their dull lives by signing on with a failing road show called the Dinky Doos. Providing financial and other assistance (as well as a name change), the company finds a potential star in Susie Dean (Matthews) and then tries to get noticed by an impresario. Adaptation of the J.B. Priestley novel. **93m/B; DVD.** *UK* Jessie Matthews; Edmund Gwenn; John Gielgud; Mary Glynne; Finlay Currie; Percy Parsons; ***D:*** Victor Saville; ***W:*** Angus MacPhail; Ian Dalrymple; ***C:*** Bernard Knowles; ***M:*** George Posford.

Good Day for a Hanging ☌☌ ½ **1958** Marshal Ben Cutler (MacMurray) finds unexpectedly opposition from the townspeople when he captures killer Eddie Campbell (Vaughn). The charismatic outlaw gains their sympathy and Cutler is going to have trouble when Campbell is sentenced to hang. **85m/C; VHS, DVD.** Fred MacMurray; Robert Vaughn; Joan Blackman; Margaret (Maggie) Hayes; James Drury; Wendell Holmes; Emile Meyer; Bing (Neil) Russell; ***D:*** Nathan "Jerry" Juran; ***W:*** Daniel Ullman; Maurice Zimm; ***C:*** Henry Freulich.

Good Day for It ☌☌ **2011 (R)** Good acting helps out a familiar plot. Luke (Patrick) steals from his crime boss employer to pay for his baby daughter's operation. Forced to leave his family for their own safety, Luke finally returns 15 years later for a reunion but the bad guys haven't forgotten about him. **93m/C; DVD.** Robert Patrick; Mika Boorem; Robert Englund; Lance Henriksen; Kathy Baker; Hal Holbrook; Joe Flanigan; Christian Kane; ***D:*** Nick Stagliano; ***W:*** Nick Stagliano; ***C:*** Stephen Kazmierski; ***M:*** Matthew Ryan.

A Good Day to Die ☌☌ ½ *Children of the Dust* **1995 (R)** Western made-for-TV saga, set during the 1880s land rush of the Oklahoma Territory, and adapted from the novel by Clancy Carlile. Half-black, half-Cherokee gunslinger Gypsy Smith (Poitier) reluctantly agrees to lead a wagon train of freed slaves west to found their own community. Naturally, there's trouble with the Klan and Gypsy isn't the only one involved—young Cherokee brave White Wolf (Wirth), who has been raised among whites, has a forbidden romance with his foster sister, Rachel (Going), leading to lots of heartbreak. Fawcett has a brief role as the young Rachel's high-strung mother. Filmed in Alberta, Canada. **120m/C; VHS, DVD.** Sidney Poitier; Michael Moriarty; Joanna Going; Billy Wirth; Regina Taylor; Hart Bochner; Shirley Knight; Robert Guillaume; Farrah Fawcett; ***D:*** David Greene; ***W:*** Joyce Eliason; ***C:*** Ronald Orieux; ***M:*** Mark Snow. **TV**

A Good Day to Die Hard ☌ **2013 (R)** John McClane (Willis) is back in the fifth installment of a franchise that has gone so far afield from its roots that it barely resembles the original. The 2013 McClane is a super-hero, a bullet-dodging, building-jumping superman who goes to Russia to find his son Jack (Courtney) before realizing he's been caught up in an international conspiracy. It's all an excuse for mind-numbing car chases, building explosions, and endless gunfire. Some action movies give you a thrill, this one sends you searching for aspirin. **98m/C; DVD, Blu-Ray.** Bruce Willis; Jai Courtney; Sebastian Koch; Mary Elizabeth Winstead; Cole Hauser; Amaury Nolasco; Yuliya Snigir; Rasha Bukvic; ***D:*** John Moore; ***W:*** Skip Woods; ***C:*** Jonathan Sela; ***M:*** Marco Beltrami.

Good Dick ☌ **2008 (R)** Multi-hyphenate Palka is apparently using her feature film debut to work out some personal issues best left to a shrink's couch. A creepy nameless L.A. video store clerk (Ritter) is intrigued when a troubled nameless young woman (Palka) starts renting porn videos. He stalks her and talks his way into her life despite her constantly humiliating him. Maybe that's part of the attraction but viewers won't have the same interest. **86m/C; DVD.** Marianna Palka; Jason Ritter; Tom Arnold; ***D:*** Marianna Palka; ***W:*** Marianna Palka; ***C:*** Andre Lascaris; ***M:*** Jared Nelson Smith.

The Good Dinosaur ☌☌ **2015 (PG)** This very troubled 3D-animated production went through numerous versions and directors, and the multiple cooks in the kitchen have done what often happens—delivered a bland dish. The film takes place in an alternate universe in which the dinosaurs never died, actually developing a unique society. It focuses on a family of Apatosaurus, and the runt Arlo (Raymond Ochoa), who is separated from his clan and partners with a feral boy. The journey home is basically a riff on a Western with the dinosaur in the role of the cowboy and the boy his horse or dog. Parts of it look beautiful, but it's pretty boring. **100m/C; DVD, Blu-Ray.** Jeffrey Wright; Frances McDormand; Marcus Scribner; Raymond Ochoa; Jack Bright; ***D:*** Peter Sohn; ***W:*** Meg LeFauve; ***M:*** Jeff Danna; Mychael Danna.

The Good Doctor **2011 (PG-13)** This odd and inert blend of mystery and drama stars a miscast Bloom as a young doctor who gets embroiled with an 18-year-old patient (Keough). There's an interesting drama somewhere here about a young man who struggles to find acceptance when he moves to the States and the lengths he's willing to go to for the admiration he so desperately covets. But Bloom is not the engaging lead this story needs and the attempt to go for the thriller in the final act leads to a lack of tension in this overly clinical doctor's visit. **91m/C; DVD, Blu-Ray.** Orlando Bloom; Riley Keough; Rob Morrow; Troy Garity; J.K. Simmons; Taraji P. Henson; Michael Peña; ***D:*** Lance Daly; ***W:*** John Enbom; ***C:*** Yaron Orbach; ***M:*** Bryan Burne.

The Good Earth **1/2 1937** Pearl S. Buck's classic re-creation of the story of a simple Chinese farm couple beset by greed and poverty. Outstanding special effects. MGM's last film produced by master Irving Thalberg and dedicated to his memory. Rainer won the second of her back-to-back Best Actress Oscars for her portrayal of the self-sacrificing O-Lan. **138m/B; VHS, DVD.** Paul Muni; Luise Rainer; Charley Grapewin; Keye Luke; Walter Connolly; ***D:*** Sidney Franklin; ***C:*** Karl Freund. Oscars '37: Actress (Rainer), Cinematog.

Good Evening, Mr. Wallenberg **1/2 1993** Raoul Wallenberg was an upper-class Swede who imported luxury goods from Hungary. He was also responsible for saving thousands of Hungarian Jews from extermination by the Nazis. Using phony documents he first has small groups of Jews smuggled to safety but when he learns that the 65,000 Jews of the Budapest ghetto are to be killed he uses a bluff to prevent the deaths. Later taken prisoner by the Soviet Army, Wallenberg's fate has never been determined. Characters are dwarfed by the immensity of the events and Wallenberg remains an enigma. In Swedish, German, and Hungarian with English subtitles. **115m/C; VHS, DVD.** *SW* Stellan Skarsgard; Erland Josephson; Katharina Thalbach; ***D:*** Kjell Grede; ***W:*** Kjell Grede.

The Good Fairy **1935** Charming romantic comedy based on the play by Ferenc Molnar and given the stardust touch of screenwriter Sturges. Luisa (a charming Sullavan) has just left a Budapest orphanage for a job where she attracts the amorous advances of millionaire Konrad (a scene-stealing Morgan). She pretends to be married and picks the first name out of the phone book as her "husband," that of struggling Max Sporum (Marshall), who goes along with the deception because he's instantly smitten with Luisa. She decides she can play "good fairy" to Max by using Konrad's bankroll but it's not that simple. Remade as 1947's "I'll Be Yours" with Deanna Durbin in the lead. **98m/B; VHS, DVD, Blu-Ray.** Margaret Sullavan; Herbert Marshall; Frank Morgan; Reginald Owen; Alan Hale; Beulah Bondi; Cesar Romero; ***D:*** William Wyler; ***W:*** Preston Sturges; ***C:*** Norbert Brodine.

The Good Father **1987 (R)** An acclaimed British TV movie about a bitter divorced man trying to come to terms with his son, his ex-wife, and his own fury by supporting the courtroom divorce battle of a friend. **90m/C; VHS, DVD.** *GB* Anthony Hopkins; Jim Broadbent; Harriet Walter; Frances Viner; Joanne Whalley; Simon Callow; Michael Byrne; ***D:*** Mike Newell; ***W:*** Christopher Hampton; ***C:*** Michael Coulter; ***M:*** Richard Hartley.

Good Fences **1/2 2003 (R)** In the mid-1970s, upwardly mobile black lawyer Tom Spader (Glover) moves with his wife Mabel (Goldberg) and their kids into a posh Greenwich, Connecticut, suburb and embraces all sorts of WASP-y behavior—much to Mabel's disgust. Self-indulgent and simplistic satire. Based on the novel by Ericka Ellis. **119m/C; VHS, DVD.** Danny Glover; Whoopi Goldberg; Mo'Nique; ***D:*** Ernest R. Dickerson; ***W:*** Trey Ellis; ***C:*** Jonathan Freeman; ***M:*** George Duke. **CABLE**

The Good Fight **1/2 1992** Grace Cragin (Lahti) is a lawyer at a small firm who's asked by her son's best friend to represent him in a tough case against a powerful corporation. The young man is dying of mouth cancer and he wants to sue the tobacco company that makes the chewing tobacco he blames for his illness. Grace is wary of the high-powered litigation necessary but with the increasingly personal aid of her prominent lawyer ex-husband (O'Quinn), she is ready to battle the odds. Another fine performance by Lahti in this cable drama. **91m/C; VHS, DVD.** Christine Lahti; Terry O'Quinn; Kenneth Welsh; Lawrence Dane; Adam Trese; Tony Rosato; Andrea Roth; Jonathan Crombie; ***D:*** John David Coles; ***W:*** Beth Gutcheon; ***M:*** W.G. Snuffy Walden. **CABLE**

The Good German **1/2 2006 (R)** A throwback to 1940s noir, director Soderbergh makes it the real deal by only using technology of the era, with mixed results. The black-and-white drama begins during WWII as war correspondent Jake (Clooney) has an affair with the married Lena (an intense Blanchett). After the war ends he returns on assignment with hopes of finding her but is disheartened to see that she's taken up hooking with Tully (Maguire), a boyish pimp who fronts as a motor-pool soldier and becomes Jake's driver. The desolate Lena is desperate to leave Germany and her misery behind but can't because the U.S. and Russian governments are searching for her possibly dead husband—a Nazi scientist—who's disappeared. Visually nifty tribute to classic Hollywood might have pulled it off if the story were better. Based on Joseph Kanon's 2001 novel of the same name. **107m/B; DVD.** George Clooney; Cate Blanchett; Tobey Maguire; Beau Bridges; Tony Curran; Leland Orser; Jack Thompson; Robin Weigert; Christian Oliver; Ravil Isyanov; Don Pugsley; ***D:*** Steven Soderbergh; ***W:*** Paul Attanasio; ***C:*** Steven Soderbergh; ***M:*** Thomas Newman.

The Good Girl **2002 (R)** Justine (Aniston) spends her days in the retail hell of Retail Rodeo, a West Texas discount mart, and her nights with her pothead housepainter hubby (Reilly), while longing for something better in director Arteta's excellent and biting indie dramedy. She finds just that in college dropout and new employee, the self-named Holden (as in Caufield) played by Gyllenhaal. Justine and the brooding, malcontent (read: would-be writer) embark on an affair with interesting results. Small-screen star Aniston gives an excellent, convincing performance. Deschanel is a standout as Cheryl, who makes creative use of the store's PA system for the benefit of the unaware, zombie-like customers. Nelson is the narrow-minded boss who provides a good portion of the comedy. Successful re-teaming of Arteta and actor/writer White. **93m/C; VHS, DVD.** Jennifer Aniston; Jake Gyllenhaal; John C. Reilly; Tim Blake Nelson; Zooey Deschanel; Mike White; Deborah Rush; John Carroll Lynch; John Doe; Roxanne Hart; ***D:*** Miguel Arteta; ***W:*** Mike White; ***C:*** Enrique Chediak. Ind. Spirit '03: Screenplay.

The Good Guy **2010 (R)** The twist in DePietro's romantic comedy directorial debut is that Beth's (Bledel) boyfriend Tommy (Porter) is a shallow, loathsome cad who loses the girl to much more worthy sweetheart of a guy Daniel (Greenberg). Wall Street broker/shark Tommy needs to fill a job vacancy quickly and offers a promotion to office computer whiz Daniel. He also introduces shy Daniel to Beth, which is the beginning of the end of Tommy and Beth's oppressive relationship. **90m/C; On Demand.** Alexis Bledel; Scott Porter; Anna Chlumsky; Aaron Yoo; Bryan Greenberg; Andrew McCarthy; Andrew Stewart-Jones; ***D:*** Julio DePietro; ***W:*** Julio DePietro; ***C:*** Seamus Tierney; ***M:*** tomandandy.

The Good Guys and the Bad Guys **1/2 1969 (PG)** When Kennedy is abandoned by his gang of outlaws for being too old to keep up, he finds himself being hunted by lifelong marshall nemesis Mitchum. **91m/C; VHS, DVD.** Robert Mitchum; George Kennedy; David Carradine; Tina Louise; Douglas Fowley; Lois Nettleton; Martin Balsam; John Carradine; ***D:*** Burt Kennedy; ***W:*** Ronald M. Cohen; ***C:*** Harry Stradling, Jr.

Good Guys Wear Black **1978 (PG)** A mild-mannered professor keeps his former life as leader of a Vietnam commando unit under wraps until he discovers that he's number one on the CIA hit list. Sequel is "A Force of One." **96m/C; VHS, DVD.** Chuck Norris; Anne Archer; James Franciscus; ***D:*** Ted Post; ***W:*** Mark Medoff; ***M:*** Craig Safan.

Good Hair **1/2 2009 (PG-13)** Documentary was sparked when one of comedian Chris Rock's young daughters asked why she didn't have 'good' hair. Rock then offers diverse interviews from the black community about hair and societal expectations, the lucrative hair care industry (relaxers and weaves included), and visiting the Bronner Bros. International Hair Show, the annual Atlanta-based convention for hair stylists. **95m/C; DVD.** Chris Rock; ***D:*** Jeff Stilson; ***W:*** Chris Rock; Jeff Stilson; Lance Crouther; Chuck Sklar; ***C:*** Cliff Charles; ***M:*** Marcus Miller.

The Good Heart **1/2 2009** Sentimental twaddle worth a look because of Brian Cox's curmudgeonly performance as Skid Row bar owner Jacques. Drinking and smoking himself to death, Jacques decides he needs an heir to take over his bar so he chooses homeless Lucas (Dano) as his protege. Jacques has three rules: no serving walk-ins, no socializing with customers, no women. But when stranded April (Le Besco) shows up, Lucas insists they help her. The two fall in love and Jacques is determined to thwart their romance so Lucas won't leave. **98m/C; DVD.** *IC DK FR* Brian Cox; Paul Dano; Islid Le Besco; ***D:*** Dagur Kari; ***W:*** Dagur Kari; ***C:*** Rasmus Videbaek; ***M:*** Slowblow.

The Good Humor Man **2005 (R)** Coming of age story set in 1976. Under-achieving high school buddies Jay (Stevens) and Mt. Rushmore (Garcia) kill time smoking weed and playing pranks. They and their buddies crash a party where Jay meets Wendy (Robinson) and there's a brawl with some jocks that results in a stabbing. When the boy later dies, suspicions point to Mt. Rushmore as the culprit and Jay tries to stay loyal through a bad situation. **112m/C; DVD.** Jorge Garcia; Cameron Richardson; Jason Segel; Kelsey Grammer; Nathan Stevens; James Ransone; Elise Robertson; ***D:*** Tenney Fairchild; ***W:*** Tenney Fairchild; ***C:*** Scott Henriksen; ***M:*** Robin Trower.

Good Intentions **1/2 2010 (PG-13)** Southern housewife Etta Milford (Hendrix) is just scrapping by since her liquor store-owning hubby Chester (Perry) keeps wasting their money on his crazy inventions. Etta finally decides to get some much-needed dough by disguising herself and robbing some of the local stores (including Chester's). This doesn't exactly work out as intended and the film is almost as inept as Etta's schemes. **85m/C; DVD.** Luke Perry; Gary Grubbs; LeAnn Rimes; Jimmi Simpson; Jon(athan) Gries; Gregory Alan Williams; ***D:*** Jim Issa; ***W:*** Anthony Stephenson; ***C:*** Jordan McMonagle. **VIDEO**

Good Kids **2016 (R)** A coming-of-age comedy about reinvention. When four friends made the best of high school by being "good kids," they did well and were admitted to the college of their choice. After graduation, however, the four realize that they missed out on all the fun aspects of the high school experience. The summer before heading off to college, they decide to redefine themselves and their lives by having all the sexual, alcohol, and other experiences in a few short months. **86m/C; DVD, Streaming, Download.** Zoey Deutch; Nicholas Braun; Mateo Arias; Israel Broussard; Ashley Judd; ***D:*** Chris McCoy; ***W:*** Chris McCoy; ***C:*** Jimmy Lindsey; ***M:*** Lucian Piane.

Good Kill **2015 (R)** What happens to a man who goes to war but never leaves his hometown? This is a question worth asking in the era of drone combat, which allows Major Thomas Egan (Hawke) to sit in a chair and make life-or-death decisions around the world with the click of a button. Sadly, writer/director Niccol seems afraid of the moral and ethical implications involved, resulting in a surprisingly matter-of-fact and even dull film, despite its important subject matter. However the leads – Hawke, Bruce Greenwood, and Zoe Saldana, as colleagues – give solid performances. **102m/C; DVD.** Ethan Hawke; Bruce Greenwood; Jake Abel; Ryan Montano; Dylan Kenin; ***D:*** Andrew Niccol; ***W:*** Andrew Niccol; ***C:*** Amir M. Mokri; ***M:*** Christophe Beck.

The Good Liar **1/2 2019 (R)** In 2009 London, Roy (McKellan) and recent widow Betty (Mirren) meet through a dating website. Though both used fake names online, they quickly became companions. Betty's protective grandson Steven (Torvy) is suspicious of Roy and concerned that his grandmother is being taken advantage of. His fears are true as Roy is a con man and a thief. In this case, however, the situation becomes more complicated because Roy develops real feelings for Betty. An interesting yet rambling story, Mirren and McKellan are exquisite, as usual. **109m/C; DVD, Blu-Ray.** Dame Helen Mirren; Ian McKellen; Russell Tovey; Jim Carter; Mark Lewis Jones; ***D:*** Bill Condon; ***W:*** Jeffrey Hatcher; ***C:*** Tobias A. Schliessler; ***M:*** Carter Burwell.

The Good Lie **1/2 2014 (PG-13)** This heartwarming true story is admittedly manipulative but subtly handled enough to be effective. Director Falardeau wisely doesn't turn his drama into another story about a white woman who saves black people, even with Witherspoon in the role of one of the Americans who helped four of the Lost Boys of Sudan find sanctuary in the United States. Instead it focuses on the actual men, detailing the difficulty in going from one of the most violent, dangerous parts of the world to Middle America. It's a bit forgettable but well-made and acted well-enough to work. **110m/C; DVD, Blu-Ray.** Reese Witherspoon; Ger Duany; Emmanuel Jal; Arnold Oceng; Kuoth Wiel; Corey Stoll; ***D:*** Philippe Falardeau; ***W:*** Margaret Nagle; ***C:*** Ronald Plante; ***M:*** Martin Leon.

The Good Life **1/2 2007 (R)** A misfit in his football-mad Nebraska town, Jason Prayer (Webber) works minimum-wage jobs to support his mom and finds pleasure in helping out his aging friend Gus (Stanton) run his neighborhood cinema and watching old movies. And who walks into the joint? Why Frances (Deschanel), the perfect film noir babe who wouldn't know the truth if it slapped her across the kisser. Jason is instantly smitten and Frances is kind enough to encourage him to get out of town and start a new life, but can Jason really do it? **89m/C; DVD.** Mark Webber; Zooey Deschanel; Harry Dean Stanton; Bill Paxton; Chris Klein; Patrick Fugit; Drea De Matteo; Bruce McGill; Donal Logue; ***D:*** Steve Berra; ***W:*** Steve Berra; ***C:*** Patrice Lucien Cochet; ***M:*** Don Davis; Joel Peterson.

Good Luck **1/2 1996 (R)** Inspirational buddy movie that manages to avoid the worst of sentimental excess. Tony Olezniak (D'Onofrio) is a football player left blind because of a game injury. He's on a downward spiral and winds up in jail, which is where paraplegic Bernard Lemley (Hines), once Tony's tutor, finds him. Bernard wants to enter a rigorous whitewater raft race held on Oregon's Rogue River and he needs Tony's strength to help him do it. The emotional payoff comes as the two bicker and bond. Lots of charm. **95m/C; VHS, DVD.** Vincent D'Onofrio; Gregory Hines; Max Gail; James Earl Jones; Sarah Trigger; Joe Theismann; ***D:*** Richard LaBrie; ***W:*** Bob Comfort; ***C:*** Maximo Munzi; ***M:*** Tim Truman.

Good Luck Chuck **WOOF! 2007 (R)** Charlie Logan (Cook) is a successful dentist whose office is conveniently adjacent to that of his long-time buddy, boob-obsessed plastic surgeon Stu (Fogler). Charlie's requisite fatal flaw is that he carries a curse placed on him during his preteen years by a rebuffed goth girl. As a result every woman he dates dumps him and immediately meets the man of her dreams. So legendary is the curse that heaps of women pursue him to ensure Mr. Right's arrival. When he meets klutzy but sweet beauty Cam (Alba), he faces a double dilemma: what to do with the Mr. Right-seeking bimbos, and how to hang on to Cam in light of the curse. Charlie and Cam are cute, but the gags are crude and the sex scenes are gross. **96m/C; DVD, Blu-Ray.** Dane Cook; Jessica Alba; Dan Fogler; Ellia English; Chelan Simmons; Lonny Ross; ***D:*** Mark Helfrich; ***W:*** Josh Stolberg; ***C:*** Anthony B. Richmond; ***M:*** Aaron Zigman.

A Good Man **2014 (R)** An action crime thriller about a former special ops who is forced to achieve reconciliation with his past. Alexander (Seagal) had an exceptional career in special ops, but its end was less than ideal. Choosing to live a quiet life far from the bustle of the United States, Alexander becomes a handyman for an apartment complex in Romania. He is drawn into a war between local gangs after one of his tenants and her family become oppressed by a local gangster. In the process of defending her family, Alexander also must face his own old foe and tries to gain peace of mind for himself. **100m/C; DVD, Blu-Ray, Streaming, Download.** Steven Seagal; Victor Webster; Iulia Verdes; Tzi Ma; Sofia Nicolaescu; ***D:*** Keoni Waxman; ***W:*** Keoni Waxman; Jason Rainwater; ***C:*** Nathan Wilson; ***M:*** Brian Jackson Harris; Justin Raines; Michael Wickstrom. **VIDEO**

A Good Man in Africa **1994 (R)** Bumbling low-level British diplomat gets caught up in the high-level political turmoil of a newly independent African state. Confusing plot has borderline incompetent blackmailed by corrupt politician into bribing respected doctor for local land rights. Wow, corrupt officials, ineffectual bureaucrats—go figure! Does to the British diplomatic corps what "A Fish Called Wanda" did to England's legal community, without the humor. Performances by Connery, Gossett and Lithgow almost make up for shortcomings in key areas such as writing and direction. Adapted from the novel by William Boyd. **95m/C; VHS, DVD.** Colin Friels; Sean Connery; Louis Gossett, Jr.; John Lithgow; Joanne Whalley; Diana Rigg; ***D:*** Bruce Beresford; ***W:*** William Boyd; ***C:*** Andrzej Bartkowiak.

A Good Marriage *Stephen King's A Good Marriage* **2014 (R)** Bob and Darcy Anderson (LaPaglia and Allen) share 25 years of wedded bliss, but when Bob leaves on a business trip, Darcy begins to find clues that he may not be who he seems. Darcy eventually learns that Bob is the suburban serial killer who's terrorizing the neighborhood and must decide what to do next. Unfortunately, it's a flat thriller even though King adapted his own novella. Despite the terrific performances, the big screen possibilities of this darkly comic domestic nightmare work much better on the page. **102m/C; DVD, Blu-Ray, Streaming.** Joan Allen; Anthony LaPaglia; Stephen Lang; Cara Buono; Kristen Connolly; ***D:*** Peter Askin; ***W:*** Stephen King; ***C:*** Frank DeMarco; ***M:*** Danny Bensi; Saunder Jurriaans.

Good Morning *Ohayo* **1959** One of Ozu's first color efforts, "Good Morning" is a light social comedy revolving around two young Japanese boys who try to talk their parents into buying them one of those newfangled television sets. Not likely, since the Dad feels that the boob tube will dull the senses of the Japanese youth...talk about your ESP. The kids feel that there's too much small talk going on. Ozu keeps the camera at kids' eye-level, emphasizing the sympathetic perspective of the children and giving a unique look to the film. Bold colors populate the screen and Ozu keeps the story whimsical while commenting on Japanese society (very much like Juzo Itami would years later). The characters are well-fleshed out and likable. **94m/C; DVD, Blu-Ray.** *JP* Masahiko Shimazu; Koji Shigaragi; Chishu Ryu; Kuniko Miyake; ***D:*** Yasujiro Ozu; ***W:*** Yasujiro Ozu; Kogo Noda; ***C:*** Yuuharu Atsuta; ***M:*** Toshiro Mayuzumi.

Good Morning, Boys **1937** An art thief hides out at his son's boarding school, which is run by inept headmaster Benjamin Twist (Hay). His lazy, gambling pupils manage to succeed in an academic competition, earning them all a trip to Paris. This happens to be where the thief and his gang plan to steal the Mona Lisa until Twist and the boys accidentally intervene. **78m/B; DVD.** *GB* Will Hay; Graham Moffatt; Martita Hunt; Peter Gawthorne; Mark Daly; Peter Godfrey; Lilli Palmer; Charles Hawtrey; ***D:*** Marcel Varnel; ***W:*** Val Guest; Marriott Edgar; Leslie Arliss; ***C:*** Arthur Crabtree; ***M:*** Louis Levy.

Good Morning, Miss Dove 1/2 **1955** Warmly sentimental adaptation of the Frances Gray Patton novel. Prim, well-respected New England spinster schoolteacher, Miss Dove (Jones), reflects back on her life when she's taken seriously ill. As the townsfolk rally around her, Miss Dove realizes the influence she had on the lives of her students, including Dr. Tom Baker (Stack), whose use of a new procedure could save her life. **107m/C; DVD.** Jennifer Jones; Robert Stack; Marshall Thompson; Chuck Connors; Mary Wickes; Kipp Hamilton; Peggy Knudsen; Jerry Paris; ***D:*** Henry Koster; ***W:*** Eleanore Griffin; ***C:*** Leon Shamroy; ***M:*** Leigh Harline.

Good Morning, Vietnam **1987 (R)** Based on the story of Saigon DJ Adrian Cronauer, although Williams' portrayal is reportedly a bit more extroverted than the personality of Cronauer. Williams spins great comic moments that may have been scripted but likely were not as a man with no history and for whom everything is manic radio material. The character ad-libs, swoops, and swerves, finally accepting adult responsibility. Engaging all the way with an outstanding period soundtrack. **121m/C; VHS, DVD.** Robin Williams; Forest Whitaker; Bruno Kirby; Richard Edson; Robert Wuhl; J.T. Walsh; Noble Willingham; Floyd Vivino; Tung Thanh Tran; Chintara Sukapatana; Richard Portnow; Juney Smith; Cu Ba Nguyen; Dan Stanton; Don Stanton; ***D:*** Barry Levinson; ***W:*** Mitch Markowitz; ***C:*** Peter Sova; ***M:*** Alex North. Golden Globes '88: Actor--Mus./Comedy (Williams).

The Good Mother 1/2 **1988 (R)** A divorced mother works at creating a fulfilling life for herself and her daughter, with an honest education for her daughter about every subject, including sex. But her ex-husband, unsure of how far this education is being taken, fights her for custody of their eight-year-old daughter after allegations of sexual misconduct against the mother's new lover. Based on Sue Miller's bestselling novel. Well acted, weakly edited and scripted. **104m/C; VHS, DVD, Blu-Ray.** Diane Keaton; Liam Neeson; Jason Robards, Jr.; Ralph Bellamy; James Naughton; Teresa Wright; Asia Vieira; Joe Morton; Katey Sagal; Tracy Griffith; Charles Kimbrough; Matt Damon; ***D:*** Leonard Nimoy; ***W:*** Michael Bortman; ***C:*** David Watkin; ***M:*** Elmer Bernstein.

The Good Neighbor **2016** A dramatic crime-thriller about a prank that gets out of control. Playing a trick on a grumpy, loner neighbor without his knowledge, two high school students makes it seem like the neighbor is being haunted by using electronic devices in his home. As the pair keeps watch on the neighbor's every reaction to their manipulations with cameras for weeks, they soon see more than they ever intended about his nature, personality, and traits. **98m/C; DVD, Streaming, Download.** James Caan; Logan Miller; Keir Gilchrist; Laura Innes; Edwin Hodge; ***D:*** Kasra Farahani; ***W:*** Mark Bianculli; Jeff Richard; ***C:*** Alexander Alexandrov; ***M:*** Andrew Hewitt.

Good Neighbor Sam **1964** A married advertising executive (Lemmon) agrees to pose as a friend's husband in order for her to collect a multimillion-dollar inheritance. Complications ensue when his biggest client mistakes the friend for his actual wife and decides they're the perfect couple to promote his wholesome product—milk. **130m/C; VHS, DVD.** Jack Lemmon; Romy Schneider; Dorothy Provine; Mike Connors; Edward G. Robinson; Joyce Jameson; David Swift; Louis Nye; Edward Andrews; Robert Q. Lewis; Anne Seymour; Charles Lane; Peter Hobbs; Tristram Coffin; Neil Hamilton; William Forrest; Bernie Kopell; ***D:*** David Swift; ***W:*** David Swift; James Fritzell; Everett Greenbaum; ***C:*** Burnett Guffey; ***M:*** Frank DeVol.

Good Neighbors **2010 (R)** During the Montreal winter of 1995, waitress and cat lover Louise is obsessed with everything concerning the serial killer victimizing young women in the neighborhood. She shares her theories with wheelchair-bound, widowed apartment neighbor Spencer. Both are suspicious when seemingly mild-mannered schoolteacher Victor moves into their building, as well as their friendship, when he develops a crush on Louise. But all three turn out to be hiding secrets. **99m/C; DVD, Blu-Ray.** *CA* Scott Speedman; Emily Hampshire; Jay Baruchel; Anne-Marie Cadieux; Gary Farmer; Micheline Lanctot; ***D:*** Jacob Tierney; ***W:*** Jacob Tierney; ***C:*** Guy Dufaux.

Good News 1/2 **1947** A vintage Comden-Green musical about the love problems of a college football star, who will flunk out if he doesn't pass his French exams. Revamping of the 1927 Broadway smash features the unlikely sight of Lawford in a song-and-dance role. **92m/C; VHS, DVD.** June Allyson; Peter Lawford; Joan McCracken; Mel Torme; ***D:*** Charles Walters; ***W:*** Betty Comden; ***C:*** Charles E. Schoenbaum; ***M:*** Hugh Martin; Ralph Blane; Roger Edens.

The Good Night 1/2 **2007 (R)** Has-been pop star Gary (Freeman) composes commercial jingles and lives in Manhattan with his nagging girlfriend Dora (Paltrow). But Gary transcends his humdrum existence in his own mind with Anna (Cruz), literally the girl of his dreams—and she's more than happy to cater to his every whim. After a frustrated Dora skips town, Gary hires dream expert Mel (DeVito) to find Anna. Mel delivers model Melodia, who hardly lives up to her dreamy counterpart. Director Jake Paltrow's (yes, Gwyneth's brother) feature debut has some clever moments and film-student charm, but never quite manages to keep the rest of us awake. **93m/C; On Demand.** Martin Freeman; Penelope Cruz; Gwyneth Paltrow; Simon Pegg; Danny DeVito; ***D:*** Jake Paltrow; ***W:*** Jake Paltrow; ***C:*** Giles Nuttgens; ***M:*** Alec Puro.

Good Night, and Good Luck 1/2 **2005 (PG)** Nearly flawless portrayals and script combine with smoky black and white shooting to transport you back to the McCarthy era, where television newsman Edward R. Murrow (Strathairn) faces off with Senator Joseph McCarthy and the House Un-American Activities Committee. Murrow is pressured to back down, but he and CBS staff are intent on exposing McCarthy's fear-based witch-hunt for communist activity. McCarthy plays his own role by way of archival footage; performances by Jeff Daniels and Robert Downey Jr. don't disappoint. A labor of love for George Clooney, he co-wrote and directed, and plays Fred Friendly, Murrow's producer at CBS. Though spare, the dialogue and acting create a scene and mood that, whether you remember the era or not, makes it completely real and utterly believable. **93m/B; DVD, Blu-Ray, UMD, HD-DVD.** *US GB FR JP* David Strathairn; Patricia Clarkson; George Clooney; Jeff Daniels; Robert Downey, Jr.; Frank Langella; Ray Wise; Robert John Burke; Reed Edward Diamond; Tate Donovan; Grant Heslov; Thomas (Tom) McCarthy; Matt Ross; Alex Borstein; Peter Jacobson; Robert Knepper; Dianne Reeves; Rose Abdoo; John David (J.D.) Cullum; Glenn Morshower; ***D:*** George Clooney; ***W:*** George Clooney; Grant Heslov; ***C:*** Robert Elswit. Ind. Spirit '06: Cinematog.; L.A. Film Critics '05: Cinematog.; Natl. Bd. of Review '05: Film.

The Good Old Boys 1/2 **1995** Debuting as both director and co-writer, Jones also stars as aging cowpoke Hewey Calloway. The n'er-do-well Hewey makes a surprise visit to the hardscrabble 1906 Texas farm of brother Walter (Kinney), whose wife Eve (McDormand) is none too happy to see the wanderer. But Walter needs help, the local banker (Brimley) is about to foreclose, and Hewey is also taken with spirited schoolmarm Spring Renfro (Spacek, who also starred with Jones in "Coal-Miner's Daughter"). And even Hewey realizes that the 20th century is going to change his way of life forever. Easy-going drama with a fine cast. **118m/C; DVD.** Tommy Lee Jones; Sissy Spacek; Terry Kinney; Frances McDormand; Wilford Brimley; Sam Shepard; Walter Olkewicz; Matt Damon; Bruce McGill; Park Overall; Richard Jones; ***D:*** Tommy Lee Jones; ***W:*** Tommy Lee Jones; J.T. Allen; ***C:*** Alan Caso; ***M:*** John McEuen.

A Good Old Fashioned Orgy **2011 (R)** A group of friends stuck in their quarter-life crises are bummed that Eric's (Sudeikis) family vacation home at which they've spent years in prolonged adolescence will soon be sold. So he plans the ultimate final bash—an orgy—until he falls for one of its listing agents (Bibb) and questions whether or not to go through with his super-party. It's almost striking how little the film understands about friendship or sex, turning every chance at actual character development into a series of flaccid punchlines—making it hard to care whether these people go through with the titular deed or not. **95m/C; DVD, Blu-Ray.** Jason Sudeikis; Leslie Bibb; Lindsay Sloane; Tyler Labine; Lake Bell; Lucy Punch; Lin Shaye; Will Forte; Don Johnson; Michelle Borth; Nick Kroll; ***D:*** Peter Huyek; Alex Gregory; ***W:*** Peter Huyek; Alex Gregory; ***C:*** John Thomas; ***M:*** Jonathan Sadoff.

Good People 1/2 **2014 (R)** Marcus Sakey's acclaimed novel turns into a disappointingly average crime movie about two people who stumble upon something clearly too good to be true. When the basement apartment owned by married couple Anna (Hudson) and Tom Wright (Franco) is quickly vacated, the pair finds a cache of cash in the empty abode. Should they keep it? Of course, everything good comes with strings attached, and the original owners of the stolen money come looking for it. The plots that work in a crime novel are sometimes implausible in filmmaking, and such is the case here, despite strong work from the leads. **90m/C; DVD, Blu-Ray.** James Franco; Kate Hudson; Tom Wilkinson; Omar Sy; Sam Spruell; Anna Friel; ***D:*** Henrik Ruben Genz; ***W:*** Kelly Masterson; ***C:*** Jorgen Johansson; ***M:*** Neil Davidge.

Good People, Bad Things 1/2 **2008** Architect Danny (Redman) finds his wife Angie (Regis) in bed with another man and goes out and gets drunk. While driving under the influence, he hits and kills a pedestrian and leaves the scene, which was witnessed by Bryan (Lennarson). Soon Bryan is blackmailing Danny to help him in a series of cons and robberies until finally Danny has had enough. **90m/C; DVD.** *CA* Dean Redman; Nels Lennarson; Nadine Wright; Marsha Regis; ***D:*** Patrick Phillips; ***W:*** Patrick Phillips; Myra Mero; ***C:*** David Puff; ***M:*** Neale Ramakrishnan. **VIDEO**

Good Sam **1948** An incurable "Good Samaritan" finds himself in one jam after another as he tries too hard to help people. Lots of missed opportunities for laughs with McCrarey's mediocre direction. **116m/B; DVD, Blu-Ray.** Gary Cooper; Ann Sheridan; Ray Collins; Edmund Lowe; Joan Lorring; Ruth Roman; ***D:*** Leo McCarey; ***W:*** Ken Englund; ***C:*** George Barnes; ***M:*** Robert Emmett Dolan.

The Good Samaritan 1/2 **2012 (R)** Con man Foley (Jackson) did 25 years in prison for murdering his partner and is determined to go straight on his release. But the outside world pulls him back as Foley feels obligated to do right by wannabe hood Ethan (Kirby) whose father he killed. Drug-addicted hooker Iris (Negga) gets involved as Ethan's scheme goes astray, which means Foley has to take charge. Jackson is certainly worth watching although the plot turns out to be familiar. **90m/C; DVD, Blu-Ray.** *CA* Samuel L. Jackson; Luke Kirby; Ruth Negga; Tom Wilkinson; Deborah Kara Unger; Martha Burns; Tom McCamus; ***D:*** David Weaver; ***W:*** David Weaver; Elan Mastai; ***C:*** Francois Dagenais; ***M:*** Todor Kobakov.

The Good Shepherd **2006 (R)** The birth of the CIA was apparently accomplished by a bunch of gray-faced, unassuming men from the same social milieu, who wore dull suits and neglected their private lives for the good of their country. Edward Wilson (Damon) knocks up and then marries senator's daughter Clover (Jolie), but that is about the most human behavior he'll show in decades as he moves from WWII through the Cold War with paranoia as his distinguishing characteristic. De Niro's second directorial effort is a long slog through the spy biz where everyone lies and betrays. If you want to see a spymaster at work, watch Alec Guinness in any of his incarnations as George Smiley; at least he's more human than robotic. **160m/C; DVD, Blu-Ray, HD-DVD.** Matt Damon; Angelina Jolie; Alec Baldwin; Tammy Blanchard; Billy Crudup; Michael Gambon; William Hurt; Timothy Hutton; Keir Dullea; John Turturro; Joe Pesci; Gabriel Macht; Eddie Redmayne; Lee Pace; John Sessions; Robert De Niro; Martina Gedeck; Mark Ivanir; ***D:*** Robert De Niro; ***W:*** Eric Roth; ***C:*** Robert Richardson; ***M:*** Marcelo Zarvos; Bruce Fowler.

The Good Son **1993 (R)** In a grand departure from cute, Culkin tackles evil as a 13-year-old obsessed with death and other unseemly hobbies. During a stay with his uncle, Mark (Wood) watches as his cousin (Culkin) gets creepier and creepier, and tries to alert the family. But will they listen? Nooo'they choose to ignore the little warning signs like the doll hanging by a noose in Culkin's room. And then there's the untimely death of a sibling. Hmmm. Culkin isn't as bad as expected, but doesn't quite get all the way down to bone-chilling terror either. Original star Jesse Bradford was dropped when Papa Culkin threatened to pull Mac off "Home Alone 2" if he wasn't cast in the lead. **87m/C; VHS, DVD, Blu-Ray.** Macaulay Culkin; Elijah Wood; Wendy Crewson; David Morse; Daniel Hugh-Kelly; Quinn Culkin;

D: Joseph Ruben; *W:* Ian McEwan; *C:* John Lindley; *M:* Elmer Bernstein.

The Good Student 1/2 **2008 (R)** The sudden disappearance of a popular teen-aged girl spells trouble for the unpopular high school teacher who was too interested in her. But is the obvious suspect too obvious? **77m/C; DVD.** Hayden Panettiere; Timothy Daly; William Sadler; Sarah Steele; *D:* David Ostry; *W:* Adam Targum. **VIDEO**

The Good, the Bad and the Ugly 1/2 **1967** Leone's grandiloquent, shambling tribute to the American Western. Set during the Civil War, it follows the seemingly endless adventures of three dirtbags in search of a cache of Confederate gold buried in a nameless grave. Violent, exaggerated, beautifully crafted, it is the final and finest installment of the "Dollars" trilogy: a spaghetti Western chef d'oeuvre. **161m/C; VHS, DVD, Blu-Ray.** *IT* Clint Eastwood; Eli Wallach; Lee Van Cleef; Chelo Alonso; Luigi Pistilli; Rada Rassimov; Livio Lorenzon; Mario Brega; *D:* Sergio Leone; *W:* Sergio Leone; Sergio Donati; Furio Scarpelli; Luciano Vincenzoni; Agenore Incrocci; *C:* Tonino Delli Colli; *M:* Ennio Morricone.

The Good, the Bad, the Weird **2008 (R)** A sort of Korean spaghetti western set in 1930s Japanese-occupied Manchuria. Killer Chang-yi (the Bad) is hired to steal a treasure map hidden on a train that's being robbed by bandit Tae-goo (the Weird), who gets the map. Then bounty hunter Do-won (the Good) comes after them both and there are various shoo-touts until the final showdown. Korean with subtitles. **139m/C; DVD.** *NK* Woo-sung Jung; Byung-hun Lee; Kang-ho Song; Seung-su Ryu; Young-chang Song; *D:* Jee-won Kim; *W:* Jee-won Kim; Min-suk Kim; *C:* Mo-gae Lee; *M:* Yeong-gyu Chang.

The Good Thief **2003 (R)** Jordan's stylish remake of Jean-Pierre Melville's "Bob le Flambeur" serves as a showcase for Nolte's magnificent performance. Nolte is Bob, an American inveterate gambler, heroin addict, and master thief whom everyone likes, including the French cop (Karyo) who wants to save him from himself. When Bob loses the last of his money at the track, he's talked into masterminding an art heist at a casino with the usual band of multinational partners. Along the way, he rescues a young waitress from a pimp, taking her under his wing. Jordan provides plenty of atmosphere and noir-heist dialogue, although the plot gets a little tricky and may induce some head-scratching at the end. **109m/C; DVD.** *FR UK IR* Nick Nolte; Tcheky Karyo; Said Taghmaoui; Gerard Darmon; Nutsa Kukhianidze; Emir Kusturica; Marc Lavoine; Mark Polish; Michael Polish; Ouassini Embarek; Ralph Fiennes; Sarah Bridges; *D:* Neil Jordan; *W:* Neil Jordan; *C:* Chris Menges; *M:* Elliot Goldenthal.

Good Time **2017 (R)** This kinetic, stylized exploration of a heist gone bad directed by the Safdie brothers, Ben and Josh, features an impressive performance by the almost unrecognizable Robert Pattinson. Connie Niklas (Pattinson) and his mentally challenged brother Nick (Safdie) rob a bank in New York City together. Though the pair get away with the cash, the situation soon deteriorates, and Nick is arrested for the crime and sent to Rikers Island. Rightfully worried about his brother—who is beaten in jail—Connie does all he can to get Nick out during the course of one long night in New York's underworld. A distinctive indie genre film enhanced by its dark look and electric feel. **101m/C; DVD, Blu-Ray.** Robert Pattinson; Benny Safdie; Taliah Webster; Jennifer Jason Leigh; Barkhad Abdi; *D:* Benny Safdie; Josh Safdie; *W:* Benny Safdie; Josh Safdie; *C:* Sean Price Williams; *M:* Oneohtrix Point Never.

Good Times 1/2 **1967** Pop silliness as Sonny and Cher (playing themselves) are offered a movie deal by an eccentric tycoon (Sanders). Sonny thinks the script is terrible and dreams up various parts that he and Cher could play. Friedkin's directorial debut. **91m/C; VHS, DVD, Blu-Ray.** Cher; Sonny Bono; George Sanders; Norman Alden; Edy Williams; China Lee; Larry Duran; Kelly Thordsen; *D:* William Friedkin; *W:* Tony Barrett; *C:* Robert Wyckoff; *M:* Sonny Bono.

The Good Wife 1/2 *The Umbrella Woman* **1986 (R)** A bored and sexually frustrated wife scandalizes her small Australian town by taking up with the new hotel barman. There's no denying Ward's sexuality, but overall the movie is too predictable. **97m/C; VHS, DVD.** *AU* Rachel Ward; Bryan Brown; Sam Neill; Steven Vidler; Bruce Barry; Jennifer Claire; *D:* Ken Cameron; *W:* Peter Kenna; *C:* James Bartle; *M:* Cameron Allan.

Good Will Hunting 1/2 **1997 (R)** Good, if predictable, first effort from screenwriting actors Damon and Affleck. Troubled, young Will Hunting (Damon) is a janitor at MIT who also happens to be an unsung mathematical genius. This gift is discovered by big-shot Professor Lambeau (Skarsgard), who must vouch for Will with the parole board by giving him weekly math sessions and taking him to a therapist to work on his anger. Naturally, only the equally troubled shrink Sean Maguire (Williams) is willing to help Hunting get beyond his blue-collar roots. But Will resists the help—not sure that he wants to leave his neighborhood and best friends behind. The Damon/Williams scenes are affecting but the southie Boston accents offer an unexpected challenge. **126m/C; VHS, DVD, Blu-Ray.** Matt Damon; Ben Affleck; Robin Williams; Minnie Driver; Stellan Skarsgard; Casey Affleck; Cole Hauser; George Plimpton; Scott Winters; *D:* Gus Van Sant; *W:* Matt Damon; Ben Affleck; *C:* Jean-Yves Escoffier; *M:* Danny Elfman. Oscars '97: Orig. Screenplay, Support. Actor (Williams); Golden Globes '98: Screenplay; Screen Actors Guild '97: Support. Actor (Williams); Broadcast Film Critics '97: Breakthrough Perf. (Damon), Orig. Screenplay.

The Good Witch 1/2 **2008** Cassandra Nightingale (Bell) moves into a small town's haunted mansion, intending to open a shop selling crystals, charms, and other odd paraphernalia. At least odd to the conservative members of the community who are sure Cassie is a witch and want to run her out of town. Of course, since she has a romance going with town sheriff Jake (Potter), he might object to that notion. A Hallmark Channel original movie. **89m/C; DVD.** Catherine Bell; Chris Potter; Catherine Disher; Peter MacNeill; Allan Royal; *D:* Craig Pryce; *W:* Rod C. Spence. **CABLE**

The Good Witch's Charm 1/2 **2012** The 5th film in the Hallmark Channel series. Cassie is now the Mayor of Middleton and she and Jake have a newborn daughter. She plans a family vacation but a series of robberies occur and stepdaughter Lori is accused. To add to Cassie's troubles, a snoopy reporter may unmask her magical abilities. **88m/C; DVD.** Catherine Bell; Chris Potter; Hannah Endicott-Douglas; Geordie Johnson; Matthew Knight; *D:* Craig Pryce; *W:* G. Ross Parker; *C:* John Berrie. **CABLE**

The Good Witch's Family 1/2 **2011** The 4th film in the Hallmark Channel series. Cassie Nightingale is settling into marriage with police chief Jake and as a stepmom to Lori and Brandon. Then her witchy cousin Abigail comes to town and begins to cause trouble just as Cassie is drafted to run for mayor. **88m/C; DVD.** Catherine Bell; Chris Potter; Sarah Power; Matthew Knight; Hannah Endicott-Douglas; *D:* Craig Pryce; *W:* G. Ross Parker; *C:* John Berrie. **CABLE**

The Good Witch's Garden 1/2 **2009** In this Hallmark Channel sequel, Cassie Nightingale is remodeling the Grey House into a B&B in time for Middleton's bicentennial. However, her first guest, Nick Chasen, claims to actually own the property as the heir to the home's original builder. Cassie's boyfriend, police chief Jake Russell, is suspicious and urges Cassie to disprove Chasen's claim before she loses the property. Followed by "The Good Witch's Gift." **86m/C; DVD.** Catherine Bell; Chris Potter; Rob Stewart; Catherine Disher; Peter MacNeill; Matthew Knight; *D:* Craig Pryce; *W:* G. Ross Parker; *C:* John Dyer. **CABLE**

The Good Witch's Gift 1/2 **2010** Sweet Hallmark Channel pic that's the third to follow the romance of Cassandra Nightingale and widowed small-town sheriff Jake Russell. They're rushing to get everything in place for their Christmas Eve wedding but complications abound--Cassie's heirloom wedding ring goes missing, Jake's kids are squabbling, Grandpa O'Hanrahan isn't feeling needed and thinks about moving away, and a robber Jake sent to prison is released and returns to town but does he want to reconnect with his own family or cause trouble for Jake? **88m/C; DVD, Streaming.** Catherine Bell; Chris Potter; Peter MacNeill; James McGowan; Matthew Knight; Hannah Endicott-Douglas; *D:* Craig Pryce; *W:* Rod C. Spence; G. Ross Parker; *C:* John Berrie; *M:* Jack Lenz. **CABLE**

A Good Woman 1/2 **2004 (PG)** Lackluster reworking of Oscar Wilde's 1892 drawing room comedy "Lady Windermere's Fan" that is now set on Italy's Amalfi coast in 1930. Penniless adventuress Mrs. Erlynne (Hunt) sets her apparently greedy eyes on wealthy American newlywed Robert Windermere (Umbers), who's honeymooning with wife Meg (Johansson). Meanwhile, devilish Lord Darlington (Campbell Moore) has designs on the naive bride. But appearances generally deceive. Hunt and Johansson are miscast and can't comfortably manage Wilde's arch bon mots, though the British actors do much better. Pic at least looks very good. **99m/C; DVD.** *US GB IT SP* Helen Hunt; Scarlett Johansson; Mark Umbers; Stephan Campbell Moore; Tom Wilkinson; Milena Vukotic; Roger Hammond; John Standing; Diana Hardcastle; *D:* Mike Barker; *W:* Howard Himelstein; *C:* Ben Seresin; *M:* Richard G. Mitchell.

A Good Year **2006 (PG-13)** Certainly everyone involved had a wonderful time swilling wine and eating foie gras in Provence, but Crowe should be forbidden from taking any role that calls for him to play a Hugh Grant-ish floppy-haired Brit. Max is a London bonds trader who lives life on the fast track. When he unexpectedly inherits his Uncle Max's (Finney) vineyard, he travels down to the property with the intention of selling it quickly. That is until all that wine, not to mention French babe Fanny (Cotillard), start Max thinking he's missing out on life's true pleasures. The setting is really, really pretty. **118m/C; DVD.** Russell Crowe; Albert Finney; Marion Cotillard; Abbie Cornish; Tom Hollander; Freddie Highmore; Kenneth Cranham; Archie Panjabi; Didier Bourdon; Isabelle Candelier; *D:* Ridley Scott; *W:* Marc Klein; *C:* Philippe Le Sourd; *M:* Marc Streitenfeld.

Goodbye Baby 1/2 **2007** Flimsy dramedy find Melissa moving in with her jazz musician brother Robert and his actor boyfriend Miller while she tries to figure out a direction for her life. She gets a job waitressing at a comedy club and starts studying the stage acts before being encouraged to try out her own material. Offstage, Melissa gets involves in a complicated love triangle and confronts a family secret—all of which she works into her act. **87m/C; DVD.** Jerry Adler; Christine Evangelista; Ivan Sandomire; Kane Manera; Kevin Corrigan; Vincent Piazza; Michael Mosley; Alan Ruck; *D:* Daniel Schechter; *W:* Daniel Schechter; *C:* Josh Silfen; *M:* Stephane Wremble.

Goodbye Christopher Robin 1/2 **2017 (PG)** A literary biopic about Winnie-the-Pooh author A.A. Milne. After becoming severely shell shocked during World War I, posh author Alan Milne (Gleeson) can no longer produce the same witty works as before. After his socialite wife Daphne (Robbie) gives birth to their son Christopher (Tilston), the family moves to the country. There, father and son bond in the outdoors with Christopher's stuffed animals. Alan is inspired to create his well-known literary characters, though his success comes with a problematic celebrity. Featuring a sweeping score, the mix of upbeat and darker themes is awkward resulting in something less crowd pleasing than expected. **107m/C; Blu-Ray.** *UK* Domhnall Gleeson; Margot Robbie; Kelly McDonald; Will Tilston; Alex Lawther; *D:* Simon Curtis; *W:* Frank Cottrell Boyce; Simon Vaughan; *C:* Ben Smithard; *M:* Carter Burwell.

Goodbye, Columbus **1969 (PG)** Philip Roth's novel about a young Jewish librarian who has an affair with the spoiled daughter of a nouveau riche family is brought to late-'60s life, and vindicated by superb performances all around. Benjamin and McGraw's first starring roles. **105m/C; VHS, DVD.** Richard Benjamin; Ali MacGraw; Jack Klugman; Nan Martin; Jaclyn Smith; *D:* Larry Peerce; *W:* Arnold Schulman; *C:* Gerald Hirschfeld; *M:* Charles Fox. Writers Guild '68: Adapt. Screenplay.

Goodbye, Dragon Inn *Bu san* **2003** Long on atmosphere and short on plot, this slow-moving drama is centered around a decaying movie palace in Taiwan that appears to have become a gay cruising spot. A Japanese tourist wanders in to get in out of the rain (or maybe for other reasons), the crippled ticket girl decides to finally act on her crush on the film projectionist, and two elderly patrons weep as they watch the feature, King Hu's 1966 epic, "Dragon Inn." Melancholy rules. Chinese with subtitles. **81m/C; VHS, DVD.** Kang-sheng Lee; Tien Miao; Kiyonobu Mitzmura; Shian-chyi Chen; Shih Chun; *D:* Ming-liang Tsai; *W:* Ming-liang Tsai; *C:* Liao Pen-yung.

The Goodbye Girl **1977 (PG)** Neil Simon's story of a former actress, her precocious nine-year-old daughter and the aspiring actor who moves in with them. The daughter serves as catalyst for the other two to fall in love. While Mason's character is fairly unsympathetic, Dreyfuss is great and Simon's dialogue witty. **110m/C; VHS, DVD, Blu-Ray.** Richard Dreyfuss; Marsha Mason; Quinn Cummings; Barbara Rhoades; Marilyn Sokol; *D:* Herbert Ross; *W:* Neil Simon; *M:* Dave Grusin. Oscars '77: Actor (Dreyfuss); British Acad. '78: Actor (Dreyfuss); Golden Globes '78: Actor--Mus./Comedy (Dreyfuss), Actress--Mus./Comedy (Mason), Film--Mus./Comedy, Screenplay; L.A. Film Critics '77: Actor (Dreyfuss).

Goodbye Love 1/2 **1934** Dull comedy about a group of ex-husbands who refuse to pay alimony and end up in jail. **65m/B; VHS, DVD.** Charlie Ruggles; Verree Teasdale; Sidney Blackmer; Mayo Methot; Phyllis Barry; Ray Walker; John Kelly; Hale Grace; Luis Alberni; *D:* Herbert Ross.

Goodbye, Lover **1999 (R)** Sandra (Arquette) and Ben (Johnson) are hot 'n' heavy lovers. Jake (Mulrony) is husband to one and brother to the other. Peggy (Parker) has eyes for Ben and works with Jake. Since this is a contemporary noir comedy, there's plot twists, betrayal, blackmail, murder, a fortune in insurance money, and two cops (DeGeneres and McKinnon) trying to piece it all together. Overshoots comedy and ultimately lands in silly territory, but looks good doing it. Johnson comes out the best, kicking pic up a notch whenever he's on screen. DeGeneres (as the jaded cop) and McKinnon (the wide-eyed newbie) plod through the odd-couple schtick. **104m/C; VHS, DVD.** Don Johnson; Patricia Arquette; Dermot Mulroney; Ellen DeGeneres; Mary-Louise Parker; Ray McKinnon; Alex Rocco; Andre Gregory; John Neville; Nina Siemaszko; David Brisbin; Lisa Eichhorn; George Furth; Barry Newman; Max Perlich; Frances Bay; *D:* Roland Joffé; *W:* Joel Cohen; Alec Sokolow; Ron Peer; *C:* Dante Spinotti; *M:* John Ottman.

Goodbye, Mr. Chips 1/2 **1939** An MGM classic, the sentimental rendering of the James Hilton novel about shy Latin professor Charles Chipping (Donat), who teaches in an English public school, marrying the vivacious Katherine (Garson) only to tragically lose her. He spends the rest of his life devoting himself to his students and becoming a school legend. Multi award-winning soaper featuring Garson's first screen appearance, which was Oscar nominated. Remade in 1969 as a fairly awful musical starring Peter O'Toole. **115m/B; VHS, DVD.** Robert Donat; Greer Garson; Paul Henreid; John Mills; Terence (Terry) Kilburn; *D:* Sam Wood; *W:* R.C. Sherriff; Sidney Franklin; Claudine West; Eric Maschwitz; *C:* Frederick A. (Freddie) Young. Oscars '39: Actor (Donat).

Goodbye, Mr. Chips **1969** Ross debuted as director with this big-budget (but inferior musical re-make) of the classic James Hilton novel about a gentle teacher at an English all-boys private school and the woman who helps him demonstrate his compassion and overcome his shyness. O'Toole, although excellent, is categorically a non-singer, while Clark, a popular singer at the time ("Downtown"), musters very little talent in front of the camera. The plot is altered unnecessarily and updated to the WWII era for little reason; the music is thoroughly forgettable. **151m/C; VHS, DVD.** Peter O'Toole; Petula Clark; Michael Redgrave; George Baker; Sian Phillips; Michael Bryant; Jack Hedley; Elspeth March; Herbert Ross; *D:* Herbert Ross; *C:* Oswald Morris; *M:* Leslie Bricusse; John Williams. Golden Globes '70: Actor--Mus./Comedy (O'Toole); Natl. Bd. of Review '69: Actor (O'Toole); Natl. Soc. Film Critics '69: Support. Actress (Phillips).

Goodbye, Mr. Chips 🦴🦴 1/2 **2002** Teachers don't get more dedicated than Arthur Chipping (Clunes), the Latin master at the cloistered Brookfield boys' boarding school. Shy, gruff, and somewhat eccentric, Chips' life is transformed when he meets unconventional Kathie (Hamilton) and they marry. Her devotion transforms his nature until tragedy strikes. Covers some 50 years from the late 1870s to the 1920s. Based on the novel by James Hilton. **120m/C; VHS, DVD.** *GB* Martin Clunes; Victoria Hamilton; John Wood; Conleth Hill; Patrick Malahide; Christopher Fulford; David Horovitch; *D:* Stuart Orme; *W:* Brian Finch; Frank Delaney; *C:* Martin Fuhrer; *M:* Colin Towns. **TV**

Goodbye My Fancy 🦴🦴 **1951** Congresswoman Agatha Reed (Crawford) accepts an honorary degree from her alma mater despite the fact she was expelled after an escapade with young professor James Merrill (Young), who's now president of the school. She's hoping to re-kindle their old romance but journalist Matt Cole (Lovejoy), another former flame, wants Agatha to marry him. There's also a subplot about Agatha working to bring the school's old-fashioned curriculum into the modern age. Crawford has more chemistry with Young than Lovejoy (whom she overwhelms). Second banana Arden does the wisecracking aide role to perfection. Adapted from the Fay Kanin play; title is taken from a Walt Whitman poem. **107m/B; DVD.** Joan Crawford; Robert Young; Frank Lovejoy; Eve Arden; Janice Rule; Lurene Tuttle; Howard St. John; Ellen Corby; Morgan Farley; *D:* Vincent Sherman; *W:* Ivan Goff; Ben Roberts; *C:* Ted D. McCord; *M:* Ray Heindorf.

Goodbye, My Lady 🦴🦴 **1956** Based on the novel by James Street, this is a tear-jerking film about a young Mississippi farmboy who finds and cares for a special dog that he comes to love but eventually must give up. **95m/B; VHS, DVD.** Brandon de Wilde; Walter Brennan; Sidney Poitier; Phil Harris; Louise Beavers; *D:* William A. Wellman.

Goodbye, Norma Jean 🦴 **1975 (R)** Detailed and sleazy re-creation of Marilyn Monroe's early years in Hollywood. Followed by "Goodnight, Sweet Marilyn." **95m/C; VHS, DVD.** Misty Rowe; Terrence Locke; Patch MacKenzie; *D:* Larry Buchanan; *M:* Joe Beck.

Goodbye Pork Pie 🦴 1/2 **1981 (R)** With the police on their trail, two young men speed on a 1000-mile journey in a small, brand-new, yellow stolen car. Remember: journey of thousand miles always begin in stolen car. **105m/C; VHS, DVD.** *NZ* Tony Barry; Kelly Johnson; *D:* Geoff Murphy; *C:* Alun Bollinger.

Goodbye, Raggedy Ann 🦴🦴 **1971** CBS TV movie. Neurotic actress Brooke's depressed by the failure of both her career asnd personal life and thinks about ending it all. Screenwriter neighbor Harlan tries to talk her out of those suicidal thoughts. **74m/C; DVD.** Mia Farrow; Hal Holbrook; John Colicos; Ed Flanders; Martin Sheen; Walter Koenig; *D:* Fielder Cook; *W:* Jack Sher; *C:* Earl Rath; *M:* Wladimir Selinsky. **TV**

Goodbye Solo 🦴🦴 **2008 (R)** Taciturn codger William makes a deal with Senegalese immigrant cabbie Solo, hiring Solo to take him on a one-way ride to Winston-Salem's nearby Blowing Rock National Park in two weeks time. Realizing the old man plans to commit suicide, the effusive Solo tries to change William's mind by forcibly befriending him—having William meet his family, taking him on jaunts around the city, and trying to get William to talk about his unhappy past while Solo reveals his own hopes for the future. **91m/C; DVD.** Souleymane Sy Savane; Red West; Diana Franco-Galindo; Carmen Leyva; *D:* Ramin Bahrani; *W:* Ramin Bahrani; Bahareh Azimi; *C:* Michael Simmonds.

Goodbye South, Goodbye 🦴🦴 *Nanguo Zaijian, Nanguo* **1996** Restless camera follows equally restless losers through Taiwan's sprawling suburbs. Kao (Kao) and his sidekick Flathead (Giong) are minor gangsters running gambling dens and various scams. A kickback scheme involving corrupt bureaucrats and cops goes awry, Flathead gets beaten, and retaliation is in order. Thin characters tend not to hold a viewer's interest. Taiwanese with subtitles. **116m/C; VHS, DVD.** *JP TW* Jack Kao; Lim Giong; Kuei-ying Hsu; Annie Shizuka Inoh; *D:* Hou Hsiao-hsien; *W:* Tien-wen Chu; *C:* Mark Ping Bin Lee; Hwai-en Chen; *M:* Lim Giong.

Goodbye to All That 🦴🦴 1/2 **2014** Otto Wall (Schneider, getting his first good part in way too long) is thrown back into the vicious dating pool after his wife unexpectedly informs him that she wants a divorce. Otto is not good in the dating pool. MacLachlan's film, which he wrote and directed, is admittedly episodic as it follows Otto's attempts to find love, or at least sex, again, but it has a surprising ease to it. We really get to know Otto and MacLachlan helps his actor to overcome the inherent clichés in a story about a guy trying to get his love life back together. **87m/C; DVD.** Paul Schneider; Melanie Lynskey; Heather Graham; Ashley Hinshaw; Anna Camp; Amy Sedaris; Celia Weston; Audrey P. Scott; *D:* Angus MacLachlan; *W:* Angus MacLachlan; *C:* Corey Walter.

Goodbye to Language 🦴🦴🦴 *Adieu au Langage* **2014** Even in his later years, Godard remains one of the most interesting international auteurs by taking chances, such as playing with 3D in this film, his best in many years. Recapping a Godard film is like trying to fit a square peg into a round hole. It uses a series of images as storytelling--there is a very loose plot about a married woman and a single man as witnessed by a wandering stray dog. But it matters not at all to the success of the film, which challenges viewers' expectations in film and in life. French with subtitles. **70m/C; DVD, Blu-Ray.** *FR* Heloise Godet; Kamel Abdelli; Richard Chevallier; *D:* Jean-Luc Godard; *W:* Jean-Luc Godard; *C:* Fabrice Aragno.

Goodbye World 🦴 1/2 **2014** A terrorist attack causes chaos and a group of former college friends flee the cities to James (Grenier) and Lily's (Bishe) house in the woods. Where everyone proceeds to complain about stuff they did ages ago. **101m/C; DVD, Blu-Ray, Streaming.** Adrian Grenier; Kerry Bishe; Caroline Dhavernas; Ben(jamin) McKenzie; Mark Webber; Gaby Hoffman; *D:* Denis Hennelly; *W:* Denis Hennelly; Sarah Adina Smith; *C:* Jeff Bollman; *M:* Eric D. Johnson. **VIDEO**

Goodfellas 🦴🦴🦴🦴 **1990 (R)** Quintessential picture about "wiseguys," at turns both violent and funny. A young man grows up in the mob, works hard to advance himself through the ranks, and enjoys the life of the rich and violent, oblivious to the horror of which he is a part. Cocaine addiction and many wiseguy missteps ultimately unravel his climb to the top. Excellent performances (particularly Liotta and Pesci, with De Niro pitching in around the corners), with visionary cinematography and careful pacing. Watch for Scorsese's mom as Pesci's mom. Based on the life of Henry Hill, ex-mobster now in the Witness Protection Program. Adapted from the book by Nicholas Pileggi. **146m/C; VHS, DVD, Blu-Ray, HD-DVD.** Robert De Niro; Ray Liotta; Joe Pesci; Paul Sorvino; Lorraine Bracco; Frank Sivero; Mike Starr; Frank Vincent; Samuel L. Jackson; Henny Youngman; Tony Darrow; Chuck Low; Frank DiLeo; Christopher Serrone; Jerry Vale; Illeana Douglas; Debi Mazar; Michael Imperioli; Peter Onorati; Beau Starr; Angela Pietropinto; Joseph (Joe) D'Onofrio; Catherine Scorsese; G. Anthony "Tony" Sirico; Vincent Pastore; *D:* Martin Scorsese; *W:* Nicholas Pileggi; Martin Scorsese; *C:* Michael Ballhaus. Oscars '90: Support. Actor (Pesci); AFI '98: Top 100; British Acad. '90: Adapt. Screenplay, Director (Scorsese), Film; L.A. Film Critics '90: Cinematog., Director (Scorsese), Film, Support. Actor (Pesci), Support. Actress (Bracco); Natl. Bd. of Review '90: Support. Actor (Pesci); Natl. Film Reg. '00; N.Y. Film Critics '90: Actor (De Niro), Director (Scorsese), Film; Natl. Soc. Film Critics '90: Director (Scorsese), Film.

Goodnight for Justice 🦴 1/2 **2011** In this too-familiar Hallmark Channel western, circuit judge John Goodnight (Perry) makes his way to the town of Crooked Stick. Still looking for the man who killed his parents when he was a boy, Goodnight meets his fate while coming up against a crooked landowner. **88m/C; DVD, Blu-Ray.** Luke Perry; Lara Gilchrist; Ron Lea; Winston Rekert; Daryl Shuttleworth; *D:* Jason Priestley; *W:* Neal Dobrofsky; Tippi Dobrofsky; *C:* Danny Nowak; *M:* Graeme Coleman. **CABLE**

Goodnight for Justice: Queen of Hearts 🦴🦴 **2013** In this third Hallmark Channel western, traveling judge and card dealer John Goodnight (Perry) comes to the rescue of Lucy Truffant (Isabelle), the only survivor of a stagecoach attack. John doesn't know that Lucy is a convicted con woman on the run from Cyril Knox (Schroeder), who wants her in jail. Lucy cons John into helping her travel to a gambling riverboat but will he discover her true identity first? **88m/C; DVD, Blu-Ray.** Luke Perry; Katharine Isabelle; Rick Schroder; Ryan Robbins; Kerry James; *D:* Martin Wood; *W:* Neal Dobrofsky; Tippi Dobrofsky; *C:* David Pelletier; *M:* Graeme Coleman. **CABLE**

Goodnight for Justice: The Measure of a Man 🦴 1/2 **2012** In this second Hallmark Channel movie, traveling Circuit Court Judge John Goodnight (Perry) witnesses a bank robbery by the Spradling gang, who have been terrorizing the locals. John's new friend, widow Callie Bluepoint (von Pfetten), reveals a secret to the judge about bandit Will (Bright) leading him to seek the truth behind the crime. **88m/C; DVD, Blu-Ray.** Luke Perry; Stefanie von Pfetten; Cameron Bright; Teach Grant; Eric Keenleyside; *D:* Kristoffer Tabori; *W:* Neal Dobrofsky; Tippi Dobrofsky; *C:* David Pelletier; *M:* Graeme Colman. **CABLE**

Goodnight, Mr. Tom 🦴🦴 1/2 **1999** Tom Oakley (Thaw) is an elderly widower, living reclusively in rural England at the onset of WWII. When abused, nine-year-old Londoner Willie Beech (Robinson) is evacuated to the countryside with a number of other children, he winds up in Tom's care. Naturally, the curmudgeonly old man and the wary young boy develop a strong friendship, which is threatened when Willie's mother unexpectedly turns up. Based on the novel by Michelle Magorian. **90m/C; VHS, DVD.** *GB* John Thaw; Nick Robinson; *D:* Jack Gold; *W:* Brian Finch.

Goodnight Mommy 🦴🦴 1/2 *Ich seh ich seh* **2015 (R)** This Austrian horror film displays enough style to overcome a few storytelling flaws. Also, it's terrifying. Two twin boys (Lukas & Elias Schwarz) roam around a countryside home in the middle of nowhere, when their mother (Wuest) returns from getting plastic surgery. With her heavily bandaged face, and some odd behavior, Lukas & Elias (yes, same names) start to question if the woman in their house is really their mom. Then things get really weird. Be warned that this film has a strange twist and a truly disturbing ending. **100m/C; Blu-Ray, Streaming.** *AT* Susanne Wuest; Lukas Schwarz; Karl Purker; Elias Schwarz; Hans Escher; Elfriede Schatz; *D:* Severin Fiala; Veronika Franz; *W:* Severin Fiala; Veronika Franz; *C:* Martin Gschlacht; *M:* Olga Neuwirth.

The Goods: Live Hard, Sell Hard 🦴 1/2 *The Goods: The Don Ready Story* **2009 (R)** Vulgar clunker of a comedy. Hustling Don Ready (Piven) and his free-lance team are shady used car liquidators hired to save the Temecula franchise of Ben Selleck (Brolin). Ben's import-selling rival Stu Harding (Thicke) is ready to take over Ben's failing business unless Ready can move all the merchandise off the lot over the 4th of July weekend (between drinking, strip clubs, and various sexual situations). **89m/C; On Demand.** Jeremy Piven; Ving Rhames; Tony Hale; David Koechner; Kathryn Hahn; Jordana Spiro; Ken Jeong; Ed Helms; James Brolin; Alan Thicke; Rob Riggle; Charles Napier; *D:* Neal Brennan; *W:* Andy Stock; Rick Stempson; *C:* Daryn Okada; *M:* Lyle Workman.

A Goofy Movie 🦴🦴 1/2 **1994 (G)** The dog finally gets his day. After 63 years of supporting roles, Disney's Goofy stars in his own movie along with his teenage son Max. When it comes to Goofy's attention that his rock music obsessed son is goofing off in school, Goofy decides to spend some quality time with Max via a road trip through the country. Their journey is plagued with mishaps, but through the obstacles, father and son bridge their generational gap and bond in the true Disney sense. A modest animated treat with six new songs that may induce some finger snapping and toe tapping. **78m/C; VHS, DVD.** *V:* Bill Farmer; Jason Marsden; Jim (Jonah) Cummings; Kellie Martin; Rob Paulsen; Wallace Shawn; Florence Stanley; Jo Anne Worley; *D:* Kevin Lima; *W:* Jymn Magon; Brian Pimental; Chris Matheson.

Goon 🦴🦴 1/2 **2012 (R)** Bouncer Doug Glatt (Scott) is a notorious letdown to his talented family. Until a hockey coach sees Doug's potential when he bloodies a player in a fistfight. And before he can say "eh," he's off playing for the Halifax Highlanders, though he can barely skate let alone wield a stick. His hockey-consumed best pal (Baruchel) offers the requisite hockey knowledge and support, and Doug becomes a decent enforcer. Loaded with the expected profanity and hockey-related violence, it all culminates in a foreseeable face-off that gives Doug a chance to make something of himself and his misfit team. **92m/C; DVD.** Seann William Scott; Jay Baruchel; Alison Pill; Liev Schreiber; Eugene Levy; Marc-André Grondin; Kim Coates; Nicholas (Nick) Campbell; Richard Clarkin; *D:* Michael Dowse; *W:* Jay Baruchel; Evan Goldberg; *C:* Bobby Shore; *M:* Ramachandra Borcar.

Goon: Last of the Enforcers 🦴🦴 **2017 (R)** An uninspired sequel to the clever hockey comedy. Aging hockey enforcer Doug Glatt (Scott) is knocked into early retirement by Anders Cain (Russell), an upstart enforcer who wants to impress his team owner father Hyrum (Rennie). Though Doug's wife Eva (Pill) is pregnant with their first child, he cannot stay away from hockey. Discovering an underground hockey fighting club, he convinces former nemesis Ross Rhea (Schreiber) to teach him to be a better fighter. Doug uses what he learns to plot his comeback and challenge Cain. **101m/C; DVD.** Seann William Scott; Alison Pill; Marc-André Grondin; Liev Schreiber; Wyatt Russell; *D:* Jay Baruchel; *W:* Jay Baruchel; Jesse Chabot; *C:* Paul Sarossy; *M:* Trevor Morris.

Goon Movie 🦴🦴 *Down Among the Z-Men; Down Among the Z Men* **1952** The cast of "The Goon Show," Britain's popular radio comedy series, perform some of their best routines in this, their only film appearance. **75m/B; VHS, DVD, Streaming.** Peter Sellers; Spike Milligan; Harry Secombe; Carole Carr; Michael Bentine; *D:* Maclean Rogers; *W:* Charles Francis; Jimmy Grafton; *C:* Geoffrey Faithfull; *M:* Jack Jordan.

The Goonies 🦴🦴 1/2 **1985 (PG)** Two brothers who are about to lose their house conveniently find a treasure map. They pick up a couple of friends and head for the "X." If they can recover the treasure without getting caught by the bad guys, then all will be saved. Steven Spielberg produced this high-energy action fantasy for kids of all ages. **114m/C; VHS, DVD, Blu-Ray, UMD.** Sean Astin; Josh Brolin; Jeff B. Cohen; Corey Feldman; Martha Plimpton; John Matuszak; Robert Davi; Anne Ramsey; Mary Ellen Trainor; Jonathan Ke Quan; Kerri Green; Joe Pantoliano; *D:* Richard Donner; *W:* Chris Columbus; Steven Spielberg; *C:* Nick McLean; *M:* Dave Grusin. Natl. Film Reg. '17.

The Goose and the Gander 🦴🦴 1/2 **1935** Complicated romantic farce finds Georgiana (Francis) discovering that her ex-husband Ralph's (Forbes) second wife Betty (Tobin) is planning a tryst with her would-be lover Robert (Brent). So she arranges an elaborate plot to have the twosome stranded at her home and for Ralph to catch them and realize that his wife is a hussy. Things don't quite go according to plan as fugitive jewel thieves Connie (Dodd) and Lawrence (Eldredge) also get stranded at Georgiana's. **65m/B; DVD.** Kay Francis; George Brent; Genevieve Tobin; Ralph Forbes; Claire Dodd; John Eldredge; Helen Lowell; *D:* Alfred E. Green; *W:* Charles Kenyon; *C:* Sidney Hickox.

Goosebumps 🦴🦴🦴 **2015 (PG)** R.L. Stine's mega-franchise finally gets a movie, and it's a surprisingly successful one that replicate the fun, anything-is-possible tone of the books. A teen boy named Zach (Dylan Minnette) moves to a new town and realizes that his neighbor is R.L. Stine (Jack Black), the famous author of scary children's books. Zach soon discovers that Stine keeps all of the ghosts and monsters about which he writes locked up in his basement. Of course, they accidentally get released and Zach and his friends have to track them down and imprison them again before the world becomes total chaos. It's fun and well-paced. **103m/C; DVD, Blu-Ray.** Jack Black; Dylan Minnette; Odeya Rush; Amy Ryan; Ken Marino; ***D:*** Rob Letterman; ***W:*** Darren Lemke; Scott Alexander; Larry Karaszewski; ***C:*** Javier Aguirresarobe; ***M:*** Danny Elfman.

Goosebumps 2: Haunted Halloween **2018 (PG)** High school senior Sarah (Iseman) agrees to supervise her younger brother Sonny (Taylor) and his best friend Sam (Harris) on Halloween. When the boys work on their re-sale junk business, they find Slappy the dummy (Black) in a locked book. Though Slappy helps the boys with a bully and Sarah with her cheating boyfriend, he decides the family is not enough and causes chaos when he brings to life characters from R.L. Stine books and Halloween decorations. Sarah, Sonny, and Sam try to fix the situation before trick or treating begins. Though the plot is thin, great special effects add to the film's appeal. **90m/C; DVD, Blu-Ray.** Wendi McLendon-Covey; Madison Iseman; Jeremy Ray Taylor; Caleel Harris; Ken Jeong; ***D:*** Ari Sandel; ***W:*** Rob Lieber; ***C:*** Barry Peterson; ***M:*** Dominic Lewis.

Gor **1/2 1988 (PG)** Sword and sorcery: a magic ring sends a meek college professor to "Gor," a faraway world in which survival goes to the fittest and the most brutal. Followed by "Outlaw of Gor." **95m/C; VHS, Streaming.** Urbano Barberini; Rebecca Ferratti; Jack Palance; Paul Smith; Oliver Reed; ***D:*** Fritz Kiersch; ***W:*** R.J. Marx.

Gordon Glass **1/2 2007** Oversized underdog Gordon makes a promise to his dying grandma that he'll finally pursue his dream of an acting career. He moves to L.A. but can only find work as a Hollywood studio security guard. But Gordon's positive attitude, despite his disappointments, has unexpected effects on those around him. **90m/C; DVD.** Omar Benson Miller; Jason Earles; Tamara Taylor; Noel Guglielmi; ***D:*** Omar Benson Miller; ***W:*** Omar Benson Miller; ***C:*** John L. (Ndiaga) Demps, Jr.; ***M:*** Jonny Fairy; Luis Montilla. **VIDEO**

Gordon's War **1973 (R)** When a Vietnam vet returns to his Harlem home, he finds his wife overdosing on the drugs that have infiltrated his neighborhood. He leads a vigilante group in an attempt to clean up the area, which makes for a lot of action; however, there's also an excessive amount of violence. **89m/C; VHS, DVD.** Paul Winfield; Carl Lee; David Downing; Tony King; Grace Jones; ***D:*** Ossie Davis; ***M:*** Angelo Badalamenti.

Gordy **1/2 1995 (G)** Perky talking porker Gordy manages to escape his fate as future bacon and find a couple of equally perky kids—motherless country-song-singing Jinnie Sue (Young) and lonely rich boy Hanky (Roescher), whom the pig manages to save from drowning. Plot scarcely matters and all the 25 piggies who performed as Gordy generally manage to outshine the humans, though country singer Stone (in his film debut) displays an easy charm. **90m/C; VHS, DVD.** Doug Stone; Michael Roescher; Kristy Young; James Donadio; Deborah Hobart; Tom Lester; Ted Manson; ***V:*** Justin Garms; ***D:*** Mark Lewis; ***W:*** Leslie Stevens; ***C:*** Richard Michalak; ***M:*** Tom Bahler.

The Gore-Gore Girls *Blood Orgy* **1972** Splatter horror director Lewis' final film follows a detective's search for a madman who's been mutilating and killing beautiful young bar dancers. **84m/C; VHS, DVD, Blu-Ray.** Amy Farrel; Frank Kress; Hedda Lubin; Henny Youngman; Russ Badger; Nora Alexis; Phil Laurenson; Frank Rice; Jackie Kroeger; Corlee Bew; Emily Mason; Lena Bousman; Ray Sager; ***D:*** Herschell Gordon Lewis; ***W:*** Alan J. Dachman; ***C:*** Alex Ameri.

Gore Vidal's Lincoln **1/2** *Lincoln* **1988** Waterston is a low-key but sympathetic Lincoln, with Moore as his high-strung wife Mary, in this made for TV adaptation of the Vidal best-seller. Follows the couple from their first day in Washington, through the Civil War, family tragedies, up to the day of the President's burial. **190m/C; VHS, DVD.** Sam Waterston; Mary Tyler Moore; John Houseman; Richard Mulligan; John McMartin; Ruby Dee; Cleavon Little; Jeffrey DeMunn; James Gammon; Deborah Adair; Robin Gammell; ***D:*** Lamont Johnson; ***W:*** Ernest Kinoy; ***M:*** Ernest Gold. **TV**

Gorgeous **1/2** *Glass Bottle; Bor Lei Jun* **1999 (PG-13)** Ah Bu (Shu), a young woman from a small Taiwan fishing village, finds a glass bottle with a romantic message inside. An adventurous spirit, she travels to Hong Kong to find the author of the note. Albert (Leung Chui Wai), the missive's writer, turns out to be a gay make-up artist but Ah Bu also meets millionaire businessman, C.N. Chan (Chan), who manages to fall for Ah Bu while battling corporate rival, Yi Lung (Jen). There may be romance amongst the action but Jackie is more than up to the challenge. Cantonese with subtitles. **99m/C; VHS, DVD.** *CH* Jackie Chan; Tony Leung Chiu-Wai; Qi Shu; Hsein-Chi Jen; ***D:*** Vincent Kok; ***W:*** Vincent Kok; ***C:*** Man Po Cheung; ***M:*** Dang-Yi Wong.

The Gorgeous Hussy **1936** Crawford stars in this fictionalized biography of Peggy Eaton, Andrew Jackson's notorious belle, who disgraces herself and those around her. A star-studded cast complete with beautiful costumes isn't enough to save this overly long and dull picture. **102m/B; VHS, DVD.** Joan Crawford; Robert Taylor; Lionel Barrymore; Melvyn Douglas; James Stewart; Franchot Tone; Louis Calhern; Beulah Bondi; Melville Cooper; Sidney Toler; Gene Lockhart; Alison Skipworth; Clara Blandick; Frank Conroy; Charles Trowbridge; ***D:*** Clarence Brown; ***C:*** George J. Folsey.

Gorgo **1/2 1961** An undersea explosion off the coast of Ireland brings to the surface a prehistoric sea monster, which is captured and brought to a London circus. Its irate mother appears looking for her baby, creating havoc in her wake. **76m/C; VHS, DVD, Blu-Ray.** *GB* Bill Travers; William Sylvester; Vincent Winter; Bruce Seton; Christopher Rhodes; ***D:*** Eugene Lourie; ***W:*** Daniel James; Robert L. Richards; ***C:*** Frederick A. (Freddie) Young; ***M:*** Angelo Francesco Lavagnino.

The Gorgon **1964** In pre-WWI Germany, the lovely assistant to a mad brain surgeon moonlights as a snake-haired gorgon, turning men to stone. A professor arrives in the village to investigate, only to become another victim. **83m/C; VHS, DVD, Blu-Ray.** *GB* Peter Cushing; Christopher Lee; Richard Pasco; Barbara Shelley; Michael Goodliffe; Patrick Troughton; Jack Watson; Jeremy Longhurst; Toni Gilpin; Prudence Hyman; ***D:*** Terence Fisher; ***W:*** John Gilling; ***C:*** Michael Reed; ***M:*** James Bernard.

The Gorilla **1939** Bumbling Ritzes are hired to protect a country gentleman receiving threats from a killer. Lugosi portrays the menacing butler. Derived from the play by Ralph Spence. **67m/B; VHS, DVD, Blu-Ray.** Al Ritz; Harry Ritz; Jimmy Ritz; Anita Louise; Patsy Kelly; Lionel Atwill; Bela Lugosi; ***D:*** Allan Dwan.

Gorilla **1956** A rampaging gorilla is sought by the local game warden and a journalist researching the natives. Filmed on location in the Belgian Congo. **79m/B; VHS, DVD, Streaming.** *SW* Gio Petre; Georges Galley; ***D:*** Sven Nykvist; Lar Henrik Ottoson.

Gorillas in the Mist **1988 (PG-13)** The life of Dian Fossey, animal rights activist and world-renowned expert on the African gorilla, from her pioneering contact with mountain gorillas to her murder at the hands of poachers. Weaver is totally appropriate as the increasingly obsessed Fossey, but the character moves away from us, just as we need to see and understand more about her. Excellent special effects. **117m/C; VHS, DVD, Blu-Ray; Open Captioned.** Sigourney Weaver; Bryan Brown; Julie Harris; Iain Cuthbertson; John Omirah Miluwi; Constantin Alexandrov; Waigwa Wachira; ***D:*** Michael Apted; ***W:*** Anna Hamilton Phelan; ***C:*** John Seale; ***M:*** Maurice Jarre. Golden Globes '88: Actress--Drama (Weaver); Golden Globes '89: Score.

Gorky Park **1983 (R)** Adaptation of Martin Cruz Smith's bestseller. Three strange, faceless corpses are found in Moscow's Gorky Park. There are no clues for the Russian police captain investigating the incident. He makes the solution to this crime his personal crusade, and finds himself caught in a web of political intrigue. Excellent police procedure yarn. **127m/C; VHS, DVD, Blu-Ray.** William Hurt; Lee Marvin; Brian Dennehy; Joanna Pacula; ***D:*** Michael Apted; ***W:*** Dennis Potter; ***C:*** Ralf Bode; ***M:*** James Horner.

Gosford Park **2001 (R)** Altman's ensemble take on a British country house murder mystery set in 1932 that showcases both the upstairs and downstairs inhabitants. Actually, the murder is given short shrift in this look at the manners and mores of the snobs and their servants. Sir William McCordle (Gambon), a self-made man, is giving a weekend shooting party whose guests seem mainly to be the grasping relatives of his cold, aristocratic wife, Lady Sylvia (Scott Thomas). He's the murder victim but nobody really seems to care much (he's not a very nice guy). There's even a couple of American interlopers—movie producer Morris Weissman (Balaban) and his "valet" Henry (Phillippe). Keeping who's who straight is confusing and the pacing is sedate but the cinematography is gorgeous and the cast are all-pro. **137m/C; VHS, DVD, Blu-Ray.** *GB* Michael Gambon; Kristin Scott Thomas; Maggie Smith; Dame Helen Mirren; Eileen Atkins; Alan Bates; Bob Balaban; Ryan Phillippe; Kelly Macdonald; Clive Owen; Jeremy Northam; Emily Watson; Richard E. Grant; Charles Dance; Geraldine Somerville; Tom Hollander; James Wilby; Sophie Thompson; Stephen Fry; Ron Webster; Camilla Rutherford; Claudie Blakley; Natasha Wrightman; Jeremy Swift; Teresa Churcher; ***D:*** Robert Altman; ***W:*** Julian Fellowes; ***C:*** Andrew Dunn; ***M:*** Patrick Doyle. Oscars '01: Orig. Screenplay; British Acad. '01: Costume Des., Film; Golden Globes '02: Director (Altman); N.Y. Film Critics '01: Director (Altman), Screenplay, Support. Actress (Mirren); Natl. Soc. Film Critics '01: Director (Altman), Screenplay, Support. Actress (Mirren); Screen Actors Guild '01: Cast, Support. Actress (Mirren); Writers Guild '01: Orig. Screenplay; Broadcast Film Critics '01: Cast.

Gospa **1/2 1994 (PG)** Based on the true story of Father Jozo Zovko (Sheen), who was put on trial for treason by the communist government in Yugoslavia in 1981 when he protected six Croatian children who repeatedly claimed that they saw visions of the Virgin Mary. Somewhat ponderous but well-meaning story that also suffers from a plethora of accents. "Gospa" means "Our Lady" in Croatian. **121m/C; VHS, DVD, Streaming.** Martin Sheen; Michael York; Morgan Fairchild; Frank Finlay; Paul Guilfoyle; ***D:*** Jakov Sedlar; ***W:*** Ivan Aralica; Paul Gronseth; ***C:*** Vjekoslav Vrdoljak; ***M:*** Nona Hendryx.

The Gospel **2005 (PG)** Young pals David and Frank both aspire to be ministers, but a family clash leads David on another path. Fifteen years later, David (Kodjoe) is now a hot pop star who returns to his minister father (Powell) and his father's church, which are both ailing. Not without bumps, romance, and clashes of will, David has to lead the church back to fiscal freedom. Gospel heavy hitters clinch the tunes, and American Idol finalist Tamyra Gray shows up, as well. Simple but effective (even non-preachy) plot and loads of solid gospel music will make fans very happy. **103m/C; DVD, UMD.** Boris Kodjoe; Idris Elba; Clifton Powell; Aloma Wright; Omar Gooding; Keisha Knight Pulliam; Nona Gaye; Michael J. Pagan; Donnie McClurkin; Tamyra Gray; ***D:*** Rob Hardy; ***W:*** Rob Hardy; ***C:*** Matthew MacCarthy; ***M:*** Stanley A. Smith.

The Gospel According to St. Matthew *Il Vangelo Secondo Matteo; L'Evangile Selon Saint-Matthieu* **1964** Perhaps Pasolini's greatest film, retelling the story of Christ in gritty, neo-realistic tones and portraying the man less as a divine presence than as a political revolutionary. The yardstick by which all Jesus-films are to be measured. In Italian with English subtitles or dubbed. **142m/B; VHS, DVD.** *IT* Enrique Irazoqui; Susanna Pasolini; Margherita Caruso; Marcello Morante; Mario Socrate; ***D:*** Pier Paolo Pasolini; ***W:*** Pier Paolo Pasolini; ***C:*** Tonino Delli Colli; ***M:*** Luis Bacalov.

Gospel Hill **2008** The residents of the black neighborhood of Gospel Hill are being forced out of their homes to make way for a golf development. John Malcolm (Glover) feels echoes of 30 years ago when his civil rights activist brother was murdered and racist sheriff Jack Herrod (Bower) let the investigation lapse. Now John's wife Sarah (Basset) decides to start a public protest and she rattles more than one skeleton. **98m/C; DVD.** Danny Glover; Tom Bower; Angela Bassett; Adam Baldwin; Taylor Kitsch; Julia Stiles; Samuel L. Jackson; Giancarlo Esposito; ***D:*** Giancarlo Esposito; ***W:*** Terrell Tannen; Jeff Stacy; Jeffrey Pratt Gordon; ***C:*** David Tumblety; ***M:*** Scott Bomar.

Gospel of Deceit **1/2 2006** Silly story of a repressed preacher's wife giving in to her sexual desires. Emily (Paul) is the dutiful spouse of Ted (McKenzie) who's more interested in his church and a potential expansion into televangelism than in his marriage. When hunky young drifter Luke (Sevier) shows up, he easily seduces Emily but it seems he has an agenda that includes revealing a secret from Emily's past. **90m/C; DVD.** Alexandra Paul; Corey Sevier; J.C. Mckenzie; Zoie Palmer; Jane Spidell; ***D:*** Timothy Bond; ***W:*** John Benjamin Martin; ***C:*** Alwyn Kumst; ***M:*** David Findlay. **CABLE**

The Gospel of John **1/2 2003 (PG-13)** Plodding along in this verbatim telling of the Gospel of John, Saville methodically shows Jesus as he performs miracles and guides his disciples, culminating in the Crucifixion and Resurrection. Plummer strains to add vitality via his narration. **180m/C; VHS, DVD.** Henry Ian Cusick; Stuart Bunce; Daniel Kash; Alan Van Sprang; Lynsey Baxter; Steven Russell; Diana Berriman; Scott Handy; Cedric Smith; ***Nar:*** Christopher Plummer; ***D:*** Philip Saville; ***W:*** John Goldsmith; ***C:*** Miroslaw Baszak; ***M:*** Jeff Danna.

The Gospel of John **2015** This dramatic feature is a word-for-word adaptation of the Gospel of John according to the New International Version of the Bible. In the film, the life of Jesus Christ (Rasalingam) is depicted from the perspective of the apostle John (Zaoui). The film performed in Aramaic by actors and with an English-language narrator (Harewood). **160m/C; DVD, Streaming, Download.** David Harewood; Selva Rasalingam; Mourad Zaoui; El Mahmoudi M'Barek; Abdelilah Wahbi; ***D:*** David Batty; ***C:*** Ben Hodgson; ***M:*** Amory Leader. **VIDEO**

Gossip **1999 (R)** Intriguing premise goes over-the-top. Bored rich boy Derrick (Marsden) share his pad with fellow college students Cathy (Headey) and Travis (Reedus). They all take a class where the prof (Bogosian) rants about the blurring of gossip and news. Then Derrick sees campus ice queen Naomi (Hudson) passed out a party with her jock boyfriend Beau (Jackson). So Derrick persuades his pals that they should all spread a rumor that Naomi did the wild thing with Beau and see how the slander takes on a life of its own. Only what no one anticipates is that Naomi comes to believe she's been raped and Beau gets arrested. **91m/C; DVD, Streaming.** James Marsden; Lena Headey; Norman Reedus; Kate Hudson; Joshua Jackson; Marisa Coughlan; Edward James Olmos; Sharon Lawrence; Eric Bogosian; ***D:*** Davis Guggenheim; ***W:*** Gregory Poirier; Theresa Rebeck; ***C:*** Andrzej Bartkowiak; ***M:*** Graeme Revell. **VIDEO**

Gossip **1/2 2000** Centers on the unexpectedly linked lives of nine actresses who auditioned for the title role in a remake of Queen Christina, a Swedish historical film originally starring film siren Greta Garbo. An American film producer is making a big budget version of the film, and is in search of the perfect Christina. The actresses await the decision in different ways. Rebecca (Endre) spends her fortieth birthday waiting for word, while Alexandra (Reuter) shoots a commercial. Cecilia (Richardson) and Georgina (Froling) make an appearance on a morning talk show, while Git (Roor) meets with her analyst. Not only did the nine audition for the same film, they also have entangling relationships which are explored through their decision-waiting activities. Swedish with subtitles. **126m/C; DVD.** *SW* Stina Ekblad; Marie Richardson; Lena Endre; Gunilla Roor; Helena Bergstrom; Pernilla August; Peter Andersson; Rolf Lassgard; Marika Lagercrantz; Ewa Froling; Harriet Andersson; Margareta Krook; Suzanne Reuter; Mikael Persbrandt; ***D:*** Colin Nutley; ***W:*** Colin Nutley; ***C:*** Jens Fischer; ***M:*** Per Andreasson. **VIDEO**

Gossip *The One That Got Away* **2008** Predictable romantic tale. Joanna (Williams) and her young daughter return to her small hometown after a bitter divorce. She soon learns that her high school sweetheart Scott (Holden-Reid) is married to her new friend Laura (Cadranel). The town gossips' tongues start wagging but Joanna isn't sure she wants to let a second chance at love pass her by. **90m/C; DVD.** Kelli Williams; Kris Holden-Ried; Inga Cadranel; Julia Kennedy; Fiona Carver; Brad Borbridge; Mary Walsh; ***D:*** Stacey Stewart Curtis; ***W:*** Cindy Myers; ***C:*** Russ Goozee; ***M:*** Christopher Dedrick. **CABLE**

Gotcha! 🦴🦴 ½ **1985 (PG-13)** The mock assassination game "Gotcha!" abounds on the college campus and sophomore Edwards is one of the best. What he doesn't know is that his "assassination" skills are about to take on new meaning when he meets up with a female Czech graduate student who is really an international spy. **97m/C; VHS, DVD.** Anthony Edwards; Linda Fiorentino; Alex Rocco; Jsu Garcia; Marla Adams; Klaus Lowitsch; Christopher Rydell; ***D:*** Jeff Kanew; ***W:*** Dan Gordon; ***M:*** Bill Conti.

Gotham 🦴🦴🦴 **1988** A wealthy financier hires private-eye Jones to track down beautiful wife Madsen. It seems that she keeps dunning her husband for money. Sounds easy enough to Jones until he learns that she has been dead for some time. Mystery ventures into the afterlife and back as it twists its way to its surprise ending. Intriguing throwback to '40s detective flicks. **100m/C; VHS, DVD.** Tommy Lee Jones; Virginia Madsen; Colin Bruce; Kevin Jarre; Denise Stephenson; Frederic Forrest; ***D:*** Lloyd Fonvielle; ***C:*** Michael Chapman; ***M:*** George S. Clinton. **TV**

Gothic 🦴🦴🦴 **1987 (R)** Mary Shelley (Richardson), Lord Byron (Byrne), Percy Bysshe Shelley (Sands), Claire Clairmont (Cyr), and Dr. John Polidori (Spall) spend the night of June 16, 1816 in a Swiss villa telling each other ghost stories and experimenting with laudanum and sexual partner combinations. The dreams and realizations of the night will color their lives ever after. Interesting premise, well-carried out, although burdened by director Russell's typical excesses. **87m/C; VHS, DVD, Blu-Ray.** Julian Sands; Gabriel Byrne; Timothy Spall; Natasha Richardson; Myriam Cyr; ***D:*** Ken Russell; ***W:*** Stephen Volk; ***C:*** Mike Southon; ***M:*** Thomas Dolby.

Gothika 🦴 ½ **2003 (R)** Prison psychiatrist Dr. Miranda Grey (Berry) veers off the road after seeing an apparition and wakes up three days later in her own mental ward accused of killing her husband (Dutton). Flimsy plot is further hampered by the film's indecision as to whether to be a ghost story or woman-wrongfully-accused yarn. The most perplexing part is trying to figure out why such good actors agreed to be in it. **95m/C; VHS, DVD, Blu-Ray, HD-DVD.** Halle Berry; Robert Downey, Jr.; Charles S. Dutton; Penelope Cruz; John Carroll Lynch; Bernard Hill; Dorian Harewood; Bronwen Mantel; Kathleen Mackey; ***D:*** Mathieu Kassovitz; ***W:*** Sebastian Gutierrez; ***C:*** Matthew Libatique; ***M:*** John Ottman.

Gotti 🦴🦴 ½ **1996 (R)** Follows the career of the New York mobster known as the "Teflon Don." Gotti's (Assante) mentor is Neil Dellacroce (Quinn), underboss to the aging head of the Gambino crime family. When Gambino (Lawrence) dies, Gotti is incensed that Paul Castellano (Sarafian) is named as family successor and eventually has him killed. He then grabs power (and lots of tabloid headlines), manages to beat his first federal racketeering rap, but is brought down with the aid of his own underboss, Sammy the Bull (Forsythe), whom the feds get into court. **118m/C; VHS, DVD.** Armand Assante; William Forsythe; Anthony Quinn; Richard Sarafian; Vincent Pastore; Robert Miranda; Frank Vincent; Marc Lawrence; Al Waxman; Alberta Watson; Silvio Oliviero; Nigel Bennett; Dominic Chianese; G. Anthony "Tony" Sirico; Scott Cohen; Raymond Serra; ***D:*** Robert Harmon; ***W:*** Steve Shagan; ***C:*** Alar Kivilo; ***M:*** Mark Isham. **CABLE**

Gotti 🦴 ½ **2018 (R)** A detailed biopic about New York City crime boss John Gotti (Travolta), based on a memoir written by Gotti's son. Gotti's father, a mob boss himself, introduces his son to the rules of mob life, including fighting the government at all costs, and never taking a plea. Over the years, Gotti moves from soldier to leader, beating most charges against him while carefully using his power. Gotti's relationships with his wife Victoria (Preston), son John Jr. (Lofranco), and daughter Angel (Trovillion) are also explored. Poorly directed and organized with cliched dialogue, it's all-around underwhelming. **112m/C; DVD, Blu-Ray.** *CA US* John Travolta; Spencer Lofranco; Pruitt Taylor Vince; Stacy Keach; William DeMeo; Kelly Preston; ***D:*** Kevin Connolly; ***W:*** Lem Dobbs; Leo Rossi; ***C:*** Michael Barrett; ***M:*** Jacob Bunton; Armando Christian Perez; Jorge Gomez.

The Governess 🦴🦴 ½ **1998 (R)** Rosina da Silva (Driver) is a young Jewish woman living in 1840s London. After her doting father dies, she changes her name to Mary Blackchurch in order to pass herself off as a Gentile and secure a position as a governess. Rosina then gets a job with the Cavendish family in remote Scotland, with her charges being randy teenager Henry (Rhys Meyers) and spoiled brat Clementina (Hoath). Her free-spirit entrances stodgy father Charles (Wilkinson), whom she aids in his obsession with the new art of photography. Where there's a dark room and chemistry, more than photos are bound to develop; and soon Mr. Cavendish comes up with a fixation of his own. Starts as a depiction of a woman adapting to different surroundings, but ends up like a history of the first girlie photos. In the end, her Jewishness isn't that big of a deal, leaving that portion of the story a dead end. **114m/C; VHS, DVD.** Minnie Driver; Tom Wilkinson; Harriet Walter; Florence Hoath; Jonathan Rhys Meyers; Arlene Cockburn; Emma Bird; Adam Levy; Bruce Meyers; ***D:*** Sandra Goldbacher; ***W:*** Sandra Goldbacher; ***C:*** Ashley Rowe; ***M:*** Ed Shearmur.

Government Agents vs. Phantom Legion 🦴🦴 **1951** Agent Hal Duncan must stop an evil group who is stealing uranium shipments from under the government's nose. Edited from 12 episodes of the original serial on two cassettes. **167m/B; VHS, DVD.** Walter Reed; Mary Ellen Kay; Dick Curtis; John Pickard; ***D:*** Fred Brannon; ***W:*** Ronald Davidson; ***C:*** John L. "Jack" Russell; ***M:*** Stanley Wilson.

Government Girl 🦴 ½ **1943** Detroit auto exec Ed Browne is brought to D.C. to speed up wartime bomber production. He's frustrated by all the bureaucracy and ignores the red tape, which gets him in trouble. Loyal secretary Smokey takes Ed's side when he's up before a senate committee. De Havilland didn't want to do the film, which shows in a lackluster performance, but Nichols' film is weak on many fronts. **94m/B; DVD.** Sonny Tufts; Olivia de Havilland; Anne Shirley; James Dunn; Agnes Moorehead; Harry Davenport; ***D:*** Dudley Nichols; ***W:*** Dudley Nichols; Budd Schulberg; ***C:*** Frank Redman; ***M:*** Leigh Harline.

Goya in Bordeaux 🦴🦴 **1999 (R)** On the eve of his death at age 82 in 1828, Spanish artist Fracisco De Goya Lucientes (Rabal), living in political exile in France, remembers the wild creative days of his youth, particularly his passionate affair with the Duchess of Alba (Verdu), his struggles as a court painter to King Charles of Spain, and the deafness that afflicted him from the age of 46. This is a lavish production, filled with sumptuous sets and costumes. It's also a fairly standard bio-pic that settles back on cliches in the second half. **105m/C; VHS, DVD.** *SP IT* Francisco Rabal; Jose Coronado; Maribel Verdu; Daphne Fernandez; Eulalia Ramon; ***D:*** Carlos Saura; ***W:*** Carlos Saura; ***C:*** Vittorio Storaro; ***M:*** Roque Baños.

Goya's Ghosts 🦴🦴 **2006 (R)** Fictionalized account of the life of Spanish painter Francisco Goya (Skarsgard), who lived and worked during the Inquisition. Straddling the eras of courtiers and modernists, Goya navigates the brutality and religious politics of his time. One of Goya's subjects, Ines Bibatua (Portman), is jailed under suspicion that she is Jewish. He must also take commissions from church officials, giving him a glimpse of the unholy and inhumane treatment handed out by the inquisitor and his minions. A well-crafted costume drama; lovely but light on script. **114m/C; DVD, Blu-Ray.** *SP US* Javier Bardem; Natalie Portman; Stellan Skarsgard; Randy Quaid; Jose Luis Gomez; Michael (Michel) Lonsdale; Blanca Portillo; ***D:*** Milos Forman; ***W:*** Milos Forman; Jean-Claude Carriere; ***C:*** Javier Aguirresarobe; ***M:*** Varham Bauer.

Goyokin 🦴🦴🦴 *Official Gold; Steel Edge of Revenge* **1969** The Shogunate has passed an unfair tax, and a clan on the brink of financial ruin spreads rumors about the local peasants in preparation for stealing the Shogun's gold. Unfortunately the plan requires that they silence any witnesses. One of the clan's samurai (Tatsuya Nakadai) decides to leave and turn Ronin rather than participate. Years later, he realizes that events are about to repeat themselves, and haunted by his guilt he attempts to prevent the massacre. **124m/C; DVD.** *JP* Tatsuya Nakadai; Kinnosuke Nakamura; Tetsuro Tamba; Yoko Tsukasa; Isao Natsuyagi; Koichi Sato; Hisashi Igawa; Susumu Kurobe; Kunie Tanaka; Ruriko Asaoka; Ben Hiura; Shinnosuke Ogata; Shingo Osawa; Tsuyoshi Haraguchi; Kenjiro Hoshino; Hajime Araki; Hiroyoshi Yamaguchi; Tsuyoshi Date; Kujiro Tanaka; ***D:*** Hideo Gosha; ***W:*** Hideo Gosha; Kei Tasaka; ***C:*** Kozo Okazaki; ***M:*** Masaru Sato.

Gozu 🦴 ½ *Gokudo kyofu dai-gekijo* **2003** Japanese freakmeister Miike revisits his yakuza world in this surreal adventure. Yakuza soldier Ozaki's (Aikawa) paranoia is causing trouble for his boss (Ishibashi) who decides he should be discreetly disposed of by newbie Minami (Sone). So Minami drives them into the country and then botches the job. He tries to find Ozaki's missing body and finds instead, well, a lot of really weird stuff. Title refers to a demon with a cow's head and a human body that Minami has nightmares about. You will too. Japanese with subtitles. **129m/C; DVD.** Hideki Sone; Ryo Ishibashi; Sho Aikawa; Kimika Yoshino; Shohei Hino; Keiko Tomita; Harumi Sone; ***D:*** Takashi Miike; ***C:*** Kazunari Tanaka; ***M:*** Koji Endo.

Grace 🦴 ½ **2009 (R)** Killer baby, obsessed mom, overdone horror. Madeline (Ladd) insists on carrying her dead baby to term and is rewarded with the birth of a living daughter who has an appetite for human blood (that also gives a new take on breast-feeding). Baby Grace also happens to attract flies—probably because she smells like dead flesh. Whatever happens, you don't want to threaten this new little family. **85m/C; DVD, Blu-Ray.** Jordan Ladd; Samantha Ferris; Gabrielle Rose; Malcolm Stewart; Serge House; Stephen Park; ***D:*** Paul Soles; ***W:*** Paul Soles; ***C:*** Zoran Popovic; ***M:*** Austin Wintory.

The Grace Card 🦴🦴 ½ **2011 (PG-13)** Effective inspirational drama has some melodramatic moments but is also matter-of-fact about faith and racism. African-American Sam Wright (Higgenbottom) is promoted to sergeant in the Memphis police department, though he worries it will keep him away from his calling as a church pastor. His new white partner, Bill 'Mac' McDonald (Joiner), is both envious and bitter as he struggles with long-standing anger issues that are part prejudice and part self-hatred for a past family tragedy. It takes another tragedy to give the men common ground. **101m/C; DVD.** Louis Gossett, Jr.; Michael Higgenbottom; Michael Joiner; Joy Parmer Moore; Rob Erickson; Dawntoya Thomason; Kiana McDaniel; Cindy Hodge; ***D:*** David Evans; ***W:*** Howard Klausner; ***C:*** John Paul Clark; ***M:*** Brent Rowman.

Grace Is Gone 🦴🦴🦴 **2007 (PG-13)** Stanley (Cusack) must tell his daughters—12-year-old Heidi (O'Keefe) and 8-year-old Dawn (Bednarczyk)?that their soldier mother Grace has been killed in Iraq, but he is too overcome with grief and his own insecurities. Instead, to buy himself time, he takes the girls on a road trip from Minnesota to Florida. Along the way, Stanley must confront his own demons as his daughters get more and more suspicious of that their impromptu vacation. Cusack (who also co-produced) goes against type, playing Stanley as an essential good but weak man. Movie avoids ideology to explore the powerful emotional effect of war on a family. Score was written by Clint Eastwood after he saw the movie at Sundance. **92m/C; DVD, Streaming.** John Cusack; Alessandro Nivola; Dana Gilhooley; Shelan O'Keefe; Grace Bednarczyk; ***D:*** James C. Strouse; ***W:*** James C. Strouse; ***C:*** Jean-Louis Bompoint; ***M:*** Clint Eastwood.

Grace Kelly 🦴🦴 ½ **1983** Glossy made-for-TV bio with Ladd a lovely Grace Kelly and the usual liberties taken with the facts of her life. It takes Grace from her privileged childhood growing up in Philadelphia, especially her relationship with her stern father Jack (Bridges), her movie career, and Grace's meeting and marriage to Prince Rainier of Monaco (McShane). **97m/C; DVD.** Cheryl Ladd; Lloyd Bridges; Diane Ladd; Ian McShane; Alejandro Rey; Marta DuBois; William Schallert; Salome Jens; Christina Applegate; ***D:*** Anthony Page; ***W:*** Cynthia Whitcomb; ***C:*** Woody Omens; ***M:*** John Andrew Tartaglia. **TV**

Grace of Monaco 🦴🦴 **2014** A biographical drama about the life of actress turned real life princess, Grace Kelly, directed by La Vie en Rose filmmaker Olivier Dahan. In 1956, movie star Grace (Kidman) marries Prince Rainier (Roth) of Monaco and sets aside her film career. Six years later, she is stuck in a troubled marriage but acclaimed filmmaker Alfred Hitchcock (Ashton-Griffiths) offers her a role in his next film. While Grace considers the offer, France is threatening to annex Monaco. Grace must chose between a creatively satisfying film role and her important role as the princess of Monaco. **103m/C; DVD, Blu-Ray, Streaming, Download.** Nicole Kidman; Tim Roth; Frank Langella; Paz Vega; Parker Posey; ***D:*** Olivier Dahan; ***W:*** Arash (A.E.) Amel; ***C:*** Eric Gautier; ***M:*** Christopher Gunning.

Grace of My Heart 🦴🦴 ½ **1996 (R)** Edna Buxton (Douglas), from a rich Philadelphia family, wins a song contest and winds up in New York at Manhattan's Brill Building, pop music's '60s song factory, where she's transformed into Denise Waverly and told to write the music—not sing it. She pens a lot of hits, winds up in hippie Malibu, and finally gets the courage to record her own concept album (think Carole King's "Tapestry"). Along the way there's a succession of wrong men and heartbreak before her independent triumph. Douglas does a fine job (her singing's dubbed by Kristen Vigard) but last minute melodrama turns this into typical showbiz kitsch. **116m/C; VHS, DVD.** Illeana Douglas; John Turturro; Matt Dillon; Eric Stoltz; Bruce Davison; Patsy Kensit; Bridget Fonda; Jennifer Leigh Warren; Chris Isaak; ***V:*** Peter Fonda; ***D:*** Allison Anders; ***W:*** Allison Anders; ***C:*** Jean-Yves Escoffier; ***M:*** Larry Klein.

Grace Unplugged 🦴🦴 ½ **2013 (PG)** Faith-based musical drama. Talented 18-year-old Grace has been performing alongside her dad, Johnny, a one-hit wonder who's traded his bad boy past to become the music pastor of their church. When he forbids her to pursue her dream of pop stardom, Grace leaves Alabama for L.A. to work with Johnny's former manager. There, she tries to negotiate singing success while staying true to her values. **95m/C; DVD, Blu-Ray.** Amanda (A.J.) Michalka; Kevin Pollak; James Denton; Michael Welch; Shawnee Smith; ***D:*** Brad J. Silverman; ***W:*** Brad J. Silverman; ***C:*** Stash Slionski; ***M:*** Jeff Lippencott.

Graceland 🦴🦴 **2012** Engaging thriller than explores complex issues of morality. An employee of a corrupt politician Manuel Chango (Cobarrubias), chauffeur Marlon Villar (Reyes) is driving both his daughter and his boss's daughter home from school when he is ambushed. Though the kidnappers were targeting Chango's daughter, Villar's daughter is taken instead. As Villar tries to save his daughter, he struggles with the desperate kidnappers, the corrupt Chango, and detectives who accuse him of playing a role in the kidnapping. Events soon take a dark turn for the families involved. Tagalog with subtitles. **84m/C; DVD, Blu-Ray, Streaming, Download.** Arnold Reyes; Menggie Cobarrubias; Dido De La Paz; Leon Miguel; Ella Guevara; ***D:*** Ron Morales; ***W:*** Ron Morales; ***C:*** Sung Rae Cho; ***M:*** Adam Schoenberg; Steven Schoenberg.

Gracie 🦴🦴 ½ **2007 (PG-13)** Formulaic sports drama that's still ingratiating. In 1978, the soccer-mad Bowen family suffers a tragedy when varsity star Johnny (Soffer) dies in a car crash. His rebellious 15-year-old sister Gracie (a winning Schroeder) is determined to replace him on the team. Everyone's discouraging, citing the "girls aren't tough enough to play with the boys" and "sexuality of female athletes is suspect" arguments. But Gracie is stubborn as well as talented. Loosely based on a real-life tragedy in the Shue family. **92m/C; DVD.** Carly Schroeder; Elisabeth Shue; Dermot Mulroney; Andrew Shue; Julia Garro; John Doman; Jesse Lee Soffer; Joshua Caras; Christopher Shand; ***D:*** Davis Guggenheim; ***W:*** Karen Janszen; ***C:*** Chris Manley; ***M:*** Mark Isham.

The Gracie Allen Murder Case 🦴 ½ **1939** Gracie tries to outsleuth the sleuth and ends up being no help at all to Philo Vance's murder case. Needless to say this is more comedy than mystery. **78m/B; VHS, DVD.** Gracie Allen; Warren William; Ellen Drew; Kent Taylor; Jed Prouty; Jerome Cowan; ***D:*** Alfred E. Green; ***W:*** Nat Perrin. **VIDEO**

Gracie's Choice ½ **2004** Drug-addicted Rowena (Heche) makes a lot of bad choices for herself and her kids. Broke and in trouble, the family eventually winds up with frail Grandma Lou (Ladd) for a temporary stay. But eldest child, 17-year-old Gracie (Bell), has had enough and decides to petition to become her siblings' legal guardian while she finishes high school and works to support them. Lifetime original TV movie is based on a true story. **90m/C; DVD.** Kristen Bell; Anne Heche; Diane Ladd; Roberta Maxwell; Shedrack Anderson, III; ***D:*** Peter Werner; ***W:*** Joyce Eliason; ***C:*** Neil Roach; ***M:*** Richard (Rick) Marvin. **CABLE**

Gradiva **2006 (R)** Last film for Robbe-Grillet focuses on British art historian John Locke (Wilby) who's doing research on French painter Eugene Delacroix in Morocco. Locke wants to track down a set of previously unknown prints and becomes obsessed with the same sort of erotic fetishes that occupied Delacroix. Locke's memory starts playing tricks after he encounters a mystery blonde (Dombasle) and he becomes implicated in a murder, which may have actually happened 100 years before. Title refers to a ghost or figure of death. French with subtitles. **119m/C; DVD.** *FR* James Wilby; Arielle Dombasle; Dany Verissimo; ***D:*** Alain Robbe-Grillet; Michael Scott; ***W:*** Alain Robbe-Grillet; Bruce Graham; ***C:*** Dominique Colin; ***M:*** Philip Griffin.

The Graduate **1967 (PG)** Famous, influential slice of comic Americana stars Hoffman as Benjamin Braddock, a shy, aimless college graduate who, without any idea of responsibility or ambition, wanders from a sexual liaison with a married woman (the infamous Mrs. Robinson) to pursuit of her engaged daughter. His pursuit of Elaine right to her wedding has become a film classic. Extremely popular and almost solely responsible for establishing both Hoffman and director Nichols. The career advice given to Benjamin, "plastics," became a catchword for the era. Watch for Dreyfuss in the Berkeley rooming house, Farrell in the hotel lobby, and screenwriter Henry as the desk clerk. Based on the novel by Charles Webb. **106m/C; VHS, DVD, Blu-Ray.** Dustin Hoffman; Anne Bancroft; Katharine Ross; Murray Hamilton; Brian Avery; Marion Lorne; Alice Ghostley; William Daniels; Elizabeth Wilson; Norman Fell; Buck Henry; Richard Dreyfuss; Mike Farrell; ***D:*** Mike Nichols; ***W:*** Buck Henry; Calder Willingham; ***C:*** Robert L. Surtees; ***M:*** Paul Simon; Art Garfunkel; Dave Grusin. Oscars '67: Director (Nichols); AFI '98: Top 100; British Acad. '68: Director (Nichols), Film, Screenplay; Directors Guild '67: Director (Nichols); Golden Globes '68: Actress--Mus./Comedy (Bancroft), Director (Nichols), Film--Mus./Comedy; Natl. Film Reg. '96; N.Y. Film Critics '67: Director (Nichols), Director (Nichols).

Graduation **2007** High school senior Carl (Marquette) needs a lot of dough to pay for his mother's cancer treatment, which her insurance won't cover. Polly (Lucio) is angry that her banker dad (Arkin) is having an affair so she suggests a heist of old cash that's about to be destroyed. Along with friends Tom (Lowell) and Chauncey (Smith), they plan the robbery for graduation day. Naturally the heist goes wrong, the cops surround the bank, and the story flashes back two weeks to how the whole mess got started. **82m/C; DVD.** Christopher Marquette; Shannon Lucio; Riley Smith; Adam Arkin; Chris Lowell; Glynnis O'Connor; ***D:*** Michael Mayer; ***W:*** Michael Mayer; D. Cory Turner; ***C:*** Matthew Uhry; ***M:*** Brian Ralston. **VIDEO**

Graduation ½ *Bacalaureat* **2017 (R)** A powerful drama examining the lengths a decent, honest father will go to for the sake of his daughter's future. Romeo, a doctor in Romania, wants teenaged Eliza to put down roots outside of their corrupt homeland. Her chances of doing so are severely comprised when she's attacked on the night before her exams for a scholarship to a prestigious British university. Romeo can fix the situation, but must contemplate the moral quandary of doing so. Winner of the Best Director prize at Cannes. **128m/C; DVD, Beta.** Adrian Titieni; Maria Dragus; Lia Bugnar; Malina Manovici; Vlad Ivanov; ***D:*** Cristian Mungiu; ***W:*** Cristian Mungiu; ***C:*** Tudor Vladimir Panduru.

Graduation Day **1981 (R)** Another teen slasher about the systematic murder of members of a high school track team. Notable mainly for brief appearance by Vanna White. **85m/C; VHS, DVD, Blu-Ray.** Christopher George; Patch MacKenzie; E. Danny Murphy; Vanna White; ***D:*** Herb Freed.

The Graffiti Artist ½ **2004** Street artist Nick is used to a lonely existence until he befriends fellow artisan Jesse. Romance seems to be in the air for the men when Jesse makes a quick exit, leaving a crushed Nick to scour the city for him. **79m/C; VHS, DVD.** Ruben Bansie-Snellman; Pepper Fajans; ***D:*** James Bolton; ***W:*** James Bolton; ***C:*** Sarah Levy; ***M:*** Kid Loco. **VIDEO**

Graffiti Bridge ½ **1990 (PG-13)** Prince preaches love instead of sex and the result is boring. The Lavender One is a Minneapolis nightclub owner who battles with Day over the love of a beautiful woman. Chauvinistic attitudes toward women abound, but the females in the film don't seem to mind. Which must mean they were "acting." Visually interesting, although not as experimental as "Purple Rain." Music made Top Ten. **90m/C; VHS, DVD, Blu-Ray.** Prince; Morris Day; Jerome Benton; Jill Jones; Mavis Staples; George Clinton; Ingrid Chavez; ***D:*** Prince; ***W:*** Prince; ***C:*** Bill Butler.

Grambling's White Tiger ½ **1981** The true story of Jim Gregory, the first white man to play on Grambling College's all-black football team. Jenner's a little too old, but Belafonte, in his TV acting debut, is fine as legendary coach Eddie Robinson. Based on book by Bruce Behrenberg. **98m/C; VHS, DVD.** Bruce Jenner; Harry Belafonte; LeVar Burton; Ray Vitte; Byron Stewart; ***D:*** Georg Stanford Brown; ***M:*** John D'Andrea. **TV**

Gran Torino **2008 (R)** After his wife dies, Korean War vet and retired autoworker Walt Kowalski (Eastwood) digs in his heels at his working-class Detroit neighborhood, where he is in the minority among the Hmong immigrants. He catches Thao (Vang) of the Hmong family next door trying to steal his cherished 1972 Grand Torino'a car he built while working the line—after pressure from gang members. Thao's teenage sister Sue (Ahney Her) offers Thao's services to make amends even though both are uncomfortable about it. Walt is drawn to his neighbors and becomes their defender despite his prejudices. Solid effort gives Eastwood another chance to show his directorial chops and, in perhaps his last appearance, gives him another memorable character to explore. **116m/C; Blu-Ray, On Demand.** Clint Eastwood; Brian Haley; Brian Howe; Dreama Walker; Geraldine Hughes; John Carroll Lynch; Christopher Carley; Bee Vang; Ahney Her; ***D:*** Clint Eastwood; ***W:*** Nick Schenk; ***C:*** Tom Stern; ***M:*** Kyle Eastwood; Michael Stevens.

The Grand Budapest Hotel **2014 (R)** There's an air of Marx Brothers absurdity to Anderson's comic adventure that's set in a fake mittel-European country in the aforementioned hotel during the 1930s. Told in flashback as the hotel's current owner (Abraham) relives his youth as a lobby boy (Revolori) mentored by concierge Gustave (Fiennes), who is so accommodating that he habitually seduces the very elderly female guests. One such eccentric, Madame D (Swinton), dies and leaves him a very valuable painting her greedy son (Brody) is determined to reclaim. This results in imprisonment, escapes, and chases. Fiennes' character is a sincere scoundrel while celebrity cameos abound. **99m/C; DVD, Blu-Ray.** *US GE* Ralph Fiennes; Tony Revolori; F. Murray Abraham; Saoirse Ronan; Jude Law; Tom Wilkinson; Adrien Brody; Willem Dafoe; Tilda Swinton; Edward Norton; Harvey Keitel; Mathieu Amalric; Jeff Goldblum; ***Cameo(s):*** Bill Murray; Owen Wilson; Bob Balaban; Jason Schwartzman; Fisher Stevens; ***D:*** Wes Anderson; ***W:*** Wes Anderson; ***C:*** Robert Yeoman; ***M:*** Alexandre Desplat. Oscars '14: Costume Des., Makeup, Orig. Score, Production Design; British Acad. '14: Costume Des., Makeup, Orig. Score, Orig. Screenplay, Production Design; Golden Globes '15: Film--Mus./Comedy; Writers Guild '15: Orig. Screenplay.

Grand Canyon **1991 (R)** Diverse group of characters is thrown together through chance encounters while coping with urban chaos in L.A. The main focus is the growing friendship between an immigration lawyer (Kline) and a tow-truck driver (Glover) who meet when Kline's car breaks down in a crime-ridden neighborhood. First-rate performances by the cast make up for numerous moral messages thrown at viewers with the subtlety of a brick. Sometimes funny, sometimes preachy became more relevant in light of the violence that exploded in L.A. during the summer of '92. **134m/C; VHS, DVD.** Danny Glover; Kevin Kline; Steve Martin; Mary McDonnell; Mary-Louise Parker; Alfre Woodard; Jeremy Sisto; Tina Lifford; Patrick Malone; Mary Ellen Trainor; Randle Mell; Sarah Trigger; K. Todd Freeman; Jack Kehler; Marley Shelton; ***D:*** Lawrence Kasdan; ***W:*** Lawrence Kasdan; Meg Kasdan; ***C:*** Owen Roizman; ***M:*** James Newton Howard.

Grand Canyon Trail ½ **1948** Our hero is the owner of a played-out silver mine who is the target of an unscrupulous engineer who thinks there's silver to be found if you know where to look. The first appearance of the Riders of the Purple Sage, who replaced the Sons of the Pioneers. **68m/B; VHS, DVD.** Roy Rogers; Andy Devine; Charles Coleman; Jane Frazee; Robert "Bob" Livingston; ***D:*** William Witney.

Grand Central Murder ½ **1942** Cocky private eye Rocky Custer (Heflin) becomes a suspect after actress Mida King (Dane) is murdered in a private train car in Grand Central Station. He must now race to solve the case before he's booked for the deed. Heflin shines in this mystery though unfolding the intricate plot comes at the cost of some character development. Director Simon captures the atmosphere of the famous train station well considering that it was not filmed on location. **72m/B; DVD.** Van Heflin; Patricia Dane; Cecilia Parker; Virginia Grey; Samuel S. Hinds; ***D:*** S. Sylvan Simon; ***W:*** Sue MacVeigh; Peter Ruric; ***C:*** George J. Folsey; ***M:*** David Snell.

The Grand Duel **1973** More spaghetti thrills as Lee plays a mysterious gunman who also acts as protector of a young ruffian falsely accused of murder. **98m/C; VHS, DVD, Blu-Ray.** *IT* Lee Van Cleef; Peter O'Brien; Jess Hahn; Horst Frank; ***D:*** Giancarlo Santi; ***W:*** Ernesto Gastaldi; ***C:*** Mario Vulpiani; ***M:*** Luis Bacalov.

Grand Hotel ½ **1932** A star-filled cast is brought together by unusual circumstances at Berlin's Grand Hotel and their lives become hopelessly intertwined over a 24 hour period. Adapted (and given the red-carpet treatment) from a Vicki Baum novel; notable mostly for Garbo's world-weary ballerina. Time has taken its toll on the concept and treatment, but still an interesting star vehicle. **112m/B; VHS, DVD, Blu-Ray.** Greta Garbo; John Barrymore; Joan Crawford; Lewis Stone; Wallace Beery; Jean Hersholt; Lionel Barrymore; ***D:*** Edmund Goulding; ***C:*** William H. Daniels. Oscars '32: Film; Natl. Film Reg. '07.

Grand Illusion *La Grande Illusion* **1937** Unshakably classic anti-war film by Renoir, in which French prisoners of war attempt to escape from their German captors during WWI. An indictment of the way Old World, aristocratic nobility was brought to modern bloodshed in the Great War. Renoir's optimism remains relentless, but was easier to believe in before WWII. In French, with English subtitles. **111m/B; VHS, DVD, Blu-Ray.** *FR* Jean Gabin; Erich von Stroheim; Pierre Fresnay; Marcel Dalio; Julien Carette; Gaston Modot; Jean Daste; Dita Parlo; Georges Peclet; Werner Florian; Sylvain Itkine; Jacques Becker; ***D:*** Jean Renoir; ***W:*** Jean Renoir; Charles Spaak; ***C:*** Christian Matras; ***M:*** Joseph Kosma. N.Y. Film Critics '38: Foreign Film.

Grand Larceny **1992** The daughter of a millionaire/thief has to prove that she can take over the family "business." Lots of action and stunts. **95m/C; VHS, DVD.** Marilu Henner; Omar Sharif; Ian McShane; Louis Jourdan; ***D:*** Jeannot Szwarc.

Grand National Night ½ *Wicked Wife* **1953** Gerald Coates should be basking in the fact that his horse is entered in the Grand National but his drunken wife Babs makes that impossible. When Gerald accidentally kills her, he panics and stuffs her body into the trunk of a stranger's car at the racetrack. Now he has to convince the coppers that he doesn't know anything. **75m/B; DVD.** *GB* Nigel Patrick; Moira Lister; Michael Hordern; Beatrice Campbell; Betty Ann Davies; Noel Purcell; ***D:*** Bob McNaught; ***W:*** Bob McNaught; Val Valentine; ***C:*** Jack Asher; ***M:*** Johnny Greenwood.

Grand Piano ½ **2013 (R)** Something of a potboiler thriller that's lent a certain style by Spanish director Mira. Pianist Tom Selznick (Wood) stopped performing publicly because of crippling stage fright. After five years, he agrees to a Chicago concert, but among the music lovers is a sniper who's left Tom a deadly message. The film turns ludicrous with a villain motivated by greed, a mystery Tom is expected to solve (while continuing to play), and an absurd plot twist. **90m/C; DVD, Blu-Ray.** *SP* Elijah Wood; John Cusack; Kerry Bishe; Tamsin Egerton; Don McManus; Allen Leech; Dee Wallace; Alex Winter; ***D:*** Eugenio Mira; ***W:*** Damien Chazelle; ***C:*** Unax Mendia; ***M:*** Victor Reyes.

Grand Prix **1966** A big-budget look at the world of Grand Prix auto racing, as four top competitors circle the world's most famous racing circuits. Strictly for those who like cars racing round and round; nothing much happens off the track. **161m/C; VHS, DVD, Blu-Ray, HD-DVD.** James Garner; Eva Marie Saint; Yves Montand; Toshiro Mifune; Brian Bedford; ***D:*** John Frankenheimer; ***C:*** Lionel Lindon; ***M:*** Maurice Jarre. Oscars '66: Film Editing, Sound, Sound FX Editing.

The Grand Role *Le Grande Role* **2004** A Hollywood director comes to Paris to film a Yiddish version of Shakespeare's "Merchant of Venice," setting the thespian world all atwitter. After being cast as Shylock, Maurice rushes home to tell his ailing wife of his big break. When the part ends up going to a more famous American actor, Maurice plays the role of his life in order to prolong his wife's happiness as her condition grows worse. In French with unfortunately inadequate subtitles. **90m/C; DVD.** Stephane Freiss; Peter Coyote; Lionel Abelanski; Francois Berleand; Berenice Bejo; ***D:*** Steve Suissa; ***W:*** Daniel Cohen. **VIDEO**

The Grand Seduction ½ **2013 (PG-13)** Predictable, nostalgic comedy is an English-language remake of the French-Canadian film "Seducing Dr. Lewis." A remote Newfoundland fishing village has a chance of hanging on if the residents can convince a new factory to open. But a doctor must be in residence full-time and Dr. Paul Lewis pays for some bad behavior by reluctantly agreeing to stay for a trial period. Then everyone in the community goes to great lengths to make his residency permanent. **113m/C; Streaming.** *CA* Brendan Gleeson; Taylor Kitsch; Liane Balaban; Mary Walsh; Gordon Pinsent; ***D:*** Don McKellar; ***W:*** Ken Scott; Michael Dowse; ***C:*** Douglas Koch; ***M:*** Paul-Etienne Cote.

Grand Slam ½ **1967** Mediocre heist film was a Euro co-production, which allowed for filming in Spain, Rio, Rome, London, and New York with Robinson's role only bookending the flick. Recently retired after teaching in Rio, American James Anders (Robinson) knows when a shipment of diamonds is due to be delivered to a building close to his former school. He contacts Mark (Celi), an old friend turned crime boss, who agrees to set up the heist, but things start going wonky when a new alarm system is installed. A doublecross and a final twist figure into the so-so action. **101m/C; DVD.** Edward G. Robinson; Janet Leigh; Adolfo Celi; Klaus Kinski; Jorge (George) Rigaud; Riccardo Cucciolla; Robert Hoffmann; ***D:*** Guiliano Montaldo; ***W:*** Mino Roli; Marcello Coscia; ***C:*** Antonio Macasoli; ***M:*** Ennio Morricone.

Grand Theft Auto **1977 (PG)** In Howard's initial directorial effort, a young couple elopes to Las Vegas in a Rolls Royce owned by the bride's father. The father, totally against the marriage and angered by the stolen Rolls, offers a reward for their safe return and a cross-country race ensues. **84m/C; VHS, DVD.** Ron Howard; Nancy Morgan; Marion Ross; Barry Cahill; Clint Howard; Elizabeth Rogers; Paul Bartel; Rance Howard; ***D:***

Ron Howard; *W:* Ron Howard; Rance Howard; *C:* Gary Graver; *M:* Peter Ivers.

Grand Theft Parsons 🦴🦴 **2003 (PG-13)** Phil Kaufman (Knoxville), manager of legendary country-rock singer Gram Parsons (Macht), has promised to cremate him at Joshua Tree National Monument. But the two are not together when the singer dies and Kaufman must beat out Parson's father (Forster) and greedy girlfriend (Applegate) to get the body first. He enlists the aid of a vivid hippy (Shannon), and the two abscond with the corpse in a brightly painted hearse. Supposedly based upon Kaufman's real-life story, film plays too hard for obvious laughs. Knoxville, Forster, and Shannon give confident performances, but Applegate is a shrill cartoon. Parsons himself seems to get lost somewhere along the way. Sadly, this isn't much of a memorial to the late great artist. **83m/C; DVD.** *US GB* Johnny Knoxville; Gabriel Macht; Marley Shelton; Christina Applegate; Robert Forster; Michael Shannon; *D:* David Caffrey; *W:* Jeremy Drysdale; *C:* Bob Hayes; *M:* Richard G. Mitchell.

Grand Tour: Disaster in Time 🦴🦴 **1992 (PG-13)** Greenglen is a quiet, small Midwestern town, until it is visited by a sinister group of time-traveling aliens. Daniels plays a widowed innkeeper who must save the town from destruction and save his daughter from being kidnapped by the fiends. **98m/C; VHS, DVD.** Jeff Daniels; Ariana Richards; Emilia Crow; Jim Haynie; Nicholas Guest; Marilyn Lightstone; George Murdock; *D:* David N. Twohy; *W:* David N. Twohy. **CABLE**

The Grandfather 🦴🦴 *El Abuelo* **1998 (PG)** Frail and nearly blind, old Count Albrit (Fernan-Gomez) returns to Spain from Peru, having lost the family's money. While he was away, the Count's only son died and from his belongings, the old man learned that his daughter-in-law was unfaithful and one of his lovely granddaughters is not his flesh-and-blood. He becomes determined to discover who is true heir, while his equally determined daughter-in-law wants to protect her children and what remains of their inheritance. Based on the novel by Benito Perez-Galdos. Spanish with subtitles. **145m/C; VHS, DVD.** *SP* Fernando Fernan-Gomez; Cayetana Guillen Cuervo; Rafael Alonso; Augustin Gonzalez; *D:* Jose Luis Garci; *W:* Jose Luis Garci; Horacio Valcarcel; *C:* R(aul) P. Cubero; *M:* Manuel Balboa.

Grandma 🦴🦴🦴 **2015 (R)** Elle Reid (Tomlin) just broke up with her girlfriend Olivia (Greer), but that isn't the greatest challenge she faces today. That comes when granddaughter Sage (Garner) lands on her doorstep with a bun in the oven, asking her notoriously free-thinking grandma for the money for an abortion. Elle and Sage spend the rest of this one-day film trying to get that money, visiting old acquaintances (Cox) and lovers (an amazing one-scene performance by Sam Elliott). Through it all, Tomlin grounds the piece in something real, refusing to play her character as the stereotype of the aging liberal. **82m/C; DVD, Blu-Ray.** Lily Tomlin; Julia Garner; Marcia Gay Harden; Judy Greer; Laverne Cox; *D:* Paul Weitz; *W:* Paul Weitz; *C:* Tobias Datum; *M:* Joel P. West.

Grandma's Boy 🦴 ½ **2006 (R)** Oh, Mrs. Partridge, how could you?! Slacker pothead Alex (Covert) is a 35-year-old videogame tester who moves in with his dotty grandma, Lilly (Roberts), and her two roommates—space case Bea (Knight) and easy-of-virtue Grace (Jones). Supposedly Alex is grown-up enough to actually have a girlfriend, co-worker Samantha (Cardellini), but this doesn't seem credible. Of course, neither does the flick but what do you expect since it comes from Adam Sandler's production company. Rob Schneider and David Spade cameo. **96m/C; DVD.** Allen Covert; Doris Roberts; Shirley Jones; Shirley Knight; Linda Cardellini; Joel David Moore; Kevin Nealon; Rob Schneider; David Spade; Peter Dante; Nick Swardson; Jonah Hill; Jonathan Loughran; *D:* Nicholaus Goossen; *W:* Allen Covert; Nick Swardson; Barry Wernick; *C:* Mark Irwin; *M:* Waddy Wachtel.

Grandma's House 🦴 *Grandmother's House* **1988 (R)** A brother and sister discover that the house in which they live with their grandmother is chock-full of secrets and strange happenings, including madness, incest, and murder. **90m/C; VHS, DVD, Blu-Ray.** Eric Foster; Kim Valentine; Brinke Stevens; Ida Lee; Len Lesser; *D:* Peter Rader; *W:* Peter C. Jensen; *C:* Peter C. Jensen.

The Grandmaster 🦴🦴 ½ *Yi dai zong shi* **2013 (PG-13)** Mangled in the editing process from "The Chinese Cut" to the American version, director Kar-Wai's kung fu epic keeps the visual power of its auteur even if it loses the plot courtesy of Harvey Weinstein's over-involvement. WKW's years-in-the-making martial arts extravaganza reunites him with regular collaborator Leung as the legendary Ip Man, one of the most important kung fu grandmaster's of the 20th century, in no small part because he ended up teaching Bruce Lee what he knew about the combat form. Ip Man's journey includes a romance with Gong Er (Zhang), the daughter of the grandmaster whom he deposes before their lives are torn apart by war. Mandarin and Japanese with subtitles. **108m/C; DVD, Blu-Ray.** *CH* Tony Leung Chiu-Wai; Zhang Ziyi; Chen "Chang Chen" Chang; Cung Le; Jin Zhang; *D:* Wong Kar-Wai; *W:* Wong Kar-Wai; Xu Haofeng; Zou Jingzhi; *C:* Philippe Le Sourd; *M:* Shigeru Umebayashi.

A Grandpa for Christmas 🦴🦴 ½ **2007** In this Hallmark Channel holiday film, 90-year-old Borgnine is an old-time song-and-dance man who's surprised when his young granddaughter Becca (Goglia) shows up on his doorstep. His long-estranged daughter Marie (Nelson) is in a coma after an accident and Becca needs looking after. Grandpa Bert isn't sure what to do until Becca gets involved in the school holiday show and all those showbiz instincts take over. **85m/C; DVD.** Ernest Borgnine; Katherine Helmond; Jamie Farr; Richard Libertini; Juliette Goglia; Tracy Nelson; *D:* Harvey Frost; *W:* David Alexander; *C:* Brian Shanley; *M:* David Lawrence. **CABLE**

Grandview U.S.A. 🦴🦴 ½ **1984 (R)** A low-key look at low-rent middle America, centering on a foxy local speedway owner and the derby-obsessed boys she attracts. Pre-"Dirty Dancing" choreography from Patrick Swayze and wife Lisa Niemi. **97m/C; VHS, DVD, Blu-Ray.** Jamie Lee Curtis; Patrick Swayze; C. Thomas Howell; M. Emmet Walsh; Troy Donahue; William Windom; Jennifer Jason Leigh; Ramon Bieri; John Cusack; Joan Cusack; Jason Court; *D:* Randal Kleiser; *M:* Thomas Newman.

The Grapes of Death 🦴🦴 *Les raisins de la mort; The Raisins of Death* **1978** Occasionally, director Jean Rollin puts aside making films about nude vampires for something slightly more politic, and this is one of those rare efforts. A young woman travelling France is accosted by a village of lunatics who all seem to have some disease causing them to disintegrate mentally and physically. Turns out the new pesticides her boyfriend has been spraying on the local vineyards make a nice zombie wine. **85m/C; DVD, Blu-Ray.** *FR* Marie-Georges Pascal; Serge Marquand; Felix Marten; Paul Bisciglia; Brigitte Lahaie; *D:* Jean Rollin; *W:* Jean Rollin; Christian Meunier; Jean-Pierre Bouyxou; *C:* Claude Becognee; *M:* Philippe Sissman. **VIDEO**

The Grapes of Wrath 🦴🦴🦴 ½ **1940** John Steinbeck's classic American novel about the Great Depression. We follow the impoverished Joad family as they migrate from the dust bowl of Oklahoma to find work in the orchards of California and as they struggle to maintain at least a little of their dignity and pride. A sentimental but dignified, uncharacteristic Hollywood epic. **129m/B; VHS, DVD, Blu-Ray.** Henry Fonda; Jane Darwell; John Carradine; Charley Grapewin; Zeffie Tilbury; Dorris Bowdon; Russell Simpson; John Qualen; Eddie Quillan; O.Z. Whitehead; Grant Mitchell; *D:* John Ford; *W:* Nunnally Johnson; *C:* Gregg Toland. Oscars '40: Director (Ford), Support. Actress (Darwell); AFI '98: Top 100; Natl. Film Reg. '89; N.Y. Film Critics '40: Director (Ford), Film.

The Grass Harp 🦴🦴 ½ **1995 (PG)** Rather dull retelling (with an excellent cast) of the Truman Capote novella covering the eccentricities of small town Southern life in the '30s and '40s. Teenaged Collin Fenwick (Furlong) is sent to live with his maiden aunts, artistic, impractical Dolly (Laurie) and shrewd, hard businesswoman Verena (Spacek). Charlie Cool's (Matthau) the retired judge who's sweet on Dolly, Morris Ritz (Lemmon) is a shady Chicago entrepreneur with plans for Verena's money, and there are various opinionated townspeople with stories to tell as well. Screen nostalgia directed by Matthau's son Charles. **107m/C; VHS, DVD.** Sissy Spacek; Piper Laurie; Edward Furlong; Walter Matthau; Nell Carter; Jack Lemmon; Mary Steenburgen; Roddy McDowall; Joe Don Baker; Charles Durning; Sean Patrick Flanery; Mia Kirshner; *D:* Charles Matthau; *W:* Stirling Silliphant; *C:* John A. Alonzo; *M:* Patrick Williams.

The Grass Is Greener 🦴🦴 ½ **1961** An American millionaire invades part of an impoverished Earl's mansion and falls in love with the lady of the house. The Earl, who wants to keep his wife, enlists the aid of an old girlfriend in a feeble attempt to make her jealous. The two couples pair off properly in the end. **105m/C; VHS, DVD, Blu-Ray.** Cary Grant; Deborah Kerr; Jean Simmons; Robert Mitchum; *D:* Stanley Donen; *W:* Hugh Williams; *C:* Christopher Challis; *M:* Noel Coward.

The Grasshopper 🦴🦴 **1969** The beautiful Bisset stars as a teenager who hops from man to man with unhappy results. Christine abandons her dull L.A. boyfriend when she meets comic Danny (Monica) who takes her to Vegas where she becomes a showgirl. Christine also meets former football star Tommy (Brown), now a hotel greeter, and they marry but Christine attracts the wrong kind of attention from mobster Dekker (Bieri) and things end badly. Which is how they continue. **95m/C; DVD.** Jacqueline Bisset; Jim Brown; Joseph Cotten; Corbett Monica; Ramon Bieri; Christopher Stone; Ed Flanders; *D:* Jerry Paris; *W:* Jerry Belson; Garry Marshall; *C:* Sam Leavitt; *M:* Billy Goldenberg.

Grave Encounters 2 🦴 ½ **2012** An obsessed film student visits the hospital from the original film intent on proving it was an actual documentary as opposed to just another found footage horror film. **98m/C; DVD, Blu-Ray, Streaming.** *CA US* Richard Harmon; Dylan Playfair; Stephanie Bennett; Howie Lai; Leanne Lapp; *D:* John Poliquin; *W:* The Vicious Brothers; *C:* Tony Mirza; *M:* Quynne Alana Paxa. **VIDEO**

Grave of the Fireflies 🦴🦴🦴 *Hotaru no Haka* **1988** In post-war Japan, in the city of Kobe's train station, a young boy lies dying. A janitor finds a metal canister lying next to the boy and when he opens it ashes fall out. As fireflies gather around, ghostly figures of the boy and his little sister appear, as the story flashes back to the orphaned, homeless Seita and his sister. The two youngsters struggle in the Japanese countryside but find they cannot escape the hardships of war and have no chance for survival. Stunning animated testimony to the human spirit. Based on the novel by Akiyuki Nosaka. In Japanese with English subtitles. **88m/C; VHS, DVD, Blu-Ray.** *JP D:* Isao Takahata; *W:* Isao Takahata.

Grave of the Vampire 🦴 *Seed of Terror* **1972 (R)** A vampire rapes and impregnates a modern-day girl. Twenty years later, their son, who grows up to be a bitter bloodsucker, sets out to find his father and kill him. **95m/C; VHS, DVD, Blu-Ray.** William (Bill) Smith; Michael Pataki; Lyn Peters; Diane Holden; Jay Adler; Kitty Vallacher; Jay Scott; Lieux Dressler; *D:* John Hayes.

Grave Secrets: The Legacy of Hilltop Drive 🦴🦴 **1992** The Williams family finds out their dream house is built on the site of an old graveyard. The spirits are not only restless, they're deadly. Based on a true story. **94m/C; VHS, DVD.** Patty Duke; David Selby; David Soul; Blake Clark; Jonelle Allen; *D:* John D. Patterson.

The Gravedancers 🦴 ½ **2006 (R)** School friends who have reunited at the funeral of one of their classmates get drunk and dance on some graves. The ghosts of the criminals buried in said graves get angry and decide to haunt them. **95m/C; DVD, Blu-Ray, Streaming.** Dominic Purcell; Josie Maran; Clare Kramer; Marcus Thomas; Tcheky Karyo; *D:* Mike Mendez; *W:* Brad Keene; Chris Skinner; *C:* David A. Armstrong; *M:* Joseph Bishara.

The Graves 🦴 **2010 (R)** Snarky and silly first horror feature from comic book creator Pulido has tough Megan Graves and her emotional younger sister Abby on a western road trip to check out kitschy attractions. They end up in an allegedly abandoned Arizona mining town called Skull City that's not really empty since there's a killer around who sacrifices tourists to a soul-devouring demon. **88m/C; DVD, Blu-Ray.** Bill Moseley; Tony Todd; Amanda Wyss; Patti Tindall; Jillian Murray; Clare Grant; Brian Pulido; *D:* Brian Pulido; *W:* Brian Pulido; *C:* Adam Goldfine; *M:* Jim Casella. **VIDEO**

Gravesend 🦴🦴 ½ **1997 (R)** Big cajones, puny budget: mini-Scorsese Stabile delivers the goods. Tracks a night in the life of four delinquent Brooklyn buddies who find themselves with a dead body on their hands. To avoid police involvement, the boys recruit local drug dealer JoJo (Aquilino) to aid in the body's disposal. JoJo demands $500 and a finger from the victim in return. Rest of pic deals with the fellows' quest for the cash and incorporates a deluge of dark humor which, outside of the pat, in your face dialogue and action, is the picture's real draw. Nineteen at the time of shooting, film school dropout's $5,000 auspicious first picture grabbed the attention of such heavyweights as Spielberg (Stabile now has a two picture deal with his Dreamworks SKG) and Oliver Stone. **85m/C; VHS, DVD.** Tony Tucci; Michael Parducci; Tom Malloy; Thomas Brandise; Macky Aquilino; *D:* Salvatore Stabile; *W:* Salvatore Stabile; *C:* Joseph Dell'Olio; *M:* Bill Laswell.

Graveyard of Honor 🦴🦴 ½ *Shin Jingi No Hakaba* **2002** Miike's remake of the 1975 classic follows Rikuo Ishimatsu, a lowly disherwasher, to the height of gang power, after he unknowingly saves the life of a gang leader. Well-executed script delves more deeply into the relationship Rikuo has with his heroin-addicted girlfriend and brings a comedic flair to gangster leader Ishimatsu's character. Japanese with subtitles. **131m/C; DVD.** *JP* Goro Kishitani; Shingo Yamashiro; Narumi Arimori; Ryosuke Miki; *D:* Takashi Miike; *W:* Shigenori Takechi; *C:* Hideo Yamamoto; *M:* Koji Endo.

Graveyard Shift 🦴 ½ **1987 (R)** A New York cabby on the night shift is actually a powerful vampire who uses his fares to build an army of vampires. Not to be confused with the 1990 Stephen King scripted film. Followed by "Understudy: Graveyard Shift II." **89m/C; VHS, DVD.** *IT* Silvio Oliviero; Helen Papas; Cliff Stoker; *D:* Gerard Ciccoritti.

Graveyard Shift 🦴 *Stephen King's Graveyard Shift* **1990 (R)** Just because Stephen King wrote the original story doesn't mean its celluloid incarnation is guaranteed to stand your hair on end; unless that's your response to abject boredom. When a man takes over the night shift at a recently reopened textile mill, he starts to find remnants. . .and they aren't fabric. Seems there's a graveyard in the neighborhood. **89m/C; VHS, DVD.** David Andrews; Kelly Wolf; Stephen Macht; Brad Dourif; Andrew Divoff; *D:* Ralph S. Singleton; *W:* Stephen King; John Esposito; *C:* Peter Stein; *M:* Brian Banks.

Gravity 🦴🦴🦴 ½ **2013 (PG-13)** Few films have produced the sense of wonder and excitement captured by Cuaron's masterful tale of survival in a place in which humans weren't meant to exist--outer space. Bullock stars as an astronaut left adrift after debris from a missile-damaged satellite knocks her and her fellow astronaut (Clooney) off their shuttle. For 90 minutes, audiences are kept on the edge of their seat in ways that other films haven't been able to accomplish. Movies in the modern age have lost some of their power to surprise but this film recaptures it by blending the humanity of a great central performance and a masterful directorial eye. **91m/C; DVD, Blu-Ray.** Sandra Bullock; George Clooney; Ed Harris; *D:* Alfonso Cuarón; *W:* Alfonso Cuarón; Jonas Cuarón; *C:* Emmanuel Lubezki; *M:* Steven Price. Oscars '13: Actress (Bullock), Cinematog., Director (Cuarón), Film Editing, Orig. Score, Sound, Sound FX Editing, Visual FX; British Acad. '13: Cinematog., Director (Cuarón), Orig. Score, Sound, Visual FX; Directors Guild '13: Director (Cuarón); Golden Globes '14: Director (Cuarón).

Gray Lady Down 🦴🦴 **1977 (PG)** A nuclear submarine sinks off the coast of Cape Cod and with their oxygen running out, a risky escape in an experimental diving craft seems to be their only hope. Dull, all-semi-star suspenser. **111m/C; VHS, DVD, Blu-Ray.** Charlton Heston; David Carradine; Stacy Keach; Ned Beatty; Ronny Cox; Christopher Reeve; Michael O'Keefe; Rosemary Forsyth; ***D:*** David Greene.

Gray Matters 🦴🦴 **2006 (PG-13)** Artificial screwball comedy finds loft-sharing siblings Gray (Graham) and Sam (Cavanagh) deciding they're too co-dependent and each needs to find a romantic partner—except they don't realize they'll want the same woman. Sam and beautiful Charlie (Moynahan) meet and are soon planning to elope to Vegas, with Gray as a witness. The gals share a drunken night out and an impulsive kiss (which Charlie doesn't remember) and suddenly the thirty-something Gray realizes she really, really likes girls. Fanciful if awkward debut from writer/director Kramer. **96m/C; DVD.** Heather Graham; Tom Cavanagh; Bridget Moynahan; Alan Cumming; Molly Shannon; Sissy Spacek; Rachel Shelley; ***Cameo(s):*** Gloria Gaynor; ***D:*** Sue Kramer; ***W:*** Sue Kramer; ***C:*** John Bartley; ***M:*** Andrew Hollender.

Grayeagle 🦴🦴 **1977 (PG)** When a frontier trapper's daughter is kidnapped by Cheyenne Indians, he launches a search for her recovery. More style than pace in this Western, but worth a look for fans of Johnson. **104m/C; VHS, DVD, Blu-Ray.** Ben Johnson; Iron Eyes Cody; Lana Wood; Alex Cord; Jack Elam; Paul Fix; Cindy Butler; Charles B. Pierce; ***D:*** Charles B. Pierce; ***W:*** Charles B. Pierce.

Gray's Anatomy 🦴🦴 **1/2 1996** Yet another monologue from Gray, this time about his medical crisis involving a rare eye disease. **80m/C; VHS, DVD, Blu-Ray.** Spalding Gray; ***D:*** Steven Soderbergh.

Grbavica: The Land of My Dreams 🦴🦴 **2006** In postwar Sarajevo, single mother Esma is forced to work as a waitress in a gangster-run club in order to supplement the government aid she needs to raise defiant adolescent daughter Sara. They argue over many things, including the truth about Sara's father, whom she believes died fighting for Bosnia. Title refers to the rundown district, formerly the site of a prison camp, where they live. Bosnian with subtitles. **90m/C; DVD.** *AT BH GE* Mirjana Karanovic; Bogdan Diklic; Luna Mijovic; Leon Lucev; Kenan Catic; ***D:*** Jasmila Zbanic; ***W:*** Jasmila Zbanic; ***C:*** Christine A. Maier; ***M:*** Enes Zlatar.

Grease 🦴🦴🦴 **1978 (PG)** Film version of the hit Broadway musical about summer love. Set in the 1950s, this spirited musical follows a group of high-schoolers throughout their senior year. The story offers a responsible moral: act like a tart and you'll get your guy; but, hey, it's all in fun anyway. Followed by a weak sequel. **110m/C; VHS, DVD, Blu-Ray.** John Travolta; Olivia Newton-John; Jeff Conaway; Stockard Channing; Didi Conn; Eve Arden; Frankie Avalon; Sid Caesar; Dinah Manoff; Joan Blondell; Alice Ghostley; Dody Goodman; Kelly Ward; Michael Tucci; Barry Pearl; Edd Byrnes; Susan Buckner; Lorenzo Lamas; Fannie Flagg; Eddie Deezen; Michael Biehn; ***D:*** Randal Kleiser; ***W:*** Allan Carr; ***C:*** Bill Butler; ***M:*** John Farrar; Barry Gibb.

Grease 2 🦴🦴 **1982 (PG)** Continuing saga of the T-Birds, the Pink Ladies, and young love at Rydell High. Newton-John and Travolta have graduated, leaving Pfeiffer to lead on love-struck book-neb Caulfield. Some okay tunes, though lame story lacks good-humor flair of the original. **115m/C; VHS, DVD, Blu-Ray.** Maxwell Caulfield; Michelle Pfeiffer; Adrian Zmed; Lorna Luft; Didi Conn; Eve Arden; Sid Caesar; Tab Hunter; Christopher McDonald; ***D:*** Patricia Birch; ***M:*** Artie Butler.

Greased Lightning 🦴🦴 **1/2 1977 (PG)** The story of the first black auto racing champion, Wendell Scott, who had to overcome racial prejudice to achieve his success. Slightly better-than-average Pryor comedy vehicle. **95m/C; VHS, DVD.** Richard Pryor; Pam Grier; Beau Bridges; Cleavon Little; Vincent Gardenia; ***D:*** Michael A. Schultz; ***W:*** Leon Capetanos; Melvin Van Peebles; ***M:*** Fred Karlin.

Greaser's Palace 🦴🦴 **1/2** *Zoot Suit Jesus* **1972** Seaweedhead Greaser, owner of the town's saloon, faces his arch-nemesis in this wide-ranging satiric Christ allegory from the director of "Putney Swope." **91m/C; VHS, DVD, Blu-Ray.** Albert Henderson; Allan Arbus; Michael Sullivan; Luana Anders; James Antonio; Ronald Nealy; Larry Moyer; John Paul Hudson; Herve Villechaize; ***D:*** Robert Downey; ***W:*** Robert Downey; ***C:*** Peter Powell; ***M:*** Jack Nitzsche.

The Greasy Strangler 🦴🦴 **2016** There's a brand of extreme horror-comedy that works off awkwardness and the kind of bizarre characters who just don't exist in the real world. It's a genre that could be dubbed purposefully bad, with the intention of building a cult audience. In this, the murderous Greasy Strangler is unleashed when Ronnie and his son Brayden fall for the same woman while conducting their Disco Walking Tour through the streets of Los Angeles. A crazy, strange, nearly-plotless comedy that deserves points for trying something different, but being odd only goes so far before wearing out its welcome. **93m/C; DVD, Blu-Ray.** Michael St. Michaels; Elizabeth De Razzo; ***D:*** Jim Hosking; ***W:*** Jim Hosking; ***C:*** Marten Tedin.

Great Adventure 🦴🦴 **1975 (PG)** In the severe environment of the gold rush days on the rugged Yukon territory, a touching tale unfolds of a young orphan boy and his eternal bond of friendship with a great northern dog. Based on a Jack London story. Baldanello used the pseudonym Paul Elliotts and Fred Romer is actually Fernando Romero. **90m/C; VHS, DVD.** *IT SP* Jack Palance; Joan Collins; Fred Romer; Elisabetta Virgili; Remo de Angelis; Manuel de Blas; ***D:*** Gianfranco Baldanello.

The Great Alligator 🦴 *Il Fiume del Grande Caimano; Alligators* **1981** As if you couldn't guess, this one's about a huge alligator who does what other huge alligators do...terrorizes the people at a resort. **89m/C; VHS, DVD, Blu-Ray.** Barbara Bach; Mel Ferrer; Richard Johnson; Claudio Cassinelli; Romano Puppo; ***D:*** Sergio Martino; ***W:*** Sergio Martino; Ernesto Gastaldi; Luigi Montefiore; Maria Chiaretta; ***C:*** Giancarlo Ferrando.

The Great Alone 🦴🦴 **2015** A feature-length, inspirational documentary about champion dog sled racer Lance Mackey. The first person in history to win four straight Iditarod Trail Sled Dog Races, Mackey has a passion for the sport. The documentary looks at this obsessive love as Mackey must manager health issues, his past, and managing the dogs as he prepares for his twelfth Iditarod. Drawing on his personal determination, he races for pride. The documentary also emphasizes the beauty of the Alaskan landscape. **80m/C; DVD, Blu-Ray, Streaming, Download.** ***D:*** Greg Kohs; ***W:*** Greg Kohs; ***C:*** Ross Riege; ***M:*** Craig Minowa. **VIDEO**

The Great American Broadcast 🦴🦴🦴 **1941** Two WWI vets want more than anything to strike it rich. After many failed endeavors, the two try that new-fangled thing called radio. The station takes off, as does the plot. The girlfriend of one vet falls for his partner and numerous other misunderstandings and complications ensue. Charming and crazy musical with an energetic cast. **92m/B; VHS, DVD.** Alice Faye; John Payne; Jack Oakie; Cesar Romero; James Newill; Mary Beth Hughes; ***D:*** Archie Mayo; ***C:*** Leon Shamroy.

The Great American Pastime 🦴🦴 **1/2 1956** In this mildly amusing sports comedy, Bruce Hallerton (Ewell) tries some father-son bonding by coaching his son's Little League team. Bumbling Bruce finds the parents more trouble than the kids, including being vamped by comely widow Doris (Miller) who wants her son to be the team's pitcher. **90m/B; DVD.** Tom Ewell; Ann Miller; Anne Francis; Dean Jones; Rudy Lee; ***D:*** Herman Hoffman; ***W:*** Nathaniel Benchley; ***C:*** Arthur E. Arling; ***M:*** Jeff Alexander.

The Great American Sex Scandal 🦴🦴 **1/2** *Jury Duty* **1994 (PG-13)** Sanford Lagelfust (Pinchot) is an meek accountant on trial for embezzlement, but when the prosecution's main witness turns out to be his sexy girlfriend Hope (Scoggins) the case turns into a courtroom sex scandal. Silly Canadian TV production. **94m/C; VHS, DVD.** *CA* Bronson Pinchot; Tracy Scoggins; Heather Locklear; Stephen Baldwin; Lynn Redgrave; Alan Thicke; Madchen Amick; Barbara Bosson; Ilene Graff; Mark Blankfield; Danny Pintauro; Reginald VelJohnson; Jacklyn Zeman; ***D:*** Michael A. Schultz.

Great Balls of Fire 🦴🦴 **1/2 1989 (PG-13)** A florid, comic-book film of the glory days of Jerry Lee Lewis, from his first band to stardom. Most of the drama is derived from his marriage to his 13-year-old cousin. Somewhat overacted but full of energy. The soundtrack features many of the "Killer's" greatest hits re-recorded by Jerry Lee Lewis for the film. **108m/C; VHS, DVD, Blu-Ray.** Dennis Quaid; Winona Ryder; Alec Baldwin; Trey Wilson; John Doe; Lisa Blount; Steve Allen; Stephen Tobolowsky; Lisa Jane Persky; Michael St. Gerard; Peter Cook; ***D:*** Jim McBride; ***W:*** Jack Baran; Jim McBride; ***C:*** Affonso Beato; ***M:*** Jack Baran; Jim McBride.

Great Bank Hoax 🦴🦴 **1/2** *The Great Georgia Bank Hoax; Shenanigans* **1978 (PG)** Three bank managers decide to rob their own bank to cover up the fact that all the assets have been embezzled. **89m/C; VHS, DVD.** Richard Basehart; Ned Beatty; Burgess Meredith; Michael Murphy; Paul Sand; Arthur Godfrey; ***D:*** Joseph Jacoby; ***C:*** Walter Lassally.

The Great Beauty 🦴🦴 *La grande bellezza* **2013** Title refers to the eternal city of Rome, the longtime playground of journalist and jaded bon vivant Jep Gambardella (Servillo). At his 65th birthday part, Jep realizes he's bored by his endless rounds of the city's nightlife and the cynicism of those he encounters. Pic doesn't particularly go anywhere and Jep may remind cinephile's of Marcello Mastroianni's guide to Roman extravagance in Fellini's 1960 film, "La Dolce Vita." Italian with subtitles. **142m/C; DVD, Blu-Ray.** *IT* Toni Servillo; Carlo Verdone; Sabrina Ferilli; Roberto Herlitzka; ***D:*** Paolo Sorrentino; ***W:*** Paolo Sorrentino; Umberto Contarello; ***C:*** Luca Bigazzi; ***M:*** Lele Marchitelli. Oscars '13: Foreign Film; British Acad. '13: Foreign Film; Golden Globes '14: Foreign Film.

The Great Buck Howard 🦴🦴🦴 **2009 (PG)** Charming, low-key tale of bored law school dropout Troy (Hanks the younger), who takes a job as personal assistant to small-time illusionist Buck Howard (Malkiovich), much to the chagrin of his father (Hanks the elder). Troy and Buck bond on the road and soon an entry-level publicist (Blunt) joins them, set to help launch Howard's comeback with an "amazing stunt," but the results aren't what anyone expected. Malkovich has fun with the role of a man who doesn't realize showbiz has passed him by. **87m/C; Blu-Ray, On Demand.** Colin Hanks; Tom Hanks; John Malkovich; Emily Blunt; Griffin Dunne; Tom Arnold; Patrick Fischler; Wallace (Wally) Langham; Stacey Travis; Steve Zahn; Ricky Jay; Donny Most; Jacquie Barnbrook; Matt Hoey; ***Cameo(s):*** Conan O'Brien; George Takei; ***D:*** Sean McGinly; ***W:*** Sean McGinly; ***C:*** Tak Fujimoto; ***M:*** Blake Neely.

The Great Caruso 🦴🦴 **1/2 1951** The story of opera legend Enrico Caruso's rise to fame, from his childhood in Naples, Italy, to his collapse on the stage of the Metropolitan Opera House. Lanza is superb as the singer, and there are 27 musical numbers to satisfy the opera lover. **113m/C; VHS, DVD.** Mario Lanza; Ann Blyth; Dorothy Kirsten; Angela (Clark) Clarke; Jarmila Novotna; Richard Hageman; Carl Benton Reid; Eduard Franz; Ludwig Donath; Alan Napier; Shepard Menken; Nestor Paiva; Ian Wolfe; ***D:*** Richard Thorpe; ***C:*** Joseph Ruttenberg; ***M:*** Johnny Green. Oscars '51: Sound.

The Great Challenge 🦴🦴 *Les Fils du Vent; Sons of the Wind* **2004 (PG-13)** Extreme athletes travel to Bangkok to set up a gym and explore the city. But they encounter a Thai gang who are allied with Japanese yakuza to take control of the city. For fans of the martial arts genre; French with subtitles. **93m/C; DVD.** *FR* Williams Belle; Chau Belle Dinh; Malik Diouf; Yann Hnautra; ***D:*** Julien Seri; ***W:*** Julien Seri; ***C:*** Michel Taburiaux; ***M:*** Christian Henson.

The Great Commandment 🦴 **1941** Young man throws himself into a revolution against the overbearing Roman Empire in A.D. 30. His brother joins him but is killed. The man, who has become influenced by the teachings of Christ, decides to give up his revolution and go off with his brother's widow. (He always loved her anyway.) **78m/B; VHS, DVD.** John Beal; Maurice (Moscovitch) Moscovich; Albert Dekker; Marjorie Cooley; Warren McCollum; ***D:*** Irving Pichel.

Great Dan Patch 🦴 **1/2 1949** The story of the great Dan Patch, the horse that went on to become the highest-earning harness racer in history. **92m/B; VHS, DVD.** Dennis O'Keefe; Gail Russell; Ruth Warrick; Charlotte Greenwood; Henry Hull; John Hoyt; Arthur Hunnicutt; Clarence Muse; ***D:*** Joseph M. Newman; ***W:*** John Taintor Foote; ***C:*** Gilbert Warrenton; ***M:*** Rudolph (Rudy) Schrager.

The Great Debaters 🦴🦴🦴 **2007 (PG-13)** Inspirational story focusing on the debate team from all black Wiley College in East Texas who took on—and beat—all comers, including vaunted white rivals, during the 1930s. Debate coach (and labor/civil rights organizer) Melvin B. Tolson (director Washington) winnows down his prospects to four: earnest Hamilton Burgess (Williams), debonair Henry Lowe (Parker), aspiring lawyer and rare female debater Samantha Booke (Smollett), and studious, teenaged prodigy James Farmer Jr. (Denzel Whitaker), who's trying to please his theology professor father (Forest Whitaker, no relation). Naturally in the Jim Crow south they run into lots of problems before the big confrontation with the oh-so-superior Harvard team. The pros graciously step back to allow their younger colleagues room to shine. **127m/C; Blu-Ray, On Demand.** Denzel Washington; Forest Whitaker; Nathaniel Parker; Jurnee Smollett; Denzel Whitaker; Jermaine Williams; Gina Ravera; John Heard; Kimberly Elise; ***D:*** Denzel Washington; ***W:*** Robert Eisele; ***C:*** Philippe Rousselot; ***M:*** James Newton Howard; Peter Golub.

The Great Diamond Robbery 🦴🦴 **1/2 1953** Skelton's last film for MGM is an average crime comedy. Orphaned diamond cutter Ambrose C. Park is anxious to demonstrate his expertise by cutting the rare Blue Goddess diamond. Crooks are determined to steal the gem after Ambrose finishes his work and get close to him by pretending to be his long-lost family. **70m/B; DVD.** Red Skelton; Cora Williams; James Whitmore; Kurt Kasznar; Dorothy Stickney; George Mathews; Reginald Owen; Harry Bellaver; ***D:*** Robert Z. Leonard; ***W:*** Martin Rackin; Laszlo Vadnay; ***C:*** Joseph Ruttenberg.

The Great Dictator 🦴🦴🦴🦴 **1940** Chaplin's first all-dialogue film, a searing satire on Nazism in which he has dual roles as a Jewish barber with amnesia who is mistaken for a Hitlerian dictator, Adenoid Hynkel. A classic scene involves Hynkel playing with a gigantic balloon of the world. Hitler banned the film's release to the German public due to its highly offensive portrait of him. The film also marked Chaplin's last wearing of the Little Tramp's (and Hitler's equally little) mustache. **126m/B; VHS, DVD, Blu-Ray.** Charlie Chaplin; Paulette Goddard; Jack Oakie; Billy Gilbert; Reginald Gardiner; Henry Daniell; Maurice (Moscovitch) Moscovich; Emma Dunn; Bernard Gorcey; Paul Weigel; Chester Conklin; Grace Hayle; Carter DeHaven; ***D:*** Charlie Chaplin; ***W:*** Charlie Chaplin; ***C:*** Karl Struss; Roland H. Totheroh; ***M:*** Meredith Willson. Natl. Film Reg. '97; N.Y. Film Critics '40: Actor (Chaplin).

The Great Divide 🦴 **1/2 1929** Early talkie is somewhat stymied by stagy acting. Puritanical mine owner Steven Ghent (Keith) is shocked that the brazen flapper at the local fiesta turns out to be the now-grown daughter of his long-deceased partner. He decides Ruth (Mackaill) needs some moral lessons. Adaptation of the William Vaughn Moody play "West of the Great Divide." **72m/B; DVD.** Ian Keith; Dorothy Mackaill; Myrna Loy; Lucien Littlefield; Creighton Hale; ***D:*** Reginald Barker; ***W:*** Paul Perez; Fred Myton; ***C:*** Lee Garmes; Alvin Knechtel.

The Great Escape 🦴🦴🦴 **1/2 1963** During WWII, troublesome allied POWs are thrown by the Nazis into an escape-proof camp, where they join forces in a single mass break for freedom. One of the great war movies, with a superb ensemble cast and lots of excitement. The story was true, based on the novel by Paul Brickhill. McQueen performed most of the stunts himself, against the wishes of director Sturges. Followed by a made for TV movie 25 years later. **170m/C; VHS, DVD, Blu-Ray.** Steve McQueen; James Garner; Richard Attenborough; Charles Bronson; James Coburn; Donald Pleasence; David McCallum; James Donald; Gordon Jackson; Hannes Messemer; John Leyton; Nigel Stock; Jud Taylor; Hans Reiser; Robert Freitag; Karl Otto Alberty; Angus Lennie; Robert Graf; Harry Riebauer; Tom Adams; ***D:*** John Sturges; ***W:*** James Clavell; W.R. Burnett; ***C:*** Daniel F. Fapp; ***M:*** Elmer Bernstein.

Great Expectations 🦴🦴 1/2 **1934** Weak Hollywood adaptation of the Dickens novel, easily dwarfed by the brilliant 1946 version. Holmes is Pip, the orphan who rises in the world thanks to a mysterious benefactor (Hull), with Wyatt as Pip's disdainful love, Estella. **102m/B; VHS, DVD.** Phillips Holmes; Henry Hull; Jane Wyatt; Florence Reed; Francis L. Sullivan; Alan Hale; Anne Howard; ***D:*** Stuart Walker; ***W:*** Gladys Unger; ***C:*** George Robinson.

Great Expectations 🦴🦴🦴🦴 **1946** Lean's magisterial adaptation of the Dickens tome, in which a young English orphan is graced by a mysterious benefactor and becomes a well-heeled gentleman. Hailed and revered over the years; possibly the best Dickens on film. Well-acted by all, but especially notable is Hunt's slightly mad and pathetic Miss Havisham. Remake of the 1934 film. **118m/B; VHS, DVD.** *GB* John Mills; Valerie Hobson; Anthony Wager; Alec Guinness; Finlay Currie; Jean Simmons; Bernard Miles; Francis L. Sullivan; Martita Hunt; Freda Jackson; Torin Thatcher; Hay Petrie; Eileen Erskine; George "Gabby" Hayes; Everley Gregg; O.B. Clarence; ***D:*** David Lean; ***W:*** David Lean; Ronald Neame; ***C:*** Guy Green; ***M:*** Walter Goehr. Oscars '47: Art Dir./Set Dec., B&W, B&W Cinematog.

Great Expectations 🦴🦴 **1981** Miniseries adaptation of the Dickens epic about Pip and his mysterious benefactor in Victorian London. **300m/C; VHS, DVD.** *GB* Gerry Sundquist; Stratford Johns; Joan Hickson; ***D:*** Julian Amyes; ***W:*** James Andrew Hall. **TV**

Great Expectations 🦴🦴 **1997 (R)** Expecting "Great Expectations?" The title and basic storyline are about all the filmmakers took for their contemporary updating of Dickens' story. The artistic, orphaned Finn (Hawke) is living a meager existence with his trashy sister and his "uncle" Joe in a Florida fishing town. His destiny is intertwined with an escaped convict (De Niro) he aids, the rich and loony Ms. Dinsmoor (Bancroft) and Dinsmoor's beautiful niece Estella (Paltrow). After being spurned by Estella as a teen, Finn quits painting and drawing entirely. Years later a mysterious art dealer offers him a one-man show in New York if he will move there and start creating again. Estella inevitably reappears in his life, providing more than a little inspiration. More style than substance. Although the visuals are stunning, the director should have learned that beauty on the surface isn't all it's cracked up to be from, say...hmm... "Great Expectations" by Charles Dickens maybe? **112m/C; VHS, DVD.** Ethan Hawke; Robert De Niro; Gwyneth Paltrow; Hank Azaria; Anne Bancroft; Chris Cooper; Josh Mostel; Kim Dickens; Nell Campbell; Stephen Spinella; ***D:*** Alfonso Cuarón; ***W:*** Mitch Glazer; ***C:*** Emmanuel Lubezki; ***M:*** Patrick Doyle.

Great Expectations 🦴🦴 1/2 **1999** British TV version of the Dickens story about the expectations of Pip (Gruffudd). As a boy, he helps escaped convict Magwitch (Hill), a kindness that will change the course of Pip's life, though he doesn't realize it. Also a continuing part of his life is haughty beauty, Estella (Waddell), who has been raised by the eccentric Miss Havisham (Rampling) to wreak havoc on the male gender. A respectable retelling and rather dull. **180m/C; VHS, Streaming.** Ioan Gruffudd; Justine Waddell; Charlotte Rampling; Bernard Hill; Clive Russell; Laila Morse; Nicholas Woodeson; Lesley Sharp; Emma Cunniffe; Daniel Evans; ***D:*** Julian Jarrold; ***W:*** Tony Marchant. **TV**

Great Expectations 🦴🦴 **2011** This BBC adaptation of the Dickens melodrama tweaks the novel's ending for no good reason and casts a couple of pretty-but-bland actors as the adult Pip (Booth) and Estella (Kirby). Winstone is fierce as the bitter Magwitch with Anderson somewhat sleepy as wedding-garbed Miss Havisham. It looks good but has no passion. **180m/C; DVD, Blu-Ray.** *UK* Douglas Booth; Vanessa Kirby; Gillian Anderson; Ray Winstone; David Suchet; Harry Lloyd; Shaun Dooley; Claire Rushbrook; Mark Addy; Paul Rhys; Perdita Weeks; Susan Lynch; ***D:*** Brian Kirk; ***W:*** Sarah Phelps; ***C:*** Florian Hoffmeister; ***M:*** Martin Phipps. **TV**

Great Expectations 🦴🦴 **2012 (PG-13)** The often-filmed Dickens novel gets yet another adaptation that's merely passable entertainment with a couple of supporting performances that offer some interest. The Irvine brothers play the young and adult Pip with empathy, but it's Bonham Carter as the cobwebbed Miss Havisham and Fiennes' terrifying Magwitch that stand out in this tale of an orphan thrust into London society. **128m/C; DVD, Blu-Ray.** *UK* Jeremy Irvine; Helena Bonham Carter; Ralph Fiennes; Holliday Grainger; Robbie Coltrane; Jason Flemyng; Sally Hawkins; Ben Lloyd-Hughes; Ewen Bremner; Toby Irvine; ***D:*** Mike Newell; ***W:*** David Nicholls; ***C:*** John Mathieson; ***M:*** Richard Hartley.

Great Flamarion 🦴🦴 1/2 **1945** A woman-hating trick-shot artist is nevertheless duped into murdering the husband of his femme fatale assistant after he comes to believe she loves him. He's wrong. **78m/B; VHS, DVD.** Dan Duryea; Erich von Stroheim; Mary Beth Hughes; ***D:*** Anthony Mann.

The Great Gabbo 🦴🦴 **1929** A ventriloquist can express himself only through his dummy, losing his own identity and going mad at the end. Von Stroheim's first talkie. May quite possibly be the first mentally-twisted-ventriloquist story ever put on film. Von Stroheim hated the movie, believing it to be analogous to his own life. When he tried to buy the rights to the film, presumably to destroy the prints, he found that the property had been already purchased by real-life ventriloquist, Edgar Bergen. Based on a story by Ben Hecht. **82m/B; VHS, DVD.** Erich von Stroheim; Betty Compson; Donald "Don" Douglas; Marjorie "Babe" Kane; ***D:*** James Cruze; ***W:*** Ben Hecht; F. Hugh Herbert; ***C:*** Ira Morgan; ***M:*** Howard Jackson; Charley Chase.

The Great Garrick 🦴🦴 1/2 **1937** Renowned 18th-century actor David Garrick (Aherne) leaves London's Drury Lane for Paris' Comedie Francaise but not before insulting French acting abilities. Wanting to teach the English upstart a lesson, the French troupe concocts an elaborate hoax by taking over the inn where Garrick is staying, but he's on to the prank. Except for the fact that beautiful runaway Germaine (de Havilland) isn't part of the scheme. He insults her but manages to make amends when they meet again. Whale was best-known for directing horror films but he did fine with this period farce (although the script is rickety). **89m/B; DVD.** Brian Aherne; Olivia de Havilland; Edward Everett Horton; Melville Cooper; Luis Alberni; Lionel Atwill; Etienne Girardot; Marie Wilson; Lana Turner; ***D:*** James Whale; ***W:*** Ernest Vadja; ***C:*** Ernest Haller; ***M:*** Adolph Deutsch.

The Great Gatsby 🦴🦴 1/2 **1974 (PG)** Adaptation of F. Scott Fitzgerald's novel of the idle rich in the 1920s. A mysterious millionaire crashes Long Island society, and finds his heart captured by an impetuous and emotionally impoverished girl. Skillful acting and directing captures the look and feel of this era, but the movie doesn't have the power of the book. **144m/C; VHS, DVD, Blu-Ray.** Robert Redford; Mia Farrow; Bruce Dern; Karen Black; Patsy Kensit; Sam Waterston; Howard da Silva; Edward Herrmann; ***D:*** Jack Clayton; ***W:*** Francis Ford Coppola; ***M:*** Nelson Riddle. Oscars '74: Costume Des., Orig. Song Score and/or Adapt.; Golden Globes '75: Support. Actress (Black).

The Great Gatsby 🦴🦴 1/2 **2001** Wealthy Jay Gatsby (Stephens) was a poor boy with a questionable past who fell in love with rich girl Daisy (Sorvino), who married another (Donovan). Now Jay, who wants to make it in Jazz Age Newport society, renews his involvement with superficial Daisy, which leads to tragedy. All the drama is observed by Daisy's cousin Nick (Rudd). Adapted from the 1925 F. Scott Fitzgerald novel. **100m/C; VHS, DVD.** Toby Stephens; Mira Sorvino; Martin Donovan; Paul Rudd; Francie Swift; Matt Malloy; ***D:*** Robert Markowitz; ***W:*** John McLaughlin; ***C:*** Guy Dufaux; ***M:*** Carl Davis. **CABLE**

The Great Gatsby 🦴🦴 **2013 (PG-13)** DiCaprio stars as the title character in writer/director Luhrmann's showy, 3D adaptation of the iconic F. Scott Fitzgerald book. The reclusive millionaire who believes he can rewrite history to find true love with Daisy Buchanan (Mulligan) remains an enigma in the director's overdone and surface level telling of his story. Maguire plays narrator Nick Carraway, the man who moves in next to the legendary Gatsby and become embroiled in his longing for the elusive Daisy. Luhrmann knows how to throw a party but not how to tell a story that feels real. **142m/C; DVD, Blu-Ray.** Leonardo DiCaprio; Tobey Maguire; Carey Mulligan; Joel Edgerton; Isla Fisher; Jason Clarke; Adelaide Clemens; ***D:*** Baz Luhrmann; ***W:*** Baz Luhrmann; Craig Pearce; ***C:*** Simon Duggan; ***M:*** Craig Armstrong. Oscars '13: Costume Des., Production Design; British Acad. '13: Costume Des., Production Design.

The Great Gilly Hopkins 🦴🦴 **2016 (PG)** A family comedy-drama about one foster kid's efforts to find her family, based on the novel by Katherine Paterson. For much of her young life, tween Gilly Hopkins (Nelisse) has moved from foster home to foster home. In each home, she finds a way to outwit her foster family. Gilly meets her match when she is placed with Maime Trotter (Bates). Though Gilly concocts a plan to bring her birth mother to her rescue, it goes horribly wrong and nearly ruins her chance to find love, acceptance, and a family who wants her to stay. **99m/C; DVD, Streaming, Download.** Sophie Nelisse; Kathy Bates; Glenn Close; Octavia Spencer; Julia Stiles; ***D:*** Stephen Herek; ***W:*** David Paterson; ***C:*** David M. Dunlap; ***M:*** Mark Isham. **VIDEO**

Great Guns 🦴🦴 **1941** Stan and Ollie enlist in the army to protect a spoiled millionaire's son but wind up being targets at target practice instead. Not one of their better efforts. **74m/B; VHS, DVD.** Stan Laurel; Oliver Hardy; Sheila Ryan; Dick Nelson; ***D:*** Montague (Monty) Banks.

The Great Hack 🦴🦴🦴 **2019** A documentary look at how political campaigns such as the 2016 U.S. presidential election and Brexit were influenced and affected by Cambridge Analytica, a company that collected and used thousands of pieces of information about individuals collected through social media. As part of the discussion, the filmmakers explain how the company gained the data from seemingly innocent Facebook quizzes, used this information, and faced devastating legal challenges. Through interviews with former employees, experts, and reporters who covered Cambridge Analytica, it offers clear explanations of the issues at stake and how the public was psychologically affected. It also is a cautionary tale. **113m/C; DVD.** ***D:*** Karim Amer; Jehane Noujaim; ***W:*** Karim Amer; Erin Barnett; Pedro Kos; ***C:*** Basil Childers; Ian Moubayed; ***M:*** Gil Talmi.

Great Jesse James Raid 🦴 1/2 **1949** Jesse James comes out of retirement to carry out a mine theft. Routine. **73m/C; VHS, DVD.** Willard Parker; Barbara Payton; Tom Neal; Wallace Ford; ***D:*** Reginald LeBorg.

The Great Lie 🦴🦴🦴 **1941** A great soaper with Davis and Astor as rivals for the affections of Brent, an irresponsible flyer. Astor is the concert pianist who marries Brent and then finds out she's pregnant after he's presumed dead in a crash. The wealthy Davis offers to raise the baby so Astor can continue her career. But when Brent does return, who will it be to? Sparkling, catty fun. Astor's very short, mannish haircut became a popular trend. **107m/B; VHS, DVD.** Bette Davis; Mary Astor; George Brent; Lucile Watson; Hattie McDaniel; Grant Mitchell; Jerome Cowan; ***D:*** Edmund Goulding; ***C:*** Gaetano Antonio "Tony" Gaudio; ***M:*** Max Steiner. Oscars '41: Support. Actress (Astor).

The Great Locomotive Chase 🦴🦴 1/2 *Andrews' Raiders* **1956** During the Civil War, Parker and his fellow Union soldiers head into Confederate territory to disrupt railroad supply lines. They take over a locomotive, but are pursued by Confederate Hunter, the conductor of another train; and soon a pursuit is underway. Based on the true story of Andrews' Raiders. **85m/C; VHS, DVD.** Fess Parker; Jeffrey Hunter; Kenneth Tobey; ***D:*** Francis D. Lyon; ***W:*** Lawrence Edward Watkin; ***C:*** Charles P. Boyle; ***M:*** Paul J. Smith.

The Great Los Angeles Earthquake 🦴 1/2 *The Big One: The Great Los Angeles Earthquake* **1991** Made-for-TV disaster movie is the same old story; multiple soap-opera plotlines are spun around terrifying special effects, as L.A. is devastated by three major earth tremors and attendant disasters. Condensed from a two-part miniseries. **106m/C; VHS, DVD.** Ed Begley, Jr.; Joanna Kerns; ***D:*** Larry Elikann.

The Great Lover 🦴🦴 1/2 **1949** Aboard an ocean liner, a bumbler chaperoning school kids gets involved with a gambler, a duchess and a murder. Vintage Bob Hope. **80m/B; VHS, DVD.** Bob Hope; Rhonda Fleming; Roland Young; Roland Culver; George Reeves; Jim Backus; Jack Benny; ***D:*** Alexander Hall; ***W:*** Edmund Beloin; Melville Shavelson; Jack Rose; ***C:*** Charles B(ryant) Lang, Jr.

The Great Magician 🦴🦴 *Daai mo seut si* **2011** Illusionist Zhang Xian comes to 1920's Beijing just after the overthrow of the Qing Dynasty; control of the city is being fought over by revolutionaries, a former Qing warlord, and a gang backed by a Japanese businessman. Into this chaos is thrown a competition between magicians, at least one of whom may be more than he seems. Mandarin with subtitles. **128m/C; DVD, Blu-Ray.** *CH HK* Tony Leung Chiu-Wai; Ching-Wan Lau; Xun Zhou; ***D:*** Tung-Shing Yee; ***W:*** Tung-Shing Yee; Tin Nam Chun; Ho Leung Lau; ***C:*** Nobuyasu Kita; ***M:*** Leon Ko.

The Great Man's Lady 🦴🦴 1/2 **1942** Stanwyck stars in a "stand by your man" story in which she supported and was responsible for the good deeds of a now past town hero. Told in flashback sequence, Stanwyck's character, 109-year-old Hanna Sampler, reveals to a young biographer the trials and tribulations of her life with Ethan Hoyt, founder of Hoyt City, who is being honored with the dedication of a statue in the opening of the film. The picture reveals their secrets and the truth about the woman behind the man. Based on the story "The Human Side" by Vina Delmar. **91m/B; VHS, DVD, Blu-Ray.** Barbara Stanwyck; Joel McCrea; Brian Donlevy; ***D:*** William A. Wellman; ***W:*** Seena Owen; W.L. Rivers; Adela Rogers St. John; ***C:*** William Mellor; ***M:*** Victor Young.

The Great McGinty 🦴🦴🦴 1/2 *Down Went McGinty* **1940** Sturges' directorial debut, about the rise and fall of a small-time, bribe-happy politician is an acerbic, ultra-cynical indictment of modern politics that stands, like much of his other work, as bracingly courageous as anything that's ever snuck past the Hollywood censors. Political party boss Tamiroff chews the scenery with gusto while Donlevy, in his first starring role, is more than his equal as the not-so-dumb political hack. **82m/B; VHS, DVD, Blu-Ray.** Brian Donlevy; Muriel Angelus; Akim Tamiroff; Louis Jean Heydt; Arthur Hoyt; William Demarest; ***D:*** Preston Sturges; ***W:*** Preston Sturges; ***C:*** William Mellor. Oscars '40: Orig. Screenplay.

The Great Mike 🦴🦴 1/2 **1944** Unlikely but moving story of a young boy who convinces track management that his work horse has a chance against the touted thoroughbred. Sentimental, with little innovation, but generally well-acted. **72m/B; VHS, DVD.** Stuart Erwin; Robert "Buzzy" Henry; Pierre Watkin; Gwen Kenyon; Carl "Alfalfa" Switzer; Edythe Elliott; Marion Martin; ***D:*** Wallace Fox.

The Great Moment 🦴🦴 **1944** Story of the Boston dentist who discovered ether's use as an anesthetic in 1845. Confusing at times, changing from comedy to drama and containing flashbacks that add little to the story. Surprisingly bland result from ordinarily solid cast and director. **87m/B; VHS, DVD.** Joel McCrea; Betty Field; Harry Carey, Sr.; William Demarest; Franklin Pangborn; Porter Hall; ***D:*** Preston Sturges; ***C:*** Victor Milner.

The Great Mouse Detective 🦴🦴🦴 *The Adventures of the Great Mouse Detective* **1986 (G)** Animated version of the book "Basil of Baker Street" by Eve Titus. Fun adventure concerning the Sherlock-of-the-mouse-world, Basil, who must prevent his arch nemesis, Professor Ratigan, from overthrowing Queen Moustoria. Not as good as some of the other Disney animated features, but kids will enjoy it nonetheless. **74m/C; VHS, DVD, Blu-Ray.** ***V:*** Vincent Price; Barrie Ingham; Val Bettin; Susanne Pollatschek; Candy Candido; Eve Brenner; Alan Young; Melissa Manchester; ***D:***

John Musker; Ron Clements; Dave Michener; Burny Mattinson; ***W:*** Ron Clements; Dave Michener; ***M:*** Henry Mancini.

The Great Muppet Caper **1981 (G)** A group of hapless reporters (Kermit, Fozzie Bear, and Gonzo) travel to London to follow up on a major jewel robbery. **95m/C; VHS, DVD, Blu-Ray.** Charles Grodin; Diana Rigg; John Cleese; Robert Morley; Peter Ustinov; Peter Falk; Jack Warden; ***V:*** Frank Oz; ***D:*** Jim Henson; ***W:*** Jack Rose; ***C:*** Oswald Morris.

The Great New Wonderful **1/2 2006 (R)** Five stories about neurotic New Yorkers that are linked by occurring in September 2002, a year after the terrorist attacks (which are never directly mentioned). So you're just left to guess how the characters were actually affected, making for some dull storytelling. **88m/C; DVD.** Maggie Gyllenhaal; Thomas (Tom) McCarthy; Judy Greer; Naseeruddin Shah; Tony Shalhoub; Jim Gaffigan; Olympia Dukakis; Dick Latessa; Sharat Saxena; Edie Falco; Stephen Colbert; Jeremy Shamos; Will Arnett; Rosemarie DeWitt; Seth Gilliam; Jim Parsons; Bill Donner; Ed Setrakian; Ari Graynor; Martha Millan; Priscilla Shanks; Sam Catlin; ***D:*** Danny Leiner; ***W:*** Sam Catlin; ***C:*** Harlan Bosmajian; ***M:*** John Swihart.

The Great Northfield Minnesota Raid **1/2 1972 (PG)** The Younger/James gang decides to rob the biggest bank west of the Mississippi, but everything goes wrong. Uneven, offbeat western, but Duvall's portrayal of the psychotic Jesse James and Robertson's cunning Cole Younger are notable. **91m/C; VHS, DVD, Blu-Ray.** Cliff Robertson; Robert Duvall; Elisha Cook, Jr.; Luke Askew; R.G. Armstrong; Donald Moffat; Matt Clark; ***D:*** Philip Kaufman; ***W:*** Philip Kaufman; ***C:*** Bruce Surtees; ***M:*** Dave Grusin.

The Great O'Malley **1/2 1936** Sentimental melodrama. By-the-book cop James O'Malley (O'Brien) causes John Phillips (Bogart) the chance at a job to support his family and the desperate man winds up in prison for robbery instead. After meeting John's crippled daughter Barbara (Jason) and her caring teacher Judy Nolan (Sheridan), O'Malley realizes that it's not weakness to show compssion and he strives to help the Phillips family. **71m/B; DVD.** Pat O'Brien; Ann Sheridan; Sybil Jason; Humphrey Bogart; Frieda Inescort; Donald Crisp; ***D:*** William Dieterle; ***W:*** Tom Reed; Milton Krims; ***C:*** Ernest Haller.

The Great Outdoors **1988 (PG)** Good cast is mostly wasted in another John Hughes's tale of vacation gone bad. A family's peaceful summer by the lake is disturbed by their uninvited, trouble-making relatives. Aykroyd and Candy are two funny guys done in by a lame script that awkwardly examines friendship and coming of age and throws in a giant bear when things get unbearably slow. May be fun for small fry. **91m/C; VHS, DVD, Blu-Ray.** Dan Aykroyd; John Candy; Stephanie Faracy; Annette Bening; Chris Young; Lucy Deakins; John Bloom; ***D:*** Howard Deutch; ***W:*** John Hughes; ***C:*** Ric Waite; ***M:*** Thomas Newman.

The Great Race **1/2 1965** A dastardly villain, a noble hero, and a spirited suffragette are among the competitors in an uproarious New York-to-Paris auto race circa 1908, complete with pie fights, saloon brawls, and a confrontation with a feisty polar bear. Overly long and only sporadically funny. **160m/C; VHS, DVD, Blu-Ray.** Jack Lemmon; Tony Curtis; Natalie Wood; Peter Falk; Keenan Wynn; George Macready; ***D:*** Blake Edwards; ***M:*** Henry Mancini. Oscars '65: Sound FX Editing.

The Great Raid **2005 (R)** Workmanlike retelling of the 1944 rescue of more than 500 American POWs from a Japanese prison camp located in a remote area of the Philippines. You've got the outside planners, Army Rangers Mucci (Bratt) and Prince (Franco) and their Filipino allies, led by Pajota (Montano); the insiders, led by malaria sufferer Gibson (Fiennes); and nurse Margaret (Nielsen), who's also a resistance leader. Film has a looooong build-up before the raid comes off, which dissipates the tension. Completed in 2002, flick sat on the Miramax shelves until its brief 2005 big screen release. **132m/C; DVD, Blu-Ray.** Benjamin Bratt; James Franco; Connie Nielsen; Joseph Fiennes; Marton Csokas; Robert Mammone; Natalie Mendoza; Motoki Kobayashi; Cesar Montano; Maximillian Martini; James Carpinello; Craig McLachlan; Dale Dye; Paolo Montalban; Gotaro Tsunashima; ***D:*** John Dahl; ***W:*** Carlo Bernard; Doug Miro; ***C:*** Peter Menzies, Jr.; ***M:*** Trevor Rabin.

The Great Rupert *A Christmas Wish* **1950** Durante and family are befriended by a helpful squirrel (a puppet) in obtaining a huge fortune. Good fun; Durante shines. **86m/B; VHS, DVD.** Jimmy Durante; Terry Moore; Tom Drake; Frank Orth; Sara Haden; Queenie Smith; ***D:*** Irving Pichel; ***W:*** Laszlo Vadnay; ***C:*** Lionel Lindon.

The Great St. Louis Bank Robbery **1/2 1959** Three career criminals (Denton, Clarke, Dukas) and young turk McQueen are brought together for a bank heist. They don't trust each other, which proves fatal when the heist goes bad. Based on a true story and filmed in semi-documentary style. Nineteen-year-old McQueen's follow-up to "The Blob." **86m/B; VHS, DVD.** Graham Denton; David Clarke; James Dukas; Steve McQueen; Molly McCarthy; ***D:*** Charles Guggenheim; ***W:*** Richard T. Heffron; ***C:*** Victor Duncan; ***M:*** Bernardo Segall.

The Great St. Trinian's Train Robbery **1966** Train robbers hide their considerable loot in an empty country mansion only to discover, upon returning years later, it has been converted into a girls' boarding school. When they try to recover the money, the thieves run up against a band of pestiferous adolescent girls, with hilarious results. Based on the cartoon by Ronald Searle. Sequel to "The Pure Hell of St. Trinian's." **90m/C; VHS, DVD.** *GB* Dora Bryan; Frankie Howerd; Reg Varney; Desmond Walter-Ellis; ***D:*** Sidney Gilliat; Frank Launder; ***M:*** Malcolm Arnold.

The Great Santini *Ace* **1980 (PG)** Lt. Col. Bull Meechum, the "Great Santini," a Marine pilot stationed stateside, fights a war involving his frustrated career goals, repressed emotions, and family. His family becomes his company of marines, as he abuses them in the name of discipline, because he doesn't allow himself any other way to show his affection. With a standout performance by Duvall, the film successfully blends warm humor and tenderness with the harsh cruelties inherent with dysfunctional families and racism. Based on Pat Conroy's autobiographical novel, the movie was virtually undistributed when first released, but re-released due to critical acclaim. **118m/C; DVD.** Robert Duvall; Blythe Danner; Michael O'Keefe; Julie Ann Haddock; Lisa Jane Persky; David Keith; ***D:*** Lewis John Carlino; ***W:*** Lewis John Carlino; ***C:*** Ralph Woolsey; ***M:*** Elmer Bernstein. Montreal World Film Fest. '80: Actor (Duvall).

Great Scout & Cathouse Thursday **1/2** *Wildcat* **1976 (PG)** Marvin and Reed vow to take revenge on their third partner, Culp, who made off with all their profits from a gold mine. The title refers to Marvin's May-December romance with prostitute Lenz. Already forgotten, unfunny, all-star comedy with cutesy title. **96m/C; VHS, DVD, Blu-Ray.** Lee Marvin; Oliver Reed; Robert Culp; Elizabeth Ashley; Kay Lenz; ***D:*** Don Taylor.

The Great Sinner **1/2 1949** Gardner is gorgeous as usual but Peck seems too shallow in this uncredited adaptation of Fyodor Dostoyevsky's "The Gambler." Writer Fedja (Peck) follows Russian beauty Pauline (Gardner) to a gambling resort and discovers she and her father (Huston) are compulsive players. Casino owner Armand de Glasse (Douglas) holds their markers and is willing to exchange them for marriage to Pauline. Fedja thinks he can win enough to spare Pauline that fate until the lure of the roulette wheel and the cards become his addiction as well. **110m/B; DVD.** Gregory Peck; Ava Gardner; Walter Huston; Melvyn Douglas; Ethel Barrymore; Frank Morgan; Agnes Moorehead; ***D:*** Robert Siodmak; ***W:*** Christopher Isherwood; Ladislas Fodor; ***C:*** George J. Folsey; ***M:*** Bronislau Kaper.

Great Smokey Roadblock *Last of the Cowboys* **1976 (PG)** While in the hospital, a 60-year-old truck driver's rig is repossessed by the finance company. Deciding that it's time to make one last perfect cross country run, he escapes from the hospital, steals his truck, picks up six prostitutes, heads off into the night with the police on his tail, and becomes a folk hero. **84m/C; VHS, DVD, Blu-Ray.** Henry Fonda; Eileen Brennan; Susan Sarandon; John Byner; Austin Pendleton; Robert Englund; Dub Taylor; Melanie Mayron; Leigh French; Gary Sandy; Valerie Curtin; Bibi Osterwald; Lyman Ward; Sander Vanocuer; ***D:*** John Leone; ***W:*** John Leone; ***C:*** Edward R. Brown; ***M:*** Craig Safan.

The Great Spy Chase *Les Barbouzes* **1964** In this spy comedy, an arms manufacturer leaves his valuable military patents to his lovely young widow. French intelligence agent Francis Lagneau (Ventura) is set to seduce them from Amaranthe (Darc) but he's not the only one with that idea. French with subtitles. **108m/B; DVD, Blu-Ray.** *FR* Lino Ventura; Mireille Darc; Bernard Blier; Francis Blanche; ***D:*** Georges Lautner; ***W:*** Michel Audiard; ***C:*** Maurice Fellous; ***M:*** Michel Magne.

The Great Texas Dynamite Chase **1/2** *Dynamite Women* **1976 (R)** Two sexy young women drive across Texas with a carload of dynamite. They leave a trail of empty banks with the cops constantly on their trail. **90m/C; VHS, DVD.** Claudia Jennings; Jocelyn Jones; Johnny Crawford; Chris Pennock; Tara Strohmeier; Miles Watkins; Bart Braverman; ***D:*** Michael Pressman; ***C:*** Jamie Anderson; ***M:*** Craig Safan.

The Great Train Robbery *The First Great Train Robbery* **1979 (PG)** A dapper thief arranges to heist the Folkstone bullion express in 1855, the first moving train robbery. Well-designed, fast-moving costume piece based on Crichton's best-selling novel. **111m/C; VHS, DVD, Blu-Ray.** *GB* Sean Connery; Donald Sutherland; Lesley-Anne Down; Alan Webb; ***D:*** Michael Crichton; ***W:*** Michael Crichton; ***C:*** Geoffrey Unsworth; ***M:*** Jerry Goldsmith.

The Great Waldo Pepper **1975 (PG)** Low key and (for Hill) less commercial film about a WWI pilot-turned-barnstormer who gets hired as a stuntman for the movies. Features spectacular vintage aircraft flying sequences. **107m/C; VHS, DVD, Blu-Ray.** Robert Redford; Susan Sarandon; Margot Kidder; Bo Svenson; Scott Newman; Geoffrey Lewis; Edward Herrmann; ***D:*** George Roy Hill; ***W:*** William Goldman; ***C:*** Robert L. Surtees; ***M:*** Henry Mancini.

A Great Wall *The Great Wall is a Great Wall* **1986 (PG)** A Chinese-American family travels to mainland China to discover the country of their ancestry and to visit relatives. They experience radical culture shock. Wang's first independent feature. In English and Chinese with subtitles. **103m/C; VHS, DVD, Blu-Ray.** Peter Wang; Sharon Iwai; Kelvin Han Yee; Lin Qinqin; Hy Xiaoguang; ***D:*** Peter Wang; ***W:*** Peter Wang; Shirley Sun; ***M:*** David Liang; Ge Ganru.

The Great Wall **1/2 2017 (PG-13)** Acclaimed auteur Zhang Yimou's monster movie is set on the Great Wall of China and stars, of all people, Matt Damon. Primarily for international audiences, the film was a huge hit overseas but was greeted with quizzical shoulder shrugs in the U.S. Damon plays a European mercenary during the Song Dynasty. He arrives at the Great Wall, where he meets a group of Chinese soldiers who defend the country from monsters on the other side of the wall. Yimou is a talented artist, but this one is just a bit too out there. **103m/C; DVD, Blu-Ray.** Matt Damon; Tian Jing; Pedro Pascal; Willem Dafoe; Lu Han; Andy Lau; ***D:*** Yimou Zhang; ***W:*** Carlo Bernard; Doug Miro; Tony Gilroy; ***C:*** Stuart Dryburgh; Xiaoding Zhao; ***M:*** Ramin Djawadi.

The Great Waltz **1938** The first of two musical biographies on the life of Johann Strauss sees the musician quit his banking job to pursue his dream of becoming a successful composer. A fine, overlooked production rich with wonderful music and romantic comedy. **102m/B; VHS, DVD.** Luise Rainer; Fernand Gravey; Milza Korjus; Hugh Herbert; Lionel Atwill; Curt Bois; Leonid Kinskey; Al Shean; Minna Gombell; George Houston; Bert Roach; Herman Bing; Alma Kruger; Sig Rumann; ***D:*** Julien Duvivier; ***C:*** Joseph Ruttenberg. Oscars '38: Cinematog.

The Great Water *Golemata voda; Velka voda* **2004** Aging Macedonian politician Lem Nikodinoski (Jovanovski) is rushed to the hospital after suffering a heart attack and has the time to reflect on his childhood, which was spent in a Stalinist camp intended to indoctrinate the young into proper communists. There, an orphaned 12-year-old Lem (Kekenovski) is taken under the wing of charismatic teen Isak (Stankovska, an actress cast as a boy), which ultimately leads to a wrenching betrayal. Based on the novel by Zivko Cingo; in English and Macedonian with subtitles. **90m/C; DVD.** Nikolina Kujaca; Meto Jovanovski; Saso Kekenovski; Maja Stankovska; Mitko Apostolovski; Verica Nedeska; Risto Gogovski; ***D:*** Ivo Trajkov; ***W:*** Ivo Trajkov; Vladimir Blazevski; ***C:*** Suki Medencevic; ***M:*** Kiril Dzajkovski.

The Great White Hope **1/2 1970 (PG-13)** A semi-fictionalized biography of boxer Jack Johnson, played by Jones, who became the first black heavyweight world champion in 1910. Alexander makes her film debut as the boxer's white lover, as both battle the racism of the times. Two Oscar-nominated performances in what is essentially an "opened-out" version of the Broadway play. **103m/C; VHS, DVD.** James Earl Jones; Jane Alexander; Lou Gilbert; Joel Fluellen; Chester Morris; Robert Webber; Hal Holbrook; R.G. Armstrong; Moses Gunn; Scatman Crothers; ***D:*** Martin Ritt; ***C:*** Burnett Guffey.

The Great White Hype **1/2 1996 (R)** Screenwriter Shelton, who penned "Bull Durham" and "White Men Can't Jump," returns to the sports arena with this satire of the sleazy world of boxing. Jackson's the Don King-esque promoter and manager of heavyweight champ Wayans. Noticing that pay-per-view revenues are slipping, he searches for a white boxer to generate interest and dollars and finds boxer-turned-musician Berg, who beat the champ in their Golden Glove days, and the publicity machine is cranked up for a veritable Lollapalooka. Jackson's performance as the flamboyant Rev. Fred Sultan fuels the entire movie. Concentrating on the shady wheeling and dealing, the boxing action is kept to a minimum. **95m/C; VHS, DVD.** Samuel L. Jackson; Damon Wayans; Peter Berg; Jeff Goldblum; Jon Lovitz; Corbin Bernsen; Richard "Cheech" Marin; John Rhys-Davies; Salli Richardson-Whitfield; Rocky Carroll; Jamie Foxx; Michael Jace; ***D:*** Reginald (Reggie) Hudlin; ***W:*** Ron Shelton; Tony Hendra; ***C:*** Ron Garcia; ***M:*** Marcus Miller.

Great World of Sound **2007 (R)** Martin (Healy) sees an ad to become a record producer and joins the shady company of the title. He's partnered with exuberant (and once homeless) Clarence (Holliday) to hit those southern highways and byways and audition and "sign" musical talent. It's a scam, but both men need the job too badly to let their consciences guide them. **108m/C; DVD.** Pat Healy; Kene Holliday; Rebecca Mader; Jonathan Baker; Robert Longstreet; Adam Stone; Tricia Paoluccio; ***D:*** Craig Zobel; ***W:*** Craig Zobel; George Smith; ***M:*** David Wingo.

The Great Yokai War **1/2** *The Great Goblin War; Yokai Daisenso; Spook Warfare; Hobgoblins & the Great War* **2005 (PG-13)** A young boy moves to a small town after his parents divorce, and he ends up involved in a spiritual war between the Yokai (odd monsters or spirits from Japanese folklore with magical powers) and a foreign spirit of toxic waste that moves into their territory. Shockingly this is a children's film directed by Miike, known for far less tame fare. Special effects abound and fantasy film fans will still be able to appreciate the bevy of unique monsters. **124m/C; DVD.** *JP* Ryunosuke Kamiki; Chiaki Kuriyama; Bunta Sugawara; Kaho Minami; Hiroyuki Miyasako; Etsushi Toyokawa; Naoto Takenaka; Kenichi Endo; Sadao Abe; Renji Ishibashi; Toshie Negishi; Tokitoshi Shiota; Riko Narumi; Kiyoshiro Yamawano; Mai Takahashi; Masaomi Kando; Takashi Okamura; Asumi Miwa; Hiroshi Aramata; Natsuhiko Kyogoku; Shigeru Mizuki; Toshiya Nagasawa; Minori Fujikura; Mame Yamada; Hiromasa Yaguchi; Rei Yoshii; Kanji Tsuda; ***D:*** Takashi Miike; ***W:*** Takashi Miike; Hiroshi Aramata; Mistuhiko Sawamura; Takehiko Itakura; ***C:*** Hideo Yamamoto; ***M:*** Koji Endo.

The Great Ziegfeld **1/2 1936** Big bio-pic of the famous showman; acclaimed in its time as the best musical biography ever done, still considered the textbook for how to make a musical. Look for cameo roles by many famous stars, as well as a walk-on role by future First Lady Pat Nixon. The movie would have stood up as a first-rate biography of Ziegfeld, even without the drop-dead wonderful songs. **179m/B; VHS, DVD.** William Powell; Luise Rainer; Myrna Loy; Frank Morgan; Reginald Owen; Nat Pendleton; Ray Bolger; Virginia Bruce; Harriet Hocter; Ernest Cossart; Robert Greig; Gilda Gray; Leon Errol; Dennis Morgan; Mickey Daniels; William Demarest; ***Cameo(s):*** Fanny Brice; ***D:*** Robert Z. Leonard; ***W:*** William Anthony McGuire. Oscars '36: Actress (Rainer), Film; N.Y. Film Critics '36: Actress (Rainer), Actress (Rainer).

The Greatest 1/2 **1977 (PG)** Autobiography of Cassius Clay, the fighter who could float like a butterfly and sting like a bee. Ali plays himself, and George Benson's hit "The Greatest Love of All" is introduced. **100m/C; VHS, DVD.** Muhammad Ali; Robert Duvall; Ernest Borgnine; James Earl Jones; John Marley; Roger E. Mosley; Dina Merrill; Paul Winfield; ***D:*** Tom Gries; ***W:*** Ring Lardner, Jr.; ***C:*** Harry Stradling, Jr.; ***M:*** Michael Masser.

The Greatest **2009 (R)** An earnest, sometimes confusing, death-in-the-family tearjerker. Teenagers Bennett (Johnson) and Rose (Mulligan) have sex in his car and then he gets killed in the subsequent car crash while she escapes with minor injuries. Mom Grace (Sarandon) can't stop crying, stoic husband Allen (Brosnan) holds everything inside, and Bennett's younger brother Ryan (Simmons) tries getting help from a grief support group before turning to pot. It gets more complicated when Rose turns up on their doorstep, pregnant and intending to keep the baby. The awful title is how everyone prefers to think of golden boy Bennett. **99m/C; Blu-Ray.** Pierce Brosnan; Susan Sarandon; Carey Mulligan; Johnny Simmons; Aaron Taylor-Johnson; Jennifer Ehle; Zoë Kravitz; Michael Shannon; Amy Morton; ***D:*** Shana Feste; ***W:*** Shana Feste; ***C:*** John Bailey; ***M:*** Christophe Beck.

The Greatest Game Ever Played 1/2 **2005 (PG)** Classic kid-from-the-wrong-side-of-the-tracks story tells how 20-year-old amateur golfer Francis Ouimet (LaBeouf) beat his boyhood idol and defending champ Harry Vardon (Dillane) to win the 1913 U.S. Open. Ouimet's working-class background precludes him from playing at the country club course where he caddies, but he learns to play on his own. Class barriers abound, and there's lots and lots of golfing. The draw of the underdog, the fact that it's a true story, and some fine performances, ultimately carries the day. **115m/C; DVD.** Shia LaBeouf; Stephen (Dillon) Dillane; Elias Koteas; Marnie McPhail; Stephen Marcus; Peter Firth; Michael Weaver; Josh Flitter; Peyton List; James Paxton; Matthew Knight; Len Cariou; Luke Askew; ***D:*** Bill Paxton; ***W:*** Mark Frost; ***C:*** Shane Hurlbut; ***M:*** Brian Tyler.

The Greatest Question 1/2 **1919** Gish is a girl menaced by a married couple whom she saw commit a murder years before. A rush job by Griffith to fulfill his studio obligations but Gish's performance is fine. Part of the 'The Directors: Rare Films of D.W. Griffith, Vol. 3' collection. **80m/B; Silent; VHS, DVD.** Lillian Gish; Robert "Bobbie" Harron; Ralph Graves; Eugenie Besserer; George Fawcett; George Nicholls, Jr.; Josephine Crowell; Carl Stockdale; ***D:*** D.W. Griffith.

The Greatest Show on Earth **1952** DeMille is in all his epic glory here in a tale of a traveling circus wrought with glamour, romance, mysterious clowns, a tough ringmaster, and a train wreck. **149m/C; VHS, DVD.** Betty Hutton; Cornel Wilde; James Stewart; Charlton Heston; Dorothy Lamour; Lawrence Tierney; Gloria Grahame; ***D:*** Cecil B. DeMille. Oscars '52: Film, Story; Golden Globes '53: Director (DeMille), Film--Drama.

The Greatest Showman 1/2 **2017 (PG)** A musical look at circus promoter P.T. Barnum (Jackman) through 11 infectious songs. As a child, Barnum befriends a girl who shares his dream of creating their own destiny. She grows up to be his wife Charity (Williams) and encourages him to strike out on his own. With business partner Phillip Carlyle (Efron), Barnum starts what becomes his circus by casting people with special talents and physical abnormalities. Barnum's career reaches new heights when he takes acclaimed Swedish singer Jenny Lind (Ferguson) on tour. Despite a message of diversity, the entertaining family-friendly film glosses over the darker side of Barnum's empire. **105m/C; DVD, Blu-Ray.** Hugh Jackman; Michelle Williams; Zac Efron; Zendaya; Rebecca Ferguson; ***D:*** Michael Gracey; ***W:*** Jenny Bicks; Bill Condon; ***C:*** Seamus McGarvey; ***M:*** John Debney; Joseph Trapanese. Golden Globes '18: Song ("This Is Me").

The Greatest Story Ever Told **1965** Christ's journey from Galilee to Golgotha is portrayed here in true international-all-star-epic treatment by director Stevens. A lackluster version of Christ's life, remarkable only for Heston's out-of-control John the Baptist. **196m/C; VHS, DVD, Blu-Ray.** Max von Sydow; Charlton Heston; Sidney Poitier; Claude Rains; Jose Ferrer; Telly Savalas; Angela Lansbury; Dorothy McGuire; John Wayne; Donald Pleasence; Carroll Baker; Van Heflin; Robert Loggia; Shelley Winters; Ed Wynn; Roddy McDowall; Pat Boone; ***D:*** George Stevens; ***W:*** George Stevens; James Lee Barrett; ***C:*** William Mellor; Loyal Griggs; ***M:*** Alfred Newman.

Greed In the Sun **1964** In this complicated French action-comedy, Rocco (Belmondo) and his partner Pepa (Parisy) steal a truck in the Saharan desert. Owner Castigliano (Frobe) wants his goods back and hires Rocco's friend Herve (Ventura) to go after him. They both have some setbacks. French with subtitles. **130m/B; DVD, Blu-Ray.** *FR* Jean-Paul Belmondo; Lino Ventura; Gert Frobe; Andrea Parisy; Bernard Blier; Reginald Kernan; ***D:*** Henri Verneuil; ***W:*** Henri Verneuil; Michel Audiard; ***C:*** Marcel Grignon; ***M:*** Georges Delerue.

The Greed of William Hart *Horror Maniacs* **1948** Reworking of the Burke and Hare legend has grave robbers providing Edinburgh medical students with the requisite cadavers. **78m/B; VHS, DVD.** *GB* Tod Slaughter; Henry Oscar; Jenny Lynn; Winifred Melville; ***D:*** Oswald Mitchell.

Greedy 1/2 **1994 (PG-13)** Money-grubbing family suck up to elderly millionaire uncle (Douglas) when they fear he'll leave his money to the sexy, young former pizza delivery girl (d'Abo) he's hired as his nurse. Fox is the long-lost nephew who comes to the rescue. Wicked comedy from veterans Ganz and Mandel should zing, but instead falls flat thanks to a descent into the maudlin. Fox bares his backside and Douglas has fun as the mean old miser, but check out Hartman, a riot as a snarky relative. **109m/C; VHS, DVD, Blu-Ray.** Kirk Douglas; Michael J. Fox; Olivia D'Abo; Phil Hartman; Nancy Travis; Ed Begley, Jr.; Bob Balaban; Colleen Camp; Jere Burns; Khandi Alexander; Jonathan Lynn; Mary Ellen Trainor; ***D:*** Jonathan Lynn; ***W:*** Lowell Ganz; Babaloo Mandel; ***C:*** Gabriel Beristain; ***M:*** Randy Edelman.

The Greek Tycoon 1/2 **1978 (R)** Old familiar story about widow of an American president who marries a billionaire shipping magnate and finds that money cannot buy happiness. A transparent depiction of the Onassis/Kennedy marriage, done to a turn. **106m/C; VHS, DVD.** Anthony Quinn; Jacqueline Bisset; James Franciscus; Raf Vallone; Edward Albert; ***D:*** J. Lee Thompson.

The Green **2011** Michael persuades his partner Daniel to leave Manhattan and move to a leafy, conservative Connecticut town where he gets a job teaching at a private high school and Daniel runs a cafe. Michael tries to help troubled scholarship student Jason, who's bullied at school and home, but gets a panicked rejection. The situation is escalated by skeevy janitor Leo and soon Michael is suspended for alleged inappropriate behavior. Unfortunately, Michael behaves like a doofus and causes more trouble for himself and Daniel. **90m/C; DVD.** Jason Butler Harner; Cheyenne Jackson; Christopher Bert; Bill Sage; Karen Young; Illeana Douglas; Julia Ormond; ***D:*** Steven Williford; ***W:*** Paul Marcarelli; ***C:*** Ryan Samul; ***M:*** William Brittelle.

Green Archer **1940** Fifteen episodes of the famed serial, featuring a spooked castle complete with secret passages and tunnels, trapdoors, and the mysterious masked figure, the Green Archer. **283m/B; VHS, DVD.** Victor Jory; Iris Meredith; James Craven; Robert (Fisk) Fiske; ***D:*** James W. Horne.

The Green Berets WOOF! **1968 (G)** Cliched wartime heroics co-directed by Wayne and based on Robin Moore's novel. The Duke stars as a Special Forces colonel, leading his troops against the Viet Cong. Painfully insipid pro-war propaganda, notable as the only American film to come out in support of U.S. involvement in Vietnam. Truly embarrassing but did spawn the hit single "Ballad of the Green Beret" by Barry Sadler. **135m/C; VHS, DVD, Blu-Ray.** John Wayne; David Janssen; Jim Hutton; Aldo Ray; George Takei; Raymond St. Jacques; Bruce Cabot; Jack Soo; Patrick Wayne; Luke Askew; Irene Tsu; Edward Faulkner; Jason Evers; Mike Henry; Chuck Roberson; Eddy Donno; ***D:*** John Wayne; ***W:*** James Lee Barrett; ***C:*** Winton C. Hoch; ***M:*** Miklos Rozsa.

Green Book **2018 (R)** In this true 1962 tale, Bronx bouncer Tony Lip (Mortensen) is hired to drive world-class jazz pianist Dr. Shirley (Ali) on a two-month concert tour through the segregated Deep South, navigating their roadtrip with *The Negro Motorist Green Book*, a guide to black-friendly establishments. Despite their differences (Lip is unsophisticated and brash; Shirley is refined and snobby), they form a friendship that defies the racism of the times. The lead performances are stellar, the script is funny and heartwarming, and the message is timeless. **130m/C; DVD, Blu-Ray.** Viggo Mortensen; Mahershala Ali; Linda Cardellini; Sebastian Maniscalco; Dimiter D. Marinov; ***D:*** Peter Farrelly; ***W:*** Peter Farrelly; Nick Vallelonga; Brian Currie; ***C:*** Sean Porter; ***M:*** Kris Bowers. Oscars '18: Actor--Supporting (Ali), Film, Orig. Screenplay; British Acad. '18: Actor--Supporting (Ali); Golden Globes '19: Actor--Supporting (Ali), Film--Mus./Comedy, Screenplay; Screen Actors Guild '18: Actor--Supporting (Ali).

The Green Butchers 1/2 *De Gronne Slagtere* **2003 (R)** Beware the sausage you're eating-particularly if it came from a certain Danish butcher shop. Friends and coworkers Svend (Mikkelsen) and Bjarne (Kaas) decide to open their own shop but business isn't going so well until Svend discovers the body of an electrician who accidentally froze to death in their store's meat locker. For some reason, Svend decides to add some human flesh to his sausage recipe and soon can't sell enough of the resulting delicacy. In order to keep up with demand, Svend turns to murder. It's a comedy. Danish with subtitles. **100m/C; DVD.** Mads Mikkelsen; Line Kruse; Nicolas Bro; Nikolaj Lie Kaas; ***D:*** Anders Thomas Jensen; ***W:*** Anders Thomas Jensen; ***C:*** Sebastian Blenkov; ***M:*** Jeppe Kaas.

Green Card 1/2 **1990 (PG-13)** Some marry for love, some for money, others for an apartment in the Big Apple. Refined, single MacDowell covets a rent-controlled apartment in Manhattan, but the lease stipulates that the apartment be let to a married couple. Enter brusque and burly Depardieu, who covets the elusive green card. The counterpoint between MacDowell, as a stuffy horticulturist, and Depardieu, as a French composer works well, and the two adroitly play a couple whose relationship covers the romantic continuum. Director Weir wrote the screenplay with Depardieu in mind. Depardieu's English-language debut. **108m/C; VHS, DVD, Blu-Ray.** Gerard Depardieu; Andie MacDowell; Bebe Neuwirth; Gregg Edelman; Robert Prosky; Jessie Keosian; Ann Wedgeworth; Ethan Phillips; Mary Louise Wilson; Lois Smith; Simon Jones; ***D:*** Peter Weir; ***W:*** Peter Weir; ***M:*** Hans Zimmer. Golden Globes '91: Actor--Mus./Comedy (Depardieu), Film--Mus./Comedy.

The Green Cockatoo *Four Dark Hours; Race Gang* **1937** Eileen (Ray) has just arrived in London and is still at the train station when Dave (Newton) stumbles into her. He's been stabbed by some crooks and dies and Eileen becomes a suspect. She flees the police to deliver a message to Dave's brother, nightclub entertainer Jim (Mills), and he wants revenge. Based on the book by Graham Greene. **65m/B; DVD.** *GB* John Mills; Rene Ray; Robert Newton; Charles Oliver; Bruce Seton; Frank Atkinson; Allan Jeayes; Julien Vedey; ***D:*** William Cameron Menzies; ***W:*** Arthur Wimperis; Edward Berkman; ***C:*** Mutz Greenbaum; ***M:*** Miklos Rozsa.

Green Dolphin Street 1/2 **1947** Flimsy romantic epic set in 19th century New Zealand. A young girl marries the beau she and her sister are battling over in this Oscar-winning special effects show which features one big earthquake. Based on the Elizabeth Goudge novel, this was one of MGM's biggest hits in 1947. **161m/B; VHS, DVD.** Lana Turner; Van Heflin; Donna Reed; Edmund Gwenn; ***D:*** Victor Saville; ***C:*** George J. Folsey.

Green Dragon 1/2 **2001 (PG-13)** Tai (Duong) is a former Army translator now appointed camp manager at a Vietnamese refugee camp in 1975. He brings a nephew, Minh, and a niece, Anh, as well as a boatload of guilt over leaving their mother behind. He forms a bond with his boss, Jim (Swayze) who seems gruff but has his own issues. The camp cook (Whitaker) helps Minh open up by teaching him to paint and working with him on a mural depicting an idealized American melting pot, with the titular Green Dragon at its center. Various subplots and periods of heavy-handed sentimantality threaten to overwhelm fine character study, but overall this is an engaging look at a period of American history previously ignored. **113m/C; VHS, DVD.** Don Duong; Patrick Swayze; Forest Whitaker; Hiep Thi Le; Kieu Chinh; Billinger C. Tran; Trung Hieu Nguyen; Long Nguyen; Jennifer Tran; ***D:*** Timothy Linh Bui; ***W:*** Tony Bui; Timothy Linh Bui; ***C:*** Kramer Morgenthau; ***M:*** Mychael Danna; Jeff Danna.

Green Eyes 1/2 **1934** A costume party in a country mansion sets the scene for a routine murder mystery when the guests find their host stabbed to death in a closet. Based on the novel "The Murder of Stephen Kester" by H. Ashbrook. **68m/B; VHS, DVD.** Shirley Grey; Charles Starrett; Claude Gillingwater; John Wray; Dorothy Revier; ***D:*** Richard Thorpe; ***W:*** Melville Shyer.

Green Fields 1/2 *Grine Felder; Gruner Felder* **1937** A quiet romance based on Peretz Hirschbein's legendary tale of a young scholar of the Talmud who leaves the shelter of the synagogue in order to learn about people in the real world. The search takes him to the countryside where he finds himself in the middle of a battle between two families who both want him as a tutor and a suitor for their daughters. In Yiddish with English subtitles. **95m/B; VHS, DVD.** Michael Goldstein; Herschel Bernardi; Helen Beverly; ***D:*** Jacob Ben-Ami.

Green Fire 1/2 **1955** The screen sizzles when emerald miner Granger meets plantation-owner Kelly in the exotic jungles of South America. Usual plot complications muddle the story, but who cares when the stars are this attractive? **100m/C; VHS, DVD.** Stewart Granger; Grace Kelly; Paul Douglas; John Ericson; Murvyn Vye; Jose Torvay; Robert Tafur; Nacho Galindo; ***D:*** Andrew Marton; ***W:*** Ivan Goff; Ben Roberts; ***M:*** Miklos Rozsa.

Green for Danger **1947** A detective stages a chilling mock operation to find a mad killer stalking the corridors of a British hospital during WWII. Sim's first great claim to fame (pre-"A Christmas Carol"). **91m/B; VHS, DVD.** *GB* Trevor Howard; Alastair Sim; Leo Genn; ***D:*** Sidney Gilliat.

The Green Glove 1/2 **1952** A jewel thief steals a beautiful relic from a tiny church. WWII makes it impossible for him to fence it and the church finds a relentless ally to track the thief. Excellent action sequences lift this standard plot slightly above the ordinary. **88m/B; VHS, DVD.** Glenn Ford; Geraldine Brooks; Cedric Hardwicke; George Macready; Gaby Andre; Roger Treville; Juliette Greco; Jean Bretonniere; ***D:*** Rudolph Mate; ***W:*** Charles Bennett.

Green Grow the Rushes *Brandy Ashore* **1951** The English government tries to put a stop to brandy smuggling on the coast, but the townspeople drink up the evidence. A young Burton highlights this watered-down comedy. Based on a novel by co-scripter Harold Clewes. **77m/B; VHS, DVD.** *GB* Roger Livesey; Honor Blackman; Richard Burton; Frederick Leister; ***D:*** Derek Twist.

The Green Hornet 1939 The feature version of the original serial, in which the Green Hornet and Kato have a series of crime-fighting adventures. **100m/B; VHS, DVD.** Gordon Jones; Keye Luke; Anne Nagel; Wade Boteler; Walter McGrail; Douglas Evans; Cy Kendall; ***D:*** Ford Beebe; Ray Taylor; ***W:*** George Plympton; Basil Dickey; ***C:*** Jerome Ash; William Sickner.

The Green Hornet 2011 (PG-13) After the suspicious death of his father, flighty L.A. party guy Britt Reid (Rogan) takes over the family media empire. With the help of martial arts expert and inventor Kato (Chou), Britt reinvents himself as vigilante crime-fighter The Green Hornet, posing as an actual criminal. The pair set their sights on a corrupt District Attorney and generic (though amusingly-played) city crime lord Chudnofsky (Waltz). Co-writer Rogan injects too much meaningless comic babble and slacker sensibility to the story, and along with over-the-top slo-mo action sequences and lame one-liners, takes too much of the edge off of a good concept. It's baffling why Diaz would accept the role of a meaningless female assistant. **119m/C; Blu-Ray, On Demand.** Seth Rogen; Jay Chou; Cameron Diaz; Christoph Waltz; Edward James Olmos; David Harbour; Edward Furlong; Tom Wilkinson; ***D:*** Michael Gondry; ***W:*** Evan Goldberg; ***C:*** John Schwartzman; ***M:*** James Newton Howard.

Green Ice 1/2 1981 An American electronics expert gets involved with a brutal South American government dealing with emeralds and plans a heist with his girlfriend and other cohorts. A little bit of romance, a little bit of action, a lot of nothing much. **109m/C; DVD, Streaming.** *UK* Ryan O'Neal; Anne Archer; Omar Sharif; John Larroquette; ***D:*** Ernest Day; ***W:*** Edward Anhalt; Robert De Laurentis.

Green Inferno *Tarzan and the Jungle Mystery* 1972 A wealthy eccentric who lives deep in the South American jungle incites the natives to rebel. Mercenary agents are then hired to kill him. **90m/C; VHS, DVD.** *SP* Richard Yesteran; Didi Sherman; Caesar Burner; ***D:*** Miguel Iglesias.

The Green Inferno 1/2 2014 (R) A group of university activists, led by raging egomaniac Alejandro (Levy), plans a trek deep into the Peruvian rain forests to protest a gas pipeline system that's destroying the countryside. Their plane crashes down into dangerous native territory, and the gang stumbles into a full-blown cannibal holocaust. Horrormeister Roth lights a long fuse that eventually explodes into the nastiest and bloodiest work of his career. This ultraviolent political commentary on the environment and the dangers of international relations is gruesome and disturbing in all the right ways. **100m/C; DVD, Blu-Ray.** Lorenza Izzo; Ariel Levy; Sky Ferreira; Daryl Sabara; Kirby Bliss Blanton; Aaron Burns; ***D:*** Eli Roth; ***W:*** Eli Roth; Guillermo Amoedo; ***C:*** Antonio Quercia; ***M:*** Manuel Riveiro.

Green Lantern 2011 (PG-13) Another potential superhero franchise (from DC Comics) suffers from special effects that overwhelm the sometimes self-conscious story. Pic also needs a lot of exposition to reveal that the Green Lantern Corps are an alien brotherhood committed to keeping the intergalactic peace, thanks to a ring that gives each of them superpowers. Reckless recruit Hal Jordan (Reynolds, nicely filling out his green costume) is the first human chosen for the Corps, but he has to master his abilities just as the evil Parallax threatens to take control. **114m/C; DVD, Blu-Ray, On Demand.** Ryan Reynolds; Blake Lively; Peter Sarsgaard; Mark Strong; Angela Bassett; Tim Robbins; Temuera Morrison; Jon Tenney; Amy Carlson; Jay O. Sanders; ***V:*** Geoffrey Rush; Michael Clarke Duncan; Clancy Brown; ***D:*** Martin Campbell; ***W:*** Michael Goldenberg; Greg Berlanti; Michael Green; Marc Guggenheim; ***C:*** Dion Beebe; ***M:*** James Newton Howard.

The Green Light 1937 Flynn seems an odd choice for a noble doctor role (especially one that leans heavily on religion) but the actor insisted Warner Bros. give him a break from swashbucklers. Newell Paige takes the blame when his elderly mentor Dr. Endicott botches a surgery that results in a patient's death. He resigns and heads west to help a friend who's trying to find a cure for Rocky Mountain Spotted Fever and Paige insists on testing the experimental vaccine on himself. Based on the novel by Lloyd C. Douglas. **85m/B; DVD.** Errol Flynn; Anita Louise; Margaret Lindsay; Walter Abel; Cedric Hardwicke; Henry O'Neill; Spring Byington; Erin O'Brien-Moore; ***D:*** Frank Borzage; ***W:*** Milton Krims; ***C:*** Byron Haskin; ***M:*** Max Steiner.

Green Mansions 1959 Screen adaptation of W. H. Hudson's novel suffers due to miscasting of Hepburn as Rima the Bird Girl, who is not permitted to leave her sanctuary. Perkins is good as the male lead who fled to the jungle in search of wealth and instead finds a powerful love. Hepburn was married to director Ferrer at the time. **104m/C; VHS, DVD.** Audrey Hepburn; Anthony Perkins; Lee J. Cobb; Sessue Hayakawa; Henry Silva; Nehemiah Persoff; Michael Pate; ***D:*** Mel Ferrer; ***W:*** Dorothy Kingsley; ***C:*** Joseph Ruttenberg.

The Green Mile 1/2 1999 (R) Lightning didn't exactly strike twice when Darabont directed this follow-up to "The Shawshank Redemption," another period prison drama by Stephen King. Paul Edgecomb (Hanks) is the decent head guard at Louisiana's Cold Mountain Penitentiary in 1935. He works E block, which is death row (title refers to the color of the floor). Among his prisoners is hulking black man John Coffey (Duncan), whose intimidating size belies a sweet nature. And something else—it seems Coffey has the power to heal. Overlong and watching the executions takes a strong stomach; characters are more symbols than human beings. **187m/C; VHS, DVD, Blu-Ray.** Tom Hanks; Michael Clarke Duncan; David Morse; Bonnie Hunt; Michael Jeter; Sam Rockwell; James Cromwell; Patricia Clarkson; Graham Greene; Barry Pepper; Doug Hutchison; Jeffrey DeMunn; Harry Dean Stanton; Dabbs Greer; Eve Brent; William Sadler; Gary Sinise; ***D:*** Frank Darabont; ***W:*** Frank Darabont; ***C:*** David Tattersall; ***M:*** Thomas Newman. Broadcast Film Critics '99: Adapt. Screenplay, Support. Actor (Duncan).

The Green Pastures 1936 Marc Connelly co-directed and adapted his own 1930 Pulitzer Prize-winning play, which attempts to retell Biblical stories in black English vernacular of the '30s. Southern theatre owners boycotted the controversial film which had an all-Black cast. **93m/B; DVD.** Rex Ingram; Oscar Polk; Eddie Anderson; George Reed; Abraham Graves; Myrtle Anderson; Frank Wilson; ***D:*** William Keighley; Marc Connelly; ***W:*** Marc Connelly; ***C:*** Hal Mohr.

Green Plaid Shirt 1996 In 1978, Phillip and Guy are exploring first love while their friends, Devon, Jerry, and Todd are exploring life. Ten years later, Phillip is the only one to survive the AIDS impact on the gay community as he tries to make sense of what happened and what comes next. **90m/C; VHS, DVD.** Gregory Phelan; Kevin Blair Spirtas; Russell Scott Lewis; Richard Israel; Jonathan Klein; ***D:*** Richard Natale; ***W:*** Richard Natale; ***C:*** Amit Bhattacharya; ***M:*** Norman Noll.

The Green Promise *Raging Waters* 1949 A well-meaning but domineering farmer and his four motherless children face disaster as a result of the father's obstinacy. But when he is laid up, the eldest daughter takes over, tries modern methods and equipment, and makes the farm a success. **90m/B; VHS, DVD.** Walter Brennan; Marguerite Chapman; Robert Paige; Natalie Wood; Ted Donaldson; Connie Marshall; Robert Ellis; Irving Bacon; Milburn Stone; ***D:*** William D. Russell; ***W:*** Monte (Monty) Collins, Jr.; ***C:*** John L. "Jack" Russell; ***M:*** Rudolph (Rudy) Schrager.

The Green Room *La Chambre Verte* 1978 (PG) Truffaut's haunting tale of a man who, valuing death over life, erects a shrine to all the dead he has known. Offered a chance at love, he cannot overcome his obsessions to take the risk. Based on the Henry James story "Altar of the Dead." In French with subtitles. **95m/C; VHS, DVD.** *FR* Francois Truffaut; Nathalie Baye; Jean Daste; Antoine Vitez; Jane Lobre; Marcel Berbert; ***D:*** Francois Truffaut; ***W:*** Jean Gruault; ***C:*** Nestor Almendros; ***M:*** Maurice Jaubert.

Green Room 2015 (R) As tight and effective as the punk rock anthems that inspire the band within it, Saulnier's latest thriller is one part John Carpenter, one part Michael Mann, and one part something completely fresh. A punk rock band accepts an assignment to play a small club in the Pacific Northwest, only to find that it's run by Neo-Nazi skinheads. They stumble on a murder in the green room, and it looks like they're never going to leave, especially when the Nazi's villainous leader (Stewart) shows up to clean up the mess. Brutal and unforgettable. **95m/C; DVD, Blu-Ray.** Anton Yelchin; Joe Cole; Alia Shawkat; Mark Webber; Macon Blair; ***D:*** Jeremy Saulnier; ***W:*** Jeremy Saulnier; ***C:*** Sean Porter; ***M:*** Brooke Blair; Will Blair.

Green Sails 1/2 2000 A young corporate executive discovers a conspiracy in his company to force an Indonesian tribe off their land in order to build a dam they can exploit for profits. He flees to Indonesia to see if the story is true, and must decide what he can do about it. **94m/C; DVD.** *AU* Marcus Graham; Alexandra Paul; Dennis Garber; Thomas Kretschmann; Michael Ontkean; ***D:*** Whitney Ransick; ***W:*** Gregory Widen; ***C:*** Nino Martinetti; ***M:*** Boris Zelkin.

The Green Slime WOOF! *Gamma Sango Uchu Daisakusen; Battle Beyond the Stars; Death and the Green Slime* 1968 (G) Danger and romance highlight the journey of a space ship assigned to intercept an oncoming asteroid. Little do the astronauts realize, but they have brought aboard the ship the malevolent alien creatures known as green slime (and we ain't talking jello here). Cheap, U.S./Japanese co-production will leave you feeling lousy in the morning. The title song is legendary among genre aficionados. **90m/C; VHS, DVD, Blu-Ray.** *JP* Robert Horton; Richard Jaeckel; Luciana Paluzzi; Bud Widom; Ted Gunther; Robert Dunham; ***D:*** Kinji Fukasaku; ***W:*** Ivan Reiner; Charles Sinclair; Bill Finger; ***C:*** Yoshikazu Yamasawa; ***M:*** Charles Fox; Toshiaki Tsushima.

Green Snake 1993 Combo of mysticism and action based on a Chinese fable. Green Snake (Cheung) and Son Ching (Wong) are actual reptiles who have been practicing taking human form. When self-righteous Buddhist monk Fa-Hai discovers them, he thinks it's a sin to tamper with the natural order. The snakes don't appreciate his lack of compassion and plot destruction. Cantonese with subtitles. **102m/C; VHS, DVD.** *CH* Maggie Cheung; Joey Wong; ***D:*** Tsui Hark.

Green Street Hooligans 1/2 2005 (R) Matt Buckner (Wood) is expelled from Harvard weeks before graduating when he's forced to take the fall for his wealthy roommate after cocaine is found in their room. He accepts $10,000 in hush money and takes off for London to visit his sister Shannon (Forlani) and brother-in-law Steve (Warren). Steve's younger brother Pete (Hunnam) takes Matt to a West Ham football match, where he's introduced to the violent world of the Green Street Elite, the gang of rabid fans committed to supporting the West Ham football club through bloody street warfare with supporters of opposing teams. Yank's eye view of the gritty nature of soccer hooliganism will leave you both fascinated and repelled. **106m/C; DVD.** *GB US* Elijah Wood; Charlie Hunnam; Claire Forlani; Marc Warren; Leo Gregory; Henry Goodman; Geoff Bell; Ross McCall; Rafe Spall; Kieran Bew; Francis Pope; Christopher Hehir; Terence Jay; ***D:*** Lexi Alexander; ***W:*** Lexi Alexander; Dougie Brimson; Josh Shelov; ***C:*** Alexander Buono; ***M:*** Christopher Franke.

Green Street Hooligans 2 2009 After a particularly brutal brawl, members of the Green Street Elite and their Millwall rivals end up in the same prison where the violence escalates. Almost every prison cliche you can imagine is on display to no great effect and the pic has little in common with its 2005 predecessor except for its violence. **94m/C; DVD.** *GB* Ross McCall; Nicky Holender; Luke Massy; Graham McTavish; Marina Sirtis; Treva Etienne; Terence Jay; ***D:*** Jesse Johnson; ***W:*** T. Jay O'Brien; ***C:*** Jonathan Hall; ***M:*** Terence Jay.

The Green Years 1/2 1946 Young Irish orphan Robert Shannon (Stockwell) is sent to live with his strict maternal grandparents in Scotland where his tippling great-grandfather Alexander (Coburn) provides love and sympathy. Also an eventual inheritance, which the older Robert (Drake) is supposed to use to achieve his dream of becoming a doctor despite his grandfather Leckie's (Cronyn) disapproval. Adapted from the A.J. Cronin novel. **125m/B; DVD.** Charles Coburn; Tom Drake; Beverly Tyler; Hume Cronyn; Jessica Tandy; Gladys Cooper; Dean Stockwell; Selena Royle; Richard Haydn; Andy Clyde; Norman Lloyd; Robert North; Wallace Ford; ***D:*** Victor Saville; ***W:*** Robert Ardrey; ***C:*** Sonya Levien; George J. Folsey; ***M:*** Herbert Stothart.

Green Zone 2010 (R) Reuniting the director and star of two of the "Bourne" series of action flicks, this thriller takes a more serious and realistic look at military secrecy. During the U.S.-led occupation of Baghdad, Roy Miller (Damon) is sent to find weapons of mass destruction allegedly stockpiled in the Iraqi desert. The only thing Miller discovers, however, is faulty intelligence and a region becoming increasingly unstable. Encounters with a slick State Department boss (Kinnear) and a jaded CIA agent (Gleeson) show him the dangers of less obvious minefields as well. Director Greengrass uses his patented "shaky-cam" technique once again, but the action sequences are never over-the-top and lend a real sense of the danger the troops face. **114m/C; Blu-Ray.** Matt Damon; Greg Kinnear; Amy Ryan; Jason Isaacs; Brendan Gleeson; ***D:*** Paul Greengrass; ***W:*** Brian Helgeland; ***C:*** Barry Ackroyd; ***M:*** John Powell.

Greenberg 1/2 2010 (R) Cranky, unmotivated ex-rocker-turned-carpenter Roger Greenberg (Stiller), newly released from a mental hospital, uproots from New York to housesit for his brother in Los Angeles. While there, his abrasive personality begins to win over his brother's personal assistant, Florence (Gerwig), who's been assigned to look out for him. Dry, subtle but uneven, coming-of-middle-age comedy that often fumbles, accurately expressing the pain and humor of its characters' lives. **107m/C; Blu-Ray.** Ben Stiller; Greta Gerwig; Rhys Ifans; Susan Traylor; Juno Temple; Mark Duplass; Jennifer Jason Leigh; Dave Franco; Chris Messina; Brie Larson; ***D:*** Noah Baumbach; ***W:*** Noah Baumbach; ***C:*** Harris Savides.

Greener Grass 1/2 2019 While watching a kids' soccer game, perfectly put together Lisa (Luebbe) compliments the infant of her friend Jill (DeBoer) and Jill immediately gives her the baby. Because Lisa wanted the child, no one thinks this is odd as peer approval drives this community. Jill later has mixed feelings about losing her baby, which is not permissible. As Jill's personality disintegrates, her remaining child, precocious Julian (Hilliard), experiences an unexpected transformation. The surreal comedy is a sharp satirical critique of conformity and civility extremes, though some scenes feel like improv bits strung together awkwardly. **95m/C; DVD, Blu-Ray.** Jocelyn DeBoer; Dawn Luebbe; Mary Holland; Beck Bennett; Neil Casey; ***D:*** Jocelyn DeBoer; Dawn Luebbe; ***W:*** Jocelyn DeBoer; Dawn Luebbe; ***C:*** Lowell A. Meyer; ***M:*** Samuel Nobles.

Greenfingers 1/2 2000 (R) One of those strange-but-true stories that barely stays ahead of being twee, thanks to its cast. Surly prisoner Colin Briggs (Owen) has just been transferred to Edgefield, an "open" prison that aims at building job skills. When Colin accidentally turns out to be a prime gardener (with greenfingers in British parlance), warden Hodge (Clarke) assigns him to garden detail along with his twinkly, dying, elderly cellmate Fergus (Kelly). Then the prison garden comes to the attention of TV star gardener Georgina Woodhouse (Mirren) and she sponsors their efforts in a very prestigious flower show. Remember the Brits take their gardening very seriously indeed. **90m/C; VHS, DVD.** *GB US* Clive Owen; Dame Helen Mirren; David Kelly; Warren Clarke; Danny Dyer; Paterson Joseph; Natasha Little; Adam Fogerty; ***D:*** Joel Hershman; ***W:*** Joel Hershman; ***C:*** John Daly; ***M:*** Guy Dagul.

The Greening of Whitney Brown 2011 (PG) Bratty Philadelphia tween Whitney is forced to move to the farm her grandparents once owned after her dad loses his job. Her mom settles in fine, but her dad also has issues involving his own crusty father. Whitney feels stranded but she does get to hang out with cuter-than-cute horse Odd Job Bob. Filmed in Newborn, Georgia. **87m/C; DVD.** Sammi Hanratty; Brooke Shields; Aidan Quinn; Kris Kristofferson;

D: Peter Odiorne; ***W:*** Gail Gilchriest; ***C:*** James L. Carter; ***M:*** Randy Edelman.

Greenmail **2001 (R)** A Seattle serial bomber is targeting corporations that harm the environment. Naturally, the bomb squad must stop him. Even things getting blowed up good can't save this one. **92m/C; VHS, DVD.** Stephen Baldwin; Tom Skerritt; Kelly Rowan; D.B. Sweeney; ***D:*** Jonathan Heap; ***W:*** Raul Inglis; James Makichuk; ***C:*** Michael G. Wojciechowski. **VIDEO**

Greenwich Village **1944** Would-be classical composer Kenneth Harvey (Ameche) finds his work being adapted for a musical revue by speakeasy owner Danny O'Mara (Bendix). But Harvey isn't too upset when he discovers singer Bonnie Watson (Blaine in her screen debut) is working on the show. Miranda is the club's fortune-telling comic foil. **82m/C; DVD.** Don Ameche; William Bendix; Vivian Blaine; Carmen Miranda; Felix Bressart; ***D:*** Walter Lang; ***W:*** Earl Baldwin; Ernest Pagano; Michael Fessier; Walter Bullock; ***C:*** Leon Shamroy; Harry Jackson; ***M:*** Emil Newman; Charles Henderson.

Greetings **1968 (R)** De Niro stars in this wild and crazy comedy about a man who tries to help his friend flunk his draft physical. One of DePalma's first films, and a pleasantly anarchic view of the late '60s, wrought with a light, intelligent tone. Followed by the sequel "Hi, Mom." **88m/C; VHS, DVD, Blu-Ray.** Robert De Niro; Jonathan Warden; Gerrit Graham; Allen Garfield; Megan McCormick; Bettina Kugel; Jack Cowley; Richard Hamilton; ***D:*** Brian De Palma; ***W:*** Brian De Palma; Charles Hirsch; ***C:*** Robert Fiore.

Greetings from Tim Buckley **2012** Rather too obvious retelling of a pivotal moment in the personal life and career of musician Jeff Buckley (Badgley) and his barely remembered father, folkie Tim Buckley (Rosenfield), who died of a drug overdose at 28 in 1975. The 25-year-old Jeff is asked by a New York concert promoter to perform in a 1991 tribute concert to Tim (leading to flashbacks of Tim's life) and reluctantly agrees, which also means Jeff must deal with some ambivalent feelings. Badgley does fine, especially in the musical sequences, although the character is portrayed as a sulky manchild. **103m/C; Streaming.** Penn Badgley; Ben Rosenfield; Imogen Poots; Norbert Lee Butz; Frank Wood; William Sadler; ***D:*** Daniel Algrant; ***W:*** Daniel Algrant; David Brendel; Emma Sheanshang; ***C:*** Andrij Parekh.

Gregory's Girl **1/2 1980** Sweet, disarming comedy established Forsyth. An awkward young Scottish schoolboy falls in love with the female goalie of his soccer team. He turns to his 10-year-old sister for advice, but she's more interested in ice cream than love. His best friend is no help, either, since he has yet to fall in love. Perfect mirror of teenagers and their instantaneous, raw, and all-consuming loves. Very sweet scene with Gregory and his girl lying on their backs in an open space illustrates the simultaneous simplicity and complexity of young love. **91m/C; VHS, DVD, Blu-Ray.** *GB* Gordon John Sinclair; Dee Hepburn; Jake D'Arcy; Chic Murray; Alex Norton; John Bett; Clare Grogan; ***D:*** Bill Forsyth; ***W:*** Bill Forsyth; ***C:*** Michael Coulter. British Acad. '81: Screenplay.

Gremlins **1984 (PG)** Comedy horror with deft satiric edge. Produced by Spielberg. Fumbling gadget salesman Rand Peltzer is looking for something really special to get his son Billy. He finds it in a small store in Chinatown. The wise shopkeeper is reluctant to sell him the adorable "mogwai" but relents after fully warning him "Don't expose him to bright light, don't ever get him wet, and don't ever, ever feed him after midnight." Naturally, this all happens and the result is a gang of nasty gremlins who decide to tear up the town on Christmas Eve. Followed by "Gremlins 2: The New Batch" which is less black comedy, more parody, and perhaps more inventive. **106m/C; VHS, DVD, Blu-Ray.** Zach Galligan; Phoebe Cates; Hoyt Axton; Polly Holliday; Frances Lee McCain; Keye Luke; Dick Miller; Corey Feldman; Judge Reinhold; Glynn Turman; Scott Brady; Jackie Joseph; ***V:*** Howie Mandel; ***D:*** Joe Dante; ***W:*** Chris Columbus; ***C:*** John Hora; ***M:*** Jerry Goldsmith.

Gremlins 2: The New Batch **1/2 1990 (PG-13)** The sequel to "Gremlins" is superior to the original, which was quite good. Set in a futuristic skyscraper in the Big Apple, director Dante presents a less violent but far more campy vision, paying myriad surreal tributes to scores of movies, including "The Wizard of Oz" and musical extravaganzas of the past. Also incorporates a Donald Trump parody, takes on TV news, and body slams modern urban living. Great fun. **107m/C; VHS, DVD, Blu-Ray.** Zach Galligan; Phoebe Cates; John Glover; Christopher Lee; Robert Prosky; Robert Picardo; Haviland (Haylie) Morris; Dick Miller; Jackie Joseph; Keye Luke; Belinda Balaski; Paul Bartel; Kenneth Tobey; John Astin; Henry Gibson; Leonard Maltin; Hulk Hogan; Charles S. Haas; ***Cameo(s):*** Jerry Goldsmith; ***V:*** Howie Mandel; Tony Randall; ***D:*** Joe Dante; ***W:*** Charles S. Haas; ***C:*** John Hora; ***M:*** Jerry Goldsmith.

Greta **1/2 2018 (R)** When young single Frances (Moretz) finds a designer handbag on a subway car, she returns it to its owner Greta (Huppert). Greta is a piano teacher and recent widow who lives alone, while Frances has just lost her mother. The pair become fast friends in a faux mother-daughter relationship. Frances learns that Greta has a more sinister agenda and has lured others into her trap before. Though the thriller-horror mash up is filled with jump scares, somewhat interesting details, and nearly unbelievable coincidences, its success turns on the over-the-top, totally fun performance of Huppert who effectively sells every aspect of her character. **98m/C; DVD, Blu-Ray.** *IR US* Isabelle Huppert; Chloë Grace Moretz; Maika Monroe; Jane Perry; Jeff Hiller; ***D:*** Neil Jordan; ***W:*** Neil Jordan; Ray Wright; ***C:*** Seamus McGarvey; ***M:*** Javier Navarrete.

The Grey **1/2 2012 (R)** Channeling his inner Jack London, director/writer Carnahan takes his interest in stories of alpha males to the middle of nowhere as a group of oil company workers crash lands in the snowy tundra of the Alaskan wilderness. Led by the one man (Neeson) who knows the nature of the wolves that surround them—it is his job to protect the workers from the creatures—the survivors must battle both another species and Mother Nature. Effectively bleak and unrelenting, it plays not unlike a horror movie in that it's clear that the men are going to go down one-by-one. **117m/C; DVD, Blu-Ray.** Liam Neeson; Frank Grillo; Dermot Mulroney; Dallas Roberts; Joe Anderson; James Badge Dale; Nonso Anozie; Ben Brey; ***D:*** Joe Carnahan; ***W:*** Joe Carnahan; Ian Mackenzie Jeffers; ***C:*** Masanobu Takayanagi; ***M:*** Marc Streitenfeld.

Grey Gardens **1975** For Jackie Kennedy fans, a documentary sure to shock. Filmed in her 79-year-old aunt's rotting Long Island mansion, we're allowed to witness the reclusive Big Edith and her 56-year-old daughter, Little Edie, singing, dancing, and fighting in this most bizarre of documentaries. **95m/C; VHS, DVD, Blu-Ray.** ***D:*** Albert Maysles; David Maysles; Ellen Hovde; Muffie Meyer; Susan Froemke; ***C:*** Albert Maysles; David Maysles. Natl. Film Reg. '10.

Grey Gardens **2009** Stellar performances from both Barrymore and Lange in a cable flick that was inspired by the 1973 documentary by the Maysles brothers, with director Michael Sucsy devotedly recreating a number of scenes. In the 1930s, vivacious 'Big Edie' Beale (Lange) is a party-thrower par excellence while her teenaged daughter 'Little Edie' (Barrymore) wants to be a starlet. As the years roll by, resources dwindle, eccentricities (and co-dependence) grow, and their East Hampton mansion becomes unlivable. In the early 1970s, things get so bad that the authorities raid the place and Jacqueline Kennedy Onassis (Tripplehorn), a relative, makes an ultimately unsuccessful attempt to help the recluses. **104m/C; DVD.** Drew Barrymore; Jessica Lange; Jeanne Tripplehorn; Ken Howard; Daniel Baldwin; Malcolm Gets; Arye Gross; Justin Louis; ***D:*** Michael Sucsy; ***W:*** Patricia Rozema; Michael Sucsy; ***C:*** Mike Eley; ***M:*** Rachel Portman. **CABLE**

Grey Owl **1/2 1999 (PG-13)** Interesting old-fashioned biopic suffers from miscasting (and it's not Brosnan, although he takes a little getting used to). Based on the true story of Archie Grey Owl (Brosnan), an Ojibway trapper in 1930s Canada who changes his occupation and becomes an ardent early environmentalist and celebrity lecturer and writer. Only after his death does the truth come out—Archie was in fact Englishman Archibald Belaney. Film bogs down in its romantic aspects with Galipeau, as Grey Owl's young Mohawk girlfriend, sadly out of her depths. **117m/C; VHS, DVD.** *GB CA* Pierce Brosnan; Annie Galipeau; Vlasta Vrana; Nathaniel Arcand; David Fox; Charles Powell; Renee Asherson; Stephenie Cole; Graham Greene; ***D:*** Richard Attenborough; ***W:*** William Nicholson; ***C:*** Roger Pratt; ***M:*** George Fenton. Genie '99: Costume Des.

The Grey Zone **2001 (R)** Nelson adapted his own play, which centers on the Sonderkommandos, Jewish prisoners who worked in the crematoriums (in this case at Auschwitz), disposed of remains, and were given special privileges by the Nazis. In October of 1944, the prisoners plan an uprising and blew up two of the gas chambers. The film can't transcend its theatrical origins and is both surreal and excruciating (since Nelson doesn't spare depicting the atrocities) to watch. **108m/C; VHS, DVD.** David Arquette; Daniel Benzali; Steve Buscemi; David Chandler; Allan Corduner; Harvey Keitel; Natasha Lyonne; Mira Sorvino; ***D:*** Tim Blake Nelson; ***W:*** Tim Blake Nelson; ***C:*** Russell Fine; ***M:*** Jeff Danna.

Greyfriars Bobby **1/2 1961** A true story of a Skye terrier named Bobby who, after his master dies, refuses to leave the grave. Even after being coaxed by the local children into town, he still returns to the cemetery each evening. Word of his loyalty spreads, and Bobby becomes the pet of 19th century Edinburgh. Nicely told, with fine location photography and good acting. Great for children and animal lovers. **91m/C; VHS, DVD.** Donald Crisp; Laurence Naismith; Kay Walsh; ***D:*** Don Chaffey.

Greystoke: The Legend of Tarzan, Lord of the Apes **1984 (PG)** The seventh Earl of Greystoke becomes a shipwrecked orphan and is raised by apes. Ruling the ape-clan in the vine-swinging persona of Tarzan, he is discovered by an anthropologist and returned to his ancestral home in Scotland, where he is immediately recognized by his grandfather. The contrast between the behavior of man and ape is interesting, and Tarzan's introduction to society is fun, but there's no melodrama or cliff-hanging action, as we've come to expect of the Tarzan genre. Due to her heavy southern accent, Andie MacDowell (as Jane) had her voice dubbed by Glenn Close. **130m/C; DVD, Blu-Ray.** Christopher Lambert; Ralph Richardson; Ian Holm; James Fox; Andie MacDowell; Ian Charleson; Cheryl Campbell; Nigel Davenport; ***D:*** Hugh Hudson; ***W:*** Michael Austin. N.Y. Film Critics '84: Support. Actor (Richardson).

Gridiron Gang **2006 (PG-13)** Based on the true story of correctional officer Sean Porter (The Rock), who recruits a bunch of gangbangers stuck in a juvie camp for his football team. Naturally, the teens find hope through the help of the game and their tough coach. Heavily motivational sports cliche; the documentary footage shown at the end, of the real team and the real coach, may be the best part of the movie. **125m/C; DVD, Blu-Ray.** Dwayne "The Rock" Johnson; Xzibit; Leon Rippy; Kevin Dunn; Willie Weathers; ***D:*** Phil Joanou; ***W:*** Jeff Maguire; ***C:*** Jeff Cutler; ***M:*** Trevor Rabin.

Gridlock'd **1996 (R)** Junkies and sometime-musicians Spoon (Shakur) and Stretch (Roth) decide to kick the habit after their singer Cookie (Newton) overdoses and slips into a coma. The hapless pair are thrown into the switches of social services programs and government offices where they shuffle endlessly but nothing happens. Think "Waiting for Godot" meets "Waiting for the Man." Meanwhile, their dealer is murdered and they're the prime suspects, pursued by the cops and the actual killers, who believe that they've stolen said dealer's stash. Shakur shows flashes of the brilliance that might have been as the more sensitive and sane of the pair, while Roth complements him perfectly as his bug-crazy short-sighted partner. Fellow actor Curtis-Hall's directorial debut. **91m/C; VHS, DVD.** Tim Roth; Tupac Shakur; Thandie Newton; Charles Fleischer; Howard Hesseman; James Pickens, Jr.; John Sayles; Tom Towler; Eric Payne; ***Cameo(s):*** Vondie Curtis-Hall; ***D:*** Vondie Curtis-Hall; ***W:*** Vondie Curtis-Hall; ***C:*** Bill Pope; ***M:*** Stewart Copeland.

Grief **1994** Mark (Chester) is a writer on the syndicated daytime TV show "The Love Judge." Still numb from his lover's death from AIDS the previous year, Mark begins to take an interest in fellow writer Bill (Arquette), while writer Paula (Gutteridge) desires to become the show's new producer and secretary Leslie (Douglas) wants to take her place as the new writer. Present producer Jo (Beat) tries to keep her office family in line while sorting out her personal life. Writer-director Glatzer knows his territory since he spent five years writing for "Divorce Court." **86m/C; VHS, DVD.** Craig Chester; Alexis Arquette; Lucy Gutteridge; Illeana Douglas; Jackie Beat; Carlton Wilborn; Paul Bartel; Mary Woronov; ***D:*** Richard Glatzer; ***W:*** Richard Glatzer; ***C:*** David Dechant.

Griff the Invisible **2010 (PG-13)** Quirky Aussie comedy about misfits in love. Insecure and bullied office worker Griff escapes from his daily life by assuming the role of a superhero. Equally eccentric scientist Melody sympathizes with Griff's oddball way of thinking, feeds into his ultimately harmless fantasies, and becomes a perfect romantic match. **90m/C; DVD, Blu-Ray.** *AU* Ryan Kwanten; Maeve Dermody; Patrick Brammall; Toby Schmitz; Marshall Napier; ***D:*** Leon Ford; ***W:*** Leon Ford; ***C:*** Raymond Chapman; ***M:*** Sep Caton.

Griffin & Phoenix **1/2 2006 (PG-13)** Despite the effective leads, this is a sentimental tearjerker of the worst sort (and a remake of the 1976 TV movie). Divorced workaholic Henry Griffin (Mulroney) learns that his inoperable cancer leaves him less than two years to live. While auditing a college course on death and dying, Henry meets Sarah Phoenix (Peet) and they decide to take a chance on romance. But it comes as no shocker that Sarah is hiding her own terminal secret. **102m/C; DVD.** Dermot Mulroney; Amanda Peet; Sarah Paulson; Blair Brown; Alison Elliott; Lois Smith; ***D:*** Ed Stone; ***W:*** John Hill; ***C:*** David M. Dunlap; ***M:*** Roger Neill.

Griffin and Phoenix: A Love Story **1/2 1976** A sentimental film about the mortality of two vital people. Falk deserts his family when he learns he has terminal cancer. Clayburgh, also terminally ill, meets him for a short but meaningful affair. Good performances help overcome the tear-jerker aspects of the story. **110m/C; VHS, DVD.** Peter Falk; Jill Clayburgh; Dorothy Tristan; John Lehne; ***D:*** Daryl Duke. **TV**

The Grifters **1/2 1990 (R)** Evocative rendering of a terrifying sub-culture. Huston, Cusak, and Bening are con artists, struggling to stay on top in a world where violence, money, and lust are the prizes. Bening and Huston fight for Cusak's soul, while he's determined to decide for himself. Seamless performances and dazzling atmosphere, along with superb pacing, make for a provocative film. Based on a novel by Jim Thompson. **114m/C; VHS, DVD, Blu-Ray.** Anjelica Huston; John Cusack; Annette Bening; Pat Hingle; J.T. Walsh; Charles Napier; Henry Jones; Gailard Sartain; Jeremy Piven; ***D:*** Stephen Frears; ***W:*** Donald E. Westlake; ***C:*** Oliver Stapleton; ***M:*** Elmer Bernstein. Ind. Spirit '91: Actress (Huston), Film; L.A. Film Critics '90: Actress (Huston); Natl. Soc. Film Critics '90: Actress (Huston), Support. Actress (Bening).

Grilled **1/2** *Men Don't Quit* **2006 (R)** Struggling meat salesmen Maurice (Romano) and Dave (James) have their bacon on the line if they don't make a big sale. There's also a mobster, his girl, and a couple of hitmen that also involve the guys. The duo did much better on the small screen, having misplaced their comedy chops while making this yawner. **77m/C; DVD.** Ray Romano; Kevin James; Juliette Lewis; Sofia Vergara; Michael Rapaport; Barry Newman; Burt Reynolds; Kim Coates; Eric Allen Kramer; Jack Kehler; Jon Polito; Lisa Jane Persky; Mary Lynn Rajskub; Caroline Aaron; Richard Libertini; Lisa Edelstein; ***D:*** Jason Ensler; ***W:*** William Tepper; ***C:*** Lawrence Sher; ***M:*** Adam Cohen. **VIDEO**

Grim **1995 (R)** Lives up to its title as an extremely icky and evil subterranean creature is awakened from a long sleep by miners. Apparently not long enough, since he proceeds to rip apart anyone he comes in contact with. **86m/C; VHS, DVD.** Emmanuel Xuereb; Tres Hanley; Peter Tregloan; ***D:*** Paul

Matthews; ***W:*** Paul Matthews; ***C:*** Alan M. Trow; ***M:*** Dennis Michael Tenney.

The Grim Reaper *La Commare Secca* **1962** 22-year-old Bertolucci directed his first feature with this grim and brutal treatment of the investigation of the murder of a prostitute, told via flashbacks and from the disparate perspectives of three people who knew the woman. A commercial bust, the critics were no kinder than the public at the time; not until two years later, with "Before the Revolution," did Bertolucci earn his directorial spurs. The script was written by Pasolini, with whom the erstwhile poet had collaborated on "Accattone" the previous year (as assistant). In Italian with English subtitles. **100m/B; VHS, DVD.** *IT* Francesco Rulu; Giancarlo de Rosa; ***D:*** Bernardo Bertolucci; ***W:*** Pier Paolo Pasolini.

Grim Reaper **1/2 1981 (R)** Mia Farrow's sister is one of a group of American students vacationing on a Greek island. Farrow learns of the twisted cannibalistic murderer who methodically tries to avenge the tragic deaths of his family. **81m/C; VHS, DVD.** *IT* Tisa Farrow; George Eastman; ***D:*** Joe D'Amato.

Grimm Love *Rohtenburg; Butterfly: A Grimm Love Story* **2006 (R)** American grad student Katie Armstrong is studying criminal psychology in Germany and fixates on the notorious 1998 cannibal killer Oliver Hagen for her thesis. Flashbacks show how an internet chat led to Oliver meeting lover Simon, who allowed himself to be murdered and eaten as the ultimate proof of his love. Based on the true crime case of Armin Meiwes. **85m/C; DVD.** *GE* Keri Russell; Thomas Kretschmann; Thomas Huber; ***D:*** Martin Weisz; ***W:*** T.S. Faull; ***C:*** Jonathan Sela; ***M:*** Steve Gutheinz.

Grimm's Snow White *Snow White* **2012 (PG-13)** The Asylum does its own low-budget version of the fairytale with the king getting eaten by some reptile/dragon creature, leaving the kingdom to evil Queen Gwendolyn. She's after the local elf population for their magic and--oh yeah--wants to knock off her interfering stepdaughter Snow White (who looks more like Alice in Wonderland). Like you're expecting the plot to make sense, especially when you can snicker at the bad CGI. **90m/C; DVD, Blu-Ray.** Jane March; Eliza Bennett; Jamie Thomas King; ***D:*** Rachel Goldenberg; ***W:*** Naomi L. Selfman; ***C:*** Alexander Yellen; ***M:*** Chris Ridenhour. **VIDEO**

The Grinch *Dr. Seuss' The Grinch* **2018 (PG)** A modern retelling of the classic 1966 Christmas television special, in which the titular green grouch tries to steal the holiday from the neighboring town of Whoville. With his hallmark velvety timbre traded for something weirdly nasal, Cumberbatch is wasted here. The animation, though, is bright and colorful, and the humor is silly and slapstick. Firmly middle of the road. **86m/C; DVD, Blu-Ray, Streaming.** *CH US JP FR* ***V:*** Benedict Cumberbatch; Rashida Jones; Tristan O'Hare; Scarlett Estevez; Angela Lansbury; Cameron Seely; ***D:*** Yarrow Cheney; Scott Mosier; Tommy Swerdlow; ***W:*** Michael LeSieur; ***M:*** Danny Elfman.

Grind **1996** Dysfunctional blue-collar family saga set in New Jersey. Eddie Dolan (Crudup), just out of the joint, moves in with brother Terry (Schulze) and sister-in-law Janey (Shelly). He gets a dull factory job and fixes up old cars to go drag-racing on the weekend—as well as helping out Terry, who has a sideline working with a car theft ring. Since gorgeous Eddie works nights, he and sulky stay-at-home-with-the-baby Janey get to be real close daytime buddies. Naturally their affair causes trouble for all. A paint-by-numbers plot with some decent acting. **96m/C; VHS, DVD.** Billy Crudup; Adrienne Shelly; Paul Schulze; Frank Vincent; Saul Stein; Amanda Peet; Steven Beach; Tim Devlin; ***D:*** Chris Kentis; ***W:*** Chris Kentis; Laura Lau; ***C:*** Stephen Kazmierski; ***M:*** Brian Kelly.

Grind **2003 (PG-13)** Lightweight tale of teens and their quest for fame and the booty that comes with it rides the rails of the newly-hip extreme sports genre. The straight-outta-Central Casting group of grinders consists of good-looking Eric (Vogel); ladies man Sweet Lou (Kern); goofy, sex-crazed Matt (Vieluf); and the nerdy Dustin (Brody). They follow their skateboarding hero Jimmy Wilson (London) on tour and hope to grab the pro's attention with their skateboarding antics in order to win a coveted sponsorship and ensuing fame and fortune. Pic finds moderate success when sticking to the 'board action (even if it's obviously stand-in work) while gross-out and slacker humor too often misses the mark. **100m/C; VHS, DVD.** Vince Vieluf; Mike Vogel; Adam Brody; Joey Kern; Jennifer (Jenny) Morrison; Jason London; Randy Quaid; Christopher McDonald; Summer Altice; ***D:*** Casey La Scala; ***W:*** Ralph Sall; ***C:*** Richard Crudo; ***M:*** Ralph Sall.

Grindin' **2007** Actor T.O. is constantly distracted from his work by all the pleasures Hollywood has to offer. With his career in shreds, T.O. has to find the motivation to get back on track, even if it's because he doesn't want to lose another part to rival Morris. **90m/C; DVD.** Omar Benson Miller; French Stewart; Regina King; Lawrence Adisa; Sam Sarpong; Richard Whitten; ***D:*** Marcello Thedford; ***W:*** Lawrence Adisa; ***C:*** John Savedra; ***M:*** Damone Arnold. **VIDEO**

Grindstone Road **1/2 2007** Hannah Sloan (Balk) was in a car accident that has left son Daniel in an extended coma. Hoping for a fresh start, Hannah and husband Graham (Bryk) move into an old farmhouse, but Hannah is soon insisting strange things are happening. Graham thinks all the anti-depressants his wife is popping are the problem but it's never that simple. **88m/C; DVD.** Fairuza Balk; Greg Bryk; Joan Gregson; Walter Learning; ***D:*** Melanie Orr; ***W:*** Paul Germann; ***C:*** Simon Shohet; ***M:*** Eric Cadesky; Nick Dyer. **VIDEO**

Gringo **1/2 2018 (R)** Ordinary American businessman Harold Soyinka (Oyelowo) is sent to Mexico by his company to deliver the formula for manufacturing marijuana pills. He gets kidnapped by drug lords, but his bosses back home, played by Theron and Edgerton, are reluctant to pay his ransom. Additional subplots involving international mercenaries and the DEA are tossed in, resulting in an unfunny, overly complicated, *caliente* mess. **111m/C; DVD, Blu-Ray.** David Oyelowo; Charlize Theron; Joel Edgerton; Amanda Seyfried; Thandie Newton; Sharlto Copley; ***D:*** Nash Edgerton; ***W:*** Anthony Tambakis; Matthew Stone; ***C:*** Eduard Grau; ***M:*** Christophe Beck.

Grisbi *Touchez pas au Grisbi; Honour Among Thieves* **1953** King of the French underworld, Gabin finds there's no honor among thieves when a gold heist goes wrong and the loot comes up missing. Moreau is the quintessential moll. French with subtitles. **94m/B; VHS, DVD, Blu-Ray.** *FR* Jean Gabin; Jeanne Moreau; Lino Ventura; Daniel Cauchy; Gaby Basset; ***D:*** Jacques Becker; ***W:*** Jacques Becker; Maurice Griffe; ***M:*** Jean Wiener. Venice Film Fest. '54: Actor (Gabin).

The Grissom Gang **1971 (R)** Remake of the 1948 British film "No Orchids for Miss Blandish." Darby is a wealthy heiress kidnapped by a family of grotesques, led by a sadistic mother. The ransom gets lost in a series of bizarre events, and the heiress appears to be falling for one of her moronic captors. Director Robert Aldrich skillfully blends extreme violence with dark humor. Superb camera work, editing, and 1920s period sets. **127m/C; VHS, DVD, Blu-Ray.** Kim Darby; Scott Wilson; Tony Musante; Ralph Waite; Connie Stevens; Robert Lansing; Wesley Addy; ***D:*** Robert Aldrich; ***W:*** Leon Griffiths; ***C:*** Joseph Biroc; ***M:*** Gerald Fried.

Grizzly *Killer Grizzly* **1976 (PG)** Giant, killer grizzly terrorizes a state park in this blatant "Jaws" rip-off. From the same folks who produced "Abby," a blatant "Exorcist" rip-off. Filmed in Georgia. **92m/C; VHS, DVD, Blu-Ray.** Christopher George; Richard Jaeckel; Andrew Prine; Victoria (Vicki) Johnson; Charles Kissinger; ***D:*** William Girdler; ***W:*** Harvey Flaxman; David Sheldon; ***M:*** Robert O. Ragland.

Grizzly Falls **1/2 1999 (PG)** Old-fashioned family fare, set in 1913, finds 13-year-old Harry (Clark) setting out on a wilderness adventure in the Canadian Rockies with his dad, Tyrone (Brown). Tyrone is out to capture a grizzly and bring it back (alive) for study. But when Tyrone finds a female grizzly and captures the bear's two cubs, Mom Grizzly gets back at him by making off with Harry. The boy and the bear bond but this interspecies relationship can't last and eventually boy and cubs end up with the right species of parent. **94m/C; VHS, DVD.** *CA GB* Daniel Clark; Bryan Brown; Tom Jackson; Oliver Tobias; Richard Harris; ***D:*** Stewart Raffill; ***W:*** Richard Beattie; ***C:*** Thom Best; ***M:*** Paul Zaza; David Reilly.

Grizzly Man **1/2 2005 (R)** Timothy Treadwell spent 13 summers, beginning in 1990, in the Alaskan wilderness living among grizzly bears until 2003, when he and his girlfriend were killed in a bear attack. Director Herzog is an ideal choice to tell the story of one self-absorbed man's obsession (tinged with madness) as the animals' self-appointed guardian and protector. Herzog includes amateur naturalist Treadwell's video footage as well as interviews and his own narration. **103m/C; DVD.** ***D:*** Werner Herzog; ***C:*** Peter Zeitlinger; ***M:*** Richard Thompson. Directors Guild '05: Documentary Director (Herzog); L.A. Film Critics '05: Feature Doc.; N.Y. Film Critics '05: Feature Doc.; Natl. Soc. Film Critics '05: Feature Doc.

Grizzly Mountain **1/2 1997 (G)** Dylan (Dylan Haggerty) and his sister Nicole (Lund) are camping in Oregon with their parents when they decide to explore a cave. After some mysterious rumbling and shaking, the siblings emerge in the 1870s. They meet mountain man Jeremiah (Haggerty), who promises to help them return home, but he's got problems of his own—bad guy Burt (Stephens) wants to dynamite the mountain so the railroad can come through. Pic wanders back and forth between the two time periods and the kids learn a lesson in ecology (and are reunited with their parents). Easy-going; some beautiful scenery. **96m/C; VHS, DVD.** Dan Haggerty; Dylan Haggerty; Nicole Lund; Perry Stephens; Kim Morgan Greene; Martin Kove; Robert Budaska; E.E. Bell; Marguerite Hickey; Don Borza; ***D:*** Jeremy Haft; ***W:*** Peter White; Jeremy Haft; ***C:*** Andy Parke; ***M:*** Jon McCallum.

Grizzly Rage **2007** Mama's got every right to be mad when four dumb teenagers run over and kill her baby. Ritch, Wes, Sean, and Lauren take a trip to celebrate high school graduation and wander off the main roads. After hitting the bear cub, they plow their jeep into a tree, which means they're stranded in the woods when Mother Grizzly shows up. **86m/C; DVD.** Tyler Hoechlin; Kate Todd; Graham Kosakoski; Brody Harms; ***D:*** David DeCoteau; ***W:*** Arne Olsen; ***C:*** Barry Gravelle; ***M:*** Joe Silva. **TV**

Groom Lake **1/2 2002** Minor sci-fi effort from Shatner with a not too interesting plot. Kate is dying so she and boyfriend Andy decide to visit Groom Lake (near Area 51) to see if the alien sightings are true and if outer space visitors can somehow help her. The government is keeping a UFO under wraps but it's actually part of a project that's just been cancelled, much to the anger of project leader Gossner (Shatner). **92m/C; DVD.** William Shatner; Amy Acker; Dan Gauthier; Tom Towler; Dick Van Patten; John Prosky; Dan Martin; ***D:*** William Shatner; ***W:*** William Shatner; ***C:*** Mac Ahlberg; ***M:*** Richard John Baker.

The Groom Wore Spurs **1951** Silly romantic comedy with a few laughs. Hollywood cowboy Ben (Carson) gets in big gambling trouble in Vegas and is bailed out by lawyer Abigail (Rogers). She and the fake cowpoke tie a marriage of convenience knot and then she sets out to remake Ben so he'll live up to his heroic screen image. There's a nonsensical murder plot that also takes up some time. **81m/B; DVD.** Ginger Rogers; Jack Carson; Joan Davis; Stanley Ridges; Victor Sen Yung; John Litel; ***D:*** Richard Whorf; ***W:*** Frank Burt; Robert Libott; ***C:*** J. Peverell Marley; ***M:*** Arthur Lange.

The Groomsmen **2006 (R)** Writer, director, actor Ed Burns mines familiar territory with yet another story of Irish-American males struggling with growing up. This time Burns casts himself as a reluctant father-to-be who gets together with his longtime pals to discuss, continuously, their individual plights and struggles, none of which are very interesting or extraordinary, before resigning himself to a life of monogamy and responsibility. Nearly everything is a retread of past Burns' flicks except for the excellent ensemble cast, which includes Jay Mohr as still juvenile cousin Mike and John Leguizamo as T.C., the prodigal friend who returns with a long-held secret. Burns' first version of this story, "The Brothers McMullen" (1995), is still his best. **99m/C; DVD.** Edward Burns; Donal Logue; Jay Mohr; John Leguizamo; Matthew Lillard; Shari Albert; Spencer Fox; John A. Russo; Heather Burns; Jessica Capshaw; Brittany Murphy; Arthur J. Nascarella; Marion McCorry; Joe Pistone; John F. O'Donohue; Jamie Tirelli; Kevin Kash; Catharine Bolz; Amy Leonard; ***D:*** Edward Burns; ***W:*** Edward Burns; ***C:*** William Rexer; ***M:*** Robert Gray; P.T. Walkley.

Groove **1/2 2000 (R)** Editor Greg Harrison's directorial debut is an economically paced examination of the "rave" scene. It features a terrific ensemble cast, but at heart, the film is an old-fashioned boy-meets-girl romance. The setting is an abandoned building on a San Francisco pier. That's where the squarish David (Linklater) is attending his first rave. Leyla (Glaudini) has perhaps been to too many. Over the course of the night they and the other rave kids go through a series of changes fueled by drugs, emotion, and sexual indecision. In another time, the same story with more limited sexual roles and consciousness-altering substances could have been told about a homecoming dance or spring break. The changes and discoveries the characters make have not changed. Even though the film was made on a restricted budget—actually shot in Super 16mm.?it looks very good. **86m/C; VHS, DVD.** Steve Van Wormer; Lola Glaudini; Hamish Linklater; Denny Kirkwood; Rachel True; MacKenzie Firgens; Nick Offerman; Ari Gold; ***D:*** Greg Harrison; ***W:*** Greg Harrison; ***C:*** Matthew Irving.

The Groove Tube **1/2 1972 (R)** A TV series called "The Groove Tube" is the context for these skits that spoof everything on TV from commercials to newscasts. Chevy Chase's movie debut. **75m/C; VHS, DVD.** Lane Sarasohn; Chevy Chase; Richard Belzer; Marcy Mendham; Bill Kemmill; Ken Shapiro; Alex Stephens; Berkeley Harris; Buzzy Linhart; Richmond Baier; ***D:*** Ken Shapiro; ***W:*** Lane Sarasohn; Ken Shapiro; ***C:*** Bob Bailin.

Gross Anatomy **1/2 1989 (PG-13)** Lightweight comedy/drama centers on the trials and tribulations of medical students. Modine is the very bright, but somewhat lazy, future doctor determined not to buy into the bitter competition among his fellow students. His lack of desire inflames Lahti, a professor dying of a fatal disease who nevertheless believes in modern medicine. She pushes and inspires him to focus on his potential, and his desire to help people. Worth watching, in spite of cheap laughs. Interesting cast of up-and-comers. **107m/C; VHS, DVD, Blu-Ray.** Matthew Modine; Daphne Zuniga; Christine Lahti; John Scott Clough; Alice Carter; Robert Desiderio; Zakes Mokae; Todd Field; ***D:*** Thom Eberhardt; ***W:*** Ron Nyswaner; ***M:*** David Newman.

Grosse Fatigue *Dead Tired* **1994 (R)** Diminutive comic everyman Blanc successfully takes up the challenge of a dual role of mistaken identity (as well as directing and writing chores). He first plays himself, bewildered by accusations of lechery and other escapades, who learns he has a psychopath double who's stolen his celebrity. So it's up to Michel and pal Carole (the gorgeous Bouquet) to track down the mischief-maker before Blanc's reputation is in complete tatters. French with subtitles. **85m/C; VHS, DVD.** *FR* Michel Blanc; Carole Bouquet; Philippe Noiret; Josiane Balasko; ***Cameo(s):*** Charlotte Gainsbourg; Mathilda May; Thierry Lhermitte; Roman Polanski; ***D:*** Michel Blanc; ***W:*** Michel Blanc; ***C:*** Eduardo Serra; ***M:*** Rene Marc Bini.

Grosse Pointe Blank **1997 (R)** Stressed-out Martin Q. Blank (Cusack) debates with his nervous shrink (Arkin) about whether to attend his 10-year high school reunion. He doesn't want to deal with the Debi (Driver), the girl he ditched on prom night, the incessant small talk, or the prospect of telling his classmates that he's a professional hit man. Then there's the matter of rival pro Grocer (Aykroyd), who wants to start an assassins union. Dark comedy with excellent writing, a charmingly off-center lead by Cusack, who attended his own reunion as research, and a surprising amount of action. Pasadena fills in for most of Grosse Pointe, but the Detroit shots are real. **107m/C; VHS, DVD, Blu-Ray.** John Cusack; Minnie Driver; Dan Aykroyd; Alan Arkin; Joan Cusack; Jeremy

Piven; Mitchell Ryan; Hank Azaria; Michael Cudlitz; Benny "The Jet" Urquidez; Barbara Harris; Ann Cusack; K. Todd Freeman; *D:* George Armitage; *W:* John Cusack; Tom Jankiewicz; D.V. DeVincentis; Steve Pink; *C:* Jamie Anderson; *M:* Joe Strummer.

Grotesque WOOF! 1987 (R) After slaughtering a young woman's family as they vacationed in a remote mountain cabin, a gang of bloodthirsty punks are attacked by the family secret, the deformed son. The title says it all. **79m/C; VHS, DVD.** Linda Blair; Tab Hunter; Guy Stockwell; Donna Wilkes; Nels Van Patten; Brad Wilson; Sharon Hughes; Robert Z'Dar; Billy Frank; Michelle Bensoussan; Mikel Angel; *D:* Joe Tornatore; *W:* Mikel Angel.

Ground Control ♂♂ 1998 (PG-13) Jack Harris (Sutherland) is a former air traffic controller, who retired after a fatal plane crash. Years later, a old friend asks Jack to help out during a busy night at the Phoenix airport and Jack finds himself being forced to aid a plane with no radar, contact or control. **98m/C; VHS, DVD.** Kiefer Sutherland; Robert Sean Leonard; Kelly McGillis; Henry Winkler; Michael Gross; Margaret Cho; Charles Fleischer; Farrah Forke; Bruce McGill; Kristy Swanson; *D:* Richard Howard.

The Ground Truth ♂♂ 1/2 2006 (R) Compelling but unabashedly biased, go-for-the-jugular documentary about the effect of the Iraq War on the soldiers who've fought it. Filmmaker Foulkrod interviews scores of vets about the violence of the war (especially against Iraqi civilians) and the struggle to reintegrate into American society in the face of an uncaring government bureaucracy. The movie raises important points about the effect of war on those who wage it but doesn't maintain focus, leaving some of its most effective arguments unresolved. The combination of bias and disturbing violence makes this one most effective for those who already agree with its premise, but doesn't reach out to those who think otherwise. **72m/C; DVD.** *D:* Patricia Foulkrod; *C:* Reuben Aaronson; *M:* Dave Hodge.

Groundhog Day ♂♂♂ 1993 (PG) Phil (Murray), an obnoxious weatherman, is in Punxatawney, PA to cover the annual emergence of the famous rodent from its hole. After he's caught in a blizzard that he didn't predict, he finds himself trapped in a time warp, doomed to relive the same day over and over again until he gets it right. Lighthearted romantic comedy takes a funny premise and manages to carry it through to the end. Murray has fun with the role, although he did get bitten by the groundhog during the scene when they're driving. Elliott is perfectly cast as a smart-mouthed cameraman. **103m/C; VHS, DVD, Blu-Ray.** Bill Murray; Andie MacDowell; Chris Elliott; Stephen Tobolowsky; Brian Doyle-Murray; Marita Geraghty; Angela Paton; *D:* Harold Ramis; *W:* Harold Ramis; Daniel F. Rubin; *C:* John Bailey; *M:* George Fenton. British Acad. '93: Orig. Screenplay; Natl. Film Reg. '06.

The Groundstar Conspiracy ♂♂♂ 1972 (PG) Spy thriller brings to life L.P. Davies' novel, "The Alien." After an explosion kills all but one space project scientist, Peppard is sent to investigate suspicions of a cover-up. Meanwhile, the surviving scientist (Sarrazin) suffers from disfigurement and amnesia. He pursues his identity while Peppard accuses him of being a spy. Splendid direction by Lamont Johnson. Sarrazin's best role. **96m/C; VHS, DVD.** *CA* George Peppard; Michael Sarrazin; Christine Belford; Cliff (Potter) Potts; James Olson; Tim O'Connor; James McEachin; Alan Oppenheimer; *D:* Lamont Johnson; *W:* Matthew Howard; *C:* Michael Reed; *M:* Paul Hoffert.

The Group ♂♂ 1/2 1966 Based upon the novel by Mary McCarthy, the well-acted story deals with a group of graduates from a Vassar-like college as they try to adapt to life during the Great Depression. Has some provocative subject matter, including lesbianism, adultery, and mental breakdowns. Soapy, but a good cast with film debuts of Bergen, Hackett, Pettet, Widdoes, and Holbrook. **150m/C; VHS, DVD, Blu-Ray.** Candice Bergen; Joanna Pettet; Shirley Knight; Joan Hackett; Elizabeth Hartman; Jessica Walter; Larry Hagman; James Broderick; Kathleen Widdoes; Hal Holbrook; Mary-Robin Redd; Richard Mulligan; Carrie Nye; *D:* Sidney Lumet; *C:* Boris Kaufman.

Group Sex ♂♂ *The Group* **2010 (R)** In this broad comedy, ad exec Andy has been dumped by his longtime girlfriend and is sharing the bachelor pad of his horndog buddy, Jerry. He becomes interested in dream girl Vanessa and follows her and finds out she's part of a sex addiction therapy group. Prompted to join in, Andy uses Jerry's exploits as his cover but starts feeling guilty. **90m/C; DVD.** Josh Cooke; Greg Grunberg; Odette Annable; Tom Arnold; Henry Winkler; Kym E. Whitley; Greg Germann; *D:* Lawrence Trilling; *W:* Greg Grunberg; Lawrence Trilling; *C:* Michael D. O'Shea. **VIDEO**

Groupers ♂ 1/2 2019 One morning, high school jocks Brad (Mayer-Klepchick) and Dylan (Duckett) wake up to find themselves bound together in an empty pool. Grad student Meg (Dambro) kidnapped them as revenge for the friends' bullying of her gay brother Orin (Pudles). Meg uses them for her experiment to prove that homosexuality is not a choice. During Meg's humiliating experiment, Brad realizes he doesn't know much about Dylan, while Dylan desperately needs Brad's reassurances. Though the low budget comedy horror has an intriguing premise, it's a bit gimmicky with many over-the-top performances, though the leads have moments of believable vulnerability. **109m/C; DVD, Blu-Ray.** Nicole Dambro; Peter Mayer-Klepchick; Cameron Duckett; Jesse Pudles; Max Reed, III; *D:* Anderson Cowan; *W:* Anderson Cowan; *C:* Milan Janicin; *M:* Rick Urban.

The Growing Pains Movie ♂ 1/2 2000 Made-for-TV reunion movie (the first of two) finds Jason and Maggie Seaver living in Washington, DC. Their kids come to celebrate their parents' 30th wedding anniversary and Maggie announces that she's going to run for Congress against the boss who fired her. Jason tries to convince Mike, Carol, Ben, and Chrissy to help with the campaign. **87m/C; DVD.** Alan Thicke; Joanna Kerns; Kirk Cameron; Tracey Gold; Jeremy Miller; Ashley Johnson; Chelsea Noble; Brandon Douglas; Mathew Harbour; *D:* Alan Metter; *W:* David Kendall; *C:* Yves Bélanger; *M:* Steve Dorff. **TV**

Growing Pains: Return of the Seavers ♂♂ 2004 This second TV reunion movie negates the storyline of the first to stay closer to the series. Maggie and Jason Seaver are still in the same house on Long Island but are about to retire. They want to sell the family home (son Ben is their realtor) but Chrissy's just moved back and Mike and Carol come home to talk their parents' out of the idea. And it seems Jason and Maggie have very different ideas about what happens when they retire anyway. **89m/C; DVD.** Joanna Kerns; Alan Thicke; Kirk Cameron; Tracey Gold; Jeremy Miller; Ashley Johnson; Chelsea Noble; *D:* Joanna Kerns; *W:* Christina Lynch; *C:* John C. Flinn, III; *M:* Kenneth Burgomaster. **TV**

Growing the Big One ♂♂ 1/2 2009 (PG) Predictable but sweet Hallmark Channel romance. City gal and radio show host Emma inherits her grandfather's farm and a huge debt. In order to pay it off, she enters a local pumpkin-growing contest though she knows nothing about farming. Her cute mechanic neighbor Seth needs some cash and offers to split the work and the winnings. Naturally Emma finds him annoying (but she'll learn). **89m/C; DVD.** Shannen Doherty; Kavan Smith; Stephanie Belding; Aaron Pearl; *D:* Mark Griffiths; *W:* Anna Sandor; Diane A. Mettler; *M:* Terry Frewer. **CABLE**

Growing Up Smith ♂♂ 1/2 *Good Ol' Boy* **2017 (PG-13)** A cross-cultural, coming of age comedy-drama centered on a young Indian immigrant trying to find his way in suburban America in 1979. Ten-year-old Smith Bhatnagar (Akurati) is bullied because of his accent and culture in his neighborhood and at school. He has a crush on his neighbor Amy (Sharbino), who befriends him. To pursue his own American Dream, Smith longs to become a good ol' boy. Though Amy's easy-going father Butch (Lee) has his own issues, he offers his support to Smith. Butch even takes Smith hunting, where the boy learns about guns and himself. The nostalgic film is uneven but touching and likable. **102m/C; DVD.** Jason Lee; Anjul Nigam; Brighton Sharbino; Hilarie Burton; Roni Akurati; *D:* Frank Lotito; *W:* Anjul Nigam; Paul Quinn; Gregory Scott Houghton; *C:* Thomas Scott Stanton; *M:* Michael Lira.

Grown Up Movie Star ♂ 1/2 2010 The problem is 14-year-old Ruby (Maslany) isn't grown-up at all; she's a troubled girl in a Newfoundland town with too many fantasies, a flaky mom, Lillian (White), who abandons her kids and the marriage she loathes, and a dad, Ray (Doyle), who's an ex-con with a drug conviction and is conflictedly gay. Oh yeah, Ruby's sexual explorations are creepily focused on her dad's best friend, wheelchair-bound Stuart (Harris), which leads to trouble. **95m/C; DVD.** *CA* Tatiana Maslany; Shawn Doyle; Jonny Harris; Julia Kennedy; Sherry White; Mark O'Brien; *D:* Adriana Maggs; *W:* Adriana Maggs; *C:* Jason Tan; *M:* Eliot Brood.

Grown Ups ♂♂ 1980 A newly married couple move into their first home only to discover that the wife's ditzy sister expects to live with them and that their next door neighbor was their former high school teacher. **95m/C; VHS, DVD.** *GB* Philip Davis; Lesley Manville; Sam Kelly; Lindsay Duncan; Brenda Blethyn; Janine Duvitsky; *D:* Mike Leigh; *W:* Mike Leigh. **TV**

Grown Ups ♂ 1/2 2010 (PG-13) A few laughs in a more family-oriented summer vacation comedy from Sandler. Five buddies were all pre-teen players on a championship basketball team back in 1978. When their revered coach dies, they reunite after 30 years by returning to the lake cottage where they first celebrated their victory. Now they're accompanied by wives and kids over a 4th of July weekend. **102m/C; Blu-Ray, On Demand.** Adam Sandler; Kevin James; Chris Rock; Rob Schneider; David Spade; Salma Hayek; Maria Bello; Maya Rudolph; Tim Meadows; Norm MacDonald; Joyce Van Patten; Colin Quinn; Tim Herlihy; Ebony Jo-Ann; Blake Clark; *Cameo(s):* Steve Buscemi; *D:* Dennis Dugan; *W:* Adam Sandler; Fred Wolf; *C:* Theo van de Sande; *M:* Rupert Gregson-Williams.

Grown Ups 2 WOOF! 2013 (PG-13) The first sequel in Adam Sandler's career is an utterly lazy train wreck, a movie that plays like deleted scenes from the first film or ideas rejected by smarter comedy writers on other movies. Entirely unfunny, the "plot" is just a lame excuse to get the cast of the first movie back together for gross-out jokes about adults acting like kids or just idiots. You won't see a major comedy with more pee, poo, or homophobic jokes than this disaster, a movie that's not just unfunny but offensively bad. Sandler and his friends think so little of their fans that this is what they deliver. **101m/C; DVD, Blu-Ray.** Adam Sandler; Kevin James; Chris Rock; David Spade; Salma Hayek; Maya Rudolph; Maria Bello; Steve Buscemi; Nick Swardson; Tim Meadows; Shaquille O'Neal; Georgia Engel; Taylor Lautner; *D:* Dennis Dugan; *W:* Adam Sandler; Fred Wolf; Tim Herlihy; *C:* Theo van de Sande; *M:* Rupert Gregson-Williams.

Growth ♂ 2010 Scientists esperimenting with evolutionary genetics on a remote island are wiped out. Flash forward years later, and an unsuspecting group of kids show up in order to claim an inheritance and stir things up again. **90m/C; DVD, Blu-Ray, Streaming.** Mircea Monroe; Christopher Shand; Nora Kirkpatrick; Brian Krause; Richard Riehle; *D:* Gabriel Cowan; *W:* Gabriel Cowan; Devin Zimmerman; John Suits; Charles Dahlgren; Matthew Cowan; *C:* Grisha Alasadi; Katie Boyum; Mark Putnam; Richard J. Vialet; *M:* Tim Ziesmer. **VIDEO**

The Grudge ♂ 1/2 2004 (PG-13) Shimizu remade his own 2003 horror flick "Ju-On" and there are still more groans (of disbelief) than shrieks. Studying social work as an exchange student in Tokyo, Karen (Gellar) discovers elderly Emma (Zabriskie) home alone, her family (Mapother, DuVall) missing. She sees a ghostly boy (Ozeki, who was in two of the Japanese films) and his demonic mother (Fuji, who's been in all five). Karen's scruffy boyfriend (Behr) is lured in, as is her boss (Raimi) and a local detective (Ishibashi). Pullman also appears briefly as an American professor who was an early victim of the house of horrors. Gellar's an old hand at battling things that go bump in the night but this experience isn't worth her expertise. **96m/C; DVD, Blu-Ray, UMD.** Sarah Michelle Gellar; Jason Behr; William Mapother; Clea DuVall; KaDee Strickland; Grace Zabriskie; Bill Pullman; Rosa Blasi; Theodore (Ted) Raimi; Ryo Ishibashi; Yuya Ozeki; Takako Fuji; Yoko Maki; *D:* Takashi Shimizu; *W:* Takashi Shimizu; *C:* Hideo Yamamoto.

The Grudge 2 ♂ 1/2 2006 (PG-13) Same shriek, different day. Hospitalized in Japan after her last ordeal, Karen (Gellar in a cameo) kills herself in front of her horrified sister Aubrey (Tamblyn). Naturally, Aubrey now wants to discover what lead her sis to suicide, which involves those weird mother-child demons and a haunted house best left alone. It's creepy, but lacks new ideas since writer-director Shimizu sticks to his formula, which has served him through four "Ju-On" flicks and two American remakes. **95m/C; DVD.** Amber Tamblyn; Arielle Kebbel; Sarah Michelle Gellar; Jennifer Beals; Christopher Cousins; Edison Chen; Takako Fuji; Kim Miyori; Oga Tanaka; Teresa Pálmer; Misako Uno; *D:* Takashi Shimizu; *W:* Stephen Susco; *C:* Katsumi Yanagijima; *M:* Christopher Young.

The Grudge 3 ♂ 1/2 2009 (R) Picks up where '2' left off as survivor Jake (Knight) is in a psych hospital babbling about his ordeal to Dr. Sullivan (Smith). When Jake is killed, Sullivan goes to his Chicago apartment to investigate and finds landlord Max (Mckinney) having trouble with a couple of Japanese ghosts who have gotten very, very violent. **90m/C; DVD.** Shawnee Smith; Mathew Knight; Marina Sirtis; Aiko Horiuchi; Shimba Tsuchiya; Gil McKinney; Johanna Braddy; Jadie Hobson; Emi Ikehata; *D:* Toby Wilkins; *W:* Brad Keene; *C:* Anton Bakarski; *M:* Sean McMahon. **VIDEO**

Grudge Match ♂ 1/2 2013 (PG-13) The men who cinematic history will know as Rocky and Jake LaMotta mock their own time in the film ring with this inert, predictable comedy about two over-the-hill boxers forced back into the spotlight with a reunion fight to end a decades-old rivalry. Henry "Razor" Sharp (Stallone) and Billy "The Kid" McDonnen (De Niro) were rivals in their younger days, each winning one of their two fights. Sly and De Niro have fun mocking their own personalities but it feels a little sad to watch two former icons reduced to what was clearly a movie built more around a paycheck. **113m/C; DVD, Blu-Ray.** Sylvester Stallone; Robert De Niro; Kevin Hart; Alan Arkin; *D:* Peter Segal; *W:* Tim Kelleher; Rodney Rothman; *C:* Dean Semler; *M:* Trevor Rabin.

Gruesome Twosome ♂ 1967 Another guts/cannibalism/mutilation fun-fest by Lewis, about someone who's marketing the hair of some very recently deceased college coeds. **75m/C; VHS, DVD, Blu-Ray.** Elizabeth Davis; Gretchen Wells; Chris Martell; Rodney Bedell; Ronnie Cass; Karl Stoeber; Dianne Wilhite; Andrea Barr; Dianne Raymond; Sherry Robinson; Barrie Walton; Michael Lewis; Ray Sager; *D:* Herschell Gordon Lewis; *W:* Allison Louise Downe; *C:* Roy Collodi; *M:* Larry Wellington.

Grumpier Old Men ♂♂ 1995 (PG-13) Max (Matthau) and John (Lemmon) are back at each other's throats, but with John happily married to Ariel (Ann-Margaret), he's not much of an adversary. Enter Maria (Loren), who wants to turn the boys' favorite bait shop into an Italian restaurant. In a twist that should surprise no one, Max soon falls for the beautiful Maria, and she with him. Jokes are similar but more adolescent than in the first, and subplots involving John and Max's kids' wedding and Grandpa's (Meredith) romantic interests are forced. Suffers the standard sequel fate of not measuring up to the original. **101m/C; VHS, DVD.** Jack Lemmon; Walter Matthau; Ann-Margret; Sophia Loren; Kevin Pollak; Burgess Meredith; Daryl Hannah; Ann Guilbert; *D:* Howard Deutch; *W:* Mark Steven Johnson; *C:* Tak Fujimoto; *M:* Alan Silvestri.

Grumpy Old Men ♂♂♂ 1993 (PG-13) Lemmon and Matthau team for their seventh movie, in parts that seem written just for them. Boyhood friends and retired neighbors, they have been feuding for so long that neither of them can remember why. Doesn't matter much, when it provides a reason for them to spout off at each other every morning and play nasty practical jokes every night. This, and ice-fishing, is life as they know it, until feisty younger woman Ann-Margret moves into the neighborhood and lights some long-dormant fires. 83-year-old Meredith is a special treat playing Lemmon's 90-something father. Filmed in Wabasha, Minnesota, and grumpy, in the most pleasant way. **104m/C; VHS, DVD.** Jack Lemmon; Walter Matthau; Ann-Margret; Burgess Meredith; Daryl Hannah; Kevin Pollak; Ossie Davis; Buck Henry; Christopher McDonald; *D:* Donald Petrie; *W:* Mark Steven Johnson; *C:* Johnny E. Jensen; *M:* Alan Silvestri.

Guadalcanal Diary 🦴🦴 ½ **1943** A vintage wartime flag-waver, with a typical crew of Marines battling the "Yellow Menace" over an important base on the famous Pacific atoll. Based on Richard Tregaskis' first-hand account. **93m/B; VHS, DVD.** Preston Foster; Lloyd Nolan; William Bendix; Richard Conte; Anthony Quinn; Richard Jaeckel; Roy Roberts; Minor Watson; Miles Mander; Ralph Byrd; Lionel Stander; Reed Hadley; John Archer; Eddie Acuff; Selmer Jackson; Paul Fung; *D:* Lewis Seiler; *W:* Lamar Trotti; Jerome Cady; *C:* Charles G. Clarke; *M:* David Buttolph.

Guantanamera 🦴🦴🦴 **1995** A famous singer returns to her hometown of Guantanamo for the first time in 50 years, is reunited with her first sweetheart, and promptly dies. Her niece Georgina (Ibarra) comes to take her remains back to Havana, along with her husband Adolfo (Cruz), an oafish Communist Party worker who has devised a bizarre relay system to transport corpses in order to save gasoline. Also in the caravan is Mariano (Perugorria), a former student of Georgina's who had a crush on her. Mariano attempts to seduce Georgina, while Adolfo attempts to get a clue. Celebrates the lives of everyday Cubans and skewers bumbling government bureaucrats. The final collaboration between directors Gutierrez Alea, who died in 1996, and Tabio. Spanish with subtitles. **104m/C; VHS, DVD.** *CU* Carlos Cruz; Mirta Ibarra; Jorge Perugorria; Raul Eguren; Pedro Fernandez; *D:* Tomas Gutierrez Alea; Juan Carlos Tabio; *W:* Tomas Gutierrez Alea; Juan Carlos Tabio; Eliseo Alberto Diego; *C:* Hans Burman; *M:* Jose Nieto.

Guantanamero 🦴🦴 *Arritmia* **2007 (R)** Ali awakens on a deserted beach without any idea how he got there. He's found by Good Samaritan Ivan, who takes Ali home so his dancer sister Manuela can look after him. Ali finds out he's in Cuba and then starts having flashbacks to being interrogated in prison. Well, the title kinda provided some clues, didn't it? **86m/C; DVD.** *GB SP* Rupert Evans; Natalia Verbeke; Derek Jacobi; Ismael de Diego; *D:* Vicente Penarrocha; *W:* Phillip W. Palmer; Vicente Penarrocha; *C:* Kiko de la Rica; *M:* Richard File.

The Guard 🦴🦴🦴 **2011 (R)** Trying to defy the typical traps of the American buddy comedy (and yet falling into a few of them at the same time), writer/director McDonagh's debut directorial effort works because of another strong central performance from the great Gleeson. The man who has refined his ability to play "cranky-but-lovable" takes on Sgt. Gerry Boyle, an Irish officer with his own faults (booze, hookers, a general lack of tact, etc.) who stumbles on to an international drug operation and partners with FBI agent Wendell Everett (Cheadle) to bring it down. Any flaws of the sometimes-dull storytelling are overcome by the talented leads. **95m/C; DVD, Blu-Ray.** *IR* Brendan Gleeson; Don Cheadle; Liam Cunningham; David Wilmot; Mark Strong; Rory Keenan; Fionnula Flanagan; Katarina Cas; *D:* John Michael McDonagh; *W:* John Michael McDonagh; *C:* Larry Smith; *M:* Calexico.

The Guardian 🦴 **1990 (R)** A young couple unwittingly hires a human sacrificing druid witch as a babysitter for their child. Based on the book "The Nanny" by Dan Greenburg. **92m/C; VHS, DVD, Blu-Ray.** Jenny Seagrove; Dwier Brown; Carey Lowell; Brad Hall; Miguel Ferrer; Natalija Nogulich; Pamela Brull; Gary Swanson; *D:* William Friedkin; *W:* William Friedkin; Stephen Volk; Dan Greenberg; *C:* John A. Alonzo; *M:* Jack Hues.

The Guardian 🦴 ½ **2001 (R)** Uninspired actioner finds Marine John Kross (Van Peebles) witnessing some freaky stuff during Desert Storm. He winds up in the hospital with a strange map carved on his chest. Flash-forward 12 years and Kross is an L.A. cop chasing down some new street drug that's made from a mystery powder from Iraq. And then there's something about a demon, a young prophet who needs protection, and his guardian who is Kross of course. Who cares. **89m/C; VHS, DVD.** Mario Van Peebles; James Remar; Ice-T; Daniel Hugh Kelly; Stacy Oversier; *D:* John Terlesky; *W:* John Terlesky; Jeff Yagher; Gary J. Tunnicliffe; *C:* Maximo Munzi. **VIDEO**

The Guardian 🦴🦴 ½ **2006 (PG-13)** Costner has settled comfortably into mentor mode in this familiar action story. Legendary Coast Guard rescue swimmer Ben Randall's wife has left him, his crew died during their last mission, and he's become an unwilling and unorthodox instructor to the Guard's latest recruits. Naturally, his biggest challenge is a cocky, younger version of himself—Jake Fischer (Kutcher). But Ben is just the guy to whip Jake into shape as they bond over past mistakes and insecurities. Kutcher's a surprisingly good match for Costner as the troubled newbie. **139m/C; DVD.** Kevin Costner; Ashton Kutcher; Melissa Sagemiller; Clancy Brown; Bonnie Bramlett; Sela Ward; Neal McDonough; John Heard; Brian Geraghty; Dulé Hill; Shelby Fenner; Alex Daniels; *D:* Andrew Davis; *W:* Ron L. Brinkerhoff; *C:* Stephen St. John; *M:* Trevor Rabin.

Guardian Angel 🦴🦴 ½ *Beyond Justice* **1994 (R)** Detective Christy McKay (Rothrock) quits the force after her partner/lover is killed by icy seductress Nina (Denier), who manages to escape from jail. When McKay is hired to protect playboy Lawton Hobbs (McVicar), she finds that the threat comes from a psycho ex-girlfriend. Guess who. **97m/C; VHS, DVD.** Cynthia Rothrock; Lydie Denier; Daniel McVicar; Kenneth McLeod; Marshall Teague; John O'Leary; Dale Jacoby; *D:* Richard W. Munchkin.

Guardians of the Galaxy 🦴🦴🦴 **2014 (PG-13)** Marvel movies are fun again in director/writer Gunn's action blockbuster that eases up on the self-seriousness invaded by the superhero movie genre. Pratt becomes a superstar as Peter Quill (aka Starlord), an Earthling child kidnapped into a universe of space criminals and interstellar combat. Quill acquires an object coveted by the nefarious Ronan (Pace) and ends up in a band of misfits that includes the lovely Gamora (Saldana), tough guy Drax the Destroyer (Bautista), somewhat-talking tree Groot (voiced by Diesel), and a sassy raccoon named Rocket (voiced by Cooper). It might like itself a bit too much, but who can blame it? And it has a kickin' "mixed tape" oldies soundtrack to go along for the ride. **121m/C; DVD, Blu-Ray.** Chris Pratt; Zoe Saldana; Dave Bautista; Benicio Del Toro; Lee Pace; Michael Rooker; Karen Gillan; John C. Reilly; Glenn Close; Djimon Hounsou; Wyett Oleff; Gregg Henry; Josh Brolin; *V:* Bradley Cooper; Vin Diesel; *D:* James Gunn; *W:* James Gunn; Nicole Perlman; *C:* Ben Davis; *M:* Tyler Bates.

Guardians of the Galaxy Vol. 2 🦴🦴🦴 ½ **2017 (PG-13)** The much anticipated next chapter joins the very short list of sequels that live up to the original. This one picks up and runs with the idea of family being where you find it, even when you might be looking in the wrong place. Star-Lord (Pratt) and crew are still doing a little bit of good, a little bit of bad, when they encounter Ego (Russell) a living planet who says he's Quill's dad, and who probably won't be receiving any "World's Greatest Dad" mugs on Father's Day. This outing ramps up the humor, the stakes, the action, and the heart, and it all works just like it should. **136m/C; DVD, Blu-Ray.** Chris Pratt; Zoe Saldana; Dave Bautista; Vin Diesel; Bradley Cooper; Kurt Russell; *D:* James Gunn; *W:* James Gunn; *C:* Henry Braham; *M:* Tyler Bates.

Guardians of the Lost Code 🦴 ½ *Guardians of the Lost Code 3D; Brijes 3D* **2010** Three young children are called upon to bond with their totem animal spirits to become superheroes and save the world! **90m/C; DVD, Blu-Ray, Streaming.** *MX V:* José-Luis Orozco; Jose A. Taladano; Miguel Calderon; Edgar Vivar; Carlos Espejel; *D:* Bernito Fernandez; *W:* Luis Antonio Avalos; *C:* Bernito Fernandez; *M:* Juan Manuel Langarica. **VIDEO**

Guarding Eddy 🦴 ½ **2004 (PG)** Autistic 18-year-old Eddy Patterson (Presley) runs away from home to fulfill his dream of playing basketball with the Los Angeles Clippers. He winds up in a homeless shelter and meets injured NBA hopeful Mike Jeffreys (Ellsworth), who's doing community service. Naturally, the two bond in this sappy inspirational flick. **96m/C; DVD.** Brian Presley; Kiko Ellsworth; Lee Garlington; Anna Maria Hosford; *D:* Scott McKinsey; *W:* Paul Davidson; *C:* Christopher Norr; *M:* Scott Kay. **VIDEO**

Guarding Tess 🦴🦴 **1994 (PG-13)** Long-suffering Secret Service agent Cage is nearing the end of his three-year assignment to crotchety widowed First Lady MacLaine when the Prez extends his tour of duty. Feels like a TV movie, not surprising since writers Torokvei and Wilson have several sitcoms to their credit, including "WKRP in Cinncinnati." Nice chemistry between Cage and MacLaine results in a few funny moments, but there are too many formulaic plot twists. End result: a pleasant, if somewhat slow buddy comedy. **98m/C; VHS, DVD.** Shirley MacLaine; Nicolas Cage; Austin Pendleton; Edward Albert; Richard Griffiths; Dale Dye; *D:* Hugh Wilson; *W:* Hugh Wilson; Peter Torokvei; *C:* Brian Reynolds; *M:* Michael Convertino.

The Guardsman 🦴🦴 *Yu Qian Shi Wei* **2015 (R)** Action-filled martial arts film set in historical China. To better comprehend the problems faced by the people living in his country, the emperor decides to travel China while disguised. However, his incognito identity is discovered by his enemies and he becomes the focus of an assassination plot that includes the Japanese pirates. To ensure the emperor stays alive and the kingdom stays peaceful in the face of internal conflict, warriors loyal to him serve as his protection and protect China from its enemies. Mandarin Chinese with English subtitles. **94m/C; DVD, Streaming, Download.** Pei Pei Cheng; Ma Wu; Jie Yan; Biao Yuen; *D:* Jiao Xiao-Yu. **VIDEO**

Guerillas in Pink Lace 🦴 ½ **1964** After the events of Pearl Harbor, the base at Manila is being evacuated and a gambler steals a military pass to escape while disguised as a priest. He and the plane full of showgirls crash and end up on an island controlled by the Japanese. **96m/C; DVD.** George Montgomery; Joan Shawlee; Valerie Varda; Robin Grace; *D:* George Montgomery; *W:* George Montgomery; Ferde Grofe, Jr.

Guernica 🦴🦴 ½ *Gernika* **2016 (R)** A dramatic exploration of the power the press, based on actual events in Guernica, Spain, in 1937. During the Spanish civil war, the residents of the Spanish village of Guernica feel the impact of the conflict on their lives daily in many different ways. Among them is ever increasing restrictions on the press. In this situation, Henry (D'Arcy), an American journalist covering the conflict, makes a secret alliance with the Teresa (Valverde), the local press office censor. When Nazi Germany bombs the village, the freedom of the press becomes an important weapon in the war against the German invaders. **110m/C; DVD, Download.** James D'Arcy; Burn Gorman; Jack Davenport; Maria Valverde; Hugo Silva; *D:* Koldo Serra; *W:* Carlos Clavijo Cobos; Barney Cohen; *C:* Unax Mendia; *M:* Fernando Velazquez. **VIDEO**

The Guernsey Literary & Potato Peel Pie Society 🦴🦴 ½ **2018** During World War II, the island was occupied by Nazi Germany and the film's title comes from a local book club/organized resistance led by Elizabeth (Findlay). In the post-war period, a Guernsey farmer invites London journalist and author Juliet Ashton (James) to visit the island and write about the group. Ignoring the concerns of her editor Sidney (Goode) and her new fiance Mark (Powell), Juliet visits and becomes close to the locals. In the process, she investigates the circumstances around Elizabeth's disappearance. Based on a best-selling novel, the film's length and predictability keep it from becoming a crowd pleaser. **124m/C; DVD.** Jessica Brown Findlay; Tom Courtenay; Michiel Huisman; Katherine Parkinson; Marek Oravec; *D:* Mike Newell; *W:* Don Roos; Kevin Hood; Thomas Bezucha; *C:* Zac Nicholson; *M:* Alexandra Harwood.

Guess What We Learned in School Today? **WOOF!** **1970 (R)** Parents in a conservative suburban community protest sex education in the schools. Intended as a satire, but it only reinforces stereotypes. **85m/C; VHS, DVD.** Richard Carballo; Devin Goldenberg; *D:* John G. Avildsen.

Guess Who 🦴🦴 **2005 (PG-13)** Guess who thought it was a good idea to remake the classic 1967 Spencer Tracy/Sidney Poitier drama as a tepid comedy starring two sitcom actors? Columbia Pictures, apparently, but they're definitely in the minority. On the eve of his anniversary, successful black businessman Percy Jones (Mac) is introduced to his daughter's new boyfriend, goofy white dude Simon (Kutcher). Unnerved by the interracial relationship, Percy struggles to cope, while Simon tries his best to fit in and win Percy over. Mac works overtime to rise above the material, but the repetitive "white guy" jokes and inappropriate slapstick diminish the film's message of racial tolerance, making it come across instead as a low-rent "Meet the Parents" rip-off. **105m/C; DVD, UMD.** Bernie Mac; Ashton Kutcher; Zoe Saldana; Judith Scott; Hal Williams; RonReaco Lee; Kellee Stewart; Robert Curtis Brown; Nicole Sullivan; Jessica Cauffiel; Kimberly Scott; Denise Dowse; Niecy Nash; Sherri Shepherd; David Krumholtz; Mike Epps; *D:* Kevin Rodney Sullivan; *W:* Peter Tolan; Jay Scherick; David Ronn; *C:* Karl Walter Lindenlaub; *M:* John Murphy.

Guess Who's Coming to Dinner 🦴🦴🦴 **1967** Controversial in its time. A young white woman brings her black fiance home to meet her parents. The situation truly tests their open-mindedness and understanding. Hepburn and Tracy (in his last film appearance) are wonderful and serve as the anchors in what would otherwise have been a rather sugary film. Houghton, who portrays the independent daughter, is the real-life niece of Hepburn. **108m/C; VHS, DVD, Blu-Ray.** Katharine Hepburn; Spencer Tracy; Sidney Poitier; Katharine Houghton; Cecil Kellaway; Beah Richards; Roy Glenn; Isabel Sanford; *D:* Stanley Kramer; *W:* William Rose; *C:* Sam Leavitt; *M:* Frank DeVol. Oscars '67: Actress (Hepburn), Story & Screenplay; AFI '98: Top 100; British Acad. '68: Actor (Tracy), Actress (Hepburn); Natl. Film Reg. '17.

The Guest 🦴🦴 ½ **2014** Veteran David (Stevens) arrives on the doorstep of the grieving family of his fallen comrade Caleb and quickly becomes a fixture in their home. He befriends Caleb's sister, teaches his brother how stand up for himself, and even helps dad get a promotion. And, of course, he's a sociopathic super-soldier-killing machine. Director Wingard creates a definite crowd-pleaser with this riff on John Carpenter's "Halloween" blended with James Cameron's "The Terminator." Unfortunately co-screenwriter Barrett can't quite keep up. **99m/C; DVD, Blu-Ray.** Dan Stevens; Sheila Kelley; Leland Orser; Brendan Meyer; Maika Monroe; Lance Reddick; *D:* Adam Wingard; *W:* Simon Barrett; *C:* Robby Baumgartner; *M:* Stephen Moore.

Guest in the House 🦴🦴 ½ **1944** A seemingly friendly young female patient is invited to stay in the family home of her doctor. She skillfully attempts to dissect the family's harmony in the process. **121m/B; VHS, DVD.** Anne Baxter; Ralph Bellamy; Ruth Warrick; Marie McDonald; Margaret Hamilton; Aline MacMahon; Scott McKay; Jerome Cowan; Percy Kilbride; Connie Laird; *D:* John Brahm; *W:* Ketti Frings; *C:* Lee Garmes; *M:* Werner Janssen.

Guest Wife 🦴🦴 ½ **1945** Determined to impress his sentimental boss, a quick-thinking bachelor talks his best friend's wife into posing as his own wife, but the hoax gets a bit out of hand and nearly ruins the real couple's marriage. **90m/B; DVD, Blu-Ray.** Claudette Colbert; Don Ameche; Dick Foran; Charles Dingle; Wilma Francis; *D:* Sam Wood; *W:* Bruce Manning; John Klorer; *C:* Joseph Valentine; *M:* Daniele Amfitheatrof.

A Guide for the Married Man 🦴🦴🦴 **1967** One suburban husband instructs another in adultery, with a cast of dozens enacting various slapstick cameos. Based on Frank Tarloff's novel of the same name. Followed by "A Guide for the Married Woman." **91m/C; VHS, DVD.** Walter Matthau; Robert Morse; Inger Stevens; Sue Ane Langdon; Claire Kelly; Elaine Devry; ***Cameo(s):*** Lucille Ball; Sid Caesar; Jack Benny; Wally Cox; Jayne Mansfield; Louis Nye; Carl Reiner; Phil Silvers; Terry-Thomas; Sam Jaffe; Jeffrey Hunter; Polly Bergen; *D:* Gene Kelly; *W:* Frank Tarloff; *M:* John Williams.

A Guide for the Married Woman 🦴 ½ **1978** A bored housewife tries to take the romantic advice of a girlfriend to add a little spice to her life. A poor TV follow-up to "A Guide for the Married Man." **96m/C; VHS, DVD.** Cybill Shepherd; Barbara Feldon; Eve Arden; Chuck Woolery; Peter Marshall; Charles Frank; ***D:*** Hy Averback. **TV**

A Guide to Recognizing Your Saints 1/2 **2006 (R)** More than anything Dito Montiel (LeBeouf) wants to get out of his 1986 Queens' Astoria neighborhood and away from his irascible father Monty (Palminteri). But for now, Dito hangs out with his pals, especially tough thug Antonio (Tatum) and Irish newcomer Mike (Compston), as well as girlfriend Laurie (Diaz). But the streets are changing—and not for the better. Years later, Dito (now played by Downey Jr.) returns home because his dad is dying. However, not everyone he knew is there to say hello. Based on debut writer/director Montiel's coming-of-age memoir. **98m/C; DVD, Blu-Ray.** Shia LaBeouf; Robert Downey, Jr.; Chazz Palminteri; Dianne Wiest; Channing Tatum; Melonie Diaz; Martin Compston; Eric Roberts; Rosario Dawson; ***D:*** Dito Montiel; ***W:*** Dito Montiel; ***C:*** Eric Gautier; ***M:*** Jonathan Elias.

The Guilt of Janet Ames **1947** Interesting premise, awkward and unbelievable execution. War widow Janet (Russell) was disappointed in her marriage and feels guilty since her husband died a hero. She decides to meet the five soldiers he saved to see if they were worthy of his sacrifice. After an accident causes hysterical paralysis, Janet is approached by one of the men, alcoholic reporter Smithfield Cobb (Douglas), who suggest hypnosis can help Janet overcome her difficulties (there's an extended dream sequence). **82m/B; DVD, Blu-Ray.** Rosalind Russell; Melvyn Douglas; Sid Caesar; Betsy Blair; Nina Foch; ***D:*** Harry E. Levin; ***W:*** Allen Rivkin; Devery Freeman; Louella MacFarlane; ***C:*** Joseph Walker; ***M:*** George Duning.

The Guilt Trip **2012 (PG-13)** Barbra Streisand returns to the screen for her first leading role in over fifteen years and the result is a comedy that's more surprisingly forgettable than anything else. The wacky concept of Streisand's comeback – an overbearing mother goes on the road with her inventor son (Rogen) – could have been fertile ground for clichés, contrivances, and really bad physical humor. There's certainly some of that here but Rogen and Streisand have an unforced chemistry that works beyond the silly set-up. Ultimately, fans of Babs will likely ignore the movie in favor of the prime of her career while younger audiences are more likely to think of her as the mom from Meet the Fockers. **95m/C; DVD, Blu-Ray.** Barbra Streisand; Seth Rogen; Yvonne Strahovski; Colin Hanks; Adam Scott; Brett Cullen; ***D:*** Anne Fletcher; ***W:*** Dan Fogelman; ***C:*** Oliver Stapleton; ***M:*** Christophe Beck.

The Guilty **1992** After winning a big case, London lawyer Steven Vey celebrates by getting drunk and going back to the flat of his pretty secretary Nicky. She claims their sexual encounter was a rape and the accusations could ruin Vey. Meanwhile, young ex-con Eddy comes to London to track down his birth father. The ending doesn't turn out as expected. **201m/C; DVD.** *GB* Michael Kitchen; Caroline Catz; Sean Gallagher; Lee Ross; Andrew Tiernan; Eleanor David; Carol Starks; ***D:*** Colin Gregg; ***W:*** Simon Burke; ***C:*** Derek Suter; ***M:*** Hal Lindes. **TV**

The Guilty **1999 (R)** Lawyer Callum Crane (Pullman) has a drunken sexual tryst with his new secretary, Sophie (Anwar), and suddenly his life is spiraling out-of-control. Sophie tries to blackmail him when Crane is appointed a federal judge and he decides to hire Nathan (Sawa), a young man who's just been released from prison, to bump her off. But Nathan's not exactly who he seems and, of course, nothing goes exactly as planned. It's a complex thriller with a good ensemble cast. **112m/C; VHS, DVD.** Bill Pullman; Gabrielle Anwar; Devon Sawa; Angela Featherstone; Joanne Whalley; Jaimz Woolvett; Ken Tremblett; Camilla Overbye Roos; ***D:*** Anthony Waller; ***W:*** William Davies; ***C:*** Tobias Schliessler; ***M:*** Debbie Wiseman.

The Guilty *Den skyldige* **2018 (R)** Jakob Cedergren plays Asger Holm, a demoted police officer pulling desk duty as an emergency dispatcher. When a panicked call from a kidnapped young mother gets disconnected, Holm scrambles to help her from the confines of his desk as the true scale of the crime slowly reveals itself. A slowburner bursting with tension that accelerates with each passing minute, and a thrilling submission by Denmark for the Foreign Language Film Award of the 91st Oscars. **85m/C; DVD, Blu-Ray.** Jakob Cedergren; Jessica Dinnage; Omar Shargawi; Johan Olsen; Jacob Lohmann; ***D:*** Gustav Möller; ***W:*** Gustav Möller; Emil Nygaard Albertsen; ***C:*** Jasper Spanning; ***M:*** Carl Coleman; Caspar Hesselager.

Guilty as Charged 1/2 **1992 (R)** A butcher rigs his own private electric chair and captures and executes paroled killers in his personal quest for justice. But when a politician frames an innocent man for murder how far will this vigilante go? **95m/C; VHS, DVD.** Rod Steiger; Lauren Hutton; Heather Graham; Isaac Hayes; ***D:*** Sam Irvin; ***M:*** Steve Bartek.

Guilty as Sin **1993 (R)** Johnson is a ruthless Casanova accused of murdering his very wealthy wife and decides lawyer DeMornay is just the woman to defend him. Question is, who'll defend DeMornay from him? Johnson has fun as the menacing smoothie but DeMornay's supposedly hotshot criminal attorney is just plain dumb. It sounds like "Jagged Edge" but there's no sexual involvement between client and lawyer and no thrill in this thriller. **120m/C; DVD.** Don Johnson; Rebecca De Mornay; Jack Warden; Stephen Lang; Dana Ivey; Ron White; Sean McCann; Luis Guzman; ***D:*** Sidney Lumet; ***W:*** Larry Cohen; ***C:*** Andrzej Bartkowiak.

Guilty by Association **2003** Very graphic look at street life and its consequences set in Washington, DC. A young man tries to support his girlfriend and their daughter without turning to drug dealing and other criminal activities but the local gang members show him the supposed lure of easy money and what it can buy. Although Freeman's name and face on prominently featured on the box art, his part as a good cop is small. **80m/C; VHS, DVD.** Daemon Moore; Jeff Edward; Morgan Freeman; ***D:*** Po Johns; ***W:*** Howard Gibson; ***C:*** Sean Morrison; ***M:*** Nicholas Rivera. **VIDEO**

Guilty by Suspicion 1/2 **1991 (PG-13)** Examination of the 1950s McCarthy investigations by the House Un-American Activities Committee comes off like a bland history lesson. De Niro plays a director who attended a Communist party meeting in the '30s but who otherwise doesn't have any red connections. He takes the moral high ground and refuses to incriminate his buddy (Wendt) to get off the hook and finds himself blacklisted. Characterized by average performances (excepting Wettig who goes overboard) and a lightweight script. "The Front" (1976) does a better job on this topic. Directorial debut for producer Winkler. **105m/C; VHS, DVD.** Robert De Niro; Annette Bening; George Wendt; Patricia Wettig; Sam Wanamaker; Chris Cooper; Ben Piazza; Martin Scorsese; Barry Primus; Gailard Sartain; Stuart Margolin; Barry Tubb; Roxann Biggs-Dawson; Robin Gammell; Brad Sullivan; Luke Edwards; Adam Baldwin; Stephen (Steve) Root; Tom Sizemore; Illeana Douglas; Jon Tenney; ***D:*** Irwin Winkler; ***W:*** Irwin Winkler; ***C:*** Michael Ballhaus; ***M:*** James Newton Howard.

Guilty Conscience **1985** Anthony Hopkins plays a successful attorney who plots his wife's murder, but is it fantasy or reality? Excellent cast and intricate plot combine for a satisfying mystery. **90m/C; DVD.** Anthony Hopkins; Blythe Danner; Swoosie Kurtz; ***D:*** David Greene; ***W:*** Richard Levinson; William Link; ***C:*** Stevan Larner; ***M:*** Billy Goldenberg. **TV**

The Guilty Generation **1931** Carrillo rules the pic as Mike Palmero, a New York gangster who has a bootlegging war with rival Tony Ricca (Karloff). Tony's son wants to distance himself from his family, changes his name to John Smith, and gets a legit job as an architect. Mike's daughter Maria (Cummings) also wants to leave her dad's violence behind and, naturally, the crazy kids fall in love and get married. Once Mike finds out who Maria's new husband really is, she may soon become a widow. **82m/B; DVD.** Leo Carrillo; Boris Karloff; Constance Cummings; Robert Young; Emma Dunn; Leslie Fenton; ***D:*** Rowland V. Lee; ***W:*** Jack Cunningham; ***C:*** Byron Haskin.

Guilty of Treason 1/2 **1950** A documentary on the life and times of Joszef Cardinal Mindszenty of Hungary, who was imprisoned by the communists as an enemy of the state for speaking out against the totalitarian regime. At the trial, it was revealed that the Cardinal's confession was obtained only by the use of drugs, hypnosis, and torture. A realistic look at the dark side of Communism. **86m/B; VHS, DVD.** Charles Bickford; Paul Kelly; Bonita Granville; Richard Derr; Berry Kroeger; Elisabeth Risdon; Roland Winters; John Banner; ***D:*** Felix Feist.

Guinevere 1/2 **1994** Feminist re-telling of the Arthurian legend from the perspective of Guinevere (Lee). It takes a great many liberties with both the original story and novels it's based upon. **90m/C; DVD.** Sheryl Lee; Sean Patrick Flanery; Noah Wyle; Brid Brennan; Donald Pleasence; ***D:*** Jud Taylor; ***W:*** Ronni Kern; ***C:*** Gabor Szabo; ***M:*** Johnny Harris. **TV**

Guinevere **1999 (R)** Harper (Polley) is an uncertain, inexperienced 20-year-old in San Francisco who ditches family responsibilites at her sister's wedding reception in order to talk to fortysomething photographer Connie Fitzpatrick (Rea). Worldly wise and a natural charmer, Connie soon has Harper as his latest "Guinevere," the innocent young women he beds and nurtures until they outgrow the need for his guidance. Harper certainly doesn't seem to have much personality on her own but Connie also needs something of a lifeline as his drinking increases while his job prospects decline. Polished production with compelling performances by both Polley and Rea. **104m/C; VHS, DVD.** Stephen Rea; Sarah Polley; Jean Smart; Gina Gershon; Paul Dooley; Francis Guinan; Jasmine Guy; Sandra Oh; Emily Procter; Gedde Watanabe; ***D:*** Audrey Wells; ***W:*** Audrey Wells; ***C:*** Charles Minsky; ***M:*** Christophe Beck. Sundance '99: Screenplay.

The Guitar 1/2 **2008 (R)** Fatal beauty. On the same day that Melody (Burrows) gets fired and dumped by her boyfriend, she also learns that she has inoperable throat cancer. With a definite time limit, Melody decides to max out her credit cards and enjoy herself; among her purchases is a coveted red guitar. Also apparently without friends or family, Melody then indulges herself sexually with a couple of delivery people but otherwise not much happens. **95m/C; DVD.** Saffron Burrows; Paz de la Huerta; Isaach de Bankole; ***D:*** Amy Redford; ***W:*** Amos Poe; ***C:*** Bobby Bukowski; ***M:*** David Mansfield.

Gulliver's Travels 1/2 **1939** The Fleischer Studio's animated version of Jonathan Swift's classic about the adventures of Gulliver, an English sailor who is washed ashore in the land of Lilliput, where everyone is about two inches tall. **74m/C; VHS, DVD, Blu-Ray.** ***V:*** Lanny Ross; Jessica Dragonette; ***D:*** Dave Fleischer; ***W:*** Dan Gordon; Tedd Pierce; Edmond Seward; Izzy Sparber; ***C:*** Charles Schettler.

Gulliver's Travels **1977 (G)** In this partially animated adventure the entire land of Lilliput has been constructed in miniature. Cartoon and real life mix in a 3-dimensional story of Dr. Lemuel Gulliver and his discovery of the small people in the East Indies. From the classic by Jonathan Swift. **80m/C; VHS, DVD.** *GB* Richard Harris; Catherine Schell; ***D:*** Peter Hunt.

Gulliver's Travels 1/2 **1995 (PG)** Faithful TV version of Jonathan Swift's 1726 satiric novel. Lemuel Gulliver (Danson) is confined to Bedlam, an English insane asylum, after having been lost at sea for eight years. While in the asylum he relates his very odd adventures—in the tiny land of Lilliput, among the giants of Brobdingnag, with the silly and impractical intellectuals of Laputa, and finally amidst the brutish human Yahoos, who are ruled by rational talking horses, the Houyhnhnms. Meanwhile, Gulliver's wife Mary (Steenburgen) and son Tom (Sturridge) struggle to prove his sanity and win his release. On two cassettes. **187m/C; VHS, DVD.** Ted Danson; Mary Steenburgen; Edward Fox; Thomas Sturridge; Edward Woodward; Nicholas Lyndhurst; Peter O'Toole; Phoebe Nicholls; Ned Beatty; Kate Maberly; Alfre Woodard; Geraldine Chaplin; John Gielgud; Kristin Scott Thomas; Omar Sharif; John Standing; Warwick Davis; Robert Hardy; Shashi Kapoor; Karyn Parsons; Edward Petherbridge; ***D:*** Charles Sturridge; ***W:*** Simon Moore; ***C:*** Howard Atherton; ***M:*** Trevor Jones. **TV**

Gulliver's Travels 1/2 **2010 (PG)** In this inferior slapstick update to the classic, Lemuel Gulliver (Black), a mailroom attendant at a New York City newspaper convinces the travel editor (Peet) to assign him to write a piece on the Bermuda Triangle. While traveling by boat Gulliver is magically sucked into the tiny world of Liliput, where he finds himself tied down by the wee Liliputians. Of course he frees himself, befriends the little locals, repels an invading armada and battles with a giant robot, all in the supposed-to-be charming glow of Black's lovable-loaf shtick. **85m/C; Blu-Ray.** Jack Black; Emily Blunt; Jason Segel; Amanda Peet; Billy Connolly; Catherine Tate; T.J. Miller; Nikki Harrup; Ian Porter; Richard Laing; ***D:*** Rob Letterman; ***W:*** Nicholas Stoller; Joe Stillman; ***C:*** David Tattersall; ***M:*** Henry Jackman.

Gumball Rally **1976 (PG)** An unusual assortment of people converge upon New York for a cross country car race to Long Beach, California where breaking the rules is part of the game. **107m/C; VHS, DVD, Blu-Ray.** Michael Sarrazin; Gary Busey; Raul Julia; Nicholas Pryor; Tim McIntire; Susan Flannery; ***D:*** Charles "Chuck" Bail; ***W:*** Leon Capetanos.

Gumby: The Movie 1/2 **1995 (G)** Gumby and his musical group, the Clayboys, seek to save their neighbors' farms from foreclosure by putting on a benefit concert. And yes, pal Pokey is along to help out. But 90 minutes of our gentle clay hero stretches the patience of even the most enthusiastic fan. **90m/C; VHS, DVD, Blu-Ray.** ***D:*** Art Clokey; ***W:*** Art Clokey.

Gummo **WOOF!** **1997 (R)** "Kids" scripter and first time helmer Korine shamelessly parades out the freaks and calls it entertainment. More like a series of grisly images than a cohesive narrative when nihilism pervades a group of disaffected Xenia, Ohio teens who explore every brand of atrocity for kicks. Disturbing, not only in the graphic violence of the bored juvies but also in the frightening lack of a point to this uneven and self-indulgent shock-fest. Touted as modern movie's golden-boy, 23 year-old Korine doesn't let any dark humor slip in to detract from the purely revolting scenarios. The images that do summon up some truth about growing up in a dead-end town are far overshadowed by the collection of images as a whole. Renowned French cinematographer Escoffier lends style to this lost cause. **88m/C; VHS, DVD.** Chloë Sevigny; Jacob Reynolds; Jacob Sewell; Nick Sutton; Carisa Bara; Darby Dougherty; Max Perlich; Linda Manz; ***D:*** Harmony Korine; ***W:*** Harmony Korine; ***C:*** Jean-Yves Escoffier.

Gumshoe 1/2 **1972 (G)** An homage to American hard-boiled detectives. Finney plays a small-time worker in a Liverpool nightclub who decides to become a detective like his movie heroes. He bumbles through a number of interconnecting cases, but finds his way in the end. Good satire of film noir detectives. **85m/C; VHS, DVD.** *GB* Albert Finney; Billie Whitelaw; Frank Finlay; Janice Rule; Carolyn Seymour; ***D:*** Stephen Frears; ***W:*** Neville Smith; ***C:*** Chris Menges; ***M:*** Andrew Lloyd Webber.

Gun 1/2 **2010 (R)** Typical urban gangsta fare. Detroit gun runner Rich has a weapons deal go wrong and the FBI investigating him. He's sure there's a traitor in his crew and that's before his old buddy, ex-con Angel, suddenly shows up. **82m/C; DVD.** 50 Cent; Val Kilmer; AnnaLynne McCord; James Remar; Paul Calderon; Charles Malik Whitfield; Hassan Johnson; John Laroquette; ***D:*** Jessy Terrero; ***W:*** 50 Cent; ***C:*** Zeus Morand; ***M:*** David Kitchens; Ben Zarai. **VIDEO**

A Gun, a Car, a Blonde **1997** Paraplegic Richard Spraggins (Metzler) escapes from his pain-filled life by imagining himself to be living in a '50s film noir world, where he takes on the persona of tough private eye Rick Stone. Naturally, as in all good noir worlds, he must save a femme fatale blonde (Thompson) from a killer. **101m/C; VHS, DVD.** Jim Metzler; Billy Bob Thornton; Andrea Thompson; John Ritter; Kay Lenz; Victor Love; Paula Marshall; ***D:*** Stefani Ames; ***W:*** Stefani Ames; Tom Epperson; ***C:*** Carlos Gaviria; ***M:*** Harry Manfredini.

Gun Brothers ½ **1956** Chad Santee (Crabbe) is an honest rancher while his brother Jubal (Brand) is a wanted outlaw along with his partner Shawnee Jack (Ansara). Jubal decides to go straight and joins Chad, but Shawnee feels betrayed and wants revenge. **79m/B; DVD.** Buster Crabbe; Neville Brand; Michael Ansara; Slim Pickens; Walter Sande; Ann (Robin) Robinson; ***D:*** Sidney Salkow; ***W:*** Richard Schayer; Gerald Drayson Adams; ***C:*** Kenneth Peach, Sr.; ***M:*** Irving Gertz.

Gun Crazy *Deadly Is the Female* **1949** Annie Laurie Starr—Annie Oakley in a Wild West show—meets gun-lovin' Bart Tare, who says a gun makes him feel good inside, "like I'm somebody." Sparks fly, and the two get married and live happily ever after—until the money runs out and fatal femme Laurie's craving for excitement and violence starts to flare up. The two become lovebirds-on-the-lam. Now a cult fave, it's based on a MacKinlay Kantor story. Ex-stuntman Russell Harlan's photography is daring; the realism of the impressive robbery scenes is owed in part to the technical consultation of former train robber Al Jennings. And watch for a young Tamblyn as the 14-year-old Bart. **87m/B; DVD, Blu-Ray.** Peggy Cummins; John Dall; Berry Kroeger; Morris Carnovsky; Anabel Shaw; Nedrick Young; Trevor Bardette; Russ Tamblyn; Harry Lewis; Mickey Little; Paul Frison; Dave Bair; Stanley Prager; Virginia Farmer; Anne O'Neal; Frances Irwin; Don Beddoe; Robert Osterloh; Shimen Ruskin; Harry Hayden; ***D:*** Joseph H. Lewis; ***W:*** Dalton Trumbo; ***C:*** Russell Harlan; ***M:*** Victor Young. Natl. Film Reg. '98.

Gun Duel In Durango ½ **1957** Recycled western plot. When outlaw Will Sabre decides to go straight, he also decides to go back to his given name of Dan Tomlinson, but his plans anger gang leader Dunsten who threatens him. Still, Dan returns to his hometown and former sweetheart Judy and even gets a job in the bank, which Dunsten then robs. Dunsten plants evidence pointing to Dan as an accomplice and Dan has to bring in the outlaw gang to clear his name. **74m/B; DVD.** George Montgomery; Ann (Robin) Robinson; Steve Brodie; Donald (Don "Red") Barry; Boyd 'Red' Morgan; Bobby Clark; Frank Ferguson; ***D:*** Sidney Salkow; ***W:*** Louis Stevens; ***C:*** Maury Gertsman; ***M:*** Paul Sawtell; Bert Shefter.

Gun for 100 Graves ½ *A Gun for One Hundred Graves; Una pistola per cento bare; Pistol for a Hundred Coffins* **1968** Jim Slade (Peter Lee Lawrence) returns home from the Civil War to find his family dead. Everyone says a local gang did it, but the truth quickly becomes obviously more complex. Currently only available as part of the 'Westerns Unchained' collection. **83m/C; Blu-Ray.** *IT SP* Peter Lee Lawrence; John Ireland; Gloria Osuna; Eduardo Fajardo; Raf Baldassarre; ***D:*** Umberto Lenzi; ***W:*** Marc Leto; Vittorio Salerno; Eduardo Brochero; ***C:*** Alejandro Ulloa; ***M:*** Angelo Francesco Lavagnino. **VIDEO**

Gun for a Coward **1957** Some solid performances in a formulaic western. Sensitive middle Keough brother would rather walk away from trouble but has to take a stand during a cattle drive when, beset by rustlers, tragedy strikes the family. **88m/C; DVD.** Fred MacMurray; Jeffrey Hunter; Dean Stockwell; Janice Rule; Chill Wills; Josephine Hutchinson; ***D:*** Abner Biberman; ***W:*** R. Wright Campbell; ***C:*** George Robinson.

Gun Fury ½ **1953** A panoramic western about a Civil War veteran pursuing the bandits who kidnapped his beautiful bride-to-be. First screened as a 3-D movie. **83m/C; VHS, DVD, Blu-Ray.** Rock Hudson; Donna Reed; Phil Carey; Lee Marvin; ***D:*** Raoul Walsh.

Gun Glory ½ **1957** Granger plays Tom Early, a gunslinger who returns home after three years to find the town would rather not have him. He regains the town's respect when he stops a murderer from invading the town with his cattle herd. Based on the novel "Man of the West" by Philip Yordan. **88m/C; VHS, DVD.** Stewart Granger; Rhonda Fleming; Chill Wills; Steve Rowland; James Gregory; Jacques Aubuchon; Arch Johnson; William "Bill" Fawcett; Lane Bradford; Michael Dugan; Bud Osborne; May McAvoy; Charles Herbert; Carl Pitti; ***D:*** Roy Rowland; ***W:*** William Ludwig; ***M:*** Jeff Alexander.

The Gun Hawk ½ **1963** The final film for director Ludwig is a western with a familar theme. Aging gunslinger Blaine Madden (Calhoun) visits his hometown, gets into a gun fight with the sheriff (Cameron), and escapes to the outlaw haven of Sanctuary with his hot-tempered young gun protege, Reb Roan (Lauren). Madden wants to go out on his own terms and a showdown is inevitable. **92m/C; DVD.** Rory Calhoun; Rod Cameron; Rod Lauren; Ruta Lee; Morgan Woodward; ***D:*** Edward Ludwig; ***W:*** Jo Heims; ***C:*** Paul Vogel; ***M:*** Jimmie Haskell.

Gun Hill Road **2011 (R)** Morales' character is an unfortunate cliche in writer/director Green's Bronx-set debut, but others make up for those inadequacies. Just released from the joint, Enrique (Morales) heads home expecting to resume his old life but his wife Angela (Reyes) has moved on and his teenage son Michael (Santana) now identifies as female and is saving up for surgery. While easily slipping back into his criminal ways, the enraged, bewildered dad tries to force Michael into following his own macho identity. Santana makes a strong debut, unselfconscious and mature. **86m/C; DVD.** Esai Morales; Judy Reyes; Harmony Santana; Tyrone Brown; Isiah Whitlock, Jr.; ***D:*** Rashaad Ernesto Green; ***W:*** Rashaad Ernesto Green; ***C:*** Daniel Patterson; ***M:*** Enrique Hank Feldman; Stefan Swanson.

The Gun in Betty Lou's Handbag **1992 (PG-13)** Shy, small town librarian with a dull marriage is looking for excitement when she stumbles across a gun used in a murder. She decides excitement will follow her (false) confession to the crime leaving her husband thunderstruck, the police confused, and the gossip line humming. She also intrigues the real bad guy, who comes looking for her. Lame silliness is redeemed somewhat by Miller, but there's some surprisingly nasty violence given the comedy label. **99m/C; VHS, DVD, Blu-Ray.** Penelope Ann Miller; Eric Thal; Alfre Woodard; Cathy Moriarty; William Forsythe; Julianne Moore; Xander Berkeley; Michael O'Neill; Christopher John Fields; ***D:*** Allan Moyle; ***W:*** Grace Cary Bickley; ***M:*** Richard Gibbs.

A Gun in the House **1981** While being attacked in her own home, a woman shoots one of her assailants. The police find no conclusive evidence of attack and arrest the woman for murder. Exploitive drama on gun control. **100m/C; VHS, DVD.** Sally Struthers; David Ackroyd; Joel Bailey; Jeffrey Tambor; ***D:*** Ivan Nagy. **TV**

Gun Riders ½ *Five Bloody Graves; Five Bloody Days to Tombstone; Lonely Man* **1969** Gunman must seek out and stop a murderer of innocent people. **98m/C; VHS, DVD.** Scott Brady; Jim Davis; John Carradine; ***D:*** Al Adamson.

The Gun Runners ½ **1958** Murphy does what he can, but this adaptation of the Hemingway story "To Have and Have Not" pales in comparison to the 1944 Bogie version. Key West charter boat captain Sam Martin has big financial woes and mistakenly agrees to do a job for arms dealer Hanagan (Albert). Hanagan is supposed to run illegal weapons to Cuban rebels in Havana but he plans a doublecross that could cost Martin more than his boat. **83m/B; DVD, Blu-Ray.** Audie Murphy; Eddie Albert; Patricia Owens; Everett Sloane; Richard Jaeckel; Gita Hall; Jack Elam; Carlos Romero; ***D:*** Don Siegel; ***W:*** Daniel Mainwaring; Paul Monash; ***C:*** Hal Mohr; ***M:*** Leith Stevens.

Gun Shy **2000 (R)** Psychiatry and organized crime collide again, but this time it's the cops in therapy. Well, one of 'em at least. Charlie (Neeson) is a burned-out DEA agent forced back undercover as a go-between for an Italian gangster (Platt) who knows he's a cliche and a Colombian drug cartel leader (Zuniga) who believes investing in bean futures is some sort of ethnic no-no. Charlie's work problems lead him to a men's therapy group and a nurse (Bullock) dubbed the "Enema Queen." Yep, it's mostly that kind of humor. The crime figures are thin, and Blakenly needs to work on his comic and scene timing, but Neeson fares pretty well. The group sessions are highlights, but the payoff isn't as big as one would hope. **102m/C; VHS, DVD, Blu-Ray.** Liam Neeson; Oliver Platt; Sandra Bullock; Jose Zuniga; Richard Schiff; Andrew Lauer; Mitch Pileggi; Paul Ben-Victor; Mary McCormack; Frank Vincent; Michael Mantell; Louis Giambalvo; Gregg Daniel; Michael Delorenzo; ***D:*** Eric Blakeney; ***W:*** Eric Blakeney; ***C:*** Tom Richmond; ***M:*** Rolfe Kent.

Gun Shy **2017 (R)** Aspiring to mash "This is Spinal Tap" with "Dumb and Dumber," this action-comedy brings only shame to Banderas et al. When his wife (Kurylenko) is kidnapped by pirates in Chile, aging and pampered-to-helplessness former rock star Turk Henry (Banderas) must rescue her on his own, even as the U.S. government tries to foil his attempts. Amazingly, his wig is not the worst thing about this flick; the plot is ridiculous, the jokes don't land, and his performance is desperately over-the-top. **86m/C; DVD, Blu-Ray.** Antonio Banderas; Olga Kurylenko; Mark Valley; Aisling Loftus; Ben Cura; ***D:*** Simon West; ***W:*** Toby Davies; Mark Haskell Smith; ***C:*** Alan Caudillo; ***M:*** David M Saunders.

The Gun That Won the West ½ **1955** That would be the Springfield Rifle, which provides more excitement than the actors in this routine western. Frontier scouts Jim Bridger and Jack Gaines are hired to protect railroad workers from attacks by the Sioux as they travel across Wyoming. Low-budget Sam Katzman production uses a lot of stock footage that doesn't always match-up with the new shots. **69m/C; DVD.** Dennis Morgan; Richard Denning; Robert Bice; Michael Morgan; Roy Gordon; Chris O'Brien; Paula Raymond; ***D:*** William Castle; ***W:*** Robert E. Kent; ***C:*** Henry Freulich.

Gun the Man Down ½ **1956** A tight B-western that's the directorial debut of McLaglen. Arness is on the other side of the law as Rem Anderson, who's wounded during a bank robbery. He goes to prison while his two partners and his gal make off with the money. When Rem gets out, he tracks them down but takes his time getting revenge, making the others nervous. So they hire a gunslinger for a showdown. **76m/B; Blu-Ray, Streaming.** James Arness; Robert J. Wilke; Don Megowan; Angie Dickinson; Michael Emmet; Emile Meyer; Harry Carey, Jr.; ***D:*** Andrew V. McLaglen; ***W:*** Burt Kennedy; ***C:*** William Clothier; ***M:*** Henry Vars.

Guncrazy **1992 (R)** Girl from the wrong side of the tracks, abused her entire life, finds her freedom in a gun. She winds up killing the man who raped her, takes up with an equally lost ex-con, and the two armed misfits go on the run from the law. Barrymore's convincing and the movie is another well-made variation on the lovers-on-the-run theme. Film was inspired by, but is not a remake of, the 1949 movie "Gun Crazy." **97m/C; VHS, DVD.** Drew Barrymore; James LeGros; Billy Drago; Rodney Harvey; Ione Skye; Joe Dallesandro; Michael Ironside; ***D:*** Tamra Davis; ***W:*** Matthew Bright; ***C:*** Lisa Rinzler.

A Gunfight **1971 (PG)** When Cash is stranded in a small Western town, he meets up with fellow old-time gunfighter Douglas. The two strike up a friendship, but discover the town folk expect a gun battle. Needing money, the two arrange a gunfight for paid admission—winner take all. Cash makes his screen debut. **90m/C; DVD.** Kirk Douglas; Johnny Cash; Jane Alexander; Karen Black; Dana Elcar; Keith Carradine; Raf Vallone; ***D:*** Lamont Johnson; ***W:*** Harold Jack Bloom.

Gunfight at Comanche Creek ½ **1964** In 1875, Bob Gifford (Murphy) is working as an undercover operative for the National Detective Agency. He's tracking a gang that springs other criminals from jail, uses them as fronts in robberies, and then kills the convicts for the increased reward money. Bob infiltrates the gang and gets into a lot of trouble. **90m/C; DVD.** Audie Murphy; Ben Cooper; Colleen Miller; DeForest Kelley; Jan Merlin; John Hubbard; Adam Williams; ***D:*** Frank McDonald; Edward L. Bernds; ***C:*** Joseph Biroc; ***M:*** Marlin Skiles.

The Gunfight at Dodge City **1959** Bat Masterson (McCrea) is pressured to become the sheriff of Dodge City and immediately has problems with the crooked local politicians and then more trouble when his old gang shows up in town. Typical oater that McCrea originally intended to be his final picture before his retirement from the screen. **80m/C; DVD, Blu-Ray.** Joel McCrea; Julie Adams; John McIntire; Nancy Gates; Richard Anderson; Don Haggerty; James Westerfield; ***D:*** Joseph M. Newman; ***W:*** Martin Goldsmith; Daniel Ullman; ***C:*** Carl Guthrie; ***M:*** Hans J. Salter.

Gunfight at Red Sands *Gringo; Duello Nel Texas* **1963** Landmark western in the history of Italian cinema. Long before Leone's Eastwood trilogy, this film introduced the theme of an avenging stranger to the genre. Harrison stars as the dark, brooding hero who is out for revenge after learning that his family has been attacked by a gang of bandits. **97m/C; VHS, DVD.** *SP IT* Richard Harrison; Giacomo "Jack" Rossi-Stuart; Sara Lezana; Dan (Daniel, Danny) Martin; ***D:*** Ricardo Blasco; ***W:*** Albert Band; Ricardo Blasco; ***C:*** Massimo Dallamano; ***M:*** Ennio Morricone.

Gunfight at the O.K. Corral **1957** The story of Wyatt Earp and Doc Holliday joining forces in Dodge City to rid the town of the criminal Clanton gang. Filmed in typical Hollywood style, but redeemed by its great stars. **122m/C; VHS, DVD, Blu-Ray.** Burt Lancaster; Kirk Douglas; Rhonda Fleming; Jo Van Fleet; John Ireland; Kenneth Tobey; Lee Van Cleef; Frank Faylen; DeForest Kelley; Earl Holliman; Dennis Hopper; Martin Milner; Jack Elam; Olive Carey; Joan Camden; ***D:*** John Sturges; ***W:*** Leon Uris; ***C:*** Charles B(ryant) Lang, Jr.; ***M:*** Dimitri Tiomkin.

Gunfight in Abilene ½ **1967** Guilt-stricken Confederate veteran Cal Wayne (Darin) comes home to Abilene and is appointed sheriff by cattle baron Grant Evers (Nielsen). Cal then tries to avoid violence in a dispute between the cattlemen and the farmers. Pop star Darin also did the soundtrack, which is more interesting than this generic western that's a remake of 1956's "Showdown at Abilene." **86m/C; DVD.** Bobby Darin; Emily Banks; Leslie Nielsen; Donnelly Rhodes; Don Galloway; ***D:*** William (Billy) Hale; ***W:*** Berne Giler; John D.F. Black; ***C:*** Maury Gertsman; ***M:*** Bobby Darin.

The Gunfighter ½ **1950** A mature, serious, Hollywood-western character study about an aging gunfighter searching for peace and quiet but unable to avoid his reputation and the duel-challenges it invites. One of King's best films. **85m/B; VHS, DVD.** Gregory Peck; Helen Westcott; Millard Mitchell; Jean Parker; Karl Malden; Skip Homeier; Mae Marsh; Angela (Clark) Clarke; ***D:*** Henry King; ***C:*** Arthur C. Miller.

Gunfighter **1998 (PG-13)** Gunfighter Sheen is out to avenge the murder of some townsfolk. Then an outlaw kidnaps his girlfriend and things get even more personal. **94m/C; VHS, DVD.** Robert Carradine; Martin Sheen; Clu Gulager; ***D:*** Christopher Coppola.

Gunfighters **1947** Routine western based on the Zane Grey novel "Twin Sombreros." Gunslinger Kane (Scott) retires to become a cowhand but picks up his six-shooter when a friend is killed. Kane accuses crooked cattle baron Banner (Barnett) of the murder, and Banner tries to get Kane lynched. Naturally, Kane is becomes even more determined to avenge his friend. **87m/C; DVD.** Randolph Scott; Griff Barnett; Barbara Britton; Dorothy Hart; Bruce Cabot; Grant Withers; Forrest Tucker; ***D:*** George Waggner; ***W:*** Alan LeMay; ***C:*** Fred H. Jackman, Jr.; ***M:*** Rudy Schrager.

The Gunfighters ½ **1987** Lackluster pilot of a proposed Canadian series pits three individualistic relatives against a powerful empire-builder. **100m/C; VHS, DVD.** *CA* Art Hindle; Reiner Schone; Anthony Addabbo; George Kennedy; Michael Kane; Lori Hallier; ***D:*** Clay Borris. **TV**

Gunfighter's Moon ½ **1996 (PG-13)** Legendary gunslinger Frank Morgan (Henriksen) is called on by former lover, Linda (Lenz), to help her sheriff husband prevent a jailbreak. Frank's tired of his constant challengers but can't seem to make another life for himself. **95m/C; VHS, DVD.** Lance Henriksen; Kay Lenz; David McIlwraith; Ivan Sergei; Nikki Deloach; ***D:*** Larry Ferguson; ***W:*** Larry Ferguson; ***C:*** James L. Carter; ***M:*** Lee Holdridge.

Gunfire *China 9, Liberty 37* **1978** A gunfighter is rescued from the hangman's noose by railroad tycoons who want him to kill a farmer. He doesn't kill the man, but runs off with his wife instead, and the incensed railway honchos send assassins after the double-crossing gunman. Peckinpah's part is pretty puny in this leisurely horse opera.

94m/C; VHS, DVD. *IT* Fabio Testi; Warren Oates; Jenny Agutter; Sam Peckinpah; ***D:*** Monte Hellman; ***M:*** Pino Donaggio.

Gung Ho! **1943** Carlson's Raiders are a specially trained group of Marine jungle fighters determined to retake the Pacific island of Makin during WWII. **88m/B; VHS, DVD.** Robert Mitchum; Randolph Scott; Noah Beery, Jr.; Alan Curtis; Grace McDonald; ***D:*** Ray Enright; ***C:*** Milton Krasner.

Gung Ho 1/2 **1986 (PG-13)** A Japanese firm takes over a small-town U.S. auto factory and causes major cultural collisions. Keaton plays the go-between for employees and management while trying to keep both groups from killing each other. From the director of "Splash" and "Night Shift." Made into a short-lived TV series. **111m/C; DVD.** Michael Keaton; Gedde Watanabe; George Wendt; Mimi Rogers; John Turturro; Clint Howard; Michelle Johnson; So Yamamura; Sab Shimono; ***D:*** Ron Howard; ***W:*** Babaloo Mandel; Lowell Ganz; ***C:*** Don Peterman; ***M:*** Thomas Newman.

Gunga Din **1939** The prototypical "buddy" film. Three veteran British sergeants in India try to suppress a native uprising, but it's their water boy, the intrepid Gunga Din, who saves the day. Friendship, loyalty, and some of the best action scenes ever filmed. Based loosely on Rudyard Kipling's famous poem, the story is credited to Ben Hecht, Charles MacArthur, and William Faulkner (who is uncredited). Also available colorized. **117m/B; VHS, DVD.** Cary Grant; Victor McLaglen; Douglas Fairbanks, Jr.; Sam Jaffe; Eduardo Ciannelli; Montagu Love; Joan Fontaine; Abner Biberman; Robert Coote; Lumsden Hare; Cecil Kellaway; Roland Varno; George Regas; Reginald (Reggie, Reggy) Sheffield; Clive Morgan; ***D:*** George Stevens; ***W:*** Fred Guiol; Joel Sayre; Ben Hecht; William Faulkner; ***C:*** Joseph August; ***M:*** Alfred Newman. Natl. Film Reg. '99.

The Gunman 1/2 *A Promise Kept* **2003 (R)** Already tormented by the murder of his wife, police detective Ben Simms (Flanery) is plunged further into turmoil when given the duty of catching a vigilante who enjoys offing the bad guys...and he discovers that her killer is up next. **91m/C; VHS, DVD.** Sean Patrick Flanery; Joey Lauren Adams; Mimi Rogers; Brian McNamara; Tom Wright; Jeff Speakman; Emma Nicolas; Steve Krieger; Alaina Kalanj; Daniel Millican; ***D:*** Daniel Millican; ***W:*** Daniel Millican. **VIDEO**

The Gunman 1/2 **2015 (R)** It's amazing that two actors as talented as Penn and Bardem can headline such a dull piece of nonsense as this action movie about a notorious hitman who kills a powerful figure in the Congo and is forced into hiding to survive the inevitable retaliation. He returns to the Congo years later, thinking he's safe, but learns the hard way that he is definitely not. Penn is never awful but he's miscast here in a role that feels a bit like an attempt at the "Neeson Money" of an acclaimed actor-turned-action star. **115m/C; DVD, Blu-Ray.** *SP FR* Sean Penn; Jasmine Trinca; Javier Bardem; Ray Winstone; Mark Rylance; ***D:*** Pierre Morel; ***W:*** Sean Penn; Don MacPherson; Pete Travis; ***C:*** Flavio Martinez Labiano; ***M:*** Marco Beltrami.

Gunmen **1993 (R)** A reluctant buddy team face down some bad guys. DEA agent Cole (Van Peebles) teams up with smuggler Dani (Lambert) to find stolen drug money also wanted by wheelchair-bound villain Loomis (Stewart) and his violence-loving henchman (Leary). Adds comedy to the mix as well as shameless action rip-offs from spaghetti westerns. **90m/C; VHS, DVD.** Christopher Lambert; Mario Van Peebles; Denis Leary; Patrick Stewart; Kadeem Hardison; Sally Kirkland; ***Cameo(s):*** Big Daddy Kane; Ed Lover; Eric B. Rakim; Dr. Dre; ***D:*** Deran Sarafian; ***W:*** Stephen Sommers; ***M:*** John Debney.

Gunner Palace **2004 (PG-13)** Frenetic documentary follows the 2/3 Field Artillery Division (known as "The Gunners") of the U.S. Army's First Armored Division as they serve their tour of duty in Iraq. The Gunners have set up camp in a once-opulent Iraqi palace, formerly occupied by one of Saddam Hussein's sons. Tucker and Epperlein ignore the politics behind the war, but rather emphasize the chaotic existence of the soldiers on the frontlines. We watch their daily routines, see them laugh and interact, and listen to them express their feelings about putting their lives on the line. The ugly, grainy camerawork might turn some off, but overall, it presents a compelling snapshot of life during wartime. **85m/C; DVD.** ***D:*** Michael Tucker; Petra Epperlein; ***C:*** Michael Tucker.

Guns **1990 (R)** An international gunrunner puts the moves on buxom women between hair-raising adventures. **95m/C; VHS, DVD, Blu-Ray.** Erik Estrada; Dona Speir; ***D:*** Andy Sidaris; ***W:*** Andy Sidaris.

Guns **2008 (R)** Canadian miniseries. British expat Paul Duguid (Feore) is a legitimate arms dealer who also sells illegal weapons to street thugs. His son Bobby (Smith) comes under police surveillance, is implicated in the murder of a U.S. senator's father, and has his girlfriend Frances (Cuthbert) willing to smuggle guns across the border if it'll help him out. **180m/C; DVD.** *CA* Colm Feore; Gregory Edward Smith; Elisha Cuthbert; Shawn Doyle; Lyriq Bent; Alan Van Sprang; Al Sapienza; ***D:*** David Sutherland; ***C:*** Arthur E. Cooper. **TV**

Guns at Batasi 1/2 **1964** Attenborough plays a tough British Sergeant Major stationed in Africa during the anti-colonial 1960s. Ultimately the regiment is threatened by rebel Africans. Fine performances make this rather predictable film watchable. **103m/B; VHS, DVD.** *GB* Richard Attenborough; Jack Hawkins; Mia Farrow; Flora Robson; John Leyton; ***D:*** John Guillermin; ***M:*** John Addison.

Guns Don't Argue **1957** Entertaining schlocker about the rise and fall of famous criminal Dillinger. Non-stop action also features Bonnie and Clyde, Pretty Boy Floyd and Baby Face Nelson. **92m/C; VHS, DVD.** Myron Healey; Jim Davis; Lyle Talbot; Paul Dubov; Sam Edwards; Richard Crane; ***D:*** Richard C. Kahn; Bill Karn; ***W:*** Phillips Lord; ***C:*** William Clothier; ***M:*** Paul Dunlap.

Guns for Hire *The Adventures of Beatles* **2015** A comedy-drama wrapped in a mystery centered on an assassin with an informercial. Beatle (Hicks) leads an unusual life of her own determination. A loner with limited human contact, she runs a towing business and is an assassin on the side. Beatle's life is turned upside down when she meets Athena Klendon (Carradine), a suicidal woman who has a killer after her. Athena and Beatle strike a bargain in which Beatle will be named the beneficiary of Athena's life insurance policy in exchange for Beatle killing her. As the related paperwork is processed, Athena lives with Beatle and helps her with her infomercial. Unknown to both women, a detective has been following all they have done and he believes he can finally arrest Beatle. Like life, however, his case takes an unexpected twist. **83m/C; DVD, Streaming, Download.** Michele Hicks; Ever Carradine; Jeffrey Dean Morgan; Ben Mendelsohn; Tony Shalhoub; ***D:*** Donna Robinson; ***W:*** Donna Robinson; Katherine Brooks; ***C:*** Bob Finley, III. **VIDEO**

Guns, Girls and Gambling **2011** Terribly muddled (and generally terrible) action-comedy. An Indian casino is robbed of an Apache war mask and the tribe suspects one of the Elvis impersonators gambling at the casino is responsible. The tribe sends out hitmen who shoot first and try to get the mask back. **90m/C; DVD, Blu-Ray.** Christian Slater; Jeff Fahey; Powers Boothe; Dane Cook; Sam Trammell; Gary Oldman; Helena Mattsson; Gordon Tootoosis; Chris Kattan; ***D:*** Michael Winnick; ***W:*** Michael Winnick; ***C:*** Jonathan Hale; ***M:*** Jeff Cardoni. **VIDEO**

Guns of Darkness 1/2 **1962** Dreary drama. A military coup overthrows the president of a South American country. Wounded, ex-President Rivera stumbles onto a British-owned sugar plantation where manager Tom Jordan feels obligated to help him, despite the objections of his troubled French wife, Claire. Tom decides the best thing is to make a hazardous journey with Rivera across the border. **102m/B; DVD.** *UK* David Niven; Leslie Caron; David Opatoshu; James Robertson Justice; ***D:*** Anthony Asquith; ***W:*** John Mortimer; ***C:*** Robert Krasker; ***M:*** Benjamin Frankel.

Guns of Diablo **1964** Wagon train master Bronson has to fight a gang that controls the supply depot, all the while showing his young helper (beardless boy Russell) the fascinating tricks of the trade. **91m/C; VHS, DVD.** Charles Bronson; Kurt Russell; Susan Oliver; ***D:*** Boris Sagal.

The Guns of Navarone 1/2 **1961** During WWII, British Intelligence in the Middle East sends six men to the Aegean island of Navarone to destroy guns manned by the Germans. Consistently interesting war epic based on the Alistair MacLean novel, with a vivid cast. **159m/C; VHS, DVD, Blu-Ray.** Gregory Peck; David Niven; Anthony Quinn; Richard Harris; Stanley Baker; Anthony Quayle; James Darren; Irene Papas; Gia Scala; James Robertson Justice; Bryan Forbes; Allan Cuthbertson; Michael Trubshawe; Percy Herbert; Walter Gotell; Tutte Lemkow; ***D:*** J. Lee Thompson; ***W:*** Carl Foreman; ***C:*** Oswald Morris; ***M:*** Dimitri Tiomkin. Golden Globes '62: Film--Drama, Score.

Guns of the Magnificent Seven 1/2 **1969 (G)** The third remake of "The Seven Samurai." Action-packed western in which the seven free political prisoners and train them to kill. The war party then heads out to rescue a Mexican revolutionary being held in an impregnable fortress. **106m/C; VHS, DVD.** George Kennedy; Monte Markham; James Whitmore; Reni Santoni; Bernie Casey; Joe Don Baker; Scott Thomas; Michael Ansara; Fernando Rey; ***D:*** Paul Wendkos; ***M:*** Elmer Bernstein.

Gunshy **1998 (R)** Familiar crime genre has some fine performances and an intelligent script. Journalist Jake Bridges (Petersen) heads to Atlantic City after catching his wife cheating on him. His drunken ranting gets him trouble, but Jake is rescued by likeable smalltime mob guy Frankie (Wincott) and his hot girlfriend, Melissa (Lane). Jake hangs around watching Frankie work and making passes at Melissa but it just might be that Jake has his own hidden agenda, as well. **101m/C; VHS, DVD.** William L. Petersen; Michael Wincott; Diane Lane; Kevin Gage; Michael Byrne; Meat Loaf Aday; Eric Schaeffer; Musetta Vander; John Fleck; Badja (Medu) Djola; R. Lee Ermey; Natalie Canerday; ***D:*** Jeff Celentano; ***W:*** Larry Gross; ***C:*** John Aronson; ***M:*** Hal Lindes.

The Gunslinger 1/2 **1956** A woman marshall struggles to keep law and order in a town overrun by outlaws. Unique western with a surprise ending. **83m/C; VHS, DVD.** John Ireland; Beverly Garland; Allison Hayes; Jonathan Haze; Dick Miller; Bruno VeSota; William Schallert; ***D:*** Roger Corman; ***W:*** Charles B. Griffith; Mark Hanna; ***C:*** Frederick E. West; ***M:*** Ronald Stein.

Gunslinger 1/2 *Have a Nice Funeral; Stranger's Gold; Buon Funerale, Amigos!* **1970** Armed to the teeth with weaponry, Sartana shows a mining town's heavies how to sling a gun or two. **90m/C; VHS, DVD.** *IT SP* Gianni "John" Garko; Antonio Vilar; Daniela Giordano; Ivano Staccioli; ***D:*** Giuliano Carnimeo; ***W:*** Roberto Gianviti; Robert Gianviti; Giovanni Simonelli; ***C:*** Stelvio Massi; ***M:*** Bruno Nicolai.

Gunslinger's Revenge *Il Mio West* **1998 (PG-13)** After 20 years Doc Lowen's (Pieraccioni) gun-toting, outlaw father Johnny (Keitel) resurfaces much to Doc's dismay as he's devoted his life to a peace-loving existence with his wife and young son. While they try to resolve their issues Johnny must also contend with the return of his former nemesis Jack Sikora (Bowie) who's bent on revenge. Pace is slow on the draw (even for a Western) and a dubbed-over Keitel shoots a blank though Bowie followers will want to lasso this one. In Italian with English subtitles. **87m/C; DVD.** Harvey Keitel; David Bowie; Sandrine Holt; Vincenzo Pardini; Leonardo Pieraccioni; ***D:*** Giovanni Veronesi; ***W:*** Giovanni Veronesi; Vincenzo Pardini. **VIDEO**

Gunsmoke: Return to Dodge 1/2 **1987** The first of the TV movies that reunited most of the cast of the classic TV western. Matt Dillon returns to Dodge and Miss Kitty after 12 years only to be trailed by a ruthless adversary. **100m/C; VHS, DVD.** James Arness; Amanda Blake; Buck Taylor; Fran Ryan; Earl Holliman; Steve Forrest; ***D:*** Vincent McEveety. **TV**

The Guru 1/2 **2002 (R)** Naive dance instructor Ramu Gupta (Mistry) leaves India to pursue stardom in New York. After being fired from his job as a waiter, he auditions for a movie company, but it turns out to be for a porn film. Unable to perform despite coaching from Sharrona (Graham), a porn starlet, Ramu is fired from this job as well. As luck (and script) would have it, he's re-hired by his former boss to replace the drunken swami that was scheduled to appear at a party for socialite Lexi (Tomei). Regurgitating his porn co-star's advice, Ramu becomes a hit as a sex guru. Soon Ramu is the toast of the town as the mystical sex therapist (think Deepak Chopra as Dr Ruth). The movie has some genuinely funny moments, but suffers for trying to be both a light-hearted romantic comedy and a social satire. **91m/C; VHS, DVD.** *GB FR US* Jimi Mistry; Heather Graham; Marisa Tomei; Michael McKean; Christine Baranski; Rob Morrow; Malachy McCourt; Dash Mihok; ***D:*** Daisy von Scherler Mayer; ***W:*** Tracey Jackson; ***C:*** John de Borman; ***M:*** David Carbonara.

Gus 1/2 **1976 (G)** A Disney film about the California Atoms, a football team that has the worst record in the league until they begin winning games with the help of their field goal kicking mule of a mascot, Gus. The competition then plots a donkey-napping. Enjoyable comedy for the whole family. **96m/C; VHS, DVD.** Ed Asner; Tim Conway; Dick Van Patten; Ronnie Schell; Bob Crane; Tom Bosley; ***D:*** Vincent McEveety; ***W:*** Arthur Alsberg; ***M:*** Robert F. Brunner.

Gutshot Straight **2014 (R)** Low-budget, clichéd crime drama. Hustling Vegas gambler Jack owes a loan shark big bucks. Sleazy, older player Duffy offers Jack a deal involving Duffy's young wife May and sex that Jack turns down. Jack's life then goes on even more of a losing streak. Title refers to a poker play. **85m/C; DVD.** George Eads; AnnaLynne McCord; Stephen Lang; Steven Seagal; Vinnie Jones; Ted Levine; Tia Carrere; ***D:*** Justin Steele; ***W:*** Jerry Rapp; ***C:*** Tiago Mesquita; ***M:*** Keith E. Waggoner. **VIDEO**

Guy and Madeline on a Park Bench 1/2 **2009** Talented jazz trumpeter Guy (Palmer) and hapless waitress Madeline (Garcia) end their romance on a park bench in the opening scene—the balance of the film is spent in hopes the two will reunite. Whether they do or don't, no matter; the singing, tap-dancing and trumpet playing more than make up for any unrequited feelings. Director Chazelle began work on this film as an undergrad at Harvard. Filmed in 16mm black and white, it feels period but is gorgeously hip and contemporary. **82m/B; Blu-Ray.** Jason Palmer; Desiree Garcia; Sandha Khin; Frank Garvin; Alma Prelec; Andre Hayward; ***D:*** Damien Chazelle; ***W:*** Damien Chazelle; ***C:*** Damien Chazelle; ***M:*** Justin Hurtwitz.

The Guy from Harlem **1977** He's mad, he's from Harlem, and he's not going to take it any more. **86m/C; VHS, DVD.** Loye Hawkins; Cathy Davis; Patricia Fulton; Wanda Starr; ***D:*** Rene Martinez, Jr.

A Guy Thing **2003 (PG-13)** Paul (Lee), wakes up after his bachelor party to find free spirit Becky (Stiles) besides him in bed. Of course his fiancee walks in just as Paul is able to shoo Becky out, thus avoiding a rather embarrassing situation. Or not. Becky turns out to be his fiancee's cousin and keeps popping up into Paul's life, as does her insanely possessive, cop ex-boyfriend. Lee and Stiles are likable enough, unfortunately the material is too bland to make anything out their chemistry. **101m/C; VHS, DVD.** Jason Lee; Julia Stiles; Selma Blair; Shawn Hatosy; James Brolin; Diana Scarwid; Lochlyn Munro; Julie Hagerty; Jackie Burroughs; David Koechner; Thomas Lennon; ***D:*** Chris Koch; ***W:*** Matt Tarses; Bill Wrubel; Greg Glienna; Pete Schwaba; ***C:*** Robbie Greenberg; ***M:*** Mark Mothersbaugh.

The Guyana Tragedy: The Story of Jim Jones **1980** Dramatization traces the story of the Reverend Jim Jones and the People's Temple from its beginnings in 1953 to the November 1978 mass suicide of more than 900 people. Boothe is appropriately hypnotic as the Reverend. **240m/C; VHS, DVD.** Powers Boothe; Ned Beatty; Randy Quaid; Brad Dourif; Brenda Vaccaro; LeVar Burton; Colleen Dewhurst; James Earl Jones; ***D:*** William A. Graham; ***C:*** Gil Hubbs; ***M:*** Elmer Bernstein. **TV**

The Guys 1/2 **2002 (PG)** Cinematic adaptation of Anne Nelson's timely play about September 11. A fateful introduction brings a journalist (Weaver) to collaborate with an emotionally wrought, inarticulate New York City Fire Department captain (LaPaglia) on poignant, heartfelt eulogies for his fallen brothers. Both leads do a fine job bringing their characters from stage to screen. Some archival footage feels awkwardly placed but on the whole film presents a dignified and humanistic perspective on an event whose world impact is still unfolding. Shot on location in New York, with very little budget in just two weeks, then reshot in another two weeks after discovering some lighting equipment had failed. Simpson and Weaver's daughter makes a cameo appearance along with Nelson's two sons. **98m/C; VHS, DVD.** Sigourney Weaver; Anthony LaPaglia; ***D:*** Jim Simpson; ***W:*** Ann Nelson; Jim Simpson; ***C:*** Maryse Alberti; ***M:*** Ron Carter.

Guys and Balls *Manner wie wir* **2004 (R)** Small-town baker's son Ecki (Bruckner) is the goalie on the local soccer team. After losing an important game, Ecki is discovered in a drunken embrace with another man and his teammates throw him off the squad. Vowing to get even, Ecki decides to put together an all-gay team and challenge his hometown's homophobes to a grudge match. So he heads to the city to recruit players and, naturally, finds mostly stereotypical oddballs. Lots of good-natured crass humor and rowdiness. German with subtitles. **106m/C; DVD.** *GE* Christian Berkel; Maximilian Bruckner; Rolf Zacher; Lisa Maria Potthoff; David Rott; Mariele Millowitsch; ***D:*** Sherry Hormann; ***W:*** Benedikt Gollhardt; ***C:*** Hanno Lentz; ***M:*** Martin Todsharow.

Guys and Dolls **1955** New York gambler Sky Masterson takes a bet that he can romance a Salvation Army lady. Based on the stories of Damon Runyon with Blaine, Kaye, Pully, and Silver recreating their roles from the Broadway hit. Brando's not-always-convincing musical debut. **150m/C; VHS, DVD, Blu-Ray.** Marlon Brando; Jean Simmons; Frank Sinatra; Vivian Blaine; Stubby Kaye; Sheldon Leonard; Veda Ann Borg; Regis Toomey; ***D:*** Joseph L. Mankiewicz; ***W:*** Joseph L. Mankiewicz; ***C:*** Harry Stradling, Sr.; ***M:*** Frank Loesser. Golden Globes '56: Actress--Mus./Comedy (Simmons), Film--Mus./Comedy.

The Guyver 1/2 **1991** A young college student is transformed into a super-human fighting machine thanks to his discovery of an alien device, "The Guyver." A CIA agent (Hamill) must keep the secret device from falling into the hands of human mutants, the Zoanoids. Based on a Japanese comic book. **92m/C; VHS, DVD.** Mark Hamill; Vivian Wu; David Gale; Jeffrey Combs; Michael Berryman; ***D:*** Steve Wang.

Guyver 2: Dark Hero 1/2 **1994 (R)** The Guvyer discovers an alien ship filled with weapons capable of destroying the planet. Naturally, he must battle the evil mutant Zoanoids in order to save the world. Adapted from a Japanese comic book. **127m/C; VHS, DVD.** David Hayter; Kathy Christopherson; Christopher Michael; ***D:*** Steve Wang; ***W:*** Nathan Long.

Gwen 1/2 **2019** In nineteenth century Wales, lively teen Gwen (Worthington-Cox) lives with her disciplinarian mother Elen (Peake) and sister Mari (Innes) on a hard-scrabble farm. As the family awaits the return of its missing patriarch, Elen hides her increasingly severe epilepsy from her daughters. Though Gwen tries to help her mother and keep her family going, the paymasters at the local mine are intent on taking the family's land by any means. McGregor's atmospheric film debut is an impressive hybrid of fable, gothic, and melodrama; the leading ladies prove up to the task. **84m/C; DVD.** Eleanor Worthington-Cox; Mark Lewis Jones; Richard Harrington; Maxine Peake; Kobna Holdbrook-Smith; ***D:*** William McGregor; ***W:*** William McGregor; ***C:*** Adam Etherington; ***M:*** James Edward Barker.

Gym Teacher: The Movie 1/2 **2008** This Nickelodeon family comedy stars Meloni as short shorts-wearing Dave Stewie, a former gymnast who suffered an unfortunate accident at the Olympics and never quite recovered his equilibrium. Now a suburban junior high gym teacher, Stewie is determined to win the national gym-teacher-of-the-year award and he won't be thwarted by the athletic nightmare that is uncoordinated eighth-grader Roland Waffles (Kress). **94m/C; DVD.** Christopher Meloni; Nathan Kress; Amy Sedaris; David Alan Grier; Chelah Horsdal; ***D:*** Paul Dinello; ***W:*** Steven Altiere; Daniel Altiere; ***C:*** Attila Szalay; ***M:*** Daniel Licht. **CABLE**

Gymkata **1985 (R)** A gymnast (Olympian Thomas) must use his martial arts skills to conquer and secure a military state in a hostile European country. **89m/C; VHS, DVD.** Kurt Thomas; Tetchie Agbayani; Richard Norton; Conan Lee; ***D:*** Robert Clouse; ***W:*** Charles Robert Carner.

The Gymnast 1/2 **2006** A devastating injury ended the Olympic gymnastic hopes of Jane Hawkins. Years later, the unhappily married, middle-aged Jane gets a chance at performing in Las Vegas in a cirque-style aerial act with the beautiful younger Serena. As they practice for the show, Jane is surprised to feel so close to her new partner. Great shots of the aerial fabric act and a romantic story. **98m/C; DVD.** Allison Mackie; Dreya Webber; Addie Yungmee; David De Simone; Mam Smith; ***D:*** Ned Farr; ***W:*** Ned Farr; ***C:*** Marco Fargnoli; ***M:*** Craig Richey.

Gypsy **1962** The life story of America's most famous striptease queen, Gypsy Rose Lee (Wood). Russell gives a memorable performance as the infamous Mama Rose, Gypsy's stage mother. Based on both Gypsy Rose Lee's memoirs and the hit 1959 Broadway play by Arthur Laurents. **144m/C; VHS, DVD, Blu-Ray.** Rosalind Russell; Natalie Wood; Karl Malden; Ann Jillian; Parley Baer; Paul Wallace; Betty Bruce; ***D:*** Mervyn LeRoy; ***W:*** Arthur Laurents; Leonard Spigelgass; ***C:*** Harry Stradling, Sr.; ***M:*** Jule Styne; Stephen Sondheim. Golden Globes '63: Actress--Mus./Comedy (Russell).

Gypsy **1975** A modern day gypsy-blooded Robin Hood cavorts between heists and romantic trysts. Dubbed. **90m/C; VHS, DVD.** Alain Delon; Annie Girardot; Paul Meurisse; ***D:*** Jose Giovanni.

Gypsy 1/2 **1993** If you like Bette brassy and larger than life, as only she can be, than this is the production for you. This TV re-creation of the 1959 Broadway musical stars Midler as notorious stage mother Mama Rose, who tries to realize all her frustrated ambitions by pushing her two young daughters, June and Louise, into vaudeville show biz. Her wish eventually comes true, in an unexpected fashion, when an adult Louise (Gibb) transforms herself into stripper Gypsy Rose Lee. **150m/C; VHS, DVD.** Bette Midler; Peter Riegert; Cynthia Gibb; Ed Asner; Christine Ebersole; Michael Jeter; Andrea Martin; Jennifer Beck; Linda Hart; Rachel Sweet; ***D:*** Emile Ardolino; ***W:*** Arthur Laurents; ***C:*** Ralf Bode; ***M:*** Jule Styne; ***M:*** Stephen Sondheim. **TV**

Gypsy Blood **1918** One of the first screen versions of "Carmen," closer to Prosper Merrimee's story than to the opera, depicting the fated love between a dancing girl and a matador. Lubitsch's first notable film. Silent. **104m/B; Silent; VHS, DVD.** Pola Negri; ***D:*** Ernst Lubitsch.

Gypsy 83 **2001** Rue is goth girl Gypsy Vale, a Stevie Nicks wanna-be named after her idol's famous song, who unhappily resides in decidedly un-hip Sandusky, Ohio with her hippie dad and abandoned by her still-aspiring rock star mother. Desperate to flee the quiet Midwestern berg where she and her only friend Clive (Turton) serve merely as social outcasts, the two black-clad souls head to a New York nightclub to participate in the "Night of 1000 Stevies" Nicks tribute bash. The two encounter some predictable problems along the way, including being hassled about the way they look by various small-minded locals but also meet some reassuring kindred spirits, including wash-up lounge singer Black and Amish boy Scoville. Typical rebel without a cause premise made slightly better by a decent Rue and Turton. **94m/C; VHS, DVD.** Sara Rue; Karen Black; John Doe; Paulo Costanzo; Kett Turton; Anson Scoville; ***D:*** Todd Stephens; ***W:*** Todd Stephens; ***C:*** Gina DeGirolamo; ***M:*** Marty Beller.

The Gypsy Moths **1969** It's not actually about a bug infestation. Instead, it's a Frankenheimer melodrama about three barnstorming skydivers arriving in a small Kansas town to give an exhibition. They're staying with the aunt (Kerr) and uncle (Windom) of young Malcolm (Wilson) and Aunt Elizabeth is immediately drawn to fatalistic, taciturn leader Mike Rettig (Lancaster). After their one-night stand, Rettig is scheduled to perform an extremely risky jump, but tragedy strikes. Because Malcolm and Joe (Hackman) need money to bury Mike, Malcolm decides to perform the same stunt to draw a big crowd. **106m/C; DVD.** Burt Lancaster; Deborah Kerr; Gene Hackman; Scott Wilson; William Windom; Bonnie Bedelia; Sheree North; Ford Rainey; ***D:*** John Frankenheimer; ***W:*** William Hanley; ***C:*** Philip H. Lathrop; ***M:*** Elmer Bernstein.

The Gypsy Warriors 1/2 **1978** Two Army captains during WWII infiltrate Nazi-occupied France in order to prevent the distribution of a deadly toxin and are aided by a band of Gypsies. **77m/C; VHS, DVD.** Tom Selleck; James Whitmore, Jr.; Joseph Ruskin; Lina Raymond; ***D:*** Lou Antonio. **TV**

H. **2015** When what appears to be a meteor strike hits near Troy, New York, not only do a bunch of odd happenings take place but two women react by losing their sanity. **93m/C; DVD.** Robin Bartlett; Rebecca Dayan; Will Janowitz; Julian Gamble; Roger Robinson; ***D:*** Rania Attieh; Daniel Garcia; ***W:*** Rania Attieh; Daniel Garcia; ***C:*** Daniel Garcia; ***M:*** Pablo Borghi; Jesse Gelaznik; Alex Weston. Ind. Spirit '15: Director (Someone to Watch, Rania Attieh and Daniel Garcia).

H-Man **WOOF!** *Bijo to Ekitainigen* **1959** A Japanese sci-fi woofer about a radioactive mass of slime festering under Tokyo. Extremely lame special effects get quite a few unintentional laughs. Dubbed. **79m/C; VHS, DVD.** *JP* Koreya Senda; Kenji Sahara; Yumi Shirakawa; Akihiko Hirata; ***D:*** Inoshiro Honda.

Habit **1997** A very low-budget New York vampire tale that tweaks tradition. Wastrel Sam (Fessenden) is at loose ends when he meets intriguing Anna (Snaider). This first encounter is a bust (Sam's very drunk) but a later meeting leads to an intense sexual encounter—and Sam waking up alone in Battery Park with a prominently cut lip and some hazy memories. All their encounters are similarly intense (and in public places) but Anna refuses to reveal anything about herself. Sam is soon a confused physical wreck but when Anna's around, he just doesn't care. **112m/C; VHS, DVD, Blu-Ray.** Larry Fessenden; Meredith Snaider; Aaron Beall; Heather Woodbury; Patricia Coleman; ***D:*** Larry Fessenden; ***W:*** Larry Fessenden; ***C:*** Frank DeMarco; ***M:*** Geoffrey Kidde.

Habitat 1/2 **1997 (R)** Nature goes wild when high school student Andreas (Getty) moves with his scientist parents, Hank (Karyo) and Clarissa (Krige), to the small Southwestern burg of Pleasanton. Hank's experiment with accelerated evolution takes some unexpected blips, with Hank turning into particles of matter, their house transformed into a vegetation-covered fortress, and Clarissa becoming a very earthy earth mother. Some eerie special effects. **103m/C; VHS, DVD.** Alice Krige; Balthazar Getty; Tcheky Karyo; Kenneth Welsh; Lara Harris; ***D:*** Renee Daalder; ***W:*** Renee Daalder; ***C:*** Jean Lepine; ***M:*** Ralph Grierson. **CABLE**

Hachiko: A Dog's Tale 1/2 *Hachi: A Dog's Tale* **2009 (G)** Family-friendly, sentimental tearjerker (a remake of a 1987 Japanese film) based on real events that occurred in Japan in the 1920s although the plot is much like 1961's "Greyfriars Bobby." The story has been moved to small town New England in the 1990s with a framing story set in 2007. Parker Wilson (Gere) finds a lost Akita puppy at the train station and winds up raising the rambunctious dog with the help of his wife Cate (Allen). Every morning and evening, Hachiko escorts Wilson to and from the station. One day Wilson doesn't get off the train although Hachiko continues to keep his vigil for years and becomes a local celebrity. **93m/C; DVD, Blu-Ray.** Richard Gere; Joan Allen; Cary-Hiroyuki Tagawa; Jason Alexander; Erik Avari; Kevin Decoste; ***D:*** Lasse Hallstrom; ***W:*** Stephen P. Lindsay; ***C:*** Ron Fortunato; ***M:*** Jan A.P. Kaczmarek.

Hack! **2007 (R)** Horror fans Vincent King (Kanan) and his wife Mary (Landau) want to create the ultimate slasher flick—with the unwitting participation of a group of college students. Emily (McKellar) and her pals are on a biology field trip at a remote island where they find the woods to be a lot worse than just a bad case of poison ivy. Low-budget but with a number of clever horror movie references. **100m/C; DVD.** Sean Kanan; Juliet Landau; Danica McKellar; Lochlyn Munro; Jay Kenneth Johnson; Tony Burton; Adrienne Frantz; Burt Young; William Forsythe; Kane Hodder; ***D:*** Matt Flynn; ***W:*** Matt Flynn; ***C:*** Roger Chingirian; ***M:*** Scott Glasgow. **VIDEO**

Hackers **1995 (PG-13)** Group of teenaged computer cyber-geeks surf the 'net and become the prime suspects in an industrial conspiracy when hacker Dade (Miller) breaks into the computer at Ellingson Oil Company. It's really an inside job but just try getting anyone (read "adult") to believe him. So the techno whiz kids band together, with cops and security all wanting to shut them down. Jolie (hacker Acid Burn) is the daughter of actor Jon Voight. **105m/C; VHS, DVD, Blu-Ray.** Jonny Lee Miller; Angelina Jolie; Fisher Stevens; Lorraine Bracco; Jesse Bradford; Wendell Pierce; Alberta Watson; Laurence Mason; Renoly Santiago; Matthew Lillard; Penn Jillette; Felicity Huffman; ***D:*** Iain Softley; ***W:*** Rafael Moreu; ***C:*** Andrzej Sekula; ***M:*** Simon Boswell.

Hacksaw Ridge 1/2 **2016 (R)** Director Gibson has a little difficulty reconciling his love for on-screen violence with the story of a famous wartime pacifist but star Garfield helps him immensely, giving a grounded, fantastic performance. Garfield plays Desmond T. Doss, a man who enlists in the Army in World War II but refuses to carry a weapon. He will be a medic and he doesn't believe in killing, only saving. Doss and his company find themselves in the Battle of Okinawa, where Doss saves dozens, becoming the first man in American history to be given the Medal of Honor without ever firing a shot. **139m/C; DVD, Blu-Ray.** Andrew Garfield; Vince Vaughn; Sam Worthington; Luke Bracey; Hugo Weaving; ***D:*** Mel Gibson; ***W:*** Robert Schenkkan; Andrew Knight; ***C:*** Simon Duggan; ***M:*** Rupert Gregson-Williams. Oscars '16: Film Editing; British Acad. '16: Film Editing.

The Hades Factor 1/2 *Covert One: The Hades Factor; Robert Ludlum's Covert One: The Hades Factor* **2006** Covert One, a top secret intelligence agency, must stop an air-borne virus that terrorists are planning to release throughout the U.S. Lots of running, chasing, double-crosses, snarling, and blood (it's not for the squeamish). Loosely based on the novel by Robert Ludlum and Gayle Lynds. **184m/C; DVD.** Stephen Dorff; Mira Sorvino; Blair Underwood; Colm Meaney; Danny Huston; Sophia Myles; Josh Hopkins; Jeffrey DeMunn; Kenneth Welsh; Anjelica Huston; ***D:*** Mick Jackson; ***W:*** Elwood Reid; ***C:*** Ivan Strasburg; ***M:*** J. Peter Robinson. **TV**

Haiku Tunnel **2000 (R)** Josh (Kornbluth) takes a temp job with high-powered attorney Bob Shelby (Keith) and then accepts an offer for a permanent position. This soon begins to freak commitment-phobic Josh out, resulting in his inablility to complete the simple task of mailing out 17 important letters. As his anxiety grows, Josh has even more trouble dealing with his chipper co-workers and his impatient boss. **88m/C; VHS, DVD.** Josh Kornbluth; Warren Keith; Helen Shumaker; June Lomena; Amy Resnick; ***D:*** Josh Kornbluth; Jacob Kornbluth; ***W:*** Josh Kornbluth; Jacob Kornbluth; John Bellucci; ***C:*** Don Matthew Smith.

Hail Caesar 1/2 **1994 (PG)** His job at an eraser factory is the only thing standing between Julius Caesar MacGruder (Hall) and fame and fortune as a rock 'n' roll singer. **93m/C; VHS, DVD.** Anthony Michael Hall; Robert Downey, Jr.; Frank Gorshin; Samuel L. Jackson; Judd Nelson; Nicholas Pryor; Leslie Danon; Bobbie Phillips; ***D:*** Anthony Michael Hall; ***W:*** Robert Mittenthal; ***M:*** Roger Tallman.

Hail, Caesar! **2016 (PG-13)** The Coens turn to a quasi-fictional version of Hollywood in the 1950s for their latest comedy, and the result is one of their most purely enjoyable films, buoyed by an incredible ensemble cast used perfectly. Hollywood "fixer" Eddie Mannix (Brolin) spends his days keeping the scandalous private lives of the stars of Capitol Pictures out of the press. When movie star Baird Whitlock (Clooney) is kidnapped, Mannix is called into action to fix the problem. A great supporting cast includes Johansson, Jonah Hill, Swinton, and a nearly-movie-stealing Tatum. The Coens do this kind of broad comedy better than anyone of their era. **106m/C; DVD, Blu-Ray.** Josh Brolin; George Clooney; Alden Ehrenreich; Ralph Fiennes; Scarlett Johansson; ***D:*** Ethan Coen; Joel Coen; ***W:*** Ethan Coen; Joel Coen; Carter Burwell; ***C:*** Roger Deakins.

Hail Mafia 🦴🦴 *Je Vous Salue, Mafia* **1965** American gangster Rudy (Constantine) has fled to France because his cohorts believe he's going to testify against them. So hitmen Phil (Klugmen) and Schaft (Silva) have been contracted to kill Rudy. They travel from Paris to Marseille in search of their quarry and for Schaft the job is strictly business, but for Phil it's more personal. Dubbed. **88m/C; DVD.** *FR IT* Eddie Constantine; Jack Klugman; Henry Silva; Micheline Presle; Elsa Martinelli; ***D:*** Raoul Levy; ***W:*** Raoul Levy; ***C:*** Raoul Coutard; ***M:*** Hubert Rostaing.

Hail Mary 🦴🦴 ½ *Je Vous Salue Marie* **1985 (R)** A modern-day virgin named Mary inexplicably becomes pregnant in this controversial film that discards notions of divinity in favor of the celebration of a lively, intellectual humanism. Godard rejects orthodox narrative structure and bourgeois prejudices. Very controversial, but not up to his breathless beginning work. In French with English subtitles. **107m/C; VHS, DVD, Blu-Ray.** *FR SI GB* Myriem Roussel; Thierry Rode; Philippe Lacoste; Manon Anderson; Juliette Binoche; Johan Leysen; ***D:*** Jean-Luc Godard; ***W:*** Jean-Luc Godard.

Hail Satan? 🦴🦴🦴 **2019 (R)** The documentary examines The Satanic Temple and its members, especially spokesman Lucien Greaves Detroit chapter leader Jex Blackmore. Founded in 2013, the group is an organized group of Satan worshippers on the surface but primarily focuses on ensuring the separation between church and state. The temple focuses on challenging Christian groups who want to use public funds to promote Christianity. The film shows how the group uses Satan as a means to troll dominant culture and expose the nature of power. More deeply, the filmmakers explore the philosophical conflicts within the group, the effects of its rapid growth, and its emphasis on social justice. **95m/C; DVD.** Jex Blackmore; Chalice Blythe; Nicholas Crowe; Sal De Ciccio; Stu De Haan; ***D:*** Penny Lane; ***C:*** Naiti Gámez; ***M:*** Brian McOmber.

Hail the Conquering Hero 🦴🦴🦴 ½ **1944** A slight young man is rejected by the Army. Upon returning home, he is surprised to find out they think he's a hero. Biting satire with Demarest's performance stealing the show. **101m/B; VHS, DVD.** Eddie Bracken; Ella Raines; William Demarest; Franklin Pangborn; Raymond Walburn; Freddie (Fred) Steele; ***D:*** Preston Sturges. Natl. Film Reg. '15.

Hair 🦴🦴🦴 ½ **1979 (PG)** Film version of the explosive 1960s Broadway musical about the carefree life of the flower children and the shadow of the Vietnam War that hangs over them. Great music, as well as wonderful choreography by Twyla Tharp help portray the surprisingly sensitive evocation of the period so long after the fact. Forman has an uncanny knack for understanding the textures of American life. Watch for a thinner Nell Carter. **122m/C; VHS, DVD, Blu-Ray.** Treat Williams; John Savage; Beverly D'Angelo; Annie Golden; Nicholas Ray; Nell Carter; ***D:*** Milos Forman; ***W:*** Michael Weller; ***C:*** Miroslav Ondricek; ***M:*** Galt MacDermot.

Hair Show 🦴 ½ **2004 (PG-13)** Flick could have used a can of hair spray to give its limp premise some hold. Outgoing (i.e. loud) Peaches (Mo'Nique) works at a low-rent Baltimore hair salon while her successful sister Angie (Smith) has gone up-scale out in L.A. Owing a wad of cash to the IRS, Peaches heads for the west coast to visit her estranged sis and discovers that an annual competitive hairstyling pageant offers enough money to pay off her debt should she win. Angie thinks the event is beneath her but may just be jealous that rival salon owner Marcella (Torres) has won several years in a row. Peaches has no problem jumping into the action. It's all one giant cliche. **105m/C; VHS, DVD.** Mo'Nique; Kellita Smith; Gina Torres; David Ramsey; Keiko Agena; Cee Cee Michaela; Joe Torry; Andre B. Blake; Taraji P. Henson; ***D:*** Leslie Small; ***C:*** Keith Smith; ***M:*** Kennard Ramsay.

The Hairdresser's Husband 🦴🦴 *Le Mari de la coiffeuse* **1992 (R)** Antoine (Rochefort) has had an odd obsession since boyhood—hairdressers—and in middle age he finds love with Mathilde (Galiena), a hairdresser he meets and proposes to as she cuts his hair. She accepts, and the two live their quiet lives in her barber shop as she cuts hair and he watches, occasionally breaking out in Arabian dances. A dark and odd yet refreshing film with fine performances by Rochefort and Galiena in this story about fetishism, obsession, and hair. In French with English subtitles. **84m/C; VHS, DVD.** *FR* Jean Rochefort; Anna Galiena; Roland Bertin; Maurice Chevit; Philippe Clevenot; Jacques Mathou; Claude Aufaure; ***D:*** Patrice Leconte; ***W:*** Patrice Leconte; Claude Klotz; ***C:*** Eduardo Serra; ***M:*** Michael Nyman.

Hairspray 🦴🦴🦴 **1988 (PG)** Waters' first truly mainstream film, if that's even possible, and his funniest. Details the struggle among teenagers in 1962 Baltimore for the top spot in a local TV dance show. Deals with racism and stereotypes, as well as typical "teen" problems (hair-do's and don'ts). Filled with refreshingly tasteful, subtle social satire (although not without typical Waters touches that will please die-hard fans). Lake is lovable and appealing as Divine's daughter; Divine, in his last film, is likeable as an iron-toting mom. Look for Waters in a cameo and Divine as a man. Great '60s music, which Waters refers to as "the only known remedy to today's Hit Parade of Hell." **94m/C; VHS, DVD, Blu-Ray.** Ricki Lake; Divine; Jerry Stiller; Colleen (Ann) Fitzpatrick; Sonny Bono; Deborah Harry; Ruth Brown; Leslie Ann Powers; Michael St. Gerard; Shawn Thompson; Clayton Prince; Pia Zadora; Ric Ocasek; Mink Stole; Mary Vivian Pearce; Alan J. Wendl; Susan Lowe; George Stover; Toussaint McCall; ***Cameo(s):*** John Waters; ***D:*** John Waters; ***W:*** John Waters; ***C:*** David Insley; ***M:*** Kenny Vance.

Hairspray 🦴🦴🦴 **2007 (PG)** Remake of the 1988 John Waters surprise hit that later became a Broadway musical. In spite of the rehash, this new iteration finds its freshness by upping the bounce and fun. The story remains intact, with less-than-popular teenager Tracy Turnblad (newcomer Blonsky, a treat) shaking up her 1960s-era town with her efforts to integrate the local television dance show. Supported by her mother Edna (Travolta in plus-size drag), she turns dance into social activism and has a blast doing it. **115m/C; DVD, Blu-Ray.** John Travolta; Christopher Walken; Michelle Pfeiffer; Queen Latifah; Nicole Blonsky; Amanda Bynes; James Marsden; Zac Efron; Brittany Snow; Allison Janney; Elijah Kelley; Jerry Stiller; Paul Dooley; Taylor Parks; ***D:*** Adam Shankman; ***W:*** Leslie Dixon; Thomas Meehan; Mark O'Donnell; ***C:*** Bojan Bazelli; ***M:*** Marc Shaiman.

The Hairy Ape 🦴🦴 **1944** Screen adaptation of the Eugene O'Neill play. A beast-like coal stoker becomes obsessed with a cool and distant passenger aboard an ocean liner. **90m/B; VHS, DVD, Streaming.** William Bendix; Susan Hayward; John Loder; Dorothy Comingore; Roman Bohnen; Alan Napier; ***D:*** Alfred Santell.

Hal 🦴🦴🦴 **2018** An insightful feature-length documentary about the life and work of director Hal Ashby, the creator of such classic New Hollywood Cinema films as Shampoo and Harold and Maude. Through often rare archive footage and revealing interviews with collaborators and family, director Scott reveals much about the fascinating man. After a rough childhood, Ashby dropped out of high school and became a bohemian. Eventually making his way to Hollywood, Ashby's career began as a film editor, and he moved into directing in the 1970s. Though Ashby's excesses often negatively impacted—and shortened--his life, Scott deftly explores both Ashby's complexities and his wider impact. **90m/C; DVD, Blu-Ray.** Hal Ashby; Judd Apatow; Dustin Hoffman; Norman Jewison; Lynn Stalmaster; ***D:*** Amy Scott; ***C:*** Adam Becker; Jonathon Narducci; Alexandre Naufel; ***M:*** Heather McIntosh.

Hala 🦴🦴 ½ **2019 (R)** High school senior Hala (Viswanathan) is head scarf-wearing Muslim who likes skateboarding and writing, and has a crush on kind classmate Jesse (Kilmer). She balances her traditional homelife with the western values she experiences outside of it. Her immigrant Pakistani parents, lawyer Zahid (Khan) and Eram (Joshi), consider themselves relatively modern, but are bothered by Hala's after school activities.Though Hala initially identifies with her intellectual father, she becomes closer to her mother as Eram finds her voice. Sometimes uneven coming of age drama offers a unique perspective on the life of its protagonist, with fully developed, memorable characters. **94m/C; DVD.** Geraldine Viswanathan; Jack Kilmer; Gabriel Luna; Purbi Joshi; Azad Khan; ***D:*** Minhal Baig; ***W:*** Minhal Baig; ***C:*** Carolina Costa; ***M:*** Mandy Hoffman.

Hale County This Morning, This Evening 🦴🦴🦴 **2018** A visually complex documentary exploration of African Americans residing in Alabama. Through the story of two high school students, Daniel and Quincy, who are on the basketball team coached by director Ross, he looks at their lives and their community, and subtly relates their experiences to those who came before them. At the same time, it considers ideas about how African Americans are depicted and seen by American society. The soulful film does not have a straightforward narrative but uses images, a few words, sounds, and music to capture the rhythms of the daily experiences of the African Americans at its heart. **76m/C; DVD.** ***D:*** RaMell Ross; ***W:*** RaMell Ross; Maya Krinsky; ***C:*** RaMell Ross; ***M:*** Scott Alario; Forest Kelley; Alex Somers.

Half a Hero 🦴🦴 ½ **1953** Magazine writer Ben Dobson (Skelton) has earned his boss' approval because he and his family have stayed in Manhattan instead of moving to the horrible suburbs. Except Ben has moved at the urging of his materialistic wife Martha (Hagen) and is keeping his domestic arrangements secret. To keep up with the neighbors, Ben has gone into debt, and trouble in the 'burbs just happens to be his new magazine assignment. **71m/B; DVD.** Red Skelton; Jean Hagen; Charles Dingle; Willard Waterman; Hugh Corcoran; Mary Wickes; Frank Cady; ***D:*** Don Weis; ***W:*** Max Shulman; ***C:*** Paul Vogel; ***M:*** Paul Sawtell.

Half a Loaf of Kung Fu 🦴 *Dian Zhi Gong Fu Gan Chian Chan* **1978** The worthy bodyguards of Sern Chuan are called upon to deliver a valuable jade statue. Thwarted again and again by ruthless robbers, they falter. Only Chan carries on, meeting the enemy alone. Fast action, good story. **98m/C; VHS, DVD.** *CH* Jackie Chan; James Tien; ***D:*** Chi-Hwa Chen; ***W:*** Ming Chi Tang; ***C:*** Chin-Kui Chen; ***M:*** Frankie Chen.

Half a Sixpence 🦴🦴 **1967** Former musician Sidney, who earlier directed "Showboat" and "Kiss Me Kate," shows a bit less verve in this production. Based on H.G. Wells' 1905 novel, "Kipps," it sports much of the original cast from its Broadway incarnation. Edwardian orphan Steele, a cloth-dealer-in-training, comes into a large sum of money and proceeds to lose it with great dispatch. Somewhere along the way he loses his girlfriend, too, but she takes him back because musicals end happily. **148m/B; VHS, DVD.** Tommy Steele; Julia Foster; Penelope Horner; Cyril Ritchard; Grover Dale; ***D:*** George Sidney; ***W:*** Beverley Cross; ***C:*** Geoffrey Unsworth.

Half-Baked 🦴 **1997 (R)** Four seedy roommates whose problems stem from their love of marijuana float through life with loser jobs that give them just enough money to buy their next bag. When Kenny (H.Williams) is arrested for killing a diabetic police horse during a munchies run, the three remaining friends must put their resinated brains together and come up with a way to bail him out. Thurgood (Chapelle), a custodian for a pharmaceutical company, decides to steal some high-grade grass from the lab; and along with Brian (Breuer, doing a very convincing stoned) and Scarface (Diaz), he begins dealing. This puts them afoul of the law as well as local drug lord Samson Simpson (C. Williams). Just say no. Trust me, dude, this stuff is bogus and it won't get you off. **83m/C; VHS, DVD, HD-DVD.** Harland Williams; Dave Chappelle; Jim Breuer; Guillermo Diaz; Rachel True; Clarence Williams, III; Thomas Chong; Jon Stewart; Stephen Baldwin; Willie Nelson; Janeane Garofalo; Steven Wright; Laura Silverman; Snoop Dogg; Tracy Morgan; ***D:*** Tamra Davis; ***W:*** Dave Chappelle; Neal Brennan; ***C:*** Steven Bernstein; ***M:*** Alf Clausen.

The Half-Breed 🦴🦴 **1951** Routine oater with settlers and Apaches fighting, and the obligatory half-breed stuck in the middle. **81m/B; VHS, DVD.** Robert Young; Jack Buetel; Janis Carter; Barton MacLane; Reed Hadley; Porter Hall; Connie Gilchrist; ***D:*** Stuart Gilmore.

Half Broken Things 🦴🦴 **2007** And completely broken people. Professional house-sitter Jean (Wilton) is due to retire after her last job at Walden Manor. When two strangers show up at the door—pregnant Steph (Matthews), who's run away from her abusive boyfriend, and Michael (Mays), who's helping her—lonely Jean takes them in. The troubled trio is soon lost amid delusions of family life and home until reality begins to intrude. **93m/C; DVD.** *GB* Penelope Wilton; Sinead Matthews; Daniel Mays; Nicholas Le Prevost; Sian Thomas; Lara Cazalet; Crispin Redman; ***D:*** Tim Fywell; ***W:*** Alan Whiting; ***C:*** David Odd; ***M:*** Colin Towns. **TV**

Half-Caste 🦴 **2004 (R)** See Bobby go to South Africa with his buddies to capture on film the fabled "Half-Caste"?half man, half leopard—that finds humans to be tasty treats. See Bobby's friends go bye-bye in not-at-all-surprising hideousness leaving him to persuade the coppers that he isn't the evil-doer. Look elsewhere for scary horror movie. **86m/C; VHS, DVD.** Sebastian Apodaca; Kim Te Roller; Robert Pike Daniel; Rob Zazzali; Kathy Wagner; Greg Good; Kelly Cohen; ***D:*** Sebastian Apodaca; ***W:*** Sebastian Apodaca; ***C:*** Cooper Donaldson; ***M:*** Charlie Brissette; Manu Hanu; Hanu-Manu. **VIDEO**

Half Light 🦴🦴 **2005 (R)** Rachel's (Moore) life as a well-known writer is sent spiraling when her five-year-old son accidentally drowns and she finds herself unable to write. Attempting to revive her career and escape her sorrow, she treks to a remote Scottish village where she seeks comfort from a local lighthouse operator. On cue, the tranquil setting is disrupted by not only visions of her dead child but by a shocking murder in town. Moore somewhat makes up for what's lacking in this not-quite-so-spooky tale. **102m/C; DVD.** Demi Moore; Henry Ian Cusick; Nicholas Gleaves; Beans El-Balawi; Kate Isitt; ***D:*** Craig Rosenberg; ***W:*** Craig Rosenberg. **VIDEO**

Half Moon Street 🦴🦴 *Escort Girl* **1986 (R)** A brilliant woman scientist supplements her paltry fellowship salary by becoming a hired escort and prostitute, which leads her into various incidents of international intrigue. Adapted from a story by Paul Theroux, "Dr. Slaughter." **90m/C; VHS, DVD.** Sigourney Weaver; Michael Caine; Keith Buckley; Ian MacInnes; ***D:*** Bob Swaim.

Half Nelson 🦴🦴🦴 **2006 (R)** Get high, Mr. Chips. Crackhead Brooklyn schoolteacher Dan Dunne (Gosling) manages to do the inspiring inner-city educator thing until 12-year-old Drey (Epps in a stellar debut performance), no stranger to addicts, discovers him passed out in a bathroom stall after a basketball game, pipe in hand. This leads to a tentative, complicated relationship between the two, with Dan's ironic efforts to save Drey from a drug dealer's plans to bring her into his fold somehow offering the pair the possibility of salvation. Gosling is raw and sympathetic portraying Dan's contradictions, and the film smartly avoids the usual feel-good trappings. **106m/C; DVD.** Ryan Gosling; Anthony Mackie; Tina Holmes; Deborah Rush; Shareeka Epps; Monique Gabriela Curnen; Jay O. Sanders; Karen Chilton; ***D:*** Ryan Fleck; ***W:*** Ryan Fleck; Anna Boden; ***C:*** Andrij Parekh. Ind. Spirit '07: Actor (Gosling), Actress (Epps).

Half Past Dead 🦴 **2002 (PG-13)** Steven Seagal hauls his bloated carcass through the motions in this action dud that's far past half dead. He plays Sascha, an undercover government agent working in a new-fangled Alcatraz prison. During the planned execution of thief/murderer Lester (Weitz), a corrupt government official (Chestnut) and his kickboxing henchwoman (Peeples) take a Supreme Court justice (Thorson) hostage in an effort to find out where Lester hid his loot. Seagal allies with Nick (Ja Rule), his former FBI sting target, in order to save the day. Peeples delivers the film's only standout fight scene, although the backstage duel between Seagal and the buffet table must have been quite a sight. TV producer/novelist Stephen J. Cannell appears as a prison bureau chief. **97m/C; VHS, DVD.** Steven Seagal; Morris Chestnut; Ja Rule; Nia Peeples; Michael "Bear" Taliferro; Claudia Christian; Linda Thorson; Bruce Weitz; Kurupt; Mo'Nique; Matt Battaglia; Richard Bremmer; Stephen J. Cannell; Don Michael Paul; Tony Plana; ***D:*** Don Michael Paul; ***W:*** Don Michael Paul; ***C:*** Michael Slovis; ***M:*** Tyler Bates.

Half-Shot at Sunrise 🦴🦴 **1930** Madcap vaudeville comedians play AWOL soldiers loose in 1918 Paris. Continuous one-liners, sight gags, and slapstick nonsense. First film appearance of comedy team Wheeler and Woolsey. **78m/B; VHS, DVD.** Bert Wheeler; Robert Woolsey; Dorothy Lee; Robert Rutherford; Edna May Oliver; ***D:*** Paul Sloane; ***M:*** Max Steiner.

Half Slave, Half Free 🦴🦴 ½ *Solomon Northrup's Odyssey* **1985** The true story of a free black man in the 1840s who is kidnapped and forced into slavery for 12 years. Part of the "American Playhouse" series on PBS. Followed by "Charlotte Forten's Mission: Experiment in Freedom." **113m/C; VHS, DVD.** Avery Brooks; Mason Adams; Petronia Paley; John Saxon; Joe Seneca; Michael (Lawrence) Tolan; Lee Bryant; Rhetta Greene; Janet League; ***D:*** Gordon Parks. **TV**

Halfmoon 🦴🦴 *Paul Bowles: Halbmond* **1995** Trilogy of stories by Paul Bowles. "Merkala Beach" looks at the friendship of two young Moroccan men who are both seduced by the same mysterious woman. "Call at Corazon" finds the honeymoon journey of a mismatched British couple turning into a nightmare as they sail up the Amazon on a crowded cargo boat. "Allal" is a Moroccan boy who's an outcast in his village because of his illegitimacy. He befriends an old snake dealer and steals one of his cobras in order to charm the reptile. Then Allal winds up in a magical transformation with the creature. English and Arabic with subtitles. **90m/C; VHS, DVD.** *GE* Samir Guesmi; Khalid Ksouri; Sondos Belhassan; Veronica Quilligan; Sam Cox; Said Zakir; Mohammed Belfquih; ***Nar:*** Paul Bowles; ***D:*** Irene von Alberti; Frieder Schlaich; ***W:*** Irene von Alberti; Frieder Schlaich; ***C:*** Volker Tittel; ***M:*** Roman Bunka.

Hall Pass 🦴 ½ **2011 (R)** Best friends Rick and Fred (Wilson and Sudeikis) live happily married lives, but lately have been caught with wandering eyes. Finally fed up and hoping it'll stop their curiosity, both their wives (Fischer and Applegate) decide to grant them one week of unadulterated single status, no questions asked (the "Hall Pass"). On the prowl with their bachelor buddies, the two soon find that their sexual prowess isn't what they had hoped. The Farrelly brothers' tenth outing, sticking to their signature crude, irreverent themes. Things fall apart when Rick and Fred are unnecessarily sprinkled with dull, sugary sentiment. **98m/C; Blu-Ray, On Demand.** Owen Wilson; Jason Sudeikis; Alyssa Milano; Richard Jenkins; Tyler Hoechlin; Jenna Fischer; Christina Applegate; ***D:*** Bobby Farrelly; Peter Farrelly; ***W:*** Bobby Farrelly; Peter Farrelly; Pete Jones; Kevin Barnett; ***C:*** Matthew F. Leonetti; ***M:*** Fernand Bos.

Hallelujah! 🦴🦴🦴 ½ **1929** Haynes plays an innocent young man who turns to religion and becomes a charasmatic preacher after a family tragedy. He retains all his human weaknesses, however, including falling for the lovely but deceitful McKinney. Great music included traditional spirituals and songs by Berlin, such as "At the End of the Road" and "Swanee Shuffle." Shot on location in Tennessee. The first all-black feature film and the first talkie for director Vidor was given the go-ahead by MGM production chief Irving Thalberg, though he knew the film would be both controversial and get minimal release in the deep South. **90m/B; VHS, DVD.** Daniel L. Haynes; Nina Mae McKinney; William Fontaine; Harry Gray; Fannie Belle DeKnight; Everett McGarrity; ***D:*** King Vidor; ***M:*** Irving Berlin. Natl. Film Reg. '08.

Hallelujah for Django 🦴🦴 *La più grande rapina del west; The Greatest Kidnapping in the West; The Greatest Robbery in the West* **1967** An outlaw gang finds itself trapped in a small town after a bank heist and quickly runs afoul of the locals after murdering the sheriff. Currently only available as part of the 'Westerns Unchained' collection. **107m/C; Blu-Ray.** *IT* George Hilton; Walter Barnes; Jack Betts; Sarah Ross; Erika Blanc; ***D:*** Maurizio Lucidi; ***W:*** Augusto Caminito; Augusto Finocchi; ***C:*** Riccardo (Pallton) Pallottini; ***M:*** Luis Bacalov. **VIDEO**

Hallelujah, I'm a Bum 🦴🦴 ½ *Hallelujah, I'm a Tramp; The Heart of New York; Happy Go Lucky; Lazy Bones* **1933** A happy-go-lucky hobo reforms and begins a new life for the sake of a woman. Bizarre Depression-era musical with a Rodgers and Hart score and continuously rhyming dialogue. The British version, due to the slang meaning of "bum," was retitled, substituting "tramp." **83m/B; VHS, DVD.** Al Jolson; Madge Evans; Frank Morgan; Chester Conklin; Edgar Connor; ***D:*** Lewis Milestone; ***W:*** Ben Hecht; S.N. Behrman; ***M:*** Richard Rodgers; ***M:*** Lorenz Hart.

The Hallelujah Trail 🦴🦴 **1965** Denver mining town in the late 1800s is about to batten down the hatches for a long winter, and there's not a drop of whiskey to be had. The U.S. Cavalry sends a shipment to the miners, but temperance leader Cora Templeton Massingale (Remick) and her bevy of ladies against liquor stand between the shipment and the would-be whistle whetters. Limp Western satire directed by Preston Sturges' brother, who fared much better when he kept a straight face (he also directed "The Great Escape"). Based on Bill Gulick's novel, "The Hallelujah Train." **166m/C; VHS, DVD, Blu-Ray.** Burt Lancaster; Lee Remick; Jim Hutton; Pamela Tiffin; Donald Pleasence; Brian Keith; Martin Landau; John McKee; ***Nar:*** John Dehner; ***D:*** John Sturges; ***W:*** John Gay; ***C:*** Robert L. Surtees; ***M:*** Elmer Bernstein.

The Halliday Brand 🦴🦴 **1957** Grim, violent western. Daniel Halliday (Cotten) returns home to see his despised dying father Big Dan (Bond), a bullying cattle baron and the local sheriff. Flashbacks highlight Big Dan's ruthlessness, which led to Daniel's departure. He vows to bring down his corrupt father even if it means resorting to violence himself. **79m/B; DVD.** Joseph Cotten; Ward Bond; Viveca Lindfors; Christopher Dark; Bill Williams; Jay C. Flippen; Betsy Blair; Jeannette Nolan; ***W:*** George W. George; George F. Slavin; ***C:*** Ray Rennahan; ***M:*** Joseph H. Lewis; Stanley Wilson.

Hallowed WOOF! **2005 (R)** Lame slasher flick. At 10, Gabriel witness his father murder his mother. Now, 20 years later, he believes it's his sacred duty to kill the vulnerable just like his religious daddy did. Naturally, Gabriel is a whack job. **80m/C; DVD.** Corey Foxx; Richard Lava; Rosslyn Roberson; Andrew Martin; ***D:*** Rocky Costanzo; ***W:*** Rocky Costanzo; ***C:*** Joseph Brown; ***M:*** Peter Gorritz. **VIDEO**

Halloween 🦴🦴 **2007 (R)** Director Rob Zombie trades suspense and chills for action and shock in this remake of the classic 1970s horror movie and loses what made the original so scary in the first place. The tale is essentially the same, but this time crazed serial killer Michael Myers (Mane) gets an extended backstory, complete with a good-hearted stripper mom (Moon-Zombie) and evil step-dad (Forsythe). Once we get to the actual story, in which Myers stalks and murders his long-lost sister's (Taylor-Compton) friends, it's been shortened so much that there's barely any time to build any tension, instead just going for your standard action-crazed stabfest. Diehard fans will deem it far better than most of the films in this series, but it doesn't hold a candle to the original. **110m/C; DVD, Blu-Ray.** Malcolm McDowell; Tyler Mane; Scout Taylor-Compton; Brad Dourif; Danny Trejo; William Forsythe; Danielle Harris; Hanna Hall; Sheri Moon Zombie; Dee Wallace; ***D:*** Rob Zombie; ***W:*** Rob Zombie; ***C:*** Phil Parmet; ***M:*** Tyler Bates.

Halloween 🦴🦴 **2018 (R)** During the 40 years after Laurie Strode (Curtis) survived an attack by mass murderer Michael Myers (Castle), she has prepared for the day he would be released from prison because she believes he will come after her. Obsessive Laurie turned her home into an armed bunker and taught her daughter Karen (Greer) how to survive an attack. After two podcasters go to the prison to interview Michael and bring him his mask, he escapes, returns to Laurie's hometown, and kills victims along the way. Though the film is not as scary or well-done as the original, it provides an adequate ending to the franchise. **106m/C; DVD, Blu-Ray.** Jamie Lee Curtis; Judy Greer; Andi Matichak; James Jude Courtney; Nick Castle; ***D:*** David Gordon Green; ***W:*** David Gordon Green; Jeff Fradley; Danny McBride; ***C:*** Michael Simmonds; ***M:*** Cody Carpenter; John Carpenter; Daniel A. Davies.

Halloween 🦴🦴🦴 ½ **1978 (R)** John Carpenter's horror classic has been acclaimed "the most successful independent motion picture of all time." A deranged youth returns to his hometown with murderous intent after 15 years in an asylum. Very, very scary—you feel this movie more than see it. **90m/C; VHS, DVD, Blu-Ray, UMD.** Jamie Lee Curtis; Donald Pleasence; Nancy Loomis; P.J. Soles; Charles Cyphers; Kyle Richards; Brian Andrews; John Michael Graham; Nancy Stephens; Arthur Malet; Mickey Yablans; Brent Le Page; Adam Hollander; Robert Phalen; Sandy Johnson; David Kyle; Nick Castle; ***D:*** John Carpenter; ***W:*** John Carpenter; Debra Hill; ***C:*** Dean Cundey; ***M:*** John Carpenter. Natl. Film Reg. '06.

Halloween 2: The Nightmare Isn't Over! 🦴 ½ **1981 (R)** Trying to pick up where "Halloween" left off, the sequel begins with the escape of vicious killer Michael, who continues to murder and terrorize the community of Haddonfield, Illinois. Lacking the innovative intentions of its predecessor, it relies on old-fashioned buckets of blood. No chills, just trauma. Co-scripted by Carpenter, director of the original. **92m/C; VHS, DVD, Blu-Ray.** Jamie Lee Curtis; Donald Pleasence; Jeffrey Kramer; Charles Cyphers; Lance Guest; ***D:*** Rick Rosenthal; ***W:*** John Carpenter; Debra Hill; ***C:*** Dean Cundey; ***M:*** John Carpenter.

Halloween 3: Season of the Witch 🦴🦴 **1982 (R)** Modern druid plans to kill 50 million children with his specially made Halloween masks. Produced by John Carpenter, this second sequel to the 1978 horror classic is not based on the events or characters of its predecessors or successors. Followed by Halloweens 4, 5, and 6. **98m/C; VHS, DVD, Blu-Ray.** Tom Atkins; Stacey Nelkin; Dan O'Herlihy; Ralph Strait; Michael Currie; ***D:*** Tommy Lee Wallace; ***W:*** Tommy Lee Wallace; ***C:*** Dean Cundey; ***M:*** John Carpenter.

Halloween 4: The Return of Michael Myers 🦴 **1988 (R)** The third sequel, wherein the lunatic that won't die returns home to kill his niece. **89m/C; VHS, DVD, Blu-Ray.** Donald Pleasence; Ellie Cornell; Danielle Harris; Michael Pataki; George P. Wilbur; Beau Starr; Kathleen Kinmont; Sasha Jenson; Gene Ross; ***D:*** Dwight Little; ***W:*** Alan B. McElroy; ***C:*** Peter Lyons Collister; ***M:*** Alan Howarth; John Carpenter.

Halloween 5: The Revenge of Michael Myers 🦴 ½ **1989 (R)** Fifth in the series, this Halloween is an improvement over 2, 3, and 4, thanks to a few well directed scare scenes. Unfortunately, the plot remains the same: a psycho behemoth chases down and kills more teens. An open ending promises yet another installment. **96m/C; VHS, DVD, Blu-Ray.** Donald Pleasence; Ellie Cornell; Danielle Harris; Don Shanks; Betty Carvalho; Beau Starr; Wendy Kaplan; Jeffrey Landman; ***D:*** Dominique Othenin-Girard; ***W:*** Dominique Othenin-Girard; Shem Bitterman; Michael Jacobs; ***C:*** Rob Draper; ***M:*** John Carpenter; Alan Howarth.

Halloween 6: The Curse of Michael Myers 🦴 *Halloween: The Origin of Michael Myers* **1995 (R)** First the return. Then his revenge. And now, his curse, aimed square at the viewer. Lame series entry connects Michael Meyers to an ancient Celtic ritual that drives him to murder whole families in his old stompin' grounds of Haddonfield. Before he finishes his reign of terror, Meyers has to contend with Dr. Loomis (Pleasence), the man who knows his true evil. Though still a profit-making monster (the entire franchise had a combined budget of $20 million and grossed over $200 million), Michael should probably join Freddy and Jason at the old slashers' retirement home. Film marks the final screen appearance of Pleasence, who died shortly after its completion. **88m/C; VHS, DVD, Blu-Ray.** Donald Pleasence; Mitchell Ryan; Marianne Hagan; Leo Geter; George P. Wilbur; Kim Darby; Bradford English; Devin Gardner; Paul Rudd; ***D:*** Joe Chappelle; ***W:*** Daniel Farrands; ***C:*** Billy Dickson; ***M:*** Alan Howarth.

Halloween: H20 🦴🦴🦴 *Halloween 7* **1998 (R)** Jamie Lee Curtis treads familiar water in this return to the wellspring of the slasher genre. She reprises her role as Laurie Strode, sister of relentless psycho-killer Michael Myers. After faking her own death and changing her name, she becomes the headmistress of a private school in California. Now an overprotective single mom, she battles with the spirit of her brother, as well as the spirit of vodka. Her rebellious son John (Harnett) blows off a field trip for a romantic weekend with girlfriend Molly (Williams). They are accompanied by fellow lust-ridden Michael fodder Charlie (Hann-Byrd) and Sarah (O'Keefe) on the dimly lit campus. Either Laurie extracts her final revenge or you can anticipate "Halloween 8: The Social Security Checks of Michael Myers." Also features Curtis' mother Janet Leigh in a family reunion of screaming divas. **86m/C; VHS, DVD, Blu-Ray.** Jamie Lee Curtis; Adam Arkin; Josh Hartnett; Michelle Williams; Adam Hann-Byrd; Jodi Lyn O'Keefe; Janet Leigh; LL Cool J; Joseph Gordon-Levitt; Nancy Stephens; Branden Williams; Chris Durand; ***D:*** Steve Miner; ***W:*** Matt Greenberg; Robert Zappia; ***C:*** Daryn Okada; ***M:*** John Ottman; John Carpenter.

Halloween II 🦴 ½ *H2: Halloween 2* **2009 (R)** Zombie's sequel to his "Halloween" re-do, which is a kinda remake of John Carpenter's 1981 sequel, follows the aftermath of Michael Myers's rampage through the eyes of survivor Laurie Strode. It's so gross and filled with caricatures that maybe the franchise can finally be laid to rest. Michael (Mane) returns to Haddonfield to continue his slaughter and a nightmare-plagued Laurie (Taylor-Compton) realizes she's Myers's baby sis, thanks to a bestselling book by publicity hound shrink Dr. Loomis (McDowell). Naturally this does nothing for her grip on her sanity. **101m/C; Blu-Ray, On Demand.** Scout Taylor-Compton; Tyler Mane; Malcolm McDowell; Sheri Moon Zombie; Brad Dourif; Danielle Harris; Howard Hesseman; Margot Kidder; Brea Grant; Mary Birdsong; ***D:*** Rob Zombie; ***W:*** Rob Zombie; ***C:*** Brandon Trost; ***M:*** Tyler Bates.

Halloween: Resurrection 🦴 ½ **2002 (R)** The producers would like you to ignore the fact that psycho Michael Myers has been killed about 957 times in this franchise, and that the entire genre has been parodied into the ground. You should ignore this movie instead. Internet entrepreneur Rhymes arranges for a group of stupid kids to stay in Michael Myers' house as a publicity stunt for a live webcast. Naturally, Mike doesn't like the interlopers and proceeds to permanently cut their internet connections. Nothing new is added to the series, and drug-use and sexual hi-jinks are still the best way for the young uns to get an interesting new piercing. Jamie Lee Curtis and Rosenthal, who directed "Halloween 2," also return. **86m/C; VHS, DVD, Blu-Ray.** Busta Rhymes; Sean Patrick Thomas; Jamie Lee Curtis; Bianca Kajlich; Tyra Banks; Thomas Ian Nicholas; Ryan Merriman; Luke Kirby; Brad Loree; Daisy McCrackin; Katee Sackhoff; ***Cameo(s):*** Rick Rosenthal; ***D:*** Rick Rosenthal; ***W:*** Larry Brand; Sean Hood; ***C:*** David Geddes; ***M:*** Danny Lux.

Halloweentown 🦴🦴 ½ **1998** Gwen Piper has relinquished her witchy powers to live life as a mortal. Her children don't know about her colorful past until Grandma Aggie comes to visit, wanting to start 13-year-old Marnie on her training despite her mother Gwen's objections. When Aggie returns to Halloweentown, a haven for creatures who go bump in the night, Marnie and her siblings follow and learn an evil force is threatening the peaceful residents. **84m/C; DVD.** Debbie Reynolds; Kimberly J. Brown; Judith Hoag; Joey Zimmerman; Robin Thomas; Phillip Van Dyke; Emily Roeske; ***D:*** Duwayne Dunham; ***W:*** Jon Cooksey; Ali Matheson; ***C:*** Michael Slovis; ***M:*** Mark Mothersbaugh. **CABLE**

Halloweentown 2: Kalabar's Revenge 🦴🦴 ½ **2001** Marnie has been training to be a witch and Grandma Aggie has come to live with the family to help out. Marnie is smitten by new boy in town Kal, but when he visits he steals Aggie's spell book. Aggie and Marnie return to Halloweentown and discover it's losing its magic while monsters are popping up in the mortal world. **81m/C; DVD.** Kimberly J. Brown; Debbie Reynolds; Daniel Kountz; Judith Hoag; Joey Zimmerman; Emily Roeske; Phillip Van Dyke; Robin

Thomas; Blu Mankuma; *D:* Mary Lambert; *W:* Jon Cooksey; Ali Matheson; *C:* Tony Westman; *M:* Mark Mothersbaugh. **CABLE**

Halloweentown High ½ *Halloweentown 3* **2004** Marnie asks the Halloweentown Council if some students can become part of the exchange program at her high school. Meanwhile, grandma Aggie is their eccentric new science teacher. They all participate in running the school's holiday haunted house but the magic students are threatened by a group of ancient foes for having ventured into the mortal world. **82m/C; DVD.** Kimberly J. Brown; Debbie Reynolds; Judith Hoag; Joey Zimmerman; Clifton Davis; Lucas Grabeel; Olesya Rulin; Finn Wittrock; Eliana Reyes; Todd Michael Schwartzman; *D:* Mark Dippe; *W:* Daniel Berendsen; *C:* Robert E. Seaman; *M:* Kenneth Burgomaster. **CABLE**

Halls of Anger ½ **1970** Cliched racial drama. Court-ordered desegregation in L.A. has 60 white students from a suburban high school bused into an all-black, inner-city school with 3,000 students. Teacher Quincy Davis (Lockhart) tries to defuse the tensions arising from white student Douglas (Bridges) being denied a chance to play basketball. The former high school champ takes a one-on-one challenge from b-ball player J.T. (Watson) to see who's gonna rule. **100m/C; DVD.** Calvin Lockhart; Janet MacLachlan; James A. Watson, Jr.; Jeff Bridges; Ed Asner; Rob Reiner; *D:* Paul Bogart; *W:* Al Ramus; John Herman Shaner; *C:* Burnett Guffey; *M:* Dave Grusin.

The Halls of Montezuma ½ **1950** Large, bombastic WWII combat epic. Depicts the Marines fighting the Japanese in the Pacific. **113m/C; VHS, DVD.** Richard Widmark; Jack Palance; Reginald Gardiner; Robert Wagner; Karl Malden; Richard Boone; Richard Hylton; Skip Homeier; Jack Webb; Neville Brand; Martin Milner; Bert Freed; *D:* Lewis Milestone; *W:* Michael Blankfort; *C:* Winton C. Hoch; Harry Jackson; *M:* Sol Kaplan.

The Hamburg Cell ½ **2004** Based on the events leading up to 9/11 from the hijackers' perspective. Ziad Jarrah (who will take over United Flight 93) is studying in Hamburg and begins going to the local mosque to learn how to become a better Muslim. A desire to belong somewhere soon leads to Jarrah being recruited by Al Qaeda. Alongside jihadists Mohammad Atta and Ramzi bin al Shibh, Jarrah's plans being to take shape; the story ends with the hijackers boarding their various flights. **101m/C; DVD.** *GB* Karem Saleh; Kamel; Agni Tsangaridou; Kammy Darweish; Omar Berdouni; Adnan Maral; *D:* Antonia Bird; *W:* Ronan Bennett; Alice Berman; *C:* Florian Hoffmeister; *M:* Adrian Corker; Paul Conboy. **TV**

Hamburger Hill ½ **1987 (R)** Popular war epic depicting the famous battle between Americans and Viet Cong over a useless hill in Vietnam. Made in the heyday of 1980s Vietnam backlash, and possibly the most realistic and bloodiest of the lot. **104m/C; VHS, DVD, Blu-Ray.** Michael Dolan; Daniel O'Shea; Dylan McDermott; Tommy Swerdlow; Courtney B. Vance; Anthony Barille; Michael Boatman; Don Cheadle; Tim Quill; Don James; Michael A. (M.A.) Nickles; Harry O'Reilly; Steven Weber; Tegan West; Kieu Chinh; Doug Goodman; J.C. Palmore; *D:* John Irvin; *W:* James (Jim) Carabatsos; *C:* Peter Macdonald; *M:* Philip Glass.

Hamilton **2020 (PG-13)** A cinematic film of the original Broadway production featuring most of its original cast. Immigrant Alexander Hamilton (Miranda) plays a key role in the founding of the United States, arguing for a military command and dreaming up a national banking system. As the country is being established, Hamilton also faces personal issues. He marries Eliza Schuyler (Soo), who also plays a role in the development of the U.S., despite his unrequited love for her sister Angelica (Goldsberry). A superb adaptation with stunning cinematography that captures the emotions and hard work of the performers. **160m/C; DVD.** Lin-Manuel Miranda; Daveed Diggs; Renee Goldsberry; Jonathan Groff; Chris Jackson; *D:* Thomas Kail; *W:* Lin-Manuel Miranda; *C:* Declann Quinn; *M:* Lin-Manuel Miranda. **VIDEO**

Hamlet **1948** Splendid adaptation of Shakespeare's dramatic play. Hamlet vows vengeance on the murderer of his father in this tight version of the four hour stage play. Some scenes were cut out, including all of Rosencrantz and Guildenstern. Beautifully photographed in Denmark. An Olivier triumph. Remade several times. **153m/B; VHS, DVD.** *GB* Laurence Olivier; Basil Sydney; Felix Aylmer; Jean Simmons; Stanley Holloway; Peter Cushing; Christopher Lee; Eileen Herlie; John Laurie; Esmond Knight; Anthony Quayle; *V:* John Gielgud; *D:* Laurence Olivier; *W:* Alan Dent; *C:* Desmond Dickinson; *M:* William Walton. Oscars '48: Actor (Olivier), Art Dir./Set Dec., B&W, Costume Des. (B&W), Film; British Acad. '48: Film; Golden Globes '49: Actor--Drama (Olivier); N.Y. Film Critics '48: Actor (Olivier).

Hamlet ½ **1990 (PG)** Zeffirelli—in his fourth attempt at Shakespeare—creates a surprisingly energetic and accessible interpretation of the Bard's moody play. Gibson brings charm, humor and a carefully calculated sense of violence, not to mention a good deal of solid flesh, to the eponymous role, and handles the language skillfully (although if you seek a poetic Dane, stick with Olivier). Exceptional work from Scofield and Bates; Close seems a tad hysterical (not to mention too young to play Gibson's mother), but brings insight and nuance to her role. Purists beware: this isn't a completely faithful adaptation. Beautifully costumed; shot on location in Northern Scotland. **135m/C; VHS, DVD.** Mel Gibson; Glenn Close; Alan Bates; Paul Scofield; Ian Holm; Helena Bonham Carter; Nathaniel Parker; Pete Postlethwaite; *D:* Franco Zeffirelli; *W:* Franco Zeffirelli; Christopher DeVore; *C:* David Watkin.

Hamlet **1996 (PG-13)** Branagh tackles Shakespeare once again with the uncut, four-hour long story of the melancholy Dane (played by you-know-who). Branagh's decision to use the complete text, and move the action ahead 600 years to the 19th century adds an interesting external political dimension to the palace intrigue and gives this sixth screen adaptation the stature of Olivier's 1948 masterpiece. Jacobi and Christie stand out among a very large and brilliant cast. Lemmon and Crystal, however, should stick to American comedy. A two and a half hour version was also prepared for those with shorter attention spans, but the uncut version is well worth the time invested. **242m/C; VHS, DVD, Blu-Ray, Streaming.** *GB* Kenneth Branagh; Kate Winslet; Julie Christie; Derek Jacobi; Richard Briers; Brian Blessed; Michael Maloney; Timothy Spall; Reece Dinsdale; Jack Lemmon; Nicholas Farrell; Charlton Heston; Rosemary Harris; Gerard Depardieu; Robin Williams; Billy Crystal; Simon Russell Beale; Michael Bryant; John Gielgud; Richard Attenborough; Rufus Sewell; Dame Judi Dench; Ian McElhinney; John Mills; *D:* Kenneth Branagh; *W:* Kenneth Branagh; *C:* Alex Thomson; *M:* Patrick Doyle.

Hamlet **2000 (R)** It's mopey Hawke's turn as the title character but in this update he's hardly a Danish prince. Instead he's an experimental filmmaker in New York whose murderous uncle Claudius (MacLachlan) runs the family conglomerate, Denmark, Inc. Thanks to Almereyda's respect for Shakespeare's language, as well as his excellent adaptation to present-day corporate America, this interpretation loses none of the play's power, and adds some insights that prove its timelessness. **111m/C; VHS, DVD.** Ethan Hawke; Kyle MacLachlan; Sam Shepard; Diane Venora; Bill Murray; Julia Stiles; Liev Schreiber; Karl Geary; Paula Malcomson; Steve Zahn; Dechen Thurman; Jeffrey Wright; Paul Bartel; Rome Neal; Casey Affleck; *D:* Michael Almereyda; *W:* Michael Almereyda; *C:* John de Borman; *M:* Carter Burwell.

Hamlet ½ **2001** Every actor wants to play Shakespeare's melancholy Dane and in this cable adaptation, it's Scott (co-directing as well) who takes on the title role. This version is set at the turn of the 20th century. Good cast and some clever supernatural visuals for enchancement. **179m/C; VHS, DVD.** Campbell Scott; Jamey Sheridan; Blair Brown; Roscoe Lee Browne; Lisa Gay Hamilton; John Benjamin Hickey; Roger Guenveur Smith; Sam Robards; Michael Imperioli; Byron Jennings; *D:* Campbell Scott; Eric Simonson; *C:* Dan Gillham. **CABLE**

Hamlet 2 **2008 (R)** Irreverent satire of Inspiration-teacher flicks, Middle American values, and religious views with nutty high school drama teacher Dana Marschz (Coogan), conceiving a sequel to Hamlet for his students to produce. Dana is never deterred, even at the fact that the major characters all died at the end of Shakespeare's play, even tossing in Jesus, Einstein, and Hillary Clinton for good measure. Wackiness aside, it hits on all the elements critical to amateur theatre: teacher's pets getting the leads, lousy costumes, and a dissapproving school board. Along with Coogan's neurotic brilliance, a talented supporting cast, including Elizabeth Shue as herself, makes director-writer Andrew Fleming's hilarious script come to ridiculously fun life. **92m/C; On Demand.** Steve Coogan; Catherine Keener; Marshall Bell; Amy Poehler; Skylar Astin; Phoebe Strole; Joseph Julian Soria; David Arquette; Elisabeth Shue; Melonie Diaz; Marco Rodriguez; *D:* Andrew Fleming; *W:* Andrew Fleming; Pam Brady; *C:* Alexander Grusynski; *M:* Ralph Sall.

Hamlet & Hutch **2014** Former Broadway actor Hutch moves in with his granddaughter Tatum because of his onset of Alzheimer's. He bonds with 10-year-old great-granddaughter Liv, who decides to help Hutch when he wants to mount a local production of "Hamlet." **90m/C; DVD.** Burt Reynolds; Emma Rayne Lyle; Elizabeth Leiner; *D:* Carelton Holt; *W:* Cas Sigers; *C:* Carelton Holt; *M:* Charles David Denler. **VIDEO**

The Hammer ½ **2007 (R)** After getting dumped by his girlfriend on his 40th birthday, carpenter/boxing instructor Jerry Ferro (Carolla), aka "The Hammer" quits his lousy day job for a return to the ring with Olympic hopes. He soon sparks up a romance with one of his students (Juergensen) and catches the eye of big-time boxing coach Eddie Bell (Quinn), who takes him under his wing. Not so much a spoof of triumphant sports movies, but a realistic underdog comedy that works as a goofy "Rocky" tribute. Nearly semi-autobiographical, written by Carolla, an actual former Golden Glover (and carpenter), who plays his usual self-deprecating, snarky self with surprising success. **93m/C; DVD.** Adam Carolla; Heather Juergensen; Jonathan Hernandez; Oswaldo Castillo; Tom Quinn; Raimu; *D:* Charles Herman-Wurmfeld; *W:* Kevin Hench; *C:* Marco Fagnoli; *M:* John Swihart; Matt Mariano.

The Hammer ½ *Hamill* **2011 (PG-13)** A dramatic biography of the first deaf wrestler to win an NCAA wrestling championship, Matt Hamill. Raised among the hearing, Matt (Harvard) feels like an outsider. This feeling continues when he becomes part of the deaf community. Finding solace in wrestling, he finds a way to use his deafness as an asset on the mat. Struggling throughout his teen years, Matt becomes a college wrestler and his success proves inspirational to all. He later uses his wrestling skills in the pro ranks, as a UFC fighter. **108m/C; DVD.** Russell Harvard; Raymond J. Barry; Shoshannah Stern; Michael Anthony Spady; Courtney Halverson; *D:* Oren Kaplan; *W:* Eben Kostbar; Joseph McKelheer; *C:* David Rom; *M:* Fil Eisler.

Hammerhead ½ **1968** Dull and somewhat confusing spy flick that's a poor James Bond imitation. Secret agent Charlie Hood needs to infiltrate the criminal organization of Hammerhead who's going to sell NATO secrets. He's a collector of vintage erotica so Hood poses as a product courier to get inside. **99m/C; DVD.** *GB* Vince Edwards; Peter Vaughan; Judy Geeson; Diana Dors; Michael Bates; Beverly Adams; Patrick Cargill; *D:* David Miller; *W:* William Bast; Ken Talbot; *C:* Wilkie Cooper; *M:* David Whitaker.

Hammers over the Anvil ½ **1991** Young Alan Marshall (Outhred) has a case of hero worship for local horse trainer East Driscoll (Crowe). But East has also caught the eye of the upper-class (and married) English beauty, Grace McAlister (Rampling), with whom he is having an affair, and which Alan witnesses. But East wants Grace more than just part-time and is determined to force her to run away with him—with disastrous consequences. **98m/C; VHS, DVD.** *AU* Charlotte Rampling; Russell Crowe; Alexander Outhred; John Rafter Lee; Kirsty McGregor; Jake Frost; *D:* Ann Turner; *W:* Ann Turner; Peter Hepworth; *C:* James Bartle.

Hammett **1982 (PG)** After many directors and script rewrites, Wenders was assigned to this arch neo-noir what-if scenario. Depicts Dashiell Hammett solving a complex crime himself, an experience he uses in his novels. Interesting, but ultimately botched studio exercise, like many from executive producer Francis Coppola, who is said to have reshot much of the film. **98m/C; VHS, DVD.** Frederic Forrest; Peter Boyle; Sylvia Sidney; Elisha Cook, Jr.; Marilu Henner; *D:* Wim Wenders; *C:* Joseph Biroc; *M:* John Barry.

Hampstead **2019 (PG-13)** In London, American widower Emily (Keaton) runs a vintage clothing for charity that is unsuccessful. As her resources decrease, she is on the verge of no longer being able to afford the home she shared with her late husband. One day, she witnesses a local man, Donald Horner (Gleeson), being assaulted outside of his makeshift dwelling. Emily begins to spend time with the gruff man and finds an unexpected connection as she helps him save his home. Based on a true story, this romantic dramedy features a predictable plot but has endearing moments and both Keaton and Gleeson shine in their roles. **102m/C; DVD.** Diane Keaton; Hugh Skinner; Brendan Gleeson; James Norton; Lesley Manville; *D:* Joel Hopkins; *W:* Robert Festinger; *C:* Felix Wiedemann; *M:* Stephen Warbeck.

Hamsun **1996** Highly regarded Norwegian Nobel Prize-winning writer Knut Hamsun (von Sydow) stunned his countrymen when he sided with the Nazis in WWII and urged them to stop resisting the invaders of their homeland. An ardent nationalist, the elderly Hamsun apparently heard only what he wanted to about Hitler's policies and regarded Britain as the greater threat to Europe. After the war Hamsun and his equally outspoken pro-German wife, Marie (Norby), are deemed traitors and are put on trial. Based on a book by Thorkild Hansen. Swedish, Danish, and Norwegian with subtitles. **154m/C; VHS, DVD.** *NO DK SW* Max von Sydow; Ghita Norby; Sverre Anker Ousdal; Ernst Jacobi; Anette Hoff; Erik Hivju; *D:* Jan Troell; *W:* Per Olof Enquist; *C:* Jan Troell; *M:* Arvo Part.

Hana & Alice *Hana to Arisu* **2004** Hana (Anne Suzuki) and Arisu (Yu Aoi) are best friends. When Arisu gets a boyfriend, she hooks Hana up with one of his friends so she won't feel like a third wheel. But then she breaks up with her boyfriend because she's fallen for Hana's beau. When he gets amnesia from walking into a wall, she convinces him she is his girlfriend. Originated from a series of candy commercials. **135m/C; DVD.** *JP* Anne Suzuki; Yu Aoi; Tomohiro Kaku; *D:* Shunji Iwai; *W:* Shunji Iwai; *C:* Noboru Shinoda.

Hana: The Tale of a Reluctant Samurai ½ **2007 (PG-13)** In 1702 peace has finally come to Japan, and the once bloodthirsty Samurai are putting away their swords. All except Soza (Junichi Okada), a young Samurai who has never killed a man, but who has sworn to avenge his murdered father. His fighting abilities are bad, and his tracking is even worse. He's been on his quest for three long years. Staying among the poor in the slums of Edo, he starts to find contentment after falling for a young widow. But his vow continues to bother him, along with the question of whether or not he can really kill a man. **172m/C; DVD.** *JP* Junichi Okada; Rie Miyazawa; Arata Furuta; Jun Kunimura; Katsuo Nakamura; Tadanobu Asano; Yoshio Harada; Teruyuki Kagawa; Tomoko Tabata; Yui Natsukawa; Renji Ishibashi; Ryuuhei Ueshima; Yuichi Kimura; Seiji Chihara; Ryo Kase; Susumu Terajima; *D:* Hirokazu Koreeda; *W:* Hirokazu Koreeda; *C:* Yutaka Yamasaki.

Hancock **2008 (PG-13)** John Hancock (Smith) is a crusty drunk who has superhero powers, although he doesn't know why or how. He might save the day, but he creates havoc and financial ruin in the process. After Hancock saves his life, PR guy Ray Embrey (Bateman) steps in to spiff up Hancock's image. Hancock has a history with Ray's wife Mary (Theron), only he doesn't remember and she's not talking (yet). But Mary's secret comes out, and Hancock is thrown for a loop. Some fun amid a flimsy plot, which won't matter for Smith fans anyway. **92m/C; Blu-Ray, On Demand.** Will Smith; Jason Bateman; Charlize Theron; Eddie Marsan; Johnny Galecki; Thomas Lennon; Jae

Head; *D:* Peter Berg; *W:* Vince Gilligan; Vy Vincent Ngo; *C:* Tobias Schliessler; *M:* John Powell.

The Hand 1981 **(R)** A gifted cartoonist's hand is severed in a car accident. Soon, the hand is on the loose with a mind of its own, seeking out victims with an obsessive vengeance. Stone's sophomore directorial outing is a unique, surreal psycho-horror pastiche consistently underrated by most critics. **105m/C; VHS, DVD.** *GB* Michael Caine; Andrea Marcovicci; Annie McEnroe; Bruce McGill; Viveca Lindfors; ***Cameo(s):*** Oliver Stone; *D:* Oliver Stone; *W:* Oliver Stone; *C:* King Baggot; *M:* James Horner.

Hand Gun 1/2 **1993 (R)** Jack McCallister (Cassel) is wounded in a shoot-out with police but still manages to get away with half-a-million from a robbery. When word gets out, everybody begins looking for Jack, including his two sons—gun happy George (Williams) and small time con artist Michael (Schulze). **90m/C; VHS, DVD.** Seymour Cassel; Treat Williams; Paul Schulze; Michael Rapaport; *D:* Whitney Ransick; *W:* Whitney Ransick; *C:* Michael Spiller; *M:* Douglas J. Cuomo.

The Hand that Rocks the Cradle 1/2 **1992 (R)** DeMornay is Peyton Flanders, the nanny from hell, in an otherwise predictable thriller. Sciorra's role is a thankless one as pregnant and unbelievably naive Claire Bartel, who unwittingly starts a horrific chain of events when she levels charges of molestation against her obstetrician. Transparent plot preys on the worst fears of viewers, and doesn't offer anything innovative or new. See this one for DeMornay's Jekyll and Hyde performance. **110m/C; VHS, DVD, Blu-Ray.** Annabella Sciorra; Rebecca De Mornay; Matt McCoy; Ernie Hudson; Julianne Moore; Madeline Zima; John de Lancie; Mitchell Laurance; *D:* Curtis Hanson; *W:* Amanda Silver; *C:* Robert Elswit; *M:* Graeme Revell. MTV Movie Awards '92: Villain (De Mornay).

A Handful of Dust **1988 (PG)** A dry, stately adaptation of the bitter Evelyn Waugh novel about a stuffy young aristocrat's wife's careless infidelity and how it sends her innocent husband to a tragic downfall. A well-meaning version that captures Waugh's cynical satire almost in spite of itself. Set in post-WWI England. **114m/C; VHS, DVD.** *GB* James Wilby; Kristin Scott Thomas; Rupert Graves; Alec Guinness; Anjelica Huston; Dame Judi Dench; Cathryn Harrison; Pip Torrens; John Junkin; *D:* Charles Sturridge; *W:* Charles Sturridge; Tim Sullivan; Derek Granger; *C:* Peter Hannan; *M:* George Fenton. British Acad. '88: Support. Actress (Dench).

The Handmaiden *Ah-ga-ssi* **2016** Park Chan-wook's latest is a gorgeous, mysterious, fascinating study of sexuality, class, and betrayal in Japanese-occupied Korea, based on Sarah Waters' Victorian era-set novel "Fingersmith." Count Fujiwara hires a poor pickpocket to be the handmaiden for the mysterious Lady Hideko, using her to get closer to the heiress to steal her inheritance. Little do they know what's really going on behind Hideko's closed doors, or the betrayals and double crosses ahead of them. Lots of twisting and turning with a degree of unbelievable style. **144m/C; DVD, Blu-Ray.** Jung-woo Ha; Jin-woong Jo; *D:* Chan-wook Park; *W:* Chan-wook Park; *C:* Chung-hoon Chung; *M:* Yeong-wook Jo. British Acad. '17: Foreign Film.

The Handmaid's Tale 1/2 **1990 (R)** A cool, shallow but nonetheless chilling nightmare based on Margaret Atwood's best-selling novel, about a woman caught in the machinations of a near-future society so sterile it enslaves the few fertile women and forces them into being child-bearing "handmaids." **109m/C; VHS, DVD, Blu-Ray.** Natasha Richardson; Robert Duvall; Faye Dunaway; Aidan Quinn; Elizabeth McGovern; Victoria Tennant; Blanche Baker; Traci Lind; *D:* Volker Schlondorff; *W:* Harold Pinter; *C:* Igor Luther; *M:* Ryuichi Sakamoto.

Hands Across the Border 1/2 **1943** A musical western in which Roy helps a woman find the men who killed her father. **72m/B; VHS, DVD.** Roy Rogers; Ruth Terry; Guinn "Big Boy" Williams; Onslow Stevens; Mary Treen; Joseph Crehan; *D:* Joseph Kane.

Hands Across the Table **1935** Regi Allen (Lombard) is a fortune-hunting manicurist in a swanky hotel barber shop. Has-been millionaire playboy Theodore Drew III (MacMurray) falls for her but he's about to marry money (Allwyn) and Regi's got a wheelchair-bound rich man (Bellamy) just waiting for her to say "I do." Snappy dialogue and light-hearted performances. Based on the story "Bracelets" by Vina Delmar. **80m/B; DVD.** Carole Lombard; Fred MacMurray; Ralph Bellamy; Astrid Allwyn; Ruth Donnelly; Marie Prevost; William Demarest; Edward (Ed) Gargan; *D:* Mitchell Leisen; *W:* Norman Krasna; Vincent Lawrence; Herbert Fields; *C:* Ted Tetzlaff.

Hands of a Murderer 1/2 *Sherlock Holmes and the Prince of Crime* **1990** Sherlock Holmes (Woodward) and the faithful Dr. Watson (Hillerman) are in pursuit of the great detective's most evil nemisis—the nefarious Moriarty (Andrews). This time, the fiend has escaped the gallows and stolen government secrets from the safe of Holmes' brother Mycroft. TV movie. **100m/C; VHS, DVD.** Edward Woodward; John Hillerman; Anthony Andrews; Kim Thomson; Peter Jeffrey; Warren Clarke; *D:* Stuart Orme; *W:* Charles Edward Pogue.

Hands of a Stranger **1962** Another undistinguished entry in the long line of remakes of "The Hands of Orlac." A pianist who loses his hands in an accident is given the hands of a murderer, and his new hands want to do more than tickle the ivories. Kellerman has a very small role as does former "Sheena" McCalla. **95m/B; DVD.** Paul Lukather; Joan Harvey; James Stapleton; Sally Kellerman; Irish McCalla; *D:* Newton Arnold; *W:* Newton Arnold; *C:* Henry Cronjager, Jr.

The Hands of Orlac *Orlacs Hande* **1925** Classic silent film about a pianist whose hands are mutilated in an accident. His hands are replaced by those of a murderer, and his urge to kill becomes overwhelming. Contains restored footage. **92m/B; Silent; VHS, DVD.** *AT* Conrad Veidt; Fritz Kortner; Carmen Cartellieri; Paul Askonas; Alexandra Sorina; Fritz Strassny; *D:* Robert Wiene; *W:* Ludwig Nerz; *C:* Gunther Krampf; Hans Androschin.

The Hands of Orlac *Hands of the Strangler; Hands of a Strangler* **1960** Third remake of Maurice Renard's classic tale. When a concert pianist's hands are mutilated in an accident, he receives a graft of a murderer's hands. Obsession sweeps the musician, as he believes his new hands are incapable of music, only violence. Bland adaptation of the original story. **95m/B; VHS, DVD.** *GB FR* Mel Ferrer; Christopher Lee; Felix Aylmer; Basil Sydney; Donald Wolfit; Donald Pleasence; Dany Carrel; Lucile Saint-Simon; Peter Reynolds; Campbell Singer; David Peel; *D:* Edmond T. Greville; *W:* Edmond T. Greville; John Baines; Donald Taylor; *C:* Desmond Dickinson; *M:* Claude Bolling.

Hands of Steel **WOOF! 1986 (R)** A ruthless cyborg carries out a mission to find and kill an important scientist. Terrible acting, and lousy writing: an all-around woofer! **94m/C; VHS, DVD.** Daniel Greene; John Saxon; Janet Agren; Claudio Cassinelli; George Eastman; *D:* Sergio Martino.

Hands of Stone **2016 (R)** Clearly heavily edited after production, this heavy-handed (pun intended) biopic of boxer Roberto Duran makes nearly every mistake of its genre. First, it takes on too much, trying to capture the entirety of Duran's (Ramirez) life from a poor kid in Panama to one of the most famous athletes in the world. Second, it's narrated by a bystander, Ray Arcel (De Niro), one of Duran's trainers. Third, it jumps around the "greatest hits" of Duran's life, taking a non-chronological approach that always keeps its story distant and makes it tough to care. **111m/C; DVD, Blu-Ray.** Edgar Ramirez; Robert De Niro; Usher Raymond; Ruben Blades; Ana de Armas; *D:* Jonathan Jakubowicz; *W:* Jonathan Jakubowicz; *C:* Miguel Ioann Littin Menz; *M:* Angelo Milli.

Hands of the Ripper 1/2 **1971 (R)** Jack the Ripper's daughter returns to London where she works as a medium by day and stalks the streets at night. Classy Hammer horror variation on the perennial theme. **85m/C; VHS, Blu-Ray, Streaming.** *GB* Eric Porter; Angharad Rees; Jane Merrow; Keith Bell; Derek Godfrey; Dora Bryan; Marjorie Rhodes; Norman Bird; *D:* Peter Sasdy; *W:* L.W. Davidson; *C:* Ken Talbot; *M:* Christopher Gunning.

Handsome Harry **2009** Divorced, 52-year-old Harry agrees to the deathbed request of Tom, a buddy from his long-past Navy days, to apologize to another ex-sailor whom they and others brutally attacked after suspecting he was gay. Harry decides to call on other former comrades in an effort to reconcile what happened but the denouement is all-too predictable though the talented cast do their best. **94m/C; DVD.** Jamey Sheridan; Steve Buscemi; Campbell Scott; Aidan Quinn; John Savage; Titus Welliver; Karen Young; Bill Sage; Mariann Mayberry; Asher Grodman; *D:* Bette Gordon; *W:* Nicholas T. Proferes; *C:* Nigel Buck; *M:* Anton Sanko.

Hang 'Em High 1/2 **1967 (PG-13)** A cowboy is saved from a lynching and vows to hunt down the gang that nearly killed him in this American-made spaghetti western. Eastwood's first major vehicle made outside of Europe. **114m/C; VHS, DVD, Blu-Ray.** *IT* Clint Eastwood; Inger Stevens; Ed Begley, Sr.; Pat Hingle; James MacArthur; *D:* Ted Post; *W:* Leonard Freeman; Mel Goldberg; *C:* Richard H. Kline; Leonard J. South; *M:* Dominic Frontiere.

Hangar 18 1/2 *Invasion Force* **1980 (PG)** Silly sci-fi drama about two astronauts who collide with a UFO during a shuttle flight. Later they learn that the government is hiding it in a hangar and they try to prove its existence. Shown on TV as "Invasion Force" with an entirely new ending. **97m/C; VHS, DVD, Blu-Ray.** Darren McGavin; Robert Vaughn; Gary Collins; James Hampton; Philip Abbott; Pamela Bellwood; Tom Hallick; Cliff Osmond; Joseph Campanella; *D:* James L. Conway; *W:* David O'Malley.

The Hanged Man 1/2 **1974** Gunman James Devlin (Forrest) is wrongly convicted of murder but survives the hanging a changed (and free) man. He decides to help those in trouble, beginning with young widow Carrie (Acker), whose property is coveted by a mining tycoon (Mitchell). Made as a TV pilot. **73m/C; DVD.** Steve Forrest; Sharon Acker; Cameron Mitchell; Rafael Campos; William (Bill) Bryant; Dean Jagger; Barbara Luna; John Mitchum; Will Geer; *D:* Michael Caffey; *W:* Ken Trevey; *C:* Keith C. Smith; *M:* Richard Markowitz. **TV**

Hangfire **1991 (R)** When a New Mexican prison is evacuated thanks to a nasty chemical explosion, several prisoners decide it's time for a furlough, and they elect the local sheriff's wife as a traveling companion. Another mediocre actioner from director Maris, it gets an extra bone for stunts kids shouldn't try at home. **91m/C; DVD.** Brad Davis; Yaphet Kotto; Lee DeBroux; Jan-Michael Vincent; George Kennedy; Kim Delaney; James Tolkan; Lou Ferrigno; Lyle Alzado; Collin Bernsen; *D:* Peter Maris; *W:* Brian D. Jeffries; *C:* Mark Morris.

Hangin' with the Homeboys **1991 (R)** One night in the lives of four young men. Although the Bronx doesn't offer much for any of them, they have little interest in escaping its confines, and they are more than willing to complain. Characters are insightfully written and well portrayed, with strongest work from Serrano as a Puerto Rican who is trying to pass himself off as Italian. Lack of plot may frustrate some viewers. **89m/C; VHS, DVD.** Mario Joyner; Doug E. Doug; John Leguizamo; Nestor Serrano; Kimberly Russell; Mary B. Ward; Christine Claravall; Rosemark Jackson; Reggie Montgomery; *D:* Joseph B. Vasquez; *W:* Joseph B. Vasquez; *C:* Anghel Decca. Sundance '91: Screenplay.

Hanging By a Thread 1/2 **1979** Overlong TV disaster flick from producer Irwin Allen. An electrical storm stalls a sightseeing tram 7,000 feet in the air with multiple passengers aboard. High winds hamper rescue efforts as the tram's weakened cable starts snapping. Naturally, this means that the characters begin reviewing their pasts through flashbacks. **196m/C; DVD.** Patty Duke; Donna Mills; Sam Groom; Burr DeBenning; Joyce Bulifant; Lonny (Lonnie) Chapman; Oliver Clark; Cameron Mitchell; Bert Convy; Peter Donat; Jacquelyn Hyde; *D:* Georg Fenady; *W:* Adrian Spies; *C:* John M. Nickolaus, Jr.; *M:* Richard LaSalle. **TV**

The Hanging Garden **1997 (R)** Bizarre family drama mixes the matter-of-fact and the surreal. Gay 25-year-old Sweet William (Leavins) returns to his rural Nova Scotia home and family after a 10-year absence for the marriage of his sister, Rosemary (Fox). The reunion brings up lots of painful memories and flashes back to the 15-year-old Sweet William (Veinotte), when he was emotionally and physically abused by his psycho father Whiskey Mac (MacNeill). After more crises, the teen hangs himself from a backyard tree. Oh yes, everyone in the present can still see the teen's ghost hanging there, including the adult William. You figure it out. **91m/C; VHS, DVD.** *CA* Chris Leavins; Peter MacNeill; Kerry Fox; Seana McKenna; Troy Veinotte; Sarah Polley; Christine Dunsworth; Joel S. Keller; Joan Orenstein; *D:* Thom Fitzgerald; *W:* Thom Fitzgerald; *C:* Daniel Jobin. Genie '97: Screenplay, Support. Actor (MacNeill), Support. Actress (McKenna); Toronto-City '97: Canadian Feature Film.

The Hanging Tree **1959** Cooper plays a frontier doctor who rescues a thief (Piazza) from a lynch mob and nurses a temporarily blind girl (Schell). Malden is the bad guy who tries to attack Schell and Cooper shoots him. The townspeople take Cooper out to "The Hanging Tree" but this time it's Schell and Piazza who come to his rescue. Slow-paced western with good performances. Scott's screen debut. **108m/B; VHS, DVD, Blu-Ray.** Gary Cooper; Maria Schell; Ben Piazza; Karl Malden; George C. Scott; Karl Swenson; Virginia Gregg; King Donovan; *D:* Delmer Daves; *W:* Wendell Mayes; Halsted Welles; *M:* Max Steiner.

Hanging Up 1/2 **1999 (PG-13)** Strident, schmaltzy comedy about family. Married working mom and middle sister Eve (Ryan) seems to be the one that has to deal with family dilemmas, in this case her cantankerous dying father Lou (Matthau). Older sis Georgia (Keaton) is a workaholic Manhattan magazine exec while ditzy younger sis Maddy (Kudrow) is an actress working on a soap. They check in by phone but duck out on their share of the responsibilities although sibling rivalry rears its head. Based on the novel by Delia Ephron. **93m/C; VHS, DVD.** Meg Ryan; Diane Keaton; Lisa Kudrow; Walter Matthau; Adam Arkin; Cloris Leachman; Jesse James; Duke Moosekian; Ann Bortolotti; *D:* Diane Keaton; *W:* Delia Ephron; Nora Ephron; *C:* Howard Atherton; *M:* David Hirschfelder.

The Hanging Woman 1/2 *Return of the Zombies; Beyond the Living Dead; La Orgia de los Muertos; Dracula, the Terror of the Living Dead; Orgy of the Dead; House of Terror* **1972 (R)** A man is summoned to the reading of a relative's will, and discovers the corpse of a young woman hanging in a cemetery. As he investigates the mystery, he uncovers a local doctor's plans to zombify the entire world. Not bad at all and quite creepy once the zombies are out in force. Euro-horror star Naschy plays the necrophiliac grave digger, Igor. **91m/C; VHS, DVD.** *SP IT* Stelvio Rosi; Vickie Nesbitt; Marcella Wright; Catherine Gilbert; Gerard Tichy; Paul Naschy; Dianik Zurakowska; Maria Pia Conte; Carlos Quiney; *D:* Jose Luis Merino; *W:* Jose Luis Merino.

The Hangman **1959** U.S. Marshal Mackenzie Bovard (Taylor) is notorious for always getting his man and he knows that stage driver Johnny Bishop (Lord) is a robbery suspect. Johnny's gone straight and is a respected member of the town so no one will turn him in. Mac tries to convince Johnny's ex-girlfriend Selah (Louise) to collect the reward money but he learns some lessons about loyalty and second chances instead. **87m/B; DVD, Blu-Ray.** Robert Taylor; Jack Lord; Tina Louise; Fess Parker; Mickey Shaughnessy; Gene Evans; *D:* Michael Curtiz; *W:* Dudley Nichols; *C:* Loyal Griggs; *M:* Harry Sukman.

Hangman **2000 (R)** A serial killer plays a lethal game of hangman, sending a videotape of each murder to detective Nick Roos (Phillips). Roos joins psychiatrist Grace Mitchell (Amick) to catch the killer but she may be the killer's next intended victim. **96m/C; VHS, DVD.** Lou Diamond Phillips; Madchen Amick; Dan Lauria; Mark Wilson; Vincent Corazza; *D:* Ken Girotti; *W:* Vladimir Nemirovsky; *C:* Gerald Packer; *M:* Steven Stern. **VIDEO**

Hangman 1/2 **2017 (R)** A serial killer is obsessed with the letter-guessing game hangman. In a mid-sized Southern city, homicide detective Ruiney (Urban) is still coming to terms with his wife's unsolved murder when he finds his badge number and that of retired detective Archer (Pacino) carved in a desk as part of a new investigation. The pair look into several interrelated killings, accompanied by investigative reporter Christi Davies (Snow). A formulaic, uninspiring film that wastes its marquee-worthy cast. **98m/C; DVD, Blu-Ray.** Brittany Snow; Al Pacino; Karl Urban; Sarah Shahi; Joe Anderson; *D:* Johnny Martin; *W:* Michael Caissie; Charles Huttinger; *C:* Larry Blanford; *M:* Frederik Wiedmann.

Hangman's Curse *The Veritas Project: Hangman's Curse* **2003 (PG-13)** It's the jocks vs. the Goths in a high school where the jocks are suddenly stricken with a deadly disease. No one's sure whether the deaths are caused by the ghost of a bullied student, drugs, or witchcraft, so an undercover family of occult investigators is brought in to solve the mystery. Convoluted plot with a predictable ending doesn't work as horror, because it's not all that scary, and the mystery elements don't hold up. Christians looking for a "family values thriller" might like it, though. **106m/C; VHS, DVD.** David Keith; Mel Harris; Edwin Hodge; William R. Moses; Leighton Meester; Douglas Smith; Bobby Brewer; Daniel Farber; Andrea Morris; Frank Peretti; George Humphreys; *W:* Kathy Mackel; Stan Foster.

Hangman's House **1928** Dying "hanging" judge James O'Brien (Bosworth) tries to ensure his daughter Connaught's (Collyer) future by marrying her to wealthy James D'Arcy (Foxe), even though she despises him. Meanwhile, exiled patriot Hogan (McLaglen) returns to Ireland to kill the man responsible for his sister's suicide (guess who). **72m/B; Silent; DVD.** Victor McLaglen; June Collyer; Earle Foxe; Hobart Bosworth; Larry Kent; *D:* John Ford; *W:* Malcolm Stuart Boylan; *C:* George Schneiderman.

Hangman's Knot 1/2 **1952** Members of the Confederate Cavalry rob a Union train, not knowing that the war is over. Now facing criminal charges, they are forced to take refuge in a stagecoach stop. Well-done horse opera with a wry sense of humor. **80m/C; VHS, DVD.** Randolph Scott; Donna Reed; Claude Jarman, Jr.; Frank Faylen; Glenn Langan; Richard Denning; Lee Marvin; Jeannette Nolan; *D:* Roy Huggins.

Hangmen WOOF! 1987 (R) Ex-CIA agents battle it out on the East side of New York. If you're into very violent, very badly acted films, then this one's for you. **88m/C; VHS, DVD.** Jake LaMotta; Rick Washburne; Dog Thomas; Sandra Bullock; *D:* J. Christian Ingvordsen; *W:* J. Christian Ingvordsen; Steven Kaman; *C:* Steven Kaman; *M:* Michael Montes.

Hangmen Also Die 1/2 **1942** Lang's anti-Nazi propaganda film was inspirated by the actual May, 1942 assassination of Reinhard Heydrich. Franz Svoboda (Donlevy) is the member of the Czech resistance who assassinates Heydrich. The Nazis seek revenge and begin rounding up and executing Czech citizens, aided by the traitorous Emil (Lockhart). Franz wants to give himself up to prevent further slaughter but is persuaded to turn the tables on Emil and make him appear to be the assassin. Bertolt Brecht had a hand in the original screenplay but did not receive screen credit and later said most of his work was cut out. **134m/B; DVD, Blu-Ray.** Brian Donlevy; Gene Lockhart; Walter Brennan; Anna Lee; Dennis O'Keefe; Alexander Granach; Jonathan Hale; Margaret Wycherly; Hans von Twardowski; *D:* Fritz Lang; *W:* John Wexley; *C:* James Wong Howe; *M:* Hanns Eisler.

The Hangover 1/2 **2009 (R)** The stuff of urban legend is touted in this immature-men-behaving-badly, morning-after look at a Vegas bachelor party none of the participants can remember. Despite the chicken, tiger, baby, stolen police car, missing tooth—and missing groom-to-be. Bland Doug (Bartha) is accompanied to Sin City by cynical married Phil (Cooper), milquetoast dentist Stu (Helms) and his fiancee's brother Alan (Galifianakis), none-too-bright and somewhat creepily overeager to belong. After many booze-fueled hours of debauchery, the groomsmen struggle to retrace their steps in an effort to find Doug, meeting (or re-meeting) sweet stripper/hooker Jade (Graham) as well as tiger-owning Mike Tyson and a trash-talking gangster (Jeong). Rowdy, raunchy, and more clever than it needs to be. **100m/C; Blu-Ray, On Demand.** Bradley Cooper; Ed Helms; Zach Galifianakis; Justin Bartha; Heather Graham; Ken Jeong; Jeffrey Tambor; Rachael Harris; Mike Epps; Mike Tyson; Sasha Barrese; *D:* Todd Phillips; *W:* Jon Lucas; Scott Moore; *C:* Lawrence Sher; *M:* Christophe Beck. Golden Globes '10: Film--Mus./Comedy.

The Hangover, Part 2 **2011 (R)** If you liked the first flick, this is more of the same in a setting even more exotic than Vegas, as director Todd Phillips and the main cast return for additional disastrous and unremembered debauchery involving drink, drugs, and hookers. Mild-mannered Stu (Helms) wants his bachelor party to be safe and boring, but since he, Phil (Cooper), Alan (Galifianakis), and Doug (Bartha) are in Bangkok, Thailand, the homeland of his fiancee Lauren (Chung), the chances for that to happen are nil. Bartha's role is limited but Jeong's crazy gangster Mr. Chow reappears and a capuchin monkey steals scenes. **102m/C; DVD, Blu-Ray, On Demand.** Ed Helms; Bradley Cooper; Zach Galifianakis; Justin Bartha; Ken Jeong; Juliette Lewis; Liam Neeson; Paul Giamatti; Mason Lee; Jamie Chung; Nirut Sirichanya; *D:* Todd Phillips; *W:* Todd Phillips; Scot Armstrong; Craig Mazin; *C:* Lawrence Sher; *M:* Christophe Beck.

The Hangover, Part III **2013 (R)** The law of diminishing returns means nothing to director Phillips who saw the cash cow in his surprise 2009 hit and milked it for two more awful comedies. This supposed lark to the trilogy features the gang (Helms, Cooper, Galifianakis) on the run from a deadly gangster (Goodman) who thinks they know how to find the notorious Chow (Jeong). Even darker than usual and with way too much Galifianakis, Phillips and company seem to have completely lost the "this could happen to anybody" theme of a night partying gone awry in favor of broad, stupid humor. **100m/C; DVD, Blu-Ray.** Bradley Cooper; Ed Helms; Zach Galifianakis; Ken Jeong; John Goodman; Justin Bartha; Heather Graham; Jamie Chung; Melissa McCarthy; Jeffrey Tambor; Mike Epps; *D:* Todd Phillips; *W:* Todd Phillips; Craig Mazin; *C:* Lawrence Sher; *M:* Christophe Beck.

Hangover Square 1/2 **1945** Foggy, gaslit London, 1903. High-strung composer George (Cregar) has periodic blackouts and thinks he's a murderer although the police clear him. Then he gets involved with lush music hall singer Netta (Darnell), who strings him along. When George discovers her betrayal, his blackouts get worse and he really does become a killer. And what happens to the two-timing Netta is still genuinely shocking. Cregar's last film—he died of a heart attack before its release. **77m/B; DVD, Blu-Ray.** Laird Cregar; Linda Darnell; George Sanders; Glenn Langan; Alan Napier; *D:* John Brahm; *W:* Barre Lyndon; *C:* Joseph LaShelle; *M:* Bernard Herrmann.

Hank and Asha **2014** The found-footage genre is typically reserved for horror films but Duff's romantic drama spins the idea to comment on the way technology brings people together while also keeping them apart. It's made up entirely of video messages between the title characters--a sweet Indian girl named Asha (Kakkar), living in Prague, and an outgoing NYC filmmaker named Hank (Pastides). Too many romantic movie clichés, but his leads are likable. **73m/C; DVD.** Mahira Kakkar; Andrew Pastides; *D:* James E. Duff; *W:* James E. Duff; Julia Morrison; *C:* Bianca Butti; *M:* Lara Meyerratken.

Hank and Mike **2008 (R)** You will never think about the Easter Bunny the same way again. Hank and Mike are pink, furry blue-collar Easter Bunnies who work for Easter Enterprises. (Not guys dressed up in costumes but the actual 'delivers baskets on Easter Sunday' bunnies.) When they mistakenly miss a house one Easter they get downsized by their cost-cutting corporation. The duo fail at an assortment of odd jobs, get into debt, wind up homeless, and find even their longtime friendship unraveling. **86m/C; DVD.** *CA* Thomas Michael; Paolo Mancini; Joe Mantegna; Chris Klein; Maggie Castle; Tony Nappo; Jane McLean; *D:* Matthew Klinck; *W:* Thomas Michael; Paolo Mancini; *C:* Glen Keenan; *M:* Phil Electric.

Hanky Panky 1/2 **1982 (PG)** Insipid comic thriller in which Wilder and Radner become involved in a search for top-secret plans. **107m/C; VHS, DVD.** Gene Wilder; Gilda Radner; Richard Widmark; Kathleen Quinlan; *D:* Sidney Poitier.

Hanna 1/2 **2011 (PG-13)** Hidden from society and trained by her ex-CIA father (Bana) to be the perfect assassin since birth, teenager Hanna (an energetic Ronan) enters the real world for the first time. Her first mission across Europe goes awry when she's intercepted by CIA officer Marissa (Blanchett) and her team of operatives, hell-bent on capturing the enigmatic father-daughter team despite an apparent lack of motive. In the midst of all the explosive chasing, fighting, and surviving, not unexpectedly Hanna begins doubting her life. Almost a coming-of-age action flick—though very human and intelligent. **111m/C; Blu-Ray, On Demand.** Saoirse Ronan; Cate Blanchett; Eric Bana; Tom Hollander; Vicky Krieps; *D:* Joe Wright; *W:* Joe Wright; Joe Penhall; Seth Lockhead; David Farr; *C:* Alwin Kuchler; *M:* Tom Rowlands; Ed Simons.

Hannah and Her Sisters 1/2 **1986 (PG)** Allen's grand epic about a New York showbiz family, its three adult sisters and their various complex romantic entanglements. Excellent performances by the entire cast, especially Caine and Hershey. Classic Allen themes of life, love, death, and desire are explored in an assured and sensitive manner. Witty, ironic, and heartwarming. **103m/C; VHS, DVD, Blu-Ray.** Mia Farrow; Barbara Hershey; Dianne Wiest; Michael Caine; Woody Allen; Maureen O'Sullivan; Lloyd Nolan; Sam Waterston; Carrie Fisher; Max von Sydow; Julie Kavner; Daniel Stern; Tony Roberts; John Turturro; Lewis Black; *D:* Woody Allen; *W:* Woody Allen; *C:* Carlo Di Palma. Oscars '86: Orig. Screenplay, Support. Actor (Caine), Support. Actress (Wiest); British Acad. '86: Director (Allen), Orig. Screenplay; Golden Globes '87: Film--Mus./Comedy; L.A. Film Critics '86: Film, Screenplay, Support. Actress (Wiest); Natl. Bd. of Review '86: Director (Allen), Support. Actress (Wiest); N.Y. Film Critics '86: Director (Allen), Film, Support. Actress (Wiest); Natl. Soc. Film Critics '86: Support. Actress (Wiest); Writers Guild '86: Orig. Screenplay.

Hannah Arendt **2012** Solid biopic of one particular time in the life of German philosopher/writer Hannah Arendt. She and her husband, Heinrich, are German-Jews who escaped a French detention camp during the war to live in New York where Hannah is teaching. After learning of the capture of Nazi Adolf Eichmann, Hannah convinces "The New Yorker" to let her cover the 1961 war crimes trial (actual footage is shown) being held in Jerusalem. She writes about the 'banality of evil' and Jewish collaboration, which causes a great deal of personal trouble. Sukowa gives a compelling lead performance. English, German, and Hebrew with subtitles. **113m/C; DVD, Blu-Ray.** *GE* Barbara Sukowa; Axel Milberg; Janet McTeer; Julia Jentsch; Michael Degan; Nicholas Woodeson; *D:* Margarethe von Trotta; *W:* Margarethe von Trotta; Pamela Katz; *C:* Caroline Champetier; *M:* Andre Mergenthaler.

Hannah Free 1/2 **2009** A broad tear-jerker that recalls the lifelong love binding Hannah (Gless) and Rachel (Gallagher). Cantankerous Hannah is in the same convalescent hospital as her comatose lover Rachel but Rachel's narrow-minded daughter Marge (Miller), who's never approved of the relationship, refuses to let Hannah see her. Flashbacks detail the two women growing up in the same small Michigan town and their subsequent tribulations. Claudia Allen adapted the script from her play. **86m/C; DVD.** Sharon Gless; Maureen Gallagher; Taylor Miller; Jacqui Jackson; Ann Hagemann; Kelli Strickland; *D:* Wendy Jo Carlton; *W:* Claudia Allen; *C:* Gretchen Warthen; *M:* Martie Marro.

Hannah Montana: The Movie **2009 (G)** Hannah's star continues to climb, while Miley is in danger of being lost in the shuffle. To help bring her back to Earth, Miley's dad (Billy Ray Cyrus) takes her to their hometown of Crowley Corners, Tennessee, where there's plenty of love and laughter in the air. Appealing to preteen girls who won't notice the cliches; however, their poor parents will pray for a quick end to this exercise in unabated commercialism. The goal of this big screen version of the Disney Channel series is clearly to further the franchise, with nothing original—ultimately making this an extended music video with a little "story" thrown in. Along with the usual cast, also features country singers Rascal Flatts and Taylor Swift. **102m/C; Blu-Ray.** Miley Cyrus; Emily Osment; Billy Ray Cyrus; Heather Locklear; Jason Earles; Dolly Parton; Moises Arias; Lucas Till; Vicki Lawrence; *D:* Peter Chelsom; *W:* Daniel Berendsen; *C:* David Hennings; *M:* Alan Silvestri. Golden Raspberries '09: Worst Support. Actor (Cyrus).

Hannah Takes the Stairs **2007** Part of the "mumblecore" film movement with ultra-low-budgets and improvised plot, dialogue, and camerawork, and centered around aimless twenty-somethings. Self-absorbed Hannah (Gerwig) breaks up with Mike (Duplass), hooks up with her neglectful boss Paul (Bujalski), and then turns to writer/coworker Matt (Osborne). If you're part of the demographic you might find it distracting; if not, it's tedious and banal. **83m/C; DVD.** Kent Osborne; Greta Gerwig; Mark Duplass; Andrew Bujalski; *D:* Joe Swanberg; *W:* Kent Osborne; Greta Gerwig; Joe Swanberg; *C:* Joe Swanberg; *M:* Kevin Bewersdorf.

Hannah's Law 1/2 **2012** Unbelievable Hallmark Channel western. Hannah Beaumont (Canning) is a bounty hunter in Dodge City who's still after the men who killed her family. She's mentored by Isom Dart (Glover) annd befriended by colorful Stagecoach Mary (Elise) but the final showdown with the McMurphy gang is all Hannah's own. **87m/C; DVD.** Sara Canning; John Pyper-Ferguson; Danny Glover; Kimberly Elise; Greyston Holt; Ryan Kennedy; Billy Zane; *D:* Rachel Talalay; *W:* John Fasano; *C:* Ken Krawczyk; *M:* Charles Sydnor. **CABLE**

Hannibal **2001 (R)** The long-awaited sequel to the much loved "Silence of the Lambs," and the lesser-known but equally praised "Manhunter," is more gruesome than scary, but it still managed to bring loads of people to the theatre, most likely to enjoy a heapin' helping of Hopkins's Hannibal. This time the infamous Dr. Lecter and FBI agent Clarice Starling (now played by Moore) are brought together by one of Hannibal's vengeful victims, the severely disfigured Verger (played by Oldman, under layers of prosthetics), and his trained wild pigs. Based on the novel by Thomas Harris. **131m/C; VHS, DVD, Blu-Ray.** Anthony Hopkins; Julianne Moore; Gary Oldman; Ray Liotta; Frankie Faison; Giancarlo Giannini; Francesca Neri; Zeljko Ivanek; Hazelle Goodman; David Andrews; Francis Guinan; Enrico Lo Verso; *D:* Ridley Scott; *W:* David Mamet; Steven Zaillian; *C:* John Mathieson; *M:* Hans Zimmer.

Hannibal Brooks **1969** Twee British WWII-set comedy. POW Brooks (Reed) cares for elephant Lucy at the Munich zoo. To escape Allied bombings, Lucy is being transferred to Innsbruck but Brooks decides he and Lucy can escape to freedom in Switzerland by going over the Alps instead. **102m/C; DVD.** *UK* Oliver Reed; Michael J. Pollard; Wolfgang Preiss; John Alderton; Helmut Lohner; *D:* Michael Winner; *W:* Dick Clement; Ian La Frenais; *C:* Robert Paynter; *M:* Francis Lai.

Hannibal Rising 1/2 **2007 (R)** How Hannibal became a cannibal. Harris adapts his own novel but the fiendish spark is gone. A teenaged Hannibal (Ulliel) and his family fall prey to vicious roving thugs in 1944 (his plump little sister suffers an especially nasty fate). He's then taken in by his widowed Japanese aunt, Lady Murasaki (Li), who introduces him to the ways of the samurai and a handy stash of swords. Hannibal then tracks his quarry and dispatches them in gory ways while practicing his supercilious sneer. A distinct comedown for a franchise character. **117m/C; DVD.** *US GB FR* Gaspard Ulliel; Gong Li; Rhys Ifans; Kevin McKidd; Dominic West; Aaron Thomas; Helena-Lia Tachovska; *D:* Peter Webber; *W:* Thomas Harris; *C:* Benjamin Davis; *M:* Ilan Eshkeri; Shigeru Umebay Ashi.

Hannie Caulder **1972 (R)** A woman hires a bounty hunter to avenge her husband's murder and her own rape at the hands of three bandits. Excellent casting but uneven direction. Boyd is uncredited as the preacher. **87m/C; VHS, DVD, Blu-Ray.** Raquel Welch; Robert Culp; Ernest Borgnine; Strother Martin; Jack Elam; Christopher Lee; Diana Dors; Stephen Boyd; ***D:*** Burt Kennedy; ***W:*** Burt Kennedy.

Hanoi Hilton ½ **1987 (R)** A brutal drama about the sufferings of American POWs in Vietnamese prison camps. Non-stop torture, filth, and degradation. **126m/C; VHS, DVD.** Michael Moriarty; Paul LeMat; Jeffrey Jones; Lawrence Pressman; Stephen Davies; David Soul; Rick Fitts; Aki Aleong; Gloria Carlin; ***D:*** Lionel Chetwynd; ***W:*** Lionel Chetwynd.

Hanover Street **1979 (PG)** An American bomber pilot and a married British nurse fall in love in war-torn Europe. Eventually the pilot must work with the husband of the woman he loves on a secret mission. A sappy, romantic tearjerker. **109m/C; VHS, DVD.** Harrison Ford; Lesley-Anne Down; Christopher Plummer; Alec McCowen; ***D:*** Peter Hyams; ***W:*** Peter Hyams; ***C:*** David Watkin; ***M:*** John Barry.

Hans Brinker ½ **1969** Young Hans Brinker and his sister participate in an ice skating race, hoping to win a pair of silver skates. A musical version of the classic tale. **103m/C; VHS, DVD.** Robin Askwith; Eleanor Parker; Richard Basehart; Cyril Ritchard; John Gregson; ***D:*** Robert Scheerer.

Hans Christian Andersen
1952 Sentimental musical story of Hans Christian Andersen, a young cobbler who has a great gift for storytelling. Digitally remastered editions available with stereo sound and original trailer. **112m/C; VHS, DVD, Blu-Ray.** Danny Kaye; Farley Granger; Zizi Jeanmaire; Joey Walsh; ***D:*** Charles Vidor; ***W:*** Moss Hart; ***C:*** Harry Stradling, Sr.; ***M:*** Frank Loesser.

Hansel & Gretel **2013** Modern retelling of teen siblings trapped in a house in the woods by a cannibalistic serial killer. **90m/C; DVD, Blu-Ray, Streaming.** *V/* Dee Wallace; Stephanie Greco; Brent Lydic; Sara Fletcher; ***D:*** Anthony C. Ferrante; ***W:*** Jose Prendes; ***C:*** Ben Demaree; ***M:*** Alan Howarth. **VIDEO**

Hansel & Gretel Get Baked **2013** The brother and sister track a missing friend to a suburban house where the witch lures teens inside with her special weed called "Black Forest." But it's the last high for the wasted since she cooks and eats her guests in order to maintain her youth and looks. Stoner humor mixed (badly) with generic horror/action. **100m/C; DVD, Blu-Ray.** Molly C. Quinn; Michael Welch; Lara Flynn Boyle; Andrew James Allen; Lochlyn Munro; Yancy Butler; ***D:*** Duane Journey; ***W:*** David Tillman; ***C:*** John Smith; ***M:*** Corey A. Jackson. **VIDEO**

Hansel & Gretel: Witch Hunters ½ **2012 (R)** Half-spoof, half-ultraviolent fairy tale with an adult Hansel (Renner) and Gretel (Arterton) who've turned their childhood trauma into a successful witch-hunting career. After one mission gets sidetracked, the bounty hunters befriend a good "white witch" and a troll as they become targets for an unusually foul, evil sorceress (Janssen in terrible make-up). Luckily, the two are armed with a full arsenal of shotguns, grenades, and semi-automatic crossbows. Director Wirkola's English-language debut can't pull it off as the unfunny story meanders to pointless half-baked action scenes and silly jokes. Renner is oddly out of place in this tacky goof. **88m/C; DVD, Blu-Ray.** Jeremy Renner; Gemma Arterton; Famke Janssen; Peter Stormare; Derek Mears; ***D:*** Tommy Wirkola; ***W:*** Tommy Wirkola; ***C:*** Michael Bonvillain; ***M:*** Atli Orvarsson.

The Happening ½ **2008 (R)** Shyamalan's self-proclaimed attempt at the best B-movie of all-time is another miss. One day in Central Park people begin doing inexplicably freaky things—wandering backwards, mumbling, and killing themselves. This phenomenon spreads across the Northeast and into Philadelphia, where high school teacher Elliot Moore (Wahlberg) and his wife Alma (Deschanel) pick up the kids and try to flee before they're next. It looks great, and it's jam-packed with suspense, but the payoff pales compared to any good episode of "The Twilight Zone." **91m/C; Blu-Ray, On Demand.** Mark Wahlberg; Zooey Deschanel; John Leguizamo; Spencer Breslin; Betty Buckley; Joel de la Fuente; Frank Collison; Ashlyn Sanchez; Robert Bailey, Jr.; ***D:*** M. Night Shyamalan; ***W:*** M. Night Shyamalan; ***C:*** Tak Fujimoto; ***M:*** James Newton Howard.

Happenstance ½ *The Beating of the Butterfly's Wings; Le Battement d'Ailes du Papillon* **2000 (R)** Is it fate? destiny? chance? that brings people together? Clerk Irene (Tautou) chats with a woman on the subway who tells her that she will meet her true love that day. He turns out to be Faudel (Younes) but of course the made-for-each-other duo's actually getting together is a maze of complications. Amusing romantic comedy; French with subtitles. **97m/C; VHS, DVD.** *FR* Audrey Tautou; Faudel; Eric Savin; Eric Feldman; Nathalie Besancon; Lysiane Meis; Lily Boulogne; Francoise Bertin; Frederique Bouraly; Irene Ismailoff; ***D:*** Laurent Firode; ***W:*** Laurent Firode; ***C:*** Jean-Rene Duveau; ***M:*** Peter Chase.

The Happiest Millionaire **1967** A Disney film about a newly immigrated lad who finds a job as butler in the home of an eccentric millionaire. Based on the book "My Philadelphia Father," by Kyle Chrichton. **118m/C; VHS, DVD.** Fred MacMurray; Tommy Steele; Greer Garson; Geraldine Page; Lesley Ann Warren; John Davidson; ***D:*** Norman Tokar; ***W:*** A.J. Carothers; ***C:*** Edward Colman; ***M:*** Richard M. Sherman; Robert B. Sherman.

Happily Ever After ½ **1993 (G)** Sequel to "Snow White" begins where the original ends, but isn't connected to the Walt Disney classic. Snow White and her Prince prepare for their wedding when the Wicked Queen is found dead by her brother, who vows revenge. So it's up to Snow and the Dwarfelles (Disney said no to using the Dwarfs), female cousins of the original Dwarfs, to rescue him. Interesting choices from the casting department: Diller is Mother Nature and Asner provides the voice of a rapping owl. Poorly animated drivel designed to ride in on Disney's coattails. While the kids might enjoy it, save your money for the original, finally slated for a video release. **74m/C; VHS, DVD.** *V:* Dom DeLuise; Phyllis Diller; Zsa Zsa Gabor; Ed Asner; Sally Kellerman; Irene Cara; Carol Channing; Tracey Ullman; ***D:*** John Howley; ***W:*** Martha Moran; Robby London.

Happily Ever After *Ils se Marient et Eurent Beaucoup D'Enfants; ...And They Lived Happily Ever After* **2004** The wandering eye of the married man. Vincent (writer/director Attal) is happily married to Gabrielle (Gainsbourg) but, when egged on by his horndog bachelor pal Fred (Cohen), has sex with a hot masseuse (David). When Gabrielle finds out, she's hurt but gives a Gallic shrug and decides it's nothing she can't handle, especially since infantile Vincent knows he's being stupid. And Gabrielle knows she can find someone else, too. Depp has a cameo as a tempting stranger. French with subtitles. **100m/C; DVD.** Yvan Attal; Charlotte Gainsbourg; Alain Chabat; Emmanuelle Seigner; Alain Cohen; Johnny Depp; Anouk Aimee; Claude Berri; ***D:*** Yvan Attal; ***W:*** Yvan Attal; ***C:*** Remy Chevrin.

Happily N'Ever After **2007 (PG)** Animated spoof of fairytales where the bad guys take over. A wizard (Carlin) goes on vacation and his two idiot assistants (Shawn, Dick) lose control of Fairy Tale Land to wicked stepmother Frieda (Weaver). Now, everyone from Cinderella to Rapunzel has their stories rewritten, and not for the better. Good voice work makes up for lackluster animation. **87m/C; DVD, Blu-Ray.** *US GE* Lisa Kaplan; *V:* Sarah Michelle Gellar; Freddie Prinze, Jr.; Sigourney Weaver; Andy Dick; Wallace Shawn; Patrick Warburton; George Carlin; Michael McShane; Kath Soucie; ***D:*** Paul J. Bolger; ***W:*** Rob Moreland; ***C:*** David Dulac; ***M:*** Paul Buckley.

Happiness **1932** Another zany comedy from the land of the hammer and sickle. Banned in Russia for 40 years, it was deemed to be risque and a bit too biting with the social satire. Silent with orchestral score. **69m/B; Silent; VHS, DVD.** *RU* Nikolai Cherkassov; Mikhail Gipsi; Yelena Yegorova; ***D:*** Alexander Medvedkin; ***C:*** Gleb Troyanski.

Happiness **1998** Very disturbing film made for the "love it or hate it" category. There are three middleclass New Jersey sisters—perky housewife Trish (Stevenson), underachieving Joy (Adams) and glamourous writer Helen (Boyle). Trish is married to shrink Bill (Baker) and they have an 11-year-old son, Billy (Read), who's getting curious about sex. His dad is the wrong person to ask since he's a pedophile who abuses his son's friends. Then there's Allen (Hoffman), one of Bill's patients. He makes obscene phone calls to Helen, who turns out to be turned on by the dirty talk. Suburban hell, indeed. Some riveting performances, especially Baker and Hoffman. **139m/C; VHS, DVD.** Dylan Baker; Cynthia Stevenson; Lara Flynn Boyle; Jane Adams; Philip Seymour Hoffman; Ben Gazzara; Louise Lasser; Rufus Read; Jared Harris; Jon Lovitz; Camryn Manheim; Elizabeth Ashley; Marla Maples; ***D:*** Todd Solondz; ***W:*** Todd Solondz; ***C:*** Maryse Alberti; ***M:*** Robbie Kondor.

Happiness Ahead **1934** Bored society heiress Joan Bradford (Hutchinson in her screen debut) likes it when she gets a kiss from window washer Bob Lane (Powell) on New Year's Eve, so she pretends to be working-class so they can date. Bob needs money to start his own business and Joan arranges for her father to secretly back Bob's plans but there's trouble when Bob learns who Joan really is. **86m/B; DVD.** Dick Powell; Josephine Hutchinson; John Halliday; Ruth Donnelly; Allen Jenkins; Dorothy Dare; Frank McHugh; Marjorie Gateson; ***D:*** Mervyn LeRoy; ***W:*** Harry Sauber; ***C:*** Gaetano Antonio "Tony" Gaudio.

The Happiness of the Katakuris *Katakuri-ke no kofuku* **2001 (R)** Theoretically this is a remake of the Korean film "Choyonghan kajok," and tells the story of a family opening an Inn that seems cursed with bad luck and death. But this remake is done by notorious Japanese director Takashi Miike. It slips effortlessly from genre to genre without warning, from romantic drama, to supernatural horror, to black comedy, to musical, seemingly at random. Some of it is live action, some is claymation. Not as gory or disturbing as some of his other films, but the surreal style in which it is done is an acquired taste. It has many film and pop culture references in the musical numbers, many of which will be lost as the audience stares in numbed disbelief. **113m/C; DVD, Blu-Ray.** *JP* Kenji Sawada; Keiko Matsuzaka; Shinji Takeda; Naomi Nishida; Tetsuro Tamba; Naoto Takenaka; Kenichi Endo; Yoshiyuki Morishita; Kiyoshiro Imawano; Tamaki Miyazaki; Takashi Matsuzaki; Yoshiki Arizono; Chihiro Asakawa; Yumeki Kanazawa; Tokitoshi Shiota; Masahiro Asakawa; Moeko Ezawa; Akiko Hatakeyama; Maro; Aya Meguro; Yuka Nakatani; Miho Sawada; ***D:*** Takashi Miike; ***W:*** Ai Kennedy; Kikumi Yamagishi; ***C:*** Hideo Yamamoto; ***M:*** Koji Endo; Koji Makaino.

Happiness Runs **2010** Happiness, in this unpleasant drama, is nonexistent. Victor and Becky were raised by their one-time flower children parents in a sex-and-drugs hippie commune that's now more of a cult run by guru Insley (Hauer). Casual hedonism and neglect is the norm but mopey Victor is determined that he and promiscuous Becky can escape before they self-destruct. **88m/C; DVD, Blu-Ray.** Mark L. Young; Hanna Hall; Rutger Hauer; Jesse Plemons; Andie MacDowell; Mark Boone, Jr.; Shiloh Fernandez; ***D:*** Adam Sherman; ***W:*** Adam Sherman; ***C:*** Aaron Platt; ***M:*** Reinhold Heil; Johnny Klimek.

Happy Accidents ½ **2000 (R)** Quirky sci-fi/romance offers a breath of fresh air by going against the grain of both genres. Ruby (Tomei) is a neurotic loser in romance who always tries to "fix" the men she dates. She meets Sam (D'Onofrio), who appears to be the well-adjusted guy she doesn't have to change. They fall for each other, and then Sam drops the other shoe. He claims to be a time-traveler from the year 2470, and he's come back to save her life by breaking the "causal chain of events" that will result in a fatal accident. Ruby then has to decide whether to believe him or write him off as another lunatic. D'Onofrio amusingly goes from seemingly normal to spouting surreal "history" without blinking. Light on the special effects (especially for sci-fi), but they're effective when they are used. Pic went through a time warp of its own, as it was shot in 1999, debuted at Sundance in 2000 and released in theatres in 2001. **110m/C; VHS, DVD.** Marisa Tomei; Vincent D'Onofrio; Tovah Feldshuh; Nadia Dajani; Holland Taylor; Richard Portnow; Sean Gullette; Cara Buono; Liana Pai; Tamara Jenkins; Jose Zuniga; ***Cameo(s):*** Anthony Michael Hall; ***D:*** Brad Anderson; ***W:*** Brad Anderson; ***C:*** Terry Stacey; ***M:*** Evan Lurie.

Happy as Lazzaro *Lazzaro felice* **2018 (PG-13)** In rural Italian village of Inviolata, the pleasant, helpful Lazzaro (Tardiolo) is a member of a clan of slave workers who are forced to work hard for their abusive, noble landlord Marchesa Alfonsina de Luna (Braschi). Lazzaro's personality and actions come to the attention of Tancredi (Chikovani), a young rebel noble who does not agree with his family's unlawfulness. A coward, Tancredi convinces Lazzaro to help him stage his own kidnapping, which leads to an unexpected journey for Lazzarro. The dreamy pastoral fable combines the realistic with supernatural elements as it studies class division in Italy. Italian with subtitles. **128m/C; DVD.** Adriano Tardiolo; Alba Rohrwacher; Tommaso Ragno; Luca Chikovani; Agnese Graziani; ***D:*** Alice Rohrwacher; ***W:*** Alice Rohrwacher; ***C:*** Helene Louvart.

Happy Birthday to Me ½ **1981 (R)** Several elite seniors at an exclusive private school are mysteriously killed by a deranged killer who has a fetish for cutlery. **108m/C; VHS, DVD, Blu-Ray.** *CA* Melissa Sue Anderson; Glenn Ford; Tracy Bregman; Jack Blum; Matt Craven; Lawrence Dane; Lenore Zann; Sharon Acker; Frances Hyland; Earl Pennington; David Eisner; Richard Rebrere; Lesleh Donaldson; ***D:*** J. Lee Thompson; ***W:*** Timothy Bond; Peter Jobin; John C.W. Saxton; John Beaird; ***C:*** Miklos Lente; ***M:*** Bo Harwood; Lance Rubin.

Happy Campers **2001 (R)** Director of Camp Bleeding Dove (Stormare) is sidelined by an injury, so his teen counselors take charge and seek to spice up their boring daily routines. Routine summer camp flick with a better-than-average cast. **94m/C; VHS, DVD.** Brad Renfro; Dominique Swain; Emily Bergl; Jaime King; Jordan Bridges; Peter Stormare; Justin Long; Keram Malicki-Sanchez; ***D:*** Daniel Waters; ***W:*** Daniel Waters; ***C:*** Elliot Davis; ***M:*** Rolfe Kent. **VIDEO**

Happy Christmas **2014 (R)** Jenny (Kendrick) breaks up with her boyfriend and moves in with brother Kelly (writer/director Swanberg) and his wife Kelly (Lynskey). Jenny's slacker approach to life involves a bit more drinking than responsibility, which dually aggravates and inspires her new roommates. Jenny teaches Kelly to loosen up; Kelly teaches Jenny a bit of responsibility. We've seen it before, done better. Too much of the action feels forced even if Kendrick and Lynskey are typically appealing while Swanberg's real-life toddler steals the movie. **88m/C; DVD.** Melanie Lynskey; Anna Kendrick; Lena Dunham; Mark Webber; Joe Swanberg; ***D:*** Joe Swanberg; ***W:*** Joe Swanberg; ***C:*** Ben Richardson; ***M:*** Paul Grimstad.

Happy Death Day ½ **2017 (PG-13)** Writer Scott Lobdell tossed *Scream, Mean Girls,* and *Groundhog Day* into a mixer to create this dark humored spin on the classic teen slasher. Tree Gelbman (a supremely watchable Rothe) is murdered at her birthday party by a baby-face killer, and gets stuck repeating that day until she unmasks her murderer. It's not the most original of concepts, but the jump scares, imaginative deaths, and college-level snark provide for an hour and a half of worthwhile, if somewhat shallow, entertainment. **96m/C; DVD.** Jessica Rothe; Israel Broussard; Ruby Modine; Charles Aitken; Laura Clifton; ***D:*** Christopher Landon; ***W:*** Scott Lobdell; ***C:*** Toby Oliver; ***M:*** Bear McCreary.

Happy Death Day 2U **2019 (PG-13)** The sequel to Happy Death Day finds Ryan (Vu) caught in the cycle of reliving the day of his murder at the hands of a masked killer as Tree (Rothe) did in the original. It turns out that Ryan and his friends invented the machine that created the time loops and sent Tree away. Meanwhile, Tree must manage life in an alternative reality where her mother is still alive, her boyfriend is dating someone else, and the killer is still targeting her. This film lacks the fun, humor, and strengths of the original. **100m/C; DVD, Blu-Ray.** *US JP* Jessica Rothe; Israel Broussard; Phi Vu; Suraj Sharma; Sarah Yarkin; ***D:*** Christopher Landon; ***W:*** Christopher Landon; ***C:*** Toby Oliver; ***M:*** Bear McCreary.

Happy End 🦴🦴 ½ **2017 (R)** A comedy drama about the dark side of an upper-class family in Calais. Several generations of Laurents live in a mansion there, including aged patriarch Georges (Trintignant), daughter Anne (Huppert), son Thomas (Kassovitz), and grandchildren. Despite elegant appearances, each faces serious issues. Georges is in the early stages of dementia and wants to end his life, while Anne must deal with a serious job site accident that was caused by her negligent son Pierre (Rogowski). Tensions increase with the arrival of 13-year-old Eve (Harduin), Thomas's troubled daughter from his first marriage. Quality performances add to the film's effectiveness. French with subtitles. **107m/C; DVD, Blu-Ray.** Isabelle Huppert; Jean-Louis Trintignant; Mathieu Kassovitz; Fantine Harduin; Franz Rogowski; ***D:*** Michael Haneke; ***W:*** Michael Haneke; ***C:*** Christian Berger.

The Happy Ending 🦴🦴 ½ **1969 (PG)** Woman struggles with a modern definition of herself and her marriage, causing pain and confusion for her family. Simmons is solid as the wife and mother seeking herself. Michel LeGrand's theme song "What Are You Doing With the Rest of Your Life?" was a big hit. **112m/C; VHS, Blu-Ray, Streaming.** Jean Simmons; John Forsythe; Lloyd Bridges; Shirley Jones; Teresa Wright; Dick Shawn; Nanette Fabray; Bobby Darin; Tina Louise; ***D:*** Richard Brooks; ***W:*** Richard Brooks; ***C:*** Conrad L. Hall.

Happy Endings 🦴🦴 ½ **2005 (R)** Director Roos somewhat successfully juggles several storylines about life, love, gay love, blackmail, deceit, and making babies that focus on two women whose paths eventually cross. There's Mamie (Kudrow) whose teenage fling with her unrelated stepbrother Charley (Coogan) resulted in a forsaken child and a cheerless, regret-filled life; meanwhile, vagabond Jude (a dynamic Gyllenhaal) manages to weasel her way into her gay friend Otis' home and his widowed father's heart. **128m/C; DVD.** Tom Arnold; Jesse Bradford; Bobby Cannavale; Sarah Clarke; Steve Coogan; Laura Dern; Maggie Gyllenhaal; Lisa Kudrow; Jason Ritter; David Sutcliffe; Hallee Hirsh; Eric Jungmann; Johnny Galecki; ***D:*** Don Roos; ***W:*** Don Roos; ***C:*** Clark Mathis.

Happy Ever Afters 🦴 ½ **2009** Cliched but cheerful Irish rom com. Two wedding receptions are booked into the same hotel at the same time and comedic intermingling goes on. Single mom Maura is marrying illegal African immigrant Wilson in a scam while Freddie is remarrying his crazy ex-wife Sophie though neither seems quite sure why. Since both marriages are a mistake is it any wonder that Maura and Freddie start eyeballing each other? **101m/C; DVD.** *IR* Sally Hawkins; Tom Riley; Jade Yourell; Ariyon Bakare; Tina Kellegher; Sinead Maguire; ***D:*** Stephen Burke; ***W:*** Stephen Burke; ***C:*** Jonathan Kovel.

Happy Feet 🦴🦴🦴 **2006 (PG)** Beautifully computer animated tale of Mumbles (Wood), a penguin who can't sing after being dropped as an egg by his father (Jackman). Instead, he hoofs like Savion Glover, whose moves were motion-captured for Mumbles' dance sequences. Exiled from his group and his love Gloria (Murphy), Mumbles has adventures with predators, other penguins and a certain two-legged animal that is apparently ruining the planet. Some situations may scare smaller children and the ecological message is a little ominous, so assure them that it will all work out fine and you'll remember to cut up those plastic six-pack thingies before you throw them out. **87m/C; DVD, Blu-Ray, HD-DVD.** ***V:*** Elijah Wood; Robin Williams; Brittany Murphy; Hugh Jackman; Nicole Kidman; Hugo Weaving; Anthony LaPaglia; Magda Szubanski; Elizabeth Daily; Steve Irwin; Miriam Margolyes; ***D:*** George Miller; ***W:*** George Miller; John Collee; Judy Morris; Warren Coleman; ***M:*** John Powell. Oscars '06: Animated Film; British Acad. '06: Animated Film; Golden Globes '07: Song ("The Song of the Heart").

Happy Feet Two 🦴🦴 **2011 (PG)** More is definitely less in the loud, garish sequel to the relatively-charming Oscar-winning animated film. Tells the tale of the next generation as Mumbles (Wood) watches his son Erik develop his own social phobias in the land of ice and penguins as he turns to another potential father figure. Director Miller is environmentally conscious but the cool animation can't make up for storytelling that's as flat as the ice on which its creatures dance. The reliance on modern music, such as LL Cool J and Justin Timberlake, comes off as more annoying then hip. **100m/C; DVD, Blu-Ray.** ***V:*** Elijah Wood; Elizabeth Daily; Hank Azaria; Robin Williams; Ray Winstone; Sofia Vergara; Hugo Weaving; Alecia Moore; Brad Pitt; Matt Damon; ***D:*** George Miller; ***W:*** George Miller; Gary Eck; Warren Coleman; Paul Livingston; ***C:*** David Peers; David Dulac; ***M:*** John Powell.

Happy Gilmore 🦴🦴 **1996 (PG-13)** Skating-impaired hockey player Gilmore (Sandler) translates his slap shot into a 400-yard tee shot and joins the pro golf tour. His unique style brings a new, less refined breed of fan to the game and upsets the reigning tour hotshot (McDonald). Sandler improves on "Billy Madison," which isn't saying much. There's still plenty of ammo for his many detractors, but the laughs are more frequent and consistent. Replacing bathroom humor with abusive behavior, the mis-named Happy swears at or beats up about 90% of the supporting cast, including Bob Barker in a charity pro-am. **92m/C; VHS, DVD, Blu-Ray, UMD, HD-DVD.** Adam Sandler; Christopher McDonald; Carl Weathers; Julie Bowen; Frances Bay; Ben Stiller; Richard Kiel; Joe Flaherty; Kevin Nealon; Allen Covert; Robert Smigel; Bob Barker; Dennis Dugan; ***D:*** Dennis Dugan; ***W:*** Adam Sandler; Tim Herlihy; ***C:*** Arthur Albert; ***M:*** Mark Mothersbaugh. MTV Movie Awards '96: Fight (Adam Sandler/Bob Barker).

Happy Go Lovely 🦴🦴 **1951** Chorus girl Janet (Vera-Ellen) is part of an American troupe that's in Scotland hoping to open a show. Producer Frost (Romero) needs financial backing and, after seeing Janet exit a limo, thinks she's found a rich beau and offers her the show's lead in hopes of getting her boyfriend's money. When the limo's owner, stodgy millionaire B.G. Bruno (Niven), does show up, Janet mistakes him for a reporter and falls in love with the guy. Tired plot, but good performances in this lightweight musical. **95m/C; VHS, DVD.** *GB* Vera-Ellen; David Niven; Cesar Romero; Bobby Howes; Sandra Dorne; ***D:*** H. Bruce Humberstone; ***W:*** Val Guest; ***C:*** Erwin Hillier; ***M:*** Mischa Spoliansky.

Happy-Go-Lucky 🦴🦴🦴 **2008 (R)** The title perfectly describes the lead, ever-optimistic London schoolteacher Poppy, who finds a silver lining no matter the situation. Her attitude leads her to romance, but she's tested by an obsessive, abusive driving instructor. Sounds simple, but it's actually a sophisticated character study with insidious charm. Director Leigh's famously morose mood couldn't be more different in this feel-good comedy about feeling good (without aid of chemicals). Poppy's cheerful disposition and perpetually rosy outlook are strangely contagious and not grating, thanks largely to Hawkins' memorable turn. **118m/C; On Demand.** *GB* Sally Hawkins; Eddie Marsan; Sylvestria Le Touzel; Alexis Zegerman; Samuel Roukin; Sinead Matthews; Kate O'Flynn; Sarah Niles; Karina Fernandez; ***D:*** Mike Leigh; ***W:*** Mike Leigh; ***C:*** Dick Pope; ***M:*** Gary Yershon. Golden Globes '09: Actress--Mus./Comedy (Hawkins).

Happy, Happy 🦴 ½ *Insanely Happy; Sykt Lykkelig* **2010 (R)** Excessively perky country schoolteacher Kaja is ignored by both her angry husband Eirik and young son Theodor so she's thrilled by her new sophisticated neighbors Sigve and Elisabeth and their adopted Ethiopian son Noa. Sigve confides his marital problems to Kaja and the neglected woman is eager to offer him sexual comforts. Then other secrets are revealed. Norwegian with subtitles. **85m/C; DVD.** *NO* Agnes Kittelsen; Joachim Rafaelsen; Henrik Rafaelsen; Maibritt Saerens; ***D:*** Anne Sewitsky; ***W:*** Ragnhild Tronvoll; ***C:*** Anna Myking; ***M:*** Stein Berge Svendsen.

Happy Hell Night 🦴🦴 **1992 (R)** A fraternity prank helps a crazed priest escape from a mental institution and again take up his hobby fom 25 years ago'killing local fraternity members. Oh, the irony is delicious! Unfortunately, the direction and script are not, and they bury some genuinely scary moments. Look for a pre-stardom Rockwell and pre-"CSI" Fox, along with McGavin making a mortgage payment or two. **84m/C; DVD, Blu-Ray.** Nick Gregory; Darren McGavin; Sam Rockwell; Jorja Fox; Ted Clark; Frank John Hughes; Irfan Mensur; Gala Videnovic; Laura Carney; Charles Cragin; ***D:*** Brian Owens; ***W:*** Brian Owens; ***C:*** Sol Negrin.

The Happy Hooker 🦴🦴 ½ **1975 (R)** Xaviera Hollander's cheeky (and bestselling) memoir of her transition from office girl to "working girl" has been brought to the screen with a sprightly (though sanitary) air of naughtiness, with Redgrave enjoyable in title role. Followed by "The Happy Hooker Goes to Washington" and "The Happy Hooker Goes Hollywood." **96m/C; VHS, DVD.** Lynn Redgrave; Jean-Pierre Aumont; Nicholas Pryor; ***D:*** Nicholas Sgarro.

The Happy Hooker Goes Hollywood 🦴 **1980 (R)** Third film inspired by the title of Xaviera Hollander's memoirs, in which the fun-loving Xaviera comes to Hollywood with the intention of making a movie based on her book, but soon meets up with a series of scheming, would-be producers. **86m/C; VHS, DVD, Blu-Ray.** Martine Beswick; Chris Lemmon; Adam West; Phil Silvers; ***D:*** Alan Roberts.

The Happy Hooker Goes to Washington 🦴 ½ **1977 (R)** Further adventures of the world's most famous madam. Heatherton (not Redgrave) is Xaviera Hollander this time, testifying before the U.S. Senate in defense of sex. Fairly stupid attempt to milk boxoffice of original. Second in the holy trilogy of Happy Hooker pictures, which also include "The Happy Hooker" and "The Happy Hooker Goes Hollywood." **89m/C; VHS, DVD.** Joey Heatherton; George Hamilton; Ray Walston; Jack Carter; ***D:*** William A. Levey.

Happy Hour 🦴 ½ **1987 (R)** A young brewing scientist discovers a secret formula for beer, and everyone tries to take it from him. Little turns in a good performance as a superspy. **88m/C; VHS, Streaming.** Richard Gilliland; Jamie Farr; Tawny Kitaen; Ty Henderson; Rich Little; ***D:*** John DeBello; ***W:*** John DeBello.

Happy Hour 🦴 ½ **2003** Tulley (LaPaglia) is a self-loathing drunk. A failed writer who works as a copywriter at a New York ad agency, Tulley lives in the shadow of his famous author father (Vaughn). Tulley and best bud/coworker Levine (Stoltz) spend time at their favorite watering hole where Tulley meets Natalie (Feeney) who becomes his instant girlfriend. Then Tulley gets diagnosed with advanced cirrhosis and has to decide what to do with his so-far wasted life. Not as maudlin as it could have been but if its familiarity doesn't breed contempt, it does breed boredom despite the talent involved. **93m/C; DVD.** Anthony LaPaglia; Eric Stoltz; Caroleen Feeney; Robert Vaughn; Sandrine Holt; Tom Sadoski; ***D:*** Mike Bencivenga; ***W:*** Mike Bencivenga; Richard Levine; ***C:*** Giselle Chamma; ***M:*** Jeff Taylor.

Happy Landing 🦴🦴 ½ **1938** Predictable, yet entertaining Henie vehicle about a plane that makes a forced landing in Norway near Henie's home. Romance follows with bandleader Romero and manager Ameche. **102m/B; DVD.** Sonja Henie; Don Ameche; Jean Hersholt; Ethel Merman; Cesar Romero; Billy Gilbert; Wally Vernon; El Brendel; ***D:*** Roy Del Ruth; ***W:*** Milton Sperling; Boris Ingster.

Happy New Year 🦴🦴🦴 *The Happy New Year Caper; La Bonne Annee* **1973** Charming romantic comedy in which two thieves plan a robbery but get sidetracked by the distracting woman who works next door to the jewelry store that's their target. Available in both subtitled and dubbed versions. Remade in 1987. **114m/C; VHS, DVD.** *FR IT* Francoise Fabian; Lino Ventura; Andre Falcon; Charles Gerard; ***D:*** Claude Lelouch; ***W:*** Claude Lelouch; Pierre Uytterhoeven.

Happy New Year 🦴🦴 ½ **1987 (PG)** Two sophisticated thieves plan and execute an elaborate jewel heist that goes completely awry. Remake of the 1974 French film of the same name. **86m/C; VHS, Streaming.** Peter Falk; Wendy Hughes; Tom Courtenay; Charles Durning; Joan Copeland; ***D:*** John G. Avildsen; ***W:*** Warren Lane; ***M:*** Bill Conti.

Happy People: A Year in the Taiga 🦴🦴🦴 **2013** Master documentarian Herzog continues his international examination of the way man interacts with the natural world (as he did in Grizzly Man, Cave of Forgotten Dreams, and more). This time he travels with Russian co-director Vasyukov to a remote part of the world deep in the Siberian Taiga, miles from civilization. Three hundred people inhabit a small village called Bakhtia on the river Yenisei, and, as the title makes clear, they're happy there. Herzog's lyrical, hands-off approach to his subject matter makes for another riveting piece. **90m/C; DVD.** *GE* ***Nar:*** Werner Herzog; ***D:*** Werner Herzog; Dmitry Vasyukov; ***W:*** Werner Herzog; Dmitry Vasyukov; Rudolph Herzog; ***M:*** Klaus Badelt.

The Happy Road 🦴🦴 ½ **1957** Innocuous comedy that Kelly also directed. After their children run away from their Swiss boarding school, widowed American Mike (Kelly) and French divorcee Suzanne (Laage) reluctantly team up to track them down. The kids have some harmless adventures on their way to a Paris reunion, including eluding NATO troops on maneuvers. Maurice Chevalier sings the title song. **100m/B; DVD.** Gene Kelly; Bobby Clark; Barbara Laage; Brigitte Fossey; Michael Redgrave; ***D:*** Gene Kelly; ***W:*** Arthur Julian; Harry Kurnitz; ***C:*** Robert Juillard; ***M:*** Georges Van Parys.

Happy Tears 🦴 ½ **2009 (R)** Disjointed and awkwardly handled questionable comedy about a dysfunctional family. No-nonsense Laura (Moore) and ditzy younger sister Jayne (Posey) must very reluctantly return to their Pittsburgh hometown to figure out how to handle their dementia-afflicted dad Joe (Torn) and his entrenched floozy, druggie girlfriend Shelly (Barkin). Naturally, there's a lot of past resentment to wade through and many uncomfortable moments ensue. **95m/C; DVD, Streaming.** Parker Posey; Demi Moore; Rip Torn; Ellen Barkin; Christian Camargo; Billy Magnussen; Sebastien Roche; Patti D'Arbanville; Victor Slezak; ***D:*** Mitchell Lichtenstein; ***W:*** Mitchell Lichtenstein; ***C:*** Jamie Anderson; ***M:*** Robert Miller.

Happy, Texas 🦴🦴🦴 **1999 (PG-13)** Producer/director Mark Illsley's quirky little debut hearkens back to such classic Hollywood comedies as "Some Like It Hot." Escaped prisoners Harry Sawyer (Northam) and Wayne Wayne Wayne Jr. (Zahn) steal a camper and assume the identity of its owners in order to evade the law. The trouble is that the owners are a pair of gay men who organize kiddie beauty pageants. When they arrive in the town of Happy, Texas, the populace thinks that they're there to stage the Little Miss Fresh Squeezed contest and greet them with open arms. Wayne is forced to summon up fashion and choreography skills not commonplace in your average hardened criminal, while Harry hobnobs with the local gentry while plotting to knock over the town bank. Romantic complications involving a schoolmarm (Douglas), lady banker (Walker) and a sexually confused sheriff (Macy) arise, setting the stage for a happy (but unnecessarily tidy) ending. **104m/C; VHS, DVD.** Steve Zahn; Jeremy Northam; Ally Walker; Illeana Douglas; William H. Macy; M.C. Gainey; Ron Perlman; Michael Hitchcock; Paul Dooley; ***D:*** Mark Illsley; ***W:*** Phil Reeves; Ed Stone; Mark Illsley; ***C:*** Bruce Douglas Johnson; ***M:*** Peter Harris. Ind. Spirit '00: Support. Actor (Zahn).

The Happy Thieves 🦴 ½ **1961** The thieves may be the only ones happy with this listless crime comedy. Jim Bourne (Harrison) and Eve Lewis (Hayworth) are art thieves who steal a Velasquez from Duchess Blanca (Valli). This leads to them being blackmailed by crazy art dealer Munoz (Aslan), who wants a Goya from a Madrid museum. Involving art forger Calbert (Wiseman), Bourne tries a switcheroo during a bullfight but things don't work out as planned. Adapted from Richard Condon's novel "The Oldest Confession." **88m/B; DVD.** Rex Harrison; Rita Hayworth; Gregoire Aslan; Alida Valli; Joseph Wiseman; Britt Ekland; Peter Illing; Virgilio Teixeira; ***D:*** George Marshall; ***W:*** John Gay; ***C:*** Paul Beeson; ***M:*** Mario Nascimbene.

Happy Times 🦴🦴 ½ *Xingfu Shiguang* **2000 (PG)** Underneath this light comedy hides an intimate tale of an aging loser and his unexpected relationship with a young, blind teenager. When Zhao (Bensham) tries to woo plus-sized divorcee (Lihua) by pretending to be a rich hotel owner, she demands that he give her blind stepdaughter Wu Ying (Jie) a job, unaware that Zhao's only experience in hotel management was renting out a dilapidated bus to couples by the hour. With the help of friends, Zhao sets up an elaborate ruse: outfitting an abandoned factory as the "hotel" where Wu, a masseuse, employs her craft on Zhao's friends posing as clients who pay her in phony money. Zhao finds redemption of a sort in the sullen but honest Wu, who in turn blossoms in her new job. Acclaimed Chinese director Yimou elicits excellent performances in his scaled-down allegory. In Mandarin with subtitles. **106m/C; VHS, DVD.** *CH* Benshan Zhao; Jie Dong; Xuejian Li; Lifan Dong; Qibin Leng; Biao Fu; Ben Nu; ***D:*** Yimou Zhang; ***W:*** Giu Zi; ***C:*** Hou Yong; ***M:*** San Bao.

Happy Together 🦴 **1989 (PG-13)** An eager freshman accidentally gets a beautiful, impulsive girl as his roommate. Together they meet the challenges of secondary education. **102m/C; VHS, DVD.** Helen Slater; Patrick Dempsey; Dan Schneider; Marius Weyers; Barbara Babcock; Brad Pitt; ***D:*** Mel Damski; ***M:*** Robert Folk.

Happy Together 🦴🦴 *Cheun Gwong Tsa Sit* **1996** Lovers Lai Yiu-Fai (Leung) and Ho Po-Wing (Cheung) travel to Argentina from Hong Kong looking for adventure but soon go their separate ways. Lai is working as a doorman at a tango bar when a badly beaten Ho unexpectedly re-enters his life. Lai looks after the self-destructive Ho but his restlessness causes him to desert Lai once again, even as Lai befriends young Taiwanese Chang (Chen). After Chang returns to Taipei, Lai begins to suffer from depression and serious homesickness, as well as still worrying about Ho. Edgy visuals and playful performances bely a serious nature. Chinese and Spanish with subtitles. **92m/C; VHS, DVD, Blu-Ray.** *CH* Leslie Cheung; Tony Leung Chiu-Wai; Chen "Chang Chen" Chang; ***D:*** Wong Kar-Wai; ***W:*** Wong Kar-Wai; ***C:*** Christopher Doyle; ***M:*** Danny Chung. Cannes '97: Director (Kar-Wai).

The Happy Years 🦴🦴 **1/2 1950** Based on "The Lawrenceville Stories" by Owen Johnson. Concerned dad Samuel Stover (Ames) sends his troublemaking teenaged son Dink (Stockwell) to a turn-of-the-century prep school in the hopes of turning him into a responsible young man. Bullied by some older students (who all have odd nicknames), Dink has to earn their respect in class and on the football field. **110m/C; DVD.** Dean Stockwell; Darryl Hickman; Scotty Beckett; Leon Ames; Margalo Gillmore; Leo G. Carroll; Peter Thompson; David Blair; Claudia Barrett; ***D:*** William A. Wellman; ***W:*** Harry Ruskin; ***C:*** Paul Vogel; ***M:*** Leigh Harline.

Happythankyoumoreplease 🦴 **1/2 2010 (R)** Microscopic look at the lives of a group of self-absorbed 30-something Manhattanites on the cusp of responsible adulthood. Director and writer Radnor stars as Sam, who tries to win over a barmaid with his humorous offer of a "three-night stand." His friend Mary struggles with the decision to stay with her boyfriend who's headed to the West Coast. Meanwhile, Sam's best friend Annie is going bald from a medical condition, leaving her few dating options. Radnor forces his characters to speak so obsessively and endlessly about the minutia of their emotional states that he comes off as a guy hoping to win the Woody Allen, Jr. award. Ultimately flat and overly indulgent—little more than a sitcom pilot with a horribly uncatchy title. **100m/C; Blu-Ray, On Demand.** Josh Radnor; Malin Akerman; Zoe Kazan; Michael Algieri; Pablo Schreiber; Tony Hale; Kate Mara; ***D:*** Josh Radnor; ***W:*** Josh Radnor; ***C:*** Seamus Tierney; ***M:*** Jaymay.

The Happytime Murders 🦴 **1/2 2018 (R)** When the puppet cast of an '80s children's TV show begins to get murdered one by one, a disgraced LAPD detective-turned-private eye puppet takes on the case. **92m/C; DVD, Blu-Ray, Streaming.** *US CH* Melissa McCarthy; Elizabeth Banks; Maya Rudolph; Joel McHale; ***V:*** Bill Barretta; ***D:*** Brian Henson; ***W:*** Todd Berger; Dee Austin Robertson; ***C:*** Mitchell Amundsen; ***M:*** Christopher Lennertz. Golden Raspberries '18: Worst Actress (McCarthy).

Hara-Kiri: Death of a Samurai 🦴🦴 **1/2** *Ichimei* **2011** Director Miike's remake of the similarly named 1962 film about a mysterious Samurai requesting permission to kill himself at the castle of a nobleman. All is not as it seems as it quickly becomes apparent that he has more intentions than killing himself. **126m/C; DVD, Blu-Ray, Streaming.** *JP* Koji Yakusho; Munetaka Aoki; Naoto Takenaka; Hikari Mitsushima; Eita; ***D:*** Takashi Miike; ***W:*** Kikumi Yamagishi; ***C:*** Nobuyasu Kita; ***M:*** Ryuichi Sakamoto.

Harakiri 🦴🦴🦴 **1/2** *Seppuku* **1962** An old samurai (Nakadai) wishes to commit ritual suicide on the grounds of a feudal lord, where he learns that his son-in-law, also a samurai, was forced to commit seppuku with a bamboo blade while seeking work. He tells the younger warrior's story to the assembled warlords, who abandoned the samurai when they were no longer needed. Beautifully told and shot film is a scathing indictment of the treatment of men of honor after the battles that defined them have been fought. A classic of the genre, focusing on the aftermath rather than the glory. **135m/B; VHS, DVD, Blu-Ray.** *JP* Hisashi Igawa; Yoshio Inaba; Akira Ishihama; Shima Iwashita; Rentaro Mikuni; Masao Mishima; Tatsuya Nakadai; Tetsuro Tamba; Shichisaburo Amatsu; Yoshio Aoki; Jo Azumi; Akiji Kobayashi; Ichiro Nakaya; Kei Sato; Ryo Takeuchi; ***D:*** Masaki Kobayashi; ***W:*** Shinobu Hashimoto; Yasuhiko Takiguchi; ***C:*** Yoshio Miyajima; ***M:*** Toru Takemitsu.

Hard As Nails 🦴🦴 **1/2 2001 (R)** Over-achieving video premiere is a genre piece that leaves no cliche unturned, but it also has moments of real style. Gangster Alex (Scotti) and stripper Kat (Yates) are caught between Russian and Japanese gangs in Los Angeles. A cop (Craig) and a hooker (Farentino) are involved, too. Doublecrosses abound. Some of the stunt work is wonderfully acrobatic. Director Katkin makes the most of a pocket-change budget. **88m/C; DVD.** Allen Scotti; Kim Yates; Andrew Craig; Matt Westmore; Lorissa McComas; Stella Farentino; ***D:*** Brian Katkin; ***W:*** Brian Katkin; ***C:*** Marco Cappetta; ***M:*** Chris Farrell. **VIDEO**

Hard-Boiled 🦴🦴 **1/2** *Lashou Shentan* **1992** Police Inspector Yuen (Woo regular Yun-Fat) is investigating, with his usual excessive force, the Triads organized crime syndicate and a group of gun smugglers who killed his partner. He joins forces with Tony, an undercover cop who's working as a gangster hitman. There's lots of gunplay and betrayals among all the participants. Usual Woo way with violence and action sequences although the plot is more contrived. In Mandarin and Chinese with English subtitles. **126m/C; VHS, DVD, Blu-Ray.** *CH* Chow Yun-Fat; Tony Leung Chiu-Wai; Philip Chan; Anthony Wong; Teresa Mo; Bowie Lam; Hoi-Shan Kwan; Philip Kwok; John Woo; ***D:*** John Woo; ***W:*** Barry Wong; John Woo; ***C:*** Wing-Heng Wang; ***M:*** Michael Gibbs.

Hard Bounty 🦴🦴 **1/2 1994 (R)** After five years of chasing desperadoes, bounty hunter Martin B. Kanning hangs up his guns to open a saloon—complete with frontier prostitutes. When one of his ladies is murdered, the other gals decide to chase after the killer. Naturally, Kanning can't let them go alone. **90m/C; VHS, DVD.** Matt McCoy; Kelly Le Brock; Rochelle Swanson; Felicity Waterman; Kimberly Kelley; ***D:*** Jim Wynorski; ***W:*** Karen Kelly; ***C:*** Zoran Hochstatter; ***M:*** Taj.

Hard Candy 🦴🦴 **2006 (R)** Page is scary-good as 14-year-old Hayley, a seeming Lolita out to tempt 32-year-old photographer Jeff (Wilson). They first flirt in an online chat room and then face-to-face in a coffee shop. Jeff invites pixie-ish Hayley back to his home for drinks, only whatever you think may happen, doesn't. Hayley drugs Jeff, ties him to a chair, and accuses him of being a child pornographer, pedophile, and possible murderer before threatening him with castration for his "crimes." Is she right or just a very dangerous hysteric? First feature for commercial/video director Slade. **103m/C; DVD.** Ellen Page; Patrick Wilson; Sandra Oh; Jennifer Holmes; Gilbert John; ***D:*** David Slade; ***W:*** Brian Nelson; ***C:*** Jo Willems; ***M:*** Molly Nyman; Harry Escott.

Hard Cash 🦴 **1/2** *Run for the Money* **2001 (R)** Thief Tom Taylor (Slater) wants to go legit after being released from prison but instead hooks up with a new crew for a job. When they discover the money is marked, Taylor finds himself embroiled with corrupt FBI agent Mark Cornell (Kilmer). Despite the billing, Kilmer has limited screen time and this caper film is a predictable yawner. **98m/C; VHS, DVD.** Christian Slater; Bokeem Woodbine; Val Kilmer; Daryl Hannah; Verne Troyer; Balthazar Getty; Vincent Laresca; Peter Woodward; William Forsythe; Sara Downing; ***D:*** Pedrag (Peter) Antonijevic; ***W:*** Willie Dreyfus; ***C:*** Phil Parmet; ***M:*** Stephen (Steve) Edwards.

Hard Choices 🦴🦴🦴 **1984** A 15-year-old Tennessee boy is unjustly charged as an accessory to murder, until a female social worker decides to help him. From then on, nothing is predictable. Excellent work by Klenck, McCleery, and Seitz. Don't miss Sayles as an unusual drug dealer. Intelligent, surprising, and powerful. Based on a true story, this is a low profile film that deserves to be discovered. **90m/C; VHS, DVD.** Margaret Klenck; Gary McCleery; John Seitz; John Sayles; Liane (Alexandra) Curtis; J.T. Walsh; Spalding Gray; ***D:*** Rick King; ***W:*** Rick King.

Hard Contract 🦴🦴 **1969** Cold-blooded hitman John Cunningham (Coburn) is contracted to kill three people in Europe. In Spain, bored socialite Sheila (Remick) pursues John and they begin an affair but, with his emotions engaged, John's work is affected. Then he discovers his last victim is former hitman Michael Carlson (Hayden), who retired to Madrid with his family. Now John has to decide if he can fulfill his contract or start a new life with Sheila--knowing someone could then be contracted to kill him. **105m/C; DVD.** James Coburn; Lee Remick; Sterling Hayden; Burgess Meredith; Lilli Palmer; Claude Dauphin; Patrick Magee; Karen Black; ***D:*** S. Lee Pogostin; ***W:*** S. Lee Pogostin; ***C:*** Jack Hildyard; ***M:*** Alex North.

Hard Core Logo 🦴🦴 **1996 (R)** Mockumentary about a group of Canadian veteran punk rock musicians who, at thirtysomething, have reunited for one last benefit concert. The semi-legendary Vancouver band are so pleased by how well the concert goes that they decide to head back on the road (in a decrepit van) for one last shot at glory, trailed by a documentary film crew (led by director McDonald). The documentary inserts reveal the band's ups and downs and the ego trips that ultimately drove them apart. Adapted from a novel by Michael Turner. McDonald describes "Hard Core Logo" as the last of his rock 'n' roll road trilogy, following "Roadkill" and "Highway 61." **96m/C; VHS, DVD, Blu-Ray.** *CA* Hugh Dillon; Callum Keith Rennie; John Pyper-Ferguson; Bernie Coulson; ***D:*** Bruce McDonald; ***W:*** Noel S. Baker; ***C:*** Danny Nowak; ***M:*** Shaun Tozer. Genie '96: Song ("Swamp Baby, Who the Hell Do You Think You Are?").

Hard Core Logo 2 🦴 **1/2 2010** In Bruce McDonald's original mockumentary he follows the career of fake rock band Hard Core Logo. He now finds himself in a career slump, and while filming some Wiccans he meets the lead singer of another band who claims to be possessed by the ghost of someone he knows pretty well. **100m/C; DVD.** *CA* Bruce McDonald; Care Failure; Julian Richings; Sera-Lys McArthur; Dazzer Scott; ***D:*** Bruce McDonald; ***W:*** Bruce McDonald; Dave Griffith; ***C:*** John Price; ***M:*** Justin Small. **VIDEO**

Hard Country 🦴🦴 **1/2 1981 (PG)** Caught between her best friend's success as a country singer and the old values of a woman's place, a small town girl questions her love and her life style. A warm and intelligent rural drama. Basinger's debut. **104m/C; VHS, DVD, Blu-Ray.** Jan-Michael Vincent; Kim Basinger; Michael Parks; Gailard Sartain; Tanya Tucker; Ted Neeley; Daryl Hannah; Richard Moll; ***D:*** David Greene; ***W:*** Michael Kane; ***M:*** Michael Martin Murphey.

A Hard Day's Night 🦴🦴🦴 **1/2 1964** The Beatles' first film is a joyous romp through an average "day in the life" of the Fab Four, shot in a pseudo-documentary style with great flair by Lester and noted as the first music video. **90m/B; VHS, DVD, Blu-Ray.** *GB* John Lennon; Paul McCartney; George Harrison; Ringo Starr; Wilfrid Brambell; Norman Rossington; John Junkin; Victor Spinetti; Anna Quayle; Deryck Guyler; Richard Vernon; Lionel Blair; Eddie Malin; Robin Ray; Alison Seebohm; David Saxon; Patti Boyd; ***D:*** Richard Lester; ***W:*** Alun Owen; ***C:*** Gilbert Taylor; ***M:*** John Lennon; Paul McCartney.

Hard Drive 🦴 **1/2 1994** A high tech, interactive network offers shared fantasies to Will and Delilah. Then they become obsessed with making their dreams a reality. **92m/C; VHS, DVD.** Matt McCoy; Christina (Kristina) Fulton; Edward Albert; Leo Damian; Stella Stevens; ***D:*** James Merendino; ***W:*** James Merendino; ***C:*** Sead Muhtarevic; ***M:*** Nels Cline.

Hard Drivin' 🦴 **1960** Rowdy action featuring Southern stock car drivers with well shot race scenes from the Southern 500. **92m/C; VHS, DVD.** Rory Calhoun; John Gentry; Alan Hale, Jr.; ***D:*** Paul Helmick.

Hard Eight 🦴🦴🦴 *Sydney* **1996 (R)** Performances are the highlight of this low-key story set in Reno, Nevada. Sydney (Hall) is a professional gambler who decides to take under his wing the destitute John (Reilly) and teach him the trade. John falls for waitress/hooker Clementine (Paltrow) but there has to be some snake in this gambler's would-be paradise and it shows up in the malevolent form of the scary Jimmy (Jackson), who the dim John befriends despite Sydney's warnings. Debut for writer/director Anderson. **101m/C; VHS, DVD.** Philip Baker Hall; John C. Reilly; Gwyneth Paltrow; Samuel L. Jackson; F. William Parker; Philip Seymour Hoffman; Nathanael Cooper; Wynn White; Robert Ridgely; Michael J. Rowe; Kathleen Campbell; Melora Walters; ***D:*** Paul Thomas Anderson; ***W:*** Paul Thomas Anderson; ***C:*** Robert Elswit; ***M:*** Michael Penn; Jon Brion.

Hard, Fast and Beautiful 🦴🦴 **1951** The title sounds like film noir but it's actually a sports drama with Trevor as grasping mom Milly Farley who sees her teen tennis prodigy daughter Florence (Forrest) as her meal ticket to money and fame. Florence is successful (but unhappy) on the amateur circuit while Milly accepts payola and pushes her daughter on a European tour. It's when mom tries to breakup Florence's romance with Gordon (Clarke) that Florence finally rebels. **71m/B; DVD.** Claire Trevor; Sally Forrest; Robert Clarke; Kenneth Patterson; Carleton Young; Joseph Kearns; ***D:*** Ida Lupino; ***W:*** Martha Wilkerson; ***C:*** Archie Stout; ***M:*** Roy Webb.

Hard Four 🦴 **1/2 2007** Legendary gambler Golden Hands Segal suffers a fatal heart attack shooting craps in Vegas. According to Jewish tradition, the body must have a proper funeral within 24 hours so it's up to Segal's grandson Spencer and his pal Freddy to get the body back to New Jersey. Would-be wacky misadventures are supposed to follow but don't. **85m/C; DVD.** Ross Benjamin; Samuel Gould; Ed Asner; Charlene Blaine; Hamilton Camp; Dabney Coleman; Bryan Cranston; John Getz; Paula Prentiss; ***D:*** Charles Dennis; ***W:*** Charles Dennis; ***C:*** Francis Porter; Josh Salzman; ***M:*** Larry Brown. **VIDEO**

Hard Ground 🦴🦴 **2003** In this Hallmark Channel western, Billy Bucklin (Figlioli) escapes en route to Yuma Prison and plans to recruit a gang to control the Mexican border. He starts by robbing a stagecoach, but Marshal Hutchinson (Dern) is already on his trail. **88m/C; DVD; Closed Captioned.** Bruce Dern; Burt Reynolds; David Figlioli; Seth Peterson; Amy Jo Johnson; Martin Kove; Larry Hankin; ***D:*** Frank Q. Dobbs; ***W:*** Frank Q. Dobbs; David S. Cass, Sr.; ***C:*** Maximo Munzi; ***M:*** Joe Kraemer. **CABLE**

Hard Hunted 🦴 **1/2 1992 (R)** Three macho undercover agents try to avoid death at the hands of high-tech guerillas trying to steal nuclear weapons. No-brain actioner, heavy on the display of feminine charms. **97m/C; VHS, DVD, Blu-Ray.** Dona Speir; Roberta Vasquez; Cynthia Brimhall; Bruce Penhall; R.J. (Geoffrey) Moore; Tony Peck; Rodrigo Obregon; Al Leong; Michael J. Shane; ***D:*** Andy Sidaris; ***W:*** Andy Sidaris.

Hard Justice 🦴🦴 **1995 (R)** Bureau of Alcohol, Tobacco & Firearms agent Nick Adams (Bradley) goes undercover in prison to find his partner's killer and discovers that Warden Pike (Napier) is running an illegal gun operation. Now, who's he gonna trust? Lots of action thrills in a routine story. **95m/C; VHS, DVD.** David Bradley; Charles Napier; Yuji Okumoto; Vernon Wells; ***D:*** Greg Yaitanes; ***W:*** Nicholas Amendolare; Chris Bold; ***C:*** Moshe Levin; ***M:*** Don Peake.

Hard Knox 🦴 **1983** A hard-nosed Marine pilot is dumped from the service and takes up command at a military school filled with undisciplined punks. A made-for-television movie. **96m/C; VHS, DVD.** Robert Conrad; Frank Howard; Alan Ruck; Red West; Bill Erwin; Dean Hill; Joan Sweeney; ***D:*** Peter Werner.

Hard Labour **1973** Middle-aged housekeeper is humiliated at home by her children and tyrannical daughter-in-law. **70m/C; VHS, DVD.** *GB* Alison Steadman; Ben Kingsley; Clifford Kershaw; ***D:*** Mike Leigh. **TV**

Hard Lessons 1/2 *The George McKenna Story* **1986** Washington stars as the newly appointed principal of George Washington High in Los Angeles. The school is located in South Central, a gang and drug-infested war zone where the students are armed for their own protection. The situation appears hopeless but McKenna refuses to give up. Based on a true story. **95m/C; VHS, DVD.** Denzel Washington; Lynn Whitfield; Akosua Busia; Richard Masur; ***D:*** Eric Laneuville; ***W:*** Charles Eric Johnson; ***C:*** Isidore Mankofsky; ***M:*** Herbie Hancock. **TV**

Hard Luck **2001** Trevor "Lucky" O'Donnell's life certainly doesn't live up to his nickname. He's doing time in a mental ward when his childhood sweetheart Sheryl visits to let him know that his buddy, her brother Eric, is dying of cancer. So Lucky escapes and heads to his hometown of Gold Beach, Oregon, determined that the threesome will take one last trip together to their favorite childhood haunt. Too bad they're being pursued by Sheryl's cop husband Matt and her and Eric's dad, who just happens to be the Chief of Police. **85m/C; VHS, DVD.** Kirk Harris; Renee Humphrey; Matthew Faber; Ron Gilbert; Gareth Williams; Karen Black; Joanne Baron; Darrell Bryan; Tony Longo; Luca Bercovici; Jon Jacobs; ***D:*** Jack Rubio; ***W:*** Kirk Harris.

Hard Pill **2005** Tim (Slavin) is young, lonely, and gay—uncomfortable with the club scene and the personals. So when he learns about a new pill that claims to turn homosexuals straight, he decides to be a test case and finds himself dealing with the consequences. Debut feature for Baumgartner. **94m/C; DVD.** Jonathan Slavin; Jennifer Elise Cox; Scotch Ellis Loring; Susan Slome; Mike Begovich; Jason Bushman; John Baumgartner; ***D:*** John Baumgartner; ***W:*** John Baumgartner; ***M:*** Mike Petrone.

Hard Promises **1992 (PG)** Absence doesn't necessarily make the heart fonder, as Joey finds out when he's accidentally invited to his wife's wedding. He's been away from home for so long he doesn't even realize he's been divorced and hightails it home to win his sweetheart back. Average performances and script round out this innocuous domestic comedy-drama. **95m/C; VHS, DVD.** Sissy Spacek; William L. Petersen; Brian Kerwin; Mare Winningham; Peter MacNichol; Ann Wedgeworth; Amy Wright; Lois Smith; Rip Torn; ***D:*** Martin Davidson; ***M:*** George S. Clinton. **CABLE**

Hard Rain *Flood* **1997 (R)** Armored car guards Tom (Slater) and his uncle Charlie (Asner) are transporting $3 million to high ground during a flood in a small Indiana town. When their truck gets stuck in the mud, a band of jet-skiin' motor boatin' thieves arrive and try to steal the money. Tom hides the dough and alerts the local sheriff (Quaid) who, being your normal American elected official, decides he wants to steal it, too. Tom forms an uneasy alliance with head bad guy Jim (Freeman) to thwart the lawman and his toadies. While all this is happening, Tom manages to find love interest Karen (Driver), who's there to protect her church restoration work and wear wet blouses. And now the weather report: floods are the least cinematic disasters. Everything just gets soggy and waterlogged (especially the action sequences). Director Salomon created the huge flooded town set inside a tank in Palmdale, California. **96m/C; VHS, DVD.** Morgan Freeman; Christian Slater; Randy Quaid; Minnie Driver; Ed Asner; Richard Dysart; Betty White; Mark Rolston; Peter Murnik; Dann Florek; Wayne Duvall; Michael Goorjian; ***D:*** Mikael Salomon; ***W:*** Graham Yost; ***C:*** Peter Menzies, Jr.; ***M:*** Christopher Young.

The Hard Ride 1/2 **1971 (PG)** Above average biker movie about a Vietnam vet who brings the body of a black buddy back home, then tries to persuade the dead man's white girlfriend and the leader of his motorcycle gang to attend the funeral. **93m/C; VHS, Streaming.** Robert Fuller; Sherry Bain; Tony Russell; Marshall Reed; Biff (Elliott) Elliot; William Bonner; R.L. Armstrong; ***D:*** Burt Topper; ***W:*** Burt Topper.

Hard Rock Zombies 1/2 **1985 (R)** Four heavy metal band members die horribly on the road and are brought back from the dead as zombies. This horror/heavy metal spoof is somewhat amusing in a goofy way. **90m/C; VHS, DVD.** E.J. Curcio; Sam Mann; ***D:*** Krishna Shah; ***W:*** David Ball.

Hard Target 1/2 **1993 (R)** Van Damme continues his action-hero ways as Chance Boudreaux, a Cajun (which explains the accent) merchant seaman, who comes to the rescue of Natasha (Butler), albeit with lots of violence. Brimley provides the humor as Chance's bayou uncle. It's another variation of "The Most Dangerous Game" story but it moves. American directorial debut of over-the-top Hong Kong action director Woo who had to tone down his usual stylistic effects and repeatedly cut some of the more violent scenes to earn an "R" rating. **97m/C; VHS, DVD, Blu-Ray.** Jean-Claude Van Damme; Lance Henriksen; Yancy Butler; Arnold Vosloo; Wilford Brimley; Kasi Lemmons; Eliott Keener; Theodore (Ted) Raimi; Chuck Pfarrer; ***D:*** John Woo; ***W:*** Chuck Pfarrer; ***C:*** Russell Carpenter; ***M:*** Graeme Revell.

Hard Target 2 **2016 (R)** The action-thriller sequel to Hard Target. Wes "The Jailor" Baylor (Adkins) is mixed martial artist who was once but great retired in disgrace. When he is offered a chance at a million dollar purse to fight in Myanmar, he cannot say no. However, when he arrives, he learns that he is really the target in a human hunt. With only water and a money belt filled with rubies, he must outsmart the men carrying firearms who have paid to kill him. When Wes fights for his life in the jungle, he turns the tables and the hunters become his targets. **104m/C; DVD, Blu-Ray, Download.** Scott Adkins; Robert Knepper; Rhona Mitra; Temuera Morrison; Adam Saunders; ***D:*** Roel Reine; ***W:*** Matt Harvey; Dominic Morgan; George Huang; ***C:*** Roel Reine; ***M:*** Jack Wall. **VIDEO**

Hard Ticket to Hawaii **1987 (R)** A shot-on-video spy thriller about an agent trying to rescue a comrade in Hawaii from a smuggling syndicate. Supporting cast includes many Playboy Playmates. **96m/C; VHS, DVD, Blu-Ray.** Ron Moss; Dona Speir; Hope Marie Carlton; Cynthia Brimhall; Harold Diamond; Rodrigo Obregon; Rustam Branaman; Kwan Hi Lim; ***D:*** Andy Sidaris; ***W:*** Andy Sidaris; ***C:*** Howard Wexler; ***M:*** Gary Stockdale.

Hard Times **1975 (PG)** A Depression-era drifter becomes a bare knuckle street fighter, and a gambler decides to promote him for big stakes. One of grade-B meister Hill's first genre films. A quiet, evocative drama. **92m/C; VHS, DVD, Blu-Ray.** Charles Bronson; James Coburn; Jill Ireland; Strother Martin; ***D:*** Walter Hill; ***W:*** Walter Hill; Bryan Gindoff; Bruce Henstell; ***C:*** Philip H. Lathrop; ***M:*** Barry DeVorzon.

Hard Times 1/2 *Holy Water* **2009 (R)** Irish crime comedy filled with obvious humor. A desperate village postman and his buddies plan to steal a truckload of Viagra and peddle the pills in Amsterdam. Instead, the pills get dumped in the local well, which causes problems for everyone, including the American pharmaceutical honcho who wants the merchandise back. **96m/C; DVD.** *IR* Cornelius Clarke; John Lynch; Linda Hamilton; Cian Barry; Stanley Townsend; Susan Lynch; Tommy (Tiny) Lister; ***D:*** Tom Reeve; ***W:*** Michael O'Mahony; ***C:*** Joost van Starrenburg; ***M:*** Tom Batoy.

Hard to Be a God 1/2 *Trudno Byt Bogom* **2013** Director German's sci-fi/drama is a remarkably ambitious Russian piece that took almost six years to film, runs over three hours long, and is like nothing ever seen (and marks the filmmaker's final film before his death). The adaptation of the influential '60s novel takes place on another planet that's in the Middle Ages period of its development. A group of historians from Earth goes to observe but cannot intervene in the power struggles and downright torture they witness. A fascinating commentary on history, conflict and the ruling class, conveyed with an abundance of dirt, grime, snot and other bodily fluids. **170m/B; DVD, Blu-Ray.** *RU* Leonid Yarmolnik; Aleksandr Chutko; Yuriy Tsurilo; ***D:*** Aleksey (Alexi) German; ***W:*** Aleksey (Alexi) German; Svetlana Karmalita; ***C:*** Vladimir Ilyin; Yuri Klimenko; ***M:*** Victor Lebedev.

Hard to Forget 1/2 **1998** Private eyes Max Warner (Dutton) and Doug Hart (Campbell) are hired by grieving mother Helen Applewhite (Maxwell). Her daughter Nicky (Shannon) was supposedly killed in a boat explosion but a body was never found and someone claims to have spotted Nicky in Johannesburg. So Max heads to South Africa and takes a safari with lookalike guide Sandra. Max falls in love while trying to discover the truth. From the Harlequin Romance Series; adapted from the Evelyn Crowe novel. **95m/C; DVD.** *CA* Tim Dutton; Polly Shannon; Nicholas (Nick) Campbell; Lois Maxwell; Chad Everett; Michael McManus; ***D:*** Vic Sarin; ***W:*** Gerald Wexler; ***C:*** Buster Reynolds; ***M:*** John McCarthy. **TV**

Hard to Get 1/2 **1938** Struggling architect Bill (Powell) is working at a gas station/motel when bored heiress Margaret (de Havilland) breezes in for a fill-up and then can't pay her tab. Refusing to believe she's good for the dough, Bill infuriates Margaret by making her work off the bill with maid service. She tries getting even when she realizes Bill is angling to meet her father (Winninger) and sabotages his plans. **82m/B; DVD.** Dick Powell; Olivia de Havilland; Charles Winninger; Bonita Granville; Allen Jenkins; Thurston Hall; Isabel Jeans; Penny Singleton; ***D:*** Ray Enright; ***W:*** Maurice Leo; Jerry Wald; Richard Macaulay; ***C:*** Charles Rosher.

Hard to Handle **1933** Smalltime promoter Lefty (Cagney) wants to marry Ruth (Brian), the winner of a rigged dance marathon. Lefty's partner runs off with the proceeds, and Ruth's greedy mother Lil (Donnelly) tells Lefty to blow. It's the story of their relationship: when Lefty has dough, everything's roses, when he doesn't, it's all thorns. After a number of schemes to get Ruth back, Lefty's bank account is finally acceptable to Lil, thanks to his pushing a fad grapefruit diet (a wink at Cagney's infamous grapefruit scene in 1931's "The Public Enemy"). **78m/B; DVD.** James Cagney; Mary Brian; Ruth Donnelly; Claire Dodd; Robert McWade; ***D:*** Mervyn LeRoy; ***W:*** Robert Lord; Wilson Mizner; ***C:*** Barney McGill.

Hard to Hold 1/2 **1984 (PG)** Rockin' Rick's lukewarm film debut where he falls in love with a children's counselor after an automobile accident. Springfield sings "Love Somebody" with music by Peter Gabriel. **93m/C; VHS, DVD.** Rick Springfield; Janet Eilber; Patti Hansen; Albert Salmi; Monique Gabrielle; ***D:*** Larry Peerce.

Hard to Kill **1989 (R)** Policeman Seagal is shot and left for dead in his bedroom, but survives against the odds, though his wife does not. After seven years, he is well enough to consider evening the score with his assailants. He hides while training in martial arts for the final battle. Strong outing from Seagal, with good supporting cast. **96m/C; VHS, DVD, Blu-Ray.** Steven Seagal; Kelly Le Brock; William Sadler; Frederick Coffin; Bonnie Burroughs; Zachary Rosencrantz; Dean Norris; ***D:*** Bruce Malmuth; ***W:*** Steven McKay; ***C:*** Matthew F. Leonetti; ***M:*** Charles Fox.

Hard Vice 1/2 **1994 (R)** Vice cops Joe Owens (Jones) and Andrea Thompson (Tweed) have their work cut out for them on their Las Vegas beat. When the bodies start piling up, the prime suspects turn out to be a group of high-priced hookers. **86m/C; VHS, DVD.** Shannon Tweed; Sam Jones; James Gammon; Rebecca Ferratti; ***D:*** Joey Travolta; ***W:*** Joey Travolta; ***C:*** F. Smith Martin; ***M:*** Jeff Lass.

The Hard Way 1/2 **1943** Lupino is outstanding as driven Helen who finds all her schemes coming apart. Unhappy with her life, Helen pushes her marginally talented kid sister Katie (Leslie) towards a showbiz career, thanks to a meeting with vaudeville team Albert Runkel (Carson) and Paul Collins (Morgan). The guys break up their act because of Katie and Albert's marriage and Helen sticks with being Katie's manager, but her continual bullying leads to trouble. **108m/B; DVD.** Ida Lupino; Joan Leslie; Jack Carson; Dennis Morgan; Gladys George; Paul Cavanagh; Roman Bohnen; ***D:*** Vincent Sherman; ***W:*** Daniel Fuchs; Paul Viertel; ***C:*** James Wong Howe; ***M:*** Heinz Roemheld.

The Hard Way **1991 (R)** Hollywood superstar Fox is assigned to hardened NYC cop Woods to learn the ropes as he trains for a role. Nothing special in the way of script or direction, but Woods and Fox bring such intensity and good humor to their roles that the package works. Fox pokes fun at the LA lifestyle as the annoying, self-absorbed actor, and Marshall has an entertaining appearance as his agent. Woods is on familiar over-the-edge turf as the brittle but dedicated detective. Silly finale almost destroys the film, but other small vignettes are terrific. **91m/C; VHS, DVD.** James Woods; Michael J. Fox; Annabella Sciorra; Stephen Lang; Penny Marshall; LL Cool J; John Capodice; Christina Ricci; Karen (Lynn) Gorney; Luis Guzman; ***D:*** John Badham; ***W:*** Daniel Pyne; Lem Dobbs; ***C:*** Robert Primes; ***M:*** Arthur B. Rubinstein.

The Hard Word 1/2 **2002 (R)** Pearce is Dale, the eldest of three criminal brothers who are enticed into one last job upon their release from prison. Since they've been pulling jobs all along, thanks to a "work-release" program cooked up by their slimy lawyer, Frank Malone (Taylor), and some crooked cops, it doesn't seem like a bad idea. Problems arise when Dale finds out that Frank is setting them up, and having an affair with his femme-fatale wife Carole (Griffiths). Aussie caper flick sizzles on the strength of lived-in performances by Pearce and Griffiths, as well as a grungy feel that makes the whole thing resonate with suspicion. **102m/C; VHS, DVD.** *AU GB* Guy Pearce; Rachel Griffiths; Robert Taylor; Joel Edgerton; Damien Richardson; Rhonda Findleton; Kate Atikinson; Vince Colosimo; Paul Sonkkila; Kim Gyngell; Dorian Nkono; ***D:*** Scott Roberts; ***W:*** Scott Roberts; ***C:*** Brian J. Breheny; ***M:*** David Thrussell.

Hardball **2001 (PG-13)** Loosely based on Daniel Coyle's book "Hardball: A Season in the Projects," the plot plays like a watered down "Bad News Bears" with a dark edge. Conor O'Neill (Reeves) is a gambler who owes money all over Chicago. He asks broker pal Jimmy (McGlone) for financial help, but it comes at a cost. Jimmy has him take over a baseball team from the Cabrini-Green projects as part of his company's community outreach program. Conor and the foul-mouthed little tykes inevitably get off on the wrong foot, setting up the eventual "rag-tag bunch of misfits turn into champions" scenario. Grimmer overtones show up, however, with the realities of the projects and a tragedy that deeply affects Conor and the team. The kids' teacher Elizabeth (Lane) is the guiding influence/unfulfilled love interest. The kids, especially Griffith and Warren, steal pic from the grown-ups with their performances. **106m/C; VHS, DVD.** Keanu Reeves; Diane Lane; John Hawkes; Bryan C. Hearne; Julian Griffith; A. Delon Ellis, Jr.; DeWayne Warren; Michael B. Jordan; D.B. Sweeney; Mike McGlone; Graham Beckel; Mark Margolis; ***D:*** Brian Robbins; ***W:*** John Gatins; ***C:*** Tom Richmond; ***M:*** Mark Isham.

Hardbodies **1984 (R)** Three middle-aged men hit the beaches of Southern California in search of luscious young girls. They find them. Mid-life crisis done stupidly. Followed by a sequel. **88m/C; VHS, DVD, Blu-Ray.** Grant Cramer; Teal Roberts; Gary Wood; Michael Rapport; Sorrels Pickard; Roberta Collins; Cindy Silver; Courtney Gains; Kristi Somers; Crystal Shaw; Kathleen Kinmont; Joyce Jameson; ***D:*** Mark Griffiths; ***W:*** Eric Alter.

Hardbodies 2 **WOOF!** **1986 (R)** A sequel to the original comedy hit, dealing with film crew in Greece that is distracted by hordes of nude natives. Sophomoric humor dependent on nudity and profanity for laughs. **89m/C; VHS, DVD.** Brad Zutaut; Brenda Bakke; Fabiana Udenio; James Karen; ***D:*** Mark Griffiths; ***W:*** Eric Alter; ***M:*** Eddie Arkin.

Hardcase and Fist **1989 (R)** A framed cop leaves prison with his mind on revenge. The godfather who used him is just his first target. **92m/C; VHS, DVD.** Maureen Lavette; Ted Prior; Tony Zarindast; Christine Lunde; Carter Wang; ***D:*** Tony Zarindast; ***W:*** Tony Zarindast; Bud Fleischer; ***C:*** Robert Hayes; ***M:*** Matthew Tucciarone; Tom Tucciarone. **VIDEO**

Hardcore 1/2 *The Hardcore Life* **1979 (R)** A Midwestern businessman who is raising a strict Christian family learns of his daughter's disappearance while she is on a church trip. After hiring a streetwise investigator, he learns that his daughter has become an actress in pornographic films out in California. Strong performance by Scott and glimpse into the hardcore pornography industry prove to be convincing points of this film, though it exploits what it condemns. **106m/C; VHS, DVD, Blu-Ray.** George C. Scott; Season Hubley; Peter Boyle; Dick Sargent; *D:* Paul Schrader; *W:* Paul Schrader; *C:* Michael Chapman; *M:* Jack Nitzsche.

Hardcore Henry ✂✂ 1/2 **2015 (R)** The line between video games and action cinema is decimated in this "first-person shooter movie." Much like video games like "Call of Duty," everything in this film is seen from the POV of its titular character, a mercenary who wakes with superpower and no idea where he is. Led around by a unique character named Jimmy (Copley), Henry tries to figure out his identity, save his wife, and kill a whole lot of bad guys along the way. The result is sometimes nauseating and undeniably half-baked. Not your typical action flick but it certainly accomplishes what it sets out to do. **90m/C; DVD, Blu-Ray.** Sharlto Copley; Danila Kozlovsky; Haley Bennett; Tim Roth; Andrei Dementiev; *D:* Ilya Naishuller; *W:* Ilya Naishuller; *C:* Chris W. Johnson; Pasha Kapinos; Vsevolod Kaptur; Fedor Lyass; *M:* Darya Charusha.

The Harder They Come ✂✂ 1/2 **1972 (R)** A poor Jamaican youth becomes a success with a hit reggae record after he has turned to a life of crime out of desperation. Songs, which are blended nicely into the framework of the film, include "You Can Get It If You Really Want it" and "Sitting In Limbo." **93m/C; VHS, DVD, Blu-Ray.** *JM* Jimmy Cliff; Janet Barkley; Carl Bradshaw; Bobby Charlton; Ras Daniel Hartman; Basil Keane; Winston Stona; *D:* Perry Henzell; *W:* Perry Henzell; Trevor D. Rhone; *C:* Peter Jessop; David McDonald; *M:* Jimmy Cliff; Desmond Dekker.

The Harder They Fall ✂✂✂ **1956** A cold-eyed appraisal of the scum-infested boxing world. An unemployed reporter (Bogart in his last role) promotes a fighter for the syndicate, while doing an expose on the fight racket. Bogart became increasingly debilitated during filming and died soon afterward. Based on Budd Schulberg's novel. **109m/B; VHS, DVD.** Humphrey Bogart; Rod Steiger; Jan Sterling; Mike Lane; Max Baer, Sr.; Albert "Poppy" Popwell; *D:* Mark Robson; *W:* Philip Yordan; *C:* Burnett Guffey.

Hardware ✂ 1/2 **1990 (R)** Rag-tag ripoff in which McDermott is a post-apocalyptic garbage picker who gives girlfriend Travis some robot remains he collected (ours is not to ask why), oblivious to the fact that the tidy android was a government-spawned population controller programmed to destroy warm bodies. Seems old habits die hard, and that spells danger, danger, Will Robinson. Much violence excised to avoid x-rating. **94m/C; VHS, DVD, Blu-Ray.** Dylan McDermott; Stacey Travis; John Lynch; Iggy Pop; *D:* Richard Stanley; *M:* Simon Boswell.

Hardwired ✂ 1/2 **2009 (R)** Derivative and dull sci-fi. Luke Gibson's (Gooding Jr.) family was killed in a car crash and he nearly died as well. Awakening in a hospital with amnesia, Luke learns a microchip has been implanted in his brain by a mysterious corporation headed by Virgil (Kilmer) that is monitoring him as a human guinea pig and that has the prerequisite sinister plans for their techno breakthrough. **94m/C; DVD.** Cuba Gooding, Jr.; Val Kilmer; Tatiana Maslany; Juan Riedinger; Michael Ironside; Alastair Gamble; *D:* Ernie Barbarash; *W:* Michael Hurst; *C:* Stephen Jackson; *M:* Shaun Tozer. **VIDEO**

The Hardys Ride High ✂✂ **1939** The Hardys are in line for a two million dollar inheritance, which means moving into the deceased's Detroit mansion until the situation is resolved. Disinherited playboy Philip Westcott and his showgirl girlfriend Consuela are determined to get the dough for themselves so Consuela vamps the impressionable Andy while the others go a little money crazy. The 6th film in the series gets resolved in a more unlikely way than usual. **80m/B; DVD.** Lewis Stone; Mickey Rooney; Cecilia Parker; Fay Holden; Sara Haden; Virginia Grey; John "Dusty" King; Ann Rutherford; *D:* George B. Seitz; *W:* Kay Van Riper; Agnes Christine Johnston; William Ludwig; *C:* John Seitz; Lester White; *M:* David Snell.

Harem ✂ **1985** A beautiful stockbroker gets kidnapped by a wealthy OPEC oil minister and becomes part of his harem. Kingsley stars as the lonely sheik who longs for the love of a modern woman. **107m/C; VHS, Streaming.** *FR* Ben Kingsley; Nastassja Kinski; *D:* Arthur Joffe.

Harem ✂✂ *Harem Suare* **1999 (R)** Exotic but not particularly erotic saga of young beauty Safiye (Gillain) who is sold as a concubine to the Sultan of the Ottoman Empire. She becomes his favorite and official wife but this does not prevent her from turning to palace eunuch Nadir (Descas) for affection. Nor does it protect Safiye or the rest of the harem's women when the empire falls, the Sultan flees to Europe, and the women are abandoned to fend for themselves. Turkish, French, and Italian with subtitles. **107m/C; VHS, DVD.** *IT* Marie Gillain; Alex Descas; Valeria Golino; Lucia Bose; *D:* Ferzan Ozpetek; *W:* Ferzan Ozpetek; Gianni Romoli; *C:* Pasquale Mari; *M:* Aldo De Scalzi.

Harem Girl ✂ 1/2 **1952** B-movie comedy from Columbia Pictures. Wisecracking American Susie Perkins is hired as a companion to Princess Shareen. They return to the desert kingdom, and Susie discovers a wicked sheik wants the Princess and her oil-rich lands. Susie and Shareen's sweetie, Majeed, have other ideas. **71m/B; DVD.** Joan Davis; Peggie Castle; Donald Randolph; Paul Marion; *D:* Edward L. Bernds; *W:* Edward L. Bernds; Elwood Ullman; *C:* Lester White.

Harlan County, U.S.A. ✂✂✂✂ **1976 (PG)** The emotions of 180 coal mining families are seen up close in this classic documentary about their struggle to win a United Mine Workers contract in Kentucky. Award-winning documentary. **103m/C; VHS, DVD.** *D:* Barbara Kopple; *C:* Phil Parmet. Oscars '76: Feature Doc.; Natl. Film Reg. '90.

Harlan County War ✂✂ 1/2 **2000** Ruby Kincaid (Hunter) is the wife of striking Kentucky coal miner Silas (Levine). After a court order severely restricts the union members' protests, Ruby leads the wives into action, even allowing her arrest to be used as propaganda by union rep Warren Jakopovich (Skarsgard) to her husband's dismay. Good lead performances, although the dramatic power of the story is subdued. Inspired by Barbara Kopple's 1976 documentary, "Harlan County, U.S.A." **104m/C; VHS, DVD.** Holly Hunter; Stellan Skarsgard; Ted Levine; Wayne Robson; *D:* Tony Bill; *W:* Peter Silverman; *C:* Flavio Martinez Labiano; *M:* Van Dyke Parks. **CABLE**

Harlem Aria ✂ 1/2 **1999 (R)** Irritatingly sentimental and contrived story has mentally challenged Anton (Casseus) obsessively listening and singing to operatic tenor arias. A natural tenor himself, Anton suddenly decides to leave home and try and find a way to get to Italy. Having no street smarts, he's a target for every hustler and con in New York, including Wes (Wayans) who introduces Anton to piano-playing Matthew (Camargo) as a way to make a few bucks. **100m/C; DVD.** Gabriel Casseus; Damon Wayans; Christian Camargo; Malik Yoba; Paul Sorvino; Kristen Wilson; Nicole Parker; Eyde Byrde; *D:* William Jennings; *W:* William Jennings; *C:* Keith Smith; *M:* Jeff Beal; Fabian Cooke.

Harlem Nights ✂✂ **1989 (R)** Two Harlem nightclub owners in the 1930s battle comically against efforts by the Mob and crooked cops to take over their territory. High-grossing, although somewhat disappointing effort from Murphy, who directed, wrote, produced, and starred. **118m/C; VHS, DVD.** Eddie Murphy; Richard Pryor; Redd Foxx; Danny Aiello; Jasmine Guy; Michael Lerner; Arsenio Hall; Della Reese; Eugene Robert Glazer; Berlinda Tolbert; Stan Shaw; Lela Rochon; David Marciano; Robin Harris; Vic Polizos; Charlie (Charles Q.) Murphy; Miguel A. Nunez, Jr.; Nona Gaye; *D:* Eddie Murphy; *W:* Eddie Murphy; *C:* Woody Omens; *M:* Herbie Hancock. Golden Raspberries '89: Worst Screenplay.

Harley Davidson and the Marlboro Man ✂✂ **1991 (R)** An awful rehash of "Butch Cassidy and the Sundance Kid" with blatant vulgarity and pointless sci-fi touches. The title duo are near-future outlaws who rob a bank to save their favorite bar, then find they've stolen mob money. Some action, but it's mostly talk: lewd, meant-to-be-whimsical soul-probing chats between H.D. and M.M. that would bore even the biker crowd—and did. **98m/C; VHS, DVD, Blu-Ray.** Mickey Rourke; Don Johnson; Chelsea Field; Tom Sizemore; Vanessa L(ynne) Williams; Robert Ginty; Daniel Baldwin; Kelly Hu; *D:* Simon Wincer; *W:* Don Michael Paul; *C:* David Eggby; *M:* Basil Poledouris.

A Harlot's Progress ✂✂ **2006** In London, painter William Hogarth (Jones) meets young whore Mary Collins (Tapper) in a Covent Garden brothel, and the social critic and satirist decides to use her as his muse. In 1731, Hogarth begins a series of six paintings (those of the title) that will bring him fame and fortune, featuring Mary's miserable fate from innocent country girl to city prostitute to early death. (The paintings were later destroyed in a fire but Hogarth's engravings remain.) **100m/C; DVD.** *GB* Toby Jones; Zoe Tapper; John Castle; Geraldine James; Nicholas (Nick) Rowe; Sophie Thompson; *D:* Justin Hardy; *W:* Clive Bradley; *C:* Douglas Hartington; *M:* Richard Blair-Oliphant. **TV**

Harlow ✂✂ 1/2 **1965** The more lavish of the two Harlow biographies made in 1965, both with the same title. A sensationalized "scandal sheet" version of Jean Harlow's rise to fame that bears little resemblance to the facts of her life. **125m/C; VHS, DVD, Blu-Ray, Streaming.** Carroll Baker; Martin Balsam; Red Buttons; Mike Connors; Angela Lansbury; Peter Lawford; Raf Vallone; Leslie Nielsen; *D:* Gordon Douglas; *W:* John Michael Hayes; *C:* Joseph Ruttenberg.

The Harmonists ✂✂ **1999 (R)** Actor/singer Harry Frommermann (Noethen) is frustrated by his lack of success and decides to put together his own a cappella group—a musical sextet known as "The Comedian Harmonists," who find great success in Germany. Unfortunately, as the '20s give way to the '30s and the rise of Nazism, the group begins to run into trouble since three of its members are Jewish. Eventually, the political pressures force the group to disband and send its Jewish members into exile. German with subtitles. **114m/C; VHS, DVD.** *GE* Ulrich Noethen; Ben Becker; Heino Ferch; Heinrich Schafmeister; Max Tidof; Kai Wiesinger; Meret Becker; Katja Riemann; Dana Vavrova; *D:* Joseph Vilsmaier; *W:* Klaus Richter; *C:* Joseph Vilsmaier; *M:* Harald Kloser.

Harmony Lane ✂✂ **1935** Highly romanticised rendition of the life of American composer, Stephen Collins Foster (1826-1864). Montgomery, as Foster, manages to lend a hint of credibility to the syrupy, melodramatic script. Very little attention is given to historical fact and almost every scene is orchestrated to showcase the composer's songs. The music steals the show. **84m/B; VHS, DVD.** Douglass Montgomery; Evelyn Venable; Adrienne Ames; Joseph Cawthorn; William Frawley; Florence Roberts; Smiley Burnette; Hattie McDaniel; *D:* Joseph Santley.

Harm's Way ✂ **2007** Darlene and her daughter Victoria come to Bea's isolated farmhouse, which is supposed to be a refuge for abused women. But Bea is soon co-opting Victoria, turning her against her mother. When Darlene learns that other women have disappeared and confronts Bea, she finds the woman has murder on her mind. **83m/C; DVD.** Kathleen Quinlan; Hannah Lochner; Ingrid Kavelaars; David Sparrow; Claudia Witt; *D:* Melanie Orr; *W:* William Brent Bell; *C:* Marcus Elliott; *M:* Eric Cadesky. **VIDEO**

Harold ✂ 1/2 **2008 (PG-13)** Single joke comedy and not a funny joke at that. Thirteen-year-old Harold (Breslin) suffers from premature male-pattern baldness and acts likes somebody's elderly grandpa for no discernable reason. After moving to a new town with his family, Harold comes in for a lot of ridicule at his new school while getting advice from self-confident janitor Cromer (Gooding Jr.) **90m/C; DVD.** Spencer Breslin; Cuba Gooding, Jr.; Ally Sheedy; Nicole Blonsky; Fred Willard; Chris Parnell; Rachel Dratch; Colin Quinn; Suzanne Shepherd; Stella Maeve; *D:* T. Sean Shannon; *W:* T. Sean Shannon; Greg Fields; *C:* Christopher Levasseur; *M:* Brady Harris. **VIDEO**

Harold & Kumar Escape from Guantanamo Bay ✂✂ **2008 (R)** Scatological, un-PC stoner comedy finds amiable dopers Harold (Cho) and Kumar (Penn) in federal trouble when Kumar can't resist lighting up his homemade bong in the airplane lavatory on their Amsterdam-bound flight. The bong is mistaken for a bomb and overzealous, idiotic Homeland Security dude Fox (Corddry) is sure the boys are terrorists (can you say ethnic profiling?). So they wind up at Gitmo, where predictable humiliations follow, before escaping and going on a road trip to Texas (an amiable fake Dubya makes an appearance), where they hope Harold's well-connected pal Colton (Winter) can keep them from wearing orange jumpsuits for the rest of their days. If you liked their first buddy adventure (NPH!), this is way more of the same. **102m/C; DVD, Blu-Ray.** John Cho; Kal Penn; Rob Corddry; Jack Conley; Roger Bart; Paula Garces; Neil Patrick Harris; Missi Pyle; Danneel Harris; Eric Winter; James Adomian; Beverly D'Angelo; David Krumholtz; Eddie Kaye Thomas; Ed Helms; Clyde Kusatsu; Christopher Meloni; *D:* Jon Hurwitz; Hayden Schlossberg; *W:* Jon Hurwitz; Hayden Schlossberg; *C:* Daryn Okada; *M:* George S. Clinton.

Harold and Kumar Go to White Castle ✂✂ 1/2 **2004 (R)** Uptight junior banker Harold (Cho) and his laid-back med student pal Kumar (Penn) take the edge of encroaching adulthood by getting high. A lot. One such session produces cravings for White Castle hamburgers and sets the pair on a convoluted quest, despite Harold's need to finish an important work project. The journey is complicated by broken down vehicles, side trips for weed, creepy tow-truck drivers, skateboard punks, over-enthusiastic cops, and a hilariously Ecstacy-fueled Neil Patrick Harris. The pair's odd-couple chemistry helps smooth over the more ridiculous plot twists, and the target audience, properly medicated, should enjoy themselves long after the final credits have rolled. **96m/C; DVD, Blu-Ray, UMD.** John Cho; Kal Penn; Paula Garces; David Krumholtz; Eddie Kaye Thomas; Fred Willard; Ethan (Randall) Embry; Neil Patrick Harris; Christopher Meloni; Ryan Reynolds; Anthony Anderson; Kate Kelton; Brooke D'Orsay; *D:* Danny Leiner; *W:* Jon Hurwitz; Hayden Schlossberg; *C:* Bruce Douglas Johnson; *M:* David Kitay.

Harold and Maude ✂✂✂✂ **1971 (PG)** Cult classic pairs Cort as a deadpan disillusioned 20-year-old obsessed with suicide (his staged attempts are a highlight) and a loveable Gordon as a fun-loving 80-year-old eccentric. They meet at a funeral (a mutual hobby), and develop a taboo romantic relationship, in which they explore the tired theme of the meaning of life with a fresh perspective. The script was originally the 20-minute long graduate thesis of UCLA student Higgins, who showed it to his landlady, Mildred Lewis, who was the wife of a producer and helped him get it made. Features music by the pre-Islamic Cat Stevens. **92m/C; VHS, DVD, Blu-Ray.** Ruth Gordon; Bud Cort; Cyril Cusack; Vivian Pickles; Charles Tyner; Ellen Geer; Eric Christmas; G(eorge) Wood; Gordon Devol; *D:* Hal Ashby; *W:* Colin Higgins; *C:* John A. Alonzo; *M:* Cat Stevens. Natl. Film Reg. '97.

Harold Robbins' Body Parts ✂✂ *Body Parts; Vital Parts* **1999 (R)** An unsurprising formula revenge flick. Ty Kinnick (Grieco) is double-crossed by his best friend (Stewart) and wife (Massey) during a drug deal. Five years later, he's back and finds that the intrigues are still being played out. **87m/C; DVD.** Richard Grieco; Will Foster Stewart; Athena Massey; *D:* Craig Corman; *W:* Craig Corman.

Harper ✂✂✂ *The Moving Target* **1966** A tight, fast-moving genre piece about cynical LA private eye Lew Harper (Newman) who is hired by Mrs. Sampson (Bacall) to investigate the disappearance of her wealthy husband. Along the way he gets involved with an aging actress (Winter), a junkie singer (Harris), a religious nut (Martin), and a smuggling operation. From the Ross McDonald novel "The Moving Target." Later sequelled in "The Drowning Pool." **121m/C; VHS, DVD, Blu-Ray.** Paul Newman; Shelley Winters; Lauren Bacall; Julie Harris; Robert Wagner; Janet Leigh; Arthur Hill; Pamela Tiffin; *D:* Jack Smight; *W:* William Goldman; *C:* Conrad L. Hall; *M:* Johnny Mandel.

Harper Valley P.T.A. ✂✂ **1978 (PG)** Eden raises hell in Harper Valley after the PTA questions her parental capabilities.

Brain candy was adapted from a hit song; TV series followed. **93m/C; VHS, DVD.** Barbara Eden; Nanette Fabray; Louis Nye; Pat Paulsen; Ronny Cox; Ron Masak; Audrey Christie; John Fiedler; Bob Hastings; ***D:*** Richard Bennett; ***W:*** Barry Schneider.

Harrad Experiment 🦴 1/2 **1973 (R)** Adaptation of Robert Rimmer's love-power bestseller in which an experiment-minded college establishes a campus policy of sexual freedom. Famous for the Hedren/Johnson relationship, shortly before Johnson married Hedren's real-life daughter Melanie Griffith. Followed by "The Harrad Summer." **98m/C; VHS, DVD.** James Whitmore; Tippi Hedren; Don Johnson; Bruno Kirby; Laurie Walters; Victoria Thompson; Elliot Street; Sharon Taggart; Robert Middleton; Billy (Billie) Sands; Melanie Griffith; ***D:*** Ted Post; ***W:*** Ted Cassedy; Michael Werner; ***C:*** Richard H. Kline; ***M:*** Artie Butler.

Harrad Summer 🦴🦴 **1974 (R)** Sequel to "The Harrad Experiment." College coeds take their sex-education to the bedroom where they can apply their knowledge by more intensive means. **103m/C; VHS, DVD.** Richard Doran; Victoria Thompson; Laurie Walters; Robert Reiser; Bill Dana; Marty Allen; Angela (Clark) Clarke; ***D:*** Steven Hilliard Stern.

Harriet 🦴🦴 1/2 **2019 (PG-13)** Tiny but fierce Cynthia Erivo expertly portrays Harriet Tubman, the slave turned freedom fighter who organized the Underground Railroad and freed hundreds of slaves in 19th century America. The story is inspiring and the action thrilling, but the formulaic treatment by the screenplay ensures that the film never quite rises to the anthemic level the subject deserves. **125m/C; DVD, Blu-Ray.** Cynthia Erivo; Leslie Odom, Jr.; Janelle Monáe; Joe Alwyn; Clarke Peters; ***D:*** Kasi Lemmons; ***W:*** Kasi Lemmons; Gregory Allen Howard; ***C:*** John Toll; ***M:*** Terence Blanchard.

Harriet the Spy 🦴🦴 1/2 **1996 (PG)** Sixth-grade, 11-year-old tomboy Harriet M. Welsch (Trachtenberg) spies on everyone around her and, encouraged by her nanny Ole Golly (O'Donnell), writes down everything going on in her secret notebook, because she's determined to become a great writer. Unfortunately, Harriet's imagination sometimes gets the best of her and when her notebook is found, her friends and family are not too happy about its contents. Based on the award-winning novel by Louise Fitzhugh. Lovers of the book may not be enthusiastic about some of the changes but generally it's enjoyable fare. **102m/C; VHS, DVD.** Michelle Trachtenberg; Rosie O'Donnell; Vanessa Lee Chester; Gregory Edward Smith; Robert Joy; Eartha Kitt; J. Smith-Cameron; ***D:*** Bronwen Hughes; ***W:*** Douglas Petrie; Theresa Rebeck; ***C:*** Francis Kenny; ***M:*** Jamshield Sharifi.

Harriet the Spy: Blog Wars 🦴🦴 1/2 **2010** Disney Channel movie based on the Louise Fitzhugh character. Teenaged Harriet is still spying—this time in preparation for her writing career. She wants to become the class blogger at her private school but is competing with gossip queen Marion. When Harriet's film producer father starts working on a teen movie with heartthrob Skander Hill, Harriet turns paparazzi and reveals too much for comfort's sake on the Internet (not all of it true). **87m/C; DVD.** Jennifer Stone; Vanessa Morgan; Wesley Morgan; Kristin Booth; Doug Murray; Jayne (Jane) Eastwood; Shauna Macdonald; ***D:*** Ron Oliver; ***W:*** Alexandra Clarke; Steve Hollar; ***C:*** Alwyn Kumst; ***M:*** Trevor Yuile. **CABLE**

Harrison's Flowers 🦴🦴 **2002 (R)** Sometimes goopy, sometimes harrowing story of a naive woman searching for her missing husband. Newsweek photojournalist Harrison Lloyd (Strathairn) promises wife Sarah (MacDowell) that his '91 assignment to Yugoslavia (at the beginning of the Balkan conflict) will be his last. Maybe in more ways than one, since he's reported missing, which Sarah doesn't believe. So she's takes off for Croatia and promptly gets a hard lesson in the confusion of war. Fellow correspondents Kyle (Brody), Stevenson (Gleeson), and Yeager (Koteas) agree to help Sarah even though they think she's nuts. Watch the guys, particularly Brody, since all MacDowell has to do is alternate between noble, frightened, and stubborn. **122m/C; VHS, DVD.** *FR* Andie MacDowell; David Strathairn; Elias Koteas; Adrien Brody; Brendan Gleeson; Alun Armstrong; Caroline Goodall; Diane Baker; Gerard Butler; Marie Trintignant; ***D:*** Elie Chouraqui; ***W:*** Elie Chouraqui; Didier Le Pecheur; Isabel Ellsen; ***C:*** Nicola Pecorini; ***M:*** Cliff Eidelman.

Harry and Max 🦴 **2004** Harry (Johnson) is a teenage pretty boy in a pop band, his brother Max (Williams) is a slightly younger pretty boy model. They're jealous of one another, and steal one another's sex partners, one being a quite older adult yoga teacher (Gilroy). While there is never any real sex or nudity on screen, one has to wonder what kind of audience this movie meant to please. Truly awful, in spite of cast's dire attempts to inject some believability into the absurd story. **74m/C; DVD.** Bryce Johnson; Cole Williams; Rain Phoenix; Tom Gilroy; Michelle Phillips; Katherine Ellis; Justin Zachery; Roni Deitz; ***D:*** Christopher Munch; ***W:*** Christopher Munch; ***C:*** Rob Sweeney; ***M:*** Michael Tubbs.

Harry and Snowman 🦴🦴🦴 1/2 **2016** Feature-length documentary centered on the true story of a man and a horse that unexpectedly won the triple crown of show jumping in mid-twentieth century America. After World War II, Harry deLeyer immigrated from the Netherlands to the United States. In the years after his arrival, he bought a broken down Amish plow horse for $80 at a horse auction. He saved the animal from the slaughter truck. This choice changed both their lives as within two years, the pair won the triple crown of show jumping over pedigree horses. Gaining fame, Harry and the horse he named Snowman traveled the world. Their story is told in interviews by Harry himself. **84m/C; DVD, Blu-Ray, Streaming, Download.** ***D:*** Ron Davis; ***W:*** Ron Davis; ***C:*** Clay Westervelt; ***M:*** Elik Alvarez; Joel Goodman.

Harry & Son 🦴🦴 **1984 (PG)** A widowed construction worker faces the problems of raising his son. Newman is miscast as the old man and we've all seen Benson play the young role too many times. **117m/C; VHS, Blu-Ray, Streaming.** Paul Newman; Robby Benson; Ellen Barkin; Wilford Brimley; Judith Ivey; Ossie Davis; Morgan Freeman; Joanne Woodward; ***D:*** Paul Newman; ***M:*** Henry Mancini.

Harry and the Hendersons 🦴🦴 1/2 **1987 (PG)** Ordinary American family vacationing in the Northwest has a collision with Bigfoot. Thinking that the big guy is dead, they throw him on top of the car and head home. Lo and behold, he revives and starts wrecking the furniture and in the process, endears himself to the at-first frightened family. Nice little tale efficiently told, with Lithgow fine as the frustrated dad trying to hold his Bigfoot-invaded home together. Basis for the TV series. **111m/C; VHS, DVD, Blu-Ray.** John Lithgow; Melinda Dillon; Don Ameche; David Suchet; Margaret Langrick; Joshua Rudoy; Kevin Peter Hall; Lainie Kazan; M. Emmet Walsh; John Bloom; ***D:*** William Dear; ***W:*** William Dear; William E. Martin; Ezra D. Rappaport; ***C:*** Allen Daviau; ***M:*** Bruce Broughton. Oscars '87: Makeup.

Harry and Tonto 🦴🦴🦴 **1974** A gentle comedy about an energetic septuagenarian who takes a cross-country trip with his cat, Tonto. Never in a hurry, still capable of feeling surprise and joy, he makes new friends and visits old lovers. Carney deserved his Oscar. Mazursky has seldom been better. **115m/C; VHS, DVD.** Art Carney; Ellen Burstyn; Larry Hagman; Geraldine Fitzgerald; Chief Dan George; Arthur Hunnicutt; Josh Mostel; Cliff DeYoung; Philip Bruns; Rene Enriquez; Herbert Berghof; Michael (Mick) McCleery; Melanie Mayron; Michael C. Butler; ***Cameo(s):*** Paul Mazursky; ***D:*** Paul Mazursky; ***W:*** Paul Mazursky; ***C:*** Michael C. Butler; ***M:*** Bill Conti. Oscars '74: Actor (Carney); Golden Globes '75: Actor--Mus./Comedy (Carney).

Harry & Walter Go to New York 🦴🦴 **1976 (PG)** At the turn of the century, two vaudeville performers are hired by a crooked British entrepreneur for a wild crime scheme. The cast and crew try their hardest, but it's not enough to save this boring comedy. The vaudeville team of Caan and Gould perhaps served as a model for Beatty and Hoffman in "Ishtar." **111m/C; VHS, DVD, Blu-Ray.** James Caan; Elliott Gould; Michael Caine; Diane Keaton; Burt Young; Jack Gilford; Charles Durning; Lesley Ann Warren; Carol Kane; ***D:*** Mark Rydell; ***W:*** John Byrum; ***M:*** David Shire.

Harry Brown 🦴🦴 **2009 (R)** Plays like "Get Carter" nearly 40 years later. Stoic, elderly Harry (Caine) is a retired soldier and recent widower who lives in a bleak and violence-ridden London housing estate. When local drug-dealing punks make the mistake of killing Harry's friend Leonard (Bradley) and police efforts are futile, Harry decides to put his Royal Marine experiences to effective use. Barber doesn't ignore the age-related frailties of Caine's Harry, but cunning over youthful stupidity goes a long way. **103m/C; Blu-Ray, On Demand.** *GB* Michael Caine; Emily Mortimer; Charlie Creed-Miles; Liam Cunningham; Iain Glen; David Bradley; Jack O'Connell; Ben Drew; ***D:*** Daniel Barber; ***W:*** Gary Young; ***C:*** Martin Ruhe; ***M:*** Martin Phipps; Ruth Barrett.

Harry in Your Pocket 🦴 1/2 **1973** Pickpocketing duo Harry (Coburn) and Casey (Pidgeon) employ younger Ray (Sarrazin) and Sandy (Van Devere) to distract their marks. Ray gets ambitious as well as jealous of Harry's interest in Sandy, so he turns to aging, coke-sniffing Casey to be his mentor. **103m/C; DVD, Blu-Ray.** James Coburn; Walter Pidgeon; Michael Sarrazin; Trish Van Devere; ***D:*** Bruce Geller; ***W:*** Ronald Austin; ***C:*** Fred W. Koenekamp; ***M:*** Lalo Schifrin.

Harry Potter and the Chamber of Secrets 🦴🦴🦴 1/2 **2002 (PG)** Action-packed sequel tops its predecessor with less exposition and more adventure as Harry (Radcliffe) and his friends at Hogwarts try to discover the force that's terrorizing the school. In his second year at school, the young (but obviously growing) wizard reteams with fellow school chums Ron (Grint) and Hermione (Watson) to brave new dangers posed by the Chamber of Secrets, which may lie somewhere in the halls of the school, unbeknownst to professors Rickman, Smith, and even headmaster Harris. Everything about this outing is bigger and better, including a delightfully expanded, labyrinthine Hogwarts. Sometimes over-the-top thrills may be a lot for younger viewers. Book two in Rowling's series. **161m/C; VHS, DVD, Blu-Ray, HD-DVD.** Daniel Radcliffe; Rupert Grint; Emma Watson; Kenneth Branagh; Robbie Coltrane; Richard Harris; Maggie Smith; John Cleese; Jason Isaacs; Tom Felton; Alan Rickman; Warwick Davis; Richard Griffiths; Fiona Shaw; Julie Walters; Shirley Henderson; Mark Williams; Julian Glover; Miriam Margolyes; Christian Coulson; Gemma Jones; David Bradley; Bonnie Wright; ***V:*** Toby Jones; ***D:*** Chris Columbus; ***W:*** Steve Kloves; ***C:*** Roger Pratt; ***M:*** John Williams.

Harry Potter and the Deathly Hallows, Part 1 🦴🦴🦴 **2010 (PG-13)** It's the beginning of the end as Rowling's seventh and final book in the saga was divided into two films. As the trio of Harry (Radcliffe), Hermione (Watson), and Ron (Grint) approaches adulthood they are forced to venture away from the confines of Hogwarts in search of the Horcruxes, which are the secret to Voldemort's (Fiennes) power, even as the Death Eaters seize control of Hogwarts and the Ministry of Magic. But the stress of being out in the world alone to find them, then figuring out how to destroy them, all while outrunning various attacks puts an unforeseen strain on their friendship. By far the gloomiest and most suspenseful of the series as the climactic ending looms. Not for Muggle nonbelievers. **146m/C; Blu-Ray.** *GB US* Daniel Radcliffe; Emma Watson; Rupert Grint; Ralph Fiennes; Helena Bonham Carter; Bill Nighy; John Hurt; Alan Rickman; Tom Felton; Jason Isaacs; Michael Gambon; Ciaran Hinds; Maggie Smith; Bonnie Wright; Brendan Gleeson; Robbie Coltrane; David Thewlis; Miranda Richardson; Imelda Staunton; Jamie Campbell Bower; Rhys Ifans; Warwick Davis; Evanna Lynch; Dave Legeno; Natalia Tena; Stanislav Ianevski; Richard Griffiths; Matthew Lewis; George Harris; Chris Rankin; ***D:*** David Yates; ***W:*** Steve Kloves; ***C:*** Eduardo Serra; ***M:*** Alexandre Desplat; Matt Biffa.

Harry Potter and the Deathly Hallows, Part 2 🦴🦴🦴 1/2 **2011 (PG-13)** The screen version of J.K. Rowling's wizard saga (10 years, eight movies, and an enormous cast) finds fitting and bittersweet closure—and in 3D no less. Harry (Radcliffe) must finally confront and defeat his ultimate enemy, Lord Voldemort (Fiennes), when he, Ron (Grint), and Hermione (Watson) return to Hogwarts to destroy the final horcruxes. Part 2 is more action-packed, with favorite characters given moments to shine, though others are seen only briefly as director Yates and screenwriter Kloves have taken some necessary liberties to move things along. Even those who've read the book and know how things turn out will be caught up in the tension and emotion of this blockbuster. **131m/C; DVD, Blu-Ray, On Demand.** *GB* Daniel Radcliffe; Ralph Fiennes; Emma Watson; Rupert Grint; Robbie Coltrane; Helena Bonham Carter; Michael Gambon; Jason Issacs; Tom Felton; Alan Rickman; David Thewlis; Gary Oldman; Ciaran Hinds; Warwick Davis; Emma Thompson; John Hurt; Bill Nighy; Maggie Smith; Bonnie Wright; Helen McCrory; ***D:*** David Yates; ***W:*** Steve Kloves; ***C:*** Eduardo Serra; ***M:*** Alexandre Desplat. British Acad. '11: Visual FX.

Harry Potter and the Goblet of Fire 🦴🦴🦴 1/2 **2005 (PG-13)** If you aren't already swept up in the book-turned-film craze created by Rowling, this film might just do it. Harry (Radcliffe) and his trusty pals Ron (Grint) and Hermione (Watson), now teens in their fourth year at Hogwarts, battle the forces of evil that swirl around Harry's mysterious past. Lord Voldemort makes a showing, and new character Mad Eye Moody (Gleeson) joins forces with the good guys to help Harry compete in the frightening and dangerous Tri-Wizard Tournament. Special effects are even better than the previous three films—old fans won't be disappointed; new fans will want to play catch-up. **157m/C; DVD, Blu-Ray, UMD, HD-DVD.** Daniel Radcliffe; Rupert Grint; Emma Watson; Robbie Coltrane; Ralph Fiennes; Michael Gambon; Brendan Gleeson; Jason Isaacs; Gary Oldman; Miranda Richardson; Alan Rickman; Maggie Smith; Timothy Spall; Frances de la Tour; Pedja Bjelac; David Bradley; Warwick Davis; Tom Felton; Robert Hardy; Shirley Henderson; Roger Lloyd-Pack; Mark Williams; Stanislav Ianevski; Robert Pattinson; Clarence Poesy; David Tennant; James Phelps; Oliver Phelps; Bonnie Wright; Katie Leung; Matthew Lewis; Afshan Azad; Shefali Chowhury; ***D:*** Mike Newell; ***W:*** Steve Kloves; ***C:*** Roger Pratt; ***M:*** Patrick Doyle.

Harry Potter and the Half-Blood Prince 🦴🦴 1/2 **2009 (PG)** The sixth Potter adventure lays the groundwork for the final two films (since Rowling's seventh book is being broken down into two parts) with Harry (Radcliffe) accompanying mentor Dumbledore (Gambon) to recruit retired potions professor Horace Slughorn (Broadbent) back to Hogwarts because Dumbledore wants to know how former star pupil Tom Riddle became Voldemort. Meanwhile, reptilian Severus Snape (Rickman) becomes allied with Voldemort recruit Draco Malfoy (Felton). Teen hormones also rage when Harry finds himself interested in his best friend Ron's sister, Ginny (Wright), while Hermione (Watson) pines for an oblivious Ron (Grint), who's dating Lavender Brown (Cave). As usual, Radcliffe gets stuck with the part of the rather dull straight man with a very colorful (and large) crowd surrounding him. **153m/C; Blu-Ray, On Demand.** Daniel Radcliffe; Emma Watson; Rupert Grint; Michael Gambon; Alan Rickman; Jim Broadbent; Helena Bonham Carter; Robbie Coltrane; Maggie Smith; David Thewlis; Tom Felton; Bonnie Wright; Julie Walters; Mark Williams; Helen McCrory; Fiona Shaw; Jessie Cave; Richard Griffiths; Timothy Spall; David Bradley; Warwick Davis; ***D:*** David Yates; ***W:*** Steve Kloves; ***C:*** Bruno Delbonnel; ***M:*** Nicholas Hooper.

Harry Potter and the Order of the Phoenix 🦴🦴 **2007 (PG-13)** Warner Brothers turned to Yates, their least recognizable director yet, for this fifth chapter of the Potter series and, regrettably, he doesn't bring much to the table. Angsty Potter (Radcliffe) returns to Hogwarts to discover that most of the wizarding world doesn't believe him about the Dark Lord's return, so he begins training his school chums in wizard-on-wizard combat under the nose of Ministry stooge Dolores Umbridge (Staunton). It's all quite dark and moody, but the story is nearly incomprehensible, and Yates bungles most of the sequences that made the book so much fun to read. **139m/C; DVD, Blu-Ray, HD-DVD.** Daniel Radcliffe; Emma Watson; Rupert Grint; Michael Gambon; Alan Rickman; Gary

Oldman; Imelda Staunton; Jason Isaacs; Ralph Fiennes; Helena Bonham Carter; David Thewlis; Robbie Coltrane; Fiona Shaw; Maggie Smith; Emma Thompson; Brendan Gleeson; Tom Felton; Katie Leung; Richard Griffiths; Julie Walters; Evanna Lynch; Mark Williams; Bonnie Wright; Warwick Davis; Robert Hardy; David Bradley; ***D:*** David Yates; ***W:*** Michael Goldberg; ***C:*** Slawomir Idziak; ***M:*** Nicholas Hooper.

Harry Potter and the Prisoner of Azkaban 1/2 **2004 (PG)** Harry's back at Hogwarts, but he's still dealing with evil entities trying to kill him. Sirius Black (Oldman), a rogue wizard and convicted murderer has escaped from Azkaban Prison. Harry also has to deal with the onset of puberty and the trials of being a teenager. Michael Gambon takes over the role of Dumbledore from the late Richard Harris. Cuaron is more faithful to the spirit of the books, driven more by emotion and feeling, and less by the marketing department. Cuaron was author J.K. Rowling's choice to direct the franchise from the start. **141m/C; DVD, Blu-Ray, HD-DVD.** Daniel Radcliffe; Emma Watson; Rupert Grint; Michael Gambon; Gary Oldman; Robbie Coltrane; Alan Rickman; Maggie Smith; Julie Walters; David Thewlis; Tom Felton; Emma Thompson; Julie Christie; Timothy Spall; ***D:*** Alfonso Cuarón; ***W:*** Steve Kloves; ***C:*** Michael Seresin; ***M:*** John Williams.

Harry Potter and the Sorcerer's Stone *Harry Potter and the Philosopher's Stone* **2001 (PG)** Much-anticipated screen adaptation of J.K. Rowling's first book about a Dickensian orphan who discovers his wizardly legacy, didn't disappoint its legions of built-in fans. Director Columbus remains painstakingly faithful to the book, although film plays, understandably, like a highlights version and sometimes lacks any personality of its own. This may have been intentional (directors Steven Spielberg and Terry Gilliam were perhaps passed over because their personal stamp would override the material), and it doesn't detract from the outstanding production and captivating storytelling. Stellar all-Brit cast is fun to watch, and the special effects are what you'd expect given a $125-million budget and use of no less than nine effects houses. Even those not familiar with the book will enjoy the film's many charms. Good mix of entertainment for kids and adults, although a bit long for the very young. **152m/C; VHS, DVD, Blu-Ray, UMD, HD-DVD.** Daniel Radcliffe; Rupert Grint; Emma Watson; Robbie Coltrane; Richard Harris; Maggie Smith; Zoe Wanamaker; Alan Rickman; Ian Hart; John Hurt; Tom Felton; Harry Melling; Richard Griffiths; Fiona Shaw; John Cleese; Warwick Davis; Julie Walters; Sean Biggerstaff; David Bradley; Matthew Lewis; ***D:*** Chris Columbus; ***W:*** Steve Kloves; ***C:*** John Seale; ***M:*** John Williams.

Harry Tracy 1/2 *Harry Tracy—Desperado* **1983 (PG)** Whimsical tale of the legendary outlaw whose escapades made him both a wanted criminal and an exalted folk hero. **111m/C; VHS, DVD.** *CA* Bruce Dern; Gordon Lightfoot; Helen Shaver; Michael C. Gwynne; ***D:*** William A. Graham; ***C:*** Allen Daviau.

Harry's War **1984 (PG)** A middle-class, middle-aged American declares military war on the IRS in this overdone comedy. **98m/C; VHS, DVD.** Edward Herrmann; Geraldine Page; Karen Grassle; David Ogden Stiers; ***D:*** Keith Merrill.

Harsh Times **2005 (R)** Bale's truly scary as Jim Davis, a haunted Gulf War vet who drinks and drugs too much, which only exacerbates his natural volatility. Jim also manages to drag best bud, weak-willed Mike (Rodriguez), into his twilight life, which takes a crazy turn when, after being turned down by the LAPD, Jim is offered a job with Homeland Security. But it's in Colombia, which means choosing between work and love with his Mexican honey (Trull). Since writer/director Ayer also wrote "Training Day," you know this isn't going to end well. **119m/C; DVD, HD-DVD.** Christian Bale; Freddy Rodriguez; Eva Longoria; Terry Crews; Tammy Trull; J.K. Simmons; Noel Guglielmi; ***D:*** David Ayer; ***W:*** David Ayer; ***C:*** Steve Mason; ***M:*** Graeme Revell.

Hart's War 1/2 **2002 (R)** Willis is leathery Col. McNamara, ranking U.S. POW officer in a German stalag who clashes with newly imprisoned Lt. Thomas Hart (Farrell), Yale law student and son of a U.S. Senator. Hart is recruited to lead a court martial proceeding against African-American prisoner Scott (Howard), accused of killing racist fellow prisoner Bedford (Hauser). McNamara seems to have ulterior motives for this court martial, however, and seems to be undermining Hart at every turn. Howard shines as the accused who doesn't even begin to expect a fair trial, and Iures is brilliant as the urbane, Yankee culture loving German Col. Visser, who also happens to be a Yale alum. Beautiful cinematography helps offset occasional heavy-handed direction and, at times, overwrought plot. **128m/C; VHS, DVD, Blu-Ray.** Bruce Willis; Colin Farrell; Terrence Howard; Cole Hauser; Marcel Iures; Linus Roache; Rory Cochrane; Michael Weston; Vicellous Shannon; Scott Michael Campbell; Adrian Grenier; Jonathan Brandis; Joe Spano; Sam Worthington; ***D:*** Gregory Hoblit; ***W:*** Billy Ray; Terry George; ***C:*** Alar Kivilo; ***M:*** Rachel Portman.

Harum Scarum *Harem Holiday* **1965** Elvis tune-fest time! When a movie star (Presley) travels through the Middle East, he becomes involved in an attempted assassination of the king and falls in love with his daughter. He also sings at the drop of a veil: "Shake That Tambourine," "Harem Holiday," and seven others. **95m/C; VHS, DVD.** Elvis Presley; Mary Ann Mobley; Fran Jeffries; Michael Ansara; Billy Barty; Theo Marcuse; Jay Novello; ***D:*** Gene Nelson; ***W:*** Gerald Drayson Adams; ***C:*** Fred H. Jackman, Jr.; ***M:*** Fred Karger.

Harvard Man 1/2 **2001 (R)** Dropping a metric ton of acid while getting chased by the Mafia and the FBI: it's all just a day in the life of Harvard student Alan Jensen (Grenier). Meanwhile, the busy scholar/basketball player is also juggling two girlfriends: a mobster's daughter/cheerleader (Gellar), and older philosophy professor (Adams), as well as the throwing of a basketball game. Stoltz and Gayheart play the mobster's bookies with a twist. Inspired by his own '60s acid trip, director Toback's modern coming-of-age comedy is long on mayhem-inspired action and dialogue but short on characters to care about and isn't as fun as it sounds. The all-too-real depiction of a bad trip alone, however, is worth a look. **100m/C; VHS, DVD.** Adrian Grenier; Sarah Michelle Gellar; Joey Lauren Adams; Eric Stoltz; Rebecca Gayheart; Gianni Russo; Ray Allen; Michael Aparo; Al Franken; ***D:*** James Toback; ***W:*** James Toback; ***C:*** David Ferrara; ***M:*** Ryan Shore.

The Harvest 1/2 **1992 (R)** Sultry temptress Leilani sends Miguel's internal thermometer into convulsions with her preference for ice during lovemaking. However, their tryst turns sour (for him) when she takes Miguel to the beach where mystery thugs beat him unconscious and swipe his kidney. Bizarre story sure to ignite a small cult following. **97m/C; VHS, DVD.** Miguel Ferrer; Leilani Sarelle Ferrer; Harvey Fierstein; Anthony John (Tony) Denison; Tim Thomerson; Matt Clark; Henry Silva; ***D:*** David Marconi; ***W:*** David Marconi; ***M:*** Rick Boston.

Harvest **2010 (R)** Well-acted family drama. College senior Josh Winters spends his summer unexpectedly playing peacemaker when he heads to his family's Connecticut beach house. His grandfather Siv is dying, grandmother Yetta has dementia and is being looked after by caregiver Rosita, and Josh's divorced mom Anna and her two constantly bickering brothers, Carmine and Benny, are at odds over how to handle what's happening. For the last time, Siv wants them to forgive and forget and remember what's most important. **110m/C; DVD.** Jack Carpenter; Robert Loggia; Barbara Barrie; Victoria Clark; Arye Gross; Peter Friedman; Christine Evangelista; Adrianna Sevan; ***D:*** Marc Meyers; ***W:*** Marc Meyers; ***C:*** Ruben O'Malley; ***M:*** David Poe; Duncan Sheik. **VIDEO**

Harvest *Stadt Land Fluss; City, Country, River* **2011** Teens studying agriculture are given hands-on experience through an apprenticeship program at a farm in rural Germany. Sullen and solitary Marko is close to his final exams, although he doesn't seem particularly interested in agricultural life until Jacob arrives. The affable, enthusiastic apprentice makes a point to befriend Marko, leading to some unexpected romantic moments, but writer/director Cantu's story meanders to somewhat limited purpose. Except for the two leads, the rest of the cast are amateurs. German with subtitles. **88m/C; DVD.** *GE* Lukas Steltner; Kai Michael Muller; Karin Butsch; ***D:*** Benjamin Cantu; ***W:*** Benjamin Cantu; ***C:*** Alexander Gheorghiu; ***M:*** Keith Keniff.

Harvest of Fire 1/2 **1995 (PG)** A close-knit Amish farming community in Iowa has been the target of a series of barn burnings, which come under the investigation of FBI agent Sally Russell (Davidovich). But the community doesn't want an outsider around and Sally needs some help, which she finds with Amish widow Annie Beiler (Duke). And gradually the disparate duo find some common ground. A Hallmark Hall of Frame presentation. **90m/C; VHS, DVD.** Patty Duke; Lolita Davidovich; J.A. Preston; Jean Louisa Kelly; Tom Aldredge; James Read; Craig Wasson; ***D:*** Arthur Allan Seidelman; ***W:*** Richard Alfieri; ***C:*** Neil Roach; ***M:*** Lee Holdridge. **TV**

The Harvesters 1/2 **2019** In South Africa's Free State province, 15-year-old Janno (a compelling Vermeulen) fulfills his duties on his Afrikaner family's farm but his desire to love and be loved by his family often leads to hurt feelings. The situation grows more complicated with the arrival of cocky Pieter (van Dyk), a streetwise orphan who is the same age as Janno. Though Janno's parents hope they will become brothers, Pieter fundamentally changes how Janno views the world. The moody film explores the duality of toxic masculinity and latent homosexuality through a coming of age story. Afrikaans with subtitles. **102m/C; DVD, Blu-Ray.** Brent Vermeulen; Alex van Dyk; Juliana Venter; Morné Visser; Erica Wessels; ***D:*** Etienne Kallos; ***W:*** Etienne Kallos; ***C:*** Michal Englert; ***M:*** Evgueni Galperine; Sacha Galperine.

Harvey 1/2 **1950** Straightforward version of the Mary Chase play about a friendly drunk with an imaginary six-foot rabbit friend named Harvey, and a sister who tries to have him committed. A fondly remembered, charming comedy. Hull is a standout, well deserving her Oscar. **104m/B; VHS, DVD, Blu-Ray.** James Stewart; Josephine Hull; Victoria Horne; Peggy Dow; Cecil Kellaway; Charles Drake; Jesse White; Wallace Ford; Nana Bryant; ***D:*** Henry Koster; ***W:*** Oscar Brodney; ***C:*** William H. Daniels; ***M:*** Frank Skinner. Oscars '50: Support. Actress (Hull); Golden Globes '51: Support. Actress (Hull).

The Harvey Girls **1946** Lightweight musical about a restaurant chain that sends its waitresses to work in the Old West. **102m/C; VHS, DVD.** Judy Garland; Ray Bolger; John Hodiak; Preston Foster; Angela Lansbury; Virginia O'Brien; Marjorie Main; Chill Wills; Kenny L. Baker; Selena Royle; Cyd Charisse; ***D:*** George Sidney; ***C:*** George J. Folsey; ***M:*** Harry Warren; Johnny Mercer. Oscars '46: Song ("On the Atchison, Topeka and Santa Fe").

Has Anybody Seen My Gal? **1952** It's the first film collaboration between director Sirk and Hudson, but the actor only has a small role as the soda jerk romantic interest of pretty Millicent (Laurie) in this light family comedy. Wealthy, meddling Samuel Fulton (Coburn) decides to leave his money to his long-ago love Harriet (Bari), after first giving the Blaisdells a large sum to see how they'll react. Ambitious Harriet tries some social climbing, but the rest of the family isn't happy with their new life. **88m/C; DVD.** Charles Coburn; Lynn Bari; Piper Laurie; Larry Gates; William Reynolds; Gigi Perreau; Rock Hudson; Skip Homeier; ***D:*** Douglas Sirk; ***W:*** Joseph Hoffman; ***C:*** Clifford A. Stone; ***M:*** Herman Stein.

Hatari! **1962** An adventure-loving team of professional big game hunters ventures to East Africa to round up animals for zoos around the world. Led by Wayne, they get into a couple of scuffs along the way, including one with lady photographer Martinelli who is doing a story on the expedition. Extraordinary footage of Africa and the animals brought to life by a fantastic musical score. **158m/C; VHS, DVD, Blu-Ray.** John Wayne; Elsa Martinelli; Red Buttons; Hardy Kruger; Gerard Blain; Bruce Cabot; ***D:*** Howard Hawks; ***W:*** Leigh Brackett; ***C:*** Russell Harlan; ***M:*** Henry Mancini.

Hatchet 1/2 **2007 (R)** Graphically gory slasher pic filmed in New Orleans. Clueless Mardi Gras tourists take a nighttime boat tour of a swamp that's haunted by the deformed and deadly Victor Crowley (Hodder). Writer/director Green then dispatches his interchangeable victims with a knowing humor about horror conventions. **84m/C; DVD, Blu-Ray.** Joel David Moore; Tamara Feldman; Kane Hodder; Deon Richmond; Mercedes McNab; Parry Shen; Tony Todd; Robert Englund; Joel Murray; Joleigh Fioravanti; Richard Riehle; Patrika Darbo; ***D:*** Adam Green; ***W:*** Adam Green; ***C:*** Will Barratt; ***M:*** Andy Garfield.

Hatchet 2 1/2 **2010** The sequel picks up where 2007's horror gorefest left off. After escaping deformed killer Victor Crowley, Marybeth returns to New Orleans to get help from Reverend Zombie, who agrees to lead a group of hunters back into the swamp. Green exaggerates the bloody violence again but there are a number of jokes only fans will appreciate. **89m/C; DVD, Blu-Ray.** Danielle Harris; Tony Todd; Kane Hodder; Parry Shen; Tom Holland; R.A. Mihailoff; AJ Bowen; Ed Ackerman; Alexis Peters; John Carl Buechler; ***D:*** Adam Green; ***W:*** Adam Green; ***C:*** Will Barratt; ***M:*** Andy Garfield.

Hatchet for the Honeymoon *Blood Brides; Una Hacha para la Luna de Miel; Il Rosso Segmo della Follia; An Axe for the Honeymoon; The Red Sign of Madness* **1970** A rather disturbed young man goes around hacking young brides to death as he tries to find out who murdered his wife. Typical sick Bava horror flick; confusing plot, but strong on vivid imagery. **90m/C; VHS, DVD, Blu-Ray.** *SP IT* Stephen Forsyth; Dagmar Lassander; Laura Betti; Gerard Tichy; Femi Benussi; Alan Collins; Jesus Puente; ***D:*** Mario Bava; ***W:*** Mario Bava; Santiago Moncada; Mario Musy; ***C:*** Mario Bava; ***M:*** Santa Maria Romitelli.

The Hatchet Man **1932** Get past the Occidentals-as-Oreintals casting and you'll find an intriguing, if brutal, film. San Francisco Tong assassin Wong Low Get (Robinson) is forced to execute a friend who asks him to care for his daughter. Years later, Wong is a respected member of the community, but his young wife, Toya (Young), is in love with crook Harry (Fenton). Wong sends her away but she and Harry get deported to China for opium smuggling and Harry sells Toya into a brothel. When Wong learns of her plight, he feels obligated to rescue her. **74m/B; DVD.** Edward G. Robinson; Loretta Young; Leslie Fenton; Dudley Digges; ***D:*** William A. Wellman; ***W:*** J. Grubb Alexander; ***C:*** Sidney Hickox.

The Hatching **2016 (R)** A comedy-horror film centered on a potential serial killer—not necessarily human—linked to the disappearance of several people from a small village. After learning his father has died, Tim Webber (Potts) goes back to the tight-knit community in England in which he was raised. Tim learns that Somerset is being affected by something sinister. More and more people disappear and dismembered, bloody body parts appear and it becomes clear that crocodiles are on the loose. Because of a mistake he made as a teenager, Tim is responsible for the situation and must act to save everyone. **90m/C; DVD, Streaming, Download.** Andrew Lee Potts; Thomas Turgoose; Georgia Henshaw; Muzz Khan; Laura Aikman; ***D:*** Michael Anderson; ***W:*** Michael Anderson; Nick Squire; ***C:*** Gerry Vasbenter. **VIDEO**

Hate *La Haine; Hatred* **1995** Twenty-hours in the lives of young, disenfranchised Said (Taghmaoui), Vinz (Cassel), and Hubert (Kounde), who are living in a housing project outside Paris. A riot breaks out, thanks to police brutality of an Arab resident, and Vinz finds a gun the cops lost. A Paris sojourn leads to a police interrogation of Hubert and Said, a fight with some skinheads, a return to their home turf, and an unexpected conclusion. Intelligent look at the idiocy engendered by societal oppression and a buildup of hatred. French with subtitles. **95m/B; VHS, DVD, Blu-Ray.** *FR* Vincent Cassel; Hubert Kounde; Said Taghmaoui; Francois Levantal; ***D:*** Mathieu Kassovitz; ***W:*** Mathieu Kassovitz; ***C:*** Pierre Aim; Georges Diane. Cannes '95: Director (Kassovitz); Cesar '96: Film, Film Editing.

Hate Crime 1/2 **2005** Overwrought melodrama. Robbie (Peterson) and Trey (Smith) are a contented gay couple whose new neighbor, Chris (Donella), is the homophobic son of a fundamentalist pastor

(Davison). Naturally, the neighbors soon clash. When Trey is beaten to death at a local park, Robbie is sure who's guilty, but the cops aren't. **103m/C; DVD.** Bruce Davison; Chad E. Donella; Cindy Pickett; Brian J. Smith; Seth Peterson; Susan Blakely; Giancarlo Esposito; Farah White; ***D:*** Tommy Stovall; ***W:*** Tommy Stovall; ***C:*** Ian W. Ellis; ***M:*** Ebony Tay.

Hate for Hate 🦴 **1967** In this lame, overly-plotted spaghetti western outlaw Cooper (Ireland) robs a bank, stealing artist Miguel's (Sabato) life savings. Cooper is betrayed by his psycho partner Moxon (Ellis) and lands in prison. He eventually escapes, only to discover that Moxon has kidnapped his family. Miguel still wants his money back and teams up with Cooper to get Moxon and his gang. **97m/C; DVD.** *IT* Antonio (Tony) Sabato; John Ireland; Mirko Ellis; Fernando (Fernand) Sancho; Gloria Milland; ***D:*** Domenico Paolella; ***W:*** Domenico Paolella; Fernando Di Leo; Bruno Corbucci; ***C:*** Alejandro Ulloa; ***M:*** Willy Brezza.

The Hate U Give 🦴🦴🦴 **2018 (PG-13)** In this adaptation of the young adult novel by Angie Thomas, Starr Carter (an excellent Stenberg) has dual identities, one who lives in a mostly black neighborhood and the other who attends a mostly white prep school. Her father taught her ways to navigate those two worlds, but her childhood friend Khalil (Smith) didn't learn those lessons and got shot by a white police officer. Starr must risk everything to speak up for justice. It's a social commentary with an important, timely message, and warrants forgiveness for delivering it a bit too heavy-handed at times. **133m/C; DVD.** Amandla Stenberg; Regina Hall; Russell Hornsby; Anthony Mackie; Issa Rae; ***D:*** George Tillman, Jr.; ***W:*** Audrey Wells; ***C:*** Milhai Malaimare, Jr.; ***M:*** Dustin O'Halloran.

The Hateful Eight 🦴🦴🦴 **2015 (R)** Tarantino delivers a brilliant meta-commentary on his own films and the formation of the country in this incredibly detailed Western. Hangman John Ruth (Russell) is bringing his prisoner Daisy Domergue (Leigh) to hang when a snowstorm forces him and his traveling companions to a remote cabin, which happens to be occupied by some equally unsavory characters. Tarantino's filmmaking skill is apparent in every frame, and the performances are great from top to bottom, especially Leigh, Samuel L. Jackson and Walton Goggins. Warning: the misogyny and racism may be a bit much for some. There's a reason they're called "hateful." **187m/C; DVD, Blu-Ray.** Samuel L. Jackson; Kurt Russell; Jennifer Jason Leigh; Walton Goggins; Demian Bichir; ***D:*** Quentin Tarantino; ***W:*** Quentin Tarantino; ***C:*** Robert Richardson; ***M:*** Ennio Morricone. Oscars '15: Orig. Score; British Acad. '15: Orig. Score; Golden Globes '16: Orig. Score.

Hateship Loveship 🦴🦴 **1/2 2013 (R)** Johanna Parry (Wiig), is a shy, sheltered woman who is about to be cast from her hermit-esque lifestyle. She is hired by Mr. McCauley (Nolte) to be a housekeeper and caregiver to his granddaughter Sabitha (Steinfeld). Sabitha plays a horrible trick on Johanna by convincing her that her father, Ken (Pearce), is romantically interested in her. While the result could have been played as mean-spirited and some of the story does feel false at times, the perfectly cast Wiig is gentle and real. **104m/C; DVD.** Kristen Wiig; Guy Pearce; Hailee Steinfeld; Nick Nolte; Sami Gayle; Jennifer Jason Leigh; Christine Lahti; ***D:*** Liza Johnson; ***W:*** Mark Jude Poirier; ***C:*** Kasper Tuxen; ***M:*** Dickon Hinchliffe.

Hatfields & McCoys 🦴🦴🦴 **2012** The History Channel's excellent miniseries sheds some light on a legendary but largely misunderstood family feud. Costner and Paxton are superb as the heads of the respective families. The series gets the Post-Civil War period right and allows each family's story room to be told. Large cast has menay standouts, as evidenced by multiple Emmy nominations (Costner, Paxton, Berenger, Winningham). **290m/C; DVD, Blu-Ray.** Kevin Costner; Bill Paxton; Matt Barr; Tom Berenger; Powers Boothe; Andrew Howard; Jena Malone; Sarah Parish; Lindsay Pulsipher; Ronan Vibert; Joe Absolom; Noel Fisher; Boyd Holbrook; Mare Winningham; ***D:*** Kevin Reynolds; ***W:*** Bill Kerby; Ted Mann; Ronald Parker; ***C:*** Arthur Reinhart; ***M:*** John Debney. **CABLE**

A Hatful of Rain 🦴🦴 **1959** Static and now-dated depiction of drug addiction based on co-scripter Gazzo's play. Wounded Korean War vet Johnny Pope (Murray) comes home to New York with a morphine addiction. His pregnant wife Celia (Saint) is clueless and Johnny depends on his enabling younger brother, Polo (Francisoca), for support. To make the family dynamics worse, their estranged father (Nolan) shows up and Johnny owes money to his vicious drug dealer (Silva). **109m/B; DVD.** Don Murray; Eva Marie Saint; Anthony (Tony) Franciosa; Lloyd Nolan; Henry Silva; Gerald S. O'Loughlin; William Hickey; ***D:*** Fred Zinnemann; ***W:*** Michael V. Gazzo; Alfred Hayes; Carl Foreman; ***C:*** Joseph Macdonald; ***M:*** Bernard Herrmann.

Hats Off 🦴 **1937** Clarke and Payne star as opposing press agents in this tedious musical. The only bright spot is the finale, which features white-robed girls on a cloud-covered carousel. **65m/B; VHS, DVD.** Mae Clarke; John Payne; Helen Lynd; Luis Alberni; Richard "Skeets" Gallagher; Franklin Pangborn; ***D:*** Boris L. Petroff.

Haunt 🦴🦴 **2019 (R)** Though it is Halloween, college student Harper (Stevens) is not particularly aware that roommate Bailey (McClain) has made plans for them. Harper is distracted by the black eye she received from her abusive alcoholic boyfriend Sam (Hunt). Bailey convinces Harper to join a group of friends for Halloween fun, and they find a remote haunted house in a rural area. After their cell phones are taken, they go through rooms that feature increasingly intense violence. When the friends get separated, the situation grows more extreme. Nodding to B-movie horror classics, the indie horror is a tight story with a good ensemble and creative twists. **92m/C; DVD.** Katie Stevens; Will Brittain; Lauryn McClain; Andrew Caldwell; Shazi Raja; ***D:*** Scott Beck; Bryan Woods; ***W:*** Scott Beck; Bryan Woods; ***C:*** Ryan Samul; ***M:*** tomandandy.

Haunted 🦴🦴 **1/2 1995 (R)** At their Sussex home, David Ash watches helplessly as his younger sister Juliet drowns. Flash-forward to 1925 and the grownup David (Quinn) returns to teach a university course debunking the supernatural. Still, he's drawn to a supposedly haunted mansion, inhabited by artist Robert Mariell (Andrews), his sister Christina (Beckinsale), brother Simon (Lowe), and their elderly nanny (Massey). David starts experiencing visions of his dead sister, while mysterious fires and other unexplained manifestations occur—all of which seem tied to the unholy Mariell trio. Based on a novel by James Herbert. **108m/C; VHS, DVD.** *GB* Aidan Quinn; Kate Beckinsale; Anthony Andrews; Alex Lowe; Anna Massey; Geraldine Somerville; Victoria Shalet; ***Cameo(s):*** John Gielgud; ***D:*** Lewis Gilbert; ***W:*** Lewis Gilbert; Bob Kellett; Tim Prager; ***C:*** Tony Pierce-Roberts; ***M:*** Debbie Wiseman.

The Haunted Airman 🦴 **1/2 2006 (R)** Clumsy and slow-moving BBC psychodrama loosely based on Dennis Wheatley's novel "The Haunting of Toby Jugg." Wounded and confined to a wheelchair, WWII flight lieutenant Toby Jugg (Pattinson) retreats to a convalescent home in Wales to recuperate. Suffering from terrible hallucinations, Toby comes to believe that his doctor (Sands) is actually trying to drive him crazy. **70m/C; DVD.** *GB* Robert Pattinson; Julian Sands; Rachael Stirling; Melissa Lloyd; Scott Handy; ***D:*** Chris Durlacher; ***W:*** Chris Durlacher; ***C:*** Jeff Baynes; ***M:*** Daniel Pemberton. **TV**

Haunted Echoes 🦴 **1/2 2008 (R)** After their daughter is murdered and the suspected killer commits suicide, the Dykstras decide to make a new start by moving into an old fixer-upper. However, their house is apparently haunted and their daughter contacts the couple during a seance to say her killer is still alive and somehow connected to the house. Mishmash of ghost story and family drama. **97m/C; DVD.** Sean Young; David Starzyk; M. Emmet Walsh; Lily Howe; Barbara Bain; Felix Williamson; Juliet Landau; ***D:*** Harry Bromley-Davenport; ***W:*** Rachel Calendar; ***C:*** David Scott Ikegami. **VIDEO**

Haunted Highway 🦴 *Death Ride* **2005** Photographer Greg (Gamble) has an affair with his model, Yumi (Yoshikawa), which his wife, Amanda (Putney), finds out about. Greg accidentally kills Amanda during an argument and puts her body in his car trunk for disposal in a remote location. Then Amanda starts to haunt him. Dumb rather than scary. **83m/C; DVD.** Rand Gamble; Hinano Yoshikawa; Laura Putney; ***D:*** Junichi Suzuki; ***W:*** Junichi Suzuki; ***C:*** Takuro Ishizaka. **VIDEO**

Haunted Honeymoon 🦴 **1986 (PG)** Arthritic comedy about a haunted house and a couple trapped there. Sad times for the Mel Brooks alumni participating in this lame horror spoof. **82m/C; VHS, DVD, Blu-Ray.** Gene Wilder; Gilda Radner; Dom DeLuise; Jonathan Pryce; Paul Smith; Peter Vaughan; Bryan Pringle; Roger Ashton-Griffiths; Jim Carter; Eve Ferret; ***D:*** Gene Wilder; ***W:*** Gene Wilder; Terence Marsh; ***C:*** Fred Schuler.

A Haunted House WOOF! **2013 (R)** Fart-jokes lovers unite. You know humanity has little hope when the "Scary Movie" franchise is spawning rip-offs. Camera-obsessed Malcolm (played by Wayans, surprise, surprise) moves into a new house only to discover it's haunted. His camera captures pot-smoking poltergeists and a team of incompetent ghost-busters--worse yet, his flatulent girlfriend (Atkins) is ruining his sex-drive. Filled with dated references and lame stereotypes, the Hound can't stomach the stench of this "Paranormal Activity" spoof. **87m/C; DVD, Blu-Ray.** Marlon Wayans; Essence Atkins; Cedric the Entertainer; David Koechner; Nick Swardson; ***D:*** Michael Tiddes; ***W:*** Marlon Wayans; Rick Alvarez; ***C:*** Steve Gainer.

A Haunted House 2 WOOF! **2014 (R)** Fart-jokes lovers unite. You know humanity has little hope when the "Scary Movie" franchise is spawning rip-offs. In this needless sequel, camera-obsessed Malcolm (played by Wayans, surprise, surprise) moves into a new house only to discover it's haunted. His camera captures pot-smoking poltergeists and a team of incompetent ghost-busters--worse yet, his flatulent girlfriend (Atkins) is ruining his sex-drive. Filled with dated references and lame stereotypes, the Hound can't stomach the stench of another "Paranormal Activity" spoof. **86m/C; DVD, Blu-Ray.** Marlon Wayans; Essence Atkins; Jaime Pressly; Missi Pyle; Cedric the Entertainer; ***D:*** Michael Tiddes; ***W:*** Marlon Wayans; Rick Alvarez; ***C:*** David Ortkiese; ***M:*** Jesse Voccia.

The Haunted Mansion 🦴 **1/2 2003 (PG)** Inspired by the popular Disney ride of the same name. Jim Evers (Murphy) is a workaholic real estate agent who takes his family along to see a mansion whose owner wants to sell. They soon find out that the mansion is inhabited with ghosts, lots of them. Coincidentally enough, it turns out that Evers's wife Sara (Thomason) bears a striking resemblance to the owner's long dead lover, who had committed suicide. So why wouldn't they want to live there? While the production design of the mansion is quite impressive, it still doesn't make up for the lack of an original story or dialogue. Murphy's comedic talent is largely wasted. Skip the movie, go for the ride. **99m/C; VHS, DVD, Blu-Ray.** Eddie Murphy; Marsha Thomason; Terence Stamp; Wallace Shawn; Jennifer Tilly; Nathaniel Parker; Marc John Jeffries; Aree Davis; Dina Spybey; ***D:*** Rob Minkoff; ***W:*** David Berenbaum; ***C:*** Remi Adefarasin; ***M:*** Mark Mancina.

The Haunted Palace 🦴🦴 **1/2 1963** Price plays both a 17th-century warlock burned at the stake and a descendant who returns to the family dungeon and gets possessed by the mutant-breeding forebearer. The movie has its own identity crisis, with title and ambience from Poe but story from H.P. Lovecraft's "The Case of Charles Dexter Ward." Respectable but rootless chills. **87m/C; VHS, DVD, Blu-Ray.** Vincent Price; Debra Paget; Lon Chaney, Jr.; Frank Maxwell; Leo Gordon; Elisha Cook, Jr.; John Dierkes; Barboura Morris; Bruno VeSota; ***D:*** Roger Corman; ***W:*** Charles Beaumont; Floyd Crosby; ***M:*** Ronald Stein.

The Haunted Sea 🦴🦴 **1997 (R)** The crew of the Patna discovered an abandoned ship that's filled with Aztec treasure. But when the Patna's crew members begin disappearing, those remaining must discover what's guarding the treasure. **74m/C; VHS, DVD.** James Brolin; Joanna Pacula; Krista Allen; Don Stroud; ***D:*** Dan Golden; ***C:*** John Aronson; ***M:*** David Wurst; Eric Wurst.

The Haunted Strangler 🦴🦴 **1/2** *The Grip of the Strangler* **1958** Boris Karloff is a writer investigating a 20-year-old murder who begins copying some of the killer's acts. **78m/B; VHS, DVD.** *GB* Boris Karloff; Anthony Dawson; Elizabeth Allan; Timothy Turner; Diane Aubrey; Dorothy Gordon; Jean Kent; Vera Day; ***D:*** Robert Day; ***W:*** John C. Cooper; Jan Read; ***C:*** Lionel Banes; ***M:*** Buxton Orr.

Haunted Summer 🦴🦴 **1988 (R)** Soft-focus, sex-and-drugs period piece of the bacchanalian summer of 1816 spent by free spirits Lord Byron, Percy Shelley, Mary Shelley, and John Polidori and others that led Mary Shelley to write "Frankenstein." Based on the novel of the same name by Anne Edwards. **106m/C; VHS, DVD.** Alice Krige; Eric Stoltz; Philip Anglim; Laura Dern; Alex Winter; ***D:*** Ivan Passer; ***W:*** Lewis John Carlino.

The Haunted World of El Superbeasto 🦴 **1/2 2009 (R)** Surreal and wildly over-the-top cartoon by director Zombie that references half the horror/exploitation/sci-fi films of the last 50 years. A lustful wrestler and his crazed sister try to stop a madman from gaining the powers of Satan. **77m/C; DVD, Blu-Ray, Streaming.** ***V:*** Tom Papa; Paul Giamatti; Sheri Moon Zombie; Brian Posehn; ***D:*** Rob Zombie; ***W:*** Tom Papa; Rob Zombie; Mike Bell; Joe Ekers; Tom Klein; Joe Orrantia; Carey Yost; ***M:*** Tyler Bates. **VIDEO**

Haunter 🦴🦴 **2013** A pubescent take on "Groundhog Day," with Lisa (Breslin) waking each morning--for decades--to her mom complaining about the laundry and her dad tinkering in the garage. It's 1985 and the day before her 16th birthday--and the day they are all seemingly killed. Her state of teenage boredom apparently reaches supernatural heights and she becomes desperate to break free--and to stop a serial killer (McHattie) from striking again. Suspenseful and creepy-without-the-gore, Breslin luckily turns in a performance that avoids the usual whiny teen drama, never once as annoying as the film's one-note premise. **97m/C; DVD, Blu-Ray.** *CA* Abigail Breslin; Stephen McHattie; Eleanor Zichy; Peter Outerbridge; Michelle Nolden; David Hewlett; Peter DaCunha; ***D:*** Vincenzo Natali; ***W:*** Brian King; ***C:*** Jon Joffin; ***M:*** Alex Khaskin.

The Haunting 🦴🦴🦴 **1/2 1963** A subtle, bloodless horror film about a weekend spent in a monstrously haunted mansion by a parapsychologist (Johnson), the mansion's skeptic heir (Tamblyn), and two mediums (Harris and Bloom). A chilling adaptation of Shirley Jackson's "The Haunting of Hill House," in which the psychology of the heroine is forever in question. There's a silly 1999 remake that's all special effects and no scares. **113m/B; VHS, DVD, Blu-Ray.** *GB* Julie Harris; Claire Bloom; Russ Tamblyn; Richard Johnson; Fay Compton; Rosalie Crutchley; Lois Maxwell; Valentine Dyall; Diane Clare; ***D:*** Robert Wise; ***W:*** Nelson Gidding; ***C:*** Davis Boulton; ***M:*** Humphrey Searle.

The Haunting 🦴 **1/2** *The Haunting of Hill House* **1999 (PG-13)** Tiny Lili Taylor gets to play avenging angel with an assortment of ghosties and ghoulies in this silly would-be frightener based on the novel by Shirley Jackson and originally filmed in 1963. Dr. Marrow (Neeson) enlists three subjects to stay at Hill House for a study in insomnia that's (unknown to them) actually a study in fear response. There's brash Theo (Zeta-Jones), dopey Luke (Wilson), and fragile Nell (Taylor), who turns out to have unexpected ties to the haunted mansion. Big-budget doesn't make for big frights, just big, mocking laughter from the audience—certainly not what director De Bont must have intended. Dern appears briefly as the scruffy caretaker, with Seldes his Mrs. Danvers-like wife. **114m/C; VHS, DVD.** Lili Taylor; Liam Neeson; Catherine Zeta-Jones; Owen Wilson; Bruce Dern; Marian Seldes; Virginia Madsen; Todd Field; Alix Koromzay; ***D:*** Jan De Bont; ***W:*** David Self; ***C:*** Caleb Deschanel; ***M:*** Jerry Goldsmith.

Haunting Fear 🦴 **1991** Poe's "The Premature Burial" inspired this pale cheapie about a wife with a fear of early interment. After lengthy nightmares and graphic sex, her greedy husband uses her phobia in a murder plot. **88m/C; VHS, DVD.** Jan-Michael Vincent; Karen Black; Brinke Stevens; Michael Berryman; ***D:*** Fred Olen Ray; ***W:*** Fred Olen Ray.

The Haunting in Connecticut 🦴 **2009 (PG-13)** Strange things are afoot in a spooky old house a family moves into while their son is being treated for cancer at a nearby clinic. The house has a past as a funeral home, and thanks to a clairvoyant previous occupant, a supposed way station for demons and other unsavory supernatural types. Little more than the typical haunted house-ghost story, despite being supposedly based on actual events (wasn't the same said about "The Blair Witch Project?"). More creepy than scary, pic is completely unoriginal and its scare tactics rely heavily on standard horror cliches as well as computer-generated special effects. A waste of Madsen's talent, as she sleepwalks through the overwrought script. **102m/C; Blu-Ray, On Demand.** Virginia Madsen; Kyle Gallner; Elias Koteas; Amanda Crew; Martin Donovan; Ty Wood; Adam Simon; Tim Metcalfe; Sophi Knight; Erik J. Berg; John Bluethner; ***D:*** Peter Cornwell; ***C:*** Adam Swica; ***M:*** Robert Kral.

The Haunting in Connecticut 2: Ghosts of Georgia 1/2 **2013 (R)** Based very loosely on the story of Heidi Wyrick. After moving to a new house a family makes two discoveries: It used to be part of the Underground Railroad and the youngest daughter has inherited her families ability to see dead people. **100m/C; DVD, Blu-Ray, Streaming.** Abigail Spencer; Emily Alyn Lind; Chad Michael Murray; Katee Sackhoff; Cicely Tyson; ***D:*** Tom Elkins; ***W:*** David Coggeshall; ***C:*** Yaron Levy; ***M:*** Michael Wandmacher. **VIDEO**

The Haunting of Helena 1/2 *Fairytale* **2012** More silly than scary, this update of the Tooth Fairy legend contains some strong imagery but wastes any opportunity of producing actual scares on a foolish plot with weak performances. Sophia's a single mother forced to move with young daughter Helena into a crumbling apartment. Helena loses a tooth and finds an ancient coin in its place, and Sophia starts to suspect something weird is going on and learns that, of course, it has a dark past. It's another generic haunting tale with horrendous dialogue that provokes more groans than scares. **84m/C; DVD.** *IT* Harriett MacMasters-Green; Sabrina Perez; Jarreth Merz; Matt Patresi; ***D:*** Christian Bisceglia; Ascanio Malgarini; ***W:*** Christian Bisceglia; ***C:*** Antonello Emidi; ***M:*** Michele Josia.

The Haunting of Hell House *Henry James' The Ghostly Rental; The Ghostly Rental* **1999 (R)** Remember when Hammer Studios made all those horror movies based on Edgar Allan Poe stories and they were a lot of campy fun (if not truly creepy)? Well, that's what this Victorian Gothic wants to (or should) be and isn't. Tormented James (Bowen) took his girlfriend to an abortionist and she died. James seeks advice from the mysterious Professor Ambrose (York), whose family past is also filled with tragedy. **90m/C; VHS, DVD.** Andrew Bowen; Michael York; Claudia Christian; Aideen O'Donnell; ***D:*** Mitch Marcus; ***W:*** Mitch Marcus; L.L. Shapira; ***C:*** Russ Brandt; ***M:*** Ivan Koutikov.

The Haunting of Lisa **1996** Young Lisa (Downey) experiences disturbing visions of a child being murdered and then a body is found buried in the park. Her widowed mom Ellen (Ladd), who also has psychic abilities, becomes increasingly scared when Lisa's visions continue and a second body is discovered, believing it will bring them to the attention of the killer. **89m/C; DVD.** Cheryl Ladd; Aemilia Robinson; Duncan Regehr; Don Allison; Corey Sevier; Amanda Tapping; Wayne Northrop; ***D:*** Don McBrearty; ***W:*** Don Henry; ***C:*** Francois Protat; ***M:*** Marvin Dolgay; Glenn Morley. **TV**

The Haunting of Marsten Manor 1/2 **2007 (PG)** Low-budget horror with a faith-based message. Jill (who's blind) travels with friends to the creepy mansion she inherited from a missing aunt. Dark secrets are revealed by a ghostly soldier though her friends think Jill is imagining things. **81m/C; DVD.** C. Thomas Howell; Brianne Davis; Ezra Buzzington; Ken Luckey; Janice Knickrehm; Julie Sapp; ***D:*** David Sapp; ***W:*** Julie Sapp; David Sapp; ***C:*** David Sapp; ***M:*** Julie Sapp. **VIDEO**

The Haunting of Molly Hartley **2008 (PG-13)** Misfit Molly Hartley (Bennett) has trouble adapting to her new life at a private school. As if the constant nosebleeds, headaches, and mysterious voices aren't bad enough, she's haunted by the fact that her mother's in a mental institution. As her eighteen birthday approaches, Molly begins to realize the horrible truth behind her ailments. A weak teen horror flick, knocked out quickly and cheaply in time for Halloween. The entire cast, along with first-time director Liddell (a longtime TV producer), should stick to the small screen. **86m/C; Blu-Ray, On Demand.** Haley Bennett; Chace Crawford; Shannon Marie Woodward; Nina Siemaszko; Jessica Lowndes; Marin Hinkle; Jake Weber; AnnaLynne McCord; Shanna Collins; Ron Canada; Kevin Cooney; ***D:*** Mickey Liddell; ***W:*** John Travis; Rebecca Sonnenshine; ***C:*** Sharone Meir; ***M:*** James T. Sale.

The Haunting of Morella **1991 (R)** Poe-inspired cheapjack exploitation about a an executed witch living again in the nubile body of her teen daughter. Ritual murders result, in between lesbian baths and nude swims. Producer Roger Corman did the same story with more class and less skin in his earlier anthology "Tales of Terror." **82m/C; VHS, DVD, Blu-Ray.** David McCallum; Nicole Eggert; Maria Ford; Lana Clarkson; ***D:*** Jim Wynorski; ***W:*** Jim Wynorski; R.J. Robertson.

The Haunting of Sharon Tate 1/2 **2019 (R)** Months after actress Sharon Tate (Duff) reveals that she has premonitions of her own death, she is heavily pregnant when she grows increasingly agitated and fearful of her fate. Her husband is out of the country, and friends Abigail (Hearst) and Wojciech (Szajda) have been staying with her. Paranoid that they have endangered her, Tate dreams repeatedly of her death, each time with a different outcome. Based on the 1969 murder of Tate by Charlie Manson's followers and using some real footage of Tate and the event's aftermath, the film distorts the truth and reduces the tragic events to an overwrought home invasion thriller. **94m/C; DVD, Blu-Ray.** Hilary Duff; Jonathan Bennett; Lydia Hearst; Pawel Szajda; Ryan Cargill; ***D:*** Daniel Farrands; ***W:*** Daniel Farrands; ***C:*** Carlo Rinaldi. Golden Raspberries '19: Worst Actress (Duff).

The Haunting of Winchester House **2009** Supposedly based on an actual (haunted) house once owned by the Winchester rifle family so the plot has something to do with those killed by Winchester rifles turning into vengeful spirits and infesting the mansion. The Greniers are serving as temporary caretakers while the house is undergoing renovation. Everyone starts seeing ghosts and young Haley Grenier is kidnapped by the ghost of Sarah Winchester who wants Haley's parents to figure out what happened to Sarah's long-missing sister Annie. **90m/C; DVD.** Lira Kellerman; Michael Holmes; Patty Roberts; Jennifer Smart; Tomas Boykin; Rob Ullett; ***D:*** Mark Atkins; ***W:*** Mark Atkins; ***C:*** Mark Atkins; ***M:*** Chris Ridenhour. **VIDEO**

The Haunting Passion 1/2 **1983** Newlywed Seymour moves into a haunted house only to be seduced by the ghost of the former occupant's dead lover. Effective and erotic presentation. **100m/C; VHS, DVD.** Jane Seymour; Gerald McRaney; Millie Perkins; Ruth Nelson; Paul Rossilli; Ivan Bonar; ***D:*** John Korty. **TV**

Haunting Sarah 1/2 **2005** Okay supernatural horror with a kinda strange ending. After Heather's (Raver) son David dies in an accident, her young niece Sarah (Wilson), the daughter of Heather's identical twin Erica, says she's still able to talk to him. They head to the family cabin, with Erica's maid Rosie (Sealy-Smith) insisting to a pregnant Erica that David wants to be reborn in the new baby. **90m/C; DVD.** Kim Raver; Niamh Wilson; Alison Sealy-Smith; Ryland Thiessen; Gordon Tanner; Rick Roberts; ***D:*** Ralph Hemecker; ***W:*** Tony Phelan; Joan Rater; ***C:*** Christian Sebaldt; ***M:*** Joel Goldsmith. **CABLE**

Haunts 1/2 *The Veil* **1977 (PG)** Tormented woman has difficulty distinguishing between fantasy and reality after a series of brutal slayings lead police to the stunning conclusion that dead people have been committing the crimes. **97m/C; VHS, DVD.** Cameron Mitchell; Aldo Ray; May Britt; William Gray Espy; Susan Nohr; ***D:*** Herb Freed; ***M:*** Pino Donaggio.

Hav Plenty **1997 (R)** Moving in the circles of young black professionals, Lee Plenty (Cherot) is an unemployed would-be writer who doesn't seem to care too much about getting a job. The materialistic and ambitious Havilland (Maxwell),a friend of his from college, invites him to a New Year's Eve party when she finds that her fiance Michael (Harper) is playing around on her. The sedate holiday weekend turns into a frenzy of surprises, as Lee is chased by Hav's hairdo-happy friend Caroline (Jones) and newlywed sister Leigh (Lee). Screwball romantic comedy comes off as a hybrid of Spike Lee and Woody Allen, with writer/director/editor Cherot's own personal touches thrown in. Performances are excellent, especially Cherot himself, who only starred when the actor hired to play his part bowed out as filming started. **87m/C; VHS, DVD.** Christopher Scott Cherot; Chenoa Maxwell; Hill Harper; Tammi Katherine Jones; Robine Lee; Betty Vaughn; Reginald James; Kenneth "Babyface" Edmonds; ***D:*** Christopher Scott Cherot; ***W:*** Christopher Scott Cherot; ***C:*** Kerwin Devonish; ***M:*** Wendy Melvoin; Lisa Coleman.

Havana 1/2 **1990 (R)** During the waning days of the Batista regime, a gambler travels to Havana in search of big winnings. Instead, he meets the beautiful wife of a communist revolutionary. Unable to resist their mutual physical attraction, the lovers become drawn into a destiny which is far greater than themselves. Reminiscent of "Casablanca." **145m/C; VHS, DVD.** Robert Redford; Lena Olin; Alan Arkin; Raul Julia; Tomas Milian; Tony Plana; Betsy Brantley; Lise Cutter; Richard Farnsworth; Mark Rydell; Daniel Davis; ***D:*** Sydney Pollack; ***W:*** Judith Rascoe; David Rayfiel; ***C:*** Owen Roizman; ***M:*** Dave Grusin.

Have No Fear: The Life of Pope John Paul II **2005** Cut-and-dried made-for-TV bio is told in flashback after the Pontiff (Kretschmann) begins to review his life after a pilgrimage to Jerusalem in 2000. He reflects on growing up as Karol Wojtyla in Nazi-occupied Poland and his journey from entering the clergy, up the priestly ladder to his elevation to Pope John Paul II. **87m/C; DVD.** Thomas Kretschmann; Bruno Ganz; John Albasiny; Charles Kay; Joaquim DeAlmeida; Sabrina Javor; ***D:*** Jeff Bleckner; ***W:*** Michael Hirst; Judd Parkin; ***C:*** Roberto Benvenuti; ***M:*** Carlo Siliotto. **TV**

Have Rocket Will Travel 1/2 **1959** Three janitors (guess who) help a scientist who is about to lose her job if she can't send a rocket to Venus. They accidently initiate the launch while still on board and introduce their brand of slapstick to a whole new planet. First of the late '50s-early '60s feature films to capitalize on the renewed popularity of the Three Stooges. **76m/B; DVD.** Moe Howard; Larry Fine; Joe DeRita; Anna-Lisa; Jerome Cowan; Bob Colbert; ***D:*** David Lowell Rich; ***W:*** Raphael Hayes; ***C:*** Ray Cory.

Have Sword, Will Travel 1/2 *Bao Biao; Bo biu; The Bodyguard* **1969** The leader of a caravan guarding service has fallen so ill he cannot protect the yearly caravan of silver sent to the capitol, and so entrusts the job to two young fighters in his service. They are joined by a down-on-his-luck warrior and the three quickly form a romantic triangle (one of them is a woman). Eventually bandits get the silver, and the chase is on. **103m/C; DVD.** *CH* Ching Lee; Lung Ti; David Chiang; Miao Ching; Feng Ku; Chung Wang; ***D:*** Cheh Chang; ***W:*** Kuang Ni; ***C:*** Kung Mo To; ***M:*** Fu-ling Wang.

Haven 1/2 **2004 (R)** Overly-complicated story begins with corrupt businessman Carl Ridley (Paxton) taking his daughter Pippa (Bruckner) and getting out of Miami with a suitcase full of cash just ahead of the feds. Ridley goes to the Caymans, hoping to arrange something with his double-dealing attorney Allan (Dillane). Meanwhile, dock worker Shy (Bloom) makes the mistake of romancing wealthy Andrea (Saldana), greatly upsetting her violent brother Hammer (Mackie). A local crime boss (Adoti) is clued into Ridley's money, Pippa hooks up with the wrong crowd, and things just get more confusing. **98m/C; DVD, Blu-Ray.** *US GB GE SP* Orlando Bloom; Agnes Bruckner; Bill Paxton; Zoe Saldana; Anthony Mackie; Bobby Cannavale; Stephen (Dillon) Dillane; Victor Rasuk; Raz Adoti; Robert Wisdom; ***D:*** Frank E. Flowers; ***W:*** Frank E. Flowers; ***C:*** Michael Bernard; ***M:*** Hector Pereira.

Having a Wild Weekend 1/2 **1965** Boorman's feature film debut takes the Dave Clark 5 on a crazy adventure that's less lighthearted than The Beatles romps. Instead of musicians, the five are London stuntmen working on a meat commercial starring Steve's (Clark) bored model girlfriend Dinah (Ferris). She persuades him to play hooky and they drive off to Devon for the weekend, but the ad exec in charge makes their getaway into a publicity stunt. **91m/B; DVD.** *UK* Dave Clark; Lenny Davidson; Rick Huxley; Mike Smith; Denis West Payton; Barbara Ferris; David de Keyser; ***D:*** John Boorman; ***W:*** Peter Nichols; ***C:*** Manny Wynn.

Having a Wonderful Time *Having Wonderful Time* **1938** City girl secretary Teddy (Rogers) heads to the country for some R&R, staying at a holiday camp for singles. She meets Chick (Fairbanks Jr.), who's working as a waiter to put himself through law school, and they insult each other before finding romance. Kober had to tone down the 'Jewish' elements of his play (which was originally set at a Catskills resort) to make it palatable for Hollywood. **71m/B; VHS, DVD.** Ginger Rogers; Douglas Fairbanks, Jr.; Peggy Conklin; Lucille Ball; Eve Arden; Lee Bowman; Red Skelton; Donald Meek; Jack Carson; ***D:*** Alfred Santell; ***W:*** Arthur Kober; ***C:*** Robert De Grasse.

Having Our Say: The Delany Sisters' First 100 Years 1/2 **1999** Based on the book and the Broadway play that looks at life through the aging eyes of the black Delany sisters: 103-year-old Sadie (Carroll) and 101-year-old Bessie (Dee). They share their experiences with New York Times reporter Amy Hill Hearth (Madigan), who has come to interview them in 1991. Their father was born a slave but all 12 of the Delany children graduated from college, with Bessie becoming a teacher and Sadie a dentist in Harlem. (The real Bessie died in 1995 and Sadie in 1999.) **90m/C; VHS, DVD, Streaming.** Diahann Carroll; Ruby Dee; Mykelti Williamson; Lonette McKee; Lisa Arrindell Anderson; Audra McDonald; Richard Roundtree; Della Reese; ***D:*** Lynne Littman; ***W:*** Emily Mann; ***C:*** Frank Byers. **TV**

Havoc 1/2 **2005** Bored, rich, white, and clueless suburban teens Allison (Hathaway), Emily (Phillips), and Toby (Vogel) head to East L.A. to buy weed from Latino gangbanger Hector (Rodriguez). The deal goes wrong but Allison is intrigued and she and Emily go back to party with Hector and his crew, which gets the wannabes into some serious trouble. Hathaway gets naked, which might be of interest to some viewers, but documentary filmmaker Kopple fails to make her fiction of much interest beyond its gritty look, thanks to a weak script from Gaghan. **92m/C; DVD; Closed Captioned.** Anne Hathaway; Bijou Phillips; Freddy Rodriguez; Mike Vogel; Matt O'Leary; Joseph Gordon-Levitt; Shiri Appleby; Channing Tatum; Michael Biehn; Laura San Giacomo; ***D:*** Barbara Kopple; ***W:*** Stephen Gaghan; ***C:*** Kramer Morgenthau; ***M:*** Cliff Martinez. **VIDEO**

Havoc 2: Normal Adolescent Behavior *Normal Adolescent Behavior* **2007 (R)** It's kinda scary to think that this is a realistic portrait of modern teen life. Six teens, who have known each other since kindergarten, have decided to have sexual relationships only with each other at their Saturday night parties. But Wendy (Tamblyn) falls for her new neighbor Sean (Holmes) and wants to change the rules, leaving clique leader Billie (Garner) very unhappy. **93m/C; DVD.** Amber Tamblyn; Ashton Holmes; Kelli Garner; Raviv (Ricky) Ullman; Stephen Colletti; Hilarie Burton; Daryl Sabara; Kelly Lynch; Julia Garro; Edward Tournier; ***D:*** Beth Schacter; ***W:*** Beth Schacter; ***C:*** Harlan Bosmajian; ***M:*** Craig DeLeon.

Hawaii **1966** James Michener's novel about a New England farm boy who decides in 1820 that the Lord has commanded him to the island of Hawaii for the purpose of "Christianizing" the natives. Filmed on location. Also available in a 181 minute version with restored footage. Available in director's cut version with an additional 20 minutes. **161m/C; VHS, DVD.** Max von Sydow; Julie Andrews; Richard Harris; Carroll O'Connor; Bette Midler; Gene Hackman; Jocelyn Lagarde; ***D:*** George Roy Hill; ***W:*** Daniel Taradash; Dalton Trumbo; ***M:*** Elmer Bernstein. Golden Globes '67: Score, Support. Actress (Lagarde).

Hawaii Calls ✐✐ **1938** Two young stowaways on a cruise ship are allowed to stay on after one of them (Breen) struts his stuff as a singer. The two then turn sleuth to catch a gang of spies. More ham than a can of Spam, but still enjoyable. **72m/B; VHS, DVD.** Bobby Breen; Ned Sparks; Irvin S. Cobb; Warren Hull; Gloria Holden; Pua Lani; Raymond Paige; Philip Ahn; Ward Bond; ***D:*** Edward F. (Eddie) Cline.

The Hawk ✐✐ **1/2 1993 (R)** Okay thriller about suburban housewife Annie (Mirren) who suspects that her husband Stephen (Costigan) is a serial killer known as the Hawk. Since Annie has a history of depression and her husband is a known louse, her suspicions are dismissed as delusional. Some surprise twists help the weak story along. Contains some graphic views of corpses. Based on the novel by Ransley. **84m/C; VHS, DVD.** *GB* Dame Helen Mirren; George Costigan; Owen Teale; Rosemary Leach; ***D:*** David Hayman; ***W:*** Peter Ransley; ***M:*** Nick Bicat.

The Hawk Is Dying ✐ **1/2 2006** And so's the flick. Gloomy George Gattling (Giamatti) is stuck in a boring life, helping his sister (Schwimmer) with her autistic son, Fred (Pitt). When tragedy strikes, George becomes obsessed with catching and taming a wild red-tail hawk, seeking to control something in his life, no matter the cost or consequences. Williams shows up occasionally as a stoner co-ed willing to boff George. Based on the novel by Harry Crews. **106m/C; DVD.** Paul Giamatti; Michelle Williams; Michael Pitt; Robert Wisdom; Rusty Schwimmer; Ann Wedgeworth; ***D:*** Julian Goldberger; ***W:*** Julian Goldberger; ***C:*** Bobby Bukowski; ***M:*** Julian Goldberger.

Hawk the Slayer ✐ **1/2 1981** A comic book fantasy. A good warrior struggles against his villainous brother to possess a magical sword that bestows upon its holder great powers of destruction. Violent battle scenes; Palance makes a great villain. **93m/C; VHS, DVD.** Jack Palance; John Terry; Harry Andrews; Roy Kinnear; Ferdinand "Ferdy" Mayne; William Morgan Sheppard; ***D:*** Terry Marcel.

Hawks ✐ **1/2 1989 (R)** Somewhere on the road to black-comedy this film gets waylaid by triviality. Two terminally ill men break out of the hospital, determined to make their way to Amsterdam for some last-minute fun. Mediocre at best. **105m/C; VHS, Streaming.** *GB* Anthony Edwards; Timothy Dalton; Janet McTeer; Jill Bennett; Sheila Hancock; Connie Booth; Camille Coduri; ***D:*** Robert Ellis Miller; ***W:*** Roy Clarke; ***C:*** Doug Milsome.

The Hawks & the Sparrows ✐✐ *Uccellacci e Uccellini* **1967** Shortly after "Mr. Ed" came Pasolini's garrulous crow, which follows a father and son's travels through Italy spouting pithy bits of politics. A comic Pasolinian allegory-fest full of then-topical political allusions, the story comes off a bit wooden. Worth watching to see Toto, the Italian comic, in his element. **91m/B; VHS, DVD.** *IT* Toto; Ninetto Davoli; Femi Benussi; ***D:*** Pier Paolo Pasolini; ***W:*** Pier Paolo Pasolini; ***M:*** Ennio Morricone.

Hawk's Vengeance ✐✐ **1996 (R)** While investigating his police detective stepbrother's murder British Royal Marine Lt. Eric "Hawk" Kelly (Daniels) discovers a bizarre connection between a skinhead gang called the Death Skulls, a martial arts master crime boss (Magda), and the black market organ trade. **96m/C; VHS, DVD.** Gary Daniels; Cass Magda; Jayne Heitmeyer; Vlasta Vrana; ***D:*** Marc Voizard; ***W:*** Jim Cirile; ***C:*** John Berrie; ***M:*** Eleanor Academia.

Hawmps! WOOF! 1976 (G) Idiotic comedy about a Civil War lieutenant who trains his men to use camels. When the soldiers and animals begin to grow fond of each other, Congress orders the camels to be set free. Hard to believe this was based on a real life incident. **98m/C; VHS, DVD.** James Hampton; Christopher Connelly; Slim Pickens; Denver Pyle; ***D:*** Joe Camp; ***W:*** William Bickley; ***M:*** Euel Box.

Haxan: Witchcraft through the Ages ✐✐✐ *Haxan; Witchcraft through the Ages* **1922** The demonic Swedish masterpiece in which witches and victims suffer against various historical backgrounds. Nightmarish and profane, especially the appearance of the Devil as played under much make-up by Christiansen himself. Silent. **74m/B; Silent; VHS, DVD, Blu-Ray.** *SW* Maren Pedersen; Clara Pontoppidan; Oscar Stribolt; Benjamin Christiansen; Tora Teje; Elith Pio; Karen Winther; Emmy Schonfeld; John Andersen; Astrid Holm; Gerda Madsen; ***Nar:*** William S. Burroughs; ***D:*** Benjamin Christiansen; ***W:*** Benjamin Christiansen; ***C:*** Johan Ankerstjerne.

Haywire ✐✐ **1/2 1980** Based on Brooke Hayward's Hollywood memoir about her dysfunctional family—actress mother Margaret Sullavan (Remick) and producer/agent father Leland Hayward (Robards). Despite her professional success, Sullavan desperately wanted to achieve the perfect family life while Hayward was wayward and the two would divorce with their three children caught up in their parents' career and marital troubles. Told in flashback, after Sullavan commits suicide in 1960. **184m/C; DVD.** Lee Remick; Jason Robards, Jr.; Deborah Raffin; Dianne Hull; Hart Bochner; Linda Gray; ***D:*** Michael Tuchner; ***W:*** Ivan Davis; ***C:*** Howard Schwartz; ***M:*** Billy Goldenberg. **TV**

Haywire ✐✐✐ **2012 (R)** Building a unique spy thriller around a non-actor in Carano (a Mixed Martial Arts champion, holding her own in her first movie role) may have been a risk, but the talents of director Soderbergh and his technical team make this a lean, mean action machine. Covert ops agent Mallory Kane (Carano) is betrayed and suddenly she must question everyone around her—including her former boss and lover Kenneth (McGregor) and other operatives Paul (Fassbender), Aaron (Tatum), Coblenz (Douglas) and Rodrigo (Banderas)?and must fight her way to vengeance. Globe-hopping, she boldly, beautifully, and violently confronts this gaggle of combatants in a fast-paced and purposefully enigmatic story. **93m/C; DVD, Blu-Ray.** Gina Carano; Channing Tatum; Ewan McGregor; Michael Fassbender; Antonio Banderas; Bill Paxton; Michael Douglas; Michael Angarano; ***D:*** Steven Soderbergh; ***W:*** Lem Dobbs; ***C:*** Steven Soderbergh; ***M:*** David Holmes.

The Hazing ✐ **1/2** *Dead Scared* **2004** A demon is set loose at a campus mansion where college frat students spend a grisly initiation evening possessed by the wicked dude. **87m/C; VHS, DVD.** Brad Dourif; Tiffany Shepis; Parry Shen; David Tom; Robert Donovan; Philip Andrew; Jeremy Maxwell; Nectar Rose; Charmaine DeGrate; Brooke Burke; Jeff LeBeau; ***Cameo(s):*** Robert Donovan; ***D:*** Rolfe Kanefsky; ***W:*** Rolfe Kanefsky; ***M:*** Chris Farrell. **VIDEO**

He Died With a Falafel in His Hand ✐✐ **2001** Ya gotta love the title—if nothing else about this adaptation of John Birmingham's seriocomic 1994 novel. Three distinct Australian cities play their part: subtropical Brisbane inspires indolence and wacky sunstruck behavior; cool Melbourne fosters navel-gazing and an overly-earnest dedication to causes; and seaside Sydney is dedicated to hedonism. Wannabe Brisbane writer Danny (Taylor) is looking for some kind of purpose in life and turns to friend Sam (Hamilton) for advice. The duo wind up in Melbourne after Sam's breakup with gal pal Anya (Bohringer) and finally make their way to Sydney where their chaotic lives don't become any more stable. Oh, and the title refers to one of the duo's many strange roommates. **107m/C; DVD.** *AU IT* Noah Taylor; Emily Hamilton; Romane Bohringer; Alex Menglet; Sophie Lee; Francis McMahon; Brett Stewart; ***D:*** Richard Lowenstein; ***W:*** Richard Lowenstein; ***C:*** Andrew de Groot. **VIDEO**

He Found a Star ✐ **1/2 1941** Struggling talent agent Lucky (Oliver) and his loyal secretary Ruth (Churchill) specialize in giving a break to unknowns. Lucky finally gets lucky when he changes the act of singer Frank Forrester (Atkins), which leads slinky nightclub singer Suzanne (Dall) to ask him to help her. Suzanne's a bad bet (she's troubled), so it's Ruth to the rescue when she fills in for the unreliable dame. **89m/B; DVD.** *GB* Sarah Churchill; Joan Greenwood; Gabrielle Brune; Vic Oliver; Evelyn Dall; Robert Atkins; ***D:*** Jack Paddy Carstairs; ***W:*** Bridget Boland; Austin Melford; ***C:*** Ernest Palmer.

He Got Game ✐✐ **1/2 1998 (R)** Lee hops all over the place with this basketball drama that reveals more of his love for the game than cohesive filmmaking. Actually two movies in one: High school basketball great Jesus Shuttlesworth (newcomer and Milwaukee Bucks player Allen) must decide between college or a lucrative NBA contract. Then up pops his incarcerated pops, Jake, (a haggard Washington) to pressure him to chose his warden's alma mater, which turns the film into a shallow look at a strained father-son relationship. Washington is dynamic as the embittered father and Allen is evenly effective. Yet, the reunion is never fully developed and sometimes abandoned, while Lee scores visually by beautifully photographing the glorious hoop moves. Extraneous, stereotypical characters and raunchy sex sequences drag the film further from its dramatic resonance. **134m/C; VHS, DVD, Blu-Ray.** Denzel Washington; Ray Allen; Milla Jovovich; Rosario Dawson; Hill Harper; Zelda Harris; Jim Brown; Ned Beatty; Lonette McKee; John Turturro; Michele Shay; Bill Nunn; Thomas Jefferson Byrd; ***D:*** Spike Lee; ***W:*** Spike Lee; ***C:*** Malik Hassan Sayeed.

He Is My Brother ✐ **1/2 1975 (G)** Two boys survive a shipwreck, landing on an island that houses a leper colony. **90m/C; VHS, DVD, Streaming.** Keenan Wynn; Bobby Sherman; Robbie (Reist) Rist; ***D:*** Edward Dmytryk.

He Knew He Was Right ✐ **1/2 2004** BBC melodrama based on the Anthony Trollope novel. Louis and Emily Trevelyan's first year of marriage is disturbed by the presence of Emily's godfather, Col. Osborne. He's a roue who pursues married women and Louis thinks he's unsuitable company for his wife. Emily thinks Louis is a jealous prig. There are other romantic travails in the subplots but it's generally dull fare. **240m/C; DVD.** *UK* Oliver Dimsdale; Laura Fraser; Bill Nighy; David Tennant; Christina Cole; Stephen Campbell Moore; Geoffrey Palmer; Geraldine James; ***D:*** Tom Vaughan; ***W:*** Andrew Davies; ***C:*** Mike Eley; ***M:*** Debbie Wiseman. **TV**

He Knows You're Alone ✐ **1980 (R)** Lame horror flick that focuses on a psychotic killer terrorizing a bride-to-be and her bridal party in his search for a suitable bride of his own. **94m/C; VHS, DVD.** Don Scardino; Caitlin (Kathleen Heaney) O'Heaney; Tom Rolfing; Paul Gleason; Elizabeth Kemp; Tom Hanks; Patsy Pease; Lewis Arlt; James Rebhorn; Joseph Leon; James Carroll; ***D:*** Armand Mastroianni; ***W:*** Scott Parker; ***C:*** Gerald Feil; ***M:*** Alexander Peskanov; Mark Peskanov.

He Loves Me ✐✐ **2011** Guilty pleasure psycho-thriller from the Lifetime channel. Bored Laura (Locklear) begins a compulsive affair with Sam (Martini) that threatens her marriage to Nick (Neal). To deal with her craziness, Laura begins to see shrink Dr. Browning (Rose) but the more she reveals, the more you realize that delusional Laura has a violent, paranoid past. **94m/C; DVD.** Heather Locklear; Maximillian Martini; Dylan Neal; Gabrielle Rose; Jill Teed; Adam Sliwinski; ***D:*** Jeff Renfroe; ***W:*** Joyce Heft Brotman; ***M:*** James Geldand. **CABLE**

He Loves Me . . . He Loves Me Not ✐✐ *A la Folie. . .Pas de Tout* **2002** Art student Angelique (Tautou) is obsessively enthralled with her married lover, cardiologist Loic (Le Bihan), and refuses to believe that he won't leave his pregnant wife Rachel (Carre). When Loic stands Angelique up before they are about to take a holiday, she begins to unravel and attempts suicide. Then the film takes us back to the beginning and shows Loic's very different point-of-view: Angelique is delusional and stalking Loic who barely knows the girl. And her madness just excels from there. French with subtitles. **92m/C; VHS, DVD.** *FR* Audrey Tautou; Samuel Le Bihan; Isabelle Carre; Sophie Guillemin; Clement Sibony; ***D:*** Laetitia Colombani; ***W:*** Laetitia Colombani; Caroline Thival; ***C:*** Pierre Aim; ***M:*** Jerome Coullet.

He Named Me Malala ✐✐ **1/2 2015 (PG-13)** Malala Yousafzai was shot in the head by a Taliban gunman for the role she played in trying to educate girls in Pakistan. She was just a child. The shooting didn't stop her; in fact, it gave a more prominent international voice, even wining her the Nobel Peace Prize. Davis Guggenheim's film about this young hero has an undeniably important story to tell, even if its creator tells it in a disappointingly straightforward manner with the narrow perspective of a white foreigner. We don't learn as much about Malala as one would hope, although one could argue that her courage is lesson enough. **88m/C; DVD.** *UA US* Malala Yousafzai; ***D:*** Davis Guggenheim; ***W:*** Davis Guggenheim; ***C:*** Erich Roland; ***M:*** Thomas Newman.

He Never Died ✐✐ **1/2 2015 (R)** Henry Rollins finds the film role for which he's been destined his whole career as Jack, an immortal killing machine who has literally seen it all—and just wants to be left alone. He spends most of his never-ending days in melancholy limbo—sleeping, watching TV, eating at the same diner. At that eating establishment he meets a waitress, with whom he gets invested enough to have to protect her when she needs it. This is a clever play on genre, coming off more like a hard-boiled noir than a horror movie. The protagonist this time just happens to be unkillable. **97m/C; DVD.** Booboo Stewart; Henry Rollins; Steven Ogg; James Cade; Jordan Todosey; ***D:*** Jason Krawczyk; ***W:*** Jason Krawczyk; ***C:*** Eric Billman; ***M:*** James Mark Stewart.

He Said, She Said ✐✐ **1/2 1991 (R)** Romance is the topic, but this isn't a typical dating film, instead a couple's relationship unfolds from differing points of view: first, the guy's (by Kwapis) and then the girl's (by Silver). Bacon and Perkins, Baltimore journalists and professional rivals, tell how their romance wound up on the rocks, and why (or so they say). The end result is overlong and lacks the zing of other war between the sexes movies, but real-life couple Silver and Kwapis do humorously highlight the fact that men and women often view the same incidents very differently. Bacon overacts, Perkins overreacts, and Stone shines as Bacon's ex-girl. **115m/C; VHS, DVD.** Elizabeth Perkins; Kevin Bacon; Sharon Stone; Nathan Lane; Anthony LaPaglia; Stanley Anderson; Charlaine Woodard; Danton Stone; Phil Leeds; Rita Karin; ***D:*** Marisa Silver; Ken Kwapis; ***W:*** Brian Hohlfeld; ***C:*** Stephen Burum; ***M:*** Miles Goodman.

He Sees You When You're Sleeping ✐ **1/2 2002 (PG)** Recently deceased stockbroker Sterling's superficial life doesn't pass muster with the powers-that-be at the pearly gates. But his guardian angel sets him up with one last selfless earthly task to make amends—save a single mom and her seven-year-old daughter from the evil clutches of the local mob. A Christmas-themed Mary Higgins Clark adaptation. **100m/C; VHS, DVD.** Cameron Bancroft; Erika Eleniak; Greg Evigan; Udo Kier; Sean Campbell; Pam Hyatt; David Palffy; Eli Gabay; Nickol Tschenscher; Landy Cannon; Roger Haskett; Rheta Hutton; Jason Low; Craig March; Claire Riley; ***D:*** David Winning; ***W:*** Carl Binder; ***C:*** David Pelletier; ***M:*** Michael Richard Plowman. **TV**

He Walked by Night ✐✐✐ **1/2 1948** Los Angeles homicide investigators track down cop killer Ray Morgan (Basehart) in this excellent drama. The final confrontation takes place in the L.A. County Flood Control System, consisting of some 700 miles of underground tunnels. Based on a true story from the files of the Los Angelés police, this first rate production reportedly inspired Webb to create "Dragnet." **80m/B; VHS, DVD, Blu-Ray.** Richard Basehart; Scott Brady; Roy Roberts; Jack Webb; Whit Bissell; ***D:*** Alfred Werker; Anthony Mann; ***W:*** John C. Higgins; ***C:*** John Alton; ***M:*** Leonid Raab.

He Was a Quiet Man ✐ **1/2 2007** Milquetoast Bob Maconel (Slater) is a paranoid and angry office drone who likes to keep a loaded gun in his desk. He accidentally becomes a hero when a co-worker does go postal and Bob kills him. This earns him a promotion. But he's dismayed to find out that his secret crush, Vanessa (Cuthbert), was paralyzed by a bullet and wants Bob to help her die. He can't, so they start a romance instead, or do they? Ending leaves a lot to puzzle out. **95m/C; DVD.** Christian Slater; Elisha Cuthbert; William H. Macy; Sascha Knopf; John Gulager; Jamison Jones; ***D:*** Frank A. Capello; ***W:*** Frank A. Capello; ***C:*** Brandon Trost; ***M:*** Jeff Beal.

He Who Gets Slapped ✐✐✐ **1924** Chaney portrays a brilliant scientist whose personal and professional humiliations cause him to join a travelling French circus as a masochistic clown (hence the title). There he falls in love with a beautiful circus performer and plans a spectacular revenge. Brilliant use of lighting and Expressionist devices by director Sjostrom (who used the Americanized version of his name-Seastrom-in the credits). Adapted from the Russian play "He, The One Who Gets Slapped" by Leonid Andreyev. **85m/B; Silent; VHS, DVD.** Lon Chaney, Sr.; Norma Shearer; John Gilbert; Tully Marshall; Ford Sterling; Marc McDermott; ***D:*** Victor Sjostrom; ***W:*** Carey Wilson; Victor Sjostrom. Natl. Film Reg. '17.

The Head 🦴🦴 **1959** A scientist comes up with a serum that can keep the severed head of a dog alive. Before too long, he tries the stuff out on a woman, transferring the head from her own hunchbacked body to that of a beautiful stripper. Weird German epic sports poor special effects and unintentional laughs, but is interesting nonetheless. **92m/B; VHS, DVD.** *GE* Horst Frank; Michel Simon; Paul Dahlke; Karin Kernke; Helmut Schmidt; ***D:*** Victor Trivas; ***W:*** Victor Trivas.

Head 🦴🦴🦴 **1968 (G)** Infamously plotless musical comedy starring the TV fab four of the '60s, the Monkees, in their only film appearance. A number of guest stars appear and a collection of old movie clips are also included. **86m/C; VHS, DVD.** Peter Tork; Mickey Dolenz; Davy Jones; Michael Nesmith; Frank Zappa; Annette Funicello; Teri Garr; Timothy Carey; Logan Ramsey; Victor Mature; Jack Nicholson; Bob Rafelson; Dennis Hopper; ***D:*** Bob Rafelson; ***W:*** Jack Nicholson; Bob Rafelson; ***C:*** Michel Hugo; ***M:*** Ken Thorne.

Head Above Water 🦴🦴 **1996 (PG-13)** Remake of same-titled 1993 Norwegian black comedy is now set on an island off the Maine coast where marrieds Nathalie (Diaz) and George (Keitel) are vacationing at her family's cottage. George goes off on an overnight fishing trip, but Nathalie isn't alone for long—former boyfriend Kent (Zane) shows up, the duo get drunk catching up on old times, and Nathalie wakes up the next morning with Kent's corpse. The unstable Nathalie hides the body, which is quickly found by George, who discards the corpse in a more permanent manner involving cement. Then Natalie suddenly decides George must have murdered Kent and is now after her. Plot doesn't hang together well and Keitel is frequently too low-key but Diaz is watchable. **92m/C; VHS, DVD.** Cameron Diaz; Harvey Keitel; Craig Sheffer; Billy Zane; ***D:*** Jim Wilson; ***W:*** Theresa Marie; ***C:*** Richard Bowen; ***M:*** Christopher Young.

Head Games 🦴🦴🦴 **2012 (PG-13)** Director James ("Hoop Dreams") returns to the sports documentary genre with an eye-opening examination of the cost of repeated head injuries in professional and youth sports. With an increasing number of retired football players dealing with dementia that is being more commonly tied to concussions, new light has been shed on all sports and the lasting damage people are taking on a daily basis in the name of sport. James asks some startling questions about the future of football on all levels and even extends his examination to soccer, hockey, and other games. **95m/C; DVD.** Bob Costas; Chris Nowinski; ***D:*** Steve James; ***C:*** Dana Kupper; Keith Walker; ***M:*** Billy Corgan; Craig Snider.

Head in the Clouds 🦴🦴 **2004 (R)** Beautiful Theron turns heads as hedonistic socialite Gilda, who briefly storms into the life of shy Irishman Guy (Townsend) in 1933. His torch remains ablaze as she later summons him to Paris, where Gilda is dabbling as a photographer and with a Spanish refugee named Mia (Cruz). Their triangular idyll is troubled by the political idealism displayed by both Mia and Guy, who are committed to the anti-fascist cause in the Spanish Civil War. Gilda feels betrayed when they leave her behind. When Guy finally sees her again in 1944, he's a British spy smuggled into Paris and Gilda is romancing Nazi officer Bietrich (Kretschmann). But is she really the unfeeling collaborator she seems? A plush potboiler with a pretty cast. **124m/C; DVD.** *GB CA* Charlize Theron; Penelope Cruz; Stuart Townsend; Thomas Kretschmann; Steven Berkoff; Karine Vanasse; Gabriel Hogan; David LaHaye; Peter Cockett; John Jorgenson; ***D:*** John Duigan; ***W:*** John Duigan; ***C:*** Paul Sarossy; ***M:*** Terry Frewer.

Head of State 🦴🦴 **2003 (PG-13)** Just because Rock played a director in "Jay and Silent Bob Strike Back" doesn't mean he can do it in real life, at least not yet. Rock plays Mays Gilliam, a D.C. alderman drafted to run for President after the unnamed party's candidates die in a plane crash. The party leadership doesn't want him to win, just provide diversity cred for the next election. With his brother Mitch (Mac) as running mate, Mays fights his handlers to create his own identity. Unfortunately, in the hands of writer and director Rock, candidate Rock isn't given much consistent identity to work with. Maybe with a proven director, and more than token effort at plot and characterization, this one might've been better. **95m/C; VHS, DVD.** Chris Rock; Bernie Mac; Dylan Baker; Nick Searcy; Lynn Whitfield; Robin Givens; Tamala Jones; Stephanie March; James Rebhorn; Keith David; Tracy Morgan; Robert Stanton; Jude Ciccolella; Nate Dogg; ***D:*** Chris Rock; ***W:*** Chris Rock; Ali LeRoi; ***C:*** Donald E. Thorin; ***M:*** Marcus Miller; David "DJ Quik" Blake.

Head of the Family 🦴 1/2 **1996 (R)** Lance (Bailey) moves to Nob Hollow and discovers the Stackpool family's dreadful secrets—they're telepathic quadruplets under the control of brother Myron (Perra), who just happens to be a giant head that gets around in a wheelchair. Lance decides to use the whacko family to get rid of babe girlfriend Loretta's (Lovell) inconvenient husband. **82m/C; VHS, DVD, Blu-Ray.** Blake Bailey; Jacqueline Lovell; Bob Schott; J.W. Perra; ***D:*** Robert Talbot; ***W:*** Benjamin Carr; ***C:*** Adolfo Bartoli; ***M:*** Richard Band.

Head Office 🦴🦴 **1986 (PG-13)** A light comedy revolving around the competition between corporate management and the lower echelon for the available position of chairman. **90m/C; VHS, DVD.** Danny DeVito; Eddie Albert; Judge Reinhold; Rick Moranis; Jane Seymour; ***D:*** Ken Finkleman; ***M:*** James Newton Howard.

Head On 🦴🦴🦴 **1998** Nineteen-year-old Ari (Dimitriades) is forced to confront his Greek heritage and its idea of manhood with the homosexuality he keeps secret from his traditional family. Much of his day is spent killing time with his friends until he can meet Sean (Garner), the young man Ari is attracted to, at a bar that night. Bored and restless, Ari is out to have a good time with as little pain to himself as possible. Adapted from the book "Loaded" by Christos Tsiolkas. **104m/C; VHS, DVD.** *AU* Alex Dimitriades; Paul Capsis; Julian Garner; Damien Fotiou; Elena Mandalis; Andrea Mandalis; Tony Nikolakopoulos; Eugenia Fragos; Maria Mercedes; ***D:*** Ana Kokkinos; ***W:*** Ana Kokkinos; Mira Robertson; Andrew Bovell; ***C:*** Jaems Grant; ***M:*** Ollie Olsen.

Head On 🦴🦴 *Gegen die Wand* **2004** Cahit (Unel) is a Turkish immigrant in Hamburg whose drunken, self-destructive behavior lands him in a psych ward. He meets fellow immigrant Sibel (Kekilli), a wrist-slasher who needs to escape her conservative Muslim family either by death or a marriage of convenience. Cahit figures he has nothing to lose and agrees when Sibel says she will keep him in alcohol. But their arrangement eventually spirals into mad love and violent consequences. Turkish and German with subtitles. **118m/C; DVD.** Birol Unel; Sibel Kekilli; Catrin Striebeck; Guven Kirac; Meltem Cumbul; Cem Akin; Aysel Iscan; Demir Gokgol; Stefan Gebelhoff; Hermann Lause; Adam Bousdoukos; Ralph Misske; Mehmet Kurtulus; ***D:*** Fatih Akin; ***W:*** Fatih Akin; ***C:*** Rainer Klausmann.

Head Over Heels 🦴🦴 *Head Over Heels In Love* **1937** Simple musical romance, set in Paris. Rising star Jeanne is loved by radio engineer Pierre, but she loves womanizing Marcel. Marcel runs off with American actress Norma, but shows up again when Jeanne becomes famous. Only now Pierre is willing to fight for her. **84m/B; DVD.** *UK* Jessie Matthews; Robert Flemyng; Louis Borel; Whitney Bourne; Romney Brent; ***D:*** Sonnie Hale; ***W:*** Fred Thompson; Dwight Taylor; Marjorie Gaffney; ***C:*** Glen MacWilliams.

Head Over Heels 🦴🦴🦴 **1967** A model married to an older man has an affair with a younger one and cannot decide between them. In French with subtitles. **89m/C; VHS, DVD.** *FR* Brigitte Bardot; Laurent Terzieff; Michael Sarne; ***D:*** Serge Bourguignon.

Head Over Heels 🦴 1/2 **2001 (PG-13)** New York art restorer Amanda (Potter) has sworn off men after a bad breakup, but finds herself back in the game when she meets her dashing and mysterious neighbor, Jim (Prinze). Having conveniently taken up residence in an apartment that offers a perfect view of the one occupied by Jim, her attraction grows as she and her supermodel roommates follow the young man's every move. Works well during its romantic comedy stretches, but loses points for its reliance on an ill-conceived plot point revolving around a possible murder, and for lowering itself to much crude, scatological humor. **86m/C; VHS, DVD.** Monica Potter; Freddie Prinze, Jr.; Shalom Harlow; Ivana Milicevic; China Chow; Jay Brazeau; Sarah O'Hare; Tomiko Fraser; Stanley DeSantis; ***D:*** Mark S. Waters; ***W:*** Ron Burch; David Kidd; ***C:*** Mark Plummer; ***M:*** Randy Edelman; Steve Porcaro.

Headhunter 🦴🦴 **2005** Ben Caruso (Parrillo) wants a new job and is advised to see Sarah (Clainos), a professional headhunter. Sarah gets Ben a higher-paying desk job but it's on the graveyard shift, and weird things immediately start happening. When Ben does some investigating, he learns Sarah was a murder victim who was decapitated and has been using her "clients" to find her missing head. And if they can't, they may have to look for their own. Offers some surprises for the indie horror genre. **90m/C; DVD.** Ben Parrillo; Kristi Clainos; Mark Aiken; ***D:*** Paul Tarantino; ***W:*** Paul Tarantino; ***C:*** Seth Kotok; ***M:*** Vincent Gillioz. **VIDEO**

Headhunters 🦴🦴 *Hodejegerne* **2011 (R)** Roger Brown (Hennie) is a Norwegian art thief forced into a life of crime to support his extravagant lifestyle. A chance meeting with a mercenary through his wife leads to Roger stumbling across something that puts everything he has worked for (or stolen) in jeopardy. An international hit, this streamlined, clever action thriller could teach a few American studios a thing or two about how to produce similar entertainment. Sleek, well-paced, and beautiful to look at, the final result is a bit inconsistent but nonetheless thoroughly entertaining. Based on Jo Nesbo's 2008 book. Norwegian with subtitles. **100m/C; DVD, Blu-Ray, Streaming.** *NO* Aksel Hennie; Nikolaj Coster-Waldau; Synnove Macody Lund; Eivind Sander; ***D:*** Morten Tyldum; ***W:*** Lars Gudmestad; Ulf Ryberg; ***C:*** John Andreas Andersen; ***M:*** Jeppe Kaas; Trond Bjerknaes.

Headin' for Trouble 🦴 1/2 **1931** Cowboy Cyclone Crosby comes to the aid of Mary Courtney, who's harassed by bad guy Butch Morgan. Morgan's cohort Slade has also set-up a crooked poker game and Mary's father, compulsive gambler John Courtney, keeps losing the deed to their ranch. Crosby gets it back and then sets out to prove Morgan is also the leader of a gang of cattle rustlers. **65m/B; DVD.** Bob Custer; Robert Walker; Betty Mack; Buck Connors; John Ince; Andy Shuford; Duke Lee; ***D:*** J(ohn) P(aterson) McGowan; ***W:*** George Morgan; ***C:*** Edward A. Kull.

Heading for Heaven 🦴🦴 **1947** A mistaken medical report leaves a frazzled realtor believing he has only three months to live, and when he disappears the family suspects the worst. A minor comedy based on a play by Charles Webb. **65m/B; VHS, DVD.** Stuart Erwin; Glenda Farrell; Russ Vincent; Irene Ryan; Milburn Stone; George O'Hanlon; ***D:*** Lewis D. Collins.

Heading South 🦴🦴🦴 *Vers le Sud* **2005** French pic set in the late '70s tells the story of three women "of a certain age," as the euphemism goes, who travel to an accommodating beachside resort in Haiti to satisfy their still-burning sexual needs. Each woman has her own backstory and reason for seeking out the pleasures of a more-than-willing local teenager, and each take a turn explaining this frankly and directly to the camera. The wretched conditions and dangers of life for the locals are shown in frightening, sharp contrast to the self-indulgence of the foreigners. Veteran French director Laurent Cantet elicits excellent performances from cast, most notably Charlotte Rampling as queen bee Ellen. Based on short stories by Haitian writer Dany Laferriere. **105m/C; DVD.** *CA FR* Charlotte Rampling; Karen Young; Louise Portal; Menothy Cesar; Lys Ambroise; Jackenson Pierre Olmo Diaz; Wilfried Paul; ***D:*** Laurent Cantet; ***W:*** Laurent Cantet; Robin Campillo; ***C:*** Pierre Milon.

Headless Body in Topless Bar 🦴🦴 1/2 **1996** Based on a famous New York Post headline and the crime that inspired it, this black comedy contains more than its lurid title lets on. Except for street footage at the opening and closing, the entire movie is set in a seedy strip club. After shooting the bartender in a robbery attempt, a crazed ex-con holds the patrons and employees hostage. He forces them to play a mind game called "Nazi truth," revealing the distasteful truth about the captives. Director Bruce and screenwriter Koper first worked together filming re-creations for "America's Most Wanted." The cast worked for "hostage scale," meaning if those playing captives stole the gun from the robber (a plot point), they got his pay for the day. If not, then he got their wages. **105m/C; VHS, DVD.** Raymond J. Barry; Jennifer MacDonald; David Selby; Taylor Nichols; Paul Williams; Biff Yeager; Rustam Branaman; April Grace; ***D:*** James Bruce; ***W:*** Peter Koper; ***C:*** Kevin Morrisey; ***M:*** Charles P. Barnett.

Headless Horseman 🦴 1/2 **2007 (R)** Run-of-the-mill horror flick with a group of teens who get lost on their way to a Halloween party. They wander into a cursed town that uses them as fodder for a ritual involving summoning a ghostly headhunter. **87m/C; DVD, Streaming.** *RO US* Billy Aaron Brown; Rebecca Mozo; Richard Moll; Arianne Fraser; Vasile Albinet; ***D:*** Anthony C. Ferrante; ***W:*** Anthony C. Ferrante; Zachary Weintraub; ***C:*** David Worth; ***M:*** Alan Howarth. **CABLE**

The Headless Woman 🦴 1/2 *La Mujer Sin Cabeza* **2008** Middle-aged Veronica (Onetto) is driving on a remote road when she is distracted by her ringing cell phone and hits something. She drives off but is burdened by guilt (there were children playing by the road) and finally confesses to her husband about what may have happened. Spanish with subtitles. **89m/C; DVD.** *AR* Maria Onetto; Cesar Bordon; Daniel Genoud; Claudia Cantero; Ines Efron; ***D:*** Lucrecia Martel; ***W:*** Lucrecia Martel; ***C:*** Barbara Alvarez.

Headline Woman 🦴🦴 **1935** An ongoing feud between a police commissioner and a newspaper's city editor causes a reporter to make a deal with a policeman in exchange for news. A good cast makes this otherwise tired story tolerable. **75m/B; VHS, DVD.** Heather Angel; Roger Pryor; Jack La Rue; Ford Sterling; Conway Tearle; ***D:*** William Nigh.

Headshot 🦴🦴 1/2 **2017** A violent, bloody martial arts action film. Ishmael (Uwais), the name given to a comatose man when he is taken to the hospital, gradually recovers his memory and learns that he grew up with a group of orphans turned killing machines formed by crime boss Lee (Pang). It becomes clear that Lee tortured young Ishmael and that Ishmael later betrayed him and the other orphans. When Lee escapes from prison and goes on a killing spree, Ishmael uses his skills on his own terms, not as the feral product of Lee's training. Full of quality action choreography and confident performance by Uwais **118m/C; DVD.** Iko Uwais; Chelsea Islan; Sunny Pang; Very Tri Yulisman; Julie Estelle; ***D:*** Kimo Stamboel; Timo Tjahjanto; ***W:*** Timo Tjahjanto; ***C:*** Yunus Pasolang; ***M:*** Aria Prayogi; Fajar Yuskemal.

Headspace 🦴 1/2 **2002 (R)** Something triggers Alex's (Denham) brain into hyperdrive and gives him immense mental abilities, including super-fast speed reading and chess-playing invincibility. But the drawbacks are wicked, as his repressed childhood memory of dad blowing away mom returns, along with hellish visions of ghastly monsters. To make things worse, the people around him are winding up dead, causing him the all-too-obvious concern that he's in some way responsible. **90m/C; DVD, Blu-Ray.** Sean Young; Larry Fessenden; William Atherton; Dee Wallace; Christopher Denham; Erick Kastel; Olivia Hussey; Mark Margolis; Udo Kier; ***D:*** Andrew van den Houten; ***W:*** Steve Klausner; William M. Miller; ***C:*** William M. Miller; ***M:*** Ryan Shore.

Healer 🦴 1/2 *Little Pal* **1936** A doctor forgets his pledge to help the lame and becomes a fashionable physician. A young crippled lad helps him eventually remember his original purpose was to serve others. **80m/B; VHS, DVD.** Mickey Rooney; Ralph Bellamy; Karen Morley; Judith Allen; Robert McWade; ***D:*** Reginald Barker.

The Healer *Julie Walking Home* **2002** When her cancer-stricken son is unable to take traditional treatment, Julie frantically seeks out a mystic healer in Poland to cure him. In the midst of a divorce from her cheating husband she unexpectedly finds romance there as well. **113m/C; VHS, DVD.** Miranda Otto; William Fichtner; Lothaire Bluteau; Jerzy Nowak; Ryan Smith; Bianca Crudo; Boguslawa Schubert; ***D:*** Agnieszka Holland; ***W:*** Agnieszka Holland; Arlene Sarner; ***C:*** Jacek Petrycki; ***M:*** Antoni Lazarkiewicz. **TV**

Healing **2015 (R)** A drama about unexpected redemption, inspired by true events. Viktor Khadem (Hany) has spent the last 18 years in prison and is a broken man. Nearing release, he spends his last incarcerated months in a low-security prison. There, a senior officer, Matt Perry (Weaving), has a unique program to help such men by using them as caretakers for injured birds. Matt takes an interest in Viktor, gets him into the program, and assigns him a wild but injured eagle named Yasmine. Both bird and man heal as they tame each other. **102m/C; DVD.** Hugo Weaving; Don Hany; Xavier Samuel; Mark Leonard Winter; Anthony Hayes; ***D:*** Craig Monahan; ***W:*** Craig Monahan; Alison Nisselle; ***C:*** Andrew Lesnie; ***M:*** David Hirschfelder. **VIDEO**

Hear No Evil 1/2 **1993 (R)** Below average thriller with a deaf victim (Matlin) involved in a game of cat-and-mouse with a corrupt cop (Sheen) who's looking for a valuable coin. Weak script plays up the woman in jeopardy theme but lacks the crucial element of suspense. A waste of an otherwise talented cast. **98m/C; VHS, DVD.** Marlee Matlin; D.B. Sweeney; Martin Sheen; John C. McGinley; Christina Carlisi; Greg Elam; Charley Lang; ***D:*** Robert Greenwald; ***W:*** Randall Badat; Kathleen Rowell; ***M:*** Graeme Revell.

The Hearse WOOF! **1980 (PG)** Incredibly boring horror film in which a young school teacher moves into a mansion left to her by her late aunt and finds her life threatened by a sinister black hearse. **100m/C; VHS, DVD, Blu-Ray.** Trish Van Devere; Joseph Cotten; Donald Hotton; David Gautreaux; ***D:*** George Bowers; ***W:*** William Bleich; ***C:*** Mori Kawa.

Heart 1/2 **1987 (R)** A down-and-out small-time boxer is given a chance to make a comeback, and makes the Rocky-like most of it. **93m/C; VHS, DVD.** Brad Davis; Jesse Doran; Sam Gray; Steve Buscemi; Frances Fisher; ***D:*** James (Momel) Lemmo.

Heart 1/2 **1999 (R)** Gruesome wannable thriller (told in flashback) finds Gary Ellis (Eccleston) suffering a jealousy-induced heart attack after discovering wife Tess's (Hardie) philandering with Alex (Ifans). Gary gets a heart transplant—the donor being a young man killed in a motorcycle accident—and contacts the man's mother, Maria Ann (Reeves) after he gets out of the hospital. Too bad she's crazy. **85m/C; VHS, DVD.** *GB* Christopher Eccleston; Saskia Reeves; Kate Hardie; Rhys Ifans; Bill Paterson; Anna Chancellor; Matthew Rhys; ***D:*** Charles McDougall; ***W:*** Jimmy McGovern; ***C:*** Julian Court; ***M:*** Stephen Warbeck.

Heart and Souls 1/2 **1993 (PG-13)** Reincarnation comedy casts Downey Jr. as a mortal whose body is inhabited by four lost souls who died on the night he was born. Now an adult, he must finish what they could not, no matter how outrageous it may be. Talented cast wears plot that's old hat. Downey Jr. must be looking to do a trilogy of tired reincarnated soul roles—this is his second, "Chances Are" was his first. **104m/C; VHS, DVD.** Robert Downey, Jr.; Charles Grodin; Tom Sizemore; Alfre Woodard; Kyra Sedgwick; Elisabeth Shue; David Paymer; ***D:*** Ron Underwood; ***W:*** Brent Maddock; S.S. Wilson; Gregory Hansen; Erik Hansen; ***C:*** Michael Watkins; ***M:*** Marc Shaiman.

Heart Beat 1/2 **1980 (R)** The fictionalized story of Jack Kerouac (author of "On the Road"), his friend and inspiration Neal Cassady, and the woman they shared, Carolyn Cassady. Based on Carolyn Cassady's memoirs. Strong performances, with Nolte as Cassady and Spacek as his wife, overcome the sometimes shaky narrative. **105m/C; VHS, DVD.** Nick Nolte; John Heard; Sissy Spacek; Ann Dusenberry; Ray Sharkey; Tony Bill; Steve Allen; John Larroquette; ***D:*** John Byrum; ***W:*** John Byrum; ***M:*** Jack Nitzsche.

Heart Condition 1/2 **1990 (R)** A deceased black lawyer's heart is donated to a bigoted Los Angeles cop who was stalking the lawyer when he was alive. Soon afterwards the lawyer's ghost returns to haunt the police officer, hoping the officer will help to avenge his murder. Both Hoskins and Washington display fine performances given the unlikely script. **95m/C; VHS, DVD; Open Captioned.** Bob Hoskins; Denzel Washington; Chloe Webb; Ray Baker; Ja'net DuBois; Alan Rachins; Roger E. Mosley; Jeffrey Meek; ***D:*** James D. Parriott; ***C:*** Arthur Albert.

The Heart Is a Lonely Hunter **1968 (G)** Set in the South, Carson McCuller's tale of angst and ignorance, loneliness and beauty comes to the screen with the film debuts of Keach and Locke. Arkin gives an instinctive, gentle performance as the deaf mute. **124m/C; VHS, DVD.** Alan Arkin; Cicely Tyson; Sondra Locke; Stacy Keach; Chuck McCann; Laurinda Barrett; ***D:*** Robert Ellis Miller; ***C:*** James Wong Howe; ***M:*** Dave Grusin. N.Y. Film Critics '68: Actor (Arkin).

The Heart Is Deceitful Above All Things **2004 (R)** Sarah (writer/director Argento) is the worst kind of trailer trash—an alcoholic druggie who doesn't say no to any scum's sexual advances—yet social services returns her 7-year-old boy Jeremiah to her, taking him from stable foster parents. After corrupting him with her lifestyle, she dumps him on her very religious parents for three years, but just as the damage is undone, skanky Sarah returns and takes him on the road for more misery. Based on a supposed autobiographical novel by J.T. LeRoy that was later outed as a ruse created by writer Laura Albert. **98m/C; DVD.** Asia Argento; Jimmy Bennett; Cole Sprouse; Dylan Sprouse; Peter Fonda; Ben Foster; Ornella Muti; Kip Pardue; Michael Pitt; ***D:*** Asia Argento; ***W:*** Asia Argento; Alessandro Magania; ***C:*** Eric Alan Edwards; ***M:*** Marco Castoldi; Sonic Youth.

Heart Like a Wheel 1/2 **1983 (PG)** The story of Shirley Muldowney, who rose from the daughter of a country-western singer to the leading lady in drag racing. The film follows her battles of sexism and choosing whether to have a career or a family. Bedelia's perfomance is outstanding. Fine showings from Bridges and Axton in supporting roles. **113m/C; VHS, DVD.** Bonnie Bedelia; Beau Bridges; Bill McKinney; Leo Rossi; Hoyt Axton; Dick Miller; Anthony Edwards; ***D:*** Jonathan Kaplan; ***W:*** Ken Friedman.

Heart o' the Hills **1919** Backwoods silent melodrama. Kentucky farm girl Mavis Hawn (Pickford) devotes her time to finding the man who murdered her father. The killing may be tied to the big city businessmen who want to drive the Hawns off their coal-rich property. **78m/B; Silent; DVD.** Mary Pickford; Allan Sears; Claire McDowell; Fred Huntley; Sam De Grasse; John Gilbert; W.H. Bainbridge; ***D:*** Sidney Franklin; ***W:*** Bernard McConville; ***C:*** Charles Rosher.

Heart of a Nation *Untel Pere et Fils; Immortal France* **1943** Saga of the Montmarte family and their life during three wars, beginning with the Franco-Prussian War and ending with the Nazi occupation in France. Although ordered to be destroyed by the Nazis, this film was saved, along with many others, by the French "Cinema Resistance." In French with English subtitles. **111m/B; VHS, DVD.** *FR* Louis Jouvet; Raimu; Suzy Prim; Michele Morgan; Renee Devillers; Harry Krimer; ***Nar:*** Charles Boyer; ***D:*** Julien Duvivier.

Heart of a Stranger **2002** Conservative, middle-aged Jill Maddox (Seymour) turns into a hard-drinking, flashy partier after receiving a heart transplant. She decides she must find out about her male donor and learns he was a wild-living, 22-year-old biker and Jill seems to have inherited some of his personality along with his heart. Based on a true story from the bestseller "Change of Heart" by Claire Sylvia. **90m/C; DVD.** Jane Seymour; Maggie Lawson; Donna Goodhand; Stacy Smith; ***D:*** Dick Lowry; ***W:*** Joan Taylor; ***C:*** Eric Van Haren Noman; ***M:*** Patrick Williams. **CABLE**

Heart of America WOOF! **2003 (R)** You might know Boll from his embarrassingly bad video game movies, but this school-shooting melodrama is easily the director's worst film yet. Your mind will boggle at how shamelessly Boll milks the Columbine tragedy in his desperate attempt to reinvent himself as a serious filmmaker. Set on the last day of high school, the film leaves no Afterschool Special cliche unturned as it follows various students and teachers hours before two brooding loners decide to take out their angst Charlton Heston-style. It's heady material, but Boll is no Michael Moore. Instead, he prefers to shoot inappropriate softcore T&A in a scene where a bully molests a mentally-handicapped girl known as "Slow White." Yeah, classy stuff all around. **87m/C; DVD.** *CA GE* Jurgen Prochnow; Michael Paré; Patrick Muldoon; Kett Turton; Elisabeth Moss; Maria Conchita Alonso; Clint Howard; Brendan Fletcher; Lochlyn Munro; Maeve Quinlan; Michaela Mann; Will Sanderson; ***D:*** Uwe Boll; ***W:*** Uwe Boll; Robert Dean Klein; ***C:*** Mathias Neumann; ***M:*** Reinhard Besser.

The Heart of Dixie **1989 (PG)** Three college co-eds at a southern university in the 1950s see their lives and values change with the influence of the civil rights movement. College newspaper reporter Sheedy takes up the cause of a black man victimized by racial violence. Lightweight social-conscience fare. **96m/C; VHS, DVD.** Virginia Madsen; Ally Sheedy; Phoebe Cates; Treat Williams; Kyle Secor; Francesca Roberts; Barbara Babcock; Don Michael Paul; Kurtwood Smith; Richard Bradford; ***D:*** Martin Davidson; ***W:*** Tom McCown; ***C:*** Robert Elswit; ***M:*** Kenny Vance.

Heart of Dragon **1985** Police officer Chan takes care of his mentally challenged brother Hung, who gets mistaken for a robbery suspect. So Chan has to track down the real crooks. Features a 20-minute fight finale. Chinese with subtitles or dubbed. **85m/C; VHS, DVD.** *CH* Jackie Chan; Sammo Hung; Emily Chu; ***D:*** Sammo Hung; ***W:*** Barry Wong; ***C:*** Arthur Wong Ngok Tai; ***M:*** Man Yee Lam.

Heart of Glass *Herz aus Glas* **1974** A pre-industrial Bavarian village becomes deeply troubled when their glassblower dies without imparting the secret of making his unique Ruby glass. The townspeople go to extremes, from madness to murder to magic, to discover the ingredients. From German director Herzog (who hypnotized his cast daily), this somewhat apocalyptic tale is based on legend. The colors are incredible in their intensity. In German with English subtitles. **93m/C; VHS, DVD, Blu-Ray.** *GE* Josef Bierbichler; Stefan Guttler; Clemens Scheitz; Volker Prechtel; Sonia Skiba; ***D:*** Werner Herzog; ***W:*** Werner Herzog; Herbert Achternbusch; ***C:*** Jorge Schmidt-Reitwein; ***M:*** Popul Vuh.

Heart of Light *Lysets Hjerte* **1997** Marginalized Inuit family, living in Danish-occupied Greenland, suffer from being cut off from their native culture. Teenager Nisi has a breakdown, goes on a killing spree, and then turns the gun on himself. His drunken father, Rasmus, decides to leave the community on an old dogsled and encounters a hermit who leads him on a mystical journey into the past. Filmed on location in Greenland. Inuit and Danish with subtitles. **92m/C; VHS, DVD.** *DK* Rasmus Lyberth; Anda Kristensen; Vivi Nielsen; Niels Platow; ***D:*** Jacob Gronlykke; ***W:*** Jacob Gronlykke; ***C:*** Dan Laustsen; ***M:*** Joachim Holbek.

The Heart of Me 1/2 **2002 (R)** Rather staid adaptation of Rosamond Lehmann's 1953 novel "The Echoing Grove," which follows the romantic trials of bohemian Dinah (Bonham Carter) and her adulterous affair with her chilly older sister Madeleine's (Williams) husband, Rickie (Bettany). Soapy melodrama covers approximately the midthirties to the post-war period. **96m/C; VHS, DVD.** *GB* Helena Bonham Carter; Olivia Williams; Paul Bettany; Eleanor Bron; ***D:*** Thaddeus O'Sullivan; ***W:*** Lucinda Coxon; ***C:*** Gyula Pados; ***M:*** Nicholas Hooper.

Heart of Stone **2001 (R)** Sexy L.A. mom Mary (Everhart) is suffering from a stale marriage and empty nest syndrome when her daughter goes off to college. So she's easy prey for the seductive Steve (Wilder), who becomes violently obsessed with Mary. And then there's a little problem of a killer targeting college coeds—could Mary's daughter become the next victim? And is Mary's unhinged lover the killer? **90m/C; VHS, DVD.** Angie Everhart; James Wilder; Peter J. Lucas; Gregor Toerzs; ***D:*** Dale Trevillion; Marty Pistone. **VIDEO**

Heart of the Beholder **2005 (R)** Writer/director Tipton's own experiences are the basis for this well-done and infuriating drama. In 1980, Mike Howard (Letscher) convinces his pregnant wife Diane (Brown) to open the first video rental store in their St. Louis hometown. By 1988, it's become a successful chain but Mike is targeted by fundamentalist preacher Brewer (Prosky) and his Citizens for Decency after he refuses to remove so-called "objectionable" material. The CFD increase their harassment, even threatening the Howards' young daughter. Then DA Eric Manion (Dye), who's being blackmailed by the group for his sexual indiscretions, takes Mike to court on trumped-up obscenity charges. His business and family are destroyed by the publicity but Mike eventually gets an unexpected revenge. **106m/C; DVD.** Sarah Brown; John Dye; Arden Myrin; Greg Germann; Michael Dorn; Tony Todd; Matt Letcher; John Prosky; ***D:*** Ken Tipton; ***W:*** Ken Tipton; ***C:*** George Mooradian; ***M:*** Peter Rafelson.

The Heart of the Game 1/2 **2005 (PG-13)** Filmed over seven years, director Serrill follows Bill Resler's unorthodox approach to coaching the Roughriders, the girls' varsity basketball team at Seattle's middle-class Roosevelt High School. He turns the losing team into winners over the seasons, especially after recruiting gifted and volatile Darnellia Russell, an African-American from the inner-city, to join the predominantly white team. **97m/C; DVD.** ***D:*** Ward Serrill; ***W:*** Ward Serrill; ***C:*** Ward Serrill.

Heart of the Rio Grande 1/2 **1942** Spoiled young rich girl tries to trick her father into coming to her "rescue" at a western dude ranch. **70m/B; VHS, DVD.** Gene Autry; Smiley Burnette; Fay McKenzie; Edith Fellows; Joseph Stauch, Jr.; ***D:*** William M. Morgan.

Heart of the Stag 1/2 **1984 (R)** On an isolated sheep ranch in the New Zealand outback, a father and daughter suffer the repercussions of an incestuous relationship when she becomes enamored with a hired hand. **94m/C; VHS, DVD.** *NZ* Bruno Lawrence; Mary Regan; Terence Cooper; ***D:*** Michael Firth.

Heart of the Storm 1/2 **2004** Dopey women-in-peril fare finds three violent escaped cons forcing their way into the bayou home of Cassie and her two teenage daughters when a hurricane disrupts their escape plans. **90m/C; DVD.** Melissa Gilbert; Tom Cavanagh; Azure Dawn; CiCi Hedgpeth; Ritchie Montgomery; Marcus Lyle Brown; Brian Wimmer; ***D:*** Charles Wilkinson; ***W:*** V.R. McDade; ***C:*** Mark Morris; ***M:*** Richard Bellis. **CABLE**

The Heart Specialist 1/2 *Ways of the Flesh* **2006 (R)** South Florida doctor Sidney Zachary is mentoring a new crop of hospital residents, including womanizing Ray Howard. Sidney thinks Ray has potential and makes a bet with his girlfriend Donna that he can school Ray into becoming a responsible adult. Comedy-drama with a good cast and a welcome lack of African-American stereotypes. **99m/C; DVD, Blu-Ray.** Wood Harris; Brian J. White; Zoe Saldana; Scott Paulin; David S. Lee; Mya; Marla Gibbs; Ed Asner; ***D:*** Dennis Cooper; ***W:*** Dennis Cooper; ***C:*** Yasu Tanida; ***M:*** Tree Adams. **VIDEO**

Heartbeat 1/2 **1946** If you thought pointless Hollywood remakes of French films were a new phenomenon (see "Pure Luck," for example), then note this lighthearted remake of a 1940 Gallic farce. Rogers becomes the best student in a Parisian school for pickpockets, but when she tries out her skills on a dashing diplomat they fall in love instead. **100m/B; VHS, DVD.** Ginger Rogers; Jean-Pierre Aumont; Adolphe Menjou; Basil Rathbone; Melville Cooper; Mona Maris; Henry

Stephenson; Eduardo Ciannelli; ***D:*** Sam Wood; ***C:*** Joseph Valentine.

Heartbeat Detector *La Question Humaine; The Human Question* **2007** Leisurely-paced French political thriller that raises intriguing questions about past and present actions. Cool and collected Simon (Amalric) is the in-house psychologist and human resources head at the Paris office of a German petrochemical firm. He's asked to quietly assess director Mathias Just (Lonsdale), who's been acting erratically. But, thanks to anonymous letters and company archives, Simon's investigation gets very complicated and involves the firm's past connection to the Third Reich. French with subtitles. **143m/C; DVD.** *FR* Mathieu Amalric; Michael (Michel) Lonsdale; Jean-Pierre Kalfon; Lou Castel; Delphine Chuillot; Edith Scob; Valerie Dreville; ***D:*** Nicolas Klotz; ***W:*** Elisabeth Perceval; ***C:*** Josee Deshaies; ***M:*** Syd Matters.

Heartbeats *Les Amours Imaginaires* **2011** Stylized Quebecois romantic comedy has 21-year-old Dolan (who practically did every job on the film) featured as one of two friends who fall for handsome but remote Montreal newcomer Nicolas (Schneider). Besotted Francis and his best friend Marie (Chokri) become increasingly competitive for the indifferent hunk's attentions as Nicolas flirts with them both. French with subtitles. **97m/C; Blu-Ray.** *CA FR* Xavier Dolan; Niels Schneider; Anne Dorval; Monia Chokri; ***D:*** Xavier Dolan; ***W:*** Xavier Dolan; ***C:*** Stephanie Anne Weber Biron.

Heartbeeps 1/2 **1981 (PG)** Mildly amusing romantic comedy about a couple of robot household servants (Kaufman and Peters) who fall in love, escape from domestic service, and begin a family of their own (they assemble a child robot from spare parts). **88m/C; VHS, DVD, Blu-Ray.** Andy Kaufman; Bernadette Peters; Randy Quaid; Kenneth McMillan; Melanie Mayron; Christopher Guest; Richard B. Shull; Dick Miller; Kathleen Freeman; Mary Woronov; Paul Bartel; ***D:*** Allan Arkush; ***W:*** John Hill; ***C:*** Charles Rosher, Jr.; ***M:*** John Williams.

Heartbreak Hotel 1/2 **1988 (PG-13)** Johnny Wolfe kidnaps Elvis Presley from his show in Cleveland and drives him home to his mother, a die-hard Elvis fan. Completely unbelievable, utterly ridiculous, and still a lot of fun. **101m/C; VHS, DVD, Blu-Ray.** David Keith; Tuesday Weld; Charlie Schlatter; Angela Goethals; Jacque Lynn Colton; Chris Mulkey; Karen Landry; Tudor Sherrard; Paul Harkins; ***D:*** Chris Columbus; ***W:*** Chris Columbus; ***M:*** Georges Delerue.

The Heartbreak Kid **1972 (PG)** Director May's comic examination of love and hypocrisy. Grodin embroils himself in a triangle with his new bride and a woman he can't have, an absolutely gorgeous and totally unloving woman he shouldn't want. Walks the fence between tragedy and comedy, with an exceptional performance from Berlin. Based on Bruce Jay Friedman's story. **106m/C; VHS, DVD.** Charles Grodin; Cybill Shepherd; Eddie Albert; Jeannie Berlin; Audra Lindley; Art Metrano; ***D:*** Elaine May; ***W:*** Neil Simon; ***C:*** Owen Roizman; ***M:*** Garry Sherman; Cy Coleman; Sheldon Harnick. N.Y. Film Critics '72: Support. Actress (Berlin); Natl. Soc. Film Critics '72: Support. Actor (Albert), Support. Actress (Berlin).

The Heartbreak Kid 1/2 **2007 (R)** In the hands of the increasingly uninspired Farrelly brothers, this lame remake of the 70s film about an unlikable putz who marries too quickly and finds the real girl of his dreams on his honeymoon turns into yet another showcase of gross-out jokes and Stiller-style neuroses. He plays unsympathetic Eddie, who's desperately trying to get out of his marriage to sexpot Lila (Akerman) so he can woo nice girl Miranda (Monaghan). Portrays none of the original's wit or bite, and Stiller blows what little chance the movie has with a by-the-numbers, unappealing performance. **115m/C; DVD, Blu-Ray, HD-DVD.** Ben Stiller; Michelle Monaghan; Malin Akerman; Jerry Stiller; Rob Corddry; Danny McBride; Scott Wilson; Carlos Mencia; ***D:*** Bobby Farrelly; Peter Farrelly; ***W:*** Bobby Farrelly; Peter Farrelly; Scot Armstrong; Leslie Dixon; Kevin Barnett; ***C:*** Matthew F. Leonetti; ***M:*** Bill Ryan; Brendan Ryan.

Heartbreak Ridge **1986 (R)** An aging Marine recon sergeant is put in command of a young platoon to whip them into shape to prepare for combat in the invasion of Grenada. Eastwood whips this old story into shape too, with a fine performance of a man who's given everything to the Marines. The invasion of Grenada, though, is not epic material. (Also available in English with Spanish subtitles.) **130m/C; VHS, DVD, Blu-Ray.** Clint Eastwood; Marsha Mason; Everett McGill; Arlen Dean Snyder; Bo Svenson; Moses Gunn; Eileen Heckart; Boyd Gaines; Mario Van Peebles; Vincent Irizarry; Ramon Franco; Tom Villard; Pete Koch; Richard Venture; J.C. Quinn; Peter Jason; Thom Sharp; ***D:*** Clint Eastwood; ***W:*** James (Jim) Carabatsos; ***C:*** Jack N. Green; ***M:*** Lennie Niehaus.

Heartbreaker 1/2 **1983 (R)** Eastern Los Angeles explodes with vicious turf wars when Beto and Hector battle for the affection of Kim, the neighborhood's newest heartbreaker. **90m/C; VHS, DVD.** Fernando Allende; Dawn Dunlap; Michael D. Roberts; Robert Dryer; Apollonia; ***D:*** Frank Zuniga.

Heartbreaker 1/2 *L'Arnacoeur* **2010** Alex (Duris) is a professional seducer who is paid by boyfriends to break up with their lovers. He falls into their lives, reminds them that they deserve better, and slowly dissolves the unhappy union. His latest assignment is to stop the Monaco wedding of wealthy Juliette (Paradis) and her equally wealthy fiance Jonathan (Lincoln). Not surprisingly, it doesn't go as planned. Wisely avoids heavy sexual situations and keeps the romance sweet and light. A pleasant alternative to Hollywood's cookie-cutter romantic comedies, but still relies too heavily on the genre's formula. English and French with subtitles. **105m/C; Blu-Ray.** *GB FR* Romain Duris; Vanessa Paradis; Julie Ferrier; Francois Damiens; Helena Noguerra; Andrew Lincoln; Jacques Frantz; Amandine Dewasmes; Jean-Yves Lafesse; Jean-Marie Paris; ***D:*** Paschal Chaumeil; ***W:*** Laurent Zeitoun; Jeremy Doner; Yoann Gromb; ***C:*** Thierry Arbogast; ***M:*** Klaus Badelt.

Heartbreakers 1/2 **2001 (PG-13)** Max and Page, played by Weaver and Hewitt, are a mother-daughter con-artist team who delight in seducing men right out of their bank accounts and billfolds. Tobacco billionaire William B. Tensy is Max's latest target, but proves to be a tougher case than she realized. Meanwhile, daughter Page has her sights set on Jack, the handsome Palm Beach bar owner, but can't decide if it's just another con, or true love. Hackman excels as the obnoxious Tensy. Director Mirkin's first feature since "Romy and Michelle's High School Reunion." **123m/C; VHS, DVD, Blu-Ray.** Sigourney Weaver; Jennifer Love Hewitt; Gene Hackman; Ray Liotta; Jason Lee; Anne Bancroft; Jeffrey Jones; Nora Dunn; Julio Oscar Mechoso; Ricky Jay; Stacey Travis; ***D:*** David Mirkin; ***W:*** Paul Guay; Robert Dunn; Stephen Mazur; ***C:*** Dean Semler; ***M:*** John Debney.

Heartburn **1986 (R)** Based on Nora Ephron's own semi-autobiographical novel about her marital travails with writer Carl Bernstein, this is a tepid, bitter modern romance between writers already shell-shocked from previous marriages. **109m/C; VHS, DVD.** Meryl Streep; Jack Nicholson; Steven Hill; Richard Masur; Stockard Channing; Jeff Daniels; Milos Forman; Catherine O'Hara; Maureen Stapleton; Karen Akers; Joanna Gleason; Mercedes Ruehl; Caroline Aaron; Yakov Smirnoff; Anna Maria Horsford; Wilfrid Hyde-White; Kevin Spacey; ***D:*** Mike Nichols; ***W:*** Nora Ephron; ***C:*** Nestor Almendros; ***M:*** Carly Simon.

Heartland 1/2 **1981 (PG)** Set in 1910, this film chronicles the story of one woman's life on the Wyoming frontier, when she contracts to become a housekeeper for a rancher. Elinore (Ferrell) and her young daughter arrive at the home of Clyde Stewart (Torn) and face any number of hazards, which test her courage and spirit. Stunningly realistic and without cliche. Based on the diaries of Elinore Randall Stewart. **95m/C; VHS, DVD.** Conchata Ferrell; Rip Torn; Barry Primus; Lilia Skala; Megan Folson; ***D:*** Richard Pearce; ***W:*** Beth Ferris; ***C:*** Fred Murphy. Sundance '81: Grand Jury Prize.

Heartless 1/2 **2010** If you make a deal with the devil, expect to get burned in Ridley's muddled dark fantasy. Jamie's life is a misery because of the large, red heart-shaped birthmark on his face. It gets worse when he's attacked by East End thugs wearing demon masks—only he discovers they are actual demons. Soon leader Papa B offers Jamie a bargain: he'll remove the birthmark if Jamie will agree to do some increasingly nasty things. **114m/C; DVD, Blu-Ray.** *GB* Jim Sturgess; Clemence Posey; Noel Clarke; Joseph Mawle; Eddie Marsan; Luke Treadaway; Timothy Spall; Ruth Sheen; Jack Gordon; Mistry Nikita; ***D:*** Philip Ridley; ***W:*** Philip Ridley; ***C:*** Matt Gray; ***M:*** David Julyan.

Hearts & Minds **1974** Gripping documentary about America's misguided involvement in Vietnam. **112m/C; VHS, DVD, Blu-Ray.** ***D:*** Peter Davis. Oscars '74: Feature Doc.; Natl. Film Reg. '18.

Hearts Beat Loud 1/2 **2018 (PG-13)** Frank Fisher (Offerman), a widowed record store owner, entices his daughter Sam (Clemons) to form a band with him during the summer before she leaves for college. When their one song unexpectedly gets traction online, Frank wants to continue making music, but Sam is torn between her father's dream and the freedom to pursue her own path. Offerman, cheekily playing that embarrassing yet endearing father, has true chemistry with the talented Clemons, and the duo offer up a light and heartwarming, if not earthshaking, flick. **97m/C; DVD, Blu-Ray.** Nick Offerman; Kiersey Clemons; Ted Danson; Toni Collette; Sasha Lane; ***D:*** Brett Haley; ***W:*** Brett Haley; Marc Basch; ***C:*** Eric Lin; ***M:*** Keegan DeWitt.

Hearts in Atlantis 1/2 **2001 (PG-13)** Coming-of-age tale tinged with creeps benefits from the odd combination of a story by Stephen King and direction from Scott Hicks, who also directed "Shine" and "Snow Falling on Cedars." Bobby (Yelchin) is an 11-year-old boy living in lower middle class Connecticut circa 1960 with his widowed mother Liz (Davis). When enigmatic Ted (Hopkins) rents a room in their attic, he offers the boy a job reading him the daily newspaper. He also has Bobby keep an eye out for the "low men" (CIA agents? Mafia?) he believes are pursuing him. Ted offers the male role model and adult attention Bobby craves and the two quickly become close. Ted, it seems, has some kind of psychic ability, which he also sees in Bobby. Although lushly filmed, the plot seems a bit stagnant and listless for a story about young people. **101m/C; VHS, DVD.** Anthony Hopkins; Anton Yelchin; Hope Davis; Mika Boorem; David Morse; Alan Tudyk; Tom Bower; Celia Weston; Adam LeFevre; Timothy Reifsnyder; Deirdre O'Connell; Will Rothhaar; ***D:*** Scott Hicks; ***W:*** William Goldman; ***C:*** Piotr Sobocinski; ***M:*** Mychael Danna.

Hearts of Darkness: A Filmmaker's Apocalypse **1991 (R)** This riveting, critically acclaimed documentary about the making of Francis Ford Coppola's masterpiece "Apocalypse Now" is based largely on original footage shot and directed by his wife Eleanor. Also included are recent interviews with cast and crew members including Coppola, Martin Sheen, Robert Duvall, Frederic Forrest and Dennis Hopper. **96m/C; VHS, DVD, Blu-Ray.** Sam Bottoms; Eleanor Coppola; Francis Ford Coppola; Robert Duvall; Laurence Fishburne; Frederic Forrest; Albert Hall; Dennis Hopper; George Lucas; John Milius; Martin Sheen; ***D:*** Fax Bahr; George Hickenlooper; ***W:*** Fax Bahr; George Hickenlooper; ***M:*** Todd Boekelheide. Natl. Bd. of Review '91: Feature Doc.

Hearts of the West 1/2 *Hollywood Cowboy* **1975 (PG)** A fantasy-filled farm boy travels to Hollywood in the 1930s and seeks a writing career. Instead, he finds himself an ill-suited western movie star in this small offbeat comedy-drama that's sure to charm. **103m/C; VHS, DVD.** Jeff Bridges; Andy Griffith; Donald Pleasence; Alan Arkin; Blythe Danner; ***D:*** Howard Zieff; ***W:*** Rob Thompson. N.Y. Film Critics '75: Support. Actor (Arkin).

Hearts of War 1/2 *The Poet* **2007 (R)** In 1939, reluctant (and poetical) German soldier Oscar Koenig (Scarfe) is sent to Poland where he rescues beautiful Rachel (Dobrev) during a snowstorm. She turns out to be a Rabbi's daughter and engaged to someone else. They fall in love anyway but Oscar realizes that he must let her go and tells Rachel to flee towards the Russian front to escape the Nazis atrocities. A pregnant Rachel marries Bernard (Bennett), who accepts Oscar's son as his own, and they eventually all meet again at a German camp where more sacrifices must be made. **96m/C; DVD.** *CA* Jonathan Scarfe; Nina Dobrev; Zachary Bennett; Roy Scheider; Kim Coates; Daryl Hannah; Colm Feore; ***D:*** Damian Lee; ***W:*** Jack Crystal; ***C:*** David Pelletier; ***M:*** Zion Lee.

Heartstopper *Dark Craving* **1992** Benjamin Latham, an innocent physician in Pittsburgh, was accused of being a vampire in colonial times and hung. 200 years later, he emerges from the grave, unscathed. While trying to figure out what has happened, he falls in love with a photojournalist, who helps him find his own descendent, Matthew Latham. Unfortunately, his deep freeze has left him with the compulsion to kill, but only evil members of society. **96m/B; VHS, DVD.** Moon Zappa; Tom Savini; Kevin Kindlin; ***D:*** John A. Russo; ***W:*** John A. Russo; ***C:*** John Rice.

Heartwood **1998 (PG-13)** Frank (Mills) is an outcast living in the woods of a failing lumber town. He falls for Sylvia (Swank), the daughter of the engineer hired by mill owner Logan Reese (Robards) to save the mill and the town as well. But when Frank discovers gold, he's the one who comes up with a plan. **92m/C; VHS, DVD.** Eddie Mills; Hilary Swank; Jason Robards, Jr.; Randall Batinkoff; Stanley DeSantis; ***D:*** Lanny Cotler.

Heat *Andy Warhol's Heat* **1972** Another Andy Warhol-produced journey into drug-addled urban seediness. Features a former child actor/junkie and a has-been movie star barely surviving in a run-down motel. This is one of Warhol's better film productions; even non-fans may enjoy it. **102m/C; VHS, DVD.** Joe Dallesandro; Sylvia Miles; Pat Ast; Andrea Feldman; Ray Vestal; ***D:*** Paul Morrissey; ***W:*** Paul Morrissey; ***C:*** Paul Morrissey; ***M:*** John Cale.

Heat 1/2 **1987 (R)** A Las Vegas bodyguard avenges the beating of an old flame by a mobster's son, and incites mob retaliation. Based on the William Goldman novel. **103m/C; VHS, DVD.** Burt Reynolds; Karen Young; Peter MacNichol; Howard Hesseman; ***D:*** R.M. Richards; ***W:*** William Goldman; ***M:*** Michael Gibbs.

Heat 1/2 **1995 (R)** Pacino and De Niro in the same scene. Together. Finally. Obsessive master thief McCauley (De Niro) leads a crack crew on various military-style heists across L.A. while equally obsessive detective Hanna (Pacino) tracks him. Each man recognizes and respects the other's ability and dedication, even as they express the willingness to kill each other, if necessary. Excellent script with all the fireworks you'd expect, as well as a surprising look into emotional and personal sacrifice. Beautiful cinematography shows industrial landscape to great effect. Writer-director Mann held onto the screenplay for 12 years. **171m/C; VHS, DVD, Blu-Ray, UMD.** Robert De Niro; Al Pacino; Val Kilmer; Jon Voight; Diane Venora; Ashley Judd; Wes Studi; Tom Sizemore; Mykelti Williamson; Amy Brenneman; Ted Levine; Dennis Haysbert; William Fichtner; Natalie Portman; Hank Azaria; Henry Rollins; Kevin Gage; Tone Loc; Bud Cort; Jeremy Piven; Tom Noonan; Xander Berkeley; ***D:*** Michael Mann; ***W:*** Michael Mann; ***C:*** Dante Spinotti; ***M:*** Elliot Goldenthal.

The Heat 1/2 **2013 (R)** McCarthy and Bullock carry a lackluster script by bringing their A-game comic timing to this buddy cop comedy that feels heavily inspired by '80s R-rated fare--only with a girl power angle. FBI Agent Ashburn (Bullock) doesn't play well with others, always going by the book. Tough Boston detective Mullins (McCarthy) threw out the book long ago. The two are forced to work together to stop a notorious drug lord who may be trying to take over Beantown. The script is haphazard and the flick is 30 minutes too long but both leads are funny gals. **117m/C; DVD, Blu-Ray.** Sandra Bullock; Melissa McCarthy; Demian Bichir; Marlon Wayans; Michael Rappaport; Jane Curtin; Thomas F. Wilson; ***D:*** Paul Feig; ***W:*** Katie Dippold; ***C:*** Robert Yeoman; ***M:*** Michael Andrews.

Heat and Dust **1982 (R)** A young bride joins her husband at his post in India and is inexorably drawn to the country and its prince of state. Years later her great niece journeys to modern day India in search of the truth about her scandalous and mysterious relative. More than the story of two romances, this is the tale of women rebelling against an unseen caste system which keeps them second-class citizens. Ruth Jhabvala wrote the novel and screenplay. **130m/C; VHS, DVD, Blu-Ray.** *GB* Julie Christie; Greta Scacchi; Shashi Kapoor; Christopher Cazenove; Nickolas Grace; Julian Glover; Susan Fleetwood; Patrick Godfrey; Jennifer Kendal; Madhur Jaffrey; Barry Foster; Amanda Walker; Sudha Chopra; Sajid Khan; Zakir Hussain; Ratna Pathak; Charles McCaughan; Parveen Paul; ***D:*** James Ivory; ***W:*** Ruth Prawer Jhabvala; Saeed Jaffrey; Harish Khare; ***C:*** Walter Lassally; ***M:*** Richard Robbins. British Acad. '83: Adapt. Screenplay.

Heat and Sunlight 🦴 1/2 **1987** A photographer becomes obsessively jealous of his lover as their relationship comes to an end. Director Nilsson again used a unique improvisational, video-to-film technique, as he did with his previous film, "Signal 7." **98m/B; VHS, DVD.** Rob Nilsson; Consuelo Faust; Bill Bailey; Don Bajema; Ernie Fosselius; ***D:*** Rob Nilsson; ***W:*** Rob Nilsson; ***C:*** Tomas Tucker; ***M:*** Mark Adler. Sundance '88: Grand Jury Prize.

The Heat of the Day 🦴🦴 1/2 **1991** A British officer is accused of treason. As he attempts to find those who framed him, he meets a lovely woman all too willing to help. But whose side is she really on? Set in WWII. Tense and well-acted; made for TV. **120m/C; VHS, DVD.** Michael York; Patricia Hodge; Peggy Ashcroft; Anna Carteret; Michael Gambon; ***W:*** Harold Pinter. **TV**

Heat of the Sun 🦴🦴🦴 **1999** Former Scotland Yard detective Albert Tyburn (Eve) has been sent to work in Nairobi, Kenya in the hedonistic expatriate community of the 1930s, known as "Happy Valley." But despite his disdain for the community's racial and social lines, Tyburn is soon involved in murder and mayhem. In "Private Lives," Tyburn investigates the death of Lady Ellesmere and discovers drug-running, adultery, and murder. "Hide in Plain Sight" finds Tyburn investigating the death of a native girl and the disappear of other girls from the local Christian mission. "The Sport of Kings" finds Tyburn involved in the murder of a young boy against the backdrop of Nairobi's premier social event, Race Week. **360m/C; VHS, DVD.** *GB* Trevor Eve; Michael Byrne; Susannah Harker; Tim Woodward; Daniel Betts; James Callis; Freddie Annobil-Dodoo; Kate McKenzie; Hugh Bonneville; Cathryn Harrison; Julian Rhind-Tutt; Diana Quick; Deborah Findlay; Joss Ackland; Richard McCabe; Sonya Walger; ***D:*** Adrian Shergold; Diarmuid Lawrence; Paul Seed; ***W:*** Russell Lewis; Tim Prager. **TV**

Heat Wave 🦴🦴🦴 **1990 (R)** The Watts ghetto uprising of 1965 is a proving ground for a young black journalist. Excellent cast and fine script portrays the anger and frustration of blacks in Los Angeles and the U.S. in the 1960s and the fear of change felt by blacks and whites when civil rights reform began. Strong drama with minimal emotionalism. **92m/C; VHS, DVD.** Blair Underwood; Cicely Tyson; James Earl Jones; Sally Kirkland; Margaret Avery; David Strathairn; Robert Hooks; Adam Arkin; Paris Vaughan; Charlie Korsmo; ***D:*** Kevin Hooks; ***W:*** Michael Lazarou; ***C:*** Mark Irwin; ***M:*** Thomas Newman. **CABLE**

Heater 🦴🦴 **1999** Two homeless men come into possession of an electric space heater that, despite the December cold, is useless to them since they don't have any place to plug it in. So they decide to travel from their inner city haunt to a suburban shopping mall—by foot—in hopes they can return the heater for a cash refund. **87m/C; VHS, DVD.** *CA* Gary Farmer; Stephen Ouimette; ***D:*** Terrance Odette; ***W:*** Terrance Odette; ***C:*** Arthur E. Cooper; ***M:*** Neil Clark.

Heathers 🦴🦴🦴 1/2 **1989 (R)** Clique of stuck-up girls named Heather rule the high school social scene until the newest member (not a Heather) decides that enough is enough. She and her outlaw boyfriend embark (accidentally on her part, intentionally on his) on a murder spree disguised as a rash of teen suicides. Dense, take-no-prisoners black comedy with buckets of potent slang, satire and unforgiving hostility. Humor this dark is rare; sharply observed and acted, though the end is out of place. Slater does his best Nicholson impression. **102m/C; VHS, DVD, Blu-Ray.** Winona Ryder; Christian Slater; Kim Walker; Shannen Doherty; Lisanne Falk; Penelope Milford; Glenn Shadix; Lance Fenton; Patrick Laborteaux; Jeremy Applegate; Renee Estevez; ***D:*** Michael Lehmann; ***W:*** Daniel Waters; ***C:*** Francis Kenny; ***M:*** David Newman. Ind. Spirit '90: First Feature.

Heatseeker 🦴🦴 **1995 (R)** Corporations use mechanical fighters to participate in brutal kickboxing contests in 2019 New America. Human Chance (Cooke) must battle cyborg opponent Xao if he wants to save his kidnapped trainer. Lots of action and even some intentional humor. **91m/C; VHS, Streaming.** Keith Cooke; Gary Daniels; Norbert Weisser; Thom Mathews; ***D:*** Albert Pyun.

Heaven 🦴🦴 **1987 (PG-13)** An exploration of "heaven" including the idea, the place, and people's views about it. Questions such as "How do you get there?" and "What goes on up there?" are discussed. Offbeat interviews mixed with a collage of celestial images. **80m/C; VHS, DVD.** ***D:*** Diane Keaton; ***M:*** Howard Shore.

Heaven 🦴 **1999 (R)** Robert Marling (Donovan) is an architect with a broken marriage and a compulsion to gamble (and lose) at a sleazy strip joint owned by the odious and brutal Stanner (Schiff). One of the performers is a psychic transvestite named Heaven (Edwards), who predicts that Robert will win big in the lottery. This info gets back to evil shrink Melrose (Malahide), who has both Robert and Heaven as patients, and who just happens to be having an affair with Robert's bitter wife, Jennifer (Going). And the coincidental silliness doesn't stop there. Based on a novel by Chad Taylor. **103m/C; VHS, DVD.** *NZ* Martin Donovan; Joanna Going; Patrick Malahide; Danny Edwards; Richard Schiff; ***D:*** Scott Reynolds; ***W:*** Scott Reynolds; ***C:*** Simon Raby; ***M:*** Victoria Kelly.

Heaven 🦴🦴 1/2 **2001 (R)** Themes of despair and redemption fuel this story of Philippa (Blanchett), a woman who has accidentally killed four innocent people while trying to assassinate drug lord Vendice. As she's questioned by the authorities (who are in cahoots with Vendice), young police translator Filippo (Ribisi) falls in love with her. The two escape thanks to police incompetence and go after Vendice. Directed by Tom Tykwer from a script written by late film legend Krzysztof Kieslowski ("The Decalogue" series and "Three Colors" trilogy) **96m/C; VHS, DVD, Blu-Ray.** *US GE* Cate Blanchett; Giovanni Ribisi; Stefania Rocca; Remo Girone; Mattia Sbragia; Alberto Di Stasio; Stefano Santospago; Alessandro Sperduti; ***D:*** Tom Tykwer; ***W:*** Krzysztof Kieslowski; Krzysztof Piesiewicz; ***C:*** Frank Griebe.

Heaven Ain't Hard to Find 🦴🦴 **2010 (PG-13)** Malcolm's serving time in an L.A. prison and escapes after being denied parole. Having found God in the joint (as well as being trained as a carpenter), Malcolm takes shelter in an inner-city Baptist church that's fallen on hard times. Three parish ladies think he's the answer to their prayers since they can not only use those carpenter's skills but they need a new pastor as well. Not subtle but it is inspirational. **77m/C; DVD.** Andre Pitre; Tasha Taylor; Clifton Powell; Kym E. Whitley; Jozella Reed; Samantha McSwain; ***D:*** Neema Barnette; ***W:*** Javan Johnson; Eugene McDaniel; Norris Muhammad; ***C:*** Brendon Phillips; ***M:*** John Ewings, III. **VIDEO**

Heaven & Earth 🦴🦴🦴 **1990 (PG-13)** A samurai epic covering the battle for the future of Japan between two feuding warlords. The overwhelming battle scenes were actually filmed on location in Canada. In Japanese with English subtitles. **104m/C; VHS, DVD.** *JP* Masahiko Tsugawa; Takaaki Enoki; Atsuko Asano; Tsunehiko Watase; Naomi Zaizen; Binpachi Ito; ***Nar:*** Stuart Whitman; ***D:*** Haruki Kadokawa; ***W:*** Haruki Kadokawa; ***M:*** Daisuke Hinata.

Heaven and Earth 🦴🦴 **1993 (R)** Conclusion of Stone's Vietnam trilogy (after "Platoon" and "Born on the Fourth of July") focuses on Vietnamese woman (film debut of Le) and her life under the French and American occupations. Jones is the American soldier who marries her and eventually brings her to the U.S. Not one for subtleties, Stone chases melodramatic excess with finesse of lumberjack, sawing away at guilt and remorse from a "woman's point of view." Cranky Tommy Lee shows up too late to save flick and is saddled with a perplexing I.D. to boot. Flawed, ambitious, and interesting if a student of Stone. Based on the two autobiographies of Le Ly Haslip, "When Heaven and Earth Changed Places" and "Child of War, Woman of Peace." Filmed on location in Thailand. **142m/C; VHS, DVD, Blu-Ray.** Hiep Thi Le; Tommy Lee Jones; Joan Chen; Haing S. Ngor; Debbie Reynolds; Conchata Ferrell; Dustin Nguyen; Liem Whatley; Dale Dye; ***D:*** Oliver Stone; ***W:*** Oliver Stone; ***C:*** Robert Richardson; ***M:*** Kitaro. Golden Globes '94: Score.

Heaven & Hell 🦴🦴 *Di san lei da dou; Di yu; Heaven and Hell Gate; Sha chu di yu mun; Shaolin Hellgate* **1978** Xin Ling (Yi-min Ling) is sent by the Queen of Heaven to capture an earthly couple. When he allows them to live out of mercy, the Queen kills him, and he reincarnates as a taxi driver only to die saving another couple. Sentenced to Hell, he decides to gather a few lost souls who were meant to go to heaven and fight his way out. Truly one of the most bizarre of Shaw Brothers kung-fu films, it is famous for re-uniting the cast of the "5 Deadly Venoms." **88m/C; DVD.** *CH* David Chiang; Ging Man Fung; Sheng Fu; Philip Kwok; Lin Lin Li; Chen Chi Lin; Yi-min Li; Meng Lo; Chien Sun; Yan Tsan Tang; Jenny Tseng; Dick Wei; ***D:*** Cheh Chang; ***W:*** Cheh Chang; Lang Chou; Kuang Ni; ***C:*** Fen Chen; Ying-Chaun Kuan; Mu-To Kung; ***M:*** Yung-Yu Chen; Chia Chang Liu.

Heaven Before I Die 🦴🦴 **1996 (PG)** Sheltered Jacob (Velasquez) travels from the Middle East to Toronto and is taken under the questionable wing of a small-time thief (Giannini) and a beautiful waitress (Pacula). But when Jacob finds a measure of success as a Charlie Chaplin impersonator, his innocence gets a dose of culture shock. **98m/C; VHS, DVD.** *CA* Andy Velasquez; Giancarlo Giannini; Catherine Oxenberg; ***Cameo(s):*** Joanna Pacula; Omar Sharif; Burt Young; Joseph Bologna; ***D:*** Izidore K. Musallam.

Heaven Can Wait 🦴🦴🦴 **1943** Social satire in which a rogue tries to convince the Devil to admit him into Hell by relating the story of his philandering life and discovers that he was a more valuable human being than he thought. A witty Lubitsch treat based on the play "Birthdays." **112m/C; VHS, DVD, Blu-Ray.** Don Ameche; Gene Tierney; Laird Cregar; Charles Coburn; Marjorie Main; Eugene Pallette; Allyn Joslyn; Spring Byington; Signe Hasso; Louis Calhern; Dickie Moore; Florence Bates; Scotty Beckett; Charles Halton; ***D:*** Ernst Lubitsch.

Heaven Can Wait 🦴🦴🦴 **1978 (PG)** A remake of 1941's "Here Comes Mr. Jordan." L.A. Rams quarterback Joe Pendleton (Beatty) is summoned to heaven before his time. When archangel Mr. Jordan (Mason) realizes the mistake, Joe is returned to Earth but it's in the body of a wealthy industrialist who's about to be murdered by his unfaithful wife Julia (Cannon) and his nervous secretary, Tony (Grodin). But Joe is about to let a little thing like murder prevent him from playing in the Super Bowl—new body or not. Christie's the new love interest; Warden's the gruff coach. Not to be confused with the 1943 film of the same name. **101m/C; VHS, DVD.** Warren Beatty; Julie Christie; Charles Grodin; Dyan Cannon; James Mason; Jack Warden; Buck Henry; ***D:*** Warren Beatty; Buck Henry; ***W:*** Warren Beatty; Elaine May; ***C:*** William A. Fraker; ***M:*** Dave Grusin. Oscars '78: Art Dir./Set Dec.; Golden Globes '79: Actor--Mus./Comedy (Beatty), Film--Mus./Comedy, Support. Actress (Cannon); Writers Guild '78: Adapt. Screenplay.

Heaven Help Us 🦴🦴 1/2 *Catholic Boys* **1985 (R)** Three mischievous boys find themselves continually in trouble with the priests running their Brooklyn Catholic high school during the mid-1960s. Realistic and humorous look at adolescent life. **102m/C; VHS, DVD.** Andrew McCarthy; Mary Stuart Masterson; Kevin Dillon; Malcolm Danare; Jennifer (Jennie) Dundas Lowe; Kate Reid; Wallace Shawn; Jay Patterson; John Heard; Donald Sutherland; Yeardley Smith; Sherry Steiner; Calvert Deforest; Philip Bosco; Patrick Dempsey; Christopher Durang; ***D:*** Michael Dinner; ***W:*** Charles Purpura; ***M:*** James Horner.

Heaven Is a Playground 🦴🦴 1/2 **1991 (R)** On Chicago's South Side an inner city basketball coach and an idealistic young lawyer are determined to change the fate of a group of high school boys. The men use the incentive of athletic scholarships to keep their team in school and away from drugs and gangs. **104m/C; VHS, DVD.** D.B. Sweeney; Michael Warren; Richard Jordan; Victor Love; ***D:*** Randall Fried; ***W:*** Randall Fried; ***C:*** Tom Richmond; ***M:*** Patrick O'Hearn.

Heaven Is for Real 🦴🦴 1/2 **2014 (PG)** Most faith-based movies are so desperate to spread their religious messages that they forget that they're making a movie. Fortunately, this one has a decent pedigree. Director Wallace's story, based on a popular book, follows Colin Burpo (no, really, that's his name), a four-year-old who dies for three minutes during surgery and comes back with tales of visiting Heaven and hanging out with Jesus. Kinnear plays his pastor dad who single-handedly grounds the feel-good movie with his excellent performance. It's slight and preachy, but is more inoffensive than most of its ilk. **99m/C; DVD, Blu-Ray.** Greg Kinnear; Connor Corum; Kelly Reilly; Thomas Haden Church; Margo Martindale; ***D:*** Randall Wallace; ***W:*** Chris Parker; Randall Wallace; ***C:*** Dean Semler; ***M:*** Nick Glennie-Smith.

Heaven Knows, Mr. Allison 🦴🦴🦴 **1957** Terrific two-character WWII drama finds tough (but tender-hearted) Marine corporal Allison (Mitchum) stranded with Irish nun, Sister Angela (Kerr), on a Pacific island overrun by Japanese troops. The duo hide out during the day and forage for food by night, gradually revealing their pasts to each other. He falls hard while she resists his advances and they struggle to stay alive until U.S. forces invade the island. Lots of action and good performances. Based on the novel by Charles Shaw. **106m/C; VHS, DVD, Blu-Ray.** Robert Mitchum; Deborah Kerr; ***D:*** John Huston; ***W:*** John Huston; John Lee Mahin; ***C:*** Oswald Morris; ***M:*** Georges Auric.

Heaven Knows What 🦴🦴🦴 **2015 (R)** The story goes that experimental filmmakers Ben and Joshua Safdie ran into street junkie Arielle Holmes and asked her to tell them her story. They then formed that loose, episodic narrative into a script, cast Holmes as the barely fictional version of herself named Harley, and surrounded her with other non-actors, mostly drug addicts. The result is a harrowing experience that captures the reality of young drug addicts living on the street in ways that haven't really been seen in film before—blending documentary and narrative styles. Not for everyone, but an undeniably daring one. **94m/C; DVD.** Buddy Duress; Ron Braunstein; Eleonore Hendricks; Arielle Holmes; Caleb Landry Jones; ***D:*** Ben Safdie; Josh Safdie; ***W:*** Josh Safdie; Ronald Bronstein; ***C:*** Sean Price Williams; ***M:*** Paul Grimstad; Ariel Pink.

Heaven With a Gun 🦴🦴 **1969** Gunslinger Jim Killian (Ford) becomes a preacher in an Arizona town beset by a range war between cattlemen and sheepherders. Jim tries to broker a peace, but his past is revealed leading up to a final showdown. **101m/C; DVD.** Glenn Ford; Carolyn Jones; John Anderson; David Carradine; J.D. Cannon; Noah Beery, Jr.; Barbara Hershey; ***D:*** Lee H. Katzin; ***W:*** Richard Carr; ***C:*** Fred W. Koenekamp; ***M:*** Johnny Mandel.

The Heavenly Body 🦴🦴 **1944** Stylish light comedy. Astronomer William Whitley (Powell) is so obsessed with his work that he ignores the heavenly body of wife Vicky (Lamarr) at home. Feeling unloved, Vicky turns to local astrologer Margaret Sibyll (Bainter) for advice and she predicts Vicky will fall for the new man who enters her life. Then air raid warden Lloyd Hunter (Craig) shows up at her door. When they continue to cross paths, both Lloyd and Vicky start taking their meetings more seriously and hubby William finally starts getting jealous. **95m/B; DVD.** William Powell; Hedy Lamarr; James Craig; Fay Bainter; Henry O'Neill; Spring Byington; ***D:*** Alexander Hall; ***W:*** Harry Kurnitz; Walter Reisch; Michael Arlen; ***C:*** Robert Planck; ***M:*** Bronislau Kaper.

Heavenly Creatures 🦴🦴🦴 1/2 **1994 (R)** Haunting and surreal drama chronicles the true-life case of two young schoolgirls, Pauline and Juliet, who were charged with clubbing to death Pauline's mother in Christchurch, New Zealand, in 1954. Opens two years before the murder, and follows the friendship as the two teens become obsessed with each other, retreating into a rich fantasy life. They create an elaborate, medieval kingdom where they escape to their dream lovers and romantic alter egos. Elaborate morphing and animation effects vividly express the shared inner fantasy world, while innovative camera work creates the sensations of hysteria and excitement that the girls experience as their infatuation becomes uncontrollable. Leads Lynsky and Winslet are convincing as the awkward, quiet Pauline and the pretty, intelligent, upper class Juliet. Bizarre crime story is stylish and eerily compelling, and made more so by real life events: after the film was released, mystery writer Anne Perry was revealed as Juliet Hulme. **110m/C; VHS, DVD, Blu-Ray.** *NZ* Melanie Lynskey; Kate Winslet; Sarah Pierse; Diana Kent; Clive Merrison; Simon O'Connor; *D:* Peter Jackson; *W:* Peter Jackson; Fran Walsh; *C:* Alun Bollinger; *M:* Peter Dasent.

Heavenly Days 1/2 **1944** Sentimental wartime comedy based on the Fibber McGee and Molly radio show. The couple take a trip to Washington where McGee has a disagreement with their pompous senator. He tries to tell Congress what's what and gets laughed at until a Gallup Poll reveals McGee to be the typical American. **72m/B; DVD.** Jim Jordan; Marian Jordan; Eugene Pallette; Raymond Walburn; Barbara Hale; Gordon Oliver; *D:* Howard Estabrook; *W:* Howard Estabrook; Don Quinn; *C:* J. Roy Hunt; *M:* Leigh Harline.

The Heavenly Kid **1985 (PG-13)** Leather-jacketed "cool" guy who died in a '60s hot rod crash finally receives an offer to exit limbo and enter heaven. The deal requires that he educate his dull earthly son on more hip and worldly ways. A big problem is that the soundtrack and wardrobe are 1955, whereas the cocky cool greaser supposedly died 17 years ago in 1968. Mildly entertaining. **92m/C; VHS, DVD.** Lewis Smith; Jane Kaczmarek; Jason Gedrick; Richard Mulligan; *D:* Cary Medoway; *W:* Cary Medoway; Martin Copeland.

A Heavenly Vintage 1/2 *The Vintner's Luck* **2009** Flat, confusing fantasy drama about wine and angels based on the 1998 novel by Elizabeth Knox. French peasant Sobran Jodeau (Renier) knows his winemaking skills are greater than those of the Comte he works for. He meets an angel who promises Sobran his own successful vineyard if he promises to meet him on the same night each year. The vintages differ over the years as the angel tells Sobran the wine is affected by his own joys and sorrows in life. **120m/C; DVD, Blu-Ray.** *FR NZ* Jeremie Renier; Keisha Castle-Hughes; Gaspard Ulliel; Vera Farmiga; *D:* Niki Caro; *W:* Niki Caro; *C:* Denis Lenoir; *M:* Antonio Pinto.

Heaven's a Drag 1/2 *To Die For* **1994** Low-budget British cross between a tearjerker and a supernatural comedy. HIV-positive London drag performer Mark (Williams) lives with Simon (Arklie), a TV repairman who keeps his sexuality a secret from his co-workers and his emotional distance from his stricken lover. When Mark dies, Simon is quick to get on with his life—too quick for Mark, who's ghostly presence puts a damper on Simon's dating possibilities and brings up some old resentments. **96m/C; VHS, DVD.** *UK* Thomas Arklie; Ian Patrick Williams; Dilly Keane; Tony Slattery; Jean Boht; John Altman; *Nar:* Ian McKellen; *D:* Peter MacKenzie Litten; *W:* Johnny Byrne; *C:* John Ward.

Heavens Above **1963** A sharp, biting satire on cleric life in England. Sellers stars as the quiet, down-to-earth reverend who is appointed to a new post in space. **113m/B; VHS, DVD.** *GB* Peter Sellers; Cecil Parker; Isabel Jeans; Eric Sykes; Ian Carmichael; *D:* John Boulting; Roy Boulting; *M:* Richard Rodney Bennett.

Heaven's Burning **1997 (R)** Fast-paced road movie with some unexpected twists. Midori (Kudoh) is a young Japanese woman who is honeymooning in Sydney with new hubby Yukio (Isomura). But Midori fakes her own kidnapping to wait for her lover to arrive (who doesn't show). Yukio and the cops quickly discover her plotting but, in the meantime, Midori's been caught up in the midst of a bank robbery. When the robbery goes wrong, she becomes the quasi-hostage of driver Colin (Crowe), who takes off across Australia, pursued by the cops, his ex-partners, and the humiliated husband who wants revenge. Midori and Colin bond and things get increasingly stranger. **96m/C; VHS, DVD.** *AU* Youki Kudoh; Russell Crowe; Kenji Isomura; Ray Barrett; Robert Mammone; Petru Gheorghiu; Matthew Dyktynski; Anthony Phelan; Colin Hay; Susan Prior; Norman Kaye; *D:* Craig Lahiff; *W:* Louis Nowra; *C:* Brian J. Breheny; *M:* Michael Atkinson.

Heaven's Door *Doorway to Heaven* **2012 (PG)** In this family drama, a struggling woman finds a portal to heaven. Living in a small rural community, Julie Taylor (Carpenter) has many pressures. Not only must she process a forthcoming divorce, she is also raising two children, looking for a fulfilling job, and must handle a constant stream of advice from her mother. Julie's father also recently died and her mother is of the belief that, though unseen, heaven and angels are here on Earth. Julie's daughter Riley (Dorn) soon discovers that there is a way to reach another such dimension—changing everyone's life forever. **98m/C; DVD, Streaming, Download.** Charisma Carpenter; Kirstin Dorn; Dean Cain; Joanna Cassidy; Kaden Billin; *D:* Craig Clyde; *W:* Craig Clyde; *C:* Brandon Christensen; *M:* Charlie Colin; Sean Genockey; Tom Luce; Adam Rossi. **VIDEO**

Heavens Fall 1/2 **2006 (PG-13)** Nine young blacks are pulled off an Alabama freight train in 1931, accused of raping two white women. Quickly convicted, they were all sentenced to the electric chair. Their case is appealed to the U.S. Supreme Court and, in 1933, New York attorney Sam Leibowitz (Hutton) travels to the deeply segregated South to work on their defense. Straightforward retelling of the case of the Scottsboro Boys and a landmark judicial decision. **105m/C; DVD.** Timothy Hutton; David Strathairn; Bill Sage; Leelee Sobieski; Anthony Mackie; Azura Skye; Bill Smitrovich; James Tolkan; Maury Chaykin; *D:* Terry Green; *W:* Terry Green; *C:* Paul Sanchez; *M:* David Reynolds.

Heaven's Fire **1999** Dean (Roberts) finds himself trying to prevent former co-worker Quentin (Prochnow) from stealing U.S. currency engraving plates from the treasury building. Dean foils the getaway but the crooks (and a group of tourists) are trapped in the building by a couple of explosions. So Dean then tries to protect the innocent while keeping Quentin at bay. **91m/C; VHS, DVD.** Eric Roberts; Jurgen Prochnow; Cali Timmins; *D:* David Warry-Smith; *W:* Rob Kerchner; Charles Philip Moore; *C:* Gordon Verheul; *M:* Deddy Tzur. **CABLE**

Heaven's Gate **1981 (R)** The uncut version of Cimino's notorious folly. A fascinating, plotless, and exaggerated account of the Johnson County cattle war of the 1880s. Ravishingly photographed, the film's production almost single-handedly put United Artists out of business. **220m/C; VHS, DVD, Blu-Ray.** Kris Kristofferson; Christopher Walken; Isabelle Huppert; John Hurt; Richard Masur; Mickey Rourke; Brad Dourif; Joseph Cotten; Jeff Bridges; Sam Waterston; Terry O'Quinn; Geoffrey Lewis; *D:* Michael Cimino; *W:* Michael Cimino; *C:* Vilmos Zsigmond. Golden Raspberries '81: Worst Director (Cimino).

Heaven's Prisoners 1/2 **1995 (R)** Dave Robicheaux (Baldwin) is an ex-New Orleans homicide detective and recovering alcoholic, living a quiet life on a bayou with patient wife Annie (Lynch). They witness a plane crash and Dave rescues the only survivor, a young Salvadoran girl, whom they adopt. But the crash wasn't an accident and Dave's snooping around involves him with drug runners and local crime bosses, including old high school buddy, Bubba Rocque (Roberts), and his sirenish wife, Claudette (Hatcher). Convoluted plot with some moody touches but Baldwin scores as the flawed hero. Based on the mystery series by James Lee Burke. **135m/C; VHS, DVD.** Alec Baldwin; Kelly Lynch; Mary Stuart Masterson; Eric Roberts; Teri Hatcher; Vondie Curtis-Hall; Badja (Medu) Djola; Joe (Johnny) Viterelli; Hawthorne James; Paul Guilfoyle; *D:* Phil Joanou; *W:* Scott Frank; Harley Peyton; *C:* Harris Savides; *M:* George Fenton.

Heavy **1994 (R)** Sensitive character study supported by an excellent ensemble, led by Vince as Victor, an obese, painfully withdrawn, 30-ish cook. He lives with his domineering mother (a subdued Winters) and helps her run their roadside diner, along with veteran waitress Delores (Harry). Then beautiful teenager Callie (Tyler) is hired and Victor develops a suitably massive crush. Tyler is all pout and promise as Callie, making it clear why a guy like Victor could fall hard for her. Harry brings a rich cynical and sexual edge to Delores. Director Mangold's feature debut is both eloquent and economical, though at times paced to a near standstill. **104m/C; VHS, DVD.** Pruitt Taylor Vince; Shelley Winters; Liv Tyler; Deborah Harry; Evan Dando; Joe Grifasi; *D:* James Mangold; *W:* James Mangold; *C:* Michael Barrow; *M:* Thurston Moore. Sundance '95: Special Jury Prize.

The Heavy 1/2 **2009 (R)** Ex-con Boots Mason is now a debt collector for London gangster Anawalt. He's estranged from his family, especially his smarmy politician brother Christian, who sent Boots to prison and now has a contract out on his life. There's a brutal bad cop and a not-so-innocent American woman mixed in as well. **102m/C; DVD.** *GB* Vinnie Jones; Adrian Paul; Shannyn Sossamon; Stephen Rea; Christopher Lee; Jean Marsh; Sadie Frost; Gary Strecth; Lee Ryan; *D:* Marcus Warren; *W:* Marcus Warren; *M:* Paul Oakenfold. **VIDEO**

Heavy Metal **1981 (R)** Yes, the animated cult flick is now legally available on video, its copyright disputes finally resolved. A collection of science-fiction and fantasy stories, inspired by the same-titled magazine and offered in a variety of graphic styles, that all encompass the theme of good versus evil. And don't always bet on the good. Features a soundtrack compiled from the work of many top metal artists of the time as well as Bernstein's score with the London Philharmonic Orchestra. A three-minute transitional segment, called "Neverwhere Land," that was cut from the original version has been restored as an epilogue. **90m/C; VHS, DVD, UMD.** *CA V:* John Candy; Joe Flaherty; Don Francks; Eugene Levy; Rodger Bumpass; Jackie Burroughs; Harold Ramis; Richard Romanus; Doug Kenney; *D:* Gerald Potterton; *W:* Dan Goldberg; Len Blum; *C:* Brian Tufano; *M:* Elmer Bernstein.

Heavy Metal 2000 1/2 **2000 (R)** The original 1981 film was cutting edge but this video game-ish sequel is average at best. Warrior babe Julie is tracking a group of space pirates, led by villain Lord Tyler, who destroyed her home and forced her sister into slavery. Julie assumes a new name, F.A.K.K. (Federation Assigned Ketogenic Killzone), and the usual avenger mission. **88m/C; VHS, DVD.** *V:* Julie Strain; Michael Ironside; Billy Idol; Sonja Ball; *D:* Michael Coldewey; Michel Lemire; *W:* Robert Payne Cabeen; *C:* Bruno Philip; *M:* Frederic Talgorn.

Heavy Petting 1/2 **1989** A hilarious compilation of "love scene" footage from feature films of the silent era to the '60s, newsreels, news reports, educational films, old TV shows, and home movies. **75m/C; VHS, DVD.** David Byrne; Josh Mostel; Sandra Bernhard; Allen Ginsberg; Ann Magnuson; Spalding Gray; Laurie Anderson; John Oates; Abbie Hoffman; Jacki Ochs; *D:* Obie Benz; *C:* Sandi Sissel.

Heavy Petting 1/2 **2007** Charlie (Hines) falls for Daphne (Akerman), which means he has to get along with her new dog, Babydoll. But Charlie hates dogs and Babydoll feels the same way about Charlie. The more time Charlie spends with Babydoll and her owner, the more he realizes that he really likes the dog better than the girl, so he needs to keep Daphne happy. **98m/C; DVD.** Brendan P. Hines; Malin Akerman; Kevin Sussman; *D:* Marcel Sarmiento; *W:* Marcel Sarmiento; *C:* Tim Ives; *M:* Julian Nott.

Heavy Traffic **1973** Ralph Bakshi's animated fantasy portrait of the hard-edged underside of city life. A young cartoonist draws the people, places, and paranoia of his environment. **77m/C; VHS, DVD, Blu-Ray.** Joseph Kaufmann; Beverly Hope Atkinson; Michael Brandon; Frank De Kova; Terri Haven; Mary Dean Lauria; Lillian Adams; Jamie Farr; Robert Easton; *D:* Ralph Bakshi; *W:* Ralph Bakshi; *C:* Ted C. Bemiller; Gregg Heschong; *M:* Ed Bogas.

Heavyweights **1994 (PG)** A product of Disney's sometimes assembly line approach to family entertainment (think "Mighty Ducks"). Nothing new saga of overweight youngsters sent to a fat camp run by tyrannical fitness guru Tony Perkis (Stiller). His methods cause the kids to band together and overthrow him and his "evil" tactics. Oh, by the way, there's a baseball competition with the more athletic camp kids on the other side of the lake. Guess who wins. Stiller as the fame obsessed fitness fanatic, sporting a David Copperfield make-over, is the only highlight in this exercise of excess fluff. Directorial debut of Brill. **98m/C; VHS, DVD, Blu-Ray.** Jeffrey Tambor; Ben Stiller; Jerry Stiller; Anne Meara; Shaun Weiss; Kenan Thompson; *D:* Steven Brill; *W:* Judd Apatow; Steven Brill; *C:* Victor Hammer; *M:* J.A.C. Redford.

Heckler **2008** After getting drubbed by the critics for "Son of the Mask," Kennedy and Addis decided to make this documentary of ticked off celebrities who are tired of being bullied by hecklers and critics. While it starts off pretty good, the buildup of bile starts to grate towards the end. **78m/C; DVD.** Jamie Kennedy; *D:* Michael Addis. **VIDEO**

Heck's Way Home 1/2 **1995** Heck is the Neufeld family dog and best friend of 11-year-old Luke (Krowchuk). The family is moving from Winnipeg to Australia and have a three-day layover in Vancouver. Heck is supposed to come along but instead, unbeknownst to the family, he gets captured by the local dogcatcher (Arkin) and the family are forced to leave without him. Naturally, Heck escapes and starts off on a 2000-mile journey to find his family before they fly away forever. **92m/C; VHS, DVD.** Chad Krowchuk; Alan Arkin; Michael Riley; Shannon Lawson; *D:* Michael Scott; *C:* Maris Jansons. **CABLE**

Hector and the Search for Happiness 1/2 **2014 (R)** Chelsom's dramedy likely had the best of intentions, and one can't fault the always-entertaining Pegg for trying to make something uplifting, but the attempt at inspiration here comes with a blanket of racism that one can't shake. Hector's a psychiatrist who searches the globe to try and find the secret to a happy life. Instead of a truly cultural experience, it offers incredibly broad, offensive stereotypes of always-happy Africans and rigid Asians, most of whom seem put on this planet to make a white man happy. **114m/C; DVD.** *CA GE* Simon Pegg; Rosamund Pike; Stellan Skarsgard; Jean Reno; Toni Collette; Christopher Plummer; *D:* Peter Chelsom; *W:* Peter Chelsom; Maria von Heland; Tinker Lindsay; *C:* Kolja Brandt; *M:* Dan Mangan; Jesse Zubot.

The Hedgehog *Le Herisson* **2009** Precocious 11-year-old Paloma decides to kill herself on her 12th birthday because life is too absurd. But this is before she gets to know frumpy concierge Renee, who hides her intelligence beneath a bristly exterior and prefers her cat to human company. Life changes for them all when Mr. Ozu, a sophisticated Japanese widower, becomes their new neighbor and befriends both Paloma and Renee. French with subtitles. **98m/C; DVD, Blu-Ray.** *FR* Garance Le Guillermic; Josiane Balasko; Togo Igawa; Anne Brochet; Wladimir Yordanoff; Sarah Le Picard; *D:* Mona Achache; *W:* Mona Achache; *C:* Patrick Blossier; *M:* Gabriel Yared.

Hedwig and the Angry Inch **2000 (R)** Creator-star Mitchell adapted and directed his Off Broadway stage rock musical along with composer-lyricist Trask (who's also in the film) and opened up his gender-bending '70s kitsch fantasy. Hedwig was once Hansel, an East Berlin boy, whose sex-change operation was botched and who was abandoned in a Kansas trailer park by her G.I. husband. Betrayed in love by teenaged boy toy Tommy (Pitt), who also steals Hedwig's songs, Hedwig and her band embark on a low-rent tour while Hedwig sings her life story to the disinterested and stalks a much-more successful Tommy. **95m/C; VHS, DVD, Blu-Ray.** John Cameron Mitchell; Michael Pitt; Andrea Martin; Miriam Shor; Alberta Watson; Maurice Dean Wint; Rob Campbell; Stephen Trask; Theodore Liscinski; Michael Aranov; *D:* John Cameron Mitchell; *W:* John Cameron Mitchell; *C:* Frank DeMarco; *M:* Stephen Trask.

Heidi 1/2 **1937** Johanna Spyri's classic tale puts Shirley Temple in the hands of a mean governess and the loving arms of her Swiss grandfather. Also available colorized.

Remade in 1967. **88m/B; VHS, DVD.** Shirley Temple; Jean Hersholt; Helen Westley; Arthur Treacher; Sidney Blackmer; Marcia Mae Jones; Mary Nash; *D:* Allan Dwan; *W:* Walter Ferris; *C:* Arthur C. Miller; *M:* Julien Josephson.

Heidi ✌✌ **1967** The second American adaptation of the classic Johanna Spyri novel tells the story of an orphaned girl who goes to the Swiss Alps to live with her grandfather. **100m/C; VHS, DVD.** Maximilian Schell; Jennifer Edwards; Michael Redgrave; Jean Simmons; *D:* Delbert Mann; *W:* Earl Hamner; *M:* John Williams. **TV**

Heidi ✌✌✌ **1993 (G)** Yet another version of the children's classic, from German writer Johanna Spyri's 1881 novel. Thornton is charming as the orphan shuttled from relative to relative until she happily ends up with her crotchety grandfather (Robards) in his mountain cabin. Then her cousin comes along and whisks her off to the city to be a companion to the invalid Klara (Randall). Seymour is the snobbish, scowling governess. This "Heidi" is spunky enough to keep the sugar level tolerable. Filmed on location in Austria. **167m/C; VHS, DVD.** Noley Thornton; Jason Robards, Jr.; Jane Seymour; Lexi (Faith) Randall; Sian Phillips; Patricia Neal; Benjamin Brazier; Michael Simkins; Andrew Bicknell; Jane Hazlegrove; *D:* Michael Rhodes; *W:* Jeanne Rosenberg; *M:* Lee Holdridge. **TV**

The Heidi Chronicles ✌✌ ½ **1995** Some 25 years of boomer angst and friendship are covered in this TNT cable adaptation of Wasserstein's 1988 Pulitzer Prize-winning play. Heidi Holland (Curtis) goes from prep school to Vassar to an art history career while searching for self-fulfillment, feminist ideals, and some romance along the way. The romance is on-and-off, thanks to caddish journalist Scoop (Friedman), but Heidi can always depend on soul mate, gay pediatrician Peter (Hulce), and Susan (Cattrall), her follow-the-fads confidante. Heidi's sometimes too morose for her own good but you won't mind spending a couple of hours in her company. **94m/C; DVD.** Jamie Lee Curtis; Tom Hulce; Kim Cattrall; Peter Friedman; Eve Gordon; Shari Belafonte; Sharon Lawrence; Julie White; Debra Eisenstadt; Roma Maffia; *D:* Paul Bogart; *W:* Wendy Wasserstein; *C:* Isidore Mankofsky; *M:* David Shire. **CABLE**

Height of the Sky ✌✌ ½ **1999** In rural Arkansas, 1935, the poor Jones family farms a small plot of land, which they rent from the rich Caldwells. When Gabriel Jones (Moninger) succumbs to tuberculosis, family patriarch Wendel Jones (Stewart) decides to hide Gabriel in an old cabin thereby leaving the strong-willed Leora (Weedon) in charge of the family. Jennifer must convince Mr. Caldwell (Palazzo) that all is well on their farm while she covers for her father's absence. Written and directed by Lyn Clinton, cousin of President Bill Clinton. **116m/C; DVD.** Grant Moninger; Evan Palazzo; Jackie Stewart; Jennifer Weedon; *D:* Lyn Clinton; *W:* Lyn Clinton; *C:* John R. Zilles; *M:* Boris Zelkin.

Heights ✌✌ ½ **2004 (R)** Mildly entertaining debut from Terrio follows the lives of several New Yorkers over 24 hours. Diana (Close) is an award-winning diva who gives acting classes at Juillard. Struggling Alec (Bradford) auditions for Diana and she decides to use him to console herself about her husband's latest romance by inviting Alec to her big birthday bash. Meanwhile, her photographer daughter Isabel (Banks) is worried about her upcoming wedding to handsome lawyer Jonathan (Marsden), who is dodging journalist Peter (Light) for suspicious reasons. Based on co-writer Fox's play. **93m/C; DVD.** Glenn Close; Elizabeth Banks; James Marsden; Jesse Bradford; Thomas Lennon; Matthew Davis; Isabella Rossellini; John Light; George Segal; Eric Bogosian; Michael Murphy; *D:* Chris Terrio; *W:* Amy Fox; *C:* Jim Denault; *M:* Martin Erskine; Ben Butler.

Heimat 1 ✌✌ ½ *Heimat-Eine deutsche Chronik* **1984** Sixteen-hour series follows the lives, loves, and tragedies of the German Simon family from the end of WWI to 1982. Based on Reitz's own family and his childhood. Shot over two years, the series has 28 lead performances and more than 140 speaking roles. German with subtitles. **924m/C; VHS, DVD.** *GE* Marita Breuer; *D:* Edgar Reitz; *W:* Edgar Reitz; Peter F. Steinbach; *C:* Gernot Roll; *M:* Nikos Mamangakis.

Heimat 2 ✌✌ ½ **1992** The continuation of the saga is composed of 25 half-hour segments and follows Hermann Simon's life in Munich from 1960 to 1970. A modernist musician and composer, Hermann falls in with a group of students, artists, and rebels. German with subtitles. **750m/C; VHS, DVD.** *GE* Daniel E. Smith; Henry Arnold; Salome Kammer; Hannelore Hoger; Anke Sevenich; Noemi Steuer; *D:* Edgar Reitz; *W:* Edgar Reitz; *C:* Gernot Roll; Gerard Vandenburg; Christian Reitz; *M:* Nikos Mamangakis.

The Heineken Kidnapping ✌✌ **2011** True crime story with some composite characters. In 1983, businessman Alfred Heineken (Hauer), the president of the Dutch brewing company, is kidnapped. He's held for a month before the ransom is paid and his kidnappers flee to France. Having suffered brutal treatment, Alfred uses his considerable resources to bring his abductors to justice. English and Dutch with subtitles. **118m/C; DVD, Blu-Ray.** *NL* Rutger Hauer; Reinout Scholten van Aschat; Gijs Naber; Marcel Hensema; *D:* Maarten Treurniet; *W:* Maarten Treurniet; *C:* Giulio Biccari; *M:* Tom Holkenborg.

The Heiress ✌✌✌ ½ **1949** Based on the Henry James novel "Washington Square." Catherine (de Havilland) is the plain, awkward daughter of wealthy widowed doctor Austin Sloper (Richardson), who is a belittling tyrant to his only child. Catherine has no suitors until handsome, fortune-seeking Morris Townsend (Clift) approaches her. Naturally, Dr. Sloper dismisses his interest and warns that his daughter will only end up with a broken heart. No happy endings here but the performances are superb. Remade as "Washington Square" in 1997. **115m/B; VHS, DVD, Blu-Ray.** Olivia de Havilland; Montgomery Clift; Ralph Richardson; Miriam Hopkins; Vanessa Brown; Mona Freeman; Ray Collins; Selena Royle; *D:* William Wyler; *W:* Ruth Goetz; Augustus Goetz; *C:* Leo Tover; *M:* Aaron Copland. Oscars '49: Actress (de Havilland), Art Dir./Set Dec., B&W, Costume Des. (B&W), Orig. Dramatic Score; Golden Globes '50: Actress--Drama (de Havilland); Natl. Bd. of Review '49: Actor (Richardson); Natl. Film Reg. '96; N.Y. Film Critics '49: Actress (de Havilland).

The Heirloom ✌ ½ *Zhaibian; House Transformations* **2005** A wealthy family commits mass suicide and 20 years later the mystery remains. James (Chang) inherits the abandoned Taipei mansion and decides to move in with girlfriend Yo (Kwan). Nasty things begin to happen. James' character fades into the background while Yo fights off the creepies. Chinese with subtitles. **97m/C; DVD.** *TW* Jason Chang; Terri Kwan; Yu-Chen Chang; Tender Huang; *D:* Leste Chen; *W:* Dorian Li; *C:* Pung-Leung Kwan; *M:* Jeffrey Cheng.

The Heist ✌✌ **1989** An ex-con, upon regaining his freedom, sets out to rip off the crook who framed him. Entertaining enough story with a first-rate cast. **97m/C; VHS, DVD; Open Captioned.** Pierce Brosnan; Tom Skerritt; Wendy Hughes; Noble Willingham; Tom Atkins; Robert Prosky; *D:* Stuart Orme; *C:* Jiri (George) Tirl; *M:* Arthur B. Rubinstein. **CABLE**

The Heist ✌✌ *Hostile Force* **1996** Con artist plots the hijacking of a transport company's fleet and starts out by taking the firm's employees hostage. But one of the workers is an ex-cop who failed once to stop a robbery and is not about to fail again. **99m/C; VHS, DVD.** *GE* Andrew McCarthy; Cynthia Geary; Wolf Larson; Hannes Jaenicke; Cali Timmins; *D:* Michael Kennedy; *W:* Michael January; *C:* Bruce Worrall. **TV**

Heist ✌✌✌ **2001 (R)** Hackman is Joe, a master thief who's planning to retire after his latest job, but fence Bergman (DeVito) has other ideas, holding Joe's payoff until he agrees to a big-time gold heist. And just to make things interesting, Bergman sends his nephew Silk (Rockwell) along. This complicates things even more, especially with Joe's wife, Fran (Pidgeon). In classic Mamet fashion, doublecrosses, plot twists, misdirection, great dialogue and perfect casting convene to create an excellent caper film. Lindo and Jay add plenty of spark as Joe's loyal crew members. **107m/C; VHS, DVD, Blu-Ray.** Gene Hackman; Danny DeVito; Delroy Lindo; Sam Rockwell; Rebecca Pidgeon; Ricky Jay; Patti LuPone; Jim Frangione; *D:* David Mamet; *W:* David Mamet; *C:* Robert Elswit; *M:* Theodore Shapiro.

Heist ✌✌ **2009** Erik (David) has one week to pay off a Colombian drug cartel or die and turns to his gangster brother for help. They hatch a scheme to rob an armored car on a busy street corner in broad daylight. Considering they're both professional criminals you think they'd realize this was a bad idea. **90m/C; DVD.** Rick Jordan; Christian Mendez; Erik David; Tim Aslin; Dana Fares; Edward C'Nyle Bradford; Frank Drank; Victor Dean; Emanuel Borria; Luis Alberto Aracena; Christian Castro; Cruz Chung; George Hernandez; Jason Park; Darren Thomas; Sean Ridgway; Joe Perales; David Alan Graf; Hisonni Johnson; *D:* Rick Jordan; Richard Cooper; *W:* Rick Jordan; Lee Denny; *C:* Grisha Alasadi; *M:* Emilio Kauderer.

Helas pour Moi ✌✌ *Oh Woe is Me* **1994** Perplexing, contemplative film on faith and love—and maybe a miracle. Told in flashback, publisher Alexander Klimt (Verley) travels to a Swiss lakeside town where it's rumored that the beautiful Rachel Donnadieu (Masliah) has been "visited" by God, who wishes to experience the pleasures of love, in the form of her own husband, simple fisherman Simon (Depardieu). Story is derived from the Greek myth concerning Zeus, who seduced Alcmene in the shape of her husband Amphitryon. French with subtitles. **84m/C; VHS, DVD, Blu-Ray.** *FR SI* Gerard Depardieu; Laurence Masliah; Bernard Verley; *D:* Jean-Luc Godard; *W:* Jean-Luc Godard; *C:* Caroline Champetier.

Held for Murder ✌ *Her Mad Night* **1932** When a vacationing daughter is accused of murder, her mom lovingly takes the blame. Will the daughter come back to clear her mom, or will she let her fry in the electric chair? **67m/B; VHS, DVD.** Irene Rich; Conway Tearle; Mary Carlisle; Kenneth Thomson; William B. Davidson; *D:* E. Mason Hopper.

Held Hostage ✌✌ **1991** The true story of Jerry Levin, a reporter kidnapped by terrorists while on assignment in Beirut, and his wife, Sis, who struggled with the State Department for his release. **95m/C; VHS, DVD.** Marlo Thomas; David Dukes; G.W. Bailey; Edward Winter; Robert Harper; William Schallert; *D:* Roger Young. **TV**

Held Hostage ✌ ½ **2009** Generic woman-in-peril Lifetime flick based on a true story. Bank manager Michelle Estey's home is invaded by three masked men who force Michelle to follow through with their bank heist instructions by threatening her daughter. However, when the criminals are caught, they insist Michelle was part of their crew and she goes on trial. **86m/C; DVD.** Julie Benz; Natasha Calis; Brendan Penny; Bruce McGill; Jason Schombing; Tom Carey; *D:* Grant Harvey; *W:* James Kearns; Maria Nation; *C:* Craig Wrobleski; *M:* Hal Beckett. **CABLE**

Held Up ✌ ½ *Inconvenienced* **2000 (PG-13)** Engaged couple Foxx and Long are having a hard time staying together when after they have a fight and Foxx becomes a hostage during a botched convenience store robbery in a sleepy southwestern town. Broad comedy works in all the black-guy-meets-white-yokels gags, but they've all been done before by funnier writers. Foxx has some appeal, but not enough to overcome this mess. It could've been worse: Rob Schneider bailed after four days of filming. **88m/C; VHS, DVD.** Jamie Foxx; Nia Long; Jake Busey; John Cullum; Barry Corbin; Eduardo Yanez; Mike Wiles; Sarah Paulson; Julie Hagerty; *D:* Steve Rash; *W:* Jeff Eastin; *C:* David Makin; *M:* Robert Folk.

Helen ✌✌ **2009 (R)** Affecting performance by Judd in a somber drama about mental illness. Married Helen Leonard seems to have a perfect life with her loving husband David (Visnjic), teen daughter Julie (Fast), and a successful teaching career. However, she also suffers from crippling clinical depression and her relapse causes devastating consequences for Helen and her family. **120m/C; DVD.** *CA GE* Ashley Judd; Goran Visnjic; Alexia Fast; Lauren Lee Smith; David Hewlett; Leah Cairns; Alberta Watson; *D:* Sandra Nettelbeck; *W:* Sandra Nettelbeck; *C:* Michael Bertl; *M:* Tim Despic.

The Helen Morgan Story ✌✌ **1957** Musical bio of tragic Jazz Age torch singer Helen Morgan (Blyth) from her carnival days to Broadway stardom. She's constantly loving and getting left by bootlegger Larry Maddox (Newman), a charismatic louse. Then Helen gets involved with married lawyer Russell Wade (Carlson). Booze eventually is the downfall to her career. Most of the plot is fictional anyway with a prerequisite upbeat ending tacked on. Gogi Grant dubbed Blyth's singing. **118m/B; DVD.** Ann Blyth; Paul Newman; Richard Carlson; Gene Evans; Alan King; Walter Woolf King; Cara Williams; *D:* Michael Curtiz; *W:* Oscar Saul; Stephen Longstreet; Nelson Gidding; Dean Riesner; *C:* Ted D. McCord; *M:* Larry Prinz.

Helen of Troy ✌ ½ **1956** Mythological fantasy finds Helen (Podesta), the beautiful daughter of Zeus, falling in love with Trojan prince Paris (Sernas)?an event that leads to the siege of Troy. Ignores script for lavish effects. Video includes behind-the-scenes footage. **135m/C; VHS, DVD.** Rossana Podesta; Jacques Sernas; Cedric Hardwicke; Stanley Baker; Niall MacGinnis; Nora Swinburne; Robert Douglas; Torin Thatcher; Harry Andrews; Janette Scott; Ronald Lewis; Brigitte Bardot; *D:* Robert Wise; *W:* John Twist; N. Richard Nash; *C:* Harry Stradling, Sr.; *M:* Max Steiner.

Helen of Troy ✌✌ ½ **2003** Since Helen was the face that launched a thousand ships for the Trojan War, she needs to be a looker and, in the person of Guillory, she is. Which is good, since the cable miniseries is fairly ordinary. Helen is married to weak-willed Menelaus (Callis), the King of Sparta but falls crazy in love with Paris (Marsden), a Prince of Troy. The lovers hightail it to Troy, where King Priam (Rhys-Davies) offers protection. Menelaus's brother Agamemnon (a snakey Sewell) leads the Spartans on a 10-year battle to get Helen back. Remember the Trojan Horse is a big deal. **177m/C; VHS, DVD.** Sienna Guillory; Matthew Marsden; Rufus Sewell; Stellan Skarsgard; John Rhys-Davies; Maryam D'Abo; Emilia Fox; James Callis; James Lapine; Nigel Whitmey; *D:* John Kent Harrison; *W:* Ronni Kern; *C:* Edward Pei; *M:* Joel Goldsmith. **CABLE**

Hell and Back Again ✌✌ **2011** Photojournalist Danfung Dennis is embedded with the Marines of Echo Company in southern Afghanistan in summer, 2009 when they launched an assault on a Taliban stronghold. After Sgt. Nathan Harris suffers a life-threatening injury, Dennis follows Harris back to his home in North Carolina as he and his wife Ashley face the difficulties of his rehab and transitioning back into civilian life when Harris would prefer to return to the military. **88m/C; DVD, Blu-Ray.** *US GB* Nathan Harris; Ashley Harris; *D:* Danfung Dennis; *C:* Danfung Dennis; *M:* J. Ralph.

Hell Boats ✌✌ **1970** American commander Tom Jeffords is assigned to the British Royal Navy to maintain the blockade of Malta. He must also devise a plan to destroy a Nazi arsenal located in Sicily. Jeffords' idea is a suicide mission involving a captured German E-boat, which can pass through enemy waters. Naturally, there's still time for a romantic interlude between Jeffords and Alison, the unhappy wife of the British commander. **94m/C; DVD.** James Franciscus; Ronald Allen; Elizabeth Shepherd; Reuven Bar-Yotam; Inigo Jackson; *D:* Paul Wendkos; *W:* Derek Ford; Donald Ford; *C:* Paul Beeson; *M:* Frank Cordell.

Hell Bound ✌ ½ **1957** A ship carrying a valuable supply of WWII surplus drugs is docked in L.A. Targeted by thief Jordan and his gang, the plan is threatened by a dame, romance, and betrayal. **71m/B; DVD.** John Russell; June Blair; Stuart Whitman; Margo Woode; George Mather; Frank Fenton; Stanley Adams; *D:* William Hole, Jr.; *W:* Richard H. Landau; *C:* Carl Guthrie; *M:* Les Baxter.

Hell Comes to Frogtown ✌ **1988 (R)** In a post-nuclear holocaust land run by giant frogs, a renegade who is one of the few non-sterile men left on earth must rescue some fertile women and impregnate them. Sci-fi spoof is extremely low-budget, but fun. Stars "Rowdy" Roddy Piper of wrestling fame. **88m/C; VHS, DVD, Blu-Ray.** Roddy Piper; Sandahl Bergman; Rory Calhoun; Donald G. Jackson; Cec Verrell; *D:* Donald G. Jackson; Robert J. Kizer; *W:* Randall Frakes; *C:* Donald G. Jackson.

Hell Commandos ✌ ½ **1969** Soldiers in WWII struggle to prevent the Nazis from releasing a deadly bacteria that will kill millions. Dubbed. **92m/C; VHS, DVD.** *IT* Guy Madison; Stelvio Rosi; ***D:*** Jose Luis Merino.

Hell Divers **1931** Navel airmen Windy Riker (Beery) and Steve Nelson (Gable) are stationed aboard the USS Saratoga where old pro Windy and cocky upstart Steve battle over planes and who's the best flyer. But when Steve crashes on a tiny island, it's Windy who leads the dangerous rescue mission. Portion of the pic were shot onboard and include scenes with the fighter-bomber Curtiss F8C-4 Helldiver. **109m/B; DVD.** Wallace Beery; Clark Gable; Conrad Nagel; Dorothy Jordan; Marjorie Rambeau; Marie Prevost; ***D:*** George W. Hill; ***W:*** Harvey Gates; Malcolm Stuart Boylan; ***C:*** Harold Wenstrom.

Hell Fest **2018 (R)** Six college-age friends, including Natalie (Forsyth) and her crush Gavin (Attal), are excited to spend the evening at a horror-themed amusement park called Hell Fest. What the friends don't know is that a masked presence known as The Other has also entered the park. As The Other stalks Natalie, she's distressed but her friends do not believe her. However, she is not The Other's only target. Though the horror film's premise has much promise, it fails to take advantage of its set up to full effect. **105m/C; DVD.** Cynthea Mercado; Stephen Conroy; Amy Forsyth; Bex Taylor-Klaus; Reign Edwards; ***D:*** Gregory Plotkin; ***W:*** Seth M. Sherwood; Blair Butler; Akela Cooper; ***C:*** Jose David Montero; ***M:*** Bear McCreary.

Hell Harbor **1930** Caribbean love, murder and greed combine to make this early talkie. Exterior shots were filmed on the west coast of Florida and the beauty of the Tampa area in the 1930s is definitely something to see. **65m/B; VHS, DVD.** Lupe Velez; Gibson Gowland; Jean Hersholt; John Holland; ***D:*** Henry King.

Hell High **1986 (R)** Four high schoolers plan a night of torture and humiliation for an annoying teacher, only to find she has some deadly secrets of her own. Dumber than it sounds. **84m/C; VHS, DVD.** Christopher Stryker; Christopher Cousins; Millie Prezioso; Jason Brill; ***D:*** Douglas Grossman.

Hell in the Pacific **1969 (PG)** A marvelously photographed (by Conrad Hall) psycho/macho allegory, about an American and a Japanese soldier stranded together on a tiny island and the mini-war they fight all by themselves. Overly obvious anti-war statement done with style. **101m/C; VHS, DVD, Blu-Ray.** Lee Marvin; Toshiro Mifune; ***D:*** John Boorman; ***W:*** Eric Bercovici; Alexander Jacobs; ***C:*** Conrad L. Hall; ***M:*** Lalo Schifrin.

Hell Is for Heroes **1/2 1962** McQueen stars as the bitter leader of a small infantry squad outmanned by the Germans in this tight WWII drama. A strong cast and riveting climax make this a must for action fans. **90m/B; VHS, DVD.** Steve McQueen; Bobby Darin; Fess Parker; Harry Guardino; James Coburn; Mike Kellin; Nick Adams; Bob Newhart; L.Q. Jones; Don Haggerty; Joseph Hoover; Michele Montau; Bill Mullikin; ***D:*** Donald Siegel; ***W:*** Robert Pirosh; Richard Carr; ***C:*** Harold Lipstein; ***M:*** Leonard Rosenman.

Hell Is Sold Out **1/2 1951** Successful writer Dominic Danges (Lom) is believed to have died in WWII, so novelist Valerie Martin (Zetterling) decides to appropriate his pen name. Naturally Danges is curious when 'his' new book is successfully released and decides to hide his identity when he tracks down and meets Valerie. **85m/B; DVD.** *GB* Herbert Lom; Mai Zetterling; Richard Attenborough; Hermione Baddeley; Kathleen Byron; ***D:*** Michael Anderson, Sr.; ***W:*** Guy Morgan; Moie Charles; ***C:*** Jack Ashler.

Hell Night **WOOF!** **1981 (R)** Several young people must spend the night in a mysterious mansion as part of their initiation into Alpha Sigma Rho fraternity in this extremely dull low-budget horror flick. **100m/C; VHS, DVD, Blu-Ray.** Linda Blair; Vincent Van Patten; Kevin Brophy; Peter Barton; Jenny Neumann; ***D:*** Tom De Simone; ***W:*** Randy Feldman; ***C:*** Mac Ahlberg; ***M:*** Danny Wyman.

Hell of the Living Dead **WOOF!** *Apocalipsis Canibal; Night of the Zombies; Zombie Creeping Flesh* **1983** Staff of a scientific research center are killed and then resurrected as cannibals who prey on the living. The living will suffer again if trapped into watching. Mattel is pseudonym for director Vincent Dawn. Cheap, dubbed, and possessing minimal coherence. **103m/C; VHS, DVD, Blu-Ray.** *IT SP* Margit Evelyn Newton; Frank Garfield; Selan Karay; ***D:*** Bruno Mattei; ***W:*** J.M. Cunilles; Claudio Fragasso; ***C:*** John Cabrera.

Hell on Wheels **1967** Two successful brothers in the racing industry are torn apart by the same girl. Brotherly love diminishes into a hatred so deep that murder becomes the sole purpose of both. **96m/C; VHS, DVD.** Marty Robbins; Jennifer Ashley; John Ashley; Gigi Perreau; Robert Dornan; Connie Smith; Frank Gerstle; ***D:*** Will Zens.

Hell or High Water **2016 (R)** A divorced father (Pine) and his ex-con brother (Foster) are forced by their economic situation into a life of crime. Though they think they have a unique approach – committing small-scale bank robberies and taking just enough to not be noticed by the U.S. authorities to avoid foreclosure of their family ranch. Of course, two Texas Rangers (Bridges & Birmingham) do notice and set out to stop the fraternal criminals. Mackenzie's drama is an excellent riff on Cormac McCarthy—a vision of the south in which there are no real heroes or villains. **102m/C; DVD, Blu-Ray.** Jeff Bridges; Chris Pine; Ben Foster; Buck Taylor; Gil Birmingham; ***D:*** David Mackenzie; ***W:*** Taylor Sheridan; ***C:*** Giles Nuttgens; ***M:*** Nick Cave; Warren Ellis. Ind. Spirit '17: Actor--Supporting (Foster).

Hell Ride **2008 (R)** Exploitation biker flick past its sell-by date. Bishop, a veteran of the 60s/70s genre, writes, directs, and stars as Pistolero, president of the Victors. He's still looking for revenge against the rival gang who killed his honey over stolen drug money and soon the glowering, riding, sexual exploitation of women, and killing is on! Oh yeah, apparently the similar "Grindhouse" wasn't enough for Quentin Tarantino, who is one of the executive producers. **84m/C; DVD.** Larry Bishop; Michael Madsen; Eric Balfour; Vinnie Jones; David Carradine; Dennis Hopper; Leonor Varela; ***D:*** Larry Bishop; ***W:*** Larry Bishop; ***C:*** Scott Kevan; ***M:*** Daniele Luppi.

Hell Ship Mutiny **1/2 1957** Man comes to the aid of a lovely island princess, whose people have been forced to hand over their pearls to a pair of ruthless smugglers. Excellent cast in an unfortunately tepid production. **66m/B; VHS, DVD.** Jon Hall; John Carradine; Peter Lorre; Roberta Haynes; Mike Mazurki; Stanley Adams; ***D:*** Lee Sholem; Elmo Williams.

Hell Squad **1985 (R)** Unable to release his son from the Middle Eastern terrorists who kidnapped him, a U.S. ambassador turns to the services of nine Las Vegas showgirls. These gals moonlight as vicious commandos in this low-budget action film with skin. **88m/C; VHS, DVD.** Bainbridge Scott; Glen Hartford; Tina Lederman; ***D:*** Kenneth Hartford; ***W:*** Kenneth Hartford; ***M:*** Charles P. Barnett.

Hell Swarm **2000 (R)** Implausible story about an ex-cop convicted of murdering his partner who teams with the government to take on an evil alien conspiracy. **90m/C; DVD.** Boyd Kestner; Kathryn Morris; Amanda Welles; ***D:*** Tim Matheson; ***W:*** Roderick Taylor; Bruce Taylor; ***C:*** David Connell; ***M:*** Don Davis. **VIDEO**

Hell to Eternity **1/2 1960** The true story of how WWII hero Guy Gabaldon persuaded 2,000 Japanese soldiers to surrender. Features several spectacular scenes. **132m/B; VHS, DVD.** Jeffrey Hunter; Sessue Hayakawa; David Janssen; Vic Damone; Patricia Owens; ***D:*** Phil Karlson.

Hell Up in Harlem **WOOF!** **1973 (R)** A black crime lord recuperates from an assassination attempt and tries to regain his power. Poor sequel to the decent film "Black Caesar." **98m/C; VHS, DVD, Blu-Ray.** Fred Williamson; Julius W. Harris; Margaret Avery; Gerald Gordon; Gloria Hendry; D'Urville Martin; Mindi Miller; Tony King; Bobby Ramsen; James Dixon; ***D:*** Larry Cohen; ***W:*** Larry Cohen; ***C:*** Fenton Hamilton; ***M:*** Fonce Mizell; Freddie Perren.

Hellbenders **1/2** *Il Crudeli; Los Despiadados* **1967 (PG)** A confederate veteran robs a Union train and must fight through acres of Civil War adversity. Dubbed. Poorly directed and acted. **92m/C; VHS, DVD, Blu-Ray.** *IT SP* Joseph Cotten; Norma Bengell; Julian Mateos; ***D:*** Sergio Corbucci; ***M:*** Ennio Morricone.

Hellbent **1/2 2004** Amusingly schlocky gay slasher pic, set on Halloween. Buff bad guy, wearing a devil-horn mask, stalks hunks in West Hollywood, decapitating his victims. Gay rookie cop Eddie (Fergus) is assigned to catch the killer. Debut effort for writer/director Etheredge-Ouzts ratchets up the tension at the end. **85m/C; DVD.** Bryan Kirkwood; Hank Harris; Kris Andersson; Shaun Benjamin; Miguel Caballero; Samuel Phillips; Dylan Fergus; Wren Brown; Andrew Levitas; Matt Phillips; ***D:*** Paul Etheredge-Ouzts; ***W:*** Paul Etheredge-Ouzts; ***C:*** Mark Mervis; ***M:*** Mike Shapiro.

Hellblock 13 **1/2 1997** Anthology of three low-budget short horror tales is told with grainy, raw-edged energy and a distinct regional flavor. Tara (Rochon) writes stories while she's on Death Row and shows them to her stolid guard (Hansen, "Leatherface" from "Texas Chainsaw Massacre"). Rochon brings a welcome note of humor to what might have been your basic madwoman stereotype. The individual films get better and funnier as they go along. **91m/C; VHS, DVD.** Debbie Rochon; Gunnar Hansen; J.J. North; Jennifer Peluso; David G. Holland; ***D:*** Paul Talbot; ***W:*** Paul Talbot; Jeffrey D. Miller; Michael R. Smith.

Hellbound **1/2 1994 (R)** Prosatanos (Neame), a powerful 12th-century wizard, is imprisoned and the source of his power (a scepter) is supposedly destroyed. Fast-forward several hundred years when Prosatanos manages to free himself and seek out the pieces of his scepter. Which happens to lead him to Chicago and a couple of unsuspecting cops (Norris, Levels). **95m/C; VHS, DVD.** Chuck Norris; Christopher Neame; Calvin Levels; Sheree J. Wilson; ***D:*** Aaron Norris.

Hellbound: Hellraiser 2 *Hellraiser 2* **1988 (R)** In this, the first sequel to Clive Barker's inter-dimensional nightmare, the traumatized daughter from the first film is pulled into the Cenobites' universe. Gore and weird imagery abound. An uncut, unrated version is also available. **96m/C; VHS, DVD, Blu-Ray.** *GB* Ashley Laurence; Clare Higgins; Kenneth Cranham; Imogen Boorman; William Hope; Oliver Smith; Sean Chapman; Doug Bradley; ***D:*** Tony Randel; ***W:*** Peter Atkins; ***C:*** Robin Vidgeon; ***M:*** Christopher Young.

Hellboy **1/2 2004 (PG-13)** Faithful adaptation of the cult Dark Horse comic is a success, thanks mostly to del Toro's smart direction and Perlman's amusing yet complex portrayal of the titular demon/hero. During WWII, the Nazis and Rasputin team up to try to bring about the reign of the seven gods of chaos. What they bring to earth is actually a baby demon who is found and adopted by Dr. Bruttenholm of the FBI's Bureau of Paranormal Research and Defense. Sixty years later, Hellboy is an adult working with the doc, breaking in a new handler, and pining over former bureau denizen Liz (Blair). Rasputin and his Nazi friends plan on using Hellboy to bring about the Apocalypse. Perlman gives Hellboy depth (even under all the prosthetics), but he has lots of help from a strong supporting cast. **125m/C; DVD, Blu-Ray, UMD.** Ron Perlman; John Hurt; Selma Blair; Rupert Evans; Karel Roden; Jeffrey Tambor; Biddy Hodson; Doug Jones; Ladislav Beran; Kevin Trainor; Corey Johnson; Stephen H. Fisher; ***V:*** David Hyde Pierce; ***D:*** Guillermo del Toro; ***W:*** Guillermo del Toro; Peter Briggs; ***C:*** Guillermo Navarro; ***M:*** Marco Beltrami.

Hellboy **2019 (R)** Hundreds of years after King Arthur killed evil blood queen Nimue (Jovovich) and put pieces of her body in boxes across England, Hellboy (Harbour) is a member of the Bureau of Paranormal Research and Defense. As Nimue gets put back together and her powers increase, she makes plans to harm humanity. With the help of his father Professor Broom (McShane) and others, Hellboy prepares to fight threats including Nimue. This reboot does not live up to its two stylistic predecessors, both directed by Guillermo del Toro. Instead, the filmmakers take Hellboy down a more violent and profane path that overwhelms the humor. **120m/C; DVD, Blu-Ray.** *US UK BL* David Harbour; Brian Gleeson; Mark Stanley; Nadya Keranova; Milla Jovovich; Penelope Mitchell; ***D:*** Neil Marshall; ***W:*** Andrew Cosby; ***C:*** Lorenzo Senatore; ***M:*** Benjamin Wallfisch.

Hellboy II: The Golden Army **2008 (PG-13)** Director Del Toro creates a stunning backdrop for big red monster Hellboy (Pearlman) to return. In flashback, young Hellboy hears a story of a king who assembles but disbands a golden army of elves to destroy the human world. But the elves are on a comeback, as if Hellboy didn't already have his hands full working through commitment issues with pyrokinetic girlfriend Liz (Blair) and drowning his sorrows with his scaly fish-man pal. With battles and action almost constant, lush visuals, and uber-quirky Barry Manilow-loving characters, it's near perfect for genre fans. **110m/C; Blu-Ray, On Demand.** Ron Perlman; Selma Blair; Doug Jones; Luke Goss; Roy Dotrice; John Hurt; Jeffrey Tambor; Brian Steele; Anna Walton; ***V:*** Thomas Kretschmann; Seth MacFarlane; ***D:*** Guillermo del Toro; ***W:*** Guillermo del Toro; Mike Mignola; ***C:*** Guillermo Navarro; ***M:*** Danny Elfman.

Hellbreeder **2004 (R)** Alice (Lyndie Uphill) has almost recovered from the death of her son, when the man she believes murdered him returns to town. **81m/C; DVD, Blu-Ray, Streaming.** *UK* Lyndie Uphill; Dominique Pinon; Darren Day; Tina Barnes; Harold Gasnier; ***D:*** James Eaves; Johannes Roberts; ***W:*** James Eaves; Johannes Roberts; ***C:*** John Raggett; ***M:*** Johannes Roberts. **VIDEO**

Hellcats **WOOF!** **1968 (R)** A mob of sleazy, leather-clad female bikers terrorize small Midwestern towns in this violent girl-gang thriller. Even biker movie fans might find this one unworthy. **90m/C; VHS, DVD.** Ross Hagen; Dee Duffy; Sharyn Kinzie; Del (Sonny) West; Bob Slatzer; ***D:*** Bob Slatzer.

Hellcats of the Navy **1/2 1957** Soggy true saga of the WWII mission to sever the vital link between mainland Asia and Japan. The only film that Ronald and Nancy Davis Reagan starred in together and the beginning of their grand romance. **82m/B; VHS, DVD.** Ronald Reagan; Nancy Davis; Arthur Franz; Robert Arthur; ***D:*** Nathan "Jerry" Juran; ***W:*** Bernard Gordon; David Lang.

Heller in Pink Tights **1960** Offbeast western, based on a novel by Louis L'Amour, that follows the adventures of a seedy vaudeville troupe in the 1880s. Manager Tom Healy (Quinn) stays barely ahead of his creditors, with Angela (Loren) as his leading asset (and Loren's assets are the film's highlight). She dallys with gunslinger Clint Mabry (Forest), who pursues her out of town and there's an Indian attack and more gunslinging until the troupe manages to find a safe haven. The story was hardly sophisticated director Cukor's specialty, which may account for the unbelievable characters and confused plot. **100m/C; VHS, DVD.** Sophia Loren; Anthony Quinn; Margaret O'Brien; Steve Forrest; Edmund Lowe; Ramon Novarro; Eileen Heckart; ***D:*** George Cukor; ***W:*** Walter Bernstein; ***C:*** Harold Lipstein; ***M:*** Daniele Amfitheatrof.

Hellfighters **1968 (G)** Texas oil well fire fighters experience trouble between themselves and the women they love. **121m/C; VHS, DVD, Blu-Ray.** John Wayne; Katharine Ross; Jim Hutton; Vera Miles; Bruce Cabot; Jay C. Flippen; ***D:*** Andrew V. McLaglen; ***W:*** Clair Huffaker; ***C:*** William Clothier; ***M:*** Leonard Rosenman.

Hellgate **1952** Medical man Gil Hanley (Hayden) gets caught between renegade Confederate soldiers and the Army in 1867 Kansas. A former Reb himself, Hanley gets railroaded into the military prison at Hellgate, New Mexico. Prison warden Voorhees (Bond) is determined to make everyone suffer but he doesn't expect an epidemic to sweep through, which means Hanley's doctoring skills are needed. **87m/C; DVD.** Sterling Hayden; Ward Bond; James Arness; Peter Coe; John Pickard; Joan Leslie; James Anderson; ***D:*** Charles Marquis Warren; ***W:*** Charles Marquis Warren; John C. Champion; ***C:*** Ernest Miller; ***M:*** Paul Dunlap.

Hellgate **WOOF!** **1989 (R)** A woman hitchhiking turns out to be one of the living dead. Her benefactor lives to regret picking her up. **96m/C; VHS, DVD.** Abigail Wolcott;

Ron Palillo; Carel Trichardt; Petrea Curran; Evan J. Klisser; Joanne Ward; *D:* William A. Levey; *W:* Michael O'Rourke; *C:* Peter Palmer.

Hellhounds ½ **2009** In ancient Greece, warrior Kleitos has just married Demetria, who is killed after the ceremony by jealous Theron. A seer tells Kleitos that he has three days to rescue Demetria from the underworld or she will become the bride of Hades. There's some swordplay, the rescue, and then Kleitos and his men go after Theron who somehow has control of Hades' hellhounds. Produced by RHI Entertainment and shown on the Syfy Channel as part of their Maneater series. **83m/C; DVD.** Scott Elrod; Amanda Brooks; Ben Cross; James Woods; Oltin Hurezeanu; Adam Butcher; Andrew Howard; *D:* Rick Schroder; *W:* Paul A. Birkett; Jason Bourque; *C:* Pierre Jodoin; *M:* Luc St. Pierre. **CABLE**

Hellion **2013** Jacob (a poignant Wiggins) is in a state of crisis. At 13 he spends his days getting into increasingly illegal trouble, when he's not forced to care for his younger brother because dad (Paul) is on another bender. The family is in disarray after Jacob's mother's death, and his life is at a turning point. Writer/director Candler, expanding her short film, creates a touching, moving portrait of men, young and old, stuck in emotional quicksand. Some of the ground has been covered in melodrama before but the filmmaker and her amazingly talented cast find the truth in it yet again. **98m/C; DVD.** Josh Wiggins; Aaron Paul; Juliette Lewis; Deke Garner; Jonny Mars; *D:* Kat Chandler; *W:* Kat Chandler; *C:* Brett Pawlak; *M:* Curtis Heath.

Hellions **2015** The talented McDonald misfires wildly in this trippy, surreal, unfocused, and all-around stupid movie about a teenage girl who discovers she's pregnant on Halloween and so stays home instead of going out trick-or-treating with her friends. What first seems to be little more than harmless pranks looking for more tricks than treats turns threatening, and McDonald's film turns trippy. As if he knew his story had no actual suspense, McDonald goes full-on surreal, staging some scenes David Lynch would raise an eyebrow at. And then he tacks on an arguably social message at the end just to leave a truly bad taste in your mouth. **80m/C; DVD, Blu-Ray, Streaming.** *CA* Chloe Rose; Robert Patrick; Rossif Sutherland; Rachel Wilson; Peter DaCunha; Luke Bilyk; Todor Kobakov; *D:* Bruce McDonald; *W:* Pascal Trottier; *C:* Norayr Kasper; *M:* Ian LeFeuvre.

Hellmaster **1992** Your basic sicko mad scientist experiments on some unsuspecting college students by injecting them with an addictive drug. The drug also causes some horrifying mutations and makes its victims superhuman (but also super-ugly). Lots of gore. Creative special effects and make-up will appeal to fans of horror. **92m/C; VHS, DVD, Blu-Ray.** John Saxon; David Emge; Amy Raasch; *D:* Douglas Schulze; *W:* Douglas Schulze.

Hello Again **1987 (PG)** The wife of a successful plastic surgeon chokes to death on a piece of chicken. A year later she returns to life, with comical consequences, but soon discovers that life won't be the same. **96m/C; VHS, DVD, Blu-Ray.** Shelley Long; Corbin Bernsen; Judith Ivey; Gabriel Byrne; Sela Ward; Austin Pendleton; Carrie Nye; Robert Lewis; Madeleine Potter; *D:* Frank Perry; *M:* William Goldstein.

Hello, Dolly! **1969 (G)** Widow Dolly Levi, while matchmaking for her friends, finds a match for herself. Based on the hugely successful Broadway musical adapted from Thornton Wilder's play "Matchmaker." Lightweight story needs better actors with stronger characterizations. Original Broadway score helps. **146m/C; VHS, DVD, Blu-Ray.** Barbra Streisand; Walter Matthau; Michael Crawford; Louis Armstrong; E.J. Peaker; Marianne McAndrew; Tommy Tune; *D:* Gene Kelly; *W:* Ernest Lehman; *C:* Harry Stradling, Sr.; *M:* Jerry Herman. Oscars '69: Art Dir./Set Dec., Scoring/Musical, Sound.

Hello Down There ½ **1969 (G)** Harmless—if dated—family comedy. Inventor Fred Miller (Randall) persuades his reluctant family to participate in a month-long experiment that has them living in a prototype underwater home. Wife Vivian (Leigh) is afraid of the water and his teenaged children are distressed because their pop band has a chance at a record deal. Meanwhile, the living room pool attracts sharks and an overly-friendly seal. Shot in Florida. **97m/C; DVD.** Tony Randall; Janet Leigh; Jim Backus; Ken Berry; Charlotte Rae; Richard Dreyfuss; Roddy MacDowall; *D:* Jack Arnold; *W:* Frank Telford; John McGreevey; *C:* Clifford Poland; *M:* Jeff Barry.

Hello, Frisco, Hello ½ **1943** San Francisco's wild Barbary Coast is the setting for this romantic musical. Smoothie Payne opens up a saloon that features Faye, who's in love with him, as the star singing attraction. Unfortunately, Payne is involved with a society snob and Faye heads off to European success. When she returns, it's to a sadder and wiser man. **98m/C; VHS, DVD, Blu-Ray.** Alice Faye; John Payne; Jack Oakie; Lynn Bari; Laird Cregar; June Havoc; Ward Bond; Aubrey Mather; John Archer; *D:* H. Bruce Humberstone; *W:* Robert Ellis; Helen Logan. Oscars '43: Song ("You'll Never Know").

Hello Goodbye **2008** Despite the cast, this culture clash comedy doesn't work thanks to annoying characters and situations. Gisele (Ardant) converted to Judaism to marry Alain (Depardieu) although the long-time married couple was never religious. What they are is bored and a trip to Israel impulsively convinces them to start over again in Tel Aviv. But doctor Alain's promised job falls through, their apartment isn't habitable, and most of their luggage is lost in transit. A zealous Gisele gets involved with questionable rabbi Yoshi (Ashkenazi) as Alain decides to explore his religious roots as well. English, French, and Hebrew with subtitles. **98m/C; DVD.** *FR IS* Fanny Ardant; Gerard Depardieu; Lior Ashkenazi; Jean Benguigui; Gilles Gaston-Dreyfus; Manu Payet; *D:* Graham Guit; *W:* Graham Guit; Michael Lelouche; *C:* Gerard Stein.

Hello, Hemingway **1990** Living in 1950s Havana, Larita hopes to be able to study in the United States and is inspired by Ernest Hemingway's "The Old Man and the Sea." She even tries to meet the writer but he's away hunting in Africa. However, the poverty of Larita's life may thwart her ambitions, and meanwhile the political situation in Cuba is becoming ever-more turbulent. Spanish with subtitles. **84m/C; DVD.** *CU* Laura De la Uz; Raul Paz; Herminia Sanchez; Caridad Hernande; Enrique Molina; *D:* Fernando Perez; *W:* Maydo Royero; *C:* Julio Valdes; *M:* Edesio Alejandro.

Hello I Must Be Going ½ **2012 (R)** Fresh off a divorce, 35-year-old Amy (Lynskey) is forced to move back in with her parents hoping to save a few bucks and start up a new business with her father. While trying to reassemble her life, she meets 19-year-old Jeremy (Abbott), and feels a spark again. The two pursue a romance filled with questions of age and experiences. An extremely lightweight, indie romantic comedy that relies on its excellent performances rather than its tame love story. Lynskey is pitch-perfect as a woman seen as a loser, who's out to prove everyone wrong. **94m/C; DVD.** Melanie Lynskey; Blythe Danner; John Rubinstein; Julie White; Christopher Abbott; Dan Futterman; *D:* Todd Louiso; *W:* Sarah Koskoff; *C:* Julie Kirkwood; *M:* Laura Veirs.

Hello Mary Lou: Prom Night 2 ½ *The Haunting of Hamilton High; Prom Night 2* **1987 (R)** A sequel to the successful slasher flick, wherein a dead-for-30-years prom queen relegates the current queen to purgatory and comes back to life in order to avenge herself. Wild special effects. **97m/C; VHS, DVD.** *CA* Michael Ironside; Wendy Lyon; Justin Louis; Lisa Schrage; Richard Monette; *D:* Bruce Pittman; *W:* Ron Oliver; *C:* John Herzog.

Hellraiser ½ **1987 (R)** A graphic, horror fantasy about a woman who is manipulated by the monstrous spirit of her husband's dead brother. In order for the man who was also her lover to be brought back to life, she must lure and kill human prey for his sustenance. Grisly and inventive scenes keep the action fast-paced; not for the faint-hearted. **94m/C; DVD, Blu-Ray, UMD.** *GB* Andrew (Andy) Robinson; Clare Higgins; Ashley Laurence; Sean Chapman; Oliver Smith; Robert Hines; Doug Bradley; Nicholas Vince; Dave Atkins; *D:* Clive Barker; *W:* Clive Barker; *C:* Robin Vidgeon; *M:* Christopher Young.

Hellraiser 3: Hell on Earth **1992 (R)** Pinhead is back in this film based on characters created by horrormeister Clive Barker. A strange black box holds the key to sending Pinhead back to Hell and is sought by the heroine, a TV newswoman (Farrell). But Pinhead's human henchman, a nasty nightclub owner, isn't going to make things easy. Imaginative special effects and Bradley's commanding presence as Pinhead aid this shocker, which becomes unfortunately mired in excessive gore. An unrated version at 97 minutes is also available. **91m/C; VHS, DVD, Blu-Ray.** Doug Bradley; Terry Farrell; Kevin Bernhardt; Paula Marshall; Ken Carpenter; Peter Boynton; Ashley Laurence; *D:* Anthony Hickox; *W:* Peter Atkins; *C:* Gerry Lively.

Hellraiser 4: Bloodline **1995 (R)** You can't keep a bad Pinhead in Hell, as this unfortunate sequel demonstrates. Bradley reprises his role as the big bad S&M pincushion in the latest and supposedly last installment of Clive Barker's blood drenched series. Tracing the origin of the infernal Rubik's Cube that releases Pinhead, the plot jumps between 18th century France, present day New York, and a 22nd century space station. Along the way, the Pointy One gets to flay, skewer, and impale to his evil heart's content. Special f/x guru Kevin Yeagher was so embarrassed by this outing that he took his director's credit off of the picture. Bad acting, bad plot, bad complexion. **81m/C; VHS, DVD, Blu-Ray.** Bruce Ramsay; Valentina Vargas; Doug Bradley; Kim Myers; Christina Harnos; Charlotte Chatton; Paul Perri; Mickey Cotrell; *D:* Alan Smithee; Kevin Yagher; *W:* Peter Atkins; *M:* Daniel Licht.

Hellraiser 5: Inferno **2000 (R)** Los Angeles detective Joseph (Sheffer) wakes up one day literally in hell. In order to escape he must find the puzzle box, which is in Pinhead's possession. This one is not only boring, it's confusing, and Pinhead has little more than a cameo appearance. **99m/C; VHS, DVD, Blu-Ray.** Craig Sheffer; Doug Bradley; Nicholas Turturro; James Remar; Lindsay Taylor; *D:* Scott Derrickson; *W:* Scott Derrickson; Paul Harris Boardman. **VIDEO**

Hellraiser: Deader *Hellraiser 7: Deader* **2005 (R)** Wanting to break the big story about a freaky Bucharest cult that supposedly rouses the deceased, a female reporter unearths the terrifying truth behind who they want to bring back to life. **88m/C; VHS, DVD, Blu-Ray.** Doug Bradley; Kari Wuhrer; Paul Rhys; Marc Warren; Georgina Rylance; *D:* Rick Bota; *W:* Neal Marshall Stevens; Tim(othy) Day; *M:* Henning Lohner. **VIDEO**

Hellraiser: Hellseeker **2002 (R)** The fifth sequel in the 15-year-old series looks great, thanks to debuting director Bota, who's a veteran cinematographer. But the story doesn't have enough Pinhead to please fans. Kristy (Laurence) has escaped from the Cenobites and is driving with her husband Trevor (Winters) when her body vanishes after a traffic accident. The same accident has caused Trevor to suffer from hallucinations that turn out to be real and make him a multiple murder suspect. **89m/C; VHS, DVD, Blu-Ray.** Ashley Laurence; Dean Winters; Doug Bradley; *D:* Rick Bota; *W:* Carl DuPre; Tim(othy) Day; *C:* John Drake; *M:* Stephen (Steve) Edwards. **VIDEO**

Hellraiser: Hellworld **2005 (R)** Pinhead (Bradley) and the Cenobites torment some computer hackers through the use of the hellworld.com site (possibly by manning the tech support phones). Ridiculously resilient franchise plods along, helped by the presence of Henriksen, on haitus from whatever Alien sequel they're probably working on. **91m/C; DVD, Blu-Ray.** Doug Bradley; Lance Henriksen; Henry Cavill; Katheryn Winnick; *D:* Rick Bota; *W:* Joel Soisson; Carl DuPre; *C:* Gabriel Kosuth; *M:* Lars Anderson. **VIDEO**

Hellraiser: Revelations **2011 (R)** Two guys discover the puzzle box that summons Pinhead and his minions, and one tries to escape by offering up his undeserving family members. **?m/CDVD, Blu-Ray.** Fred Tatasciore; Tracey Fairaway; Steven Brand; Nick Eversman; Stephen Smith Collins; *D:* Victor Garcia; *W:* Gary J. Tunnicliffe; *C:* David A. Armstrong; *M:* Frederik Wiedmann. **VIDEO**

Hell's Angels **1930** Classic WWI aviation movie is sappy and a bit lumbering, but still an extravagant spectacle with awesome air scenes. Studio owner Hughes fired directors Howard Hawks and Luther Reed, spent an unprecedented $3.8 million, and was ultimately credited as director (although Whale also spent some time in the director's chair). Three years in the making, the venture cost three pilots their lives and lost a bundle. Harlow replaced Swedish Greta Nissen when sound was added and was catapulted into blond bombshelldom as a two-timing dame. And the tinted and two-color scenes—restored in 1989—came well before Ted Turner ever wielded a crayola. **135m/B; VHS, DVD.** Jean Harlow; Ben Lyon; James Hall; John Darrow; Lucien Prival; Frank Clarke; Roy "Baldy" Wilson; Douglas Gilmore; Jane Winton; Evelyn Hall; *D:* Howard Hughes; *W:* Harry Behn; Howard Estabrook; Joseph Moncure March; *C:* Elmer Dyer; Harry Perry; E. Burton Steene; Dewey Wrigley; Gaetano Antonio "Tony" Gaudio; *M:* Hugo Riesenfeld.

Hell's Angels on Wheels ½ **1967** Low-budget, two-wheeled Nicholson vehicle that casts him as a gas station attendant who joins up with the Angels for a cross country trip. Laszlo Kovacs is responsible for the photography. One of the better 1960s biker films. **95m/C; VHS, DVD, Blu-Ray.** Jack Nicholson; Adam Roarke; Sabrina Scharf; Jana Taylor; John Garwood; Sonny Barger; Bruno VeSota; *D:* Richard Rush; *W:* Robert W(right) Campbell; *C:* Laszlo Kovacs; *M:* Stu Phillips.

Hell's Angels '69 **1969 (PG)** Figuring on robbing Caesar's Palace for the thrill, two wealthy brothers plot a deadly game by infiltrating the ranks of the Hell's Angels. Upon figuring out that they've been duped, the Angels seek revenge. Average biker epic filmed in Nevada features Hell's Angels Oakland chapter. **97m/C; VHS, DVD.** Tom Stern; Jeremy Slate; Conny Van Dyke; G.D. Spradlin; Sonny Barger; Steve Sandor; *D:* Lee Madden; *W:* Tom Stern; Jeremy Slate; Don Tait; *C:* Paul Lohmann.

Hell's Belles ½ *Girl in the Leather Suit* **1969** Biker has his ride stolen by a rival, who leaves a chick as payment. The two team up to get revenge, chasing the gang across the Arizona desert and picking them off one by one. **95m/C; VHS, DVD.** Jeremy Slate; Adam Roarke; Jocelyn Lane; Angelique Pettyjohn; Michael Walker; William Lucking; *D:* Maury Dexter; *W:* James Gordon White; Robert McMullen; *M:* Les Baxter.

Hell's Bloody Devils ½ *Operation M; Smashing the Crime Syndicate; Swastika Savages; The Fakers* **1970 (PG)** Mark Adams (Gabriel) is an FBI agent assigned to infiltrate a counterfeiting ring composed of bikers, right wing American Neo-Nazis, the Mafia, and an actual Nazi war criminal named Count von Delberg (Taylor). Originally produced under the titles "The Fakers" and "Operation M," the biker subplot was added (along with its more exploitative title name) when distributors balked at releasing the film. It has also been released since then without the biker footage under the name "Smashing the Crime Syndicate." **92m/C; DVD.** John Gabriel; Anne Randall; Broderick Crawford; Scott Brady; Kent Taylor; Robert Dix; Keith Andes; Jack Starrett; Erin O'Donnell; Vicki Volante; Emily Banks; *D:* Al Adamson; *W:* Jerry Evans; *C:* Gary Graver; Laszlo Kovacs; Frank Ruttencutter; *M:* Nelson Riddle; Don Ginnis.

Hell's Gate ½ *Bad Karma* **2001 (R)** Dangerous and crazy Agnes Thatcher (Kensit) believes her shrink, Dr. Trey Cambell (Muldoon), is the reincarnation of Jack the Ripper and that she was his mistress. She escapes from the looney bin and decides to eliminate Trey's family so that they can be reunited. Standard psycho-horror fare with some nudity for titillation (no pun intended). **92m/C; VHS, DVD.** Patsy Kensit; Patrick Muldoon; Amy Locane; Damian Chapa; *D:* John Hough; *C:* Jacques Haitkin; *M:* Harry Manfredini. **VIDEO**

Hell's Ground *Zibahkhana* **2008** Pakistan isn't known for its gory slasher movies, and this claims to be the first one ever (which is quite probably true). A couple of teenagers head out to a concert, and are diverted by a political protest into a forest, where their van breaks down. Apparently the local water is polluted, and causes dead people to become flesh-eating zombies. You'd think someone would have noticed and posted signs. Also attacking them are a maniac in a burkha wielding a spiked ball and chain, and a lunatic carrying a severed head. The budget isn't great, but who cares. How often do you get a film with zombies AND insane killers? **78m/C; DVD.** Kunwar Ali Roshan; Rooshanie Ejaz; Rubya Chaudhry; Haider Raza; Osmand Khalid Butt; Rehan; Najma Malik; Sultan Billa; Serim Meraj; Razia Malik; Ashfaq Bhatti; Mai Billi; Bobby Deol; Dharmendra; Lara Dutta; ***D:*** Omar Khan; ***W:*** Omar Khan; Pete Tombs; ***C:*** Najaf Bilgrami; ***M:*** Stephen Thrower.

Hell's Half Acre **1954** Somewhat clumsy noir with an interesting setting. Reformed gangster Chet Chester (Corey) lives in Honolulu with his girlfriend Sally (Gates). He takes the rap when she kills one of his ex-partners and goes to jail. Donna Williams (Keyes) arrives, looking for her husband who disappeared after Pearl Harbor. Sally is murdered, and Chet breaks out of jail to go after the killer--in the same titular slum area of the city that Donna is searching. **90m/B; DVD, Blu-Ray.** Wendell Corey; Evelyn Keyes; Nancy Gates; Elsa Lanchester; Philip Ahn; Keye Luke; Marie Windsor; Jesse White; ***D:*** John H. Auer; ***W:*** Steve Fisher; ***C:*** John L. "Jack" Russell; ***M:*** R. Dale Butts.

Hell's Heroes **1930** Off-told tale, based on the Peter B. Kyne novel "The Three Godfathers," finds three outlaws travelling through the desert who stumble on a dying woman who's just given birth. They agree to take her newborn to its father, who lives in the town they just robbed. It happens to be Christmas and it'll be a miracle if any one of them can make it back to fulfill their promise. Shot on location in the Mojave Desert and the Panamint Valley. Wyler, in his first all-sound film, keeps his story focused and stark. **65m/B; DVD.** Charles Bickford; Raymond Hatton; Fred Kohler, Sr.; Fritzi Ridgeway; Maria Alba; Joe de la Cruz; ***D:*** William Wyler; ***W:*** Tom Reed; ***C:*** George Robinson.

Hell's Hinges **1916** The next to last Hart western, typifying his good/bad cowboy character. This time he's a gunslinger who falls for the new preacher's sister, while the minister himself is led astray by a saloon gal. Perhaps Hart's best film. **65m/B; Silent; VHS, DVD.** William S. Hart; Clara Williams; Jack Standing; Robert McKim; ***D:*** William S. Hart. Natl. Film Reg. '94.

Hell's House **1932** After his mother dies, young lad Durkin goes to the city to live with relatives, gets mixed up with moll Davis and her bootlegger boyfriend O'Brien, and is sent to a brutal reform school. Interesting primarily for early appearances by Davis and O'Brien (before he was typecast as the indefatigable good guy). **80m/B; DVD, Blu-Ray.** Junior Durkin; Pat O'Brien; Bette Davis; Frank "Junior" Coghlan; Charley Grapewin; Emma Dunn; ***D:*** Howard Higgin; ***W:*** B. Harrison Orkow; Paul Gangelin; ***C:*** Allen Siegler.

Hell's Kitchen **1/2 1939** The Dead End Kids get into trouble with Hiram Crispin, the crooked warden of the Hell's Kitchen boys' shelter. Paroled racketeer Buck Caesar tries to do right by the boys, but it's up to the Kids themselves to get justice when one of their own dies. Fifth in the series. **82m/B; DVD.** Billy Halop; Bobby Jordan; Leo Gorcey; Huntz Hall; Gabriel Dell; Bernard Punsley; Ronald Reagan; Stanley Fields; Grant Mitchell; Margaret Lindsay; ***D:*** Lewis Seiler; Ewald Andre Dupont; ***W:*** Crane Wilbur; Fred Niblo, Jr.; ***C:*** Charles Rosher.

Hell's Kitchen NYC **1/2 1997 (R)** Ex-con Johnny Miles (Phifer) returns home to New York's notorious Hell's Kitchen after serving five years for a crime he did not commit. More or less a redemption drama, the film benefits from a good cast, especially Jolie as a revenge-driven street urchin and Arquette as her drugged-out mom. Despite the trappings of his "convict-into-street angel" role, Phifer exudes a quiet strength that never seems out of place, even when the action gets hysterical. Director Cinciripini scores points in creating scenes of drug addiction that invoke a kind of horrific absurdity, guiding seemingly over-the-top moments with a sure hand and a rock-solid purpose. It's in the more preachy aspects of his script where he loses control, the rising saccharine quotient potentially diluting the potency of his worthwhile message. **101m/C; DVD.** Rosanna Arquette; William Forsythe; Michael Spiller; Angelina Jolie; Mekhi Phifer; Johnny Whitworth; Michael Nicolosi; Ryan Slater; Sharif Rashed; ***D:*** Tony Cinciripini; ***W:*** Tony Cinciripini; ***C:*** Derek Wiesehahn; ***M:*** Tony Cinciripini; Nat Robinson.

The Hellstrom Chronicle **1971 (G)** A powerful quasi-documentary about insects, their formidable capacity for survival, and the conjectured battle man will have with them in the future. **90m/C; VHS, DVD, Blu-Ray.** Lawrence Pressman; ***D:*** Walon Green; ***W:*** David Seltzer. Oscars '71: Feature Doc.

Help! *Eight Arms to Hold You* **1965 (G)** Ringo's ruby ring is the object of a search by Arab cult members Clang (McKern) and Ahme (Bron) who chase the Fab Four all over the globe in order to acquire the bauble. A crazy scientist (Spinelli) and his assistant (Kinnear) also want the ring and join in the pursuit. **90m/C; VHS, DVD, Blu-Ray.** *GB* John Lennon; Paul McCartney; Ringo Starr; George Harrison; Leo McKern; Eleanor Bron; Victor Spinetti; Roy Kinnear; John Bluthal; Patrick Cargill; Alfie Bass; Warren Mitchell; Peter Copley; Bruce Lacey; ***D:*** Richard Lester; ***W:*** Charles Wood; Marc Behm; ***C:*** David Watkin; ***M:*** John Lennon; Paul McCartney; Ringo Starr; George Harrison; Ken Thorne.

The Help **2011 (PG-13)** Aspiring writer Eugenia 'Skeeter' Phelan (Stone) explores the oppressive racist culture of Mississippi in the early 1960s. Driven to sell a story that's never been told before, Skeeter persuades black housekeepers Aibileen (Davis) and Minny (Spencer) to share their personal accounts, revealing injustices they've suffered at the hands of the callous white upper class. Finding strength and courage in the face of tumultuous hardships, Aibileen and Minny ultimately alter the lives of both white and black communities. Moving, with remarkable actors (especially the extraordinary Davis) though the "empowering" aspects may be exaggerated. Based on Kathryn Scott's bestselling novel. **137m/C; Blu-Ray.** Viola Davis; Emma Stone; Sissy Spacek; Octavia Spencer; Bryce Dallas Howard; Allison Janney; Chris Lowell; Mike Vogel; Brian Kerwin; Dana Ivey; Jessica Chastain; Cicely Tyson; Aunjanue Ellis; Ashley Johnson; Ahna O'Reilly; ***D:*** Tate Taylor; ***W:*** Tate Taylor; ***C:*** Stephen Goldblatt; ***M:*** Thomas Newman. Oscars '11: Support. Actress (Spencer); British Acad. '11: Support. Actress (Spencer); Golden Globes '12: Support. Actress (Spencer); Screen Actors Guild '11: Actress (Davis), Cast, Support. Actress (Spencer).

Help Wanted Female **1968** Jo Jo, a prostitute with kung fu skills who likes to rob traveling salesmen, is in a quandary over her lesbian roommate's acid dropping friends, including Mr. Gregory, who has a penchant for murder. After recounting a previous trip in which he murdered an acquaintance, he succeeds in alienating his current companions, who must fight for their life to escape him. **71m/B; VHS, DVD.** Anthony (Tony) Vorno; Inga Olsen; ***D:*** Harold Perkins.

Helter Skelter **1/2 1976** The harrowing story of the murder of actress Sharon Tate and four others at the hands of Charles Manson and his psychotic "family." Based on the book by prosecutor Vincent Bugliosi, adapted by J.P. Miller. Features an outstanding performance by Railsback as Manson. **194m/C; VHS, DVD.** Steve Railsback; Nancy Wolfe; George DiCenzo; Marilyn Burns; Christina Hart; Alan Oppenheimer; Cathy Paine; ***D:*** Tom Gries; ***W:*** J(ames) P(inckney) Miller; ***M:*** Billy Goldenberg. **TV**

Helter Skelter Murders **WOOF! 1971 (R)** An independently made version of the Charles Manson story, with sequences filmed at Spawn Ranch. Includes Manson's own recording of his songs "Mechanical Man" and "Garbage Dump" on the soundtrack. **83m/B; VHS, DVD.** Brian Klinknett; Debbie Duff; Phyllis Estes; ***D:*** Frank Howard; ***W:*** J.J. Wilkie; Duke Howze; ***C:*** Frank Howard.

Hemel **1/2 2014** A psychological drama about an emotionally and sexually complicated young woman. Hemel (Hoekstra) is a young woman raised by her father, Gijs (Dagelet), after the early death of her mother. While father and daughter are devoted to each other, they are also both restless and sexually promiscuous. Each night, Hemel finds a new sexual partner as she tries to grasp the difference between sex and love. Hemel's world becomes more complicated when her father falls in love with Sophie (Lodeizen), an auctioneer he meets through his work at an auction house. As Hemel tries to detach from her father, she seeks love for herself. Dutch, Spanish, and Arabic with subtitles. **80m/C; DVD, Blu-Ray, Streaming, Download.** Hannah Hoekstra; Hans Dagelet; Rifka Lodeizen; Mark Reitman; Eva Duijvestein; ***D:*** Sacha Polak; ***W:*** Helena van der Meulen; ***C:*** Daniel Bouquet. **VIDEO**

Hemingway & Gelhorn **2012** HBO drama about the volatile meeting and marriage of writer Ernest Hemingway (Owen) and war correspondent Martha Gelhorn (Kidman), who became his third wife. Swaggering Hemingway met his match in the fearless, resourceful Gelhorn as they travel to Spain to cover the Civil War, then on into WWII. But eventually his machismo collides with her independence. Director Kaufman structures his romance as a narrative flashback by Gelhorn and it's well-done hooey. **155m/C; DVD, Blu-Ray.** Nicole Kidman; Clive Owen; David Strathairn; Molly Parker; Parker Posey; Rodrigo Santoro; Tony Shalhoub; Peter Coyote; Joan Chen; Robert Duvall; ***D:*** Philip Kaufman; ***W:*** Jerry Stahl; Barbara Turner; ***C:*** Rogier Stoffers; ***M:*** Javier Navarrete. **CABLE**

Hemingway's Garden of Eden **1/2** *The Garden of Eden* **2008 (R)** Miscast, clumsy adaptation of Hemingway's posthumous novel, published in 1986. In the 1920s, American writer David Bourne (Huston) and his rich wife Catherine (Suvari) are on an extended European honeymoon. While stopping on the French Riviera, Catherine becomes restless and befriends sultry Italian beauty Marita (Murino) and wants to bring her into their lives (and bed). David isn't as eager as you might think. **111m/C; DVD.** *GB SP* Jack Huston; Mena Suvari; Caterina Murino; Richard E. Grant; Carmen Maura; Matthew Modine; ***D:*** John Irvin; ***W:*** James Linville; ***C:*** Ashley Rowe; ***M:*** Roger Julia.

The Henderson Monster **1/2 1980** Experiments of a genetic scientist are questioned by a community and its mayor. A potentially controversial drama turns into typical romantic fluff. **105m/C; VHS, DVD.** Jason Miller; Christine Lahti; Stephen Collins; David Spielberg; Nehemiah Persoff; Larry Gates; ***D:*** Waris Hussein. **TV**

Hendrix **1/2 2000 (R)** Biopic of legendary rock guitarist Jimi Hendrix (Harris) from his first teenaged band to his drug overdose death in 1970. There are some fine re-creations of such notable Hendrix performances at the 1967 Monterey Pop Festival and Woodstock in 1969. **103m/C; VHS, DVD.** Wood Harris; Vivica A. Fox; Billy Zane; Christian Potenza; Dorian Harewood; Kris Holden-Ried; Christopher Ralph; Michie Mee; ***D:*** Leon Ichaso; ***W:*** Art Washington; Hal Roberts; Butch Stein; ***C:*** Claudio Chea; ***M:*** Daniel Licht. **CABLE**

Hennessy **1/2 1975 (PG)** An IRA man plots revenge on the Royal family and Parliament after his family is violently killed. Tense political drama, but slightly far-fetched. **103m/C; VHS, DVD.** *GB* Rod Steiger; Lee Remick; Richard Johnson; Trevor Howard; Peter Egan; Eric Porter; ***D:*** Don Sharp; ***W:*** John Gay.

Henri Langlois: The Phantom of the Cinematheque *Le Fantome D'henri Langlois* **2004** Documentary follows the career of the eccentric, longtime curator and film preservationist of the Cinematheque Francaise, founded by Langlois and Georges Franju in 1936. A fanatical collector, Langlois began by preserving silent films and hiding banned works from the Nazis during their occupation of Paris. Later, Langlois offered screenings of his collection, which heavily influenced such budding directors as Godard and Truffaut. Langlois also had a fractious relationship with the French government, who provided a subsidy and tried to exert control over the organization. A somewhat lengthy labor of love from director Richard; French with subtitles. **128m/B; DVD.** ***D:*** Jacques Richard; ***C:*** Jerome Blumberg; ***M:*** Nicolas Baby; Liam Farell.

Henry IV **1/2 1985** The adaptation of the Luigi Pirandello farce about a modern-day recluse who shields himself from the horrors of the real world by pretending to be mad and acting out the fantasy of being the medieval German emperor Henry IV. In Italian with English subtitles. **94m/C; VHS, DVD.** *IT* Marcello Mastroianni; Claudia Cardinale; Leopoldo Trieste; Paolo Bonacelli; Luciano Bartoli; Latou Chardons; ***D:*** Marco Bellocchio; ***W:*** Marco Bellocchio; Tonino Guerra; Astor Piazzolla.

Henry V **1944** Classic, epic adaptation of the Shakespeare play, and Olivier's first and most successful directorial effort, dealing with the medieval British monarch that defeated the French at Agincourt. Distinguished by Olivier's brilliant formal experiment of beginning the drama as a 16th Century performance of the play in the Globe Theatre, and having the stage eventually transform into realistic historical settings of storybook color. Filmed at the height of WWII suffering in Britain (and meant as a parallel to the British fighting the Nazis), the film was not released in the U.S. until 1946. **136m/C; VHS, DVD.** *GB* Laurence Olivier; Robert Newton; Leslie Banks; Esmond Knight; Renee Asherson; Leo Genn; George Robey; Ernest Thesiger; Felix Aylmer; Ralph Truman; Harcourt Williams; Max Adrian; Valentine Dyall; Russell Thorndike; Roy Emerton; Robert Helpmann; Freda Jackson; Griffith Jones; John Laurie; Niall MacGinnis; Michael Shepley; ***D:*** Laurence Olivier; ***W:*** Laurence Olivier; Alan Dent; Dallas Bower; ***C:*** Robert Krasker; ***M:*** William Walton. Natl. Bd. of Review '46: Actor (Olivier); N.Y. Film Critics '46: Actor (Olivier).

Henry V **1989** Stirring, expansive retelling of Shakespeare's drama about the warrior-king of England. Branagh stars as Henry, leading his troops and uniting his kingdom against France. Very impressive production rivals Olivier's 1945 rendering but differs by stressing the high cost of war—showing the ego-mania, doubts, and subterfuge that underlie conflicts. Marvelous film-directorial debut for Branagh (who also adapted the screenplay). Wonderful supporting cast includes some of Britain's finest actors. **138m/C; VHS, DVD, Blu-Ray.** *GB* Kenneth Branagh; Derek Jacobi; Brian Blessed; Alec McCowen; Ian Holm; Richard Briers; Robert Stephens; Robbie Coltrane; Christian Bale; Dame Judi Dench; Paul Scofield; Michael Maloney; Emma Thompson; Patrick Doyle; Richard Clifford; Richard Easton; Paul Gregory; Harold Innocent; Charles Kay; Geraldine McEwan; Christopher Ravenscroft; John Sessions; Simon Shepherd; Jay Villiers; Danny (Daniel) Webb; ***D:*** Kenneth Branagh; ***W:*** Kenneth Branagh; ***C:*** Kenneth Macmillan; ***M:*** Patrick Doyle. Oscars '89: Costume Des.; British Acad. '89: Director (Branagh); Natl. Bd. of Review '89: Director (Branagh).

Henry & June **1/2 1990 (NC-17)** Based on the diaries of writer Anais Nin which chronicled her triangular relationship with author Henry Miller and his wife June, a relationship that provided the erotic backdrop to Miller's "Tropic of Capricorn." Set in Paris in the early '30s, the setting moves between the impecunious expatriate's cheap room on the Left bank—filled with artists, circus performers, prostitutes, and gypsies—to the conservative, well-appointed home of Nin and her husband. Captures the heady atmosphere of Miller's gay Paris; no one plays an American better than Ward (who replaced Alec Baldwin). Notable for having prompted the creation of an NC-17 rating because of its adult theme. **136m/C; VHS, DVD.** Fred Ward; Uma Thurman; Maria De Medeiros; Richard E. Grant; Kevin Spacey; ***D:*** Philip Kaufman; ***W:*** Philip Kaufman; ***C:*** Philippe Rousselot; ***M:*** Mark Adler.

Henry & Verlin **1994** Verlin (Macintosh) is a nine-year-old who doesn't talk. He lives in rural Ontario (during the Depression) with his overprotective mother Minnie (Beatty) and indifferent father Ferris (Joy), as well as Ferris' childlike brother Henry (Farmer) who befriends Verlin. The misfit duo develop a strong bond that includes disabled retired prostitute Mabel (Kidder)?much to the resentment of some of the less-enlightened townsfolk. There's some melodramatic events but the performances skirt maudlin excess. **87m/C; VHS, DVD.** *CA* Gary Farmer;

Keegan Macintosh; Nancy Beatty; Robert Joy; Margot Kidder; Eric Peterson; ***Cameo(s):*** David Cronenberg; ***D:*** Gary Ledbetter; ***W:*** Gary Ledbetter.

Henry Fool ♪♪♪ **1998 (R)** Simon Grim (Urbaniak) is a socially inept garbage man treated with contempt by his depressed mother (Porter) and caustic sister (Posey). Henry Fool (Ryan), an alcoholic homeless man, claims to be a great writer and sees a bit of poet in Simon as well. After he moves Henry into the family's basement, Simon takes his first steps as a poet and Henry takes liberties with both of the women. Simon turns out to be a natural artist, and writes a poem that profoundly moves and/or shocks the public and creates a controversy on the Internet. As Simon is courted by publishers, he champions Henry's unread work as well. Their respective fortunes rise and fall as Henry's work is unveiled and the price of fame affects their lives. Director Hartley pulls very different elements such as the artistry of Samuel Beckett and the myth of Faust together to create a bizarre urban fable. **138m/C; VHS, DVD.** Thomas Jay Ryan; James Urbaniak; Parker Posey; Maria Porter; Kevin Corrigan; James Saito; ***D:*** Hal Hartley; ***W:*** Hal Hartley; ***C:*** Michael Spiller; ***M:*** Hal Hartley.

Henry Hill ♪♪ **2000** Misfit Henry (Harrold) was a childhood musical prodigy who left his rural Maine home for New York City. But his extreme stage fright means his dreams of becoming a concert violinist are remote and a failed suicide attempt finds Henry returning to his loony family who run a gas station/diner. To Henry's rescue (maybe) is Cynthia (Kelly), a troubled loner in a red car who takes an interest in Henry and decides to hang around until she can persuade him to go back to New York with her and try again. **85m/C; VHS, DVD.** Jamie Harrold; Moira Kelly; Susan Blommaert; John Griesemer; Eden Riegel; ***D:*** David G. Kantar; ***W:*** David G. Kantar; ***C:*** Luke Eder; ***M:*** Dave Eggar.

Henry Poole Is Here ♪♪♪ **2008 (PG)** Low-key comedy based on the Catholic idea of miracles and public fascination with divine imagery. Fed up with life-as-he-knows-it, Henry (Wilson) abruptly leaves his fiancee and family business, retreating to a small house in an LA suburb in search of complete isolation. However, nosy neighbors won't leave him alone, and one in particular, Esperanza (Barrazza), discovers a water stain on his house in the shape of Jesus that quickly becomes a pilgrimage destination for those looking to relieve their ailments and burdens. Soon the skeptical Henry discovers the healing power in hope. A perfectly-balanced comedy that refreshingly believes in itself, opting out of snarky punchlines and cynical jabs at religion without getting preachy or sappy. For believers and skeptical audiences alike. **100m/C; Blu-Ray, On Demand.** Luke Wilson; Radha Mitchell; George Lopez; Cheryl Hines; Adriana Barraza; Richard Benjamin; Beth Grant; Morgan Lily; Rachel Seiferth; ***D:*** Mark Pellington; ***W:*** Albert Torres; ***C:*** Eric Schmidt; ***M:*** John (Gianni) Frizzell.

Henry: Portrait of a Serial Killer ♪♪♪♪ **1990 (R)** Based on the horrific life and times of serial killer Henry Lee Lucas, this film has received wide praise for its straight-forward and uncompromising look into the minds of madmen. The film follows ex-cons Henry (Rooker) and his roommate Otis (Towles) as they set out on mindless murder sprees (one of which they videotape). Extremely disturbing and graphic film. Unwary viewers should be aware of the grisly scenes and use their own discretion when viewing this otherwise genuinely moving film. **90m/C; VHS, DVD, Blu-Ray.** Michael Rooker; Tom Towler; Tracy Arnold; David Katz; ***D:*** John McNaughton; ***W:*** John McNaughton; Richard Fire; ***C:*** Charlie Lieberman; ***M:*** Robert F. McNaughton.

Henry: Portrait of a Serial Killer 2: Mask of Sanity ♪ *Henry 2: Portrait of a Serial Killer* **1996 (R)** Michael Rooker gave a chilling performance as serial killer Henry in part 1 but Giuntoli is merely dull. A sullen drifter, Henry manages to get a job and fellow worker Kai (Komenich) invites him to crash at his place. Turns out Kai is a part-time arsonist for hire and Henry helps him out—also introducing Kai to the pleasures of casual murder. The gore is actually limited to a few bloody scenes (usually more is heard than shown) but the whole project is boring. **84m/C; VHS, DVD.** Neil Giuntoli; Rich Komenich; Kate Walsh; Carri Levinson; Penelope Milford; ***D:*** Chuck Parello; ***W:*** Chuck Parello; ***C:*** Michael Kohnhurst; ***M:*** Robert F. McNaughton.

Henry's Crime ♪ 1/2 **2010 (R)** The crime here is the dullness of the plot and performances (with the exception of charismatic Caan). Luckless Henry (Reeves) foolishly finds himself the wheelman in a bank robbery with acquaintances Eddie (Stevens) and Joe (Hoch) that lands him in the slammer when things go wrong. Henry learns a lot from cellmate Max (Caan) and when he gets out, he decides he might as well do the crime for real. Part of Henry's screwy plan involves newly-released Max, new girlfriend and aspiring actress Julie (Farmiga), and a stage production of Chekov's "The Cherry Orchard." **108m/C; DVD, Blu-Ray.** Keanu Reeves; James Caan; Vera Farmiga; Fisher Stevens; Danny Hoch; Peter Stormare; Judy Greer; Bill Duke; ***D:*** Malcolm Venville; ***W:*** Sacha Gervasi; ***C:*** Paul Cameron.

Her ♪♪♪ 1/2 **2013 (R)** A touching, beautiful, personal examination of how human beings connect and grow through relationships, Jonze's award-winning dramedy is a unique gem. Theodore (Phoenix) writes letters for other people but is unable to heal the deep emotional wounds from his pending divorce. He tries to date but fails and spends many nights playing video games on his own and perusing adult Internet chat rooms. In this near future, an "Intuitive Operating System" named Samantha (Johannson) enters his life and changes it forever. Jonze delivers despite the trickiness of a story about a man who falls in love with his OS. **126m/C; DVD, Blu-Ray.** Joaquin Rafael (Leaf) Phoenix; Amy Adams; Rooney Mara; Chris Pratt; ***V:*** Scarlett Johansson; ***D:*** Spike Jonze; ***W:*** Spike Jonze; ***C:*** Hoyte Van Hoytema; ***M:*** Owen Pallett. Oscars '13: Orig. Screenplay; Golden Globes '14: Screenplay; Writers Guild '13: Orig. Screenplay.

Her Alibi ♪♪ **1988 (PG)** When successful murder-mystery novelist Phil Blackwood runs out of ideas for good books, he seeks inspiration in the criminal courtroom. There he discovers a beautiful Romanian immigrant named Nina who is accused of murder. He goes to see her in jail and offers to provide her with an alibi. Narrated by Blackwood in the tone of one of his thriller novels. Uneven comedy, with appealing cast and arbitrary plot. **95m/C; VHS, DVD.** Tom Selleck; Paulina Porizkova; William Daniels; James Farentino; Hurd Hatfield; Patrick Wayne; Tess Harper; Joan Copeland; ***D:*** Bruce Beresford; ***W:*** Charlie Peters; ***C:*** Freddie Francis; ***M:*** Georges Delerue.

Her Best Move ♪♪ 1/2 **2007 (G)** Sara (Pipes) is a 15-year-old soccer phenom being pushed by her domineering coach dad (Patterson) to make the U.S. national team. She would really like the chance to just be a typical teen and maybe get a date and a kiss from cute Josh (Bell). Sara tries to juggle soccer, school, dance lessons, a part-time job, a best friend, her parents, and a potential boyfriend until something has to give. Cute, chipper story with a well-filmed big soccer game finale. **100m/C; DVD.** Scott Patterson; Lisa Darr; Drew Tyler Bell; Daryl Sabara; Lalaine; ***D:*** Norm Hunter; ***W:*** Norm Hunter; Tony Vidal; ***C:*** Dr. Paul Ryan; ***M:*** Didier Rachou. **VIDEO**

Her Cardboard Lover ♪♪ **1942** Shearer's last film is a cardboard romantic comedy. Wealthy divorcee Consuelo (Shearer) knows she can't resist the charms of her ex-lover, playboy Tony Barling (Sanders). So she hires Terry Trindale (Young), who needs money to pay off his gambling debts, to pretend to be her new beau. This only makes Tony jealous and then Terry actually falls in love with Consuelo. **93m/B; DVD.** Norma Shearer; Robert Taylor; George Sanders; Frank McHugh; Chill Wills; Elizabeth Patterson; ***D:*** George Cukor; ***W:*** Anthony Veiller; Jacques Deval; John Collier; William H. Wright; ***C:*** Robert Planck; Harry Stradling, Sr.; ***M:*** Franz Waxman.

Her Fatal Flaw ♪♪ **2006** Chicago defense attorney Laney Hennessy (Pratt) is engaged to businessman Robert Genaro (Spano) when he is accused of murdering city alderman Sutton (Robertson). Laney decides to defend Robert, which pits her against former boss Richard O'Brien (Davis). The evidence against Robert starts piling up but Laney tries to prove it's a very elaborate frame. **90m/C; DVD.** Victoria Pratt; Vincent Spano; William B. Davis; Keegan Connor Tracy; Fulvio Cecere; Brad Robertson; Chris Kramer; Alvin Sanders; ***D:*** George Mendeluk; ***W:*** Hans Wasserburger; ***C:*** Mahlon Todd Williams; ***M:*** Clinton Shorter. **CABLE**

Her Forgotten Past ♪♪ **1933** After falling in love with a crusading district attorney, Doris (Barbara Kent) finds she may have to confess her past in which she was ruthlessly taken advantage of by a criminal before it becomes a scandal that may derail her election campaign. **65m/C; DVD.** Monte Blue; Barbara Kent; Henry B. Walthall; Eddie (Edward) Phillips; William V. Mong; Dewey Robinson; ***D:*** Wesley Ford; ***W:*** George Morgan; ***C:*** James S. Brown, Jr. **VIDEO**

Her Highness and the Bellboy ♪♪ 1/2 **1945** A smitten Princess Veronica (Lamarr) comes to New York to see newspaperman Paul MacMillan (Anderson) and is mistaken for a maid by young bellboy Jimmy (Walker). She's amused and asks Jimmy to be her personal assistant but he assumes she's fallen for him while being oblivious to the fact that his pretty neighbor Leslie (Allyson) is in love. **112m/B; DVD.** Hedy Lamarr; Robert Walker; Warner Anderson; June Allyson; Carl Esmond; Agnes Moorehead; Rags Ragland; ***D:*** Richard Thorpe; ***W:*** Gladys Lehman; Richard Connell; ***C:*** Harry Stradling, Sr.; ***M:*** Georgie Stoll.

Her Husband's Affairs ♪ **1947** Tone is an advertising wonder and Ball is his loving wife who always gets credit for his work. Tone does the advertising for an inventor who is searching for the perfect embalming fluid in this rather lifeless comedy. **83m/B; VHS, DVD.** Lucille Ball; Franchot Tone; Edward Everett Horton; Gene Lockhart; Larry Parks; ***D:*** S. Sylvan Simon; ***M:*** George Duning.

Her Jungle Love ♪ 1/2 **1938** Creaky Technicolor adventure romance. When their plane crash-lands on a South Sea island, aviator Bob and his mechanic Jimmy meet beautiful Tuva. While Bob tries out his romantic moves, the local witch doctor wants to use them in some ritual human sacrifices involving crocodiles. Lamour looks lovely in her sarongs and a volcanic eruption saves the good guys. **81m/C; DVD.** Ray Milland; Dorothy Lamour; Lynne Overman; J. Carrol Naish; ***D:*** George Archainbaud; ***W:*** Eddie Welch; Joseph Moncure March; Lillie Hayward; ***C:*** Ray Rennahan.

Her Majesty ♪♪ **2001** Young New Zealander Elizabeth Wakefield (Andrews) can't believe it when, in 1953, she learns that her hero, Queen Elizabeth II, will be visiting her hometown during a commonwealth tour. Elizabeth is friends with Hira Mata (Haughton), an aged Maori whose shack is considered an eyesore by town busybody Virginia Hobson (Holloway). When Virginia wants to clean up the community by displacing the old woman, things take a turn for the worst thanks to Elizabeth's spiteful brother (Elliott). **105m/C; DVD.** *NZ* Vicky Haughton; Sally Andrews; Craig Elliott; Liddy Holloway; Annabel Leach; ***D:*** Mark J. Gordon; ***W:*** Mark J. Gordon; ***C:*** Stephen M. Katz; ***M:*** William Ross.

Her Night of Romance ♪♪ 1/2 **1924** Amusing silent romantic comedy. American heiress Dorothy Adams (Talmadge) heads to London with her father (Gran) to escape the fortune hunters harassing her. She meets cute with dashing but impoverished Lord Paul Menford (Coleman) although they don't realize that Mr. Adams is the one buying Menford's estate. Paul is mistaken for his doctor uncle when Dorothy has heart trouble (in more ways than one) and more romantic complications ensue. **70m/B; Silent; DVD.** Constance Talmadge; Ronald Colman; Albert Gran; Jean Hersholt; Robert Rendel; Joseph J. Dowling; Sidney Bracy; ***D:*** Sidney Franklin; ***W:*** Hans Kraly; ***C:*** Ray Binger; Victor Milner.

Her Secret ♪ **1933** Unintentionally comic romance due to both the silly story and actress Sari Maritza's attempts at a southern accent. Useless playboy Johnny Norton is disinherited by his fed-up father. He winds up a gas jockey in Tucson and falls for Georgia-born diner manager, Waffles. Mr. Norton decides to check up on Johnny and also becomes smitten by the dame who's managed to reform his wastrel son. **73m/B; DVD.** Sari Maritza; William "Buster" Collier, Jr.; Alan Mowbray; Ivan Simpson; ***D:*** Warren Millais; ***W:*** Helen Mitchell; ***C:*** J. Peverell Marley.

Her Sister from Paris ♪♪ 1/2 **1925** The spark is gone from the marriage of Helen (Talmadge) and Joseph (Colman) Weyringer. After a marital spat, Helen takes off for her mother's, only to remember that her identical twin sister Lola, a famous dancer living in Paris, is arriving in town. The siblings have a heart-to-heart and Lola decides dowdy Helen needs a makeover and a plan to teach Joseph a lesson in appreciation. **70m/B; Silent; DVD.** Constance Talmadge; Ronald Colman; George K. Arthur; Gertrude Claire; ***D:*** Sidney Franklin; ***W:*** Hans Kraly; ***C:*** Arthur Edeson.

Her Sister's Keeper ♪ 1/2 **2006** The disappearance of Kate's (Salem) sister Melissa (Ory) sends her into a tailspin. Things get more complicated when a large amount of drug money goes missing too, which puts them both in danger. **90m/C; DVD.** Dahlia Salem; Meaghan Ory; Ty Olsson; Anthony Ulc; Bruno Verdoni; ***D:*** Michael Scott; ***W:*** Michael Sloan; ***C:*** Adam Sliwinski; ***M:*** Michael Neilson. **CABLE**

Her Sister's Secret ♪♪ **1946** Unmarried Toni Dubois (Coleman) discovers she's pregnant by her soldier boyfriend Richard (Reed), who's been shipped overseas. Toni gives the baby to her married sister Renee (Lindsay) to raise. After reuniting three years later, Toni and Richard want to reclaim their child but Renee is very reluctant. **85m/B; DVD.** Nancy Coleman; Margaret Lindsay; Phillip Reed; Regis Toomey; Felix Bressart; Henry Stephenson; ***D:*** Edgar G. Ulmer; ***W:*** Anne Greene; ***C:*** Franz Planer; ***M:*** Hans Sommer.

Her Smell ♪♪ 1/2 **2019 (R)** Aging punk star Becky Something (Moss) is struggling years after her original success. In addition to distancing herself from her bandmates Ali (Rankin) and Mari (Deyn), she also has damaged relationships with her mother Becky (Madsen), exasperated ex Danny (Stevens), and young daughter Tama (Pugh-Weiss). As Becky continues to perform and create through the chaos, she undermines new relationships including those with members of a collaborating band, Akergirls (Delevigne, Benson, and Gelula), at a recording studio. The music-focused drama is harsh as it explores Becky's deterioration in stylish fashion, though Moss's performance bring energy and believability to Becky's journey. **134m/C; DVD.** Elisabeth Moss; Cara Delevingne; Dan Stevens; Agyness Deyn; Gayle Rankin; ***D:*** Alex Ross Perry; ***W:*** Alex Ross Perry; ***C:*** Sean Price Williams; ***M:*** Keegan DeWitt.

Herbie: Fully Loaded ♪♪ **2005 (G)** On her way out of town, college graduate Maggie Peyton (Lohan) spends 75 bucks to free a '63 VW Beetle from the junkyard scrap pile and has boy pal Kevin (Long) restore it. Lo and behold, it's Herbie and he helps Maggie prove her driving skills to her NASCAR champ daddy (Keaton)?who's spent his energies on his not-as-talented son—as they race against pompous archenemy Trip Murphy (Dillon). The sassy Lohan, in her third Disney venture, picks up the speed for an uninspired-and-somewhat-CGI Herbie. Fifth feature in a series that, 15 years before, seemed out of gas. **101m/C; DVD, UMD.** Lindsay Lohan; Matt Dillon; Justin Long; Breckin Meyer; Michael Keaton; Jill Ritchie; Cheryl Hines; Thomas Lennon; Jimmi Simpson; Jeremy Roberts; ***D:*** Angela Robinson; ***W:*** Robert Ben Garant; Alfred Gough; Miles Millar; Thomas Lennon; ***C:*** Greg Gardiner; ***M:*** Mark Mothersbaugh.

Herbie Goes Bananas ♪ 1/2 **1980 (G)** While Herbie the VW is racing in Rio de Janeiro, he is bothered by the syndicate, a pickpocket, and a raging bull. The fourth and final entry in the Disney "Love Bug" movies, but Herbie later made his way to a TV series. **93m/C; VHS, DVD, Blu-Ray.** Cloris Leachman; Charles Martin Smith; Harvey Korman; John Vernon; Alex Rocco; Richard Jaeckel; Fritz Feld; ***D:*** Vincent McEveety.

Herbie Goes to Monte Carlo ♪♪ **1977 (G)** While participating in a Paris-to-Monte-Carlo race, Herbie the VW takes a detour and falls in love with a Lancia. Third in the Disney "Love Bug" series. **104m/C; VHS, DVD, Blu-Ray.** Dean Jones; Don Knotts; Julie Sommars; Roy Kinnear; ***D:*** Vincent McEveety; ***W:*** Arthur Alsberg.

Herbie Rides Again 1/2 **1974 (G)** In this "Love Bug" sequel, Herbie comes to the aid of an elderly woman who is trying to stop a ruthless tycoon from raising a skyscraper on her property. Humorous Disney fare. Two other sequels followed. **88m/C; VHS, DVD, Blu-Ray.** Helen Hayes; Ken Berry; Stefanie Powers; John McIntire; Keenan Wynn; ***D:*** Robert Stevenson; ***M:*** George Bruns.

Herblock: The Black & the White 1/2 **2013** Documentary on the highly regarded, Pulitzer Prize-winning editorial cartoonist Herbert Block (he compressed his names for his signature). In his career at the "Washington Post," which began in 1946 and lasted until his death in 2001, he took illustrative aim at 13 U.S. presidents and every notable situation and personage (including coining the term 'McCarthyism' while deriding Senator Joseph McCarthy's communist witch-hunt). Filmmaker Stevens stages 'interviews' with actor Alan Marshall portraying Herblock, which are sometimes confusing, but journalists, colleagues, and admirers offer their own laudatory assessments. **95m/C; DVD.** ***D:*** Michael Stevens; ***W:*** Michael Stevens; Sara Lukinson; ***C:*** Zoran Popovic; ***M:*** Rob Mathes.

Hercules 1/2 *La Tatiche de Ercole* **1958** The one that started it all. Reeves is perfect as the mythical hero Hercules who encounters many dangerous situations while trying to win over his true love. Dubbed in English. **107m/C; VHS, DVD.** *IT* Steve Reeves; Sylva Koscina; Fabrizio Mioni; Gianna Maria Canale; Arturo Dominici; ***D:*** Pietro Francisci; ***C:*** Mario Bava.

Hercules **1983 (PG)** Lackluster remake of 1957 original finds legendary muscle guy Hercules in the person of Ferrigno's Hulkster fighting against the evil King Minos for his own survival and the love of Cassiopeia, a rival king's daughter. **100m/C; VHS, DVD, Blu-Ray.** *IT* Lou Ferrigno; Sybil Danning; William Berger; Brad Harris; Ingrid Anderson; Mindi Miller; ***D:*** Luigi Cozzi; ***W:*** Luigi Cozzi; ***M:*** Pino Donaggio. Golden Raspberries '83: Worst New Star (Ferrigno), Worst Support. Actress (Danning).

Hercules 1/2 **1997 (G)** After a couple of animated downers, Disney's latest adventure goes for a happy heroic tone by taking on Greek myths. Baby Herc is the son of Zeus, who rules on Mt. Olympus. Hades, Lord of the Underworld, plans a takeover and learns that only Hercules' strength will stand in his way. Hades manages to kidnap the tyke and turn him mortal but when the teenaged Herc learns his true origins, he also discovers that if he proves himself to be a hero he can regain his immortality and return to Mt. Olympus. He's aided by his flying horse Pegasus, satyr-like trainer Phil, and smart gal Meg, while Hades has his less-than-bright minions Pain and Panic. Lots of fun and lots of merchandising (even the movie makes fun of the inevitable tie-ins). **92m/C; VHS, DVD, Blu-Ray.** ***V:*** Tate Donovan; James Woods; Danny DeVito; Matt Frewer; Bobcat Goldthwait; Susan Egan; Rip Torn; Samantha Eggar; Paul Shaffer; Barbara Barrie; Hal Holbrook; Amanda Plummer; Carol(e) Shelley; ***Nar:*** Charlton Heston; ***D:*** John Musker; Ron Clements; ***W:*** John Musker; Ron Clements; Bob Shaw; Donald McEnery; Irene Mecchi; ***M:*** Alan Menken; ***M:*** David Zippel.

Hercules **2014 (PG-13)** Not as bad as the previews made it look but not good either, director Ratner's take on the legendary strongman feels more like a studio vehicle than a creative prospect. "Swords and Sandals" movies, games, and shows are huge in the current century, and so a 3D Hercules was only a matter of time. Johnson steps into the sandals he was born to fill as the title character, who is put through the expected 3D eye-popping trials provided by classic mythology. The result is totally forgettable but never bland, working as eye candy and succeeding slightly because of its star's undeniable charisma. **98m/C; DVD, Blu-Ray.** Dwayne "The Rock" Johnson; Rufus Sewell; Ian McShane; Ingrid Bolso Berdal; Aksel Hennie; Reece Ritchie; John Hurt; Rebecca Ferguson; Tobias Santelmann; ***D:*** Brett Ratner; ***W:*** Ryan Condal; Evan Spiliotopolos; ***C:*** Dante Spinotti; ***M:*** Fernando Velazquez.

Hercules 2 *The Adventures of Hercules* **1985 (PG)** The muscle-bound demi-god returns to do battle with more evil foes amidst the same stunningly cheap special effects. **90m/C; VHS, DVD, Blu-Ray.** *IT* Lou Ferrigno; Claudio Cassinelli; Milly Carlucci; Sonia Viviani; William Berger; Carlotta Green; ***D:*** Luigi Cozzi; ***W:*** Luigi Cozzi; ***M:*** Pino Donaggio.

Hercules Against the Mongols *Maciste Contro I Mongoli* **1963** It might be the 13th century but that doesn't meant ole Herc can't show up to battle the late Genghis Khan's three sons. They've captured the city of Tuleda and are holding Princess Bianca hostage. Herc offers himself as a slave so the princess can go free, but each of the brothers tries to get the strongman on their side so they can become sole ruler of the Mongols. **99m/C; DVD.** *IT* Mark Forest; Jose Greci; Ken Clark; Howard Ross; Nadir Moretti; ***D:*** Domenico Paolella; ***W:*** Domenico Paolella; ***C:*** Raffaele Masciocchi; ***M:*** Carlo Savina.

Hercules against the Moon Men *Maciste la Regina di Samar* **1964** It's no holds barred for the mighty son of Zeus when evil moon men start killing off humans in a desperate bid to revive their dead queen. **88m/C; VHS, DVD.** *IT FR* Alan Steel; Jany Clair; Anna Maria Polani; Nando Tamberlani; Delia D'Alberti; Jean-Pierre Honore; ***D:*** Giacomo Gentilomo; ***W:*** Arpad De Riso; Nino Scolaro; ***C:*** Oberdan Troiani; ***M:*** Carlo Franci.

Hercules and the Black Pirate 1/2 *Hercules the Avenger* **1960** This Italian swashbuckler has nothing to do with Hercules (or sword-and-sandals) since the pirate-fighting soldier is actually called Samson. He wants to marry governor's daughter Rosita but her father disapproves. A conniving courtier conspires with the Black Pirate to kill the governor so he can have the babe for himself but Samson isn't going for that. Italian with subtitles. **93m/C; DVD.** *IT* Sergio Ciani; Rosalba Neri; Nerio Bernardi; Andrea Aureli; Pierro Lulli; ***D:*** Luigi Capuano; ***W:*** Arpad DeRiso; Piero Pierotti; ***C:*** Augusto Tiezzi; ***M:*** Angelo Francesco Lavagnino.

Hercules and the Captive Women *Hercules and the Haunted Women; Hercules and the Conquest of Atlantis; Ercole Alla Conquista di Atlantide* **1963** Hercules' son is kidnapped by the Queen of Atlantis, and the bare-chested warrior goes on an all-out rampage to save the boy. Directed by sometimes-lauded Cottafavi. **93m/C; VHS, DVD.** *IT* Reg Park; Fay Spain; Ettore Manni; ***D:*** Vittorio Cottafavi.

Hercules and the Tyrants of Babylon *Ercole Contro I Tiranni di Babilonia* **1964** Babylon has been divided into three areas ruled by two brothers and their sister who are each planning to overthrow the others. Hercules doesn't like their slavery policy and needs to rescue the Queen of the Hellenes who's one of their unwitting captives. The so-called plot is just an excuse to see Herc flex, swing a club, throw papier-mache rocks, and cause the walls of Babylon to come tumbling down. **96m/C; DVD.** *IT* Peter Lupus; Helga Line; Livio Lorenzon; Tullio Altamura; Mario Petri; Anna Maria Polani; ***D:*** Domenico Paolella; ***W:*** Domenico Paolella; Luciano Martino; ***C:*** Augusto Tiezzi; ***M:*** Angelo Francesco Lavagnino.

Hercules in New York 1/2 *Hercules: The Movie; Hercules Goes Bananas* **1970 (G)** Motion picture debut of Schwarzenegger (his voice is dubbed) as a Herculean mass of muscle sent by dad Zeus to Manhattan, where he behaves likes a geek out of water and eventually becomes a professional wrestling superstar. 250 pounds of stupid, lighthearted fun. **93m/C; VHS, DVD.** Arnold Schwarzenegger; Arnold Stang; Deborah Loomis; James Karen; Ernest Graves; Taina Elg; ***D:*** Arthur Allan Seidelman; ***W:*** Aubrey Wisberg; ***C:*** Leo Lebowitz; ***M:*** John Balamos.

Hercules in the Haunted World 1/2 *Ercole al Centro Della Terra* **1964** Long before the days of 24-hour pharmacies, Hercules—played yet again by Reeves-clone Park—must journey to the depths of Hell in order to find a plant that will cure a poisoned princess. Better than most muscle operas, thanks to Bava. **91m/C; VHS, DVD.** *IT* Reg Park; Leonora Ruffo; Christopher Lee; George Ardisson; ***D:*** Mario Bava.

Hercules, Prisoner of Evil **1964** Spaghetti myth-opera in which Hercules battles a witch who is turning men into werewolves. Made for Italian TV by director Dawson (the nom-de-cinema of Antonio Margheriti). **90m/C; VHS, DVD.** *IT* Reg Park; ***D:*** Anthony M. Dawson. **TV**

Hercules, Samson and Ulysses 1/2 *Ercole Sfida Sansone; Hercules Challenges Samson* **1964** Hercules, Ulysses, and their crew are shipwrecked and imprisoned by Philistine King Seren. He'll release them if Hercules brings him Samson. Instead, the two rivals join forces against their common foe. (Ulysses doesn't have much to do.) Styrofoam rocks and pillars are flung with abandon. **86m/C; DVD.** *IT* Kirk Morris; Iloosh Khoshabe; Enzo Cerusico; Liana Orfei; Aldo Giuffre; ***D:*** Pietro Francisci; ***W:*** Pietro Francisci; ***C:*** Silvano Ippoliti; ***M:*** Angelo Francesco Lavagnino.

Hercules the Legendary Journeys, Vol. 1: And the Amazon Women 1/2 **1994** Half-man, half-god Hercules (Sorbo) and his friend Ioleus (Hurst) are summoned to a village to kill the beasts stealing livestock. Turns out those responsible are the village's women, who are mad at their husbands and have formed a band of Amazons, lead by Hippolyta (Downey), who happens to be working for Hercules' immortal enemy, the goddess Hera. Now it's up to Herc to convince Hippolyta that men and women can work together and outsmart Hera at the same time. **91m/C; VHS, DVD.** Kevin Sorbo; Michael Hurst; Roma Downey; Anthony Quinn; Lucy Lawless; ***D:*** Bill W.L. Norton; ***M:*** Joseph LoDuca. **TV**

Hercules the Legendary Journeys, Vol. 2: The Lost Kingdom 1/2 **1994** Hera has hidden the kingdom of Troy and only a magic compass can point Hercules (Sorbo) in the right direction. He rescues a sacrificial virigin (O'Connor) and the duo manage to find the compass and get into Troy where she learns her father was once its king. Turns out dad sent his daughter away so he wouldn't have to sacrifice her to Hera and lost his kingdom instead. Now she wants her kingdom back and Hera still wants her sacrifice—especially if it's Hercules. **91m/C; VHS, DVD.** Kevin Sorbo; Michael Hurst; Anthony Quinn; Renee O'Connor; Robert Trebor; ***D:*** Harley Cokliss; ***M:*** Joseph LoDuca. **TV**

Hercules the Legendary Journeys, Vol. 3: The Circle of Fire 1/2 **1994** Hera's stolen fire from mankind, which is slowly freezing to death, keeping one eternal torch for herself. A villager named Deianeira (Kitaen) enlists Hercules (Sorbo) to search for Prometheus (Ferguson), the god of fire, but Hera's stolen his flame as well. When Herc finds the torch it's encircled in a ring of fire, which Hera knows can destroy Hercules' immortality. **92m/C; VHS, DVD.** Kevin Sorbo; Michael Hurst; Anthony Quinn; Tawny Kitaen; Mark Ferguson; ***D:*** Doug Lefler; ***M:*** Joseph LoDuca. **TV**

Hercules the Legendary Journeys, Vol. 4: In the Underworld 1/2 **1994** Having married Deianeira (Kitaen), Herc's a pretty happy guy until a mysterious maiden, Iole, comes to him for help. Seems a deadly crack has opened up in the earth and is swallowing villagers. But Iole has actually been sent by Hera to destroy Hercules and when Deianeira discovers her treachery she goes to warn her husband. Only Hera manages to trick her into walking off a clift and falling to her death. Hercules must go into the underworld to save the world from Hera but when he learns Deianeira's fate, he accepts an impossible challenge from Hades (Ferguson) to bring his wife back to life. **91m/C; VHS, DVD.** Kevin Sorbo; Michael Hurst; Anthony Quinn; Tawny Kitaen; Mark Ferguson; ***D:*** Bill W.L. Norton; ***M:*** Joseph LoDuca. **TV**

Hercules Unchained *Ercole e la Regina de Lidia* **1959** Sequel to "Hercules" finds superhero Reeves must use all his strength to save the city of Thebes and the woman he loves from the giant Antaeus. **101m/C; VHS, DVD.** *IT* Steve Reeves; Sylva Koscina; Silvia Lopel; Primo Carnera; ***D:*** Pietro Francisci.

Hercules vs. the Sons of the Sun 1/2 *Hercules Against the Sons of the Sun; Ercole Contro I Figli del Sole* **1964** Herc (Forest) battles the evil King of the Incas by building unstoppable fighting machines. Typical of the genre. **91m/C; VHS, DVD.** *IT SP* Mark Forest; Giuliano Gemma; Riccardo Valle; Andrea Scotti; Anna Maria Pace; Angela Rhu; Giulio Donnini; ***D:*** Osvaldo Civirani; ***W:*** Osvaldo Civirani; ***C:*** Osvaldo Civirani; Julio Ortas; ***M:*** Coriolano Gori.

Here 1/2 **2012** Lol Crawley's outstanding cinematography almost makes up for the tediousness of this avant-garde road movie. Will (Foster) is an American satellite-mapping engineer who needs to reconcile ground objects to satellite images in some disputed Armenian territory. He meets photographer Gadarine (Azabal), returning to her homeland from a long stay abroad, who serves as Will's interpreter while shooting the rapidly-changing countryside. They're little more than symbols and a narration given to abstractions is pretentious. English and Armenian with subtitles. **126m/C; DVD.** Ben Foster; Lubna Azabal; ***D:*** Braden King; ***W:*** Braden King; Dani Valent; ***C:*** Lol Crawley; ***M:*** Michael Krassner.

Here Come the Co-Eds 1/2 **1945** Bud & Lou are the caretakers of an all-girl college which is about to go bankrupt unless the boys can find a way to pay off the mortgage. And come to the rescue they do, including Bud getting into the wrestling ring with the "Masked Marvel" (Chaney Jr. as the villain). There's also a classic silent scene with Lou served a bowl of oyster stew containing a live oyster, which promptly grabs his tie, bites his fingers, and squirts in his face. **90m/B; VHS, DVD.** Bud Abbott; Lou Costello; Lon Chaney, Jr.; Peggy Ryan; Martha O'Driscoll; June Vincent; Donald Cook; Charles Dingle; ***D:*** Jean Yarbrough; ***W:*** Arthur T. Horman; John Grant.

Here Come the Girls 1/2 **1953** An unfunny musical-comedy about a chorus boy (Hope) fired for incompetence and then rehired to set a trap when the new singer (Martin) is stalked by a killer. Weak script, weak songs. **100m/C; VHS, Streaming.** Bob Hope; Tony Martin; Arlene Dahl; Rosemary Clooney; Millard Mitchell; William Demarest; Fred Clark; Robert Strauss; ***D:*** Claude Binyon; ***W:*** Hal Kanter.

Here Come the Waves **1945** Easy-going wartime musical finds Der Bingle as a singing idol drafted into the Navy, assigned to direct WAVE shows. The crooner meets identical twins (both played by Hutton) and falls hard. Only problem is he can't tell the gals apart—and one twin can't stand him. Amusing romantic complications mix well with some spoofing of a star's life. **99m/B; VHS, DVD.** Bing Crosby; Betty Hutton; Sonny Tufts; Ann Doran; Noel Neill; Mae Clarke; Gwen Crawford; Catherine Craig; ***D:*** Mark Sandrich; ***W:*** Zion Myers.

Here Comes Cookie 1/2 **1935** Amusing farce finds Gracie (Allen) the daughter of wealthy Harrison Allen (Barbier), who's afraid of the fortune hunters eyeing other daughter Phyllis (Furness). So he temporarily turns over the family fortune to Gracie, who promptly turns their Park Avenue mansion into a home for down-on-their-luck vaudevillians. Lots of specialty acts and Burns is around as straight man. **65m/B; VHS, DVD.** Gracie Allen; George Burns; George Barbier; Betty Furness; ***D:*** Norman Z. McLeod; ***W:*** Don Hartman; Sam Mintz; ***C:*** Gilbert Warrenton.

Here Comes Mr. Jordan **1941** Montgomery is the young prizefighter killed in a plane crash because of a mix-up in heaven. He returns to life in the body of a soon-to-be murdered millionaire. Rains is the indulgent and advising guardian angel. A lovely fantasy/romance remade in 1978 as "Heaven Can Wait." **94m/B; VHS, DVD, Blu-Ray.** Robert Montgomery; Claude Rains; James Gleason; Evelyn Keyes; Edward Everett Horton; Rita Johnson; John Emery; ***D:*** Alexander Hall; ***W:***

Sidney Buchman; Seton I. Miller; ***M:*** Frederick "Friedrich" Hollander. Oscars '41: Screenplay, Story.

Here Comes Santa Claus 1/2 **1984** A young boy and girl travel to the North Pole to deliver a very special wish to Santa Claus. **78m/C; VHS, DVD.** Karen Cheryl; Armand Meffre; ***D:*** Christian Gion.

Here Comes the Boom 1/2 **2012 (PG)** Push comes to shove when lazy, but lovable high school teacher Scott (James) learns that the music department and his mentor's job, are threatened with budget cuts. The former collegiate wrestler's sudden life-goal takes him into the cage to single-handedly raise the money by winning a mixed-martial-arts tournament. The overweight oaf hits the gym and in a mere four months, we're led to believe he's now a serious UFC contender. (Yes, we're still talking about Kevin James.) What starts out as a fun, witty comedy, spirals into a sappy, absurd underdog story too absurd to believe. **105m/C; DVD, Blu-Ray.** Kevin James; Henry Winkler; Salma Hayek; Melissa Peterman; ***D:*** Frank Coraci; ***W:*** Allan Loeb; Kevin James; ***C:*** Phil Meheux; ***M:*** Rupert Gregson-Williams.

Here Comes the Groom **1951** Late, stale Capra-corn, involving a rogue journalist who tries to keep his girlfriend from marrying a millionaire by becoming a charity worker. Includes a number of cameos. **114m/B; DVD.** Bing Crosby; Jane Wyman; Franchot Tone; Alexis Smith; James Barton; Connie Gilchrist; Robert Keith; Anna Maria Alberghetti; Charles Halton; ***Cameo(s):*** Dorothy Lamour; Phil Harris; Louis Armstrong; ***D:*** Frank Capra. Oscars '51: Song ("In the Cool, Cool, Cool of the Evening").

Here Comes the Navy 1/2 **1934** Dated military comedy was the first pairing between Cagney and O'Brien. Cocky Chesty O'Connor loses a fight, his job, and a dame because of Chief Petty Officer Biff Martin. So Chesty joins the Navy, thinking he can get back at Martin, especially after he starts romancing Martin's sister, Dorothy (Stuart). Scenes were filmed on the USS Arizona, which would be sunk in 1941 at Pearl Harbor. **86m/B; DVD.** James Cagney; Pat O'Brien; Gloria Stuart; Frank McHugh; Robert Barrat; ***D:*** Lloyd Bacon; ***W:*** Earl Baldwin; Ben Markson; ***C:*** Arthur Edeson.

Here is My Heart 1/2 **1934** It's a classic plot: someone pretends to be someone they're not, all for love. In this musical comedy a famous (and wealthy) singer pretends to be a waiter, all to position himself nearer to the woman of his dreams. Only she's a European princess. Will she even notice him? **77m/B; VHS, DVD.** Bing Crosby; Kitty Carlisle Hart; Roland Young; Alison Skipworth; Reginald Owen; William Frawley; ***D:*** Frank Tuttle; ***W:*** Alfred Savoir; ***M:*** Leo Robin; Ralph Rainger.

Here on Earth **2000 (PG-13)** Predictable teary teen romantic drama with a very pretty cast doing what they can with one-note roles. Smalltown beauty Samantha (Sobieski) waits tables at the family diner and hangs out with long-time boyfriend Jasper (Hartnett), who's rivals with snotty prep, Kelley (Klein). Their rivalry causes a disaster for Sam and her family that the boys must rectifiy, even as Kelley and Sam turn to each other. Oh yeah, and then Sam's recurring knee problems turn out to be cancer and everyone has to pull together. **96m/C; VHS, DVD.** Chris Klein; Leelee Sobieski; Josh Hartnett; Michael Rooker; Annie Corley; Bruce Greenwood; Annette O'Toole; Stuart Wilson; Tac Fitzgerald; ***D:*** Mark Piznarski; ***W:*** Michael Seitzman; ***C:*** Michael D. O'Shea; ***M:*** Andrea Morricone.

Here We Go Again! **1942** Fibber McGee and Molly are planning a cross-country trip for their 20th anniversary celebration, but complications abound. Based on the popular NBC radio series. **76m/B; DVD.** Marian Jordan; Jim Jordan; Harold (Hal) Peary; Gale Gordon; Edgar Bergen; Ray Noble; ***D:*** Allan Dwan.

Hereafter 1/2 **2010 (PG-13)** American construction worker George (Damon), French journalist Marie (De France), and British schoolboy Marcus (McLaren) find their lives intersecting after being touched by death. George has psychic abilities that enable him to communicate with the dead; Marcus reads about George and wants to talk to his dead twin brother; and Marie survived a near-death experience that provided a possible glimpse into the afterlife. Director Eastwood controls the hokey and the skepticism to offer a thoughtful drama. **129m/C; DVD, Blu-Ray.** Matt Damon; Cecile de France; Frankie McLaren; Richard Kind; Bryce Dallas Howard; Jay Mohr; George McLaren; Thierry Neuvic; Lyndsey Marshal; Jenifer Lewis; Marthe Keller; ***D:*** Clint Eastwood; ***W:*** Peter Morgan; ***C:*** Tom Stern; ***M:*** Clint Eastwood.

Hereditary **2018 (R)** The death of the family matriarch sends her grieving descendants down a path of sinister discovery. The stellar movie delivers scene after scene of scares, but also pulses with dread, slowly burning toward a terrifying conclusion. Collette is a master of her craft, acting her socks off in a performance that's genuine and unsettling. Writer-director Ari Aster's feature debut. **127m/C; DVD, Blu-Ray.** Toni Collette; Gabriel Byrne; Alex Wolff; Milly Shapiro; Ann Dowd; ***D:*** Ari Aster; ***W:*** Ari Aster; ***C:*** Pawel Pogorzelski; ***M:*** Colin Stetson.

Hero **1992 (PG-13)** Interesting twist on Cinderella fable and modern media satire has TV reporter Davis looking for the man who saved her life, expecting a genuine hero, and accepting without question the one who fits her vision. Critically considered disappointing, but wait—Garcia and Hoffman make a great team, and Davis is fetching as the vulnerable media person. Strong language and dark edges may keep away some of the kids, but otherwise this is a fine fable. **116m/C; VHS, DVD.** Geena Davis; Dustin Hoffman; Andy Garcia; Joan Cusack; Kevin J. O'Connor; Chevy Chase; Maury Chaykin; Stephen Tobolowsky; Christian Clemenson; Tom Arnold; Warren Berlinger; Susie Cusack; James Madio; Richard Riehle; Don Yesso; Darrell Larson; ***D:*** Stephen Frears; ***W:*** David Peoples; ***C:*** Oliver Stapleton; ***M:*** George Fenton.

Hero *Ying Xiong* **2002 (PG-13)** Visually stunning movie combines martial arts, tragedy, historical drama, and philosophy into one complex, satisfying epic. Set in 3rd century B.C. China, the story revolves around swordsman Nameless (Li), who hunts down three assassins for the ruthless King (Chen), who used brutal methods to bring the various states of China under his leadership. Told mostly in flashback, Nameless unveils his encounters with the warriors (Leung, Cheung, and Yen) to the King, but all is not as it seems, and in the end Nameless faces a choice of what his place in the King's newly unified China should be. Features meticulous, creative cinematography (each segment has its own color theme) and beautiful martial arts sequences, but is hindered by inconsistent performances. The most expensive Chinese production ever made at $30 million, it has been criticized for appearing to endorse the government's stance on a unified China. **98m/C; DVD, Blu-Ray, UMD.** *CH CH* Jet Li; Maggie Cheung; Donnie Yen; Ziyi Zhang; Tony Leung Chiu-Wai; Daoming Chen; ***D:*** Yimou Zhang; ***W:*** Yimou Zhang; Feng Li; Bin Wang; ***C:*** Christopher Doyle; ***M:*** Tan Dun.

The Hero 1/2 **2017 (R)** A star of Westerns whose best real work was decades earlier, Lee Hayden's (Elliott) life as a pot smoking, hard drinking voiceover artist changes dramatically after learning he is terminally ill. He tries to reconnect with his estranged daughter Lucy (Ritter) and forms an unexpected romantic relationship with a stand-up comedian, Charlotte (Prepon). Through it all, Lee explores his mortality by looking back at his best film role. Sentimental and unfocused, the film succeeds only because of Elliott's formidable presence as an actor. **93m/C; DVD.** Sam Elliott; Laura Prepon; Nick Offerman; Krysten Ritter; Katharine Ross; ***D:*** Brett Haley; ***W:*** Brett Haley; Marc Basch; ***C:*** Rob Givens; ***M:*** Keegan DeWitt.

A Hero Ain't Nothin' but a Sandwich 1/2 **1978 (PG)** A young urban black teenager gets involved in drugs and is eventually saved from ruin. Slow-moving, over-directed and talky. However, Scott turns in a fine performance. Based on Alice Childress' novel. **107m/C; VHS, DVD.** Cicely Tyson; Paul Winfield; Larry B. Scott; Helen Martin; Glynn Turman; David Groh; ***D:*** Ralph Nelson.

Hero and the Terror 1/2 **1988 (R)** Perennial karate guy Norris plays a sensitive policeman who conquers his fear of a not-so-sensitive maniac who's trying to kill him. Plenty of action and a cheesy subplot to boot. **96m/C; VHS, DVD, Blu-Ray.** Chuck Norris; Brynn Thayer; Steve James; Jack O'Halloran; Ron O'Neal; Billy Drago; ***D:*** William (Bill) Tannen; ***W:*** Michael Blodgett; ***C:*** Eric Van Haren Noman; ***M:*** David Michael Frank.

Hero at Large 1/2 **1980 (PG)** An unemployed actor foils a robbery while dressed in a promotional "Captain Avenger" suit, and instant celebrity follows. Lightweight, yet enjoyable. **98m/C; VHS, DVD.** John Ritter; Anne Archer; Bert Convy; Kevin McCarthy; Kevin Bacon; ***D:*** Martin Davidson; ***W:*** A.J. Carothers.

Hero of Rome **1963** Rome has many who could be called "hero," but one stands biceps and pecs above the rest. Cheesy sword and sandal epic with political intrigue and battles galore, along with plenty of wooden acting and ridiculous dialogue. **90m/C; VHS, DVD.** *IT* Gordon Scott; Gabriella Pallotta; Massimo Serato; Gabriele Antonini; ***D:*** Giorgio Ferroni; ***W:*** Alberta Montanti; Antonino Visont; ***C:*** Augusto Tiezzi; ***M:*** Angelo Francesco Lavagnino.

Hero Wanted **2008 (R)** Garbage collector Liam Case (Gooding) becomes a local hero when he rescues a young girl from a burning car, but that one moment doesn't bring the changes to his life Liam anticipates. He happens to be at the bank, flirting with a pretty teller, when a heist is attempted. Liam and the teller are among the shooting victims and Liam vows revenge. But the detective (Liotta) on the case gets suspicious about Liam's true role in the bank job. Lots of flashbacks and a few plot twists. **95m/C; DVD.** Cuba Gooding, Jr.; Ray Liotta; Christa Campbell; Jean Smart; Norman Reedus; Tommy Flanagan; Kim Coates; Ben Cross; ***D:*** Chad Law; ***W:*** Evan Law; ***C:*** Larry Blanford; ***M:*** Kenneth Burgomaster. **VIDEO**

Herod the Great **1960** Biblical epic of the downfall of Herod, the ruler of ancient Judea. Scantily clad women abound. Dubbed. **93m/C; VHS, DVD.** *IT* Edmund Purdom; Sandra Milo; Alberto Lupo; ***D:*** Arnaldo Genoino.

Heroes **1977 (PG)** An institutionalized Vietnam vet (Winkler) escapes, hoping to establish a worm farm which will support all his crazy buddies. On the way to the home of a friend he hopes will help him, he encounters Field. Funny situations don't always mix with serious underlying themes of mental illness and post-war adjustment. **97m/C; VHS, DVD, Blu-Ray.** Henry Winkler; Sally Field; Harrison Ford; ***D:*** Jeremy Paul Kagan; ***W:*** James (Jim) Carabatsos; ***M:*** Jack Nitzsche.

Heroes for Sale **1933** Fascinating melodrama about a WWI veteran who returns home and manages to survive one disaster after another. Barthelmess is great in his performance as an American Everyman who must deal with everything from morphine addiction to finding work during the Depression. Fast-paced, patriotic film is helped by ambitious script and the expert direction of Wellman. **72m/B; VHS, DVD.** Richard Barthelmess; Loretta Young; Aline MacMahon; Robert Barrat; Grant Mitchell; Douglass Dumbrille; Charley Grapewin; Ward Bond; ***D:*** William A. Wellman; ***W:*** Robert Lord; Wilson Mizner.

The Heroes of Telemark 1/2 **1965** In 1942, Norway is under Nazi occupation and Nazi scientists are dangerously close to producing an essential element for making an atomic bomb in a secret factory. Underground leader Knut Straud (Harris) enlists the help of Norwegian scientist Rolf Pedersen (Douglas) and a group of saboteurs to destroy the factory. But their raid only provides a short delay and our heroes must now prevent shipment of the component from ever reaching Germany. Filmed on location in Norway, with former members of the underground serving as technical advisors for director Mann. **130m/C; VHS, DVD, Blu-Ray.** *GB* Richard Harris; Kirk Douglas; Michael Redgrave; Ulla Jacobsson; David Weston; Sebastian Breaks; Alan Howard; Roy Dotrice; Patrick Jordan; Anton Diffring; Eric Porter; Ralph Michael; ***D:*** Anthony Mann; ***W:*** Ben Barzman; ***C:*** Robert Krasker; ***M:*** Malcolm Arnold.

Heroes of the Alamo 1/2 **1937** Remember the Alamo...but forget this movie. Dull, threadbare dramatization of the battle that was scorned even back in '37. **75m/B; VHS, DVD.** Rex Lease; Lane Chandler; Roger Williams; Earle Hodgins; Julian Rivero; ***D:*** Harry Fraser.

Heroes of the East *Challenge of the Ninja Shaolin; Challenges Ninja; Zhong hua zhang fu; Drunk Shaolin Challenges Ninja* **2008** Chinese Martial Arts master Ho Tao (Chia Hui Liu) has been arranged to marry Yumiko Koda (Yuka Mizuno), and inadvertently insults her and her entire family when he suggests that the Japanese fighting arts are inferior to Chinese Kung Fu. She leaves him, and his attempts to win her back are so misunderstood her family challenges him to a duel. Karate vs Kung Fu. It's one of the few Shaw Brothers martial arts films where revenge isn't a theme, and no one dies or gets bloodied in a fight. It might even be called family friendly. **100m/C; DVD.** *CH* Chia Hui Liu; Yuka Mizuno; Kang-Yeh Cheng; Norman Chu; ***D:*** Chia-Liang Liu; ***W:*** Kuang Ni; ***C:*** Arthur Wong; ***M:*** Yung-Yu Chen.

Heroes of the Heart 1/2 **1994** Residents ofa West Viriginia trailer park are devastated when their homes are destroyed in a flood. But then Basquette claims she was visited by God, who's directed her to bring the poor community together so that each can be granted their most secret wish. Nicely eccentric characters, serious theme with some whimsical touches, and a country-music soundtrack. **102m/C; VHS, DVD.** Lena Basquette; Larry Groce; Dusty Rhodes; Webb Wilder; John McIntire; Jennifer Gurney; Johnny Paycheck; ***D:*** Daniel Boyd; ***W:*** Daniel Boyd; ***C:*** Larry Kopelman; ***M:*** Michael Lipton.

Heroes Shed No Tears *Ying Xiong Wei Lei; The Sunset Warrior* **1986** Chinese mercenaries are hired by the Thai government to capture a drug lord from the Golden Triangle. Cantonese with subtitles. **93m/C; VHS, DVD, Blu-Ray.** *CH* Eddy Ko; Ching-Ying Lam; Chen Yue Sang; Kuo Sheng; ***D:*** John Woo; ***W:*** John Woo.

Heroes Two 1/2 *Fang Shiyu yu Hong Xiguan; The Blood Brothers; Bloody Fists; Kung Fu Invaders; Temple of the Dragon* **1973** Shaw Brothers martial arts film centering on martial artists Fang Shih-yu (Sheng Fu) and Hung His-kuan (Kuan Tai Chen) determined to get revenge on the destroyers of the Shaolin temple. Tricked into fighting each other by an evil Manchurian general, Fang is attacked by the local rebels after he helps the general imprison Hung. Finally realizing he has been a naive fool, he attempts to rescue Hung and gain his help to defeat the Manchurians once and for all. **91m/C; DVD.** *CH* Kuan Tai Chen; Sheng Fu; ***D:*** Cheh Chang; ***W:*** Cheh Chang; Kuang Ni; ***C:*** Mu-To Kung.

The Heroic Ones *Shi San Tai Bo* **1970** At the end of the Tang Dynasty, two warlords band together against a common enemy. One has 13 generals, whom he's adopted and treats like sons, and he chooses the youngest to lead the battle. This causes resentment and betrayal within the clan. Mandarin with subtitles or dubbed. **94m/C; DVD.** *CH* David Chiang; Han Chin; Lung Ti; James Nam; Chung Wang; Feng Ku; Sing Chen; ***D:*** Chen Chang; ***W:*** Chen Chang; ***C:*** Mu-To Kung; ***M:*** Fu-ling Wang.

The Heroic Trio 1/2 *Dong Fang San Xia* **1993** Three superheroines battle the Lord of the Underground to prevent him from stealing any more human babies. Lots of martial arts and supernatural action. Chinese with subtitles or dubbed. **87m/C; VHS, DVD.** *CH* Michelle Yeoh; Maggie Cheung; Anita (Yim-Fong) Mui; Anthony Wong; Damian Lau; ***D:*** Ching Siu Tung; Johnny To; ***W:*** Sandy Shaw; ***C:*** Hang-Seng Poon; Tom Lau; ***M:*** William Hu.

Hero's Island 1/2 **1962** Good swashbuckling adventure. In the early 1700s, the Mainwarings inherit Bull Island off the Carolina coast, but the fisherman already occupying the property turn to violence to force the family to leave. A castaway—who turns out to be Blackbeard the pirate—washes ashore and comes to the aid of the family. **94m/C; DVD.** James Mason; Kate Manx; Brendan Dillon; Rip Torn; Neville Brand; Warren Oates; Harry Dean Stanton; Darby Hinton; ***D:*** Leslie Stevens; ***W:*** Leslie Stevens; ***C:*** Ted D. McCord; ***M:*** Dominic Frontiere.

He's Just Not That Into You ☆☆ **2009 (PG-13)** Comic take on the relationship book by Greg Behrendt and Liz Tuccillo, set in Baltimore, following five women through their struggles with modern-day relationships. Beth (Aniston) has been living with the perfect man for years who won't commit to marriage. Gigi (Goodwin) waits by the phone all day, hoping the dream guy who asked for her number will call. Janine (Connelly) is upset that her new husband Ben isn't excited by home decor. Mary (Barrymore) is surrounded by great guys, problem is, they're all gay. Then there's Anna (Johansson), who's being pursued by Mr. Right, but she's already committed to a married man who won't commit back. Cute and harmless, but doesn't think too highly of these five women with its paper-thin material. **129m/C; Blu-Ray.** Drew Barrymore; Jennifer Aniston; Kevin Connolly; Jennifer Connelly; Bradley Cooper; Ginnifer Goodwin; Justin Long; Scarlett Johansson; Ben Affleck; Wilson Cruz; Kris Kristofferson; Cory Hardrict; Leonardo Nam; ***D:*** Ken Kwapis; ***W:*** Abby Kohn; Marc Silverstein; ***C:*** John Bailey; ***M:*** Cliff Eidelman.

He's My Girl ☆ ½ **1987 (PG-13)** When a rock singer wins a trip for two to Hollywood, he convinces his agent to dress up as a woman so they can use the free tickets. **104m/C; VHS, Streaming.** David Hallyday; T.K. Carter; Misha McK; Jennifer Tilly; ***D:*** Gabrielle Beaumont; ***W:*** Terence H. Winkless; Taylor Ames; Charles F. Bohl; ***C:*** Peter Lyons Collister.

Hesher ☆☆ **2010 (R)** Creepy and funny in an anarchist sort of way, but it's hard to know just what director/co-writer Susser was going for, although lead Gordon-Levitt was obviously game for anything. Depressed Paul Forney (Wilson) is mourning the recent car accident death of his wife while his 13-year-old son T.J. (Brochu) is obsessed with getting the auto back from the salvage yard and grandma Madeleine (Laurie) tries to look after them. T.J. meets antisocial, violent, foul-mouthed, tattooed Hesher (Gordon-Levitt) who suddenly shows up, moves in, and makes himself completely at home. **105m/C; DVD, On Demand.** Joseph Gordon-Levitt; Devin Brochu; Rainn Wilson; Piper Laurie; Natalie Portman; John Carroll Lynch; ***D:*** Spencer Susser; ***W:*** Spencer Susser; David Michod; ***C:*** Morgan Susser; ***M:*** Francois (Frank) Tetaz.

The Hessen Conspiracy ☆ ½ *The Hessen Affair* **2009** In 1945, victorious U.S. Army officers occupy Castle Kronberg in Frankfort, Germany, which once belonged to the German royal family. Col. Jack Durant and Lt. Kathleen Nash uncover the crown jewels and manage to smuggle them into the U.S., where they run into trouble trying to fence them. German Princess Sophie Von Hessen complains to the Army about the missing gems and now Durant and Nash have even more trouble. **113m/C; DVD.** Billy Zane; Lyne Renee; Rudolph Segers; Michael Bowen; ***D:*** Paul Breuls; ***W:*** Nicholas Meyer; Ronald Roose; ***C:*** Kees Van Oostrum; ***M:*** Stephen Warbeck. **VIDEO**

Hester Street ☆☆☆ ½ **1975** Set at the turn of the century, the film tells the story of a young Jewish immigrant who ventures to New York City to be with her husband. As she re-acquaints herself with her husband, she finds that he has abandoned his Old World ideals. The film speaks not only to preserving the heritage of the Jews, but to cherishing all heritages and cultures. Highly regarded upon release, unfortunately forgotten today. **92m/B; VHS, DVD, Blu-Ray.** Carol Kane; Doris Roberts; Steven Keats; Mel Howard; Dorrie Kavanaugh; Stephen Strimpell; ***D:*** Joan Micklin Silver; ***W:*** Joan Micklin Silver; ***C:*** Kenneth Van Sickle; ***M:*** William Bolcom. Natl. Film Reg. '11.

Hexed ☆ ½ **1993 (R)** Walter Mitty lives in the person of bellboy Matthew Welsh, who enjoys masquerading as a debonair bon vivant. He finagles his way into the life of Hexina, a beautiful psychotic model who has checked into the hotel where Matthew works in order to murder her blackmailer. She tries to kill Matthew, apparently getting in a little practice, but he'll still follow her anywhere. Inane, charmless comedy that intends to satirize "Fatal Attraction" and similar films. **93m/C; VHS, DVD.** Arye Gross; Claudia Christian; Adrienne Shelly; R. Lee Ermey; Norman Fell; Michael E. Knight; ***D:*** Alan Spencer; ***W:*** Alan Spencer.

Hey Arnold! The Movie ☆☆ **2002 (PG)** Kidpic based on the Nickelodeon series has the cranial oddity cast getting civic-minded about saving their endangered 'hood from an evil corporate developer. Eerily upbeat Arnold battles strangely Ronald Reagan-sounding Scheck who wants to raze their inner-city neighborhood. Together with his more realistic, flat-topped friend Gerald, Arnold employs a variety of ways to save his diverse urban home, from organizing a block party (good) to breaking and entering (hmm. . .this is for kids?). Castellaneta is the voice of Grandpa, who has explosive plans of his own to save the street. Big names (well, their voices) cameo. Some of the charm of the series remains but lacks feature-length punch. Animation suffers from the big screen treatment, as well. **76m/C; VHS, DVD.** ***V:*** Spencer Klein; Francesca Marie Smith; Jamil Walker Smith; Dan Castellaneta; Tress MacNeille; Paul Sorvino; Jennifer Jason Leigh; Christopher Lloyd; Vincent Schiavelli; Maurice LaMarche; ***D:*** Tuck Tucker; ***W:*** Craig Bartlett; Steve Viksten; ***M:*** Jim Lang.

Hey, Babu Riba ☆☆ ½ **1988 (R)** A popular Yugoslavian fit of nostalgia about four men convening at the funeral of a young girl they all loved years before, and their happy, Americana-bathed memories therein. In Serbo-Croatian with English subtitles. **109m/C; VHS, DVD.** *YU* Gala Videnovic; Nebojsa Bakocevic; Dragan Bjelogric; Marko Todorovic; Goran Radakovic; Relja Basic; Milos Zutic; ***D:*** Jovan Acin; ***W:*** Jovan Acin.

Hey Good Lookin' ☆☆ ½ **1982** Ralph Bakshi's irreverent look at growing up in 1950s Brooklyn bears the trademark qualities that distinguish his other adult animated features, "Fritz the Cat" and "Heavy Traffic." **87m/C; DVD, Streaming.** ***D:*** Ralph Bakshi; ***W:*** Ralph Bakshi.

Hey, Happy! ☆☆ **2001** Camp comedy set in a post-apocalyptic Winnipeg where survivors of some type of environmental plague seem blase about a coming flood of biblical proportions. So enterprising DJ Sabu (Yuen) decides to hold an end-of-the-world rave party on the appropriately named Garbage Hill. That is after he fulfills his sexual quest of sleeping with 2,000 men. And his choice for the magic number is schizo Happy (Aftanas), who hears alien voices on his radio urging him to give in. But the path to sexual conquest does not run smooth as Sabu has a stalker/rival in pierced punk Spanky (Godson). Sometimes slick, sometimes outrageous, sometimes surreal and just plain weird. **75m/C; VHS, DVD.** *CA* Jeremie Yuen; Craig Aftanas; Clayton Godson; ***D:*** Noam Gonick; ***W:*** Noam Gonick; ***C:*** Paul Suderman.

Hey Hey It's Esther Blueberger ☆ ½ **2008 (PG-13)** Nerdy Jewish Esther Blueburger is frequently humiliated at her private girls' school. Things change when she is befriended by older teen Sunni and they secretly plan for Esther to switch to Sunni's public school where Esther will pass herself off as a Swedish exchange student. The secrets strain the film's credibility and there's some cringe-worthy happenings that make this more suitable for older teens. **103m/C; DVD.** *AU* Danielle Catanzariti; Keisha Castle-Hughes; Essie Davis; Russell Dykstra; Christin Byers; Toni Collette; ***D:*** Cathy Randall; ***W:*** Cathy Randall; ***C:*** Anna Howard; ***M:*** Guy Gross.

Hey! Hey! USA! ☆ ½ **1938** Ocean liner porter Benjamin Twist (Hays) masquerades as an education expert for bored millionaire's son Bertie (Bupp) and discovers gangster Bugs (Kennedy) is a stowaway aboard ship. Twist winds up in Chicago when Bertie is kidnapped and he's asked to deliver the ransom, which involves Bugs and rival gangsters. **89m/B; DVD.** *GB* Will Hay; Edgar Kennedy; David Burns; Edmon Ryan; Tommy Bupp; Fred Duprez; Paddy Reynolds; ***D:*** Marcel Varnel; ***W:*** Val Guest; Marriott Edgar; J.O.C. Orton; ***C:*** Arthur Crabtree; ***M:*** R. E. Dearing.

Hey There, It's Yogi Bear ☆☆ **1964** When Yogi Bear comes out of winter hibernation to search for food, he travels to the Chizzling Brothers Circus. The first feature-length cartoon to come from the H-B Studios. **98m/C; VHS, DVD.** ***V:*** Daws Butler; James Darren; Mel Blanc; J. Pat O'Malley; Julie Bennett; ***D:*** William Hanna; Joseph Barbera; ***W:*** William Hanna; Joseph Barbera; ***M:*** Marty Paich.

The Heyday of the Insensitive Bastards ☆☆ **2017** Based on Robert Boswell's short story collection, seven vignettes that explore the human condition. In one story, a father (Modine) faces a life-changing dilemma, while his son is hounded by bullies. A lighter segment centers on a maid (Wiig) who daydreams while working for her rich employers. Another part features teenage boys telling stories they made up about their first sexual encounters. Created in collaboration with University of California Los Angeles graduate film students, the film's quality is uneven but each segment offers a meaningful moment about the impact of the pursuit of happiness in contemporary America on lives and life choices. **97m/C; DVD.** Rico Rodriguez; Matthew Modine; James Franco; Abigail Spencer; Kate Mara; ***D:*** Mark Columbus; Lauren Hoekstra; Sarah Kruchowski; Ryan Moody; Simon Savelyev; Vanita Shastry; Shadae Lamar Smith; Jeremy David White; ***W:*** Roxanne Beck; Neville Kiser; Marissa Matteo; Mona Nahm; Jessica Nikkel; Nicole Riegel; Teresa Sullivan; Jacqueline Vleck; ***C:*** Alejandro Salinas Albrecht; Phil Carter; Dylan Chapgier; Justin Perkinson; Ivan Rodriguez; Andrew Wesman; Ragland Williamson; ***M:*** Joshua Theroux.

H.G. Wells' War of the Worlds ☆☆ *War of the Worlds* **2005** Low-budget but not nearly the usual 'let's cash in on another current film release' Asylum studio production. Modern retelling of the Martian invasion of Earth where the baddies are annihilating humanity. Astronomer George Herbert (Howell) is trying to meet up with family in DC and instead encounters the aliens. Followed by 2008's "War of the Worlds 2: The Next Wave." **100m/C; DVD.** C. Thomas Howell; Peter Greene; Andrew Lauer; Rhett Giles; Dashiell Howell; Jake Busey; Tinarie Van Wyk-Loots; Kim Little; ***D:*** David Michael Latt; ***W:*** David Michael Latt; Carlos De Los Rios; ***C:*** Steven Parker; Lucia Diaz Sas; ***M:*** Ralph Rieckermann. **VIDEO**

Hi Diddle Diddle ☆☆ ½ *Diamonds and Crime; Try and Find It* **1943** Topsy-turvy comedy features young lovers who long for conventional happiness. Instead they are cursed with con-artist parents who delight in crossing that law-abiding line. **72m/B; VHS, DVD.** Adolphe Menjou; Martha Scott; Dennis O'Keefe; Pola Negri; ***D:*** Andrew L. Stone.

Hi-Jacked ☆ **1950** When a parolee trucker's cargo is stolen, he inevitably becomes a suspect and must set out to find the true culprits. **66m/B; VHS, DVD.** Jim Davis; Paul Cavanagh; Marsha Jones; Sid Melton; David Bruce; Ralph Sanford; Iris Adrian; George Eldredge; ***D:*** Sam Newfield; ***W:*** Orville H. Hampton; Fred Myton; Raymond L. Schrock; ***C:*** Philip Tannura; ***M:*** Paul Dunlap.

Hi-Life ☆☆ ½ **1998 (R)** Talky, Christmastime, Manhattan-set ensemble comedy finds compulsive gambler and out of work actor Jimmy (Stoltz) owing bookie Fatty (Durning) $900. To get the money, he tells girlfriend Susan (Kelly) it's to finance an abortion for his slutty sis Maggie (Hannah). Then Maggie's ex-boyfriend Ray (Scott) gets involved and Fatty's associate Miner (Reigart) and numerous other players who all wind up at the Hi-Life Bar and discover Jimmy's scams. **82m/C; VHS, DVD.** Eric Stoltz; Moira Kelly; Daryl Hannah; Campbell Scott; Peter Riegert; Katrin Cartlidge; Charles Durning; Saundra Santiago; Anne DeSalvo; Bruce MacVittie; Tegan West; ***D:*** Roger Hedden; ***W:*** Roger Hedden; ***C:*** John Thomas; ***M:*** David Lawrence.

The Hi-Lo Country ☆☆ ½ **1998 (R)** For years, Sam Peckinpah wanted to make this movie. It took Martin Scorsese to resurrect the project and to secure Walon Green to adapt the 1961 Max Evans novel for the screen. Pete Calder (Crudup) returns to New Mexico from WWII. While waiting for buddy Big Boy Matson (Harrelson) to return from the Marines, Pete falls for Mona (Arquette), a saucy woman whose husband works for the area's biggest rancher, Jim Love (Elliott). When Big Boy does return, it becomes obvious that he and Mona are hot for each other, so Pete bows out. Big Boy is the last real cowboy (a favorite Peckinpah theme), who loves the land, fears no one, and knows his times are coming to an end. Director Frears may not completely understand the American mythic West, but thanks to Oliver Stapleton's cinematography, the film has a look close to what a Peckinpah or a Ford might have given it. **114m/C; VHS, DVD.** Woody Harrelson; Patricia Arquette; Billy Crudup; Penelope Cruz; Sam Elliott; Cole Hauser; Darren E. Burrows; Jacob Vargas; James Gammon; Lane Smith; Katy Jurado; John Diehl; Enrique Castillo; Rosaleen Linehan; ***D:*** Stephen Frears; ***W:*** Walon Green; ***C:*** Oliver Stapleton; ***M:*** Carter Burwell.

Hi, Mom! ☆☆☆ *Confessions of A Peeping John; Blue Manhattan* **1970 (R)** DePalma's follow-up to "Greetings" finds amateur pornographer/movie maker De Niro being advised by a professional in the field (Garfield) of sleazy filmmaking. De Niro films the residents of his apartment building and eventually marries one of his starlets. One of De Palma's earlier and better efforts with De Niro playing a crazy as only he can. **87m/C; VHS, DVD, Blu-Ray.** Robert De Niro; Charles Durnham; Allen Garfield; Lara Parker; Jennifer Salt; Gerrit Graham; ***D:*** Brian De Palma; ***W:*** Brian De Palma.

Hi, Nellie! ☆☆ ½ **1934** A fast-paced crime comedy with a familiar plot. Newspaper editor Bradshaw is demoted to the despised lonelyhearts advice column after a fight with his publisher. This means reporter Gerry, whom Bradshaw had demoted, goes back to the news. He unexpectedly becomes a success, but then gets a lead on a big story with ties to a lonelyhearts killer, a missing man, and a crime boss that Gerry is also working. **75m/B; DVD.** Paul Muni; Glenda Farrell; Douglass Dumbrille; Robert Barrat; Ned Sparks; Hobart Cavanaugh; ***D:*** Mervyn LeRoy; ***W:*** Abem Finkel; Sidney Sutherland; ***C:*** Sol Polito.

Hi-Riders ☆ **1977 (R)** A revenge-based tale about large, mag-wheeled trucks and their drivers. **90m/C; VHS, DVD.** Mel Ferrer; Stephen McNally; Neville Brand; Ralph Meeker; ***D:*** Greydon Clark.

Hiawatha ☆ ½ **1952** Low-budget drama very loosely based on the Longfellow poem. After being attacked by a bear, Ojibway warrior Hiawatha (Edwards) is nursed by Minnehaha (Duguay) from the rival Dacotah tribe. They marry, but Hiawatha may be forced to make a choice between the two tribes when a hot-headed young Ojibway (Larsen) incites a war. **80m/C; DVD.** Vince Edwards; Yvette Duguay; Keith Larsen; Eugene Iglesias; Armando Silvestre; ***D:*** Kurt Neumann; ***W:*** Arthur Strawn; Daniel Ullman; ***C:*** Harry Neumann; ***M:*** Marlin Skiles.

Hick WOOF! **2011 (R)** Desperate Nebraska teen Luli (Moretz) starts hitchhiking to Vegas to escape her drunken parents. Gratingly awful with a group of improbable characters, including a good-hearted grifter (Lively) and a creepy cowboy (Redmayne). Based on screenwriter Portes' 2007 novel. **99m/C; DVD; Closed Captioned.** Chloë Grace Moretz; Blake Lively; Eddie Redmayne; Alec Baldwin; Rory Culkin; Juliette Lewis; Anson Mount; ***D:*** Derick Martini; ***W:*** Andrea Portes; ***C:*** Frank Godwin; ***M:*** Larry Campbell. **VIDEO**

Hickey & Boggs ☆☆ **1972 (PG)** Culp reunites with Cosby to play a pair of down on their luck P.I.s, who inadvertently set in motion a tragic set of events while trying to rescue a little girl. Notable for being much darker than their usual work and for being Culp's only turn as a director. **111m/C; DVD, Blu-Ray, Streaming.** Bill Cosby; Robert Culp; Rosalind Cash; Michael Moriarty; James Woods; ***D:*** Robert Culp; ***W:*** Walter Hill; ***C:*** Bill Butler; ***M:*** Ted Ashford.

Hidalgo ☆☆ ½ **2004 (PG-13)** Inspired by real-life U.S. Calvary horseman Frank T. Hopkins (Mortensen)?meaning it takes liberties with the truth (which Hopkins himself has been accused of). Old-fashioned adventure story hows the devotion he had for his mixed-breed horse, Hidalgo, as they travel 3,000 miles in 1890 to the "Ocean of Fire" endurance race, going against thoroughbreds and the wild elements of Arabia per the invitation of Sheikh Riyadh (Sharif). Mortensen looks stunning riding his steed, the elegant Sharif stirs up wonderful memories of Lawrence of

Arabia, and the visual effects of sandstorms, colossal locusts, and the competition are captivating; however, this kind of story has been told before, with more dramatic twists and turns. **135m/C; VHS, DVD.** Viggo Mortensen; Omar Sharif; Louise Lombard; Said Taghmaoui; Peter Mensah; J.K. Simmons; Adoni Maropis; Floyd "Red Crow" Westerman; Zuleikha Robinson; Adam Alexi-Malle; Silas Carson; Harsh Nayyar; Elizabeth Berridge; Victor Talmadge; Frank Collison; Jerry Hardin; C. Thomas Howell; Malcolm McDowell; ***D:*** Joe Johnston; ***W:*** John Fusco; ***C:*** Shelly Johnson; ***M:*** James Newton Howard.

The Hidden **1987 (R)** A seasoned cop (Nouri) and a benign alien posing as an FBI agent (MacLachlan) team up to track down and destroy a hyper-violent alien who survives by invading the bodies of humans, causing them to go on murderous rampages. Much acclaimed, high velocity action film with state-of-the-art special effects (at least for the time). Followed by a minor 1994 sequel with a different cast. **98m/C; VHS, DVD, Blu-Ray.** Kyle MacLachlan; Michael Nouri; Clu Gulager; Ed O'Ross; Claudia Christian; Clarence Felder; Richard Brooks; William Boyett; Chris Mulkey; ***D:*** Jack Sholder; ***W:*** Bob Hunt; Jim Kouf; ***C:*** Jacques Haitkin; ***M:*** Michael Convertino.

Hidden 1/2 *Cache* **2005 (R)** Georges Laurent (Auteuil) and his wife Anne (Binoche) are upper middle class professionals living a comfortable life with their young son in Paris when suddenly a disturbing surveillance video tape of their own home is left at their front door, followed by another and another. This invasion plunges Georges into a world of repressed memories and disquieting dreams as he tries to make sense of these events as well as his past. On the surface a whodunit mystery not unlike any other from the post modern era. However, this is in post-9/11 modern-age France, and the story unfolds as a metaphor for personal and societal responsibility to those previously held under thumb. **121m/C; DVD.** Daniel Auteuil; Juliette Binoche; Annie Girardot; Maurice Benichou; Bernard Le Coq; Lester Makedonsky; Walid Afkir; ***D:*** Michael Haneke; ***W:*** Michael Haneke; ***C:*** Christian Berger. L.A. Film Critics '05: Foreign Film.

Hidden *Skjult* **2009 (R)** Unsettling Norwegian psycho-horror has jittery Kai (Joner) returning (after nearly 20 years) to his creepy childhood home in the woods to settle his crazy/cruel mother's estate. He's beset by delusions (or maybe they're not), hostile locals, and then Kai becomes the prime suspect when a couple of campers go missing. Norwegian with subtitles. **96m/C; DVD.** *NO* Kristoffer Joner; Arthur Berning; Knut Morten Brekke; Marco (Marko Iversen) Kanic; Eivind Sander; Agnes Karin Haaskjold; ***D:*** Pal Oie; ***W:*** Pal Oie; ***C:*** Sjur Aarthun; ***M:*** Trond Bjerknaes.

Hidden 1/2 **2011** BBC miniseries suffers from too many plot holes and improbabilities to be successful. Soliciter Harry Venn is asked by Gina Hawkes to find a missing alibi witness for her client. This leads back to the death of Harry's brother 20 years before and a conspiracy involving the collapse of Britain's coalition government that puts both Harry and Gina's lives in danger. **240m/C; DVD.** *UK* Philip Glenister; Thekla Reuten; David Suchet; Anna Chancellor; Richard Dormer; ***D:*** Niall MacCormick; ***W:*** Ronan Bennett; Walter Bernstein; ***C:*** Jan Jonaeus; ***M:*** Rob Lane. **TV**

The Hidden 2 1/2 **1994 (R)** The hyper-violent alien of the 1987 movie returns. With its love of fast cars, high-caliber weapons, and heavy metal music, this body-possessing creature appears to be unstoppable. **91m/C; VHS, DVD.** Raphael Sbarge; Kate Hodge; Michael Nouri; ***D:*** Seth Pinsker; ***W:*** Seth Pinsker; ***M:*** David McHugh.

Hidden Agenda 1/2 **1990 (R)** A human rights activist and an American lawyer uncover brutality and corruption among the British forces in Northern Ireland. Slow-paced but strong performances. The Northern Irish dialect is sometimes difficult to understand as are the machinations on the British police system. Generally worthwhile. **108m/C; VHS, DVD.** Frances McDormand; Brian Cox; Brad Dourif; Mai Zetterling; John Benfield; Des McAleer; Jim Norton; Maurice Roeves; ***D:*** Ken Loach; ***W:*** Jim Allen; ***C:*** Clive Tickner; ***M:*** Stewart Copeland. Cannes '90: Special Jury Prize.

Hidden Agenda **1999 (R)** Arriving in Berlin, American tourist Dillon learns his brother has been murdered. He decides to do some investigating on his own and winds up caught between CIA spies and the German secret police. **97m/C; VHS, DVD.** Kevin Dillon; Christopher Plummer; Andrea Roth; Michael Wincott; J.T. Walsh; ***D:*** Iain Paterson; ***W:*** Iain Paterson; ***C:*** Thom Best; ***M:*** Harry Manfredini. **VIDEO**

Hidden Agenda 1/2 **2001 (R)** Former NSA agent Jason Price (Lundgren) is still doing covert government work by making people vanish. His latest client is a mobster (Houde) but Price finds that a legendary hit man (Roy) has taken an unhealthy interest in his operation. **94m/C; VHS, DVD.** Dolph Lundgren; Maxim Roy; Brigitte Paquette; Serge Houde; Patrick Kerton; Christian Paul; ***D:*** Marc S. Grenier; ***W:*** Les Weldon; ***C:*** Sylvain Brault. **VIDEO**

Hidden Assassin *The Shooter* **1994 (R)** French hit woman Simone (Detmers) supposedly shoots the Cuban ambassador to the U.N. and escapes back to her home base in Prague, followed by Czech-born U.S. Marshal Mickey Dane (Lundgren). Mickey starts to doubt that Simone is the killer (she claims she's long retired and is being set up) and the duo try to find the truth amid lots of double-crosses. Doesn't make much sense in any case. **89m/C; VHS, DVD, Blu-Ray.** Dolph Lundgren; Maruschka Detmers; Assumpta Serna; Gavan O'Herlihy; John Ashton; Simon Andreu; ***D:*** Ted Kotcheff; ***W:*** Meg Thayer; Billy Ray; Yves Andre Martin; ***C:*** Fernando Arguelles; ***M:*** Stefano Mainetti.

Hidden Away **2013** Basic Lifetime woman-in-peril flick. Stephanie wants out of her abusive marriage to Andrew so she fakes her death and that of young daughter, Sage. !0 years later, they've renamed themselves Alexandra and Rachel and have new lives in Palm Springs where Rachel has a job as a guide on the Palm Springs Tramway. The peril comes to an end there when Andrew finally tracks them down. **90m/C; DVD.** Emmanuelle Vaugier; Ivan Sergei; Allie Gonino; Sean Patrick Flanery; Elisabeth Rohm; Thomas Calabro; ***D:*** Peter Sullivan; ***W:*** Jeff Barmash; ***C:*** Roberto Schein; ***M:*** Matthew Janszen. **CABLE**

The Hidden Blade 1/2 *Kakushi Ken: Oni No Tsume* **2004 (R)** Set in 1861, Katagiri (Nagase) is a lower-caste samurai who has a forbidden love for serving girl Kie (Matsu), who he rescues from domestic abuse. He's also troubled by being ordered to kill an old comrade, Hazama (Ozawa), who plotted against the Shogunate and has escaped from confinement. Based on the short stories of Shuhei Fujisawa. The Japanese title, "Hidden Blade: The Devil's Claw," refers to a unique sword maneuver. Japanese with subtitles. **132m/C; DVD, Blu-Ray.** *JP* Masatoshi Nagase; Min Tanaka; Nenji Kobayashi; Ken Ogata; Takako Matsu; Hidetaka Yoshioka; Yukioshi Ozawa; Tomoko Obata; Reiko Takashima; ***D:*** Yoji Yamada; ***W:*** Yoji Yamada; Yishitaka Yamamoto; ***C:*** Mutsuo Naganuma; ***M:*** Isao Tomita.

Hidden City **1987** A film archivist and a statistician become drawn into a conspiracy when a piece of revealing film is spliced onto the end of an innocuous government tape. **112m/C; VHS, DVD.** Charles Dance; Cassie Stuart; Alex Norton; Tusse Silberg; Bill Paterson; ***D:*** Stephen Poliakoff.

Hidden Figures **2017 (PG)** This surprise crowd pleaser tells the untold story of three African-American women crucial in the formative years of America's space program. Henson, Monae, and Spencer headline a fantastic ensemble as the mathematician trio working on the launch of John Glenn into orbit in 1962, and, more treacherously, his return to Earth. Of course, the ladies face institutional sexism and racism, but director Melfi balances the message with a truly entertaining piece of drama. It helps that his cast is uniformly talented, even winning the Screen Actors Guild award for Best Ensemble. **127m/C; DVD, Blu-Ray.** Taraji P. Henson; Octavia Spencer; Janelle Monáe; Kevin Costner; Kirsten Dunst; Jim Parsons; ***D:*** Theodore Melfi; ***W:*** Theodore Melfi; Allison Schroeder; ***C:*** Mandy Walker; ***M:*** Benjamin Wallfisch; Pharrell Williams; Hans Zimmer. Screen Actors Guild '16: Cast.

The Hidden Fortress 1/2 *Kakushi Toride No San Akunin; Three Rascals in the Hidden Fortress; Three Bad Men in the Hidden Fortress* **1958** Kurosawa's tale of a warrior who protects a princess from warring feudal lords. An inspiration for George Lucas' "Star Wars" series and deserving of its excellent reputation. In Japanese with English subtitles. **139m/B; VHS, DVD, Blu-Ray.** *JP* Toshiro Mifune; Misa(ko) Uehara; Kamatari (Keita) Fujiwara; Susumu Fujita; Eiko Miyoshi; Takashi Shimura; Kichijiro Ueda; Koji Mitsui; Minoru Chiaki; Toshiko Higuchi; Shiten Ohashi; ***D:*** Akira Kurosawa; ***W:*** Akira Kurosawa; Shinobu Hashimoto; Ryuzo Kikushima; Hideo Oguni; ***C:*** Kazuo Yamazaki; ***M:*** Masaru Sato. Berlin Intl. Film Fest. '59: Director (Kurosawa).

Hidden Guns **1956** Above-average tale of father-and-son lawmen out to reform a town and put the bad guys away. When dad is killed, son goes up against the villain alone. A Greek chorus adds an interesting twist to the action. Erich von Stroheim Jr. is listed as assistant director. **66m/B; VHS, DVD.** Bruce Bennett; Richard Arlen; John Carradine; Faron Young; Angie Dickinson; Guinn "Big Boy" Williams; ***D:*** Albert C. Gannaway.

The Hidden Hand 1/2 **1942** The fun is in seeing the crazy brother/sister Channings carry out their deadly plans. Wealthy Lorinda fakes her death just to watch her heirs battle it out. She wants her brother John's help in killing off their greedy relatives and, fortunately for her, he's just escaped from an insane asylum and is returning home. Peter Thorne is the spoilsport who's out to stop the murders. **67m/B; DVD.** Craig Stevens; Milton Parsons; Cecil Cunningham; Elisabeth Fraser; Frank Wilcox; Roland Drew; Tom Stevenson; Julie Bishop; Ruth Ford; Willie Best; ***D:*** Ben Stoloff; ***W:*** Raymond L. Schrock; Anthony Coldeway; ***C:*** Henry Sharp.

Hidden in America 1/2 **1996 (PG-13)** Bill Januson (Bridges) has lost his autoplant job because of downsizing and his wife to cancer. His savings exhausted and his prospects bleak, Januson struggles to put food on the table for his two kids, who increasingly begin to suffer the effects of poverty. Produced in conjunction with the End Hunger Network, whose co-founder, Jeff Bridges, has a cameo. **96m/C; VHS, DVD.** Beau Bridges; Bruce Davison; Jena Malone; Shelton Dane; Alice Krige; Josef Sommer; Frances McDormand; ***Cameo(s):*** Jeff Bridges; ***D:*** Martin Bell; ***W:*** Peter Silverman; Michael deGuzman; ***C:*** James R. Bagdonas; ***M:*** Mason Daring. **CABLE**

Hidden in Silence **1996** Lifetime movie based on a true story. Before the Germans invade Poland and the Nazis set up the Jewish ghetto, the Diamant family transfer their goods to their teenaged Christian maid, Stefania 'Fusia' Podgorska (Martin). She ends up hiding 13 Polish Jews in her apartment attic for more than two years until two German nurses are assigned to board with her and it seems all will be revealed. **90m/C; DVD.** Kellie Martin; Marc Warren; Tom Radcliffe; Marion Ross; Jan Nemejovsky; David Nykl; Anna Geislerova; ***D:*** Richard A. Colla; ***W:*** Stephanie Liss; ***C:*** Michael D. Margulies; ***M:*** Dennis McCarthy. **CABLE**

Hidden in the Woods **2016** A thriller about two sisters who struggle to escape their abusive past. In an isolated region of Chile, two sisters and their mentally challenged brother have been kept from society and tormented by their father, a drug dealer. Their efforts to escape his clutches results in the murders of two police officers. Though their father is jailed, the siblings must face their uncle, Costello, a drug kingpin who is also mentally unhinged. The siblings face his wrath because he believes that they know where his merchandise is hidden. To find them, he sends trained killers who find them an unexpected challenge. **98m/C; DVD, Streaming, Download.** Michael Biehn; William Forsythe; Jennifer Blanc; Chris Browning; Nick Bateman; ***D:*** Patricio Valladares; ***W:*** Bradley Marcus; Kevin Marcus; ***C:*** Patricio Valladares; Shawn Welling; ***M:*** Luigi Seviroli. **VIDEO**

A Hidden Life 1/2 **2019 (PG-13)** During World War II, German farmer Franz Jagerstatter (Diehl) lives a hardscrabble life as a farmer with his wife in a small Alpine village. After being drafted and serving in the German army early in the conflict, the devout Catholic is called up again in 1943 by which time he has two young daughters. Because of the nature of Nazi Germany's campaign, including genocide, Franz becomes a conscientious objector and pays a heavy price for defying the state. Based on a true story, the drama is slow-paced but brilliantly complex and masterfully edited. **173m/C; DVD, Blu-Ray.** August Diehl; Valerie Pachner; Tobias Moretti; Bruno Ganz; Matthias Schoenaerts; ***D:*** Terrence Malick; ***W:*** Terrence Malick; ***C:*** Jörg Widmer; ***M:*** James Newton Howard.

Hidden Places **2006** Widowed mom Eliza (Penny) is struggling through the Depression on her father-in-law's farm when he suddenly dies. Eliza has to get in the orange crop or risk foreclosure on the debt-ridden property. Her Aunt Batty (Jones) says to have faith and when charming veteran Gabe (Gedrick) shows up, he may be the answer to their prayers. Gabe agrees to help out with the harvest and falling in love with the young widow may be his bonus. Based on the novel by Lynn Austin. **?m/CDVD.** Sydney Penny; Jason Gedrick; Shirley Jones; Barry Corbin; Tom Bosley; John Diehl; ***D:*** Yelena Lanskaya; ***W:*** Robert Tate Miller; ***C:*** James W. Wrenn; ***M:*** Roger Bellon. **CABLE**

The Hidden Room *Obsession* **1949** A doctor finds out about his wife's affair and decides to get revenge on her lover. He kidnaps him, imprisons him in a cellar, and decides to kill him—slowly. Tense melodrama. **98m/B; VHS, DVD.** *GB* Robert Newton; Sally Gray; Naunton Wayne; Phil Brown; Olga Lindo; Russell Waters; James Harcourt; Allan Jeayes; Stanley Baker; ***D:*** Edward Dmytryk; ***W:*** Alec Coppel; ***C:*** C.M. Pennington-Richards; ***M:*** Nino Rota.

The Hide **2008** Fussy, middle-aged bird-watcher Roy Tunt has come to a remote shack on the Suffolk marshes in order to spot the last native bird species on his checklist. Apparently the place isn't remote enough since Roy's quiet day is interrupted by menacing Dave, who carries a gun and may be a killer. Bad weather forces the two men to remain in the hide, so they start talking. Adapted by Tim Whitnall from his play "The Sociable Plover." **82m/C; DVD.** *GB* Alex MacQueen; Phil Campbell; ***D:*** Marek Losey; ***W:*** Tim Whitnall; ***C:*** George Richmond; ***M:*** Debbie Wiseman.

Hide 1/2 **2008 (R)** Part torture porn, part crime drama. Betty and Billy fancy themselves the modern-day Bonnie and Clyde until Billy is captured after gunning down an innocent victim during a bank robbery. An eventual prison transfer leads to Betty springing her lover but Billy has gotten remorseful over the years and tells Betty someone is violently targeting those close to him in revenge for their crimes. **93m/C; DVD.** *CA* Rachel Miner; Christian Kane; Polly Shannon; Beth Grant; ***D:*** K.C. Bascombe; ***W:*** Greg Rosati; ***C:*** Pablo Schverdfinger; ***M:*** Eliane Katz. **VIDEO**

Hide and Go Shriek **1987 (R)** Several high school seniors are murdered one by one during a graduation party. Also available in an unrated, gorier version. **90m/C; VHS, DVD, Blu-Ray.** Annette Sinclair; Brittain Frye; Rebunkah Jones; ***D:*** Skip Schoolnik.

Hide and Seek 1/2 *Cord* **2000 (R)** Pregnant Ann (Hannah) is kidnapped by a crazy childless couple (Tilly and Gallo) and it's no kids' game when husband Jack (Greenwood) tries to find her. **100m/C; VHS, DVD.** Daryl Hannah; Jennifer Tilly; Vincent Gallo; Bruce Greenwood; Johanna Black; ***D:*** Sidney J. Furie; ***W:*** Joel Hladecek; Yas Takata; ***M:*** Robert Carli. **VIDEO**

Hide and Seek **2005 (R)** Nine-year-old Emily (Fanning) witnesses her mother's bloody suicide. Her father (De Niro), a psychologist, decides to take the traumatized girl from bustling Manhattan to a peaceful, rural community to help her cope. Once settled in, it's pretty clear that Emily isn't coping very well. Her issues manifest in the form of an imaginary friend named Charlie, who does some rather scary things when he's angry. Stellar cast and high production values can't hide the fact that it's still a run-of-the-mill horror movie. Fanning sports the best child goth look since Christina Ricci's Wednesday Addams. **100m/C; DVD.** Robert De Niro; Dakota Fanning; Famke Janssen; Elisabeth Shue; Amy Irving; Dylan Baker; Melissa Leo; Robert John Burke; David Chandler; Molly Grant Kallins; ***D:*** John Polson; ***W:*** Ari Schlossberg; ***C:*** Dariusz Wolski; ***M:*** John Ottman.

Hide Away *A Year In Mooring* **2011 (PG-13)** Meditative, somewhat pretentious character drama where the characters are nameless. After suffering a traumatic event, a businessman tries to cope by attempting to fix up a decrepit sailboat docked in a Northern Michigan harbor town. **88m/C; DVD.** Josh(ua) Lucas; Ayelet Zurer; James Cromwell; Jon Tenney; Taylor Nichols; ***D:*** Chris Eyre; ***W:*** Peter Vanderwall; ***C:*** Elliot Davis; ***M:*** Tony Morales; Edward Rogers.

Hide in Plain Sight **1980 (PG)** A distraught blue-collar worker searches for his children who disappeared when his ex-wife and her mobster husband are given new identities by federal agents. Caan's fine directorial debut is based on a true story. **96m/C; VHS, DVD.** James Caan; Jill Eikenberry; Robert Viharo; Kenneth McMillan; Josef Sommer; Danny Aiello; ***D:*** James Caan.

Hideaway **1994 (R)** Hodge podge movie finds Hatch Harrison (Goldblum) brought back from the other side after suffering injuries from a near-fatal car accident. He returns with the ability to psychically connect with Vassago (Sisto), a sadistic serial killer of young girls. Coincidentally, Harrison has a teenage daughter, Regina (Silverstone), and Vassago has her lined up as his next victim. The visual effects of spirits floating down a cosmic vortex are entertaining, but plot originality must have been hidden away to make room for the nifty special effects. Based on a novel by Dean R. Koontz. **103m/C; VHS, DVD.** Jeff Goldblum; Christine Lahti; Alicia Silverstone; Jeremy Sisto; Rae Dawn Chong; ***D:*** Brett Leonard; ***W:*** Andrew Kevin Walker; Neal Jimenez; ***C:*** Gale Tattersall; ***M:*** Trevor Jones.

Hideaway *The Refuge* **2009** Minor Ozon has heroin addict Mousse (Carre) awakening from a coma after an OD to learn that her junkie boyfriend Louis (Poupaud) is dead and she is pregnant. The moody Mousse semi cleans up and decides to go through with the pregnancy. She's staying in the country when Louis' gay younger brother Paul (Choisy) shows up in an effort at family bonding though nothing terribly unexpected happens. French with subtitles. **88m/C; DVD.** *FR* Isabelle Carre; Louis-Ronan Choisy; Pierre Louis-Calixte; Melvil Poupaud; ***D:*** Francois Ozon; ***W:*** Francois Ozon; Mathieu Hippeau; ***C:*** Mathias Raafluab; ***M:*** Louis-Ronan Choisy.

The Hideaways 1/2 *From the Mixed-Up Files of Mrs. Basil E. Frankweiler* **1973 (G)** A 12-year-old girl and her younger brother run away and hide in the Metropolitan Museum of Art. The girl becomes enamored of a piece of sculpture and sets out to discover its creator. Based on the children's novel by E.L. Konigsburg. **105m/C; VHS, DVD.** Richard Mulligan; George Rose; Ingrid Bergman; Sally Prager; Johnny Doran; Madeline Kahn; ***D:*** Fielder Cook.

Hideous 1/2 **1997 (R)** Eccentric collector's greatest prize is a seemingly petrified toxic waste mutant that's not so petrified afterall. It manages to come to life and even spawn little mutants to go on a killing spree. **82m/C; VHS, DVD, Blu-Ray.** Jacqueline Lovell; Michael Citrinti; Rhonda Griffin; Mel Johnson, Jr.; Traci May; Jerry O'Donnell; ***D:*** Charles Band; ***W:*** Benjamin Carr; ***M:*** Richard Band.

Hideous Kinky 1/2 **1999 (R)** Julia (Winslet) is a free-spirited single mom who decides to leave London and take her two daughters, Bea and Lucy, to live in Morocco in 1972. She gets by on sales of homemade dolls and the occasional check from the girls' father. Julia believes that a conversion to the Sufi life will solve her problems, while Bea would rather they settle into a "normal" life. Julia meets, and has a passionate affair with, juggler and sometime con man Bilal, whom the girls adopt as a surrogate father figure. Winslet plays her character's mixture of naivete and motherly concern well, and looks good doing it, as does the whole movie. The Moroccan locales are brilliantly displayed. Character development and consistent narrative are sometimes lacking. **97m/C; VHS, DVD.** *GB FR* Kate Winslet; Said Taghmaoui; Bella Riza; Carrie Mullan; Pierre Clementi; Abigail Cruttenden; Sira Stampe; ***D:*** Gilles Mackinnon; ***W:*** Billy Mackinnon; ***C:*** John de Borman; ***M:*** John Keane.

Hideous Sun Demon 1/2 *Blood on His Lips; Terror from the Sun; The Sun Demon* **1959** A physicist exposed to radiation must stay out of sunlight or he will turn into a scaly, lizard-like creature. Includes previews of coming attractions from classic sci-fi films. **75m/B; VHS, DVD.** Robert Clarke; Patricia Manning; Nan Peterson; Patrick Whyte; Peter Similuk; Fred La Porta; Robert Garry; Del Courtney; ***D:*** Robert Clarke; Thomas Bontross; ***W:*** Doane R. Hoag; E. S. Seeley, Jr.; ***C:*** Vilis Lapenieks; John Morrill; Stan Follis; ***M:*** John Seely.

Hiding Out **1987 (PG-13)** A young stockbroker testifies against the Mafia and must find a place to hide in order to avoid being killed. He winds up at his cousin's high school in Delaware, but can he really go through all these teenage troubles once again? **99m/C; VHS, DVD.** Jon Cryer; Keith Coogan; Gretchen Cryer; Annabeth Gish; Tim Quill; ***D:*** Bob Giraldi; ***W:*** Jeff Rothberg; Joe Menosky; ***C:*** Daniel Pearl; ***M:*** Anne Dudley.

The Hiding Place **1975** True story of two Dutch Christian sisters sent to a concentration camp for hiding Jews during WWII. Film is uneven but good cast pulls it through. Based on the Corrie Ten Boom book and produced by Billy Graham's Evangelistic Association. **145m/C; VHS, DVD.** Julie Harris; Eileen Heckart; Arthur O'Connell; Jeanette Clift; ***D:*** James F. Collier.

High & Low 1/2 *Tengoku To Jigoku* **1962 (R)** Fine Japanese film noir about a wealthy businessman who is being blackmailed by kidnappers who claim to have his son. When he discovers that they have mistakenly taken his chauffeur's son he must decide whether to face financial ruin or risk the life of a young boy. Based on an Ed McBain novel. In Japanese with English subtitles. **143m/B; VHS, DVD, Blu-Ray.** *JP* Toshiro Mifune; Tatsuya Mihashi; Tatsuya Nakadai; ***D:*** Akira Kurosawa; ***W:*** Akira Kurosawa; Evan Hunter; Ryuzo Kikushima; Hideo Oguni; ***C:*** Asakazu Nakai; Takao Saito; ***M:*** Masaru Sato.

The High and the Mighty **1954** One of Wayne's most sought-after films finally makes it to DVD, as it took 10 years for Wayne's daughter-in-law to restore a negative found in a pool of water in a warehouse. Wayne is Dan Roman, who steps up to the situation on a trans-Pacific airline flight in deep trouble. In a device that'll be familiar to viewers of "Lost," many flashbacks give backstory on passengers and crew. Unfortunately, this serves mostly to slow down the action and suspense of their current situation. Excellent performance by an all-star cast cover for some of the more dated elements of the film, which was, after all, a precursor to the popular disaster flicks of the 70s. **148m/C; DVD.** John Wayne; Claire Trevor; Laraine Day; Robert Stack; Jan Sterling; Phil Harris; Robert Newton; David Brian; Paul Kelly; Sidney Blackmer; Julie Bishop; John Howard; Wally Brown; William Campbell; Ann Doran; John Qualen; Paul Fix; Joy Kim; George Chandler; Douglas Fowley; Regis Toomey; Carl "Alfalfa" Switzer; William Hopper; William Schallert; Julie Mitchum; ***D:*** William A. Wellman; ***W:*** Ernest K. Gann; ***C:*** Archie Stout; ***M:*** Dimitri Tiomkin. Oscars '54: Orig. Dramatic Score; Golden Globes '55: Support. Actress (Sterling).

High Anxiety **1977 (PG)** Brooks tries hard to please in this low-brow parody of Hitchcock films employing dozens of references to films like "Psycho," "Spellbound," "The Birds," and "Vertigo." Tells the tale of a height-fearing psychiatrist caught up in a murder mystery. The title song performed a la Sinatra by Brooks is one of the film's high moments. Brooks also has a lot of fun with Hitchcockian camera movements. Uneven (What? Brooks?) but amusing tribute. **92m/C; VHS, DVD, Blu-Ray.** Mel Brooks; Madeline Kahn; Cloris Leachman; Harvey Korman; Ron Carey; Howard Morris; Dick Van Patten; ***D:*** Mel Brooks; ***W:*** Mel Brooks; Ron Clark; Barry Levinson; Rudy DeLuca.

High Art **1998 (R)** A trio of women play romantic games in New York's art community. Ambitious magazine editor-in-training Syd (Mitchell) has a boyfriend, James (Mann), but feels something's missing. Noticing a leak in her apartment ceiling, Syd heads upstairs to confront her neighbor and meets Lucy Berliner (Sheedy), a once-celebrated, now-retired photographer with a heroin problem and an equally hooked girlfriend, Greta (Clarkson). Syd and Lucy begin a friendship that leads to an affair, while Syd also wants to revitalize Lucy's career. Ex-Brat Packer Sheedy's the real revelation with her standout performance. **102m/C; VHS, DVD.** Radha Mitchell; Ally Sheedy; Patricia Clarkson; Tammy Grimes; Gabriel Mann; William Sage; David Thornton; Anh Duong; ***D:*** Lisa Cholodenko; ***W:*** Lisa Cholodenko; ***C:*** Tami Reiker; ***M:*** Craig Wedren. Ind. Spirit '99: Actress (Sheedy); L.A. Film Critics '98: Actress (Sheedy); Natl. Soc. Film Critics '98: Actress (Sheedy); Sundance '98: Screenplay.

High Barbaree 1/2 **1947** Ponderous romantic drama. Navy pilot Alec Brooke's (Johnson) plane is shot down during a Pacific bombing mission and only he and wounded comrade Joe Moore (Mitchell) survive. As they drift in the ocean, hoping to be rescued, Alec tells Joe his grandfather's stories about the mythic title island and about his on-and-off romance with Nancy (Allyson). **91m/B; DVD.** Van Johnson; June Allyson; Cameron Mitchell; Thomas Mitchell; Marilyn Maxwell; Henry Hull; Claude Jarman, Jr.; ***D:*** Jack Conway; ***W:*** Whitfield Cook; Anne Morrison Chapin; Cyril Hume; ***C:*** Sidney Wagner; ***M:*** Herbert Stothart.

The High Bright Sun 1/2 *McGuire, Go Home!* **1965** Weakly-developed drama with a good cast. In 1954, American archeology student Juno (Strasberg) is in Cyprus as guerrillas are attacking occupying British forces. She accidentally learns the whereabouts of fighter Haghios (Chakiris), but doesn't tell British intelligence officer McGuire (Bogarde). Haghios is certain Juno has betrayed him and wants to kill her, so McGuire helps her hide and the two fall in love. More trouble follows. **115m/C; DVD.** *UK* Dirk Bogarde; Susan Strasberg; George Chakiris; Denholm Elliott; George Pastell; Gregoire Aslan; ***D:*** Ralph Thomas; ***W:*** Ian Stuart Black; ***C:*** Ernest Steward; ***M:*** Angelo Francesco Lavagnino.

High Command 1/2 **1937** To save his daughter from an ugly scandal, the British general of an isolated Colonial African outpost traps a blackmailer's killer. **84m/B; VHS, DVD.** *GB* Lionel Atwill; Lucie Mannheim; James Mason; ***D:*** Thorold Dickinson.

The High Cost of Living **2010** Nathalie (Blais), a young pregnant woman, loses her child in a hit-and-run accident caused by drunken prescription-drug dealer, Henry (Braff). Her husband Michel (Labbe) is unable to cope with the tragedy, leaving Nathalie alone and devastated. When she encounters Henry, she unknowingly views him as an engaging guardian angel in her hour of need. Suspense builds with the police on Henry's heels. Director (and writer) Chow's first feature is a melancholy exploration of the painful sacrifices in life. The likeable leads struggle to overcome a lack in cinematic style. **92m/C; On Demand.** *CA* Zach Braff; Isabelle Blais; Patrick Labbe; Aimee Lee; Julian Lo; ***D:*** Deborah Chow; ***W:*** Deborah Chow; ***C:*** Claudine Sauve; ***M:*** Normand Corbeil.

High Crimes 1/2 **2002 (PG-13)** Military courtroom thriller is only average but does have Freeman, who's always worth watching. He's reteamed with "Kiss the Girls" co-star Judd, who plays spunky California attorney Claire Kubik. Claire gets a big surprise when her contractor hubby Tom (Caviezel) is suddenly arrested by the FBI and sent to a military prison. Turns out Tom, then known as Ron Chapman, was in an elite Marine special unit and is accused of a 1988 civilian massacre in El Salvador. She looks to recovering alcoholic and ex-JAG lawyer Charlie Grimes (Freeman) for assistance but sinister plots are afoot. Based on the 1998 novel by Joseph Finder. **115m/C; VHS, DVD.** Ashley Judd; James (Jim) Caviezel; Morgan Freeman; Amanda Peet; Tom Bower; Adam Scott; Bruce Davison; Michael Gaston; Juan Carlos Hernandez; Jude Ciccolella; Michael Shannon; ***D:*** Carl Franklin; ***W:*** Yuri Zeltser; Cary Bickley; ***C:*** Theo van de Sande; ***M:*** Graeme Revell.

The High Crusade 1/2 **1992 (PG-13)** A group of 13th-century English crusaders are heading for the Holy Land when they're interrupted on their journey by an alien spacecraft. They overpower the space guys and take over the vessel, hoping it will take them to Jerusalem, but since the spacecraft's on autopilot, the knights wind up heading for the aliens' home planet instead. **100m/C; VHS, DVD.** *GB GE* John Rhys-Davies; Michael Des Barres; Rick Overton; ***D:*** Holger Neuhauser.

High Fidelity **2000 (R)** Frears, Cusack, and the writing team from "Grosse Pointe Blank" successfully bring Nick Hornby's 1995 novel to the screen, transplanting it from London to Chicago in the process. Cusack is Rob, a stuck-in-adolescence record store owner who just broke up with Laura (Hjejle), his long-time, live-in love. This gets him to thinking about his Top Five All-Time Breakups. Cue flashbacks. It also sends him on some hilarious conversations with his employees: know-it-all Barry (Black) who wields his musical tastes like a weapon, and Dick (Louiso), who's bashful to the point of invisibility. Cusack does his usual fine job, but Black and Louiso take over whenever they're on screen. **113m/C; VHS, DVD, Blu-Ray.** John Cusack; Todd Louiso; Jack Black; Iben Hjejle; Tim Robbins; Joan Cusack; Lisa Bonet; Catherine Zeta-Jones; Lili Taylor; Natasha Gregson Wagner; Sara Gilbert; Chris Rehmann; Ben Carr; Joelle Carter; Bruce Springsteen; ***D:*** Stephen Frears; ***W:*** John Cusack; D.V. DeVincentis; Steve Pink; Scott Rosenberg; ***C:*** Seamus McGarvey; ***M:*** Howard Shore.

High Flyers 1/2 **1937** The last film for the Wheeler & Woolsey team (Woolsey died in 1938) has some comic moments but is generally dull. Jerry and Pierre operate an airplane amusement park ride and are amateur pilots. A shady friend asks them to fly his seaplane to pick up a package but when the boys snoop, they discover stolen diamonds and cocaine, which they accidentally snort. This causes them to crash the plane on the Arlington estate and while things are being sorted out, the family dog buries the jewels! **70m/B; DVD.** Bert Wheeler; Robert Woolsey; Lupe Velez; Marjorie Lord; Margaret Dumont; Paul Harvey; Jack Carson; ***D:*** Edward F. (Eddie) Cline; ***W:*** Bert Granet; Byron Morgan; Benny Rubin; ***C:*** Jack MacKenzie; ***M:*** Roy Webb.

High Flying Bird 1/2 **2019** High powered player's agent Ray (Holland) is struggling financially during an NBA lockout. He is not getting paid because the players he represents, including number one draft pick Erick (Gregg), are not getting paid. When Ray learns that his salary and expense accounts have been frozen for the duration of the lockout, he puts a plan into action involving the NBA players union, owners, and other players to end the labor standoff. Shot on iPhones, it is an energetic and timely reflection on the concerns of modern athletes. **90m/C; DVD.** Andre Holland; Melvin Gregg; Zazie Beetz; Bill Duke; Zachary Quinto; ***D:*** Steven Soderbergh; ***W:*** Tarell McCraney; ***C:*** Steven Soderbergh; ***M:*** David Wilder Savage. **VIDEO**

High Heels *Tacones Lejanos* **1991 (R)** An outrageous combination murder-melodrama-comedy from Almodovar. Rebecca is a TV anchorwoman in Madrid whose flamboyant singer/actress mother has returned to the city for a concert. Rebecca happens to be married to one of her mother's not-so-ex-flames. When her husband winds up dead, Rebecca confesses to his murder during her newscast—but is she telling the truth or just covering up for mom? Mix in a drag queen/judge, a dancing chorus of women prison inmates, and a peculiar police detective, and see if the plot convolutions make sense. In Spanish with English subtitles. **113m/C; VHS, DVD.** *SP* Victoria Abril; Marisa Paredes; Miguel Bose; Feodor Atkine; Bibi Andersen; Rocio Munoz; ***D:*** Pedro Almodóvar; ***W:*** Pedro Almodóvar; ***C:*** Alfredo Mayo; ***M:*** Ryuichi Sakamoto. Cesar '93: Foreign Film.

High Heels and Low Lifes **2001 (R)** Brit nurse Shannon (Driver) and American actress Frances (McCormack) overhear a plot to rob a London safe deposit box center and immediately go to the cops. When the cops seem uninterested, the girls decide to blackmail the crooks into giving them a cut. Nice premise and an enjoyable performance by Driver are wasted by Smith's flat direction, which misses almost all comic payoff opportunities in the script. **85m/C; VHS, DVD, Blu-Ray.** *US GB* Minnie Driver; Mary McCormack; Kevin McNally; Mark Williams; Danny

Dyer; Michael Gambon; Kevin Eldon; Len Collin; Darren Boyd; Julian Wadham; *D:* Mel Smith; *W:* Kim Fuller; *C:* Steven Chivers; *M:* Charlie Mole.

High Hopes 1988 A moving yet nasty satiric comedy about a pair of ex-hippies maintaining their counterculture lifestyle in Margaret Thatcher's England, as they watch the signs of conservative "progress" overtake them and their geriatric, embittered Mum. Hilarious and mature. **110m/C; VHS, DVD.** *GB* Philip Davis; Ruth Sheen; Edna Dore; Philip Jackson; Heather Tobias; Lesley Manville; David Bamber; *D:* Mike Leigh; *W:* Mike Leigh; *C:* Roger Pratt; *M:* Andrew Dixon; Rachel Portman.

High Life **2009 (R)** Ensemble crime comedy (set in 1983) with a bunch of ex-con loser/drug abusers who decide to rob a bank ATM. Since their brains (presuming they ever had any) are fried, the inexpertly-planned criminal enterprise goes wrong. Based on Lee MacDougall's 1996 play, which he adapted for the screen. Filmed in Winnipeg, Manitoba though the city goes unnamed. **80m/C; DVD.** *CA* Timothy Olyphant; Stephen McIntyre; Joe Anderson; Rossif Sutherland; Sarah Constible; Brittany Scobie; Mark McKinney; Ernesto Griffiths; *D:* Gary Yates; *W:* Lee MacDougall; *C:* Michael Marshall; *M:* Jonathan Goldsmith.

High Life ½ **2018 (R)** In deep space, astronaut Monte (Pattinson) is the lone adult on a ship he is trying to keep going while caring for toddler Willow (Lindsay). It is revealed that he was part a group of prisoners, primarily younger offenders, who were sent into deep space to do studies intended to benefit humanity. Led by the immoral Dr. Dibs (Binoche), Monte, Boyse (Goth), Tcherny (Benjamin), and others must do her bidding on experiments, often related to sex and reproduction, despite an uncertain fate. A thoughtful work of arthouse sci fi, the film is at once challenging, meaningful, and disturbing. **110m/C; DVD, Blu-Ray.** *UK FR GE PL US* Robert Pattinson; Juliette Binoche; Andre Benjamin; Mia Goth; Agata Buzek; *D:* Claire Denis; *W:* Claire Denis; Jean-Pol Fargeau; Geoff Cox; *C:* Yorick Le Saux; *M:* Stuart A. Staples; Tindersticks.

High Lonesome ½ **1950** Barrymore is a drifter in Big Bend country, suspected in a series of mysterious murders. While he is being held captive, the real killers—thought dead—return to exact revenge on those they hold responsible for the range war in which they were wounded. This was LeMay's only stint as a director. **80m/C; VHS, DVD.** John Drew (Blythe) Barrymore, Jr.; Chill Wills; John Archer; Lois Butler; Kristine Miller; Basil Ruysdael; Jack Elam; *D:* Alan LeMay; *W:* Alan LeMay; *C:* William Howard Greene; *M:* Rudolph (Rudy) Schrager.

High Noon **1952** Landmark Western about Hadleyville town marshal Will Kane (Cooper) who faces four professional killers alone, after being abandoned to his fate by the gutless townspeople who profess to admire him. Cooper is the ultimate hero figure, his sheer presence overwhelming. Note the continuing use of the ballad written by Dimitri Tiomkin, "Do Not Forsake Me, Oh My Darlin'" (sung by Tex Ritter) to heighten the tension and action. **85m/B; VHS, DVD, Blu-Ray.** Gary Cooper; Grace Kelly; Lloyd Bridges; Lon Chaney, Jr.; Thomas Mitchell; Otto Kruger; Katy Jurado; Lee Van Cleef; Harry (Henry) Morgan; Robert J. Wilke; Sheb Wooley; *D:* Fred Zinnemann; *W:* Carl Foreman; *C:* Floyd Crosby; *M:* Dimitri Tiomkin. Oscars '52: Actor (Cooper), Film Editing, Orig. Dramatic Score, Song ("High Noon (Do Not Forsake Me, Oh My Darlin')"); AFI '98: Top 100; Golden Globes '53: Actor--Drama (Cooper), Score, Support. Actress (Jurado); Natl. Film Reg. '89; N.Y. Film Critics '52: Director (Zinnemann), Film.

High Noon ½ **2000 (PG-13)** Generally faithful but needless TV remake of the 1952 western classic. Stoic marshal Will Kane (Skerritt), having just married the Quaker Amy (Thompson), is about to give up his badge when he learns that outlaw Frank Miller (Madsen) will be coming in on the noon train with revenge on his mind. Everyone thinks Will should just skedaddle out of town and save them all some grief but, hey, he's a hero and has to do what's right! **93m/C; VHS, DVD.** Tom Skerritt; Susanna Thompson; Reed Edward Diamond; Maria Conchita Alonso; Michael Madsen; Dennis Weaver; August Schellenberg; *D:* Rod Hardy; *W:* Carl Foreman; T.S. Cook; *C:* Robert McLachlan; *M:* Allyn Ferguson. **CABLE**

High Noon **2009** Phoebe McNamara (de Ravin) is trying to juggle her high-pressure job as a police hostage negotiator with her life as a single mother and caregiver to her own agoraphobic mother, Essie (Shepherd). So she's not interested when bar owner Duncan (Sergei) starts flirting. Then Phoebe gets threatening messages and realizes that dealing with a psycho (who's obsessed with the Gary Cooper movie "High Noon") means getting some help. Romantic suspense from Lifetime that's based on the book by Nora Roberts. **90m/C; DVD.** emile de ravin; Ivan Sergei; Cybill Shepherd; Brian Markinson; Ty Olsson; Olivia Cheng; Patrick Sabongui; *D:* Peter Markle; *W:* Terri Kopp; *C:* Joel Ransom; *M:* Stuart M. Thomas. **CABLE**

High Plains Drifter ½ **1973 (R)** A surreal, violent western focusing on a drifter who defends a town from gunmen intent on meting out death. One of Eastwood's most stylistic directorial efforts, indebted to his "Man with No Name" days with Sergio Leone. Laser format is letterboxed and includes chapter stops and the original theatrical trailer. **105m/C; VHS, DVD, Blu-Ray.** Clint Eastwood; Verna Bloom; Mitchell Ryan; Marianna Hill; Jack Ging; Stefan Gierasch; Walter Barnes; *D:* Clint Eastwood; *W:* Ernest Tidyman; Dean Riesner; *C:* Bruce Surtees; *M:* Dee Barton.

High Plains Invaders **2009** Generally dull sci fi western—with bad CGI—that's part of the "Maneater" cable movie series. Train robber Sam Danville (Marsters) has a noose around his neck when the town is besieged by a spaceship full of nasty but not-too-bright aliens. The human survivors hide out in the jail while trying to figure out how to defeat the creatures. **97m/C; DVD.** James Marsters; Cindy Sampson; Sanny Van Heteren; Sebastian Knapp; Adrianna Butoi; Angus MacInnes; Antony Byrne; *D:* Kristoffer Tabori; *W:* Richard Beattie; *C:* Pierre Jodoin; *M:* James Gelfand.

High-Rise **2016 (R)** Working from J.G. Ballard's hit 1975 novel of the same name, Wheatley makes a gorgeous film, with a great cast, but it feels hollow. The title refers to the building in which the most well-off, wealthy residents reside on the top floors and the poorest occupy the lower floors. The architectural symbol of society collapses on itself as the occupants of the high-rise resort to infighting and revolution. Hiddleston is typically fantastic but there's never much of a reason to care about what's happening here outside of how pretty its vision of the end of society happens to be. **119m/C; DVD, Blu-Ray.** Tom Hiddleston; Jeremy Irons; Sienna Miller; Luke Evans; Elisabeth Moss; *D:* Ben Wheatley; *W:* Amy Jump; *C:* Laurie Rose; *M:* Clint Mansell.

High Risk ½ **1981 (R)** Improbable action-adventure of four unemployed Americans who battle foreign armies, unscrupulous gunrunners, and jungle bandits in a harrowing attempt to steal $5 million from an expatriate American drug dealer living in the peaceful splendor of his Columbian villa. Interesting in its own run-on way. **94m/C; VHS, DVD.** James Brolin; Anthony Quinn; Lindsay Wagner; James Coburn; Ernest Borgnine; Bruce Davison; Cleavon Little; Chick Vennera; *D:* Stewart Raffill; *W:* Stewart Raffill; *C:* Alex Phillips, Jr.; *M:* Mark Snow.

High Road to China **1983 (PG)** A hard-drinking former WWI air ace is recruited by a young heiress who must find her father before his ex-partner takes over his business. Post-"Raiders of the Lost Ark" thrills and romance, but without that tale's panache. **105m/C; VHS, DVD, Blu-Ray.** Bess Armstrong; Tom Selleck; Jack Weston; Robert Morley; Wilford Brimley; Brian Blessed; *D:* Brian G. Hutton; *M:* John Barry.

High Rolling in a Hot Corvette *High Rolling* **1977 (PG)** Two carnival workers leave their jobs and hit the road in search of adventure and excitement, eventually turning to crime. **82m/C; VHS, DVD.** *AU* Joseph Bottoms; Greg Taylor; Judy Davis; Wendy Hughes; *D:* Igor Auzins.

High School ½ **1940** Rambunctious Texas teen Jane Wallace is used to behaving as she pleases on her family's cattle ranch. Her father is tired of Jane bamboozling her tutors and sends her to the San Antonio high school run by his brother. Jane's behavior continues to cause trouble, especially for football star Slats Roberts, until she learns some difficult lessons. **74m/B; DVD.** Jane Withers; Joe Brown, Jr.; Lloyd Corrigan; Paul Harvey; Lynne Roberts; *D:* George Nicholls, Jr.; *W:* Harold Tarshis; Jack Jungmeyer; *C:* Lucien N. Andriot.

High School **2010 (R)** The latest entry in a subgenre littered with comedic failures gets another low point as talented actors like Brody, Hanks, and Chiklis toke up in a stoner flick. When the school valedictorian (Bush) discovers that he's going to fail a drug test, he concocts a plan to get the whole school high (they can't expel everyone, right?) With few laughs and a miscast ensemble, it can't get beyond its predictable set-up of stoned teachers and students. **99m/C; DVD, Blu-Ray.** Adrien Brody; Sean Marquette; Matthew Bush; Colin Hanks; Michael Chiklis; Adhir Kalyan; Yeardley Smith; *D:* Jon Stalberg, Jr.; *W:* Jon Stalberg, Jr.; Stephen Susco; *C:* Mitchell Amundsen; *M:* The Newton Brothers.

High School Big Shot ½ **1959** The title is what lonely, brainy, and poor high school senior Marv (Pittman) wants to be in this typical '50s juvie drama. He's easy pickings when hot bad girl Betty (Aldridge) flirts so Marv will write her English term paper. After getting dumped, Marv is sure Betty will come back if he has a lot of dough but his cockamamie plan to rob a drug deal is a disaster waiting to happen. **90m/B; DVD.** Tom Pittman; Virginia Aldridge; Howard Veit; Malcolm Atterbury; Stanley Adams; Louis Quinn; *D:* Joel Rapp; *W:* Joel Rapp; *C:* John M. Nickolaus, Jr.; *M:* Gerald Fried.

High School Caesar **1960** A seedy teenage exploitation flick about a rich teenager, with no parental supervision, who starts his own gang to run his high school. **75m/B; VHS, DVD.** John Ashley; Steve Stevens; Lowell Brown; Gary Vinson; Judy Nugent; Daria Massey; *D:* O'Dale Ireland; *W:* Ethelmae Wilson Page; Robert Slaven; *C:* Harry Birch; *M:* Nicholas Carras.

High School Confidential *Young Hellions* **1958** Teen punk Tamblyn transfers to Santo Bello high school from Chicago and causes havoc among the locals. He soon involves himself in the school drug scene and looks to be the top dog in dealing, but what no one knows is that he's really a narc! A must for midnight movie fans thanks to high camp values, "hep cat" dialogue and the gorgeous Van Doren as Tamblyn's sex-crazed "aunt." **85m/B; VHS, DVD, Blu-Ray.** Russ Tamblyn; Jan Sterling; John Drew (Blythe) Barrymore, Jr.; Mamie Van Doren; Diane Jergens; Jerry Lee Lewis; Ray Anthony; Jackie Coogan; Charles Chaplin, Jr.; Burt Douglas; Michael Landon; Jody Fair; Phillipa Fallon; Robin Raymond; James Todd; Lyle Talbot; William Wellman, Jr.; *D:* Jack Arnold; *W:* Robert Blees; Lewis Meltzer; *C:* Harold Marzorati.

High School High ½ **1996 (PG-13)** Idealistic teacher Richard Clark (Lovitz) leaves the private school world for notorious inner city Marion Barry High. This school is so bad it has its own cemetery (it's a parody, folks), but Clark is determined to get through to the kids. "Clockers" star Phifer shows up as a helpful student. Penned by David Zucker of "Airplane!" fame, so don't expect a "Mr. Holland's Opus." **86m/C; VHS, DVD, Blu-Ray.** Jon Lovitz; Tia Carrere; Mekhi Phifer; Louise Fletcher; Malinda Williams; *D:* Hart Bochner; *W:* David Zucker; Robert Locash; Pat Proft; *C:* Vernon Layton; *M:* Ira Newborn.

High School Musical ½ **2006 (PG)** Bouncy musical with catchy tunes, made for the Disney Channel, finds high school basketball star Troy (Efron) falling for studious Gabriella (Hudgens) on vacation (they do karaoke together). When they realize they go to the same school, Troy is pressured to stay with the status quo'especially when he wants to try out for the school musical with Gabriella against the very ambitious Evans siblings. **98m/C; DVD.** Zac Efron; Ashley Tilsdale; Lucas Grabeel; Bart Johnson; Monique Coleman; Vanessa Anne Hudgens; Alyson Reed; Corbin Bleu; *D:* Kenny Ortega; *W:* Peter Barosocchini; *C:* Gordon C. Lonsdale; *M:* David Lawrence. **CABLE**

High School Musical 2 ½ **2007 (G)** Just as lively (if not as fresh) as its predecessor. Gabriella is hoping to enjoy the summer with Troy but he needs to save some cash for college. The Wildcats get jobs at the Lava Springs Country Club, which happens to be owned by the parents of scheming Sharpay and Ryan. Sharpay dangles basketball perks and other incentives for Troy to sing with her in the club talent contest, which leaves Gabriella feeling neglected, but none of it is anything that a few song-and-dance numbers can't solve. **111m/C; DVD, Blu-Ray.** Zac Efron; Vanessa Anne Hudgens; Ashley Tisdale; Corbin Bleu; Lucas Brabeel; Monique Coleman; *D:* Kenny Ortega; *W:* Peter Barsocchini; *C:* Daniel Aranyo; *M:* David Lawrence. **CABLE**

High School Musical 3: Senior Year **2008 (G)** The Disney juggernaut churns out the third installment of the wildly popular and squeaky clean teen musical series in as many years, this time cashing in with the big-screen debut of Zac and Vanessa. It's the utopian high-school experience, complete with all of the trappings: the big game, spring musical, prom, graduation, and puppy-love angst, as Troy and Gabriela are facing the prospect of, gulp, being separated as they plan on attending different colleges. Tweens will go ga-ga despite the forgettable tunes, logic-defying plot, and utter lack of edge. **100m/C; Blu-Ray.** Zac Efron; Vanessa Anne Hudgens; Ashley Tisdale; Lucas Grabeel; Corbin Bleu; Monique Coleman; Bart Johnson; Olesya Rulin; *D:* Kenny Ortega; *W:* Peter Barsocchini; *C:* Daniel Aranyo; *M:* David Lawrence.

High School USA ½ **1984** A high-school class clown confronts the king of the prep-jock-bullies. Antics ensue in this flick that features many stars from '50s and '60s sitcoms. **96m/C; VHS, DVD.** Michael J. Fox; Nancy McKeon; Bob Denver; Angela Cartwright; Elinor Donahue; Dwayne Hickman; Lauri Hendler; Dana Plato; Tony Dow; David Nelson; *D:* Rod Amateau; *M:* Miles Goodman. **TV**

High Season ½ **1988 (R)** A satire about a beautiful English photographer (Bisset) stranded on an idyllic Greek island with neither money nor inspiration, and the motley assembly of characters who surround her during the tourist season. **95m/C; DVD.** *UK* Jacqueline Bisset; James Fox; Irene Papas; Sebastian Shaw; Kenneth Branagh; Robert Stephens; Lesley Manville; *D:* Clare Peploe; *W:* Mark Peploe; Clare Peploe; *C:* Chris Menges; *M:* Jason Osborn.

High Sierra **1941** Bogart is Roy "Mad Dog" Earle, an aging gangster whose last job goes bad, so he's hiding out from the police in the High Sierras with a dame and a dog. He's also juggling a soft spot for a down-on-their luck farm family that reminds him of home. Bogart's first starring role. Based on the novel by W.R. Burnett. Remade in 1955 as "I Died A Thousand Times." Also available colorized. **96m/B; VHS, DVD.** Humphrey Bogart; Ida Lupino; Arthur Kennedy; Joan Leslie; Cornel Wilde; Henry Travers; Henry Hull; Jerome Cowan; Minna Gombell; Barton MacLane; Elisabeth Risdon; Alan Curtis; Donald MacBride; Paul Harvey; Willie Best; Spencer Charters; George Meeker; *D:* Raoul Walsh; *W:* John Huston; W.R. Burnett; *C:* Gaetano Antonio "Tony" Gaudio; *M:* Adolph Deutsch.

High Society **1956** A wealthy man attempts to win back his ex-wife who's about to be remarried in this enjoyable remake of "The Philadelphia Story." **107m/C; VHS, DVD.** Frank Sinatra; Bing Crosby; Grace Kelly; Louis Armstrong; Celeste Holm; Sidney Blackmer; Louis Calhern; *D:* Charles Walters; *C:* Paul Vogel; *M:* Cole Porter.

High Spirits **1988 (PG-13)** An American inherits an Irish castle and a sexy 200-year-old ghost. A painful, clumsy comedy by the fine British director that was apparently butchered by the studio before its release. **99m/C; VHS, DVD, Blu-Ray.** Daryl Hannah; Peter O'Toole; Steve Guttenberg; Beverly D'Angelo; Liam Neeson; Martin Ferrero; Peter Gallagher; Jennifer Tilly; *D:* Neil Jordan; *W:* Neil Jordan; *C:* Alex Thompson; *M:* George Fenton.

High Stakes 🦴🦴 ½ *The Disappearance of Nora* **1993** Nora Fremont (Hamel) wakes up in the Nevada desert bloodied and bruised from a beating and suffering from amnesia. She makes it to Vegas where she meets Denton (Farina), who does casino security, and he agrees to help her find out who she is. But when her husband (Collins) comes to claim her, Nora's nightmare is really just beginning. **98m/C; VHS, DVD.** Veronica Hamel; Dennis Farina; Stephen Collins; Stan Ivar; Bryan Cranston; ***D:*** Joyce Chopra; ***W:*** Tom Cole; Alan Ormsby; ***C:*** James Glennon; ***M:*** Mark Snow. **TV**

High Strung 🦴🦴 ½ **2016 (PG)** A music-centered romantic drama about pursuing your dreams. The subway in New York City proves to be where love blooms when Johnnie (xxx), a hip-hip violinist who makes money performing there, meets Ruby, a dancer training on scholarship in Manhattan. However, Johnnie is an illegal alien and when his violin gets stolen, he is bereft. Ruby learns about a competition that pairs a dancer with a string musician for a prize that includes a scholarship and a student visa. Working with Ruby and a hip hop crew, Johnnie competes and hopes he can find his future. **97m/C; DVD, Streaming, Download.** Keenan Kampa; Nicholas Galitzine; Jane Seymour; Sonoya Mizuno; Richard Southgate; ***D:*** Michael Damian; ***W:*** Michael Damian; Janeen Damian; ***C:*** Viorel Sergovici, Jr.; ***M:*** Nathan Lanier.

High Tension WOOF! *Haute tension* **2003 (R)** French splatter exploitation film finds college friends Marie (De France) and Alex (Maiwenn) spending the weekend at the isolated farmhouse of Alex's parents. Your standard gross killer (Nahon), who enjoys decapitation, kills Alex's family and kidnaps Alex so he can torture her at his leisure. Marie sets out to rescue her. There's a lot more gore and even more bad dubbing. Americans do these things much better. **91m/C; DVD, Blu-Ray, UMD.** *FR* Cecile de France; Maiwenn Le Besco; Philippe Nahon; Franck Khalfoun; Andrei Finti; Oana Pellea; Marco Claudiu Pascu; ***D:*** Alexandre Aja; ***W:*** Alexandre Aja; Gregory Levasseur; ***C:*** Maxime Alexandre; ***M:*** Francois Eudes.

High Tide 🦴🦴 **1980** Peter Curtis (McShane) was convicted of manslaughter and has just been released from prison. While travelling to Cornwall, Peter realizes he's being followed and the man wants to know the last words spoken by Peter's victim. When Peter does remember, he tries to figure out what they mean and discovers that hidden gold (liberated from WWII France) is involved. **98m/C; DVD.** *GB* Ian McShane; Wendy Morgan; Terence Rigby; Kika Markham; John Bird; Malcolm Terris; ***D:*** Colin Buckley; ***W:*** Andrew Brown; ***C:*** Peter Jessop; ***M:*** Richard Hartley.

High Tide 🦴🦴🦴 **1987 (PG-13)** A strong and strange drama once again coupling the star and director of "My Brilliant Career." A small-time rock 'n' roll singer who is stranded in a small, beach town fortuitously meets up with her previously abandoned teenage daughter. Acclaimed. **120m/C; VHS, Streaming.** *AU* Judy Davis; Jan Adele; Claudia Karvan; Colin Friels; John Clayton; Mark Hembrow; Frankie J. Holden; Monica Trapaga; ***D:*** Gillian Armstrong; ***W:*** Laura Jones; ***C:*** Russell Boyd; ***M:*** Peter Best; Ricky Fataar; Mark Moffatt. Australian Film Inst. '87: Actress (Davis); Natl. Soc. Film Critics '88: Actress (Davis).

High Time 🦴 ½ **1960** Innocuous campus comedy in which widowed Harvey Howard (Crosby), a 51-year-old successful businessman, returns to college for the education he lacks. Assigned to a dorm room with young roommates Gil (Fabian), Bob (Beymer), and T.J. (Adiarte), Harvey proves that he's both a serious student and a fun guy. Film follows him through his four years and as Harvey starts a discreet romance with French professor Helene Gauthier (Maurey). **103m/C; DVD, Blu-Ray.** Bing Crosby; Fabian; Richard Beymer; Patrick Adiarte; Tuesday Weld; Nicole Maurey; Gavin MacLeod; Yvonne Craig; ***D:*** Blake Edwards; ***W:*** Tom Waldman; Frank Waldman; ***C:*** Ellsworth Fredericks; ***M:*** Henry Mancini.

High Voltage 🦴🦴 **1998 (R)** Tough guy Johnny Clay (Sabato Jr.) winds up in unexpected trouble when he and his cohorts rob a bank that's laundering money for the Asian mob. Mob boss Cheung decides they need to be taught a lesson. **92m/C; VHS, DVD.** Antonio Sabato, Jr.; Lochlyn Munro; William Zabka; George Kee Cheung; Amy Smart; James Lew; Antonio (Tony) Sabato; Shannon Lee; ***D:*** Isaac Florentine; ***W:*** Mike Mains; ***C:*** Philip D. Schwartz; ***M:*** Stephen (Steve) Edwards. **VIDEO**

High Wall 🦴🦴 ½ **1947** Ex-Army pilot Steven Kenet (Taylor) returns home suffering blackouts from a head injury and then discovers his wife Helen (Patrick) is cheating on him with her smug boss Whitcombe (Marshall). When Helen is strangled, Steven is accused of murder but is sent to a mental hospital for observation under the care of shrink Ann Lorrison (Totter). Steven escapes to prove his innocence but the very cold-blooded killer has other ideas. **100m/B; DVD.** Robert Taylor; Audrey Totter; Herbert Marshall; Dorothy Patrick; H.B. Warner; Vince Barnett; Warner Anderson; Moroni Olsen; Morris Ankrum; ***D:*** Curtis Bernhardt; ***W:*** Sydney (Sidney) Boehm; Lester Cole; ***C:*** Paul Vogel; ***M:*** Bronislau Kaper.

High, Wide and Handsome 🦴🦴 ½ **1937** Overstuffed dramatic musical mishmash with some great tunes, courtesy of Jerome Kern and Oscar Hammerstein. In 1859, Doc Watterson and his daughter Sally are stuck in Pennsylvania when their medicine show wagon breaks down. They're offered shelter by farmer-turned oil prospector Peter Cortlandt. Sally and Peter marry, Peter strikes a gusher, but he and the locals have trouble from a conniving railroad baron. The Cortlandt marriage is shaky, so Sally joins the circus and she and her new circus pals (including the elephants) come to the rescue. **110m/B; DVD.** Irene Dunne; Randolph Scott; Dorothy Lamour; Raymond Walburn; Alan Hale; Charles Bickford; Akim Tamiroff; ***D:*** Rouben Mamoulian; ***W:*** Oscar Hammerstein; George O'Neil; ***C:*** Theodor Sparkuhl; ***M:*** Jerome Kern.

Highball 🦴🦴🦴 **1997 (R)** Newlyweds try to expand their social life by throwing a series of theme parties. Charmingly low-key indie. **90m/C; VHS, DVD.** Justine Bateman; Peter Bogdanovich; Rae Dawn Chong; Christopher Eigeman; Annabella Sciorra; Ally Sheedy; Eric Stoltz; Catherine Kellner; Dean Cameron; Andrea Bowen; ***D:*** Noah Baumbach; ***W:*** Noah Baumbach; ***C:*** Steven Bernstein. **VIDEO**

Higher and Higher 🦴🦴 **1944** Bankrupt aristocrat conspires with servants to regain his fortune, and tries to marry his daughter into money. Sinatra's first big-screen role. **90m/B; VHS, DVD.** Frank Sinatra; Leon Errol; Michele Morgan; Jack Haley; Mary McGuire; ***D:*** Tim Whelan.

Higher Ground 🦴 ½ **1988** Bland TV fare with Denver as an unlikely FBI agent. Disillusioned fed Jim Clayton (Denver) quits the Bureau and takes buddy Rick's (Kove) offer to become a pilot for his Alaskan air freight business. However, Rick is in financial trouble and has been taking work from local bootlegger McClain (Masur). When Rick tries quitting, he ends up dead and Jim is out to get justice. **96m/C; DVD.** John Denver; Martin Kove; Meg Wittner; Richard Masur; John Rhys-Davies; Brandon Marsh; ***D:*** Robert Day; ***W:*** Michael Eric Stein; ***C:*** Richard Leiterman; ***M:*** Lee Holdridge. **TV**

Higher Ground 🦴🦴🦴 **2011 (R)** Farmiga directs and takes the lead role in the story of Corinne, who experiences an ongoing crisis of faith, as she struggles to navigate a world defined by her evangelical religion. Once a teenage bride, Corinne later finds herself seriously questioning her spiritual and personal beliefs as she lives in a born-again community. The story finds strength in character development, and Farmiga is impressive as a first-time director in this sensitive and insightful portrayal of a conflicted woman. Adaptation of "This Dark World: A Memoir of Salvation Found and Lost," the memoir of Carolyn S. Briggs. **109m/C; DVD.** Vera Farmiga; Dagmara Dominczyk; Joshua Leonard; John Hawkes; Ebon Moss-Bachrach; Bill Irwin; Norbert Lee Butz; Donna Murphy; Taissa Farmiga; Nina Arianda; Boyd Holbrook; ***D:*** Vera Farmiga; ***W:*** Tim Metcalfe; Carolyn S. Briggs; ***C:*** Michael McDonough; ***M:*** Alec Puro.

Higher Learning 🦴🦴 **1994 (R)** Racism, idealism, and the struggle for identity converge in this stylistically shot but rarely enlightening commentary on campus life and strife, focusing on three very different freshmen at fictional Columbus University—a bright track star (Ebbs) who questions the exploitation of black student athletes; a sheltered, sexually confused beauty from the 'burbs (Swanson); and a goony, paranoid loner who falls in with a group of skinheads (Rapaport). Singleton's honorable intention—to make a movie that makes a difference—is marred by cardboard supporting characters, a penchant for in-your-face irony, and a predictable, simplistic conclusion. **127m/C; VHS, DVD, Blu-Ray.** Omar Epps; Kristy Swanson; Michael Rapaport; Laurence Fishburne; Jennifer Connelly; Ice Cube; Tyra Banks; Jason Wiles; Cole Hauser; Regina King; Colleen (Ann) Fitzpatrick; ***D:*** John Singleton; ***W:*** John Singleton; ***C:*** Peter Lyons Collister.

Higher Power 🦴 ½ **2018 (R)** When humankind faces the threat of extinction from a massive gamma energy burst, angry widower Joseph Steadman (Eldard) must decide if he will act to save everyone. Joseph learns that that he has superpowers and must follow the directions of an enigmatic mad scientist (Feore) to use them to save Earth as well as his estranged daughter Zoe (Hinson). However, as Joseph becomes more powerful, his anger issues only grows, which puts the scientist's plan in jeopardy. Despite a miniscule budget and a mediocre narrative, the low-fi indie features impressive visual special effects and interesting take on the superhero genre. **93m/C; DVD.** Ron Eldard; Jordan Hinson; Austin Stowell; Colm Feore; Jade Tailor; ***D:*** Matthew Santoro; ***W:*** Matthew Santoro; Julia Fair; ***C:*** Dallas Sterling; ***M:*** Kevin Riepl.

Highland Park 🦴 ½ **2013** Predictable dramedy. High school principal Lloyd Howard (Burke) wonders how he can cut his budget any further to avoid layoffs in a troubled city where the corrupt mayor (Posey) has completely mismanaged its finances. The faculty decide to play their lottery pool numbers one last time and think they've finally hit it big with Howard vowing to use his share to help the school. Only, thanks to Ed's (Glover) last minute decision, they didn't win after all. **94m/C; DVD.** Billy Burke; Danny Glover; Parker Posey; Eric Ladin; Rockmond Dunbar; John Carroll Lynch; Kimberly Elise; Michelle Forbes; ***D:*** Andrew Meieran; ***W:*** Andrew Meieran; Christopher Keyser; ***C:*** Daniel (Danny) Moder; ***M:*** Jane Antonia Cornish. **VIDEO**

Highlander 🦴🦴🦴 **1986 (R)** A strange tale about an immortal 16th-century Scottish warrior who has had to battle his evil immortal enemy through the centuries. The feud comes to blows in modern-day Manhattan. Connery makes a memorable appearance as the good warrior's mentor. Spectacular battle and death scenes. A cult favorite which spawned a weak sequel and a TV series. Based on a story by Gregory Widen. **110m/C; VHS, DVD, Blu-Ray.** Christopher Lambert; Sean Connery; Clancy Brown; Roxanne Hart; Beatie Edney; Alan North; Sheila Gish; Jon Polito; ***D:*** Russell Mulcahy; ***W:*** Gregory Widen; Peter Bellwood; Larry Ferguson; ***C:*** Gerry Fisher; ***M:*** Michael Kamen.

Highlander 2: The Quickening 🦴 ½ *Highlander 2: Renegade Version* **1991 (R)** The saga of Connor MacLeod and Juan Villa-Lobos continues in this sequel set in the year 2024. An energy shield designed to block out the sun's harmful ultraviolet rays has left planet Earth in perpetual darkness, but there is evidence that the ozone layer has repaired itself. An environmental terrorist and her group begin a sabotage effort and are joined by MacLeod and Villa-Lobos in their quest to save Earth. Stunning visual effects don't make up for the lack of substance. The Renegade version is a director's cut, which has been reedited and contains some 19 additional minutes of footage. **90m/C; VHS, DVD, Blu-Ray.** Christopher Lambert; Sean Connery; Virginia Madsen; Michael Ironside; John C. McGinley; ***D:*** Russell Mulcahy; ***W:*** Peter Bellwood; ***C:*** Phil Meheux; ***M:*** Stewart Copeland.

Highlander: Endgame 🦴🦴 ½ **2000 (R)** Fourth series installment ignores the two middle films but harkens back to the 1985 original. Lambert returns as immortal Connor MacLeod, teaming up with his equally immortal clansman, Duncan (TV "Highlander" Paul), to battle baddie Jacob Kell (Payne). Kell has a long-standing grudge against Connor and doesn't follow the rules of the "game." Numerous flashbacks could be confusing for newcomers but fans will find enjoyment and there is much action and sword-play. Story is so fast-paced that some subplots and characters are left in the dust for the exploits of the three main immortals. The video release contains 12 more minutes of footage and a new ending. **101m/C; VHS, DVD.** Christopher Lambert; Adrian Paul; Bruce Payne; Lisa Barbuscia; Peter Wingfield; Jim Byrnes; Donnie Yen; Beatie Edney; Sheila Gish; ***D:*** Douglas Aarniokoski; ***W:*** Joel Soisson; ***C:*** Doug Milsome; ***M:*** Stephen Graziano.

Highlander: The Final Dimension 🦴 ½ *Highlander 3: The Magician; Highlander 3: The Sorcerer* **1994 (R)** Immortal Conner MacLeod (Lambert) battles master illusionist Kane (Van Peebles), who seeks to rule the world. Aiding MacLeod is Alex Smith (Unger), a research scientist who discovers Kane was once buried beneath a mystical mountain along with three other immortal warriors some 300 years before. MacLeod returns to his old Scottish stomping grounds to prepare for battle. Lots of action and special effects, really dumb storyline and overacting—even for a fantasy film. Original theatrical release was PG-13 and 94 minutes; the director's cut has been re-edited and footage added. **99m/C; VHS, DVD.** Christopher Lambert; Mario Van Peebles; Deborah Kara Unger; Mako; ***D:*** Andrew Morahan; ***W:*** Paul Ohl; ***C:*** Steven Chivers; ***M:*** J. Peter Robinson.

Highlander: The Gathering 🦴🦴 ½ **1992 (PG-13)** Re-edited episodes from the syndicated TV series finds good immortals Connor MacLeod (Lambert) and distant relative Duncan (Paul) battling against an evil immortal (Moll as a particularly nasty villain) and a misguided human (Vanity). Lots of sword-play and a little bit of romance (courtesy of Vandernoot). **98m/C; VHS, DVD.** Christopher Lambert; Adrian Paul; Richard Moll; Vanity; Alexandra Vandernoot; Stan Kirsch; ***D:*** Thomas J. Wright; Ray Austin; ***W:*** Lorain Despres; Dan Gordon. **TV**

Highlander: The Source 🦴 ½ **2007 (R)** The fifth sequel takes its cues from the syndicated TV series rather than the original films, although the parameters of the myth change once again to conform to the confines of mindless action. Duncan MacLeod (Paul) learns that the Source—the cosmic dimension that resulted in the first immortal—has been located. Only the mutated immortal (Solimeno) who guards the spot won't let anyone near without a fight. **86m/C; DVD.** Adrian Paul; Jim Byrnes; Peter Wingfield; Thekla Reuten; Cristian Solimeno; Stephen Wight; ***D:*** Brett Leonard; ***W:*** Stephen Kelvin Watkins; Mark Bradley; ***C:*** Steve Arnold; ***M:*** George Kalis. **VIDEO**

Highly Dangerous 🦴 ½ **1950** Silly spy adventure. Entomologist Frances Gray (Lockwood) is sent by the British Secret Service to an Eastern European country where the scientists are working on germ warfare using insects as carriers. There's a murder and Frances is given truth serum by the government bad guy (Goring), which causes her to hallucinate. **89m/B; DVD.** *UK* Margaret Lockwood; Dane Clark; Marius Goring; Wilfrid Hyde-White; Naunton Wayne; ***D:*** Roy Ward Baker; ***W:*** Eric Ambler; ***C:*** Reg Wyer; ***M:*** Richard Addinsell.

Highway 🦴🦴 **2001 (R)** Vegas pool cleaner Jack Hayes (Leto) decides to make make a quick getaway when he gets caught in bed with a mobster's wife. So he and best pal Pilot Kelson (Gyllenhaal) score some drugs and head out on the road, along with hitchhiking hooker Cassie (Blair). And they even have a destination—to attend a vigil for the recently deceased Kurt Cobain in Seattle. **97m/C; VHS, DVD.** Jared Leto; Selma Blair; Jake Gyllenhaal; Kimberley Kates; Jeremy Piven; John C. McGinley; ***D:*** James Cox; ***W:*** Scott Rosenberg; ***C:*** Mauro Fiore. **VIDEO**

Highway Hitcher 🦴🦴 *The Pass* **1998 (R)** Comic strip salesman Charles Duprey (Forsythe) is in the midst of a mid-life crisis, including having his wife Shirley (Allen) leave him. Charles' friend Willie (McKean) convinces him to hit the road to Reno for a little R&R. On a backroad Charles crosses paths with Hunter (LeGros), who's having car trouble, and reluctantly offers him a ride. He should have trusted his instincts, since this is only the beginning of trouble. **93m/C; VHS, DVD.** William Forsythe; James LeGros; Elizabeth Pena; Jamie Kennedy; Nancy Allen; Michael McKean; Jaason Simmons; John Doe; *D:* Kurt Voss; *W:* Kurt Voss; *C:* Denis Maloney; *M:* Vinnie Golia. **VIDEO**

The Highway Man 🦴🦴 **1999 (R)** Middleaged Frank Drake (McHattie) is running telephone scams and winds up getting framed by his nasty boss (Gossett) for fraud and then accused of murder. Into this mess strolls Ziggy (Harris), who thinks Frank is her daddy, along with her boyfriend/thief Walter (Priestly), who's just made a big score. It plays more like two separate stories that never really come together. **97m/C; VHS, DVD.** Jason Priestley; Louis Gossett, Jr.; Stephen McHattie; Laura Harris; Callum Keith Rennie; Gordon Michael Woolvett; Bernie Coulson; *D:* Keoni Waxman; *W:* Richard Beattie.

Highway Patrolman 🦴🦴 *El Patrullero* **1991** Young Pedro Rojas (Sosa) has just graduated from the National Highway Patrol Academy and he and best friend Anibal (Bichir) have been assigned to the isolated roads of northern Durango. He quickly learns that most of the people he stops for minor violations are too poor to pay for licenses and fines. What Pedro does get is a wife, Griselda (Gutierrez), who's soon complaining about Pedro's meager wages. Pedro's resistance to bribery begins to weaken and he becomes more depressed as his ideals are destroyed and his rage increases. Spanish with subtitles. **104m/C; VHS, DVD, Blu-Ray.** *MX* Roberto Sosa; Zaide Silvia Gutierrez; Bruno Bichir; Vanessa Bauche; *D:* Alex Cox; *W:* Lorenzo O'Brien; *C:* Miguel Garzon; *M:* Zander Schloss.

Highway 61 🦴🦴 **1991 (R)** Shy barber Pokey Jones lives in the small Canadian town of Pickerel Falls and becomes a celebrity when he discovers the frozen corpse of an unknown young man in his backyard. Jackie Bangs, a rock roadie who's stolen her band's stash of drugs, finds herself stranded in the same small town. So begins a wild road trip. Lackluster direction undercuts much of the first-rate acting and amusing story quirks. **110m/C; VHS, DVD.** Valerie Buhagiar; Don McKellar; Earl Pastko; Peter Breck; Art Bergmann; *D:* Bruce McDonald; *W:* Don McKellar.

Highway 301 🦴🦴 **1950** Crime noir told from the crooks' POV. Four bank robbers, known as the Tri-State Gang and led by ruthless George (Cochran), go on a crime spree through Virginia, North Carolina, and Maryland. Accompanied by their gun molls (who don't fare well either), the quartet are relentlessly pursued by the cops until the crime doesn't pay ending. **83m/B; DVD.** Steve Cochran; Robert Webber; Richard Egan; Wally Cassell; Virginia Grey; Aline Towne; Gaby Andre; *D:* Andrew L. Stone; *W:* Andrew L. Stone; *C:* Carl Guthrie; *M:* William Lava.

Highwaymen 🦴🦴 **2003 (R)** Rennie (Caviezel) uses a fast car and a police scanner to get a bead on the serial killer who murdered his wife by running her down with a '72 El Dorado. Along for the ride is Molly (Mitra), the one woman to survive the attacks. Intriguing premise is run off the road by the short run-time, which doesn't leave much time to make the plot very cohesive. **80m/C; DVD.** James (Jim) Caviezel; Rhona Mitra; Frankie Faison; Gordon Currie; Colm Feore; *D:* Robert Harmon; *W:* Hans Bauer; Craig Mitchell; *C:* Rene Ohashi; *M:* Mark Isham.

The Highwaymen 🦴🦴 **1/2 2019 (R)** In 1934, outlaws Bonnie (Brobst) and Clyde (Bossert) are robbing banks in the South and becoming increasingly famous. Texas governor Ma Ferguson (Bates) believes the only way to stop them is to revive the Texas Rangers. To that end, she convinces retired law enforcement officer Frank Hamer (Costner) to bring the duo to justice. Working with old partner Maney Gault (Harrelson), Frank tracks Bonnie and Clyde throughout the South as their crime spree continues. Costner and Harrelson play well off each other, smoothly leading us down the inevitable path leading to outlaws' demise. **132m/C; DVD.** Kevin Costner; Woody Harrelson; Kathy Bates; John Carroll Lynch; Thomas Mann; *D:* John Lee Hancock; *W:* John Fusco; *C:* John Schwartzman; *M:* Thomas Newman.

Hijack Highway 🦴🦴 *Gas-Oil* **1955** Trucker Jean (Gabin) discovers a dead body on a rural highway and informs the cops, which promptly gets him into trouble. Gangsters think Jean stole loot from the corpse and go after him while his schoolteacher girlfriend Alice (Moreau) and his trucker friends come to his rescue. French with subtitles. **88m/B; DVD.** *FR* Jean Gabin; Jeanne Moreau; Gaby Basset; Marcel Bozzuffi; Robert Dalban; *D:* Gilles Grangier; *W:* Michel Audiard; *C:* Pierre Montazel; *M:* Henri Crolla.

Hijacked 🦴 **1/2 2012 (R)** Generic, low-budget action with a wooden lead performance from Couture. Rogue special agent Ross is after criminal business tycoon Lieb (Fairbrass) and takes a job as security on Lieb's private jet. Ross is hoping this also gets him the chance to reconcile with his ex, Olivia (Dupont), who's working for Lieb. Romance will have to wait when the plane is hijacked by another criminal element. **90m/C; DVD, Blu-Ray.** Randy Couture; Craig Fairbrass; Tiffany DuPont; Dominic Purcell; Holt McCallany; Gina Phillips; Vinnie Jones; *D:* Brandon Nutt; *W:* Brandon Nutt; *C:* Adam Biddle. **VIDEO**

A Hijacking 🦴🦴🦴 *Kapringen* **2013 (R)** Lindholm's internationally acclaimed true story of the hijacking of a Danish cargo ship by Somali pirates alternates between heart-rending action on the vessel and the boardrooms in which men had to negotiate for the lives of their own employees. Asbaek plays the chef on the ship, one of the men who survived the longest purely because the pirates needed to eat and because he became a go-between in the negotiations for ransom money. Malling shines as the executive who ignored advice to get counsel from people more experienced in hostage negotiations and whose mistakes arguably led to the loss of life. **103m/C; DVD, Blu-Ray.** *DK* Pilou Asbaek; Soren Malling; *D:* Tobias Lindholm; *W:* Tobias Lindholm; *C:* Magnus Nordenhof Jønck; *M:* Hildur Guonadottir.

Hijacking Catastrophe: 9/11, Fear and the Selling of America 🦴🦴 **1/2 2004** Another in a series of Anti-Bush documentaries to come out in 2004. This one suggests a much larger and darker conspiracy behind the Bush administration's agenda post-9/11. Hermann Goering is quoted at the start, offering a frightening parallel that may or may not be too out there, depending on your party affiliation. Many partisan and non-partisan authorities are interviewed, notably Noam Chomsky and Norman Mailer. **68m/C; DVD.** *D:* Jeremy Earp; Sut Jhally; *C:* David Rabinovitz; *M:* Thom Monahan.

Hijacking Hollywood 🦴🦴 **1997** Modest Hollywood satire finds naive Kevin Conroy (Thomas) using family ties to land a menial job with distant relative Michael Lawrence (Metcalf), a tyrannical producer. Kevin's supervisor is the petty Russell (Thompson), who enjoys sending the kid on useless errands. Kevin's one important task is to pick up film rushes at the airport and he tells hustling roommate Tad (Mandt) that if someone took the dailies, a production could be held hostage. Naturally, Tad is all for the idea. **91m/C; VHS, DVD.** Henry Thomas; Scott Thompson; Mark Metcalf; Paul Hewitt; Art LaFleur; Neil Mandt; *D:* Neil Mandt; *W:* Neil Mandt; Jim Rossow; *C:* Anton Floquet.

Hilary and Jackie 🦴🦴🦴 **1998 (R)** Based on the true story of cover girl cellist Jacqueline Du Pre (Watson) and her relationship with her sister Hilary (Griffiths). As Jackie takes the world of classical music by storm, Hilary gives up her musical ambitions and marries conductor Kiffer (Morrissey). The story switches perspectives between the two women after Jackie arrives at Hilary's doorstep and asks if she may sleep with her husband. Hilary reluctantly agrees, and there go all those stereotypes you had about girls who play classical music. The second half details Jackie's decline and eventual death from multiple sclerosis and the sisters' mutual bonds developed during her illness. Excellent performances and music, including some actual Du Pre performances, make this a pleaser for those who liked "Shine." **124m/C; VHS, DVD.** *GB* Emily Watson; Rachel Griffiths; James Frain; David Morrissey; Charles Dance; Celia Imrie; Rupert Penry-Jones; Nyree Dawn Porter; Bill Paterson; Vernon Dobtcheff; Auriol Evans; Keeley Flanders; *D:* Anand Tucker; *W:* Frank Cottrell-Boyce; *C:* David C(lark) Johnson; *M:* Barrington Pheloung.

The Hill 🦴🦴 **1/2 1965** British soldiers in a WWII North African military prison are subjected to the brutal discipline of the sadistic Staff Sgt. Williams (Hendry). One of the harshest punishments is the "Hill" a man-made sand wall that the men must climb in full gear. When one of the men dies, it provokes a confrontation between the prisoners, led by Connery, and Williams and his C.O. (Andrews). Harrowing, disturbing look at British Army life and discipline excels on the strength of taut script and great work by the fine cast. **121m/B; VHS, DVD.** *GB* Sean Connery; Harry Andrews; Ian Hendry; Ian Bannen; Ossie Davis; Alfred Lynch; Jack Watson; Roy Kinnear; Michael Redgrave; Norman Bird; Neil McCarthy; Howard Goorney; Tony Caunter; *D:* Sidney Lumet; *W:* Ray Rigby; R.S. (Ray) Allen; *C:* Oswald Morris.

Hillary's America: The Secret History of the Democratic Party **WOOF! 2016 (PG-13)** Political allegiances aside, this is as incompetent and horrendous a documentary as has been theatrically released in years. In fact, most amateur productions are better. Director D'Souza pretends to chronicle the history of the Democratic Party in a way that casts doubt on Hillary Clinton's past and her plans for the future. Again, while almost all of it can be dismissed with a fact check, it's jaw-dropping just how poorly edited, written, technically made and directed it is. He puts in no effort when preaching to his choir. **100m/C; DVD.** Dinesh D'Souza; Jonah Goldberg; Peter Schweizer; Rebekah Turner; Michael Clemmons; *D:* Dinesh D'Souza; Bruce Schooley; *W:* Dinesh D'Souza; Bruce Schooley; *M:* Stephen Limbaugh. Golden Raspberries '16: Worst Actor (D'Souza), Worst Actress (Turner), Worst Director (D'Souza), Worst Picture.

Hillbillies in a Haunted House **WOOF!** *Hillbillys in a Haunted House* **1967** Two country and western singers en route to the Nashville jamboree encounter a group of foreign spies "haunting" a house. Features Rathbone's last film performance. Sequel to "Las Vegas Hillbillies" (1966). Giant step down for everyone involved. **88m/C; VHS, DVD.** Ferlin Husky; Joi Lansing; Don Bowman; John Carradine; Lon Chaney, Jr.; Basil Rathbone; Merle Haggard; Sonny James; Linda Ho; Molly Bee; George Barrows; *D:* Jean Yarbrough; *W:* Duke Yelton; *C:* Vaughn Wilkins; *M:* Hal Borne.

The Hills Have Eyes 🦴 **1/2 2006 (R)** Unnecessary remake of Wes Craven's 1977 lunatic-fest. Not much has been altered in way of the storyline—family stranded in the desert with a pack of inbred killers on their tail, but this time around there's an actual budget. Most of it's blown on fake blood. Slick and humorless, desperate to cash in on the (hopefully) short-lived sadism genre resurrected by Rob Zombie. Thanks, Rob. **107m/C; DVD, Blu-Ray, UMD.** Aaron Stanford; Emilie de Ravin; Vinessa Shaw; Kathleen Quinlan; Ted Levine; Desmond Askew; Dan Byrd; Tom Bower; Billy Drago; Robert Joy; Michael Bailey Smith; Laura Ortiz; *D:* Alexandre Aja; *W:* Gregory Levasseur; *C:* Maxime Alexandre; *M:* tomandandy.

The Hills Have Eyes WOOF! 1977 (R) Desperate family battles for survival and vengeance against a brutal band of inbred hillbilly cannibals. Craven gore-fest followed by Hills II. **83m/C; VHS, DVD, Blu-Ray.** Susan Lanier; Robert Houston; Martin Speer; Dee Wallace; Russ Grieve; John Steadman; James Whitworth; Michael Berryman; Virginia Vincent; Janus Blythe; *D:* Wes Craven; *W:* Wes Craven; *C:* Eric Saarinen; *M:* Don Peake.

The Hills Have Eyes 2 🦴 **2007 (R)** The unnecessary sequel to the unnecessary 2006 remake (not to be confused with 1984's unnecessary sequel to the gory 1977 original). The inbred mutant cannibal Carter clan were unfortunately not quite wiped out and are hiding in some New Mexico caves just waiting to pick off the members of a National Guard patrol and feed on their intestines. The Craven father and son screenwriting team isn't showing us anything we haven't seen before—or want to see again. **89m/C; DVD, Blu-Ray.** Flex Alexander; Jacob Vargas; Michael Bailey Smith; Lee Thompson Young; Michael McMillian; Jessica Stroup; Daniella Alonso; Eric Edelstein; *D:* Martin Weisz; *W:* Wes Craven; Jonathan Craven; *C:* Sam McCurdy; *M:* Trevor Morris.

The Hills Have Eyes, Part 2 🦴 **1984** Craven reprises Hills with Eyes number one to ill effect. Ignorant teens disregard warnings of a "Hills Have Eyes" refugee, and go stomping into the grim reaper's proving grounds. Predictably bad things happen. **86m/C; VHS, DVD, Blu-Ray.** Michael Berryman; Kevin Blair Spirtas; John Bloom; Janus Blythe; John Laughlin; Tamara Stafford; Peter Frechette; *D:* Wes Craven; *W:* Wes Craven; *C:* David Lewis.

The Hills of Home 🦴🦴🦴 *Master of Lassie* **1948 (G)** Warm sentimental tale about a Scottish doctor and his beloved pet collie. One of the better films in the "Lassie" series. **97m/C; VHS, DVD.** Edmund Gwenn; Donald Crisp; Tom Drake; Janet Leigh; *D:* Fred M. Wilcox; *W:* William Ludwig.

The Hills Run Red 🦴 *River of Dollars; Un Fiume di Dollari* **1967** Violent, dubbed spaghetti western set in the post-Civil War years has best friends Jerry and Ken trying to get back to Texas with a stolen army payroll. Jerry gets caught and lands in prison while Ken uses the money to become a power in their town at the expense of Jerry's family. When Jerry is released, all he wants is revenge. **89m/C; DVD.** *IT* Thomas Hunter; Nando Gazzolo; Henry Silva; Dan Duryea; *D:* Carlo Lizzani; *W:* Piero Regnoli; *C:* Antonio Secchi; *M:* Ennio Morricone.

The Hillside Stranglings 🦴 **1/2 2004 (R)** Okay dramatization of the serial murder cases that occurred over a 14-month period in California in 1977-78 and were originally thought to have been the work of one man. Instead, the crimes were committed by cousins Kenneth Bianchi (Howell) and Angelo Buono (Turturro) after their try at running an escort service went bad and Bianchi strangled one of the hookers. Flick ignores the police investigation in favor of showing the murders. Both lead actors are gung-ho about their roles but this is hardly Oscar-worthy material. **97m/C; DVD.** Nicholas Turturro; C. Thomas Howell; Allison Lange; Lin Shaye; Aimee Brooks; Julia Lee; *D:* Chuck Parello; *C:* John Pirozzi.

Himalaya 🦴🦴🦴 *Himalaya - L'Enfance d'un Chef; Himalaya - The Youth of a Chief; Caravan* **1999** The age-old struggle of generations deciding between tradition and progress plays itself out once more against the spectacular scenery of the Tibetan mountains. Although the story is nothing new, the film gives a detailed look into a traditional lifestyle that is fast dying out, using non-professional actors, location shooting, and not an ounce of special effects. A bit of the film's grandeur is lost on the small screen, but it is still breathtaking. **104m/C; VHS, DVD, Blu-Ray.** *FR SI GB* Thinlen Lhondup; Karma Wangiel; Lhakpa Tsamchoe; *D:* Eric Valli; *W:* Eric Valli; Olivier Dazat; *C:* Eric Guichard; Jean-Paul Meurisse; *M:* Bruno Coulais.

The Hindenburg 🦴🦴 **1975 (PG)** A dramatization of what might have happened on the fateful night the Hindenburg exploded. Scott plays an investigator who is aware that something is up, and has numerous suspects to interrogate. The laser edition features widescreen format, digital Stereo Surround, the original trailer, and chapter stops. **126m/C; VHS, DVD, Blu-Ray.** George C. Scott; Anne Bancroft; William Atherton; Roy Thinnes; Gig Young; Burgess Meredith; Charles Durning; Richard Dysart; *D:* Robert Wise; *W:* Nelson Gidding; Richard Levinson; William Link; *C:* Robert L. Surtees; *M:* David Shire. Oscars '75: Sound FX Editing, Visual FX.

Hindle Wakes 🦴🦴 *Fanny Hawthorne* **1927** Lancashire factory girls Fanny and Mary are on holiday in Blackpool where Fanny is secretly meeting with her lover Allan, the son of factory owner Nathaniel Jeffcote. Their liaison is discovered and Allan's father expects him to marry Fanny despite their class differences, but Fanny's decision is unexpected. Silent drama adapted from Stanley Houghton's 1912 play. **117m/B; Silent; DVD.** *GB* Estelle Brody; John Stuart; Norman McKinnel; Humberston Wright; Peggy Carlisle; Marie Ault; Gladys Jennings; Arthur Chesney; ***D:*** Maurice Elvey; ***W:*** Victor Saville; ***C:*** Jack Cox.

Hip Hop 4 Life 🦴🦴 **2002 (PG-13)** Devon is an eloquent wordsmith at the crossroads of life: pursue college or battle rap his way to the top? Despite his girlfriend and father pushing for college, Devon's dreams of becoming an mc drive him to the stage. Half-baked storyline begins to drag quickly, but to its credit, the film avoids the cliched misogyny and profanity that so many urban dramas cling to. Rough enough to keep younger audiences watching, but nice enough to satisfy the older crowd. Features a slew of Cleveland, Ohio's lesser-known, but decent, rap acts contributing stage time. **98m/C; VHS, DVD.** Michael Bell; Q-Nice; Danielle Green; ***D:*** David Velo Stewart; ***W:*** Dâvid Velo Stewart. **VIDEO**

Hired Hand 🦴🦴 ½ **1971** Two drifters settle on a farm belonging to one of their wives, only to leave again seeking to avenge the murder of a friend. TV prints include Larry Hagman in a cameo role. **93m/C; VHS, DVD, Blu-Ray.** Peter Fonda; Warren Oates; Verna Bloom; Severn Darden; Robert Pratt; ***Cameo(s):*** Larry Hagman; ***D:*** Peter Fonda; ***W:*** Alan Sharp; ***C:*** Vilmos Zsigmond; ***M:*** Bruce Langhorne.

Hired to Kill 🦴 ½ *The Italian Connection* **1973 (R)** A pair of Mafia hoods plot against each other over a $6 million drug shipment. **90m/C; VHS, DVD.** Henry Silva; Woody Strode; Adolfo Celi; Mario Adorf; ***D:*** Fernando Di Leo; ***W:*** Fernando Di Leo; ***C:*** Franco Villa; ***M:*** Armando Trovajoli.

Hired to Kill 🦴 ½ **1991 (R)** The granite-hewn Thompson plays a male-chauvinist commando grudgingly leading a squad of beautiful mercenary-ettes on an international rescue mission. Not as bad as it sounds (mainly because the ladies aren't complete bimbos), but between senseless plotting, gratuitous catfights, and a love scene indistinguishable from rape, there's plenty to dislike. **91m/C; VHS, DVD, Blu-Ray.** Brian Thompson; George Kennedy; Jose Ferrer; Oliver Reed; Penelope Reed; Michelle Moffett; Barbara Niven; Jordanna Capra; ***D:*** Nico Mastorakis; Peter Rader; ***W:*** Nico Mastorakis.

The Hireling 🦴🦴 **1973** In 1923, widowed Lady Helen Franklin (Miles) suffers a nervous breakdown after her husband's death. She becomes dependent on her new chauffeur, Ledbetter (Shaw), and the two begin a flirtation with the servant believing they've overcome their class differences. But as Lady Helen recovers, she finds a more suitable companion in an upcoming politician (Egan) to Ledbetter's rage. Based on L.P. Hartley's novel although the ending has been changed to the melodramatic. **95m/C; DVD.** *UK* Sarah Miles; Robert Shaw; Peter Egan; Caroline Mortimer; ***D:*** Alan Bridges; ***W:*** Wolf Mankowitz; ***C:*** Michael Reed; ***M:*** Marc Wilkinson.

Hiroshima 🦴🦴🦴 **1995 (PG)** Haunting depiction re-reates the circumstances surrounding the dropping of the first atomic bomb in 1945. Juxtaposes scenes between the U.S., Japan, and their leaders—President Truman (Welsh) and Emperor Hirohito (Umewaka)?with the development of the Manhattan Project, the bombing itself, and its consequences. Filmed primarily in B&W, with newsreel and contemporary witness interviews in color; Japanese sequences are subtitled in English. Filmed on location in Montreal and Tokyo. **180m/C; VHS, DVD.** *JP CA* Kenneth Welsh; Naohiko Umewaka; Wesley Addy; Richard Masur; Hisashi Igawa; Ken Jenkins; Jeffrey DeMunn; Leon Pownall; Saul Rubinek; Timothy West; Koji Takahashi; Kazuo Kato; ***D:*** Roger Spottiswoode; Koreyoshi Kurahara; ***W:*** John Hopkins; Toshiro Ishido; ***C:*** Pierre Mignot; Shohei Ando. **CABLE**

Hiroshima, Mon Amour 🦴🦴🦴🦴 **1959** Presented in a complex network of flashbacks, this profoundly moving drama explores the shadow of history over the personal lives of a lonely French actress (Riva), who's working in Hiroshima, and the Japanese architect (Okada) with whom she's having an affair. She has suffered during the war in occupied France, while his parents were in Hiroshima when the atomic bomb was dropped—and their pasts deeply affect their present. Resnais' first feature film and highly influential; adapted by Marguerite Duras from her book. French with subtitles. **88m/B; DVD, Blu-Ray.** *JP FR* Emmanuelle Riva; Eiji Okada; Bernard Fresson; Stella Dassas; Pierre Barbaud; ***D:*** Alain Resnais; ***W:*** Marguerite Duras; ***C:*** Sacha Vierny; Michio Takahashi; ***M:*** Georges Delerue; Giovanni Fusco. N.Y. Film Critics '60: Foreign Film.

His and Her Christmas 🦴🦴 ½ **2005** Columnist Tom Lane (Sutcliffe) works for a major San Francisco news conglomerate and is about to get his own TV show until rival columnist Liz Madison (Meyer) suddenly becomes more popular. Liz works for a small community paper that's about to be bought out by the conglomerate and she starts writing about the true meaning of Christmas. Tom counters with a practical holiday message and the battle, as well as romance, is on. **90m/C; DVD.** Dina Meyer; David Sutcliffe; April Telek; Kyle Cassie; Alistair Abell; Paula DeVicq; Garry Chalk; ***D:*** Farhad Mann; ***W:*** Peter Sullivan; ***C:*** Anthony C. Metchie; ***M:*** Peter Allen. **CABLE**

His Butler's Sister 🦴🦴 **1944** Bachelor composer Charles Gerard (Tone) lives a sybarite's life in his Manhattan penthouse, which is run by his butler Martin Murphy (O'Brien). When Murphy's stepsister Ann Carter (Durbin) arrives unexpectedly, she's delighted to hear who Murphy works for because she's a singer and wants an audition—an absolute taboo in Gerard's household. So she fools him into thinking she's the new maid until she can get her big break. Nothing new but Durbin does get to work her pretty pipes. **87m/B; VHS, DVD.** Deanna Durbin; Franchot Tone; Pat O'Brien; Evelyn Ankers; Akim Tamiroff; Alan Mowbray; Frank Jenks; Walter Catlett; Hans Conried; Florence Bates; Roscoe Karns; Franklin Pangborn; ***D:*** Frank Borzage; ***W:*** Samuel Hoffenstein; Bety Reinhardt; ***C:*** Elwood "Woody" Bredell; ***M:*** Hans J. Salter.

His Double Life 🦴🦴 ½ **1933** When a shy gentleman's valet dies, his master assumes the dead man's identity and has a grand time. From the play "Buried Alive" by Arnold Bennett. Remade in 1943 as "Holy Matrimony." **67m/B; VHS, DVD.** Roland Young; Lillian Gish; Montagu Love; ***D:*** Arthur Hopkins.

His Girl Friday 🦴🦴🦴🦴 **1940** Classic, unrelentingly hilarious war-between-the-sexes comedy. Cynical newspaper editor Walter Burns (Grant) wants to get a big scoop on political corruption, which involves convincing star reporter (and ex-wife) Hildy Johnson (Russell), to come back to work and put off her marriage to dull Bruce Baldwin (Bellamy). Hildy can't resist covering a good story, even when it mean helping a condemned man (Qualen) escape the law. One of Hawks's most furious and inventive screen combats in which women are given uniquely equal (for Hollywood) footing, with staccato dialogue and wonderful performances. Based on the Hecht-MacArthur play "The Front Page," which was filmed in 1931, remade in 1974, and again in 1988 (as "Switching Channels"). **92m/B; VHS, DVD, Blu-Ray.** Cary Grant; Rosalind Russell; Ralph Bellamy; Gene Lockhart; John Qualen; Porter Hall; Roscoe Karns; Abner Biberman; Cliff Edwards; Billy Gilbert; Helen Mack; Ernest Truex; Clarence (C. William) Kolb; Frank Jenks; ***D:*** Howard Hawks; ***W:*** Charles Lederer; ***C:*** Joseph Walker; ***M:*** Morris Stoloff. Natl. Film Reg. '93.

His Greatest Gamble 🦴 ½ **1934** Tearjerker. Philip Eden (Dix) escapes from prison after 15 years when he learns his estranged daughter, Alice (Wilson), has become a neurotic wimp under the thumb of her vengeful mother, Florence (O'Brien-Moore). And that's no way to treat daddy's little girl. **72m/B; DVD.** Richard Dix; Dorothy Wilson; Bruce Cabot; Erin O'Brien-Moore; Shirley Grey; Leonard Carey; ***D:*** John S. Robertson; ***W:*** Sidney Buchman; Harry Hervey; ***C:*** Ted Tetzlaff.

His Kind of Woman 🦴🦴🦴 **1951** Sleazy, campy crime drama that turns out to be compelling fun. Unlucky gambler Dan Milner (Mitchum) accepts a big payday for an unknown job that takes him to a Mexican resort. He gets an eyeful of chanteuse Lenore (Russell) and the hot twosome hook-up, even though her married boyfriend, Mark (Price), is also hanging around. Then Dan learns his job is to be the fall guy for racketeer Nick Ferraro (Burr), who wants to get back into the States, and he doesn't go for the idea. **120m/B; VHS, DVD.** Robert Mitchum; Jane Russell; Vincent Price; Tim Holt; Charles McGraw; Raymond Burr; Jim Backus; Marjorie Reynolds; ***D:*** John Farrow; ***W:*** Frank Fenton; Jack Leonard; ***C:*** Harry Wild; ***M:*** Leigh Harline.

His Majesty O'Keefe 🦴🦴 ½ **1953** Lancaster stars as a South Seas swashbuckler dealing in the lucrative coconut-oil trade of the mid-1800s. The natives see him as a god and allow him to marry a beautiful maiden. When his reign is threatened by unscrupulous traders, Lancaster springs into action to safeguard his kingdom. Based on a real-life American adventurer, this was the first movie ever filmed in the Fiji Islands. **92m/C; VHS, DVD.** Burt Lancaster; Joan Rice; Benson Fong; Philip Ahn; Grant Taylor; ***D:*** Byron Haskin.

His Majesty, the American 🦴🦴 ½ **1919** William Brooks (Fairbanks) is a young man whose heritage is unknown to him. It turns out he's an heir to a small European kingdom. When Brooks arrives in Alaine he discovers the war minister is trying to overthrow the present king. With his usual dash, our hero saves the day and also wins the hand of a beautiful princess. First picture released by United Artists studios, formed by Fairbanks, Mary Pickford, Charles Chaplin, and D.W. Griffith. **100m/B; Silent; VHS, DVD.** Douglas Fairbanks, Sr.; Marjorie Daw; Lillian Langdon; Frank Campeau; ***D:*** Joseph Henabery.

His Name Was King WOOF! *Lo Chiamavano King* **1971** A man goes after the gang who murdered his brother and raped his young wife in the old West. **90m/C; VHS, DVD, Blu-Ray.** *IT* Klaus Kinski; Anne Puskin; Richard Harrison; ***D:*** Giancarlo Romitelli; ***W:*** Renato Savino; ***C:*** Guglielmo Mancori; ***M:*** Luis Bacalov.

His Picture in the Papers 🦴🦴 **1916** An early silent comedy wherein the robust, red-meat-eating son of a health food tycoon must get his father's permission to marry by getting his picture favorably in the paper for advertising's sake. **68m/B; Silent; VHS, DVD.** Douglas Fairbanks, Sr.; Clarence Handysides; Rene Boucicault; Jean Temple; Charles Butler; Homer Hunt; Loretta Blake; Helena Rupport; ***D:*** John Emerson; ***W:*** John Emerson; Anita Loos.

His Private Secretary 🦴 ½ **1933** Wayne plays the jet-setting son of a wealthy businessman who wants his boy to settle down. And he does—after he meets the minister's beautiful daughter. **68m/B; VHS, DVD.** John Wayne; Evalyn Knapp; Alec B. Francis; Reginald Barlow; Natalie Kingston; Arthur Hoyt; Al "Fuzzy" St. John; ***D:*** Philip H. (Phil, P.H.) Whitman.

His Secret Life 🦴🦴🦴 *Fate Ignoranti; Blind Fairies; Ignorant Fairies* **2001 (R)** Antonia (Buy) is devastated when her husband Massimo (Renzi) is killed in a car accident. But her grief turns to shock when she accidentally discovers he was having a longtime affair. She goes to confront her husband's mistress and learns it's a mister—Michele (Accorsi), who resents Antonia's interference in his life. But Antonia is desperate to learn about her husband's secret life and other love and they are finally drawn together by their mutual bereavement and curiosity. Italian with subtitles. **105m/C; VHS, DVD.** *FR IT* Margherita Buy; Stefano Accorsi; Serra Yilmaz; Andrea Renzi; Erika Blanc; Gabriel Garko; Rosario De Cicco; Lucrezia Valia; Koray Candemir; ***D:*** Ferzan Ozpetek; ***W:*** Ferzan Ozpetek; Gianni Romoli; ***C:*** Pasquale Mari; ***M:*** Andrea Guerra.

The History Boys 🦴🦴 ½ **2006 (R)** Bennett adapted his own play, which also features the same cast and director and may seem more stagebound than cinematic. In 1983, at a Sheffield grammar school, eight senior boys are being specially tutored in history for a chance to pass the entrance exams to Oxford and Cambridge. To this end, the headmaster (Merrison) has brought in recent Oxford history grad Irwin (Campbell Moore) to tailor their studies, much to the dismay of portly general studies teacher Hector (Griffiths), who prefers a broader method of learning, and tart-tongued longtime teacher Dorothy (de la Tour). Except for class stud Dakin (Cooper) and the Jewish Posner (Barnett), who has a crush on him, the boys serve as background while the grownups show off. But Bennett can write some very good monologues. **109m/C; DVD.** *US GB* Richard Griffiths; Frances de la Tour; James Corden; Samuel Anderson; Stephan Campbell Moore; Samuel Barnett; Dominic Cooper; Jamie Parker; Sacha Dhawan; Russell Tovey; Georgia Taylor; Andrew Knott; Clive Merrison; Penelope Wilton; Adrian Scarborough; ***D:*** Nicholas Hytner; ***W:*** Alan Bennett; ***C:*** Andrew Dunn; ***M:*** George Fenton.

History Is Made at Night 🦴🦴🦴 **1937** A wife seeks a divorce from a jealous husband while on an Atlantic cruise; she ends up finding both true love and heartbreak in this story of a love triangle at sea. **98m/B; VHS, DVD.** Charles Boyer; Jean Arthur; Leo Carrillo; Colin Clive; ***D:*** Frank Borzage; ***C:*** Gregg Toland.

The History of Mr. Polly 🦴🦴 ½ **2007** Victorian everyman Alfred Polly (Evans) finds himself desperately unhappy since he's stuck with a nagging wife (Duff) and a failing business. So he decides to take drastic action to transform himself from a downtrodden loser into a hero. Based on a novel by H.G. Wells. **93m/C; DVD.** *GB* Lee Evans; Anne-Marie Duff; Julie Graham; Richard Coyle; Roger Lloyd-Pack; Trevor Cooper; ***D:*** Gilles Mackinnon; ***W:*** Adrian Hodges; ***C:*** Nigel Willoughby; ***M:*** James Edward Barker; Tim Despic. **TV**

History of the World: Part 1 🦴🦴 **1981 (R)** More misses than hits in this Brooks parody of historic epics. A bluntly satiric vision of human evolution, from the Dawn of Man to the French Revolution told in an episodic fashion. Good for a few laughs. **90m/C; VHS, DVD, Blu-Ray.** Mel Brooks; Dom DeLuise; Madeline Kahn; Harvey Korman; Cloris Leachman; Gregory Hines; Pamela Stephenson; Paul Mazursky; Bea Arthur; Fritz Feld; John Hurt; Jack Carter; John Hillerman; John Gavin; Barry Levinson; Ron Carey; Howard Morris; Sid Caesar; Jackie Mason; Charlie Callas; Henny Youngman; Hugh Hefner; ***Nar:*** Orson Welles; ***D:*** Mel Brooks; ***W:*** Mel Brooks; ***C:*** John Morris; Woody Omens; ***M:*** Shecky Greene.

A History of Violence 🦴🦴🦴 **2005 (R)** Unassuming small-town diner owner and family man Tom Stall foils a robbery, killing the hold-up men, and becomes a hero. This new status brings the unwanted attention of a trio of men who claim to be from Tom's past. And a very violent past it turns out to be. Cronenberg, with the exceptional help of a great cast, deftly and cleverly plays with the notion of identity and reality, while he takes a jab at the audience's knowledge of and expectations for action movies and their conventions. It's all very cool and engrossing, but he makes you squirm a little for enjoying the ride. **96m/C; DVD, Blu-Ray.** Viggo Mortensen; Maria Bello; William Hurt; Stephen McHattie; Peter MacNeill; Ed Harris; Ashton Holmes; Heidi Hayes; ***D:*** David Cronenberg; ***W:*** Josh Olson; ***C:*** Peter Suschitzky; ***M:*** Howard Shore. L.A. Film Critics '05: Support. Actor (Hurt); N.Y. Film Critics '05: Support. Actor (Hurt), Support. Actress (Bello); Natl. Soc. Film Critics '05: Director (Cronenberg), Support. Actor (Harris).

Hit! 🦴🦴 **1973 (R)** When the 15-year-old daughter of a government agent dies of a drug overdose, he deals his revenge to top French heroin traffickers. **135m/C; VHS, Blu-Ray, Streaming.** Billy Dee Williams; Richard Pryor; Gwen Welles; Paul Hampton; Warren Kemmerling; Sid Melton; ***D:*** Sidney J. Furie; ***W:*** Alan R. Trustman; David M. Wolf; ***M:*** Lalo Schifrin.

The Hit 🦴🦴 ½ **1985 (R)** A feisty young hooker gets mixed-up with two strong-armed hired killers as they escort an unusual stoolpigeon from his exile in Spain to their angry mob bosses. Minor cult-noir from the director of "My Beautiful Launderette" and "Dangerous Liaisons." **105m/C; VHS, DVD.** *GB* Terence Stamp; John Hurt; Laura Del Sol; Tim Roth; Fernando Rey; Bill Hunter; ***D:*** Stephen Frears; ***W:*** Peter Prince; ***C:*** John A. Alonzo; ***M:*** Eric Clapton.

The Hit 🦴 ½ **2001** A not-very-thrilling thriller that finds Baltimore reporter Keith (Caulfield) furious when he learns of wife

Sonia's (Pacula) infidelity. He gets drunk and arranges a contract hit on her but, after sobering up, realizes that's a little extreme and tries to call the whole thing off. Of course, Keith discovers he can't. Oh, and Lithuania fills in for Baltimore as a location site. **86m/C; VHS, DVD.** Maxwell Caulfield; Joanna Pacula; Christine Elise; Lucky Vanous; ***D:*** Vincent Monton; ***W:*** Vincent Monton; ***C:*** Raphael Smadja. **VIDEO**

The Hit 2006 Rising record exec Hen (Underwood) wants to unite all rival rap labels under one black-owned company that will also be a community power. But he crosses the mob, bent on shutting down Hen's efforts. **97m/C; DVD.** Blair Underwood; DeRay Davis; Ernest Harden, Jr.; James Russo; Michelle Flowers; Nicki Norris; ***D:*** Ryan Combs; ***W:*** Ryan Combs; ***C:*** Daniel (Danny) Moder; ***M:*** Chris Winston. **VIDEO**

Hit and Run 1/2 **2012 (R)** Comedy star Shepard steps behind the camera and in front of the typewriter for this uneven Tarantino-esque action comedy about a couple on a cross-country adventure. Charles Bronson (Shepard) happens to have been in Witness Protection for the last several years but he agrees to take his girlfriend Annie (Bell) to L.A. for a new job. A bad move since his former criminal compatriots want to kill him. **100m/C; DVD, Blu-Ray.** Dax Shepard; Kristen Bell; Bradley Cooper; Tom Arnold; Beau Bridges; Kristin Chenoweth; Michael Rosenbaum; Joy Bryant; ***D:*** Dax Shepard; David Palmer; ***W:*** Dax Shepard; ***C:*** Bradley Stonesifer; ***M:*** Julian Wass.

Hit and Runway 2001 **(R)** Alex (Parducci) works at his family's restaurant, although he really wants to be a screenwriter. He comes up with the idea for a movie for a big action star named Jagger Stevens (Richards), although Alex has no writing talent at all. So, Alex turns to playwright Elliot (Jacobson), whom he meets at the restaurant, for professional help. In return, Alex promises to help Elliot win the body of cute waiter Joey (Smith). It's all cute and predictable. **90m/C; VHS, DVD.** Michael Parducci; Peter Jacobson; Kerr Smith; Judy Prescott; J.K. Simmons; Teresa De Priest; Hoyt Richards; John Fiore; Steve Singer; ***D:*** Christopher Livingston; ***W:*** Christopher Livingston; Jaffe Cohen; ***C:*** David Tumblety; ***M:*** Frank Piazza.

Hit By Lightning 2014 A romantic comedy about finding love ... that demands murder. Middle-aged single fast food manager Ricky Miller (Cryer) longs to fall in love. Having no success in other ways, he turns to online dating and meets Danita (Szostak). Though she has no pictures on line, she wants to go on a date with Ricky and he finds her to be beautiful, charming, and intelligent. Though Danita seems very interested in him and his friend Seth (Sasso) encourages him to pursue her, Ricky believes there is a catch because she is out of his league. One day, Danita tells him she is in an unhappy marriage with a crime novelist who was accused of murdering an ex-wife. To be free of him and not lose her own life to her husband, Danita asks Ricky to murder him. **89m/C; DVD, Blu-Ray, Streaming, Download.** Jon Cryer; Jed Rees; Stephanie Szostak; Will Sasso; Nathaly Thibault; ***D:*** Ricky Blitt; ***W:*** Ricky Blitt; ***C:*** Arthur E. Cooper; ***M:*** Joel Campbell; Chantal Chamandy.

Hit Lady 1974 An elegant cultured woman becomes a hit lady for the syndicate in this predictable, yet slick gangster movie. **74m/C; VHS, DVD.** Yvette Mimieux; Dack Rambo; Clu Gulager; Keenan Wynn; ***D:*** Tracy Keenan Wynn; ***W:*** Yvette Mimieux; ***M:*** George Aliceson Tipton. **TV**

The Hit List 1/2 **2011 (R)** Disgruntled businessman Allan Campbell (Hauser) gets drunk with stranger Jonas Arbor (Gooding Jr.), who claims to be a hitman. Campbell facetiously creates a list of five people that Jonas is willing to take out for free. The next day they start turning up dead with all the evidence pointing to Allan committing the crimes. **90m/C; DVD.** Cole Hauser; Cuba Gooding, Jr.; Jonathan LaPaglia; Ginny Weirick; Sean Cook; Drew Waters; Michael (Mike) Papajohn; ***D:*** William Kaufman; ***W:*** Chad Law; Evan Law; ***C:*** Mark Rutledge; ***M:*** Deane Ogden. **VIDEO**

Hit Man 1/2 **1972** Blaxploitation version of 1971's "Get Carter" (based on the same novel) with lots of violence (and nudity by the ladies). Tyrone (Casey) arrives in L.A. for the funeral of his brother Cornell, believing he was murdered. Turns out Tyrone's niece Rochelle was forced into a porn picture and her daddy found out and wanted revenge. Now Tyrone is after the same thing—by any means and no matter who gets in his way. **91m/C; DVD.** Bernie Casey; Pam Grier; Lisa Moore; Bhetty Waldron; Sam Laws; Candy All; Don Diamond; Ed Cambridge; ***D:*** George Armitage; ***W:*** George Armitage; ***C:*** Andrew Davis; ***M:*** H.B. Barnum.

Hit Me 1/2 **1996 (R)** Bleak neo-noir based on Jim Thompson's novel "A Swell-Looking Babe." Sonny (Koteas) is a thirty-something bellhop at the downscale Stillwell hotel who goes home to a scuzzy apartment and the responsibilities of caring for his retarded brother Leroy (Leggett). His first slip is falling for troubled guest Monique (Marsac)?the femme fatale of the flick. And then Sonny makes an even bigger mistake by agreeing to help his "friend" Del (Ramsay) rob the hotel's safe deposit boxes of cash intended for a big poker game. **125m/C; VHS, DVD.** Elias Koteas; Laure Marsac; Bruce Ramsay; Jay Leggett; Kevin J. O'Connor; Philip Baker Hall; J.C. Quinn; Haing S. Ngor; William H. Macy; ***D:*** Steven Shainberg; ***W:*** Denis Johnson; ***C:*** Mark J. Gordon.

Hit Parade 2010 Quirky crime comedy. Retired hitman Jerome Archer is working as a bookstore manager when he's tracked down by two oddball Census Bureau employees. They insist Jerome resume his previous profession and go after crazy young killer Speed Razor, who's offed a CIA agent. **105m/C; DVD.** Jonathan Browning; Nicholas Lanier; Scott Brick; Mariah Robinson; Roger McDonald; Ned Mochel; Leslie McManus; ***D:*** Joe Casey; ***W:*** Joe Casey; ***C:*** Tom Camarda. **VIDEO**

Hit Parade of 1937 1937 Radio talent agent Pete (Regan) is fired after getting society girl singer Monica (Henry) a contract. So he decides to get even by finding a new singer to take Monica's spot on the radio show. Unfortunately, chosen singer Ruth (Langford) has a shady past that Monica is happy to reveal. Followed by four "Hit Parade of" sequels. **77m/B; DVD.** Phil Regan; Frances Langford; Louise Henry; Pert Kelton; Monroe Owsley; Edward Brophy; Max Terhune; ***D:*** Gus Meins; ***W:*** Bradford Ropes; ***C:*** Ernest Miller.

Hit the Deck 1/2 **1955** Second-rate studio musical about sailors on leave and looking for romance. Based on the 1927 Broadway musical. **112m/C; VHS, DVD, Blu-Ray.** Jane Powell; Tony Martin; Debbie Reynolds; Walter Pidgeon; Vic Damone; Gene Raymond; Ann Miller; Russ Tamblyn; J. Carrol Naish; Kay Armen; Richard Anderson; ***D:*** Roy Rowland; ***C:*** George J. Folsey.

Hit the Dutchman 1992 **(R)** Routine gangster flick about Dutch Schultz trying to rise to the top of the New York crime community—with or without the help of underworld pals Legs Diamond and Lucky Luciano. An unrated version is also available. **116m/C; VHS, DVD.** Bruce Nozick; Sally Kirkland; Will Kempe; Jenny (Jennifer) McShane; ***D:*** Menahem Golan.

Hit the Ice 1943 Newspaper photographers Bud and Lou are mistaken as gangsters in Chicago and the usual complications ensue. Includes an appearance by Johnny Long & His Orchestra. **89m/C; VHS, DVD.** Bud Abbott; Lou Costello; Patric Knowles; Elyse Knox; Ginny Simms; ***D:*** Charles Lamont.

Hitch 1/2 **2005 (PG-13)** The charming Smith tackles romantic comedy to amiable effect as the title character. Alex "Hitch" Hitchens is a professional dating doctor, the hero of schlubs everywhere. This time his client is shy, hefty accountant Albert (James), who's in love with Allegra (Valletta), a wealthy beauty far out of his league. While Hitch works on Albert, he's also falling for cynical gossip columnist Sara (Mendes) but his every smooth move turns disastrous in her hot babe presence. Everyone pulls their weight and looks like they're having fun. So should the audience. **119m/C; DVD, Blu-Ray, UMD.** Will Smith; Eva Mendes; Amber Valletta; Michael Rapaport; Adam Arkin; Kevin James; Julie Ann Emery; ***D:*** Andy Tennant; ***W:*** Kevin Bisch; ***C:*** Andrew Dunn; ***M:*** George Fenton.

The Hitch-Hiker 1953 Two young men off on the vacation of their dreams pick up a psychopathic hitchhiker with a right eye that never closes, even when he sleeps. Taut suspense makes this flick worth seeing. **71m/B; DVD, Blu-Ray.** Edmond O'Brien; Frank Lovejoy; William Talman; Jose Torvay; ***D:*** Ida Lupino; ***W:*** Ida Lupino; Daniel Mainwaring; Lucille Fletcher; Robert L. Joseph; ***C:*** Nicholas Musuraca; ***M:*** Leith Stevens. Natl. Film Reg. '98.

Hitchcock 1/2 **2012 (PG-13)** Iconic director Alfred Hitchcock remains an enigma to most who know his films but know little about the man. Hitchcock (Hopkins) and his wife Alma Reville (Mirren) are partners in life as well as in filmmaking--she offers her opinions on casting, writing, editing, and other aspects of filmmaking. In this love story, the pair ride the highs and lows of filming one of Hitchcock's most well-known films, "Psycho." And while Hopkins and Mirren make quite a pair, the storytelling doesn't equal up to its subject. In other words, it's nothing to go nuts about. **98m/C; DVD, Blu-Ray.** Anthony Hopkins; Dame Helen Mirren; Scarlett Johansson; Danny Huston; Toni Collette; Michael Stuhlbarg; Michael Wincott; Jessica Biel; James D'Arcy; ***D:*** Sacha Gervasi; ***W:*** John J. McLaughlin; ***C:*** Jeff Cronenweth; ***M:*** Danny Elfman.

Hitchcock/Truffaut 1/2 **2015 (PG-13)** New York critical luminary Kent Jones turns his documentary lens to a loose adaptation of one of the most influential critical theory books of all time, which shares the same title as the film. In an era when much of the critical establishment saw Hitchcock as purely an entertainer (believe it or not) and not a real filmmaker, Truffaut knew otherwise, sitting with the man and releasing their conversations. The film is a tribute to both filmmakers, although one wishes it wasn't 100% white men interviewed. While everyone here clearly adores and has been inspired by Hitch, no doubt that female directors were as well. **79m/C; DVD.** Mathieu Amalric; Wes Anderson; Olivier Assayas; Peter Bogdanovich; Arnaud Desplechin; ***D:*** Kent Jones; ***W:*** Kent Jones; Serge Toubiana; ***C:*** Nick Bentgen; Daniel Cowen; Eric Gautier; Mihai Malaimare, Jr.; Lisa Rinzler; Genta Tamaki; ***M:*** Jeremiah Bornfield.

Hitched 2001 Housewife Eve (Lee) doesn't suspect that her salesman hubby Ed (Hall) is cheating on her. But then he winds up in the hospital after a drunk-driving accident that also involved his lady friend of the moment. So Eve decides to get even by shackling him in their soundproof basement and filing a missing person's report. Detective Cary Grant (Carter) is immediately smitten and makes his move on Eve but gets confused when Ted reappears and Eve goes missing. **89m/C; VHS, DVD.** Sheryl Lee; Anthony Michael Hall; Alex Carter; ***D:*** Wesley Strick; ***W:*** Wesley Strick; ***C:*** Jonathan Freeman; ***M:*** Randy Miller. **CABLE**

Hitched for the Holidays 1/2 **2012** This Hallmark Channel rom com extends the holiday spirit by including Hanukkah. Rob Marino's family calls him on his inability to keep a girlfriend, so he tries to make his dying grandma happy by finding a honey to bring home for Christmas. To please her meddling Jewish mom, Julie wants a temporary boyfriend for the family's Hanukkah festivities. Rob and Julie meet online and agree to pose as a couple, but things get complicated. **90m/C; DVD.** Joseph Lawrence; Emily Hampshire; Marilu Henner; Paula Shaw; Serge Houde; ***D:*** Michael M. Scott; ***W:*** Gary Goldstein; ***C:*** Adam Sliwinski; ***M:*** James Jandrisch. **CABLE**

The Hitcher 1/2 **1986 (R)** A young man picks up a hitchhiker on a deserted stretch of California highway only to be tormented by the man's repeated appearances: is he real or a figment of his imagination? Ferociously funny, sadomasochistic comedy with graphic violence. **98m/C; VHS, DVD.** Rutger Hauer; C. Thomas Howell; Jennifer Jason Leigh; Jeffrey DeMunn; John M. Jackson; Billy Green Bush; ***D:*** Robert Harmon; ***W:*** Eric Red; ***C:*** John Seale; ***M:*** Mark Isham.

The Hitcher 1/2 **2007 (R)** Bean can't out-spook Rutger Hauer's title character from the 1986 original as this remake gets gutted (and not in a scary way) into generic action-horror. Jim (Knighton) and girlfriend Grace (Bush) are traveling that lonely desert highway, only to have repeated run-ins with psychopath John Ryder. Many of the original's set action pieces are recreated but, except for the addition of the nubile Bush, the '86 version is a lot more terrifying (if not as loud). **83m/C; DVD, Blu-Ray, HD-DVD.** Sean Bean; Sophia Bush; Zachery Knighton; Neal McDonough; ***W:*** Jake Wade Wall; Eric Bernt; ***C:*** Dave Meyers; James Hawkinson; ***M:*** Steve Jablonsky.

The Hitcher 2: I've Been Waiting 2003 **(R)** Jim Halsey (Howell reprises his role from the 1986 film) goes back to West Texas to confront his fear of the past accompanied by his girlfriend Maggie (Wuhrer). They travel the same stretch of desolate road and—surprise!?encounter a psycho hitchhiker, Jake (Busey, who certainly looks the part). **93m/C; VHS, DVD.** C. Thomas Howell; Kari Wuhrer; Jake Busey; ***D:*** Louis Morneau; ***W:*** Molly Meeker; Charles Meeker; Leslie Scharf; ***C:*** George Mooradian; ***M:*** Joe Kraemer. **VIDEO**

The Hitchhiker's Guide to the Galaxy 1981 The six-episode BBC TV adaptation of Douglas Adams's hilarious science-fiction books. Features the intergalatic Ford Prefect, sent to Earth to update its planetary listing in the Hitchhiker's Guide; hapless hero Arthur Dent, a typical Englishman caught up in space mayhem; and an odd assortment of aliens, including Marvin the Paranoid Android. The show's sheer cheesiness is part of the charm. **194m/C; VHS, DVD.** *UK* Simon Jones; David Dixon; Sandra Dickinson; Mark Wing-Davey; ***D:*** Alan Bell; ***W:*** Douglas Adams. **TV**

The Hitchhiker's Guide to the Galaxy **2005 (PG)** Douglas Adams' absurdist sci-fi classic finally makes it to the big screen. When the Earth is demolished, Arthur Dent (Freeman) hitches a ride off the planet with Ford Prefect (Def), a writer for the HGTG, a Fodors-esque guidebook to the universe. Arthur and Ford fall in with Zaphod Beeblebrox (Rockwell), the sublimely dense President of the Galaxy, and his girlfriend, Trillian (Deschanel), in their quest to find the Ultimate Question to life, the universe, and everything. The script's slavish devotion to Adams' text weighs down certain scenes, making them sound more like audiobook recitations, but Jennings does a praiseworthy job of bringing the author's eccentric vision to life. The cast is uniformly strong, particularly Rockwell, who gleefully chews the scenery as two-headed egotist Zaphod. **110m/C; DVD, UMD.** *GB US* Martin Freeman; Mos Def; Sam Rockwell; Zooey Deschanel; John Malkovich; Bill Nighy; Warwick Davis; Simon Jones; Anna Chancellor; Albie Woodington; Jason Schwartzman; Dominique Jackson; Jack Stanley; ***V:*** Alan Rickman; Thomas Lennon; Dame Helen Mirren; Stephen Fry; Richard Griffiths; Ian McNeice; ***D:*** Garth Jennings; ***W:*** Douglas Adams; Karey Kirkpatrick; ***C:*** Igor Jadue-Lillo; ***M:*** Joby Talbot.

Hitler 1/2 *Women of Nazi Germany* **1962** The true story of the infamous Nazi dictator's rise to power and his historic downfall. **107m/B; DVD.** Richard Basehart; Maria Emo; Cordula Trantow; Martin Kosleck; ***D:*** Stuart Heisler; ***W:*** Sam Neuman; ***C:*** Joseph Biroc; ***M:*** Hans J. Salter.

Hitler: Beast of Berlin 1/2 *Beasts of Berlin* **1939** German intellectual Hans, his wife Elsa, and their patriotic friends print and distribute anti-Nazi propaganda. Hans and some of the others are captured and taken to a concentration camp where they are tortured, but he has a chance to escape. Film was drastically edited before its release because of isolationist protests since America had yet to enter the war. **87m/B; DVD.** Roland Drew; Steffi Duna; Greta Granstedt; Alan Ladd; Lucien Prival; Hans Joby; Walter O.Stahl; John Ellis; Vernon Dent; ***D:*** Sam Newfield; ***W:*** Fred Myton; ***C:*** Jack Greenhalgh.

Hitler: The Last Ten Days 1973 **(PG)** Based on an eyewitness account, the story of Hitler's last days in an underground bunker gives insight to his madness. **106m/C; VHS, DVD.** Alec Guinness; Simon Ward; Adolfo Celi; Phyllida Law; Diane Cilento; Gabriele Ferzetti; Eric Porter; Doris Kunstmann; Joss Ackland; John Bennett; John Barron; Barbara Jefford; Julian Glover; Michael Goodliffe; Mark Kingston; Philip Stone; ***D:*** Ennio de Concini; *W:* Ennio de Concini; *C:* Ennio Guarnieri; *M:* Mischa Spoliansky.

Hitler: The Rise of Evil 🦴🦴 **2003** General overview of the insecure but ambitious Hitler (Carlyle) during his rise to power. He goes from World War I soldier to member of the nationalistic German Worker's Party and leader of the Nazi Party. Filmed on location in Vienna and Prague. **186m/C; DVD.** Robert Carlyle; Stockard Channing; Liev Schreiber; Peter O'Toole; Jena Malone; Julianna Margulies; Matthew Modine; Peter Stormare; Chris Larkin; *D:* Christian Duguay; *W:* John Pielmeier; G. Ross Parker; *C:* Pierre Gill; *M:* Normand Corbeil. **TV**

The Hitman 🦴🦴 **1991 (R)** Norris plays a cop undercover as a syndicate hit man in Seattle, where he cleans up crime by triggering a three-way mob bloodbath between beastly Italian mafiosi, snooty French-Canadian hoods, and fanatical Iranian scum. But he teaches a black kid martial arts, so you know he's politically correct. Action addicts will give this a passing grade; all others need not apply. **95m/C; VHS, DVD.** Chuck Norris; Michael Parks; Al Waxman; Alberta Watson; Salim Grant; Ken Pogue; Marcel Sabourin; Bruno Gerussi; Frank Ferrucci; *D:* Aaron Norris; *C:* Joao Fernandes.

Hitman WOOF! 2007 (R) Just like the videogame on which the film is based, orphaned kids are recruited by a top-secret organization that trains them as assassins. Grown, the killers are all bald with their heads tattooed with large bar codes, and they roam around the rest of the world with large guns, knocking off whomever needs knocking off. One of these guys, known only as "47" (Olyphant), is on task to murder Russian President Belicoff (Thomsen), which he does with brutal (and predictable) violence. But when Belicoff later shows up alive on television, 47 realizes he's been had, and now he's running from police, Interpol, and worse yet, a handful of his old cronies. Somehow gorgeous Nika (Kurylenko) gets tossed into the mix and is on the lam with 47. She lends some eye-candy and a touch of humanity, but that's about it. The violence is over the top, the plot is less than thin, and the acting perfunctory at best. **100m/C; Blu-Ray, On Demand.** Timothy Olyphant; Olga Kurylenko; Dougray Scott; Robert Knepper; Ulrich Thomsen; Henry Ian Cusack; Michael Offei; *D:* Skip Woods; Xavier Gens; *C:* Laurent Bares; *M:* Geoff Zanelli.

Hitman: Agent 47 🦴 **2015 (R)** Another movie adaptation of a video game that feels made by people who never even played the source material. Eight years after adapting the Square-Enix hit failed with Timothy Olyphant in the lead, it fails even harder with Rupert Friend as the title character, a factory-produced killing machine who revolts against the system that created him. Agent 47 teams up with mysterious woman Katia (Ware) to find her father, who designed the program and may be the only person who can stop it. Slow-motion action scenes can't disguise a complete lack of creativity here. Who knew video games were this boring? **96m/C; DVD, Blu-Ray.** Rupert Friend; Zachary Quinto; Emilio Rivera; Hannah Ware; Thomas Kretschmann; *D:* Aleksander Bach; *W:* Skip Woods; Michael Finch; *C:* Ottar Gudnason; *M:* Marco Beltrami.

The Hitman Diaries 🦴 1/2 *Charlie Valentine* **2009 (R)** Aging gangster Charlie Valentine (Barry) decides to fund his retirement by stealing from his boss Rocco (Russo). When his plan fails, Charlie hides out with his estranged son Danny (Weatherly) who inexplicably decides he wants his old man to teach him to be a tough guy. Too bad Rocco has put out a hit on Charlie. **96m/C; DVD.** Raymond J. Barry; Michael Weatherly; James Russo; Tom Berenger; Steven Bauer; Maxine Bahns; Keith David; *D:* Jesse Johnson; *W:* Jesse Johnson; *C:* Jonathan Hall; *M:* Wagner Fluco. **VIDEO**

The Hitman's Bodyguard 🦴🦴 **2017 (R)** A precise man whose reputation as the world's leading bodyguard was shattered by one protection gig gone bad, a beleaguered Michael Bryce (Reynolds) is forced to guard his enemy, assassin Darius Kincaid (Jackson), over the course of one long day. Kincaid is the key witness in the trial of a notorious Eastern European dictator, Vladislav Dukhovich (Oldman), for international war crimes at The Hague, and Bryce is tasked with getting Kincaid to court in time to testify. Combining high speed car and boat chases, loads of violence and gunfire, and topical political concerns, the film makes the most of what would have been a overdone summer flick with lesser actors. **118m/C; DVD, Blu-Ray.** Ryan Reynolds; Elodie Yung; Richard E. Grant; Gary Oldman; Rod Hallett; *D:* Patrick Hughes; *W:* Tom O'Connor; *C:* Jules O'Loughlin; *M:* Atli Orvarsson.

Hitman's Journal 🦴🦴 *18 Shades of Dust* **1999 (R)** Vincent Dianni (Aiello) is a mob enforcer for Don Cucci and his son Tommy (Forsythe). But when info leaked to the feds gets the Don life in prison, Vincent comes under suspicion as the squealer. All Vincent wants to do is quietly retire but first he has to square things with his bosses. **95m/C; VHS, DVD.** Danny Aiello; William Forsythe; Polly Draper; Vincent Pastore; Aida Turturro; *D:* Danny Aiello, III. **VIDEO**

Hitman's Run 🦴🦴 **1999 (R)** Former Mafia hitman Roberts has double-crossed his bosses and is now in the FBI's Witness Protection Program. However, his safety is hardly guaranteed. **93m/C; VHS, DVD.** Eric Roberts; Damian Chapa; Esteban Louis Powell; *D:* Mark L. Lester; *W:* Eric Barker; *C:* Zoltan David; *M:* Roger Bellon. **VIDEO**

The Hive 🦴🦴 **2008** Tries to be more than your typical creature feature but you can only do so much with killer ants. Exterminators Len (Weber) and Bill (Wopat) are dispatched by their company to eradicate a mass of flesh-eating ants in the jungles of Ben Tao, Thailand. Entomologist Claire (Healy) has discovered that the hive displays a disturbing collective intelligence. The team is actually captured by the ants and learn about their origin and intentions from the hive queen herself. Let's just say no one is going to be stepping on these babies anytime soon! **90m/C; DVD.** Tom Wopat; Elizabeth Healey; Kal Weber; Jessica Reavis; Mark Ramsey; *D:* Peter Manus; *W:* T.S. Cook; *C:* Kittiwat Sawmaret; *M:* Mark Ryder; Charles Olins. **CABLE**

H.M. Pulham Esquire 🦴🦴 **1941** His 25th Harvard reunion (and an encounter with an old flame) has stuffy Bostonian Harry Pulham (Young) contemplating his conventional life. The scion of a wealthy family remembers the one time he went against society's strictures by falling for Iowa-born Marvin (Lamarr) when they worked together in New York. With his father disapproving of their romance, Harry scuttles home to marry suitable Kay (Hussey) while Marvin goes on to a successful career. Lamarr's heavy Viennese accent is distracting but so is her beauty. Adapted from the John P. Marquand novel. **119m/B; DVD.** Robert Young; Hedy Lamarr; Ruth Hussey; Charles Coburn; Van Heflin; Fay Holden; Bonita Granville; Leif Erickson; *D:* King Vidor; *W:* King Vidor; Elizabeth Hill; *C:* Ray June; *M:* Bronislau Kaper.

The Hoarder 🦴 1/2 **2015** A horror film centered on a predator who **84m/C; DVD, Streaming, Download. VIDEO**

The Hoax 🦴🦴 **2006 (R)** In 1971, egocentric writer Clifford Irving's (Gere) dreams collapse when his book deal falls through. To bolster his bruised ego, Irving tells his publisher (Davis) that his new tome will be a sensation—and then has to come up with an idea. With the help of loyal researcher Dick Suskind (Molina), Irving schemes to sell a bogus autobiography of recluse Howard Hughes and greed wins out over corporate suspicions before Irving's scam is exposed. Hallstrom and his cast do well but this long-forgotten hoax has to work hard to attract the interest of a casual viewer. **115m/C; DVD, Blu-Ray.** Richard Gere; Alfred Molina; Hope Davis; Marcia Gay Harden; Stanley Tucci; Julie Delpy; *D:* Lasse Hallstrom; *W:* William Wheeler; *C:* Oliver Stapleton; *M:* Carter Burwell.

Hoax for the Holidays 🦴 1/2 *Faith, Fraud and Minimum Wage* **2010** Bored, rebellious Nova Scotia teen Casey feels responsible for the accident that put her sister Meg into a coma. Bills are piling up and her dad Donald spends most of his time at the hospital. Casey gets mad at her donut shop boss Uncle Bob, flings a cup of coffee at an outside wall, and alters the results so the stain looks like Jesus. Since she does this at Christmas, her hoax starts drawing crowds and spins out of control. **98m/C; DVD.** *CA* Martha MacIsaac; Callum Keith Rennie; Don Allison; Ricky Mabe; Andrew Bush; *D:* George Mihalka; *W:* Josh MacDonald; *C:* Norayr Kasper.

The Hobbit 🦴🦴🦴 **1978** An animated interpretation of J.R.R. Tolkien's novel of the same name. The story follows Bilbo Baggins and his journeys in Middle Earth and encounters with the creatures who inhabit it. He joins comrades to battle against evil beings and creatures. **76m/C; VHS, DVD.** *V:* Orson Bean; John Huston; Otto Preminger; Richard Boone; Cyril Ritchard; Brother Theodore; Paul Frees; Donald E. Messick; Hans Conried; Thurl Ravenscroft; *D:* Arthur Rankin, Jr.; Jules Bass; *M:* Maury Laws. **TV**

The Hobbit: An Unexpected Journey 🦴🦴 1/2 **2012 (PG-13)** A true disappointment following the artistic success of Peter Jackson's The Lord of the Rings trilogy, this first of three films based on J.R.R. Tolkien's prequel to the adventures of Frodo Baggins in Middle Earth is overlong, bloated, and generally dull. Freeman works as Bilbo and the return of McKellen as Gandalf is welcome but Jackson loses the pacing and urgency that made his first adventures in this fantasy world so accomplished. There enough creative hints to suggest that the sequels will work better but this prologue could easily lose an hour and not suffer in the plot department. Strong visuals only slightly compensate. **169m/C; DVD, Blu-Ray.** Ian McKellen; Martin Freeman; Richard Armitage; Elijah Wood; Hugo Weaving; Cate Blanchett; Christopher Lee; Sylvester McCoy; Manu Bennett; *V:* Andy Serkis; *D:* Peter Jackson; *W:* Peter Jackson; Fran Walsh; Philippa Boyens; Guillermo del Toro; *C:* Andrew Lesnie; *M:* Howard Shore.

The Hobbit: The Battle of the Five Armies 🦴 1/2 **2014 (PG-13)** Dividing J.R.R. Tolkien's books into three chapters leads to the inevitable fate of a final film in this saga that is basically all epilogue. The drama of this installment could be distilled to half an hour and added on to the end of the last film. The biggest problem is that Thorin Oakenshield (Armitage) is forced to take center stage as the dwarves take control of the Lonely Mountain and their leader goes crazy from his obsession with gold, and Thorin just isn't an engaging enough protagonist. And so all we're left with is the CGI battles, which are admittedly well-staged and executed, but become so repetitious that it's impossible to care. **144m/C; DVD, Blu-Ray.** Martin Freeman; Richard Armitage; Ian McKellen; Lee Pace; Orlando Bloom; Billy Connolly; Luke Evans; Evangeline Lilly; Aidan Turner; Cate Blanchett; Christopher Lee; Hugo Weaving; *V:* Benedict Cumberbatch; *D:* Peter Jackson; *W:* Peter Jackson; Fran Walsh; Philippa Boyens; Guillermo del Toro; *C:* Andrew Lesnie; *M:* Howard Shore.

The Hobbit: The Desolation of Smaug 🦴🦴🦴 **2013 (PG-13)** Now that we're getting closer to the meat of the story, the second film based on J.R.R. Tolkien's "The Hobbit" at least connects in terms of pure spectacle and action-adventure storytelling--even if it doesn't quite yet justify the expansion of the book into three films. Bilbo (Freeman) and the gang are still headed to Lonely Mountain and the lair of Smaug (Cumberbatch), a gloriously-rendered dragon. The art direction, the characters, and the action set-pieces--every element feels more confident than the first Hobbit and ends on a note that should get viewers excited for the final chapter. **161m/C; DVD, Blu-Ray.** Ian McKellen; Martin Freeman; Richard Armitage; Orlando Bloom; Evangeline Lilly; Luke Evans; *V:* Benedict Cumberbatch; *D:* Peter Jackson; *W:* Peter Jackson; Philippa Boyens; Fran Walsh; Guillermo del Toro; *C:* Andrew Lesnie; *M:* Howard Shore.

Hobgoblins 🦴 **1987** Little creatures escape from a studio vault and wreak havoc. **92m/C; VHS, DVD, Blu-Ray.** Jeffrey Culver; Tom Bartlett; *D:* Rick Sloane.

Hobo With a Shotgun 🦴🦴 **2011** Gleeful entry in the trash/midnight movie genre complete with lots of guns and gore. Nameless grizzled hobo (Hauer) panhandles at local crime boss Drake's (Downey) sleazy hangout, whose two psycho sons (Smith & Bateman) get their jollies by mutilation and death. They target the hobo but instead of being their victim he gets a shotgun, teams up with pretty hooker Abby (Dunsworth), and decides to get even and then some. Director Eisener got the chance to make his feature film after winning a fake trailer contest for Robert Rodriguez and Quentin Tarantino's "Grindhouse." **86m/C; DVD, Blu-Ray, Download.** Rutger Hauer; Molly Dunsworth; Brian Downey; Gregory Edward Smith; Nick Bateman; *D:* Jason Eisener; *W:* John Davies; *C:* Karim Hussain; *M:* Adam Burke; Darius Hobert.

Hobo's Christmas 🦴🦴 **1987** A man who left his family to become a hobo comes home for Christmas 25 years later. Hughes turns in a delightful performance as the hobo. **94m/C; VHS, DVD.** Barnard Hughes; William Hickey; Gerald McRaney; Wendy Crewson; *D:* Will MacKenzie. **TV**

Hobson's Choice 🦴🦴🦴 **1953** A prosperous businessman in the 1890s tries to keep his daughter from marrying, but the strong-willed daughter has other ideas. **107m/B; VHS, DVD.** *GB* Charles Laughton; John Mills; Brenda de Banzie; *D:* David Lean; *C:* Jack Hildyard; *M:* Malcolm Arnold. British Acad. '54: Film.

Hobson's Choice 🦴🦴 **1983** Remake of the old family comedy about a crusty, penny-pinching businessman whose headstrong daughter proves to him she'll not become an old maid. Instead she marries one of his employees. Not bad, but not as good as the original. **95m/C; VHS, DVD.** Jack Warden; Sharon Gless; Richard Thomas; Lillian Gish; *D:* Gilbert Cates. **TV**

Hockey Night 🦴🦴 1/2 **1984** A movie for pre- and early teens in which a girl goalie makes the boys' hockey team. **77m/C; VHS, DVD.** *CA* Megan Follows; Rick Moranis; Gail Youngs; Martin Harburg; Henry Ramer; *D:* Paul Shapiro.

Hocus Pocus 🦴🦴 1/2 **1993 (PG)** The divine Miss M is back, but this time she's not so sweet. Midler, Najimy, and Parker are 17th century witches accidentally conjured up in the 20th century, appropriately enough on Halloween in Salem, Massachusetts. Seems they were hung 300 years back and they take their revenge in some surprisingly gruesome ways, given the Disney label. They rant, they rave, they sing (only once), they fly. See this one for the three stars who make up for the lack of substance with their comedic talents. **95m/C; VHS, DVD, Blu-Ray.** Bette Midler; Kathy Najimy; Sarah Jessica Parker; Thora Birch; Doug Jones; Omri Katz; Vinessa Shaw; Stephanie Faracy; Charles Rocket; ***Cameo(s):*** Penny Marshall; Garry Marshall; *D:* Kenny Ortega; *W:* Neil Cuthbert; Mick Garris; *M:* John Debney.

Hoffa 🦴🦴🦴 **1992 (R)** The story of union organizer James R. Hoffa, who oversaw the rise of the Teamsters, a labor union composed mostly of truck drivers, from its fledgling infancy during the Great Depression to a membership of two million by the 1970s. Powerful performances by Nicholson in the title role and DeVito, who plays a union aide, a fictitious composite of several men who actually served Hoffa. This almost affectionate biographical treatment stands out in contrast from a career bristling with tension and violence. Proceeds through a series of flashbacks from the day Hoffa disappeared, July 30, 1975. **140m/C; VHS, DVD, Blu-Ray.** Jack Nicholson; Danny DeVito; Armand Assante; J.T. Walsh; Frank Whaley; Kevin Anderson; John P. Ryan; Robert Prosky; Natalija Nogulich; Nicholas Pryor; John C. Reilly; Karen Young; Cliff Gorman; Paul Guilfoyle; Jennifer Nicholson; Richard Schiff; *D:* Danny DeVito; *W:* David Mamet; *C:* Stephen Burum; *M:* David Newman.

Hoffman 🦴 1/2 **1970** Lonely, middle-aged business Benjamin Hoffman (Sellers) has a yen for his secretary Janet (Cusack). When he discovers her boyfriend Tom (Mitchell) is involved in some illegal activities, Hoffman blackmails her into spending the weekend with him. Very minor Sellers and not very funny. Gebler adapted from his own novel. **113m/C; VHS, DVD.** *GB* Peter Sellers; Sinead Cusack; Jeremy Bulloch; *D:* Alvin Rakoff; *W:* Ernest Gebler; *C:* Gerry Turpin; *M:* Ron Grainer.

Hogfather 🦴🦴 1/2 **2006** Adapted from the 20th book in Terry Pratchett's Discworld series, this is a more-or-less stand-alone

Christmas story. It's the night before Hogswatch, the mid-winter festival where the Hogfather delivers presents to the kiddies. But the wraith-like Auditors have decided that Discworld's humans are destroying their perfect vision of the universe. They want assassin Mr. Teatime to eliminate Hogfather and destroy the idea of hope in the world. But Death decides to take over for the missing Hogfather while his granddaughter Susan investigates. **189m/C; DVD, Blu-Ray.** *GB* David Jason; Joss Ackland; Marc Warren; David Warner; Ian Richardson; Michelle Dockery; ***V:*** Ian Richardson; ***D:*** Vadim Jean; ***W:*** Vadim Jean; ***C:*** Gavin Finney; Jan Pester; ***M:*** David A. Hughes. **TV**

The Holcroft Covenant **1985 (R)** Based upon the complex Robert Ludlum novel. Details the efforts of a man trying to release a secret fund that his Nazi father humanistically set up to relieve the future sufferings of Holocaust survivors. Confusing, and slow, but interesting, nonetheless. **112m/C; VHS, DVD, Blu-Ray.** *GB* Michael Caine; Victoria Tennant; Anthony Andrews; Lilli Palmer; Mario Adorf; Michael (Michel) Lonsdale; ***D:*** John Frankenheimer; ***W:*** Edward Anhalt; John Hopkins; George Axelrod.

Hold Back the Dawn **1/2 1941** Unable to enter the United States during WWII after escaping Nazi Europe, philandering immigrant George (an immensely charismatic Boyer) encounters former love interest Anita (Goddard) who shares the method she used to circumvent the process: marry an American citizen, get in the country, and then bail out on them. Enter demure, wide-eyed schoolteacher Emmy (de Havilland), who takes George's bait. But George and Anita's future might not be so certain. Director Leisen's romance is imperfect yet pleasing, highlighted by superb performances by the attractive leads. Told in flashbacks, writers Wilder and Brackett aptly adapted from a 1941 novel by Ketti Frings. **116m/B; DVD, Blu-Ray.** Charles Boyer; Olivia de Havilland; Paulette Goddard; Victor Francen; Walter Abel; ***D:*** Mitchell Leisen; Arthur Hornblow, Jr.; ***W:*** Charles Brackett; Billy Wilder; ***C:*** Leo Tover; ***M:*** Victor Young.

Hold 'Em Jail **1/2 1932** Some good laughs with Wheeler and Woolsey starting a competitive football team at Kennedy's Bidemore Prison. **65m/B; VHS, DVD.** Bert Wheeler; Robert Woolsey; Edgar Kennedy; Betty Grable; Edna May Oliver; ***D:*** Norman Taurog.

Hold On! **1966** Goofy, campy musical-comedy stars Brit pop-rockers Herman's Hermits. The band is on a U.S. tour and might get a space capsule named after them if they pass inspection by NASA scientist Lindquist (Anderson). Complicating matters are a couple of chicks. It all ends with a Rose Bowl concert. **85m/C; DVD.** Peter Noone; Shelley Fabares; Herbert Anderson; Sue Ane Langdon; Bernard Fox; Hortense Petra; ***D:*** Arthur Lubin; ***W:*** Robert Kent; ***C:*** Paul Vogel; ***M:*** Fred Karger.

Hold That Ghost *Oh, Charlie* **1941** Abbott and Costello inherit an abandoned roadhouse where the illicit loot of its former owner, a "rubbed out" mobster, is supposedly hidden. **86m/B; VHS, DVD.** Bud Abbott; Lou Costello; Joan Davis; Richard Carlson; Mischa Auer; Andrews Sisters; Shemp Howard; Evelyn Ankers; Nestor Paiva; ***D:*** Arthur Lubin; ***W:*** Robert Lees; Frederic Rinaldo; John Grant; ***C:*** Elwood "Woody" Bredell; ***M:*** Hans J. Salter.

Hold the Dark **1/2 2018** Russell Core (Wright), a retired naturalist and wolf expert, is summoned to remote Alaska (is there any other kind of Alaska?) to hunt the wolf responsible for killing a small boy. Things are not what they seem, but good luck figuring out what's going on, other than the conclusion that wolves may be the most benign creatures involved. An unexplained supernatural presence also confuses matters, leaving you wondering what was left on the editing room floor. The cinematography is gorgeous and the acting is fine, but for answers, read the book by William Giraldi. **125m/C; Streaming.** Jeffrey Wright; Alexander Skarsgård; James Badge Dale; Riley Keough; Julian Black Antelope; ***D:*** Jeremy Saulnier; ***W:*** Macon Blair; ***C:*** Magnus Nordenhof Jonck; ***M:*** Brooke Blair; Will Blair. **VIDEO**

Hold the Dream **1/2 1986** Barbara Taylor Bradford's sequel to "A Woman of Substance." Kerr plays the adult Emma Harte while Seagrove, who played young Emma in the original miniseries, now plays her granddaughter Paula, who has been chosen to take over the family's retailing empire. But will her ambitions clash with her romantic possibilities? **200m/C; VHS, DVD.** Jenny Seagrove; Deborah Kerr; Claire Bloom; James Brolin; Stephen Collins; Nicholas Farrell; Nigel Havers; John Mills; Liam Neeson; Valentine Pelka; ***D:*** Don Sharp; ***C:*** John Coquillon; ***M:*** Barrie Guard. **TV**

Hold Your Breath *#HOLDYOURBREATH* **2012 (R)** Teens confront an urban myth that if you don't hold your breath when passing a cemetery that you can be possessed by ghosts. **87m/C; DVD, Blu-Ray, Streaming.** Katrina Bowden; Randy Wayne; Erin Marie Hogan; Steve Hanks; Seth Cassell; ***D:*** Jared Cohn; ***W:*** Geoff Meed; Kenny Zinn; ***C:*** Stuart Brereton; ***M:*** Chris Ridenhour. **VIDEO**

Hold Your Man **1933** Great star vehicle that turns from comedy to drama with Harlow falling for hustler Gable. Harlow and Gable are at their best in this unlikely story of a crooked couple. Direction drags at times, but snappy dialogue and the stars' personalities more than make up for it. **86m/B; DVD.** Jean Harlow; Clark Gable; Stuart Erwin; Dorothy Burgess; Garry Owen; Paul Hurst; Elizabeth Patterson; Laura La Plante; ***D:*** Sam Wood; ***W:*** Anita Loos; Howard Emmett Rogers.

Hold Your Peace **2011** Too-predictable gay indie rom com. Aidan still isn't over his breakup with ex Max, though it's clear Max has moved on when he asks Aidan to be his best man at his commitment ceremony to Forrest. Aidan refuses to be the lonely single guy and persuades Lance to pretend to be his boyfriend. However, Aidan still wants Max, Max and Forrest are quarreling, and Lance makes it clear he's willing to help Forrest with any romantic troubles. **99m/C; DVD.** Chad Ford; Tyler Brockington; Scott Higgins; Blair Dickens; Aleisha Force; ***D:*** Wade McDonald; ***W:*** Wade McDonald; ***C:*** Wade McDonald. **VIDEO**

Holding Trevor **1/2 2007 (R)** Disaffected 20-somethings try to find meaning in their L.A. lives. Trevor dutifully takes his heroin-addicted boyfriend Darrell to the hospital when he overdoses again. Once he finds out Darrell will be okay, Trevor decides he's done with the drama and turns to intern Ephram for stability. But when Trevor and his friends, alcoholic Andie and promiscuous Jake, decide to throw a party, it turns out to be an unexpectedly dramatic affair. **88m/C; DVD.** Brent Gorski; Eli Ktanski; Melissa Searing; Jay Brannan; ***D:*** Christopher Wyllie; Rosser Goodman; ***W:*** Brent Gorski; ***C:*** Kara Stephens.

The Hole *The Last Dance; Dong* **1998** Originally conceived as an entry for a French TV series of end-of-the-millennium dramas, this award-winning film crosses several genres and might not be immediately accessible to most. Seven days before the end of the 21st century the rain simply will not let up, and a new virus is causing odd mutations in behavior (and sometimes bodies). Despite evacuation orders the tenants of one run down apartment building stay, and indulge in stockpiling toilet paper, performing odd musical numbers, and pretending to be roaches. If you like weird, drawn-out art films, this is for you. **95m/C; DVD.** *TN FR* Kang-sheng Lee; Tien Miao; Kuei-Mei Yang; Hui-Chin Lin; Hsiang-Chu Tong; ***D:*** Ming-liang Tsai; ***W:*** Ming-liang Tsai; Pi-ying Yang; ***C:*** Pen-jung Liao; ***M:*** Grace Chang.

The Hole **1/2 2001** Teen psycho-drama offers cheap thrills. A terrified Liz (Birch) is discovered to be the only survivor of four students who have been missing for 18 days. Liz talks to psychologist Philippa Horwood (Davidtz) as flashbacks reveal the nightmare. Liz has a crush on Mike (Harrington), which she revealed to confidante Martin (Brocklebank), who has an unrequited crush on her. Seeking to escape a school trip, Liz persuades Martin to let her and Mike and their friends Geoff (Fox) and Frankie (Knightley) spend the time in a disused WWII underground steel bunker he's discovered. Only jealous Martin locks them in. Or does he? Liz's story is full of holes and the police investigation offers another theory of what happened. Based on the novel "After the Hole" by Guy Burt. **102m/C; VHS, DVD, Blu-Ray.** *GB* Thora Birch; Desmond Harrington; Embeth Davidtz; Daniel Brocklebank; Keira Knightley; Steven Waddington; Laurence Fox; ***D:*** Nick Hamm; ***W:*** Ben Court; Caroline Ip; ***C:*** Denis Crossan; ***M:*** Clint Mansell.

A Hole in One **2004** It's not about golf. Anna (Williams) is a sweet but troubled small-town girl in the 1950s whose boyfriend is the pathologically jealous and violent Billy (Aday). Emotionally fragile, Anna becomes convinced that the way out of her troubles is to undergo that ice pick cure-all—a lobotomy—at the hands of crackpot Dr. Ashton (Raymond). Billy ropes in diffident employee Tom (Guinee) to pose as a rival doc and dissuade Anna but the twosome end up falling in love. **97m/C; DVD.** Michelle Williams; Meat Loaf Aday; Tim Guinee; Bill Raymond; Wendell Pierce; ***D:*** Richard Ledes; ***W:*** Richard Ledes; ***C:*** Stephen Kazmierski; ***M:*** Stephen Trask.

The Hole in the Ground **2019 (R)** To escape an abusive relationship and start anew, Sarah (Kerslake) moves with her young son Chris (Markey) to rural Ireland. They settle into a small cabin near the woods, which contains a sinister sinkhole. Soon, Chris acts differently and his odd behavior seems to be linked by his closeness to the sinkhole. As Sarah grows progressively more disturbed by Chris and his behavior, she tries to understand what is happening to him through others do not believe what she is experiencing. While the horror film features an excellent soundtrack and some interesting story ideas, it missing the necessary tension. **90m/C; DVD.** Seana Kerslake; James Quinn Markey; Kati Outinen; David Crowley; Simone Kirby; ***D:*** Lee Cronin; ***W:*** Lee Cronin; Stephen Shields; ***C:*** Tom Comerford; ***M:*** Stephen McKeon.

A Hole in the Head **1/2 1959** A comedy-drama about a shiftless but charming lout who tries to raise money to save his hotel from foreclosure and learn to be responsible for his young son. Notable for the introduction of the song "High Hopes." **120m/C; VHS, DVD, Blu-Ray; Open Captioned.** Frank Sinatra; Edward G. Robinson; Thelma Ritter; Carolyn Jones; Eleanor Parker; Eddie Hodges; Keenan Wynn; Joi Lansing; ***D:*** Frank Capra; ***W:*** Arnold Schulman; ***C:*** William H. Daniels. Oscars '59: Song ("High Hopes").

Hole in the Sky **1/2** *The Ranger, The Cook and a Hole in the Sky* **1995 (PG)** Teenaged Mac (O'Connell) is working for the Montana forestry service in the summer of 1919 under the tutelage of taciturn legend Bill Bell (a mustache-less Elliott). Mac learns some lessons about growing up, first love, card-playing—and never to rile the camp cook. Based on an autobiographical story by Norman MacLean. Made for TV; filmed on location in British Columbia. **94m/C; VHS, DVD.** Sam Elliott; Jerry O'Connell; Ricky Jay; Molly Parker; ***D:*** John Kent Harrison; ***W:*** Robert W. Lenski. **TV**

The Holes **1/2** *Les Gaspards* **1972 (PG)** A Parisian book shop owner's daughter vanishes along with other local citizens and American tourists, and he decides to investigate when the police won't. In French with subtitles. **92m/C; VHS, DVD.** *FR* Philippe Noiret; Charles Denner; Michel Serrault; Gerard Depardieu; ***D:*** Pierre Tchernia; ***W:*** Pierre Tchernia; Rene Goscinny; ***C:*** Jean Tournier; ***M:*** Gerard Calvi.

Holes **1/2 2003 (PG)** Poor Stanley Yelnats VI. As a result of a family curse, he's just been convicted of a crime he didn't commit and sent to a juvenile facility in the middle of the Texas desert. While there, he's met with a nasty overseer, Mr. Sir (Voight, at his best), a proverb-spouting counselor (Nelson), and scariest of all, the Warden (Weaver) an intimidating figure who makes the kids dig holes in the desert to "build character." She's really looking for an Old West outlaw's treasure, and her ancestors' past may be connected to Stanley's family. Faithfully adapted by Sachar, from his own award-winning children's book, the movie keeps all the elements that make the book so popular with the early adolescent crowd: it doesn't talk down to the audience, it has an involving, complex plot, the characters are not caricatures, and it handles real issues with honesty. You won't find that in many movies aimed at any age nowadays. **111m/C; VHS, DVD, Blu-Ray.** Sigourney Weaver; Jon Voight; Patricia Arquette; Shia LaBeouf; Tim Blake Nelson; Dulé Hill; Henry Winkler; Nathan Davis; Khleo Thomas; Jake M. Smith; Byron Cotton; Brendan Jefferson; Miguel Castro; Max Kasch; Noah Poletiek; Rick Fox; Scott Plank; Roma Maffia; Eartha Kitt; Siobhan Fallon Hogan; ***D:*** Andrew Davis; ***W:*** Louis Sachar; ***C:*** Stephen St. John; ***M:*** Joel McNeely.

Holiday **1/2** *Free to Live; Unconventional Linda* **1938** The classically genteel screwball comedy about a rich girl who steals her sister's fiance. A yardstick in years to come for sophisticated, urbane Hollywood romanticism. Based on the play by Philip Barry who later wrote "The Philadelphia Story." **93m/B; VHS, DVD, Blu-Ray.** Cary Grant; Katharine Hepburn; Doris Nolan; Edward Everett Horton; Ruth Donnelly; Lew Ayres; Binnie Barnes; ***D:*** George Cukor; ***W:*** Donald Ogden Stewart; Sidney Buchman.

The Holiday **1/2 2006 (PG-13)** Chick romance lite. LA careerist Amanda (Diaz) has just discovered her boyfriend (Burns) cheating; London journalist Iris (Winslet) loves Jasper (Sewell), who's just announced his engagement. Naturally, Christmas joy is the furthest thing from their minds, until, thanks to an Internet site, the two women decide to swaps digs for the holidays. Iris gets Beverly Hills luxury and Amanda gets cozy, snowy English countryside cottage. At least the cottage is soon adorned with Iris's oh-so-attractive brother Graham (Law). Back in LA, Iris is stuck with goofy romancer Miles (Black). Well, three out of four attractive, charming characters is pretty good and Black is at least low-key (although that crazy gleam in his eye should give Iris pause). Happy holidays to all. **135m/C; DVD, Blu-Ray.** Cameron Diaz; Kate Winslet; Jude Law; Jack Black; Eli Wallach; Edward Burns; Rufus Sewell; Shannyn Sossamon; Bill Macy; Shelley Berman; Kathryn Hahn; John Krasinski; ***D:*** Nancy Meyers; ***W:*** Nancy Meyers; ***C:*** Dean Cundey; ***M:*** Hans Zimmer.

Holiday Affair **1/2 1949** Hollywood yuletide charmer about a pretty widow being courted by two very different men. **86m/B; VHS, DVD.** Robert Mitchum; Janet Leigh; Griff Barnett; Wendell Corey; Esther Dale; Henry O'Neill; Harry (Henry) Morgan; Larry J. Blake; ***D:*** Don Hartman.

Holiday Baggage **1/2** *Baggage* **2008 (PG)** Sarah (Ladd) receives a visit from her long-estranged husband Pete (Bostwick), who wants her to finally sign their divorce papers so he can marry his silly, much-younger fiance. She agrees if he'll stay during the holidays and make a sincere effort to reconcile with their two grown daughters, who aren't happy with dad's choices. Bostwick's character is such an irresponsible nitwit that you'll wonder why Ladd would even consider getting back together with him. **96m/C; DVD.** Cheryl Ladd; Barry Bostwick; Julia Sobaski; Leah Wagner; Rachel Dayne; Stephen Polk; ***D:*** Stephen Polk; ***W:*** Stephen Polk; ***C:*** Ben Kufrin; ***M:*** Kurt Oldman. **VIDEO**

Holiday Breakup **1/2 2016** Eminently predictable rom-com, in which the two protagonists decide to break up right before the holidays but pretend to be together to 'spare their families'. As if fibbing to them for 60 days or so, before informing them of said fibbing spree, will somehow make them less angry. Only by the rules in a rom-com universe is this remotely a plausible idea. **89m/C; DVD, Blu-Ray, Streaming.** Manon Mathews; Shawn Roe; Katie Leclerc; Jordan James Smith; Derek DuChesne; ***D:*** Temple Mathews; ***W:*** Temple Mathews; ***C:*** Carmen Cabana; ***M:*** Michael J. Lloyd. **VIDEO**

Holiday Engagement **1/2 2011** Hallmark Channel rom com. Thirty-something Hillary (Somerville) thinks she finally has a chance to please her critical mother Meredith (Long) by bringing her fiance, Jason (McKenna), to the family Thanksgiving weekend. Only Jason breaks up with Hillary and, desperate, she hires out-of-work actor David (Bridges) to play the part. Naturally, the fake couple finds themselves having some real feelings. **87m/C; DVD.** Bonnie Somerville; Jordan Bridges; Shelley Long; Haylie Duff; Sam

McMurray; Carrie Wiita; Chris(topher) McKenna; **D:** Jim Fall; **W:** Jim Fall; Barbara Kymlicka; **C:** John Matysiak; **M:** Kerry Muzzey. **CABLE**

Holiday for Lovers 🦴🦴 1/2 **1959** Lighthearted family comedy. Proper Boston shrink Robert Dean (Webb) gets worried when his college daughter Meg (St. John), who's studying in Brazil, seems to be too enthusiastic about her teacher, Eduardo Barroso (Henreid). Robert, wife Mary (Wyman), and teen daughter Betsy (Lynley) head to Rio to see what's happening. **103m/C; DVD.** Clifton Webb; Jane Wyman; Jill St. John; Carol Lynley; Paul Henreid; Nico Minardos; Gary Crosby; **D:** Henry Levin; **W:** Luther Davis; **C:** Charles G. Clarke; **M:** Leigh Harline.

Holiday Heart 🦴🦴 **2000 (R)** Macho big man Rhames may not be the first actor to spring to mind to play a drag queen but he does a fine job in this melodramatic adaptation of the play by West. Holiday Heart (Rhames) comes to the rescue of ex-addict Wanda (Woodard) who has a 12-year-old daughter, Niki (Reynolds), and lousy taste in men. Wanda just can't make that final break with her dealer boyfriend Silas (Williamson), even though it leads to her sliding back into crack addiction and means that Heart has to draw on his maternal skills to give Niki a stable home. **97m/C; VHS, DVD.** Ving Rhames; Alfre Woodard; Mykelti Williamson; Jesika Reynolds; **D:** Robert Townsend; **W:** Cheryl L. West; **C:** Jan Kiesser; **M:** Stephen James Taylor. **CABLE**

A Holiday Heist 🦴 **2011** Typically silly and sappy TV Christmas fare. College kids working at the school's art gallery over the holiday break are held hostage by a trio of inept thieves on Christmas Eve. Of course everyone has to work together to teach the crooks the error of their ways. **90m/C; DVD.** Lacey Chabert; Vivica A. Fox; Chris Kattan; Rick Malambri; Preston Lacy; **D:** Christie Will; **W:** Christie Will; **M:** Frederik Wiedmann. **TV**

Holiday in Handcuffs 🦴🦴 1/2 **2007** Struggling waitress Trudie (Hart) goes a little nuts when dumped by her boyfriend right before the holidays. Desperate to make Christmas perfect and have her family believe that everything is going her way, Trudie kidnaps customer Clay (Lopez) and takes him home with her to pass off as her new beau. Rather than calling the cops, Clay eventually decides to go along and you know what happens next in this ABC Family movie. **90m/C; DVD.** Melissa Joan Hart; Mario Lopez; June Lockhart; Markie Post; Timothy Bottoms; Kyle Howard; Vanessa Lee Evigan; **D:** Ron Underwood; **W:** Sara Endsley; **C:** Derick Underschultz; **M:** Danny Lux. **CABLE**

Holiday in Mexico 🦴🦴 1/2 **1946** Pidgeon plays the U.S. ambassador to Mexico whose teenage daughter (Powell) tries to run his life along with his household. He falls for a singer while she develops a crush on an older, respected pianist (Iturbi playing himself). Lots of lively production numbers featuring Xavier Cugat and his orchestra. **127m/C; VHS, DVD.** Walter Pidgeon; Jane Powell; Ilona Massey; Jose Iturbi; Roddy McDowall; Xavier Cugat; Hugo Haas; **D:** George Sidney; **W:** Isobel Lennart; **C:** Harry Stradling, Sr.; **M:** Georgie Stoll.

Holiday in the Wild 🦴🦴 *Christmas in the Wild* **2019** After the workaholic husband (Moss) of Kate (Davis) announces their marriage is over moments after their son Luke (J. O. Lowe) leaves for college, the couple divorces and she travels to Zambia to go on an already-planned safari. There, Kate meets womanizing bush pilot Derek (R. Lowe), who flies her on a tour of a game preserve. A veterinarian, Kate puts her skills to use at an elephant orphanage, funded by Derek's girlfriend Leslie (Owen), and finds unexpected chemistry with the roguish pilot. Though the holiday-themed romantic comedy is predictable and cheesy, it also has feel-good moments involving elephants and Lowe. **85m/C; DVD.** Rob Lowe; Kristin Davis; Fezile Mpela; John Owen Lowe; Colin Moss; **D:** Ernie Barbarash; **W:** Neal Dobrofsky; Tippi Dobrofsky; **C:** Hein de Vos; **M:** Alan Ari Lazar. **VIDEO**

Holiday Inn 🦴🦴🦴 **1942** Fred Astaire and Bing Crosby are rival song-and-dance men who decide to work together to turn a Connecticut farm into an inn, open only on holidays. Remade in 1954 as "White Christmas." **101m/B; VHS, DVD, Blu-Ray.** Bing Crosby; Fred Astaire; Marjorie Reynolds; Walter Abel; Virginia Dale; **D:** Mark Sandrich. Oscars '42: Song ("White Christmas").

Holiday Rush 🦴 1/2 **2019** Rush Williams (Malco) is a successful New York hip-hop radio DJ, widower, and father to four spoiled children. Just before Christmas, he loses his job and must move his family out of their wealthy suburban neighborhood. The Williams clan returns to its first home in Queens, which they must share with current occupant, Aunt Jo (Love). At the same time, Rush faces his feelings for his producer and love interest Roxy (Martin-Green) considering the death of his wife Paula (Anthony) to cancer. The holiday film is enjoyable, despite the simplistic moral messages. **93m/C; DVD.** Romany Malco; Sonequa Martin-Green; Darlene Love; Amarr M. Wooten; Deysha Nelson; **D:** Leslie Small; **W:** Sean Dwyer; Greg Cope White; **C:** Keith L. Smith; **M:** Kathryn Bostic. **VIDEO**

Holiday Spin 🦴 1/2 **2012** Holiday drama from Lifetime. Ruben is a former dance champ, long sidelined by injury, whose Miami dance studio is in financial trouble. He reunites with his estranged 17-year-old son, Blake, who enters a ballroom dance contest that takes place on Christmas Eve since the winners' prize money could save the business. **96m/C; Streaming.** Ralph Macchio; Garrett Clayton; Allie Bertram; Karen Olivo; Benji Schwimmer; Julia Harnett; Erika Eleniak; **D:** Jonathan A. Rosenbaum; **W:** Albert Leon; **C:** Kamal Derkaoui; **M:** Jeff Toyne. **CABLE**

Holiday Switch 🦴🦴 **2007** Paula is struggling with bills, children, and her marriage to Gary when her high school beau Nick returns to town a wealthy man. Paula wonders if she made a mistake and gets a do-over Christmas wish, seeing what her life would be like as Nick's wife. But the holly isn't so jolly, especially when Gary and her daughters are happy and Paula isn't. **90m/C; DVD.** Nicole Eggert; Bret Anthony; Brett Le Bourveau; Stefanie von Pfetten; **W:** Gayle Decoursey; **C:** Paul Suderman; **M:** Christopher Ward. **CABLE**

Holiday Wishes 🦴🦴 **2006** Pampered rich girl Britney and orphaned foster kid Rachel have a body switch thanks to a mall visit with Santa. Now it's up to professional party planner Danni to help them find some true holiday spirit before the switcheroo gets undone. **90m/C; DVD.** Amber Benson; Britt Mckillip; Katie Keating; Tygh Runyan; Gwynyth Walsh; Barclay Hope; **D:** David Weaver; **W:** Peter Mohan; **C:** Anthony C. Metchie; **M:** Michael Richard Plowman. **CABLE**

Holidays 🦴🦴 **2016** Anthology horror take on various holidays. Drawing on folklore and tradition, each part of the anthology takes a unique, usually dark perspective on beloved holidays including Christmas, Easter, Halloween, St. Patrick's Day, and Father's Day. Through each story, a bizarre aspect or unexpected twist is given to the story presented related to a holiday celebration. Many tales are quirky with a touch of macabre or haunting. **105m/C; DVD, Blu-Ray.** Harley Quinn Smith; Lorenza Izzo; Seth Green; Ruth Bradley; Jocelin Donahue; **D:** Anthony Scott Burns; Kevin Kölsch; Nicholas Mccarthy; Adam Egypt Mortimer; Ellen Reid; Gary Shore; Kevin Smith; Sarah Adina Smith; Scott Stewart; Dennis Widmyer; **W:** Anthony Scott Burns; Kevin Kölsch; Gary Shore; Kevin Smith; Sarah Adina Smith; Scott Stewart; Dennis Widmyer; **C:** Benji Bakshi; Stuart Brereton; Adam Bricker; David Grennan; Kevin Joelson; James Laxton; Bridger Nielson; Shaheen Seth; **M:** Robert Allaire; Mark De Gli Antoni; Christopher Drake; Ronen Landa; Leo Pearson; Pilotpriest; Jonathan Snipes; Mister Squinter.

The Hollars 🦴🦴 **2016 (PG-13)** Krasinski directs and stars in this well-meaning but clichéd melodrama. He plays John Hollar, a man who goes home to help take care of his sick mother Sally (the great Martindale) and try to manage his irresponsible brother Ron (Copley) and emotional father Don (Jenkins). He also has a pregnant girlfriend (Kendrick) and an old flame back in his hometown. Yes, this is one of those films about a dying mother and pregnant woman that's more about what the dude thinks and feels. We've seen that a few too many times, even if this cast is likable. **88m/C; DVD, Blu-Ray.** Margo Martindale; Sharlto Copley; Richard Jenkins; John Krasinski; Anna Kendrick; **D:** John Krasinski; **W:** James C. Strouse; **C:** Eric Alan Edwards; **M:** Josh Ritter.

The Hollow 🦴 1/2 **2004 (R)** Updated remake of the classic Legend of Sleepy Hollow. Ian (Zegers), who is the great-great-grandson of Ichabod Crane, moves to town. Once he learns of his lineage, chaos ensues for the teens of Sleepy Hollow on Halloween eve, and it's up to Ian to settle the score with the Headless Horseman. Love interest Karen (Cuoco), nemesis Brody (Carter) and Claus Van Ripper (Keach) are among the cast. Strangely enough this film first aired on the ABC Family channel in 2004, though the violence would preclude many families from watching it. **82m/C; DVD.** Kevin Zegers; Kaley Cuoco; Nick Carter; Ben Scott; Stacy Keach; Judge Reinhold; Nicholas Turturro; Eileen Brennan; **D:** Kyle Newman; **W:** Hans Rodionoff; **C:** Scott Kevan; **M:** Todd Haberman. **CABLE**

Hollow 🦴 1/2 *Dunwich* **2011** Four friends on vacation in Britain encounter local folklore about an evil, suicide inducing spirit that lives in a hollow tree. **89m/C; DVD, Blu-Ray, Streaming.** *UK* Emily Plumtree; Sam Stockman; Jessica Ellerby; Matthew Stokoe; Simon Roberts; **D:** Michael Axelgaard; **W:** Matthew Holt; **C:** Mark James. **VIDEO**

Hollow Man 🦴🦴 **2000 (R)** Scientist Caine (Bacon) heads a team that discovers the ability to make humans invisible. He decides to test it on himself and the process works, in fact it's irreversible, and his new-found power has unexpected side effects when he gives into his worst impulses and terrorizes his colleagues, including ex-girlfriend Linda (Shue) and her new beau (Brolin). Stunning visual effects can't hide script's lack of imagination and creepy sexual kink. Degenerates into body-count slasher flick as the intriguing moral questions are dropped in favor of cheap scares. **114m/C; VHS, DVD, Blu-Ray, UMD.** Kevin Bacon; Elisabeth Shue; Josh Brolin; William Devane; Kim Dickens; Greg Grunberg; Mary Jo Randle; Joey Slotnick; **D:** Paul Verhoeven; **W:** Andrew Marlowe; **C:** Jost Vacano; **M:** Jerry Goldsmith.

Hollow Man 2 🦴 1/2 **2006 (R)** Volunteer soldier/assassin Michael Griffin (Slater) goes mad when he becomes invisible thanks to a research project. He needs certain drugs to stay alive so Michael goes after scientist Maggie Dalton (Regan), who's being protected by cop Frank Turner (Facinelli). Slater has little actual screen time since his character's invisible and does mostly voice work. **91m/C; DVD, Blu-Ray.** Christian Slater; Peter Facinelli; Laura Regan; David McIlwraith; Sarah Deakins; William Macdonald; **D:** Claudio Fah; **W:** Joel Soisson; **C:** Peter Wunstorf; **M:** Marcus Trump. **VIDEO**

Hollow Point 🦴🦴 **1995 (R)** After FBI agent Diane Norwood (Carrere) and DEA agent Max Perish (Griffith) get in each other's way, they reluctantly team up to bring down crime kingpin Oleg Krezinsky (Hemblen). Only Krezinsky and his partner Livingston (Lithgow) learns she's a fed and hire assassin Lawton (Sutherland) to teach her a lesson. **103m/C; VHS, DVD.** Thomas Ian Griffith; Tia Carrere; John Lithgow; Donald Sutherland; David Hemblen; **D:** Sidney J. Furie; **C:** David Franco; **M:** Brahm Wenger.

The Hollow Point 🦴🦴 **2016 (R)** A violent indie drama that focuses on drug-related crime in an Arizona border town. Locals make extra money by selling ammunition to a drug cartel. This trade becomes an issue when straight-arrow Wallace (Wilson) returns to the community to replace the cynical Leland (McShane) as sheriff. After being caught in the crossfire of a delivery gone bad, Wallace must protect his community, especially used car dealer Shepard (Belushi) and Wallace's ex-wife Marla (Collins), from determined hit man Atticus (Leguizamo). Save for a few twists and an awesomely over-the-top performance by McShane, it's typical genre fare. **97m/C; DVD.** Lynn Collins; Ian McShane; Patrick Wilson; Jim Belushi; John Leguizamo; **D:** Gonzalo Lopez-Gallego; **W:** Nils Lyew; **C:** Jose David Montero; **M:** Juan Navazo.

Holly 🦴🦴 **2007 (R)** American ex-pat gambler Patrick (Livingston) is working in Phnom Penh when he's contacted by criminal buddy Freddie (Penn) to move stolen artifacts across the border. Patrick's motorcycle breaks down in a red-light district and he spends the night in one of the brothels, which is where he meets 12-year-old Holly (Nguyen). She's been sold by her Vietnamese family into the sex trade and the madam is just waiting for the right customer so she can sell the girl's virginity for a high price. Spending (platonic) time with the damaged Holly gives Patrick the urge to rescue her. English, Khmer, and Vietnamese with subtitles. **114m/C; DVD.** Ron Livingston; Christopher Penn; Udo Kier; Virginie Ledoyen; Thuy Nguyen; **D:** Guy Moshe; **W:** Guy Moshe; Guy Jacobsen; **C:** Yaron Orbach; **M:** Ton That Tiet.

Holly's Holiday 🦴 1/2 **2012** Lifetime holiday rom com. Ad exec Holly is strangely drawn to the handsome mannequin in a holiday display window. After she's knocked unconscious by a falling icicle, the mannequin apparently comes to life as her 'perfect' boyfriend--only he's not so ideal after all. **96m/C; DVD.** Claire Coffee; Ryan McPartlin; Robin Riker; Gabrielle Dennis; **D:** Jim Fall; **W:** Andrea Janakas; Justine Cogan; **C:** John Matysiak; **M:** Christopher Farrell. **CABLE**

Hollywood after Dark 🦴 **1965** McClanahan plays a young starlet trying to make it big in Hollywood. Pure exploitation schlock. Not released theatrically until 1968. **74m/C; VHS, DVD.** Anthony (Tony) Vorno; Rue McClanahan; Paul Bruce; Ernest Macias; John Barrick; **D:** John Patrick Hayes; **W:** John Patrick Hayes; **C:** Vilis Lapenieks; **M:** Bill Marx.

Hollywood Boulevard 🦴🦴 1/2 **1976 (R)** Behind-the-scenes glimpse of shoestring-budget movie making offers comical sex, violence, sight gags, one-liners, comedy bits, and mock-documentary footage. Commander Cody and His Lost Planet Airmen are featured. **93m/C; VHS, DVD, Blu-Ray.** Candice Rialson; Mary Woronov; Rita George; Jonathan Kaplan; Jeffrey Kramer; Dick Miller; Paul Bartel; Charles B. Griffith; Richard Doran; **D:** Joe Dante; Allan Arkush; **W:** Patrick Hobby; **C:** Jamie Anderson; **M:** Andrew Stein.

Hollywood Canteen 🦴🦴🦴🦴 **1944** Star-studded extravaganza with just about every Warner Bros. lot actor in this tribute to love and nationalism. Lovesick G.I. Hutton falls for Leslie, wins a date with her in a phony raffle set up at the Hollywood Canteen, and the sparks fly right away. But he thinks she tricked him as he boards his train and she's not there to see him off. Lame story is redeemed by the talented cast and wonderful musical numbers which make this picture fly with charm and style. Before production began there were arguments over "unpatriotic" actors—labeled as such due to their lack of participation in this, and other similar movies produced at the time. **124m/B; DVD.** Robert Hutton; Dane Clark; Janis Paige; Jonathan Hale; Barbara Brown; James Flavin; Eddie Marr; Ray Teal; Bette Davis; Joan Leslie; Jack Benny; Jimmy Dorsey; Joan Crawford; John Garfield; Barbara Stanwyck; Ida Lupino; Eddie Cantor; Jack Carson; Eleanor Parker; Alexis Smith; S.Z. Sakall; Peter Lorre; Sydney Greenstreet; Helmut Dantine; **D:** Delmer Daves; **W:** Delmer Daves.

Hollywood Cavalcade 🦴🦴 1/2 **1939** This Technicolor Fox drama is basically the Hollywoodized story of director Mack Sennett and actress Mabel Normand. Silent screen director Michael Linnett Connors (Ameche) discovers Molly Adair (Faye) and offers her a sweet movie deal, making her a comic star in her first film opposite Buster Keaton (playing himself). Molly loves Connors but he's too wrapped up in his career to notice so she eventually marries co-star Nicky Hayden (Curtis). Connors notices that and fires them both. While their careers rise, Connors's goes on the skids until Molly offers him another chance. A number of Sennett's (who also appears) original silent stars have cameos. **100m/C; DVD.** Alice Faye; Don Ameche; Alan Curtis; J. Edward Bromberg; Stuart Erwin; Donald Meek; Jed Prouty; Russell Hicks; Irving Cummings; **D:** Irving Cummings; **W:** Ernest Pascal; **C:** Ernest Palmer; Allen Davey.

Hollywood Chainsaw Hookers 🦴🦴 **1988 (R)** A campy, sexy, very bloody parody about attractive prostitutes who dismember their unsuspecting customers. **90m/C; VHS, DVD, Blu-Ray.** Linnea Quigley; Gunnar Hansen; Jay Richardson; Michelle (McClellan) Bauer; Dawn Wildsmith; Dennis Mooney; Jerry Fox; **D:** Fred Olen

Ray; *W:* Fred Olen Ray; T.L. Lankford; *C:* Scott Ressler; *M:* Michael Perilstein.

Hollywood Confidential **1997 (R)** TV movie stars Olmos as former LAPD cop Stan Navarro, who now runs a struggling detective agency specializing in the seamier sides of Hollywood. His latest cases involve getting dirt on a studio acting coach, seeing if a bartender at the newest hotspot is skimming the receipts, and "persuading" the mistress of a well-known director to take a hike. **90m/C; VHS, DVD.** Edward James Olmos; Anthony Yerkovich; Rick Aiello; Richard T. Jones; Charlize Theron; Angela Alvarado; Christina Harnos; Thomas Jane; Amanda Pays; *D:* Reynaldo Villalobos; *W:* Anthony Yerkovich; *C:* Reynaldo Villalobos; *M:* Marc Bonilla. **TV**

Hollywood Cop ½ **1987 (R)** A tough cop in Hollywood goes up against the mob for the sake of a kidnapped boy. **101m/C; VHS, DVD.** Jim Mitchum; David Goss; Cameron Mitchell; Troy Donahue; Aldo Ray; *D:* Amir Shervan.

Hollywood Dreams ½ **1994 (R)** Starlet on the Hollywood casting couch saga of a midwestern gal that comes to California with dreams of making it big. **90m/C; VHS, DVD.** Kelly Cook; Danny Smith; Debra Beatty; *D:* Ralph Portillo.

Hollywood Ending **2002 (PG-13)** Allen continues two recent disturbing trends: making mediocre comedies, and making creepy casting choices when picking his female leads. This time he's Val Waxman, a a down-on-his-luck, nuerotic director about ten years past his prime with a hot ex-wife, Ellie (Leoni) who's engaged to a smarmy studio head (Williams). He's also managed to snag a hot dim-bulb wannabe-actress girlfriend (Messing). When Ellie uses her connections to get Val a job directing an "Ode to New York" pic, his hypochodriac tendencies go into haywire and he goes blind. Woody's made some great comedies in the past, and if this was 10-15 years ago, this one might've been great, too. But his overwhelmingly annoying screen persona, and the missed execution of some pretty good setups, this one goes to the forgettable file. Leoni, Williams, and Rydell do well with what they're given. **114m/C; VHS, DVD.** Woody Allen; Tea Leoni; Treat Williams; Debra Messing; George Hamilton; Tiffani(-Amber) Thiessen; Mark Rydell; Isaac Mizrahi; Marian Seldes; Peter Gerety; Greg Mottola; Mark Webber; Lu Yu; Barney Cheng; Jodie Markell; *D:* Woody Allen; *W:* Woody Allen; *C:* Wedigo von Schultzendorff.

Hollywood High, Part 2 **1981 (R)** Ignored by their boyfriends for the lure of sun and surf, three comely high school students try their best to regain their interest. **86m/C; VHS, DVD.** April May; Donna Lynn; Camille Warner; Lee Thomburg; *D:* Caruth C. Byrd.

Hollywood Homicide **2003 (PG-13)** In 2003, director Shelton released the hard-edged corrupt cop film "Dark Blue." And then this buddy cop comedy. The first works, this doesn't (much), although the premise had possibilities. Veteran L.A. homicide detective Joe Gavilan (Ford) has three exwives, a couple of kids he never sees, money troubles thanks to his off-duty job peddling real estate, and an Internal Affairs investigator (Greenwood) dogging him. His dewy partner, K.C. Calden (Hartnett) isn't sure he even wants to be a detective—he'd rather be an actor. Meanwhile, he moonlights as a yoga instructor. Their on-and-off duty jobs collide as they investigate multiple homicides at a rap club. Ford's relaxed and grumpy; Hartnett's naive and cute but they don't have much rapport and the story's generally weak. **111m/C; VHS, DVD, Blu-Ray.** Harrison Ford; Josh Hartnett; Lena Olin; Master P; Bruce Greenwood; Keith David; Isaiah Washington, IV; Lolita Davidovich; Martin Landau; Dwight Yoakam; Kurupt; Lou Diamond Phillips; Gladys Knight; Meredith Scott Lynn; James MacDonald; Clyde Kusatsu; Frank Sinatra, Jr.; Smokey Robinson; Robert Wagner; *Cameo(s):* Eric Idle; *D:* Ron Shelton; *W:* Ron Shelton; Robert Souza; *C:* Barry Peterson; *M:* Alex Wurman.

Hollywood Hotel ½ **1937** Singer/saxophonist Ronnie Bowers (Powell) wins a talent contest with a prize of a Hollywood film contract. When diva Mona (Lola Lane) refuses to attend her movie premiere, Ronnie escorts her stand-in Virginia (Rosemary Lane) and they fall in love. Ronnie learns he's dubbing the singing for actor Alex (Mowbray) in a film with Mona, but when Alex is supposed to sing on Louella Parson's radio program, Ronnie refuses to go along. Thanks to some showbiz maneuvers, Ronnie goes on the show himself and becomes a hit. The Berkeley-directed musical features Johnny Mercer's industry anthem "Hooray for Hollywood." **100m/B; DVD.** Dick Powell; Rosemary Lane; Lola Lane; Alan Mowbray; Hugh Herbert; Ted Healy; Glenda Farrell; Mabel Todd; Lee Dixon; *D:* Busby Berkeley; *W:* Richard Macaulay; Jerry Wald; Johnnie Davis; *C:* George Barnes; Charles Rosher.

Hollywood, Je T'Aime *Hollywood, I Love You* **2009** Gay Frenchman Jerome Beaunez (Debets) goes on a solo Christmas vacation to L.A., vaguely deciding to try his luck as an actor in Hollywood to escape the romantic heartbreak of his life in Paris (those scenes are set in black-and-white). He makes a number of tourist mistakes, bewilderingly goes to auditions, and is taken under the wing of Silverlake drag queen Norma Desire (Airington) before realizing there's no place like home. The supporting characters are more colorful than the lead, who's at least likeable. English and French with subtitles. **95m/C; DVD.** Eric Debets; Jonathan Blanc; Chad Allen; Michael Arlington; Diarra Kilpatrick; *D:* Jason Bushman; *W:* Jason Bushman; *C:* Alison Kelly; *M:* Timo Chen.

Hollywood Kills ½ **2006** Horrible showbiz horror. Four struggling actors become pawns in a reclusive director/producer's sick games. He 'casts' them in a horror reality film that proves deadly. **90m/C; DVD.** Dominic Keating; Zack (Zach) Ward; Happy Mahaney; Angela DiMarco; Matthew Scollon; Gillian Shure; *D:* Sven Pape; *W:* Nicholas Brandt; *C:* Dave Cramer; *M:* Gerhard Daum.

The Hollywood Knights **1980 (R)** Cheap imitation of "American Graffiti" is not without its funny moments. Beverly Hills teens, lead by Newbomb Turk (Wuhl), are displeased that their hangout—Tubby's Drive-in—is being shut down by those no-fun adults. So they decide to retaliate. Set on Halloween Night, 1965. **91m/C; VHS, DVD.** Robert Wuhl; Michelle Pfeiffer; Tony Danza; Fran Drescher; Leigh French; Gary (Rand) Graham; James Jeter; Stuart Pankin; Gailard Sartain; Mike Binder; T.K. Carter; Moosie Drier; Debra Feuer; Garry Goodrow; Joyce Hyser; Roberta Wallach; Doris Hargrave; Walter Janovitz; Art LaFleur; Glenn Withrow; Sandy Helberg; *D:* Floyd Mutrux; *W:* Floyd Mutrux; *C:* William A. Fraker.

Hollywood Man **1976 (R)** A Hollywood actor wants to make his own film but when his financial support comes from the mob there's trouble ahead. **90m/C; VHS, DVD.** William (Bill) Smith; Don Stroud; Jennifer Billingsley; Mary Woronov; *D:* Jack Starrett.

Hollywood North ½ **2003 (R)** Amusing satire on Canadian filmmaking when the government offered tax incentives for films made in Canada. Novice film producer Bobby Meyers (Modine) is trying to raise money to film a classic Canadian novel. But he needs a name actor and winds up with gun-toting paranoid Michael (Bates). Things just get worse—he's stuck with oversexed actress Gillian (Tilly), and numerous script changes turn Bobby's vision into something unrecognizable. All the while his trials are being documented by director Sandy (Unger). **89m/C; VHS, DVD.** *CA* Matthew Modine; Alan Bates; Deborah Kara Unger; Jennifer Tilly; Alan Thicke; John Neville; Kim Coates; Clare Coulter; Joe Cobden; Saul Rubinek; Lindy Booth; *D:* Peter O'Brian; *W:* Barry Healey; John Hunter; Tony Johnston; *C:* Barry Stone; *M:* Terence Gowan; Blair Packham.

Hollywood or Bust ½ **1956** The zany duo take their act on the road as they head for Tinsel Town in order to meet Lewis' dream girl Ekberg. This was the last film for the Martin & Lewis team and it's not the swan song their fans would have hoped for. **95m/C; DVD.** Dean Martin; Jerry Lewis; Anita Ekberg; Pat(ricia) Crowley; Maxie "Slapsie" Rosenbloom; Willard Waterman; *D:* Frank Tashlin; *W:* Erna Lazarus; *C:* Daniel F. Fapp.

Hollywood Party ½ **1934** Durante plays a film star who decides to throw a Hollywood bash. Any plot is incidental as it is mainly an excuse to have numerous stars of the day appear in brief comic bits or musical numbers. Mickey Mouse and the Big Bad Wolf of Disney fame also appear in color animated footage combined with live action. Numerous MGM directors worked on parts of the film but Dwan was given the task of trying to pull the various scenes together (he is uncredited onscreen). **72m/B; VHS, DVD.** Jimmy Durante; Stan Laurel; Oliver Hardy; Lupe Velez; Ted Healy; Moe Howard; Curly Howard; Larry Fine; Robert Young; Charles Butterworth; Polly Moran; George Givot; Tom Kennedy; Arthur Treacher; *V:* Walt Disney; Billy Bletcher; *D:* Allan Dwan; Richard Boleslawski; *W:* Howard Dietz; Arthur Kober; *C:* James Wong Howe.

Hollywood Revue of 1929 **1929** Whether or not the film is actually good is irrelevant (tastes obviously change) since it's a time capsule of the era's stars and popular bits. It was the first talkie showcase from MGM for a number of their previously silent stars, including comedians Laurel & Hardy and Buster Keaton, a dancing and singing Joan Crawford, and Norma Shearer and John Gilbert doing a Shakespeare spoof. There's also a big 'Singin' in the Rain' song and dance number. **118m/C; DVD.** *D:* Charles Reisner; *W:* Al Boasberg; Robert Hopkins; *C:* John Arnold; Maximilian Fabian; Irving Reis.

Hollywood Safari ½ **1996 (PG)** Jane (Boone) and Troy (Leisure) Johnson train animals for the movies. But Kensho the mountain lion escapes into the woods after a transport accident and is eventually captured by the police who think it's the wild cat that recently attacked a local teen. The Johnsons try to prevent the sheriff's deputy (Savage) from having Kensho killed before they can prove their claims, but their best defense would be to find the renegade cougar. It's a pleasant enough time-waster, with Muddy, the Johnson's dog, providing some fine heroics. **89m/C; VHS, DVD.** John Savage; Ted Jan Roberts; David Leisure; Debbie Boone; Ken Tigar; Don "The Dragon" Wilson; *D:* Henri Charr; *W:* Robert Newcastle; *C:* Guido Verweyen. **VIDEO**

Hollywood Shuffle ½ **1987 (R)** Townsend's autobiographical comedy about a struggling black actor in Hollywood trying to find work and getting nothing but stereotypical roles. Written, directed, financed by Townsend, who created this often clever and appealing film on a $100,000 budget. **81m/C; VHS, DVD, Blu-Ray.** Robert Townsend; Anne-Marie Johnson; Starletta DuPois; Helen Martin; Keenen Ivory Wayans; Damon Wayans; Craigus R. Johnson; Eugene Robert Glazer; *D:* Robert Townsend; *W:* Robert Townsend; Keenen Ivory Wayans; *C:* Peter Deming; *M:* Patrice Rushen; Udi Harpaz.

The Hollywood Sign **2001 (R)** Tom Greener (Berenger) and Kage Mulligan (Reynolds) have seen their acting careers fade away as has that of veteran actor Floyd Benson (Steiger). The three get together to drink and talk at the foot of the Hollywood sign where they happen to stumble across the body of a dead gangster. Doing some investigating, the trio discover a plot to steal millions from a Vegas casino. They include Tom's girlfriend Paula (Kim) in their plan to get the money, finance Paula's script, and jump start their careers. **93m/C; VHS, DVD.** *US GE NL* Rod Steiger; Burt Reynolds; Tom Berenger; Jacqueline Kim; Al Sapienza; David Proval; *Cameo(s):* Garry Marshall; *D:* Soenke Wortmann; *W:* Leon de Winter; *C:* Wedigo von Schultzendorff; *M:* Peter Wolf.

Hollywood Story **1951** Somewhat too twisted script hampers this whodunit. Independent producer Larry O'Brien comes to Hollywood and decides to make a movie about the murder of a silent screen director. He tracks down details to the unsolved crime and finds himself in danger from the killer. **76m/B; DVD, Blu-Ray.** Richard Conte; Henry Hull; Julie Adams; Richard Egan; Jim Backus; Fred Clark; *D:* William Castle; *W:* Fred Brady; Frederick Kohner; *C:* Carl Guthrie.

The Hollywood Strangler Meets the Skid Row Slasher **WOOF!** *The Model Killer* **1979 (R)** Voiced-over narration, canned music, and an unfathomable plot are but a few of this would-be fright fest's finer points. Uninhibited by any narrative connection, two terrors strike fear in the heart of Tinseltown. While a psycho photographer cruises L.A. taking pictures of models he subsequently strangles, a woman working in a bare-bums magazine store takes a stab (with a knife) at lowering the city's derelict population. There's a word for this sort of dribble, and it isn't versimilitude. Steckler used an alias (not surprisingly) for this one—Wolfgang Schmidt. **72m/C; VHS, DVD.** Pierre Agostino; Carolyn Brandt; Forrest Duke; Chuck Alford; *D:* Ray Dennis Steckler.

Hollywood Vice Sqaud **1986 (R)** Explores the lives of Hollywood police officers and the crimes they investigate. Contains three different storylines involving prostitution, child pornography, and organized crime. The film can't decide to be a comedy send-up of crime stories or a drama and is also crippled by a poor script. Written by the real-life chief of the Hollywood Vice Squad. **90m/C; VHS, DVD.** Trish Van Devere; Ronny Cox; Frank Gorshin; Leon Isaac Kennedy; Carrie Fisher; Ben Frank; Robin Wright; *D:* Penelope Spheeris; *W:* James J. Docherty; *M:* Michael Convertino.

Hollywood Wives: The New Generation *Jackie Collins' Hollywood Wives: The New Generation* **2003** Hollywood star Lissa Roman (Fawcett) hires PI Michael (Scalia) to find out if her younger hubby is cheating on her. Lissa gets support from gal pals Kyndra (Givens), a singer who's trying to get closer to her daughter Saffron (McClure), and married Taylor (Gilbert), who's fooling around with a younger writer while trying to develop a screenplay. Then Lissa's daughter Nikki (Hutton) gets kidnapped and Michael comes to the rescue. Unfortunately the flick doesn't fall into the campy-bad category but into the bad-bad category with some terrible acting and ridiculous situations, even by Collins' standards. Originally shown on CBS. **95m/C; DVD.** Farrah Fawcett; Robin Givens; Jack Scalia; Kandyse McClure; Pascale Hutton; Dorian Harewood; Jeff Kaake; Stewart Bick; Robert Moloney; Greg Lawson; Melissa Gilbert; *D:* Joyce Chopra; *W:* Nicole Avril; *C:* Derick Underschultz; *M:* Mark Korven. **TV**

Hollywoodland ½ **2006 (R)** Lowrent detective Louis Simo (Brody) is hired by the mother (Smith) of actor George Reeves (Affleck) to investigate his suspicious death. In 1959, middle-aged Reeves allegedly shot himself in his bedroom—probably because of his failing career and his frustration at being typecast as TV's Superman. But Louis isn't so sure; George had dumped his longtime lover, fading beauty Toni Mannix (Lane), for young starlet Leonore (Tunney). Maybe Toni's protective tough hubby Eddie (Hoskins), an MGM exec, arranged something. Louis' poking around doesn't sit well with those in power and if he's not careful he may end up like Reeves. The self-aware Lane is the cast standout, though Affleck is comfortably capable while Brody is overly twitchy. **126m/C; DVD, HD-DVD.** Adrien Brody; Diane Lane; Ben Affleck; Bob Hoskins; Lois Smith; Robin Tunney; Jeffrey DeMunn; Brad William Henke; Dash Mihok; Molly Parker; Kathleen Robertson; Joe Spano; *D:* Allen Coulter; *W:* Paul Bernbaum; *C:* Jonathan Freeman; *M:* Marcelo Zarvos.

Holmes & Watson **2018 (PG-13)** Art. What drives artists to create? Is it an innate need to give sensory expression to a light that burns brightly within their soul? To appease a muse who bestows slavish inspiration? Or do they figure, hey, we're getting paid, so whatever. One guess as to which applies to this "comedy." In between the vomiting, heroin jokes, and outdated anachronisms (is that even a thing?), there's a plot, but who cares. Any laughter derived from this mess is from Ferrell, O'Reilly, Fiennes, et al., en route to the bank. **90m/C; Blu-Ray, Streaming.** Will Ferrell; John C. Reilly; Rebecca Hall; Rob Brydon; Kelly Macdonald; *D:* Etan Cohen; *W:* Etan Cohen; *C:* Oliver Wood; *M:* Christophe Beck; Mark Mothersbaugh. Golden Raspberries '18: Worst Director (Cohen), Worst Picture, Worst Remake/Sequel, Worst Support. Actor (Reilly).

Holocaust ½ **1978** The war years of 1935 to 1945 are relived in this account of the Nazi atrocities, focusing on the Jewish Weiss family, destroyed by the monstrous crimes, and the Dorf family, Germans who thrived under the Nazi regime. Highly acclaimed riveting miniseries with an exceptional cast. Won eight Emmys. **475m/C;**

VHS, DVD, Blu-Ray. Michael Moriarty; Fritz Weaver; Meryl Streep; James Woods; Joseph Bottoms; Tovah Feldshuh; David Warner; Ian Holm; Michael Beck; Marius Goring; *D:* Marvin J. Chomsky. **TV**

Holocaust Survivors. . . Remembrance of Love *Remembrance of Love* **1983** A concentration camp survivor and his daughter attend the 1981 World Gathering of Holocaust Survivors in Tel-Aviv and both find romance. **100m/C; VHS, DVD.** Kirk Douglas; Pam Dawber; Chana Eden; Yoram Gal; Robert Clary; *D:* Jack Smight; *M:* William Goldstein. **TV**

A Hologram for the King 1/2 **2016 (R)** Based on a Dave Eggers' book of the same name, Tykwer's dramedy has some issues but the always-great Tom Hanks carries viewers over many of them. Hanks plays a washed-up, frustrated salesman sent to Saudi Arabia to try to sell them a holographic teleconferencing system. He's depressed, going through a divorce, has recently lost his house, and Saudi Arabia feels like another planet. Tykwer's film (he also adapted) is a little too meandering for its own good—something easier to do in literature than it is in movies—but Hanks keeps viewers engaged in this shaggy dog story. **98m/C; DVD, Blu-Ray.** Tom Hanks; Alexander Black; Sarita Choudhury; Sidse Babett Knudsen; Tracey Fairaway; *D:* Tom Tykwer; *W:* Tom Tykwer; *C:* Frank Griebe; *M:* Tom Tykwer; Johnny Klimek.

Hologram Man **1995 (R)** Futuristic thriller finds psycho/terrorist Slash Gallagher (Lurie) captured by rookie cop Kurt Decoda (Lara). His prison term is to be served in Holographic Stasis, which means his mind is stored on a computer. Slash's gang manges to break his mind out of the computer but since his body is destroyed, Slash roams as a powerful electro-magnetic hologram. And it's up to cop Decoda to get Slash back. **96m/C; VHS, DVD.** Joe Lara; Evan Lurie; William Sanderson; Tommy (Tiny) Lister; Michael Nouri; John Amos; *D:* Richard Pepin; *W:* Evan Lurie; *M:* John Gonzalez.

Holt of the Secret Service **1942** Secret service agent runs afoul of saboteurs and fifth-columnists in this 15-episode serial. **290m/B; VHS, DVD.** Jack Holt; Evelyn Brent; C. Montague Shaw; Tristram Coffin; John Ward; George Chesebro; *D:* James W. Horne.

Holy Flame of the Martial World 1/2 *Wu len shing huo jin; Mou lam sing foh gam* **1983** Bizarre fantasy film from the Shaw Brothers about two siblings whose parents are killed by villains. Separated at birth they are raised by rival martial artist wizards (one of whom is their parents' killer), and trained to duel each other at 18 to determine who will gain control of the Yin and Yang Holy Flame swords. It's quite possibly the only film to ever feature a villain who kills people with his laughing, and a woman who practices "snake bladder kung fu". **83m/C; DVD.** *CH* Hsueh-hua Liu; Siu Chung Mok; Jason Pai Piao; Jing-Jing Yung; Hsueh-erh Wen; Tao Chiang; Ching Ho Wang; *D:* Chin-Ku Lu; *W:* Chin-Ku Lu; Kwok-Yuen Cheung; Sheng Hsiao; *C:* Chin Chiang Ma; *M:* Chin Yung Shing; Chenhou Su.

Holy Girl *La Nina Santa; The Holy Child* **2004 (R)** Martel's second feature film, in Spanish with English subtitles, explores themes of sexual power, shame and longing through the comings and goings and chance encounters of doctors and hotel staff during an otolaryngologists (ear, nose, & throat specialists) conference. At the center is the hotel manager's teenage and very Catholic daughter who is discovering the vulnerability and power of her own sexuality. The story unfolds in a not-so-orderly fashion but patience finds an intricate and startling conclusion. **106m/C; DVD.** *AR NL SP IT* Mercedes Morán; Carlo Belloso; Alejandro Urdapilleta; Maria Alche; Julieta Zylberberg; *D:* Lucrecia Martel; *W:* Lucrecia Martel; *C:* Felix Monti; *M:* Andres Gerszenzon.

Holy Hell **2016** Director Allen spent 22 years with the Buddhafield, a Los Angeles spiritual group, as the cult's videographer. He assembled the footage of his time in the cult so secretly that the film's director wasn't even revealed when the film premiered at Sundance for fear of retaliation. The documentary is a damning portrait of the group's narcissistic leader, Michel. It's easy to see it as a commentary on how quickly average people can be seduced by community and leadership, but Allen's position within the cult creates an interesting conflict. It's hard to take him seriously given his role in what he now condemns. **103m/C; DVD.** *D:* Will Allen; *C:* Will Allen; Polly Morgan; *M:* Giles Lamb; Cody Westheimer.

Holy Man **1998 (PG)** This satire of home shopping networks is supposed to shell American consumerism, but ends up shooting itself in the foot instead. Murphy is G, a New Age-babble spouting wise man who is used by home shopping execs Goldblum and Preston to boost flagging sales. G lectures about the joy of spiritual over material happiness, but sales soar anyway. Misuses Murphy's wisecracking ability in what could have been a good premise, and reduces his character to a sight gag. **113m/C; VHS, DVD, Blu-Ray.** Eddie Murphy; Jeff Goldblum; Kelly Preston; Robert Loggia; Jon Cryer; Eric McCormack; Marc Macaulay; Sam Kitchin; Robert Small; Morgan Fairchild; *D:* Stephen Herek; *W:* Tom Schulman; *C:* Adrian Biddle; *M:* Alan Silvestri.

Holy Matrimony **1943** Sophisticated, amusing comedy. Reclusive, publicity-shy artist Priam Farli (Woolley) assumes the identity of his dead valet, Henry Leek (Blore), upon his return to England. Trouble comes along when Priam discovers that A) Henry arranged to marry Alice (Fields), B) Henry abandoned his first wife, Sarah (O'Connor), and C) art dealer Clive (Cregar) is selling Priam's new paintings and there are doubts about his death. **87m/B; DVD.** Monty Woolley; Gracie Fields; Una O'Connor; Laird Cregar; Franklin Pangborn; Alan Mowbray; Eric Blore; *D:* John M. Stahl; *W:* Nunnally Johnson; *C:* Lucien Ballard; *M:* Cyril Mockridge.

Holy Matrimony 1/2 **1994 (PG-13)** Mild-mannered and pleasant comedy in spite of its potentially salacious plot. Thieves Peter (Donovan) and Havana (Arquette) take off to Canada to hide out in the Hutterite religious community where Peter grew up and where he's welcomed as the prodigal son. Peter hides their stolen loot but neglects to pass the word on before he's killed in an accident. Wanting to stay and search for the money, Havana uses the colony's reliance on biblical law to marry Peter's brother, Zeke (Gordon-Levitt). Only problem is Zeke is 12 and doesn't even like girls. Strictly brother-sister affection develops between the two. Amusing performances by both. **93m/C; VHS, DVD, Blu-Ray.** Patricia Arquette; Joseph Gordon-Levitt; Armin Mueller-Stahl; Tate Donovan; John Schuck; Lois Smith; Courtney B. Vance; Jeffrey Nordling; Richard Riehle; *D:* Leonard Nimoy; *W:* David Weisberg; Douglas S. Cook; *C:* Bobby Bukowski; *M:* Bruce Broughton.

Holy Motors **2012** What to make of director/writer Carax's defiantly strange film that opens with the director himself in a surreal sequence and ends with limousines literally talking to each other? In between, Carax chronicles the tale of a man (a brilliant Lavant) who goes to a series of "appointments" in which he takes on completely different personalities. In one, he is a dying man being comforted. In another, he is a homeless woman. The various characters combine for a mesmerizing journey through a Parisian night as driven by an interesting international filmmaker. French with subtitles. **115m/C; DVD, Blu-Ray.** *FR* Denis Lavant; Edith Scob; Eva Mendes; Kylie Minogue; Elise Lhomeau; *D:* Leos Carax; *W:* Leos Carax; *C:* Caroline Champetier.

The Holy Mountain **1973** A thief is one of various immortal beings who are being trained by an alchemist to find a spiritual something hidden by monks at the summit of the Holy Mountain. Jodorowsky delights in elaborate visuals, settings, and pyrotechnics as well as a bunch of bombast about Tarot and a Jesus parable. Except it doesn't make that much sense. English and Spanish with subtitles. **113m/C; DVD, Blu-Ray.** *MX* Alejandro Jodorowsky; Horacio Salinas; *D:* Alejandro Jodorowsky; *W:* Alejandro Jodorowsky; *C:* Rafael Corkidi; *M:* Ronald Frangipane; Don Cherry.

Holy Rollers **2010 (R)** Based on a true story set in 1998. Brooklyn Hasidic Jew Sam Gold (Eisenberg) suffers a crisis of faith about the life his family has planned for him. Instead, Sam is persuaded by neighbor Yosef (Bartha) to transport medicine from Amsterdam to New York. The medicine turns out to be ecstasy pills and Sam uses his business acumen to temporarily find a more exciting double life until community suspicions are raised. **89m/C; Blu-Ray.** Jesse Eisenberg; Justin Bartha; Ari Graynor; Danny A. Abeckaser; Mark Ivanir; Elizabeth Marvel; Jason Fuchs; *D:* Kevin Asch; *W:* Antonio Macia; *C:* Ben Kutchins; *M:* MJ Mynarski.

Holy Smoke **1999 (R)** Free-spirited Ruth (Winslet) travels to India and finds would-be spiritual enlightenment with an Indian guru. Her behavior terrifies her parents and her mother (Hamilton) manages to lure Ruth back home to Australia. They've hired American cult specialist, macho PJ Waters (Keitel), to rescue and deprogram her. Isolated in the Australian bush, the balance of power between Ruth and PJ begins to shift as sexual obsession takes hold. Complex characters but the strident storytelling gets annoying and some scenes seem staged for needless shock value. Based on the novel by the Campion sisters. **114m/C; VHS, DVD.** *AU* Harvey Keitel; Kate Winslet; Julie Hamilton; Tim Robertson; Sophie Lee; Pam Grier; Paul Goddard; Daniel Wyllie; *D:* Jane Campion; *W:* Jane Campion; Anna Campion; *C:* Dion Beebe; *M:* Angelo Badalamenti.

Homage **1995 (R)** Archie's (Whaley) an emotionally disturbed mathematical nerd who needs a break from academia and persuades widowed ex-teacher Katherine Samuel (Danner) to hire him as caretaker for her New Mexico ranch. The duo achieve a strange serenity that shatters when Katherine's TV star daughter, self-absorbed Lucy (Lee), arrives seeking shelter because of her drug and drinking problems. A nasty triangle ensues as Lucy makes the mistake of sexually enticing, then rejecting, the needy Archie. In fact, the mistake's fatal. Based on Medoff's play "The Homage That Follows." **100m/C; VHS, DVD.** Frank Whaley; Blythe Danner; Sheryl Lee; Bruce Davison; Danny Nucci; *D:* Ross Kagen Marks; *W:* Mark Medoff; *C:* Tom Richmond; *M:* W.G. Snuffy Walden.

Hombre **1967** A white man in the 1880s, raised by a band of Arizona Apaches, is forced into a showdown. In helping a stagecoach full of settlers across treacherous country, he not only faces traditional bad guys, but prejudice as well. Based on a story by Elmore Leonard. **111m/C; VHS, DVD, Blu-Ray.** Paul Newman; Fredric March; Richard Boone; Diane Cilento; Cameron Mitchell; Barbara Rush; Martin Balsam; *D:* Martin Ritt; *W:* Harriet Frank, Jr.; Irving Ravetch; *C:* James Wong Howe.

Hombres Armados *Men with Guns* **1997 (R)** Fiercely independent filmmaker John Sayles' men with guns are not characters; they're an inevitable force like time or the weather that the characters have learned to accept. Set in a fictional Latin American country, story follows a well-to-do physician (Luppi) who trains doctors to work in the countryside among the local Mayan Indians. What he doesn't realize is that a civil war is engulfing his country, the Indians are practically enslaved, and his students have been murdered by the government that trained them. He picks up a ragged bunch of stragglers whose lives have been shattered by ever-present soldiers from either side of the war. Together they trudge through the jungle, searching for a place devoid of war or politics. Sayles based his idea on the 36-year-long civil war in Guatemala, which began in 1960. Spanish with subtitles. **128m/C; VHS, DVD.** Federico Luppi; Damian Delgado; Dan Rivera Gonzalez; Tania Cruz; Damian Alcazar; Iguandili Lopez; Nandi Luna Ramirez; Rafael De Quevedo; Mandy Patinkin; Kathryn Grody; Roberto Sosa; *D:* John Sayles; *W:* John Sayles; *C:* Slawomir Idziak; *M:* Mason Daring.

Home 1/2 **2005** Roommates Susan and Rose throw a party in their Brooklyn brownstone one hot summer night. Bobby shows up in hopes of re-connecting with his ex Harper, who's more interested in making a play for Rose's crush, Tommy. So Bobby gets to know Susan until HER ex shows up. Frankly, this is a pretty dull gathering although the situations and conversations will sound familiar. **91m/C; DVD.** Nicol Zanzarella; E. Jason Liebrecht; Erin Stacey Visslailli; Minerva Scelza; T. Stephen Neave; Bradley Spinelli; *D:* Matt Seitz; *W:* Matt Seitz; *C:* Jonathan Wolff.

Home 1/2 **2008** Pennsylvania farm wife Inga (Harden) is recovering from breast cancer and her illness has caused fissures in her marriage to the distant Herman (Gaston). Inga is also worried how her illness has affected her eight-year-old daughter Indigo (Scheel, Harden's own daughter). When Inga learns an elderly neighbor (Seldes) wishes to sell her house, she fantasizes about buying and restoring the property, which reminds her of her childhood home and her relationship with her own mother, who died from cancer. **84m/C; DVD.** Marcia Gay Harden; Michael Gaston; Marian Seldes; Eulala Scheel; *D:* Mary Haverstick; *W:* Mary Haverstick; *C:* Richard Rutkowski; *M:* Michele Mercure.

Home **2009** A bohemian family of five live happily in rural isolation on the edge of an abandoned four-lane highway. Except the highway is reopened and the family refuses to relocate despite the increasing intrusions and strains as more than their home starts to crack. French with subtitles. **98m/C; DVD.** *FR SI* Isabelle Huppert; Olivier Gourmet; Adelaide Leroux; Madeleine Budd; Kacey Mottet Klein; *D:* Ursula Meier; *W:* Ursula Meier; *C:* Agnes Goddard.

Home **2015 (G)** DreamWorks' animated offering is just too familiar and too redundant to matter to anyone outside of a very young demo. Parsons ably voices Oh, an alien who lands on Earth and forms a friendship with a girl named Tip (Rihanna), who is worried about the fate of the human race by impending alien attack. Two outcasts from different worlds uniting as friends? Only solid voice work by the leads keeps it engaging, and some of the visuals are hyperactive enough to keep little ones entertained. Based on "The True Meaning of Smekday" by Adam Rex. **93m/C; DVD, Blu-Ray.** *UK V:* Jim Parsons; Rhianna; Steve Martin; Jennifer Lopez; Matt Jones; *D:* Tim Johnson; *W:* Tom J. Astle; Matt Ember; *M:* Lorne Balfe; Stargate.

Home Again 1/2 **2013** A dramatic exploration of the impact of deportation orders on the lives of three young individuals from three countries whose lives intersect in their native country. All three deportees are sent back to their native Jamaica, where they have not lived since they were children. They must begin new lives in the unfamiliar city of Kingston while facing their own personal issues and re-discovering their Jamaican roots. A single mother from Toronto, Marva (Ali) must cope with life without her children. British teenager Everton (James) is appealing his deportation order, but must wait for news. A young man from New York City, Dunston (Bent) tries to distance himself from his years as a criminal. **104m/C; DVD, Streaming, Download.** Tatyana Ali; CCH Pounder; Stephan James; Lyriq Bent; Eugene Clark; *D:* David Sutherland; *W:* David Sutherland; Jennifer Holness; *C:* Arthur E. Cooper; *M:* Mischa Chillak. **VIDEO**

Home Again **2017 (PG-13)** Newly separated Alice moves cross country with her two daughters, hooks up with a young filmmaker (Wolff) on her 40th birthday, and, obviously not vying for mother of the year, decides to move him and his two buddies into her guesthouse, thereby setting up a Three's Company situation for the inevitable appearance of hubby. Predictable and bland, with no major hardships for the characters to overcome. The first feature film written and directed by Hallie Meyers-Shyer, daughter of veteran rom-com writer Nancy Meyers. **97m/C; DVD, Blu-Ray.** Reese Witherspoon; Michael Sheen; Lake Bell; Nat Wolff; Candice Bergen; *D:* Hallie Meyers-Shyer; *W:* Hallie Meyers-Shyer; *C:* Dean Cundey; *M:* John Debney.

Home Alone **1990 (PG)** Eight-year-old Kevin is accidentally left behind when his entire (and large) family makes a frantic rush for the airport. That's the plausible part. Alone and besieged by burglars, Culkin turns into a pint-sized Rambo defending his suburban castle with the wile and resources of a boy genius with perfect timing and unlimited wherewithal. That's the implausible part. Pesci and Stern, the targets of Macauley's wrath, enact painful slapstick with considerable vigor, while Candy has a small but funny part as the leader of a polka band traveling cross-country with mom O'Hara. The highest-grossing picture of 1990, surpassing "Ghost" and "Jaws." **105m/C; VHS, DVD, Blu-Ray.** Macaulay Culkin; Catherine O'Hara; Joe Pesci; Daniel Stern; John Heard; Roberts Blossom; John Candy; Billie Bird; Angela Goethals; Devin Ratray; Kieran Culkin; ***D:*** Chris Columbus; ***W:*** John Hughes; ***C:*** Julio Macat; ***M:*** John Williams.

Home Alone 2: Lost in New York ½ **1992 (PG)** In an almost exact duplication of the original blockbuster, the harebrained McCallister family leaves Kevin behind in the shuffle to start their Florida vacation. Boarding the wrong plane, Kevin lands in NYC, where wonder of wonders, he meets crooks Pesci and Stern, prison escapees who somehow survived the torture meted out in the first film. And they want revenge. Loaded with cartoon violence and shameless gag replicas from HA1, mega-hit still produces genuine laughs and manages to incorporate fresh material. Culkin is as adorable as ever, with supporting cast all delivering fine performances. Filmed in New York City. **120m/C; VHS, DVD, Blu-Ray.** Macaulay Culkin; Joe Pesci; Daniel Stern; Catherine O'Hara; John Heard; Tim Curry; Brenda Fricker; Devin Ratray; Hillary Wolf; Eddie Bracken; Dana Ivey; Rob Schneider; Kieran Culkin; Gerry Bamman; Donald Trump; ***D:*** Chris Columbus; ***W:*** John Hughes; ***C:*** Julio Macat; ***M:*** John Williams.

Home Alone 3 **1997 (PG)** Regardless of the new faces, the story and cartoon violence seems all too familar. Linz (taking over for the teenaged Culkin) is stricken with the chicken pox but able to booby trap his suburban house with to foil the plans of international criminals trying to recover a microchip stashed in a toy car. Film fails to carry the charm of its predecessors and sends the wrong messages: it's okay for parents to leave underaged kids home by themselves and electrocuting people is fun. Writer Hughes should be left home alone to rethink his skills as a screenwriter. **102m/C; VHS, DVD.** Alex D. Linz; Kevin Kilner; Olek Krupa; Rya Kihlstedt; Lenny Von Dohlen; David Thornton; Haviland (Haylie) Morris; Marian Seldes; Scarlett Johansson; Christopher Curry; Baxter Harris; Seth Smith; ***D:*** Raja Gosnell; ***W:*** John Hughes; ***C:*** Julio Macat; ***M:*** Nick Glennie-Smith.

Home Alone: The Holiday Heist **2012** ABC Family slapstick comedy. After moving from California to Maine, 10-year-old Finn Baxter is certain that their new home is haunted. When Finn and his sister Alexis are home alone, Finn rigs up a series of booby traps to protect the property. Just in time to confuse some inept thieves after a valuable painting hidden in a secret room by the home's previous owner. **90m/C; DVD.** Christian Martyn; Jodelle Ferland; Malcolm McDowell; Eddie Steeples; Ed Asner; Debi Mazar; Doug Murray; ***D:*** Peter Hewitt; ***W:*** Aaron Ginsburg; Wade McIntyre; ***C:*** Peter Benison; ***M:*** David Kitay. **CABLE**

A Home at the End of the World ½ **2004 (R)** Cunningham adapted his 1990 novel, but the beauty of his prose gets lost in the transition. Sweet-but-awkward Bobby Morrow (Farrell) meets shy outsider Jonathan Glover (Roberts) in 1967 Cleveland. When Bobby is orphaned, he moves in with the Glovers (Spacek, Frewer) and stays with them even after Jonathan takes off for gay life in the New York. Bobby later follows and then bunks with Jonathan and his older, platonic roommate Clare (Wright Penn). Jonathan is in love with Bobby but it's Clare who seduces him and gets pregnant. When the threesome move out of the city and try to raise the baby together, Clare soon realizes that the emotional intimacy between the two men leaves no room for her. Farrell is tender, but the storytelling is disjointed and the ending somewhat abrupt. Farrell's controversial frontal nude scene, allegedly cut for being distracting, was not restored for the DVD release. **95m/C; VHS, DVD.** Colin Farrell; Robin Wright; Dallas Roberts; Sissy Spacek; Matt Frewer; Erik Smith; Harris Allan; Andrew Chalmers; Ryan Donowho; ***D:*** Michael Mayer; ***W:*** Michael Cunningham; ***C:*** Enrique Chediak; ***M:*** Duncan Sheik.

Home Before Dark **1958** Overly-long psycho-drama with no clear ending. Charlotte (Simmons) returns home from a mental hospital still in a fragile state after a breakdown. Her meddling stepmother Inez (Anderson) and stepsister Joan (Fleming) are living there with Charlotte's college prof husband Arnold (O'Herlihy). Since Charlotte suspected Joan and Arnold were fooling around, this isn't a happy situation. Charlotte finds her own comfort with visiting professor Jacob Diamond (Zimbalist Jr.), who runs into anti-Semitic prejudice on campus. **137m/B; DVD.** Jean Simmons; Dan O'Herlihy; Efrem Zimbalist, Jr.; Rhonda Fleming; Mabel Albertson; Steve (Stephen) Dunne; ***D:*** Mervyn LeRoy; ***W:*** Robert Bassing; Eileen Bassing; ***C:*** Joseph Biroc; ***M:*** Franz Waxman.

Home Before Midnight ½ **1984** A young songwriter falls in love with a 14-year-old, is discovered, and is subsequently charged with statutory rape. **115m/C; VHS, DVD, Blu-Ray.** James Aubrey; Alison Elliott; ***D:*** Pete Walker.

Home By Christmas **2006** When Julie (Hamilton) discovers husband George (Sanford) is an adulterer, she gets a divorce but not much money and things just get worse. Daughter Andie (Wilson) decides she'd rather be with dad and Julie hits a financial rock bottom as she tries to get her daughter home for Christmas. **90m/C; DVD.** Linda Hamilton; Brittney Wilson; Garwin Sanford; Rob Stewart; Brenda Crichlow; Laura Soltis; Serge Houde; ***D:*** Gail Harvey; ***W:*** Nancey Silvers; ***C:*** Larry Lynn; ***M:*** Ron Ramin. **CABLE**

Home for Christmas ½ **1990** An elderly homeless man, with the love of a young girl, teaches a wealthy family the spirit of Christmas. **96m/C; VHS, DVD.** Mickey Rooney; Joel Kaiser; ***D:*** Peter McCubbin.

Home for Christmas ½ *Little Miss Millions* **1993 (PG)** A 12-year-old has run away from her wicked stepmom who hires a bounty hunter to bring her back—for a half a million bucks. Only when he finds the girl stepmom doesn't want to pay up and she tells anyone who will listen that the bounty hunter actually kidnapped the girl. Bounty hunter turns to friends, including the 12-year-old who isn't a fool and knows stepmom is a lying witch, for help. **90m/C; VHS, DVD.** Howard Hesseman; Anita Morris; Jennifer Love Hewitt; James Avery; Steve Landesberg; Terri Treas; Deanna (Dee) Booher; ***D:*** Jim Wynorski; ***W:*** Jim Wynorski; R.J. Robertson; ***C:*** Zoran Hochstatter; ***M:*** Joel Goldsmith.

Home for the Holidays ½ **1995 (PG-13)** Frantic dysfunctional family saga finds eldest daughter Claudia Larson (Hunter) on her way to Baltimore to spend Thanksgiving with her family. Frazzled Claudia must deal with badly bewigged mom Adele (Bancroft), genial dad Henry (Durning), and her siblings—frenzied gay brother Tommy (Downey Jr.) and self-righteous sister Joanne (Stevenson), as well as screwy Aunt Glady (Chaplin) and Tommy's handsome friend Leo Fish (McDermott). Yes, there are moments of deja vu about your very own family holidays but the film seems badly paced and ultimately irritating. Adapted from a short story by Chris Radant. **103m/C; VHS, DVD, Blu-Ray.** Holly Hunter; Anne Bancroft; Charles Durning; Robert Downey, Jr.; Dylan McDermott; Cynthia Stevenson; Geraldine Chaplin; Steve Guttenberg; Claire Danes; David Strathairn; Austin Pendleton; ***D:*** Jodie Foster; ***W:*** W.D. Richter; ***C:*** Lajos Koltai; ***M:*** Mark Isham.

Home Fries **1998 (PG-13)** Things go from bad to worse for pregnant fast-food cashier, Sally (Drew Barrymore), as she learns that the father of her child is not only married, but dead! The catch is that the philanderer's stepsons are responsible and believe that Sally may have overheard their dastardly deed on her drive-through headset. Brother Dorian (Luke Wilson) takes a job at the Burger-Matic to find out just what Sally knows, but predictably falls in love with her instead. Tries to be a quirky dark comedy in a sweet love story, but the result is a bad mix of bleak humor and saccharine-sweet puppy love. Barrymore's cute and convincing performance manages to keep the whole thing from spoiling. Unfortunately, first-time director Parisot leaves the audience thinking, "this isn't what I ordered." **94m/C; VHS, DVD.** Drew Barrymore; Luke Wilson; Catherine O'Hara; Jake Busey; Shelley Duvall; Kim Robillard; Daryl (Chill) Mitchell; Lanny Flaherty; Chris Ellis; Edward "Blue" Deckert; ***D:*** Dean Parisot; ***W:*** Vince Gilligan; ***C:*** Jerzy Zielinski; ***M:*** Rachel Portman.

Home from the Hill **1960** A solemn, brooding drama about a southern landowner and his troubled sons, one of whom is illegitimate. This one triumphs because of casting. **150m/C; VHS, DVD, Blu-Ray.** Robert Mitchum; George Peppard; George Hamilton; Eleanor Parker; Everett Sloane; Luana Parker; Constance Ford; ***D:*** Vincente Minnelli; ***W:*** Harriet Frank, Jr.; Irving Ravetch; ***C:*** Milton Krasner. Natl. Bd. of Review '60: Actor (Mitchum).

The Home Front ½ *The Scoundrel's Wife* **2002 (R)** During World War II, Camille (O'Neal), a Louisiana widow with two kids, Blue (McCullough) and Florida (Chabert), takes a job as an assistant to an exiled German doctor. They are both outcasts, she because of an incident years before involving her husband, and he because he is German. When German U-boats begin attacking ships in the harbor, they both fall under suspicion. Complicating matters is Florida's romance with a Nazi-hunting Coast Guard ensign. A little disjointed, and the conclusion isn't exactly believable, but the movie looks good, and has a great sense of the time and place. It should, as director/writer Pitre based it on stories he heard growing up in the same town in which the tale is set. **102m/C; VHS, DVD.** Tatum O'Neal; Julian Sands; Tim Curry; Lacey Chabert; Eion Bailey; Rudolf Martin; Patrick McCullough; ***D:*** Glen Pitre; ***W:*** Glen Pitre; Michelle Benoit; ***C:*** Uta Briesewitz; ***M:*** Ernest Troost.

Home In Indiana ½ **1944** Homespun story with some notable Technicolor cinematography. Troubled city kid Sparke (McCallister) is sent to live with his aunt and uncle who own a rundown horse breeding farm. He's shown that country life isn't so bad by a couple of local gals (Crain, Havoc) and becomes interested in horses. Sparke gets the opportunity to raise and train a filly and decides to try his hand at harness racing to help out his family. Remade as 1957's "April Love." **106m/C; DVD.** Lon (Bud) McCallister; Walter Brennan; Charlotte Greenwood; Jeanne Crain; June Havoc; Ward Bond; Charles Dingle; ***D:*** Henry Hathaway; ***W:*** Winston Miller; ***C:*** Edward Cronjager; ***M:*** Hugo Friedhofer.

Home in Oklahoma **1947** A boy will be swindled out of his inheritance and a killer will escape justice until Roy comes to the rescue. Standard series fare. **72m/B; VHS, DVD.** Roy Rogers; Dale Evans; George "Gabby" Hayes; Carol Hughes; ***D:*** William Witney.

Home Invasion **2016 (PG-13)** A psychological thriller centered on a robbery gone bad. Residing in a mansion in a remote location, a rich woman, Chloe Paige (Henstridge), and her stepson Jacob (Dickinson) live a quiet life. Their world is shattered when three determined, expert thieves arrive to rob a safe and murder her friend. To escape the situation, she must rely on the security systems agent, Mike (Patric) who answers her distress call. As the situation grows worse, Chloe must chose between the connection with the faraway specialist and her own fear when trying to find safety. **85m/C; DVD, Download.** Natasha Henstridge; Liam Dickinson; Jason Patric; Scott Adkins; Kyra Zagorsky; ***D:*** David Tennant; ***W:*** Peter Sullivan; ***C:*** Toby Gorman; ***M:*** Robert Smart. **VIDEO**

Home Movie ½ **2008 (R)** Shrink Clare Poe (McClain) and her minister husband David (Pasdar) move their two children into an isolated home and quickly come to realize that their offspring are deeply disturbed. Clare uses a video camera in her work and tries to document all the awful things they do instead of getting them some serious help since she's completely ineffectual. Dad drinks and goofs around because he was abused as a child and can't cope. The parents act so stupidly that you root for their vicious little brats. **80m/C; DVD.** Cady McClain; Adrian Pasdar; Austin Williams; Amber Joy Williams; ***D:*** Christopher Denham; ***W:*** Christopher Denham; ***C:*** William M. Miller; ***M:*** Ryan Shore.

Home Movies ½ **1979 (PG)** Brian DePalma and his film students at Sarah Lawrence College devised this loose, sloppy comedy which hearkens back to DePalma's early films. Tells the story of a nebbish who seeks therapy to gain control of his absurdly chaotic life. **89m/C; VHS, DVD.** Kirk Douglas; Nancy Allen; Keith Gordon; Gerrit Graham; Vincent Gardenia; Mary Davenport; ***D:*** Brian De Palma; ***W:*** Brian De Palma; ***C:*** James L. Carter; ***M:*** Pino Donaggio.

A Home of Our Own ½ **1975** An American priest sets up a home in Mexico for orphan boys and changes their lives for the better. A true story of Father William Wasson. **100m/C; VHS, DVD.** Jason Miller; Pancho Cordova; Pedro Armendariz, Jr.; Carmen Zapāta; Enrique Novi; Richard Angarola; ***D:*** Robert Day; ***W:*** Blanche Hanalis; ***C:*** Jacques "Jack" Marquette; ***M:*** Laurence Rosenthal.

A Home of Our Own ½ **1993 (PG-13)** Semi-autobiographical tearjerker based on screenwriter Duncan's childhood. Widowed and poor mother of six (Bates) is fired from her job at a Los Angeles potato chip factory, packs up the tribe and heads for a better life and a home to call their own. They end up in Idaho, in a ramshackle house owned by lonely Mr. Moon (Oh) and what follows is a winter of discontent. Bates provides an intense performance as a poor but proud woman with a tough exterior. Furlong provides the story's narration as the eldest son. A story of spiritual triumph, this one is sure to make your heart weep. **104m/C; VHS, DVD, Blu-Ray.** Kathy Bates; Edward Furlong; Soon-Teck Oh; Amy Sakasitz; Tony Campisi; ***D:*** Tony Bill; ***W:*** Patrick Duncan; ***C:*** Jean Lepine; ***M:*** Michael Convertino.

Home of the Brave **2006 (R)** Iraqi war vets from the same National Guard unit return home to Spokane and have trouble readjusting to civilian life in Winkler's conventional drama. Medic Will Marsh (Jackson) turns to alcohol and lashing out at his wife (Rowell) and son (Jones). Single mom Vanessa (Biel) lost a hand and discovers her prosthesis makes everyone uncomfortable while Tommy (Presley) can't get past the death of his best friend. Actors do as well as can be expected with the cliched material. **105m/C; DVD, Blu-Ray.** Samuel L. Jackson; Jessica Biel; 50 Cent; Sam Jones, III; Victoria Rowell; Chad Michael Murray; Christina Ricci; Brian Presley; ***D:*** Irwin Winkler; ***W:*** Mark Friedman; ***C:*** Tony Pierce-Roberts; ***M:*** Stephen Endelman.

Home of the Giants **2007 (PG-13)** It's a sports drama, teen flick, and thriller with a twist. The Giants are the champion high-school basketball team in their obsessed Indiana community. School newspaper reporter Gar is best friends with star player Matt, who has the chance to impress some scouts with the state finals coming up. However, Matt falls under the influence of his brother Keith, who's just been released from prison, and goes along with a stupid plan to rip off a drug dealer that also gets Gar involved. **101m/C; DVD.** Haley Joel Osment; Ryan Merriman; Danielle Panabaker; Kenneth Mitchell; Brent Briscoe; Mike Harding; Stephen Michael Ayers; ***D:*** Rusty Gorman; ***W:*** Rusty Gorman; ***C:*** Rodney Taylor; ***M:*** Michael Suby. **VIDEO**

Home on the Range ½ **2004 (PG)** Disney kicks this 2-D cartoon old-school style—which would be great if there was anything new, fresh, or very funny going on. Three gal cow pals (Barr, Dench, and Tilly) trying to save their farm from foreclosure go after the bounty on the evil rustler Alameda Slim (Quaid). Lots of hyped-up action and gags will keep the kids amused; however, it wants oh-so-much to mimic the classic Looney Tunes but, like Daffy to Bugs, it just doesn't measure up. Oscar winner Alan Menken produces some pleasant if not memorable music with singers k.d. lang, Bonnie Raitt, and Tim McGraw. **75m/C; VHS, DVD, Blu-Ray.** ***V:*** Roseanne; G.W. Bailey; Steve Buscemi; Dame Judi Dench; Randy Quaid; Lance LeGault; Charles Haid; Cuba Gooding, Jr.; Joe Flaherty; Carole Cook; Charles Dennis; Marshall Efron; Charlie Dell; Richard Riehle; Jennifer Tilly; Patrick Warburton; Mark Walton; Estelle Harris; Dennis Weaver; Edie McClurg; Samm Levine; Gov. Ann Richards; ***D:*** John Sanford; Will Finn; ***W:*** John Sanford; Will Finn; Samm Levine; Michael LaBash; Mark Kennedy; Robert Lence; ***C:*** H. Lee Peterson; ***M:*** Alan Menken.

Home Room **2002 (R)** Philipps and Christensen shine in this riveting story of two girls on opposite end of the high school social spectrum who survive a Columbine-type massacre. Popular, affluent Deanna (Christensen) was seriously injured in the attack and is hospitalized. Alienated loner Alicia (Philipps) was near the perpetrator when he was killed, and is believed to be somehow involved. When Alicia is forced to visit Deanna in the hospital, the two eventually form a friendship and learn to cope with the aftermath of the incident. The two leads are excellent, with a breakout performance by Philipps, and the film wisely sticks to the story of their unlikely friendship, pushing other plotlines to the background. **133m/C; VHS, DVD.** Busy Philipps; Erika Christensen; Victor Garber; Raphael Sbarge; Ken Jenkins; Holland Taylor; Arthur Taxier; James Pickens, Jr.; Constance Zimmer; Richard Gilliland; Roxanne Hart; Agnes Bruckner; Nathan West; Ben Gould; Jenette Goldstein; Vernee Watson-Johnson; ***D:*** Paul F. Ryan; ***W:*** Paul F. Ryan; ***C:*** Mike Shapiro; ***M:*** Rebecca Baehler.

Home Run 🦴🦴 **2013 (PG-13)** Cory Brand (Elrod) was a big-deal baseball player who boozed his success away. Ordered by his agent (Fox) back to his hometown to get his bearings, he's not particularly overjoyed when given the task of coaching some little leaguers. But of course the kids prove to be just what he needs--along with the fellow coach who assumes the usual "lost-love" role. Injected with heavy religious overtones, it's an overplayed yet harmless story of one man's struggle to recapture what's important in life. And Elrod and Fox are a lively pair. **113m/C; On Demand.** Scott Elrod; Dorian Brown; Vivica A. Fox; Charles Henry Wyson; James Devoti; ***D:*** David Boyd; ***W:*** Brian Brightley; Candace Lee; Eric Newman; Melanie Wistar; ***C:*** David Boyd; ***M:*** Scott Allan Mathews.

Home Run Showdown 🦴 1/2 **2010** When 12-year-old Lorenzo (Kirk) fails to make the youth baseball team, he joins a new ragtag squad with former minor leaguer Joey Deluca (Lillard) as coach. This starts up a sibling rivalry with Joey's ex-Major League brother Rico (Cain) as they become home run competitors. **94m/C; DVD, Blu-Ray.** Dean Cain; Matthew Lillard; Annabeth Gish; Kyle Kirk; Barry Bostwick; ***D:*** Oz Scott; ***W:*** John Bella; Tim Cavanaugh; ***C:*** David Stockton; ***M:*** Austin Wintory. **VIDEO**

Home Sick 🦴 1/2 **2008** A young girl goes home to meet her friends and party when some nutjob with a suitcase full of razor blades walks in and forces them all to name someone they hate while cutting himself. One guy doesn't take it seriously and names everyone there, and the bloodbath begins. You'd think someone would've beat the crap out of the kid who named everyone but between getting high and being murdered they're a little bit distracted. **89m/C; DVD.** Lindley Evans; Bill Moseley; Tiffany Shepis; William M. Akers; Forrest Pitts; Brandon Carroll; Tom Towler; Matt Lero; Jeff Dylan Graham; L.C. Holt; Patrick Engel; Shaina Fewell; ***D:*** Adam Wingard; ***W:*** E.L. Katz; ***C:*** Andor Becsi; Michael 'Bear' Praytor; ***M:*** Zombi. **VIDEO**

Home Sweet Home 🦴 1/2 *Slasher in the House* **1980** A murdering psychopath escapes from the local asylum, and rampages through a family's Thanksgiving dinner. **84m/C; VHS, DVD.** Jake Steinfeld; Sallee Elyse; Peter DePaula; ***D:*** Nettie Pena.

Home Sweet Home 🦴🦴 **1982** Postman Stan fancies himself a ladies man, but his wife has left him. So Stan decides to assuage his loneliness by seducing his co-workers' wives. Black comedy look at British social classism. **90m/C; VHS, DVD.** *GB* Eric Richard; Timothy Spall; Tim Barker; Su Elliot; Frances Barber; Kay Stonham; ***D:*** Mike Leigh; ***W:*** Mike Leigh. **TV**

Home Team 🦴🦴 1/2 **1998 (PG)** Gambling addict and ex-con Henry Butler (Guttenberg) is required to perform community service as part of his parole. Since he's a former soccer coach, he finds a job at a boys' home where administor Karen (Lorain) figures a soccer team will teach the kids teamwork and sportsmanship. Familiar plot but that's not necessarily bad. **94m/C; VHS, DVD.** Steve Guttenberg; Sophie Lorain; Ryan Slater; Johnny Morina; ***D:*** Allan Goldstein; ***C:*** Barry Gravelle. **CABLE**

Homeboy 🦴 1/2 *Black Fist* **1975** A Black boxer owes his career to the mob. When he tries to break free his wife is murdered—and he seeks revenge. **93m/C; VHS, DVD.** Dabney Coleman; Philip Michael Thomas; Richard Lawson; ***D:*** Timothy Galfas; Richard Kaye; ***W:*** Tim Kelly; ***C:*** William Larrabure; ***M:*** Ed Townsend.

Homeboy 🦴🦴 **1988 (R)** A small-time club boxer who dreams of becoming middleweight champ is offered his big break, but the opportunity is jeopardized by his dishonest manager's dealings. Never released theatrically. **118m/C; VHS, DVD, Blu-Ray.** Mickey Rourke; Christopher Walken; Debra Feuer; Kevin Conway; Antony Alda; Ruben Blades; ***D:*** Michael Seresin; ***M:*** Eric Clapton; Michael Kamen.

Homecoming 🦴🦴 **1948** Average soap opera starring Gable and Turner set amidst the trenches of WW II. Gable plays a selfish doctor who leaves behind his wife and colleague to enlist in the Medical Corps as a major. Turner is the battlefield nurse who forever changes his life. Film is hindered by a story which is far below the talents of the excellent cast. Although voted by the New York Critics as one of the ten worst movies of 1948, the public loved it. Based on the story "The Homecoming of Ulysses" by Sidney Kingsley. **113m/B; VHS, DVD.** Clark Gable; Lana Turner; Anne Baxter; John Hodiak; Ray Collins; Gladys Cooper; Cameron Mitchell; Art Baker; Lurene Tuttle; ***D:*** Mervyn LeRoy; ***W:*** Paul Osborn; Jan Lustig.

The Homecoming 🦴🦴🦴 1/2 **1973** Excellent adaptation of the Pinter stage play has Teddy, a philosophy professor, bringing his wife home to meet his repugnant family after a nine-year absence. Teddy's two brothers, his father, and his uncle live together and battle verbally and, on occasion, physically. Teddy's wife becomes involved in all forms of the family's dysfunction. **114m/C; DVD, Blu-Ray.** *GB CA* Cyril Cusack; Ian Holm; Michael Jayston; Vivien Merchant; Terence Rigby; Paul Rogers; ***D:*** Peter Hall; ***W:*** Harold Pinter; ***C:*** David Watkin; ***M:*** Thelonious Monk.

Homecoming 🦴🦴 1/2 **1996 (PG)** Mentally ill mother abandons her four children at a Connecticut shopping mall in the care of 13-year-old eldest daughter Dicey (Peterson). The children slowly make their way to a relative's (Bedelia) home in Bridgeport, but when she proves equally uncaring Dicey decides to continue the family trek to their maternal grandmother Ab's (Bancroft) house in Chrisfield, Maryland. No surprise when crazy grandma doesn't want them either but this time Dicey is determined to make them all a home. Based on the Newbery Medal-winning children's novel by Cynthia Voight. **105m/C; VHS, DVD.** Anne Bancroft; Kimberlee Peterson; Bonnie Bedelia; Trever O'Brien; Hanna Hall; William Greenblatt; ***D:*** Mark Jean; ***W:*** Mark Jean; Christopher Carlson; ***C:*** Toyomichi Kurita; ***M:*** W.G. Snuffy Walden. **CABLE**

Homecoming 🦴 **2009** Predictable psycho dreck with stupid characters. High school honey Shelby (Barton) is in total denial that her bland jock boyfriend Mike (Long) dumped her when he went off to college. Now it's Christmas vacation and Matt comes back to their small hometown with his new squeeze, dull-but-wealthy Elizabeth (Stroup). Low-class Shelby is not pleased and when Elizabeth is accidentally injured, Shelby holds her captive in her rundown house outside of town. Elizabeth makes lame escape attempts and Shelby gets increasingly violent. **90m/C; DVD.** Mischa Barton; Jessica Stroup; Matt Long; Michael Landes; ***D:*** Morgan J. Freeman; ***W:*** Katie Fetting; Jake Goldberger; Frank Hannah; ***C:*** Stephen Kazmierski; ***M:*** Jack Livesey.

Homecoming 🦴🦴 1/2 **2013** A reunion of college friends two decades after graduation leads to an exploration of the importance of forgiveness and love. After attending a historically black college in the early 1990s, a group of five friends comes together for homecoming weekend twenty years later in the house that was once their off-campus home. Though the members happily renew their friendship, they also remember a recently deceased friend. In the process, the friends remember hidden secrets, lingering emotions, many regrets, and reconsider their lives, as well as the power of their friendship. **96m/C; DVD, Streaming, Download.** Duane Allen Robinson; Nina Bena-Ashe; Jerry Ford; Nydia Simone; Ruby Thomas; ***D:*** Eugene Ashe; ***W:*** Eugene Ashe; ***C:*** Will Vaultz. **VIDEO**

Homecoming: A Christmas Story 🦴🦴 1/2 **1971** Heart-tugger that inspired the television series "The Waltons." A depression-era Virginia mountain family struggles to celebrate Christmas although the whereabouts and safety of their father are unknown. Adapted from the autobiographical novel by Earl Hamner Jr. **98m/C; VHS, DVD.** Richard Thomas; Patricia Neal; Edgar Bergen; Cleavon Little; Ellen Corby; ***D:*** Fielder Cook. **TV**

Homefront 🦴 1/2 **2013 (R)** Statham brings out his tough-guy persona for yet more B-movie nonsense in this story of a former DEA agent who crosses paths with a deadly meth lord, played with reckless abandon by Franco. Phil retires and moves away from his dangerous life to take care of his daughter Maddy, but finds out that crime and evil still exist even in small-town America when a bullying incident puts him on the wrong side of a dealer named Gator. Written by Stallone (originally as a vehicle for himself), it's a movie you've seen a hundred times before and really only worth a look for the most hardcore Statham fans. **100m/C; DVD, Blu-Ray.** Jason Statham; Iszabela Vidovic; Kate (Catherine) Bosworth; Winona Ryder; ***D:*** Gary Fleder; ***W:*** Sylvester Stallone; ***C:*** Theo van de Sanda; ***M:*** Mark Isham.

Homegrown 🦴🦴 1/2 **1997 (R)** Engaging comedy-noir has three dense Norther California pot growers (Thornton, Azaria, Phillippe) witness their Boss's (Lithgow) murder. Seeing this as a bad omen, they take off, with the crop, to the operation's packaging department (Lynch) and decide to carry on as if the boss is still alive. Amid many cameos (Danson, Curtis) they set up a big deal with a seemingly laid-back wholesaler (Bon Jovi). **101m/C; VHS, DVD.** Billy Bob Thornton; Hank Azaria; Ryan Phillippe; Kelly Lynch; Jon Bon Jovi; John Lithgow; Jon Tenney; Matt Clark; ***Cameo(s):*** Ted Danson; Jamie Lee Curtis; Judge Reinhold; ***D:*** Stephen Gyllenhaal; ***W:*** Stephen Gyllenhaal; Nicholas Kazan; ***C:*** Greg Gardiner; ***M:*** Trevor Rabin.

Homeless to Harvard: The Liz Murray Story 🦴🦴 **2003** Based on a true story. Young Liz grows up with drug-addicted parents in a filthy Bronx apartment until her schizophrenic mother is institutionalized. She's taken away from her indifferent father to a horrifying group home and winds up living on the streets at 15. Her mother's AIDS-related death inspires Liz to make something of her life so she decides to go back to high school. It's inspirational but the ending may not be what you expect. **90m/C; DVD.** Thora Birch; Kelly Lynch; Michael Riley; Robert Bockstael; Makyla Smith; Jennifer Pisana; Aron Tager; ***D:*** Peter Levin; ***W:*** Ronni Kern; ***C:*** Uta Beiesewitz; ***M:*** Louis Febre. **CABLE**

Homer and Eddie 🦴 **1989 (R)** A witless road comedy with Goldberg as a dying sociopath and a mentally retarded Belushi. They take off cross-country to make a little trouble, learn a little about life, and create a less than entertaining movie. **100m/C; VHS, DVD; Open Captioned.** Whoopi Goldberg; James Belushi; Karen Black; ***D:*** Andrei Konchalovsky; ***W:*** Patrick Cirillo; ***C:*** Lajos Koltai; ***M:*** Eduard Artemyev.

The Homesman 🦴🦴 1/2 **2014 (R)** After three women have been driven so mad by the brutality of life that their husbands have given up on them, the depressed and single Mary Bee Cuddy (Swank) agrees to transport them back east to their families, with the assistance of a lowlife named George Briggs (Jones). The torturous existence of life on the plains of the Old West, especially for women, has rarely been captured like this but director Jones' dark tale falls apart by its end. **122m/C; DVD, Blu-Ray.** Tommy Lee Jones; Hilary Swank; Grace Gummer; Miranda Otto; Sonja Richter; John Lithgow; Meryl Streep; James Spader; ***D:*** Tommy Lee Jones; ***W:*** Tommy Lee Jones; Kieran Fitzgerald; Wesley Oliver; ***C:*** Rodrigo Prieto; ***M:*** Marco Beltrami.

Hometown Legend 🦴🦴 1/2 **2002 (PG)** The local high school football team in Rachel Sawyer's (Chabert) Alabama hometown hasn't won a game in 12 years—ever since then-coach Buster Schuler's (O'Quinn) son died on the playing field. Rachel figures it wouldn't hurt to pray for a miracle and her prayers are answered when Coach Schuler returns and agrees to coach the team again. **106m/C; VHS, DVD.** Terry O'Quinn; Lacey Chabert; Nick Cornish; Kirk B.R. Woller; Ian Bohen; ***D:*** James Anderson; ***W:*** Shawn Hoffman; Michael Patwin; ***C:*** Mark Petersen; ***M:*** Dan Haseltine. **VIDEO**

Hometown U.S.A. **WOOF!** **1979 (R)** Set in L.A. in the late '50s, this teenage cruising movie is the brainchild of director Baer, better known as Jethro from that madcap TV series "The Beverly Hillbillies." **97m/C; VHS, DVD.** Brian Kerwin; Gary Springer; David Wilson; Cindy Fisher; Sally Kirkland; ***D:*** Max Baer, Jr.

Homeward Bound: The Incredible Journey 🦴🦴🦴 **1993 (G)** Successful remake of the 1963 Disney release "The Incredible Journey." Two dogs and a cat once again try to find their way home after their family relocates, armed with greater depth of character than the original. Hard not to shed a tear for the brave animal trio who develop a trusting bond through assorted misadventures. Based on the novel by Sheila Burnford. Superior family fare. **85m/C; VHS, DVD.** Robert Hays; Kim Greist; Jean Smart; Benj Thall; Veronica Lauren; Kevin Timothy Chevalia; ***V:*** Don Ameche; Michael J. Fox; Sally Field; ***D:*** Duwayne Dunham; ***W:*** Linda Woolverton; Caroline Thompson; ***C:*** Reed Smoot; ***M:*** Bruce Broughton.

Homeward Bound 2: Lost in San Francisco 🦴🦴 1/2 **1996 (G)** House pets Chance, the feisty bulldog (Fox), Sassy the sophisticated feline (Field), and Shadow the sage golden retriever (Waite) find themselves on the loose again, this time in the tough streets of San Francisco. The animals escape from the airport as the family departs for a Canadian holiday, and on their way back home, encounter some tough mutts—a gang of streetwise dogs, (most notably comedian Sinbad as Riley) and, of course, some dog nappers. Chance even finds romance along the way with Delilah (Gugino). Not too scary for the little ones, flick carries the same charm of the first adventure. **88m/C; VHS, DVD.** Robert Hays; Kim Greist; Veronica Lauren; Kevin Timothy Chevalia; Michael Rispoli; Max Perlich; ***V:*** Michael J. Fox; Sally Field; Ralph Waite; Al Michaels; Tommy Lasorda; Bob Uecker; Jon Polito; Adam Goldberg; Sinbad; Carla Gugino; ***D:*** David R. Ellis; ***W:*** Julie Hickson; Chris Hauty; ***C:*** Jack Conroy.

Homework 🦴 **1982 (R)** Young man's after-school lessons with a teacher are definitely not part of the curriculum. Yawning sexploitation. **90m/C; VHS, DVD.** Joan Collins; Michael Morgan; Betty Thomas; Shell Kepler; Wings Hauser; Lee Purcell; ***D:*** James Beshears.

Homework 🦴🦴 *La Tarea* **1990** Film student Virginia (Rojo) decides to record her prearranged meeting with her ex-lover Marcelo (Alonso). When Marcelo discovers that their sexual tryst has been videotaped, he eventually decides to help Virginia with her work. Spanish with subtitles. **85m/C; VHS, DVD.** *MX* Maria Rojo; Jose Alonso; ***D:*** Jaime Humberto Hermosillo; ***W:*** Jaime Humberto Hermosillo; ***C:*** Toni Kuhn.

Homicidal 🦴🦴🦴 **1961** Castle's "Psycho" imitation makes a belated debut on home video. He takes all the key elements of Hitchcock's original and reshuffles them: the big old house with the steep staircase, the creepy invalid older woman, a troubled young man, the blonde who's up to something, the cheap hotel, the vaguely threatening cops, the unexpectedly graphic knife violence, the young couple who investigates. And a central gimmick which is cheesily transparent; most viewers will tumble to it early on and that's part of the fun, too. With enthusiastic overacting from all the leads, the whole thing becomes a minor camp masterpiece. **87m/B; DVD, Blu-Ray.** Glenn Corbett; Patricia Breslin; Alan Bunce; James Westerfield; ***D:*** William Castle; ***W:*** Robb White; ***C:*** Burnett Guffey; ***M:*** Hugo Friedhofer.

Homicide 🦴 1/2 **1949** LAPD detective Michael Landers (Douglas) goes undercover as an insurance investigator when a suicide turns out to be a homicide instead. This takes him to a desert resort and a gambling syndicate run by gangster Andy (Alda). **77m/B;**

DVD. Robert Douglas; Helen Westcott; Robert Alda; Monte Blue; Warren Douglas; John Harmon; James Flavin; Richard Benedict; *D:* Felix Jacoves; *W:* William Sackheim; *C:* J. Peverell Marley; *M:* William Lava.

Homicide ½ **1991 (R)** Terrific police thriller with as much thought as action; a driven detective faces his submerged Jewish identity while probing an anti-Semitic murder and a secret society. Playwright/filmmaker Mamet creates nail-biting suspense and shattering epiphanies without resorting to Hollywood glitz. Rich (often profane) dialogue includes a classic soliloquy mystically comparing a lawman's badge with a Star of David. **100m/C; VHS, DVD.** Joe Mantegna; William H. Macy; Natalija Nogulich; Ving Rhames; Rebecca Pidgeon; *D:* David Mamet; *W:* David Mamet; *C:* Roger Deakins.

Homicide: The Movie **2000 (PG-13)** Rather a disappointment for fans of the intelligent NBC cop series but at least the TV movie tied up some loose ends. Giardello (Kotto) is gunned down at a rally where he's campaigning for mayor of Baltimore. While G hovers between life and death, the tragedy brings Pembleton (Braugher) back to town and gets Giardello's old squad—some of whom have retired or been re-assigned—back to work on his case. A somewhat surreal ending has cameos by cast members from previous seasons. **89m/C; VHS, DVD.** Yaphet Kotto; Andre Braugher; Kyle Secor; Richard Belzer; Giancarlo Esposito; Peter Gerety; Clark Johnson; Zeljko Ivanek; Michael Michele; Reed Edward Diamond; Michelle Forbes; Isabella Hofmann; Melissa Leo; Callie (Calliope) Thorne; Jon Seda; Max Perlich; Jason Priestley; Daniel Baldwin; Ned Beatty; Jon Polito; Toni Lewis; *D:* Jean De Segonzac; *W:* Eric Overmyer; Tom Fontana; James Yoshimura; *C:* Jean De Segonzac; *M:* Douglas J. Cuomo. **TV**

Homo Sapiens ½ **2016** A revealing feature-length documentary about the future of Earth. Through images of empty spaces, ruins, and abandoned cities, the film explores what is happening as humanity withdraws from areas. As nature reclaims such spaces, a glimpse at the post-human, post-industrial age world emerges. Though this outcome is by no means a certainty, the film shows how it could be. **94m/C; DVD.** *D:* Nikolaus Geyrhalter; *W:* Nikolaus Geyrhalter; *C:* Nikolaus Geyrhalter.

Hondo **1953** In 1874, whites have broken their treaty with the Apache nation who are now preparing for war. Cavalry dispatch rider Hondo Lane (Wayne) encounters Angie (Page) and her young son at an isolated ranch and warns her of the danger but she refuses to leave. After various Indian attacks, Hondo persuades Angie (they've fallen in love) to leave for California with him. Based on the story "The Gift of Cochise" by Louis L'Amour. **84m/C; VHS, DVD, Blu-Ray.** John Wayne; Geraldine Page; Ward Bond; Michael Pate; James Arness; Rodolfo Acosta; Leo Gordon; Lee Aaker; Paul Fix; *D:* John Farrow; *W:* James Edward Grant; *C:* Robert Burks; Archie Stout; *M:* Hugo Friedhofer; Emil Newman.

Honey **2003 (PG-13)** Honey Daniels (Alba) shakes her tail feathers as a hip-hop dancer with a heart of gold. Honey is plucked out of clubland obscurity by slimy music director Michael Ellis (Moscow) and her career as a video choreographer skyrockets. Alba shines as Honey shows a lot of bare midriffs, romances the local good-guy barber (Phifer), and tries to prevent two local kids from falling in with the wrong crowd. Energetic dancing and hip-hop soundtrack couldn't prevent the formulaic cliches from popping up (does every dance movie need to put on a show to save the kids?). Could also be called "Save the Last Electric Boogaloo Flashdance." Cameos by Jadakiss, Ginuwine and Missy Elliott. **94m/C; VHS, DVD.** Jessica Alba; Mekhi Phifer; Joy Bryant; Lil' Romeo; David Moscow; Lonette McKee; Zachary Isaiah Williams; Laurie Ann Gibson; Anthony Sherwood; ***Cameo(s):*** Missy Elliott; *D:* Bille Woodruff; *W:* Alonzo Brown; Kim Watson; *C:* John R. Leonetti; *M:* Mervyn Warren.

Honey 2 ½ **2014 (PG-13)** The second entry in the Honey series finds a street kid finding solace in dance after dealing with difficulties in her life. Maria Ramirez (Graham) is a 17-year-old talented dancer from an impoverished background in the Bronx. After a brush with the law and spending time in juvenile detention, Maria tries to rebuild her life in street dance. Returning to the rec center where she became passionate about dance because of Honey Daniels, Maria lives with Connie's mother (McKee) and has a job to pay the bills. When Maria gets a chance to lead an underdog dance crew at a national competition, she learns the importance of never giving up. **110m/C; DVD, Blu-Ray, Streaming, Download.** Kat Graham; Lonette McKee; Gerry Bednob; Kimberly Brooks; Seychelle Gabriel; *D:* Bille Woodruff; *W:* Alyson Fouse; Blayne Weaver; *C:* David Klein; *M:* Tim Boland; Sam Retzer. **VIDEO**

Honey 3: Dare to Dance **2016 (PG-13)** The third entry in the Honey series features more dance, romance, and music. Though Melea (Ventura) has found love at her prestigious South African school, she is forced to leave when she cannot pay her tuition. Believing that she has a destiny to fulfill, she convinces the community to believe in her and her aspirations. When rehearsals for her show fall apart because of clashing egos, she does all she can to put on a memorable performance and fulfill her dreams. **97m/C; DVD, Blu-Ray, Streaming, Download.** Cassie Ventura; Kenny Wormald; Dena Kaplan; Sibongile Mlambo; Bobby Lockwood; *D:* Bille Woodruff; *W:* Catherine Cyran; *C:* Michael Cleary; *M:* Mark Killian. **VIDEO**

Honey Boy **2019 (R)** Eleven-year-old Otis (Jupe) is a working Hollywood actor who keeps his broken family financially afloat. His mother (Lyonne) comes in and out of Otis's life, and he primarily lives with his father James (LaBeouf), a former clown, a convicted sex offender, and former alcoholic, in a motel room. Emotionally abused by his father, Otis grows into an angry young adult (Hedges). Though a successful actor, he has mental health issues that result in arrests and court-ordered therapy that compels him to face his past. Based on LaBeouf's own childhood, it's authentic and powerful. **93m/C; DVD.** Shia LaBeouf; Lucas Hedges; Noah Jupe; Byron Bowers; Laura San Giacomo; *D:* Alma Har'el; *W:* Shia LaBeouf; *C:* Natasha Braier; *M:* Alex Somers. Directors Guild '19: First Feature (Har'el).

Honey, I Blew Up the Kid ½ **1992 (PG)** Screwball suburban inventor Moranis reverses his shrinking process and this time manages to enlarge his two-year-old into a 112-foot giant who gets bigger every time he comes in contact with electricity. Yikes! Loaded with great special effects, this is a charming and funny film that's fit for the whole family. Sequel to "Honey I Shrunk the Kids." **89m/C; VHS, DVD, Blu-Ray.** Rick Moranis; Marcia Strassman; Robert Oliveri; Daniel Shalikar; Joshua Shalikar; Lloyd Bridges; John Shea; Keri Russell; Gregory Sierra; Julia Sweeney; Kenneth Tobey; Peter Elbling; *D:* Randal Kleiser; *W:* Thom Eberhardt; Garry Goodrow; *M:* Bruce Broughton.

Honey, I Shrunk the Kids ½ **1989 (G)** The popular Disney fantasy about a suburban inventor. His shrinking device accidentally reduces his kids to 1/4 inch tall, and he subsequently throws them out with the garbage. Now they must journey back to the house through the jungle that was once the back lawn. Accompanied by "Tummy Trouble," the first of a projected series of Roger Rabbit Maroon Cartoons. Followed by "Honey, I Blew Up the Kids." **101m/C; VHS, DVD, Blu-Ray.** Rick Moranis; Matt Frewer; Marcia Strassman; Kristine Sutherland; Thomas Wilson Brown; Jared Rushton; Amy O'Neill; Robert Oliveri; *V:* Charles Fleischer; Kathleen Turner; Lou Hirsch; April Winchell; *D:* Joe Johnston; Rob Minkoff; *W:* Ed Naha; Tom Schulman; Stuart Gordon; *C:* Hiro Narita; *M:* James Horner.

The Honey Pot ½ *It Comes Up Murder; Anyone for Venice?; Mr. Fox of Venice* **1967** A millionaire feigns death to see the reaction of three of his former lovers. Amusing black comedy with fine performances from all. Based on Moliere's "Volpone." **131m/C; VHS, DVD.** Rex Harrison; Susan Hayward; Cliff Robertson; Capucine; Edie Adams; Maggie Smith; Adolfo Celi; *D:* Joseph L. Mankiewicz; *W:* Joseph L. Mankiewicz; *M:* John Addison.

Honey, We Shrunk Ourselves ½ **1997 (PG)** Scientist Wayne Szalinsky (Moranis) manages to shrink himself, his wife, his brother, and his sister-in-law. The kids just think their parents are out of town for the weekend (so they go nuts). The third in the "Honey" series, this one was released directly to video. Though adults may find it dull, it was made with the kids in mind. **76m/C; VHS, DVD.** Rick Moranis; Stuart Pankin; Robin Bartlett; Eve Gordon; Bug Hall; *D:* Dean Cundey; *W:* Karey Kirkpatrick; Nell Scovell; Joel Hodgson; *C:* Raymond N. Stella. **VIDEO**

Honeybaby **1974 (PG)** A smooth international soldier of fortune and a bright, sexy American interpreter are entangled in Middle-Eastern turbulence when they must rescue a politician kidnapped by terrorists. **94m/C; VHS, DVD.** Calvin Lockhart; Diana Sands; *D:* Michael A. Schultz.

Honeydripper **2007 (PG-13)** Sayles rarely is predictable, but this time the showbiz story seems all too familiar. In rural 1950s Alabama, Tyrone Purvis (Glover) is going to lose his debt-ridden roadhouse, the Honeydripper, unless he can come up with a surefire way to make money. He decides to advertise that local legend Guitar Sam will appear on Saturday night, though he hasn't actually booked the performer. Riding the rails into town to save the day is young blues upstart Sonny Blake (Clark), who brings along his solid wood-body electric guitar. **123m/C; On Demand.** Danny Glover; Lisa Gay Hamilton; Yaya DaCosta; Charles S. Dutton; Gary Clark, Jr.; Vondie Curtis-Hall; Stacy Keach; Mable John; *D:* John Sayles; *W:* John Sayles; *C:* Dick Pope; *M:* Mason Daring.

Honeyland **2019** In remote Macedonia, wild beekeeper Hatidze works alone, harvesting honey with mindfulness, while also caring for her partially paralyzed mother and her own animals. Hatidze's only break comes when she travels to Skopje to sell her harvest and purchase supplies. Her life is changed when a family moves in next door. In addition to adding children, animals, and noise to Hatidze's life, they affect her beekeeping by encroaching on her business and disrupting the natural balance she works so hard to maintain. The documentarians eloquently capture Hatidze and her wild bees while making a meaningful statement about the relationship between humanity and nature. Turkish with subtitles. **87m/C; DVD.** *D:* Tamara Kotevska; Ljubomir Stefanov; *C:* Fejmi Daut; Samir Ljuma; *M:* Foltin.

Honeymoon ½ **1947** Teenage Temple stars in this sweet, slight rom com set in Mexico City. Barbara and her G.I. fiancé Phil want to elope since he only has a two-day pass. Mix-ups occur and Barbara turns to American counsel David Flanner for help, causing him many tribulations, including interfering in his own romance. **74m/B; DVD.** Shirley Temple; Guy Madison; Franchot Tone; Lina Romay; Gene Lockhart; *D:* William Keighley; *W:* Michael Kanin; *C:* Edward Cronjager; *M:* Leigh Harline.

Honeymoon **2014 (R)** How much do you really know about the person you married? Such a question has become a staple of the horror genre for decades and gets a neat riff in Janiak's festival hit. Bea (Leslie) and Paul (Treadaway) are newly married, off to a remote cabin for their honeymoon. After a few foreboding shots of light in the middle of the night, Bea disappears, returning a bit "off." She doesn't remember how to do basic things, or some of the details of her relationship with Paul. Something's clearly wrong. It could have been tighter but the leads carry it well. **87m/C; DVD, Blu-Ray.** Harry Treadaway; Rose Leslie; *D:* Leigh Janiak; *W:* Leigh Janiak; Phil Graziadel; *C:* Kyle Klutz; *M:* Heather McIntosh.

Honeymoon in Vegas ½ **1992 (PG-13)** Romantic comedy turns frantic after Cage loses his fiancee to Caan in a high stakes Vegas poker game. Cage displays lots of talent for manic comedy as the distraught young groom-to-be who encounters numerous obstacles on his way to the altar. Lightweight and funny, featuring a bevy of Elvis impersonators in every size, shape, and color and new versions of favorite Elvis tunes. Look for former UNLV basketball coach Jerry Tarkanian as one of Caan's gambling buddies. **95m/C; VHS, DVD.** James Caan; Nicolas Cage; Sarah Jessica Parker; Noriyuki "Pat" Morita; John Capodice; Robert Costanzo; Anne Bancroft; Peter Boyle; Seymour Cassel; Tony Shalhoub; Ben Stein; Angela Pietropinto; *D:* Andrew Bergman; *W:* Andrew Bergman; *C:* William A. Fraker; *M:* David Newman.

Honeymoon Killers *The Lonely Hearts Killers* **1970 (R)** A grim, creepy dramatization of a true multiple-murder case wherein an overweight woman and slimy gigolo living on Long Island seduce and murder one lonely woman after another. Independently made and frankly despairing. **103m/C; VHS, DVD.** Tony LoBianco; Shirley Stoler; Mary Jane Higby; Dortha Duckworth; Doris Roberts; Marilyn Chris; Kip McArdle; Mary Breen; Barbara Cason; Ann Harris; Guy Sorel; *D:* Leonard Kastle; *W:* Leonard Kastle; *C:* Oliver Wood.

The Honeymoon Machine ½ **1961** A lightweight comedy about two American sailors and a computer scam. McQueen and Mullaney hook up with computer expert Hutton to use their ship's computer to beat the gambling odds at an Italian casino. Their commander misinterprets the signals and thinks the ship is being attacked. Fast paced and the computer angle was new territory in '61. **87m/C; VHS, DVD.** Steve McQueen; Jack Mullaney; Jim Hutton; Dean Jagger; Paula Prentiss; Brigid Bazlen; Jack Weston; *D:* Richard Thorpe; *W:* George Wells; *C:* Joseph LaShelle; *M:* Leigh Harline.

Honeymoon with Mom **2006** Lifetime rom com. Shannon gets dumped at the altar and since the luxury honeymoon is already paid for, she asks her divorced mom, who owns a gossip magazine, to accompany her to the remote resort. Mom has an ulterior motive for agreeing—the resort is owned by a reclusive ex-astronaut and she wants to get an exclusive interview. **89m/C; DVD.** Virginia Williams; Shelley Long; Jack Scalia; Edward Finlay; Eric Johnson; Mike Coleman; *D:* Paul A. Kaufman; *W:* Duane Poole; *C:* Harris Done; *M:* Ethan Holzman. **CABLE**

The Honeymooners **2003** Modest romantic comedy. When David is jilted at the altar, he gets drunk and decides to go on his honeymoon anyway. He meets Claire, who's just been fired and whose married lover keeps breaking his promises. She's anxious to get out of Dublin and David's too drunk to drive, so he pays her to take him to his brand-new cottage in Donegal where they can both recover from being betrayed. **86m/C; DVD.** *IR GB* Jonathan Byren; Justine Mitchell; Alex Reid; Conor Mullen; *D:* Karl Golden; *W:* Karl Golden; *C:* Darran Tiernan; *M:* Niall Byrne.

The Honeymooners **2005 (PG-13)** The classic '50s TV series, which starred Jackie Gleason and Art Carney, is given an update—but why bother? Bus driver Ralph Kramden (Cedric the Entertainer) involves best pal, sewer worker Ed Norton (Epps), in various get-rich-quick schemes that always go wrong, exasperating both Ralph's wife Alice (Union) and Ed's wife Trixie (Hall). At least this time Ralph wants to give Alice the moon instead of sending her there, but the story should have been left in the TV vault where it belonged. **90m/C; DVD.** Cedric the Entertainer; Mike Epps; Gabrielle Union; Regina Hall; John Leguizamo; Jon Polito; Eric Stoltz; Carol Woods; Ajay Naidu; Kim Chan; *D:* John Schultz; *W:* Don Rhymer; Barry W. Blaustein; David Sheffield; Danny Jacobson; *C:* Shawn Maurer; *M:* Richard Gibbs.

Honeysuckle Rose ½ *On the Road Again* **1980 (PG)** A road-touring country-Western singer whose life is a series of one night stands, falls in love with an adoring young guitar player who has just joined his band. This nearly costs him his marriage when his wife, who while waiting patiently for him at home, decides she's had enough. Easygoing performance by Nelson, essentially playing himself. **120m/C; VHS, DVD.** Willie Nelson; Dyan Cannon; Amy Irving; Slim Pickens; Joey Floyd; Charles Levin; Priscilla Pointer; *D:* Jerry Schatzberg; *W:* William D. Wittliff; John Binder; Carol Sobieski; *M:* Willie Nelson; Richard Baskin. Golden Raspberries '80: Worst Support. Actress (Irving).

Hong Kong 1941 ½ **1984** Yip Kim Fay (Yun-Fat) arrives in Hong Kong on the eve of war in 1941 and befriends peasant Wong Hak Keung (Man). Fay and Keung plan to leave Hong Kong with Keung's girlfriend, Ah Nam (Yip), but fall victim to the Japanese invasion. An early role for Yun-Fat, who's the romantic hero here rather than the action star he later became. Chinese with subtitles. **118m/C; VHS, DVD.** *CH* Chow Yun-Fat; Cecilia Yip; Alex Man; ***D:*** Po-Chih Leung; ***W:*** Koon-Chung Chan.

Honky Tonk **1941** A western soap opera in which ne'er do well Clark marries Lana and tries to live a respectable life. In this, the first of several MGM teamings between Gable and Turner, the chemistry between the two is evident. So much so in fact that Gable's then wife Carole Lombard let studio head Louis B. Mayer know that she was not at all thrilled. The public was pleased however, and made the film a hit. **106m/B; VHS, DVD.** Clark Gable; Lana Turner; Frank Morgan; Claire Trevor; Marjorie Main; Albert Dekker; Chill Wills; Henry O'Neill; John Maxwell; Morgan Wallace; Betty Blythe; Francis X. Bushman; Veda Ann Borg; ***D:*** Jack Conway.

Honky Tonk Freeway **1981 (PG)** An odd assortment of people become involved in a small town Mayor's scheme to turn a dying hamlet into a tourist wonderland. You can find better things to do with your evening than watch this accident. **107m/C; VHS, DVD.** Teri Garr; Howard Hesseman; Beau Bridges; Hume Cronyn; William Devane; Beverly D'Angelo; Geraldine Page; David Rasche; Peter Billingsley; Daniel Stern; Deborah Rush; George Dzundza; Jessica Tandy; Joe Grifasi; Frances Bay; John Ashton; Celia Weston; Anne Ramsay; ***D:*** John Schlesinger; ***W:*** Edward Clinton; ***C:*** John Bailey; ***M:*** Elmer Bernstein; Steve Dorff.

Honkytonk Man **1982 (PG)** Unsuccessful change-of-pace Eastwood vehicle set during the Depression. Aging alcoholic country singer tries one last time to make it to Nashville, hoping to perform at the Grand Ole Opry. This time he takes his nephew (played by Eastwoood's real-life son) with him. **123m/C; VHS, DVD.** Clint Eastwood; Kyle Eastwood; John McIntire; Alexa Kenin; Verna Bloom; ***D:*** Clint Eastwood; ***W:*** Clancy Carlile; ***C:*** Bruce Surtees; ***M:*** Steve Dorff.

Honolulu **1/2 1939** A screwball comedy with Powell providing the musical numbers. Young takes on the dual role of a Hollywood star who meets his exact double, a Hawaii plantation owner. They decide to switch identities to give their lives a little oomph. The star sails to Hawaii, falling for fellow passenger Powell, only to discover he's expected to get married upon his arrival in Honolulu. Anderson and Burns and Allen provide the comic relief. **83m/B; VHS, DVD.** Robert Young; Eleanor Powell; George Burns; Gracie Allen; Rita Johnson; Eddie Anderson; Clarence (C. William) Kolb; ***D:*** Edward Buzzell; ***W:*** Frank Partos; Herbert Fields; ***M:*** Franz Waxman.

Honor **1/2 2006 (R)** Standard martial arts showdown between two neighborhood friends, Raymond (Wong) and Gabriel (Barry), who wind up on dueling gangs when a vicious police conflict sends Raymond to the slammer and Gabriel to the military and an overseas war. After returning home, it's a natural end game for the now more callous pair. **85m/C; DVD.** Jason Barry; Russell Wong; Roddy Piper; Remy Bonjasky; Linda Park; ***D:*** David Worth; ***W:*** Larry Felix, Jr. **VIDEO**

Honor Among Thieves **1/2** *Farewell, Friend; Adieu, l'ami* **1968 (R)** Two former mercenaries reteam for a robbery that doesn't come off as planned. Not as fast paced as others in Bronson canon. **115m/C; VHS, DVD, Blu-Ray.** *FR IT* Charles Bronson; Alain Delon; Brigitte Fossey; Olga Georges-Picot; Bernard Fresson; ***D:*** Jean Herman; ***W:*** Sebastien Japrisot; ***C:*** Jean-Jacques Tarbes; ***M:*** Francois de Roubaix.

Honor Thy Father **1973** The everyday life of a real-life Mafia family as seen through the eyes of Bill Bonanno, the son of mob chieftain Joe Bonanno. Adapted from the book by Gay Talese. **97m/C; DVD.** Raf Vallone; Richard S. Castellano; Brenda Vaccaro; Joseph Bologna; ***D:*** Paul Wendkos; ***M:*** George Duning. **TV**

Hood Vengeance **1/2** *Venganza de Barrio* **2009** Smokes (Huen) is a missing drug kingpin. Much to everyone's surprise he turns back up one day. Much to his surprise, his best friend has taken over his empire in his absence. You can pretty much guess what happens next. Granted it's his own fault, because drug dealers probably shouldn't take vacations. **90m/C; DVD.** Justin Huen; Robert Arevalo; Joey Gaytan; Kadyr Gutierrez; Jacqueline Calderon-Guido; Aurelio Bocanegra; West Liang; Nidia Urrea; Fernando Luis; Richard Villa; Lauren Renee Martinez; Chris Banda; ***D:*** Carlos Santillan; ***W:*** Jacqueline Calderon-Guido; Carlos Santillan; Oskar Toruno; ***C:*** Patrick Russo; ***M:*** Danny G; Dj Cooch; Walter Reyes.

Hooded Angels *Glory Glory* **2000 (R)** Westrogen features six women out for revenge after enduring mistreatment by a gang of renegade soldiers shortly after the Civil War. Male posse, led by brothers Bauer and Johansson, don't realize their outlaws are female at first but they learn these ladies give as good as they get. **95m/C; VHS, DVD.** Amanda Donohoe; Steven Bauer; Paul Johansson; Chantel Stander; Gary Busey; Juliana Venter; ***D:*** Paul Matthews; ***W:*** Paul Matthews; ***C:*** Vincent Cox.

The Hooded Terror *Sexton Blake and the Hooded Terror* **1938** A merciless group of murderers take on a G-man. **70m/B; VHS, DVD.** *GB* Tod Slaughter; Greta Gynt; George Curzon; Tony Sympson; Charles Oliver; David Farrar; ***D:*** George King; ***W:*** A.R. Rawlinson; ***C:*** Hone Glendinning.

The Hoodlum **1/2 1919** In this silent comedy, tantrum-throwing rich girl Amy Burke (Pickford) lives with her grandfather in a New York mansion. Bored, Amy tries slumming with her sociologist father (Crittenden) in an East Side tenement when grandad goes abroad. The culture shock is great but Amy tries to fit in by becoming a street urchin. **92m/B; Silent; DVD, Blu-Ray.** Mary Pickford; T.D. Crittenden; Ralph Lewis; Kenneth Harlan; Buddy Messinger; ***D:*** Sidney Franklin; ***W:*** Julie Mathilde Lippmann; ***C:*** Charles Rosher.

Hoodlum **1/2** *Gangster; Hoods* **1996 (R)** Highly fictionalized tale of '30s gangster "Bumpy" Johnson (Fishburne, reprising his role from "The Cotton Club"), who refuses to allow Dutch Schultz (Roth) and Lucky Luciano (Garcia) to muscle into the Harlem numbers rackets. Duke makes the proceedings nice to look at, and does well by the eclectic cast, but the uneven screenplay occasionally lets everybody down, especially during the cheesy time-passage montage (complete with Tommy Gun fire and flipping calendar pages). Roth is ruthless as ever and Garcia is smooth as ever. But it's definitely Fishburne's show, as he explores Johnson's professional triumphs and the personal toll they take. Fishburne previously worked with director Duke on "Deep Cover." Singer Michael McCary from Boyz II Men makes his film debut as an explosives expert. **130m/C; VHS, DVD, Blu-Ray.** Laurence Fishburne; Tim Roth; Andy Garcia; Vanessa L(ynne) Williams; Cicely Tyson; Clarence Williams, III; William Atherton; Chi McBride; Richard Bradford; Loretta Devine; Queen Latifah; Paul Benjamin; Mike Starr; Beau Starr; Joe Guzaldo; Ed O'Ross; ***D:*** Bill Duke; ***W:*** Chris Brancato; ***C:*** Frank Tidy; ***M:*** Elmer Bernstein.

Hoodlum & Son **1/2 2003 (PG-13)** Charlie's a 1930s gangster who neglects his ten-year-old trouble-prone son Archie. The kid then gets in dad's way when he's trying to do a job for mob boss Benny and collect on a debt. Stolen money and a beautiful widow also figure in to the good-natured plot. Shot (though not set) in South Africa. **92m/C; DVD.** *GB* T. W. (Ted) King; Ron Perlman; Myles Jeffrey; Mia Sara; Robert Vaughn; ***D:*** Ashley Way; ***W:*** Ashley Way; ***C:*** Buster Reynolds; ***M:*** Mark Thomas.

Hoodlum Empire **1952** A senator enlists the aid of a former gangster, now a war hero, in his battle against the syndicate. Loosely based on the Kefauver investigations of 1950-51. **98m/B; DVD, Blu-Ray.** Brian Donlevy; Claire Trevor; Forrest Tucker; Vera Hruba Ralston; Luther Adler; John Russell; Gene Lockhart; Grant Withers; Taylor Holmes; Roy Barcroft; Richard Jaeckel; ***D:*** Joseph Kane; ***W:*** Robert Considine; Bruce Manning; ***C:*** Reggie Lanning; ***M:*** Nathan Scott.

The Hoodlum Priest **1961** Biography of the Rev. Charles Dismas Clark (Murray), a Jesuit priest who dedicated his life to working with juvenile delinquents and ex-cons in St. Louis. Dullea made his screen debut as Billy Lee Jackson, a thief who finds the straight and narrow is a hard road with more detours than he can handle. Fine performances with Murray co-scripting under the pseudonym Don Deer. **101m/B; DVD.** Don Murray; Keir Dullea; Larry Gates; Logan Ramsey; Cindi Wood; ***D:*** Irvin Kershner; ***W:*** Don Murray; Joseph Landon; ***C:*** Haskell Wexler.

Hoodrats 2 *Hoodrat Warriors* **2008** After one of their friends is nearly beaten to death by a gangster, three women decide to give him the same treatment. Since they're foolish enough to let him live, he puts a bounty on their heads and the local gangs come to collect. Astonishingly the local gangs all have the same number of members, are all women, and all of them prefer some sort of melee weapon theme (bats, chains, etc) to guns. **90m/C; DVD.** Donnabelle Mortel; June Marie; Arden Cho; ***D:*** Edgar Arellano; ***W:*** Edgar Arellano; ***C:*** Eugenio Canas; ***M:*** Dave Bouza.

Hoods **1/2 1998 (R)** Mob comedy features a bunch of pros that make it worth watching. Smalltime mobster Martinelli (Mantegna) suffers a midlife crisis on his 50th birthday when he learns that his floozy girlfriend (Tilly) is cheating on him and his aging father wants him to whack someone named Carmine—who turns out to be a nine-year-old boy. **92m/C; VHS, DVD.** Joe Mantegna; Kevin Pollak; Joe Pantoliano; Jennifer Tilly; ***D:*** Mark Malone; ***W:*** Mark Malone; ***C:*** Tobias Schliessler; ***M:*** Anthony Marinelli.

Hoodwinked **2005 (PG)** "Rashamon" meets the brothers Grimm as the Weinsteins introduce the kiddies to police procedurals and action flicks by way of "The Thin Man" and extreme sports. Red Riding Hood (Hathaway), Granny (Close), the Wolf (Warburton), and the Woodsman (Belushi) all get to tell their side of the famous story when the cops bust in on the proceedings. Plenty of references to genres and movies old and new ensure that adults will enjoy this one as much as, if not more than, the kids. Somewhat clunky animation is the only flaw. **89m/C; DVD, Blu-Ray.** ***V:*** Anne Hathaway; Glenn Close; James Belushi; Patrick Warburton; Anthony Anderson; David Ogden Stiers; Xzibit; Chazz Palminteri; Andy Dick; Cory Edwards; Benjy Gaither; ***D:*** Cory Edwards; ***W:*** Cory Edwards; Todd Edwards; Tony Leech; ***M:*** Todd Edwards.

Hoodwinked Too! Hood vs. Evil *Hoodwinked 2: Hood vs. Evil* **2011 (PG)** Lousy sequel to the excellent 2005 predecessor is irritatingly shrill and filled with bad puns and obvious film references that will go over the heads of children but make their parents yawn. Red is training with the Sisters of the Hood while Granny, the Big Bad Wolf, and Twitchy the squirrel are working for the Happily Ever After Agency. Their latest rescue mission is to save Hansel and Gretel from witch Verushka who is really after another target. The animation is colorful but clunky and the 3D adds nothing. **86m/C; DVD, Blu-Ray, On Demand.** Cory Edwards; ***V:*** Hayden Panettiere; Patrick Warburton; Glenn Close; David Ogden Stiers; Andy Dick; Martin Short; Brad Garrett; Joan Cusack; Bill Hader; Amy Poehler; Cheech Marin; Thomas Chong; Heidi Klum; Wayne Newton; ***D:*** Mike Disa; ***W:*** Mike Disa; Cory Edwards; Todd Edwards; Tony Leech; ***M:*** Murray Gold.

The Hook **1/2 1963** Military drama based on a true story. At the end of the Korean War, Sgt. Briscoe and two of his men are aboard a neutral civilian charter ship that's returning them to their lines when they rescue a North Korean pilot who's crashed into the sea. Briscoe alerts the authorities and is told by the South Korean commander to execute his prisoner. However, the three soldiers argue about the difference between executing a POW and killing a man in combat. A ceasefire lets the men off the hook (hence the title) but that doesn't prevent a tragedy. **97m/B; DVD.** Kirk Douglas; Nick Adams; Robert Walker, Jr.; Pancho Magalona; Nehemiah Persoff; ***D:*** George Seaton; ***W:*** Henry Denker; ***C:*** Joseph Ruttenberg; ***M:*** Larry Adler.

Hook **1991 (PG)** Although he said he was never gonna to do it, Peter Pan has grown up. Uptight Peter Banning places work before family and has forgotten all about Neverland and the evil Captain Hook, until Hook kidnaps the Banning kids and takes them to Neverland. With the help of Tinkerbell, her magic pixie dust, and happy thoughts, Peter rescues his kids and rediscovers his youth while visiting with the Lost Boys. The sets and special effects are spectacular; the direction less so. Big-budget fantasy lacks the charm it needs to really fly. Still, kids seem to love it. You'll have to look hard to spot pirates Crosby and Close. Futurizes the J.M. Barrie classic. **142m/C; VHS, DVD, Blu-Ray.** Dustin Hoffman; Robin Williams; Julia Roberts; Bob Hoskins; Maggie Smith; Charlie Korsmo; Caroline Goodall; Amber Scott; Phil Collins; Arthur Malet; Dante Basco; Gwyneth Paltrow; Glenn Close; David Crosby; ***D:*** Steven Spielberg; ***W:*** Nick Castle; ***C:*** Dean Cundey; ***M:*** John Williams.

Hook, Line and Sinker **1930** A couple of insurance investigators try to help a young woman restore a hotel, and they find romance and run-ins with crooks. Directed by Cline, who later directed W.C. Fields in "The Bank Dick," "My Little Chickadee," and "Never Give a Sucker an Even Break." **75m/B; VHS, DVD.** Bert Wheeler; Robert Woolsey; Dorothy Lee; Jobyna Howland; Ralf Harolde; Natalie Moorhead; George F. Marion, Sr.; Hugh Herbert; ***D:*** Edward F. (Eddie) Cline; ***W:*** Rod Amateau.

The Hooked Generation **1969 (R)** A group of drug pushers kidnap defenseless victims, rape innocent girls, and even murder their own Cuban drug contacts (and all without the aid of a cohesive plot). Many gory events precede their untimely deaths; few will be entertained. **92m/C; VHS, DVD.** Jeremy Slate; Steve Alaimo; ***D:*** William Grefe; ***W:*** William Grefe; ***C:*** Gregory Sandor; ***M:*** Chris Martell.

Hoop Dreams **1994 (PG-13)** Exceptional documentary follows two innercity basketball phenoms' lives through high school as they chase their dreams of playing in the NBA. We meet Arthur Agee and William Gates as they prepare to enter St. Joseph, a predominantly white Catholic school that has offered them partial athletic scholarships. The coach tabs Gates as the "next Isiah Thomas," alluding to the school's most famous alum. There's plenty of game footage, but the more telling and fascinating parts of the film deal with the kids' families and home life. Both players encounter dramatic reversals of fortune on and off the court, demonstrating the incredibly long odds they face. **169m/C; DVD, Blu-Ray.** Arthur Agee; William Gates; ***D:*** Steve James; ***C:*** Peter Gilbert. L.A. Film Critics '94: Feature Doc.; Natl. Bd. of Review '94: Feature Doc.; Natl. Film Reg. '05; N.Y. Film Critics '94: Feature Doc.; Natl. Soc. Film Critics '94: Feature Doc.; Sundance '94: Aud. Award.

Hooper **1/2 1978 (PG)** Lightweight behind-the-scenes satire about the world of movie stuntmen. Reynolds is a top stuntman who becomes involved in a rivalry with an up-and-coming young man out to surpass him. Dated good-ole-boy shenanigans. **94m/C; VHS, DVD, Blu-Ray.** Burt Reynolds; Jan-Michael Vincent; Robert Klein; Sally Field; Brian Keith; John Marley; Adam West; ***D:*** Hal Needham; ***W:*** Bill Kerby; Thomas (Tom) Rickman; ***C:*** Bobby Byrne; ***M:*** Bill Justis.

Hooray for Love **1/2 1935** Lackluster RKO comedy-musical. After Doug Tyler (Raymond) loses his job for flirting with singer Pat Thatcher (Sothern), her con artist daddy (Hall) convinces Doug to produce a Broadway show starring Pat. Doug's plans fall flat when he finally realizes his backer is broke, but Pat finds a way to make everyone's dreams come true. Bill 'Bojangles' Robinson, Fats Waller, and dancer Jeni Le Gon are among the stage performers. **72m/B; DVD.** Gene Raymond; Ann Sothern; Thurston Hall; Georgia Caine; Pert Kelton; Lionel Stander; ***D:*** Walter Lang; ***W:*** Ray Harris; Lawrence Hazard; ***C:*** Lucien N. Andriot.

Hoosiers **1986 (PG)** In Indiana, where basketball is the sport of the gods, a small town high school basketball team gets a new, but surprisingly experienced coach. He makes the team, and each person in it, better than they thought possible. Classic plot rings true because of Hackman's complex and sensitive performance coupled with Hopper's touching portrait of an alcoholic basketball fanatic. **115m/C; VHS, DVD, Blu-Ray, UMD.** Gene Hackman; Barbara Hershey;

Dennis Hopper; David Neidorf; Sheb Wooley; Fern Parsons; Brad Boyle; Steve Hollar; Brad Long; ***D:*** David Anspaugh; ***W:*** Angelo Pizzo; ***C:*** Fred Murphy; ***M:*** Jerry Goldsmith. L.A. Film Critics '86: Support. Actor (Hopper); Natl. Film Reg. '01.

Hoot 1/2 **2006 (PG)** Mild eco-tale based on Carl Hiaasen's young-adult novel. Young teen Roy (Lerman) is the new kid at his Coconut Cove, Florida, school. After tangling with a bully, Roy is grateful to befriend tomboy Beatrice (Larson) and runaway Mullet Fingers (Linley). Mullet spends his time sabotaging a construction site that is the habitat of the endangered burrowing owl (which is small and cute while the corporation destroying it is big and greedy). Naturally, Roy decides to help out (the owls of course). **90m/C; DVD.** Luke Wilson; Logan Lerman; Tim Blake Nelson; Brie Larson; Cody Linley; Neil Flynn; Clark Gregg; Kiersten Warren; Jessica Cauffiel; Dean Collins; Robert Wagner; Eric Phillips; Jimmy Buffett; John Archie; Kin Shriner; ***D:*** Will Shriner; ***W:*** Will Shriner; ***C:*** Michael Chapman; ***M:*** Phil Marshall; Michael Utley; Mac McAnally.

Hootch Country Boys *Redneck County; The Great Lester Boggs* **1975 (PG)** A film packed with moonshine, sheriffs, busty country girls, and chases. **90m/C; VHS, DVD.** Alex Karras; Scott MacKenzsie; Dean Jagger; Willie Jones; Bob Ridgely; Susan Denbo; Bob Ginnaven; David Haney; ***D:*** Harry Z. Thomason.

Hop 1/2 **2011 (PG)** In this hyper, candy-fueled animated/live action combo romp, the Easter Bunny's teenage son, E.B. (voiced by Brand), rejects taking over the Easter family business in favor of pursuing his dream of being a drummer. He leaves Easter Island for Hollywood and stays with unemployed slacker Fred (Marsden) after Fred injures him in a car accident. With E.B. gone a power-hungry chick plots to take over the Easter Bunny job. Can E.B. save Easter? The CGI/live action combo works well enough and it's cute enough but with a lack of imagination and humor it's not fun for the whole family. **90m/C; DVD, Blu-Ray.** James Marsden; Kaley Cuoco; Chelsea Handler; Hank Azaria; Gary Cole; Elizabeth Perkins; David Hasselhoff; ***V:*** Russell Brand; Hank Azaria; Hugh Laurie; ***D:*** Tim Hill; ***W:*** Cinco Paul; Ken Daurio; Brian Lynch; ***C:*** Peter Lyons Collister; ***M:*** Christopher Lennertz.

Hopalong Cassidy Returns 1/2 **1936** In the seventh entry in the "Hopalong Cassidy" series, Hoppy (Boyd) faces a lady outlaw, Lilli Marsh (Brent), who, of course, falls hard for our stalwart hero. If this is not one of the best in the series, it maintains the high production standards, and it contains the debut of series regular Morris Ankrum as a villain. **74m/B; DVD.** William Boyd; George "Gabby" Hayes; Evelyn Brent; Morris Ankrum; William Janney; ***D:*** Nate Watt; ***W:*** Doris Schroeder; ***C:*** Archie Stout.

Hopalong Cassidy: Riders of the Deadline **1943** Hoppy turns into a baddie in this episode in order to infiltrate a treacherous gang and apprehend their leader. **70m/B; VHS, DVD.** William Boyd; Andy Clyde; Jimmy Rogers; Robert Mitchum; ***D:*** Lesley Selander.

Hopalong Cassidy: The Devil's Playground **1946** Strange things are afoot in a peaceful valley adjacent to a desolate, forbidding wasteland. When Hoppy and a young woman set out across the wasteland to make a gold delivery, they encounter a band of desperados and begin to unravel the secrets of a dishonest political ring. **65m/B; VHS, DVD.** William Boyd; Andy Clyde; Rand Brooks; Elaine Riley; ***D:*** George Archainbaud.

Hope and Glory 1/2 **1987 (PG-13)** Boorman turns his memories of WWII London into a complex and sensitive film. Father volunteers, and mother must deal with the awakening sexuality of her teenage daughter, keep her son in line, balance the ration books, and try to make it to the bomb shelter in the middle of the night. Seen through the boy's eyes, war creates a playground of shrapnel to collect and wild imaginings come true. Nice companion film to "Empire of the Sun" and "Au Revoir Les Enfants," two more 1987 releases that explore WWII from the recollections of young boys. **97m/C; VHS, DVD, Blu-Ray.** *GB* Sebastian Rice-Edwards; Geraldine Muir; Sarah Miles; Sammi Davis; David Hayman; Derrick O'Connor; Susan Wooldridge; Jean-Marc Barr; Ian Bannen; Jill Baker; Charley Boorman; Annie Leon; Katrine Boorman; Gerald James; Amelda Brown; Colin Higgins; ***D:*** John Boorman; ***W:*** John Boorman; ***C:*** Philippe Rousselot; ***M:*** Peter Martin. British Acad. '87: Film, Support. Actress (Wooldridge); Golden Globes '88: Film--Mus./Comedy; L.A. Film Critics '87: Director (Boorman), Film, Screenplay; Natl. Soc. Film Critics '87: Cinematog., Director (Boorman), Film, Screenplay.

Hope Floats 1/2 **1998 (PG-13)** Former small town Texas beauty queen Birdee Pruitt (Bullock) finds out her husband Bill (Pare) is having an affair with her best friend (Arquette) live on TV, thanks to a tabloid talk show expose. Completely humiliated, she takes her daughter Bernice (Whitman) and heads home to her own rather spaced-out mom Ramona (Rowlands). She's trying to gain some perspective on her life—and maybe, slowly, find a new love with the help of handsome cowpoke Justin (Connick Jr.) Movie is sweet, sentimental, obvious, and has an appealing cast and a happy ending. Perfect girlfriend fare. **114m/C; VHS, DVD.** Sandra Bullock; Harry Connick, Jr.; Gena Rowlands; Mae Whitman; Cameron Finley; Michael Paré; Rosanna Arquette; Kathy Najimy; Bill Cobbs; ***D:*** Forest Whitaker; ***W:*** Steven Rogers; ***C:*** Caleb Deschanel; ***M:*** Dave Grusin.

Hope Gap 1/2 **2020 (PG-13)** A son (O'Connor) returns to his English seaside home, where he witnesses the dissolution of his parents' (Bening and NIghy) 29-year marriage. Neither the fine acting of the three leads (particularly Bening) nor the gorgeous cinematography could elevate this film from dull sentimentality. **100m/C; DVD.** Annette Bening; Bill Nighy; Josh O'Connor; Aiysha Hart; Rose Keegan; ***D:*** William Nicholson; ***W:*** William Nicholson; ***C:*** Anna Valdez-Hanks; ***M:*** Alex Heffes.

Hope Ranch **2002 (PG-13)** J.T Hope (Boxleitner), an ex-cop and Marine, runs a ranch designed to rehabilitate juvenile delinquents. When three street-wise but troubled kids arrive, J.T. and his staff are put to the test. Uplifting family fare blends action and message smoothly. Produced for the Animal Planet network. **100m/C; VHS, DVD.** Bruce Boxleitner; Lorenzo Lamas; Barry Corbin; Gail O'Grady; Laura Johnson; Richard Lee Jackson; Brian Gross; J.D. Pardo; Isabell Howell; Brad Hawkins; ***D:*** Rex Piano; ***W:*** C. Thomas Howell; Jim Snider; ***C:*** Howard Wexler; ***M:*** Bruce Lynch. **CABLE**

Hope Springs **2012 (PG-13)** After three decades of marriage, Kay (Streep) is feeling alone and taken for granted by her grumpy accountant husband Arnold (Jones). She signs them up from a week of intensive couples' with counselor Dr. Feld (Carell). Arnold reluctantly goes along, growling all the while, but some hard truths are revealed during their sessions and the marriage exercises Feld has them attempt. Carell is the straight man to touching performances from Streep and a surprisingly tender Jones. Some humor arises from the situations, but this is more drama than comedy about people of a certain age and their expectations. **100m/C; DVD, Blu-Ray.** Meryl Streep; Tommy Lee Jones; Steve Carell; Elisabeth Shue; Jean Smart; Brett Rice; Mimi Rogers; ***D:*** David Frankel; ***W:*** Vanessa Taylor; ***C:*** Florian Ballhaus; ***M:*** Theodore Shapiro.

Hopelessly in June 1/2 **2011 (R)** African-American financial analyst Daleon Myers (Brantley) falls in love with L.A. businesswoman June Flowers (Neff) but a big clash in upbringing and family values exists. His meddling parents are staunch conservative Baptists and adopted June's two dads are liberal--and white. **93m/C; DVD; Closed Captioned.** Vincent Brantley; Carolyn Neff; Peter Jason; Stuart Pankin; Keith David; Ella Joyce; Tommy (Tiny) Lister; Ed Asner; ***D:*** Vincent Brantley; ***W:*** Vincent Brantley; ***C:*** Seth Johnson; ***M:*** Silas Hite. **VIDEO**

Hoppity Goes to Town *Mr. Bug Goes to Town* **1941** Full-length animated feature from the Max Fleischer studios tells the story of the inhabitants of Bugville, who live in a weed patch in New York City. **77m/C; VHS, DVD.** ***D:*** Dave Fleischer; ***M:*** Frank Loesser; Hoagy Carmichael.

Hoppy Serves a Writ **1943** In this last of the series to be based on the writings of the original author, Texas sheriff Cassidy tries to bring a gang of outlaws to justice. Look for a young Robert Mitchum as one of the villains. **67m/B; VHS, DVD.** William Boyd; Andy Clyde; Jay Kirby; Victor Jory; George Reeves; Hal Taliaferro; Robert Mitchum; Byron Foulger; Earle Hodgins; Roy Barcroft; ***D:*** George Archainbaud.

Hopscotch **1980 (R)** A C.I.A. agent drops out when his overly zealous chief demotes him to a desk job. When he writes a book designed to expose the dirty deeds of the CIA, he leads his boss and KGB pal on a merry chase. Amiable comedy well-suited for Matthau's rumpled talents. **107m/C; VHS, DVD, Blu-Ray.** Walter Matthau; Glenda Jackson; Ned Beatty; Sam Waterston; Herbert Lom; ***D:*** Ronald Neame.

Horatio Hornblower **1999** Adventure on the high seas in these adaptations of C.S. Forester's popular novels, which are set in the late 18th-century. Hornblower (Gruffudd) is a young recruit who rises through the ranks of the King's Navy as the British battle the French. "The Duel" provides the introduction to Hornblower and his mentor, Captain Pellew (Lindsay). "The Fire Ships" has Hornblower preparing for his lieutenant's exam. "The Duchess and the Devil" finds Hornblower escorting the Duchess of Wharfedale (Lunghi) to England with important naval dispatches. "The Wrong War" finds the Brits preparing a coup against the French Republican government. **400m/C; VHS, DVD.** *GB* Ioan Gruffudd; Robert Lindsay; Denis Lawson; Cherie Lunghi; Anthony Sher; Samuel West; Andrew Tiernan; Ronald Pickup; ***D:*** Andrew Grieve; ***W:*** Russell Lewis; Mike Cullen; Patrick Harbinson; ***C:*** Alec Curtis; Neve Cunningham. **TV**

Horatio Hornblower: The Adventure Continues **2001** The adventures of young British naval officer Hornblower (Gruffud) continue with two linked stories: "Mutiny" and "The Retribution." Horatio recounts to his mentor, Captain Pellew (Lindsay), the reasons for his imprisonment on mutiny charges after confining his insane captain (Warner) to his quarters to prevent his sending the crew into a suicidal battle. But Hornblower must also lead a force to recapture an enemy fort. Based on C.S. Forrester's novel, "Lieutenant Hornblower." **200m/C; VHS, DVD.** *GB* Ioan Gruffudd; Robert Lindsay; David Warner; Jamie Bamber; Paul McGann; Nicholas Jones; Philip Glenister; David Rintoul; ***D:*** Andrew Grieve; ***C:*** Chris O'Dell; ***M:*** John Keane. **TV**

Horizons West 1/2 **1952** Two brothers go their separate ways after the Civil War. One leads a peaceful life as a rancher but the other, corrupted by the war, engages in a violent campaign to build his own empire. Ryan's outstanding performance eclipses that of the young Hudson. **81m/C; DVD.** Robert Ryan; Julie Adams; Rock Hudson; Raymond Burr; James Arness; John McIntire; Dennis Weaver; Frances Bavier; ***D:*** Budd Boetticher; ***W:*** Louis Stevens; ***C:*** Charles P. Boyle; ***M:*** Henry Mancini.

The Horizontal Lieutenant 1/2 **1962** Hutton and Prentiss team up again in this moderately funny romantic-comedy about an officer's escapades during WWII. Based on the novel "The Bottletop Affair" by Gordon Cotler. **90m/C; VHS, DVD.** Jim Hutton; Paula Prentiss; Jack Carter; Jim Backus; Charles McGraw; Miyoshi Umeki; ***D:*** Richard Thorpe; ***W:*** George Wells.

The Horn Blows at Midnight **1945** A band trumpeter falls asleep and dreams he's a bumbling archangel, on Earth to blow the note bringing the end of the world. But a pretty girl distracts him, and...A wild, high-gloss, well-cast fantasy farce, uniquely subversive in its lighthearted approach to biblical Doomsday. Benny made the film notorious by acting ashamed of it in his later broadcast routines. **78m/B; DVD.** Jack Benny; Alexis Smith; Dolores Moran; Allyn Joslyn; Reginald Gardiner; Guy Kibbee; John Alexander; Margaret Dumont; ***D:*** Raoul Walsh; ***W:*** Sam Hellman; James V. Kern; ***C:*** Sidney Hickox; ***M:*** Franz Waxman.

Hornets' Nest **1970** Third-rate WWII adventure pic with fading star Hudson starring as American commando Capt. Turner. His team parachutes into Italy where they must blow up a dam, but only a wounded Turner survives a German ambush. He's rescued by some urchins whose parents were murdered by the Nazis. They force Bianca, a German medic, to doctor Turner, who responds in a despicable manner. The boys agree to help Turner with the dam in return for his help wiping out the enemy soldiers. **110m/C; VHS, DVD.** Rock Hudson; Sylva Koscina; Mark Colleano; Sergio Fantoni; Giacomo "Jack" Rossi-Stuart; Andrea Bosic; Jacques Sernas; Gerard Herter; Tom Felleghi; ***D:*** Phil Karlson; ***W:*** S.S. Schweitzer; ***C:*** Gabor Pogany; ***M:*** Ennio Morricone.

Horns **2013 (R)** Ig Perrish (Radcliffe) is having a bad week. His girlfriend is raped and murdered and he's the prime suspect. Add to that, he wakes up one day to find actual demon's horns growing out of his head. Good people can't see Ig's horns, but they reveal their darkest secrets to the young man, giving him remarkable power. Based on a hit book by Stephen King's son, Joe Hill, Aja's horror-comedy jumps back and forth in haphazard, inconsistent ways for its bloated running time. Again, Radcliffe does his best but can't quite make up for what lacks. **120m/C; DVD, Blu-Ray, Streaming.** Daniel Radcliffe; Max Minghella; Juno Temple; Kelli Garner; David Morse; Heather Graham; James Remar; Kathleen Quinlan; ***D:*** Alexandre Aja; ***W:*** Keith Bunin; ***C:*** Frederick Elmes; ***M:*** Robin Coudert.

Horrible Bosses 1/2 **2011 (R)** Resentful buddies Nick (Bateman), Kurt (Sudekis), and Dale (Day) work for truly horrible people: manager Nick is constantly abused by his sneering control freak supervisor Dave Harken (Spacey); dental hygienist Dale (Day) is sexually harassed by his nympho boss Dr. Julia Harris (a dark-haired Aniston); and accountant Kurt's (Sudeikis) superior Bobby Pellitt (Farrell with a bad comb-over) is an idiot who's risking his family's business to fund his hooker and coke-loving lifestyle. A chance meeting with crook Jones (Foxx) spurs an inept plan to kill the loathsome threesome but the tasteless, crude, and sometimes amusing comedy isn't quite black enough. **98m/C; Blu-Ray, On Demand.** Jason Bateman; Jason Sudeikis; Charlie Day; Jamie Foxx; Jennifer Aniston; Colin Farrell; Donald Sutherland; Kevin Spacey; Julie Bowen; John Francis Daley; ***D:*** Seth Gordon; ***W:*** John Francis Daley; Jonathan M. Goldstein; Michael Markowitz; ***C:*** David Hennings.

Horrible Bosses 2 1/2 **2014 (R)** Proving the fact that a joke is only really funny the first time you hear it, this follow-up to the 2011 hit is a stale, loud, obnoxious affair that gets overly slapsticky and annoying. Buddies Nick (Bateman), Kurt (Sudeikis), and Dale (Day) are swindled by a nefarious investor (Waltz), so they plot to kidnap his rebellious son (Pine). Aniston, Spacey, and Foxx return to reprise their most popular bits from the first movie, but none of it has the same energy or charm. **108m/C; DVD, Blu-Ray.** Jason Bateman; Charlie Day; Jason Sudeikis; Christoph Waltz; Chris Pine; Jamie Foxx; Kevin Spacey; Jennifer Aniston; Jonathan Banks; ***D:*** Sean Anders; ***W:*** Sean Anders; John Morris; ***C:*** Julio Macat; ***M:*** Christopher Lennertz.

The Horrible Dr. Bones **2000 (R)** Dr. Bones (Igus) is a record producer who gives the young Urban Protectors band their big break, but it turns out that he's exploiting them in a supernatural scheme involving human sacrifice and zombies. The plotting is amateurish. Some of the effects have shock value. The low-budget horror doesn't rise much above the studio's bare-bones production. **72m/C; DVD.** Darrow Igus; Larry Bates; Sarah Scott; Rhonda Claebaut; Nathaniel Lamar; ***D:*** Art Carnage; ***W:*** Raymond Forchon; ***C:*** Adolfo Bartoli.

The Horrible Dr. Hichcock 1/2 *L'Orribile Segreto del Dr. Hichcock* **1962** A sicko doctor, who accidentally killed his first wife while engaged in sexual antics, remarries to bring the first missus back from the dead using his new wife's blood. Genuinely creepy. Sequelled by "The Ghost." **76m/C;**

VHS, DVD, Blu-Ray. *IT* Robert Flemyng; Barbara Steele; Silvano Tranquilli; Harriet Medin; Ernesto Gastaldi; Maria Teresa Vianello; ***D:*** Riccardo Freda; ***W:*** Perry (Ernesto Gastaldi) Julyan; ***C:*** Raffaele Masciocchi; ***M:*** Roman Vlad.

A Horrible Way to Die **2010 (R)** Low-budget indie with too many camera tricks that nearly ruin a decent serial killer flick. Charming psycho Garrick Turrell (Bowen) escapes from prison and makes his bloody way cross-country to get to ex-girlfriend Sarah (Seimetz), who turned him in. She's relocated to a small town to start over with a waitress job, attending AA meetings and starting a tentative romance with nice guy Kevin (Swanberg). **87m/C; DVD, Blu-Ray.** AJ Bowen; Amy Seimetz; Joe Swanberg; Brandon Carroll; Lane Hughes; ***D:*** Adam Wingard; ***W:*** Simon Barrett; ***C:*** Chris Hilleke; ***M:*** Jasper Justice Leigh.

The Horror at 37,000 Feet 1/2 **1973** An altar from an English abbey--that was supposedly built over a Druidic sacrificial site--is in the cargo hold of a 747 flying from London to L.A. A demon escapes from the altar and causes inflight panic. Shatner plays a defrocked priest and this telepic is silly rather than scary although it's filled with familiar faces. **73m/C; DVD.** Roy Thinnes; Jane Merrow; Chuck Connors; William Shatner; Buddy Ebsen; Tammy Grimes; Paul Winfield; Russell Johnson; Darleen Carr; France Nuyen; ***D:*** David Lowell Rich; ***W:*** Ronald Austin; ***C:*** Earl Rath; ***M:*** Morton Stevens. **TV**

The Horror Chamber of Dr. Faustus 1/2 *Eyes without a Face; Les Yeux sans Visage; Occhi senza Volto* **1959** A wickedly intelligent, inventive piece of Grand Guignol about a mad doctor who kills young girls so he may graft their skin onto the face of his accidentally mutilated daughter. In French with English subtitles. **84m/B; VHS, DVD, Blu-Ray.** *FR* Alida Valli; Pierre Brasseur; Edith Scob; Francois Guerin; Juliette Mayniel; Alex(andre) Rignault; Claude Brasseur; Charles Blavette; ***D:*** Georges Franju; ***W:*** Jean Redon; ***C:*** Eugen Shufftan; ***M:*** Maurice Jarre.

Horror Express 1/2 *Panic on the Trans-Siberian Express; Panico en el Transiberiano; Panic in the Trans-Siberian Train* **1972 (R)** A creature from prehistoric times, that was removed from its tomb, is transported on the Trans-Siberian railroad. Passengers suddenly discover strange things happening—such as having their souls sucked out of them. **88m/C; VHS, DVD, Blu-Ray.** *SP GB* Christopher Lee; Peter Cushing; Telly Savalas; Alberto De Mendoza; Silvia Tortosa; Julio Pena; Angel Del Pozo; Helga Line; Jorge (George) Rigaud; Jose Jaspe; ***D:*** Eugenio (Gene) Martin; ***W:*** Julian Zimet; Arnaud d'Usseau; ***C:*** Alejandro Ulloa.

Horror Hospital *Computer Killers; Doctor Blood Bath* **1973 (R)** Patients are turned into zombies by a mad doctor in this hospital where no anesthesia is used. Those who try to escape are taken care of by the doctor's guards. **91m/C; VHS, DVD.** *GB* Michael Gough; Robin Askwith; Vanessa Shaw; Ellen Pollock; Skip Martin; Dennis Price; ***D:*** Antony Balch; ***W:*** Antony Balch; Alan Watson; ***C:*** David McDonald.

Horror Hotel 1/2 *The City of the Dead* **1960** A young witchcraft student visits a small Massachusetts town which has historic ties to witch burnings and discovers a new, and deadly, coven is now active. Well done and atmospheric. **76m/B; VHS, DVD, Blu-Ray.** *GB* Christopher Lee; Patricia Jessel; Betta St. John; Dennis Lotis; Venetia Stevenson; Valentine Dyall; ***D:*** John Llewellyn Moxey; ***W:*** George L. Baxt; ***C:*** Desmond Dickinson.

Horror House on Highway 5 **WOOF! 1986** Someone in a Nixon mask kills people in this extremely cheap dud. **90m/C; VHS, DVD, Blu-Ray.** Phil Therrien; Max Manthey; Susan Leslie; ***D:*** Richard Casey; ***W:*** Richard Casey; ***C:*** David Golia.

Horror in the Wind 1/2 **2008** A violent fundamentalist religious lunatic wins the U.S. presidency and begins a war on sex, blaming it for all of society's ills. Hearing of a formula that may suppress sexual desire he orders it stolen, copied, and sprayed via plane over the entire world. Unfortunately the formula hadn't finished testing and instead of turning people against sex it changes their sexual orientation. **90m/C; DVD, Streaming.** Perren Hedderson; Morse Bicknell; Courtney Bell; Jiji Hise; ***D:*** Max Mitchell; ***W:*** Max Mitchell; ***C:*** John Graham. **VIDEO**

The Horror of Dracula 1/2 *Dracula* **1958** The first Hammer Dracula film, in which the infamous vampire is given a new, elegant and ruthless persona, as he battles Prof. Van Helsing after coming to England. Possibly the finest, most inspired version of Bram Stoker's macabre chestnut, and one that single-handedly revived the horror genre. **82m/C; VHS, DVD, Blu-Ray.** *GB* Peter Cushing; Christopher Lee; Michael Gough; Melissa Stribling; Carol Marsh; John Van Eyssen; Valerie Gaunt; Charles Lloyd-Pack; Miles Malleson; ***D:*** Terence Fisher; ***W:*** Jimmy Sangster; ***C:*** Jack Asher; ***M:*** James Bernard.

The Horror of Frankenstein **1970** Spoof of the standard Frankenstein story features philandering ex-med student Baron Frankenstein, whose interest in a weird and esoteric branch of science provides a shocking and up-to-date rendition of the age-old plot. Preceded by "Frankenstein Must Be Destroyed" and followed by "Frankenstein and the Monster from Hell." **93m/C; VHS, DVD, Blu-Ray.** *GB* Ralph Bates; Kate O'Mara; Dennis Price; David Prowse; Veronica Carlson; Joan Rice; Bernard Archard; Graham James; ***D:*** Jimmy Sangster; ***W:*** Jimmy Sangster; Jeremy Burnham; ***C:*** Moray Grant.

Horror of Party Beach **WOOF!** *Invasion of the Zombies* **1964** Considered to be one of the all-time worst films. Features a mob of radioactive seaweed creatures who eat a slew of nubile, surf-minded teenagers. **71m/C; VHS, DVD, Blu-Ray.** John Scott; Alice Lyon; Allen Laurel; Marilyn Clarke; Augustin Mayer; Eulabelle Moore; ***D:*** Del Tenney; ***W:*** Richard Hilliard; ***C:*** Richard Hilliard; ***M:*** Bill Holmes.

Horror of the Blood Monsters **WOOF!** *Vampire Men of the Lost Planet; Horror Creatures of the Prehistoric Planet; Creatures of the Prehistoric Planet; Creatures of the Red Planet; Flesh Creatures of the Red Planet; The Flesh Creatures; Space Mission of the Lost Planet* **1970 (PG)** John Carradine made a career out of being in bad movies, and this one competes as one of the worst. This is an editor's nightmare, made up of black & white film spliced together and colorized. Vampires from outer space threaten to suck all the blood from the people of Earth. **85m/C; VHS, DVD.** *PH* John Carradine; Robert Dix; Vicki Volante; Jennifer Bishop; ***D:*** Al Adamson; George Joseph.

Horror Rises from the Tomb *El Espanto Surge de la Tumba* **1972** A 15th century knight and his assistant are beheaded for practicing witchcraft. Five hundred years later, they return to possess a group of vacationers and generally cause havoc. **89m/C; VHS, DVD, Blu-Ray.** *SP* Paul Naschy; Vic Winner; Emma Cohen; Helga Line; Cristina Suriani; ***D:*** Carlos Aured; ***W:*** Paul Naschy.

The Horror Show *House 3* **1989 (R)** Serial killer fries in electric chair, an event that really steams him. So he goes after the cop who brought him in. Standard dead guy who won't die and wants revenge flick. **95m/C; VHS, DVD, Blu-Ray; Open Captioned.** Brion James; Lance Henriksen; Rita Taggart; Dedee Pfeiffer; Aron Eisenberg; Matt Clark; Thom Bray; Terry Alexander; David Oliver; ***D:*** James Isaac; ***W:*** Alan Smithee; Leslie Bohem; ***C:*** Mac Ahlberg.

Horrors of Burke & Hare **1971** A gory tale about the exploits of a bunch of 19th-century grave robbers. **94m/C; VHS, DVD.** Derren Nesbitt; Harry Andrews; Yootha Joyce; ***D:*** Vernon Sewell.

Horrors of the Black Museum **1959** Gruesome, though camp, Brit horror. Frustrated crime writer Edmond Bancroft (Gough) decides his latest opus must have accurate murder descriptions so he uses Scotland Yard's "Black Museum" for inspiration. He hypnotizes his assistant Rick (Curnow) and has him kill using various tortuous gadgets with Bancroft disposing of the bodies in a vat of acid. Will Scotland Yard catch Bancroft or will the abused Rick snap out of his trance first? Director Crabtree's last film was released in "Hypnovision" as a promotional gimmick. **95m/C; DVD.** *GB* Michael Gough; Graham Curnow; June Cunningham; Shirley Anne Field; Geoffrey Keen; John Warwick; Gerald Anderson; Beatrice Varley; ***D:*** Arthur Crabtree; ***W:*** Aben Kandel; Herman Cohen; ***C:*** Desmond Dickinson; ***M:*** Gerard Schurmann.

Horrors of the Red Planet *The Wizard of Mars* **1964** Cheapo epic sees astronauts crash on Mars, meet its Wizard, and stumble into a few Oz-like creatures. Technically advised by Forrest J. Ackerman. **81m/C; VHS, DVD.** John Carradine; Roger Gentry; Vic McGee; ***D:*** David L. Hewitt.

Hors Satan 1/2 *Outside Satan* **2011** Internationally renowned writer/director Dumont's enigmatic piece defies categorization, interpretation, or even recap. A man and woman (credited only as The Guy and The Girl) live in a seaside town near Boulogne sure Mer in France. They walk and walk and walk as Dumont punctuates long sequences of complete inactivity with scenes of extreme violence. Perhaps the filmmaker is balancing God and Satan, good and evil, or perhaps he is making it up as he goes along. Either way, it gives the audience no easy answers, playing with theme and captivating visuals instead of traditional plot. **110m/C; DVD.** *FR* David Dewaele; Alexandra Lematre; ***D:*** Bruno Dumont; ***W:*** Bruno Dumont; ***C:*** Yves Cape.

The Horse 1/2 *Horse, My Horse* **1982** A moving, mature Turkish film about a father and son trying to overcome socioeconomic obstacles and their own frailties in order to make enough money to send the boy to school. In Turkish with English subtitles. **116m/C; VHS, DVD.** *TU* Genco Erkal; ***D:*** Ali Ozgenturk; ***W:*** Isil Ozgenturk; ***C:*** Kenan Ormanlar; ***M:*** Okay Temiz.

Horse Camp **2014 (PG)** A family film about friendship, mean girls, and horses. Excited at the prospect of going to horse camp, teen Kathy (Trovillion) soon discovers the depth of personal and competitive rivalries. She is especially vexed by resident mean girl Stacy (Ryda). When the competition at the camp grows more intense, Kathy finds out that true friendships have real power. **108m/C; DVD, Streaming, Download.** Jordan Trovillion; Kristen Ryda; Dean Cain; Annelyse Ahmad; Kristin Mellian; ***D:*** Joel Paul Reisig; ***W:*** Joel Paul Reisig; ***C:*** Jeffrey T. Morgan; Joel C. Warren; ***M:*** Todd Maki.

Horse Feathers 1/2 **1932** Huxley College has to beef up its football team to win the championship game which has been rigged by local gamblers in the opposition's favor, and the corrupt new college president (Groucho) knows just how to do it. Features some of the brothers' classic routines, and the songs "Whatever It Is, I'm Against It" and "Everyone Says I Love You." **67m/B; VHS, DVD, Blu-Ray.** Groucho Marx; Chico Marx; Harpo Marx; Zeppo Marx; Thelma Todd; David Landau; Nat Pendleton; ***D:*** Norman Z. McLeod; ***W:*** Bert Kalmar; S.J. Perelman; Harry Ruby; ***C:*** Ray June; ***M:*** Harry Ruby.

A Horse for Danny 1/2 **1995 (G)** Horse trainer Eddie (Urich), dogged by bad luck, and his 11-year-old niece Danny (Sobieski), come across a thoroughbred named Tom Thumb, who may be their chance at racing's winners circle. TV movie. **92m/C; VHS, DVD.** Robert Urich; Leelee Sobieski; Ron Brice; Karen Carlson; Gary Basaraba; ***D:*** Dick Lowry; ***C:*** Steven Fierberg.

Horse Girl 1/2 **2020 (R)** Socially awkward Sarah (Brie) works in a craft store and is suffering from declining mental health. Though her family has a long history of mental illness, especially her grandmother, Sarah cannot see that her issues are affecting her even as her dreams begin to merge with her reality. As she goes about her daily life, even as she wakes up in random places, Sarah slowly comes to believe she is a time traveling clone of her grandmother and suffers a mental breakdown. The complicated, ambitious drama depicts mental illness in creative ways, grounded by Brie's memorable performance. **104m/C; DVD.** Alison Brie; Molly Shannon; John Ortiz; Lauren Weedman; Robin Tunney; ***D:*** Jeff Baena; ***W:*** Alison Brie; Jeff Baena; ***C:*** Sean McElwee; ***M:*** Josiah Steinbrick; Jeremy Zuckerman.

The Horse in the Gray Flannel Suit 1/2 **1968 (G)** Disney comedy portrays an advertising executive who links his daughter's devotion to horses with a client's new ad campaign. **114m/C; VHS, DVD.** Dean Jones; Ellen Janov; Fred Clark; Diane Baker; Lloyd Bochner; Kurt Russell; ***D:*** Norman Tokar; ***W:*** Louis Pelletier; ***M:*** George Bruns.

The Horse Soldiers 1/2 **1959** An 1863 Union cavalry officer is sent 300 miles into Confederate territory to destroy a railroad junction and is accompanied by a fellow officer who is also a pacifist doctor. Based on a true Civil War incident. **114m/C; VHS, DVD, Blu-Ray.** John Wayne; William Holden; Hoot Gibson; Constance Towers; Russell Simpson; Strother Martin; Anna Lee; Judson Pratt; Denver Pyle; Jack Pennick; Althea Gibson; William Forrest; Willis Bouchey; Bing (Neil) Russell; Ken Curtis; O.Z. Whitehead; Walter Reed; Hank Worden; Carleton Young; Cliff Lyons; ***D:*** John Ford; ***W:*** John Lee Mahin; Martin Rackin; ***C:*** William Clothier; ***M:*** David Buttolph.

A Horse Tale **2015 (G)** A man unexpectedly finds redemption at a horse farm. With foreclosure on their stable looming, a family approaches accountant Michael Thompson (Muldoon) for assistance. Living in the city and possessing inflexible personality, Michael agrees to help them only reluctantly. However, his quest to save the farm results in profound life changes for him and his teenage daughter Chloe (Carlson) as they find new hope and a brighter future in the country. **85m/C; DVD, Streaming, Download.** Charisma Carpenter; Patrick Muldoon; Dominique Swain; Billy Tilk; Mandalynn Carlson; ***D:*** Brad Keller; ***W:*** Lori Twichell; ***C:*** Michael Redding; ***M:*** Nathaniel Smith. **VIDEO**

The Horse Whisperer 1/2 **1997 (PG-13)** After her teenaged daughter Grace (Johansson) is injured in a riding accident, determined mom Annie (Thomas), believeing that the girl's recovery is tied to the horse's, takes child and horse to Montana to seek the help of horse healer Tom (Redford) in the big-screen adaptation of the Nicholas Evans novel. While there, chilly New York editor Annie warms up to Tom and the possibility of love. Like "The Bridges of Madison County," this adaptation removes the overwrought syrupy melodrama of its source novel to concentrate on mature themes like fidelity, trust, and fate. Fine performances by all (although Redford could be seen as a bit self-indulgent at times) and the beautiful Montana backdrop make up for the lack of sustained dramatic impact, which is probably due to the almost three-hour run time and some dramatic changes from the book. **168m/C; VHS, DVD, Blu-Ray.** Robert Redford; Kristin Scott Thomas; Scarlett Johansson; Sam Neill; Chris Cooper; Dianne Wiest; Cherry Jones; Jeannette Nolan; Don Edwards; Ty Hillman; Kate (Catherine) Bosworth; Steve Frye; ***D:*** Robert Redford; ***W:*** Eric Roth; Richard LaGravenese; ***C:*** Robert Richardson; ***M:*** Thomas Newman.

The Horse Without a Head 1/2 **1963** Stolen loot has been hidden in a discarded toy horse which is now the property of a group of poor children. The thieves, however, have different plans. Good family fare from the Disney TV show. **89m/C; VHS, DVD.** Jean-Pierre Aumont; Herbert Lom; Leo McKern; Pamela Franklin; Vincent Winter; ***D:*** Don Chaffey. **TV**

The Horseman on the Roof 1/2 *Le Hussard sur le Toit* **1995 (R)** Lavish costume drama set in Provence in the 1830s, during a cholera epidemic. Italian officer/revolutionary Angelo (Martinez) is on the run and eventually meets up with beautiful Pauline de Theus (Binoche), who hides him in a quarantined French village. Pauline's in search of her husband and Angelo reluctantly agrees to help her. Together they manage to escape a military cordon and travel to another plague town. There's lots of riding through the countryside and hiding out and not much actually happens. Nice scenery, attractive stars. Based on the 1951 novel by Jean Giono. French with subtitles; originally released at 135 minutes. **119m/C; VHS, DVD.** *FR* Olivier Martinez; Juliette Binoche; Francois Cluzet; Isabelle Carre; Jean Yanne; Claudio Amendola; Pierre Arditti; ***Cameo(s):*** Gerard Depardieu; ***D:*** Jean-Paul Rappeneau; ***W:*** Jean-Paul Rappeneau; Jean-Claude Carriere;

Nina Companeez; **C:** Thierry Arbogast; **M:** Jean-Claude Petit. Cesar '96: Cinematog., Sound.

The Horsemen ♂ 1/2 **1970 (PG)** An Afghani youth enters the brutal buzkashi horse tournament to please his macho-minded father. Beautifully shot in Afghanistan and Spain by Claude Renoir. **109m/C; DVD.** Omar Sharif; Leigh Taylor-Young; Jack Palance; David De; Peter Jeffrey; **D:** John Frankenheimer; **W:** Dalton Trumbo; **M:** Georges Delerue.

Horsemen ♂ 1/2 **2009 (R)** Gory and slapdash horror-thriller. Forensic dentist Aidan Breslin (Quaid) realizes that a series of mutilated corpses is related to the biblical passage about the 'Four Horsemen of the Apocalypse.' The domestic scenes with Breslin's estranged sons (and a good performance by Quaid) at least offer something slightly different. **88m/C; DVD.** Dennis Quaid; Ziyi Zhang; Lou Taylor Pucci; Clifton (Gonzalez) Collins, Jr.; Liam James; Peter Stormare; Patrick Fugit; Eric Balfour; **D:** Jonas Akerlund; **W:** David Callaham; **C:** Eric Broms; **M:** Jan A.P. Kaczmarek.

The Horse's Mouth ♂♂♂ *The Oracle* **1958** An obsessive painter discovers that he must rely upon his wits to survive in London. A hilarious adaptation of the Joyce Cary novel. **93m/C; VHS, DVD.** *GB* Alec Guinness; Kay Walsh; Robert Coote; Renee Houston; Michael Gough; **D:** Ronald Neame; **W:** Alec Guinness; **C:** Arthur Ibbetson; **M:** Kenneth V. Jones. Natl. Bd. of Review '58: Support. Actress (Walsh).

The Horses of McBride ♂♂ 1/2 *Christmas Rescue* **2012** Feel-good family film made for Canadian TV. Bratty teenager Nicki is having trouble dealing with her family's financial hardships that may result in her dad selling their ranch in McBride, British Columbia. When she discovers two starving horses stranded in the snow on Renshaw Mountain, she's determined to rescue them. With few options, Nicki starts digging a path so the horses can be led out, which galvanizes the entire community. Inspired by a true story. **85m/C; DVD.** *CA* Mackenzie Porter; Aidan Quinn; Kari Matchett; Edward Ruttle; Scott Hylands; Greyston Holt; **D:** Anne Wheeler; **W:** Anne Wheeler; **C:** Peter Woeste; **M:** Louis Natale. **TV**

Horsey ♂♂ **1999** Young Delilah makes no apologies for any of her passions—those of her art or the men or women she chooses to love. Then she starts a relationship with volatile Ryland Yale, a rock 'n' roller with a heroin addiction who still manages to fill all Delilah's emotional and physical needs. But is Delilah ready to deal with what Ryland will cost her? **93m/C; VHS, DVD.** Holly Ferguson; Todd Kerns; Ryan Robbins; Victoria Deschanel; **D:** Kirsten Clarkson; **W:** Kirsten Clarkson; **C:** Glen Winter; **M:** Helen Keller.

Horton Foote's Alone ♂♂ 1/2 *Alone* **1997** John Webb (Cronyn) is an elderly Texas farmer, lost after the death of his wife of 52 years. His nephews (Forrest, Cooper) want him to sell his land to an interested oil company and his daughters (Miles, Hart) want to cry on his shoulder. Then Webb's former tenant farmer (Jones) comes back to visit and is the only one to ask the old man what he wants to do. **107m/C; VHS, DVD.** Hume Cronyn; James Earl Jones; Chris Cooper; Frederic Forrest; Joanna Miles; Roxanne Hart; Shelley Duvall; Hallie Foote; Ed Begley, Jr.; David Selby; Piper Laurie; **D:** Michael Lindsay-Hogg; **W:** Horton Foote; **C:** Jeffrey Jur; **M:** David Shire. **CABLE**

The Hospital ♂♂♂ 1/2 **1971 (PG)** Cult favorite providing savage, unrelentingly sarcastic look at the workings of a chaotic metropolitan hospital beset by murders, witchdoctors, madness, and plain ineptitude. Scott's suicidal chief surgeon Herbert Bock, who falls in love with free-spirited Barbara Drummond (Riggs), a patient's daughter. **101m/C; VHS, DVD, Blu-Ray.** George C. Scott; Diana Rigg; Barnard Hughes; Stockard Channing; Nancy Marchand; Richard Dysart; Stephen Elliott; Rehn Scofield; Katherine Helmond; Roberts Blossom; **D:** Arthur Hiller; **W:** Paddy Chayefsky; **C:** Victor Kemper. Oscars '71: Story & Screenplay; Berlin Intl. Film Fest. '72: Silver Prize; British Acad. '72: Screenplay; Golden Globes '72: Screenplay; Natl. Film Reg. '95; Writers Guild '71: Orig. Screenplay.

Hospital of Terror ♂♂ *Nurse Sherri; Terror Hospital; Beyond the Living* **1978 (R)** A transmigratory religious fanatic who died on the operating table manages to possess a nurse (Jacobson) before he kicks the bucket, and once in his candystripe incarnation, vents his spleen on the doctors who botched his operation. It's got a little more plasma than Adamson's "AstroZombies," considered by many to be a world-class boner. **88m/C; VHS, DVD, Blu-Ray.** Jill Jacobson; Geoffrey Land; Marilyn Joi; Mary Kay Pass; Prentiss Moulden; Clayton Foster; **D:** Al Adamson.

The Host ♂♂♂ *Gwoemul* **2006 (R)** An overgrown mutant tadpole is on a man-eating bender along the Han River in South Korea, but that's not the most peculiar thing going on in this genre-stomping thriller. The family of one of the monsters would-be victims, high-schooler Park Hyeon-seo (Ko A-sung), is kookier than the monster. The story simultaneously lampoons and exploits the monster-on-the-loose genre to great effect. Fantastic visual effects, oddly juxtaposed humor and a super-stylie monster. . . it doesn't get much better. **119m/C; DVD.** *NK* Du-na Bae; Kang-ho Song; Hie-bon Byeon; Hae-il Park; Ah-sung Ko; **D:** Joon-ho Bong; **W:** Joon-ho Bong; Chul-hyan Baek; **C:** Hyung-ku Kim; **M:** Byung-woo Lee.

The Host ♂ **2013 (PG-13)** Another nauseatingly awful fantasy for young adults that hopes to jump on the Twilight bandwagon, this one courtesy of that franchise's source material author, Stephenie Meyer. Melanie Stryder (Ronan) will do whatever it takes to protect her family from an impending alien attack by forces that can take over their bodies and erase their memories. All potentially interesting sci-fi is trampled by awful dialogue, poor storytelling, and a number of scenes that play as comedy even though they weren't intended as such. Ronan is too talented for this knock-off junk and one hopes the Twilight rip-off genre ends soon. **125m/C; DVD, Blu-Ray, HD-DVD.** Saoirse Ronan; Max Irons; Diane Kruger; Jake Abel; William Hurt; Frances Fisher; **D:** Andrew Niccol; **W:** Andrew Niccol; **C:** Roberto Schaefer; **M:** Antonio Pinto.

The Hostage ♂♂ 1/2 **1967 (PG)** A young teenager is witness to a gruesome and clandestine burial. The two murderers responsible take it upon themselves to see that their secret is never told. **84m/C; VHS, DVD.** Don O'Kelly; Harry Dean Stanton; John Carradine; Danny Martins; **D:** Russell S. Doughten, Jr.

Hostage ♂♂ 1/2 **2005 (R)** Burnt-out hostage negotiator (Willis) retreats to the suburbs hoping for calm, only to find himself pulled into the middle of a deadly crisis. Three delinquents take over the house of an underworld accountant (Pollack), whose shadowy employers then kidnap Willis's family, forcing him to retrieve their vital info hidden inside. Very violent, exciting, and grim melodrama with a dizzying number of twists and turns. Ben Foster is memorably sick as the psycho leader of the young thugs. **113m/C; DVD, Blu-Ray.** Bruce Willis; Kevin Pollak; Ben Foster; Jonathan Tucker; Jimmy Bennett; Tina Lifford; Kim Coates; Serena Scott Thomas; Marshall Allman; Michelle Horn; Robert Knepper; Rumer Willis; Marjean Holden; Johnny Messner; Glenn Morshower; Chad Smith; **D:** Florent Emilio Siri; **W:** Doug Richardson; **C:** Giovanni Fiore Coltellacci; **M:** Alexandre Desplat.

Hostage Flight ♂♂ 1/2 **1985** A domestic DC-10 flight with its crew and 65 passengers is hijacked by four international terrorists who demand that their imprisoned leader be freed. They kill some passengers to make sure everyone knows they're serious but when the others onboard realize they have nothing to lose, they decide to regain control of the aircraft. NBC (the TV movie's broadcaster) was so disturbed by the movie's original ending, which had the passengers taking a judge, jury, and executioner revenge, that a second, milder ending was filmed and shown instead. **96m/C; DVD.** Ned Beatty; Barbara Bosson; Rene Enriquez; Jack Gilford; John Karlen; Frank McRae; Mitchell Ryan; Dee Wallace; Kristina Wayborn; Michael Alldredge; Ina Balin; **D:** Steven Hilliard Stern; **W:** Felix Culver; Stephen Zito; **C:** King Baggot; **M:** Fred Karlin. **TV**

Hostage High ♂♂ *Detention: The Siege at Johnson High* **1997 (R)** Jason Copeland (Schroeder) returns to his former high school with a gun in order to take revenge on the teachers who failed him. The students, including Aaron (Prinze Jr.), he holds hostage inside the building have entirely different tactics for negotiation from the adults who are outside. Based on a true story. **93m/C; VHS, DVD.** Rick Schroder; Henry Winkler; Freddie Prinze, Jr.; Ren Woods; Katie Wright; Alexis Cruz; Patrick Malone; **D:** Michael W. Watkins; **W:** Larry Golin; **C:** Bill Roe; **M:** Brian Adler. **TV**

Hostage Hotel ♂♂ **2000 (R)** Ex-cop Logan McQueen (Reynolds) tries to outmanouever a kidnapper who's holding a congressman's daughter and McQueen's old partner hostage in an abandoned old hotel. **95m/C; VHS, DVD.** Burt Reynolds; Charles Durning; Keith Carradine; David Rasche; **D:** Hal Needham; **W:** Nicholas Factor. **CABLE**

Hostel ♂♂ **2006 (R)** Just another brick in the faux-snuff genre wall. This time around some hot-to-trot American dudes are led to a Slovakian hostel after several splurges into red-light debauchery and uninhibited misogyny. (They probably got distracted on the way to the history museums.) Much to their chagrin, they find that the Russian mafia has converted their lodging quarters into a pleasuredome for sickos looking to get their sadism on. Since our heroes have been developed as mindless hornballs, we're expected to almost cheer their pain and agony. The creators try, rather unsuccessfully, to disguise the charade as a parody of the snuff and torture films it actually reproduces. **95m/C; DVD, Blu-Ray, UMD.** Jay Hernandez; Derek Richardson; Jan Vlasak; Eythor Gudjonsson; Barbara Nedeljakova; Jana Kaderabkova; Jennifer Lim; Lubomir Bukovy; Petr Janis; Josef Bradna; Keiko Seiko; Rick Hoffman; **D:** Eli Roth; **W:** Eli Roth; **C:** Milan Chadima; **M:** Nathan Barr.

Hostel: Part 2 ♂ **2007 (R)** You can add (or subtract) your own bones to the rating, depending on your appetite for torture porn. Roth out-does the gross and gore of his original, and switches his victims to the female gender, also making them slightly more sympathetic. American tourists Beth (German), Whitney (Phillips), and Lorna (Matarazzo) wind up at a Slovakian hostel where scummy businessmen pay top dollar to turn their snuff fantasies into reality, with Sasha (Knazko) the operational mastermind (and ripe for leading further sequels). **94m/C; DVD, Blu-Ray.** Lauren German; Bijou Phillips; Heather Matarazzo; Vera Jordanova; Roger Bart; Richard Burgi; Stanislav Ianevski; Jay Hernandez; Jordan Ladd; Edwige Fenech; Milan Knazko; **D:** Eli Roth; **W:** Eli Roth; **C:** Milan Chadima; **M:** Nathan Barr.

Hostel: Part 3 **WOOF!** **2011 (R)** Direct-to-video dreck moves the torture porn series from Europe to the U.S. Carter, Mike, and Justin join pal Scott in Las Vegas for his bachelor party. Besides the booze and hookers, the four become involved with a rich men's club that pays for the privilege of torturing and murdering people. **88m/C; DVD.** Kip Pardue; Brian Hallisay; John Hensley; Skyler Stone; Chris Coy; Thomas Kretschmann; **D:** Scott Spiegel; **W:** Michael D. Weiss; **C:** Andrew Strahorn; **M:** Frederik Wiedmann. **VIDEO**

Hostile Border ♂♂ *Pocha: Manifest Destiny* **2016 (R)** An engrossing drama about a young woman's problematic American dream. An undocumented immigrant who spent nearly the whole of her life in the United States, Claudia (Sixtos) lives beyond her means, is arrested by the FBI for credit card fraud, and deported to Mexico. Though she speaks no Spanish and no real understanding about her native country, she finds a place to live with her estranged, difficult father Andres (Cedillo) on his ranch. Desperate to return to the United States, she becomes involved with a smuggler who makes grandiose promises, Ricky (Urbina). As circumstances become more difficult, Claudia is forced to consider the effects of her actions. **83m/C; DVD, Streaming, Download.** Veronica Sixtos; Julio Cesar Cedillo; Roberto Urbina; Jorge A. Jimenez; Jesse Garcia; **D:** Michael Dwyer; **W:** Kaitlin McLaughlin; **C:** Michael Dwyer; **M:** John Kirby; Kenneth Pattengale.

Hostile Guns ♂♂ 1/2 **1967** A law man discovers a woman he once loved is now an inmate he is transporting across the Texas badlands. Routine with the exception of cameos by veteran actors. Based on a story by Sloan Nibley and James Edward Grant. **91m/C; VHS, Streaming.** George Montgomery; Yvonne De Carlo; Tab Hunter; John Russell; **Cameo(s):** Brian Donlevy; Richard Arlen; Fuzzy Knight; Donald (Don "Red") Barry; **D:** R.G. Springsteen; **W:** Steve Fisher; Sloan Nibley.

Hostile Intent ♂♂ **1997 (R)** Computer whiz Mike Cleary (Lowe) has designed a new program to counter a computer chip that will allow the government access to everyone's computer. Naturally, this does not make the feds happy and when Mike and his team are off in the woods playing wargames for relaxation, someone is using real bullets to pick off the workers. **90m/C; VHS, DVD.** Rob Lowe; John Savage; Sofia Shinas; James Kidnie; **D:** Jonathan Heap; **W:** Manny Coto; **C:** Gerald R. Goozie; **M:** Christophe Beck. **VIDEO**

Hostile Makeover ♂♂ **2009** Lifetime's second adaptation of an Ellen Byerrum mystery following "Killer Hair." D.C. fashion columnist Lacey Smithsonian gets involved in the murder of reality TV star, Amanda Manville, who underwent a celebrated makeover leading to a modeling career. Lacey's romance with Vic unexpectedly hits a bump. **87m/C; Streaming.** Maggie Lawson; Victor Webster; Sadie LeBlanc; Sarah Edmondson; James McDaniel; Mark Consuelos; Sarah Strange; Serinda Swan; Mario Cantone; **D:** Jerry Ciccoritti; **W:** Kelli Pryor; **C:** Danny Nowak; **M:** James Gelfand. **CABLE**

Hostile Waters ♂♂ 1/2 **1997 (PG)** Based on Soviet accounts of an October 1986 incident that nearly set off a nuclear holocaust. A Russian and a U.S. sub play a game of cat-and-mouse 500 miles east of Bermuda. There's a collision and a fire aboard the Soviet sub threatens their cargo of thermonuclear missiles. Soviet captain Igor Britanov (Hauer) tries to control the situation while the U.S. skipper (Sheen) tries to figure out just what's going on. **92m/C; VHS, DVD.** Rutger Hauer; Martin Sheen; Colm Feore; Rob Campbell; Harris Yulin; Max von Sydow; Regina Taylor; John Rothman; **D:** Dr. David Drury; **W:** Troy Kennedy-Martin; **C:** Alec Curtis; **M:** David Ferguson. **CABLE**

Hostile Witness ♂♂ **1968** Psychological courtroom drama, with Milland as director and star, has a few too many twists. The police can't find the driver of the car that killed his daughter Joanna and barrister Simon Crawford vows to get revenge on his own although the stress first causes a mental breakdown. His elderly neighbor, a high court judge who appears to have been involved in the hit-and-run, is killed in a staged burglary. Crawford is accused and goes on trial. **95m/C; DVD.** *GB* Ray Milland; Sylvia Sims; Felix Aylmer; Raymond Huntley; Geoffrey Lumsden; Percy Marmont; **D:** Ray Milland; **W:** Jack Roffey; **C:** Gerald Gibbs; **M:** Wilfred Josephs.

Hostiles ♂♂ 1/2 **2017 (R)** A revisionist Western that explores the bitter anger between Native Americans and the white people who invaded their land. Captain Joseph Blocker (Bale) is given the assignment of escorting dying captive Cheyenne chief Yellow Hawk (Studi) to his Montana tribal home. Though Blocker initially refuses the assignment because of his deep hatred for Indians, he eventually agrees but humiliates Yellow Hawk by keeping him in chains. During their journey, they find the only survivor of a Comanche massacre, Rosalee Quaid (Pike), who joins them and helps Blocker change his perspective. The film's beautiful cinematography and Bale's outstanding performance compensate for an unfocused plot. **133m/C; DVD, Blu-Ray.** Scott Shepherd; Rosamund Pike; David Midthunder; Christian Bale; Rory Cochrane; **D:** Scott Cooper; **W:** Scott Cooper; **C:** Masanobu Takayanagi; **M:** Max Richter.

Hot Blood ♂ 1/2 **1956** Luridly colorful, oddball musical/romance with director Ray not above focusing on the physical assets of his leads. Rival families in an L.A. gypsy community arrange for the marriage of Annie (Russell) and Stephano (Wilde) though both are reluctant. Stephano makes his new wife miserable until she finally asks the gypsy council for a divorce. **85m/C; DVD.** Jane Russell; Cornel Wilde; Luther Adler; Joseph Calleia; Mikhail Rasumny; James H. Russell; Helen Westcott; **D:** Nicholas Ray; **W:** Jesse Lasky, Jr.; **C:** Ray June; **M:** Les Baxter.

Hot Blooded ♂ *Hit & Run; Red Blooded American Girl 2* **1998 (R)** Trent Colbert (Winters) is a naive college freshman driving back to his family at Thanksgiving. Pulling into a truck stop he's makes the mistake of offering alluring hooker Miya (Wuhrer) a ride. But Miya's a twisted soul and all this means for the libidinous Trent is trouble. **95m/C; VHS, DVD.** Kari Wuhrer; Kristoffer Ryan Winters; David Keith; Burt Young; ***D:*** David Blyth; ***W:*** Nicolas Stiliadis; ***C:*** Edgar Egger; ***M:*** Paul Zaza. **VIDEO**

Hot Box WOOF! 1972 (R) A Filipino-shot, low budget woofer. Prison flick about women who break out and foment a revolution. Currently only available as part of a collection. **85m/C; VHS, DVD.** Andrea Cagan; Margaret Markov; Rickey Richardson; Laurie Rose; ***D:*** Joe Viola; ***W:*** Joe Viola; Jonathan Demme.

Hot Cars ♂ ½ **1956** To finance an operation for his sick son, used car salesman Nick Dunn (Bromfield) gets involved in a mob-run stolen car ring. Moll Karen (Lansing) vamps Nick, a police detective gets murdered, and Nick gets framed and goes on the lam. There's a rather silly final confrontation between Nick and the crime ringleader at an amusement park on a roller coaster. **61m/B; DVD.** John Bromfield; Joi Lansing; Ralph Clanton; Mark Dana; Carol Shannon; Robert Osterloh; George Sawaya; Dabbs Greer; Charles Keane; ***D:*** Donald McDougall; ***W:*** Richard H. Landau; Don Martin; ***C:*** William Margulies; ***M:*** Les Baxter.

The Hot Chick ♂♂ **2002 (PG-13)** Snotty high school queen Jessica (MacAdams) magically switches bodies with 30-ish shlub Clive (Schneider) and finds the true meaning of "bad hair day." As you'd expect from a movie starring and co-written by Schneider and produced by Adam Sandler, it does take a few dips in the gutter, but manages to have heart, much like Sandler's surprising "Wedding Singer" a few years back. Strings together enough laughs to make you forget "Like Father, Like Son" ever happened. **101m/C; VHS, DVD.** Rob Schneider; Anna Faris; Matthew Lawrence; Eric Christian Olsen; Robert Davi; Melora Hardin; Alexandra Holden; Rachel McAdams; Fay Hauser; Tamera Mowry; Tia Mowry; Lee Garlington; Michael O'Keefe; ***Cameo(s):*** Adam Sandler; ***D:*** Tom Brady; ***W:*** Tom Brady; ***C:*** Tim Suhrstedt; ***M:*** John Debney.

Hot Dog. . . The Movie! ♂ ½ **1983 (R)** There's an intense rivalry going on between an Austrian ski champ and his California challenger during the World Cup Freestyle competition in Squaw Valley. Snow movie strictly for teens or their equivalent. **96m/C; VHS, DVD, Blu-Ray.** David Naughton; Patrick Houser; Shannon Tweed; Tracy N. Smith; ***D:*** Peter Markle; ***M:*** Peter Bernstein.

Hot Enough for June ♂♂ *Agent 8 3/4* **1964** Mediocre British spy spoof. Unemployed writer Nicholas Whistler (Bogarde) is living on the dole when the Labour Exchange gets him a translator position in Prague. It turns out the messages he innocently sends back are coded for the Foreign Office and Nicholas is unknowingly a spy. He tangles with the Soviets and learns his chauffeur Vlasta (Koscina) is a Russian agent, but by now they've fallen in love. **98m/C; DVD.** *GB* Dirk Bogarde; Sylva Koscina; Robert Morley; Leo McKern; Roger Delgado; John Le Mesurier; ***D:*** Ralph Thomas; ***W:*** Lukas Heller; ***C:*** Ernest Steward; ***M:*** Angelo Francesco Lavagnino.

The Hot Flashes ♂ ½ **2013 (R)** Pandering, contrived comedy about a group of middle-aged women in Texas. The town's mobile mammogram clinic is about to go bust until housewife Beth (Sheilds) persuades her old high school basketball teammates to reunite. They'll play the current girls' high school champs in a series of charity matches but naturally there's problems within and without the team. Their comedic quest gets them media attention but it turns out to be less inspirational than most of its ilk although the actresses try hard. **99m/C; DVD, On Demand.** Brooke Shields; Daryl Hannah; Virginia Madsen; Camryn Manheim; Wanda Sykes; Eric Roberts; Mark Povinelli; ***D:*** Susan Seidelman; ***W:*** Brad Hennig; ***C:*** Frank DeMarco; ***M:*** Marcelo Zarvos.

Hot Fuzz ♂♂♂ **2007 (R)** Wright and Pegg, the lads who revitalized the zombie genre with "Shaun of the Dead", offer this decidedly English take on the over-the-top Hollywood action genre. Constable Nick Angel (Pegg) is the best cop in London, but when his over-achieving starts making the force look bad, he's transferred to the quiet village of Sandford and saddled with a lump of a partner, Danny Butterman (Frost). However, once Angel discovers the secret behind Sandford's surprisingly high "accident" rate, he and Danny team up Riggs and Murtaugh-style to take down the town fathers, vicar and all. Such a smart premise, and Pegg sells every moment, but it veers off into parody occasionally due to some regrettably broad supporting players. **121m/C; DVD, Blu-Ray, HD-DVD.** *GB US* Simon Pegg; Nick Frost; Jim Broadbent; Paddy Considine; Timothy Dalton; Billie Whitelaw; Edward Woodward; Rafe Spall; Olivia Colman; Paul Freeman; Martin Freeman; Bill Nighy; Steve Coogan; Cate Blanchett; Peter Jackson; Kevin Eldon; Stuart Wilson; ***D:*** Edgar Wright; ***W:*** Simon Pegg; Edgar Wright; ***C:*** Jess Hall; ***M:*** David Arnold.

Hot Lead & Cold Feet ♂♂ **1978 (G)** Twin brothers (one a gunfighter, the other meek and mild) compete in a train race where the winner will take ownership of a small western town. Dale not only plays both brothers, but also their tough father. Standard Disney fare. **89m/C; VHS, DVD.** Jim Dale; Don Knotts; Karen Valentine; ***D:*** Robert Butler; ***W:*** Arthur Alsberg; ***M:*** Buddy (Norman Dale) Baker.

Hot Millions ♂♂♂ **1968** Hysterical comedy about high-class swindling operation with Ustinov as a refined embezzler. Excellent cast and sharp script. Although it didn't do well at the boxoffice, this amusing romp became one of the biggest sleepers of the year. **106m/C; VHS, DVD.** *GB* Peter Ustinov; Maggie Smith; Karl Malden; Bob Newhart; Robert Morley; Cesar Romero; Melinda May; Ann Lancaster; Margaret Courtenay; Lynda Baron; Billy Milton; Peter Jones; Raymond Huntley; Kynaston Reeves; ***D:*** Eric Till; ***W:*** Peter Ustinov; Ira Wallach; ***C:*** Ken Higgins.

Hot Moves ♂ **1984 (R)** Four high school boys make a pact to lose their virginity before the end of the summer. **89m/C; VHS, DVD.** Michael Zorek; Adam Silbar; Jill Schoelen; Deborah Richter; Monique Gabrielle; Tami Holbrook; Virgil Frye; ***D:*** Jim Sotos.

Hot Potato ♂ **1976 (PG)** Black Belt Jones rescues a senator's daughter from a megalomaniacal general by using skull-thwacking footwork. **87m/C; VHS, DVD.** Jim Kelly; George Memmoli; Geoffrey Binney; ***D:*** Oscar Williams.

Hot Pursuit ♂ ½ **1984 (PG)** A woman who has been framed for murder runs from the law and a relentless hitman. **94m/C; VHS, DVD.** Mike (Michael) Preston; Dina Merrill; Kerrie Keane; ***D:*** Kenneth Johnson; ***W:*** Kenneth Johnson; ***C:*** John McPherson; ***M:*** Joseph Harnell.

Hot Pursuit ♂ ½ **1987 (PG-13)** A prep-school bookworm resorts to Rambo-like tactics in tracking down his girlfriend and her family after being left behind for a trip to the tropics. **93m/C; VHS, DVD.** John Cusack; Robert Loggia; Jerry Stiller; Wendy Gazelle; Monte Markham; Shelley Fabares; Ben Stiller; ***D:*** Steven Lisberger; ***W:*** Steven W. Carabatsos; ***C:*** Frank Tidy; ***M:*** Joseph Conlan.

Hot Pursuit ♂ **2015 (PG-13)** Cooper (Witherspoon) is the by-the-numbers cop who always gets her man. Daniella (Vergara) is the drug lord's boss who needs her protection. The two head out on a road trip, pursued by crooked cops and hired killers. Witherspoon's uptight style and Vergara's loose comic timing must have seemed like a perfect oil-and-water buddy comedy formula on paper. But someone forgot to write a script. Loud, annoying, repetitive, and sexist junk, the only thing you'll feel is pity for the two talented stars stuck in it. **87m/C; DVD, Blu-Ray.** Reese Witherspoon; Sofia Vergara; Matthew Del Negro; Michael Mosley; Robert Kazinsky; ***D:*** Anne Fletcher; ***W:*** David Feeney; John Quaintance; ***C:*** Oliver Stapleton; ***M:*** Christophe Beck.

The Hot Rock ♂♂♂ *How to Steal a Diamond in Four Easy Lessons* **1970 (PG)** A motley crew of bumbling thieves conspire to steal a huge, priceless diamond; a witty, gritty comedy that makes no moral excuses for its characters and plays like an early-'70s crime thriller gone awry. Adapted from the novel by Donald E. Westlake. The sequel, 1974's "Bank Shot," stars George C. Scott in the role created by Redford. **97m/C; VHS, DVD, Blu-Ray.** Robert Redford; George Segal; Ron Leibman; Zero Mostel; Moses Gunn; William Redfield; Charlotte Rae; Topo Swope; ***M:*** Quincy Jones.

Hot Rod ♂♂ **2007 (PG-13)** Twenty-seven year old moped-riding stuntman-wannabe Rod Kimble (Samberg) lives at home with mom Marie (Spacek) and stepdad Frank (McShane). Rod's real dad, now dead, is a legend as a former Evel Kneivel second-hand man who is said to have performed all of Evel's stunts himself in order to test the bikes. Rod dreams of making his father proud; meanwhile he and stepdad go at it like archrivals, and Rod's always on the losing side of their jousts. Rod sees his chance when they learn that Frank needs a $50,000 heart transplant—money they don't have. He'll raise the money by jumping over 15 buses on his moped, fix Frank's heart, and then beat him to a pulp. Loaded with goofy gags, and aimed at "Napoleon Dynamite," "Saturday Night Live" (several of the film's cast are from SNL,) and Will Ferrell fans, but never nails the landing. Has some moments, but that's about it. **88m/C; DVD, Blu-Ray, HD-DVD.** Isla Fisher; Andy Samberg; Jorma Taccone; Bill Hader; Sissy Spacek; Ian McShane; Will Arnett; Chris Parnell; Brittney Irvin; Danny McBride; ***D:*** Akiva Shaffer; ***W:*** Pam Brady; ***C:*** Andrew Dunn; ***M:*** Trevor Rabin.

Hot Rod Girl ♂ *Hot Car Girl* **1956** A concerned police officer (Conners) organizes supervised drag racing after illegal drag racing gets out of hand in his community. **75m/B; VHS, DVD.** Lori Nelson; Chuck Connors; John Smith; ***D:*** Leslie Martinson; ***W:*** John McGreevey; ***C:*** Sam Leavitt.

Hot Rods to Hell WOOF! *52 Miles to Terror* **1967** Originally made for television, this film was put into drive-ins in the '60s when the TV stations wouldn't touch it. Tom Phillips (Andrews) is moving his family to the desert to take over an Inn when they are run off the road by some teenage hell-raisers in a hot rod. Upon arriving they find the owner wants to sell because those same teens hang out there and make trouble. **92m/C; DVD.** Dana Andrews; Jeanne Crain; Mimsy Farmer; Paul Bertoya; Gene Kirkwood; Jeffrey Byron; Charles P. Thompson; Laurie Mock; George Ives; Paul Genge; Harry Hickox; ***D:*** John Brahm; ***W:*** Robert E. Kent; Alex Gaby; ***C:*** Lloyd Ahern; ***M:*** Fred Karger.

Hot Saturday ♂♂ **1932** Small-town bank clerk Ruth (Carroll) has a reputation for being fast. She and some friends are invited for a Saturday shindig at the home of notorious playboy Romer Sheffield (Grant) and Ruth winds up spending quality alone time (platonically) with their host. Gossip is rampant, Ruth loses her job and her straight arrow beau Bill (Scott), but Romer steps in to set the record straight and offer Ruth an out. **72m/B; DVD.** Nancy Carroll; Cary Grant; Randolph Scott; Edward (Eddie) Woods; William Collier, Sr.; Jane Darwell; Lillian Bond; ***D:*** William A. Seiter; ***W:*** Seton I. Miller; ***C:*** Arthur L. Todd.

Hot Shot ♂ ½ **1986 (PG)** An inspirational tale involving a young soccer player who goes to great lengths to take training from a soccer star, played—of course—by Pele. **90m/C; VHS, DVD.** Pele; Jim Youngs; Billy Warlock; Weyman Thompson; Mario Van Peebles; David Groh; ***D:*** Rick King.

Hot Shots! ♂♂♂ **1991 (PG-13)** Another entry from "The Naked Gun" team of master movie parodists, this has lots of clever sight gags but the verbal humor often plummets to the ground. Spoofs "Top Gun" and similar gung-ho air corps adventures but doesn't forget other popular films including "Dances with Wolves" and "The Fabulous Baker Boys." Sheen is very funny as ace fighter pilot Sean "Topper" Harley who's to avenge the family honor. Great when you're in the mood for laughs that don't require thought. **83m/C; VHS, DVD.** Charlie Sheen; Cary Elwes; Valeria Golino; Lloyd Bridges; Kevin Dunn; Jon Cryer; William O'Leary; Kristy Swanson; Efrem Zimbalist, Jr.; Bill Irwin; Heidi Swedberg; Judith Kahan; Pat Proft; ***Cameo(s):*** Charles Barkley; Bill Laimbeer; ***D:*** Jim Abrahams; ***W:*** Pat Proft; Jim Abrahams; ***C:*** Bill Butler; ***M:*** Sylvester Levay.

Hot Shots! Part Deux ♂♂ ½ **1993 (PG-13)** Second "Hot Shots" outing doesn't live up to the first, but it's not bad either. Admiral Tug Benson (Bridges) is elected President (yes, of the U.S.) and calls on Sheen's newly pumped-up Topper to take on Saddam Hussein Rambo-style. Love interest Ramada (Golino), returns but this time she's competing with Michelle (Bakke), a sexy CIA agent. Crenna spoofs his role in the "Rambo" films as Sheen's mentor; look for real-life dad Martin in a take-off of "Apocalypse Now." Shtick flies as fast and furious as the bodies, with Bridges getting a chance to reprise his glory days of "Sea Hunt." Don't miss the credits. **89m/C; VHS, DVD.** Charlie Sheen; Lloyd Bridges; Valeria Golino; Brenda Bakke; Richard Crenna; Miguel Ferrer; Rowan Atkinson; Jerry Haleva; Mitchell Ryan; Gregory Sierra; Ryan Stiles; Michael Colyar; ***Cameo(s):*** Martin Sheen; Bob Vila; ***D:*** Jim Abrahams; ***W:*** Pat Proft; Jim Abrahams; ***M:*** Basil Poledouris.

The Hot Spot ♂♂ ½ **1990 (R)** An amoral drifter arrives in a small Texas town and engages in affairs with two women, including his boss's over-sexed wife and a young woman with her own secrets. Things begin to heat up when he decides to plot a bank robbery. Based on Charles Williams' 1952 novel "Hell Hath No Fury." **120m/C; VHS, DVD, Blu-Ray.** Don Johnson; Virginia Madsen; Jennifer Connelly; Charles Martin Smith; William Sadler; Jerry Hardin; Barry Corbin; Leon Rippy; Jack Nance; ***D:*** Dennis Hopper; ***W:*** Charles Williams; Nona Tyson; ***C:*** Ueli Steiger; ***M:*** Jack Nitzsche.

Hot Stuff ♂ **1980 (PG)** Officers on a burglary task force decide the best way to obtain convictions is to go into the fencing business themselves. **91m/C; VHS, DVD.** Dom DeLuise; Jerry Reed; Suzanne Pleshette; Ossie Davis; ***D:*** Dom DeLuise; ***W:*** Donald E. Westlake; Michael Kane.

Hot Summer in Barefoot County ♂♂ **1974 (R)** A state law enforcement officer on the search for illegal moonshiners finds more than he bargained for. **90m/C; VHS, DVD.** Sherry Robinson; Tonia Bryan; Dick Smith; ***D:*** Will Zens.

Hot Tamale ♂♂ ½ **2006 (R)** Amusing action-comedy finds naive musician Harlan Woodriff (Spelling) traveling from Wyoming to LA so he can play in a salsa band. Along the way, a con man (Priestley) hides some stolen diamonds in Harlan's car. In LA, Harlan meets sexy neighbor Tuesday (Baird) while unwittingly being targeted by thugs after the loot. **98m/C; DVD.** Jason Priestley; Carmen Electra; Mike Starr; Beth Grant; Randy Spelling; Diora Baird; Matt Cedeno; ***D:*** Michael Damian; ***W:*** Michael Damian; Janeen Damian; ***C:*** Fred Iannone; ***M:*** Mark Thomas.

Hot to Trot! ♂ **1988 (PG)** A babbling idiot links up with a talking horse in an updated version of the "Francis, the Talking Mule" comedies, by way of Mr. Ed. The equine voice is provided by Candy. Some real funny guys are wasted here. **90m/C; VHS, DVD.** Bobcat Goldthwait; Dabney Coleman; Virginia Madsen; Jim Metzler; Cindy Pickett; Tim Kazurinsky; Santos Morales; Barbara Whinnery; Garry Kluger; ***V:*** John Candy; ***D:*** Michael Dinner; ***W:*** Charlie Peters; ***M:*** Danny Elfman.

Hot Tub Time Machine ♂♂ **2010 (R)** A group of bored, struggling middle-aged buddies have lost their mojo. But thanks to vodka, Red Bull, and a hot tub they travel back in time 20 years and rediscover their young and stupider selves. Better-than-it-should-be flick keeps the frat-boy humor and era/culture shock jokes coming as it winks at the audience, never failing to acknowledge how ridiculous it all is. **101m/C; DVD, Blu-Ray.** John Cusack; Rob Corddry; Craig Robinson; Crispin Glover; Sebastian Stan; Chevy Chase; Lizzy Caplan; Lyndsy Fonseca; William Zabka; Charlie McDermott; Clark Duke; ***D:*** Steve Pink; ***W:*** Josh Heald.

Hot Tub Time Machine 2 ♂ **2015 (R)** A sequel to the surprisingly successful 2010 comedy is not an unwelcome thing in theory but this louder, grosser, dumber version just never should have happened. John Cusack wisely jumped ship, leaving Corddry, Duke, and Robinson to jump back into the titular sci-fi apparatus after Lou (Corddry) gets shot and the gang has to go back to change history to save him. They accidentally go the wrong way into the future (picking up Adam Scott) and wacky hijinks ensue. As is often the case with comedy sequels, jokes are never funny once you've heard them, and it doesn't help that the guys here just aren't as likable, especially Corddry. **93m/C; DVD, Blu-Ray.** Rob Corddry; Craig Robinson; Clark Duke; Adam Scott; Chevy Chase; Gillian Jacobs; ***D:*** Steve Pink; ***W:*** Josh Heald; ***C:*** Declan Quinn; ***M:*** Christophe Beck.

Hot Type: 150 Years of The Nation 1/2 *The Nation* **2015** A feature-length documentary look at the long-running newsweekly The Nation and the state of American journalism. In considering the oldest continuously published newsweekly in the United States, the documentary focuses on its editor, writers, and the daily pressures of putting the magazine together. The history of The Nation, its impact, and changes over time are included as well. **93m/C; DVD.** ***D:*** Barbara Kopple; ***C:*** Gary Keith Griffin; ***M:*** Max Avery Lichtenstein. **VIDEO**

Hotel 1/2 **1967 (PG)** A pale rehash of the "Grand Hotel" formula about an array of rich characters interacting in a New Orleans hotel. From the Arthur Hailey potboiler; basis for the TV series. **125m/C; VHS, DVD.** Rod Taylor; Catherine Spaak; Karl Malden; Melvyn Douglas; Merle Oberon; Michael Rennie; Richard Conte; Kevin McCarthy; ***D:*** Richard Quine; ***W:*** Wendell Mayes; ***C:*** Charles B(ryant) Lang, Jr.

Hotel **2001 (R)** Using a Dogme 95 approach, Director Figgis gathers a bunch of celebs and lets them aimlessly make things up as they go along. Follows the filming of John Webster's play "The Duchess of Malfi" by an English production crew at a hotel in Venice, Italy that has call girls, a murderer, and cannibalistic hotel staffers lurking about while the entire fiasco is caught on film by a brash documentarian. Fans of Figgis' work or the Dogme movement will want to check in on this one. **112m/C; VHS, DVD.** *GB IT* Rhys Ifans; John Malkovich; Saffron Burrows; Salma Hayek; Max Beesley; Lucy Liu; Julian Sands; David Schwimmer; Jason Isaacs; ***D:*** Mike Figgis; ***W:*** Mike Figgis; ***C:*** Patrick Alexander Stewart; ***M:*** Mike Figgis; Anthony Marinelli.

Hotel America *Hotel des Ameriques* **1981** Techine's drama meanders to little purpose and often less interest despite its leads. Layabout Gilles (Dewaere) is sponging off his mother Elise (Haudepin), who owns a small hotel. Helene (Deneuve), depressed after her lover's accidental death, is high from popping pills and nearly runs Gilles down in the street. They begin a haphazard relationship that lessens Helene's depression but Gilles is jealous of her architect lover's renown and pushes her away to pine for self-absorbed musician Bernard (Chicot) instead. French with subtitles. **95m/C; DVD.** *FR* Catherine Deneuve; Patrick Dewaere; Etienne Chicot; Sabine Haudepin; Dominque Lavanant; Josiane Balasko; Jean-Louis Vitrac; ***D:*** Josiane Balasko; Andre Techine; ***W:*** Josiane Balasko; Andre Techine; Gilles Taurand; ***C:*** Bruno Nuytten; ***M:*** Philippe Sarde.

Hotel Artemis **2018 (R)** A sci-fi B-movie thriller set in futuristic Los Angeles. In 2028, criminals pay a fee to be treated with no questions asked at an underground medical facility called the Hotel Artemis. All members must follow rules enforced by The Nurse (Foster) and her assistant Everest (Bautista). One night, tensions run high because of a riot outside and the issues among the patients. The situation grows more complicated when two people with close connections to The Nurse arrive, a cop (Slate) and a crime boss (Goldblum). Though the film obviously lifts ideas from such films as John Wick, it is witty and stylish. **94m/C; Blu-Ray, Streaming.** *UK US* Jodie Foster; Sterling K. Brown; Sofia Boutella; Jeff Goldblum; Brian Tyree Henry; ***D:*** Drew Pearce; ***W:*** Drew Pearce; ***C:*** Chung-hoon Chung; ***M:*** Cliff Martinez; Eric Craig; Brian McNelis.

Hotel de Love 1/2 **1996 (R)** Seventeen-year-old fraternal twin brothers Rick (Young) and Stephen Dunne (Bossell) both fall for beautiful Melissa (Burrows) and she has a short-lived romance with the more-aggressive Rick. Ten years later, mopey stockbroker Stephen shows up at the tacky theme honeymoon hotel Rick now manages and who should show up (besides the twins bickering parents) but Melissa and her fiance Norman (O'Brien). So the twins renew their competition while Melissa decides if Norman is the right guy for her, Mrs. Dunne gets mash notes from a secret admirer, and fortuneteller Alison (Grandison), who happens to be Rick's ex-girlfriend, offers romantic advice to Stephen. **93m/C; VHS, Streaming.** *AU* Aden Young; Simon Bossell; Saffron Burrows; Julia Blake; Ray Barrett; Pippa Grandison; Alan Hopgood; Peter O'Brien; ***D:*** Craig Rosenberg; ***W:*** Craig Rosenberg; ***C:*** Stephen F. Windon; ***M:*** Brett Rosenberg.

Hotel for Dogs 1/2 **2009 (PG)** Orphaned teenager Andi and her younger brother Bruce are living in a new foster home with a strict no pets rule, which means Andi has to find a place for their beloved dog Friday. When they spot an abandoned hotel nearby, it becomes the perfect solution not only for Friday but also dozens of neighborhood strays (as long as the neighbors don't find out). Despite star-filled supporting roles by the likes of Don Cheadle, Matt Dillon and Lisa Kudrow, the numerous trained dogs are the best part of this woofer (no canine bias by the Hound!). Purely a kids' movie with ample silly sweetness courtesy of the dogs. Based on the novel by Lois Duncan. **100m/C; Blu-Ray, On Demand.** Emma Roberts; Jake T. Austin; Lisa Kudrow; Don Cheadle; Kevin Dillon; Kyla Pratt; Troy Gentile; Johnny Simmons; Robine Lee; ***D:*** Thor Freudenthal; ***W:*** Jeff Lowell; Robert Schooley; Mark McCorkle; ***C:*** Michael Grady; ***M:*** John Debney.

Hotel Imperial **1927** Set in 1917 Budapest, six Hungarian soldiers ride into a frontier town and find it occupied by Russians. Hall plays Lieutenant Almasy, who takes refuge in the Hotel Imperial. Orchestra scored. **84m/B; Silent; VHS, DVD.** Pola Negri; James Hall; George Siegmann; Max Davidson; ***D:*** Mauritz Stiller.

Hotel Mumbai 1/2 **2018 (R)** One day in Mumbai, India, jihadists attacked key places in the city, including a transportation center, restaurant, and finally, the Hotel Mumbai. Before the attack, hotel employee Arjun (Patel) fears the wrath of his boss Hermant Oberoi (Kher) because of misplaced shoes. Guests for the evening include VIPs such as a Russian businessman (Isaacs) and a wealthy family headed by architect David (Hammer). During the attack, all at the hotel struggle to survive. The debut film by Maras effectively depicts the events that happened at the hotel, giving viewers an unflinching look at the violence and its effects. **123m/C; DVD, Blu-Ray.** *AU US IN* Dev Patel; Anupam Kher; Armie Hammer; Nazanin Boniadi; Amandeep Singh; ***D:*** Anthony Maras; ***W:*** Anthony Maras; John Collee; ***C:*** Nick Remy Matthews; ***M:*** Volker Bertelmann.

The Hotel New Hampshire **1984 (R)** The witless, amoral adaptation of John Irving's novel about a very strange family's adventures in New Hampshire, Vienna and New York City, which include gang rape, incest, and Kinski in a bear suit. **110m/C; VHS, DVD, Blu-Ray.** Jodie Foster; Rob Lowe; Beau Bridges; Nastassja Kinski; Wallace Shawn; Wilford Brimley; Amanda Plummer; Anita Morris; Matthew Modine; Lisa Banes; Seth Green; Jennifer (Jennie) Dundas Lowe; ***D:*** Tony Richardson; ***W:*** Tony Richardson; ***C:*** David Watkin.

Hotel Rwanda 1/2 **2004 (PG-13)** Cheadle gives a remarkable performance in a drama that covers a too-little-known episode in recent history. In 1994 Rwanda, a former Belgian colony, members of the Hutu tribe killed some 800,000 members of the once-dominant Tutsi tribe. Paul Rusesabagina (Cheadle) is a Hutu, who manages a four-star hotel in Kigali. When the genocide begins, he fears for his own family since his wife, Tatiana (Okonedo), is a Tutsi. Unable to escape or to get any help, Paul decides his safety depends on business as usual (and bribing the military) even as he comes to shelter some 1,200 refugees within the hotel. Film focuses on Paul and not on what is happening in Rwanda in general. Without some historical background, the general viewer will likely be somewhat confused. **110m/C; DVD.** *GB IT SA* Don Cheadle; Sophie Okonedo; Joaquin Rafael (Leaf) Phoenix; Nick Nolte; Desmond Dube; David O'Hara; Jean Reno; Cara Seymour; ***D:*** Terry George; ***W:*** George Pearson; ***C:*** Robert Fraisse; Naomi Geraghty; ***M:*** Andrea Guerra; Rupert Gregson-Williams.

Hotel Transylvania **2012 (PG)** Dear daddy Dracula (Sandler) throws a big bash for daughter Mavis' 118th birthday but things go awry when a normal guy happens along and--of course--falls for her. The film goes awry too as a potentially modern update of the Universal Monster comedies like "Abbott & Costello Meet Frankenstein" instead comes off like a bad "Saturday Night Live" sketch. This horrendous animated comedy turns Dracula, Frankenstein, The Mummy, and the rest of the iconic characters into little more than the butt of fart jokes. Sandler's voice work annoys while his group of buddies (James, Buscemi, Samberg) tell a tale that wallows in clichés and bodily fluids. **91m/C; DVD, Blu-Ray.** ***V:*** Adam Sandler; Selena Gomez; Andy Samberg; Kevin James; Cee-Lo Green; David Spade; David Koechner; Molly Shannon; Fran Drescher; Steve Buscemi; ***D:*** Genndy Tartakovsky; ***W:*** Dan Hageman; Kevin Hageman; ***M:*** Mark Mothersbaugh.

Hotel Transylvania 2 **2015 (PG)** More animated horror hijinks from Sandler and his buddies in this defiantly senseless sequel. Sandler voices Dracula, the caretaker of the titular hotel, which has opened its doors to human visitors as well. When half-human grandson Dennis isn't showing signs of being a vampire, Dracula and his buddies (including James' Frankenstein) put the little tyke through Monster Academy to make him one of the gang. Messages of acceptance are nice and all, but Sandler's increased laziness when it comes to his work reaches new lows with each effort. This is one of his worst films, which is really saying something. **89m/C; DVD, Blu-Ray.** ***V:*** Adam Sandler; Kevin James; Selena Gomez; Steve Buscemi; Mel Brooks; Andy Samberg; ***D:*** Genndy Tartakovsky; ***W:*** Adam Sandler; Robert Smigel; ***M:*** Mark Mothersbaugh.

Hotel Transylvania 3: Summer Vacation 1/2 **2018 (PG)** Hotel manager Dracula (Sandler) is suffering a bout of ennui and romantic loneliness, so his daughter Mavis (Gomez) surprises him--and the whole Drac pack--with a cruise vacation. Onboard, his lifeless heart begins beating for the ship's captain, Ericka, who's harboring a secret lineage that may spell doom for Dracula and his pals. This third installment is just as colorful and energetic as its predecessors, although the bathroom humor is getting tiresome. **97m/C; DVD, Blu-Ray.** ***V:*** Adam Sandler; Andy Samberg; Selena Gomez; Kevin James; David Spade; ***D:*** Genndy Tartakovsky; ***W:*** Genndy Tartakovsky; Michael McCullers; ***M:*** Mark Mothersbaugh.

Hothead **1963** Angry teenaged punk blames all his troubles on his dead-beat dad and takes it out on a boozy transient. Along the way his story intersects with that of a young hooker and a runaway husband. **74m/B; DVD.** Barbara Joyce; Steve Franklin; Robert Glen; John Delgar; ***D:*** Edward Andrew (Santos Alcocer) Mann; ***W:*** Milton Mann; ***C:*** Edward Nicholson.

H.O.T.S. *T & A Academy* **1979 (R)** A sex-filled sorority rivalry film, starring a slew of ex-Playboy Playmates in wet shirts. Screenplay co-written by exploitation star Caffaro. **95m/C; VHS, DVD.** Susan Kiger; Lisa London; Kimberly Cameron; Danny Bonaduce; Steve Bond; ***D:*** Gerald Seth Sindell; ***W:*** Cheri Caffaro; Joan Buchanan; ***C:*** Harvey Genkins; ***M:*** David Davis.

The Hottest State **2006 (R)** Sarah Garcia (Moreno), a young girl with dreams of the big city, sets out for New York to begin her singing career. Enter romantic William Harding (Webber), an aspiring actor transplanted from Texas. They fall in love, and then as often happens with young love, someone gets dumped. But Harding can't seem to move on, pining and yearning insufferably for his lost love, and in doing so annoys everyone around him. Mom Jesse (Linney) offers sympathy, but it's not until distant dad (Hawke) shows up that the lovesick puppy gets some clarity and maturity about the situation. Hawke serves as writer/director/actor in this self-indulgent and overly talky bit about young (and unrequited) love based on Hawke's own semi-biographical novel of the same name. **117m/C; DVD.** Mark Webber; Catalina Sandino Moreno; Laura Linney; Michelle Williams; Sonia Braga; Jesse Harris; Ethan Hawke; ***D:*** Ethan Hawke; ***W:*** Ethan Hawke; ***C:*** Christopher Norr; ***M:*** Jesse Harris.

The Hottie and the Nottie **2008 (PG-13)** Despite Hilton's blonde banality this comedy isn't quite as bad as you might expect. Geeky Joel fell in love with Cristabel when they were kids. Now an adult, he's come to L.A. to pursue romance. Only problem is Cristabel (Hilton) won't put out until Joel (Moore) finds her incredibly ugly best friend June (Lakin) a boyfriend. June's a decent gal in need of a makeover and you have to wonder why Cristabel didn't think of that herself. Maybe because once June's inner beauty is reflected outwardly, Joel's attentions waver. **91m/C; DVD.** Paris Hilton; Christine Lakin; Joel David Moore; Johann Urb; Adam Kulbersh; ***D:*** Tom Putnam; ***W:*** Heidi Ferrer; ***C:*** Alex Vendler; ***M:*** David E. Russo. Golden Raspberries '08: Worst Actress (Hilton).

Houdini 1/2 **1953** Historically inaccurate but entertaining biopic of the infamous magician and escapologist. Chronicles his rise to stardom, his efforts to contact his dearly departed mother through mediums (a prequel to "Ghost"?), and his heart-stopping logic-defying escapes. First screen teaming of Leigh and Curtis, who had already been married for two years. **107m/C; VHS, DVD, Blu-Ray.** Tony Curtis; Janet Leigh; Torin Thatcher; Angela (Clark) Clarke; Stefan Schnabel; Ian Wolfe; Sig Rumann; Michael Pate; Connie Gilchrist; Mary Murphy; Tor Johnson; ***D:*** George Marshall; ***W:*** Philip Yordan; ***C:*** Ernest Laszlo; ***M:*** Roy Webb.

Houdini 1/2 **1998** New York Jewish youth Erich Weiss transforms himself into vaudeville magician/illusionist Harry Houdini (Schaech) and marries Bess (Edwards), who becomes his assistant. Houdini soon becomes a famed escape artist, pushing himself into ever-more dangerous stunts. After his beloved mother's death, Houdini then goes on a crusade to expose fake spiritualists who had promised him contact with her. **94m/C; DVD.** Johnathon Schaech; Stacy Edwards; Grace Zabriskie; Paul Sorvino; Rhea Perlman; George Segal; David Warner; Mark Ruffalo; Ron Perlman; Judy Geeson; ***D:*** Pen Densham; ***W:*** Pen Densham; ***C:*** Gordon C. Lonsdale; ***M:*** Don Harper. **CABLE**

Houdini 1/2 **2014** An overly- long History Channel miniseries on the life of master magician and escape artist Harry Houdini with Brody giving a masterful lead performance. A voiceover ties together the bio as Houdini works on his act and gets ever more reckless over his evolving tricks, jeopardizing his marriage to former assistant Bess. **325m/C; DVD, Blu-Ray.** Adrien Brody; Kristen Connolly; Evan Jones; Tim Pigott-Smith; ***D:*** Uli Edel; ***W:*** Nicholas Meyer; ***C:*** Karl Walter Lindenlaub; ***M:*** John Debney. **CABLE**

The Houdini Serial *The Master Mystery* **1920** Quentin Locke (Houdini) is a Justice Department agent investigating a powerful crime cartel in this silent chapter serial. The cartel is protected by a "robot" armed with a deadly gas weapon and at the end of each chapter Locke is trapped in some perilous situation from which he is able to astonishingly escape. While the plot is rather tedious, Houdini's performance is an absolute delight. **?m/B; Silent; DVD.** Harry Houdini; Marguerite Marsh; Ruth Stonehouse; Edna Britton; William Pike; Charles Graham; ***D:*** Harry Grossman; Burton King; ***W:*** Arthur B. Reeve; Charles Logue.

The Hound of the Baskervilles **1939** The curse of a demonic hound threatens descendants of an English noble family until Holmes and Watson solve the mystery. **80m/B; VHS, DVD.** *GB* Basil Rathbone; Nigel Bruce; Richard Greene; John Carradine; Wendy Barrie; Lionel Atwill; E.E. Clive; ***D:*** Sidney Lanfield.

The Hound of the Baskervilles 1/2 **1959** Cushing's not half bad as Sherlock Holmes as he investigates the mystery of a supernatural hound threatening the life of a Dartmoor baronet. Dark and moody. **86m/C; VHS, DVD, Blu-Ray.** *GB* Peter Cushing; Christopher Lee; Andre Morell; ***D:*** Terence Fisher; ***W:*** Peter Bryan; ***C:*** Jack Asher; ***M:*** James Bernard.

The Hound of the Baskervilles **WOOF! 1977** Awful spoof of the Sherlock Holmes classic with Cook as Holmes and Moore as Watson (and Holmes' mother). Even the cast can't save it. **84m/C; VHS, DVD.** Dudley Moore; Peter Cook; Denholm Elliott; Joan Greenwood; Spike Milligan; Jessie Matthews; Roy Kinnear; ***D:*** Paul Morrissey; ***W:*** Dudley Moore; Peter Cook; Paul Morrissey; ***C:*** Dick Bush; ***M:*** Dudley Moore.

The Hound of the Baskervilles 1983 Another remake of the Sherlock Holmes story which finds the great detective investigating the murder of Sir Charles Baskerville and a mysterious haunted moor. **100m/C; VHS, DVD.** *GB* Ian Richardson; Donald Churchill; Martin Shaw; Nicholas Clay; Denholm Elliott; Brian Blessed; Ronald Lacey; ***D:*** Douglas Hickox; ***W:*** Charles Edward Pogue; ***C:*** Ronnie Taylor; ***M:*** Michael Lewis.

The Hound of the Baskervilles 1/2 **2000** Frewer takes on the role of Sherlock Holmes, emphasizing the character's cynical humor as well as his sometimes insufferable intelligence. Welsh ably backs him up as Watson and this version closely follows the Conan Doyle story. Sir Henry Baskerville (London) has inherited an estate with a curse and a devilish hound that terrorizes the moors. Holmes investigates. **90m/C; VHS, DVD.** *CA* Matt Frewer; Kenneth Welsh; Jason London; Emma Campbell; Robin Wilcock; Arthur Holden; Leni Parker; Gordon Masten; ***D:*** Rodney Gibbons; ***W:*** Joe Wiesenfeld; ***C:*** Eric Cayla; ***M:*** Marc Ouellette. **CABLE**

The Hound of the Baskervilles **2002** The umpteenth version of the Sherlock Holmes story about an inheritance and a vicious dog out on the moors is distinguished by its cast with Roxburgh's Holmes and Hart's Watson ably playing off each other. **100m/C; VHS, DVD.** *GB* Richard Roxburgh; Ian Hart; Matt(hew) Day; Richard E. Grant; Neve McIntosh; John Nettles; Geraldine James; Ron Cook; Danny (Daniel) Webb; ***D:*** David Attwood; ***W:*** Allan Cubitt; ***C:*** James Welland; ***M:*** Robert (Rob) Lane. **TV**

Hounddog 1/2 **2008 (R)** Grimy fairy tale set in a 1950's ramshackled Southern town, home to high-spirited 14-year-old tomboy Lewellen (Fanning), who has a rotten family and a budding Elvis obsession. Most of her time is taken up at the local swimming hole with her best friend Buddy, as the two begin teaching each other the differences between boys and girls. Lewellen's glow quickly fades after an older boy takes advantage of her curiosity, leaving her silent and afraid. Somehow revived by a mysterious midnight snake infestation, she again turns to Elvis to save her soul. Unfortunately, most of Fanning's mature performance, in which she proves she's more Jodie Foster than Lindsay Lohan, is lost on Southern cliches and aimless coming-of-age nonsense. Despite the controversy, the rape scene is restrained and brief. **93m/C; Blu-Ray.** Dakota Fanning; Piper Laurie; David Morse; Afemo Omilami; Cody Hanford; Robin Wright; Jill Scott; Christoph Sanders; ***D:*** Deborah Kampmeier; ***W:*** Deborah Kampmeier; ***C:*** Edward Lachman; Jim Denault.

Hour of the Gun **1967** Western saga chronicles what happens after the gunfight at the OK Corral. Garner plays the grim Wyatt Earp on the trail of vengeance after his brothers are killed. Robards is excellent as the crusty Doc Holliday. **100m/C; VHS, DVD, Blu-Ray.** James Garner; Jason Robards, Jr.; Robert Ryan; Albert Salmi; Charles Aidman; Steve Ihnat; Jon Voight; Robert Phillips; ***D:*** John Sturges; ***W:*** Edward Anhalt; ***M:*** Jerry Goldsmith.

The Hour of the Star 1/2 *A Hora Da Estrela* **1985** The poignant, highly acclaimed feature debut by Amaral, about an innocent young woman moving to the city of Sao Paulo from the impoverished countryside of Brazil, and finding happiness despite her socioeconomic failures. Based on Clarice Lispector's novel. In Portuguese with English subtitles. **96m/C; VHS, DVD.** *BR* Marcelia Cartaxo; ***D:*** Suzana Amaral. Berlin Intl. Film Fest. '85: Actress (Cartaxo).

Hour of the Wolf 1/2 *Vargtimmen* **1968** An acclaimed, surreal view into the tormented inner life of a painter as he and his wife are isolated on a small northern island. In Swedish with English subtitles. **89m/B; VHS, DVD, Blu-Ray.** *SW* Max von Sydow; Liv Ullmann; Ingrid Thulin; Erland Josephson; Gertrud Fridh; Gudrun Brost; Georg Rydeberg; Naima Wifstrand; Bertil Anderberg; Ulf Johansson; ***D:*** Ingmar Bergman; ***W:*** Ingmar Bergman; ***C:*** Sven Nykvist; ***M:*** Lars Johan Werle. Natl. Bd. of Review '68: Actress (Ullmann); Natl. Soc. Film Critics '68: Director (Bergman).

The Hour of 13 **1952** In 1890s London, suave jewel thief Nicholas Revel (Lawford) runs into trouble just after he steals an emerald at a party. A cop-killer has just claimed another victim and Scotland Yard inspector Connor (Culver) mistakenly believes both crimes are the work of the same man. This means Revel must bring the real killer to justice before he's captured himself. Remake of the 1934 thriller "The Mystery of Mr. X." **79m/B; DVD.** *GB* Peter Lawford; Roland Culver; Dawn Addams; Michael Hordern; Colin Gordon; Derek Bond; Leslie Dwyer; Richard Shaw; ***D:*** Harold French; ***W:*** Leon Gordon; Howard Emmett Rogers; ***C:*** Guy Green; ***M:*** John Addison.

Hourglass **1995 (R)** Fashion industry honcho Michael Jardine (Howell) risks his reputation and his life when he becomes involved with deadly, revenge-minded seductress Dara (Shinas), who blames the Jardines for her father's suicide. Another in a long line of be careful who you sleep with movies. **91m/C; VHS, Streaming.** C. Thomas Howell; Sofia Shinas; Ed Begley, Jr.; Timothy Bottoms; Anthony Clark; ***D:*** C. Thomas Howell; ***W:*** C. Thomas Howell; Darren Dalton; ***C:*** John Lambert; ***M:*** Chris Saranec.

The Hours 1/2 **2002 (PG-13)** In 1923 Virginia Woolf (Kidman) is recovering from a mental collapse while writing her novel "Mrs. Dalloway." In the 1950s, Laura Brown (Moore) is reading said novel, and in 2001, Clarissa (Streep) eerily embodies Woolf's character Dalloway. All three are facing questions of fulfillment in their lives and examining whether it's worth living, and all have issues with their own sexuality and the current men in their lives. Parallel gestures and words from era to era wonderfully enhance the illusion the three are indeed one. Many felt Cunningham's Pulitzer Prize-winning novel would not translate well to the screen, but Hare's screenplay and Daldry's direction superbly present this quilt of tales. **114m/C; VHS, DVD.** Nicole Kidman; Julianne Moore; Meryl Streep; Stephen (Dillon) Dillane; Miranda Richardson; John C. Reilly; Ed Harris; Allison Janney; Claire Danes; Jeff Daniels; Toni Collette; Eileen Atkins; Jack Rovello; Margo Martindale; Linda Bassett; ***D:*** Stephen Daldry; ***W:*** David Hare; ***C:*** Seamus McGarvey; ***M:*** Philip Glass. Oscars '02: Actress (Kidman); British Acad. '02: Actress (Kidman), Score; Golden Globes '03: Actress--Drama (Kidman), Film--Drama; L.A. Film Critics '02: Actress (Moore); Natl. Bd. of Review '02: Film; Writers Guild '02: Adapt. Screenplay.

Hours 1/2 **2013 (PG-13)** In 2005, regular guy Nolan (Walker) is sitting in a new Orleans hospital with his premature newborn daughter, who's on a ventilator. Mom died during childbirth (she's seen in flashbacks), so the guy's a mess even before Hurricane Katrina hits. The power goes out, the hospital is evacuated, but the baby can't be moved (just go with it). Nolan also has an apparently faulty ventilator battery with only a few minutes of charge at a time that he needs to deal with as the desperate dad tries to keep the baby alive while also trying to get help. It's basically a one-man show and Walker does an admirable job even if you've seen this story before. **96m/C; Blu-Ray, On Demand.** Paul Walker; Genesis Rodriguez; ***D:*** Eric Heisserer; ***W:*** Eric Heisserer; ***C:*** Jason Presant; ***M:*** Benjamin Wallfisch.

House **1986 (R)** Horror novelist Roger Cobb (Katt) moves into his dead aunt's supposedly haunted house only to find that the monsters don't necessarily stay in the closets. His worst nightmares come to life as he writes about his Vietnam experiences and is forced to relive the tragic events, but these aren't the only visions that start springing to life. It sounds depressing, but is actually a funny, intelligent "horror" flick. Followed by several lesser sequels. **93m/C; VHS, DVD, Blu-Ray.** William Katt; George Wendt; Richard Moll; Kay Lenz; Michael Ensign; Mary Stavin; Susan French; ***D:*** Steve Miner; ***W:*** Ethan Wiley; ***C:*** Mac Ahlberg; ***M:*** Harry Manfredini.

The House 1/2 **2017 (R)** Should've been called The Gym out of respect for the heavy-lifting Poehler and Ferrell exert to elevate the script. To pay for their daughter's college tuition, two parents open an underground casino in their basement. The premise has potential, but the characters are reduced to stereotypes and the laughs are more the exception than the rule. **88m/C; DVD, Blu-Ray.** Will Ferrell; Amy Poehler; Jason Mantzoukas; Ryan Simpkins; Nick Kroll; ***D:*** Andrew Jay Cohen; ***W:*** Andrew Jay Cohen; Brendan O'Brien; ***C:*** Jas Shelton; ***M:*** Andrew Feltenstein; John Nau.

House 2: The Second Story **1987 (PG-13)** The flaccid sequel to the haunted-house horror flick concerns two innocent guys who move into the family mansion and discover Aztec ghosts. Has none of the humor which helped the first movie along. **88m/C; VHS, DVD, Blu-Ray.** John Ratzenberger; Arye Gross; Royal Dano; Bill Maher; Jonathan Stark; Lar Park-Lincoln; Amy Yasbeck; Devin Devasquez; ***D:*** Ethan Wiley; ***W:*** Ethan Wiley; ***C:*** Mac Ahlberg.

House Across the Bay 1/2 **1940** Raft, an imprisoned nightclub owner, finds that he is being duped by his attorney who's eager to get his hooks into the lingerie-clad prisoner's wife. But prison isn't going to stop the bitter husband from getting his revenge. **88m/B; VHS, DVD.** George Raft; Walter Pidgeon; Joan Bennett; Lloyd Nolan; Gladys George; ***D:*** Archie Mayo.

House Arrest 1/2 **1996 (PG)** Another tired kids-think-they-know-best formula film. When Grover Beindorf (Howard) and his younger sister learn that their constantly fighting parents (Curtis and Pollak) are separating, they lock them in the basement so they'll be forced to sort things out. Word gets around and some school pals kidnap their problem parents and stash them in the basement with the Beindorfs. Most of the movie was actually shot in a basement; watch for Curtis hanging upside down in a laundry chute "True Lies" style. **107m/C; VHS, DVD.** Jamie Lee Curtis; Kevin Pollak; Christopher McDonald; Jennifer Tilly; Caroline Aaron; Wallace Shawn; Sheila McCarthy; Ray Walston; Kyle Howard; Amy Sakasitz; Jennifer Love Hewitt; ***D:*** Harry Winer; ***W:*** Michael Hitchcock; ***C:*** Ueli Steiger; ***M:*** Bruce Broughton.

House at the End of the Street 1/2 **2012 (PG-13)** Stop the Hound if you've heard this before--a girl (Lawrence) befriends the awkward kid (Thierot) down the street, the one with the dark past who's mocked by all the other locals, but is he being bullied or more dangerous? Despite the best efforts by the always-stellar Lawrence, what could have been a reasonably interesting suspense film about the nightmare that could be going on right next door in middle America becomes cliche. The only reason to check it out is to see how much a talented actress can do with a horrendous script. **101m/C; DVD, Blu-Ray.** Jennifer Lawrence; Max Thieriot; Elisabeth Shue; Gil Bellows; ***D:*** Mark Tonderai; ***W:*** David Loucka; ***C:*** Miroslaw Baszak; ***M:*** Theo Green.

The House Bunny **2008 (PG-13)** Playboy Bunny Shelly (Faris) is tossed from the mansion after turning the ripe old age of 27 (which is like 59 in Playboy years, she's told). Oblivious to the outside world, she wanders the streets like some Pinocchio Barbie until the geeky sorority girls of Zeta Alpha Zeta take her in as "house mom." Shelly slowly convinces the girls to get makeovers and let their hair down, transforming the ugly ducklings into tarted-up swans. Meanwhile, to win over sweet, brainy co-ed Oliver (Hanks), the girls help Shelly undergo her own makeover via books and less hairspray. Brainless and shallow (shocking!). Faris's considerable comic talents deserve more than what she's given to work with here. She really needs a new agent. **97m/C; Blu-Ray, On Demand.** Anna Faris; Colin Hanks; Emma Stone; Kat Dennings; Katharine McPhee; Rumer Willis; Tyson Ritter; Kiely Williams; Dana Min Goodman; Monet Mazur; Christopher McDonald; Kimberly Makkouk; Beverly D'Angelo; Charles Robinson; Jonathan Loughran; ***Cameo(s):*** Hugh Hefner; ***D:*** Fred Wolf; ***W:*** Karen McCullah Lutz; Kirsten Smith; ***C:*** Shelly Johnson; ***M:*** Waddy Wachtel.

The House by the Cemetery *Quella Villa Accanto Al Cimitero* **1983 (R)** When a family moves into a house close to a cemetery, strange things start to happen to them. **84m/C; VHS, DVD, Blu-Ray.** *IT* Katherine (Katriona) MacColl; Paolo Malco; Giovanni Frezza; ***D:*** Lucio Fulci; ***W:*** Lucio Fulci; Dardano Sacchetti; ***C:*** Sergio Salvati; ***M:*** Walter Rizzati.

House Calls **1978 (PG)** A widowed surgeon turns into a swinging bachelor until he meets a witty but staid English divorcee. Wonderful dialogue. Jackson is exceptional. Made into a short-lived TV series. **98m/C; VHS, DVD.** Walter Matthau; Glenda Jackson; Art Carney; Richard Benjamin; Candice Azzara; ***D:*** Howard Zieff; ***W:*** Charles Shyer; ***M:*** Henry Mancini.

The House I Live In **2012** Director Jarecki's well-intentioned and earnest documentary of the politics and policies of America's losing war on drugs, from President Nixon's declaration in 1971 to the present day. Includes a recap of the antidrug movement as well as interviews with various law enforcement officers and officials, historians, writers, and others though it doesn't offer much that's new. **108m/C; DVD.** ***D:*** Eugene Jarecki; ***W:*** Eugene Jarecki; ***C:*** Sam Cullman; Derek Hallquist; ***M:*** Robert Miller.

The House Next Door **2001** Lori (Cook) and Tom (Harrison) Peterson move into their dream house, meeting next-door neighbors Helen (Russell) and Carl (Russo) Schmidt. Carl seems rowdy but friendly but Lori comes to realize that he's a wife-beater and when Helen disappears she suspects the worse. Tom doesn't take his wife seriously and leaves on a business trip, with Lori's friend Monica (Young) coming to visit. So Lori persuades Monica to help her investigate Carl. **93m/C; VHS, DVD.** A.J. Cook; James Russo; Theresa Russell; Sean Young; Frederic Forrest; Matthew Harrison; ***D:*** Joey Travolta; ***W:*** John Benjamin Martin; ***C:*** Pieter Stathis; ***M:*** John Sereda. **VIDEO**

The House Next Door 1/2 **2006** Not as creepy as it should be and a late plot swerve is confusing. Col (Boyle) and Walker (Ferguson) have their doubts about the out-of-place modern house built by architect Kim (Goselaar) next to their standard suburban property. The house is soon showing its evil influence when each new owner begins behaving in a bizarre and often violent manner. Based on the 1979 Anne Rivers Siddons novel. **90m/C; DVD.** Lara Flynn Boyle; Colin Ferguson; Mark Paul Goselaar; Charlotte Sullivan; Stephen Arnell; Aidan Devin; Julie Stewart; Noam Jenkins; Emma Campbell; Niamh Wilson; ***D:*** Jeff Woolnough; ***W:*** Suzette Couture; ***C:*** David Herrington; ***M:*** Andrew Lockington. **CABLE**

House of Bamboo 1/2 **1955** A ruthless gang in Tokyo is holding up U.S. ammunition trains and will stop at nothing to cover their tracks, including killing their own. Stack is an undercover cop who infiltrates the gang, led by Ryan's vicious crime boss. Although Ryan does not disappoint, Stack's not at his best, and love scenes between him and Shirley Yamaguchi are stilted and uncomfortable to watch. The real star in this remake of "The Street with No Name" (1948) is the Cinemascope view of post war Japan and the finale in a Tokyo amusement park. **102m/C; DVD, Blu-Ray.** Robert Ryan; Robert Stack; Yoshiko (Shirley) Yamaguchi; Cameron Mitchell; Brad Dexter; Sessue Hayakawa; Biff (Elliott) Elliot; Harry Carey, Jr.; John Doucette; Barry Coe; DeForest Kelley; ***D:*** Samuel Fuller; ***W:*** Harry Kleiner; ***C:*** Joe MacDonald; ***M:*** Leigh Harline.

House of Bodies **2013** A bunch of college girls run a chat website where they do porny murder re-enactments at a home previously owned by a serial killer. When the girls get offed by a copycat, Detective Starks (Howard)goes to the imprisoned killer (Fonda) for some answers. The name actors have little to do in this dull, amateur splatterfest. **80m/C; DVD, Blu-Ray.** Terrence Howard; Peter Fonda; Alexz Johnson; Harry Zittel; Queen Latifah; ***D:*** Alex Merkin; ***W:*** Eddie Harris; ***C:*** Lukasz Pruchnik. **VIDEO**

House of Bones 1/2 **2009 (R)** Generally dull horror courtesy of the Syfy Channel. A failing reality TV series about ghost hunters goes on location to a New Orleans haunted house. Also along is guest psychic Heather who's convinced the place is reeking with a malevolent force. Arrogant host Quentin only believes her when crew members start disappearing and the house won't let anyone leave. **90m/C; DVD.** Charisma Carpenter; Corin "Corky" Nemec; Rick Robinson, Jr.; Marcus Lyle Brown; Kyle Russell Clements; Stephanie Honore; *D:* Jeffrey Scott Lando; Griff Furst; *W:* Jay Frasco; Anthony C. Ferrante; *C:* Andrew Strahorn; *M:* Miles Hankin. **CABLE**

House of Cards **1990** Depicts the political machinations of Machiavellian Tory whip Francis Urquhart (Richardson), who schemes to bring down the present government so that he can become the next Prime Minister. And there's absolutely nothing "F.U." (as he's appropriately known) won't do to achieve power. Followed by "To Play the King" and "The Final Cut"; based on the novel Michael Dobbs. On two cassettes. **200m/C; VHS, DVD.** *GB* Ian Richardson; Susannah Harker; Miles Anderson; David Lyon; Malcolm Tierney; Nicholas Selby; James Villiers; Diane Fletcher; *D:* Paul Seed; *W:* Andrew Davies; *C:* Ian Punter; Jim Fyans; *M:* Jim Parker.

House of Cards 1/2 **1992 (PG-13)** Precocious six-year-old Sally (Menina) suddenly stops talking after her father is killed in an accident at an archeological site in Mexico. Mom Ruth (Turner) fights to bring her daughter out of her fantasy world and seeks medical advice from a psychiatrist (a sympathetic Jones) but ignores it when it clashes with her own theories. The ethereal Menina, in her acting debut, gives the best performance in this weakly plotted and confusing family saga. **109m/C; VHS, DVD.** Kathleen Turner; Asha Menina; Tommy Lee Jones; Shiloh Strong; Esther Rolle; Park Overall; Michael Horse; Anne Pitoniak; *D:* Michael Lessac; *W:* Michael Lessac; *C:* Victor Hammer.

House of D **2004 (PG-13)** First time writer/director Duchovny is Tom Warshaw. He recounts for his son the events of his own early adolescence that shaped his life. In the early '70s, young Tommy has recently lost his father, his mother is suffering from depression, his best friend is Pappas, the retarded janitor at his school, he gets life advice from an inmate at the nearby Women's House of Detention, and he is just now noticing girls, particularly neighbor Melissa. This last development leads a jealous Pappas to petty theft to win back Tommy's friendship. Cloying, overly sentimental, and shamelessly sappy, this tale works much better as nostalgia for the carefree Greenwich Village Duchovny grew up in than the coming of age fable he obviously intended. **96m/C; DVD.** *US FR* David Duchovny; Anton Yelchin; Erykah Badu; Robin Williams; Zelda Williams; Magali Amadei; Tea Leoni; Frank Langella; Harold Cartier; Orlando Jones; Alice Drummond; *D:* David Duchovny; *W:* David Duchovny; *C:* Michael Chapman; *M:* Geoff Zanelli.

House of Dark Shadows **1970 (PG)** Gory, intense feature-film version of the gothic TV daytime soap "Dark Shadows." Released from his coffin by a handyman seeking treasure, 150-year-old vampire Barnabas Collins (Frid) avails himself of the hospitality of his descendents and moves into a house on their property. As a series of vampire attacks plague the area, Barnabas finds himself involved with a love-smitten doctor who wants to cure him (Hall) and a young girl who resembles his lost love, Josette (Scott). A violent and exciting film, long on shocks but short on continuity and character development. **97m/C; VHS, Blu-Ray, Streaming.** Jonathan Frid; Joan Bennett; Grayson Hall; Kathryn Leigh Scott; Roger Davis; Nancy Barrett; John Karlen; Thayer David; Louis Edmonds; *D:* Dan Curtis; *W:* Sam Hall; Gordon Russell; *C:* Arthur Ornitz.

House of Darkness 1/2 **1948** Psycho-thriller opens with a narrative by composer Melachrino explaining how the inspiration for a symphony came from his visit to a haunted house. Greedy Francis Merryman (Harvey) wants to inherit his stepbrother John's (Archdale) lavish mansion. Knowing John has a severe heart condition, Francis smashes John's prized violin, which brings on a fatal attack. Driven to paranoia and madness by his actions, Francis thinks he hears violin music (and possibly sees John's ghost). Director Mitchell's last film. **77m/B; DVD.** *GB* Laurence Harvey; John Stuart; Lesley Brook; Lesley Osmond; Alexander Archdale; Grace Arnold; George Melachrino; John Teed; *D:* Oswald Mitchell; *W:* John Gilling; *C:* Cyril Bristow.

The House of Dies Drear 1/2 **1988** A modern-day African American family moves into an old house that turns out to be haunted by the ghost of a long dead abolitionist. The family is transported back to the days of slavery as they interact with the ghost. Based on the story by Virginia Hamilton. Aired on PBS as part of the "Wonderworks" family movie series. **107m/C; VHS, DVD.** Howard E. Rollins, Jr.; Moses Gunn; Shavar Ross; Gloria Foster; Clarence Williams, III; *D:* Allan Goldstein.

House of Dracula **1945** Sequel to "House of Frankenstein" features several of the Universal monsters. Overly ambitious story gets a bit hokey, but it's entertaining, nonetheless. **67m/B; VHS, DVD, Blu-Ray.** Lon Chaney, Jr.; Martha O'Driscoll; John Carradine; Lionel Atwill; Onslow Stevens; Glenn Strange; Jane Adams; Ludwig Stossel; *D:* Erle C. Kenton; *W:* Edward T. Lowe; *C:* George Robinson.

House of Dreams **1964** Berry is a blocked writer coping with domestic difficulties whose dreams reveal a disturbing future. Contains a bit part for Goodnow, now a CNN talking head. **80m/B; VHS, DVD.** Robert Berry; Pauline Elliott; Charlene Bradley; Lance Bird; David Goodnow; *D:* Robert Berry.

House of Fear 1/2 **1945** Holmes and Watson investigate the murders of several members of the Good Comrades Club, men who were neither good nor comradely. **69m/B; VHS, DVD.** Basil Rathbone; Nigel Bruce; Dennis Hoey; Aubrey Mather; Paul Cavanagh; Gavin Muir; *D:* Roy William Neill.

House of Flying Daggers *Shimian Maifu* **2004** Zhang continues his interest in swordplay and chivalry following 2002's "Hero." Set in 859 A.D., during a period of unrest in the Tang Dynasty, the film follows three main characters. Police captains Leo (Lau) and Jin (Kaneshiro) are assigned to uncover the leader of the Flying Daggers, an anti-government rebel group. An elaborate set piece introduces beautiful blind dancer Mei (Zhang), the apex of the triangle. Jin poses as a sympathizer and hopes Mei will lead him to the rebel headquarters but doesn't expect to fall in love with her. A bamboo forest scene is among the film's action highlights. Mandarin with subtitles. Film is dedicated to actress Anita Mui who died from cancer before filming her role. **120m/C; DVD, Blu-Ray, UMD.** *CH* Takeshi Kaneshiro; Andy Lau; Ziyi Zhang; Song Dandan; *D:* Yimou Zhang; *W:* Yimou Zhang; Feng Li; Bin Wang; *C:* Xiaoding Zhao; *M:* Shingeru Umebayashi.

House of Fools *Dom Durakov* **2002 (R)** Janna (Vysotsky) is a young psychiatric patient in an old mansion located near the border of Chechnya. The cheerful Janna believes herself to be the fiancee of Canadian singer Bryan Adams (who appears as himself in the young woman's fantasies). The everyday activities of the childlike patients are disrupted when the fighting between the Russians and the Chechens comes closer. The staff flee and the doctor (Bagdonas) leaves to find buses to evacuates his patients. Meanwhile, the inmates are left to fend for themselves—and are soon joined by a group of Chechen soldiers, including handsome Akhmed (Isalmov) who Janna falls in love with. The film was inspired by an incident that happened in 1996. Russian with subtitles. **104m/C; VHS, DVD.** *RU FR* Julia Vysotsky; Sultan Iskamov; Bryan Adams; Vladas Bagdonas; Stanislav Varkki; Marina Politseimako; *D:* Andrei Konchalovsky; *W:* Andrei Konchalovsky; *C:* Sergei Kozlov; *M:* Eduard Artemyev.

House of Frankenstein 1/2 **1944** An evil scientist (Karloff) escapes from prison, and, along with his hunchback manservant, revives Dracula, Frankenstein's monster, and the Wolfman to carry out his dastardly deeds. An all-star cast helps this horror fest along. **71m/B; VHS, DVD, Blu-Ray.** Boris Karloff; J. Carrol Naish; Lon Chaney, Jr.; John Carradine; Elena Verdugo; Anne Gwynne; Lionel Atwill; Peter Coe; George Zucco; Glenn Strange; Sig Rumann; *D:* Erle C. Kenton; *W:* Edward T. Lowe; *C:* George Robinson.

House of Fury *Jing Mo Gaa Ting* **2005** Yue (Anthony Wong) is a former secret agent turned chiropractor who annoys his rebellious children with far-fetched tales of the good old days. That is until they're proven true when an old nemesis kidnaps their father, and the family is required to rescue him. Fortunately he's trained them in kung fu since early childhood. Suspending disbelief helps. **102m/C; DVD, Blu-Ray, UMD.** *CH* Anthony Wong Chau-Sang; Stephen Fung; Charlene (Cheuk-Yin) Choi; Gillian (Yan-Tung) Chung; Michael Wong; Daniel Wu; Winnie Leung; Ma Wu; Jon Foo; Philip Ng; *D:* Stephen Fung; *W:* Stephen Fung; Yui Fai Lo.

House of Games **1987 (R)** The directorial debut of playwright Mamet is a tale about an uptight female psychiatrist who investigates the secret underworld of conartistry and becomes increasingly involved in an elaborate con game. She's led along her crooked path by smooth-talking con-master Mantegna. A taut, well plotted psychological suspense film with many twists and turns. Stylishly shot, with dialogue which has that marked Mamet cadence. Most of the leads are from Mamet's theatre throng (including his wife, Crouse). **102m/C; VHS, DVD, Blu-Ray.** Joe Mantegna; Lindsay Crouse; Lilia Skala; J.T. Walsh; Meshach Taylor; Ricky Jay; Mike Nussbaum; Willo Hausman; *D:* David Mamet; *W:* David Mamet; *C:* Juan Ruiz-Anchia; *M:* Alaric Jans.

House of Horrors 1/2 **1946** Deformed murderer "The Creeper" (Hatton) is used by a mad sculptor in a twisted revenge plot. Marcel De Lange (Kosleck) believes his work has been vilely abused by art critics so he uses his friend's homicidal urges to get rid of anyone who stands in his way. **76m/B; VHS, DVD, Blu-Ray.** Martin Kosleck; Rondo Hatton; Robert Lowery; Virginia Grey; Bill Goodwin; Alan Napier; Joan Shawlee; Howard Freeman; *D:* Jean Yarbrough; *W:* George Bricker.

House of Mirth **2000 (PG-13)** The treacherous world of high society is the backdrop for savvy social climber Lily Bart (Anderson), who seeks to match her wits with an eligible bachelor's money in early 20th-century N.Y.C. Stoltz plays friend Selden who is not quite up to snuff financially for Lily, and Aykroyd, a well-heeled and seemingly well-meaning married "friend" who offers her investment advice. . .but at a hefty price. To make matter worse, a high-profile social maven (Linney) uses Lily to distract her husband from her own infidelities which puts Lily's reputation in jeopardy. With powerful friends lining up against her and her gambling debts piling up, the innocent Lily soon finds her once promising social position compromised. Disturbing but involving story made all the more so by Anderson's performance. Based on the novel by Edith Wharton. **140m/C; VHS, DVD.** *GB US* Gillian Anderson; Eric Stoltz; Dan Aykroyd; Eleanor Bron; Terry Kinney; Anthony LaPaglia; Laura Linney; Jodhi May; Elizabeth McGovern; *D:* Terence Davies; *W:* Terence Davies; *C:* Remi Adefarasin.

House of 9 **2005 (R)** So how familiar does this sound? Nine strangers wake up trapped in a creepy mansion without any idea how they got there. A voice tells them that only one will survive and that last person gets five million bucks for their trouble. Not as grisly as "Saw" or "Cube" but still nasty. **86m/C; DVD.** *GB* Dennis Hopper; Hippolyte Girardot; Peter Capaldi; Raffaello Degruttola; Kelly Brook; Ashley Walters; Susie Amy; Morven Christie; Julienne Davis; *D:* Stephen R. Monroe; *W:* Philippe Vidal; *C:* Damian Bromley; *M:* Mark Ryder.

House of 1000 Corpses WOOF! **2003 (R)** Disjointed and thoroughly confusing homage to horror films akin to "The Texas Chainsaw Massacre." Director Zombie has an honest affection for the films he references and recreates. Unfortunately, his movie is a hodge-podge of stories with no clear direction. It's stylish enough to be a popular cult film, but it lacks tangible scares or real drama. None of the episodes really fit together in this failure paved by good intentions. Hype may lead you to think this will be a gorefest. It isn't. **88m/C; VHS, DVD, Blu-Ray.** Sid Haig; Bill Moseley; Karen Black; Sheri Moon Zombie; Chris Hardwick; Erin Daniels; Dennis Fimple; Jennifer Jostyn; Walton Goggins; Tom Towler; Michael J. Pollard; Harrison Young; *D:* Rob Zombie; *W:* Rob Zombie; *C:* Tom Richmond; Alex Poppas; *M:* Rob Zombie; Scott Humphrey.

The House of 1000 Dolls *Haus Der Tausend Freuden* **1967** Doleful, not dollful, exploitation thriller as magician Price drugs young girls and sells them to slavery rings. An international production set in Tangiers; dialogue is dubbed. **79m/C; VHS, DVD, Blu-Ray.** *GE SP GB* Vincent Price; Martha Hyer; George Nader; Ann Smyrner; Maria Rohm; *D:* Jeremy Summers.

House of Saddam 1/2 **2008** HBO miniseries depicting power-mad Saddam Hussein's (Naor) rise and fall through his reliance on family ties to keep his country under control. His paranoia and megalomania aren't attractive traits and there's no one else to root for either as the biography focuses on the Iraqi side of the various conflicts that lead to the American invasion. **260m/C; DVD.** Igal Naor; Shohreh Aghdashloo; Said Taghmaoui; Makram Khoury; Uri Gavriel; Philip Arditti; Christine Stephen-Daly; *D:* Alex Holmes; Jim O'Hanlon; *W:* Alex Holmes; Stephen Butchard; *C:* Florian Hoffmeister; *M:* Samuel Sim. **CABLE**

House of Sand *Casa de Areia* **2005 (R)** In 1910, Aurea (Torres) and her mother Maria (Montenegro, Torres' real-life mom) are transplanted to the oblivion of northern Brazil by Aurea's delusioned husband, who is intent on turning the barren land into a farm. She quickly finds her pregnant self widowed and stranded, but she is befriended by Massu (Moldia), a former slave from a nearby settlement who helps the women make their way. The story unfolds over three generations (Torres and Motenegro eventually shift roles, with Montenegro as Aurea and Torres as daughter Maria) as the house slowly fills with sand, symbolizing the effects of gradual but inevitable passage of time. Not much happens save the occasional opportunity for escape from the desolate desert life, but for those with patience, it's a visual and dramatic treat. Portuguese with English subtitles. **115m/C; DVD.** *BR* Fernanda Montenegro; Fernanda Torres; Ruy Gerra; Luiz Melodia; Emiliano Queiroz; Enrique Diaz; *D:* Andrucha Waddington; *W:* Elena Soarez; *C:* Ricardo Della Rosa; *M:* Joao Barone.

House of Sand and Fog 1/2 **2003 (R)** Kathy (Connolly) is a recovering alcoholic whose husband recently left her. Because of a bureaucratic mix-up, she finds her house has been auctioned off from beneath her to Colonel Massoud Behrani (Kingsley), a former Iranian officer desperate to live the American dream. What follows is the conflict and struggle between the two, neither of which are evil or wrong in their viewpoints. Superb acting all around, combined with an interesting story. Based on the best-selling novel by Andre Dubus III. **126m/C; VHS, DVD.** Jennifer Connelly; Ben Kingsley; Ron Eldard; Shohreh Aghdashloo; Frances Fisher; Kim Dickens; Jonathan Ahdout; Navi Rawat; Carlos Gomez; *D:* Vadim Perelman; *W:* Vadim Perelman; Shawn Otto; *C:* Roger Deakins; *M:* James Horner. Ind. Spirit '04: Support. Actress (Aghdashloo); L.A. Film Critics '03: Support. Actress (Aghdashloo); N.Y. Film Critics '03: Support. Actress (Aghdashloo).

The House of Secrets **1937** A Yank travels to Britain to collect an inheritance and stays in a dusty old mansion filled with an odd assortment of characters. **70m/B; VHS, DVD.** Leslie Fenton; Muriel Evans; Noel Madison; Sidney Blackmer; Morgan Wallace; Holmes Herbert; *D:* Roland D. Reed.

The House of Seven Corpses **1973 (PG)** A crew attempts to film a horror movie in a Victorian manor where seven people died in a variety of gruesome manners. Things take a turn for the ghoulish when a crew member becomes possesed by the house's evil spirits. Good, low budget fun with a competent "B" cast. Filmed in what was the Utah governor's mansion. **90m/C; VHS, DVD, Blu-Ray.** John Ireland; Faith Domergue; John Carradine; Carole Wells; *D:* Paul Harrison; *W:* Paul Harrison; Thomas J. Kelly.

House of Strangers 1/2 **1949** Conte, in a superb performance, swears vengeance on his brothers, whom he blames for his father's death. Robinson, in a smaller part than you'd expect from his billing, is nevertheless excellent as the ruthless banker father who sadly reaps a reward he didn't count on. Based on Philip Yordan's "I'll Never Go There Again." **101m/B; VHS, DVD.** Edward G. Robinson; Susan Hayward; Richard Conte; Luther Adler; Efrem Zimbalist, Jr.; Debra Paget; ***D:*** Joseph L. Mankiewicz; ***W:*** Philip Yordan; ***C:*** Milton Krasner. Cannes '49: Actor (Robinson).

The House of the Arrow 🦴🦴🦴 **1953** Investigating the murder of a French widow, who was killed by a poisoned arrow, a detective must sort through a grab bag of potential suspects. Superior adaptation of the A.E.W. Mason thriller. **73m/B; VHS, DVD.** *GB* Oscar Homolka; Yvonne Furneaux; Robert Urquhart; ***D:*** Michael Anderson, Sr.

House of the Black Death 🦴 ½ *Blood of the Man Devil; Night of the Beast* **1965** Horror titans Chaney and Carradine manage to co-star in this as warring warlocks, yet they share no scenes together! Chaney is the evil warlock (the horns are a giveaway) holding people hostage in the title edifice. **89m/B; VHS, DVD.** Lon Chaney, Jr.; John Carradine; Katherine Victor; Tom Drake; Andrea King; ***D:*** Harold Daniels; Reginald LeBorg.

House of the Dead 🦴 *Alien Zone* **1978** Man is trapped inside a haunted house. Scary. **100m/C; VHS, DVD, Blu-Ray.** John Ericson; Charles Aidman; Bernard Fox; Ivor Francis; ***D:*** Sharron Miller; ***W:*** David O'Malley; ***C:*** Ken Gibb; ***M:*** Stan Worth.

House of the Dead WOOF! **2003 (R)** Cinematic trainwreck Uwe Boll attempts to make the filmmakers behind "Super Mario Brothers" feel better about themselves by directing one of the worst video game movies ever (and that's saying something). Four actors you could care less about travel to a remote island for the lamest rave ever captured on film (it has a baked goods tent... honestly) and, surprise, surprise, hordes of the undead start chomping on the extras. B-movie mainstays like Jurgen Prochnow and Clint Howard sleepwalk past the camera occasionally, but the real star is Boll's near-legendary technical ineptitude. Take a shot every time you notice a glaring gaffe and, trust us, you'll be dead long before the movie's over. **90m/C; VHS, DVD, UMD.** *GE CA US* Jonathan Cherry; Tyron Leitso; Clint Howard; Ellie Cornell; Will Sanderson; Sonya Salomaa; Michael Eklund; David Palffy; Jurgen Prochnow; Erica Durance; Anthony Harrison; Ona Grauer; Enuka Okuma; Kira Clavell; ***D:*** Uwe Boll; ***W:*** Mark Altman; David Parker; ***C:*** Mathias Neumann; ***M:*** Reinhard Besser; Oliver Lieb.

House of the Dead 2: Dead Aim 🦴 ½ **2005 (R)** Tongue-in-cheek horror about a college prof (Haig) whose experiments unleash a zombie infestation on campus. A couple of scientists try to find a cure before the bomb-happy military decides to solve the problem by blowing up the area. **95m/C; DVD.** Emmanuelle Vaugier; Edward Quinn; Kirk "Sticky Fingaz" Jones; Victoria Pratt; Sid Haig; Steve Monroe; ***D:*** Michael Hurst; ***W:*** Michael Roesch; ***C:*** Raymond N. Stella; ***M:*** Joe Kraemer. **VIDEO**

The House of the Devil 🦴🦴🦴 **2009 (R)** Retro horror homage set in the 1980s as college sophomore Samantha (Donahue) takes a babysitting job for a strange family. Samantha soon realizes that weirdoes Mr. And Mrs. Ulman, who live in a creepy Victorian mansion out in the woods, hired her not to watch young children, but instead, the father's aged mother on the night of the total lunar eclipse. Refreshingly free of the sadistic torture that mars so many modern horror flicks, relying instead on good old-fashioned suspense. Genuinely scary stuff, understanding that it's not what you see, but what you don't see. **95m/C; Blu-Ray, On Demand.** Jocelin Donahue; AJ Bowen; Dee Wallace; Tom Noonan; Mary Woronov; Greta Gerwig; Heather Robb; ***D:*** Ti West; ***W:*** Ti West; ***C:*** Eliot Rockett; ***M:*** Jeff Grace.

House of the Living Dead 🦴 *Doctor Maniac* **1973 (PG)** Brattling Manor harbors a murderous and flesh-eating secret ready to lure the unsuspecting. Don't you be one. **87m/C; VHS, DVD.** *SA* Mark Burns; Shirley Anne Field; David Oxley; ***D:*** Ray Austin.

House of the Rising Sun 🦴 **2011 (R)** Former wrestler-turned-. . . well, Bautista is no actor, though it doesn't matter so much when there's some action onscreen. Ex-cop, ex-con Ray gets a job working security at a mob-owned strip club. The club gets robbed and the owner's son is killed, with Ray accused of being the inside man. He's got the mob and the cops targeting him and has to prove who was really responsible. **90m/C; DVD, Blu-Ray.** Amy Smart; Dominic Purcell; Danny Trejo; Dave Bautista; Craig Fairbrass; Lyle Kanouse; Brian Vander Ark; Tim Fields; ***D:*** Brian A. Miller; ***W:*** Brian A. Miller; Chuck Hustmyre; ***C:*** William Eubank; ***M:*** Norman Orenstein. **VIDEO**

The House of the Seven Gables 🦴🦴 ½ **1940** Nathaniel Hawthorne's brooding novel about greed and a family curse. Jaffrey Pyncheon (Sanders) frames his brother Clifford (Price) for the murder of their father so that he can search in peace for the fortune Jaffrey believes is hidden somewhere in the family mansion, Seven Gables. But, eventually, Clifford gets out of prison and returns to claim his birthright. The studio built an exact duplicate of the original Salem house. **89m/B; VHS, DVD.** George Sanders; Vincent Price; Margaret Lindsay; Dick Foran; Nan Grey; Cecil Kellaway; Alan Napier; ***D:*** Joe May; ***W:*** Harold Greene; ***C:*** Milton Krasner.

The House of the Seven Hawks 🦴 ½ **1959** Lackluster Brit crime/suspense. Charter boat captain John Nordley's (Taylor) willing to bend the rules for the right price. When Nordley's passenger dies on the trip from England to Holland, Nordley takes a map off the body before reporting the death to the Dutch police. The dead man was actually a police inspector and the map is supposed to lead to stolen Nazi treasure. **92m/B; DVD.** *UK* Robert Taylor; Nicole Maurey; Linda Christian; Donald Wolfit; David Kossoff; Eric Pohlmann; ***D:*** Richard Thorpe; ***W:*** Jo Eisinger; ***C:*** Edward (Ted) Scaife; ***M:*** Clifton Parker.

The House of the Spirits 🦴🦴 **1993 (R)** Star-studded adaptation of the novel by Isabel Allende is a multi-generational saga following the fortunes of the powerful Trueba family. The ambitious Esteban (Irons) marries the clairvoyant Clara (Streep), exploits the peasants on his property, and becomes a conservative senator. Their rebellious daughter Blanca (Ryder) falls for rabble-rousing peasant Pedro (Banderas), and the country undergoes a bloody revolution. Magical realism of the novel is lost in screen melodrama, with the international cast ill-served by tepid direction. The child Clara is played by Streep's daughter, Mary Willa (listed in the credits as Jane Gray). **109m/C; VHS, DVD.** Meryl Streep; Jeremy Irons; Glenn Close; Winona Ryder; Antonio Banderas; Armin Mueller-Stahl; Vanessa Redgrave; Sarita Choudhury; Maria Conchita Alonso; Vincent Gallo; Miriam Colon; Jan Niklas; Teri Polo; Jane Gray; ***D:*** Bille August; ***W:*** Bille August; ***C:*** Jorgen Persson; ***M:*** Hans Zimmer.

The House of Tomorrow 🦴🦴 ½ **2018** Sixteen-year-old Sebastian (Butterfield) lives a strange life: in a geodesic dome house/tourist attraction with his Nana (Burstyn). There, he meets Jared (Wolff), a punk rocker with a transplanted heart and an overprotective father (Offerman), and the two new pals form a band and woo the ladies. Based on the novel by Peter Bognanni, this coming of age tale isn't as punk as it aims to be, but it's a charming enough bromance, finely acted by its two young leads. **85m/C; DVD, Blu-Ray.** Asa Butterfield; Alex Wolff; Nick Offerman; Ellen Burstyn; Maude Apatow; ***D:*** Peter Livolsi; ***W:*** Peter Livolsi; ***C:*** Corey Walter; ***M:*** Rob Simonsen.

House of Traps 🦴🦴 *Chong xiao lou; Chung siu lau* **1981** In this last film reuniting director Chang Cheh and (most of) the cast of the "5 Deadly Venoms," a rebellious nephew wishes to usurp his uncle's throne. All of the people conspiring with him (along with all the goods and treasure he has stolen) are placed in a pagoda loaded with death traps. When the judge investigating the case is murdered, a group of avengers set out to recover the treasure and put an end to the rebellion. **95m/C; DVD.** *CH* Feng Lu; Li Wang; Tien Hsiang Lung; Chien Sun; Siu-hou Chin; Philip Kwok; Ke Chu; Sheng Chiang; Tien-chi Ching; ***D:*** Cheh Chang; ***W:*** Cheh Chang; Kuang Ni; ***C:*** Hui-chi Tsao; ***M:*** Eddie Wang.

The House of Usher 🦴 ½ **2006 (R)** Jill arrives at Usher House, which comes complete with a sinister housekeeper, to attend the funeral of her friend Maddy. She also encounters Roderick, her former lover and Maddy's twin brother, who's suffering the same inherited illness that claimed his sister's life. Jill becomes drawn to Rick once again, despite menacing warnings and curiosity that could get her killed. Another very loose adaptation of the famed Poe story. **81m/C; DVD.** Izabella Miko; Austin Nichols; Beth Grant; Danielle McCarthy; Stephen Fischer; ***D:*** Hayley Cloake; ***W:*** Colin Chang; ***C:*** Eric Trageser. **VIDEO**

House of Versace 🦴 ½ **2013** Despite the seriousness of the overall subject, this true story begs for a camp retelling it doesn't get from Lifetime. Gianni Versace (Colantoni) was a flamboyant fashion designer in a family-run company. After his 1997 murder, the design work is taken on by his oh-so-blonde sister Donatella (Gershon), who turns to drugs to find the confidence to carry on in the fickle business. She's eventually forced into rehab before making a comeback. Although Gershon certainly makes the most of the melodrama, the pic is still a flimsy knock-off. **90m/C; DVD.** Gina Gershon; Enrico Colantoni; Colm Feore; Donna Murphy; Raquel Welch; Alex Carter; ***D:*** Sara Sugarman; ***W:*** Rama Laurie Stagner; ***C:*** John Dyer; ***M:*** Michel Corriveau. **CABLE**

House of Wax 🦴🦴🦴 **1953 (PG)** A deranged sculptor (Price, who else?) builds a sinister wax museum which showcases creations that were once alive. A remake of the early horror flick "Mystery of the Wax Museum," and one of the '50s most popular 3-D films. This one still has the power to give the viewer the creeps, thanks to another chilling performance by Price. Look for a very young Charles Bronson, as well as Carolyn "Morticia Addams" Jones as a victim. **88m/C; VHS, DVD, Blu-Ray.** Vincent Price; Frank Lovejoy; Carolyn Jones; Phyllis Kirk; Paul Cavanagh; Charles Bronson; Paul Picerni; Angela (Clark) Clarke; ***D:*** Andre de Toth; ***W:*** Crane Wilbur; ***C:*** Bert Glennon; ***M:*** David Buttolph. Natl. Film Reg. '14.

House of Wax 🦴 ½ **2005 (R)** Based on, but not very faithful to, the creepy 1953 3-D horror flick that starred Vincent Price. In this dismal dumbed-down remake, your usual gang of stupid college students are stranded by car trouble on their way to a football game. They wind up in the very small town of Ambrose and make the mistake of seeking help from the curator of a strange museum, Trudy's House of Wax, filled with wax figures that seem suspiciously lifelike. Said students include Hilton (making her legit film debut) who everyone will be happy to see encased in wax, which should actually make her more lifelike. **113m/C; DVD, Blu-Ray, UMD, HD-DVD.** *US AU* Elisha Cuthbert; Chad Michael Murray; Brian Van Holt; Jared Padalecki; Jon Abrahams; Robert Ri'chard; Paris Hilton; ***D:*** Jaume Collet-Serra; ***W:*** Carey Hayes; Chad Hayes; ***C:*** Stephen F. Windon; ***M:*** John Ottman. Golden Raspberries '05: Worst Support. Actress (Hilton).

House of Whipcord WOOF! **1975** Beautiful young women are kidnapped and tortured in this British gore-o-rama. Awful and degrading. **102m/C; VHS, DVD, Blu-Ray.** *GB* Barbara Markham; Patrick Barr; Ray Brooks; Penny Irving; Anne Michelle; Ivor Salter; Robert Tayman; ***D:*** Pete Walker; ***W:*** David McGillivray; ***C:*** Peter Jessop; ***M:*** Stanley Myers.

House of Women 🦴🦴 **1962** Pregnant young Erica (Knight) is sent to the joint for a five-year stretch but at least the inmates are allowed to keep their children until age three. Warden Frank Cole (Duggan) takes a very personal interest in Erica but then uses his lovesick passion to deny her parole to keep Erica around. This means no mother-child reunion, which leads to a riot. **85m/B; DVD.** Shirley Knight; Andrew Duggan; Constance Ford; Jeanne Cooper; Barbara Nichols; Margaret (Maggie) Hayes; Virginia Gregg; ***D:*** Walter Doniger; ***W:*** Crane Wilbur; ***C:*** Harold E. Stine; ***M:*** Howard Jackson.

The House of Yes 🦴🦴 **1997 (R)** Thanksgiving certainly brings out the worst in families although the Pascal clan is dysfunction personified. Marty (Hamilton) brings home fiancee Lesley (Spelling) to meet his eccentric mom (Bujold) and siblings. Younger brother Anthony's (Prinze) a dropout with no direction and Marty's twin sister Jackie-O (Parker) is bonkers. She's recreated herself as Jackie Kennedy Onassis and has had a very intimate relationship with Marty that Lesley probably doesn't know about. **90m/C; VHS, DVD.** Parker Posey; Josh Hamilton; Tori Spelling; Freddie Prinze, Jr.; Genevieve Bujold; Rachael Leigh Cook; ***D:*** Mark S. Waters; ***W:*** Mark S. Waters; ***C:*** Michael Spiller; ***M:*** Jeff Rona.

The House on 56th Street 🦴🦴 ½ **1933** Thirty years of plot are crammed into the brief run time of this tearjerker. In 1905, New York chorus girl Peggy (Francis) marries wealthy Monte (Raymond), leaving sugar daddy Lyndon (Halliday) behind. The couple move into the titular house, have a daughter, and are happy until Lyndon shows up. A shooting has Peggy doing 20 in the slammer. Now widowed, Peggy's kept from daughter Eleanor (Lindsay) so she takes up with card sharp Bill (Cortez), learning that her old home has been turned into a gambling den and speakeasy. More heartache follows. **70m/B; DVD.** Kay Francis; Gene Raymond; John Halliday; Ricardo Cortez; Margaret Lindsay; Hardie Albright; William "Stage" Boyd; Frank McHugh; ***D:*** Robert Florey; ***W:*** Sheridan Gibney; Austin Parker; Sheridan Gibney; ***C:*** Ernest Haller.

The House on Carroll Street 🦴 ½ **1988 (PG)** New York 1951, the middle of the McCarthy era. A young woman overhears a plot to smuggle Nazi war criminals into the U.S. She's already lost her job because of accusations of subversion, and it's not easy persuading FBI agent Daniels that she knows what she's talking about. Contrived plot and melodramatic finale help sink this period piece. **111m/C; VHS, DVD, Blu-Ray.** Kelly McGillis; Jeff Daniels; Mandy Patinkin; Jessica Tandy; ***D:*** Peter Yates; ***W:*** Walter Bernstein; ***C:*** Michael Ballhaus; ***M:*** Georges Delerue.

The House on Garibaldi Street 🦴🦴 ½ **1979** Spy drama about the capture of Nazi war criminal Adolph Eichmann in Argentina and his extradition to Israel for trial. Based on the book by Isser Harel. **96m/C; VHS, Streaming.** Topol; Nick Mancuso; Martin Balsam; Janet Suzman; Leo McKern; Charles Gray; Alfred Burke; ***D:*** Peter Collinson; ***M:*** Charles Bernstein. **TV**

House on Haunted Hill 🦴🦴 ½ **1958** A wealthy man throws a haunted house party and offers $10,000 to anyone who can survive the night there. Vintage cheap horror from the master of the macabre Castle. Remembered for Castle's in-theatre gimmick of dangling a skeleton over the audiences' heads in the film's initial release. **75m/B; VHS, DVD, Blu-Ray.** Vincent Price; Carol Ohmart; Richard Long; Alan Marshal; Carolyn Craig; Elisha Cook, Jr.; Julie Mitchum; Howard Hoffman; ***D:*** William Castle; ***W:*** Robb White; ***C:*** Carl Guthrie; ***M:*** Von Dexter.

House on Haunted Hill 🦴🦴 ½ **1999 (R)** This remake of William Castle's 1958 B-movie doesn't reach too far above its predecessor. In an homage to original star Vincent Price, Geoffrey Rush plays mincing amusement park tycoon Stephen Price, who invites a few friends over for his wife Evelyn's (Janssen) birthday. However, he invites them to a haunted former insane asylum, and offers them a million bucks if they can stick it out for the entire night. Stephen and the scheming Evelyn have a few tricks rigged for the guests, who all end up having some connection to the horrors that went on in the house in the bad old days. Soon, however, actual supernatural creepiness starts thinning the ranks of the guests. Unashamedly bloody and cheesy. **96m/C; VHS, DVD, Blu-Ray.** Geoffrey Rush; Famke Janssen; Taye Diggs; Peter Gallagher; Chris Kattan; Ali Larter; Bridgette Wilson-Sampras; Max Perlich; Jeffrey Combs; ***D:*** William Malone; ***W:*** Dick Beebe; ***C:*** Rick Bota; ***M:*** Don Davis.

House on 92nd Street 🦴🦴🦴 **1945** Documentary-style thriller finds federal investigator George Briggs (Nolan) contacted by German-American student Bill Dietrich (Eythe), who's been sought out by Nazi spies. Briggs encourages Dietrich to play along and report their nefarious activities to the feds. What Dietrich discovers is that a scientist, working on the atomic bomb project, is actually a Nazi agent. Lots of atmosphere and action, with director Hathaway incorporating newsreel footage to highlight the true-to-life feel. Title refers to the house where the head of the Nazi spies resides. **89m/B; VHS, DVD, Blu-Ray.** William Eythe; Lloyd Nolan; Signe Hasso; Gene Lockhart; Leo G. Carroll; William Post, Jr.; Harry Bellaver; ***D:*** Henry Hathaway; ***W:*** Barre Lyndon; John Monks, Jr.; Charles G. Booth; ***C:*** Norbert Brodine; ***M:*** David Buttolph. Oscars '45: Story.

The House on Skull Mountain 🦴 1/2 **1974 (PG)** The four surviving relatives of a deceased voodoo priestess are in for a bumpy night as they gather at the House on Skull Mountain for the reading of her will. **85m/C; VHS, DVD.** Victor French; Janee Michelle; Mike Evans; Jean Durand; ***D:*** Ron Honthaner.

The House on Sorority Row 🦴 1/2 *House of Evil; Seven Sisters* **1983** Less-than-harrowing story of what happens when seven sorority sisters have a last fling and get back at their housemother at the same time. **90m/C; VHS, DVD, Blu-Ray.** Eileen Davidson; Kate McNeil; Robin Meloy; Lois Kelso Hunt; Christopher Lawrence; Janis Zido; ***D:*** Mark Rosman; ***W:*** Mark Rosman; ***C:*** Tim Suhrstedt; ***M:*** Richard Band.

The House on Tombstone Hill 🦴 1/2 **1992** An old, abandoned mansion seems like a good investment to a group of friends. Wrong! The original owner is still around and doesn't like strangers coming to visit. **95m/C; VHS, DVD, Blu-Ray.** Doug Gibson; John Dayton (J.D.) Cerna; Sarah Newhouse; ***D:*** J. Reifel; ***W:*** J. Reifel.

House Party 🦴🦴🦴 **1990 (R)** Lighthearted, black hip-hop version of a '50s teen comedy with rap duo Kid 'n' Play. After his father grounds him for fighting, a high-schooler attempts all sorts of wacky schemes to get to his friend's party. Sleeper hit features real-life music rappers and some dynamite dance numbers. **100m/C; VHS, DVD; Open Captioned.** Christopher Reid; Christopher Martin; Martin Lawrence; Tisha Campbell; Paul Anthony; A.J. (Anthony) Johnson; Robin Harris; ***D:*** Reginald (Reggie) Hudlin; ***W:*** Reginald (Reggie) Hudlin; ***C:*** Peter Deming; ***M:*** Marcus Miller. Sundance '90: Cinematog.

House Party 2: The Pajama Jam 🦴🦴 1/2 **1991 (R)** Rap stars Kid 'N' Play are back in this hip-hop sequel to the original hit. At Harris University Kid 'N' Play hustle up overdue tuition by holding a campus "jammie jam jam." A stellar cast shines in this rap-powered pajama bash. **94m/C; VHS, DVD.** Christopher Reid; Christopher Martin; Tisha Campbell; Iman; Queen Latifah; Georg Stanford Brown; Martin Lawrence; Eugene Allen; George Anthony Bell; Kamron; Tony Burton; Helen Martin; William Schallert; ***D:*** Doug McHenry; George Jackson; ***W:*** Rusty Cundieff; Daryl G. Nickens; ***M:*** Vassal Benford.

House Party 3 🦴 **1994 (R)** Kid is engaged to be married and Play tries to set up a blowout bachelor party. The duo are also working on their record producer careers by trying to sign a feisty female rap group (real life TLC). Strikes out early for easy profanity while never coming within spitting distance of first two flicks. **93m/C; VHS, DVD.** Christopher Reid; Christopher Martin; Angela Means; Tisha Campbell; Bernie Mac; Barbara (Lee) Edwards; Michael Colyar; David Edwards; Betty Lester; Chris Tucker; ***D:*** Eric Meza; ***W:*** Takashi Bufford; ***M:*** David Allen Jones.

The House that Dripped Blood 🦴🦴 1/2 **1971 (PG)** A Scotland Yard inspector discovers the history of an English country house while investigating an actor's disappearance. Four horror tales comprise the body of this omnibus creeper, following the successful "Tales from the Crypt" mold. Duffell's debut as director. **101m/C; VHS, DVD, Blu-Ray.** *GB* Christopher Lee; Peter Cushing; Jon Pertwee; Denholm Elliott; Ingrid Pitt; John Bennett; Tom Adams; Joss Ackland; Chloe Franks; ***D:*** Peter Duffell; ***W:*** Robert Bloch.

The House That Jack Built 🦴🦴 **2018 (R)** Jack, creepily played by Matt Dillon, recounts key "incidents" from his 12-year serial killer rampage to Verge (short for Virgil, the hell-guide in *Dante's Inferno*). The film is so gory and disturbing that many Cannes viewers walked out, but audiences with strong stomachs may find art and dark humor among the psychopathy. **152m/C; DVD, Blu-Ray.** Matt Dillon; Bruno Ganz; Uma Thurman; Siobhan Fallon Hogan; Sofie Gråbol; ***D:*** Lars von Trier; ***W:*** Lars von Trier; ***C:*** Manuel Alberto Claro; ***M:*** Mikkel Maltha.

House Where Evil Dwells 🦴 1/2 **1982 (R)** An American family is subjected to a reign of terror when they move into an old Japanese house possessed by three deadly samurai ghosts. The setting doesn't upgrade the creepiness of the plot. Based on a novel by James Hardiman. **88m/C; VHS, DVD, Blu-Ray.** Edward Albert; Susan George; Doug McClure; Amy Barrett; Mako Hattori; Toshiya Maruyama; Henry Mitowa; Tsuyako Okajima; Tsuiyuki Sasaki; ***D:*** Kevin Connor; ***W:*** Robert Subotsky; ***C:*** Jacques Haitkin.

The House with a Clock in Its Walls 🦴🦴 1/2 **2018 (PG)** After his parents die, pre-teen Lewis (Vaccaro) moves in with his offbeat uncle Jonathan (Black) in his magical home. Magical, Lewis learns, because the home is haunted by a ticking doomsday clock. He also becomes close with Jonathan's spinster neighbor Mrs. Zimmerman (Blanchett). Though Jonathan helps young Lewis become a magical warlock, the pre-teen does not fit in at his new school and abuses his powers to impress a friend, Tarby (Suljic). An adaptation of a novel by John Bellairs, this kid-friendly horror fantasy has some humor and well-done computer imagery but is overwhelmed by Black's smothering performance. **104m/C; DVD, Blu-Ray.** Jack Black; Cate Blanchett; Owen Vaccaro; Kyle MacLachlan; Renee Goldsberry; ***D:*** Eli Roth; ***W:*** Eric Kripke; ***C:*** Rogier Stoffers; ***M:*** Nathan Barr.

A House Without a Christmas Tree 🦴🦴 1/2 **1972** A frustrated middle-aged man denies his young daughter her one desire—a Christmas tree. Charming TV holiday fare. **90m/C; VHS, DVD.** Jason Robards, Jr.; Lisa Lucas; Mildred Natwick; Kathryn Walker; Alexa Kenin; ***V:*** Patricia Hamilton; ***D:*** Paul Bogart. **TV**

Houseboat 🦴🦴 1/2 **1958** Widower Grant with three precocious kids takes up residence on a houseboat with Italian maid Loren who is actually a socialite, incognito. Naturally, they fall in love. Light, fun Hollywood froth. **110m/C; DVD.** Cary Grant; Sophia Loren; Martha Hyer; Eduardo Ciannelli; Murray Hamilton; Harry Guardino; ***D:*** Melville Shavelson; ***W:*** Melville Shavelson; Jack Rose; ***M:*** George Duning.

Housebroken **WOOF!** **2009 (R)** Miserably unfunny gross-out comedy. Fire Captain Cathkart (DeVito) retires and finally notices that his two worthless, 20-something sons Elliot (Hansen) and Quinn (Stone) are mooching off him and their mom (Sagal). To teach them a lesson, Mr. and Mrs. C. take off in the family RV, leaving the guys behind to pay the bills and keep the household going. The bros first idea is to rent a room to your basic babe and then, when they need more cash, the schemes get even cruder. **84m/C; DVD.** Danny DeVito; Katey Sagal; Ryan Hansen; Skyler Stone; Brie Larson; Thomas F. Wilson; Caitlin Crosby; ***D:*** Sam Harper; ***W:*** Sam Harper; ***C:*** Robert M. Stevens; ***M:*** Timothy Andrew Edwards. **VIDEO**

Houseguest 🦴🦴 **1994 (PG)** Dumb comedy about mistaken identity finds hard luck dreamer Kevin Franklin (Sinbad) on the run from loan sharks. Fortunately, while trying to make a getaway at the airport, he's mistaken for the childhood buddy (who's also an eminent dentist prompting some hygiene humor) of family guy/lawyer Gary Young (Hartman), who opens his suburban home to his long lost pal. Street smart Kevin naturally manages to solve every dysfunctional family problem that arises while avoiding some inept Mafia thugs. Everyone is oh-so-good-natured but there's nothing new to hold much interest. **109m/C; VHS, DVD.** Sinbad; Phil Hartman; Jeffrey Jones; Kim Greist; Stan Shaw; Tony Longo; Mason Adams; Paul Ben-Victor; Chauncey Leopardi; Ron Glass; Talia Seider; Kim Murphy; ***D:*** Randall Miller; ***W:*** Michael J. Di Gaetano; Laurence Gay; ***C:*** Jerzy Zielinski; ***M:*** John Debney.

The Householder 🦴🦴 *Gharbar* **1963** An early Merchant-Ivory collaboration featuring a young Indian schoolteacher whose widowed mother arranges his marriage to a woman he doesn't know. The immature couple find their adjustment to marriage fraught with, sometimes amusing, complications. **101m/B; VHS, DVD.** *IN* Shashi Kapoor; Leela Naidu; Durga Khote; ***D:*** James Ivory; ***W:*** Ruth Prawer Jhabvala.

The Housekeeper 🦴🦴 *Une Femme de Menage* **2002 (R)** When his wife (Breillat) walks out on him after 15 years, middle-aged Jacques (Bacri) can't manage to keep his Paris apartment clean, so he hires young and energetic Laura (Dequenne) as a housekeeper. Soon she is taking on more domestic responsibilities and Jacques grows increasingly used to her presence, even when she shows up in his bed. Laura assumes they have a relationship and Jacques even agrees to take her along on a summer holiday, but soon their differences are making themselves very clear. Based on the novel by Christian Oster. French with subtitles. **86m/C; DVD.** *FR* Jean-Pierre Bacri; Emilie Dequenne; Brigitte Catillon; Jacques Frantz; Catherine Breillat; Axelle Abbadie; ***D:*** Claude Berri; ***W:*** Claude Berri; ***C:*** Eric Gautier; ***M:*** Frederic Botton.

Housekeeping 🦴🦴🦴 **1987 (PG)** A quiet but bizarre comedy by Forsyth (his first American film). A pair of orphaned sisters are cared for by their newly arrived eccentric, free-spirited aunt in a small and small-minded community in Oregon in the 1950s. Conventional townspeople attempt to intervene, but the sisters' relationship with their offbeat aunt has become strong enough to withstand the coercion of the townspeople. May move too slowly for some viewers. Based on novel by Marilynne Robinson. **117m/C; VHS, DVD, Streaming.** Christine Lahti; Sarah Walker; Andrea Burchill; ***D:*** Bill Forsyth; ***W:*** Bill Forsyth; ***C:*** Michael Coulter; ***M:*** Michael Gibbs.

The Housemaid 🦴🦴 *Hanyo* **2010** Im's melodramatic reimaging rather than a straight-up remake of Ki-young Kim's 1960 classic psycho-drama. Naive Euny (Jeon) is hired to help out at the home of wealthy businessman Hoon (Lee) and his pregnant wife Hera (Woo). Hoon thinks nothing of seducing his young servant but passive Euny winds up pregnant and, when the affair is discovered, Hera's cold-blooded mother decides to use money to solve the problem and protect their pampered lives. Korean with subtitles. **106m/C; On Demand.** *NK* Do-yeon Jeon; Jung-jae Lee; Seo Woo; Yeo-Jong Yun; Ji-yeon Park; ***D:*** Sang-soo Im; ***W:*** Sang-soo Im; ***C:*** Lee Hyung-deok; ***M:*** Hong-jip Kim.

The Houses October Built 🦴🦴 1/2 **2014** A haunted house horror-thriller. Five friends who love Halloween and haunted houses take a road trip to find the best haunted house. Though they keep finding every day haunted houses with fake blood, they soon learn of something better. They focus their search on the Haunt, a very realistic alternative to these less frightening haunted houses. Though they initially cannot find this underground attraction, they soon start experiencing the unexpected. As more more odd and disturbing events occur, the friends realize the Haunt may have found them and some people will go too far for a thrill. **91m/C; DVD, Blu-Ray, Streaming, Download.** Brandy Schaefer; Zack Andrews; Mikey Roe; Jeff Larson; ***Cameo(s):*** Bobby Roe; ***D:*** Bobby Roe; ***W:*** Zack Andrews; Bobby Roe; Jason Zada; ***C:*** Andrew Strahorn; ***M:*** Mark Binder.

Housesitter 🦴🦴 1/2 **1992 (PG)** Newton Davis (Martin), an architect/dreamer, builds his high school sweetheart (Delany) a beautiful house and surprises her with a marriage proposal. She says no, so he has a one-night stand with Gwen (Hawn), who moves into his empty house and assumes the position of Davis's wife, unbeknownst to him. Gwen spins whopper lies and soon has the entire town, including Davis's parents and ex-girlfriend, believing her wacky stories. This romantic screwball comedy is a delight, not only because of Martin and Hawn, but also because of the array of other characters who complicate the stories they spin. **102m/C; VHS, DVD, Blu-Ray.** Steve Martin; Goldie Hawn; Dana Delany; Julie Harris; Donald Moffat; Peter MacNichol; Richard B. Shull; Laurel Cronin; Christopher Durang; ***D:*** Frank Oz; ***W:*** Mark Stein; Brian Grazer; ***C:*** John A. Alonzo; ***M:*** Miles Goodman.

Housewife 🦴🦴 **1934** Melodrama finds milquetoast office manager William Reynolds (Brent) being urged to start his own ad agency by his supportive wife Nan (Dvorak). It's only successful thanks to a campaign engineered by his ex-girlfriend, copywriter Patricia (Davis), who turns their working-late-at-the-office into an adulterous romance. Nan has to decide if William is worth fighting for. **70m/B; DVD.** George Brent; Ann Dvorak; Bette Davis; John Halliday; Robert Barrat; Hobart Cavanaugh; Ruth Donnelly; ***D:*** Alfred E. Green; ***W:*** Manuel Seff; Lillie Hayward; ***C:*** William Rees.

Housewife 🦴🦴 *Bone; Beverly Hills Nightmare; Dial Rat for Terror* **1972 (R)** Bone (Kotto) is a vengeful black man, who holds an unhappily married Beverly Hills couple (Duggan and Van Patten) hostage in their home. **96m/C; VHS, DVD.** Yaphet Kotto; Andrew Duggan; Joyce Van Patten; Jeannie Berlin; ***D:*** Larry Cohen; ***W:*** Larry Cohen; ***C:*** George Folsey, Jr.; ***M:*** Gil Melle.

How About You 🦴🦴 1/2 **2007** Widowed Kate Harris (Brady) operates a financially-shaky Irish retirement home. Her feisty younger sister Ellie (Atwill) comes to help out and Kate must leave her in charge over the Christmas holidays when their mother becomes ill. The four most difficult residents (two alcoholics and two spinster sisters) are left in Ellie's less-than-tender care and they all find something to learn about each other. Less twee than might be indicated (probably because the cast is terrific). Based on a short story by Maeve Binchy. **90m/C; DVD.** Hayley Atwell; Vanessa Redgrave; Joss Ackland; Imelda Staunton; Brenda Fricker; Orla Brady; Joan O'Hara; ***D:*** Anthony Byrne; ***W:*** Jean Pasley; ***C:*** Des Whelan; ***M:*** Niall Byrne.

How Do You Know 🦴 1/2 *Everything You've Got* **2010 (PG-13)** All too familiar and uninspired romantic comedy about two men—business executive George (Rudd) and major league baseball player/philanderer Matty (Wilson)?who vie for the love of a recently retired softball player Lisa (Witherspoon). Meanwhile, George contends with accusations of shady dealings and is hounded by his father (Nicholson) and the government. Although cast with bankable and likeable leads, the story is at times as stale as a day-old hot dog and the business scandal though appealing feels out of place. Director Brooks' effort might not entirely strike out but can't quite reach base either. **116m/C; Blu-Ray, On Demand.** Reese Witherspoon; Owen Wilson; Paul Rudd; Jack Nicholson; Kathryn Hahn; Dean Norris; Brian O'Halloran; Shelley Conn; Domenick Lombardozzi; Mark Linn-Baker; Molly Price; Daniel Benzali; Lenny Venito; Ron McLarty; ***D:*** James L. Brooks; ***W:*** James L. Brooks; ***C:*** Janusz Kaminski; ***M:*** Hans Zimmer.

How Green Was My Valley 🦴🦴🦴🦴 **1941** Compelling story of the trials and tribulations of a Welsh mining family, from the youthful perspective of the youngest child (played by a 13-year-old McDowall). Spans 50 years, from the turn of the century, when coal mining was a difficult but fair-paying way of life, and ends, after unionization, strikes, deaths, and child abuse, with the demise of a town and its culture. Considered by many to be director Ford's finest work. When WWII prevented shooting on location, producer Zanuck built a facsimile Welsh valley in California (although Ford, born Sean Aloysius O'Fearna, was said to have been thinking of his story as taking place in Ireland rather than Wales). Based on the novel by Richard Llewellyn. **118m/C; VHS, DVD, Blu-Ray.** Walter Pidgeon; Maureen O'Hara; Donald Crisp; Anna Lee; Roddy McDowall; John Loder; Sara Allgood; Barry Fitzgerald; Patric Knowles; Rhys Williams; Arthur Shields; Ann E. Todd; Mae Marsh; ***Nar:*** Irving Pichel; ***D:*** John Ford; ***W:*** Philip Dunne; ***C:*** Arthur C. Miller; ***M:*** Alfred Newman. Oscars '41: B&W Cinematog., Director (Ford), Film, Support. Actor (Crisp); Natl. Film Reg. '90; N.Y. Film Critics '41: Director (Ford).

How Harry Became a Tree 🦴🦴 1/2 *Bitter Harvest* **2001 (R)** Harry, an embittered farmer (Meany) declares war on the most powerful man in town, who happens to be the town matchmaker. In order to marry off his dim but handsome son, Harry finds himself again indebted to his nemesis, which only fuels his anger and proves he is his own worst enemy. Engaging Irish drama with a dark comedic edge. **100m/C; DVD.** *IR IT GB FR* Colm Meaney; Adrian Dunbar; Cillian Murphy; Kerry Condon; Pat Laffan; ***D:*** Goran Paskalyevic; ***W:*** Goran Paskalyevic; Christine Gentet; Stephen Walsh; ***C:*** Milan Spasic; ***M:*** Stefano Arnaldi.

How High 1/2 **2001 (R)** Genial stoner comedy finds tokers Silas (Method Man) and Jamal (Redman) smoking some extra-potent "smart" ganja that magically gets them into Harvard. There the laid back homeboys clash with uptight Dean Cain (Babatunde) but find time for some fine chicks. **93m/C; VHS, DVD.** Method Man; Redman; Obba Babatunde; Chuck Davis; Anna Maria Horsford; Fred Willard; Lark Voorhies; Essence Atkins; Jeffrey Jones; Mike Epps; Hector Elizondo; Chris Elwood; Spalding Gray; Tracey Walter; Louis Freese; Al Shearer; ***D:*** Jesse Dylan; ***W:*** Dustin Lee Abraham; ***C:*** Francis Kenny; ***M:*** Rockwilder.

How I Ended This Summer **2010** Veteran meteorologist Sergei and his unseasoned new partner Pavel are stationed on the Russian Arctic island of Chukotka with their only link to the outside world a two-way radio. Sergei likes to relieve the boredom by going fishing and, during one of his trips, Pavel gets a personal and tragic message for his partner that he's supposed to relay. Wimpy Pavel can't do it and when Sergei takes off again, the base station orders Pavel to get Sergei back, which means he must travel into polar-bear territory. Russian with subtitles. **130m/C; DVD.** *RU* Sergey Puskepalis; Grigory Dobrygin; ***D:*** Aleksey Popgrebsky; ***W:*** Aleksey Popgrebsky; ***C:*** Pavel Kostomarov; ***M:*** Dmitriy Katkhanov.

How I Got into College **1989 (PG-13)** A slack, uninspired satire about doofus high school senior Marion Browne (Parker) who is eager to attend the same college as brainy Jessica (Boyle). But both run into problems from the snooty college recruiter (Rocket). More interesting for what the cast went on to do in the nineties. **87m/C; VHS, DVD.** Corey Parker; Lara Flynn Boyle; Christopher Rydell; Anthony Edwards; Phil Hartman; Brian Doyle-Murray; Nora Dunn; Finn Carter; Charles Rocket; ***D:*** Savage Steve Holland; ***W:*** Terrel Seltzer; ***C:*** Robert Elswit; ***M:*** Joseph Vitarelli.

How I Got Lost **2009** A quarter-life crisis by two New Yorkers feels familiar and a little overly earnest; the story is also bookended by 9/11 and the mass Northeast blackout in August 2003. Best buds, sportswriter Jake (Fishel) and banker Andrew (Stanford) are moving aimlessly through their lives. After one drunken night, Andrew persuades Jake to blow everything off for awhile and take a road trip with him that turns out to be to Andrew's Ohio hometown where his father has just died. **87m/C; DVD.** Aaron Stanford; Jacob Fishel; Rosemarie DeWitt; Nicole Vicius; Jill Flint; Emily Wickersham; ***D:*** Joe Leonard; ***C:*** Christopher Chambers; ***M:*** Kaki King.

How I Killed My Father *Comment J'ai Tue Mon Pere* **2003** No fathers were actually killed in the making of this film. Grim, dry melodrama about a man whose life is upset when the father who deserted him as a boy reappears in his life. Jean-Luc (Berling) is an aloof doctor with a seemingly perfect life but very little passion for his work or his family, and he's afraid of having children. Enter his father, Maurice (Bouquet), who storms back in and starts to wear away at his son's appearance of perfection. The result is a metaphorical tug-of-war between the two men. Fontaine's direction is both effective and ruthless as she questions the nature of the relationship between father and son, but it's occasionally heavy-handed and predictable, giving the sense that the characters are doomed before they get a chance to start. **100m/C; DVD.** *FR SP* Michel Bouquet; Charles Berling; Natacha Regnier; Amira Casar; Hubert Kounde; Stephane Guillon; ***D:*** Anne Fontaine; ***W:*** Anne Fontaine; Jacques Fieschi; ***C:*** Jean-Marc Fabre; ***M:*** Jocelyn Pook.

How I Live Now **2013 (R)** Hostile American teen Daisy (Ronan) is sent to spend the summer with her cousins in the English countryside. With Aunt Penn (Chancellor) away in Geneva at peace talks, the kids are mainly left to enjoy a momentary idyll as Daisy falls for her older cousin, Edmond (MacKay). When terrorists strike London (a prelude to World War III), Daisy and young Piper (Bird) are separated from the family when martial law is declared and they are sent to a labor camp. But Daisy is determined to survive and reunite them. Her interior monologues get tiresome but Ronan makes a fine lead in this adaptation of Meg Rosoff's young adult novel. **101m/C; DVD, Blu-Ray.** *UK* Saoirse Ronan; George MacKay; Tom Holland; Harley Bird; Danny McEvoy; Anna Chancellor; ***D:*** Kevin MacDonald; ***W:*** Jeremy Brock; Tony Grisoni; ***C:*** Franz Lustig; ***M:*** Jon Hopkins.

How I Married My High School Crush 1/2 *The Wedding Wish* **2007** Be careful what you wish for. In 1990, brainiac 17-year-old Sara is paired up with her crush, oblivious football star Brian, in a high school life class where you pretend to be married to learn about adult issues. A wish from Sara and a solar eclipse sends them to 2007 on their wedding day but because Sara and Brian are still teens on the inside adjusting to their new lives is difficult and very confusing. **90m/C; DVD.** Katee Sackhoff; Sage Brocklebank; Tommy Lioutas; Kim Poirier; Elyse Levesque; Nikki Elek; ***D:*** David Winkler; ***W:*** Nancey Silvers; Ron Fassler; ***C:*** Mark Dobrescu; ***M:*** Todd Bryanton; Rob Bryanton. **CABLE**

How I Spent My Summer Vacation **1997** Squabbling college sweethearts Perry (Lee) and Stephanie (Davis) have decided their battles have blighted their romance and they split up right before their senior year. Perry moves into an apartment with a couple of buddies and pines for his ex, who's independently getting on with her life, although the dating scene turns out to be trying for them both. Sweetly amusing debut for writer/director Fisher. **75m/C; VHS, DVD.** RonReaco Lee; Deanna Davis; E. Roger Mitchell; Mike Ngaujah; Jade Janise Dixon; ***D:*** John Fisher; ***W:*** John Fisher; ***C:*** Charles Mills; ***M:*** Johnny Barrow.

How I Won the War **1967 (PG)** An inept officer must lead his battalion out of England into the Egyptian desert to conquer a cricket field. Indulgent, scarcely amusing Richard Lester comedy; Lennon, in a bit part, provides the brightest moments. **111m/C; VHS, DVD, Blu-Ray.** *GB* John Lennon; Michael Crawford; Michael Hordern; Roy Kinnear; ***D:*** Richard Lester; ***W:*** Charles Wood; ***C:*** David Watkin; ***M:*** Ken Thorne.

How It All Went Down 1/2 **2003** Inspired by the true story of Carmine Cavelli, a would-be filmmaker (Pollio) who needs financing for his next movie idea and turns to selling cocaine to get the money. Quickly becoming one of the top dealers in his area he becomes addicted himself and his life begins a quick downward spiral. **93m/C; DVD.** *CA* Silvio Pollio; Daniella Evangelista; Franco Valenti; Paige Gray; Jay Kramer; Joe Pascual; Horace Morris; Paul Anderson; Alistair Abell; Jim Bremner; Jane Sowerby; John B. Destry; Woody Jeffreys; David Lewis; Nadia Polio; Kristina Copeland; Maria Luisa Cianni; Tasha Michelin; Mike Goodheart; Antonio Sorace; John Vranic; Hamid Nazemzadeh; Rahi Ashraf; Romaeo Jahroudi; Behram Khosravi; Ray Abraham; ***D:*** Silvio Pollio; ***W:*** Silvio Pollio.

How Many Miles to Babylon? **1982** During WWI, two young men become friends despite their different backgrounds. But one is court-martialed for desertion, and the other is supposed to oversee his execution. **106m/C; DVD.** *UK* Daniel Day-Lewis; Christopher Fairbank; Sian Phillips; Alan MacNaughton; Barry Foster; David Gwillim; ***D:*** Moira Armstrong; ***W:*** Derek Mahon; ***C:*** John Hooper; ***M:*** Geoffrey Burgon. **TV**

How Much Do You Love Me? *Combien Tu M'Aimes?* **2005** Downtrodden, ordinary office worker Francois (Campan) tells gorgeous hooker Daniela (Bellucci) that he's won the lottery and invites her to live with him and help him spend his windfall. Naturally, she agrees despite her threatening gangster boyfriend Charly (Depardieu) and the fact that Francois' heart condition flairs up when he gets too, uh, stimulated. French with subtitles. **95m/C; DVD.** *FR* Monica Bellucci; Gerard Depardieu; Jean-Pierre Darroussin; Bernard Campan; ***D:*** Bernard Blier; ***W:*** Bernard Blier; ***C:*** Francois Catonne.

How She Move 1/2 **2008 (PG-13)** Talented dancer Raya (Wesley) returns to her inner-city Toronto neighborhood from private school after her sister dies of a drug overdose. Desperate for a new route out, she uses her dance talents to earn a spot in an all-male dance troupe, where she must constantly prove herself to be as good as the boys. Film's grit, depth, and excellent choreography make it a cut above the average hip-hop dance movie. **94m/C; DVD.** *CA* Melanie Nicholls-King; Rutina Wesley; Tre Armstrong; Dwain Murphy; Brennan Gademans; Shawn Desman; Kevin Duhaney; ***D:*** Ian Iqbal Rashid; ***W:*** Annmarie Morais; ***C:*** Andre Pienaar; ***M:*** Andrew Lockington.

How Stella Got Her Groove Back **1998 (R)** Underneath the flawless physique and upscale way of life, fortyish single mom Stella (Bassett) is sad; too much work and no love life is to blame. Coaxed by her best friend Delilah (Goldberg), Stella takes a trip to Jamaica where she falls in love with 20-year-old islander Winston (Diggs in his film debut). A flipside to the May-December romance that is purely more gloss (picturesque shots of the Carribean landscape) than grit. Bassett glows in a tailor-made role and muscular hunk Diggs is a find, but perfection in casting can't rescue this hollow romance that woefully missteps after a promising beginning. Based on the novel by Terry McMillan. **124m/C; VHS, DVD.** Angela Bassett; Whoopi Goldberg; Taye Diggs; Regina King; Suzzanne Douglass; Richard Lawson; Michael J. Pagan; Barry (Shabaka) Henley; Sicily; ***D:*** Kevin Rodney Sullivan; ***W:*** Ronald Bass; Terry McMillan; ***C:*** Jeffrey Jur; ***M:*** Michel Colombier.

How Sweet It Is! **1968** Typical American family takes a zany European vacation. Looks like a TV sitcom and is about as entertaining. National Lampoon's version is a lot more fun. **99m/C; VHS, DVD.** James Garner; Debbie Reynolds; Maurice Ronet; Paul Lynde; Erin Moran; Marcel Dalio; Terry-Thomas; Jenie Jackson; ***D:*** Jerry Paris; ***W:*** Jerry Belson; ***C:*** Lucien Ballard.

How Tasty Was My Little Frenchman *Como Era Gostoso O Meu Frances* **1971** French explorer is captured by a cannibal tribe in the jungles of Brazil. He's treated very well and attempts to learn tribal customs to avoid his fate—he's going to be the main course in a ceremonial dinner. French and Tupi with subtitles. **80m/C; VHS, DVD.** *BR* Arduino Colasanti; Ana Maria Magalhaes; Ital Natur; Eduardo Embassahy; ***D:*** Nelson Pereira dos Santos.

How the Garcia Girls Spent Their Summer **2005 (R)** During a sweltering summer in an Arizona border town, Dona Genoveva (Gallardo), the 70-year-old matriarch of the Garcia family, buys a car and announces she's going to learn to drive, with gardener Don Pedro (Cervera Jr.) happy to offer lessons. Her middle-aged divorced daughter Lolita (Pena) breaks off an affair with a married man (Bauer) only to become interested in fellow butcher shop employee Jose (Najera). And Lolita's 17-year-old daughter Blanca (Ferrera) is discovering first love with Sal (Minaya), a boy with a bad reputation. English and Spanish with subtitles. **128m/C; DVD.** Lucy Gallardo; Elizabeth Pena; America Ferrera; Steven Bauer; Leo Minaya; Jorse Cervera, Jr.; Rick Najera; ***D:*** Georgina Garcia Riedel; ***W:*** Georgina Garcia Riedel; ***C:*** Tobias Datum.

How the West Was Fun 1/2 **1995** The Olsen gals are visiting great godmother Natty's dude ranch, which is in financial difficulty, and must outsmart her greedy son Bart (Mull), a land grabber who wants to turn the ranch into an environmentally unfriendly western theme park. Made for TV. **93m/C; VHS, DVD.** Mary-Kate Olsen; Ashley (Fuller) Olsen; Martin Mull; Michele Greene; Patrick Cassidy; Leon Pownall; Margaret "Peg" Phillips; ***D:*** Stuart Margolin; ***M:*** Richard Bellis. **TV**

How the West Was Won **1963 (G)** A panoramic view of the American West, focusing on the trials, tribulations and travels of three generations of one family, set against the background of wars and historical events. Particularly notable for its impressive cast list and expansive western settings. **165m/C; VHS, DVD, Blu-Ray.** John Wayne; Carroll Baker; Lee J. Cobb; Spencer Tracy; Gregory Peck; Karl Malden; Robert Preston; Eli Wallach; Henry Fonda; George Peppard; Debbie Reynolds; Carolyn Jones; Richard Widmark; James Stewart; Walter Brennan; Andy Devine; Raymond Massey; Agnes Moorehead; Harry (Henry) Morgan; Thelma Ritter; Russ Tamblyn; ***D:*** John Ford; Henry Hathaway; George Marshall; ***W:*** James R. Webb; ***C:*** Milton Krasner; Charles B(ryant) Lang, Jr. Oscars '63: Film Editing, Sound, Story & Screenplay; Natl. Film Reg. '97.

How to Be 1/2 **2008** Dumped by his girlfriend and forced to move back in with his parents, depressed London supermarket clerk and would-be musician Art (Pattinson) hires a self-help author to be his life coach. Navel-gazing aimlessness. **85m/C; DVD.** *GB* Robert Pattinson; Rebecca Pidgeon; Powell Jones; Jeremy Hardy; Michael Irving; Alisa Arnah; Mike Pearce; Johnny White; ***D:*** Oliver Irving; ***W:*** Oliver Irving; ***C:*** Paul Swann; ***M:*** Joe Hastings.

How to Be a Latin Lover **2017 (PG-13)** Mexican star Derbez goes for stateside success as Maximo, who gets the boot from his 80-year-old sugar momma when she turns him in for a younger model. Broke and homeless, he moves in with his sister and nephew, Hugo. Maximo sees a chance to get back to the good life through the billionaire grandmother of Hugo's first crush. Some moments are inspired, and the stellar supporting cast is game (especially Lowe as a fellow gold digger), but the uneven pacing, silly dialogue, and whiplash changes in tone mostly sabotage the whole thing. Premise and execution smack of 1980s-era sex romp comedy, wrapped in a PG-13 package. **115m/C; DVD, Blu-Ray.** Eugenio Derbez; Salma Hayek; Rob Lowe; Kristen Bell; Raphael Alejandro; ***D:*** Ken Marino; ***W:*** Chris Spain; Jon Zack; ***C:*** John Bailey; ***M:*** Craig Wedren.

How to be a Serial Killer **2008** Genial serial killer Mike Wilson has developed his own ten-step program and seminar, including ethics, killing methods, body disposal, and balancing your work and personal life. Mike needs an apprentice so he takes on vulnerable video store clerk Bart to test his theories. **91m/C; DVD.** Laura Regan; George Wyner; Dameon Clarke; Matthew Gray; ***D:*** Luke Ricci; ***W:*** Luke Ricci; ***C:*** H. Michael Otano; ***M:*** Nicholas O'Toole.

How to Be a Woman and Not Die in the Attempt *How to Be a Woman and Not Die Trying; Como ser Mujer y No Morir en El* **1991** Carmen has just turned 42, is married to her third husband, and is raising three children. She's also very serious about her journalistic career on the local paper. So, she's a modern woman with too much to do and too little time, trying to juggle her home and her work and still keep a sense of humor. Based on the novel by Carmen Rico-Godoy. Spanish with subtitles. **96m/C; VHS, DVD.** *SP* Carmen Maura; Antonio Resines; ***D:*** Ana Belen; ***W:*** Carmen Rico Godoy; ***C:*** Juan Amoros.

How to Be Single 1/2 **2016 (R)** Another advice book is turned into a cheap rom-com, wasting a talented cast on manipulative clichés and dumb set-ups. Alice (Johnson) is newly single and in New York City, the biggest dating pool in the world. She moves in with her sister (Mann), who is also struggling to meet people. When Alice befriends Robin (Wilson), the requisite one-stand fan of the film, her eyes are opened to the dating scene. A supporting cast of recognizable faces flit by in this movie that feels more like a failed pilot for an NBC comedy than a feature film. **110m/C; DVD, Blu-Ray.** Dakota Johnson; Rebel Wilson; Leslie Mann; Damon Wayans, Jr.; Anders Holm; ***D:*** Christian Ditter; ***W:*** Abby Kohn; Marc Silverstein; Dana Fox; ***C:*** Christian Rein; ***M:*** Fil Eisler.

How to Beat the High Cost of Living 1/2 **1980 (PG)** Three suburban housewives decide to beat inflation by taking up robbery, and they start by planning a heist at the local shopping mall. Comedic talent can't salvage whipped script and direction. **105m/C; VHS, DVD, Blu-Ray.** Jessica Lange; Susan St. James; Jane Curtin; Richard

Benjamin; Eddie Albert; Dabney Coleman; Fred Willard; Cathryn Damon; Art Metrano; ***D:*** Robert Scheerer.

How to Build a Girl **2020 (R)** In early '90s London, Johanna (Feldstein) is a broke 16 year old living with her large family in an unfashionable part of the city. Shy Johanna is a loner who wants to write about music professionally. To achieve her goal and overcome her inner doubts, she creates a new persona, Dolly Wilde, complete with a new look. Quickly, Johanna finds that her dreams are coming true and that she has much internal strength despite the many challenges she faces. An adaptation of the Caitlin Moran best-selling novel, it's charming, sweet, and full of humor, with a star-making performance by Feldstein. **102m/C; DVD.** Beanie Feldstein; Paddy Considine; Laurie Kynaston; Sarah Solemani; Michael Sheen; ***D:*** Coky Giedroyc; ***W:*** Caitlin Moran; ***C:*** Hubert Taczanowski; ***M:*** Oli Julian.

How to Commit Marriage **1/2 1969 (PG)** Hope and Wyman have been married for 20 years when they decide to divorce—just when their daughter (Cameron) decides to marry her college boyfriend (Matheson). His father (Gleason) tries to stop the wedding, fails, but sticks around to cause more trouble. Subplots involve the divorced duo's new loves and the fact that they're about to become grandparents but the comedy is completely uninspired. **96m/C; VHS, DVD.** Bob Hope; Jane Wyman; Jackie Gleason; Joanna Cameron; Tim Matheson; Bea Arthur; Leslie Nielsen; Tina Louise; Paul Stewart; Prof. Irwin Corey; ***D:*** Norman Panama; ***W:*** Ben Starr; Michael Kanin; ***C:*** Charles B(ryant) Lang, Jr.; ***M:*** Joseph J. Lilley.

How to Deal **1/2 2003 (PG-13)** High schooler Halley (Moore) decides love is a crock when she hits some speed bumps on the road of life. Her parents split when DJ dad Len (Gallagher) has a midlife crisis and romances a younger woman. Bitter mom Lydia (Janney) copes by getting involved with the wedding plans of older daughter Ashley (Garrison), whose fiance (Astin) seems dominated by his wealthy parents. Then Halley's best friend Scarlett (Holden) finds out she's preggers after her boyfriend is killed in an accident. So Halley is none too receptive to romance when sensitive hunk Macon (Ford) comes around. Adapted from the young adult novels "Someone Like You" and "That Summer" by Sarah Dessen. **101m/C; VHS, DVD.** Mandy Moore; Allison Janney; Peter Gallagher; Trent Ford; Alexandra Holden; Dylan Baker; MacKenzie Astin; Connie Ray; Nina Foch; Sonja Smits; Mary Catherine Garrison; ***D:*** Clare Kilner; ***W:*** Neena Beber; ***C:*** Eric Alan Edwards; ***M:*** David Kitay.

How to Eat Fried Worms **1/2 2006 (PG)** New kid in school tries to put the class bully in his place by meeting the challenge of eating 10 worms—each served up in increasingly creative but decidedly unappetizing ways—in one day without ralphing. The 1973 kid-lit classic of the same name by Thomas Rockwell is sliced and diced to fit its over-the-top big-screen rendering (really, what kids know their way around a kitchen like these do?). But with decent performances by the kiddie cast, it's big-time gross-out fun for the younguns, tied up with a positive (if equally barf-inducing) message about standing up for yourself—if you can get to the end without wretching, that is. **98m/C; DVD.** Luke Benward; Hallie Kate Eisenberg; Alexander Gould; James Rebhorn; Adam Hicks; Austin Rogers; Tom Cavanagh; Kimberly Williams; ***D:*** Bob Dolman; ***W:*** Bob Dolman; ***C:*** Richard Rutkowski; ***M:*** Mark Mothersbaugh; Bob Mothersbaugh.

How to Eat Your Watermelon in White Company (and Enjoy It) **1/2 2005** Full-bodied documentary paying tribute to the life and times of Melvin Van Peebles, the famed black filmmaker most noted for 1971's "Sweet Sweetback's Baadasssss Song." Van Peebles was also an Air Force navigator, cable car operator, novelist in two languages, composer, recording artist, and floor trader at the American Stock Exchange. Title comes from an essay written by Van Peebles. **85m/C; On Demand.** ***D:*** Joe Angio; ***C:*** Michael Solomon; Joe Angio; ***M:*** Jeremy Parise.

How to Fall in Love **1/2 2012** Predictable Hallmark Channel rom com. Shy accountant Harold White (Mabius) has no confidence about his romantic life and hires a dating coach. This happens to be his high school crush, Annie Hayes (D'Orsay), but neither of them is willing to admit they have feelings for each other. **86m/C; DVD.** Eric Mabius; Brooke D'Orsay; Kathy Najimy; Gina Holden; Kurt Evans; ***D:*** Mark Griffiths; ***W:*** Bart Fisher; ***C:*** Eric Goldstein; ***M:*** Lawrence Shragge. **CABLE**

How to Frame a Figg **1/2 1971 (G)** Bookkeeper Hollis A. Figg (Knotts) is working at Dalton's corrupt city hall where he's setup to be the patsy in the fradulent doings of the mayor and city council. But his best friends Prentiss (Welker) and Ema Letha (Joyce) set out to prove the bumbler's innocence. **103m/C; VHS, DVD, Blu-Ray.** Don Knotts; Elaine Joyce; Frank Welker; Joe Flynn; Edward Andrews; Yvonne Craig; Parker Fennelly; Fay DeWitt; ***D:*** Alan Rafkin; ***W:*** George Tibbles; ***C:*** William Margulies; ***M:*** Vic Mizzy.

How to Get Ahead in Advertising **1989 (R)** A cynical, energetic satire about a manic advertising idea man who becomes so disgusted with trying to sell a pimple cream that he quits the business. Ultimately he grows a pimple of his own that talks and begins to take over his life. Acerbic and hilarious. **95m/C; VHS, DVD; Open Captioned.** *GB* Richard E. Grant; Rachel Ward; Susan Wooldridge; Mick Ford; Richard Wilson; John Shrapnel; Jacqueline Tong; ***D:*** Bruce Robinson; ***W:*** Bruce Robinson; ***C:*** Peter Hannan; ***M:*** David Dundas; Rick Wentworth.

How to Go Out on a Date in Queens **2006 (R)** Interesting cast, lame story involving three romantic crises set in a Queens restaurant called Mandatori's. Self-proclaimed dating expert Stan (Drillinger) sets up a double date with his widowed friend Artie (Estes) that turns into a disaster. Bookie Johnny (Alexander) finds out that he owes a lot of money to the Russian mob and must blow town just as his gal Ann Marie (Dunford) tells him she's pregnant. And assistant manager Elizabeth (Lynn) is sure her boyfriend Frankie (Morales) is going to propose but he wants to use their life savings to bet on the Super Bowl. **90m/C; DVD.** Rob(ert) Estes; Jason Alexander; Esai Morales; Brian Drillinger; Kimberly Williams; Christine Dunford; Meredith Scott Lynn; Ron Perlman; Alison Eastwood; Enrique Murciano; Bjorn Johnson; Michelle Danner; ***D:*** Michelle Danner; ***W:*** Richard Vetere; ***C:*** Jens Sturup; ***M:*** Shark.

How to Kill a Judge *Perche si uccide un magistrato; Why Does One Kill a Magistrate?* **1975** Giacomo (Nero) has just finished his new film about a judge in bed with the Mafia. A real judge orders it seized, but then dies in a manner similar to the film's character before it can be done. All of a sudden corrupt politicians come out of the woodwork, and Giacomo realizes he may have stepped in a nest of vipers as his friends start dying. **109m/C; DVD.** *IT* Franco Nero; Francoise Fabian; Pierluigi Apra; Giancarlo Badessi; Luciano Catenacci; Giorgio Cerioni; Tano Cimarosa; Eva Czemerys; Marco Guglielmi; Salvatore Moscardini; Renzo Palmer; Elio Zamuto; Gianni Zavota; Sergio Valentini; Elio Di Vincenzo; Vincenzo Norvese; Giovanni Lo Cascio; ***D:*** Damiano Damiani; ***W:*** Damiano Damiani; Enrico Dimarco; ***C:*** Mario Vulpiani; ***M:*** Riz Ortolani.

How to Kill Your Neighbor's Dog **2001 (R)** Critically acclaimed playwright Peter McGowen (Branagh) has fallen on hard times after a string of flops and is feeling the pressure from his sunny-natured wife Melanie (Wright Penn) to have kids. He's trying to fix his latest work but his neighbor's incessantly barking dog keeps him awake nights. The grouch also finds he must befriend a neighbor's daughter, Amy (Hofrichter), because he needs a model for the child role in his play, although Amy's presence does some not entirely unexpected reexamination of Peter and Melanie's marriage. Branagh is amusingly sharp-tongued but the film has a squishy center. **108m/C; VHS, DVD.** Kenneth Branagh; Robin Wright; Jared Harris; Suzi Hofrichter; Johnathon Schaech; Peter Riegert; Lynn Redgrave; ***D:*** Michael Kalesniko; ***W:*** Michael Kalesniko; ***C:*** Hubert Taczanowski; ***M:*** David Robbins.

How to Lose a Guy in 10 Days **2003 (PG-13)** Andie (Hudson) is a columnist who needs to date Ben (McConaughey) and then be so obnoxious that he will dump her in 10 days so she can write an article about it for Composure magazine. Ben has placed a bet with his colleagues that he can get any woman to fall in love with him in 10 days so he can get an account he wants. So while Andie is being the needy, clingy narcissic woman from hell, Ben patiently puts up with it for his own reasons. It's a universal rule that such contrivances in a romantic comedy guarantee that the two will genuinely fall in love. Unfortunately, the laughs are far too sparse and both characters too distasteful in their deceit for you to care. **112m/C; VHS, DVD, Blu-Ray.** Kate Hudson; Matthew McConaughey; Adam Goldberg; Michael Michele; Shalom Harlow; Bebe Neuwirth; Robert Klein; Kathryn Hahn; Thomas Lennon; Annie Parisse; ***D:*** Donald Petrie; ***W:*** Kristen Buckley; Brian Regan; Burr Steers; ***C:*** John Bailey; ***M:*** David Newman.

How to Lose Friends & Alienate People **1/2 2008 (R)** Smart aleck British writer Sydney Young (Pegg) struggles to fit in at his new job in a high-profile New York magazine. Constantly irritating his boss Lawrence (Huston) and eventually blowing a connection with one of Hollywood's most powerful publicists Eleanor Johnson (Anderson), Sydney can't go ten minutes without ruining someone's day. Unfortunately, Johnson represents Sophie Maes (Fox), an up-and-coming starlet who also happens to be the object of Sydney's lustful affection, leaving co-worker Alison (Dunst), who's in love with their boss, as his only hope in the Big Apple. Pegg is great, as usual, but miscast as a romantic lead, again. Funny in places, but the movie suffers from tone problems, unable to decide if it wants be a gooey romantic comedy or a vicious satire. Based on the 2001 memoir by Toby Young, who briefly worked for "Vanity Fair." **110m/C; Blu-Ray, On Demand.** *GB* Simon Pegg; Kirsten Dunst; Megan Fox; Jeff Bridges; Gillian Anderson; Danny Huston; Max Minghella; Miriam Margolyes; ***D:*** Robert B. Weide; ***W:*** Peter Straughan; ***C:*** Oliver Stapleton; ***M:*** David Arnold.

How to Lose Your Lover **1/2** *50 Ways to Leave Your Lover* **2004** Owen (Schneider) lives in L.A. and writes trashy celebrity biographies. He decides to break free and move to New York to find intellectual fulfillment. So he won't be tempted to return, Owen crudely breaks all ties to friends and family. Of course, just as he's leaving, he meets the girl of his dreams, Val (Westfeldt), and decides to put her through various romantic trials to see if it could be true love. Val should personally put Owen on that plane instead. **95m/C; DVD.** Paul Schneider; Jennifer Westfeldt; Poppy Montgomery; Tori Spelling; Fred Willard; ***D:*** Jodan Hawley; ***W:*** Jodan Hawley; ***C:*** Dino Parks; ***M:*** Stephen Trask.

How to Make a Monster **1958** In-joke from the creators of youth-oriented '50s AIP monster flicks; a mad makeup man's homebrew greasepaint brainwashes the actors. Disguised as famous monsters, they kill horror-hating movie execs. Mild fun if—and only if—you treasure the genre. Conway repeats his role as Teenage Frankenstein, but the studio couldn't get Michael Landon for the Teenage Werewolf. **73m/B; VHS, DVD.** Robert H. Harris; Paul Brinegar; Gary Conway; Gary Clarke; Malcolm Atterbury; Dennis Cross; John Ashley; Morris Ankrum; Walter Reed; Heather Ames; ***D:*** Herbert L. Strock.

How to Make a Monster **2001 (R)** Computer game company hires three ambitious programmers to finish a game and bring it to market in four weeks. A telemetry suit is used to render a 3-D version of the game's villain but a power-surge brings the program to life. Now the game's killer cyborg (AKA the telemetry suit) goes after the threesome, thinking they're players in the game. Basically takes only the title from the 1958 A.I.P. flick. **90m/C; VHS, DVD.** Steven Culp; Clea DuVall; Jason Marsden; Tyler Mane; Julie Strain; Karim Prince; ***D:*** George Huang; ***W:*** George Huang; ***C:*** Steven Finestone; ***M:*** David Reynolds. **CABLE**

How to Make an American Quilt **1/2 1995 (PG-13)** Slow-moving take on female friendship and marriage revolves around perennial grad student Finn (the mopey Ryder), who is frantic to both finish her third attempted thesis and to answer a marriage proposal from practically perfect beau Sam (Mulroney). She takes a summer refuge with her grandmother (Burstyn), where a variety of family friends work on her wedding quilt as they tell stories of loves lost and won. Lots of (somewhat overextended) flashbacks and with so many characters, naturally some get the short end of the script. Based on the novel by Whitney Otto. **109m/C; VHS, DVD, Blu-Ray.** Winona Ryder; Ellen Burstyn; Anne Bancroft; Lois Smith; Jean Simmons; Kate Nelligan; Maya Angelou; Alfre Woodard; Dermot Mulroney; Kate Capshaw; Rip Torn; Derrick O'Connor; Loren Dean; Samantha Mathis; Joanna Going; Tim Guinee; Johnathon Schaech; Claire Danes; Jared Leto; Esther Rolle; Melinda Dillon; Alicia (Lecy) Goranson; Maria Celedonio; Mykelti Williamson; ***D:*** Jocelyn Moorhouse; ***W:*** Jane Anderson; ***C:*** Janusz Kaminski; ***M:*** Thomas Newman.

How to Make Love to a Woman **2009 (R)** First, don't use this lame, predictable rom com as a template. Clueless Andy thinks he's not satisfying girlfriend Lauren in bed but she's really complaining about his lack of communications skills (he doesn't listen). He goes on a sexual info quest and she decides to break up, leave L.A., and take a new job in Chicago. **91m/C; DVD.** Krysten Ritter; Ian Somerhalder; Eugene Byrd; Ken Jeong; Josh Meyers; Lindsay Richards; James Kyson-Lee; ***D:*** Scott Culver; ***W:*** Dennis Kao; ***C:*** Dallas Sterling; ***M:*** Nathan Wong. **VIDEO**

How to Marry a Millionaire **1/2 1953** Three models pool their money and rent a lavish apartment in a campaign to trap millionaire husbands. Clever performances by three lead women salvage a vehicle intended primarily to bolster Monroe's career. The opening street scene, with the accompanying theme music, was a state-of-the-art achievement of screen and sound in the one of the first movies to be filmed in CinemaScope ("The Robe" was the first). Remake of "The Greeks Had a Word for Them." **96m/C; VHS, DVD, Blu-Ray.** Lauren Bacall; Marilyn Monroe; Betty Grable; William Powell; David Wayne; Cameron Mitchell; Charlotte Austin; ***D:*** Jean Negulesco; ***W:*** Nunnally Johnson; ***C:*** Joe MacDonald; ***M:*** Alfred Newman.

How to Murder Your Wife **1964** While drunk, a cartoonist marries an unknown woman and then frantically tries to think of ways to get rid of her—even contemplating murder. Frantic comedy is tailored for Lemmon. **118m/C; VHS, DVD, Blu-Ray.** Jack Lemmon; Terry-Thomas; Virna Lisi; Eddie Mayehoff; Sidney Blackmer; Claire Trevor; Mary Wickes; Jack Albertson; ***D:*** Richard Quine; ***W:*** George Axelrod; ***C:*** Harry Stradling, Sr.

How to Rob a Bank **2007** Tedious crime caper that tries too hard to be clever. Jinx (Stahl) and Jessica (Christensen) are trapped in a bank vault during a robbery they may or may not be a part of. The bank robbers are holding hostages in the lobby, the cops are outside, and the guy (Carradine) who planned the heist is none too pleased that things have gone wrong. **81m/C; DVD.** Nick Stahl; Erika Christensen; Gavin Rossdale; David Carradine; Terry Crews; Leo Fitzpatrick; Adriano Aragon; ***D:*** Andrew Jenkins; ***W:*** Andrew Jenkins; ***C:*** Joseph Meade; ***M:*** Didier Rachou.

How to Steal a Million *How to Steal a Million Dollars and Live Happily Ever After* **1966** Sophisticated comedy-crime caper involving a million-dollar heist of a sculpture in a Paris art museum. Hepburn and O'Toole are perfectly cast as partners in crime and Griffith gives a good performance as Hepburn's art-forging father. A charming, lightweight script and various Parisian locales combine for fun, above-average fluff. Based on the story "Venus Rising" by George Bradshaw. **127m/C; VHS, DVD, Blu-Ray.** Audrey Hepburn; Peter O'Toole; Eli Wallach; Hugh Griffith; Charles Boyer; Fernand Gravey; Marcel Dalio; Jacques Marin; ***D:*** William Wyler; ***W:*** Harry Kurnitz; ***C:*** Charles B(ryant) Lang, Jr.; ***M:*** John Williams.

How to Stuff a Wild Bikini **1965** Tired next to last feature in the overlong tradition of Frankie and Annette doing the beach thing, featuring a pregnant Funicello (though this is hidden and not part of the plot). Avalon actually has only a small role as the jealous boyfriend trying to see if Annette will remain faithful while he's away on military duty. Keaton is the witch doctor who helps Frankie keep Annette true. "Playboy" playmates wander about in small swimsuits, garage band extraordinare "The Kingsmen" play themselves, and Brian Wilson of the "Beach Boys" drops by. Followed by "Ghost in the Invisible Bikini," the only movie in the series that isn't on video. **90m/C; VHS, DVD, Blu-Ray.** Annette Funicello; Dwayne Hickman; Frankie Avalon; Beverly Adams; Buster Keaton; Harvey Lembeck; Mickey Rooney; Brian Donlevy; Jody McCrea; John Ashley; Marianne Gaba; Len Lesser; Irene Tsu; Bobbi Shaw; Luree Holmes; ***D:*** William Asher; ***W:*** William Asher; Leo Townsend; ***C:*** Floyd Crosby; ***M:*** Les Baxter.

How to Succeed in Business without Really Trying 🦴🦴🦴 1/2 **1967** Classic musical comedy about a window-washer who charms his way to the top of a major company. Robert Morse repeats his Tony winning Broadway role. Loosely based on a non-fiction book of the same title by Shepherd Mead, which Morse purchases on his first day of work. Excellent transfer of stage to film, with choreography by Moreda expanding Bob Fosse's original plan. Dynamite from start to finish. **121m/C; VHS, DVD, Blu-Ray.** Robert Morse; Michele Lee; Rudy Vallee; Anthony Teague; George Fenneman; Maureen Arthur; ***D:*** David Swift; ***W:*** David Swift; Abe Burrows; ***C:*** Burnett Guffey; ***M:*** Frank Loesser.

How to Survive a Plague 🦴🦴🦴 1/2 **2012** There have been dozens of documentaries about the AIDS crisis but few have more deftly put the viewer right on the front line of the battle for survival in a more complete and effective way. Using mostly archival footage of protests, meetings, conferences, and newsreels from the '80s, director France brilliantly captures a largely untold aspect of how the gay community banded together not merely for support but to fight a system that worked against them. Protests that led to increased speed in drug trials have a fire and passion to survive that's inspiring for any cause. **120m/C; DVD, Blu-Ray.** ***D:*** David France; ***W:*** David France; Todd Richman; Tyler H. Walk; ***C:*** Derek Wiesehahn; ***M:*** Stuart Bogie.

How To Talk To Girls At Parties 🦴🦴 1/2 **2017 (R)** An energetic adaptation of a Neil Gaiman short story about punk rock and aliens. In 1980s England, punk Enn (Sharp) meets alien Zan (Fanning) one night while looking for an after party. Zan is on vacation on Earth with members of her conformist alien race. Zan becomes fascinated by Enn, and spends two days exploring the city with him. Through Enn, Zan learns the power of youth rebellion. Enn's two friends also have their own life-changing alien encounters. Though ambitious and likable, the film derails in its second half as the story gets blurry while and the humor falls flat. **102m/C; DVD, Blu-Ray, Streaming.** *US UK* Elle Fanning; Nicole Kidman; Ruth Wilson; Alex Sharp; Abraham Lewis; ***D:*** John Cameron Mitchell; ***W:*** John Cameron Mitchell; Philippa Goslett; ***C:*** Frank G. DeMarco; ***M:*** Nico Muhly; Jamie Stewart.

How to Train Your Dragon 🦴🦴 1/2 **2010 (PG)** A 3D animated lesson in friendship, inspired by Cressida Cowell's multi-book children's series. Small and awkward, teenager Hiccup isn't much of a Viking to his warrior clan on the Isle of Berk, which is beset by fire-breathing dragons. Hiccup is more curious than frightened by the beasties and when he accidentally wounds a feared black Night Fury (that looks more like a flying gargoyle), he befriends and cares for the creature, which he calls Toothless, and then learns to ride. Good visuals and a simple story make for some fine family entertainment. **98m/C; DVD, Blu-Ray.** ***V:*** Jay Baruchel; Gerard Butler; America Ferrera; Jonah Hill; Christopher Mintz-Plasse; Craig Ferguson; Kristen Wiig; ***D:*** Chris (Christopher) Sanders; Dean DeBlois; ***W:*** Chris (Christopher) Sanders; Dean DeBlois; ***M:*** John Powell.

How to Train Your Dragon 2 🦴🦴 1/2 **2014 (PG)** Not quite as magical as the first film, the animated follow-up to the massive 2010 hit is still an impressive accomplishment if just for its visual beauty and the fact that its creators refuse to talk down to its target audience. Hiccup (voiced by Baruchel) is older and physically handicapped but remains confident as ever. Working with his dragon Toothless, he helps his people foil the nefarious plans of a dragon collector named Drago and even reunites with his mother in the process. Displacement, death, and power struggles are not common themes in kid's entertainment but this is a film that treats kids with uncommon trust. **102m/C; DVD, Blu-Ray.** ***V:*** Jay Baruchel; Gerard Butler; America Ferrera; Cate Blanchett; Jonah Hill; Christopher Mintz-Plasse; T.J. Miller; Kristen Wiig; Djimon Hounsou; Craig Ferguson; ***D:*** Dean DeBlois; ***W:*** Dean DeBlois; ***C:*** Roger Deakins; ***M:*** John Powell. Golden Globes '15: Animated Film.

How to Train Your Dragon: The Hidden World 🦴🦴🦴 **2019 (PG)** After the death of his father, Viking Hiccup (Baruchel) has become chief of Berk and faces challenges caring for the many dragons and people in his community. Hiccup's dragon Toothless was believed to be the last of his species until a female named Light Fury shows up. It is revealed that she is part of a plot by dragon hunter Grimmel the Grisley (Abraham) to kills as many dragons as he can, and the residents of Berk must act to protect the dragons. The final entry in the series offers a satisfying conclusion that includes beautiful visuals and an emotionally pleasing story. **104m/C; DVD, Blu-Ray.** *US JP* Jay Baruchel; America Ferrera; F. Murray Abraham; Cate Blanchett; Gerard Butler; ***D:*** Dean DeBlois; ***W:*** Dean DeBlois; ***M:*** John Powell.

How U Like Me Now? 🦴🦴🦴 **1992 (R)** Comedy set on Chicago's south side focuses on Thomas, an attractive but unmotivated guy with low earning potential, and his girl Valerie, a pretentious overachiever who wants much more than he's able to offer. Robert's second directorial effort offers a fresh look at African Americans on film with plenty of lively supporting characters and witty dialogue. Filmed on a $600,000 budget. **109m/C; VHS, DVD.** Darnell Williams; Salli Richardson-Whitfield; Daniel Gardner; Raymond Whitefield; Debra Crable; Jonelle Kennedy; Byron Stewart; Charnele Brown; Daryll Roberts; ***D:*** Daryll Roberts; ***W:*** Daryll Roberts; ***M:*** Kahil El Zabar; Chuck Webb.

How You Look to Me 🦴🦴 **2005 (R)** William Marshall (Romans), the son of a wealthy Kentucky horse racing family, reluctantly heads back to graduate school to prevent being cut off financially. He falls for classmate Jane Webb (Allen), who's not interested in a wannabe playboy, and is encouraged to find his potential by his writing teacher, Professor Driskoll (Langella). Shot on location at Churchill Downs. **101m/C; DVD.** Laura Allen; Frank Langella; Bruce Marshall Romans; Kevin Butler; David S. Jung; ***D:*** J. Miller Tobin; ***W:*** Bruce Marshall Romans; ***C:*** Michael Caporale; ***M:*** Veigar Margeirsson. **VIDEO**

Howard the Duck 🦴 **1986 (PG)** Big-budget Lucasfilm adaptation of the short-lived Marvel comic book about an alien, resembling a cigar-chomping duck, who gets sucked into a vortex, lands on Earth and saves it from the Dark Overlords. While he's at it, he befriends a nice young lady in a punk rock band and starts to fall in love. A notorious boxoffice bomb and one of the '80s' worst major films, although it seems to work well with children, given the simple storyline and good special effects. **111m/C; VHS, DVD, Blu-Ray.** Lea Thompson; Jeffrey Jones; Tim Robbins; Elizabeth Sagal; Thomas Dolby; Paul Guilfoyle; Dominique Davalos; Holly Robinson Peete; Tommy Swerdlow; Richard Edson; Miguel (Michael) Sandoval; David Paymer; ***V:*** Chip Zien; Richard Kiley; ***D:*** Willard Huyck; ***W:*** Willard Huyck; Gloria Katz; ***C:*** Richard H. Kline; ***M:*** John Barry; Sylvester Levay. Golden Raspberries '86: Worst Picture, Worst Screenplay.

Howard's End 🦴🦴🦴🦴 **1992 (PG)** E.M. Forster's 1910 novel about property, privilege, class differences, and Edwardian society is brought to enchanting life by the Merchant Ivory team. A tragic series of events occurs after two impulsive middle-class sisters, Margaret (Thompson) and Helen (Bonham Carter), become involved with the working class Basts (West, Duffett), and the wealthy Wilcox family (Hopkins, Redgrave). Tragedy aside, this is a visually beautiful effort with subtle performances where a glance or a gesture says as much as any dialog. The winner of numerous awards and wide critical acclaim. Thompson is especially notable as the compassionate Margaret, while Hopkins plays the repressed English gentleman brilliantly. **143m/C; VHS, DVD, Blu-Ray.** *GB* Anthony Hopkins; Emma Thompson; Helena Bonham Carter; Vanessa Redgrave; James Wilby; Samuel West; Jemma Redgrave; Nicola Duffett; Prunella Scales; Joseph Bennett; ***Cameo(s):*** Simon Callow; ***D:*** James Ivory; ***W:*** Ruth Prawer Jhabvala; ***C:*** Tony Pierce-Roberts; ***M:*** Richard Robbins. Oscars '92: Actress (Thompson), Adapt. Screenplay, Art Dir./Set Dec.; British Acad. '92: Actress (Thompson); Golden Globes '93: Actress--Drama (Thompson); L.A. Film Critics '92: Actress (Thompson); Natl. Bd. of Review '92: Actress (Thompson), Director (Ivory), Film; N.Y. Film Critics '92: Actress (Thompson); Natl. Soc. Film Critics '92: Actress (Thompson).

The Howards of Virginia 🦴🦴 1/2 *Tree of Liberty* **1940** A lavish Hollywood historical epic, detailing the adventures of a backwoodsman and the rich Virginia girl he marries as their families become involved in the Revolutionary War. **117m/B; VHS, DVD.** Cary Grant; Martha Scott; Cedric Hardwicke; Alan Marshal; Richard Carlson; Paul Kelly; Irving Bacon; Tom Drake; Anne Revere; Ralph Byrd; Alan Ladd; ***D:*** Frank Lloyd.

Howl 🦴🦴 1/2 **2010** Smart biopic about the early days of Beat Generation's unofficial spokesman, Allen Ginsberg (Franco). Focuses on the '50s as the insecure poet looks to make a name for himself, not yet the mystical outspoken frontman of a literary revolution, and meets Jack Karouac and now-legendary "On the Road" inspiration, Neal Cassady. The landmark 1957 trial of Ginsberg's "Howl" on obscenity charges is convincingly recreated word-for-word. Franco is restrained and understanding of the budding poet's fragile nature, as is the writing and directing team of Epstein and Friedman. Nothing radical here, but a must for anyone even mildly intrigued by this era. **84m/C; Blu-Ray.** James Franco; David Strathairn; Jon Hamm; Bob Balaban; Jeff Daniels; Mary-Louise Parker; Treat Williams; Alessandro Nivola; Todd Rotondi; John Prescott; Aaron Tveit; ***D:*** Robert Epstein; Jeffrey Friedman; ***W:*** Robert Epstein; Jeffrey Friedman; ***C:*** Edward Lachman; ***M:*** Carter Burwell.

The Howling 🦴🦴🦴 **1981 (R)** A pretty TV reporter takes a rest at a clinic and discovers slowly that its denizens are actually werewolves. Crammed with inside jokes, this horror comedy pioneered the use of the body-altering prosthetic makeup (by Rob Bottin) now essential for on-screen man-to-wolf transformations. At last count, followed by six sequels. **91m/C; VHS, DVD, Blu-Ray.** Dee Wallace; Patrick Macnee; Dennis Dugan; Christopher Stone; Belinda Balaski; Kevin McCarthy; John Carradine; Slim Pickens; Elisabeth Brooks; Robert Picardo; Dick Miller; Kenneth Tobey; Meshach Taylor; ***Cameo(s):*** John Sayles; Roger Corman; Forrest J Ackerman; ***D:*** Joe Dante; ***W:*** John Sayles; Terence H. Winkless; ***C:*** John Hora; ***M:*** Pino Donaggio.

Howling 2: Your Sister Is a Werewolf 🦴 *Howling 2: Stirba—Werewolf Bitch* **1985 (R)** A policeman (the brother of one of the first film's victims) investigates a Transylvanian werewolf-ridden castle and gets mangled for his trouble. Followed by four more sequels. **91m/C; VHS, DVD, Blu-Ray.** *FR IT* Sybil Danning; Christopher Lee; Annie McEnroe; Marsha A. Hunt; Reb Brown; Ferdinand "Ferdy" Mayne; Judd Omen; Jimmy Nail; ***D:*** Philippe Mora; ***W:*** Gary Brandner; Robert Sarno; ***C:*** Geoffrey Stephenson.

Howling 3: The Marsupials 🦴🦴 *The Marsupials: Howling 3* **1987 (PG-13)** Australians discover a pouch-laden form of lycanthrope. Third "Howling" (surprise), second from Mora and better than his first. **94m/C; VHS, DVD, Blu-Ray.** *AU* Barry Otto; Imogen Annesley; Dasha Blahova; Max Fairchild; Ralph Cotterill; Leigh Biolos; Frank Thring, Jr.; Michael Pate; ***D:*** Philippe Mora; ***W:*** Philippe Mora; ***C:*** Louis Irving; ***M:*** Allan Zavod.

Howling 4: The Original Nightmare 🦴 **1988 (R)** A woman novelist hears the call of the wild while taking a rest cure in the country. This werewolf tale has nothing to do with the other sequels. **94m/C; VHS, DVD.** Romy Windsor; Michael T. Weiss; Antony (Tony) Hamilton; Susanne Severeid; Lamya Derval; Dennis Folbigge; ***D:*** John Hough.

Howling 5: The Rebirth 🦴 **1989 (R)** The fifth in the disconnected horror series, in which a varied group of people stranded in a European castle are individually hunted down by evil. **99m/C; VHS, DVD.** Philip Davis; Victoria Catlin; Elizabeth She; Ben Cole; William Shockley; ***D:*** Neal Sundstrom; ***C:*** Arledge Armenaki.

Howling 6: The Freaks 🦴 1/2 **1990 (R)** Hideous werewolf suffers from multiple sequels, battles with vampire at freak show, and discovers that series won't die. Next up: "Howling 7: The Nightmare that Won't Go Away." **102m/C; VHS, DVD, Blu-Ray.** Brendan Hughes; Michelle Matheson; Sean Gregory Sullivan; Antonio Fargas; Carol Lynley; Jered Barclay; Bruce Payne; ***D:*** Hope Perello.

Howl's Moving Castle 🦴🦴 1/2 *Hauru no ugoku shiro* **2004 (PG)** More eye-popping anime from Miyazaki. Young wizard Howl (Bale) and his moveable castle travel around the countryside to avoid his enemy, the Witch of the Waste (Bacall). When Howl rescues Sophie (Mortimer) from thugs, the jealous Witch turns her into an old woman (now voiced by Simmons). Sophie appoints herself the castle housekeeper and encounters various strange characters and many adventures. There's a lot of plot but it's the visuals that will keep attention riveted. Adapted from Diana Wynne Jones' 2000 fantasy novel. There is also a Japanese-language version. **120m/C; DVD, Blu-Ray.** *JP* ***V:*** Emily Mortimer; Jean Simmons; Christian Bale; Lauren Bacall; Blythe Danner; Josh Hutcherson; Billy Crystal; Jena Malone; Liliana Mumy; ***D:*** Hayao Miyazaki; ***W:*** Hayao Miyazaki; ***C:*** Atsushi Okui; ***M:*** Joe Hisaishi. L.A. Film Critics '05: Orig. Score; N.Y. Film Critics '05: Animated Film.

H.P. Lovecraft's The Color Out of Space 🦴 1/2 *Die Farbe* **2010** Jonathan (Heise) is looking for news of his grandfather who disappeared in a small village after WWII. He discovers a blasted landscape and a secret involving a meteorite that landed long ago. **86m/C; DVD, Blu-Ray.** *GE* Ingo Heise; Philipp Jacobs; Olaf Kratke; ***D:*** Huan Vu; ***W:*** Huan Vu; ***C:*** Martin Kolbert. **VIDEO**

Huck and the King of Hearts 🦴🦴 1/2 **1993 (PG)** When a cardshark and his young friend Huck travel the country searching for Huck's long-lost grandfather, they find adventure everywhere from Hannibal, Missouri to L.A. to Vegas. Loose, contemporary adaptation of Mark Twain's "The Adventures of Huckleberry Finn." **103m/C; VHS, DVD.** Chauncey Leopardi; Graham Greene; Dee Wallace; Joe Piscopo; John Astin; Gretchen Becker; ***D:*** Michael Keusch; ***W:*** Christopher Sturgeon; ***M:*** Chris Saranec.

Huckleberry Finn 🦴🦴 **1974 (G)** The musical version of the Mark Twain story about the adventures a young boy and a runaway slave encounter along the Mississippi River. **114m/C; VHS, Blu-Ray, Streaming.** Jeff East; Paul Winfield; Harvey Korman; David Wayne; Arthur O'Connell; Gary Merrill; Natalie Trundy; Lucille Benson; ***D:*** J. Lee Thompson.

The Hucksters 🦴🦴🦴 **1947** Account of a man (Gable) looking for honesty and integrity in the radio advertising world and finding little to work with. All performances are excellent; but Greenstreet, as the tyrannical head of a soap company, is a stand out. Deborah Kerr's American debut. Based on the novel by Frederic Wakeman. **115m/B; VHS, DVD.** Clark Gable; Deborah Kerr; Sydney Greenstreet; Adolphe Menjou; Ava Gardner; Keenan Wynn; Edward Arnold; ***D:*** Jack Conway; ***W:*** Edward Chodorov; Luther Davis; George Wells; ***C:*** Harold Rosson; ***M:*** Lennie Hayton.

Hud 🦴🦴🦴🦴 **1963** Newman is a hard-driving, hard-drinking, woman-chasing young man whose life is a revolt against the principles of stern father Douglas. Neal is outstanding as the family housekeeper. Excellent photography. Based on the Larry McMurtry novel "Horseman, Pass By." **112m/B; VHS, DVD.** Paul Newman; Melvyn Douglas; Patricia Neal; Brandon de Wilde; John

Ashley; *D:* Martin Ritt; *W:* Irving Ravetch; Harriet Frank, Jr.; *C:* James Wong Howe; *M:* Elmer Bernstein. Oscars '63: Actress (Neal), B&W Cinematog., Support. Actor (Douglas); British Acad. '63: Actress (Neal); Natl. Bd. of Review '63: Actress (Neal), Support. Actor (Douglas); Natl. Film Reg. '18; N.Y. Film Critics '63: Actress (Neal), Screenplay.

Huddle 1932 Gary, Indiana steel-worker's son Tony Amatto (Navarro) gets a scholarship to Yale but can't overcome Ivy League prejudices even with his prowess on the gridiron. He sticks out the tough times with some difficulty, learns some hard lessons, and proves himself in his final big game. **104m/B; DVD.** Ramon Novarro; Madge Evans; Kane Richmond; Ralph Graves; Una Merkel; John Arledge; Frank Albertson; Martha Sleeper; *D:* Sam Wood; *W:* Robert Lee Johnson; Arthur S. Hyman; *C:* Harold Wenstrom.

Hudson Hawk 1991 (R) A big-budget star vehicle with little else going for it. Willis plays a master burglar released from prison, only to find himself trapped by the CIA into one last theft. Everyone in the cast tries to be extra funny, resulting in a disjointed situation where no one is. Weakly plotted, poorly paced. **95m/C; VHS, DVD, Blu-Ray.** Bruce Willis; Danny Aiello; Andie MacDowell; James Coburn; Sandra Bernhard; Richard E. Grant; Frank Stallone; *D:* Michael Lehmann; *W:* Steven E. de Souza; Daniel Waters; *C:* Dante Spinotti; *M:* Michael Kamen; Robert Kraft. Golden Raspberries '91: Worst Director (Lehmann), Worst Picture, Worst Screenplay.

Hudson's Bay 1/2 1940 Fictionalized adventure story about the founding of the Hudson Bay Trading Company. In 17th century Canada, fur trapper Radisson (Muni) has big plans for establishing a trading post. After teaching British aristocrat Edward Crewe (Sutton) some frontier skills, Crewe takes Radisson back to England with him to meet King Charles II (Price). The trapper convinces the king to fund his venture but there's trouble with the local tribe when Radisson gets started. **95m/B; DVD.** Paul Muni; John Sutton; Laird Cregar; Vincent Price; Gene Tierney; Morton Lowry; Nigel Bruce; Virginia Field; *D:* Irving Pichel; *W:* Lamar Trotti; *C:* J. Peverell Marley; George Barnes; *M:* Alfred Newman.

The Hudsucker Proxy 1993 (PG) In an effort to scare off would-be investors in a public stock offering dim bulb mailboy Robbins is installed as the Prez of Hudsucker Industries (in 1958) by Board Director Newman after corporate magnate Hudsucker (Durning) takes a swan dive from the 44th floor. First truly mainstream effort from the maverick Coen brothers is peppered with obscure references to numerous points on the historical map of cinematic style, and trots out an equally old but instantly recognizable story. Will delight Coen fans, but may be too dark for others. Destined to keep art history profs busy for decades. **115m/C; VHS, DVD, Blu-Ray.** Tim Robbins; Paul Newman; Jennifer Jason Leigh; Charles Durning; John Mahoney; Jim True-Frost; Bill Cobbs; Bruce Campbell; Steve Buscemi; *Cameo(s):* Peter Gallagher; *D:* Joel Coen; *W:* Ethan Coen; Joel Coen; Sam Raimi; *C:* Roger Deakins; *M:* Carter Burwell.

Hue and Cry 1947 Nobody believes a young boy when he discovers crooks are sending coded messages in a weekly children's magazine. A detective writer finally believes his story and they set off to capture the crooks. **82m/B; VHS, DVD, Blu-Ray.** *GB* Alastair Sim; Jack Warner; Frederick Piper; Jack Lambert; Joan Dowling; *D:* Charles Crichton.

Hugh Hefner: Once Upon a Time 1992 (R) Fascinating look at the "Bunny" king and Playboy Enterprises. His celebrated life of isolation and excess at the Playboy mansions is portrayed as is the founding of "Playboy" magazine in 1953 and the Playboy clubs (with their notorious Bunnies). Includes interviews, home movies, and photographs. Admiring yet not without a few sharp edges. **91m/C; VHS, DVD.** Hugh Hefner; *Nar:* James Coburn; *D:* Robert Heath.

Hugh Hefner: Playboy, Activist and Rebel 2009 (R) Canadian director Berman's puff-piece chronicling the ups, not many of the downs, of "Playboy" magazine founder Hugh Hefner. Traces his early life, his status as a ladies' man, and his work on various liberal causes. All his celeb friends chime in on his wonderfulness while only briefly covering the opposition from right-wing conservatives and feminist leaders—controversy that launched and has followed the brand's popularity. Nothing new here though Hef's history is fascinating and this one plays like his premature eulogy. **124m/C; On Demand.** Hugh Hefner; Joan Baez; Tony Bennett; Pat Boone; Jim Brown; James Caan; Dick Cavett; Tony Curtis; Jesse Jackson; George Lucas; Bill Maher; Jenny McCarthy; Pete Seeger; Gene Simmons; David Steinberg; Shannon Tweed; Mike Wallace; *D:* Brigitte Berman; *W:* Brigitte Berman; *C:* John Westheuser; *M:* James Mark Stewart.

Hugo 2011 (PG) Technically well-crafted and a daring use of 3D, director Scorsese's adaptation of Brian Selznick's "The Invention of Hugo Cabret" feels somewhat sterile given its fairy tale story but is nonetheless evidence of a great filmmaker expanding his craft. The title character (Butterfield) lives in a Parisian train station and stumbles upon a great mystery when he realizes there's a connection between the automaton found by his father (Law) and the toymaker (Kingsley) who works in the station. It's not unlike a snow globe, glorious to look at but we never get to live it. **127m/C; DVD, Blu-Ray.** Asa Butterfield; Chloë Grace Moretz; Christopher Lee; Ben Kingsley; Helen McCrory; Richard Griffiths; Ray Winstone; Emily Mortimer; Sacha Baron Cohen; Jude Law; Frances de la Tour; Michael Stuhlbarg; *D:* Martin Scorsese; *W:* John Logan; *C:* Robert Richardson; *M:* Howard Shore. Oscars '11: Art Dir./Set Dec., Cinematog., Sound, Sound FX Editing, Visual FX; Golden Globes '12: Director (Scorsese).

Hugo Pool 1/2 1997 (R) Pool cleaner Hugo Dugay (Milano) has to clean the pools of 44 backyard eccentrics. Reluctantly, she must enlist the aid of her gambler mom (Moriarty) and drug addict father (McDowell). Bizarre characters abound, including Downey Jr. overacting as Hungarian film director Franz Mazur, whose accent changes with each line. Most interesting is Dempsey as ALS-afflicted Floyd Galen. The romance between Floyd and Hugo supplies the most sensitive and well-acted sequences. Disappointing, long-anticipated outing from director Downey Sr. (this is his first directorial effort in six years) who shared writing duties with wife Laura, who died of ALS in 1994. **92m/C; VHS, DVD.** Alyssa Milano; Patrick Dempsey; Robert Downey, Jr.; Malcolm McDowell; Cathy Moriarty; Sean Penn; Richard Lewis; Chuck Barris; *D:* Robert Downey; *W:* Laura Downey; *C:* Joe Montgomery; *M:* Danilo Perez.

Hula Girls *Hula garu* 2006 Based on the true story of the rural Japanese coal mining town of Iwaki in 1965. After the Korean War, demand for coal has plummeted, and Iwaki is dying. To rescue their city the natives decide to rebuild as a tourist town with a Hawaiian themed spa resort using the hot springs that were the bane of the mine. But this means they need Hula girls, and Japan is still pretty conservative. One of the female characters is based on famous hula dancer Kaleinani Hayakawa who founded a hula school in Japan, and also did the choreography for the film. **120m/C; DVD.** *JP* Etsushi Toyokawa; Yu Aoi; Ittoku Kishibe; Yasuko Matsuyuki; Shizuyo Yamazaki; Eri Tokunaga; Junko Fuji; *D:* Sang-il Lee; *W:* Sang-il Lee; Daisuke Habara; *C:* Hideo Yamamoto; *M:* Jake Shimabakuro.

Hulk 1/2 2003 (PG-13) Hulk SMASH! Hulk explore Oedipal relationship. Hulk confused! Scientist Bruce Banner (Bana) gets zapped by gamma rays during an experiment gone wrong, and finds out that it's harder than ever to control his temper. Ang Lee classes up the summer superhero blockbuster genre by going beyond the special effects and action (but he doesn't leave 'em behind, either) to explore Banner's troubled relationships with girlfriend/colleague Betty (Connolly) and wacked-out former scientist dad David (Nolte). The extra depth may be jarring for the target fan-boy audience, but it should play better to people looking for a little thought with their thrills. Solid performances by Bana, Connolly, and Elliot as Betty's aloof, gung-ho military man father help Lee pull off the more angst-ridden moments. **138m/C; VHS, DVD, Blu-Ray, HD-DVD.** Eric Bana; Jennifer Connelly; Josh(ua) Lucas; Sam Elliott; Nick Nolte; Paul Kersey; Cara Buono; Mike Erwin; Celia Weston; *Cameo(s):* Lou Ferrigno; Stan Lee; *D:* Ang Lee; *W:* James Schamus; Michael France; John Turman; *C:* Frederick Elmes; *M:* Danny Elfman.

Hullabaloo 1/2 1940 MGM musical/comedy finds ex-vaudevillian Frank Merriweather (Morgan) trying to restore his career by going into radio. Frank is also trying to reunite with his three estranged children while fending off his three ex-wives who want their alimony. **78m/B; DVD.** Frank Morgan; Dan Dailey; Virginia Grey; Billie Burke; Donald Meek; Nydia Westman; Sara Haden; Reginald Owen; Connie Gilchrist; *D:* Edwin L. Marin; *W:* Nat Perrin; *C:* Charles Lawton, Jr.

Hullabaloo over Georgie & Bonnie's Pictures 1/2 1978 A young maharajah has inherited a priceless collection of Indian miniature paintings he doesn't appreciate and which his greedy sister is anxious for him to sell. They're beseiged by art dealers and collectors who learn about the treasure trove and will do anything to possess it. Among them are the British Ashcroft, who wants the art for the British Museum, and competing American collector Pine. **85m/C; VHS, DVD.** *GB* Victor Banerjee; Aparna Sen; Larry Pine; Saeed Jaffrey; Peggy Ashcroft; *D:* James Ivory; *W:* Ruth Prawer Jhabvala; *C:* Walter Lassally. **TV**

Human Beasts 1980 Jewel robbers face a tribe of hungry cannibals. **90m/C; VHS, DVD, Blu-Ray.** *SP JP* Paul Naschy; Eiko Nagashima; *D:* Paul Naschy; *W:* Paul Naschy.

The Human Centipede: First Sequence WOOF! 2010 Whatever Dutch director Six's intentions, this freakish fetish exploitation flick is as icky as you might suspect from its title. A couple of female American tourists get lost traveling in some German woods and find the home of mad Dr. Heiter who could outdo the Nazis for loathsome medical experiments. The Americans, along with a Japanese hostage, are to be subjected to some truly disgusting surgery to fulfill Heiter's twisted fantasies. English, German, and Japanese with subtitles. **92m/C; DVD, Blu-Ray.** *NL* Dieter Laser; Ashley Williams; Ashlynn Yennie; Akhiro Kitamura; Andreas Leupold; *D:* Tom Six; *W:* Tom Six; *C:* Goof de Koning; *M:* Patrick Savage; Holeg Spies.

The Human Centipede 2: Full Sequence WOOF! 2011 This piece of black-and-white offal is even more vile, perverted, and pretentious than the first flick. The nominal plot has crazy, obese mama's boy Martin becoming obsessed with the movie and deciding to make his own human centipede. He leaves a bunch of corpses behind (including his unlamented mom) and then collects 12 unfortunates for his experiments. Writer/director Six insists it'll be a trilogy so there's more stupid grossness to follow. **88m/B; DVD, Blu-Ray.** *GB* Laurence R. Harvey; Vivien Bridson; Bill Hutchens; *D:* Tom Six; *W:* Tom Six; *C:* David Meadows; *M:* James Edward Barker.

The Human Centipede 3: The Final Sequence WOOF! *The Human Centipede 3* 2015 One of the most remarkable wastes of time, digital camera HD space, acting, sets, etc. in the history of movies. This film is the equivalent of Internet trolling. Tom Six doesn't want you to like his horror films. He wants to annoy you. He wants to make critics angry. And so he's made a meta-movie about a warden who takes inspiration from Six's Human Centipede films and creates his own 500-person chain in a prison yard. Reportedly the last film in the Human Centipede series, it should also be the last film that everyone involved in its production is allowed to make. **102m/C; DVD, Blu-Ray.** Bree Olson; Eric Roberts; Tom Six; Robert LaSardo; Tommy (Tiny) Lister; *D:* Tom Six; *W:* Tom Six; *C:* David Meadows; *M:* Misha Segal.

The Human Comedy 1/2 1943 A small-town boy experiences love and loss and learns the meaning of true faith during WWII. Straight, unapologetically sentimental version of the William Saroyan novel. **117m/B; VHS, DVD.** Mickey Rooney; Frank Morgan; James Craig; Fay Bainter; Ray Collins; Donna Reed; Van Johnson; Barry Nelson; Robert Mitchum; Jackie "Butch" Jenkins; *D:* Clarence Brown; *W:* William Saroyan; *C:* Harry Stradling, Sr. Oscars '43: Story.

The Human Condition: A Soldier's Prayer 1961 A Japanese pacifist escapes from his commanders and allows himself to be captured by Russian troops, hoping for better treatment as a P.O.W. The final part of the trilogy preceded by "The Human Condition: No Greater Love" and "The Human Condition: Road to Eternity." In Japanese with English subtitles. **190m/B; VHS, DVD.** *JP* Tatsuya Nakadai; Michiyo Aratama; Yusuke Kawazu; Tamao Nakamura; Chishu Ryu; Taketoshi Naito; Reiko Hitomi; Kyoko Kishida; Keijiro Morozumi; Koji Kiyomura; Nobuo Kaneko; Fujio Suga; *D:* Masaki Kobayashi.

The Human Condition: No Greater Love 1958 First of a three-part series of films. A pacifist is called into military service and subsequently sent to a run a military mining camp. A gripping look at one man's attempt to retain his humanity in the face of war. Followed by "The Human Condition: Road to Eternity" and "The Human Condition: A Soldier's Prayer." In Japanese with English subtitles. **200m/B; VHS, DVD.** *JP* Tatsuya Nakadai; Michiyo Aratama; So Yamamura; Eitaro (Sakae, Saka Ozawa) Ozawa; Akira Ishihama; Chikage Awashima; Ineko Arima; Keiji Sada; Shinji Nambara; Seiji Miyaguchi; Toru Abe; Masao Mishima; Eijiro Tono; Yasushi Nagata; Yoshio Kosugi; *D:* Masaki Kobayashi; *W:* Masaki Kobayashi; Zenzo Matsuyama; *C:* Yoshio Miyajima; *M:* Chuji Kinoshita.

The Human Condition: Road to Eternity *No Greater Love; Ningen No Joken* 1959 A Japanese pacifist is on punishment duty in Manchuria where he is beaten by sadistic officers who try to destroy his humanity. The second part of the trilogy, preceded by "The Human Condition: No Greater Love" and followed by "The Human Condition: A Soldier's Prayer." In Japanese with English subtitles. **180m/B; VHS, DVD.** *JP* Tatsuya Nakadai; Michiyo Aratama; Kokinji Katsura; Jun Tatara; Michio Minami; Keiji Sada; Minoru Chiaki; Ryohei Uchida; Kan Yanagidani; Kenjiro Uemura; Yusuke Kawazu; Susumu Fujita; *D:* Masaki Kobayashi; *W:* Masaki Kobayashi; Zenzo Matsuyama; *C:* Yoshio Miyajima; *M:* Chuji Kinoshita.

The Human Contract 2008 (R) Pinkett Smith makes her screenwriting and directing debut. Uptight businessman Julian (Clarke) allows his life to be turned upside down when he meets beautiful Michael (Vega), a woman who believes in abandon rather than control. **107m/C; DVD.** Jason Clarke; Paz Vega; Idris Elba; Steven Brand; Joanna Cassidy; Ted Danson; T.J. Thyne; Jada Pinkett Smith; *D:* Jada Pinkett Smith; *W:* Jada Pinkett Smith; *C:* Darren Genet; *M:* Anthony Marinelli.

Human Desire 1/2 1954 Femme fatale Grahame and jealous husband Crawford turn out the lights on Crawford's boss (seems there's some confusion about how Miss Gloria managed to convince the guy to let her hubby have his job back). Ford's wise to them but plays see no evil because he's gone crackers for Grahame, who by now has decided she'd like a little help to rid herself of an unwanted husband. Bleak, melodramatic, full of big heat, its Lang through and through. Based on the Emile Zola novel "La Bete Humaine," which inspired Renoir's 1938 telling as well. **90m/B; VHS, DVD.** Glenn Ford; Gloria Grahame; Broderick Crawford; Edgar Buchanan; Kathleen Case; *D:* Fritz Lang; *C:* Burnett Guffey.

Human Desires 1997 (R) A lingerie beauty contest provides a bevy of beauties for P.I. Dean Thomas (Noble) to investigate when one of them turns up dead. The death is ruled a suicide but a fellow contestant thinks it was murder and Thomas is around to check things out—very closely. **95m/C; VHS, DVD.** Shannon Tweed; Christian Noble; Dawn Ann Billings; Duke Stroud; *D:* Ellen Earnshaw; *W:* Todd Smith; *C:* Carl Oakwood; *M:* Ed Korvin.

The Human Duplicators 1/2 1964 Kiel is an alien who has come to Earth to make androids out of important folk, thus allowing the "galaxy beings" to take over. Cheap stuff, but earnest performances make this more fun than it should be. **82m/C; VHS, DVD.** George Nader; Barbara Nichols; George Macready; Dolores Faith; Hugh Beaumont; Richard Kiel; Richard Arlen; *D:* Hugo Grimaldi.

The Human Factor ♂ 1/2 **1975 (R)** Kennedy stars as a computer expert who tracks down his family's murderers using technology. Bloody and violent. **96m/C; VHS, DVD.** *GB IT* George Kennedy; John Mills; Raf Vallone; Rita Tushingham; Barry Sullivan; Arthur Franz; *D:* Edward Dmytryk; *M:* Ennio Morricone.

The Human Factor ♂♂ 1/2 **1979 (R)** Unexciting spy caper has a British Secret Service agent (Williamson) betraying his country in order to aid a friend. As a result of his actions an innocent man is killed and Williamson is forced to defect to the Soviet Union. Based on a novel by Graham Greene. **115m/C; DVD.** *UK* Nicol Williamson; Richard Attenborough; John Gielgud; Derek Jacobi; Robert Morley; Ann Todd; Richard Vernon; Iman; *D:* Otto Preminger; *W:* Tom Stoppard; *C:* Mike Molloy; *M:* Gary Logan; Richard Logan.

The Human Monster ♂♂ 1/2 *Dark Eyes of London* **1939** Scotland Yard inspector investigates five drownings of the blind patients a phony Dr. Orloff (Lugosi) is exploiting for insurance money. Superior Lugosi effort that's modestly violent and tasteless. Based on the Edgar Wallace novel. **73m/B; VHS, DVD, Blu-Ray.** *GB* Bela Lugosi; Hugh Williams; Greta Gynt; *D:* Walter Summers; *W:* Walter Summers.

Human Nature ♂♂ 1/2 **2002 (R)** Offbeat and charming screwball comedy stars Arquette as Lila, a sweet kid with a hairy problem—extreme hirsutism—which forces her to become a reclusive nature writer living in the woods. Her sex drive finally forces her back to civilization, where she finds a sympathetic electrologist (Perez) who sets her up with repressed scientist Nathan (Robbins). As a result of his uber-repressed upbringing, Nathan is on a quest to teach mice good table manners, but when the couple finds a woods-dwelling wildman (Ifans), he has something new to experiment on and tries to teach nature-boy to be civilized, despite his raging libido. Eccentric feature debut of Gallic director Gondry is a quirky study of three characters at odds with their own true nature and trying to fit into a judgmental society. In keeping with the offbeat humor of writer/co-producer Kaufman's "Being John Malkovich." **96m/C; VHS, DVD.** *US FR* Tim Robbins; Rhys Ifans; Patricia Arquette; Miranda Otto; Robert Forster; Mary Kay Place; Miguel (Michael) Sandoval; Toby Huss; Peter Dinklage; Rosie Perez; *D:* Michel Gondry; *W:* Charlie Kaufman; *C:* Tim Maurice-Jones; *M:* Graeme Revell. Natl. Bd. of Review '02: Screenplay.

The Human Race ♂ **2014** After a sudden, unexplained burst of light, a group of Los Angeles strangers are magically transported to a battle zone and telepathically given instructions to finish this death race or be killed. A couple of Army vets, a pro cyclist, and two deaf friends emerge as the strongest contenders, but must then face gangbangers who take pleasure in causing extreme pain. Production took over three years, as actors came and went, leaving gaping gaps in logic along the way. This inept low budget sci-fi spin on survival thrillers plays less like "Hunger Games", and more like straight-to-Mystery Science Theater 3000 fodder. **87m/C; DVD.** *UK* Eddie McGee; Paul McCarthy-Boyington; Fred Coury; *D:* Paul Hough; *W:* Paul Hough; *C:* Matt Fore; *M:* Marinho Nobre.

The Human Stain ♂♂ **2003 (R)** Anthony Hopkins is a professor in the middle of a racial controversy who's passing as a white Jew and Nicole Kidman is the sorrowful, down-on-her-luck janitor with whom he becomes involved in Benton's watered-down adaptation of Philip Roth's 2000 novel. The book is an angry expose of America's struggles with issues of race, age, and sexuality, but the film falls short of conveying that anger. Excellent cast does what it can to compensate. **106m/C; VHS, DVD, Blu-Ray.** Anthony Hopkins; Nicole Kidman; Ed Harris; Gary Sinise; Wentworth Miller; Harry J. Lennix; Anna Deavere Smith; Jacinda Barrett; Phyllis Newman; Kerry Washington; Margo Martindale; Ron Canada; Mili Avital; Mimi Kuzyk; *D:* Robert Benton; *W:* Nicholas Meyer; *C:* Jean-Yves Escoffier; *M:* Rachel Portman.

Human Traffic ♂ 1/2 **1999 (R)** It's kinda like "Groove" only these club kids are spending their oblivious weekend in Cardiff, Wales. They have various personal dilemmas that they try to overcome by taking E and dancing the hours away and they're all one step away from insufferable. Writer/director Kerrigan was just 25 when he recorded his debut film so he's got time to grow up. Or maybe the Hound is just getting old. **84m/C; VHS, DVD.** *GB* John Simm; Lorraine Pilkington; Shaun Parkes; Nicola Reynolds; Danny Dyer; Dean Davies; *D:* Justin Kerrigan; *W:* Justin Kerrigan; *C:* David Bennett; *M:* Matthew Herbert; Rob Mellow.

Human Trafficking ♂♂ 1/2 **2005** Kate Morozov (Sorvino) and Bill Meehan (Sutherland) are agents for Immigrations and Customs Enforcement. They're trying to bring down Russian gangster Sergei (Carlyle) who poses as the owner of a modeling agency while actually running a sex-slave ring, bringing in desperate young women from Eastern Europe to work for him. Tawdry and moralizing but still compelling. Montreal substitutes for Washington, D.C. **180m/C; DVD.** *US CA* Mira Sorvino; Donald Sutherland; Robert Carlyle; Remy Girard; Isabelle Blais; Vlasta Vrana; Celine Bonnier; *D:* Christian Duguay; *W:* Carol Doyle; Agatha Dominik; *C:* Christian Duguay; *M:* Normand Corbeil. **CABLE**

Humanity ♂♂ *L'Humanite* **1999** Overly long and raw look at a few days in the life naive cop Pharon De Winter (Schotte), who suffers from an overabundance of empathy for the pain of others. His latest assignment is certain to plunge Pharon into despair as he investigates the rape and murder of an 11-year-old girl. Pharon is also hopelessly attracted to his young neighbor Domino (Caneele), whose sexual interludes with boyfriend Joseph (Tullier) leave nothing to the viewers' imagination. French with subtitles. **142m/C; VHS, DVD, Blu-Ray.** *FR* Emmanuel Schotte; Severine Caneele; Philippe Tullier; Ghislain Ghesquiere; Ginette Allegre; *D:* Bruno Dumont; *W:* Bruno Dumont; *C:* Yves Cape; *M:* Richard Cuvillier. Cannes '99: Actor (Schotte), Actress (Caneele), Grand Jury Prize.

Humanoids from the Deep **WOOF!** *Monster* **1980 (R)** Mutated salmon-like monsters rise from the depths of the ocean and decide to chomp on some bikinied babes. Violent and bloody. **81m/C; VHS, DVD, Blu-Ray.** Doug McClure; Ann Turkel; Vic Morrow; Cindy Weintraub; Anthony Penya; Denise Balik; Hoke Howell; Meegan King; Rob Bottin; *D:* Barbara Peeters; *W:* Frank Arnold; Frederick James; Martin B. Cohen; *C:* Daniel Lacambre; *M:* James Horner.

Humanoids from the Deep ♂♂ *Roger Corman Presents: Humanoids from the Deep* **1996 (R)** Remake of the 1980 Corman culter finds fishery manager Wade Parker (Carradine) and researcher Dr. Drake (Samms) dealing with a coastal town's battle against killers whose DNA has been genetically combined with that of fish. When the fish monsters escape the lab, their mutations are further altered by toxic waste and they go on a rampage. **90m/C; VHS, DVD.** Robert Carradine; Emma Samms; Mark Rolston; Clint Howard; Kaz Garas; Warren Burton; Bert Remsen; *D:* Jeff Yonis; *W:* Jeff Yonis; *C:* Christopher Baffa; *M:* Christopher Lennertz. **CABLE**

Humble Pie ♂♂ *American Fork* **2007** Melancholy rules in this quirky comedy. Grocery store clerk Tracy Orbison has a huge heart and a binge-eating body to match. Mom Agnes is bitter and nagging and his sister Peggy is more than a little odd, while dad is long gone. His life gets a shake-up (in a low-key way) when Tracy decides to take acting classes with vain teacher Truman Hope and learns to stand up for himself. **84m/C; DVD.** Hubbel Palmer; Kathleen Quinlan; Mary Lynn Rajskub; William Baldwin; Vincent Caso; Nick Lashaway; Bruce McGill; *D:* Chris Bowman; *W:* Hubbel Palmer; *C:* Douglas Chamberlain; *M:* Bobby Johnston.

Humboldt County ♂ 1/2 **2008 (R)** A failing grade leads to stodgy medical student Peter getting drunk in a club where he attracts the attention of singer Bogart. He later wakes up in a northern California community of hippies and pot farmers who live off-the-grid. Peter is offered a place to stay by Jack and his wife Rosie, whose son Max runs the family's business. Peter decides to hang out and then gets involved in a family conflict when Max plans a big score that could bring too much interest from the DEA. **97m/C; DVD.** Fairuza Balk; Brad Dourif; Frances Conroy; Chris Messina; Jeremy Strong; Madison Davenport; Peter Bogdanovich; *D:* Darren Grodsky; Danny Jacobs; *W:* Darren Grodsky; Danny Jacobs; *C:* Ernest Holtzman; *M:* Izler.

The Hummingbird Project ♂♂ **2018 (R)** In 2011, Eva Torres (Hayek) is a tough power broker who hires the best traders and programmers, including coder Anton Zaleski (Skarsgard) and his obnoxious cousin Vincent (Eisenberg), for her trading company. Eva is upset when the pair abruptly quit, but unknown to her, they have gained financing for a fiber optic cable project that will allow them to get trading data quicker than Eva. It comes to light that the data will not be transmitted any faster unless Anton can improve his code, which Eva claims to own. The solid performances by the leads can't overcome this disorganized mess. **111m/C; DVD, Blu-Ray.** *BE CA* Jesse Eisenberg; Alexander Skarsgård; Salma Hayek; Michael Mando; Johan Heldenbergh; *D:* Kim Nguyen; *W:* Kim Nguyen; *C:* Nicolas Bolduc; *M:* Yves Gourmeur.

Humongous **WOOF!** **1982 (R)** Brain-dead bevy of teens shipwreck on an island where they encounter a deranged mutant giant who must kill to survive. You'll be rooting for the monster. **93m/C; VHS, DVD, Blu-Ray.** *CA* Janet (Johnson) Julian; David Wallace; Janit Baldwin; Joy Boushel; Page Fletcher; *D:* Paul Lynch; *W:* William Gray; *C:* Brian R.R. Hebb.

Humor Me ♂♂ 1/2 **2017** Narcissistic, undisciplined playwright Nick (Clement) has reached career and personal lows. The production of his latest play was shut down because he could not commit to an ending, and his wife is leaving him for a French billionaire and taking their son Gabe (Lappin). Unable to pay his own rent, he moves in with his father Bob (Gould) at his retirement community. There, Nick gains personal insight, self-respect, and opens himself up to others. Amidst many mediocre performances and stereotypical characters, only Clement's transcends the uninspired script. **93m/C; DVD, Blu-Ray.** Jemaine Clement; Elliott Gould; Ingrid Michaelson; Maria Dizzia; Priscilla Lopez; *D:* Sam Hoffman; *W:* Sam Hoffman; *C:* Seamus Tierney; *M:* Gabriel Mann.

Humoresque ♂♂♂ 1/2 **1946** Talented but struggling young musician Paul Boray (Garfield) finds a patron in the married, wealthy, and older Helen Wright (Crawford). His appreciation is not as romantic as she hoped. Stunning performance from Crawford, with excellent supporting cast (Levant supplies the witty comebacks), including a young Robert Blake as a young Paul. Fine music sequences (Isaac Stern dubbed the violin), and lush production values. **123m/B; VHS, DVD.** Joan Crawford; John Garfield; Oscar Levant; J. Carrol Naish; Joan Chandler; Tom D'Andrea; Peggy Knudsen; Ruth Nelson; Craig Stevens; Paul Cavanagh; Richard Gaines; John Abbott; Robert (Bobby) Blake; *D:* Jean Negulesco; *W:* Clifford Odets; Zachary Gold; *C:* Ernest Haller; *M:* Franz Waxman. Natl. Film Reg. '15.

Humpday ♂ 1/2 **2009 (R)** Best pals in college, Ben and Andrew have drifted apart over the last decade. Ben has a job, wife, and home in Seattle while Andrew has lived the life of a deliberately scruffy vagabond artist. When Andrew suddenly turns up, they fall back into their macho male-bonding pretensions. Andrew takes Ben to a bohemian party where they hear about Humpfest, an experimental homemade porn film festival and, during their drunken evening, they vow to enter the contest with the two straight men having sex together on camera. Male bluster makes them determined not to wimp out despite their increasing discomfort, but how is Ben going to explain such shenanigans to his exasperated wife Anna? **94m/C; On Demand.** Mark Duplass; Joshua Leonard; Alycia Delmore; Trina Willard; Lynn Shelton; *D:* Lynn Shelton; *W:* Lynn Shelton; *C:* Benjamin Kasulke; *M:* Vinny Smith.

The Hunchback ♂♂ 1/2 **1997** Cable version of Victor Hugo's ever-popular "The Hunchback of Notre Dame." In 15th-century Paris, hunchbanked Notre Dame bell-ringer Quasimodo (Patinkin) loves spirited and kind gypsy Esmeralda (Hayek), who's the lustful obsession of evil archdeacon Frollo (Harris). Properly melodramatic, with Harris stealing the film as the cold cleric. **98m/C; DVD.** Mandy Patinkin; Richard Harris; Salma Hayek; Jim Dale; Edward Atterton; *D:* Peter Medak; *W:* John Fasano; *C:* Elemer Ragalyi; *M:* Ed Shearmur. **CABLE**

The Hunchback of Notre Dame ♂♂♂ **1923** The first film version of Victor Hugo's novel about the tortured hunchback bellringer of Notre Dame Cathedral, famous for the contortions of Lon Chaney's self-transformations via improvised makeup. Also available at 68 minutes. **100m/B; Silent; VHS, DVD, Blu-Ray.** Lon Chaney, Sr.; Patsy Ruth Miller; Norman Kerry; Ernest Torrence; Kate Lester; Brandon Hurst; *D:* Wallace Worsley, II; *W:* Edward T. Lowe; *C:* Tony Kornman; Robert S. Newhard.

The Hunchback of Notre Dame ♂♂♂♂ **1939** Best Hollywood version of the Victor Hugo classic, infused with sweep, sadness, and an attempt at capturing a degree of spirited, Hugoesque detail. Laughton is Quasimodo, a deformed Parisian bellringer, who provides sanctuary to young gypsy Esmeralda (O'Hara) accused by church officials of being a witch. The final scene of the townspeople storming the cathedral remains a Hollywood classic. Great performances all around; the huge facade of the Notre Dame cathedral was constructed on a Hollywood set for this film. Remake of several earlier films, including 1923's Lon Chaney silent, and followed by several remakes for both the big screen (included an animated Disney version) and for TV. **117m/B; VHS, DVD, Blu-Ray.** Charles Laughton; Maureen O'Hara; Edmond O'Brien; Cedric Hardwicke; Thomas Mitchell; George Zucco; Alan Marshal; Walter Hampden; Harry Davenport; Curt Bois; George Tobias; Rod La Rocque; *D:* William Dieterle; *W:* Sonya Levien; Bruno Frank; *C:* Joseph August; *M:* Alfred Newman.

The Hunchback of Notre Dame ♂♂ 1/2 *Notre Dame de Paris* **1957 (PG)** Slow retelling of the Victor Hugo novel, filmed entirely in France in CinemaScope. Quinn's the tragic Quasimodo with bombshell Lollobrigida appropriatley hot-blooded as gypsy Esmerelda. **104m/C; VHS, DVD.** *FR* Anthony Quinn; Gina Lollobrigida; Alain Cuny; Jean Danet; Robert Hirsch; Jean Tissier; *D:* Jean Delannoy; *W:* Jacques Prevert; Jean Aurenche; *C:* Michel Kelber; *M:* Georges Auric.

The Hunchback of Notre Dame ♂♂♂ *Hunchback* **1982 (PG)** It's not often that a classic novel is remade into a classic movie that's remade into a made-for-TV reprise, and survives its multiple renderings. But it's not often a cast so rich in stage trained actors is assembled on the small screen. Hopkins gives a textured, pre-Hannibal Lecter interpretation of Quasimodo, the Hunchback in Hugo's eponymous novel. Impressive model of the cathedral by production designer John Stoll. **102m/C; VHS, DVD.** Anthony Hopkins; Derek Jacobi; Lesley-Anne Down; John Gielgud; Tim Pigott-Smith; Rosalie Crutchley; Robert Powell; *D:* Michael Tuchner.

The Hunchback of Notre Dame ♂♂♂ **1996 (G)** Animated/musical version of Victor Hugo's story about deformed bellringer Quasimodo (Hulce) and his love for the beautiful gypsy Esmerelda (Moore). The original isn't exactly fun fare but you expect Disney to find a way to leave everybody humming (and happy). The sweeping music was provided by "Pocahontas" tunesmiths Menken and Schwartz. Comic relief is supplied by three gargoyles, companions to Quasimodo, who are voiced wonderfully by Alexander, Kimbrough and Wickes. Wickes, 85, died six weeks after voicing her role. Looks like another boatload of boxoffice, merchandising, and video sale cash is making its way into old Walt's vaults. **91m/C; VHS, DVD, Blu-Ray.** *V:* Tom Hulce; Demi Moore; Kevin Kline; Tony Jay; Charles Kimbrough; Jason Alexander; Mary Wickes; David Ogden Stiers; *D:* Kirk Wise; Gary Trousdale; *W:* Irene Mecchi; Tab Murphy; Jonathan Roberts; Bob Tzudiker; Noni White; *M:* Stephen Schwartz; Alan Menken.

The Hundred-Foot Journey 🦴🦴 **2014 (PG)** Cultural clashes and fine cuisine are given the Disney treatment in director Hallstrom's latest dramedy based on the book by Richard C. Morais. An Indian family moves to France and opens a restaurant across the street (hence the title) from a world-famous eatery run by the legendary Madame Mallory (Mirren). It's the kind of movie you can write in your head just from that description alone. But the cast is likable, and the story occasionally heartwarming. It's a predictable meal but sometimes it's a filling one. **122m/C; DVD, Blu-Ray.** Dame Helen Mirren; Om Puri; Manish Dayal; Charlotte Le Bon; Michel Blanc; ***D:*** Lasse Hallstrom; ***W:*** Steven Knight; ***C:*** Linus Sandgren; ***M:*** A.R. Rahman.

Hungarian Rhapsody 🦴🦴 *Ungarische Rhapsodie* **1928** Silent German romantic melodrama. Well-born but impoverished Austrian Army officer Franz makes a fool of himself with Camilla, the bored wife of an elderly aristocrat. His reputation is saved by commoner Marika who really loves him. **70m/B; Silent; DVD.** *GE* Willy Fritsch; Lil Dagover; Dita Parlo; Leopold Kramer; Erich Kaiser-Titz; ***D:*** Hanns Schwarz; ***W:*** Hans Szekely; ***C:*** Carl Hoffmann.

Hunger 🦴🦴 *Sult* **1966** In the late 1800s, a starving Norwegian writer, unable to sell his work, rejects charity out of pride, and retains his faith in his talent. Based on a novel "Sult" by Knut Hamsun. In Danish with English subtitles. **115m/B; VHS, DVD.** *DK* Per Oscarsson; Gunnel Lindblom; ***D:*** Henning Carlsen; ***W:*** Henning Carlsen. Cannes '66: Actor (Oscarsson); Natl. Soc. Film Critics '68: Actor (Oscarsson).

The Hunger 🦴🦴 **1983 (R)** A beautiful 2000-year-old vampire needs new blood when she realizes that her current lover, Bowie, is aging fast. Visually sumptuous but sleepwalking modern vampire tale, complete with soft-focus lesbian love scenes between Deneuve and Sarandon. **100m/C; VHS, DVD, Blu-Ray.** Catherine Deneuve; David Bowie; Susan Sarandon; Cliff DeYoung; Ann Magnuson; Dan Hedaya; Willem Dafoe; Beth Ehlers; Suzanne Bertish; Rufus Collins; James Aubrey; ***D:*** Tony Scott; ***W:*** Michael Thomas; Ivan Davis; ***C:*** Stephen Goldblatt; Tom Mangravite; ***M:*** Denny Jaeger; Michel Rubini.

Hunger 🦴🦴 **2008** Focuses on the last months of Irish Republican Army member Bobby Sands (Fassbender), who instigated a hunger strike in Belfast's Maze prison. He eventually starved himself to death in 1981 to protest the British government's refusal to recognize convicted IRA members as political prisoners. The story begins with fellow inmates Davey Gillen (Milligan) and Gerry Campbell (McMahon) and their 'blanket protest' refusal to wear prison uniforms but soon shifts to Sands and the ethical dialogue between Sands and Catholic priest Father Moran (Cunningham) over being a martyr to the cause. **96m/C; DVD.** Michael Fassbender; Liam Cunningham; Brian Milligan; Liam McMahon; Stuart Graham; ***D:*** Steve McQueen; ***W:*** Steve McQueen; Enda Walsh; ***C:*** Sean Bobbitt; ***M:*** David Holmes; Leo Abrahams.

The Hunger Games 🦴🦴🦴½ **2012 (PG-13)** Director/writer Ross' adaptation of the hit 2008 young adult sci-fi novel by Suzanne Collins is a smashing success. The title refers to a to-the-death battle among two dozen teenagers used as reality TV entertainment for a dystopian future. Playing one of the most striking heroines in years in Katniss Everdeen, Lawrence perfectly injects her memorable character with just the right balance of toughness and vulnerability. With superb technical elements (including a fantastic score and stylish cinematography), this mega-hit (the third highest-grossing opening weekend in history) is one of the rare box office blockbusters that connects creatively as well. **142m/C; DVD, Blu-Ray.** Jennifer Lawrence; Josh Hutcherson; Liam Hemsworth; Wes Bentley; Elizabeth Banks; Stanley Tucci; Woody Harrelson; Toby Jones; Donald Sutherland; Lenny Kravitz; Amandla Stenberg; Paula Malcomson; Alexander Ludwig; Isabelle Fuhrman; Brooke Bundy; Willow Shields; Kiniko Gelman; Nelson Ascencio; Dayo Okeniyi; Leven Rambin; Jack Quaid; Latarsha Rose; Jacqueline Emerson; ***D:*** Gary Ross; ***W:*** Gary Ross; Suzanne Collins; Billy Ray; ***C:*** Tom Stern; ***M:*** James Newton Howard; T-Bone Burnett.

The Hunger Games: Catching Fire 🦴🦴🦴½ **2013 (PG-13)** The massively successful franchise, based on the hit books by Suzanne Collins, continues with this transitional chapter between the first book/film and the two-film finale, "Mockingjay." Katniss (Lawrence) and Peeta (Hutcherson) are forced back into action after the power structure (led by a charismatic Sutherland) realizes that they have become idols for a revolution. Director Lawrence has crafted a stellar piece of action filmmaking, driven by an incredible cast and perfectly plotted source material. It's ultimately more complex than the original but just as entertaining a piece of blockbuster escapism. **146m/C; DVD, Blu-Ray.** Jennifer Lawrence; Josh Hutcherson; Woody Harrelson; Donald Sutherland; Liam Hemsworth; Sam Claflin; Jena Malone; Elizabeth Banks; Stanley Tucci; Philip Seymour Hoffman; Lynn Cohen; Jeffrey Wright; Amanda Plummer; Lenny Kravitz; ***D:*** Francis Lawrence; ***W:*** Simon Beaufoy; Michael Arndt; ***C:*** Jo Willems; ***M:*** James Newton Howard.

The Hunger Games: Mockingjay--Part 1 🦴🦴½ **2014 (PG-13)** Setting up the grand finale of Suzanne Collins' third book, Katniss (Lawrence) wakes up to find her District 12 extinct and Peeta (Hutcherson) taken by President Snow (Sutherland). Taking refuge in the believed-destroyed District 13, Katniss recovers from her injuries from the last Games with her family and Gale (Hemsworth). Still the face of the rebellion, she is reluctantly forced into battle with her cohorts under the direction of the covert district's President Coin (Moore). Like most stories that are divided into two films, it focuses more on explaining what's to come and packs less punch as a result, though fans might not notice. **123m/C; DVD, Blu-Ray.** Jennifer Lawrence; Josh Hutcherson; Liam Hemsworth; Donald Sutherland; Julianne Moore; Philip Seymour Hoffman; Stanley Tucci; Woody Harrelson; Elizabeth Banks; Sam Claflin; Natalie Dormer; Jeffrey Wright; ***D:*** Francis Lawrence; ***W:*** Peter Craig; Danny Strong; ***C:*** Jo Willems; ***M:*** James Newton Howard.

The Hunger Games: Mockingjay—Part 2 🦴🦴½ **2015 (PG-13)** Jennifer Lawrence's time with one of the '10s most successful franchises ends on something of a whimper as Suzanne Collins' final book has been lessened by breaking it into two parts. Lawrence is still great as Katniss Everdeen, as she leads the final revolution against the Capitol, finally united with the men on her side and with the power of a country behind her. But, in the end, Francis Lawrence gets all of the major beats of the story right, leading to a satisfying finale for the franchise's faithful. **136m/C; DVD, Blu-Ray.** Jennifer Lawrence; Josh Hutcherson; Liam Hemsworth; Woody Harrelson; Donald Sutherland; Elizabeth Banks; Natalie Dormer; ***D:*** Francis Lawrence; ***W:*** Peter Craig; Danny Strong; ***C:*** Jo Willems; ***M:*** James Newton Howard.

Hunger Point 🦴½ **2003** Unfortunately cliched look at eating disorders. Weight-obsessed Marsha Hunter (Hershey) ridicules her two daughters when they don't adhere to her rigid diet and exercise regimes. Naturally, both Shelly (Pratt) and Frannie (Hendricks) have food issues with Shelly winding up in a mental hospital, but the tragedy doesn't stop there. **90m/C; DVD.** Barbara Hershey; Christina Hendricks; Susan May Pratt; John Getz; Stephanie Mills; ***D:*** Joan Micklin Silver; ***W:*** Deborah Amelon; ***C:*** Pierre Letarte; ***M:*** Richard (Rick) Marvin. **CABLE**

The Hungover Games 🦴½ **2014 (R)** A satiric parody of Hollywood that combines The Hangover with The Hunger Games. The morning after the bachelor party for Doug (Livingston), Bradley (Nathan), Ed (Begley), and Zach (Russell) find themselves in a strange room in an unknown world—without Doug. After meeting Effing (Reid) and Justmitch (Kennedy), they realize they are to take part in the Hungover Games. As part of the games, they must compete with other pop culture districts, including the Superhero district. If they prepare well enough with the help of Effing and Justmitch, victory could be within reach. **85m/C; DVD, Blu-Ray, Streaming, Download.** Ross Nathan; Ben Begley; Herbert Russell; John Livingston; Tara Reid; Jamie Kennedy; ***D:*** Josh Stolberg; ***W:*** Kyle B. Anderson; David Bernstein; ***C:*** Andrew Strahorn; ***M:*** Todd Haberman. **VIDEO**

The Hungry Ghosts 🦴½ **2009 (R)** Vignettes about the search for spiritual fulfillment by various New Yorkers are weakly strung together in Imperioli's director/writer debut. Irresponsible coke-addicted gambler Frank is a lousy parent to teenage son Matthew, who disappears from his therapy session while Frank battles with ex-wife Sharon. Meanwhile, Nadia refuses to get back together with ex-boyfriend Gus, who's just out of alcohol rehab and doesn't take her rejection well. **106m/C; DVD.** Steve Schirripa; Aunjanue Ellis; Nick Sandow; Sharon Angela; Emory Cohen; Paul Calderon; John Ventimiglia; Angelica Torn; ***D:*** Michael Imperioli; ***W:*** Michael Imperioli; ***C:*** Dan Hersey; ***M:*** Elijah Amitin.

Hungry Hearts 🦴🦴½ **2015** What begins innocently enough, as a playful romcom, devolves into a something of a dark surprise. After an obligatory meet-cute, young lovers Jude (Driver) and Mina (Rohrwacher), eventually take the plunge, rings, kids, and all. The years bring out a disturbing side of Mina, as she constantly puts her baby at risk, out of the fear for its safety. Jude must decide how far he'll go to save his child, while taking down his wife. A chilling portrait of paranoia that tries its best to walk the line of thriller and relationship drama, never quite succeeding in either. **109m/C; DVD, Blu-Ray, Streaming.** *IT* Adam Driver; Alba Rohrwacher; Roberta Maxwell; Al Roffe; Geisha Otero; ***D:*** Saverio Costanzo; ***W:*** Saverio Costanzo; ***C:*** Fabio Cianchetti; ***M:*** Nicola Piovani.

Hunk 🦴🦴 **1987 (PG)** A computer nerd sells his soul to the devil for a muscular, beach-blonde physique. Answers the question, "Was it worth it?" **102m/C; VHS, DVD.** John Allen Nelson; Steve Levitt; Deborah Shelton; Rebecca Bush; James Coco; Avery Schreiber; ***D:*** Lawrence Bassoff; ***W:*** Lawrence Bassoff; ***C:*** Bryan England.

The Hunley 🦴🦴½ **1999** Based on the true story of the Confederate submarine that was used to defend Charleston harbor against Union forces in 1864. The experimental craft has already claimed the lives of two crews but General Beauregard (Sutherland) is desperate to break the blockade of the city and gives command to Lt. George E. Dixon (Assante), an engineer. As usual, Dixon's crew is a ragged bunch of misfits but Dixon perseveres. **120m/C; VHS, DVD.** Armand Assante; Donald Sutherland; Alex Jennings; Sebastien Roche; Michael Dolan; Chris Bauer; Michael Stuhlbarg; Jack Baun; Kevin Robertson; ***D:*** John Gray; ***W:*** John Gray; ***C:*** John Thomas; ***M:*** Randy Edelman. **CABLE**

The Hunt 🦴🦴🦴 *La Caza* **1965** A teenage boy accompanies three Spanish Civil War veterans on what is supposed to be a friendly rabbit hunt. Things turn violent, however, when old rivalries and tensions begin to surface. In Spanish with English subtitles. **87m/B; VHS, DVD.** *SP* Alfredo Mayo; Ismael Merlo; Jose Maria Prada; Emilio Gutierrez-Caba; Fernando Sanchez Polack; ***D:*** Carlos Saura.

The Hunt 🦴🦴🦴 *Jagten* **2013 (R)** Mikkelsen won the Best Actor Award at the 2012 Cannes Film Festival for his portrayal of a Danish schoolteacher caught up in mass hysteria after being falsely accused of sexually assaulting a child. Lucas (Mikkelsen) works at a day care attended by Klara, the daughter of his good friend Theo (Larsen). After Klara's older brother playfully shows Klara an explicit picture, she says something about it that leads the community to hunt Lucas as a sexual predator. Lucas proclaims his complete innocence but the stigma of child abuse hunts him even after he's vindicated. Danish with subtitles. **115m/C; DVD, Blu-Ray.** *DK* Mads Mikkelsen; Thomas Bo Larsen; Annika Wedderkopp; Lasse Fogelstrom; Susse Wold; ***D:*** Thomas Vinterberg; ***W:*** Thomas Vinterberg; Tobias Lindholm; ***C:*** Charlotte Bruus Christensen; ***M:*** Nikolaj Egelund.

The Hunt 🦴🦴½ **2020 (R)** A random group of poor conservatives is kidnapped from various parts of the United States, drugged, and transported to a remote location. When they awake, they find themselves the prey of a group of wealthy liberals armed with guns. Among the kidnapped is Crystal (Gilpin), a car rental agency worker who previously served in the military and draws on those skills as she tries to survive and better understand the situation she is in. An uneven social satire of politics with many stereotypical characters, though Gilpin is impressive as are a handful of well-executed, suspenseful sequences. **90m/C; DVD.** Betty Gilpin; Hilary Swank; Ike Barinholtz; Wayne Duvall; Ethan Suplee; ***D:*** Craig Zobel; ***W:*** Nick Cuse; Damon Lindelof; ***C:*** Darran Tiernan; ***M:*** Nathan Barr.

The Hunt for Eagle One: Crash Point 🦴 **2006 (R)** Routine military action pic. The Strike Force team returns when terrorists steal an anti-hijack device. Lt. Matt Daniels (Dacascos) and his crew must get the device back and also prevent the bad guys from crashing a jetliner into a military base. **86m/C; DVD.** Mark Dacascos; Theresa Randle; Gary Kasper; Rutger Hauer; Zach McGowan; Joe Suba; Jeff Fahey; ***D:*** Henry Crum; ***W:*** Michael Henry Carter; ***C:*** Andrea V. Rossotto; ***M:*** Mel Lewis. **VIDEO**

The Hunt for Red October 🦴🦴🦴 **1990 (PG)** Based on Tom Clancy's blockbuster novel, a high-tech Cold War yarn about a Soviet nuclear sub (commanded by Connery) turning rogue and heading straight for U.S. waters, as both the U.S. and the U.S.S.R. try to stop it. Complicated, ill-plotted potboiler that succeeds breathlessly due to the cast and McTiernan's tommy-gun direction. Introduces the character of CIA analyst Jack Ryan (Baldwin) who returns in "Patriot Games," though in the guise of Harrison Ford. **137m/C; VHS, DVD, Blu-Ray.** Sean Connery; Alec Baldwin; Richard Jordan; Scott Glenn; Joss Ackland; Sam Neill; James Earl Jones; Peter Firth; Tim Curry; Courtney B. Vance; Jeffrey Jones; Fred Dalton Thompson; ***D:*** John McTiernan; ***W:*** Larry Ferguson; Donald Stewart; ***C:*** Jan De Bont; ***M:*** Basil Poledouris. Oscars '90: Sound FX Editing.

The Hunt for the I-5 Killer 🦴 **2011** Tedious Lifetime true crime drama based on the manhunt for a serial killer who used the I-5 corridor from California to Washington state as his hunting grounds in 1981. Adaptaion of the Ann Rule book. **89m/C; Streaming.** John Corbett; Sara Canning; Tygh Runyan; Bo Derek; Garry Chalk; ***D:*** Allan Kroeker; ***W:*** Teena Booth; ***C:*** C. Kim Miles; ***M:*** James Jandrisch. **CABLE**

Hunt for the Wilderpeople 🦴🦴🦴 **2016 (PG-13)** Ricky Baker (Dennison) is a troubled teenager sent to live with the latest in a line of foster parents in the New Zealand outback. When his new guardian passes away, he's forced on the run with a man he calls Uncle Hec (Neill). Becoming local celebrities, the story of Ricky and Hec defies all predictable conventions of the coming-of-age story, as writer/director Waititi so deftly balances comedy and drama. It's a movie you watch with a smile plastered on your face from first frame to last. **101m/C; DVD, Blu-Ray.** Sam Neill; Julian Dennison; Rima Te Wiata; Rachel House; Tioreore Ngatai-Melbourne; ***D:*** Taika Waititi; ***W:*** Taika Waititi; ***C:*** Lachlan Milne; ***M:*** Lukasz Pawel Buda; Samuel Scott; Conrad Wedde.

Hunt the Man Down 🦴🦴½ **1950** An innocent man is charged with murder, and a public defender must find the real killer before time runs out. **68m/B; VHS, DVD.** Gig Young; Lynne Roberts; Gerald Mohr; ***D:*** George Archainbaud.

Hunt to Kill 🦴 **2010 (R)** Remarkably dumb and not very action-oriented despite Austin's lead role. Rhodes is a border agent in Montana whose rebellious teen daughter Kim becomes the hostage of a gang of thieves. They're after their double-crossing partner, who's headed to Canada with the loot, and they need Rhodes as a wilderness guide. **98m/C; DVD, Blu-Ray.** Steve Austin; Gil Bellows; Gary Daniels; Michael Hogan; Michael Eklund; Adrian Holmes; Donnelly Rhodes; Eric Roberts; Marie Avgeropoulos; ***D:*** Keoni Waxman; ***W:*** Frank Hannah; ***C:*** Thomas M. (Tom) Harting; ***M:*** Michael Richard Plowman. **VIDEO**

The Hunted 🦴🦴 **1948** Laura Mead (Belita) blames her incompetent lawyer for getting her convicted and sent to prison for a crime she swears she didn't commit. To make it worse, her own boyfriend, police detective Johnny Saxon (Foster), was the one who turned her in. After Laura gets out on parole, the lawyer winds up dead after Laura threatened him and Saxon is once again pursuing his ex-lover. But this time he seems to believe that Laura is being framed in this atmospheric B-noir. **84m/B; DVD.** Belita; Preston Foster; Pierre Watkin; Russell Hicks; Edna Holland; ***D:*** Jack Bernhard; ***W:*** Steve Fisher; ***C:*** Harry Neumann; ***M:*** Edward Kay.

Hunted *The Stranger In Between* **1952** Bleak, intense drama. Young Robbie (Whiteley) runs away from his abusive home and accidentally crosses path with fugitive Chris Lloyd (Bogarde), who's on the lam for killing his wife's lover. The boy is soon devoted to the brusque Chris as the two flee London and make a difficult journey into Scotland, but Chris must make a hard choice when Robbie becomes ill. **85m/B; DVD.** *UK* Dirk Bogarde; Jon Whiteley; Elizabeth Sellars; Kay Walsh; Geoffrey Keen; ***D:*** Charles Crichton; ***W:*** Jack Whittingham; ***C:*** Eric Cross; ***M:*** Hubert Clifford.

The Hunted 1/2 **1994 (R)** American businessman in Japan meets, beds, and witnesses the assassination of a mysterious woman and is forced on the run by the modern-day ninja clan that committed the crime. Only a notch above the low-budget, badly dubbed martial arts flicks of the '70s, this shameless bloodfest features unintentionally campy performances by Lambert and Lone and lots of silly dialogue. Beware, the cliches pile up as quickly as the bodies. **110m/C; VHS, DVD.** Christopher Lambert; John Lone; Joan Chen; Yoshio Harada; Yoko Shimada; Mari Natsuki; Tak Kubota; ***D:*** J.F. Lawton; ***W:*** J.F. Lawton; ***C:*** Jack Conroy; ***M:*** Motofumi Yamaguchi.

The Hunted **2003 (R)** "First Blood" meets "The Fugitive" in Friedkin's newest chase thriller. Ex-Special Forces member Hallam (Del Toro) comes back from Kosovo severely messed up and heads to the Oregon woods, fileting hunters who use high-powered scopes to stalk their prey. Apparently he's joined PETA's paramilitary wing. Jones is Bonham, the man who trained him in the arts of stalking, killing, and surviving, and must now stop him. He's teamed with female FBI agent Durrell (Nielsen), who doesn't realize she's brought a gun to knife fight. She (as well as plot) is basically window dressing, as Friedkin is clearly more concerned with the grunt-inducing mano-a-mano action scenes and car chases. It's a good thing they're well done, because the meditation of the good and evil that men do doesn't cut it. **94m/C; VHS, DVD.** Tommy Lee Jones; Benicio Del Toro; Connie Nielsen; Leslie Stefanson; John Finn; Jose Zuniga; Ron Canada; Mark Pellegrino; Lonny (Lonnie) Chapman; Rex Linn; Eddie Velez; ***D:*** William Friedkin; ***W:*** David Griffiths; Peter Griffiths; Art Monterastelli; ***C:*** Caleb Deschanel; ***M:*** Brian Tyler.

The Hunter 1/2 **1980 (PG)** Action drama based on the real life adventures of Ralph (Papa) Thorson, a modern day bounty hunter who makes his living by finding fugitives who have jumped bail. McQueen's last. **97m/C; VHS, DVD.** Steve McQueen; Eli Wallach; Kathryn Harrold; LeVar Burton; ***D:*** Buzz Kulik; ***W:*** Peter Hyams; ***C:*** Fred W. Koenekamp; ***M:*** Charles Bernstein.

The Hunter **2012 (R)** Allegorical adventure-drama. Loner mercenary Martin David (an impressive Dafoe) is hired by a military-biotech company to go on a hunt in the Tasmanian rainforest for a probably extinct tiger species that would be commercially valuable if it did still exist. There is a dispute between the local loggers and environmentalists and David is unwillingly involved because he's rooming with the shattered family of a missing eco-activist. The best moments are those of Dafoe alone in the woods; the rest is filler. Based on the 1999 novel by Julia Leigh. **101m/C; DVD, Blu-Ray, Streaming.** *AU* Willem Dafoe; Sam Neill; Frances O'Connor; Morgana Davies; Finn Woodlock; ***D:*** Daniel Nettheim; ***W:*** Alice Addison; ***C:*** Robert Humphreys; ***M:*** Matteo Zingales; Andrew Lancaster; Michael Lira.

Hunter in the Dark **1980** Set in 18th-century Japan, where power, betrayal, and corruption are the dark side of the samurai world. Tanuma is a powerful shogunate minister who becomes involved with Gomyo, the leader of a secret underworld organization of thieves and murderers with a violent honor code. In Japanese with English subtitles. **138m/C; VHS, Streaming.** *JP* Tatsuya Nakadai; Tetsuro Tamba; Sonny Chiba; ***D:*** Hideo Gosha.

Hunter Killer **2018 (R)** An untested American submarine captain teams with U.S. Navy Seals to rescue the Russian president, who has been kidnapped by a rogue general. **121m/C; DVD, Blu-Ray, Streaming.** *CH US UK* Gerard Butler; Gary Oldman; Common; Michael Nyqvist; Linda Cardellini; ***D:*** Donovan Marshall; ***W:*** Arne L. Schmidt; Jamie Moss; ***C:*** Tom Marais; ***M:*** Trevor Morris.

The Hunters 1/2 **1958** A motley crew of pilots learn about each other and themselves in this melodrama set during Korean war. Incredible aerial photography sets this apart from other films of the genre. **108m/C; VHS, DVD.** Robert Mitchum; Robert Wagner; Richard Egan; May Britt; Lee Philips; John Gabriel; Stacy Harris; John Doucette; Jay Jostyn; Leon Lontoc; Ralph Manza; Alena Murray; Robert Reed; Victor Sen Yung; Candace Lee; ***D:*** Dick Powell; ***W:*** Wendell Mayes; ***C:*** Charles G. Clarke; ***M:*** Paul Sawtell. Natl. Film Reg. '03.

The Hunters **2011 (R)** Yet another hunt-the-humans pic. Hikers in a nature preserve come across an abandoned fort that's covered in blood and filled with body parts. When police officer Le Saint investigates, he becomes a target for the hunters. **107m/C; DVD.** Chris Briant; Steven Waddington; Tony Becker; Terrence Knox; Dianna Agron; ***D:*** Chris Briant; ***W:*** Michael Lehman; ***C:*** John Aronson; ***M:*** Mark Snow. **VIDEO**

The Hunters 1/2 **2013** Family adventure from the Hallmark Channel. Carter and Jordan Flynn are let in on some family secrets when their parents go missing. The Flynn's assistant, Dylan, tells the brothers that mom and dad are protectors of fairytale objects, including the magic mirror from the Snow White story. Now, the job falls to the brothers to save the mirror and their parents. **86m/C; DVD, Blu-Ray.** Robbie Amell; Keenan Tracey; Alexa Vega; Victor Garber; Dan Payne; Michelle Forbes; ***D:*** Nisha Ganatra; ***W:*** Matthew Huffman; Jeff Schechter; ***C:*** C. Kim Miles; ***M:*** Brent Belke. **CABLE**

Hunter's Moon 1/2 **1997 (R)** Reynolds plays a very bad guy (very well) as a Depression era, Kentucky backwoods moonshiner who has no intention of letting his lovely daughter, Flo (Du Mond), fall for a city boy (Carradine) who's trying to make a new life for himself. **104m/C; VHS, DVD.** Burt Reynolds; Keith Carradine; Hayley Du Mond; Ann Wedgeworth; Pat Hingle; Brion James; Charles Napier; ***D:*** Richard Weinman; ***W:*** Richard Weinman; L. Ford Neale; John Huff; William Kemper; ***C:*** Suki Medencevic.

The Hunting Ground **2015 (PG-13)** A revealing documentary look at the impact of rape on college campuses in the United States. Following several survivors of such sexual assaults, the filmmakers chronicle their efforts to continue their educations and to pursue justice. The challenges faced by these survivors is examined as well, including retaliation and denial by higher authorities. Through it all, the effect of this fight for justice on survivors and their families remains at the film's heart. The result is thought provoking but sometimes painful to watch. **103m/C; DVD.** ***D:*** Kirby Dick; ***W:*** Kirby Dick; ***C:*** Aaron Kopp; Thaddeus Wadleigh; ***M:*** Miriam Cutler.

Hunting Humans **2002 (R)** Unlikely story about a serial killer being stalked by a rival serial killer who murders potential victims before he can as a way of cheesing him off. And you thought your workplace rivalry was bad. **89m/C; DVD, Streaming.** Rick Ganz; Bubby Lewis; Jeff Kipers; Lisa Michele; ***D:*** Kevin Kangas; ***W:*** Kevin Kangas; ***C:*** David Maurice Gil; ***M:*** Evan Evans. **VIDEO**

The Hunting of the President **2004** Documentary about the extreme Right's attempts to smear and destroy the presidency of Bill Clinton. Covers events from Whitewater-gate to the impeachment proceedings. Partisan slam against Starr and company co-written and directed by Thomason, a close friend of the Clintons. In the year of partisan political docs, acceptance will depend on party affiliation and ideology. Techniques used are overly arch and comic at times. **88m/C; VHS, DVD.** ***D:*** Nickolas Perry; Harry Z. Thomason; ***W:*** Nickolas Perry; Harry Z. Thomason; ***C:*** Jim Roberson; ***M:*** Bruce Miller.

The Hunting Party 1/2 **2007 (R)** What could be funnier than a couple of journalists tromping through postwar Bosnia hunting a war criminal? Simon Hunt (Gere) is a former big-time television reporter, fallen from grace after an on-camera meltdown. Now a freelancer covering tragedies around the globe, he and his journalist buddies improbably find themselves mistaken as a hit squad on the lookout for a brutal war criminal, Bosnian Serb leader Radovan Karadzic (Kerekes). Based on Scott Anderson's 2000 article in "Esquire" magazine about five journalists who found themselves in just that situation, although sans the goofy and madcap tone. Doesn't work as a war comedy, as the story just doesn't translate, particularly with oddly-cast Gere. **104m/C; DVD.** Richard Gere; Terrence Howard; Jesse Eisenberg; Diane Kruger; James Brolin; Dylan Baker; Ljubomir Kerekes; ***D:*** Richard Shepard; ***W:*** Richard Shepard; ***C:*** David Tattersall; ***M:*** Rolfe Kent.

The Huntsman: Winter's War 1/2 **2016 (PG-13)** It's almost unfathomable to waste the talents of three of the most charismatic actresses of their generation—Theron, Blunt, and Chastain. It's the only movie magic you'll find in this sequel nobody asked for without the star of the last movie. Hemsworth returns as the title character, who has a secret love with Chastain's Sara, and that fires up the ire of Blunt's Queen Freya and her sister Ravenna, played by Theron. One hopes these women at least got a good paycheck out of the deal because they sure didn't get a good movie. **123m/C; DVD, Blu-Ray.** Chris Hemsworth; Charlize Theron; Jessica Chastain; Emily Blunt; Nick Frost; ***D:*** Cedric Nicolas-Troyan; ***W:*** Evan Spiliotopoulos; Craig Mazin; ***C:*** Phedon Papamichael; ***M:*** James Newton Howard.

Hurlyburly **1998 (R)** Casting agents Eddie (Penn) and Mickey (Spacey) share a Hollywood apartment with out-of-work actor Phil (Palminteri). Eddie uses cocaine almost constantly, Phil has just been dumped by his wife, and Mickey (Spacey), although more low key, is himself ready to explode. They're all desperate to be huge "Hollywood" successes. Plot pretty much consists of the men venting their spleens and treating women like crap, particularly Bonnie (Ryan), a slutty exotic dancer traded between the boys. Snappy dialogue-happy script might have worked on the stage, but here, with the camera in close, the mean spirit becomes tiring very quickly. Paquin shows confidence in her first adult role, as a drifter girl-toy. **122m/C; VHS, DVD.** Sean Penn; Kevin Spacey; Chazz Palminteri; Meg Ryan; Robin Wright; Anna Paquin; Garry Shandling; ***D:*** Tony Drazan; ***W:*** David Rabe; ***C:*** Gu Changwei; ***M:*** David Baerwald.

The Hurricane **1937** A couple on the run from the law are aided by a hurricane and are able to build a new life for themselves on an idyllic island. Filmed two years before the Academy's "special effects" award came into being, but displaying some of the best effects of the decade. Boringly remade in 1979. **102m/B; VHS, DVD, Blu-Ray.** Jon Hall; Dorothy Lamour; Mary Astor; Sir C. Aubrey Smith; Raymond Massey; Thomas Mitchell; John Carradine; ***D:*** John Ford; ***W:*** Oliver H.P. Garrett; Dudley Nichols; ***C:*** Bert Glennon; Paul Eagler; Archie Stout; ***M:*** Alfred Newman. Oscars '37: Sound.

Hurricane **1974** TV's answer to the disaster movie craze of the early 1970s. Realistic hurricane footage and an adequate cast cannot save this catastrophe. **78m/C; VHS, DVD.** Larry Hagman; Martin Milner; Jessica Walter; Barry Sullivan; Will Geer; Frank Sutton; ***D:*** Jerry Jameson. **TV**

Hurricane **WOOF!** *Forbidden Paradise* **1979 (PG)** And the wind cried, "turkey." Robards is the governor of a tropical island beset with environmental and personal concerns. Virginal daughter Farrow falls for hunky native, standard colonial power/indigenous people complications ensue, vital explanatory footage is cut, and overacting reaches epidemic heights. Then too late the big wind blows in, leveling the place. Expensive (most of the $22 million must have gone to catering) and essentially misdirected remake of the 1937 semi-classic. **120m/C; VHS, DVD.** Mia Farrow; Jason Robards, Jr.; Trevor Howard; Max von Sydow; Timothy Bottoms; James Keach; ***D:*** Jan Troell; ***C:*** Sven Nykvist; ***M:*** Nino Rota.

The Hurricane *Lazarus and the Hurricane* **1999 (R)** Moving, albeit truncated account of the true story of middleweight boxing champ Rubin "Hurricane" Carter (Washington—in peak physical and professional form), who was falsely accused and convicted of murder and who spent 20 years in prison. Anchored by a transcendent performance by Washington, pic came under fire for its liberal rearrangement of the facts behind the case. If you want a full lowdown on the case, read one of several books written about this unique court battle by Carter himself ("The Sixteenth Round") or "Lazurus and the Hurricane," which served as the basis for the film; but if you want to see acting that can lift one to a higher spirtual plane, give "The Hurricane" a look. Carter was immortalized in Bob Dylan's 1976 protest song, "Hurricane." **125m/B; VHS, DVD, Blu-Ray, HD-DVD.** Denzel Washington; Vicellous Shannon; Deborah Kara Unger; Liev Schreiber; John Hannah; David Paymer; Dan Hedaya; Debbi (Deborah) Morgan; Clancy Brown; Harris Yulin; Vincent Pastore; Rod Steiger; ***D:*** Norman Jewison; ***W:*** Armyan Bernstein; Dan Gordon; ***C:*** Roger Deakins; ***M:*** Christopher Young. Golden Globes '00: Actor--Drama (Washington).

Hurricane Express **1932** Twelve episodes of the vintage serial, in which the Duke pits his courage against an unknown, powerful individual out to sabotage a railroad. **223m/B; VHS, DVD, Blu-Ray.** John Wayne; Joseph Girard; Conway Tearle; Shirley Grey; ***D:*** J(ohn) P(aterson) McGowan; Armand Schaefer.

The Hurricane Heist 1/2 **2018 (PG-13)** Despite its misleading title, this flick is not about the theft of a hurricane (would that it were). Instead, thieves take advantage of an impending hurricane to steal $600 million from the U.S. Treasury, but are foiled by a meteorologist (Kebbell) and a Treasury Agent (Grace) who use the storm against them. Subtlety is not in the wheelhouse of Rob Cohen, creator of *The Fast & the Furious* franchise. The action and special effects are big and loud, but the dialogue is absurd and the plot holes are Category 5. Take cover. **103m/C; DVD, Blu-Ray.** Toby Kebbell; Maggie Grace; Ryan Kwanten; Ralph Ineson; Melissa Bolona; ***D:*** Rob Cohen; ***W:*** Jeff Dixon; Scott Windhauser; ***C:*** Shelly Johnson; ***M:*** Lorne Balfe.

Hurricane Season 1/2 **2009 (PG-13)** Sports drama based on a true story that's inspirational but on the dull side and without any surprises. Al Collins (Whitaker) is the basketball coach at Marrero, Louisiana's John Ehret High School. The school is basically destroyed by Hurricane Katrina in 2005 and his players scattered, so Collins tries to rebuild the Patriots by forming a new team with players from rival schools and pushing them towards a state championship. **102m/C; DVD.** Forest Whitaker; Bow Wow; Robbie Jones; Eric D. Hill, Jr.; Lil Wayne; Taraji P. Henson; Courtney B. Vance; Michael Gaston; Isaiah Washington, IV; Bonnie Hunt; Irma P. Hall; ***D:*** Tim Story; ***W:*** Robert Eisele; ***C:*** Larry Blanford; ***M:*** Mark Mancina. **VIDEO**

Hurricane Smith **1992 (R)** Weathers stars as a roughneck Texan who travels to Australia's Gold Coast in search of his missing sister. While in the land of Oz, he gets entangled in a Mafia-style drug and prostitution ring around the "Surfer's Paradise" section of the Gold Coast. Packed with mind-blowing stunts and a good performance from Weathers, this fast-paced action thriller won't disappoint fans of this genre. **86m/C; DVD.** Carl Weathers; Jurgen Prochnow; Tony Bonner; Cassandra Delaney; ***D:*** Colin Budds; ***W:*** Peter Kinloch; ***C:*** John Stokes; ***M:*** Brian May.

Hurricane Streets 1/2 *Hurricane* **1996** Freeman's directorial debut centers on a group of young teenagers getting into trouble in lower Manhattan. 15-year-old Marcus (Sexton) is on the edge—his dad is dead, his mother's in jail, he's being ineffectually looked after by his working grandma, and the authorities are already eyeing this petty thief. He hangs with three buddies, one of whom, Chip (Frank), wants to start them stealing cars. Meanwhile, Marcus falls for 14-year-old Melena (Vega), whose father is both possessive and abusive, and tries to plan an escape for them both. **89m/C; DVD.** Brendan Sexton, III; Isidra Vega; David Roland Frank; L.M. Kit Carson; Jose Zuniga; Lynn Cohen; Edie Falco; Shawn Elliot; Heather Matarazzo; Terry Alexander; ***D:*** Morgan J. Freeman; ***W:*** Morgan J. Freeman; ***C:*** Enrique Chediak. Sundance '97: Aud. Award, Cinematog., Director (Freeman).

Hurry Sundown **1967** Controversial Preminger racial drama based on the book by K.B. Gilden. In 1946, vets Rad McDowell (Law) and Reeve Scott (Hooks) are neighboring sharecroppers in Georgia. Real estate developer Henry Warren (Caine) needs their land to finish a deal but neither man will sell. He puts on the pressure, using his unhappy wife Julie (Fonda), a crooked, racist judge (Meredith), and even the KKK to force things to go his way. **142m/C; DVD, Blu-Ray.** Michael Caine; Jane Fonda; John Phillip Law; Diahann Carroll; Robert Hooks; Faye Dunaway; Burgess Meredith; Loring Smith; George Kennedy; Luke Askew; Beah Richards; Madeline Sherwood; Frank Converse; Robert Reed; Jim Backus; ***D:*** Otto Preminger; ***W:*** Horton Foote; Thomas C. Ryan; ***C:*** Loyal Griggs; Milton Krasner; ***M:*** Hugo Montenegro.

Hurry Up or I'll Be Thirty **1973** A Brooklyn bachelor celebrates his 30th birthday by becoming morose, depressed, and enraged. His friends try to help; they fail, but he finds love anyway. For those seeking a better life through celluloid. **87m/C; VHS, DVD.** Danny DeVito; John Lefkowitz; Steve Inwood; Linda DeCoff; Ronald Anton; Maureen Byrnes; Francis Gallagher; ***D:*** Joseph Jacoby.

Hurt **1/2 2009 (R)** When Helen's husband Robert is killed in a car crash, she and her two teenaged children are forced by financial circumstances to move in with her strange brother-in-law Darryl, who lives in an Arizona junkyard. Artistic son Conrad readily adjusts but popular Lenore is upset. Then young, orphaned Sarah moves in as well, after telling the family that Robert promised to protect her from her own abusive family. However, Sarah isn't as innocent as she seems. **97m/C; DVD.** Melora Walters; William Mapother; Sofia Vassilieva; Jackson Rathbone; Johanna Braddy; ***D:*** Barbara Stepansky; ***W:*** Barbara Stepansky; Alison Lea Bingeman; ***C:*** Ralph Kachele; ***M:*** Dana Niu. **VIDEO**

The Hurt Locker **2008 (R)** Set in Baghdad in 2004, Bigelow's unconventional Iraq war film offers disorienting anxiety and fear centering on a three-man Army bomb-disposal unit. Staff Sgt. William James (Renner, in an effortlessly breakout performance) arrives to take the place of his deceased predecessor with 38 days left in the unit's rotation. Vulnerable Specialist Owen Eldridge (Geraghty) and by-the-book professional Sgt. J.T. Sanborn (Mackie) aren't sure they'll make it since the new guy is a wild card—an adrenaline cowboy consumed by his work. There's mutual distrust between the American occupiers and Iraqi citizens, but Bigelow isn't interested in the rights or wrongs of the conflict itself as much as the small, sometimes terrifying moments. Military "experts" can squawk all they want about technical accuracy (this is hardly the first war film to take artistic liberties), but the film succeeds in providing 'twisting your guts' tension. Based on screenwriter Boal's embedded reports from his time in Baghdad. **131m/C; Blu-Ray, On Demand.** Jeremy Renner; Anthony Mackie; Brian Geraghty; Guy Pearce; Ralph Fiennes; David Morse; Evangeline Lilly; Christian Camargo; Christopher Sayegh; Nabil Koni; ***D:*** Kathryn Bigelow; ***W:*** Mark Boal; ***C:*** Barry Ackroyd; ***M:*** Marco Beltrami; Buck Sanders. Oscars '09: Director (Bigelow), Film, Film Editing, Orig. Screenplay, Sound, Sound FX Editing; British Acad. '09: Cinematog., Director (Bigelow), Film, Orig. Screenplay, Sound; Directors Guild '09: Director (Bigelow); Writers Guild '09: Orig. Screenplay.

Husbands **1/2 1970 (PG-13)** When Stuart (Rowlands) dies suddenly of a heart attack, his three equally middleaged buddies—Harry (Gazzara), Archie (Falk), and Gus (Cassavettes)?are reluctantly confronted with their own mortality. These suburban married men decide to cut loose and go on a spree, with Harry even persuading his buddies they should carry their frantic merriment across the pond in a trip to London. Meanders on a bit too long, thanks to Cassavettes usual reliance on improv and reluctance to edit. **140m/C; VHS, DVD, Blu-Ray.** Ben Gazzara; Peter Falk; John Cassavetes; Jenny Runacre; David Rowlands; Jenny Lee Wright; Noelle Kao; ***D:*** John Cassavetes; ***W:*** John Cassavetes; ***C:*** Victor Kemper.

Husbands and Wives **1/2 1992 (R)** Art imitates life as Allen/Farrow relationship dissolves onscreen (and off) and Woody becomes involved with young student. Mature, penetrating look at modern pair bonding and loneliness offers more painful honesty and sadness than outright laughs, though still retains essential Allen charm. Stylistically burdened by experiment with pseudo-documentary telling of tale and spasmodic hand-held cameras that annoy more than entertain. Excellent, intriguing cast, notably Davis as the overwhelming, overbearing wife/friend. Trailers became unintentionally funny in light of the highly publicized personal problems of Allen and Farrow. **107m/C; VHS, DVD, Blu-Ray.** Woody Allen; Mia Farrow; Judy Davis; Sydney Pollack; Liam Neeson; Juliette Lewis; Lysette Anthony; Blythe Danner; ***D:*** Woody Allen; ***W:*** Woody Allen; ***C:*** Carlo Di Palma. British Acad. '92: Orig. Screenplay; L.A. Film Critics '92: Support. Actress (Davis); Natl. Bd. of Review '92: Support. Actress (Davis); Natl. Soc. Film Critics '92: Support. Actress (Davis).

Hush **1/2** *Kilronan; Bloodline* **1998 (PG-13)** Stinky thriller stars Paltrow as a working-class gal who marries wealthy dreamboat Jackson (Schaech) and moves to his family's Kentucky estate, Kilronan. There, smother-in-law Lange camps it up (albeit unknowingly) as she turns psycho on the pregnant bride while coming on to her dim-witted son who doesn't have a clue. Apparently, neither did filmmaker Darby, whose film was held from release pending two years of pasting Band-Aids on this gaping wound of a movie. Foch's crusty grandmother is the sole highlight of this horror of a film. **96m/C; VHS, DVD.** Gwyneth Paltrow; Jessica Lange; Johnathon Schaech; Nina Foch; Debi Mazar; Kaiulani Lee; David Thornton; Hal Holbrook; ***D:*** Jonathan Darby; ***W:*** Jonathan Darby; Jane Rusconi; ***C:*** Andrew Dunn; ***M:*** Christopher Young.

Hush, Hush, Sweet Charlotte **1965** A fading southern belle finds out the truth about her married lover's murder when the case is reopened 37 years later by her cousin in an elaborate plot to drive her crazy. Grisly, superbly entertaining Southern Gothic horror tale, with vivid performances from the aging leads. **134m/B; VHS, DVD, Blu-Ray.** Bette Davis; Olivia de Havilland; Joseph Cotten; Agnes Moorehead; Mary Astor; Bruce Dern; Cecil Kellaway; Victor Buono; ***D:*** Robert Aldrich; ***W:*** Lukas Heller; Henry Farrell; ***C:*** Joseph Biroc. Golden Globes '65: Support. Actress (Moorehead).

Hush Little Baby **1/2 1993** Susan Nolan (Meldrum), with a husband and family of her own, is shocked when the biological mother she had thought was dead tries to contact her. Turns out that Edie Landers (Ladd) is another of those female psychos who were so popular in suspense films of the late '80s and '90s. This made-for-TV variation connects the dots competently enough. **91m/C; DVD.** Diane Ladd; Wendel Meldrum; Geraint Wyn Davies; Ilya Woloshyn; Ingrid Veninger; ***D:*** Jorge Montesi. **TV**

Hush Little Baby **2007** Predictable supernatural thriller. Jamie Ashford's (Pratt) first daughter drowned and two years later, after a difficult second pregnancy and birth, Jamie has daughter Caitlin. But after a series of accidents, Jamie believes that Caitlin is possessed...or is Jamie suffering from post-partum psychosis? **90m/C; DVD.** Victoria Pratt; Tom Carey; Barbara Wilson; Ari Cohen; Lorena Gale; Johanna Black; ***D:*** Holly Dale; ***W:*** Philip Levens; Ian Kessner; ***C:*** Craig Wrobleski; ***M:*** Zack Ryan. **CABLE**

Hussy **1980 (R)** Hooker and her boyfriend find themselves trapped in a web of gangsters and drugs. **95m/C; VHS, DVD, Blu-Ray.** *GB* Dame Helen Mirren; John Shea; Jenny Runacre; ***D:*** Matthew Chapman; ***W:*** Matthew Chapman; ***M:*** George Fenton.

The Hustle **1975 (R)** Gritty urban adventure with Reynolds as an L.A. detective investigating a young call girl's death. He becomes romantically entangled with high-priced call girl Deneuve. **120m/C; VHS, DVD.** Burt Reynolds; Catherine Deneuve; ***D:*** Robert Aldrich; ***C:*** Joseph Biroc.

Hustle **1/2 2004** Slight, sometimes laughable, story of Pete Rose's banishment from Major League Baseball as a result of his gambling on games his team was playing. Traces the beginnings and escalation of his gambling problem and the investigation that brought him down. Sizemore's ridiculous portrayal of Rose does nothing to help the situation. **90m/C; DVD.** Tom Sizemore; Dash Mihok; Melissa Di Marco; George DiCenzo; Paul Fauteux; ***D:*** Peter Bogdanovich; ***W:*** Christian Darren; ***C:*** James Gardner; ***M:*** Lou Natale. **CABLE**

The Hustle **1/2 2008 (R)** Bug exterminator Freddie Manning and his best friend Junior are in serious trouble since they owe an Asian mob boss $10,000. They have one week to pay the money back and when the two are mistaken for the new pastors at a struggling Baptist church, Freddie decides to hustle the congregation for the dough. As usual, he comes to see the error of his ways. **97m/C; DVD.** Al Shearer; Charlie (Charles Q.) Murphy; David Alan Grier; Tamala Jones; Kym E. Whitley; Bai Ling; John Witherspoon; ***D:*** Deon Taylor; ***W:*** Deon Taylor; Sarah Connolly; Candice Jean Walker; ***C:*** Philip Lee. **VIDEO**

The Hustle **2019 (PG-13)** Josephine (Hathaway) is a stylish, successful con artist who has made millions swindling the wealthy from her base in the French Riviera town of Beaumont-sur-Mer. Meeting brash, low stakes con artist Penny (Wilson) on a train, Penny tries to get in on Josephine's action and learn from her ways. They ultimately bet on who can con an unsuspecting tech billionaire (Sharp) out of $500,000 for the right to stay in the town. A gender swap remake of the 1988 con comedy Dirty Rotten Scoundrels, the film has moments of humor but the leads don't quite mesh. **94m/C; DVD, Blu-Ray.** Anne Hathaway; Rebel Wilson; Alex Sharp; Nicholas Woodeson; Timothy Simons; ***D:*** Chris Addison; ***W:*** Stanley Shapiro; Paul Henning; Dale Launer; Jac Schaeffer; ***C:*** Michael Coulter; ***M:*** Anne Dudley.

Hustle & Flow **2005 (R)** After reuniting with an old buddy who's a sound engineer, Djay, an aging pimp (Howard), decides to go after a dream he let slide and use his talent as a wordsmith to make rap songs. The plan includes giving the demo to Skinny Black (Ludacris) a big-time rap star who Djay claims to know. The film's heart is in the second act where they create a make-shift recording studio and enlist a hooker to sing backup, daring to move beyond their current situations into one dreams are made of. Easy to see why this won the Audience Award at the 2005 Sundance Film Festival, earning Singleton and Allain a hefty distribution deal. **114m/C; DVD, Blu-Ray, UMD, HD-DVD.** Terrence Howard; Taryn Manning; Taraji P. Henson; Paula Jai Parker; Elise Neal; Isaac Hayes; DJ Qualls; Chris Bridges; Anthony Anderson; ***D:*** Craig Brewer; ***W:*** Craig Brewer; ***C:*** Amy Vincent; ***M:*** Scott Bomar. Oscars '05: Song ("It's Hard Out Here for a Pimp"); Natl. Bd. of Review '05: Breakthrough Perf. (Howard); Broadcast Film Critics '05: Song ("Hustle and Flow").

The Hustler **1961** The original story of Fast Eddie Felsen and his adventures in the seedy world of professional pool. Newman plays the naive, talented and self-destructive Felsen perfectly, Laurie is outstanding as his lover, and Gleason epitomizes the pool great Minnesota Fats. Rivetingly atmospheric, and exquisitely photographed. Parent to the reprise "The Color of Money," made 25 years later. **134m/B; VHS, DVD, Blu-Ray.** Paul Newman; Jackie Gleason; Piper Laurie; George C. Scott; Myron McCormick; Murray Hamilton; Michael Constantine; Jake LaMotta; Vincent Gardenia; ***D:*** Robert Rossen; ***W:*** Robert Rossen; ***C:*** Eugen Shufftan. Oscars '61: Art Dir./Set Dec., B&W, B&W Cinematog.; British Acad. '61: Actor (Newman), Film; Natl. Bd. of Review '61: Support. Actor (Gleason); Natl. Film Reg. '97; N.Y. Film Critics '61: Director (Rossen).

Hustler Squad **1976 (R)** U.S. Army major and Philippine guerrilla leader stage a major operation to help rid the Philippines of Japanese Occupation forces: they have four combat-trained prostitutes infiltrate a brothel patronized by top Japanese officers. Verrrrry clever. **98m/C; VHS, DVD.** John Ericson; Karen Ericson; Lynda Sinclaire; Nory Wright; ***D:*** Ted V. Mikels.

Hustler White **1996** Outrageous underground actor/filmmaker LaBruce stars as pretentious German writer Jurgen Anger, who comes to Hollywood to research the gay scene for a book. Cruising Santa Monica Boulevard he becomes obsessively intrigued by local hustler Montgomery Ward (Ward), who serves as a tour guide to the city's sexual kinks. Yes, it's racy, but it's also not as hardcore as the subject matter might imply. **80m/C; VHS, DVD, Blu-Ray.** Tony Ward; Bruce La Bruce; ***D:*** Bruce La Bruce; Rick Castro; ***W:*** Bruce La Bruce; Rick Castro; ***C:*** James Carman.

Hustlers **2019 (R)** Inspired by a New York Magazine article, Hustlers tells the true story of strippers who plot to steal from their greedy, slimy, arrogant Wall Street clients. Beyond the G-strings and lap dances is a feminist Robin Hood flick, in which the women hold the power and the men are relegated to supporting roles. As the group's matriarch, Lopez (requisite mention of her age: 50) delivers the performance of her acting career, and writer/director Scafaria showcases the women's morality, strength, and camaraderie more than their bodies. **110m/C; DVD, Blu-Ray.** Constance Wu; Jennifer Lopez; Julia Stiles; Cardi B.; Madeline Brewer; ***D:*** Lorene Scafaria; ***W:*** Lorene Scafaria; ***C:*** Todd Banhazl.

Hustling **1975** A reporter writing a series of articles on prostitution in New York City takes an incisive look at their unusual and sometimes brutal world. Notable performance by Remick as the reporter and Clayburgh as a victimized hooker. Made for TV and based on a novel by Gail Sheehy. **96m/C; VHS, DVD.** Jill Clayburgh; Lee Remick; Alex Rocco; Monte Markham; ***D:*** Joseph Sargent. **TV**

Hybrid **1/2 1997 (R)** Another bleak apocalyptic future flick, which finds a handful of survivors stumbling across a remote desert lab where they decide to take shelter. Big mistake since the lab still houses a living alien hybrid that's bent on reproduction and destruction. **87m/C; VHS, DVD.** Brinke Stevens; Tim Abell; John Barrymore, III; ***D:*** Fred Olen Ray; ***W:*** Sean O'Bannon; ***C:*** James Lawrence Spencer; ***M:*** Jeff Walton.

Hybrid **2007** Low-budget horror hokum. After being blinded in an explosion, Aaron (Monteith) comes under the care of Dr. Andrea Hewitt (Bateman), whose latest medical experiment involves cross-species transplants. Hewitt uses a wolf's eyes to replace Aaron's and suddenly he has exceptional night vision, acute hearing, a taste for raw meat, and a desire to hunt prey. Native American Lydia (Korey) has learned to control her own feral instincts with the help of a shaman (Tootoosis) but Hewitt's colleagues think Aaron should just be destroyed. Won't be easy—don't they know wolves hunt in packs? **90m/C; DVD.** Cory Monteith; Justine Bateman; Gordon Tootoosis; Gordon Tanner; Tinsel Korey; Aaron Hughes; Brett Sorensen; ***D:*** Yelena Lanskaya; ***W:*** Arne Olsen; ***C:*** Barry Gravelle; ***M:*** Terry Frewer. **TV**

The Hybrids Family **2016** A family comedy focused on two siblings who are the product of a marriage between a vampire and a witch. When vampire Todor (Willingham) and witch Valantina (Leighton) marry have children, they keep their hybrid children, Blaz (Aria) and Velana (Agmon), hidden away for years. They are first hybrid vampire/witch beings. When they reach their teens, they run away to have a normal life and pursue filmmaking and singing careers. As their parents try to find them, the siblings must also outpace the warlock that is pursuing them and the outfall from the ongoing wars between vampires and witches. **95m/C; DVD, Streaming, Download.** Mojean Aria; Leanne Agmon; Carolyn Hennesey; Philip Willingham; Paul Sorvino; **D:** Tony Randel; **W:** Tony Schweikle; **C:** David Rakoczy; **M:** Corey Wallace. **VIDEO**

Hyde Park on Hudson 🦴 1/2 **2012 (R)** Bill Murray plays Franklin Delano Roosevelt in this dull biopic that focuses on the time that the President played host to British royalty. In June 1939, King George VI (West) and Queen Elizabeth (Olivia Colman) stayed at FDR's country estate in Hyde Park, New York. It was the first time that a British monarch had ever visited the States and it was on the eve of WWII. Surely, this could make fertile ground for a dramatic screenwriter and a stellar cast. Maybe it will next time as Michell's film is oddly unfocused and inert despite Murray's best efforts in it. **94m/C; DVD, Blu-Ray.** *UK* Bill Murray; Laura Linney; Samuel West; Olivia Colman; Olivia Williams; **D:** Roger Michell; **W:** Richard Nelson; **C:** Lol Crawley; **M:** Jeremy Sams.

Hydra 🦴 1/2 **2009** Chomp! A quartet of super-rich men travel to a remote island to hunt human prisoners but the island is already inhabited by the multi-headed mythical dragon/snake monster of the title. And it has its own plans for them. **103m/C; DVD.** Polly Shannon; Alex McArthur; George Stults; Roark Critchlow; Texas Battle; Dawn Olivieri; James Wlcek; Michael Shamus Wiles; **D:** Andrew Prendergast; **W:** Peter Sullivan; **M:** Gregory Tripi. **CABLE**

Hyena 🦴 1/2 **2015** A movie that makes you want to shower when it's done to wash off the grime of such deeply unlikable characters. Michael (Ferdinando) is a semi-corrupt cop in the seedy underworld of London who gets in way over his head after witnessing the brutal killings of some Albanian criminals. Suddenly, he's a lynchpin in an all-out gang war. Gerard Johnson mistakes gore and ugliness for grit, thinking he's making a variation on "Bad Lieutenant" or TV's "The Shield" but lacking the depth of the great stories of criminal enterprise. The result is an ugly movie without a single redeemable character. **112m/C; DVD.** *UK* Peter Ferdinando; Stephen Graham; Neil Maskell; Elisa Lasowski; MyAnna Buring; **D:** Gerard Johnson; **W:** Gerard Johnson; **C:** Benjamin Kracun; **M:** Matt Johnson.

Hyena of London 🦴🦴 **1962** A doctor steals the hyena of London's corpse and injects the rabid protoplasm into his own brain with deadly results. **79m/C; VHS, DVD.** Tony Kendall; Bernard Price; Alan Collins; Claude Dantes; **D:** Gino Mangini; **W:** Gino Mangini.

Hyena Road 🦴🦴 1/2 **2016 (R)** A war drama inspired by actual events. In Taliban-held Afghanistan, circumstances force sniper Ryan Sanders (Sutherland) and his team to hide in a village. There, they meet The Ghost (xx), a well-know freedom fighter who is hiding from the Taliban. Intelligence officer Pete Mitchell (Gross) learns of the encounter and instructs Sanders and his squad to locate The Ghost so the United States can make an alliance with him. **120m/C; DVD, Blu-Ray, Streaming, Download.** Paul Gross; Rossif Sutherland; Allan Hawco; Christine Horne; Clark Johnson; **D:** Paul Gross; **W:** Paul Gross; **C:** Karim Hussain; **M:** Asher Lenz.

Hyenas WOOF! **2010 (R)** Cheap and ridiculous. Gannon's (Mandylor) family was slaughtered by the title beasts, who turn out to be shape-shifting humans. He recruits hunter Crazy Briggs (Taylor) to help him get revenge. **92m/C; DVD.** Costas Mandylor; Meshach Taylor; Christa Campbell; Joshua Alba; Rudolf Martin; **D:** Eric Weston; **W:** Eric Weston; **C:** Curtis Peterson; **M:** Lawrence Shragge. **VIDEO**

Hyper Space 🦴 1/2 *Black Forest* **1989** Six people awaken from cryogenic sleep to discover that their spaceship has become marooned lightyears from earth and only a single passenger shuttle is available to get someone home. Naturally, everyone wants that one chance. **90m/C; VHS, DVD, On Demand.** Richard Norton; Don Stroud; Lynn-Holly Johnson; James Van Patten; Ron O'Neal; Rebecca Cruz; **D:** David Huey; **W:** Richard Dominguez; **C:** Roger Olkowski.

Hypersonic 🦴 *Hypersonic: The Ultimate Rush* **2002 (R)** Incomprehensibly bad film about an air race from Buenos Aires to Paris done with fighter jets as a hurricane awaits on the horizon. If any of you have ever actually flown a fighter jet (or even a regular plane for that matter), watch this film and see how little the producers actually know of your profession. Some might like Sabato Jr.'s shirtlessness though. **94m/C; DVD.** Antonio Sabato, Jr.; Adam Baldwin; Alex Jolig; Michael Sutton; Amanda Reyne; Julian Vergov; **D:** Phillip J. Roth; **W:** Phillip J. Roth; Sam Wells; **C:** Todd Baron; **M:** Rich McHugh.

The Hypnotic Eye 🦴 1/2 **1960** Stage hypnotist The Great Desmond uses post-hypnotic suggestions to force pretty women audience volunteers to horribly mutilate themselves. Detective Kennedy isn't too bright but his girlfriend Marcia picks up on the clues and allows herself to be used as bait. **77m/B; DVD.** Jacques Bergerac; Allison Hayes; Marcia Henderson; Joseph Patridge; Merry Anders; Guy Prescott; **D:** George Blair; **W:** Gitta Woodfield; William Read Woodfield; **C:** Arch R. Dalzell; **M:** Marlin Skiles; Eve Newman.

Hysteria 🦴 1/2 **1964 (PG)** When an American becomes involved in an accident and has amnesia, a mysterious benefactor pays all his bills and gives the man a house to live in. But a series of murders could mean he's the murderer—or the next victim. **85m/B; VHS, DVD.** *GB* Robert Webber; Sue Lloyd; Maurice Denham; **D:** Freddie Francis; **W:** Jimmy Sangster; **M:** Don Banks.

Hysteria 🦴🦴 1/2 **2011 (R)** Costume romantic comedy set in Victorian England in the 1880s, which is based on actual events. Doctors Mortimer Granville (Dancy) and Robert Dalrymple (Pryce) specialize in treating ladies supposedly afflicted with hysterical disorders, which leads to the somewhat accidental invention of the vibrator. More to the point, though, is the sexism of the day as Dalrymple's feisty daughter Charlotte (a lively Gyllenhaal) not only helps the poor but supports suffrage at a time when it was unpopular to do so. Director Wexler's film chooses to make that story secondary, instead focusing on romance and comedy. **100m/C; DVD, Blu-Ray, Streaming; Closed Captioned.** *UK FR GE LU* Hugh Dancy; Maggie Gyllenhaal; Jonathan Pryce; Felicity Jones; Rupert Everett; Ashley Jensen; **D:** Tanya Wexler; **W:** Stephen Dyer; Jonah Lisa Dyer; **C:** Sean Bobbitt; **M:** Gast Waltzing.

Hysterical 🦴🦴 **1983 (PG)** Odd little attempt at a horror flick parody features the Hudson Brothers and involves a haunted lighthouse occupied by the vengeful spirit of a spurned woman. Late-night fun. **86m/C; VHS, DVD.** Brett Hudson; Bill Hudson; Mark Hudson; Cindy Pickett; Richard Kiel; Julie Newmar; Bud Cort; **D:** Chris Bearde; **W:** Brett Hudson; Bill Hudson; Mark Hudson; Trace Johnston; **C:** Thomas Del Ruth; **M:** Robert Alcivar.

Hysterical Blindness 🦴🦴 1/2 **2002** It's 1987 in Bayonne, New Jersey where Debby (Thurman) and her best friend Beth (Lewis) like to hang out at the local bar and pick up guys. Despite her looks, Debby, who lives with her waitress mom Virginia (Rowlands), comes off as so needy that she can't find anything more stable than a one-night stand. Meanwhile, Beth neglects her young daughter for non-committal barender Bobby (de Sando) and Viriginia gets a second chance with nice-guy customer Nick (Gazzara). Overly familiar and somewhat shrill; the best reason to watch are veterans Rowlands and Gazzara. Cahill adapted from her play. **99m/C; VHS, DVD.** Uma Thurman; Juliette Lewis; Gena Rowlands; Ben Gazzara; Justin Chambers; Anthony De Sando; Jolie Peters; **D:** Mira Nair; **W:** Laura Cahill; **C:** Declan Quinn; **M:** Lesley Barber. **CABLE**

I, a Woman 🦴🦴 *Jag, en Kvinna* **1966** Siv (Persson) is a seductive young nurse who likes to have sex with every man she meets—and then leave them after they fall in love with her. Based on the novel by the pseudonoromous Siv Holm. Dubbed. **90m/B; VHS, DVD.** *SW* Essy Persson; Jorgen Reenberg; Preben Mahrt; **D:** Mac Ahlberg; **W:** Peer Guldbrandsen; **C:** Mac Ahlberg.

I Accidentally Domed Your Son 🦴🦴 **2004 (R)** Uneven urban comedy has four friends trying to score some pot from the local kingpin's son. When the kid ends up dead, the over-protective boss sends his killers after the guys, so they head underground to try to change their appearance and get away. Fans of the genre and star Kurupt may be the only ones pleased by this one. **89m/C; VHS, DVD.** Ryan Combs; Tony Cox; Kurupt; Pedro (Pete) Pano; **D:** Ryan Combs; **W:** Ryan Combs. **VIDEO**

I Accuse My Parents 🦴 1/2 **1945** Juvenile delinquent tries to blame a murder and his involvement in a gang of thieves on his mom and dad's failure to raise him properly. **70m/B; VHS, DVD.** Mary Beth Hughes; Robert Lowell; John Miljan; Edward Earle; Patricia Knox; George Meeker; George Lloyd; **D:** Sam Newfield; **W:** Marjorie Dudley; **C:** Robert E. Cline; **M:** Lee Zahler.

I Am 🦴🦴 **2011** Successful director and producer Shadyac enters the documentary arena seeking the meaning of life by reaching out to a wide range of community members—from his own father (Richard Shadyac, formerly CEO of St. Jude Hospital's fundraising division) to linguist Noam Chomsky and Archbishop Desmond Tutu. After building a career on somewhat juvenile comedy, a serious bike accident left him physically and emotionally struggling and he purposely abandoned his wealthy way of life. A very likeable and funny guy at heart, his efforts here are admirable yet a bit lacking and slightly inane. **76m/C; On Demand.** Tom Shadyac; Noam Chomsky; Coleman Barks; Howard Zinn; Desmond Tutu; **D:** Tom Shadyac.

I Am a Fugitive from a Chain Gang 🦴🦴🦴🦴 *I Am a Fugitive From the Chain Gang* **1932** WWI veteran Muni returns home with dreams of traveling across America. After a brief stint as a clerk, he strikes out on his own. Near penniless, Muni meets up with a tramp who takes him to get a hamburger. He becomes an unwilling accomplice when the bum suddenly robs the place. Convicted and sentenced to a Georgia chain gang, he's brutalized and degraded, though he eventually escapes and lives the life of a criminal on the run. Based on the autobiography by Robert E. Burns. Brutal docu-details combine with powerhouse performances to create a classic. Timeless and thought-provoking. **93m/B; VHS, DVD.** Paul Muni; Glenda Farrell; Helen Vinson; Preston Foster; Edward Ellis; Allen Jenkins; **D:** Mervyn LeRoy; **W:** Howard J. Green. Natl. Film Reg. '91.

I Am Bolt 🦴🦴🦴 **2016 (PG)** This feature-length documentary explores the life and influence of the fastest man in history, Jamaican sprinter Usain Bolt. Offering a behind-the-scenes look at his life on and off the track, Bolt's family life, grueling training regime, competitions, and periods of relaxation are revealed in depth. Interviews with international figures including Serena Williams, Pele, and Ziggy Marley offer insight into Bolt's status as a global icon. **107m/C; DVD, Blu-Ray, Streaming, Download.** Usain Bolt; **D:** Benjamin Turner; Gabe Turner; **C:** Patrick Smith; **M:** Ian Arber. **VIDEO**

I Am Cuba 🦴🦴 *Soy Cuba; Ja Cuba* **1964** Agitprop Russian-Cuban co-production illustrates different aspects of the Cuban revolution from the toppling of Batista's decadent Havana to idealistic soldiers and student revolutionaries. Lots of oratory and deliberate artificiality combined with cinematographer Urusevky's stunning high-contrast photography. Spanish and Russian with subtitles. **141m/B; VHS, DVD.** *CU RU* Luz Maria Collazo; Jose Gallardo; Sergio Corrieri; Jean Bouise; Raul Garcia; Celia Rodriguez; **D:** Mikhail Kalatozov; **W:** Yevgeny Yevtushenko; Enrique Pineda Barnet; **C:** Sergei Urusevsky; **M:** Carlos Farinas.

I Am Curious (Yellow) 🦴🦴 1/2 *Jag ar nyfiken-gul; Jag ar nyfiken-en film i gult* **1967** A woman sociologist is conducting a sexual survey on Swedish society, which leads her to have numerous sexual encounters in all sorts of places. Very controversial upon its U.S. release because of the nudity and sexual content but tame by today's standards. Followed by "I Am Curious (Blue)" which was filmed at the same time. In Swedish with English subtitles. **95m/B; VHS, DVD.** *SW* Lena Nyman; Peter Lindgren; Borje Ahlstedt; Marie Goranzon; Magnus Nilsson; **D:** Vilgot Sjoman; **W:** Vilgot Sjoman; **M:** Bengt Ernryd.

I Am David 🦴🦴 **2004 (PG)** Unlikely adventure story follows the travails of a 12-year-old orphan named David (Tibber), who escapes from a 1952 Stalinist labor camp in Bulgaria and makes his way across Greece, Italy, and Switzerland to safety in Denmark. He gets really lucky—first his nice camp friend Johannes (Caviezel) helps him, then nice Italian Roberto (De Vito), and then nice Swiss grandmother Sophie (Plowright). Based on the novel "North to Freedom" by Anne Holm. **95m/C; VHS, DVD.** Ben Tibber; Joan Plowright; James (Jim) Caviezel; Maria Bonnevie; Paco Reconti; Hristo Naumov Shopov; Alessandro Sperduti; Viola Carinci; Silvia De Santis; **D:** Paul Feig; **M:** Stewart Copeland.

I Am Legend 🦴🦴🦴 **2007 (PG-13)** Third adaptation of Richard Matheson's 1954 classic novel, following "The Last Man on Earth" and "The Omega Man," about Robert Neville (Smith), a scientist who is the last man standing after a massive plague wipes out the entire world population. However, after three years of biological research and wandering the desolate streets of Manhattan with his dog, he discovers he may not be alone. Will Smith holds his own, with some big special effects carrying the rest. Entertaining as it is, apparently logic and coherency were lost in the plague as well. **100m/C; Blu-Ray, On Demand.** Will Smith; Dash Mihok; Salli Richardson-Whitfield; Alice Braga; Charlie Tahan; Willow Smith; **D:** Francis Lawrence; **W:** Mark Protosevich; Akiva Goldsman; **C:** Andrew Lesnie; **M:** James Newton Howard.

I Am Love 🦴🦴🦴 *Lo Sono L'Amore* **2009 (R)** Deep and rich depiction of an oppressed Russian woman who is never completely accepted into the wealthy Italian family she married into. As her husband is given control of the family's textile business, Emma (Swinson), struggles to find liberation in a culture so steeped in centuries of Italian tradition. Although looking the part of an untouchable aristocratic wife, Emma's facade begins to crack when she discovers her daughter is a lesbian. Director Guadagnino brings style to a very human melodrama without a trace of camp or irony. Brit starlet Swinson learned to speak Italian with a Russian accent for her role. English, Italian, and Russian with subtitles. **119m/C; Blu-Ray, On Demand.** *IT* Tilda Swinton; Gabriele Ferzetti; Alba Rohrwacher; Diane Fleri; Waris Ahluwalia; Marisa Berenson; Flavio Parenti; Edoardo Gabbriellini; Pippo Delbono; Maria Paiato; **D:** Luca Guadagnino; **W:** Ivan Cotroneo; Walter Fasano; Luca Guadagnino; Barbara Alberti; **C:** Yorick Le Saux; **M:** John Adams.

I Am Michael 🦴🦴 1/2 **2017** Justin Kelly adapts Benoit Denizet-Lewis' New York Times Magazine's article about Michael Glatze, a famous gay activist who became even more famous when he denounced homosexuality and became a Christian pastor. There's an admirable desire to not demonize a man who arguably betrayed and rejected the young men he encouraged to embrace their sexuality, but this is still too often a flat, TV-esque drama, elevated only through Franco's committed performance as the lead. As hard as it may be to understand Glatze's about-face, Franco tries to do just that, finding something truthful in something generally unimaginable. **98m/C; DVD, Streaming.** James Franco; Zachary Quinto; Emma Roberts; Daryl Hannah; Leven Rambin; **D:** Justin Kelly; **W:** Justin Kelly; **C:** Christopher Blauvelt; **M:** Tim Kvasnosky; Jake Shears.

I Am Not A Serial Killer 🦴🦴 1/2 **2016** A serial killer who may be a supernatural monster has hit town, and only angsty teen John (Max Records) has any idea how to find and stop him. Unfortunately for the town, John is not the cliché kid in every horror movie no one believes. John is a barely restrained psychopath who feels a deep seated need to murder people himself, and only retains his humanity by closely adhering to a set of rules. Rules he will need to break in order to stop the killer. **104m/C; DVD, Blu-Ray, Streaming.** *IR UK*

I Am Not a Witch 🦴🦴 1/2 **2018** In a Zambian village, young Shula (Mulubwa) is accused of being a witch. Several villagers report her to Officer Josephine (Mumanonga), without any evidence of black magic. One villager reports that Shula cut off one of his arms with an ax, though he has both of his arms as he tells his story. Josephine relays information about Shula to Mr. Banda (Phiri), a government official in charge of witch camps where the accused are used as unpaid labor. Though Banda eagerly punishes Shula, the older accused try to protect her. Carefully balancing satire and drama, the film is driven by Mulubwa's nuanced performance. **90m/C; DVD.** Maggie Mulubwa; Henri B.J. Phiri; Nancy Murilo; Gloria Huwiler; Travers Merrill; ***D:*** Rungano Nyoni; ***W:*** Rungano Nyoni; ***C:*** David Gallego; ***M:*** Matthew James Kelly.

I Am Not Your Negro **2017 (PG-13)** Based on James Baldwin's incendiary and phenomenal unfinished manuscript for "Remember This House," Peck's documentary captures race relations in the 2010s by using words written a half-century earlier. Baldwin's account of the deaths of Medgar Evers, Malcolm X, and Martin Luther King Jr. is read by Samuel L. Jackson over footage of the fight for Civil Rights from not just the era of those leaders but today. The result is a striking picture of how much that was relevant then is still relevant today. It's a daring and complex approach to non-fiction filmmaking that works. **95m/C; DVD, Blu-Ray.** Samuel L. Jackson; James Baldwin; Dick Cavett; ***D:*** Raoul Peck; ***W:*** James Baldwin; ***M:*** Alexei Aigui. British Acad. '17: Feature Doc.

I Am Number Four **2011 (PG-13)** Nine alien teens come to Earth after their planet is destroyed, blending in as typical high school students. After enemies zap away aliens Number One through Three, John (Pettyfer)?AKA Number Four—turns to alien refugee Henri (Olyphant) for protection. A fling with Earth girl Sarah (Agron) gives him more reason to fight back against his extra-terrestrial predators. Nothing more than a cash-in on the "Twilight" phenomenon, only with big, noisy battle sequences. Devoid of original thought while masking gaping plot holes by parading fresh flesh for its teen girl target audience. Adapted from the 2010 YA novel by Pittacus Lore (pseudonym of authors James Frey and Jobie Hughes). **104m/C; Blu-Ray.** Alex Pettyfer; Timothy Olyphant; Dianna Agron; Kevin Durand; Teresa Palmer; ***D:*** D.J. Caruso; ***W:*** Alfred Gough; Miles Millar; Marti Noxon; ***C:*** Guillermo Navarro; ***M:*** Trevor Rabin.

I Am Omega **2007** Sci Fi Channel horror that's a rip-off of "I Am Legend." L.A. has been overrun with cannibal survivors of a plague and non-infected Renchard (Dacascos) is setting bombs to blow up the city, apparently in an effort to stop the contagion (or maybe he just likes things to go boom). Brianna (Wiggins), another non-infected survivor, shows up claiming to know about a cure and wanting to get to Antioch, a town the non-infected have allegedly made their own. Two soldiers then come along with bad intentions. Low-budget and with plot holes bigger than the explosions Renchard likes. **90m/C; DVD, Blu-Ray.** Mark Dacascos; Jennifer Lee Wiggins; Ryan Llody; Geoff Mead; ***D:*** Griff Furst; ***W:*** Geoff Mead; ***C:*** Alexander Yellen; ***M:*** David Raiklen. **CABLE**

I Am Potential **2015** An uplifting drama based on the true story of Patrick Henry Hughes (Bellinger). Born with eyes and improperly formed joints, Patrick Henry cannot walk and endures multiple surgeries. Yet, he is a gifted musician and singer, and longs to be a member of a marching band. To help him achieve his goal, his father (Jenkins) must let go of his own dreams and goals and plans for his son. **94m/C; DVD.** Jimmy Bellinger; Burgess Jenkins; Jama Williamson; Judge Reinhold; Lance E. Nichols; ***D:*** Zach Meiners; ***W:*** Zach Meiners; ***C:*** Austin Brooks; ***M:*** B.J. Davis.

I Am Sam **1/2 2001 (PG-13)** Single father Penn has the mental capacity of a seven-year-old which makes authorities question his ability to raise young daughter Fanning. Pfeifer's the hard-edged lawyer who comes to his aid and becomes a better person for it. Overly sentimental and sweet, with not much new to offer except the obvious talent of Fanning. **93m/C; VHS, DVD.** Sean Penn; Michelle Pfeiffer; Dakota Fanning; Dianne Wiest; Loretta Devine; Richard Schiff; Laura Dern; Brad Allan Silverman; Stanley DeSantis; Doug Hutchison; Joseph Rosenberg; Mary Steenburgen; ***D:*** Jessie Nelson; ***W:*** Jessie Nelson; Kristine Johnson; ***C:*** Elliot Davis; ***M:*** John Powell.

I Am the Cheese **1983** An institutionalized boy undergoes psychiatric treatment; with the aid of his therapist (Wagner) he relives his traumatic childhood and finds out the truth about the death of his parents. A bit muddled, but with its moments. Adapted from a Robert Cormier teen novel. **95m/C; VHS, DVD.** Robert MacNaughton; Hope Lange; Don Murray; Robert Wagner; Sudie Bond; Cynthia Nixon; John Fiedler; ***D:*** Robert Jiras; ***M:*** Jonathan Tunick.

I Am Vengeance **1/2** *Vengeance* **2018 (R)** British military veteran John Gold (Bennett) makes his living as a gun for hire. When his best friend is killed, he goes to the small town of Devotion to investigate. John finds that former soldiers are involved in organized crime activities organized by Hatcher (Daniels). John has violent encounters with locals and gets closer to the high-end estate where Hatcher trains the soldiers. This British action film has positives, including exploring the effects of small town drug use, displaying a sense of humor, and infusing energy into fight scenes. However, it's pure B-movie quality. **93m/C; DVD.** Stu Bennett; Fleur Keith; Alan Calton; Gary Daniels; Keith Allen; ***D:*** Ross Boyask; ***W:*** Ross Boyask; ***C:*** Simon Rowling; ***M:*** Greenhaus.

I Am Vengeance: Retaliation **1/2 2020 (R)** John Gold (Bennett) is a former British special ops soldier turned mercenary and seeker of revenge. Because of his skill set and background, he is recruited by his former commander, Frost (Griffin), to take charge of a commando unit on a mission. Gold and his team are charged with capturing his former fellow soldier Sean Teague (Jones), who once betrayed Gold and their special ops group while on a failed mission in Eastern Europe years before. A ho-hum low-budget sequel with endless hand-to-hand combat and fighting sequences and very little plot. **90m/C; DVD.** Stu Bennett; Vinnie Jones; Sam Benjamin; Lee Charles; Tony Cook; ***D:*** Ross Boyask; ***W:*** Ross Boyask; ***C:*** Simon Rowling; ***M:*** Thomas Andrew Gallegos. **VIDEO**

I Am Wrath **2016 (R)** An action crime drama about a vigilante seeking justice for his wife's murder. A former member of Black Ops, Stanley Hill (Travolta) has suffered through a difficult tragedy. He his wife being murdered by a street gang. Though the police arrest a prime suspect, he is allowed to go free. An enraged Stanley takes the law into his own hands. With the help of a former comrade, Stanley learns of a far-reaching conspiracy and takes part in a showdown for justice. **?m/CDVD, Blu-Ray, Streaming, Download.** John Travolta; Christopher Meloni; Amanda Schull; Sam Trammell; Patrick St. Esprit; ***D:*** Chuck Russell; ***W:*** Paul Sloan; ***C:*** Andrzej Sekula; ***M:*** Haim Mazar.

I Am Zozo **1/2 2012** Based on real experiences, a psychological horror-thriller centered on an encounter with an ancient evil. On Halloween night, five teens play with an Ouija board. In the course of the evening, they make contact with a malicious demon from ancient times called ZoZo. According to the legend of ZoZo, this spirit becomes attached to people through Ouija board. The five soon learn the extent of the darkness brought forth by this heinous force. **85m/C; DVD, Streaming, Download.** Kelly McLaren; Courtney Foxworthy; Demetrius Sager; Caleb Courtney; Caleb Debattista; ***D:*** Scott Di Lalla; ***W:*** Scott Di Lalla; ***C:*** Scott Di Lalla; ***M:*** B.C. Smith. **VIDEO**

I Bury the Living **1958** A cemetery manager sticks pins in his map of a graveyard and people mysteriously start to die. Well-done suspense film. **76m/B; VHS, DVD, Blu-Ray.** Richard Boone; Theodore Bikel; Peggy Maurer; Herbert Anderson; Howard Smith; Robert Osterloh; Russ Bender; Matt Moore; Ken Drake; Glenn Vernon; Lynn Bernay; Cyril Delevanti; ***D:*** Albert Band; ***W:*** Louis Garfinkle; ***C:*** Frederick Gately; ***M:*** Gerald Fried.

I Can Do Bad All By Myself **1/2** *Tyler Perry's I Can Do Bad All By Myself* **2009 (PG-13)** Tyler Perry's Madea franchise continues, but this time Madea (Perry) offers up some laughs and then steps aside, allowing the real story to develop. Don't expect any surprises, though. In this installment, Madea finds three teens robbing her home, and after learning that their druggy mom is dead and grandma is missing, she sends them to live with hard-drinking, tough-living nightclub singer Aunt April. April's life and outlook are transformed with the help of church lady Miss Wilma (Knight) and a nightclub owner (Blige), who both belt out powerful vocal performances. It's never in doubt that April will embrace her lessons in caring and generosity, but fans of Perry will absolutely love the journey. **113m/C; Blu-Ray, On Demand.** Tyler Perry; Taraji P. Henson; Gladys Knight; Brian White; Adam Rodriguez; Hope Olaide Wilson; Mary J. Blige; Marvin Winans; Kwesi Boakye; Frederick Siglar; ***D:*** Tyler Perry; ***W:*** Tyler Perry; ***C:*** Alexander Grusynski.

I Can Get It For You Wholesale **1951** Hayward's character is unlikeable and her change of heart is abrupt but the look at New York's rag trade is interesting in this adaptation of the Jerome Weidman novel. Ambitious Harriet (Hayward) wants to be more than a showroom model. She recruits salesman Teddy (Dailey) and manager Sam (Jaffe) to start their own fashion design company. Harriet is wooed by department store owner Noble (Sanders) to design exclusive evening wear, which Teddy insists isn't their market. Harriet's pride is greater than her common sense. **91m/B; DVD.** Susan Hayward; Dan Dailey; George Sanders; Sam Jaffe; Randy Stuart; ***D:*** Michael Gordon; ***W:*** Abraham Polonsky; Vera Caspary; ***C:*** Milton Krasner; ***M:*** Sol Kaplan.

I Can Only Imagine **1/2 2018 (PG)** This faith-based biopic explains the origins of the titular song by Christian band MercyMe. In small town Texas, Bart Millard (Finley) grows up with an abusive father (Quaid), and, after age 13, absent mother. At praise camp, Bart discovers his Christian faith and a childhood sweetheart, both of which help him cope with his father's beatings. As the talented Bart seriously pursues music after high school, he forms MercyMe, gains help from manager Brickell (Adkins) and singer Amy Grant (DuPort), and writes his famous song, which becomes the best-selling Christian single ever. The optimistic film offers a heart-felt message about inspiration and forgiveness. **110m/C; DVD, Blu-Ray.** Dennis Quaid; J. Michael Finley; Trace Adkins; Madeline Carroll; Cloris Leachman; ***D:*** Andrew Erwin; Jon Erwin; ***W:*** Jon Erwin; Brent McCorkle; ***C:*** Kristopher S. Kimlin; ***M:*** Brent McCorkle.

I Can't Sleep *J'ai Pas Sommeil* **1993** Serial killers, French style. Gay, black Camille (Courcet), an immigrant from Martinique, and his white lover Raphael (Dupont) live in a Paris hotel and murder elderly women. Though they also rob them, the motive for their horrific crimes is vague (seemingly even to themselves). Not much actually happens—Camille visits his brother, who longs to return home, and their status as outsiders is juxtaposed against another immigrant, Daiga (Golubeva) from Lithuania, who takes little interest in the crimes but unwittingly crosses paths with Camille. Atmospheric if nothing else. Based on the 1987 "Granny Killer" slayings of 20 women. French with subtitles. **110m/C; VHS, DVD.** ***FR*** Richard Courcet; Vincent Dupont; Yekaterina (Katia) Golubeva; Alex Descas; Beatrice Dalle; Laurent Grevill; ***D:*** Claire Denis; ***W:*** Claire Denis; Jean-Pol Fargeau; ***C:*** Agnes Godard; ***M:*** Jean Murat.

I Capture the Castle **1/2 2002 (R)** First, the R rating is dumb—it's for a bit of nudity that wouldn't shock a country vicar. Second, the film is based on the book by Dodie Smith (who wrote "101 Dalmatians") and is a coming-of-age tale set in 1936 in the Suffolk countryside. The Mortmains rent a small crumbling castle and times are hard. Dad James (Nighy) ignores his family and hides away to "write," leaving flaky second wife Topaz (Fitzgerald) to cope. Cassandra (Garai) is 17, smart, and pretty but overshadowed by her ambitious, beautiful older sister Rose (Bryne) who is determined to marry well. She gets her chance when two wealthy American brothers, Simon (Thomas) and Neil (Blucas), arrive to claim their inheritance, which includes the castle. Quite a romantic tangle ensues. Fine acting, particularly by Garai who gives the story its point of view. **113m/C; VHS, DVD.** ***GB*** Romola Garai; Rose Byrne; Henry Thomas; Marc Blucas; Bill Nighy; Tara Fitzgerald; Sinead Cusack; Henry Cavill; James Faulkner; Sarah Woodward; ***D:*** Tim Fywell; ***W:*** Heidi Thomas; ***C:*** Richard Greatrex; ***M:*** Dario Marianelli. L.A. Film Critics '03: Support. Actor (Nighy).

I Come in Peace *Dark Angel* **1990 (R)** A tough, maverick Texas cop embarks on a one-way ride to Nosebleed City when he attempts to track down a malevolent alien drug czar who kills his victims by sucking their brains. Mindless thrills. **92m/C; VHS, DVD, Blu-Ray, Streaming.** Dolph Lundgren; Brian Benben; Betsy Brantley; Jesse Vint; Michael J. Pollard; ***D:*** Craig R. Baxley; ***M:*** Jan Hammer.

I Confess **1/2 1953** Interesting but overly serious mid-career Hitchcock, adapted from Paul Anthelme's 1902 play, "Our Two Consciences." Father Michael Logan (Clift) is a young curate in Quebec, who hears the murder confession of Otto Keller (Hasse). Keller knows Father Logan can tell no one because of the sanctity of the confessional, even when Logan himself comes under suspicion for the crime. Unfortunately, the resolution to the conflict is not up to the master's usual standards. **95m/B; VHS, DVD, Blu-Ray.** Montgomery Clift; Anne Baxter; Karl Malden; Brian Aherne; O.E. Hasse; Dolly Haas; Roger Dann; ***D:*** Alfred Hitchcock; ***W:*** William Archibald; George Tabori; ***C:*** Robert Burks; ***M:*** Dimitri Tiomkin.

I Could Go on Singing **1/2 1963** An aging American songstress, on a tour in Britain, becomes reacquainted with her illegitimate son and his British father, but eventually goes back to the footlights. Garland's last film. Songs include "By Myself" and "It Never Was You." A must for Garland fans. Letterboxed. **99m/C; DVD, Blu-Ray.** Judy Garland; Dirk Bogarde; Jack Klugman; Aline MacMahon; ***D:*** Ronald Neame; ***W:*** Mayo Simon; ***C:*** Arthur Ibbetson; ***M:*** Mort Lindsey.

I Could Never Be Your Woman **1/2 2006 (PG-13)** Not terribly romantic or funny although Pfeiffer is as gorgeous as ever. Divorced and frazzled, 40-something TV sitcom producer Rosie (Pfeiffer) is shocked when she falls for the show's newest cast member, the years-younger Adam (Rudd). Meanwhile, Rosie's teen daughter Izzy (Ronan) is in the throes of first love. Thrown into the mix—and an uneasy addition—is Ullman's Mother Nature, who appears as Rosie's conscience, offering unsolicited and unwelcome romantic advice. **97m/C; DVD.** Michelle Pfeiffer; Paul Rudd; Stacey Dash; Tracey Ullman; Fred Willard; Henry Winkler; Sally Kellerman; Jon Lovitz; Saoirse Ronan; Sarah Alexander; Brittany Benson; Jed Bernard; ***D:*** Amy Heckerling; ***W:*** Amy Heckerling; ***C:*** Brian Tufano.

I Cover the Waterfront **1/2 1933** A reporter is assigned to write about a boatman involved in a fishy scheme to smuggle Chinese immigrants into the country wrapped in shark skins. While trying to get the story, the journalist falls in love with the fisherman's daughter. Torrance passed away before its release. **70m/B; VHS, DVD.** Claudette Colbert; Ben Lyon; Ernest Torrence; Hobart Cavanaugh; ***D:*** James Cruze.

I, Daniel Blake **2016 (R)** After suffering a heart attack that renders him unable to work as a carpenter, Londoner Daniel Blake (an impressive Johns) befriends unemployed single mother Katie (an equally impressive Squires) as they navigate the welfare nightmare that is literally killing him. Blake has been destroyed by a system of red tape that can't give him a disability payment or a job, but finds solace in trying to help Katie. Director Loach is back in this groove with another story of the put-upon working class. He manages to make you care despite the moments of undeniable heartstring tugging. **100m/C; DVD, Blu-Ray.** Dave Johns; Hayley Squires; Sharon Percy; Briana Shann; Dylan McKiernan; ***D:*** Ken Loach; ***W:*** Paul Laverty; ***C:*** Robbie Ryan; ***M:*** George Fenton.

I Declare War **2012** A captivating comedy-adventure-drama that explores human nature through child's play. One afternoon, a group of friends decide to play the game "capture the flag" in nearby woods. The 13 year olds keep it simple, with sticks, rules, and imagination. But the game takes a dark turn as feelings like jealousy and betrayal emerge during the battle for victory. Imaginations take over and fantasy becomes reality, and the disturbing side of human nature emerges among the child/warriors. **94m/C; DVD, Blu-Ray, Streaming, Download.** Siam Yu; Gage Munroe; Michael Friend; Aidan Gouveia; Mackenzie Munro; ***D:*** Jason Lapeyre; ***W:***

Jason Lapeyre; *C:* Ray Dumas; *M:* Eric Cadesky; Nick Dyer.

I Died a Thousand Times ✍✍ **1955** Aging gangster Mad Dog Earle (pushup prince Palance) plans one last death-defying heist while hiding from police in the mountains. Meanwhile, the hard boiled gangster softens a bit thanks to surgery-needing girlfriend, but moll Winters doesn't seem to think that three's company. A low rent "High Sierra." From the novel by W.R. Burnett. **109m/C; VHS, DVD.** Jack Palance; Shelley Winters; Lori Nelson; Lee Marvin; Earl Holliman; Lon Chaney, Jr.; Howard St. John; *D:* Stuart Heisler; *W:* W.R. Burnett.

I Dismember Mama WOOF! *Poor Albert and Little Annie* **1974 (R)** Classless story of an asylum inmate who escapes to kill his mother. Although he hates women, he likes little girls as evidenced by his nine-year-old love interest. Notably lacking in bloody scenes. **81m/C; VHS, DVD.** Zooey Hall; Joanne Moore Jordan; Greg Mullavey; Marlene Tracy; Geri Reischl; Frank Whiteman; *D:* Paul Leder; *W:* William W. Norton, Sr.; *C:* Andreas Mannkopff; *M:* Herschel Burke Gilbert.

I Do ✍ 1/2 *Prete-Moi ta Main* **2006** Overplayed and obvious romantic comedy. Middle-aged Luis (Chabat) is happily single since his over-protective mother and multiple sisters care for him. But when they finally insist he get married, Luis decides to hire a fiance to charm them and then leave him at the altar. Emma's (Gainsbourg) a hit, but when she dumps Luis, his family insist he win back the perfect woman. The original French title translates to "lend me your hand." French with subtitles. **90m/C; DVD.** *FR* Alain Chabat; Charlotte Gainsbourg; Bernadette LaFont; Gregoire Oestermann; Wladimir Yordanoff; *D:* Eric Lartigau; *W:* Laurent Zeitoun; Laurent Tiraud; Philippe Mechelen; Gregoire Vigeron; *C:* Regis Blondeau; *M:* Erwann Kermorvant.

I Do ✍✍✍ **2013** Gaylord's pic could have been little more than a gay version of Peter Weir's "Green Card," but it finds truth in its admittedly clichéd set-up. Screenwriter Ross also stars as Jack Edwards, a Brit living in NYC who learns that the renewal of his work visa is denied and he'll be deported. Though Jack's fallen in love with Spainard Mano (Compte), a gay marriage would have no impact on his immigration situation. He opts for a green card marriage to his lesbian friend Ali (Sigler) and, of course, things get complicated. Strong performances throughout an an emotionally volatile end scenario. **91m/C; DVD.** David W. Ross; Jamie-Lynn Sigler; Alicia Witt; Maurice Compte; Grant Bowler; *D:* Glenn Gaylord; *W:* David W. Ross; *C:* David Maurice Gil; *M:* Jordan Balagot; Gabriel Isaac Mounsey.

I Do & I Don't ✍✍ **2007 (R)** Bob and Cheryl must complete pre-marital instruction before being allowed to wed in the Catholic Church. The priest at Cheryl's family parish suggests one-on-one counseling with long-time marrieds Dick and Nora but is apparently unaware that the crazy couple is seriously considering divorce and not likely to be inspirational (except for what not to do). **83m/C; DVD.** Bryan Callen; Alexie Gilmore; Matt Servitto; Jane Lynch; Eric Zuckerman; Cynthia Harris; James Murtaugh; Adam LeFevre; *D:* Steve Blair; *W:* Steve Blair; *C:* Todd Evans; *M:* Adam Jones. **VIDEO**

I Do (But I Don't) ✍✍ 1/2 **2004** Type-A wedding planner Lauren Crandall is convinced that handsome fireman Nick is engaged to her wealthy bridezilla client Darla. Naturally, this is only the first in a series of misunderstandings. Adapted from the Cara Lockwood novel. **88m/C; DVD.** Denise Richards; Dean Cain; Karen Cliche; Jessica Walter; Mimi Kuzyk; David Lipper; Yannick Bisson; *D:* Kelly Makin; *W:* Eric Charmelo; Nicole Snyder; *C:* Serge Landouceur; *M:* Danny Lux. **CABLE**

I Don't Buy Kisses Anymore ✍✍ 1/2 **1992 (PG)** Heartwarming story starring Alexander and Peeples as two mismatched lovers who end up realizing that they're made for each other. Alexander plays Bernie Fishbine, an overweight Jewish shoe store owner who falls for a psychology graduate student (Peeples). Little does he know, but Peeples is studying him for her term paper, appropriately titled "The Psychological Study of an Obese Male." Alexander gives a great performance, as do Kazan and Jacobi who play Bernie's parents. **112m/C; VHS, DVD.** Jason Alexander; Nia Peeples; Lainie Kazan; Lou Jacobi; Eileen Brennan; Larry Storch; Arleen (Arlene) Sorkin; *D:* Robert Marcarelli; *W:* Jonnie Lindsell; *C:* Michael Ferris; *M:* Cobb Bussinger. **TV**

The I Don't Care Girl ✍✍ **1953** In this musical bio, producer George Jessel (playing himself) is unhappy with the screen treatment of vaudeville star Eva Tanguay (Gaynor). So he sends the writers to talk to her first partner, Ed McCoy (Wayne), leading to other interviews and showbiz stories. This allows Gaynor to show off her singing and dancing skills without having to worry about the plot, espeically since the film was badly recut, allegedly at the behest of Fox studio head Dary F. Zanuck. **78m/C; DVD.** Mitzi Gaynor; David Wayne; Oscar Levant; Bob Graham; Warren Stevens; George Jessel; *D:* Lloyd Bacon; *W:* Walter Bullock; *C:* Arthur E. Arling.

I Don't Feel at Home in This World Anymore ✍✍✍ **2017** This Sundance Grand Jury Award winner is the directorial debut of "Blue Ruin" star Macon Blair, and he learned a thing or two about dark, witty tension from that film. Ruth (the always-great Lynskey) is a fed-up nursing assistant who reaches her breaking point after she finds her house robbed. After tracking down her stolen laptop, Ruth asks her quirky, martial-arts lovin' neighbor Tony (Wood) to help her hunt down the criminals, going down a rabbit hole of increasingly dangerous behavior. While this isn't without some debut director flaws, Lynskey and Wood are so much fun that it doesn't matter. **93m/C; DVD, Streaming.** Melanie Lynskey; Elijah Wood; Jane Levy; Devon Graye; Christine Woods; *D:* Macon Blair; *W:* Macon Blair; *C:* Larkin Seiple; *M:* Brooke Blair; Will Blair. **VIDEO**

I Don't Kiss ✍✍ *J'embrasse Pas* **1991** An episodic pic about Pierre (Blanc), a young man from the country who has dreams of finding success as an actor in Paris. But he soon finds himself making a living as a hustler with only fellow prostie Ingrid (Beart) offering genuine friendship. French with subtitles. **116m/C; DVD.** *FR* Manuel Blanc; Emmanuelle Beart; Philippe Noiret; Helene Vincent; Ivan Desny; Roschdy Zem; Jacques Nolot; Christophe Bernard; *D:* Andre Techine; *W:* Jacques Nolot; *C:* Thierry Arbogast; *M:* Philippe Sarde.

I Don't Know How She Does It ✍ 1/2 **2011 (PG-13)** Apparently she can't really do it all as this cliche-ridden pic, an adaptation of Allison Pearson's 2002 novel, shows. Frazzled and frequently humiliated Boston working mom Kate Reddy (Parker) tries to maintain a delicate balancing act between her high-finance career and home lives. But her downsized architect husband Richard (Kinnear) gets his ideal job just as Kate gets a big promotion that means frequent trips to New York where she has to work with flirty, appreciative associate Jack (Brosnan). The leads all do professional work (and have charm to spare) but the flick is so predictable it's a mostly-wasted effort. **95m/C; DVD.** Sarah Jessica Parker; Pierce Brosnan; Greg Kinnear; Christina Hendricks; Olivia Munn; Kelsey Grammer; Seth Meyers; Jane Curtin; Busy Philips; Sarah Shahi; Mark Blum; Jessica Szohr; *D:* Douglas McGrath; *W:* Aline Brosh McKenna; *C:* Stuart Dryburgh; *M:* Aaron Zigman.

I Don't Want to Be Born ✍ *The Devil Within Her* **1975 (R)** It's got all the right ingredients for overnight camp: a spurned dwarf, a large, howling baby-thing, slice and dice murder and mayhem, and Collins. It could've been so bad. Instead, this "Rosemary's Baby" rehash is just stupid bad. **90m/C; VHS, DVD, Blu-Ray.** *GB* Joan Collins; Eileen Atkins; Donald Pleasence; Ralph Bates; Caroline Munro; *D:* Peter Sasdy.

I Don't Want to Talk About It ✍✍ 1/2 *De Eso No Se Habla* **1994** Fable set in a small South American town in the '30s. The widowed Leonor (Brando) is the community leader, a woman determined to see that her daughter Charlotte (Podesta) be as happy and accomplished as possible. Leonor refuses to acknowledge Charlotte is a dwarf and size is never permitted to be mentioned in her presence. Her zealous protectiveness is challenged by worldly and charming newcomer Ludovico (Mastroianni) who becomes entranced by Charlotte. Mastroianni is masterly as always but the moody film proves slight. Based on story by Julio Llinas. Spanish with subtitles. **102m/C; VHS, Streaming.** *AR* Marcello Mastroianni; Luisina Brando; Alejandra Podesta; *D:* Maria-Luisa Bemberg; *W:* Maria-Luisa Bemberg; Jorge Goldenberg.

I Dood It ✍✍ *By Hook or By Crook* **1943** Young tailor's assistant Skelton falls hard for young actress Powell working near his shop. She agrees to date, and eventually marry him, but only to spite her boyfriend who has just run off with another woman. All's well however, when Skelton stumbles across a spy ring, is hailed a hero and helps Powell realize she really loves him. **102m/B; VHS, DVD.** Red Skelton; Eleanor Powell; Richard Ainley; Patricia Dane; Sam Levene; Thurston Hall; Lena Horne; Butterfly McQueen; *D:* Vincente Minnelli.

I Downloaded a Ghost ✍✍ 1/2 **2004 (PG)** Amusing family-oriented Halloween TV movie. Misfit 12-year-old Stella (Page) wants to create the ultimate spooky haunted house for Halloween and repeatedly uses a ghost-oriented website for some tips. This leads to Stella accidentally contacting a ghost (who needs to make amends) who travels into her world. Now, unless she and her best pal Albert (Kaney) can help him, they've just made a new friend who they really don't want hanging around. **90m/C; DVD.** *CA* Ellen Page; Michael Kaney; Carlos Alazraqui; Gary Hudson; Barbara Alyn Woods; Vincent Corazza; Tim Progosh; Krista Mitchell; *D:* Kelly Sandefur; *W:* Jeff Phillips; *C:* Ken Krawczyk; *M:* Timothy S. (Tim) Jones. **TV**

I Dream of Jeannie ✍ **1952** The third and worst bio of Stephen Foster has Foster as a bookkeeper-cum-songwriter alternating between writing tunes and chasing Lawrence. When she dumps him, he goes into a funk. Will he be able to complete the title song? The suspense will kill you. Lots of singing, but not much else. **90m/C; VHS, DVD.** Ray Middleton; Bill (William) Shirley; Muriel Lawrence; Lynn Bari; Rex Allen; *D:* Allan Dwan.

I Dream of Murder ✍✍ **2006** Therapist Joanna (Blalock), on the verge of a midlife crisis, is horrified when a patient who dreamed of her own murder is killed. She risks her marriage and career to get overly involved in solving the crime, including getting close to her married patient's boyfriend. **90m/C; DVD.** Jolene Blalock; Martin Cummins; Greg Lawson; Carrie Colak; Judith Buchan; Eliabeth Lavender; *D:* Neill Fearnley; *W:* Cynthia Whitcomb; *C:* Craig Wrobleski; *M:* Bruce Leitl. **CABLE**

I Dreamed of Africa ✍✍ 1/2 **2000 (PG-13)** Okay the scenery is beautiful (it was filmed in Kenya), including blonde Basinger, but the story is predictable and trite despite being based on the autobiography of Italian socialite Kuki Gallmann. Gallmann (Basinger) trades in her designer duds for safari khaki when she, her young son, Emanuele (Aiken), and her second husband, Paolo (Perez), decide they need a fresh start. The somewhat irresponsible Paolo likes to go big game hunting with his friends, leaving Kuki alone, and she eventually becomes a conservationist after some personal tragedies. Most of the roles, except Basinger's, are one-dimensional. **114m/C; VHS, DVD.** Kim Basinger; Vincent Perez; Eva Marie Saint; Daniel Craig; Lance Reddick; Liam Aiken; Garrett Strommen; *D:* Hugh Hudson; *W:* Paula Milne; Susan Shilliday; *C:* Bernard Lutic; *M:* Maurice Jarre.

I Drink Your Blood ✍ 1/2 **1971 (R)** Hippie satanists looking for kicks spike an old man's drink with LSD. To get revenge, the old codger's grandson sells the nasty flower children meat pies injected with the blood of a rabid dog. The hippies then turn into cannibalistic maniacs, infecting anyone they bite. From the man responsible for "I Spit on Your Grave"; originally played on a double bill with "I Eat Your Skin." **83m/C; VHS, DVD, Blu-Ray.** Bhasker; Jadine Wong; Ronda Fultz; Elizabeth Marner-Brooks; George Patterson; Riley Mills; Iris Brooks; John Damon; Bruno Damon; *D:* David E. Durston; *W:* David E. Durston; *C:* Jacques Demarecaux; *M:* Clay Pitts.

I Eat Your Skin WOOF! *Voodoo Blood Bath; Zombie; Zombies* **1964** Cannibalistic zombies terrorize a novelist and his girlfriend on a Caribbean island. Blood and guts, usually shown on a gourmet double bill with "I Drink Your Blood." **82m/B; VHS, DVD.** William Joyce; Heather Hewitt; Betty Hyatt Linton; Robert Stanton; Dan Stapleton; *D:* Del Tenney; *W:* Del Tenney; *C:* Francois Farkas; *M:* Lon Norman.

I Escaped from the Gestapo ✍ 1/2 **1943** Wartime crime drama with a luridly misleading title. Nazi agents bust forger Torgen Lane (Jagger) out of prison and take him to their L.A. hideout.They force him to make counterfeit U.S. currency but he manages to engrave a message on one of the plates to alert the Feds to the funny money. **75m/B; DVD.** Dean Jagger; John Carradine; Mary Brian; Sidney Blackmer; Edward (Ed Kean, Keene) Keane; Anthony Warde; *D:* Harold Young; *W:* Martin Mooney; *C:* Ira Morgan; *M:* W. Franke Harling.

I Feel Pretty ✍✍ **2018 (PG-13)** A somewhat effective, modern fairy tale that explores issues related to women's self-esteem. When the unconfident Renee (Schumer) hits her head in a spin class accident, she believes she has been transformed into the beautiful bombshell she has longed to be. The newly confident Renee gains a coveted job at a high-end cosmetics company and a boyfriend (Scovel) because of her inner transformation. Schumer's surprisingly layered, inspired performance make the directing debut of screenwriters Kohn and Silverstein work despite a mixed message by the end of the film. **110m/C; DVD, Blu-Ray, Streaming.** *US CH* Amy Schumer; Michelle Williams; Rory Scovel; Emily Ratajkowski; Aidy Bryant; *D:* Abby Kohn; Marc Silverstein; *W:* Abby Kohn; Marc Silverstein; *C:* Florian Ballhaus; *M:* Michael Andrews.

I, Frankenstein WOOF! **2013 (PG-13)** Another tragically awful release, based on a graphic novel, with a lack of creativity or pure entertainment that should have Mary Shelley spinning in her grave. This effects-heavy nonsense recasts Frankenstein (Eckhart) as a centuries-spanning action hero who fights against the demons who have pursued him since the monster buried his creator. Reasonably talented people like Nighy and Otto are caught up in a film that aspires to nothing more challenging than an "Underworld" sequel, and yet it somehow fails to jump over even that incredibly low bar of quality. Loud and obnoxious, it should have been left for dead. **93m/C; DVD, Blu-Ray.** *US AU* Aaron Eckhart; Bill Nighy; Yvonne Strahovski; Miranda Otto; Jai Courtney; *D:* Stuart Beattie; *W:* Stuart Beattie; *C:* Ross Emery; *M:* Johnny Klimek; Reinhold Heil.

I Give It a Year ✍ 1/2 **2013 (R)** Awkward, racy Brit anti-rom com. Uptight ad exec Nat (Byrne) and layabout novelist Josh (Spall) have just gotten married despite friends and family being certain the mismatched Londoners won't last. After nine months, the newlyweds are seeking marital counseling and flashbacks reveal what's been going wrong, including them both being attracted to more suitable lovers. **97m/C; DVD, Blu-Ray, Streaming.** *UK* Rose Byrne; Rafe Spall; Anna Faris; Simon Baker; Minnie Driver; Stephen Merchant; Olivia Colman; Jason Flemyng; *D:* Dan Mazer; *W:* Dan Mazer; *C:* Ben Davis; *M:* Ilan Eshkeri.

I Got Five on It ✍ **2005** Absurd partying flick begins with Jimmy (Bridges) behind bars for buying dope, leaving his three spacey pals to fend for themselves. As they scavenge about town to score weed, trouble seems to be all they can find, even after Jimmy returns. **76m/C; DVD.** Todd Bridges; Jose Rosette; Chris Angelo; Carl Washington; *D:* Eduardo Quiroz; Jose Quiroz; *W:* Eduardo Quiroz; Jose Quiroz. **VIDEO**

I Got the Hook-Up ✍ 1/2 **1998 (R)** Inner-city hustlers Black (Master P) and Blue (Johnson) have their own "department store" in a vacant lot where they sell various goods of dubious quality and origin. When a truckload of cell phones is mistakenly delivered to them, it ushers them into a new business venture. All hell breaks loose when a thug (Lister) has a money pick-up go bad because of the defective phones. Sporadically amusing comedy plays gang violence and misogyny for laughs, while the leads do nothing to make their characters interesting or even likable. **93m/C; VHS, DVD.** Mark Zuelzke; A.J. (Anthony) Johnson; Gretchen Palmer; Frantz Turner; Tommy (Tiny) Lister; Helen Martin; John Witherspoon; Harrison White; Ice Cube; Anthony Boswell; Lola Mae; ***D:*** Michael Martin; ***W:*** Mark Zuelzke; ***C:*** Antonio Calvache; ***M:*** Tommy Coster; Brad Fairman.

I Hate Valentine's Day 1/2 **2009 (PG-13)** Vardalos' appeal comes from her everywoman qualities but she keeps undermining it by trying too hard to be the center of flattering attention. Brooklyn flower shop owner Genevieve is the one everyone turns to for romantic advice despite her stupid rule that she only dates a guy five times so the romantic infatuation will last (she says she's not interested in a relationship). Then along comes hunky new neighbor Greg (Corbett), they hit it off really well, and Genevieve starts rethinking her situation. **89m/C; DVD.** Nia Vardalos; John Corbett; Zoe Kazan; Gary Wilmes; Mike Starr; Judah Friedlander; Rachel Dratch; Jay O. Sanders; Stephen Guarino; Amir Arison; ***D:*** Nia Vardalos; ***W:*** Nia Vardalos; ***C:*** Brian Przypek; ***M:*** Keith Power.

I Heart Huckabees **2004 (R)** Director Russell's existential comedy has a cast willing to take chances with material that is too clever for its own good—and a viewers' enjoyment. Environmentalist/poet Albert (Schwartzman), fighting giant retail chain Huckabees, takes his search for enlightenment to the offices of existential detectives Bernard and Vivian Jaffe (Hoffman, Tomlin), who believe everything in life is connected. Albert thinks his nemesis is Huckabee's golden exec Brad Stand (Law) and Brad's gorgeous spokesmodel girlfriend Dawn (Watts) until they also become the Jaffes' clients. Then Albert befriends Tommy Corn (Wahlberg), a firefighter, who has become involved with French nihilist Caterine (Huppert), who believes everything is meaningless and...okay, things get even more convoluted, although Tomlin and Hoffman, at least, seem to be having a grand time. **105m/C; VHS, DVD.** Jason Schwartzman; Isabelle Huppert; Dustin Hoffman; Lily Tomlin; Jude Law; Mark Wahlberg; Naomi Watts; ***D:*** David O. Russell; ***W:*** David O. Russell; Jeff Baena; ***C:*** Peter Deming.

I Hope They Serve Beer in Hell **2009 (R)** With friends like these... Based on the true life stories of Tucker Max (Czuchry), who has his best bud Dan (Stults) lying to fiancee Kristy (Pratt) so Tucker can take Dan to an impromptu bachelor party at a strip club where things invariably go out of control. Disinvited from the wedding (and the friendship), Tucker has to figure out a way to get back into everyone's good graces. Unfortunately, main character Tucker is completely unlikable and narcissistic-to-the-nth degree and succeeds in making a supposed raunchy romp quite unfunny. **105m/C; Blu-Ray.** Matt Czuchry; Marika Dominczyk; Geoff Stults; Jesse Bradford; Keri Lynn Pratt; ***D:*** Bob Grosse; ***W:*** Tucker Max; Nils Parker; ***C:*** Suki Medencevic; ***M:*** James L. Venable.

The I Inside **2004 (R)** Simon (Phillipe) awakens in the hospital with no memory of the past two years. While trying to piece things together he finds he has the ability to travel from 2002 to the year 2000. It goes without saying this complicates his situation enormously as he discovers that he might not have been such a great guy before. **91m/C; DVD.** *GE* Ryan Phillipe; Sarah Polley; Piper Perabo; Stephen Rea; Robert Sean Leonard; Stephen Lang; Peter Egan; Stephen Graham; Rakie Ayola; ***D:*** Roland Suso Richter; ***W:*** Michael Cooney; Timothy Scott Bogart; ***C:*** Martin Langer; ***M:*** Adam F; Nicholas Pike.

I Killed My Mother *J'ai Tue Ma Mere* **2009** Flawed but bold debut for Dolan, who was 20 when he wrote, directed, starred, and produced. Self-absorbed and constantly angry high schooler Hubert can't abide anything about his single mom Chantal and doesn't tell her anything about his life (including the fact that he's gay). As their squabbles increase and his outbursts towards her become more aggressive, Chantal is forced to respond. Set in Montreal; French with subtitles. **96m/C; DVD.** *CA* Suzanne Clément; Patricia Tulasne; Xavier Dolan; Anne Dorval; François Arnaud; Niels Schneider; Monique Spaziani; ***D:*** Xavier Dolan; ***W:*** Xavier Dolan; ***C:*** Stephanie Anne Weber Biron; ***M:*** Nicholas Savard-L'Herbier.

I Killed That Man 1/2 **1942** A prisoner scheduled to die in the electric chair is given an early ticket out when he is found poisoned. Evidence points to an unusual group of suspects. Effective low-budget thriller offers a few unexpected surprises. **72m/B; VHS, DVD.** Ricardo Cortez; Joan Woodbury; Iris Adrian; George Pembroke; Herbert Rawlinson; Pat Gleason; Ralf Harolde; Jack Mulhall; Vince Barnett; Gavin Gordon; John Hamilton; ***D:*** Phil Rosen.

I Know My First Name Is Steven **1989** Heart-wrenching and infuriating true crime story. In 1972, serial child molester Kenneth Parnell (Howard) picks up 7-year-old Steven Stayner (Edwards) and convinces the child that his family has abandoned him. He then becomes the boy's 'father,' subjecting him to continual sexual abuse. When Steven is 14 (now played by Nemec), Parnell brings home a 5-year-old boy and Steven knows the youngster's fate. So he takes the child and escapes. Steven is reunited with his family but the adjustment is difficult and what follows is worse. **185m/C; DVD.** Corin "Corky" Nemec; Arliss Howard; Luke Edwards; Cindy Pickett; John Ashton; Pruitt Taylor Vince; Ray Walston; Gregg Henry; Jim Haynie; ***D:*** Larry Elikann; ***W:*** J.P. Miller; Cynthia Whitcomb; ***C:*** Eric Van Haren Noman; ***M:*** David Shire. **TV**

I Know What You Did Last Summer **1997 (R)** Four teens get involved in a fatal hit-and-run accident and think they've managed to keep it a secret. Good girl Julie (Hewitt), beauty queen Helen (Gellar), arrogant jock Barry (Philippe), and regular guy Ray (Prinze) make a pact to take the secret to their graves, which may be sooner than they thought. One year later, the quartet receive letters which give the movie its title and set them against each other. After a few youngsters are made into bait on rather large fishing hooks, they band together to stop the bloodthirsty killer. Hint: It's not Mrs. Paul. Another quality slasher throwback written by Kevin Williamson, the man who made you "Scream." **100m/C; VHS, DVD, Blu-Ray.** Jennifer Love Hewitt; Sarah Michelle Gellar; Ryan Phillippe; Freddie Prinze, Jr.; Muse Watson; Anne Heche; Bridgette Wilson-Sampras; Johnny Galecki; Dan Albright; ***D:*** Jim Gillespie; ***W:*** Kevin Williamson; ***C:*** Denis Crossan; ***M:*** John Debney.

I Know Where I'm Going **1945** A young woman (Hiller), who believes that money brings happiness, is on the verge of marrying a rich old man, until she meets a handsome naval officer (Livesey) and finds a happy, simple life. Early on the female lead appears in a dream sequence filmed in the mode of surrealist painter Salvador Dali and avant garde director Luis Bunuel. Scottish setting and folk songs give a unique flavor. Brown provides a fine performance as a native Scot. **91m/B; VHS, DVD.** *GB* Roger Livesey; Wendy Hiller; Finlay Currie; Pamela Brown; George Carney; Walter Hudd; ***D:*** Michael Powell; Emeric Pressburger; ***W:*** Michael Powell; Emeric Pressburger; ***C:*** Erwin Hillier; ***M:*** Allan Gray.

I Know Who Killed Me **2007 (R)** Upper middle class high school student Aubrey Fleming (Lohan) goes missing. Her distraught parents (Ormond and McDonough) cooperate with the police but have little insight into the disappearance. When Aubrey's found beside a rural road near death and mutilated in the M.O. of a local serial killer, the case seems pretty simple, until Aubrey awakes and thinks she's actually stripper Dakota Moss, who is the subject of a story Aubrey was writing for a class. Flashbacks, dream sequences and semi-plausible cinematic gimmicks bring this to a tidy conclusion, with unfortunate results. With her career in shambles, this might be your last chance to see Lohan (outside a courthouse) for a while. **108m/C; DVD, Blu-Ray.** Lindsay Lohan; Julia Ormond; Neal McDonough; Garcelle Beauvais; Brian Geraghty; Spencer Garrett; Gregory Itzin; Rodney Rowland; Paula Marshall; Eddie Steeples; Kenya Moore; Donovan Scott; Bonnie Aarons; Thomas Tofel; David Figlioni; Michael (Mike) Papajohn; Michelle Page; ***D:*** Chris Sivertson; ***W:*** Jeffrey Hammond; ***C:*** John R. Leonetti; ***M:*** Joel McNeely. Golden Raspberries '07: Worst Actress (Lohan), Worst Director (Sivertson), Worst Picture, Worst Remake, Worst Screenplay.

I Like It Like That **1994 (R)** Chaotic family life and loves in the Bronx are the setting for this tale of a Cinderella in the record industry. Strong-willed black-Latina Lisette (Velez) has been married for 10 years to macho Latin, Chino (Seda), who has a wandering eye. When Chino is jailed for looting during a blackout, Lisette, needing to support their three kids, talks her way into a job with WASP record promoter Stephen Price (Dunne). When local gossips make it seem Lisette is having an affair, the newly sprung Chino retaliates by turning to lusty Magdalena (Vidal). Lisette, meanwhile, gathers support from her transvestite brother and proves to have inner resources previously unnoticed. Great Latino soundtrack illuminates the complications. Modest-budget sleeper quickly exited the theatre but proves to be a strong debut for director/writer Martin, reputed to be the first African-American woman to be given the reins by a major studio. **106m/C; VHS, DVD.** Lauren Velez; Jon Seda; Lisa Vidal; Jesse Borrego; Griffin Dunne; Rita Moreno; Tomas Melly; Desiree Casado; Isaiah Garcia; ***D:*** Darnell Martin; ***W:*** Darnell Martin; ***C:*** Alexander Grusynski; ***M:*** Sergio George.

I Like to Play Games 1/2 **1995 (R)** Michael is looking for a woman who enjoys playing sexual games—and he seems to have the perfect partner in Suzanne. But just how far will their kinks take them? Also available unrated. **95m/C; VHS, DVD.** Lisa Boyle; Ken Steadman; ***D:*** Moctezuma Lobato; ***W:*** David Keith Miller; ***C:*** Kim Haun; ***M:*** Herman Beeftink.

I Live in Fear *Record of a Living Being; Kimono No Kiroku* **1955** Nakajima, an elderly, wealthy owner of a foundry, becomes increasingly fearful of atomic war and the threats to his family's safety. He tries to persuade them to leave Japan and move with him to Brazil but they fear the family will be ruined financially. Nakajima then burns down his foundry to force his children to move but instead they go to court and have him declared mentally incompetent. He is placed in an institution where he finds peace in the delusion that he has escaped to another planet and that the Earth has indeed suffered a nuclear holocaust. Provocative look at the fear of atomic warfare and radiation. In Japanese with English subtitles. **105m/C; VHS, DVD.** *JP* Toshiro Mifune; Takashi Shimura; Eiko Miyoshi; Haruko Togo; ***D:*** Akira Kurosawa; ***W:*** Akira Kurosawa; Shinobu Hashimoto; Hideo Oguni; ***C:*** Asakazu Nakai; ***M:*** Fumio Hayasaka.

I Live in Grosvenor Square *A Yank In London* **1946** An American soldier in Great Britain falls in love with a major's fiancee. Entertaining if a bit drawn out. **106m/B; VHS, DVD.** *GB* Anna Neagle; Rex Harrison; Dean Jagger; Robert Morley; Jane Darwell; ***D:*** Herbert Wilcox.

I Live My Life 1/2 **1935** Stylish glossy flick with Crawford playing a bored New York debutante who travels to Greece and meets a dedicated archaelogist (Aherne). A love/hate relationship ensues in this typical Crawford vehicle where she is witty and parades around in sophisticated fashions, but there is little substance here. **92m/B; DVD.** Joan Crawford; Brian Aherne; Frank Morgan; Aline MacMahon; Eric Blore; Fred Keating; Jessie Ralph; Arthur Treacher; Frank Conroy; Sterling Holloway; Vince Barnett; Hedda Hopper; Lionel Stander; ***D:*** W.S. Van Dyke; ***W:*** Joseph L. Mankiewicz; Gottfried Reinhardt; Ethel B. Borden; ***C:*** George J. Folsey.

I Lost My Body *J'ai perdu mon corps* **2019** One night in Paris, a severed hand escapes from a medical bag and the medical refrigerator in which it is being held. Crawling outside, the hand makes its way through city streets and out to the countryside, dodging threats like traffic, trains, and rats, clearly trying to get somewhere. Intercut with the hand's journey is the story of a pizza delivery boy with a tragic past, Naoufel (Faris), who develops a crush and pursues one of his customers, Gabrielle (Du Bois). The powerful animated feature depicts many memorable, dream-like moments. French with subtitles. **81m/C; DVD.** Hakim Faris; Victoire Du Bois; Patrick D'Assumcao; Alfonso Arfi; Hichem Mesbah; ***D:*** Jeremy Clapin; ***W:*** Jeremy Clapin; Guillaume Laurant; ***M:*** Dan Levy.

I Love Budapest **2001** Teenaged Aniko leaves her village to have a better life in Budapest. She gets a factory job and becomes smitten with security guard Miki. Aniko's new friend, the more sophisticated Moni, gets her boyfriend Krisztian to offer Miki a better job to impress Aniko. The problem is the job is part of Krisztian's underground criminal world, which will effect everyone's relationships. Hungarian with subtitles. **85m/C; VHS, DVD.** *HU* Gabriella Hamori; Sandor Csanyi; Martina Kovacs; Tamas Lengyel; ***D:*** Agnes Incze; ***W:*** Agnes Incze; ***C:*** Gergely Poharnok; ***M:*** Laszlo Fogarasi.

I Love Melvin 1/2 **1953** Reynolds wants to be a Tinseltown goddess, and O'Connor just wants Reynolds; so he passes himself off as chief lenseman for a famous magazine and promises her a shot at the cover of "Look." Seems he has a little trouble on the follow through. Choreographed by Robert Alton, it's got a best ever football ballet (with Reynolds as pigskin). **77m/C; VHS, DVD.** Donald O'Connor; Debbie Reynolds; Una Merkel; Richard Anderson; Jim Backus; Allyn Joslyn; Les Tremayne; Noreen Corcoran; Robert Taylor; Howard Keel; Helen Winston; ***D:*** Don Weis.

I Love N.Y. **1987** A young metropolitan couple struggles to find true love amidst disapproving parents and doubting friends. Choppy direction and poor writing contribute to its failure. **100m/C; VHS, DVD.** Scott Baio; Kelley Van Der Velden; Christopher Plummer; Jennifer O'Neill; Jerry Orbach; Virna Lisi; ***D:*** Alan Smithee; ***M:*** Bill Conti.

I Love Trouble 1/2 **1994 (PG)** Veteran reporter Peter Brackett (sexy veteran Nolte) and ambitious cub reporter Sabrina Petersen (young and sexy Roberts) are competitors working for rival Chicago newspapers. When they begin to secretly exchange information on a big story, they find their lives threatened and their rivalry turning to romance. Some action, simplistic retro script, one big star, one sorta big star, and you've got the perfect movie package for the Prozac decade. Written, produced and directed by husband/wife team Meyers and Shyer. **123m/C; VHS, DVD.** Julia Roberts; Nick Nolte; Saul Rubinek; Robert Loggia; James Rebhorn; Dan E. Butler; Kelly Rutherford; Olympia Dukakis; Marsha Mason; Eugene Levy; Charles Martin Smith; Paul Gleason; Jane Adams; Lisa Lu; Nora Dunn; Clark Gregg; Kevin Breznahan; Dorothy Lyman; Keith Gordon; Joseph (Joe) D'Onofrio; Barry Sobel; Frankie Faison; Stuart Pankin; Megan Cavanagh; Jessica Lundy; Nestor Serrano; Robin Duke; ***D:*** Charles Shyer; ***W:*** Nancy Meyers; Charles Shyer; ***C:*** John Lindley; ***M:*** David Newman.

I Love You Again 1/2 **1940** A classic screwball comedy with Powell and Loy working together (wonderfully) in something other than their "Thin Man" series. Powell is a gloomy businessman who's about to be divorced by Loy. But after an accident it turns out Powell had been suffering from amnesia and has now regained his memory (which he keeps a secret). It seems Mr. Respectable used to be a con man and he decides to revert to his criminal ways. He also doesn't remember Loy but falls instantly in love with her and must decide what kind of life he wants. Witty dialog, amusing situations, fine direction. **97m/B; VHS, DVD.** William Powell; Myrna Loy; Frank McHugh; Edmund Lowe; ***D:*** W.S. Van Dyke.

I Love You, Alice B. Toklas! 1/2 *Kiss My Butterfly* **1968** A straight uptight lawyer decides to join the peace and love generation in this somewhat maniacal satire of the hippie culture. Pretty dated now. Authored by Paul Mazursky and Larry Tucker. Incidentally, the title's Alice B. Toklas was actually the lifemate of "Lost Generation" author Gertrude Stein. **94m/C; DVD.** Peter Sellers; Jo Van Fleet; Leigh Taylor-Young; Joyce Van Patten; David Arkin; Herb Edelman; Salem Ludwig; ***D:*** Hy Averback; ***W:*** Paul Mazursky; Larry Tucker; ***C:*** Philip H. Lathrop; ***M:*** Elmer Bernstein.

I Love You Baby **2001** Absurd romantic comedy with an implausible premise (even for the genre) and a mis-cast leading actor in Sanz, who seems too old matched against his co-stars. Marcos (Sanz) has hooked up with Daniel (Magill). They're happy until a mirror ball falls on Marcos's head in a disco and he wakes up thinking he's straight. So he falls for Marisol (Scanda) and they settle down together. Meanwhile Daniel will do anything to get his boyfriend back. Spanish with subtitles. **110m/C; DVD.** *SP* Jorge Sanz; Santiago Magill; Tiare Scanda; Veronica Forque; Boy George; *D:* Alfonso Albacete; David Menkes; *W:* Alfonso Albacete; David Menkes; Lucia Etxeberria; *C:* Gonzalo Fernandez-Berridi; *M:* Paco Ortega; Miguel Angel Collado.

I Love You, Beth Cooper ✐ 1/2 **2009 (PG-13)** During his graduation speech, ubernerdy high school valedictorian Denis Cooverman (Rust) publicly declares his love for popular cheerleader Beth Cooper (Panettiere). Intrigued, somewhat bored, and having just dumped her loser macho boyfriend, Beth and her two best friends wind up at Denis' and proceed to show him that his dream girl is not the right one for him at all during an evening of rather brutal humiliations. A rehash of teen cliches based on the novel by Doyle, who also wrote the screenplay. **102m/C; Blu-Ray, On Demand.** Hayden Panettiere; Shawn Roberts; Lauren Storm; Lauren London; Paul Rust; Jack Carpenter; Alan Ruck; Cynthia Stevenson; *D:* Chris Columbus; *W:* Larry Doyle; *C:* Phil Abraham; *M:* Christophe Beck.

I Love You, Don't Touch Me! ✐✐ 1/2 **1997 (R)** Katie (Schafel) is a smart-mouthed, 25-year-old would-be singer in L.A., who also happens to be a virgin. She wants everything to be perfect her first time but all the guys she meets are just wrong. Her best friend Ben (Whitfield) would like to be the one, but Katie just can't see him in a romantic like. Then Katie finally gets involved with an older composer (Webber) who takes an interest in her career and all the romantic complications just get worse. **85m/C; VHS, DVD.** Maria Schaffel; Mitchell Whitfield; Michael (M.K.) Harris; Nancy Sorel; Meredith Scott Lynn; Darryl Theirse; *D:* Julie Davis; *W:* Julie Davis; *C:* Mark Putnam.

I Love You, I Love You Not ✐✐ 1/2 **1997 (PG-13)** The Holocaust becomes a metaphor for one teen's survival of her first painful romance. Daisy (Danes) is a Jewish student at a snobby and anti-Semetic Manhattan prep school, where she falls in love with the ultimate gentile, Ethan (Law) in a "Kids" meets "The Way We Were" spin. Moreau is Nana, Daisy's grandmother and a Holocaust survivor, whom Daisy visits every weekend. The two share their painful stories (Danes also plays Nana as a young girl). Danes does what she does best as a misunderstood teen coming of age. Moreau shines in her role as the beloved grandmother. What misfires is the trite handling of the serious subject matter as Daisy's romance scores far more screen time than Nana's suffering. Hopkins, an established casting director, makes his feature debut. **92m/C; VHS, DVD.** *FR GE GB* Claire Danes; Jeanne Moreau; Jude Law; James Van Der Beek; Robert Sean Leonard; Kris Park; Lauren Fox; Emily Burkes-Nossiter; Carrie Slaza; *D:* Billy Hopkins; *W:* Wendy Kesselman; *C:* Maryse Alberti; *M:* Gil Goldstein.

I Love You, Man ✐✐✐ *Let's Make Friends* **2009 (R)** Peter (Rudd) discovers proposing to his girlfriend might have been the easiest part of getting married. Now he has to find a male friend to be his best man and embarks on a series of "man dates" to find Mr. Right in time for his wedding. Formulaic but funny, thanks mainly to the excellent performances by Rudd and Segel, who strike a perfect mix and complement each other's comedic strong suit a la the original buddy movie, "The Odd Couple." Full of the apparently requisite gross-out and sex jokes that the young, male target audience won't mind but may be a little much for their dates. Another solid entry in the booming "bromance" category. **105m/C; Blu-Ray, On Demand.** Paul Rudd; Jason Segel; Jon Favreau; Rashida Jones; Andy Samberg; Jaime Pressly; J.K. Simmons; Jane Curtin; *D:* John Hamburg; *W:* John Hamburg; Larry Levin; *C:* Lawrence Sher; *M:* Theodore Shapiro.

I Love You Phillip Morris ✐✐ 1/2 **2010 (R)** Based on a true story and the novel by Steve McVicker. Steven Russell (Carrey) goes from law-abiding family man to charming gay con man, which eventually lands him in prison. He falls in love with cellmate Phillip Morris (McGregor) and they set up a home together when they're released, but Steven just can't let go of his criminal ways. Part farce, part romantic comedy, featuring a fine performance from centerpiece Carrey and good support from MacGregor. Story is charming but erratic, relying more on Carrey's considerable comic talent than solid pacing and traditional structure. **100m/C; Blu-Ray, On Demand.** Jim Carrey; Ewan McGregor; Leslie Mann; Rodrigo Santoro; *D:* Glenn Ficarra; John Requa; *W:* Glenn Ficarra; John Requa; *C:* Xavier Perez Grobet; *M:* Nick Urata.

I Love You Rosa ✐✐ 1/2 **1972** Rosa, a young Jewish widow, wrestles big time with old world values. Required by custom to marry her dearly departed's eldest brother, she's not enamored with her newly betrothed. Not that he's not a nice guy; he seems to plan to take his marital duties very seriously. It's just that he's a tad youthful (11 years old, to be exact). Much rabbi consulting and soul searching. **90m/C; VHS, DVD.** Michal Bat-Adam; Gabi Oterman; Joseph Shiloah; *D:* Moshe Mizrahi; *W:* Moshe Mizrahi.

I Love You to Death ✐✐ 1/2 **1990 (R)** Dry comedy based on a true story, concerns a woman who tries to kill off her cheating husband. Lots of stars, but they never shine. Hurt and Reeves are somewhat amusing as drugged up hit men who struggle with the lyrics to the National Anthem. Watch for director Kasdan as Devo's lawyer. Cates, Kline's real-life wife, has an unbilled part as one of his one-night stands. **110m/C; VHS, DVD.** Kevin Kline; Tracey Ullman; Joan Plowright; River Phoenix; William Hurt; Keanu Reeves; James Gammon; Victoria Jackson; Miriam Margolyes; Heather Graham; Jack Kehler; *Cameo(s):* Phoebe Cates; *D:* Lawrence Kasdan; *W:* John Kostmayer; *C:* Owen Roizman; *M:* James Horner.

I Love Your Work ✐✐ **2003 (R)** Goldberg tries to highlight the glamour and fake fabulousness of modern Hollywood celebrity, not always successfully, but at times interestingly. Loft-dwelling Gray Evans (Ribisi) and his wife Mia Lang (Potente) are famous, paparazzi-stalked actors living in Los Angeles. Gray's navel-gazing and paranoia turn into obsession with a young artist who reminds him of his pre-fame days. May be tedious for those not well-versed in the L.A. vibe. **111m/C; DVD.** Marisa Coughlan; Judy Greer; Shalom Harlow; Jared Harris; Joshua Jackson; Nicky Katt; Jason Lee; Franka Potente; Giovanni Ribisi; Christina Ricci; Vince Vaughn; *Cameo(s):* Elvis Costello; *D:* Adam Goldberg; *W:* Adam Goldberg; Adrian Butchart; *C:* Mark Putnam; *M:* Adam Goldberg; Steven Drozd.

I, Madman ✐✐ **1989 (R)** A novel-loving horror actress is stalked by the same mutilating madman that appears in the book she's presently reading. We call that bad luck. **90m/C; VHS, DVD, Blu-Ray.** Jenny Wright; Clayton Rohner; William Cook; *D:* Tibor Takacs; *W:* David Chaskin; *C:* Bryan England.

I Married a Centerfold ✐✐ **1984** Fluff about a young man's amorous pursuit of a model. **100m/C; VHS, DVD.** Teri Copley; Timothy Daly; Diane Ladd; Bert Remsen; Anson Williams; *D:* Peter Werner. **TV**

I Married a Monster from Outer Space ✐✐ 1/2 **1958** The vintage thriller about a race of monster-like aliens from another planet who try to conquer earth. Despite its head-shaking title, an effective '50s sci-fi creeper. **78m/B; DVD.** Tom Tryon; Gloria Talbott; Maxie "Slapsie" Rosenbloom; Mary Treen; Ty Hardin; Ken Lynch; John Eldridge; Jean-Philippe Carson; Alan Dexter; *D:* Gene Fowler, Jr.; *W:* Louis Vittes; *C:* Haskell Boggs.

I Married a Vampire ✐✐ **1987** A country girl in the city is romanced and wed by a dashing vampire. Troma-produced hypercamp. **85m/C; VHS, DVD.** Rachel Gordon; Brendan Hickey; Ted Zalewski; Deborah Carroll; Temple Aaron; *D:* Jay Raskin; *W:* Jay Raskin; *C:* Oren Rudavsky.

I Married an Angel ✐ 1/2 **1942** The last MacDonald/Eddy film. A playboy is lured away from his usual interests by a beautiful angel. Adapted from Rodgers and Hart Broadway play. Strange and less than compelling. **84m/C; VHS, DVD.** Jeanette MacDonald; Nelson Eddy; Binnie Barnes; Edward Everett Horton; Reginald Owen; Mona Maris; Janis Carter; Inez Cooper; Douglass Dumbrille; Leonid Kinskey; Marion Rosamond; Anne Jeffreys; Marek Windheim; Veda Ann Borg; *D:* W.S. Van Dyke; *W:* Anita Loos; *M:* Richard Rodgers; *M:* Lorenz Hart.

I Me Wed ✐✐ 1/2 **2007** Successful 30-year-old career woman Isabel, tired of her mom and friends insisting she find Mr. Right, jokes that the person who knows and loves her best is herself and she decides she'll plan a wedding and marry, well, herself. The story makes her a media dream bride and that's when Isabel actually meets a dream guy. **88m/C; DVD.** Erica Durance; Paul Popowich; Cara Pifko; Thom Allison; Janet-Laine Green; Vlasta Vrana; Thelma Farmer; *D:* Craig Pryce; *W:* Julie Wolfe; *C:* Stephen Reizes; *M:* James Gelfand. **CABLE**

I Melt With You ✐ **2011 (R)** Like a drug-fueled version of "The Big Chill," Pellington's film chronicles four friends (Jane, Piven, Lowe, McKay) who get together annually for a reunion at a Big Sur rental home. Past dramas come to life as these four self-indulgent jerks bicker, drink, do drugs, and eventually come to actual tragedy as a local Sheriff (Gugino) becomes drawn to their unusual behavior. It's an obnoxious, shockingly narcissistic piece about people with such massive egos that no one comes off as likable or worth following—especially for a runtime of over two hours. **129m/C; DVD, Blu-Ray.** Thomas Jane; Jeremy Piven; Rob Lowe; Christian McKay; Carla Gugino; Sasha Grey; Arielle Kebbel; Tom Bower; *D:* Mark Pellington; *W:* Glenn Porter; *C:* Eric Schmidt; *M:* tomandandy.

I Met Him in Paris ✐✐ 1/2 **1937** The three leads have a fine time romping through a lighthearted romance. Kay (Colbert) dumps boring fiance Berk (Bowman) and takes off to Paris. She's attracted to playboy Gene (Young) and his equally attractive friend, playwright George (Douglas). The three go on a Swiss holiday but Gene is keeping a secret that's sure to upset their fun. Lots of slapstick sight gags involving snow, skates, skis, and bobsleds (scenes were filmed in Sun Valley, Idaho). **85m/B; DVD.** Claudette Colbert; Melvyn Douglas; Robert Young; Lee Bowman; Mona Barrie; *D:* Wesley Ruggles; *W:* Claude Binyon; *C:* Leo Tover.

I, Mobster ✐✐ 1/2 **1958** Cochran tells a Senate Sub-Committee of his rise in the ranks of the Underworld—from his humble beginning as a bet collector for a bookie to his position as kingpin of the crime syndicate. **80m/B; VHS, DVD.** Steve Cochran; Lita Milan; Robert Strauss; Celia Lovsky; *D:* Roger Corman; *C:* Floyd Crosby.

I, Monster ✐✐✐ **1971** The character names may have changed but this is still Robert Louis Stevenson's "Dr. Jekyll and Mr. Hyde." Lee tackles the title characters with his usual sinister savoir faire as Dr. Marlowe, who is obsessed with the nature of the id, the ego, and the superego and whether they can be separated within an individual. He injects himself with his secret formula and is transformed into Mr. Blake, who prowls the seedy sections of Victorian London to satisfy his violent desires. Frequent co-star Cushing shows up as a suspicious colleague. **74m/C; VHS, DVD.** *GB* Christopher Lee; Peter Cushing; Mike Raven; George Merritt; Richard Hurndall; Kenneth J. Warren; Michael Des Barres; Susan Jameson; *D:* Stephen Weeks; *W:* Milton Subotsky; *C:* Moray Grant; *M:* Carl Davis.

I Never Promised You a Rose Garden ✐✐✐ **1977 (R)** A disturbed 16-year-old girl spirals down into madness and despair while a hospital psychiatrist struggles to bring her back to life. Based on the Joanne Greenberg bestseller. Compelling and unyielding exploration of the clinical treatment of schizophrenia. **90m/C; VHS, DVD.** Kathleen Quinlan; Bibi Andersson; Sylvia Sidney; Diane Varsi; Dennis Quaid; Jeff Conaway; *D:* Anthony Page; *W:* Gavin Lambert; Lewis John Carlino; *C:* Bruce Logan; *M:* Paul Chihara.

I Never Sang for My Father ✐✐✐ 1/2 **1970 (PG)** A devoted son must choose between caring for his cantankerous but well-meaning father, and moving out West to marry the divorced doctor whom he loves. While his mother wants him to stay near home, his sister, who fell out of her father's favor by marrying out of the family faith, argues that he should do what he wants. An introspective, stirring story based on the Robert Anderson play. **90m/C; VHS, DVD.** Gene Hackman; Melvyn Douglas; Estelle Parsons; Dorothy Stickney; *D:* Gilbert Cates; *W:* Robert Anderson. Writers Guild '70: Adapt. Screenplay.

I Now Pronounce You Chuck and Larry ✐ **2007 (PG-13)** In an effort to game the benefits system two Brooklyn firefighters pose as gay life partners. Larry's (James) spouse has died and he must name a new beneficiary, so of course he turns to his womanizing buddy Chuck (Sandler), who owes him one for saving his life. They have to make the whole gay couple thing believable, pulling out all of the cringe-worthy stereotypical gags while they're at it. Once their scam comes under suspicion they have to up the ante, which proves difficult while being represented by super hot (female) lawyer Alex (Biel). If you chuckle at bum jokes, or want to see Biel in a PVC catwoman costume, this is the movie to see. **115m/C; DVD, Blu-Ray, HD-DVD.** Adam Sandler; Kevin James; Jessica Biel; Ving Rhames; Steve Buscemi; Dan Aykroyd; Nicholas Turturro; Dennis Dugan; Allen Covert; Richard Chamberlain; Rob Schneider; Rachel Dratch; Mary Pat Gleason; Rob Corddry; Nick Swardson; Jonathan Loughran; Chandra West; Blake Clark; Richard Kline; *D:* Dennis Dugan; *W:* Barry Fanaro; Alexander Payne; Jim Taylor; Brooks Arthur; *C:* Dean Semler; *M:* Rupert Gregson-Williams.

I Only Want You to Love Me ✐✐ *Ich Will Doch Nur, Dass Ihr Mich Liebt* **1976** Peter's (Zeplichal) been denigrated by his family his entire life, so he decides to move with his wife (Aberle) to Munich and show them he can make something of himself. But his desires become compulsions and he falters under the strain of work and marriage, leading to a terrifying crackup. A true story, based on the book "Life Sentence" by Klaus Antes and Christine Eberhardt. Originally produced for TV; German with subtitles. **104m/C; VHS, DVD.** *GE* Vitus Zeplichal; Elke Aberle; Ernie Mangold; Joanna Hole; Alexander Allerson; *D:* Rainer Werner Fassbinder; *W:* Rainer Werner Fassbinder; *C:* Michael Ballhaus; *M:* Peer Raben.

I Origins ✐✐ 1/2 **2014 (R)** Dr. Ian Grey (Pitt) is trying to prove the evolution of the human eye, in part to debunk the religious association with the way it defines us uniquely. While doing so, he falls in love with a model with a perfect set of peepers named Sofi (Berges-Frisbey), who challenges his lack of faith and belief in a power greater than him. As his story evolves, Ian learns that there may be something to the concept of the eye as the window to the soul. Writer/director Cahill has a grounded, distinct approach to sci-fi that makes for memorable viewing. **107m/C; DVD, Blu-Ray.** Michael Pitt; Brit Marling; Astrid Berges-Frisbey; Steven Yuen; *D:* Mike Cahill; *W:* Mike Cahill; *C:* Markus Forderer; *M:* Will Bates; Phil Mossman.

I Really Hate My Job ✐ 1/2 **2007** Some days, don't we all. Five women all hold down mundane, low-paying jobs at the same London restaurant while dreaming of better opportunities ahead. They struggle through a somewhat atypical series of mishaps during their evening shift, with things going wrong at the worst possible times. **89m/C; DVD.** *GB* Neve Campbell; Shirley Henderson; Alexandra Maria Lara; Oana Pellea; Danny Huston; Barry Morse; *D:* Oliver Parker; *W:* Jennifer Higgie; *C:* Tony Miller; *M:* Charlie Mole.

I Remember Mama ✐✐✐ 1/2 **1948** A true Hollywood heart tugger chronicling the life of a Norwegian immigrant family living in San Francisco during the early 1900s. Dunne triumphs as the mother, with a perfect Norwegian accent, and provides her family with wisdom and inspiration. A kindly father and four children round out the nuclear family. A host of oddball characters regularly pop in on the household—three high-strung aunts and an eccentric doctor who treats a live-in uncle. Adapted from John Van Druten's stage play, based on Kathryn Forbes memoirs, "Mama's Bank Account"; a TV series ran from 1946-57. **95m/B; VHS, DVD.** Irene Dunne; Barbara

Bel Geddes; Oscar Homolka; Ellen Corby; Cedric Hardwicke; Edgar Bergen; Rudy Vallee; Barbara O'Neil; Florence Bates; *D:* George Stevens; *W:* DeWitt Bodeen. Golden Globes '49: Support. Actress (Corby).

I Remember Nelson ♪♪ **1982** Made-for-TV historical drama examines the life of brave, ruthless, hedonistic, ambitious Vice-Admiral Horatio Nelson through the eyes of several people around him, including his neglected wife, the husband of his mistress, and those who served with him at the battle of Trafalgar. **208m/C; DVD.** *UK* Kenneth Colley; Geraldine James; Tim Pigott-Smith; John Clements; Michael Harbour; Raf Vallone; Anna Massey; *D:* Simon Langton; *W:* Hugh Whitemore; *M:* Patrick Gowers. **TV**

I, Robot ♪♪ **2004 (PG-13)** Very loose adaptation of Asimov's seminal 1950 sci-fi collection of short stories has action-hero Smith as Chicago detective Del Spooner, who's investigating the murder of robotic pioneer, Dr. Alfred Lanning (Cromwell). It's 2035, and robots are as common a household appliance as a toaster, and supposedly just as safe. But Spooner thinks those 'bots have minds (and plans) of their own and that one of them offed the good doctor. When Spooner persists in his theory that a robot committed the crime, he gets bumped from the force, which doesn't stop his investigation. The robots are creepily cool but there's no shock of the new in this crime caper. **115m/C; DVD, Blu-Ray, UMD.** Will Smith; Bridget Moynahan; Bruce Greenwood; Chi McBride; Alan Tudyk; James Cromwell; Shia LaBeouf; Adrian L. Ricard; *D:* Alex Proyas; *W:* Akiva Goldsman; Jeff Vintar; *C:* Simon Duggan; *M:* Marco Beltrami.

I Saw the Devil ♪♪ *Akamreul Boatda* **2010** Artistic psycho-thriller torture from South Korea. After special agent Soo-hyun's fiancee falls victim to vicious serial killer Kyung-chul, he takes a leave of absence to get his own particular kind of justice. This involves catching the killer, hurting him, and letting him go'only to recapture him, up the torture, and resume his sadistic revenge game. By the end, you won't know who the devil really is. Korean with subtitles. **142m/C; DVD, Blu-Ray.** *NK* Byung-hun Lee; Min-Sik Choi; San-ha Oh; Kook-haun Chun; Ho-jin Chun; Moo-seong Choi; Yoon-Seo Kim; In-seo Kim; *D:* Jee-woon Kim; *W:* Hoon-jung Park; *C:* Lee Mogae; *M:* Mowg.

I See a Dark Stranger ♪♪♪ *The Adventuress* **1946** Cynical yet whimsical post-war British spy thriller about an angry Irish lass who agrees to steal war plans for the Nazis in order to battle her native enemies, the British—then she falls in love with a British officer. A sharply performed, decidedly jaded view of nationalism and wartime "heroism." **112m/B; VHS, DVD.** *GB* Deborah Kerr; Trevor Howard; Raymond Huntley; *D:* Frank Launder.

I-See-You.Com ♪ 1/2 **2006** And I really wish I hadn't. After single parents Harvey and Lydia marry, they discover they can't make ends meet with their blended families. Entrepreneurial teenager Colby buys some webcams and installs them around the house (without his family's knowledge), uploads the footage to the Internet, and makes them a reality show sensation. Only their 15 minutes of fame proves to be a problem. **94m/C; DVD.** Beau Bridges; Rosanna Arquette; Mathew Botuchis; Shiri Appleby; Dan Castellaneta; Doris Roberts; Hector Elizondo; Victor Alfieri; Baelyn Neff; Tracee Ellis Ross; *D:* Eric Steven Stahl; *W:* Eric Steven Stahl; Sean McLain; *C:* Ricardo Jacques Gale; *M:* Kevin Kiner.

I Sell the Dead ♪♪ **2009** Horror comedy about Victorian-era grave-robbing. Willy Grimes (Fessenden) and his new partner Arthur (Monaghan) sell most of their exhumed corpses to sinister Dr. Quint (Scrimm). However, not only is their trade illegal but the bodies have a nasty habit of coming back to life. Looks like a Hammer studio horror homage (and that's a good thing.) **85m/C; DVD, Blu-Ray.** Dominic Monaghan; Larry Fessenden; Angus Scrimm; Ron Perlman; Eileen Colgan; John Speredakos; Brenda Cooney; Aidan Redmond; *D:* Glenn McQuaid; *W:* Glenn McQuaid; *C:* Richard Lopez; *M:* Jeff Grace.

I Served the King of England ♪♪♪ 1/2 *Obsluhoval Jsem Anglickeho Krale* **2007 (R)** Well-acted portrayal of the life of Jan Dite (Barnev), a waiter in Prague's finest hotel restaurant with aspirations of wealth during a time when Czechoslovakia was controlled by Germany and later the Soviet Union. An older Dite (Kaiser) flashes back to his younger days - the dissident gets out of prison and is so seduced by his desire for material success that he weds Aryan Liza (Jentsch) and has no hesitation using wealth looted from Jewish households to purchase the hotel he has worked in. Dite's relatively unremarkable life provides a perfect backdrop for a satirical jab at Nazis and Commies alike. Put on your thinking cap to extract the many-layered dark humor from this one, but in the end what's better than disarming tyrants with brainy laughter? In Czech with English subtitles. **120m/C; On Demand.** *CZ* Oldrich Kaiser; Julia Jentsch; Martin Huba; Jiri Labus; Ivan Barnev; Marian Lasica; Josef Abrham; Jaromir Dulava; *D:* Jiri Menzel; *W:* Jiri Menzel; *C:* Jaromir Sofr; *M:* Ales Brezina.

I Shot Andy Warhol ♪♪♪ **1996 (R)** Based on a true story, this black comedy focuses on the 15 minutes of fame achieved by Valerie Solanas, the woman who shot pop artist Andy Warhol for ignoring her in 1968. Taylor manages to recreate the more unpleasant aspects of Solanas without making her completely unsympathetic. Writer/director Harron, making her feature film debut, does a wonderful job of recreating the drugged-out world Warhol and his cohorts inhabited. Her script succeeds by attempting to understand Solanas's actions, while not excusing or sensationalizing them. Features music by former Velvet Underground member, John Cale. **100m/C; VHS, DVD.** Lili Taylor; Jared Harris; Stephen Dorff; Martha Plimpton; Donovan Leitch; Tahnee Welch; Michael Imperioli; Lothaire Bluteau; Anna Thomson; Peter Friedman; Jill(ian) Hennessey; Craig Chester; James Lyons; Reginald Rodgers; Jamie Harrold; Edoardo Ballerini; Lynn Cohen; Myriam Cyr; Isabel Gillies; Eric Mabius; *D:* Mary Harron; *W:* Mary Harron; Daniel Minahan; *C:* Ellen Kuras; *M:* John Cale.

I Shot Jesse James ♪♪♪ **1949** In his first film, director Fuller breathes characteristically feverish, maddened fire into the story of Bob Ford (Ireland) after he killed the notorious outlaw. An essential moment in Fuller's unique, America-as-tabloid-nightmare canon, and one of the best anti-westerns ever made. **83m/B; VHS, DVD.** John Ireland; Barbara Britton; Preston Foster; Reed Hadley; *D:* Samuel Fuller; *W:* Samuel Fuller.

I Smile Back ♪♪ 1/2 **2015 (R)** Sarah Silverman gives a challenging, breakthrough performance as Laney, a woman dealing with depression, mental illness and addiction. From all appearances, Laney would have what everyone wants, including two loving children, a kind man for her husband, and enough money that she need not worry. But Laney isn't satisfied. She battles both depression and extremely destructive behavior, crying out for help with every action until it's too late. The script for Adam Salky's film is a bit thin but Silverman really elevates it with her committed work. She's the reason to see the film, even if the rest doesn't live up to her performance. **85m/C.** Josh Charles; Skylar Gaertner; Shayne Coleman; Sarah Silverman; Mia Barron; Thomas Sadoski; *D:* Adam Salky; *W:* Paige Dylan; Amy Koppelman; *C:* Eric Lin; *M:* Zack Ryan.

I Spit on Your Corpse WOOF! *Girls for Rent* **1974 (R)** A vicious female hired killer engages in a series of terrorist activities. Stars Spelvin in a non-pornographic role. **90m/C; VHS, DVD.** Georgina Spelvin; Susan McIver; Kent Taylor; Rosalind Miles; Preston Pierce; Robert "Bob" Livingston; *D:* Al Adamson.

I Spit on Your Grave WOOF! *Day of the Woman* **1977 (R)** Woman vacationing at a Connecticut lake house (on the Housatonic River) is brutally attacked and raped by four men. Left for dead, she recovers and seeks revenge. Not to be confused with the 1962 film of the same title, this one is worth zero as a film; lots of violent terror and gory death, totally irresponsibly portrayed. Also available in a 102-minute version. **98m/C; VHS, DVD, Blu-Ray.** Camille Keaton; Eron Tabor; Richard Pace; Anthony Nichols; Gunter Kleeman; Alexis Magnotti; *D:* Mier Zarchi; *W:* Mier Zarchi; *C:* Yuri Haviv.

I Spit on Your Grave WOOF! **2010 (R)** Loathsome and abhorrent remake of the equally exploitative 1979 cult revenge horror pic. City gal Jennifer Hills (Butler) retreats to a cabin in the woods to write and is instead repeatedly raped and brutalized by a depraved group of locals. She fakes her death and then wants her revenge to equal what she went through. Only for fans of torture porn. **108m/C; DVD, Blu-Ray.** Sarah Butler; Rodney Eastman; Jeff Branson; Daniel Franzese; Chad Lindberg; Andrew Howard; Tracey Walter; *D:* Stephen R. Monroe; Steven R. Monroe; *W:* Stuart Morse; *C:* Neil Lisk; *M:* Corey A. Jackson.

I Spit on Your Grave 2 ♪♪ **2013 (R)** A dramatic horror-thriller about a modeling job gone very, very bad. Living in New York City and trying to make it as a model, Kate (Dallender) accepts an offer to pose for new photos for her portfolio. The shoot is not as it seems as she is beaten, battered, and broken, and must draw on her deep internal strength to survive. Not only does she live, she finds the strength to exact her own form of revenge. **106m/C; DVD, Blu-Ray, Download.** Jemma Dallender; Joe Absolom; Yavor Baharov; George Zlatarev; Mary Stockley; *D:* Steven R. Monroe; *W:* Neil Elman; Thomas Fenton; *C:* Damian Bromley; *M:* Corey A. Jackson.

I Spit on Your Grave: Vengeance Is Mine ♪ 1/2 *I Spit on Your Grave 3: Vengeance Is Mine* **2015** The third installment in the thematically related I Spit on Your Grave series and the true sequel to the series' first film. Though Jennifer Hills (Butler) survives her brutal sexual and physical assault, the crime against her still haunts her years later. With a new identity and living in a new city, she joins a support group of other survivors. Though Jennifer was reluctant to join, she experiences some much needed healing with the group's members and makes new friends. After a friend is murdered and her killer goes free, however, she decides to take the law into her own hands and enact her own form of justice on the attackers of her friends and fellow survivors. **110m/C; DVD, Blu-Ray, Download.** Sarah Butler; Jennifer Landon; Doug McKeon; Gabriel Hogan; Harley Jane Kozak; *D:* R.D. Braunstein; *W:* Daniel Gilboy; *C:* Richard J. Vialet; *M:* Edwin Wendler.

I Spy ♪♪ **2002 (PG-13)** Bland adaptation of the Robert Culp/Bill Cosby TV series falls short of the cool vibe of the original. Second-banana spy Alex Scott (Wilson) is teamed up with heavyweight boxing champion Kelly Robinson (Murphy) to catch illegal arms dealer Gundars (McDowell), who has stolen a prototype stealth fighter from the U.S. government. Along the way, the duo engage in familiar buddy picture jokiness, and Kelly helps Alex woo mysterious spygirl Rachel (Janssen). Gary Cole is a scene stealer as faux-Spanish superagent Carlos. **96m/C; VHS, DVD, Blu-Ray.** Eddie Murphy; Owen Wilson; Famke Janssen; Malcolm McDowell; Gary Cole; Phill Lewis; Viv Leacock; *D:* Betty Thomas; *W:* Cormac Wibberley; Marianne S. Wibberley; Jay Scherick; David Ronn; *C:* Oliver Wood; *M:* Richard Gibbs.

I Stand Alone ♪♪ *Seul contre tous* **1998 (R)** Loud and RE-PUL-SIVE drama has unemployed butcher Chevalier (Nahon) descending into madness at warp speed when he can't find work. The brutal approach Noe takes distracts, rather than intrigues, as the "hero" is such a low-life loser. His hate-filled narration is accompanied by wild camera moves and loud gun-shot booms ending each scene. A 30-second warning plastered before the film's grisly climax is not only unique but warranted when the least of Chevalier's crimes is maliciously kicking his pregnant girlfriend in the stomach. Considered a continuation to Noe's 1991 short feature entitled "Carne." French with English subtitles. **93m/C; VHS, DVD.** Philippe Nahon; Blandine Lenoir; Frankye Pain; Martine Audrain; *D:* Gaspar Noé; *W:* Gaspar Noé; *C:* Dominique Colin.

I Stand Condemned ♪♪ 1/2 *Moscow Nights* **1936** A Russian officer is tricked into borrowing money from a spy and is condemned for treason. He's saved when a girl who loves him gives herself to a profiteer. Worth seeing only for young Olivier's performance. **90m/B; VHS, DVD.** *GB* Laurence Olivier; Penelope Dudley Ward; Robert Cochran; *D:* Anthony Asquith.

I Still Know What You Did Last Summer ♪♪ **1998 (R)** You know what the real problem with teenagers is? It's not the loud music or the messy room; it's that they can't finish off psycho-killers who show up annually on a major holiday to wield the axe they've been grinding for the rest of the year. Perky survivor Julie James (Hewitt) and new best friend Karla (Brandy) win a vacation in the Bahamas, and take boyfriends Tyrell (Phifer) and Will (Settle) along for some fun in the monsoon. Along with the hurricane, the kids must cope with fish stick guy/killer Ben Willis, who's still pretty cranky. The scares come at such a regular interval, and sometimes with such a lame premise, that the viewer becomes numb to them. The young cast, especially the wet t-shirt adorned Hewitt, help to keep it afloat, however. **100m/C; VHS, DVD, Blu-Ray.** Jennifer Love Hewitt; Freddie Prinze, Jr.; Brandy Norwood; Mekhi Phifer; Muse Watson; Matthew Sattle; Bill Cobbs; Jeffrey Combs; John Hawkes; Jennifer Esposito; Jack Black; *D:* Danny Cannon; *W:* Trey Callaway; *C:* Vernon Layton; *M:* John (Gianni) Frizzell.

I Take This Woman ♪♪ **1940** Lonely Dr. Karl Decker (Tracy) saves beautiful Georgi Gragore (Lamarr) from a shipboard suicide attempt after Georgi discovers her married lover Phil (Taylor) hasn't divorced his wife (Barrie) as promised. A smitten Decker, who works with the poor, eventually persuades Georgi to marry him and he trades in his clinic work for an uptown practice to support her in style. But Georgi (who possibly sees the older Karl as more father figure than husband material) can't get Phil out of her heart. **98m/B; DVD.** Spencer Tracy; Hedy Lamarr; Kent Taylor; Verree Teasdale; Mona Barrie; Laraine Day; Paul Cavanagh; Louis Calhern; Jack Carson; Marjorie Main; *D:* W.S. Van Dyke; *W:* James Kevin McGuinness; *C:* Harold Rosson; *M:* Bronislau Kaper; Artur Guttmann.

I Thank a Fool ♪ 1/2 **1962** Over-the-top psychological drama. Convicted of a mercy killing, Dr. Christine Allison (Hayward) can't practice medicine. She takes a job as a nurse to mentally ill Liane (Cilento) even though it was her husband, prosecutor Stephen Dane (Finch), who sent Christine to prison. Tragedy strikes and suspicion falls on Christine. But what role did Liane's sleazy father (Cusack) play? **100m/C; DVD.** *UK* Susan Hayward; Peter Finch; Diane Cilento; Cyril Cusack; Kieron Moore; *D:* Robert Stevenson; *W:* Karl Tunberg; *C:* Harry Waxman; *M:* Ronald Goodwin.

I, the Jury ♪♪ **1982 (R)** A remake of the 1953 Mike Hammer mystery in which the famed PI investigates the murder of his best friend. Assante mopes around as Hammer and looks out of place in this slowed-down version. **111m/C; VHS, Blu-Ray, Streaming.** Armand Assante; Barbara Carrera; Laurene Landon; Alan King; Geoffrey Lewis; Paul Sorvino; Jessica James; Leigh Anne Harris; Lynette Harris; *D:* Richard T. Heffron; *W:* Larry Cohen; *M:* Bill Conti.

I, the Worst of All ♪♪ *Yo, la Peor de Todas* **1990** Portrayal of 17th-century Mexican poet, Sister Juana Ines del la Cruz (Serna). She develops a passionate but chaste friendship with Maria Luisa (Sanda), the wife of the Spanish viceroy in Mexico, and writes love poems to her. However, the newly appointed archbishop (Murua) is a religious fanatic who condemns Juana's work, burns her books, and proceeds to persecute her. Adapted from the novel, "The Traps of Faith," by Octavio Paz. Spanish with subtitles. **105m/C; VHS, DVD.** *SP* Assumpta Serna; Dominique Sanda; Lautaro Murua; Hector Alterio; *D:* Maria-Luisa Bemberg; *W:* Maria-Luisa Bemberg; Antonio Larreta; *C:* Felix Monti; *M:* Luis Maria Serra.

I Think I Do ♪♪ **1997** Gay Bob (Arquette) has always had an unrequited crush on college roomie, Brendan (Maelen). Five years after graduation, the duo meet up at the wedding of mutual friends, Carol (Velez) and Matt (Harrold). Bob's brought along his boyfriend, Sterling (Watkins), and doesn't know that Brendan has come out and is anticipating their reunion. It seems no one's sure about any of their romantic entanglements and someone's bound to be disappointed. **92m/C; VHS, DVD.** Alexis Arquette; Christian Maelen; Maddie Corman; Guillermo Diaz; Lauren Velez; Jamie Harrold; Marianne Hagan; Tuc Watkins; Marni Nixon; Dechen Thurman; ***D:*** Brian Sloan; ***W:*** Brian Sloan; ***C:*** Milton Kam; ***M:*** Gerry Gershman.

I Think I Love My Wife 🦴🦴 **2007 (R)** Redo of Eric Rohmer's 1972 French film "Chloe in the Afternoon." Rock directs and stars as bored, frustrated middle-class hubby Richard Cooper, who's not getting any loving from his beautiful wife Brenda (Torres), leaving him vulnerable to the wanton charms of Nikki (Washington), the ex of an old pal. Richard's conscience won't quite let him actually indulge (all the guilt, none of the pleasure). Rock does manage some humorous takes on modern marriage and Washington is smokin' hot. **94m/C; DVD.** Chris Rock; Kerry Washington; Gina Torres; Steve Buscemi; Edward Herrmann; Michael K(enneth) Williams; Wendell Pierce; Cassandra Freeman; Welker White; ***D:*** Chris Rock; ***W:*** Chris Rock; Louis CK; ***C:*** William Rexer; ***M:*** Marcus Miller.

I Think We're Alone Now 🦴🦴 ½ **2018 (R)** After an apocalypse, Del (Dinklage) is the only survivor in his upstate New York community. He spends his days going from home to home to find and bury the dead while locating necessary supplies that he uses to survive. Though he is alone, he is not lonely, but his solitude ends when another survivor arrives. Unlike the cautious, quiet Del, lively Grace (Fanning) is free spirited and joyful. They change each other for the better, but their new lives are unexpectedly challenged. The film's plot is uneven, but Dinklage's performance and the chemistry between the actors makes it compelling. **93m/C; DVD, Blu-Ray.** Peter Dinklage; Elle Fanning; Charlotte Gainsbourg; Paul Giamatti; ***D:*** Reed Morano; ***W:*** Mike Makowsky; ***C:*** Reed Morano; ***M:*** Adam Taylor.

I, Tonya 🦴🦴🦴 **2017 (R)** A darkly comic yet sympathetic look at the tragic life of disgraced figure skating champion, Tonya Harding (an inspired Robbie). Raised in a working class, unstable family, Tonya reaches the height of her sport despite long odds. Along the way, her mother, LaVona (Janney), emotionally and physically abuses her daughter as part of her effort to make Tonya a champion. Tonya's poor choices, including marrying the abusive Jeff Gillooly (Stan), contribute to her eventual downfall. Jeff and Shawn Eckhardt (Hauser) attempt to remove Tonya's main competition but instead ends her career. Some stuff you just can't make up. **119m/C; DVD, Blu-Ray.** Margot Robbie; Sebastian Stan; Allison Janney; Caitlin Carver; Bobby Cannavale; ***D:*** Craig Gillespie; ***W:*** Steven Rogers; ***C:*** Nicolas Karakatsanis; ***M:*** Peter Nashel. Oscars '17: Actress--Supporting (Janney); British Acad. '17: Actress--Supporting (Janney); Golden Globes '18: Actress--Supporting (Janney); Ind. Spirit '18: Actress--Supporting (Janney), Film Editing; Screen Actors Guild '17: Actress--Supporting (Janney).

I, Vampiri 🦴🦴 ½ *The Devil's Commandment; Lust of the Vampires* **1956** Original vampire film which started the classic Italian horror cycle. A gorgeous Countess needs blood to stay young, otherwise she reverts to a 200-year-old vampire. **81m/B; VHS, DVD.** *IT* Gianna Maria Canale; Carlo D'Angelo; Dario Michaelis; Wandisa Guida; Renato Tontini; ***D:*** Riccardo Freda; ***W:*** Riccardo Freda; Piero Regnoli; ***C:*** Mario Bava; ***M:*** Franco Mannino; Roman Vlad.

I Vitelloni 🦴🦴🦴 ½ *The Young and the Passionate; Vitelloni; Spivs* **1953** Fellini's semi-autobiographical drama, argued by some to be his finest work. Five young men grow up in a small Italian town. As they mature, four of them remain in Romini and limit their opportunities by roping themselves off from the rest of the world. The characters are multi-dimensional, including a loafer who is supported by his sister and a young stud who impregnates a local woman. The script has some brilliant insights into youth, adulthood and what's in between. **104m/B; VHS, DVD.** *IT* Alberto Sordi; Franco Interlenghi; Franco Fabrizi; Leopoldo Trieste; Riccardo Fellini; ***D:*** Federico Fellini; ***W:*** Federico Fellini; Ennio Flaiano; ***C:*** Carlo Carlini; Otello Martelli; ***M:*** Nino Rota.

I Wake Up Screaming 🦴🦴🦴 *Hot Spot* **1941** An actress' promoter is accused of her murder. Entertaining mystery with a surprise ending. Remade as "Vicki." **82m/B; VHS, DVD, Blu-Ray.** Betty Grable; Victor Mature; Carole Landis; Laird Cregar; William Gargan; Alan Mowbray; Allyn Joslyn; Elisha Cook, Jr.; Chick Chandler; Cyril Ring; Morris Ankrum; Charles Lane; May (Mae) Beatty; Frank Orth; ***D:*** H. Bruce Humberstone; ***W:*** Steve Fisher; Dwight Taylor; ***C:*** Edward Cronjager; ***M:*** Cyril Mockridge.

I Walk Alone 🦴🦴 ½ **1948** Moody crime drama with Douglas and Lancaster starring as former bootleggers. After spending 14 years in prison, Frankie (Lancaster) expects his one-time partner Noll (Douglas) to cough up his half of the profits from their nightclub as promised. But Noll uses his meek accountant Dave (Corey) to give Frankie the financial runaround and distracts him with singer Kay (Scott). Frankie is determined to get what's owed him, no matter the cost. Solid performances by all in a gritty, if familiar, story. **97m/B; Blu-Ray, Streaming.** Burt Lancaster; Kirk Douglas; Lizabeth Scott; Wendell Corey; Mike Mazurki; ***D:*** Byron Haskin; ***W:*** Charles Schnee; John Bright; ***C:*** Leo Tover; ***M:*** Victor Young.

I Walk the Line 🦴🦴 ½ **1970 (PG-13)** Tennessee sheriff Henry Tawes (Peck) is known for his inflexible upholding of the law and his moral character. But even he can't resist the tawdry charms of wild nymphet Alma (Weld), the daughter of local moonshiner Carl McCain (Meeker). Tawes crosses all lines to be with Alma, even leaving his family and ignoring McCain's crimes with tragic consequences. Johnny Cash sings the title track. **95m/C; DVD.** Gregory Peck; Tuesday Weld; Ralph Meeker; Estelle Parsons; Charles Durning; Lonny (Lonnie) Chapman; ***D:*** John Frankenheimer; ***W:*** Alvin Sargent; ***C:*** David M. Walsh; ***M:*** Bobby Johnston.

I Walked with a Zombie 🦴🦴🦴 ½ **1943** The definitive and eeriest of the famous Val Lewton/Jacques Tourneur horror films. Dee, a young American nurse, comes to Haiti to care for the catatonic matriarch of a troubled family. Local legends bring themselves to bear when the nurse takes the ill woman to a local voodoo ceremony for "healing." Superb, startling images and atmosphere create a unique context for this serious "Jane Eyre"-like story; its reputation has grown through the years. **69m/B; VHS, DVD.** Frances Dee; Tom Conway; James Ellison; Christine Gordon; Edith Barrett; Darby Jones; Sir Lancelot; ***D:*** Jacques Tourneur; ***W:*** Curt Siodmak; Ardel Wray; ***C:*** J. Roy Hunt; ***M:*** Roy Webb.

I Wanna Hold Your Hand 🦴🦴 ½ **1978 (PG)** Teenagers try to crash the Beatles' appearance on the Ed Sullivan show. **104m/C; VHS, DVD, Blu-Ray.** Nancy Allen; Bobby DiCicco; Wendie Jo Sperber; Marc McClure; Susan Kendall Newman; Theresa Saldana; Eddie Deezen; William Jordan; ***D:*** Robert Zemeckis; ***W:*** Robert Zemeckis.

I Want Candy 🦴🦴 **2007 (R)** Juvenile Brit sex comedy. Joe (Riley) and Baggy (Burke) are two struggling film students in Leatherhead, England, who have been working on a feature-length script for their graduation thesis, only to learn they are supposed to film a several-minute short. They decide to flog their script in London but Doug (Marsan) the producer is only interested if they turn it into a porno and cast adult star Candy Fiveways (Electra). The boys manage to get Candy to agree but the only place they have to film is in Joe's parents' house, which makes the sex scenes (including one with a pear) a little awkward. More nudge-nudge, wink-wink than sleazy. **86m/C; DVD.** *GB* Tom Riley; Tom Burke; Carmen Electra; Michelle Ryan; Eddie Marsan; Mackenzie Crook; Philip Jackson; John Standing; Felicity Montagu; ***D:*** Stephen Surjik; ***W:*** Peter Hewitt; Phil Hughes; ***C:*** Crighton Bone; ***M:*** Murray Gold.

I Want Someone to Eat Cheese With 🦴🦴 ½ **2006** Garlin adapts his one-man stage show into a full-length movie about overeating comedian James (Garlin), who's trying to find love while still living at home with his mother (Kolb). His best options are a sweet but weird schoolteacher (Hunt) or a possibly crazy ice cream store worker (Silverman). Self-deprecating but sweet, Garlin's debut relies on the improvisation skills of his cast to flesh out a thin but charming story. **80m/C; DVD.** Jeff Garlin; Sarah Silverman; Bonnie Hunt; Amy Sedaris; Wallace (Wally) Langham; Joey Slotnick; Richard King; Gina Gershon; Mina Kolb; David Pasquesi; ***D:*** Jeff Garlin; ***W:*** Jeff Garlin; ***C:*** Pete Biagi; ***M:*** Rob Kolson.

I Want to Get Married 🦴 ½ **2011** Over-long gay rom com. Ultra-nerd ad exec Paul Roll meets the perfect man at his lesbian friends' wedding. Jim is a political activist and Paul knows he won't approve of Paul's latest client—an ultra-conservative, anti-gay organization. Since it's also just six days before Proposition 8 is put before California voters, if Paul intends to get married, he's got to do it now. **115m/C; DVD.** Matthew Montgomery; Peter Stickles; Ashleigh Sumner; Jane Wiedlin; ***D:*** William Clift; ***W:*** William Clift; ***C:*** John Lore. **VIDEO**

I Want to Go Home 🦴 ½ *Je Veux Rentrer a la Maison* **1989** Crass comedy about culture shock and family ties. Cranky Cleveland cartoonist Joey Wellman (Green) agrees to attend an exhibition of his work in Paris in an effort to reunite with his estranged daughter Elsie (Benson), who's studying at the Sorbonne. Elsie is ashamed of her dad but the scholar she's trying to impress, Christian Gauthier (Depardieu), is a big fan of American comic books and is thrilled to befriend Joey, who can't adjust to French culture. Joey's cartoon cat characters pop up in animated thought balloons to offer their own comments. English and French with subtitles. **100m/C; DVD.** *FR* Adolph Green; Gerard Depardieu; Linda Lavin; Geraldine Chaplin; Micheline Presle; John Aston; Laura Benson; ***D:*** Alain Resnais; ***W:*** Jules Feiffer; ***C:*** Charlie Van Damme; ***M:*** John Kander.

I Want to Live! 🦴🦴🦴 **1958** Based on a scandalous true story, Hayward gives a riveting, Oscar-winning performance as a prostitute framed for the murder of an elderly woman and sentenced to death in the gas chamber. Producer Walter Wanger's seething indictment of capital punishment. **120m/B; VHS, DVD, Blu-Ray.** Susan Hayward; Simon Oakland; Theodore Bikel; Virginia Vincent; Wesley Lau; ***D:*** Robert Wise; ***W:*** Nelson Gidding; Don Mankiewicz; ***C:*** Lionel Lindon; ***M:*** Johnny Mandel. Oscars '58: Actress (Hayward); Golden Globes '59: Actress--Drama (Hayward); N.Y. Film Critics '58: Actress (Hayward).

I Want What I Want 🦴🦴 **1972 (R)** A young Englishman wants a sex-change, lives as a woman, falls in love, complications ensue. Not as shocking to watch as it might seem, but more a melodramatic genderbender. **91m/C; VHS, DVD.** *GB* Anne Heywood; Harry Andrews; Jill Bennett; ***D:*** John Dexter.

I Was a Communist for the FBI **WOOF! 1951** Pure paranoid propaganda made when Hollywood was running scared of Joe McCarthy and his communists-under-the-bed witch hunt. Pittsburgh steelworker Matt (Lovejoy) is recruited by the feds to infiltrate his labor union, which is just a Communist front, despite the trouble it causes since his family think he's a pinko. Matt also opens the eyes of naive teacher Dorothy (Merrick), saving her from the evil clutches of red recruiters. Based on a "Saturday Evening Post" article. **82m/B; DVD.** Frank Lovejoy; Dorothy Hart; Phil Carey; Richard Webb; James Millican; Paul Picerni; ***D:*** Gordon Douglas; ***W:*** Crane Wilbur; ***C:*** Edwin DuPar.

I Was a Male War Bride 🦴🦴🦴 **1949** Hilarious WWII comedy. French officer Grant falls in love with and marries WAC lieutenant Sheridan in occupied Europe. Planning to leave the continent and settle down in the U.S., the couple hits a roadblock of red tape and Grant must cross-dress in order to accompany his bride on the troop ship taking her home. Worth watching for Grant's performance alone. Based on the novel by Henri Rochard. **105m/B; VHS, DVD.** Cary Grant; Ann Sheridan; Randy Stuart; Kenneth Tobey; William Neff; Marion Marshall; ***D:*** Howard Hawks; ***W:*** William Neff; Charles Lederer; Leonard Spigelgass; ***M:*** Cyril Mockridge.

I Was a Teenage TV Terrorist **WOOF!** *Amateur Hour* **1987** Two teenagers pull on-the-air pranks at the local cable television, blaming it all on an imaginary terrorist group. Poorly acted, cheaply made, and pointless. **85m/C; VHS, DVD.** Adam Nathan; Julie Hanlon; John MacKay; ***D:*** Stanford Singer; ***W:*** Stanford Singer; Kevin McDonough; ***C:*** Lisa Rinzler; ***M:*** Cengiz Yaltkaya.

I Was a Teenage Zombie 🦴 **1987** Spoof of high school horror films features a good zombie against a drug-pushing zombie. Forget the story and listen to the music by Los Lobos, the Fleshtones, the Waitresses, Dream Syndicate, and Violent Femmes. **92m/C; VHS, DVD.** Michael Rubin; Steve McCoy; Cassie Madden; Allen Rickman; ***D:*** John E. Michalakis; ***W:*** Steve McCoy; George Seminara; ***C:*** Peter Lewnes; ***M:*** Jonathan Roberts; Craig Seeman.

I Was a Zombie for the FBI 🦴 ½ **1982** Intelligence agency toughens its hiring criteria. Much McCarthyian mirth. **105m/B; VHS, DVD.** James Raspberry; Larry Raspberry; John Gillick; Christina Wellford; Anthony Isbell; Laurence Hall; Rick Crowe; ***D:*** Maurice Penczner; ***W:*** Maurice Penczner; John Gillick; ***C:*** Rick Dupree.

I Was an American Spy 🦴🦴 ½ **1951** Entertainer Claire Phillips (Dvorak) becomes a spy during the Japanese occupation of Manila after her American soldier husband is killed. She opens a nightclub to get info that she passes on to guerilla fighter Boone (Evans) but is eventually caught and imprisoned. Can she be rescued before her scheduled execution? Based on a true story. **84m/B; DVD.** Ann Dvorak; Douglas Kennedy; Gene Evans; Richard Loo; Philip Ahn; ***D:*** Lesley Selnder; ***W:*** Samuel Roeca; ***C:*** Harry Neumann; ***M:*** Edward Kay.

I Was Born But. . . 🦴🦴🦴 *Umarete Wa Mita Keredo* **1932** Two young brothers (Sugahara and Tokkankozo) are the leaders of the neighborhood gang of kids. Their office clerk father (Saito), who is trying to advance his position by playing up to the boss, insists the boys accompany him to his boss' house for a visit. The sons are embarassed by their father's ingratiating behavior, especially when they realize that the boss' son is a minor member of their gang. In retaliation, the brothers decide to go on a hunger strike. Charming social satire. Japanese with subtitles. **89m/B; VHS, DVD.** *JP* Tatsuo Saito; Hideo Sugahara; Tokkankozo; Mitsuko Yoshikawa; Takeshi Sakamoto; ***D:*** Yasujiro Ozu; ***W:*** Akira Fushimi; Geibei Ibushiya; ***C:*** Hideo Shigehara.

I Was Happy Here 🦴🦴 *Time Lost and Time Remembered* **1966** In a 'the grass is always greener' story, Cass (Miles) leaves her Irish seaside village for the bright lights of London, believing her beau Colin (Caffrey) will follow. He doesn't and lonely Cass soon finds herself married to pompous doctor Michael (Glover). Cass goes back to her village one Christmas, finds Colin has gotten engaged, and also realizes how much she's changed. When Michael comes to collect her, Cass has some life-changing decisions to make. Based on Edna O'Brien's story "A Woman by the Seaside." **91m/B; DVD.** *GB* Sarah Miles; Julian Glover; Sean Caffrey; Cyril Cusack; Eve Belton; ***D:*** Desmond Davis; ***W:*** Desmond Davis; Edna O'Brien; ***C:*** Manny Wynn; ***M:*** John Addison.

I Will Fight No More Forever 🦴🦴🦴 **1975** A vivid recounting of the epic true story of the legendary Chief Joseph who led the Nez Perce tribe on a 1600-mile trek to Canada in 1877. Disturbing and powerful. **100m/C; VHS, DVD.** James Whitmore; Ned Romero; Sam Elliott; ***D:*** Richard T. Heffron. **TV**

I Will, I Will...for Now 🦴🦴 **1976 (R)** Tacky sex clinic comedy with Keaton and Gould trying to save their marriage through kinky therapy. **109m/C; DVD.** Diane Keaton; Elliott Gould; Paul Sorvino; Victoria Principal; Robert Alda; Warren Bellinger; ***D:*** Norman Panama; ***W:*** Norman Panama; ***C:*** John A. Alonzo; ***M:*** John Cameron.

I Wish 🦴🦴🦴 *Kiseki* **2011 (PG)** Two brothers (Koki and Ohshiro Maeda, also brothers in real life) are divided by not just the separation of their parents but each other as their musician father has moved the younger brother to a new city. The older brother reads that a wish can be made at the point where two bullet trains pass and sets out with some friends to find that spot. A sweet tale about childhood expectations from international master filmmaker Kore-eda isn't his best--a little too slow for its own good--but he continues to have a way with getting exceptional performances from his young actors. **128m/C; DVD; Closed Captioned.** *JP* Koki Maeda; Oshiro Maeda; Nene Ohtsuka; Joe Odagiri; Isao Hashizume; Kirin Kiki; ***D:*** Hirokazu Kore-eda; ***W:*** Hirokazu Kore-eda; ***C:*** Yutaka Yamasaki.

I Witness 🦴🦴 **2003 (R)** Greed and corruption lead to a single culprit in three separate crimes: 27 people are found dead in a collapsed tunnel at a Mexican border town, two American college boys on holiday go missing and are later found murdered, and human rights observer James (Daniels) is monitoring a union election taking place at a chemical plant owned by a multinational corporation. Spader is typecast as an oily rep who keeps those third-world wheels greased and turning for the sake of the American economy. **95m/C; DVD.** Jeff Daniels; James Spader; Portia de Rossi; Clifton (Gonzalez) Collins, Jr.; Wade Andrew Williams; Jordi Caballero; ***D:*** Rowdy Herrington; ***W:*** Colin Greene; Robert Ozn; ***C:*** Michael G. Wojciechowski; ***M:*** David Kitay.

I Wonder Who's Killing Her Now? 🦴🦴 *Kill My Wife. . . Please!* **1976 (PG)** Scuzzy husband pays to have his wife murdered for the insurance money, then changes his mind. On-again, off-again comedy. **87m/C; VHS, DVD.** Bob (Robert) Dishy; Joanna Barnes; Bill Dana; Vito Scotti; Severn Darden; Harvey Jason; Richard Libertini; Noriyuki "Pat" Morita; ***D:*** Steven Hilliard Stern; ***W:*** Mickey Rose; ***C:*** Richard H. Kline; ***M:*** Patrick Williams.

I Wouldn't Be in Your Shoes 🦴 ½ **1948** Down-and-out dance duo Tom (Castle) and Ann (Knox) find some much-needed money—but it gets them into a heap of trouble when they're simultaneously found with the cash and a local recluse is found dead—with prints from Tom's dancing shoes near the murder scene. It looks like an open-and-shut case, but Ann has to unravel the mystery before Tom's execution date. **70m/B; DVD.** Don Castle; Elyse Knox; Regis Toomey; Charles D. Brown; ***D:*** William Nigh; ***W:*** Cornell Woolrich; Steve Fisher; ***C:*** Mack Stengler; ***M:*** Edward Kay.

Icarus 2017 121m/C; Streaming. *US RU* ***D:*** Bryan Fogel; ***W:*** Bryan Fogel; Jon Bertain; Mark Monroe; Timothy Rode; ***C:*** Timothy Rode; Jake Swantko; ***M:*** Adam Peters. Oscars '17: Feature Doc. **VIDEO**

Ice 🦴🦴 ½ **1993 (R)** Charley and Ellen Reed are thieves whose latest heist is $60 million in diamonds from mob boss Vito Malta. There's trouble when they try to fence the goods and Ellen is left with the merchandise and on the run from Malta's henchmen. **91m/C; VHS, DVD.** Traci Lords; Phillip Troy; Zach Galligan; Jorge (George) Rivero; Michael Bailey Smith; Jamie Alba; Jean Pflieger; Floyd Levine; ***D:*** Brook Yeaton; ***W:*** Sean Dash.

Ice Age 🦴🦴🦴 **2002 (PG)** Director Wedge (also the voice of Scrat the squirrel) crafts a smart, sophisticated and touching animated comedy/adventure about a group of prehistoric beasts who find a human baby and then try to restore the tyke to his tribe. During the long march south during an ice age, the cuddly Manfred the Mammoth (Romano) and Sid the Sloth (the already animated Leguizamo) are joined by Diego the scheming Sabertooth Tiger (Leary) whose bond is solidified after the two save Diego's life. Amazing computer-animation technology and artistry are top-notch. Characters are likeable but sometimes spew overly glib dialogue. Although not quite of the same caliber story-wise, this one fits right in with "Shrek," "Monsters, Inc." and "Toy Story." **81m/C; VHS, DVD, Blu-Ray, UMD.** ***V:*** John Leguizamo; Denis Leary; Ray Romano; Goran Visnjic; Jack Black; Cedric the Entertainer; Stephen (Steve) Root; Tara Strong; Diedrich Bader; Alan Tudyk; Lorri Bagley; Jane Krakowski; Chris Wedge; ***D:*** Chris Wedge; ***W:*** Michael Berg; Michael J. Wilson; Peter Ackerman; ***M:*** David Newman.

Ice Age: Collision Course 🦴 **2016 (PG)** In this fifth installment of the franchise, even the voice cast and writers seem to be asking "Why bother?" as it unfolds. This time around, the physical comedy of Scrat takes place in outer space, believe it or not, pushing into action a meteor shower that threatens to make the creatures extinct. They must outrace the carnage and figure out a way to stop the biggest meteor from wiping out the entire planet. Playing like deleted scenes from previous installments, it's uninspired and shockingly boring, even for the little ones. **94m/C; DVD, Blu-Ray.** Ray Romano; John Leguizamo; Denis Leary; Queen Latifah; Jennifer Lopez; Adam Devine; ***D:*** Michael Thurmeier; ***W:*** Michael J. Wilson; Michael Berg; Yoni Brenner; ***C:*** Renato Falcao; ***M:*** John Debney.

Ice Age: Continental Drift 🦴🦴 ½ **2012 (PG)** In this fourth animated comedy (in 3D), Scrat's pursuit of his ever-elusive acorn causes an earthquake that starts splitting apart the continents and Manny (Romano), Diego (Leary), Sid (Leguizamo), and Sid's crazy Granny (Sykes) are set adrift on an ice floe. They literally run into a pirate ship, led by oranutan Captain Gutt (Dinklage), and have various adventures while trying to reunite Manny and his family. Nothing particularly memorable but it's still pleasant fun. **88m/C; DVD, Blu-Ray.** ***V:*** Ray Romano; Denis Leary; John Leguizamo; Queen Latifah; Seann William Scott; Josh Peck; Keke Palmer; Jennifer Lopez; Wanda Sykes; Peter Dinklage; ***D:*** Steve Martino; Michael Thurmeier; ***W:*** Michael Berg; Jason Fuchs; ***C:*** Renato Falcao; ***M:*** John Powell.

Ice Age: Dawn of the Dinosaurs 🦴🦴 ½ **2009 (PG)** Animated 3-D sequel is content to coast along on the strengths of the previous two films. Anxiety-ridden Manny and fun-loving Ellie are awaiting the birth of their baby mammoth, which causes jealousy in sloth Sid who decides he needs a family of his own. So he adopts three dinosaur eggs but momma T-Rex is none too pleased and leaves her subterranean tropical jungle world to retrieve her offspring—taking Sid back with her. This means the rest of the crew, including saber-toothed tiger Diego who fears he's been domesticated, go on a rescue mission. Underground, they meet swashbuckling (and crazy) one-eyed weasel Buck and his albino dino nemesis. Meanwhile, squirrel/rat Scrat must guard his beloved acorn from a flirtatious rival, Scratte. **94m/C; Blu-Ray, On Demand.** John Leguizamo; ***V:*** Ray Romano; Queen Latifah; Denis Leary; Chris Wedge; Simon Pegg; Seann William Scott; Josh Peck; Bill Hader; ***D:*** Carlos Saldanha; ***W:*** Michael Berg; Peter Ackerman; Mike Reiss; Yoni Brenner; ***M:*** John Powell.

Ice Age: The Meltdown 🦴🦴 ½ **2006 (PG)** Okay, so global warming gets its licks in but this is hardly an environmental diatribe. Anyway, the glaciers are melting, the water is rising, and the animals are on the move to higher, drier ground. Manny (Romano) believes he's the last wooly mammoth left until he meets flirty Ellie (Queen Latifah), who thinks she's actually a possum like her two foster brothers (Scott & Peck). Fast-talking Sid (Leguizamo) and grumpy Diego (Leary) are part of the mix as is acorn-chasing, scene-stealing Scrat. The animation still rocks even if the adventures are a mild retread. **90m/C; DVD, Blu-Ray.** ***V:*** Ray Romano; John Leguizamo; Denis Leary; Seann William Scott; Josh Peck; Queen Latifah; Will Arnett; Jay Leno; Joseph Bologna; Renee Taylor; Stephen (Steve) Root; Mindy Sterling; Alan Tudyk; Clea Lewis; ***D:*** Carlos Saldanha; ***W:*** Peter Gaulke; Gerry Swallow; Jim Hecht; ***C:*** Harry Hitner; ***M:*** John Powell.

Ice Blues: A Donald Strachey Mystery 🦴🦴 ½ **2008** In this 4th cable installment, adapted from the Richard Stevenson novel, Albany PI Donald Strachey's (Allen) latest client is his lover Tim (Spence). Tim, a NY State Senate aide, receives a donation of $3 million to fund a teen shelter from donor Jake Lenigan. Jake is murdered and Donald suspects there's a tie-in to the unsolved murder of Jake's father. Meanwhile, Tim is being threatened by several people who want the money back. **98m/C; DVD.** Chad Allen; Sebastian Spence; Daryl Shuttleworth; Nelson Wong; Sherry Miller; Sebastien Roberts; Myron Natwick; Jason Poulsen; Adrian Holmes; Brittney Wilson; P. Lynn Johnson; ***W:*** Ron Oliver; ***C:*** Ron McGee; ***M:*** C. Kim Miles; Rick Whitfield. **CABLE**

Ice Castles 🦴🦴 **1979 (PG)** A young figure skater's Olympic dreams are dimmed when she is blinded in an accident, but her boyfriend gives her the strength, encouragement, and love necessary to perform a small miracle. Way too schmaltzy. **110m/C; VHS, DVD.** Robby Benson; Lynn-Holly Johnson; Tom Skerritt; Colleen Dewhurst; Jennifer Warren; David Huffman; ***D:*** Donald Wrye; ***W:*** Donald Wrye; Gary L. Bain; ***C:*** Bill Butler; ***M:*** Marvin Hamlisch.

Ice Castles 🦴🦴 ½ **2010 (PG)** Remake of the 1978 tearjerker. Alexis (figure skater Firth) skates for fun back home in Iowa while boyfriend Nick (Mayes) plays college hockey. Then Alexis enters a competition and gets noticed by bigtime scout and trainer Aiden Reynolds (Kelly). She becomes ambitious and reckless, leading to a serious injury that leaves Alexis blind, but Nick and her family encourage her to compete again. **95m/C; DVD.** Taylor Firth; Rob Mayes; Henry Czerny; Morgan Kelly; Eve Crawford; Tattiawana Jones; ***D:*** Donald Wyre; ***W:*** Donald Wyre; Gary L. Baim; Karen Bloch Morse; ***C:*** Eric Cayla; ***M:*** David Williams. **VIDEO**

Ice Cream Man 🦴 **1995 (R)** Quite disgusting horror tale of a dweeby, demented ice cream man who delivers gore and death along with his frozen treats. **96m/C; VHS, DVD, Blu-Ray.** Clint Howard; Sandahl Bergman; Olivia Hussey; Lee Majors, II; David Naughton; Jan-Michael Vincent; David Warner; Steve Garvey; ***D:*** Norman Apstein.

Ice Follies of 1939 🦴🦴 **1939** The marriage of skating team Mary (Crawford) and Larry (Stewart) is in trouble when she gets a Hollywood film contract and he can't make it on his own. Egged on by Mary, producer Tolliver (Stone) offers Larry the chance to produce an ice revue extravaganza. The only highlight (besides watching Crawford) is the finale—a Technicolor Cinderella fantasy performed by the International Ice Follies. **82m/B; DVD.** Joan Crawford; James Stewart; Lewis Stone; Lionel Stander; Lew Ayres; ***D:*** Reinhold Schunzel; ***W:*** Florence Ryerson; Edgar Allan Woolf; Leonard Praskins; ***C:*** Joseph Ruttenberg; Oliver Marsh; ***M:*** Roger Edens.

The Ice Harvest 🦴🦴 ½ **2005 (R)** It's Christmas Eve in Wichita, and mob lawyer Charlie (Cusack) still has a pretty long to-do list. But things got complicated when he and his partner Vic (Thornton) skimmed $2.2 million from crime lord Bill Guerrard (Quaid). Now, in the midst of an ice storm, Charlie has to dodge Bill's hit man Roy (Starr), withstand the dangerous charms of topless bar manager/femme fatale Renata (Nielson), baby-sit his drunken brother-in-law Pete (a hilariously over-the-top Platt), and finish his shopping. A lovely bit of screwball comedic film noir, but with a director like Ramis, things should have been funnier. **88m/C; DVD, Blu-Ray.** John Cusack; Billy Bob Thornton; Connie Nielsen; Randy Quaid; Oliver Platt; ***D:*** Harold Ramis; ***W:*** Richard Russo; Robert Benton; ***C:*** Alar Kivilo; ***M:*** David Kitay.

The Ice House 🦴🦴🦴 **1997** Chilling TV adaptation of Minette Walters' first mystery. Ten years ago Phoebe Maybury's (Downie) abusive husband David disappeared. Locally condemned as a murderess, she and her friends Diana (Barber) and Anne (Aldridge) have been shunned by their small-minded community. Now a body has been discovered in an ice house located on Maybury property. Is it David? Inspector Walsh (Redgrave), who couldn't prove anything against Phoebe before, certainly thinks so, but his on-the-edge associate Sgt. McLoughlin (Craig) isn't so certain. **180m/C; DVD.** *UK* Daniel Craig; Penny Downie; Corin Redgrave; Kitty Aldridge; Frances Barber; ***D:*** Tim Fywell; ***W:*** Elizabeth (Lizzie) Mickery; ***C:*** John Daly; ***M:*** David Ferguson. **TV**

Ice Men 🦴🦴 **2004** Uptight Vaughn (Cummins) decides to throw a birthday party for buddy Bryan (Hewlett) at the lakeside cabin he's inherited. He also invites Jon (Spottiswood) and Steve (Thomas) for a weekend of hunting and drinking. Unfortunately, there's some uninvited guests as well: Vaughn's drunken black sheep brother Trevor (Tracey) and his ex-girlfriend Renee (Ledford), who both cause problems. Some sexual shenanigans and revealed secrets don't make for relaxation either, although the plot tends to meander. **108m/C; DVD.** *CA* Martin Cummins; David Hewlett; Greg Spottiswood; Ian Tracey; James Thomas; Brandy Ledford; ***D:*** Thom Best; ***W:*** Michael Lewis MacLennan; ***C:*** Gavin Smith; ***M:*** Michael Shields; Russell Broom.

Ice Palace 🦴🦴 **1960** Two rugged adventurers maintain a lifelong rivalry in the primitive Alaskan wilderness, their relationship dramatizing the development of the 49th state. Silly but entertaining. Based on Edna Ferber's novel. **143m/C; VHS, DVD.** Richard Burton; Robert Ryan; Carolyn Jones; Shirley Knight; Martha Hyer; Jim Backus; George Takei; ***D:*** Vincent Sherman; ***C:*** Joseph Biroc; ***M:*** Max Steiner.

Ice Pirates 🦴 ½ **1984 (PG)** Space pirates in the far future steal blocks of ice to fill the needs of a thirsty galaxy. Cool plot has its moments. **91m/C; VHS, DVD, Blu-Ray.** Robert Urich; Mary Crosby; Michael D. Roberts; John Matuszak; Anjelica Huston; Ron Perlman; John Carradine; Robert Symonds; ***D:*** Stewart Raffill; ***W:*** Stewart Raffill; ***M:*** Bruce Broughton.

Ice Princess 🦴🦴 ½ **2005 (G)** Casey Carlyle (Trachtenberg) is a high school science whiz kid who needs a stellar science project to get into Harvard. She decides to analyze the science of figure skating by observing a bunch of local elite skaters at a nearby rink. Casey is not satisfied with simply observing, so she straps on a pair of skates and starts taking lessons. She soon realizes that she has a natural talent for it, but her feminist mother (Joan Cusack) disapproves. While the movie holds no surprises, it's still enjoyable for the target audience. Go figure. **92m/C; VHS, DVD.** Michelle Trachtenberg; Joan Cusack; Kim Cattrall; Hayden Panettiere; Trevor Blumas; Kirsten Olson; Connie Ray; Juliana Cannarozzo; ***Cameo(s):*** Brian Boitano; Michelle Kwan; ***D:*** Tim Fywell; ***W:*** Hadley Davis; Meg Cabot; ***C:*** David Hennings; ***M:*** Christophe Beck.

Ice Quake 🦴 ½ **2010 (PG)** Typically mediocre Syfy Channel disaster pic finds a gigantic ice shelf collapsing in the Russian Arctic. This causes massive shockwaves and starts melting the permafrost, which is a very bad thing. Military geologist Michael Webster is recruited to find a way to stop the planet from being destroyed. **90m/C; DVD, Blu-Ray.** Brendan Fehr; Victor Garber; Jodelle Ferland; Holly Dignard; Ryan Grantham; Rob LaBelle; ***D:*** Paul Ziller; ***W:*** Paul Ziller; David Ray; ***C:*** Anthony C. Metchie; ***M:*** Anthony Neilson. **CABLE**

The Ice Rink 🦴🦴 *La Patinoire* **1999** A director (Novembre) decides to make a movie about the romance between a French ice skater (Chaplin) and an American hockey player (Campbell) that is to be filmed on an ice skating rink. However, most of the cast and crew can't skate, the ice keeps melting, the supporting hockey players are Lithuanian and don't speak French, the two leads are having a torrid (and disruptive) affair, and that's just the beginning. A generally playful look at the tribulations of making a movie. French with subtitles. **80m/C; VHS, DVD.** *FR* Tom Novembre; Marie-France Pisier; Bruce Campbell; Dolores Chaplin; Mireille Perrier; Jean-Pierre Cassel; ***D:*** Jean-Philippe Toussaint; ***W:*** Jean-Philippe Toussaint; ***C:*** Jean-Francois Robin.

The Ice Runner 🦴🦴 ½ **1993 (R)** Low-key Cold War thriller, filmed in 1991, about a U.S. spy who escapes from the Soviet gulag. Jeffrey West (Albert) gets caught in a botched payoff to a Soviet minister and when the diplomats wash their hands of him a rigged trial has West sentenced to 12 years hard labor. A convenient train wreck lets him assume a different prisoner's name which gets him to a minimum security camp under the eyes of a suspicious commander. Now West needs to escape and cross 39 miles of icy tundra separating his Russian prison from American freedom. **116m/C; VHS, DVD.** Edward Albert; Eugene (Yevgeny) Lazarev; Olga Kabo; Victor Wong; Alexander Kuznitsov; Basil Hoffman; Bill Bordy; Sergei Ruban; ***D:*** Barry Samson; ***W:*** Joyce Warren; Clifford Coleman; Joshua Stallings.

Ice Soldiers 🦴🦴 **2013 (R)** Cheesy but watchable actioner with a plot that seems cobbled together from similar flicks. Genetically modified Soviet soldiers from the Cold War era wind up buried in Canadian Arctic ice. Years later, at least one of these super-soldier is thawed out and willing to kill the unfortunate crew that stumbles upon him as a prelude to restarting his original mission. **95m/C; DVD, Blu-Ray.** Dominic Purcell; Adam Beach; Michael Ironside; Benz Antoine; Gabriel

Hogan; Camille Sullivan; *D:* Sturla Gunnarsson; *W:* Jonathan Tydor; *C:* Stephen Reizes; *M:* Jonathan Goldsmith. **VIDEO**

Ice Spiders 🦴🦴 1/2 **2007 (R)** Pure camp and gore from the Sci-Fi Channel. Olympic ski hopefuls head to a remote resort in Utah where Dash (Muldoon) is the head instructor. He has the hots for Dr. April (Williams), who works at a secret government lab where they're doing military experiments on gigantic spiders with ravenous appetites who get loose and don't mind the cold as they go looking for their next meal. **86m/C; DVD.** Patrick Muldoon; Vanessa Williams; Thomas Calabro; Stephen J. Cannell; David Millbern; Noah Bastien; Carleigh King; *D:* Tibor Takacs; *W:* Eric Miller; *C:* Barry Gravelle. **CABLE**

Ice Station Zebra 🦴🦴 1/2 **1968 (G)** A nuclear submarine races Soviet seamen to find a downed Russian satellite under a polar ice cap. Suspenseful Cold War adventure based on the novel by Alistair MacLean. **148m/C; VHS, DVD, Blu-Ray.** Rock Hudson; Ernest Borgnine; Patrick McGoohan; Jim Brown; Lloyd Nolan; Tony Bill; *D:* John Sturges; *W:* Douglas Heyes; W.R. Burnett; *C:* Daniel F. Fapp; *M:* Michel Legrand.

The Ice Storm 🦴🦴🦴 1/2 **1997 (R)** Excellent family drama/period piece (the 1970s!) directed by Ang Lee and based on the book by Rick Moody. Kline plays a husband and father too self-absorbed to notice his marriage (to Allen) unraveling into crisis, and his children (Maguire and Ricci) mimicking the sordid behavior that surrounds them. Skillfully fuses together a frank, unsympathetic look at family psychology, while also making a comment on the social situation of the early 1970s. Flirts with being overpoweringly negative and moody, but is elevated by Lee's insight and direction. Excellent job by the entire cast, especially Weaver, frighteningly dead-on as an emotionally reckless wife and mother, and Hann-Byrd and Wood as her eerie sons. **113m/C; VHS, DVD, Blu-Ray.** Kevin Kline; Sigourney Weaver; Joan Allen; Christina Ricci; Tobey Maguire; Elijah Wood; Katie Holmes; Henry Czerny; Adam Hann-Byrd; David Krumholtz; Jamey Sheridan; Maia Danziger; Kate Burton; John Benjamin Hickey; Allison Janney; Byron Jennings; *D:* Ang Lee; *W:* James Schamus; *C:* Frederick Elmes; *M:* Mychael Danna. British Acad. '97: Support. Actress (Weaver).

Ice Twisters 🦴 **2009 (PG-13)** Syfy Channel disaster flick. In order to counteract the effects of a drought, a couple of Federal Science Foundation employees develop a new device for seeding clouds for rain. The unexpected consequences are freezing flash tornadoes that controversial author and former FSF employee Charlie Price (Moses) investigates. **91m/C; DVD.** Mark Moses; Camille Sullivan; Alex Zahara; Kaj-Erik Eriksen; Ryan Kennedy; Luisa D'Oliveira; Robert Moloney; Chelan Simmons; *D:* Stephen R. Monroe; *W:* Andrew C. Erin; *C:* Anthony C. Metchie; *M:* Michael Richard Plowman. **CABLE**

Iceland 🦴🦴 **1942** Labored romance of an Iceland girl and a Marine with plenty of skating thrown in for good measure. Skating and singing interludes are the best part of an otherwise average film. **79m/B; DVD.** Sonja Henie; John Payne; Jack Oakie; Felix Bressart; Osa Massen; Fritz Feld; *D:* H. Bruce Humberstone; *W:* Robert Ellis; Helen Logan.

Iceman 🦴🦴🦴 **1984 (PG)** A frozen prehistoric man is brought back to life, after which severe culture shock takes hold. Underwritten but nicely acted, especially by Lone as the primal man. **101m/C; VHS, DVD, Blu-Ray.** *CA* Timothy Hutton; Lindsay Crouse; John Lone; David Strathairn; Josef Sommer; Danny Glover; *D:* Fred Schepisi; *W:* Chip Proser; *C:* Ian Baker; *M:* Bruce Smeaton.

The Iceman 🦴🦴 **2012 (R)** Notorious mob hitman Richard Kuklinski (Shannon) earned his titular nickname not only because he would keep his victims on ice to make their time of death harder to determine but also because he was as cold as the substance. With an oblivious wife (Ryder) and kids, Kuklinski lived an unusual double life. Sadly, while Shannon gives yet another great performance, director Vromen too often asks viewers to identify with a serial killer, a maniac of the highest degree. The result is a film with shady morality. Based on a true story covered in Philip Carlo's 2009 book of the same name. **103m/C; DVD, Blu-Ray.** Michael Shannon; Winona Ryder; Chris Evans; Ray Liotta; David Schwimmer; Robert Davi; Stephen Dorff; James Franco; *D:* Ariel Vromen; *W:* Ariel Vromen; Morgan Land; *C:* Bobby Bukowski; *M:* Haim Mazar.

Iceman 🦴🦴 1/2 *Der Mann aus dem Eis* **2019** A member of the mountain tribe during the Neolithic era, Kelab (Vogel) is a farmer, head of a family, and caretaker of caretaker of the tribe's box-sized shrine, Tineka. His world is turned upside down when marauders burn down the village, murder nearly all of his family, and steal Tineka while he is away hunting. Taking his surviving infant and a goat, he begins a journey through the mountains seeking vengeance and retribution. Inspired by a slain Copper Age hunter whose body was found in Central Europe in 1991, the film is visually stunning but its story and plot do not match. **96m/C; DVD.** Jurgen Vogel; Andre Hennicke; Susanne Wuest; Sabin Tambrea; Martin Augustin Schneider; *D:* Felix Randau; *W:* Felix Randau; *C:* Jakub Bejnarowicz; *M:* Beat Soler.

The Iceman Cometh 🦴🦴🦴 **1960** A recording of CBS' live version (flubs and all) of Eugene O'Neill's searing drama. Traveling salesman Hickey (Robards) comes to visit his old pals, the no-hopers who populate Harry Hope's (Pelly) Greenwich Village saloon, circa 1912. But something's changed about the glad-handing Hickey as he seeks to strip the bar's denizens of all their so-called pipe dreams. This is the role that made Robards a star in a 1956 off-Broadway revival; he would eventually embody many of O'Neill's characters. Originally shown in kinescope. **210m/B; DVD.** Jason Robards, Jr.; Myron McCormick; Tom Pedi; James Broderick; Robert Redford; Ronald Radd; Roland Winters; Michael Strong; Sorrell Booke; Hilda Brawner; Julie Bovasso; Joan Copeland; Farrell Pelly; Harrison Dowd; *D:* Sidney Lumet. **TV**

The Iceman Cometh 🦴🦴 1/2 **1973** American Film Theater version of the Eugene O'Neill play with Marvin starring as salesman Hickey, who's found an unsettling peace of mind after—it's slowly revealed to the drunks of Harry Hope's bar—committing a terrible crime. However, it's Ryan who steals the picture as former anarchist Larry, a man simply waiting to die. Ryan was ill with terminal cancer, as was March (who plays Harry Hope); this would be the last appearance for both men. **239m/C; DVD, Blu-Ray.** Lee Marvin; Fredric March; Robert Ryan; Jeff Bridges; Martyn Green; George Voskovec; Moses Gunn; Tom Pedi; Evans Evans; Bradford Dillman; Sorrell Booke; John McLiam; Hildy Brooks; Clifton James; *D:* John Frankenheimer; *W:* Thomas Quinn Curtiss; *C:* Ralph Woolsey.

Ichi 🦴🦴 **2008 (R)** The story of Zatoichi the Blind Swordsman is one of the most venerable movie franchises in Japan, spawning 29 films, a television series, and inspiring the Rutger Hauer film "Blind Fury". In this latest incarnation, Ichi (Haruka Ayase) is a blind woman who travels looking for the equally blind swordsman who taught her to fight. Along the way she helps out a pacifist Samurai who is being swindled by gamblers, and in the process they bring the wrath of a bandit lord on an innocent village. **120m/C; DVD, Blu-Ray.** *JP* Haruka Ayase; Shido Nakamura; Yosuke Kubozuka; Takao Osawa; *D:* Fumihiko Sori; *W:* Kan Shimosawa; *C:* Keiji Hashimoto; *M:* Michael Edwards; Lisa Gerrard.

Ichi the Killer 🦴🦴 *Koroshiya Ichi* **2001** Based on the comic of the same name, this film centers around Kakihara, a sadistic yakuza killer in Shinjuku. His boss Anjo has disappeared, so Kakihara kidnaps a rival boss to torture the information of Anjo's whereabouts from him. A hostess from a club later informs him that his boss is dead, slain by a mysterious superhuman killer known only as Ichi. Unable to find the pain he craves (Kakihara is a masochist) that he used to get from his boss, Kakihara sets out to find the murderer in a quest to assuage his needs, and find out why Anjo was killed. Director Takashi Miike is known for over the top films, and Ichi is truly one of those. **128m/C; DVD, Blu-Ray.** *JP* Tadanobu Asano; Shinya Tsukamoto; Paulyn Sun; Susumu Terajima; Shun Sugata; Jun Kunimura; Nao Omori; Toru Tezuka; Yoshiki Arizano; Kiyohiko Shibukawa; Satoshi Nizuma; Suzuki Matsuo; Hiroyuki Tanaka; Moro Morooka; Houka Kinoshita; Hiroshi Kobayashi; Mai Goto; Rio Aoki; Yuki Kazamatsuri; *D:* Takashi Miike; *W:* Hideo Yamamoto; Sakichi Sato; *C:* Hideo Yamamoto; *M:* Seiichi Yamamoto; Karera Musication.

iCrime 🦴 1/2 **2011** Fletcher is good as a tough babe involved in Hollywood sleaze to protect her family. Beauty queen-turned-pinup model Stefy calls on her cousin Carrie to help her when she's threatened by video blogger Evelyn Echo over a sex tape. Carrie does a deal with Evelyn by offering a new target: a reality star who faked her own kidnapping for publicity. Only then the kidnapping turns real. **111m/C; DVD.** Sara Fletcher; Kelly Noonan; Leah Mckendrick; Travis Brorsen; Griff Furst; *D:* Bears Fonte; *W:* Bears Fonte; *C:* Matt Egan; *M:* Richard Ford. **VIDEO**

Icy Breasts 🦴🦴🦴 **1975** A French psychiatrist tries to prevent his beautiful but psychotic patient from continuing her murdering spree. Dubbed. **105m/C; VHS, DVD.** *FR* Alain Delon; Mireille Darc; *D:* Georges Lautner.

I'd Climb the Highest Mountain 🦴🦴🦴 **1951** Sincere, sentimental piece of Americana about a country preacher (Lundigan) and his city wife (Hayward) as they adjust to life in a small town in Southern hill country. Filmed on location in Georgia. Film was a big hit, especially in the South. Based on the novel by Corra Harris. **88m/C; DVD.** Susan Hayward; William Lundigan; Rory Calhoun; Gene Lockhart; Ruth Donnelly; Barbara Bates; Lynn Bari; Alexander Knox; *D:* Henry King; *W:* Lamar Trotti; *C:* Edward Cronjager; *M:* Sol Kaplan.

I'd Give My Life 🦴 1/2 **1936** A gangster's ex-wife is presently married to the governor. He tries to use their honest but framed son to blackmail her. **73m/B; VHS, DVD.** Guy Standing; Frances Drake; Tom Brown; Janet Beecher; *D:* Edwin L. Marin.

Ida 🦴🦴🦴 **2013** Orphan Anna (Trzebuchowska) is raised in a convent and is about to take her vows to enter the nunnery. The sisters finally contact a living relative of hers, an aunt named Wanda, and advise that she visit her to learn about her past before starting her life as a nun. The journey reveals that Anna's parents were Jews killed in World War II, leaving Anna on the church steps. Polish writer/director Pawlikowski crafts a haunting, soulful look at faith, history, and the changing face of Poland in the '60s that lingers long after the credits roll. Polish with subtitles. **80m/B; DVD, Blu-Ray.** *PL* Agata Trzebuchowska; Agata Kulesza; *D:* Pawel Pawlikowski; *W:* Pawel Pawlikowski; Rebecca Lenkiewicz; *C:* Lukasz Zal; Ryszard Lenczewski; *M:* Kristian Eidnes Andersen. Oscars '14: Foreign Film; British Acad. '14: Foreign Film; Ind. Spirit '15: Foreign Film.

Idaho 🦴 1/2 **1943** On a mission to close down houses of ill repute, Rodgers teams up with Autry's old sidekick Burnette. **70m/B; VHS, DVD.** Roy Rogers; Harry Shannon; Virginia Grey; Smiley Burnette; Ona Munson; *D:* Joseph Kane.

Idaho Transfer WOOF! *Deranged* **1973 (PG)** Fonda's second directorial effort; Carradine's first screen appearance. An obnoxious group of teens travel through time to Idaho in the year 2044. Environmental wasteland story is dull and confused. **90m/C; VHS, DVD.** Keith Carradine; Kelley Bohanan; *D:* Peter Fonda.

An Ideal Husband 🦴🦴 1/2 **1947** Adventuress Laura Cheveley (Goddard) slithers back into the life of former schoolmate Gertrude Chiltern (Wynyard) with the intention of blackmailing her husband Robert (Williams). Robert is a rising politician, known for his honesty, but he committed a financial indiscretion in his youth that Laura is happy to exploit. Elegantly witty version of the Oscar Wilde play; remade in 1999. **96m/C; DVD.** *GB* Paulette Goddard; Hugh Williams; Diana Wynyard; Michael Wilding; Sir C. Aubrey Smith; Glynis Johns; Constance Collier; *D:* Alexander Korda; *W:* Lajos Biro; *C:* Georges Perinal; *M:* Arthur Benjamin.

An Ideal Husband 🦴🦴🦴 **1999 (PG-13)** Victorian comedy of manners adapted from the play by Oscar Wilde. The very proper Lady Gertrud Chiltern (Blanchett) discovers that her husband, Sir Robert (Northam), a member of Parliament, attained their fortune and power through questionable means. Robert is being blackmailed over a shady business deal by Gertrud's loathed ex-school mate, Laura Cheveley (Moore). Cynical social butterfly, Lord Arthur Goring (Everett), is drawn into the fray because of his friendship with Chiltern. It's rather exaggerated and very witty, as one would expect of Wilde. **96m/C; VHS, DVD.** *GB* Cate Blanchett; Jeremy Northam; Minnie Driver; Rupert Everett; Julianne Moore; Jeroen Krabbe; Lindsay Duncan; Peter Vaughan; John Wood; Marsha Fitzalan; Benjamin Pullen; *D:* Oliver Parker; *W:* Oliver Parker; *C:* David C(lark) Johnson; *M:* Charlie Mole. Natl. Bd. of Review '99: Support. Actress (Moore).

The Identical 🦴 **2014 (PG)** Just a weird, weird drama, this quasi-inspirational musical film stars the fantastically named Blake Rayne as identical twins Ryan Wade and Drexel Hemsley. The twins were separated shortly after birth. Hemsley went on to be a superstar musician while Wade struggled in a church-loving household to find his own identity. Wade never lost his musical passion either. What could have been a story of how much chance impacts our fate is a flat, Lifetime TV movie affair with almost nothing but bad performances, paper-thin characters, and even music that feels lackluster. **107m/C; DVD, Blu-Ray.** Blake Rayne; Ray Liotta; Ashley Judd; Erin Cottrell; Brian Geraghty; Joe Pantoliano; Seth Green; Amanda Crew; *D:* Dustin Marcellino; *W:* Howard Klausner; *C:* Karl Walter Lindenlaub; *M:* Klaus Badelt; Christopher Carmichael.

Identicals 🦴🦴 *Brand New-U* **2016 (R)** A science fiction exploration of ideas about identity and self-discovery. In the future, Brand New-U is a company that finds people that walk and talk like you with better lives and gives their clients an upgraded life. Though Slater (Nieboer) seems to have it all, his life is turned upside down when his girlfriend is taken by Brand New-U and a corpse is left in her place. To find his girlfriend, he becomes an Identical, moves through many parallel lives, and learns more about himself. **100m/C; DVD, Streaming, Download.** Lachlan Nieboer; Nora-Jane Noone; Nick Blood; Tony Way; Andrew Buckley; *D:* Simon Pummell; *W:* Simon Pummell; *C:* Reinier van Brummelen; *M:* Roger Goula Sarda.

Identification of a Woman 🦴🦴 *Identificazione di una Donna* **1982** Niccolo (Milian) is a middle-aged film director who is searching for the perfect female image as the focus for his new movie. But his personal search alienates the flesh-and-blood women already in his life. Lots of visuals give the film a slow, dreamlike quality. Italian with subtitles. **131m/C; VHS, DVD, Blu-Ray.** *IT* Tomas Milian; Christine Boisson; Daniela Silverio; Sandra Monteleoni; *D:* Michelangelo Antonioni; *W:* Michelangelo Antonioni; Gerard Brach; *C:* Carlo Di Palma; *M:* John Foxx.

Identity 🦴🦴 1/2 **2003 (R)** See if this premise sounds familiar—ten strangers, an ex-cop turned chauffeur; his movie star passenger; a family with a wounded wife; a newlywed couple; a cop transporting a prisoner; and an ex-hooker are brought together (because of a severe rainstorm) at a desolate motel run by a creepy clerk. One by one they start to die in various icky and/or disturbing ways. A possibly-connected subplot involves a man on death row getting a last-minute, late-night hearing. Well-executed, if unspectacular, suspenser provides a satisfyingly twisty thrill. **90m/C; VHS, DVD, Blu-Ray.** John Cusack; Rebecca De Mornay; Ray Liotta; Jake Busey; Amanda Peet; Clea DuVall; William Lee Scott; John C. McGinley; Leila Kenzle; Bret Loehr; John Hawkes; Pruitt Taylor Vince; Alfred Molina; Matt Letscher; Carmen Argenziano; Marshall Bell; Holmes Osborne; Frederick Coffin; *D:* James Mangold; *W:* Michael Cooney; *C:* Phedon Papamichael; *M:* Alan Silvestri.

Identity Crisis 🦴 **1990 (R)** Campy fashion maven and flamboyant rapper switch identities causing much tedious overacting. Lifeless murder comedy from father and son Van Peebles. **98m/C; VHS, DVD.** Mario Van Peebles; Ilan Mitchell-Smith; Nicholas Kepros; Shelly Burch; Richard Clarke; *D:* Melvin Van Peebles.

Identity Theft: The Michelle Brown Story 🦴🦴 **2004** Michelle Brown's (Williams-Paisley) identity is stolen by crazy Connie Volkos (Sciorra) with devastating consequences to her life. She's even mistakenly arrested when a warrant is issued for the imposter but it leads Michelle to fight for stronger identity theft laws. Based on a true story. **90m/C; DVD.** Kimberly Williams; Annabella Sciorra; Jason London; Stephen Strachan; ***D:*** Robert Dornhelm; ***W:*** Deena Goldstone; ***C:*** Derick Underschultz; ***M:*** J. Peter Robinson. **CABLE**

Identity Thief 🦴 ½ **2013 (R)** Diana (McCarthy) is an identity thief who takes the ID of Sandy Bigelow Patterson (Bateman), who comes after her in an attempt to enact revenge. Often dull and obnoxious comedy puts McCarthy's abrasive character too front and center to stay entertaining. Bateman excels at playing the straight man and McCarthy has perfect comic timing, but their rapport here is just bluntly forced and juvenile and gets tiring quickly. It's another oil-and-water road-trip comedy that's been made 100 times before, 99 of them funnier. **111m/C; DVD, Blu-Ray.** Jason Bateman; Melissa McCarthy; Jon Favreau; Amanda Peet; John Cho; Eric Stonestreet; Morris Chestnut; Genesis Rodriguez; Robert Patrick; ***D:*** Seth Gordon; ***W:*** Craig Mazin; ***C:*** Javier Aguirresarobe; ***M:*** Christopher Lennertz.

Identity Unknown 🦴🦴 ½ **1945** Shell-shocked veteran goes AWOL to discover who he is, meeting grieving relatives along the way. Interesting premise is sometimes moving. **70m/B; VHS, DVD.** Richard Arlen; Cheryl Walker; Roger Pryor; Bobby Driscoll; ***D:*** Walter Colmes.

The Ides of March 🦴🦴 ½ **2011 (R)** Stephen Myers (Gosling) is the whiz kid political player who gets caught up in a moral scandal involving the candidate (Clooney) most assume will be the next President and one of his young campaign workers (Wood). Very loosely based on the play "Farragut North" by Beau Willimon of Howard Dean's 2004 presidential run, Clooney proves to yet again be a great director with ensemble, drawing strong work from Gosling, Wood, Hoffman, Tomei, and Giamatti. Ultimately tripped up a bit by unrealistic political machinations and a lackluster pace. **101m/C; DVD, Blu-Ray.** George Clooney; Ryan Gosling; Philip Seymour Hoffman; Marisa Tomei; Paul Giamatti; Max Minghella; Evan Rachel Wood; ***D:*** George Clooney; ***W:*** George Clooney; Grant Heslov; ***C:*** Phedon Papamichael; ***M:*** Alexandre Desplat.

Idiocracy 🦴🦴 **2006 (R)** Mike Judge's "Office Space" became a cult hit after being rudely dumped during its studio release, and this satirical flick may obtain the same status. Everyman soldier Joe (Wilson) and hooker Rita (Rudolph) are selected by the Pentagon to take part in a hibernation experiment. Thanks to a snafu, they wake up 500 years later in an America so completely dumbed-down that they are now the smartest couple alive, with Joe given a presidential appointment to turn this mess around. The ultimate "what if" movie, with Wilson at his clueless, curious best. **84m/C; DVD.** Luke Wilson; Maya Rudolph; Dax Shepard; Terry Crews; David Herman; Justin Long; Thomas Haden Church; Stephen (Steve) Root; ***V:*** Earl Mann; ***D:*** Mike Judge; ***W:*** Mike Judge; Etan Cohen; ***C:*** Tim Suhrstedt; ***M:*** Theodore Shapiro.

The Idiot 🦴🦴🦴🦴 **1951** Dostoevski's Russian novel is transported by Kurosawa across two centuries to post-war Japan, where the madness and jealousy continue to rage. In Japanese with English subtitles. **166m/B; VHS, DVD.** Toshiro Mifune; Masayuki Mori; Setsuko Hara; Yoshiko Kuga; Takashi Shimura; ***D:*** Akira Kurosawa.

Idiot Box 🦴🦴 **1997** Crazy youth comedy about lazy, brainless Kev (Mendelsohn) and Mick (Sims) who spend most of their unemployed time watching violent cop shows on TV and drinking beer. It's from the "idiot box" that the dim duo get the idea that they've learned enough to rob a bank, but it just so happens that a pair of crooks, who wear clown masks, are already on a bank crime spree. Naturally, both sets of robbers choose the same bank as their target and the cops just happen to be waiting. **83m/C; VHS, DVD.** *AU* Ben Mendelsohn; Jeremy Sims; John Polson; Robyn Loau; Graeme Blundell; Deborah Kennedy; Stephen Rae; Andrew S. Gilbert; Amanda Muggleton; Paul Gleeson; Susie Porter; ***D:*** David Caesar; ***W:*** David Caesar; ***C:*** Joseph Pickering; ***M:*** Tim Rogers; Nick Launay.

The Idiots 🦴🦴 *Idioterne* **1999 (R)** Von Trier uses the stripped back camerawork of Dogma 95 to tell an annoying, pointless story involving a commune-like group of middle-class drop-outs around Copenhagen who spend their time deliberately acting like idiots in public places. They're trying to get in touch with their wounded inner child while you'll want to slap some sense into them. Film provoked controversy because of a group sex scene that (at least) borders on porn. Danish with subtitles. **115m/C; VHS, DVD.** *DK* Bodil Jorgensen; Jens Albinus; Anne Louise Hassing; Troels Lyby; Nikolaj Lie Kaas; Henrik Prip; Luis Mesonero; Louise Mieritz; Knud Romer Jorgensen; Trine Michelsen; ***D:*** Lars von Trier; ***W:*** Lars von Trier; ***C:*** Lars von Trier.

Idiot's Delight 🦴🦴🦴 **1939** At an Alpine hotel, a song and dance man meets a gorgeous Russian countess who reminds him of a former lover. Incredibly, Gable sings and dances through "Puttin' on the Ritz," the film's big highlight. Based on the Pulitzer Prize-winning play by Robert Sherwood. **107m/B; VHS, DVD.** Clark Gable; Norma Shearer; Burgess Meredith; Edward Arnold; Charles Coburn; Joseph Schildkraut; ***D:*** Clarence Brown; ***C:*** William H. Daniels.

Idle Hands 🦴 ½ **1999 (R)** Pothead slacker Anton (Sawa) finds that his very idle hand is possessed by a demon, making him do things he doesn't want to do, like get up off the couch and kill his friends Mick (Green) and Pnub (Henson). When Anton cuts off the offending appendage, it's free to terroroze his girlfriend Molly (Alba). With the help of a Druid priestess (Fox) and his now undead friends, Anton must stop the hand from taking Molly's soul to Hell. Even if the release hadn't coincided with the Littleton tragedy, this tasteless horror-comedy wouldn't be funny. Relentless overacting tries to cover up for a lame script filled with pot jokes and gory high school slasher conventions. Green and Henson are the only bright spots. **90m/C; VHS, DVD, Blu-Ray.** Devon Sawa; Seth Green; Elden (Ratliff) Henson; Jessica Alba; Christopher Hart; Vivica A. Fox; Jack Noseworthy; Sean M. Whalen; Nicholas Sadler; Fred Willard; Katie Wright; Connie Ray; ***D:*** Rodman Flender; ***W:*** Terri Hughes; Ron Milbauer; ***C:*** Christopher Baffa; ***M:*** Graeme Revell.

The Idle Rich 🦴🦴 **1929** It's a case of reverse class snobbery in this early talkie that suffers from problems with sound and staginess. Millionaire William Van Luyn marries his secretary Joan and doesn't object when Joan insists they move into the crowded apartment of her middle-class family. The family continues to disdain William's fortune until he shrewdly announces that he's giving his money away. **80m/B; DVD.** Conrad Nagel; Leila Hyams; James Neill; Edythe Chapman; Bessie Love; Robert Ober; Kenneth Gibson; ***D:*** William de Mille; ***W:*** Clara Beranger; ***C:*** Leonard Smith.

Idlewild 🦴🦴 **2006 (R)** OutKast bandmates star in a genre-bending tale of two buddies in 1930s Georgia, creating an anachronistic but entertaining jumble of eye- and ear-candy. Percival (Benjamin), a mortician by day, reserved piano player by night, and Rooster (Patton), a club-owning family man and musician in his own right, escape their ho-hum lives at Church, a lively speakeasy that encapsulates the flick's mash-up of jazz-era nostalgia with a contemporary vibe. Soon love and murder and lots of stars making cameos come to town for a mix of lavish production numbers and murder. It's all as gutsy and confusing as it sounds. **120m/C; DVD, Blu-Ray.** Andre Benjamin; Antwan Andre Patton; Paula Patton; Terrence Howard; Malinda Williams; Macy Gray; Ben Vereen; Ving Rhames; Faizon Love; ***D:*** Bryan Barber; ***W:*** Bryan Barber; ***C:*** Pascal Rabaud; ***M:*** John Debney.

The Idol 🦴🦴🦴 *Ya Tayr El Tayer* **2015** This Palestinian drama is a feel-good, fictionalized version of the life of Mohammed Assaf, a wedding singer from a refugee camp in Gaza, who earned international fame when he won the 2013 iteration of Arab Idol. Mohammed learns to how to sing playing with his sister in a band in Gaza before becoming a wedding singer. When he learns that his sister is dying of kidney failure, Mohammed decides to use his voice to make enough money to pay for a transplant. Years later, he travels to Egypt from Gaza to audition for Arab Idol, changing his life forever. **95m/C; DVD.** Tawfeek Barhom; Eyad Hourani; Nadine Labaki; Hiba Attalah; Kais Attalah; ***D:*** Hany Abu-Assad; ***W:*** Hany Abu-Assad; Sameh Zoabi; ***C:*** Ehab Assal; ***M:*** Hani Asfari.

The Idol Dancer 🦴🦴 ½ **1920** Romance and adventure in the South Seas with a drunken American beachcomber inspired by love to change his ways. There's also a native uprising for added excitement. Minor Griffith but nice Nassau scenery. **93m/B; Silent; VHS, DVD.** Richard Barthelmess; Clarine Seymour; Creighton Hale; George MacQuarrie; Kate Bruce; Anders Randolph; Walter James; Thomas Carr; ***D:*** D.W. Griffith.

Idol on Parade 🦴 ½ **1959** It's the Brit version of Elvis being drafted into the Army. Pop singer Jeep Jackson disrupts military discipline when he's called up for his National Service. Newley gets to sing a few tunes. **88m/B; DVD.** *GB* Anthony Newley; William Bendix; Lionel Jeffries; Anne Aubrey; Sidney James; William Kendall; ***D:*** John Gilling; ***W:*** Bill Shepherd; John Antrobus; ***C:*** Ted Moore.

Idolmaker 🦴🦴 ½ **1980 (PG)** A conniving agent can make a rock star out of anyone. Well-acted fluff with Sharkey taking a strong lead. The first film by hack-meister Hackford and somewhat based on true-life teen fab Fabian. **119m/C; VHS, DVD, Blu-Ray.** Ray Sharkey; Tovah Feldshuh; Peter Gallagher; Paul Land; Joe Pantoliano; Maureen McCormick; John Aprea; Richard Bright; Olympia Dukakis; Steven Apostlee Peck; ***D:*** Taylor Hackford; ***C:*** Adam Holender; ***M:*** Jeff Barry. Golden Globes '81: Actor--Mus./Comedy (Sharkey).

If. . . 🦴🦴🦴🦴 **1969 (R)** Three unruly seniors at a British boarding school refuse to conform. A popular, anarchic indictment of staid British society, using the same milieu as Vigo's "Zero de Conduite," with considerably more violence. The first of Anderson and McDowell's trilogy, culminating with "O Lucky Man!" and "Britannia Hospital." In color and black and white. **111m/C; VHS, DVD.** *GB* Malcolm McDowell; David Wood; Christine Noonan; Richard Warwick; Robert Swann; Arthur Lowe; Mona Washbourne; Graham Crowden; Hugh Thomas; Guy Rose; Peter Jeffrey; Geoffrey Chater; Mary MacLeod; Anthony Nicholls; Ben Aris; Charles Lloyd-Pack; Rupert Webster; Brian Pettifer; Sean Bury; Michael Cadman; ***D:*** Lindsay Anderson; ***W:*** David Sherwin; ***C:*** Miroslav Ondricek; ***M:*** Marc Wilkinson. Cannes '69: Film.

If a Man Answers 🦴 ½ **1962** Dated rom com has young couple Chantal (Dee) and Eugene (Darin) already having marital issues since Chantal thinks Eugene takes her for granted. Her mom (Presle) gives her some bad advice about how to train Eugene to be the perfect husband by pretending to have a lover (this involves the telephone title). However, Eugene soon catches on and decides to turn the tables on his wife when his father (Romero), whom Chantal has apparently never seen, shows up unexpectedly. **102m/C; DVD.** Sandra Dee; Bobby Darin; Micheline Presle; John Lund; Cesar Romero; Stefanie Powers; Christopher Knight; ***D:*** Henry Levin; ***W:*** Richard Morris; ***C:*** Russell Metty; ***M:*** Hans J. Salter.

If a Tree Falls: A Story of the Earth Liberation Front 🦴🦴 **2011** Director Curry examines the roots of the radical environmental group the Earth Liberation Front (ELF) and why its members are regarded by the U.S. government as eco-terrorists and prosecuted under anti-terrorism statutes. Curry's 'in' is the arrest of former-ELF member Daniel McGowan, whom he interviewed after McGowan is placed under house arrest while awaiting trial. While the various ELF info is often compelling, the focus on McGowan slows down the narrative. **85m/C; DVD.** Daniel McGowan; Jake Ferguson; Tim Lewis; ***D:*** Marshall Curry; Sam Cullman; ***W:*** Marshall Curry; Matthew Hamachek; ***C:*** Sam Cullman; ***M:*** James Baxter.

If Beale Street Could Talk 🦴🦴🦴 **2018 (R)** James Baldwin's treasured 1974 novel comes to cinematic glory in the hands of writer/director Barry Jenkins. Lush visuals and a spot-on soundtrack provide perfect accompaniments to the story told through the eyes of Tish (newcomer Layne), a 19-year-old bride-to-be who aches to free her fiancé from prison, where he's incarcerated for a crime he didn't commit. Racism, injustice, and family bonds are running themes, but the overarching subject is lyrical romance. **119m/C; DVD, Blu-Ray.** KiKi Layne; Stephan James; Regina King; Colman Domingo; Teyonah Parris; ***D:*** Barry Jenkins; ***W:*** Barry Jenkins; ***C:*** James Laxton; ***M:*** Nicholas Britell. Oscars '18: Support. Actress (King); Golden Globes '19: Actress--Supporting (King); Ind. Spirit '19: Actress--Supporting (King), Director (Jenkins), Film.

If I Die Before I Wake **WOOF!** **1998 (R)** Suburban family become the grisly victims of three intruders who enjoy terrorizing, torturing, and killing until teenaged LoriBeth (Jones), who has been hiding from the bad guys, gets revenge. Ick, ick, ick. **77m/C; VHS, DVD.** Michael (Mick) McCleery; Muse Watson; Stephanie Jones; Anthony Nicosia; ***D:*** Brian Katkin; ***W:*** Brian Katkin; ***C:*** Zoran Hochstatter; ***M:*** Thomas Morse. **VIDEO**

If I Had a Million 🦴🦴 **1932** Paramount put a number of familiar faces to work in this anthology of eight stories from seven directors (MacLeod did two) and a multitude of screenwriters. Dying steel tycoon John Glidden (Bennett) is disgusted with his greedy relatives and randomly picks eight names from the phone book, giving each person a one million dollar check. He proceeds to sit back to see what they do with the money. **88m/B; DVD.** Richard Bennett; Charlie Ruggles; Wynne Gibson; George Raft; W.C. Fields; Alison Skipworth; Charles Laughton; Gary Cooper; Jack Oakie; Roscoe Karns; ***D:*** James Cruze; H. Bruce Humberstone; Ernst Lubitsch; Norman Z. McLeod; Stephen Roberts; William A. Seiter; Norman Taurog; ***C:*** John Leipold.

If I Had My Way 🦴🦴 **1940** When their best friend Fred is killed in an accident, buddies Buzz (Crosby) and Axel (Brendel) vow to take his teenaged daughter Patricia (Jean) to find her relatives in New York. Joe (Dodd) and his wife Marian (Bryant) are a couple of kind-hearted but penniless vaudevillians and Buzz is horrified when Axel uses Patricia's inheritance to buy a failing restaurant. So he decides to make lemonade out of lemons and convert the eatery into a nightclub in hopes of providing for the family. **82m/B; DVD.** Bing Crosby; Gloria Jean; El Brendel; Claire Dodd; Nana Bryant; Charles Winninger; Allyn Joslyn; Donald Woods; William Conselman; James V. Kern; ***D:*** David Butler; ***C:*** George Robinson; ***M:*** Charles Previn.

If I Stay 🦴🦴 **2014 (PG-13)** Teenager Mia Hall (Moretz) is a girl caught between life and death after a car accident puts her in a coma. Trying to cope with the tragedy that surrounds her, Mia has an out-of-body experience in this YA variation on "It's a Wonderful Life." She relives the meaningful moments of her life with her idyllic family and boyfriend (a flat Blackley) as she envisions how the world would change if she doesn't make it back from the other side. Moretz is effective, but the melodrama too often washes away the truthful emotions in director Cutler's adaptation of Gayle Forman's hit Young Adult novel. **106m/C; DVD, Blu-Ray.** Chloë Grace Moretz; Jamie Blackley; Mireille Enos; Joshua Leonard; Jakob Davies; Gabrielle Cerys Haslett; Stacy Keach; Gabrielle Rose; ***D:*** R.J. Cutler; ***W:*** Shauna Cross; ***C:*** John de Borman; ***M:*** Heitor Pereira.

If I Want to Whistle, I Whistle 🦴🦴 **2010** Tough teen Silvu is two weeks away from being released from a juvenile detention facility when his beloved younger brother Marius tells him that their wayward mother is taking Marius to Italy with her. The warden refuses Silvu a day pass, and he resorts to a desperate act. Romanian with subtitles. **94m/C; DVD.** *RO* George Pistereanu; Ada Condeescu; Marian Bratu; Mihai Constantin; Clara Voda; ***D:*** Florin Serban; ***W:*** Florin Serban; ***C:*** Marius Panduru.

If I Were Free 🦴🦴 ½ **1933** Sarah Casanove's (Dunne) abusive husband Tono (Asther) leaves her for another woman and, after a chance meeting in Paris, she finds solace in the arms of unhappily married barrister Gordon Evers (Brook). Gordon's wife Catherine (MacLean) stayed in their marriage through her own affair, so she doesn't want to give him a divorce. Based on the John Van Druten play "Behold, We Live." **66m/B; DVD.** Irene Dunne; Clive Brook; Lorraine MacLean; Nils Asther; Henry Stephenson; Vivian Tobin; Laura Hope Crews; ***D:*** Elliott Nugent; ***W:*** Dwight Taylor; ***C:*** Edward Cronjager.

If I Were You 🦴 1/2 **2012 (R)** A woman discovers her husband has been unfaithful after saving his mistress from suicide and finds herself drawn into a pact to fix their lives by each of them following orders given by the other in the world's most unlikely scenario. **114m/C; DVD, Streaming.** *UK CA* Marcia Gay Harden; Leonor Watling; Joseph Kell; Aidan Quinn; Valerie Mahaffey; ***D:*** Joan Carr-Wiggin; ***W:*** Joan Carr-Wiggin; ***C:*** Bruce Worrall; ***M:*** Guy Farley; Paolo Buonvino.

If I'm Lucky 🦴🦴 **1946** Bandleader Earl Gordon (James) gets a gig working for a corrupt political campaign by playing concerts to lure in voters. The politicos decide that the band's squeaky clean singer, Allen Clark (Como), would be a better promoter than their own candidate. But when Allen doesn't want to go along, the politicians threaten to ruin everyone's reputations. A remake of 1935's "Thanks a Million." **80m/B; DVD.** Perry Como; Vivian Blaine; Harry James; Carmen Miranda; Phil Silvers; Edgar Buchanan; Reed Hadley; ***D:*** Lewis Seiler; ***W:*** Helen Logan; George Bricker; Robert Ellis; Snag Werris; ***C:*** Glen MacWilliams; ***M:*** Emil Newman.

If It's Tuesday, This Must Be Belgium 🦴🦴🦴 **1969 (G)** A fast-paced, frantic, and funny look at a group of Americans on a whirlwind European tour. The group does a nine-country, 18-day bus tour with clashing, comic personalities and lots of romantic possibilities. Remade in 1987 for TV. **99m/C; VHS, DVD, Blu-Ray.** Suzanne Pleshette; Ian McShane; Mildred Natwick; Norman Fell; Michael Constantine; Peggy Cass; Murray Hamilton; Marty Ingels; Sandy Baron; Pamela Britton; Luke Halpin; ***D:*** Mel Stuart.

If Looks Could Kill 🦴🦴 1/2 **1991 (PG-13)** TV stud Grieco makes film debut as a high school class cutup who travels to France with his class to parlez vous for extra credit. Mistaken for a CIA agent, he stumbles into a plot to take over all the money in the whole wide world, and much implausible action and eyelash batting follows. Extra kibbles for supporting characterizations. Oh, and don't be put off by the fact that the Parisian scenes were shot in Montreal. **89m/C; VHS, DVD.** Richard Grieco; Linda Hunt; Roger Rees; Robin Bartlett; Gabrielle Anwar; Roger Daltrey; Geraldine James; Carole (Raphaelle) Davis; ***D:*** William Dear; ***W:*** Fred Dekker; ***M:*** David Foster.

If Lucy Fell 🦴🦴 **1995 (R)** Schaeffer serves as writer/director/star of this predictable 90s-style romantic comedy. Ludicrous premise has psychotherapist Lucy (Parker) bent on realizing a 10-year-old pact with longtime friend Joe (Schaeffer) that stipulates they both jump off the Brooklyn Bridge if neither one has found true love by age 30. With the big birthday approaching, Lucy takes a desperate shot with eccentric painter Bwick (Stiller), while Joe finally goes for the object of his desire, asking beautiful neighbor Jane (MacPherson) to a showing of his paintings. Highlights come in the casting, with Parker a solid and energetic neurotic and MacPherson showing that there's something beyond her more obvious talents. **92m/C; VHS, DVD.** Sarah Jessica Parker; Eric Schaeffer; Ben Stiller; Elle Macpherson; James Rebhorn; Dominic Chianese; ***D:*** Eric Schaeffer; ***W:*** Eric Schaeffer; Tony Spiridakis; ***C:*** Ron Fortunato; ***M:*** Amanda Kravat; Charles Pettis.

If Only 🦴🦴 1/2 **2004 (PG-13)** Sappy romantic drama finds perky American Samantha Andrews (Hewitt) studying music in London. She and her British businessman boyfriend Ian (Nicholls) are constantly at odds and finally break up. Samantha is immediately killed in a car accident before Ian can come to his senses and reunite with her. But when Samantha appears the next morning, Ian realizes he's reliving their last day together. However, the more he tries to change the outcome, the more inevitable it seems. **92m/C; DVD.** *GB* Jennifer Love Hewitt; Paul Nicholls; Tom Wilkinson; Diana Hardcastle; Lucy Davenport; ***D:*** Gil Junger; ***W:*** Christian Welsh; ***C:*** Giles Nuttgens; ***M:*** Adrian Johnston.

If There's a Hell Below 🦴🦴 **2016** A suspenseful mystery-thriller which explores what happened when too much political power gets in the wrong hands. Abe (Marx) is a young journalist in search of the story that will move his career from a Chicago newsweekly to a major newspaper. When he arranges a meeting with Debra (Roscoe), a woman who says she works for the government in national security. Paranoid, Debra claims she is a whistleblower who has important information. An hour after they meet in desolate place, one of them is dead. **94m/C; DVD, Streaming, Download.** Carol Roscoe; Conner Marx; Mark Carr; Paul Budraitis; ***D:*** Nathan Williams; ***W:*** Nathan Williams; ***C:*** Christopher Messina. **VIDEO**

If These Walls Could Talk 🦴🦴 1/2 **1996 (R)** Covers four decades, from the '50s to the present, telling the stories of three women and the different ways they deal with unexpected pregnancies. "1952" finds recently widowed nurse Claire (Moore) discovering she's pregnant—and it's not her late husband's. In some graphic scenes she tries to end the pregnancy herself with a knitting needle and later through a back-alley abortion. Happily married Barbara (Spacek) already has four children in "1974" and has just returned to college. Then she discovers she's pregnant again. Abortion's an option but does Barbara want one? Finally, college student Christine (Heche) gets pregnant by her married professor in "1996" and reluctantly opts for an abortion at a family planning clinic, which is besieged by pro-lifers and on the edge of some violent confrontations. **109m/C; VHS, DVD.** Demi Moore; Catherine Keener; Jason London; Shirley Knight; Kevin Cooney; CCH Pounder; Robin Gammell; Sissy Spacek; Xander Berkeley; Joanna Gleason; Harris Yulin; Anne Heche; Jada Pinkett Smith; Cher; Diana Scarwid; Lindsay Crouse; Lorraine Toussaint; Rita Wilson; Eileen Brennan; Craig T. Nelson; ***D:*** Cher; Nancy Savoca; ***W:*** Nancy Savoca; Susan Nanus; I. Marlene King; ***C:*** Ellen Kuras; Bobby Bukowski; John Stanier; ***M:*** Cliff Eidelman. **CABLE**

If These Walls Could Talk 2 🦴🦴 1/2 **2000 (R)** Anthology features the stories of three lesbian couples in America. "1961" shows the sedate lives of retired schoolteachers Edith (Redgrave) and Abby (Seldes), who have lived together for decades. But when Abby suddenly dies, Edith discovers she will be dispossessed by Abby's greedy nephew. "1972" finds Linda (Williams) living with a group of lesbian feminists who disapprove of butch-femme couples. But Linda is still drawn to the butch Amy (Sevigny), who refuses to apologize for how she chooses to live. "2000" has thirtysomething couple Fran (Stone) and Kal (DeGeneres) deciding to have a baby and having some comical problems with the sperm issue. **96m/C; VHS, DVD.** Vanessa Redgrave; Marian Seldes; Paul Giamatti; Elizabeth Perkins; Michelle Williams; Chloë Sevigny; Nia Long; Natasha Lyonne; Heather McComb; Sharon Stone; Ellen DeGeneres; Regina King; Kathy Najimy; Mitchell Anderson; George Newbern; Amy Carlson; ***D:*** Jane Anderson; Martha Coolidge; Anne Heche; Alex Sichel; ***W:*** Jane Anderson; Sylvia Sichel; Anne Heche; ***C:*** Paul Elliott; Robbie Greenberg; Peter Deming; ***M:*** Basil Poledouris. **CABLE**

If They Tell You I Fell 🦴 1/2 *Si Te Dicen Que Cai; Aventis* **1989** The corpse of a man famous from the Spanish Civil War and in local folk stories (called "aventis") is found by a doctor and nurse and spawns revelations that clash with the tall tales. Based on Juan Marse's 1976 novel, spans several decades in muddled flashbacks with actors taking on multiple roles. Spanish, with English subtitles. **120m/C; VHS, DVD.** Victoria Abril; Antonio Banderas; Juan Diego Botto; Maria Botto; Marc Barahoma; Javier Gurruchaga; Lluis Homar; Guillermo Montesinos; Margarita Calahorra; Jose Cerro; Pep Cruz; Teresa Cunille; Cesareo Estebanez; Luis Giralte; Aitor Merino; Joan Miralles; Montserrat Salvador; Jorge Sanz; Rosa Morata; Ariadna Novarro; Ferran Rane; Merce Sans; Carlos Tristancho; ***D:*** Vicente Aranda; ***W:*** Vicente Aranda; Juan Marse; ***C:*** Juan Amoros; ***M:*** Jose Nieto. **VIDEO**

If Tomorrow Comes 🦴🦴 1/2 *Sidney Sheldon's If Tomorrow Comes* **1986** CBS miniseries adapted from Sidney Sheldon's novel. Tracy Whitney (Smith) wants revenge after she's pardoned and released from prison for a crime she didn't commit. She's mentored by Gunther Hartog (Kiley), who teaches Tracy how to be an international jewel thief. Tracy finds a professional and romantic partner in Jeff Stevens (Berenger). But every criminal needs a nemesis and theirs is single-minded insurance investigator Daniel Cooper (Keith). **315m/C; DVD.** Madolyn Smith; Tom Berenger; Richard Kiley; David Keith; Liam Neeson; Jack Weston; Lane Smith; Jeffrey Jones; ***D:*** Jerry London; ***W:*** Carmen Culver; ***C:*** Dennis C. Lewiston; Paul Lohmann; ***M:*** Nick Bicat. **TV**

If Winter Comes 🦴🦴 **1941** Romantic tearjerker based on the A.S.M. Hutchinson novel. Two married, middle-aged former lovers (Pidgeon, Kerr) try to rekindle their star-crossed romance that includes a bitter wife (Lansbury), a pregnancy, false accusations, and the shadow of war. **119m/B; DVD.** Walter Pidgeon; Deborah Kerr; Angela Lansbury; Janet Leigh; Binnie Barnes; May Whitty; Reginald Owen; Hugh French; ***D:*** Victor Saville; ***W:*** Marguerite Roberts; Arthur Wimperis; ***C:*** George J. Folsey; ***M:*** Herbert Stothart.

If You Could Only Cook 🦴🦴 1/2 **1936** Down-and-out Joan (Arthur) is looking for work when she meets Jim (Marshall) on a park bench and assumes he needs a job too. Jim is actually an auto exec who's fed up with his board of directors and thinks it would be fun to play hooky for awhile. He agrees to Joan's idea to pretend to be a married so they can apply for the cook and butler positions at mobster (and gourmet) Mike Rossini's (Carrillo) mansion. Confusion follows. **70m/B; DVD.** Jean Arthur; Herbert Marshall; Leo Carrillo; Lionel Stander; Frieda Inescort; Alan Edwards; ***D:*** William A. Seiter; ***W:*** Howard J. Green; Gertrude Purcell; ***C:*** John Stumar.

If You Don't Stop It. . . You'll Go Blind 🦴 1/2 **1977 (R)** A series of gauche and tasteless vignettes from various little-known comedians. **80m/C; VHS, DVD, Streaming.** Pat McCormick; George Spencer; Patrick Wright; ***D:*** I. Robert Levy; Keefe Brasselle.

If You Knew Susie 🦴🦴 **1948** Two retired vaudeville actors find a letter from George Washington which establishes them as descendants of a colonial patriot and the heirs to a $7 billion fortune. **90m/B; VHS, DVD.** Eddie Cantor; Joan Davis; Allyn Joslyn; Charles Dingle; Charles Halton; ***D:*** Gordon Douglas.

If You Only Knew 🦴🦴 **2000** Struggling New York writer (are there any other kind?) Parker (Schaech) falls for painter Samantha (Eastwood) when he answers her ad for someone to share her loft. She has no problem rooming with a guy—as long as he's gay. So Parker moves in and finds the pretense an increasing struggle. Formulaic but Eastwood is a real charmer. **111m/C; VHS, DVD.** Johnathon Schaech; Alison Eastwood; Gabrielle Anwar; James LeGros; Lainie Kazan; Paul Sampson; Frank Vincent; Annie Corley; Miguel A. Nunez, Jr.; ***D:*** David Snedeker.

Igby Goes Down 🦴🦴🦴 **2002 (R)** Steers's directorial debut is a smart, dark comedy. Modern-day Holden Caufield Igby (Culkin) rebels against his privileged upbringing, dropping out of countless prep and, finally, military schools. Adrift, Igby heads to the boho pad of his rich godfather (Goldblum) and his beautiful, drug-addled girlfriend (Peet) and is initiated into their degenerate "arty" scene. While in a questionable relationship with Peet, Igby falls for soulful college dropout Sookie Sapperstein (Danes) who's also the target of his slick older brother Oliver's (Phillippe) affection. The matriarch of Igby's dysfunctional family is Sarandon, in a humorously unlikable role. Thoughtful, satiric view of the emptiness of the American Dream. **98m/C; VHS, DVD.** Kieran Culkin; Ryan Phillippe; Susan Sarandon; Claire Danes; Jeff Goldblum; Bill Pullman; Amanda Peet; Jared Harris; Rory Culkin; Cynthia Nixon; Eric Bogosian; ***D:*** Burr Steers; ***W:*** Burr Steers; ***C:*** Wedigo von Schultzendorff; ***M:*** Uwe Peterson.

Ignition 🦴🦴 1/2 **2001 (R)** The U.S. Army is preparing a major rocket launch just as Federal Judge Faith Matheson (Olin) begins a corruption and treason trial that involves the military. Is it any surprise that there are links between the launch and her case? When Faith is threatened, she turns to former Marine helicopter pilot Conor Gallagher (Pullman) for help. **95m/C; VHS, DVD.** *US CA* Lena Olin; Bill Pullman; Colm Feore; Nicholas Lea; Peter Kent; Michael Ironside; Roger Dunn; Scott Hylands; Benjamin Ratner; ***D:*** Yves Simoneau; ***W:*** William Davies; ***C:*** Jonathan Freeman.

Igor 🦴🦴 **2008 (PG)** Looney and colorful animated tale about Igor (Cusack), the hunchbacked assistant to mad scientist Dr. Glickenstein (Cleese) who secretly longs to be a scientist himself. In the hopes of winning the Evil Science Fair, Igor builds his own female monster, Eva (Shannon), who turns out to be a sweet, gentle giant. After learning of Igor's creation, even more evil than most evil scientists, Dr. Schadenfreude (Izzard) tries to steal Eva and take the credit. At Igor's side are best friends Scamper (Buscemi), a road-kill rabbit on two feet, and clueless Brain (Hayes), a literal brain floating in a jar with eyes. Not nearly as witty or technically sharp as Pixar's CGI releases, but nonetheless, pulls off an entertaining gothic fable in the vein of a Tim Burton cartoon. **86m/C; DVD, Blu-Ray.** ***V:*** John Cusack; Steve Buscemi; John Cleese; Sean P. Hayes; Molly Shannon; Jennifer Coolidge; Eddie Izzard; Jay Leno; Arsenio Hall; Christian Slater; James Lipton; ***D:*** Anthony Leondis; ***W:*** Chris McKenna; ***M:*** Patrick Doyle.

Igor & the Lunatics 🦴 **1985 (R)** Tasteless tale of a cannibal cult leader released from prison who picks up where he left off. **79m/C; VHS, DVD.** Joseph Eero; Joe Niola; T.J. Michaels; ***D:*** Billy Parolini.

Iguana 🦴🦴 **1989** The videocassette box art makes this look like a horror movie, but it's really a stiff, solemn period drama about a deformed sailor with lizardlike features. After a life of mistreatment he reigns mercilessly over a handful of island castaways. An international coproduction with mostly English dialogue, some Spanish and Portuguese with subtitles. **88m/C; VHS, DVD, Blu-Ray.** *SI IT* Everett McGill; Michael Madsen; Joseph Culp; Fabio Testi; ***D:*** Monte Hellman; ***W:*** Monte Hellman; Jaime Comas Gil; Steven Gaydos; ***C:*** Josep Civit.

Ike: Countdown to D-Day 🦴🦴 1/2 **2004 (PG)** Selleck shaves off the signature mustache—and the rest of his hair—to star in this low-key (meaning no battle scenes) biopic of Gen. Dwight D. Eisenhower that gives a behind-the-scenes account of the war-room planning for the pivotal D-Day invasion. **89m/C; VHS, DVD.** Tom Selleck; James Remar; Timothy Bottoms; Gerald McRaney; Ian Mune; Bruce Phillips; John Bach; Nick Blake; Kevin J. Wilson; Christopher Baker; George Shevtsov; Gregor McLennan; Paul Gittins; Craig Hall; Stephen Brunton; Paul Barrett; Mickey Rose; Carole Seay; ***D:*** Robert Harmon; ***W:*** Lionel Chetwynd; ***C:*** David Gribble; ***M:*** Jeff Beal. **TV**

Ikiru 🦴🦴🦴🦴 *To Live; Doomed; Living* **1952** When a clerk finds out he is dying of cancer, he decides to build a children's playground and give something of himself back to the world. Highly acclaimed, heartbreaking drama from the unusually restrained Kurosawa; possibly his most "eastern" film. In Japanese with English subtitles. **134m/B; VHS, DVD, Blu-Ray.** *JP* Takashi Shimura; Nobuo Kaneko; Kyoko Seki; Miki Odagari; Yunosuke Ito; ***D:*** Akira Kurosawa; ***W:*** Akira Kurosawa; Shinobu Hashimoto; Hideo Oguni; ***C:*** Asakazu Nakai; ***M:*** Fumio Hayasaka.

Il Bidone 🦴🦴 *The Swindle* **1955** Three Italian conmen pull capers in Rome trying to make a better life for themselves. Dark overtones permeate one of Fellini's lesser efforts. Good cast can't bring up the level of this film. In Italian with English subtitles. **92m/C; VHS, DVD.** *IT* Broderick Crawford; Giulietta Masina; Richard Basehart; Franco Fabrizi; ***D:*** Federico Fellini; ***W:*** Federico Fellini; Tullio Pinelli; Ennio Flaiano; ***C:*** Otello Martelli; ***M:*** Nino Rota.

Il Divo 🦴🦴 **2008** Complicated political bio of seven-time Italian Prime Minister Giulio Andreotti. Pic focuses on his seventh election in the 1990s to his later trial for corruption and conspiracy with the Mafia in a series of political assassinations, including that of political rival Aldo Moro by the Red Brigade. (Andreotti was first convicted and then later acquitted.) Italian with subtitles. **110m/C; DVD.** *IT* Toni Servillo; Anna Bonaiuto; Guilio Bosetti; Flavio Bucci; Carlo Buccirosso; Giorgio Colangeli; *D:* Poalo Sorrentino; *W:* Poalo Sorrentino; *C:* Luca Bigazzi; *M:* Teho Teardo.

Il Futuro *The Future* **2013** In this atmospheric drama, orphaned teen siblings, Bianca (Martelli) and Tomas (Ciardo), try to survive in Rome with the "help" of a couple of unlikely acquaintances. They come up with an elaborate plot to use Bianca's sexual wiles on an aging, now blind, former Mr. Universe (Hauer), who starred in some muscleman flicks as Maciste (the Italian version of Hercules). Supposedly, his crumbling mansion hides a fortune and Bianca is sent to find it, but seduction (the actress is frequently nude and oiled like a bodybuilder) turns to friendship and Bianca comes up with her own plan. English and Italian with subtitles. **94m/C; DVD.** *IT CL* Manuela Martelli; Rutger Hauer; Luigi Ciardo; Nicolas Vaporidis; Alessandro Giallocosta; *D:* Alicia Scherson; *W:* Alicia Scherson; *C:* Ricardo De Angelis; *M:* Eduardo Henriquez.

Il Grido *The Cry; The Outcry* **1957** A jilted husband takes his young daughter from village to village in search of the woman who deserted them for another man. Set in the desolate Po Valley of director Antonioni's childhood. In Italian with English subtitles. **116m/B; VHS, DVD.** *IT* Steve Cochran; Alida Valli; Dorian Gray; Betsy Blair; Gabriella Pallotta; *D:* Michelangelo Antonioni; *W:* Michelangelo Antonioni; Ennio de Concini; *C:* Gianni Di Venanzo; *M:* Giovanni Fusco.

Il Sorpasso 1/2 **1963** A braggart, who has failed at everything, spends all his time traveling around Italy in his sportscar. He takes a repressed law student under his wing and decides to teach him how to have fun. In Italian with English subtitles. **116m/B; DVD, Blu-Ray.** *IT* Vittorio Gassman; Jean-Louis Trintignant; Catherine Spaak; *D:* Dino Risi; *W:* Dino Risi; Ettore Scola; Ruggero Maccari; *C:* Alfio Contini; *M:* Riz Ortolani.

I'll Be Home for Christmas 1/2 **1998 (PG)** Snotty college kid Jake (Thomas) wants to teach his Dad a lesson by boycotting Christmas and stealing away to Mexico with his girlfriend (Biel). Jake thinks his Dad remarried too soon after his mother's death, but is bribed home with his Dad's prized Porshe (now there's a lesson for the kids) if he can arrive for Christmas Eve dinner. A series of absurd mishaps ensue (almost all of which occur because Jake is a lying, cheating jerk) as he makes his away cross-country while glued inside of a Santa suit. The characters are superficial and at times downright annoying. This run of the mill holiday stinker will likely only appeal to Thomas' legion of teenage groupies. **86m/C; VHS, DVD, Blu-Ray.** Jonathan Taylor Thomas; Jessica Biel; Adam LaVorgna; Gary Cole; Eve Gordon; Sean O'Bryan; Andrew Lauer; *D:* Arlene Sanford; *W:* Harris Goldberg; Tom Nursall; *C:* Hiro Narita; *M:* John Debney.

I'll Be Seeing You 1/2 **1944** Not exactly your typical Christmas fare, although the schmaltz is laid on as thickly as icing on cookies. Mary (Rogers) meets Zachary (Cotten) on a train as she's traveling to Texas to spend the holidays with her family. They've both got secrets: she's on a good behavior furlough from the pen where she's serving time for manslaughter, and he's a shell-shocked soldier on leave from the psych ward. Mary takes Zach home for a family Xmas and they fall in love but she doesn't want to make his shaky hold on his sanity worse by admitting she's going back to jail. 17-year-old Temple plays curious cousin Barbara. Adapted from the radio play "Double Furlough" by Charles Martin. **83m/B; VHS, DVD, Blu-Ray.** Ginger Rogers; Joseph Cotten; Shirley Temple; Spring Byington; Tom Tully; Chill Wills; John Derek; *D:* William Dieterle; *W:* Marion Parsonnet; *C:* Gaetano Antonio "Tony" Gaudio; *M:* Daniele Amfitheatrof.

I'll Be There 1/2 **2003 (PG-13)** Aging pop idol (Ferguson) sobers up and discovers he has a teenage daughter (Church). The two start to develop a relationship in spite of Mother's reservations. Of course, the kid can sing and catches the attention of Dad's slimy manager. Church's acting has a way to go to catch up to her singing, but she's better than Britny or Mariah (at both). Scottish comic Ferguson seems to have taken on more (co-writing/directing/acting) than he can currently handle, but gets points for effort. **104m/C; VHS, DVD.** Craig Ferguson; Jemma Redgrave; Joss Ackland; Charlotte Church; Ralph Brown; Ian McNeice; Imelda Staunton; Anthony Head; *D:* Craig Ferguson; *W:* Craig Ferguson; Philip McGrade; *C:* Ian Wilson; *M:* Trevor Jones.

I'll Believe You 1/2 **2007 (PG)** Genial Dale Sweeney is the late-night host of a low-rated radio show in Melbourne, Florida that's devoted to UFO sightings and conspiracy theories. Threatened with cancellation, Dale decides he needs one legitimate alien encounter to save his job and maybe one of his strange callers is actually from another world. **81m/C; DVD.** David Alan Basche; Patrick Warburton; Patrick Gallo; Fred Willard; Doc Dougherty; Thomas Gibson; Mo Rocca; Chris Elliott; Cece Pleasants; Paul Sullivan; *D:* Paul Sullivan; *W:* Ted Sullivan; Sean McPharlin; Gregory Lee; Paul Sullivan; *C:* John Mans; *M:* J.J. McGeehan. **VIDEO**

I'll Bury You Tomorrow 1/2 **2002** Low-budget indie horror is a true creepfest. Beech Funeral Home attracts whack jobs, including new assistant mortician Delores (Chlanda), who keeps a big secret in a steamer trunk. This is discovered by fellow employee Jake (Murdock), who is into illegal organ donations. So he tries blackmailing Delores into helping him, which is a really bad idea. **119m/C; DVD.** Zoe Daelman Chlanda; Jerry Murdock; Bill Corry; Katherine O'Sullivan; Kristen Overdurf; Renee West; Alan Rowe Kelly; Tom Burns; *D:* Alan Rowe Kelly; *W:* Alan Rowe Kelly; *C:* Tom Cadawas; Gary Malick; *M:* Tom Burns.

I'll Cry Tomorrow **1955** Hayward brilliantly portrays actress Lillian Roth as she descends into alcoholism and then tries to overcome her addiction. Based on Roth's memoirs. **119m/B; VHS, DVD.** Susan Hayward; Richard Conte; Eddie Albert; Jo Van Fleet; Margo; Don Taylor; Ray Danton; Veda Ann Borg; *D:* Daniel Mann; *M:* Alex North. Oscars '55: Costume Des. (B&W); Cannes '56: Actress (Hayward).

I'll Do Anything 1/2 **1993 (PG-13)** Hollywood satire finds unemployed actor Matt (Nolte) suddenly forced to care for his six-year-old daughter Jeannie (Wright), whom he hasn't seen in three years. Matt also finally gets a job—as a chauffeur to an obnoxious producer (well played by Brooks) whose company winds up making the manipulative demon Jeannie into a hot child star. Great work by Kavner as the owner of a test-screening service who romances Brooks. Originally intended as a musical, the test screenings were so disastrous that the numbers were axed. What's left is less jerky than expected; Brooks reportedly based his character in part on mega-mogul Joel Silver. **115m/C; VHS, DVD.** Nick Nolte; Albert Brooks; Julie Kavner; Whittni Wright; Joely Richardson; Tracey Ullman; *D:* James L. Brooks; *W:* James L. Brooks; *C:* Michael Ballhaus; *M:* Hans Zimmer.

I'll Follow You Down 1/2 **2013** An interesting premise falls victim to directorial inexperience and a pedestrian production. Physicist Gabe leaves for a conference and doesn't return, so wife Marika contacts her father, Sal, who was Gabe's mentor, but all he finds in the missing man's hotel room is a strange, non-working apparatus. Years pass and Sal has figured out that Gabe was working on a time machine, which Sal now thinks he can get working with the help of grandson Erol, a troubled young scientist following in the men's footsteps. **92m/C; DVD, Blu-Ray.** *CA* Haley Joel Osment; Victor Garber; Gillian Anderson; Susanna Fournier; Rufus Sewell; *D:* Richie Mehta; *W:* Richie Mehta; *C:* Tico Poulakakis; *M:* Andrew Lockington.

I'll Get You *Escape Route* **1953** In this dull, slow-paced crime drama FBI agent Steve Rossi heads to London and teams up with intelligence agent Joan Miller. They're after kidnapped nuclear scientists who have been smuggled behind the Iron Curtain. **79m/B; DVD.** George Raft; Sally Gray; Clifford Evans; Frederick Piper; Reginald Tate; *D:* Seymour Friedman; *W:* Nicholas Phipps; John Baines; *C:* Eric Cross; *M:* Hans May.

Ill Met By Moonlight 1/2 *Night Ambush* **1957** Decent WWII adventure based on the memoirs of Moss, who's depicted as one of the two British soldiers who capture arrogant Nazi General Kriepe from his headquarters on Crete. They intend to transport him to British-occupied Cairo, which means they have to get him over the mountains to a waiting boat, aided by Cretan partisans and with Kriepe's soldiers after them. **104m/B; DVD.** *GB* Dirk Bogarde; David Oxley; Marius Goring; Cyril Cusack; Dimitri Andreas; Wolfe Morris; Laurence Payne; Michael Gough; *D:* Michael Powell; Emeric Pressburger; *W:* Michael Powell; Emeric Pressburger; *C:* Christopher Challis; *M:* Mikis Theodorakis.

I'll Name the Murderer **1936** Suspense film in which a gossip columnist starts his own investigation into the murder of a club singer. **66m/B; VHS, DVD.** Ralph Forbes; Marion Shilling; *D:* Bernard B. Ray.

I'll Never Forget What's 'Isname **1967** To some tastes, this overwrought and long-unseen comedy from the swinging '60s will be completely dated with characters whose mindsets are totally alien. Protagonist Andrew Quint (Reed) is a piggish young ad executive who tries to leave his even more piggish boss (Welles), and his two mistresses, though he's not sure he wants to divorce his wife. Why? He wants to go back to do something meaningful with his life, something like working for a literary magazine. It's actually a long midlife crisis (though the phrase did not exist when the film was made) that set standards for frankness in its sexual material. **99m/C; DVD.** Oliver Reed; Orson Welles; Carol White; Marianne Faithfull; Michael Hordern; Frank Finlay; *D:* Michael Winner; *W:* Peter Draper; *C:* Otto Heller; *M:* Francis Lai.

I'll Never Forget You *The House in the Square* **1951** American atomic physicist Peter Standish (Power) has inherited a London house. His friend Roger (Rennie) tells him about an American ancestor who lived there in the 18th century. According to Standish's theory of time and space, he should be able to switch places and—with the help of a lightning strike—Peter wakes up in the past, engaged to Kate (Campbell). Too bad Peter actually falls in love with her younger sister Helen (Blyth). Another storm eventually propels Peter back to the 20th century, but can his love transcend time as well? Some scenes are filmed in Technicolor. Adapted from the play by John Baldeston and previously filmed in 1933 as "Berkeley Square." **89m/B; DVD.** *GB* Tyrone Power; Michael Rennie; Ann Blyth; Beatrice Campbell; Dennis Price; Kathleen Byron; Raymond Huntley; *D:* Roy Ward Baker; *W:* Ranald MacDougall; *C:* Georges Perinal; *M:* William Alwyn.

I'll Remember April 1/2 **1999** In the days following the bombing of Pearl Harbor rumors abound that Japanese submarines are patrolling the Pacific and four 10-year-old California boys like to pretend they are Marines in search of the Japanese enemy. Imagine their surprise when they discover a Japanese soldier who washed up on the beach and is hiding out in their clubhouse. They keep him their prisoner while trying to decide what to do but when the soldier rescues one of the boys from drowning, the boys decide that they have to save him. **90m/C; VHS, DVD.** Haley Joel Osment; Trevor Morgan; Richard Taylor Olson; Yuki Tokuhiro; Mark Harmon; Pam Dawber; Noriyuki "Pat" Morita; Yuji Okumoto; Troy Evans; Paul Dooley; *D:* Bob (Benjamin) Clark; *W:* Mark Sanderson; *C:* Stephen M. Katz; *M:* Paul Zaza.

I'll See You in My Dreams 1/2 **1951** Hokey but fun musical biography of songwriter Gus Kahn (Thomas) and his wife Grace LeBoy (Day). Kahn gets his start in Ziegfeld shows but loses both his career and wife after the 1929 crash. However, she soon returns and everything ends happily ever after. **109m/B; VHS, DVD.** Danny Thomas; Doris Day; Frank Lovejoy; Patrice Wymore; James Gleason; Mary Wickes; Jim Backus; Minna Gombell; William Forrest; *D:* Michael Curtiz; *W:* Melville Shavelson; Jack Rose.

I'll See You in My Dreams 1/2 **2015 (PG-13)** The legendary Danner gets the best role she's had in years and proves that she deserves more in this gentle, wonderful drama about how much life continues to surprise us, even late in it. Danner plays Carol Petersen, a former singer and widow, pushed by her three loyal friends (Perlman, Squibb and Place) to get back into life before it's too late. She forms a unique friendship with her pool man (Starr), a new love interest (Elliott) and even contacts her estranged daughter (Akerman). While it sounds clichéd, Danner makes every emotional beat feel real. **92m/C; DVD.** Blythe Danner; June Squibb; Rhea Perlman; Mary Kay Place; Martin Starr; *D:* Brett Haley; *W:* Brett Haley; Marc Basch; *C:* Rob Givens; *M:* Keegan DeWitt.

I'll Sleep When I'm Dead **2003 (R)** Will Graham (Owen) thinks he has escaped the horrors of urban life for the great outdoors. Unfortunately, his hipster drug-dealing younger brother (Rhys Meyers) has been found dead from an apparent suicide. Shady businessman Boad (McDowell) took a nasty fancy to him and, with the help of his stooges, raped him quite brutally. Now Will has to return to London and make the bad men pay. Extra dark and mean contemporary noir from Hodges looks and acts like a remake of his classic "Get Carter," with Clive Owen ably filling Michael Caine's shoes (unlike a certain American action star). Story is a bit muddled and confusing at times, but the onslaught of action makes up for it. The rape scene is one of the most agonizing sequences you'll see. Not for the faint of heart. **102m/C; DVD.** *US GB* Clive Owen; Charlotte Rampling; Malcolm McDowell; Jamie Foreman; Ken Stott; Sylvia Syms; Geoff Bell; Desmond Baylis; Kirris Riviere; Brian Croucher; Ross Boatman; Marc O'Shea; *D:* Mike Hodges; *W:* Trevor Preston; *C:* Mike Garfath; *M:* Simon Fisher Turner.

I'll Take Sweden 1/2 **1965** Overprotective father Hope disapproves of teenaged daughter Weld's guitar-playing boyfriend (Avalon). So to keep her out of harm's way he finagles a company transfer to Sweden. Dad falls for an interior decorator (Merrill) while Weld gets involved with a Swedish playboy (Slate). Deciding Avalon is the lesser of two evils, Hope schemes to get the two back together. **96m/C; VHS, DVD, Blu-Ray.** Bob Hope; Tuesday Weld; Frankie Avalon; Dina Merrill; Jeremy Slate; Walter Sande; John Qualen; Roy Roberts; Maudie Prickett; *D:* Fred de Cordova; *W:* Arthur Marx; Bob Fisher; Nat Perrin; *C:* Daniel F. Fapp.

I'll Take You There **1999 (R)** Lightweight, somewhat schizophrenic romantic comedy-road flick-drama has despondent Bill (Rogers) trying to recover from a failed relationship. His sister sets him up with old school friend Bernice (Sheedy), but he viciously insults her on the date. She shows up a few days later, and kidnaps him on a road trip that begins with the heist of a prom dress. More outlandish events ensue, but the unbelievable plot almost sinks the whole enterprise. Solid work by a strong cast mostly save the day. **93m/C; VHS, DVD.** Ally Sheedy; Reg Rogers; Lara Harris; John Pyper-Ferguson; Alice Drummond; Alan North; Ben Vereen; Adrienne Shelly; *D:* Adrienne Shelly; *W:* Adrienne Shelly; *C:* Vanja Cernjul; *M:* Andrew Hollander.

I'll Wait for You **1941** Racketeer Lucky Wilson (Sterling) goes on the lam and finds love with farmer's daughter Pauline (Hunt) after he lies about his identity and the Millers give him a place to stay. Pauline's kind, upstanding family even has Lucky deciding to go straight, but the cops haven't stopped looking and Lucky's luck finally runs out. Remake of the 1934 pic "Hideout." **73m/B; DVD.** Robert Sterling; Marsha Hunt; Fay Holden; Henry Travers; Virginia Weidler; Paul Kelly; Reed Hadley; *D:* Robert B. Sinclair; *W:* Guy Trosper; *C:* Sidney Wagner; *M:* Bronislau Kaper.

Illegal 1/2 **1955** Crime melodrama stars Robinson as an attorney who risks all to acquit his assistant of murder. Early Mansfield appearance. Remake of "The Mouthpiece." **88m/B; VHS, DVD.** Edward G. Robinson; Nina Foch; Hugh Marlowe; Jayne Mansfield; Albert Dekker; Ellen Corby; DeForest Kelley; Howard St. John; *D:* Lewis Allen; *W:* W.R. Burnett.

Illegal **2010** Russian Tania is working illegally in Belgium when she is caught and detained at a rundown immigration detention center, though her 14-year-old son Ivan gets away. Constantly worrying about Ivan, she refuses to give her name and has burned off her fingerprints so she can't be identified. This frustrates the authorities who can't legally deport Tania if they don't know who she is, which leads to increasingly harsh treatment. Russian and French with subtitles. **90m/C; DVD.** *BE* Anne Coesens; Alexandre Gontcharov; Esse Lawson; Christelle Cornil; Tomasz Bialkowski; Olga Zhdanova; Gabriela Perez; ***D:*** Olivier Masset-Depasse; ***W:*** Olivier Masset-Depasse; ***C:*** Tomasso Fiorilli; ***M:*** Andre Dziezuk; Marc Mergen.

Illegal Affairs **1996** The kind of film that almost makes you feel sorry for lawyers. The sleazy firm of Grimes and Peterson specializes in divorce cases—and seem personally responsible for any number of them on account of adultery. **87m/C; VHS, DVD.** Jay Richardson; Monique Parent; Christian Noble; ***D:*** Michael Paul Girard; ***W:*** Michael Paul Girard; ***C:*** Denis Maloney; ***M:*** Miriam Cutler. **VIDEO**

Illegal Business **2006 (R)** Tony (Rosete) is a mob henchman who feels the need to make more money, and sells drugs behind his boss' back to do so. A spat with a dirty cop soon pits him against his boss, his partner, his drug connection, and the police. Somehow you're expected to sympathize with him, which is sort of where the film goes wrong. **91m/C; DVD.** Jose Roseto; David Peterson; Victor Zaragoza; Chris Angelo; Raul Martinez; Carl Washington; Refugio Franco; Hiram Zagala; Ryan Mac; Daniel Landeros; Tom Uyeda; Eduardo Quiroz; ***D:*** Eduardo Quiroz; Jose Quiroz; ***W:*** Eduardo Quiroz; Jose Quiroz; ***C:*** Rocky Robinson.

Illegal Tender 1/2 **2007 (R)** Twenty-one-year-old Wilson (Gonzalez) enjoys his upper-middle class lifestyle until his mother (De Jesus) informs him that his dead father was a drug dealer and hands him a gun. Turns out they need to defend themselves from his father's murderer, who's still after them and the money Dad stole. Wilson is mostly adequate as the reluctant heir to his father's legacy but is overshadowed by De Jesus's two-gun Pam Grier-style performance. You'll find yourself wishing you saw more of Mom and a lot less of Wilson. John Singleton produced what is, essentially, a blaxploitation film gone Latino (Laxploitation?). Nothing really distinguishes it from any other mediocre B-movie revenge flick. **107m/C; DVD.** Wanda De Jesus; Rick Gonzalez; Dania Ramirez; Antonio Ortiz; Manny Perez; Tego Calderon; ***D:*** Franc Reyes; ***W:*** Franc Reyes; ***C:*** Frank Byers; ***M:*** Hector Pereira.

Illegally Yours **1987 (PG)** Miscast comedy about a college student serving on the jury in trial of old girlfriend. Bring down the gavel on this one. **94m/C; VHS, DVD.** Rob Lowe; Colleen Camp; Kenneth Mars; ***D:*** Peter Bogdanovich.

Illicit **1931** In love, Stanwyck fears that marrying Rennie will only ruin their wonderful relationship. Two years after their marriage her fears are realized when each searches for happiness with a past lover. A melodramatic performance that doesn't quite hit its mark. Remade two years later as "Ex-Lady" with Bette Davis in the lead. Based on the play by Edith Fitzgerald and Robert Riskin. **76m/B; VHS, DVD.** Barbara Stanwyck; Ricardo Cortez; Natalie Moorhead; Charles Butterworth; Joan Blondell; Claude Gillingwater; ***D:*** Archie Mayo; ***W:*** Harvey Thew.

Illuminata **1998 (R)** Comedy-drama about a struggling theatre troupe in turn-of-the-century New York. Tuccio (Turturro) is the company's playwright—in love with manager/leading lady, Rachel (Turturro's wife Borowitz), and worried about the reception for his new work. Also involved are self-centered aging diva Celimene (Sarandon), theatre owner Astergourd (D'Angelo), foppish critic Bevalaqua (Walken) and the unlikely object of his affections, the troupe's clown, Marco (Irwin), among many others. Adapted from the play by Brandon Cole. **111m/C; VHS, DVD.** John Turturro; Katherine Borowitz; Christopher Walken; Susan Sarandon; Beverly D'Angelo; Bill Irwin; Rufus Sewell; Georgina Cates; Ben Gazzara; Donal McCann; Aida Turturro; Matthew Sussman; Leo Bassi; ***D:*** John Turturro; ***W:*** John Turturro; Brandon Cole; ***C:*** Harris Savides; ***M:*** William Bolcom; Arnold Black.

The Illusionist 1/2 **2006 (PG-13)** Eisenheim (Norton) is a wildly popular magician in 1900 Vienna where he is reunited with his childhood love, the aristocratic Sophie (Biel). She's now engaged to suspicious Crown Prince Leopold (Sewell) who sics police chief Inspector Uhl (Giamatti) on Eisenheim in an effort to debunk his illusions. You won't find anyone pulling doves out of their sleeves to the tune of "Final Countdown" in Burger's icy turn-of-the-century romance, but there's still a lot to like, particularly the always-intriguing Norton and Giamatti. Unfortunately, no illusion can make the audience believe there's any spark between Eisenheim and Sophie, which is mostly the fault of the lovely, though vacant, Ms. Biel. **110m/C; DVD, Blu-Ray.** Edward Norton; Jessica Biel; Rufus Sewell; Paul Giamatti; Eddie Marsan; Aaron Taylor-Johnson; ***D:*** Neil Burger; ***W:*** Neil Burger; ***C:*** Dick Pope; ***M:*** Philip Glass.

The Illusionist 1/2 *L'Illusioniste* **2010 (PG)** Based on a 1956 script by French comedian Jacques Tati (intended for live-action), Chomet's animated tale tells the story of magician Monsieur Tatischeff who travels to a remote Scottish island in the 1950s and befriends teenage domestic Alice in the pub where he performs. Later, he allows her to accompany him to his next booking in Edinburgh, resulting in adventures that will change their lives forever. A charming, engaging, and bittersweet story—though Tati's writing was apparently semi-autobiographical, Chomet's version doesn't make this apparent. French with subtitles. **78m/C; Blu-Ray, On Demand.** *GB FR* ***V:*** Jean-Claude Donda; Eilidh Rankin; ***D:*** Sylvain Chomet; ***W:*** Sylvain Chomet; ***M:*** Sylvain Chomet; Malcolm Ross.

The Illustrated Man **1969 (PG)** A young drifter meets a tattooed man. Each tattoo causes a fantastic story to unfold. A strange, interesting, but finally limited attempt at literary sci-fi. Based on the story collection by Ray Bradbury. **103m/C; DVD, Blu-Ray.** Rod Steiger; Claire Bloom; Robert Drivas; Don Dubbins; ***D:*** Jack Smight; ***W:*** Howard B. Kreitsek; ***C:*** Philip H. Lathrop; ***M:*** Jerry Goldsmith.

Ilsa, Harem Keeper of the Oil Sheiks **WOOF!** **1976 (R)** The naughty Ilsa works for an Arab sheik in the slave trade. More graphic violence and nudity. Plot makes an appearance. **90m/C; VHS, DVD.** Dyanne Thorne; Max (Michael) Thayer; Victor Alexander; Elke Von; Sharon Kelly; Haji; Tanya Boyd; Marilyn Joy; Bobby Woods; ***D:*** Don Edmonds; ***W:*** Langton Stafford; ***C:*** Dean Cundey; Glenn Roland.

Ilsa, the Wicked Warden **WOOF!** *Ilsa, the Absolute Power; Greta the Mad Butcher* **1978 (R)** Ilsa is now a warden of a woman's prison in South America, behaving just as badly as she always has, until the prisoners stage an uprising. Lots of skin, no violence, no acting. Also: no plot. **90m/C; VHS, DVD.** Dyanne Thorne; Lina Romay; Tania Busselier; Howard Maurer; Jess (Jesus) Franco; ***D:*** Jess (Jesus) Franco; ***W:*** Jess (Jesus) Franco; Erwin C. Dietrich; ***C:*** Ruedi Kuttel; ***M:*** Walter Baumgartner.

I'm All Right Jack **1959** Sellers plays a pompous communist union leader in this hilarious satire of worker-management relations. Based on Alan Hackney's novel "Private Life." **101m/B; VHS, DVD.** Peter Sellers; Ian Carmichael; Terry-Thomas; Victor Maddern; ***D:*** John Boulting. British Acad. '59: Actor (Sellers), Screenplay.

I'm Dancing as Fast as I Can **1982 (R)** A successful TV producer hopelessly dependent on tranquilizers tries to stop cold turkey. Good story could be better; based on Barbara Gordon's memoirs. **107m/C; VHS, DVD.** Jill Clayburgh; Nicol Williamson; Dianne West; Joe Pesci; Geraldine Page; John Lithgow; Daniel Stern; ***D:*** Jack Hofsiss; ***W:*** David Rabe; ***C:*** Jan De Bont.

I'm for the Hippopotamus 1/2 *Io sto con gli ippopotami* **1979** Brothers Slim (Hill) and Tom (Spencer) are living the good life in Africa when they must stop an evil German nut from catching all of the local wildlife and selling it to zoos in Canada. An odd plot, but that's the usual for most of the films pairing Hill and Spencer. **105m/C; DVD.** *IT* Terence Hill; Bud Spencer; Joe Bugner; May Dlamini; Dawn Jurgens; Ben Masinga; ***D:*** Italo Zingarelli; ***W:*** Italo Zingarelli; Barbara Alberti; Amedeo Pagani; Vincenzo Mannino; ***C:*** Aiace Parolini; ***M:*** Walter Rizzati.

I'm from Arkansas **1944** The little town of Pitchfork, Arkansas, goes nuts when a pig gives birth to ten piglets. **68m/B; VHS, DVD.** El Brendel; Slim Summerville; Iris Adrian; Harry Harvey; Bruce Bennett; ***D:*** Lew Landers.

I'm Glad My Mother Is Alive 1/2 *Je Suis Heureux que Ma Mere Soit Vivante* **2009** Troubled Thomas becomes obsessed with tracking down his restless birth mother Julie Martino, who gave him and his younger brother Patrick up for adoption. Eventually, Thomas finds Julie, a single mom with another son, and introduces himself. He's resentful, insecure, and violent; she's now tired and trying to live a more-stable life. Their continuing reunion doesn't end well. French with subtitles. **90m/C; DVD.** *FR* Vincent Rottiers; Sophie Cattani; Maxime Renard; ***D:*** Claude Miller; Nathan Miller; ***W:*** Claude Miller; Nathan Miller; ***C:*** Aurelien Devaux; ***M:*** Vincent Sagal.

I'm Going Home *Je Rentre a la Maison* **2000** Distinguished, elderly actor Gilbert Valence (Piccoli) is dealt a devastating blow when his wife, daughter, and son-in-law are killed in a car accident. Coping with dignity, he looks after his young grandson and works in the theatre (playing Prospero in "The Tempest"). His agent urges Valance to take his first role in an English-language film directed by an American (Malkovich) and he struggles mightily to cope with his part. Title refers to Valance's simple statement when he realizes that his time is past. French with subtitles. **90m/C; VHS, DVD.** *PT FR* Michel Piccoli; Catherine Deneuve; John Malkovich; Leonor Silveira; Antoine Chappey; Leonor Baldaque; Jean Koeltgen; ***D:*** Manoel de Oliveira; ***W:*** Manoel de Oliveira; ***C:*** Sabine Lancelin.

I'm Gonna Git You Sucka **1988 (R)** Parody of "blaxploitation" films popular during the '60s and '70s. Funny and laced with out-right bellylaughs. A number of stars who made "blaxploitation" films, including Jim Brown, take part in the gags. **89m/C; VHS, DVD, Blu-Ray.** Keenen Ivory Wayans; Bernie Casey; Steve James; Isaac Hayes; Jim Brown; Ja'net DuBois; Dawnn Lewis; Anne-Marie Johnson; John Vernon; Antonio Fargas; Eve Plumb; Clu Gulager; Kadeem Hardison; Damon Wayans; Gary Owens; Clarence Williams, III; David Alan Grier; Kim Wayans; Robin Harris; Chris Rock; Jester Hairston; Eugene Robert Glazer; Peggy Lipton; Robert Townsend; ***D:*** Keenen Ivory Wayans; ***W:*** Keenen Ivory Wayans; ***C:*** Tom Richmond; ***M:*** David Michael Frank.

I'm Losing You **1998 (R)** Confusing story with too many shocks and no point of view, which wastes a good cast. TV producer Perry Krohn (Langella) learns that he is dying of cancer. His wife, Diantha (Jens), takes the news badly, as do his wayward children Bertie (McCarthy) and Rachel (Arquette). But it seems everyone has a doom-laden revelation to deal with. Wagner adapts from his own novel. **102m/C; VHS, DVD.** Frank Langella; Salome Jens; Rosanna Arquette; Andrew McCarthy; Amanda Donohoe; Elizabeth Perkins; Gina Gershon; Buck Henry; Ed Begley, Jr.; ***D:*** Bruce Wagner; ***W:*** Bruce Wagner; ***C:*** Rob Sweeney; ***M:*** Daniel Catan.

I'm No Angel **1933** "Beulah, peel me a grape." Well, you'd be hungry too if you spent your time eyeing playboy Grant as West does. She's a circus floozy who's prone to extorting money from her men (after hashing over their shortcomings with her seen-it-all-maid, the aforementioned Beulah). However, after wooing Grant, she sues for breach of promise. This leads to a comic courtroom scene with Grant bringing in all West's exlovers as witnesses. Grant's second film with West, following "She Done Him Wrong." **88m/B; DVD.** Mae West; Cary Grant; Gregory Ratoff; Edward Arnold; Ralf Harolde; Kent Taylor; Gertrude Michael; Russell Hopton; Dorothy Peterson; William B. Davidson; Gertrude Howard; Hattie McDaniel; ***D:*** Wesley Ruggles; ***W:*** Mae West; Lowell Brentano; ***C:*** Leo Tover; ***M:*** Harvey Brooks.

I'm Not Ashamed **2016 (PG-13)** Faith-based drama about 17-year-old Rachel Scott (McLain), the first person killed in the 1999 Columbine High School massacre. Though Rachel longs to have a positive impact on others, she also wants to fit in at school and have a real boyfriend so she sneaks out of the house and goes to parties. After a summer with devout relatives in Louisiana, Rachel becomes more involved with a church youth group and changes the life of Nathan (Davies), a young homeless man, before the tragedy. Though the earnest film's message may appeal to its intended audience, its quality is more television movie than feature film. **112m/C; DVD.** Masey McLain; Ben Davies; Cameron McKendry; Terri Minton; Victoria Staley; ***D:*** Brian Baugh; ***W:*** Philipa Booyens; Robin Hanley; Kari Redmond; Bodie Thoene; ***C:*** John Matysiak; ***M:*** Tim Williams.

I'm Not Here **2019** As painfully thin Steve (Simmons) wanders his home in a worn out bathrobe, he contemplates his past while considering suicide because he has lost everything that matters to him. As he thinks and looks in mirrors, he has flashbacks to his past including his time as child Stevie (Armitage) who does not understand his parents' divorce and his father's alcoholism. Other flashbacks feature young adult Steve (Stan) who faces his own struggles with drinking. The complex script, co-written by the director who is also Simmons' wife, allows Simmons to shine while showing the depth of Steve's alcoholic destruction regret. **81m/C; DVD.** J.K. Simmons; Sebastian Stan; Maika Monroe; Mandy Moore; Max Greenfield; ***D:*** Michelle Schumacher; ***W:*** Michelle Schumacher; Tony Cummings; ***C:*** Pete Villani; ***M:*** Nima Fakhrara.

Mission of Honor *Hurricane* **2019** During World War II, Polish pilot Jan Zumbach (Rheon) steals a plane and flies from Nazi-occupied France to exile in Britain. There, he joins unit 303 Squadron, a Royal Air Force unit that includes other exiled Poles. Though the unit plays a key role in battles for Britain, the Polish pilots face xenophobia from some British pilots and must manage conflict among themselves. The pilots also must come to terms with the idea that their Nazi-occupied country is already lost to them. Though melancholy in tone, the CGI-heavy film features a strong performance by Rheon and echoes contemporary British concerns about Poles in Britain. **107m/C; DVD, Blu-Ray.** Iwan Rheon; Milo Gibson; Stefanie Martini; Krystof Hadek; Marcin Dorocinski; ***D:*** David Blair; ***W:*** Robert Ryan; Alastair Galbraith; ***C:*** Piotr Sliskowski; ***M:*** Laura Rossi.

I'm Not Rappaport **1996 (PG-13)** Matthau does some comic grump schtick as irascible, unrepentent 81-year-old New York Jewish radical Nat. He likes to vent his considerable opinions in Central Park and carries on a grumbling friendship with fellow octogenarian Midge (Davis), who stills works as a building superintendent, tending an equally ancient boiler. But Nat's fed-up daughter Clara (Irving) is threatening to put him in a home and Midge seems likely to lose his job when the boiler is scheduled for replacement. Gardner's 1986 stage play tends to show its weaknesses on the big screen. **135m/C; VHS, DVD, Blu-Ray.** Walter Matthau; Ossie Davis; Amy Irving; Martha Plimpton; Craig T. Nelson; Boyd Gaines; Guillermo Diaz; Elina Lowensohn; Ron Rifkin; ***D:*** Herb Gardner; ***W:*** Herb Gardner; ***C:*** Adam Holender; ***M:*** Gerry Mulligan.

I'm Not Scared *Io Non Ho Paura* **2003 (R)** Ten-year-old Michele (Cristiano) lives in a remote and poor village in southern Italy. As he pokes around an abandoned house one hot summer day, he discovers a trapdoor that leads to a pit where a traumatized kidnapped boy, Filippo (Di Pierro), is being held prisoner. Michele's afraid to tell his parents--rightly so as it becomes clear his father (Abbrescia) is involved--but he also can't abandon Filippo, returning to him again and again with food and water. Just what Michele does do becomes the crux of this disturbing thriller. Based on the novel by co-screenwriter Ammaniti. Italian with subtitles. **110m/C; DVD.** *GB IT SP* Aitana Sanchez-Gijon; Diego Abatantuono; Dino Abbrescia; Giorgio Careccia; Giuseppe Cristiano; Mattia Di Perro; ***D:*** Gabriele Salvatores; ***W:*** Francesca Marciano; Niccolo Ammaniti; ***C:*** Italo Petriccione; ***M:*** Pepo Scherman; Ezio Bosso.

I'm Not There **2007 (R)** Sort of a symbolist musical history pic loaded with real-life clips and acted by no less than six separate actors and actresses representing different identities of poet/musician/revolutionary Bob Dylan. There's 11-year-old Woody (Franklin) who hops trains and tells far-fetched stories; Jack Rollins (Bale) personifies Dylan's first look at fame in folk-song roots; Jude (Blanchett) represents Dylan's shift to electric rock, a divisive move that alienated many of his fans. Richard Gere shows up as Billy, a personification of Dylan exiled in Missouri. Arthur (Whishaw), yet another Dylan, narrates and brings the sequences somewhat into focus. It's long and rambling and dreamlike, but Dylan fans will delight at the many references that their less-obsessed friends will miss. **135m/C; Blu-Ray.** *GE US* Christian Bale; Heath Ledger; Cate Blanchett; Ben Whishaw; Marcus Carl Franklin; Richard Gere; Charlotte Gainsbourg; Julianne Moore; Michelle Williams; David Cross; Bruce Greenwood; Lisa Bronwyn Moore; ***D:*** Todd Haynes; ***W:*** Todd Haynes; Oren Moverman; ***C:*** Edward Lachman. Golden Globes '08: Support. Actress (Blanchett); Ind. Spirit '08: Support. Actress (Blanchett).

I'm Reed Fish **2006 (PG)** Reed Fish (Baruchel), a talk jock on the small local radio station in Mud Meadows, is about to marry his high school sweetheart, Kate (Bledel). But Reed questions his carefully planned-out world when former school chum/aspiring musician Jill (Fisk) blows back into town. Reed decides to quit his job and make a movie about his life. Yeah, this quirky comedy is based on the life of screenwriter—wait for it—Reed Fish. **93m/C; DVD.** Jay Baruchel; Alexis Bledel; Schuyler Fisk; DJ Qualls; Shiri Appleby; Katey Sagal; Victor Rasuk; Chris Parnell; A.J. Cook; ***D:*** Zackary Adler; ***W:*** Reed Fish; ***C:*** Douglas Chamberlain; ***M:*** Roddy Bottum.

I'm So Excited *Los amantes pasajeros* **2013 (R)** Retro-looking bawdiness from Almodovar. A packed passenger jet has a mechanical problem and the pilots search for a place to make an emergency landing. The economy class passengers are sedated while three tres gay male flight attendants offer a unique brand of in-flight entertainment and solace by spiking the other passengers' drinks with mescaline to keep them from worrying, which happens to release everyone's sexual kinks. The director also works in some satire about Spain's political and business corruption that doesn't interrupt the good time. Title refers to The Pointer Sisters song. Spanish with subtitles. **90m/C; DVD, Blu-Ray.** *SP* Javier Camara; Raul Arevalo; Carlos Areces; Lola Duenas; Cecilia (Celia) Roth; Guillermo Toledo; Jose Luis Torrijo; Jose Maria Yazpik; ***D:*** Pedro Almodóvar; ***W:*** Pedro Almodóvar; ***C:*** Jose Luis Alcaine; ***M:*** Alberto Iglesias.

I'm Still Here **1/2** *I'm Still Here: The Lost Years of Joaquin Phoenix* **2010 (R)** Directorial debut of actor Casey Affleck, who follows his Oscar-nominated actor brother-in-law Joaquin Phoenix around for a year. Of course, this happens to be the year that Phoenix trades in a Hollywood career for hip hop. The new MC is seemingly having a severe personal crisis and the camera captures every awkward and painful moment—parties with hookers, demanding a record contract from P. Diddy, and an infamously bizarre appearance on David Letterman. It's never revealed whether Phoenix is truly suffering a meltdown; still, it's an intriguing glimpse on the ego of stardom, although some of the intrigue was lost when Affleck and Phoenix revealed that it was, if fact, all an elaborate hoax. **108m/C; Blu-Ray, On Demand.** Joaquin Rafael (Leaf) Phoenix; Casey Affleck; Antony Langdon; David Letterman; Edward James Olmos; Ben Stiller; ***D:*** Casey Affleck; ***C:*** Magdalena Gorka.

I'm with Lucy **1/2** **2002 (R)** Cutesy romantic comedy. Lucy (Potter) gets publicly dumped by her boyfriend but still believes her soulmate is out there somewhere. So she goes on five blind dates (Hannah, Bernal, LaPaglia, Thomas, Boreanaz) but can only see her would-be suitors' flaws and not their good points. Still, it all comes out right in the end. **90m/C; VHS, DVD.** Monica Potter; John Hannah; Gael Garcia Bernal; Anthony LaPaglia; Henry Thomas; David Boreanaz; Julianne Nicholson; Harold Ramis; Julie Christie; ***D:*** Jon Sherman; ***W:*** Eric Pomerance; ***C:*** Tom Richmond; ***M:*** Stephen Endelman.

The Image **1/2** **1989** Anchorman Finney, the unscrupulous czar of infotainment, does a little soul delving when a man he wrongly implicated in a savings and loan debacle decides to check into the hereafter ahead of schedule. Seems the newsmonger's cut a few corners en route to the bigtime, and his public is mad as hell and. . .oops, wrong movie (need we say there are not a few echoes of "Network"?). Finney's great. **91m/C; VHS, DVD.** Albert Finney; John Mahoney; Kathy Baker; Swoosie Kurtz; Marsha Mason; Spalding Gray; ***D:*** Peter Werner; ***M:*** James Newton Howard. **CABLE**

Imagemaker **1/2** **1986 (R)** Uneven story of a presidential media consultant who bucks the system and exposes corruption. **93m/C; VHS, DVD.** Michael Nouri; Jerry Orbach; Jessica Harper; Farley Granger; ***D:*** Hal Wiener.

Images **1972 (R)** Minor Altman is a confusing mish-mash with the scenery more dramatic than the flick. Hugh (Auberjonois) has taken his anxiety-ridden wife Cathryn (York) for a weekend at their country retreat on the Irish coast. Cathryn is having hallucinations about dead lovers but Hugh doesn't seem to realize his wife is going nuts until it's too late. **101m/C; DVD, Blu-Ray.** Susannah York; Rene Auberjonois; Marcel Bozzuffi; Hugh Millais; Cathryn Harrison; ***D:*** Robert Altman; ***W:*** Robert Altman; ***C:*** Vilmos Zsigmond; ***M:*** John Williams.

The Imaginarium of Doctor Parnassus **2009 (PG-13)** Traveling showman Dr. Parnassus (Plummer) made a very long ago deal with the devil (Waits) for immortality but barters his teenage daughter Valentina's (Cole) soul in exchange. That is, unless he can deliver five other souls to an alternate world of the imagination that's entered through a looking glass (shades of Lewis Carroll). When Tony (Ledger et al) is saved from suicide by the travelers, Parnassus sees him as being a possible way to win the bet. Since Heath Ledger died during production, director Gilliam had actors Depp, Law, and Farrell play variations of the same character to melancholy effect. It's fool-the-eye, existential smoke and mirrors from Gilliam's obviously overloaded and exhausting imagination. **122m/C; Blu-Ray, On Demand.** *GB CA* Christopher Plummer; Heath Ledger; Johnny Depp; Jude Law; Colin Farrell; Tom Waits; Lily Cole; Verne Troyer; Andrew Garfield; ***D:*** Terry Gilliam; ***W:*** Terry Gilliam; Charles McKeown; ***C:*** Nicola Pecorini; ***M:*** Mychael Danna; Jeff Danna.

Imaginary Crimes **1994 (PG)** Ray Weiler (Keitel) is a well-meaning salesman with dreams much bigger than his reach. After the death of his wife (Lynch), Ray tries to raise his two daughters, Sonya (Balk) and Greta (Moss). But gifted high school senior (in 1962) Sonya is resentful of being her sister's maternal anchor and having her father's schemes come to nothing even as she acknowledges how much Ray cares and how he wants to improve their lives. Remarkable performances by Keitel and Balk. From the novel by Sheila Ballantyne. **106m/C; VHS, DVD.** Harvey Keitel; Fairuza Balk; Kelly Lynch; Vincent D'Onofrio; Elisabeth Moss; Diane Baker; Christopher Penn; Seymour Cassel; Annette O'Toole; ***D:*** Tony Drazan; ***W:*** Kristine Johnson; Davia Nelson; ***C:*** John J. Campbell; ***M:*** Stephen Endelman.

Imaginary Heroes **2005 (R)** Painfully cliche-ridden story of a dysfunctional, angst-ridden suburban family. When her superjock son kills himself, Sandy (Weaver) descends into a weed-smoking haze while the rest of her family struggles to deal with Matt's death as well as their own problems. Drugs, anger, bisexual experimentation, eating disorders, and cancer scares ensue. Writer/director Harris piles on the plot twists and tragedies to remind you of how bad these people have it. Weaver and Hirsch (as younger son Tim) are convincing, but the film's combination of grief-stricken melodrama and wry irony is awkward and contrived, and the movie just ends up feeling like a cheap knock-off of many superior films. **112m/C; DVD.** Sigourney Weaver; Emile Hirsch; Jeff Daniels; Michelle Williams; Kip Pardue; Deirdre O'Connell; Ryan Donowho; Jay Paulson; Suzanne Santo; ***D:*** Daniel P. "Dan" Harris; ***W:*** Daniel P. "Dan" Harris; ***C:*** Tim Orr; ***M:*** John Ottman; Deborah Lurie.

Imaginary Playmate **2006** After moving into a new home, stepmom Suzanne isn't too concerned when young Molly suddenly starts talking about her imaginary friend Candace. Odd occurrences and Molly talking about things she couldn't possibly know, has Suzanne believing that Candace is actually the troubled spirit of a girl who died in the house. **90m/C; DVD.** Dina Meyer; Cassandra Sawtell; Rick Ravanello; Nancy Sivak; Kurt Evans; Nicole Munoz; ***D:*** William Fruet; ***W:*** Christine Gallagher; ***M:*** Hal Beckett. **CABLE**

Imagine Me & You **1/2** **2006 (R)** In this London-set confection, Rachel (Perabo) is walking up the aisle to marry longtime sweetie Heck (Goode) when she catches the eye of attractive florist Luce (Headey). Newlywed Rachel and Luce are then repeatedly thrown together and soon admit to their mutual attraction. Heck eventually realizes that something is amiss in his marriage even as Luce despairs at being the other woman. Bland and boring, despite, or maybe because of, the attractive cast. **93m/C; DVD.** Piper Perabo; Lena Headey; Matthew Goode; Celia Imrie; Anthony Head; Darren Boyd; Eva Birthistle; Bo Jackson; Sue Johnston; Sharon Horgan; ***D:*** Ol Parker; ***W:*** Ol Parker; ***C:*** Benjamin Davis; ***M:*** Alex Heffes.

Imagine That **1/2** *Nowhereland* **2009 (PG)** Murphy as family man. Evan Danielson is a workaholic investment advisor who discovers his bonding with his adorable seven-year-old daughter Olivia (Shahidi) leads literally to an unexpected payoff. Olivia's imaginary world (that is accessed through her security blanket Goo-Gaa) consists of three princesses, a queen, and a dragon that provide exceptionally accurate financial advice. Of course, Evan has to make a fool of himself (to placate Olivia's invisible playmates) and his business rival—fake Native American Johnny Whitefeather (Church)?is jealous and suspicious of Evan's sudden success. **107m/C; Blu-Ray, On Demand.** Eddie Murphy; Nicole Ari Parker; Thomas Haden Church; Vanessa Williams; Ronny Cox; Yara Shahidi; Martin Sheen; ***D:*** Karey Kirkpatrick; ***W:*** Edward Solomon; Chris M. Theson; ***C:*** John Lindley; ***M:*** Mark Mancina.

Imagining Argentina **2004 (R)** In 1970s Argentina, Banderas is Carlos Rueda, a childrens' theater director whose journalist wife (Thompson) has disappeared after trying to investigate the fate of thousands of people who have been taken away by government agents. He soon discovers psychic abilities and is able to tell the fates of many of the victims, but is only able to divine obscure clues to his wife's disappearance. The introduction of the pshychic element is jarring to the political and personal story of the toll of totalitarian persecution, and derails the entire production. **108m/C; DVD.** Antonio Banderas; Emma Thompson; Ruben Blades; Maria Canals; Claire Bloom; John Wood; ***D:*** Christopher Hampton; ***W:*** Christopher Hampton; ***C:*** Guillermo Navarro; ***M:*** George Fenton.

The Imitation Game **2014 (PG-13)** Cumberbatch is phenomenal as Alan Turing, a socially awkward genius whose work was so important and influential that it helped end World War II and led to the invention of the personal computer. To say the 20th century wouldn't be the same without him would be a massive understatement. However, Turing was also gay, which was a crime in his lifetime in Britain, leading to persecution and tragedy, despite the fact that he had assisted England in cracking the Nazi Enigma code, allowing the Allies to intercept enemy transmissions and save lives. It is a relatively standard wartime drama but well-made. **113m/C; DVD, Blu-Ray.** *UK US* Benedict Cumberbatch; Keira Knightley; Matthew Goode; Charles Dance; Rory Kinnear; Mark Strong; Allen Leech; ***D:*** Morten Tyldum; ***W:*** Graham Moore; ***C:*** Oscar Faura; ***M:*** Alexandre Desplat. Oscars '14: Adapt. Screenplay; Writers Guild '14: Adapt. Screenplay.

Imitation General **1/2** **1958** WWII military comedy. In 1944 France, a battle has left a ragtag group of American soldiers surrounded by German troops. When their commanding officer is killed, Master Sgt. Savage (Ford) is mistaken for the dead general and decides to impersonate the officer so he can rally the remaining soldiers and counterattack. Only a disgruntled private (Andrews) could expose the ruse and wreak havoc with the plan. **88m/B; DVD.** Glenn Ford; Red Buttons; Dean Jones; Tige Andrews; Taina Elg; John Wilder; Kent Smith; ***D:*** George Marshall; ***W:*** William Bowers; ***C:*** George J. Folsey.

Imitation of Life **1/2** **1934** Fannie Hurst novel tells the story of widowed Beatrice Pullman (Colbert) who uses maid Delilah's (Beaver) recipe for pancakes in order to have the women open a restaurant, which becomes a success. Both mothers suffer at the hands of their willfull teenaged daughters. Delilah's lightskinned daughter Peola (Washington) breaks away from her mother so she can continue to pass for white and Bea's daughter Jessie (Hudson) has a serious crush on her mother's beau, Stephen (William). Weepie was also successfully filmed in 1959. **106m/B; VHS, DVD, Blu-Ray.** Claudette Colbert; Louise Beavers; Rochelle Hudson; Fredi Washington; Warren William; Ned Sparks; Alan Hale; ***D:*** John M. Stahl; ***W:*** Preston Sturges; William Hurlbut; ***C:*** Merritt B. Gerstad. Natl. Film Reg. '05.

Imitation of Life **1959** Remake of the successful 1934 Claudette Colbert outing of the same title, and based on Fanny Hurst's novel, with a few plot changes. Turner is a single mother, more determined to achieve acting fame and fortune than function as a parent. Her black maid, Moore, is devoted to her own daughter (Kohner), but loses her when the girl discovers she can pass for white. When Turner discovers that she and her daughter are in love with the same man, she realizes how little she knows her daughter, and how much the two of them have missed by not having a stronger relationship. Highly successful at the boxoffice. **124m/C; VHS, DVD, Blu-Ray.** Lana Turner; John Gavin; Troy Donahue; Sandra Dee; Juanita Moore; Susan Kohner; ***D:*** Douglas Sirk; ***C:*** Russell Metty. Golden Globes '60: Support. Actress (Kohner); Natl. Film Reg. '15.

Immediate Family **1/2** **1989 (PG-13)** Childless couple contact a pregnant, unmarried girl and her boyfriend in hopes of adoption. As the pregnancy advances, the mother has doubts about giving up her baby. A bit sugar-coated in an effort to woo family trade. **112m/C; VHS, DVD.** Glenn Close; James Woods; Kevin Dillon; Mary Stuart Masterson; Linda Darlow; Jane Greer; Jessica James; Mimi Kennedy; ***D:*** Jonathan Kaplan; ***W:*** Barbara Benedek; ***M:*** Brad Fiedel. Natl. Bd. of Review '89: Support. Actress (Masterson).

The Immigrant **2013 (R)** It is 1921 and Ewa Cybulska (Cotillard) and her sister Magda sail to New York from Poland. Like so many other immigrants in the first part of the century, they are processed through Ellis Island and Ewa is separated from her sister and thrown alone into the streets of Manhattan. She falls prey to Bruno (Phoenix), who introduces her to a life of prostitution, but she could be saved from her nightmare by Orlando (Renner). Gorgeously shot, deeply personal, and with strikingly genuine performances, James Gray has crafted a lovely, old-fashioned drama. It drags sometimes but always beautifully so. **120m/C; DVD, Blu-Ray.** *US FR* Marion Cotillard; Joaquin Rafael (Leaf) Phoenix; Jeremy Renner; Dagmara Dominczyk; Angela Sarafyan; ***D:*** James Gray; ***W:*** James Gray; Richard Menello; ***C:*** Darius Khondji; ***M:*** Chris Spelman.

Immigration Tango **2011 (R)** Two green card marriages test the limits of friendship in Morris' slight-but-attractive rom com. In Miami, Russian immigrant Elena (Portnoy) and her Colombian boyfriend Carlos (Leon) have run out of legal options to remain in the U.S. Their best friends, American couple Betty (Wolfe) and Mike (Burnett), agree to a partner switch and not-so-convenient marriages. This puts a strain on everyone's relationships as they lie to family, friends, and a suspicious immigration agent (Sommers). **92m/C; DVD.** Carlos Leon; McCaleb Burnett; Elika Portnoy; Ashley Wolfe; Avery Sommers; Beth Glover; Steve DuMouchel; ***D:*** David Burton Morris; ***W:*** David Burton Morris; Martin Kelley; Todd Norwood; ***C:*** Taylor Gentry; Angel Barroeta; ***M:*** Dan Wool.

Immortal **1/2** *Immortal Ad Vitam* **2004 (R)** Writer/director Bilal uses CGI and blue screen to depict a devastated New York in 2095 in this visually arresting but completely confusing (and very loose) adaptation of two of his graphic novels. An interstellar pyramid invisibly hovers over the city, housing several Egyptian gods, including Horus (Pollard), who is about to lose his immortality. He has seven days to find a human vessel to host his spirit long enough so that he may impregnate a mate who will give birth to a new immortal. Horus chooses the rebellious Alcide Nikopol (Kretschmann) and the blue-haired Jill (Hardy), only there are a lot of complications to overcome, including the fact that Jill isn't exactly human. **102m/C; DVD, Blu-Ray.** *GB FR IT* Linda Hardy; Thomas Pollard; ***D:*** Enki Bilal; ***W:*** Enki Bilal; Joe Sheridan; Serge Lehman; ***C:*** Pascal Gennesseaux; ***M:*** Goran Vejvoda.

Immortal Battalion *The Way Ahead* **1944** Entertaining wartime psuedo-documentary follows newly recruited soldiers as they are molded from an ordinary group of carping civilians into a hardened battalion of fighting men by Niven. Some prints run to 116 minutes. **89m/B; VHS, DVD.** *GB* David Niven; Stanley Holloway; Reginald Tate; Raymond Huntley; William Hartnell; James Donald; Peter Ustinov; John Laurie; Leslie Dwyer; Hugh Burden; Jimmy Hanley; Leo Genn; Renee Asherson; Mary Jerrold; Tessie O'Shea; Raymond Lovell; A.E. Matthews; Jack Watling; ***D:*** Carol Reed; ***W:*** Peter Ustinov; Eric Ambler; ***C:*** Guy Green; ***M:*** William Alwyn.

Immortal Beloved **1994 (R)** The death of Ludwig van Beethoven prompts his loyal secretary to seek the identity of a mystery love to whom the composer has bequeathed his estate. While Beethoven's genius is awesome and his music breathtaking, his lovelife is neither, and the ensuing confessions of the maestro's former loves only get in the way of flashbacks that hint at his torment and triumph. Oldman is darkly intense, and a scene in which the aged Beethoven remembers his terrifying childhood amid the strains of "Ode to Joy" is simply stunning, but an unfocused script undoes what might have been a fine tribute to the master. The London Symphony Orchestra and soloists Murray Perahia, Emanuel Ax, and Yo Yo Ma contributed to the splendid soundtrack. **121m/C; VHS, DVD, Blu-Ray.** Gary Oldman; Jeroen Krabbe; Isabella Rossellini; Johanna Ter Steege; Marco Hofschneider; Miriam Margolyes; Barry Humphries; Valeria Golino; Christopher Fulford; ***D:*** Bernard Rose; ***W:*** Bernard Rose; ***C:*** Peter Suschitzky.

Immortal Combat **1/2 1994 (R)** An army of men trained in ninja and guerilla warfare have seemingly immortal powers. Can our two violent heroes find an equally destructive way to stop the killing? **109m/C; VHS, DVD.** Roddy Piper; Sonny Chiba; Tommy (Tiny) Lister; Meg Foster; ***D:*** Daniel Neira; ***W:*** Daniel Neira; Robert Crabtree; ***C:*** Henner Hofmann.

Immortal Sergeant **1/2 1943** After the battle death of the squad leader, an inexperienced corporal takes command of North African troops during WWII. Fonda gives a strong performance. Based on a novel by John Brody. **91m/B; VHS, DVD.** Henry Fonda; Thomas Mitchell; Maureen O'Hara; Allyn Joslyn; Reginald Gardiner; Melville Cooper; Morton Lowry; Peter Lawford; John Banner; Bud Geary; James Craven; ***D:*** John M. Stahl; ***W:*** Lamar Trotti; ***C:*** Clyde De Vinna; Arthur C. Miller; ***M:*** David Buttolph.

Immortality *The Wisdom of Crocodiles* **1998 (R)** The vampire myth undergoes yet another postmodern twist. Steven Grlscz (Law) is a medical researcher, living in London, who stops Maria (Fox) from committing suicide and then sets out to seduce her. When he's convinced she's in love with him, he kills her and takes her blood. His next would-be victim is Anne (Lowensohn), but she's reluctant to commit to Steven and soon he becomes ill, which leads him to confess to Anne that his bloodsucking tendencies can only be satiated when he believes his victims love him. While Law is a charming seducer, he fails to chill as a vampire killer. **98m/C; VHS, DVD, Blu-Ray.** *GB* Jude Law; Elina Lowensohn; Timothy Spall; Kerry Fox; Jack Davenport; Colin Salmon; ***D:*** Po-Chih Leung; ***W:*** Paul Hoffman; ***C:*** Oliver Curtis; ***M:*** John Lunn; Orlando Gough.

The Immortalizer **1989 (R)** A mad doctor transfers people's brains into young bodies for a price, although it's not as simple as it sounds. **85m/C; VHS, Blu-Ray, Streaming.** Ron Kay; Chris Crone; Melody Patterson; Clarke Lindsley; Bekki Armstrong; ***D:*** Joel Bender.

The Immortals **1995 (R)** Nightclub owner Jack (Roberts) recruits eight terminally ill criminals in an elaborate heist that calls for simultaneously hitting targets city-wide. But when they compare notes, the team fear a doublecross. **92m/C; VHS, DVD.** Eric Roberts; Tia Carrere; William Forsythe; Joe Pantoliano; Clarence Williams, III; Tony Curtis; Chris Rock; Kieran Mulroney; Kevin Bernhardt; Louis Lombardi; ***D:*** Brian Grant; ***W:*** Kevin Bernhardt; ***C:*** Anthony B. Richmond.

Immortals **1/2 2011 (R)** Easily, one of the best-looking bad movies ever. Tyrannous king Hyperion (Rourke) sets out to conquer ancient Greece, but the oracle Phaedra gives word to scrappy stonemason Theseus (Cavill) that his destiny is to stop the king and save the fate of the Olympian gods. He first must find the Epirus Bow, which can summon arrows from thin air and strike its target without aim. From here, a dizzying barrage of battles erupt in a parade of CGI wizardry. Too bad the story is confusing and incoherent. It's like a classical bronze statue beautiful, but lifeless. **110m/C; DVD, Blu-Ray.** Henry Cavill; Freida Pinto; Mickey Rourke; Stephen Dorff; Isabel Lucas; Luke Evans; Kellan Lutz; Corey Sevier; Joseph Morgan; Stephen McHattie; John Hurt; ***D:*** Tarsem Singh; ***W:*** Charles Parlapanides; Vlas Parlapanides; ***C:*** Brendan Galvin; ***M:*** Trevor Morris.

L'Immortelle **1963** A man known only a 'N' is at a loss when he comes to Istanbul for a new job. A mysterious, beautiful woman--let's call her 'L'--comes to his aid, but she remains a cypher despite the man's increasing obsession with her. Surreal, nonlinear Nouvelle Vague drama that's the directorial debut of writer Robbe-Grillet. French with subtitles. **101m/B; DVD, Blu-Ray.** *FR* Francoise Brion; Jacques Doniol-Valcroze; ***D:*** Alain Robbe-Grillet; ***W:*** Alain Robbe-Grillet; ***C:*** Maurice Barry; ***M:*** Georges Delerue.

Impact **1949** A woman and her lover plan the murder of her rich industrialist husband, but the plan backfires. More twists and turns than a carnival ride. **111m/B; VHS, DVD.** Brian Donlevy; Ella Raines; Charles Coburn; Helen Walker; Anna May Wong; Philip Ahn; Art Baker; Tony Barrett; Harry Cheshire; Lucius Cooke; Joel Friedkin; Sheilah Graham; Tom Greenway; Hans Herbert; Linda Johnson; Joe (Joseph) Kirk; Clarence (C. William) Kolb; Mary Landa; Mae Marsh; ***D:*** Arthur Lubin; ***W:*** Dorothy Davenport Reid; Jay Dratler; ***C:*** Ernest Laszlo; ***M:*** Michel Michelet.

Impact **1/2 2009** Typical made-for-TV disaster miniseries with a big meteor hitting the Moon, causing bits of it to break off and crash into Earth, which is not a good thing. A couple of hot-looking astrophysicists (Henstridge and Elliott) must save our planet from a host of increasingly worsening disturbances. Since it's a co-production with Germany, you at least get a 'we're all in this together' world vibe. **180m/C; DVD.** David James Elliott; Natasha Henstridge; Benjamin Sadler; Florentine Lahme; Steven Culp; James Cromwell; Colin Cunningham; Michael Kopsa; ***D:*** Mike Rohl; ***W:*** Michael Vickerman; ***C:*** Gordon Verheul; ***M:*** Michael Richard Plowman. **TV**

Impact Point **1/2 2008 (R)** Popular pro beach volleyball player Kelly Reyes (Keller) has only cared about her game until mysterious reporter Holden (Green) shows up. A series of bizarre events threaten to derail her career and then things turn even more sinister. **85m/C; DVD.** Melissa Keller; Linden Ashby; Joe Manganiello; Brian Austin Green; Eddie Alfano; ***D:*** Hayley Cloake; ***W:*** Brett Merryman; ***C:*** Thomas M. (Tom) Harting; ***M:*** Steven Stern. **VIDEO**

Impasse **1/2 1969** Four WWII Army vets know the location of some government gold hidden from the advancing Japanese on Corregidor Rock in the Philippines. Morrison (Reynolds) and his salvage team put together a plan to retrieve it but there are multiple problems since the vets have not stayed friends. **100m/C; DVD.** Burt Reynolds; Anne Francis; Charles Gordon; Lyle Bettger; Rodolfo Acosta; Jeff Corey; ***D:*** Richard Benedict; ***W:*** John C. Higgins; ***C:*** Nonong Rasca; ***M:*** Philip Springer.

The Impatient Years **1944** A rushed wartime marriage leads to problems for Sgt. Andy Anderson (Bowman) and his wife Janie (Arthur) when he returns to his postwar home. Basically strangers, they decide to divorce but their judge decrees the couple should retrace their San Francisco courtship to find out why they got together in the first place. **91m/B; DVD.** Jean Arthur; Lee Bowman; Charles Coburn; Edgar Buchanan; Phil Brown; Charley Grapewin; ***D:*** Irving Cummings; ***W:*** Virginia Van Upp; ***C:*** Joseph Walker; ***M:*** Marlin Skiles.

Imperial Venus *Venere Imperiale* **1963 (PG)** Biography of Napoleon's sister, Paolina Boneparte—with particular focus on her many loves, lusts and tribulations. **121m/C; VHS, DVD.** *FR IT* Gina Lollobrigida; Stephen Boyd; Raymond Pellegrin; ***D:*** Jean Delannoy; ***W:*** Jean Delannoy; ***C:*** Gabor Pogany; ***M:*** Angelo Francesco Lavagnino.

Imperium **1/2 2016 (R)** Radcliffe plays an FBI agent who goes undercover in a white supremacist group. Initially set to destroy and bring down the group from within, the agent discovers that these are sometimes good people too, often caught up in something they don't understand that's beyond their control. Then he discovers they're planning to destroy a dirty bomb. Director Ragussis delivers this tense undercover cop thriller inspired by true events, carried not only by high-quality filmmaking but a great, committed performance from Radcliffe. **109m/C; DVD, Blu-Ray.** Daniel Radcliffe; Toni Collette; Tracy Letts; Sam Trammell; Nestor Carbonell; ***D:*** Daniel Ragussis; ***W:*** Daniel Ragussis; ***C:*** Bobby Bukowski; ***M:*** Will Bates.

Implicated **1998 (R)** Tom (McNamara) asks his new girlfriend Ann (Locane) to help him out by babysitting his boss' young daughter, Katie. But Ann soon realizes that Tom's kidnapped Katie and they're both pawns in an elaborate scheme that has gone out of control. Based on the book "Wishful Thinking" by Frank Wyka. **95m/C; VHS, DVD.** Amy Locane; William McNamara; Frederic Forrest; Priscilla Barnes; ***D:*** Irving Belateche; ***W:*** Webb Millsaps; Irving Belateche. **VIDEO**

Impolite **1/2 1992** After getting on the wrong side during a police corruption story, alcoholic reporter Jack (Wisden) has been demoted to writing obits. When he gets a tip that rich and powerful O'Rourke (an uncredited Plummer who also plays the character's twin brother, a priest) has died, Jack decides to investigate the rumor by interviewing the strange group who surrounded O'Rourke. **90m/C; VHS, DVD.** *CA* Robert Wisden; Kevin McNulty; Stuart Margolin; Jill Teed; Susan Hogan; Christopher Plummer; ***D:*** David Hauka; ***W:*** Michael McKinley; ***C:*** Robert McLachlan; ***M:*** Braun Farnon; Robert Smart.

The Importance of Being Earnest **1952** Fine production of classic Oscar Wilde comedy-of-manners. Cast couldn't be better or the story funnier. **95m/C; VHS, DVD.** Michael Redgrave; Edith Evans; Margaret Rutherford; Michael Denison; Joan Greenwood; Dorothy Tutin; ***D:*** Anthony Asquith; ***W:*** Anthony Asquith; ***C:*** Desmond Dickinson; ***M:*** Benjamin Frankel.

The Importance of Being Earnest **2002 (PG)** Jack Worthing (Firth) has invented a brother, Earnest, in order to leave the dull country and visit lovely Gwendolyn (O'Connor), the daughter of the formidable Lady Bracknell (Dench), in London. His best friend Algernon Montcrieff (Everett), who is Gwendolyn's cousin, also has a make-believe chum named Bunbury to get Algy out of boring situations. Then Algy decides to pose as Earnest in order to woo Jack's country ward, Cecily (Witherspoon). But when everyone ends up together, chaos threatens. Based on the play by Oscar Wilde and filled with bon mots, director Parker felt compelled to "open up" the production, which only works some of the time. But the performances are all delightful and Witherspoon manages her English accent quite nicely. **100m/C; VHS, DVD.** *US GB* Colin Firth; Rupert Everett; Frances O'Connor; Reese Witherspoon; Dame Judi Dench; Tom Wilkinson; Anna Massey; Edward Fox; Patrick Godfrey; Charles Kay; Finty Williams; ***D:*** Oliver Parker; ***W:*** Oliver Parker; ***C:*** Tony Pierce-Roberts; ***M:*** Charlie Mole.

The Imported Bridegroom **1989** A comedy set at the turn of the century about a man who returns to Poland in order to find his daughter a proper husband. **93m/C; VHS, DVD.** Eugene Troobnick; Avi Hoffman; Greta Cowan; Annette Miller; ***D:*** Pamela Berger; ***W:*** Pamela Berger.

The Impossible **1/2 2012 (PG-13)** J.A. Bayona directs this emotionally wrenching true story of a family's fight for survival during and after the 2004 tsunami in Thailand. Watts and McGregor play the parents of three boys and the family is split in two after the air is filled with water on a Christmas vacation to one of the most beautiful resorts in the world. Watts is devastatingly good and Bayona's direction approaches Spielberg in his grasp of unimaginable horror and how it can still lead to inspirational truth. The film is a technical accomplishment, especially with the best sound design of the year, but Bayona never forgets that it's about a family that never refuses to believe reunion and survival are possible. **114m/C; DVD, Blu-Ray.** *SP* Naomi Watts; Ewan McGregor; Tom Holland; Samuel Joslin; Oaklee Pendergast; ***D:*** Juan Antonio Bayona; ***W:*** Sergio G. Sanchez; ***C:*** Oscar Faura; ***M:*** Fernando Velazquez.

The Impossible Elephant **1/2 2002** When you wish upon a star...you get a baby elephant. At least that's what Daniel gets when he wishes for a cool, loyal pet that will never forget him. But a pachyderm in the suburbs proves to be an awkward fit. Only Lumpy turns out to have magical powers as well—he can fly! **95m/C; DVD.** *CA* Mark Rendall; Alex Doduk; Nicholas Lea; Mia Sara; William Taylor; Jordan Becket; ***D:*** Martin Wood; ***W:*** Robert Cooper; ***C:*** Michael Storey; ***M:*** Michael Richard Plowman.

The Impossible Spy **1987** True story of Elie Cohen, an unassuming Israeli who doubled as a top level spy in Syria during the 1960s. Cohen became so close to Syria's president that he was nominated to become the Deputy Minister of Defense before his double life was exposed. Well-acted spy thriller and is worth a look for espionage fans. **96m/C; VHS, DVD.** *GB* John Shea; Eli Wallach; Michal Bat-Adam; Rami Danon; Sasson Gabray; Chaim Girafi; ***D:*** Jim (James) Goddard; ***M:*** Richard Hartley. **CABLE**

The Impossible Years **1968** Unattractive, leering sex farce about psychiatrist Nivens who has problems with his own young daughter. Dismal adaptation of the hit Broadway play by Bob Fisher and Arthur Marx. **97m/C; VHS, DVD.** David Niven; Lola Albright; Chad Everett; Ozzie Nelson; Christina Ferrare; Jeff Cooper; John Harding; ***D:*** Michael Gordon; ***W:*** George Wells.

The Imposter **1/2 2012 (R)** Director Layton expertly mixes cinematic recreations with insightful interviews in this true crime doc with a twist. When a missing Texan boy ends up in France with a remarkable story about being kidnapped and held as a sex slave, his family embraces him with open arms...even though he is quite obviously not their son. Frederic Bourdin offers little enlightenment as to why someone would take advantage of a grieving family's quest for answers but the film takes a startling left turn in the final act when Layton and Bourdin suggest there are other questions that we should be asking. Expertly made and as riveting as any fictional thriller. **95m/C; DVD.** *UK* ***D:*** Bart Layton; ***C:*** Erik Alexander Wilson; Lynda Hall; ***M:*** Anne Nikitin.

The Imposters *Ship of Fools* **1998 (R)** Its the 1930s, and third-rate actors Arthur and Maurice (Tucci and Platt, respectively) are out of work. Inadvertently forced into hiding on a cruise ship, they encounter a virtual ship of fools while slinking around in an array of costumes. The wacky story unfolds as the stowaways run into various characters: the Nazi-like, crop-wielding head steward (Scott), a gay Scottish wrestler (Connolly), an anarchist bomber from an unnamed Eastern European nation (Shalhoub), his country's deposed queen (Rossellini), and a pair of murderous con artists posing as French tourists. Written and directed by Tucci, pic reunites much of the cast from Tucci and Scott's "Big Night." Unfortunately, they weren't as successful this time. Too much free-reign hamming by the big-name indie cast sinks this homage to Buster Keaton and the Marx Brothers. **101m/C; VHS, DVD.** Stanley Tucci; Oliver Platt; Elizabeth Bracco; Steve Buscemi; Billy Connolly; Allan

Corduner; Hope Davis; Dana Ivey; Allison Janney; Richard Jenkins; Matt McGrath; Alfred Molina; Isabella Rossellini; Campbell Scott; Tony Shalhoub; Lili Taylor; Lewis J. Stadlen; Woody Allen; *D:* Stanley Tucci; *W:* Stanley Tucci; *C:* Ken Kelsch; *M:* Gary DeMichele.

Impostor **2002 (PG-13)** When a movie is shelved for a year and a half, there's usually a reason. Earth in 2079 is dystopian and paranoid, and the neon-blue cave lighting makes it difficult to see. Which is not a huge loss. Talented cast is reduced to a collection of archetypes, including the usually solid Sinise as an elite military scientist accused of fighting (as a replicant) for the wrong team, namely, the sinister aliens who are laying waste to our earth. Citizens are monitored via spinal identification chips, yet a hooded sweatshirt and sunglasses are enough to shield public enemy #1 from detection. Tired sci-fi themes of soul and identity are not enough to keep things interesting. Adapted (and yawningly stretched) from a short story by perennial sci-fi source Philip K. Dick. **96m/C; VHS, DVD, Blu-Ray.** Gary Sinise; Madeleine Stowe; Vincent D'Onofrio; Tony Shalhoub; Mekhi Phifer; Tim Guinee; Lindsay Crouse; Gary Dourdan; Erica Gimpel; Elizabeth Pena; *D:* Gary Fleder; *W:* Ehren Kruger; David N. Twohy; Caroline Case; *C:* Robert Elswit; *M:* Mark Isham.

Impostor **1/2 2002 (R)** A sci-fi drama based on a short story by Philip K. Dick. In the year 2079, war between Earth and aliens has been going on for years. The aliens deploy androids as bombs on Earth. Just as respected government weapons specialist Spencer Olham (Sinise) announces a project that may save everyone on the planet, he is accused of being an alien spy and forced into hiding. While being pursued by the government, he realizes that he needs to prove his identity to the secret police and to himself. **102m/C; DVD, Streaming, Download.** Gary Sinise; Madeleine Stowe; Vincent D'Onofrio; Tony Shalhoub; Tim Guinee; *D:* Gary Fleder; *W:* Caroline Case; Ehren Kruger; David N. Twohy; *C:* Robert Elswit; *M:* Mark Isham.

The Impostors **1998 (R)** In this homage to classical farce, two out of work actors hide in a crate to avoid being killed by a coworker and accidentally end up as stowaways on a cruise ship surrounded by their would-be killer, a terrorist, and a great many fools. **101m/C; DVD, Streaming.** Oliver Platt; Stanley Tucci; Alfred Molina; Steve Buscemi; Tony Shalhoub; *D:* Stanley Tucci; *W:* Stanley Tucci; *C:* Ken Kelsch; *M:* Gary DeMichele.

Impromptu **1990 (PG-13)** A smart, sassy, romantic comedy set in 1830s Europe among the era's artistic greats—here depicted as scalawags, parasites and early beatniks. The film's ace is Davis in a lusty, dynamic role as mannish authoress George Sand, obsessively in love with the dismayed composer Chopin. Though he's too pallid a character for her attraction to be credible, a great cast and abundant wit make this a treat. Beautiful score featuring Chopin and Liszt. Film debut of stage director Lapine; screenplay written by his wife, Sarah Kernochan. **108m/C; VHS, DVD, Blu-Ray.** Judy Davis; Hugh Grant; Mandy Patinkin; Bernadette Peters; Julian Sands; Ralph Brown; Georges Corraface; Anton Rodgers; Emma Thompson; Anna Massey; John Savident; Elizabeth Spriggs; *D:* James Lapine; *W:* Sarah Kernochan; *C:* Bruno de Keyzer. Ind. Spirit '92: Actress (Davis).

Impulse **WOOF!** *Want a Ride, Little Girl?; I Love to Kill* **1974 (PG)** Shatner, a crazed killer, is released from prison and starts to kill again in this low-budget, predictable, critically debased film about child-molesting. **85m/C; VHS, DVD.** William Shatner; Ruth Roman; Harold Sakata; Kim Nicholas; Jennifer Bishop; James Dobson; *D:* William Grefe; *W:* Tony Crechales; *C:* Edwin Gibson; *M:* Lewis Perles.

Impulse **1984 (R)** Small town residents can't control their impulses, all because of government toxic waste in their milk. A woman worried about her mother's mental health returns to town with her doctor boyfriend to discover most of the inhabitants are quite mad. Starts strong but... **95m/C; VHS, DVD, Blu-Ray.** Tim Matheson; Meg Tilly; Hume Cronyn; John Karlen; Bill Paxton; Amy Stryker; Claude Earl Jones; Sherri Stoner; *D:* Graham Baker; *W:* Don Carlos Dunaway; Nicholas Kazan; *C:* Thomas Del Ruth; *M:* Paul Chihara.

Impulse **1/2 1990 (R)** A beautiful undercover vice cop poses as a prostitute, and gives in to base desires. Russell gives a fine performance in this underrated sleeper. **109m/C; DVD.** Theresa Russell; Nicholas Mele; Eli Danker; Charles McCaughan; Jeff Fahey; George Dzundza; Alan Rosenberg; Lynne Thigpen; Shawn Elliott; *D:* Sondra Locke; *W:* John DeMarco; Leigh Chapman; *M:* Michel Colombier.

Impulse **2008 (R)** Utterly preposterous, not-so-erotic thriller. Clair (Ford) is an advertising manager, married to older psychologist Jonathan (Macfayden). Wanting to spice up their love life, Clair suggests a hotel fantasy while she's on a business trip. Clair's happily surprised when Jonathan picks her up in the bar, only to find out that the man in bed with her is not her husband but a lookalike named Simon. Upset when Clair suddenly rejects him without explanation, Simon begins stalking her. **101m/C; DVD.** Angus MacFadyen; Ingrid Torrance; Willa Ford; *D:* Charles Kanganis; *W:* Charles Kanganis; *C:* Gordon Verheul; *M:* Stu Goldberg. **VIDEO**

iMurders **2008** A serial killer targets a group of friends who chat nightly on a social network. A couple of FBI agents show up before the group realizes they're losing members to more than boredom and the crime relates back to a secret in someone's past. Actually the movie makes little to no sense with characters popping in and out for no discernable reason. **98m/C; DVD.** Terri Colombino; Frank Grillo; Joanne Baron; Gabrielle Anwar; Billy Dee Williams; Tony Todd; Brooke Lewis; Wilson Jermaine Heredia; Shannon Ivey; Charles Durning; William Forsythe; Margaret Colin; Justin Deas; *D:* Robbie Bryan; *W:* Robbie Bryan; Ken Del Vecchio; *C:* Hiroo Takaoka. **VIDEO**

In a Better World *Haevnen* **2010** Two unwittingly neglectful fathers try to teach their troubled sons moral lessons in Bier's family drama. Pacifist Anton divides his time between his work as a doctor in a Kenyan refugee camp and his life with estranged wife Marianne and son Elias in a Danish town. Recent widower Claus and his son Christian are newcomers to the same town and the boys become friends. When Christian sees Elias being harassed by the school bully, he intervenes (a knife is involved), shocking the adults who miss the implication that the boys' idea of violent retribution is not so isolated. Danish with subtitles. **113m/C; Blu-Ray, On Demand.** *DK* Mikael Persbrandt; Ulrich Thomsen; Trine Dyrholm; Kim Bodnia; Markus Rygaard; William Johnk Nielsen; *D:* Suzanne (Susanne) Bier; *W:* Anders Thomas Jensen; *C:* Morten Soborg; *M:* Johan Soderqvist. Oscars '10: Foreign Film; Golden Globes '11: Foreign Film.

In a Class of His Own **1/2 1999** School janitor Rich Donato (Phillips) is an ex-teen bad boy who has formed a close relationship with both the teachers and the students at the high school where he works. However, in order to keep his job, he learns he must pass his GED and this isn't an easy task. When his wife appeals for help, Rich finds himself becoming a school project. Based on a true story. **94m/C; VHS, DVD.** Lou Diamond Phillips; Cara Buono; Joan Chen; Nathaniel DeVeaux; *D:* Robert Munic; *W:* Robert Munic; *C:* Ron Stannett; *M:* Sharon Farber. **CABLE**

In a Day **2006** Ashley (Pilkington) is waiting at a London bus stop when a crazy stranger throws coffee all over her. Michael (Robertson), whom Ashley recognizes as a frequent customer at the sandwich shop where she works, comes to her aid and persuades her to let him make things better with a gourmet lunch and a makeover though Ashley wants to know what he wants in return. **81m/C; DVD.** *GB* Lorraine Pilkington; Finlay Robertson; Rose Keegan; Jake Broder; Nolan Hemmings; *D:* Evan Richards; *W:* Evan Richards; *C:* Gareth Pritchard; *M:* George M. Young.

In a Glass Cage **1/2** *Tras el Cristal* **1986** A young boy who was tortured and sexually molested by a Nazi official seeks revenge. Years after the war, he shows up at the Nazi's residence in Spain and is immediately befriended by his tormentor's family. Confined to an iron lung, the official is at the mercy of the young man who tortuously acts out the incidents detailed in the Nazi's journal. Suspenseful and extremely graphic, it's well crafted and meaningful but may be just too horrible to watch. Sexual and violent acts place it in the same league as Pasolini's infamous "Salo, or The 120 Days in Sodom." Definitely not for the faint of heart. In Spanish with English subtitles. **110m/C; VHS, DVD, Blu-Ray.** *SP* Gunter Meisner; David Sust; Marisa Paredes; Gisela Echevarria; *D:* Agustin Villaronga; *W:* Agustin Villaronga.

In a Lonely Place **1/2 1950** Bogart is outstanding as Dixon Steele, a hard-drinking and volatile Hollywood screenwriter, who becomes the prime suspect in the murder of a hat-check girl, last seen alive leaving his apartment. New neighbor Laurel Gray (Grahame) alibis the guy because she doesn't think he's a killer and he's grateful. Enough so to begin a romance with the cool beauty. But the investigating detectives still have the writer on their A-list and his paranoia kicks in. Dix begins to question Laurel's loyalty and violently over-reacts to his suspicions. Offbeat, yet superb film noir, expertly directed by Ray. Based on the novel by Dorothy B. Hughes. Ray's disintegrating marriage to Grahame seemingly played out onscreen; they split after filming. **93m/B; VHS, DVD, Blu-Ray.** Humphrey Bogart; Gloria Grahame; Frank Lovejoy; Carl Benton Reid; Art Smith; Jeff Donnell; *D:* Nicholas Ray; *W:* Andrew Solt; *C:* Burnett Guffey. Natl. Film Reg. '07.

In a Stranger's Hand **1/2 1992** Urich stars a respected businessman who happens to find a doll which belongs to a kidnapped young girl. The police have their suspicions but Urich teams up with the child's mother to find the girl and winds up uncovering a child-selling ring. **93m/C; VHS, DVD.** Robert Urich; Megan Gallagher; Brett Cullen; Vondie Curtis-Hall; Dakin Matthews; Alan Rosenberg; Maria O'Brien; *D:* David Greene. **TV**

In a Valley of Violence **1/2 2016 (R)** A western set in Denton, Texas, in which the spirit of revenge encompasses the whole town. Paul (Hawke) and his dog are drifters moving from Mexico to parts north. They stop in the nearly empty town of Denton, which was once a thriving mining town. The town is now essentially controlled by the violent Gilly (Ransone), the son of the town's powerful marshal (Travolta). Paul and Gilly become violent, and bring the whole town into their conflict. Though some cooler heads try to prevail, a secret from Paul's past makes the situation worse. **104m/C; DVD, Blu-Ray, Streaming, Download.** Ethan Hawke; John Travolta; Taissa Farmiga; James Ransone; Karen Gillan; *D:* Ti West; *W:* Ti West; *C:* Eric Robbins; *M:* Jeff Grace.

In a World... **2013 (R)** Lake Bell writes, directs, and stars in this equal parts wacky and delightful satire with a feminist bent that won a major award at the 2013 Sundance Film Festival. The charming Bell plays Carol Solomon, daughter of legendary voiceover star Sam Soto (Melamed). When Carol steals a coveted voiceover spot from the titan of the industry, Gustav Warner (Marino), she's forced to deal with an inherently sexist industry that thinks viewers only want to hear male voices. An authentic and clever effort from its young and talented creator. **93m/C; DVD, Blu-Ray.** Lake Bell; Fred Melamed; Demetri Martin; Ken Marino; Rob Corddry; Michaela Watkins; Alexandra Holden; Geena Davis; Nick Offerman; *D:* Lake Bell; *W:* Lake Bell; *C:* Seamus Tierney; *M:* Ryan Miller.

In a Year of 13 Moons *In a Year with 13 Moons; In Einem Jahr Mit 13 Monden* **1978** Notorious Fassbinder tale of Erwin who becomes Elvira and is subjected to a series of humiliating relationships with men. Finally, with the aid of his/her ex-wife and a prostitute, Elvira looks into the past in an effort to resolve the present. Alternatingly depressing and pretentious. German with subtitles. **119m/C; VHS, DVD.** *GE* Volker Spengler; Ingrid Caven; Gottfried John; Elisabeth Trissenaar; Eva Mattes; Gunther Kaufman; *D:* Rainer Werner Fassbinder; *W:* Rainer Werner Fassbinder; *C:* Rainer Werner Fassbinder; *M:* Peer Raben.

In America **2002 (PG-13)** After their 2-year old son dies from a brain tumor, Johnny (Considine) and Sarah (Morton) Sheridan leave Ireland with their family and head for America. The family deals with poverty and personal struggles while trying to create a better life. Real life sisters Sarah and Emma Bolger steal every scene they're in as the young Sheridans, not an easy task with this top-notch group. Honsou stands out as a dying artist neighbor. Based on the experiences of director Jim Sheridan, who co-wrote with daughters Kirsten and Naomi. Well-paced and uplifting. **103m/C; VHS, DVD.** *IR GB* Paddy Considine; Samantha Morton; Sarah Bolger; Emma Bolger; Djimon Hounsou; *D:* Jim Sheridan; *W:* Jim Sheridan; Naomi Sheridan; Kirsten Sheridan; *C:* Declan Quinn; *M:* Gavin Friday; Maurice Seezer. Ind. Spirit '04: Cinematog., Support. Actor (Hounsou).

In and Out **1997 (PG-13)** See what an Oscar can do? When Tom Hanks thanked, and inadvertently outed, his high school drama teacher during his Academy Awards speech (for "Philadelphia"), it lead to this feature. Popular high school English teacher Howard Brackett (Kline) has his sexuality come into question on the eve of his wedding thanks to a former-student-turned-movie-star (Dillon). As a media circus converges on the small town, Howard is forced to examine his sexuality by openly gay reporter Selleck (out to prove Howard's gay), his mother Reynolds (who wants the wedding to go on regardless of his orientation) and his tightly wound fiancee Cusack (who wants to put a serious hurtin' on Barbra Striesand). All-around excellent performances, especially by Kline and Cusack. **92m/C; VHS, DVD.** Kevin Kline; Joan Cusack; Matt Dillon; Debbie Reynolds; Wilford Brimley; Bob Newhart; Tom Selleck; Deborah Rush; Lewis J. Stadlen; J. Smith-Cameron; Zak Orth; Gregory Jbara; Shalom Harlow; Kate McGregor-Stewart; Shawn Hatosy; Lauren Ambrose; Alexandra Holden; *D:* Frank Oz; *W:* Paul Rudnick; *C:* Rob Hahn; *M:* Marc Shaiman. N.Y. Film Critics '97: Support. Actress (Cusack); Broadcast Film Critics '97: Support. Actress (Cusack).

In Bloom **2013** A heartfelt exploration of the impact of a romantic breakup on both partners in a long-term relationship. Living in Boystown in Chicago, Kurt (xx) and Paul (xx) have been together for two years. After a summer-time party, their relationship is deeply impacted after Kurt meets Kevin (xxx). Kevin tries to seduce Kurt, who resists for a time. His decision changes when Kevin takes up this same profession as Kurt—selling marijuana. Full of desire for Kevin, Kurt impulsively breaks up Paul and focuses on partying and what he does not have in life. In the meantime, Paul spirals downward into empty, painful feelings. Both their worlds are changed forever when Kurt attracts a serial killer looking for new victims. **87m/C; DVD, Streaming, Download.** Kyle Wigent; Tanner Rittenhouse; Adam Fane; Jake Andrews; Steve Casillas; *D:* Chris Michael Birkmeier; *W:* Chris Michael Birkmeier; *C:* Dustin Supencheck. **VIDEO**

In Bruges **1/2 2008 (R)** Ray (Farrell) and Ken (Gleeson), two Irish hitmen, are sent to the picturesque medieval berg of Bruges, Belgium, to hide out following a partially botched job that targeted a priest but accidentally offed a young boy, hardly a premise for comedy. But writer/director McDonagh's debut mostly hits the mark with this pitch-black fish-out-of-water tale of tough guys laying low in the quaint town, a feat made impossible by their involvement with a local hottie and a filmmaking dwarf and the arrival of their cool boss (Fiennes). Snappy repartee and postcard scenery offset an abundance of inner torment and blood, and it's all almost too hip for its own good, but Farrell and Gleeson are terrific. **107m/C; DVD.** *GB* Colin Farrell; Brendan Gleeson; Ralph Fiennes; Clarence Poesy; Jeremie Renier; Thekla Reuten; Jordan Prentice; *D:* Martin McDonagh; *W:* Martin McDonagh; *C:* Eigil Bryld; *M:* Carter Burwell. British Acad. '08: Orig. Screenplay; Golden Globes '09: Actor--Mus./Comedy (Farrell).

In Caliente **1935** New York magazine critic Larry MacArthur (O'Brien) has the bad habit of panning performances without ever seeing them. His friend Harold (Horton) hustles Larry to a Mexican resort to get him away from gold-digging Clara (Farrell) and Larry soon falls for Mexican dancer Rita (Del Rio). Unfortunately, he doesn't realize he savaged her act in print but Rita certainly knows who Larry is and wants to get even.

84m/B; DVD. Pat O'Brien; Dolores Del Rio; Edward Everett Horton; Glenda Farrell; Leo Carrillo; Phil Regan; *D:* Lloyd Bacon; *W:* Jerry Wald; Julius J. Epstein; *C:* George Barnes; Sol Polito.

In Celebration **1975 (PG)** Three successful brothers return to the old homestead for their parents' 40th wedding celebration. Intense drama but somewhat claustrophobic. Based on a play by David Storey. **131m/C; VHS, DVD, Blu-Ray.** *GB CA* Alan Bates; James Bolam; Brian Cox; Constance Chapman; Gabrielle Daye; Bill Owen; *D:* Lindsay Anderson; *W:* David Storey; *C:* Dick Bush.

In Cold Blood ½ **1967** Truman Capote's supposedly factual novel provided the basis for this hard-hitting docu-drama about two ex-cons who ruthlessly murder a Kansas family in 1959 in order to steal their non-existent stash of money. Blake is riveting as one of the killers. **133m/B; VHS, DVD, Blu-Ray.** Robert (Bobby) Blake; Scott Wilson; John Forsythe; Paul Stewart; Gerald S. O'Loughlin; Jeff Corey; Will Geer; James Flavin; John Gallaudet; John Collins; Charles McGraw; John McLiam; *D:* Richard Brooks; *W:* Richard Brooks; *C:* Conrad L. Hall; *M:* Quincy Jones. Natl. Bd. of Review '67: Director (Brooks); Natl. Film Reg. '08.

In Cold Blood **1996** Tv miniseries version of the Truman Capote true crime classic, which follows the 1959 murders of the four members of the Clutter family in Holcomb, Kansas by ex-cons Dick Hickock (Edwards) and Perry Smith (Roberts). The TV version covers more of the background of both the killers and the Holcombs, the relentless hunt by Al Dewey (Neill) of the Kansas Bureau of Investigation, and the duo's time on death row. **180m/C; VHS, DVD.** Anthony Edwards; Eric Roberts; Sam Neill; Kevin Tighe; Gillian Barber; Robbie Bowen; Margot Finley; Bethel Leslie; Gwen Verdon; Stella Stevens; L.Q. Jones; Louise Latham; Campbell Lane; Leo Rossi; *D:* Jonathan Kaplan; *W:* Benedict Fitzgerald. **TV**

In Country ½ **1989 (R)** Based on Bobbie Ann Mason's celebrated novel, the story of a young Kentucky high schooler (perfectly played by Lloyd) and her search for her father, killed in Vietnam. Willis plays her uncle, a veteran still struggling to accept his own survival, and crippled with memories. Moving scene at the Vietnam Veterans Memorial. **116m/C; VHS, DVD; Open Captioned.** Bruce Willis; Emily Lloyd; Joan Allen; Kevin Anderson; Richard Hamilton; Judith Ivey; Peggy Rea; John Terry; Patricia Richardson; Jim Beaver; *D:* Norman Jewison; *W:* Frank Pierson; Cynthia Cidre; *C:* Russell Boyd; *M:* James Horner.

The In Crowd **1988 (PG)** A bright high school student gets involved with a local TV dance show circa 1965, and must choose between uncertain fame and an Ivy League college. A fair nostalgic look at the period. Leitch is the son of psychedelic folk singer Donovan. **96m/C; VHS, Streaming.** Donovan Leitch; Jennifer Runyon; Scott Plank; Joe Pantoliano; *D:* Mark Rosenthal; *W:* Mark Rosenthal.

The In Crowd **2000 (PG-13)** Having been cured of her "erotomania," pretty, young Adrien (Heuring) is released from a psychiatric hospital, and, on the advice of her doctor, gains employment for the summer at a seaside country club. There Adrien is confronted by the in crowd, which is led by the ultra bitchy (what other name would suffice?) Brittany (Ward), who, with clearly ulterior motives, befriends the lovely Adrien. As Adrien is introduced to the ways of the privileged, things become stranger and stranger as our heroine discovers some unpleasant things about her new acquaintance. **98m/C; VHS, DVD.** Susan Ward; Lori Heuring; Matthew Settle; Nathan Bexton; Tess Harper; Laurie Fortier; Kim Murphy; *D:* Mary Lambert; *W:* Mark Gibson; Philip Halprin; *C:* Tom Priestley; *M:* Jeff Rona.

In Custody *Hifazaat* **1994 (PG)** Producer Merchant makes his feature directorial debut with this dreamy tale of small-town teacher Deven (Puri) who's urged by a publishing friend to interview Nur (Kapoor), the greatest living poet in the disappearing Urdu language. The worshipful Deven is dismayed to find his idol a wreck, surrounded by sycophants and a shrewish second wife who's plagiarizing her husband's work, and soon finds himself hopelessly entangled in the writer's life. Unabashedly literary (the poetry recited is by Faiz Ahmed Faiz) with a star cast. Based on the 1987 novel by Anita Desai. Urdu with subtitles. **123m/C; VHS, DVD.** *IN* Shashi Kapoor; Om Puri; Shabana Azmi; Sushma Seth; Neena Gupta; Ajay Sahni; Tinnu Anand; *D:* Ismail Merchant; *W:* Anita Desai; Shahrukh Husain; *C:* Larry Pizer; *M:* Zakir Hussain; Ustad Sultan Khan.

In Dark Places **1997 (R)** Seductive artist Chapelle (Severance) visits long-estranged brother Chazz (Kestner) with more than familial feelings on her mind. As things between them heat up, Chazz loses his girl, best friend, and job before discovering his sister's true agenda. This one actually has a story to go along with the eroticism. **96m/C; VHS, Streaming.** Joan Severance; Bryan Kestner; John Vargas; Suzanne Turner; *D:* James Burke.

In Darkness **2011 (R)** Holland's overlong Holocaust drama is based on a true story and adapted from "In the Sewers of Lvov" by Robert Marshall. Leopold Socha is a former sewer inspector turned scavenger and petty criminal after the Nazis occupy the town of Lvov. The sewer system has served as his escape route and he's shocked to find parts are now occupied by a group of Jews escaping Nazi persecution. Though an anti-Semite, Socha first helps because they pay him and then because of a gradual moral awakening. Polish, German, and Yiddish with subtitles. **145m/C; DVD, Blu-Ray.** *PL* Benno Furmann; Robert Wieckiewicz; Krzysztof Skonieczny; Marcin Bosak; Julia Kijowska; Agnieszka Grochowska; Maria Schrader; Herbert Knaup; Michal Zurawski; *D:* Agnieszka Holland; *W:* David F. Shamoon; *C:* Jolanta Dylewska; *M:* Antoni Komasa-Lazarkiewicz.

In Desert and Wilderness *W Pustyni I W Puszczy* **2001** Children's adventure story has problems for what should be its target audience since it is in Polish with subtitles—maybe the stunning visuals will interest the kids. Set in North Africa at the end of the 19th century, Stas and Nel are children of engineers working on the Suez Canal. They are kidnapped by rebels but escape from their captors, along with two African children, Mea and Kali, who were slaves. Their journey across the beautiful but desolate country is fraught with hardship and unexpected adventures. Based on the novel by Henryk Sienkiewicz. **111m/C; VHS, DVD.** *PL* Adam Fidusiewicz; Karolina Sawka; Lingile Shongwe; Mzwandile Ngubeni; Krzystof Kowalewski; Krzysztof Kolberger; *D:* Gavin Hood; *W:* Gavin Hood; *C:* Paul Gilpin; *M:* Krzesinir Debski.

In Dreams ½ *Blue Vision* **1998 (R)** Bening is a small town wife and mother with a psychic connection to twisted child killer Downey, causing her to dream of his gruesome crimes before he commits them. After she dreams that her daughter is killed, her life begins to unravel, causing those around her to suspect her of insanity. Draws its chills from a more cerebral standpoint, so fans of big action may want to pass. The unnerving dream sequences are suitable murky and ominous thanks to cinematographer Darius Khondji, who also filmed "Seven." **99m/C; VHS, DVD.** Annette Bening; Robert Downey, Jr.; Aidan Quinn; Stephen Rea; Paul Guilfoyle; Dennis Boutsikaris; Pamela Payton-Wright; Margo Martindale; Prudence Wright Holmes; Katie Sagona; Krystal Benn; *D:* Neil Jordan; *W:* Neil Jordan; Bruce Robinson; *C:* Darius Khondji; *M:* Elliot Goldenthal.

In Dubious Battle **2017 (R)** Franco adapts an early novel from John Steinbeck that's essentially about the formation of unions reflected through contentious labor movements for fruit workers in California in the 1930s. A few incredible actors have a few great moments in this sprawling tale, including D'Onofrio, Harris, and Duvall, but the typically adventurous Franco plays this tale remarkably straight, making an old-fashioned ensemble piece with old-fashioned energy. He's more mature than ever as a director here, but one wishes he would have taken a few more risks rather than produce a Cliff Notes version of the book. **110m/C; DVD, Blu-Ray.** Nat Wolff; James Franco; Vincent D'Onofrio; Selena Gomez; Robert Duvall; Ed Harris; Bryan Cranston; Sam Shepard; *D:* James Franco; *W:* Matthew Rager; *C:* Bruce Thierry Cheung; *M:* Volker Bertelmann.

In Enemy Hands *U-Boat* **2004** Germans take an American submarine crew captive during WWII but the POWs face greater threats from a meningitis outbreak and a U.S. vessel posed to attack. **98m/C; VHS, DVD.** Til Schweiger; Thomas Kretschmann; Connor Donne; Matt Lindquist; Andy Gatjen; Rene Heger; Alex Prusmack; Sascha Rosemann; Sven-Ole Thorsen; Scott Caan; Clark Gregg; A.J. Buckley; William H. Macy; Jeremy Sisto; Ian Somerhalder; Carmine D. Giovinazzo; Sam Huntington; Lauren Holly; Xander Berkeley; Chris Ellis; James Burke; Roy Werner; Justin Thomson; Braden R. Morgan; Patrick Gallagher; Tom DeGrezia; William Gregory Lee; Doug Biolchini; *D:* Tony Giglio; *W:* Tony Giglio; John Hartmann; John E. Deaver; *C:* Gerry Lively; *M:* Steven Bremson. **VIDEO**

In Fabric ½ **2018 (R)** Divorced bank teller Sheila (Jean-Baptiste) struggles with a hostile work environment, a bratty art student son Vince (Ayeh) at home, and forgettable dates. To treat herself, she goes shopping at a boutique where the mysterious Miss Luckmore (Mohamed) essentially forces Sheila to buy a red dress that is both flattering and cursed. The dress changes her life in unexpected ways. Also linked to the store is Reg (Bill), a washing machine repairman who can hypnotize anyone by explaining which parts of their machine may be broken. The horror comedy's inspired, mesmerizing moments are best appreciated with an eye for its twisted humor. **118m/C; DVD, Blu-Ray.** Sidse Babett Knudsen; Marianne Jean-Baptiste; Julian Barratt; Steve Oram; Jaygann Ayeh; *D:* Peter Strickland; *W:* Peter Strickland; *C:* Ari Wegner; *M:* Cavern of Anti-Matter.

In Fear ½ **2013 (R)** Tom (De Caestecker) and Lucy (Englert) are an average couple on a vacation in a wooded part of the country far away from civilization. What could go wrong, right? Director Lovering's Sundance midnight entry essentially plays like a home invasion film in a car as the poor pair gets lost and then becomes convinced that they're not alone on these roads where no one can get a cell phone signal. Of course, they're right. Sadly, this is one of those horror flicks that's a slow burn that fizzles out instead of staying aflame. **85m/C; DVD, Blu-Ray.** *UK* Alice Englert; Iain de Caestecker; Allen Leech; *D:* Jeremy Lovering; *W:* Jeremy Lovering; *C:* David Katznelson; *M:* Roly Porter; Daniel Pemberton.

In God's Country **2007** Judith takes her five children and escapes from the polygamous, fundamentalist sect where she grew up. Struggling to make a life on the outside, Judith is horrified when her naive eldest daughter goes back, thinking she'll be allowed to marry the boy she left behind. Judith knows that the girl will be forced into a marriage with her one-time stepfather and she is determined to get her daughter back. **90m/C; DVD.** Kelly Rowan; Richard Burgi; Martha MacIsaac; Hannah Lochner; Peter Outerbridge; Marc Strange; *D:* John L'Ecuyer; *W:* Esta Spalding; *C:* Thomas M. (Tom) Harting; *M:* Christopher Dedrick. **CABLE**

In God's Hands **1998 (PG-13)** Dude! Check it out! Three surfers (Dorian, George, and Liu) travel the world looking for (what else?) the perfect wave. Disjointed, plot-deprived, but beautifully shot flick has the trio busting out of prison (why they're there is never explained) to begin their quest. Moving from Madagascar to Bali to Hawaii, one finds love with a girl from Ipanema (!), another contracts malaria, and the other succumbs to the surf. What happens to whom doesn't really matter, because as actors, they're really great surfers. Besides, the "story" is just connective tissue for the killer surfing scenes. Gnarly. **98m/C; VHS, DVD.** Patrick Shane Dorian; Matt George; Matty Liu; Brion James; Shaun Thompson; Maylin Pultar; Bret Michaels; Brian L. Keaulana; Darrick Doerner; *D:* Zalman King; *W:* Matt George; Zalman King; *C:* John Aronson.

In Good Company **2004 (PG-13)** Writer-director Weitz scores with this wry commentary on the effect of corporate politics on the modern family. Seasoned ad-exec Dan Foreman (Quaid) arrives at work to discover he's been demoted to make room for his new boss, 26-year-old Carter Duryea (Grace). Carter is the golden boy of the office's new corporate owners, but his work success barely masks his unfulfilling personal life. Carter finds himself drawn to family-man Dan, particularly Dan's fetching daughter Alex (Johansson), and the two men reluctantly teach each other about the vagaries of workplace ethics. Lapses into sentimentality and the end comes a bit easy, but strong performances by Quaid and Grace save the day. **131m/C; DVD, Blu-Ray, HD-DVD.** Dennis Quaid; Topher Grace; Scarlett Johansson; Marg Helgenberger; David Paymer; Clark Gregg; Philip Baker Hall; Selma Blair; Frankie Faison; Ty Burrell; Kevin Chapman; Amy Aquino; Zena Grey; Colleen Camp; *D:* Paul Weitz; *W:* Paul Weitz; *C:* Remi Adefarasin; *M:* Stephen Trask.

In Harm's Way **1965** Overdone story about two naval officers and their response to the Japanese attack at Pearl Harbor. Even the superb cast members (and there are plenty of them) can't overcome the incredible length and overly intricate plot. **165m/B; VHS, DVD.** John Wayne; Kirk Douglas; Tom Tryon; Patricia Neal; Paula Prentiss; Brandon de Wilde; Burgess Meredith; Stanley Holloway; Henry Fonda; Dana Andrews; Franchot Tone; Jill Haworth; George Kennedy; Carroll O'Connor; Patrick O'Neal; Slim Pickens; Bruce Cabot; Larry Hagman; Hugh O'Brian; Jim Mitchum; Barbara Bouchet; Stewart Moss; Tod Andrews; *D:* Otto Preminger; *W:* Wendell Mayes; *C:* Loyal Griggs; *M:* Jerry Goldsmith. British Acad. '65: Actress (Neal).

In Hell *The Savage* **2003 (R)** An American engineer working in Russia, Kyle LeBlanc (Van Damme) kills his wife's murderer and is convicted and sent to a remote prison run by corrupt officials. The warden likes to organize and take bets on fights between the prisoners and Kyle soon turns himself into a champion in order to survive. Now, he's pitted against his most vicious opponent—Valya (Smith). **98m/C; VHS, DVD.** Jean-Claude Van Damme; Michael Bailey Smith; Lawrence Taylor; Marnie Alton; Malakai Davidson; Billy Reick; *D:* Ringo Lam; *W:* Eric James Virgets; *C:* John Aronson; *M:* Alexander Bubenheim. **VIDEO**

In Her Line of Fire ½ **2006 (R)** Vice President Walker's (Keith) jet crashes on a South American island dominated by insurgents who hold the Yankee dog for ransom. Having evaded capture, Walker's sinewy secret service agent Lynn Delaney (Hemingway) and press secretary Sharon Serrano (Bennett) devise their own rescue plan. The two are lesbians who kinda have a maybe thing going on but romance is put on hold until they free their boss. **88m/C; DVD.** Mariel Hemingway; Jill Bennett; David Keith; David Millbern; Sydney Jackson; *D:* Brian Trenchard-Smith; *W:* Paula Goldberg; Anna Lorenzo; *C:* Neil Cervino; *M:* David Reynolds. **CABLE**

In Her Mother's Footsteps **2006** Kate (Caulfield) inherits a mansion from her wealthy estranged father and thinks life with her daughter Emma (Fedor) and second husband Buddy (Orth) will finally be settled. Except Kate suddenly sees the ghosts of murdered women and realizes she inherited her dead mom's psychic abilities. Or maybe greedy Buddy is trying to drive her crazy so he can control Kate's money. Or maybe it's a little bit of both. Overstuffed plot, but Caulfield is a good lead. **90m/C; DVD.** Emma Caulfield; David Orth; Matreya Fedor; Tracy Waterhouse; Daryl Shuttleworth; Adrien Dorval; Jody Thompson; *D:* Farhad Mann; *W:* Steven A. Finly; *C:* Brian Johnson; *M:* Michael Neilson. **CABLE**

In Her Shoes **2005 (PG-13)** Despite its sometimes-embarrassing stereotypes and implausible situations, sappy but fun chick-flick works as a story of two very different sisters navigating the bonds of family. Rose (Colette) seemingly has life buttoned up, while Maggie (Diaz) is a mess who shows up homeless and drunk at Rose's door. Maggie manages to continually screw things up and Rose finally tosses her out. Maggie ends up at long-lost grandma Ella's door, where she rather comically falls in with Ella's senior friends as relationships eventually get mended. **129m/C; DVD.** Cameron Diaz; Toni Collette; Shirley MacLaine; Mark Feuerstein; Ken Howard; Candice Azzara; Francine Beers; Norman Lloyd; Jerry Adler; Brooke Smith; Richard Burgi; Anson Mount; *D:* Curtis Hanson; *W:* Susannah Grant; *C:* Terry Stacey; *M:* Mark Isham.

In Her Skin *I Am You* **2009** True crime story that happened in 1999 in Melbourne. Fifteen-year-old Rachel Barber is everything her psychotically jealous 20-year-old former babysitter/neighbor Caroline is not: pretty, popular, talented, with a boyfriend and a great relationship with her parents. Rachel disappears and the cops think she's just a runaway—until she turns out to be a murder victim. Writer/director North divides her film into three perspectives: Rachel's parents, her killer, and Rachel herself. **97m/C; DVD.** *AU* Kate Bell; Ruth Bradley; Guy Pearce; Miranda Otto; Sam Neill; Rebecca Gibney; Khan Chittenden; ***D:*** Simone North; ***W:*** Simone North; ***C:*** Jules O'Loughlin; ***M:*** Ben Frost.

In His Father's Shoes ½ **1997 (PG)** After his father (Gossett) dies, 15-year-old Clay (Ri'chard) takes a literal journey of self-discovery. Slipping on a pair of his dad's old wingtips, the teen is transported back to the '60s to revisit his father's past, and then further back to his grandfather's (Gossett again) day. Clay learns his granddad was a hard-working man who gave up his own dreams to support his family, which later caused a generational rift. Touching drama. **105m/C; VHS, DVD.** Louis Gossett, Jr.; Robert Ri'chard; Rachael Crawford; ***D:*** Vic Sarin; ***W:*** Gary Gelt; ***C:*** Michael Storey; ***M:*** John Welsman. **CABLE**

In His Life: The John Lennon Story ½ **2000** Focuses on seven years in the life of John Lennon—from the purchase of his first guitar to the Beatles arrival in America. Flashbacks show a teenage John (McQuillian) in 1957 Liverpool teaming up with art school pal Stu Sutcliffe (Williams) and meeting Paul (McGowan) and George (Rice-Oxley). There's the trip to Hamburg, the group's meeting with eventual manager Brian Epstein (Glover), Ringo (Ealey) becoming the band's drummer, and the first recordings. Skims the surface but, of course, the music is excellent. **87m/C; VHS, DVD.** Phillip McQuillan; Daniel McGowan; Mark Rice-Oxley; Lee Williams; Jamie Glover; Scot Williams; Blair Brown; Kristian Ealey; Christine Kavanagh; Gillian Kearney; Palina Jonsdottir; ***D:*** David Carson; ***W:*** Michael O'Hara; ***C:*** Lawrence Jones; ***M:*** Dennis McCarthy. **TV**

In Hot Pursuit ½ *Polk County Pot Plane* **1977** Convicted for drug smuggling, two young men stage a daring but not too exciting escape from a southern prison. **90m/C; VHS, DVD.** Bob Watson; Debbie Washington; ***D:*** Jim West.

The In-Laws **1979 (PG)** A wild comedy with Falk, who claims to be a CIA agent, and Arkin, a dentist whose daughter is marrying Falk's son. The fathers foil a South American dictator's counterfeiting scheme in a delightfully convoluted plot. **103m/C; VHS, DVD, Blu-Ray.** Peter Falk; Alan Arkin; Richard Libertini; Nancy Dussault; Penny Peyser; Arlene Golonka; Michael Lembeck; Ed Begley, Jr.; Rosanna Desoto; Art Evans; Eduardo Noriega; ***D:*** Arthur Hiller; ***W:*** Andrew Bergman; ***M:*** John Morris.

The In-Laws ½ **2003 (PG-13)** According to Douglas and Brooks this isn't really a remake of the 1979 Peter Falk/Alan Arkin comedy. They're right. That one was funny. Douglas is the groom's (Reynolds) dad, a CIA operative on the trail of a French weapons dealer and Brooks is the bride's neurotic podiatrist pop, who's shanghaied for the mission and becomes the object of the bad guy's affections. The tedious script avoids laughter at every turn, while Brooks and Douglas never seem to click as a comic duo. Bergen is amusing in her too few scenes as Douglas's New Age ex, while Reynolds does well with what little he's given to do. **98m/C; VHS, DVD.** Michael Douglas; Albert Brooks; Candice Bergen; Robin Tunney; Ryan Reynolds; Lindsay Sloane; David Suchet; Maria Ricossa; Russell Andrews; ***D:*** Andrew Fleming; ***W:*** Nat Mauldin; Edward Solomon; ***C:*** Alexander Grusynski; ***M:*** Jocelyn Pook.

In Like Flint ½ **1967** Sequel to "Our Man Flint" sees our dapper spy confronting an organization of women endeavoring to take over the world. Spy spoofery at its low-level best. **107m/C; VHS, DVD, Blu-Ray.** James Coburn; Lee J. Cobb; Anna Lee; Andrew Duggan; Jean Hale; ***D:*** Gordon Douglas; ***W:*** Hal Fimberg; ***C:*** William H. Daniels; ***M:*** Jerry Goldsmith.

In Love and War ½ **1958** Unmemorable war drama. Three young men join the Marines at the beginning of World War II, experiencing romance and fighting in the Pacific. Wrong side of the tracks Frankie (Wagner) is worried about being a coward in battle; rich kid Alan (Dillman) leaves his drunken socialite girlfriend (Wynter) for romance with native nurse Kalai (Nuyen) in Hawaii; and patriotic Nico (Hunter) marries his pregnant girlfriend (Lange) but is afraid he'll be killed in action. **106m/C; DVD.** Robert Wagner; Jeffrey Hunter; Bradford Dillman; Sheree North; Dana Wynter; Hope Lange; France Nuyen; Mort Sahl; ***D:*** Philip Dunne; ***W:*** Edward Anhalt; ***C:*** Leo Tover; ***M:*** Hugo Friedhofer.

In Love and War ½ **1991 (R)** Woods plays Navy pilot Jim Stockdale, whose plane was grounded over hostile territory and who endured nearly eight years of torture as a POW. Meanwhile, wife Sybil is an organizer of POW wives back in the States. Low octane rendering of the US Navy Commander's true story. Aaron earlier directed "The Miracle Worker," and you may recognize Ngor from "The Killing Fields." **96m/C; VHS, DVD.** James Woods; Jane Alexander; Haing S. Ngor; Concetta Tomei; Richard McKenzie; James Pax; ***D:*** Paul Aaron; ***W:*** Carol Schreder.

In Love and War ½ **1996 (PG-13)** Tells the story of 19-year-old Ernest Hemingway's (O'Donnell) romance with 27-year-old Red Cross nurse Agnes (Bullock) while both were stationed in Italy during WWI. This romance later served as the basis for Hemingway's novel "A Farewell to Arms." Here's a thought. Read the book instead. The boyish O'Donnell is so miscast as testosterone-junkie Hemingway, the only analogy would be having Sylvester Stallone play Truman Capote. The lack of passion and chemistry between the two stars is unsettling, and the action is just plain clunky. Bullock looks great in a nurse's uniform, though. Adapted from "Hemingway in Love and War: The Lost Diary of Agnes Von Kurowsky" by Henry Villard and James Nagel. **115m/C; VHS, DVD.** Chris O'Donnell; Sandra Bullock; MacKenzie Astin; Ingrid Lacey; Emilio Bonucci; Margot Steinberg; Colin Stinton; Ian Kelly; Richard Blackburn; ***D:*** Richard Attenborough; ***W:*** Allan Scott; Anna Hamilton Phelan; Clancy Sigal; Dimitri Villard; ***C:*** Roger Pratt; ***M:*** George Fenton.

In Love and War ½ **2001** British commando Eric Newby (Blue) is captured by the Italian army in 1942 and held as a POW until the Italian Armistice in 1943. He is released just before the advancing German forces and is rescued by a group of anti-fascist farmers, including lovely Wanda (Bobulova). They fall in love but Eric is betrayed and Wanda risks her life to warn him so he can escape. But can he bear to leave her behind? Based on Newby's autobiography "Love and War in the Apennines." **98m/C; VHS, DVD.** Callum Blue; Barbara Bobulova; Peter Bowles; Nick Reding; John Warnaby; Toby Jones; Robert Weatherby; Nicholas Gallagher; ***D:*** John Kent Harrison; ***W:*** John Mortimer; ***C:*** Giovanni Fiore Coltellacci; ***M:*** Nicola Piovani. **TV**

In Love We Trust *Zuo You* **2007** Mei Zhu and Xiao Lu are divorced and both have remarried with Mei Zhu having custody of their five-year-old daughter Hehe. When they learn that Hehe is dying from leukemia, the doctor informs them that the best chance for Hehe's survival is for Mei Zhu and Xiao Lu to have another child (via in-vitro fertilization) and use the baby's umbilical cord blood for a transplant. Naturally, this is a shock to both their spouses but Mei Zhu becomes obsessed with doing anything that will save her child, regardless of the upset to everyone's lives. Mandarin with subtitles. **115m/C; DVD.** *CH* Weiwei Liu; Jia-yi Zhang; Nan Yu; Taisheng Chen; Chuqian Zhang; ***D:*** Xiaoshuai Wang; ***W:*** Xiaoshuai Wang; ***C:*** Di Wu; ***M:*** Wei Dou.

In My Country *Country of My Skull* **2004 (R)** High-minded, well-intentioned, and oh-so-serious neocolonial drama. Based on the memoir "Country of My Skull" by Afrikaans poet Antjie Krog, a personal account of the 1996 Truth and Reconciliation Commission, investigating human rights abuses under apartheid. Washington Post reporter Langston Whitfield (Jackson) covers the hearings and meets poet/journalist Anna Malan (Binoche), who's doing daily radio broadcasts about the event. They each have their prejudices; they argue and, no surprise, find romance. The strongest moments are actually between Whitfield and his interviewee, Col. De Jager (Gleeson), a brutal cop who tries to explain his actions. Binoche seems merely bewildered. **100m/C; DVD, Blu-Ray.** *US GB IR* Samuel L. Jackson; Juliette Binoche; Brendan Gleeson; Menzi "Ngubs" Ngubane; Sam Ngakane; Aletta Bezuidenhout; Lionel Newton; Langley Kirkwood; Owen Sejake; Harriet Manamela; Louis Van Niekirk; Jeremiah Ndlovu; Fiona Ramsay; Charley Boorman; ***D:*** John Boorman; ***W:*** Ann Peacock; ***C:*** Seamus Deasy.

In My Dreams ½ **2014** Sweet romantic fantasy from Hallmark Hall of Fame. Cutie pie Natalie (McPhee) and hunky Nick (Vogel) are both having professional and romantic issues. They happen to each toss a coin into a park fountain and then suddenly start dreaming about each other. Of course they don't realize that their dream lover is an actual person as other romantic possibilities pop up to confuse the when-will-they-ever-meet issue. **90m/C; DVD.** Katharine McPhee; Mike Vogel; JoBeth Williams; Antonio Cupo; Rachel (Racheal) Skarsten; Jessalyn Wanlim; ***D:*** Kenny Leon; ***W:*** Teena Booth; Suzette Couture; ***C:*** James Chressanthis; ***M:*** William Ross. **TV**

In My Father's House **2015 (R)** This moving, insightful feature-length documentary looks at issues such as identity and legacy in the African-American family. The film centers on Grammy Award-winning rapper Che "Rhymefest" Smith, who was raised in a broken home on the South Side of Chicago. He did not see his father, Brian, for more than two decades and assumed he was dead, until he bought his father's childhood home. Trying to find out what happened to his father, Che learns that Brian is a homeless alcoholic living nearby. As the father and son reconnect, they try to build a new relationship and create a new legacy. **93m/C; DVD, Download.** ***D:*** Ricki Stern; Anne Sundberg; ***W:*** Ricki Stern; Anne Sundberg; Pax Wassermann; ***C:*** Charles Miller; ***M:*** Paul Brill; Elizabeth Ziman.

In My Pocket ½ **2011** Stephen Jameson thinks of himself as a functioning addict but after nearly dying from an overdose, his parents send him to rehab. There Stephen meets rock star Rob Vills, who's also struggling to stay clean while his band goes on tour without him. Now both men have to decide what to do next. **90m/C; DVD.** Gregory Edward Smith; Zack (Zach) Ward; Shantel VanSanten; Brendan Sexton, III; Jamie McShane; Kaylee DeFer; ***D:*** David Lisle Johnson; ***W:*** David Lisle Johnson; ***C:*** Miguel Bunsten; ***M:*** Christopher Kemp Fredie. **VIDEO**

In Name Only ½ **1939** Somber drama about a heartless woman who marries for wealth and prestige and holds her husband to a loveless marriage. Based on "Memory of Love" by Bessie Brewer. **102m/B; VHS, DVD.** Carole Lombard; Cary Grant; Kay Francis; Charles Coburn; ***D:*** John Cromwell.

In Old California ½ **1942** Plucky story of a young Boston pharmacist who searches for success in the California gold rush and runs into the local crime boss. Also available colorized. **88m/B; VHS, DVD, Blu-Ray.** John Wayne; Patsy Kelly; Binnie Barnes; Albert Dekker; Charles Halton; ***D:*** William McGann.

In Old Chicago **1937** The O'Leary family travels to Chicago to seek their fortune, with mom working as a washerwoman to support her sons. Brothers Power and Ameche become power-broking rivals and when mom comes to break up a brawl between the two, she neglects to properly restrain the family cow. This leads to the great Chicago fire of 1871, supposedly started when the cow kicks over a latern and sets the barn ablaze. The city burns down in a spectacular 20-minute sequence. Based on the story "We the O'Learys" by Niven Busch. **115m/B; VHS, DVD.** Tyrone Power; Alice Faye; Don Ameche; Alice Brady; Andy Devine; Brian Donlevy; Phyllis Brooks; Tom Brown; Sidney Blackmer; Gene Reynolds; Berton Churchill; Bobs Watson; ***D:*** Henry King; ***W:*** Lamar Trotti; Sonya Levien. Oscars '37: Support. Actress (Brady).

In Old Kentucky ½ **1935** The Shattucks and the Martingales are fussing, feuding race horse owners. Steve Tapley (Rogers) is the Shattucks' trainer but gets fired for helping out crazy old coot Ezra Martingale (Sellon). So Steve decides to train the Martingale's horse Greyboy to run against the Shattucks' horse Emperor in a big race. Rogers' last released film. **86m/B; DVD.** Will Rogers; Dorothy Wilson; Charles Sellon; Louise Henry; Russell Hardie; Charles Richman; Alan Dinehart; Esther Dale; Gladys Lehman; ***D:*** George Marshall; ***W:*** Sam Hellman; ***C:*** L. William O'Connell; ***M:*** Arthur Lange.

In Order of Disappearance ½ *Kraftidioten* **2014 (R)** A Norway-set action crime thriller centered on one father's quest for revenge. A snow plower in Norwegian winters, Nils (Skasgard) undergoes a profound change after his son is murdered for something he did not do. When Nils seeks revenge for his death, he starts a war between the vegan gangster known as "The Count" (Hagen) and Papa (Ganz), a Serbian crime boss. Nils remains in it to win it using the tools he has at hand to ensure those responsible for his son's death suffer. Norwegian, Swedish, Danish, Serbian, and German with subtitles. **116m/C; DVD, Blu-Ray, Streaming, Download.** Stellan Skarsgard; Bruno Ganz; Pal Sverre Hagen; Peter Andersson; Jakob Oftebro; ***D:*** Hans Petter Moland; ***W:*** Kim Fupz Aaekson; ***C:*** Philip Ogaard; ***M:*** Brian Batz; Kaspar Kaae; Kare Vestrheim.

In Praise of Love *Eloge de L'Amour; Eulogy of Love* **2001** The aged New Wave pioneer has made a generally incomprehensible, didactic, visually interesting film that will be mostly of interest to Godard completists. Director Edgar (Putzulu) is in the process of casting his latest production (which is about the stages of love) but discovers the young woman, Berthe, he wants for his lead has committed suicide. The film then flashes back a couple of years to Edgar interviewing an elderly couple who fought in the Resistance and who are thinking of selling their story for an American film. Their granddaughter, who turns out to be Berthe, is present at the interview. French with subtitles. **98m/C; VHS, DVD.** *FR SI* Bruno Putzulu; Cecile Camp; Jean Davy; Francoise Verney; Audrey Klebaner; Jeremy Lippman; Claude Baigneres; ***D:*** Jean-Luc Godard; ***W:*** Jean-Luc Godard; ***C:*** Christophe Pollock; Julien Hirsch.

In Praise of Older Women **1978** Berenger is just right as a young Hungarian who is corrupted by WWII and a large number of older women. Based on a novel by Stephen Vizinczey. **110m/C; VHS, DVD.** *CA* Karen Black; Tom Berenger; Susan Strasberg; Helen Shaver; Alexandra Stewart; ***D:*** George Kaczender.

In Pursuit **2000 (R)** Attorney Rick Alvarez (Baldwin) is accused of murdering his lover Katherine's (Schiffer) rich husband (Stockwell) and goes on the lam to Mexico. Routine thriller. **91m/C; VHS, DVD.** Daniel Baldwin; Claudia Schiffer; Coolio; Sarah Lassez; Dean Stockwell; ***D:*** Peter Pistor; ***W:*** Peter Pistor; John Penney; ***C:*** Richard Crudo. **VIDEO**

In Pursuit of Honor ½ **1995 (PG-13)** Based on the true story of five American cavalry soldiers who find themselves being phased out in the 1935 Army. Ordered by General Douglas MacArthur to destroy their horses, they instead try to outrun an elite tank division to get some 400 horses to safety in Canada. Rugged performances and the violence towards the horses is aptly disturbing. Filmed on location in Australia and New Zealand. **110m/C; VHS, DVD.** Don Johnson; Craig Sheffer; Gabrielle Anwar; Bob Gunton; Rod Steiger; James B. Sikking; John Dennis Johnston; Robert Coleby; ***D:*** Ken Olin; ***W:*** Dennis Lynton Clark; ***C:*** Stephen F. Windon; ***M:*** John Debney. **CABLE**

In Search of a Golden Sky **1984 (PG)** Following their mother's death, a motley group of children move in with their secluded cabin-dwelling uncle, much to the righteous chagrin of the welfare department. **94m/C; VHS, DVD.** Charles Napier; George "Buck" Flower; Cliff Osmond; ***D:*** Jefferson (Jeff) Richard.

In Search of Fellini ½ **2017 (R)** A coming of age travel movie inspired by the movies. In 1993, Lucy (Solo) has grown up insulated from reality by her mother Claire

(Bello). Lucy's worldview is forever changed when she attends a screening of Fellini's La Strada and seeks out more of his films...and then him. She calls Fellini's office in Rome and is offered an appointment with him the following afternoon. Because her secretly ill mother cannot travel, she encourages Lucy to go alone. In Italy, Lucy experiences the unexpected. Though the idealized premise is sentimental and incredulous, the film is polished and features a thoughtful performance by Solo. **93m/C; DVD.** Maria Bello; Ksenia Solo; David O'Connell; Mary Lynn Rajskub; Beth Riesgraf; ***D:*** Taron Lexton; ***W:*** Nancy Cartwright; Peter Kjenaas; ***C:*** Kevin Garrison; ***M:*** David Campbell.

In Search of Greatness 2018 **(PG-13)** An insightful documentary exploration of greatness in sports by filmmaker Polsky who considers the careers of sports legends such as Rocky Marciano, Wayne Gretzky, Jerry Rice, and Pele. Through interviews with athletes, parents, and coaches, Polsky emphasizes and illustrates the importance of factors such as vision, innovation, knowledge, and imagination over technique and training. By looking at how these athletes approached problem-solving, were extremely determined, and loved their sports, Polsky shows that success is not usually measurable in ways that are often used by professional sports such as the NFL Scouting Combine. **77m/C; DVD.** ***D:*** Gabe Polsky; ***W:*** Gabe Polsky; ***C:*** Svetlana Cvetko; ***M:*** Leo Birenberg.

In Search of the Castaways **1962** Stirring adventure tale of a teenage girl and her younger brother searching for their father, a ship's captain lost at sea years earlier. Powerful special effects and strong cast make this a winning Disney effort. Based on a story by Jules Verne. **98m/C; VHS, DVD, Blu-Ray.** *GB* Hayley Mills; Maurice Chevalier; George Sanders; Wilfrid Hyde-White; Michael Anderson, Jr.; ***D:*** Robert Stevenson.

In Secret *Therese* **2013 (R)** Yawn. Well-staged and beautifully cast, one still can't help but feel lulled into sleep by this overblown drama based on Emile Zola's novel, "Therese Raquin." The great Olsen plays Raquin, a sexually repressed young woman who is stuck in a horrible marriage with her dull cousin (Felton). Of course, Therese's life changes when she meets a childhood friend of her husband's, Laurent (Isaac). Her affair with Laurent should be a sexually charged, scandalous bit of filmmaking but the film's too familiar and too boring to be effective. **101m/C; DVD, Blu-Ray.** Elizabeth Olsen; Oscar Isaac; Jessica Lange; Tom Felton; Shirley Henderson; Matt Lucas; ***D:*** Charles (Charlie) Stratton; ***W:*** Charles (Charlie) Stratton; ***C:*** Florian Hoffmeister; ***M:*** Gabriel Yared.

In Society 1/2 **1944** The duo play dim-witted plumbers who are mistakenly invited to a high society party, where they promptly create catastrophe. **84m/B; VHS, DVD.** Bud Abbott; Lou Costello; Marion Hutton; Kirby Grant; Ann Gillis; Arthur Treacher; Thomas Gomez; Steven Geray; Margaret Irving; Thurston Hall; ***Cameo(s):*** Sid Fields; ***D:*** Jean Yarbrough; ***W:*** Sid Fields; Hal Fimberg; Edmund L. Hartmann; John Grant.

In the Aisles 1/2 *In Den Gangen* **2019** Shy, slightly awkward Christian (Rogowski) begins his new job as the night shift head of the beverage department of a big box grocery store. Over time, Christian slowly becomes part of the store's community of workers who often socialize with each other. He even develops a crush on his married coworker Marion (Huller), and the pair flirt. Through sometimes difficult events, the workers retain a sense of camaraderie that is the heart of the film. Though the slice-of-life drama is set in Germany, its themes are universal and the filmmaker successfully emphasizes his characters' humanity. German with subtitles. **125m/C; DVD.** Sandra Hüller; Franz Rogowski; Peter Kurth; Henning Peker; Gerdy Zint; ***D:*** Thomas Stuber; ***W:*** Thomas Stuber; Clemens Meyer; ***C:*** Peter Matjasko; ***M:*** Milena Fessmann.

In the Arms of My Enemy 1/2 *Voleurs de Chevaux; Horse Thieves* **2007** An eastern western. In the early 1800s, brothers Jakub (Jolivet) and Valdimir (Leprince-Rinquet) escape their lives of poverty by joining the vicious Cossack army. Meanwhile, gypsy brothers Roman (Colin) and Elias (Dupont) are horse thieves and their lives intersect when Vladimir is killed by Roman, who's stealing their horses. Now a vengeful Jakub is after him. Little dialogue, lots of violence. French with subtitles. **87m/C; DVD.** *FR BE CA* Gregoire Colin; Gregoire Leprince-Ringuet; Adrien Jolivet; Francois-Rene Dupont; ***D:*** Micha Wald; ***W:*** Micha Wald; ***C:*** Jean-Paul de Zaeytijd; ***M:*** Stephan Micus; Johann Johannsson; Jef Mercelis.

In the Army Now **1994 (PG)** Pauly dude gets his head shaved, man. Service comedy about a slacker who joins the Army hoping to cash in on military benefits but who winds up in combat instead. Shore drops the Valley Guy shtick and ventures into the land of action when he gets sent on a mission to the Sahara. Strictly for Shore's fans. **92m/C; VHS, DVD.** Pauly Shore; Esai Morales; Lori Petty; David Alan Grier; Ernie Hudson; Andy Dick; ***D:*** Daniel Petrie, Jr.; ***W:*** Daniel Petrie, Jr.; Ken Kaufman; Fax Bahr; Stu Krieger; Adam Small; ***M:*** Robert Folk.

In the Bedroom 1/2 **2001 (R)** Spacek and Wilkinson are a middle age couple who lose their son to violence. The numbing grief, paralyzing emotional swirl, and long-simmering but long-denied marital resentments that follow combine to drastically alter their marriage and lives. Field's impressive, if gut-wrenching directorial debut shows trust for the script and in the actors by not overplaying the obvious emotional moments, or the dramatic twists. This trust is rewarded with exceptional performances by Spacek, Wilkinson, and Tomei (in her best performance to date), and by a film that doesn't miss a chance to be subtle when it's called for, or explosive when it's needed. **131m/C; VHS, DVD.** Sissy Spacek; Tom Wilkinson; Nick Stahl; Marisa Tomei; William Mapother; William Wise; Celia Weston; Karen Allen; ***D:*** Todd Field; ***W:*** Todd Field; Rob Festinger; ***C:*** Antonio Calvache; ***M:*** Thomas Newman. Golden Globes '02: Actress--Drama (Spacek); Ind. Spirit '02: Actor (Wilkinson), Actress (Spacek), First Feature; L.A. Film Critics '01: Actress (Spacek), Film; Natl. Bd. of Review '01: Director (Field), Screenplay; N.Y. Film Critics '01: Actor (Wilkinson), Actress (Spacek), First Feature; Broadcast Film Critics '01: Actress (Spacek).

In the Blood **2006** Campy, low-budget gay horror played, uh, straight. A serial killer is attacking pretty blonde co-eds, which has pretty, blonde Jessica (Flynn) freaked out. Especially since her sexually confused brother Cassidy (Hanes) keeps having vague visions of her bloody corpse, which are followed by his suffering wicked nose bleeds. It seems Cassidy could get a much clearer image (and stop his blood loss) if he would just come out of the closet. **82m/C; DVD.** Carlos Valencia; Tyler Hanes; James Katherine Flynn; Graeme Malcolm; Robert Dionne; Alison Fraser; ***D:*** Lou Peterson; ***W:*** Lou Peterson; ***C:*** Aaron Medick; ***M:*** Sasha Gordon. **VIDEO**

In the Blood **2013 (R)** Carano stars in this essentially straight-to-DVD piece of garbage about a woman whose husband goes missing on their Caribbean honeymoon after a zip-lining accident. Was it the tough guy they got into a fight with the night before? The clearly corrupt cops and other people who put no effort into finding him? Or someone else entirely? You won't care at all. Better question: Why did someone make a Carano action movie with almost no action? **108m/C; DVD, Blu-Ray.** Gina Carano; Cam Gigandet; Danny Trejo; Luis Guzman; Stephen Lang; Amaury Nolasco; Treat Williams; ***D:*** John Stockwell; ***W:*** James Robert Johnson; Bennett Yellin; ***C:*** P.J. Lopez; ***M:*** Paul Haslinger.

In the City of Sylvia 1/2 *En La Ciudad de Sylvia* **2007** An artist's quest to find his former love/muse is at the heart of this poetic, meditative drama. Six years ago, El (Latiffe) was in Strasbourg and fell in love. He returns to find te love he cannot forget amidst the winding streets of this German city. As part of his quest, he sketches diners of an outdoor cafe. Though El believes he has sighted her, he wants to make sure he does not lose her or love this time. French and Spanish with subtitles. **90m/C; DVD.** Pilar Lopez de Ayala; Xavier Lafitte; Laurence Cordier; Tanja Czichy; Eric Dietrich; ***D:*** Jose Luis Guerin; ***W:*** Jose Luis Guerin; ***C:*** Natasha Braier.

In the Cold of the Night **1989 (R)** Another drowsy entry into the "to sleep perchance to have a nightmare genre." A photographer with a vivid imagination dreams he murders a woman he doesn't know, and when said dream girl rides into his life on the back of a Harley, Mr. Foto's faced with an etiquette quandary: haven't they met before? Cast includes Hedren (Hitchcock's Marnie and Melanie Griffith's mother). **112m/C; VHS, DVD, Blu-Ray.** Jeff Lester; Adrienne Sachs; Shannon Tweed; David Soul; John Beck; Tippi Hedren; Marc Singer; ***D:*** Nico Mastorakis; ***W:*** Nico Mastorakis; ***C:*** Andreas Bellis.

In the Company of Men **1996 (R)** A couple of dissatisfied Yuppies, Chad (Eckhart) and Howard (Malloy), are sent on a six-week job out of town by their home office. Grumbling about the lack of control in their lives (and blaming it on women), Chad formulates a nasty plan (to which Howard eventually agrees)?they'll deliberately get involved with the same girl, secretary Christine (Edwards), string her along, and then abandon her when their job is done. But Chad actually has his own agenda and bigger corporate ideas in mind. Think misogynistic satire. **93m/C; VHS, DVD.** Matt Malloy; Aaron Eckhart; Stacy Edwards; Mark Rector; Jason Dixie; Emily Cline; Michael Martin; Chris Hayes; ***D:*** Neil LaBute; ***W:*** Neil LaBute; ***C:*** Anthony P. Hettinger; ***M:*** Ken Williams. Ind. Spirit '98: Debut Perf. (Eckhart), First Screenplay; Sundance '97: Filmmakers Trophy.

In the Cool of the Day 1/2 **1963** Ho-hum soap opera based on the Susan Ertz novel. Christine Bonner (Fonda) is the unhappy young wife of overprotective Sam (Hill). He asks his friend Murray (Finch) to help him but since Murray is in a long loveless marriage to Sybil (Lansbury), he can't offer romantic advice. The two couples plan a vacation to Athens but, ultimately, it's Christine and Murray who get to enjoy the romantic atmosphere. **88m/C; DVD.** Jane Fonda; Peter Finch; Arthur Hill; Angela Lansbury; Constance Cummings; Alexander Knox; ***D:*** Robert Stevens; ***W:*** Meade Roberts; ***C:*** Peter Newbrook; ***M:*** Francis Chagrin.

In the Custody of Strangers **1982** A teenager's parents refuse to help when he is arrested for being drunk and he ends up spending the night in jail. Realistic handling of a serious subject. Real-life father and son Sheen and Estevez play father and son. **100m/C; VHS, Streaming.** Martin Sheen; Jane Alexander; Emilio Estevez; Kenneth McMillan; Ed Lauter; Matt Clark; John Hancock; ***D:*** Robert Greenwald. **TV**

In the Cut **2003 (R)** Meg Ryan, in an attempt to break out of her sweet, blond, comic romance roles takes on the part of a sexually repressed teacher who engages in an affair with a suspected serial killer. The sex scenes are appropriately steamy, but a weak plot and so-so acting conspire to undercut the suspense. Based on the Susanna Moore novel. **113m/C; VHS, DVD, Blu-Ray.** *US AU* Meg Ryan; Mark Ruffalo; Jennifer Jason Leigh; Kevin Bacon; Nick Damici; Sharrieff Pugh; ***D:*** Jane Campion; ***W:*** Jane Campion; Susanna Moore; ***C:*** Dion Beebe; ***M:*** Hilmar Orn Hilmarsson.

In the Days of the Thundering Herd & the Law & the Outlaw **1914** In the first feature, a pony express rider sacrifices his job to accompany his sweetheart on a westward trek to meet her father. In the second show, a fugitive falls in love with a rancher's daughter and risks recognition. **76m/B; Silent; VHS, DVD.** Tom Mix; Myrtle Stedman; ***D:*** Colin Campbell.

In the Dead of Space 1/2 **1999 (R)** Confusing sci fier has the space station Tesla becoming the target of saboteurs, who are determined to crash the ship into Los Angeles. **85m/C; VHS, DVD.** Michael Paré; Lisa Bingley; Tony Curtis Blondell; ***D:*** Eli Necakov. **VIDEO**

In the Deep Woods **1991** Children's author Joanna Warren (Arquette) gets too close to mayhem when a childhood friend is murdered by the Deep Woods Killer. A mysterious private detective (Perkins) is on the killer's trail but when Joanna comes into the picture will she be a suspect or a victim? Based on the book by Nicholas Conde. **96m/C; VHS, DVD.** Rosanna Arquette; Anthony Perkins; Will Patton; D.W. Moffett; Christopher Rydell; Harold Sylvester; Kimberly Beck; ***D:*** Charles Correll; ***W:*** Robert Nathan; Robert Rosenbaum; ***C:*** James Glennon.

In the Electric Mist 1/2 **2008 (R)** Generally disappointing adaptation of the James Lee Burke novel "In the Electric Mist with Confederate Dead," which features his veteran detective Dave Robicheaux. Robicheaux (Jones) thinks a series of murders are linked to New Orleans mobster Balboni (Goodman). But he has other problems: back in New Iberia, the star (Sarsgaard) of a Civil War film shooting in the area claims he found the corpse of a black man in a swamp and there are reports of ghostly Confederate soldiers making an appearance. Corruption and long-buried secrets surface to threaten Robicheaux's own family. It helps to be familiar with the mystery series to understand the characters, and the various plot threads don't hang together very well. **102m/C; DVD, Blu-Ray.** Tommy Lee Jones; John Goodman; Peter Sarsgaard; Kelly Macdonald; Mary Steenburgen; Justina Machado; Ned Beatty; James Gammon; Pruitt Taylor Vince; Levon Helm; Buddy Guy; ***D:*** Bertrand Tavernier; ***W:*** Jerzy Kromolowski; ***C:*** Bruno de Keyzer; ***M:*** Marco Beltrami.

In the Eyes of a Killer **2009** Routine psycho-thriller. Jack Newman feels he's adjusted to being blind after an accident until he's offered a chance to regain his sight with experimental surgery. His fiancée Gwen is soon noticing personality changes as Jack struggles with violent impulses. Then they find out the donor was an executed psychopath killer. **96m/C; DVD.** Louis Mandylor; Gwendolyn Edwards; Costas Mandylor; Randy Colton; ***D:*** Louis Mandylor; ***W:*** Mamie Jean Calvert; ***C:*** Ted Caloroso; ***M:*** Deane Ogden. **VIDEO**

In the Fade 1/2 *Aus dem Nichts* **2017 (R)** A vigilante justice film that examines immigrant tensions in Germany. One day, Katja (Kruger) drops off her young son Rocco (Santana) with her husband, Turkish immigrant Nuri (Acar), at their tax consulting firm. When she returns, she learns that the office was destroyed in an explosion and her loved ones are dead. Though Katja is convinced that neo-Nazis are involved, the police believe the bombing is related to Nuri's drug dealing past. As Katja deeply struggles, the police ultimately arrest a neo-Nazi couple, but justice remains elusive. Though the plotting is muddled, the film is stylish, detailed, and powerful. German with subtitles. **106m/C; DVD, Blu-Ray.** Diane Kruger; Denis Moschitto; Numan Acar; Samia Muriel Chancrin; Johannes Krisch; ***D:*** Fatih Akin; ***W:*** Fatih Akin; Hark Bohm; ***C:*** Rainer Klausmann; ***M:*** Joshua Homme. Golden Globes '18: Foreign Film.

In the Family 1/2 **2011** A hot-button topic is handled with fair-mindedness, dignity, and restraint in Wang's lengthy debut feature. Joey Williams and his partner Cody Hines have raised Cody's son Chip together in their conservative Tennessee community since the boy was an infant. When Cody is killed in a car crash, Joey expects to continue raising six-year-old Chip until Cody's sister Eileen reveals Cody never updated his will and she and her husband Dave are Chip's guardians. They immediately remove Chip and, despite the odds and his emotions, Joey pursues his custody case with the help of retired lawyer Paul Hawks. **169m/C; DVD, Blu-Ray.** Kelly McAndrew; Patrick Wang; Sebastian Banes; Trevor St. John; Brian Murray; Park Overall; Susan Kellerman; Peter Hermann; Elaine Bromka; ***D:*** Patrick Wang; ***W:*** Patrick Wang; ***C:*** Frank Barrera; ***M:*** Chip Taylor; Andy Wagner.

In the Flesh **1997** Closeted Atlanta police detective Philip (Corbin) is working an undercover drug operation that puts him in a gay bar. Which is where he meets Oliver (Ritter), a student by day/hustler by night. When Oliver witnesses a murder, it's Philip who provides him with an alibi, a place to stay, and a new relationship, even though it nearly destroys his own career. But then it seems Philip and Oliver have other connections besides sex. **105m/C; VHS, DVD.** Dane Ritter; Ed Corbin; Roxzane T. Mims; Adrian Roberts; ***D:*** Ben Taylor; ***W:*** Ben Taylor; ***C:*** Brian Gurley; ***M:*** Eddie Horst.

In the French Style 🦴🦴 **1963** American Christina (Seberg) is studying art in Paris and has a series of romances before falling for correspondent Walter Beddoes (Baker). Their continuous separations take their toll and when Christina's wealthy father (Powell) visits, he finally convinces her that she's not so much a free-spirit as a kept woman and needs to rethink her life. Shaw wrote the novel and the screenplay. **105m/B; DVD, Blu-Ray.** Jean Seberg; Stanley Baker; Addison Powell; Philippe Forquet; James Leo Herlihy; Maurice Teynac; ***D:*** Robert Parrish; ***W:*** Irwin Shaw; ***C:*** Michel Kelber; ***M:*** Joseph Kosma.

In the Good Old Summertime 🦴🦴🦴 **1949** This pleasant musical version of "The Shop Around the Corner" tells the story of two bickering co-workers who are also anonymous lovelorn pen pals. Minnelli made her second screen appearance at 18 months in the final scene. **104m/C; VHS, DVD.** Judy Garland; Van Johnson; S.Z. Sakall; Buster Keaton; Spring Byington; Liza Minnelli; Clinton Sundberg; ***D:*** Robert Z. Leonard; ***C:*** Harry Stradling, Sr.

In the Heart of the Sea 🦴🦴 **2015 (PG-13)** Who knew Moby Dick was really about difficulties in the whaling industry? Howard delivers one of the most miscalculated films of his career, a 3D piece that feels like Oscar bait that even the Academy turned their nose away from en masse. It is winter in New England in 1820 when the whaling ship Essex sets sail. Before long, they are overtaken by a massive whale, leaving the surviving crew clinging to what remains of the ship. As conditions get worse, the captain (Hemsworth) has to keep his men fighting to survive while his first mate still wants to get that elusive whale. **?m/C; DVD, Blu-Ray.** Chris Hemsworth; Benjamin Walker; Cillian Murphy; Brendan Gleeson; Ben Whishaw; ***D:*** Ron Howard; ***W:*** Charles Leavitt; ***C:*** Anthony Dod Mantle; ***M:*** Roque Baños.

In the Heat of the Night 🦴🦴🦴 ½ **1967** A wealthy industrialist in a small Mississippi town is murdered. A black homicide expert is asked to help solve the murder, despite resentment on the part of the town's chief of police. Powerful script with underlying theme of racial prejudice is served well by taut direction and powerhouse performances. Poitier's memorable character Virgil Tibbs appeared in two more pictures, "They Call Me Mister Tibbs" and "The Organization." **109m/C; VHS, DVD, Blu-Ray.** Sidney Poitier; Rod Steiger; Warren Oates; Lee Grant; ***D:*** Norman Jewison; ***W:*** Stirling Silliphant; ***C:*** Haskell Wexler; ***M:*** Quincy Jones. Oscars '67: Actor (Steiger), Adapt. Screenplay, Film, Film Editing, Sound; British Acad. '67: Actor (Steiger); Golden Globes '68: Actor--Drama (Steiger), Film--Drama, Screenplay; Natl. Film Reg. '02; N.Y. Film Critics '67: Actor (Steiger), Film; Natl. Soc. Film Critics '67: Actor (Steiger), Cinematog.

In the Lake of the Woods 🦴🦴 ½ **1996** Senatorial candidate John Waylan (Strauss) finds his political campaign crashing down when a journalist reveals his part in a Vietnam massacre of civilians. He and wife Kathy (Quinlan) retire to a lakeside cottage to lick their wounds and repair their tattered marriage. But Kathy finds it difficult to reach her distant and increasingly disturbed husband, who's having wartime flashbacks. Then Kathy disappears and the local police, as well as Kathy's sister, suspect that John killed her. Very disturbing TV movie, adapted from the novel by Tim O'Brien. **90m/C; VHS, DVD.** Peter Strauss; Kathleen Quinlan; Peter Boyle; Richard Anderson; Ken Pogue; Nancy Sorel; ***D:*** Carl Schenkel; ***W:*** Philip Rosenberg; ***C:*** Dietrich Lohmann; ***M:*** Don Davis.

In the Land of Blood and Honey 🦴🦴 **2011 (R)** Longtime humanitarian Jolie makes her competent writer/director debut in a harrowing drama set during the Bosnian War in the 1990s. An affair between Bosnian Muslim Ajla and Serbian Christian commander Danijel is fraught with tragedy as artist Ajla is sent to a prison camp where Danijel protects her for his own purposes while justifying (and carrying out) the policy of ethnic cleansing. Although Jolie simultaneously filmed an English-language version, it was decided to only release the Bosnian/Serbian version with subtitles. **127m/C; DVD.** Zana Marjanovic; Goran Kostic; Rade Serbedzija; ***D:*** Angelina Jolie; ***W:*** Angelina Jolie; ***C:*** Dean Semler; ***M:*** Gabriel Yared.

In the Land of Women 🦴🦴 **2006 (PG-13)** Sensitive 26-year-old aspiring screenwriter Carter Webb (Brody) escapes a failed relationship and a nowhere career in L.A. to visit his grouchy ailing grandma, Phyllis (Dukakis), in Michigan. Carter then becomes involved in the lives of neighbors Sarah (Ryan) and Lucy (Stewart) Hardwicke. Sarah's just been diagnosed with breast cancer and has a troubled marriage, while 16-year-old Lucy is acting like an obnoxious brat. Carter becomes the confidante of each, which leads to some emotional fireworks, although the pic is so low-key and familiar it's hard to get involved. Kasdan, making his feature debut, is the son of director Lawrence and younger brother of director Jake. **97m/C; DVD.** Adam Brody; Kristen Stewart; Meg Ryan; Olympia Dukakis; Makenzie Vega; Elena Anaya; Gregg Henry; JoBeth Williams; Dustin Milligan; Ginnifer Goodwin; Clark Gregg; Gina Mantegna; ***D:*** Jonathan Kasdan; ***W:*** Jonathan Kasdan; ***C:*** Paul Cameron; ***M:*** Stephen Trask.

In the Line of Duty: Ambush in Waco 🦴🦴 ½ *Ambush in Waco* **1993 (R)** Insta-TV movie made by NBC even before the fire which engulfed the Texas compound and ended the standoff between self-proclaimed "prophet" David Koresh and the federal government. Daly does well as the manipulative, charasmatic Branch Davidian cult leader whose stockpiling of illegal weapons lead to an investigation by the Bureau of Alcohohol, Tobacco and Firearms and a botched raid which caused the ultimately fatal siege. Filmed on location outside Tulsa, Oklahoma. **93m/C; VHS, DVD.** Timothy Daly; Dan Lauria; William O'Leary; ***D:*** Dick Lowry; ***W:*** Phil Penningroth. **TV**

In the Line of Duty: The FBI Murders 🦴🦴🦴 *The FBI Murders* **1988** A fact-based chiller about the bloody 1986 shootout between Miami FBI agents and a pair of violent killers (Soul and Gross playing against type). **95m/C; VHS, DVD.** David Soul; Michael Gross; Ronny Cox; Bruce Greenwood; Doug Sheehan; Teri Copley; ***D:*** Dick Lowry; ***W:*** Tracy Keenan Wynn. **TV**

In the Line of Fire 🦴🦴🦴 ½ **1993 (R)** Aging Secret Service agent Frank Horrigan (Eastwood) meets his match in a spooky caller, ex-CIA assassin Mitch Leary (Malkovich), who threatens his honor and the president in an exciting, fast-paced cat and mouse game. Terrific performance by Eastwood includes lots of dry humor and an unscripted emotional moment, but is nearly overshadowed by Malkovich's menacing bad guy. Russo is agent Lily Raines, who begins a charmingly tentative romance with Horrigan. Eerie special effects add to the mood. The Secret Service cooperated and most scenes are believable, with a few Hollywood exceptions; the end result clearly pays homage to the agents who protect our presidents. **128m/C; VHS, DVD, Blu-Ray.** Clint Eastwood; John Malkovich; Rene Russo; Dylan McDermott; Gary Cole; Fred Dalton Thompson; John Mahoney; Gregory Alan Williams; John Heard; Tobin Bell; Clyde Kusatsu; Steve Hytner; Bob Schott; Eric Bruskotter; Joshua Malina; Steve Railsback; ***D:*** Wolfgang Petersen; ***W:*** Jeff Maguire; ***C:*** John Bailey; ***M:*** Ennio Morricone.

In the Loop 🦴🦴 **2009** In this British political satire, fumbling development minister Simon Foster (Hollander) gives a radio interview that sends communications minister Malcolm Tucker (Capaldi) apoplectic because the British government is trying to downplay its involvement with the Americans in the imminent invasion of Iraq. Timid Simon is thrust into a media frenzy where his every utterance is analyzed. It's decided he can do less damage by getting shuttled off to Washington, where the Americans decide to use Simon for their own ends. **105m/C; DVD.** *GB* Tom Hollander; Peter Capaldi; Gina McKee; James Gandolfini; Chris Addison; Anna Chlumsky; Paul Higgins; Mimi Kennedy; David Rasche; Steve Coogan; Alex MacQueen; ***D:*** Armando Iannucci; ***W:*** Armando Iannucci; Jesse Armstrong; Simon Blackwell; Tony Roche; ***C:*** Jaimie Cairney; ***M:*** Adem Ilhan.

In the Meantime, Darling 🦴 ½ **1944** Preminger's an odd directorial choice for a light comedy that's only semi-successful. Socialite Maggie (Craine) falls for Army lieutenant Daniel (Latimore) but struggles to adjust to life as a military spouse. She fights with the other wives in their boardinghouse and tries to use her family influence to get her hubby a stateside wartime position. **72m/B; DVD.** Jeanne Crain; Frank Latimore; Eugene Pallette; Mary Nash; Stanley Prager; Gale Robbins; ***D:*** Otto Preminger; ***W:*** Michael Uris; Arthur Kober; ***C:*** Joseph Macdonald; ***M:*** David Buttolph.

In the Mix WOOF! **2005 (PG-13)** This one's a straight-up vehicle for recording artist Usher. If that just made you wonder "Who?" stop here. Darrell (Usher) is a New York City DJ/chick magnet who, as a result of a family friendship, must step in as body guard to a Jersey mobster's daughter, Dolly (Chriqui). A romantic flame ignites between the two. With nowhere else to go, the film becomes a handful of mafia and racial jokes. **97m/C; DVD.** Usher Raymond; Chazz Palminteri; Emmanuelle Chriqui; Robert Davi; Robert Costanzo; Geoff Stults; K.D. Aubert; Kevin Hart; Matt Gerald; Anthony Fazio; ***D:*** Ron Underwood; ***W:*** Jacqueline Zambrano; ***C:*** Clark Mathis; ***M:*** Aaron Zigman.

In the Mood 🦴🦴 ½ **1987 (PG-13)** Based on fact, this is the story of teenager Sonny Wisecarver, nicknamed "The Woo Woo Kid," who in 1944, seduced two older women and eventually landed in jail after marrying one of them. Look for Wisecarver in a cameo role as a mailman in the film. **98m/C; VHS, DVD.** Patrick Dempsey; Beverly D'Angelo; Talia Balsam; Michael Constantine; Betty Jinnette; Kathleen Freeman; Peter Hobbs; Edith Fellows; ***Cameo(s):*** Ellsworth Wisecarver; ***D:*** Phil Alden Robinson; ***W:*** Phil Alden Robinson; ***M:*** Ralph Burns.

In the Mood for Love 🦴🦴 ½ **2000 (PG)** Romantic melodrama set in the Shanghai community of Hong Kong in 1962. Newspaper editor Chow (Leung Chiu-Wai) and his wife have just moved into a new apartment across the hall from Li-zhen (Cheung) and her husband. Both their respective spouses are away from home a great deal, traveling on business, so the lonely duo begin a tentative friendship. Then Chow begins to suspect his wife is having an affair and it quickly becomes apparent that it's with Li-zhen's husband. Gorgeous to look at, melancholy in tone, if somewhat oblique. Chinese with subtitles. **98m/C; VHS, DVD, Blu-Ray.** *CH* Tony Leung Chiu-Wai; Maggie Cheung; Rebecca Pan; Lai Chen; Siu Ping-Lam; ***D:*** Wong Kar-Wai; ***W:*** Wong Kar-Wai; ***C:*** Christopher Doyle; Mark Ping Bin Lee; ***M:*** Michael Galasso; Shingeru Umebayashi. Cannes '00: Actor (Leung Chiu-Wai); N.Y. Film Critics '01: Cinematog., Foreign Film.

In the Mouth of Madness 🦴🦴 **1995 (R)** Standard horror flick pays homage to or pokes fun at Stephen King (you decide) with story of successful horror novelist whose fans become a bit too engrossed in his stories—seems his readers tend to slip into dementia and carry out the grisly acts depicted within the pages. Neill plays an insurance investigator who must track down the missing author while combating the psychotic, axe-wielding residents of the seemingly quiet east coast hamlet where the author resides. Worth a look for the above-average special effects and makeup provided by Industrial Light and Magic (ILM). **95m/C; VHS, DVD, Blu-Ray.** Sam Neill; Jurgen Prochnow; Julie Carmen; Charlton Heston; David Warner; John Glover; Bernie Casey; Peter Jason; Frances Bay; Wilhelm von Homburg; ***D:*** John Carpenter; ***W:*** Michael De Luca; ***C:*** Gary B. Kibbe; ***M:*** John Carpenter; Jim Lang.

In the Name of the Father 🦴🦴🦴 ½ **1993 (R)** Compelling true story of Gerry Conlon and the Guildford Four, illegally imprisoned in 1974 by British officials after a tragic IRA bombing near London. The British judicial system receives a black eye, but so does the horror and cruelty of IRA terrorism. Politics and family life in a prison cell share the focus, as Sheridan captures superior performances from Day-Lewis and Postlethwaite (beware the thick Belfast brogue). Thompson was accused of pro-IRA sympathies in the British press for her role as the lawyer who believed in Conlon's innocence. Adapted from "Proved Innocent," Conlon's prison memoirs; reunites Sheridan and Day-Lewis after "My Left Foot." Includes original songs by U2's Bono, with a haunting theme sung by Sinead O'Connor. **127m/C; VHS, DVD, Blu-Ray.** *GB IR* Daniel Day-Lewis; Pete Postlethwaite; Emma Thompson; John Lynch; Corin Redgrave; Beatie Edney; John Benfield; Paterson Joseph; Marie Jones; Gerard McSorley; Frank Harper; Mark Sheppard; Don Baker; Britta Smith; Aidan Grennell; Daniel Massey; Tom Wilkinson; Bosco Hogan; ***D:*** Jim Sheridan; ***W:*** Jim Sheridan; Terry George; ***C:*** Peter Biziou; ***M:*** Trevor Jones; Bono; Sinead O'Connor. Berlin Intl. Film Fest. '94: Golden Berlin Bear.

In the Name of the King: A Dungeon Siege Tale WOOF! **2008 (PG-13)** It's just like "Lord of the Rings"... only much, much worse. German schauenfreude-specialist Uwe Boll is at it again with yet another video game adaptation, this time with his biggest budget ever. But money doesn't mean a thing if you don't have the talent to spend it wisely, and Boll squanders his wad on unconvincing FX and Peter Jackson-esque helicopter shots. In ye olden times, a man named Farmer (Statham, who is, guess what... a farmer) rallies a nation to defend Burt Reynolds' kingdom (King Bandit the IV) against evil wizard and not-so-goodfella Ray Liotta. The rest is a mish-mash of boring battles, orc knock-offs, and inexplicable ninjas. What in the name of the king was Boll thinking? **124m/C; DVD, Blu-Ray.** *GE CA* Jason Statham; John Rhys-Davies; Ray Liotta; Leelee Sobieski; Matthew Lilliard; Burt Reynolds; Ron Perlman; Claire Forlani; Kristanna Loken; Will Sanderson; Brian White; Mike Dopud; ***D:*** Uwe Boll; ***W:*** Doug Taylor; ***C:*** Mathias Neumann; ***M:*** Jessica de Rooij; Henning Lohner. Golden Raspberries '08: Worst Director (Boll).

In the Name of the King 2: Two Worlds 🦴 **2011 (R)** Campy fantasy (complete with CGI dragon) from director Boll. Ex-special forces op Granger (Lundgren) is transported back in time and finds himself in the war-torn kingdom of Ehb. He learns he's the guy meant to fulfill a prophecy to save the kingdom from evil. **96m/C; DVD, Blu-Ray.** Dolph Lundgren; Lochlyn Munro; Natassia Malthe; Heather Doerksen; Aleks Paunovic; ***D:*** Uwe Boll; ***W:*** Michael Nachoff; ***C:*** Mathias Neumann; ***M:*** Jessica de Rooij. **VIDEO**

In the Name of the King 3: The Last Mission 🦴 **2014 (R)** Hitman Hazen Kaine (Purcell) takes one last job for his Bulgarian employers--a kidnapping gig that ultimately transports him back to the Middle Ages thanks to a mysterious medallion and a tattoo. The symbol figures into the mythology of a couple of princesses who are battling their evil uncle for the throne. There's also a dragon. Hey, it's a Uwe Boll flick--just go with it. **86m/C; DVD, Blu-Ray.** Dominic Purcell; Ralitsa Paskaleva; Daria Simeonova; Bashar Rahal; Nikolai Sotirov; ***D:*** Uwe Boll; ***W:*** Joel Ross; ***C:*** Mathias Neumann; ***M:*** Jessica de Rooij. **VIDEO**

In the Navy 🦴🦴 ½ *Abbott and Costello in the Navy* **1941** Abbott and Costello join the Navy in one of four military-service comedies they cranked out in 1941 alone. The token narrative involves about a singing star (Powell) in uniform to escape his female fans, but that's just an excuse for classic A & C routines. With the Andrews Sisters. **85m/B; VHS, DVD.** Lou Costello; Bud Abbott; Dick Powell; Andrews Sisters; ***D:*** Arthur Lubin; ***W:*** Arthur T. Horman; John Grant; ***C:*** Joseph Valentine.

In the Pit 🦴🦴 ½ *En el Hoyo* **2006** Rulfo filmed a single crew, who were building the second level of Mexico City's Periferico freeway, from March 2003 to December 2005. He focuses primarily on the distinctly different attitudes of two workers: Shorty's live-and-let-live philosophy and El Grande's disgust with corruption and the lack of credit given the working man. Spanish with subtitles. **84m/C; DVD.** *MX* ***D:*** Juan Carlos Rulfo; ***C:*** Juan Carlos Rulfo; ***M:*** Leonardo Heiblum.

In the Presence of Mine Enemies 🦴🦴 ½ **1997 (PG-13)** Remake of Rod Serling's 1960 script for "Playhouse 90." Rabbi Adam Heller (Mueller-Stahl) and his daughter Rachel (Lowensohn) are living in the Warsaw ghetto in 1942, trying to deal with Nazi oppression. But the Rabbi's faith is put the test when his son Paul (McKellar), who's escaped from the Treblinka labor camp, returns for vengeance and Rachel becomes the sexual victim of a vicious German officer (Dance). **100m/C; VHS, DVD.** Armin Mueller-Stahl; Elina Lowensohn; Don McKellar; Charles Dance; Chad Lowe; ***D:*** Joan Micklin Silver; ***W:*** Rod Serling. **CABLE**

In the Realm of the Senses 🦴🦴🦴 *Ai No Corrida* **1976 (NC-17)** Taboo-breaking story of a woman and man who turn their backs on the militaristic rule of Japan in the mid-1930s by plunging into an erotic and sensual world all their own. Striking, graphic work that was seized by U.S. customs when it first entered the country. Violent with explicit sex, and considered by some critics as pretentious, while others call it Oshima's masterpiece. In Japanese with English subtitles. **105m/C; VHS, DVD, Blu-Ray.** *JP FR* Tatsuya Fuji; Eiko Matsuda; Aio Nakajima; Meika Seri; ***D:*** Nagisa Oshima; ***W:*** Nagisa Oshima; ***C:*** Hideo Ito; ***M:*** Minoru Miki.

In the Realms of the Unreal 🦴🦴🦴 1/2 **2004** Rich documentary study of the life of outsider artist Henry Darger, who lived most of his life as a harmless oddball janitor. When he died in 1973, his neighbors discovered a huge cache of paintings and writings showing a bizarre, oceanic imaginary world. If you can get beyond Darger's obsession with naked hermaphroditic little girls, and that's not so easy, film is an awesome exploration of the power of the human mind. One of a kind. **82m/C; DVD.**

In the Shadow of the Moon 🦴🦴🦴 1/2 **2007 (PG)** Using original (and some never-before-seen) footage, this exceptional documentary examines the triumphs and failures of America's race to the moon, from the beginnings of the Apollo program to its end in 1972. Movie focuses on the astronauts who were on the missions, capturing the wonder and unique perspective of the men who looked at Earth from the surface of another world. Notably absent is the legendary (and incredibly private) Neil Armstrong. Through interviews and remastered footage, Sington creates a compelling, moving film about a time when humanity reached for the skies and technology equaled hope for the future. **100m/C; DVD.** ***D:*** David Sington; ***C:*** Clive North; ***M:*** Philip Sheppard.

In the Shadow of the Moon 🦴🦴 **2019** In Philadelphia in 1988, cop Tom Lockhart's (Holbrook) life changes forever when he begins to investigate an unusual case. Three people die at the exact same moment in different locations with their brains seeping out of their heads. Tom and his partner Maddox (Woodbine) locate a suspect, Rya (Coleman), but her knowledge of Tom's life, including his pregnant wife's forthcoming delivery of a girl, unsettles him. Every nine years, the same situation occurs again, driving Lockhart to extremes as he becomes obsessed with the case and its meaning. An ambitious mix of noir, action, and science fiction loses steam as it plods along. **115m/C; DVD.** Boyd Holbrook; Cleopatra Coleman; Bokeem Woodbine; Michael C. Hall; Rudi Dharmalingam; ***D:*** Jim Mickle; ***W:*** Gregory Weidman; Geoffrey Tock; ***C:*** David Lanzenberg; ***M:*** Jeff Grace. **VIDEO**

In the Shadows 🦴🦴 1/2 *Under Heaven* **1998 (R)** Modern update of Henry James' 1902 novel "The Wings of the Dove." Lonely, wealthy divorcee Eleanor (Richardson) is dying from cancer and needs a caregiver. Cynthia (Parker) moves in along with her weak-willed boyfriend Buck (Young), who passes himself off as Cynthia's brother and takes a job as a gardener. Avaricious Cynthia decides Buck should make Eleanor fall in love and marry him, so they can inherit her fortune. Of course this menage is made for misery. **115m/C; VHS, DVD.** Joely Richardson; Molly Parker; Aden Young; ***D:*** Meg Richman; ***W:*** Meg Richman; ***C:*** Claudio Rocha; ***M:*** Marc Olsen.

In the Shadows 🦴🦴 **2001 (R)** New York hitman Eric O'Byrne (Modine) is sent to Miami to kill veteran Hollywood stunt coordinator Lance Huston (Caan) in retaliation for an accident that killed stuntman Jimmy (Brancato), a mobster's nephew. But before he died, Jimmy managed to steal money and drugs from an undercover FBI agent (Gooding Jr.) who's posing as a dealer. So both the mob and the feds want to reclaim their property. And then Eric goes and falls for the doctor daughter (Adams) of his target just to complicate things further. **104m/C; VHS, DVD.** James Caan; Joey Lauren Adams; Matthew Modine; Cuba Gooding, Jr.; Lillo Brancato; Jeffrey Chase; ***D:*** Ric Roman Waugh; ***W:*** Ric Roman Waugh; ***C:*** Chuck Cohen; ***M:*** Adam Gorgoni.

In the Soup 🦴🦴 1/2 **1992 (R)** Adolpho is a naive New York filmmaker barely scraping by. He decides to sell his script in a classified ad which is answered by the fast-talking Joe, a would-be film producer who's true profession is as a con artist. The two then try numerous (and humorous) ways to raise the money to begin filming. Also available colorized. **93m/B; VHS, DVD.** Steve Buscemi; Seymour Cassel; Jennifer Beals; Will Patton; Pat Moya; Stanley Tucci; Sully Boyar; Rockets Redglare; Elizabeth Bracco; Ruth Maleczech; Debi Mazar; Steven Randazzo; Francesco Messina; ***Cameo(s):*** Jim Jarmusch; Carol Kane; ***D:*** Alexandre Rockwell; ***W:*** Tim Kissell; Alexandre Rockwell; ***C:*** Phil Parmet; ***M:*** Mader. Sundance '92: Grand Jury Prize.

In the Spider's Web 🦴 **2007** The only reason to see this mess is to watch Henriksen in one of his whacko roles. A group of backpackers are traveling in a remote area of India when one is bitten by a poisonous spider. The others carry their stricken friend to the closest village where American physician Dr. Lecorpus (guess who) lives. The villagers actually worship the lethal arachnids at a nearby temple. Turns out a spider bite is the least of the friends' worries. **90m/C; DVD.** Lance Henriksen; Michael Rogers; Emma Catherwood; Cian Barry; Michael Smiley; Lisa Livingstone; Jane Perry; Sohrab Ardeshir; ***D:*** Terry Winsor; ***W:*** Gary Dauberman; ***M:*** Charles Olins; Mark Ryder. **TV**

In the Tall Grass 🦴🦴 **2019** On a road trip, Cal (Whitted) and his sister Becky (De Oliveira) make a stop near a vast field of tall grass. When they hear a boy crying for help, they walk into the grass. The duo gets lost in the field and realize it is a moving maze that defies the laws of physics. Though they find the boy, Tobin (Buie), and his father Ross (Wilson), their disturbing behavior makes the siblings wonder if they will ever get out. Adapted from a Stephen King/Joe Hill book, it's well-crafted but meanders a bit too long to manage the suspense. **101m/C; DVD.** Laysla De Oliveira; Avery Whitted; Patrick Wilson; Will Buie, Jr.; Harrison Gilbertson; ***D:*** Vincenzo Natali; ***W:*** Vincenzo Natali; ***C:*** Craig Wrobleski; ***M:*** Mark Korven. **VIDEO**

In the Time of the Butterflies 🦴🦴 1/2 **2001 (PG-13)** Based on the novel by Julia Alvarez, which was inspired by the true story of the three Mirabal sisters (collectively known as Las Mariposas) who fought against the Trujillo dictatorship in the Dominican Republic. After their father is murdered, Minerva (Hayek) persuades her sisters Mate (Maestro) and Patria (Cavazos) to join with the rebels in overthrowing the government to ultimately tragic consequences for the women. **92m/C; VHS, DVD.** Salma Hayek; Lumi Cavazos; Mia Maestro; Edward James Olmos; Marc Anthony; Pilar Padilla; Demian Bichir; Fernando Becerril; ***D:*** Mariano Barroso; ***W:*** Judy Klass; David Klass; ***C:*** Xavier Perez Grobet; ***M:*** Van Dyke Parks. **CABLE**

In the Valley of Elah 🦴🦴🦴 **2007 (R)** Retired army sergeant and Vietnam vet Hank Deerfield (Jones) and wife Joan (Sarandon) learn that their soldier son is actually back from Iraq, but they haven't yet heard from him. Hank goes looking and finds that his son has been killed, not in the line of duty but stateside at his New Mexico base—and drugs may be involved. Army investigators and local police are anything but helpful, until Hank hooks up with detective Emily Sanders (Theron). Then the pieces begin to fall into place and Hank delves into his son's experience in the Middle East. Part exploration into the senselessness of war and part exploration into the depths of pain a family can encounter when losing a son to the terror and tragedy that comes with, and out of, fighting. Gritty and raw, Jones' intensity makes it all work. **121m/C; DVD.** Tommy Lee Jones; Charlize Theron; Susan Sarandon; Jason Patrick; Jonathan Tucker; James Franco; Barry Corbin; Josh Brolin; Frances Fisher; Wes Chatham; Jake McLaughlin; Victor Wolf; Devin Brochu; ***D:*** Paul Haggis; ***W:*** Paul Haggis; ***C:*** Roger Deakins; ***M:*** Mark Isham.

In the Weeds 🦴 **2000 (R)** A series of obvious situations (and obvious characters) render this ensemble comedy unfit for human consumption. Spend an evening shift with the wait staff at an upscale Manhattan eatery as their obnoxious boss castigates them, they avoid the psychotic chef, deal with rude diners, and whine about their lives. **90m/C; DVD.** Molly Ringwald; Joshua Leonard; Eric Bogosian; John Paul (J.P.) Pitoc; Ellen Pompeo; Michael B. Silver; Sam Harris; Kirk Acevedo; Bonnie Root; Peter Riegert; Bridget Moynahan; ***D:*** Michael Rauch; ***W:*** Michael Rauch; ***C:*** Horacio Marquinez; ***M:*** Douglas J. Cuomo.

In the Winter Dark 🦴🦴 **1998** The isolation of a remote valley community (filmed in Australia's Blue Mountains) is enhanced by the discovery of a woman's body and the slaughter of livestock. Maurice (Barrett) and Ida (Blethyn) have scratched out a farm living but personally never recovered from the death of their baby son long before. Outcast Laurie (Roxburgh) spends his time drifting through the countryside while pregnant Ronnie (Otto) has been abandoned by her lover. The four are brought together by death and what (or who) might be causing it. Based on the novel by Tim Winton. **92m/C; VHS, DVD.** *AU* Ray Barrett; Brenda Blethyn; Richard Roxburgh; Miranda Otto; ***D:*** James Bogle; ***W:*** James Bogle; Peter Rasmussen; ***C:*** Martin McGrath; ***M:*** Peter Cobbin.

In Their Skin 🦴 1/2 **2012** What starts as a potentially interesting variation on the new millennial fear of identity theft by first-time director Regimbal becomes little more than a cookie cutter of other home invasion films that have been done significantly better. Writer Close pens his own role of Mark, the emotionally damaged patriarch of a family that includes Mary (Blair) and a young son. As they cope with the loss of their daughter, another nuclear trio (including D'Arcy & Miner) stops by their isolated home and acts creepy right from the get-go. **97m/C; DVD.** *CA* Selma Blair; Joshua Close; James D'Arcy; Rachel Miner; Quinn Lord; Alex Ferris; ***D:*** Jeremy Power Regimbal; ***W:*** Joshua Close; ***C:*** Norm Li; ***M:*** Keith Power.

In This House of Brede 🦴🦴🦴 **1975** A sophisticated London widow turns her back on her worldly life to become a cloistered Benedictine nun. Rigg is outstanding as the woman struggling to deal with the discipline of faith. Based on the novel by Rumer Godden. **105m/C; VHS, DVD.** Diana Rigg; Pamela Brown; Gwen Watford; Denis Quilley; Judi Bowker; ***D:*** George Schaefer; ***M:*** Peter Matz. **TV**

In This Our Life 🦴🦴 1/2 **1942** Histrionic melodrama handled effectively by Huston about a nutsy woman who steals her sister's husband, rejects him, manipulates her whole family and eventually leads herself to ruin. Vintage star vehicle for Davis, who chews scenery and fellow actors alike. Adapted by Howard Koch from the Ellen Glasgon novel. **101m/B; VHS, DVD.** Bette Davis; Olivia de Havilland; Charles Coburn; Frank Craven; George Brent; Dennis Morgan; Billie Burke; Hattie McDaniel; Lee Patrick; Walter Huston; Ernest Anderson; ***D:*** John Huston; ***M:*** Max Steiner.

In This World 🦴🦴 1/2 *M1187511* **2003 (R)** Torabi and Enayatullah star as themselves as the film recounts their journey as Afghan refugees from Pakistan to London. Winterbottom's most political film is powerful and effectively balances the personal issues and travails of its characters with the larger issues it illustrates. The lack of a script (they used mostly outlines) hurts the film in the end, but the performances of the mostly non-professional cast balance that weakness. Shot in documentary style on digital video. **88m/C; DVD.** *GB* Jamal Udin Torabi; Enayatullah; Imran Paracha; Hiddayatullah; Jamau; Wakeel Khan; Lal Zarin; Mirwais Torabi; Amanullah Torabi; ***D:*** Michael Winterbottom; ***W:*** Tony Grisoni; ***C:*** Marcel Zyskind; ***M:*** Dario Marianelli. British Acad. '03: Foreign Film.

In Time 🦴 1/2 *Now* **2011 (PG-13)** A clever idea—that we stop aging at 25 and are given one year to live in a future where time literally becomes money—is poorly played out in this pedestrian sci-fi thriller. Will Salas (Timberlake) becomes a Robin Hood of time after being gifted over a century and turning it into much more. Chased by men who want to regulate what is essentially a paper-thin metaphor for money, Salas kidnaps a beautiful heiress (Seyfried) and he naturally falls in love (despite the poor chemistry between the leads). **109m/C; DVD, Blu-Ray.** Justin Timberlake; Amanda Seyfried; Cillian Murphy; Vincent Kartheiser; Alex Pettyfer; Johnny Galecki; Olivia Wilde; Matt Bomer; ***D:*** Andrew Niccol; ***W:*** Andrew Niccol; ***C:*** Roger Deakins; ***M:*** Craig Armstrong.

In Too Deep 🦴🦴 **1999 (R)** Omar Epps and LL Cool J rise above the tired formula in this by-the-book undercover cop/paranoid drug dealer crime drama. Young Cincinnati cop Jef Cole (Epps) is working undercover in a drug ring run by a none-too-humble crime lord who calls himself God (LL Cool J). As he tries to gain the confidence of God, Cole becomes so deeply mired in the gangster life that his commander Boyd (Tucci) begins to question his loyalty. Epps does an excellent job conveying the tension in his character's position, although the script is totally devoid of any kind of plot twist to help him out. Also shining in minor parts are Pam Grier as a veteran detective and Nia Long as the standard issue love interest. **104m/C; VHS, DVD, Blu-Ray.** Omar Epps; Stanley Tucci; LL Cool J; Pam Grier; Veronica Webb; Nia Long; David Patrick Kelly; Hill Harper; Kirk "Sticky Fingaz" Jones; ***D:*** Michael Rymer; ***W:*** Paul Aaron; Michael Henry Brown; ***C:*** Ellery Ryan; ***M:*** Christopher Young.

In Tranzit 🦴 1/2 **2007** Intriguing premise (supposedly based on fact) but obvious execution. In the aftermath of WWII, some 50 German POWs in Russian hands are sent to a female-run Soviet prison camp. The commander has been informed that some prisoners were SS officers and they need to find out just who, but circumstances aren't exactly what they seem. **113m/C; DVD.** *GB RU* Thomas Kretschmann; Vera Farmiga; Daniel Brühl; Nathalie Press; John Malkovich; Ingeborga Dapkounaite; ***D:*** Tom Roberts; ***W:*** Natalia Portnova; Simon van der Borgh; ***C:*** Sergei Astakhov; ***M:*** Dan (Daniel) Jones.

In Which We Serve 🦴🦴🦴 1/2 **1943** Much stiff upper-lipping in this classic that captures the spirit of the British Navy during WWII. The sinking of the destroyer HMS Torrin during the Battle of Crete is told via flashbacks, with an emphasis on realism that was unusual in wartime flag-wavers. Features the film debuts of Johnson and Attenborough, and the first Lean directorial effort. Coward received a special Oscar for his "outstanding production achievement," having scripted, scored, codirected, and costarred. **114m/B; VHS, DVD.** *GB* Noel Coward; John Mills; Bernard Miles; Celia Johnson; Kay Walsh; James Donald; Richard Attenborough; Michael Wilding; George Carney; Gerald Case; John Varley; ***D:*** Noel Coward; David Lean; ***W:*** Noel Coward; ***C:*** Ronald Neame; ***M:*** Noel Coward. N.Y. Film Critics '42: Film.

In Your Dreams 🦴🦴 **2007** Unhappy Albert Ross suffers an accident and suddenly can see the future in his dreams, including a sexy girl named Olivia who's interested in him. But first Albert teams up with amateur sleuth Georgie to figure out why his dreams (good and bad) are coming true and if he can prevent one particular vision in which someone dies. **90m/C; DVD.** *GB* Dexter Fletcher; Linda Hamilton; Parminder K. Nagra; Susan George; Elize du Toit; Robert Portal; Beatie Edney; ***D:*** Gary Sinyor; ***W:*** Gary Sinyor; ***C:*** Jean-Philippe Gossart; ***M:*** David A. Hughes.

In Your Eyes 🦴 1/2 **2014** Minor romantic dramedy that writer Whedon first tinkered with back in the '90s (and it shows). Rebecca had a psychic connection with Dylan when they were kids. 20 years later, it's suddenly back but now she's unhappily married, he's an ex-con on parole, and they live across the country from each other. The connection grows (although everyone around them thinks they're nuts) and the pic takes an unfortunate sharp left turn into crisis in the third act. **106m/C; DVD.** Zoe Kazan; Michael Stahl-David; Mark Feuerstein; Jennifer Grey; Steve Howey; ***D:*** Brin Hill; ***W:*** Joss Whedon; ***C:*** Elisha Christian; ***M:*** Tony Morales. **VIDEO**

In Your Face 🦴 1/2 *Abar, the First Black Superman* **1977 (R)** Little known blaxploitation film about a black family harrassed in a white suburb. A black motorcycle gang comes to their rescue. **90m/C; VHS, DVD.** J. Walter Smith; Tobar Mayo; Roxie Young; Tina James; ***D:*** Frank Packard.

InAlienable 🦴 ½ **2008** Cheesy morality tale (with a lot of familiar faces) wrapped in a sci-fi story. Scientist Eric Norris (Hatch) has an alien parasite growing inside him and he fights to protect what he comes to see as a surrogate offspring for his son, who died years before. Turns into a courtroom debate on whether the alien can be considered a human being with rights or if it should be destroyed as a threat to mankind. **105m/C; DVD.** Richard Hatch; Walter Koenig; Courtney Peldon; Erik Avari; Marina Sirtis; Jay Acovone; Alan Ruck; Judy Levitt; ***D:*** Robert Dyke; ***W:*** Walter Koenig; ***C:*** Jonathan Hall; ***M:*** Justin Durban. **VIDEO**

Incantato 🦴 ½ *Enchanted; Il Cuore Altroe; The Heart Is Elsewhere* **2003** Meek Nello is a 35-year-old classics teacher in 1920s Rome. He's sent to Bologna by his exasperated father in hopes that a change of scene will finally lead Nello into marriage. Nello meets society beauty Angela and thinks he has a chance because she has been recently blinded in an accident and hasn't resumed her wild ways. But Angela is just leading the poor schlub on. Italian with subtitles. **107m/C; DVD.** *IT* Neri Marcore; Vanessa Incontrada; Guilio Bosetti; Nino D'Angelo; Sandra Milo; Giancarlo Giannini; ***D:*** Pupi Avati; ***W:*** Pupi Avati; ***C:*** Pasquale Rachini; ***M:*** Riz Ortolani.

Incendiary 🦴🦴 **2008** Williams is the nameless London working-class mother of a young son whose marriage to a bomb disposal expert is in trouble. So she starts up with charming if slightly sleazy journalist Jasper (McGregor) and while they are canoodling one afternoon, terrorists set off a bomb in a soccer stadium and her husband and son are killed. Her husband's friend Terrence (Macfadyen) is taking part in the investigation, and takes a very personal interest in the new widow, who manages to learn that one of the bomber's wives, the mother of a young son, works nearby. Story doesn't hold together particularly well and some of the narration is risible but Williams is watchable no matter what. **100m/C; DVD, Blu-Ray.** *GB* Michelle Williams; Ewan McGregor; Matthew Macfadyen; Nicholas Greaves; Sidney Johnston; Sasha Behar; Usman Khokhar; ***D:*** Sharon Maguire; ***W:*** Sharon Maguire; ***C:*** Benjamin Davis; ***M:*** Shingeru Umebayashi.

Incendies 🦴🦴🦴 *Scorched* **2010 (R)** Fraternal twins Jeanne (Desormeaux-Poulin) and Simon (Gaudette) are shocked when their mother Nawal's (Azabal) will reveals startling family secrets—their father is alive and they have a brother. Traveling to the Middle East to seek them out, they discover their family history is rife with animosity, wars, and turmoil. The journey also shows them their mother's brave spirit and enduring love. An eloquent and powerful tragedy that is definitely worth the despair it invokes. Loose adaptation of the Wajdi Mouawad play. Arabic and French with subtitles. **130m/C; Blu-Ray.** *CA FR* Lubna Azabal; Melissa Desormeaux-Poulin; Maxim Gaudette; Remy Girard; Abdelghafour Elaaziz; Allen Altman; Mohamed Majd; Nadim Sawalha; Baya Belal; ***D:*** Denis Villenueve; ***W:*** Denis Villenueve; ***C:*** Andre Turpin; ***M:*** Gregoire Hetzel.

Inception 🦴🦴🦴 ½ **2010 (PG-13)** When entering and extracting from the dreams of others becomes reality, the world becomes a very dangerous place. And thief Dom Cobb (DiCaprio) is an expert at doing just that, though he is plagued by visions of the beautiful Mal (Cotillard), which often interrupt the process though he tries to keep this secret from his team. The game changes though when Japanese businessman Saito (Watanabe) hires Cobb for a different kind of assignment. As the dreams layer upon—and crumble and tumble around—each other the question of what's real gets muddled. Writer/director Nolan conceives an elaborate sci fi thriller experience at its most brilliant (on an equally astounding $160 million budget), with stunning visuals that are most appreciated in IMAX format. Worthy of repeat viewing. **148m/C; Blu-Ray.** Leonardo DiCaprio; Ken(saku) Watanabe; Ellen Page; Joseph Gordon-Levitt; Marion Cotillard; Tom (Thomas) Hardy; Cillian Murphy; Tom Berenger; Michael Caine; Lukas Haas; ***D:*** Christopher Nolan; ***W:*** Christopher Nolan; ***C:*** Wally Pfister; ***M:*** Hans Zimmer. Oscars '10: Cinematog., Sound, Sound FX Editing, Visual FX; British Acad. '10: Sound, Visual FX; Writers Guild '10: Orig. Screenplay.

Inch'Allah 🦴🦴 **2012 (R)** French-Canadian obstetrician Chloe (Brochu) is living in Jerusalem while daily crossing the border into occupied Ramallah to do volunteer work at a refugee camp. She tries to be sensitive to both sides of the conflict, maintaining a friendship with Israeli soldier Ava (Levy) and pregnant Palestinian, Rand (Ouazani), whose husband is in an Israeli jail. But when tragedy strikes, an overwhelmed Chloe acts unexpectedly. Brochu is something of a blank lead, but the supporting cast makes up for her. English, French, Arabic, and Hebrew with subtitles. **102m/C; DVD.** *CA FR* Evelyne Brochu; Sabrina Ouazani; Sivan Levy; Yousef (Joe) Sweid; ***D:*** Anais Barbeau-Lavalette; ***W:*** Anais Barbeau-Lavalette; ***C:*** Philippe Lavalette; ***M:*** Levon Minassian.

The Incident 🦴🦴🦴 **1989** Political thriller set during WWII in Lincoln Bluff, Colorado. Matthau is excellent in his TV debut as a small-town lawyer who must defend a German prisoner of war accused of murder at nearby Camp Bremen. An all-star cast lends powerful performances to this riveting made for TV drama. **95m/C; VHS, DVD.** Walter Matthau; Susan Blakely; Harry (Henry) Morgan; Robert Carradine; Barnard Hughes; Peter Firth; William Schallert; ***D:*** Joseph Sargent. **TV**

Incident at Loch Ness 🦴🦴🦴 ½ **2004 (PG-13)** Famously difficult German director Werner Herzog is followed by a documentary crew ala "Burden of Dreams" as he tries to film his meditation on humanity's obsession with the Loch Ness monster. Whole production is wonderfully tongue-in-cheek mockumentary within a mockumentary. Game and lively cast pokes unrelenting fun at themselves and the task at hand in this humorous exploration of filmmaking and unmaking. Though nodding to such films as "Waiting for Guffman" and "Blair Witch Project," film is thoroughly and enjoyably one of a kind. **90m/C; DVD.** ***D:*** Zak Penn; ***C:*** John Bailey; ***M:*** Henning Lohner.

Incident at Oglala: The Leonard Peltier Story 🦴🦴🦴 **1992 (PG)** Offers a detailed account of the violent events leading to the murder of two FBI agents in Oglala, South Dakota in 1975. American Indian activist Leonard Peltier was convicted of the murders and is presently serving two consecutive life sentences, but he's cited as a political prisoner by Amnesty International. The documentary examines the highly controversial trial and the tensions between the government and the Oglala Nation stemming back to the Indian occupation of Wounded Knee in 1973. Director Apted is sympathetic to Peltier and offers reasons why he should be allowed a retrial; he examined similar incidents in his film "Thunderheart." **90m/C; VHS, DVD.** ***Nar:*** Robert Redford; ***D:*** Michael Apted; ***M:*** John Trudell; Jackson Browne.

Incident in an Alley 🦴 ½ **1962** Cop Bill Joddy is investigating a robbery when a scream in a dark alley leads to the death of a 14-year-old boy. A media frenzy results in pressure to charge him with manslaughter. There's a trial and Joddy becomes a pariah within and without his precinct until he can clear his name. **85m/B; DVD.** Chris Warfield; Erin O'Donnell; Harp McGuire; Willis Bouchey; Don Keefer; Virginia Christine; Michael Vandever; ***D:*** Edward L. Cahn; ***W:*** Harold Medford; Orville H. Hampton; ***C:*** Gilbert Warrenton; ***M:*** Richard LaSalle.

Lazy Eye 🦴🦴 **2016** A romantic comedy-drama about unexpected romance and changes in perspective. Dean (Near-Verbrugghe) is graphic designer in Los Angeles experiencing sudden changes in his vision. Just as he is absorbing this news, Alex (Costa Ganis) gets in touch with him. The pair were involved 15 years earlier and he is interested in rekindling their romance. When Dean and Alex meet at a vacation home near Joshua Tree, the secrets that come to light and passions that emerge leave both of their lives changed forever. **87m/C; DVD, Streaming, Download.** Lucas Near-Verbrugghe; Aaron Costa Ganis; Michaela Watkins; Drew Barr; Simon Petrie; ***D:*** Tim Kirkman; ***W:*** Tim Kirkman; ***C:*** Gabe Mayhan; ***M:*** Steven Argila. **VIDEO**

Incognito 🦴 ½ **1997 (R)** Art forger Harry Donovan (Patric) is approached by a couple of British art dealers and a Japanese broker to forge a Rembrandt for a Japanese client. He checks out the painter's style by traveling to Amsterdam and Paris, where he falls for art expert Marieke (Jacob). Harry forges the painting and then gets doublecrossed and caught up in murder. Convoluted plot; lots of cliches. Original director Peter Weller was replaced by Badham after two weeks of filming. **107m/C; VHS, DVD.** Jason Patric; Irene Jacob; Rod Steiger; Thomas Lockyer; Simon Chandler; Michael Cochrane; Ian Richardson; Pip Torrens; Togo Igawa; ***D:*** John Badham; ***W:*** Jordan Katz; ***C:*** Denis Crossan; ***M:*** John Ottman.

Incognito 🦴🦴 **1999** After exec Erin Courtland (Dean) is raped by Derek Scanlon (Morris), he eludes prosecution and begins stalking her. So Erin's wealthy daddy (Glass) hires bodyguard Jake Hunter (Jones) to protect his little girl. **95m/C; DVD.** Allison Dean; Richard T. Jones; Phil Morris; Ron Glass; Vanessa Williams; Joan Pringle; Roger Guenveur; ***D:*** Julie Dash; ***W:*** Shirley Pierce; ***C:*** David West. **CABLE**

Inconceivable 🦴 **2017 (R)** Married woman (Gershon) befriends new lady in town, hires her as a nanny, moves her into the guest house, and asks her to become surrogate for her and her husband...what could go wrong? Doesn't thrill enough to be a decent psychological thriller. Lindsay Lohan was initially attached as producer and star, but the studio wasn't having it. **105m/C; DVD, Blu-Ray.** Gina Gershon; Faye Dunaway; Nicolas Cage; Nicky Whelan; Natalie Eva Marie; ***D:*** Jonathan Baker; ***W:*** Chloe King; ***C:*** Brandon Cox; ***M:*** Kevin Kiner.

An Inconvenient Sequel: Truth to Power 🦴🦴 ½ **2017 (PG)** A follow-up to 2006's "An Inconvenient Truth." Al Gore travels the globe, pointing out evidence of climate change and speaking with experts on the issue. But he also delivers hope, showcasing the citizen activists and technological advancements that are having an impact on curtailing, possibly even reversing, the negative effects of human activities on the planet. Gore himself is a bit lionized in the film, but he's an effective messenger. **98m/C; DVD, Blu-Ray.** Al Gore; George W. Bush; John Kerry; Angela Merkel; Vladimir Putin; ***D:*** Bonni Cohen; Jon Shenk; ***C:*** Jon Shenk; ***M:*** Jeff Beal.

An Inconvenient Truth 🦴🦴🦴 ½ **2006 (PG)** Former Vice President Al Gore speaks out on his personal cause—the dangers of global warming. Guggenheim follows Gore on the lecture circuit as he tries to raise awareness and state his case in an effective (and alarming) multimedia presentation that he has been giving, with a certain confident and professorial charm, since 1989. **100m/C; DVD.** ***D:*** Davis Guggenheim; ***C:*** Davis Guggenheim; Bob Richman; ***M:*** Michael Brook. Oscars '06: Feature Doc., Song ("I Need to Wake Up").

The Incredible Burt Wonderstone 🦴 **2013 (PG-13)** A cast filled with miscast comedy stars sputter to the screen in this limp movie magic act that's about as much fun as a restaurant magician who can't pick the right card. Carell doesn't fit as the smug lead character, a Las Vegas relic who refuses to change his act even as a street magician (Carrey) is threatening to steal the spotlight. Wonderstone breaks up with his partner (Buscemi) and needs the help of a retired star (Arkin) and his former assistant (Wilde) to get his name back in lights. **100m/C; DVD, Blu-Ray.** Steve Carell; Jim Carrey; Steve Buscemi; Olivia Wilde; James Gandolfini; Alan Arkin; Jay Mohr; ***D:*** Don Scardino; ***W:*** John Francis Daley; Jonathan M. Goldstein; ***C:*** Matthew Clark; ***M:*** Lyle Workman.

The Incredible Hulk 🦴🦴 ½ **1977** Bixby is a scientist who achieves superhuman strength after he is exposed to a massive dose of gamma rays. But his personal life suffers, as does his wardrobe. Ferrigno is the Hulkster. Pilot for a TV series; based on the Marvel Comics character. **94m/C; VHS, DVD.** Bill Bixby; Susan Sullivan; Lou Ferrigno; Jack Colvin; ***D:*** Kenneth Johnson. **TV**

The Incredible Hulk 🦴🦴 ½ **2008 (PG-13)** Hulk SMASH! A re-do for the Hulk franchise, with the studio hoping to get off to a better start than Ang Lee's overly thoughtful "Hulk." The story's more or less the same: mild-mannered scientist Bruce Banner (now played by Norton) inherits the wild-mannered Hulk gene from his old man and falls in love with Betty Ross (Tyler). Betty's military father (Hurt), plans to breed a whole infantry of Hulk soldiers, and tests his scheme out on bloodthirsty marine Emil Blonsky (Roth). Very little to think or care about, but lots of fun with the usual CGI overloading all of the action. **112m/C; DVD, Blu-Ray.** Edward Norton; Tim Roth; Liv Tyler; William Hurt; Tim Blake Nelson; Ty Burrell; Christina Cabot; Peter Mensah; Robert Downey, Jr.; ***D:*** Louis Leterrier; ***W:*** Zak Penn; ***C:*** Peter Menzies, Jr.; ***M:*** Craig Armstrong.

The Incredible Hulk Returns 🦴 ½ **1988** The beefy green mutant is back and this time he wages war against a Viking named Thor. Very little substance in this made for TV flick, so be prepared to park your brain at the door. Followed by "The Trial of the Incredible Hulk." **100m/C; VHS, DVD.** Bill Bixby; Lou Ferrigno; Jack Colvin; Lee Purcell; Charles Napier; Steve Levitt; ***D:*** Nicholas J. Corea. **TV**

The Incredible Journey 🦴🦴 ½ **1963** A labrador retriever, bull terrier and Siamese cat mistake their caretaker's intentions when he leaves for a hunting trip, believing he will never return. The three set out on a 250 mile adventure-filled trek across Canada's rugged terrain. Entertaining family adventure from Disney taken from Sheila Burnford's book. **80m/C; VHS, DVD, Streaming.** ***D:*** Fletcher Markle.

The Incredible Journey of Dr. Meg Laurel 🦴🦴🦴 **1979** A young doctor returns to her roots to bring modern medicine to the Appalachian mountain people during the 1930s. Features Wagner in a strong performance. **143m/C; VHS, DVD.** Lindsay Wagner; Jane Wyman; Dorothy McGuire; James Woods; Gary Lockwood; ***D:*** Guy Green. **TV**

The Incredible Journey of Mary Bryant 🦴🦴 ½ *Mary Bryant* **2005 (R)** Mary (Garai) is convicted of theft in 1786 and becomes one of the first British convicts transported to Australia's Botany Bay colony. She marries fellow convict Will Bryant (O'Loughlin) but when the colony faces starvation, Mary wants to save her family by escaping and reaching safety in the Dutch colony of Timor. True story was originally broadcast as an Australian miniseries. **185m/C; DVD.** *AU* Romola Garai; Alex O'Loughlin; Jack Davenport; Sam Neill; Tony (Anthony) Martin; ***D:*** Peter Andrikidis; ***W:*** Peter Berry; ***C:*** Joseph Pickering; ***M:*** Iva Davies. **TV**

Incredible Melting Man WOOF! **1977 (R)** Two transformations change an astronaut's life after his return to earth. First, his skin starts to melt, then he displays cannibalistic tendencies. Hard to swallow. Special effects by Rick Baker. Look for director Jonathan Demme in a bit part. Gross-out remake of 1958's "First Man Into Space." **85m/C; VHS, DVD, Blu-Ray.** Alex Rebar; Burr de Benning; Cheryl "Rainbeaux" Smith; ***Cameo(s):*** Jonathan Demme; ***D:*** William Sachs.

The Incredible Mrs. Ritchie 🦴🦴 *L'Incroyable Mme. Ritchie* **2003 (PG-13)** Sentimental "After-school-Special"influenced drama has troubled kid Charlie fall in with the wrong crowd, get in trouble, and find himself helping an eccentric old lady in her garden as punishment. This is one of those sappy dramas in which everyone who is not a part of Charlie's dysfunctional family is gentle, quirky, insightful, and always right. Of course, everone in his family is none of these things, and desperately in need of these kinds of people to point out what they were doing wrong and help them mend their ways. As if that wasn't bad enough, there's a puppy drowning. **102m/C; VHS, DVD.** *CA* Kevin Zegers; Gena Rowlands; James Caan; Brenda James; Leslie Hope; Justin Chatwin; ***D:*** Paul Johansson; ***W:*** Paul Johansson; ***C:*** Paul Sarossy. **TV**

The Incredible Mr. Limpet 🦴🦴
1964 Limp comedy about a nebbish bookkeeper who's transformed into a fish, fulfilling his aquatic dreams. Eventually he falls in love with another fish, and helps the U.S. Navy find Nazi subs during WWII. Partially animated, beloved by some, particularly those under the age of seven. Based on Theodore Pratt's novel. **99m/C; VHS, DVD, Blu-Ray.** Don Knotts; Jack Weston; Carole Cook; Andrew Duggan; Larry Keating; Elizabeth McRae; ***D:*** Arthur Lubin; ***W:*** Jameson Brewer.

The Incredible Petrified World
WOOF! 1958 Divers are trapped in an underwater cave when volcanic eruptions begin. Suffocating nonsense. **78m/B; VHS, DVD.** John Carradine; Allen Windsor; Phyllis Coates; Lloyd Nelson; George Skaff; ***D:*** Jerry Warren.

The Incredible Shrinking Man 🦴🦴🦴 ½ **1957** Adapted by Richard Matheson from his own novel, the sci-fi classic is a philosophical thriller about a man who is doused with radioactive mist and begins to slowly shrink. His new size means that everyday objects take on sinister meaning and he must fight for his life in an increasingly hostile, absurd environment. A surreal, suspenseful allegory with impressive special effects. Endowed with the tension usually reserved for Hitchcock films. **81m/B; VHS, DVD.** Grant Williams; Randy Stuart; April Kent; Paul Langton; Raymond Bailey; William Schallert; Frank Scanell; Billy Curtis; ***D:*** Jack Arnold; ***W:*** Richard Matheson; ***C:*** Ellis W. Carter. Natl. Film Reg. '09.

The Incredible Shrinking Woman 🦴🦴 ½ **1981 (PG)** "...Shrinking Man" spoof and inoffensive social satire finds household cleaners producing some strange side effects on model homemaker Tomlin, slowly shrinking her to doll-house size. She then encounters everyday happenings as big tasks and not so menial. Her advertising exec husband has a hand in the down-sizing. Sight gags abound but the cuteness wears thin by the end. **89m/C; VHS, DVD, Blu-Ray.** Lily Tomlin; Charles Grodin; Ned Beatty; Henry Gibson; ***D:*** Joel Schumacher; ***W:*** Jane Wagner.

The Incredible Two-Headed Transplant WOOF! 1971 (PG) Mad scientist Dern has a criminal head transplanted on to the shoulder of big John Bloom and the critter runs amuck. Low-budget special effects guaranteed to give you a headache or two. Watch for Pat "Marilyn Munster" Priest in a bikini. **88m/C; VHS, DVD, Blu-Ray.** Bruce Dern; Pat Priest; Casey Kasem; Albert Cole; John Bloom; Berry Kroeger; ***D:*** Anthony M. Lanza; ***W:*** John Lawrence; James Gordon White; ***C:*** Glen Gano; Paul Hipp; Jack Steely; ***M:*** John Barber.

The Incredibles 🦴🦴🦴 ½ **2004 (PG)** Pixar's final feature as a Disney partner ends the relationship on a high note with this story of a retired superhero family and their difficulties adjusting to "normal" life. Bob Parr (Nelson) is the former Mr. Incredible, who, because of multiple lawsuits, has been forced, along with all other costumed heroes, including wife Helen (Hunter) and best friend Lucius (Jackson), into the Hero Relocation Program. He's stuck in a soul-sucking corporate job where he can't save anyone, he misses the old crimefighting days, and his kids Dash and Violet aren't allowed to use their powers. That is, until someone from Mr. Incredible's past returns to endanger them all. Director/writer Bird's script is smart, funny, and insightful. There's plenty for the kids to enjoy, to be sure, but Bird makes some pointed and poignant observations about marriage, middle class values, and the rise of mediocrity in a self-esteem obsessed society. No wonder the screenplay was nominated for an Oscar. **115m/C; VHS, DVD, Blu-Ray, UMD.** ***V:*** Craig T. Nelson; Holly Hunter; Samuel L. Jackson; Jason Lee; Wallace Shawn; Sarah Vowell; Spencer Fox; Brad Bird; Elizabeth Pena; Dominique Louis; ***D:*** Brad Bird; ***W:*** Brad Bird; ***C:*** Janet Lucroy; Patick Lin; Andrew Jimenez; ***M:*** Michael Giacchino. Oscars '04: Animated Film, Sound FX Editing.

Incredibles 2 🦴🦴🦴 **2018 (PG)** Despite a gap of 14 years between movies, the plot picks up immediately where the original left off: suburban life is humdrum for the Parr family, who are forced to hide their illegal super powers. While Elastigirl works with a PR pro to change the public's perception of superheroes, stay-at-home dad Mr. Incredible discovers that it takes more than super strength to parent Violet, Dash, and especially Jack-Jack, the scene-stealing toddler whose emerging powers are unpredictable, uncontrollable, and hilarious. Another Pixar work of art, entertaining for viewers of all ages. **118m/C; DVD, Blu-Ray.** ***V:*** Craig T. Nelson; Holly Hunter; Sarah Vowell; Huckleberry Milner; Catherine Keener; ***D:*** Brad Bird; ***W:*** Brad Bird; ***C:*** Mahyar Abousaeedi; Erik Smitt; ***M:*** Michael Giacchino.

Incredibly Strange Creatures Who Stopped Living and Became Mixed-Up Zombies WOOF! *The Teenage Psycho Meets Bloody Mary; The Incredibly Strange Creatures* **1963** The infamous, super-cheap horror spoof that established Sheckler (for whom Cash Flagg is a pseudonym), about a carny side show riddled with ghouls and bad rock bands. Assistant cinematographers include the young Laszlo Kovacs and Vilmos Zsigmond. A must-see for connoisseurs of cult and camp. **90m/C; VHS, DVD.** Ray Dennis Steckler; Carolyn Brandt; Brett O'Hara; Atlas King; Sharon Walsh; Toni Camel; Erina Enyo; ***D:*** Ray Dennis Steckler; ***W:*** Gene Pollock; Robert Silliphant; ***C:*** Laszlo Kovacs; Vilmos Zsigmond; Joseph Mascelli; ***M:*** Andre Brummer.

The Incredibly True Adventure of Two Girls in Love 🦴🦴 ½ **1995 (R)** Gentle low-budget romantic comedy about first love between two high school girls. Tomboyish working-class Randy (Holloman) lives with her lesbian aunt and works part-time at the local gas station where she spots the rich and beautiful Evie (Parker), one of the popular girls in school. Some sparks fly but Evie's confused, though she's willing to be wooed and, later, defend her new relationship. The issue of race (Randy's white, Evie's black) is only briefly alluded to'more is made of the differences between the girls' social classes and their vulnerability. Directorial debut for Maggenti. **95m/C; VHS, DVD.** Laurel Holloman; Nicole Ari Parker; Kate Stafford; Stephanie Berry; ***D:*** Maria Maggenti; ***W:*** Maria Maggenti.

Incubus 🦴🦴 **1965** One of the very few films made in the artificial language of Esperanto (so it's subtitled in English). Beautiful Kia (Ames) and Amael (Hardt) are sisters who retain their youth and beauty by sucking the life out of the corrupted souls who visit a supposedly magic well. Then Kia discovers the uncorrupted soldier Mark (Shatner) and falls big time. But her succubis sis doesn't like what's going on and casts a spell that calls an incubus to wreak havoc. Creepily atmospheric with striking cinematography by Hall. **76m/B; VHS, DVD.** William Shatner; Allyson Ames; Eloise Hardt; Ann Atmar; Robert Fortier; Milos Milos; ***D:*** Leslie Stevens; ***W:*** Leslie Stevens; ***C:*** Conrad L. Hall; ***M:*** Dominic Frontiere.

Incubus WOOF! 1982 (R) A doctor and his teenaged daughter settle in a quiet New England community, only to encounter the incubus, a terrifying, supernatural demon who enjoys sex murders. Offensive trash. **90m/C; VHS, DVD, Blu-Ray.** *CA* John Cassavetes; Kerrie Keane; Helen Hughes; Erin Flannery; John Ireland; Duncan McIntosh; ***D:*** John Hough; ***W:*** George Franklin; ***C:*** Conrad L. Hall; Albert J. Dunk; ***M:*** Stanley Myers.

Incubus 🦴 **2005** Getting stranded in the middle of nowhere never seems to end well. When Jay (Reid) and her college pals have a car accident, they find refuge in an ominous looking (for a reason!) building that is, indeed, filled with lots of dead folks and a killer in a coma who can enter people's minds as they sleep. No, he is NOT named Freddy but rather, um, cleverly "The Sleeper." Once in their dreams they themselves begin hunting one another so Jay tries really, really super hard not to snooze, as does the unfortunate viewer. **89m/C; DVD.** Tara Reid; Akemnji Ndifernyan; Alice O'Connell; Russell Carter, II; Christian Brassington; ***D:*** Anya Camilleri; ***W:*** Gary Humphreys. **VIDEO**

Indecent Behavior 2 🦴 ½ **1994 (R)** Sex therapist Rebecca is targeted for blackmail as she finds out all sorts of unhealthy things about her patients. Meanwhile, she's practicing her technique with a fellow therapist. Also available unrated. **96m/C; VHS, DVD.** Shannon Tweed; James Brolin; Chad McQueen; Elizabeth Sandifer; Craig Stepp; Rochelle Swanson; ***D:*** Carlo Gustaff.

Indecent Proposal 🦴🦴 ½ **1993 (R)** High-gloss movie that had couples everywhere discussing the big question: Would you let your wife sleep with a billionaire in exchange for a million bucks? Probably, if all were as goodlooking as the weathered, yet ever gorgeous Redford. Moore and Harrelson are the financially down on their luck, but happy, couple who venture to Vegas on a last-ditch gambling effort. Surreally slick direction from Lyne, but an ultimately empty film that explores the values of marriage in a terribly angst-ridden fashion. Based on the novel by Jack Engelhard. Proof that average movies can make a killing at the boxoffice, landing in sixth place for 1993. **119m/C; VHS, DVD, Blu-Ray.** Robert Redford; Demi Moore; Woody Harrelson; Seymour Cassel; Oliver Platt; Billy Bob Thornton; Rip Taylor; Billy Connolly; Joel Brooks; Sheena Easton; Herbie Hancock; ***D:*** Adrian Lyne; ***W:*** Amy Holden Jones; ***C:*** Howard Atherton; ***M:*** John Barry. MTV Movie Awards '94: Kiss (Demi Moore/Woody Harrelson); Golden Raspberries '93: Worst Picture, Worst Screenplay, Worst Support. Actor (Harrelson).

Independence Day 🦴🦴🦴 **1996 (PG-13)** The biggest of the new wave of disaster flicks paying tribute to the Irwin Allen celebrity-fests of the '70s finds an alien armada descending on Earth to create some fireworks on the July 4th weekend. The fate of the world rests in the hands of an unlikely band of Earthlings led by President Whitmore (Pullman), a computer expert (Goldblum), and a Marine fighter pilot (Smith). Special effects, despite forgoing some of the more expensive newer technology, don't disappoint. Strong (if not A-list) cast and plenty of action. Devlin and Emmerich wrote the script while promoting "Stargate," after a reporter asked Emmerich if he believed in aliens. **135m/C; VHS, DVD, Blu-Ray, UMD.** Bill Pullman; Will Smith; Jeff Goldblum; Judd Hirsch; Margaret Colin; Randy Quaid; Mary McDonnell; Robert Loggia; Brent Spiner; James Rebhorn; Vivica A. Fox; James Duval; Harry Connick, Jr.; Harvey Fierstein; Richard Speight, Jr.; Adam Baldwin; Bill Smitrovich; Mae Whitman; Kiersten Warren; Giuseppe Andrews; Devon Gummersall; Leland Orser; Raphael Sbarge; Bobby Hosea; Dan Lauria; Robert Pine; John Capodice; Lyman Ward; ***D:*** Roland Emmerich; ***W:*** Dean Devlin; Roland Emmerich; ***C:*** Karl Walter Lindenlaub; ***M:*** David Arnold. Oscars '96: Visual FX; MTV Movie Awards '97: Kiss (Vivica A. Fox/Will Smith).

Independence Day: Resurgence 🦴 ½ **2016 (PG-13)** Beyond the craven attempt to milk an audience's nostalgia, no one involved in this production ever seemed to ask "why bother?" returning to the film that made Will Smith a star. A lot has changed in the blockbuster in the last two decades and director Emmerich embraces all of the problems with the CGI-heavy, apocalypse-crazy genre, failing to give us any characters worth caring about and focusing so much on visual effects that all story gets as destroyed as the White House notoriously did in the original movie. The Hound almost wants the aliens to win! **120m/C; DVD, Blu-Ray.** Liam Hemsworth; Jeff Goldblum; Jessie T. Usher; Bill Pullman; Maika Monroe; Sela Ward; ***D:*** Roland Emmerich; ***W:*** Roland Emmerich; James A. Woods; Nicolas Wright; James Vanderbilt; Dean Devlin; ***C:*** Markus Forderer; ***M:*** Harald Kloser; Thomas Wander.

Independence Daysaster 🦴 **2013 (PG-13)** Typical Syfy Channel nonsense. The President plans to spend the 4th of July in his hometown but Air Force One is shot down by an alien force. Small town first responders and some geek scientists come up with a plan to stop the invasion. **90m/C; DVD.** Ryan Merriman; Emily Holmes; Tom Everett Scott; Keenan Tracey; Andrea Brooks; Garwin Sanford; ***D:*** W.D. Hogan; ***W:*** Sydney Roper; Rudy Thauberger; ***C:*** Michael Blundell; ***M:*** Michael Neilson. **CABLE**

The Independent 🦴🦴 **2000** Affectionate spoof of low-budget, schlock cinema. Morty Fineman (Stiller) has directed more than 400 "B" movies, which has made him a legend in certain circles. His latest project has gone bust, leaving him facing bankruptcy once again, but he's sure he has a hit with his next idea—the rights to the life story of serial killer William Henry Ellis (Hankin). Now Morty just has to convince his exasperated, estranged daughter Paloma (Garofalo) to help him raise the cash for his new opus. Faux trailers from some of Morty's epics and interviews with various co-workers, admirers, and cast are among the inspired bits. **93m/C; VHS, DVD.** Jerry Stiller; Janeane Garofalo; Max Perlich; Larry Hankin; Ginger Lynn Allen; Billy Burke; Andy Dick; Fred (John F.) Dryer; Ethan (Randall) Embry; Jonathan Katz; John (Johnny Rotten) Lydon; Anne Meara; ***Cameo(s):*** Ben Stiller; Fred Williamson; Karen Black; Peter Bogdanovich; Nick Cassavetes; Roger Corman; Ron Howard; Ted (Edward) Demme; ***D:*** Stephen Kessler; ***W:*** Stephen Kessler; Mike Wilkins; ***C:*** Amir Hamed; ***M:*** Ben Vaughn.

The Indestructible Man 🦴 **1956** Chaney, electrocuted for murder and bank robbery, is brought back to life by a scientist. Naturally, he seeks revenge on those who sentenced him to death. Chaney does the best he can with the material. **70m/B; VHS, DVD.** Lon Chaney, Jr.; Marian Carr; Max (Casey Adams) Showalter; Ross Elliott; Ken Terrell; Robert Shayne; ***D:*** Jack Pollexfen; ***W:*** Sue Bradford; Vy Russell; ***C:*** John L. "Jack" Russell; ***M:*** Albert Glasser.

The Indian 🦴🦴 ½ **2007 (PG-13)** Skip is dying and needs a transplant. His most likely match is his teenaged son Danny, whom he abandoned years before. So Skip hires beautiful mechanic Shelby to manipulate Danny into helping restore a 1917 Indian motorcycle, hoping the developing bond between the three of them will save his life. **91m/C; DVD.** Matt Dallas; Sal Landi; Alison Haislip; Jane Higginson; Angela Lanza; Richard Portnow; Robert Miano; ***D:*** James R. Gorrie; ***W:*** James R. Gorrie; ***C:*** David Palmieri; ***M:*** Frederik Wiedmann. **VIDEO**

The Indian Fighter 🦴🦴🦴 **1955** Exciting actioner has Douglas as a scout hired to lead a wagon train to Oregon in 1870. The train must past through dangerous Sioux territory and Douglas tries to make peace with the Sioux leader but a secret Indian gold mine and romance cause friction and keep things lively. **88m/C; VHS, DVD, Blu-Ray.** Kirk Douglas; Elsa Martinelli; Walter Abel; Walter Matthau; Diana Douglas; Lon Chaney, Jr.; Eduard Franz; Alan Hale, Jr.; Elisha Cook, Jr.; Harry Landers; ***D:*** Andre de Toth; ***W:*** Ben Hecht; Robert L. Richards.

The Indian in the Cupboard 🦴🦴 ½ **1995 (PG)** On his ninth birthday, Omri receives a three-inch plastic indian named Little Bear and an old wooden medicine cabinet. (Guess they were out of Power Rangers.) When placed in the cabinet, Little Bear magically comes to life, taking Omri on adventures and teaching him important lessons. Blue screen techniques allow them to appear together on-screen although they were actually shot together only once. Based on the best-selling children's book by Lynne Reid Banks. **97m/C; VHS, DVD.** Hal Scardino; Litefoot; Lindsay Crouse; Richard Jenkins; Rishi Bhat; David Keith; Michael (Mike) Papajohn; ***D:*** Frank Oz; ***W:*** Melissa Mathison; ***C:*** Russell Carpenter; ***M:*** Miles Goodman.

Indian Paint 🦴🦴 **1964** A pleasant children's film about an Indian boy's love for his horse and his rite of passage. Silverheels was Tonto on TV's "The Lone Ranger," while Crawford was the "Rifleman's" son. **90m/C; VHS, DVD.** Jay Silverheels; Johnny Crawford; Pat Hogan; Robert Crawford, Jr.; George Lewis; ***D:*** Norman Foster.

Indian Point 🦴🦴 ½ **2016** A feature-length documentary consideration of the issues related to nuclear energy in a post-Fukushima disaster era. Focusing on the Indian Point Nuclear Power Plant near New York City, the documentary examines related controversies over its operation and federal government regulation. Because of the Fukushima disaster, many of the millions living near the Indian Point plant are concerned that the same thing could happen in the United States. The uncertainty of America's nuclear future is considered as well. **94m/C;**

DVD. ***D:*** Ivy Meeropol; ***W:*** Ivy Meeropol; ***C:*** Rob Featherstone; Daniel B. Gold; Brett Wiley; ***M:*** Nathan Halpern; Chris Ruggiero.

The Indian Runner 1/2 **1991 (R)** Penn's debut as a writer-director tells the story of two brothers in Nebraska during the late '60s, who are forced to change their lives with the loss of their family farm. Joe is a good cop and family man who can't deal with the rage of his brother Frank, who has just returned from Vietnam and is turning to a life of crime. Penn does a decent job of representing the struggle between the responsible versus the rebellious side of human nature. Quiet and very stark. Based on the song "Highway Patrolman" by Bruce Springsteen. **127m/C; VHS, DVD, Blu-Ray.** David Morse; Viggo Mortensen; Sandy Dennis; Charles Bronson; Valeria Golino; Patricia Arquette; Dennis Hopper; Benicio Del Toro; ***D:*** Sean Penn; ***W:*** Sean Penn.

The Indian Scarf **1963** Heirs to a dead man's fortune are being strangled one by one at the benefactor's country estate. An Edgar Wallace suspense tale. **85m/C; VHS, DVD.** *GE* Heinz Drache; Gisela Uhlen; Klaus Kinski; ***D:*** Alfred Vohrer.

Indian Summer **1993 (PG-13)** Yet another addition to the growing 30-something nostalgia genre. Delete the big house, add a crusty camp director (Arkin), change the characters' names (but not necessarily their lives) and you feel like you're experiencing deja vu. This time seven friends and the requisite outsider reconvene at Camp Tamakwa, the real-life summer camp to writer/director Binder. The former campers talk. They yearn. They save Camp Tamakwa and experience personal growth. A must see for those who appreciate listening to situational jokes that are followed by "I guess you had to be there." **108m/C; VHS, DVD, Blu-Ray.** Alan Arkin; Matt Craven; Diane Lane; Bill Paxton; Elizabeth Perkins; Kevin Pollak; Sam Raimi; Vincent Spano; Julie Warner; Kimberly Williams; Richard Chevolleau; ***D:*** Mike Binder; ***W:*** Mike Binder; ***M:*** Miles Goodman.

The Indian Tomb 1/2 *The Mission of the Yogi; The Tiger of Eschanapur* **1921** Silent film fare in two parts. Ayan (Veidt) is the Maharajah of Eschanapur. But all his wealth and power has not prevented Ayan's wife, Princess Savitri, from falling in love with British officer MacAllan. Ayan plots to built a massive tomb to imprison the woman who betrayed him but yogi Ramigani prophesizes that such revenge will destroy the prince's life. Huge budget (for the time) and lavish spectacle, which was all created at director May's German studio. Adapted from the novel by Thea von Haubou. **212m/B; Silent; VHS, DVD.** *GE* Conrad Veidt; Paul Richter; Olaf Fonss; Mia May; Bernhard Goetzke; Lya de Putti; Erna Morena; ***D:*** Joe May; ***W:*** Fritz Lang; ***C:*** Werner Brandes.

Indiana Jones and the Kingdom of the Crystal Skull 1/2 **2008 (PG-13)** Lucas and Spielberg again team up to bring Harrison Ford back in the fedora in a hugely hyped return that lives up to its adventurous roots, but suffers from the vices of its day. The Soviets are hot on Indy's trail as they both race deep into the Amazon to recover a legendary crystal skull with potentially extraterrestrial powers. Indy's joined by a young greaser named Mutt Williams (LaBeouf), who shares Jones's thrill for danger and possibly his gene structure. The thrill and excitement are constant, but suffer from CGI overload and many lapses in credibility in the second half. Allen is back as Indy's long-lost love and LaBeouf brings a spirit of youth to the journey. **122m/C; DVD, Blu-Ray.** Harrison Ford; Shia LaBeouf; Karen Allen; Cate Blanchett; Ray Winstone; Jim Broadbent; John Hurt; Andrew Divoff; Igor Jijikine; Neil Flynn; Ernie Reyes, Jr.; ***D:*** Steven Spielberg; ***W:*** David Koepp; ***C:*** Janusz Kaminski; ***M:*** John Williams. Golden Raspberries '08: Worst Sequel/Prequel.

Indiana Jones and the Last Crusade **1989 (PG)** In this, the third and last (?) Indiana Jones adventure, the fearless archaeologist is once again up against the Nazis in a race to find the Holy Grail. Connery is perfectly cast as Indy's father; opening sequence features Phoenix as a teenage Indy and explains his fear of snakes and the origins of the infamous fedora. Returns to the look and feel of the original with more adventures, exotic places, dastardly villains, and daring escapes than ever before; a must for Indy fans. **126m/C; VHS, DVD, Blu-Ray.** Harrison Ford; Sean Connery; Denholm Elliott; Alison Doody; Julian Glover; John Rhys-Davies; River Phoenix; Michael Byrne; Alex Hyde-White; ***D:*** Steven Spielberg; ***W:*** Jeffrey Boam; ***C:*** Douglas Slocombe; ***M:*** John Williams.

Indiana Jones and the Temple of Doom **1984 (PG)** Daredevil archaeologist Indiana Jones is back. This time he's on the trail of the legendary Ankara Stone and a ruthless cult that has enslaved hundreds of children. More gore and violence than the original; Capshaw's whining character is an irritant, lacking the fresh quality that Karen Allen added to the original. Enough action for ten movies, special effects galore, and the usual booming Williams score make it a cinematic roller coaster ride, but with less regard for plot and pacing than the original. Though second in the series, it's actually a prequel to "Raiders of the Lost Ark." Followed by "Indiana Jones and the Last Crusade." **118m/C; VHS, DVD, Blu-Ray.** Harrison Ford; Kate Capshaw; Ke Huy Quan; Amrish Puri; ***D:*** Steven Spielberg; ***W:*** Willard Huyck; Gloria Katz; ***C:*** Douglas Slocombe; ***M:*** John Williams. Oscars '84: Visual FX.

Indictment: The McMartin Trial **1995 (R)** Woods stars as attorney Danny Davis, who has the unenviable task of providing a defense in the notorious McMartin child molestation trial. In 1983, Manhattan Beach, California was rocked by reports that some 60 preschoolers had been abused at a day-care center. Seven defendants were accused thanks to lurid videotaped interviews with the children. The trial lasted six years (the longest and most expensive on record) and all charges were eventually dismissed. It's clear from this telepic that public hysteria and media hype lead to a grave miscarriage of justice that put the legal system on trial as well. **132m/C; VHS, DVD.** James Woods; Henry Thomas; Mercedes Ruehl; Shirley Knight; Sada Thompson; Mark Blum; Alison Elliott; Chelsea Field; Richard Bradford; Lolita Davidovich; ***D:*** Mick Jackson; ***W:*** Abby Mann; Myra Mann; ***C:*** Rodrigo Garcia; ***M:*** Peter Melnick.

Indignation 1/2 **2016 (R)** Award-winning writer Schamus makes his directorial debut with this confidently made adaptation of Philip Roth's 2008 novel set in 1950's Ohio. While many young men his age are serving in the Korean War, Marcus (Lerman) opts for college where he contends with both anti-Semitism and a sexual awakening after meeting the gorgeous Olivia (Gadon). Religion, academia, sexism, and sexuality all play roles in Roth's complex tale. While a bit overloaded, Schamus and his talented cast do their best to keep it entertaining, particularly Tracy Letts in a supporting role. **110m/C; DVD, Blu-Ray.** Logan Lerman; Sarah Gadon; Tracy Letts; Linda Emond; Danny Burstein; ***D:*** James Schamus; ***W:*** James Schamus; ***C:*** Christopher Blauvelt; ***M:*** Jay Wadley.

Indiscreet 1/2 **1931** Empty-headed romantic comedy about a fashion designer whose past catches up with her when her ex-lover starts romancing her sister. No relation to the classic 1958 film with Cary Grant and Ingrid Bergman. **81m/B; VHS, DVD.** Gloria Swanson; Ben Lyon; Barbara Kent; ***D:*** Leo McCarey.

Indiscreet **1958** A charming American diplomat in London falls in love with a stunning actress, but protects himself by saying he is married. Needless to say, she finds out. Stylish romp with Grant and Bergman at their sophisticated best. Adapted by Norman Krasna from his stage play "Kind Sir." **100m/C; VHS, DVD, Blu-Ray.** Cary Grant; Ingrid Bergman; Phyllis Calvert; ***D:*** Stanley Donen; ***W:*** Norman Krasna; ***C:*** Frederick A. (Freddie) Young; ***M:*** Richard Rodney Bennett.

Indochine **1992 (PG-13)** Soapy melodrama follows the fortunes of Eliane (Deneuve), a Frenchwoman born and reared in Indochina, from 1930 to the communist revolution 25 years later. She contends with the changes to her country as well as her adopted daughter as she grows up and becomes independent. Deneuve's controlled performance (and unchanging beauty) is eminently watchable. Filmed on location in Vietnam with breathtaking cinematography by Francois Catonne. In French with English subtitles. **155m/C; VHS, DVD.** *FR* Catherine Deneuve; Linh Dan Pham; Vincent Perez; Jean Yanne; Dominique Blanc; Henri Marteau; Carlo Brandt; Gerard Lartigau; ***D:*** Regis Wargnier; ***W:*** Erik Orsenna; Louis Gardel; Catherine Cohen; Regis Wargnier; ***C:*** Francois Catonne; ***M:*** Patrick Doyle. Oscars '92: Foreign Film; Cesar '93: Actress (Deneuve), Art Dir./Set Dec., Cinematog., Sound, Support. Actress (Blanc); Golden Globes '93: Foreign Film; Natl. Bd. of Review '92: Foreign Film.

Inequality For All **2013 (PG)** Robert Reich is a public policy professor and longtime Washington insider who understands the widening gap between the haves and have-nots better than nearly anyone in the world. His dissertation about the decline of the middle class plays not unlike Al Gore's "An Inconvenient Truth" in that the film basically serves as a podium for its central subject to reveal his statistics and use them to sketch a disturbing portrait of where the world's economy may be going. It's undeniably a one-sided affair, but Reich makes a convincing enough case that his side is the only one that needs to be heard--if one doesn't mind the lack of counterpoint. **89m/C; DVD, Blu-Ray.** ***D:*** Jacob Kornbluth; ***W:*** Jacob Kornbluth; ***C:*** Svetlana Cvetho; Dan Krauss; ***M:*** Marco d'Ambrosio.

The Inevitable Defeat of Mister & Pete 1/2 **2013 (R)** It's a hard-knocked life for young Mister and Pete. Not only is Mister (Brooks) constantly in trouble at school, but the 8th grader also has to sort out his mother's prostitution and heroin hang-ups. Same goes for his sworn enemy Pete (Dizon). But after the law snatches up much of their family, the two are forced to team up and survive on their own in a gloomy Brooklyn housing project. As solid and realistic as the child actors may be, they're stuck with a clunky, melodramatic coming-of-age script that's unfortunately just as awkward as its title. **108m/C; DVD.** Skylan Brooks; Ethan Dizon; Jennifer Hudson; Adewale Akinnuoye-Agbaje; Jordin Sparks; Anthony Mackie; Jeffrey Wright; ***D:*** George Tillman, Jr.; ***W:*** Michael Starrbury; ***C:*** Reed Morano; ***M:*** Alicia Keys; Mark Isham.

Infamous **2006 (R)** The other Truman Capote movie, which was filmed at the same time as the more successful (both financially and artistically) "Capote." Englishman Jones is at least physically more suited to the role of the fey author, who revels in his Gotham society milieu. Still, you've got Truman and his best friend Harper Lee (an understated Bullock) traipsing off to Kansas to work on his true-crime story. Daniels is solid as lawman Alvin Dewey while Craig (the new James Bond) is a mixed blessing as killer Perry Smith; he's physically wrong and overwhelming for the part but you still can't take your eyes off him. Would that the same could be said of McGrath's glossy film. **118m/C; DVD.** Toby Jones; Sandra Bullock; Daniel Craig; Lee Pace; Peter Bogdanovich; Jeff Daniels; Hope Davis; Sigourney Weaver; Isabella Rossellini; Juliet Stevenson; Gwyneth Paltrow; John Benjamin Hickey; ***D:*** Douglas McGrath; ***W:*** Douglas McGrath; ***C:*** Bruno Delbonnel; ***M:*** Rachel Portman.

Infamous 1/2 **2020 100m/C; DVD.** Bella Thorne; Jake Manley; Amber Riley; Michael Sirow; Marisa Coughlan; ***D:*** Joshua Caldwell; ***W:*** Joshua Caldwell; ***C:*** Eve Cohen; ***M:*** Bill Brown.

Infected 1/2 **2008** Ben (Bellows) and Lisa (Roy) are working at a Boston newspaper when an informant of Lisa's says a big bad corporation is actually a front for an alien plague (the precursor to an invasion) and the toxins are delivered to humans through—wait for it!?designer bottled vitamin water! See—all those environmentalists were right about it being bad for you! But maybe not as bad as this SciFi Channel effort, which is boring. **84m/C; DVD.** Gil Bellows; Maxim Roy; Judd Nelson; Isabella Rossellini; Jesse Todd; ***D:*** Adam Weissman; ***W:*** Joshua Hale Failkov; Mark Wheaton; ***C:*** Daniel Villeneuve; ***M:*** Ned Bouhalassa. **CABLE**

Infected 1/2 *The Dead Inside* **2013** The survivors of a zombie apocalypse try to find out if they are the last people who are still human on Earth. In an every day suburb, the world changes overnight as it becomes ground zero for a global pandemic that makes people become flesh-eating zombies. Those few who have evaded this fast-spreading infection in this community have taken refuge with some army personnel in an elementary school's emergency shelter. With of little food and few weapons, those in the shelter soon come into conflict, though they soon realize they will begin to die there. They eventually make the decision to escape and find out if other infected humans can be located on Earth. **120m/C; DVD, Streaming, Download.** Luke Hobson; Nicky Paul Barton; Roger Fowler; Samuel Hogarth; David Wayman; ***D:*** Andrew Gilbert; ***W:*** Andrew Gilbert; Julian Hundy; ***C:*** Julian Hundy; James Mann; ***M:*** Stephen Currell. **VIDEO**

Infernal Affairs *Mogan Do; Wu jian dao* **2002 (R)** Claustrophobic cat-and-mouse, cops-and-robbers noir. Lau (Lau) is a Triad member who's sent by his boss Hon Sam (Tsang) to the police academy so he can become a deep cover mole. Chan (Leung Chui-wai) is a cop whose boss, Supt. Wong (Wong), has sent him into the mob as a police informer. Each boss knows he has a mole and each mole knows it's only a matter of time before a slip-up will prove fatal. Lau is sent by Internal Affairs to investigate the Triad mole while Chan is told to find out who the police stoolie is. Talk about your identity crisis! Cantonese with subtitles. There's also a prequel and a sequel. **100m/C; DVD.** Tony Leung Chiu-wai; Andy Lau; Anthony Wong; Eric Tsang; Lam Ka-tung; Ng Ting-yip; Wan Chi-keung; Sammi Cheng; ***D:*** Wai Keung (Andrew) Lau; ***W:*** Felix Chong; ***C:*** Lai Yui-fai Lang; ***M:*** Chan Kwong-wing.

Infernal Affairs 2 1/2 *Infernal Affairs II; Mou gaan dou II; Wu jian dao 2* **2003** In this prequel, a Triad boss is murdered and his son takes over the empire before all out war is declared. Meanwhile Yan (now played by Shawn Yue), has just been thrown out of the police academy for violating the rules, and then quickly drafted to infiltrate the Triads undercover when it's discovered that he's the new boss's half-brother. **119m/C; DVD.** *CH* Anthony Wong Chau-Sang; Eric Tsang; Carina Lau; Frances Ng; Edison Chen; Peter Ngor; Arthur Wong; Teddy Chan; Roy Cheung; Chapman To; Shawn Yue; Jun Hu; Tung Cho 'Joe' Cheung; Henry Fong; Chung-yue Chiu; Phorjeat Keanpetch; Shipin Ye; Ping Hui Tay; Alexander Chan; Chi Keung Wan; ***D:*** Wai Keung (Andrew) Lau; Siu Fai Mak; ***W:*** Felix Chong; Siu Fai Mak; ***C:*** Wai Keung (Andrew) Lau; Man-Ching Ng; ***M:*** Kwong Wing Chan.

Infernal Affairs 3 *Mou gaan dou III: Jung mik mou gaan; Infernal Affairs III; Infernal Affairs: End Inferno 3; Wu jian dao III: Zhong ji wu jian* **2003** Picking up where the first film left off, Ming (Andy Lau) is cleared of all charges of killing a fellow officer, and is somehow inexplicably promoted to Internal Affairs. He discovers a corrupt cop who may be a Triad mole, and tries to expose him while covering up the fact that he used to be one himself. Unfortunately the aforementioned mole has the same idea about Ming. **118m/C; DVD.** *CH* Anthony Wong Chau-Sang; Eric Tsang; Carina Lau; Chi Keung Wan; Andy Lau; Leon Lai; Daoming Chen; Tony Leung Chiu-Wai; Kelly Chen; Sammi Cheng; Chapman To; Waise Lee; Ka-tung Lam; Ting Yip Ng; Huang Zhi Zhong; ***D:*** Wai Keung (Andrew) Lau; Siu Fai Mak; ***W:*** Siu Fai Mak; Felix Chong; ***C:*** Man-Ching Ng; ***M:*** Kwong Wing Chan.

Inferno **1980 (R)** Uneven occult horror tale about a young man who arrives in New York to investigate the mysterious circumstances surrounding his sister's death. Dubbed. **106m/C; VHS, DVD, Blu-Ray.** *IT* Leigh McCloskey; Elenora Giorgi; Irene Miracle; Sacha (Sascha) Pitoeff; ***D:*** Dario Argento; ***W:*** Dario Argento; ***C:*** Romano Albani; ***M:*** Keith Emerson.

Inferno 1/2 **1999 (R)** Jack Conley awakens in the middle of the desert with no idea who he is or what's happened to him. Taken in by a reclusive artist, Jack suffers violent flashbacks as he tries to piece together his identity, only remembering that he had a lot of money in his possession and it's gone. Then two of Jack's former associates track him down and he learns the dangerous truth about himself. **94m/C; VHS, DVD.** Ray Liotta; Gloria Reuben; Armin Mueller-Stahl; ***D:***

Harley Cokliss; ***C:*** Stephen McNutt; ***M:*** Fred Mollin. **VIDEO**

Inferno ½ **2001** Darcy Hamilton (Gunn) is an expert firejumper who leads her team in controlling a forest fire that Darcy suspects was arson. A second blaze erupts and heads for the nearest town and the local fire chief accuses Darcy's daughter and her boyfriend of being fire bugs. Now Darcy not only has to fight the fire but prove her daughter's innocence. **91m/C; VHS, DVD.** Janet Gunn; Jeff Fahey; Dean Stockwell; ***D:*** Dusty Nelson; ***M:*** Jeff Marsh.

Inferno **2016 (PG-13)** Years after most of the world gave up on caring about Dan Brown books, director Howard and star Hanks reunite for another adaptation of one of his novels, a sequel to "The DaVinci Code" and "Angels & Demons." Hanks returns as Professor Robert Langdon, this time joined by Dr. Sienna Brooks (Jones) on a globetrotting journey to stop a madman from releasing a plague that will decimate the human race. These movies are made for the international audience, and make a fortune overseas because of their location-hopping, but this one is total nonsense. It seems that Hanks is even getting bored making it. **121m/C; DVD, Blu-Ray.** Tom Hanks; Felicity Jones; Omar Sy; Irrfan Khan; Sidse Babett Knudsen; ***D:*** Ron Howard; ***W:*** David Koepp; ***C:*** Salvatore Totino; ***M:*** Hans Zimmer.

Infestation ½ **2009 (R)** Funny and fast-paced horror comedy that finds slacker Cooper waking up cocooned in webbing as the next meal for huge, mutant flesh-eating bugs. Freeing himself, Cooper also unwraps those around him and the would-be meals decide to fight back by going after the queen of the bugs and saving the world! **93m/C; DVD.** Christopher Marquette; Brooke Nevin; Ray Wise; Wesley Thompson; Deborah Geffner; Kinsey Packard; E. Quincy Sloan; ***D:*** Kyle Rankin; ***C:*** Thomas Ackerman; ***M:*** Steve Gutheinz. **VIDEO**

Infested: Invasion of the Killer Bugs **2002 (R)** It's a boomer reunion with bugs! Yuppie friends gather for a funeral and have their reminiscing disturbed by mutant flies that transform their victims into zombies. This one is meant to be cheesy. **84m/C; VHS, DVD, Blu-Ray.** Zach Galligan; Amy Jo Johnson; Robert Duncan McNeill; Mark Margolis; Lisa Ann Hadley; Daniel H. Jenkins; ***D:*** Josh Olson; ***W:*** Josh Olson; ***C:*** M. David Mullen; ***M:*** Rodney Whittenberg. **VIDEO**

The Infidel **2010** Blunt Brit comedy with a few too many stereotypes (but some funny sight gags). Londoner Mahmud Nassir (Djalili), a lapsed Muslim, discovers he was adopted, his birth mother was Jewish, and he was born Solly Shimshillewitz. This puts a crimp in the plans of his son Rashid (Shah), who wants to marry Uzma (Radford). She's the daughter of fundamentalist Islamic preacher Arshad Al-Masri (Naor) who's dividing the ethnic communities with his rhetoric of hate. Embarrassed by his newly-found Hebrew ties, Mahmud turns to cabbie Lenny Goldberg (Schiff), a former neighbor of his mother's, for advice and then decides to try and embrace his new faith. **104m/C; DVD.** *GB* Omid Djalili; Richard Schiff; Amit Shah; Yigal Naor; Soraya Radford; Archie Panjabi; Mina Anwar; ***D:*** Josh Appignanesi; ***W:*** David Baddiel; ***C:*** Natasha Braier; ***M:*** Erran Baron Cohen.

The Infiltrator ½ **1995 (R)** Based on the true story of Yaron Svoray (Platt), an Israeli journalist and the son of Holocaust survivors, whose latest assignment is to go to Berlin and investigate the rising Neo-Nazi movement. Eventually, Svoray manages to meet leaders of the Nationalist Front and then finds himself enmeshed in a worldwide political network. Based on the book "In Hitler's Shadow" by Yaron Svoray and Nick Taylor. **102m/C; VHS, DVD.** Oliver Platt; Arliss Howard; Peter Riegert; Alan King; Tony Haygarth; Michael Byrne; Julian Glover; Alex Kingston; ***D:*** John MacKenzie; ***W:*** Guy Andrews; ***M:*** Hal Lindes. **CABLE**

The Infiltrator **2016 (R)** There's a shade of irony in watching an actor who became famous playing television's most notorious drug dealer taking on the role of the man who helped take down one of history's drug kingpins. Cranston plays Robert Mazur, the U.S. Customs official who figured out that the only way to stop Colombian drug lord Pablo Escobar was to go undercover in his organization. Furman's real-life drama from the mid-1980s offers some interesting details when it comes to the war on drugs but it's really only worth seeing for Cranston's performance. He's consistently engaging and believable, even when the film is predictable. **127m/C; DVD, Blu-Ray.** Bryan Cranston; Diane Kruger; John Leguizamo; Benjamin Bratt; Yul Vazquez; ***D:*** Brad Furman; ***W:*** Ellen Brown Furman; ***C:*** Joshua Reis; ***M:*** Chris Hajian.

The Infiltrators ½ **2020** Documentary about the for-profit Broward Transitional Center, which detains immigrants without a trial or representation. Relates the stories of prisoners there, including a political refugee from Venezuela and a domestic violence victim from the Congo, and the work of immigrant rights activists. With the help of the National Immigrant Youth Alliance, activists reveal details about the corruption in such centers and the power of the U.S. Customs and Border protection agency. They also work from the inside to help free the immigrant detainees. Though featuring sympathetic subjects and powerful stories, its use of recreations negatively impacts the message. **95m/C; DVD.** Maynor Alvarado; Dino Nicandros; Chelsea Rendon; Juan Gabriel Pareja; Fernando Martinez; ***D:*** Cristina Ibarra; Alex Rivera; ***W:*** Cristina Ibarra; Alex Rivera; Aldo Velasco; ***C:*** Lisa Rinzler; ***M:*** tomandandy.

The Infinite Worlds of H.G. Wells ½ **2001** Hallmark TV miniseries about sci fi writer H.G. Wells. Journalist Ellen McGillivray interviews Wells in 1946 in London on how he was inspired to write his fiction. In flashback, Wells details his meeting and love for scientist Jane Robbins and, thanks to various experiemnts, how they learned to slip through time, so his stories are from his actual life experience. Ellen's not surprised because she's keeping some secrets herself. **240m/C; DVD.** *UK US* Tom Ward; Katy Carmichael; Eve Best; Nicholas (Nick) Rowe; Matthew Cottle; ***D:*** Robert Young; ***W:*** Clive Exton; Matthew Faulk; Chris Harrald; Mark Skeet; ***C:*** John McGlashan; ***M:*** Stanislas Syrewicz. **CABLE**

Infinitely Polar Bear **2014** Cameron (Ruffalo), a father of two girls, suffers from bipolar disorder in this frustratingly episodic and inconsistent dramedy that uses mental illness as a manipulative plot device. His wife Maggie (Saldana) has done most of the parenting of their children but everyone's life is upended when she gets a scholarship to pursue her MBA in New York, leaving the girls in the care of their careless father. The film was supposedly inspired by writer/director Forbes' upbringing, and so it has a personal touch but it lacks focus. Boring when it's not maddening. **90m/C; DVD, Blu-Ray.** Mark Ruffalo; Zoe Saldana; Imogene Wolodarsky; Ashley Aufderheide; Keir Dullea; Beth Dixon; ***D:*** Maya Forbes; ***W:*** Maya Forbes; ***C:*** Bobby Bukowski; ***M:*** Theodore Shapiro.

Infinity ½ **1996 (PG)** Based on memoirs covering the early years of Nobel Prize-winning physicist Richard Feynman (Broderick) and his romance with aspiring artist Arline Greenbaum (Arquette). They marry despite the fact that Arline is diagnosed with tuberculosis, at this time in the '30s a contagious and incurable disease. Richard's recruited to work on the Manhattan Project at Los Alamos, New Mexico, and the narrative travels between his scientific endeavors and Arline's worsening illness in an Albuquerque hospital. Problem is it's neither a character study or a love story but a weak combo. Directing debut of Broderick; screenplay is written by his mother. **119m/C; VHS, DVD.** Matthew Broderick; Patricia Arquette; James LeGros; Peter Riegert; Dori Brenner; Peter Michael Goetz; Zeljko Ivanek; ***D:*** Matthew Broderick; ***W:*** Patricia Broderick; ***C:*** Toyomichi Kurita; ***M:*** Bruce Broughton.

The Informant! **2009 (R)** Damon gained 30 pounds and a goofy mustache in this seriously nutzoid tale that's based on a true story. In 1992, Mark Whitacre (Damon) turns whistleblower when he exposes multinational agri-giant Archer Daniels Midland's price-fixing schemes to the FBI. Whitacre wears a wire and collects documents to make their case, but the feds discover Whitacre's hands aren't exactly clean. Then the pressure from doing undercover work causes Whitacre to crack (although he doesn't seem very stable to begin). Adapted from the nonfiction book by Kurt Eichenwald. **108m/C; Blu-Ray, On Demand.** Matt Damon; Scott Bakula; Melanie Lynskey; Patton Oswalt; Joel McHale; Edward Jemison; Rick Overton; Tom Papa; ***Cameo(s):*** Tom Smothers; Dick Smothers; ***D:*** Steven Soderbergh; ***W:*** Scott Burns; ***C:*** Steven Soderbergh; ***M:*** Marvin Hamlisch.

The Informer ½ **1929** Hanson wants to flee Ireland's poverty for America, using the reward money he gets for turning in an IRA comrade. But things don't turn out as planned and instead he's haunted by the guilt of his betrayal. Based on the novel by Liam O'Flaherty and filmed to much greater effect by John Ford in 1935. **83m/B; VHS, DVD, Blu-Ray.** *GB* Lars Hanson; Lya de Putti; Warwick Ward; Dennis Wynham; ***D:*** Arthur Robison; ***W:*** Benn W. Levy; Rolfe E. Vanlo.

The Informer **1935** Based on Liam O'Flaherty's novel about the Irish Sinn Fein Rebellion of 1922, it tells the story of a hard-drinking Dublin man (McLaglen) who informs on a friend (a member of the Irish Republican Army) in order to collect a 20-pound reward. When his "friend" is killed during capture, he goes on a drinking spree instead of using the money, as planned, for passage to America. Director Ford allowed McLaglen to improvise his lines during the trial scene in order to enhance the realism, leading to excruciating suspense. Wonderful score. **91m/B; VHS, DVD.** Victor McLaglen; Heather Angel; Wallace Ford; Margot Grahame; Joseph (Joe) Sawyer; Preston Foster; Una O'Connor; J.M. Kerrigan; Donald Meek; ***D:*** John Ford; ***W:*** Dudley Nichols; ***M:*** Max Steiner. Oscars '35: Actor (McLaglen), Director (Ford), Score, Screenplay; Natl. Film Reg. '18; N.Y. Film Critics '35: Director (Ford), Film.

The Informers **2009 (R)** Hedonism in 1980s L.A. courtesy of a Bret Easton Ellis novel and screenplay. Movie honcho William (Thornton) is having an affair with newscaster Cheryl (Ryder) as wife Laura (Basinger) pops pills. Their son Graham (Foster) deals drugs and parties with his pretty friends. Working-class Jack (Renfro in his last role) gets disastrously involved in a kidnapping scheme orchestrated by his perverted surrogate father Peter (Rourke) and the shallowness just keeps getting more apparent. Disturbing, generally unlikeable characters and situations (especially those involving Rourke) make this a waste. **100m/C; Blu-Ray, On Demand.** Billy Bob Thornton; Kim Basinger; Mickey Rourke; Winona Ryder; Jon Foster; Amber Heard; Austin Nichols; Lou Taylor Pucci; Chris Isaak; Rhys Ifans; Bryan Metro; ***D:*** Gregor Jordan; ***W:*** Bret Easton Ellis; Nicholas Jarecki; ***C:*** Petra Korner; ***M:*** Christopher Young.

Infra-Man **WOOF!** *Super Inframan; The Super Inframan; The Infra Superman; Zong guo chhao ren; Chinese Superman* **1976 (PG)** If you're looking for a truly bad, hokey flick, this could be it. Infra-man is a superhero who must rescue the galaxy from the clutches of the evil Princess Dragon Mom and her army of prehistoric monsters. Outlandish dialogue (delivered straight) combines with horrible special effects and costumes to create what may well be one of the best camp classics to date. Poorly dubbed in English. **92m/C; VHS, DVD.** *CH* Li Hsiu-hsien; Danny Lee; Wang Hsieh; Bruce Le; Yuan Mantzu; Terry Liu; Tsen Shu-yi; Huang Chien-lung; Lu Sheng; Hsieh Wang; Man-Tzu Yuan; Wen-wei Lin; ***D:*** Shan Hua; ***W:*** Kuang Ni; ***C:*** Tadashi Nishimoto; ***M:*** Yung-Yu Chen.

The Inglorious Bastards *Quel Maldetto Treno Blindato* **1978** Resembles "The Dirty Dozen" only with less prisoners (and a lesser cast). In 1944, five American soldiers facing time in a military prison escape custody to head for the Swiss border. Having accidentally foiled an Allied plan for stopping a German train carrying an advanced rocket, the quintet must step in and complete the mission, which means a lot of fighting and blowing things up. An in-name-only remake by Quentin Tarantino (with a deliberately misspelled title) was done in 2009. **89m/C; DVD.** *IT* Bo Svenson; Fred Williamson; Peter Hooten; Michael Pergolani; Jackie Basehart; Raimund Harmstorf; Ian Bannen; ***D:*** Enzo G. Castellari; ***W:*** Sandro Continenza; Sergio Grieco; Laura Toscano; ***C:*** Giovanni Bergamini; ***M:*** Francesco De Masi.

Inglourious Basterds **2009 (R)** Tarantino's sorta remake of the 1978 Italian-produced action pic set in WWII. American Lt. Aldo Raine (Pitt) puts together a squad of Jewish soldiers to attack the Nazis in brutal guerrilla raids. Meanwhile, teenager Shosanna (Laurent) has witnessed her family's extermination by the Nazis and vows revenge. All are pursued by an icily charming SS officer (Waltz, in a brilliant performance). Ten years in the making, the screenplay shows off Tarantino's legendary ear for dialogue, and he does a fantastic job of building tension and atmosphere. Pacing is a bit of a problem, and those who are looking for non-stop action will be disappointed. The violence, when it does show up, is swift and graphic. All of Tarantino's strengths and weaknesses are on full display, giving plenty of ammo to both his admirers and detractors. **153m/C; Blu-Ray, On Demand.** Brad Pitt; Diane Kruger; Melanie Laurent; Christoph Waltz; Samm Levine; B.J. Novak; Eli Roth; Daniel Brühl; Til Schweiger; Mike Myers; Cloris Leachman; Michael Fassbender; Maggie Cheung; Rod Taylor; Gedeon Burkhard; Omar Doom; August Diehl; Julie Dreyfus; Martin Wuttke; Michael Bacall; Bo Svenson; Jacky Ido; Denis Menochet; Sylvester Groth; Anne-Sophie Franck; ***Nar:*** Samuel L. Jackson; ***D:*** Quentin Tarantino; ***W:*** Quentin Tarantino; ***C:*** Robert Richardson. Oscars '09: Support. Actor (Waltz); British Acad. '09: Support. Actor (Waltz); Golden Globes '10: Support. Actor (Waltz); Screen Actors Guild '09: Cast, Support. Actor (Waltz).

Ingrid Goes West ½ **2017 (R)** An insightful, satirical comedy that explores on the power of social media through the unbalanced stalker Ingrid Thorburn, whose lost yet needy obsessiveness is played with empathy by Aubrey Plaza. After a stay in a psychiatric hospital and her mother's death, Ingrid uses the money she inherits to go to Los Angeles and worm her way into the life of Taylor Sloane (Olsen), an Instagram star and influencer. Ingrid's time as Taylor's BFF is short-lived as she learns the hard way that the perfect life on social media does not translate into a real, meaningful relationship. The debut directorial effort by Matt Spicer features on-point dialogue, sharp commentary on the culture of Los Angeles, and a savvy performance by Plaza. **98m/C; DVD, Blu-Ray.** Aubrey Plaza; Elizabeth Olsen; O'Shea Jackson, Jr.; Wyatt Russell; Billy Magnussen; ***D:*** Matt Spicer; ***W:*** Matt Spicer; David Branson Smith; ***C:*** Bryce Fortner; ***M:*** Jonathan Sadoff; Nick Thorburn.

Inhale ½ **2010** Unbelievable situations distract from this thriller's potential. Distraught parents Paul and Diane Stanton will do anything for their dying teenage daughter Chloe who needs a lung transplant. Paul heads to Juarez, Mexico's black market, and soon discovers that illegal organ trafficking can be very dangerous, especially when it involves murder. **84m/C; DVD.** Dermot Mulroney; Diane Kruger; Rosanna Arquette; Vincent Perez; Sam Shepard; Jordi Molla; Mia Stallard; David Selby; ***D:*** Baltasar Kormakur; ***W:*** John Claflin; Walter A. Doty, III; ***C:*** Ottar Gudnason; ***M:*** James Newton Howard. **VIDEO**

Inherent Vice **2014 (R)** Anderson adapts Thomas Pynchon's most accessible (but still generally considered unfilmable) novel about Doc Sportello (Phoenix), a Los Angeleno in the '70s who gets caught up in a web of intrigue and possibly murder. Sorta. Not really. The plot of PTA's fantastic work is entirely secondary to the mood it sets and carries throughout. Those who try to follow its story are missing the point, man. It's about getting lost in a changing world, and every element of the film, down to even the smallest performances and technical choices, could be studied in a film class. **148m/C; DVD, Blu-Ray.** Joaquin Rafael (Leaf) Phoenix; Josh Brolin; Owen Wilson; Reese Witherspoon; Joanna Newsom; Jena Malone; Sasha Pieterse; Katherine Waterston; Eric Roberts; Maya Rudolph; Benicio Del Toro; Martin Short; ***D:*** Paul Thomas Anderson; ***W:*** Paul Thomas Anderson; ***C:*** Robert Elswit; ***M:*** Jonny Greenwood. Ind. Spirit '15: Cast.

Inherit the Wind **1960** Powerful courtroom drama, based on the Broadway play, is actually a fictionalized version of the infamous Scopes "Monkey Trial" of 1925. Tracy is the defense attorney for the schoolteacher on trial for teaching Darwin's Theory of Evolution to a group of students in a small town ruled by religion. March is the prosecutor seeking to put the teacher behind bars and restore religion to the schools. **128m/B; VHS, DVD, Blu-Ray.** Spencer Tracy; Fredric March; Florence Eldridge; Gene Kelly; Dick York; Donna Anderson; Harry (Henry) Morgan; Elliott Reid; Philip Coolidge; Claude Akins; Noah Beery, Jr.; Norman Fell; ***D:*** Stanley Kramer; ***W:*** Nedrick Young; Harold Jacob Smith; ***C:*** Ernest Laszlo; ***M:*** Ernest Gold. Berlin Intl. Film Fest. '60: Actor (March).

Inherit the Wind 1/2 **1999 (PG)** Adaptation of the 1955 play by Jerome Lawrence and Robert E. Lee, previously filmed in 1960 and based on the 1925 Scopes Monkey Trial. Tennessee science teacher Bertram Cates (Tom Everett Scott) is being prosecuted for teaching evolution. Agnostic attorney Henry Drummond (Lemmon) comes to town to defend Cates against respected, conservative prosecutor Matthew Harrison Brady (George C. Scott) who wants to keep religious teachings in the school. **113m/C; DVD.** Jack Lemmon; George C. Scott; Tom Everett Scott; Piper Laurie; Beau Bridges; John Cullum; Kathryn Morris; Lane Smith; Brad Greenquist; David Wells; Royce D. Applegate; Dirk Blocker; Russ Tamblyn; Steve Monroe; ***D:*** Daniel Petrie; ***W:*** Nedrick Young; Harold Jacob Smith; ***C:*** James Bartle; ***M:*** Laurence Rosenthal. **CABLE**

Inheritance *Uncle Silas* **1947** Victorian-era melodrama of a young heiress endangered by her guradian, who plots to murder his charge for her inheritance. Chilling and moody story based on a novel by Sheridan Le Fanu. **103m/B; VHS, DVD.** *GB* Jean Simmons; Katina Paxinou; Derrick DeMarney; Derek Bond; ***D:*** Charles Frank.

The Inheritance 1/2 *L'Eredita Ferramonti* **1976 (R)** Wealthy partiarch becomes sexually involved with scheming daughter-in-law. Tawdry tale is nonetheless engaging. **121m/C; VHS, DVD.** *IT* Anthony Quinn; Fabio Testi; Dominique Sanda; ***D:*** Mauro Bolognini; ***W:*** Sergio Bazzini; ***C:*** Ennio Guarnieri; ***M:*** Ennio Morricone. Cannes '76: Actress (Sanda).

The Inheritance *Arven* **1976** Christoffer (Thomsen) is bullied by his manipulative mother Annelise (Norby) to take over the family's near-bankrupt steel company in Copenhagen after his father commits suicide. Doing this means making hard decisions, both personally and professionally, that torment Christoffer and cause serious problems within his family. Danish and Swedish with subtitles. **115m/C; DVD.** *CZ* Ulrich Thomsen; Ghita Norby; Lisa Welinder; Lars Brygmann; Karina Skands; ***D:*** Per Fly; ***W:*** Per Fly; Kim Leona; ***C:*** Harald Gunnar Paalgard.

The Inheritance 1/2 **1997** Loose adaptation of a novella by a teenage Louisa May Alcott. Orphaned Edith Adelon is the longtime companion of Amy Hamilton, living on her wealthy family's Massachusetts estate. Cousin Ida comes to visit with matrimonial intentions towards two of the local bachelors but Edith turns out to be more appealing, especially to rich James Percy. Ida's jealous manipulations, a horse race, Edith's lesser social standing, and Hamilton family secrets all play a part in the drama. **95m/C; DVD.** Cari Shayne; Thomas Gibson; Tom Conti; Meredith Baxter; Brigitta Dau; Brigid Brannagh; Paul Anthony Stewart; Max Gail; ***D:*** Bobby Roth; ***W:*** Maria Nation; ***C:*** Shelly Johnson; ***M:*** Christopher Franke. **TV**

The Inheritance 1/2 **2010** Compelling story and good acting although not as much horror as a viewer might expect. Five cousins are called to a cabin for a reunion only to discover just how their families have prospered over the generations. African witch doctor Chakabazz became a southern slave and revives after a lynching. He offers other slaves freedom and wealth if they will sacrifice their brightest children to him so that he can keep his powers alive—and they have agreed for more than a century. **84m/C; DVD.** Keith David; Novella Nelson; Adriane Lenox; Golden Brooks; DB Woodside; Darrin Dewitt Henson; Rochelle Aytes; Shawn Michael Howard; Lanre Idewu; ***D:*** Robert O'Hara; ***W:*** Robert O'Hara; ***C:*** Tommy Maddox-Upshaw; ***M:*** Nathan Furst.

The Inheritors 1/2 **1982** Not-too-subtle tale of a young German boy who becomes involved with a Nazi youth group as his home life deteriorates. Heavy-going anti-fascism creates more message than entertainment. In German with English subtitles or dubbed. **89m/C; VHS, DVD, Blu-Ray.** *GE* Nikolas Vogel; Roger Schauer; Klaus Novak; Johanna Tomek; ***D:*** Walter Bannert; ***W:*** Walter Bannert.

The Inheritors *Die Siebtelbauern* **1998 (R)** Seven peasants in 1930s rural Austria unexpectedly inherit the farm they've been working from its misanthropic owner, who was murdered by an elderly peasant woman. The foreman (Pruckner) tries to bully the others to sell the farm to the neighboring gentry, Danniger (Wildgruber). When they refuse, the twosome try to sabotage the property, which leads to the foreman's death and places the peasants in the murderous path of the intolerant locals. German with subtitles. **94m/C; VHS, DVD.** *GE* Tilo Pruckner; Ulrich Wildgruber; Simon Schwarz; Sophie Rois; Lars Rudolph; Julia Gschnitzer; ***D:*** Stefan Ruzowitzky; ***W:*** Stefan Ruzowitzky; ***C:*** Peter von Haller.

Inhuman Resources 1/2 *Fangoria Presents: Inhuman Resources; Redd Inc.* **2012 (R)** A former office manager convicted of being a serial killer kidnaps 5 people and tells them to prove he is innocent or die a slow, horrifyingly painful death. **93m/C; DVD.** *AU* Nicholas Hope; Kelly Paterniti; Sam Reid; Alan Dukes; James Mackay; ***D:*** Daniel Krige; ***W:*** Jonathon Green; Anthony O'Connor; ***C:*** Richard Bradshaw; ***M:*** Michael Yezerski. **VIDEO**

Inhumanity **2000** Serial killer thriller is indescribably inept. Though the lead performances are mostly all right, supporting work is amateur. The film is padded with shots of traffic and buildings in Dallas. Lighting, writing, and directing are substandard. **90m/C; DVD.** Todd Bridges; Faizon Love; Carl Jackson; Georgia Foy; Billy Davis; ***D:*** Carl Jackson; ***W:*** Carl Jackson; ***C:*** Kurt Ugland; ***M:*** Damon Criswell.

The Initiation **1984 (R)** Trying to rid herself of a troublesome nightmare, a coed finds herself face-to-face with a psycho. Gory campus slaughterfest. **97m/C; VHS, DVD.** Vera Miles; Clu Gulager; James Read; Daphne Zuniga; ***D:*** Larry Stewart.

Initiation **1987** Danny (Harvey) leaves America for Australia after the death of his mother. His father has fallen on hard times and has been reduced to smuggling drugs, and the local Aborigine mystic makes a few unsettling predictions about his future. Sure enough when he goes with his dad on a run tragedy strikes, and Danny has to navigate a few hundred miles of bush country to get help. **100m/C; DVD.** *AU* Bruno Lawrence; Rodney Harvey; Anna-Maria Winchester; Miranda Otto; Bobby Smith; Tony Barry; Luciano Catenacci; David Tyler; Mladen Mladenov; Sandra Stewart; Katrina Sedgwick; ***D:*** Michael Pearce; ***W:*** James Barton; ***C:*** Geoffrey Simpson; ***M:*** Stephen Matters.

Initiation of Sarah **1978** College freshman joins a sorority, undergoes abusive initiation, and gains a supernatural revenge. "Carrie" rip-off. **100m/C; VHS, DVD.** Kay Lenz; Shelley Winters; Kathryn Crosby; Morgan Brittany; Tony Bill; Tisa Farrow; Robert Hays; Morgan Fairchild; ***D:*** Robert Day. **TV**

The Initiation of Sarah 1/2 **2006** Dull ABC Family remake of the 1978 TV frightener. Fraternal twin sisters, nonconformist Sarah (Boorem) and insecure Lindsey (Glau), are freshmen at Temple Hill University. Their domineering mother Trina (Fairchild) is determined that they pledge her old sorority Alpha Nu Gamma, who happen to be a coven of witches. They need a virgin blood sacrifice to keep their mojo working and Sarah seems to be the chosen one. However, Sarah prefers Pi Epsilon Delta (also witches, only good ones) and making out with boyfriend Finn (Ziff), so that whole virgin thing may be moot. **90m/C; DVD.** Mika Boorem; Summer Glau; Morgan Fairchild; Joanna Garcia; Jennifer Tilly; Tessa Thompson; Ben Ziff; ***D:*** Stuart Gillard; ***W:*** Daniel Berendsen; ***C:*** Manfred Guthe; ***M:*** John Van Tongeren.

Inkheart **2009 (PG)** As a "silvertongue," Mo (Fraser) has the power to bring book characters to life simply by reading aloud. He travels the world with teenaged daughter, Meggie (Bennett), as a professional book buyer in search of an exceptionally rare medieval tale that wreaked havoc on their lives. Years earlier, while reading that book Mo unleashed the nefarious characters Dustfinger (Bettany) and Capricorn (Serkis) while accidentally banishing his wife into the book, because when a silvertongue draws a character out someone must be sent in. As he tries to bring her back and return Dustfinger and Capricorn to their dusty pages, Capricorn employs all manner of magical powers to interfere and conquer the world. Based on the novel by Cornelia Funke, the special effects are thrilling but the complicated story struggles on the big screen. **105m/C; Blu-Ray.** Brendan Fraser; Eliza Bennett; Paul Bettany; Andy Serkis; Dame Helen Mirren; Sienna Guillory; Rafi Gavron; Jim Broadbent; ***D:*** Iain Softley; ***W:*** David Lindsay-Abaire; ***C:*** Roger Pratt; ***M:*** Javier Navarrete.

The Inkwell 1/2 **1994 (R)** Quiet teenager Drew Tate finds first love when his family spends their vacation with relatives on Martha's Vineyard. Drew is drawn into the party atmosphere of the Inkwell, the area where affluent black professionals have summered for decades. Meanwhile, political differences between Drew's former Black Panther father and his conservative uncle threaten family harmony. Everything about the film has a sugary aura, with conflicts handled tastefully. Rich directs broadly, leading to some overacting. Film is set in 1976. **112m/C; VHS, DVD, Blu-Ray.** Larenz Tate; Joe Morton; Phyllis Stickney; Jada Pinkett Smith; ***D:*** Matty Rich; ***W:*** Paris Qualles; Trey Ellis; ***C:*** John L. (Ndiaga) Demps, Jr.; ***M:*** Terence Blanchard.

Inland Empire **2006 (R)** Lynch has taken his film experiments to a whole new level of weirdness with this digital-video effort. Nikki (Dern) is a married actress who is warned by her sinister new neighbor (Zabriskie), who may be a Polish Gypsy, that she shouldn't take the part in a new film because bad things will happen, but she doesn't listen. Nikki and married co-star Devon (Theroux) are playing characters (Sue and Billy) that have an affair, which leaks over into their real lives. And then they find out that their film is a remake of a Polish movie where the two leads were murdered. Giant talking rabbits and Polish hookers are also involved and there's something about an alternate reality—or maybe Lynch'. **172m/C; DVD.** *US PL FR* Laura Dern; Justin Theroux; Jeremy Irons; Harry Dean Stanton; Grace Zabriskie; Peter J. Lucas; Diane Ladd; Julia Ormond; Ian Abercrombie; Laura Elena Harring; ***V:*** Scott Coffey; Naomi Watts; ***D:*** David Lynch; ***W:*** David Lynch; ***C:*** Odd Geir Saether.

Inn of the Damned 1/2 **1974** Detective looks into an inn where no one ever gets charged for an extra day; they simply die. Anderson is watchable. **92m/C; VHS, DVD.** *AU* Alex Cord; Judith Anderson; Tony Bonner; Michael Craig; John Meillon; ***D:*** Terry Burke.

The Inn of the Sixth Happiness **1958** Inspiring story of Gladys Aylward, an English missionary in 1930s' China, who leads a group of children through war-torn countryside. Donat's last film. **158m/C; VHS, DVD, Blu-Ray.** Ingrid Bergman; Robert Donat; Curt Jurgens; ***D:*** Mark Robson; ***C:*** Frederick A. (Freddie) Young; ***M:*** Malcolm Arnold. Natl. Bd. of Review '58: Actress (Bergman).

Inn on the River 1/2 **1962** Scotland Yard investigates a series of murders taking place on the waterfront by the "Shark's" gang. Remake of "The Return of the Frog." **95m/C; VHS, DVD.** *GE* Klaus Kinski; Joachim Fuchsberger; Brigitte Grothum; Richard Much; ***D:*** Alfred Vohrer.

The Inner Circle **1991 (PG-13)** Ivan Sanshin is a meek, married man working as a movie projectionist for the KGB in 1935 Russia. Sanshin is taken by the KGB to the Kremlin to show movies, primarily Hollywood features, to leader Joseph Stalin, a job he cannot discuss with anyone, even his wife. Under the spell of Stalin's personality, Sanshin sees only what he's told and overlooks the oppression and persecution of the times. Based on the life of the projectionist who served from 1935 until Stalin's death in 1953. Filmed on location at the Kremlin. **122m/C; VHS, Streaming.** Tom Hulce; Lolita Davidovich; Bob Hoskins; Alexandre Zbruev; Maria Baranova; Feodor Chaliapin, Jr.; Bess Meyer; ***D:*** Andrei Konchalovsky; ***W:*** Andrei Konchalovsky; Anatoli Usov; ***M:*** Eduard Artemyev.

Inner Sanctum WOOF! 1991 (R) Cheating husband hires sensuous nurse to tend invalid wife. You can guess the rest; in fact, you have to because the plot ultimately makes no sense. Available in R-rated and sex-drenched unrated editions. **87m/C; VHS, DVD.** Tanya Roberts; Margaux Hemingway; Joseph Bottoms; Valerie Wildman; William Butler; Brett (Baxter) Clark; ***D:*** Fred Olen Ray.

Innerspace 1/2 **1987 (PG)** A space pilot, miniaturized for a journey through a lab rat a la "Fantastic Voyage," is accidentally injected into a nebbish supermarket clerk, and together they nab some bad guys and get the girl. Award-winning special effects support some funny moments between micro Quaid and nerdy Short, with Ryan producing the confused romantic interest. **120m/C; VHS, DVD, Blu-Ray.** Dennis Quaid; Martin Short; Meg Ryan; Kevin McCarthy; Fiona Lewis; Henry Gibson; Robert Picardo; John Hora; Wendy Schaal; Orson Bean; Chuck Jones; William Schallert; Dick Miller; Vernon Wells; Harold Sylvester; Kevin Hooks; Kathleen Freeman; Kenneth Tobey; ***D:*** Joe Dante; ***W:*** Jeffrey Boam; Chip Proser; ***M:*** Jerry Goldsmith. Oscars '87: Visual FX.

The Innkeepers 1/2 **2011 (R)** Indie wunderkind director West's best horror film to date is a clever nod to the subgenre in which people looking for ghosts should be careful what they wish for. Using the hotel they stayed in when they shot House of the Devil as inspiration, West tells the story of two employees (Paxton, Healy) on the last night of the Yankee Pedlar Inn. Trying to prove it's haunted before it closes for good, the pair stumbles across something truly terrifying. A slow build leads to a big payoff with a chilling final act even the most hardened horror veteran will enjoy. **100m/C; DVD, Blu-Ray.** Sara Paxton; Pat Healy; Kelly McGillis; Lena Dunham; Alison Bartlett; Jake Ryan; ***D:*** Ti West; ***W:*** Ti West; ***C:*** Eliot Rockett; ***M:*** Jeff Grace.

Innocence 1/2 **2000 (R)** Sweet tale of lasting love has postwar teenaged Belgian lovers meeting again 45 years later in Australia. Andreas is an affable widower who finds out his long-lost love, Claire, is living in his town and looks her up. Claire is still married, but soon the old feelings are rekindled between the two and they begin an affair. Film deals honestly and beautifully with the endurance of true love, and how the routines and expectations of everyday life are affected by it. The role of Andreas was originally written for Kaye, but illness forced him to take a smaller, supporting role. **96m/C; VHS, DVD.** *AU* Julia Blake; Charles "Bud" Tingwell; Terry Norris; Robert Menzies; Chris Haywood; Norman Kaye; Joey Kennedy; Marta Dusseldorp; Kristien Van Pellicom; Kenny Aernouts; ***D:*** Paul Cox; ***W:*** Paul Cox; ***C:*** Tony Clark; ***M:*** Paul Grabowsky.

Innocence Unprotected 1/2 **1968** A film collage that contains footage from the 1942 film "Innocence Unprotected," the story of an acrobat trying to save an orphan from her wicked stepmother, newsreels from Nazi-occupied Yugoslavia, and interviews from 1968 with people who were in the film. Confiscated by the Nazis during final production, "Innocence Unprotected" was discovered by director Makavejev, who worked it into the collage. Filmed in color and black and white; in Serbian with English subtitles. **78m/C; VHS, DVD.** *YU* Dragoljub Aleksic; Ana Milosavljevic; Vera Jovanovic; ***D:*** Dusan Makavejev; ***W:*** Dusan Makavejev.

The Innocent *L'Innocente* **1976** Visconti's final film is a stately costume drama adapted from Gabriele D'Annunzio's 1892 novel. Aristocrat Tullio (Giannini) is openly carrying on an affair with manipulative Teresa (O'Neill) and expects his wife Guilliana (Antonelli) not only to understand but to help him when he returns to her. However, he's not so understanding when he discovers Guilliana had her own lover and is now pregnant. Italian with subtitles. **112m/C; DVD.** *IT* Giancarlo Giannini; Laura Antonelli; Jennifer O'Neill; Massimo Girotti; Marc Porel; Rina Morelli; ***D:*** Luchino Visconti; ***W:*** Suso Cecchi D'Amico; Enrico Medioli; ***C:*** Pasqualino De Santis; ***M:*** Franco Mannino.

The Innocent 1/2 **1993 (R)** Cold War thriller has naive British engineer Leonard Markham (Scott) sent to Berlin in 1955 by

Brits who are warily cooperating with the U.S. forces. He's turned over to CIA operator Bob Glass (Hopkins) and asked to intercept communications between East Germany and the Soviet Union. Glass continually warns Markham not to trust anyone, including Maria (Rossellini), the married German woman with whom he begins an affair. Failure to build necessary suspense and performances leads to disappointing one-note display. Based on the novel by McEwan. **97m/C; VHS, DVD.** *GE GB* Anthony Hopkins; Campbell Scott; Isabella Rossellini; Hart Bochner; James Grant; Jeremy Sinden; Ronald Nitschke; ***D:*** John Schlesinger; ***W:*** Ian McEwan; ***M:*** Gerald Gouriet.

Innocent Blood **1992 (R)** A mediocre modern-day vampire/gangster combo with the beautiful (though red-eyed) Parillaud as the woman with a taste for someone "Italian." Unfortunately, she doesn't finish off her latest meal—mobster Loggia—who finds being undead very useful to his vicious work. LaPaglia plays the bewildered, love-struck cop involved with the vamp. Parillaud appears nude in several scenes and the gore and violence are stomach-turning. **112m/C; VHS, DVD, Blu-Ray.** Anne Parillaud; Anthony LaPaglia; Robert Loggia; David Proval; Don Rickles; Rocco Sisto; Kim Coates; Chazz Palminteri; Angela Bassett; Tom Savini; Frank Oz; Forrest J Ackerman; Sam Raimi; Dario Argento; Linnea Quigley; ***D:*** John Landis; ***W:*** Michael Wolk; ***C:*** Mac Ahlberg; ***M:*** Ira Newborn.

Innocent Bystanders **1972** Quasi-Bondian spy adventure. Aging Brit spy John Craig (Baker) is given one last chance by boss Loomis (Pleasence), who assigns him to find a Russian scientist who escaped a Siberian gulag. Craig has to contend with two younger colleagues, a CIA agent, and a woman with information as he travels to New York, Turkey, and Cypress. Betrayal is close at hand. **111m/C; DVD, Blu-Ray.** *UK* Stanley Baker; Donald Pleasence; Geraldine Chaplin; Dana Andrews; Sue Lloyd; Derren Nesbitt; ***D:*** Peter Collinson; ***W:*** James Mitchell; ***C:*** Brian Probyn; ***M:*** Johnny Keating.

Innocent Lies 1/2 **1995 (R)** In 1938, British policeman Alan Cross (Dunbar) heads for an island off the French coast to look into the suicide of a colleague who was investigating the expatriate Graves family. There are family tensions, skeletons in the closet, and some Nazi-sympathizers all mixed together in an old-fashioned but satisfying stew. **88m/C; VHS, DVD.** *FR GB* Adrian Dunbar; Stephen Dorff; Gabrielle Anwar; Joanna Lumley; ***D:*** Patrick Dewolf; ***W:*** Kerry Crabbe; Patrick Dewolf; ***C:*** Patrick Blossier; ***M:*** Alexandre Desplat.

An Innocent Man 1/2 **1989 (R)** Uneven story of Selleck, an ordinary family man and airline mechanic, framed as a drug dealer and sent to prison. **113m/C; VHS, DVD, Blu-Ray.** Tom Selleck; F. Murray Abraham; Laila Robins; David Rasche; Richard Young; Badja (Medu) Djola; ***D:*** Peter Yates; ***W:*** Larry Brothers; ***M:*** Howard Shore.

The Innocent Sleep 1/2 **1995 (R)** Adequate thriller that stays true to genre cliches. Homeless drunk Alan Terry (Graves) witnesses an execution (by hanging) from London's Tower Bridge, near where he's bedded down. He's spotted but manages to escape. When he tries to report the crime, Terry realizes that one of the killers is police investigator Matheson (Gambon). Terry then goes to tabloid journalist Billie Hayman (Sciorra) for help but her probing into the death leads to even more danger. **96m/C; VHS, DVD.** *GB* Rupert Graves; Annabella Sciorra; Michael Gambon; Franco Nero; Graham Crowden; John Hannah; ***D:*** Scott Michell; ***W:*** Ray Villis; ***C:*** Alan Dunlop; ***M:*** Mark Ayres.

Innocent Sorcerers *Niewinni Czarodzieje* **1960** Ironic comedy about aimless '60s Polish youth that finds a young doctor having trouble committing himself to his superficial girlfriend and coping with the problems of his cynical friends. Polish with subtitles. **86m/B; VHS, DVD.** *PL* Tadeusz Lomnicki; Zbigniew Cybulski; Roman Polanski; Krystyna Stypulkowska; Jerzy Skolimowski; ***D:*** Andrzej Wajda; ***W:*** Jerzy Skolimowski; Andrzej Wajda; ***M:*** Krzysztof Komeda.

Innocent Voices *Voces inocentes* **2004 (R)** In the 1980's, Chava (Padilla) is the 11-year-old man of the family, trying to help his mother Kella (Varela) and his siblings survive during El Salvador's protracted civil war. Things are going to get worse since 12 is the legal age for conscription into the right-wing government's army. The horrifying and bewildering events are seen through Chava's eyes and are based on the experiences of co-writer Torres. Spanish with subtitles. **120m/C; DVD.** Leonor Varela; Jose Maria Yazpik; Ofelia Medina; Daniel Gimenez Cacho; Jesus Ochoa; Carlos Padilla; Gustavo Munoz; ***D:*** Luis Mandoki; ***W:*** Oscar Torres; ***C:*** Juan Ruiz-Anchia; ***M:*** Andre Abujamra.

The Innocents 1/2 **1961** Incredibly creepy version of Henry James' "The Turn of the Screw." Minister's daughter, Miss Giddens (Kerr), is hired by Redgrave (known only as "The Uncle") as governess to young Flora (Franklin) and her brother Miles (Stephens) at his country estate. Miss Giddens begins to see the specters of a man and a woman and is told her descriptions match that of former estate manager Peter Quint and the last governess, his mistress, whose influence on the children was thought to be malevolent. Indeed, Miss Giddens believes the children are possessed by evil—but is it true or a product of her own hysteria? **85m/B; VHS, DVD, Blu-Ray.** *GB* Deborah Kerr; Michael Redgrave; Pamela Franklin; Martin Stephens; Peter Wyngarde; Megs Jenkins; Clytie Jessop; Isla Cameron; Eric Woodburn; ***D:*** Jack Clayton; ***W:*** Truman Capote; William Archibald; John Mortimer; ***C:*** Freddie Francis; ***M:*** Georges Auric.

Innocents 1/2 *Dark Summer* **2000** Boring thriller about French cellist Gerard (Anglade) who gets involved with beautiful Megan (Nielsen) and her disturbed younger sister, Dominique (Kirshner). After the sisters' father (Langella) dies, the trio head to Seattle to tell mom (Archer) she's now a widow. The road trip takes a turn for the worst when a judge (Culp) gets killed and Gerard gets blamed. Never does make much sense. **90m/C; VHS, DVD.** *CA* Jean-Hugues Anglade; Connie Nielsen; Mia Kirshner; Robert Culp; Anne Archer; Keith David; Joseph Culp; ***Cameo(s):*** Frank Langella; ***D:*** Gregory Marquette; ***W:*** Gregory Marquette; ***C:*** Bruce Worrall; ***M:*** Michel Colombier.

The Innocents *Les innocentes* **2016 (PG-13)** Based on a true story in 1945 Poland, a young French Red Cross worker Mathilde (de Laage) is called upon to visit a local convent, where she discovers several pregnant nuns. The women were violated by the occupying Red Army, but despite their situation many rebuff Mathilde's assistance since she's not of the faith. A compelling look at those who hold true to their religion despite having every reason not to, and at those who view the world from a purely scientific perspective. Is there something in between? A nearly all-female cast portrays the sensitive material with grace. With Polish and French subtitles. **115m/C; DVD.** Lou de Laâge; Agata Buzek; Agata Kulesza; Vincent Macaigne; Joanna Kulig; ***D:*** Anne Fontaine; ***W:*** Anne Fontaine; Pascal Bonitzer; ***C:*** Caroline Champetier; ***M:*** Gregoire Hetzel.

Innocents with Dirty Hands *Les Innocents aux Mains Sales; Dirty Hands* **1976** A woman and her lover conspire to murder her husband. A must for fans of the sexy Schneider. Cinematography provides moments that are both interesting and eerie. **102m/C; VHS, DVD.** *FR* Rod Steiger; Romy Schneider; Paul(o) Giusti; Jean Rochefort; Hans-Christian Blech; ***D:*** Claude Chabrol.

Inquisition 1/2 **1976** Naschy is a 16th century witch hunting judge who finds himself accused of witchcraft. **85m/C; VHS, DVD, Blu-Ray.** *SP* Paul Naschy; Daniela Giordano; Juan Gallardo; Monica Randall; ***D:*** Paul Naschy; ***W:*** Paul Naschy.

Insanitarium **2008 (R)** Ooh, blood, gore and flesh-eating psychos! How much fun is that? Well, more than you might expect from Buhler's directorial debut, which doesn't take itself too seriously. Lily (Sanchez) is institutionalized after a suicide attempt and when her equally troubled brother Jack (Metcalfe) can't contact her, he decides to get himself committed as well. He discovers the real loon is doc-in-charge Gianetti (Stomare), who's been experimenting on his patients with a drug "therapy" that turns them into gleeful, blood-thirsty cannibals. **89m/C; DVD.** Jesse Metcalfe; Lisa Arturo; Armin Shimerman; Carla Gallo; Kevin Sussman; Kiele Sanchez; Peter Stomare; ***D:*** Jeff Buhler; ***W:*** Jeff Buhler; ***C:*** Robert Hauer; ***M:*** Paul D'Amour. **VIDEO**

Insanity *Striptease* **1976** A film director becomes violently obsessed with a beautiful actress. **101m/C; VHS, DVD.** *SP* Terence Stamp; Fernando Rey; Corinne Clery; ***D:*** German Lorente; ***W:*** German Lorente; ***C:*** Antonio Ballesteros; ***M:*** Francis Lai.

The Insatiable **2006** Shy Harry (Flanery) witnesses a murder by beautiful vampire Tatiana (Ayanna). Since no one believes his story, Harry decides to track her down before she can strike again. But when he gets up close and personal, Harry can't kill Tatiana. Instead he puts her in a cage in his basement, trying to figure out what to do. But she'll die without fresh blood, so Harry has to find a way to keep her fed and satisfied. **103m/C; DVD.** Sean Patrick Flanery; Charlotte Ayanna; Michael Biehn; Josh Hopkins; Boyd Kestner; Jon Huertas; Brad Rowe; ***D:*** Chuck Konzelman; Cary Solomon; ***W:*** Chuck Konzelman; Cary Solomon; ***C:*** Mike Washlesky; ***M:*** Christopher Tin. **VIDEO**

The Insect Woman *The Insect; Nippon Konchuki* **1963** Chronicles 45 years in the life of a woman who must work with the diligence of an ant in order to survive. Thoughtfully reflects the exploitation of women and the cruelty of human nature in Japanese society. Beautiful performance from Hidari, who ages from girlhood to middle age. In Japanese with English subtitles. **123m/B; VHS, DVD.** *JP* Sachiko Hidari; Jitsuko Yoshimura; Hiroyuki Nagaes; Sumie Sasaki; ***D:*** Shohei Imamura.

Insecticidal **2005 (R)** Oy. A science experiment by sorority girl Cami in insect intelligence goes wrong and giant mutant insects attack the sorority house. Girls run around in their scanties being bugged by really bad CGI. **81m/C; DVD, Blu-Ray.** Meghan Heffern; Rhonda Dent; Samantha McLeod; Vicky Huang; ***D:*** Jeffrey Scott Lando; ***W:*** Jeff O'Brien; ***C:*** Pieter Stathis; ***M:*** Chris Nickel. **VIDEO**

Inseminoid **WOOF!** *Horror Planet* **1980 (R)** Alien creature needs a chance to breed before moving on to spread its horror. When a group of explorers disturbs it, the years of waiting are over, and the unlucky mother-to-be will never be the same. Graphic and sensationalistic, capitalizing on the popularity of "Aliens." **93m/C; VHS, DVD, Blu-Ray.** *GB* Robin Clarke; Jennifer Ashley; Stephanie Beacham; Judy Geeson; Stephen Grives; Victoria Tennant; ***D:*** Norman J. Warren; ***W:*** Gloria Maley; Nick Maley; ***C:*** John Metcalfe; ***M:*** John Scott.

Inserts **1976 (R)** A formerly successful director has been reduced to making porno films in this pretentious, long-winded effort set in a crumbling Hollywood mansion in the 1930s. Affected, windbaggish performances kill it. **99m/C; VHS, DVD, Blu-Ray.** *GB* Richard Dreyfuss; Jessica Harper; Veronica Cartwright; Bob Hoskins; ***D:*** John Byrum; ***W:*** John Byrum.

Inside **1996 (R)** Harrowing anti-apartheid drama finds university professor and white Afrikaaner Peter Martin Strydom (Stoltz) being held in a Johannesburg government prison. He's being interrogated by Col. Kruger (Hawthorne), head of the prison security force, supposedly for conspiracy against the South African regime. Tortured, Strydom's will begins to break as the drama flashes forward ten years, with Colonel Kruger now subjected to interrogation by a nameless black questioner (Gossett Jr.) investigating human rights crimes, including Strydom's fate. **94m/C; VHS, DVD.** Eric Stoltz; Nigel Hawthorne; Louis Gossett, Jr.; ***D:*** Arthur Penn; ***W:*** Bima Stagg; ***C:*** Jan Weincke; ***M:*** Robert Levin. **CABLE**

Inside 1/2 **2006** Reclusive Alex (D'Agosto) likes to spy on people. He follows folks to observe their daily routines and becomes extremely interested in Alice (White) and Mark (Kilner) Smith because of the sadness they project. Alex goes too far and is caught in their home but the Smiths don't call the cops. Seems their only child—a son—has died and Alex looks like him. They start to bond (Alex's own parents are dead) and when he's in a car accident, the Smiths take him in to recover. Only the grieving Alice is now convinced that Alex IS her son returned from the grave and won't ever let him leave. Despite Meester's prominence on the box art, she only has a small role as a kleptomaniac, would-be friend of Alex's. **103m/C; DVD.** Nicholas D'Agosto; Kevin Kilner; Leighton Meester; Cheryl White; ***D:*** mahler Jeff; ***W:*** mahler Jeff; ***C:*** Michael Marius Pessah; ***M:*** Jason Brandt. **VIDEO**

Inside Daisy Clover 1/2 **1965** Wood is the self-sufficient, junior delinquent waif who becomes a teenage musical star and pays the price for fame in this Hollywood saga set in the 1930s. Discovered by tyrannical studio head Plummer, Daisy is given her big break and taken under his wing for grooming as Swan Studio's newest sensation. She falls for fellow performer, matinee idol Redford, who has some secrets of his own, and eventually has a breakdown from the career pressure. Glossy melodrama is filled with over-the-top performances but its sheer silliness makes it amusing. **128m/C; VHS, DVD, Blu-Ray.** Natalie Wood; Christopher Plummer; Robert Redford; Ruth Gordon; Roddy McDowall; Katharine Bard; ***D:*** Robert Mulligan; ***W:*** Gavin Lambert; ***C:*** Charles B(ryant) Lang, Jr.; ***M:*** Andre Previn. Golden Globes '66: Support. Actress (Gordon).

Inside Deep Throat **2005 (NC-17)** Respectable documentary about the landmark porno blockbuster "Deep Throat." Mixes old and new interviews, newsreel footage, and, yes, full-on, full-frontal clips to tell the story of an enterprising hairdresser, Gerard Damiano, who dared to make a porno "film," not a porno "flick." He set out to build a story, create some characters, and inject some (admittedly pretty dumb) humor. He wasn't marketing to the old men in raincoats out for a quick peep, but aiming at couples looking to goose their relationship. It worked. Made for only $25,000, it went on to become the most profitable movie in history, grossing over $600 million. Since Universal produced the documentary, we're thankfully spared gratuitous reenactments. **90m/C; DVD, Streaming.** ***D:*** Fenton Bailey; Randy Barbato; ***W:*** Fenton Bailey; Randy Barbato; ***C:*** Teodoro Maniaci; David Kempner; ***M:*** David Steinberg.

Inside Job **2010 (PG-13)** Ferguson's relentless, incriminating but matter-of-fact documentary examines the global economic crisis from the private sector financial service executives and lobbyists to the government officials who repeatedly neglected financial reforms. Includes archival footage, giving a 30-year overview of Wall Street machinations. Narrated by actor Matt Damon. **120m/C; Blu-Ray, On Demand.** ***Nar:*** Matt Damon; ***D:*** Charles Ferguson; ***W:*** Charles Ferguson; ***C:*** Kalyanee Mam; Svetlana Cvetko; ***M:*** Alex Heffes. Oscars '10: Feature Doc.; Directors Guild '10: Documentary Director (Ferguson); Writers Guild '10: Documentary Screenplay.

Inside Llewyn Davis **2013 (R)** The Coen brothers transport viewers back to Greenwich Village in 1961 in this acquired-taste character study, a film that chronicles not necessarily a hidden talent but someone whose artistic integrity seems to be a tightening noose around his neck. The unlikable title character, played poignantly by Isaac, struggles with unfulfilled career aspirations (and a cat) over the course of a few days in a snow-covered New York. The movie unfolds like a folk album, punctuated by full songs from Isaac and other talented cast members like Mulligan and Timberlake. **105m/C; DVD, Blu-Ray.** Oscar Isaac; Carey Mulligan; Justin Timberlake; Adam Driver; John Goodman; Garrett Hedlund; ***D:*** Ethan Coen; Joel Coen; ***W:*** Ethan Coen; Joel Coen; ***C:*** Bruno Delbonnel.

The Inside Man 1/2 **1984** Double agents struggle to find a submarine-detecting laser device. Based on true incidents in which a soviet sub ran aground in Sweden. Made in Sweden; dubbed. **90m/C; VHS, DVD.** *SW* Dennis Hopper; Hardy Kruger; Gosta Ekman, Jr.; David Wilson; ***D:*** Tom Clegg; ***W:*** Alan Plater; ***C:*** Jorgen Persson; ***M:*** Stefan Nilsson.

Inside Man **2006 (R)** Lee spins the conventional in this over-extended, gabby but well-played crime thriller. Dalton Russell (Owen) and his gang enter a Manhattan bank, apparently to rob the vault. They take hostages but aren't in a hurry to negotiate with slick detective Keith Frazier (Washington). Frazier suspects more is up when icy fixer Madeline White appears, at nervous bank chairman Arthur Case's (Plummer) request, saying Russell must be prevented at any cost from obtaining the contents of a particular safety deposit box. Many twists and turns follow to a satisfying conclusion. **129m/C; DVD, Blu-Ray, HD-DVD.** Denzel Washington; Clive Owen; Jodie Foster; Christopher Plummer; Willem Dafoe; Chiwetel Ejiofor; Peter Gerety; Daryl (Chill) Mitchell; Kim Director; Marcia Jean Kurtz; Waris Ahluwalia; Amir Ali Said; ***D:*** Spike Lee; ***W:*** Russell Gewirtz; ***C:*** Matthew Libatique; ***M:*** Terence Blanchard.

Inside Men 2012 Overextended Brit crime miniseries. It starts with the heist of 250 million pounds at a money-counting firm in Bristol, then flashes back to the planning of the crime by the three inside men. John is a seemingly mild-mannered manager who confronts a couple of employees about filching small amounts of cash and suggests they go for a big score. The action slows down for subplots about their private lives and troubles, then goes back to the crime and its aftermath. **240m/C; DVD.** *UK* Steven Mackintosh; Warren Brown; Ashley Walters; Nicola Walker; Kierston Wareing; Leila Mimmack; ***D:*** James Kent; ***W:*** Tony Basgallop; ***C:*** Tim Fleming; ***M:*** Paul Englishby. **TV**

Inside Monkey Zetterland 1993 **(R)** Monkey Zetterland (Antin) is a screenwriter and former actor with an eccentric family. His actress mother is neurotically insecure and a nag; his father is an aging hippie who only shows up at Thanksgiving; his lesbian sister Grace is trying to get over a failed relationship; and his brother Brent is totally self-absorbed. Add to this menage his equally lunatic friends: Imogene, the compulsive talker and exhibitionist; his vicious girlfriend Daphne; and frightening married couple Sophie and Sasha. Meanwhile, Monkey tries to survive amidst the chaos. Interesting cast but lots of camera tricks do not a successful film make and the effort to be hip is all too apparent. **92m/C; VHS, DVD.** Steve Antin; Patricia Arquette; Sandra Bernhard; Sofia Coppola; Tate Donovan; Katherine Helmond; Bo Hopkins; Debi Mazar; Martha Plimpton; Rupert Everett; Ricki Lake; Lance Loud; Frances Bay; Luca Bercovici; ***D:*** Jefery Levy; ***W:*** Steve Antin; John Boskovich; ***C:*** Christopher Taylor; ***M:*** Rick Cox; Jeff Elmassian.

Inside Moves 1/2 **1980 (PG)** A look at handicapped citizens trying to make it in everyday life, focusing on the relationship between an insecure, failed suicide and a volatile man who is only a knee operation away from a dreamed-about basketball career. **113m/C; VHS, DVD, Blu-Ray.** John Savage; Diana Scarwid; David Morse; Amy Wright; ***D:*** Richard Donner; ***W:*** Valerie Curtin; Barry Levinson; ***M:*** John Barry.

Inside Out 1/2 *The Golden Heist; Hitler's Gold* **1975 (PG)** An ex-GI, a jewel thief and a German POW camp commandant band together to find a stolen shipment of Nazi gold behind the Iron Curtain. To find the gold, they help a Nazi prisoner who knows the secret to break out of prison. Good action caper. **97m/C; VHS, DVD.** *GB* Telly Savalas; Robert Culp; James Mason; Aldo Ray; Doris Kunstmann; ***D:*** Peter Duffell.

Inside Out 1/2 **2005 (R)** Bored in the 'burbs. Neighbors suffer ennui until a mysterious single guy, shrink Dr. Peoples, moves in and antagonizes everyone with his peculiarities. Then the new guy gets suspected of murder. Dull, including the last-minute revelation. **95m/C; DVD.** Eriq La Salle; Steven Weber; Kate Walsh; Russell Wong; Nia Peeples; Tim Maculan; Tyler Posey; ***D:*** David Ogden; ***W:*** David Ogden; ***C:*** Steven Douglas Smith; ***M:*** Jamie Christopherson.

Inside Out 1/2 **2011 (PG-13)** After having served over a decade in prison for manslaughter, AJ (Levesque) looks forward to a life of freedom, including starting a small business. Naturally, small-time mobster and long-time best friend Jack (Rapaport) exposes AJ to an accidental shooting death hours after his release. Evading the authorities, Jack skips town, leaving AJ to protect Jack's wife Claire (Posey) and her daughter Pepper from Jack's violent father, Dr. Vic (Dern). AJ is again forced to become involved with criminal elements, as he also grows closer to Claire, a woman he'd loved for many years. **93m/C; DVD, Blu-Ray.** Paul Levesque; Michael Rapaport; Parker Posey; Michael Cudlitz; Julie White; Bruce Dern; Jency Griffin; ***D:*** Artie Mandelberg; ***W:*** Dylan Schaffer; ***C:*** Kenneth Zunder; ***M:*** James Alan Johnston. **VIDEO**

Inside Out **2015 (PG)** Pixar's first true masterpiece, perfectly weaving grown-up ideas into a brightly-colored package for kids. On the surface, the story follows 11-year-old tomboy hockey player Riley (voiced by Dias) as her parents opt to relocate from comfortable Minnesota to an unfriendly San Francisco. But the real story takes place inside Riley's frustrated, angry, confused, sad head. Her emotions all have a mind and body of their own (voiced by Poehler, Hader, Kaling, Black), trying their best to sort everything out for the bummed Riley. Besides being Pixar's crowning achievement, it's easily one of the most sneaky art films ever, taking as much inspiration from Bugs Bunny as it does the French New Wave. **102m/C; DVD, Blu-Ray, Streaming.** ***V:*** Amy Poehler; Phyllis Smith; Mindy Kaling; Bill Hader; Lewis Black; ***D:*** Pete Docter; Ronnie Del Carmen; ***W:*** Pete Docter; Meg LaFauve; Ronnie Del Carmen; Josh Cooley; ***M:*** Michael Giacchino. Oscars '15: Animated Film; British Acad. '15: Animated Film; Golden Globes '16: Animated Film.

Inside Paris 1/2 *Dans Paris* **2006** Depressed, heartbroken Paul (Duris) moves into his father's apartment after a breakup and immediately confines himself to bed. His father (Marchand), himself divorced, worries that Paul's depression will have tragic results, while Paul's brother Jonathan (Garrel) goofs his way through life and his brother's trauma. All three men struggle to find common ground and understanding in light of Paul's ongoing depression. Tone alternates between fanciful and somber as characters break into song and jump into rivers. For fans of French cinema. **93m/C; DVD.** *FR* Louis Garrel; Guy Marchand; Joana Preiss; Romain Duris; Alice Butaud; ***D:*** Christophe Honore; ***W:*** Christophe Honore; ***C:*** Jean-Louis Vialard; ***M:*** Alexandre Beaupain.

Inside the Lines **1930** A WWI tale of espionage and counter-espionage. **73m/B; VHS, DVD.** Betty Compson; Montagu Love; Mischa Auer; Ralph Forbes; Ivan Simpson; Wilhelm von Brinken; Reginald Sharland; Betty Carter; Evan Thomas; ***D:*** Roy Pomeroy; ***W:*** Ewart Adamson; ***C:*** Nicholas Musuraca; ***M:*** Roy Webb.

Inside the Walls of Folsom Prison **1951** Prison cliches aside, this is a fast-paced drama from Warner Bros. that was filmed on location. In the 1920s, sadistic Warden Rickey routinely brutalizes prisoners and encourages his guards to do the same. College-educated new head guard Benson institutes reforms that get the prisoners on his side and Rickey fires him. This infuriates a group of cons who put an ill-fated escape plan into motion that then leads to further violence. **87m/B; DVD.** Ted de Corsia; David Brian; Steve Cochran; Scott Forbes; Philip Carey; Paul Picerni; Michael (Lawrence) Tolan; Edward Norris; ***D:*** Crane Wilbur; ***W:*** Crane Wilbur; ***C:*** Edwin DuPar; ***M:*** William Lava.

The Insider 1/2 **1999 (R)** Riveting and controversial film that caused a real-life snit at "60 Minutes" over the facts and portrayals in the story. After Jeffrey Wigand (Crowe) is fired from his top-level tobacco company job, he turns whistleblower, claiming his former employers lied about the dangers of cigarettes. Veteran "60 Minutes" producer Lowell Bergman (Pacino) and newsman Mike Wallace (Plummer) pursue the story—only to be shot down by their own network. The fallout causes ethical consequences for all involved. Performances are outstanding—from the chameleon Crowe to the relatively subdued Pacino and the slyly pompous Plummer. Based on a "Vanity Fair" magazine article. **157m/C; VHS, DVD, Blu-Ray.** Russell Crowe; Al Pacino; Christopher Plummer; Gina Gershon; Philip Baker Hall; Diane Venora; Lindsay Crouse; Debi Mazar; Stephen Tobolowsky; Colm Feore; Bruce McGill; Michael Gambon; Rip Torn; Lynne Thigpen; Hallie Kate Eisenberg; Michael Paul Chan; Wings Hauser; Pete Hamill; Nestor Serrano; Michael Moore; ***D:*** Michael Mann; ***W:*** Michael Mann; Eric Roth; ***C:*** Dante Spinotti; ***M:*** Graeme Revell. L.A. Film Critics '99: Actor (Crowe), Cinematog., Film, Support. Actor (Plummer); Natl. Bd. of Review '99: Actor (Crowe); Natl. Soc. Film Critics '99: Actor (Crowe), Support. Actor (Plummer); Broadcast Film Critics '99: Actor (Crowe).

Insidious 1/2 **2010 (PG-13)** Borderline camp horror (that's not played for laughs) enlivens this story of possession. The Lambert family move into a new home that soon appears to be haunted. When young Dalton has an accident and falls into a coma, his even-younger brother starts seeing his hospitalized sibling walking around the house at night. There's a pair of ineffectual ghostbusters and a much-more competent exorcist hired by the Lamberts to find out what ghoulie has taken over their child. **103m/C; DVD, Blu-Ray.** Patrick Wilson; Rose Byrne; Ty Simpkins; Lin Shaye; Andrew Astor; Angus Sampson; Leigh Whannell; ***D:*** James Wan; ***W:*** Leigh Whannell; ***C:*** David M. Brewer; ***M:*** Joseph Bishara.

Insidious: Chapter 2 1/2 **2013 (PG-13)** Give director Wan credit for not merely repeating what led to the success of the first film--yet this still feels like a step back. It's a movie full of interesting ideas but none of them are delivered in a remotely effective way. Part of the problem is that it's all second-act as it picks up literally at the end of the first film with Josh Lambert (Wilson) having returned from the other side to haunt his wife Renai (Byrne) and their kids. More "The Shining" than the previous film, it repeats itself before getting to a final act that's more ridiculous than terrifying. **106m/C; DVD, Blu-Ray.** Patrick Wilson; Rose Byrne; Ty Simpkins; Lin Shaye; Barbara Hershey; Leigh Whannell; ***D:*** James Wan; ***W:*** Leigh Whannell; James Wan; ***C:*** John R. Leonetti; ***M:*** Joseph Bishara.

Insidious: Chapter 3 **2015 (PG-13)** Despite the title, this third entry is actually a prequel, following the gradual demon-possession of high schooler Quinn (Scott), from an apparition living in her apartment's vent system. Her widowed father (Mulroney) calls in the familiar spiritual medium Elise Rainier (Shaye) and her goofball ghostbusters to clean house. Predictable as it may be, breaking zero new ground, there are a few genuine scares to be had. Does its job, but by no means do we need a fourth. **97m/C; DVD, Blu-Ray, Streaming.** Dermot Mulroney; Stefanie Scott; Angus Sampson; Leigh Whannell; Lin Shaye; ***D:*** Leigh Whannell; ***W:*** Leigh Whannell; ***C:*** Brian Pearson; ***M:*** Joseph Bishara.

Insidious: The Last Key **2018 (PG-13)** Professional medium and spookhunter Dr. Elise Rainier (Shaye) revisits her creepy childhood home when the current owners complain of supernatural pestering. In case you didn't notice in the first three installments, there's nothing terribly original in them -- they rely on jump-scares and grotesque ghouls instead of acting and plot. Here's hoping this last key will firmly lock the door on the tired franchise. **103m/C; DVD.** Lin Shaye; Leigh Whannell; Angus Sampson; Kirk Acevedo; Caitlin Gerard; ***D:*** Adam Robitel; ***W:*** Leigh Whannell; ***C:*** Toby Oliver; ***M:*** Joseph Bishara.

InSight 1/2 **2011 (R)** Obvious supernatural thriller with no real scares. ER nurse Kaitlyn is accidentally electrocuted on the job. When she awakens, Kaitlyn experiences the memories of the young woman she was helping, who died of stab wounds. As Kaitlyn investigates the woman's past to figure out what she's experiencing, she teams up with Det. Peter Rafferty, who's sure the woman's killer will come after Kaitlyn next. **90m/C; DVD.** Natalie Zea; Sean Patrick Flanery; Christopher Lloyd; Thomas Ian Nicholas; Adam Baldwin; Veronica Cartwright; Juliet Landau; Max Perlich; ***D:*** Richard Gabai; ***W:*** Wade McIntyre; Aaron Ginsburg; ***C:*** Scott Peck; ***M:*** Lisa Gerrard. **VIDEO**

Insignificance **1985** A film about an imaginary night spent in a New York hotel by characters who resemble Marilyn Monroe, Albert Einstein, Joe McCarthy, and Joe DiMaggio. Entertaining and often amusing as it follows the characters as they discuss theory and relativity, the Russians, and baseball among other things. **110m/C; VHS, DVD.** *GB* Gary Busey; Tony Curtis; Theresa Russell; Michael Emil; Will Sampson; ***D:*** Nicolas Roeg; ***W:*** Terry Johnson; ***C:*** Peter Hannan; ***M:*** Hans Zimmer.

Insomnia **1997** After a young girl is murdered in northern Norway, Oslo detective Jonas Engstrom (Skarsgard) and his partner Erik Vik (Ousdal) are called in to solve the crime, aided by local cop Hilde Hagen (Armand). Engstrom accidentally shoots and kills his partner during a stakeout in the fog and attempts to cover up one killing while uncovering another. He begins to unravel when his conscience and the unrelenting sun cause not only insomnia, but a moral breakdown. His nerves jangle as he comes under suspicion from Hilde. He is also forced into a face-to-face climax with the killer, who witnessed the shooting. Excellent feature debut for Norwegian director Erik Skjoldbjaerg. **97m/C; VHS, DVD, Blu-Ray.** *NO* Stellan Skarsgard; Sverre Anker Ousdal; Maria Bonnevie; Bjorn Floberg; Gisken Armand; Marianne O. Ulrichsen; Maria Mathiesen; ***D:*** Erik Skjoldbjaerg; ***W:*** Nikolaj Frobenius; ***C:*** Erling Thurmann-Andersen; ***M:*** Geir Jenssen.

Insomnia 1/2 **2002 (R)** American remake of a 1997 Norwegian films finds veteran police detective Will Dormer (Pacino), under Internal Affairs investigation back home, sent to a small Alaskan town to investigate the murder of a 17-year-old girl. Primary suspect Walter Finch (Williams) plays a game of psychological chicken after witnessing a moment of Dormer's increasing weakness. Pacino, in service to an excellent script, gives an outstanding performance as the guilt-ridden, exhausted supercop, and Swank impresses (again) as the idol-worshipping but self-assured local deputy. "Memento" helmer Nolan proves there doesn't have to be a letdown after a breakout, groundbreaking hit. **116m/C; VHS, DVD, Blu-Ray.** Al Pacino; Robin Williams; Hilary Swank; Maura Tierney; Martin Donovan; Nicky Katt; Paul Dooley; Jonathan Jackson; Katharine Isabelle; Larry Holden; Crystal Lowe; Tasha Simms; ***D:*** Christopher Nolan; ***W:*** Hillary Seitz; ***C:*** Wally Pfister; ***M:*** David Julyan.

Inspector Bellamy *Bellamy* **2009** Director Claude Chabrol's final film is a relaxed mystery with famed Parisian detective, Paul Bellamy (Depardieu), on vacation with his wife Francoise (Bunel) when trouble occurs. There's a wrecked car, an unidentified body, an insurance scam, a wronged wife, a duplicitous mistress, and Bellamy's own trials with his angry deadbeat half-brother Jacques (Cornillac) just to keep the plot moving leisurely along in various directions. French with subtitles. **110m/C; DVD.** *FR* Gerard Depardieu; Marie Bunel; Clovis Cornillac; Vahina Giocante; Marie Matheron; Jacques Gamblin; ***D:*** Claude Chabrol; ***W:*** Claude Chabrol; Odile Barski; ***C:*** Eduardo Serra; ***M:*** Matthieu Chabrol.

Inspector Clouseau **1968 (G)** The bumbling French detective (Arkin) goes to England to help break up a daring robbery ring that uses Clouseau masks to hide their identity. Arkin gives it a fine effort, but he's no Peter Sellers. This makes the absence of the usual band of comic foils like Cato, Dreyfus, and Hercule (as well as director Blake Edwards) that much more glaring. The same writing team remains, but maybe they needed Sellers as their muse, because the entire script falls flat. **98m/C; VHS, DVD, Blu-Ray.** Alan Arkin; David Bauer; Patrick Cargill; Anthony Ainley; Delia Boccardo; Barbara Dana; Frank Finlay; Barry Foster; Beryl Reid; John Bindon; Tutte Lemkow; Bud Yorkin; ***W:*** Frank Waldman; Tom Waldman; ***C:*** Arthur Ibbetson; ***M:*** Ken Thorne.

Inspector Gadget **1999 (PG)** Go-go gadget script rewrite! The popular cartoon character goes live-action with Broderick in the title role. Blown to pieces by the evil Dr. Claw (Everett), a naive security guard is put back together by scientist Brenda Bradford (Fisher) with a vast array of grafted-on gizmos. Gadget becomes the world's top detective and discovers that Claw also murdered Brenda's father. In his battle against Claw, he is forced to fight his evil robot twin in order to clear his own name. The computer generated effects are eye-catching but far too brief, and Broderick is forced to react lamely to them most of the time. **77m/C; VHS, DVD.** Matthew Broderick; Rupert Everett; Joely Fisher; Michelle Trachtenberg; Dabney Coleman; Andy Dick; Michael G. (Mike)

Hagerty; Rene Auberjonois; Frances Bay; *V:* Don Adams; D.L. Hughley; *D:* David Kellogg; *W:* Kerry Ehrin; Zak Penn; *C:* Adam Greenberg; *M:* John Debney.

Inspector Gadget 2 🦴🦴 **2002 (G)** A female agent called G2 is competing with Inspector Gadget (Stewart) to stop Claw from using a time-freezing device to rob a bank. **88m/C; VHS, DVD.** French Stewart; Elaine Hendrix; Caitlin Wachs; Tony (Anthony) Martin; Mark Mitchell; Sigrid Thornton; Bruce Spence; *D:* Alex Zamm; *W:* Alex Zamm. **VIDEO**

Inspector Gadget's Biggest Caper Ever 🦴🦴 ½ **2005** Bionic detective Gadget must stop a flying dinosaur, under the control of the evil Dr. Claw, from destroying Metro City. Animated adventure has some slow patches but should still satisfy Gadget's kiddie fans. **70m/C; VHS, DVD.** *V:* Maurice LaMarche; Bernie Mac; Tegan Moss; Ezekiel Norton; Brian Drummond; *W:* Phil Harnage. **VIDEO**

The Inspector General 🦴🦴🦴 *Happy Times* **1949** Classic Kaye craziness of mistaken identities with the master comic portraying a carnival medicine man who is mistaken by the villagers for their feared Inspector General. If you like Kaye's manic performance, you'll enjoy this one. **103m/C; VHS, DVD.** Danny Kaye; Walter Slezak; Barbara Bates; Elsa Lanchester; Gene Lockhart; Walter Catlett; Alan Hale; *D:* Henry Koster; *W:* Harry Kurnitz; Philip Rapp; *C:* Elwood "Woody" Bredell; *M:* Johnny Green. Golden Globes '50: Score.

Inspector Hornleigh 🦴🦴 ½ **1939** A pair of bumbling detectives arrive on the scene when a Chancellor's fortune is stolen. Fine comedy, although the Scottish and British accents can be rather thick now and again. **76m/B; VHS, DVD.** *GB* Gordon Harker; Alastair Sim; Miki Hood; Wally Patch; Steven Geray; Edward Underdown; Hugh Williams; Gibb McLaughlin; *D:* Eugene Forde.

The Inspectors 🦴 ½ **1998** Remarkably dull thriller about postal inspectors Silverman and Gossett Jr., who are tracking a mail bomber. **91m/C; VHS, DVD.** Louis Gossett, Jr.; Jonathan Silverman; *D:* Brad Turner; *W:* Bruce Zimmerman; *C:* Albert J. Dunk; *M:* Terry Frewer. **CABLE**

The Inspectors 2: A Shred of Evidence 🦴🦴 **2000** Con man is using the mail to assume other identities and must be stopped by our two intrepid postal inspectors. Standard made-for-TV suspense. **95m/C; DVD.** Louis Gossett, Jr.; Jonathan Silverman; Michael Madsen; *D:* Brad Turner; *W:* Bruce Zimmerman; *C:* Albert J. Dunk; *M:* Terry Frewer. **CABLE**

Instant Family 🦴🦴 ½ **2018 (PG-13)** A dramedy that strikes the precarious balance between silly and schmaltzy. Mark Wahlberg and Rose Byrne have great chemistry together as a childless couple who decide to foster three kids, two more than they bargained for: a 15-year-old girl and her younger siblings. The challenges of becoming a spontaneous family, alongside the laughs from getting it wrong, feel genuine and earnest, undoubtedly because they're inspired by writer/director Sean Anders's own experiences. **118m/C; DVD.** Mark Wahlberg; Rose Byrne; Isabela Moner; Gustavo Quiroz; Julianna Gamiz; *D:* Sean Anders; *W:* Sean Anders; John Morris; *C:* Brett Pawlak; *M:* Michael Andrews.

Instant Karma 🦴 ½ **1990** Would be comedy depicts young man's far fetched attempts to score babewise. Ask no more what happened to erstwhile teen heart throb Cassidy: he suffers from a major bout of bad karma. **94m/C; VHS, Streaming.** Craig Sheffer; Chelsea Noble; David Cassidy; Alan Blumenfeld; Glen Hirsch; Marty Ingels; Orson Bean; *D:* Roderick Taylor.

Instinct 🦴🦴 **1999 (R)** Primatologist Ethan Powell (Hopkins) has been in the African jungle studying gorillas a little too long, and has turned apeman, killing poachers threatening his primate friends. Since he's been returned to the U.S. and incarcerated in a Miami prison ward for for the insane, he's taken a vow of silence. Theo Caulder (Gooding) is an ambitious shrink who's sent to see if Powell is still (or ever was) a clinical whacko. Hopkins mainly gets to chew the scenery and leave Gooding wide-eyed in his wake. "Suggested" by the novel "Ishmael" by Daniel Quinn. **123m/C; VHS, DVD.** Anthony Hopkins; Cuba Gooding, Jr.; Donald Sutherland; George Dzundza; Maura Tierney; John Ashton; Paul Bates; John Aylward; *D:* Jon Turteltaub; *W:* Gerald Di Pego; *C:* Philippe Rousselot; *M:* Danny Elfman.

Instinct to Kill 🦴🦴 **2001 (R)** Abused wife Tess (Crider) helps put her husband Jim (Abell) in prison after discovering he's a killer. But when he escapes, Tess hires martial arts expert J.T. Dillon (Dacascos) to teach her how to defend herself and waits for her hubby to come after her. Based on the novel "The Perfect Husband" by Lisa Gardner. **92m/C; VHS, DVD.** Missy (Melissa) Crider; Tim Abell; Mark Dacascos; Kadeem Hardison; *D:* Gustavo Graef-Marino; *W:* Randall Frakes. **VIDEO**

Institue Benjamenta or This Dream People Call Human Life 🦴🦴 **1995** The Brothers Quay's first live-action feature is a surreal nightmareish fairytale based on the 1905 novel "Jakob von Gunten" by Robert Waiser. Jakob (Rylance) arrives at the secluded Institute Benjamenta, which is run by Lisa (Krige) and her brother Johannes (John), to train as a servant. He becomes a favorite of the enigmatic duo and tries to decide what is real and what isn't. Eccentric and wonderfully photographed by Knowland. **105m/B; VHS, DVD.** *GB* Mark Rylance; Alice Krige; Gottfried John; *D:* Stephen Quay; Timothy Quay; *W:* Stephen Quay; Timothy Quay; Allan Passes; *C:* Nicholas D. Knowland; *M:* Lech Jankowski.

The Insult 🦴🦴🦴 *L'insulte* **2017 (R)** A gripping exploration of divisions in Lebanon through a courtroom drama. Construction crew chief Yasser Salameh (El Basha) fixes an illegal pipe on mechanic Tony's (Karam) apartment for free, despite Tony's protestations. When Tony smashes the new pipe, Yasser hurls an insult. A confrontation ensues that includes further insults, apologies, and violence, deepened by the fact that Tony is a right-leaning Christian while Yasser is a Palestinian. At their trials, the pair become sectarian symbols in the national media. The well-crafted film explores timely issues in the Middle East with a fearless eye, while featuring universally recognizable themes. Arabic with subtitles. **112m/C; DVD, Blu-Ray, Streaming.** *BE CY FR LB US* Kamel El Basha; Adel Karam; Camille Salameh; Diamond Bou Abboud; Rita Hayek; *D:* Ziad Doueiri; *W:* Ziad Doueiri; Joelle Touma; *C:* Tommaso Fiorilli; *M:* Eric Neveux.

The Insurance Man 🦴🦴 **1986** Surreal BBC TV drama. The story is told in flashbacks as an elderly man explains the origins of his illness to his doctor. Franz works in a dye factory in Prague. He develops a spreading rash and runs into a bureaucratic nightmare when he attempts to get workers' compensation until he meets sympathetic insurance clerk Kakfa. **77m/C; DVD.** *UK* Robert Hines; Daniel Day-Lewis; Trevor Peacock; Alan MacNaughton; Jim Broadbent; *D:* Richard Eyre; *W:* Alan Bennett; *C:* Nat Crosby; *M:* Ilona Sekacz. **TV**

Insurgent 🦴🦴 ½ *The Divergent Series: Insurgent* **2015 (PG)** This sequel picks up three days after the end of Divergent and further proves that this series will not quite be "another Hunger Games" but should keep the fans of the books happy enough. Tris Prior (Woodley) and Four (James) are on the run after escaping the takeover by the Erudite on Initiation Day. The power struggle in futuristic Chicago leads to turmoil, as even the city crumbles to the ground now that its carefully-structured society begins to collapse. The whole thing looks great and Woodley and Winslet make rousing adversaries, but the story is weighed down with unearned self-importance. The trilogy will follow current trends and be split into two parts. **93m/C; DVD, Blu-Ray.** Kate Winslet; Jai Courtney; Mekhi Phifer; Shailene Woodley; Theo James; Ansel Elgort; Miles Teller; *D:* Robert Schwentke; *W:* Brian Duffield; Akiva Goldsman; Mark Bomback; *C:* Florian Ballhaus; *M:* Joseph Trapanese.

The Insurgents 🦴🦴 ½ **2006 (R)** Thought-provoking look at post-9/11 paranoia and homegrown terrorism. A radical author persuades a small-time crook, an ex-hooker, and an angry Iraq War vet to become a terrorist cell, build a truck bomb, and detonate it on U.S. soil. **85m/C; DVD.** John Shea; Henry Simmons; Juliette Marquis; Michael Mosley; Mary Stuart Masterson; *D:* Scott Dacko; *W:* Scott Dacko; *M:* Ben Butler; Mario Grigorov; Learan Kahanov.

Intacto 🦴🦴 **2001 (R)** Samuel Berg (von Sydow) has survived the Nazi death camps and believes that he not only possesses good luck but runs a remote Spanish casino where the patrons bet their good luck against his own in a version of Russian roulette. When Sam steals the luck of his one-time confidante (and earthquake survivor) Federico (Poncela), the man goes looking for a protege to pit against his former boss and eventually finds Tomas (Sbaraglia), the only person to survive a plane crash. But Tomas is also a bank robber trailed by police officer Sara (Lopez), who survived a car crash. So luck gets pitted against luck—winner takes all. English and Spanish with subtitles. **108m/C; VHS, DVD.** *SP* Max von Sydow; Leonardo Sbaraglia; Eusebio Poncela; Monica Lopez; Antonio Dechent; Paz Gomez; *D:* Juan Carlos Fresnadillo; *W:* Juan Carlos Fresnadillo; Andres M. Koppel; *C:* Xavier Jimenez; *M:* Lucio Godoy.

The Intended 🦴🦴 **2002 (R)** Period melodrama set in steamy 1920s Indochina. Ambitious young surveyor (Feild) heads upriver with his older fiancee (McTeer) in hopes of starting a new life at a colonial trading post. Of course, all is not right when they arrive. They find the post run by scary militant widow Fricker, surrounded by a freakshow of family and hangers-on. Her son, a disgustingly oily slacker (Maudsley), is angry when mommy decides to pass control over to a nephew instead of him and starts scheming. While Maudsley's unhinged nanny (Dukakis) creepily fawns over him, he casts a greedy eye towards McTeer. Wonderfully twisted over-the-top horror show reminds at times of Old Dark House thrillers of the '30s, minus the knowing, tongue-in-cheek humor. Takes itself way too seriously, but it's good fun for fans of unintentional camp. **110m/C; DVD.** *GB DK* Janet McTeer; J.J. Feild; Olympia Dukakis; Brenda Fricker; Tony Maudsley; David Bradley; Philip Jackson; Robert Pugh; *D:* Kristian Levring; *W:* Kristian Levring; *C:* Jens Schlosser; *M:* Matthew Herbert.

Intent to Kill 🦴🦴 **1958** British doctor Bob McLaurin (Todd), who's working at a Montreal hospital, is chosen to perform surgery on incognito South American dictator Juan Menda (Lom), who's been targeted for assassination. That ends with a hospital shoot-out. There's also a melodramatic subplot about Bob and his shrewish wife Margaret (Boyle), who wants them to move back to London and is threatening to expose Bob's relationship with fellow doctor Nancy Ferguson (Drake) if he doesn't agree. **89m/B; DVD.** *UK* Richard Todd; Herbert Lomas; Betsy Drake; Catherine Boyle; Warren Stevens; Lisa Gastoni; Carlo Giustini; *D:* Jack Cardiff; *W:* Jimmy Sangster; *C:* Desmond Dickinson; *M:* Kenneth V. Jones.

Interception 🦴 **2008** The usual super secret prototype weapon of mass destruction is stolen, and a software engineer gets the data disk needed to make it work by mistake. So he gets teamed up with the usual suspended lawman in a race to stop the evil terrorists. Any part of this plot sound familiar? **107m/C; DVD.** John Will Clay; Ashley Morgan; Bret Hopkins; Buck Rodgers; *D:* John Will Clay; Turner Clay; *W:* John Will Clay; Turner Clay; *M:* Turner Clay.

Interceptor 🦴🦴 **1992 (R)** Hijackers attempt to steal a Stealth Bomber in this action-adventure saga which features virtual reality computer-generated imagery in its combat sequences. **92m/C; VHS, DVD.** Jurgen Prochnow; Andrew Divoff; Elizabeth Morehead; *D:* Michael Cohn; *W:* John Brancato; Michael Ferris; *M:* Richard (Rick) Marvin.

Interceptor Force 🦴🦴 **1999 (R)** The Interceptors are a top-secret group of soldiers trained for encounters with aliens. Their latest assignment involves a UFO in a remote community and a species that's capable of morphing into any form. And if they can't clean up the mess in 24 hours, the military will nuke the region. **91m/C; VHS, DVD.** Olivier Gruner; Brad Dourif; Glenn Plummer; Ernie Hudson; Ken Olandt; Angel Boris; Holly Fields; *D:* Phillip J. Roth; *W:* Phillip J. Roth; Martin Lazarus. **VIDEO**

Interceptor Force 2 🦴 **2002 (R)** In the near future an elite team of soldiers, led by stone-faced Sean Lambert (Gruner), combat a shape-shifting female alien that has taken over a Russian nuclear plant and is threatening a nuclear winter. Things get personal when the alien learns it was Lambert who killed her mate (in the first bad pic). A Sci-Fi Channel original. **89m/C; DVD.** Olivier Gruner; Roger R. Cross; Elizabeth (Ward) Gracen; Nigel Bennett; Adrienne Wilkinson; Eve Scheer; *D:* Phillip J. Roth; *W:* Patrick Phillips; *C:* Todd Barron; *M:* Tony Riparetti. **CABLE**

Interiors 🦴🦴🦴 ½ **1978 (R)** Ultra serious, Bergmanesque drama about three neurotic adult sisters, coping with the dissolution of their family. When Father decides to leave mentally unbalanced mother for a divorcee, the daughters are shocked and bewildered. Depressing and humorless, but fine performances all the way around, supported by the elegant camera work of Gordon Willis. **95m/C; VHS, DVD, Blu-Ray.** Diane Keaton; Mary Beth Hurt; E.G. Marshall; Geraldine Page; Richard Jordan; Sam Waterston; Kristin Griffith; Maureen Stapleton; *D:* Woody Allen; *W:* Woody Allen; *C:* Gordon Willis. British Acad. '78: Support. Actress (Page); L.A. Film Critics '78: Support. Actress (Stapleton).

Interlocked 🦴 ½ *A Bold Affair* **1998 (R)** Another psycho-babe thriller. Pregnant Emily Anderson (Ferguson) and happy hubby Michael (Trachta) befriend Eva (Harrison), which turns into trouble. Harrison and Trachta previously worked together on TV soap "The Bold & the Beautiful." **94m/C; VHS, DVD.** Jeff Trachta; Schae Harrison; Sandra Ferguson; George Alvarez; Bruce Kirby; *D:* Rick Jacobson; *W:* Al Sophianopoulos; *C:* Jesse Weathington. **VIDEO**

Interlude 🦴 ½ **1968** Temperamental, middle-aged conductor Stefan Zelter (Werner) ignores his family for his work. Some injudicious comments during an interview with young journalist Sally Carter (Ferris) leave Stefan with too much time on his hands and they begin an affair. Sally eventually realizes that they can't stay together. **113m/C; DVD.** *UK* Oskar Werner; Barbara Ferris; Virginia Maskell; Donald Sutherland; *D:* Kevin Billington; *W:* Lee Langley; Hugh Leonard; *C:* Gerry Fisher; *M:* Georges Delerue.

Intermezzo 🦴🦴🦴 *Interlude* **1936** Married violinist Ekman meets pianist Bergman and they fall in love. He deserts his family to tour with Bergman, but the feelings for his wife and children become too much. When Bergman sees their love won't last, she leaves him. Shakily, he returns home and as his daughter runs to greet him, she is hit by a truck and he realizes that his family is his true love. One of the great grab-your-hanky melodramas. In Swedish with English subtitles. 1939 English re-make features Bergman's American film debut. **88m/B; VHS, DVD.** *SW* Gosta Ekman; Inga Tidblad; Ingrid Bergman; Erik "Bullen" Berglund; Anders Henrikson; Hasse (Hans) Ekman; Britt Hagman; Hugo Bjorne; *D:* Gustaf Molander; *W:* Gustaf Molander; Gosta Stevens; *C:* Ake Dahlqvist; *M:* Heinz Provost.

Intermezzo 🦴🦴🦴 *Intermezzo: A Love Story* **1939** Fine, though weepy, love story of a renowned, married violinist who has an affair with his stunningly beautiful protege (Bergman), but while on concert tour realizes that his wife and children hold his heart, and he returns to them. A re-make of the 1936 Swedish film, it's best known as Bergman's American debut. Howard's violin playing was dubbed by Toscha Seidel. **70m/B; VHS, DVD, Blu-Ray.** *IT* Ingrid Bergman; Leslie Howard; Edna Best; Ann E. Todd; *D:* Gregory Ratoff; *C:* Gregg Toland; *M:* Max Steiner.

Intermission 🦴🦴🦴 **2003 (R)** Smashingly fast-paced action and snappy dialogue dominate this lively ensemble piece set in Dublin and led by ruffian Colin Farrell who kicks off the mayhem with—quite literally—a doozy of a punch that sets the tone. Writer O'Rowe swirls around many plotlines but eventually connects all the players in stories involving love, infidelity, kidnapping, and bank robbery—although the latter is the crux. There's violence and obscenities aplenty and some may feel they're superfluous but removing them would leave this wild ride devoid of its appealingly shocking qualities. **103m/C; DVD.** *IR* Colin Farrell; Neili Conroy; Shirley Henderson; Conleth Hill; Pat Laffan; Kelly Macdonald; Colm Meaney; Cillian Murphy; Brian F. O'Byrne; Ger Ryan; David Wilmot; Kerry Condon; Emma Bolger; David Herlihy; Michael McElhatton; Deirdre O'Kane; Owen Roe; Tomas D. Sullivan; ***D:*** John Crowley; ***W:*** Mark O'Rowe; ***C:*** Ryszard Lenczewski; ***M:*** John Murphy.

Intern 🦴 1/2 **2000** Satire on the fashion industry is filled with insider chit-chat and cameos from fashionistas and designers, takes a lot of well-placed digs, and is finally as superficial and throw away as the world it depicts. Naive Jocelyn (Swain) is an intern at fashion magazine Skirt who is desperate to fit in. But everyone is more paranoid and mean-spirited than usual because there's an insider giving the rag's best ideas to archrival Vogue. **93m/C; VHS, DVD.** Dominique Swain; Benjamin Pullen; Peggy Lipton; Joan Rivers; David Deblinger; Dwight Ewell; Billy Porter; Anna Thomson; Paulina Porizkova; Kathy Griffin; ***D:*** Michael Lange; ***W:*** Caroline Doyle; Jill Kopelman; ***C:*** Rodney Charters; ***M:*** Jimmy Harry.

The Intern 🦴🦴 **2015 (PG-13)** Seventy-year-old widower Ben Whittaker (De Niro) is bored with life and decides it's time to go back to work, becoming a Senior Intern at an online fashion site run by the glamorous Jules Ostin (Hathaway). Of course, generation cop hilarity ensues. Most of you can probably close your eyes and imagine the trajectory of Meyers' latest comedy, but De Niro and Hathaway keep the predictability engaging. He puts more effort in here than he has of late, and she's always charming. Rene Russo also shines in a small role, although one wishes she would get bigger ones. **121m/C; DVD, Blu-Ray.** Anne Hathaway; Robert De Niro; Adam Devine; Anders Holm; Andrew Rannells; ***D:*** Nancy Meyers; ***W:*** Nancy Meyers; ***C:*** Stephen Goldblatt; ***M:*** Theodore Shapiro.

Internal Affairs 🦴🦴 1/2 **1990 (R)** Wild, sexually charged action piece about an Internal Affairs officer for the L.A.P.D. (Garcia) who becomes obsessed with exposing a sleazy, corrupt street cop (Gere). Drama becomes illogical, but boasts excellent, strung out performances, especially Gere as the creepy degenerate you'd love to bust. **114m/C; VHS, DVD, Blu-Ray.** Richard Gere; Andy Garcia; Laurie Metcalf; Ron Vawter; Marco Rodriguez; Nancy Travis; William Baldwin; Richard Bradford; Annabella Sciorra; Michael Beach; Mike Figgis; Elijah Wood; Arlen Dean Snyder; Faye Grant; John Capodice; Xander Berkeley; John Kapelos; ***D:*** Mike Figgis; ***W:*** Henry Bean; ***C:*** John A. Alonzo; ***M:*** Brian Banks; Mike Figgis.

The International 🦴🦴 **2009 (R)** Interpol agent Louis Salinger (Owen) and Manhattan ADA Eleanor Whitman (Watts) uncover myriad illegal activities at one of the world's most powerful financial institutions, sending them on a death-defying global chase to expose the truth. Flick takes enough liberties to make Dick and W proud while going for the international espionage vibe, a la Jason Bourne, but with a timely financial twist. Ultimately doesn't offer enough to differentiate itself from the superior Bourne series and follows a predictable, paint-by-numbers approach. A lowlight on the considerable resumes of Owen and Watts. **118m/C; Blu-Ray, UMD.** *US GE* Clive Owen; Naomi Watts; Armin Mueller-Stahl; Brian F. O'Byrne; Ulrich Thomsen; Jack McGee; James Rebhorn; ***D:*** Tom Tykwer; ***W:*** Eric Singer; ***C:*** Frank Griebe; ***M:*** Tom Tykwer; Reinhold Heil; Johnny Klimek.

International House 🦴🦴 1/2 **1933** A wacky Dada-esque Hollywood farce about an incredible array of travelers quarantined in a Shanghai hotel where a mad doctor has perfected television. Essentially a burlesque compilation of skits, gags, and routines. Guest stars Rudy Vallee, Baby Rose Marie, and Cab Calloway appear on the quaint "TV" device, in musical sequences. **72m/B; VHS, DVD.** W.C. Fields; Peggy Hopkins Joyce; Rudy Vallee; George Burns; Cab Calloway; Sari Maritza; Gracie Allen; Bela Lugosi; Sterling Holloway; Baby Rose Marie; ***D:*** Edward Sutherland.

International Settlement 🦴 1/2 **1938** Gunrunner Del Forbes is working in Shanghai but gets into trouble over an impersonation, a dead contact, and missing money. He's on the run when the Japanese start bombing the city and is rescued by French singer Lenore. The duo falls in love while trying to flee. **75m/B; DVD.** Dolores Del Rio; George Sanders; John Carradine; Leon Ames; June Lang; Dick Baldwin; Keye Luke; ***D:*** Eugene Forde; ***W:*** John Patrick; Lou Breslow; ***C:*** Lucien N. Andriot.

International Velvet 🦴 1/2 **1978 (PG)** Why did they bother? This dismal and long overdue sequel to "National Velvet," finds the adult Velvet, with live-in companion (Plummer), grooming her orphaned niece (O'Neal) to become an Olympic champanion horsewoman. O'Neal's way out of her league although Plummer and Hopkins give good performances and the sentiment is kept at a trot. **126m/C; VHS, DVD.** *GB* Tatum O'Neal; Anthony Hopkins; Christopher Plummer; ***D:*** Bryan Forbes.

Internecine Project 🦴🦴 1/2 **1973 (PG)** Stylistic espionage tale with Coburn's English professor acting as the mastermind behind an unusual series of murders where industrial spies kill each other, so Coburn can garner a top government job in D.C. Unexpected ending is worth the viewing. Based on Mort Elkind's novel. **89m/C; VHS, DVD, Blu-Ray.** *GB* James Coburn; Lee Grant; Harry Andrews; Keenan Wynn; ***D:*** Ken Hughes; ***W:*** Barry Levinson; ***C:*** Geoffrey Unsworth.

Internes Can't Take Money 🦴🦴 1/2 **1937** With the help of McCrea and gangster Nolan, widow Stanwyck is desperately trying to find the daughter her bank robber husband hid before he died. Young doctor McCrea must save the life of another gangster who knows the whereabouts of the toddler. The first film featuring writer Max Brand's Dr. Kildare characters, which later became part of a series starring Lew Ayres and Laraine Day. **79m/B; VHS, DVD, Blu-Ray.** Barbara Stanwyck; Joel McCrea; Lloyd Nolan; Stanley Ridges; Lee Bowman; Irving Bacon; ***D:*** Alfred Santell; ***W:*** Rian James; Theodore Reeves; ***C:*** Theodor Sparkuhl; ***M:*** Gregory Stone.

Internet Dating 🦴 1/2 **2008** Lonely, unprepossessing single guy Mikey creates a false profile on an Internet dating service claiming to be a professional basketball player. Imagine how many doors get slammed in his face when he shows up and his would-be date gets a look at him. **86m/C; DVD.** Katt Micah Williams; Clifton Powell; Master P; Lil' Romeo; Reynaldo Rey; Liana Mendoza; Jessica Meza; ***D:*** Master P; ***W:*** Master P; ***M:*** Ramon Balcazar. **VIDEO**

The Internet's Own Boy: The Story of Aaron Swartz 🦴🦴🦴 **2014** Aaron Swartz committed suicide in 2013 at the age of 26, allegedly because of an ongoing federal prosecution case about hacking and freedom of speech. In 2010, the political activist and co-founder of the social news site Reddit mass downloaded millions of documents from the subscription-based digital library JSTOR and was charged with violating the 1986 Computer Fraud and Abuse Act. Was the Justice Department zealously pursuing the case as a warning to fellow hactivists? Director Knappenberger includes interviews and archival footage. **105m/C; Streaming.** ***D:*** Brian Knappenberger; ***W:*** Brian Knappenberger; ***C:*** Lincoln Else; Scott Sinkler; ***M:*** John Dragonnetti. Writers Guild '14: Documentary Screenplay.

The Interns 🦴🦴 1/2 **1962** Finessed hospital soaper about interns on the staff of a large city hospital, whose personal lives are fraught with trauma, drugs, birth, death, and abortion. Good performances and direction keep this medical melodrama moving in a gurney-like manner. Followed by the "The New Interns" and the basis for a TV series. Adapted from a novel by Richard Frede. **120m/C; VHS, DVD.** Cliff Robertson; James MacArthur; Michael Callan; Nick Adams; Stefanie Powers; Suzy Parker; Buddy Ebsen; Telly Savalas; Haya Harareet; Angela (Clark) Clarke; ***D:*** David Swift; ***W:*** David Swift; Walter Newman; ***C:*** Russell Metty; ***M:*** Leith Stevens.

The Internship 🦴 **2013 (PG-13)** Working from a script that might have been effective ten years ago, stars Vaughn and Wilson are way past their prime in this bland, unfunny comedy about man-children who really should know better by now. Perhaps commenting on their increased lack of popularity, the two play salesmen left behind by the digital age who are forced to take an internship at Google, resulting in a world record for product placement in a Hollywood film. **119m/C; DVD, Blu-Ray.** Vince Vaughn; Owen Wilson; Rose Byrne; Max Minghella; Aasif Mandvi; Dylan O'Brien; Jessica Szohr; Josh Gad; ***Cameo(s):*** John Goodman; ***D:*** Shawn Levy; ***W:*** Vince Vaughn; Shawn Levy; Jared Stern; ***C:*** Jonathan Brown; ***M:*** Christophe Beck.

The Interpreter 🦴🦴🦴 1/2 **2005 (PG-13)** White, native African U.N. interpreter Sylvia Broome (Kidman) accidently overhears a plot to kill the corrupt and murderous president of a small African country, a man with whom her family has a past. Tobin Keller (Penn) is the burned-out, recently-widowed Secret Service agent assigned to investigate her claim and, if necessary, protect her as a possible witness. Pollack's taut thriller is well-paced and full of twists and revelations that succeed in keeping the resolution in doubt right up to the end. Kidman and Penn are excellent, as is Keener in the thankless role of Keller's level-headed partner. **128m/C; DVD, Blu-Ray, HD-DVD.** Nicole Kidman; Sean Penn; Catherine Keener; Jesper Christensen; Yvan Attal; Michael Wright; Earl Cameron; George Harris; Tsai Chin; Clyde Kusatsu; Hugo Speer; Maz Jobrani; Eric Keenleyside; Christopher Evan Welch; David Zayas; Sydney Pollack; Curtiss Cook; Byron Utley; ***D:*** Sydney Pollack; ***W:*** Charles Randolph; Scott Frank; Steven Zaillian; ***C:*** Darius Khondji; ***M:*** James Newton Howard.

Interrogation 🦴🦴 **2016 (R)** An action-thriller centered on a city under siege by a madman. After a criminal mastermind sends a threat to the FBI, interrogator Lucas (Copeland) and I.T. specialist Becky (Perry) must follow the criminal's mind games to understand the threat to a city. As FBI agents try to discern the mastermind's real agenda, they must protect the thousands of people at risk because of the plot. **93m/C; DVD, Blu-Ray, Streaming, Download.** Adam Copeland; C.J. Perry; Julia Benson; Erica Carroll; Mitchell Kummen; ***D:*** Stephen Reynolds; ***W:*** Michael Finch; Adam Rodin; ***M:*** Nathan Whitehead. **VIDEO**

The Interrogation of Michael Crowe 🦴🦴 **2002** Family drama based on a true story. In 1998, 14-year-old Michael Crowe is coerced by police into confessing to the murder of his younger sister after a prolonged videotaped interrogation. The confession spins even more out of control to involve an alleged conspiracy with two of Michael's friends who are accused of helping him. Michael's parents then hire lawyer Dorothy Sorenson to battle for their son's legal rights and find the true killer. **86m/C; DVD.** Mark Rendall; Ally Sheedy; Michael Riley; Rosemary Dunsmore; John Bourgeois; Karl Pruner; Richard Banel; Christopher Behnisch; ***D:*** Don McBrearty; ***W:*** Alan Hines; ***C:*** Rhett Morita; ***M:*** Alexina Louie; Alex Pauk. **CABLE**

Interrupted Journey 🦴🦴 1/2 **1949** A married man runs away to start a new life with another woman. When she is killed in a train accident, he becomes the prime suspect in her murder. Lots of action and speed, but a disappointing ending. **80m/B; VHS, DVD, Streaming.** *GB* Richard Todd; Valerie Hobson; ***D:*** Daniel Birt.

Interrupted Melody 🦴🦴🦴 **1955** True story of opera diva Marjorie Lawrence's courageous battle with polio and her fight to appear once more at the Metropolitan Opera. Parker was nominated for an Oscar in her excellent portrayal of the Australian singer who continues her career despite her handicap. Vocals dubbed by opera star Eileen Farrell. Based on the book by Marjorie Lawrence. **106m/C; VHS, DVD.** Glenn Ford; Eleanor Parker; Roger Moore; Cecil Kellaway; Evelyn Ellis; Walter Baldwin; ***D:*** Curtis Bernhardt; ***W:*** William Ludwig; Sonya Levien; ***C:*** Paul Vogel. Oscars '55: Story & Screenplay.

The Interrupters 🦴🦴🦴 1/2 **2011** Gripping documentary by director James focusing on the efforts of a group called Cease-Fire, made up of reformed ex-convicts (dubbed "The Interrupters") who take their anti-violence message to Chicago gang members. Trailing the men for about a year, the film is a sobering and stark portrayal of the effects of violence on a community. Based on a highly lauded "New York Times" article by co-producer Alex Kotlowitz. **125m/C; DVD, Blu-Ray.** ***D:*** Steve James; ***W:*** Alex Kotlowitz. Ind. Spirit '12: Feature Doc.

Intersection 🦴 1/2 **1993 (R)** Successful architect Vincent (Gere) is torn between his aloof wife/partner, Sally (Stone), and a sexy journalist mistress, Olivia (Davidovitch). Whom to choose? Since he's a completely self-involved boor, you won't care either way. Another retooling of a French film ("Les Choses de la Vie") as a Hollywood star vehicle that doesn't work. Lousy dialogue doesn't help. Does boast some nice location shots of Vancouver, B.C. **98m/C; VHS, DVD.** Richard Gere; Sharon Stone; Lolita Davidovich; Martin Landau; David Selby; Jennifer (Jenny) Morrison; ***D:*** Mark Rydell; ***W:*** Marshall Brickman; David Rayfiel; ***C:*** Vilmos Zsigmond; ***M:*** James Newton Howard. Golden Raspberries '94: Worst Actress (Stone).

Interstate 🦴 **2007** Montreal DJ Edgar (Fernandez), who proves to be amazingly stupid, is driving across the U.S. to meet his girlfriend in L.A. He can't pay for the repairs after having car trouble, so Edgar starts hitching. He's picked up by speed freak Allan (Pena), but soon Edgar is alone with the car. Not having had enough trouble, Edgar picks up his own hitchers, skanky weird sisters Veronica (Ackerman) and Gloria (Stanford). Veronica slips Edgar some acid and they wind up in a seedy interstate motel where Veronica tries out her blackmail scheme only it's not over for Edgar yet. **89m/C; DVD.** Shiloh Fernandez; Alexandra Ackerman; Jodi Stanford; Walter Pena; Chase Mallen; ***D:*** Marc-Andre Samson; ***W:*** Marc-Andre Samson; ***C:*** Pascal Chappuis; ***M:*** David Bawal; Daniel Fowler. **VIDEO**

Interstate 60 🦴🦴 **2002 (R)** Weird road trip down a highway that doesn't exist. College grad Neil (Marsden) is being pressured to follow his dad into the law but thinks he may want to become an artist instead. After an accidental conk on the head, Neil's perceptions are skewed—his dream girl talks to him from billboards and he meets the oddball O.C. (Oldman), who persuades Neil to take a trip in his new convertible on (nonexistant) Interstate 60 to deliver a mysterious package. **112m/C; VHS, DVD, On Demand.** James Marsden; Gary Oldman; Chris Cooper; Amy Smart; Christopher Lloyd; Ann-Margret; ***Cameo(s):*** Kurt Russell; Michael J. Fox; ***D:*** Bob Gale; ***W:*** Bob Gale; ***C:*** Denis Maloney; ***M:*** Christophe Beck.

Interstellar 🦴🦴 1/2 **2014 (PG-13)** McConaughey plays the leader of a small group of space travelers seeking a new planet for the human race in the last days of the life-sustaining viability of Earth. As he shuttles across the universe, he remains tied to the memory and continued existence of his daughter back at home. Director Nolan's ambitious film is bloated and overly sentimental, but is also daring as it conveys a cinematic vision of the importance of love. Unabashedly emotional, it never allows the big budget CGI to overwhelm the humanity of the story. **169m/C; DVD, Blu-Ray.** Matthew McConaughey; Anne Hathaway; Wes Bentley; Michael Caine; David Gyasi; Jessica Chastain; Casey Affleck; John Lithgow; Matt Damon; William Devane; Ellen Burstyn; Mackenzie Foy; ***V:*** Bill Irwin; ***D:*** Christopher Nolan; ***W:*** Christopher Nolan; Jonathan Nolan; ***C:*** Hoyte Van Hoytema; ***M:*** Hans Zimmer. Oscars '14: Visual FX; British Acad. '14: Visual FX.

The Intervention 🦴🦴 **2016 (R)** Four couples head off on a weekend getaway, but one of them—Peter (Piazza) and Ruby (Smulders)—have no idea that the other couples are there to essentially break them up. They're not happily married, and their friends are going to fix their problem in Duvall's directorial debut. The actress also stars with Jason Ritter, Ben Schwartz, Natasha Lyonne, and a movie-stealing Melanie Lynskey. As good as Lynskey is here, Duvall can't quite handle the Big Chill-esque ensemble, losing some of the rhythm as she jumps from couple to couple. **90m/C; DVD.** Cobie Smulders; Vincent Piazza; Ben Schwartz; Alia Shawkat; Clea DuVall; Natasha Lyonne; Melanie Lynskey; Jason Ritter; ***D:*** Clea DuVall; ***W:*** Clea DuVall; ***C:*** Polly Morgan; ***M:*** Sara Quin.

The Interview 🦴🦴🦴 **1998** Eddie Fleming (Weaving) is a seemingly ordinary bloke who is rudely awakened when armed police burst into his apartment and haul him off for questioning. His interrogators are tenacious Detective Steele (Martin) and his younger partner, Prior (Jeffery). It slowly becomes clear that the cops are interested in a serial killer and that Fleming isn't the only one under investigation. It seems the two detectives are being watched by an internal affairs unit who are suspicious of Steele himself. And maybe Fleming isn't quite as innocent as he protests. **101m/C; VHS, DVD.** *AU* Hugo Weaving; Tony (Anthony) Martin; Aaron Jeffery; Paul Sonkkila; Michael Caton; Peter McCauley; ***D:*** Craig Monahan; ***W:*** Craig Monahan; Gordon Davie; ***C:*** Simon Duggan; ***M:*** David Hirschfelder. Australian Film Inst. '98: Actor (Weaving), Film, Orig. Screenplay.

Interview ☙☙☙ 1/2 **2007 (R)** A White House scandal is breaking, but ace political reporter Pierre (Buscemi) is stuck in Manhattan profiling beautiful but vacuous starlet Katya (Miller). He waits an hour for the unapologetic diva, and once she shows up he's had enough and they argue. Name-calling ensues and the interview ends with Katya running outside, Pierre on her heels. He's injured and she insists he come to her nearby loft for a cold compress. Here the two posture, drink, flirt and eventually reveal their darkest truths to each other. As in life, both characters are more complex than one initially assumes. Script, camera work and editing are top notch. **83m/C; DVD.** Steve Buscemi; Sienna Miller; ***D:*** Steve Buscemi; ***W:*** Steve Buscemi; David Schechter; ***C:*** Thomas Kist; ***M:*** Evan Lurie.

The Interview ☙☙ **2014 (R)** The most controversial film of 2014 almost started World War III when someone hacked into Sony's servers and threatened terrorist actions of it was released. After finally being released, it's hard to see what all the fuss was about given that the film itself is pretty mediocre and ineffective. Rogen (as a TV producer) and Franco (as a smarmy talk show host) are approached by the government to assassinate North Korea's Kim Jong-Un. Of course, this is a concept designed for broad comedy but Franco strikes the wrong tone, almost as if he's laughing along with the jokes. It gets annoying fast. **112m/C; DVD, Blu-Ray.** James Franco; Seth Rogen; Randall Park; Diana Bang; Lizzy Caplan; James Yi; ***D:*** Seth Rogen; Evan Goldberg; ***W:*** Dan Sterling; ***C:*** Brandon Trost; ***M:*** Henry Jackman.

Interview With a Hitman ☙ 1/2 **2012** Grim, violent thriller. Romanian Viktor (Goss) has been a stone-cold contract killer since childhood. Betrayed by the men who trained him, Viktor fakes his death and escapes to London. Since he knows nothing else, Viktor joins a new crime family, but there's no escaping the past. **96m/C; DVD, Blu-Ray.** *UK* Luke Goss; Stephen Marcus; Danny Midwinter; Caroline Tillette; ***D:*** Perry Bhandal; ***W:*** Perry Bhandal; ***C:*** Richard Swingle; ***M:*** Dan Teicher.

Interview with the Assassin ☙☙ 1/2 **2002 (R)** Ron Kobeleski (Haggerty) is an unemployed video cameraman who needs cash, so Ron agrees when his loner neighbor Walter Ohlinger (Barry) wants to hire him to record a confession. What ex-Marine Walter confesses to is being the second gunman on the grassy knoll in Dallas and the one who actually fired the fatal shot killing President Kennedy. His story turns out to have enough truth that Ron accompanies Walter to Dallas for a re-enactment. But just what did the people who hired Walter want? Character actor Barry is formidable as the ambiguous assassin. **85m/C; VHS, DVD.** Raymond J. Barry; Dylan Haggerty; Darrell Sandeen; Kate Williamson; ***D:*** Neil Burger; ***W:*** Neil Burger; ***C:*** Richard Rutkowski.

Interview with the Vampire ☙☙ **1994 (R)** Portrayal of the elegantly decadent world of vampires and their prey, which features the perverse Lestat (Cruise) who decides to make 18th-century New Orleans aristocrat Louis (Pitt) his latest recruit. Only problem is Louis is horrified by his blood-sucking nature and whines about it for 200 years (it does get tedious). Lestat even makes a child-vampire, Claudia (Dunst), for their own very dysfunctional family but this doesn't turn out well. Director Jordan brings some much needed humor to the dark mix along with some overdone gore. The first book in Anne Rice's "The Vampire Chronicles" was a 17-year film project beset by controversy, including the casting of Cruise (who looks nothing like Rice's description of the character, although Pitt does), leading to an outcry among the cult book's fans though Rice finally came around. Slater replaced the late River Phoenix as the interviewer. **123m/C; VHS, DVD, Blu-Ray.** Tom Cruise; Brad Pitt; Kirsten Dunst; Christian Slater; Antonio Banderas; Stephen Rea; Domiziana Giordano; ***D:*** Neil Jordan; ***W:*** Anne Rice; ***C:*** Philippe Rousselot; ***M:*** Elliot Goldenthal. MTV Movie Awards '95: Breakthrough Perf. (Dunst), Male Perf. (Pitt), Most Desirable Male (Pitt).

Intervista ☙☙☙ *Federico Fellini's Intervista* **1987** A pseudo-documentary look at director Fellini's love of the movies, "Intervista" is a mixture of recollection, parody, memoir, satire, self-examination and fantasy. Fellini himself is the master of ceremonies in this joyous celebration of the studio community that features actors, actresses, bit players, make-up artists, scene painters, publicity agents, technicians, and gate-crashers. The high point of the film arrives with the stars of "La Dolce Vita" re-screening the Fellini masterpiece at Ekberg's country villa. It's a special moment of fantasy vs. reality in this glorious tribute to cinema history. In Italian with English subtitles. **108m/C; VHS, DVD.** *IT* Marcello Mastroianni; Anita Ekberg; Sergio Rubini; Lara Wendel; Antonio Cantafora; Antonella Ponziani; Maurizio Mein; Paola Liguori; Nadia Ottaviani; Federico Fellini; ***D:*** Federico Fellini; ***W:*** Federico Fellini; Gianfranco Angelucci; ***C:*** Tonino Delli Colli; ***M:*** Nicola Piovani.

Intimacy ☙☙ **2000** Furtive and explicit; the first English-language pic from director Chereau. Jay (Rylance), who's walked away from his wife and kids, is managing a bar and living in a basement hovel. Unhappily married Claire (Fox) has sexual trysts with Jay every Wednesday afternoon, although neither seem interested in learning anything about one another. Then Jay decides to follow Claire and discovers she's married and an amateur actress; Jay then befriends Claire's taxi-driving husband, Andy (Spall). When Claire finds out, she skips her trysts and Jay becomes resentful, leading to more emotional upheavals. Based on two stories by Hanif Kureishi. **119m/C; DVD, Blu-Ray.** *GB FR* Mark Rylance; Kerry Fox; Timothy Spall; Alastair Galbraith; Marianne Faithfull; Susannah Harker; Philippe Calvario; Rebecca Palmer; Fraser Ayres; ***D:*** Patrice Chereau; ***W:*** Patrice Chereau; Anne-Louise Trividic; ***C:*** Eric Gautier; ***M:*** Eric Neveux.

Intimate Affairs ☙ 1/2 *Investigating Sex* **2001 (R)** In 1929, academician Edgar (Mulroney) is determined to take a clinical, psychological approach to examining the heterosexual male libido. He hires two attractive women, Alice (Campbell) and Zoe (Tunney), as stenographers, but his approach soon goes awry as his subjects don't cooperate as expected. **101m/C; DVD.** Dermot Mulroney; Neve Campbell; Robin Tunney; Alan Cumming; Nick Nolte; Til Schweiger; John Light; Julie Delpy; Terrence Howard; Jeremy Davies; Tuesday Weld; ***D:*** Alan Rudolph; ***W:*** Alan Rudolph; Michael Henry Wilson; ***C:*** Florian Ballhaus; ***M:*** Ulf Skogsbergh.

Intimate Betrayal ☙ 1/2 **1996 (R)** Mack (Brown) is surprised when ex-friend Charlie (Edson) crashes his bachelor party. Charlie still wants the bride-to-be, Katie (Hecht), and has hired a hooker, Shelley (Conaway), to seduce Mack and then tell Katie all the dirty details. The wedding's off, Charlie makes his play, Shelley confesses the scam, blah, blah, blah. Neither of these guys is worth the time. **90m/C; VHS, DVD, Streaming.** Dwier Brown; Richard Edson; Cristi Conaway; Jessica Hecht; ***D:*** Andrew Behar; ***W:*** Sara Sackner; ***C:*** Hamid Shams; ***M:*** Peter Fish.

Intimate Confessions of a Chinese Courtesan ☙☙ 1/2 *Ai nu; Body and Sword* **1972** Ai Nu (Lily Ho) is kidnapped and sold into prostitution. Fortunately the brothel owner Chun Yi (Betty Pei Ti) is a devoted lesbian, and so enthralled by Ai Nu that she teaches her a secret martial arts skill. Unfortunately Ai immediately begins using it to quietly murder all the men who force themselves on her at the brothel, most of them are very high-ranking members of society. In its time was groundbreaking for its depiction of two women lovers. **86m/C; DVD.** *HK* Shen Chan; Mien Fang; Wen Chung Ku; Mui Sang Fan; Hua Yueh; Lily Ho; Betty Pei Ti; ***D:*** Yuen Tat Chor; ***W:*** Kang Chien Chiu; ***C:*** Chia Chu; ***M:*** Fu-liang Chow.

Intimate Power ☙☙ 1/2 **1989 (R)** True story of French schoolgirl sold into slavery to an Ottoman sultan who becomes the harem queen. She bears an heir and begins to teach her son about his people's rights, in the hope that he will bring about reform in Turkey where he grows up to be a sultan. Good cast supports the exotic storytelling in this cable drama. **104m/C; VHS, DVD.** F. Murray Abraham; Maud Adams; Amber O'Shea; ***D:*** Jack Smight. **CABLE**

Intimate Stranger ☙ 1/2 **2006** Based on a true story. Single mom Karen Reese (Matchett) breaks off her relationship with Denis Teague (Outerbridge) when he becomes too controlling. He's obsessed and uses his intelligence background to terrorize Karen while she fights back. **90m/C; DVD.** Kari Matchett; Peter Outerbridge; Matthew Knight; Jonas Chernick; Robert Benz; ***W:*** Michael Vickerman; ***C:*** Mark Dobrescu; ***M:*** Rob Bryanton. **CABLE**

Intimate Strangers ☙☙☙ 1/2 *Confidences trop intimes* **2004 (R)** French suspense thriller in the vein of Alfred Hitchcock. William Faber (Luchini) is visited in his office by a beautiful woman named Anna (Bonnaire), who begins to unload her personal problems, mistaking him for a therapist. William, who is actually a tax consultant, is bewildered but also drawn into Anna's world. Stylish and sophisticated flick excellent makes use of two very talented and mesmerizing leads. **104m/C; VHS, DVD.** Sandrine Bonnaire; Fabrice Luchini; Michel Duchaussoy; Anne Brochet; Gilbert Melki; Helene Surgere; Urbain Cancellier; Laurent Gamelon; ***D:*** Patrice Leconte; ***W:*** Patrice Leconte; Jerome Tonnerre; ***C:*** Eduardo Serra; ***M:*** Pascal Esteve.

Into Temptation ☙☙ 1/2 **2009 (R)** Father John Burlien (Sisto) is hearing confessions when abused call girl Linda (Chenoweth) tells him she's going to commit suicide. Hoping to save her, the priest plunges into a morass of Catholic sin and guilt (over celibacy and his vocation) when he checks out the seedier environs of Minneapolis hoping to find Linda before it's too late. Things don't play out as you might imagine. **95m/C; DVD.** Jeremy Sisto; Kristin Chenoweth; Brian Baumgartner; Amy Matthews; Bruce A. Young; ***D:*** Patrick Coyle; ***W:*** Patrick Coyle; ***C:*** David Doyle; ***M:*** Russell Holsapple. **VIDEO**

Into the Abyss ☙☙☙ 1/2 **2011 (PG-13)** Master documentarian Herzog offers one of his most memorable and powerful works as he illustrates the emotional minefield that presents itself when one believes that capital punishment is morally unjust. Focusing on the case of Michael Perry, a young man accused of killing three people in Texas, he presents candid interviews with the men and women destroyed by Perry's actions with clear sympathy and yet still asserts that the death penalty is not the answer. **107m/C; DVD, Blu-Ray.** Richard Lopez; Fred Allen; Jason Burkett; Lisa Stotler-Balloun; Eddie Lee Sausage; Jeremy Richardson; ***Nar:*** Werner Herzog; ***D:*** Werner Herzog; ***C:*** Peter Zeitlinger; ***M:*** Mark De Gli Antoni.

Into the Arms of Strangers ☙ 1/2 **2007** Several years ago, Andy Barker (Carey) suffered brain damage and memory loss in a car accident. Now some memories are re-surfacing and they seem to have something to do with his hometown. So Andy insists that he and wife Erin (Wade) move back (over her objections), but he soon realizes that he doesn't like what he's finding out. **101m/C; DVD.** Ron Carey; April Wade; Juliana Dever; Alison Haislip; Justin Lawrence; Robert T. Bruce; Mark Shady; Lee Perkins; ***D:*** Chris Harris; ***W:*** Chris Harris; Andrew Putnam-Nelson; ***C:*** Chris Harris; ***M:*** Luke McQueen. **VIDEO**

Into the Arms of Strangers: Stories of the Kindertransport ☙☙☙ **2000 (PG)** Academy Award-winning documentary based on the true story of some 10,000 children--most of them German-Jews--who were sent by their parents to foster families in Great Britain to escape Nazi persecution in the late 1930s. Includes archival footage and interviews. **122m/B; DVD.** ***Nar:*** Dame Judi Dench; ***D:*** Mark Jonathan Harris; ***W:*** Mark Jonathan Harris; ***C:*** Don Lenzer; ***M:*** Lee Holdridge. Oscars '00: Feature Doc.

Into the Badlands ☙☙ **1992 (R)** Mild thriller presents three suspense tales in "Twilight Zone" fashion, linked by the appearance of a mysterious Man in Black. No, it's not Johnny Cash, but Dern as a sinister bounty hunter in the old west, who inspires strange events on the trail. **89m/C; VHS, DVD.** Bruce Dern; Mariel Hemingway; Helen Hunt; Dylan McDermott; Lisa Pelikan; Andrew (Andy) Robinson; ***D:*** Sam Pillsbury; ***W:*** Dick Beebe; Marjorie David; Gordon Dawson. **CABLE**

Into the Blue ☙☙ 1/2 **1997** Harry Barnett (Thaw) is a bankrupt businessman now working as a caretaker at a friend's estate on the Greek isle of Rhodes. He has a one-nighter with young Englishwoman Heather Mallender (Cruttenden) and when she mysteriously disappears, Harry becomes a suspect. Then he learns she was investigating the drowning death of her sister, which involves people Harry knows, and he returns to London to try and sort out the mess he's in. **120m/C; VHS, DVD.** *GB* John Thaw; Abigail Cruttenden; Miles Anderson; Michael Culkin; Celia Imrie; ***D:*** Jack Gold. **TV**

Into the Blue ☙☙ **2005 (PG-13)** Sam (Alba) works for an entertainment venture, bobbing about in a bikini and feeding sharks all day. Jared (Walker) has a similar affinity to water, earning his keep as a scuba instructor. Together they hunt for buried treasure, instead finding a cocaine stash buried at the bottom of the ocean in a crashed plane. Of course, the drug dealers aren't too happy to have them sniffing around the goods. Amazingly, there is a bit of a plot behind what first appears to be a video swimsuit catalog. Sure, attractive young people in bathing suits are the focus, but flick surprises with a decent dose of adventure, action, suspense, and some interesting underwater scenes. **110m/C; DVD, Blu-Ray, UMD.** Paul Walker; Jessica Alba; Scott Caan; Ashley Scott; Josh Brolin; James Frain; Tyson Beckford; ***D:*** John Stockwell; ***W:*** Matt Johnson; ***C:*** Shane Hurlbut; ***M:*** Paul Haslinger.

Into the Blue 2: The Reef ☙ **2009** Scuba divers Sebastian (Carmack) and Dani (Vandervoort) are hired by suspicious Eurotrash couple Azra (Thomason) and Carlton (Anders) to search a dangerous Hawaiian reef for Christopher Columbus' lost treasure ship. But really the duo are interested in some cargo that smugglers were forced to abandon. Low-rent and uninteresting with two bland, blonde, albeit hard-bodied, leads. **92m/C; DVD.** Chris Carmack; Marsha Thomason; David Anders; Mircea Monroe; Laura Vandervoort; Michael Graziadel; ***D:*** Stephen Herek; ***W:*** Mitchell Kapner; ***C:*** Thomas Yatsko; ***M:*** Robert Duncan. **VIDEO**

Into the Fire ☙ **1988 (R)** Thriller about a young drifter who, against the backdrop of a Canadian winter, happens upon a roadside lodge and diner, where he gets involved in sex and murder. Title gives a good idea of what to do with this one. **88m/C; VHS, DVD.** *CA* Susan Anspach; Art Hindle; Olivia D'Abo; Lee Montgomery; ***D:*** Graeme Campbell.

Into the Fire ☙ **2005** Ernest, overwrought, and depressing drama examines the crack up of police lieutenant Walter Hartwig Jr. (Flanery) who's with the NYC Harbor Patrol. Bad times ensue when a jumbo jet crashes into the ocean before it can land at Kennedy Airport and Walter searches for survivors. Walter has family issues (including a sister who drowned) that lead him to try to comfort distraught June (Williams) and Catrina (Kanakaredes). **90m/C; DVD.** Melina Kanakaredes; JoBeth Williams; Sean Patrick Flanery; Ron McLarty; Lydia Grace Jordan; Ed Lauter; Pablo Schreiber; Talia Balsam; ***D:*** Michael Phelan; ***W:*** Michael Phelan; ***C:*** Christopher Norr; ***M:*** Steve O'Reilly; Matt Anthony.

Into the Forest ☙☙ **2016 (R)** Page and Wood shine as sisters who live deep in a Canadian forest, generally off the grid, but totally out of touch when there's a continent-wide power outage. After tragedy strikes, the sisters must pull together to face the elements, intruders, and a lack of resources. Great performances and an intriguing set-up are undermined by an ending that's not so much ambiguous as non-existent. Writer/director Rozema writes herself into a corner from which she finds no way out. A minor recommendation for the leads but otherwise the movie goes nowhere. **101m/C; DVD, Blu-Ray.** Ellen Page; Evan Rachel Wood; Max Minghella; Callum Keith Rennie; Michael Eklund; Wendy Crewson; ***D:*** Patricia Rozema; ***W:*** Patricia Rozema; ***C:*** Daniel Grant; ***M:*** Max Richter.

Into the Inferno **2016** One of the best documentarians of the natural world turns his eye to one of nature's most fascinating subjects: the volcano. Working with co-director and volcanologist Clive Oppenheimer, Werner Herzog explores active volcanoes in Indonesia, Iceland, North Korea, and Ethiopia. Of course, Herzog is fascinated by something so destructive coming from Mother Nature, and the fact that people live next door to certain death. His environmentally focused documentaries have been some of the best work of the second half of his career, and this one shows Herzog in an adventurous, exploratory mood. It may not be transcendent but it's certainly fascinating. **104m/C; DVD.** Werner Herzog; Clive Oppenheimer; Maurice Krafft; Katia Krafft; James Hammond; ***D:*** Werner Herzog; ***W:*** Werner Herzog; ***C:*** Peter Zeitlinger.

Into the Night **1985 (R)** Campy, off-beat thriller about a middle-aged, jilted deadbeat (Goldblum), who meets a beautiful woman (Pfeiffer) when she suddenly drops onto the hood of his car, with a relentless gang of Iranians pursuing. During their search through L.A. and other parts of California for the one person who can help her out of this mess, a whole crew of Hollywood directors make cameo appearances, making this a delight for film buffs, but occasionally tedious for general audiences. B.B. King sings the title song. **115m/C; VHS, DVD, Blu-Ray.** Jeff Goldblum; Michelle Pfeiffer; David Bowie; Carl Perkins; Richard Farnsworth; Dan Aykroyd; Paul Mazursky; Roger Vadim; Irene Papas; Bruce McGill; Vera Miles; Clu Gulager; Don Steel; Kathryn Harrold; ***Cameo(s):*** Jim Henson; Paul Bartel; David Cronenberg; Jack Arnold; Jonathan Demme; Lawrence Kasdan; Amy Heckerling; Donald Siegel; Richard Franklin; Colin Higgins; Andrew Marton; ***D:*** John Landis; ***W:*** Ron Koslow; ***M:*** Ira Newborn.

Into the Storm ½ **2009** Follows 2002's "The Gathering Storm" with a charismatic Gleeson starring as prime minister Winston Churchill during the World War II years. The rhetoric is familiar and the story moves swiftly as Churchill realizes when the war ends that peacetime leadership means he won't be needed anymore and it's back to the political wilderness. **100m/C; DVD.** Brendan Gleeson; Janet McTeer; Len Cariou; James D'Arcy; Iain Glen; Patrick Malahide; Alexei Petrenko; Bill Paterson; Donald (Don) Sumpter; ***D:*** Thaddeus O'Sullivan; ***W:*** Hugh Whitemore; ***C:*** Michel Amathieu; ***M:*** Howard Goodall. **CABLE**

Into the Storm **2014 (PG-13)** It's been a couple decades since "Twister," so why not do it again? In an era that turns The Weather Channel personalities into household names, it makes sense that director Quale would try and mine the obsession with Mother Nature's fury into action escapism. His film is mostly found-footage, chronicling a series of legendary tornadoes in the heartland through the videos of those caught in the storms and those chasing them. Any commentary on how we're obsessed with capturing all of life's major events is discarded by the loud, annoying end. To say it could have been worse is not really a compliment. **89m/C; DVD, Blu-Ray.** Matt Walsh; Richard Armitage; Jeremy Sumpter; Sarah Wayne Callies; Kyle Davis; Jon Reep; Max Deacon; Alycia Debnam-Carey; ***D:*** Steven Quale; ***W:*** John Swetnam; ***C:*** Brian Pearson; ***M:*** Brian Tyler.

Into the Sun ½ **1992 (R)** Hall plays a Hollywood star who encounters real-life danger while hanging out with an Air Force pilot (Pare) to prepare for an upcoming role. Spectacular aerial scenes steal the show, which isn't hard to do in this lackluster movie. **101m/C; VHS, Blu-Ray, Streaming.** Anthony Michael Hall; Michael Paré; Terry Kiser; Deborah Maria Moore; ***D:*** Fritz Kiersch; ***W:*** John Brancato; Michael Ferris.

Into the West **1992 (PG)** Enchanting horse tale set amid the mystic isle of Eire. Brooding, drunken Riley (Byrne), once the leader of a band of travelers (the Irish version of gypsies), leaves the road after his wife's death and settles in a Dublin slum with his two boys. The boys are enraptured when their grandfather turns up with a beautiful white horse, but their happiness is shattered when the police take it away. Boys and horse eventually escape in a wild ride across Ireland and into the west. Spiritual and mythic, with an awe-inspiring performance by the horse. Fitzgerald and Conroy make a run at best performances by kids, while Byrne is convincingly sodden and sulky. Meany and Barkin shine in small parts as sibling travellers. **97m/C; VHS, DVD.** *IR* Gabriel Byrne; Ellen Barkin; Ciaran Fitzgerald; Ruaidhri Conroy; David Kelly; Colm Meaney; ***D:*** Mike Newell; ***W:*** Jim Sheridan; ***M:*** Patrick Doyle.

Into the White ½ *Cross of Honour* **2012 (R)** Bland, predictable WWII adventure based on a true story. In April 1940, two aircrews--one German, one British--are shot down over a snowy Norwegian wasteland. The survivors find their way to the same deserted hunting lodge and the Germans try to hold the Brits hostage until everyone realizes that they must all work together. English, Norwegian, and German with subtitles. **101m/C; DVD, Blu-Ray.** *NO SW* Florian Lukas; David Kross; Stig Henrik Hoff; Lachlan Nieboer; Rupert Grint; ***D:*** Petter Naess; ***W:*** Petter Naess; Ole Meldgaard; ***C:*** Dave Mango; Daniel Voldheim.

Into the Wild **2007 (R)** Director Sean Penn tells the true story of Christopher McCandless' (Hirsch) heady journey from 22-year-old middle class college grad to a state of romanticized independence in wild and free Alaska, where McCandless finds the wilderness as brutally indifferent to his high-minded ideals as it is stunningly beautiful. Adapted from Jon Krakauer's book of the same name, the film follows McCandless from Virginia through the American West, where he dons the moniker "Alexander Supertramp." Scenes cut between his journey, his last weeks in the wild, and his personal journal entries to effectively paint a picture of McCandless' thoughts and motivations as he tries to drop off the grid. Quintessential American film for adventurers and non-adventurers alike. **140m/C; DVD, Blu-Ray, HD-DVD.** Emile Hirsch; Marcia Gay Harden; William Hurt; Jena Malone; Catherine Keener; Vince Vaughn; Kristen Stewart; Hal Holbrook; Brian Dierker; ***D:*** Sean Penn; ***W:*** Sean Penn; ***C:*** Eric Gautier; ***M:*** Michael Brook; Edward Vedder; Kaki King. Golden Globes '08: Song ("Guaranteed").

Into the Woods **2014 (PG)** Writer/director Marshall goes back to the musical well with another adaptation of a Broadway hit with expectedly routine, mixed results. A super-talented cast, including Blunt and Streep, keep the story moving. The premise of the musical is simple enough as a Baker (Corden) and his wife (Blunt) encounter legendary characters in a magical woods. Kendrick plays Cinderella, Depp plays a wolf, Streep plays a witch—it's all a bit too whimsical and flat, especially given the source material's darker tones. **124m/C; DVD, Blu-Ray.** Meryl Streep; Emily Blunt; James Corden; Anna Kendrick; Chris Pine; Johnny Depp; Lilla Crawford; Mackenzie Mauzy; Billy Magnussen; Christine Baranski; Daniel Huttlestone; Tracey Ullman; Frances de la Tour; ***D:*** Rob Marshall; ***W:*** James Lapine; ***C:*** Dion Beebe; ***M:*** Stephen Sondheim.

Into Thin Air **1985** A mother searches tirelessly for her college bound son who disappeared on a cross-country drive. Well-done TV drama with a good performance from Burstyn. **100m/C; VHS, DVD.** Ellen Burstyn; Robert Prosky; Sam Robards; Tate Donovan; Caroline McWilliams; Nicholas Pryor; John Dennis Johnston; ***D:*** Roger Young; ***W:*** George Rubio; Larry Cohen; ***M:*** Brad Fiedel. **TV**

Into Thin Air: Death on Everest **1997** Based on the book by Jon Krakauer (played in the telepic by McDonald) about the tragic May, 1996 climbing expedition to Mount Everest that resulted in the deaths of eight climbers. **90m/C; VHS, DVD.** Peter Horton; Christopher McDonald; Nathaniel Parker; Richard Jenkins; ***D:*** Robert Markowitz; ***W:*** Robert J. Avrech. **TV**

Intolerable Cruelty ½ **2003 (PG-13)** The Coens are back with another impeccably cast and written comedy. This time they tackle the genre of screwball comedy, with the formidable help of stars Clooney and Zeta-Jones. He is Miles Massey, an unbeatable divorce attorney, and she's Marilyn Rexroth, a gold-digging serial divorcee. They meet when Miles is hired by Marilyn's soon-to-be-ex, Rex, who's been caught cheating but doesn't want to pay up. When Miles beats her out of her settlement, they begin a dance of mutual attraction and escalating acts of...well, you know. In addition to the genuine movie-star spark of the leads, plenty of hilarious supporting characters inhabit the Coens' over-the-top L.A. landscape. Film's fascination with the characters' charming amorality results in great moments, but contributes to a weak ending by draining the warmth that the romance portion requires. **100m/C; VHS, DVD, Blu-Ray.** George Clooney; Catherine Zeta-Jones; Geoffrey Rush; Cedric the Entertainer; Edward Herrmann; Richard Jenkins; Billy Bob Thornton; Paul Adelstein; Irwin Keyes; Julia Duffy; Tom Aldredge; Jonathan Hadary; Stacey Travis; Royce D. Applegate; ***D:*** Joel Coen; ***W:*** Joel Coen; Ethan Coen; Robert Ramsey; Matthew Stone; ***C:*** Roger Deakins; ***M:*** Carter Burwell.

Intolerance **1916** Griffith's largest film in every aspect. An interwoven, four-story epic about human intolerance, with segments set in Babylon, ancient Judea, and Paris. One of the cinema's grandest follies, and greatest achievements. Silent with music score; B&W with some restored color footage. **175m/B; Silent; VHS, DVD, Blu-Ray.** Lillian Gish; Mae Marsh; Constance Talmadge; Bessie Love; Elmer Clifton; Erich von Stroheim; Eugene Pallette; Seena Owen; Alfred Paget; ***D:*** D.W. Griffith; ***W:*** D.W. Griffith; Tod Browning; ***C:*** Billy (G.W.) Bitzer; Karl Brown. Natl. Film Reg. '89.

The Intouchables ½ **2012 (R)** Millionaire Parisian quadriplegic Philippe (Cluzet) hires ex-con Driss (Sy) as his caretaker. Driss isn't particularly interested in the position and has only applied to satisfy a requirement of collecting unemployment. At first Philippe is no prize to get along with yet eventually a friendship blossoms despite their differences and dissimilar backgrounds. Based on a true story (by Phillippe Pozzo di Borgo titled "A Second Wind"), the film was a major box office success in its native France, but its saccharin qualities and obvious turns (the swapping of race and culture roles) may be a bit too sweet for some. French with subtitles. **112m/C; DVD, Blu-Ray.** *FR* Francois Cluzet; Omar Sy; Anne LeNy; Audrey Fleurot; Cyril Mendy; Christian Ameri; Gregoire Oestermann; ***D:*** Oliver Nakache; Eric Toledano; ***W:*** Oliver Nakache; Eric Toledano; ***C:*** Mathieu Vadepied; ***M:*** Ludovico Einaudi.

Introducing Dorothy Dandridge **1999 (R)** Beautiful, sexy singer/actress Dorothy Dandridge (Berry) was the first African-American woman to be nominated for a best actress Oscar for her title role in 1955's "Carmen Jones." Ten years later, at the age of 42, she was dead from an overdose of antidepressants after suffering a lifetime of tragedies—an abusive childhood, two failed marriages, a brain-damaged child, tumultuous affairs, limited career choices, and bad financial decisions. Based on the book by Dandridge's loyal manager, Earl Mills. **115m/C; VHS, DVD.** Halle Berry; Brent Spiner; Obba Babatunde; Loretta Devine; Cynda Williams; LaTanya Richardson Jackson; Tamara Taylor; Klaus Maria Brandauer; D.B. Sweeney; William Atherton; ***D:*** Martha Coolidge; ***W:*** Scott Abbott; Shonda Rhimes; ***C:*** Robbie Greenberg; ***M:*** Elmer Bernstein. **CABLE**

Introducing the Dwights ½ *Clubland* **2007 (R)** Jean Dwight (Blethyn) and grown sons Tim (Chittenden) and Mark (Wilson) live in Sydney, Australia, where Jean laments her lost career as a comedienne, which she left behind in her native England after relocating with ex-husband and one-hit-wonder musician John (Holden). Self-absorbed Jean works in a cafeteria by day while attempting to resurrect her comedy career by night, leaving little room for helping the boys sort out adulthood. Mark, brain damaged at birth, is addled and precocious. Tom, overcoming his shyness enough to pursue romance with blonde beauty Jill (Booth), sparks conflicts. Feel-good comedy drama strikes a good balance. **105m/C; On Demand.** *AU* Brenda Blethyn; Frankie J. Holden; Rebecca Gibney; Philip Quast; Russell Dykstra; Khan Chittenden; Emma Booth; Katie Wall; ***D:*** Cherie Nowlan; ***W:*** Keith Thompson; ***C:*** Mark Wareham; ***M:*** Martin Armiger.

Intruder **1988 (R)** A psychotic killer stalks an all-night convenience store shopping for fresh meat (customers beware). Slasher movie fans should get a kick out of the plot twist at the end. **90m/C; VHS, DVD, Blu-Ray.** Elizabeth Cox; Renee Estevez; Alvy Moore; ***D:*** Scott Spiegel; ***W:*** Lawrence Bender.

The Intruder *L'Intrus* **2004** Spurred on by a mild heart attack, Louis Trebor (Subor), a troubled and aging loner living in a forest near the French-Swiss border, sets out on a journey to bring meaning to his self-serving life. He first arranges a black market heart transplant then travels to South Korea to purchase a boat, which he sails to a remote island near Tahiti were he lived and fathered a son many years prior. As his health begins to deteriorate, his dreams, visions, memories and reality all blur to create a metaphor for Louis's inner turmoil. Denis creates a stunning piece dripping with impressionistic imagery. **130m/C; DVD.** Michel Subor; Beatrice Dalle; Gregoire Colin; Florence Loiret-Caille; Yekaterina (Katia) Golubeva; ***D:*** Claire Denis; ***W:*** Claire Denis; Jean-Pol Fargeau; ***C:*** Agnes Godard; ***M:*** S. A. Staples.

Intruder ½ **2016** Elizabeth (Louise Linton) is a cliché lone woman in a dark house during a violent storm. Unsurprisingly, an equally cliché murderer is on the loose and stalking her neighborhood. For a home invasion film it has a disappointing lack of action, and manages to lather on so many conventions of the genre it becomes stifled by them. **95m/C; DVD, Blu-Ray, Streaming.** Louise Linton; John Robinson; Mary McDonald-Lewis; Zach Myers; Susannah Mars; ***D:*** Travis Zariwny; ***W:*** Travis Zariwny; ***C:*** Bradley Sellers; ***M:*** Nathaniel Levisay. **VIDEO**

The Intruder **2019 (PG-13)** A young couple's dream house turns nightmarish when its former owner (Quaid) won't let go. The premise is predictable, but the result is enjoyable...enjoyably bad, that is. In typical horror flick fashion, the protagonists remain clueless until it's nearly too late. But it's worth the price of admission to revel in Quaid, with his creepy Joker-esque grin, who chews the scenery with psychopathic gusto. **102m/C; DVD, Blu-Ray.** Dennis Quaid; Meagan Good; Michael Ealy; Joseph Sikora; Alvina August; ***D:*** Deon Taylor; ***W:*** David Loughery; ***C:*** Daniel Pearl; ***M:*** Geoff Zanelli; Paul Stewart.

Intruder in the Dust ½ **1949** A small southern community develops a lynch mob mentality when a black man is accused of killing a white man. Powerful, but largely ignored portrait of race relations in the South. Solid performances from the whole cast; filmed in Mississippi. Adapted from a novel by William Faulkner. **87m/B; VHS, DVD, Streaming.** David Brian; Claude Jarman, Jr.; Juano Hernandez; Porter Hall; Elizabeth Patterson; ***D:*** Clarence Brown; ***C:*** Robert L. Surtees.

Intruders **2011 (R)** Fitfully creepy but mostly unsatisfying psycho-thriller with a faceless monster that's not very scary. Young Juan (Corchero) lives in Madrid while Mia (Purnell) lives in London. Both have nightmares about a scary man that they each write about called Hollowface, who wants to steal a face for his own. Juan's mom Luisa (Lopez de Ayala) goes to a priest for help while Mia's dad John (Owen), who can also see the spook, tries to fend off the creature himself. The end twist is just a gimmick. English and Spanish with subtitles. **100m/C; DVD, Blu-Ray.** *SP* Clive Owen; Ella Purnell; Izan Corchero; Pilar Lopez de Ayala; Carice van Houten; Daniel Brühl; Kerry Fox; ***D:*** Juan Carlos Fresnadillo; ***W:*** Nicolas Casariego; Jaime Marques; ***C:*** Enrique Chediak; ***M:*** Roque Baños.

Intruders *Shut In* **2016 (R)** In this dramatic thriller, a trio of criminals pick the wrong target for a home invasion. Living in an old Victorian home on the edge of town, Anna (Riesgraf) suffers from severe agoraphobia and avoids nearly all human contact. She is not completely isolated, however. She has a terminally ill boyfriend, Conrad (McKinney), and is friendly to her likable Meals on Wheels driver Dan (Culkin). The day of her brother's funeral, three criminals break into her home in search of cash they believe is there. When they tie Anna up, the trio soon learn Anna and the house have many secrets. **90m/C; DVD, Streaming, Download.** Beth Riesgraf; Timothy T. McKinney; Rory Culkin; Jack Kesy; Joshua Mikel; ***D:*** Adam Schindler; ***W:*** T.J. Cimfel; David White; ***C:*** Eric Leach; ***M:*** Frederik Wiedmann.

Intruso 🦴🦴 ½ *Intruder* **1993** Gloomy story set in a coastal city in northern Spain. Luisa (Abril) spots her destitute ex-husband Angel (Arias) and persuades him to stay with her and her new family, husband Ramiro (Valero)?once Angel's good friend—and their two young children. Angel turns out to be terminally ill and decides to wreak vengeance on Ramiro by reclaiming Luisa for himself. In Spanish with English subtitles. **85m/C; VHS, DVD.** *SP* Victoria Abril; Imanol Arias; Antonio Valero; ***D:*** Vicente Aranda; ***W:*** Vicente Aranda; Alvaro del Amo.

Inugami 🦴🦴🦴 **2001** Inugami (literal translation "dog spirit") are familiar spirits created by burying a dog up to his neck and letting it starve to death. Their owners receive wealth and success, at the expense of being shunned by other people. But the Inugami are fickle, and if their owners offend them they will turn on them instead of their enemies. Akira Nutahara is a young grade-school teacher who gets transferred to a school in a remote mountain village. There he falls in love with lonely spinster and paper maker Miki Bonomiya. It isn't long before he discovers the Bonomiya family is shunned due to their connection to the Inugami, and because of other, darker family secrets. **106m/C; DVD.** *JP* Yuki Amami; Atsuro Watabe; Kenichi Yajima; Keiko Awaji; Koichi Sato; Eugene Harada; Shiho Fujimara; Kazuhiro Yamaji; Kanako Fukaura; Shion Machida; Masato Irie; Makoto Tagashi; Torahiko Yamada; Miyu Watase; ***D:*** Masato Harada; ***W:*** Masato Harada; Masako Bando; ***C:*** Junichi Fujisawa; ***M:*** Takatsugu Muramatsu.

Invader 🦴🦴 **1991 (R)** When a news reporter is sent to cover a mysterious massacre, he begins to realize that the culprits are vicious aliens thirsty for blood...and now they're after him! **95m/C; VHS, DVD.** Hans Bachman; A. Thomas Smith; Rich Foucheux; John Cooke; Robert Diedermann; Allison Sheehy; Ralph Bluemke; ***D:*** Phillip Cook.

The Invader 🦴🦴 ½ **1996** School-teacher Annie (Young) discovers she's pregnant by a mystery man (Cross), who turns out to be an alien from a dying race—and Annie's child may be their salvation. Only her ex-cop boyfriend (Baldwin) is on their trail as is an intergalactic bounty hunter (Mancuso). This one is on the romance rather than the action side. **97m/C; VHS, DVD.** Sean Young; Ben Cross; Nick Mancuso; Daniel Baldwin; ***D:*** Mark Rosman; ***W:*** Mark Rosman; ***C:*** Gregory Middleton; ***M:*** Todd Hayen. **VIDEO**

The Invaders 🦴🦴 *Erik the Conqueror; Gli Invasori; La Ruee Des Vikings; Fury of the Vikings* **1963** Two Viking brothers battle each other and the Britons. **88m/C; VHS, DVD, Blu-Ray.** *FR IT* Cameron Mitchell; George Ardisson; Andrea Checchi; Francoise Christophe; Joe Robinson; ***D:*** Mario Bava; ***M:*** Les Baxter.

Invaders from Mars 🦴🦴 ½ **1953** Young boy cries "martian" in this sci-fi cheapy classic. He can't convince the townspeople of this invasion because they've already been possessed by the alien beings. His parents are zapped by the little green things first, making this perhaps an allegory for the missing Eisenhower/Stepford years. Includes previews of coming attractions from classic science-fiction films. Remade in 1986 by Tobe Hooper. **78m/C; VHS, DVD.** Helena Carter; Arthur Franz; Jimmy Hunt; Leif Erickson; Hillary Brooke; Morris Ankrum; Lock Martin; ***D:*** William Cameron Menzies; ***W:*** Richard Blake; John Tucker Battle; ***C:*** John Seitz; ***M:*** Raoul Kraushaar.

Invaders from Mars 🦴 ½ **1986 (PG)** A high-tech remake of Menzies' 1953 semi-classic about a Martian invasion perceived only by one young boy and a sympathetic (though hysterical) school nurse, played by mother and son Black and Carson. Instant camp. **102m/C; VHS, DVD, Blu-Ray.** Hunter Carson; Karen Black; Louise Fletcher; Laraine Newman; Timothy Bottoms; Bud Cort; Dale Dye; ***D:*** Tobe Hooper; ***W:*** Dan O'Bannon; Don Jakoby; ***C:*** Daniel Pearl; ***M:*** Sylvester Levay; David Storrs; Christopher Young.

Invasion! 🦴🦴 ½ *Top of the Food Chain* **1999 (PG-13)** Deliberately tacky and frequently amusing spoof of alien invasion flicks. Atomic scientist Dr. Karel Lamonte (Scott) comes to the town of Exceptional Vista just after the local TV tower is hit by a big meteor. It's hard to tell if aliens have invaded since the townspeople are so weird to begin with, but they have. And they turn out to be the cannibalistic kind who take to munching on the locals. Oh, and it turns out that TV is the key to the aliens' destruction. **99m/C; VHS, DVD.** *CA* Campbell Scott; Fiona Loewi; Tom Everett Scott; Hardee T. Lineham; Bernard Behrens; Nigel Bennett; Peter Donaldson; Robert Bockstael; Lorry Ayers; Ron Gabriel; James Allodi; Maggie Butterfield; Kathryn Kirkpatrick; ***D:*** John Paizs; ***W:*** Phil Bedard; Larry Lalonde; ***C:*** Bill Wong; ***M:*** David Krystal.

The Invasion 🦴 ½ **2007 (PG-13)** In this "Body Snatchers" for the 21st century, Kidman and friends must fight infection by an alien species that takes hold while people are asleep, leaving zombies with no individual thought and no conflict. The only way to prevent the infection is to stay awake, which leads to sleep-deprived paranoia as they struggle to fight the alien menace. Never manages to settle on a consistent theme or tone, as director Hirschbiegel's original version was extensively reshot and recut by the Wachowski/McTeigue team. The end result is a movie that doesn't make any sense, switches from moody thriller to absurd high-impact actioner with no warning, and lacks any standout performances to redeem it. The worst of many versions of the classic "Invasion of the Body Snatchers" story. **93m/C; DVD, Blu-Ray, HD-DVD.** Nicole Kidman; Daniel Craig; Jeremy Northam; Jackson Bond; Jeffrey Wright; Veronica Cartwright; Malin Akerman; John M. Jackson; Josef Sommer; Celia Weston; Jeff Wincott; Alexis Raben; Roger Rees; ***D:*** Oliver Hirschbiegel; ***W:*** David Kajganich; ***C:*** Rainer Klausmann; ***M:*** John Ottman.

Invasion 🦴 ½ *Infection* **2007 (R)** An experimental found-footage horror movie done as a continuous shot entirely in real time. A meteorite lands outside a small town carrying an alien virus, and the locals have to deal with the infected who become violent. **81m/C; DVD.** Jenny Dare Paulin; Morgan Weisser; Alan Abelew; Norbert Weisser; Scott Paulin; ***D:*** Albert Pyun; ***W:*** Cynthia Cuman; ***C:*** Jim Hagopian; ***M:*** Tony Riparetti. **VIDEO**

Invasion: Earth 🦴🦴 ½ **1998** Britain's Royal Air Force and U.S. Air Force officers discover that two alien races have invaded earth and only one of them is amenable to letting the current inhabitants remain. British sci-fi miniseries on 3 cassettes. **270m/C; VHS, DVD.** *GB* Fred Ward; Maggie O'Neill; Phyllis Logan; Vincent Regan; ***D:*** Richard Laxton; Patrick Lau. **TV**

Invasion Earth: The Aliens Are Here! 🦴 **1987** A cheap spoof of monster movies, as an insectoid projectionist takes over the minds of a movie audience. Clips of Godzilla, Mothra and other beasts are interpolated. **84m/C; VHS, DVD.** Janice Fabian; Christian Lee; ***D:*** George Maitland.

Invasion for Flesh and Blood 🦴 **1994** In this sequel to "Flesh Eaters from Outer Space," the old gang must once again foil the plot of carnivorous aliens, this time with the help of a soccer-mom-turned-cyborg death machine. **90m/C; DVD.** Kathy Monks; Warren Disbrow, Sr.; James Cironnella; Adrienne D' Accardi; ***D:*** Warren F. Disbrow; ***W:*** Warren F. Disbrow; ***C:*** Warren F. Disbrow; ***M:*** James Cironella; Anthony Annunziata; Lorenzo Conte; Paul Krautheim; Nick Primiano. **VIDEO**

The Invasion of Carol Enders 🦴 ½ **1974** A woman, almost killed by a prowler, awakens with an expanded consciousness, and tries to convince her husband that her near death wasn't an accident. Currently only available as part of a collection. **72m/C; VHS, DVD.** Meredith Baxter; Christopher Connelly; Charles Aidman; ***D:*** Burt Brinckerhoff; ***W:*** Gene R. Kearney; ***M:*** Robert Colbert.

The Invasion of Johnson County 🦴🦴 **1976** TV movie based on the events of the Johnson County War in 1892. Bostonian Sam Lowell (Bixby) heads to Wyoming and joins with a group of homesteaders who are fighting off cattle barons determined to stop the interlopers from settling in. **100m/C; DVD.** Bill Bixby; Bo Hopkins; John Hillerman; Billy Green Bush; Stephen Elliott; M. Emmet Walsh; Lee De Broux; ***D:*** Jerry Jameson; ***W:*** Nicholas E. Baehr; ***C:*** Rexford Metz; ***M:*** Peter Carpenter; Mike Post. **TV**

Invasion of the Animal People
WOOF! *Terror in the Midnight Sun; Space Invasion of Lapland; Horror in the Midnight Sun; Space Invasion from Lapland* **1962** Hairy monster from outer space attacks Lapland. Narrated by Carradine, the only American in the cast. Pretty silly. **73m/B; VHS, DVD.** *SW* Robert Burton; Barbara Wilson; John Carradine; ***D:*** Virgil W. Vogel; Jerry Warren; ***W:*** Arthur C. Pierce; ***C:*** Hilding Bladh; ***M:*** Harry Arnold; Allan Johansson.

Invasion of the Bee Girls 🦴🦴🦴 *Graveyard Tramps* **1973** California girls are mysteriously transformed into deadly nymphomaniacs in this delightful campy science fiction romp. Written by Meyer who later directed "Star Trek II: The Wrath of Khan." **85m/C; VHS, DVD, Blu-Ray.** William (Bill) Smith; Anitra Ford; Cliff Osmond; Victoria Vetri; Wright King; Ben Hammer; Cliff Emmich; Anna Aries; Tom Pittman; ***D:*** Denis Sanders; ***W:*** Nicholas Meyer; ***C:*** Gary Graver; ***M:*** Charles Bernstein.

Invasion of the Blood Farmers
WOOF! 1972 (PG) In a small New York town, members of an ancient Druidic cult murder young women, taking their blood in the hope of finding the precise, rare blood type to keep their queen alive. A real woofer. **86m/C; VHS, DVD, Blu-Ray.** Norman Kelley; Tanna Hunter; Bruce Detrick; Jack Neubeck; Cythia Fleming; Paul Craig Jennings; ***D:*** Ed Adlum; ***W:*** Ed Adlum; Ed Kelleher.

Invasion of the Body Snatchers 🦴🦴🦴🦴 *Sleep No More* **1956** The one and only post-McCarthy paranoid sci-fi epic, where a small California town is infiltrated by pods from outer space that replicate and replace humans. A chilling, genuinely frightening exercise in nightmare dislocation. Based upon a novel by Jack Finney. Remade in 1978. **80m/B; VHS, DVD, Blu-Ray.** Kevin McCarthy; Dana Wynter; Carolyn Jones; King Donovan; Larry Gates; Jean Willes; Whit Bissell; Richard Deacon; Pat O'Malley; Bobby Clark; Sam Peckinpah; Donald Siegel; Dabbs Greer; ***D:*** Donald Siegel; ***W:*** Sam Peckinpah; Daniel Mainwaring; ***C:*** Ellsworth Fredericks; ***M:*** Carmen Dragon. Natl. Film Reg. '94.

Invasion of the Body Snatchers 🦴🦴🦴 ½ **1978 (PG)** One of the few instances where a remake is an improvement on the original, which was itself a classic. This time, the "pod people" are infesting San Francisco, with only a small group of people aware of the invasion. A ceaselessly inventive, creepy version of the alien-takeover paradigm, with an intense and winning performance by Sutherland. Features cameos by Don Siegel and Kevin McCarthy from the original, as well as an uncredited appearance by Robert Duvall. **115m/C; VHS, DVD, Blu-Ray.** Donald Sutherland; Brooke Adams; Veronica Cartwright; Leonard Nimoy; Jeff Goldblum; Kevin McCarthy; Donald Siegel; Art Hindle; Robert Duvall; ***D:*** Philip Kaufman; ***W:*** W.D. Richter; ***C:*** Michael Chapman.

Invasion of the Girl Snatchers
WOOF! 1973 Aliens from another planet, in cahoots with a cult kingpin, subdue young earth girls and force them to undergo bizarre acts that may just rob them of their dignity. Save a bit of your own dignity by staying away. Cheap look, cheap feel, cheap thrills. **90m/C; VHS, DVD, Streaming.** Elizabeth Rush; Ele Grigsby; David Roster; ***D:*** Lee Jones.

Invasion of the Neptune Men 🦴 *Uchu Kaisoku-sen* **1961** Aliens from Neptune invade Japan only to find their schemes put in jeopardy by local superhero Space Chief. Space Chief's superpowers include driving a flying car, supernaturally bad karate, befriending small children, and making awkward slow-moving aliens fall down. Currently only available as part of a collection. **74m/B; DVD.** *JP* Sonny Chiba; Kappei Matsumoto; Ryuko Mizukami; ***D:*** Koji Ota; ***W:*** Shin Morita; Akihiro Watanabe; ***M:*** Michiaki Watanabe. **VIDEO**

Invasion of the Pod People 🦴 **2007** After a meteor shower hits California, Melissa notices that her friends and co-workers at the modeling agency have extreme personality changes after receiving a weird plant. When Melissa disposes of her own plant in a garbage disposal, it bleeds. Think aliens are involved? Actually think umpteenth would-be version of "Invasion of the Body Snatchers." **85m/C; DVD.** Erica Roby; Jessica Bork; Danae Nason; Marat Glazer; Amanda Ward; Michael Tower; Sarah Lieving; Shaley Scott; ***D:*** Justin Jones; ***W:*** Leigh Scott; ***C:*** Leigh Scott; Bianca Bahena. **VIDEO**

Invasion of the Space Preachers 🦴🦴 *Strangest Dreams: Invasion of the Space Preachers* **1990** Hideous creatures from outer space arrive on Earth with plans for conquest. Led by the seemingly human Reverend Lash, they prey on the innocent and trusting, fleecing God-fearing folk out of their hard earned cash! **100m/C; VHS, DVD.** Jim Wolfe; Guy Nelson; Eliska Hahn; Gary Brown; Jesse Johnson; John Riggs; Jimmie Walker; ***D:*** Daniel Boyd; ***W:*** Daniel Boyd; ***C:*** Bill Hogan; ***M:*** Michael Lipton.

Invasion of the Star Creatures
WOOF! 1963 Barely good for a giggle, this sci-fi comedy is a clunker in every possible way. A couple of dimwit army privates get separated from their patrol while investigating a mysterious crater. They are captured by VegeMonsters, taken to a spaceship hidden in a cave, and find the aliens are your typical Amazonian babes who just need a little earthly smooching to get over that whole invasion thing. Ewwwww. **70m/B; DVD.** Frankie Ray; Robert Ball; Gloria Victor; Dolores Reed; Mark Ferris; ***D:*** Bruno VeSota; ***W:*** Jonathan Haze; ***C:*** Basil Bradbury; ***M:*** Jack Cookerly; Elliott Fisher.

Invasion Quartet 🦴 ½ **1961** Disabled officers escape from a Dover military hospital in order to cross into France and destroy a Nazi weapon that's aimed at the port. Since they're disguised as Germans, they eventually get captured by the French Resistance until the slapstick comedic complications get sorted out. **87m/B; DVD.** *GB* Bill Travers; Spike Milligan; John Le Mesurier; Gregoire Aslan; Maurice Denham; Millicent Martin; Thorley Walters; Cyril Luckham; ***D:*** Jay Lewis; ***W:*** Jack Trevor Story; John Briley; ***C:*** Gerald Moss; Geoffrey Faithfull; ***M:*** Ronald Goodwin.

Invasion U.S.A. 🦴 ½ **1952** Cheap Red Scare movie using tons of stock footage showing actual bombings and air battles. O'Herlihy is a stranger who visits a New York bar and convinces the patrons that the H-bomb has been unleashed on America, while Mohr romances Castle. Full of propaganda and overacting. Based on a story by Robert Smith and Franz Spencer. **73m/B; VHS, DVD.** Gerald Mohr; Peggy Castle; Dan O'Herlihy; Robert Bice; Tom Kennedy; Phyllis Coates; Erik Blythe; Wade Crosby; William Schallert; Noel Neill; ***D:*** Alfred E. Green; ***W:*** Robert Smith; ***C:*** John L. "Jack" Russell; ***M:*** Albert Glasser.

Invasion U.S.A. 🦴 **1985 (R)** A mercenary defends nothing less than the entire country against Russian terrorists landing in Florida and looking for condos. A record-setting amount of people killed. Count them—it's not like you'll miss anything important. Norris is a bit less animated than a wooden Indian, and the acting is more painful to endure than the violence. Glasnost saved the movie industry from additional paranoia movies of this kind. **108m/C; VHS, DVD, Blu-Ray.** Chuck Norris; Richard Lynch; Melissa Prophet; Alex Colon; Billy Drago; ***D:*** Joseph Zito; ***W:*** James Bruner; ***C:*** Joao Fernandes; ***M:*** Jay Chattaway.

Inventing the Abbotts 🦴🦴 **1997 (R)** Appealing cast populates this sleepy, bittersweet coming-of-age story set in small town Illinois in 1957. Alice (Going), Eleanor (Connelly) and Pamela (Tyler) are the lovely daughters of wealthy Lloyd Abbott (Patton) who's determined that they'll marry well despite the temptations offered by the two working-class Holt boys. Surly stud Jacey (Crudup) holds a grudge against Lloyd for possibly cheating his deceased father in a business deal and causing whispers about his schoolteacher mother Helen's (Baker) reputation, while sweet-natured younger brother Doug (Phoenix) has his romantic ideals fixed on Pamela, who loves him in return. Not memorable, but not a complete waste of time, either. Based on the story by Sue Miller. **110m/C; VHS, DVD.** Billy Crudup; Joaquin Rafael (Leaf) Phoenix; Liv Tyler; Will Patton; Kathy Baker; Jennifer Connelly; Joanna Going; Barbara Williams; ***D:*** Pat O'Connor; ***W:*** Ken Hixon; ***C:*** Kenneth Macmillan; ***M:*** Michael Kamen.

The Invention of Lying 🦴🦴 1/2 *This Side of the Truth* **2009 (PG-13)** Jobless filmmaker Mark Bellison (Gervais) lives in a rather drab world where lying, in all its forms (embellishment, flattery, storytelling, religion, and presumably politics) has yet to be discovered. During the course of a particularly bad day, Mark discovers that the untruth can set you free. Interesting and funny concept takes on some big issues in an amusing way, but falters after a brilliant opening. Gervais leavens some potentially offensive (to some) and cringe-worthy spots with genuine warmth and, well, honesty. **99m/C; Blu-Ray, On Demand.** Ricky Gervais; Jennifer Garner; Fionnula Flanagan; Rob Lowe; Jonah Hill; Tina Fey; Christopher Guest; Jason Bateman; Jeffrey Tambor; Louis CK; Stephanie March; Philip Seymour Hoffman; Nathan (Nate) Corddry; Conner Rayburn; Edward Norton; ***Nar:*** Patrick Stewart; ***D:*** Ricky Gervais; Matt Robinson; ***W:*** Ricky Gervais; Matt Robinson; ***C:*** Tim Suhrstedt; ***M:*** Tim Atack.

The Inventor: Out For Blood In Silicon Valley 🦴🦴 1/2 **2019** Theranos founder and CEO Elizabeth Holmes claimed to have developed a revolutionary way of doing blood testing, even though she was not a scientist. She stated that her compact, portable blood analysis machine could quickly conduct 200 different kinds of tests using a pinprick of blood. Holmes' company was suddenly worth billions before hitting the market. Though her own experts said it was not physically possible to build such a device, Holmes convinced many that her product worked even when she was deceiving them all. The documentary offers in-depth information on the company and its claims, but does not go deep enough into Holmes herself. **119m/C; DVD.** Alex Gibney; ***D:*** Alex Gibney; ***W:*** Alex Gibney; ***C:*** Lincoln Else; Antonio Rossi; ***M:*** Will Bates. Writers Guild '19: Documentary Screenplay. **VIDEO**

The Inveterate Bachelor 🦴🦴 1/2 *Il Zitelloni* **1958** Young sales clerk Marcello ignores the advice of 'Professor' Luigi and decides to marry his landlady's beautiful daughter. But he's soon driven crazy by his new wife and mother-in-law and is arrested for murder. Don't believe everything you see—this is a comedy. Italian with subtitles. **98m/B; DVD.** *IT* Vittorio De Sica; Walter Chiari; Rina Morelli; Maria Luz Galicia; Mario Riva; ***D:*** Giorgio Bianchi; ***W:*** Silvio Amadio; Antonio Amurri; ***C:*** Manuel Berenguer; ***M:*** Italo Greco.

Invictus 🦴🦴🦴 **2009 (PG-13)** Director Eastwood tells the true story of political prisoner-turned-President Nelson Mandela (Freeman), who in an effort to unite South Africa after years of apartheid joins with the captain (Damon) of the country's underdog rugby team to try to win the 1995 World Cup. The leads are solid as two men from very different worlds working towards a common goal. And Eastwood delivers—in this case, with the compelling tale of how a sport can pull together people for the greater good—though glossing over much of the historical figures and times. Adapted from the 2008 book by John Carlin "Playing the Enemy: Nelson Mandela and the Game That Made a Nation." **134m/C; DVD, Blu-Ray.** Morgan Freeman; Matt Damon; Robert Hobbs; Langley Kirkwood; Grant Roberts; ***D:*** Clint Eastwood; ***W:*** Anthony Peckham; ***C:*** Tom Stern; ***M:*** Steve Juliani.

Invincible 🦴🦴 **2001 (PG-13)** Herzog's stylized and operatic exploration of a true story is his first dramatic feature in 10 years. In 1932, naive Polish blacksmith Zishe (Ahola) is hired as a strongman to perform at the Palace of the Occult in Berlin, which is owned by showman Hanussen (Roth), who outfits Zishe to resemble German hero Siegfried. Hanussen wishes to be a significant player in the emerging Nazi party but when Zishe reveals himself to be Jewish, he takes it in stride and revels in Zishe's money-making abilities as a "new Samson." But politics and entertainment prove to be a volatile mix. **135m/C; VHS, DVD.** *GB GE* Tim Roth; Jouko Ahola; Anna Gourari; Max Raabe; Udo Kier; Jacob Wein; Gustav Peter Wohler; ***D:*** Werner Herzog; ***W:*** Werner Herzog; ***C:*** Peter Zeitlinger; ***M:*** Hans Zimmer; Klaus Badelt.

Invincible 🦴🦴🦴 **2006 (PG)** True-ish story of not-quite over-the-hill South Philly substitute teacher and part-time bartender Vince Papale (Wahlberg), who gives it a go when new Philadelphia Eagles coach Dick Vermeil (Kinnear) holds open tryouts. Of course the otherwise down-and-out Papale makes the team, much to the delight of his football-crazy buds and the dismay of other players. Papale's on-screen gridiron accomplishments are a Disneyfied exaggeration of his real-life experience, but just try not to root for another underdog sports hero. Exceptional cinematography and cool soundtrack make up for any schmaltz. **104m/C; DVD, Blu-Ray.** Mark Wahlberg; Greg Kinnear; Elizabeth Banks; Kevin Conway; Michael Rispoli; Kirk Acevedo; Michael Nouri; Jack Kehler; Lola Glaudini; Paige Turco; Michael Kelly; ***D:*** Ericson Core; ***W:*** Brad Gann; ***C:*** Ericson Core; ***M:*** Mark Isham.

The Invincible Gladiator 🦴 1/2 *Il Gladiatore Invincible* **1962** A cut above the usual gladiator pics because star Harrison is fun to watch. Rezius (Harrison) is recruited by evil regent Rabirius (Anchoriz) to wipe out some annoying bandits. Imagine his surprise when Rezius figures out they're lead by babe Sira (Boni), the sister of the boy king whom Rabirius wants dead. Rezius winds up back in the arena fighting for the good guys. Dubbed. **90m/C; VHS, DVD.** *IT SP* Richard Harrison; Isabel Corey; Luisella Boni; Leo Anchoriz; Joseph Marco; Livio Lorenzon; Ricardo Canales; ***D:*** Frank Gregory; Alberto De Martino; Antonio Momplet; ***W:*** Alberto De Martino; Antonio Momplet; ***C:*** Eloy Mella; ***M:*** Carlo Franci.

The Invincible Iron Man 🦴🦴 **2007 (PG-13)** In an animated re-telling of the comic character Iron Man's origins, billionaire Tony Stark is digging up an ancient Chinese city when he unwittingly releases the Mandarin, an evil sorcerer. To fight him he creates a suit of armor with powerful weapons. Some longtime comic fans may twitch at this recreation. **83m/C; DVD, Blu-Ray.** ***V:*** Marc Worden; Gwendoline Yeo; Fred Tatasciore; Elisa Gabrielli; Rodney Saulsberry; John McCook; James Sie; Stephen Mendillo; John DeMita; ***D:*** Patrick Archibald; Jay Oliva; Frank Paur; ***W:*** Avi Arad; Greg Johnson; Craig Kyle; Stan Lee; Larry Lieber; ***M:*** Guy Michelmore.

Invisible 🦴 **2006** An improvised, bare bones indie that turns from marital drama to psychos in the woods. Joe and Jane squabble all the way to their secluded cabin. Just as they finally relax, they encounter a couple of crazies who insist that Jane is their long-lost mother. **86m/C; DVD.** James Tupper; Kit Pongetti; David Mongentale; Joe Mellis; ***D:*** Adam Watstein; ***W:*** Adam Watstein; ***C:*** Adam Watstein; Tim Nuttall; ***M:*** Steve Bias.

The Invisible 🦴 1/2 **2007 (PG-13)** Supernatural mystery of no particular distinction. Unhappy teen Nick Powell (Chatwin) is beaten by bad seed Annie (Levieva) and she dumps his body in the woods, but he's not dead. Now Nick's spirit is hovering around, hoping he's found before he does become a homicide case. although he can't do anything useful like spirit writing or move objects. Based on the 2002 Swedish film (and novel) "Den Osynlige." **97m/C; DVD, Blu-Ray.** Justin Chatwin; Marcia Gay Harden; Christopher Marquette; Alex O'Loughlin; Margarita Levieva; Callum Keith Rennie; Michelle Harrison; Ryan Kennedy; Serge Houde; ***D:*** David S. Goyer; ***W:*** Mick Davis; Christine Roum; ***C:*** Gabriel Beristain; ***M:*** Marco Beltrami.

Invisible Adversaries 🦴🦴 **1977** A photographer uncovers an extra-terrestrial plot to cause excessive aggression in humans. She and her lover attempt to hold on to their crumbling humanity. Movies like this make you mad enough to tear something up. Enjoyed a meek cult following. In German with English subtitles. **112m/C; VHS, DVD.** *AT* Susanne Widl; Peter Weibel; ***D:*** Valie Export.

Invisible Agent 🦴🦴 **1942** Hall plays an agent using the secret formula to outwit the Nazis in this third sequel to "The Invisible Man." Especially enjoyable for the kids. Based on characters suggested in H.G. Wells' "The Invisible Man." **83m/B; VHS, DVD, Blu-Ray.** Ilona Massey; Jon Hall; Peter Lorre; Cedric Hardwicke; J. Edward Bromberg; Albert Bassermann; John Litel; Holmes Herbert; ***D:*** Edwin L. Marin; ***W:*** Curt Siodmak.

Invisible Child 🦴 **1999** Annie (Wilson) is a wife and mother who believes she has three children—only the third happens to be invisible. Her husband and kids go along with her delusions with the hope of keeping the family together but then Annie decides to hire nanny Gillian (Bergen) to help out. Since no reason is given for Annie's delusions, this film is just silly. **93m/C; VHS, DVD.** Rita Wilson; Victor Garber; Tushka Bergen; Mae Whitman; David Dorfman; ***D:*** Joan Micklin Silver; ***W:*** David Field; ***C:*** Ken Kelsch; ***M:*** Victoria Dolceamore. **CABLE**

Invisible Circus 🦴 1/2 **2000 (R)** Coming-of-age drama set in 1976 of a young woman, Phoebe (Brewster), who treks through Europe in an attempt to solve the mystery of her older sister Faith (Diaz), a radical hippie who died there seven years ago. Her Nancy Drew-like sleuthing leads her to the big, bad Wolf (Eccleston) in Paris, Faith's old boho boyfriend, now a bourgeois married. Somewhat unlikely tales emerge about Faith's dealings with German terrorists gone bad and bring Phoebe closer to the truth and danger. Story told much like many a late 1960s memory, in confusing flashback fashion, and lacks adequate pacing. Brewster has inspired moments, along with Danner as the girls' mother, while Diaz seems an unlikely terrorist. Based on the novel by Jennifer Egan. **98m/C; VHS, DVD.** Cameron Diaz; Jordana Brewster; Christopher Eccleston; Blythe Danner; Patrick Bergin; Moritz Bleibtreu; Isabelle Pasco; ***D:*** Adam Brooks; ***W:*** Adam Brooks; ***C:*** Henry Braham; ***M:*** Nick Laird-Clowes.

Invisible Dad 🦴🦴 **1997 (PG)** Doug Baily's dad invents a machine that makes him invisible and uses it to foil the evil designs of a co-worker. Unfortunately, the machine isn't perfect, and Mr. Baily tends to reappear at inopportune moments. When Doug discovers his dad is in danger, he figures it's time to help out. **90m/C; VHS, DVD.** Daran Noris; William Meyers; Mary Elizabeth McGlynn; Charles Dierkop; Karen Black; ***D:*** Fred Olen Ray; ***W:*** Steve Latshaw; ***C:*** Gary Graver; ***M:*** Jeff Walton. **VIDEO**

The Invisible Dr. Mabuse 🦴🦴🦴 *The Invisible Horror; Die Unsichtbaren Krallen des Dr. Mabuse* **1962** Possibly the best of the Dr. Mabuse series sees the mad scientist using an invisibility agent in an attempt to take over the world. Preiss also played the title villian in Fritz Lang's "The Thousand Eyes of Dr. Mabuse." **89m/B; VHS, DVD.** *GE* Lex Barker; Karin Dor; Siegfried Lowitz; Wolfgang Preiss; Rudolf Fernau; ***D:*** Harald Reinl.

The Invisible Ghost 🦴 1/2 **1941** A man carries out a series of grisly stranglings while under hypnosis by his insane wife. Typically bad low-budget exploiter about a fun-lovin' crazy couple bringing down property values in the neighborhood. **70m/B; VHS, DVD, Blu-Ray.** Bela Lugosi; Polly Ann Young; John McGuire; Clarence Muse; Betty Compson; ***D:*** Joseph H. Lewis; ***W:*** Helen Martin; Al Martin; ***C:*** Marcel Le Picard.

Invisible Invaders 🦴 **1959** Short, cheap, and silly aliens-try-to-take-over-the-earth flick. This time they're moonmen who use the bodies of dead earthlings (ugh) to attack the living until Agar can save the day. Carradine has a brief role as a formerly dead scientist. **67m/B; VHS, DVD, Blu-Ray.** John Agar; Robert Hutton; Hal Torey; Jean Byron; Philip Tonge; John Carradine; ***D:*** Edward L. Cahn; ***W:*** Samuel Newman; ***C:*** Maury Gertsman.

The Invisible Man 🦴🦴🦴🦴 **1933** The vintage horror-fest based on H. G. Wells' novella about scientist Jack Griffin (Rains) whose formula for invisibility slowly drives him insane. His mind definitely wandering, Jack plans to use his recipe to rule the world. Rains' first role; though his body doesn't appear until the final scene, his voice characterization is magnificent. The visual detail is excellent, setting standards that are imitated because they are difficult to surpass; with special effects by John P. Fulton and John Mescall. **71m/B; VHS, DVD, Blu-Ray.** Claude Rains; Gloria Stuart; Dudley Digges; William Harrigan; Una O'Connor; E.E. Clive; Dwight Frye; Henry Travers; Holmes Herbert; John Carradine; Walter Brennan; ***D:*** James Whale; ***W:*** R.C. Sherriff; ***C:*** Arthur Edeson; ***M:*** W. Franke Harling. Natl. Film Reg. '08.

The Invisible Man 🦴🦴🦴 **2020 (R)** Universal dusts off another of its classic monsters in this sharp, timely, and truly terrifying remake. Elisabeth Moss is utterly captivating in her role as Cecilia, a woman controlled and abused by her husband (Jackson-Cohen). She seemingly escapes and he seemingly dies, but she is convinced that he used his scientific acumen to render himself invisible in order to toy with - and ultimately kill - her and her loved ones. **124m/C; DVD, Blu-Ray, Streaming.** Elisabeth Moss; Oliver Jackson-Cohen; Harriet Dyer; Aldis Hodge; Storm Reid; ***D:*** Leigh Whannell; ***W:*** Leigh Whannell; ***C:*** Stefan Duscio; ***M:*** Benjamin Wallfisch.

The Invisible Man Returns 🦴🦴🦴 **1940** Price stars as the original invisible man's brother. Using the same invisibility formula, Price tries to clear himself after being charged with murder. He reappears at the worst times, and you gotta love that floating gun. Fun sequel to 1933's classic "The Invisible Man." **81m/B; VHS, DVD, Blu-Ray.** Cedric Hardwicke; Vincent Price; John Sutton; Nan Grey; ***D:*** Joe May; ***W:*** Lester Cole; Curt Siodmak; ***C:*** Milton Krasner.

The Invisible Man's Revenge 🦴🦴 1/2 **1944** Left for dead on a safari five years before, Robert Griffin (Hall) seeks revenge against wealthy English couple Lady Irene (Sondergaard) and Sir Jasper (Matthews) Herrick by taking over their estate and marrying their daughter, Julie (Akers). He's aided by scientist Peter Drury (Carradine) who renders Griffin invisible. Only problem is he doesn't stay that way. Fifth in Universal's "Invisible Man" film series. **78m/B; VHS, DVD, Blu-Ray.** Jon Hall; John Carradine; Gale Sondergaard; Lester Matthews; Evelyn Ankers; Alan Curtis; Leon Errol; Doris Lloyd; ***D:*** Ford Beebe; ***W:*** Bertram Millhauser; ***C:*** Milton Krasner; ***M:*** Hans J. Salter.

Invisible Mom 🦴🦴 1/2 **1996 (PG)** Dad (Livingston) invents an invisibility potion that his 10-year-old son decides will make him popular at school. Too bad Mom (Wallace Stone) accidentally swallows the concoction instead. **80m/C; VHS, DVD.** Dee Wallace; Barry Livingston; Trenton Knight; Russ Tamblyn; Stella Stevens; Justin Berfield; Mary Woronov; Mickey Dolenz; ***D:*** Fred Olen Ray; ***W:*** William C. Martell; Sean O'Bannon; ***C:*** Gary Graver; ***M:*** Jeff Walton.

Invisible Mom 2 🦴🦴 **1999 (PG)** Newly adopted 12-year-old discovers his mom can literally disappear and has to deal with cousins trying to get in on his good fortune. Harmless family fare may entertain fans of the original, or the not-too-discerning preadolescent. **80m/C; VHS, DVD.** Dee Wallace; Justin Berfield; Barry Livingston; Mickey Dolenz; Mary Woronov; ***D:*** Fred Olen Ray; ***W:*** Sean O'Bannon; ***C:*** Jesse Weathington. **VIDEO**

The Invisible Monster 🦴🦴 *Slaves of the Invisible Monster* **1950** Special investigators Lane Carlson and Carol Richards battle a mad scientist ready to take over the world with his invisible army. Twelve episodes of the original serial edited onto two cassettes. **167m/B; VHS, DVD.** Richard Webb; Aline Towne; Lane Bradford; Stanley Price; John Crawford; George Meeker; ***D:*** Fred Brannon.

The Invisible Ray 🦴🦴 1/2 **1936** For a change, this horror film features Lugosi as the hero, fighting Karloff, a scientist who locates a meteor that contains a powerful substance. Karloff is poisoned and becomes a murdering megalomaniac. Watching Karloff and Lugosi interact, and the great special effects—including a hot scene where a scientist bursts into flames—helps you ignore a generally hokey script. **82m/B; DVD, Blu-Ray.** Boris Karloff; Bela Lugosi; Frances Drake; Frank Lawton; Beulah Bondi; Walter Kingsford; ***D:*** Lambert Hillyer; ***W:*** John Colton; ***C:*** George Robinson.

Invisible Scars 🦴🦴 **2015** A feature-length documentary exploration of the long-term impact of childhood sexual abuse.

Though Johanna Janis appears strong and confident, the life-long scars of being sexual abused by her father as a child are always present for her. In addition to sharing her struggles, the documentary follows her as she talks about sexual abuse with other survivors as well as scholars and experts on the topic. **84m/C; DVD.** ***D:*** Johnna Janis; Sergio Myers; ***W:*** Johnna Janis; Sergio Myers; ***C:*** Sergio Myers; ***M:*** John Mark Harris. **VIDEO**

An Invisible Sign 1/2 **2011** The whimsy goes out of control in Agrelo's unbelievable adaptation of the Aimee Bender novel "An Invisible Sign of My Own." Young Mona (Madison) enjoys a close relationship with her math-loving dad (Shea) until he has a breakdown. She makes math-related deals with God that never work out except for Mona becoming obsessive-compulsive. Later hired as a math teacher at her old elementary school thanks to some lying by her mom (Braga), the socially inept childlike woman is unable to concentrate and keep her unruly class in order although science teacher Ben (Messina) takes an more-than professional interest. **96m/C; Blu-Ray.** Jessica Alba; J.K. Simmons; Chris Messina; Bailee Madison; John Shea; Sonia Braga; Sophie Nyweide; Marylouise Burke; ***D:*** Marilyn Agrelo; ***W:*** Pamela Falk; Michael Ellis; ***C:*** Lisa Rinzler; ***M:*** Andrew Hollander.

The Invisible Strangler 1/2 *The Astral Factor* **1976 (PG)** A death-row murderer can make himself invisible and rubs out witnesses who helped put him away; woman risks her life to expose him when the police fail to see the problem. Very violent collection of brutal scenes. Not released theatrically until 1984. **85m/C; VHS, DVD.** Robert Foxworth; Stefanie Powers; Elke Sommer; Sue Lyon; Leslie Parrish; Marianna Hill; ***D:*** John Florea; ***W:*** Arthur C. Pierce; ***C:*** Alan Stensvold; ***M:*** Richard Hieronymous; Alan Oldfield.

Invisible Stripes 1/2 **1939** Cliff (Raft) and Chuck (Bogart) just got out of the pen. Cliff is determined to go straight but Chuck goes right back to his criminal ways. Cliff's kid brother Tim (Holden) needs dough to marry sweetheart Peggy (Bryan) and Cliff (who has job problems as an ex-con) winds up pulling some heists with Chuck. Chuck then hides out at Tim's, who is arrested for harboring a fugitive, and Cliff makes a deal with the cops. It doesn't end well. **82m/B; DVD.** George Raft; Humphrey Bogart; William Holden; Jane Bryan; Paul Kelly; Marc Lawrence; Flora Robson; Lee Patrick; Joe Downing; ***D:*** Lloyd Bacon; ***W:*** Warren Duff; ***C:*** Ernest Haller; ***M:*** Heinz Roemheld.

Invisible: The Chronicles of Benjamin Knight 1/2 **1993 (R)** Scientist Benjamin Knight is rendered invisible during a terrible laboratory accident. His only hope of regaining his visible form is a desperate search by Knight and his fellow scientists for just the right chemical antidote. Part of the 'Full Moon Classics, Vol. 2' collection. **80m/C; VHS, DVD.** Brian Cousins; Jennifer Nash; Michael DellaFemina; Curt Lowens; David Kaufman; Alan Oppenheimer; Aharon Ipale; ***D:*** Joakim (Jack) Ersgard; ***W:*** Earl Kenton.

The Invisible Woman **1940** Above average comedy about zany professor Gibbs (Barrymore) discovering the secret of invisibility and making luscious model Kitty (Bruce) transparent during his experiments. She tries some romance with Richard (Howard), the guy who financed the invention, and then gets involved with crooks who want to steal the machine for their own illicit gain. A very likeable movie with a good cast. Based on a story by Curt Siodmak and Joe May, the same team that wrote "The Invisible Man Returns." **73m/B; VHS, DVD, Blu-Ray.** John Barrymore; Virginia Bruce; John Howard; Charlie Ruggles; Oscar Homolka; Margaret Hamilton; Donald MacBride; Edward Brophy; Shemp Howard; Charles Lane; Thurston Hall; ***D:*** Edward Sutherland; ***W:*** Robert Lees; Frederic Rinaldo; Gertrude Purcell; ***C:*** Elwood "Woody" Bredell.

The Invisible Woman **2013 (R)** Fiennes does a generally masterful job as director and star as married (and father of 10), middle-aged author, Charles Dickens. While on tour with a play in 1857, Dickens meets 18-year-old Nelly (Jones), an aspiring actress. Though she tries to keep to the proprieties of the hypocritical Victorian era, they embark upon a very clandestine affair as Dickens belittles his long-suffering wife (Scanlan) and craves his public's adoration. The story moves between their early romance and married Nelly's life in 1883 as she is troubled by her own past's secrets. **111m/C; DVD, Blu-Ray.** *UK* Ralph Fiennes; Felicity Jones; Kristin Scott Thomas; Tom Hollander; Joanna Scanlan; John Kavanagh; Tom Burke; Perdita Weeks; Amanda Hale; ***D:*** Ralph Fiennes; ***W:*** Abi Morgan; ***C:*** Rob Hardy; ***M:*** Ilan Eshkeri.

The Invisibles 1/2 **1999** Likeable actors in unlikeable roles and a rather pretentious script. Rock star Jude (Goorjian) and supermodel Joy (De Rossi) share more than a romance, they share a heroin habit. So they take off for a Paris flat to kick drugs (what's wrong with going into rehab?). They're spoiled and childish and not much happens that you'll care about. **89m/C; VHS, DVD.** Michael Goorjian; Portia de Rossi; Terry Camillieri; Jonathan Segel; ***D:*** Noah Stern; ***W:*** Noah Stern; ***C:*** Robert Humphreys; ***M:*** Jonathan Segel.

Invitation 1/2 **1951** Ellen (McGuire) is dying of a heart condition and her wealthy father Simon (Calhern) decides it would make his little girl happy to be married. So he pays playboy Dan (Johnson) to woo and wed her. However, Dan has dumped Maud (Roman) to do so and she gets back at him by not-so-subtly hinting to Ellen that her new husband was bought and paid for. This news devastates Ellen but Dan is now actually in love with his wife and must convince her of that fact. The lovely, classy McGuire steals the picture. **85m/B; DVD.** Dorothy McGuire; Van Johnson; Ruth Roman; Louis Calhern; Ray Collins; Michael Chekhov; ***D:*** Gottfried Reinhardt; ***W:*** Paul Osborn; ***C:*** Ray June; ***M:*** Bronislau Kaper.

The Invitation **2003 (R)** Clunky thriller has wealthy writer Roland Levy (Henriksen) inviting six friends to his island for what turns out to be a deadly dinner invitation. Seems after a near-death experience, Roland poisons his guests so they can too can experience the bliss he felt. He promises the antidote—if they'll reveal their deepest, darkest secrets. **85m/C; VHS, DVD.** Lance Henriksen; Christopher Shyer; Sarah Jane Redmond; Stefanie von Pfetten; Doug O'Keefe; Fred Henderson; ***D:*** Patrick Bermel; ***W:*** Patrick Bermel; ***C:*** Barney Donlevy; ***M:*** Michael Richard Plowman. **VIDEO**

The Invitation **2016** An intense psychological thriller about paranoia and the uncomfortable space between the perception and reality of an uncomfortable situation. Though he has not seen her in many years, Will (Marshall-Green) attends a dinner party hosted by his ex-wife Eden (Blanchard) and her new husband David (Huisman) at their home in the Hollywood Hills. Will and Eden have a difficult, tragic past, and Will begins to believe that the invitation to the party comes with a hidden agenda. Kusama's thriller is a notable entry in the new movement of horror greats. **100m/C; Blu-Ray, Streaming, Download.** Logan Marshall-Green; Tammy Blanchard; Michiel Huisman; Michelle Krusiec; Aiden Lovekamp; ***D:*** Karyn Kusama; ***W:*** Phil Hay; Matt Manfredi; ***C:*** Bobby Shore; ***M:*** Theodore Shapiro.

Invitation to a Gunfighter **1964** Small town politics change when a paid assassin ambles into town and creates a lot of talk among the neighbors. Like a long joke in which the teller keeps forgetting the important details, the plot grows confusing though it's not complicated. Brynner is interesting as an educated, half-black/half-creole, hired gun. **92m/C; VHS, DVD, Blu-Ray.** Yul Brynner; George Segal; Strother Martin; William Hickey; Janice Rule; Mike Kellin; Pat Hingle; John Alonzo; ***D:*** Richard Wilson.

Invitation to Hell **WOOF!** **1982** Tormented maiden has a devil of a time discovering a secret power that can enable her to gracefully decline a satanic summoning. The cliched evil is tormenting. **100m/C; VHS, DVD.** Becky Simpson; Joseph Sheahan; Colin Efford; ***D:*** Michael J. Murphy; ***W:*** Carl Humphrey; ***M:*** Terence Mills.

Invitation to Hell 1/2 **1984** "Faust" meets "All My Children" in celluloid suburbia. Never Emmied Lucci is the devil's dirty worker, persuading upwardly mobile suburbanites to join a really exclusive country club in exchange for a little downward mobility. Urich, a space scientist, and family are new in town, and soul searching Lucci's got her devil vixen sights set on space jock and brood. Bound to disappoint both fans of Craven's early independent work ("Last House on the Left") and his later high gloss ("Nightmare on Elm Street") formulas. Made for the small screen. **100m/C; VHS, DVD.** Susan Lucci; Robert Urich; Joanna Cassidy; Kevin McCarthy; Patty McCormack; Joe Regalbuto; Soleil Moon Frye; Barret Oliver; ***D:*** Wes Craven. **TV**

Invitation to the Dance 1/2 **1956** Three classic dance sequences, "Circus," "Ring Around the Rosy," and "Sinbad the Sailor." For dance lovers, featuring excellent performances by Kelly. **93m/C; VHS, DVD.** Gene Kelly; Igor Youskevitch; Tamara Toumanova; ***D:*** Gene Kelly. Berlin Intl. Film Fest. '56: Golden Berlin Bear.

The Invoking 1/2 *Sader Ridge* **2013** Problematic horror centered on questions of sanity, brutality, family, and origins. Samantha (Miller) never knew her family, but finds herself inheriting a remote house from them. With three friends, Sam travels to her inherited property to see what it is like. After she gets there, Sam notices changes. She and her friends experience jealous and tension that threatens their friendship. Sam also finds memories from long ago flooding into her subconscious as she loses her sanity. Her world falls apart as she struggles with brutal, evil visions and an inability to differentiate between reality and what she sees. She soon learns that these experiences may explain her forgotten past and buried secrets. **82m/C; DVD, Streaming, Download.** Trin Miller; Brandon Anthony; Carson Holden; D'Angelo Midili; Andi Norris; ***D:*** Jeremy Berg; ***W:*** Jeremy Berg; John Portanova; ***C:*** Jeremy Berg; ***M:*** Trip Like Animals. **VIDEO**

The Invoking 2 1/2 **2015** A sequel to the horror flick The Invoking in name only, this outing is an anthology of stories related to the paranormal. In the six unrelated stories, a central character faces a struggle for his or her soul with some sort of of evil or paranormal force such as a demon or poltergeist. One story includes a haunted asylum, while another centers on a woman being driven mad by a scratching noise. **83m/C; DVD, Streaming, Download.** Andrew Fleming; Allen Lowman; William McMichael; Erin Meyer; Deanna Nelson; ***D:*** Jamie DeWolf; Jay Holben; Corey Norman; Adam O'Brien; Patrick Rea; Jamie Root; ***W:*** Jamie DeWolf; Jay Holben; Corey Norman; Patrick Rea; Jamie Root; Trevor Botkin; Julien Maisonneuve; Haley Norman; Dave Shepherd; ***C:*** Hanuman Brown-Eagle; Jayson Crothers; Arnaud Dumas; Ken Gonneville; ***M:*** Aldon Baker; Julian Bickford; Christian Clermont; Richard DeCosta. **VIDEO**

IO **2019** After Earth has become essentially uninhabitable, most humans have left for a floating colony located outside Jupiter's moon IO. Among those left on Earth is Susan (Qualley), a scientist who believes that sustaining life on Earth must be possible. As she experiments with different elements and lifeforms to find a solution, her lover Elon (Payne) begs her to take one of the last shuttles to the colony. Susan's solitude is disrupted by the arrival of Micah (Mackie), who wants to meet her famous scientist father (Huston). The minimalist sci fi film explores familiar themes but is dry and serious, and features little chemistry between the leads. **96m/C; DVD.** Margaret Qualley; Anthony Mackie; Danny Huston; Tom Payne; Emma Fitzgerald; ***D:*** Jonathan Helpert; ***W:*** Clay Jeter; Charles Spano; Will Basanta; ***C:*** Andre Chemetoff; ***M:*** Alex Belcher; Henry Jackman. **VIDEO**

Iowa **2005** Low-budget indie that's an overly-familiar tale of drug addiction and crime. Esper (Farnsworth) and his girlfriend Donna (Foster) begin manufacturing crystal meth so they can get the money to hightail it out of their Iowa hometown. Instead, they become addicts. Esper also has a problem with his floozy mom (Arquette) and her psychotic cop boyfriend (Weiss) who are after an inheritance due from Esper's late dad. **97m/C; DVD.** Matt Farnsworth; Dianne Foster; Michael T. Weiss; Rosanna Arquette; John Savage; Muse Watson; ***D:*** Matt Farnsworth; ***W:*** Matt Farnsworth; ***C:*** Andy Parke; John Houghton; ***M:*** Elia Cmiral. **VIDEO**

Ip Man 1/2 *Yip Man* **2008 (R)** In mid-1930s Foshan, wealthy Ip Man (Yen) is the top master of the martial art Wing Chun but will not establish his own school. When he is challenged to a private duel by the dandy Master Li (Zhihui), he easily defeats him. The situation becomes more complicated when Japan invades China and takes over. Ip Man is compelled to seek employment, protect his family, and avenge his country. The first in a series of films, the kung fu epic is based on the true life of Ip Man. Featuring a memorable performance by Yen, it successfully balances drama with excellently staged fights. Cantonese, Mandarin, and Japanese with subtitles. **106m/C; DVD.** Donnie Yen; Simon Yam; Lynn Xiong; Hiroyuki Ikeuchi; Ka Tung Lam; ***D:*** Wilson (Wai-Shun) Yip; ***W:*** Edmond Wong; Tai-Lee Chan; ***C:*** Sing-Pui O; ***M:*** Kenji Kawai.

Ip Man 2 1/2 *Ip Man 2: Legend of the Grandmaster; Yip Man 2* **2010 (R)** In 1949 Hong Kong, Ip Man (Yen) is a family man with a second child on the way when he opens up a martial arts academy. Though Ip Man's talents as a Wing Chun master are not in doubt, the syndicate that controls the sport oppose the move. After defeating a series of the best fighters controlled by the syndicate, Ip Man establishes his school but ultimately finds himself fighting something bigger: Chinese home rule against the British colonizers. Like the original, the sequel to Ip Man includes well-crafted, impactful fight scenes and Yen's athletic, disciplined performance. Cantonese and Mandarin with subtitles. **108m/C; DVD.** Donnie Yen; Xiaoming Huang; Sammo Hung; Lynn Xiong; Kent Cheng; ***D:*** Wilson (Wai-Shun) Yip; ***W:*** Tai-Lee Chan; Hiu-Yan Choi; Edmond Wong; ***C:*** Hang-Sang Poon; ***M:*** Kenji Kawai.

Ip Man 3 1/2 *Yip Man 3* **2016 (PG-13)** Donnie Yen's unexpected franchise gets a robust, fun installment, complete with a cameo by the one and only Mike Tyson, who actually gets a fighting scene. Before then, we get a pretty standard martial-arts movie set-up—there are bad guys who look like gangsters and, of course, there's only one man who can stop them—Yen's Master Ip. What people really care about here is the fight choreography and it's surprisingly great. The martial arts genre may be well past its prime, but this is a fun late installment that doesn't break any new ground but does kick some butt. Chinese with subtitles. **105m/C; DVD, Blu-Ray.** Donnie Yen; Lynn Hung; Jin Zhang; Mike Tyson; Patrick Tam; ***D:*** Wilson (Wai-Shun) Yip; ***W:*** Lai-Yin Leung; Chan Tai-Li; Edmond Wong; ***C:*** Kenny Tse; ***M:*** Kenji Kawai.

Ip Man 4: The Finale 1/2 *Yip Man 4* **2019** As Ip Man (Wong) reaches later stages of life, he is no longer the prominent, popular Wing Chun martial arts master he once was. Though he may no longer be an in-demand teacher, he stubbornly lives his life with virtue and strength. While helping others and fighting enemies, Ip Man also mentors his young disciple, Tang Shing (Chan), who tries to do the same. Despite Wong's charismatic performance as Ip Man, there is an overall lethargy in the film's execution. Cantonese and Mandarin with subtitles. **107m/C; DVD.** Donnie Yen; Scott Adkins; Kwok-Kwan Chan; Vanness Wu; Jim Liu; ***D:*** Wilson (Wai-Shun) Yip; ***W:*** Tai-Lee Chan; Hiroshi Fukazawa; Lai-Yin Leung; Edmond Wong; ***C:*** Siu-keung Cheng; ***M:*** Kenji Kawai.

The Ipcress File **1965** The first of the Harry Palmer spy mysteries that made Caine a star. Based upon the bestseller by Len Deighton, it features the flabby, nearsighted spy investigating the kidnapping of notable British scientists. Solid scenes, including a scary brainwashing session, and tongue-firmly-in-British-cheek humor. Lots of camera play to emphasize Caine's myopia. Two sequels: "Funeral in Berlin" and "Billion Dollar Brain." **108m/C; VHS, DVD, Blu-Ray.** *GB* Michael Caine; Nigel Green; Guy Doleman; Sue Lloyd; Gordon Jackson; ***D:*** Sidney J. Furie; ***W:*** Bill Canaway; James Doran; ***C:*** Otto Heller; ***M:*** John Barry. British Acad. '65: Film.

Iphigenia **1977** Based on the classic Greek tragedy by Euripides, this story concerns the Greek leader Agamemnon, who plans to sacrifice his lovely daughter, Iphigenia, to please the gods. Mere mortals protest and start a save-the-babe movement, but Euripides' moral—you can't please 'em all—is devastatingly realized. Fine adaptation that becomes visually extravagant at times, with an equally fine musical score. In Greek with English subtitles. **130m/C; VHS, DVD, Blu-Ray.** *GR* Irene Papas; Costa Kazakos; Tatiana Papamoskou; Costas Carras; Christos Tsangas; Panos Michalopoulas; ***D:*** Michael Cacoyannis; ***W:*** Michael Cacoyannis; ***C:*** Yorgos Arvanitis; ***M:*** Mikis Theodorakis.

I.Q. 1/2 **1994 (PG)** Albert Einstein (the irascible Matthau) thinks his co-ed niece (Ryan) is in need of a little romance, so he engineers a plan to get her into the arms of Robbins, a local auto mechanic. Robbins and Ryan are comfortable in their comic roles, although they're both above the material. Matthau shines as the famous physicist. Plot gets a little farfetched with its central contrivance of making Robbins look like a brilliant scientist, which leaves second half of story flat. However, chemistry between leads is undeniable and you can't help but cheer on the inevitable. Visually pleasing with Ryan costumed in cool, elegant '50s fashions. Filmed in Princeton, New Jersey. **95m/C; VHS, DVD.** Tim Robbins; Meg Ryan; Walter Matthau; Lou Jacobi; Gene Saks; Joseph Maher; Stephen Fry; Tony Shalhoub; Frank Whaley; ***D:*** Fred Schepisi; ***W:*** Michael Leeson; Andy Breckman; ***C:*** Ian Baker; ***M:*** Jerry Goldsmith.

Ira & Abby **2006 (R)** Jewish Ira (Messina) is the neurotic, underachieving son of two analysts (Klein, Light) while shiksa Abby (Westfeldt) is a free spirit, thanks to her hipster parents (Willard, Conroy). They impulsively get married but discover exes and in-laws, affairs and insecurities, and too many therapists cause them lots of trouble. Manhattan looks great, the parents are great, but the flick is Woody Allen-lite via an episode of "Dharma & Greg" with swearing and overt sexual content. **105m/C; DVD.** Jennifer Westfeldt; Judith Light; Jason Alexander; Fred Willard; Chris Messina; Frances Conroy; Robert Klein; Darrell Hammond; Chris Parnell; ***D:*** Robert Cary; ***W:*** Jennifer Westfeldt; ***C:*** Harlan Bosmajian; ***M:*** Marcelo Zarvos.

Irene 1/2 **1940** Based on the 1919 Broadway musical comedy. Shopgirl Irene (Neagle) is supposed to model a couture gown at a charity function but it gets ruined. So she substitutes a vintage blue gown and goes to the party (which is shown in Technicolor) where she's mistaken for a royal heiress. Dress shop manager Mr. Smith (Young) continues the charade so Irene can promote the shop's fashions but this causes problems for her new romance with Don Marshall (Milland), who's hiding a secret of his own. The Oscar-nominated score contains the song "Alice Blue Gown." **100m/B; DVD.** Anna Neagle; Ray Milland; Roland Young; Billie Burke; Alan Marshal; May Robson; Marsha Hunt; Arthur Treacher; ***D:*** Herbert Wilcox; ***W:*** Alice Duer Miller; ***C:*** Russell Metty; ***M:*** Anthony Collins.

Irene in Time 1/2 **2009 (PG-13)** Typically loose production from Jaglom focusing on the neurotic title character who has daddy issues. Irene's (Frederick) father was a philandering gambler who disappeared from her life, causing her to have romantic problems with men. However, Irene's self-absorption (and the endless discussions with her girlfriends) quickly becomes tiresome, as does the film. **95m/C; DVD.** Andrea Marcovicci; Tanna Frederick; Victoria Tennant; Karen Black; David Proval; Jack Maxwell; Lanre Idewu; Kelly De Sarla; ***D:*** Henry Jaglom; ***W:*** Henry Jaglom; ***C:*** Hanania Baer; ***M:*** Harriet Schock.

Irina Palm **2007 (R)** Provincial middle-aged widow Maggie (Faithfull) is happy to care for her seriously ill grandson Olly (Burke) and play bridge with her girlfriends. Olly's parents learn about an experimental new treatment but it's impossibly expensive and Maggie decides to get a job in London but is constantly rejected until she answers an advert at a Soho sex club. When she learns what she'll be paid, Maggie accepts the job—using the professional name Irina Palm, which hints at her sexual specialty—and is an unexpected success. However, her son Tom (Bishop) is soon wondering why his mother is so secretive. **103m/C; DVD.** *FR BE* Marianne Faithfull; Miki (Predrag) Manojlovic; Kevin Bishop; Siobhan Hewlett; Jenny Agutter; Corey Burke; Dorka Gryllus; ***D:*** Sam Garbarski; ***W:*** Philippe Blasband; Martin Herron; ***C:*** Christophe Beaucarne; ***M:*** Ghinzu.

Iris **2001 (R)** Enduring love story between novelist/philosopher Iris Murdoch and her husband John Bayley from their days at Oxford in the 1950s to Murdoch's long decline from Alzheimer's and death in 1999. Winslet and Bonneville play the young duo while Dench and Broadbent play the mature marrieds. The ladies have the showier roles, especially Winslet, since the young Iris was a sexual free-spirit and disdained conventional morality while John comes across as shy and rather awed by Murdoch's talents. Based on Bayley's memoirs "Iris: A Memoir" and "Elegy for Iris." **90m/C; VHS, DVD.** *GB US* Dame Judi Dench; Jim Broadbent; Kate Winslet; Hugh Bonneville; Penelope Wilton; Juliet Aubrey; Timothy West; Samuel West; Eleanor Bron; ***D:*** Richard Eyre; ***W:*** Richard Eyre; Charles Wood; ***C:*** Roger Pratt; ***M:*** James Horner. Oscars '01: Support. Actor (Broadbent); British Acad. '01: Actress (Dench); Golden Globes '02: Support. Actor (Broadbent); L.A. Film Critics '01: Support. Actor (Broadbent), Support. Actress (Winslet); Natl. Bd. of Review '01: Support. Actor (Broadbent).

Iris Blond 1/2 **1998 (R)** Bittersweet romantic comedy about a sadsack piano player named Romeo (Verdone), who's pushing 50 and is unlucky in love. Having been cuckholded by his girlfriend, Romeo asks a fortuneteller (Fumo) for some help. She tells him his future resides with a singer who has the name of a flower. Naturally, Romeo picks the wrong chick (Ferrerol), only to soon meet red-hot maneater, Iris (Gerini). Eventually things work out as they should. French and Italian with subtitles. **100m/C; VHS, DVD.** *IT* Carlo Verdone; Andrea Ferreol; Claudia Gerini; Nuccia Fumo; ***D:*** Carlo Verdone; ***W:*** Carlo Verdone; Francesca Marciano; Pasquale Plastino; ***C:*** Giuseppe Di Biase.

The Iris Effect **2004 (R)** Confusing thriller. Sarah Hathaway's (Archer) troubled son Thomas disappeared 10 years ago. Unexpectedly, Sarah sees an art catalog that contains paintings similar to those Thomas did, so she travels to St. Petersburg, Russia, to find the art gallery and the artist—which isn't Thomas. Or is it? Something strange is happening as Sarah is followed by a mute street kid (Alan) who seems to know a lot about her son. **90m/C; DVD.** Anne Archer; Agnes Bruckner; Mia Kirshner; Kip Pardue; Gregory Hlady; Devon Alan; Yuri Kolokol; ***D:*** Nikolai Lebedev; ***W:*** Kam Miller; ***C:*** Irek Hartowicz; ***M:*** Alexey Rybnikov. **VIDEO**

Iris Johansen's The Killing Game *The Killing Game* **2011** Lifetime movie based on Johansen's novel, published in 2000. Forensic sculptor Eve Duncan suffered her own tragedy when her 7-year-old daughter Bonnie was kidnapped and murdered. Her body was never found so when a number of skeletons are unearthed, including that of a child, Eve believes it might be Bonnie. The psycho serial killer behind the crimes contacts Eve, taunting her that he's going to kill another little girl if she can't stop him. **90m/C; DVD.** Laura Prepon; Naomi Judd; Ty Olsson; Teryl Rothery; Kavan Smith; Brian Markinson; ***D:*** Bobby Roth; ***W:*** Jill Blotevogel; ***C:*** Rick Bota; ***M:*** James Gelfand. **CABLE**

Irish Eyes Are Smiling **1944** Uninspired and typically fictious showbiz bio of sentimental songwriter Ernest R. Ball. Ball (Haymes) falls for burlesque performer Mary 'Irish' O'Brien (Haver) and follows her to New York where he gets some nightclub work. He sings a coupleof his own tunes and impresses local celebrity Lucille Lacey (Whitney), becomes a success, and renews his romance with Mary. **89m/C; DVD.** Dick Haymes; June Haver; Monty Woolley; Anthony Quinn; Beverly Whitney; Maxie "Slapsie" Rosenbloom; Veda Ann Borg; ***D:*** Gregory Ratoff; ***W:*** Earl Baldwin; John Tucker Battle; ***C:*** Harry Jackson; ***M:*** Alfred Newman.

The Irish in Us 1/2 **1935** Brothers Pat, Danny, and Mike O'Hara share a tenement flat with their Ma although cop Pat wants to move out after marry his gal, Lucille. Too bad she's actually fallen for feisty boxing promoter Danny. Lots of enjoyable blarney and Cagney gets the opportunity to get into the ring when Danny's boxer gets drunk before his big match. **84m/B; DVD.** James Cagney; Pat O'Brien; Olivia de Havilland; Frank McHugh; Allen Jenkins; Mary Gordon; J. Farrell MacDonald; ***D:*** Lloyd Bacon; ***W:*** Earl Baldwin; ***C:*** George Barnes.

Irish Jam **2005** Con man Jimmy (Griffin) has a tough life in L.A. and sees a small Irish town's poetry contest as a way out. After lifting some rap lyrics he wins the grand prize and becomes the town's new pub owner, not knowing the locales concocted the whole thing to keep a filthy rich developer at bay. Usual "worlds colliding" confusion plus an unlikely romance with a lonely widowed mother. **90m/C; DVD.** Eddie Griffin; Anna Friel; Kevin McNally; Mo'Nique Imes; ***D:*** John Eyres; ***W:*** John Eyres; Max Myers. **VIDEO**

The Irishman 1/2 **1978** Set in 1920s Australia, the tale of a proud North Queensland family and their struggles to stay together. The Irish immigrant father is a teamster whose horse-drawn wagons are threatened by progress. His fight to preserve old ways is impressive, but gives way to sentimentality. **108m/C; VHS, DVD.** *AU* Lou Brown; Michael Craig; Simon Burke; Robyn Nevin; Bryan Brown; ***D:*** Donald Crombie; ***W:*** Donald Crombie; ***C:*** Peter James; ***M:*** Charles Marawood.

The Irishman **2019 (R)** A biopic of Frank "The Irishman" Sheeran (De Niro), who recounts his days as a mob hitman for the Bufalino crime family, with particular focus on his role in the 1975 disappearance of Teamsters' president Jimmy Hoffa. Feeling both nostalgic and fresh, this NY crime epic features an impeccable cast of veteran heavy-hitters and Scorsese's trademark mashup of humor and violence. Based on the book by Charles Brandt. **209m/C; DVD.** Robert De Niro; Al Pacino; Joe Pesci; Jesse Plemons; Bobby Cannavale; ***D:*** Martin Scorsese; ***W:*** Steven Zaillian; ***C:*** Rodrigo Prieto; ***M:*** Robbie Robertson.

Irma La Douce 1/2 **1963** A gendarme pulls a one-man raid on a back-street Parisian joint and falls in love with one of the hookers he arrests. Lemmon is great as a well-meaning, incompetent boob, and MacLaine gives her all as the hapless hooker. A plodding pace, however, robs it of the original's zip, though it was a boxoffice smash. Broadway musical is lost without the music. **144m/C; VHS, DVD, Blu-Ray.** Jack Lemmon; Shirley MacLaine; Herschel Bernardi; ***D:*** Billy Wilder; ***W:*** Billy Wilder; I.A.L. Diamond; ***M:*** Andre Previn. Oscars '63: Adapt. Score; Golden Globes '64: Actress--Mus./Comedy (MacLaine).

Irma Vep **1996** Satiric tweaking of French filmmaking begins with has-been director Rene Vidal (Leaud) hiring Hong Kong star Maggie Cheung to take the lead role of Irma Vep in a remake of the 1915 silent French classic "Les Vampires." But from the moment the actress arrives in Paris, it's one disaster after another. Cheung has trouble with the language barrier, Vidal is having a breakdown, lesbian costumer Zoe (Richard) is instantly smitten by Cheung and has her interest humiliatingly conveyed to everyone on the production. Then there's Jose Murano (Castel), a snobbish auteur who replaces Vidal and believes the Chinese actress can't play a French thief, not knowing that Cheung has become obsessed with her role and is practicing stealing from other hotel guests. English and French with subtitles. **96m/C; VHS, DVD.** *FR* Maggie Cheung; Jean-Pierre Leaud; Nathalie Richard; Bulle Ogier; Lou Castel; Antoine Basler; Nathalie Boutefeu; Arsinee Khanjian; Alex Descas; ***D:*** Olivier Assayas; ***W:*** Olivier Assayas; ***C:*** Eric Gautier.

Iron & Silk 1/2 **1991 (PG)** A young American searches for himself while he teaches English and learns martial arts in mainland China. Based on the true story of Salzman's travels. His studies of martial arts and Chinese culture provide a model for his students in their studies of American language and culture. Beautiful photography. Fine performances. **94m/C; VHS, DVD.** Mark Saltzman; Pan Qingfu; Jeanette Lin Tsui; Vivian Wu; ***D:*** Shirley Sun; ***W:*** Mark Saltzman; Shirley Sun; ***M:*** Michael Gibbs.

Iron Angel 1/2 **1964** During the Korean War a squadron sets out to silence North Korean guns. They do. Judging by their eternal bickering they must have put the enemy to sleep. **84m/B; VHS, DVD.** Jim Davis; Margo Woode; Donald (Don "Red") Barry; L.Q. Jones; ***D:*** Ken Kennedy; ***W:*** Ken Kennedy.

Iron Cowboy **1968** Actor finds romance with film editor while audience stifles yawns. Filmed on the set of "Blue," this pre-"Deliverance" Reynolds comedy never made it to the theaters. (Smithee is actually director Jud Taylor.) **86m/C; VHS, DVD.** Burt Reynolds; Barbara Loden; Terence Stamp; Noam Pitlik; Ricardo Montalban; Patricia Casey; Jane Hampton; Joseph V. Perry; ***D:*** Alan Smithee.

Iron Eagle 1/2 **1986 (PG-13)** A teenager teams with a renegade fighter pilot to rescue the youth's father from captivity in the Middle East. Predictable but often exciting. Followed by two sequels. **117m/C; VHS, DVD.** Louis Gossett, Jr.; Jason Gedrick; Tim Thomerson; David Suchet; Larry B. Scott; Caroline Lagerfelt; Jerry Levine; Michael Bowen; Robbie (Reist) Rist; Bobby Jacoby; Melora Hardin; ***D:*** Sidney J. Furie; ***W:*** Kevin Elders; Sidney J. Furie; ***M:*** Basil Poledouris.

Iron Eagle 2 **1988 (PG)** Lower-budget extended adventures of a maverick fighter pilot after he is reinstated in the Air Force. This time he links with an equally rebellious commie fighter and blasts away at nuke-happy Ivan. Yahoo fun for all overt Yankees! Followed by "Aces: Iron Eagle 3." Available in Spanish. **102m/C; VHS, DVD.** *CA IS* Louis Gossett, Jr.; Mark Humphrey; Stuart Margolin; Alan Scarfe; Maury Chaykin; Sharon H. Brandon; ***D:*** Sidney J. Furie; ***W:*** Sidney J. Furie; Kevin Elders; ***C:*** Alan Dostie; ***M:*** Amin Bhatia.

Iron Eagle 4 1/2 **1995 (PG-13)** Series has gotten old and tired though Gossett Jr. shows professionalism in his father figure role of retired Air Force General "Chappy" Sinclair. He's running the Iron Eagle Flight School—a training center/holding cell for troubled teens—along with pilot Doug Masters (Cadieux). Masters and his would-be pilots discover suspicious activities at a local air base, leading to biological weapons and an Air Force conspiracy. **95m/C; VHS, DVD.** *CA* Louis Gossett, Jr.; Jason Cadieux; Al Waxman; Joanne Vannicola; Rachel Blanchard; Sean McCann; Ross Hill; Karen Gayle; ***D:*** Sidney J. Furie; ***W:*** Michael Stokes; ***C:*** Curtis Petersen; ***M:*** Paul Zaza.

The Iron Giant 1/2 **1999 (PG)** After a giant robot falls from the sky and frightens a small town, only a young boy is willing to befriend the iron man. With his new friend, he teaches the townspeople a lesson about being afraid of what is different. Jennifer Aniston provides the voice for the boy's mother, and Harry Connick Jr. that of the town beatnik. Great animation and story propel this tale above the level of most kiddie fare. Based on the 1968 children's book by Ted Hughes, which was also used for a 1989 concept album by Pete Townshend. **86m/C; VHS, DVD, Blu-Ray.** ***V:*** Vin Diesel; Eli Marienthal; Jennifer Aniston; Harry Connick, Jr.; John Mahoney; M. Emmet Walsh; Cloris Leachman; James Gammon; Christopher McDonald; ***D:*** Brad Bird; ***W:*** Tim McCanlies; ***M:*** Michael Kamen.

The Iron Horse **1924** Davy Brandon is a frontiersman and scout who learned about western trails from his surveyor father. His childhood sweetheart Miriam is traveling with her fiance Jesson, who is working on the route for the new transcontinental railway. Davy says he knows a shortcut but a jealous Jesson (who's been bribed by land speculators) tries to kill him. There's lots more action (and Abraham Lincoln!) before the railroad is finished and the sweethearts reunited. Ford's epic western was filmed on location and was his first major studio success. **119m/B; Silent; DVD, Blu-Ray.** George O'Brien; Madge Bellamy; Cyril Chadwick; Fred Kohler, Jr.; Charles Edward Bull; Gladys Hullette; ***D:*** John Ford; ***W:*** Charles Kenyon; John Russell; Charles Denton; ***C:*** George Schneiderman. Natl. Film Reg. '11.

The Iron Ladies 1/2 *Satree Lex* **2000** The true story of a 1996 Thai volleyball team that made it to national competition. When the governor asks the coach to assemble a dream team to compete in volleyball, the addition of a transvestite and a drag queen so offend the team all of them quit except for one guy. So the coach rounds the team out with assorted gays, drag queens, transvestites, and a transsexual. Definitely a new take on the underdog sports comedy genre, and Thailand's second-highest grossing film. **104m/C; DVD.** *TH* Jesdaporn Pholdee; Sahaphap Tor; Ekachai Buranapanit;

Giorgio Maiocchi; Chaicham Nimpulsawasdi; Kokkorn Benjathikoon; Shiriohona Hongsopon; Phomsit Sitthijamroenkhun; Sutthipong Sitthijamroenkhun; Anucha Chatkaew; *D:* Youngyooth Thongkonthun; *W:* Youngyooth Thongkonthun; Visuttchai Boonyakarnjawa; Jira Maligool; *C:* Jira Maligool.

The Iron Ladies 2 🦴🦴 ½ *Satree lek 2; The Iron Ladies 2: Before and After; The Iron Ladies II: The Early Years* **2003** Both a sequel and a prequel, the film begins with the background stories of how the various Iron Ladies met. Fast-forward to the present after their success in the first film, and one of the teammates has joined up with a promoter attempting to copy the Iron Ladies. Sensing he is dishonest, the group splits, but they ponder a reunion when they learn the promoter's copycat team is going to be captained by an infamous homophobe. **100m/C; DVD.** *TH* Anucha Chatkaew; Shiriohona Hongsopon; Chaicham Nimpulsawasdi; Phomsit Sitthijamroenkhun; Sutthipong Sitthijamroenkhun; Sahaphap Tor; Sujira Arunpipat; Kokkorn Benjathikoon; Surapun Chatkaew; Giorgio Maiocchi; Peter Maiocchi; Jesdaporn Pholdee; Aphichart Vongkavee; Hathairat Jaroenchaichana; *D:* Youngyooth Thongkonthun; *W:* Youngyooth Thongkonthun; *C:* Jira Maligool; Sayombhu Mukdeeprom.

The Iron Lady 🦴 ½ **2011 (PG-13)** Meryl Streep proves her laudable skills at impersonation yet again by stepping into the historically gigantic shoes of the United Kingdom's first—and so far only—woman Prime Minister, Margaret Thatcher. Director Lloyd focuses largely on the later years of her life as she remembers key moments of her reign through senility-infused flashback and has imaginary conversations with her dead husband (Broadbent). Cluttered, it feels like a wasted opportunity to bring to life one of the more politically controversial figures of the 20th century. **105m/C; DVD, Blu-Ray.** Meryl Streep; Jim Broadbent; Anthony Head; Richard E. Grant; Roger Allam; Julian Wadham; Iain Glen; John Sessions; Alexandra Roach; Harry Lloyd; Olivia Colman; Nicholas Farrell; Victoria Bewick; *D:* Phyllida Lloyd; *W:* Abi Morgan; *C:* Elliot Davis; *M:* Justine Wright; Thomas Newman. Oscars '11: Actress (Streep), Makeup; British Acad. '11: Actress (Streep), Makeup; Golden Globes '12: Actress--Drama (Streep).

Iron Man 🦴🦴🦴 **2008 (PG-13)** Sadly, this film is not based on the Black Sabbath song, but this big-screen version of Marvel Comics' B-list armored avenger is one of the better movies to emerge from the bloated, nerd-fed superhero genre. Billionaire weapons-maker/media playboy Tony Stark (Downey Jr.) builds an amazing suit of armor to help him escape from terrorists and decides to make a go of it as a card-carrying hero, much to the confusion of his flirty assistant (Paltrow) and chagrin of his business partner (Bridges). There's some great FX and sharp dialogue, but 95 percent of the movie's appeal comes from Downey, who brings a ridiculous charm and energy to the whole affair. On the flip side, the plot is paper-thin, and you probably saw all the best bits in the trailer. Not exactly iron, but solid summer fun, nonetheless. **126m/C; DVD, Blu-Ray.** Robert Downey, Jr.; Gwyneth Paltrow; Terrence Howard; Jeff Bridges; Samuel L. Jackson; Shaun Toub; Leslie Bibb; Bill Smitrovich; Clark Gregg; Tim Guinee; Faran Tahir; Ahmed Ahmed; Joshua Harto; Peter Billingsley; Jon Favreau; Sayed Badreya; *V:* Paul Bettany; *D:* Jon Favreau; *W:* Mark Fergus; Art Marcum; Mat Holloway; Hawk Ostby; *C:* Matthew Libatique; *M:* Ramin Djawadi.

Iron Man 2 🦴🦴🦴 **2010 (PG-13)** In the Marvel Comics sequel, billionaire industrialist/inventor Tony Stark (Downey Jr.) has a business rival (Rockwell) and the government to deal with while his alter-ego Iron Man has trouble with the vengeful Whiplash (Rourke). There's a lot going on, but not enough that the whole things goes off the rails (a la "Spider Man 3"). Downey's charm, and the well-staged action sequences, help keep this one just as enjoyable as the original. Rourke and Rockwell are fun as the villains. Don Cheadle does well with the thankless job of replacing Terrence Howard as Stark's bud Col. James Rhodes. **117m/C; Blu-Ray, On Demand.** Robert Downey, Jr.; Gwyneth Paltrow; Don Cheadle; Mickey Rourke; Scarlett Johansson; Sam Rockwell; Samuel L. Jackson; Kate Mara; Leslie Bibb; John Slattery; Clark Gregg; Garry Shandling; Tim Guinee; Helena Mattsson; Jon Favreau; *V:* Paul Bettany; *D:* Jon Favreau; *W:* Justin Theroux; *C:* Matthew Libatique; *M:* John Debney.

Iron Man 3 🦴🦴🦴 **2013 (PG-13)** Tony Stark/Iron Man (Downey, Jr.) returns in his first outing since he saved New York City with his costumed buddies in "The Avengers" and the result is a thoroughly enjoyable summer blockbuster, arguably the best standalone Iron Man film. Writer/director Black brings a better sense of action choreography and pacing to the story of the Mandarin (Kingsley) and his attempts to bring chaos to the world and destroy Iron Man in the process. With a stronger supporting cast, clever script, and some amazing action sequences, this escapist superhero movie outmuscles much of its competition. **130m/C; DVD, Blu-Ray.** Robert Downey, Jr.; Ben Kingsley; Gwyneth Paltrow; Guy Pearce; Don Cheadle; Rebecca Hall; Jon Favreau; James Badge Dale; William Sadler; Miguel Ferrer; Bingbing Fan; *V:* Paul Bettany; *D:* Shane Black; *W:* Shane Black; Drew Pearce; *C:* John Toll; *M:* Brian Tyler.

The Iron Mask 🦴🦴 ½ **1929** Early swashbuckling extravaganza with a master swordsman defending the French king from a scheme involving substitution by a lookalike. Still fairly exciting, thanks largely to director Dwan's flair. Based on Alexandre Dumas's "Three Musketeers" and "The Man in the Iron Mask" with talking sequences. **103m/B; Silent; VHS, DVD.** Douglas Fairbanks, Sr.; Nigel de Brulier; Marguerite de la Motte; Ullrich Haupt; William "Billy" Bakewell; *D:* Allan Dwan; *W:* Douglas Fairbanks, Sr.; *C:* Henry Sharp.

Iron Maze 🦴 ½ **1991 (R)** A fascinating notion forms the center of this dramatic scrapheap; the classic Japanese "Rashomon" plot shifted to a rusting Pennsylvania steel town. When a Tokyo businessman is found bludgeoned, witnesses and suspects (including his American-born wife) tell contradictory stories. It's too convoluted and contrived to work, with a hollow happy ending tacked on. Oliver Stone helped produce. **102m/C; VHS, DVD.** Jeff Fahey; Bridget Fonda; Hiroaki Murakami; J.T. Walsh; Gabriel Damon; John Randolph; Peter Allas; *D:* Hiroaki Yoshida; *W:* Tim Metcalfe; *C:* Morio Saegusa; *M:* Stanley Myers.

The Iron Mistress 🦴🦴 **1952** Lots of action but hardly a historically accurate bio of frontiersman Jim Bowie. Bowie (Ladd) comes to New Orleans to run the family's lumber business and is made a fool of by Creole beauty Judalon (Mayo), who's stringing along several beaus. Bowie turns to gambling to get the money to woo Judalon, who marries another man (Kjellin) anyway. However, the femme still has Bowie in her clutches, which leads to his design of the titular double-edged knife. **109m/C; DVD.** Alan Ladd; Virginia Mayo; Alf Kjellin; Joseph Calleia; Anthony Caruso; Phyllis Kirk; Douglas Dick; *D:* Gordon Douglas; *W:* James R. Webb; *C:* John Seitz; *M:* Max Steiner.

Iron Monkey 🦴🦴 ½ *Siunin Wong Feihung Tsi Titmalau; Shao Nian Huang Fei Hong Zhi Tie Ma Liu; Iron Monkey: The Young Wong Fei-hung* **1993 (PG-13)** Historical fantasy martial arts is built around the Iron Monkey (Rongguang Yu), a Robin-Hood figure who defeats whole armies of opponents and can leap tall buildings in a single bound. The humor and outstanding choreography of the fight scenes put this one a cut above the usual martial arts action flick. **87m/C; VHS, DVD, Blu-Ray.** *CH* Rongguang Yu; Donnie Yen; Yam Sai-kun; Tsing-ying Wong; *D:* Woo-ping Yuen; *W:* Tseng Pik-Yin; Tsui Hark; Tai-Muk Lau; Cheung Tan; Pik-yin Tang; *C:* Arthur Wong Ngok Tai; *M:* James L. Venable.

The Iron Orchard 🦴🦴 **2019 (R)** To win over the mother of his love Mazie (Harrison), young Jim (Garrison) seeks his fortune in the Texas oilfields in late 1930s Texas. At his first job with Bison Oil, he endures the harsh words of industry veterans while becoming involved with Lee (Cobrin), the wife of a colleague. After saving money, he runs off with Lee and seeks his own oil fortune. As he achieves success, he must come to terms with girl he left behind. Based on a novel by Edmund Van Zandt and his well-known Texas oil family, the film has many fine period details but the characters aren't very interesting. **112m/C; DVD, Blu-Ray.** Lane Garrison; Hassie Harrison; Austin Nichols; Ali Cobrin; Allan McLeod; *D:* Ty Roberts; *W:* Gerry De Leon; *C:* Mathieu Plainfosse; *M:* Duncan Thum.

The Iron Petticoat 🦴 **1956** Ghastly attempt at a Cold War comedy. Soviet pilot Vinka (Hepburn, with an uncertain accent) gets in a snit and flies into the American sector in Berlin. Army Major Chuck Lockwood (Hope, doing schtick) is assigned to convince her to defect. She wants to convert him to communism but a trip to London has her enjoying capitalist pleasures. Her superiors back in Moscow think a kidnapping is in order. **87m/C; DVD, Blu-Ray.** *UK* Bob Hope; Katharine Hepburn; Noelle Middleton; James Robertson Justice; Robert Helpmann; *D:* Ralph Thomas; *W:* Ben Hecht; *C:* Ernest Steward; *M:* Benjamin Frankel.

Iron Road 🦴 ½ **2008** Canadian miniseries. In 1882, Alfred Nichol sends his son James to Hong Kong to secure Chinese workers for the railroad being built through the Canadian Rockies. Little Tiger diisguises herself as a boy to get chosen, doing menial tasks. Having worked in a fireworks factory, she wants to join the better-paying, but dangerous, explosives crew. Little Tiger also falls in love with James but if her identity is revealed, their interracial romance would be forbidden. **180m/C; DVD.** *CA* Betty Sun; Luke Macfarlane; Sam Neill; Tony Leung Ka-Fai; Peter O'Toole; Ian Tracey; *D:* David Wu; *W:* Barry Pearson; *C:* Attila Szalay; *M:* Lawrence Shragge. **TV**

The Iron Sheriff 🦴🦴 **1957** Sheriff Samuel Galt's (Hayden) son Benjie (Hickman) is accused of murdering a stagecoach driver during a robbery. Wanting to keep Benjie away from his daughter Kathi (Nolan), Eugene Walden (Jolley) makes a false deathbed confession to Sam implicating the young man and Benjie is convicted. Realizing some evidence doesn't add up, Sam hunts the real killer. **73m/B; DVD.** Sterling Hayden; Constance Ford; John Dehner; Kent Taylor; Darryl Hickman; I. Stanford Jolley; Kathleen Nolan; *D:* Sidney Salkow; *W:* Seeleg Lester; *C:* Kenneth Peach, Sr.; *M:* Emil Newman.

The Iron Triangle 🦴🦴 **1989 (R)** A U.S. officer taken prisoner by the Viet Cong forms a bond with one of his captors. Film lends the viewer an opportunity to see things from the other sides perspective. **94m/C; VHS, DVD.** Beau Bridges; Haing S. Ngor; Liem Whatley; *D:* Eric Weston; *W:* John Bushelman.

Iron Will 🦴🦴 ½ **1993 (PG)** Okay Disney family movie based on a true story. Will Stoneman is a 17-year-old farm kid from South Dakota. It's 1917 and because of his father's death there's no money to send Will to college. So he decides to enter the 500 mile winner-take-all dog sled race, with its $10,000 prize. Lots of obstacles, several villains, but Will perseveres. **109m/C; VHS, DVD.** MacKenzie Astin; Kevin Spacey; David Ogden Stiers; August Schellenberg; George Gerdes; John Terry; *D:* Charles Haid; *W:* John Michael Hayes; Jeffrey Arch; Djordje Milicevic; *M:* Joel McNeely.

Ironclad 🦴 ½ **2011 (R)** This ambitious and bloody historical drama (set in 1215) suffers from a relatively low budget and some scenery-chewing by the actors. Britain's King John is forced by his barons to sign the Magna Carta, which undermines his royal power. Very unhappy, John hires mercenaries to wipe out the barons who thwarted him, leading to a siege of Rochester Castle that involves the usual boiling oil and sword fights. **121m/C; DVD.** *GB* James Purefoy; Brian Cox; Paul Giamatti; Kate Mara; Derek Jacobi; Charles Dance; Jason Flemyng; *D:* Jonathan English; *W:* Jonathan English; *C:* David Eggby; *M:* Lorne Balfe. **VIDEO**

Ironclad: Battle for Blood 🦴 **2014** The squire from the original film has grown into a mercenary and is now being begged to help save his homeland from the vengeful Celts. Jerky camera action and blood abound. **108m/C; DVD, Blu-Ray.** *UK* Roxanne Mckee; Michelle Fairley; Tom Austen; Rosie Day; Andy Beckwith; *D:* Jonathan English; *W:* Jonathan English; Stephen McDool; *C:* Zoran Popovic; *M:* Andreas Weidinger. **VIDEO**

Ironweed 🦴🦴🦴 **1987 (R)** Grim and gritty drama about bums living the hard life in Depression-era Albany. Nicholson excels as a former ballplayer turned drunk bothered by visions of the past, and Streep is his equal in the lesser role of a tubercular boozer. Waits also shines. Another grim view from "Pixote" director Babenco. Kennedy scripted based on his Pulitzer Prize-winning tragedy. **135m/C; VHS, DVD, Blu-Ray.** Jack Nicholson; Meryl Streep; Tom Waits; Carroll Baker; Michael O'Keefe; Fred Gwynne; Diane Venora; Margaret Whitton; Jake Dengel; Nathan Lane; James Gammon; Joe Grifasi; Bethel Leslie; Ted Levine; Frank Whaley; *D:* Hector Babenco; *W:* William Kennedy; *M:* John Morris. L.A. Film Critics '87: Actor (Nicholson); N.Y. Film Critics '87: Actor (Nicholson).

Irreconcilable Differences 🦴🦴 ½ **1984 (PG)** When her Beverly Hills parents spend more time working and fretting than giving hugs and love, a ten-year-old girl sues them for divorce on the grounds of "irreconcilable differences." The media has a field day when they hear that she would rather go live with the maid. Well cast, with well-developed characterizations. The script, by the creators of "Private Benjamin," is humanely comic rather than uproariously funny. **112m/C; VHS, DVD, Blu-Ray.** Ryan O'Neal; Shelley Long; Drew Barrymore; Sam Wanamaker; Allen Garfield; Sharon Stone; Luana Anders; *D:* Charles Shyer; *W:* Charles Shyer; Nancy Meyers.

Irreplaceable You 🦴🦴 **2018** A romantic drama about a couple facing a cancer diagnosis. Together since childhood, Abbie (Raw) and Sam (Huisman) are engaged to be married when they learn that Abbie has stage 4 cancer. After she is diagnosed, Abbie's reaction is find Sam a new mate to take care of him after she is gone. Abbie also finds solace in her support group, where she befriends the terminally ill Myron (Walken) who does not support her plan. Though Abbie's journey from denial to acceptance of her illness has its charms, the lack of authenticity in--Abbie never seems sick--and depth in the story undermines its message. **96m/C; DVD.** Gugu Mbatha-Raw; Michiel Huisman; Steve Coogan; Timothy Simons; Jacki Weaver; *D:* Stephanie Laing; *W:* Bess Wohl; *C:* Magdalena Gorka; *M:* Lesley Barber.

Irresistible 🦴🦴 ½ **2006** Sophie Harley (Sarandon) is convinced she's being stalked by her husband Craig's (Neill) beautiful coworker Mara (Blunt) because she wants Sophie's life for herself. But the truth will shock Sophie even more. Formulaic psycho-thriller redeemed by expert cast. **109m/C; DVD.** *AU* Susan Sarandon; Sam Neill; Emily Blunt; Charles "Bud" Tingwell; William McInnes; *D:* Ann Turner; *W:* Ann Turner; *C:* Martin McGrath; *M:* David Hirschfelder. **VIDEO**

Irresistible 🦴🦴 **2020 (R) 101m/C; DVD.** Steve Carell; Rose Byrne; Chris Cooper; Brent Sexton; Will Sasso; *D:* Jon Stewart; *W:* Jon Stewart; *C:* Bobby Bukowski; *M:* Bryce Dessner.

Irreversible 🦴 ½ **2002** The rape scene is nine minutes long. If you're still willing to sit through this abrasive flick after knowing that, here's the story (which is told backwards). Marcus (Cassel) and Pierre (Dupontel) are being led away from a gay S&M club where a murder has occurred. They have sought revenge for what happened to Marcus's lover Alex (Bellucci). Earlier, Marcus fought with Alex at a party and she leaves alone—to be brutalized into a coma by a thug (Prestia) in an underground pedestrian tunnel. Then we see the trio, Pierre is an old friend of Alex's and is jealous of Marcus, going to the party and expecting to have fun. Everyone's destined to be disappointed. French with subtitles. **99m/C; VHS, DVD.** *FR* Monica Bellucci; Vincent Cassel; Albert Dupontel; Jo Prestia; Philippe Nahon; *D:* Gaspar Noé; *W:* Gaspar Noé; *C:* Gaspar Noé; *M:* Thomas Bangalter.

Is Anybody There? 🦴🦴 ½ **2008 (PG-13)** And the answer would be 'not anymore.' Elderly traveling magician Clarence Parkinson (Caine) has ended up at a rundown seaside retirement home. Despite his general grumpiness, Clarence befriends lonely 10-year-old Edward (Milner), the son of the home's harried owners. Clarence starts teaching Edward magic tricks but the magic Clarence would like is a chance to visit his late wife's grave before his dementia takes control of his life—and Edward wants to help. Notable, vanity-free performance by Caine. **94m/C; DVD.** *GB* Michael Caine; Bill Milner; Anne-Marie Duff; David Morrissey; Rosemary Harris; Peter Vaughan; Elizabeth Spriggs; *D:*

John Crowley; **W:** Peter Harness; **C:** Rob Hardy; **M:** Joby Talbot.

Is Paris Burning? 𝒮𝒮𝒮 *Paris Brule-t-il?* **1966** A spectacularly star-studded but far too sprawling account of the liberation of Paris from Nazi occupation. The script, in which seven writers had a hand, is based on Larry Collins and Dominique Lapierre's best-seller. **173m/C; VHS, DVD.** *FR* Jean-Paul Belmondo; Charles Boyer; Leslie Caron; Jean-Pierre Cassel; George Chakiris; Claude Dauphin; Alain Delon; Kirk Douglas; Glenn Ford; Gert Frobe; Daniel Gelin; E.G. Marshall; Yves Montand; Anthony Perkins; Claude Rich; Simone Signoret; Robert Stack; Jean-Louis Trintignant; Pierre Vaneck; Orson Welles; Bruno Cremer; Suzy Delair; Michael (Michel) Lonsdale; **D:** Rene Clement; **W:** Gore Vidal; Francis Ford Coppola; **C:** Marcel Grignon; **M:** Maurice Jarre.

Is There Life Out There? 𝒮𝒮 ½ **1994** Wife, mother, and waitress Lily Marshall (McEntire) decides it's time to do something for herself—so she goes to work on her college degree. But there's unexpected family resentments, a breast cancer scare, and the interest of a young teaching assistant to turn her head away from her studies. Filmed in Nashville, Tennessee. Based on a song by McEntire; made for TV. **92m/C; VHS, DVD.** Reba McEntire; Keith Carradine; Mitchell Anderson; Donald Moffat; Genia Michaela; **D:** David Hugh Jones; **W:** Dalene Young. **TV**

Is There Sex After Death? 𝒮𝒮𝒮 **1971 (R)** Often funny satire on the sexual revolution is constructed as a behind-the-scenes view of the porn film world. Odd cast includes Henry and Warhol superstar Woodlawn. Originally rated "X." **97m/C; VHS, DVD.** Buck Henry; Alan Abel; Marshall Efron; Holly Woodlawn; Earl Doud; **D:** Alan Abel; Jeanne Abel.

Isaac Asimov's Nightfall 𝒮𝒮 *Nightfall* **2000 (R)** The planet Aeon has six suns and has never experienced night. But with an eclipse approaching, religious cultists are predicting catastrophe. Scientist Carradine tries to allay the population's fear. Low-budget and bland adaptation of Asimov's 1941 short story. **85m/C; VHS, DVD.** David Carradine; Jennifer Burns; Joseph Hodge; **D:** Gwyneth Gibby; **W:** Gwyneth Gibby; John W. Corrington; Michael B. Druxman; **C:** Abhik Mukhopadhyay; **M:** Nicolas Tenbroek; Brad Segal. **VIDEO**

Isabelle 𝒮𝒮 **2019** Happily married Matt (Brody) and Larissa (Crew) Kane have moved into a new neighborhood ahead of the birth of their first child. While getting the mail one day, the skittish Larissa sees a neighbor, Isabel (Belkin), staring at her. Larissa immediately starts bleeding. She briefly flat lines at the hospital and her child is stillborn. As she recovers, Larrisa sees and hears her baby everywhere and notices Isabel is still watching her. The couple soon learn that devil worshipping took place at the house next door. Though labeled horror, the film does not have many horror moments nor particularly engaging performances. **81m/C; DVD.** Amanda Crew; Adam Brody; Zoe Belkin; Sheila McCarthy; Booth Savage; **D:** Robert Heydon; **W:** Donald Martin; **C:** Pasha Patriki; **M:** Mark Korven.

Ishtar 𝒮𝒮 **1987 (PG-13)** Two astoundingly untalented performers have a gig in a fictional Middle Eastern country and become involved in foreign intrigue. A big-budget boxoffice bomb produced by Beatty offering few laughs, though it's not as bad as its reputation. Considering the talent involved, though, it's a disappointment, with Beatty and Hoffman laboring to create Hope and Crosby chemistry. Anyone for a slow night? **107m/C; VHS, Blu-Ray.** Dustin Hoffman; Warren Beatty; Isabelle Adjani; Charles Grodin; Jack Weston; Tess Harper; Carol Kane; Matt Frewer; **D:** Elaine May; **W:** Elaine May; **C:** Vittorio Storaro; **M:** Dave Grusin; Bahjawa. Golden Raspberries '87: Worst Director (May).

The Island **WOOF!** **1980 (R)** New York reporter embarks on a Bermuda triangle investigation, only to meet with the murderous but sterile descendants of 17th century pirates on a deserted island. Caine is designated as stud service for the last remaining fertile woman. Almost surreal in its badness. Adapted by Benchley from his novel. **113m/C; VHS, DVD, Blu-Ray, Streaming.** Michael Caine; David Warner; Angela Punch McGregor; Frank Middlemass; Don Henderson; **D:** Michael Ritchie; **W:** Peter Benchley; **C:** Henri Decae; **M:** Ennio Morricone.

The Island 𝒮𝒮 ½ **2005 (PG-13)** In 2019, folks at the sterile, white-uniform-only, underground community believe that they've been spared from a cataclysmic disaster and await a lottery pick that's supposedly a ticket to "The Island," the last uncontaminated place on the planet. Among the placid group is troublemaker Lincoln Six Echo (McGregor), who discovers they're clones created by evil scientist Merrick (Bean) to serve as donors for their human counterparts. Lincoln flees with fellow resident Jordan Two Delta (Johansson) but Merrick's henchman Laurent (Hounsou) isn't far behind. Initially intriguing plot becomes a typical Bay blow'em up, kill'em all action fest. Interesting (at least to the original's producer) similarity to "Parts: The Clonus Horror" adds another dimension to all the cloning around, and became fodder for some controversy. Partially filmed in Detroit. **136m/C; DVD, Blu-Ray, UMD.** Ewan McGregor; Scarlett Johansson; Djimon Hounsou; Steve Buscemi; Michael Clarke Duncan; Shawnee Smith; Sean Bean; Ethan Phillips; Max Baker; Kim Coates; **D:** Michael Bay; **W:** Caspian Tredwell-Owen; Alex Kurtzman; Roberto Orci; **C:** Mauro Fiore; **M:** Steve Jablonsky.

The Island at the Top of the World 𝒮𝒮 ½ **1974 (G)** A rich Englishman, in search of his missing son, travels to the Arctic Circle in 1908. The rescue party includes an American archeologist, a French astronaut, and an Eskimo guide. Astonishingly, they discover an unknown, "lost" Viking kingdom. This Jules Verne-style adventure doesn't quite measure up, but kids will like it. **93m/C; VHS, DVD.** David Hartman; Donald Sinden; Jacques Marin; Mako; David Gwillim; **D:** Robert Stevenson; **W:** John Whedon; **C:** Frank V. Phillips; **M:** Maurice Jarre.

Island in the Sky 𝒮𝒮𝒮 **1953** When a transport plane crashes in an isolated area of Labrador, the captain (Wayne) must keep his crew alive long enough for them to be rescued. Long-awaited release has all the rugged manliness you'd expect of a Wayne flick. Faithful adaptation successfully conveys the increasing desperation and sense of doom of the crew and the would-be rescuers. **109m/B; DVD.** John Wayne; Lloyd Nolan; Walter Abel; James Arness; Andy Devine; Allyn Joslyn; Jimmy Lydon; Harry Carey, Jr.; Hal Baylor; Sean McClory; Wally Cassell; Gordon Jones; Frank Fenton; Regis Toomey; Paul Fix; George Chandler; Louis Jean Heydt; Darryl Hickman; Mike Connors; Carl "Alfalfa" Switzer; Ann Doran; Fess Parker; **D:** William A. Wellman; **W:** Ernest K. Gann; **C:** Archie Stout; **M:** Emil Newman.

Island in the Sun 𝒮𝒮 **1957** Racial tension pulls apart the lives of the residents of a Caribbean island. Good cast, but a very poor adaptation of Alec Waugh's novel. Marvelous location shots. **119m/C; VHS, DVD.** James Mason; Joan Fontaine; Dorothy Dandridge; John Williams; Harry Belafonte; **D:** Robert Rossen; **C:** Frederick A. (Freddie) Young; **M:** Malcolm Arnold.

Island Monster 𝒮 ½ *Monster of the Island* **1953** Deals with ruthless, kidnapping drug-smugglers led by "monster" Karloff, and the efforts to bring them to justice. **87m/B; VHS, DVD.** *IT* Boris Karloff; Renata Vicario; Franca Marzi; **D:** Robert Bianchi Montero.

Island of Desire 𝒮 *Saturday Island* **1952** An Army nurse, a doctor, and a young Navy Adonis are trapped on a deserted island. Not surprisingly, a love triangle develops. **93m/C; VHS, DVD.** *GB* Tab Hunter; Linda Darnell; Donald Gray; **D:** Stuart Heisler.

The Island of Dr. Moreau 𝒮𝒮 ½ **1977 (PG)** This remake of the "Island of the Lost Souls" (1933) is a bit disappointing but worth watching for Lancaster's solid performance as the scientist who has isolated himself on a Pacific island in order to continue his chromosome research—he can transform animals into near-humans and humans into animals. Neat-looking critters. Adaptation of the H.G. Wells novel of the same title. **99m/C; VHS, DVD, Blu-Ray.** Burt Lancaster; Michael York; Nigel Davenport; Barbara Carrera; Richard Basehart; Nick Cravat; **D:** Don Taylor; **W:** John Herman Shaner; Al Ramrus; **C:** Gerry Fisher.

The Island of Dr. Moreau 𝒮 ½ **1996 (PG-13)** What were they thinking? Not even the frightening "manimals" could prevent the unintentional laughs from this abomination of the horrifying 1896 H.G. Wells novel. Brando's enormous presence as the mad scientist Moreau walks a tight rope between puzzling and campy, especially as he explains his ghastly DNA experiments on a remote Pacific to a miscast Thewlis. A wasted Kilmer is the doctors's right-hand hybrid who often seems to be acting in a different movie. Filming hit some big rocks when "creative differences" caused original director Richard Stanley to be replaced and Rob Morrow (originally the lawyer) to ask for his release. Previously filmed under the same title in 1977 and (terrifically) as "Island of Lost Souls" in 1933. **91m/C; VHS, DVD, Blu-Ray.** Marlon Brando; Val Kilmer; David Thewlis; Fairuza Balk; Marco Hofschneider; Temuera Morrison; Ron Perlman; **D:** John Frankenheimer; **W:** Richard Stanley; Ron Hutchinson; **C:** William A. Fraker; **M:** Gary Chang.

Island of Lost Souls 𝒮𝒮𝒮 ½ **1932** Horrifying adaptation of H.G. Wells's "The Island of Dr. Moreau" was initially banned in parts of the U.S. because of its disturbing contents. Dr. Moreau (Laughton) is a mad scientist who lives on a remote island and is obsessed with making men out of jungle animals. When shipwreck survivor Edward Parker (Arlen) gets stranded on the island, little does he know that Moreau wants to mate him with Lota (Burke), the Panther Woman, to produce the first human-animal child. As unsettling today as it was in the '30s. Lugosi has the notable role of the hybrid "Sayer of the Law" while Burke beat out more than 60,000 young women in a nationwide search to play the Panther Woman, winning the role because of her "feline" look. Remade as "The Island of Dr. Moreau" in both 1977 and 1996. **71m/B; VHS, DVD, Blu-Ray.** Charles Laughton; Bela Lugosi; Richard Arlen; Leila Hyams; Kathleen Burke; Stanley Fields; Robert F. (Bob) Kortman; Arthur Hohl; **Cameo(s):** Alan Ladd; Randolph Scott; Buster Crabbe; **D:** Erle C. Kenton; **W:** Philip Wylie; Waldemar Young; **C:** Karl Struss.

Island of Lost Women 𝒮 ½ **1959** Known mostly for being a subtly homoerotic rip-off of "Forbidden Planet." Two men crash-land on an island inhabited by a mad scientist and his three lovely daughters who have never met anyone but their father. When the men take time out of oiling each others' backs and claiming to love the girls they notice the scientist is experimenting with nuclear energy and has the ability to blow up the island. And one would assume non-island portions of the world as well. **71m/B; DVD.** Jeff Richards; Venetia Stevenson; John Smith; Diane Jergens; June Blair; Alan Napier; Gavin Muir; George Brand; **D:** Frank Tuttle; **W:** Ray Buffum; Prescott Chaplin; **C:** John Seitz; **M:** Raoul Kraushaar; Dave Kahn.

Island of Love 𝒮 **1963** Remarkably unfunny comedy with wince-making performances and only the Greek scenery offering any relief. Con men Steve (Preston) and Paul (Randall) convince gangster Tony Dallas (Matthau) to invest in their movie take on Adam & Eve, starring Tony's stripper girlfriend (Bruce). When it's a complete disaster, the partners hightail it to a Greek isle where Steve's next idea is to turn the rundown tourist spot into a lover's playground. Too bad Tony finds out where they are. **101m/C; DVD.** Robert Preston; Tony Randall; Georgia Moll; Walter Matthau; Betty Bruce; Vassili Lambrinos; Titos Vandis; Michael Constantine; **D:** Morton DaCosta; **W:** David R. Schwartz; **C:** Harry Stradling, Sr.; **M:** George Duning.

Island of the Burning Doomed 𝒮𝒮 ½ *Island of the Burning Damned; Night of the Big Heat* **1967** A brutal heat wave accompanies invading aliens in this British-made outing. Lee and Cushing carry the picture. **94m/C; VHS, DVD.** *GB* Christopher Lee; Peter Cushing; Patrick Allen; Sarah Lawson; Jane Merrow; **D:** Terence Fisher.

Island of the Dead 𝒮𝒮 **2000 (R)** Now here's a storyline sure to be entertaining. One business tycoon, one policewoman, one prison warden, and three convicts are all trapped on a island burial ground. Just when the dead (in the form of maggots and killer flies) decide to rise up and strike a little terror. **91m/C; VHS, DVD.** Malcolm McDowell; Talisa Soto; Bruce Ramsay; Mos Def; **D:** Tim Southam; **W:** Peter Koper; Tim Southam. **VIDEO**

Island of the Hungry Ghosts 𝒮𝒮 ½ **2018** On the remote Christmas Island, located in the Indian Ocean, Australia operates a detention center for refugees. The documentary follows grief and trauma therapist Poh Lin Lee, who counsels those detained at the compound. This task deeply affects her and colors her relationship with her family. Filmmaker Brady contrasts these experiences with rituals conducted by the island's permanent residents for the "hungry ghosts," the spirits of Chinese migrants who came to the island a century ago as indentured servants. Telling its story through poetic visuals gives it more meaning, despite the slow pace. **98m/C; DVD.** **D:** Gabrielle Brady; **W:** Gabrielle Brady; **C:** Michael Latham; **M:** Aaron Cupples. **VIDEO**

Island of the Lost 𝒮 ½ **1968** An anthropologist's family must fight for survival when they become shipwrecked on a mysterious island. **92m/C; VHS, DVD.** *GB* Richard Greene; Luke Halpin; Mart Hulswit; Jose De Vega; Robin Mattson; Irene Tsu; Sheilah Wells; **D:** John Florea; Ricou Browning; **W:** Richard Carlson; Ivan Tors; **C:** Howard Winner; **M:** George Bruns.

The Island on Bird Street 𝒮𝒮 ½ **1997 (PG-13)** Eleven-year-old Jewish Alex (Kiziuk) is forced to live in the Warsaw ghetto with his father Stefan (Bergin) and great-uncle Boruch (Warden). When the Gestapo round up the inhabitants to send them to concentration camps, Alex manages to elude capture. Inspired by his favorite book, "The Adventures of Robinson Crusoe," he hides out in an abandoned building on Bird Street with only his pet mouse Snow for company. Alex struggles with daily survival as he awaits his father's promised return. Based on the autobiographical children's book by Uri Orlev. **102m/C; DVD.** *GB DK GE* Patrick Bergin; Jack Warden; Soeren Kragh-Jacobsen; Jordan Kiziuk; **W:** John Goldsmith; Tony Grisoni; **C:** Ian Wilson; **M:** Zbigniew Preisner.

The Islander 𝒮 **1988** Sixteen-year-old Inga comes of age among the commercial fishermen of Lake Michigan. **99m/C; VHS, DVD.** Kit Wholihan; Jeff Weborg; Celia Klehr; Jacob Mills; Julie Johnson; Mary Ann McHugh; Michael Rock; Sheri Parish; **D:** Phyllis Berg-Pigorsch.

Islander 𝒮𝒮 **2006 (R)** Lobster fisherman Eben Cole lives in a tight-knit community on a small island off the Maine coast. A tragedy leads to Eben's 5-year imprisonment and he returns to find himself shunned as other fisherman now consider him bad luck. Eben tries to rebuild his life, getting a second chance at what he does best from elderly trawler Popper. **100m/C; DVD.** Amy Jo Johnson; Philip Baker Hall; Judy Prescott; Ron Canada; Larry Pine; Thomas Hildreth; Mark Kiely; Emma Ford; **D:** Ian McCrudden; **W:** Thomas Hildreth; **C:** Dan Coplan; **M:** Billy Mallery.

Islands in the Stream 𝒮𝒮 ½ **1977 (PG)** Based on Ernest Hemingway's novel, this film is actually two movies in one. An American painter/sculptor, Thomas Hudson, lives a reclusive life on the island of Bimini shortly before the outbreak of WWII. The first part is a sensitive story of a broken family and the coming of the artist's three sons to live with their father after a four-year separation. The second part is a second rate action-adventure. **105m/C; DVD.** George C. Scott; David Hemmings; Claire Bloom; Susan Tyrrell; Gilbert Roland; **D:** Franklin J. Schaffner; **W:** Denne Bart Petitclerc; **C:** Fred W. Koenekamp; **M:** Jerry Goldsmith.

The Isle 𝒮𝒮 *Seom* **2001** For those who like their arthouse features on the kinky side. The isle is a series of small huts anchored in a river that's part of a remote fishing area. But the male guests don't just come for the fishing—they bring their own female company or take what's offered by mute manager Hee-Jin. She becomes obsessed with Hyun-Shik, an ex-cop who murdered his unfaithful lover and who's hiding out while contemplating suicide. She saves him, protects him from the police, and shares a very intimate relationship with the unstable man. Korean with subtitles. **89m/C; VHS, DVD.** *NK* Suh Jung; Yoo-Suk Kim; Sung-Hee Park; ***D:*** Ki-Duk Kim; ***W:*** Ki-Duk Kim; ***C:*** Seo-Shik Hwang; ***M:*** Sang-Yun Jeon.

Isle of Dogs **2018 (PG-13)** A stop-motion animated tale of a boy who hunts for his beloved Spots among the canine population on Trash Island, where all dogs from the Japanese city of Megasaki have been banished. Wes Anderson's trademark quirk and imagination are in full glory, with beautifully crafted animation and clever attention to detail. **101m/C; DVD, Blu-Ray.** ***V:*** Bryan Cranston; Koyu Rankin; Edward Norton; Bob Balaban; Bill Murray; ***D:*** Wes Anderson; ***W:*** Wes Anderson; ***C:*** Tristan Oliver; ***M:*** Alexandre Desplat.

Isle of Forgotten Sins *Monsoon* **1943** Deep sea divers and an evil ship's captain vie for treasure. Good cast and direction but unremarkable material. **82m/B; VHS, DVD.** John Carradine; Gale Sondergaard; Sidney Toler; Frank Fenton; Veda Ann Borg; ***D:*** Edgar G. Ulmer.

Isle of the Dead **1/2 1945** A Greek general is quarantined with seemingly all manner of social vermin on a plague-infested island in the early 1900s. The fear is that vampires walk among them. Characteristically spooky Val Lewton production with some original twists. **72m/B; VHS, DVD.** Boris Karloff; Ellen Drew; Marc Cramer; Katherine Emery; Helen Thimig; Alan Napier; Jason Robards, Sr.; Skelton Knaggs; ***D:*** Mark Robson; ***W:*** Josef Mischel; Ardel Wray; ***C:*** Jack MacKenzie; ***M:*** Leigh Harline.

Isn't It Romantic **2019 (PG-13)** Natalie (Wilson) is a young single woman living in a drab New York City apartment while working for a company that does not appreciate her. Her world is turned upside down after she suffers a head injury and wakes up in the hospital. Everything is transformed, including the city, her friends, and her now spacious apartment with endless closet space. As Natalie enjoys a romance with attractive real estate developer Blake (Hemsworth), she tries to figure out what to do to get back to her regular life. Wilson's deadpan-yet-sly delivery adds to a strong performance that carries the high concept, yet somewhat flawed, film. **89m/C; DVD.** Rebel Wilson; Liam Hemsworth; Adam Devine; Priyanka Chopra; Betty Gilpin; ***D:*** Todd Strauss-Schulson; ***W:*** Erin Cardillo; Dana Fox; Katie Silberman; ***C:*** Simon Duggan; ***M:*** John Debney.

Isn't She Great **2000 (R)** Irreverant biopic about the queen of '60s trash novels, Jacqueline Susann (Midler), and her hungry quest for flashy fame. Lane plays her ever-loyal husband and manager, Irving Mansfield. Susann's life was no bed of roses as she fought a long battle with breast cancer and had an austistic child, although she never let her personal tragedies become public fodder. Midler gives an overripe performance while Channing (as best friend Florence) proves to be the true scene-stealer. Unfortunately, the film is even more shallow than a Susann novel and lot less fun. Based on a memoir by Susann's editor, Michael Korda. **96m/C; VHS, DVD.** Bette Midler; Nathan Lane; Stockard Channing; David Hyde Pierce; John Cleese; John Larroquette; Amanda Peet; Lisa Bronwyn Moore; Dina Spybey; ***D:*** Andrew Bergman; ***W:*** Paul Rudnick; ***C:*** Karl Walter Lindenlaub; ***M:*** Burt Bacharach.

The Ister **2004** Rookie writers/directors Barison and Ross document their thought-provoking five-year trek up the 2,000-mile-long Danube River (ancient Greek name "The Ister") from its mouth in the Black Sea to its origin in Germany's Black Forest. Along the way, the Australian philosophy students visit with prominent European philosophers who discuss the 1942 lecture of German existentialist Martin Heidegger (their inspiration and author of "Time and Being") while capturing such images as an ancient Greek city, war-torn Serbian towns, and the Mauthausen-Gusen concentration camp. **189m/C; DVD.** ***D:*** Daniel Ross; David Barison; ***C:*** Daniel Ross; David Barison.

It **1/2 1927** The film that established Bow as a prominent screen siren. Betty Lou (Bow) is a saucy lingerie sales clerk who sets her sights on department store owner Cyrus (Moreno), despite the fact that he has a fiancee. Adapted by Elinor Glyn from her own story; Glyn also makes an appearance. **71m/B; Silent; VHS, DVD.** Clara Bow; Antonio Moreno; Jacqueline Gadsdon; William Austin; Gary Cooper; Julia Swayne Gordon; ***D:*** Clarence Badger; Josef von Sternberg; ***W:*** Hope Loring; Louis D. Lighton; ***C:*** Kinley Martin. Natl. Film Reg. '01.

I.T. **1/2 2016** Mike Regan (Pierce Brosnan) hires a company Internet guy to fix up his home, which is a fabulous new smart house with oodles of technology. Predictably Mike tosses the guy out on his butt when the dude puts the moves on his daughter, but by that time his former employee has total digital control of their lives. An update of equally flawed films about digital invasion of privacy, it falls as flat as its predecessors. **95m/C; DVD, Blu-Ray, Streaming.** *FR IR US* Pierce Brosnan; Anna Friel; Stefanie Scott; James Frecheville; Michael Nyqvist; ***D:*** John Moore; ***W:*** Dan Kay; William Wisher; ***C:*** Ekkehart Pollack; ***M:*** Tim Williams. **VIDEO**

It **2017 (R)** In 1989, a group of bullied kids band together to face Pennywise, an evil clown who's been murdering the children of Derry, Maine. In a terrifying throwback to classic horror, Skarsgård's appearance and performance is the stuff of nightmares. And the Hound thinks you won't find a better group of young actors. Based on the first half, "The Loser's Club," of Stephen King's iconic novel. Part two, set 27 years later, is scheduled to be released in 2019. **135m/C; DVD, Blu-Ray.** Bill Skarsgård; Jaeden Lieberher; Jeremy Ray Taylor; Sophia Lillis; Finn Wolfhard; ***D:*** Andy Muschietti; ***W:*** Chase Palmer; Cary Fukunaga; Gary Dauberman; ***C:*** Chung-hoon Chung; ***M:*** Benjamin Wallfisch.

It Ain't Hay **1/2 1943** Grover (Abbott) and buddy Wilbur (Costello) accidentally kill their friend King O'Hara's (Kellaway) horse, so they steal a horse from the racetrack. Only the horse turns out to be a champion racer. Remake of the 1935 film "Princess O'Hara" and based on a Damon Runyon story. **79m/B; DVD.** Bud Abbott; Lou Costello; Cecil Kellaway; Grace McDonald; Eugene Pallette; Shemp Howard; Eddie Quillan; ***D:*** Erle C. Kenton; ***W:*** Allen Boretz; John Grant; ***C:*** Charles Van Enger.

It All Came True **1940** Awkward crime comedy/musical. Piano playing songwriter Tommy (Lynn) is falsely accused of a crime committed by gangster Chips Maguire (Bogart). He hides Chips at the theatrical boardinghouse where he lives, which is filled with eccentrics and run by Maggie (O'Connor) and Nora (Busley), the mother of Tommy's singer girlfriend Sarah Jane (Sheridan). She recognizes Chips as a nightclub owner and doesn't know about his criminal ties. When Chips takes a liking to the ladies, he comes up with a plan to turn part of the boardinghouse into a club to help pay their back taxes. **97m/B; DVD.** Humphrey Bogart; Ann Sheridan; Jeffrey Lynn; Una O'Connor; Jessie Busley; Zasu Pitts; Felix Bressart; John Litel; Grant Mitchell; ***D:*** Lewis Seiler; ***W:*** Michael Fessier; Lawrence Kimble; ***C:*** Ernest Haller; ***M:*** Heinz Roemheld.

It All Starts Today **1/2** *Ca commence aujourd'hui* **1999** A drama by filmmaker Bertrand Tavernier centered on social commitment and power of one person to make changes. In a once vital mining village in northern France, unemployment, economic depression, and despair are the norm. Schoolteacher Daniel (Torreton) faces challenges such as institutional paralysis, indifferent bureaucracy, and students facing poor living conditions. Instead of accepting the worst, Daniel acts to make a difference within the system and for his students. In the process, he makes profound changes in their lives and the wider community. French with subtitles. **118m/C; DVD.** Philippe Torreton; Maria Pitarresi; Emmanuelle Bercot; Francoise Bette; Christine Citti; ***D:*** Bertrand Tavernier; ***W:*** Bertrand Tavernier; Dominique Sampiero; Tiffany Tavernier; ***C:*** Alain Choquart; ***M:*** Louis Sclavis.

It Always Rains on Sunday **1/2 1947** Slice-of-life snapshot of several lives intertwining on a rainy Sunday in post-war London. Tommy Swann (McCallum) has just escaped from prison and hopes to hide out with ex Rose (Withers), but she's moved on and is now married. Tommy's arrival brings up Rose's own unhappiness, and the family is thrown into turmoil. **92m/B; DVD, Blu-Ray.** Googie Withers; Edward Chapman; Susan Shaw; Patricia Plunkett; David Lines; Sydney Tafler; Betty Ann Davies; John Slater; Jane Hylton; Meier Tzelniker; John McCallum; Jimmy Hanley; John Carol; Alfie Bass; Jack Warner; ***D:*** Robert Hamer; ***W:*** Henry Cornelius; ***C:*** Douglas Slocombe; ***M:*** Georges Auric.

It Came From Another World **1/2 2007** Professor Jackson (Craig) is once again required to save the world in another homage to 50s sci-fi movies. This time a meteorite has unleashed a mysterious force that may be responsible for the disappearance of a local scientist. **93m/B; DVD, Streaming.** Josh Craig; Shannon McDonough; Mike Mason; Michael Cook; M. Scott Taulman; Deanne McDonald; ***D:*** Christopher R. Mihm; ***W:*** Christopher R. Mihm; ***C:*** Christopher R. Mihm. **VIDEO**

It Came from Beneath the Sea **1955** A giant octopus arises from the depths of the sea to scour San Francisco for human food. Ray Harryhausen effects are special. **80m/B; VHS, DVD, Blu-Ray.** Kenneth Tobey; Faith Domergue; Ian Keith; Donald Curtis; ***D:*** Robert Gordon.

It Came from Outer Space **1953** Aliens take on the form of local humans to repair their spacecraft in a small Arizona town. Good performances and outstanding direction add up to a fine science fiction film. Based on the story "The Meteor" by Ray Bradbury, who also wrote the script. Originally filmed in 3-D. **81m/B; VHS, DVD, Blu-Ray.** Richard Carlson; Barbara Rush; Charles Drake; Russell Johnson; Kathleen Hughes; ***D:*** Jack Arnold; ***W:*** Harry Essex; Ray Bradbury; ***C:*** Clifford Stine; ***M:*** Henry Mancini; Herman Stein; Irving Gertz.

It Came from the Sky **1998 (R)** Eccentric strangers Jarvis Moody (Lloyd) and his girlfriend Pepper (Bleeth) invade the lives of bitter Donald (Ritter), his long-suffering wife Alice (Williams), and their brain-damaged teenage son (Zegers). Has fate sent the strange duo to intervene for good or is disaster about to strike? **92m/C; VHS, DVD.** John Ritter; Christopher Lloyd; Yasmine Bleeth; JoBeth Williams; Kevin Zegers; ***D:*** Jack Bender.

It Came Upon a Midnight Clear **1/2 1984** A heavenly miracle enables a retired (and dead) New York policeman to keep a Christmas promise to his grandson. **96m/C; VHS, DVD.** Mickey Rooney; Scott Grimes; George Gaynes; Annie Potts; Lloyd Nolan; Barrie Youngfellow; ***D:*** Peter H. Hunt; ***C:*** Dean Cundey. **TV**

It Chapter Two **1/2 2019 (R)** Twenty-seven years after the kids of the Losers Club escaped from the clutches of evil clown Pennywise (Skarsgard), they have grown up and gone their separate ways. When Pennywise resurfaces, Mike Hanlon (Mustafa), the only member who stayed in Derry, Maine, brings the group together again to get rid of him -- for good. At the same time, each member of the club works to reconcile with his or her past. An overly long adaptation of the second part of Stephen King's classic novel, though the casting and monster effects are impeccable. **169m/C; DVD, Blu-Ray.** Jessica Chastain; James McAvoy; Bill Hader; Isaiah Mustafa; Jay Ryan; ***D:*** Andy Muschietti; ***W:*** Gary Dauberman; ***C:*** Checco Varese; ***M:*** Benjamin Wallfisch.

It Comes at Night **1/2 2017 (R)** A minimalist, character-driven horror movie about the terror of the unknown and the evil within. After an unexplained illness wipes out much of the human race, Paul (Edgerton) protects his family inside a remote cabin, but when they take in another family, their relative security is replaced with distrust and paranoia. A movie that leaves you with lingering questions -- that everything might not be what it seems. **91m/C; DVD, Blu-Ray.** Joel Edgerton; Christopher Abbott; Carmen Ejogo; Riley Keough; Kelvin Harrison, Jr.; ***D:*** Trey Edward Shults; ***W:*** Trey Edward Shults; ***C:*** Drew Daniels; ***M:*** Brian McOmber.

It Could Happen to You **1/2** *Cop Tips Waitress $2 Million* **1994 (PG)** NYC cop Charlie Lang (Cage) doesn't have any change to leave coffee shop waitress Yvonne (Fonda) a tip, so he promises to split his lottery ticket with her. When he nets $4 million, he makes good on the promise, much to the chargrin of his upwardly mobile wife (Perez). Capra-corn for the X-crowd is pleasant dinnertime diversion as Cage and Perez shine as henpecked nice guy and the wife committed to making him miserable. Don't look for the diner on your next trip to NYC; it was specially built in TriBeCa and dismantled after the shoot. **101m/C; VHS, DVD.** Bridget Fonda; Nicolas Cage; Rosie Perez; Red Buttons; Isaac Hayes; Seymour Cassel; Stanley Tucci; J.E. Freeman; Richard Jenkins; Ann Dowd; Wendell Pierce; Angela Pietropinto; Vincent Pastore; Peter Jacobson; ***D:*** Andrew Bergman; ***W:*** Andrew Bergman; Jane Anderson; ***C:*** Caleb Deschanel; ***M:*** Carter Burwell.

It Felt Like Love **1/2 2014** A tender, heartfelt festival hit about the vulnerable days when young people's emotional and physical needs often go haywire. Lila (Piersanti) is a sweet girl who is fascinated by the idea of losing her virginity but somewhat terrified at the same time. Her friend Chiara (Salimeni) knows a boy named Sammy (Rubinstein) who the girls believe will help get the "big event" out of the way but feelings and maybe even love intercede. Director/writer Hittman's film can be a little too low-energy but its simplicity allows for a welcome emphasis on character and table-turning on gender roles. **82m/C; DVD.** Gina Piersanti; Giovanna Salimeni; Ronen Rubinstein; Jesse Cordasco; Kevin Anthony Ryan; ***D:*** Eliza Hittman; ***W:*** Eliza Hittman; ***C:*** Sean Porter.

It Follows **2015 (R)** After a quick hook-up with her boyfriend, Jay (Monroe) is told she now has the curse her beau once held, in which a creature in human form will "follow" her. What exactly happens when it catches her is unclear, but it is obviously very dangerous, and the only way to pass it on is to have sex with someone else. Using rundown Detroit nearly as a haunted village, writer/director Mitchell becomes an important voice in independent horror, crafting strong visual compositions instead of just jump scares. **94m/C; DVD, Blu-Ray.** Keir Gilchrist; Olivia Luccardi; Lili Sepe; Maika Monroe; Jake Weary; ***D:*** David Robert Mitchell; ***W:*** David Robert Mitchell; ***C:*** Mike Gioulakis; ***M:*** Rich Vreeland.

It Had to Be You **1/2 2000 (PG)** Elementary school teacher Anna (Henstridge) is engaged to marry advertising exec David (Healy). Ex-cop Charlie (Vartan) is engaged to busy editor Claire (Parker). Both find themselves staying at the Plaza Hotel—without their fiancees who have opted to work—planning their mutual weddings. As Charlie and Anna discuss flowers and entertainment, it becomes clear that the duo are marrying the wrong people. But what will they do about it? Charming and lightweight romantic comedy. **95m/C; VHS, DVD.** Natasha Henstridge; Michael Vartan; Joelle Carter; Frankie Muniz; Phyllis Newman; Faith Prince; Olivia D'Abo; G. Anthony "Tony" Sirico; ***D:*** Steven Feder; ***W:*** Steven Feder; ***C:*** Ken Kelsch; ***M:*** Luis Bacalov.

It Happened at Nightmare Inn *A Candle for the Devil; Nightmare Hotel* **1970** Average thriller in which Geeson travels to Spanish inn and confronts two mad sisters who run the hotel. **95m/C; VHS, DVD, Blu-Ray.** *SP* Judy Geeson; Aurora Bautista; Esperanza Roy; Victor Alcocer; Lone Fleming; ***D:*** Eugenio (Gene) Martin.

It Happened at the World's Fair **1/2 1963** Fun and light romance comedy has Elvis and a companion (O'Brien) being escorted through the Seattle World's Fair by a fetching Chinese girl. **105m/C; VHS, DVD.** Elvis Presley; Joan O'Brien; Gary Lockwood; Kurt Russell; Edith Atwater; Yvonne Craig; ***D:*** Norman Taurog.

It Happened in Brooklyn **1947** Former sailor with blue eyes bunks with janitor with big nose in Brooklyn. Sailor and cronies encounter many musical opportunities. Lots of songs and falling in love, little entertainment. **104m/B; VHS, DVD.** Frank Sinatra; Kathryn Grayson; Jimmy Durante; Peter Lawford; Gloria Grahame; ***D:*** Richard Whorf.

It Happened in Hollywood **1937** Fading silent western stars Tim (Dix) and Gloria (Wray) try to make the transition to sound but Tim's drawl is dubbed unappealing. Gloria is more successful but she doesn't like working without her old partner. Meanwhile, Tim has gone broke but tries to keep up appearances when a sick child, who idolizes the white-hatted cowboy, makes a surprise appearance at his ranch. **67m/B; DVD.** Richard Dix; Fay Wray; Victor Kilian; Franklin Pangborn; Charles Arnt; Granville Bates; ***D:*** Harry Lachman; ***W:*** Ethel Hill; Samuel Fuller; Harvey Fergusson; ***C:*** Joseph Walker.

It Happened in New Orleans 1/2 *Rainbow on the River* **1936** A young boy is cared for by a former slave in post-Civil War New Orleans until his Yankee grandmother claims him and takes him to New York. The boy is resented by his family but manages to overcome their hostilities. **86m/B; VHS, DVD.** Bobby Breen; May Robson; Alan Mowbray; Benita Hume; Charles Butterworth; Louise Beavers; Henry O'Neill; Marilyn Knowlden; ***D:*** Kurt Neumann; ***W:*** Harry Chandlee; William Hurlbut; ***C:*** Charles E. Schoenbaum; ***M:*** Karl Hajos; Hugo Riesenfeld.

It Happened on 5th Avenue 1/2 **1947** Mysterious hobo Aloyious T. McKeever (Moore) makes his home in the vacant 5th Ave. mansion of wealthy Michael O'Connor (Ruggles), who's gone south for the winter. It's Christmas and McKeever plays Santa to evicted war veteran Jim Bullock (DeFore) and his friends. Runaway Trudy O'Connor (Storm) returns home and lets everyone stay, but then her father shows up. Michael decides to pass himself off as the new butler so he can figure out what's going on but when the inhabitants realize who he is, they hope he'll remember what happened to that guy Scrooge and change his hard-hearted ways. **116m/B; DVD.** Victor Moore; Don DeFore; Gale Storm; Charlie Ruggles; Ann Harding; Alan Hale, Jr.; Eddie Ryan; Edward Brophy; Grant Mitchell; Dorothea Kent; Cathy Carter; ***D:*** Roy Del Ruth; ***W:*** Everett Freeman; ***C:*** Henry Sharp; ***M:*** Edward Ward.

It Happened One Night **1934** Classic Capra comedy about an antagonistic couple determined to teach each other about life. Colbert is an unhappy heiress who runs away from her affluent home in search of contentment. On a bus she meets newspaper reporter Gable, who teaches her how "real" people live. She returns the favor in this first of the 1930s screwball comedies. The plot is a framework for an amusing examination of war between the sexes. Colbert and Gable are superb as affectionate foes. Remade as the musicals "Eve Knew Her Apples" and "You Can't Run Away From It." **105m/B; DVD, Blu-Ray.** Clark Gable; Claudette Colbert; Roscoe Karns; Walter Connolly; Alan Hale; Ward Bond; ***D:*** Frank Capra; ***W:*** Robert Riskin; ***C:*** Joseph Walker. Oscars '34: Actor (Gable), Actress (Colbert), Adapt. Screenplay, Director (Capra), Film; AFI '98: Top 100; Natl. Film Reg. '93.

It Happened to Jane 1/2 **1959** Sunny comedy with a spunky Day as a widowed working mom battling a bullying railroad tycoon. Jane runs a live lobster business but her reputation is ruined thanks to penny-pinching Harry Foster Malone (Kovacs). When he refuses to pay proper compensation, Jane turns to longtime friend and lawyer George (Lemmon) to sue Malone and she becomes a media sensation when Malone gets nasty. **100m/C; DVD.** Doris Day; Jack Lemmon; Ernie Kovacs; Steve Forrest; Mary Wickes; Ted Rooney; Russ Brown; ***D:*** Richard Quine; ***W:*** Norman Katkov; ***C:*** Charles Lawton, Jr.; ***M:*** George Duning.

It Happened Tomorrow 1/2 **1944** Now-familiar plotline will remind TV viewers of "Early Edition." Whimsical fantasy finds obituary writer Larry Stevens (Powell) receiving the next day's newspaper from his paper's librarian (Philliber). Stevens uses his knowledge of coming events to get some major scoops, win at the track, and impress beautiful spiritualist Sylvia (Darnell). Then, he reads his own obituary and tries to avoid his fate. **84m/B; VHS, DVD.** Dick Powell; Linda Darnell; Jack Oakie; John Philliber; Edgar Kennedy; Edward Brophy; Sig Rumann; George Cleveland; Paul Guilfoyle; Eddie Acuff; ***D:*** Rene Clair; ***W:*** Rene Clair; Dudley Nichols; ***C:*** Archie Stout.

It Might Get Loud 1/2 **2009 (PG)** Slick documentary that acknowledges the ties between three generations of electric guitar rock music virtuosos: "Led Zeppelin"'s Jimmy Page, "U2"'s The Edge, and Jack White of the "White Stripes" (and numerous side projects). Director Guggenheim gets the three together for the first time at an L.A. soundstage jam session and then profiles them individually (in London, Dublin, and Tennessee), including how the guitarists developed their signature styles. Numerous performance clips and concert footage are included. **97m/C; DVD, Blu-Ray.** Jimmy Page; Edge; Jack White; ***D:*** Davis Guggenheim; ***C:*** Erich Roland; Guillermo Navarro.

It Rains In My Village 1/2 *Bice Skoro Propast Sveta* **1968** Simple-minded Goca marries swineherd Trisa. He's resigned to his familiar village life until bored big-city teacher Reza shows up to paint portraits of the local rustics. She seduces Trisa because she can and then abandons him, and he takes out his dashed dreams on his happy wife. Serbian with subtitles. **80m/C; DVD.** *YU* Ivan Paluch; Eva Ras; Annie Girardot; Mija Aleksic; ***D:*** Aleksandar Petrovic; ***W:*** Aleksandar Petrovic; ***C:*** Djordje Nikolic; ***M:*** Aleksandar Petrovic.

It Runs in the Family 1/2 **2003 (PG-13)** The curiosity factor is at least high, even if the family drama seems familiar. Michael Douglas co-stars with father Kirk, as well as mom Diana (Kirk's first wife), and Cameron, the son from his first marriage. They're the Grombergs, a Jewish upper-middle class professional family living in Manhattan. Alex (Michael) is a lawyer; dad Mitchell (Kirk) founded the firm. Alex's marriage to Rebecca (Peters) is strained and their older son Asher (Cameron) is troubled. Only Mitchell and wife Evelyn (Diana) seem to have found a measure of peace despite Mitchell's still recovering from a stroke. There's a lot of bickering until the true meaning of family comes through. **101m/C; VHS, DVD, Blu-Ray.** Michael Douglas; Kirk Douglas; Diana Douglas; Cameron Douglas; Rory Culkin; Bernadette Peters; Michelle Monaghan; Geoffrey Arend; Sarita Choudhury; Annie Golden; Irene Gorovaia; Mark Hammer; Audra McDonald; ***D:*** Fred Schepisi; ***W:*** Jesse Wigutow; ***C:*** Ian Baker; ***M:*** Paul Grabowsky.

It Seemed Like a Good Idea at the Time *Good Idea* **1975** Newley is an artist whose gold-digging wife leaves him for a dim rich guy. Of course he embarks on a covoluted scheme to get her back. Canadian producton wastes a decent cast and premise with undervelped writing. Candy's feature premiere, which got him a sequel, "Find the Lady." **106m/C; VHS, DVD.** *CA* Anthony Newley; Stefanie Powers; Isaac Hayes; Lloyd Bochner; John Candy; Yvonne De Carlo; Henry Ramer; Lawrence Dane; ***D:*** John Trent; ***W:*** David Main; Claude Harz; ***C:*** Harry Makin; ***M:*** William McCauley.

It Should Happen to You **1954** An aspiring model attempts to boost her career by promoting herself on a New York City billboard. The results, however, are continually surprising. Fine comedy teamwork from master thespians Holliday and Lemmon in this, the latter's first film. **87m/B; VHS, DVD.** Judy Holliday; Jack Lemmon; Peter Lawford; ***D:*** George Cukor; ***W:*** Ruth Gordon; Garson Kanin; ***C:*** Charles B(ryant) Lang, Jr.

It Shouldn't Happen to a Dog 1/2 **1946** The dog steals the movie (naturally) although lovely Landis is a close second. Police detective Julia Andrews is partnered with a former military canine named Rodney. Somehow, she and the Doberman are accused of a stick-up and Rodney is dognapped by racketeers. Reporter Henry needs a hot story and thinks this is it, so he and Julia team up, but it's Rodney who's the hero. **70m/B; DVD.** Carole Landis; Allyn Joslyn; Margo Woode; Harry (Henry) Morgan; Reed Hadley; John Ireland; ***D:*** Herbert I. Leeds; ***W:*** Eugene Ling; ***C:*** Glen MacWilliams; ***M:*** David Buttolph.

It Started in Naples **1960** Good performances by both Gable and Loren in this comedy-drama about an American lawyer in Italy who, upon preparing his late brother's estate, finds that his brother's nephew is living with a stripper. A custody battle ensues, but love wins out in the end. Loren is incredible in nightclub scenes. **100m/C; VHS, DVD.** Clark Gable; Sophia Loren; Marietto; Vittorio De Sica; Paolo Carlini; Claudio Ermelli; Giovanni Filidoro; ***D:*** Melville Shavelson; ***W:*** Melville Shavelson; Jack Rose.

It Started with a Kiss 1/2 **1959** Reynolds plays a showgirl who impulsively marries an Air Force sargeant (Ford). When he's transfered to Spain they try to make a go of their hasty marriage among numerous comic complications. Flimsy farce with likeable leads. **104m/C; VHS, DVD, Blu-Ray.** Debbie Reynolds; Glenn Ford; Eva Gabor; Gustavo Rojo; Fred Clark; Edgar Buchanan; Robert Warwick; Harry (Henry) Morgan; Frances Bavier; ***D:*** George Marshall.

It Started with Eve **1941** Funny comedy about grumpy old millionaire Jonathan Reynolds (Laughton) whose dying wish is to meet the young lady his son Johnny (Cummings) is to wed. Unfortunately, the bride-to-be is unavailable, so Johnny finds a replacement in hatcheck girl Anne (Durbin). Of course, Anne steals the old man's heart and he miraculously makes a full-blown recovery, which means big trouble for Johnny. Remade in 1964 as "I'd Rather Be Rich." Based on the story "Almost An Angel" by Hans Kraly. **92m/B; DVD.** Deanna Durbin; Charles Laughton; Robert Cummings; Guy Kibbee; Margaret Tallichet; Catherine Doucet; Walter Catlett; Charles Coleman; Clara Blandick; ***D:*** Henry Koster; ***W:*** Norman Krasna; Leo Townsend; ***C:*** Rudolph Mate; ***M:*** Hans J. Salter.

It Takes a Thief *The Challenge* **1960** Tough cookie Jayne's a buxom gangstress who does the hokey pokey with her criminal minions. A former lover who's been released from the big house seems to think she's been minding the mint for him. Au contraire. **93m/B; DVD.** *GB* Jayne Mansfield; Anthony Quayle; Carl Mohner; Peter Reynolds; John Bennett; Barbara Mullen; Robert Brown; Dermot Walsh; Patrick Holt; ***D:*** John Gilling; ***W:*** John Gilling; ***C:*** Gordon Dines; ***M:*** Bill McGuffie.

It Takes Two **1995 (PG)** Vapid sugary comedy finds the nine-year-old Olsen twins playing a duo from opposite sides of the tracks who change identities in an effort to get their respective adults (Guttenberg and Alley) together. See "The Parent Trap" instead. **100m/C; VHS, DVD.** Ashley (Fuller) Olsen; Mary-Kate Olsen; Kirstie Alley; Steve Guttenberg; Philip Bosco; Jane Sibbett; Lawrence Dane; Gerard Parkes; ***D:*** Andy Tennant; ***W:*** Deborah Dean Davis; ***C:*** Kenneth Zunder; ***M:*** Sherman Foote; Ray Foote.

It! The Terror from Beyond Space 1/2 *It! The Vampire from Beyond Space* **1958** The sole survivor of a Martian expedition is believed to have murdered his colleagues. He's arrested and brought back to Earth via space ship. En route, a vicious alien, the actual culprit, is discovered on board and begins killing the crew members. A fun science fiction thriller which, 20 years later, would provide Ridley Scott with the plot for "Alien." **68m/B; VHS, DVD.** Marshall Thompson; Shawn Smith; Kim Spalding; Ann Doran; Dabbs Greer; Paul Langton; Ray Corrigan; ***D:*** Edward L. Cahn; ***W:*** Jerome Bixby; ***C:*** Kenneth Peach, Sr.; ***M:*** Paul Sawtell; Bert Shefter.

It Waits WOOF! **2005** And you'll wish it hadn't. Silly spooker finds alcoholic forest ranger Danielle (Vincent, she of the bouncy breasts and tight tank tops) goes into the woods after the creature that has ripped apart her boyfriend. It turns out to be a Native American spirit that was entombed in a cave until some stupid college kids released it. **88m/C; DVD, Blu-Ray.** Cerina Vincent; Dominic Zamprogna; Eric Schweig; ***D:*** Stephen R. Monroe; ***W:*** Richard Christian Matheson; Thomas Szollosi; Stephen J. Cannell; ***C:*** Jon Joffin; ***M:*** Corey A. Jackson. **VIDEO**

It Was One of Us 1/2 **2007** Five former college roommates have a reunion and each reveals a secret to the group. A week later, they all receive blackmail threats Long-standing jealousies surface since they assume that one of them must be the blackmailer. **90m/C; DVD.** Sarah Brown; Jordan Ladd; Elisa Donovan; Marissa Jaret Winokur; Kira Clavell; Susan Hogan; Kurt Evans; ***D:*** Nell Sovell; ***W:*** Nell Sovell; Claire Lazebnik; ***C:*** Adam Sliwinski; ***M:*** Justin Melland. **CABLE**

The Italian **1915** The story of an Italian immigrant family living in the slums of New York during the turn of the century. **78m/B; Silent; VHS, DVD.** George Beban; Clara Williams; Leo Wills; J. Frank Burke; Fanny Midgley; ***D:*** Reginald Barker; ***W:*** Thomas Ince. Natl. Film Reg. '91.

The Italian *Italianetz* **2005 (PG-13)** Tough story based on a true incident and best seen by adults despite its MPAA rating. Six-year-old Vanya (solemnly appealing Spiridonov) has been deposited in a bleak Russian orphanage by his mother. His luck is apparently changing when a rich Italian couple offer to buy him from the home's corrupt adoption broker, known only as Madam (Kuznetsova). While waiting for the red tape to untangle, Vanya decides he wants to find his birth mom and, armed with an old address from his stolen files, he hits the road pursued by Madam and her lackey, who don't want to lose a sale. Russian with subtitles. **99m/C; DVD.** *RU* Kolya Spiridonov; Denis Moiseenko; Sasha Syrotkin; Olga Shuvalova; Dima Zemlyanko; Maria Kuznetsova; Yuri Itskov; ***D:*** Andrei Kravchuk; ***W:*** Andrei Romanov; ***C:*** Alexander Burov; ***M:*** Alexander Knaifel.

The Italian Connection *La Mala Ordina; Manhunt; Black Kingpin; Hit Men* **1973** Pulp crime melodrama from Di Leo. A heroin shipment goes missing on its way to New York and likeable Milanese pimp Luca (Adorf) becomes the scapegoat for the theft. The real thieves want him dead before U.S. hitmen Dave (Silva) and Frank (Strode) show up, but Luca's family become collateral damage instead. So the sneaky criminal, who understands survival, decides to take care of anyone who done him wrong. Italian with subtitles. **95m/C; VHS, DVD.** *IT* Mario Adorf; Henry Silva; Woody Strode; Adolfo Celi; Luciana Paluzzi; Franco Fabrizi; Sylva Koscina; Femi Benussi; Cyril Cusack; ***D:*** Fernando Di Leo; ***W:*** Fernando Di Leo; Augusto Finocchi; Ingo Hermes; ***C:*** Franco Villa; ***M:*** Armando Trovajoli.

Italian for Beginners 1/2 *Italiensk for Begyndere* **2001 (R)** Director Scherfig is the first woman to use the strict Dogma 95 filmmaking rules (hand-held cameras, natural light, live music, no studios scenes, no costumes, and no special effects) of her Danish colleagues. She's also the first to try to do a romantic comedy in the Dogma style, and she pulls it off nicely. Her tale brings together six quirky lonelyhearts: Andreas (Berthlesen), newly widowed minister; Hall-Finn (Kaalund), a soccer-obsessed restaurant manager; his best friend Jorgen (Gantzler), who's convinced he's impotent; Olympia (Stovelbaek), who likes Andreas and cares for her abusive, ill father; Karen (Jorgensen) who cuts Hal-Finn's hair and cares for her alcoholic shrew of a mother; and Giulia (Jensen), an Italian waitress with a crush on Jorgen, in a Conversational Italian class. The seemingly lightweight plot is anchored by insight into everyday misery and hurt amid the giddy matchmaking and likeable characters. **112m/C; VHS, DVD.** *DK* Anders W. Berthelsen; Peter Gantzler; Anette Stovelbaek; Ann Eleonora Jorgensen; Lars Kaalund; Sara Indrio Jensen; ***D:*** Lone Scherfig; ***W:*** Lone Scherfig; ***C:*** Jorgen Johansson.

The Italian Job 1/2 **1969 (G)** Caine and Coward pair up to steal $4 million in gold by causing a major traffic jam in Turin, Italy. During the jam, the pair steals the gold from an armored car. Silliness and chases through the Swiss mountains ensue, culminating in a hilarious ending. **99m/C; VHS, DVD.** *GB* Michael Caine; Noel Coward; Benny Hill; Raf Vallone; Tony Beckley; Rossano Brazzi; Margaret Blye; ***D:*** Peter Collinson; ***M:*** Quincy Jones.

The Italian Job **2003 (PG-13)** Typically cool crew of expert theives, led by Charlie (Wahlberg), pulls off a heist of $35 million worth of gold bars in Venice, only to be doublecrossed by crewmember Steve (Norton), who kills Charlie's mentor John (Sutherland) and leaves the rest for dead. When the group find Steve a year later in L.A., John's daughter Stella (Theron), an exceptional safecracker in her own right, joins the gang for revenge. Amiable caper flick succeeds on the multiple strengths of understated cool, superbly orchestrated action, pitch-perfect humor, and an excellent cast doing a great job. Green, as computer geek Lyle, stands out, while Wahlberg boosts his leading man appeal. Remake of the 1969 Michael Caine vehicle copies original's use of Mini Coopers, but not much else. **111m/C; VHS, DVD, Blu-Ray, UMD, HD-DVD.** Mark

Wahlberg; Edward Norton; Charlize Theron; Mos Def; Seth Green; Jason Statham; Donald Sutherland; Christina Cabot; Franky G.; Olek Krupa; *D:* F. Gary Gray; *W:* Wayne Powers; Donna Powers; *C:* Wally Pfister; *M:* John Powell.

Italian Movie ✓✓ **1993** First-generation Italian immigrant Leonardo decides to become a male escort to pay off his gambling debts and support his large family but things get quite complicated. **95m/C; VHS, DVD.** Michael DellaFemina; Rita Moreno; James Gandolfini; Caprice Benedetti; *D:* Roberto Monticello.

The Italian Stallion ✓ *The Party at Kitty and Stud's* **1973** Stallone plays a man with only one thing on his mind...sex! **90m/C; VHS, DVD.** Sylvester Stallone; Henrietta Holm; *D:* Morton Lewis; *W:* Morton Lewis; *C:* Rolph Laube; *M:* Kay Leodel.

Italian Straw Hat ✓✓✓ *Un Chapeau de Paille d'Italie* **1927** Classic silent about the chain of errors that ensues when a man's horse eats a woman's hat. His vast, unending struggle to replace the hat is the source of continual comedy. From Eugene Labiche's play. **114m/B; Silent; VHS, DVD.** *FR* Albert Prejean; Olga Tschekowa; *D:* Rene Clair.

Ithaca ✓✓ ½ **2016 (PG)** A coming-of-age drama set in the American homefront during World War II, based on the novel The Human Comedy by William Saroyan. In 1942, 14-year-old Homer Macauley (Neustaedter) has many responsibilities in his home city of Ithaca, New York. His older brother is fighting in the war, and Homer is left to look after his widowed mother and two siblings. He works as a bicycle telegraph messenger, and wants to be the best one possible. He spends much of his time delivering messages that contain messages about love, death, hope, and difficulties. One message profoundly impacts him for the rest of his life. **96m/C; DVD, Streaming, Download.** Alex Neustaedter; Tom Hanks; Meg Ryan; Sam Shepard; Jack Quaid; *D:* Meg Ryan; *W:* Erik Jendresen; *C:* Andrew Dunn; *M:* John Cougar Mellencamp.

It's a Big Country ✓ ½ **1951** And apparently it's very boring too if you go by these eight inconsistent vignettes that are set throughout the then-48 states. A professor lectures a fellow train passenger about USA diversity to link the tales together. The best is the tongue-in-cheek humor of Cooper's laconic cowboy as he tackles the stereotypes of Texas and the worst is the overextended story of a boy whose immigrant father refuses to believe he needs to get glasses for school. **89m/B; DVD.** William Powell; James Whitmore; Gary Cooper; Ethel Barrymore; Keenan Wynn; George Murphy; Gene Kelly; Janet Leigh; S.Z. Sakall; Van Johnson; Keefe Brasselle; Marjorie Main; Fredric March; Robert Hyatt; Nancy Davis; *D:* William A. Wellman; Clarence Brown; Richard Thorpe; Charles Vidor; John Sturges; Don Weis; *W:* Allen Rivkin; Dorothy Kingsley; William Ludwig; George Wells; Dore Schary; Helen Deutsch; Isobel Lennart; *C:* John Alton; William Mellor; Joseph Ruttenberg; Ray June; *M:* Charles Wolcott; Adolph Deutsch; Bronislau Kaper; David Rose; David Raskin; Lennie Hayton.

It's a Boy Girl Thing ✓✓ ½ **2006 (PG-13)** Good girl brainiac Nell (Armstrong) and high school QB Woody (Zegers) grew up next door to each other and are lifelong enemies. Thanks to one of those goofy movie contrivances, they wake up one morning in each other's bodies. After dealing with their different—ah—equipment, the antagonistic duo first try to trash each other's reputations and then realize they have to work together to get back to normal. There's more juvenile raunch than you might expect, but the leads are likeable and it's good for a giggle. **95m/C; DVD.** *GB* Samaire Armstrong; Kevin Zegers; Sherry Miller; Robert Joy; Maury Chaykin; Sharon Osbourne; Mpho Koaho; Brooke D'Orsay; Emily Hampshire; *D:* Nick Hurran; *W:* Geoff Deane; *C:* Steve Danyluk; *M:* Christian Henson.

It's a Disaster ✓✓ **2012 (R)** Modest black comedy with the title referring to a literal disaster and not just the uncomfortable Sunday gathering of four couples. Longtime-marrieds Pete (Miller) and Emma (Hayes) are using their weekly brunch to announce that they're splitting up. Forever-engaged couple Shane (Grace) and Hedy (Ferrera), free-spirited Buck (Brennan) and Lexi (Boston), and single Tracy (Stiles) don't know how to react while Tracy's new boyfriend Glen (Cross) is just bewildered. At least until an apparent bomb detonates in L.A. and the subsequent nerve-gas cloud drifting their way gives everyone something more dramatic to obsess about. **88m/C; DVD, Blu-Ray.** Blaise Miller; Erinn Hayes; David Cross; Julia Stiles; Kevin M. Brennan; Rachel Boston; Jeff Grace; America Ferrera; *D:* Todd Berger; *W:* Todd Berger; *C:* Nancy Schreiber.

It's a Dog's Life ✓✓ ½ *The Bar Sinister* **1955** The hero and narrator of this story is a wily bull terrier called Wildfire. Wildfire is a tough dog on the mean streets of the Bowery in turn-of-the-century New York. His master has him in dog fights in the local saloon but eventually abandons him. Wildfire is then taken in by the kindly employee of the rich and dog-hating Jagger but naturally manages to win the codger over. Based on the short story "The Bar Sinister" by Richard Harding Davis. **87m/C; VHS, DVD.** Jeff Richards; Edmund Gwenn; Dean Jagger; *D:* Herman Hoffman; *W:* John Michael Hayes; *M:* Elmer Bernstein.

It's a Gift ✓✓✓ ½ **1934** A grocery clerk moves his family west to manage orange groves in this classic Fields comedy. Several inspired sequences. The supporting cast shines too. A real find for the discriminating comedy buff. Remake of the silent "It's the Old Army Game." **71m/B; VHS, DVD.** W.C. Fields; Baby LeRoy; Kathleen Howard; Jean Rouverol; Julian Madison; Tammany Young; Tommy Bupp; *D:* Norman Z. McLeod; *W:* Jack Cunningham; *C:* Henry Sharp. Natl. Film Reg. '10.

It's a Great Feeling ✓✓ ½ **1949** Another Carson and Day team-up where Carson plays a camera-hogging show-off whom no one wants to direct. He's such an industry piranha that he ends up directing himself! He cons Day, a waitress and would-be actress, by promising her a part in his new film. Some executives hear her sing before she heads back home to Wisconsin, fed up with Hollywood. They make Carson track her down to star in the new picture, but when he arrives she is at the altar with her high school sweetheart. **85m/C; VHS, DVD.** Dennis Morgan; Doris Day; Jack Carson; Bill Goodwin; Errol Flynn; Gary Cooper; Joan Crawford; Ronald Reagan; Sydney Greenstreet; Danny Kaye; Eleanor Parker; Edward G. Robinson; Jane Wyman; *D:* David Butler.

It's a Great Life ✓ ½ **1929** It's also a pretty lousy movie. The only talkie-era film for the Duncan sisters, who play sisters working at a department store. They get fired and start a vaudeville act but split up when Babe marries piano player Jimmy whom sister Casey can't stand. The sisters eventually reunite when they're a flop on their own. Includes two-color sequences. Since the film wasn't successful the Duncans returned to vaudeville themselves. **93m/C; DVD.** Rosetta Duncan; Vivian Duncan; Lawrence Gray; Jed Prouty; Benny Rubin; *D:* Sam Wood; *W:* Al Boasberg; Willard Mack; *C:* J. Peverell Marley.

It's a Mad, Mad, Mad, Mad World ✓✓ **1963** Overblown epic comedy with a cast of notables desperately seeking the whereabouts of stolen money. Ultimately exhausting film undone by its length and overbearing performances. **155m/C; VHS, DVD, Blu-Ray.** Spencer Tracy; Sid Caesar; Milton Berle; Ethel Merman; Jonathan Winters; Jimmy Durante; Buddy Hackett; Mickey Rooney; Phil Silvers; Dick Shawn; Edie Adams; Dorothy Provine; Buster Keaton; Terry-Thomas; Moe Howard; Larry Fine; Joe DeRita; Jim Backus; William Demarest; Peter Falk; Leo Gorcey; Edward Everett Horton; Joe E. Brown; Carl Reiner; Zasu Pitts; Eddie Anderson; Jack Benny; Jerry Lewis; Norman Fell; Stan Freberg; Don Knotts; *D:* Stanley Kramer; *W:* William Rose; Tania Rose; *C:* Ernest Laszlo; *M:* Ernest Gold. Oscars '63: Sound FX Editing.

It's a Pleasure ✓✓ ½ **1945** Henie in Technicolor splendor. Ice skater Chris wants to help out hockey player Don Martin (O'Shea) who gets thrown out of the league for punching out a ref. He becomes her skating partner and they get married but Don's also an alcoholic and is soon bringing Chris problems on and off the ice. When she gets a shot at stardom, is he man enough to let her go? **90m/C; DVD.** Sonja Henie; Michael O'Shea; Bill Johnson; Marie McDonald; Gus Schilling; Arthur Loft; *D:* William A. Seiter; *W:* Elliot Paul; Lynn Starling; *C:* Ray Rennahan; *M:* Arthur Lange.

It's a Small World ✓ ½ **1950** Castle's film about midgets depicts the problems Harry experiences growing up and the exploitation he undergoes (he becomes a criminal) until his love for another little person has him finding a new refuge. **69m/B; DVD.** Paul Dale; Lorraine Miller; Anne Sholter; Will Geer; Nina Koshetz; Steve Brodie; Todd Karns; *D:* William Castle; *W:* William Castle; Otto Schreiber; *C:* Karl Struss; *M:* Karl Hajos.

It's a Wonderful Life ✓✓✓✓ **1946** American classic about a man saved from suicide by a considerate angel, who then shows the hero how important he's been to the lives of loved ones. Corny but inspirational and heartwarming, with an endearing performance by Travers as angel Clarence. Stewart and Reed are typically wholesome. Perfect film for people who want to feel good, joyfully teetering on the border between Hollywood schmaltz and genuine heartbreak. Available colorized. Also available in a 160-minute Collector's Edition with original preview trailer, "The Making of 'It's a Wonderful Life,'" and a new digital transfer from the original negative. **125m/B; VHS, DVD, Blu-Ray.** James Stewart; Donna Reed; Henry Travers; Thomas Mitchell; Lionel Barrymore; Samuel S. Hinds; Frank Faylen; Gloria Grahame; H.B. Warner; Ellen Corby; Sheldon Leonard; Beulah Bondi; Ward Bond; Frank Albertson; Todd Karns; Mary Treen; Charles Halton; Carl "Alfalfa" Switzer; *D:* Frank Capra; *W:* Frances Goodrich; Albert Hackett; Jo Swerling; *C:* Joseph Biroc; Joseph Walker; *M:* Dimitri Tiomkin. AFI '98: Top 100; Golden Globes '47: Director (Capra); Natl. Film Reg. '90.

It's a Wonderful World ✓✓ **1939** Moderately amusing screwball comedy although the two leads don't have much chemistry. Guy Johnson (Stewart) is a rude, neophyte PI who goes on the lam after his trouble-prone millionaire client Willie Heyward (Truex) gets them both falsely convicted of murder and conspiracy. Guy steals the car of eccentric poet Edwina Corday (Colbert)?with her in it—and she's soon charmed by the lug and eager to help him find the real killer. Guy's fond of trying out goofy disguises, including posing as a Boy Scout leader in short pants and coke-bottle glasses. **86m/B; DVD.** James Stewart; Claudette Colbert; Guy Kibbee; Ernest Truex; Nat Pendleton; Frances Drake; Edgar Kennedy; *D:* W.S. Van Dyke; *W:* Ben Hecht; *C:* Oliver Marsh; *M:* Edward Ward.

It's Alive! ✓ **1968** Slow-moving dud about a farmer feeding passersby to the area's cave-dwelling lizard man. The ping pong ball-eyed monster puts in a belated appearance that's not worth the wait. **80m/C; VHS, DVD.** Tommy Kirk; Shirley Bonne; Bill (Billy) Thurman; Annabelle MacAdams; Corveth Osterhouse; *D:* Larry Buchanan; *W:* Larry Buchanan; *C:* Robert Alcott.

It's Alive ✓✓✓ **1974 (PG)** Cult film about a mutated baby, born to a normal Los Angeles couple, who escapes and goes on a bloodthirsty, murderous rampage. It's a sight to behold. Fantastic score by Bernard Herrmann makes this chilling film a memorable one. **91m/C; VHS, DVD, Blu-Ray.** John P. Ryan; Sharon Farrell; Andrew Duggan; Guy Stockwell; James Dixon; Michael Ansara; William Wellman, Jr.; Shamus Locke; *D:* Larry Cohen; *W:* Larry Cohen; *C:* Fenton Hamilton; *M:* Bernard Herrmann.

It's Alive 2: It Lives Again WOOF! *It Lives Again* **1978 (R)** In this sequel to "It's Alive," the original hellspun baby meets up with two more of the same and all three terrorize the city, murdering everyone they can find. Truly horrendous. **91m/C; VHS, DVD, Blu-Ray.** Frederic Forrest; Kathleen Lloyd; John P. Ryan; Andrew Duggan; John Marley; Eddie Constantine; James Dixon; Bobby Ramsen; *D:* Larry Cohen; *W:* Larry Cohen; *C:* Fenton Hamilton.

It's Alive 3: Island of the Alive ✓ *Island of the Alive* **1987 (R)** The second sequel to the tongue-in-cheek horror film, in which the infant mutant of the previous films has been left with other mutations to spawn on a desert island. **94m/C; VHS, DVD, Blu-Ray.** Michael Moriarty; Karen Black; Laurene Landon; Gerrit Graham; James Dixon; Neal Israel; MacDonald Carey; *D:* Larry Cohen; *W:* Larry Cohen; *C:* Daniel Pearl; *M:* Laurie Johnson.

It's All About Love ✓ **2003** Danish director Vinterberg, one of the founders of Dogme 95, tries on a futuristic romantic thriller with dismal results. John (Phoenix) arrives in New York to sign final divorce papers with his estranged wife Elena (Danes), an ice-skating superstar. Elena is in some kind of mysterious trouble and the twosome elude her flunkies to be together, later learning that Elena has been cloned for insurance purposes. They then go on the run. And Penn is around as John's brother who muses while constantly flying around the world (and no, it doesn't make any sense). Both American leads have really bad, allegedly Polish, accents and although it's supposed to be New York it was filmed in a Swedish movie studio. **104m/C; DVD.** Joaquin Rafael (Leaf) Phoenix; Claire Danes; Sean Penn; Douglas Henshall; Alun Armstrong; Margo Martindale; Mark Strong; Geoffrey Hutchings; *D:* Thomas Vinterberg; *C:* Anthony Dod Mantle; *M:* Zbigniew Preisner.

It's All Gone, Pete Tong WOOF! **2004 (R)** "Pete Tong" is a Cockney rhyming slang for 'wrong.' Frankie Wilde (Kaye) is a DJ with a major coke habit and the club world at his feet when, after years of audio at excessive levels, he loses his hearing. Dropping out of sight he hires a beautiful deaf woman to teach him lip-reading and learns the properties of vibration from a flamenco dancer, all to eventually reclaim his King of the Club DJ status. Too little hilarity and an unfocused script. **88m/C; DVD.** *GB CA* Paul Kaye; Beatriz Batarda; Mike Wilmot; Paul J. Spence; Kate Magowan; Dave Lawrence; *D:* Michael Dowse; *W:* Michael Dowse; *C:* Balasz Bolygo; *M:* Graham Massey.

It's All So Quiet ✓✓ ½ *Boven is het stil* **2013** Based on the novel Boven is het Stil by Gerbrand Bakker, this drama explores themes such as dying, families, communication, and carving your own path. Living in the Dutch countryside with his elderly, bedridden father, stoic Helmer (Willems) is an unmarried farmer. Through his work, he comes in daily contact with milk collector, who is Helmer's age and fascinates him. One day, Helmer begins to make changes by renovating the house, buying himself a new, bigger bed, and moving his father upstairs. As Helmer prepares to live his own life after his father passes, his domineering, but dying, father clashes with him. Once Helmer finds his voice, his world opens up in unexpected ways. The last film role for Willems and one that shows the depth of his talents. Dutch with subtitles. **94m/C; DVD.** Jeroen Willems; Henri Garcin; Wim Opbrouck; Martijn Lakemeier; Lies Visschedijk; *D:* Nanouk Leopold; *W:* Nanouk Leopold; *C:* Frank van den Eeden; *M:* Paul M. van Brugge.

It's All True ✓✓ **1993 (G)** A look at auteur Welles' ill-fated WWII filmmaking project. Welles served as a special cultural ambassador to South America and, in 1942, began a documentary covering the area's complex political and social issues. Includes footage from "Four Men on a Raft," Welles' recreation about the peasant fishermen of Brazil; surviving excerpts from "The Story of Samba," a Technicolor musical about Carnaval in Rio de Janeiro; and footage from "My Friend Bonito," set against a backdrop of bullfighting in Mexico. **85m/C; VHS, DVD.** *Nar:* Miguel Ferrer; *D:* Richard Wilson; Bill Krohn; Myron Meise; Orson Welles; *W:* Richard Wilson; Bill Krohn; Myron Meise; *C:* Gary Graver; George Fanto; *M:* Jorge Arriagada.

It's Always Fair Weather ✓✓ **1955** Three WWII buddies meet again at a 10-year reunion and find that they don't like each other very much. A surprisingly cynical film. Director Donen produced "Seven Brides for Seven Brothers" the previous year. **102m/C; DVD.** Gene Kelly; Cyd Charisse; Dan Dailey; Michael Kidd; *D:* Stanley Donen; *W:* Betty Comden; Adolph Green; *M:* Betty Comden; Adolph Green; Andre Previn.

It's Complicated ✓✓ ½ **2009 (R)** Meyers' comfortable film is probably best appreciated by a specific and generally neglected audience—middle-aged (and older) women looking to relax into a dazzling, if shallow, world of consumerism and romantic possibilities. Radiant Santa Barbara bakery/ restaurant owner Jane Adler (Streep) has been divorced from Jake (Baldwin) for 10 years, thanks to his cheating and subsequent marriage to younger, pouty beauty Agness (Bell). They maintained a civilized relationship for the sake of their three now-grown kids and it's the kids' lives (and too much alcohol) that brings Jane and Jake closer together than expected. As Jane rather gleefully exclaims to her gal pals, she's now the 'other woman.' Of course the smarmily charming Jake is suddenly not Jane's only suitor as she hires gentlemanly architect Adam (Martin) for a kitchen re-do and some wooing of his own. Oh, romance among actual adults! Even though they may not act like it. **118m/C; Blu-Ray.** Meryl Streep; Alec Baldwin; Steve Martin; John Krasinski; Zoe Kazan; Hunter Parrish; Lake Bell; Rita Wilson; Mary Kay Place; Nora Dunn; Alexandra Wentworth; Caitlin FitzGerald; ***D:*** Nancy Meyers; ***W:*** Nancy Meyers; ***C:*** John Toll; ***M:*** Hans Zimmer; Hector Pereira.

It's Good to Be Alive 1/2 **1974** The true story of how Brooklyn Dodgers' catcher Roy Campanella learned to face life after an automobile accident left him a quadriplegic. Good performances. **100m/C; VHS, DVD.** Paul Winfield; Ruby Dee; Louis Gossett, Jr.; Ramon Bieri; Joe De Santis; ***D:*** Michael Landon; ***M:*** Michel Legrand. **TV**

It's in the Bag! 1/2 *The Fifth Chair* **1945** Cheap indie comedy. Fred (Allen), a shiftless flea circus owner, sells chairs he has inherited, not knowing that a fortune is hidden in one of them. Allen's schtick with Jack Benny--a holdover from their radio days--is a highlight. **87m/B; DVD, Blu-Ray.** Fred Allen; Don Ameche; Jack Benny; William Bendix; Binnie Barnes; Robert Benchley; ***D:*** Richard Wallace; ***W:*** Jay Dratler; Alma Reville; ***C:*** Russell Metty; ***M:*** Werner R. Heymann.

It's In the Water **1996** Small, conservative Azalea Springs, Texas is rocked by the opening of an AIDS hospice. The homophobia outrages society wife Alex, who begins working at the hospice alongside best friend (soon to be more) Grace. Then a rumor starts that the local drinking water turns you gay and things really get wild. Fast-moving and funny. **100m/C; VHS, DVD.** Keri Jo Chapman; Teresa Garrett; Barbara Lasater; Larry Randolph; ***D:*** Kelli Herd.

It's Kind of a Funny Story 1/2 **2010 (PG-13)** Stressed-out and depressed, 16-year-old Craig (Gilchrist) checks himself into a psychiatric hospital unbeknownst to his parents. Stuck in the adult ward with truly troubled personalities, he quickly realizes he's normal but has a minimum five-day stay. Luckily, he's befriended by fellow patient Bobby (Galifanakis), who understands what Craig is going through. Despite Galifanakis's presence, this is more of a funny drama then a dramatic comedy. Offbeat and completely human, the cast never goes big but maintains a somber yet still silly mood. Based on the Ned Vizzini novel. **101m/C; Blu-Ray.** Keir Gilchrist; Zach Galifianakis; Emma Roberts; Viola Davis; Aasif Mandvi; Zoë Kravitz; Lauren Graham; Jim Gaffigan; ***D:*** Anna Boden; Ryan Fleck; ***W:*** Anna Boden; Ryan Fleck; ***C:*** Andrij Parekh; ***M:*** Broken Social Scene.

It's Love Again 1/2 **1936** In a light music-hall comedy gossip columnist Peter invents a celebrity to write about--tiger-hunting adventurer Mrs. Smythe-Smythe who's just arrived in London from India. Everyone in society wants to meet the mystery woman, so actress Elaine decides to impersonate her in order to get her big break. This confuses Peter and may ruin their budding romance when he discovers the truth. **83m/B; DVD.** *UK* Jessie Matthews; Robert Young; Sonnie Hale; Ernest Milton; Sara Allgood; ***D:*** Victor Saville; ***W:*** Lesser Samuels; Marion Dix; Austin Melford; ***C:*** Glen MacWilliams; ***M:*** Bretton Byrd; Louis Levy.

It's Love I'm After 1/2 **1937** Screwball romp has egotistical matinee idol Basil Underwood (Howard) and his jealous leading lady Joyce Arden (Davis) involved on and off the stage and constantly breaking and making up. Star struck debutante Marcia West (de Havilland) thinks she's in love, flatters Basil, and neglects her own fiance, Henry (Knowles), who tries to rectify the situation and only makes it worse. Blore is a comic delight as Basil's inventive valet Digges. **90m/B; DVD.** Leslie Howard; Bette Davis; Olivia de Havilland; Patric Knowles; Eric Blore; George Barbier; Spring Byington; Bonita Granville; Veda Ann Borg; ***D:*** Archie Mayo; ***W:*** Casey Robinson; ***C:*** James Van Trees; ***M:*** Heinz Roemheld.

It's My Party 1/2 **1995 (R)** When L.A. architect Nick Stark (Roberts) learns that he's developed untreatable brain lesions from AIDS that will essentially leave him helpless, he decides to throw himself a monumental farewell bash before taking a drug overdose. Friends and family all turn up as does, awkwardly enough, Brandon Theis (Harrison), Nick's former live-in who couldn't handle his HIV-positive diagnosis but would like a last reapproachment. Fine, sympathetic performances, espcially by the two leads, and yes, it's a weepie. Based on a true story. **120m/C; VHS, DVD.** Eric Roberts; Gregory Harrison; Marlee Matlin; Lee Grant; George Segal; Bronson Pinchot; Bruce Davison; Devon Gummersall; Roddy McDowall; Margaret Cho; Paul Regina; Olivia Newton-John; Christopher Atkins; Dennis Christopher; Ron Glass; Eugene Robert Glazer; ***D:*** Randal Kleiser; ***W:*** Randal Kleiser; ***C:*** Bernd Heinl; ***M:*** Basil Poledouris.

It's My Turn **1980 (R)** A mathematics professor (Clayburgh) struggles in her relationship with live-in lover (Grodin) who sells real-estate in Chicago. She meets retired baseball player (Douglas) and falls in love. "Ho-hum" just about describes the rest. **91m/C; VHS, Streaming.** Jill Clayburgh; Michael Douglas; Charles Grodin; Beverly Garland; Steven Hill; Dianne Wiest; Daniel Stern; ***D:*** Claudia Weill; ***W:*** Eleanor Bergstein; ***C:*** Bill Butler.

It's Only Money 1/2 **1962** Slapstick Lewis comedy is the 6th collaboration between the comedian and director Tashlin. TV repairman and would-be PI Lester March hears elderly Cecilia Albright (Questel) make a televised plea to locate her long-lost nephew, who's the heir to the family fortune. Lester goes to see Albright, hoping to work on the case, and is recognized as the heir (no surprise there) by greedy attorney DeWitt (Scott) who wants the money himself. He has to get rid of Lester for good. **83m/B; DVD, Blu-Ray.** Jerry Lewis; Zachary Scott; Joan O'Brien; Mae Questel; Jesse White; Jack Weston; ***D:*** Frank Tashlin; ***W:*** John Fenton Murray; ***C:*** W. Wallace Kelley; ***M:*** Walter Scharf.

It's Pat: The Movie **WOOF!** **1994 (PG-13)** This movie is so bad, let's pray it sounds the death knell to big-screen versions of "Saturday Night Live" sketch characters—who possessed little humor to begin with. For what it's worth, the androgynous Pat (Sweeney) falls for the equally gender-suspect Chris (Foley, from Canada's version of SNL, "Kids in the Hall") and all sorts of embarrassing situations arise. Pat's quest to find Pat's self is sketch material stretched see-through thin. **78m/C; VHS, DVD, Blu-Ray.** Julia Sweeney; Dave Foley; Charles Rocket; Kathy Griffin; Julie Haydon; Tim Meadows; Arleen (Arlene) Sorkin; ***Cameo(s):*** Sally Jesse Raphael; Kathy Najimy; ***D:*** Adam Bernstein; ***W:*** Julia Sweeney; Jim Emerson; Stephen Hibbert.

It's the Old Army Game **1926** Classic Fields gags in three of his best Ziegfeld Follies sketches: "The Drug Store," "A Peaceful Morning," and "The Family Flivver." The beautiful Brooks serves as his comic foil. **75m/B; Silent; VHS, DVD, Blu-Ray.** W.C. Fields; Louise Brooks; Blanche Ring; William Gaxton; ***D:*** Edward Sutherland.

It's the Rage 1/2 *All the Rage* **1999 (R)** Glib ensemble comedy about the collision of guns and anger, with an interesting cast. Warren (Daniels) shoots an intruder who turns out to be his business partner, who may have been fooling around with Warren's prim wife, Helen (Allen). His lawyer, Tim (Braugher), has just been given a gun by his boyfriend (Schwimmer), and he has another client (Paquin) whose brother (Ribisi) is trigger-happy. Meanwhile, Helen takes a job with paranoid billionaire, Mr. Morgan (Sinise), while Warren's being investigated by a couple of detectives (Forster, Woodbine) for whom guns are job accessories. Reddin scripted from his play. **97m/C; VHS, DVD.** Jeff Daniels; Joan Allen; Andre Braugher; David Schwimmer; Anna Paquin; Giovanni Ribisi; Gary Sinise; Josh Brolin; Robert Forster; Bokeem Woodbine; ***D:*** James D. Stern; ***W:*** Keith Reddin; ***C:*** Alex Nepomniaschy; ***M:*** Mark Mothersbaugh.

It's Tough to Be Famous **1932** Navy captain Scotty McClenahan (Fairbanks Jr.) saves his submarine crew from disaster and becomes an overnight hero. A private man hounded by celebrity and publicity, Scotty fears his new marriage to Janet (Brian) won't survive the intrusions. Said to be based on the fame that surrounded Charles Lindbergh. **79m/B; DVD.** Douglas Fairbanks, Jr.; Mary Brian; Walter Catlett; Oscar Apfel; J. Carrol Naish; ***D:*** Alfred E. Green; ***W:*** Robert Lord; ***C:*** Sol Polito; Byron Haskin.

Itty Bitty Titty Committee 1/2 **2007** Recent high school grad Anna (Diaz) has just been dumped by her first girlfriend and is working a monotonous job with no direction to her life. Then she meets guerilla grrl Sadie (Vicius) and her group of radical femmes who stage public art protests. Anna joins in, but the eventual romance between her and Sadie upsets a delicate balance within the group. **87m/C; DVD.** Melonie Diaz; Nicole Vicius; Carly Pope; Guinevere Turner; Jenny Shimizu; Deak Evgenikos; Lauren Mollica; Daniela Sea; Melanie Myron; ***D:*** Jamie Babbit; ***W:*** Tina Mabry; Abigail Shafran; ***C:*** Christine A. Maier.

Ivan the Terrible, Part 1 *Ivan Groznyi* **1944** Contemplative epic of Russia's first czar is a classic, innovative film from cinema genius Eisenstein. Visually stunning, with a fine performance by Cherkassov. Ivan's struggles to preserve his country is the main concern of the first half of Eisenstein's masterwork (which he originally planned as a trilogy). In Russian with English subtitles. **100m/B; VHS, DVD.** *RU* Nikolai Cherkassov; Lyudmila Tselikovskaya; Serafina Birman; Piotr Kadochnikev; ***D:*** Sergei Eisenstein; ***W:*** Sergei Eisenstein; ***C:*** Eduard Tisse; ***M:*** Sergei Prokofiev.

Ivan the Terrible, Part 2 1/2 *Ivan the Terrible, Part 2: The Boyars' Plot; Ivan Groznyi 2* **1946** Landed gentry conspire to dethrone the czar in this continuation of the innovative epic. More stunning imagery from master Eisenstein, who makes no false moves in this one. Slow going, but immensely rewarding. Russian dialogue with English subtitles; contains color sequences. **87m/B; VHS, DVD.** *RU* Nikolai Cherkassov; Lyudmila Tselikovskaya; Serafina Birman; Piotr Kadochnikev; ***D:*** Sergei Eisenstein; ***W:*** Sergei Eisenstein; ***C:*** Eduard Tisse; Andrei Moskvin; ***M:*** Sergei Prokofiev.

Ivanhoe **1952** Knights fight each other and woo maidens in this chivalrous romance derived from the Sir Walter Scott classic. Taylor is suitably noble, while Sanders is familiarly serpentine. Remade in 1982. **107m/C; VHS, DVD.** Robert Taylor; Elizabeth Taylor; Joan Fontaine; George Sanders; Finlay Currie; Felix Aylmer; ***D:*** Richard Thorpe; ***W:*** Marguerite Roberts; Noel Langley; ***C:*** Frederick A. (Freddie) Young; ***M:*** Miklos Rozsa.

Ivanhoe 1/2 **1982** A version of Sir Walter Scott's classic novel of chivalry and knighthood in 12th-century England. Remake of the 1953 film classic. **142m/C; VHS, DVD.** Anthony Andrews; James Mason; Lysette Anthony; Sam Neill; Olivia Hussey; Michael Hordern; Julian Glover; George Innes; Ronald Pickup; John Rhys-Davies; Chloe Franks; ***D:*** Douglas Camfield. **TV**

Ivanhoe **1997** TV miniseries version of Sir Walter Scott's epic tale of knights, chivalry, romance, and daring. Saxon knight Wilfred of Ivanhoe (Waddington), having fought for Richard the Lionheart (Edwards) during the Crusades, returns to England to battle the scheming Prince John (Brown) and sinister Grand Master of the Templars, Lucas De Beaumanoir (Lee) in order to regain his honor. His childhood sweetheart, Saxon heiress Rowena (Smurfit), is betrothed to another but Ivanhoe's also drawn to Jewish healer Rebecca (Lynch) as is scheming Knight Templar, Sir Brian Bois-Guilbert (Hinds). Lots of action. On six cassettes. **292m/C; VHS, DVD.** *GB* Steven Waddington; Susan Lynch; Ciaran Hinds; Victoria Smurfit; Ralph Brown; Rory Edwards; Ronald Pickup; David Horovitch; Trevor Cooper; Valentine Pelka; Nick Brimble; Jimmy Chisholm; Christopher Lee; Aden (John) Gillett; James Cosmo; Sian Phillips; Ciaran Madden; ***D:*** Stuart Orme; ***W:*** Deborah Cook; ***C:*** Clive Tickner; ***M:*** Colin Towns. **TV**

I've Always Loved You 1/2 *Concerto* **1946** The drama of love and jealousy explored in an extravagant production filled with classical music. **117m/C; DVD, Blu-Ray.** Philip Dorn; Catherine McLeod; Maria Ouspenskaya; Felix Bressart; ***D:*** Frank Borzage; ***W:*** Borden Chase; ***C:*** Gaetano Antonio "Tony" Gaudio.

I've Been Waiting for You 1/2 **1998 (PG-13)** California teen Sarah Zoltanne (Chalke), who has an interest in the occult, moves with her family to a New England town. Her fellow teens begin to believe that she's a witch out for revenge on the descendents of the townspeople who burned another witch, who had the same name. Then on Halloween, Sarah begins to see events beyond her knowledge or control. Based on the novel "Gallows Hill" by Lois Duncan. **90m/C; VHS, DVD.** Sarah Chalke; Soleil Moon Frye; Markie Post; Christian Campbell; Tom Dugan; ***D:*** Christopher Leitch; ***W:*** Duane Poole. **TV**

I've Got Your Number **1934** In this sassy comedy, telephone switchboard operator Marie (Blondell) gets fired after unwittingly doing a favor for gangster Nicky (Westcott). Telephone repairmen Terry (O'Brien) and Johnny (Jenkins) help her out by getting Marie a job with financier J.P. Schuyler (O'Neill) but Nicky thinks he can use this angle for his own profit. **70m/B; DVD.** Joan Blondell; Pat O'Brien; Allen Jenkins; Gordon Westcott; Henry O'Neill; Glenda Farrell; ***D:*** Ray Enright; ***W:*** Warren Duff; ***C:*** Arthur L. Todd.

I've Heard the Mermaids Singing **1987** Independent Canadian semi-satiric romantic comedy details the misadventures of a klutzy woman who suddenly obtains a desirable job in an art gallery run by a lesbian on whom she develops a crush. Good-natured tone helped considerably by McCarthy's winning performance. **81m/C; VHS, DVD.** *CA* Sheila McCarthy; Paule Baillargeon; Ann-Marie MacDonald; John Evans; ***D:*** Patricia Rozema; ***M:*** Mark Korven. Genie '88: Actress (McCarthy), Support. Actress (Baillargeon).

I've Loved You So Long *Il Y a Longtemps Que Je T'aime* **2008 (PG-13)** A quiet slice of life family drama from debuting director Claudel that features outstanding (but not showy) work from the female leads. Careworn and self-contained Juliette (Scott Thomas) has just moved in with her anxious younger sister Lea (Zylberstein) and her family. Everyone seems wary of each other but Claudel only lets the past be revealed in snippets: Juliette's estrangement is because she's spent 15 years in prison for murder. That fact is something no one cares to broadcast to curious friends in their provincial town. Both sisters slowly learn to trust while Juliette also struggles to make a full life for herself. French with subtitles. **115m/C; Blu-Ray, On Demand.** *FR GE* Elsa Zylberstein; Laurent Grevill; Frederic Pierrot; Kristin Scott Thomas; Serge Hazanavicius; Lise Segur; Jean-Claude Arnaud; Mouss Zouheyri; ***D:*** Philippe Claudel; ***W:*** Philippe Claudel; ***C:*** Jerome Almeras; ***M:*** Jean-Louis Aubert. British Acad. '08: Foreign Film.

The Ivory Handled Gun **1935** The Wolverine Kid wants Buck Ward (Jones) dead because the Kid's father, John Plunkett, was rejected by Buck's mother in favor of Buck's dad, Bill, who killed the interloper in a fight. Bill also happens to be in possession of one of Plunkett's ivory-handed guns and the Kid wants that back as well. In chapter 2 of "Gordon of Ghost City," Gordon and Mary Gray are observed by a mysterious, threatening figure and Mary gets caught in a stampede. **81m/B; VHS, DVD.** Buck Jones; Charlotte Wynters; Walter Miller; Frank Rice; Carl Stockdale; Joseph Girard; Madge Bellamy; ***D:*** Ray Taylor.

Ivory Tower **1997** Anthony Daytona (Van Horn) is a hotshot marketing exec in charge of launching a new computer product. But then his new boss arrives and suddenly not only the project but Anthony's career and the company itself is in jeopardy.

107m/C; VHS, DVD. Patrick Van Horn; James Wilder; Kari Wuhrer; Michael Ironside; Donna Pescow; Keith Coogan; Ian Buchanan; *D:* Darin Ferriola; *W:* Darin Ferriola; *C:* Maida Sussman.

Izzy & Moe 1/2 **1985** Carney and The Great One are reunited for the last time on screen as former vaudevillians who become federal agents and create havoc amid speak-easies and bathtub gin during Prohibition. Based on true stories. **92m/C; VHS, DVD.** Jackie Gleason; Art Carney; Cynthia Harris; Zohra Lampert; Drew Snyder; Dick Latessa; *D:* Jackie Cooper. **TV**

J. Edgar **2011 (R)** Driven by strong attention to detail and a fully committed performance from DiCaprio, director Eastwood's period piece comes off more like a shallow history lesson than a chapter of it brought to life. Covering large chunks of FBI Director J. Edgar Hoover's history, from his controversial private life to the formation of the bureau to the Lindbergh kidnapping to his general state of paranoia, the storytelling never gains traction, failing to find the emotion beneath the recreation. DiCaprio is impressive, particularly when not encumbered by old-age makeup, but he gets lost in the tedious script. **137m/C; DVD, Blu-Ray.** Leonardo DiCaprio; Naomi Watts; Armie Hammer; Josh(ua) Lucas; Dame Judi Dench; Lea Thompson; Dermot Mulroney; Jeffrey Donovan; Ed Westwick; Josh Hamilton; Jessica Hecht; Ken Howard; Geoffrey Pierson; Cheryl Lawson; Gunner Wright; David A. Cooper; *D:* Clint Eastwood; *W:* Dustin Lance Black; *C:* Tom Stern; *M:* Clint Eastwood.

J-Men Forever! **1979 (PG)** A spoof on early sci-fi/spy serials in which an alien takeover is attempted via rock-n-roll (your parents warned you). Employs an amusing technique of dubbing footage from dozens of Republic dramas intercut with new film featuring the "Firesign Theater" crew. **73m/B; VHS, DVD.** Peter Bergman; Phil(ip) Proctor; *D:* Richard Patterson.

Jabberwocky 1/2 **1977 (PG)** Pythonesque chaos prevails in the medieval cartoon kingdom of King Bruno the Questionable, who rules with cruelty, stupidity, lust and dust. Jabberwocky is the big dragon mowing everything down in its path until hero Palin decides to take it on. Uneven, but real funny at times. **104m/C; VHS, DVD, Blu-Ray.** *GB* Michael Palin; Max Wall; Deborah Fallender; Terry Jones; John Le Mesurier; Annette Badland; Warren Mitchell; Harry H. Corbett; David Prowse; Neil Innes; *D:* Terry Gilliam; *W:* Terry Gilliam; Charles Alverson; *C:* Terry Bedford; *M:* De Wolfe.

J'accuse! 1/2 *I Accuse!* **1919** Filmed before the WWI armistice, director (and soldier) Gance was able to use actual footage of trench warfare in his anti-war, love-triangle melodrama that features some stunning scenes. Francois Laurin (Severi-Mars) is married to the younger Edith (Dauvray), a marriage forced on her by her father (Desjardins). She loves, and is loved by, poet Jean Diaz (Joube), who is a pacifist until Marie is captured by German soldiers. Diaz enlists and winds up in the trenches where he and Laurin become friends. Much heartbreak follows as Diaz goes mad and has visions of dead soldiers rising out of their graves. **166m/B; Silent; DVD.** *FR* Romuald Joube; Maryse Dauvray; Severin Mars; Maxime Desjardins; Angele Guys; *D:* Abel Gance; *W:* Abel Gance; *C:* Marc Bujard; Leonce-Henri Burel; Maurice Foster.

Jack 1/2 **1996 (PG-13)** Ten-year-old Jack Powell (Williams) suffers from a rare genetic disorder that causes him to age at four times the normal rate so he looks like a 40-year-old. His family, fearing ridicule, has kept him isolated but since Jack's so lonely, they finally agree to let him attend school. This new fourth grader isn't the only one with a lot to learn. **111m/C; VHS, DVD.** Robin Williams; Bill Cosby; Diane Lane; Brian Kerwin; Fran Drescher; Michael McKean; Jennifer Lopez; Don Novello; Todd Bosley; *D:* Francis Ford Coppola; *W:* James DeMonaco; Gary Nadeau; *C:* John Toll; *M:* Michael Kamen.

Jack and Diane **2012 (R)** Stylized strangeness (with animated sequences by the Quay Brothers) revolving around the teen romance of British waif Diane and tomboyish Jack. Diane is staying in New York with her aunt for the summer and there's an instant attraction between the girls. Diane undergoes bizarre physical changes, apparently related to her emotional state. None of it really makes any sense nor will you likely care. **105m/C; DVD, Blu-Ray.** Riley Keough; Juno Temple; Cara Seymour; Kylie Minogue; Leo Fitzpatrick; Dane DeHaan; *D:* Bradley Rust Gray; *W:* Bradley Rust Gray; *C:* Anne Misawa.

Jack and Jill 1/2 **2011 (PG)** Unfortunate backslide for Sandler, pulling an Eddie Murphy, playing both Jack and his twin sister Jill. Jack is a successful ad exec living with his family in L.A., dreading the annual Thanksgiving visit from his nutty, loudmouth sister from the Bronx. She's nothing but annoying. The best bits involve Jack trying to close a Dunkin' Donuts commercial deal with the one and only Al Pacino. Sandler is best as Jack, the smart straight man he plays so well in the second half of his career. It's the first half of his career as Jill that doesn't know when to shut up. **93m/C; DVD, Blu-Ray.** Adam Sandler; Katie Holmes; Al Pacino; Elodie Tougne; Rohan Chand; Eugenio Derbez; David Spade; Nick Swardson; Tim Meadows; *D:* Dennis Dugan; *W:* Steve Koren; Robert Smigel; Ben Zook; *C:* Dean Cundey; *M:* Rupert Gregson-Williams. Golden Raspberries '11: Worst Actor (Sandler), Worst Actress (Sandler), Worst Director (Dugan), Worst Ensemble Cast, Worst Picture, Worst Remake/Sequel (Ripoff of "Glen or Glenda"), Worst Screenplay, Worst Support. Actor (Pacino), Worst Support. Actress (Spade).

Jack and Jill vs. the World **2008 (PG-13)** Predictable mix of romantic comedy with some tears thrown in. Control freak Jack (Prinze) is a New York ad exec who meets cute but naive newcomer Jill (Manning). Soon they are friends with benefits, negotiating their relationship with a generally light-hearted nine-rule manifesto. Except Jill breaks the honesty rule in a big way when she doesn't tell Jack that she has cystic fibrosis. **87m/C; DVD.** Freddie Prinze, Jr.; Taryn Manning; Peter Stebbings; Kelly Rowan; Vanessa Parise; Hannah Lochner; Robin Dunne; Charles Martin Smith; Robert Forster; *D:* Vanessa Parise; *W:* Vanessa Parise; *C:* Manfred Guthe; *M:* Jeremy Parise.

Jack and Sarah 1/2 **1995 (R)** Widowed London lawyer (Grant) hires American waitress (Mathis), to help raise his infant daughter Sarah. Complications arise because Amy has no child rearing skills and Jack's parents and in-laws disapprove of the whole situation. Performances are nice (especially the scene-stealing infants), and there's some fine moments combining tragedy with romance, but the plot is a little thin and the whole film is slow moving (it takes more than half the movie to get the three protagonists in place). An edited version is rated PG. **110m/C; VHS, DVD.** *GB* Richard E. Grant; Samantha Mathis; Ian McKellen; Dame Judi Dench; Cherie Lunghi; Eileen Atkins; Imogen Stubbs; *D:* Tim Sullivan; *W:* Tim Sullivan; *C:* Jean-Yves Escoffier; *M:* Simon Boswell.

Jack & the Beanstalk **1952** While baby-sitting, Lou falls asleep and dreams he's Jack in this spoof of the classic fairy tale. **78m/C; VHS, DVD.** Bud Abbott; Lou Costello; Buddy Baer; Dorothy Ford; Barbara Brown; William Farnum; *D:* Jean Yarbrough; *W:* Nathaniel Curtis; *C:* George Robinson; *M:* Heinz Roemheld.

Jack and the Beanstalk 1/2 **2009 (G)** In this modern update, Jack (Ford) has only one weekend left to perform a heroic deed before flunking out of fairytale school. So he trades his computer for some magic beans that grown into a beanstalk for Jack to climb and discover a magical world of possibilities. **94m/C; DVD, Blu-Ray.** Colin Ford; Chloë Grace Moretz; Gilbert Gottfried; Chevy Chase; Katey Sagal; Christopher Lloyd; Wallace Shawn; Madison Davenport; *V:* James Earl Jones; *D:* Gary J. Tunnicliffe; *W:* Flip Kobler; Cindy Marcus; *C:* Brian Baugh; *M:* Randy Miller. **VIDEO**

Jack and the Beanstalk: The Real Story 1/2 *Jim Henson's Jack and the Beanstalk* **2001** Attenuated and dull take on the familiar fairytale finds Modine's Jack a modern-day descendant of the Jack who stole the golden goose. That's how his family built an empire but it's payback time and Jack needs to climb that beanstalk and make reparations for his ancestor's crimes. **184m/C; VHS, DVD.** Matthew Modine; Vanessa Redgrave; Mia Sara; Jon Voight; Daryl Hannah; Richard Attenborough; *D:* Brian Henson; *W:* James V. Hart; Brian Henson. **TV**

Jack Be Nimble **1994 (R)** Siblings Jack (Arquette) and Dora (Kennedy) were separated as children and adopted by different families. Jack's family turns out to be sadistic and he suffers much abuse, until he enacts a violent revenge; Dora begins to hear voices and soon realizes it's Jack crying out to her. The duo finally reunite but between Jack's rage and Dora's telepathic abilities, life takes on further bizarre twists. Much psychological terror rather than gore. **93m/C; VHS, DVD.** *NZ* Alexis Arquette; Sarah Smuts-Kennedy; Bruno Lawrence; *D:* Garth Maxwell; *W:* Garth Maxwell; *C:* Donald Duncan; *M:* Chris Neal.

Jack Brown, Genius **1994 (PG-13)** Offbeat fantasy, written by Peter Jackson and Fran Walsh, concerns a medieval monk named Elmer (Devenie) who tried to fly (shades of Icarus) and wound up killing himself instead. Somehow Elmer briefly gets his spirit out of Hell and into the modern mind of inventor Jack Brown (Balme). Now he has to get Jack to invent a contraption that will allow man himself to fly so Elmer's soul can get into Heaven instead. **90m/C; DVD.** *NZ* Timothy Balme; Stuart Devenie; Marton Csokas; Nicola Murphy; Edward Campbell; *D:* Tony Hiles; *W:* Peter Jackson; Fran Walsh; *C:* Allen Guilford; *M:* Michelle Scullion.

The Jack Bull 1/2 **1999 (R)** Cusack's father adapted a 19th-century German novel, "Michael Kohlhaas" by Heinrich Von Kleist, into a 19th-century American western, set in Wyoming. Myrl Redding (Cusack) is a peaceful horse trader who demands justice when wealthy landowner Henry Ballard (Jones) beats two of Redding's horses and their Indian caretaker. Since Ballard has the local law in his pocket, Redding gets no satisfaction. Becoming obsessed, he decides to form a vigilante posse to get Ballard to pay for his actions. **120m/C; VHS, DVD.** John Cusack; L.Q. Jones; John Goodman; Rodney A. Grant; Miranda Otto; John C. McGinley; John Savage; Jay O. Sanders; Scott Wilson; Drake Bell; Glenn Morshower; Ken Pogue; *D:* John Badham; *W:* Richard (Dick) Cusack; *C:* Gale Tattersall; *M:* Lennie Niehaus. **CABLE**

Jack Frost **1997 (R)** Convicted serial killer Jack Frost (McDonald) mutates after accidental exposure to an experimental liquid DNA, becomes a killer snowman, and terrorizes a town preparing for the annual Snowman Festival. Snickering seasonal gore with a killer who uses icicles and a carrot nose to dispatch some of his latest victims. **89m/C; VHS, DVD, Blu-Ray.** Scott McDonald; Christopher Allport; F. William Parker; *D:* Michael Cooney; *W:* Michael Cooney; *C:* Dean Lent. **VIDEO**

Jack Frost **1998 (PG)** As emotionally realistic and cool as soap flake snow, alleged family feature has Keaton playing Jack Frost, a struggling musician who spends too much time away from wife Gabby (Preston) and son Charlie (Cross). He decides to blow off a Christmas Day gig to spend more time with the family, only to be killed on his way to their mountain cabin. One year later, forlorn Charlie makes a snowman, dresses it in his dead dad's duds, and blows a note on Jack's harmonica. Bingo! Now his dead father is back to life as a creepy-looking talking snowman! Keaton tries his best with the lame material; but with the use of four confused screenwriters, he didn't have a snowball's chance. Additional warning: Keaton sings. Not to be confused with the straight-to-video release of the same name about a murderous deranged talking snowman. **95m/C; VHS, DVD.** Michael Keaton; Kelly Preston; Joseph Cross; Mark Addy; Eli Marienthal; Dweezil Zappa; Henry Rollins; Andrew (Andy) Lawrence; Ahmet Zappa; Jeff Cesario; *D:* Troy Miller; *W:* Mark Steven Johnson; Steven L. Bloom; Jeff Cesario; Jonathan Roberts; *C:* Laszlo Kovacs; *M:* Trevor Rabin.

Jack Frost 2: Revenge of the Mutant Killer Snowman WOOF! **2000 (R)** Snowy horror is returned to his evil ways by a lab accident that also makes him impervious to heat, bullets, and antifreeze. So Jack decides to get revenge on Sheriff Sam (who defeated him previously), who just happens to be on vacation in a tropical paradise. But Chilly Boy doesn't have to worry about that. **91m/C; VHS, DVD.** Christopher Allport; David Allan Brooks; Chip Heller; Eileen Seeley; Adrienne Barbeau; *D:* Michael Cooney; *W:* Michael Cooney. **VIDEO**

Jack Goes Boating **2010 (R)** Hoffman makes his directorial debut in this adaptation of Bob Glaudini's play in which he also starred onstage. Insecure, overweight 40something New York limo driver Jack (Hoffman) is set up for romance with can't-catch-a-break Connie (Ryan) by his best married friends Clyde (Ortiz) and Lucy (Rubin-Vega). But both are inclined to take any romance very, very slowly, as shown by Jack's intention to give Connie a summer rowboat ride (it's now winter) as he does some other self-improvements using his feelings to finally make some changes. **90m/C; DVD, Blu-Ray.** John Ortiz; Philip Seymour Hoffman; Amy Ryan; Daphne Rubin-Vega; Thomas (Tom) McCarthy; *D:* Philip Seymour Hoffman; *W:* Bob Glaudini; *C:* W. Mott Hupfel, III; *M:* Grizzly Bear; Evan Lurie.

Jack Goes Home **2016 (R)** A suspenseful psychological thriller about one man learning unexpected truths about himself and his family after the sudden death of his father. Jack Thurlowe (Culkin) finds his world turned upside down after his parents are involved in a car crash. His father loses his life and his mother Teresa (Shaye) is seriously injured. When the grief-stricken Jack returns to his childhood home to take care of his mother, the revelations about his parents, family, friends and identity forever alter his perspective and impact his already shaky mental stability. **100m/C; DVD, Streaming, Download.** Rory Culkin; Lin Shaye; Britt Robertson; Nikki Reed; Natasha Lyonne; *D:* Thomas Dekker; *W:* Thomas Dekker; *C:* Austin F. Schmidt; *M:* Ceiri Torjussen.

Jack London 1/2 *The Adventures of Jack London; The Life of Jack London* **1944** Dramatizes London's most creative years during his careers as oyster pirate, prospector, war correspondent and author. Based on "The Book of Jack London" by Charmian London. **94m/B; VHS, DVD.** Michael O'Shea; Susan Hayward; Harry Davenport; Virginia Mayo; Frank Craven; *D:* Alfred Santell.

Jack London's The Call of the Wild 1/2 *The Call of the Wild: Dog of the Yukon* **1997 (PG)** Adaptation of Jack London's 1903 adventure story is told from the view of Buck, an intelligent St. Bernard-Labrador mix who's kidnapped from his California home. He's sold in the Yukon and eventually winds up with prospector John Thornton (Hauer) but Buck is increasingly drawn to running free. **90m/C; VHS, DVD.** Rutger Hauer; Luc Morrissette; Bronwyn Booth; *Nar:* Richard Dreyfuss; *D:* Peter Svatek; *W:* Graham Ludlow; *C:* Sylvain Brault; *M:* Alan Reeves. **CABLE**

Jack-O 1/2 **1995 (R)** Halloween nightmares in the small town of Oakmoor Crossing. When warlock Walter Machen (Carradine) was hung 100 years before, he invoked a demon creature to take his revenge. Now partyers, fooling around in the local cemetery, have stumbled onto horrific Jack-O's remains and manage to once again unleash the evil within. Cheesy grade-Z horror features old footage of deceased actors Carradine and Mitchell incorporated into what little plot there is. **90m/C; VHS, DVD.** Linnea Quigley; Ryan Latshaw; Cameron Mitchell; John Carradine; Dawn Wildsmith; Brinke Stevens; *D:* Steve Latshaw; *W:* Patrick Moran; *C:* Maxwell J. Beck; *M:* Jeff Walton.

The Jack of Diamonds 1/2 **1949** Good location shooting and a quick pace help move this routine Brit programmer along. Roger and Joan agree to lease their yacht to Alan Butler, who says he's after diamonds he lost when his transport was sunk during the evacuation of Belgium in 1940. But is he telling the truth? **65m/B; DVD.** *GB* Nigel Patrick; Cyril Raymond; Joan Carroll; Dolly Bouwmeester; John Basings; Darcy Conyers; *D:* Vernon Sewell; *W:* Nigel Patrick; Cyril Raymond; *C:* Moray Grant.

Jack of the Red Hearts **2015 (PG)** A family drama centered on a teenage runaway who cons a family into hiring her as a live-in companion for their autistic daughter, but both parties find their lives forever positively changed by her presence. Streetwise teen Jacquelyn "Jack" has (Robb) has run away from her probation officer, but wants to make money, avoid the law, and gain stability to remove her 11-year-old sister Coke (Caruso) from foster care. Using her hustling skills, Jack gets herself hired by a suburban family seeking a live-in caregiver for their 11-year-old nonverbal autistic daughter Glory (Richardson). To the surprise of everyone, Jack finds a close bond with Glory and a mother figure in Kay (Janssen). She also finds love with Glory's 17-year-old brother Robert (Broussard). When law enforcement finds Jack and the truth is revealed, she must choose between who she should save. **102m/C; DVD, Streaming, Download.** AnnaSophia Robb; Sophia Anne Caruso; Taylor Richardson; Famke Janssen; Israel Broussard; ***D:*** Janet Grillo; ***W:*** Jennifer Deaton; ***C:*** Hilary Spera; ***M:*** Danny Bensi; Saunder Jurriaans.

Jack O'Lantern 🦴 **2004 (R)** Inept, miniscule-budgeted horror flick finds Jack (Watkins) still suffering nightmares a year after a deadly car crash. Only his nightmares are now resulting in murder. Oh, and the monster has a jack o'lantern for a head. **94m/C; VHS, DVD.** David R. Watkins; Kevin L. Powers; Tracy Yarkoni; Justice Leak; Brian Avenet-Bradley; Ron McLellen; Sacha A. Dzuba; ***D:*** Ron McLellen; ***W:*** Ron McLellen; ***M:*** Sacha A. Dzuba. **VIDEO**

Jack Reacher 🦴🦴 **1/2** *One Shot* **2012 (PG-13)** Based on Lee Child's hit 2005 book One Shot, Tom Cruise's latest action vehicle is a modest success but the title character is an odd fit for the Oscar nominee and some tonal imbalances keep it from really clicking like the best multiplex fare from Mr. Cruise. A sniper is terrorizing a community but Jack Reacher (Cruise) is convinced the cops have the wrong guy. Cruise is miscast as a tough-as-nails, take-no-prisoners action hero, forgetting that he plays smooth better than he plays gruff. A strong supporting cast that includes Pike, Jenkins, and a beautifully-malevolent Werner Herzog keeps it entertaining enough, but just barely. **130m/C; DVD, Blu-Ray.** Tom Cruise; Rosamund Pike; Richard Jenkins; David Oyelowo; Werner Herzog; Alexia Fast; Robert Duvall; ***D:*** Christopher McQuarrie; ***W:*** Christopher McQuarrie; ***C:*** Caleb Deschanel; ***M:*** Joe Kraemer.

Jack Reacher: Never Go Back 🦴🦴 **2016 (PG-13)** The first Jack Reacher film was a smart, efficient thriller featuring a strong but silent performance from Tom Cruise. Cruise returns as Reacher, now a vigilante drifter framed for murder and forced on the run with Major Susan Turner (a miscast Smulders) and her daughter Samantha. Some of the action is still well-choreographed but there are flat attempts at comedy and the whole thing feels a bit off. It's never once as thrilling as the original. And who thought it was a good idea to turn the sequel into a family road trip movie? You really can never go back. **118m/C; DVD, Blu-Ray.** Tom Cruise; Cobie Smulders; Aldis Hodge; Danika Yarosh; Patrick Heusinger; ***D:*** Edward Zwick; ***W:*** Edward Zwick; Richard Wenk; Marshall Herskovitz; ***C:*** Oliver Wood; ***M:*** Henry Jackman.

Jack Ryan: Shadow Recruit 🦴🦴 **1/2 2014 (PG-13)** Another attempt to reboot the Tom Clancy franchise that started with "The Hunt for Red October" and now sees its fourth gentleman in Ryan's shoes in Pine. The first Ryan film not based on a Clancy book sees Ryan as a young CIA analyst caught up in a web after going undercover on Wall Street to stop terrorist activity at the source of its funding. Pine, the star of the "Star Trek" reboots, proves adequate enough here as an action star. Coupled with director Branagh, who also cast himself as the villain, and co-stars Knightley and Costner make for a reasonable degree of entertainment. **105m/C; DVD, Blu-Ray.** *US RU* Chris Pine; Keira Knightley; Kevin Costner; Colm Feore; Peter Andersson; Kenneth Branagh; ***D:*** Kenneth Branagh; ***W:*** Adam Cozad; David Koepp; ***C:*** Haris Zambarloukos; ***M:*** Patrick Doyle.

Jack Squad 🦴 **2008** Three women who have been lifelong friends find themselves devoid of cash and decide to drug and rob men after offering them sex. In what will come as a shock to no one they eventually rob someone working for a crime lord who is none too happy about the situation. **128m/C; DVD.** Dawnisha Halfkenny; Onira Tares; Patshreba Villegas; Benjamin Anderson; Michael Angelo; Tabitha Christopher; Qiana Nichol; Damian Oliver; Jerry Brown; Qiana Harps; Carol Warrick; Jerome N. Brooks; Jeronique Bartley; Jon Chaffin; Jevocas Green; Marcus Chase; Terrance Campbell; Louie Love; ***D:*** Simuel Rankins; ***W:*** Simuel Rankins; ***C:*** Christopher Peters.

Jack the Bear 🦴 **1/2 1993 (PG-13)** Exercise in misery centers on a father and his two sons, trying to pick up the pieces after the death of wife and mother Marcovicci. Dad DeVito is the host of a late-night horror show who's cuddly as a bear—when he's not drinking. While the talent and circumstances might have been enough to create a sensitive study, the emotion is completely overwrought by contrived plot twists, including a kidnapping by the local Nazi. TV's "thirtysomething" director Herskovitz creates an effect not unlike a cement block being dropped on a card house. Point made, but so much for subtlety. Based on a novel by Dan McCall. **98m/C; VHS, DVD.** Danny DeVito; Robert J. Steinmiller, Jr.; Miko Hughes; Gary Sinise; Art LaFleur; Andrea Marcovicci; Julia Louis-Dreyfus; Reese Witherspoon; ***D:*** Marshall Herskovitz; ***W:*** Steven Zaillian; ***C:*** Fred Murphy; ***M:*** James Horner.

Jack the Giant Killer 🦴🦴🦴 **1962 (G)** A young farmer joins a medieval princess on a journey to a distant convent. Along the way, they combat an evil wizard, dragons, sea monsters, and other mystical creatures, and are assisted by leprechauns, a dog, and a chimp. Generally considered a blatant rip-off of "The Seventh Voyage of Sinbad," the film nonetheless delivers plenty of fun and excitement. Jim Danforth of "Gumby" fame provided the stop-motion animation. **95m/C; VHS, DVD, Blu-Ray.** Kerwin Mathews; Judi Meredith; Torin Thatcher; Walter Burke; Roger Mobley; Barry Kelley; Don Beddoe; Anna Lee; Robert Gist; ***D:*** Nathan "Jerry" Juran; ***W:*** Nathan "Jerry" Juran; Orville H. Hampton; ***C:*** David S. Horsley; ***M:*** Paul Sawtell; Bert Shefter.

Jack the Giant Killer 🦴 *The Giant Killer* **2013** A giant beanstalk brings Jack (Atkins) to a land in the clouds, but all the giants from the old fairy tale have been killed by his father. As a consequence, giant reptilian beasts are multiplying and a witch who wants revenge on the world leads them to Earth. **90m/C; DVD, Blu-Ray.** Jane March; Ben Cross; Jamie Atkins; Harry Dyer; Vicki Glover; ***D:*** Mark Atkins; ***W:*** Mark Atkins; ***C:*** Mark Atkins; ***M:*** Chris Ridenhour; Andrew Morgan Smith. **VIDEO**

Jack the Giant Slayer 🦴🦴 **2013 (PG-13)** Ten years after medieval commoner Jack (Hoult) climbed the beanstalk and saved the day, he's again called to duty in the name of a damsel in distress (Tomlinson) not realizing she's Princess Isabelle. The king and his men, led by valiant knight Elmont (McGregor), recruit Jack to once again ascend the beanstalk and go head-to-head with hordes of grotesque CGI giants and overthrow the evil captor Roderick (Tucci). With a title hinting at some kind of brutal onslaught, the entire undertaking feels uninspired and tame. An obvious attempt to cash-in on the 3D steroid fairy tale trend. **114m/C; DVD, Blu-Ray.** Nicholas Hoult; Eleanor Tomlinson; Stanley Tucci; Ian McShane; Bill Nighy; Ewan McGregor; Eddie Marsan; Ewen Bremner; ***D:*** Bryan Singer; ***W:*** Darren Lemke; Christopher McQuarrie; ***C:*** Newton Thomas (Tom) Sigel; ***M:*** John Ottman.

Jack the Ripper 🦴🦴 **1960** An American detective joins Scotland Yard in tracking down the legendary and elusive Jack the Ripper. More gory than most. The last scene is in color. **88m/B; VHS, DVD, Blu-Ray.** *GB* Lee Patterson; Betty McDowall; Barbara Burke; John Le Mesurier; George Rose; ***D:*** Monty Berman; Robert S. Baker; ***M:*** Stanley Black.

Jack the Ripper 🦴🦴 *Der Dirnenmoerder von London* **1976 (R)** The inimitable Kinski assumes the role of the most heinous criminal of modern history—Jack the Ripper. **82m/C; VHS, DVD.** *SI GE* Klaus Kinski; Josephine Chaplin; Herbert (Fuchs) Fux; Ursula von Wiese; Lina Romay; Andreas Mannkopff; ***D:*** Jess (Jesus) Franco; ***W:*** Jess (Jesus) Franco; ***C:*** Peter Baumgartner.

Jack the Ripper 🦴🦴🦴 **1988** Another retelling of the life of the legendary serial killer. Caine is the Scotland Yard inspector who tracks down the murderer. Ending is based on recent evidence found by director/co-writer Wickes. Extremely well done TV film. **200m/C; VHS, DVD.** Michael Caine; Armand Assante; Ray McNally; Susan George; Jane Seymour; Lewis Collins; Ken Bones; ***D:*** David Wickes; ***W:*** David Wickes. **TV**

The Jackal 🦴🦴 **1/2 1997 (R)** The plot has more holes than Swiss cheese but thanks to a pro cast this film manages to be at least a workmanlike thriller. Willis stars as a killer-for-hire known only as "The Jackal." His latest employer, a Russian gangster, wants revenge for FBI interference in his business, and the Jackal's target is apparently the FBI's Director. Few know what the Jackal looks like and the most available is Declan Mulqueen (Gere), an IRA gunman imprisoned in the U.S. He's given a deal by good FBI guy Preston (Poitier) and the hunt is on. Unfortunately, the Jackal's elaborate preparations don't raise the tension, though they do provide some gross-out moments. The end game (in the D.C. subway) between the Jackal and Mulqueen provides a satisfying conclusion and Willis does excell as the ice-cold killer. Started off as a heavily reworked version of the 1973 assassination thriller "The Day of the Jackal" but most of the associations have been cut. **124m/C; VHS, DVD, Blu-Ray.** Bruce Willis; Richard Gere; Sidney Poitier; Diane Venora; Mathilda May; Stephen Spinella; John Cunningham; J.K. Simmons; Tess Harper; Richard Lineback; Jack Black; David Hayman; Steve Bassett; ***D:*** Michael Caton-Jones; ***W:*** Chuck Pfarrer; ***C:*** Karl Walter Lindenlaub; ***M:*** Carter Burwell.

The Jackals 🦴🦴 **1967** Six bandits threaten miner Price and his granddaughter in order to get his gold. Set in South Africa. **105m/C; VHS, DVD.** Vincent Price; Diana Ivarson; Robert Gunner; Bob Courtney; Patrick Mynhardt; ***D:*** Robert D. Webb; ***W:*** W.R. Burnett.

Jackass 3D 🦴🦴 **2010 (R)** Older but no wiser, Knoxville and his buddies are back with their stupidity fully exposed in 3D as they humiliate themselves nonstop. Puke, poop, and male genitalia are on display although most of the stunts are just variations on what's gone on in the previous two flicks. **94m/C; Blu-Ray, On Demand.** Johnny Knoxville; Bam Margera; Steve-O; Ryan Dunn; Jason "Wee Man" Acuna; Chris Pontius; Preston Lacy; ***D:*** Jeff Tremaine; ***W:*** Preston Lacy; ***C:*** Dimitry Elyashkavich.

Jackass Number Two 🦴🦴 **2006 (R)** With the TV series iced, the Jackass posse is back with four years' worth of new gags, stunts, and bad ideas. There's less talk, more shock and if you're familiar with the curiously charismatic Knoxville, you'll know what to expect—men are stupid and eager to risk their body parts in even more insane contests. By the way, the title is not just an indication that it's a sequel, it's a literal warning of what to expect. **95m/C; DVD, Blu-Ray.** Johnny Knoxville; Bam Margera; Chris Pontius; Ryan Dunn; Steve-O; Dave England; Preston Lacy; Ehren McGhehey; ***D:*** Jeff Tremaine; ***W:*** Preston Lacy; Sean Cliver; ***C:*** Dimitry Elyashkavich; Lance Bangs; Rick Kosick.

Jackass Presents: Bad Grandpa 🦴🦴 **2013 (R)** Who would have imagined a world where spin-offs of the Jackass franchise, started so many years ago on MTV and transitioning to three hit films, would even exist? The Jackass boys show no signs of slowing down as Johnny Knoxville expands the universe of his juvenile stunt work by taking one of the characters from his films and show and giving him his own twisted spotlight. Knoxville dresses up like an old man and gets into trouble with a young kid at his side--the arrogance being that we let old people and children get away with more than average adults. Funny but stupid. **92m/C; DVD, Blu-Ray.** Johnny Knoxville; Jackson Nicoll; Gregory Harris; Georgina Cates; ***D:*** Jeff Tremaine; ***W:*** Johnny Knoxville; Jeff Tremaine; ***C:*** Lance Bangs; ***M:*** Sam Spiegel.

Jackass: The Movie 🦴🦴 **2002 (R)** The ultimate critic-proof movie. Those who love the TV show will also love the fact that these guys can swear and be as gross as they wanna be, and indulge in even bigger, dumber, if not always more elaborate stunts. Those who think the whole thing is stupid and childish will continue to think so. In case you don't know the drill, Johnny Knoxville and his crew perform homemade or made-up stunts to a) get laughs, b) get a reaction out of people, c) gross out bystanders, d) see if they can be done, and e) all of the above. Watch it to bring out your inner 12-year-old with ADHD. **87m/C; VHS, DVD.** Johnny Knoxville; Bam Margera; Steve "Steve-O" Glover; Chris Pontius; Ryan Dunn; Jason "Wee Man" Acuna; ***D:*** Jeff Tremaine; ***C:*** Dimitry Elyashkavich.

Jacked Up 🦴 **1/2** *Jacked* **2001 (R)** Bleak, depressing film about a young gangsta wannabe who accidentally kills a man and then helps his victim's family out of remorse. Of course he doesn't tell them he's responsible for the man's death, which will cause complications when the daughter falls for him and his old gang comes calling. **96m/C; DVD.** RonReaco Lee; Alexis Fields; Anna Maria Horsford; Bizzy Bone; T-Low; Tweety; Brandon Thomas; Andrew Ford; Bobbie Bowman; Tenika Early; Toni Jones; Pamela Lowery; Roderick Paulette; ***D:*** Timothy Wayne Folsome; ***W:*** Timothy Wayne Folsome; ***C:*** Wayne Sells.

The Jacket 🦴🦴 **1/2 2005 (R)** A gulf vet (Brody) is falsely convicted of murder. Having no memory of the crime, he's sentenced to a mental institution instead of prison. The chief psychiatrist's therapy consists of drugs, a straitjacket, and sensory deprivation in a morgue drawer. Vet's reaction to this is, of course, to time-travel, allowing him to confront the ghosts of his present in the future and effect changes for the general good of all. Interesting premise, but handled with a lead foot and little originality. Think "Jacob's Ladder" meets "Twelve Monkeys" meets "One Flew Over the Cuckoo's Nest." Fairly entertaining with good performances by solid cast. **102m/C; DVD.** Adrien Brody; Keira Knightley; Kris Kristofferson; Jennifer Jason Leigh; Kelly Lynch; Brad Renfro; Daniel Craig; MacKenzie Phillips; ***D:*** John Maybury; ***W:*** Massy Tadjedin; ***C:*** Peter Deming; ***M:*** Brian Eno.

Jackie 🦴🦴 **2012** 30-something Dutch twin sisters Sofie and Daan learn that their American birth mother, Jackie, has been in an accident. So they come to the U.S. and find her in the hospital, needing a ride to a rehabilitation facility. This leads to hopping into an RV on a 500-mile road trip across New Mexico accompanied by a predictable amount of emotional clashes and bonding along their route. Dutch and English with subtitles. **100m/C; Streaming.** *NL* Holly Hunter; Carice van Houten; Jelka van Houten; ***D:*** Antoinette Beumer; ***W:*** Marnie Blok; Karin van Holst Pellekaan; ***C:*** Danny Elsen.

Jackie 🦴🦴🦴 **2016 (R)** Portman gives the best performance of her career as Jackie Kennedy, captured in the days and weeks after the death of John F. Kennedy. Jumping back and forth between several key conversations in this period, director Larrain's unique approach to the biopic details a woman who knew that she was writing the final chapter of her husband's legacy. While making sure JFK's story ended the way she wanted, she was also dealing with unimaginable grief, and doing so in the glare of a blinding, international spotlight. Larrain's style is mesmerizing as we watch a woman close Camelot forever. **100m/C; DVD, Blu-Ray.** Natalie Portman; Peter Sarsgaard; Greta Gerwig; Billy Crudup; John Hurt; ***D:*** Pablo Larrain; ***W:*** Noah Oppenheim; ***C:*** Stephane Fontaine; ***M:*** Mica Levi. British Acad. '16: Costume Des.

Jackie Bouvier Kennedy Onassis 🦴 **1/2 2000** CBS TV miniseries covers the high points of a typical Jackie bio with Whalley shallow in the title role. Most of the story is focused on her marriage to JFK (Matheson) and her attempts to fit in with the Kennedy clan. Jackie tires of being a presidential widow constantly in the public eye and seeks the questionable security of being the trophy wife of wealthy Greek Aristotle Onassis (Hall) instead. **113m/C; DVD.** Joanne Whalley; Tim Matheson; Philip Baker Hall; Tom Skerritt; Diane Baker; Andrew McCarthy; Frances Fisher; Fred Ward; ***D:*** David Burton Morris; ***W:*** Eric Overmyer; Tina Andrews; ***C:*** Paul Elliott; ***M:*** Joseph Conlan. **TV**

Jackie Brown **1997 (R)** Tarantino finally climbs back into the director's chair with his leisurely but satisfying adaptation of Elmore Leonard's "Rum Punch." No, it's not "Pulp Fiction," but it could do for Pam Grier what "Pulp" did for John Travolta. Grier stars as out-of-luck-and-options stewardess Jackie Brown, who runs money to Mexico for ruthless arms dealer Ordell (Jackson). Busted on one of her errands, she comes up with an intricate plan to get out from under, hopefully with the money and without getting caught or killed. Slower and less bloody than Quentin fans are used to, but as usual, he gets killer performances from everybody. Cool dialogue and chronological shifts are again key ingredients, along with a hightened sense of character development. Fonda and De Niro make the most of small (but crucial) roles, but it's Forster (another '70s whatever-happened-to refugee) who provides the standout performance. The look and feel of the movie reflects the dingy world it inhabits, as well as Tarantino's love of '70s blaxploitation flicks. **155m/C; VHS, DVD, Blu-Ray.** Pam Grier; Robert Forster; Samuel L. Jackson; Robert De Niro; Bridget Fonda; Michael Keaton; Michael Bowen; Chris Tucker; Lisa Gay Hamilton; Tommy (Tiny) Lister; Hattie Winston; Aimee Graham; Sid Haig; ***D:*** Quentin Tarantino; ***W:*** Quentin Tarantino; ***C:*** Guillermo Navarro; ***M:*** Mary Ramos; Michelle Kuznetsky.

Jackie Chan's First Strike *First Strike; Police Story 4* **1996 (PG-13)** Plot, schmot. The human hurricane that is Jackie Chan is once again amazing in this kung-fu comedy homage to '60s James Bond movies. Half Bruce Lee and half Charlie Chaplin, Chan reprises the role of the Hong Kong supercop named Jackie, who is this time loaned out by his superior officer "Uncle Bill" (Tung) to the CIA. He is sent to the Ukraine to spy on a beautiful young woman involved in smuggling nuclear weapons along with rogue CIA agent Tsui (Lou). He follows the villains to Australia, where he secures justice, peace, and sharp blows to the head. Enough about the plot. Listen to this! He holds bad guys at bay by whirling an aluminum stepladder like it was a drum major's baton! He kicks somebody off of a second story ledge while on stilts! He sings and dances while wearing koala bear underwear! Dubbed in English. **87m/C; VHS, DVD.** *CH* Jackie Chan; Bill Tung; Jackson Lou; Annie (Chen Chun) Wu; Jouri (Yuri) Petrov; Grishajeva Nonna; ***D:*** Stanley Tong; ***W:*** Stanley Tong; Greg Mellott; Nick Tramontane; Elliot Tong; ***C:*** Jingle Ma; ***M:*** J. Peter Robinson.

Jackie Chan's The Myth **1/2** *San wa; Shen hua; The Myth; Time Breaker; Titanium Rain* **2005 (PG-13)** Jack (Chan) is an archeologist who travels the world looking for a gemstone that supposedly has the power to defy gravity. At night in his dreams he is the loyal general to China's first emperor (whose tomb his studies lead him to find). The truth quickly becomes obvious in a plot fans of Chinese cinema will recognize as the usual romance-via-reincarnation theme. **118m/C; DVD.** *CH* Jackie Chan; Hee-seon Kim; Tony Leung Ka Fai; Mallika Sherawat; Ken Lo; Rongguang Yu; ***D:*** Stanley Tong; ***W:*** Stanley Tong; Hai-Shu Li; Hui-Ling Wang; ***C:*** Wing-Hung Wong; ***M:*** Garry Chase; Nathan Wang.

Jackie Chan's Who Am I **1/2** *Who Am I; Ngo Hai Sui* **1998 (PG-13)** Jackie (Chan) is recruited by the CIA to join a team of commandos leading a raid on a secret weapons research lab in South Africa. The team hijack a piece of highly explosive experimental material and are betrayed by their leader. Only Jackie survives but he's got amnesia. When he finally returns home, he's still wondering who he is—an important question since he's being pursued by the bad guys who want him to stay dead. **108m/C; VHS, DVD.** *CH* Jackie Chan; Ed Nelson; Ron Smerczak; Michelle Ferre; Mirai Yamamoto; ***D:*** Jackie Chan; Benny Chan; ***W:*** Jackie Chan; Lee Reynolds; Susan Chan; ***C:*** Hang-Seng Poon; ***M:*** Nathan Wang.

Jackie, Ethel, Joan: The Kennedy Women **1/2** *Jackie, Ethel, Joan: Women of Camelot* **2001** TV miniseries focuses on the Kennedy wives: Jackie (Hennessy), Ethel (Holly), and Joan (Stefanson) rather than on their husbands and the toll that politics and the spotlight took on them as individuals. Sudser follows the period from 1960 to 1980; based on the bestseller by J. Randy Taraborrelli. **172m/C; VHS, DVD.** Jil-l(ian) Hennessey; Lauren Holly; Leslie Stefanson; Daniel Hugh-Kelly; Robert Knepper; Matt Letscher; Harve Presnell; Charmion King; Thom Christopher; ***D:*** Larry Shaw; ***W:*** David Stevens; ***C:*** Frank Byers; ***M:*** Martin Davich. **TV**

The Jackie Robinson Story **1950** Chronicles Robinson's rise from UCLA to his breakthrough as the first black man to play baseball in the major league. Robinson plays himself; the film deals honestly with the racial issues of the time. **76m/B; VHS, DVD.** Jackie Robinson; Ruby Dee; Minor Watson; Louise Beavers; Richard Lane; Harry Shannon; Joel Fluellen; Ben Lessy; ***D:*** Alfred E. Green; ***W:*** Arthur Mann; Lawrence Taylor; ***C:*** Ernest Laszlo; ***M:*** David Chudnow.

Jackie's Back **1/2 1999 (R)** Mockumentary follows the stumbling comeback of forgotten pop diva, Jackie Washington (Lewis). Spoiled and temperamental, Jackie is followed by a supersilicious British documentary filmmaker, Edward Whatsett St. John (Curry), as she prepares for a big concert as everything is in chaos around her. Flashbacks reflect on Jackie's early career. **91m/C; VHS, DVD.** Jenifer Lewis; Tim Curry; Tangie Ambrose; Whoopi Goldberg; David Hyde Pierce; Tom Arnold; Julie Hagerty; JoBeth Williams; Dolly Parton; Grace Slick; Liza Minnelli; ***D:*** Robert Townsend; ***W:*** Mark Brown; Dee La Duke; ***C:*** Charles Mills; ***M:*** Marc Shaiman. **CABLE**

Jacknife **1989 (R)** The well-crafted story of a Vietnam veteran who visits his old war buddy and tries to piece together what's happened to their lives since their homecoming. During his visit he encounters anger and hostility from the other veteran, and tenderness from his friend's sister. A masterfully acted, small-scale drama, adapted by Stephen Metcalfe from his play. **102m/C; VHS, DVD.** Robert De Niro; Kathy Baker; Ed Harris; Loudon Wainwright, III; Charles S. Dutton; ***D:*** David Hugh Jones; ***W:*** Stephen Metcalfe; ***M:*** Bruce Broughton.

The Jackpot **1950** An average Joe wins a bushel of money from a radio quiz show but can't pay the taxes. Maybe that was funny before the age of read-my-lips economics, but the all-star cast doesn't deliver on its promise. Lang, noted for mostly mediocre pictures, went on to direct "The King and I." **87m/C; DVD.** James Stewart; Natalie Wood; Barbara Hale; James Gleason; Fred Clark; Patricia Medina; ***D:*** Walter Lang; ***W:*** Phoebe Ephron; Henry Ephron; ***C:*** Joseph LaShelle; ***M:*** Lionel Newman.

Jackpot **2001 (R)** Brothers Mark and Michael Polish follow up their critically lauded debut "Twin Falls Idaho" with this road tale of karaoke and crackpots. Sunny Holiday (Gries) is an aspiring country singer riding the back roads of the remote West with his manager Les (Morris), trying to break into Nashville via the untraveled karaoke route. Neither one seems to realize the futility of his dreams, but Bobbi (Hannah), the wife he's abandoned with their young child, does. The "Jackpot" of the title is his dream of making it big, the way he hopes to support his family (he sends them a lottery ticket each week in lieu of child support) and the name of the Nevada town where he hopes to be discovered. Tries way too hard to be arty in a folksy "look at these eccentric characters" way, but it's not without its own weird charm. **100m/C; VHS, DVD.** Jon(athan) Gries; Garrett Morris; Daryl Hannah; Peggy Lipton; Adam Baldwin; Mac Davis; Crystal Bernard; Anthony Edwards; ***V:*** Patrick Bauchau; ***D:*** Michael Polish; ***W:*** Michael Polish; Mark Polish; ***C:*** M. David Mullen; ***M:*** Stuart Matthewman.

Jackson County Jail **1/2 1976 (R)** While driving cross-country, a young woman is robbed, imprisoned, and raped by a deputy, whom she kills. Faced with a murder charge, she flees, with the law in hot pursuit. Also known by its later remade-for-TV name, "Outside Chance," this is a minor cult film. **84m/C; VHS, DVD.** Yvette Mimieux; Tommy Lee Jones; Robert Carradine; Severn Darden; Howard Hesseman; Mary Woronov; Ed Marshall; Cliff Emmich; Betty Thomas; ***D:*** Michael Miller; ***W:*** Donald Stewart; ***C:*** Bruce Logan; ***M:*** Loren Newkirk.

The Jacksons: An American Dream **1/2 1992** Miniseries covering the career of the Jackson 5, the working-class family from Gary, Indiana, who became a celebrated show business success. The series begins with the courtship of Joseph and Katherine Jackson and ends with the group's farewell tour in 1984, covering both family and career turmoils. Simplistic, glossy biography. **225m/C; VHS, DVD.** Lawrence-Hilton Jacobs; Angela Bassett; Wylie Draper; Angel Vargas; Jacen Wilkerson; Terrence Howard; Jason Weaver; Jermaine Jackson, II; Billy Dee Williams; Vanessa L(ynne) Williams; Holly Robinson Peete; Margaret Avery; ***D:*** Karen Arthur. **TV**

Jacob **1/2 1994** Jacob (Modine), second son of Isaac (Ackland), tricks his father into giving him the blessing meant for eldest son Esau (Bean). Jacob is forced to run away to his Uncle Laban (Giannini), where he promptly falls in love with his cousin Rachel (Boyle). But Laban tricks Jacob into marrying eldest daughter Leah (Aubrey), before allowing his marriage to Rachel. Finally, Jacob settles on his own land with his wives and children (who will become the tribes of Israel). Diginified retelling of the biblical story; filmed on location in Morocco. **120m/C; VHS, DVD.** Matthew Modine; Lara Flynn Boyle; Sean Bean; Juliet Aubrey; Giancarlo Giannini; Joss Ackland; Irene Papas; Christoph Waltz; ***D:*** Peter Hall; ***W:*** Lionel Chetwynd; ***M:*** Marco Frisina. **CABLE**

Jacob **2011** When his little sister is murdered by their drunken step-father, autistic Jacob (Dylan Horne) goes on an unstoppable killing spree. **90m/C; DVD, Blu-Ray.** Grace Powell; Dylan Home; Krystyn Caldwell; Larry Wade Carrell; Leo D. Wheeler; ***D:*** Larry Wade Carrell; ***W:*** Larry Wade Carrell; ***C:*** Stacy Davidson; ***M:*** Iain Kelso. **VIDEO**

Jacob the Liar *Jakob der Lugner* **1974 (PG-13)** When Jacob Heim is stopped for being out of the Jewish ghetto after curfew, he is sent to see the police commander. On the police radio, he hears that the Red Army is advancing and he returns to the ghetto to pass along the news, pretending that he heard it on his own hidden radio. Soon, Jacob is inventing news reports to give his fellow Jews hope. German with subtitles. A sentimental American remake came out in 1999. **101m/C; VHS, DVD.** *GE* Armin Mueller-Stahl; Vlastimil Brodsky; Erwin Geschonneck; Henry Hubchen; Blanche Kommerell; Manuela Simon; ***D:*** Frank Beyer; ***W:*** Jurek Becker; ***C:*** Gunter Marczinkowski.

Jacob Two Two Meets the Hooded Fang **1/2 1999** Edgy kids fantasy based on the book by Mordecai Richler. Jacob (Morrow) is nicknamed Jacob Two Two because he repeats everything since no one every listens to him the first time he says something. Because of this Jacob gets into unexpected trouble when shopping at the corner store, runs into the store basement, and knocks himself out in the darkness. Jacob dreams he's now on trial and is sentenced to Slimers' Island, which is run by a bizarre creature called the Hooded Fang (Busey) and his equally strange henchmen. **96m/C; VHS, DVD.** *CA* Max Morrow; Gary Busey; Miranda Richardson; Ice-T; Mark McKinney; Maury Chaykin; ***D:*** George Bloomfield; ***W:*** Tim Burns; ***C:*** Gerald Packer; ***M:*** Jono Grant.

Jacob's Ladder **1/2 1990 (R)** A man struggles with events he experienced while serving in Vietnam. Gradually, he becomes unable to separate reality from the strange, psychotic world into which he increasingly lapses. His friends and family try to help him before he's lost forever. Great story potential is flawed by too many flashbacks, leaving the viewer more confused than the characters. **116m/C; VHS, DVD, Blu-Ray.** Tim Robbins; Elizabeth Pena; Danny Aiello; Matt Craven; Pruitt Taylor Vince; Jason Alexander; Patricia Kalember; Ving Rhames; Eriq La Salle; Macaulay Culkin; Lewis Black; ***D:*** Adrian Lyne; ***W:*** Bruce Joel Rubin; ***C:*** Jeffrey L. Kimball; ***M:*** Maurice Jarre.

Jada **1/2 2008 (PG)** Uninspired though well-meaning drama about a woman's faith in troubled times. After Jada's husband dies, she and her two teenage children are forced to move into the gang-run projects. Jada turns to the church for guidance and to helpful ex-con Simon as well. **89m/C; DVD.** Siena Goines; Rockmond Dunbar; Jennifer Freeman; Jason Weaver; Clifton Powell; ***D:*** Robert Johnson; ***W:*** Daniel Chavez; ***C:*** Christopher Gosch. **VIDEO**

Jade **1/2 1995 (R)** Sleazy whodunnit scraped from the bottom of the Eszterhas barrel (and it's a deep one) has hot-shot San Francisco Assistant D.A. David Corelli (Caruso) tracking a trail of pubic hairs across San Francisco. Seems he's caught up in the murder of a millionaire that points to his ex-lover, psychologist Katrina Gavin (Fiorentino), as the killer. Oh yeah, she's also a kinky call girl of choice to California's rich and famous, and happens to be married to Corelli's best friend (Palminteri). Psycho-thriller with little of either injects lots of lurid details (and a car chase scene that Friedkin has done much better elsewhere) in an attempt to curtail boredom; it doesn't work. Combine it with "Showgirls" for the No Self-Respect Film Festival, then go to confession. **94m/C; VHS, DVD.** David Caruso; Linda Fiorentino; Chazz Palminteri; Michael Biehn; Richard Crenna; Kenneth King; Angie Everhart; ***D:*** William Friedkin; ***W:*** Joe Eszterhas; ***C:*** Andrzej Bartkowiak; ***M:*** James Horner.

The Jade Mask **1/2 1945** Chan discovers a murderer and his wife use puppets and masks to make it appear their victims are still alive. Another in the detective series with nothing noteworthy about it. Luke, the brother of actor Keye Luke, takes on the role of Chan's Number Four son. **66m/B; VHS, DVD.** Sidney Toler; Mantan Moreland; Edwin Luke; Janet Warren; Hardie Albright; Edith Evanson; ***D:*** Phil Rosen.

Jade Warrior *Jadesoturi* **2006 (PG-13)** Cross-cultural martial arts mythology from Finland and China. A blacksmith in modern-day Finland, Kai (Eronen) is asked by anthropologist Berg (Peltola) to unlock a metal box he believes is an ancient magical artifact that has been discovered in the ice alongside two mummified bodies. The story's rather convoluted and unclear (unless you know the folklore it's based on) but director Annila's combo of swordplay and legend generally works well. Mandarin and Finnish with subtitles. **105m/C; DVD.** *FI CH* Tommi Eronen; Markku Peltola; Jingchu Zhang; Krista Kosonen; Hao Dang; Elle Kull; Taisheng ("Cheng Tai Shen") Cheng; ***D:*** Antti-Jussi Annila; ***W:*** Antti-Jussi Annila; Petri Jokiranta; ***C:*** Henri Blomberg; ***M:*** Kimmon Pohjonen; Samuli Kosminen.

Jaded **1/2 1996 (R)** Seemingly innocent Meg (Gugino) is befriended by a couple of uninhibited babes (Kihlstedt, Thompson) at the local bar and goes with them to a party where she's sexually assaulted. The two women are accused of rape and the case goes to trial but Meg's past secrets come to light and things don't seem so cut-and-dried anymore. The box art is the real tease since the film isn't the erotic thriller it might appear to be. **95m/C; VHS, DVD.** Carla Gugino; Anna Thomson; Rya Kihlstedt; Christopher McDonald; Lorraine Toussaint; ***D:*** Caryn Krooth. **VIDEO**

Jafar Panahi's Taxi *Taxi; Taxi Tehran* **2015** Jafar Panahi has been imprisoned in his own home, denied the right to make films in his own country of Iran by a dictatorial government that sees his work as dangerous. And yet he's made three films since being put under house arrest. His latest is also his best, as Panahi drives around Tehran, filming both himself and his customers as they discuss everything from bootleg films to torture. Taxi has the structure of a documentary, but one quickly realizes that Panahi's passengers are scripted actors as well. The result is a daring act of cinematic defiance, a film that shouldn't exist taking place all over the country's biggest city. **82m/C.** *IA* Jafar Panahi; ***D:*** Jafar Panahi; ***W:*** Jafar Panahi; ***C:*** Jafar Panahi.

JAG **1/2 1995** TV pilot episode features Navy pilot-turned-lawyer Lt. Harmon Rabb, Jr. (Elliott) assigned to investigate the case of a young female pilot who disappears from an aircraft carrier. Seems some of her fellow sailors resented having women on board so was it an accident or murder? JAG stands for the office of the Judge Advocate General, whose Navy lawyers serve as investigators, prosecutors, and defense attorneys. **94m/C; VHS, DVD.** David James Elliott; Andrea Parker; Terry O'Quinn; John Roselius; Katie Rich; Scott Jaeck; Patrick Laborteaux; Cliff DeYoung; Kevin Dunn; ***D:*** Donald P. Bellisario;

W: Donald P. Bellisario; *C:* Thomas Del Ruth; *M:* Bruce Broughton. **TV**

The Jagged Edge ½ **1985 (R)** The beautiful wife of successful newspaper editor, Jack Forester, is killed and the police want to point the guilty finger at Jack. Attorney Teddy Barnes is brought in to defend him and accidentally falls in love. Taut murder mystery will keep you guessing "whodunit" until the very end. **108m/C; VHS, DVD.** Jeff Bridges; Glenn Close; Robert Loggia; Peter Coyote; John Dehner; Leigh Taylor-Young; Lance Henriksen; James Karen; Karen Austin; Michael Dorn; Guy Boyd; Marshall Colt; Louis Giambalvo; *D:* Richard Marquand; *W:* Joe Eszterhas; *C:* Matthew F. Leonetti; *M:* John Barry.

Jaguar Lives **1979 (PG)** A high-kicking secret agent tracks down bad boy drug kings around the world. **91m/C; VHS, DVD.** Joe Lewis; Barbara Bach; Christopher Lee; Woody Strode; Donald Pleasence; Joseph Wiseman; John Huston; Capucine; *D:* Ernest Pintoff.

Jail Bait ½ *Hidden Face* **1954** Early Wood film about a group of small-time crooks who are always in trouble with the law; they blackmail a plastic surgeon into using his talents to help them ditch the cops. Not as "bad" as Wood's "Plan 9 From Outer Space," but still bad enough for camp fans to love (check the cheesy score leftover from an equally cheesy Mexican mad-scientist flick). **80m/B; VHS, DVD.** Timothy Farrell; Clancy Malone; Lyle Talbot; Steve Reeves; Herbert Rawlinson; Dolores Fuller; Theodora Thurman; Conrad Brooks; Mona McKinnon; *D:* Edward D. Wood, Jr.; *W:* Edward D. Wood, Jr.; Alex Gordon; *C:* William C. Thompson.

Jail Party **2004** Urban spoof tries to put the funny into ex-con Yusef Porter's (Sharp) desire to flee his Atlanta 'hood in search of a better life with girlfriend Elise (Terry) after his prison time wraps up. Things go expectedly sour at his homecoming party when his past, naturally, catches up to him. **90m/C; DVD.** Shane Sharp; Richard Player; Trina Braxton; Antonette Terry; Rashaun Murdaugh; *D:* Bernie Calloway; *W:* Redd Claiborne; Donnie Leapheart; Jason Upson. **VIDEO**

Jailbait! **2000 (R)** Popular high school jock Adam (Mundy), who's 18, cheats on his girlfriend and gets wrong side of the tracks 16-year-old Gynger (Purrott) preggers leading to a charge of statutory rape. Satire on teen sex, political platforms, and society. First original movie made for MTV. **94m/C; VHS, DVD.** Kevin Mundy; Mo Gaffney; Alycia Purrott; Melody Johnson; Matt Frewer; Mary Gross; Reagan Pasternak; *D:* Allan Moyle. **CABLE**

Jailbait: Betrayed By Innocence ½ **1986 (R)** A man is on trial for statutory rape. **90m/C; VHS, DVD.** Barry Bostwick; Lee Purcell; Paul Sorvino; Cristen Kauffman; Isaac Hayes; *D:* Elliot Silverstein. **TV**

Jailbreakers **1994 (R)** Another remake from Showtime's "Rebel Highway" series that takes little but the title from the 1960 A.I.P. flick. Cheerleader Angel (Doherty) falls for bad boy Tony (Sabato Jr.) and gets busted by the cops while they're out on a little crime spree. He goes to prison, she and her family must leave town. But boy can't get girl out of his head and he busts out of the big house to reunite with his true love. Then the crazy kids hit the road for the Mexican border. **76m/C; VHS, DVD.** Shannen Doherty; Antonio Sabato, Jr.; Adrienne Barbeau; Adrien Brody; Vince Edwards; George Gerdes; *D:* William Friedkin; *W:* Debra Hill; Gigi Vorgan; *C:* Cary Fisher; *M:* Hummie Mann. **CABLE**

Jailbreakin' *The Ballad of Billie Blue* **1972** A faded country singer and a rebellious youth team up to break out of jail. **90m/C; VHS, DVD, Streaming.** Erik Estrada; Jason Ledger; Marty Allen; Ray Danton; Sherry Bain; Sherry Miles; *D:* Ken Osborne.

Jailhouse Rock **1957 (G)** While in jail for manslaughter, teenager Vince Everett (Presley) learns to play the guitar. After his release, he slowly develops into a top recording star. Probably the only film that captured the magnetic power of the young Elvis Presley; an absolute must for fans. Also available in a colorized version. **96m/B; VHS, DVD, Blu-Ray, HD-DVD.** Elvis Presley; Judy Tyler; Vaughn Taylor; Dean Jones; Mickey Shaughnessy; William Forrest; Glenn Strange; Jennifer Holden; Anne Neyland; *D:* Richard Thorpe; *W:* Guy Trosper; *C:* Robert J. Bronner; *M:* Jeff Alexander. Natl. Film Reg. '04.

Jake Speed ½ **1986 (PG)** Comic-book mercenary Jake and his loyal associate Remo rescue a beautiful girl from white slave traders. Supposedly a parody of the action adventure genre. **93m/C; VHS, DVD.** Wayne Crawford; John Hurt; Karen Kopins; Dennis Christopher; *D:* Andrew Lane; *W:* Wayne Crawford; *C:* Bryan Loftus; *M:* Mark Snow.

Jake's Corner ½ **2008 (PG)** Sensitive family issues are addressed with some intelligence although lead Tyson is a rather dull mope. Ex-football player Johnny Dunn (Tyson) buys the bar in the small desert town of Jake's Corner, Arizona. His young nephew, Spence (Rodgers), can't remember the car accident that injured him and killed his parents and still thinks they are hospitalized. So Uncle John asks the quirky townsfolk to go along with the story until he can figure out a way to deal with the situation (and his own grief). **97m/C; DVD.** Richard Tyson; Diane Ladd; Danny Trejo; B.J. Thomas; Tony Longo; Colton Rodgers; Karla Basile; Sanel Budlimic; Ky Moni Abraham; *D:* Jeff Santo; *W:* Jeff Santo; *C:* Paul Sanchez; *M:* Steve Dorff. **VIDEO**

Jakob the Liar **1999 (PG-13)** Robin Williams reins in his usual manic personality in this touching tale set during the Holocaust. Jakob (Williams) is a Jew confined to the Polish ghetto by the Nazis. After he hears a radio broadcast describing German defeats while in a Nazi commandant's office, he relates the news to his friend Mischa (Schreiber). This leads to rumors that he owns a contraband radio, which is an offense punishable by death. He sees the excitement and hope that his news has brought and begins to make up new stories to encourage his oppressed community. Finally, the men become courageous enough to start a resistance movement, with Jakob as the leader. The realities of the Holocaust are shown with no attempt to sugarcoat them, and the performances are excellent all around. **114m/C; VHS, DVD.** Robin Williams; Armin Mueller-Stahl; Alan Arkin; Bob Balaban; Michael Jeter; Liev Schreiber; Hannah Taylor Gordon; Nina Siemaszko; Mathieu Kassovitz; Mark Margolis; *D:* Peter Kassovitz; *W:* Peter Kassovitz; Didier Decoin; *C:* Elemer Ragalyi; *M:* Ed Shearmur.

Jalsaghar *The Music Room* **1958** Bisambhar Roy is the last in his aristocratic line and has inherited nothing but debts. But his position in society demands a certain style and he pawns family heirlooms in order to host expensive private concerts, even after tragedy strikes his family. Bengali with subtitles. **100m/B; VHS, DVD, Blu-Ray.** *IN* Chhabi Biswas; Padma Devi; Tulsi Lahnin; Pinaki Sen Gupta; Kali Sarkar; *D:* Satyajit Ray; *W:* Satyajit Ray; *C:* Subrata Mitra; *M:* Satyajit Ray.

Jam **2006** That's jam as in traffic, not food product, or Phish concert. Sitcom characters and situations abound as 15 weary souls are trapped in their cars after an accident on a mountain road. It's Father's Day—so everyone can exchange trite stories. A woman goes into labor (ah, that old chestnut!). There's a couple of bumbling crooks and even a kitchen sink 'cause someone's driving a camper. **91m/C; DVD.** Jeffrey Dean Morgan; William Forsythe; Gina Torres; Amanda Detmer; Jonathan Silverman; Marianne Jean-Baptiste; Dan Byrd; David DeLuise; Elizabeth Bogush; Tess Harper; Alex Rocco; Christopher Amitrano; Julie Claire; Amanda Foreman; *D:* Craig Sterling; *W:* Craig Sterling; Nicole Lonner; *C:* Jeff Venditti; *M:* Andy Kubiszewski. **VIDEO**

Jamaica Inn **1939** In old Cornwall, an orphan girl becomes involved with smugglers. Remade in 1982; based on the story by Daphne Du Maurier. **98m/B; VHS, DVD, Blu-Ray.** *GB* Charles Laughton; Maureen O'Hara; Leslie Banks; Robert Newton; *D:* Alfred Hitchcock; *W:* Sidney Gilliat; Joan Harrison; *C:* Harry Stradling, Sr.; *M:* Eric Fenby.

Jamaica Inn ½ **1982** Miniseries based on the old Daphne Du Maurier adventure about highwaymen and moor-lurking thieves in Cornwall. Remake of the 1939 Hitchcock film. **192m/C; VHS, DVD.** Patrick McGoohan; Jane Seymour; *D:* Lawrence Gordon-Clark. **TV**

James and the Giant Peach **1996 (PG)** Terrific combo of live action and stop-motion animation highlights this adaptation of Roald Dahl's 1961 children's book. Orphaned James is sent to live with his wicked aunts. When magic "crocodile tongues," given to James by a hobo, spill at the base of a peach tree, one fruit grows to such a tremendous size that James crawls inside, meets six insect friends, and goes on numerous adventures, all the while trying to face his fears. Dahl's books are creepy and since the people who brought you "Nightmare Before Christmas" are also doing "James," expect the visuals to be astonishing but too scary for the little ones. **80m/C; VHS, DVD, Blu-Ray.** *V:* Paul Terry; Pete Postlethwaite; Joanna Lumley; Miriam Margolyes; Richard Dreyfuss; Susan Sarandon; David Thewlis; Simon Callow; Jane Leeves; *D:* Henry Selick; *C:* Pete Kozachik; Hiro Narita; *M:* Randy Newman.

James Dean *The Legend* **1976** Dean's friend Bast wrote this behind-the-scenes look at the short life of the enigmatic movie star. **99m/C; VHS, DVD.** Stephen McHattie; Michael Brandon; Candy Clark; Amy Irving; Brooke Adams; Dane Clark; Jayne Meadows; Meg Foster; *D:* William Bast; Robert Butler; *W:* William Bast; *M:* Billy Goldenberg. **TV**

James Dean ½ **2001** The original rebel without a cause gets a superficial biopic treatment that doesn't have much time to explore the appeal of the young legend who died at the age of 24. Dean's (Franco) troubles stem from his unhappy relationship with his distant father (Moriarty) and even his impressive acting talents can't save him from self-destruction. Film focuses on the making of "East of Eden" and Dean's romance with fragile actress Pier Angeli (Cervi). Franco does well in the title role. **95m/C; VHS, DVD.** James Franco; Michael Moriarty; Valentina Cervi; Enrico Colantoni; Edward Herrmann; Barry Primus; Mark Rydell; Joanne Linville; John Pleshette; *D:* Mark Rydell; *W:* Israel Horovitz; *C:* Robbie Greenberg. **CABLE**

James Dean: Live Fast, Die Young *James Dean: Race with Destiny* **1997 (PG-13)** Lightweight biopic of legendary acting rebel with a cause Dean (Van Dien). Film finds Dean troubled when girlfriend Pier Angeli (Carrie Mitchum, Robert's granddaughter) marries another, and in trouble with studio boss Jack Warner (Connors) and director George Stevens (Mitchum). **105m/C; VHS, DVD.** Casper Van Dien; Robert Mitchum; Mike Connors; Carrie Mitchum; Diane Ladd; Connie Stevens; Monique Parent; Casey Kasem; Joseph Campanella; *D:* Marti Rustam; *W:* Dan Sefton; *C:* Gary Graver; Irv Goodnoff. **TV**

James' Journey to Jerusalem *Massa'ot James Be'eretz Hakodesh* **2003** Idealistic James (Shibe) is a young African Christian who is sent on a pilgrimage to the promised land of Zion. Only the promise starts out tarnished when the innocent is thrown into a Tel Aviv jail by a cynical immigration official who thinks he's just another illegal. James gets bailed out by shady businessman Shimi (Daw) to be used as cheap labor and he begins to learn—and work—the system, which leads James into some very secular temptation. English, Zulu, and Hebrew with subtitles. **87m/C; DVD.** Siyabonga Melongisi Shibe; Salim Dau; Arie Elias; Sandra Schonwald; Hugh Masebenza; Gregory Tal; *D:* Ra'anan Alexandrowicz; *W:* Ra'anan Alexandrowicz; Sami Duenias; *C:* Shark (Sharon) De Mayo; *M:* Ehud Banay.

James Joyce: A Portrait of the Artist as a Young Man **1977** A moving, lyrical adaptation of the author's autobiography, told through the character of Stephen Dedalus. Joyce's characterizations, words, and scenes are beautifully translated to the medium of film. Excellent casting. **93m/C; VHS, DVD, Streaming.** John Gielgud; T.P. McKenna; Bosco Hogan; *D:* Joseph Strick.

James White **2015 (R)** Josh Mond's writing/directing debt is a deeply personal piece about his own history with cancer but it's more universal. Christopher Abbott (of HBO's "Girls") gives a devastating performance as the title character, a man embraced by anger and addiction who has used defense mechanisms to avoid honest emotion and responsibility most of his life. Then his mother's (Nixon) cancer returns and he's faced with a situation from which he can no longer run. Abbott and Nixon are incredible as Mond pulls no punches in his representation of the life-changing power of death. **85m/C; DVD.** Christopher Abbott; Cynthia Nixon; Scott Mescudi; Ron Livingston; Makenzie Leigh; *D:* Josh Mond; *W:* Josh Mond; *C:* Mátyás Erdély.

Jamesy Boy **2014** In this familiar scenario, teen delinquent James (Lofranco) winds up doing time in an adult prison after some flashback scenes of him making all the wrong choices. In the joint, hardened con Conrad (Rhames) becomes his reluctant mentor. Rhames maintains his dignity but this pic deserves to be locked up. **109m/C; DVD, Blu-Ray.** Spencer Lofranco; Ving Rhames; James Woods; Ben Rosenfield; Mary-Louise Parker; Taissa Farmiga; Michael Trotter; *D:* Trevor White; *W:* Trevor White; Lane Shadgett; *C:* Robert Lam; *M:* Jermaine Stegall.

Jamie Marks is Dead **2013** Writer/director Smith adapts Christopher Barzak's novel "One For Sorrow" with an artist's eye but a lack of genuine characters that makes this indie ineffective. The title character is found mostly naked on the side of a river, returning a few days later to haunt a popular boy named Adam (Monaghan), who is one of only two people who can see the shivering ghost. The allegory is that no one saw Jamie when he was alive, nicknaming him Mooney Marks and generally ignoring him. The blend of ghost story and message movie about bullying might work in young adult fiction but feels overcooked in a film. **100m/C; DVD.** Cameron Monaghan; Morgan Saylor; Noah Silver; Madisen Beaty; Liv Tyler; Judy Greer; Ryan Munzert; *D:* Carter Smith; *W:* Carter Smith; *C:* Darren Lew; *M:* Francoise-Eudes Chanfrault.

Jane **2017 (PG)** Mining more than 100 hours of unseen footage, writer/director Morgen presents an intimate look into the life and work of Jane Goodall, who pioneered the study of chimpanzees in the wild. Shot on 16mm film by renowned wildlife photographer (and Goodall's eventual husband) Hugo van Lawick, the video captures the lush African foliage while lending a home-movie feel to the portraits, actions, and relationships of and among the chimps and Goodall herself. Her intelligence, passion, and courage shed light on the understanding of these apes, and, as the species most closely related to them, that of humans as well. **90m/C; DVD.** Jane Goodall; *D:* Brett Morgen; *W:* Brett Morgen; *C:* Ellen Kuras; *M:* Philip Glass. Writers Guild '17: Documentary Screenplay.

Jane & the Lost City ½ **1987 (PG)** A British farce based on the age-old, barely dressed comic-strip character, Jane, as she stumbles on ancient cities, treasures, villains, and blond/blue-eyed heroes. Low-budget camp fun. **94m/C; VHS, DVD.** *GB* Kirsten Hughes; Maud Adams; Sam Jones; *D:* Terry Marcel; *W:* Mervyn Haisman; *C:* Paul Beeson; *M:* Harry Robertson.

The Jane Austen Book Club **2007 (PG-13)** Why yes, this is a chick flick, and unabashedly so. A group of Jane Austen devotees gather monthly to discuss six Jane Austen books, but end up revealing themselves in the process. The characters are not unlike Austen's, albeit living in the dizzying pace of the modern world. There's Bernadette (Baker), a wise and carefree divorcee; free-spirit dog-breeder Jocelyn (Bello); Sylvia (Brenneman), whose 20-plus-year marriage has abruptly ended, and her lesbian daughter (Grace); uptight teacher Prudie (Blunt); and a token man, software geek Grigg (Dancy). Austen's spirit floats (figuratively) in and out of the clubber's lives, losses, and romances as they navigate the passages Austen penned two centuries ago. **106m/C; DVD, Blu-Ray.** Kathy Baker; Maria Bello; Emily Blunt; Amy Brenneman; Maggie Grace; Hugh Dancy; Lynn Redgrave; Jimmy Smits; Marc Blucas; Kevin Zegers; Nancy Travis; Parisa Fitz-Henley; *D:* Robin Swicord; *W:* Robin Swicord; *C:* John Toon; *M:* Aaron Zigman.

Jane Austen in Manhattan 1/2 **1980** Two acting-teachers vie to stage a long-lost play written by a youthful Jane Austen. Dreary, despite the cast. Hodiak is the real-life daughter of Baxter. **108m/C; VHS, DVD.** Anne Baxter; Robert Powell; Michael Wager; Sean Young; Kurt Johnson; Katrina Hodiak; ***D:*** James Ivory; ***W:*** Ruth Prawer Jhabvala.

Jane Doe 1/2 **1983** Valentine plays a young amnesia victim who is linked to a series of brutal slayings. Quite suspenseful for a TV movie. **100m/C; VHS, DVD.** Karen Valentine; William Devane; Eva Marie Saint; Stephen E. Miller; Jackson Davies; ***D:*** Ivan Nagy. **TV**

Jane Doe *Pictures of Baby Jane Doe* **1996 (R)** Jane Doe (Flockhart) is a drug addict who's getting seriously involved with shy writer Horace (Peditto). Only her addictions begin to cause some serious trouble for this odd couple. Adapted from a play. **92m/C; VHS, DVD.** Calista Flockhart; Elina Lowensohn; Joe Ragno; Christopher Peditto; ***D:*** Paul Peditto; ***W:*** Paul Peditto.

Jane Eyre **1934** Stiff, early version of Charlotte Bronte's classic gothic romance. English orphan grows up to become the governess of a mysterious manor. Notable as the first talkie version. Remade several times. **67m/B; VHS, DVD.** Virginia Bruce; Colin Clive; Beryl Mercer; Jameson Thomas; Aileen Pringle; David Torrence; Clarissa Selwynne; Anne Howard; ***D:*** Christy Cabanne; ***W:*** Adele Comandini; ***C:*** Robert Planck; ***M:*** Mischa Bakaleinikoff.

Jane Eyre **1944** Excellent adaptation of the Charlotte Bronte novel about the plain governess with the noble heart and her love for the mysterious and tragic Mr. Rochester. Fontaine has the proper backbone and yearning in the title role but to accommodate Welles' emerging popularity the role of Rochester was enlarged. Excellent bleak romantic-Gothic look. Taylor, in her third film role, is seen briefly in the early orphanage scenes. **97m/B; VHS, DVD, Blu-Ray.** Joan Fontaine; Orson Welles; Margaret O'Brien; Peggy Ann Garner; John Sutton; Sara Allgood; Henry Daniell; Agnes Moorehead; Aubrey Mather; Edith Barrett; Barbara Everest; Hillary Brooke; Elizabeth Taylor; ***D:*** Robert Stevenson; ***W:*** John Houseman; Aldous Huxley; Robert Stevenson; ***C:*** George Barnes; ***M:*** Bernard Herrmann.

Jane Eyre **1983** Miniseries based on the famed Charlotte Bronte novel about the maturation of a homeless English waif, her love for the tormented Rochester, and her quest for permanent peace. **239m/C; VHS, DVD.** *GB* Timothy Dalton; Zelah Clarke; ***D:*** Julian Amyes. **TV**

Jane Eyre **1996 (PG)** Zeffirelli creates an eloquent yet spare interpretation of Charlotte Bronte's 1847 masterpiece, about a meek governess and her mysterious employer, in its fourth film incarnation. Everything about it, from the lighting to the score, is muted and somber. Still a beautiful film, it seems to lack a certain passion that earlier versions (especially the 1944 classic) brought to the screen. Strong performances all around, including Oscar-winner Paquin and French star Gainsbourg as the younger and older Jane, and Hurt as the tormented Rochester. **116m/C; VHS, DVD, Blu-Ray.** William Hurt; Anna Paquin; Charlotte Gainsbourg; Joan Plowright; Elle Macpherson; Geraldine Chaplin; Fiona Shaw; John Wood; Amanda Root; Maria Schneider; Josephine Serre; Billie Whitelaw; ***D:*** Franco Zeffirelli; ***W:*** Franco Zeffirelli; Hugh Whitemore; ***C:*** David Watkin; ***M:*** Alessio Vlad; Claudio Capponi.

Jane Eyre 1/2 **1997** Charlotte Bronte's dark romance between meek-yet-strong-willed governess Jane (Morton) and her tormented-yet-dashing employer, Mr. Rochester (Hinds). This version dispenses quickly with many of the subplots to concentrate on the main duo. **108m/C; VHS, DVD.** *GB* Samantha Morton; Ciaran Hinds; Gemma Jones; Abigail Cruttenden; Richard Hawley; ***D:*** Robert M. Young; ***W:*** Kay Mellor; ***M:*** Richard Harvey. **CABLE**

Jane Eyre 1/2 **2006** Yet another version (from the BBC) of Charlotte Bronte's novel, complete with gothic romance, naive but undaunted governess Jane (Wilson, properly plain), and secretive aristocrat Edward Rochester (Stephens, more grumpy than brooding). Well done but unnecessary; didn't Charlotte write anything else worth filming? **247m/C; DVD.** *GB* Toby Stephens; Francesca Annis; Christina Cole; Tara Fitzgerald; Ruth Wilson; Claudia Coulter; Pam Ferris; Andrew Buchan; ***D:*** Susanna White; ***W:*** Sandy Welch; ***C:*** Mike Eley; ***M:*** Robert (Rob) Lane. **TV**

Jane Eyre 1/2 **2011 (PG-13)** Director Fukunaga's version of the Charlotte Bronte novel succeeds with the perfect casting of teenaged Wasikowska in the title role of the naive but steadfast governess. Fassbender is the slightly less brooding, much less sinister than usual, wealthy Edward Rochester, the master of Thornfield House and its many secrets. Dench is also perfect as the voluble housekeeper Mrs. Fairfax. The director wisely shifts the story around so Jane's miserable childhood is shown in brief flashbacks rather than dragged out and you get to the romantic drama right away. **115m/C; Blu-Ray, On Demand.** *GB* Mia Wasikowska; Michael Fassbender; Jamie Bell; Dame Judi Dench; Imogen Poots; Valentina Cervi; Harold Lloyd, Jr.; Sally Hawkins; Sophie Ward; Holliday Grainger; Tamzin Merchant; Rosie Cavaliero; Simon McBurney; ***D:*** Cary Fukunaga; ***W:*** Moira Buffini; ***C:*** Adriano Goldman; ***M:*** Dario Marianelli.

Jane Got a Gun **2016 (R)** Jane Hammond (Portman) has built a quiet, secluded life with her husband Bill (Emmerich) after being a victim of the Bishop Boys gang in the old West, but they find her and shoot poor Bill. Led by the ultra-violent Colin (McGregor), the Bishop Boys come after Jane, who has turn to her ex-fiance Dan (Edgerton) for help. The Weinstein Company didn't like the cut of this that came in and so sat on it for years and barely released it in theaters. It's too bad because it's not horrible, just not a particular stand-out either. **?m/CDVD, Blu-Ray.** Natalie Portman; Joel Edgerton; Ewan McGregor; Rodrigo Santoro; Noah Emmerich; ***D:*** Gavin O'Connor; ***W:*** Joel Edgerton; Brian Duffield; Anthony Tambakis; ***C:*** Mandy Walker; ***M:*** Marcello De Francisci; Lisa Gerrard.

Janice Beard **1999** Eccentric comedy about a social misfit that's overwhelmed by whimsey. Janice (Walsh) moves from her Scottish town to London in hopes of making enough money to help her agoraphobic mother Mimi (Voe). Living in her own fantasy world (she videotapes letters to her mother that are mostly fabrications of how swell things are going), Janice gets a temp job at a car manufacturing company and gets unwittingly involved in corporate espionage with sneaky office assistant Sean (Ifans). Walsh is endearing but the office antics get tedious. **80m/C; DVD.** *GB* Eileen Walsh; Rhys Ifans; Patsy Kensit; Sandra Voe; David O'Hara; Frances Gray; ***D:*** Clare Kilner; ***W:*** Clare Kilner; Ben Hopkins; ***C:*** Richard Greatrex; Peter Thwaites; ***M:*** Paul Carr.

Janie Jones 1/2 **2010** Likeable cast but hackneyed story. Ex-groupie and current addict, Mary Ann (Shue) decides it's time 13-year-old Janie's (Breslin) alt-rock dad Ethan Brand (Nivola) do some parenting while she goes into rehab. He's on tour and claims he didn't even know about the kid but is stuck with her anyway. The heavy-drinking Ethan nearly blows his dwindling career but Janie proves to have inherited his musical talent and a surprisingly stable character as they warily explore their new relationship. **101m/C; DVD.** Abigail Breslin; Alessandro Nivola; Elisabeth Shue; Brittany Snow; Joel David Moore; Frances Fisher; Frank Whaley; Peter Stormare; ***D:*** David M. Rosenthal; ***W:*** David M. Rosenthal; ***C:*** Anastas Michos; ***M:*** Eef Barzelay.

The Janky Promoters 1/2 **2009 (R)** Decidedly non-PC comedy about a couple of blustering, shady, cash-poor would-be rap concert promoters in Modesto, California. Russell (Ice Cube) and Jellyroll (Epps) are trying to present a concert by Young Jeezy (playing himself) despite skepticism over their abilities from all concerned. Profane dialogue and numerous sexual references earn the pic its rating. **85m/C; DVD.** Ice Cube; Mike Epps; Darris Love; Julio Oscar Mechoso; Glenn Plummer; Young Jeezy; Little JJ; Tamala Jones; Juanita Jennings; ***D:*** Marcus Raboy; ***W:*** Ice Cube; ***C:*** Tom Priestly, Jr.; ***M:*** John Murphy.

The January Man **1989 (R)** An unorthodox cop, previously exiled by a corrupt local government to the fire department, is brought back to the force in New York City to track down a serial killer. Written by the "Moonstruck" guy, Shanley, who apparently peaked with the earlier movie. **97m/C; VHS, DVD, Blu-Ray.** Kevin Kline; Susan Sarandon; Mary Elizabeth Mastrantonio; Harvey Keitel; Rod Steiger; Alan Rickman; Danny Aiello; ***D:*** Pat O'Connor; ***W:*** John Patrick Shanley; Pat O'Connor; ***C:*** Jerzy Zielinski; ***M:*** Marvin Hamlisch.

Japan Japan 1/2 **2007** A brief look at the life of aimless teen Imri who moves to Tel Aviv and idly fantasizes about emigrating to Japan despite his misconceptions about the country. There's a rather confusingly random, improvised feel and writer/director Shamriz likes to break the fourth wall and have his actors speak directly to the camera and audience. Hebrew with subtitles. **67m/C; DVD.** *IS* Imri Kahn; Amnon Friedman; Irit Gidron; Neema Yuria; ***D:*** Lior Shamriz; ***W:*** Lior Shamriz; ***C:*** Lior Shamriz.

Japanese Story **2003 (R)** Headstrong Sandy (Collette) is a geologist by trade and part owner of a software firm who is obliged to entertain a potential client, Hiromitsu (Tsunashima), an uptight Japanese businessman looking to experience the Australian landscape. Despite her objections he insists that they drive into the desert where they end up stranded for a night amid the harsh elements. Their struggle to endure brings them closer but their eventual affair (he's married) is marred by a dramatic plot twist midstream that shakes Sandy to her core. Gorgeous scenery provides a striking backdrop for Brooks' passionate piece while Collette displays great depth as a woman challenged by a gamut of emotions. **105m/C; DVD.** *AU* Toni Collette; Matthew Dyktynski; Lynette Curran; John Howard; Gotaro Tsunashima; Yukimo Tanaka; Kate Atkinson; Bill Young; George Shevtsov; Justine Clarke; ***D:*** Sue Brooks; ***W:*** Alison Tilson; ***C:*** Ian Baker; ***M:*** Elizabeth Drake.

Japanese War Bride **1952** When he's wounded and hospitalized in Japan, Korean War vet Jim is cared for by Japanese nurse Tae and they fall in love and marry. Jim brings his bride home to the farming community of Salinas, California, and is met with lingering anti-Japanese sentiment, particularly from his own family, while Tae tries to maintain her dignity amidst the hostility. **91m/B; DVD.** Don Taylor; Cameron Mitchell; Marie Windsor; Yoshiko (Shirley) Yamaguchi; James Bell; Louise Lorimer; Philip Ahn; ***D:*** King Vidor; ***W:*** Catherine Turney; ***C:*** Lionel Lindon; ***M:*** Arthur Lange; Emil Newman.

Jarhead 1/2 **2005 (R)** Solid adaptation of Anthony Swofford's memoir is not so much an anti-war film as an absence-of-war film. Gyllenhaal is excellent as "Swoff," a Marine recruit trained as a sniper and sent to fight in the first Gulf War. Only when he gets there, there's no fighting, just waiting and preparing. Mendes's deft touch is put to good use in showing the frustration and boredom of the Marines, using other war movies as touchstones and keeping politics in the background while focusing on the characters. The drawback of this approach is that the audience becomes just as frustrated as the soldiers with all the inaction. **122m/C; DVD, Blu-Ray, UMD, HD-DVD.** Jake Gyllenhaal; Peter Sarsgaard; Lucas Black; Brian Geraghty; Jacob Vargas; Laz Alonso; Evan Jones; Ivan Fenyo; Chris Cooper; Dennis Haysbert; Scott MacDonald; Jamie Foxx; Jamie Martz; Kareem Grimes; Peter Gail; Jocko Sims; John Krasinski; ***D:*** Sam Mendes; ***W:*** William Broyles, Jr.; ***C:*** Roger Deakins; ***M:*** Thomas Newman.

Jarhead 2: Field of Fire WOOF! **2014 (R)** Cpl. Chris Merrimette and his unit are on their way to resupply an outpost in hostile Helmand province. A Navy SEAL enlists their help in getting an Afghani woman, who's been openly defying the Taliban, out of the country to safety. Tacky actioner has absolutely nothing to do with the original 2005 movie. **103m/C; DVD, Blu-Ray.** Josh Kelly; Jesse Garcia; Esai Morales; Stephen Lang; Bokeem Woodbine; Cole Hauser; Ralitsa Paskaleva; ***D:*** Don Michael Paul; ***W:*** Berkeley Anderson; Ellis Black; ***C:*** Alexander Krumov; ***M:*** Frederik Wiedmann. **VIDEO**

Jarhead 3: The Siege **2016 (R)** The third entry in the Jarhead series focuses on the Marines' response to an unexpected militant attack on a U.S. embassy. When Corporal Evan Albright (Weber) joins the elite Marine Corps Security Guards, his first assignment is protecting a U.S. embassy in relatively safe Middle Eastern country. The workdays are slow until well armed and well trained militants launch a surprise attack in front of the embassy. Albright and his colleagues must rely on courage and firepower to manage the situation before it turns into all-out war. **95m/C; DVD, Blu-Ray, Streaming, Download.** Charlie Weber; Scott Adkins; Tom Ainsley; Erik Valdez; Dante Basco; ***D:*** William Kaufman; ***W:*** Chad Law; Michael D. Weiss; ***C:*** Mark Rutledge. **VIDEO**

Jason and the Argonauts **1963 (G)** Jason, son of the King of Thessaly, sails on the Argo to the land of Colchis, where the Golden Fleece is guarded by a seven-headed hydra. Superb special effects and multitudes of mythological creatures; fun for the whole family. **104m/C; VHS, DVD.** *GB* Todd Armstrong; Nancy Kovack; Gary Raymond; Laurence Naismith; Nigel Green; Michael Gwynn; Honor Blackman; Niall MacGinnis; Douglas Wilmer; Jack (Gwyllam) Gwillim; ***D:*** Don Chaffey; ***W:*** Jan Read; Beverley Cross; ***C:*** Wilkie Cooper; ***M:*** Bernard Herrmann.

Jason and the Argonauts 1/2 **2000** Elaborate retelling of the Greek myth of Jason and his quest for the golden fleece. Young Prince Jason (London) has had his heritage usurped by his evil Uncle Pelias (Hopper in braids), who has killed Jason's father and taken his throne. In order to reclaim it, Jason must retrieve the magical golden fleece from distant Colchis and bring it to Pelias. So Jason assembles the usual motley crew of would-be heroes and sets sail on the Argos for uncharted waters and numerous adventures. TV saga with lots of action and some good special effects. **179m/C; VHS, DVD.** Jason London; Dennis Hopper; Angus MacFadyen; Olivia Williams; Brian Thompson; Adrian Lester; Derek Jacobi; Jolene Blalock; Frank Langella; Natasha Henstridge; Ciaran Hinds; Kieran O'Brien; Charles Cartmell; ***D:*** Nick Willing; ***W:*** Matthew Faulk; Mark Skeet; ***C:*** Sergei Kozlov; ***M:*** Simon Boswell. **TV**

Jason Bourne 1/2 **2016 (PG-13)** A tragic cash-in on a hit franchise, Damon and Greengrass reunite for a reboot of the Bourne series without any of the wit or even thrilling action of the other four films. Damon's take on Jason Bourne this time is more like Charles Bronson—strong, deadly, and silent (he has 25 lines in the entire film). More damagingly, the script re-asks questions already answered about Bourne's past, going back to the origin story closed out in "Ultimatum." Vikander makes a minor impact but Tommy Lee Jones and Vincent Cassel are wasted. **123m/C; DVD, Blu-Ray.** Matt Damon; Tommy Lee Jones; Alicia Vikander; Vincent Cassel; Julia Stiles; Riz Ahmed; ***D:*** Paul Greengrass; ***W:*** Paul Greengrass; Christopher Rouse; ***C:*** Barry Ackroyd; ***M:*** David Buckley; John Powell.

Jason Goes to Hell: The Final Friday WOOF! **1993 (R)** The supposed last, at least so far, in the "Friday the 13th" gore series. Only through the bodies—dead or alive—of his Vorhees kin can supernatural killer Jason be reborn, and only at their hands can he truly die. One can only hope that this is finally true. An unrated, even gorier, version is also available. **89m/C; VHS, DVD, Blu-Ray.** Kane Hodder; John D. LeMay; Kari Keegan; Steven Williams; Steven Culp; Erin Gray; Richard Gant; Leslie Jordan; Billy Green Bush; Rusty Schwimmer; Allison Smith; Julie Michaels; ***D:*** Adam Marcus; ***W:*** Dean Lorey; Jay Huguely-Cass; ***M:*** Harry Manfredini.

Jason X **2001 (R)** This time it's Jason in space. The tenth installment of the "Friday the 13th" franchise is set in 2455, when Earth has been abandoned because of toxic damage. An archeological expedition discovers the cryogenically frozen Jason and a young woman and brings them back to their spaceship. Of course, if they'd just leave him on Earth with no one to kill, he'd die a horrible existential death that'd be really cool to see. Unfortunately, there's a passel of horny med students that needs killin' so here we go again. The space setting does give the series a bunch of new franchises to rip off, but that doesn't really help. **93m/C; VHS, DVD, Blu-Ray.** Lexa Doig; Lisa Ryder; Kane Hodder; Jonathan Potts; Chuck Campbell; Peter Mensah; Melyssa Ade; Melody Johnson; Dov Tiefenbach; David Cronenberg; Derwin Jordan; ***D:*** James Isaac; ***W:*** Todd Farmer; ***C:*** Derick Underschultz; ***M:*** Harry Manfredini.

Jason's Lyric 1994 **(R)** A romantic triangle, sibling rivalry, family bonds, and neighborhood violence all set on the wrong side of the Houston tracks. Jason (Payne) is the responsible young man who works hard and helps out his mom; younger brother Joshua (Woodbine) has just gotten out of jail and is headed straight for more trouble. Between the two is Lyric (Pinkett), a soul-food waitress whose bad news half-brother Alonzo (Treach) is naturally one of Joshua's homies. Good-looking but ultimately empty storytelling. **119m/C; VHS, DVD.** Allen Payne; Bokeem Woodbine; Jada Pinkett Smith; Suzzanne Douglass; Forest Whitaker; Treach; ***D:*** Doug McHenry; ***W:*** Bobby Smith, Jr.; ***M:*** Matt Noble.

Jasper, Texas 1/2 **2003** Dramatization of the 1998 hate crime that shook the small Texas town. When black James Byrd Jr. dies after being chained to the back of a pickup truck and dragged for three miles, the town's citizens find themselves at the center of a nationwide political and media frenzy. It's up to Sheriff Billy Rowles (Voight) and Jasper's first black mayor, R.C. Horn (Gossett Jr.) to portray the murder as an isolated incident, but the subsequent trial force the townsfolk to take a hard look at their community. Some Hollywood platitudes remain but the story is neither white-washed nor sensationalized. **120m/C; DVD.** Jon Voight; Louis Gossett, Jr.; Joe Morton; Emily Yancy; Bokeem Woodbine; Blu Mankuma; Karen Robinson; Ron White; Eugene Clark; ***D:*** Jeff Byrd; ***W:*** Jonathan Estrin; ***C:*** Ousama Rawi. **CABLE**

Jauja 1/2 **2014** A father (Mortensen) and his daughter (Villbjork Malling Agger) travel from the safety of Denmark to some unidentified, daunting desert landscape in this trippy, bizarre period piece. Shot in full frame, almost like looking at old photographs, Alonso's film is boldly thoughtful as the daughter disappears and the father goes deeper into the unknown and unfamiliar to find her. Made up more of careful compositions, it's almost like paintings than narrative. Though it can get self-indulgent, it's also hard to forget. Mortensen also deserves credit again for trying something different. **108m/C; DVD.** Viggo Mortensen; Ghita Norby; Villbjork Malling Agger; Esteban Bigliardi; Adrian Fondari; ***D:*** Lisandro Alonso; ***W:*** Lisandro Alonso; Fabian Casas; ***C:*** Timo Salminen; ***M:*** Viggo Mortensen.

Java Heat 1/2 **2013 (R)** Generic actioner finds American Jake Travers (bland Lutz) witnessing a terrorist attack in Indonesia. When questioned by devout Muslim detective Hashim (Bayu), Jake reveals he's an undercover FBI agent tracking evil, mumbling mastermind Malik (Rourke, tres bizarre), who's kidnapped the Sultana (Hasiholan) in order to pull of a royal jewel heist. Shootouts, explosions, and chases follow. English and Indonesian with subtitles. **99m/C; DVD, Blu-Ray, Streaming.** Kellan Lutz; Ario Bayu; Mickey Rourke; Frans Tumbuan; Atiqah Hasiholan; ***D:*** Conor Allyn; ***W:*** Conor Allyn; Rob Allyn; ***C:*** Shane Daly; ***M:*** Justin Caine Burnett.

Jawbreaker **1998 (R)** Writer-director Darren Stein steals the plot from "Heathers" and adds a dash of S&M for this black comedy about high school clique queens. Courtney (McGowan) is the leader of a group of glam princesses who accidentally kill one of their own during a mock kidnapping. Fellow beautiful people Julie (Gayheart) and Marcie (Benz) help her cover up, but class nerd Fern (Greer) is a witness. Further complicating things are nosy detective Vera Cruz (Grier) and the upcoming prom, which provides a "Carrie" style finale. Although the movie treads familiar ground, McGowan's performance keeps it interesting. Cameo by rocker Marilyn Manson, billed as Brian Warner. **87m/C; VHS, DVD, Blu-Ray.** Rose McGowan; Rebecca Gayheart; Julie Benz; Charlotte Roldan; Judy Greer; Chad Christ; Carol Kane; Pam Grier; William Katt; P.J. Soles; Jeff Conaway; Ethan Erickson; ***D:*** Darren Stein; ***W:*** Darren Stein; ***C:*** Amy Vincent.

Jaws 1/2 **1975 (PG)** Early directorial effort by Spielberg from the Peter Benchley potboiler. A tight, very scary, and sometimes hilarious film about the struggle to kill a giant great white shark that is terrorizing an eastern beach community's waters. The characterizations by Dreyfuss, Scheider, and Shaw are much more enduring than the shock effects. Memorable score. Sequelled by "Jaws 2" in 1978, "Jaws 3" in 1983, and "Jaws: The Revenge" in 1987. Look for Benchley as a TV reporter. **124m/C; VHS, DVD, Blu-Ray.** Roy Scheider; Robert Shaw; Richard Dreyfuss; Lorraine Gary; Murray Hamilton; Carl Gottlieb; Peter Benchley; ***D:*** Steven Spielberg; ***W:*** Carl Gottlieb; Peter Benchley; ***C:*** Bill Butler; ***M:*** John Williams. Oscars '75: Film Editing, Orig. Score, Sound; AFI '98: Top 100; Golden Globes '76: Score; Natl. Film Reg. '01.

Jaws 2 1/2 **1978 (PG)** Unsatisfactory sequel to "Jaws." It's been four years since the man-eating shark feasted on the resort town of Amity; suddenly a second shark stalks the waters and the terror returns. Scheider—who must by now wonder at his tendancy to attract large aquatic carnivores with lunch on their minds—battles without his compatriots from the original. And we haven't seen the last of the mechanical dorsal fin yet; two more sequels follow. **116m/C; VHS, DVD, Blu-Ray.** Roy Scheider; Lorraine Gary; Murray Hamilton; Joseph Mascolo; Jeffrey Kramer; Collin Wilcox-Paxton; Keith Gordon; ***D:*** Jeannot Szwarc; ***W:*** Carl Gottlieb; Howard Sackler; ***C:*** Michael C. Butler; ***M:*** John Williams.

Jaws 3 *Jaws 3-D* **1983 (PG)** Same monster, new setting: in a Sea World-type amusement park, a great white shark escapes from its tank and proceeds to cause terror and chaos. Little connection to the previous "Jaws" sagas. Followed by one more sequel, "Jaws: The Revenge." **98m/C; VHS, DVD, Blu-Ray.** Dennis Quaid; Bess Armstrong; Louis Gossett, Jr.; Simon MacCorkindale; Lea Thompson; John Putch; ***D:*** Joe Alves; ***W:*** Richard Matheson; Carl Gottlieb; ***C:*** James A. Contner; ***M:*** John Williams.

Jaws of Death *Mako: The Jaws of Death* **1976** "Jaws"-like saga of shark terror. Jaeckel illogically strikes out to protect his "friends," the sharks. **91m/C; VHS, DVD.** Richard Jaeckel; Harold Sakata; Jennifer Bishop; John Chandler; Buffy Dee; ***D:*** William Grefe.

Jaws of Satan **WOOF!** *King Cobra* **1981 (R)** Weaver is terrorized by a slimy snake who is, in actuality, the Devil. Not released for two years after it was filmed, and generally considered a bomb of the first caliber. Unfortunate work for usually worthwhile Weaver. **92m/C; VHS, Blu-Ray, Streaming.** Fritz Weaver; Gretchen Corbett; Jon Korkes; Norman Lloyd; Christina Applegate; ***D:*** Bob Claver; ***C:*** Dean Cundey.

Jaws: The Revenge **1987 (PG-13)** The third sequel, in which Mrs. Brody is pursued the world over by a seemingly personally motivated Great White Shark. Includes footage not seen in the theatrical release. Each sequel in this series is progressively inferior to the original. **87m/C; VHS, DVD, Blu-Ray.** Lorraine Gary; Lance Guest; Karen Young; Mario Van Peebles; Michael Caine; Judith Barsi; Lynn Whitfield; ***D:*** Joseph Sargent; ***W:*** Michael deGuzman; ***C:*** John McPherson; ***M:*** Michael Small.

Jay and Silent Bob Reboot 1/2 **2019 (R)** The now middle-aged Jay (Mewes) and Silent Bob (K. Smith) travel across the country to attend Chronic-Con, a celebration of their stoner superhero alter-egos, Bluntman and Chronic. Still hard-core potheads, the duo also manages Jay's teenage daughter Milly (H. Smith) and her three friends because they are also going to the convention. The girls are also hardcore marijuana smokers who do not trust authority figures and are obsessed with sex. The third film featuring Jay & Silent Bob by Kevin Smith, the stoner comedy has a younger and more diverse cast than previous outings but offers not much else that is new. Targeted at die-hard fans. **95m/C; DVD, Blu-Ray.** Kevin Smith; Jason Mewes; Harley Quinn Smith; Val Kilmer; Melissa Benoist; ***D:*** Kevin Smith; ***W:*** Kevin Smith; ***C:*** Yaron Levy; ***M:*** James L. Venable.

Jay and Silent Bob Strike Back 1/2 **2001 (R)** The fifth in Smith's series of movies with ties to Red Bank, New Jersey, is a road movie as the boys go after Miramax studio (which produced the film) when it makes a movie based on the comic book characters that are based on them without their permission. It makes more sense (and is probably more enjoyable) if you've seen Smith's entire ouvre. Besides Jay (Mewes) and Silent Bob (Smith himself), many of the characters and jokes are from Smith's previous movies. Subplots and detours abound for our heroes, allowing Smith to effectively parody and lampoon recent summer blockbusters, his own stars, and Hollywood in general. **95m/C; VHS, DVD, Blu-Ray.** Kevin Smith; Jason Mewes; Jason Lee; Ben Affleck; Shannon Elizabeth; Eliza Dushku; Ali Larter; Jennifer Schwalbach Smith; Chris Rock; Will Ferrell; Brian O'Halloran; Seann William Scott; George Carlin; Carrie Fisher; Judd Nelson; Jon Stewart; Mark Hamill; Diedrich Bader; Renee Humphrey; Joey Lauren Adams; Dwight Ewell; Eli Marienthal; Marc Blucas; ***Cameo(s):*** Wes Craven; Gus Van Sant; Matt Damon; Shannen Doherty; Jason Biggs; James Van Der Beek; Alanis Morissette; ***D:*** Kevin Smith; ***W:*** Kevin Smith; ***C:*** Jamie Anderson; ***M:*** James L. Venable.

The Jayhawkers **1959** Chandler and Parker battle for power and women in pre-Civil War Kansas. **100m/C; VHS, DVD, Blu-Ray, Streaming.** Jeff Chandler; Fess Parker; Nicole Maurey; Henry Silva; Herbert Rudley; Frank De Kova; Don Megowan; Leo Gordon; ***D:*** Melvin Frank.

The Jayne Mansfield Story *Jayne Mansfield: A Symbol of the '50s* **1980** Recounts the blond bombshell's career from her first career exposure, through her marriage to a bodybuilder, to the famous car crash that beheaded her. **97m/C; VHS, DVD.** Loni Anderson; Arnold Schwarzenegger; Raymond Buktenica; Kathleen Lloyd; G.D. Spradlin; Dave Shelley; ***D:*** Dick Lowry. **TV**

Jayne Mansfield's Car **2013 (R)** Old-fashioned storytelling from director Thornton, with a notable cast somewhat lost in a dysfunctional melodrama set in 1969 in Morrison, Alabama. WWI vet Jim Caldwell (Duvall), who has a thing for car wrecks, raised his four kids after wife Naomi divorced him to marry an Englishman. Jim learns that his ex has died and wants to be buried in Morrison, so her second husband, Kingsley Bedford (Hurt), and his two grown children come for the funeral. Rather than showing a two-family throwdown, the focus stays with the conflicts between the dads and their male offspring, who are troubled WWII vets (the daughters take a back seat). **122m/C; DVD, Blu-Ray.** Robert Duvall; John Hurt; Kevin Bacon; Robert Patrick; Katherine LaNasa; Ray Stevenson; Frances O'Connor; Billy Bob Thornton; ***D:*** Billy Bob Thornton; ***W:*** Billy Bob Thornton; Tom Epperson; ***C:*** Barry Markowitz; ***M:*** Owen Easterling Hatfield.

Jazz on a Summer's Day **1959** Filmed version of the 1958 Newport Jazz Festival. Performers include Louis Armstrong, Dinah Washington, Mahalia Jackson, Thelonius Monk, Anita O'Day, and Chuck Berry. Jazz fans won't want to miss this fabulous production. **85m/C; VHS, DVD.** ***D:*** Bert Stern; ***C:*** Bert Stern; Courtney Hafela; Ray Phealan. Natl. Film Reg. '99.

The Jazz Singer 1/2 **1927** A Jewish cantor's son breaks with his family to become a singer of popular music. Of historical importance as the first successful part-talkie; a very early Loy performance. With the classic line "You ain't heard nothing yet!" Remade several times. **89m/B; VHS, DVD, Blu-Ray.** Al Jolson; May McAvoy; Warner Oland; William Demarest; Eugenie Besserer; Myrna Loy; ***D:*** Alan Crosland; ***C:*** Hal Mohr. AFI '98: Top 100; Natl. Film Reg. '96.

The Jazz Singer **1952** Updated remake of the 1927 Al Jolson hit with comedian Thomas starring as the cantor's son. Returning to his Philly hometown after his Korean War service, Jerry Golding (Thomas) longs to try his chances singing on Broadway while his father (Franz) wants Jerry to take over his duties as cantor in their synagogue. Jerry chooses the bright lights and is taken under the wing of established songbird Judy (Lee), causing a family break. Thomas certainly isn't a singer and the flick is still so much schmaltz; followed by the even worse 1980 version. **107m/C; DVD.** Danny Thomas; Peggy Lee; Eduard Franz; Mildred Dunnock; Tom Tully; Alex Gerry; Allyn Joslyn; ***D:*** Michael Curtiz; ***W:*** Frank Davis; Lewis Meltzer; Leonard Stern; ***C:*** Carl Guthrie; ***M:*** Max Steiner; Ray Heindorf.

The Jazz Singer **WOOF!** **1980 (PG)** Flat and uninteresting (if not unintentionally funny) remake of the 1927 classic about a Jewish boy who rebels against his father and family tradition to become a popular entertainer. Stick with the original, this is little more than a vehicle for Diamond to sing. **115m/C; VHS, DVD.** Neil Diamond; Laurence Olivier; Lucie Arnaz; Catlin Adams; Franklin Ajaye; Ernie Hudson; ***D:*** Richard Fleischer; ***W:*** Herbert Baker; Stephen H. Foreman; ***C:*** Isidore Mankofsky; ***M:*** Neil Diamond; Leonard Rosenman. Golden Raspberries '80: Worst Actor (Diamond), Worst Support. Actor (Olivier).

J.D.'s Revenge 1/2 **1976 (R)** Attorney in training Glynn Turman is possessed by the spirit of a gangster who was murdered on Bourbon Street in the early 1940s and grisly blaxploitation results. Ever so slightly better than others of the genre. Shot in New Orleans, with a soundtrack by a then-unknown Prince. **95m/C; VHS, DVD, Blu-Ray.** Louis Gossett, Jr.; Glynn Turman; Joan Pringle; David McKnight; James L. Watkins; ***D:*** Arthur Marks; ***W:*** Jaison Starkes; ***C:*** Harry J. May; ***M:*** Prince.

Je Tu Il Elle 1/2 *I You She He* **1974** A hyperactive young woman desperately seeking the answers to life gradually gains experience and maturity as she travels around France. The directorial debut of Ackerman. In French with English subtitles. **90m/B; VHS, DVD.** *FR* Niels Arestrup; Claire Wauthion; Chantal Akerman; ***D:*** Chantal Akerman.

Jealousy *Celos* **1999** Antonio (Giminez Cacho) and Carmen (Sanchez-Gijon) seem to be happily engaged and making wedding plans when Antonio finds an old photo of Carmen with another man. Although he has no reason to be suspicious, he begins to investigate Carmen's past and becomes consumed by a jealous obsession that threatens to tear the couple apart. Spanish with subtitles. **105m/C; VHS, DVD.** *SP* Daniel Gimenez Cacho; Aitana Sanchez-Gijon; Maria Botto; Luis Tosar; ***D:*** Vicente Aranda; ***W:*** Vicente Aranda; Alvaro del Amo; ***C:*** Jose Luis Alcaine; ***M:*** Jose Nieto.

Jealousy *La jalousie* **2013** An intimate look at the wide impact of a man leaving his family for new relationships, by acclaimed French filmmaker Philippe Garrel. Louis (Garrel), an actor, leaves his wife and daughter to live with move in with a fellow actress, Claudia (Mouglalis). As his wife and daughter struggle in the wake of the abandonment and betrayal, Louis and Claudia must deal with their own fidelity issues. They also question if they should remain actors or live an easier life. The film emphasizes physical gestures and appearances to illustrate the emotional turmoil of the story. French with subtitles. **77m/B; DVD, Streaming, Download.** Louis Garrel; Anna Mouglalis; Rebecca Convenant; Olga Milshtein; Esther Garrel; ***D:*** Philippe Garrel; ***W:*** Philippe Garrel; Marc Cholodenko; Caroline Deruas-Garrel; Arlette Langmann; ***C:*** Willy Kurant; ***M:*** Jean-Louis Aubert.

Jean de Florette 1/2 **1987 (PG)** The first of two films (with "Manon of the Spring") based on Marcel Pagnol's novel. A single spring in drought-ridden Provence, France is blocked by two scheming countrymen (Montand and Auteuil). They await the imminent failure of the farm nearby, inherited by a city-born hunchback, whose chances for survival fade without water for his crops. A devastating story with a heartrending performance by Depardieu as the hunchback. Lauded and awarded; in French with English subtitles. **122m/C; VHS, DVD, Blu-Ray.** *FR* Gerard Depardieu; Yves Montand; Daniel Auteuil; Elisabeth Depardieu; Ernestine Mazurowna; Margarita Lozano; Armand Meffre; ***D:*** Claude Berri; ***W:*** Claude Berri; Gerard Brach; ***C:*** Bruno Nuytten; ***M:*** Jean-Claude Petit. British Acad. '87: Adapt. Screenplay, Film, Support. Actor (Auteuil); Cesar '87: Actor (Auteuil).

Jean-Michel Basquiat: The Radiant Child 2010 Definitive documentary on painter Jean-Michel Basquiat and New York's influential downtown art scene in the late '70s, exploding throughout the '80s. Crafted by friend Tamra Davis, who knew Basquiat from his rise to international stardom in 1983 at the age of 23 until his tragic heroin overdose in 1988. Unlike many gushy docs that focus on the uber-cool attitude of this period, Davis centers the footage on an interview she filmed with her friend in 1985 and recalls specific details that defined the movement. **93m/C; On Demand.** ***D:*** Tamra Davis; ***C:*** Tamra Davis; David Koh; Harry Geller; ***M:*** J. Ralph; Adam Horowitz; Mike Diamond.

Jeanne and the Perfect Guy *Jeanne et le Garcon Formidable* **1998** Jeanne (Ledoyen) is a hopeless romantic looking for her perfect love and having a lot of sex as she "auditions" her would-be Romeos. Then she meets Olivier (Demy) in the subway and decides he's the one. Only Olivier tells Jeanne that he has AIDS. Oh yeah, and it's a musical, with everyone breaking into song and dancing through the Parisian streets. It's gawky romanticism is strangely appealing and Ledoyen has a lot of charisma. French with subtitles. **98m/C; VHS, DVD.** ***FR*** Virginie Ledoyen; Mathieu Demy; Frederic Gorny; Jacques Bonnaffe; Valerie Bonneton; ***D:*** Olivier Ducastel; Jacques Martineau; ***W:*** Olivier Ducastel; Jacques Martineau; ***C:*** Mathieu Poirot-Delpech; ***M:*** Philippe Miller.

Jeanne Eagels 1957 Usual unreliable showbiz bio about the ill-fated 1920s actress. Jeanne (Novak) starts off as a hootchie-coochie dancer for carnival owner Sal Satori (Chandler). She's desperate to become a star and heads to Broadway where Jeanne takes acting lessons and then gets her chance by ruthlessly betraying another actress. Lover Sal is jealous of her success and won't help her when the booze and drugs take over. **108m/B; DVD.** Kim Novak; Jeff Chandler; Agnes Moorehead; Virginia Grey; Larry Gates; Murray Hamilton; Charles Drake; ***D:*** George Sidney; ***W:*** John Fante; Daniel Fuchs; Sonya Levien; ***C:*** Robert Planck; ***M:*** George Duning.

Jeanne la Pucelle *Joan the Maid: The Battles; Joan the Maid: The Prisons; Jeanne la Pucelle: Les Batailles; Jeanne la Purcelle: Les Prisons* **1994** Rivette's ambitious two-part production on the life of Joan of Arc. The first section, "The Battles," follows Joan (Bonnaire) as she becomes convinced that God has spoken to her, and that only she can lead the Dauphin's soldiers and end the English siege of Orleans. "The Prisons" finds the Dauphin crowned King Charles VII and no longer needing Joan's aid—in fact she becomes a hindrance to his plans and is sold to the English for trial and execution. French with subtitles. **241m/C; VHS, DVD, Blu-Ray.** ***FR*** Sandrine Bonnaire; Andre Marcon; Jean-Louis Richard; Jean-Pierre Lorit; ***D:*** Jacques Rivette; ***W:*** Christine Laurent; Pascal Bonitzer; ***C:*** William Lubtchansky; ***M:*** Jordi Savall.

Jeepers Creepers 2001 (R) Uneven horror entry that slips from mocking trite slasher flicks to becoming a trite slasher flick itself. Trish (Phillips) and her brother Darry (Long) are driving home from college during spring break when they're almost run down by a dilapidated cargo hauler. Further on down the abandoned desolate road, they see the driver of the van dumping what looks to be squirming human bodies into a drain pipe near a creepy church. They turn around to see if anyone needs help. Well, no one needs help, but a horror movie needs victims and they've just volunteered. The storyline then degrades into demonic, prophecy-laden voodoo nonsense while trying to keep its tongue firmly in cheek. Creature effects and make-up take over in no time. **89m/C; VHS, DVD, Blu-Ray.** Gina Philips; Justin Long; Jonathan Breck; Patricia Belcher; Brandon Smith; Eileen Brennan; ***D:*** Victor Salva; ***W:*** Victor Salva; ***C:*** Don E. Fauntleroy; ***M:*** Bennett Salvay.

Jeepers Creepers 2 1/2 2003 (R) Sequel finds teen football players and cheerleaders stranded on a bus somewhere in the sticks, looking like the next batch of victims of the titular Creeper, who apparently didn't get dead enough in the original. While the stereotypical, cardboard cast chews on the uninspired dialogue within the doomed bus, grizzled local farmer Jack Taggart (Wise) prepares to do battle with the thing that ate his son some 23 years ago. Although pic furnishes this beast with more special effects, including wings, it loses some of the low tech charm of the original in the process. Apparently the extra money spent on amping up the monster came out of the wardrobe budget, as a host of well-developed football players frequently, and inexplicably, walk around shirtless. **103m/C; VHS, DVD, Blu-Ray.** Ray Wise; Jonathan Breck; Deaundre "Double D" Davis; Eric Nenninger; Nicki Aycox; Travis Schiffner; Lena Cardwell; Billy Aaron Brown; Drew Tyler Bell; Marieh Delfino; ***D:*** Victor Salva; ***W:*** Victor Salva; ***C:*** Don E. Fauntleroy; ***M:*** Bennett Salvay.

Jeepers Creepers 3 2017 Set in the time period between the first and second installments, a group of fed-up farmers try to unearth the origins of the flying, cannibalistic Creeper in the hopes of finding his Achilles heel. High enough in body count to satisfy fans of the cult franchise, despite its shortcomings in acting and special effects. And as close to direct-to-video as they come -- it was screened in theaters for a single day. **100m/C; DVD, Blu-Ray.** Jonathan Breck; Gina Philips; Meg Foster; Stan Shaw; Chester Rushing; ***D:*** Victor Salva; ***W:*** Victor Salva; ***C:*** Don E. FauntLeRoy; ***M:*** Andrew Morgan Smith.

Jeff, Who Lives at Home 1/2 2012 (R) Jeff (Segel) is a slacker who lives in his mother's (Sarandon) basement and one day decides to "go with the flow" as life presents it to him. After convincing himself that the wrong number call he keeps getting is meant to guide him in a certain direction, Jeff follows the signs he sees around him and ends up crossing paths with his brother (Helms) and potentially-cheating sister-in-law (Greer). The Duplass brothers find an easygoing charm in the story, and there are some strong performances, but it ultimately feels a little too thin, and Helms seems miscast. **83m/C; DVD, Blu-Ray.** Jason Segel; Ed Helms; Susan Sarandon; Judy Greer; Rae Dawn Chong; Steve Zissis; Evan Ross; ***D:*** Jay Duplass; Mark Duplass; ***W:*** Jay Duplass; Mark Duplass; ***C:*** Jas Shelton; ***M:*** Michael Andrews.

Jefferson in Paris 1/2 1994 (PG-13) Costume drama explores the impact Thomas Jefferson's (Nolte) five years in pre-revolutionary Paris (as American ambassador to Versailles) had on his private life. Jefferson confronts the personal and political issues of slavery in America, as well as his feelings for Sally Hemings (Newton), a Monticello slave brought to Paris by Jefferson's daughter. The Jefferson-Hemings legend may or may not be true (more likely not, according to many historians), but it seems to be the central theme here. Merchant Ivory's trademark tasteful production values and earnest characters can't camouflage the fact that they're playing fast and loose with the historical facts. **139m/C; VHS, DVD, Blu-Ray.** Nick Nolte; Greta Scacchi; Gwyneth Paltrow; Thandie Newton; Jean-Pierre Aumont; Seth Gilliam; Todd Boyce; James Earl Jones; ***D:*** James Ivory; ***W:*** Ruth Prawer Jhabvala; ***M:*** Richard Robbins.

Jeffrey 1/2 1995 (R) AIDS-fearing Jeffrey (Weber) decides to give celibacy a try until a trip to the gym brings Mr. Right into the picture. Steve (Weiss) is a hunk, but he happens to be HIV-positive, which prompts Jeffrey to do some serious soul-searching. Hence the message: AIDS sucks, but don't let it destroy life's joys. Musical fantasy numbers, phallic fireworks, and a game show are a bit crass and the high theatrics can get annoying, but wicked barbs and one-liners score lots of laughs. Scene-stealer Stewart is caustically funny as Jeffrey's flamboyantly effeminate best friend Sterling, who works as an interior decorator and dates a "Cats" chorus boy. Adapted from the Paul Rudnick play. **92m/C; VHS, DVD, Blu-Ray.** Steven Weber; Patrick Stewart; Michael T. Weiss; Bryan Batt; Sigourney Weaver; Olympia Dukakis; Kathy Najimy; Nathan Lane; ***Cameo(s):*** Victor Garber; Christine Baranski; ***D:*** Christopher Ashley; ***W:*** Paul Rudnick; ***C:*** Jeffery Tufano; ***M:*** Stephen Endelman.

Jekyll 2007 A modern retelling of the Robert Louis Stevenson tale of the ultimate split personality. Using modern technology Dr. Tom Jackson (Nesbitt), the last descendent of Jekyll/Hyde, is determined to keep his dangerous alter ego under control. But he doesn't realize that someone else is monitoring him (or them, as the case may be). As usual, Hyde has a great deal more fun than his responsible other half. **300m/C; DVD.** ***GB*** James Nesbitt; Gina Bellman; Denis Lawson; Michelle Ryan; Meera Syal; Fenella Woolgar; ***D:*** Douglas Mackinnon; Matt Lipsey; ***W:*** Steven Moffatt; ***C:*** Adam Suschitzky; ***M:*** Debbie Wiseman. **TV**

Jekyll and Hyde 1/2 1990 Unmemorable remake of the Robert Louis Stevenson tale of a doctor whose scientific experiments lead to a horrifyingly violent split personality. Caine does have a good time with his dual role. Made for TV. **100m/C; VHS, DVD.** Michael Caine; Cheryl Ladd; Joss Ackland; Ronald Pickup; Kim Thomson; Lionel Jeffries; Kevin McNally; Lee Montague; Diane Keen; David Schofield; ***D:*** David Wickes; ***W:*** David Wickes; ***C:*** Norman G. Langley. **TV**

Jekyll & Hyde. . . Together Again 1982 (R) New Wave comic version of the classic story. This time, a serious young surgeon turns into a drug-crazed punk rocker after sniffing a mysterious powder. Mad scientist Blankfield fires and misfires, occasionally eliciting a snort. **87m/C; VHS, DVD, Blu-Ray.** Mark Blankfield; Bess Armstrong; Krista Errickson; Tim Thomerson; Michael McGuire; Cassandra Peterson; Peter Brocco; Lin Shaye; Corinne Bohrer; George Wendt; Michael Ensign; Sam Whipple; Tony Cox; Art LaFleur; ***D:*** Jerry Belson; ***W:*** Jerry Belson; Monica Johnson; Michael Leeson; Harvey Miller; ***C:*** Philip H. Lathrop; ***M:*** Barry DeVorzon.

Jem and the Holograms 2015 (PG) Jon M. Chu's adaptation of the hit 1980s TV series is so strange that one almost has to admire it for its sheer oddity, even as it totally alters its source material and angers its fan base. However, oddity only gets a movie so far. Aubrey Peeples plays Jerrica Benton, a singer who becomes an internet sensation and forms the titular band with her two foster sisters. They end up embarking on a truly odd quest at the behest of a robot named 51N3RG.Y (pronounced Synergy). The odd combination of coming-of-age drama and cartoon source material doesn't quite blend, but it could become a cult hit. **118m/C; DVD, Blu-Ray.** Aubrey Peeples; Stefanie Scott; Aurora Perrineau; Hayley Kiyoko; Molly Ringwald; Ryan Guzman; ***D:*** Jon M. Chu; ***W:*** Ryan Landels; ***C:*** Alice Brooks; ***M:*** Nathan Lanier.

Jennifer 8 1992 (R) Mix of familiar genres results in a film about a burned-out cop moving to the suburbs where he finds the eighth victim of a serial killer and falls in love with the chief witness. Garcia is John Berlin, the cop who discovers the hand of the blind female victim, which leads him to her school and Helena Robertson (Thurman), another blind woman who may have the information he needs. Dark and mysterious atmosphere is dramatic, but plot lacks logic and sense of thrill. **127m/C; VHS, DVD, Blu-Ray.** Andy Garcia; Uma Thurman; Lance Henriksen; Kathy Baker; Graham Beckel; Kevin Conway; John Malkovich; ***D:*** Bruce Robinson; ***W:*** Bruce Robinson.

Jennifer On My Mind WOOF! 1971 Ghastly would-be youth pic told in flashback. Marcus (Brandon) meets hippie chick Jennifer (Walker) on vacation in Venice and follows her back to New York. She goes from smoking weed to shooting heroin in record time. Tragedy strikes and Marcus has to deal with the aftermath. The acting is terrible and United Artists' re-edit did nothing to help the plot make sense. Robert de Niro has a small part as a gypsy cab driver. **90m/C; DVD.** Michael Brandon; Tippy Walker; Chuck McCann; Peter Bonerz; Renee Taylor; Robert De Niro; ***D:*** Noel Black; ***W:*** Erich Segal; ***C:*** Andrew Laszlo; ***M:*** Stephen Lawrence.

Jennifer's Body 2009 (R) Campy, messy (in many ways), self-referential teen horror comedy. Bitchy high school sex bomb/cheerleader Jennifer (Fox) gets transformed into a succubus-type demon who munches on the flesh of teenaged boys. Her best friend—sensible, smart Needy (Seyfried)--discovers Jennifer's bloody afterschool pursuits and decides to put a stop to the mayhem when Jennifer goes after Needy's sweetie, Chip (Simmons). **102m/C; Blu-Ray, On Demand.** Megan Fox; Amanda Seyfried; Johnny Simmons; Adam Brody; J.K. Simmons; Amy Sedaris; Chris Pratt; Kyle Gallner; Allison Janney; ***D:*** Karyn Kusama; ***W:*** Diablo Cody; ***C:*** M. David Mullen; ***M:*** Theodore Shapiro; Stephen Barton.

Jenny Lamour *Quai des Orfevres* **1947** A dark mystery thriller about a singer accused of murdering a man he thought was stealing his woman. Acclaimed genre piece, dubbed into English. **95m/B; VHS, DVD, Blu-Ray.** ***FR*** Louis Jouvet; Suzy Delair; Bernard Blier; Simone Renant; ***D:*** Henri-Georges Clouzot.

The Jensen Project 1/2 2010 Innocuous family adventure. Claire and husband Matt used to work for a covert research organization called the Jensen Project—a fact their bored teenaged son Brody never knew until the Thompsons are contacted once again. Seems Claire's mentor Edwin has stolen nanobot technology and is going to use it for nefarious purposes unless Brody and trainee Samantha (Diaz) can help foil his plans. **90m/C; DVD.** Justin Kelly; Alyssa Diaz; Kellie Martin; LeVar Burton; Brady Smith; Patricia Richardson; David Andrews; ***D:*** Douglas Barr; ***W:*** Monica Macer; ***C:*** Pierre Jodoin; ***M:*** Randy Jackson; Eric Allaman. **TV**

Jeopardy 1/2 1953 Sunlit noirish thriller with an intriguingly crazed performance by Meeker and Stanwyck doing some vamping. While vacationing on a remote beach spot in Baja, Mexico, Doug Stilwin (Sullivan) gets trapped by a piling on a rotted pier with the tide coming in. Leaving their young son (Aaker) to comfort dad, mom Barb (Stanwyck) takes off in the car to get help. She's thankful to run into an American along the deserted road, except Lawson (Meeker) turns out to be a dangerous escaped con who takes her hostage and steals the car. Barb eventually persuades Lawson that she'll run away with him if only he'll rescue her hubby first. Ya know, sometimes crime does pay. **69m/C; DVD.** Barbara Stanwyck; Ralph Meeker; Barry Sullivan; Lee Aaker; ***D:*** John Sturges; ***W:*** Mel Dinelli; ***C:*** Victor Milner; ***M:*** Dimitri Tomkin.

Jeremiah 1/2 1998 The prophet Jeremiah abandons his family and the woman he loves in order to proclaim God's message that the people of Judah must change their ways or be overcome by the Babylonians. He's deemed a traitor but the prophecy is fulfilled when Jerusalem is destroyed. **96m/C; VHS, DVD.** Patrick Dempsey; Oliver Reed; Klaus Maria Brandauer; ***D:*** Harry Winer. **CABLE**

Jeremiah Johnson 1972 (PG) The story of a man (Redford) who turns his back on civilization, circa 1830, and learns a new code of survival (thanks to a trapper, played by Geer) in a brutal land of isolated mountains and hostile Indians. In the process, Jeremiah becomes part of the wilderness, eventually taking an Indian wife and adopting a son. When hostile Crow warriors kill them, he begins a one-man revenge mission, gaining legendary status as a warrior. Based on the novel "Mountain Man" by Vardis Fisher and the story "Crow Killer" by Raymond W. Thorp and Robert Bunker. A notable and picturesque movie, filmed in Utah. **107m/C; VHS, DVD, Blu-Ray.** Robert Redford; Will Geer; Stefan Gierasch; Allyn Ann McLerie; Joaquin Martinez; Charles Tyner; Paul Benedict; Josh Albee; Delle Bolton; ***D:*** Sydney Pollack; ***W:*** Edward Anhalt; John Milius; ***C:*** Duke Callaghan; ***M:*** John Rubinstein.

Jeremy's Family Reunion 2004 Jeremy is a young, successful, African American attorney in New York City. He and his attractive white fiancee, Lisa, attend Jeremy's annual family reunion in New Orleans, where his colorful kin embarrass Jeremy. The family shows their disapproval of Jeremy's relationship and his city lifestyle, and Lisa flirts with the relatives—ultimately ending up in the bathroom with one. Unapologetically urban farce with unapologetically cheap story line and production values. **88m/C; DVD.** Jedda Jones; Gavin Lewis; Chauvon Higgins; Nolan Powell; ***D:*** Abel Garcia; ***W:*** Abel Garcia. **VIDEO**

Jericho *Dark Sands* **1938** Jericho Jackson (Robeson) is a corporal in the black unit of the U.S.'s Expeditionary Forces in WWI France. After a fight with his sergeant leads to the man's accidental death, Jackson is court-martialed and sentenced to die. He manages to escape to North Africa and begin a new life but military authorities eventually discover his whereabouts. Despite the military drama, Robeson's vocal talents are still showcased. **77m/B; VHS, DVD.** *GB* Paul Robeson; Henry Wilcoxon; Wallace Ford; ***D:*** Thornton Freeland.

Jericho 1/2 **2001 (PG-13)** When a robbery goes wrong in the town of Jericho, the three bandits—one of whom has suffered a serious head wound—leave a dead sheriff behind as they head out of town. The wounded thief is soon left to die but is found and nursed back to health by freed slave turned preacher Joshua (Coffee), who names the amnesiac "Jericho." As the two travel the countryside, bits and pieces of Jericho's past surface and he's drawn to his namesake town, where his past is finally revealed. The surprise ending feels tacked on rather than a part of the ordinary script but the two men's friendship is a bonus as is Coffee's affecting performance. **102m/C; VHS, DVD.** Mark Valley; R. Lee Ermey; Leon Coffee; Lisa Stewart; Buck Taylor; Mark Collie; ***D:*** Merlin Miller; ***W:*** Robert Avard Miller; ***C:*** Jerry Holway; ***M:*** Mark Haffner. **VIDEO**

Jericho Mansions 1/2 **2003 (R)** Longtime apartment building super Leonard (Caan) becomes involved in a murder investigation when a tenant turns up dead. He's already having a rough time, with complaints from other tenants and a theft accusation. Director Sciamma takes a much cooler, smarter path to the surprise ending than most mystery/thriller tales these days. Caan is in fine form. **98m/C; VHS, DVD.** James Caan; Jennifer Tilly; Genevieve Bujold; Maribel Verdu; Peter Keleghan; Bruce Ramsay; Susan Glover; Mark Camacho; ***D:*** Alberto Sciamma; ***W:*** Alberto Sciamma; Harriet Sand; ***C:*** Alastair Meux; ***M:*** Dan (Daniel) Jones. **VIDEO**

Jerichow **2015** A thriller inspired by such classic film noirs as The Postman Always Rings Twice. Set a bleak village in northeastern Germany, a love triangle forms between a Turkish immigrant businessman, his gorgeous but unhappy German wife, and a good looking former solider who has recently returned from Afghanistan after being dishonorably discharged. The soldier, Thomas (Furmann), is hired by Ali (Sozer) as a driver, and soon meets Ali's wife Laura (Hoss) Thomas and Laura eventually fall in love and begin to make plans to run away together, but nothing works out as it should. German and Turkish with subtitles. **93m/C; DVD.** Benno Furmann; Nina Hoss; Hilmi Sozer; Andre Hennicke; Claudia Geisler; ***D:*** Christian Petzold; ***W:*** Christian Petzold; ***C:*** Hans Fromm; ***M:*** Stefan Will.

The Jerk 1/2 **1979 (R)** A jerk tells his rags-to-riches-to-rags story in comedic flashbacks, from "I was born a poor Black child," through his entrepreneurial success in his invention of the "Optigrab," to his inevitable decline. Only film in history with a dog named "Shithead." Martin's first starring role, back in his wild and crazy days; his ridiculous misadventures pay tribute to Jerry Lewis movies of the late '60s. Followed by a TV version released in 1984 as "The Jerk Too," with Mark Blankfield as the Jerk. **94m/C; VHS, DVD, Blu-Ray, HD-DVD.** Steve Martin; Bernadette Peters; Catlin Adams; Bill Macy; Jackie Mason; Carl Gottlieb; Mabel King; Richard Ward; M. Emmet Walsh; Dick O'Neill; Maurice Evans; Pepe Serna; Trinidad Silva; Lenny Montana; ***Cameo(s):*** Carl Reiner; Rob Reiner; ***D:*** Carl Reiner; ***W:*** Steve Martin; Carl Gottlieb; Michael Elias; ***C:*** Victor Kemper; ***M:*** Jack Elliott.

The Jerk Theory **2011 (PG-13)** A teen romantic comedy about the importance of being yourself. After being dumped by his girlfriend as she searches for someone more exciting, nice guy Adam (Henderson) decides to make a major life change to get a new girl. He's going to be a jerk because every girl loves a bad boy. Initially, his plan works and Adam becomes one of the most popular guys in school. However, Adam is forced to question his new attitude when he meets Molly (Dewan Tatum) who has had some bad experiences of her own and only gives her number to nice guys. Adam soon learns that he has to be himself to really find love. **93m/C; DVD.** Josh Henderson; Jenna Dewan; Lauren Storm; Derek Lee Nixon; Jesse Heiman; ***D:*** Scott S. Anderson; ***W:*** Scott S. Anderson; Abraham Taylor; ***C:*** T.C. Christensen; ***M:*** Josh Aker.

The Jerky Boys **WOOF!** **1995 (R)** Quick! Let's make a Jerky Boys movie and exploit their popularity before everyone realizes what a lame, one-joke act it is! Too late, guys. In what passes for a plot, Johnny and Kamal prank call an irritable mob boss (Arkin), pretending to be Chicago hitmen in need of a hideout. The wiseguys soon figure out the truth, but the requisite dumb cop (Sullivan) pads the film by not catching on. All these "twists" serve only one purpose—to get our heroes to the next phone. Don't accept the charges for this one. **82m/C; VHS, Streaming.** Johnny Brennan; Kamal Ahmed; Alan Arkin; William Hickey; Alan North; James Lorinz; Brad Sullivan; Vincent Pastore; Ozzy Osbourne; Paul Bartel; Suzanne Shepherd; ***Cameo(s):*** Tom Jones; ***D:*** James Melkonian; ***W:*** Johnny Brennan; Kamal Ahmed; Rich Wilkes; James Melkonian.

Jerome **1998** Well-acted indie with a compelling story that deserves a wider audience. After 15 soul-sucking years as a factory welder in California, Wade Hampton (Pillsbury) decides to just walk away from his life. He picks Jerome, Arizona as his destination because he's heard it has an artists' colony and Wade has secretly been making miniature metal sculptures. So Wade heads out on the highway and encounters restless hitchhiker, Jane (Malick), who has no destination in mind at all. The film is interspersed with interviews with people from Wade's past, so the viewer also anticipates trouble coming for the travelers as well. **91m/C; VHS, DVD.** Wendie Malick; Drew Pillsbury; Scott McKenna; Beth Kennedy; James Keeley; ***D:*** Thomas Johnston; David Elton; Eric Tignini; ***W:*** Thomas Johnston; David Elton; Eric Tignini; ***C:*** Gina DeGirolamo.

Jerry and Tom **1998 (R)** Tom (Mantegna) is a veteran hitman breaking in an impatient protege, Jerry (Rockwell), on various assignments for a couple of old-time mobsters. The most important thing to remember is that it's just a job—nothing personal—but that kind of emotional vacuum isn't easy to maintain. Familiar story but it has the advantage of a talented cast and good direction. **97m/C; VHS, DVD.** Joe Mantegna; Sam Rockwell; Maury Chaykin; Charles Durning; Peter Riegert; William H. Macy; Ted Danson; ***D:*** Saul Rubinek; ***W:*** Rick Cleveland; ***C:*** Paul Sarossy; ***M:*** David Buchbinder.

Jerry Maguire 1/2 **1996 (R)** Romantic sports comedy focuses on the off-field action and makes an agent the good guy. Risky business in an era of strikes, lockouts, and astronomical salaries, but writer/director Crowe manages to pull it off. Cruise is well-used as the title character in the story of a shark-like sports agent who sees the error of his ways and transforms into...a more moral sports agent. Somewhat regretting his momentary twinge of honor (which gets him fired from his ultra-huge agency), he allies himself with his obnoxious and least important client Rod Tidwell (Gooding Jr.), as well as Dorothy, an adoring young accountant (Zellweger) with a lovable young son (Lipnicki, making a strong bid for Culkin-like stardom). Famously well-researched, film sports great dialogue, talented leads, great supporting cast and a mega-star currently riding a wave of $100-million-plus films (talk about "Show me the money!"). Pop culture bonus points for coining 1996's most memorable catch phrase, which Crowe took from real life ex-Phoenix Cardinal Tim McDonald, and is now being used to sell everything from magazines to t-shirts. **135m/C; VHS, DVD, Blu-Ray, UMD.** Tom Cruise; Cuba Gooding, Jr.; Renée Zellweger; Kelly Preston; Bonnie Hunt; Jerry O'Connell; Jay Mohr; Regina King; Glenn Frey; Jonathan Lipnicki; Todd Louiso; Mark Pellington; ***Cameo(s):*** Eric Stoltz; ***D:*** Cameron Crowe; ***W:*** Cameron Crowe; ***C:*** Janusz Kaminski; ***M:*** Nancy Wilson. Oscars '96: Support. Actor (Gooding); Golden Globes '97: Actor--Mus./Comedy (Cruise); MTV Movie Awards '97: Male Perf. (Cruise); Natl. Bd. of Review '96: Actor (Cruise); Screen Actors Guild '96: Support. Actor (Gooding); Broadcast Film Critics '96: Breakthrough Perf. (Zellweger), Support. Actor (Gooding).

Jersey Boys 1/2 **2014 (R)** Eastwood wisely chooses to stick closely to the Broadway hit musical about the life of Frankie Valli and the rise of The Four Seasons, casting actors who played the crooners on stage, including the Tony Award-winning star. However, Eastwood can't seem to find a way to make the scenes when they're not singing hearts out work like they did in a theater. Luckily, there aren't too many of those and the "Boys" have an infectious energy. It also deserves points for appealing to an audience that isn't targeted much in the superhero-centric era of Hollywood. **134m/C; DVD, Blu-Ray.** John Lloyd Young; Vincent Piazza; Michael Lomenda; Erich Bergen; Christopher Walken; Joseph Russo; Mike Doyle; ***D:*** Clint Eastwood; ***W:*** Marshall Brickman; Rick Elice; ***C:*** Tom Stern; ***M:*** Bob Gaudio.

Jersey Girl 1/2 **1992 (PG-13)** Toby Mastellone (Gertz) is a bright single gal from the Jersey shore who wants something better in her life. Her hard-working dad (Bologna) has fixed her up with an apprentice plumber but she wants a Manhattan guy. And then Toby meets cute with Sal (McDemott), who seems just the ticket, but can you really take the Jersey out of the girl? **95m/C; VHS, DVD.** Jami Gertz; Dylan McDermott; Joseph Bologna; Aida Turturro; Star Jasper; Sheryl Lee; Joseph Mazzello; Molly Price; ***D:*** David Burton Morris; ***W:*** Gina Wendkos; ***M:*** Stephen Bedell.

Jersey Girl 1/2 **2004 (PG-13)** Big shot music PR man Ollie (Affleck) is widowed when wife Gertrude (Lopez) dies in childbirth and must raise his daughter Gertie (Castro) on his own. But this proves too challenging as he loses his job and is forced to crash with dear old dad (Carlin) in New Jersey. After seven years, he's still struggling with his loss. Celibate, he frequents the video shop for porno flicks where he meets the shoot-from-the-hip clerk, Maya (Tyler). Ah, and there the romance begins, along with the "should I be a good parent or have a great career" dilemma. Writer-director Smith's considerable comedic talents emerge unevenly in his foray into the dramatic-comedy genre. Granted, it's probably not what Smith's fans are used to, but it's still enjoyable. Castro is a fresh, sassy presence in her feature debut. **102m/C; VHS, DVD, Blu-Ray.** Ben Affleck; Jennifer Lopez; George Carlin; Liv Tyler; Raquel Castro; Stephen (Steve) Root; Mike Starr; Jason Biggs; S. Epatha Merkerson; Jennifer Schwalbach Smith; Jason Lee; Matt Damon; Paulie (Litowsky) Litt; ***Cameo(s):*** Will Smith; ***D:*** Kevin Smith; ***W:*** Kevin Smith; ***C:*** Vilmos Zsigmond; ***M:*** James L. Venable.

Jersey Shore Shark Attack **2012 (R)** In this goofy creature feature from the Syfy Channel, Seaside, New Jersey is the place to party on the 4th of July. A bunch of (lame CGI) red-eyed, albino, human-munching sharks feel the same way. Much to the disgust of viewers, the parodied "Jersey Shore" dimwits who are out to stop the sea killers don't become shark bait. **87m/C; DVD, Blu-Ray.** Jeremy Luke; Melissa Molinaro; Daniel Booko; Alex Mauriello; Joey Russo; Audie Resendez; Jack Scalia; William Atherton; Tony Sirico; Paul Sorvino; ***D:*** John Shepphird; ***W:*** Michael Ciminera; Richard Gnolfo; ***C:*** Theo Angell; ***M:*** Andres Boulton. **CABLE**

Jesse **2011 (R)** A sibling's death compels a cop to become a vigilante in this action drama. Jesse (Finochio) is a gifted Nassau County, New York, police detective who does all she can to ensure justice is served among the criminal element in her area and protect her family. She is pushed to her limit when her brother is murdered during a drug deal gone bad and when her mother is beaten nearly to death. Known for having a temper, she takes matters into her own hands to ensure punishment is delivered one way or another. She fights the crime, the system, and the corruption therein to ensure justice is fully served. **120m/C; DVD, Streaming, Download.** Stephanie Finochio; William Forsythe; Armand Assante; Eric Roberts; Michael Wright; ***D:*** Fred Carpenter; ***W:*** Fred Carpenter; Joanne Tamburro; ***C:*** Al Rodgers; ***M:*** Douglas Brown. **VIDEO**

Jesse James **1939** One of director King's best efforts is this Hollywood biography of the notorious outlaw. 24-year-old Power showed he was more than just his good looks in the title role but Fonda truly became a star in the role of brother Frank James. Screenwriter Johnson also focused more on the legend than the reality of the outlaw's career in post-Civil War Missouri. **105m/C; VHS, DVD, Blu-Ray.** Henry Fonda; Tyrone Power; Randolph Scott; Henry Hull; Jane Darwell; Brian Donlevy; Charles Halton; John Carradine; Donald Meek; Slim Summerville; ***D:*** Henry King; ***W:*** Nunnally Johnson; ***C:*** George Barnes; William Howard Greene; ***M:*** Louis Silvers.

Jesse James Meets Frankenstein's Daughter 1/2 **1965** The gunslinger and Frankenstein's granddaughter, Maria, meet up in the Old West in this wacky combination of western and horror genres. **95m/C; VHS, DVD.** John Lupton; Cal Bolder; Narda Onyx; Steven Geray; Estelita; Jim Davis; William "Bill" Fawcett; Nestor Paiva; Rayford Barnes; Roger Creed; ***D:*** William Beaudine; ***W:*** Carl K. Hittleman; ***C:*** Lothrop Worth; ***M:*** Raoul Kraushaar.

Jesse James Rides Again **1947** Originally a serial, this feature depicts the further adventures of the West's most notorious outlaw. **181m/B; VHS, DVD.** Clayton Moore; Linda Stirling; Roy Barcroft; Tristram Coffin; ***D:*** Fred Brannon; Thomas Carr.

Jesse James' Women **1954** Only directorial effort for leading man Barry is a very low-budget, mediocre western. Outlaw Jesse heads to Mississippi where he proceeds to use every woman he meets in various robberies and swindles. Has a prerequisite catfight--this one between singer Delta (Baron) and saloonkeeper Waco (Castle). **86m/C; DVD.** Donald (Don "Red") Barry; Peggie Castle; Lita Baron; Jack Buetel; ***D:*** Donald (Don "Red") Barry; ***W:*** D.D. Beauchamp; ***C:*** Kenneth Peach, Sr.; ***M:*** Walter Greene.

The Jesse Owens Story **1984** The moving story of the four-time Olympic Gold medal winner's triumphs and misfortunes. **174m/C; VHS, DVD.** Dorian Harewood; Debbi (Deborah) Morgan; Georg Stanford Brown; LeVar Burton; George Kennedy; Tom Bosley; Ben Vereen; ***D:*** Richard Irving; ***W:*** Harold Gast. **TV**

Jesse Stone: Benefit of the Doubt **2012** In Selleck's eighth appearance as Jesse Stone, the ex-police chief of Paradise is called back to work when his successor and his deputy are blown up in their patrol car. The case involves money and drugs and a lot of drinking, brooding, and occasional conversation from Stone. He's also working without deputies Rose and Luther since they've left the force. These are always slow-paced character studies but there's some action in the final minutes that leaves a few unanswered questions. **90m/C; DVD.** Tom Selleck; Saul Rubinek; Gloria Reuben; Stephen McHattie; William Devane; William Sadler; Robert Carradine; Kohl Sudduth; Jeff Geddis; Jeremy Akerman; Kathy Baker; ***D:*** Robert Harmon; ***W:*** Tom Selleck; Michael Brandman; ***C:*** David Gribble; ***M:*** Jeff Beal. **TV**

Jesse Stone: Death in Paradise 1/2 *Death in Paradise; Robert B. Parker's Jesse Stone: Death in Paradise* **2006** Jesse (Selleck) is reluctantly seeing a shrink (Devane) to help him with his drinking problem but his bad habits don't interfere with his investigating skills. When the body of a pregnant teenage girl is found floating in a lake, he wants to know why no one reported her missing. Jesse's investigation soon leads him to a best-selling local author (Basaraba) and a Boston mob boss (Flynn). The third in the series of TV movies. Based on a novel by Robert B. Parker. **87m/C; DVD.** Tom Selleck; Viola Davis; Kohl Sudduth; Stephen McHattie; William Devane; Edward Edwards; Gary Basaraba; Matthew F. Barr; Steve Flynn; John Diehl; Debra Christofferson; Orla Brady; Mae Whitman; ***D:*** Robert Harmon; ***W:*** J.T. Allen; Michael Brandman; ***C:*** David Gribble; ***M:*** Jeff Beal. **TV**

Jesse Stone: Innocents Lost **2011** Jesse (Selleck) is brooding even more than usual in this seventh TV movie, based on characters created by Robert B. Parker. No longer the sheriff of Paradise, Jesse is bored, drinking, and depressed (even his dog is depressed) when a college student he busted and then befriended is found dead of a drug overdose. Jesse suspects there's more to the case but his pressing the matter puts him on the wrong side of a lot of people (as usual). A slow-paced story although the recurring characters add colorful bits and

Selleck is always worth watching. **90m/C; DVD.** Tom Selleck; Kathy Baker; Kohl Sudduth; Stephen McHattie; William Sadler; Saul Rubinek; William Devane; Gloria Reuben; Jeff Geddis; Eileen April Boylan; ***D:*** Dick Lowry; ***W:*** Tom Selleck; Michael Brandman; ***C:*** David Gribble; ***M:*** Jeff Beal. **TV**

Jesse Stone: Night Passage 🦴🦴 1/2 *Night Passage; Robert B. Parker's Jesse Stone: Night Passage* **2006** In this prequel, we see how Jesse Stone (Selleck), a former L.A. homicide detective with a drinking problem and an ex-wife he still loves, gets his last chance by taking on the job of police chief of Paradise. Town councilor Hasty Hardaway (Rubinek) thinks Stone will be easy to push around but he learns differently. Jesse is soon investigating the suspicious death of his recently retired predecessor, which leads to a money laundering scheme and mob ties. Second in the series of TV movies. Based on the book by Robert B. Parker. **89m/C; DVD.** Tom Selleck; Viola Davis; Kohl Sudduth; Polly Shannon; Stephen McHattie; Saul Rubinek; Stephanie March; Stephen Baldwin; Mike Starr; ***D:*** Robert Harmon; ***W:*** Tom Epperson; ***C:*** David Gribble; ***M:*** Jeff Beal. **TV**

Jesse Stone: No Remorse 🦴🦴 1/2 **2010** In this leisurely-paced sixth outing, Selleck gets even more comfortable in the role of contemplative, boozing Paradise sheriff Jesse Stone. Except Jesse has been suspended by the town council for his unorthodox behavior and is not supposed to have any contact with his harried deputies (Baker, Sudduth) who are dealing with a robbery spree. So his old Boston pal Healy (McHattie) asks Jesse to look into three murders, which brings him back into contact with mobster Gino Fish (Sadler). Based on characters created by Robert B. Parker. **90m/C; DVD.** Tom Selleck; Kathy Baker; Kohl Sudduth; Stephen McHattie; William Sadler; Todd Hofley; William Devane; Saul Rubinek; Krista Allen; ***D:*** Robert Harmon; ***W:*** Tom Selleck; Michael Brandman; ***C:*** David Gribble; ***M:*** Jeff Beal. **TV**

Jesse Stone: Sea Change 🦴🦴 1/2 *Sea Change* **2007** In this fourth TV movie (based on the novel by Robert B. Parker), Paradise sheriff Jesse Stone (Selleck) is bored, brooding, and drinking too much. So bored that he recruits deputy Rose (Baker) and reopens a cold case—a bank robbery, shooting, and missing teller from 15 years ago. Then things heat up when a young local woman claims to have been raped aboard a visitor's yacht and some Boston thug is tailing Jesse with bad intent. **87m/C; DVD.** Tom Selleck; Kathy Baker; William Devane; Rebecca Pidgeon; Sean Young; Saul Rubinek; Viola Davis; Kohl Sudduth; Nigel Bennett; ***D:*** Robert Harmon; ***W:*** Ronni Kern; ***C:*** Rene Ohashi; ***M:*** Jeff Beal. **TV**

Jesse Stone: Stone Cold 🦴🦴 1/2 *Stone Cold; Robert B. Parker's Jesse Stone: Stone Cold* **2005** Jesse Stone (Selleck) is settling into his life as police chief of Paradise, a small New England fishing/tourist community. But his quiet, which is usually spent with a bottle of scotch, is disturbed by a series of murders—one of which hits too close to home. The first in a series of TV movies. Based on the book by Robert B. Parker. **87m/C; DVD.** Tom Selleck; Viola Davis; Kohl Sudduth; Polly Shannon; Stephen McHattie; Jane Adams; Mimi Rogers; ***D:*** Robert Harmon; ***W:*** John Fasano; Michael Brandman; ***C:*** Rene Ohashi; ***M:*** Jeff Beal. **TV**

Jesse Stone: Thin Ice 🦴🦴 1/2 *Thin Ice* **2009** In Selleck's fifth outing as Robert B. Parker's sheriff of smalltown Paradise, Jesse is hitting the booze a little harder than usual before two investigations occupy his time. First, his Boston buddy Capt. Healy (McHattie) is nearly murdered, and second, desperate Elizabeth Blue (Manheim) visits the town looking for her long-missing son. And as usual, Jesse's unorthodox policing has the town council threatening to suspend or fire him. **88m/C; DVD.** Tom Selleck; Kathy Baker; Kohl Sudduth; Leslie Hope; Stephen McHattie; Camryn Manheim; William Sadler; Jessica Hecht; William Devane; Joanna Miles; ***D:*** Robert Harmon; ***W:*** Ronni Kern; ***C:*** Rene Ohashi; ***M:*** Jeff Beal. **TV**

The Jesse Ventura Story 🦴 1/2 **1999** Cheap quickie TV movie capitalizes on Ventura's unlikely career path. Smalltown boy Ventura becomes a Navy SEAL, a professional wrestler known as "The Body" (among other jobs), and eventually winds up in an upset victory as the governor of Minnesota. A dull, unauthorized whitewash that would probably bore even Ventura himself. **95m/C; VHS, DVD.** Nils Allen Stewart; Nancy Sakovich; Thomas Brandise; Christopher Bondy; Nola Auguston; ***D:*** David S. Jackson; ***W:*** Patricia Jones; Donald Reiker; ***C:*** John Holosko; ***M:*** Richard Gibbs. **TV**

Jesus 🦴🦴 1/2 **2000** Not completely reverential look at the life and teachings of Jesus (Sisto) from a historical, political, and religious viewpoint. Jesus is kind of a fun-loving 30-year-old who knows he has a destiny to fulfill. He and his parents (Bissett and Mueller-Stahl) struggle to deal with that as his followers seek the best course of resistance to Roman oppression, embodied by the political savvy Pontius Pilate (Oldman). The only truly disconcerting note is a slick Satan (Krabbe), who dresses like a contemporary wiseguy, and his temptation of Jesus in the wilderness. **174m/C; VHS, DVD.** Jeremy Sisto; Jacqueline Bisset; Armin Mueller-Stahl; Debra Messing; Gary Oldman; Jeroen Krabbe; David O'Hara; G.W. Bailey; Thomas Lockyer; Luca Zingaretti; Stefania Rocca; Claudio Amendola; ***D:*** Roger Young; ***W:*** Suzette Couture; ***C:*** Raffaele Mertes; ***M:*** Patrick Williams. **TV**

Jesus Camp 🦴🦴 1/2 **2006 (PG-13)** Follows several children at an evangelical Christian summer camp that serves as a training ground for the youth to become advocates and assume leadership roles in a born-again religious revival. **84m/C; DVD.** ***D:*** Heidi Ewing; Rachel Grady.

Jesus Christ, Superstar 🦴🦴🦴 **1973 (G)** A rock opera that portrays, in music, the last seven days in the earthly life of Christ, as reenacted by young tourists in Israel. Outstanding musical score was the key to the success of the film, although Elliman and Anderson are standouts as, respectively, Mary Magdalene and Judas. Based on the stage play by Tim Rice and Andrew Lloyd Webber, film is sometimes stirring while exhibiting the usual heavy-handed Jewison approach. **108m/C; VHS, DVD, Blu-Ray.** Ted Neeley; Carl Anderson; Yvonne Elliman; Josh Mostel; Barry Dennen; Bob Bingham; Larry T. Marshall; ***D:*** Norman Jewison; ***W:*** Melvyn Bragg; ***C:*** Douglas Slocombe; ***M:*** Andrew Lloyd Webber; Andre Previn; Herbert W. Spencer.

Jesus Christ Superstar 🦴🦴 1/2 **2000** This new version updates the Tim Rice-Andrew Lloyd Webber rock opera for the MTV generation. The musical numbers have a rock video look and feel. The production is based on a stage version and so it doesn't feel or look like a real film. **112m/C; VHS, DVD, Blu-Ray.** Glenn Carter; Jerome Pradon; Renee Castle; Rik Mayall; ***D:*** Nick Morris; Gale Edwards; ***W:*** Tim Rice; Andrew Lloyd Webber; ***C:*** Nicholas D. Knowland; Anthony Van Laast; ***M:*** Simon Lee; Tim Rice; Andrew Lloyd Webber.

Jesus Christ Vampire Hunter 🦴 1/2 **2001** Bizarre cult comedy pitting a Kung Fu practicing Jesus and a Mexican Wrestler against an army of atheists, mad scientists, and lesbian vampires. **85m/C; DVD, Blu-Ray.** *CA* Phil Caracas; Murielle Varyelhi; Maria Moulton; Tim Devries; Ian Driscoll; ***D:*** Lee Demarbre; ***W:*** Ian Driscoll; ***M:*** Graham Collins. **VIDEO**

Jesus Henry Christ 🦴 1/2 **2012 (PG-13)** Good performances save this indie comedy from being merely peculiar. Henry James Herman is a 10-year-old genius conceived via sperm donor. His feminist mother Patricia has given him outspoken tendancies that make him a social outcast. Henry finally tracks down his biological father, mild-mannered academic Slavkin, whose furious adolescent daughter, Audrey, was also a 'test tube' baby. Some uneasy family bonding occurs. **95m/C; DVD.** Jason Spevack; Toni Collette; Michael Sheen; Samantha Weinstein; Frank Moore; ***D:*** Dennis Lee; ***W:*** Dennis Lee; ***C:*** Daniel (Danny) Moder.

Jesus of Montreal 🦴🦴🦴 1/2 *Jesus de Montreal* **1989 (R)** A vagrant young actor (stage-trained Canadian star Bluteau) is hired by a Montreal priest to produce a fresh interpretation of an Easter passion play. Taking the good book at its word, he produces a contemporized literal telling that captivates audiences, inflames the men of the cloth, and eventually wins the players' faith. Quebecois director Arcand (keep an eye out for him as the judge) tells a compelling, acerbically satirical and haunting story that never forces its Biblical parallels. In French with English subtitles. **119m/C; VHS, DVD.** *FR CA* Gilles Pelletier; Lothaire Bluteau; Catherine Wilkening; Robert Lepage; Johanne-Marie Tremblay; Remy Girard; Marie-Christine Barrault; ***D:*** Denys Arcand; ***W:*** Denys Arcand; ***C:*** Guy Dufaux; ***M:*** Jean-Marie Benoit; Francois Dompierre; Yves Laferriere. Cannes '89: Special Jury Prize; Genie '90: Actor (Girard), Director (Arcand), Film, Support. Actor (Girard).

Jesus of Nazareth 🦴🦴🦴 **1977** An all-star cast vividly portrays the life of Christ in this miniseries. Wonderfully directed and sensitively acted. **371m/C; VHS, DVD, Blu-Ray.** Robert Powell; Anne Bancroft; Ernest Borgnine; Claudia Cardinale; James Mason; Laurence Olivier; Anthony Quinn; ***D:*** Franco Zeffirelli; ***W:*** Franco Zeffirelli; Anthony Burgess; Suso Cecchi D'Amico; ***M:*** Maurice Jarre. **TV**

Jesus' Son 🦴🦴 **1999 (R)** Crudup gives a fine performance as a sweet, passive, bungling druggie known only as FH (which stands for F***head). He falls for reckless heroin-addict Michelle (Morton), ODs, gets saved, gets dumped, gets in a car wreck, and eventually cleans up and finds some kind of peace working in an Arizona nursing home. There's really not much plot; it's the characters that carry things along. Film is set in the '70s and based on Dennis Johnson's 1992 collection of short stories. **109m/C; VHS, DVD.** Billy Crudup; Samantha Morton; Denis Leary; Holly Hunter; Dennis Hopper; Jack Black; Will Patton; Greg Germann; ***D:*** Alison Maclean; ***W:*** Elizabeth Cuthrell; David Urrutia; Oren Moverman; ***C:*** Adam Kimmel; ***M:*** Joe Henry.

The Jesus Trip 🦴 1/2 **1971** Hunted motorcyclists take a young nun hostage in the desert. **86m/C; VHS, DVD.** Robert Porter; Tippy Walker; ***D:*** Russ Mayberry.

Jet Lag 🦴🦴 *Decalage Horaire* **2002 (R)** Lightweight romance finds beautician Rose (Binoche) stuck at Charles de Gaulle airport thanks to an unexpected strike. She is heading on a solo holiday away from her abusive boyfriend Sergio (Lopez). Also stuck is Felix (Reno), a former chef turned frozen-food businessman on his way to Munich. Rose loses her cell phone and asks to borrow Felix's. They wind up sharing the last available room in an airport hotel and compare lives. Felix cooks dinner for Rose, they argue, leave, get together again—it's creaky but watchable because of the two leads. French with subtitles. **81m/C; VHS, DVD.** *FR GB* Juliette Binoche; Jean Reno; Sergi Lopez; ***D:*** Daniele Thompson; ***W:*** Daniele Thompson; Christopher Thompson; ***C:*** Patrick Blossier; ***M:*** Éric Serra.

Jet Li's Fearless 🦴🦴 *Fearless; Huo Yuan Jia* **2006 (PG-13)** Touted as Jet Li's final go at traditional Chinese martial arts (wushu) cinema. Li plays famed mainland fighter Huo Yuanjia in this elaborate bio, which begins in 1910, with flashbacks and flashforwards that document Yuanjia's childhood and gradual ascent to martial arts stardom. Yuanjia's initial arrogance costs him much and he must learn humility in order to achieve true harmony (or something like that). Director Yu wisely avoids wasting much time in between fight scenes and takes an almost purist approach with very little CGI and cable work. English and Chinese with subtitles. **103m/C; DVD, Blu-Ray, HD-DVD.** *CH CH* Jet Li; Shido Nakamura; Betty Sun; Yong Dong; Collin Chou; Nathan Jones; Yun Qu; ***D:*** Ronny Yu; ***W:*** Wang Bin; Chris Chow; Christine To; Li Feng; ***C:*** Hang-Seng Poon; ***M:*** Mei Linmao.

Jet Li's The Enforcer 🦴🦴 1/2 *The Enforcer; My Father Is a Hero; Letter to Daddy; Gei Ba Ba de Xin* **1995** Chinese cop Li goes undercover to infiltrate a Hong Kong gang. His son (Miu) has been told dad is a crook but he has faith. When Li's wife dies, cop Mui brings the boy to Hong Kong and the kid (a fighting fiend just like his father) winds up helping dad with his police work. Dubbed from Cantonese. **100m/C; VHS, DVD.** *CH* Jet Li; Anita (Yim-Fong) Mui; Damian Lau; Tse Miu; Rongguang Yu; Collin Chou; ***D:*** Corey Yuen.

Jet Pilot 🦴🦴 **1957** An American Air Force colonel (Wayne) in charge of an Alaskan Air Force base falls in love with a defecting Russian jet pilot (Leigh). They marry, but Wayne suspects Leigh is a spy planted to find out top U.S. secrets. He pretends to defect with her back to Russia to see what he can find out, but they again flee. Ludicrous plot is saved only by spectacular flying scenes, some performed by Chuck Yeager. Although this was filmed in 1950, it took seven more years to be released because producer Hughes couldn't keep his hands off it. **112m/B; VHS, DVD.** John Wayne; Janet Leigh; Jay C. Flippen; Paul Fix; Richard Rober; Roland Winters; Hans Conried; Ivan Triesault; ***D:*** Josef von Sternberg; ***C:*** Winton C. Hoch.

Jetsons: The Movie 🦴🦴 **1990 (G)** The famous outer space family of '60s TV is given a new silver-screened life. George gets a promotion that puts him in charge of an asteroid populated by furry creatures. Ecological concerns are expressed; while this is rare for a cartoon, the story is overall typical. **82m/C; VHS, DVD.** ***V:*** George O'Hanlon; Mel Blanc; Penny Singleton; Tiffany; Patric Zimmerman; Donald E. Messick; Jean Vander Pyl; Ronnie Schell; Patti Deutsch; Dana Hill; Russi Taylor; Paul Kreppel; Rick Dees; ***D:*** William Hanna; Joseph Barbera; ***M:*** John Debney.

The Jewel in the Crown 🦴🦴🦴 **1984** Epic saga of the last years of British rule in India from 1942-47 concentrating on a controversial love affair between the Indian Hari Kumar and the English Daphne Manners, which profoundly affects the lives of many. Based on "The Raj Quartet" by Paul Scott. Originally shown on British TV, it aired in the U.S. on the PBS series "Masterpiece Theatre." An excellent miniseries that was shown in 14 segments. **750m/C; VHS, DVD.** *GB* Charles Dance; Susan Wooldridge; Art Malik; Tim Pigott-Smith; Geraldine James; Peggy Ashcroft; Judy Parfitt; ***D:*** Christopher Morahan; Jim O'Brien; ***M:*** George Fenton. **TV**

The Jewel of the Nile 🦴🦴 1/2 **1985 (PG)** Sequel to "Romancing the Stone" with the same cast but new director. Romance novelist Joan thought she found her true love in Jack but finds that life doesn't always end happily ever. After they part ways, Jack realizes that she may be in trouble and endeavors to rescue her from the criminal hands of a charming North African president. Of course, he can always check out this "jewel" at the same time. Chemistry is still there, but the rest of the film isn't quite up to the "Stone's" charm. **106m/C; VHS, DVD, Blu-Ray.** Michael Douglas; Kathleen Turner; Danny DeVito; Avner Eisenberg; The Flying Karamazov Brothers; Spiros Focas; Holland Taylor; ***D:*** Lewis Teague; ***W:*** Mark Rosenthal; Larry Konner; ***C:*** Jan De Bont; ***M:*** Jack Nitzsche.

Jewel Robbery 🦴🦴 **1932** In this naughty pre-code crime comedy, a debonair jewel thief (Powell) charms a bored, adulterous Viennese baroness (Francis) even after he robs her. Oh yes, the thief gives his victims reefer to smoke, making them too passive to bother about the thefts. **70m/B; DVD.** William Powell; Kay Francis; Henry Kolker; Hardie Albright; Alan Mowbray; Helen Vinson; ***D:*** William Dieterle; ***W:*** Erwin Gelsey; ***C:*** Robert B. Kurrle.

The Jeweller's Shop 🦴🦴 **1990** A highly spiritual tale of two married couples in Poland whose children meet and fall in love much later in Canada. Based on a play by Karol Wojtyla—who later became Pope Jean-Paul II. Adapted under strict Vatican supervision. **90m/C; VHS, DVD.** Burt Lancaster; Ben Cross; Olivia Hussey; ***D:*** Michael Anderson, Sr.; ***W:*** Jeff Andrus; ***C:*** Franco Di Giacomo; ***M:*** Michel Legrand.

Jewels 🦴🦴 1/2 *Danielle Steel's Jewels* **1992** Sarah and her second husband the Duke of Whitfield—as a goodwill gesture after WWI—start buying jewelry from war survivors, which eventually leads to a successful jewelry store business. After William dies, Sarah struggles to keep control of her children and the family business. Classic soap-opera mini-series drama. **228m/C; DVD.** Annette O'Toole; Anthony Andrews; Jurgen Prochnow; Sheila Gish; Simon Oates; Robert Wagner; Ursula Howells; Geoffrey Whitehead; Corinne Touzet; ***D:*** Roger Young; ***W:*** Shelley List; Jonathan Estrin; ***M:*** Patrick Williams. **CABLE**

Jewtopia **WOOF!** **2012** Oy vey. Working-class lunkhead Christian has a thing for Jewish girls. So to impress rabbi's daughter

Alison, he gives her a fake name--Avi Rosenberg--and pretends to be a Jewish doctor with coaching from his friend Adam, who has his own romantic issues. Broad humor and offensive stereotypes date this would-be rom com. **90m/C; DVD, Blu-Ray.** Ivan Sergei; Jennifer Love Hewitt; Joel David Moore; Jamie-Lynn Sigler; Nicolette Sheridan; Peter Stormare; Jon Lovitz; Rita Wilson; ***D:*** Bryan Fogel; ***W:*** Bryan Fogel; Sam Wolfson; ***C:*** Sandra Valde-Hansen; ***M:*** Nathan Wang. **VIDEO**

Jexi **2019 (R)** Millennial Phil (Devine) is a digital native whose smartphone is a key part of his life. When his phone breaks, he buys a cheaper model with an interface called Jexi (Byrne). To improve Phil's life, pushy Jexi uses her ability to control his email, social media, and bank accounts to make better choices for him than watching Netflix and ordering food to eat alone. When Jexi's efforts pay off, she reacts in unexpected ways. While making appropriate fun of smartphone addictions and how the devices have changed human interaction, the depiction of gender dynamics is clichéd and the jokes are outdated. **84m/C; DVD, Blu-Ray.** Adam Devine; Alexandra Shipp; Rose Byrne; Ron Funches; Charlyne Yi; ***D:*** Jon Lucas; Scott Moore; ***W:*** Jon Lucas; Scott Moore; ***C:*** Ben Kutchins; ***M:*** Christopher Lennertz; Philip White.

Jezebel **1/2 1938** Davis is a willful Southern belle who loses fiance Fonda through her selfish and spiteful ways in this pre-Civil War drama. When he becomes ill, she realizes her cruelty and rushes to nurse him back to health. Davis' role won her an Oscar for Best Actress, and certainly provided Scarlett O'Hara with a rival for most memorable female character of all time. **105m/B; VHS, DVD, Blu-Ray.** Bette Davis; George Brent; Henry Fonda; Margaret Lindsay; Fay Bainter; Donald Crisp; Spring Byington; Eddie Anderson; ***D:*** William Wyler; ***W:*** Clements Ripley; Abem Finkel; John Huston; Robert Buckner; ***C:*** Ernest Haller; ***M:*** Max Steiner. Oscars '38: Actress (Davis), Support. Actress (Bainter); Natl. Film Reg. '09.

Jezebel's Kiss **1990 (R)** A sizzling young beauty returns to the town where she grew up and proceeds to destroy any man she pleases. **96m/C; VHS, DVD.** Meg Foster; Malcolm McDowell; Meredith Baxter; Everett McGill; Katherine Barrese; ***D:*** Harvey Keith; ***W:*** Harvey Keith.

Jezebeth **2011** The immortal vampiric child of a demon and a Satan worshiper is offended when a foul-mouthed, Christian tarot card reader moves into her house. **80m/C; DVD, Blu-Ray.** Bree Michaels; ***D:*** Damien Dante; ***W:*** Damien Dante; ***C:*** Dan Manzella; ***M:*** Avery Watts; David Tedeschi. **VIDEO**

JFK **1/2 1991 (R)** Highly controversial examination of President John F. Kennedy's 1963 assassination, from the viewpoint of New Orleans district attorney Jim Garrison. Hotly debated because of Stone's conspiracy theory, it sparked new calls to open the sealed government records from the 1977 House Select Committee on Assassinations investigation. Outstanding performances from all-star principal and supporting casts, stunning cinematography, and excellent editing. Even Garrison himself shows up as Chief Justice Earl Warren. Considered by some to be a cinematic masterpiece, others see it as revisionist history that should be taken with a grain of salt. Extended version adds 17 minutes. **189m/C; VHS, DVD, Blu-Ray.** Kevin Costner; Sissy Spacek; Kevin Bacon; Tommy Lee Jones; Laurie Metcalf; Gary Oldman; Michael Rooker; Jay O. Sanders; Beata Pozniak; Joe Pesci; Donald Sutherland; John Candy; Jack Lemmon; Walter Matthau; Ed Asner; Vincent D'Onofrio; Sally Kirkland; Brian Doyle-Murray; Wayne Knight; Tony Plana; Tomas Milian; Sean Stone; Dale Dye; ***Cameo(s):*** Lolita Davidovich; Frank Whaley; Jim Garrison; ***D:*** Oliver Stone; ***W:*** Oliver Stone; Zachary Sklar; ***C:*** Robert Richardson; ***M:*** John Williams. Oscars '91: Cinematog., Film Editing; Golden Globes '92: Director (Stone).

JFK: Reckless Youth **1/2 1993** Dempsey does a fine job as the young John F. Kennedy Jr. TV flick covers the first 30 years of his life and the family ties and influences that shape him up to his 1946 election to Congress. Based on the book by Nigel Hamilton. **183m/C; DVD.** Patrick Dempsey; Terry Kinney; Loren Dean; Robin Tunney; Diana Scarwid; Malachy McCourt; Claire Forlani; Yolanda Jilot; James Rebhorn; Natalie Radford; Stan Cahill; Andrew Lowery; Cedric Smith; Greg Spottiswood; Nicole de Boer; Barry Morse; ***D:*** Harry Winer; ***W:*** William Broyles, Jr.; ***C:*** Jean Lepine; ***M:*** Cameron Allan. **TV**

Jigsaw *Gun Moll* **1949** Crime drama with a smattering of cameos by Hollywood favorites. A newspaper reporter is murdered. The dead man's friend, an assistant district attorney, seeks the punks responsible. They send in a seductress to keep the D.A. busy, but she too is murdered. Action and tension in a well-made flick. Based on a story by John Roeburt. **70m/B; VHS, DVD.** Franchot Tone; Jean Wallace; Myron McCormick; Marc Lawrence; Winifred Lenihan; Betty Harper; Robert Gist; ***Cameo(s):*** Marlene Dietrich; Henry Fonda; Burgess Meredith; John Garfield; ***D:*** Fletcher Markle.

Jigsaw **1/2 1999 (R)** Convential neo-noir is weak in both plot and performances. Vicky (Ehm) asks her boyfriend, Jules (Corno), to pick up $5000 that's owed her. Vicky winds up dead and Jules is on the lam from both cops and drug dealers. **83m/C; VHS, DVD.** *CA* William Corno; Erica Ehm; Edgar George; ***D:*** Paul Shoebridge. **VIDEO**

Jigsaw **1/2 2017 (R)** The seventh sequel in the Saw franchise continues its signature look and feel, though is less sadistic overall. As in earlier films, a group of strangers have been kidnapped by serial killer John "Jigsaw" Carter (Bell) and taken to a locked mystery room on a farm. There, they must confess to secret sins only Jigsaw knows about. When they refuse, they are forced to do obstacle courses that include painful death traps. The result is a stack of bodies and a police investigation into the cause of their demise. Despite a lack of subtlety, the film can be enjoyed for its glorious cheesiness. **92m/C; DVD, Blu-Ray.** Matt Passmore; Tobin Bell; Callum Keith Rennie; Hannah Emily Anderson; Cle Bennett; ***D:*** Michael Spierig; Peter Spierig; ***W:*** Peter Goldfinger; Josh Stolberg; ***C:*** Ben Nott; ***M:*** Charlie Clouser.

Jill the Ripper **2000 (R)** Alcoholic ex-cop Matt Wilson launches his own investigation after his brother is murdered. This takes him into a world of political corruption and kinky sex, circa 1977 in Boston. **94m/C; VHS, DVD.** Dolph Lundgren; Danielle Brett; ***D:*** Anthony Hickox; ***W:*** Kevin Bernhardt; Gareth Wardell; ***C:*** David Pelletier; ***M:*** Steve Gurevitch; Thomas Barquee. **VIDEO**

Jim Hanvey, Detective **1/2 1937** Portly retired police detective Jim Hanvey is hired by an insurance company to recover the emeralds stolen from Adelaide Frost. It all turns out to be a prank perpetuated by Joan Frost's writer boyfriend Don Terry who was looking for a book plot. The jewels get returned, stolen again, the butler's killed, and Don is the prime suspect unless Hanvey can solve the case. **71m/B; DVD.** Guy Kibbee; Lucie Kaye; Tom Brown; Catherine Doucet; Howard Hickman; Edward (Ed) Gargan; Edward Brophy; Theodore von Eltz; ***D:*** Phil Rosen; ***W:*** Olive Cooper; Joseph Krumgold; ***C:*** Jack A. Markta.

Jim Thorpe: All American **1/2** *Man of Bronze* **1951** The life story of Thorpe, a Native American athlete who gained international recognition for his excellence in many different sports. A must for sports fans. **105m/B; VHS, DVD.** Burt Lancaster; Phyllis Thaxter; Charles Bickford; Steve Cochran; Dick Wesson; ***D:*** Michael Curtiz; ***W:*** Douglas S. Morrow; ***M:*** Max Steiner.

Jimi: All Is by My Side **2014 (R)** Writer/director Ridley was so set on making a film about Jimi Hendrix that he didn't let the fact the legendary guitarist's estate didn't license him any of the rights to Hendrix's music get in his way. And so this biopic chooses to go the origin route, detailing the life of Hendrix before he became a musician so popular that he could be recognized only by his surname. The result is like the opening act for the band you really came to see—it has its moments, most of them courtesy of strong lead work by Benjamin, but it's a bit unsatisfying overall. **118m/C; DVD, Blu-Ray.** Andre Benjamin; Imogen Poots; Andrew Buckley; Hayley Atwell; Clare-Hope Ashitey; ***D:*** John Ridley; ***W:*** John Ridley; ***C:*** Tim Fleming; ***M:*** Waddy Wachtel; Danny Bramson.

Jiminy Glick in LaLa Wood **1/2 2005 (R)** Obsequious smalltime entertainment critic Jiminy Glick (Short) and his clueless wife Dixie (Hooks) are in showbiz heaven at the Toronto Film Festival. Granted an exclusive interview with rising young star Ben DiCarlo (Pearson), Jiminy is wined and dined and catches the eye of fading diva Miranda Coolidge (Perkins). When Miranda is murdered, Jiminy inexplicably investigates. Short's grating Comedy Central character is unsuccessfully carried to the big screen, seemingly so Short will have a showcase for his dead-on David Lynch impersonation. The only other reason to take a look is Higgins's turn as Eurotrash snob Andre. **90m/C; DVD.** *US CA* Martin Short; Jan Hooks; Elizabeth Perkins; John Michael Higgins; Linda Cardellini; Janeane Garofalo; Carlos Jacott; Corey Pearson; Aries Spears; Robert Trebor; Gary Anthony Williams; Larry Joe Campbell; Mo Collins; DeRay Davis; Landon Hansen; Jake Hoffman; ***Cameo(s):*** Kiefer Sutherland; Whoopi Goldberg; Steve Martin; Kevin Kline; Sharon Stone; Forest Whitaker; Susan Sarandon; Kurt Russell; Rob Lowe; ***D:*** Vadim Jean; ***W:*** Martin Short; Paul Flaherty; ***C:*** Mike J. Fox; ***M:*** David Lawrence.

Jimmy & Judy **2006 (R)** Social misfits Jimmy (Furlong) and Judy (Bella) turn into lover/losers on the lam after setting out from suburbia on one wild ride—of all which is naturally documented by video camera. Derivative drivel trying way too hard. **100m/C; DVD.** Edward Furlong; Rachael Bella; William Sadler; James Eckhouse; A.J. Buckley; A. J. Buckley; ***D:*** Randall K. Rubin; Jon Schroder; ***W:*** Jon Schroder; ***C:*** Ben Kufrin; ***M:*** Benoit Grey.

Jimmy Hollywood **1/2 1994 (R)** Wanna-be Hollywood actor Pesci has never acted in his life but longs for stardom—which he gets after he accidentally becomes a community vigilante. Burned-out sidekick Slater helps create the videotapes that will bring Jimmy his 15 minutes of fame. Although appropriately desperate, Pesci's role comes off as mostly shtick; two dogs in a row for the usually talented Levinson (after "Toys"). **118m/C; VHS, DVD.** Joe Pesci; Christian Slater; Victoria Abril; ***Cameo(s):*** Barry Levinson; Rob Weiss; ***D:*** Barry Levinson; ***W:*** Barry Levinson; ***C:*** Peter Sova; ***M:*** Robbie Robertson.

Jimmy Neutron: Boy Genius **1/2 2001 (G)** Huge-brained and grease-haired Jimmy Neutron is a retro geek hero for the new millennium in this bright and flashy computer animated feature. The child-inventor is young enough to think a sugar rush is the ultimate taboo but smart enough to have created a toaster-satellite that makes contact with an alien race. When said alien race respond by stealing all the parents in Retroville, Jimmy and his band of nerds endeavor to rescue them. Though mildly targeted at adults, it prefers gas gags to pop culture reference; even the new-wave songs are covered by kiddie bands. Frenetic pacing and onslaught of images may tire older (than teenage) viewers, although the animation is pleasant enough and there are some inventive lines that will go over the young-uns' heads. Short and Stewart are amusing as a pair of egg-shaped space invaders. **90m/C; VHS, DVD.** ***V:*** Debi Derryberry; Carolyn Lawrence; Rob Paulsen; Martin Short; Patrick Stewart; Megan Cavanagh; Mark DeCarlo; Jeff Garcia; Candi Milo; Andrea Martin; ***D:*** John A. Davis; ***W:*** David N. Weiss; J. David Stem; Steve Oedekerk; John A. Davis; ***M:*** John Debney.

Jimmy P. **2013** Del Toro gives an intense lead performance in this true story. Blackfoot Indian Jimmy Picard is a WWII vet suffering from mental issues that find him a patient in the Menninger Clinic in 1948. He's labeled a schizophrenic, but Dr. Karl Menninger (Pine) calls in anthropologist and psychoanalyst Georges Devereaux (Amalric) to review the case. Devereaux has been studying Native American culture and forms a relationship with Jimmy that leads him to dealing with his traumatic past. **117m/C; On Demand.** *FR* Benicio Del Toro; Mathieu Amalric; Larry Pine; Gina McKee; Joseph Cross; Gary Farmer; Michelle Thrush; ***D:*** Arnaud Desplechin; ***W:*** Arnaud Desplechin; Julie Peyr; Kent Jones; ***C:*** Stephanie Fontaine; ***M:*** Howard Shore.

The Jimmy Show **1/2 2001 (R)** Average Jimmy O'Brien (Whaley) vents the frustrations of his humble daily life at open mike night at a comedy club. But his routine isn't about jokes—his monologues are painful confessions about thwarted dreams, which only get worse when his fed-up wife Annie (Gugino) leaves. Whaley's at his best in the club scenes but they tend to overwhelm the rest of film. **93m/C; VHS, DVD.** Frank Whaley; Carla Gugino; Ethan Hawke; Lynn Cohen; ***D:*** Frank Whaley; ***W:*** Frank Whaley; ***C:*** Mike Mayers; ***M:*** Robert Whaley; Anthony Grimaldi.

Jimmy, the Boy Wonder **1/2 1966** Goremeister Lewis' attempt at a "family" film turns out just as weird as expected. A young boy goes on a magical trip to find out who stopped time and meets an absent-minded astronomer, the evil Mr. Fig, and then discovers what happens at world's end. **69m/C; VHS, DVD.** Dennis Jones; David Blight, Jr.; Nancy Jo Berg; ***D:*** Herschell Gordon Lewis; ***W:*** Hal Berg; ***C:*** Andy Romanoff.

Jimmy the Gent **1934** Fast-paced crime comedy. Joan Martin (Davis) works with boss Jimmy Corrigan (Cagney) to find missing heirs to unclaimed estates, taking a cut of the inheritance. But Jimmy sometimes cheats by supplying phony heirs and Joan gets disgusted and goes to work for Jimmy's seemingly honest and smooth rival James Wallingham (Dinehart). **67m/B; DVD.** James Cagney; Bette Davis; Alan Dinehart; Allen Jenkins; Arthur Hohl; Alice White; Mayo Methot; Phillip Reed; ***D:*** Michael Curtiz; ***W:*** Bertram Millhauser; ***C:*** Ira Morgan.

Jimmy Vestvood: Amerikan Hero **2016** Iranian comedian Maz Jobrani stars as the titular Jimmy Vestvood, a poor Iranian who wins the Green Card lottery and moves to America to pursue his dream of being a P.I. Quickly mistaken for a terrorist, only a corrupt millionaire gives him a chance by hiring him on to spy on his wife. It's billed as "Borat Meets the Pink Panther," but thankfully isn't nearly as vulgar or needlessly offensive as Sacha Baron Cohen. **83m/C; DVD, Blu-Ray, Streaming.** Maz Jobrani; John Heard; Deanna Russo; Marshall Manesh; Mathew Glave; ***D:*** Jonathan Kesselman; ***W:*** Maz Jobrani; Amir Ohebsion; ***C:*** Armando Salas; ***M:*** Michael Cohen.

Jimmy Zip **2000 (R)** Jimmy (Fletcher) is a pyromaniac abused runaway who gets a job working for drug dealing pimp Rick (Mulkey). He goes on a fireworks spree, which is how Jimmy meets down-and-out sculptor Horace (Gossett), who encourages him to channel his energies in more productive directions. But Jimmy fuels his new interests by stealing money from Rick, which puts him and girlfriend Sheila (Frantz) in a very dangerous position. **112m/C; VHS, DVD.** *CA* Brendan Fletcher; Chris Mulkey; Robert Gossett; Adrienne Frantz; James Russo; Kim (Kimberly Dawn) Dawson; ***D:*** Robert McGinley; ***W:*** Robert McGinley; ***C:*** Christopher Tufty; ***M:*** Geoff Levin.

Jindabyne **1/2 2006 (R)** Director Lawrence transports this Raymond Carver story from the Pacific Northwest to the mountainous southwest of Australia. Working-class buddies Stewart (Byrne), Carl (Howard), Rocco (Yiakmis), and Billy (Stone) go off for a weekend fishing trip. They quickly find a dead Aboriginal girl floating in the river and tie the body to a tree while they continue with their plans. When they finally report their discovery, all hell breaks loose: Stewart's wife Claire (Linney) is appalled at their callousness, there's the racial aspect (would they have left the body if she had been white?), and it turns out that the girl was murdered. Despite some strong performances, pic tends to be sluggish and underdeveloped. **123m/C; DVD.** *AU* Gabriel Byrne; Laura Linney; John Howard; Stelios Yiakmis; Deborra-Lee Furness; Leah Purcell; Chris Haywood; Alice Garner; Simon Stone; Sean Rees-Wemyss; Eva Lazzaro; Tatea Reilly; ***D:*** Ray Lawrence; ***W:*** Beatrix Christian; ***C:*** David Williamson; ***M:*** Paul Kelly; Dan Luscombe.

Jingle All the Way **1996 (PG)** Producer Chris Columbus grabs the reins of the slapstick and sentiment sleigh from mentor John Hughes in this farce of holiday capitalism. Any parent who has searched frantically for that Mighty Morphin' Cabbage Elmo will understand hapless Howard Langston (Schwarzenegger), a workaholic dad who was supposed to secure the coveted Turbo Man action figure for his son Jamie (Lloyd).

Unfortunately, it slips his mind until Christmas Eve and all the Turbo Men have blasted off with more mindful parents. In his panic-stricken quest for the toy, he is confronted by a crazed postman (Sinbad) hunting Turbo Man, a pack of sleazy Santas, and a vicious reindeer attack. Meanwhile, Howard's slimy neighbor Ted (Hartman) is attempting to get into his wife Liz's (Wilson) stockings with great care. Although aimed at a younger audience, there's a definite lack of kids; which leaves it too grown-up for the kids and too childish for the adults. There is some satisfaction in seeing the Mall of America torn to shreds, however. Ho ho hum. **88m/C; VHS, DVD, Blu-Ray.** Arnold Schwarzenegger; Phil Hartman; Sinbad; Rita Wilson; James Belushi; Robert Conrad; Martin Mull; Jake Lloyd; Harvey Korman; Laraine Newman; ***D:*** Brian Levant; ***W:*** Randy Kornfield; ***C:*** Victor Kemper; ***M:*** David Newman.

Jingle All the Way 2 **2014 (PG)** Lightweight holiday pic without the slapstick fun of the original. Divorced dad Larry's young daughter Noel only wants Harrison the Talking Bear for Christmas. Naturally, this hot toy is nowhere to be found--in part because Noel's wealthy new stepdad Victor is buying up all the available bears so he can be the big present-giving hero over laid-back Larry. **93m/C; DVD, Blu-Ray.** Larry the Cable Guy; Brian Stepanek; Kennedi Clements; Kirsten Robek; ***D:*** Alex Zamm; ***W:*** Stephen Mazur; ***C:*** Barry Donlevy; ***M:*** Chris Hajian. **VIDEO**

Jinn **2014 (PG-13)** It's hard to think of a supernatural creature that doesn't have its own horror franchise yet, but this lame attempt to turn a "Jinn" (a spooky version of a genie with less singing) into the new Candyman or Freddy Krueger is an absolute dud. Dominic Rains tries his hardest to sell his cursed husband-hero as a butt-kicking demon knight, desperate to save his pregnant wife from the Middle Eastern mythological monsters, but only genre favorites William Atherton (Walter Peck!) and Ray Park (Darth Maul!) seem to be having any fun with the schlocky material. **97 minutwam/C; DVD, Download.** Dominic Rains; Serinda Swan; Ray Park; William Atherton; Faran Tahir; ***D:*** Ajmal Zaheer Ahmad; ***W:*** Ajmal Zaheer Ahmad; ***C:*** Robert Mehnert; ***M:*** Noah Sorota.

Jinn **1/2 2018** High school senior Summer (Renee) seems to have everything together. She has close friends, applied to colleges, and plans to study dance after she graduates. Summer's personal identity is challenged when her mother Jade (Missick) converts to Islam. Brought to the mosque by her mother, Summer is forced to wear a headscarf. Through this experience, Summer questions who she should be. At the same time, Jade faces discrimination in her workplace for her choice. The debut film by director Mu'min features a low-key exploration of a complex mother-daughter relationship and the challenges faced by both people because of Jade's conversion. **91m/C; DVD.** Simone Missick; Zoe Renee; Hisham Tawfiq; Kelvin Harrison, Jr.; Dorian Missick; ***D:*** Nijla Mu'min; ***W:*** Nijla Mu'min; ***C:*** Bruce Francis Cole; ***M:*** Jesi Nelson.

Jinxed **1982 (R)** Las Vegas nightclub singer tries to convince a gullible blackjack dealer to murder her crooked boyfriend, but the plan backfires when the gangster electrocutes himself while taking a shower. Offscreen cast disputes were probably much more interesting than onscreen comedy. **104m/C; VHS, DVD, Blu-Ray.** Bette Midler; Ken Wahl; Rip Torn; ***D:*** Donald Siegel; ***W:*** David Newman; Frank D. Gilroy; ***M:*** Miles Goodman.

Jirga **1/2 2019** Former Australian soldier Mike Wheeler (Smith) returns to Afghanistan three years after he accidentally killed a married father during a raid. Anxious and full of guilt, Mike wants to make monetary amends to the man's widow and sons. During his journey to them, he ends up captured by a small Taliban squad in their cave hideout. Explaining why he is there, the group decides his fate. An engaging tale of life and morality set against the backdrop of stunning scenery. **78m/C; DVD.** Sam Smith; Sher Alam Miskeen Ustad; Basheer Safi; Arzo Weda; Inam Khan; ***D:*** Benjamin Gilmour; ***W:*** Benjamin Gilmour; ***C:*** Benjamin Gilmour; ***M:*** AJ True.

Jiro Dreams of Sushi **1/2** *Jiro sni o sushi* **2012 (PG)** Hailed as the world's greatest sushi chef, 85-year-old Jiro Ono tirelessly pursues his process of creating the perfect piece of sushi at his world-renowned Tokyo restaurant. Director Gelb shows us more an art form than a man as he presents a snapshot into Jiro's restaurant and his relationships with his two sons--Yoshikazu, who prepares to take the restaurant reins one day, and the other who owns his own sushi bar. Very exclusive, Jiro's place seats only 10, has three Michelin stars, and costs a diner (who must wait months to get in) about $300. This documentary is far less costly, but nearly as delicious. In Japanese, with subtitles. **81m/C; DVD, Blu-Ray.** Jiro Ono; Yoshikazu Ono; ***D:*** David Gelb; ***C:*** David Gelb.

Jitters *Oroi* **2010** Reasonably effective coming of age drama. Icelandic teens Gabriel and Markus attend a foreign exchange program in England and it gives shy Gabriel a chance to explore his sexuality with his anything-goes roomie. Back home, Gabe would like to step out of the closet a little more but finds it difficult since his friends, who are dealing with their own emotional issues, still expect him to be their shoulder to lean on. English and Icelandic with subtitles. **93m/C; DVD.** *IC* Atli Oskar Fjalarson; Haraldur Ari Stefansson; Elias Kofoed Ansen; Hreindis Yiva Gardarsdottir; ***D:*** Baldvin Zophoniasson; ***W:*** Baldvin Zophoniasson; ***C:*** Johann Johannsson; ***M:*** Olafur Arnalds.

Jo Jo Dancer, Your Life Is Calling **1/2 1986 (R)** Pryor directed and starred in this semi-autobiographical rise-and-fall-of-fame story of a comic, hospitalized for a drug-related accident, who must re-evaluate his life. A serious departure from Pryor's slapstick comedies that doesn't quite make it as a drama; Pryor nevertheless deserves credit for the honesty he demonstrates in dealing with his real-life problems. **97m/C; VHS, DVD.** Richard Pryor; Debbie Allen; Art Evans; Fay Hauser; Barbara Williams; Paula Kelly; Wings Hauser; Carmen McRae; Diahnne Abbott; Scoey Mitchell; Billy Eckstine; Virginia Capers; Dennis Farina; ***D:*** Richard Pryor; ***W:*** Richard Pryor; Rocco Urbisci; ***C:*** John A. Alonzo; ***M:*** Herbie Hancock.

Joan of Arc **1/2 1948** A touching and devout look at the life of Joan of Arc. Perhaps unfortunately, the film is accurately based on the play by Maxwell Anderson, and adds up to too much talk and too little action. **100m/C; VHS, DVD, Blu-Ray.** Ingrid Bergman; Jose Ferrer; John Ireland; Leif Erickson; ***D:*** Victor Fleming; ***C:*** Joseph Valentine. Oscars '48: Color Cinematog., Costume Des. (C).

Joan of Arc **1/2 1999** Earnest biopic of legendary 15th-century French heroine, Joan of Arc (Sobieski). Joan is a peasant girl, born during France's Hundred Years War with England. She hears saints' voices telling her to help the Dauphin Charles (Harris) claim the French throne and drive out the English. Charles persuades Joan to proclaim herself the legendary Maid of Lorraine and raise an army to battle the Brits. But after her success, Joan is betrayed by the King, sold to the English, and put on trial for heresy. **240m/C; VHS, DVD.** Leelee Sobieski; Neil Patrick Harris; Peter O'Toole; Robert Loggia; Jacqueline Bisset; Powers Boothe; Shirley MacLaine; Olympia Dukakis; Maury Chaykin; Jonathan Hyde; Maximilian Schell; Peter Strauss; ***D:*** Christian Duguay; ***W:*** Ronald Parker; Michael Miller; ***C:*** Pierre Gill; ***M:*** Asher Ettinger; Tony Kosinec. **TV**

Joan of Paris **1/2 1942** A French resistance leader dies so that Allied pilots can escape from the Nazis. A well done, but obviously dated propaganda feature. **91m/B; VHS, DVD.** Michele Morgan; Paul Henreid; Thomas Mitchell; Laird Cregar; May Robson; Alexander Granach; Alan Ladd; ***D:*** Robert Stevenson; ***W:*** Charles Bennett.

Joan Rivers: A Piece of Work **2010 (R)** Directors Stern and Sundberg follow a year in the life of 75-year-old Joan Rivers, who's been a trailblazing comedian for more than 40 years. The focus is on workaholic Rivers' still-intense career preparation and how she keeps it going, including TV appearances and performing nightclub gigs. The comedian doesn't shy away from controversy, her own foibles (including her insecurity) or what her career has personally cost her. **84m/C; DVD, Blu-Ray.** Joan Rivers; Melissa Rivers; ***D:*** Ricki Stern; Annie Sundberg; ***C:*** Charles Miller; ***M:*** Paul Brill.

The Job **2003 (R)** Hitwoman CJ (Hannah) has agreed to one last job before she leaves her violent life behind her. Only she has a crisis of conscience and finds it difficult to pull the trigger on the target—young wannabe gangster Troy (Renfro), who stole a drug shipment from the wrong people. However, if CJ doesn't follow through, it'll be her life on the line. **86m/C; VHS, DVD.** Daryl Hannah; Brad Renfro; Dominique Swain; Eric Mabius; Alex Rocco; ***D:*** Kenny Golde; ***W:*** Kenny Golde; ***C:*** Scott Kevan. **VIDEO**

The Job **1/2 2009 (R)** Unemployed Bubba gets a tip about a job from drifter Jim and meets with Mr. Perriman, who owns a very specialized employment agency. The job is to kill a guy who cheated a gangster and it pays a lot, but Bubba isn't sure he can go through with it. **99m/C; DVD.** Patrick Fleuger; Ron Perlman; Joe Pantoliano; Taryn Manning; Gregory Itzin; Katie Lowes; Mark Harelik; ***D:*** Shem Bitterman; ***W:*** Shem Bitterman; ***C:*** John Foster; ***M:*** Enis Rotthoff. **VIDEO**

A Job to Kill For **1/2 2006** Senior ad exec Jennifer Kamplen's (Young) workaholic attitude is causing problems in her marriage to artist Patrick (Cohen). But that's nothing compared to what happens when she hires a new assistant, Stacy Sherman (Craig), who is literally willing to do anything (including murder) to anyone she thinks is standing in Jennifer's way. This ironically doesn't bode well when Jennifer has a change of heart. **90m/C; DVD.** Sean Young; Georgia Craig; Ari Cohen; Lucia Walters; Bill Dow; Jason Schombing; ***D:*** Bill Corcoran; ***W:*** Peter Baloff; Dave Wollert; ***C:*** Adam Sliwinski; ***M:*** Terry Frewer. **CABLE**

Jobs **2013 (PG-13)** Biopic of Steve Jobs, circa 1971-2001, from his days as a college dropout to Apple founder and the firm's subsequent trials and resurgence. Even as a young man, Jobs (Kutcher), is uncompromising in his creative vision which leads him to start Apple in a garage with his friend Steve Wozniak (Gad) Under his direction, he drives Apple to the front of a new era in computing but manages to alienate many on his road to success. Primarily focusing on his professional rise and trials, the story is reverent in its depiction of Jobs as an experimental genius although it does detail some of the more troubling aspects of his personal life, including his failings as a father. However, the film lacks the creative vision of its subject, instead opting for a very straightforward biopic that doesn't get broader than its main subject, barely touching on the technological revolution that Apple and its competitors defined. **122m/C; DVD, Blu-Ray.** Ashton Kutcher; Josh Gad; Dermot Mulroney; Ron Eldard; Lukas Haas; Matthew Modine; J.K. Simmons; James Woods; ***D:*** Joshua Michael Stern; ***W:*** Matthew Whiteley; ***C:*** Russell Carpenter; ***M:*** John Debney.

Jocks **1/2 1987 (R)** A whiz-kid tennis team competes in a pro meet in Las Vegas, and paints the town red. **90m/C; VHS, DVD.** Christopher Lee; Perry Lang; Richard Roundtree; Scott Strader; ***D:*** Steve Carver; ***W:*** Jeff Buhai.

Jodi Picoult's Salem Falls *Salem Falls* **2011** Lifetime original based on Picoult's 2002 novel. Former teacher Jack is trying to start over in the small New England town of Salem Falls after being falsely accused and convicted of sexual assault. Manipulative 17-year-old Gillian tries to get Jack's attention with Wiccan spells, which fail. But when she's raped, Jack becomes the target of a modern-day witch hunt. **90m/C; DVD.** James Van Der Beek; Sarah Carter; Amanda (A.J.) Michalka; Allie MacDonald; Zoe Belkin; ***D:*** Bradley Walsh; ***W:*** Teena Booth; Craig Bolotin; ***C:*** Rudolf Blahacek; ***M:*** Gary Koftinoff. **CABLE**

Jodorowsky's Dune **2013 (PG-13)** In the '70s, Alejandro Jodorowsky was riding a wave of international acclaim as an innovative and daring director who could do no wrong. And so he started to assemble a dream project, a film VERY loosely based on the unfilmable sci-fi book "Dune." Jodorowsky hadn't even read it but he liked the idea of a sci-fi extravaganza that recreated the impact of hallucinogenic drugs on a viewer without actually taking them. The amount of pre-production and design work that went into his Dune was staggering. And then it never got made. This is a wistful, clever doc about a cinematic dream deferred. **90m/C; DVD, Blu-Ray.** *US FR* Alejandro Jodorowsky; ***D:*** Frank Pavich; ***C:*** David Cavallo; ***M:*** Kurt Stenzel.

Joe **1/2 1970 (R)** An odd friendship grows between a businessman and a blue-collar worker as they search together for the executive's runaway daughter. Thrust into the midst of the counter-culture, they react with an orgy of violence. **107m/C; VHS, DVD, Blu-Ray.** Peter Boyle; Susan Sarandon; Dennis Patrick; ***D:*** John G. Avildsen; ***W:*** Norman Wexler; ***C:*** John G. Avildsen; Henri Decae; ***M:*** Bobby Scott.

Joe **2013 (R)** Joe (Cage) is a hard-drinking, hard-fighting, hard-living guy who doesn't get attached but sees something in the young Gary (Sheridan) that needs saving. Gary's father is an alcoholic, abusive sociopath (played by non-actor Poulter), and Joe inadvertently becomes the only man in Gary's life who could save him from eventual ruin. Cage handles the role with remarkable subtlety, while director Gordon Green's drama is a delicate, challenging piece that plays not unlike an old-fashioned Western set on the edge of poverty outside Austin, Texas in 2013. **117m/C; DVD, Blu-Ray.** Nicolas Cage; Tye Sheridan; Gary Poulter; Ronnie Gene Blevins; Adriene Mishler; ***D:*** David Gordon Green; ***W:*** Gary Hawkins; ***C:*** Tim Orr; ***M:*** David Wingo; Jeff McIlwain.

Joe and Max **2002 (PG-13)** That would be heavyweight boxing champs Joe "the Brown Bomber" Louis and Max Schmeling. In 1936, Max defeats Joe in a title match, although the two become friends. Joe has to put up with his country's racism (the whites in the audience cheer for Schmeling) while Max has to endure the Nazi's using him as a symbol of Aryan superiority. In 1938, the tables are turned in a rematch at Yankee Stadium—this time it's Louis that's the people's choice and the victor. Not only does the film relate the duo's celebrity (and symbolism) but their alternating fortunes after WWII. Both leads do fine work, although Schweiger seems more comfortable in his role. **113m/C; VHS, DVD.** *US GE* Til Schweiger; Leonard Roberts; Peta Wilson; Richard Roundtree; David Paymer; John Toles-Bey; Bruce Weitz; ***D:*** Steve James; ***W:*** Jason Horwitch; ***C:*** Bill Butler; ***M:*** Jeff Beal. **CABLE**

Joe Dirt **2001 (PG-13)** Spade plays the hapless, well-meaning personification of every trailer-trash joke you've ever heard or told. He sports a robo-mullet, earns his keep with degrading, sub-minimum wage jobs, drives a beat-up muscle car, and grooves to '70s arena-rock. He's also searching for his parents, who bailed on him during a trip to the Grand Canyon when he was eight. Too bad he isn't funny. Co-writers Spade and Wolf spend too much time on the heart strings and not enough on the funny bone, which results in an unholy hybrid of Jerry Springer and the Lifetime Network. Miller's shock-jock and Walken's crazed janitor add some genuine laughs to the proceedings, but not enough. **91m/C; VHS, DVD, Blu-Ray, UMD.** David Spade; Dennis Miller; Adam Beach; Christopher Walken; Jaime Pressly; Caroline Aaron; Fred Ward; Brittany Daniel; Kid Rock; Erik Per Sullivan; Megan Taylor Harvey; ***D:*** Dennie Gordon; ***W:*** David Spade; Fred Wolf; ***C:*** John R. Leonetti; ***M:*** Waddy Wachtel.

Joe Gould's Secret **1/2 2000 (R)** Tucci directed, co-wrote, and stars as Joe Mitchell, famed "New Yorker" columnist who chronicled, among many others, the peculiar life of Greenwich Village eccentric Joe Gould in the 1940s. Gould (Holm) lived on the streets of New York for 26 years, regaling the intelligensia with wild stories and behavior while claiming to be writing the "Oral History of Our Time," which he said was two million words long and contained the fruits of 20,000 overheard conversations. The film quietly (except when Holm's Gould is onscreen) and effectively explores the relationship between Mitchell and Gould, and the reasons for Mitchell's fascination with his subject. **108m/C; VHS, DVD.** Stanley Tucci; Ian Holm; Hope Davis; Patricia Clarkson; Steve Martin; Susan Sarandon; Celia Weston; Allan Corduner; Alice Drummond; Julie Halston; Hallee Hirsh; Ben Jones; John Tormey; David Wohl; Patrick Tovatt; Sarah Hyland; ***D:*** Stanley Tucci; ***W:*** Stanley Tucci; Howard A. Rodman; ***C:*** Maryse Alberti; ***M:*** Evan Lurie.

Joe Kidd 1/2 **1972 (PG)** A land war breaks out in New Mexico between Mexican natives and American land barons. Eastwood, once again portraying the "mysterious stranger," must decide with whom he should side, all the while falling in love with Garcia. Lackluster direction results in a surprisingly tedious western, in spite of the cast. One of Eastwood's lowest money grossers. **88m/C; VHS, DVD, Blu-Ray.** Clint Eastwood; Robert Duvall; John Saxon; Don Stroud; Stella Garcia; James Wainwright; Paul Koslo; Gregory Walcott; Dick Van Patten; Lynn(e) Marta; ***D:*** John Sturges; ***W:*** Elmore Leonard; ***C:*** Bruce Surtees; ***M:*** Lalo Schifrin.

The Joe Louis Story **1953** The story of Joe Louis' rise to fame as boxing's Heavyweight Champion of the world. **88m/B; VHS, DVD.** Coley Wallace; Paul Stewart; Hilda Simms; Albert "Poppy" Popwell; ***D:*** Robert Gordon; ***W:*** Robert Sylvester; ***C:*** Joseph Brun; ***M:*** George Bassman.

Joe Maddison's War **2010** A veteran of WWI, Newcastle shipyard worker Joe Maddison is depressed when he's deemed too old for active service in 1939. So he, his best pal Harry, and fellow worker Eddie all decide to join the Home Guard, which is locally commanded by martinet Mr. Simpson. Joe finds himself fending off more than the Germans as the war begins to take its toll on the homefront. **86m/C; DVD.** *GB* Kevin Whately; Robson Green; Trevor Fox; Derek Jacobi; Angela Lonsdale; Melinda Hill; John Woodvine; ***D:*** Patrick Collerton; ***W:*** Alan Plater; ***C:*** Chris Seager; ***M:*** Kevin Sargent. **TV**

The Joe McDoakes Collection 1/2 **1942** Sixty-three one-reelers released by Warner Bros. from 1942-1956 that starred George O'Hanlon as frustrated everyman Joe McDoakes whose every plan, challenge, and ambition went wrong in a comedic way. **648m/B; DVD.** George O'Hanlon; Phyllis Coates; ***D:*** Richard Bare; ***W:*** Richard Bare.

Joe Panther **1976 (G)** Family drama about a young Seminole Indian who stakes his claim in the Anglo world by wrestling alligators. Montalban plays a wise old chieftain who helps the youth handle the conflict between Indian and white societies. **110m/C; VHS, DVD.** Brian Keith; Ricardo Montalban; Alan Feinstein; Cliff Osmond; A. Martinez; Robert Hoffman; ***D:*** Paul Krasny.

Joe Somebody **2001 (PG)** By-the-numbers dud feels like an after-school special with ten times the budget and half the brains or heart. Tim Allen again plays the allegedly likable Average Joe, only this time, his name is actually Joe. Trouble is, he doesn't look nerdy or ineffectual, even if he's wearing glasses and getting beat up in the parking lot. After Joe's daughter (Panettiere) witnesses his turn as punching bag for the office bully (Warburton), he slides into a depression. But after a visit from sure-to-be romantic interest Meg (Bowen), Joe decides he wants a rematch. He enlists the help of a faded martial arts guru (Belushi) and becomes popular, but his daughter and love interest like the old Joe better. Tries to have a moral message about rejecting violence while also giving a good dose of it. Joe's precocious, sage-like daughter makes the Olsen twins pleasant by comparison. **97m/C; VHS, DVD.** Tim Allen; Julie Bowen; Hayden Panettiere; Kelly Lynch; James Belushi; Patrick Warburton; Greg Germann; Robert Joy; Ken Marino; ***D:*** John Pasquin; ***W:*** John Scott Shepherd; ***C:*** Daryn Okada; ***M:*** George S. Clinton.

Joe the King **1999 (R)** Undistinguished coming of age pic, set in the mid-'70s, about a boy caught up in violence. Fourteen-year-old Joe (Fleiss) and his older brother Mike (Ligosh) are subjected to the constant drunken abuse of their father Bob (Henry) and the indifference of their overworked mother Theresa (Young). Joe begins stealing to get by but his crimes gradually becomes less than petty. A troubled student as well, Joe is befriended by guidance counselor Len (Hawke), whose attempts to help only result in a stint for Joe in a juvie center. Slow-paced and developmentally challenged. **101m/C; VHS, DVD.** Noah Fleiss; Val Kilmer; Ethan Hawke; Karen Young; John Leguizamo; Austin Pendleton; Max Ligosh; James Costa; ***D:*** Frank Whaley; ***W:*** Frank Whaley; ***C:*** Mike Mayers; ***M:*** Robert Whaley; Anthony Grimaldi. Sundance '99: Screenplay.

Joe Versus the Volcano **1990 (PG)** Expressionistic goofball comedy about a dopey guy who, after finding out he has only months to live, contracts with a millionaire to leap into a volcano alive. Imaginative farce with great "Metropolis"-pastiche visuals that eventually fizzle out. Watch for Ryan in not one, but three roles, and mysterious symbolism throughout. Special effects courtesy of Industrial Light and Magic. **106m/C; VHS, DVD, Blu-Ray; Open Captioned.** Tom Hanks; Meg Ryan; Lloyd Bridges; Robert Stack; Amanda Plummer; Abe Vigoda; Dan Hedaya; Barry McGovern; Ossie Davis; Nathan Lane; Carol Kane; ***D:*** John Patrick Shanley; ***W:*** John Patrick Shanley; ***C:*** Stephen Goldblatt; ***M:*** Georges Delerue.

Joe's Apartment **1996 (PG-13)** Fresh-from-Iowa Joe (O'Connell) comes to New York, finds a squalid apartment, and then discovers its other occupants are hordes of singing, joking cockroaches. Lucky for Joe, his unwelcome roommates are on his side, even helping out with his love life, when necessary. Gross but interesting, throw in Vaughn as a panty-wearing politician and you've got yourself a potential cult-movie favorite. Neat freaks probably won't enjoy it much. Flick took three years to finish as computer-animated roaches had to do all the dancing and singing. Feature directorial debut for writer Payson, who created the original 1992 live-action/animation MTV short. **82m/C; DVD.** Jerry O'Connell; Megan Ward; Robert Vaughn; Jim Turner; Don Ho; Sandra "Pepa" Denton; Shiek Mahmud-Bey; ***V:*** Billy West; Reginald (Reggie) Hudlin; ***D:*** John Payson; ***W:*** John Payson; ***C:*** Peter Deming.

Joey 1/2 **1985 (PG)** Daddy, a former doo-wopper, looks back on his years of musical success as a waste of time. His son takes to the world of rock guitar with blind fervor. Their argument plays against the backdrop of the "Royal Doo-Wopp Show" at New York City's Radio Music Hall. Features multi-generational rock songs. **90m/C; VHS, DVD.** Neill Barry; James Quinn; Ellen Hammill; Dan Grimaldi; ***D:*** Joseph Ellison; ***W:*** Ellen Hammill; Joseph Ellison; ***C:*** Oliver Wood; ***M:*** Jim Roberge.

Joey 1/2 **1998 (PG)** Young Billy (Croft) rescues a baby kangaroo (known as a joey) who was left behind when an evil hunter captures a group of kangaroos and hauls them off to Sydney for nefarious purposes. So Billy puts Joey in his backpack and heads off to the city to reunite the little family—aided by the rebellious daughter (McKenna) of the newly appointed U.S. ambassador (Begley). **96m/C; VHS, DVD.** *AU* Jamie Croft; Alex McKenna; Ed Begley, Jr.; Rebecca Gibney; Ruth Cracknell; Harold Hopkins; ***D:*** Ian Barry; ***W:*** Stuart Beattie; ***C:*** David Burr; ***M:*** Roger Mason.

John Adams 1/2 **2008** Enjoyment rests on whether you can buy Giamatti as the titular founding father and second president of the U.S. Based on the best-selling bio by David McCullough, Adams is intelligent, impatient, irascible, resentful, and deeply devoted to both his country and his wife, the equally resourceful Abigail (Linney). Most of the familiar historical figures are present and accounted for—George Washington (Morse), Benjamin Franklin (Wilkinson), and Thomas Jefferson (Dillane)?as well as such events as the Continental Congress and the Declaration of Independence, but Adams isn't particularly likeable and you'll probably find out more than you could ever want to know. **560m/C; DVD.** Paul Giamatti; Laura Linney; David Morse; Tom Wilkinson; Stephen (Dillon) Dillane; Zeljko Ivanek; Danny Huston; Sarah Polley; Rufus Sewell; Justin Theroux; ***D:*** Tom Hooper; ***W:*** Kirk Ellis; ***C:*** Tak Fujimoto; ***M:*** Robert (Rob) Lane; Joseph Vitarelli. **CABLE**

John Carpenter Presents Vampires: Los Muertos 1/2 *Vampires: Los Muertos* **2002 (R)** It's mostly a yawner because it's so predictable. Vamp hunter Derek (Bon Jovi) loses his team to the bloodsuckers but hooks up with a rag tag crew, including Father Rodrigo (De La Fuente), to go a-hunting in Mexico. This time the head biter is a vampire babe (Jover). Pretty tame even in comparison to the first flick. **94m/C; VHS, DVD.** Jon Bon Jovi; Cristian de la Fuente; Arly Jover; Darius McCrary; Natasha Gregson Wagner; Diego Luna; ***D:*** Tommy Lee Wallace; ***W:*** Tommy Lee Wallace; ***C:*** Jack Lorenz; ***M:*** Brian Tyler.

John Carpenter's Ghosts of Mars *Ghosts of Mars* **2001 (R)** John Carpenter unashamedly fires up his B-movie machine to maximum cheese factor in this tale of space babes and zombies. Henstridge is a police lieutenant on the matriarchal Mars colony in 2025 sent to retrieve murderer "Desolation" Williams (Ice Cube). The job turns from get the bad guy to simple survival when long-dormant Martian warriors begin taking over the bodies of the Earth intruders, turning them into zombies. So do you think the bad guys and the good guys have to team up to win one for the humans? At its best during the action sequences, but probably a bad choice to follow "A Room with a View" for a Saturday night double feature. **98m/C; VHS, DVD, Blu-Ray.** Natasha Henstridge; Ice Cube; Clea DuVall; Pam Grier; Jason Statham; Joanna Cassidy; Rosemary Forsyth; Liam Waite; Richard Cetrone; ***D:*** John Carpenter; ***W:*** John Carpenter; Larry Sulkis; ***C:*** Gary B. Kibbe; ***M:*** John Carpenter.

John Carpenter's Vampires 1/2 *Vampires* **1997 (R)** Vatican-sponsored vampire hunter Jack Crow (Woods) leads his team of mercenaries into the American Southwest to battle master bloodsucker Valek (Griffith) and his hordes. After destroying a vampire hideout, Crow and company are ambushed at a post-stake party. The only survivors are Crow, his buddy Montoya (Baldwin), and a hooker (Lee) with a psychic link to the vampires. Satisfying horror-western packs plenty of action and gore (along with just enough humor) to hold attention until the inevitable showdown. Woods does a good job of toning down from his usual bug-eyed crazy to merely borderline disturbed here. Based on the novel "Vampires" by John Steakley. **108m/C; VHS, DVD, Blu-Ray.** James Woods; Thomas Ian Griffith; Sheryl Lee; Daniel Baldwin; Tim Guinee; Maximilian Schell; Cary-Hiroyuki Tagawa; Mark Boone, Jr.; Tom Rosales; ***D:*** John Carpenter; ***W:*** John Carpenter; Don Jacoby; ***C:*** Gary B. Kibbe; ***M:*** John Carpenter.

John Carter **2012 (PG-13)** Bloated, incoherent, and misguided, the mega-budgeted John Carter turns out to be all spectacle and no substance. Based on the highly-influential book by Edgar Rice Burroughs (which allegedly inspired both Star Wars and Avatar), this Disney-fied, 3D Christ allegory tells the story of John Carter (Riggins), a Civil War-era captain, who is mysteriously transported to the red planet, where he essentially unites the various warring inhabitants that live there. Too long and too uninspired, it never develops a personality of its own. Director/writer Stanton pulls off a few action sequences to keep it from total disaster, but it's still a major disappointment. **132m/C; DVD, Blu-Ray.** Taylor Kitsch; Willem Dafoe; Lynn Collins; Samantha Morton; Mark Strong; Ciaran Hinds; Dominic West; James Purefoy; Polly Walker; Bryan Cranston; Thomas Haden Church; ***D:*** Andrew Stanton; ***W:*** Andrew Stanton; Mark C. Andrews; Michael Chabon; ***C:*** Dan(iel) Mindel; ***M:*** Michael Giacchino.

John Cleese on How to Irritate People *How to Irritate People* **1968** Cleese, a master at causing irritation, demonstrates how to take care of all those annoying people who irritate you, including job interviewers, bank clerks, waiters, and salesmen. Monty Python alumni Palin and Chapman also join Cleese in the "Airline Pilots" sketch about bored pilots deliberately trying to terrify their passengers. **65m/C; VHS, DVD.** John Cleese; Michael Palin; Graham Chapman; Connie Booth.

John Dies at the End **2012 (R)** Grisly, wacky horror comedy. Twenty-something buddies Dave (Williamson) and John (Mayes) are in the paranormal/ghostbusting biz, tripping out on the latest illegal--a substance nicknamed soy sauce. The drug allows them to read each others' minds and mess with the space/time continuum and invading aliens. As told in a framing story by Dave to a world-weary newspaper reporter (Giamatti). Well, you kinda know what happens to John. **99m/C; DVD, Blu-Ray.** Chase Williamson; Rob Mayes; Paul Giamatti; Clancy Brown; Glynn Turner; Doug Jones; ***D:*** Don A. Coscarelli; ***W:*** Don A. Coscarelli; ***C:*** Michael Gioulakis; ***M:*** Brian Tyler.

John Doe: Vigilante **2014 (R)** A crime thriller about an ordinary guy who finds and kills criminals. After becoming disenchanted with a legal system that often sets violent criminals free, John Doe (Bamber) begins to take justice into his own hands. As he locates and murders such crime doers, John becomes a media sensation and is labeled both a hero and a villain. When his actions become more widely known, copycats spring up leading some to wonder who the real John Doe is and the truth about his actions. **93m/C; DVD, Blu-Ray, Streaming, Download.** Jamie Bamber; Daniel Lissing; Lachy Hulme; Ditch Davey; Fletcher Humphrys; ***D:*** Kelly Dolen; ***W:*** Stephen M. Coates; ***C:*** David Parker; ***M:*** David Hirschfelder.

John Grisham's The Rainmaker 1/2 *The Rainmaker* **1997 (PG-13)** Yet another legal drama from the successful pen of John Grisham. Baylor (Damon) is a young lawyer whose job disappears when his firm is absorbed by a giant company. He fills his time giving legal advice to indigents and mooning over Kelly (Danes), a young abused wife. Then he takes on the case of a couple whose leukemia-stricken son was denied treatment by their insurance company, coincidentally represented by the firm that booted Baylor. Pre-"Jack," Coppola probably wouldn't have gone anywhere near such formulaic franchise fare, and if he did, he could've directed it in his sleep. As it is he creates a serviceable, if not spectacular, piece of entertainment. His main allies are Voight's insurance company mouthpiece and DeVito's ambulance chaser. Damon plays the hero with much less bravado than previous Grisham protagonists. **137m/C; VHS, DVD.** Matt Damon; Claire Danes; Danny DeVito; Jon Voight; Danny Glover; Virginia Madsen; Mary Kay Place; Mickey Rourke; Johnny Whitworth; Teresa Wright; Dean Stockwell; Red West; Roy Scheider; Randy Travis; Andrew Shue; Sonny Shroyer; ***D:*** Francis Ford Coppola; ***W:*** Francis Ford Coppola; Michael Herr; ***C:*** John Toll; ***M:*** Elmer Bernstein.

John John in the Sky **2000 (PG-13)** Ten-year-old John John (Craft) is living with a lot of tension in 1968. His good ol' boy dad (Travis) is abusive and angry at the changes going on around him, especially the fact that his wife (Rosemont) wants to take her kid and flee to San Francisco to join a commune. And John John also doesn't know how to deal with the unwanted friendship of the disabled Zeola (Schwimmer). Title comes from the boy's dream to build his own airplane. Sometimes confusing story with its series of flashbacks and flash-forwards. **101m/C; VHS, DVD.** Randy Travis; Christian Craft; Romy Rosemont; Rusty Schwimmer; Matt Letscher; ***D:*** Jefferson Davis; ***W:*** Keri Skogland; Jefferson Davis; ***C:*** Joel David; ***M:*** Christopher Ward.

John Loves Mary **1948** Wartime marriage dilemmas. Soldier John (Reagan) owes buddy Fred (Carson) bigtime for saving his life so he agrees to an in-name-only marriage to Fred's English girlfriend Lily (Field) so she can get to the States. But by the time that happens, fickle Fred has actually married another gal and John must keep his marriage a secret from his own fiancee, Mary (Neal), until he can get that Reno divorce. But John's waffling has left Mary believing that he doesn't love her anymore. **96m/B; DVD.** Ronald Reagan; Patricia Neal; Jack Carson; Virginia Field; Edward Arnold; Wayne Morris; Katherine Alexander; Paul Harvey; ***D:*** David Butler; ***W:*** Henry Ephron; Phoebe Ephron; ***C:*** J. Peverell Marley; ***M:*** David Buttolph.

John Q **2002 (PG-13)** "Dog Day Afternoon" lite is essentially a two hour tirade against the U.S. health system (who can blame them?) which casts Washington as the title's everyman hero who's desperate and gutsy enough to bypass medical bureaucracy altogether to get his 10-year old son Mike (Smith) the heart transplant he desperately needs to live. John Quincy Archibald's plant has just cut his hours, and when his HMO gives him the run-around, he is forced to come up with the $75,000 for his son's operation. Unable to come up with it, John Q. takes over the ER and demands his son be placed at the top of the transplant list. Talented cast, including Duvall as the sympathetic police negotiator, Woods as the cynical doctor, and Liotta, as the boldly drawn police chief, is generally wasted on the sentimental and melodramatic one-note premise. **118m/C; VHS, DVD, Blu-Ray.** Denzel Washington; Robert Duvall; James Woods; Anne Heche; Eddie Griffin; Kimberly Elise; Shawn Hatosy; Ray Liotta; Daniel E. Smith; David Thornton; Ethan Suplee; Kevin Connolly; Paul Johansson; Troy Beyer; Obba Babatunde; Laura Elena Harring; *D:* Nick Cassavetes; *W:* James Kearns; *C:* Rogier Stoffers; *M:* Aaron Zigman.

John Rabe ⅆⅆ **2009** Old-fashioned historical epic based of the true story of John Rabe (Tukur), a Nazi German industrialist running the Chinese branch of a German engineering conglomerate in Nanking, China. A longtime resident, he is credited with saving the lives of more than 200,000 Chinese during the 1937 massacre in the second Sino-Japanese war. German, Cantonese, Mandarin, and Japanese with subtitles. **130m/C; DVD.** Ulrich Tukur; Daniel Brühl; Anne Consigny; Dagmar Manzel; Steve Buscemi; Jingchu Zhang; Teruyuki Kagawa; Mathias Herrmann; *D:* Florian Gallenberger; *W:* Florian Gallenberger; *C:* Jurgen Jurges; *M:* Laurent Petitgand; Annette Focks.

John Tucker Must Die ⅆⅆ **2006 (PG-13)** Title character (Metcalfe) is the resident B.M.O.C. who uses his looks and status to triple-time the three hottest girls in school, who end up learning about his cheating ways. The hotties plot unsuccessfully for revenge until they enlist the help of the ugly-duckling new girl, Kate (Snow), and the requisite makeover-to-lure-the-jerk ensues. Pic backfires in its girl-power message by resorting to cliches about female sensitivity, self-image, and estrogen side-effects and never gets as mean as "Mean Girls" or as darkly original as "Heathers." **82m/C; DVD.** Jesse Metcalfe; Ashanti; Arielle Kebbel; Brittany Snow; Sophia Bush; Jenny McCarthy; Fulvio Cecere; Penn Badgley; *D:* Betty Thomas; *W:* Jeff Lowell; *C:* Anthony B. Richmond; *M:* Richard Gibbs.

John Wick ⅆⅆ ½ **2014 (R)** The title character (Reeves) gets a gift of a puppy posthumously from his recently deceased wife. The dog means a lot to him. When a trio of Russian mobsters kills the dog, John Wick goes off the edge. And you don't want John Wick off the edge. He embarks upon a campaign of destruction, taking out those who wronged him in violent, butt-kicking ways. Stahelski's action flick is a clever throwback to the stunt-driven films of the '80s and '90s, before CGI took over the genre. In fact, the stunt choreography makes the film, and that's a compliment. You can hear the bones crunch. **96m/C; DVD, Blu-Ray.** Keanu Reeves; Willem Dafoe; Alfie Allen; Michael Nyqvist; John Leguizamo; Adrianne Palicki; Ian McShane; Dean Winters; Bridget Moynahan; *D:* Chad Stahelski; *W:* Derek Kolstad; *C:* Jonathan Sela; *M:* Tyler Bates; Joel J. Richard.

John Wick: Chapter 2 ⅆⅆⅆ **2017 (R)** The follow-up to the cult hit that reinvigorated the action career of Reeves picks up pretty much right where the last one left off, continuing the story of that film about a man getting vengeance for the death of his dog. After what John did in chapter one, a bounty is placed on his head, which leads to waves of incompetent bad guys for him to dispatch in his beautifully choreographed, balletic style. With director Stahelski's streamlined, efficient approach to action, it's just as much fun as you want it to be. **122m/C; Blu-Ray.** Keanu Reeves; Common; Laurence Fishburne; Riccardo Scamarcio; Ruby Rose; *D:* Chad Stahelski; *W:* Derek Kolstad; *C:* Dan Laustsen; *M:* Tyler Bates; Joel J. Richard.

John Wick: Chapter 3—Parabellum ⅆⅆⅆ **2019 (R)** The third entry in the John Wick action series picks up where the second ends. After killing a member of the High Table of assassins on the safe grounds of the Continental Hotel, Wick (Reeves) loses all related rights and privileges. An open contract, which includes multimillion dollar payoff, is issued for Wick's death. Given an hour hour head start, Wick seeks help from people in his past as he tries to reach the secretive leader of the High Table to personally atone for his transgression. Anchored by a memorable performance by Reeves, the stylistic film features memorable details and intense fight sequences. **130m/C; DVD, Blu-Ray.** Keanu Reeves; Halle Berry; Ian McShane; Laurence Fishburne; Mark Dacascos; *D:* Chad Stahelski; *W:* Derek Kolstad; Chad Stahelski; Shay Hatten; Chris Collins; Marc Adams; *C:* Dan Laustsen; *M:* Tyler Bates; Joel J. Richard.

Johnnie Gibson F.B.I. ⅆ *Johnnie Mae Gibson: FBI* **1987** Supposedly based on a true story, the adventures of a beautiful, black FBI agent who falls in love with a man she's investigating. **96m/C; VHS, DVD.** Howard E. Rollins, Jr.; Lynn Whitfield; William Allen Young; Richard Lawson; *D:* Bill Duke; *M:* Billy Goldenberg.

Johnny Allegro ⅆ ½ **1949** Ex-gangster Johnny Allegro (Raft) now works undercover for the Treasury Department. Wealthy criminal Morgan Vallin (Macready) is planning to flood the U.S. with bogus money in an effort to overthrow the government so the feds send Johnny to Vallin's private. The bad guy likes to hunt humans and decides Johnny will be next if the feds can't rescue him first. **81m/B; DVD, Blu-Ray.** George Raft; George Macready; Nina Foch; Will Geer; Gloria Henry; Ivan Triesault; *D:* Ted Tetzlaff; *W:* Karen DeWolf; Guy Endore; *C:* Joseph Biroc; *M:* George Duning.

Johnny Apollo ⅆⅆ ½ **1940** Upright college student Power keeps his nose clean until Dad's sent to jail for playing with numbers. Scheming to free his old man (Arnold) from the big house, he decides crime will pay for the stiff price tag of freedom. Predictable and melodramatic, but well directed. **93m/B; VHS, DVD.** Tyrone Power; Dorothy Lamour; Lloyd Nolan; Edward Arnold; Charley Grapewin; Lionel Atwill; Marc Lawrence; Jonathan Hale; Russell Hicks; Selmer Jackson; Charles Trowbridge; *D:* Yves Allegret; *W:* Rowland Brown; Philip Dunne; Samuel G. Engel; *C:* Arthur C. Miller; *M:* Cyril Mockridge; Alfred Newman; Lionel Newman.

Johnny B. ⅆⅆ ½ **2000 (R)** College dropout Johnny B. has become a smalltime hustler with no ambitions since the murder of his older brother. Then he learns his ex-girlfriend, who's also the mother of his young daughter, has gotten engaged to a successful lawyer. Now, Johnny has some tough decisions to make. **98m/C; VHS, DVD.** Richard Brooks; Vonetta McGee; Richard Gant; Kent Masters King; Tempestt Bledsoe; *D:* Richard Brooks; *W:* Gwendolyn J. Lester; *C:* Pancho Gonzales.

Johnny Be Good ⅆ **1988 (R)** A too-talented high school quarterback is torn between loyalty to his best friend and to his girlfriend amid bribery and schemings by colleges eager to sign him up. **91m/C; VHS, DVD, Blu-Ray.** Anthony Michael Hall; Robert Downey, Jr.; Paul Gleason; Uma Thurman; John Pankow; Steve James; Seymour Cassel; Michael Greene; Marshall Bell; Deborah May; *D:* Bud Smith; *W:* Jeff Buhai; *M:* Jay Ferguson.

Johnny Belinda ⅆⅆⅆ **1948** A compassionate physician cares for a young deaf mute woman and her illegitimate child. Tension builds as the baby's father returns to claim the boy. **103m/B; VHS, DVD.** Jane Wyman; Lew Ayres; Charles Bickford; Agnes Moorehead; Jan Sterling; *D:* Jean Negulesco; *M:* Max Steiner. Oscars '48: Actress (Wyman); Golden Globes '49: Actress--Drama (Wyman), Film--Drama.

Johnny Come Lately ⅆⅆ ½ *Johnny Vagabond* **1943** An elderly editor helps out an ex-newspaperman with a police charge. The two then team up to expose political corruption despite threats from a rival newspaperman. **97m/B; DVD, Blu-Ray.** James Cagney; Grace George; Marjorie Main; Marjorie Lord; Hattie McDaniel; Edward McNamara; *D:* William K. Howard; *W:* John Van Druten; *C:* Theodor Sparkuhl; *M:* Leigh Harline.

Johnny Cool ⅆⅆ **1963** Violent crime drama. Gangster Johnny Colini (Lawrence) is deported back to Sicily thanks to some rivals. He grooms Salvatore Giordano (Silva) into becoming his assassin, giving him his own 'Johnny Cool' nickname. Colini then sends him to the States to take out those who betrayed him. Johnny hooks up with wealthy divorcee Dare (Montgomery), who becomes his accomplice until the violence gets to be too much. Executive producer Peter Lawford offered pals parts, which accounts for so many familiar faces in small roles. **102m/B; DVD, Blu-Ray.** Henry Silva; Elizabeth Montgomery; Marc Lawrence; Brad Dexter; Telly Savalas; Jim Backus; John McGiver; Wanda Hendrix; Mort Sahl; Joey Bishop; Sammy Davis, Jr.; *D:* William Asher; *W:* Joseph Landon; *C:* Sam Leavitt; *M:* Billy May.

Johnny Dangerously ⅆⅆ **1984 (PG-13)** A gangster spoof about Johnny Dangerously, who turned to crime in order to pay his mother's medical bills. Now, Dangerously wants to go straight, but competitive crooks would rather see him dead than law-abiding and his mother requires more and more expensive operations. Crime pays in comic ways. **90m/C; VHS, DVD.** Michael Keaton; Joe Piscopo; Danny DeVito; Maureen Stapleton; Marilu Henner; Peter Boyle; Griffin Dunne; Glynnis O'Connor; Dom DeLuise; Richard Dimitri; Ray Walston; Dick Butkus; Alan Hale, Jr.; Bob Eubanks; *D:* Amy Heckerling; *W:* Norman Steinberg; Harry Colomby.

Johnny Doesn't Live Here Any More ⅆⅆ **1944** The Washington, DC housing shortage, caused by an influx of WWII workers, finds Kathie without a place to live. She convinces Marine Johnny Moore, who's about to ship out, to let her sublet his apartment. What she doesn't know is Johnny has a generous open-door policy with his friends, including buddy Mike who takes a shine to the new occupant. Last film for director May. **78m/B; DVD.** Simone Simon; James Ellison; William Terry; Minna Gombell; Robert Mitchum; *D:* Joe May; *W:* Philip Yordan; *C:* Ira Morgan; *M:* W. Franke Harling.

Johnny Eager ⅆⅆⅆ **1942** Glossy crime melodrama starring Taylor as an unscrupulous racketeer and Turner as the daughter of D.A. Arnold who falls for him and ends up becoming a pawn in his schemes. Heflin won an Oscar for his outstanding performance as Taylor's alcoholic confidant. Excellent direction by LeRoy makes this a top-rate gangster film. Based on a story by James Edward Grant. **107m/B; VHS, DVD.** Robert Taylor; Lana Turner; Edward Arnold; Van Heflin; Robert Sterling; Patricia Dane; Glenda Farrell; Barry Nelson; Henry O'Neill; Charles Dingle; Cy Kendall; *D:* Mervyn LeRoy; *W:* James Edward Grant; John Lee Mahin. Oscars '42: Support. Actor (Heflin).

Johnny English ⅆ ½ **2003 (PG)** Johnny English (Atkinson) is a deskbound member of the espionage community who's promoted to active status due to some unfortunate circumstances that he caused. The klutz must then prevent an evil French businessman (Malkovich) from dethroning the Queen and taking over. Anglophiles, fans of Rowan Atkinson, and toilet/slapstick humor lovers will enjoy this stale crumpet, but there's not much here for anyone else Stateside. Atkinson manages to squeeze some laughs from a poor script with his supreme gift for physical comedy, however, and Malkovich gleefully throws himself over the top. Imbruglia, making her feature debut, is game, but doesn't have much to do. **86m/C; VHS, DVD, Blu-Ray.** *GB US* Rowan Atkinson; John Malkovich; Natalie Imbruglia; Ben Miller; Kevin McNally; Tim Pigott-Smith; Douglas McFerran; Greg Wise; Oliver Ford Davies; *D:* Peter Howitt; *W:* Neal Purvis; Robert Wade; William Davies; *C:* Remi Adefarasin; *M:* Ed Shearmur.

Johnny English Reborn ⅆⅆ **2011 (PG)** Atkinson reprises the role that brought him a new American audience in 2003 as the world's most unlikely spy, Johnny English. This time around English is assigned to prevent the assassination of the Chinese premier, despite the misgivings of his new boss (Anderson). English bumbles his way through the mission by either kicking or getting kicked in the groin repeatedly and incorrectly deploying an arsenal of high-tech gadgets. Although Atkinson's brilliant slapstick persona is in top form, the material feels somewhat tired eight years on. **101m/C; DVD, Blu-Ray.** *GB* Rowan Atkinson; Gillian Anderson; Dominic West; Daniel Kaluuya; Richard Schiff; *D:* Oliver Parker; *W:* Hamish McColl; William Davies; *C:* Daniel Cohen; *M:* Ilan Eshkeri.

Johnny English Strikes Again ⅆⅆ *Johnny English 3.0* **2018 (PG)** The third entry in the Johnny English (Atkinson) comedy franchise finds the bumbling yet overconfident British spy teaching at a British boarding school in retirement. When a cyber-attack exposes every British agent in the field ahead of the G12 meeting of world leaders, the British prime minster (Thompson) calls on retired spies for help. She ultimately must rely on Johnny to discover the source of the destructive attacks. With sidekick Bough (Miller), Johnny goes undercover in France to save his country. While there are amusing sequences and Thompson is an admirable prime minister, the film's one-joke premise wears thin. **89m/C; DVD, Blu-Ray.** Rowan Atkinson; Emma Thompson; Adam James; Kevin Eldon; Kendra Mei; *D:* David Kerr; *W:* William Davies; *C:* Florian Hoffmeister; *M:* Howard Goodall.

Johnny Firecloud ⅆ **1975** A modern Indian goes on the warpath when the persecution of his people reawakens his sense of identity. **94m/C; VHS, DVD.** Victor Mohica; Ralph Meeker; Frank De Kova; Sacheen Little Feather; David Canary; Christina Hart; *D:* William Allen Castleman; *W:* Wilton Denmark; *M:* William Loose.

Johnny Got His Gun ⅆⅆⅆ **1971 (R)** Dalton Trumbo's story of a young WWI veteran (Bottoms) who meets a bomb with his name on it and is rendered armless, legless, and more or less faceless, as well as deaf, dumb, and blind. Regarded as a vegetable and stuck in a lightless hospital utility room, he dreams and fantasizes about life before and after the bomb, and tries vainly to communicate with the staff. Wrenching and bleak anti-war diatribe made at the climax of the Vietnam War. **111m/C; VHS, DVD.** Timothy Bottoms; Jason Robards, Jr.; Donald Sutherland; Diane Varsi; Kathy Fields; Donald (Don "Red") Barry; Peter Brocco; Judy Chaikin; Eric Christmas; Maurice Dallimore; Robert Easton; Eduard Franz; Anthony Geary; Edmund Gilbert; Ben Hammer; Wayne Heffley; Marsha Hunt; Joseph Kaufmann; Charles McGraw; Byron Morrow; David Soul; *D:* Dalton Trumbo; *W:* Dalton Trumbo; *C:* Jules Brenner; *M:* Jerry Fielding. Cannes '71: Grand Jury Prize.

Johnny Guitar ⅆⅆⅆ ½ **1953** Women strap on six-guns in Nicholas Ray's unintentionally hilarious, gender-bending western. A guitar-playing loner wanders into a small town feud between lovelorn saloon owner Crawford and McCambridge, the town's resident lynch mob-leading harpy. This fascinating cult favorite has had film theorists arguing for decades: is it a parody, a political McCarthy-era allegory, or Freudian exercise? The off-screen battles of the two female stars are equally legendary. Stick around for the end credits to hear Peggy Lee sing the title song. **116m/C; VHS, DVD, Blu-Ray.** Joan Crawford; Ernest Borgnine; Sterling Hayden; Mercedes McCambridge; Scott Brady; Ward Bond; Royal Dano; John Carradine; Ben Cooper; Frank Ferguson; Paul Fix; Denver Pyle; *D:* Nicholas Ray; *W:* Philip Yordan; *C:* Harry Stradling, Sr.; *M:* Victor Young. Natl. Film Reg. '08.

Johnny Handsome ⅆⅆⅆ **1989 (R)** An ugly, deformed hood, after he's been double-crossed and sent to prison, volunteers for a reconstructive surgery experiment and is released with a new face, determined to hunt down the scum that set him up. A terrific modern B-picture based on John Godey's "The Three Worlds of Johnny Handsome." **96m/C; VHS, DVD, Blu-Ray.** Mickey Rourke; Ellen Barkin; Lance Henriksen; Elizabeth McGovern; Morgan Freeman; Forest Whitaker; Scott Wilson; Blake Clark; *D:* Walter Hill; *W:* Ken Friedman; *M:* Ry Cooder.

Johnny Mnemonic ⅆⅆ **1995 (R)** Robo-yuppie data courier Johnny (Reeves), has over extended the storage capacity in his head and must download his latest job before his brain turns to applesauce. Aided by an implant-enhanced bodyguard (Meyer), underground hacker rebels called LoTeks, and a former doctor (Rollins) battling a technology-induced epidemic, Johnny is on the run from the corporation that wants his head (literally). Freshman director Longo can't seem to get a handle on the plot and doesn't get much help from Gibson, who combined characters and scenarios from his other books. Action sequences and computer effects are appropriately spiffy, preventing a total system crash. **98m/C; VHS, DVD.** Keanu Reeves; Dina Meyer; Ice-T; Takeshi "Beat" Kitano; Dolph Lundgren; Henry Rollins; Udo Kier; Barbara Sukowa; Denis Akayama; *D:* Robert

Longo; *W:* William Gibson; *C:* Francois Protat; *M:* Brad Fiedel.

Johnny O'Clock 🦴🦴 **1947** Slick film noir that's the directorial debut of Rossen. Johnny and Pete operate a casino and crooked cop Chuck wants in. When Chuck's girlfriend, Harriet, allegedly commits suicide, her sister Nancy wants Johnny to help her prove it was actually a murder. Then Chuck turns up dead and Inspector Koch is ready to pin the crime on Johnny. **95m/B; DVD.** Dick Powell; Evelyn Keyes; Lee J. Cobb; Thomas Gomez; Jim Bannon; Ellen Drew; Nina Foch; *D:* Robert Rossen; *W:* Robert Rossen; Milton Holmes; *C:* Burnett Guffey; *M:* George Duning.

Johnny 100 Pesos 🦴🦴 **1993** Seventeen-year-old Johnny (Araiza) walks into a video store that is a front for an illegal currency exchange operation. He's the advance man for a quartet of criminals who are planning to rob the place but before they can escape with the cash, the police show up and the crooks take the store's inhabitants hostage. Now there's a standoff, with the media shamelessly broadcasting all events and the Chilean authorities struggling to control the escalating situation. Based on a true 1990 incident. Spanish with subtitles. **90m/C; VHS, DVD.** Armando Araiza; Patricia Rivera; Willy Semler; Sergio Hernandez; *D:* Gustavo Graef-Marino; *W:* Gustavo Graef-Marino; Gerardo Caceres; *C:* Jose Luis Arredondo; *M:* Andres Pollak.

Johnny Reno 🦴 ½ **1966** Laughable western that has U.S. Marshal Andrews trying to save an accused killer from lynching. Of interest for star-watching only. Based on a story by Steve Fisher, A.C. Lyles, and Andrew Craddock. **83m/C; VHS, DVD.** Dana Andrews; Jane Russell; Lon Chaney, Jr.; John Agar; Lyle Bettger; Tom Drake; Richard Arlen; Robert Lowery; *D:* R.G. Springsteen; *W:* Steve Fisher.

Johnny Shiloh 🦴🦴 **1963** An underage youth becomes a heroic drummer during the Civil War. Originally a two-part Disney TV show. **90m/C; VHS, DVD.** Kevin Corcoran; Brian Keith; Darryl Hickman; Skip Homeier; *D:* James Neilson. **TV**

Johnny Skidmarks 🦴🦴 **1997 (R)** Johnny (Gallagher) is a burned-out freelance crime-scene photographer who moonlights for blackmailers by shooting incriminating pics of prominent citizens in seedy motels. Then the blackmailers start winding up dead and Johnny checks out his photos to see if he can figure out who's doing the crime before he becomes the next target. **96m/C; VHS, DVD.** Peter Gallagher; Frances McDormand; John Lithgow; Jack Black; Charlie Spradling; *D:* John Raffo; *W:* John Raffo; William Preston Robinson; *C:* Bernd Heinl; *M:* Brian Langsbard.

Johnny Suede 🦴🦴 ½ **1992 (R)** Hip kid with big hair wanders the city seeking an identity via retro black suede elevator shoes. Sleepy surreal comedy walks Pitt through two romantic entanglements and a rendezvous with his own rock idol in his quest for musical talent and pop singer nirvana (not necessarily in that order). Candidate for induction into the David Lynch Movie Musuem of the Weird. **97m/C; VHS, DVD.** Brad Pitt; Calvin Levels; Nick Cave; Wilfredo Giovanni Clark; Alison Moir; Peter McRobbie; Tina Louise; Michael Mulheren; Catherine Keener; Samuel L. Jackson; *D:* Tom DiCillo; *W:* Tom DiCillo; *M:* Jim Farmer.

Johnny Tremain & the Sons of Liberty 🦴🦴 **1958** The story of the gallant American patriots who participated in the Boston Tea Party. **85m/C; VHS, DVD.** Sebastian Cabot; Hal Stalmaster; Luana Patten; Richard Beymer; *D:* Robert Stevenson.

Johnny 2.0 🦴 ½ **1999 (PG-13)** Contrived thriller about a genetic scientist, Johnny Dalton (Fahey), who awakens from a 15-year coma and discovers his memory has been transplanted into a clone, Johnny 2.0. Now Dalton has six days to find his duplicate before the Corporation, the group behind the procedure, decides on termination. **95m/C; VHS, DVD.** Jeff Fahey; Michael Ironside; Tahnee Welch; *D:* Neill Fearnley. **CABLE**

Johnny Was 🦴 ½ **2005 (R)** Johnny Doyle (Jones) escapes his IRA past by hiding out in London's tough Brixton neighborhood, trapped between a pirate reggae radio station and a crack-dealing gangster. His life gets tougher when former mentor Flynn (Bergin) escapes from prison and is determined to derail the Irish peace process with a new bombing campaign. Good soundtrack but inept thriller. **90m/C; DVD.** *GB IR* Vinnie Jones; Patrick Bergin; Roger Daltrey; Samantha Mumba; Lennox Lewis; Eriq La Salle; *D:* Mark Hammond; *W:* Brendan Foley; *C:* Mark Moriarty.

Johnny Winter: Down & Dirty 🦴🦴 ½ **2014** A feature-length documentary about the life, work, and influence of Texas-born blues icon Johnny Winter. Shot during the last two years of Winter's life with the help of Winter's family, the film includes extensive interviews with family members and his many peers. Also examined is the making of his album Step Back and many tour dates including his last live performance ever. Along the way, the documentary features information on Winter's life from his earliest years in Texas to his coming to fame in the 1960s to his work until his unexpected death while on tour in Switzerland in 2014. **104m/C; DVD, Streaming, Download.** *D:* Greg Olliver; *C:* Greg Olliver. **VIDEO**

Johnny Yuma 🦴 ½ **1966** Gunslinger Johnny (Damon) has been named the heir to his wealthy uncle Thomas Felton's ranch, much to the disgust of Felton's greedy wife Samantha (Neri) and her shifty brother Pedro (Vannucchi). After Pedro kills Felton, they try to frame someone else for the crime until Johnny shows up. Spaghetti western gets an extra half bone for Neri's sultry presence. **75m/C; DVD.** *IT* Mark Damon; Rosalba Neri; Luigi Vannucchi; Lawrence (Larry) Dobkin; Leslie Daniels; *D:* Romolo Guerrieri; *W:* Romolo Guerrieri; Fernando Di Leo; *C:* Mario Capriotti; *M:* Nora Orlandi.

johns 🦴🦴 ½ **1996 (R)** A gritty, yet predictable tale of street hustling in L.A. redeemed by intense performances by its two lead actors. It's Christmas Eve and John (Arquette) has only one thing in mind: recover his stolen money and celebrate his birthday in style. On the way, he mentors crony Donnor (Haas), who's love for John blinds him to the rules of hustling, which can only lead to tragedy. Arquette's controlled performance is on target for the cynical male lead and Haas's doe-eyed look is perfect for the slightly dim-witted naivete his character revels in. Downfall comes when first-time director Silver fails to maintain actors' intensity with uneven editing and out of place symbolism. Still, not a bad first try. **96m/C; VHS, DVD.** David Arquette; Lukas Haas; Arliss Howard; Keith David; Elliott Gould; Christopher Gartin; Joshua Schaefer; Wilson Cruz; Terrence Howard; Nicky Katt; Alanna Ubach; *D:* Scott Silver; *W:* Scott Silver; *C:* Tom Richmond; *M:* Charles D. Brown.

Johnson County War 🦴🦴 **2002** The Hammett brothers, Cain (Berenger), Harry (Perry), and Dale (Storke) struggle to protect their ranch against greedy cattle barons after their property and that of other homesteaders. And in this case, the "law" in the guise of trigger-happy Hunt Lawton (Reynolds) is on the side of the bad guys. Based on the novel "Riders of Judgment" by Frederic Manfred. The story of this 1890s Wyoming range war was also covered in the film "Heaven's Gate." **178m/C; VHS, DVD.** Tom Berenger; Luke Perry; Adam Storke; Burt Reynolds; Rachel Ward; Michelle Forbes; Christopher Cazenove; Jack Conley; Fay Masterson; Blu Mankuma; Silas Weir Mitchell; Ken Pogue; *D:* David S. Cass, Sr.; *W:* Larry McMurtry; Diana Ossana; *C:* Doug Milsome; *M:* Sheldon Mirowitz. **CABLE**

Johnson Family Vacation 🦴 ½ **2004 (PG-13)** Slapdash road comedy will have viewers whining miles before the end, "Are we there yet?" At a crisp 97 minutes, that is no easy feat but one managed with uninspired, corny dialogue, and not one ounce of originality as the Johnson family, headed by patriarch Nate (Cedric the Entertainer) hit the road in search of a decent premise—er, family reunion in Missouri. Recently separated from wife Dorothy (Williams), Nate hopes the trip with their three children (Bow Wow, Knowles, and Soleil) will bring them closer together and hopefully snatch the coveted reunion "family of the year" trophy from regular winner Mack (Harvey), Nate's older bro. Cedric's natural charisma somewhat elevates this washed-out "Vacation." **97m/C; DVD, Blu-Ray.** Cedric the Entertainer; Vanessa L(ynne) Williams; Bow Wow; Steve Harvey; Solange Knowles; Shannon Elizabeth; Aloma Wright; Shari Headley; Jennifer Freeman; Lee Garlington; Gabby Soleil; Philip Daniel Bolden; Rodney B. Perry; Christopher B. Duncan; *Cameo(s):* Kurupt; *D:* Christopher Erskin; *W:* Todd R. Jones; Earl Richey Jones; *C:* Shawn Maurer; *M:* Richard Gibbs.

Join the Marines 🦴 ½ **1937** New York cop Phil resigns from the force to try out for the U.S. Olympic boxing team but then gets involved with Paula, the daughter of Marine Colonel Denbrough. Phil gets kicked off the team when he's falsely accused of being drunk and joins the Marines to win his future father-in-law's approval. Somehow everyone winds up on a South Seas island facing a native uprising and a plague. **70m/B; DVD.** Paul Kelly; June Travis; Purnell Pratt; Reginald Denny; Warren Hymer; Irving Pichel; Sterling Holloway; Ray Corrigan; *D:* Ralph Staub; *W:* Olive Cooper; Joseph Krumgold; *C:* Ernest Miller.

Joint Body 🦴🦴 **2011** Recent parolee Nick (Pellegrino) is trying to move on with his life. But he gets involved with stripper Michelle (Witt), who's being threatened by someone from her past. Nick gets on the wrong side of the law again when he tries to help. **85m/C; DVD.** Mark Pellegrino; Alicia Witt; Tom Guiry; Bellamy Young; Ryan O'Nan; *D:* Brian Jun; *W:* Brian Jun; *C:* Ryan Samul; *M:* Alec Puro. **VIDEO**

Jojo Rabbit 🦴🦴🦴 **2019 (PG-13)** As World War II nears its end in Germany, ten-year-old Jojo (Davis) attends a camp where he is indoctrinated into Nazism. Embracing its doctrines, he often talks to his bumbling imaginary friend, Adolf Hitler (Waititi). Jojo's perspective changes when he finds an older Jewish girl (McKenzie) that his mother (Johansson), a member of the resistance, is hiding in their attic. As Jojo gets to know the girl, his feelings about Jews and Nazis become conflicted. The coming-of-age comedy is an original, mostly convincing satire with an impressive cast, especially the child actors. **108m/C; DVD, Blu-Ray.** Roman Griffin Davis; Thomasin McKenzie; Scarlett Johansson; Taika Waititi; Sam Rockwell; *D:* Taika Waititi; *W:* Taika Waititi; *C:* Mihai Malaimare, Jr.; *M:* Michael Giacchino. Oscars '19: Adapt. Screenplay; British Acad. '19: Adapt. Screenplay; Writers Guild '19: Adapt. Screenplay.

Joker 🦴🦴🦴 **2019 (R)** This unsettling origin story of Batman's nemesis, the Joker. As struggling comedian Arthur Fleck succumbs to mental illness, he embodies a violent alter ego that avenges the mistreatment and apathy he endured in Gotham City. Phoenix's disturbing yet humanizing performance was universally hailed. Yet the film's release was met with protests over the glorification of violence and the collective memory of the 2002 mass shooting during a screening of "Dark Knight Rises" in Aurora, Colorado; as a result, costumes and masks were banned for "Joker" audiences by AMC Theatres and Landmark Theatres. **122m/C; DVD, Blu-Ray.** Joaquin Rafael (Leaf) Phoenix; Robert De Niro; Zazie Beetz; Frances Conroy; Brett Cullen; *D:* Todd Phillips; *W:* Todd Phillips; Scott Silver; *C:* Lawrence Sher; *M:* Hildur Guonadottir. Oscars '19: Orig. Score; Oscars '20: Actor (Phoenix); British Acad. '19: Actor (Phoenix), Orig. Score; Golden Globes '20: Actor--Drama (Phoenix), Orig. Score; Screen Actors Guild '19: Actor (Phoenix).

Jolene 🦴 **2008** Exploitative adaptation of the E.L. Doctorow short story. Fifteen-year-old orphan Jolene gets out of the South Carolina foster care system by becoming a child bride and then continues over a 10-year period to make bad judgments about jobs, including pole-dancing, and men, by taking a succession of skeevy and/or self-centered lovers. **120m/C; DVD.** Jessica Chastain; Frances Fisher; Rupert Friend; Dermot Mulroney; Zeb Newman; Denise Richards; Theresa Russell; Michael Vartan; Chazz Palminteri; *D:* Dan Ireland; *W:* Dennis Yares; *C:* Claudio Rocha; *M:* Harry Gregson-Williams.

The Jolly Boys' Last Stand 🦴🦴 **2000** Spider (Serkis) is leaving behind his loutish, hard-drinking mates, known as the Jolly Boys, after proposing to girlfriend Annie (Craig). His best man Des (Twomey) decides to make a pre-wedding video for the groom as a gift. Then Vinnie (Baron Cohen) also goes domestic, which throws the rest of the gang into a tizzy and the video turns into a group effort with unexpected results. Ragged (and amiable) debut for writer/director Payne that was shot in 1998. **88m/C; DVD.** *GB* Andy Serkis; Sacha Baron Cohen; Milo Twomey; Rebecca Craig; Jo Martin; *D:* Christopher Payne; *W:* Christopher Payne; *C:* Will Jacob; Robin Cox; *M:* Jeremy Panufnik.

Jolson Sings Again 🦴🦴 **1949** This sequel to "The Jolson Story" brings back Larry Parks as the ebullient entertainer, with Jolson himself dubbing Parks's voice for the songs. Picking up where the other film ended, the movie chronicles Jolson's comeback in the 1940s and his tireless work with the USO overseas during WWII and the Korean War. **96m/C; VHS, DVD.** Larry Parks; William Demarest; Barbara Hale; Bill Goodwin; *D:* Henry Levin; *M:* George Duning.

The Jolson Story 🦴🦴🦴 **1946** A smash Hollywood bio of Jolson, from his childhood to super-stardom. Features dozens of vintage songs from Jolson's parade of hits. Jolson himself dubbed the vocals for Parks, rejuvenating his own career in the process. **128m/C; VHS, DVD.** Larry Parks; Evelyn Keyes; William Demarest; Bill Goodwin; Tamara Shayne; John Alexander; Jimmy Lloyd; Ludwig Donath; Scotty Beckett; *D:* Alfred E. Green; *M:* Morris Stoloff. Oscars '46: Scoring/Musical, Sound.

Jonah Hex 🦴 ½ **2010 (PG-13)** Having survived death, Jonah Hex (Brolin), a scarred, gunslinging bounty hunter, has ties to both the natural and supernatural worlds. Shortly after the Civil War, veteran Hex was forced to watch as sadistic voodoo practitioner Quentin Turnbull (Malkovich) murdered his family then branded his face, leaving him for dead. Years later, without much explanation, Hex finds himself on a military mission to prevent Turnbull from unleashing Hell on Earth. Starts off sizzling, but soon loses all steam, struggling to maintain focus for its pathetically short runtime with Fox serving mostly as eye candy as Hex's hooker girlfriend. **84m/C; Blu-Ray.** Josh Brolin; John Malkovich; Megan Fox; Michael Shannon; Michael Fassbender; Aidan Quinn; David Patrick Kelly; Luke James Fleischmann; Julia Jones; Will Arnett; *D:* Jimmy Hayward; *W:* Mark Neveldine; Brian Taylor; *C:* Mitchell Amundsen; *M:* Marco Beltrami; Mastodon.

Jonas Brothers: The 3D Concert Experience 🦴🦴 ½ **2009 (G)** Disney flick, showcasing the squeaky-clean pop trio, is tailor-made for the brothers' squealing young teen girl demographic. The performance part is taken mainly from their 2008 Anaheim, CA arena show (which is also where the 3D effects appear) with some brief New York appearances and the usual mayhem with Joe, Nick, and Kevin being chased by their rabid fans. Demi Lovato and Taylor Swift drop by to do a couple of songs. **76m/C; On Demand.** Joe Jonas; Kevin Jonas; Nick Jonas; *D:* Bruce Hendricks; *C:* Mitchell Amundsen; Reed Smoot. Golden Raspberries '09: Worst Actor (Jonas), Worst Actor (Jonas), Worst Actor (Jonas).

Jonathan 🦴🦴 ½ **2019** Prim Jonathan (Elgort) is considered gifted by the architectural firm where he works, though he cannot ever stay for a full day there. The reason is that he shares his body with his more laid-back "brother" Jon (also Elgort) in what is called "single body multi-consciousness." The pair have rules to ensure both can survive, including strict limits on activities and no romantic involvement. When Jon becomes entangled with a barmaid named Elena (Waterhouse), Jonathan must take action keep them both alive. Director and co-screenwriter Oliver focuses on a study of their characters rather than the mechanism of their existence to the movie's benefit. **101m/C; DVD, Blu-Ray.** Ansel Elgort; Suki Waterhouse; Patricia Clarkson; Matt Bomer; Douglas Hodge; *D:* Bill Oliver; *W:* Bill Oliver; Peter Nickowitz; Gregory Davis; *C:* Zach Kuperstein; *M:* Brooke Blair; Will Blair.

Jonathan Livingston Seagull 🦴🦴 ½ **1973 (G)** Based on the best-selling novella by Richard Bach, this film quietly envisions a world of love, understanding, achievement, hope and individuality. Jonatan Livingston Seagull (voiced by

Franciscus) is bored with his seagull clan and his independent ways get him thrown out. So he decides to fly solo. **99m/C; DVD.** ***V:*** James Franciscus; Juliet Mills; David Ladd; Dorothy McGuire; Richard Crenna; ***D:*** Hall Bartlett; ***W:*** Hall Bartlett; ***C:*** Jack Couffer; ***M:*** Neil Diamond; Lee Holdridge. Golden Globes '74: Score.

The Joneses **2009 (R)** Mean-spirited satire about consumerism. A fake family is commissioned by a marketing company to move into an upscale suburban neighborhood and extol new luxury goods to the envious neighbors in an effort to make them popular. Steve's (Duchovny) the newbie salesman with something of a conscience, Kate's (Moore) his gung-ho boss/fake wife, and they're the 'parents' of teenagers (who aren't)?nympho Jenn (Heard) and closeted Mick (Hollingsworth). But "keeping up with the Joneses" proves problematic for both the Joneses and their neighbors. **93m/C; Blu-Ray, On Demand.** David Duchovny; Demi Moore; Amber Heard; Gary Cole; Chris(topher) Williams; Glenne Headly; Lauren Hutton; ***D:*** Derrick Borte; ***W:*** Derrick Borte; ***C:*** Yaron Orbach; ***M:*** Nick Urata.

Joni **1979 (G)** An inspirational story based on the real life of Tada (playing herself) who was seriously injured in a diving accident, and her conquering of the odds. A born-again feature film based on the book by Tada. **75m/C; VHS, DVD.** Joni Eareckson Tada; Bert Remsen; Katherine De Hetre; Cooper Huckabee; ***D:*** James F. Collier.

Jory **1972 (PG)** A young man's father is killed in a saloon fight, and he must grow up quickly to survive. **96m/C; VHS, DVD.** Robby Benson; B.J. Thomas; John Marley; ***D:*** Jorge Fons.

Joseph **1/2 1995** Following "Abraham" and "Jacob" comes the Old Testament story of young Joseph (Mercurio), beloved son of Jacob, who's sold into slavery by his envious older brothers. Joseph is bought by the Pharoah's chief steward, Potiphar (Kingsley), and, after a long series of tribulations, rises to become a power in Egypt, which unexpectedly leads Joseph to hold the fate of his long-lost family in his hands. Filmed in Morocco. **240m/C; VHS, DVD.** Paul Mercurio; Ben Kingsley; Martin Landau; Lesley Ann Warren; Warren Clarke; Alice Krige; Dominique Sanda; Stefano Dionisi; Valeria Cavalli; Peter Eyre; Timothy Bateson; Jamie Glover; Michael Attwell; ***D:*** Roger Young; ***W:*** Lionel Chetwynd; James Carrington; ***C:*** Raffaele Mertes; ***M:*** Marco Frisina.

Joseph and the Amazing Technicolor Dreamcoat **2000** Something more than a filmed stage presentation of the Webber-Rice musical, but something less than a real movie. It begins with a school assembly hall where the narrator (Friedman) bursts into song and tells the biblical story of Joseph (Osmond). Then the scene shifts to soundstages. The catchy songs often seem to be on the verge of morphing into "Cats" or "Phantom of the Opera." Overall, the production values are good and the sound is excellent. **78m/C; VHS, DVD.** Donny Osmond; Richard Attenborough; Joan Collins; Maria Friedman; ***D:*** David Mallet; Steven Pimlott; ***C:*** Nicholas D. Knowland; ***M:*** Andrew Lloyd Webber; Tim Rice. **VIDEO**

Joseph Andrews **1977 (R)** This adaptation of a 1742 Henry Fielding novel chronicles the rise of Joseph Andrews from servant to personal footman (and fancy) of Lady Booby. **99m/C; DVD.** *UK* Ann-Margret; Peter Firth; Jim Dale; Michael Hordern; Beryl Reid; ***D:*** Tony Richardson; ***W:*** Chris Bryant; Allan Scott; ***C:*** David Watkin; ***M:*** John Addison.

Joseph Pulitzer: Voice of the People **1/2 2018** A biographical documentary about Joseph Pulitzer and his impact on modern journalism. Born in Hungary in 1847, Pulitzer escaped turmoil by coming to the United States during the Civil War to serve in the place of rich Americans who paid him to fight. After the war, he settled in St. Louis, where he bought the newspapers that became his empire's base. As Pulitzer expanded his influence, he used techniques like public shaming, campaigns, and crusades, visual storytelling, and sensationalism to sell newspapers. Narrated by Adam Driver, it tries to be comprehensive but does not shy away from controversies involving Pulitzer. **84m/C; DVD.** ***D:*** Oren Rudavsky; ***W:*** Oren Rudavsky; Robert Seidman; ***C:*** Wolfgang Held; ***M:*** Clare Manchon; Olivier Manchon.

The Josephine Baker Story **1990 (R)** Biopic of exotic entertainer/activist Josephine Baker, an Afro-American woman from St. Louis who found superstardom in pre-WWII Europe, but repeated racism and rejection in the U.S. At times trite treatment turns her eventful life into a standard rise-and-fall showbiz tale, but a great cast and lavish scope pull it through. Whitfield recreates Baker's (sometimes topless) dance routines; Carol Dennis dubs her singing. Filmed on location in Budapest. **129m/C; VHS, DVD.** Lynn Whitfield; Ruben Blades; David Dukes; Craig T. Nelson; Louis Gossett, Jr.; Kene Holliday; Vivian Bonnell; ***D:*** Brian Gibson; ***M:*** Ralph Burns. **CABLE**

Josette **1938** Two brothers are upset that their wealthy father has feelings for the title character--a gold-digging New Orleans singer. They're determined to confront the hussy but go after the wrong girl. To make matters worse, they both fall for her. **74m/B; DVD.** Don Ameche; Robert Young; Simone Simon; Tala Birell; William Collier, Sr.; Bert Lahr; ***D:*** Allan Dwan; ***W:*** James Edward Grant; ***C:*** John Mescall.

Josh and S.A.M. **1993 (PG-13)** Road movie for youngsters with a twist: the driver can barely see over the dashboard. Josh and Sam are brothers whose parents are splitting. They cope by taking off on their own. Sam, meanwhile has been convinced by Josh that he's not a real boy at all, but rather a S.A.M.: Strategically Altered Mutant. Weber's directorial debut will appeal to young kids, but adults will see over the dashboard and through the transparent plot. **97m/C; VHS, Streaming.** Jacob Tierney; Noah Fleiss; Martha Plimpton; Joan Allen; Christopher Penn; Stephen Tobolowsky; Ronald Guttman; ***D:*** Billy Weber; ***W:*** Frank Deese; ***C:*** Don Burgess; ***M:*** Thomas Newman.

Josh Kirby. . .Time Warrior: Chapter 1, Planet of the Dino-Knights **1/2 1995 (PG)** Time-traveling 14-year-old Josh Kirby is accidently zapped to the 25th-century where fierce warriors ride dinosaurs and a madman is out to destroy the universe. The first tale in a fantasy series designed as an old-fashioned movie serial, complete with cliff-hanger ending. **88m/C; VHS, DVD.** Corbin Allred; Jennifer Burns; Derek Webster; John De Mita; ***D:*** Ernest Farino; ***W:*** Ethan Reiff; Cyrus Voris; Paul Callisi.

Josh Kirby. . . Time Warrior: Chapter 2, The Human Pets **1/2 1995 (PG)** Josh and his friends now find themselves in the year 70, 370—held hostage by the enormous Fatlings, who regard their human finds as pet-like action toys. **90m/C; VHS, DVD.** Corbin Allred; Jennifer Burns; ***D:*** Frank Arnold; ***W:*** Ethan Reiff; Cyrus Voris; Paul Callisi.

Josh Kirby. . . Time Warrior: Chapter 3, Trapped on Toyworld **1/2 1995 (PG)** Josh is stranded away from his friends on the strange planet of Toyworld and must rely on the lifelike creations of a toy magnate to defend himself from the villainous Dr. Zoetrope. **90m/C; VHS, DVD.** Corbin Allred; Jennifer Burns; Derek Webster; Sharon Lee Jones; Buck Kartalian; Barrie Ingham; ***D:*** Frank Arnold; ***W:*** Nick Paine.

Josh Kirby. . . Time Warrior: Chapter 4, Eggs from 70 Million B.C. **1/2 1995 (PG)** Josh and his pals finds themselves in a military compound that is under attack and encounter some very hungry alien worms. **93m/C; VHS, DVD.** Corbin Allred; Jennifer Burns; Derek Webster; Gary Kasper; Barrie Ingham; ***D:*** Mark Manos.

Josh Kirby. . . Time Warrior: Chapter 5, Journey to the Magic Cavern **1/2 1996 (PG)** Josh and pals find themselves in the center of a planet where they are befriended by the weird Mushroom People who are under siege by a monster known as "the Muncher." **93m/C; VHS, DVD.** Corbin Allred; Jennifer Burns; Derek Webster; Michael Hagiwara; Barrie Ingham; ***D:*** Ernest Farino; ***W:*** Ethan Reiff; Cyrus Voris.

Josh Kirby. . . Time Warrior: Chapter 6, Last Battle for the Universe **1/2 1996 (PG)** Josh is ready to get back to his own time but first he must survive a battle between long-feuding rivals of the timebelt. **90m/C; VHS, DVD.** Corbin Allred; Jennifer Burns; Derek Webster; Barrie Ingham; ***D:*** Frank Arnold; ***W:*** Ethan Reiff; Cyrus Voris.

Joshua *Black Rider* **1976 (R)** Western drama about a vigilante who tracks down the group of outlaws that killed his mother. **75m/C; VHS, DVD.** Fred Williamson; Isela Vega; ***D:*** Larry Spangler.

Joshua **1/2 2002 (G)** Joshua (Goldwyn) is a stranger to the 19th-century midwestern community of Auburn. He rents a barn and sets himself up as a woodworker and all-around helpful guy. Seeing that the black community's church is damaged, Joshua sets out to rebuild it and soon has the entire town pitching in to help. But traditionalist priest Father Tardone (Abraham) is askance when townsfolk begin to think Joshua has miraculous powers. Spiritually uplifting without being preachy; based on the novel by Father Joseph Girzone. **90m/C; VHS, DVD.** Tony Goldwyn; F. Murray Abraham; Kurt Fuller; Giancarlo Giannini; Stacy Edwards; Colleen Camp; ***D:*** Jon Purdy; ***W:*** Brad Mirman; Keith Giglio; ***C:*** Bruce Surtees; ***M:*** Michael W. Smith.

Joshua **2007 (R)** New twist on the creepy-kid movie trades demon possession for subtle psychological twists and turns. Joshua (Kogan) is a tidy, disconnected child prodigy who goes from simply odd to creepy after the birth of his sister. Meanwhile, his mother Abby (Farmiga) descends into postpartum depression and dad Brad (Rockwell) struggles to hold his family together as pets die and Granny has an accident. Director Ratliff maintains suspense by never showing all his cards, but it leaves you with a question: is there a method to the madness, or is this just a series of events in the lives of some screwed-up people? **105m/C; DVD.** Sam Rockwell; Vera Farmiga; Dallas Roberts; Celia Weston; Michael McKean; Jacob Kogan; ***D:*** George Ratliff; ***W:*** George Ratliff; David Gilbert; ***C:*** Benoît Debie; ***M:*** Nico Muhly.

Joshy **2016 (R)** Josh's (Middleditch) engagement ends suddenly when his fiancé kills herself. Determined to save Josh from the associated depression with such a horrible event, his buddies spend his bachelor party weekend with their best buddy. Writer/director Baena assembles a top-notch cast of indie comedy stars, including Adam Pally, Jenny Slate, and Nick Kroll, but he doesn't quite give them enough to do, and he really can't handle the shifts from comedy to heartbreaking grief. **93m/C; DVD, Beta.** Thomas Middleditch; Adam Pally; Alex Ross Perry; Nick Kroll; Brett Gelman; Jenny Slate; ***D:*** Jeff Baena; ***W:*** Jeff Baena; ***C:*** Patrice Lucien Cochet; ***M:*** Devendra Banhart.

Josie and the Pussycats **2001 (PG-13)** This Josie and company have almost as many dimensions as the cartoon from whence they came. Simple plot has Josie's band looking for their big break when record company exec Wyatt Frame, looking for a new sound, spots our heroines and remakes them as teen sensations. Wyatt is partnered with Fiona (Posey, chewing scenery like a starving dog in an Alpo factory) in a scheme to use pop music to control the minds of teens. Basically harmless parody of the pop music biz chokes on its own product-placing hypocrisy, but gets by on the obvious charms of leads Cook, Reid, and Dawson. **99m/C; VHS, DVD.** Rachael Leigh Cook; Tara Reid; Rosario Dawson; Parker Posey; Alan Cumming; Gabriel Mann; Paulo Costanzo; Tom Butler; Missi Pyle; Carson Daly; ***Cameo(s):*** Seth Green; Breckin Meyer; Donald Adeosun Faison; ***D:*** Deborah Kaplan; Harry Elfont; ***W:*** Deborah Kaplan; Harry Elfont; ***C:*** Matthew Libatique; ***M:*** John (Gianni) Frizzell.

The Journey **1959** A group of international refugees escape Russian-occupied Budapest during the 1956 uprising. They travel by bus to the Austrian border where they are stopped by Soviet Major Surov (Brynner), who is looking for Hungarian rebels. Since Paul Kedes (Robards) is using a fake passport, his British friend Diana Ashmore (Kerr) tries to distract the lonely Surov to allow them to escape. **126m/C; DVD.** Deborah Kerr; Yul Brynner; Jason Robards, Jr.; Robert Morley; E.G. Marshall; Anne Jackson; Ron Howard; Kurt Kasznar; Anouk Aimee; ***D:*** Anatole Litvak; ***W:*** George Tabori; ***C:*** Jack Hildyard; ***M:*** Georges Auric.

Journey 2: The Mysterious Island **1/2 2012 (PG)** A crude yet family friendly sequel to the surprisingly successful original has Hutcherson returning as teenager Sean Anderson, a 'Vernian'?someone who believes that author Jules Vernes' works were non-fiction. Sean received a coded message from Grandpa (Caine) that the titular location that allegedly inspired Jonathan Swift and Robert Louis Stevenson has been found. He travels with stepdad Hank (Johnson, replacing Brendan Fraser's paternal role) and obligatory "pretty girl," stepsister Kailani (Hudgens), to the middle of the ocean only to find that the island is sinking. Giant bees, gold volcanoes, and lame 3D jokes make this a journey not worth taking. Luckily, Caine and Johnson are at least an amiable pair. **94m/C; DVD, Blu-Ray.** Josh Hutcherson; Dwayne "The Rock" Johnson; Vanessa Anne Hudgens; Luis Guzman; Michael Caine; Kristin Davis; ***D:*** Brad Peyton; ***W:*** Mark Gunn; Brian Gunn; ***C:*** David Tattersall; ***M:*** Andrew Lockington.

Journey Back to Oz **1/2 1971** Animated special features Dorothy and Toto returning to visit their friends in the magical land of Oz. **90m/C; VHS, DVD.** ***V:*** Liza Minnelli; Ethel Merman; Paul Lynde; Milton Berle; Mickey Rooney; Danny Thomas; Herschel Bernardi; Margaret Hamilton; ***D:*** Hal Sutherland; ***W:*** Fred Ladd; Norm Prescott; ***M:*** Walter Scharf; James Van Heusen.

Journey Beneath the Desert *Antinea, l'Amante Della Citta Sepolta* **1961** Three engineers discover the lost-but-always-found-in-the-movies kingdom of Atlantis when their helicopter's forced down in the sunny Sahara. A poor hostess with a rotten disposition, the mean sub-saharan queen doesn't roll out the welcome mat for her grounded guests, so a beautiful slave babe helps them make a hasty exit. Dawdling Euro production with adequate visuals. **105m/C; VHS, DVD.** *FR IT* Haya Harareet; Jean-Louis Trintignant; James Westmoreland; Amedeo Nazzari; George Riviere; Giulia Rubini; Gabriele Tinti; Gian Marie Volonte; ***D:*** Edgar G. Ulmer; Giuseppe Masini; Frank Borzage.

Journey for Margaret **1942** Young and Day star as an expectant American couple living in London during WWII so Young can cover the war for a newspaper back home. After she loses her baby during an air raid, Day heads back to the States. Young stays in London where he meets two young orphans and takes them under his wing. He decides to take them back to the United States and adopt them, but problems arise. A real tearjerker and a good story that shows the war through the eyes of children. O'Brien's first film. Based on the book by William L. White. **81m/B; VHS, DVD.** Robert Young; Laraine Day; Fay Bainter; Signe Hasso; Margaret O'Brien; Nigel Bruce; G.P. (Tim) Huntley, Jr.; William Severn; Doris Lloyd; Halliwell Hobbes; Jill Esmond; ***D:*** W.S. Van Dyke.

The Journey Home **1/2** *The Midnight Sun* **2014 (PG)** A Canada-set family adventure about a boy and his desperate attempt to get a polar bear cub home. Young Luke Mercier (Goyo) finds a young polar bear cub who has been separated from his mother outside his home. Ignoring the advice of his family and friends to leave the cub alone, Luke takes a snowmobile and the cub into the wilderness. While he searches for the cub's mother in the tundra, a storm hits. As he protects the cub, Luke's mother (Moynahan) and a family friend Muktuk (Visnjic) search for Luke and the cub in the dangerous cold so they can both get home. **120m/C; DVD, Blu-Ray, Streaming, Download.** Dakota Goyo; Goran Visnjic; Bridget Moynahan; Duane Murray; Peter MacNeill; ***D:*** Roger Spottiswoode; Brando Quilici; ***W:*** Bart Gavigan; Hugh

Hudson; ***C:*** Peter Wunstorf; ***M:*** Lawrence Shragge. **VIDEO**

The Journey of August King 🦴🦴 1/2 **1995 (PG-13)** Adapted by Ehle from his own 1971 novel, set in 1815, about a runaway slave (Newton) protected by a lonely farmer against the landowner and posse tracking her down. August King (Patric), a widower on his way home from town, comes upon Annalees (Newton), prize possession of powerful slaveowner Olaf Singletary (Drake). August, a highly principled man, resists helping her at first, for fear of breaking the law and losing his farm and only remaining possessions. But he rises to higher moral ground, deciding to help her find freedom, whatever the consequences. Director Duigan ("Sirens") crafts a thoughtful, but not particularly suspenseful, period piece of early American history. Patric/Newton relationship reflects the gradual feel of the film. Drake booms as slaveowner. Includes brief brutal scene of slave torture. **91m/C; VHS, DVD.** Jason Patric; Thandie Newton; Larry Drake; Sam Waterston; ***D:*** John Duigan; ***W:*** John Ehle; ***C:*** Slawomir Idziak; ***M:*** Stephen Endelman.

Journey of Hope 🦴🦴🦴 1/2 **1990 (PG)** Powerful drama about Kurdish family that sells its material possessions in hopes of emigrating legally to Switzerland, where life will surely be better. During the perilous journey, smugglers take their money and the family must attempt crossing the formidable slopes of the Swiss Mountains on foot. Based on a true story. In Turkish with English subtitles. **111m/C; VHS, DVD.** *SI* Necmettin Cobanoglu; Nur Surer; Emin Sivas; Yaman Okay; Mathias Gnaedinger; Dietmar Schoenherr; ***D:*** Xavier Koller; ***W:*** Xavier Koller. Oscars '90: Foreign Film.

The Journey of Jared Price 🦴🦴 1/2 **2000** Sweet-natured but predictable gay coming of age tale. 19-year-old Jared (Spears) leaves Georgia for California and self-discovery, winding up in a youth hostel where he's befriended by Robert (Jacobson), who wants to be more than buddies. Jared eventually gets a job as a caretaker to elderly, blind Mrs. Haines (Craigg) and is soon pulled into a destructive relationship with the older Matthew (Tyler), Mrs. Haines son. **96m/C; VHS, DVD.** Corey Spears; Josh Jacobson; Steve Tyler; Rocki Craigg; ***D:*** Dustin Lance Black; ***W:*** Dustin Lance Black; ***C:*** Tony Croll; ***M:*** Damon Intrabartolo.

The Journey of Natty Gann 🦴🦴🦴 1/2 **1985 (PG)** With the help of a wolf (brilliantly portrayed by a dog) and a drifter, a 14-year-old girl travels across the country in search of her father in this warm and touching film. Excellent Disney representation of life during the Great Depression. **101m/C; VHS, DVD, Blu-Ray.** Meredith Salenger; John Cusack; Ray Wise; Scatman Crothers; Lainie Kazan; Verna Bloom; ***D:*** Jeremy Paul Kagan; ***W:*** Jeanne Rosenberg; ***C:*** Dick Bush; ***M:*** James Horner.

Journey of the Doomed 🦴 *Shui Ngai Miu Si* **1985** A girl raised in a brothel learns she's actually the illegitimate daughter of a prince, and her father decides it's time she should embrace her heritage. This idea doesn't go over well with others in the court, and assassins are sent to eliminate her. The girl finds a protector in a fisherman with some major fighting skills. Mandarin with subtitles or dubbed. **93m/C; DVD.** *CH* Tony Leung Ka-Fai; Alex Man; Kara Hui; Tien-Lang Li; ***D:*** Chuen-yee Cha; ***C:*** Hui-chi Tsao; ***M:*** Dik-Man Chan.

Journey to Promethea 🦴 **2010 (PG-13)** Cliched and low-budget fantasy fare from the Syfy Channel. An ancient prophecy foretells that a young man will start a violent rebellion against a tyrannical king and lead the people to the promised land of Promethea. **83m/C; DVD.** Billy Zane; Louis Herthum; James DuMont; Jerry Katz; Jessica Heap; Marcelle Baer; Natacha Itzel; ***D:*** Dan Garcia; ***W:*** Dan Garcia; ***C:*** John Lands; ***M:*** Andrew Markus. **CABLE**

Journey to the Center of the Earth 🦴🦴🦴 **1959** A scientist and student undergo a hazardous journey to find the center of the earth and along the way they find the lost city of Atlantis. Based upon the Jules Verne novel. **132m/C; VHS, DVD, Blu-Ray.** James Mason; Pat Boone; Arlene Dahl; Diane Baker; Thayer David; Alan Napier; Peter Ronson; ***D:*** Henry Levin; ***W:*** Charles Brackett; Robert Gunter; Walter Reisch; ***C:*** Leo Tover; ***M:*** Bernard Herrmann.

Journey to the Center of the Earth 🦴🦴 **1988 (PG)** A young nanny and two teenage boys discover Atlantis while exploring a volcano. **83m/C; VHS, DVD.** Nicola Cowper; Paul Carafotes; Ilan Mitchell-Smith; ***D:*** Rusty Lemorande; ***W:*** Rusty Lemorande; Kitty Chalmers.

Journey to the Center of the Earth **WOOF! 1993** Laughably bad NBC movie that's a very loose adaptation of the Jules Verne adventure novel about a group who descend into an active volcano, this time via a nuclear-powered craft, and discover a lost world. Meant as a TV pilot, it didn't tie up many plot points, further frustrating unwary viewers. **91m/C; DVD.** F. Murray Abraham; John Neville; Kim Miyori; Farrah Forke; Jeffrey Nordling; Tim Russ; ***D:*** William Dear; ***W:*** David Mickey Evans; Robert Gunter; ***C:*** Ron Garcia; ***M:*** Christopher Franke. **TV**

Journey to the Center of the Earth 🦴🦴 **1999** Jules Verne's 1864 fantasy made its way to cable in this adventurous retelling. Geologist Theodore Lytton (Williams) is hired by wealthy Alice Hastings (Bergen) to find her husband, Casper (Brown), who disappeared seven years earlier during an expedition to a volcano in New Zealand. Lytton and his compatriots descend into deep caverns and discover a tunnel system leading to the planet's center and a new civilization that Hastings has usurped for his own greedy purposes. There's derring-do and even babes in animal-hide bikinis. **139m/C; VHS, DVD.** Treat Williams; Jeremy London; Tushka Bergen; Hugh Keays-Byrne; Bryan Brown; Sarah Chadwick; Petra Yared; Tessa Wells; ***D:*** George Miller; ***W:*** Thomas Baum; ***C:*** John Stokes; ***M:*** Bruce Rowland. **CABLE**

Journey to the Center of the Earth 🦴🦴 1/2 **2008** Edward Dennison (Fonda) vanished four years ago while on an expedition to find an Alaskan passage leading into the center of the earth. His wealthy wife Martha (Pratt) hires anthropologist Jonathan Brock (Schroder) to find Edward, accompanied by his journalist nephew Abel (Grayhm) and Russian miner Sergei (Dopud) whose brother disappeared on the same journey. After discovering the passage, the four find it leads to an evolving prehistoric world and a primitive tribe that worships the now power-mad Edward. But a rival tribe could prove deadly to them all. Loose adaptation of the Jules Verne adventure. **89m/C; DVD.** Rick Schroder; Victoria Pratt; Peter Fonda; Mike Dopud; Jonathan Brewer; Tim James; Steve Grahym; ***W:*** Thomas Baum; ***C:*** Philip Linzey; ***M:*** Rene Dupere. **TV**

Journey to the Center of the Earth 🦴🦴 1/2 **2008 (PG)** Volcanologist Trevor Anderson ventures to Iceland with some young charges to continue the research of his missing brother Max, whose notes in the margins of a tattered copy of Jules Verne's classic sci-fi fantasy novel help guide the group. Soon they're battling ancient flora and fauna in, you guessed it, the earth's core. Only problem is they have to find their way out or risk being trapped. The CGI is wild, with carnivorous plants, flying piranhas, dinosaurs and other creepy creatures, and affable Fraser keeps it all cheery, but the plot's a bit thin and the premise is, well, silly. Just enjoy the thrill-ride and don't think too much. **92m/C; DVD, Blu-Ray, Streaming.** Brendan Fraser; Josh Hutcherson; Anita Briem; ***D:*** Eric Brevig; ***W:*** Michael D. Weiss; Jennifer Flackett; Marc Levin; ***C:*** Chuck Shuman; ***M:*** Andrew Lockington.

Journey to the Center of Time 🦴 1/2 **1967** A scientist and his crew are hurled into a time trap when a giant reactor explodes. **83m/C; VHS, DVD.** Lyle Waggoner; Scott Brady; Gigi Perreau; Anthony Eisley; ***D:*** David L. Hewitt.

Journey to the End of the Night 🦴🦴 **2006 (R)** Rosso (Glenn) is a shady ex-pat American who owns a brothel in Sao Paulo, Brazil, that he runs with his gambler son Paul (Fraser). A drug deal is meant to get them out of the sex business and Rosso into a nicer life with his squeeze Angie (Sandino Moreno) and their young kid (who may actually be Paul's because Angie used to be a hooker). Paul is planning a doublecross but the deal starts going south when the drug mule dies and Rosso presses their Nigerian dishwasher Wemba (Mos Def) into service. Sleazy crime thriller that has its moments although it doesn't hang together. **98m/C; DVD.** Scott Glenn; Brendan Fraser; Mos Def; Catalina Sandino Moreno; Alice Braga; ***D:*** Eric Eason; ***W:*** Eric Eason; ***C:*** Ulrich Burtin; ***M:*** Elia Cmiral.

Journey to the Far Side of the Sun 🦴🦴🦴 *Doppelganger* **1969 (G)** Chaos erupts in the Earth's scientific community when it is discovered that a second, identical Earth is on the other side of the Sun. Both planets end up sending out identical exploratory missions. The denouement is worth the journey. **92m/C; VHS, DVD, Blu-Ray.** *GB* Roy Thinnes; Ian Hendry; Lynn Loring; Patrick Wymark; Loni von Friedl; Herbert Lom; Ed Bishop; ***D:*** Robert Parrish; ***W:*** Gerry Anderson; ***C:*** John Read; ***M:*** Barry Gray.

Journey to the Lost City 🦴 1/2 *Tiger of Bengal* **1958** Architect living in India happens upon a lost city, the rulership of which is being contested by two brothers. In the midst of fighting snakes and tigers, he falls in love with Paget, a beautiful dancer. This feature is actually a poorly edited hybrid of two Lang German adventures, "Der Tiger von Eschnapur" and "Das Indische Grabmal" merged for U.S. release. **95m/C; VHS, DVD.** *FR IT GE* Debra Paget; Paul (Christian) Hubschmid; Walter Reyer; Claus Holm; Sabine Bethmann; Valeri Inkizhinov; Rene Deltgen; Luciana Paluzzi; ***D:*** Fritz Lang.

Journey to the Seventh Planet 🦴 1/2 **1962** Astronauts go to the frozen world of Uranus, only to find upon landing, a warm forest filled with pretty women, and places and people from their past. Obviously something isn't kosher. **77m/C; DVD, Blu-Ray.** *DK US* John Agar; Greta Thyssen; Carl Ottosen; peter monch; Louis Miehe-Renard; ***D:*** Sidney W. Pink; ***W:*** Sidney W. Pink; Ib Melchior; ***C:*** Aage Wiltrup; ***M:*** Ib Glindemann; Ronald Stein. **VIDEO**

Journey to the West 🦴🦴 1/2 **2014 (PG-13)** A very loose adaptation of the Chinese classic from nearly manic writer/director Chow, who has arguably never been more over the top as he throws his numerous genres—action, period, drama, comedy, and even horror—into a blender and hits puree. Zhang Wen plays Xuan Zang, a demon fighter who, well, you kind of need to see it to believe it. Demons, martial arts, and slapstick comedy—Chow's film is defiantly weird as he stretches the boundaries of the genre. **110m/C; DVD, Blu-Ray.** *CH* Zhang Wen; Qi Shu; Bo Huang; ***D:*** Stephen (Chiau) Chow; Chi-kin Kwok; ***W:*** Stephen (Chiau) Chow; Chi-kin Kwok; ***C:*** Sung Fai Choi; ***M:*** Ying-wah Wong.

Journey's End 🦴🦴 1/2 **2018 (R)** World War I drama focusing on tensions, anxieties, and comraderies of British soldiers in the trenches, based on R.C. Sheriff's 1928 play. In 1918 France, teenage Second Lieutenant Raleigh (Butterfield) gets himself assigned to the battle zone command of Captain Stanholpe (Claflin), a schoolmate once in love with Raleigh's sister. Raleigh finds that the war-hardened Stanholpe has changed, and is now a troubled alcoholic. These men and others in their unit have learned that a massive German offensive is expected to begin soon and are sent on a seemingly suicidal mission to retrieve intelligence. This well-crafted film features strong performances and realistic visuals. **107m/C; DVD, Blu-Ray.** Paul Bettany; Sam Claflin; Stephen Graham; Asa Butterfield; Toby Jones; ***D:*** Saul Dibb; ***W:*** Simon Reade; ***C:*** Laurie Rose; ***M:*** Hildur Guonadottir.

Journeys with George 🦴🦴 1/2 **2002** On the road with George W. Bush's 2000 presidential campaign, NBC News producer Alexandra Pelosi—daughter of California congresswoman Nancy Pelosi—offers a day-in-the-grinding-life view of a pool reporter captured via camcorder yet stops short of any meaty behind-the-scenes strategy sessions. Allows W to show off his easy-going manner while sidestepping any heavy topics. **76m/C; VHS, DVD.** ***Cameo(s):*** Alexandra Pelosi; ***D:*** Alexandra Pelosi; ***W:*** Alexandra Pelosi; ***C:*** Alexandra Pelosi. **TV**

Joy 🦴🦴 **2015 (PG-13)** Joy Mangano (Lawrence) is the kind of larger than life real person who makes for great Hollywood filmmaking. She went from a blue collar Italian-American family background to stunning success when she invented the Miracle Mop, of all things, but she also lived a complex life of betrayals, family, and her driven passion. Lawrence carries every element of her third collaboration with David O. Russell, but she feels miscast here, way too young for the part's demands as Mangano ages through multiple decades of storytelling. Russell is great with actors yet again (including De Niro and Cooper), but this story gets away from him. **120m/C; DVD, Blu-Ray.** Jennifer Lawerence; Edgar Ramirez; Robert De Niro; Dascha Polanco; Isabella Rossellini; Bradley Cooper; Elisabeth Rohm; ***D:*** David O. Russell; ***W:*** David O. Russell; ***C:*** Linus Sandgren; ***M:*** West Dylan Thordson; David Campbell. Golden Globes '16: Actress--Mus./Comedy (Lawerence).

Joy House 🦴🦴 *The Love Cage; Les Felins* **1964** French playboy Marc (Delon) seduces the wife of an American mobster who sends his goons after him. Marc hides out by becoming the chauffeur to Barbara (Albright) at her chateau, which is also where he meets his employer's niece, Melinda (Fonda). Soon, Marc is part of a romantic triangle—or is it quartet since Barbara's lover, Vincent (Oumansky), is also living there. And don't forget the gangsters, who certainly haven't forgotten Marc. Complicated plot with no particular payoff. **98m/B; VHS, DVD.** Jane Fonda; Alain Delon; Lola Albright; Andre Oumansky; Sorrell Booke; ***D:*** Rene Clement; ***W:*** Rene Clement; ***C:*** Henri Decae; ***M:*** Lalo Schifrin.

The Joy Luck Club 🦴🦴🦴 **1993 (R)** Universal themes in mother/daughter relationships are explored in a context Hollywood first rejected as too narrow, but which proved to be a modest sleeper hit. Tan skillfully weaves the plot of her 1989 best-seller into a screenplay which centers around young June's (Ming-Na) going-away party. Slowly the stories of four Chinese women, who meet weekly to play mah-jongg, are unraveled. Each vignette reveals life in China for the four women and the tragedies they survived, before reaching into the present to capture the relationships between the mothers and their daughters. Powerful, relevant, and moving. **136m/C; VHS, DVD, Blu-Ray.** Tsai Chin; Kieu Chinh; France Nuyen; Rosalind Chao; Tamlyn Tomita; Lisa Lu; Lauren Tom; Ming Na; Michael Paul Chan; Andrew McCarthy; Christopher Rich; Russell Wong; Victor Wong; Vivian Wu; Jack Ford; Diane Baker; ***D:*** Wayne Wang; ***W:*** Amy Tan; Ronald Bass.

The Joy of Knowledge 🦴 1/2 *Le Gai Savoir* **1965** Godard's experimental use of language and image in a plotless narrative. Berto and Leaud sit together on a bare sound stage and are exposed to popular culture through images, word association, and conversation. In French with English subtitles. **96m/C; VHS, DVD, Blu-Ray.** *FR* Juliet Berto; Jean-Pierre Leaud; ***D:*** Jean-Luc Godard; ***W:*** Jean-Luc Godard.

Joy of Living 🦴🦴🦴 **1938** Vintage screwball farce finds successful songstress Maggie (Dunne) the sole support of her n'er-do-well family. Maggie's aggressively courted by playboy Dan Brewster (Faribanks Jr.) and finally (after numerous silly complications) they fall in love. **90m/B; VHS, DVD.** Irene Dunne; Douglas Fairbanks, Jr.; Alice Brady; Guy Kibbee; Jean Dixon; Eric Blore; Lucille Ball; Warren Hymer; Billy Gilbert; Frank Milan; ***D:*** Tay Garnett; ***W:*** Graham Baker; Allan Scott; Gene Towne; ***C:*** Joseph Walker; ***M:*** Jerome Kern; Dorothy Fields.

Joy Ride 🦴🦴🦴 **2001 (R)** Released about the same time as fellow road thriller/horror entry "Jeepers Creepers," this superior outing benefits from better humor, pacing, and performances. Nice guy Lewis (Walker), a college freshman, offers to drive friend/potential squeeze Venna (Sobieski) back home from Colorado for the holidays. Unfortunately for Lewis, roguish brother Fuller (Zahn) calls Lewis to bail him out of jail in Utah and sticks around for the ride. Fuller instigates a CB radio prank in which Lewis, imitating a woman's voice, invites a trucker with the handle Rusty Nail to the hotel room next to theirs. The next day, the man in the room is found close to death in the middle of the road, and the trio has a very angry trucker on their tail. Taut countrywide chase thrills are reminiscent of Spielberg's "Duel." Great mixture of shocks and black humor. **96m/C; VHS, DVD, Blu-Ray.** Paul Walker; Steve Zahn; Leelee Sobieski; Jessica Bowman; Stuart Stone; Basil Wallace; Brian Leckner; ***V:*** Ted Levine; ***D:*** John Dahl; ***W:*** J.J. (Jeffrey) Abrams; Clay Tarver; ***C:*** Jeffrey Jur; ***M:*** Marco Beltrami.

Joy Ride 2: Dead Ahead 🦴 **2008** Truck driver Rusty Nails had found someone new to slaughter. Four friends traveling to Vegas get into trouble when their car breaks down. They find a seemingly abandoned farmhouse with a working vehicle in the barn and borrow it, not knowing it belongs to the trucker/psycho, who then comes after them. **91m/C; DVD.** Nick Zano; Nicki Aycox; Kyle Schmid; Laura Jordan; ***D:*** Louis Morneau; ***W:*** James Johnston; Bennett Yellin; ***C:*** Robert New. **VIDEO**

Joy Ride 3: Road Kill 🦴 **2014 (R)** Unnecessary sequel in which a group of street racers confront a pissed off truck driver who just happens to be a serial killer. Just like these folks should have avoided the shortcut, you should steer clear of this gore-fest. **96m/C; DVD, Blu-Ray, Streaming.** Ken Kirzinger; Jesse Hutch; Ben Hollingsworth; Kirsten Prout; Dean Armstrong; ***D:*** Declan O'Brien; ***W:*** Declan O'Brien; ***C:*** Michael Marshall; ***M:*** Claude Foisy. **VIDEO**

Joy Sticks **WOOF!** *Joysticks* **1983 (R)** Joy sticks in question are down at the arcade. Businessman wants to shut down local video game palace. Inhabitants just say no. **88m/C; VHS, DVD, Blu-Ray.** Joe Don Baker; Leif Green; Jim Greenleaf; Scott McGinnis; Jon(athan) Gries; ***D:*** Greydon Clark.

Joyeux Noel 🦴🦴🦴 *Merry Christmas* **2005 (PG-13)** On Christmas Eve, during World War I in France, troops on both sides of the battlefield laid down their weapons in unified holiday spirit for a performance of "Silent Night" by a German soldier, and famed tenor named Sprink, along with his wife. Drinking, cheering, and even some soccer followed, right there in the trenches. This really happened, and it makes for the perfect centerpiece in this postmodern French Christmas miracle movie. WWI is a backdrop to the human turmoil faced by German, French, and Scottish troops at war. An almost ironically surreal melodrama that's just as sad as it is joyous. Nominated for Best Foreign Film Oscar. **110m/C; DVD.** *FR GE GB BE RO* Diane Kruger; Benno Furmann; Guillaume Canet; Gary Lewis; Daniel Brühl; Steven Robertson; Lucas Belvaux; Bernard Le Coq; Ian Richardson; Robin Laing; Suzanne Flon; Michel Serrault; Dany Boon; Alex Ferns; Frank Witter; Thomas Schmauser; Joachim Bissmeier; ***D:*** Christian Carion; ***W:*** Christian Carion; ***C:*** Walther Vanden Ende; ***M:*** Philippe Rombi.

Joyful Noise 🦴🦴 **1/2 2012 (PG-13)** Inspirational musical in which the singing matters more than the formulaic story and the good-natured performances (yes, Dolly Parton allows—and makes—wisecracks about her numerous nips-and-tucks). Pacashau Sacred Divinity Choir's choirmaster Bernard (Kristofferson) dies, and Pastor Dale (Vance) asks conventional-but-mouthy Vi Rose Hill (Queen Latifah) to take over rather than Bernard's tiny, strong-willed widow G.G. (Parton). The women struggle to work together even as Vi Rose's daughter Olivia (Palmer) and G.G.'s grandson Randy (Jordan) fall in love. Naturally there's a national choir competition that could change the fortunes of their economically-strapped choir if they win. **118m/C; DVD, Blu-Ray.** Queen Latifah; Dolly Parton; Kris Kristofferson; Keke Palmer; Jeremy Jordan; Courtney B. Vance; Dexter Darden; Jesse L. Martin; Kirk Franklin; ***D:*** Todd Graff; ***W:*** Todd Graff; ***C:*** David Byrd; ***M:*** Mervyn Warren.

Joyless Street 🦴🦴🦴 **1/2** *Street of Sorrow; Die Freudlosse Gasse* **1925** Silent film focuses on the dismal life of the middle class in Austria during an economic crisis. Lovely piano score accompanies the film. **96m/B; Silent; VHS, DVD.** *GE* Greta Garbo; Werner Krauss; Asta Nielson; Jaro Furth; Loni Nest; Max Kohlhase; Silva Torf; Karl Ettlinger; Ilka Gruning; Agnes Esterhazy; Alexander Musky; Valeska Gert; ***D:*** G.W. Pabst; ***W:*** Willi Haas; ***C:*** Guido Seeber; Curt Oertel; Walter Robert Lach.

Joyride 🦴 **1/2 1977 (R)** Mistreated by a union official, three friends steal a car for a joy ride and plummet into a life of crime. **91m/C; VHS, DVD.** Desi Arnaz, Jr.; Robert Carradine; Melanie Griffith; Anne Lockhart; ***D:*** Joseph Ruben.

Joyride 🦴🦴 **1997 (R)** Three friends make the mistake of stealing a car that belongs to a beautiful blonde assassin, who'll stop at nothing to get her wheels back (her latest victim is stashed in the trunk). **92m/C; VHS, DVD.** Tobey Maguire; Wilson Cruz; Amy Hathaway; Chrisstina Naify; James Karen; Adam West; Benicio Del Toro; Judson Mills; ***D:*** Quinton Peeples; ***W:*** Quinton Peeples; ***C:*** S. Douglas Smith. **VIDEO**

JSA: Joint Security Area 🦴🦴🦴 **1/2** *J.S.A. Joint Security Area; Gongdong gyeongbi guyeok JSA* **2000** A group of North and South Korean soldiers befriend each other when the troops from the South stray across the border into the North after getting lost one evening. Later invited to return, one of the men from the South ends up dead, and a Korean national raised in Switzerland (apparently this makes her a neutral party somehow) is asked to investigate the affair before it mushrooms into a war. **107m/C; DVD.** *NK* Yeong-ae Lee; Byung-hun Lee; Kang-ho Song; Ha-Kyun Shin; Tae-woo Kim; ***D:*** Chan-wook Park; ***W:*** Chan-wook Park; Mu-yeong Lee; Seong-san Jeong; Sang-yeon Park; Hyeon-seok Kim; ***C:*** Sung-bok Kim; ***M:*** Yeong-wook Jo; Jun-Seok Bang.

Ju Dou 🦴🦴🦴🦴 **1990 (PG-13)** Breathtaking story of an aging factory owner in search of an heir. He takes a third wife, but she finds caring in the arms of another man, when her husband's brutality proves too much. Beautiful color cinematography, excellent acting, and epic story. Oscar nominee for Best Foreign Film. In Chinese with English subtitles. **98m/C; VHS, DVD.** *CH* Gong Li; Baotian Li; Li Wei; Zhang Yi; Zheng Jian; ***D:*** Yimou Zhang; ***W:*** Liu Heng; ***C:*** Gu Changwei; Yang Lun; ***M:*** Xia Ru-jin; Jiping Zhao.

Ju-On: The Grudge 🦴 **1/2** *The Grudge* **2003** This is the third in the Shimizu's Japanese horror series, following "Ju-On: The Curse" and "Jun-On 2: The Curse 2," which all revolve around (in a convoluted manner) a horrific event occurring in the same house. Social worker Rika (Okina) discovers her elderly patient mute, terrified, and alone. Then Rika finds a ghostly boy hiding in a closet—the victim of previous violence. Premise is that great rage leaves an evil presence behind, which drives new inhabitants mad and causes them to commit more acts of violence, leaving more evil behind. Or something like that. Lots of interlocking flashbacks and intermittent shocks. Best left to fanciers of Asian horror; Japanese with subtitles. The 2004 American remake, "The Grudge," holds no surprises. **92m/C; VHS, DVD.** *JP* Misa(ko) Uehara; Megumi Okina; Misaki Ito; Yuya Ozeki; Takako Fuji; ***D:*** Takashi Shimizu; ***W:*** Takashi Shimizu; ***C:*** Tokusho Kikumura; ***M:*** Shiro Sato.

Ju-On 2 🦴🦴 **2000** Pregnant horror movie actress Kyoko miscarries in a tragic road accident in front of the cursed house from the first "Ju-On" where she encounters the ghosts. Despite this she goes through with starring in the documentary a film crew is making about the house's curse, and the ghosts that dwell in it. You can pretty much guess what happens from here. Eventually she falls ill, and a doctor tells her that not only hasn't she miscarried, her pregnancy is progressing smoothly. Not as effective as the original, as it is marred by scenes of camp that seem entirely out of place, and too much time is spent recapping the events of the first film. Several scenes will inspire much confusion. **76m/C; DVD.** *JP* Yuko Daike; Makoto Ashikawa; Kahori Fujii; Yurei Yanagi; Takako Fuji; Taro Suwa; Reita Serizawa; Kiriko Shimizu; Mayoko Saito; Dankan; Tomohiro Kaku; Ryota Koyama; Denden; Taizo Mizumura; Harumi Matsukaze; Takashi Matsuyama; Hue Rong Weng; Yuue; Miyako Nakatsuka; Kenta Ishikawa; Ganko Fuyu; Takemura Nagisa; Hayato Ichihara; Akihiro Toyotome; Shiori Yonezawa; Mashio Miyazaki; ***D:*** Takashi Shimizu; ***W:*** Takashi Shimizu; ***C:*** Nobuhito Kisuki; ***M:*** Gary Ashiya.

Juanita 🦴🦴 **2019** Juanita (Woodard) is unhappy with her life in Columbus, Ohio. She is drained by her job at a hospital and babysitter for her young granddaughter, disappointed by her three children, and unable even to zone out to enjoy a sexual fantasy without getting interrupted. To address the situation, Juanita randomly takes a trip to Butte, Montana. There, she gains an unexpected perspective on life as she connects with new friends and lovers. Based on a novel by Sheila Williams, the story is uneven but Woodard's stellar performance brings Juanita and the film to life. **90m/C; DVD.** Alfre Woodard; Bonnie Johnson; Jordan Nia Elizabeth; Acorye' White; Blair Underwood; ***D:*** Clark Johnson; ***W:*** Roderick M. Spencer; ***C:*** Luc Montpellier; ***M:*** Kevin Lax. **VIDEO**

Juarez 🦴🦴 **1939** A revolutionary leader overthrows the Mexican government and then becomes President of the country. Based on the true story of Benito Pablo Juarez. **132m/B; VHS, DVD.** Paul Muni; John Garfield; Bette Davis; Claude Rains; Gale Sondergaard; Charles Halton; Brian Aherne; Donald Crisp; Joseph Calleia; Gilbert Roland; Henry O'Neill; Harry Davenport; Louis Calhern; Montagu Love; Walter Kingsford; ***D:*** William Dieterle; ***W:*** John Huston; Aeneas MacKenzie; ***C:*** Gaetano Antonio "Tony" Gaudio; ***M:*** Erich Wolfgang Korngold.

Jubal 🦴🦴 **1956** A rancher (Borgnine) seeks advice from a cowhand (Ford) about pleasing his wife, but another cowhand (Steiger) implies that Ford is "advising" Borgnine's wife, as well. A western take on "Othello." **101m/C; DVD, Blu-Ray.** Glenn Ford; Rod Steiger; Ernest Borgnine; Felicia Farr; Charles Bronson; Valerie French; Noah Beery, Jr.; ***D:*** Delmer Daves; ***W:*** Delmer Daves; Russell S. Hughes; ***C:*** Charles Lawton, Jr.; ***M:*** David Raskin.

Jud Suess 🦴🦴🦴 **1940** Classic, scandalous Nazi anti-Semitic tract about a Jew who rises to power under the duchy of Wuerttemberg by stepping on, abusing, and raping Aryans. A film that caused riots at its screenings and tragedy for its cast and crew, and the Third Reich's most notorious fictional expression of policy. In German with English subtitles. **100m/B; VHS, DVD.** *GE* Ferdinand Marian; Werner Krauss; Heinrich George; Kristina Soderbaum; Eugene Klopfer; ***D:*** Veit Harlan.

Judas Kiss 🦴 **1/2 2011** One-time college filmmaking whiz Zachary Wells has let the Hollywood party lifestyle turn him into a never-was. He returns to his alma mater as a film festival judge but gets a spooky wake-up call when he meets Danny Reyes (Zach's birth name) and discovers other similarities between them. Is there some glitch in time giving Zach a chance to start over? The cast is attractive but the fantasy narrative doesn't hold up. **94m/C; DVD, Blu-Ray.** Charlie David; Richard Harmon; Sean Paul Lockhart; Timo Descamps; ***D:*** J.T. Tepnapa; ***W:*** J.T. Tepnapa; Carlos Pedraza; ***C:*** David Berry; ***M:*** Brad Anthony Laina.

The Judas Project: The Ultimate Encounter 🦴 **1/2 1994 (PG-13)** Religious fantasy finds Jesse battling corruption and pseudo-religious figures in a fight to save a violent and decaying world. But Jesse's destroyed by his own disciple, Jude. Sound familiar? (There's even a cruxifixion scene.) **98m/C; VHS, DVD.** John O'Banion; Ramy Zada; Richard Herd; ***D:*** James H. Barden; ***C:*** Bryan England.

Jude 🦴🦴🦴 *Jude the Obscure* **1996 (R)** Engrossing retelling of Thomas Hardy's depressing 1896 novel "Jude the Obscure," set in his fictional Wessex. Country stonemason Jude (Eccleston) hopes to improve his impoverished lot in life by becoming a student at Christminister University. But first he's distracted into an unwise marriage with lively Arabella (Griffiths), who soon leaves him, and then into an ill-fated romance with his capricious cousin Sue Brideshead (Winslet). Class and societal barriers prove impossible for the couple to overcome and lead to a shocking tragedy. Hardy's book was so badly received by critics that he never wrote another novel and stuck to poetry for the rest of his life. **123m/C; VHS, DVD.** *GB* Christopher Eccleston; Kate Winslet; Liam Cunningham; Rachel Griffiths; ***D:*** Michael Winterbottom; ***W:*** Hossein Amini; ***C:*** Eduardo Serra; ***M:*** Adrian Johnston.

Jude the Obscure 🦴🦴 **1/2 1971** Thomas Hardy's last novel is a tragic, bleak story of mismatched lovers and blighted ambitions. Jude is a poor stonemason whose dream is to get a proper education and marry his beloved cousin. Failing to get into Oxford he is seduced by a farm girl, whom he marries and fathers a child by (a gnome-like creature named "Father Time"). Meanwhile, his cousin marries a schoolteacher who disgusts her. Finally, the two thwarted lovers marry, only to find themselves living in poverty and hopelessness. After this novel (said to be Hardy's favorite), he devoted the rest of his long life to poetry. On three cassettes. **262m/C; VHS, DVD.** *GB* Robert Powell; Daphne Heard; Alex Marshall; John Franklyn-Robbins; Fiona Walker; ***D:*** Hugh David; ***W:*** Harry Green. **TV**

Judex 🦴🦴 *Justice* **1916** Feuillade's 12-episode serial finds the mysterious (and morally suspect hero) Judex torn between his quest for revenge against wealthy, greedy banker Favraux and his love for Favraux's daughter, Jacqueline. Musidora does some vamping as Favraux's wicked assistant. **300m/B; Silent; DVD.** *FR* rene creste; Louis Leubas; Yvette Andreyor; Musidora; Marcel Levesque; Bout de-zan; Edouard Mathe; ***D:*** Louis Feuillade; ***W:*** Arthur Bernede; ***C:*** Andre Glatti; Leon Klausse.

Judex 🦴🦴 **1/2 1964** Judex, a sensitive cloaked hero-avenger, fights master criminal gangs. In French with English subtitles. Remake of the silent French serial. **103m/B; VHS, DVD, Blu-Ray.** *FR IT* Channing Pollock; Francine Berge; Jacques Jouanneau; ***D:*** Georges Franju; ***M:*** Maurice Jarre.

The Judge 🦴 **1/2 1949** A courtroom crime-drama about the consequences of infidelity. A lawyer sends an acquitted hit man to kill his wife and her lover. Things go amiss and the lawyer winds up dead. **69m/B; VHS, DVD.** Milburn Stone; Katherine DeMille; Paul Guilfoyle; Jonathan Hale; ***D:*** Elmer Clifton.

The Judge 🦴🦴 **2014 (R)** Always under the thumb of his loudmouth father, and town judge (Duvall), Hank Palmer (Downey, Jr.) has grown up to be a misfit attorney. The night of his wife's death, the judge goes on a grief-stricken bender, capped off by slamming his vehicle into the village idiot, who coincidentally caused one of the few blemishes to the judge's career. Hank steps in to defend his father against the evil prosecutor (Thornton), but their history complicates things. Melodramatic, bloated morality play tries too hard to be a big movie with big feelings and big scenes, but comes off as a second-rate courtroom drama. **141m/C; DVD, Blu-Ray.** Robert Downey, Jr.; Robert Duvall; Vincent D'Onofrio; Jeremy Strong; Billy Bob Thornton; Dax Shepard; Vera Farmiga; Leighton Meester; Ken Howard; Grace Zabriskie; ***D:*** David Dobkin; ***W:*** Nick Schenk; Bill Dubuque; ***C:*** Janusz Kaminski; ***M:*** Thomas Newman.

Judge & Jury 🦴 **1/2 1996 (R)** Convicted killer Joseph Miller (Keith) dies in the electric chair but then manages to return from the dead to get revenge. So how do you kill someone who's already dead? Well, Michael Silvano (Kove) will have to find a way to send Miller back where he belongs. **98m/C; VHS, DVD.** David Keith; Martin Kove; Laura Johnson; Thomas Ian Nicholas; Paul Koslo; ***D:*** John Eyres; ***W:*** John Eyres; John Cianetti; Amanda I. Kirpaul; ***C:*** Bob Paone; ***M:*** Johnathon Flood. **VIDEO**

Judge Dredd 🦴 **1/2 1995 (R)** Futuristic lawman Dredd (Stallone), who acts as cop, judge, jury, and executioner, is framed for murder by his "brother" Rico (Assante), a renegade misfit. With the help of a female Judge (Lane) and an ex-con (Schneider), Dredd fights to clear his name and save the people of Mega City One. Big names, big bangs, big budget—big disappointment. Dialogue makes "Rambo" sound like Shakespeare, and the choppy, convoluted plot doesn't help. Schneider provides a rare bright spot while acting circles around Sly, who hoped (in vain) that the project would provide him with another profitable action franchise. The source comic book has been a cult favorite in England for 20 years. **96m/C; VHS, DVD, Blu-Ray.** Sylvester Stallone; Armand Assante; Diane Lane; Rob Schneider; Joan Chen; Jurgen Prochnow; Max von Sydow; ***D:*** Danny Cannon; ***W:*** Steven E. de Souza; Michael

De Luca; William Wisher; **C:** Adrian Biddle; **M:** Alan Silvestri.

Judge Hardy and Son 🦴🦴 **1939** The eighth film in the series takes a somber turn when Andy needs a lesson in honesty and Mrs. Hardy becomes seriously ill with pneumonia. The Judge wants Andy to help him find the estranged daughter of an old couple facing home foreclosure, but Andy is more interested in claiming a cash prize in an essay contest even if it means cheating. **89m/B; DVD.** Mickey Rooney; Lewis Stone; Fay Holden; Cecilia Parker; Sara Haden; Ann Rutherford; Maria Ouspenskaya; Egon Brecher; Henry Hull; June Preisser; Martha O'Driscoll; **D:** George B. Seitz; **W:** Carey Wilson; **C:** Lester White; **M:** David Snell.

Judge Hardy's Children 🦴🦴 ½ **1938** The 3rd film in the series. Judge Hardy and his family go to DC when the Judge is asked to sit on an important public committee. Naive Marian turns into a snob, thanks to her questionable new friends, and Andy tries to impress Suzanne, the French ambassador's daughter. The pic has some fun when Andy livens up a stuffy cotillion with a swing dance. **78m/B; DVD.** Lewis Stone; Mickey Rooney; Fay Holden; Cecilia Parker; Betty Ross Clarke; Jacqueline Laurent; Ruth Hussey; Leonard Penn; Robert Frost Whitney; **D:** George B. Seitz; **W:** Kay Van Riper; **C:** Lester White; **M:** David Snell.

Judge Priest 🦴🦴🦴 **1934** Small-town judge in the old South stirs up the place with stinging humor and common-sense observances as he tangles with prejudices and civil injustices. Funny, warm slice-of-life is occasionally defeated by racist characterizations. Ford remade it later as "The Sun Shines Bright." Taken from the Irvin S. Cobb stories. **80m/B; VHS, DVD.** Will Rogers; Stepin Fetchit; Anita Louise; Henry B. Walthall; **D:** John Ford.

The Judge Steps Out 🦴🦴 ½ **1949** Pleasant, light comedy about a hen-pecked, Bostonian judge who decides he's had enough and heads for balmy California. There he finds a job in a restaurant and, more importantly, a sympathetic friend in its female owner. He soon finds himself falling for the woman, and realizes he faces an important decision. **91m/B; VHS, DVD.** Alexander Knox; Ann Sothern; George Tobias; Sharyn Moffett; Florence Bates; Frieda Inescort; Myrna Dell; Ian Wolfe; H.B. Warner; **D:** Boris Ingster.

Judgementall Hai Kya 🦴🦴 ½ **2019** After suffering a trauma in childhood and being diagnosed with acute psychosis in adulthood, Bobby (Ranaut) has a career as a dubbing artist. Because of her mental health issues, she often imagines herself in place of the characters she is voicing and the people she encounters in real life, blurring fiction and reality. This tendency becomes problematic after she gets new tenants, a young married couple named Reema (Dastur) and Keshav (Rao). After becoming overinvolved in their romantic relationship, a murder sends Bobby over the edge. A dark, quirky comedy-thriller with impressive performances. Hindi with subtitles. **121m/C; DVD.** Kangana Ranaut; Rajkummar Rao; Amyra Dastur; Jimmy Sheirgill; Brijendra Kala; **D:** Prakash Kovelamudi; **W:** Kanika Dhillon; **C:** Pankaj Kumar.

Judgment 🦴🦴🦴 **1990 (PG-13)** A devout Catholic couple are shocked to learn that their young son has been molested by the popular priest of their small Louisiana parish. When they find out their son is not the first victim, and other families have been coerced into silence, they vow to fight back. Tasteful treatment of a real court case. **89m/C; VHS, DVD.** Keith Carradine; Blythe Danner; Jack Warden; David Strathairn; Bob Gunton; Mitchell Ryan; Michael Faustino; **D:** Tom Topor; **W:** Tom Topor. **CABLE**

Judgment at Nuremberg 🦴🦴🦴🦴 **1961** It's 1948 and a group of high-level Nazis are on trial for war crimes. Chief Justice Tracy must resist political pressures as he presides over the trials. Excellent performances throughout, especially by Dietrich and Garland. Considers to what extent an individual may be held accountable for actions committed under orders of a superior officer. Consuming account of the Holocaust and WWII; deeply moving and powerful. Based on a "Playhouse 90" TV program. **178m/B; VHS, DVD, Blu-Ray.** Spencer Tracy; Burt Lancaster; Richard Widmark; Montgomery Clift; Maximilian Schell; Judy Garland; Marlene Dietrich; William Shatner; Edward Binns; Werner Klemperer; Torben Meyer; Martin Brandt; Kenneth MacKenna; Alan Baxter; Ray Teal; Karl Swenson; **D:** Stanley Kramer; **W:** Abby Mann; **C:** Ernest Laszlo; **M:** Ernest Gold. Oscars '61: Actor (Schell), Adapt. Screenplay; Golden Globes '62: Actor--Drama (Schell), Director (Kramer); Natl. Film Reg. '13; N.Y. Film Critics '61: Actor (Schell), Screenplay.

Judgment Day 🦴🦴 **1999 (R)** A meteor collides with an asteroid in deep space and if fragments from the mishap should hit Earth, it's goodbye planet. One scientist has an idea how to prevent disaster but he's kidnapped by a cult leader who thinks the planet's doom is foretold. Now the government has to get the scientist back before it's too late. **90m/C; VHS, DVD.** Mario Van Peebles; Ice-T; Suzy Amis; Tommy (Tiny) Lister; Coolio; **D:** John Terlesky; **W:** William Carson; **C:** Maximo Munzi; **M:** Joseph Williams. **VIDEO**

Judgment in Berlin 🦴🦴 ½ *Escape to Freedom* **1988 (PG)** East German family hijacks a U.S. airliner into West Germany, and then must stand trial in Berlin before a troubled American judge. Based on a true 1978 incident and the book by Herbert J. Stern. **92m/C; VHS, DVD.** Martin Sheen; Sam Wanamaker; Max Gail; Sean Penn; Heinz Hoenig; Carl Lumbly; Max Volkert Martens; Harris Yulin; Jutta Speidel; Juerger Hemrich; **D:** Leo Penn; **W:** Joshua Sinclair; **M:** Peter Goldfoot.

Judgment Night 🦴🦴 **1993 (R)** Four macho buddies on their way to a boxing match detour a highway traffic jam via surface streets and find themselves witnesses to a murder. The rest of their guys-night-out is spent trying to escape a gloomy ghetto and determined killer (played convincingly by Leary). All of the action takes place after dark on the streets and in the sewers and, subsequently, the scenes are extremely dark with only a burnt orange lighting. Lots of action and a little oomph. Based on a story by Lewis Colick and Jere Cunningham. **109m/C; VHS, DVD, Blu-Ray.** Emilio Estevez; Cuba Gooding, Jr.; Stephen Dorff; Denis Leary; Jeremy Piven; Peter Greene; **D:** Stephen Hopkins; **W:** Lewis Colick; **C:** Peter Levy; **M:** Alan Silvestri.

Judicial Indiscretion 🦴🦴 **2007** Widowed federal judge Monica Barrett (Archer) is about to be nominated to fill a vacancy on the U.S. Supreme Court. While on vacation in San Francisco, she meets charming Jack Sullivan (Shanks) and wakes up the next morning to learn she's been drugged and filmed in a compromising manner that could destroy her career. Will she give in or expose the threats instead? **90m/C; DVD.** Anne Archer; Michael Shanks; Matthew Harrison; William B. Davis; Erin Karpluk; Anna Hagan; Sean Allan; **D:** George Mendeluk; **C:** Kamal Derkaoui; **M:** Clinton Shorter. **CABLE**

Judith of Bethulia 🦴🦴🦴 **1914** A young widow uses her charm and wits to save her city from attack by the Assyrians. Based on the Apocrypha, this is the last film Griffith directed for Biograph. It was re-released as "Her Condoned Sin" in 1971, including two reels of Griffith's outtakes. **65m/B; Silent; VHS, DVD.** Blanche Sweet; Henry B. Walthall; Mae Marsh; Robert "Bobbie" Harron; Lillian Gish; Dorothy Gish; Kate Bruce; Harry Carey, Sr.; **D:** D.W. Griffith; **W:** D.W. Griffith.

Judy 🦴🦴🦴 **2019 (PG-13)** Though Judy Garland (Zellweger) had been a movie star since her youth, she is struggling in Los Angeles and London. Though still an enthusiastic performer, she is broke and needs a break to stay solvent. Leaving her two younger children with their father Sidney (Sewell), she goes on a tour of England to hopefully revitalize her finances and her professional reputation. Based on a play by Peter Quilter, it follows the last few months of Judy's life while providing backstory about her abusive, unhappy childhood. Zellweger's impassioned performance of the Hollywood legend takes the spotlight, overshadowing any flaws in the filmmaking. **118m/C; DVD, Blu-Ray.** Renée Zellweger; Jessie Buckley; Finn Wittrock; Rufus Sewell; Michael Gambon; **D:** Rupert Gold; **W:** Tom Edge; **C:** Ole Bratt Birkeland; **M:** Gabriel Yared. Oscars '19: Actress (Zellweger); British Acad. '19: Actress (Zellweger); Golden Globes '20: Actress--Drama (Zellweger); Ind. Spirit '20: Actress (Zellweger); Screen Actors Guild '19: Actress (Zellweger).

Judy & Punch 🦴🦴 ½ **2020** In rustic village of Seaside in 17th century England, puppeteers/romantic partners Punch (Herriman) and Judy (Wasikowska) attract boisterous crowds for their often violent puppet shows. Behind the scenes, Punch is a charismatic narcissist with a drinking problem and Judy is the real puppeting talent who also parents their infant daughter. Punch's belief that a talent scout will find them and take them to the big time leads to a series of bad decisions that affect his family and his act, and results in Punch's empowerment. The sometimes surreal revenge drama/fantasy struggles to find the right tone and consistency but includes Wasikowska's memorable performance. **105m/C; DVD.** Mia Wasikowska; Damon Herriman; Benedict Hardie; Jacek Koman; Tom Budge; **D:** Mirrah Foulkes; **W:** Mirrah Foulkes; **C:** Stefan Duscio; **M:** Francois (Frank) Tetaz.

Judy Berlin 🦴🦴 ½ **1999** It's a school day in the placid suburb of Babylon, Long Island. Teacher Sue (Barrie) likes to flirt with weary principal Arthur (Dishy) who has a high-maintenance wife, Alice (Kahn), and a mopey grown son, David (Harnick), whose homecoming visit has gone on too long. Sue has her own offspring problems with sunnily ditsy, aspiring actress daughter Judy (Falco). Then Judy and David meet cute and a solar eclipse seems to inspire strange behavior. **97m/B; VHS, DVD.** Barbara Barrie; Bob (Robert) Dishy; Edie Falco; Aaron Harnick; Madeline Kahn; Carlin Glynn; Julie Kavner; Anne Meara; **D:** Eric Mendelsohn; **W:** Eric Mendelsohn; **C:** Jeffrey Seckendorf; **M:** Michael Nicholas. Sundance '99: Director (Mendelsohn).

Judy Moody and the Not Bummer Summer 🦴 ½ **2011 (PG)** Undemanding girl-oriented comedy based on the children's book series by Megan McDonald. Third-grader Judy (Beatty) is determined to have an exciting summer despite her best friends being away, being stuck with her Bigfoot-obsessed little brother Stink (Mosteller), and under the care of Aunt Opal (Graham), who turns out to be the free-spirited, artistic type. Which is good, since Judy and Aunt Opal come up with a 'thrill chart' to assign points to the summer adventures a moody Judy isn't sure she's going to have. **91m/C; DVD, Blu-Ray, On Demand.** Jordana Beatty; Parris Mosteller; Heather Graham; Jaleel White; Preston Bailey; Janet Varney; Kristoffer Ryan Winters; **D:** John Schultz; **W:** Kathy Waugh; Megan McDonald; **C:** Shawn Maurer; **M:** Richard Gibbs.

Jug Face 🦴🦴 ½ **2013 (R)** Ada (Carter) is a member of a backwoods community that still practices sacrifice to ward off bad fortune since their allegiance to "the pit" saved their people from disease decades earlier. A sculptor named Dawai (Bridgers) chooses the subject of sacrifice by crafting their face on a jug and Ada discovers that she's the next to die for the greater good. A stylish, consistent horror thriller that nonetheless ends up being something unsatisfactory as it feels like a short film stretched to feature running time. Great performances and an eerie setting overcome a distinct lack of story. **81m/C; DVD, Blu-Ray.** Sean Young; Lauren Ashley Carter; Daniel Manche; Mathieu Whitman; Sean Bridgers; Larry Fessenden; **D:** Chad Crawford Kinkle; **W:** Chad Crawford Kinkle; **C:** Chris Heinrich; **M:** Sean Spillane.

Juggernaut 🦴🦴🦴 **1974 (PG-13)** Well-done drama about a doomed luxury liner. A madman plants bombs aboard a cruise ship and mocks the crew about his plan over the wireless. The countdown ensues, while the bomb experts struggle to find the explosives. Suspenseful with good direction. **109m/C; DVD, Blu-Ray.** *UK* Richard Harris; Omar Sharif; David Hemmings; Anthony Hopkins; Shirley Knight; Ian Holm; Roy Kinnear; Freddie Jones; **D:** Richard Lester; **W:** Richard DeKoker; **C:** Gerry Fisher; **M:** Ken Thorne.

The Juggler 🦴 ½ **1953** A once-famous juggler in Germany, Hans Muller (Douglas) survives a concentration camp but is psychologically damaged. He emigrates to Israel but panics and attacks a policeman he fears will send him back. Running away, Hans hides out in a kibbutz where he's befriended by the widowed Ya'el (Vitale). Douglas comes across as too much of a he-man to make his character's mental fragility believable. **85m/B; DVD.** Kirk Douglas; Milly Vitale; Joseph Walsh; Paul Stewart; Charles Lane; Richard Benedict; Alf Kjellin; **D:** Edward Dmytryk; **W:** Michael Blankfort; **C:** J. Roy Hunt; **M:** George Antheil.

Juice 🦴🦴 ½ **1992 (R)** Day-to-day street life of four Harlem youths as they try to earn respect ("juice") in their neighborhood. Q, an aspiring deejay, is talked into a robbery by his friends but everything takes a turn for the worse when one of the others, Bishop, gets hold of a gun. The gritty look and feel of the drama comes naturally to Dickerson in his directorial debut. Prior to his first film, Dickerson served as cinematographer for Spike Lee's "Do the Right Thing" and "Jungle Fever." **95m/C; VHS, DVD, Blu-Ray.** Omar Epps; Jermaine "Huggy" Hopkins; Tupac Shakur; Khalil Kain; Cindy Herron; Vincent Laresca; Samuel L. Jackson; **D:** Ernest R. Dickerson; **W:** Gerard Brown; Ernest R. Dickerson; **C:** Larry Banks.

Juke Girl 🦴🦴 ½ **1942** Friends Steve (Reagan) and Danny (Whorf) are working the tomato fields of Cat Tail, Florida but wind up on opposite sides of a labor dispute when Steve sides with independent grower Nick (Tobias) and Danny takes a job with ruthless plant owner Henry (Lockhart). Sheridan comes into the picture as juke joint hostess Lola, who falls for Steve and loses her job for helping him. Nick gets murdered and the lovebirds wind up in more trouble. Reagan and Sheridan were previously paired in the much-better "Kings Row" (1942) but this is a good, if melodramatic, social issues pic, although it certainly seems oddly titled since Sheridan's character isn't the focus. **90m/B; DVD.** Ronald Reagan; Ann Sheridan; Richard Whorf; Gene Lockhart; George Tobias; Alan Hale; Betty Brewer; Faye Emerson; **D:** Curtis Bernhardt; **W:** A(lbert) I(saac) Bezzerides; Kenneth Garmet; **C:** Bert Glennon; **M:** Adolph Deutsch.

Jules and Jim 🦴🦴🦴🦴 *Jules et Jim* **1962** Beautiful film with perfect casting, particularly Moreau. Spanning from 1912 to 1932, it is the story of a friendship between two men and their 20-year love for the same woman. Werner is the shy German Jew and Serre the fun-loving Frenchman, who meet as students. The two men discover and woo the bohemian, destructive Moreau, although it is Werner she marries. After WWI, the friends are reunited but the marriage of Moreau and Werner is in trouble and she has an affair with Serre, which leads to tragedy for all three. Adapted from the novel by Henri-Pierre Roche. In French with English subtitles. **104m/B; VHS, DVD, Blu-Ray.** *FR* Jeanne Moreau; Oskar Werner; Henri Serre; Marie DuBois; Vanna Urbino; **D:** Francois Truffaut; **W:** Jean Gruault; Francois Truffaut; **C:** Raoul Coutard; **M:** Georges Delerue.

Jules Verne's Mysterious Island 🦴 *Mysterious Island* **2010** A nonsensical adventure that has little-to-nothing to do with the Jules Verne tale despite its title. Five Union POWs escape their Civil War prison by hijacking a hot air balloon. They drift all night and find themselves on a strange island, lost in time, that's home to other wrecked survivors, including Captain Nemo. He's got a plan to get everyone off the island before a volcanic eruption sinks it. **91m/C; DVD.** William Morgan Sheppard; Lochlyn Munro; Susie Arbromeit; Gina Holden; J.D. Evermore; Edrick Browne; Pruitt Taylor Vince; **D:** Mark A. Sheppard; **W:** Cameron Larson; **C:** Dave McFarland; **M:** Kenneth Hampton. **VIDEO**

Julia 🦴🦴🦴 ½ **1977 (PG)** The story recounted in Lillian Hellman's fictional memoir "Pentimento." Fonda plays Hellman as she risks her life smuggling money into Germany during WWII for the sake of Julia, her beloved childhood friend (Redgrave), who is working in the Resistance. All cast members shine in their performances; watch for Streep in her screen debut. **118m/C; VHS, DVD, Blu-Ray.** Jane Fonda; Jason Robards, Jr.; Vanessa Redgrave; Maximilian Schell; Hal Holbrook; Rosemary Murphy; Meryl Streep; Lisa Pelikan; John Glover; Mark Metcalf; Lambert Wilson; **D:** Fred Zinnemann; **W:** Alvin Sargent; **C:** Douglas Slocombe; **M:** Georges Delerue. Oscars '77:

Adapt. Screenplay, Support. Actor (Robards), Support. Actress (Redgrave); British Acad. '78: Actress (Fonda), Film, Screenplay, Support. Actress (Redgrave); Golden Globes '78: Actress--Drama (Fonda), Support. Actress (Redgrave); L.A. Film Critics '77: Cinematog., Support. Actor (Robards), Support. Actress (Redgrave); N.Y. Film Critics '77: Support. Actor (Schell); Writers Guild '77: Adapt. Screenplay.

Julia 2008 **(R)** Self-absorbed, self-destructive alcoholic Julia (Swinton) has obviously lost a few too many brain cells to the booze when she agrees to a kidnapping plan proposed by a virtual stranger. Elena (Del Castillo), who Julia meets at an AA meeting, claims that she is forbidden to see her son who lives in Mexico with his wealthy grandfather. She proposes they kidnap the boy and split the ransom and Julia thinks this is a great idea. Watching Swinton in action makes the lengthy run time go by faster than it should. English and Spanish with subtitles. **144m/C; Blu-Ray.** *FR* Tilda Swinton; Saul Rubinek; Kate del Castillo; Jude Ciccolella; Bruno Bichir; Kevin Kilner; Aidan Gould; Horacio Garcia Rojas; ***D:*** Erick Zonca; ***W:*** Erick Zonca; Aude Py; ***C:*** Yorick Le Saux; ***M:*** Pollard Berrier; Darius Keeter.

Julia Misbehaves 1948 Charming comedy that has Garson returning to ex-husband Pidgeon and daughter Taylor after an 18-year absence. Taylor is about to be married at a chateau in France and wants Garson to be there. While traveling to France from England, Garson encounters a bunch of colorful circus characters who are taking their act to Paris. Wonderful slapstick scenes give the stars a chance to have some real fun. Based on the novel "The Nutmeg Tree" by Margery Sharp. **99m/B; VHS, DVD.** Greer Garson; Walter Pidgeon; Peter Lawford; Cesar Romero; Elizabeth Taylor; Lucile Watson; Nigel Bruce; Mary Boland; Reginald Owen; Veda Ann Borg; Joi Lansing; ***D:*** Jack Conway.

Julian Po 1/2 *The Tears of Julian Po* **1997 (PG-13)** Nondescript bookkeeper Julian Po (Slater) has his car break down near an isolated mountain community and immediately comes under suspicion when he checks into the local boarding house, which never gets any guests. And the next day Julian's car has vanished, stranding him in nowherestown. The locals become convinced he's a hit man and demand explanations. Julian unexpectedly blurts out that the only person he's planning to kill is himself. Immediately the center of attention, Julian becomes confessor to everyone's darkest secrets and a recipient of their constant kindnesses but since he really doesn't intend to off himself, he's also got some unexpected problems. **82m/C; VHS, DVD.** Christian Slater; Robin Tunney; Michael Parks; Frankie Faison; Harve Presnell; Allison Janney; Cherry Jones; LaTanya Richardson Jackson; Dina Spybey; Zeljko Ivanek; ***D:*** Alan Wade; ***W:*** Alan Wade; ***C:*** Bernd Heinl; ***M:*** Patrick Williams.

Julia's Eyes *Los Ojos de Julia* **2010** In this atmospheric, although ultimately disappointing, chiller from Spain, Julia is convinced that her twin sister Sara did not commit suicide despite both women suffering from a degenerative eye condition that leads to blindness. Julia then tries reconstructing Sara's recent activities, including discovering Sara had a secret boyfriend. Is the mystery man the killer as well? Spanish with subtitles. **112m/C; DVD, Blu-Ray.** *SP* Beten Rueda; Lluis Homar; Pablo Derqui; Francesc Orella; ***D:*** Guillem Morales; ***W:*** Guillem Morales; Oriol Paulo; ***C:*** Oscar Faura; ***M:*** Fernando Velazquez.

Julie 1956 Widowed stewardess Julie (Day) remarries but soon discovers insanely jealous new hubby Lyle Benton (Jourdan) is responsible for her first husband's death. She tries to escape but even the skies aren't safe when Lyle boards her plane, which eventually results in a lot of unbelievable in-flight excitement. Day sings the Oscar-nominated title song. **97m/B; DVD.** Doris Day; Louis Jourdan; Barry Sullivan; Frank Lovejoy; John Gallaudet; Jack Kruschen; Harlan Warde; Jack Kelly; ***D:*** Andrew L. Stone; ***W:*** Andrew L. Stone; ***C:*** Fred H. Jackman, Jr.; ***M:*** Leith Stevens.

Julie & Julia **2009 (PG-13)** Yum. You may not find your inner chef but you'll definitely develop an appetite as foodie Ephron combines Julia Child's memoir "My Life in France" and Julie Powell's memoir "Julie & Julia" into a somewhat disjointed delight. Julie Powell (Adams) is tired of her boring job, her Queens apartment with its tiny kitchen, and her life in general. To break the monotony, Julie vows to use her mother's 1961 copy of Julia Child's "Mastering the Art of French Cooking" and make all 524 recipes in one year, while blogging about her experiences, encouraged by her usually-supportive husband Eric (Messina). The ever-enthusiastic Streep stars as the ever-enthusiastic Child, shown in flashbacks, as she lives and cooks in Paris in the late 1940s and 50s while her always-supportive husband Paul (an equally delightful Tucci) was stationed at the U.S. Embassy. Unfortunately for Adams, her New Yorker Julie is rather neurotic and dull, especially out of the kitchen. Bon appetit! **123m/C; Blu-Ray, On Demand.** Amy Adams; Meryl Streep; Stanley Tucci; Jane Lynch; Chris Messina; Mary Lynn Rajskub; Vanessa Ferlito; Joan Juliet Buck; Linda Emond; Helen Carey; Frances Sternhagen; ***D:*** Nora Ephron; ***W:*** Nora Ephron; ***C:*** Stephen Goldblatt; ***M:*** Alexandre Desplat. Golden Globes '10: Actress--Mus./Comedy (Streep).

Julien Donkey-boy 1/2 **1999 (R)** Harmony Korine's story of a schizophrenic young man and his disturbed family is the first American movie to be filmed using the principles of the restrictive Danish filmmaking method known as Dogma '95. Apparently, there must be some kind of restriction on the plot and narrative as well, because the audience is merely shown disturbing images of the mentally ill Julien (Bremner), his pregnant sister Pearl (Sevigny), his jock brother Chris (Neumann) and their abusive father (Herzog). Largely improvised and shot using hand-held digital video cameras, this unsettling project is for the cinematically adventurous only. **101m/C; VHS, DVD.** Ewen Bremner; Chloë Sevigny; Werner Herzog; Evan Neumann; Joyce Korine; Chrissy Kobylak; Alvin Law; ***D:*** Harmony Korine; ***W:*** Harmony Korine; ***C:*** Anthony Dod Mantle.

Juliet, Naked 1/2 **2018 (R)** Duncan (O'Dowd) is more into Tucker Crowe (Hawke), an indie-rocker who disappeared from the music scene decades earlier, than he is his long-time girlfriend, Annie (Byrne). Burning with resentment over her boyfriend's obsession, Annie posts a scathing review of Tucker's tunes, leading to an unlikely bond/romance with the music man himself. The three leads are engaging and appealing, but their sum is only humdrum. Based on the 2009 novel by Nick Hornby. **105m/C; DVD, Blu-Ray.** Rose Byrne; Ethan Hawke; Chris O'Dowd; Lily Newmark; Jimmy O. Yang; ***D:*** Jesse Peretz; ***W:*** Tamara Jenkins; Evgenia Peretz; Phil Alden Robinson; Jim Taylor; ***C:*** Remi Adefarasin; ***M:*** Nathan Larson.

Juliet of the Spirits *Giulietta Degli Spiriti* **1965** Fellini uses the sparse story of a woman (Fellini's real-life wife) deliberating over her husband's possible infidelity to create a wild, often senseless surrealistic film. With a highly symbolic internal logic and complex imagery, Fellini's fantasy ostensibly elucidates the inner life of a modern woman. In Italian with English subtitles. **142m/C; VHS, DVD.** *IT* Giulietta Masina; Valentina Cortese; Sylva Koscina; Mario Pisu; Sandra Milo; Caterina Boratto; Valeska Gert; ***D:*** Federico Fellini; ***W:*** Federico Fellini; Tullio Pinelli; Ennio Flaiano; Brunello Rondi; ***C:*** Gianni Di Venanzo; ***M:*** Nino Rota. N.Y. Film Critics '65: Foreign Film.

Julieta 1/2 **2016 (R)** Almodovar's twentieth feature as he approached 70 years old proves that the writer/director is losing almost nothing when it comes to his incredible eye and strong storytelling ability. Suarez and Ugarte star as older and younger versions of the title character in this adaptation of three short stories from "Runaway" by Alice Munro. The older Julieta lives in Madrid with her boyfriend, and she runs into a former best friend of her estranged daughter one day. The interaction sends Julieta into a flashback story about Julieta's teenage years. An episodic drama that's so remarkably well done that you won't care. **99m/C; DVD, Blu-Ray.** Emma Suarez; Adriana Ugarte; Daniel Grao; Inma Cuesta; Dario Grandinetti; ***D:*** Pedro Almodóvar; ***W:*** Pedro Almodóvar; ***C:*** Jean-Claude Larrieu; ***M:*** Alberto Iglesias.

Julius Caesar 1/2 **1953** All-star version of the Shakespearean tragedy, heavily acclaimed and deservedly so. Working directly from the original Shakespeare, director Mankiewicz produced a lifelike, yet poetic production. **121m/B; VHS, DVD; Open Captioned.** James Mason; Marlon Brando; John Gielgud; Greer Garson; Deborah Kerr; Louis Calhern; Edmond O'Brien; George Macready; John Hoyt; Michael Pate; ***D:*** Joseph L. Mankiewicz; ***W:*** Joseph L. Mankiewicz; ***C:*** Joseph Ruttenberg; ***M:*** Miklos Rozsa. Oscars '53: Art Dir./Set Dec., B&W; British Acad. '53: Actor (Brando), Actor (Gielgud); Natl. Bd. of Review '53: Actor (Mason).

Julius Caesar **1970** Subpar adaptation of the Shakespeare play about political greed and corruption within the Roman Empire. **116m/C; VHS, DVD, Blu-Ray.** *GB* Charlton Heston; John Gielgud; Jason Robards, Jr.; Richard Chamberlain; Robert Vaughn; Diana Rigg; ***D:*** Stuart Burge.

Jumanji 1/2 **1995 (PG)** For the past 26 years Alan Parish (Williams) has been stuck in the netherworld of Jumanji, a jungle-themed board game that sucks players into its alternate universe. When unsuspecting youngsters Judy (Dunst) and Peter (Pierce) happen upon the game and begin to play, they release Williams and a jungle full of rampaging beasts from the game and into the present. Loosely based on Chris Van Allsburg's children's book, the film version relies too heavily on cutting-edge special effects to make up for a thin story. Many of the creatures and effects are utterly too bizarre and unsettling for younger audiences. With a $65 million pricetag, Jumanji is definitely a roll of the dice. **104m/C; VHS, DVD, Blu-Ray, UMD.** Robin Williams; Kirsten Dunst; Bonnie Hunt; Bradley Michael Pierce; Bebe Neuwirth; Jonathan Hyde; David Alan Grier; Adam Hann-Byrd; ***D:*** Joe Johnston; ***W:*** Jonathan Hensleigh; ***C:*** Thomas Ackerman; ***M:*** James Horner.

Jumanji: The Next Level 1/2 **2019 (PG-13)** College freshman Spencer (Wolff) is struggling in NYC and unsure if he is still in a relationship with Martha (Turner). When he returns home for Christmas break, Spencer finds his grandfather Eddie (DeVito) is staying with his mother while he recovers from surgery. To regain the confidence he had as video game avatar Dr. Smolder Bravestone (Johnson), Spencer goes back inside the Jumanji video game. When Spencer goes missing, his friends enter the game as well, unexpectedly along with his grandfather and grandfather's estranged friend Milo (Glover). The sequel to the 2017 hit is an enjoyable mesh of fantasy, action-adventure, and comedy while celebrating friendships and courage. **100m/C; DVD, Blu-Ray.** Dwayne "The Rock" Johnson; Jack Black; Kevin Hart; Karen Gillan; Nick Jonas; ***D:*** Jake Kasdan; ***W:*** Jake Kasdan; Jeff Pinkner; Scott Rosenberg; ***C:*** Gyula Pados; ***M:*** Henry Jackman.

Jumanji: Welcome to the Jungle 1/2 **2017 (PG-13)** An updated reboot of the 1995 hit "Jumanji." While in high school detention, the brainy Spender (Wolff), the spoiled Bethany (Iseman), the athletic Fridge (Blain), and loner Martha (Turner) discover a Jumanji video game cartridge. When they play, they are sucked into the video game world as their game avatars. Spencer becomes the heroic Dr. Smolder Bravestone (Johnson), Fridge becomes the diminutive Moose Finabar (Hart), Bethany becomes the portly cartographer (Black), and Martha the warrior Ruby Roundhouse (Gillan). The teens cannot escape until they reach the top level of the game. Appealing and endearing, the crowd-pleasing film is full of spot-on humor. **119m/C; DVD, Blu-Ray.** Dwayne "The Rock" Johnson; Kevin Hart; Jack Black; Karen Gillan; Rhys Darby; ***D:*** Jake Kasdan; ***W:*** Chris McKenna; Erik Sommers; Scott Rosenberg; Jeff Pinkner; ***C:*** Gyula Pados; ***M:*** Henry Jackman.

Jump In! 1/2 **2007** Relentlessly chipper Disney Channel movie finds Izzy (Bleu) taking up boxing to please his dad, a former Golden Gloves champ. When his sister takes Izzy to a double-dutch competition, he's surprised to see cutie girl-next-door Mary (Palmer) on a team. Mary convinces Izzy to take his moves to her sport when they need a replacement jumper, but the guy's worried about not appearing cool at school. But he soon learns, of course, that first you have to be true to yourself. **85m/C; DVD.** Corbin Bleu; Keke Palmer; David Reivers; Shanica Knowles; Patrick Johnson, Jr.; ***D:*** Paul Hoen; ***W:*** Doreen Spicer; Regina Hicks; Karin Gist; ***C:*** David Makin; ***M:*** Frank Fitzpatrick. **CABLE**

Jump Into Hell 1/2 **1955** In 1954, Viet Cong are overrunning north Indochina and French troops are surrounded at the fort of Dien Bien Phu. French paratroopers volunteer to reinforce the cutoff troops in this war drama that includes newsreel footage of the actual conflict. **93m/B; DVD.** Jacques Sernas; Kurt Kasznar; Peter Van Eyck; Norman Dupont; Arnold Moss; Marcel Dalio; Lawrence (Larry) Dobkin; Patricia Blair; ***D:*** David Butler; ***W:*** Irving Wallace; ***C:*** J. Peverell Marley; ***M:*** David Buttolph.

Jumper 1/2 **2008 (PG-13)** Picked-on kid David (Christensen) discovers that he has the ability to teleport at will, and he uses his gift to flit around the world, rob banks, and basically do what he pleases, including pursuing his childhood crush Millie (Bilson). Enter Roland (Jackson), a member of a mysterious group that hunts and kills "jumpers" like David. Heavy action fails to cover up the weak plot and David's brattiness. Loosely based on a series of young adult novels by Steven Gould. **88m/C; DVD, Blu-Ray.** Hayden Christensen; Jamie Bell; Samuel L. Jackson; Rachel Bilson; Diane Lane; Michael Rooker; AnnaSophia Robb; Max Thieriot; ***D:*** Doug Liman; ***W:*** David S. Goyer; Simon Kinberg; Jim Uhls; ***C:*** Barry Peterson; ***M:*** John Powell.

Jumpin' at the Boneyard **1992 (R)** Gritty family drama about the trials of two dispossessed brothers, set on the streets of New York. Deeply depressed, out-of-work, divorced Manny hates his recently deceased father, adores his mother, and is estranged from his younger brother, Danny. Danny is a scared crack addict who's supported by a hooker/girlfriend. The two brothers reunite for a trip into their scarred past when Danny tries to rob his brother's apartment to get dope money. Manny starts to believe that the only way to redeem his own life is to get his brother into a rehab program. Good acting helps to overcome some script weaknesses but this is one depressing movie. **107m/C; VHS, Streaming.** Tim Roth; Alexis Arquette; Danitra Vance; Samuel L. Jackson; Kathleen Chalfant; Luis Guzman; ***D:*** Jeff Stanzler; ***W:*** Jeff Stanzler.

Jumpin' Jack Flash 1/2 **1986 (R)** A bank worker is humorously embroiled in international espionage when her computer terminal picks up distress signals from a British agent in Russia. Marshall's directing debut. Good performances from a fun cast and a particularly energetic effort by Goldberg are held back by an average and predictable script. **98m/C; VHS, DVD, Blu-Ray.** Whoopi Goldberg; Stephen Collins; Carol Kane; Annie Potts; Jonathan Pryce; James Belushi; Jon Lovitz; John Wood; ***Cameo(s):*** Michael McKean; Tracey Ullman; Roscoe Lee Browne; Sara Botsford; Jeroen Krabbe; Phil Hartman; Tracy Reiner; Paxton Whitehead; Jamey Sheridan; Garry Marshall; Peter Michael Goetz; ***D:*** Penny Marshall; ***W:*** David Franzoni; ***C:*** Jan De Bont; ***M:*** Thomas Newman.

Jumping Jacks **1952** Martin and Lewis are a couple of nightclub performers who wind up in the paratroop corps instead of performing their act for the soldiers. Martin gets to sing and Lewis gets to parachute into enemy territory and capture a general. **96m/B; DVD.** Dean Martin; Jerry Lewis; Mona Freeman; Don DeFore; Robert Strauss; Ray Teal; ***D:*** Norman Taurog; ***C:*** Daniel F. Fapp.

Jumping the Broom **2011 (PG-13)** A brassy African-American family comedy not made by Tyler Perry. Rich Sabrina (Patton) and working guy Jason (Alonso) are getting hitched in Martha's Vineyard and as can be expected the paradoxical families have a less-than-harmonious first meeting. And naturally it trickles down to the couple. The concept is classic but tackles way too many stereotypes for one movie and tries too hard to be over-the-top. Disappointing for an otherwise sincere and likeable cast. The title alludes to the tradition of literally stepping over a broom at weddings. **107m/C; Blu-Ray, On Demand.** Paula Patton; Laz Alonso;

Meagan Good; Pooch Hall; Angela Bassett; Mike Epps; Loretta Devine; Julie Bowen; Gary Dourdan; *D:* Salim Akil; *W:* Arlene Gibbs; Elizabeth Hunter; *C:* Anastas Michos; *M:* Ed Shearmur.

The Junction Boys ♂♂ **2002** A look at one phase in the career of legendary tough-guy college football coach Paul "Bear" Bryant (well-played by Berenger). Film starts in 1954 with Bryant's arrival at Texas A&M as he drives his players, eventually known as the Junction Boys, to make the team. (Drama sticks to football practice not competition.) The focus is on three key players (who, of course, have personal problems to overcome)?Skeet Keeler (Humphrys), Claude Gearheart (Kwanten), and Johnny Haynes (Curry). **93m/C; VHS, DVD.** Tom Berenger; Bernard Curry; Fletcher Humphrys; Ryan Kwanten; Nick (Nicholas) Tate; Mark Lee; Andy Anderson; *D:* Mike Robe; *W:* Mike Robe; *C:* Stephen F. Andrich; *M:* Steve Dorff. **CABLE**

Juncture ♂ 1/2 **2007 (R)** Anna Carter (Blackport) is the director of a foundation that funds programs to help abused children. Learning she has terminal brain cancer and only three months to live, Anna takes a proactive approach and decides to get justice for those damaged kids by offing pedophile criminals who have slipped through the justice system. **106m/C; DVD.** Andrew Porter; Kristine Blackport; John Hutton; Bill LeVasseur; Jeff Nicholson; *D:* James Seale; *W:* Robert Gosnell; *C:* Richard Lerner; *M:* Neal Acree. **VIDEO**

June ♂♂ **2015** A suspenseful horror/science fiction thriller about a possessed child and a fight to save humanity. June (Brice) has been in foster care for most of her nine years in this world, and always seems to attract chaos despite her efforts to be a well-behaved child. After June is sent to live with Dave (Van Dien) and Lily (Pratt), it comes to light that the innocent-looking child is possessed by an ancient angry demon that controls her soul. June must find her true self and defeat the spirit to save herself, her new family, and the world. **84m/C; DVD, Blu-Ray, Streaming, Download.** Kennedy Brice; Casper Van Dien; Victoria Pratt; Eddie Jemison; Lance E. Nichols; *D:* L. Gustavo Cooper; *W:* L. Gustavo Cooper; Sharon Y. Cobb; *C:* Ryan Patrick Dean; *M:* Juliette Beavan; Sean Beavan. **VIDEO**

June Night ♂♂ *Juninatten* **1940** A woman who was victimized by a shooting incident cannot escape the public eye due to her former promiscuous behavior. In Swedish with English subtitles. **90m/C; VHS, DVD.** *SW* Ingrid Bergman; Marianne Lofgren; Gunnar Sjoberg; Olaf Widgren; *D:* Per Lindberg; *W:* Ragnar Hylten-Cavalius; *C:* Ake Dahlqvist; *M:* Jules Sylvain.

Junebug ♂♂♂ **2005 (R)** Sophisticated Chicago art dealer Madeleine (Davidtz) has impulsively married enigmatic, ex-small town North Carolinian George (Nivola) and is finally about to meet her in-laws. George's homecoming is reluctant at best: his mom, Peg (Weston), is a busybody who immediately dislikes her new daughter-in-law; dad Eugene (Wilson) lives in his own quiet world; younger brother Johnny (McKenzie) is moody and resentful; and only his young and very pregnant bride Ashley (Adams) is happy and welcoming. It's a cultural and familial clash without being condescending. Pic is stolen by the delightful Adams as a sweetly wise chatterbox. **107m/C; DVD.** Embeth Davidtz; Alessandro Nivola; Amy Adams; Celia Weston; Ben(jamin) McKenzie; Scott Wilson; Frank Hoyt Taylor; Joanne Pankow; *D:* Phil Morrison; *W:* Angus MacLachlan; *C:* Peter Donahue; *M:* Yo LaTengo. Ind. Spirit '06: Support. Actress (Adams); Natl. Soc. Film Critics '05: Support. Actress (Adams); Broadcast Film Critics '05: Support. Actress (Adams).

Jungle ♂ **1952** A princess and an American adventurer lead an expedition into the Indian wilds to discover the source of recent elephant attacks. Currently released as 'The Jungle' in a collection only. **74m/B; VHS, DVD.** Rod Cameron; Cesar Romero; Marie Windsor; *D:* William Berke; *C:* Clyde De Vinna.

Jungle ♂♂ 1/2 **2017 (R)** An arresting thriller about one man's quest for survival, based on a true story. In November 1981, former Israeli soldier Yossi Ghinsberg (Radcliffe) and two friends explore the Bolivian jungle with the help of arrogant guide Karl (Kretschmann). After friction between them, the group breaks up, then Yossi finds himself alone after a river accident. As Yossi becomes gaunt and broken to a primal state, he remembers key moments in his life before the trip and struggles to make it out alive. Though the story is intense and powerful, an injection of melodrama and obvious attempts to please viewers makes the film less incredible. **115m/C; DVD.** Daniel Radcliffe; Alex Russell; Thomas Kretschmann; Lily Sullivan; Yasmin Kassim; *D:* Greg McLean; *W:* Justin Monjo; *C:* Stefan Duscio; *M:* Johnny Klimek.

The Jungle Book ♂♂ *Rudyard Kipling's Jungle Book* **1942** A lavish version of Rudyard Kipling's stories about Mowgli, the boy raised by wolves in the jungles of India. **109m/C; VHS, DVD.** Sabu; Joseph Calleia; Rosemary DeCamp; Ralph Byrd; John Qualen; *D:* Zoltan Korda; *W:* Laurence Stallings; *C:* Lee Garmes; *M:* Miklos Rozsa.

The Jungle Book ♂♂♂ **1967** Based on Kipling's classic, a young boy raised by wolves must choose between his jungle friends and human "civilization." Along the way he meets a variety of jungle characters including zany King Louie, kind-hearted Baloo, wise Bagherra and the evil Shere Khan. Great, classic songs including "Trust in Me," "I Wanna Be Like You," and Oscar-nominated "Bare Necessities." Last Disney feature overseen by Uncle Walt himself and a must for kids of all ages. **78m/C; VHS, DVD, Blu-Ray.** *V:* Phil Harris; Sebastian Cabot; Louis Prima; George Sanders; Sterling Holloway; J. Pat O'Malley; Verna Felton; Darleen Carr; *D:* Wolfgang Reitherman; *M:* George Bruns.

The Jungle Book ♂♂♂ 1/2 **2016 (PG)** Favreau's live-action update of the Rudyard Kipling book and Disney animated classic is a surprisingly robust and entertaining success, a film that really works for kids and their parents. Neel Sethi plays Mowgli in this update of the classic tale of the boy raised by wolves, and he's the only actual human being in the film, as CGI animals (voiced by Murray, Kingsley, Elba, and others) interact with the young man in surprisingly believable ways. The special effects are stunning but it's Favreau's understanding of what makes this story timeless that makes it work. **106m/C; DVD, Blu-Ray.** Neel Sethi; Bill Murray; Ben Kingsley; Idris Elba; Lupita Nyong'o; *D:* Jon Favreau; *W:* Justin Marks; *C:* Bill Pope; *M:* John Debney. Oscars '16: Visual FX; British Acad. '16: Visual FX.

The Jungle Book 2 ♂♂ **2003 (G)** Sequel to the classic Disney version, it picks up where the original left off. Mowgli (voice by Osment) is now living in the village with a warmhearted human family. He misses the excitement of the jungle and sneaks back to his old pal, Baloo the Bear (a decent enough Goodman, but the original voice of Phil Harris is a tough act to follow). Two of the village children follow him and many adventures ensue. Although the animation is quite good, the plot merely recycles old material, even going so far as reprising the classic song "Bare Necessities" three times. Adults will find the movie tiresome, but the younger set won't be as picky. **72m/C; VHS, DVD, Blu-Ray.** *V:* John Goodman; Haley Joel Osment; Mae Whitman; Tony Jay; Connor Funk; Bob Joles; John Rhys-Davies; Phil Collins; *D:* Steve Trenbirth; *W:* Karl Guers; *M:* Joel McNeely.

Jungle Boy ♂♂ **1996 (PG)** After being lost in the jungles of India, Manling (Seth) is raised by a monkey and an elephant. Able to communicate with the animals, Manling uses his talents to defeat the evil poacher, Hook (Roberts), who's out to steal a sacred statue. **88m/C; VHS, DVD.** Asif Mohammed Seth; Jeremy Roberts; Lea Moreno; *D:* Allan Goldstein; *W:* Allan Goldstein; John Lawson; Damian Lee; *C:* Nicholas Josef von Sternberg.

Jungle Drums of Africa ♂♂ *U-238 and the Witch Doctor* **1953** Jungle adventures abound as Moore and Coates encounter lions, wind tunnels, voodoo and enemy agents in deepest Africa. A 12-episode serial re-edited onto two cassettes. **167m/B; VHS, DVD.** Clayton Moore; Phyllis Coates; Roy Glenn; John Cason; *D:* Fred Brannon.

Jungle Fever ♂♂♂ **1991 (R)** Married black architect's affair with his white secretary provides the backdrop for a cold look at interracial love. Focuses more on the discomfort of friends and families than with the intense world created by the lovers for themselves. Provides the quota of humor and fresh insight we expect from Lee, but none of the joyous sexuality experienced by the lovers in "She's Gotta Have It." In fact, Lee tells viewers that interracial love is unnatural, never more than skin deep, never more than a blind obsession with the allure of the opposite race. Very fine cast but if you don't agree with Lee, a real disappointment as well. **131m/C; VHS, DVD, Blu-Ray.** Wesley Snipes; Annabella Sciorra; John Turturro; Samuel L. Jackson; Ossie Davis; Ruby Dee; Lonette McKee; Anthony Quinn; Spike Lee; Halle Berry; Tyra Ferrell; Veronica Webb; Frank Vincent; Tim Robbins; Brad Dourif; Richard Edson; Michael Imperioli; Nicholas Turturro; Steven Randazzo; Joseph (Joe) D'Onofrio; Michael Badalucco; Debi Mazar; Gina Mastrogiacomo; Phyllis Stickney; Theresa Randle; Pamela Tyson; Rick Aiello; Miguel (Michael) Sandoval; Doug E. Doug; Queen Latifah; *D:* Spike Lee; *W:* Spike Lee; *C:* Ernest R. Dickerson; *M:* Terence Blanchard. N.Y. Film Critics '91: Support. Actor (Jackson).

Jungle Hell ♂♂ **1955** Sabu comes to the rescue of an Indian tribe being harassed by flying saucers, death rays and radioactive debris. **78m/B; VHS, DVD.** Sabu; David Bruce; George E. Stone; K.T. Stevens; *D:* Norman A. Cerf.

Jungle Man-Eaters ♂ **1954** No man-eating is apparent in the 13th film in the Jungle Jim series. Jungle Jim (Weissmuller) faces off against a diamond smuggler who is willing to destroy a local tribe in order to control their diamond mine. **68m/B; DVD.** Johnny Weissmuller; Karin (Karen, Katharine) Booth; Richard Wyler; Bernie Hamilton; Lester Matthews; Gregory Gay; Vince Townsend, Jr.; Paul Thompson; *D:* Lee Sholem; *W:* Samuel Newman; *C:* Henry Freulich.

Jungle Manhunt ♂ **1951** In Jungle Jim's 7th adventure, L.A. journalist Anne Lawrence (Ryan) asks the guide (Weissmuller) to find missing football star Bob Miller (Waterfield). But it's Miller who must come to their rescue then they are attacked by a tribe under the control of evil Dr. Heller (Talbot) who's forcing them to be slave labor in his mines so he can create synthetic diamonds. **66m/B; DVD.** Johnny Weissmuller; Sheila Ryan; Bob Waterfield; Lyle Talbot; Rick Vallin; *D:* Lew Landers; *W:* Samuel Newman; *C:* William F. Whitley.

Jungle Moon Men ♂ **1955** Johnny Weissmuller plays himself but this is still the 15th entry in the Jungle Jim series. This time the safari he's guiding is captured by a pygmy tribe who worship the moon and their immortal priestess Oma (Stanton). **70m/B; DVD.** Johnny Weissmuller; Jean Byron; William Henry; Helene Stanton; Billy Curtis; Myron Healey; Michael Granger; *D:* Charles S. Gould; *W:* Dwight Babock; Jo Pagano; *C:* Henry Freulich.

Jungle Patrol ♂ 1/2 **1948** In 1943 New Guinea, a squadron of entrapped fliers are confronted with a beautiful USO entertainer. Romance and show tunes follow. **72m/B; VHS, DVD.** Kristine Miller; Arthur Franz; Richard Jaeckel; Ross Ford; Tommy Noonan; Gene Reynolds; *D:* Joseph M. Newman.

Jungle 2 Jungle ♂♂ 1/2 **1996 (PG)** Remake of French farce released as "Little Indian, Big City," changes little of the "wild child" premise. Workaholic Wall Streeter Michael Cromwell (Allen) decides to finalize the divorce from his long-estranged doctor wife, Patricia (Williams), who happens to have been ministering to a tribe in the Amazon rain forest for many years. He gets more than the divorce when he meets the 13-year-old son, Mimi-Siku (Huntington), he never knew he had. Although the boy speaks English, he's been raised as a tribal native, which causes quite a culture shock when he returns with Michael to the jungles of Manhattan. Of course the kid's more than a match for any situation. **105m/C; VHS, DVD, Blu-Ray.** Tim Allen; Sam Huntington; Martin Short; JoBeth Williams; Lolita Davidovich; David Ogden Stiers; Bob (Robert) Dishy; Valerie Mahaffey; Leelee Sobieski; Luis Avalos; Frankie J. Galasso; *D:* John Pasquin; *W:* Bruce A. Evans; Raynold Gideon; *C:* Tony Pierce-Roberts; *M:* Michael Convertino.

Jungle Warriors ♂ 1/2 **1984 (R)** Seven fashion models are abducted by a Peruvian cocaine dealer. To escape him, they must become Jungle Warriors. **96m/C; VHS, DVD.** *GE MX* Sybil Danning; Marjoe Gortner; Nina Van Pallandt; Paul Smith; John Vernon; Alex Cord; Woody Strode; Kai Wulff; *D:* Ernst R. von Theumer.

Junglee ♂♂ **2019** Mumbai veterinarian Raj Nair (Jammwal) blames his conservationist father for his mother's death and has not spoken to him in years. As the tenth anniversary of her death nears, Raj returns to his father's elephant sanctuary. Though Raj reunites with childhood friends human and elephant, he is distressed by the sanctuary's downturn. Raj's concern only increases when former teacher Gaja (Deshpande) warns that poachers have invaded the forest. The actions of big game hunter Keshav (Kulkarni) force Raj to take steps to protect those he loves. The film is an action film with a message and effectively features elephants in their natural habitat. Hindi with subtitles. **115m/C; DVD.** Vidyut Jammwal; Thalaivasal Vijay; Atul Kulkarni; Makrand Deshpande; Pooja Sawant; *D:* Chuck Russell; *W:* Chuck Russell; Adam Prince; *C:* Mark Irwin; *M:* Sameer Uddin.

Jungleground ♂ 1/2 **1995 (R)** Jungleground is a urban wasteland controlled by rival gangs. Lt. Jake Cornel (Piper) gets caught in a shoot-out when a sting operation goes bad and winds up before psychotic gang leader Odin. Odin offers him one chance—Cornel's going to be hunted in Jungleground's abandoned streets and if he can escape before dawn, he gets to live. **90m/C; VHS, DVD.** *CA* Roddy Piper; Torri Higginson; Peter Williams; *D:* Don Allan; *W:* Michael Stokes; *C:* Gilles Corbeil; *M:* Varouje.

Junior ♂♂ **1994 (PG-13)** Out of the way women! Schwarzenegger trades the war room for the delivery room to experience the miracle of birth. As scientists, he and DeVito take a dip in the gene pool once again to test an anti-miscarriage drug. Thompson provides the egg and some surprisingly good physical comedy as the klutzy cryogenics expert who moves into their university digs. Every pregnancy cliche is explored as Schwarzenegger and DeVito bring the concept to term. Sorry, action fans. . .nothing blows up except Arnold. **109m/C; VHS, DVD.** Arnold Schwarzenegger; Danny DeVito; Emma Thompson; Frank Langella; Pamela Reed; Judy Collins; James Eckhouse; Aida Turturro; *D:* Ivan Reitman; *W:* Kevin Wade; Chris Conrad; *C:* Adam Greenberg; *M:* James Newton Howard.

Junior Bonner ♂♂♂ **1972 (PG)** A rowdy modern-day western about a young drifting rodeo star who decides to raise money for his father's new ranch by challenging a formidable bull. **100m/C; VHS, DVD, Blu-Ray.** Steve McQueen; Robert Preston; Ida Lupino; Ben Johnson; Joe Don Baker; Barbara Leigh; *D:* Sam Peckinpah; *W:* Jeb Rosebrook; *C:* Lucien Ballard; *M:* Jerry Fielding.

Jr. Detective Agency ♂ 1/2 *Sam Steele and the Jr. Detective Agency* **2009 (G)** Mildly entertaining kids fare. Thirteen-year-old Sam Steele Jr. wants to be like his Des Moines police detective dad. He decides to help his dad catch an elusive jewel thief nicknamed 'The Cat' by opening his own agency, complete with receptionist Emma and Emma's beagle Doug to nose out clues. **90m/C; DVD.** Luke Perry; Jacob Hays; Katherine McNamara; Darren Kennedy; M. Emmet Walsh; *D:* Tom Whitus; *W:* Tom Whitus; *C:* Jeffrey McLeid; *M:* Nathan Lanier. **VIDEO**

Junior G-Men ♂♂ **1940** The Dead End Kids fight Fifth Columnists who are trying to sabotage America's war effort. Twelve episodes. **237m/B; VHS, DVD.** Billy Halop; Huntz Hall; Gabriel Dell; Bernard Punsley; Harris Berger; Hal E. Chester; Kenneth Howell; Kenneth Lundy; *D:* Ford Beebe; John Rawlins; *W:* Basil Dickey; George Plympton; Rex Taylor; *C:* Jerome Ash; *M:* Charles Previn.

Junior G-Men of the Air ♂ 1/2 **1942** The Dead End Kids become teenage flyboys in this 12-episode serial adventure. **215m/B; VHS, DVD.** Billy Halop; Huntz Hall; Gene Reynolds; Lionel Atwill; Frank Albertson; Richard Lane; Gabriel Dell; Bernard Punsley; Frankie Darro; David Gorcey; Turhan Bey; Vinton (Hayworth) Haworth; *D:* Lewis D. Collins; Ray Taylor; *W:* George Plympton; Griffin Jay; Paul Huston; *C:* William Sickner.

Junior Miss ♂♂ 1/2 **1945** Well-meaning New York teen Judy Graves (Garner) manages to throw her family into chaos over the

Christmas holidays. She tries matchmaking her Uncle Willis (Dunne) with Ellen Curtis (Marlowe), the daughter of her dad's boss, and nearly gets her dad (Joslyn) fired. **94m/B; DVD.** Peggy Ann Garner; Stephen Dunne; Allyn Joslyn; Faye Marlowe; Mona Freeman; John Alexander; Barbara Whiting; ***D:*** George Seaton; ***W:*** George Seaton; ***C:*** Charles G. Clarke; ***M:*** David Buttolph.

Junior's Groove 🦴🦴 *The Planet of Junior Brown* **1997 (R)** Young piano prodigy grows up in a tough neighbor with a caring mom, eccentric piano teacher, and a group of street-smart friends. Based on the novel by Virginia Hamilton. **91m/C; VHS, DVD.** Lynn Whitfield; Clark Johnson; Margot Kidder; Sarah Polley; Martin Villafana; ***D:*** Clement Virgo; ***W:*** Clement Virgo; Cameron Bailey; ***C:*** Jonathan Freeman; ***M:*** Christopher Dedrick. **VIDEO**

The Juniper Tree 🦴 1/2 **1987** Based on a tale by the Brothers Grimm, this Icelandic curio finds sisters Margit (Bjork) and Katla (Bragadottir) fleeing across the medieval countryside after their mother is burned at the stake for witchcraft. The sisters have their own special powers, which they turn on each other when they become romantic rivals over a young widower (Flygenring). **78m/B; VHS, DVD, Blu-Ray.** *IC* Bjork; Bryndis Petra Bragadottir; Vladimar Orn Flygenring; ***D:*** Nietzchka Keene.

The Junkman 🦴 1/2 **1982 (R)** Movie maker whose new film is about to be premiered is being chased by a mysterious killer. Promoted as "the ultimate car chase film" since the production used and destroyed over 150 automobiles. From the makers of "Gone in 60 Seconds." **97m/C; VHS, DVD.** H.B. Halicki; Christopher Stone; Lynda Day George; Hoyt Axton; ***D:*** H.B. Halicki.

Juno 🦴🦴🦴 1/2 **2007 (PG-13)** Ultra-sassy Juno (Page) realizes she may not know it all after she finds herself facing teenage motherhood, with her goofy, lovable best friend Paulie (Cera) as the expectant dad. Her parents are concerned, but not angry, almost like they've been there before. Juno opts for adoption rather than abortion, but has trouble following through after she's met with the childless yuppie couple Venessa (Garner) and Mark (Bateman) who are first in line to snatch up her baby. Note-perfect performances all around, especially by Page as the girl unwillingly rocketing into womanhood. Director Jason Reitman retains expert balance for this very smart, funny, offbeat, and touching story, which easily could've come out as another lame teen comedy. **92m/C; Blu-Ray, On Demand.** Ellen Page; Michael Cera; Jennifer Garner; Jason Bateman; Allison Janney; J.K. Simmons; Olivia Thirlby; ***D:*** Jason Reitman; ***W:*** Diablo Cody; ***C:*** Eric Steelberg; ***M:*** Mateo Messina. Oscars '07: Orig. Screenplay; British Acad. '07: Orig. Screenplay; Ind. Spirit '08: Actress, Film, First Screenplay; Writers Guild '07: Orig. Screenplay.

Juno and the Paycock 🦴🦴 1/2 **1930** Perhaps if Hitchcock hadn't been so faithful to O'Casey this early effort would have been less stagey and more entertaining. In Dublin during the civil uprising, a poor family is torn apart when they receive news of an imminent fortune. Hitchcock's reported to have said that "drama is life with the dull bits left out," though here too many dull bits remain. **96m/B; VHS, DVD.** Sara Allgood; Edward Chapman; John Longden; John Laurie; Maire O'Neill; ***Nar:*** Barry Fitzgerald; ***D:*** Alfred Hitchcock; ***W:*** Alfred Hitchcock.

Jupiter Ascending 🦴 1/2 **2015 (PG-13)** The Wachowski siblings continue to frustrate their legion of fans hoping for another "The Matrix" but only getting bloated, CGI nonsense. Jupiter Jones (Kunis) is an average cleaning woman who is contacted by an interplanetary warrior (Tatum) who basically tells her that she's the key to the fate of the universe. It turns out that the human race is little more than a breeding ground for the most powerful alien dynasties across the stars, who will use it to harvest "youth serum" to live forever. Of course, Jupiter is the only one who can stop them. Loud, annoying, and ridiculous. **125m/C; DVD, Blu-Ray.** Mila Kunis; Channing Tatum; Eddie Redmayne; Tuppence Middleton; Douglas Booth; Sean Bean; Nikki Amuka-Bird; ***D:*** Lilly Wachowski; Lana Wachowski; ***W:*** Lilly Wachowski; Lana Wachowski; ***C:*** John Toll; ***M:*** Michael Giacchino. Golden Raspberries '15: Worst Support. Actor (Redmayne).

Jupiter's Darling 🦴🦴 **1955** This spoof of Hannibal (Keel) and Amytis (Williams) gravely misses the mark in making funny the world of the Roman Empire. Amytis has the job of distracting Hannibal from attacking the Eternal City, and does so through musical interludes and unfunny jokes. **96m/C; DVD.** Esther Williams; Howard Keel; George Sanders; Gower Champion; Marge Champion; Norma Varden; Richard Haydn; William Demarest; Douglass Dumbrille; Michael Ansara; Martha Wentworth; Chris Alcaide; William Tannen; ***D:*** George Sidney; ***C:*** Charles Rosher.

Jurassic Park 🦴🦴🦴 1/2 **1993 (PG-13)** Crichton's spine-tingling thriller translates well (but not faithfully) due to its main attraction: realistic, rampaging dinosaurs. Genetically cloned from prehistoric DNA, all is well until they escape from their pens—smarter and less predictable than expected. Contrived plot and thin characters (except Goldblum), but who cares? The true stars are the dinos, an incredible combination of models and computer animation. Violent, suspenseful, and realistic with gory attack scenes. Not for small kids, though much of the marketing was aimed at them. At the time, Spielberg knocked his own "E.T." out of the box office top spot, making "JP" the highest grossing movie ever. The T-Rex has since been bested by an iceberg and Celine Dion. **127m/C; VHS, DVD, Blu-Ray.** Sam Neill; Laura Dern; Jeff Goldblum; Richard Attenborough; Bob Peck; Martin Ferrero; B.D. Wong; Joseph Mazzello; Ariana Richards; Samuel L. Jackson; Wayne Knight; ***V:*** Richard Kiley; ***D:*** Steven Spielberg; ***W:*** David Koepp; Michael Crichton; ***C:*** Dean Cundey; ***M:*** John Williams. Oscars '93: Sound, Sound FX Editing, Visual FX; Natl. Film Reg. '18.

Jurassic Park 3 🦴🦴 **2001 (PG-13)** Neill (who skipped JP2) is back as Dr. Alan Grant, reluctantly leading a seach-and-rescue mission when a plane crash-lands on an island populated by his old nemeses, the dinos. Another new dinosaur species, the Spinosaurus, shows up and to make some more humans into snack food. The talented, and probably over-qualified, group of writers mercifully makes this trip a short one, making sure that any dialogue is mostly expository or in-joke amusing while glossing over the dumb-as-a-box-of-fossils plot and characters. The dinosaurs are, once again, impressive, if you haven't gotten enough of the computer-generated ferocity in the first two outings. Warning: Just because this franchise is getting progressively worse doesn't mean they didn't set up JP4. **90m/C; VHS, DVD, Blu-Ray.** Sam Neill; William H. Macy; Tea Leoni; Alessandro Nivola; Michael Jeter; Trevor Morgan; John Diehl; Bruce A. Young; Taylor Nichols; Mark Harelik; Julio Oscar Mechoso; Laura Dern; ***D:*** Joe Johnston; ***W:*** Peter Buchman; Alexander Payne; Jim Taylor; ***C:*** Shelly Johnson; ***M:*** Don Davis.

Jurassic World 🦴🦴 **2015 (PG-13)** Fast-forward twenty-some years from Jurassic Park horrifically failing its test run, to Jurassic World raking in the dough as the world's coolest theme park. Still, even in the modern era, just because you can doesn't mean you should. Bored teenager Zach (Robinson) and his eager young brother Gray (Simpkins) get the VIP treatment from their park manager Aunt Claire (Howard), ushered through gyro globe rides, T-Rex photos, and meet their aunt's super studly raptor whisperer once-boyfriend, Owen (Pratt), who steps up as superhero after Mother Nature starts to rear her ugly head. A fast-paced thrill ride that feels more like an action flick than its scarier predecessor. Trumps the previous limp sequels, but never quite rises to the original's sense of awe. **130m/C; DVD, Blu-Ray, Streaming.** Chris Pratt; Bryce Dallas Howard; Vincent D'Onofrio; Judy Greer; Jake Johnson; ***D:*** Colin Trevorrow; ***W:*** Colin Trevorrow; Derek Connolly; Rick Jaffa; Amanda Silver; ***C:*** John Schwartzman; ***M:*** Mike Giacchino.

Jurassic World: Fallen Kingdom 🦴🦴 **2018 (PG-13)** Three years after the destruction of the Jurassic World theme park, Owen (Pratt) and Claire (Howard) return to the island to rescue the remaining dinosaurs from an impending volcano blast. While there, they uncover a conspiracy that threatens to revert the entire planet to a prehistoric state. Let's face it: none of these sequels are going to hold a candle to the original Jurassic Park. But this installment is exciting, if dumb, and at least Howard's wearing more appropriate footwear. **129m/C; DVD, Blu-Ray.** Chris Pratt; Bryce Dallas Howard; Rafe Spall; Justice Smith; Daniella Pineda; ***D:*** J.A. Bayona; ***W:*** Derek Connolly; Colin Trevorrow; ***C:*** Oscar Faura; ***M:*** Michael Giacchino.

The Juror 🦴 1/2 **1996 (R)** Plucky single mom (Moore) ends up on the jury in the trial of a powerful mobster and draws the attention of the smooth enforcer (Baldwin) who muscles her into providing a certain verdict. The usual good-vs.-evil, family-in-danger action ensues. Despite boasting a fine cast and impressive attention to detail, flick is guilty of ludicrous situations, a mechanical plot and a dopey ending. Based on the novel by George Dawes Green. **107m/C; VHS, DVD.** Demi Moore; Alec Baldwin; Joseph Gordon-Levitt; Anne Heche; James Gandolfini; Lindsay Crouse; Tony LoBianco; Michael Constantine; Matt Craven; Polly Adams; ***D:*** Brian Gibson; ***W:*** Ted Tally; ***C:*** Jamie Anderson; ***M:*** James Newton Howard.

Jury Duty 🦴 **1995 (PG-13)** Mama's boy loser Tommy Collins (Shore) gets jury duty on a serial-killer case and tries to keep what seems to be an open-and-shut case going so he can continue to get free room and board. He falls for babe juror Monica (Carrere) and really drags the trial (and the film) out in a pathetic attempt to woo her. Shore is even more annoying and unfunny than ever. Lowrent bastardization of "Twelve Angry Men" tries to pass off lame O.J. references and Shore falling out of chairs as humor. Creates reasonable doubt as to Shore's talent and movie execs' judgment. **88m/C; VHS, DVD, Blu-Ray.** Pauly Shore; Tia Carrere; Shelley Winters; Brian Doyle-Murray; Abe Vigoda; Stanley Tucci; Charles Napier; Richard Edson; ***Cameo(s):*** Andrew Silverstein; ***D:*** John Fortenberry; ***W:*** Fax Bahr; Barbara Williams. Golden Raspberries '95: Worst Actor (Shore).

Just a Kiss 🦴🦴 **2002 (R)** Actor Stevens' clever directorial debut shows the dark side of 30-something NYC hipsters whose infidelity and jealousy rival any low-brow talk show fodder. Chain of perilous events is set off by Dag (Eldard), who cheats on his live-in Halley (Sedgwick) with suicidal ballerina Rebecca (Shelton), the girlfriend of Dag's best friend Peter (Breen). When the secret is revealed, more cheating takes place with newcomers Diggs, Choudhury, and Tomei—who plays a hilarious bowling alley waitress. A quirky singles mixer/romantic comedy with a twist, characters are given the chance to go back in time and change their actions. Good performances and writing keep this a few notches above melodramatic send-up, even with somewhat gimmicky use of an animation technique called rotomation. **89m/C; VHS, DVD.** Ron Eldard; Kyra Sedgwick; Patrick Breen; Marisa Tomei; Marley Shelton; Taye Diggs; Sarita Choudhury; Zoe Caldwell; ***D:*** Fisher Stevens; ***W:*** Patrick Breen; ***C:*** Terry Stacey; ***M:*** Sean Dinsmore.

Just a Little Harmless Sex 🦴🦴 **1999 (R)** Alan (Mailhouse) has spent the evening with his buddies, Danny (Silverman) and Brent (Ragsdale), at a topless bar. Driving home, he offers help to a stranded motorist (who turns out to be a hooker) and winds up getting arrested. Alan's wife, Laura (Eastwood), is, naturally, not happy about the situation and discusses her plight with her gal pals while Alan and his buddies discuss his fractured marriage. Angsty but not particularly novel. **98m/C; VHS, DVD.** Robert Mailhouse; Alison Eastwood; Jonathan Silverman; William Ragsdale; Lauren Hutton; Kimberly Williams; Jessica Lundy; Rachel Hunter; Michael Ontkean; Tito Larriva; ***D:*** Rick Rosenthal; ***W:*** Roger Miller; Marti Noxon; ***C:*** Bruce Surtees; ***M:*** Tito Larriva.

Just About Famous: A Film About Celebrity Impersonators 🦴🦴 **2015** A hilarious documentary look into the world of celebrity impersonators. Centered on the Convention for Celebrity Tribute Artists, the perspectives and intimate lives of the impersonators are examined. How they manage the attention, how they were discovered, and how they handle their resemblance to someone famous is considered as well. **95m/C; DVD, Streaming, Download.** ***D:*** Jason Kovacsev; Matt Mamula; ***C:*** Matt Mamula; Aaron Hose; John Schaub. **VIDEO**

Just Add Water 🦴🦴 **2007 (R)** Mild-mannered, blue-collar Ray Tuckby (Walsh) lives in the dead-end desert community of Trona, California, in a lousy marriage and with a nothing job. The community has fallen prey to a slimy real estate speculator and a violent teenage meth dealer. But somewhere along the way, Ray decides it's time for a change—for himself and the town. **91m/C; DVD.** Dylan Walsh; Tracy Middendorf; Danny DeVito; Justin Long; Jonah Hill; Anika Noni Rose; Brad Hunt; ***D:*** Hart Bochner; ***W:*** Hart Bochner; ***C:*** Aaron Barnes; ***M:*** John Swihart.

Just Another Girl on the I.R.T. 🦴🦴 1/2 **1993 (R)** Double debut from two African American women, writer/director Harris, and actress Johnson, captures the sass and wit of a girl from the projects. Seventeen-year-old Chantal has a plan for her life and challenges authority with assurance, even after an unexpected pregnancy puts a twist into her plan. Strong initial statement tends to become weak and cloudy as Chantal loses her focus. This doesn't dismiss the remarkable realism and raw talent portrayed in a picture filmed in just seventeen days for $130,000. Winner of a special jury prize at the Sundance Film Festival. **96m/C; VHS, DVD.** Ariyan Johnson; Kevin Thigpen; Ebony Jerido; Jerard Washington; Chequita Jackson; William Badget; ***D:*** Leslie Harris; ***W:*** Leslie Harris; ***C:*** Richard Conners. Sundance '93: Special Jury Prize.

Just Another Love Story 🦴 1/2 *Kaerlighed Pa Film* **2008** Danish potboiler is an overdone romantic thriller about identity. Despite his work as a crime-scene photographer, married Jonas' (Berthelsen) life is average and predictable. Until he and his family are involved in a serious car accident. They are fine but Julia (Hemse), the driver of the other car, is in a coma. Jonas lets her family believe that he is her mysterious boyfriend, wanting to help in her recovery, and when the troubled young woman regains consciousness, she allows the deception to continue. Of course the real boyfriend (Lie Kaas) will show up and trouble will escalate. Danish with subtitles. **104m/C; DVD.** *DK* Anders W. Berthelsen; Nikolaj Lie Kaas; Bent Mejding; Rebecka Hemse; Charlotte Fich; Dejan Cukic; Karsten Jansfort; Ewa Frohling; ***D:*** Ole Bornedal; ***W:*** Ole Bornedal; ***C:*** Dan Laustsen; ***M:*** Joachim Holbek.

Just Another Secret 🦴 1/2 **1989** CIA agent Jack Grant poses as an East German citizen when five American agents go missing behind the Iron Curtain. With help from a German agent, Jack figures out Soviet premier Gorbachev is targeted for assassination, which will be blamed on the missing Americans. There are various double-crosses and Jack doesn't know who to trust. Adapted from a Frederick Forsyth story. **98m/C; DVD.** *UK* Beau Bridges; James Faulkner; Kenneth Cranham; Beatie Edney; Alan Howard; ***D:*** Lawrence Gordon Clark; ***W:*** Murray Smith; ***C:*** Cristiano Pogany; ***M:*** Paul Chihara. **TV**

Just Around the Corner 🦴 1/2 **1938 (G)** Temple helps her Depression-poor father get a job after she befriends a cantankerous millionaire. Temple duets with Bill "Bojangles" Robinson with the fourth time. Also available colorized. **71m/B; VHS, DVD.** Shirley Temple; Charles Farrell; Bert Lahr; Joan Davis; Bill Robinson; Cora Witherspoon; Franklin Pangborn; ***D:*** Irving Cummings.

Just Ask My Children 🦴🦴 **2001** Appalling true story from Lifetime. In 1982, Brenda and Scott Kniffen testify for friends in a child custody hearing. A vindictive relative of the losing side then accuses the Kniffens of abusing their two sons and a vicious prosecutor pursues the patently unbelievable case, even badgering the sons into giving false testimony. The Kniffens spend some 12 years in prison trying to prove their innocence as their sons go into the foster care system. **91m/C; DVD.** Virginia Madsen; Jeffrey Nordling; Cody Dorkin; Ryan Wilson, MS III; Scott Bailey; Gregory Edward Smith; Robert Joy; John Billingsley; Maree Cheatham; Scott Paulin; Graham Beckel; ***D:*** Arvin Brown; ***W:*** Deborah Serra; ***C:*** Lowell Peterson; ***M:*** Patrick Williams. **CABLE**

Just Before Dawn 1980 (R) Another murderers stalk campers story; humans resort to their animal instincts in their struggle for survival. Not to be confused with the William Castle film (1946) from the "Crime Doctor" series. **90m/C; VHS, DVD, Blu-Ray.** Chris Lemmon; Deborah Benson; Gregg Henry; George Kennedy; ***D:*** Jeff Lieberman; ***M:*** Brad Fiedel.

Just Before I Go 1/2 **2015 (R)** A comedy-drama about the power of confrontation to change one man's life. For much of his life, Ted Morgan (Scott) has been living an incomplete life. When he is dumped by his wife, he decides he has nothing to live for and decides to confront his demons in his hometown to achieve closure. He believes that certain people have made him into the shell of a person he has become. As he tries to confront these people and gain the closure he needs so he can withdraw from his family, Ted finds himself pulled more deeply into situations in their lives. Just as he prepares for suicide, he discovers that life has something to offer. **95m/C; DVD, Blu-Ray, Download.** Seann William Scott; Olivia Thirlby; Garret Dillahunt; Kate Walsh; Kyle Gallner; ***D:*** Courteney Cox; ***W:*** David Flebotte; ***C:*** Mark Schwartzbard; ***M:*** Erran Baron Cohen.

Just Before Nightfall 1/2 *Juste Avant la Nuit* **1971** Charles (Bouquet) is having an affair with Laura (Douking), the domineering wife of his best friend Francois (Tellier). Laura dies (apparently during a sex game) and Charles goes home to his wife Helene (Audran), pretending nothing has happened. Then the police investigation starts and Charles's guilt begins to gnaw at him. First he confesses to Helene—and then to Francois—but their bourgeois reactions are more shocking to Charles than Laura's death. French with subtitles. **100m/C; DVD.** *FR* Stephane Audran; Michel Bouquet; Francois Perier; Jean Carmet; Anna Douking; Henri Attal; ***D:*** Claude Chabrol; ***W:*** Claude Chabrol; ***C:*** Jean Rabier; ***M:*** Pierre Jansen.

Just Between Friends 1986 (PG-13) Two women become friends, not knowing that one is having an affair with the husband of the other. Allan Burns directorial debut. **110m/C; DVD.** Mary Tyler Moore; Christine Lahti; Sam Waterston; Ted Danson; Jim MacKrell; Jane Greer; ***D:*** Allan Burns; ***W:*** Allan Burns; ***C:*** Jordan Cronenweth.

Just Buried 1/2 **2007** Misanthropic would-be black comedy. N'er-do-well Oliver learns that he's inherited his dad's failing mortuary business, which he intends to sell until he gets interested in fixated embalmer Roberta. Accidentally killing a hiker in a car mishap, Oliver uses the funeral home to dispose of the body, which gives Roberta the idea that they should drum up clientele through murderous means. **94m/C; DVD.** *CA* Jay Baruchel; Rose Byrne; Graham Greene; Nigel Bennett; Thomas Gibson; Reagan Pasternak; Sergio Di Zio; ***D:*** Chaz Thorne; ***W:*** Chaz Thorne; ***C:*** Christopher Porter; ***M:*** Darren Fung.

Just Business 1/2 **2008** Elizar Perla (Pastko) can't resist coming out of cat burglar retirement to go after the art collection of David Gray (Watton). But when Perla disappears, his daughter Marty (Gershon) is forced to accept help from Gray to recover the art work, which may lead to her father's whereabouts. But it seems the rarest of the stolen pieces is beyond monetary value, so expect some complications. **85m/C; DVD.** Gina Gershon; Jonathan Watton; John Robinson; Zachary Bennett; Earl Pastko; ***D:*** Jonathan Dueck; ***W:*** David Robinson; ***C:*** Mick Reynolds; ***M:*** Ryan Latham. **VIDEO**

Just Cause 1994 (R) Incoherent mystery/thriller set in the Florida Everglades. Retired attorney, Paul Armstrong, now a Harvard law professor, decides to defend Bobby Earl (Underwood), on death row for the murder of a white girl. As Armstrong investigates the case, he discovers that the arresting officer Tanny Brown, (Fishburne) is corrupt and tortured the confession out of Bobby. Starts off promising with the electricity of Connery's and Fishburne's presence and a frigthening cameo by Ed Harris as an incarcerated serial killer, but once the barrage of plot twists start, creating gator size holes in the plot, the movie drifts into a murkey swamp of absurdity. Adapted from the legal thriller by John Katzenbach. **102m/C; VHS, DVD, Blu-Ray.** Sean Connery; Laurence Fishburne; Kate Capshaw; Blair Underwood; Ruby Dee; Daniel J. Travanti; Ned Beatty; Lynne Thigpen; George Plimpton; Chris Sarandon; Kevin McCarthy; Ed Harris; ***D:*** Arne Glimcher; ***W:*** Jeb Stuart; Robert Stone; ***C:*** Lajos Koltai; ***M:*** James Newton Howard.

Just Eat It 1/2 **2014** This insightful feature-length documentary looks at the issue of food waste and global consequences. Noting that almost 50 percent of the food in the world goes to waste, the filmmakers specifically explore how much edible food is tossed from farms, retail establishments, and household, and why this situation occurs. The filmmakers themselves then pledge to stop grocery shopping for six months and only consume food that would otherwise be thrown away, and film the results of this experience. Also included are revealing interviews with experts in food science and the perspective of activists. **75m/C; DVD, Streaming, Download.** Jenny Rustemeyer; Grant Baldwin; ***D:*** Grant Baldwin; ***W:*** Jenny Rustemeyer; Grant Baldwin; ***C:*** Jenny Rustemeyer; Grant Baldwin; ***M:*** Grant Baldwin. **VIDEO**

Just for Fun 1/2 **1963** Silly Brit teen musical. British teens get the right to vote, politicians try to get them on their side. Instead, the teens decide to form their own political party and use popular recording artists to sway their fellow young voters to take over the country. **85m/B; DVD.** *UK* Mark Wynter; Cherry Roland; Richard Vernon; Reginald Beckwith; John Wood; Jeremy Lloyd; ***D:*** Gordon Flemyng; ***W:*** Milton Subotsky; ***C:*** Nicolas Roeg; ***M:*** Tony Hatch.

Just for the Hell of It WOOF! *Destruction, Inc.* **1968** A quartet of teenage punks ruthlessly terrorize their suburban Miami 'hood while an innocent kid gets blamed. More exploitation from schlock king Lewis, who also wrote the theme song, "Destruction, Inc." (pic's alternate title). Essentially the same cast as the director's "She Devils on Wheels," filmed simultaneously. **85m/C; VHS, DVD.** Rodney Bedell; Ray Sager; Nancy Lee Noble; Agi Gyenes; Steve White; ***D:*** Herschell Gordon Lewis; ***W:*** Allison Louise Downe; ***C:*** Roy Collodi; ***M:*** Larry Wellington.

Just for You 1/2 **1952** Entertaining musical about producer Crosby who doesn't have time for his kids until Wyman steps in and shows him the way. Based on Stephen Vincent Benet's novel "Famous." **95m/C; DVD.** Bing Crosby; Jane Wyman; Ethel Barrymore; Robert Arthur; Natalie Wood; Cora Witherspoon; ***D:*** Elliott Nugent; ***W:*** Robert Carson.

Just Friends 2005 (PG-13) No surprises in this romantic comedy, but it's sweet enough anyway. Chris (Reynolds), the chubby Jersey kid, is in love with his high school chick friend Jamie (Smart) but he's overweight, shy, and in the "friend zone." Chris moves to L.A., where he transforms into a super hot So-Cal babe collector before returning to his hometown 10 years later. **94m/C; DVD.** Ryan Reynolds; Amy Smart; Anna Faris; Julie Hagerty; Christopher Marquette; Stephen (Steve) Root; Chris Klein; Fred Ewanuick; ***D:*** Roger Kumble; ***W:*** Adam "Tex" Davis; ***C:*** Anthony B. Richmond; ***M:*** Jeff Cardoni.

Just Getting Started 1/2 **2017 (PG-13)** An uneven romantic comedy/caper which lacks enough story for its formidable star power. Duke Diver (Freeman) manages a Palm Springs retirement community, but has secrets in his past. As someone tries to kill him, he also must deal with Texas big man Leo McKay (Jones), who comes to the resort with an unknown agenda. Leo challenges Duke on several fronts, including his sexual entanglements with a trio of residents When Suzie Quince (Russo) arrives to audit Duke's books, Duke and Leo vie for her affections. Though the film marks Ron Shelton's return to directing, it does not live up to its comic potential. **91m/C; DVD, Blu-Ray.** Glenne Headly; Rene Russo; Morgan Freeman; Jane Seymour; Tommy Lee Jones; ***D:*** Ron Shelton; ***W:*** Ron Shelton; ***C:*** Barry Peterson; ***M:*** Alex Wurman.

Just Go With It 2011 (PG-13) Danny (Sandler), a plastic surgeon, enlists his assistant Katherine (Aniston) to pretend to be his soon-to-be-ex-wife, in order to cover up a lie he told to the (much younger) girl of his dreams, Palmer (Decker). About to be divorced in real life, Katherine and her kids suddenly find themselves on a Hawaii vacation with Danny and Palmer. Sandler's silly antics will satisfy his fans, and Aniston plays well off of him. Decker does well in her big-screen debut while Kidman makes a splash as Katherine's long-ago friend. Nothing spectacular but an amiable remake of 1969's "Cactus Flower." **117m/C; Blu-Ray, On Demand.** Adam Sandler; Jennifer Aniston; Nicole Kidman; Dave Matthews; Bailee Madison; Brooklyn Decker; Kevin Nealon; Nick Swardson; Griffin Gluck; Rachel Dratch; ***D:*** Dennis Dugan; ***W:*** Adam Sandler; Allan Loeb; Timothy Dowling; ***C:*** Theo van de Sande; ***M:*** Rupert Gregson-Williams. Golden Raspberries '11: Worst Actor (Sandler), Worst Director (Dugan).

Just Henry 1/2 **2011** ITV drama adapted from Michelle Magorian's novel. In 1950, troubled 15-year-old Henry Dodge is living with his mother Maureen and his new stepfather Bill as his father Joey was supposedly killed in the war. A man suddenly appears, claiming to be Joey Dodge and saying he lost his memory but something sinister is going on that puts Joey and his mother in danger. **100m/C; DVD.** *UK* Josh Bolt; Elaine Cassidy; Dean Andrews; Stephen Campbell Moore; Sheila Hancock; ***D:*** David Moore; ***W:*** Michael Chaplin; ***C:*** Balazs Bolygo; ***M:*** Dominik Scherrer. **TV**

Just Like a Woman 1/2 **2013 (R)** Meandering road pic that director Bouchareb intends as the first in a cross-cultural trilogy. Mona is an Egyptian-born immigrant whose husband owns a Chicago party store where Marilyn is a regular customer. Marilyn loses her job and cheating husband just as Mona flees after her hateful mother-in-law dies. The women bond and head to Santa Fe where Marilyn wants to join a belly-dancing troupe. Mona turns out to have some expertise so the two take some dancing gigs to pay their way but it's seedy not generally desperate. Farahani and Miller work well together but it's mild fare. **88m/C; Blu-Ray, On Demand.** *UK US FR* Sienna Miller; Golshifteh Farahani; Bahar Soomekh; Tim Guinee; Roschdy Zem; Jesse Bob Harper; Chafia Boudraa; Marion Doussot; ***D:*** Rachid Bouchareb; ***W:*** Joelle Touma; ***C:*** Christophe Beaucarne; ***M:*** Eric Neveux.

Just like Heaven 2005 (PG-13) David Abbott (Ruffalo) tragically loses his wife, sending him into a tailspin of depression. Looking to start anew, Abbott moves into a new apartment, which just happens to be occupied—by a ghost, Elizabeth (Witherspoon), who doesn't know she's dead Actually she's only mostly dead—she's in limbo, in a coma after a car accident. Mindless romantic fluff worth it for fans of that sort of thing, or for those of you with a crash on one of the attractive leads. **101m/C; VHS, DVD.** Reese Witherspoon; Mark Ruffalo; Dina Spybey; Donal Logue; Ben Shenkman; Jon Heder; Ivana Milicevic; Rosalind Chao; Ron Canada; ***D:*** Mark S. Waters; ***W:*** Peter Tolan; Leslie Dixon; ***C:*** Daryn Okada; ***M:*** Rolfe Kent.

Just Like the Son 2006 (PG-13) Petty criminal Daniel (Webber) is performing community service at a Brooklyn elementary school, which is where he meets eight-year-old Boone (Ortiz). When his mom is hospitalized, Boone is sent to a foster school upstate and Daniel decides he needs rescuing. So he steals a car, grabs the kid, and they embark on a cross-country road trip to find Boone's sister who's supposed to be living in Dallas. Has sentimental written all over the plot (and Ortiz is adorable) but Freeman doesn't overindulge in the schmaltz. **86m/C; DVD.** Mark Webber; Antonio Ortiz; Rosie Perez; Brendan Sexton, III; Bruce MacVittie; Adrian Martinez; ***D:*** Morgan Freeman; ***W:*** Morgan Freeman; ***C:*** Yaron Orbach; ***M:*** Dean Wareham; Britta Phillips.

Just Looking 1/2 *Cherry Pink* **1999 (R)** A comedy about teenaged voyeurism set in 1955. 14-year-old Lenny (Merriman) has only one thing on his mind for summer vacation in his Bronx neighborhood. He's determined to figure out what sex is all about by watching some adults "do it." Well, Lenny's mom decides to send him to stay in suburban Queens with her sister but that doesn't change his plans. Predictable coming of age comedy with Alexander making his directorial debut. **97m/C; VHS, DVD.** Ryan Merriman; Gretchen Mol; Patti LuPone; Peter Onorati; Ilana Levine; Richard V. Licata; John Bolger; Joey Franquinha; ***D:*** Jason Alexander; ***W:*** Marshall Karp; ***C:*** Fred Schuler; ***M:*** Michael Skloff.

Just Married 1/2 **2003 (PG-13)** Mismatched newlyweds Tom (Kutcher) and Sarah (Murphy) find slapstick situations and jealousy instead of romantic bliss on their European honeymoon. Tom's a sports-lovin' regular guy, and Sarah's the well-educated daughter of a Beverly Hills tycoon. In Europe, they must deal with that, along with every ugly American and snooty European stereotype in the book, er, script. Kutcher plays his usual pretty-boy doofus, but Murphy is wasted in a stupid movie seemingly designed to give Kutcher pin-up status. **94m/C; VHS, DVD, Blu-Ray.** Ashton Kutcher; Brittany Murphy; Christian Kane; David Moscow; Monet Mazur; David Rasche; Veronica Cartwright; Raymond J. Barry; Thad Luckinbill; David Agranov; Taram Killam; ***D:*** Shawn Levy; ***W:*** Sam Harper; ***C:*** Jonathan Brown; ***M:*** Christophe Beck.

Just Mercy 2019 (PG-13) Activist lawyer Bryan Stevenson (Jordan) takes the case of Walter McMillian (Foxx), a black death row inmate who was convicted of murdering a white woman. Walter swears he did not commit the crime and presented 17 alibis at trial but was convicted on the basis of an ex-con's testimony. Bryan uses the CBS news magazine 60 Minutes to try to get the case re-opened after a judge refuses to accept the ex-con's admission that he had lied under oath. Based on a true story, the compassionate storytelling along with Jordan and Foxx's performances overcome any clichés along the way. **136m/C; DVD, Blu-Ray.** Brie Larson; Michael B. Jordan; O'Shea Jackson, Jr.; Jamie Foxx; Tim Blake Nelson; ***D:*** Destin Daniel Cretton; ***W:*** Destin Daniel Cretton; Andrew Lanham; ***C:*** Brett Pawlak; ***M:*** Joel P. West.

Just My Luck 1/2 **1935** Former silent screen star Ray's comeback attempt turned out to be unlucky as this workplace comedy flopped. Chemist Homer Crew is certain his new rubber formula will be a success even after getting fired. Someone must agree since there are repeated attempts to steal his invention. **70m/B; DVD.** Charles Ray; Edward J. Nugent; Anne Grey; Quentin Smith; Snub Pollard; ***D:*** Ray Heinz; ***W:*** Wallace Sullivan; ***C:*** Arthur Martinelli.

Just My Luck 1/2 **2006 (PG-13)** Bland romantic fantasy finds Lohan growing up and trying to escape the teen queen ghetto. Ashley, a junior exec in Manhattan, is just the luckiest gal ever. Her opposite is cutie-pie Jake (Pine), whose life is one continuous calamity. They meet at a costume party, kiss, and their worlds turn—Jake can do no wrong and Ashley, well, life is just so not fair! Now she needs to kiss Jake again and do another switcheroo. Lohan's game for slapstick humiliation, but this one's just another rung up the acting ladder. **108m/C; DVD.** Lindsay Lohan; Chris Pine; Samaire Armstrong; Bree Turner; Faizon Love; Missi Pyle; Makenzie Vega; Tovah Feldshuh; Jaqueline Fleming; Carlos Ponce; ***D:*** Donald Petrie; ***W:*** I. Marlene King; Amy Harris; ***C:*** Dean Semler; ***M:*** Teddy Castellucci.

Just Off Broadway 1/2 **1942** Private eye Michael Shayne (Nolan) is on the jury in the murder trial when a witness who could clear the accused is killed by a knife hurled from within the courtroom. Shayne hides the knife and, overnight, traces the knife to the thrower, but that's only the beginning of the trail. Shayne's back in the court the next morning and he's got the scoop, although he's in the hot seat for skipping out on jury duty. **65m/B; DVD.** Lloyd Nolan; Marjorie Weaver; Phil Silvers; Janis Carter; Richard Derr; ***D:*** Herbert I. Leeds; ***W:*** Brett Halliday; Arnaud d'Usseau; ***C:*** Lucien N. Andriot; ***M:*** David Raksin.

Just One Night 1/2 **2000 (PG-13)** College professor Isaac Adler (Hutton) is spending the night before his wedding in San Francisco. His taxi collides with that of beautiful, married Aurora (Cucinotta) and maybe the collision shook them up more than they thought, since they decide to spend the evening getting to know each other better. **90m/C; VHS, DVD.** Timothy Hutton; Maria Grazia Cucinotta; Udo Kier; Michael O'Keefe; Robert Easton; Don Novello; Seymour Cassel; Natalie Shaw; ***D:*** Alan Jacobs; ***W:*** Alan Jacobs; ***C:*** John J. Campbell; ***M:*** Anthony Marinelli.

Just One of the Girls 1/2 **1993 (R)** Teen star Haim transfers to a new high school where he dresses in drag in order to avoid the itinerant leader of the school's toughest gang whom he has unwittingly enraged. Palling around with Eggert becomes one of his costume's unexpected perks. Sort of a cross between "Some Like It Hot" and "90210." **94m/C; VHS, DVD.** Corey Haim; Nicole Eggert; Cameron Bancroft; ***D:*** Michael Keusch; ***M:*** Amin Bhatia.

Just One of the Guys 1985 **(PG-13)** When the school newspaper refuses to accept the work of an attractive young girl, she goes undercover as a boy to prove that her work is good. She goes on to befriend the school's nerd, and even helps him grow out of his awkward stage, falling for him in the process. Very cute, but predictable. **100m/C; VHS, DVD, Blu-Ray.** Joyce Hyser; Clayton Rohner; Billy Jacoby; Toni Hudson; Leigh McCloskey; Sherilyn Fenn; William Zabka; ***D:*** Lisa Gottlieb.

Just One Time 2000 **(R)** New York-set romantic comedy about fulfilling fantasies. Fireman Anthony (Janger) is about to marry lawyer Amy (Carter) but can't resist telling her about his sexual dream to see her make out with another woman—just once—before the wedding. Distraught, Amy confides in their gay neighbor, Victor (Diaz), who admits to a crush on Anthony. So she offers a quid pro quo to her beau—she'll indulge him with sultry lesbian Michelle (Esposito) if Anthony will do the same for her with Victor, and he has to go first. **94m/C; VHS, DVD.** Lane Janger; Joelle Carter; Guillermo Diaz; Jennifer Esposito; Vincent Laresca; David Lee Russek; Domenick Lombardozzi; ***D:*** Lane Janger; ***W:*** Lane Janger; Jennifer Vandever; ***C:*** Michael St. Hilaire; ***M:*** Edward Bilous.

Just Peck 2009 Michael Peck is an undersized, awkward high school sophomore who's befriended by kind-hearted and beautiful senior Emily. Peck's overachieving parents force him to compete in the science fair making his natural nerd come out and he decides to come up with a project so outlandish that it will get him both noticed and respected. **93m/C; DVD.** Keir Gilchrist; Brie Larson; Kyle Kaplan; Andrew McFarlane; Adam Arkin; Marcia Cross; Camryn Manheim; Don McManus; Tom McGowan; ***D:*** Michael A. (M.A.) Nickles; ***W:*** Marc Arneson; ***C:*** Mark Petersen; ***M:*** Benjamin Wynn; Jeremy Zuckerman. **VIDEO**

Just Tell Me What You Want 1/2 1980 **(R)** A wealthy, self-made married man finally drives his longtime mistress away when he refuses to let her take over the operation of a failing movie studio he has acquired. After she falls for another man, the tycoon does everything he can to win her back. The department store battle between MacGraw and King is priceless. **112m/C; VHS, DVD.** Alan King; Ali MacGraw; Myrna Loy; Keenan Wynn; Tony Roberts; ***D:*** Sidney Lumet; ***W:*** Jay Presson Allen; ***C:*** Oswald Morris.

Just the Ticket *The Scalper* 1998 **(R)** Romantic comedy set in the seedy world of ticket scalpers should have skipped the trite love story and centered on the ducat slingers. Gary (Garcia) is a fast talking huckster trying to win back ex-girlfriend Linda (MacDowell). He's also hoping for the ever-popular last big score before he goes legit. His opportunity arrives when the Pope announces a visit to Yankee Stadium, but he must out-hustle competitor Casino (Blake). Garcia wrote many of the Salsa-flavored songs used in the movie. **115m/C; VHS, DVD.** Andy Garcia; Andie MacDowell; Richard Bradford; Laura Harris; Andre B. Blake; Elizabeth Ashley; Patrick Breen; Ron Leibman; Chris Lemmon; Don Novello; Abe Vigoda; Bill Irwin; Ronald Guttman; Donna Hanover; Irene Worth; Fred Asparagus; Louis Mustillo; Paunita Nichols; Joe Frazier; Lenny Venito; ***D:*** Richard Wenk; ***W:*** Richard Wenk; ***C:*** Ellen Kuras; ***M:*** Rick Marotta.

Just the Way You Are 1984 **(PG)** An attractive musician struggles to overcome a physical handicap and winds up falling in love while on vacation in the French Alps. **96m/C; VHS, DVD.** Kristy McNichol; Robert Carradine; Kaki Hunter; Michael Ontkean; Alexandra Paul; Lance Guest; Timothy Daly; Patrick Cassidy; ***D:*** Edouard Molinaro; ***W:*** Allan Burns; ***M:*** Vladimir Cosma.

Just Visiting 2001 **(PG-13)** Remake of the 1993 French flick "Les Visiteurs" has Reno and Clavier reprising their roles as a medieval knight and his servant who find themselves in modern-day Chicago. Original was a huge hit in France, but bombed here. This one should do much better here, since there's much less reading of subtitles involved, and this one makes good use of the excellent leads and the transplanted Chicago locales. **88m/C; VHS, DVD, Blu-Ray.** Jean Reno; Christian Clavier; Christina Applegate; Tara Reid; Matt Ross; Bridgette Wilson-Sampras; John Aylward; George Plimpton; Malcolm McDowell; Sarah Badel; Richard Bremmer; Robert Glenister; ***D:*** Jean-Marie Poire; ***W:*** Christian Clavier; Jean-Marie Poire; John Hughes; ***C:*** Ueli Steiger; ***M:*** John Powell.

Just Wright 1/2 2010 **(PG)** A serious injury forces NBA star Scott McKnight (Common) to seek the aide of physical therapist Leslie Wright (Latifah). She unexpectedly falls for him and the two seem to be a perfect match, but Leslie has competition from her childhood pal Morgan (Patton) who is determined to become an NBA trophy wife. Leslie and Scott complement each other so well that Morgan's interference is farfetched at best. Film puts a sports-insider twist on the standard romantic comedy, but doesn't do much besides that. **100m/C; Blu-Ray.** Queen Latifah; Common; Paula Patton; Pam Grier; James Pickens, Jr.; Mehcad Brooks; Michael Landes; Phylicia Rashad; ***D:*** Sanaa Hamri; ***W:*** Michael Elliot; ***C:*** Terry Stacey; ***M:*** Lisa Coleman; Wendy Melvoin.

Just Write 1/2 1997 **(PG-13)** Sweet and slight romantic comedy about making your dreams come true. Harold (Piven) is a Hollywood tour bus driver who works for his well-meaning but overbearing father (Rocco). He meets cute with rising star Amanda (Fenn), who is mistakenly lead to believe Harold is a screenwriter. And Amanda just happens to have a script that needs some work. They begin to fall in love but sooner or later the truth is bound to come out. Leads play well together and the supporting cast is fine, especially Williams as a hard-charging agent. **95m/C; VHS, DVD.** Jeremy Piven; Sherilyn Fenn; JoBeth Williams; Alex Rocco; Jeffrey D. Sams; Wallace Shawn; Costas Mandylor; Yeardley Smith; Holland Taylor; ***Cameo(s):*** Nancy McKeon; Ed McMahon; ***D:*** Andrew Gallerani; ***W:*** Stan Williamson; ***C:*** Michael Brown; ***M:*** Leland Bond.

Justice for Natalee 2011 Okay follow-up to Lifetime's 2009 pic "Natalee Holloway" finds Natalee's mother Beth (Pollan) still working with the FBI to build a case against Joran van der Sloot (Amell), the prime suspect in her daughter's disappearance in Aruba in 2005. Then Joran is accused and jailed for murdering a young woman in a hotel in Peru. **86m/C; DVD.** Tracy Pollan; Stephen Amell; Scott Cohen; Michael Beach; Francesco Quinn; Julio Oscar Mechoso; Grant Show; Amy Gumenick; ***D:*** Stephen Kay; ***W:*** Teena Booth; ***C:*** Jamie Barber; ***M:*** Tree Adams. **CABLE**

Justice League 1/2 2017 **(PG-13)** An appealing entry in the DC Comics movie franchise explains the origins of the Justice League but struggles to balance screen time for its many superhero characters. When the very existence of Earth is in peril at the hands of the powerful Steppenwolf (Hinds), Batman (Affleck), Wonder Woman (Gadot), and another revived superhero (guess who!) recruit three new major characters to the fight--The Flash (Miller), Aquaman (Momoa), and Cyborg (Fisher). As the league forms and does their thing, there are moments of humor, warmth, and emotion that are satisfying enough. **120m/C; DVD, Blu-Ray.** Ben Affleck; Henry Cavill; Amy Adams; Gal Gadot; Ezra Miller; ***D:*** Zack Snyder; ***W:*** Chris Terrio; Joss Whedon; ***C:*** Fabian Wagner; ***M:*** Danny Elfman.

Justin Bieber: Never Say Never 1/2 2011 **(G)** Goes behind the scenes of teenage pop music sensation Justin Bieber's 2010 concert tour, including his sold-out show at Madison Square Garden. Follows his rise to fame along with lots of home video footage of his early life. Love him or leave him, this doesn't pretend to be anything other than it is—an over-the-top celebration of all that is Justin, to the delight of his multitude of adoring (mostly preteen girl) fans. Somewhat bearable to all others. **105m/C; Blu-Ray, On Demand.** Justin Bieber; Miley Cyrus; Chris Bridges; Boyz II Men; Sean Kingston; Jaden Smith; Usher Raymond; ***D:*** Jon M. Chu; ***C:*** Reed Smoot; ***M:*** Deborah Lurie.

Justin Morgan Had a Horse 1981 The true story of a colonial school teacher in post-Revolutionary War Vermont who first bred the Morgan horse, the first and most versatile American breed. **91m/C; VHS, DVD.** Don Murray; Lana Wood; Gary Crosby; ***D:*** Hollingsworth Morse.

Justine *Marquis de Sade's Justine* 1969 In the 1930s, a prostitute who marries an Egyptian banker becomes involved with a variety of men and a plot to arm Palestinian Jews in their revolt against English rule. A condensed film version of Lawrence Durrell's "The Alexandria Quartet." **115m/C; VHS, DVD, Blu-Ray.** *IS* Anouk Aimee; Michael York; Dirk Bogarde; Philippe Noiret; Michael Constantine; John Vernon; Jack Albertson; ***D:*** George Cukor; ***W:*** Lawrence B. Marcus; ***C:*** Leon Shamroy; ***M:*** Jerry Goldsmith.

Juwanna Mann 2002 **(PG-13)** Cross-dressing comedy plays like a "Tootsie" retread in sneakers. Jamal (Nunez) is an obnoxious pro basketball player booted out of the league after mooning a ref while protesting a call. Facing total bankruptcy and realizing his only skills are on the basketball court, Jamal dons make-up and falsies and joins a pro women's league as Juwanna Mann. Predictable situations occur, including Jamal falling for beautiful teammate Michelle (Fox) and being hit on by clueless suitor Puff Smokey Smoke (Davidson), but performances save what could have been a complete disaster. **91m/C; VHS, DVD.** Miguel A. Nunez, Jr.; Vivica A. Fox; Kevin Pollak; Tommy Davidson; Kim Wayans; Jenifer Lewis; Kimberly (Lil' Kim) Jones; Annie Corley; Ginuwine; ***D:*** Jesse Vaughan; ***W:*** Bradley Allenstein; ***C:*** Reynaldo Villalobos; ***M:*** Wendy Melvoin; Lisa Coleman.

K-11 2011 A record executive (Visnjic) awakes from a drug blackout to find himself inexplicably imprisoned in a ward reserved for LGBT inmates and sex offenders. **88m/C; DVD, Blu-Ray.** Goran Visnjic; Kate del Castillo; D.B. Sweeney; Portia Doubleday; ***D:*** Jules Stewart; ***W:*** Jules Stewart; Jared Kurt; ***C:*** Adam Silver; ***M:*** Phil Marshall. **VIDEO**

K-9 1/2 1989 **(PG-13)** After having his car destroyed by a drug dealer, "I work alone" Belushi is forced to take on a partner—a German Shepherd. Together they work to round up the bad guys and maybe chew on their shoes a little. Sometimes amusing one-joke comedy done in by a paper-thin script. Both the dog and Belushi are good, however. **111m/C; VHS, DVD, Blu-Ray.** James Belushi; Mel Harris; Kevin Tighe; Ed O'Neill; Cotter Smith; James Handy; Jerry Lee; ***D:*** Rod Daniel; ***W:*** Steven Siegel; Scott Myers; ***C:*** Dean Semler; ***M:*** Miles Goodman.

K-9 3: P.I. 1/2 2001 **(PG-13)** Detective Dooley (Belushi) and Jerry Lee are heading for retirement and new careers as private eyes. But when they try stopping a crime in progress, they wind up as the prime suspects and now must try to find the real culprits. Oh, and Dooley thinks he can earn some extra cash by having Jerry Lee serve as a German Shepard stud for a dog breeder. Family friendly fun. **95m/C; VHS, DVD.** James Belushi; Jason Schombing; Barbara Tyson; Gary Basaraba; Kymberley Huffman; Christopher Shyer; ***D:*** Richard J. Lewis; ***W:*** Gary Scott Thompson; Ed Horowitz. **VIDEO**

K-911 1/2 1999 **(PG-13)** Ten years after the original film, Belushi returns to his role of LAPD Detective Dooley, along with his German Sheperd partner, Jerry Lee. The aging duo are now reluctantly partnered with a younger K-9 unit—no-nonsense detective Welles (Tucci) and her partner, a Doberman named Zeus. But Dooley has some other things on his mind—some kook is trying to kill him. **91m/C; VHS, DVD.** James Belushi; James Handy; Christine Tucci; Wade Andrew Williams; J.J. Johnston; Vincent Castellanos; ***D:*** Charles Kanganis; ***W:*** Gary Scott Thompson; ***C:*** George Mooradian; ***M:*** Stephen (Steve) Edwards. **VIDEO**

K-9000 1989 The Hound salutes the idea behind this standard sci-fi crime-fighter; a cyberdog fights the forces of evil with the aid of a cop, a lady reporter, and the usual cliches. **96m/C; VHS, DVD.** Chris Mulkey; Catherine Oxenberg; ***D:*** Kim Manners; ***M:*** Jan Hammer. **TV**

K-19: The Widowmaker 2002 **(PG-13)** Cold War tensions abound in this aptly claustrophobic submarine suspenser involving the Soviet Union's first nuclear ballistic sub, which suffers a reactor malfunction during a test voyage in the North Atlantic. Ford plays the tough Russian captain, who takes command from the more-popular Neeson, and must deal with rebellion in the ranks in order to save his sub and crew, and prevent an all out World War. Sarsgaard is the panicky, inexperienced reactor officer who's every nuke sub captain's nightmare. Strong performances by the lead actors almost overshadows their flimsy Russian accents. Bigelow shot on a set built to scale, with parts salvaged from an old diesel sub. Loosely based on a military incident that happened in 1961 but wasn't publicly revealed until the 1990s. **138m/C; VHS, DVD, Blu-Ray.** Harrison Ford; Liam Neeson; Peter Sarsgaard; Joss Ackland; John Shrapnel; Donald (Don) Sumpter; Tim Woodward; Ravil Isyanov; Christian Camargo; Steve Nicholson; ***D:*** Kathryn Bigelow; ***W:*** Christopher Kyle; ***C:*** Jeff Cronenweth; ***M:*** Klaus Badelt.

K-PAX 1/2 2001 **(PG-13)** Spacey plays his patented "smirky guy with a secret" again in this tale of aliens and the humans who love them. Prot (Spacey) is admitted to a psychiatric hospital when he claims to be from outer space. Dr. Powell (Bridges) is assigned his case and soon finds himself intrigued by Prot. It seems that he's going around helping the patients in the hospital to actually get better. His other quirks include an astounding knowledge of astrophysics and an amazing tolerance to Thorazine. After Powell hypnotizes Prot, a deeply hidden personality is unmasked, but the actual truth about his identity is left open to interpretation. Bridges and Spacey work well together, and they save this sentimental E.T. tale from turning to schmaltzy mush. **120m/C; VHS, DVD.** Kevin Spacey; Jeff Bridges; Mary McCormack; Alfre Woodard; David Patrick Kelly; Saul Williams; Peter Gerety; Celia Weston; Ajay Naidu; John Toles-Bey; Kimberly Scott; Mary Mara; Aaron Paul; William Lucking; ***D:*** Iain Softley; ***W:*** Charles Leavitt; ***C:*** John Mathieson; ***M:*** Ed Shearmur.

Kaaterskill Falls 2001 Indie horror flick suffers from its obvious low budget and stilted improvisations. Yuppie couple Mitchell (Riggs) and Ren (Howard) are driving to a cabin in upstate New York where they hope to rekindle their disintegrating marriage. Ren decides to offer monosyllabic hitchhiker Lyle (Leslie) a ride to a nearby motel. But Lyle soons makes an appearance at their cabin and they decide to extent their hospitality to inviting him in for dinner. This is the first of many mistakes. **87m/C; VHS, DVD.** Mitchell Riggs; Hilary Howard; Anthony Leslie; ***D:*** Josh Apter; Peter Olsen; ***W:*** Mitchell Riggs; Hilary Howard; Anthony Leslie; Josh Apter; Peter Olsen; ***C:*** Peter Olsen.

Kabei: Our Mother 2008 Director Yamada's 80th film follows the vicissitudes of the Nogami family after professor Shigeru Nogami is thrown in prison in 1940 for protesting Japan's invasion of China. This leaves his delicate wife Kayo to support their two young daughters with the unexpected help of Shigeru's former student, clumsy, bumptious Toru. Narrow and soapy exploration about a paragon of motherhood. Japanese with subtitles. **133m/C; DVD.** *JP* Sayuri Yoshinago; Mitsugoro Bando; Tsurube Shofukutei; Umenosuke Nakamura; Tadanobu Asano; ***D:*** Yoji Yamada; ***W:*** Emiko Hiramatsu; Yoji Yamada; ***C:*** Mutsuo Naganuma; ***M:*** Isao Tamita.

Kaboom 1/2 2011 Araki's surreal, haphazard college campus-set paranoid comedy follows a group of sexually-ambiguous, drug-taking students who discover an apocalyptic plot, which may be just in their overly-active imaginations. Bisexual freshman Smith (Dekker) begins having weird dreams that could be psychic visions introducing him to a series of mysterious characters, cults, and death. **86m/C; Blu-Ray.** *US FR* Thomas Dekker; Haley Bennett; Roxane Mesquida; Chris Zylka; Juno Temple; Andy Fischer-Price; Jason Olive; Brennan Mejia; James Duval; Kelly Lynch; Nicole LaLiberte; ***D:*** Gregg Araki; ***W:*** Gregg Araki; ***C:***

Sandra Valde-Hansen; ***M:*** Ulrich Schnauss; Mark Peters.

Kadosh **1999** Meir (Hattab) and his wife Rivka (Abecassis) are ultra-Orthodox Jews living in the Mea Shearim quarter of Jerusalem. They have been married for 10 years and are still childless, so Meir is being pressured by his rabbi father to divorce his wife (though they love each other) and remarry. Rivka learns the fertility problem is with her husband but can do nothing because of religious tenets and she leaves their home. Meanwhile, Rivka's younger sister, Malka (Barda), contemplates abandoning her unhappy arranged marriage to be with the man she loves. Hebrew with subtitles. **110m/C; VHS, DVD.** *IS* Yael Abecassis; Yoram Hattab; Meital Barda; Sami Hori; Uri Klauzner; Yussef Abu-Warda; ***D:*** Amos Gitai; ***W:*** Amos Gitai; Eliette Abecassis; ***C:*** Renato Berta; ***M:*** Louis Sclavis.

Kaena: The Prophecy ½ *Kaena: La Prophetie* **2003 (PG-13)** Sci-fi fantasy epic about a brave young humanoid girl (Dunst) who resists her society's groveling submission to its tyrannical "gods." Once cast out, she discovers many hidden secrets about her world. She meets an old astronaut/scientist (Harris) who is the last survivor of the ancient spaceship-wreck that formed her world, and who may possess the power to revive or destroy it as well. Visually stunning movie is France's first entry into full-length CGI animation. Texture is so rich and intricate, it should hold up well to multiple viewings. Characters are a bit thin, and the dubbed dialogue is annoyingly flat and unnatural. It would be interesting to see the French version. One of Richard Harris' last performances. **91m/C; DVD.** *FR CA* ***V:*** Kirsten Dunst; Richard Harris; Anjelica Huston; Michael McShane; Greg Proops; Keith David; ***D:*** Chris Delaporte; Pascal Pinon; ***W:*** Chris Delaporte; Tarik Hamdine; ***M:*** Farid Russlan.

Kagemusha ½ *The Shadow Warrior; The Double* **1980 (PG)** A thief is rescued from the gallows because of his striking resemblance to a warlord in 16th Century Japan. When the ambitious warlord is fatally wounded, the thief is required to pose as the warlord. In Japanese with English subtitles. **160m/C; VHS, DVD, Blu-Ray.** *JP* Tatsuya Nakadai; Tsutomu Yamazaki; Kenichi Hagiwara; Hideji Otaki; ***D:*** Akira Kurosawa; ***W:*** Akira Kurosawa; Masato Ide; ***C:*** Kazuo Miyagawa; Masaharu Ueda; ***M:*** Shinichiro Ikebe. British Acad. '80: Director (Kurosawa); Cannes '80: Film; Cesar '81: Foreign Film.

Kahlil Gibran's The Prophet **2015 (PG)** Animated adapation of the poems found in Lebanese poet Khalil Gibran's classic book The Prophet (1923), interspersed with a story about a poet-artist (Neeson) who leaves his life in exile and goes back to his native country with the help of his housekeeper (Hayek) and her daughter (Wallis). Hayek has been trying to produce this animated retelling of the beloved anthology for years, finally assembling a talented and diverse array of animators to bring Gibran's work to life. Roger Allers, who headed Disney animation in its renaissance in the late '80s and early '90s, serves as writer and producer of the story. The result is a beautiful, lyrical film that feels more like poetry than prose. **85m/C; DVD.** Liam Neeson; Salma Hayek; John Krasinski; Quvenzhane Wallis; Alfred Molina; ***D:*** Roger Allers; ***W:*** Roger Allers; ***M:*** Gabriel Yared.

Kalamity ½ **2010 (R)** Insecure Billy (Stahl) returns to his North Virginia hometown after breaking up with his longtime girlfriend Alice (Garrett). He reunites with childhood friend Stanley (Jackson), whose flirty girlfriend Ashley (Tal) has disappeared. Billy may not have noticed, but Stanley's nerdy roommate Christian (Clark) warns Billy that Stanley's hostility is growing and he's become dangerous. **98m/C; DVD.** Nick Stahl; Jonathan Jackson; Christopher M. Clark; Alona Tal; Beau Garrett; Robert Forster; Patricia Kalember; ***D:*** James Hausler; ***W:*** James Hausler; ***C:*** Jim Hunter; ***M:*** Chistopher Mangum. **VIDEO**

Kaleidoscope ½ **1966** Playboy Barney Lincoln (Beatty) likes to get into trouble for the thrill of it and his latest scheme is cheating the casinos at cards. This raises the suspicions of ex-flame Angel (York), who tells her Scotland Yard daddy (Revill). He offers Barney a chance at redemption if he'll help financially ruin illegal drug importer Dominion (Porter). Beatty is attractive but wooden and is constantly shown up by his Brit co-stars in this crime caper flop. **103m/C; VHS, DVD.** *GB* Warren Beatty; Susannah York; Clive Revill; Eric Porter; Murray Melvin; George Sewell; ***D:*** Jack Smight; ***W:*** Robert B. Carrington; Jane-Howard Carrington; ***C:*** Christopher Challis; ***M:*** Howard Myers.

Kalifornia ½ **1993 (R)** "Badlands" meets the '90s in a road trip with the hitchhikers from hell. Early Grayce (Pitt) is your average slimeball who murders his landlord and hops a ride with his waifish girlfriend Adele (Lewis) from Kentucky to California with Brian (Duchovny), a yuppie writer interested in mass murderers, and his sultry photographer girlfriend Carrie (Forbes). Pitt and Lewis were still an item when they made this. Pitt reportedly wanted to play against type, and as pretty boy gone homicidal, he succeeds. Extremely violent and disturbing. Also available in an unrated version. **117m/C; VHS, DVD, Blu-Ray, UMD.** Brad Pitt; Juliette Lewis; David Duchovny; Michelle Forbes; Sierra Pecheur; Lois Hall; Mars Callahan; ***D:*** Dominic Sena; ***W:*** Tim Metcalfe; ***C:*** Bojan Bazelli; ***M:*** Carter Burwell.

Kama Sutra: A Tale of Love **1996** Erotic but flawed fantasy covering the sexual and political wiles of palace life in 16th-century India. Princess Tara (Choudhury) and girlhood friend/servant Maya (Varma) are close until the Princess becomes jealous of the even-more beautiful Maya. In revenge for a public humiliation, Maya seduces Tara's dissolute fiance, Raj Singh (Andrews), and is banished from the palace after the wedding. She becomes involved with handsome royal sculptor Jai Kumar (Tikaram) and later learns the sexual arts of the Kama Sutra, becoming the chief courtesan to the Raj. Messy, somewhat overwrought plot, extremely attractive cast. Also available in an R-rated version. **117m/C; VHS, DVD.** *IN* Indira Varma; Sarita Choudhury; Ramon Tikaram; Naveen Andrews; Devi Rekha; ***D:*** Mira Nair; ***W:*** Mira Nair; Helena Kriel; ***C:*** Declan Quinn; ***M:*** Mychael Danna. Ind. Spirit '98: Cinematog.

Kamikaze Girls ½ *Shimotsuma monogatari* **2004** Momoko (Kyoko Fukada), is hit by a cabbage truck and her life is told in flashback. Her Yakuza father is abandoned by her mom for the doctor who delivered her, and instead of living in the fashion district they now live in a country backwater. Being devoted to Japanese Lolita fashion she is disgusted by the local rednecks who are proud of buying their clothes at the Japanese version of Walmart. Against all odds she befriends Ichigo (Anna Tsuchiya) a half Russian, half Japanese female biker. They go on a road trip to meet a legendary tailor for a special jacket for the retiring leader of Ichigo's gang. **103m/C; DVD.** *JP* Kyoko Fukada; Sadao Abe; Anna Tsuchiya; Eiko Koike; Shin Yazawa; ***D:*** Tetsuya Nakashima; ***W:*** Tetsuya Nakashima; Nobara Takemoto; ***C:*** Masakazu Ato; ***M:*** Yoko Kanno.

Kampai! For the Love of Sake **2016** This feature-length documentary offers an in-depth look at sake, the fermented rice wine. Most closely identified with Japanese culture and cuisine, sake has been produced for centuries. The documentary examines the production process from rice paddies in Japan to breweries in a number of countries around the world. The bulk of the documentary focuses on the perspectives and experiences of three promoters of sake, including the first foreign master brewer in Japan, an American journalist, and a fifth-generation Japanese brewer who wants to adapt to the changing global market. **95m/C; DVD, Streaming, Download.** ***D:*** Mirai Konishi; ***C:*** Mirai Konishi; Masami Inomoto; ***M:*** Stephen Viens.

Kanal ½ *They Loved Life* **1956** Wajda's first major success, a grueling account of Warsaw patriots, upon the onset of the Nazis toward the end of the war, fleeing through the ruined city's sewers. Highly acclaimed. Part 2 of Wajda's "War Trilogy," preceded by "A Generation" and followed by "Ashes and Diamonds." In Polish with English subtitles or dubbed. **96m/B; VHS, DVD.** *PL* Teresa Izewska; Tadeusz Janczar; Vladek Sheybal; Emil Karewicz; Wienczylaw Glinski; ***D:*** Andrzej Wajda; ***W:*** Jerzy Stefan Stawinski; ***C:*** Jerzy Lipman; ***M:*** Jan Krenz. Cannes '57: Grand Jury Prize.

Kandahar **2001** Nafas (Pazira) and her family emigrated to Canada from Afghanistan, although they were forced to leave behind Nafas's crippled sister. Now, the sister has vowed to commit suicide rather than live any longer under Taliban rule and Nafas returns to try and save her. But journeying to Kandahar is a maze of obstacles and restrictions. Farsi and English. **85m/C; VHS, DVD.** *IA* Nelofer Pazira; Hassan Tantai; Sadou Teymouri; ***D:*** Mohsen Makhmalbaf; ***W:*** Mohsen Makhmalbaf; ***C:*** Ebraheem Ghafouri; ***M:*** Mohammad Reza Darvishi.

The Kane Files ½ **2010 (R)** Competent, low-budget action flick. Hitman Scott Kane (Fuller) has gone straight, but his young son needs expensive medical treatment and he turns to crime boss Daniel Morgan (Atherton) for one last job. Morgan doublecrosses him by sending crooked cop Olsen (Embry) to kill Kane, which is a big mistake as Kane doesn't have a problem upping the body count to keep his family safe. **91m/C; DVD.** Drew Fuller; Ethan (Randall) Embry; William Atherton; William Devane; Whitney Able; Eve Mauro; ***D:*** Benjamin Gourley; ***C:*** Ty Arnold; ***M:*** Jason Livesay. **VIDEO**

Kangaroo Jack **2002 (PG)** Pals O'Connell and Anderson are forced to deliver mob money to Australia, but it's accidentally stolen from them by a kangaroo. If this sounds like a sad excuse for a movie, it is. Aside from some beautiful shots of the Australian landscape, there's little redeeming value. Jokes are lowbrow and (even worse) not funny, script is bland and mainly uninspired. Walken must've owed producer Jerry Bruckheimer a favor. The kangaroo was computer-generated, but still had more charisma than any of the leading actors. **88m/C; VHS, DVD.** Jerry O'Connell; Anthony Anderson; Estella Warren; Michael Shannon; Christopher Walken; Bill Hunter; Marton Csokas; David Ngoombujarra; ***D:*** David McNally; ***W:*** Steve Bing; Scott Rosenberg; ***C:*** Peter Menzies, Jr.

The Kansan **1943** The marshall in a Kansas town won't rest until he's stamped out all traces of corruption. **79m/B; VHS, DVD.** Richard Dix; Victor Jory; Albert Dekker; Jane Wyatt; Eugene Pallette; Robert Armstrong; Beryl Wallace; Clem Bevans; Hobart Cavanaugh; Francis McDonald; George Reeves; Willie Best; ***D:*** George Archainbaud; ***W:*** Harold Shumate; ***C:*** Russell Harlan; ***M:*** Gerard Carbonara.

Kansas **1988 (R)** Two young men, one a lawless rebel, the other a rational loner, stage a bank heist, and then go on the lam. Lame plot and very weak acting combine to make this film a dud. **111m/C; VHS, DVD; Open Captioned.** Matt Dillon; Andrew McCarthy; Leslie Hope; Kyra Sedgwick; ***D:*** David Stevens; ***W:*** Spencer Eastman; ***C:*** David Eggby; ***M:*** Pino Donaggio.

Kansas City **1995 (R)** Altman mixes music, politics, crime and the movies in this bittersweet homage to his hometown, set in the jazz-driven 1930s. Star-struck, tough-talking Blondie (Leigh) kidnaps Carolyn Stilton (Richardson), a self-sedating wife of a political shaker (Murphy), in a hairbrained scheme to save her husband from a local mobster (Belafonte). Styled to imitate the brilliant jazz scores played by the likes of Joshua Redman and James Carter, the action can become a bit confusing and Leigh is beyond irritating with her derivative dame routine. Belafonte, however, is brilliant, relishing the part of the legendary Seldom Seen, a real-life K.C. gangster. **110m/C; VHS, DVD, Blu-Ray.** Jennifer Jason Leigh; Miranda Richardson; Harry Belafonte; Michael Murphy; Dermot Mulroney; Steve Buscemi; Brooke Smith; Jane Adams; ***D:*** Robert Altman; ***W:*** Frank Barhydt; Robert Altman; ***C:*** Oliver Stapleton; ***M:*** Hal Willner. N.Y. Film Critics '96: Support. Actor (Belafonte).

Kansas City Bomber **1972** The only explosions here are the tempermental kind. Divorced mom Diane "K.C." Carr (Welch) is a roller derby gal who signs on with the team of ambitious owner Burt Henry (McCarthy). Since she's fooling around with Burt, most of her teammates don't like K.C. much, especially team captain Jackie (Kallianiotes), a mean drunk who's afraid of losing her palce to the new girl, which results in a showdown match. Sometimes cheesy entertainment that's all grind and no glamor. Welch was game to do her own stunts and Foster has an early role as K.C.'s daughter, Rita. **96m/C; DVD.** Raquel Welch; Kevin McCarthy; Helena Kallianiotes; Jeanne Cooper; Norman Alden; Mary Kay Pass; Jodie Foster; ***D:*** Jerrold Freedman; ***W:*** Thomas (Tom) Rickman; Calvin Clements, Sr.; ***C:*** Fred W. Koenekamp; ***M:*** Don Ellis.

Kansas City Confidential **1952** An ex-cop on the wrong side of the law launches a sophisticated armored car heist. A disgruntled ex-con gets arrested for the crime on circumstantial evidence. When released, he scours the underworld for the real thieves. **98m/B; VHS, DVD, Blu-Ray.** John Payne; Coleen Gray; Preston Foster; Neville Brand; Lee Van Cleef; Jack Elam; Carleton Young; ***D:*** Phil Karlson; ***W:*** Rowland Brown; George Bruce; Harry Essex; Harold Greene; ***C:*** George E. Diskant; ***M:*** Paul Sawtell.

Kansas Pacific **1953** A group of Confederate sympathizers try to stop the Kansas Pacific Railroad from reaching the West Coast in the 1860s. **73m/C; VHS, DVD.** Sterling Hayden; Eve Miller; Barton MacLane; Reed Hadley; Douglas Hadley; ***D:*** Ray Nazarro.

Kansas Raiders **1950** Young outlaws Jesse and Frank James, along with Kit Dalton and Cole and James Younger, join up with Col. William Quantrill and his guerilla raiders in Kansas during the Civil War. Jesse refuses to believe that Quantrill, who's assumed the role of surrogate father, is merely a murderous thief even after the others have had enough. It's pure fiction but fast-paced with lots of gunplay. **80m/C; DVD.** Audie Murphy; Brian Donlevy; Richard Long; Tony Curtis; James Best; Dewey Martin; Marguerite Chapman; David Wolfe; Scott Brady; ***D:*** Ray Enright; ***W:*** Robert L. Richards; ***C:*** Irving Glassberg; ***M:*** Milton Rosen.

Kaos *Chaos* **1985 (R)** The Taviani brothers adaptation of four stories by Luigi Pirandello ("The Other Son," "Moonstruck," "The Jar," and "Requiem"), which look at peasant life in Sicily, ranging from the comic to the tragic. A fictional epilog, "Conversing with Mother," has Pirandello talking with the spirit of his dead mother. As with any anthology some stories are stronger than others but all possess the Taviani's great visual style and some fine acting. In Italian with English subtitles. **188m/C; VHS, DVD.** *IT* Margarita Lozano; Claudio Bigagli; Massimo Bonetti; Omero Antonutti; Enrica Maria Modugno; Ciccio Ingrassia; Franco Franchi; Biagio Barone; Salvatore Rossi; Franco Scaldati; Pasquale Spadola; Regina Bianchi; ***D:*** Paolo Taviani; Vittorio Taviani; ***W:*** Paolo Taviani; Vittorio Taviani; ***C:*** Giuseppe Lanci; ***M:*** Nicola Piovani.

Kapo **1959** A 14-year-old Jewish girl and her family are imprisoned by the Nazis in a concentration camp. There, the girl changes identities with the help of the camp doctor, and rises to the position of camp guard. She proceeds to become taken with her power until a friend commits suicide and jolts the girl back into harsh reality. An Academy Award nominee for Best Foreign Film (lost to "The Virgin Spring"). Primarily English dialogue, with subtitles for foreign language. **116m/B; VHS, DVD.** *IT FR YU* Susan Strasberg; Laurent Terzieff; Emmanuelle Riva; Gianni "John" Garko; ***D:*** Gillo Pontecorvo; ***W:*** Gillo Pontecorvo.

Karate Cop ½ **1991 (R)** In a future without law or order John Travis (Marchini) is the last cop on earth. He saves Rachel, a beautiful scientist, from a band of scavengers and together they hunt for a hidden crystal with mysterious powers. Only first John has to defeat a gladiator in a martial arts fight to the death. **90m/C; VHS, DVD.** Ron Marchini; Carrie Chambers; David Carradine; Michael Bristow; D.W. Landingham; Michael Foley; Dana Bentley; ***D:*** Alan Roberts.

Karate Dog **2004** Totally inept comedy finds wisecracking dog Cho-Cho (voiced by Chase) teaming up with a geeky detective (Rex) to investigate the murder of his Zen karate master (Morita). Presumably everyone involved had bills to pay. **?m/CDVD.** Simon Rex; Jon Voight; Jaime Pressly; Noriyuki "Pat" Morita; Thomas Kretschmann; ***V:*** Chevy Chase; Lori Petty; Nicolette Sheridan; ***D:*** Bob

(Benjamin) Clark; *W:* Steven Paul; *C:* Brian Pearson. **VIDEO**

The Karate Kid 1/2 **1984 (PG)** A teenage boy finds out that Karate involves using more than your fists when a handyman agrees to teach him martial arts. The friendship that they develop is deep and sincere; the Karate is only an afterthought. From the director of the original "Rocky," this movie is easy to like. **126m/C; VHS, DVD, Blu-Ray.** Ralph Macchio; Noriyuki "Pat" Morita; Elisabeth Shue; Randee Heller; Martin Kove; Chad McQueen; William Zabka; Larry B. Scott; Robert Garrison; Tony O'Dell; Frances Bay; Peter Jason; Andrew Shue; *D:* John G. Avildsen; *W:* Robert Mark Kamen; *M:* Bill Conti.

The Karate Kid 1/2 **2010 (PG)** Ingratiating, formulaic (too long) martial arts/family drama. Will Smith's kid, skinny and charismatic, takes on Ralph Macchio's role of the bullied boy learning how to defend himself, with Chan as his wise but eccentric mentor. Twelve-year-old Dre and his mom move to Beijing, China for her work and Dre is constantly (and brutally) beaten up by the school bullies. When he's rescued by quiet janitor Mr. Han, Dre wants to learn kung fu from this unassuming master. First he must learn discipline, focus, and inner strength before the big martial arts tournament. **140m/C; DVD, Blu-Ray.** *US CH* Jaden Smith; Jackie Chan; Taraji P. Henson; Han Wenwen; Rongguang Yu; Wang Zhenwei; *D:* Harald Zwart; *W:* Christopher Murphey; Robert Mark Kamen; *C:* Roger Pratt; *M:* James Horner.

The Karate Kid: Part 2 1/2 **1986 (PG)** Sequel to the first film wherein our high-kicking hero tests his mettle in real-life karate exchanges in Okinawa, and settles a long-standing score. Followed by a second sequel. **95m/C; VHS, DVD.** Ralph Macchio; Noriyuki "Pat" Morita; Danny Kamekona; Martin Kove; Tamlyn Tomita; Nobu McCarthy; Yuji Okumoto; William Zabka; *D:* John G. Avildsen; *W:* Robert Mark Kamen; *C:* James A. Crabe; *M:* Bill Conti.

The Karate Kid: Part 3 1/2 **1989 (PG)** Second sequel takes a tired plot and doesn't do much to perk it up. Macchio again battles an evil nemesis and learns about himself, but this time Morita refuses to be a part of his training until, of course, Macchio desperately needs his help. Followed by "The Next Karate Kid," which introduces a new kid—a girl. **105m/C; VHS, DVD, Blu-Ray.** Ralph Macchio; Noriyuki "Pat" Morita; Thomas Ian Griffith; Martin Kove; Sean Kanan; Robin (Robyn) Lively; Gabe Jarret; Frances Bay; *D:* John G. Avildsen; *W:* Robert Mark Kamen; *C:* Steve Yaconelli; *M:* Bill Conti.

Karla 1/2 **2006 (R)** Routine true crime saga based on the story of Canadian serial killers Paul Bernardo and Karla Homolka, the girls they murdered through sexual torture, and the sensational trial that followed. Told in flashback as Karla talks to her shrink in an effort to mitigate her part in the crimes. **101m/C; DVD.** Laura Prepon; Misha Collins; Tess Harper; Patrick Bauchau; Alexandra Boyd; Shawn Hoffman; Emilie Jacobs; Cherilyn Hayres; Adam Lieberman; *D:* Joel Bender; *W:* Joel Bender; Michael D. Sellers; Manette Beth Rosen; *C:* Charles Mills; *M:* Timothy S. (Tim) Jones.

Karma Police 1/2 **2008** The karma police are a secret organization that believe in rewarding the good and punishing the bad. Newest recruit Charles West is happy with his job but finds that his own past may prove karma is not on his side. **90m/C; DVD.** John Wesley Shipp; David Sullivan; Jessica Turner; Chamblee Ferguson; Nicole Leigh; Dan Forsythe; *D:* John Venable; *W:* John Venable; *C:* Red Sanders; *M:* Benjamin Stanton. **VIDEO**

Kaspar Hauser **1993** Historical epic based on the true story of Kaspar Hauser (Eisermann), a 16-year-old found abandoned in Nuremberg, Germany in 1828, who was unable to walk, write, or speak. Entrusted to the scientific concerns of Professor Daumer (Samel), rumors begin to circulate that the boy is actually the Crown Prince of Baden. Supposedly, Kaspar was abducted as a baby and substituted for a child who died so his Uncle Ludwig (Oscsenknecht) could become Grand Duke. Court intrigue and threats abound as Kaspar struggles to survive. German with subtitles. **137m/C; VHS, DVD.** *GE* Andre Eisermann; Jeremy Clyde; Katharina Thalbach; Udo Samel; Uwe Ochsenknecht; *D:* Peter Sehr; *W:* Peter Sehr; *C:* Gernot Roll; *M:* Nikos Mamangakis.

Kate & Leopold 1/2 **2001 (PG-13)** Cute but underwhelming romantic comedy involving time travel. Eccentric scientist Stuart (Schreiber) finds a portal that allows him to visit New York City in 1876. But his presence is noticed by dashing Leopold, the Duke of Albany (Jackman), who unwittingly follows Stuart to present-day Manhattan. The Duke manages the adjustment quite well, especially after meeting business exec Kay McKay (Ryan), Stuart's ex-girlfriend. Kate's more interested in a big promotion than romance, though she finds Leopold charming if strange. Too bad Leopold can't hang around, he has to go back to 1876 but can Kate be persuaded to go with him? This is familiar territory for Ryan (who's more brittle than perky) but Jackman does chivalry with the best of them. **121m/C; VHS, DVD, Blu-Ray.** Meg Ryan; Hugh Jackman; Liev Schreiber; Breckin Meyer; Natasha Lyonne; Bradley Whitford; Paxton Whitehead; Spalding Gray; Philip Bosco; David Aaron Baker; *D:* James Mangold; *W:* James Mangold; Steven Rogers; *C:* Stuart Dryburgh; *M:* Rolfe Kent. Golden Globes '02: Song ("Until").

The Kate Logan Affair **WOOF! 2010** Truly stupid Canadian thriller. How did rookie Kate Logan even become a cop when she's incompetent and crazy? She makes abject apologies to married French businessman Benoit Gando after accusing him of being a rapist and then seduces him so he won't report her mistake. After an incident with her service revolver, Kate gets Benoit to run away with her and the situation just gets worse (and more unbelievable) from there. **85m/C; DVD.** *CA* Alexis Bledel; Laurent Lucas; Serge Houde; Alan Fawcett; *D:* Noel Mitrani; *W:* Noel Mitrani; *C:* Natalie Moliavko-Visotzky; *M:* James Gelfand.

Kate Plays Christine **2016** Robert Greene's masterful documentary tells the story of Christine Chubbuck, mostly in documentary form. He parallels what he tells us about Chubbuck, a woman news anchor who killed herself on live television in Florida decades ago, with the journey of an actress named Kate Lyn Sheil as she endeavors to play Christine. The result is a fascinating example of performance and depression. Why would a woman do something that horrifying when she knew children and families would be watching? Why would an actress seek to get in the mind of such a sad person? It's a fantastic examination of mental illness and craft. **112m/C; DVD.** Kate Lyn Sheil; Steve Zurk; David Mackey; Michael Ray Davis; Holland Hayes; *D:* Robert Greene; *W:* Robert Greene; *C:* Sean Price Williams; *M:* Keegan DeWitt.

Kate's Addiction **1999 (R)** Kate (Wuhrer) comes to L.A. in search of an old friend (Forke) but she's really interested in more than hanging around. And anyone who gets in her way may not live to regret it. **95m/C; VHS, DVD.** Kari Wuhrer; Farrah Forke; Matt Borlenghi; *D:* Eric De La Barre. **VIDEO**

Kate's Secret **1986** An NBC TV movie. Living in looks-conscious southern California, Kate Stark (Baxter) tries to be the perfect suburban wife and mother. She hides her eating disorder from everyone close to her. As her bulimia worsens, Kate gets into therapy and her fellow patients help her confront her problems. **96m/C; DVD.** Meredith Baxter; Ben Masters; Ed Asner; Shari Belafonte; Tracy Nelson; MacKenzie Phillips; Summer Phoenix; *D:* Arthur Allan Seidelman; *W:* Susan Seeger; *C:* Dennis Dalzell; *M:* J. Peter Robinson. **TV**

Katherine *The Radical* **1975** A young heiress rejects her pampered lifestyle and becomes a violent revolutionary, rebelling against social injustices and the system that spawned them. **98m/C; VHS, DVD.** Sissy Spacek; Art Carney; Jane Wyatt; Henry Winkler; Julie Kavner; Hector Elias; Jenny Sullivan; *D:* Jeremy Paul Kagan. **TV**

Kathleen 1/2 **1941** Temple stars in the title role as a neglected, somewhat bratty 12-year-old who wants her busy widowed dad John to remarry so she can have a stepmom and be a real family. But she's strongly opposed when her father chooses icy Lorraine. Kathleen acts out and child shrink A. Martha Kent comes in as a temporary governess leading Kathleen to play matchmaker. Not bad but a big boxoffice flop for MGM. **88m/B; DVD.** Shirley Temple; Herbert Marshall; Laraine Day; Gail Patrick; Felix Bressart; Nella Walker; *D:* Harold Bucquet; *W:* Mary C. McCall; *C:* Sidney Wagner; *M:* Franz Waxman.

Katie Tippel *Katie's Passion; Cathy Tippel; Hot Sweat; Keetje Tippel* **1975 (R)** In 1881 Amsterdam, a young Dutch prostitute works her way out of poverty and enters a world of education and wealth. A Victorian tale of exploitation with a tough and intelligent Cinderella heroine. In Dutch with English subtitles. **104m/C; VHS, DVD.** *NL* Monique Van De Ven; Rutger Hauer; Eddie Brugman; Hannah De Leeuwe; Andrea Domburg; *D:* Paul Verhoeven; *W:* Gerard Soeteman; *C:* Jan De Bont; *M:* Roger van Otterloo.

Katy Perry: Part of Me 1/2 **2012 (PG)** Pop star Perry offers an inside look into her seemingly fairytale life, as well as a backstage pass to her recent major worldwide tour. She shares her journey to success, which is far from the overnight sensation she seemed to be, and exposes the side of herself that isn't just the fairytale dream. Viewers see how difficult it is to put on a major tour while maintaining personal relationships and remaining a positive role model for young women as a celebrity in the public eye. A real treat for Perry fans and those who enjoy behind-the-music style biopics. **93m/C; DVD, Blu-Ray.** Katy Perry; Adam Marcello; Casey Hopper; Patrick Matera; Max Hart; Joseph Moreau; *D:* Dan Cutforth; Jane Lipsitz; *M:* Deborah Lurie.

Katyn **2007** In 1939, Joseph Stalin and Adolf Hitler signed a nonaggression pact that allowed both countries to destroy Polish sovereignty. In 1940, Stalin ordered the massacre of 15,000 Polish officers, who were buried in the Katyn Forest, and then officially blamed the Nazis when the mass graves were discovered. Director Wajda dispenses with sentimentality, using restraint to tell the story from various viewpoints, including that of Anna (Ostaszewska), who's searching for her husband Andrzej (Zmijewski), who's in an internment camp and destined to be killed; Jerzy (Chyra), a guilt-ridden survivor; and two sisters (Cielecka, Glinska) who take opposite stances in the postwar Soviet regime. Polish, Russian, and German with subtitles. **121m/C; Blu-Ray.** *PL* Jan Englert; Maja Ostaszewska; Artur Zmijewski; Andrzej Chyra; Magdalena Cielecka; Agnieszka Glinska; *D:* Andrzej Wajda; *W:* Andrzej Wajda; Wladyslaw Pasikowski; Przemyslaw Nowarkowski; *C:* Pawel Edelman; *M:* Krzysztof Penderecki.

Kavik the Wolf Dog 1/2 *The Courage of Kavik, the Wolf Dog* **1980** Heartwarming story of a courageous dog's love and suffering for the boy he loves. **99m/C; VHS, DVD.** Ronny Cox; Linda Sorensen; Andrew Ian McMillian; Chris Wiggins; John Ireland; *D:* Peter Carter. **TV**

Kawa **2011** An adult coming-out drama from New Zealand based on Witi Ihimaera's novel "Nights in the Garden of Spain." Successful Maori businessman Kawa has a wife, two kids, and a commitment to another man, Chris. With his father retiring, Kawa's expected to take over the family business and legacy but he can't take the pressure of leading a double life anymore. The situation finally comes to the breaking point as Chris arrives at his father's birthday celebration. **77m/C; DVD.** *NZ* Calvin Tuteao; Natalie Boltt; Dean O'Gorman; George Henare; Vicky Haughton; *D:* Katie Wolfe; *W:* Kate McDermott; *C:* Fred Renata; *M:* Joel Haines.

Kazaam 1/2 **1996 (PG)** Twelve-year-old Max (Capra) is having problems—bullies are chasing him and his single mom's just found a new boyfriend. But his luck seems ready to change when a battered boombox reveals a seven-foot rappin' genie named Kazaam (O'Neal). The kid's beyond obnoxious and Shaq shouldn't plan to give up b-ball anytime soon (at least for an acting career), even though director Glaser did think up the part for the tall guy just before he met him at an NBA All-Star Game. **93m/C; VHS, DVD, Blu-Ray.** Francis Capra; Shaquille O'Neal; Ally Walker; John A. Costelloe; Marshall Manesh; James Acheson; *D:* Paul Michael Glaser; *W:* Christian Ford; Roger Soffer; *C:* Charles Minsky; *M:* Christopher Tyng.

Keane **2004 (R)** Unflinching, unsettling, and intense portrait of grief, and one man's struggle to regain his sanity. William Keane (Lewis), a wanders an NYC bus terminal, searching for his daughter, who may or may not have disappeared from there a year earlier while in his care. He struggles to hold himself together to continue his search when he meets, and helps, a fellow lost soul, Lynn (Ryan), who trusts him enough to ask him to watch her seven year old daughter Kira. Lewis's performance more than stands up to the constant scrutiny director/writer keeps on his character, as the tension of his inner struggle with himself mounts. **100m/C; DVD.** Damian Lewis; Abigail Breslin; Amy Ryan; *D:* Lodge Kerrigan; *W:* Lodge Kerrigan; *C:* John Foster.

Keanu 1/2 **2016 (R)** The first feature film from the comedy duo behind Comedy Central's hilarious "Key & Peele" is a hit-and-miss affair, filled with big laughs but also reminiscent of a sketch from their show stretched out to feature length. Rell (Peele) is a sad sack just dumped by his girlfriend who finds an adorable kitten on his front step who he names Keanu. Michael-Key plays his cousin Clarence. When they're out one day, Rell's place is ransacked and Keanu is stolen. The guys have to go deep into the world of drug dealers to get their kitty back. **100m/C; DVD, Blu-Ray.** Jordan Peele; Keegan Michael Key; Tiffany Haddish; Method Man; Darrell Britt-Gibson; *D:* Peter Atencio; *W:* Jordan Peele; Alex Rubens; *C:* Jas Shelton; *M:* Steve Jablonsky; Nathan Whitehead.

Keaton's Cop **1990 (R)** Another cheap cop comedy involving the mistaken identity of an important mob witness. **95m/C; VHS, DVD.** Lee Majors; Abe Vigoda; Don Rickles; *D:* Robert Burge.

Kedi **2017** A documentary about the cats of Istanbul probably sounds like something you'd rather watch on PBS in short form, if it all, but this film does a lot with its very simple premise. It's a work not so much about feline life in Turkey as it is about the people around these animals and the world they inhabit. The filmmakers keep their cameras at cat level, but they capture a city of people who respect and admire the animals they allow so freely to wander in and out of their buildings and homes. It's a delicate, fascinating film. **80m/C; DVD, Blu-Ray.** Bülent Üstün; *D:* Ceyda Torun; *C:* Alp Korfali; Charlie Wuppermann; *M:* Kira Fontana.

Keep 'Em Flying **1941** Bud and Lou star in the this wartime morale-booster that hasn't aged well. The duo follow their barnstorming friend into flight academy; a not-too-taxing plot includes five musical numbers and two Martha Rayes (she plays twins). **86m/B; VHS, DVD.** Bud Abbott; Lou Costello; Martha Raye; *D:* Arthur Lubin.

Keep My Grave Open *The House Where Hell Froze Over* **1980 (R)** A woman lives in an isolated house where a series of strange murders take place. She attributes them to her brother, but does he really exist? Made cheaply, but not without style; filmed in Harrison County, Texas. **85m/C; VHS, DVD.** Camilla Carr; Gene Ross; Stephen Tobolowsky; Ann Stafford; Sharon Bunn; Chelcie Ross; *D:* S.F. Brownrigg.

Keep the Faith, Baby 1/2 **2002 (PG)** Showtime drama about larger than life congressman Adam Clayton Powell Jr. (Lennix). The story is told in flashbacks when a young journalist comes to interview the retired Powell. The flamboyant politician started out as a Harlem preacher before being elected to Congress in 1945. He fought the inherent racism of the times but came to grief over charges of misconduct. Williams plays Powell's second wife, jazz pianist Hazel Scott. **107m/C; DVD.** Harry J. Lennix; Vanessa L(ynne) Williams; Russell Hornsby; *D:* Doug McHenry; *W:* Art Washington; *C:* Francis Kenny; *M:* Todd Cochran. **CABLE**

Keep the Lights On **2012** Writer/director Sachs tells an intimate and harrowing tale of doomed love in his semi-autobiographical work about two men with a strong sexual connection but increasingly different lives. Erik (Lindhardt) is a documentary filmmaker who meets closeted lawyer Paul (Booth), who has a significant and increasing drug addiction. As Paul's demons begin to dominate their relationship, Sachs' film takes on the feeling of memory as he chronicles the few highs and many lows of a long-term relationship. The lead performances are brutally honest and fearless. **101m/C; DVD, Blu-Ray.** Thure Lindhardt; Zachary Booth; Paprika Steen; Julianne Nicholson; Sebastian La Cause; ***D:*** Ira Sachs; ***W:*** Ira Sachs; Mauricio Zacharias; ***C:*** Thimios Bakatakis; ***M:*** Arthur Russell.

Keep Walking *Cammina Cammina* **1982 (R)** Respected Italian filmmaker Ermanno Olmi offers his take on the Biblical story of the journey of the Magi. In this interpretation, one of the Magi views a comet in the sky and believes it is a divine message. With a caravan of assistants, soldiers, merchants, and villagers, he travels the direction of the star. Along the way, two more Maji join. For all involved, the journey becomes a test of faith and strength. **171m/C; DVD.** Alberto Fumagalli; Antonio Cucciarre; Eligio Martellucci; Renzo Samminiatesi; Marco Bartolini; ***D:*** Ermanno Olmi; ***W:*** Ermanno Olmi; ***C:*** Ermanno Olmi; Gianni Maddaleni; ***M:*** Bruno Nicolai.

Keep Your Powder Dry 1/2 **1945** Valerie (Turner), Leigh (Day), and Ann (Peters) join the Women's Army Corp for different reasons: party girl Valerie has been financially cut off and has to prove herself to the family trustees, Leigh is an Army brat looking to become an officer, and Ann just wants to be closer to her enlisted husband. Then the trio learns they need to rally around each other as well as the flag. **93m/B; DVD.** Lana Turner; Laraine Day; Susan Peters; Agnes Moorehead; Michael Kirby; Bill Johnson; Natalie Schafer; June Lockhart; Lee Patrick; ***D:*** Edward Buzzell; ***W:*** George Bruce; Mary C. McCall; ***C:*** Ray June; ***M:*** David Snell.

Keeper **1976** Wealthy patients at Underwood Asylum suffer unspeakable horrors while under the care of Lee. Detective Dick Driver investigates. Obscure horror spoof. **96m/C; VHS, DVD.** *CA* Christopher Lee; Tell Schreiber; Sally Gray; ***D:*** Tom Drake; ***W:*** Tom Drake.

The Keeper 1/2 **1996** Disillusioned Paul Lamott (Esposito) is a corrections officer at the King's County House of Detention in Brooklyn. Nevertheless, Paul, who's earning a law degree, is moved by the pleas of Haitian prisoner Jean Baptiste (de Bankole), who swears he's been wrongly accused of rape. Paul, who's father was Haitian, manages to help Jean make bail and then invites him home—to the strong dismay of Paul's teacher wife Angela (Taylor). However, Angela begins warming to Jean's charm—but beware the stranger. **97m/C; VHS, DVD.** Giancarlo Esposito; Regina Taylor; Isaach de Bankole; ***D:*** Joe Brewster; ***W:*** Joe Brewster; ***C:*** Igor Sunara; ***M:*** John Petersen.

The Keeper 1/2 **2009 (R)** Typical B-actioner from Seagal. Forcibly retired from the LAPD, Roland Sallinger gets a call from old friend Connor Wells (DuVall) asking him to become the bodyguard of Connor's trouble-attracting daughter Nikita (Carstens). So Roland heads to Texas where he learns Nikita has survived one kidnapping attempt and Connor hasn't exactly told him everything. **94m/C; DVD.** Steven Seagal; Steph Duvall; Liezl Carstens; Aaron Shivers; Luce Rains; Brian Gamble; ***D:*** Keoni Waxman; ***W:*** Paul A. Birkett; ***C:*** Nathaniel Wilson; ***M:*** Philip White. **VIDEO**

The Keeper 1/2 *Trautmann* **2018** Near the end of World War II, German soldier Bert Traumann (Kross) is captured and sent to a prisoner of war camp in northern England. There, his skills as a soccer goalie are discovered by the coach of a local amateur team. He is allowed to play for the team as long as he returns to the camp each night. Bert's abilities eventually capture the attention of a leading professional team, Manchester City, after the war. He signs with the team but struggles to gain acceptance. Based on a true story, the uplifting sports drama features a balanced script and strong performances. **120m/C; DVD.** David Kross; Freya Mavor; John Henshaw; Harry Melling; Michael Socha; ***D:*** Marcus H. Rosenmuller; ***W:*** Marcus H. Rosenmuller; Nicholas J. Schofield; ***C:*** Daniel Gottschalk; ***M:*** Gerd Baumann. **VIDEO**

The Keeper of the Bees 1/2 **1935** Elderly backwoods faith healer Margaret, her daughter Molly and young niece Scout offer disillusioned artist and WWI vet Jamie a lesson in humanity that also involves Michael, the local bee keeper. Based on the 1875 novel by Gene Stratton-Porter; remade in 1947. **76m/B; DVD.** Emma Dunn; Neil Hamilton; Betty Furness; Edith Fellows; Hobart Bosworth; Lafe (Lafayette) McKee; ***D:*** Christy Cabanne; ***W:*** Adele Buffington; George Waggner; ***C:*** Harry Neumann.

Keeper of the Flame 1/2 **1942** Tracy and Hepburn manage to keep the murk of this story at bay as war correspondent Steven O'Malley (Tracy) is assigned to write about super patriot Robert V. Forrest, who's just died in an accident. Reclusive widow Christine Forrest (Hepburn) finally agrees to help O'Malley out but what our intrepid reporter discovers is that the hero was really a heel—something Christine still doesn't want known. Based on the novel by I.A.R. Wylie. **100m/B; VHS, DVD, Streaming.** Spencer Tracy; Katharine Hepburn; Richard Whorf; Margaret Wycherly; Donald Meek; Stephen McNally; Audrey Christie; Frank Craven; Forrest Tucker; Percy Kilbride; Howard da Silva; Darryl Hickman; ***D:*** George Cukor; ***W:*** Donald Ogden Stewart; ***C:*** William H. Daniels; ***M:*** Bronislau Kaper.

The Keeper: The Legend of Omar Khayyam **2005 (PG)** Account of 11th century poet-astronomer Omar Khayyam and his love triangle in 11th century Persia. First-time director Mashayekh intercuts an autobiographical tale of 12-year-old Kkayyam descendent Kamran (Echahly) in modern Houston. Respectable labor of love is an indie that looks quite epic. Unfortunately, the movie comes off more like an after-school special with a flair for bright costumes. Surprise cameo from Vanessa Redgrave sparks things only for as long as she's on the screen. **95m/C; DVD.** Bruno Lastra; Moritz Bleibtreu; Rade Serbedzija; Vanessa Redgrave; C. Thomas Howell; Diane Baker; Christopher Simpson; Adam Echahly; Marie Espinosa; ***D:*** Kayvan Mashayekh; ***W:*** Kayvan Mashayekh; Belle Avery; ***C:*** Dusan Joksimovic; Matt Cantrell; ***M:*** Elton Ahi.

Keepin' It Real WOOF! **2001** A dishonest rapper convinces his girlfriend to steal a master tape of a rival's song from her father and bring it to him on the other side of the country. She quickly ends up on a bizarre road trip being chased by thugs and would-be rappers. No-budget loser with rapper Kurupt, prominently featured on the box art, barely seen at the end in a couple of scenes. **83m/C; DVD.** Portia Realer; Sean Blakemore; Tommy (Tiny) Lister; ***D:*** Brian Cox; ***W:*** Brian Cox; ***C:*** Luc G. Nicknair.

Keeping Mum 1/2 **2005 (R)** Smith steals the show in this black comedy as homicidal housekeeper Grace. She's just taken a job with harried, oblivious vicar Walter Goodfellow (Atkinson) and his neglected family. Bored wife Gloria (Scott Thomas) is flirting with her brash American golf pro Lance (Swayze); teen daughter Holly is a nympho; and younger son Petey (Parkes) is beset by bullies. But tart-tongued Grace will make everything all right since her lurid past (a stint in a prison for the criminally insane) has not made her squeamish about getting things done. **103m/C; DVD.** *GB* Maggie Smith; Rowan Atkinson; Patrick Swayze; Kristin Scott Thomas; Emilia Fox; James Booth; Liz Smith; Tamsin Egerton; Toby Parkes; ***D:*** Niall Johnson; ***W:*** Niall Johnson; Richard Russo; ***C:*** Gavin Finney; ***M:*** Dickon Hinchliffe.

The Keeping Room 1/2 **2015 (R)** Just when you think there are no more angles to explore regarding cinematic depictions of the Civil War, along comes this film which could be described as a Feminist Western. Three women (Marling, Steinfeld, Otaru) are stuck in their large home as the men in their lives are off fighting the war. When one reveals their predicament in front of a couple of low-lives in a bar (Worthington, Soller), an assault ensues in which they must protect their property and lives from the men coming to take both. It's an effective, memorable piece of work, carried by another strong performance from Marling. **95m/C; DVD, Blu-Ray.** Brit Marling; Hailee Steinfeld; Sam Worthington; Muna Otaru; Ned Dennehy; ***D:*** Daniel Barber; ***W:*** Julia Hart; ***C:*** Martin Ruhe; ***M:*** Martin Phipps.

Keeping the Faith 1/2 **2000 (PG-13)** Norton's directorial debut sounds like a bad bar joke but turns out to be a slick, if meandering, romantic comedy. He's a priest, Brian, whose longtime best friend Jake (Stiller) is a rabbi with a congregation that wants him married to a nice Jewish girl. As kids, their mutual best pal was Anna, who returns to New York as a workaholic corporate exec (Elfman). The friendship is re-established but so is something more—both men fall for the lady and, unbeknownst to Brian, Anna and Jake begin an affair. More than sparks fly. **127m/C; VHS, DVD.** Edward Norton; Ben Stiller; Jenna Elfman; Anne Bancroft; Eli Wallach; Milos Forman; Ron Rifkin; Holland Taylor; Rena Sofer; Lisa Edelstein; Bodhi (Pine) Elfman; ***D:*** Edward Norton; ***W:*** Stuart Blumberg; ***C:*** Anastas Michos; ***M:*** Elmer Bernstein.

Keeping Track **1986 (R)** Two tourists witness a murder and robbery and find the stolen $5 million on a New York-bound train. The two are relentlessly pursued by everyone, including the CIA and Russian spies. **102m/C; VHS, DVD.** Michael Sarrazin; Margot Kidder; Alan Scarfe; Ken Pogue; Vlasta Vrana; Donald Pilon; ***D:*** Robin Spry.

Keeping Up with the Joneses **2016 (PG-13)** Jeff and Karen Gaffney (Galifianakis & Fisher) are an average couple in middle America, but their lives are thrown into upheaval when they get a pair of gorgeous new neighbors: Tim & Natalie Jones (Hamm & Gadot). They become obsessed with the pair, soon discovering that the gorgeous couple are actually international spies, and going on a madcap adventure. If you're looking for a comedy rental, you could do a lot worse, but you could also do a lot better, especially given the talented cast here. Everyone here is comedically talented, but the script isn't funny enough. **105m/C; DVD, Blu-Ray.** Zach Galifianakis; Jon Hamm; Isla Fisher; Gal Gadot; Patton Oswalt; ***D:*** Greg Mottola; ***W:*** Michael LeSieur; ***C:*** Andrew Dunn; ***M:*** Jake Monaco.

Keeping Up with the Steins **2006 (PG-13)** Benjamin Fiedler (Sabara) finds his bar mitzvah being turned into a chance for his Hollywood agent dad Adam (Piven) to one-up rival agent Arnie Stein (Miller) and the Steins' Titanic-themed event for their own son. But Ben sees it as the opportunity to reconcile his dad and his crazy, hippie grandfather, Irwin (Marshall). Director Scott Marshall, making his feature debut, is Garry's son. Flails wildly between sweet and cynical, with lessons learned in a "very special sitcom" way. Subtract at least a bone for the sight of Garry Marshall's naked backside. **99m/C; DVD.** Daryl Sabara; Jeremy Piven; Garry Marshall; Jami Gertz; Cheryl Hines; Daryl Hannah; Doris Roberts; Larry Miller; Carter Jenkins; Richard Benjamin; Miranda Cosgrove; Adam Goldberg; Sandra Taylor; ***Cameo(s):*** Neil Diamond; ***D:*** Scott Marshall; ***W:*** Mark Zakarin; ***C:*** Charles Minsky; ***M:*** John Debney.

Keillers Park **2005** A true hate crime story told in flashbacks. Peter sits in jail accused of a murder in Gothenburg's Keillers Park. Engaged and involved in the family business, Peter catches the eye of young street vendor Nassim and soon the two are lovers. Peter becomes obsessive and his life unravels with devastating consequences. Swedish with subtitles. **87m/C; DVD.** *SW* Marten Klingberg; Piotr Giro; Karin Bergquist; Gosta Bredefeldt; ***D:*** Susanna Edwards; ***W:*** Pia Gradvall; ***C:*** Robert Nordstrom; ***M:*** Peter Adolfsson.

Keith 1/2 **2008** A weepie made for teenaged girls. High-school senior Natalie (Harnois) has set her path and thinks she knows exactly what she wants, which isn't free-spirited new student Keith (McCartney). Keith keeps trying to shake up her world and he tells Natalie stuff about his life that turns out to be untrue. Still, she's attracted to him and starts snooping, soon discovering that Keith is seriously ill. **95m/C; DVD.** Elisabeth Harnois; Jesse McCartney; Jennifer Grey; Ignacio Serricchio; Tim Halligan; Zack Rockefeller; ***D:*** Todd A. Kessler; ***W:*** Todd A. Kessler; David Zabel; ***C:*** Darko Suvak; ***M:*** Tree Adams. **VIDEO**

Kelly's Heroes 1/2 **1970 (PG)** A misfit band of crooks are led by Eastwood on a daring mission: to steal a fortune in gold from behind enemy lines. In the process, they almost win WWII. Sutherland is superb, as is McLeod, in his pre-Love Boat days. **145m/C; VHS, DVD, Blu-Ray.** Clint Eastwood; Donald Sutherland; Telly Savalas; Gavin MacLeod; Don Rickles; Carroll O'Connor; Stuart Margolin; Harry Dean Stanton; Jeff Morris; Richard (Dick) Davalos; Perry Lopez; Tom Troupe; Len Lesser; David Hurst; George Savalas; Tom Signorelli; ***D:*** Brian G. Hutton; ***W:*** Troy Kennedy-Martin; ***C:*** Gabriel Figueroa; ***M:*** Lalo Schifrin.

Kennedy **1983** NBC historical drama starring Martin Sheen as John F. Kennedy and focusing on events such as the abortive invasion of Cuba, national racial conflicts, America's growing involvment in Vietnam and the Cuban Missle Crisis. In addition to political aspirations, it also reveals parts of the man's private life, family tragedies, and chronic womanizing. **278m/C; VHS, DVD.** Martin Sheen; Blair Brown; Vincent Gardenia; Geraldine Fitzgerald; E.G. Marshall; John Shea; Kevin Conroy; Nesbitt Blaisdell; John Glover; Kelsey Grammer; David Schramm; Trey Wilson; Jimmie Ray Weeks; ***D:*** Jim (James) Goddard; ***W:*** Reg Gadney; ***C:*** Ernest Vincze; ***M:*** Richard Hartley. **TV**

The Kennedys 1/2 **2011** Shallow depiction of a too-familiar family dooms this cable miniseries to boredom. Beginning with JFK's (Kinnear) election in 1960, story flashes back to ruthless patriarch Joe Kennedy's (Wilkinson) push to power and into politics. Then attention focuses on Jack and brother Bobby (Pepper) in the White House and the various crises his presidency faces. Holmes is inordinately whispery as long-suffering Jackie. **360m/C; DVD.** Greg Kinnear; Tom Wilkinson; Barry Pepper; Katie Holmes; Diana Hardcastle; Kristin Booth; Enrico Colantoni; Charlotte Sullivan; Chris Diamantopoulos; ***D:*** Jon Cassar; ***W:*** Stephen Kronish; ***C:*** David Moxness; ***M:*** Sean Callery. **CABLE**

The Kennel Murder Case **1933** Debonair detective Philo Vance suspects that a clear-cut case of suicide is actually murder. Powell is considered the best of the many actors to portray Vance in this adaptation of the S.S. Van Dine mysteries. Loosely remade as "Calling Philo Vance" in 1940. **73m/B; DVD.** William Powell; Mary Astor; Jack La Rue; Ralph Morgan; Eugene Pallette; ***D:*** Michael Curtiz; ***W:*** Robert Presnell, Sr.; Robert N. Lee; Peter Milne; ***C:*** William Rees; ***M:*** Bernhard Kaun.

Kenner 1/2 **1973** Bombay locations make up for sometimes sappy drama. Roy Kenner follows dope smuggler Tom Jordan to Bombay to get revenge for the murder of his partner. While searching, he's befriended by young Saji, who introduces Kenner to his single mom and later saves him from an ambush. Jordan turns out to be a fan of cricket fighting as is Saji, so Kenner is able to find Jordan's hideout. **92m/C; DVD.** Jim Brown; Ricky Cordell; Charles Horvath; Madlyn Rhue; Robert Coote; ***D:*** Steve Sekely; ***W:*** John Loring; ***C:*** Dieter Liphardt; ***M:*** Piero Piccioni.

Kenny Rogers as the Gambler 1/2 **1980** Rogers stars as Brady Hawkes, debonair gambler searching for a son he never knew he had. Based on the Rogers song of the same name. One of the highest rated TV movies ever. Followed by several sequels. **94m/C; VHS, DVD.** Kenny Rogers; Christine Belford; Bruce Boxleitner; Harold Gould; Clu Gulager; Lance LeGault; Lee Purcell; Noble Willingham; ***D:*** Dick Lowry. **TV**

Kenny Rogers as the Gambler, Part 2: The Adventure Continues 1/2 **1983** The surprise success of the made-for-TV western based on the popular Kenny Rogers' song spawned this equally popular sequel. Rogers returns as Brady Hawkes, this time searching for his kidnapped son. Followed by two more sequels. **195m/C; VHS, DVD.** Kenny Rogers; Bruce Boxleitner; Linda Evans; Harold Gould; David Hedison; Clu Gulager; Johnny Crawford; ***D:*** Dick Lowry. **TV**

Kenny Rogers as the Gambler, Part 3: The Legend Continues **1987** Roger's third attempt at humanizing the gambler from his hit '70s song. This time, the Gambler gives a hand with the mediating between the warring U.S. government and the Sioux nation. Sitting Bull and Buffalo Bill add credibility to this average undertaking. Made for TV. **190m/C; VHS, DVD.** Kenny Rogers; Bruce Boxleitner; Linda Gray; Melanie Chartoff; Matt Clark; George Kennedy; Dean Stockwell; Charles Durning; Jeffrey Jones; George American Horse; ***D:*** Dick Lowry. **TV**

The Kentuckian ✗✗ 1/2 **1955** Burt Lancaster stars as a rugged frontiersman who leaves with his son to go to Texas. On their journey the two are harassed by fighting mountaineers. **104m/C; VHS, DVD, Blu-Ray.** Burt Lancaster; Walter Matthau; Diana Lynn; John McIntire; Dianne Foster; Una Merkel; John Carradine; ***D:*** Burt Lancaster; ***C:*** Ernest Laszlo.

Kentucky ✗✗ 1/2 **1938** The horses are the real stars of this Technicolor romantic drama. A family feud dating back to the Civil War affects the lives of would-be lovers Sally (Young) and Jack (Greene). The Goodwins breed and train thoroughbreds but, after financial difficulties, are left with only one horse they claim on a bet from their hated rivals, the Dillons. Disgusted by his family, Jack Dillon keeps his identity a secret as he offers to train Sally's horse for the Kentucky Derby. Brennan won a Best Supporting Actor Oscar for his role as cantankerous Uncle Peter Goodwin. **96m/C; DVD.** Loretta Young; Richard Greene; Walter Brennan; Moroni Olsen; ***D:*** David Butler; ***W:*** Lamar Trotti; John Taintor Foote; ***C:*** Ray Rennahan; Ernest Palmer. Oscars '38: Actor--Supporting (Brennan).

Kentucky Fried Movie ✗✗✗ **1977 (R)** A zany potpourri of satire about movies, TV, commercials, and contemporary society. Written by Abrahams and the Zuckers, who later gave us "Airplane!" **85m/C; VHS, DVD, Blu-Ray.** Bill Bixby; Jerry Zucker; Jim Abrahams; David Zucker; Donald Sutherland; Henry Gibson; George Lazenby; Tony Dow; Uschi Digart; Rick Baker; Marilyn Joi; Forrest J Ackerman; ***D:*** John Landis; ***W:*** Jerry Zucker; Jim Abrahams; David Zucker; ***C:*** Stephen M. Katz.

Kentucky Jubilee ✗ 1/2 **1951** At the jubilee, a movie director is kidnapped and the master of ceremonies, among others, decides to find him. **67m/B; VHS, DVD.** Jerry Colonna; Jean Porter; James Ellison; Raymond Hatton; Fritz Feld; Vince Barnett; Michael Whalen; Archie Twitchell; Russell Hicks; Margia Dean; Si Jenks; Ralph Sanford; Jack Reitzen; ***D:*** Ron Ormond; ***W:*** Ron Ormond; Maurice Tombragel; ***C:*** Jack Greenhalgh.

Kentucky Kernels ✗✗ *Triple Trouble* **1934** A pair of down and out magicians ('30s comic duo Wheeler and Woolsey) happen upon a young boy (Little Rascal Spanky) who happens to be heir to a fortune. The three head for the rascal's Kentucky home, where they're welcomed with southern inhospitality. Much feuding and slapsticking. **75m/B; VHS, DVD.** Bert Wheeler; Robert Woolsey; Mary Carlisle; George "Spanky" McFarland; Noah Beery, Sr.; Lucille LaVerne; Willie Best; ***D:*** George Stevens; ***M:*** Max Steiner.

Kentucky Moonshine ✗ 1/2 **1938** Mild showbiz comedy filled with southern cliches. Radio star Jerry Wade (Martin) needs a new idea to boost his falling ratings and looks for a hillbilly act. Wannabe performer Caroline (Weaver) hears about the plan and she and her friends, the Ritz Brothers, head to her Kentucky hometown so Jerry can give them their big break. Comic foolery before they all head back to the Big Apple. **87m/B; DVD.** Tony Martin; Marjorie Weaver; Harry Ritz; Jimmy Ritz; Al Ritz; Slim Summerville; John Carradine; ***D:*** David Butler; ***W:*** Art Arthur; ***C:*** Robert Planck.

Kentucky Rifle ✗ 1/2 **1955** A Comanche Indian tribe will let a group of stranded pioneers through their territory only if they agree to sell the Kentucky rifles aboard their wagon. **80m/C; VHS, DVD.** Chill Wills; Lance Fuller; Cathy Downs; Jess Barker; Sterling Holloway; Jeanne Cagney; ***D:*** Carl K. Hittleman.

Kept ✗✗ **2001 (R)** Struggling architectural student Kyle Griffin thinks his worries are over when he lands a job at the firm owned by Barbara Weldon and her husband. But Barbara is a very hands-on employer and soon Kyle is involved in an affair and is a suspect in a murder. Now he has to save himself from being the fall guy. **98m/C; VHS, DVD.** Ice-T; Yvette Nipar; Christian Oliver; Paul Michael Robinson; Michelle Von Flotow; Laura Rose; Art Hingle; ***D:*** Fred Olen Ray; ***W:*** Richard Uhug; Kimberly A. Ray; ***C:*** Theo Angell; ***M:*** Herman Jackson; Michael van Blum; Barry Taylor. **VIDEO**

Kept Husbands ✗✗ **1931** A factory worker saves two lives in an industrial accident, and the boss invites him home to dinner. When he meets the boss' daughter, romance blooms. But their different backgrounds cause difficulties. A bit dull, and dated by its chauvinism. **76m/B; VHS, DVD, Blu-Ray.** Dorothy Mackaill; Joel McCrea; Robert McWade; Florence Roberts; Clara Kimball Young; Mary Carr; Ned Sparks; Bryant Washburn; ***D:*** Lloyd Bacon; ***M:*** Max Steiner.

Kes ✗✗✗ **1969** Loach's social realism is mixed with humor and adapted from Barry Hines' novel "A Kestrel for a Knave." Sullen, scrawny teenager Billy is bullied at home and school and thought useless everywhere. His working-class Yorkshire family live in poverty; Billy doesn't want to join his older brother in the coal mines but doesn't have any plans until he catches a kestrel chick. This gives Billy the idea to raise and train the bird, which also gives him a personal identity and respect. **111m/C; DVD, Blu-Ray.** *GB* David Bradley; Colin Welland; Freddie Fletcher; Lynne Perrie; Brian Glover; Bob Bowes; ***D:*** Ken Loach; ***W:*** Ken Loach; Tony Garnett; Barry Hines; ***C:*** Chris Menges; ***M:*** John Cameron.

Kesari ✗✗ 1/2 **2019** In 1897 British-controlled India, Saragarhi serves as a signalling post between Fort Gulistan and Fort Lockhart. A small regiment of 21 Sikh soldiers, members of the British Indian Army, are stationed at Saragarhi, led by Havildar Ishar Singh (Kumar) by fall. One September day, thousands of Afghan soldiers attack to capture Saragarhi to cut off communication between the forts. However, they find unexpected resistance from the Sikh soldiers, who valiantly fight. Based on true events, the patriotic war drama is full of authentic details and impressive visuals though the story is dragged down by uninspired writing and unnecessary plot devices. Hindi with subtitles. **150m/C; DVD.** Akshay Kumar; Parineeti Chopra; Suvinder Vicky; Vansh Bhardwaj; Sumeet Basran; ***V:*** Girish Kohli; ***D:*** Anurag Singh; ***W:*** Anurag Singh; ***C:*** Anshul Chobey.

Kettle of Fish ✗✗ **2006 (R)** Jazz sax man Mel (Modine) decides it's time to act like an adult and he moves in with his girlfriend—subletting his apartment to nerdy biologist Ginger (Gershon). But when Mel becomes obsessed with another woman, he gets tossed out on his ear, and is forced to beg Ginger to allow him to share the apartment. Romantic complications follow. Familiar story, rather engaging performances. **97m/C; DVD.** Matthew Modine; Gina Gershon; Fisher Stevens; Isiah Whitlock, Jr.; Christy Scott Cashman; Kevin J. O'Connor; ***D:*** Claudia Myers; ***W:*** Claudia Myers; ***C:*** Neil Lisk; ***M:*** David Tobocman.

The Kettles in the Ozarks ✗✗ 1/2 **1956** Since Kilbride retired after the seventh comedy, Hunnicutt played a new male character, Uncle Sledge, in the eighth film. Ma (Main) takes the young'uns to visit their uncle in the Ozarks and finds she must help him and fiancee Bedelia (Merkel) save the failing farm from bootleggers. Sold as part of the 'Ma & Pa Kettle Complete Comedy Collection'. **81m/B; VHS, DVD.** Marjorie Main; Arthur Hunnicutt; Una Merkel; Ted de Corsia; Richard Eyer; Joseph (Joe) Sawyer; Richard Deacon; ***D:*** Charles Lamont; ***W:*** Kay Lenard.

The Kettles on Old MacDonald's Farm ✗✗ 1/2 **1957** The ninth and last in the series finds Ma (Main in her final film) and Pa (Kennelly replacing the retired Kilbride) playing matchmakers for humble lumberman Brad (Smith). Seems he wants to marry the boss' spoiled daughter, Sally (Talbott), whom Ma decides needs a little backwoods seasoning before she'll make the proper wife. Sold as part of the 'Ma & Pa Kettle Complete Comedy Collection'. **82m/B; VHS, DVD.** Marjorie Main; Parker Fennelly; John Smith; Gloria Talbott; Claude Akins; Roy Barcroft; Patricia Morrow; George Dunn; ***D:*** Virgil W. Vogel; ***W:*** Herbert Margolis; William Raynor.

Kevin & Perry Go Large ✗ 1/2 **2000 (R)** The Brits can make bad teen sex comedies adapted from TV shows just as easily as Americans can. Kevin (Enfield) and Perry (Burke in drag) are a couple of gormless teenage boys who have only one thing on their teeny brains. And since the Brits all seem to go to Spain to be naughty, the boys decide to take their summer holidays in party capital Ibiza and get some chicks. Only problem is Kevin's parents decide to accompany them. Bummer (or whatever the Brit equivalent would be). May make more sense if you've seen the characters on TV. **83m/C; VHS, DVD.** *GB* Harry Enfield; Kathy Burke; Rhys Ifans; Laura Fraser; Tabitha Wady; James Fleet; Louisa Rix; ***D:*** Ed Bye; ***W:*** Harry Enfield; David Cummings; ***C:*** Alan Almond.

Kevin Hart: Let Me Explain ✗✗ 1/2 **2013 (R)** Kevin Hart's ego runs rampant in this stand-up comedy film, one that takes the usually smart comedian in directions more abrasive than his previous hits. The energetic Hart stalks the stage not unlike Chris Rock and Eddie Murphy at their peaks, commanding a crowd of 30,000 sold-out fans at Madison Square Garden. He's still an amazing, engaging performer but his material this time isn't as strong as previous stand-up outings. The title refers to the intro, in which Hart is told by friends that he's changed and he stages the stand-up act to explain what he's been through lately. **75m/C; DVD, Blu-Ray.** ***D:*** Leslie Small; Tim Story; ***C:*** Larry Blanford; ***M:*** Kennard Ramsey.

Kevin Hart: What Now? ✗✗ **2016 (R)** The stand-up portion of Hart's latest stand-up concert film is as sharp and energetic as to be expected from the stadium-filling superstar, but it's intercut with a simply horrendous spy movie spoof starring himself, Halle Berry, Don Cheadle and Ed Helms. The idea is that Hart is really an agent for MI6, and the writers try to incorporate the idea that this superspy has to do a stand-up show as a part of a mission. It's amateur and downright horrible but Hart's stand-up is clever and as insightful as ever. Just fast-forward through any of the moments he's not on stage. **96m/C; DVD.** Kevin Hart; Halle Berry; Don Cheadle; Ed Helms; David Meunier; ***D:*** Leslie Small; ***W:*** Kevin Hart; Joey Wells; Harry Ratchford; ***C:*** Cameron Barnett.

The Key ✗✗ 1/2 **1958** A long, slow WWII drama about the key to an Italian girl's apartment that gets passed from tugboat skipper to tugboat skipper before dangerous missions. Ultimately she finds true love, or does she? Based on the novel "Stella" by Jan de Hartog. **125m/B; DVD, Streaming.** *UK* William Holden; Sophia Loren; Trevor Howard; Oscar Homolka; Kieron Moore; ***D:*** Carol Reed; ***W:*** Carl Foreman; ***C:*** Oswald Morris; ***M:*** Malcolm Arnold. British Acad. '58: Actor (Howard).

Key Largo ✗✗✗ 1/2 **1948** WWII vet Bogart travels to the run-down Florida hotel owned by Barrymore and Bacall who are, respectively, the father and widow of a war buddy. Bogart notes the other guests are of a decidedly criminal bent, but as a hurricane threatens, no one can leave. One-time mob kingpin Robinson lords it over the others while Bogart keeps his usual cynical cool. Trevor, who plays Robinson's alcoholic ex-singer moll, deservedly won an Oscar for her role. Based on a play by Maxwell Anderson. **101m/B; VHS, DVD, Blu-Ray.** Humphrey Bogart; Lauren Bacall; Claire Trevor; Edward G. Robinson; Lionel Barrymore; Thomas Gomez; Marc Lawrence; Dan Seymour; ***D:*** John Huston; ***W:*** Richard Brooks; John Huston; ***C:*** Karl Freund; ***M:*** Max Steiner. Oscars '48: Support. Actress (Trevor).

Key to the City ✗✗ 1/2 **1950** Light comedy featuring Gable and Young as two small town mayors who meet and fall in love at a convention in San Francisco. Throw in some sharp lines, a little slapstick, and a bit of satire for an amusing picture. Based on the story by Albert Beich. **99m/B; DVD.** Clark Gable; Loretta Young; Frank Morgan; Marilyn Maxwell; Raymond Burr; James Gleason; Lewis Stone; Raymond Walburn; ***D:*** George Sidney; ***W:*** Robert Riley Crutcher; ***C:*** Harold Rosson; ***M:*** Bronislau Kaper.

Key Witness ✗ 1/2 **1947** Familiar Columbia Pictures B-movie crime drama. Would-be inventor Milton Higby (Beal) is accused of murdering his girlfriend but the only apparent witness who can prove his innocence has disappeared. Milton makes things worse by disguising himself and going on the lam and then gets into more trouble when he stumbles across another murder victim and decides to switch identities with the dead man. **67m/B; DVD.** John Beal; Trudy Marshall; Jimmy Lloyd; Helen Mowery; Barbara Read; Charles Trowbridge; Wilton Graff; ***D:*** David Ross Lederman; ***W:*** Edward Bock; Raymond L. Schrock; ***C:*** Philip Tannura.

Keyhole ✗✗ **2011 (R)** Gangster Ulysses (Patric) returns to his men after a shoot-out at his former home, which is surrounded by police, where presumably his wife (Rossellini) is being held captive. The story is told by Ulysses' father-in-law--who is dead--who proclaims that the house is now haunted. The ghosts of gangsters lurk about. Director Maddin's unique film is part noir, part ghost story, part nightmare. And a little too off the beaten path for most. **94m/B; DVD, Blu-Ray.** *CA* Jason Patric; Isabella Rossellini; Udo Kier; Brooke Palsson; David Wontner; Louis Negin; ***D:*** Guy Maddin; ***W:*** Guy Maddin; George Toles; ***C:*** Benjamin Kasulke; ***M:*** Jason Staczek.

The Keys of the Kingdom ✗✗✗ **1944** An earnest adaptation of A.J. Cronin's novel about a young Scottish missionary spreading God's word in 19th Century China. **137m/B; VHS, DVD, Blu-Ray.** Gregory Peck; Thomas Mitchell; Edmund Gwenn; Vincent Price; Roddy McDowall; Cedric Hardwicke; Peggy Ann Garner; James Gleason; Anne Revere; Rose Stradner; Sara Allgood; Abner Biberman; Arthur Shields; ***D:*** John M. Stahl; ***W:*** Joseph L. Mankiewicz; Nunnally Johnson; ***C:*** Arthur C. Miller.

Keys to Tulsa ✗✗ 1/2 **1996 (R)** After losing his job as a lowly movie reviewer (gasp!), Richter Bourdreau (Stoltz), the black-sheep son of a wealthy Tulsa family, is lured into a blackmail scheme by his ex-flame Vicky (Unger) and her perpetually stoned husband Ronnie (Spader). When the tables are turned on him, Richter finally gets up off of his slacker butt for some revenge. Excellent cast includes Moore as his flinty mother and Coburn as a wealthy redneck patriarch. Stoltz's performance holds the spiraling story of class distinction, murder and deceit together, and Spader's Elvis-helmeted loser is fun to watch. Based on the novel by Brian Fair Berkey. **112m/C; VHS, DVD.** Eric Stoltz; James Spader; Mary Tyler Moore; Joanna Going; Cameron Diaz; James Coburn; Michael Rooker; Peter Strauss; Deborah Kara Unger; ***D:*** Leslie Greif; ***W:*** Harley Peyton; ***C:*** Robert Fraisse; ***M:*** Stephen Endelman.

Khartoum ✗✗ 1/2 **1966** A sweeping but talky adventure epic detailing the last days of General "Chinese" Gordon as the title city is besieged by Arab tribes in 1884. **134m/C; DVD, Blu-Ray.** Charlton Heston; Laurence Olivier; Ralph Richardson; Richard Johnson; Alexander Knox; Hugh Williams; Nigel Green; Michael Hordern; Johnny Sekka; ***D:*** Basil Dearden; ***W:*** Robert Ardrey; ***C:*** Edward (Ted) Scaife; ***M:*** Frank Cordell.

Kibakichi ✗✗ *Kinakichi: Bokko-yokaiden; Werewolf Warrior* **2004 (R)** Part traditional samurai film, part spaghetti western, and part monster movie, the titular Kibakichi is a vagabond samurai werewolf—an unusual critter for an Asian horror movie. When the government decides to wipe out the Yokai (traditional Japanese spirit monsters), the Yokai flee to the rural villages disguised as humans. In one village, a criminal boss proposes to the Yokai that if they will use their powers to help further his schemes, he will feed them people. Kibakichi agrees to be his bodyguard, unaware of what is truly going on. When the boss betrays the Yokai, Kibakichi defends the monsters against a human militia, while trying to bring the boss to justice. **95m/C; DVD.** *JP* Ryuuji Harada; Nozomi Ando; Miki Tanaka; ***D:*** Tomoo Haraguchi; ***W:*** Mugi Kamio; ***C:*** Shoji Ebara; ***M:*** Kenji Kawai.

Kibakichi 2 ✗ 1/2 *Kinakichi: Bokko-yokaiden 2* **2004 (R)** In this poor sequel, Kibakichi is helping a blind girl and her village gain revenge on a sadistic madman while being stalked by a female werewolf. Eventually all three of them team up to defeat a bad guy more evil than themselves. Notable for being a martial arts film wherein no one seems to be very accomplished at martial arts, and a horror film that seems confused as to actually how to scare an audience. The first film wasn't exactly great, but it had its uniqueness going for it. Even naked women dancing under the moon with polar bears doesn't save this thing. **80m/C; DVD.** *JP*

Ryuuji Harada; Miki Tanaka; *D:* Tomoo Haraguchi; Daiji Hattori; *W:* Baku Kamio; *C:* Shinji Watanabe; *M:* Kenji Kawai.

Kichiku: Banquet of the Beasts 🦴🦴 1/2 *Kichiku Dai Enkai; Kichiku Satanic Banquet* **2004** A leftist political group's leader is imprisoned, with dire consequences for the rest of them. Instead of leaving his second in charge, he turns the group over to his slutty, megalomaniacal girlfriend, who proceeds to either control the members by sleeping with them and then blackmailing them, or just plain alienating them. When the group's leader dies, everyone isolates themselves in the mountains, and their ever increasing paranoia leads them to commit acts that would make the average street thug flinch. **103m/C; DVD.** *JP* Yuji Hashimoto; Tomohiro Zaizen; Sumiko Mikami; *D:* Kazuyoshi Kumakiri; *W:* Kazuyoshi Kumakiri; *C:* Kiyoaki Hashimoto.

Kick-Ass 🦴🦴🦴 **2010 (R)** Comic book fanboy teen Dave Lizewski (Johnson) wants to become a superhero. Of course he has no actual powers but that doesn't stop him from getting a costume and an alter ego. Dave then attracts the crazies, including 11-year-old vigilante Hit Girl (Moretz) and her father, Big Daddy (Cage, better than he's been in years), as well as bad guys with real weapons. Ultra-violent and controversial, it's also funny, well acted and directed, and satisfying as parody and straight-up action flick. Definitely not for the kiddies. Adapted from the Mark Millar comic book series. **117m/C; Blu-Ray, On Demand.** Aaron Taylor-Johnson; Nicolas Cage; Chloë Grace Moretz; Lyndsy Fonseca; Mark Strong; Christopher Mintz-Plasse; Xander Berkeley; Clark Duke; Evan Peters; Elizabeth McGovern; Sophie Wu; Michael Rispoli; Randall Batinkoff; Jason Flemyng; Garrett M. Brown; Yancy Butler; *D:* Matthew Vaughn; *W:* Matthew Vaughn; Jane Goldman; *C:* Benjamin Davis; *M:* Marius De Vries; Ilan Eshkeri; Henry Jackman; John Murphy.

Kick-Ass 2 🦴 **2013 (R)** This superhero satire sequel makes the original look like a masterpiece in comparison. Misguided and offensive, it mistakes vulgarity for style. The action of the first film has opened the world to the potential of real-life superheroes but Kick-Ass (Taylor-Johnson) and Hit Girl (Moretz) are forced to go back into their normal lives of adolescence until a darker version of Red Mist (Mintz-Plasses) seeks vengeance. Cluttered and remarkably stupid, only another charismatic turn from the always-good Moretz keeps it from total disaster. **103m/C; DVD, Blu-Ray.** Aaron Taylor-Johnson; Chloë Grace Moretz; Christopher Mintz-Plasse; Jim Carrey; Morris Chestnut; John Leguizamo; Donald Adeosun Faison; Robert Emms; Lindy Booth; Olga Kurkulina; Yancy Butler; *D:* Jeff Wadlow; *W:* Jeff Wadlow; *C:* Tim Maurice-Jones; *M:* Henry Jackman; Matthew Margeson.

Kickboxer 🦴 1/2 **1989 (R)** The brother of a permanently crippled kickboxing champ trains for a revenge match. **97m/C; VHS, DVD, Blu-Ray; Open Captioned.** Jean-Claude Van Damme; Rochelle Ashana; Dennis Chan; Dennis Alexio; *D:* Mark DiSalle; *W:* Jean-Claude Van Damme; Mark DiSalle; Glenn A. Bruce; *C:* Jon Kranhouse; *M:* Paul Hertzog.

Kickboxer 2: The Road Back 🦴 1/2 **1990 (R)** Mitchell takes over for Van Damme in this action sequel which finds our athletic hero seeking revenge on the kickboxer who murdered his brother. **90m/C; VHS, DVD.** Sasha Mitchell; Peter Boyle; John Diehl; *D:* Albert Pyun.

Kickboxer 3: The Art of War 🦴 1/2 **1992 (R)** Mitchell returns in this second sequel. This time the American kickboxing champ flies to Rio for a big match which turns out to be fixed by a local mobster. For a little more fun our hero saves a kidnapped girl and fights a hired killer. **92m/C; VHS, DVD.** Sasha Mitchell; Dennis Chan; Richard Comar; Noah Verduzco; Althea Miranda; Ian Jacklin; *D:* Rick King.

Kickboxer 4: The Aggressor 🦴🦴 1/2 **1994 (R)** Martial arts expert David Sloan (Mitchell) was framed by sworn enemy Tong Po but now he's back and looking for revenge. **90m/C; VHS, DVD.** Sasha Mitchell; Kamal Krifia; Nicholas Guest; Deborah Mansy; Brad Thornton; *D:* Albert Pyun.

Kickboxer: Vengeance 🦴🦴 **2016** An action film related to the 1989 cult classic Kickboxer. After his martial arts champion brother Eric (Shahlavi) is killed by Tong Po (Bautista) during a free-for-all match in Thailand, Kurt Sloan (Moussi) begins a quest for redemption and revenge. To that end, he trains with a master (Van Damme) and ultimately gains his chance to face Tong himself. **90m/C; DVD, Blu-Ray, Streaming, Download.** Alain Moussi; Dave Bautista; Darren Shahlavi; Jean-Claude Van Damme; T.J. Storm; *D:* John Stockwell; *W:* Dimitri Logothetis; Jim McGrath; *C:* Mateo Londono; *M:* Adam Dorn.

Kicked in the Head 🦴🦴 **1997 (R)** Redmond, a loser who dreams of the Hindenburg disaster, is newly jobless, homeless and loveless. He decides to go on a "spiritual quest", which unfortunately consists of bad poetry and worse trouble, through Manhattan's Lower East Side. His Uncle Sam (Woods) wants him to deliver a package, his buddy Stretch (Rapaport) wants him to work for his shady (and sometimes violent) beer business and stewardess Megan (Fiorentino) wants him to leave her alone. It's all settled in a hail of gunfire and car chases, because that's how things are solved in the movies. Director Harrison did more with much less in debut "Rhythym Thief." **97m/C; VHS, DVD.** Kevin Corrigan; Linda Fiorentino; James Woods; Lili Taylor; Michael Rapaport; Burt Young; Olek Krupa; *D:* Matthew Harrison; *W:* Kevin Corrigan; Matthew Harrison; *C:* John Thomas; Howard Krupa; *M:* Stephen Endelman.

Kickin' It Old Skool 🦴 **2007 (PG-13)** Lame comedy has breakdancing Justin (Calvert) starring his 1986 school talent show until an accident puts him in a 20-year coma. Naturally, there's a big adjustment when Justin (an annoying Kennedy) wakes up, complicated by the fact that he thinks like a 13-year-old. Realizing his parents have gone broke paying for his care, Justin decides to get his old crew back together and enter a hip-hop dance contest, despite the fact that time has definitely marched on. **108m/C; DVD.** Jamie Kennedy; Miguel A. Nunez, Jr.; Maria Menounos; Michael Rosenbaum; Debra Jo Rupp; Christopher McDonald; Vivica A. Fox; Alan Ruck; Bobby Lee; Aris Alvarado; Alexander Calvert; Michelle Trachtenberg; Kira Clavell; Alexia Fast; *Cameo(s):* David Hasselhoff; Erik Estrada; Roddy Piper; *D:* Harvey Glazer; *W:* Trace Slobotkin; Josh Siegal; Dylan Morgan; *C:* Robert M. Stevens; *M:* Richard Glasser.

Kicking and Screaming 🦴🦴🦴 **1995 (R)** Baumbach's deft, though slightly self-conscious directorial debut examines the post-college grad angst of Grover (Hamilton) and his three other slacker roomies. In denial of their recently achieved non-student status, the four bond together in pursuit of the inane and trivial, while their various girlfriends slip more easily into adulthood. Funny and tender flashback scenes of Grover and girlfriend Jane (D'Abo) add depth without all the dialogue, well-written though it is. Hilarious highlight occurs as roommate Otis interviews for that most popular of low-budget, Gen-X movie jobs—video store clerk. **96m/C; VHS, DVD.** Josh Hamilton; Olivia D'Abo; Carlos Jacott; Christopher Eigeman; Eric Stoltz; Jason Wiles; Parker Posey; Cara Buono; Elliott Gould; *D:* Noah Baumbach; *W:* Oliver Berkman; Noah Baumbach; *C:* Steven Bernstein; *M:* Phil Marshall.

Kicking & Screaming 🦴🦴 1/2 **2005 (PG)** Anemic family sports comedy that never would have been greenlit without a powerhouse like Ferrell in the lead. And it's to his sole credit that a movie this derivative works as well as it does. Mild-mannered Phil (Ferrell) is the anxiety-prone son of Buck (Duvall), a ridiculously competitive junior soccer coach who traded his own grandson, Phil's son Sam (McLaughlin), to another team. Determined to prove himself to Buck, Phil takes over coaching Sam's new soccer team, filled with losers and misfits, with the help of Buck's arch-rival Mike Ditka (yes, that Mike Ditka). Ferrell screaming at kids never stops being funny, but there's not an original moment in the entire film. **95m/C; DVD, Blu-Ray.** Will Ferrell; Robert Duvall; Steven Anthony Lawrence; Musetta Vander; Elliot Cho; Josh Hutcherson; Dylan McLaughlin; Eric Walker; Dallas McKinney; Jeremy Bergman; Kate Walsh; Francesco Liotti; Alessandro Ruggiero; Laura Kightlinger; Rachael Harris; *Cameo(s):* Mike Ditka; *D:* Jesse Dylan; *W:* Leo Benvenuti; Steve Rudnick; *C:* Lloyd Ahern, II; *M:* Mark Isham.

Kicking It 🦴🦴 **2008** In 2006, four dozen soccer teams participated in the fourth annual World Homeless Cup, and this doc follows six of the players as they struggle with their personal demons while preparing for the tournament. The results are inspiring and depressing: the idea of staging a sporting event to bring attention to the homeless plight is interesting, as are the tales of participants who are said to have made their way off the streets, but the fates of most of the players remain iffy at best. **99m/C; DVD.** *D:* Susan Koch; Jeff Warner; *W:* Susan Koch. **VIDEO**

Kicks 🦴🦴 1/2 **2016 (R)** A coming-of-age adventure drama that follows the efforts of teens to retrieve the Air Jordans stolen from one of them. At the age of 15, Brandon (Guillory) lives in poverty and is often picked on. He wants a pair of Air Jordans more than anything. After he works hard to obtain them, Brandon becomes a target and his new sneakers are stolen by a local hood. With two friends, Brandon goes on a dangerous journey to Oakland to retrieve them and has unexpected experiences along the way. **80m/C; DVD, Blu-Ray, Streaming, Download.** Jahking Guillory; Christopher Jordan Wallace; Christopher Meyer; Kofi Siriboe; Mahershala Ali; *D:* Justin Tipping; *W:* Justin Tipping; Joshua Beirne-Golden; *C:* Michael Ragen; *M:* Brian Reitzell.

The Kid 🦴🦴 1/2 **1997 (PG)** High schooler Jimmy Albright (Saumier) is secretly taking boxing lessons from trainer Harry Sloan (Steiger) since his parents don't approve. Jimmy is a natural and is ready to compete in the amateur championship match. Then Harry dies and fellow boxer Trey (Brochu) schemes to have Jimmy's parents find out about his secret life and forbid him to box. **89m/C; VHS, DVD.** *CA* Jeff Saumier; Rod Steiger; Ray Aranha; Mark Camacho; Jane Wheeler; Tod Fennell; Daniel Brochu; Jason Tremblay; *D:* John Hamilton; *W:* Seymour Blicker; *M:* Normand Corbeil.

The Kid 🦴🦴 **2019 (R)** After 14-year-old Rio (Schur) shoots his abusive father to try and save his mother from being beaten to death, the teen's plan to run away is stopped by his cruel Uncle Grant (Pratt). Unsure who to trust, Rio is impressed when he meets outlaw Billy the Kid (DeHaan), and Bill manipulates Rio for his own purposes. After Rio meets Sheriff Pat Garrett (Hawke), he must choose between living as a bandit or a virtuous man. A different spin on the Billy the Kid story, the film successfully explores the effects of domestic violence through common Western tropes and features a complex performance by Hawke. **99m/C; DVD, Blu-Ray.** Chris Pratt; Vincent D'Onofrio; Ethan Hawke; Leila George; Dane DeHaan; *D:* Vincent D'Onofrio; *W:* Andrew Lanham; *C:* Matthew J. Lloyd; *M:* Latham Gaines; Shelby Gaines.

The Kid and I 🦴🦴 **2005 (PG-13)** A film about the making of a film, built around Aaron Roman (Gores) who, although born with cerebral palsy, dreams of starring in action movies like his favorite, "True Lies." Since his father (Mantegne) is a wealthy and powerful Los Angeles business mogul, Aaron gets his chance. Bill Williams (Arnold), whose acting career is floundering, is hired to write and co-star with Aaron. Actor Gores, who actually has cerebral palsy, is great as Aaron. Uplifting and fun, if you have a high schmaltz tolerance. **93m/C; DVD.** Tom Arnold; Linda Hamilton; Henry Winkler; Richard Edson; Joe Mantegna; Shannon Elizabeth; Arielle Kebbel; Brenda Strong; Eric Gores; *Cameo(s):* Penelope Spheeris; *D:* Penelope Spheeris; *W:* Tom Arnold; *C:* Robert E. Seaman.

The Kid Brother 🦴🦴🦴 1/2 **1927** The shy, weak son of a tough sheriff, Harold fantasizes about being a hero like his father and big brothers, falls in love with a carnival lady, and somehow saves the day. Classic silent comedy. **84m/B; Silent; VHS, DVD, Blu-Ray.** Harold Lloyd; Walter James; Jobyna Ralston; *D:* Ted Wilde.

Kid Cannabis 🦴 1/2 **2014** A revenge of the drug-dealing nerds underdog story, based on the life of Nate Norman (Brown). Fat and dorky, Nathan teamed up with fellow dropout Topher (Wormald) in 2005 to smuggle mass quantities of marijuana from Canada into Idaho. Nate's daring exploits with the police, dangerous investors, and a quick-witted supplier (McGinley) is whole-hearteded endorsed and celebrated by the filmmakers. This half-baked fantasy, however, is loaded with cliches, playing out like a stoned Scorsese reading about the origins of Facebook. **110m/C; DVD, Blu-Ray.** Jonathan Daniel Brown; Kenny Wormald; John C. McGinley; Ron Perlman; Aaron Yoo; *D:* John Stockwell; *W:* John Stockwell; *C:* John Sejdinaj; *M:* Irv Johnson.

Kid Colter 🦴🦴 1/2 **1985** Enjoyable family film about a city kid who goes to visit his dad in a remote wilderness area of the Pacific Northwest. While there he is abducted by two grizzly mountain men and left for dead, but survives and pursues his abductors relentlessly. Received the Film Advisory Board Award of Excellence and the Award of Merit from the Academy of Family Films. **101m/C; VHS, DVD.** Jim Stafford; Jeremy Shamos; Hal Terrance; Greg Ward; Jim Turner; *D:* David O'Malley; *W:* David O'Malley.

Kid Dynamite 🦴🦴 *Queen of Broadway* **1943** A Bowery Boys series episode. Gorcey is a boxer who is kidnapped to prevent his participation in a major fight. The real fighting occurs when his brother is substituted, and Gorcey is smitten. **73m/B; VHS, DVD.** Leo Gorcey; Huntz Hall; Bobby Jordan; Gabriel Dell; Pamela Blake; *D:* Wallace Fox.

A Kid for Two Farthings 🦴🦴 1/2 **1955** An episodic, sentimental portrait of the Jewish quarter in London's East End, centered on a boy with a malformed goat he thinks is a magic unicorn capable of granting wishes and bringing happiness to his impoverished 'hood. Acclaimed adaptation of a novel by screenwriter Wolf Mankowitz. **96m/C; VHS, DVD.** *GB* Diana Dors; David Kossoff; Celia Johnson; Jonathan Ashmore; Joe Robinson; Brenda de Banzie; Primo Carnera; Lou Jacobi; Irene Handl; *D:* Carol Reed; *W:* Wolf Mankowitz; *C:* Edward (Ted) Scaife; *M:* Benjamin Frankel.

The Kid from Brooklyn 🦴🦴 **1946** A shy, musically inclined milkman becomes a middleweight boxer by knocking out the champ in a street brawl. Remake of "The Milky Way" by Harold Lloyd. Available with digitally remastered stereo and original movie trailer. **113m/C; DVD.** Danny Kaye; Virginia Mayo; Eve Arden; Fay Bainter; Walter Abel; *D:* Norman Z. McLeod; *W:* Don Hartman; Melville Shavelson; *C:* Gregg Toland; *M:* Carmen Dragon.

The Kid From Cleveland 🦴🦴 1/2 **1949** Troubled teen Johnny (Tamblyn) is taken under the wing of sports announcer Mike Jackson (Brent) who introduces him to the owner and players of the Cleveland Indians. They do their best to set the kid on the straight and narrow as the baseball team enters the 1948 World Series. A real nostalgia piece. **89m/B; DVD, Blu-Ray.** George Brent; Russ Tamblyn; Lynn Bari; Tommy Cook; Louis Jean Heydt; Ann Doran; Bill Veeck; *D:* Herbert Kline; *W:* John Bright; *C:* Jack Marta; *M:* Nathan Scott.

Kid from Spain 🦴🦴 1/2 **1932** Early Busby Berkeley choreography highlights this fun, if nonsensical, musical. Thanks to the usual mixups, college boy Eddie (Cantor) witnesses a bank robbery and flees to his friend Ricardo's (Young) home in Mexico, with the crooks on his trail. Then he gets mistaken for a famous bullfighter and is even forced into the ring. Oh, and there's some romantic complications as well. **96m/B; VHS, Streaming.** Eddie Cantor; Robert Young; Lyda Roberti; Ruth Hall; John Miljan; Noah Beery, Sr.; J. Carrol Naish; Robert Emmett O'Connor; *D:* Leo McCarey; *W:* William Anthony McGuire; Bert Kalmar; Harry Ruby; *C:* Gregg Toland.

Kid Galahad 🦴🦴🦴 *The Battling Bellhop* **1937** Well-acted boxing drama with Robinson playing an honest promoter who wants to make Morris into a prize fighter. Davis plays the girl they both want. Remade as "The Wagons Roll at Night" and then made again as an Elvis Presley vehicle. **101m/B; VHS, DVD.** Edward G. Robinson; Bette Davis; Humphrey Bogart; Wayne Morris; Jane Bryan; Harry Carey, Sr.; Veda Ann Borg; *D:* Michael Curtiz; *W:*

Seton I. Miller; ***C:*** Gaetano Antonio "Tony" Gaudio; ***M:*** Max Steiner.

Kid Galahad 🦴🦴 **1962** The King plays a young boxer who weathers the fight game, singing seven songs along the way. **95m/C; VHS, DVD, Blu-Ray.** Elvis Presley; Lola Albright; Charles Bronson; Ned Glass; Joan Blackman; Ed Asner; Gig Young; ***D:*** Phil Karlson; ***C:*** Burnett Guffey.

A Kid in Aladdin's Palace 🦴🦴 ½ **1997 (PG)** Burger flipper Calvin (Nicholas) time travels to anicent Arabia thanks to a mischief-making genie (Negron). He meets Princess Scheherazade (Mitra), who wants Calvin's help in fighting evil Luxor (Faulkner), who's overthrown her father, King Aladdin (Ipale). **89m/C; VHS, DVD.** Thomas Ian Nicholas; Rhona Mitra; Taylor Negron; James Faulkner; Aharon Ipale; ***D:*** Robert L. Levy; ***W:*** Michael Part; ***C:*** Wally Pfister; ***M:*** David Michael Frank.

A Kid in King Arthur's Court 🦴 ½ **1995 (PG)** Lame adaptation of Mark Twain's "A Connecticut Yankee in King Arthur's Court" finds insecure California teen Calvin Fuller (Nicholas), falling down a hole created by an earthquake and landing in Camelot. Arthur's (Ackland) a doddering old man with a cute teen daughter, Princess Katey (Baeza), who needs some help in defeating the evil Lord Belasco (Malik). Naturally, Calvin helps out and gains confidence in himself. Okay time-waster for the kids. **91m/C; DVD.** Thomas Ian Nicholas; Joss Ackland; Art Malik; Paloma Baeza; Kate Winslet; Ron Moody; Daniel Craig; ***D:*** Michael Gottlieb; ***W:*** Robert L. Levy; Michael Part; ***C:*** Elemer Ragalyi; ***M:*** J.A.C. Redford.

A Kid Like Jake 🦴 ½ **2018 (R)** Daniel Pearle's uneven adaption of his own 2013 play tackles gender identification issues in children via four-year-old Jake (Davis). When his loving parents (Danes and Parsons) search for the right school for him in Brooklyn, they realize that Jake might identify as a girl given his preference for "girl" toys over "boy" toys. The dilemma of whether they acknowledge it and label Jake at such a young age arises. The leads are well-suited for their roles but Jake, for being the title character, is oddly in the background. **92m/C; DVD, Blu-Ray, Streaming.** Claire Danes; Jim Parsons; Octavia Spencer; Priyanka Chopra; Amy Landecker; ***D:*** Silas Howard; ***W:*** Daniel Pearle; ***C:*** Steven Capitano Calitri; ***M:*** Roger Neill.

Kid Millions 🦴🦴 ½ **1934** Vintage musical comedy in which a dull-witted Brooklyn boy must travel to exotic Egypt to collect an inherited fortune. The finale is filmed in early three-strip Technicolor. Lucille Ball appears as a Goldwyn Girl. **90m/C; DVD.** Eddie Cantor; Ethel Merman; Ann Sothern; George Murphy; ***D:*** Roy Del Ruth; ***W:*** Nunnally Johnson; Nat Perrin; Arthur Sheekman; ***C:*** Ray June; Ray Rennahan.

Kid Monk Baroni 🦴🦴 ½ **1952** Street punk Baroni (Nimoy) leaves his gang behind when a good-guy priest (Rober) introduces him to boxing. The kid rises to success thanks to a cagey manager (Cabot) and despite the presence of organized crime. Typical B-movie melodrama. **80m/B; VHS, DVD.** Leonard Nimoy; Bruce Cabot; Richard Rober; Kathleen Freeman; ***D:*** Harold Schuster.

The Kid Stays in the Picture 🦴🦴🦴 **2002 (R)** Documentary covers the up-and-down career and life of one-time actor and '70s-super film producer Robert Evans. Evans narrates the film memoir that is taken from his 1994 autobiography—so don't expect objectivity (or, necessarily, accuracy). Evans discusses not only his career but his marriages, romances, drug problems, involvement in a murder investigation, and his rise-fall-rise life. **93m/C; VHS, DVD. *Nar:*** Robert Evans; ***D:*** Brett Morgen; Nanette Burstein; ***W:*** Brett Morgen; ***C:*** John Bailey; ***M:*** Jeff Danna.

Kid Vengeance 🦴 ½ **1975 (R)** After witnessing the brutal slaying of his family, a boy carries out a personal vendetta against the outlaws. **90m/C; VHS, DVD.** Leif Garrett; Jim Brown; Lee Van Cleef; John Marley; Glynnis O'Connor; ***D:*** Joseph Manduke.

The Kid Who Would Be King 🦴🦴🦴 **2019 (PG)** Twelve-year-old Alex (Serkis) is a loyal friend with a strong code of honor. He defends his best friend Bedders (Chaumoo) even when bullied by older teens Lance (Taylor) and Kaye (Dorris). Alex's life changes forever when he gains the Excalibur and is trained to fight evil by a young Merlyn (Imrie). Alex then must organize other tweens and teens to fight the recently revived evil sorceress Morgana (Ferugson), who has long waited to take over England. Though the film does not live up to its potential, it has moments of fun and strong, endearing performances by the young actors. **120m/C; DVD.** Louis Ashbourne Serkis; Dean Chaumoo; Tom Taylor; Rhianna Dorris; Nathan Stewart-Jarrett; ***D:*** Joe Cornish; ***W:*** Joe Cornish; ***C:*** Bill Pope; ***M:*** Electric Wave Bureau.

The Kid with a Bike 🦴🦴 *Le gamin au velo* **2011** Desperate, angry 11-year-old Cyril refuses to believe his deadbeat dad has not only abandoned him to an orphanage but sold his bike. He regularly breaks out of its confines to try to find him, which leads to Cyril being befriended by hairdresser Samantha. She agrees to foster the boy on the weekends and patiently tries to give him something of a normal childhood. Cyril does track down his dad but can't believe the man doesn't want him, and rejection leads Cyril down a dangerous path. French with subtitles. **87m/C; DVD, Blu-Ray.** *BE FR* Thomas Doret; Cecile de France; Jeremie Renier; Egon Di Mateo; ***D:*** Jean-Pierre Dardenne; Luc Dardenne; ***W:*** Jean-Pierre Dardenne; Luc Dardenne; ***C:*** Alain Marcoen.

The Kid with the X-Ray Eyes 🦴🦴 **1999 (PG)** Twelve-year-old Bobby wants to be a spy when he grows up. Then he finds a strange pair of glasses that allow him to see through anything. He attracts the attentions of the C.I.A., the police, and a pair of theives who all want his special specs. **84m/C; VHS, DVD.** Justin Berfield; Robert Carradine; Mark Collie; Diane Salinger; Griffin (Griffen) Drew; Brinke Stevens; ***D:*** Fred Olen Ray; ***W:*** Sean O'Bannon; ***C:*** Theo Angell; ***M:*** Jay Bolton. **VIDEO**

Kidco 🦴🦴 **1983 (PG)** The true story of a money-making corporation headed and run by a group of children ranging in age from 9 to 16. **104m/C; VHS, Streaming.** Scott Schwartz; Elizabeth Gorcey; Cinnamon Idles; Tristen Skylar; ***D:*** Ronald F. Maxwell.

Kidnap 🦴🦴 ½ **2017 (R)** When her son gets kidnapped from a park, Karla eschews police assistance and chases down the abductors in her car, desperate to keep them in sight. The action starts 10 minutes in, and never takes its foot off the accelerator. Berry is excellent as a normal mom fueled only by tank of gas and maternal determination. **95m/C; DVD, Blu-Ray.** Halle Berry; Sage Correa; Chris McGinn; Lew Temple; Jason Winston George; ***D:*** Luis Prieto; ***W:*** Knate Lee; ***C:*** Flavio Martinez Labiano; ***M:*** Federico Jusid.

Kidnap Syndicate 🦴 ½ **1976 (R)** Kidnappers swipe two boys, releasing one—the son of a wealthy industrialist who meets their ransom demands. When they kill the other boy, a mechanic's son, the father goes on a revengeful killing spree. Italian with subtitles. **98m/C; DVD, Blu-Ray.** *IT* Luc Merenda; James Mason; Valentina Cortese; Irina Maleeva; Vittorio Caprioli; Marino (Martin) Mase; ***D:*** Fernando Di Leo; ***W:*** Fernando Di Leo; ***C:*** Erico Menczer; ***M:*** Luis Bacalov.

Kidnapped 🦴🦴 ½ **1938** Lots of derring-do even if 20th Century Fox took liberties with the Robert Louis Stevenson novel. Young David Balfour (Bartholomew), the heir to a fortune, is set up to be kidnapped and sent to sea by his greedy uncle. He's rescued by Alan Breck (Baxter), a fugitive because he's part of the Scottish rebellion against the British crown. They join together to get justice and restore David to his proper place. **93m/B; DVD.** Freddie Bartholomew; Warner Baxter; Arleen Whelan; Sir C. Aubrey Smith; Reginald Owen; Nigel Bruce; Miles Mander; John Carradine; ***D:*** Alfred Werker; ***W:*** Sonya Levien; Edwin Blum; Eleanor Harris; Ernest Pascal; ***C:*** Gregg Toland; ***M:*** Arthur Lange.

Kidnapped 🦴🦴 **1948** Low-budget version of the Robert Louis Stevenson classic from independent Monogram Studios. David (McDowall) comes to claim his inheritance only to be kidnapped and sold into slavery. He's rescued by adventurer Alan Breck (O'Herlihy) and the duo make their way across the Scottish Highlands to claim David's heritage from his greedy uncle. **81m/B; DVD.** Roddy McDowall; Dan O'Herlihy; Sue England; Roland Winters; Jeff Corey; Houseley Stevenson; ***D:*** William Beaudine; ***W:*** Scott Darling; ***C:*** William Sickner; ***M:*** Edward Kay.

Kidnapped 🦴🦴 ½ **1960** A young boy is sold by his wicked uncle as a slave, and is helped by an outlaw. A Disney film based on the Robert Louis Stevenson classic. **94m/C; VHS, DVD, Streaming.** Peter Finch; James MacArthur; Peter O'Toole; ***D:*** Robert Stevenson.

Kidnapped 🦴 ½ *Rabid Dogs; Cani Arrabbiati* **1974** The Italian title of "Rabid Dogs" is much more apt for this violent crime drama. Three vicious criminals have a getaway problem after a bank robbery. First they take a female hostage and then they force their way into a car driven by an old man who has an unconscious child in the back seat. Much sadistic behavior follows as they make their way to a safe house and an unexpected turn of events. Italian with subtitles. Bava's film fell into a financial black hole and was not completed (by others) and released until 1998. **96m/C; DVD, Blu-Ray.** *IT* Maurice Poli; George Eastman; Don Backy; Lea Lander; Riccardo Cucciolla; Erika Dario; ***D:*** Mario Bava; ***W:*** Alessandro Parenzo; ***C:*** Emilio Varriano; ***M:*** Stelvio Cipriani.

Kidnapped 🦴🦴 ½ **1995** Cable adaptation of Robert Louis Stevenson's 1886 novel. In 1751 shanghaied young David Balfour (McCardie) and Highland patriot Aln Breck Stewart (Assante) escape from a slave ship and return to Scotland to battle the British. **142m/C; VHS, DVD.** Armand Assante; Brian McCardie; Michael Kitchen; Brian Blessed; Patrick Malahide; ***D:*** Ivan Passer; ***W:*** John Goldsmith. **CABLE**

Kidnapped 🦴🦴🦴 **2005** This BBC version of the Robert Louis Stevenson adventure tale finds orphaned Davie Balfour (Pearson) trying to claim his inheritance from his eccentric Uncle Ebeneezer (Dunbar). Instead, Davie gets kidnapped and imprisoned on a slave ship. Fortunately, he joins forces with exiled rebel Alan Breck (Glen) and the two wind up shipwrecked and running from evil English soldier Colonel McNabb (McGann) and his bounty hunters in the Scottish Highlands circa the 1750s. Exciting swashbuckling abounds. **150m/C; VHS, DVD.** *GB* Iain Glen; Adrian Dunbar; Paul McGann; Gregor Fisher; John Bach; John Leigh; James Anthony Pearson; Kirstin Coulter Smith; ***D:*** Brendan Maher; ***W:*** Bev Doyle; Richard Kurti; ***C:*** Geoffrey Hall; ***M:*** David Hirschfelder. **TV**

Kidnapped 🦴 ½ *Secuestrados* **2010** Stylish but sadistic home invasion drama from Spain. Three thugs break into the upper-middle class home of Jaime, his wife Marta, and their 18-year-old daughter Isa. While Jefe drives Jaime around to ATMs to clean out his bank account, his two accomplices terrify the women. Spanish with subtitles. **85m/C; DVD.** *SP* Fernando Cayo; Ana Wagener; Manuela Valles; Dritan Biba; Martijn Kuiper; Guillermo Barrienttos; ***D:*** Miguel Angel Vivas; ***W:*** Miguel Angel Vivas; Javier Garcia; ***C:*** Pedro J. Marquez; ***M:*** Sergio Moure.

The Kidnapping of the President 🦴🦴 ½ **1980 (R)** The U.S. president is taken hostage by Third World terrorists. The Secret Service is on the ball trying to recover the nation's leader. Well-integrated subplot involves the vice president in a scandal. Engrossing political thriller. Based on novel by Charles Templeton. **113m/C; VHS, DVD.** *CA* William Shatner; Hal Holbrook; Van Johnson; Ava Gardner; Miguel Fernandes; ***D:*** George Mendeluk.

Kids 🦴🦴 **1995** Very controversial docudrama about 24 hours in the lives of some aimless New York teenagers. The sullen Telly (Fitzpatrick) enjoys bragging about his skill in deflowering virgins but his promiscuity has lead Jennie (Sevigny) to test H.I.V. positive—something Telly is as yet unaware of. Telly'd rather hang around with best friend Casper (Pierce) anyway, out on the streets, being generally profane and obnoxious. Can either be regarded as a brutally realistic look at teen life today or a lot of fuss about nothing. Korine was 19 when he wrote the screenplay. The MPAA rated the film NC-17, after a protest the distributors chose to release it unrated. **90m/C; VHS, DVD.** Leo Fitzpatrick; Justin Pierce; Chloë Sevigny; Rosario Dawson; Sarah Henderson; Harold Hunter; Yakira Peguero; Joseph Knafelmacher; Jon Abrahams; ***D:*** Larry Clark; ***W:*** Harmony Korine; ***C:*** Eric Alan Edwards; ***M:*** Louis Barlow. Ind. Spirit '96: Debut Perf. (Pierce).

The Kids Are All Right 🦴🦴🦴 **2010 (R)** Straight 15-year-old Nick (Hutcherson) has no problem with his lesbian moms Jules (Moore) and Nic (Bening) except he feels the need for a guy's outlook. So he persuades older sister Joni (Wasikowska) to search out their sperm-donating, bio dad—very laid-back organic chef Paul (Ruffalo). This throws uptight doc Nic and underachieving Jules into something of a panic when Paul starts hanging out a little too much for their comfort. Great performances by all and the story hits a lot of emotional highs about true family values and culture clashes even among L.A.'s upper-middle class. **104m/C; Blu-Ray.** Julianne Moore; Annette Bening; Mark Ruffalo; Mia Wasikowska; Josh Hutcherson; Kunal Sharma; Yaya DaCosta; Joaquin Garrido; Eddie Hassell; Zosia Mamet; ***D:*** Lisa Cholodenko; ***W:*** Lisa Cholodenko; Stuart Blumberg; ***C:*** Igor Jadue-Lillo; ***M:*** Craig Wedren; Nathan Larson. Golden Globes '11: Actress--Mus./Comedy (Bening), Film--Mus./Comedy; Ind. Spirit '11: Screenplay.

The Kids Are Alright 🦴🦴🦴 ½ **1979 (PG)** A feature-length compilation of performances and interviews spanning the first 15 years of the rock group, The Who. Includes rare footage from the "Rolling Stones Rock and Roll Circus" film. Songs include: "My Generation," "I Can't Explain," "Young Man's Blues," "Won't Get Fooled Again," "Baba O' Reilly," and excerpts from "Tommy." **106m/C; VHS, DVD.** Roger Daltrey; Pete Townshend; Keith Moon; John Entwhistle; Ringo Starr; Keith Richards; Steve Martin; Tom Smothers; Rick Danko; ***D:*** Jeff Stein; ***W:*** Jeff Stein; ***C:*** Anthony B. Richmond; Norman Wexler; ***M:*** Roger Daltrey; Pete Townshend; Keith Moon; John Entwhistle.

Kids in America 🦴 ½ **2005 (PG-13)** Self-satisfied satire finds ambitious, control-freak high school principal Donna Weller (Bowen) clamping down on various activities organized by her mildly-rebellious suburban students. They finally get fed up by her dictatorial policies and decide to fight back. Richie makes her film debut as a (what else?) bimbette cheerleader. **91m/C; DVD.** Andrew Shaifer; Gregory Edward Smith; Caitlin Wachs; Crystal Grant; Stephanie Sherrin; Chris Morris; Emy Coligado; Julie Bowen; Malik Yoba; George Wendt; Adam Arkin; Jeffrey Chase; Nicole Richie; Rosanna Arquette; Elizabeth Perkins; Charles Shaughnessy; Samantha Mathis; Rain Phoenix; Amy Hill; Michelle Phillips; ***D:*** Josh Stolberg; ***W:*** Josh Stolberg; Andrew Shaifer; ***C:*** Guy Livneh; ***M:*** B.C. Smith.

Kids in the Hall: Brain Candy 🦴🦴 *Brain Candy; The Drug* **1996 (R)** The Canadian Kids bring their Monty Python-meets-SCTV humor to the big screen with moderate success. Dr. Cooper (McDonald), facing corporate downsizing, allows his new, untested anti-depressant to be released to the public after it shows promise. The drug, Gleemonex, sweeps the country by forcing the user's mind to focus on a favorite memory. As befits the troupe's twisted vision, these happy memories aren't always pleasant to the "Family Values" crowd. The easily offended should be warned—there's a character named "Cancer Boy." The story wanders a bit, giving everyone a chance to show their versatility (these Kids collectively play 32 different roles). Sophomore director Makin served the same duty on many of the TV episodes. **88m/C; DVD.** Dave Foley; Bruce McCulloch; Kevin McDonald; Scott Thompson; Mark McKinney; Janeane Garofalo; ***D:*** Kelly Makin; ***W:*** Bruce McCulloch; Kevin McDonald; Scott Thompson; Mark McKinney; Norm Hiscock; ***C:*** David Makin; ***M:*** Craig Northey.

Kids of the Round Table 🦴🦴 ½ **1996** Eleven-year-old Alex (Morina) and his buddies like to have mock sword battles, pretending to be King Arthur and his knights. When their games are broken up by the local bully, Alex takes off into the woods where he discovers a sword in a stone. It's the legendary Excalibur and when Alex removes it, Merlin (McDowell) appears, explaining the sword will give the boy special powers. Of course, Alex abuses his newfound strength until he comes to the rescue of his friends. **89m/C; VHS, DVD.** *CA* Johnny Morina; Michael Ironside; Malcolm McDowell; Peter Aykroyd; Rene Simard; *D:* Robert Tinnell; *W:* David Sherman; *C:* Roxanne Di Santo; *M:* Normand Corbeil.

Kika 🦴🦴 **1994** Another flamboyant comedy from Almodovar finds irrepressible beautician Kika (Forque) involved with kinky photographer Ramon (Casanovas) and his stepfather Nicholas (Coyote), a sinister American pulp novelist. There's also Andrea Scarface (Jean-Paul Gaultier-costumed Abril), the host of a vile tabloid TV show called "Today's Worst," and Kika's lesbian maid Juana (de Palma) whose brother happens to be an escaped con/porn star, leading to an outlandish rape and...well, it's all pretty nonsensical, anyway. Spanish with subtitles. **115m/C; VHS, DVD.** *SP* Veronica Forque; Peter Coyote; Victoria Abril; Alex Casanovas; Rossy de Palma; *D:* Pedro Almodóvar; *W:* Pedro Almodóvar; *C:* Alfredo Mayo; *M:* Enrique Granados.

Kiki 🦴🦴 **1926** The 30-something Talmadge was a little old to be playing a Parisian waif but she gave it a spritely shot. Kiki sells newspapers on the street while dreaming of making it in showbiz. When she hears about a chorus girl opening in theater manager Victor Renal's (Colman) new show, she finagles her way into the job. She can sing but her lack of experience causes problems and angers leading lady Paulette (Astor) and Kiki gets fired. However, Victor takes pity on her when he discovers Kiki is homeless but by now she's in love with Victor and he can't get rid of her. **108m/B; Silent; DVD.** Norma Talmadge; Ronald Colman; Gertrude Astor; Marc McDermott; George K. Arthur; Frankie Darro; William Orlamond; *D:* Clarence Brown; *W:* Hans Kraly; *C:* Oliver Marsh.

Kiki's Delivery Service 🦴🦴 ½ **1998 (G)** Young witch Kiki, accompanied by her outspoken cat Jiji, tries to find her place in the world. She becomes the resident witch in a small town and uses her flying-broom to create a bakery delivery service, while making some new friends. Voice cast listed is for the American (dubbed) version. **104m/C; VHS, DVD, Blu-Ray.** *JP V:* Kirsten Dunst; Phil Hartman; Debbie Reynolds; Janeane Garofalo; Matthew Lawrence; Jeff Glenn Bennett; Tress MacNeille; Debi Derryberry; Pamela Segall; Lewis Arquette; *D:* Hayao Miyazaki; *W:* Hayao Miyazaki. **VIDEO**

Kikujiro 🦴🦴 **1999 (PG-13)** Eight-year-old Masao (Sekiguchi) lives with his grandmother. His father is dead and his mother lives in a distant town due to her job. Bored on his summer vacation, the boy decides to visit his mother—accompanied by the tough-guy husband, Kikujiro (Kitano), of a neighbor. Only this guy doesn't have much of an idea about kids and their travels lead to some unpredictable adventures. Clumsy and protracted; Japanese with subtitles. **116m/C; VHS, DVD.** *JP* Takeshi "Beat" Kitano; Yusuke Sekiguchi; *D:* Takeshi "Beat" Kitano; *W:* Takeshi "Beat" Kitano; *C:* Katsumi Yanagishima; *M:* Joe Hisaishi.

Kilimanjaro 🦴 ½ **2013** Ineffectual 20-something New Yorker Brian (Geraghty) is already stuck in a self-made rut until his frustrated girlfriend Clare (Rasmussen) breaks up with him. After watching a TV program on Mt. Kilimanjaro, Brian inexplicably decides he should climb Africa's tallest peak. Of course, he lacks practical experience as well as gumption, so he's easily derailed when his everyday life interferes with his impulsive decision. **80m/C; On Demand.** Brian Geraghty; Abigail Spencer; Christopher Marquette; Jim Gaffigan; Bruce Altman; Alexia Rasmussen; *D:* Walter Stafford; *W:* Walter Stafford; *C:* Gavin Kelly; *M:* Jake Monaco.

Kill! 🦴🦴 ½ *Kiru* **1968** A black comedy parody of Samurai films, this one will be a bit difficult to get the humor if you aren't well-versed in the genre. Two wandering Ronin come into a town fallen on hard times ruled by two warring factions of Yakuza. Each crime family hires one of them as muscle expecting them to kill each other as their first job. **115m/B; DVD.** *JP* Tatsuya Nakadai; Etsushi Takahashi; Yuriko Hoshi; Naoko Kubo; Tadao Nakamaru; Akira Kubo; Shigeru Koyama; Eijiro Tono; Nami Tamura; Yoshio Tsuchiya; Isao Hashimoto; Akira Hamada; Takeo Chii; Sishiro Kuno; Ben Hiura; Emiko Suzuki; Haruo Suzuki; *D:* Kihachi Okamoto; *W:* Kihachi Okamoto; Akira Murao; Shugoro Yamamoto; *C:* Rokuro Nishigaki; *M:* Masaru Sato.

Kill a Dragon 🦴 **1967** Unbelievable crime/martial arts combo. Mercenary Rick (Palance) operates out of Hong Kong and is hired by Chinese locals from a nearby island when they have trouble with crime boss Patrai (Lamas). A valuable cargo of nitro has washed ashore and Patrai is claiming the goods for himself and threatening the villagers if they interfere. **91m/C; DVD.** Jack Palance; Fernando Lamas; Aldo Ray; Aliza Gur; Kam Tom; *D:* Michael D. Moore; *W:* George Schenck; William Marks; *C:* Emmanuel I. Rojas; *M:* Philip Springer.

Kill and Kill Again 🦴🦴 ½ **1981 (PG)** A martial arts champion attempts to rescue a kidnapped Nobel Prize-winning chemist who has developed a high-yield synthetic fuel. Colorful, tongue-in-cheek, and fun even for those unfamiliar with the genre. **100m/C; VHS, DVD, Blu-Ray.** James Ryan; Anneline Kriel; Stan Schmidt; Bill Flynn; Norman Robinson; Ken Gampu; John Ramsbottom; *D:* Ivan Hall; *W:* John Crowther; *C:* Tai Krige.

Kill, Baby, Kill 🦴🦴🦴 *Curse of the Living Dead; Operacione Paura* **1966** A small Transylvania town is haunted by the ghost of a seven-year-old witchcraft victim, and the town's suicide victims all seem to have hearts of gold (coins, that is). Lots of style and atmosphere in this Transylvanian tale from horror tongue in cheekster Bava. Considered by many genre connoisseurs to be the B man's finest, except that it bears early symptoms of the director's late onset infatuation with the zoom shot. **83m/C; VHS, DVD, Blu-Ray.** *IT* Erika Blanc; Giacomo "Jack" Rossi-Stuart; Fabienne Dali; Giana Vivaldi; *D:* Mario Bava; *W:* Mario Bava; *C:* Antonio Rinaldi; *M:* Carlo Rustichelli.

Kill Bill Vol. 1 🦴🦴🦴 ½ **2003 (R)** Tarantino is back with a vengeance. In the first of two volumes of what originally was supposed to be a single film, Uma Thurman is spectacular as The Bride, a former assassin, betrayed and left for dead at her wedding by her associates and mysterious boss, Bill. When she awakens from a coma four years later she begins a mission of revenge that takes her from suburban L.A. to Okinawa, to Tokyo. Tarantino joyfully and masterfully immerses the audience in the different styles and ultraviolence of the Asian cinema he loves so much, even using anime for one backstory sequence, with some spaghetti western and '70s TV added for spice. His trademark sharp dialogue is not as plentiful as in the past, but what's here is layered, sometimes moving, and often humorous. Tarantino fave Chiba delivers as a master samurai swordmaker. **110m/C; VHS, DVD, Blu-Ray, UMD.** Uma Thurman; Lucy Liu; Vivica A. Fox; Michael Madsen; Daryl Hannah; Gordon (Chia Hui) Liu; Sonny Chiba; Michael Parks; Chiaki Kuriyama; Jun Kunimura; Julie Dreyfus; Larry Bishop; Michael Bowen; *V:* David Carradine; *D:* Quentin Tarantino; *W:* Quentin Tarantino; *C:* Robert Richardson; *M:* RZA.

Kill Bill Vol. 2 🦴🦴🦴 ½ **2004 (R)** The Bride continues to work her way through her former associates on the way to the big showdown with Bill, where she discovers some unexpected developments. This volume has less action than the first, but it is just as intense. All that was hidden in Vol. 1 is revealed, and it's done with more of the character development and dialogue-driven scenes that some thought were lacking in the first installment. The two volumes are so vastly different in tone and style that it seems odd that they were intended as one (very) long movie, but the idea of seeing them united into one film is intriguing. Carradine gives what might be the finest performance of his career as the enigmatic Bill. Thurman proves that her work on set was more than just physical, and that she can carry a movie even when she isn't carrying a sword. **137m/C; DVD, Blu-Ray, UMD.** Uma Thurman; David Carradine; Lucy Liu; Michael Madsen; Vivica A. Fox; Daryl Hannah; Michael Parks; Julie Dreyfus; Chiaki Kuriyama; Sonny Chiba; Gordon (Chia Hui) Liu; LaTanya Richardson Jackson; Bo Svenson; Samuel L. Jackson; Jeannie Epper; Perla Haney-Jardine; Caitlin Keats; Christopher Allen Nelson; Stevo Polyi; Venessia Valentino; *D:* Quentin Tarantino; *W:* Uma Thurman; Quentin Tarantino; *C:* Robert Richardson; *M:* RZA; Robert Rodriguez.

Kill by Inches 🦴🦴 **1999** Strange and stylized story follows traumatized tailor Thomas Klamm (Salinger) who, as a child, was forced by his authortarian father (Powell) to literally eat a tape measure as punishment for a dispute with his sister. Since then, Tom finds a sexual thrill in the measurement of human bodies. Sister Vera (Cyr), also a tailor, suddenly shows up at Thomas' Brooklyn shop with her own special gifts and they play out their odd sibling rivalry. **85m/C; VHS, DVD.** *FR* Emmanuel Salinger; Myriam Cyr; Marcus Powell; Peter McRobbie; *D:* Diane Doniol-Valcroze; Arthur Flam; *W:* Diane Doniol-Valcroze; Arthur Flam; *C:* Richard Rutkowski; *M:* Geir Jenssen.

Kill Castro 🦴 **1980 (R)** Ever hear the one about the exploding cigar? Key West boat skipper is forced to carry a CIA agent to Cuba on a mission to assassinate Castro. Low-budget adventure that's deadly dull. **90m/C; VHS, DVD.** Sybil Danning; Albert Salmi; Michael V. Gazzo; Raymond St. Jacques; Woody Strode; Stuart Whitman; Robert Vaughn; Caren Kaye; *D:* Chuck Workman.

Kill Cruise 🦴🦴 **1990 (R)** The depressed and alcoholic skipper of the yacht Bella Donna gives up sailing until he meets two beautiful young women who want to sail to Bermuda for a taste of the good life. The calm of the Atlantic is disturbed when they are plagued by bad weather and fierce storms, and tensions rise as the two women's jealousies erupt. Will it set the climate for murder? **99m/C; VHS, DVD.** Jurgen Prochnow; Patsy Kensit; Elizabeth Hurley; *D:* Peter Keglevic; *W:* Peter Keglevic; *C:* Edward Klosinski; *M:* Brynmor Jones.

Kill Django 🦴🦴 *Kill Django...Kill First ; Uccidi Django... uccidi per primo!!!* **1971** A gunfighter takes on a banker trying to acquire all the local mines in a land grab. Currently only available as part of the 'Westerns Unchained' collection. **97m/C; Blu-Ray.** *IT SP* Giacomo "Jack" Rossi-Stuart; George Wang; Aldo Sambrell; Krista Nell; Silvio Bagolini; *D:* Sergio Garrone; *W:* Sergio Garrone; Ambrogio Molteni; Victoria Andres Catena; *C:* Francisco Sánchez; *M:* Elsio Mancuso. **VIDEO**

Kill 'Em All 🦴 **2012** A madman kidnaps the world's top assassins and traps them in a bunker. To leave they must fight one another and their tormentor's pet ninjas. **86m/C; DVD, Blu-Ray, Streaming.** Johnny Messner; Chia Hui Liu; Ammara Siripong; Joe Lewis; Brahim Achabbakhe; *D:* Raimund Huber; *W:* Ken Miller; *C:* Vardhana Wachuplao; *M:* Alec Puro. **VIDEO**

Kill Factor WOOF! *Death Dimension; Black Eliminator; The Freeze Bomb* **1978 (R)** Something stupid about a killer bomb tht could freeze the planet. So inept your brain cells will also be frozen if you watch it. **91m/C; VHS, DVD.** Jim Kelly; George Lazenby; Aldo Ray; Harold Sakata; Terry Moore; *D:* Al Adamson.

Kill for Me 🦴 ½ **2012 (R)** Slow-paced thriller with too many obvious plot twists. Amanda and new roommate Hailey share abusive pasts--Amanda from an ex-boyfriend and Hailey from her father. Amanda's ex shows up, and Hailey helps her out but wants a favor in return. **95m/C; DVD.** *CA* Katie Cassidy; Tracy Spiridakos; Donal Logue; Adam DiMarco; Ryan Robbins; *D:* Michael Greenspan; *W:* Michael Greenspan; Christopher Dodd; *C:* James Liston; *M:* Michael Brook. **VIDEO**

The Kill Hole 🦴 ½ **2012** Disjointed thriller. Former Marine Samuel Drake suffers from PTSD and is having problems adjusting to his civilian life in Oregon. Drake is approached by two intelligence agents who coerce him into tracking crazy vet Devon Carter, who's off in the wilderness plotting terrorist acts. Carter may be crazy but he's right that a shadowy government organization is out to get him. **98m/C; DVD.** Chadwick Boseman; Tory Kittles; Peter Greene; Billy Zane; Dennis Adkins; Ted Rooney; *D:* Mischa S. Webley; *W:* Mischa S. Webley; *C:* Eric Billman; *M:* Jason Wells. **VIDEO**

Kill Katie Malone 🦴 **2010 (R)** Clumsy, innocuous horror. College students Kyle, Jim, and Ginger buy a ghost in an online auction though they're sure it's a prank. However, the antique box contains the vengeful spirit of a servant girl who starts upping the campus body count. **91m/C; DVD, Blu-Ray.** Jonathan McDaniel; Stephen Colletti; Masiela Lusha; Sylvia Panacione; Dean Cain; *D:* Carlos Ramos, Jr.; *W:* Carlos Ramos, Jr.; Mark Onspaugh; *C:* Aaron Moorhead. **VIDEO**

Kill Line 🦴🦴 **1991 (R)** Kim stars as Joe, a street fighter who seeks to clear his name after serving a 10-year prison sentence for a crime he didn't commit. When he finds his brother's family has been murdered by criminals looking for the millions he supposedly stole, Joe wages a one-man martial arts war against a corrupt police force and the gang of thugs who are looking for the money. **93m/C; VHS, DVD.** Bobby Kim; Michael Parker; Marlene Zimmerman; H. Wayne Lowery; C.R. Valdez; Mark Williams; Ben Pfeifer; *D:* Richard H. Kim; *W:* Richard H. Kim.

Kill List 🦴🦴 ½ **2012** Defiantly bizarre, director/writer Wheatley's thriller is practically three films in one. The first act details the rough home life of a former soldier named Jay (Maskell) and his wife Shel (Buring). It is revealed that Jay and his friend Gal (Smiley) are hired killers and the second act plays not unlike a Quentin Tarantino film. Finally, it turns into a horror flick. Unabashedly original, yet still a bit too incoherent to be completely effective. **95m/C; DVD, Blu-Ray.** *GB* Neil Maskell; Michael Smiley; MyAnna Buring; Emma Fryer; *D:* Ben Wheatley; *W:* Ben Wheatley; Amy Jump; *C:* Laurie Rose; *M:* Jim Williams.

Kill Me Again 🦴🦴 ½ **1989 (R)** Director Dahl does the contemporary noir thing through the Nevada desert with Whalley as a beautiful femme fatale. She asks a detective (then husband Kilmer) to fake her death, which gets him targeted not only by the police, but also the mob and her psychoboyfriend (Madsen). Fun and full of plot twists that will satisfy fans of the noir persuasion. **93m/C; VHS, DVD, Blu-Ray.** Val Kilmer; Joanne Whalley; Michael Madsen; Jon(athan) Gries; Bibi Besch; *D:* John Dahl; *W:* John Dahl; David Warfield; *C:* Jacques Steyn.

Kill Me Later 🦴🦴 **2001 (R)** Loan officer Shawn (Blair) has just broken up with her married lover/boss (Moffett) and decides to kill herself by jumping off the bank's roof. However, she's just in time to become the hostage of British thief Charlie (Beesley) whose robbery of the bank has gone wrong. Shawn agrees to help Charlie escape if he will agree to kill her later. An unlikely romance blossoms as the on the lam duo are tracked by a couple of FBI agents. **89m/C; VHS, DVD.** Selma Blair; Max Beesley; Lochlyn Munro; O'Neal Compton; Brendan Fehr; D.W. Moffett; *D:* Dana Lustig; *W:* Annette Goliti Gutierrez; *C:* David Ferrara; *M:* Tal Bergman; Renato Neto.

Kill Me Quick, I'm Cold 🦴 ½ **1967** Crime comedy finds lovers Giovanna and Franco pretending to be brother and sister as they scam wealthy marks at luxury hotels. While traveling, they meet Christina who tells them she's being threatened by her brother, Sergio, who wants to be the sole heir to the family fortune. But things aren't as they seem. Italian with subtitles. **98m/B; DVD.** *IT* Monica Vitti; Jean Sorel; Daniela Surina; Roberto Bisacco; *D:* Francesco Maselli; *W:* Francesco Maselli; *C:* Alfio Contini; *M:* Gianni Marchetti.

Kill Me Tomorrow 🦴🦴 **1957** Hard-drinking, widowed reporter Bart Crosbie loses his job just when he learns his son needs an expensive operation. He finds his ex-boss murdered and diamond smuggler Webber, who did the crime, makes a deal to pay Crosbie to take the fall. Only Scotland Yard doesn't believe Crosbie when he tries to confess and Webber starts thinking Crosbie reneged on their deal. **80m/B; DVD.** *GB* Lois Maxwell; Wensley Pithey; George Coulouris; Pat O'Brien; Freddie Mills; Claude Kingston; *D:* Terence Fisher; *W:* Robert Falconer; Paddy Manning O'Brine; *C:* Geoffrey Faithfull; *M:* Temple Abady.

Kill Me Tomorrow 🦴 ½ **1999** Teenaged witch Holly (Vamshon) sets her sights on hunk Russell (Sheppard), which doesn't sit well with his present girlfriend Tricia (Shafia). So Holly decides to get even by stealing his soul. The inexperience of the cast shows up bigtime but they're very earnest. **80m/C; VHS, DVD.** Louisa Shafia; Gregory Sheppard; Lyndee Yamshon; ***D:*** Patrick McGuinn; ***W:*** Patrick McGuinn. **VIDEO**

The Kill-Off **1989 (R)** Bedridden Luanne (Gross), married to janitor Ralph (Monroe), manages to cause dissension in her isolated New Jersey community with her vicious gossip. But when Luanne learns Ralph's involved with a stripper (Haase), it puts her own life in danger. Based on a story by Jim Thompson. **100m/C; DVD.** Loretta Gross; Andrew Lee Barrett; Cathy Haase; Jackson Sims; Jorja Fox; ***D:*** Maggie Greenwald; ***W:*** Maggie Greenwald; ***C:*** Declan Quinn; ***M:*** Evan Lurie.

Kill or Be Killed *Kill or Die* **1966 (PG)** Martial arts champion is lured to a phony martial arts contest by a madman bent on revenge. **90m/C; VHS, DVD, Blu-Ray.** James Ryan; Charlotte Michelle; Norman Coombes; ***D:*** Ivan Hall.

Kill or Be Killed ½ **1993** Michael Julian just spent eight years in jail for saving his brother Charlie's life. He must wonder why he bothered since Charlie has stolen his girl Beth and set up a drug empire. Michael ambushes Charlie's men and steals $1 million to use as leverage but Charlie thinks rival drug lords are out to get him and starts a street war. **97m/C; VHS, DVD.** David Heavener; Joseph Nuzzolo; Paulo Tocha; Lynn Levand; ***D:*** Joe Straw; ***W:*** Joseph Nuzzolo.

Kill or Be Killed **2015** Texas-set western focused on a desperate gang of outlaws and the men in search of them. Known for their daring robberies, Claude "Sweet Tooth" Barbee (Meeks) and his group of outlaws once committed a very bold, but botched, railroad heist and buried the fortune they acquired. Now Barbee wants out of the game and gang members are the most wanted men in Texas. To put Barbee's "retirement plan" into motion, they are riding hundreds of miles across the vastness to recover the hidden loot. Their journey soon becomes more urgent as the gang is pursued by those in search of the "dead or alive" bounty on each of their heads. As more members of the gang get picked off, the rest seek both the money and survival. **103m/C; DVD, Streaming, Download.** Justin Meeks; Paul McCarthy-Boyington; Greg Kelly; Deon Lucas; Bridger Zadina; ***D:*** Justin Meeks; Duane Graves; ***W:*** Justin Meeks; Duane Graves; ***C:*** Brandon Torres; ***M:*** John Constant; Nick Durham.

Kill or Cure ½ **1962** Minor Brit comedy set at a health spa. A wealthy dowager hires PI J. Barker-Rynde to investigate suspicious goings-on at Green Glades. He arrives to find his client has been poisoned and must endure various indignities to find the killer. **98m/B; DVD.** *UK* Terry-Thomas; Eric Sykes; Dennis Price; Lionel Jeffries; Ronnie Barker; Moira Redmond; Derren Nesbitt; ***D:*** George Pollock; ***W:*** Jack Seddon; David Pursall; ***C:*** Geoffrey Faithfull; ***M:*** Ronald Goodwin.

Kill Switch *A Higher Form of Learning* **2008 (R)** Typically lumbering Seagal effort. Homicide detective Jacob King (Seagal) is so successful at apprehending serial killers that the FBI assigns naive agent Frankie Miller (Dignard) to study his methods. But King may have met his match in Lazereus (Filipowich), the current psycho terrorizing Memphis, who plants evidence that makes it look like King has finally gone over to the dark side. **96m/C; DVD, Blu-Ray.** Steven Seagal; Chris Thomas King; Michael Filipowich; Mark Collie; Holly Dignard; Isaac Hayes; ***D:*** Jeff King; ***W:*** Steven Seagal; ***C:*** Thomas M. (Tom) Harting; ***M:*** John Sereda. **VIDEO**

Kill the Irishman **2011 (R)** By-the-numbers true crime wiseguy movie set in 1970s Cleveland, based on the book by district police chief Rick Porrello. Danny Greene (Stevenson) goes from longshoreman to corrupt union boss to mob enforcer. Then Greene teams up with local gangster John Nardi (D'Onforio) in a turf war with New York-based Tony Salerno (Sorvino) that results in 36 bombings in the summer of 1976 and repeated attempts on Greene's life. **106m/C; DVD, Blu-Ray.** Ray Stevenson; Vincent D'Onofrio; Paul Sorvino; Val Kilmer; Christopher Walken; Robert Davi; Vinnie Jones; Tony Lo Bianco; Tony Darrow; Mike Starr; Steve Schirripa; Linda Cardellini; Fionnula Flanagan; Laura Ramsey; ***D:*** Jonathan Hensleigh; ***W:*** Jonathan Hensleigh; Jeremy Walters; ***C:*** Karl Walter Lindenlaub; ***M:*** Patrick Cassidy.

Kill the Messenger **2014 (R)** Cuesta's true story drama stars Renner as Gary Webb, a reporter whose life was ruined after he exposed the role between the Contras in Nicaragua, cocaine, and the CIA. Renner embraces the role and for that alone the film is worth seeing even if it gets a little cluttered and loses some of the human story underneath the international espionage and location jumping. Cuesta can't quite find the right tone for such a challenging story, but Renner infuses every frame with the perfect balance of character and righteous indignation over our broken system. **112m/C; DVD, Blu-Ray.** Jeremy Renner; Michael K(enneth) Williams; Andy Garcia; Michael Sheen; Yul Vazquez; Rosemarie DeWitt; Lucas Hedges; Ray Liotta; Tim Blake Nelson; Barry Pepper; Oliver Platt; Paz Vega; ***D:*** Michael Cuesta; ***W:*** Peter Landesman; ***C:*** Sean Bobbitt; ***M:*** Nathan Johnson.

Kill the Poor **2003** When Joe's wife becomes pregnant, it's clear that their marriage of convenience will suddenly take emotional root and they'd better grow up, right now. Rather than moving out of their New York squatter building in the Lower East Side, Joe decides to become its co-op president, fighting off crackheads with a baseball bat and sleeping in the lobby as night security. Dark comedies normally only work if the comedy part is exercised. This one needs to lighten up. Labor of love for director Alan Taylor, who struggled to adapt Joel Rose's tragicomic novel for 15 years. **84m/C; DVD.** David Krumholtz; Clara Bellar; Paul Calderon; Larry (Lawrence) Gilliard, Jr.; Jon Budinoff; Cliff Gorman; Damian Young; Heather Burns; Otto Sanchez; Zak Orth; ***D:*** Alan Taylor; ***W:*** Daniel Handler; ***C:*** Harlan Bosmajian; ***M:*** Michel Delory; Anna Domino.

Kill the Umpire ½ **1950** Baseball comedy with much shtick and sight gags. Bill Johnson (Bendix) keeps losing jobs because he's always skipping work to go to baseball games. With his wife (Merkel) threatening to take the kids and leave, Bill's father-in-law Jonah (Collins), a retired ump, comes up with a solution and sends him to umpire school despite Bill's contempt for the guy the fans love to hate. After graduation, Bill is assigned to the Texas Interstate League where he discovers a couple of gamblers are trying to fix the pennant race. **78m/B; DVD.** William Bendix; Una Merkel; Jeff Richards; Ray Collins; Gloria Henry; Connie Marshall; William Frawley; Tom D'Andrea; Jeff York; Robert J. Wilke; ***D:*** Lloyd Bacon; ***W:*** Frank Tashlin; ***C:*** Charles Lawton, Jr.; ***M:*** Heinz Roemheld.

Kill Your Darlings **2006 (R)** Swede Erik (Wilson) is a failed Hollywood screenwriter. In an attempt to jump-start his life, Erik allows crazy free spirit Lola (Davidovich) to talk him into a road trip into the desert but she has ulterior motives. Meanwhile, celebrity shrink Dr. Bagley (Larroquette) has arranged for some of his suicidal patients to attend his book signing in Vegas. Think the two parallel plots will combine? **94m/C; DVD.** *US SW* Andreas Wilson; Lolita Davidovich; John Larroquette; Julie Benz; Alexander Skarsgård; Greg Germann; Skye McCole Bartusiak; Benito Martinez; Fares Fares; John Savage; Stellan Skarsgard; Terry Moore; ***D:*** Bjorne Larson; ***W:*** Bjorne Larson; Johan Sandstrom; Lisa Taube; ***C:*** Irek Hartowicz; ***M:*** Jon Rekdal.

Kill Your Darlings ½ **2013 (R)** Beat writers, the early years. Sensitive Columbia freshman Allen Ginsberg (Radcliffe) secretly falls for troublemaking, headstrong poet Lucien Carr (DeHaan), who introduces the timid writer to the nitrous-huffing William Burroughs (Foster) and swaggering journeyman Jack Kerouac (Huston). But besides conflicted sexual dynamics and drugs, Carr has an older, love-stricken stalker (Hall) and this leads to a shocking act. Radcliffe does his best but is overmatched by his supporting cast. An informed literary melodrama, based on a true incident, which never betters the source material. **104m/C; DVD, Blu-Ray.** Daniel Radcliffe; Dane DeHaan; Ben Foster; Jack Huston; Michael C. Hall; David Cross; Jennifer Jason Leigh; Elizabeth Olsen; ***D:*** John Krokidas; ***W:*** John Krokidas; Austin Burn; ***C:*** Reed Morano; ***M:*** Nico Muhly.

Kill Your Friends **2016** Steven Stelfox (Hoult) is an A&R man in '90s England—the heyday of Oasis and Blur—and he's willing to do absolutely anything to get ahead in this blend of a traditional office comedy and "American Psycho." When it looks like one of his dumber colleagues (Corden) is going to catch an undeserved break, Steven strangles him with a dog leash. And his crimes get more intense from there..and the movie gets less interesting. Carried by Hoult's charisma, the first half works. As it gets darker, it gets less interesting and less funny, fatally so. **103m/C; DVD, Blu-Ray.** Nicholas Hoult; James Corden; Georgia King; Craig Roberts; Jim Piddock; ***D:*** Owen Harris; ***W:*** John Niven; ***C:*** Gustav Danielsson; ***M:*** Junkie XL.

Kill Zone ½ **2008** Fugitive Prescott Roeh has bounty hunters on his trail but he decides he must return to his hometown to make amends for his crimes. But not everyone is ready to forgive and forget. **110m/C; DVD.** Brandon Chase; Troy Davidson; Ryan Michael Jones; ***D:*** Vitor Santos; ***W:*** Vitor Santos; Chris Carberg; ***C:*** Vitor Santos; ***M:*** Assaf Rinde. **VIDEO**

Killa Season ½ **2006 (R)** A completely un-original film that's a semi-autobiographical wish fulfillment story written and directed by a rapper (Giles, aka Cam'ron) who wants to portray himself as a drug dealing gangster who flouts the law. **126m/C; DVD.** Cam'ron; Michael Williams; Durrel Mohammad; Juelz Santana; Flexmaster Flex; Malcolm Ross; James Roach; Leshawn Rogers; DJ Megatron; Big Joe; Osas Ighodaro; ***D:*** Cam'ron; ***W:*** Cam'ron; ***M:*** Kerry Muzzey.

The Killer ½ *Die Xue Shuang Xiong* **1990 (R)** Jeffrey Chow is a gangster gunman who wants out. He's hired by his best friend to perform one last killing, but it doesn't go as smoothly as he wanted. He's almost caught by "Eagle" Lee, a detective who vows to hunt him down using Jennie, a singer blinded by Chow in crossfire. Lots of action and gunfights, but also pretty corny and sentimental. Very similar to American action movies, but using Chinese and Asian cultural conventions. A good introduction to the Chinese gangster-flick genre. Available with subtitles or dubbed in English. **110m/C; VHS, DVD, Blu-Ray.** *CH* Chow Yun-Fat; Sally Yeh; Danny Lee; Kenneth Tsang; Chu Kong; Fui-On Shing; ***D:*** John Woo; ***W:*** John Woo; ***C:*** Wing-Hung Wong; Peter Pau; ***M:*** Lowell Lo.

Killer: A Journal of Murder **1995 (R)** Young, idealistic Jewish guard Henry Lesser (Leonard) befriends prisoner Carl Panzram (Woods) and encourages the man to write his life story. Then he must deal with the consequences of discovering the brutality behind Panzram's murderous crimes. The leads do fine but there's nothing new here. Inspired by true events and set in the 1920s. **91m/C; VHS, DVD.** James Woods; Robert Sean Leonard; Ellen Greene; Cara Buono; Robert John Burke; Steve Forrest; John Bedford Lloyd; Harold Gould; ***D:*** Tim Metcalfe; ***W:*** Tim Metcalfe; ***C:*** Ken Kelsch; ***M:*** Graeme Revell.

A Killer Among Friends ½ *Friends For Life* **1992** Effective CBS TV true crime drama. Jean Monroe (Duke) is devastated when her teenage daughter Jenny (Thiessen) is murdered. Jean takes some solace when Jenny's best friend Ellen (Welsh) moves into the Monroe home, vowing to help Jean find the killer. **96m/C; DVD.** Patty Duke; Margaret Welsh; Loretta Swit; Tiffani(-Amber) Thiessen; Angie Ray McKinney; David Cubitt; ***D:*** Charles Robert Carner; ***W:*** Charles Robert Carner; Christopher Lofton; ***C:*** Richard Leiterman; ***M:*** Richard Bellis. **TV**

Killer Bees **2002** Many films have been made on invasions of Africanized killer bees, and most of them have been predictably bad low budget bombs. This one is made for television so the budget is lower than usual. The typical small town law enforcement officer tries to figure out what's killing the townsfolk while the audience gets bored waiting for him to play catch-up. **90m/C; DVD.** C. Thomas Howell; Tracy Nelson; Fiona Loewi; Noel Fisher; Emily Tennant; Doug Abrahams; Tom Heaton; Chris Lovick; Michael P. Northey; Betty Linde; Natasha Wilson; Ralph J. Alderman; ***D:*** Penelope Buitenhuis; ***W:*** Dana Stone; ***C:*** Mahlon Todd Williams; ***M:*** John Sereda; Michael Thomas. **TV**

Killer Bud ½ **2000 (R)** Best buds Waylon (Nemec) and Buzz (Faustino) get fired and decide to to go on a road trip to score babes and marijuana. They're incredibly dumb—as is the movie—but it's funny in a stupid, I can't believe I'm watching this, kinda way. **92m/C; VHS, DVD.** Corin "Corky" Nemec; David Faustino; Robert Stack; Danielle Harris; Caroline Keenan; ***D:*** Karl T. Hirsch; ***W:*** Greg DePaul; Hank Nelken; ***C:*** David Lewis; ***M:*** Russ Landau.

Killer by Nature **2010** Nature vs. nurture debate figures in when the son of a serial killer, who's a serial killer himself, is days away from execution. Meanwhile, troubled Owen Whitmore has a sleep disorder leading to violent dreams and sleepwalking. Before long there are dead bodies with Owen as a suspect as well as shrinks, hypnosis, and various plot twists. **90m/C; DVD.** Zachary Ray Sherman; Ron Perlman; Armand Assante; Lin Shaye; Richard Riehle; Svetlana Efremova; ***D:*** Douglas S. Younglove; ***W:*** Douglas S. Younglove; ***C:*** Ben Kufrin; ***M:*** Veigar Margeirsson. **VIDEO**

Killer by Night **1972** CBS TV movie. Virologist Larry Ross (Wagner) is worried that a woman hospitalized with diptheria has spread the contagious disease. When he goes to the cops for help, Capt. Benson (Morris) is using his resources to find a cop killer. Naturally, the two investigations soon tie together. **96m/C; DVD.** Robert Wagner; Greg Morris; Diane Baker; Theodore Bikel; Robert Lansing; Mercedes McCambridge; ***D:*** Bernard McEveety; ***W:*** David Harmon; ***C:*** Robert B. Hauser; ***M:*** Quincy Jones. **TV**

Killer Cop ½ **2002 (R)** A TV crew doing a reality show on police is bored and disappointed when nothing seems to be happening so they hire officer Rick Callahan (Williams) to catch a few thugs. To make a good impression he arranges for a few to escape so he can catch them, and oddly enough things don't go according to plan. **91m/C; DVD, Blu-Ray.** Adam Clark; Adam Ambruso; Aaron Braxton; Valentino Ferreira; Brad Heller; Carrie Janisse; Thomas Fuhler; Angela Ho; James Quinn; Mario Quinonez, Jr.; Shane Scalco; Scott Rocco Shonts; Wade Williams; Peter Spinella; ***D:*** Mark Rylewski; ***W:*** Mark Rylewski; ***C:*** Armand Gazarian; Michel Thiriet; ***M:*** Daniel Walker.

Killer Deal ½ **1999** A worldwide economic collapse creates a two-class system of haves—who live in the walled community of Parkland—and have-nots who struggle to survive. The poor are useful as paid organ donors so the rich can live longer. An exception is heroic police detective James Quinn (Rossovich) and his family, who are allowed to live in Parkland, but his situation changes when he turns out to be a perfect organ match for the desperate creator of the donor program. **90m/C; DVD.** Rick Rossovich; Claudette Mink; Ellen Dubin; Peter MacNeill; Richard Eden; Udo Kier; Desiree Nosbuch; Joseph Scoren; ***D:*** Clay Borris; ***W:*** Peter Hankoff; William Gray; ***C:*** Adam Swica; ***M:*** Jim McGrath. **TV**

Killer Dill ½ **1947** Also killer dull. A meek salesman is misidentified as a death-dealing gangster, and the comic mixups begin. **71m/B; VHS, DVD.** Stuart Erwin; Anne Gwynne; Frank Albertson; Mike Mazurki; Milburn Stone; Dorothy Granger; ***D:*** Lewis D. Collins.

Killer Diller ½ **1948** All-black musical revue featuring Nat King Cole and his Trio. **70m/B; VHS, DVD.** Dusty Fletcher; Nat King Cole; Butterfly McQueen; Moms (Jackie) Mabley; George Wiltshire; ***D:*** Josh Binney.

Killer Diller **2004 (PG-13)** Trouble-making, guitar-playing Wesley (Scott) is sentenced to a halfway house located on a Baptist college campus where he's supposed to join in the gospel ensemble. But when he meets autistic Vernon (Black), a piano prodigy, he decides to form a blues group instead and convinces everyone to sneak away to play at the local honky-tonk. **95m/C; DVD.** William Lee Scott; Lucas Black; Fred Willard; W. Earl Brown; Robert Wisdom; Mary Kay Place; Taj Mahal; Ashley Johnson; RonReaco Lee; ***D:*** Tricia Brock; ***W:*** Tricia Brock; ***C:*** Matthew Jensen; ***M:*** Tree Adama.

The Killer Elite 🦴🦴 1/2 **1975 (PG)** Straight-ahead Peckinpah fare examining friendship and betrayal. Two professional assassins begin as friends but end up stalking each other when they are double-crossed. This minor Peckinpah effort is murky and doesn't have a clear resolution, but is plenty bloody. Lots of Dobermans roam through this picture too. **120m/C; VHS, DVD, Blu-Ray.** James Caan; Robert Duvall; Arthur Hill; Gig Young; Burt Young; Mako; Bo Hopkins; Helmut Dantine; ***D:*** Sam Peckinpah; ***W:*** Marc Norman; Stirling Silliphant; ***C:*** Peter Lathrop; ***M:*** Jerry Fielding.

Killer Elite 🦴 **2011 (R)** With yet another lethargic performance from Statham (and an even drowsier one from De Niro), the action star's latest shoot-'em-up is dull and absurd even by his standards. The bald icon plays a British special ops agent who is tasked with killing three of his countrymen in order to save the life of his former mentor (De Niro). As he's being tracked by an equally deadly agent (Owen), it becomes harder and harder to care about these ho-hum characters. The cliches are so tired and outdated that the result is nothing but deadly boredom. **116m/C; DVD, Blu-Ray.** Jason Statham; Clive Owen; Robert De Niro; Yvonne Strahovski; Dominic Purcell; ***D:*** Gary McKendry; ***W:*** Matt Sherring; ***C:*** Simon Duggan; ***M:*** Reinhold Heil; Johnny Klimek.

Killer Hair 🦴🦴 **2009** One of two unimpressive Lifetime adaptations of Ellen Byerrum's "Crime of Fashion" mysteries although Lawson does fine as D.C. reporter Lacey Smithsonian and Webster is appropriately hunky as Vic Donovan. Hairdresser Angela is an apparent suicide but fellow stylist, and Lacey's BFF, Stella is positive she was murdered and asks Lacey to snoop around. Followed by "Hostile Makeover." **87m/C; Streaming.** Maggie Lawson; Victor Webster; Sadie LeBlanc; Sarah Edmondson; James McDaniel; Mark Consuelos; Mario Cantone; Finola Hughes; ***D:*** Jerry Ciccoritti; ***W:*** Elisa Bell; ***C:*** Danny Nowak; ***M:*** James Gelfand. **CABLE**

Killer Image 🦴 **1992 (R)** A photographer unwittingly sees more than he should and becomes involved in a lethal political coverup. At the same time a wealthy senator targets him and he must fight for his life. Viewers might feel they have to fight their boredom. **97m/C; VHS, DVD.** John Pyper-Ferguson; Michael Ironside; M. Emmet Walsh; Krista Errickson; ***D:*** David Winning.

A Killer in the Family 🦴🦴 **1983** Convicted killer Gary Tison (Mitchum) convinces his three sons to bust him and cellmate Randy Greenwalt (Margolin) out of prison. Then psycho dad makes sure they are all part of his Southwest crime spree. Based on the true story of the 1978 escape of Tison and Greenwalt from the Arizona State Prison. **95m/C; DVD.** Robert Mitchum; James Spader; Eric Stoltz; Lance Kerwin; Stuart Margolin; Salome Jens; Lynn Carlin; Arliss Howard; ***D:*** Richard T. Heffron; ***W:*** Robert Aller; ***C:*** Hanania Baer; ***M:*** Gerald Fried. **TV**

The Killer Inside Me 🦴🦴 **1976 (R)** The inhabitants of a small Western town are unaware that their mild-mannered deputy sheriff is actually becoming a crazed psychotic murderer. From the novel by Jim Thompson. **99m/C; VHS, DVD.** Stacy Keach; Susan Tyrrell; Tisha Sterling; Keenan Wynn; John Dehner; John Carradine; Don Stroud; Charles McGraw; Julie Adams; Royal Dano; ***D:*** Burt Kennedy; ***W:*** Robert Chandlee; ***C:*** William A. Fraker; ***M:*** Tim McIntire; John Rubinstein.

The Killer Inside Me 🦴🦴 1/2 **2010 (R)** Set in 1950's West Texas. Lou Ford (Affleck) is a mild-mannered deputy sheriff—and homicidal nutjob—who is sent to resolve a domestic concern between a prostitute (Alba) and the son of a wealthy developer. After a brief chat, the wacko deputy and prostitute burst into sudden rough sex, resulting in an affair and eventual bloody crime scene. Meanwhile his naive girlfriend (Hudson) waits in the wings. Clumsy adaptation of Jim Thompson's pulpy 1952 crime novel. A rare misfire from normally sharp director Winterbottom with little more than a ferocious performance from Affleck. **108m/C; Blu-Ray.** Casey Affleck; Kate Hudson; Jessica Alba; Simon Baker; Bill Pullman; Ned Beatty; Elias Koteas; Tom Bower; Jay R. Ferguson; Liam Aiken; Mathew Maher; ***D:*** Michael Winterbottom; ***W:*** John Curran; ***C:*** Marcel Zyskind; ***M:*** Mark Tildesley; Lynette Meyer; Melissa Parmenter; Joel Cadbury. Golden Raspberries '10: Worst Support. Actress (Alba).

Killer Instinct 🦴🦴 **2000 (R)** A bunch of teens attempt to spend the night in a creepy abandoned mental hospital, with predictably bloody results. Meanwhile, an outsider trying to broker the sale of a factory, the small town's main employer, finds out deadly secrets about the place. Somehow, the two stories are related and tied up nicely. **87m/C; DVD.** Corbin Bernsen; Paige Moss; Jeannie Meyers; Brigitte Brooks; Dee Wallace; ***D:*** Ken Barbet; ***W:*** Christopher Stone; Bruce Cameron; ***C:*** Richard Ashbury; ***M:*** Timothy S. (Tim) Jones.

Killer Instinct: From the Files of Agent Candice DeLong 🦴🦴 **2003** Deciding to retire after 15 years as a profiler with the FBI, Candice DeLong (Smart) takes on one last case when a friend becomes the victim of a Chicago rapist/serial killer. But her investigation leads to the perp targeting Candice and her son Ryan (Sutton). **90m/C; DVD.** Jean Smart; A. Martinez; Robert Joy; Jeff Sutton; Peter MacNeill; Robin Brule; Joy Tanner; ***D:*** Peter Werner; ***W:*** Lynn Mamet; ***C:*** Neil Roach; ***M:*** Hector Pereira. **CABLE**

The Killer Is Loose 🦴🦴 **1956** Effectively-told noir. Det. Sam Wagner (Cotten) accidentally kills the wife of Leon Poole (Corey) while arresting him for being the inside man in a bank robbery. At his trial, Poole vows to get revenge and eventually escapes from a prison farm. He's now a trigger-happy psycho aiming to kill Wagner's wife Lila (Fleming) and Wagner is asked to let the cops use Lila as bait so Poole can be recaptured. **73m/B; DVD, Blu-Ray.** Joseph Cotten; Wendell Corey; Rhonda Fleming; Alan Hale, Jr.; Michael Pate; Virginia Christine; John Larch; ***D:*** Budd Boetticher; ***W:*** Harold Medford; ***C:*** Lucien Ballard; ***M:*** Lionel Newman.

Killer Joe 🦴🦴 1/2 *Killer Joe: A Twisted Redneck Trailer Park Murder Story* **2011 (R)** Desperately needing some quick dough, young drug dealer Chris (Hirsch) talks it over with dad (Hayden Church) and they decide to hire a hitman to off his ex-wife for the insurance money. "Killer" Joe Cooper (McConaughey) gets the job and requires Chris' sweet younger sister Dottie's (Temple) sexual favors in the interim until the money comes in. Life inside the trailer filled with idiots spirals out of control until a brutal climax ties everything together in a ballet of gunfire. Powerful and darkly hilarious, director Friedkin's adaptation of writer Letts' screenplay gives McConaughey the best role of his career to date. **102m/C; DVD, Blu-Ray; Closed Captioned.** Matthew McConaughey; Emile Hirsch; Juno Temple; Thomas Haden Church; Gina Gershon; ***D:*** William Friedkin; ***W:*** Tracy Letts; ***C:*** Caleb Deschanel; ***M:*** Tyler Bates.

Killer Klowns from Outer Space 🦴🦴 1/2 **1988 (PG-13)** Bozo-like aliens resembling demented clowns land on earth and set up circus tents to lure Earthlings in. Visually striking, campy but slick horror flick that'll make you think twice about your next visit to the big top. Mood is heightened by a cool title tune by the Dickies. Definitely has cult potential! **90m/C; VHS, DVD, Blu-Ray.** Grant Cramer; Suzanne Snyder; John Allen Nelson; Royal Dano; John Vernon; Peter Licassi; Michael Siegel; Charles Chiodo; ***D:*** Stephen Chiodo; ***W:*** Stephen Chiodo; Charles Chiodo; ***C:*** Alfred Taylor; ***M:*** John Massari.

Killer Leopard 🦴 **1954** The leopard hunt is only part of Bomba's adventures in the 11th film in the sputtering series. Garland's an asset as actress Linda Winters, who's trying to find her missing husband with Bomba's help. However, Fred isn't missing, he's actually an embezzler looking to buy illicit diamonds. **70m/B; DVD.** John(ny) Sheffield; Beverly Garland; Donald Murphy; Leonard Mudie; ***D:*** Ford Beebe; ***W:*** Ford Beebe; ***C:*** Harry Neumann; ***M:*** Marlin Skiles.

Killer Likes Candy 🦴 **1978** An assassin stalks the King of Kafiristan, and a CIA operative tries to stop him. **86m/C; VHS, DVD.** Kerwin Mathews; Marilu Tolo; ***D:*** Richard Owens.

Killer McCoy 🦴🦴 **1947** Remake of 1938's "Crowded House" with Rooney in his first adult role. Hardworking Tommy McCoy does a boxing benefit with his drunken dad Brian (Dunn) and becomes intrigued by boxing champ Johnny Martin (Knox). Martin offers to mentor Tommy who turns out to be a natural. Eventually, Tommy must fight opposite Johnny and a horrible accident occurs, which earns Tommy his nickname. To makes matters worse, his dad is deeply in debt to gambler Jim Caighn (Donlevy) and has sold Tommy's contract to the ruthless man. Tommy's only bright spot is secretly dating Caighn's daughter Sheila (Blyth), who tries to keep Tommy honest. **104m/B; DVD.** Mickey Rooney; Brian Donlevy; Ann Blyth; James Dunn; Mickey Knox; Sam Levene; Tom Tully; ***D:*** Roy Rowland; ***W:*** Frederick Hazlitt Brennan; ***C:*** Joseph Ruttenberg; ***M:*** David Snell.

Killer Me 🦴🦴 **2001** George (Foster) is a college student who takes criminology classes and works in the library—the kind of quiet kid nobody notices. Except for fellow loner Anna (Kew), who pratically stalks George in order to befriend him. Perhaps not the best of ideas since George had an abusive childhood and suffers from hallucinations in which he kills people with a straight-edged razor. Of course, they might not be just delusions at all. **80m/C; VHS, DVD.** George Foster; Kirk B.R. Woller; Christina Kew; ***D:*** Zachary Hansen; ***W:*** Zachary Hansen; ***C:*** Neal Fredericks; ***M:*** Zachary Hansen.

Killer Movie 🦴🦴 **2008 (R)** Horror/showbiz comedy about the subjects and crew of a reality TV show who get stranded in a small North Dakota town. The town has an eerie history of deadly accidents and the outsiders soon become victims. Stereotypes deliberately abound, including the down-on-his-luck director, the diva, and the ruthless producer. **92m/C; DVD.** Paul Wesley; Nestor Carbonell; Kaley Cuoco; Jason London; Cyia Batten; Leighton Meester; Robert (Bob) Buckley; Andy Fischer-Price; J.C. Chasez; ***D:*** Jeff Fisher; ***W:*** Jeff Fisher; ***C:*** Dino Parks; ***M:*** Todd Haberman. **VIDEO**

The Killer Must Kill Again 🦴🦴 *Il Ragno; The Spider* **1975** After cheating hubby Giorgio Mainardi (Hilton) witnesses nameless killer (a very scary Antoine) dumping a body, he blackmails him into offing his rich wife while he sets up his alibi. The killer has the bad luck to have his car stolen—with the wife's body in the trunk. He goes after the joyriding teen thieves while Giorgio tries to convince the cops that his wife's been kidnapped. Italian with subtitles or dubbed. **90m/C; DVD.** *IT FR* Teresa Velazquez; Eduardo Fajardo; ***D:*** Luigi Cozzi; ***W:*** Luigi Cozzi; Daniele Del Giudice; ***C:*** Riccardo (Pallton) Pallottini; ***M:*** Nand De Luca.

Killer of Sheep 🦴🦴🦴🦴 **1977** Age does nothing to date this seminal examination of urban poverty and race in 1970's Watts. Stan (Sanders) is a slaughterhouse worker plagued by insomnia who becomes increasingly disconnected from the rest of the world, including his wife (Moore). Nothing seems to help as a series of events just serves to compound Stan's sense of futility. Burnett wrote and directed as a student on a budget of $10,000. A popular part of the festival circuit that took 30 years to be released theatrically, in part because of the time and expense in licensing the music used in the soundtrack. **80m/B; DVD.** Henry Sanders; Kaycee Moore; Eugene Cherry; Charles Bracy; ***D:*** Charles Burnett; ***W:*** Charles Burnett; ***C:*** Charles Burnett. Natl. Film Reg. '90.

Killer Pad 🦴 1/2 **2006 (R)** Silly horror comedy about three not-too-bright buddies who don't bother to question their luck when they get an exceptional deal on a Hollywood Hills mansion. But their dream pad is a nightmare since it's also a direct portal to Hell. **84m/C; DVD.** Daniel Franzese; Eric Jungmann; Andy Milonakis; Hector Jimenez; Shane McRae; Joseph Lawrence; Jennifer Lyons; ***D:*** Robert Englund; ***W:*** Dan Stoller; ***C:*** David G. Stump; ***M:*** Timothy Andrew Edwards. **VIDEO**

Killer Party **WOOF!** **1986 (R)** Three coeds pledge a sorority and are subjected to a hazing that involves a haunted fraternity house. Standard horror plot; Paul Bartel ("Eating Raoul"; "Lust in the Dust") is the only significant element. **91m/C; VHS, DVD.** Elaine Wilkes; Sherry Willis-Burch; Joanna Johnson; Paul Bartel; Martin Hewitt; Ralph Seymour; Woody Brown; Alicia Fleer; ***D:*** William Fruet; ***W:*** Barney Cohen; ***C:*** John Lindley; ***M:*** John Beal.

The Killer Shrews 🦴🦴 *Attack of the Killer Shrews* **1959** Lumet (Sidney's father) creates a serum that causes the humble shrew to take on killer proportions. The creatures are actually dogs in makeup. Goude was 1957's Miss Universe. **70m/B; VHS, DVD, Blu-Ray.** James Best; Ingrid Goude; Baruch Lumet; Ken Curtis; Alfredo DeSoto; Gordon McLendon; ***D:*** Ray Kellogg; ***W:*** Jay Simms; ***C:*** Wilfred M. Cline; ***M:*** Emil Cadkin; Harry Bluestone.

The Killer That Stalked New York 🦴 1/2 *Frightened City* **1947** Married couple Sheila (Keyes) and Matt (Korvin) arrive in New York City with $40,000 worth of smuggled diamonds. Sheila's not feeling so hot, and cheating Matt has his own plans for the diamonds, involving Sheila's sister. But Sheila's got bigger problems—she's brought home something far more sinister. Will the health department find the person who's spreading smallpox before the police catch the diamond thief? **79m/B; DVD, Blu-Ray.** Evelyn Keyes; William Bishop; Charles Korvin; Dorothy Malone; Lola Albright; Carl Benton Reid; Barry Kelley; Ludwig Donath; ***D:*** Earl McEvoy; ***W:*** Milton Lehman; Harry Essex; ***C:*** Joseph Biroc; ***M:*** Hans J. Salter.

Killer Tomatoes Eat France 🦴 1/2 **1991** Professor Gangrene takes his tomato fetish to France, where the giant vegetables try to take over the streets. The fourth in the killer-vegetable series. **94m/C; VHS, DVD.** John Astin; Marc Price; Steve Lundquist; John DeBello; Rick Rockwell; Angela Visser; Kevin West; Tom Ashworth; Suzanne Dean; Mary Egan; Debra Fares; Arnie Miller; J.R. Morley; ***D:*** John DeBello; ***W:*** John DeBello; Steve Peace; Constantine Dillon; ***C:*** Kevin Morrisey.

Killer Tomatoes Strike Back 🦴🦴 **1990** The third "Killer Tomatoes" movie isn't in the league of "The Naked Gun" satires, but it's still bright parody for the Mad Magazine crowd, as tomato-mad scientist Astin harnesses the powers of trash-TV in a planned vegetable invasion. Perhaps due to a 'Killer Tomatoes' cartoon series at the time, this isn't as saucy as its predecessors and is acceptable for family audiences. Followed by "Killer Tomatoes Eat France." **87m/C; VHS, DVD.** John Astin; Rick Rockwell; Crystal Carson; Steve Lundquist; John Witherspoon; John DeBello; Tom Ashworth; Frank Davis; Debra Fares; Rock Peace; Constantine Dillon; Kevin West; Spike Sorrentino; D.J. Sullivan; ***D:*** John DeBello; ***W:*** Rick Rockwell; John DeBello; Constantine Dillon; ***C:*** Stephen F. Andrich; ***M:*** Neal Fox.

Killer Tongue 🦴 *La Lengua Asesina* **1996 (R)** Okay, now here's a story (but not a good story, mind): Candy (Clarke) and Johnny (Durr) pull off a heist but Johnny winds up in jail while Candy hides out with the loot. She winds up in a desert hotel, near where a meteorite has landed. Somehow, Candy ingests a piece of the meteorite and an alien parasite (in the form of the titular killer tongue) takes over. The tongue is big on human sacrifices and Candy can't seem to do anything to stop it. Oh, and Candy's four poodles also get a meteorite taste and turn into drag queens. Just as gross as you may imagine it to be. **98m/C; VHS, DVD.** *GB SP* Melinda (Mindy) Clarke; Jason Durr; Robert Englund; Mapi Golan; Doug Bradley; Jonathan Rhys Meyers; ***D:*** Alberto Sciamma; ***W:*** Alberto Sciamma; ***C:*** Denis Crossan.

Killer Wave 🦴 1/2 **2007** A series of tidal waves have left the major cities on the east coast of the U.S. in ruins. Maverick scientist John McAdams (Macfadyen) has his doubts that the waves are natural occurrences, believing that they are man-made disasters. The more McAdams investigates, the more dangerous his life becomes, especially when he learns who's behind all the destruction (it's not too hard to figure out). **175m/C; DVD.** Angus MacFadyen; Tom Skerritt; Stephen McHattie; John Robinson; Louis-Philippe Dandenault; ***D:*** Bruce McDonald; ***W:*** William Gray; ***C:*** Pierre Jodoin; ***M:*** Normand Corbeil. **TV**

Killerman 🦴 1/2 **2019 (R)** Criminal partners Moe (Hemsworth) and Skunk (Cohen) are partners in the middle of making a drug deal with money from their boss Perico (Buric) that could take them to the big time, except the deal goes wrong. On top of that, the pair gets into a horrific car accident and Moe suffers from a concussion that gives him amnesia. As Skunk tries to make things right, Moe has no idea who he is or what he does and learns more about himself in the process. Exhilarating at times with its raw, unflinching violence, the crime thriller is too routine and drawn out for its own good. **112m/C; DVD.** Liam Hemsworth; Emory Cohen; Diane Guerrero; Zlatko Buric; Suraj Sharma; ***D:*** Malik Bader; ***W:*** Malik Bader; ***C:*** Ken Seng; ***M:*** Julian DeMarre; Heiko Maile.

The Killers **1946** Classic film noir based on a Hemingway story. Lancaster's film debut comes as an ex-boxer, "The Swede," who's murdered in a contract hit. Insurance investigator Jim Reardon (O'Brien) reconstructs the young man's life, discovering his involvement with crime boss Big Jim Colfax (Dekker) and double-crossing femme fatale Kitty Collins (Gardner). So Reardon sets out to set up Colfax and Kitty. Rosza's musical score may sound familiar—it was later used on the TV series "Dragnet." **105m/B; VHS, DVD, Blu-Ray.** Edmond O'Brien; Albert Dekker; Ava Gardner; Burt Lancaster; Sam Levene; William Conrad; Charles McGraw; Virginia Christine; ***D:*** Robert Siodmak; ***W:*** Anthony Veiller; John Huston; ***C:*** Elwood "Woody" Bredell; ***M:*** Miklos Rozsa. Natl. Film Reg. '08.

The Killers *Ernest Hemingway's the Killers* **1964** After two hired assassins kill a teacher, they look into his past and try to find leads to a $1,000,000 robbery. Reagan's last film. Remake of 1946 film of the same name, which was loosely based on a short story by Ernest Hemingway. Originally intended for TV, but released to theatres instead due to its violence. **95m/C; VHS, DVD, Blu-Ray.** Lee Marvin; Angie Dickinson; John Cassavetes; Ronald Reagan; Clu Gulager; Claude Akins; Norman Fell; Don Haggerty; Seymour Cassel; Robert Phillips; ***D:*** Donald Siegel; ***W:*** Gene L. Coon; ***C:*** Richard L. Rawlings; ***M:*** John Williams.

Killers **1988** Remote jungles of southern Africa are the scene of a military coup. **83m/C; VHS, DVD.** Cameron Mitchell; Alicia Hammond; Robert Dix; ***D:*** Ewing Miles Brown.

Killers **2010 (PG-13)** Heigl and Kutcher are really pretty people but this clueless action/romantic comedy is all flash and no payoff. Heartbroken after being dumped, uptight Jen Kornfeldt is vacationing on the French Riviera with her parents when she meets cute with shirtless Spencer Aimes. Before you can blink, they are three years married when Jen suddenly discovers that Spencer is a CIA assassin with a bounty on his head. Now they have to survive until Spencer can figure out who wants him dead while Jen freaks and tries to help. **100m/C; Blu-Ray, On Demand.** Ashton Kutcher; Katherine Heigl; Katheryn Winnick; Rob Riggle; Kevin Sussman; Tom Selleck; Catherine O'Hara; Martin Mull; Alex Borstein; ***D:*** Robert Luketic; ***W:*** Ted Griffin; Bob DeRosa; ***C:*** Russell Carpenter. Golden Raspberries '10: Worst Actor (Kutcher).

Killers **2014** Mr. Nomura is a serial killer. He is a sharp-dressed man who kidnaps women, tortures them, kills them, and does it all on camera. He draws the attention of a more average guy, a journalist named Bayu, who is forced to kill in self-defense when a robbery goes very wrong. It turns out that Bayu likes it and Mr. Nomura sees in him something common. One of the most bloated horror flicks in a long time. English, Japanese, and Indonesian with subtitles. **137m/C; DVD, Blu-Ray.** *ID JP* Kazuki Kitamura; Oka Antara; Rin Takanashi; ***D:*** Kimo Stamboel; Timo Tjahjanto; ***W:*** Timo Tjahjanto; ***C:*** Gunnar Nimpuno; ***M:*** Aria Prayogi.

Killers Anonymous **2019 (R)** The Man (Oldman) is a quick-tempered hitman who organizes meetings of Killers Anonymous, a therapy group for hitmen and hitwomen. When a meeting is called by unknown persons, attendees, including first timer Alice (Brown), paranoid Markus (Flanagan), and smooth-talking Leandro (Socha), are concerned. They are on edge because someone has issued a big bounty the hitperson responsible for the death of a US senator. Over the course of the meeting, secrets are revealed and the attendees offer personal revelations as tensions rise. An overly slick crime drama-thriller, the film tries to be high concept and energetic but is not particularly inventive or funny. **96m/C; DVD, Blu-Ray.** Gary Oldman; Jessica Alba; Rhyon Nicole Brown; Tommy Flanagan; Michael Socha; ***D:*** Martin Owen; ***W:*** Martin Owen; Seth Johnson; Elizabeth Morris; ***C:*** Havard Helle; ***M:*** Roger Goula.

The Killer's Edge ½ *Blood Money* **1990 (R)** Cop is caught between rock and hard place in L.A. when he's forced to confront criminal who once saved his life in 'Nam. Plenty of gut busting and soul wrenching. **90m/C; VHS, DVD.** Wings Hauser; Robert Z'Dar; Karen Black.

Killers from Space WOOF! **1954** Cheap sci-fi flick in which big-eyed men from beyond Earth bring scientist Graves back to life to assist them with their evil plan for world domination. **80m/B; VHS, DVD.** Peter Graves; Barbara Bestar; James Scay; ***D:*** W. Lee Wilder.

Killer's Kiss ½ **1955** A boxer and a dancer set out to start a new life together when he saves the woman from an attempted rape. Gritty, second feature from Kubrick was financed by friends and family and shows signs of his budding talent. **67m/C; VHS, DVD.** Frank Silvera; Jamie Smith; Irene Kane; Jerry Jarrett; ***D:*** Stanley Kubrick; ***W:*** Stanley Kubrick; ***C:*** Stanley Kubrick; ***M:*** Gerald Fried.

The Killing **1956** The dirty, harsh, street-level big heist epic that established Kubrick and presented its genre with a new and vivid existentialist aura, as an ex-con engineers the rip-off of a racetrack with disastrous results. Displays characteristic nonsentimental sharp-edged Kubrick vision. Based on the novel "Clean Break" by Lionel White. **83m/B; VHS, DVD, Blu-Ray; Open Captioned.** Sterling Hayden; Marie Windsor; Elisha Cook, Jr.; Jay C. Flippen; Vince Edwards; Timothy Carey; Coleen Gray; Joseph (Joe) Sawyer; Ted de Corsia; James Edwards; Jay Adler; Kola Kwarian; Joe Turkel; ***D:*** Stanley Kubrick; ***W:*** Stanley Kubrick; Jim Thompson; ***C:*** Lucien Ballard; ***M:*** Gerald Fried.

A Killing Affair **1985 (R)** Set in West Virginia, 1943, this is the story of a widow who takes in a drifter who she believes is the man who killed her husband. She begins to fall for him, but cannot be sure if she should trust him. Vague and melodramatic. From the novel "Monday, Tuesday, Wednesday" by Robert Houston. Saperstein's directorial debut. **100m/C; VHS, DVD.** Peter Weller; Kathy Baker; John Glover; Bill Smitrovich; ***D:*** David Saperstein; ***M:*** John Barry.

Killing Bono **2011 (R)** Over-long, awkward Britcom loosely based on Neil McCormick's 2004 memoir "I Was Bono's Doppelganger." Actually, McCormick wished to be anything close to a rock star as he and his brother Ivan were Dublin schoolmates of Paul Hewson, who would rename himself Bono as the lead singer of U2. But they stay musical wannabes and Neil becomes more antic and deluded as he decides to confront his old mate at U2's 1987 Dublin concert. **114m/C; DVD, Blu-Ray.** *GB* Ben Barnes; Robert Sheehan; Martin McCann; Krysten Ritter; Stanley Townsend; Pete Postlethwaite; Justine Waddell; ***D:*** Nick Hamm; ***W:*** Dick Clement; ***C:*** Kieran McGuigan; ***M:*** Stephen Warbeck.

The Killing Club ½ *You're Killing Me* **2001 (R)** When timid Jamie (Bowen) accidentally kills her controlling boyfriend, her tough best friend Laura (Lords) decides they should dispose of the body and give themselves an alibi. When this works, the ladies decide there's lots of losers who need disposing of—starting with the leering boss (McDonough) of another pal, Arlene (Maxey). There's neither enough black comedy nor suspense to make this anything but ordinary. **86m/C; DVD.** Julie Bowen; Traci Lords; Dawn Maxey; Neal McDonough; David Packer; ***D:*** Antoni Stutz; ***W:*** Amy Kiehl; ***C:*** James Lawrence Spencer; ***M:*** Tom Hiel. **VIDEO**

The Killing Device ½ **1992** Two government scientists lose their funding on a covert political assassination project and decide to eliminate the government officials responsible. When two journalists attempt to solve the murders they become the next targets. **93m/C; VHS, DVD.** Clu Gulager; Antony Alda; Gig Rauch; ***D:*** Paul MacFarlane; ***W:*** Kliff Keuhl; ***C:*** Paul MacFarlane.

Killing Down **2006 (R)** Six years before, the present Steven Down (Tompkins) was an operative in Nicaragua who was caught and tortured. It had some not so nice implications for his future mental health but six years later he's rebuilding his life and getting a new job. Until he thinks he sees one of the men who tortured him. **108m/C; DVD.** Sheree J. Wilson; Matthew Tompkins; Natalie Raitano; Burton Gilliam; Julio Cesar Cedillo; Maurice Ripke; Oliver Tull; ***D:*** Blake Calhoun; ***W:*** Blake Calhoun; Steve Mahone; ***C:*** Alan Lefebvre; ***M:*** Roy Machado.

Killing Emmett Young *Emmett's Mark* **2002 (R)** Homicide detective Emmett Young (Wolf) has been told by his doctor that he has a terminal illness and only a short time to live. To avoid the disease's debilitating effects, Emmett takes up the offer of a mysterious stranger (Byrne) to arrange for a hit man (Roth) to do the job quickly. Of course, Emmett discovers he's not really dying (ALWAYS get a second opinion about a terminal disease) and tries to call the hit off. **104m/C; VHS, DVD, On Demand.** Scott Wolf; Tim Roth; Gabriel Byrne; Khandi Alexander; John Doman; Wayne Duvall; ***D:*** Keith Snyder; ***W:*** Keith Snyder; ***C:*** Lawrence Sher; ***M:*** Steve Porcaro.

The Killing Fields ½ **1984 (R)** Based on the New York Times' Sydney Schanberg's account of his friendship with Cambodian interpreter Dith Pran. They separated during the fall of Saigon, when Western journalists fled, leaving behind countless assistants who were later accused of collusion with the enemy by the Khmer Rouge and killed or sent to re-education camps during the bloodbath known as "Year Zero." Schanberg searched for Pran through the Red Cross and U.S. government, while Pran struggled to survive, finally escaping and walking miles to freedom. Ngor's own experiences echoed those of his character Pran. Malkovich's debut is intense. Joffe's directorial debut shows a generally sure hand, with only a bit of melodrama at the end. **142m/C; VHS, DVD, Blu-Ray.** *GB* Sam Waterston; Haing S. Ngor; John Malkovich; Athol Fugard; Craig T. Nelson; Julian Sands; Spalding Gray; Bill Paterson; ***D:*** Roland Joffé; ***W:*** Bruce Robinson; ***C:*** Chris Menges. Oscars '84: Cinematog., Film Editing, Support. Actor (Ngor); British Acad. '84: Actor (Ngor), Adapt. Screenplay, Film; Golden Globes '85: Support. Actor (Ngor); L.A. Film Critics '84: Cinematog.; N.Y. Film Critics '84: Cinematog.; Natl. Soc. Film Critics '84: Cinematog.; Writers Guild '84: Adapt. Screenplay.

The Killing Floor ½ **2006 (R)** David Lamont (Blucas), a literary agent who specializes in horror writers, has just moved into a lavish Manhattan penthouse, but weird things start happening. A young man turns up, claiming he inherited the place from his father. David is sent bloody crime scene photos that show his apartment, only the police have no record of any crimes, and he receives videotapes showing him sleeping. Obsessed, David will go to any length to find his stalker. **98m/C; DVD.** Marc Blucas; Shiri Appleby; Reiko Aylesworth; John Bedford Lloyd; Joel Leffert; Andrew Weems; Jeff Carlson; ***D:*** Gideon Raff; ***W:*** Gideon Raff; Ryan Swanson; ***C:*** Martina Radwan; ***M:*** Michael Wandmacher. **VIDEO**

The Killing Game ½ *All Weekend Lovers; Jeu de Massacre* **1967** A husband-wife cartoonist team link up with an unhinged playboy and act out a murder-mystery comic they produce together. In French with subtitles. **95m/C; VHS, DVD.** *FR* Jean-Pierre Cassel; Claudine Auger; Michel Duchaussoy; Anna Gaylor; ***D:*** Alain Jessua.

The Killing Game **1987** A slew of Californians kill and betray each other for lustful reasons. **90m/C; VHS, DVD.** Chard Hayward; Cynthia Killion; Geoffrey Sadwith; ***D:*** Joseph Merhi.

The Killing Gene ½ *WAZ* **2007 (R)** New York cop Eddie (Skarsgard) and his partner Helen (George) are called in for a couple of mutilated bodies that have the initials WAZ carved on them. Eddie thinks it's all gang-related (other pairs of victims with gang connections turn up) but the letters are actually W Delta Z, the beginning of something called the Price equation that's too convoluted to explain. Anyway, you find out the who and why about the killer early on so then you get to watch the cops play catch up. Lots of torture and gore but slightly more interesting than "Saw" and its spawn because it's got better actors. **104m/C; DVD.** *GB* Stellan Skarsgard; Melissa George; Selma Blair; Ashley Walters; Tom (Thomas) Hardy; Paul Kaye; ***D:*** Tom Shankland; ***W:*** Clive Bradley; ***C:*** Morten Soborg; ***M:*** David Julyan.

The Killing Grounds ½ **1997 (R)** Killers Vince (Gains) and Art (Hall) are searching in the mountains for a missing plane that carried $3 million in gold. But it's already been found by a group of hikers, who think finders keepers. Boy, are they wrong. **93m/C; VHS, DVD.** Anthony Michael Hall; Courtney Gains; Priscilla Barnes; Charles Rocket; Rodney A. Grant; Cynthia Geary; ***D:*** Kurt Anderson; ***W:*** Thomas Ritz. **VIDEO**

Killing Gunther **2017 (R)** A mockumentary about rival assassins. Blake (Killam) is an elite career assassin who is on a quest to kill his greatest rival, Gunther (Schwarzenegger). Blake's quest for retribution has a personal component because Gunther had a fling with Blake's ex-girlfriend Lisa (Smulders), whom he still loves, after their relationship ended. Putting together a bumbling crew that includes explosives expert Donnie (Moynihan), poison guru Yong (Yoo), sharpshooter Sanaa (Simone), and her overprotective father Rahmat (Kelamis), Blake threatens the lives of a documentary crew so that their escapades are recorded. Despite the comic talents involved, the film lacks imagination, save for Schwarzenegger's enthusiastic performance. **92m/C; DVD, Blu-Ray.** Arnold Schwarzenegger; Cobie Smulders; Hannah Simone; Allison Tolman; Taran Killam; ***D:*** Taran Killam; ***W:*** Taran Killam; ***C:*** Blake Mcclure; ***M:*** Dino Meneghin.

Killing Heat ½ *The Grass is Singing* **1984 (R)** An independent career woman living in South Africa decides to abandon her career to marry a struggling jungle farmer. Based on Doris Lessing's novel "The Grass is Singing." **104m/C; VHS, DVD.** *GB SW* Karen Black; John Thaw; John Kani; John Moulder-Brown; ***D:*** Michael Raeburn.

Killing Hour *The Clairvoyant* **1984 (R)** A psychic painter finds that the visions she paints come true in a string of grisly murders. Her ability interests a TV reporter and a homicide detective. **97m/C; VHS, DVD.** Elizabeth Kemp; Perry King; Norman Parker; Kenneth McMillan; ***D:*** Armand Mastroianni; ***W:*** Armand Mastroianni; ***M:*** Alexander Peskanov.

A Killing in a Small Town *Evidence of Love* **1990 (R)** Candy Morrison seems like the perfect member of her small Texas community—but appearances can be deceiving, particularly after she's charged with killing a fellow church-goer by striking her 41 times with an axe (shades of Lizzie Borden)! Dennehy is her skeptical lawyer who isn't sure if it was self-defense or a peculiar sort of revenge. Good performances by Hershey and Dennehy lift this above the usual tawdry made-for-TV level. Based on a true story. **95m/C; VHS, DVD.** Barbara Hershey; Brian Dennehy; Hal Holbrook; Richard Gilliland; John Terry; Lee Garlington; ***D:*** Stephen Gyllenhaal; ***C:*** Robert Elswit; ***M:*** Richard Gibbs. **TV**

The Killing Jar ½ **1996 (R)** Michael Sanford (Cullen) has taken his pregnant wife Diane (Tomita) back to the California wine country to take over the failing family vineyard. A series of vicious murders occur in the area, one of which Michael may have witnessed. Hypnosis brings up a lot of Michael's repressed childhood memories, he begins to unravel, and becomes the prime suspect in the killings. **101m/C; VHS, DVD.** Brett Cullen; Tamlyn Tomita; Wes Studi; Brion James; M. Emmet Walsh; Tom Bower; Xander Berkeley; ***D:*** Evan Crooke; ***W:*** Mark Mullin; ***C:*** Michael G. Wojciechowski; ***M:*** David Williams.

The Killing Jar **2010** Young's repetitive, talky, wannabe thriller hits every boring hostage cliche imaginable and is also hindered by a bunch of generally listless performances. A group of diners are at a rural truck stop when a radio announcer reports that a local farm family has been murdered. Soon afterwards, sneering Doe (Madsen) shows up and takes everyone hostage. Killing ensues but did he really murder the farm family or was the real killer already there? **90m/C; On Demand.** Michael Madsen; Harold Perrineau, Jr.; Amber Benson; Jake Busey; Kevin Gage; Lew Temple; Danny Trejo; Talan Torriero; Lindsey Axelsson; ***D:*** Mark H. Young; ***W:*** Mark H. Young; ***C:*** Gregg Easterbrook; ***M:*** Elia Cmiral.

Killing Kennedy **1/2 2013** This cable drama from the National Geographic Channel eschews conspiracy theories in the Kennedy assassination for a chillingly straightforward lone gunman approach. It tracks the lives, including their marriages, of both president (Lowe) and killer (Rothaar) until their fateful meeting in Dallas in November 1963. Based on the bestseller by Bill O'Reilly and Martin Dugand. **88m/C; DVD, Blu-Ray.** Rob Lowe; Will Rothhaar; Ginnifer Goodwin; Michelle Trachtenberg; Jack Noseworthy; Casey Siemaszko; Francis Guinan; Mary Pat Gleason; ***D:*** Nelson McCormick; ***W:*** Kelly Masterson; ***C:*** Stephen St. John; ***M:*** Geoff Zanelli. **CABLE**

The Killing Kind **1/2 1973** Man released from prison is obsessed with wreaking vengeance on his daft lawyer and his accuser. His vendetta eventually draws his mother into the fray as well. Fine performance by Savage. **95m/C; VHS, DVD, Blu-Ray.** Ann Sothern; John Savage; Ruth Roman; Luana Anders; Cindy Williams; ***D:*** Curtis Harrington; ***M:*** Andrew Belling.

Killing Lincoln **1/2 2013** Docudrama from the National Geographic Channel, based on Bill O'Reilly's book, that has its form working against the story as Hanks' onscreen narration slows the pace and takes the focus off the leads. Assassin John Wilkes Booth (Johnson) comes off as a delusional egotist while Lincoln (Campbell) is weary and burdened by the presidency. **120m/C; DVD, Blu-Ray.** Billy Campbell; Jesse Johnson; Graham Beckel; Geraldine Hughes; ***Nar:*** Tom Hanks; ***D:*** Adrian Moat; ***W:*** Erik Jendresen; ***C:*** Jeremy Benning; ***M:*** David Buckley. **CABLE**

The Killing Machine **2009 (R)** Lundgren plays (and directs) to his action strengths as Edward Genn, an investment broker in Vancouver, who was once a feared KGB assassin known as Icarus. When his identity is exposed, Russian gangsters want to settle some old scores but make a big mistake by coming after his family. Now Icarus will show them that he hasn't forgotten how to kill. **88m/C; DVD, Blu-Ray.** Dolph Lundgren; Bo Svenson; Stefanie von Pfetten; Samantha Ferris; John Tench; Lindsay Maxwell; David Lewis; ***D:*** Dolph Lundgren; ***W:*** Raul Inglis; ***C:*** Marc Windon; ***M:*** James Jandrisch. **VIDEO**

The Killing Man **1994 (R)** Former mobster tries going legit by changing his identity and working for the government. **91m/C; VHS, DVD.** Jeff Wincott; Terri Hawkes; Michael Ironside; David Bolt; Jeff Pustil; ***D:*** David Mitchell; ***W:*** David Mitchell; Damian Lee; ***C:*** David Pelletier.

Killing Me Softly **2001 (R)** Chinese director Kaige's English-lanugage debut turned out to be an unfortunate choice—a turgid, sexual melodrama based on the novel by the pseudonymous Nicci French. American Alice (Graham) is living in London, seemingly content with boyfriend Jake (Hughes). Then she meets mysterious and intense mountaineer Adam (Fiennes) and she's soon agreeing to marry him despite evidence of his violent temper and how little she knows about him. Bouts of S&M sex follow but it's when Alice learns that her new hubby's previous lover disappeared that she decides maybe she's made a mistake. An unrated version is also available. **100m/C; VHS, DVD, Blu-Ray.** Heather Graham; Joseph Fiennes; Jason Hughes; Natascha (Natasha) McElhone; Ulrich Thomsen; Ian Hart; ***D:*** Chen Kaige; ***W:*** Kara Lindstrom; ***C:*** Michael Coulter; ***M:*** Patrick Doyle.

The Killing Mind **1990** A young girl witnesses a grisly murder that is never solved. Twenty years later she (Zimbalist) becomes a cop who specializes in trapping psychos. Haunted by her memories, she and a reporter (Bill) team up to find the killer, never suspecting that she is his next victim. **96m/C; VHS, DVD.** Stephanie Zimbalist; Tony Bill; Daniel Roebuck; Lee Tergesen; Danielle Harris; ***D:*** Michael Rhodes. **CABLE**

Killing Mr. Griffin **1/2 1997** If this sounds suspiciously akin to the plot for 1999's "Teaching Mrs. Tingle," it's not just your imagination. However, this TV movie is based on the novel by Lois Duncan. Evil high school teacher Mr. Griffin antagonizes all his students, who wind up kidnapping and humiliating him—leaving him tied up in the woods. But when Mr. G turns up dead, the students are all suspects unless they can point the cops in another direction. **108m/C; VHS, DVD.** Scott Bairstow; Amy Jo Johnson; Mario Lopez; Chris Young; Michelle Williams; Jay Thomas; Scott Jaeck; Denise Dowse; ***D:*** Jack Bender; ***W:*** Michael Angeli; Kathleen Rowell; ***C:*** David Geddes; ***M:*** Christophe Beck. **TV**

Killing Moon **WOOF! 2000** Abysmal air disaster flick features an airborne (on a plane!) virus that makes it's victims bleed from the eyes before dying and a mean G-man trying to weaponize the disease. On the ground, government doctor Miller is trying to stop the illness and get the passengers to stop oozing. Has all the elements of an "Airplane" spoof, but the comedy is purely unintentional. **95m/C; DVD.** Penelope Ann Miller; Daniel Baldwin; Kim Coates; Daniel Kash; Denis Akayama; Tracy Cook; Christopher Bolton; Natalie Radford; Mark Camacho; ***D:*** John Bradshaw; ***W:*** Tony Johnston; ***C:*** Nicholas Josef von Sternberg. **TV**

Killing Obsession **1/2 1994** Albert (Savage) has been locked in the Parkview State Psychiatric Facility for 20 years, ever since he murdered 11-year-old Annie's mother. Annie is Albert's obsession and in his mind she's always remained a young girl. So when Albert is released, he goes looking for Annie—murdering along the way. Now that the real Annie is an adult will Albert finally accept the passage of time or will she be just another victim? **95m/C; VHS, DVD.** John Savage; Kimberly Chase; John Saxon; Bernie (Bernard) White; Bobby DiCicco; ***D:*** Paul Leder; ***W:*** Paul Leder; ***C:*** Francis Grumman; ***M:*** Dana Walden.

The Killing of a Chinese Bookie **1976 (R)** Gazzara runs a Sunset Strip nightclub and is in hock to loan sharks. When he can't come up with the cash, he's offered a deal—get rid of a troublesome Chinese bookie and all debts will be forgiven. But it turns out the bookie is highly connected in the Asian mob and nothing goes as planned. Cassavette's improv technique makes for a self-indulgent and endless film. **109m/C; VHS, DVD, Blu-Ray.** Ben Gazzara; Jean-Pierre Cassel; Zizi Johari; Soto Joe Hugh; Robert Phillips; Timothy Carey; Morgan Woodward; ***D:*** John Cassavetes; ***W:*** John Cassavetes; ***C:*** Frederick Elmes.

The Killing of a Sacred Deer **1/2 2017 (R)** A disturbing psycho-thriller that's part morality tale, part revenge quest, and part *Sophie's Choice.* The lives of Dr. Steven Murphy (Farrell) and his idyllic family are catastrophically upended when Martin (Keoghan), a fatherless teen, inserts himself into them. After his children are stricken with a mysterious illness, the doctor must confront his past and make a difficult decision. Fine acting from the leads, particularly Kidman, combined with Lanthimos's uniquely unsettling style set this film apart from the typical fox-in-the-henhouse thriller, and it will reverberate with you long after the credits roll. **120m/C; DVD, Blu-Ray.** Nicole Kidman; Colin Farrell; Barry Keoghan; Alicia Silverstone; Raffey Cassidy; ***D:*** Yorgos Lanthimos; ***W:*** Yorgos Lanthimos; Efthymis Filippou; ***C:*** Thimios Bakatakis.

The Killing of Sister George **1969 (R)** Racy, sensationalized film based on the Frank Marcus black comedy/melodrama about a lesbian love triangle between a television executive, the soap opera star she's about to fire, and the soap star's girlfriend. **138m/C; VHS, DVD, Blu-Ray.** Beryl Reid; Susannah York; Coral Browne; Ronald Fraser; Patricia Medina; Hugh Paddick; Cyril Delevanti; Brendan Dillon; Sivi Aberg; William Beckley; Elaine Church; Mike Freeman; Maggie Paige; Jack Raine; Dolly Taylor; ***D:*** Robert Aldrich; ***W:*** Lukas Heller; Frank Marcus; ***C:*** Joseph Biroc; ***M:*** Gerald Fried.

The Killing Room **2009 (R)** Four strangers sign up for a paid research study only to learn they've become part of a classified government program that's supposed to have been terminated. Confined to a white room, the quartet discover that the study is designed to find out what will break the human mind. The first step is a shocking violent act. **93m/C; DVD, Blu-Ray.** Clea DuVall; Nick Cannon; Timothy Hutton; Peter Stormare; Chloë Sevigny; Shea Whigham; ***D:*** Jonathan Liebesman; ***W:*** Gus Krieger; Ann Peacock; ***C:*** Lukas Ettlin; ***M:*** Brian Tyler. **VIDEO**

Killing Season **2013 (R)** Generally offensive, graphically violent actioner with the actors spouting tedious dialogue in cartoonish accents when they aren't trying to torture or kill each other. Back in the '90s, during the Bosnian war, Col. Benjamin Ford (De Niro) was part of a force that executed Serbian war criminals (sans trials), except that Emil Kovacs (Travolta) didn't die. Years later, Kovacs shows up at Ford's hermetic Appalachian retreat where the two men trade war stories and decide to go hunting together. Only Ford doesn't realize he's going to be the prey. Travolta chews the scenery and De Niro looks tired. **90m/C; DVD, Blu-Ray.** Robert De Niro; John Travolta; Milo Ventimiglia; Elizabeth Olin; ***D:*** Mark Steven Johnson; ***W:*** Evan Daugherty; ***C:*** Peter Menzies, Jr.; ***M:*** Christopher Young.

A Killing Spring **2002 (R)** Former cop turned reporter, Joanne Kilbourn (Crewson), who once taught at Lanholme College, is pulled into the investigation of the suspicious death of the disliked dean of the School of Journalism. Ambition, jealousy, and corruption run rampant in academia. **85m/C; VHS, DVD.** *CA* Wendy Crewson; Shawn Doyle; Michael Ontkean; Zachery Ty Bryan; Sherry Miller; John Furey; Bruce Gray; ***D:*** Stephen Williams; ***W:*** Joe Wiesenfeld; Jeremy Hole; ***C:*** David Herrington; ***M:*** Robert Carli. **TV**

Killing Them Softly **1/2 2012 (R)** Professional hitman Jackie Cogan (Pitt) becomes increasingly frustrated when he's hired to clean up the mess left by aging, sloppy gangsters, including Markie (Liotta) and a drunken Mickey (Gandolfini). He's ordered to take out two bottom-feeding goons who robbed a mob-run poker game but things get messy. The gun play, when it finally happens, is stylish and almost romantic. An unconventional mob flick, never going for the car chase or an easy shoot-out, focusing as much attention on its 2008 financial crisis landscape as it does the actual cost to kill a man. Based on the 1974 bestseller, "Cogan's Trade." **97m/C; DVD, Blu-Ray.** Brad Pitt; Scoot McNairy; Ben Mendelsohn; Ray Liotta; James Gandolfini; Sam Shepard; Richard Jenkins; Vincent Curatola; ***D:*** Andrew Dominik; ***W:*** Andrew Dominik; ***C:*** Greig Fraser; ***M:*** Rachel Fox.

The Killing Time **1987 (R)** A minor, effective murder thriller about a quiet small resort town suddenly beset by a web of murder, double-crossings, blackmail, and infidelity. They seem to coincide with the appearance of a mysterious stranger posing as the town's deputy sheriff just as the new sheriff is about to take up the badge. **94m/C; VHS, DVD, Blu-Ray.** Kiefer Sutherland; Beau Bridges; Joe Don Baker; Wayne Rogers; ***D:*** Rick King; ***W:*** Don Bohlinger.

Killing Zoe **1994 (R)** American safecracker travels to Paris for a little rest, recreation, and robbery. At the request of a childhood friend, he involves himself in an ill-conceived daytime bank heist, but not before enjoying a night with a local call girl and participating in some good ol' fashioned heroin-induced debauchery with the other bank robbers on the night before the job. Surprising no one (except maybe the still-stoned crooks), things don't go exactly as planned. Visually impressive debut for Tarantino collaborator Avary, who had his actors read "Beowulf" for its portrayal of Viking excess. **97m/C; VHS, DVD.** Eric Stoltz; Julie Delpy; Jean-Hugues Anglade; Gary Kemp; Bruce Ramsay; Kario Salem; Carlo Scandiuzzi; ***D:*** Roger Avary; ***W:*** Roger Avary; ***C:*** Tom Richmond.

The Killing Zone **1/2 1990** Convict nephew of onetime Drug Enforcement agent rewrites zoning ordinances to hunt for Mexican drug lord south of the border. **90m/C; VHS, DVD.** Daron McBee; James Dalesandro; Melissa Moore; Armando Silvestre; Augustine Beral; Sydne Squire; Debra Dare; ***D:*** Addison Randall.

Killjoy **1/2** ***Who Murdered Joy Morgan?*** **1981 (PG)** A sleazy surgeon's daughter is the prey in this CBS TV thriller. The plot twists are led by the array of people who become involved. A clever suspense mystery. **100m/C; DVD.** Kim Basinger; Robert Culp; Stephen Macht; Nancy Marchand; John Rubinstein; Ann Dusenberry; Ann Wedgeworth; Helene Winston; ***D:*** John Llewellyn Moxey; ***W:*** Sam Rolfe; ***C:*** Robert B. Hauser; ***M:*** Bruce Broughton. **TV**

Killpoint **1/2 1984 (R)** Special task force is assembled to catch the criminals who robbed a National Guard armory for its weapons. **89m/C; VHS, DVD.** Leo Fong; Richard Roundtree; Cameron Mitchell; ***D:*** Frank Harris.

Killshot **1/2 2009 (R)** Another unsuccessful adaptation of an Elmore Leonard novel that's primarily a routine crime thriller. Troubled contract killer Degas (Rourke) makes the mistake of hooking up with trigger-happy Richie Nix (Gordon-Levitt) and a botched job is witnessed by Carmen (Lane) and her estranged husband Wayne Colson (Jane). Degas is known for never leaving witnesses alive and the Colsons aren't going to be the exception. The film underwent numerous re-shoots and re-edits, which show in the uneven pacing and now-you-see-them, now-you-don't characters. **95m/C; DVD.** Diane Lane; Mickey Rourke; Thomas Jane; Joseph Gordon-Levitt; Rosario Dawson; Hal Holbrook; ***D:*** John Madden; ***W:*** Hossein Amini; ***C:*** Caleb Deschanel; ***M:*** Klaus Badelt.

Kilma, Queen of the Amazons **WOOF! 1975** A shipwrecked sailor finds himself on an island populated by man-hating Amazons. When a shipload of lusty sailors arrive to rescue him, carnage ensues. **90m/C; VHS, DVD.** *SP* Francisco (Frank) Brana; Eva Miller; Claudia Gravy; ***D:*** Miguel Iglesias; ***W:*** Miguel Iglesias; ***C:*** Francisco Sanchez.

Kilroy Was Here **1947** Johnny Kilroy (Cooper) gets out of the service and wants to attend college but is a credit short for admission. So coed Connie (Harcourt) an his buddy Pappy (Coogan) make it seem like Johnny is the soldier behind the popular 'Kilroy Was Here' wartime graffitti and the publicity gets him enrolled and into a snobbish fraternity. But what happens when the truth comes out? **70m/B; DVD.** Jackie Cooper; Jackie Coogan; Wanda McKay; Frank Jenks; Rand Brooks; ***D:*** Phil Karlson; ***W:*** Louis Quinn; Dick Irving Hyland; ***C:*** William Sickner.

Kim **1950** A colorful Hollywood adaptation of the Rudyard Kipling classic about an English boy disguised as a native in 19th Century India, and his various adventures. **113m/C; VHS, DVD.** Errol Flynn; Dean Stockwell; Paul Lukas; Cecil Kellaway; ***D:*** Victor Saville; ***M:*** Andre Previn.

Kim **1/2 1984** Kim (Sheth) is a 15-year-old boy living by his wits on the streets of 1890s India. Trying to discover his true identity, Kim's befriended by a Buddhist monk who wishes the boy to be his disciple and a British spy, who trains him for a daring mission against the Russians. Rousing TV adaptation of the Rudyard Kipling novel. **135m/C; VHS, DVD.** Ravi Sheth; Peter O'Toole; Bryan Brown; John Rhys-Davies; Julian Glover; ***D:*** John Davies.

Kim Possible **1/2 2019** Talented over-achiever Kim (Stanley) believes high school will be easy but discovers that the reality is more difficult on the first day. Essentially pushed out of the soccer team by rival Bonnie (Tham), Kim is late to everything despite her best laid plans. Though she survives with the help of sidekick Ron Stoppable (Giambrone) and new friend Athena (Wilson), they must balance high school with her teen superhero missions including fighting the evil Dr. Drakken (Stashwick) and his mastermind assistant (Ortega). Based on the popular Disney Channel cartoon, the film is mostly an exercise in nostalgia. **86m/C; DVD.** Sadie Stanley; Sean Giambrone; Ciara Riley Wilson; Todd Stashwick; Taylor Ortega; ***D:*** Zach Lipovsky; Adam B. Stein; ***W:*** Josh A. Cagan; Mark McCorkle; Robert Schooley; ***C:*** Christopher Baffa; ***M:*** Jim Dooley. **VIDEO**

Kimjongilia **2009** Documentary on North Korean's dangerous despotic leader Kim Jong-Il, whose father Kim Il-Sung established North Korea as a Marxist state, invaded the south, and started the Korean War. He is still a revered figure in the north and his legacy of brutality and repression is followed by his son who puts offenders in concentration camp-like prisons. Director Heikin's interview subjects were all victims of Kim's purges who escaped North Korea. The title refers to the country's national flower, a hybrid begonia. Korean with subtitles. **75m/C; DVD.** *US FR NK* ***D:*** N.C. Heiken; ***C:*** Kyle Saylors; ***M:*** Michael Gordon.

Kin **2018 (PG-13)** Troubled 14-year-old Eli (Truitt) is being raised in Detroit by a loving adoptive father Hal (Quaid) facing his own challenges, including the imprisonment of his adult son Jimmy (Reynor). After Eli steals a mysterious hi-tech gun from an abandoned building, he unintentionally becomes caught up in a scheme involving Jimmy and stolen money, and a crime lord Taylor (Franco). Taken on a road trip to Tahoe by Jimmy, the brothers are being pursued by the police, Taylor, and the futuristic soldiers who own the gun. Unfortunately the story never really comes together and clumsily combines too many genres. **102m/C; DVD, Blu-Ray.** Myles Truitt; Jack Reynor; Dennis Quaid; Zoë Kravitz; James Franco; ***D:*** Jonathan Baker; Josh Baker; ***W:*** Daniel Casey; ***C:*** Larkin Seiple; ***M:*** Mogwai.

Kind Hearts and Coronets 1/2 **1949** Black comedy, set in 1900, in which ambitious young Louis (Price) sets out to bump off eight relatives in an effort to claim a family title. Guinness is wonderful in his role as all eight (male and female) of the fated relations. There are a number of clever twists and turns and it proves that writing one's memoirs can be fatal. Very loosely based on Roy Horiman's novel "Israel Rank." **104m/B; VHS, DVD, Blu-Ray.** *GB* Alec Guinness; Dennis Price; Valerie Hobson; Joan Greenwood; Audrey Fildes; Miles Malleson; Clive Morton; Cecil Ramage; John Penrose; Hugh Griffith; John Salew; Eric Messiter; Anne Valery; Arthur Lowe; Jeremy Spenser; ***D:*** Robert Hamer; ***W:*** Robert Hamer; John Dighton; ***C:*** Douglas Slocombe; ***M:*** Ernest Irving.

A Kind of Murder **2016 (R)** This adaptation of the Patricia Highsmith novel "The Blunderer" effectively portrays turmoil in a wintry Northeast in 1960, but lacks the punch to make it an effective thriller. Architect Walter Stackhouse (Wilson) is part-time fiction writer obsessed with a woman's unsolved murder. After visiting with the deceased woman's enraged husband (Marsan), both Stackhouse and the detective (Kartheiser) on the case believe he did it. Stackhouse also has his own marital struggles with his emotionally unstable wife Clara (Biel) and desire for another woman (Bennett). The film's superficial direction and plot undermine the story. **95m/C; DVD.** Patrick Wilson; Jessica Biel; Haley Bennett; Eddie Marsan; Vincent Kartheiser; ***D:*** Andy Goddard; ***W:*** Susan Boyd; ***C:*** Chris Seager; ***M:*** Danny Bensi; Saunder Jurriaans.

Kindergarten Cop 1/2 **1990 (PG-13)** Pectoral perfect cop Kimble (Schwarzenegger) stalks mama's boy/criminal Crisp (Tyson) by locating the drug lord's ex and his six-year-old son. When the pec man's female partner succumbs to a nasty bout of food poisoning, he's forced to take her place as an undercover kindergarten teacher in the drowsy Pacific northwest community where mother and son reside incognito. A cover all the bases Christmas release, it's got romance, action, comedy and cute. And boxoffice earnings to match Arnie's chest measurements. A bit violent for the milk and cookie set. **111m/C; VHS, DVD, Blu-Ray.** Arnold Schwarzenegger; Penelope Ann Miller; Pamela Reed; Linda Hunt; Richard Tyson; Carroll Baker; Cathy Moriarty; Park Overall; Richard Portnow; Jayne Brook; ***D:*** Ivan Reitman; ***W:*** Murray Salem; Herschel Weingrod; Timothy Harris; ***C:*** Michael Chapman; ***M:*** Randy Edelman.

Kindergarten Cop 2 **2016 (PG-13)** The sequel to Kindergarten Cop featuring Dolph Lundgren in the role similar to the one played by Arnold Schwarzenegger. Gruff FBI agent Reed (Lundgren) goes undercover as a kindergarten teacher in order to recover sensitive stolen data. Though his mission is challenging, he finds it harder to work in the school's politically correct environment. **100m/C; DVD, Blu-Ray, Streaming, Download.** Dolph Lundgren; Darla Taylor; Bill Bellamy; Aleks Paunovic; Sarah Strange; ***D:*** Don Michael Paul; ***W:*** David H. Steinberg; ***C:*** Kamal Derkaoui; ***M:*** Jake Monaco.

Kindergarten Ninja 1/2 **1994** Football star is sentenced to community service after a drunk-driving arrest and is guided by a kung fu angel into helping a group of children. **80m/C; VHS, DVD.** Dwight Clark; ***D:*** Anthony Chan.

King **1978** Docudrama with terrific cast follows the life and career of one of the greatest non-violent civil rights leaders of all time, Martin Luther King. **272m/C; DVD, Blu-Ray.** Paul Winfield; Cicely Tyson; Roscoe Lee Browne; Ossie Davis; Art Evans; Ernie Banks; Howard E. Rollins, Jr.; William Jordan; Cliff DeYoung; ***D:*** Abby Mann; ***W:*** Abby Mann; ***M:*** Billy Goldenberg. **TV**

The King 1/2 **2005 (R)** Illegitimate Elvis Valderez (Garcia Bernal) heads to Corpus Christi to meet his dad, David Sandow (Hurt), who's now a Baptist preacher. Elvis insinuates himself into the family (with no one else knowing who he really is) and seduces his sheltered 16-year-old half-sister, Malerie (James). When Sandow's son Paul (Dano) disappears, the preacher reaches out to Elvis. Only his wife, Twyla (Harring), suspects that the pleasant young man isn't what he seems at all. The sins of the father come back in a big way. **105m/C; DVD.** Gael Garcia Bernal; Pell James; Paul Dano; William Hurt; Laura Elena Harring; Milo Addica; ***D:*** James Marsh; ***W:*** Milo Addica; James Marsh; ***C:*** Eigil Bryld; ***M:*** Max Lichtenstein.

The King 1/2 *Deoking* **2018** A young prosecutor in South Korea quickly ascends the political ranks, and soon finds himself immersed in backroom shenanigans and organized crime. Well-acted and visually appealing, with real-life relevance, but it drags in the middle and would benefit from better English subtitles. **134m/C; DVD.** In-sung Jo; Seong-Woo Bae; Woo-sung Jung; Ryoo Joon-Yeol; Jeong Eun-Chae; ***D:*** Jae-rim Han; ***M:*** Mowg.

The King **2019 (R)** The heir to the English throne, young Prince Hal (Chalamet) prefers drinking and womanizing with his friend and mentor, Falstaff (Edgerton) to focusing on matters of state. While Hal's severe father Henry IV (Mendelsohn) is a war enthusiast, Hal prefers peace, if pressed. When Hal unexpectedly becomes King Henry V in 1413 upon the battlefield death of his father, he is torn between his new responsibilities and has pacifist beliefs, and must learn how to make good decisions and who he can trust. Loosely based on Shakespeare's history plays, the medieval epic presents events in appealing fashion and features an exceptional performance by Chalamet. **140m/C; DVD.** Timothée Chalamet; Ben Mendelsohn; Joel Edgerton; Tom Glynn-Carney; Steven Elder; ***D:*** David Michod; ***W:*** Joel Edgerton; David Michod; ***C:*** Adam Arkapaw; ***M:*** Nicholas Britell.

King and Country **1964** Aristocratic army officer, Capt. Hargreaves (Bogarde), serves as the defense lawyer for troubled Private Arthur Hamp (Courtenay), whose wartime experiences have caused him to desert. Hargreaves at first ignores the uneducated Hamp's obvious shell-shock but soon begins to feel sympathy for his confused client. Director Losey shows the effects of war rather than the war itself and provides a sincere and bitter condemnation of military mentality. Based on the play "Hamp" by John Wilson. **86m/B; DVD, Blu-Ray.** *UK* Dirk Bogarde; Tom Courtenay; Leo McKern; Barry Foster; James Villiers; Peter Copley; ***D:*** Joseph Losey; ***W:*** Evan Jones; ***C:*** Denys Coop; ***M:*** Larry Adler. British Acad. '64: Film.

The King and Four Queens 1/2 **1956** Gable, on the run from the law, happens upon a deserted town, deserted, that is, except for a woman and her three daughters. Clark soon discovers that the women are looking for $100,000 in gold that one of their missing husbands had stolen. True to form, conniving Clark wastes no time putting the moves on each of them to find the whereabouts of the loot. **86m/C; VHS, DVD, Blu-Ray.** Clark Gable; Eleanor Parker; Jo Van Fleet; Jean Wiles; Barbara Nichols; Sara Shane; Roy Roberts; Arthur Shields; Jay C. Flippen; ***D:*** Raoul Walsh; ***M:*** Alex North.

The King and I **1956** Wonderful adaptation of Rodgers and Hammerstein's Broadway play based on the novel "Anna and the King of Siam" by Margaret Landon. English governess Kerr is hired to teach the King of Siam's many children and bring them into the 20th century. She has more of a job than she realizes, for this is a king, a country, and a people who value tradition above all else. Features one of Rodgers and Hammerstein's best-loved scores. Brynner made this role his, playing it over 4,000 times on stage and screen before his death. Kerr's voice was dubbed when she sang; the voice you hear is Marni Nixon, who also dubbed the star's singing voices in "West Side Story" and "My Fair Lady." **133m/C; VHS, DVD, Blu-Ray.** Deborah Kerr; Yul Brynner; Rita Moreno; Martin Benson; Terry Saunders; Rex Thompson; Alan Mowbray; Carlos Rivas; Patrick Adiate; ***D:*** Walter Lang; ***W:*** Ernest Lehman; ***C:*** Leon Shamroy; ***M:*** Richard Rodgers; Oscar Hammerstein. Oscars '56: Actor (Brynner), Art Dir./Set Dec., Color, Costume Des. (C), Scoring/Musical, Sound; Golden Globes '57: Actress--Mus./Comedy (Kerr), Film--Mus./Comedy.

The King and I **1999 (G)** Animated musical tries, but fails, to split the difference between faithfulness to the Broadway version and the action needed to entertain kids. Tells the story of Anna (Richardson), an English woman who travels to Siam in order to tutor the children of the King (Vidnovic). The evil Kralahome and stereotypical comic relief sidekick Master Little (Hammond) plan to use Anna to capture the throne. The ending is given a kid-friendly twist, but eight of the original 20 Broadway songs were slashed to keep it brief for the short attention span set. **87m/C; VHS, DVD.** ***V:*** Miranda Richardson; Martin Vidnovic; Ian Richardson; Darrell Hammond; Allen D. Hong; Armi Arabe; Adam Wylie; Sean Smith; ***D:*** Richard Rich; ***W:*** Jacqueline Feather; David Seidler; Peter Bakalian.

King Arthur 1/2 **2004 (PG-13)** The noble knights are recast as centurions fighting for Rome in Britain circa 500 A.D. Arthur is Artorius, a mercenary from a backwater colony fighting to earn back his freedom by pacifying Celts. He and his men don't like this one bit, especially when sent to rescue a rich brat favored by the Pope from encroaching Saxon invaders. The filmmakers claim historical accuracy. Well. . .maybe, but it's still just an excuse to recycle a classic western/war story: corrupt command sends band of hardened roughnecks on suicide mission. Nothing feels very novel about this novel idea, but it is a fun ride. Owen is a terrific Arthur, all brooding and steely. Knightley is perhaps the sexiest (and most proactive) Guinevere ever. Skarsgard hams it up as a nasty proto-fascist villain. **130m/C; DVD, Blu-Ray, UMD.** *GB IR* Clive Owen; Stephen (Dillon) Dillane; Keira Knightley; Ioan Gruffudd; Stellan Skarsgard; Ray Winstone; Hugh Dancy; Ray Stevenson; Charlie Creed-Miles; Joel Edgerton; Ken Stott; Til Schweiger; Mads Mikkelsen; Sean Gilder; Ivano Marescotti; Lorenzo De Angelis; ***D:*** Antoine Fuqua; ***W:*** David Franzoni; ***C:*** Slawomir Idziak; ***M:*** Hans Zimmer.

King Arthur: Legend of the Sword **2017 (PG-13)** Ritchie's gritty reboot of the Arthurian legend is loud, vulgar, packed with wall-to-wall action, and decidedly unsentimental. Spirited away from danger as an infant when his uncle Vortigern (Law) betrayed his father Uthur (Bana), Arthur (Hunnam) grows up in a brothel and hangs with tough back-alley mates. Eventually he pulls Excalibur from the stone and learns of his birthright. Epic brutal swashbuckling ensues. While it may not be dull, and is sometimes clever, it is also repetitive and clichéd. Law is excellent in his villainous turn and Hunnam carries the weight of the lead duties well. **126m/C; DVD, Blu-Ray.** Charlie Hunnam; Jude Law; Astrid Berges-Frisbey; Djimon Hounsou; Eric Bana; ***D:*** Guy Ritchie; ***W:*** Guy Ritchie; Joby Harold; Lionel Wigram; ***C:*** John Mathieson; ***M:*** Daniel Pemberton.

King Arthur, the Young Warlord **1975 (PG)** The struggle that was the other side of Camelot—the campaign against the Saxon hordes. The early, somewhat violent years of King Art. **90m/C; VHS, DVD.** Oliver Tobias; Michael Gothard; Jack Watson; Brian Blessed; Peter Firth; ***D:*** Sidney Hayers; Pat Jackson; Peter Sasdy.

King Boxer 1/2 *5 Fingers of Death; Tian xia di yi quan; Hand of Death; Shaolin Avenger* **1972 (R)** More commonly known in the U.S. as "Five Fingers of Death", this Shaw Brothers film's international success is said to be responsible for introducing kung fu films to the world at large and creating the martial arts craze of the 1970s. An old master sends his pupil Chao (Lo Lieh) to a martial arts school to learn the Iron Palm technique. Unfortunately a rival school has hired Japanese mercenaries to cripple Chao's teachers and has killed his master. He enters the All China Tournament in order to compete against them and get revenge with his new techniques. **98m/C; DVD.** *CH* Lieh Lo; Feng Tien; James Nam; Bolo Yeung; Ping Wang; Hsiung Chiao; Chin-Feng Wang; Mien Fang; Shen Chan; Wen Chung Ku; Lung Yu; Yukio Sumeno; Chi Chu Chin; Bong-jin Jin; ***D:*** Chang-hwa Jeong; ***W:*** Yeung Kong; ***C:*** Yung-lung Wang; ***M:*** Yung-Yu Chen.

King Cobra 1/2 **1998 (PG-13)** If you like big snakes, this low-budgeter is for you! A mutant cobra/rattlesnake hybrid, having escaped its lab environment, threatens the populace of a small California town. **93m/C; VHS, DVD.** Noriyuki "Pat" Morita; Hoyt Axton; Kasey Fallo; Scott Brandon; Joseph Ruskin; Courtney Gains; ***D:*** David Hillenbrand; Scott Hillenbrand; ***W:*** David Hillenbrand; Scott Hillenbrand; ***C:*** Philip D. Schwartz. **VIDEO**

King Cobra 1/2 **2016** Based on true events, a biographical crime drama that explores dark events in the life of gay pornography star Brent Corrigon (Clayton). In his suburban home, the career of middle-aged gay pornographer Stephen (Slater) takes off after he signs a blond 18-year-old Brent and makes him an internet star. When Brent realizes that Stephen has been exploiting him, he leaves and wants to work with troubled pornographer Joe (Franco) and his boy star Harlow (Allen). Because Stephen threatens legal action if Brent acts under that name for anyone else, Joe and Harlow take violent action. Soulful performances overcome the uneven scripting. **91m/C; DVD.** Garrett Clayton; Christian Slater; Molly Ringwald; James Kelley; Keegan Allen; ***D:*** Justin Kelly; ***W:*** Justin Kelly; ***C:*** Benjamin Loeb; ***M:*** Tim Kvasnosky.

King Creole 1/2 **1958 (PG)** The King goes film noir as a teenager with a criminal record who becomes a successful pop singer in New Orleans but is threatened by his ties to crime, represented by Walter Matthau. One of the better Elvis films, based on Harold Robbins' "A Stone for Danny Fisher." Features Elvis's last film appearance before his service in the Army. **115m/B; VHS, DVD, Blu-Ray.** Elvis Presley; Carolyn Jones; Walter Matthau; Dean Jagger; Dolores Hart; Vic Morrow; Paul Stewart; Brian G. Hutton; Liliane Montevecchi; Jan Shepard; Jack Grinnage; ***D:*** Michael Curtiz; ***W:*** Herbert Baker; Michael V. Gazzo; ***C:*** Russell Harlan; ***M:*** Walter Scharf.

King David 1/2 **1985 (PG-13)** The story of David, the legendary Biblical hero whose acts of bravery paved the way for him to become king of Israel. **114m/C; DVD.** Richard Gere; Alice Krige; Cherie Lunghi; Hurd Hatfield; Edward Woodward; ***D:*** Bruce Beresford; ***W:*** Andrew Birkin; James Costigan; ***C:*** Donald McAlpine; ***M:*** Carl Davis.

A King in New York **1957** Chaplin plays the deposed king of a European minimonarchy who comes to the United States in hope of making a new life. Looks critically at 1950s-era America, including Cold War paranoia and over reliance on technology. Containing Chaplin's last starring performance, this film wasn't released in the U.S. until 1973. Uneven but interesting. **105m/B; VHS, DVD.** *GB* Charlie Chaplin; Dawn Addams; Michael Chaplin; Oliver Johnston; Maxine Audley; Harry Green; ***D:*** Charlie Chaplin; ***W:*** Charlie Chaplin; ***C:*** Georges Perinal; ***M:*** Charlie Chaplin.

The King Is Alive 1/2 **2000 (R)** A tourist bus traveling in Namibia strays off-course and runs out of gas. The passengers stumble into a deserted mining town with little food or water and only a small chance at survival. Retired actor Henry (Bradley) begins to think their situation resembles that of "King Lear" and he gradually begins to convince the others to rehearse the play as a way to pass the time. Much lunacy ensues. **118m/C; VHS, DVD.** *DK* Miles Anderson; Romane Bohringer; David Bradley; David Calder; Bruce Davison; Brion James; Vusi Kunene; Peter Kubheka; Jennifer Jason Leigh; Janet McTeer; Lia Williams; Chris Walker; ***D:*** Kristian Levring; ***W:*** Anders Thomas Jensen; Kristian Levring; ***C:*** Jens Schlosser.

King Jack **2016** A coming-of-age drama about a small-town teen facing difficulties but finding joy. Trapped in a run-down community, 15-year-old Jack (Plummer) not only has to manage his violent conflict with an older bully but also is stuck going to summer school again. His situation seems only grow worse when his aunt becomes sick and his younger cousin must stay with his family for a weekend. Though Jack has no real interest in looking after the boy, he experiences unexpected friendship and happiness. **81m/C; DVD, Streaming, Download.** Charlie Plummer; Cory Nichols; Christian Madsen; Danny Flaherty; Erin Davie; ***D:*** Felix Thompson; ***W:*** Felix Thompson; ***C:*** Brandon Roots; ***M:*** Bryan Senti.

King Kong **1933** The original beauty and the beast film classic tells the story of Kong, a giant ape captured in Africa by filmmaker Carl Denham (Armstrong) and brought to New York as a sideshow attraction. Kong falls for starlet Ann (Wray), escapes from his captors, and rampages through the city, ending up on top of the newly built Empire State Building. Moody Steiner score adds color, and Willis O'Brien's stop-motion animation still holds up well. Scenes were cut during the 1938 re-release because of the Hays production code, including one where a curious Kong strips Wray of her clothes. Remade numerous times with various theme derivations. **105m/B; VHS, DVD, Blu-Ray.** Fay Wray; Bruce Cabot; Robert Armstrong; Frank Reicher; Noble Johnson; Sam Hardy; James Flavin; Ernest B. Schoedsack; Merian C. Cooper; ***D:*** Ernest B. Schoedsack; Merian C. Cooper; ***W:*** James A. Creelman; Ruth Rose; Edgar Wallace; ***C:*** Edward Linden; J.O. Taylor; Vernon Walker; ***M:*** Max Steiner. AFI '98: Top 100; Natl. Film Reg. '91.

King Kong **1976 (PG)** Oil company official travels to a remote island to discover it inhabited by a huge gorilla. The transplanted beast suffers unrequited love in classic fashion: monkey meets girl, monkey gets girl and brandishes her while atop the World Trade Center. An updated remake of the 1933 movie classic that also marks the screen debut of Lange. Impressive sets and a believable King Kong romp around New York City in this film. Watch for Joe Piscopo, and quickly for Corbin Bernsen as a reporter. **135m/C; VHS, DVD.** Jeff Bridges; Charles Grodin; Jessica Lange; Rene Auberjonois; John Randolph; Ed Lauter; Jack O'Halloran; Dennis Fimple; John Agar; Rick Baker; Joe Piscopo; Corbin Bernsen; ***D:*** John Guillermin; ***W:*** Lorenzo Semple, Jr.; ***C:*** Richard H. Kline; ***M:*** John Barry. Oscars '76: Visual FX.

King Kong 1/2 **2005 (PG-13)** In this remake of the 1933 classic, Depression-era filmmaker Carl Denham (Black) lures starving ingenue Ann Darrow (Watts) and screenwriter Jack Driscoll (Brody) to the uncharted Skull Island to shoot his masterpiece. However, once they arrive, the crew meets angry natives, rampaging dinosaurs, and a massive, menacing monkey named Kong. We all know where the story goes from there, but Jackson enlivens the familiar with thrilling action sequences (Kong vs. T. Rexes equals awesome) and the most expressive simian ever put to film (WETA deserves an acting Oscar for Kong's face alone). Regrettably, the three-hour flick drags whenever Kong isn't on-screen, and Jackson spends way too much time with his so-so supporting cast. But, as always, Kong remains king. **187m/C; DVD, Blu-Ray, HD-DVD.** Naomi Watts; Jack Black; Adrien Brody; Thomas Kretschmann; Colin Hanks; Jamie Bell; Evan Dexter Parke; Kyle Chandler; Andy Serkis; Lobo Chan; ***D:*** Peter Jackson; ***W:*** Peter Jackson; Fran Walsh; Philippa Boyens; ***C:*** Andrew Lesnie; ***M:*** James Newton Howard. Oscars '05: Sound, Visual FX; British Acad. '05: Visual FX.

King Kong Escapes WOOF! *Kingu Kongu no gyakushu* **1967** After the success of "King Kong vs Godzilla" Rankin-Bass decided to have a cartoon series on Kong produced in Japan (for which this film was the lead-in). They got Toho to do a kid-friendly Kong film about a mad scientist who plans to kidnap the giant ape in order to mine a radioactive element in a plot to take over the world, because apparently radiation made his own giant robot ape shut off. So the robot ape is repaired and sent to hypnotize Kong as a replacement. How many films feature a giant robot gorilla hypnotist? At least it's unique. **96m/C; DVD, Blu-Ray.** *JP* Rhodes Reason; Mie Hama; Linda Miller; Akira Takarada; Eisei Amamoto; ***D:*** Ishio Honda; ***W:*** Takeshi Kimura; ***C:*** Hajime Koizumi; ***M:*** Akira Ifukube.

King Kong Lives **1986 (PG-13)** Unnecessary sequel to the 1976 remake of "King Kong," in which two scientists get the big ape, now restored after his asphalt-upsetting fall, together with a lady ape his size and type. **105m/C; VHS, DVD.** Brian Kerwin; Linda Hamilton; John Ashton; Peter Michael Goetz; ***D:*** John Guillermin; ***W:*** Steven Pressfield; Ronald Shusett.

King Kong vs. Godzilla 1/2 *King Kong tai Godzilla; KinguKongu tai Gojira* **1963** The planet issues a collective shudder as the two mightiest monsters slug it out for reasons known only to themselves. Humankind can only stand by and watch in impotent horror as the tide of the battle sways to and fro, until one monster stands alone and victorious. **105m/C; VHS, DVD, Blu-Ray.** *JP* Michael Keith; Tadao Takashima; Mie Hama; Kenji Sahara; Yu Fujiki; Akihiko Hirata; Jun Tazaki; Akiko Wakabayashi; Ichiro Arishima; Haruo Nakajima; Katsumi Tezuka; ***Nar:*** Les Tremayne; ***D:*** Inoshiro Honda; ***W:*** Shinichi Sekizawa; ***C:*** Hajime Koizumi; ***M:*** Akira Ifukube; Robert Emmett Dolan; Henry Mancini; Herman Stein; Milton Rosen.

King Kung Fu **1987 (G)** A karate master raises a gorilla, and sends it from Asia to the U.S. There, two out-of-work reporters decide to release it from captivity and then recapture it so they can get the story and some needed recognition. The background they don't have on the gorilla is that its master taught it kung fu. **90m/C; VHS, DVD.** John Balee; Tom Leahy; Maxine Gray; Bill Schwartz; ***D:*** Bill Hayes.

King Lear **1998** Holm gives a powerful performance as the deluded monarch. The King comes to rue the day he banished faithful daughter Cordelia (Hamilton) in favor of dividing his kingdom between her manipulative siblings Goneril (Flynn) and Regan (Redman). As war engulfs his country, Lear descends into despair and madness. **150m/C; VHS, DVD.** Ian Holm; Victoria Hamilton; Barbara Flynn; Amanda Redman; Michael Bryant; Paul Rhys; Timothy West; Finbar Lynch; David Burke; ***D:*** Richard Eyre; ***W:*** Richard Eyre; ***C:*** Roger Pratt; ***M:*** Dominic Muldowney. **TV**

King of California 1/2 **2007 (PG-13)** Charlie (Douglas), a bipolar jazz musician, leaves his hospital in order to find the horde of Spanish treasure he's convinced is buried in his old neighborhood. His teenage daughter Miranda (Wood), abandoned by her mother, reluctantly joins him on his quest, and the two must seek clues as to the treasure's location amongst a sea of box stores and chain restaurants. Douglas is excellent as the erratic, Quixote-like Charlie in search of meaning in an alienated world, but the movie fails to dig much deeper than the superficial world it satirizes. **93m/C; DVD, Blu-Ray, HD-DVD.** Michael Douglas; Evan Rachel Wood; Willis Burks, II; ***D:*** Mike Cahill; ***W:*** Mike Cahill; ***C:*** Jim Whitaker; ***M:*** David Robbins.

King of Comedy **1982 (PG)** An unhinged would-be comedian haunts and eventually kidnaps a massively popular Johnny Carson-type TV personality. A cold, cynical farce devised by Scorsese seemingly in reaction to John Hinckley's obsession with his film "Taxi Driver." Controlled, hard-hitting performances, especially by De Niro and Lewis. **101m/C; VHS, DVD, Blu-Ray.** Robert De Niro; Jerry Lewis; Sandra Bernhard; Tony Randall; Diahnne Abbott; Shelley Hack; Liza Minnelli; ***D:*** Martin Scorsese; ***W:*** Paul Zimmerman; ***C:*** Fred Schuler; ***M:*** Robbie Robertson. British Acad. '83: Orig. Screenplay; Natl. Soc. Film Critics '83: Support. Actress (Bernhard).

King of Devil's Island *Kongen av Bastoy* **2010** Based on a 1915 uprising at the brutally-run Bastoy Boys Home where the Norwegian Army was called in to quell the rioting. Living on an isolated island, the young men are used as cheap manual labor and endure cruel punishments. Newcomer Erling, who's determined to escape, immediately clashes with both the hypocritical school governor and his dorm leader, who sexually abuses weaker boys. Erling gradually rallies the others to defiance. Norwegian with subtitles. **100m/C; DVD.** *NO* Stellan Skarsgard; Benjamin Helsted; Trond Nilssen; Kristoffer Joner; ***D:*** Marius Hoist; ***W:*** Dennis Magnusson; ***C:*** John Andreas Andersen; ***M:*** Johan Soderqvist.

The King of Hearts *Le Roi de Coeur* **1966** In WWI, a Scottish soldier finds a battle-torn French town evacuated of all occupants except a colorful collection of escaped lunatics from a nearby asylum. The lunatics want to make him their king, which is not a bad alternative to the insanity of war. Bujold is cute as ballerina wanna-be; look for Serrault ("La Cage aux Folles") as, not surprisingly, a effeminate would-be hairdresser. Light-hearted comedy with a serious message; definitely worthwhile. **101m/C; VHS, DVD, Blu-Ray.** *FR GB IT* Alan Bates; Genevieve Bujold; Adolfo Celi; Francoise Christophe; Micheline Presle; Michel Serrault; Julien Guiomar; Pierre Brasseur; Jean-Claude Brialy; Pier Paolo Capponi; Jacques Balutin; Marc Dudicourt; Daniel Boulanger; ***D:*** Philippe de Broca; ***W:*** Daniel Boulanger; ***C:*** Pierre Lhomme; ***M:*** Georges Delerue.

King of Kings 1/2 **1927** DeMille depicts the life of Jesus Christ in this highly regarded silent epic. The resurrection scene appears in color. Remade by Nicholas Ray in 1961. **115m/B; Silent; VHS, DVD.** H.B. Warner; Dorothy (Dorothy G. Cummings) Cumming; Ernest Torrence; Joseph Schildkraut; Jacqueline Logan; Victor Varconi; William Boyd; James Neill; Robert Edeson; Charles Belcher; Montagu Love; Monte (Monty) Collins; ***D:*** Cecil B. DeMille; ***C:*** J. Peverell Marley.

The King of Kings **1961** The life of Christ is intelligently told, with an attractive visual sense and a memorable score. Remake of Cecil B. DeMille's silent film, released in 1927. **170m/C; VHS, DVD.** Jeffrey Hunter; Siobhan McKenna; Hurd Hatfield; Robert Ryan; Rita Gam; Viveca Lindfors; Rip Torn; ***Nar:*** Orson Welles; ***D:*** Nicholas Ray; ***W:*** Philip Yordan; ***C:*** Milton Krasner; ***M:*** Miklos Rozsa.

The King of Kong: A Fistful of Quarters 1/2 **2007 (PG-13)** Documentary follows the intense rivalry of two men battling to be declared the undisputed King of Donkey Kong, and you couldn't ask for two more intriguing characters. Hot-sauce tycoon and idly rich Billy Mitchell is at the top of the arcade champ heap, holding the high score in Donkey Kong for over 25 years until lowly, humble high school teacher Steve Wiebe appears on the scene with an even higher score. A battle on multiple fronts ensues as Mitchell challenges the validity of Weibe's score to respected video game authority Walter Day, but refuses a head-to-head battle with Weibe. Throughout, there's not a moment in which each man sees their dispute as anything but a conflict of epic proportions. Director Gordon skillfully takes us inside a competition few people (even video game enthusiasts) care about and turns it into an exploration of egoism, rivalry, and what it means to be a champion. The movie clearly roots for underdog Weibe, but the obvious slant is half the fun. **79m/C; On Demand.** ***D:*** Seth Gordon; ***C:*** Seth Gordon; ***M:*** Craig Richey.

King of Kong Island WOOF! **1978** Intent on world domination, a group of mad scientists implant receptors in the brains of gorillas on Kong Island, and the monster apes run amok. **92m/C; VHS, DVD.** *SP* Brad Harris; Marc Lawrence; ***D:*** Robert Morris.

The King of Marvin Gardens 1/2 **1972 (R)** Nicholson stars as a radio personality who prefers to reminisce about his life and family back home rather than play records. When Nicholson returns for a visit he finds brother Dern, king of the get-rich-quick schemers, working for a black crime syndicate. Dern is involved in another scheme which means embezzling money from his boss—not a smart idea although Nicholson can't disuade him. Talky drama also features Burstyn as Dern's neglected girlfriend. **104m/C; VHS, DVD.** Jack Nicholson; Bruce Dern; Ellen Burstyn; Scatman Crothers; Julia Anne Robinson; Charles Lavine; Arnold Williams; Josh Mostel; ***D:*** Bob Rafelson; ***W:*** Jacob Brackman.

The King of Masks **1999** Wang (Xu) is an elderly street performer in 1930s China who practices the ancient art of face-changing with masks. Tradition has it that he pass his secrets to a male heir, which Wang doesn't have. So, he decides to purchase a boy child on the black market, only to later discover that his clever protege (Ren-ying) is actually a little girl. Chinese with subtitles. **101m/C; VHS, DVD.** *CH* Zhu Xu; Zhou Renying; ***D:*** Wu Tianming; ***W:*** Wei Minglung; ***C:*** Mu Dayuan; ***M:*** Jiping Zhao.

King of New York **1990 (R)** Drug czar Frank White (Walken), recently returned from a prison sabbatical, regains control of his New York drug empire with the aid of a loyal network of black dealers. How? Call it dangerous charisma, an inexplicable sympatico. Headquartered in Manhattan's chic Plaza hotel, he ruthlessly orchestrates the drug machine, while funneling the profits into a Bronx hospital for the poor. As inscrutable as White himself, Walken makes the drug czar's power tangible, believable, yet never fathomable. **106m/C; VHS, DVD, Blu-Ray, UMD.** Christopher Walken; Laurence Fishburne; David Caruso; Victor Argo; Wesley Snipes; Janet (Johnson) Julian; Joey Chin; Giancarlo Esposito; Steve Buscemi; ***D:*** Abel Ferrara; ***W:*** Nicholas St. John; ***C:*** Bojan Bazelli; ***M:*** Joe Delia.

The King of Staten Island 1/2 **2020 (R) 136m/C; DVD.** Pete Davidson; Bel Powley; Ricky Velez; Lou Wilson; Moises Arias; ***D:*** Judd Apatow; ***W:*** Pete Davidson; Judd Apatow; Dave Sirus; ***C:*** Robert Elswit; ***M:*** Michael Andrews.

King of Texas **2002** Shakespeare's "King Lear" set in 1840s Texas with Stewart as John Lear, the patriarch rancher who gives his property to greedy daughters Susannah (Harden) and Rebecca (Holly) instead of to sweet daughter Claudia (Cox). Then the bad girls kick him out into the wilderness. Powerful performance by Stewart does the Bard proud. **120m/C; DVD.** Patrick Stewart; Marcia Gay Harden; Lauren Holly; Julie Cox; David Alan Grier; Roy Scheider; Colm Meaney; Matt Letscher; Steven Bauer; Patrick Bergin; Liam Waite; ***D:*** Uli Edel; ***W:*** Stephen Harrigan; ***C:*** Paul Elliott; ***M:*** John Altman. **CABLE**

King of the Ants 1/2 **2003** Handyman Sean (McKenna) could stand a little excitement but he gets more than he bargained for when Duke (Wendt, convincing in quite the anti-"Norm" role) steers him to crooked businessman Ray (Baldwin) who wants Sean to clip a city accountant who's getting too close for comfort. He jumps at the chance but the feel-good ends there when Ray and Duke cut him loose and have his face rearranged. Whereupon, it becomes a standard revenge tale. Screenwriter Charlie Higson adapted from his 1992 novel of the same name. **103m/C; VHS, DVD.** Kari Wuhrer; Daniel Baldwin; George Wendt; Ron Livingston; Chris(topher) McKenna; Timm Sharp; Vernon Wells; Lionel Mark Smith; Carlie Westerman; ***D:*** Stuart Gordon; ***W:*** Charles Higson; ***C:*** Mac Ahlberg. **VIDEO**

King of the Corner **2004 (R)** Leo (Riegert) has hit the middle-age wall and can hardly hold back his angst. He abhors his lifelong VP status at a Manhattan marketing job, wife Rachel (Rossellini) appears mentally unstable, and teenage daughter Elena (Johnson) just started dating. Adding to the stress are every-other-weekend treks to Arizona to visit his dying father Sol, whose sage advice for Leo teaches him the real meaning about being a "good Jew." Adapted from the short-story collection "Bad Jews and Other Stories" by Gerald Shapiro, who co-wrote the screenplay along with actor/director Riegert. **93m/C; VHS, DVD.** Peter Riegert; Isabella Rossellini; Beverly D'Angelo; Eli Wallach; Ashley Johnson; Eric Bogosian; Dominic Chianese; Rita Moreno; Peter Friedman; Harris Yulin; Frank Wood; ***D:*** Peter Riegert; ***W:*** Peter Riegert; ***C:*** Mauricio Rubinstein.

King of the Grizzlies 🦴 1/2 **1969 (G)** The mystical relationship between a Cree Indian and a grizzly cub is put to the test when the full grown bear attacks a ranch at which the Indian is foreman. **93m/C; VHS, DVD.** Chris Wiggins; John Yesno; *D:* Ron Kelly.

King of the Gypsies 🦴🦴 1/2 **1978 (R)** Interesting drama. A young man, scornful of his gypsy heritage, runs away from the tribe and tries to make a life of his own. He is summoned home to his grandfather's deathbed where he is proclaimed the new king of the gypsies, thus incurring the wrath of his scorned father. From Peter Maas's best-selling novel. **112m/C; VHS, DVD, Blu-Ray.** Sterling Hayden; Eric Roberts; Susan Sarandon; Brooke Shields; Shelley Winters; Annie Potts; Annette O'Toole; Judd Hirsch; Michael V. Gazzo; Roy Brocksmith; Anthony Holland; Antonia Rey; Stephen Mendillo; Matthew Laborteaux; Patti LuPone; Rachel Ticotin; *D:* Frank Pierson; *W:* Frank Pierson; *C:* Sven Nykvist; *M:* David Grisman.

King of the Jungle 🦴🦴 **2001 (R)** Contrived story with an energized performance by Leguizamo. He's Seymour, a mentally challenged man with the intellectual and emotional capacity of a preadolescent. He lives with his long-divorced Puerto Rican mother Mona (Carmen) and her lover Joanne (Perez). His dad, Jack (Gorman), is a deadbeat poet who has never accepted his son's limitations. Seymour spends his time on the streets playing basketball until his mother is fatally shot and he wants revenge. **87m/C; VHS, DVD.** John Leguizamo; Cliff Gorman; Julie Carmen; Rosie Perez; Michael Rapaport; Rosario Dawson; Marisa Tomei; Annabella Sciorra; *D:* Seth Zvi Rosenfeld; *W:* Seth Zvi Rosenfeld; *C:* Fortunato Procopio; *M:* Harry Gregson-Williams.

King of the Khyber Rifles 🦴🦴 1/2 **1953** Rousing adventure, filmed in CinemaScope, that's a remake of 1929's "The Black Watch." Capt. Alan King (Power) and his escort fend off an ambush by rebel Karram Khan (Rolfe) on their way to the British garrison near the Khyber Pass. When it's revealed King's a half-caste, he's subjected to prejudice except from commanding officer Maitland (Rennie) and his daughter Susan (Moore). To prove his loyalty, King offers to stop Khan. The seasoned Power was ill-matched with young Moore and their pairing lacked romance. **100m/C; DVD.** Tyrone Power; Guy Rolfe; Michael Rennie; Terry Moore; John Justin; *D:* Henry King; *W:* Ben Roberts; Ivan Goff; *C:* Leon Shamroy; *M:* Bernard Herrmann.

King of the Lost World 🦴 1/2 **2006 (R)** Blatant cash-in on the "King Kong" remake which was released about the same time despite claiming to be based on Sir Arthur Conan Doyle's "The Lost World." A group of plane passengers crash land in a jungle full of giant scorpions and reptiles and encounter the inevitable crazed primitives and a giant ape. **85m/C; DVD.** Bruce Boxleitner; J.J. Denton; Rhett Giles; Sarah Lieving; Steve Railsback; Chriss Anglin; Christina Rosenberg; Amanda Wad; Andrew Lauer; Boni Yanagisawa; Thomas Downey; Amanda Barton; James Ferris; Jennifer Lee Wiggins; Angela Horvath; Eliza Swenson; Leigh Scott; Yoshie Morino; Tony Thomas; Ava Bellamy; Brian J. Garland; Shaun Lavery; *D:* Leigh Scott; *W:* Leigh Scott; Sir Arthur Conan Doyle; David Michael Latt; Carlos De Los Rios; *C:* Steven Parker; *M:* Ralph Riekermann.

King of the Newsboys 🦴 1/2 **1938** Working-class newsboy Jerry Flynn can't compete with the flash and cash of gangster Wire Arno when it comes to wooing poor beauty Mary Ellen. Jerry succeeds in turning his newsstand into a major distribution center but discovers (as does Mary Ellen) that money can't buy happiness. Can their mutual dissatisfaction bring Jerry and Mary Ellen back together? **65m/B; DVD.** Lew Ayres; Helen Mack; Victor Varconi; Alison Skipworth; Sheila Mannors; Alice White; Horace McMahon; *D:* Bernard Vorhaus; *W:* Peggy Thompson; Louis Weitzenkorn; *C:* Jack Marta; *M:* Alberto Colombo.

The King of the Roaring '20s: The Story of Arnold Rothstein 🦴🦴 1/2 *The Big Bankroll* **1961** "True" story of infamous gangster, Arnold Rothstein, a brilliant and ruthless gambler who practically ran New York in the '20s. This version of his life focuses on his rise to power, the dealings with his enemies, and his crumbling personal life. Superficial due mostly to the weak screenplay. Adapted from the book "The Big Bankroll" by Leo Katcher. **106m/B; VHS, DVD.** David Janssen; Dianne Foster; Mickey Rooney; Jack Carson; Diana Dors; Dan O'Herlihy; Mickey Shaughnessy; Keenan Wynn; *D:* Joseph M. Newman.

King of the Rocketmen 🦴🦴 *Lost Planet Airmen* **1949** Jeff King thwarts an attempt by traitors to steal government scientific secrets. Serial in 12 episodes. Later released as a feature titled "Lost Planet Airmen." **156m/B; VHS, DVD.** Tristram Coffin; Mae Clarke; I. Stanford Jolley; *D:* Fred Brannon.

King of the Underworld 🦴 1/2 **1939** Physician Carol Nelson (Francis) has problems with gangster Joe Gurney (Bogart) after he comes expecting the doc to take care of his bullet wound. Fearing she could lose her medical license, Carol tries to outsmart the hoodlum. Francis' stardom was waning and Jack Warner took advantage to play up Bogart in this routine crime drama. **67m/B; DVD.** Kay Francis; Humphrey Bogart; James Stephenson; John Eldredge; Arthur Aylesworth; *D:* Lewis Seiler; *W:* Vincent Sherman; George Bricker; *C:* Sidney Hickox; *M:* Heinz Roemheld.

King of the Wild Stallions 🦴 1/2 **1959** Widowed rancher Martha (Brewster) needs $500 to pay off cattle baron Matt Maguire (Meyer), which happens to be the same amount he's put up for the capture of the wild black stallion roaming the hills. When Martha's son Bucky (Hartleben) captures the horse, he wants to keep him and it's up to ranch foreman Randy (Montgomery)?who's sweet on Martha—to settle the matter. **76m/C; DVD.** George Montgomery; Diane Brewster; Emile Meyer; Edgar Buchanan; Denver Pyle; Jerry Hartleben; *D:* R.G. Springsteen; Ford Beebe; *W:* Ford Beebe; *C:* Carl Guthrie; *M:* Marlin Skiles.

King of the Wind 🦴🦴 1/2 **1993 (PG)** An epic adventure featuring the true story of a legendary Arabian horse and a poor stable boy who gave the most precious gift of all: love. **101m/C; VHS, DVD.** Richard Harris; Glenda Jackson.

King of the Zombies WOOF! **1941** Mad scientist creates his own zombies without souls, to be used as the evil tools of a foreign government. Zombie nonsense. **67m/B; VHS, DVD, Blu-Ray.** John Archer; Dick Purcell; Mantan Moreland; Henry Victor; Joan Woodbury; *D:* Jean Yarbrough; *W:* Edmond Kelso; *C:* Mack Stengler; *M:* Edward Kay.

King of Thieves 🦴🦴 *Konig der Diebe* **2004** Poor Ukrainian circus kids, 10-year-old Barbu and his 13-year-old sister Mimma, are sold to one-time circus performer Caruso who makes a lot of promises about a better life. After smuggling them into Berlin, the siblings are separated and Barbu learns to be a pickpocket. But when he discovers that Mimma is forced to work in a brothel, he tries to free her. German with subtitles. **101m/C; DVD.** *GE* Lazar Ristovski; Paulus Manker; Katharina Thalbach; Iakov Kultiasov; Julia Khanverdieva; *D:* Ivan Fila; *W:* Ivan Fila; *C:* Vladimir Smutny; *M:* Michael Kocab.

King Ralph 🦴🦴 **1991 (PG)** When the rest of the royal family passes away in a freak accident, lounge lizard Ralph finds himself the only heir to the throne. O'Toole is the long-suffering valet who tries to train him for the job. Funny in spots and Goodman is the quintessential good sport, making the whole outing pleasant. Sometimes too forced. **96m/C; VHS, DVD.** John Goodman; Peter O'Toole; Camille Coduri; Joely Richardson; John Hurt; *D:* David S. Ward; *W:* David S. Ward; *C:* Kenneth Macmillan; *M:* James Newton Howard.

King Rat 🦴🦴🦴 **1965** Drama set in a WWII Japanese prisoner-of-war camp. Focuses on the effect of captivity on the English, Australian, and American prisoners. An American officer bribes his Japanese captors to live more comfortably than the rest. Based on James Clavell's novel. **134m/B; VHS, DVD.** George Segal; Tom Courtenay; James Fox; James Donald; Denholm Elliott; Patrick O'Neal; John Mills; Todd Armstrong; Gerald Sim; Leonard Rossiter; John Standing; Alan Webb; Sam Reese; Wright King; Joe Turkel; Geoffrey Bayldon; Reg Lye; Arthur Malet; Richard Dawson; William "Bill" Fawcett; John Warburton; John Ronane; Michael Lees; Hamilton Dyce; Hedley Mattingly; Dale Ishimoto; *D:* Bryan Forbes; *W:* Bryan Forbes; James Clavell; *C:* Burnett Guffey; *M:* John Barry.

King Richard and the Crusaders 🦴 1/2 **1954** Laughable costume epic with Sanders as Richard the Lionheart, who survives an assassination attempt during the Crusades. Harvey is a loyal knight sworn to find the traitors with Harrison as the noble leader of the Arab forces. Mayo plays Harvey's object of affection. Even the battle scenes are boring. Based on "The Talisman" by Sir Walter Scott. **113m/C; DVD.** George Sanders; Rex Harrison; Laurence Harvey; Virginia Mayo; Robert Douglas; Michael Pate; Paula Raymond; Lester Matthews; *D:* David Butler; *W:* John Twist; *M:* Max Steiner.

King Solomon's Mines 🦴🦴🦴 **1937** The search for King Solomon's Mines leads a safari through the treacherous terrain of the desert, fending off sandstorms, Zulus, and a volcanic eruption. Adapted from the novel by H. Rider Haggard and remade twice. **80m/B; VHS, DVD.** Cedric Hardwicke; Paul Robeson; Roland Young; John Loder; Anna Lee; *D:* Robert Stevenson; *W:* Michael Hogan; Roland Pertwee; *C:* Cyril Knowles; Glen MacWilliams; *M:* Mischa Spoliansky.

King Solomon's Mines 🦴🦴🦴 **1950** Hunter Allan Quartermain (Granger) is hired by Elizabeth Curtis (Kerr) and her brother John (Carlson) to find Elizabeth's missing husband who was searching for the legendary diamond mines of King Solomon. Naturally, there are numerous adventures during their expedition. Filmed on location in Nairobi, Tanganyika and the Belgian Congo. A lavish version of the classic H. Rider Haggard novel; remake of the 1937 classic and remade again in 1985. **102m/C; VHS, DVD; Open Captioned.** Stewart Granger; Deborah Kerr; Richard Carlson; Hugo Haas; Lowell Gilmore; *D:* Compton Bennett; *W:* Helen Deutsch; *C:* Robert L. Surtees. Oscars '50: Color Cinematog., Film Editing.

King Solomon's Mines 🦴 1/2 **1985 (PG-13)** The third remake of the classic H. Rider Haggard novel about a safari deep into Africa in search of an explorer who disappeared while searching for the legendary diamond mines of King Solomon. Updated but lacking the style of the previous two films. Somewhat imperialistic, racist point of view. **101m/C; VHS, DVD, Blu-Ray.** Richard Chamberlain; John Rhys-Davies; Sharon Stone; Herbert Lom; *D:* J. Lee Thompson; *W:* Gene Quintano; *M:* Jerry Goldsmith.

King Solomon's Treasure 🦴 **1976** The great white adventurer takes on the African jungle, hunting for hidden treasure in the Forbidden City. Ekland stars as a Phoenician Queen—need we say more?? **90m/C; VHS, DVD.** *CA GB* David McCallum; Britt Ekland; Patrick Macnee; Wilfrid Hyde-White; *D:* Alvin Rakoff.

The Kingdom 🦴🦴🦴 1/2 *Riget* **1995** Danish director von Trier serves up what must be the first four-and-a- half-hour long hospital soap opera/ghost story/comedy/satire. Elderly Mrs. Drusse checks herself into a hospital known as the Kingdom, which is inhabited by the usual medical suspects: Pompous surgeons, incompetent buraucrats, and quirky residents. She hears the ghostly call of a child from an elevator shaft and sticks around to investigate. Made for Danish TV but released theatrically there and in the States, film owes a great deal to "Twin Peaks" and B-movie horror flicks. Doesn't take itself too seriously, but probably can't be watched all in one sitting. Danish and Swedish with subtitles. **279m/C; VHS, DVD.** *DK* Kirsten Rolffes; Ghita Norby; Udo Kier; Ernst-Hugo Jaregard; Soren Pilmark; Holger Juul Hansen; Baard Owe; Birgitte Raaberg; Peter Mygind; Solbjorg Hojfeldt; *D:* Lars von Trier; *W:* Lars von Trier; Tomas Gislason; Niels Vorsel; *C:* Eric Kress; *M:* Joachim Holbek.

The Kingdom 🦴🦴 **2007 (R)** After a suicide bombing in Saudi Arabia kills over 100 Americans, FBI agent Ronald Fleury (Foxx) leads a hotshot team (Cooper, Garner, and a particularly obnoxious Bateman) to investigate, although officials from both governments aren't exactly happy about the situation. Fleury and company arrive on Saudi soil ready to open a can of American whoop-ass, but not everything is as simple as it seems for them or their Saudi handler Col. al Ghazi (Barhom). Culture clashes, personal agendas, and political intrigue prove complicated while they track the terrorist suspected of planning the bombing. Big-budget actioner strives for relevance with its true-life backdrop, but too often settles for exploitation, and director Berg never seems at ease with his subject until the movie's final explosion-fest. **110m/C; DVD, Blu-Ray, HD-DVD.** Jamie Foxx; Chris Cooper; Jennifer Garner; Jason Bateman; Ashraf Barhoum; Ali Suliman; Jeremy Piven; *D:* Peter Berg; *W:* Matthew Carnahan; *C:* Mauro Fiore; *M:* Danny Elfman.

The Kingdom 2 🦴🦴🦴 1/2 *Riget II* **1997** In the continuation of Von Trier's hospital soap/supernatural/satire, madness runs rampant through Copenhagen's Kingdom hospital. Spiritualist Mrs. Drosse comes back to life after dying during surgery. A baby, sired by a demon, grows at a monstrous rate. Pompous Swedish neurosurgeon Helmer returns from Haiti with voodoo potions and is beseiged by his unbalanced lover and on and on it goes in its quirky, bizarre way. Swedish and Danish with subtitles. **286m/C; VHS, DVD.** *DK* Kirsten Rolffes; Ghita Norby; Udo Kier; Ernst-Hugo Jaregard; Soren Pilmark; Holger Juul Hansen; Baard Owe; Birgitte Raaberg; Peter Mygind; Solbjorg Hojfeldt; *D:* Lars von Trier; *W:* Lars von Trier; Niels Vorsel; *C:* Eric Kress; *M:* Joachim Holbek.

Kingdom Come 🦴🦴 **2001 (PG)** The death of an African-American family's patriarch brings archetypical relatives from near and far for the funeral. There's the wise, saintly widow (Goldberg), the stoic, hard-working son (LL Cool J) and his eager-to-please wife (Fox), the ne'er-do-well son (Anderson) and his shrewish wife (Pinkettt-Smith), the Bible-thumper (Devine), and the gold-digger (Braxton). Throw in an over-officious and unfortunately flatulent preacher (Cedric), let simmer, and bring to a boil. Most of the humor comes from the over-the-top renditions of the characters, as well as the aforementioned gastrointestinal distress, but it keeps getting in the way of the serious, and well-done drama between the at-odds family members. The swings in tone and mood are jarring, but the ride is made easier by the stellar performances, highlighted by LL Cool J's breakout as the eldest son. **89m/C; VHS, DVD.** LL Cool J; Jada Pinkett Smith; Vivica A. Fox; Loretta Devine; Anthony Anderson; Cedric the Entertainer; Darius McCrary; Whoopi Goldberg; Toni Braxton; Masasa; Clifton Davis; Richard Gant; Doug McHenry; *D:* Doug McHenry; *W:* Jessie Jones; David Bottrell; *C:* Francis Kenny; *M:* Tyler Bates.

Kingdom of Blood: The Final Battle 🦴🦴 *The Four 3; Si da ming bu 3* **2016 (R)** The third and final entry in a Chinese-language action series set in historical China. After the death of an aristocrat, two members of the six members leave Six Doors, the Divine Constabulary. The group still has a strong reputation, however. When issues emerge in the imperial palace, they band with allies to successfully stage a rescue and take part in a military operation with the emperor. Ultimately though, they must face a deadly kung fu master to save the empire. Mandarin and Cantonese with subtitles. **106m/C; DVD, Streaming, Download.** Yuki Li; Emma Wu; Xiubo Wu; Collin Chou; Chao Deng; *D:* Gordon Chan; *W:* Koon-nam Lui; Frankie Tam; Maria Wong. **VIDEO**

Kingdom of Heaven 🦴🦴🦴 **2005 (R)** Scott successfully moves from Roman epic "Gladiator" to the 12th century of the Crusades. Godfrey of Ibelin (Neeson) is a knight in the service of dying King Baldwin IV (Norton) of Jerusalem. He returns to France to recruit for a crusade and to seek out his illegitimate son, blacksmith Balian (Bloom). During his quest, Balian becomes a knight, falls in love with Baldwin's sister, Princess Sibylla (Green), and tries to protect Jerusalem from the conspirators within the city and the amassing forces of Saladin (Massoud) without. Of course, as the smart screenplay deftly points out, it's the self-interested extremists on both sides that cause most of the trouble. Despite the epic scale, Scott pays ample attention to the human aspect. **145m/C; DVD, Blu-Ray, UMD.** *GB SP US GE* Orlando Bloom; Eva Green; Liam Neeson;

Jeremy Irons; David Thewlis; Brendan Gleeson; Marton Csokas; Michael Sheen; Edward Norton; Alexander Siddig; Kevin McKidd; Jon Finch; Ghassan Massoud; Velibor Topi; Ulrich Thomsen; Nikolaj Coster-Waldau; Iain Glen; *D:* Ridley Scott; *W:* William Monahan; *C:* John Mathieson; *M:* Harry Gregson-Williams.

Kingdom of the Spiders 🦴🦴 1/2 **1977 (PG)** A desert town is invaded by swarms of killer tarantulas, which begin to consume townspeople. **90m/C; VHS, DVD, Blu-Ray.** William Shatner; Tiffany Bolling; Woody Strode; *D:* John Cardos; *W:* Alan Caillou; Richard Robinson; *C:* John Morrill.

The Kingmaker 🦴🦴🦴 **2019 (R)** A revelatory documentary about Imelda Marcos, the controversial Filipino political figure. Formed around interviews with Marcos, her son, experts on the Marcos regime, and Filipinos who suffered under it, it explores the wide corruption that led to the fall of her husband Ferdinand's regime. While the Marcos family stole an estimated $10 billion from the Filipino people and their political enemies were raped, tortured, and killed, Marcos claims to have used her wealth for their benefit. Offers a powerful portrait of how wealth and privilege allows sociopathic behavior to go unchecked and its far-reaching effects on a society. **101m/C; DVD.** Imelda Marcos; *D:* Lauren Greenfield; *W:* Lauren Greenfield; *C:* Shana Hagan; Lars Skree; *M:* Jocelyn Pook.

Kingpin 🦴🦴 1/2 **1996 (PG-13)** Bowling epic serves up social satire while showcasing some of the worst hair ever seen at the cinema. Roy Munson (a very bald Harrelson, reasonably subdued in relation to rest of cast) is a former bowling champ who, thanks to his sleazy ways, lost a hand and is reduced to selling bowling equipment while wearing a crude rubber prosthetic (on his hand). That is until he meets innocent Amish phenom Ishmael (Quaid), resplendent in a dutch boy wig, whom he persuades to hit the road to a big money tournament in Reno, where Roy can confront an old nemesis (Murray) and compare shampoos, while Ish attempts to win enough money to save the family farm. Claudia (Angel) is around as the highly decorative love interest of Roy. Co-written by "Dumb & Dumber" writers the brothers Farrelly. Look for Amish sensations Blues Traveler at the credit roll. **107m/C; VHS, DVD, Blu-Ray.** Woody Harrelson; Randy Quaid; Vanessa Angel; Bill Murray; Chris Elliott; Mike Cerrone; William Jordan; Richard Tyson; Lin Shaye; Zen Gesner; Prudence Wright Holmes; Rob Moran; *D:* Peter Farrelly; Bobby Farrelly; *W:* Bobby Farrelly; Mort Nathan; *C:* Mark Irwin; *M:* Freedy Johnston.

Kings 🦴🦴 **2007** In 1977, six friends leave Connemara, Ireland, for London to realize their dreams. Thirty years later, they reunite at the pub for the wake of Jackie, who's died under questionable circumstances. The years have left most of these middle-aged men bitter, drink-sodden, and resentful. Based on the play "The Kings of Kilburn High Road" by Jimmy Murphy. In English and Gaelic with subtitles. **89m/C; DVD.** *IR* Colm Meaney; Donal O'Kelly; Barry Barnes; Donncha Crowley; Brendan Conroy; Sean O'Tarpaigh; Peadar O'Treasaigh; *D:* Tom Collins; *W:* Tom Collins; *C:* P.J. Collins; *M:* Pol O'Brennan.

Kings 🦴 **2017 (R)** A crime drama that purports to explore the 1992 Los Angeles riots and its causes through an unexpected set of characters. In South Central LA, white drunken foreigner Obie (Craig) acts out when angry and dislikes children. He lives opposite of Millie (Berry), who has taken in numerous kids and works as a cake baker to support them. As the riots break out and violent acts begin to occur, Obie helps Millie escape, while some of her wards take their survival into their own hands. Despite the star presence and relevant archive footage, its a muddled mess. **92m/C; DVD.** Halle Berry; Daniel Craig; Lamar Johnson; Kaalan Walker; Rachel Hilson; *D:* Deniz Gamze Erguven; *W:* Deniz Gamze Erguven; *C:* David Chizallet; *M:* Nick Cave; Warren Ellis.

Kings and Queen 🦴🦴🦴 *Rois et reine* **2004** French portrait of seemingly ordinary life, steeped with hints at a dark reality that refuses to admit the truth. Nora is a dwice-divorced, hip, intelligent art gallery owner, and mother to an 11-year-old boy. She's now engaged to a very rich man, and has a father dying of stomach cancer. A standard set-up to any Hollywood melodrama, but Hollywood doesn't exist in France. Therefore, Nora may not care about any of them the way we think she should. Ismael is Nora's most recent lover, stuck in a mental institution only because of poor judgment. These characters talk for real, and walk right past the emotional traps that any Hollywood screenplay might fall into. Stunning conclusion leaves an almost dirty taste in the mouth. **150m/C; DVD.** *FR* Emmanuelle Devos; Mathieu Amalric; Catherine Deneuve; Magali Woch; Olivier Rabourdin; Maurice Garrel; Nathalie Boutefeu; Hippolyte Girardot; Joachim Salinger; *D:* Arnaud Desplechin; *W:* Arnaud Desplechin; Roger Bohbot; *C:* Eric Gautier.

Kings Go Forth 🦴🦴 1/2 **1958** Hormones and war rage in this love triangle set against the backdrop of WWII France. Sinatra loves Wood who loves Curtis. When Sinatra asks for her hand in marriage she refuses because she is mixed—half black, half white. He says it doesn't matter, but she still declines because she's in love with Curtis. When Sinatra tells Curtis that Wood is mixed, Curtis says that it doesn't matter to him either because he'd never planned on marrying her. Meanwhile, the war continues. Not particularly satisfying on either the war or race front. Based on a novel by Joe David Brown. **109m/B; VHS, DVD, Blu-Ray.** Frank Sinatra; Tony Curtis; Natalie Wood; Leora Dana; *D:* Delmer Daves; *W:* Merle Miller; *C:* Daniel F. Fapp; *M:* Elmer Bernstein.

The King's Guard 🦴🦴 1/2 **2001 (PG-13)** Captain Reynolds (St. John) and his men must accompany betrothed Princess Gwendolyn (Jones)?and her dowry of gold—to her intended's kingdom. But two traitors (Roberts, Perlman) seek both the princess and the treasure. Low-budget but the fast paced action helps keep things interesting. **94m/C; VHS, DVD.** Ashley Jones; Eric Roberts; Ron Perlman; Trevor St. John; Lesley-Anne Down; *D:* Jonathan Tydor; *W:* Jonathan Tydor. **VIDEO**

Kings in Grass Castles 🦴🦴 1/2 **1997** Aussie miniseries based on the memoirs of Dame Mary Durack and her immigrant family who leave famine-stricken Ireland in the 1850s for Australia. After dealing with an eight-year indenture, the family become Queensland cattle barons, lose everything, and struggle to rebuild, all the while dealing with more prejudice from the British colonials. **200m/C; VHS, DVD.** *AU* Stephen (Dillon) Dillane; Essie Davis; Fionnula Flanagan; David Ngoombujarra; Susan Lynch; Ernie Dingo; James Fox; Max Cullen; Des McAleer; *D:* John Woods; *W:* Tony Morphett; *C:* Roger Lanser; *M:* Shaun Davey. **TV**

Kings of South Beach 🦴 **2007** Remarkably dull and cliched crime drama based on a true story. Chris Troiano (Gedrick) is a thuggish but popular Miami club owner in the 1990s, with Andy Burnett (Wahlberg) as his right-hand man. But Troiano's clubs are actually fronts for laundering mob money and the feds already have an op in motion to bring him down. **90m/C; DVD.** Jason Gedrick; Donnie Wahlberg; Steven Bauer; Nadine Velazquez; Ricardo Chavira; Sean Poolman; Frank John Hughes; Maria Valentina Bove; *D:* Tim Hunter; *W:* Nicholas Pileggi; *C:* Patrick Cady; *M:* Rob Mounsey. **VIDEO**

The Kings of Summer 🦴 1/2 **2013 (R)** Mannered and annoying, Vogt-Roberts's coming-of-age comedy has echoes of other such pics but nothing that approaches reality. The overly stylized sense of humor makes for an abrasive experience that feels more intentionally hip than honest. Joe (Robinson) and Patrick (I Basso) run away from home and build their own lodging in the woods with odd hanger-on Biaggio (Arias). The three guys learn that the early days of freedom will give way to many of the problems of the real world, especially when the girl that Joe likes takes an interest in Patrick. **93m/C; DVD, Blu-Ray.** Nick Robinson; Gabriel Basso; Moises Arias; Nick Offerman; Erin Moriarty; *D:* Jordan Vogt-Roberts; *W:* Chris Galletta; *C:* Ross Riege; *M:* Ryan Miller.

Kings of the Evening 🦴🦴 **2008 (PG)** Inspirational but unsubtle story finds Homer homeless upon his release from a Southern chain gang and willing to let new friend Benny find him a room at Grace's boardinghouse. The men gather on Sunday night at the local hall for an all-male fashion show that brings prize money or food and some social standing for the winner as they try to maintain their dignity through hard times. **99m/C; DVD.** Tyson Beckford; Lynn Whitfield; Glynn Turner; Reginald T. Dorsey; Linara Washington; James Russo; Steven Williams; Bruce McGill; *D:* Andrew P. Jones; *W:* Andrew P. Jones; Robert Page Jones; *C:* Warren Yeager; *M:* Kevin Toney.

Kings of the Sun 🦴 1/2 **1963** Balam (Chakiris), the newly crowned king of the Mayans, decides to resettle his people in another area of Mexico, thus angering the locals who are led by Black Eagle (Brynner). But the two make peace when a greater threat emerges. Brynner always has presence but Chakiris is solemn and lightweight and this story is more foolish than fact. **108m/C; DVD, Blu-Ray.** Yul Brynner; George Chakiris; Shirley Anne Field; Richard Basehart; Brad Dexter; Barry Morse; Leo Gordon; *D:* J. Lee Thompson; *W:* Elliott Arnold; James R. Webb; *C:* Joe MacDonald; *M:* Elmer Bernstein.

King's Ransom 🦴 **2005 (PG-13)** Perennial comic sidekick Anderson proves that some actors are only funny in small doses with his first leading role as obnoxious self-obsessed billionaire Malcolm King. The deceitful mogul ignores his gold-digging wife (Smith), harasses his good-natured secretary (Devine), and makes life a living hell for the employees at his Chicago-based marketing firm. His enemies all get the same idea—kidnap King and teach him a lesson—and painfully unfunny hijinks ensue. Even King gets involved with faking his own kidnapping, which was amusing back when it was originally done in "Ruthless People." The cast features an ensemble of legitimately funny actors who are cast adrift in this pointless, humorless wreck. **97m/C; DVD.** Anthony Anderson; Jay Mohr; Kellita Smith; Nicole Ari Parker; Regina Hall; Loretta Devine; Donald Adeosun Faison; Charlie (Charles Q.) Murphy; Lisa Marcos; Brooke D'Orsay; Leila Arcieri; Jackie Burroughs; *D:* Jeff Byrd; *W:* Wayne Conley; *C:* Robert McLachlan.

Kings Row 🦴🦴🦴 **1941** The Harry Bellamann best-selling Middle American potboiler comes to life. Childhood friends grow up with varying degrees of success, in a decidedly macabre town. All are continually dependent on and inspired by Parris (Cummings) a psychiatric doctor and genuine gentleman. Many cast members worked against type with unusual success. Warner held the film for a year after its completion, in concern for its dark subject matter, but it received wide acclaim. Shot completely within studio settings—excellent scenic design by William Cameron Menzies, and wonderful score. **127m/B; DVD.** Ann Sheridan; Robert Cummings; Ronald Reagan; Betty Field; Charles Coburn; Claude Rains; Judith Anderson; Nancy Coleman; Karen Verne; Maria Ouspenskaya; *D:* Sam Wood; *W:* Casey Robinson; *C:* James Wong Howe; *M:* Erich Wolfgang Korngold.

The King's Speech 🦴🦴🦴🦴 **2010 (R)** Britain's King George VI (Firth), afflicted with a stammer since childhood, seeks help from irreverent and unconventional speech therapist Lionel Logue (Rush). The King's ascension to the throne was neither expected nor desired, but in the wake of his brother Edward's (Pearse) abdication he finds himself pressed into service, yet utterly unable to address a world headed toward war. Both Firth and Rush deliver riveting performances, pulling back the curtain on an intimate and pivotal moment in the world of royalty. **111m/C; Blu-Ray, On Demand.** *GB* Colin Firth; Geoffrey Rush; Helena Bonham Carter; Guy Pearce; Derek Jacobi; Timothy Spall; Michael Gambon; Jennifer Ehle; Anthony Andrews; *D:* Tom Hooper; *W:* David Seidler; *C:* Danny Cohen; *M:* Alexandre Desplat. Oscars '10: Actor (Firth), Director (Hooper), Film, Orig. Screenplay; British Acad. '10: Actor (Firth), Film, Orig. Score, Orig. Screenplay, Support. Actor (Rush), Support. Actress (Bonham Carter); Directors Guild '10: Director (Hooper); Golden Globes '11: Actor--Drama (Firth); Ind. Spirit '11: Foreign Film; Screen Actors Guild '10: Actor (Firth), Cast.

The King's Thief 🦴🦴 1/2 **1955** Costume swashbuckler with Niven as the bad guy. He's a duke at the court of 17th-century English King Charles II and is involved in a plot to steal the crown jewels. **78m/C; DVD.** David Niven; Edmund Purdom; George Sanders; Ann Blyth; Roger Moore; John Dehner; Sean McClory; Melville Cooper; Alan Mowbray; *D:* Robert Z. Leonard; *W:* Christopher Knopf; *M:* Miklos Rozsa.

The King's Whore 🦴🦴 **1990 (R)** Dalton stars as a 17th-century king who falls obsessively in love with the wife of one of his courtiers. His passions lead him to make a decision between the woman and the throne. Good-looking costume epic with obligatory sword fights. **111m/C; VHS, DVD.** Timothy Dalton; Valeria Golino; Feodor Chaliapin, Jr.; Margaret Tyzack; *W:* Daniel Vigne; Frederic Raphael.

Kingsman: The Golden Circle 🦴🦴 **2017 (R)** A sequel with less humor, dignity, and satirical bite than the original, but with 100% more lasso jokes. When the British headquarters of the super-secret spy agency Kingsman gets blown up, its operatives seek help from its U.S. counterpart, the Statesman. There are a few sparks of fun, but writer/director Vaughn added big names (Moore, Berry, John, Tatum, Bridges) to mask his smug laziness with this one. **141m/C; DVD, Blu-Ray.** Colin Firth; Julianne Moore; Taron Egerton; Mark Strong; Halle Berry; Sir Elton John; Channing Tatum; Jeff Bridges; *D:* Matthew Vaughn; *W:* Matthew Vaughn; Jane Goldman; *C:* George Richmond; *M:* Henry Jackman; Matthew Margeson.

Kingsman: The Secret Service 🦴🦴 1/2 **2015 (R)** Firth plays Harry Hart, the 007-esque power broker for the titular group, an ultra-covert collection of superspies who protect us from threats we don't ever hear about. Hart recruits a young man named Eggsy (Edgerton) to join, just as a madman named Valentine (Jackson) threatens the safety of all mankind. Director Vaughn creates a cluttered and hyperactive flick that is also remarkably, unnecessarily violent, with a poorly-developed villain. Only a truly fun, almost self-referential performance from Firth keeps the film afloat. Based on the comic book by Mark Millar and Dave Gibbons. **129m/C; DVD, Blu-Ray.** *UK* Colin Firth; Taron Egerton; Samuel L. Jackson; Michael Caine; Sofia Boutella; Mark Strong; Sophie Cookson; Jack Davenport; Mark Hamill; *D:* Matthew Vaughn; *W:* Matthew Vaughn; Jane Goldman; *C:* George Richmond; *M:* Henry Jackman; Matthew Margeson.

Kinjite: Forbidden Subjects 🦴🦴 **1989 (R)** A cop takes on a sleazy pimp whose specialty is recruiting teenage girls, including the daughter of a Japanese business man. Slimy, standard Bronson fare. **97m/C; VHS, DVD, Blu-Ray.** Charles Bronson; Juan Fernandez; Peggy Lipton; *D:* J. Lee Thompson.

Kinky Boots 🦴🦴 1/2 **2006 (PG-13)** Title says it all in this slight Brit comedy that's based on a true story. Charlie Price (Edgerton) reluctantly takes over the failing family shoe factory after his dad dies. They need a specialty product to save the day, and Charlie receives unexpected inspiration when he comes to the aid of big black drag queen Lola (a sweet Ejiofor), who bemoans that the average stiletto wasn't made to support someone of his size. With Lola offering expertise, Charlie and his workers find their new market in cross-dressers. A big fashion show finale adds to the feel-good fantasy. **106m/C; DVD.** *GB* Joel Edgerton; Chiwetel Ejiofor; Sarah-Jane Potts; Jemima Rooper; Linda Bassett; Nick Frost; Ewan Hooper; Robert Pugh; Geoffrey Streatsfield; *D:* Julian Jarrold; *W:* Tim Firth; Geoff Deane; *C:* Eigil Bryld; *M:* Adrian Johnston.

Kinsey 🦴🦴🦴 **2004 (R)** Well-written, well-acted, and provocative biopic on the life of still-controversial sex researcher Alfred Kinsey. Trained as a zoologist, Kinsey (Neeson) found his true calling when his own sexual ignorance and that of his equally inexperienced bride Clara (Linney) caused them marital problems. The Indiana U professor began by offering his students factual and explicit information on human sexuality and then embarked on a massive research project that involved interviewing thousands about their sexual histories. Rumpled but charismatic, Kinsey's own complicated sexual feelings, especially towards young associate Clyde Martin (Sarsgaard), offer emotional consequences Kinsey is unprepared for. Nor is he prepared for the increasingly shrill notoriety his published works bring him. Lynn Redgrave offers a striking cameo. **118m/C; DVD.** Liam Neeson; Laura Linney; Chris O'Donnell; Peter Sarsgaard; Timothy Hutton; John Lithgow; Tim Curry; Oliver Platt; Dylan Baker; Julianne Nicholson; William Sadler; Heather Goldenhersch; John McMartin; Veronica Cartwright; Kathleen Chalfant; Dagmara Dominczyk; Lynn Redgrave; John Krasinski; ***D:*** Bill Condon; ***W:*** Bill Condon; ***C:*** Joe Dunton; ***M:*** Carter Burwell.

Kippur **2000** Set during Israel's 1973 Yom Kippur War—named after the Jewish holiday on which Egypt and Syria launched a surprise attack. Director Gitai's (a veteran himself) war drama concerns friends Weinraub (Levo) and Ruso (Ruso), who are in a rush to join their reserve unit. But their unit has already left, so they wind up in the company of Klauzner (Klauzner), a medic, and join a helicoptor rescue squad in evacuating the dead and wounded. It's a striking combination of commitment, tedium, frustration, fear, and disillusionment. Hebrew with subtitles. **117m/C; VHS, DVD.** *IS* Uri Klauzner; Liron Levo; Tomer Ruso; ***D:*** Amos Gitai; ***W:*** Amos Gitai; Marie-Jose Sanselme; ***C:*** Renato Berta; ***M:*** Jan Garbarek.

Kira's Reason—A Love Story *En Kaerlighedshistorie* **2001** Uneven depiction of mental illness and a marriage in crisis. Thirtysomethings Kira (Stenegade) and Mads (Mikkelsen) have a seemingly comfortable life with a happy marriage and kids—until Kira has a breakdown and is committed to an institution. Even after returning to her family, Kira's behavior is erratic, disruptive, and sometimes publicly humiliating. Mads continues to stand by his troubled wife but though their love survives, can their lives together? Danish with subtitles. **94m/C; VHS, DVD.** *DK* Stine Stengade; Lars Mikkelsen; Sven Wollter; ***D:*** Ole Christian Madsen; ***W:*** Ole Christian Madsen; ***C:*** Jorgen Johansson; ***M:*** Oyvind Ougaard; Cesar Berti.

Kismet **1920** Original screen version of the much filmed lavish Arabian Nights saga (remade in '30, '44 and '55). A beggar is drawn into deception and intrigue among Bagdad upper-crusters. Glorious sets and costumes; silent with original organ score. **98m/B; Silent; VHS, DVD.** Otis Skinner; Elinor Fair; Herschel Mayall; ***D:*** Louis Gasnier; ***C:*** Gaetano Antonio "Tony" Gaudio.

Kismet **1/2 1944** Colman stars a Hafiz, King of Beggars, in this Technicolor Arabian fantasy. He's posing as a prince to slip into the palace and woo Jamilla (Dietrich), the favorite wife of evil Mansur (Arnold), the Grand Vizier. Meanwhile, the young Caliph (Craig) poses as a gardener's son to escape the palace, falling in love with a beautiful peasant girl (Page) who turns out to be Hafiz's daughter. Mansur wants to kill the Caliph and involves Hafiz-the-fake-prince in the plot. Dietrich—her famous legs painted gold—gets to shimmy in a sultry dance number too. Based on a play by Edward Knoblock and previously filmed in 1920 and 1930; also remade as the 1955 musical. **100m/C; DVD.** Ronald Colman; Marlene Dietrich; Edward Arnold; James Craig; Joy Page; Hugh Herbert; Florence Bates; Harry Davenport; ***D:*** William Dieterle; ***W:*** John Meehan; ***C:*** Charles Rosher; ***M:*** Herbert Stothart.

Kismet **1955** A big-budget Arabian Nights musical drama of a Baghdad street poet who manages to infiltrate himself into the Wazir's harem. The music was adapted from Borodin by Robert Wright and George Forrest. **113m/C; VHS, DVD, Blu-Ray.** Howard Keel; Ann Blyth; Dolores Gray; Vic Damone; ***D:*** Vincente Minnelli; ***W:*** Charles Lederer; Luther Davis; ***C:*** Joseph Ruttenberg; ***M:*** Andre Previn.

The Kiss **1929** Garbo, the married object of earnest young Ayres' lovelorn affection, innocently kisses him nightly night since a kiss is just a kiss. Or so she thought. Utterly misconstrued, the platonic peck sets the stage for disaster, and murder and courtroom anguish follow. French Feyder's direction is stylized and artsy. Garbo's last silent and Ayres' first film. **89m/B; Silent; VHS, DVD.** Greta Garbo; Conrad Nagel; Holmes Herbert; Lew Ayres; Anders Randolph; ***D:*** Jacques Feyder; ***C:*** William H. Daniels.

The Kiss **1988 (R)** A kind of "Auntie Mame from Hell" story in which a mysterious aunt visits her teenage niece in New York, and tries to apprentice her to the family business of sorcery, demon possession, and murder. Aunt Felicity's kiss will make you appreciate the harmless cheek-pinching of your own aunt; your evening would be better spent with her, rather than this movie. **98m/C; VHS, DVD; Open Captioned.** Pamela Collyer; Peter Dvorsky; Joanna Pacula; Meredith Salenger; Mimi Kuzyk; Nicholas Kilbertus; Jan Rubes; ***D:*** Pen Densham; ***W:*** Tom Ropelewski.

Kiss and Kill *Blood of Fu Manchu; Against All Odds* **1968 (R)** Lee returns in his fourth outing as Fu Manchu. This time the evil one has injected beautiful girls with a deadly poison that reacts upon kissing. They are then sent out to seduce world leaders. Not on par with the previous movies, but still enjoyable. Sequel to "Castle of Fu Manchu." **91m/C; VHS, DVD, Blu-Ray.** Christopher Lee; Richard Greene; Shirley Eaton; Tsai Chin; Maria Rohm; Howard Marion-Crawford; ***D:*** Jess (Jesus) Franco.

Kiss and Make Up **1/2 1934** Grants stars as suave Dr. Maurice Lamar—a purveyor of beauty creams, fad diets, and cosmetic surgery. He marries his best patient—Eve (Tobin)?without realizing that her beauty really is only skin deep since she's shallow and selfish. Meanwhile, Eve's sweet ex-husband Marcel (Horton) is charmed by the natural beauty of Lamar's loyal secretary Ann (Mack). Still a remarkably prescient, offbeat comedy where Grant winds up with "a" girl but not the "right" girl for a change. **78m/B; DVD.** Cary Grant; Helen Mack; Genevieve Tobin; Edward Everett Horton; Lucien Littlefield; Mona Maris; ***D:*** Harlan Thompson; ***W:*** Harlan Thompson; Jane Hinton; George Marion, Jr.; ***C:*** Leon Shamroy; ***M:*** Ralph Rainger.

Kiss and Tell **1996** Lonely undercover policewoman Jude (Rowell) tries to get a confession from a man suspected of murdering his wife. Becoming attracted to her quarry, Jude's previous relationship with her supervising officer (Craig) also clouds her judgment until Jude isn't sure what she believes. **110m/C; DVD.** *GB* Rosie Rowell; Daniel Craig; Peter Howitt; David Bradley; Ralph Ines; Nicola Stephenson; ***D:*** David Richards; ***W:*** Heidi Thomas; ***C:*** Alan Almond; ***M:*** Hal Lindes. **TV**

A Kiss Before Dying **1991 (R)** Botched adaptation of Ira Levin's cunning thriller novel (filmed before in 1956). This flick serves up an exploded head in the first few minutes. So much for subtlety. The highlight is Dillon's chilly role as a murderous opportunist bent on marrying into a wealthy family. Young plays two roles (not very well) as lookalike sisters on his agenda. The ending was hastily reshot and it shows. **93m/C; VHS, DVD.** Matt Dillon; Sean Young; Max von Sydow; Diane Ladd; James Russo; Martha Gehman; Ben Browder; Joy Lee; Adam Horovitz; ***D:*** James Dearden; ***W:*** James Dearden. Golden Raspberries '91: Worst Actress (Young), Worst Support. Actress (Young).

Kiss Daddy Goodbye **1/2** *Revenge of the Zombie; The Vengeful Dead* **1981 (R)** A widower keeps his two children isolated in order to protect their secret telekinetic powers. When he is killed by bikers, the kids attempt to raise him from the dead. **81m/C; VHS, DVD.** Fabian; Marilyn Burns; Jon Cedar; Marvin Miller; ***D:*** Patrick Regan.

Kiss Daddy Goodnight **1987 (R)** A Danish-made thriller about a beautiful young girl who seduces men, drugs them and takes their money. One man turns the tables on her, however, and decides that she will only belong to him. **89m/C; VHS, DVD.** *DK* Uma Thurman; Paul Dillon; Paul Richards; David Brisbin; ***D:*** P.I. Huemer; ***C:*** Bobby Bukowski.

A Kiss in the Dark **1949** Slight, silly comedy saved by Niven's charm. Snobbish concert pianist Eric Phillips (Niven) has an apartment house as a business investment but he's an absentee landlord. Persuaded to check out the property, Eric is introduced to the tenants and is smitten by the charms of perky photograph's model, Polly (Wyman), and suddenly moving in is appealing. **88m/B; DVD.** David Niven; Jane Wyman; Broderick Crawford; Victor Moore; Wayne Morris; Maria Ouspenskaya; ***D:*** Delmer Daves; ***W:*** Harry Kurnitz; ***C:*** Robert Burks; ***M:*** Max Steiner.

Kiss Kiss Bang Bang **1/2 2005 (R)** Making his directorial debut, Black—the screenwriter responsible for such awesome cinematic machismo as "Lethal Weapon" and "Last Boy Scout"--reinvents crime noir with this hilarious riff on hardboiled detective fiction and vapid LA culture. Harry Lockhart (Downey Jr.) is a two-bit thief who stumbles into an acting audition after a robbery gone wrong. The producers fly him to Hollywood where he takes private eye lessons from a gay PI named Perry (Kilmer) and gets embroiled in a complicated conspiracy involving a dead body and a femme fatale from his past (Monaghan). Kilmer and Downey have never been funnier, thanks to Black's sharp-as-a-laser dialogue, and Monaghan is insanely easy on the eyes. Sam Spade never had it this good. **103m/C; DVD, Blu-Ray, HD-DVD.** Robert Downey, Jr.; Val Kilmer; Michelle Monaghan; Corbin Bernsen; Dash Mihok; Larry Miller; Shannyn Sossamon; Angela Lindvall; Rockmond Dunbar; ***D:*** Shane Black; ***W:*** Shane Black; ***C:*** Michael Barrett; ***M:*** John Ottman.

Kiss Kiss Kill Kill *Kommissar X-Jagd auf Unbekant* **1966** Odd little '60s European Bond rip-off in which a super spy and his assistant must defeat a criminal mastermind with an army of brainwashed women. It's currently only available in the U.S. as part of the 'Kommissar X' series. **86m/C; DVD.** *GE IT YU* Tony Kendall; Brad Harris; Maria Perschy; Christa Linder; Danielle Godet; Nikola Popovic; Giuseppe Mattei; Jacques Bezard; Olivera Katarina; Liliane Dulovic; ***D:*** Gianfranco Parolini; ***W:*** Gianfranco Parolini; Werner Hauff; Paul Alfred Muller; Giovanni Simonelli; ***C:*** Francesco Izzarelli; ***M:*** Mladen Gutesa.

Kiss Me Again **2006 (R)** Dull and unsexy sexual drama. Self-centered Julian and his wife Chalice share their expensive loft with her bisexual best friend Malika. After spying Malika in a threesome, Julian convinces his wife they should indulge as well and persuades exchange student Elena to join them. Only it gets complicated when Chalice becomes more interested in Elena than her marriage. And Julian isn't the only one who's jealous. **103m/C; DVD.** Jeremy London; Katheryn Winnick; Mirelly Taylor; Elisa Donovan; ***D:*** William Tyler Smith; ***W:*** William Tyler Smith; ***C:*** Christopher LaVasseur; ***M:*** Justin Samaha.

Kiss Me Deadly **1/2 1955** Aldrich's adaptation of Mickey Spillane's private eye tale takes pulp literature high concept. Meeker, as Mike Hammer, is a self-interested rough-and-tumble all-American dick (detective, that is). When a woman to whom he happened to give a ride is found murdered, he follows the mystery straight into a nuclear conspiracy. Aldrich, with tongue deftly in cheek, styles a message through the medium; topsy-turvy camera work and rat-a-tat-tat pacing tell volumes about Hammer, the world he orbits, and that special '50s kind of paranoia. Now a cult fave, it's considered to be the American grandaddy to French New Wave. **105m/B; VHS, DVD, Blu-Ray.** Ralph Meeker; Albert Dekker; Paul Stewart; Wesley Addy; Cloris Leachman; Strother Martin; Marjorie Bennett; Jack Elam; Maxine Cooper; Gaby Rodgers; Nick Dennis; Jack Lambert; Percy Helton; ***D:*** Robert Aldrich; ***W:*** A(lbert) I(saac) Bezzerides; ***C:*** Ernest Laszlo; ***M:*** Frank DeVol. Natl. Film Reg. '99.

Kiss Me Deadly **2008 (R)** Ex-spy Jacob Keane (Gant) is pulled away from his boyfriend and back into the espionage game when his former partner Marta (Doherty) suddenly reappears with her memory erased. They have to determine what classified info the villains want and avoid the pair of assassins who are hunting her. **91m/C; DVD.** Robert Gant; Shannen Doherty; John Rhys-Davies; Fraser Brown; ***D:*** Ron Oliver; ***W:*** George Schenck; Frank Cardea; ***C:*** Neil Cervin; ***M:*** Claude Foisy. **CABLE**

Kiss Me Goodbye **1982 (PG)** Young widow Fields can't shake the memory of her first husband, a charismatic but philandering Broadway choreographer, who's the antithesis of her boring but devoted professor fiance. She struggles with the charming ghost of her first husband, as well as her domineering mother, attempting to understand her own true feelings. Harmless but two-dimensional remake of "Dona Flor and Her Two Husbands." **101m/C; VHS, DVD.** Sally Field; James Caan; Jeff Bridges; Paul Dooley; Mildred Natwick; Claire Trevor; ***D:*** Robert Mulligan; ***W:*** Charlie Peters; ***M:*** Ralph Burns; Peter Allen.

Kiss Me, Guido **1/2 1997 (R)** Heterosexual and handsome Frankie (Scotti) is a Bronx-born and -raised pizza maker and De Niro wanna-be who's not too bright. Apartment hunting in Manhattan, he thinks an ad listing "GWM" stands for "guy with money" and mistakenly moves in with gay actor Warren (Barrile). Pokes fun at both Italian-American and gay stereotypes without offending or canonizing either group. Vitale and an excellent, if largely unknown, cast inject enough energy and humor to rise above the often predictable story. Low-budget independent sex farce that offers a promising start for first-time filmmaker Vitale. **90m/C; VHS, DVD.** Nick Scotti; Anthony Barrile; Craig Chester; Anthony De Sando; Christopher Lawford; Molly Price; ***D:*** Tony Vitale; ***W:*** Tony Vitale; ***C:*** Claudia Raschke; ***M:*** Randall Poster.

Kiss Me Kate **1953** A married couple can't separate their real lives from their stage roles in this musical-comedy screen adaptation of Shakespeare's "Taming of the Shrew," based on Cole Porter's Broadway show. Bob Fosse bursts from the screen—particularly if you see the 3-D version—when he does his dance number. **110m/C; VHS, DVD, Blu-Ray.** Kathryn Grayson; Howard Keel; Ann Miller; Tommy (Thomas) Rall; Bob Fosse; Bobby Van; Keenan Wynn; James Whitmore; ***D:*** George Sidney; ***C:*** Charles Rosher; ***M:*** Andre Previn.

Kiss Me, Kill Me **1/2** *Devil's Witch; Baba Yaga; So Sweet, So Perverse; Cosi Dolce...Cosi Perversa; Baba Yaga—Devil Witch* **1973 (R)** Confused woman is on the run after she may have murdered someone. **91m/C; VHS, DVD, Blu-Ray.** *IT* Carroll Baker; George Eastman; Isabelle DeFunes; Ely Gallo; ***D:*** Corrado Farina; ***W:*** Corrado Farina.

Kiss Me, Stupid! **1964 (PG-13)** Once condemned as smut, this lesser Billy Wilder effort now seems no worse than an average TV sitcom. Martin basically plays himself as a horny Vegas crooner stranded in the boondocks. A local songwriter wants Dino to hear his tunes but knows the cad will seduce his pretty wife, so he hires a floozy to pose as the tempting spouse. It gets better as it goes along, but the whole thing suffers from staginess, being an adaptation of an Italian play "L'Ora Della Fantasia" by Anna Bonacci. **126m/B; DVD, Blu-Ray.** Dean Martin; Kim Novak; Ray Walston; Felicia Farr; Cliff Osmond; Barbara Pepper; Doro Merande; Howard McNear; Henry Gibson; John Fiedler; Mel Blanc; ***D:*** Billy Wilder; ***W:*** Billy Wilder; I.A.L. Diamond; ***C:*** Joseph LaShelle; ***M:*** Andre Previn.

KISS Meets the Phantom of the Park **1/2** *Attack of the Phantoms* **1978** The popular '70s rock band is featured in this Dr. Jekyll-esque Halloween horror tale, interspersed with musical numbers. **96m/C; VHS, DVD.** Peter Criss; Ace Frehley; Gene Simmons; Paul Stanley; Anthony Zerbe; Carmine Caridi; Deborah Ryan; John Dennis Johnston; John Lisbon Wood; Lisa Jane Persky; Brion James; Bill Hudson; ***D:*** Gordon Hessler; ***W:*** J. Michael Sherman; Albert (Don) Buday; ***C:*** Robert Caramico; ***M:*** Hoyt Curtin; Fred Karlin.

Kiss Me...Kill Me **1976** Tediously dated ABC TV movie that's more talk than action. When handicapped teacher Maureen Coyle is murdered, a note from D.A. investigator Stella Stafford is found in her apartment. Stella interviewed Coyle after she was beaten up by one of her kinky sex partners although charges were never filed. Stella teams up with former mentor Harry Grant to find out whodunit. **90m/C; DVD.** Stella Stevens; Claude Akins; Robert Vaughn; Alan Fudge; Dabney Coleman; Bruce Boxleitner; Tisha Sterling; ***D:*** Michael O'Herlihy; ***W:*** Robert E. Thompson; ***C:*** Meredith Nicholson; ***M:*** Richard Markowitz. **TV**

Kiss of Death **1947** Paroled when he turns state's evidence, Mature must now watch his back constantly. Widmark, in his film debut, seeks to destroy him. Police chief Donlevy tries to help. Filmed on location in New York, this gripping and gritty film is a vision of the most terrifying sort of existence, one where nothing is certain, and everything is dangerous. Excellent. **98m/B; VHS, DVD, Blu-Ray.** Victor Mature; Richard Widmark; Coleen Gray; Brian Donlevy; Karl Malden; ***D:*** Henry Hathaway.

Kiss of Death 1977 Weird comedy about a shy undertaker's assistant and his attempts at first romance. **80m/C; VHS, DVD.** *GB* David Threlfall; John Wheatley; Kay Adshead; Angela Curran; ***D:*** Mike Leigh; ***W:*** Mike Leigh. **TV**

Kiss of Death 1/2 **1994 (R)** Very loose contemporary remake of the 1947 film noir classic of the same name. Jimmy Kilmartin (Caruso) is a paroled car thief turned informant. He soon finds himself trapped in a web of deceit involving corrupt district attorneys and ruthless hoodlums like Little Junior (Cage, pumped up and playing against type), with no one to trust. Crime drama keeps the far-fetched genre conventions in check until the end. Caruso makes the transition from TV cop on "NYPD Blue" by not straying far from his small screen persona. Cage's standout performance may not be as chilling as Widmark's unforgettable debut in the original, but he's able to convey a level of mercilessness and depth that'll make you wince. **100m/C; VHS, DVD.** David Caruso; Nicolas Cage; Samuel L. Jackson; Helen Hunt; Stanley Tucci; Michael Rapaport; Ving Rhames; Anthony Heald; Anne Meara; Hope Davis; Kathryn Erbe; Philip Baker Hall; Kevin Corrigan; Michael Artura; Jay O. Sanders; Joe Lisi; ***D:*** Barbet Schroeder; ***W:*** Richard Price; ***M:*** Trevor Jones.

Kiss of Fire *Claudine's Return* **1998 (R)** Stefano (Dionisi) gets a job as the handyman at a Georgia motel and gets involved with laundress/stripper Claudine (Applegate) in what proves to be a dangerous relationship. And despite her role, Applegate does not get naked. **92m/C; VHS, DVD.** Stefano Dionisi; Christina Applegate; Matt Clark; Gabriel Mann; Perry Anzilotti; Tom Nowicki; ***D:*** Antonio Tibaldi; ***W:*** Antonio Tibaldi; Heidi A. Hall; ***C:*** Luca Bigazzi; ***M:*** Michel Colombier. **VIDEO**

Kiss of the Damned 1/2 **2012 (R)** Lonely house-bound vampire Djuna (de La Baume) wastes away her days weeping at old movies and longing for the excitement of a normal life. Her blood gets pumping again after hooking-up with hunky writer Paolo (Ventimiglia) who puts his neck on the line for an eternity of domestic bliss. The union is disrupted when Djuna's trashy sister Mimi (Mesquida) comes to visit after a stint in rehab for blood addiction. A loving tribute (and send-up) of '70s Euro gothic horror films, aiming for sensuality over gore. A respectfully fleshed-out (wink, wink) feature debut from John's daughter, Xan Cassavetes. **97m/C; DVD, Blu-Ray.** Josephine de la Baume; Milo Ventimiglia; Roxane Mesquida; Anna Mouglalis; Michael Rapaport; Riley Keough; ***D:*** Xan Cassavetes; ***W:*** Xan Cassavetes; ***C:*** Tobias Datum; ***M:*** Steven Hufsteter.

Kiss of the Dragon 1/2 **2001 (R)** Li is Chinese super-cop Liu who is sent to Paris to help stop a Chinese drug lord. Once there, he learns that the cop, Richard (Karyo), he was sent to help is actually running the drug ring, and has set Liu up for the dealer's murder. Fonda is the hooker/addict who helps Lui in order to free herself and her daughter from Richard. Spectacular action sequences, as well as Li's martial art skills and charisma more than make up for a pretty lame script which is little more than connective tissue anyway. Besson and Li co-produced the feature debut of director Nahon, who comes from the video/commercials world. **98m/C; VHS, DVD, Blu-Ray, UMD.** *FR US* Jet Li; Bridget Fonda; Tcheky Karyo; Burt Kwouk; ***D:*** Chris Nahon; ***W:*** Luc Besson; Robert Mark Kamen; ***C:*** Thierry Arbogast; ***M:*** Craig Armstrong.

Kiss of the Spider Woman *O Beijo da Mulher Aranha* **1985 (R)** From the novel by Manuel Puig, an acclaimed drama concerning two cell mates in a South American prison, one a revolutionary, the other a homosexual. Literate, haunting, powerful. **119m/C; VHS, DVD, Blu-Ray.** *BR* William Hurt; Raul Julia; Sonia Braga; Jose Lewgoy; Milton Goncalves; Nuno Leal Maia; Denise Dumont; Antonio Petrim; Miriam Pires; Fernando Torres; ***D:*** Hector Babenco; ***W:*** Leonard Schrader; ***C:*** Rodolfo Sanchez; ***M:*** John Neschling; Wally Badarou. Oscars '85: Actor (Hurt); British Acad. '85: Actor (Hurt); Cannes '85: Actor (Hurt); Ind. Spirit '86: Foreign Film; L.A. Film Critics '85: Actor (Hurt); Natl. Bd. of Review '85: Actor (Hurt), Actor (Julia).

Kiss of the Tarantula **1975 (PG)** Teen girl who lives with her family in a mortuary battles inner torment and vents anxiety by releasing her deadly pet spiders on those whom she despises. Eight-legged "Carrie" rip-off. **85m/C; VHS, DVD, Blu-Ray.** Eric Mason; ***D:*** Chris Munger; ***W:*** Warren Hamilton.

Kiss of the Vampire 1/2 *Kiss of Evil* **1962** Newlywed couple is stranded in Bavaria near a villa of vampires and are invited in by its charmingly evil owner. Fortunately, hubby manages to escape and finds a knowledgeable professor who unleashes a horde of bats to rout the bloodsuckers. Properly creepy; producer Hinds used the pseudonym John Elder for his screenplay. **88m/C; VHS, DVD, Blu-Ray.** *GB* Clifford Evans; Noel Willman; Edward De Souza; Jennifer Daniel; Barry Warren; Jacqueline Wallis; Peter Madden; Isobel Black; Vera Cook; Olga Dickie; ***D:*** Don Sharp; ***W:*** John (Anthony Hinds) Elder; ***C:*** Alan Hume; ***M:*** James Bernard.

Kiss Shot **1989** Goldberg is a struggling single mother who loses her job but still must make the mortgage payments. She takes a job as a waitress but realizes it isn't going to pay the bills so she tries her hand as a pool hustler. Frantz is the promoter who finances her bets and Harewood, the pool-shooting playboy whose romantic advances are destroying her concentration. **88m/C; VHS, DVD.** Whoopi Goldberg; Dennis Franz; Dorian Harewood; David Marciano; Teddy Wilson; ***D:*** Jerry London; ***C:*** Chuy Elizondo; ***M:*** Steve Dorff.

Kiss the Bride 1/2 **2007 (R)** Though Spelling is game, her co-stars don't have the light touch this featherweight gay comedy needs. Bride-to-be Alex runs into an unexpected complication when she meets Matt, her fiance Ryan's best friend from high school. Seems Matt and Ryan were very close indeed (wink, wink) and Matt has decided he should see if those youthful sparks can be rekindled before Ryan walks down the aisle. **100m/C; DVD.** Tori Spelling; Philipp Karner; Robert Foxworth; Tess Harper; James O'Shea; Joanna Cassidy; Amber Benson; Steve Sandvoss; ***D:*** C. Jay Cox; ***W:*** Tyler Lieberman; ***C:*** Carl F. Bartels; ***M:*** Ben Holbrook.

Kiss the Bride **2010 (PG-13)** Thomas and Robin have the usual assortment of problems with their wedding, including feuding mothers. However, Thomas feels guilty over a past indiscretion and his revelation has Robin learning her groom-to-be isn't perfect. They both need to find understanding and forgiveness before they take their marriage vows. **90m/C; DVD.** Darrin Dewitt Henson; Reagan Gomez; Jedda Jones; Evangeline Gabriel Young; Darnell Thibodeaux; ***D:*** Ibrahim Yilla; ***W:*** Dan Garcia; ***C:*** John Lands; ***M:*** Andrew Markus. **VIDEO**

Kiss the Girls **1997 (R)** After his niece is abducted, forensic psychologist Alex Cross (Freeman) joins the hunt for a lunatic who's kidnapping and collecting successful young women. After doctor Kate McTiernan (Judd), who also happens to be a kickboxer, escapes the sicko's love dungeon, she helps Cross track him down. Borrowing heavily from "Silence of the Lambs" and "Seven," this psycho-killer thriller falls far short of both. Adapted from the novel by James Patterson. **117m/C; VHS, DVD, Blu-Ray.** Morgan Freeman; Ashley Judd; Cary Elwes; Tony Goldwyn; Jay O. Sanders; Bill Nunn; Brian Cox; Alex McArthur; Richard T. Jones; Jeremy Piven; William Converse-Roberts; Gina Ravera; Roma Maffia; ***D:*** Gary Fleder; ***W:*** David Klass; ***C:*** Aaron Schneider; ***M:*** Mark Isham.

Kiss the Sky **1998 (R)** Suffering from midlife crises, Jeff (Petersen) and Marty (Cole) head off on a business trip to the Philippines. Once there, they decide to abandon their settled lives and families in order to experiment with recapturing their lost youth. In their case, it's by becoming a menage a trois with sexy Oxford grad, Andy (Lee). Provocative but hardly gratuitous. **105m/C; VHS, DVD.** William L. Petersen; Gary Cole; Sheryl Lee; Terence Stamp; Patricia Charbonneau; Season Hubley; ***D:*** Roger Young; ***W:*** Eric Lerner; ***C:*** Donald M. Morgan; ***M:*** Patrick Williams.

Kiss Them for Me **1957** Glib and glossy military comedy. It's 1944, and before three heroic Navy fly boys head back into combat, they are given a four-day leave in San Francisco. They score a hotel suite and decide to throw a major party. Enticed into the fun is buxom blonde Alice (Mansfield)and socialite Gwinnith (Parker). There's an alternate motive for Gwinnith's appearance since she's the fiancé of a shipping tycoon the Navy is trying to impress. Instead, Cmdr. Crewson decides to steal Gwinnith away (well, it's Cary Grant after all). **105m/C; DVD.** Cary Grant; Suzy Parker; Jayne Mansfield; Ray Walston; Larry Blyden; Leif Erickson; Werner Klemperer; ***D:*** Stanley Donen; ***W:*** Julius J. Epstein; ***C:*** Milton Krasner; ***M:*** Lionel Newman.

Kiss Toledo Goodbye **2000 (R)** Young man finds out his biological dad is the local head mobster just before pops is rubbed out. The kid inherits the job (which he tries to keep a secret from his fiancee) as well as his father's enemies. **96m/C; VHS, DVD.** Michael Rapaport; Christine Taylor; Christopher Walken; Robert Forster; Nancy Allen; Paul Ben-Victor; Bill Smitrovich; ***D:*** Lyndon Chubbuck; ***W:*** Robert Easter; ***C:*** Frank Byers; ***M:*** Phil Marshall. **VIDEO**

Kiss Tomorrow Goodbye **1950** A brutal, murderous escaped convict rises to crime-lord status before his inevitable downfall. Based on a novel by Horace McCoy. **102m/B; VHS, DVD, Blu-Ray.** James Cagney; Barbara Payton; Ward Bond; Luther Adler; Helena Carter; Steve Brodie; Rhys Williams; ***D:*** Gordon Douglas.

Kiss Tomorrow Goodbye **2000 (R)** Based on 1942's "Moontide" this updated would-be modern noir suffers from unappealing characters. Dustin Yarma (Lea) is an arrogant, hard-partying Hollywood film exec who wakes up on the beach after a night of debauchery to find that his nameless female companion is dead. Suspicious drifter Minnow (McCallany) says he saw Dustin murder the girl in a drunken rage but will take care of the matter—for a price. The price turns out to be Dustin's life as Minnow moves in on his career and his girlfriend, D'Arcy (Wuhrer). Then Dustin discovers things aren't exactly as they seem. Director Priestley plays the small role of Dustin's buddy Jarred. **90m/C; VHS, DVD.** Nicholas Lea; Holt McCallany; Kari Wuhrer; Jason Priestley; Philip Casnoff; Jennifer Blanc; ***D:*** Jason Priestley; ***W:*** Ozzie Cheek; ***C:*** Bruce Logan; ***M:*** Harald Kloser. **TV**

Kissed **1996 (R)** The subject matter (necrophilia) is sure to give one pause though debut director Stopkewich hardly dwells on the prurient. Sandra Larson (Parker) has been obsessed with death and its rituals since childhood. So as a young adult it seems natural when she gets a job in a funeral home, preparing the bodies for embalming. Only Sandra's obsession leads her to begin making love (shown through a gauzy white light) to the corpses. She does attract the attentions of a very alive medical student, Matt (Outerbridge), who becomes fascinated by Sandra's fetish and determined to make himself as appealing to her as the dead. Adapted from Barbara Gowdy's short story "We So Seldom Look on Love." **78m/C; VHS, DVD.** *CA* Molly Parker; Peter Outerbridge; Jay Brazeau; ***D:*** Lynne Stopkewich; ***W:*** Lynne Stopkewich; Angus Fraser; ***C:*** Gregory Middleton; ***M:*** Don MacDonald. Genie '97: Actress (Parker).

Kisses **2008** Tough, foul-mouthed 11-year-old Dylan and his equally brattish best friend Kylie run away from home during Christmas break, heading to Dublin in search of Dylan's brother, who escaped his abusive home two years earlier. Their bleak, depressive suburban outlook bursts into colors and sounds as they enter the big city, realizing quickly that there is life elsewhere. The music of Bob Dylan is their totem, projecting the mystery and magic of the city streets. Gripping and just emotional enough without becoming mawkish or gushy. Much of the snarling Irish brogue is subtitled. **76m/C; On Demand.** *IR* Kelly O'Neill; Shane Curry; Paul Roe; Neili Conroy; ***D:*** Lance Daly; ***W:*** Lance Daly; ***C:*** Lance Daly; ***M:*** GoBlimpsGo.

Kisses for My President 1/2 **1964** Silly comedy about the first woman elected President and her trials and tribulations. MacMurray is the husband who has to adjust to the protocol of being "First Man." Bergen is miscast, but the other performances are just fine. **113m/C; VHS, DVD.** Fred MacMurray; Polly Bergen; Arlene Dahl; Edward Andrews; Eli Wallach; Donald May; ***D:*** Curtis Bernhardt.

Kisses in the Dark **1997** Four short award-winning films. "Coriolis Effect" finds two daredevil tornado-chasers falling in love. "Solly's Diner" has a vagrant becoming a hero during a diner hold-up. "Looping" finds an egotistic Italian director deciding in the middle of shooting his big-budget Mafia musical that the material isn't worthy of him. "Joe" finds solace in his daily routine in a psych ward when an interloper disturbs his refuge. **75m/C; VHS, DVD.** Jennifer Rubin; James Wilder; Dana Ashbrook; Corinne Bohrer; Katherine Wallach; Ronald Guttman; Quentin Tarantino; ***D:*** Larry Hankin; Louis Venosta; Roger Paradiso; Sasha Wolf; ***W:*** Louis Venosta; Roger Paradiso; Sasha Wolf.

Kissin' Cousins 1/2 **1964** Air Force officer on a secluded base in the South discovers a local hillbilly is his double. Presley quickie that includes country tunes such as "Smokey Mountain Boy" and "Barefoot Ballad" as well as the title song. **96m/C; VHS, DVD.** Elvis Presley; Arthur O'Connell; Jack Albertson; Glenda Farrell; Pam(ela) Austin; Yvonne Craig; Cynthia Pepper; Donald Woods; Tommy Farrell; Beverly (Hills) Powers; ***D:*** Gene Nelson.

Kissing a Fool 1/2 **1998 (R)** Movie asks the titillating question: Who will smart, pretty Sam marry? The unctuous Schwimmer character, Max, or the sensitive writer guy Max sets up with Sam to test her fidelity? Who cares. Hunt sets up the utterly lame opening premise as Sam's boss, who is throwing her a wedding and explains to guests how Sam and her intended met while the rote triangle scenario plays out in flashback. Schwimmer, as a Chicago sportscaster with a roving eye, plays nicely (and wisely) against type while Lee's novelist Jay, a supposedly close friend of Max, occupies a less gratifying role. Avital has little to do but does is well. **93m/C; VHS, DVD.** David Schwimmer; Jason Lee; Mili Avital; Bonnie Hunt; Vanessa Angel; Kari Wuhrer; Frank Medrano; Bitty Schram; Judy Greer; ***D:*** Doug Ellin; ***W:*** Doug Ellin; James Frey; ***C:*** Thomas Del Ruth; ***M:*** Joseph Vitarelli.

The Kissing Bandit 1/2 **1948** A misbegotten MGM musical that's minor Sinatra. Mild-mannered, Boston-bred Ricardo inherits his father's inn in California. When he decides to take it over, he learns that dad was also a thief whose trademark was kissing his female victims. Dad's old gang wants Ricardo to carry on but he's more interested in Theresa (Grayson), the governor's daughter. Ricardo Montalban, Cyd Charisee, and Ann Miller are the dancers performing the number "Dance of Fury," which is the most exciting thing in the flick. **102m/B; DVD.** Frank Sinatra; Kathryn Grayson; J. Carrol Naish; Mildred Natwick; Mikhail Rasumny; Billy Gilbert; ***D:*** Laszlo Benedek; ***W:*** Isobel Lennart; John Harding; ***C:*** Robert L. Surtees.

Kissing Cousins **2008** A confirmed bachelor, Amir (Chakrabarti) has fashioned himself as a "relationship termination specialist." To show his friends that he can have a relationship, he has his beautiful British cousin, Zara (Hazelwood) pose as his girlfriend. The plan does not go accordingly. **98m/C; DVD, Streaming, Download.** Maggie Eilertson; Samrat Chakrabarti; David Alan Grier; Manish Goyal; Brian Kent; Rebecca Hazlewood; ***D:*** Amyn Kaderali; ***W:*** Amyn Kaderali; ***C:*** Alison Kelly; ***M:*** Timo Chen. **VIDEO**

Kissing Jessica Stein 1/2 **2002 (R)** Neurotic, Jewish, and straight Jessica (Westfeldt) is tired of blind dates with loser guys so she decides to respond to a personal ad that was placed by Helen (Jurgensen). Much to Jessica's surprise, the two have a lot in common and awkwardly begin a relationship, even though Jessica is skittish when it comes to sex. However, Jessica can't 'fess up to her family about Helen so they have some other issues to work out. Feldshuh, who plays Westfeldt's doting Jewish mama steals the film. **96m/C; VHS, DVD, Blu-Ray.** Jennifer Westfeldt; Heather Juergensen; Tovah Feldshuh; Scott Cohen; Jackie Hoffman; Michael Mastro; Carson Elrod; David Aaron Baker; ***D:*** Charles Herman-Wurmfeld; ***W:*** Jennifer Westfeldt; Heather Juergensen; ***C:*** Lawrence Sher; ***M:*** Marcelo Zarvos.

Kit Carson 1/2 **1940** Frontiersman Kit Carson joins up with John C. Fremont and his troops to lead a wagon train to California, fighting off marauding Indians and the elements. Their troubles continue as General Castro and his soldiers are determined to keep California a Mexican province rather than let it be claimed by the U.S. Historically inaccurate but entertaining western. **97m/B; DVD.** Jon Hall; Dana Andrews; Lynn Bari; C. Henry Gordon; Raymond Hatton; Ward Bond; Harold Huber; Clayton Moore; ***D:*** George B. Seitz; ***W:*** George Bruce; ***C:*** John Mescall; Robert Pittack; ***M:*** Edward Ward.

Kit Kittredge: An American Girl 1/2 **2008 (G)** In Depression-era Cincinnati, young Kit Kittredge (Breslin) is an aspiring reporter with a penchant for bringing home strays. Tough times hit, and Dad (O'Donnell) is forced to seek work elsewhere while Mom (Ormond) and Kit grow vegetables and take in a colorful cast of boarders to help pay the bills. A crime spree hits town and Kit and company set out defend a group of hobo suspects and find the real criminals, uncovering an even bigger plot than they imagined. Squeaky-clean minus any cloying sugar-sweet subtext adds up to worthwhile family viewing. First American Girl feature film, based on a doll in the product line. **100m/C; DVD, Blu-Ray.** Abigail Breslin; Julia Ormond; Chris O'Donnell; Joan Cusack; Madison Davenport; Jane Krakowski; Zach Mills; Max Thieriot; Stanley Tucci; Wallace Shawn; Willow Smith; Colin Mochrie; Glenne Headly; ***D:*** Patricia Rozema; ***W:*** Ann Peacock; ***C:*** David Boyd; Julie Rogers; ***M:*** Joseph Vitarelli.

The Kitchen **2012 (R)** Jennifer's 30th birthday party, planned by her best friend Stan, who has a crush, turns into a disaster. She's quit her job and dumped her cheating boyfriend Paul, who shows up at the party anyway to put the moves on her female friends. Then Jen's sister Penny announces she's pregnant, talks about getting an abortion, and flirts with Jen's roommate, Kenny. Further chaos follows. **80m/C; DVD, Blu-Ray.** Laura Prepon; Bryan Greenberg; Matthew Bush; Dreama Walker; Tate Ellington; ***D:*** Ishai Setton; ***W:*** Jim Beggarly; ***C:*** Josh Silfen. **VIDEO**

The Kitchen **2019 (R)** In gritty 1970s New York City, three members of the Irish gang the Westies are arrested and sent to jail. While they are serving their time, their long-suffering wives suffer financial difficulties when interim gang leader Little Jackie (Watford) shorts them on their take. Led by Kathy (McCarthy), Ruby (Haddish) and Claire (Moss) take matters into their hands and take over for their husbands themselves. Based on a comic book, what could have been an interesting, female-centered twist on the gangster genre ends up in shambles. **102m/C; DVD, Blu-Ray.** Melissa McCarthy; Tiffany Haddish; Elisabeth Moss; Domhnall Gleeson; James Badge Dale; ***D:*** Andrea Berloff; ***W:*** Andrea Berloff; ***C:*** Maryse Alberti; ***M:*** Bryce Dessner.

Kitchen Privileges 1/2 *Housebound* **2000 (R)** Rape victim Marie (Wressnig) now suffers from agoraphobia and hasn't left her house in a year. Still, she didn't take down her roommate-wanted sign and agrees to rent to chef Tom (Sarsgaard), who tempts her with gourmet meals. However, Tom's oddly secretive, and paranoid Marie becomes convinced he is the L.A. serial killer currently in the news. Must be all those sharp knives he's so good with. Not a horror or suspense flick despite the premise and not very interesting either. **89m/C; DVD.** Peter Sarsgaard; Angeline Ball; Liz Stauber; Ann Magnuson; Katharina Wressnig; Geoffrey Lower; ***D:*** Mari Kornhauser; ***W:*** Mari Kornhauser; ***C:*** Garrett Fisher; ***M:*** Mark Binder.

Kitchen Stories *Salmer fra Kjokkenet* **2003** Subversive Scandinavian comedy set in the 1950s. A number of scientific observers from Sweden's Home Research Institute are sent to collect data from the homes of confirmed bachelors living in the rural community of Landstad, Norway. The idea is to track domestic habits and then standardize the average household kitchen for maximum efficiency. Folke (Norstrom) is sent to the tiny home of codger Isak (Calmeyer), who initially makes things as difficult as possible. The men slowly begin to bond even as the study begins to fall apart. Swedish and Norwegian with subtitles. **95m/C; DVD.** *NO SW* Bjorn Floberg; Reine Brynolfsson; Joachim Calmeyer; Tomas Norstrom; ***D:*** Bent Hamer; ***W:*** Bent Hamer; Jorgen Bergmark; ***C:*** Philip Ogaard; ***M:*** Hans Mathisen.

The Kitchen Toto **1987 (PG-13)** Set in 1950 Kenya as British rule was being threatened by Mau Mau terrorists. A young black boy is torn between the British for whom he works and the terrorists who want him to join them. Complex and powerful story of the Kenyan freedom crusade. **96m/C; VHS, Streaming.** *GB* Bob Peck; Phyllis Logan; Robert Urquhart; Edward Judd; Edwin Mahinda; Kirsten Hughes; ***D:*** Harry Hook; ***W:*** Harry Hook; ***C:*** Roger Deakins; ***M:*** John Keane.

The Kite Runner 1/2 **2007 (PG-13)** Amir and Hassan spend their days flying kites in a safe and peaceful Afghanistan, before it descended into war and terror. But after secretly witnessing Hussan's brutal assault from neighborhood bullies, Amir turns to shame and eventual resentment. Hussan and his father leave the country, and the two friends never reconcile. Over the next twenty years Afghanistan is torn apart by war, and Amir, now living in the U.S., continues to struggle with his past, until an urgent phone call opens a window for his redemption. Majority of the story focuses on the boys, with each showing incredible range and emotion. A realistic and moving experience, based on the popular novel by Khaled Hosseini. **122m/C; Blu-Ray, On Demand.** Khalid Abdalla; Homayon Ershadi; Shaun Toub; Zekiria Ebrahimi; Ahmad Khan Mahmoodzada; ***D:*** Marc Forster; ***W:*** David Benioff; ***C:*** Roberto Schaefer; ***M:*** Alberto Iglesias.

Kitten with a Whip 1/2 **1964** Whatever the film's original intentions, it's now become pure camp. Jody (Ann-Margaret) is a juvenile delinquent who's broken out of a girls' reformatory and breaks into the home of wannabe politician David Patton (Forsythe), who's separated from his wife. Jody works her considerable wiles and soon Patton's life is filled with wild parties, rampant teen lust, and violence. Too bad it wasn't filmed in the lurid color it deserved. Based on the book by Wade Miller. **84m/B; VHS, DVD, Blu-Ray.** Ann-Margret; John Forsythe; Peter Brown; Patricia Barry; Richard Anderson; Diane Sayer; Ann Doran; Patrick Whyte; Audrey Dalton; Leo Gordon; ***D:*** Douglas Heyes; ***W:*** Douglas Heyes; ***C:*** Joseph Biroc.

Kitty Foyle **1940** From the novel by Christopher Morley, Rogers portrays the white-collar working girl whose involvement with a married man presents her with both romantic and social conflicts. **108m/B; VHS, DVD.** Ginger Rogers; Dennis Morgan; James Craig; Gladys Cooper; Ernest Cossart; Eduardo Ciannelli; ***D:*** Sam Wood. Oscars '40: Actress (Rogers).

The Klansman *Burning Cross; KKK* **1974 (R)** Race relations come out on the short end in this film about a sheriff trying to keep the lid on racial tensions in a southern town. Even the big-name cast can't save what comes off as a nighttime soaper rather than a serious drama. **112m/C; VHS, DVD, Blu-Ray.** Lee Marvin; Richard Burton; Cameron Mitchell; Lola Falana; Luciana Paluzzi; Linda Evans; O.J. Simpson; ***D:*** Terence Young; ***W:*** Samuel Fuller.

Klaus 1/2 **2019 (PG)** Spoiled Jesper (Schwartzman) is slacking through the Postal Academy, ready to live off the money and connections of his politically powerful family. To improve his attitude, he is sent to remote Smerensburg, where mail has not been sent or received in years. Jesper finds the hostile town is full of clannish conflicts as he tries desperately to find someone to send a letter. His perspective is altered when he meets burly craftsman Klaus (Simmons) who has a gift for toy making. The animated Santa Claus origin story shines brightly with a stylized look and personality that sets it apart from more recent full-length cartoons. **96m/C; DVD.** Jason Schwartzman; J.K. Simmons; Rashida Jones; Will Sasso; Neda Margrethe Labba; ***D:*** Sergio Pablos; ***W:*** Sergio Pablos; Jim Mahoney; Zach Lewis; ***M:*** Alfonso Gonzalez Aguilar. British Acad. '19: Animated Film.

Klepto **2003** Emily (Bishop) is a kleptomaniac. When ex-con/department store security guard Nick (Garcia) catches her stealing on camera, he decides to use Emily's talents to further a drug deal so that he can get enough money together to open his own private security business. Naturally, things don't go as planned. Okay crime thriller that's rough around the edges. **82m/C; DVD.** Jsu Garcia; Leigh Taylor-Young; Henry Czerny; Michael Nouri; Meredith Bishop; ***D:*** Thomas Trail; ***W:*** Thomas Trail; Ethan Gross; ***C:*** Peter Rieveschl; ***M:*** David DeLaski.

Klimt 1/2 **2006** Unwieldy and unenlightening biopic of Austrian artist Gustav Klimt (Malkovich) that starts with him on his deathbed (in 1918), hallucinating as he's dying from syphilis. Jumps back to 1900 where Klimt scandalizes proper Viennese society with his fin-de-siecle style. Klimt also has a lot of mistresses, including Parisian muse Lea (Burrows), who highlight the eroticism of his work. English, German, and French with subtitles. **97m/C; DVD.** *AT GB FR GE* John Malkovich; Saffron Burrows; Stephen (Dillon) Dillane; Nikolai Kinski; Veronica Ferres; ***D:*** Raoul Ruiz; ***C:*** Ricardo Aronovich; ***M:*** Jorge Arriagada.

Klondike Annie 1/2 **1936** West stars as a woman on the lam for a murder (self-defense) who heads out for the Yukon aboard McLaglen's ship. He falls for her, finds out about her problems, and helps her with a scam to pass herself off as a missionary, only she begins to take her saving souls seriously (although in her own risque style). **77m/B; VHS, DVD.** Mae West; Victor McLaglen; Phillip Reed; Helen Jerome Eddy; Harry Beresford; Harold Huber; Conway Tearle; Esther Howard; ***D:*** Raoul Walsh; ***W:*** Mae West; ***C:*** George T. Clemens.

Klondike Fever 1/2 *Jack London's Klondike Fever* **1979 (PG)** Join the young Jack London as he travels from San Francisco to the Klondike fields during the Great Gold Rush of 1898. **118m/C; VHS, DVD.** Rod Steiger; Angie Dickinson; Lorne Greene; ***D:*** Peter Carter; ***M:*** Hagood Hardy.

Klondike Fury **1942** A failed operation on a friend leads surgeon John Mandre to give up his medical career and become a wilderness pilot in Alaska. His plane crashes in the Klondike and Mandre is looked after by Peg. Coincidentally, Peg's friend Jim needs just the same operation Mandre botched before. **68m/B; DVD.** Edmund Lowe; Lucille Fairbanks; William Henry; Ralph Morgan; Mary Forbes; Jean Brooks; ***D:*** William K. Howard; ***W:*** Henry Blankfort; ***C:*** L. William O'Connell; ***M:*** Edward Kay.

Klown 1/2 *Klovn: The Movie* **2012 (R)** Based on a long-running Danish television series also named Klown, this awkward comedic romp through Denmark is centered on the antics of two amazingly inappropriate friends. Partnered with a doubting pregnant girlfriend, Frank (Hvam) tries to prove he is ready for fatherhood by kidnapping her nephew and taking on adventures. Accompanying Frank is his randy friend Casper (Christensen), whose goal is visit a famous brothel. Along the way the friends and their young companion circumvent the standards of society and experience memorable interpersonal encounters. Danish with subtitles. **93m/C; DVD, Blu-Ray, Streaming, Download.** Frank Hvam; Casper Christensen; Marcuz Jess Petersen; Mia Lyhne; Iben Hjejle; ***D:*** Mikkel Norgaard; ***W:*** Frank Hvam; Casper Christensen; ***C:*** Jacob Banke Olesen; ***M:*** Kristian Eidnes Andersen.

Klute 1/2 **1971 (R)** A small-town policeman (Sutherland) comes to New York in search of a missing friend and gets involved with a prostitute/would-be actress (Fonda) being stalked by a killer. Intelligent, gripping drama. **114m/C; VHS, DVD, Blu-Ray.** Jane Fonda; Donald Sutherland; Charles Cioffi; Roy Scheider; Rita Gam; Jean Stapleton; ***D:*** Alan J. Pakula; ***W:*** Andy Lewis; Dave Lewis; ***C:*** Gordon Willis; ***M:*** Michael Small. Oscars '71: Actress (Fonda); Golden Globes '72: Actress--Drama (Fonda); N.Y. Film Critics '71: Actress (Fonda); Natl. Soc. Film Critics '71: Actress (Fonda).

The Klutz **1973** A bumbling fool, on the way to visit his girlfriend, becomes accidentally embroiled in a bank robbery and other ridiculous mishaps. Light French comedy; dubbed. **87m/C; VHS, DVD.** *FR* Claude Michaud; Louise Portal; Guy Provost; ***D:*** Pierre Rose.

Km. 0 1/2 *Kilometer Zero* **2000 (R)** Good-natured romantic comedy takes its title from the marker in Madrid's Puerta del Sol plaza that designates the spot from which all road travel is measured. It's a popular meeting place as this mixed bag of stories show. Actress Silvia (Pons) forgets she's to meet her sister's friend, Pedro (Fuentes), and Pedro mistakes hooker Tatiana (Matilla) for Silvia. Tatiana thinks Pedro is her new client, but that's actually virginal Sergio (San Juan), who's comforted instead by kindly gay Maximo (del Rio). Lonely Benjamin (Garcia) is mistaken for the Internet date of hottie Bruno (Ullate) and neglected wife Marga (Velasco) finds her meeting with escort Miguel (Cabrero) doesn't go as planned. Amor in all its follies. Spanish with subtitles. **108m/C; DVD.** *SP* Carlos Fuentes; Merce Pons; Georges Corraface; Elisa Matilla; Armando Del Rio; Jesus Cabrero; Tristan Ulloa; Alberto San Juan; Concha Velasco; Victor Ullate, Jr.; Miguel Garcia; ***D:*** Juan Luis Iborra; Yolanda Garcia Serrano; ***W:*** Juan Luis Iborra; Yolanda Garcia Serrano; ***C:*** Angel Luis Fernandez; ***M:*** Joan Bibiloni.

The Knack *The Knack. . .and How to Get It* **1965** Amusing, fast-paced adaptation of the play by Ann Jellicoe. Schoolteacher Crawford is baffled by his tenant Brooks' extreme luck with the ladies so Brooks decides to teach him the "knack" of picking up women. Crawford promptly falls for the first woman (Tushingham) he meets. Swinging London at its most mod. **84m/B; VHS, DVD, Blu-Ray.** *GB* Michael Crawford; Ray Brooks; Rita Tushingham; Donal Donnelly; ***D:*** Richard Lester; ***W:*** Charles Wood; ***C:*** David Watkin; ***M:*** John Barry.

Knife Fight 1/2 **2013 (R)** Political dramedy gets absolutely no update at all in this practically straight-to-video offering with a decent cast given nothing to do by lackluster director/co-writer Guttentag. Paul Turner (Lowe) is an expert at maneuvering slimy politicians out of scandalous situations. His new assistant (Chung) and main operative (Schiff) work with Turner to protect his clients, including a Kentucky governor (McCormick), California senator (Haborur), and gubernatorial candidate (Moss). Of course, Paul has a crisis of conscience and learns how to bring humanity to the cruel world of politics. There would be no movie otherwise. **100m/C; DVD, Streaming.** Rob Lowe; Jamie Chung; Jennifer Morrison; Eric McCormack; Julie Bowen; Carrie-Anne Moss; Saffron Burrows; Richard Schiff; ***D:*** Bill Guttentag; ***W:*** Bill Guttentag; Chris Lehane; ***C:*** Stephen Kazmierski.

Knife in the Water *Noz w Wodzie* **1962** A journalist, his wife and a hitchhiker spend a day aboard a sailboat. Sex and violence can't be far off. Tense psychological drama. Served as director Polanski's debut. In Polish with English subtitles. **94m/B; VHS, DVD.** *PL* Leon Niemczyk; Jolanta Umecka; Zygmunt Malandowicz; ***D:*** Roman Polanski; ***W:*** Jerzy Skolimowski; Roman Polanski; Jakub Goldberg; ***C:*** Jerzy Lipman; ***M:*** Krzysztof Komeda.

Knight and Day 1/2 **2010 (PG-13)** Disappointingly routine action-spy comedy with some glamour thanks to its stars and locations. June (Diaz) chats up airline passenger Roy Miller (Cruise) and finds herself in a world of adventure since Roy is a CIA super spy who's being chased for some sort of new energy source. Roy keeps drugging June for her own safety, which gets really annoying, and he's manic to the point that June thinks maybe he's just crazy but hey, he's attractive and she gets to shoot a machine gun. **109m/C; Blu-Ray.** Cameron Diaz; Tom Cruise; Peter Sarsgaard; Maggie Grace; Jordi Molla; Viola Davis; Paul Dano; Marc Blucas; Celia Weston; Dale Dye; ***D:*** James Mangold; ***W:*** Patrick O'Neil; ***C:*** Phedon Papamichael; ***M:*** John Powell.

The Knight Before Christmas ✂✂ **2019** Cole (Whitehouse) is a knight in 14th century England who is given a special quest of the heart to become a true knight. He is transported to 2019 Ohio and lands in the middle of a community Christmas festival. Confused, Cole is hit by a car driven by Brooke (Hudgens), a high school teacher who has been unlucky in love. Believing that Cole has amnesia, Brooke lets him stay in her guest house and he spends the week before Christmas with her. The premise is certainly preposterous, but it also has a certain kind of holiday allure. **92m/C; DVD.** Vanessa Anne Hudgens; Josh Whitehouse; Emmanuelle Chriqui; Ella Kenion; Harry Jarvis; ***D:*** Monika Mitchell; ***W:*** Cara J. Russell; ***C:*** Greg Gardiner; ***M:*** Roger Bellon. **VIDEO**

A Knight in Camelot ✂✂ 1/2 **1998** Oft told Mark Twain tale this time finds computer expert Vivien (Goldberg) conducting an experiment that transports her back to medieval England and the court of King Arthur (York). Lucky for Viv, she's travelling with her laptop, unluckily the kingly court think the tart-tongued woman is a witch. Bossy Vivien makes Merlin (Richardson) jealous and antagonizes everyone until lessons are learned by all. Engaging fluff. **88m/C; VHS, DVD.** Whoopi Goldberg; Michael York; Amanda Donohoe; Ian Richardson; Robert Addie; Simon Fenton; Paloma Baeza; James Coombes; ***D:*** Roger Young; ***W:*** Joe Wiesenfeld; ***C:*** Elemer Ragalyi; ***M:*** Patrick Williams. **TV**

Knight Moves ✂✂ **1993 (R)** Suspenseful thriller about a series of murders which take place at an international resort where a championship chess match is underway. The prime suspect is a chess master who has an unlikely affair with a beautiful police psychologist called in to decipher the mind of the murderer. Filmed in the Pacific Northwest. **105m/C; VHS, DVD.** Christopher Lambert; Diane Lane; Tom Skerritt; Daniel Baldwin; ***D:*** Carl Schenkel; ***W:*** Brad Mirman; ***C:*** Dietrich Lohmann; ***M:*** Anne Dudley.

Knight of Cups ✂✂ 1/2 *Vitez se peharom* **2015 (R)** Terrence Malick continues to make films like only he could make, complete with elusive plot points, characters who disappear from the story, and a style that more accurately feels like poetry than prose. Recapping the plot of a Malick film is increasingly fruitless. In this one, Rick (Bale) is a writer who journeys around Los Angeles and Las Vegas. Perhaps this is a commentary on the quality of both cities or the film industry or just life in the modern age. Malick continues to mesmerize, even if the intent of this one is a bit blurrier than the rest. **118m/C; DVD, Blu-Ray.** Christian Bale; Cate Blanchett; Natalie Portman; Wes Bentley; Brian Dennehy; ***D:*** Terrence Malick; ***W:*** Terrence Malick; ***C:*** Emmanuel Lubezki; ***M:*** Hanan Townshend.

Knight Without Armour ✂✂✂ **1937** A journalist opposed to the Russian monarchy falls in love with the daughter of a czarist minister in this classic romantic drama. **107m/B; VHS, DVD.** *GB* Marlene Dietrich; Robert Donat; ***D:*** Jacques Feyder; ***C:*** Harry Stradling, Sr.; ***M:*** Miklos Rozsa.

Knightriders ✂✂ 1/2 **1981 (R)** The story of a troupe of motorcyclists who are members of a traveling Renaissance Fair and look and act like modern-day Knights of the Round Table. Their battles center around who is the bravest and strongest, and who deserves to be king. **145m/C; VHS, DVD.** Ed Harris; Gary Lahti; Tom Savini; Amy Ingersoll; ***D:*** George A. Romero; ***W:*** George A. Romero; ***C:*** Michael Gornick; ***M:*** Donald Rubinstein.

Knights of Badassdom ✂ 1/2 **2013 (R)** When a magic book lands in the lap of Eric (Zahn), a geeky LARPer ("Live Action Role Players"--those guys parading around waving duct tape swords), his intentions are to simply use it as a prop in his fantasy play world. After reading some passages, however, the book awakens a bloodthirsty succubus who stalks the forests in search for fresh LARPer meat. This mindless gorefest should satisfy the cult enthusiasts. But its cheapo digital effects, and tone that drifts from comedic to awkwardly brutal, highlights its three-year post-production nightmare. And that title. The Hound says yuck. **86m/C; DVD.** Ryan Kwanten; Peter Dinklage; Steve Zahn; Margarita Levieva; Summer Glau; ***D:*** Joe Lynch; ***W:*** Kevin Dreyfuss; Matt Wall; ***C:*** Sam McCurdy; ***M:*** Bear McCreary.

Knights of Bloodsteel ✂ **2009** Muddled and dull fantasy flick with elves, goblins, and humans forced to work together when evil Dragon Eye (Gibbon) tries to grab all of Mirabilis' supply of the magical ore bloodsteel by gaining control of the Crucible. Sorcerer Tesselink (Lloyd) knows the only way to stop that from happening is through four warrior knights—Serragoth (Elliott), Perfidia (Malthe), Adric (Jacot), and Ber-Lak (Viergever). The makeup effects on the humans are decent enough but the CGI dragons look silly. **175m/C; DVD.** ***D:*** Philip Spink; ***W:*** Sam Egan; ***C:*** David Moxness. **CABLE**

Knights of the Round Table ✂✂ 1/2 **1953** The story of the romantic triangle between King Arthur, Sir Lancelot, and Guinevere during the civil wars of 6th-century England. **106m/C; VHS, DVD.** Robert Taylor; Ava Gardner; Mel Ferrer; Anne Crawford; Felix Aylmer; Stanley Baker; ***D:*** Richard Thorpe; ***C:*** Frederick A. (Freddie) Young; ***M:*** Miklos Rozsa.

Knights of the South Bronx ✂✂ 1/2 **2005 (PG)** Middle-aged and recently unemployed, Richard Mason (Danson) decides to return to teaching and works at an inner-city school with fourth-graders. He begins using chess to motivate his students and finds them responding—and becoming champions. Based on a true story and an ongoing project that uses chess as an educational tool. **90m/C; DVD.** Ted Danson; Keke Palmer; Antonio Ortiz; Malcolm David Kelly; Yucini Diaz; ***D:*** Allen Hughes; ***W:*** Dianne Houston; Jamal Joseph; ***C:*** Derick Underschultz; ***M:*** Stephen Endelman. **CABLE**

A Knight's Tale ✂✂ 1/2 **2001 (PG-13)** Peasant squire William Thatcher (hunky Ledger) takes the identity of his recently deceased master in 14th-century France so that he may enter the jousting tournaments, which are only open to nobility. He also falls in love with Jocelyn (newcomer Sossamon), a noble lady who would be out of his league given his lowly birth. Count Adhemar (Sewell) is the bad guy rival and a young Geoffrey Chaucer (Bettany), pre-"Canterbury Tales," aids William. The soundtrack is strictly contemporary and filled with anthem rock—depending on your tolerance it's either weirdly complementary or a complete distraction. The movie's strictly popcorn entertainment for the teen set. **132m/C; VHS, DVD.** Heath Ledger; Mark Addy; Rufus Sewell; Shannyn Sossamon; Paul Bettany; Laura Fraser; Christopher Cazenove; Alan Tudyk; James Purefoy; ***D:*** Brian Helgeland; ***W:*** Brian Helgeland; ***C:*** Richard Greatrex; ***M:*** Carter Burwell.

Knives of the Avenger ✂ 1/2 *Viking Massacre; I Coltelli Del Vendicatore* **1965** Brutal ax-bearing Vikings ruin the days of hundreds in this primitive story of courage and desperation. John Hold is the pseudonym for director Mario Bava. **85m/C; VHS, DVD, Blu-Ray.** *IT* Cameron Mitchell; Elissa Pichelli; Luciano Pollentin; Fausto Tozzi; Giacomo "Jack" Rossi-Stuart; ***D:*** Mario Bava; ***W:*** Mario Bava; Alberto Liberati; Giorgio Simonelli; ***M:*** Marcello Giombini.

Knives Out ✂✂✂ 1/2 **2019 (PG-13)** When successful mystery writer Harlan Thrombey (Plummer) dies unexpectedly, the conclusion of suicide is investigated by two local law officers (Stanfield, Segan) to be sure nothing has been missed. The case may have been closed except that a famous detective, Southerner Benoit Blanc (Craig), is sent money and a copy of a story about the death. With Blanc taking charge, the investigation continues, focusing on members of Thrombey's family and Harlan's trusted caregiver Marta (de Armas) and revealing unexpected twists. Reminiscent of an Agatha Christie story, the entertaining mystery expertly weaves in sharp social commentary while also featuring charismatic performances, especially from Craig. **130m/C; DVD, Blu-Ray.** Daniel Craig; Chris Evans; Ana de Armas; Jamie Lee Curtis; Michael Shannon; ***D:*** Rian Johnson; ***W:*** Rian Johnson; ***C:*** Steve Yedlin; ***M:*** Nathan Johnson.

Knock Down the House ✂✂ 1/2 **2019 (PG)** A dynamic documentary following four Democratic women who challenged incumbent politicians in the 2018 primary elections for the House of Representatives. Documentarian Lears follows Queens' Alexandra Ocasio-Cortez, Missouri's Cori Bush, West Virginia's Paula Jean Swearengin, and Nevada's Amy Vilea through the election cycle, emphasizing their self awareness, anti-establishment perspective, and grassroots support. Showing their campaigns gain momentum, Lears reveals how their strategies and ideologies evolved in the face of difficult challenges. Though not all the women won their elections, it highlights the value of making your voice heard and the potential long-term impact of their campaigns. **86m/C; DVD.** ***D:*** Rachel Lears; ***W:*** Rachel Lears; Robin Blotnick; ***C:*** Rachel Lears; ***M:*** Ryan Blotnick.

Knock Knock ✂✂ **2015 (R)** Eli Roth returns to the horror genre with a domestic thriller about an everyman who makes a series of very bad decisions. As he has done before, Roth sketches a world in which sex leads men down dangerous roads. Evan Webber (Keanu Reeves) is happily married with a wife and kids who are out of town while he heals from a shoulder injury. Late one night, two women named Genesis (Lorenza Izzo) and Bel (Ana de Armas) knock on his door, looking for a party and lost on a rainy night. Eventually, Evan succumbs to temptation, but he discovers the girls won't leave after. **111m/C; DVD, Blu-Ray, Streaming.** *CL US* Keanu Reeves; Lorenza Izzo; Ana de Armas; Aaron Burns; Ignacia Allamand; Colleen Camp; ***D:*** Eli Roth; ***W:*** Eli Roth; Guillermo Amoedo; Nicolas Lopez; ***C:*** Antonio Quercia; ***M:*** Manuel Riveiro.

Knock Off ✂✂ **1998 (R)** As if anyone really cares whether the plot makes any sense (no) but a lot of booty is certainly kicked. Marcus Ray (Van Damme) and Tommy Hendricks (Schneider) are partners in a Hong Kong business that manufactures designer jeans. Marcus was once involved in the shady fashion "knock-off" business and still knows people in low places, where he hears about a Russian mob plot to sell bombs to terrorists. Oh yeah, seems Tommy has a little secret too'he's actually working undercover for the CIA. It's action schlock and you won't mind a bit. **91m/C; VHS, DVD.** Jean-Claude Van Damme; Rob Schneider; Lela Rochon; Paul Sorvino; Michael Wong; Carman Lee; Wyman Wong; ***D:*** Tsui Hark; ***W:*** Steven E. de Souza; ***C:*** Arthur Wong Ngok Tai; ***M:*** Ron Mael; Russell Mael.

Knock on Any Door ✂✂ **1949** A young hoodlum from the slums is tried for murdering a cop. He is defended by a prominent attorney who has known him from childhood. Part of the 'Humphrey Bogart: The Columbia Pictures Collection'. **100m/B; VHS, DVD.** Humphrey Bogart; John Derek; George Macready; ***D:*** Nicholas Ray; ***W:*** Daniel Taradash; John Monks, Jr.; ***C:*** Burnett Guffey.

Knock on Wood ✂✂ 1/2 **1954** Comic spy thriller finds ventriloquist Jerry (Kaye) losing control of how his dummies speak and behave. His manager tells him to see a shrink and Jerry falls for beautiful doctor Ilse (Zetterling). Then there's the subplot about dollmaker Papinek (Biberman) hiding the plans for a new weapon in the heads of Jerry's dummies, which sets rival spy rings after the papers. Michael Kidd choreographed Kaye's wild Russian ballet number. **103m/C; DVD, Blu-Ray.** Danny Kaye; Mai Zetterling; Torin Thatcher; Abner Biberman; Leon Askin; Steven Geray; Virginia Huston; ***D:*** Norman Panama; Melvin Frank; ***W:*** Norman Panama; Melvin Frank; ***C:*** Daniel F. Fapp.

Knock Outs ✂ **1992** Samantha not only loses her shirt at a sorority strip poker marathon but she loses her tuition money to a gang of biker chicks. Then Samantha and a bevy of bikini-clad friends decide to pose for a swimsuit calendar to earn some cash but are secretly videotaped in the nude by some local sleaze promoters. Tired of being taken advantage of these lovelies take up martial arts and challenge their nefarious girl biker rivals to a winner-take-all wrestling match, not forgetting about the purveyors of the not-so-secret videotape. **90m/C; VHS, DVD.** Chona Jason; Cindy Rome; Brad Zutaut; ***D:*** John Bowen.

Knockaround Guys ✂✂ 1/2 **2001 (R)** Matty (Pepper), the son of mobster Benny Chains (Hopper), finds it difficult to find normal work due to his notorious heritage. He pesters his dad to give him a chance, and with the backing of his uncle Teddy (Malkovich) is given an assignment to pick up a bag of cash in Spokane. His unreliable pal Johnny Marbles (Green) botches the job by losing the loot in a rural Wyoming town. Matty is forced to call in friends Chris (Davoli) and Taylor (Diesel) as muscle to deal with a couple of skate punks and a crooked sheriff (Noonan). Collected dust on the shelf for two years at New Line until executives noticed the cash that Diesel's "XXX" was making. **93m/C; VHS, DVD.** Barry Pepper; Seth Green; Dennis Hopper; Vin Diesel; Andrew Davoli; John Malkovich; Tom Noonan; ***D:*** Brian Koppelman; David Levien; ***W:*** Brian Koppelman; David Levien; ***C:*** Tom Richmond; ***M:*** Clint Mansell.

Knockdown ✂ 1/2 *The Bad Penny* **2011 (R)** In this drama, a boxer's efforts to escape his past prove futile. Though Jack "The Ripper" Stemmons (Evans) was an undefeated boxer with a rising career, it was destroyed by a bookie six years ago. Unknown to Jack, the bookie fixed the biggest fight of his career to date. The angry Jack physically attacked the bully, then disappeared to Bangkok, Thailand. Though life in Thailand seemed to have its perks, he soon learns the woman he loves has been put in his path by a Russian gangster who wants him to take part in the underground fighting clubs in the city. The situation grows only more complicated when a mysterious fan arrives in Bangkok, bringing Jack's past, present, and future together. **89m/C; DVD, Blu-Ray.** Casey T. Evans; Tom Arnold; Nick Faltas; Bai Ling; Josh Randall; ***D:*** Todd Bellanca; ***W:*** Todd Bellanca; Sasha Levinson; ***C:*** Patrick Cady; Vincent Passeri; ***M:*** Human; Michael Lee Jackson; Scott M. Miller.

Knocked Up ✂✂ 1/2 **2007 (R)** Alison Scott (Heigl) is an ambitious blonde entertainment show producer who celebrates her promotion by getting drunk. This makes teddy-bearish chronic slacker Ben (Rogen) look appealing and they hook up—much to his amazement. And hers, when she winds up pregnant. Ben's initially horrified when she decides to have the baby and expects some type of commitment from him. They bond cute, although the situation remains uncertain, with Ben's equally clueless stoner buds and Alison's control-freak married sister Debbie (Mann) offering opinions and running commentary. Apatow has an ear for just the right line and pop-culture reference and knows how to cast his flicks to have quirky appeal. **132m/C; DVD, Blu-Ray, HD-DVD.** Katherine Heigl; Seth Rogen; Leslie Mann; Paul Rudd; Tim Bagley; Jay Baruchel; Jonah Hill; Alan Tudyk; J.P. Manoux; B.J. Novak; Kristen Wiig; Harold Ramis; Martin Starr; Craig Robinson; ***D:*** Judd Apatow; ***W:*** Judd Apatow; ***C:*** Eric Alan Edwards; ***M:*** Loudon Wainwright, III; Joe Henry.

Knocking on Death's Door ✂✂ **1999 (R)** Newlyweds Bloom and Rowe are students of the supernatural and head to a Maine town in order to document the ghosts haunting creepy Hillside House. Their investigation leads them to even more creepy doctor Carradine. Actually filmed in Ireland. **92m/C; VHS, DVD.** David Carradine; Brian Bloom; Kimberly Rowe; John Doe; ***D:*** Mitch Marcus. **VIDEO**

Knockout ✂✂ **2011** A boxing version of "The Karate Kid." New student Matthew (Magder) gets bullied, especially by high school boxing champ Hector (Bartlett). Retired boxer turned school janitor Dan (Austin) becomes Matthew's mentor, teaching him the sweet science and preparing him for a ring match with his tormentor. **95m/C; DVD.** Steve Austin; Daniel Magder; Jaren Bradnt Barlette; Emma Grabinksy; Janet Kidder; Scott Hylands; ***D:*** Anne Wheeler; ***W:*** Evan Jacobs; ***C:*** Peter Woeste; ***M:*** Daniel Seguin. **VIDEO**

Knots ✂ **2005 (R)** Troubled married couple calls it quits when they turn to a seductive lawyer to sort things out. Meanwhile, one of the hubby's friends loses his girlfriend, while another can't even get anything going. A fizzling comedy that can't drive home the punchlines, so it turns to absurd "shocks" hoping to kickstart a reaction. **93m/C; VHS, DVD.** Scott Cohen; John Stamos; Michael Leydon Campbell; Annabeth Gish; Tara Reid; KaDee Strickland; Paulina Prizkova; ***D:*** Guy Lombardo; ***W:*** Guy Lombardo; ***C:*** Michael Fimognari; ***M:*** Joseph Saba. **VIDEO**

Knowing **2009 (PG-13)** History professor Ted Myles (Cage) winds up with a mysterious page filled with seemingly random numbers. He soon discovers that the numbers represent every major disaster of the last 50 years with frightening accuracy. And, naturally, he also learns that he is part of the enigma, and the only one who can prevent further catastrophes, the last being the end of the world. Dark, dreary, sci-fi, quasi-religious, peri-apocalyptic pabulum is so bad, you will wish for the world to end rather than endure another painful minute. Various aspects make this flick laughable, including Cage, as usual, taking himself way too seriously and the movie opening with a flaming moose running in slow motion (seriously). **121m/C; Blu-Ray, On Demand.** Nicolas Cage; Rose Byrne; Ben Mendelsohn; Chandler Canterbury; Lara Robinson; Nadia Townsend; ***D:*** Alex Proyas; ***W:*** Juliet Snowden; Stiles White; Ryne Pearson; ***C:*** Simon Duggan; ***M:*** Marco Beltrami.

Knuckle **2011 (R)** This powerful documentary follows three clans in an Irish Traveler community over 12 years, especially the Quinn brothers fight to defend their family name. Focusing on secret, harsh bare-knuckle bouts without flinching, the film also explores the years of violent, bloody conflicts between the families. In the process, much is revealed about the wider Traveler culture. **97m/C; DVD.** ***Nar:*** Ian Palmer; ***D:*** Ian Palmer; ***C:*** Ian Palmer; ***M:*** Jessica Dannheiser; Ilan Eshkeri. **VIDEO**

Knuckle Sandwich **2004** Leaving his small town behind, Carter Simms (Callan), a high school football star, finds success in Los Angeles with a lucrative, fast-track job and gorgeous girlfriend (Burke) from a prominent family. During one very bad hour, Simms finds his world turned upside down when he is fired and discovers his girlfriend has been cheating on him. Returning home to regroup and get advice from his parents, Simms tries to rediscover his friends and reconnect with an old love. A dramatic comedy with a little heart. **94m/C; DVD.** Douglas Callan; Andrea Andes; Brooke Burke; Norman Lehnert; Kirk Zipfel; Morgan Fairchild; John O'Hurley; ***D:*** Ryan Minigham; ***W:*** Ryan Minigham; John Fordham; ***C:*** Keith Solomon; ***M:*** Tree Adams. **VIDEO**

Knucklehead **2010 (PG-13)** Boxing/road-trip comedy finds its minimal laughs in the plight of con artist/boxing coach Eddie (Feuerstein), who not only is in deep debt to his bookie but also suffers the loss of his latest fighter. His fortunes seem to turn when he comes across Walter (Wight, AKA Big Show), a gentle seven-feet-tall, 400-pound man who has spent his whole life in an orphanage. Eddie convinces Walter to team up with him so the large man can win $100, 000 at an annual Pro-AM MMA tournament to square a related debt. **100m/C; DVD, Blu-Ray.** Mark Feuerstein; Melora Hardin; Paul Wight; Dennis Farina; Wendie Malick; Rebecca Creskoff; ***D:*** Michael W. Watkins; ***W:*** Bear Aderhold; Tomas D. Sullivan; Adam Rifkin; ***C:*** Kenneth Zunder; ***M:*** Jim Johnston. **VIDEO**

Knucklehead **2015** A moving drama about a mentally challenged man's efforts to improve himself and escape his life. Though Langston Bellows (Akinnagbe) is mentally disabled, he has stability in the housing projects of Brooklyn because of his brother. When his brother disappears, Langston is left at the mercy of his abusive mother (Woodard). Seeking a cure, Langston places his faith in a celebrity magazine columnist doctor who promotes prescription drugs of dubious use and quality. Though Langston longs to be independent from everything in his life—including his disability—his quest to find the doctor does not go as planned and he learns some hard truths about pharmaceutical marketing and the people around him. **83m/C; DVD, Streaming, Download.** Gbenga Akinnagbe; Alfre Woodard; Amari Cheatom; Carla Duren; Justin S. Myrick; ***D:*** Ben Bowman; ***W:*** Ben Bowman; Bryan Adams; ***C:*** Soopum Sohn; ***M:*** Michael Shobe; Benjamin Wright. **VIDEO**

Knute Rockne: All American ***A Modern Hero*** **1940** Life story of Notre Dame football coach Knute Rockne, who inspired many victories with his powerful speeches. Reagan, as the dying George Gipp, utters that now-famous line, "Tell the boys to win one for the Gipper." **96m/B; VHS, DVD.** Ronald Reagan; Pat O'Brien; Gale Page; Donald Crisp; John Qualen; ***D:*** Lloyd Bacon. Natl. Film Reg. '97.

Koch **2013** Filmed just before his 2013 passing, director Barsky's documentary captures the still-irascible former Mayor of New York City, Ed Koch, and paints a portrait of one of the most important politicians of the '80s. As the Big Apple was crumbling in waves of crime, graffiti, and general decay, Koch was put in charge of turning it around. Whether or not one agrees with his policies, he was a crucial figure in the recovery of one of the most important cities in the world. Barsky's doc finds a very private man publically examining his legacy. **100m/C; DVD.** ***D:*** Neil Barsky; ***C:*** Tom Hurwitz; ***M:*** Mark De Gli Antoni.

Kolberg ***Burning Hearts*** **1945** The true story of a Prussian town heroically withstanding Napoleon. Produced by Joseph Goebbels in the last days of the Third Reich, it is best remembered as the film whose expensive production and momentous use of real German soldiers, supplies, and ammunition eventually helped to fell the Axis war machine. In German with English subtitles. **118m/C; VHS, DVD.** *GE* Kristina Soderbaum; Heinrich George; Horst Caspar; Paul Wegener; ***D:*** Veit Harlan.

Kolobos **1999** Kyra and her fellow actors report to a remote filming location only to discover it's all a set-up. They've been lured into a fight for survival by a mutilated maniac—or have they? Low-budget hardcore gore. **87m/C; VHS, DVD, Blu-Ray.** Amy Weber; Promise LeMarco; Linnea Quigley; ***D:*** Daniel Liatowitsch; David Todd Ocvirk. **VIDEO**

Kolya **1996 (PG-13)** Set in the late '80s, just before the Velvet Revolution ended Soviet domination of Czechoslovakia, womanizing Prague cellist Louka (Sverak) agrees to marry (for money) the Russian Klara (Safrankova) who wants Czech papers. She soon clears out to join her lover in Berlin and Louka finds himself saddled with her five-year-old son, Kolya (Chaliman). Grumpy Louka isn't obvious dad material and they don't even speak the same language but the kid (who's adorable without being cloying) manages to worm his way into his new life. Czech with subtitles or dubbed. **105m/C; VHS, DVD.** *CZ* Zdenek Sverak; Andrej Chalimon; Libuse Safrankova; ***D:*** Jan Sverak; ***W:*** Zdenek Sverak; ***C:*** Vladimir Smutny; ***M:*** Ondrej Soukup. Oscars '96: Foreign Film; Golden Globes '97: Foreign Film.

Komodo **1/2** **1999 (PG-13)** Komodo dragons are pretty impressive in the wild but are they really scary? This low-budgeter tries to assure you that at least these animatronic/computer-generated versions are. The displaced lizards are breeding on an island off the North Carolina coast where teen Patrick (Zegers) and his aunt (Landis) have unwisely ventured. **85m/C; VHS, DVD.** *AU* Kevin Zegers; Nina Landis; Jill(ian) Hennessey; Paul Gleeson; Billy Burke; ***D:*** Michael Lantieri; ***W:*** Hans Bauer; Craig Mitchell; ***C:*** David Burr; ***M:*** John Debney.

Komodo vs. Cobra ***KVC: Komodo vs. Cobra*** **2005 (PG-13)** Environmentalists hire a boat crew to take them to an island where they suspect military testing is being done and encounter gigantic, poorly done CGI animals. Apparently the govenment has been turning regular animals into giant fiends in their latest effort to waste the taxpayers' money. **94m/C; DVD, Streaming.** Michael Paré; Michelle Borth; Jerri Manthey; ***D:*** Jim Wynorski; ***W:*** Jim Wynorski; Bill Munroe; ***C:*** Andrea V. Rossotto; ***M:*** Chuck Cirino. **CABLE**

Kon-Tiki **2012** Norwegian blend of adventure and biography that dramatizes Thor Heyerdahl's Pacific Ocean voyage. The anthropologist sets out to prove his theory that native Polynesians arrived from the Americas and not Asia. After building a raft of indigenous materials, Thor and five crewmates set out on a 4,300-mile voyage from Peru to Polynesia that proves a lesson in endurance. A true sight to behold even if its substance floats around a bit much. English, Norwegian, and French with subtitles. **118m/C; DVD, Blu-Ray.** *NO* Pal Sverre Hagen; Agnes Kittelsen; Gustaf Skarsgard; Anders Baasmo Christiansen; Odd Magnus Williamson; Tobias Santelmann; Jakob Oftebro; ***D:*** Joachim Roenning; Espen Sandberg; ***W:*** Petter Skavlan; ***C:*** Geir Hartly Andreassen; ***M:*** Johan Soderqvist.

Kona Coast **1/2** **1968** Tedious and rather silly adaptation of John D. MacDonald's "Bimini Gal." Gruff fishing boat captain Sam Moran (Boone) learns daughter Dee has died of a drug overdose, thanks to drug-dealing playboy Kryder (Ihnat). Naturally he wants revenge, which takes Sam to the Kona Coast. **93m/C; DVD.** Richard Boone; Steve Ihnat; Vera Miles; Joan Blondell; Chips Rafferty; Kent Smith; Gloria Nakea; Duane Eddy; ***D:*** Lamont Johnson; ***W:*** Gilbert Ralston; ***C:*** Joseph LaShelle; ***M:*** Jack Marshall.

Kong: Skull Island **1/2** **2017 (PG-13)** Director Vogt-Roberts reimagines a monster movie classic through the lens of the Vietnam War, creating a wildly entertaining blockbuster that feels different than most modern Hollywood films in that fun is what matters most. The plot is refreshingly simple enough: scientists and Vietnam vets travel to an island in the Pacific and find evolution to be notably different there, including deadly monsters and the mighty Kong himself. Some of the social commentary of its predecessors is absent here, but it's been replaced by a fantastic cast who is clearly having such a riot that it's infectious. **118m/C; DVD, Blu-Ray.** Tom Hiddleston; Samuel L. Jackson; Brie Larson; John C. Reilly; John Goodman; ***D:*** Jordan Vogt-Roberts; ***W:*** Dan Gilroy; Max Borenstein; Derek Connolly; ***C:*** Larry Fong; ***M:*** Henry Jackman.

Kongo **1932** Loony, sleazy Pre-Hays Code horror that's a remake of 1928's "West of Zanzibar." Wheelchair-bound Flint, a former magician, uses stage magic to rule superstitious local Africans while he plots against Gregg, the man who paralyzed him and stole his wife. This leads Flint to abuse Ann, whom he believes is Gregg's daughter. He also gets the new doctor (who loves Ann) addicted to drugs and debases his own mistress Tula, who loves Flint anyway. **86m/B; DVD.** Walter Huston; Lupe Velez; Virginia Bruce; C. Henry Gordon; Conrad Nagel; Mitchell Lewis; Forrester Harvey; Curtis Nero; ***D:*** William J. Cowen; ***W:*** Leon Gordon; ***C:*** Harold Rosson.

Konrad **1985** Konrad, an "instant" child made in a factory, is accidentally delivered to an eccentric woman. The factory wants him back when the mistake is discovered, but Konrad stands up against it. Includes a viewers' guide. Part of the "Wonderworks" series. **110m/C; VHS, DVD.** Ned Beatty; Polly Holliday; Max Wright; Huckleberry Fox; ***D:*** Nell Cox; ***W:*** Malcolm Marmorstein.

Kontroll ***Control*** **2003 (R)** Hungary's claustrophobic, dimly fluorescent lit subways employ "kontrollers"?ticket inspectors roaming train to train without much inspiration, not many friends, and zero sunlight. Bulscu (Csanyi) is a kontroller stuck in endless catacomb searching for meaning and trying to fill his quota. Then one day a lovely young something happens to catch his eye. Just his luck, that same day he manages to catch the eye of a hooded killer stalking the trains. First time director Antal does a bang-up job on a limited budget. There's no digital effects, no bluescreens, no bungees, and that's precisely why it's so effective. Watching actors jump from train to train and narrowly avoid death looks much more real when it is real. **106m/C; DVD.** *HU* Sandor Csanyi; Lajos Kovacs; Sandor Badar; Csaba Pindroch; Zsolt Nagy; Eszter Balla; Bence Matyassy; Szabo Gyozo; Balazs Mihalyfi; ***D:*** Nimrod Antal; ***W:*** Nimrod Antal; ***C:*** Gyula Pados; ***M:*** NEO.

The Korean **2008** A top crime lord has been fingered by his associates and with his arrest imminent he summons his top assassin to get revenge for him. Told in a very nonlinear style through flashbacks that probably will be a little confusing for action fans. **98m/C; DVD.** Josiah D. Lee; Jennifer Vos; John Yost; Jack Erdie; Rik Billock; ***D:*** Thomas Dixon; ***W:*** Thomas Dixon; ***C:*** Andrzej Krol; ***M:*** Jace Vek.

Kotch **1971 (PG)** An elderly man resists his children's attempts to retire him. Warm detailing of old age with a splendid performance by Matthau. Lemmon's directorial debut. **113m/C; VHS, DVD, Blu-Ray.** Walter Matthau; Deborah Winters; Felicia Farr; ***D:*** Jack Lemmon; ***M:*** Marvin Hamlisch. Golden Globes '72: Song ("Life Is What You Make It"); Writers Guild '71: Adapt. Screenplay.

Kounterfeit **1996 (R)** Hopscotch (Hawkes) finds three million in counterfeit cash and tries to get some real cash for the fake stuff with his topless-bar owner buddy Frankie (Payne) serving as muscle. But things go bad. Bernsen has little more than a cameo role as Hopscotch's brother. **87m/C; VHS, DVD.** Andrew Hawkes; Bruce Payne; Hilary Swank; Michael Gross; Mark-Paul Gosselaar; Corbin Bernsen; ***D:*** John Mallory Asher; ***W:*** Jay Irwin; David Chase; ***C:*** Karl Herrmann. **VIDEO**

The Kovak Box **2006 (R)** Best-selling sci-fi author David Norton (Hutton) arrives on a Mediterranean island for a conference. His fiancee receives a mysterious phone call and inexplicably commits suicide. That's only the beginning as David's fictional world and his real world overlap, with a government conspiracy thrown in. Dull and confusing, with Hutton's acting consisting of a furrowed brow and grimaces. **102m/C; DVD.** Timothy Hutton; Lucia Jimenez; David Kelly; Georgia Mackenzie; Gary Piquer; Annette Badland; ***D:*** Daniel Monzon; ***W:*** Daniel Monzon; ***C:*** Carlos Gusi; ***M:*** Roque Baños.

Koyaanisqatsi **1983** A mesmerizing film that takes an intense look at modern life (the movie's title is the Hopi word for "life out of balance"). Without dialogue or narration, it brings traditional background elements, landscapes and cityscapes, up front to produce a unique view of the structure and mechanics of our daily lives. Riveting and immensely powerful. A critically acclaimed score by Glass, and Reggio's cinematography prove to be the perfect match to this brilliant film. Followed by "Powaqqatsi." **87m/C; VHS, DVD, Blu-Ray.** ***D:*** Godfrey Reggio; ***W:*** Godfrey Reggio; Ron Fricke; Michael Hoenig; ***C:*** Godfrey Reggio; Ron Fricke; ***M:*** Philip Glass; Michael Hoenig. L.A. Film Critics '83: Score; Natl. Film Reg. '00.

Kraa! the Sea Monster **1998 (PG)** The Planet Patrol sends an agent to Earth to stop a giant sea monster sent to take over the world by an intergalactic criminal. **69m/C; DVD.** Michael Guerin; Teal Marchande; Robert Garcia; ***V:*** Jerry Lentz; ***D:*** Aaron Osborne; ***W:*** Benjamin Carr; ***C:*** Joe C. Maxwell; ***M:*** Carl Dante. **VIDEO**

Krakatoa East of Java **1969 (G)** Oversized disaster pic was produced in Cinerama, an ultra-widescreen process that utilized three projectors. It immediately became the butt of jokes when people realized that the volcano Krakotoa had been west of Java. The plot is filled with potentially intriguing elements--sunken treasure, hot air balloons, erupting volcano, tidal wave--but they're never compelling. The film fared poorly in its initial theatrical run and was shortened for wider distribution in conventional theatres. (Even so, it can be seen as a precursor to the early '70s disaster pictures which which were built on the same combination of all-star casts and splashy special effects.) **131m/C; DVD, Blu-Ray.** Maximilian Schell; Diane Baker; Brian Keith; Barbara Werle; John Leyton; Rossano Brazzi; Sal Mineo; J.D. Cannon; Jacqueline "Jackie" Chan; Marc Lawrence; Geoffrey Holder; Niall MacGinnis; Peter Graves; ***D:*** Bernard L. Kowalski; ***W:*** Bernard Gordon; Clifford Gould; ***M:*** Frank DeVol.

Kraken: Tentacles of the Deep **2006 (R)** Cheap CGI and an over-familiar story make this big beastie tale mostly a yawn. Ray (O'Connell) wants revenge on the multi-tentacled creature that killed his parents so he tracks it down with the help of underwater archeologist Nicole (Pratt, looking very—uh—fit in her scanty attire). But the creature is guarding a treasure that mobster Maxwell (Scalia) is determined to have. **87m/C; DVD.** Charlie O'Connell; Victoria Pratt; Jack Scalia; Kristi Angus; Cory Monteith; ***D:*** Tibor Takacs; ***W:*** Sean Keller; ***C:*** George Campbell; ***M:*** Rich Walters. **CABLE**

Kramer vs. Kramer **1/2** **1979 (PG)** Highly acclaimed family drama about an advertising executive husband and child left behind when their wife and mother leaves on a quest to find herself, and the subsequent courtroom battle for custody when she returns. Hoffman and Streep give exacting performances as does young Henry. Successfully moves you from tears to laughter and back again. Based on the novel by Avery Corman. **105m/C; VHS, DVD.** Dustin Hoffman; Meryl Streep; Jane Alexander; Justin Henry; Howard Duff; JoBeth Williams; ***D:*** Robert Benton; ***W:*** Robert Benton; ***C:*** Nestor Almendros. Oscars '79: Actor (Hoffman), Adapt. Screenplay, Director (Benton), Film, Support. Actress (Streep); Directors Guild '79: Director (Benton); Golden Globes '80: Actor--Drama (Hoffman), Film--Drama, Screenplay, Support. Actress (Streep); L.A. Film Critics '79: Actor (Hoffman), Director (Benton), Film, Screenplay, Support. Actress (Streep); Natl. Bd. of Review '79: Support. Actress (Streep); N.Y. Film Critics '79: Actor (Hoffman), Film, Support. Actress (Streep); Natl. Soc. Film Critics '79: Actor (Hoffman), Director (Benton), Support. Actress (Streep); Writers Guild '79: Adapt. Screenplay.

Krampus 1/2 **2015** Max (Anthony) is tired of his family around the holidays. All they do is bicker and bring him down. So he turns his back on Christmas, decidedly losing that holiday spirit. Little does he know that this action unleashes the wrath of Krampus, a legendary beast rumored to destroy non-believers. Beloved holiday icons come to life and try to destroy Max and his family in this Gremlins-esque dark season comedy. For a while, the horror-comedy works, but it gets repetitive and silly before it gets over. Kind of like the actual holidays, you just want it to end. **98m/C; DVD, Blu-Ray.** Adam Scott; Toni Collette; David Koechner; Allison Tolman; Conchata Ferrell; ***D:*** Michael Dougherty; ***W:*** Michael Dougherty; Todd Casey; Zach Shields; ***C:*** Jules O'Loughlin; ***M:*** Douglas Pipes.

The Kremlin Letter **1970** Based on the novel by Noel Behn, Huston's complicated, cynical spy thriller has some dated—and unpleasant—psycho-sexual implications, including pimps, prostitutes, transvestites, and various sexcapades. There are double agents, doublecrosses, red herrings, and murder as newbie spy Charles Rone (O'Neal) is sent to retrieve an unauthorized and inflammatory anti-Chinese letter, written by an American official, from the Kremlin. **118m/C; DVD.** Patrick O'Neal; Richard Boone; Nigel Green; Dean Jagger; George Sanders; Max von Sydow; Orson Welles; Barbara Parkins; Bibi Andersson; Ronald Radd; Lila Kedrova; Raf Vallone; Micheal MacLiammoir; ***D:*** John Huston; ***W:*** John Huston; Gladys Hill; ***C:*** Edward (Ted) Scaife; ***M:*** Robert Drasnin.

The Kreutzer Sonata 1/2 **2008 (R)** Adaptation of Leo Tolstoy's 1889 novella was written as a morality tale about the dangers of too much carnal love but doesn't exactly play that way in Rose's version. Edgar (Huston) hooks up with classical pianist Abby (Rohm) the night they first meet and they keep it up until they are married with kids and a Beverly Hills mansion. Abby is bored, so Edgar urges her to do a charity gig with violinist Aiden (King) but gets fiercely jealous the more the duo rehearse. Since the pic begins with a bloody flashback you know things won't end well. **99m/C; DVD.** Danny Huston; Elisabeth Rohm; Matthew Yang King; Anjelica Huston; ***D:*** Bernard Rose; ***W:*** Bernard Rose; Lisa Enos; ***C:*** Bernard Rose.

Krews 1/2 **2010** Henry and Peter are a couple of white-collar criminals who specialize in currency manipulation. An L.A. deal goes south and things get worse when street thugs Slate and Wishbone try to carjack them. The four all end up in deep trouble and find themselves at gangsta boss Rebob's crib while trying to figure out what to do next. **105m/C; DVD.** Brian Geraghty; Jonathan Cake; Sam Jones, III; Ty Hodges; Charles Malik Whitfield; Faune A. Chambers; ***D:*** Hilbert Hakim; ***W:*** Joshua Leibner; ***C:*** Robert Benavides; ***M:*** Trevor Morris. **VIDEO**

Kriemhilde's Revenge *Die Nibelungen* **1924** The second film, following "Siegfried," of Lang's "Die Nibelungen," a lavish silent version of the Teutonic legends Wagner's "Ring of the Nibelungen" was based upon. In this episode, Kriemhilde avenges Siegfried's death by her marriage to the Kings of the Huns, thus fulfilling a prophecy of destruction. **95m/B; Silent; VHS, DVD.** *GE* Paul Richter; Margareta Schoen; Theodore Loos; Hanna Ralph; Rudolf Klein-Rogge; ***D:*** Fritz Lang.

Krippendorf's Tribe **1998 (PG-13)** James Krippendorf (Dreyfuss), a widowed anthropology professor, returns from an expedition to New Guinea after squandering all his grant money on his kids. Since he didn't find the rare tribe he was sent there for, he makes up tribal stories based on his own kids. When skeptic Tomlin demands proof of his amazing discoveries, the Krippendorf clan and an over-eager colleague (Elfman) go native in front of the camera. Works best when at its silliest, and in fact, could have been a fun family film. Unfortunately, most of the humor is of the smutty variety, involving mating rituals, tribal sex toys, circumcision jokes, and so on. **94m/C; VHS, DVD.** Richard Dreyfuss; Jenna Elfman; Natasha Lyonne; Gregory Edward Smith; Stephen (Steve) Root; Elaine Stritch; Tom Poston; David Ogden Stiers; Lily Tomlin; Doris Belack; Julio Oscar Mechoso; Barbara Williams; Zakes Mokae; Carl Michael Lindner; Siobhan Fallon Hogan; ***D:*** Todd Holland; ***W:*** Charlie Peters; ***C:*** Dean Cundey; ***M:*** Bruce Broughton.

Krisha 1/2 **2015 (R)** Trey Edward Shults' deeply personal film was made for almost nothing (five figures) and became a gigantic festival hit after its SXSW premiere, earning an indie release a year later. The drama stars Krisha Fairchild as the title character, a woman coming home to an estranged family on Thanksgiving after a decade away. The less you know, the better. Why was she gone? Why is she coming back now? Shults' style is both artistic and genuine. **83m/C; DVD, Blu-Ray.** Alex Dobrenko; Krisha Fairchild; Olivia Grace Applegate; Trey Edward Shults; Bryan Casserly; ***D:*** Trey Edward Shults; ***W:*** Trey Edward Shults; Brian McOmber; ***C:*** Drew Daniels.

Kronos 1/2 **1957** A giant robot from space drains the Earth of all its energy resources. A good example of this genre from the 50s. Includes previews of coming attractions from classic science fiction films. **78m/B; VHS, DVD.** Jeff Morrow; Barbara Lawrence; John Emery; ***D:*** Kurt Neumann; ***W:*** Lawrence Louis Goldman; ***C:*** Karl Struss; ***M:*** Paul Sawtell; Bert Shefter.

Krull **1983 (PG)** Likeable fantasy adventure set in a world peopled by creatures of myth and magic. A prince embarks on a quest to find the Glaive (a magical weapon) and then rescues his young bride, taken by the Beast of the Black Fortress. **121m/C; VHS, DVD, Blu-Ray.** *GB* Ken Marshall; Lysette Anthony; Freddie Jones; Francesca Annis; Liam Neeson; ***D:*** Peter Yates; ***W:*** Stafford Sherman; ***C:*** Peter Suschitzky; ***M:*** James Horner.

Krush Groove **1985 (R)** The world of rap music is highlighted in this movie, the first all-rap musical. **95m/C; VHS, DVD.** Blair Underwood; Lisa Gay Hamilton; Kurtis Blow; Sheila E; John MacKay; Richard Gant; LL Cool J; ***D:*** Michael A. Schultz.

K2: The Ultimate High **1992 (R)** Two men, one a skirt-chasing lawyer, the other a happily married physicist, tackle the world's second largest mountain—the K-2 in Kashmir, northern Pakistan. They encounter a number of dangers, including an ascent of sheer rock face, an avalanche, and a fall down perpendicular mountain ice, but even the exciting mountain-climbing scenes can't hold up this watered down movie. The film was actually shot on Canada's Mount Waddington. Based on the play by Patrick Meyers. **104m/C; VHS, Streaming.** Michael Biehn; Matt Craven; Raymond J. Barry; Luca Bercovici; Patricia Charbonneau; Julia Nickson-Soul; Hiroshi Fujioka; Jamal Shah; ***D:*** Franc Roddam; ***W:*** Patrick Meyers; Scott Roberts.

Kubo and the Two Strings **2016 (PG)** Kubo is a boy on a fantastic journey to locate a suit of armor that his warrior father once wore to save his village. He befriends a monkey and a beetle along the way, voiced perfectly by Theron and McConaughey. The talented people at LAIKA (Coraline, ParaNorman) deliver another superb piece of family entertainment. It's difficult to explain the plot, which is one of its greatest strengths. A tale of loss and legacy; a beautiful fable that challenges children with its themes instead of coddling them. **101m/C; DVD, Blu-Ray.** Charlize Theron; Art Parkinson; Ralph Fiennes; Rooney Mara; George Takei; Matthew McConaughey; ***D:*** Travis Knight; ***W:*** Marc Haimes; Chris Butler; ***C:*** Frank Passingham; ***M:*** Dario Marianelli. British Acad. '16: Animated Film.

Kuffs **1992 (PG-13)** Slater stars as George Kuffs, a young guy who reluctantly joins his brother's highly respected private security team in this original action comedy. After his brother is gunned down in the line of duty, George finds himself the new owner of the business. Out to avenge his brother, George pursues a crooked art dealer as he battles crime on the streets of San Francisco. Worthwhile premise is hampered by a predictable plot and mediocre acting. **102m/C; VHS, DVD, Blu-Ray.** Christian Slater; Tony Goldwyn; Milla Jovovich; Bruce Boxleitner; Troy Evans; George de la Pena; Leon Rippy; Mary Ellen Trainor; ***D:*** Bruce A. Evans; ***W:*** Bruce A. Evans; Raynold Gideon; ***M:*** Harold Faltermeyer.

Kuhle Wampe, Or Who Owns the World? *Kuhle Wampe, Oder Wen Gehort die Welt?* **1932** An avant-garde narrative about how hard times affect a working-class Berlin family. Anni's family is forced to move to a lakeside camp for the unemployed on the outskirts of the city. Anni eventually moves back to Berlin and gets involved in the workers' youth movement. German with subtitles. The film was banned by the Nazis in 1933 for its communist leanings. **69m/B; DVD.** *GE* Hertha Thiele; Adolf Fischer; Martha Wolter; Lilli Schonborn; ***D:*** Slatan Dudow; ***W:*** Bertolt Brecht; Ernst Ottwalt; ***C:*** Gunther Krampf; ***M:*** Hanns Eisler.

Kull the Conqueror 1/2 **1997 (PG-13)** Sorbo goes from TV's heroic Hercules to action-fantasy hero Kull, a slave who becomes the warrior king of a mythic land. Overthrown by a corrupt nobility, Kull begins a perilous journey to find the one weapon that will destroy the she-demon Akivasha (Carrere) and save the land of Valusia. Lots of action, although the PG-13 rating keeps some of the mayhem less bloody than might be expected for this genre. Based on the '30s character created by pulp writer Robert E. Howard, who also originated "Conan the Barbarian." **96m/C; VHS, DVD, Blu-Ray.** Kevin Sorbo; Tia Carrere; Thomas Ian Griffith; Karina Lombard; Litefoot; Harvey Fierstein; Roy Brocksmith; Douglas Henshall; Sven-Ole Thorsen; Terry O'Neill; ***D:*** John Nicolella; ***W:*** Charles Edward Pogue; ***C:*** Rodney Charters; ***M:*** Joel Goldsmith.

Kumiko the Treasure Hunter **2014** Kumiko (Kikuchi) is a quiet, lonely young woman living in crowded Tokyo with her pet rabbit, Bunzo. She lives an ordinary life that is shattered by her obsession with the Coen brothers' "Fargo," which she not only believes is based on a true story but is showing her the way to the money buried in a snowy field by Steve Buscemi's character. She leaves her Japanese life behind and heads to Minnesota, in winter, to find the treasure. The Zellner brothers deliver a memorable character study that comments on cultural confusion while maintaining their quirky cinematic personality. English and Japanese with subtitles. **105m/C; DVD, Blu-Ray.** Rinko Kikuchi; David Zellner; ***D:*** David Zellner; ***W:*** Nathan Zellner; ***C:*** Sean Porter.

The Kumite *Star Runner* **2003 (PG-13)** So it takes 40 minutes to get to any martial arts competition, as the first part of the flick is taken up by the romance between Hong Kong student Bond (Wu) and his young Korea-born teacher Mei (Kim). Bond wants to enter the Star Runner competition but has trouble finding the right mentor and then lets love get in the way of his training. Wu and Kim are both popular Asian pop stars but that doesn't mean they can act (not that it seems to be a requirement). Korean and Cantonese with subtitles. **104m/C; DVD.** *CH NK* Hyung-koo Kim; David Chiang; Vanessa Wu; Andy On; Shawn Tam; ***D:*** Daniel Lee; ***W:*** Daniel Lee; ***M:*** Henry Lai.

Kundun **1997 (PG-13)** Scorsese's cinematic portrait of the life of the young 14th Dalai Lama from 1937 through 1959, when he was forced to flee Chinese-occupied Tibet and live in exile in India. The incredibly detailed and sumptuous Tibetan journey begins with the discovery of the young boy as the Buddha reborn and uses different actors to portray him through young adulthood. Dramatic depiction of the Chairman Mao-ordered slaughter of Tibetan nuns and monks around the young Kundun illustrates theme of the dilemmas facing a nonviolent man in an increasingly violent world. The adult Dalai Lama's (Tsarong) meeting with cartoonishly evil incarnate Chairman Mao Zedong (Lin) mars an otherwise realistic and honest portrayal. Made with the cooperation of the 14th Dalai Lama, the story reflects the director's yen for accuracy and integrity. Scorsese's gamble on using a cast of non-professional Tibetan refugees pays off. Beautiful scenery and dreamy Philip Glass score set the proper mood. **134m/C; VHS, DVD, Blu-Ray.** Tanzin Thuthob Tsarong; Robert Lin; ***D:*** Martin Scorsese; ***W:*** Melissa Mathison; ***C:*** Roger Deakins; ***M:*** Philip Glass. N.Y. Film Critics '97: Cinematog.; Natl. Soc. Film Critics '97: Cinematog.

Kung Fu 1/2 **1972** A fugitive Buddhist quasi-Asian martial arts master accused of murder in his native land, roams across the Old West fighting injustice. Pilot for the successful TV series; was reincarnated 14 years later in the sequel, "Kung Fu: The Movie." **75m/C; VHS, DVD.** Keith Carradine; David Carradine; Barry Sullivan; Keye Luke; ***D:*** Jerry Thorpe; ***C:*** Richard L. Rawlings. **TV**

Kung Fu Hustle *Gong fu* **2004 (R)** Writer/director Chow casts himself as the lead in this goofy kung-fu comedy. Sing (Chow), a good-natured con man, desperately wants to join the evil Axe Gang. Posing as a gangster, Sing tries to shake down the poor residents of Pig Sty Alley, but a number of hapless martial arts masters have retired to the slum. Sing's scam starts an all-out war between the Axe Gang and Pig Sty Alley, resulting in a series of larger-than-life, CGI-enhanced battles that more closely resemble Looney Tunes than Bruce Lee. While the unrelenting action might cross cultural borders, Chow's sense of humor doesn't seem to. In Cantonese and Mandarin with English subtitles. **99m/C; DVD, Blu-Ray, UMD.** Stephen (Chiau) Chow; Yuen Wah; Kwok-Kwan Chan; Feng Xiao Gang; Lam Suet; Leung Siu Lung; Dong Zhi Hua; Chiu Chi Ling; Yuen Qui; Xing Yu; Huang Sheng Yi; Lam Tze Chung; ***D:*** Stephen (Chiau) Chow; ***W:*** Stephen (Chiau) Chow; Kan-Cheung (Sammy) Tsang; Chan Man-keung; Lola Huo; ***C:*** Hang-Seng Poon; ***M:*** Raymond Wong.

Kung Fu Killer *The White Crane Chronicles; Kung Fu Kingdom* **2008** White Crane (Carradine) is the orphaned son of western missionaries raised by monks in China and taught Kung Fu. When a crook destroys the temple he journeys to Shanghai where he and a lounge singer with her own score to settle set out for revenge. **88m/C; DVD.** David Carradine; Daryl Hannah; Kay Tong Lim; Yu Beng Lim; Pei Pei Cheng; Christian Lee; Anya; Yan Wu Yan; Vasilios E.; Gilbert Kupsami; Gary Peterman; Osric Chau; James Taenaka; Rosalind Pho; Nic Rhind; ***D:*** Philip Spink; ***W:*** Jacqueline Feather; John Mandel; David Seidler; ***C:*** Man-Ching Ng; ***M:*** Jim Guttridge.

Kung Fu Panda **2008 (PG)** The title pretty much sums it up. Po (voiced by Black), a chubby panda working for his father's noodle shop, slowly learns of his secret kung fu prowess while bumbling through his daily routine. He comes across a contest held by the wise Shifu (voiced by Hoffman) that draws huge crowds to watch five chosen competitors battle it out for the title of Dragon Warrior. Somehow, Po is selected as the final competitor, and from there, he becomes a big furry Rocky. Kiddies and young teens will love it, while mom and dad may get sleepy. **90m/C; Blu-Ray, On Demand.** ***V:*** Jack Black; Dustin Hoffman; Jackie Chan; Angelina Jolie; Lucy Liu; Ian McShane; Seth Rogen; David Cross; Michael Clarke Duncan; James Hong; Dan Fogler; Randall Duk Kim; ***D:*** Dr. John Stevenson; Mark Osborne; ***W:*** Jonathan Aibel; Glenn Berger; ***C:*** Yong Duk Jhun; ***M:*** Hans Zimmer; John Powell.

Kung Fu Panda 2 **2011 (PG)** Skadoosh! The now-Dragon Warrior Po (voiced by Black) is back and, along with his Furious Five pals—Tigress (Jolie), Mantis (Rogen), Monkey (Chan), Viper (Liu), and Crane (Cross)?they rally to ward off the nefarious peacock Lord Shen (Oldman) from overtaking their Valley of Peace with a weapon intended to destroy kung fu forever. And if that's not enough, Po is perplexed by childhood flashbacks that may, perhaps, answer the question of his heritage. Hilarious and engaging with a gifted group of voice actors that all age groups can appreciate, while the visuals and 3-D effects are truly spectacular. **91m/C; Blu-Ray, On Demand.** ***V:*** Jack Black; Dustin Hoffman; Angelina Jolie; Jackie Chan; Seth Rogen; Lucy Liu; David Cross; James Hong; Gary Oldman; Jean-Claude Van Damme; Victor Garber; Michelle Yeoh; ***D:*** Jennifer Yuh; ***W:*** Jonathan Aibel; Glenn Berger; ***M:*** John Powell; Hans Zimmer.

Kung Fu Panda 3 **2016 (PG)** Less eager to please and nimbler than the last installment in this DreamWorks franchise, the arguable closing chapter of this trilogy finds Po (Black) reunited with his biological father (Cranston), who introduces him to the rest of the pandas in China, which Po and his new friends thought long-dead. The new crew of oversized creatures has to band together when a legendary villain (Simmons) returns from the spirit world set to steal the chi of the Dragon Warrior. This is a surprisingly sweet and funny flick that doesn't forget to bring the martial arts action either. Great voice work too. **95m/C; DVD, Blu-Ray.** Jack Black; Bryan Cranston; Dustin Hoffman; Angelina Jolie; J.K. Simmons; ***D:*** Alessandro Carloni; Jennifer Yuh; ***W:*** Jonathan Aibel; Glenn Berger; ***M:*** Hans Zimmer.

Kung Fu: The Movie **1/2 1986** Carradine reprises his role as Kwai Chang Caine from the TV show of the '70s. Now, he's hunted by evil warlord Mako, who's involved in the California opium trade. Mako sends assassin Lee (son of martial-arts star Bruce) after Caine. Luke appears in flashbacks as the young Grasshopper's blind mentor, Master Po. **93m/C; DVD.** David Carradine; Mako; Brandon Lee; Keye Luke; Kerrie Keane; Martin Landau; William Lucking; Luke Askew; Benson Fong; ***D:*** Richard Lang; ***W:*** Durrell Royce Crays; ***C:*** Robert Seaman; ***M:*** Lalo Schifrin. **TV**

Kung Pow! Enter the Fist **1/2 2002 (PG-13)** Oedekerk, the "mind" behind such comedies as "Ace Ventura: When Nature Calls" and "Patch Adams," opts to put himself in front of the camera in this painfully boring kung-fu spoof. He splices new footage into a 1970s martial arts movie, making himself the lead character and adding in a liberal helping of scatological humor. It's "What's Up, Tiger Lily" meets "Dead Men Don't Wear Plaid," only without the comedic genius or even an elementary grasp of basic filmmaking. Leave this fist closed, grasshopper. **81m/C; VHS, DVD.** Steve Oedekerk; Tad Horino; Simon Rhee; Lin Yan; Jennifer Tung; Lo Ming; ***D:*** Steve Oedekerk; ***W:*** Steve Oedekerk; ***C:*** John J. Connor; ***M:*** Robert Folk.

Kuroneko *Black Cat* **1968** Stunning and eerie horror tale from director/writer Shindo about revenge (and cat demons). During a feudal civil war, Yone and her daughter-in-law Shige are raped and murdered by rogue samurai. Thanks to their pet cat, they are given the chance to return as demons who rip out the throats of itinerant samurai passing through their village. Young samurai Gintoki is sent to deal with the supernatural problem. Japanese with subtitles. **99m/B; DVD, Blu-Ray.** *JP* Kichiemon Nakamura; Nobuko Otowa; Kei Sato; Kiwako Taichi; ***D:*** Kaneto Shindo; ***W:*** Kaneto Shindo; ***C:*** Kiyomi Kuroda; ***M:*** Hiraku Hayashi.

Kwaidan **1964** A haunting, stylized quartet of supernatural stories, each with a surprise ending. Adapted from the stories of Lafcadio Hearn, an American author who lived in Japan just before the turn of the century. The visual effects are splendid. In Japanese with English subtitles. **164m/C; VHS, DVD, Blu-Ray.** *JP* Michiyo Aratama; Rentaro Mikuni; Katsuo Nakamura; Keiko Kishi; Tatsuya Nakadai; Takashi Shimura; ***D:*** Masaki Kobayashi; ***W:*** Yoko Mizuki; ***C:*** Yoshio Miyajima; ***M:*** Toru Takemitsu. Cannes '65: Grand Jury Prize.

LA Apocalypse **WOOF! 2014** The Syfy Channel needs some new plots. The Earth's core begins a meltdown and devastation follows. L.A. is being evacuated but Calvin must first rescue fiancée Ashley, who's been kidnapped. **83m/C; DVD.** David Cade; Gina Holden; Raymond J. Barry; Eric Allen Kramer; Kamar De Los Reyes; Christopher Judge; ***D:*** Michael J. Sarna; ***W:*** Neil Elman; Erik Estenberg; ***C:*** Erick Crespo; ***M:*** Mario Salrucci. **CABLE**

La Balance **1982 (R)** An underworld stool pigeon is recruited by the Parisian police to blow the whistle on a murderous mob. Baye, as a prostitute in love with the pimp-stoolie, is a standout. Critically acclaimed; French with subtitles. **103m/C; VHS, DVD.** *FR* Philippe Leotard; Nathalie Baye; Bob Swaim; ***D:*** Reymond LePlont; ***M:*** Roland Bocquet. Cesar '83: Actor (Leotard), Actress (Baye), Film.

La Bamba **1987 (PG-13)** A romantic biography of the late 1950s pop idol Ritchie Valens, concentrating on his stormy relationship with his half-brother Bob (Morales), his love for his WASP girlfriend Donna (Von Zerneck) for whom he wrote a hit song, and his tragic, sudden death in the famed plane crash that also took the lives of Buddy Holly and the Big Bopper. Soundtrack features Setzer, Huntsberry, Crenshaw, and Los Lobos as, respectively, Eddie Cochran, the Big Bopper, Buddy Holly, and a Mexican bordello band. **99m/C; VHS, DVD, Blu-Ray.** Lou Diamond Phillips; Esai Morales; Danielle von Zerneck; Joe Pantoliano; Brian Setzer; Marshall Crenshaw; Howard Huntsberry; Rosanna Desoto; Elizabeth Pena; Rick Dees; ***D:*** Luis Valdez; ***W:*** Luis Valdez; ***C:*** Adam Greenberg; ***M:*** Carlos Santana; Miles Goodman. Natl. Film Reg. '17.

La Belle Noiseuse **1/2** *Divertimento; The Beautiful Troublemaker* **1990** Beautiful (and long) drama about art and life. Creatively crippled, an aging painter has left a masterwork unfinished for ten years. When an admiring younger artist and his beautiful lover arrive for a visit, the painter is inspired and makes the young woman his model and muse. The film details every nuance of the work from the first to the last brushstroke and the battle of wills between artist and model over the symbiotic creative process. Based on an Honore Balzac novella. French with subtitles. "Divertimento" is a recut and shortened version (126 minutes) of the original film. **240m/C; DVD, Blu-Ray.** *FR* Michel Piccoli; Emmanuelle Beart; Jane Birkin; David Bursztein; Marianne (Cuau) Denicourt; ***D:*** Jacques Rivette; ***W:*** Jacques Rivette; Christine Laurent; Pascal Bonitzer; ***C:*** William Lubtchansky. Cannes '91: Grand Jury Prize; L.A. Film Critics '91: Foreign Film.

La Bete Humaine **1/2** *The Human Beast* **1938** A dark, psychological melodrama about human passion and duplicity, as an unhinged trainman plots with a married woman to kill her husband. Wonderful performances and stunning photography. Based on the Emile Zola novel. In French with English subtitles. 1954 Hollywood remake, "Human Desire," was directed by Fritz Lang. **90m/B; VHS, DVD.** *FR* Jean Gabin; Simone Simon; Julien Carette; Fernand Ledoux; ***D:*** Jean Renoir; ***W:*** Jean Renoir; ***C:*** Curt Courant; ***M:*** Joseph Cosma.

La Boheme **1/2 1926** Tragic story of seamstress Mimi (Gish) and aspiring playwright Rodolphe (Gilbert) who live and love in the Bohemian district of 1830s Paris, beset by poverty, ambition, jealousy, separation, and death. It's not based on the Puccini opera (the film company could not obtain the rights) but Henri Murgi's 1851 novel "Life in the Latin Quarter." Gish's first film for MGM; she went 'Method' long before the technique was known by depriving herself of water so she could appear appropriately weak. **93m/B; Silent; DVD.** Lillian Gish; John Gilbert; Renee Adoree; George Hassell; Roy D'Arcy; Edward Everett Horton; Gino Corrado; ***D:*** King Vidor; ***W:*** Fred de Gresac; ***C:*** Hendrik Sartov.

La Boum **1/2 1981** A teenager's adjustment to the changes brought about by a move to Paris is compounded by her parents' marital problems. Followed by "La Boum 2." **90m/C; VHS, DVD.** *FR* Sophie Marceau; Claude Brasseur; Brigitte Fossey; Denise Grey; Bernard Giraudeau; ***D:*** Claude Pinoteau; ***M:*** Vladimir Cosma.

La Buche **2000** The title refers to a special Christmas cake, fashioned in the shape of a yule log. The holiday season is proving to be particularly tiresome for three sisters: nightclub singer Louba (Azema) who's pregnant with her married lover's child; homemaker Sonia (Beart) whose husband is leaving her for a younger woman; and career-driven Milla (Gainsbourg) who becomes intrigued by melancholy Joseph (Thompson, the director's son). Family crises start with the funeral of the sisters' stepfather, leading to a reunion between their parents who haven't spoken in 25 years, and get more complicated from there. French with subtitles. **106m/C; VHS, DVD.** *FR* Sabine Azema; Emmanuelle Beart; Charlotte Gainsbourg; Francoise Fabian; Claude Rich; Christopher Thompson; Jean-Pierre Darroussin; ***D:*** Daniele Thompson; ***W:*** Christopher Thompson; Daniele Thompson; ***C:*** Robert Fraisse; ***M:*** Michel Legrand.

La Cage aux Folles **1/2** *Birds of a Feather* **1978 (R)** Adaption of the popular French play. Gay Saint-Tropez nightclub owner Renato (Tognazzi) and his drag queen lover Albin (Serrault) try to play it straight when Renato's son (Laurent) from a long-ago liaison brings his fiancee and her conservative parents home for dinner. Charming music and lots of fun. So successful, it was followed by two sequels in 1980 and 1985, a Broadway musical, and a 1995 American remake, "The Birdcage." French with subtitles. **91m/C; VHS, DVD, Blu-Ray.** *FR* Ugo Tognazzi; Michel Serrault; Michel Galabru; Claire Maurier; Remy Laurent; Benny Luke; Carmen Scarpitta; Luisa Maneri; ***D:*** Edouard Molinaro; ***W:*** Edouard Molinaro; Francis Veber; Jean Poiret; Marcello Danon; ***C:*** Armando Nannuzzi; ***M:*** Ennio Morricone. Cesar '79: Actor (Serrault); Golden Globes '80: Foreign Film.

La Cage aux Folles 2 **1/2 1981 (R)** Albin sets out to prove to his companion that he still has sex appeal, and gets mixed up in some espionage antics. This sequel to the highly successful "La Cage aux Folles" loses some steam, but is still worth seeing. Followed by "La Cage Aux Folles 3: The Wedding." **101m/C; VHS, DVD.** *FR* Ugo Tognazzi; Michel Serrault; Marcel Bozzuffi; Michel Galabru; Benny Luke; ***D:*** Edouard Molinaro; ***W:*** Francis Veber; ***C:*** Armando Nannuzzi; ***M:*** Ennio Morricone.

La Cage aux Folles 3: The Wedding **1/2 1986 (PG-13)** The flamboyant drag queen Albin must feign normalcy by marrying and fathering a child in order to collect a weighty inheritance. Final segment of the trilogy; inferior to the previous films. In French with English subtitles. **88m/C; VHS, Streaming.** *FR* Michel Serrault; Ugo Tognazzi; Michel Galabru; Benny Luke; Stephane Audran; ***D:*** Georges Lautner; ***M:*** Ennio Morricone.

La Ceremonie *A Judgment in Stone* **1995** Sullen maid Sophie (Bonnaire) is hired by the rich Lelievre family to work at their country estate. She's befriended by independent postmistress Jeanne (Huppert), who's disliked by Sophie's employers, and who encourages Sophie into small defiant actions. Something's off about the entire situation and there's violence beneath the seemingly calm surface. Based on Ruth Rendell's chiller "Judgment in Stone." French with subtitles. **109m/C; VHS, DVD.** *FR GE* Sandrine Bonnaire; Isabelle Huppert; Jacqueline Bisset; Jean-Pierre Cassel; Virginie Ledoyen; Valentine Merlet; Julien Rochefort; Dominique Frot; Jean-Francois Perrier; ***D:*** Claude Chabrol; ***W:*** Claude Chabrol; Caroline Eliacheff; ***C:*** Bernard Zitzermann; ***M:*** Matthieu Chabrol. Cesar '96: Actress (Huppert); L.A. Film Critics '96: Foreign Film; Natl. Soc. Film Critics '96: Foreign Film.

La Chartreuse de Parme **1/2** *Charterhouse at Parma* **1948** Nineteenth century period piece featuring an Archbishop willing to break his vows for the woman he loves, and the aunt who will make sure that if she can't have him only God will. French adaptation of the novel by Stendahl. Available dubbed. **170m/B; VHS, DVD.** *FR* Gerard Philipe; Maria Casares; Renee Faure; ***D:*** Christian-Jaque; ***W:*** Christian-Jaque.

La Chevre **1/2** *The Goat* **1981** A screwball French comedy about two policemen (Richard and Depardieu—picture Gene Wilder and Nick Nolte with accents) stumbling along the path of a missing heiress who suffers from chronic bad luck. Contains a hilarious scene with chairs used to test the luck of the investigative team; based on one partner's ability to sit on the only broken chair in a rather large collection, he is judged to be sufficiently jinxed to allow them to re-create the same outrageous misfortunes that befell the heiress in her plight. In French with English subtitles. **91m/C; VHS, DVD.** *FR* Gerard Depardieu; Pierre Richard; Corynne Charbit; Michel Robin; Pedro Armendariz, Jr.; ***D:*** Francis Veber; ***M:*** Vladimir Cosma.

La Chinoise *The Chinese* **1967** Godard's study in French intellectualism and the young left's discontent. Over a summer five students form a radical communist cell devoted to the teachings of Chairman Mao. The nominal leaders are uncompromising idealist Guillaume (Leaud) and his girlfriend Veronique (Wiazemsky), a daughter of the bourgeoisie. Henri (Semeniako) gets expelled for not being a true believer, but while the others stay in the apartment talking revolution, Henri is in the Paris streets taking action. French with subtitles. **93m/C; DVD, Blu-Ray.** *FR* Jean-Pierre Leaud; Anna Wiazemsky; Juliet Berto; Michel Semeniako; Lex De Bruijn; ***D:*** Jean-Luc Godard; ***W:*** Jean-Luc Godard; ***C:*** Raoul Coutard.

La Cicada **1/2** *The Cricket* **1983** The sparks fly when a woman and her 17-year-old daughter become rivals for the affections of the same man. Currently sold as 'The Cricket.' **90m/C; VHS, DVD.** *IT* Clio Goldsmith; Virna Lisi; Anthony (Tony) Franciosa; Renato Salvatori; ***D:*** Alberto Lattuada.

La Collectionneuse *The Gentleman Tramp* **1967** The third of Rohmer's "Moral Tales" finds an artist (Bachau) and an antiques dealer (Pommereulle) vacationing in St. Tropez and sharing a villa with a young woman (Politoff) who picks a different man to sleep with each night. Both try to resist the sexual temptations of being added to her collection of lovers. French with subtitles. **88m/C; VHS, DVD, Blu-Ray.** *FR* Patrick Bauchau; Daniel Pommereulle; Haydee Politoff; Alain Jouffroy; ***D:*** Eric Rohmer; ***W:*** Eric Rohmer; ***C:*** Nestor Almendros.

L.A. Confidential **1997 (R)** Director Hanson does a masterful job in this adaptation of James Ellroy's hard-boiled, complex crime novel. Fifties Hollywood is ripe with corruption, including journalistic sleaze in the persona of Sid Hudgens (DeVito), editor of a tabloid rag. Sid's police contact is fame-loving Sgt. Jack Vincennes (Spacey), who gets tangled in a bloodbath murder case along with brutal cop Bud White (Crowe), ruthlessly ambitious neophyte Ed Exley (Pearce), and their veteran boss, Capt. Dudley Smith (Cromwell). There's also wealthy pimp/businessman Pierce Patchett (Strathairn) and his movie-star look-alike hookers, including Lynn (Basinger), who gets involved with Bud, who... Well, Hanson ties up the loose ends and still leaves you wanting more. **136m/C; DVD, Blu-Ray.** Kevin Spacey; Russell Crowe; Guy Pearce; Danny DeVito; Kim Basinger; James Cromwell; David Strathairn; Ron Rifkin; Graham Beckel; Matt McCoy; Simon Baker; Paul Guilfoyle; Amber Smith; John Mahon; Paolo Seganti; Gwenda Deacon; ***D:*** Curtis Hanson; ***W:*** Curtis Hanson; Brian Helgeland; ***C:*** Dante Spinotti; ***M:*** Jerry Goldsmith. Oscars '97: Adapt. Screenplay, Support. Actress (Basinger); Australian Film Inst. '98: Foreign Film; British Acad. '97: Film Editing, Sound; Golden Globes '98: Support. Actress (Basinger); L.A. Film Critics '97: Cinematog., Director (Hanson), Film, Screenplay; Natl. Bd. of Review '97: Director (Hanson), Film; Natl. Film Reg. '15; N.Y. Film Critics '97: Director (Hanson), Film, Screenplay; Natl. Soc. Film Critics '97: Director (Hanson), Film, Screenplay; Screen Actors Guild '97: Support. Actress (Basinger); Writers Guild '97: Adapt. Screenplay; Broadcast Film Critics '97: Adapt. Screenplay, Film.

La Cucaracha **1999 (R)** Ex-office worker Walter (Roberts) has hightailed it to Mexico to become a writer—or so he says. Instead, he's a drunk practically immobilized by night terrors. Then the local big shot (de Almeida) suddenly offers Walter money to kill someone. Things don't go as expected. **95m/C; VHS, DVD.** Eric Roberts; Joaquim de Almeida; Tara Crespo; James McManus; ***D:*** Jack Perez; ***W:*** James McManus; ***C:*** Shawn Maurer; ***M:*** Martin Davich.

La Cucina **1/2 2007** The kitchen is at the heart of these food-oriented romantic vignettes. Lily is preparing a simple meal for her older lover as they try to figure out their new relationship. Pregnant Shelly's lasagna is a disaster and she has a hormonal breakdown, turning to friend Jude for sympathy.

However, Jude is preparing a complicated dinner for lover Celia who won't be home because she is filming an elaborate kitchen scene while her hungry crew watches. **89m/C; DVD.** Joaquim de Almeida; Leisha Hailey; Oz (Osgood) Perkins, II; Rachel Hunter; Clare Carey; Christina Hendricks; Kala Savage; ***D:*** Allison Hebble; Zed Starkovich; ***W:*** A.W. Gryphon; ***C:*** Alan Caudillo; ***M:*** Ian Ball.

L.A. Dicks ½ **2005** Two private eyes fall victim to predictions about their own futures when their current job involves tracking a psychic while they also compete with some of L.A.'s finest to drum up Hollywood interest in their cases. **90m/C; DVD.** Anthony Guidera; Michael Madsen; Sarah Wynter; Erik Palladino; Dean Alioto; Kym E. Whitley; ***D:*** Dean Alioto; ***W:*** Dean Alioto; ***C:*** Tim Gibbons; ***M:*** Ryan Beveridge. **VIDEO**

La Dolce Vita **1960** In this influential and popular work a successful, sensationalistic Italian journalist covers the show-biz life in Rome, and alternately covets and disdains its glitzy shallowness. The film follows his dealings with the "sweet life" over a pivotal week. A surreal, comic tableaux with award-winning costuming; one of Fellini's most acclaimed films. In this film Fellini called his hungry celebrity photographers the Paparazzo'and it is as the paparazzi they have been ever since. In Italian with English subtitles. **174m/B; VHS, DVD, Blu-Ray.** *IT* Marcello Mastroianni; Anita Ekberg; Anouk Aimee; Alain Cuny; Lex Barker; Yvonne Furneaux; Barbara Steele; Nadia Gray; Magali Noel; Walter Santesso; Jacques Sernas; Annibale Ninchi; ***D:*** Federico Fellini; ***W:*** Tullio Pinelli; Ennio Flaiano; Brunello Rondi; Federico Fellini; ***M:*** Nino Rota. Oscars '61: Costume Des. (B&W); Cannes '60: Film; N.Y. Film Critics '61: Foreign Film.

La Femme Infidele ½ *The Unfaithful Wife* **1969** When Charles (Bouquet) learns that his wife (Audran) has found the passion that their marriage now lacks in the arms of another man (Ronet), he confronts and kills him. This rekindles his wife's interest in him. Chabrol at his best. **98m/C; VHS, DVD.** *FR* Stephane Audran; Michel Bouquet; Michel Duchaussoy; Henri Marteau; Maurice Ronet; Dominique Zardi; ***D:*** Claude Chabrol; ***W:*** Claude Chabrol; ***C:*** Jean Rabier; ***M:*** Pierre Jansen.

La Femme Musketeer **2003** The daughter of D'Artagnan joins up with the sons of her old friends the Three Musketeers to go on her own adventures to protect the King of France from an evil Cardinal and an equally vile noble woman who intend to blackmail him. She also has to fetch the king's bride-to-be before she ends up dead or kidnapped. It helps that everyone assumes she can't use a sword because she's a woman. **171m/C; DVD.** *CR GE* Gerard Depardieu; Michael York; Nastassja Kinski; Susie Amy; John Rhys-Davies; Allan Corduner; Christopher Casenove; Casper Zafer; Marcus Jean Pirae; Freddie Sayers; Clemency Burton-Hill; ***D:*** Steve Boyum; ***W:*** Sandra Weintraub; ***C:*** David Connell; ***M:*** Mader. **TV**

La Femme Nikita **1991 (R)** Stylish French noir version of Pygmalion. Having killed a cop during a robbery, young sociopath Nikita (Parillaud) is reprieved from a death sentence for a government program that trains her in both etiquette (by Moreau) and assasination (by Karyo). Released after three years, Nikita's schizophrenic life consists of a beau (Anglade) and agency-mandated murders. Parillaud is excellent as the once-amoral street urchin transformed into a woman of depth and sensitivity—a bitterly ironic moral evolution for a contract killer. Remade as "Point of No Return." **117m/C; DVD, Blu-Ray.** *FR* Anne Parillaud; Jean-Hugues Anglade; Tcheky Karyo; Jeanne Moreau; Jean Reno; Jean Bouise; ***D:*** Luc Besson; ***W:*** Luc Besson; ***C:*** Thierry Arbogast; ***M:*** Éric Serra. Cesar '91: Actress (Parillaud).

La France ½ **2007** After Camille receives a disquieting letter from her husband, who's on the French front lines in WWI, she disguises herself as a boy in order to find him. She crosses paths with a small group of soldiers and their lieutenant eventually allows Camille to join them as they head towards the French-Dutch border. The soldiers have a habit of breaking into song, which is jarring at first but then adds to the story. French with subtitles. **102m/C; DVD.** *FR* Sylvie Testud; Pascal Greggory; Guillaume Verdier; Jean-Christophe Bouvet; Guillaume Depardieu; ***D:*** Serge Bozon; ***W:*** Axelle Ropert; ***C:*** Celine Bozon; ***M:*** Medhi Zannad; Benjamin Esdraffo.

La Grande Bouffe *The Blow-Out* **1973** Four middle-aged men, bored with life, meet at a secluded mansion for one last excessive fling and to literally eat themselves to death. Four very fine actors in a vulgar feast. French with subtitles. **125m/C; VHS, DVD.** *FR* Marcello Mastroianni; Philippe Noiret; Michel Piccoli; Ugo Tognazzi; Andrea Ferreol; ***D:*** Marco Ferreri; ***W:*** Marco Ferreri; Rafael Azcona; ***C:*** Mario Vulpiani; ***M:*** Philippe Sarde.

La Grande Vadrouille *Don't Look Now, We've Been Shot At* **1966** In 1943 German-occupied France, three Allied parachutists drop in on a Paris Opera conductor and a house painter. If the pair wish to find some peace, they must help the trio get to the free zone. France's number one boxoffice hit for almost 30 years. Also available dubbed. **122m/C; VHS, DVD.** *FR* Louis de Funes; Andre Bourvil; Terry-Thomas; ***D:*** Gerard Oury.

La Guerre Est Finie ½ *The War Is Over; Kriget ar Slut* **1966** Alain Resnais's understated suspense film makes a belated debut on home video. It's the story of Diego (Montand), a revolutionary who comes to wonder if he can still fight the good fight against the fascists who control Spain. Montand, one of the most deceptively effortless actors ever to appear on screen, is a commanding presence in this low-keyed exercise. **121m/C; DVD.** *FR SW* Yves Montand; Michel Piccoli; Ingrid Thulin; Genevieve Bujold; Jean Daste; Dominique Rozan; Jean-Francois Remi; ***Nar:*** Jorge Semprun; ***D:*** Alain Resnais; ***W:*** Jorge Semprun; ***C:*** Sacha Vierny; ***M:*** Giovanni Fusco.

L.A. Heat ½ **1988** When a vice cop's partner is killed, he seeks revenge on the murderers, only to find that his own department may have been involved. Followed by "L.A. Vice." **90m/C; VHS, DVD.** Jim Brown; Lawrence-Hilton Jacobs; ***D:*** Joseph Merhi.

La La Land ½ **2016 (PG-13)** Damien Chazelle's hit musical is a love letter to dreamers, captured in the story of Mia (Stone) and Seb (Gosling), a couple of star-crossed lovers in Los Angeles just trying to make their dreams come true. Seb's dream is to open his own jazz club; Mia is an aspiring actress bitter at years of failed auditions. Gosling and Stone are dynamic and lovable in this unique vision, a musical that actually pays attention to choreography and music more than lyrics. It's a lovable, inspirational, fantastic piece of work, a musical for the dreamers in all of us. **128m/C; DVD, Blu-Ray.** Ryan Gosling; Emma Stone; John Legend; Rosemarie DeWitt; J.K. Simmons; ***D:*** Damien Chazelle; ***W:*** Damien Hurzelle; ***C:*** Linus Sandgren; ***M:*** Justin Hurwitz. Oscars '16: Actress (Stone), Cinematog., Director (Chazelle), Orig. Score, Orig. Song Score and/or Adapt. ("City of Stars"), Production Design; British Acad. '16: Actress (Stone), Cinematog., Director (Chazelle), Film, Orig. Score; Directors Guild '16: Director (Chazelle); Golden Globes '17: Actor--Mus./Comedy (Gosling), Actress--Mus./Comedy (Stone), Director (Chazelle), Film--Mus./Comedy, Score, Screenplay, Song ("City of Stars"); Screen Actors Guild '16: Actress (Stone).

La Leon *The Lion* **2007** Beautifully photographed in black and white, this debut feature by Otheguy is a story of loneliness and isolation. Alvaro (Roman) works cutting reeds on a marshy Argentine island. The community's main contact with the outside world comes courtesy of Turu (Valenzuela), the captain of the Lion water taxi. Alvaro is even more isolated by the fact that he is gay and Turu is openly hostile although there's more than anger causing the tension between the two men. Spanish with subtitles. **85m/B; DVD.** *AR* Daniel Valenzuela; Jorge Roman; Jose Munoz; ***D:*** Santiago Otheguy; ***W:*** Santiago Otheguy; ***C:*** Paula Grandio; ***M:*** Vincent Artaud.

La Marseillaise ½ **1937** Sweeping epic by Renoir made before he hit his stride with "Grand Illusion." It details the events of the French Revolution in the summer of 1789 using a cast of thousands. The opulent lifestyle of the French nobility is starkly contrasted with the peasant lifestyle of poverty and despair. The focus is on two new recruits who have joined the Marseilles division of the revolutionary army as they begin their long march to Paris, the heart of France. As they travel, they adopt a stirring and passionate song that embodies the spirit and ideals of the revolution known as "La Marseillaise," now France's national anthem. In French with English subtitles. **130m/B; VHS, DVD, Blu-Ray.** *FR* Pierre Renoir; Lisa (Lise) Delamare; Louis Jouvet; Aime Clariond; Andrex Andrisson; Paul Dullac; ***D:*** Jean Renoir; ***W:*** Jean Renoir; ***C:*** Jean (Yves, Georges) Bourgoin.

An L.A. Minute ½ **2018 (R)** Novelist Ted Gould (Byrne) seems to have it all. He won a Pulitzer, lives in a mansion in Malibu, and is minting money for his best-selling potboilers. One day, he accidentally gives his good luck charm to a homeless man (Marinaro) with some change. Ted tries to get his charm back but is beaten and robbed by muggers. He then meets Velocity (Clemons), a young homeless performing artist. Taken by her artistic integrity, he vows to follow her ways. Their lives change forever when he brings her on a television talk show with him. This comedy lacks cleverness and satirizes Hollywood in unconvincing cliches. **86m/C; DVD.** Gabriel Byrne; Kiersey Clemons; Bob Balaban; Lyne Renee; Ed Marinaro; ***D:*** Daniel Adams; ***W:*** Daniel Adams; Larry Sloman; ***C:*** Denise Brassard.

La Mission **2009 (R)** Hot-tempered, widowed ex-con Che Rivera (Bratt) is trying to go straight while living in San Francisco's Mission District barrio with his honor student son Jesse (Valdez). But Che can't accept it when he finds out Jesse's gay and throws him out. Jesse's taken in by his Uncle Rene (Borrego) but it becomes common neighborhood gossip, which leads to violence. Benjamin and his writer/director brother Peter Bratt grew up in and around the Mission district so there's a certain authenticity in a rather familiar plot. **117m/C; Blu-Ray, On Demand.** Jeremy Ray Valdez; Benjamin Bratt; Jesse Borrego; Kevin M. Richardson; Patrick Shining-Elk; Max Rosenak; Rene Quinones; Erika Alexander; Talisa Soto; ***D:*** Peter Bratt; ***W:*** Peter Bratt; ***C:*** Hiro Narita; ***M:*** Mark Killian.

La Moustache *The Moustache* **2005** Carree adapts and directs his 1986 novel in which architect Marc (Lindon) decides to shave off the moustache he's had most of his life. He's taken aback when his wife Agnes (Devos) doesn't notice. Nor does anyone else. Marc first thinks it's an elaborate practical joke but then suspects everyone of more sinister motives. His marriage unravels as, perhaps, does Marc's sanity. French with subtitles. **86m/C; DVD.** *FR* Vincent Lindon; Emmanuelle Devos; Mathieu Amalric; Hippolyte Girardot; Cylia Malki; Macha Polikarpova; ***D:*** Emmanuel Carrere; ***W:*** Jerome Beaujour; Emmanuel Carrere; ***C:*** Patrick Blossier.

La Notte *The Night; La Nuit* **1960** A middle-class writer (Mastroianni) and his wife (Moreau) are questioning staying together any longer as they spend one long and lonely night observing the city around them, trying to make sense of a seemingly chaotic and uncaring world. By dawn, the couple have indeed come to an understanding, but it's not the simple Hollywood solution of staying or leaving. Antonioni's concern is with coping with the modern world while not living in denial amidst a certain postwar/cold war angst. French with subtitles. **122m/B; VHS, DVD, Blu-Ray.** *IT* Marcello Mastroianni; Jeanne Moreau; Monica Vitti; Bernhard Wicki; Grigor Taylor; Maria Pia Luzi; Rosy Mazzacurati; ***D:*** Michelangelo Antonioni; ***W:*** Michelangelo Antonioni; Ennio Flaiano; Tonino Guerra; ***C:*** Gianni Di Venanzo; ***M:*** Giorgio Gaslini.

La Petite Jerusalem *Little Jerusalem* **2005** Two sisters live in a drab housing project in a Paris suburb home to such a number of Orthodox Jewish immigrants that it's known as "Little Jerusalem." Philosophy student and skeptic Laura (Valette) is attracted to Algerian Muslim Djamel (Tillette de Clermont-Tonnerre) while her religious married sister Mathilde (Zylberstein) figures out that her devotions to God are causing her frustrated husband, Ariel (Todeschini), to stray. The sisters have trouble reconciling intimacy with their cultural upbringing but debut writer/director Albou really doesn't go anywhere with her story. French and Hebrew with subtitles. **96m/C; DVD.** *FR* Fanny Valette; Elsa Zylberstein; Bruno Todeschini; Hedi Tillette de Clermont-Tonerre; Michael Cohen; Francois Marthouret; Sonia Tahar; Saida Bekkouche; Salah Teskouk; ***D:*** Karin Albou; ***W:*** Karin Albou; ***C:*** Laurent Brunet; ***M:*** Cyril Morin.

La Petite Lili ½ *Little Lili* **2003** Miller develops a freeform adaptation of Chekhov's 1895 "The Seagull," moving it from 19th-century Russia to 21st-century rural France and shifting the literature/theater emphasis to filmmaking. What transpires is much unrequited love, geriatric loathing, and opinions about making art. In French with subtitles. **104m/C; DVD.** *FR CA* Nicole Garcia; Bernard Giraudeau; Jean-Pierre Marielle; Ludivine Sagnier; Robinson Stevenin; Julie Depardieu; Yves Jacques; Anne LeNy; Marc Betton; ***D:*** Claude Miller; ***C:*** Gerard de Battista.

La Piscine *The Swimming Pool; The Sinners* **1969** Jean-Paul (Delon) and his wife Marianne (Schneider) are on vacation at a villa near St. Tropez. Marianne invites her ex-lover Harry (Ronet) and his teenaged daughter Penelope (Birkin) to join them and the foursome spend most of their time lounging around the pool. But tensions develop and the consequences are dramatic when Jean-Paul decides to seduce the nubile Penelope. French with subtitles. **120m/C; DVD.** *FR* Alain Delon; Romy Schneider; Maurice Ronet; Jane Birkin; ***D:*** Jacques Deray; ***W:*** Jacques Deray; Jean-Claude Carriere; ***C:*** Jean-Jacques Tarbes; ***M:*** Michel Legrand.

La Promesse *The Promise* **1996** Fifteen-year-old Igor (Renier) helps his disreputable father Roger (Gourmet) run an illegal immigrant operation in the Beligan town of Liege. African immigrant Amidou (Ouedraogo) has just been joined by his wife Assita (Ouedraogo) and their baby. When Amidou dies in an accident, Roger forces Igor to help him bury the body secretly and tells the bewildered wife that her husband has left her. But Igor is caught in the middle—he'd promised the dying Amidou to look after Assita and he still has enough conscience to want to help—but it also puts Igor into a dangerous conflict with his father. French with subtitles. **93m/C; DVD, Blu-Ray.** *FR BE* Jeremie Renier; Olivier Gourmet; Assita Ouedraogo; Rasmane Ouedraogo; ***D:*** Jean-Pierre Dardenne; Luc Dardenne; ***W:*** Jean-Pierre Dardenne; Luc Dardenne; ***C:*** Alain Marcoen; ***M:*** Jean-Marie Billy. L.A. Film Critics '97: Foreign Film; Natl. Soc. Film Critics '97: Foreign Film.

La Ronde ½ **1951** A classic comedy of manners and sharply witty tour-de-farce in which a group of people in 1900 Vienna keep changing romantic partners until things wind up where they started. Ophuls' swirling direction creates a fast-paced farce of desire and regret with wicked yet subtle style. Based on Arthur Schnitzler's play and remade as "Circle of Love." In French with English subtitles. **97m/B; VHS, DVD.** *FR* Simone Signoret; Anton Walbrook; Simone Simon; Serge Reggiani; Daniel Gelin; Danielle Darrieux; Jean-Louis Barrault; Fernand Gravey; Odette Joyeux; Isa Miranda; Gerard Philipe; ***D:*** Max Ophuls. British Acad. '51: Film.

La Roue *The Wheel* **1923** Locomotive engineer Sisif saves the infant Norma from a train wreck and raises her as his daughter. When she becomes a beautiful young woman, Sisif realizes he has romantic feelings for her as does his son Elie so a horrified Norma (who finally learns she was adopted) goes off to marry Jacques. Tragedy strikes, leaving Sisif embittered and blind but a widowed Norma secretly cares for him. Gance's epic was primarily filmed on location and his experimental techniques, including rapid montage, were taken up by numerous other filmmakers. **270m/B; Silent; DVD.** *FR* Severin Mars; Ivy Close; Gabriel de Gravone; Pierre Magnier; ***D:*** Abel Gance; ***W:*** Abel Gance; ***C:*** Leonce-Henri Burel; Gaston Burn.

La Rupture ½ *The Breakup* **1970** Thriller about a wife trying to protect her child from her husband's unsavory family. Audran and her son are attacked by her husband (Drouot), who's high on drugs. She fights back and he winds up in the hospital. Her father-in-law (Bouquet), who wants his grandson to live with him, then hires a seedy investigator (Cassel) to spy on Audran. Based on the Charlotte Armstrong novel. In French with English subtitles. **124m/C; VHS, DVD.** *FR* Stephane Audran; Jean-Claude Drouot; Michel Bouquet; Jean-Pierre Cassel; Catherine Rouvel; Jean Carmet; Annie Cordy; ***D:*** Claude Chabrol; ***W:*** Claude Chabrol; ***M:*** Pierre Jansen.

La Scorta 🦴🦴🦴 1/2 *The Bodyguards; The Escorts* **1994** Slick, fact-based political thriller focuses on four carabinieri (state police officers) who struggle to maintain some semblance of their normal lives after they are assigned to protect a judge investigating government corruption and a related murder in a Sicilian town. A crackling alternative to Americanized mobster melodrama, marked by taut direction, meaty characters, and coolly understated performances that seamlessly portray brotherhood, heroism, suspicion, and betrayal amid the battle for power between the Italian state and the Mafia. In Italian with English subtitles. **92m/C; VHS, DVD.** *IT* Claudio Amendola; Enrico Lo Verso; Tony Sperandeo; Ricky Memphis; Carlo Cecchi; Leo Gullotta; Angelo Infanti; ***D:*** Ricky Tognazzi; ***W:*** Graziano Diana; Simona Izzo; ***M:*** Ennio Morricone.

La Sentinelle 🦴🦴 *The Sentinel* **1992** Morose Mathias (Salinger) is traveling by train from Germany to France to attend medical school. The sinister Bleicher (Richard), who seems to be a customs official, grills Mathias but lets him go. In his hotel, Mathias finds a strange package in his luggage and discovers it contains the shrunken head of a man. He keeps his discovery a secret but tests samples of the head in the school laboratory on a quest to figure out who the man was. May sound like a thriller but it's too talky and paced too slowly to hold complete interest. French with subtitles. **139m/C; DVD.** *FR* Emmanuel Salinger; Jean-Louis Richard; Thibault de Montalembert; Valerie Dreville; Marianne (Cuau) Denicourt; Bruno Todeschini; Jean-Luc Boutte; ***D:*** Arnaud Desplechin; ***W:*** Arnaud Desplechin; ***C:*** Caroline Champetier; ***M:*** Marc Oliver Sommer.

La Separation 🦴🦴🦴 **1998** Pierre (Auteuil) and Anne (Huppert) share a long-term relationship and a 15-month-old son. What they no longer seem to have is any passion for each other as they go through their daily routine. Anne decides to have an affair—but doesn't see any reason it should break up her household. However, the increasingly miserable Pierre doesn't share her belief. Based on the 1991 novel "Separation" by Franck. French with subtitles. **85m/C; VHS, DVD.** *FR* Daniel Auteuil; Isabelle Huppert; Karin Viard; Jerome Deschamps; ***D:*** Christian Vincent; ***W:*** Christian Vincent; Dan Franck; ***C:*** Denis Lenoir.

L.A. Story 🦴🦴🦴 **1991 (PG-13)** Livin' ain't easy in the city of angels. Martin, starring as a weatherman in a city where the weather never changes, wrestles with the meaning of life and love while consorting with beautiful people, distancing from significant other Henner, cavorting with valley girl Parker, and falling for newswoman Tennant. Written by the comedian, the story's full of keen insights into the everyday problems and ironies of living in la-la-land. It's no wonder the script's full of so much thoughtful detail: Martin supposedly worked on it for some seven years. Charming, fault-forgiving but not fault-ignoring portrait. **98m/C; DVD.** Steve Martin; Victoria Tennant; Richard E. Grant; Marilu Henner; Sarah Jessica Parker; Sam McMurray; Patrick Stewart; Iman; Kevin Pollak; ***D:*** Mick Jackson; ***W:*** Steve Martin; ***C:*** Andrew Dunn; ***M:*** Peter Melnick.

La Strada 🦴🦴🦴🦴 *The Road* **1954** Simple-minded girl, played by Fellini's wife, Masina, is sold to a brutal, coarse circus strongman and she falls in love with him despite his abuse. They tour the countryside and eventually meet up with a gentle acrobat, played by Basehart, who alters their fate. Fellini masterwork was the director's first internationally acclaimed film, and is, by turns, somber and amusing as it demonstrates the filmmaker's sensitivity to the underprivileged of the world and his belief in spiritual redemption. Subtitled in English. **107m/B; VHS, DVD.** *IT* Giulietta Masina; Anthony Quinn; Richard Basehart; Aldo Silvani; ***D:*** Federico Fellini; ***W:*** Ennio Flaiano; Brunello Rondi; Tullio Pinelli; Federico Fellini; ***M:*** Nino Rota. Oscars '56: Foreign Film; N.Y. Film Critics '56: Foreign Film.

La Terra Trema 🦴🦴🦴 1/2 *Episoda Del Mare; The Earth Will Tremble* **1948** The classic example of Italian neo-realism, about a poor Sicilian fisherman, his family and their village. A spare, slow-moving, profound and ultimately lyrical tragedy, this semi-documentary explores the economic exploitation of Sicily's fishermen. Filmed on location with the villagers playing themselves; highly acclaimed though not commercially successful. In Sicilian with English subtitles. Some radically cut versions may be available, but are to be avoided. Franco Zefferelli was one of the assistant directors. **161m/B; VHS, DVD.** *IT* Antonio Pietrangeli; ***D:*** Luchino Visconti.

La Truite 🦴🦴🦴 *The Trout* **1983 (R)** A young woman leaves her family's rural trout farm and a loveless marriage to seek her fortune in high finance and corporate mayhem. The complicated plot, full of intrigue and sexual encounters, sometimes lacks focus. Slickly filmed. **80m/C; VHS, DVD.** *FR* Isabelle Huppert; Jean-Pierre Cassel; Daniel Olbrychski; Jeanne Moreau; Jacques Spiesser; Ruggero Raimondi; Alexis Smith; Craig Stevens; ***D:*** Joseph Losey. Cesar '83: Cinematog.

L.A. Twister 🦴 **2004** Sloppy buddy comedy has unemployed actor Lenny (Ward) convincing his best friend Ethan (Daly) to produce a movie about their misadventures in Hollywood. It's showbiz cliches all the way with a couple of disagreeable leads. **92m/C; DVD.** Zack (Zach) Ward; Jennifer Aspen; Susan Blakely; Tony Daly; Wendy Worthington; ***D:*** Sven Pape; ***W:*** Geoffrey Saville-Reed; ***C:*** Patrice Lucien Cochet; ***M:*** Ben Moody. **VIDEO**

L.A. Vice 🦴 1/2 **1989** A detective is transferred to the vice squad, where he must investigate a series of murders. Sequel to "L.A. Heat." **90m/C; VHS, DVD.** Jim Brown; Lawrence-Hilton Jacobs; William (Bill) Smith; ***D:*** Joseph Merhi.

La Vie en Rose 🦴🦴🦴 *La Mome; The Kid* **2007 (PG-13)** Think Judy Garland—only French. Somewhat old-fashioned, nonchronological biopic follows the triumphs and tragedies of Edith Piaf (Cotillard), France's famous "little sparrow." Dirt-poor little Edith grows up in a brothel, sings on street corners, gets discovered (by Depardieu's oily impresario), and finds success in cabaret with her astonishing voice. She also finds alcohol and drug addiction, ill health, and a tragic love with married boxer Marcel Cerdan (Martins). Cotillard is amazing in the lead, getting both Piaf's gestures and attitude just right (she lip-synchs her vocals). French with subtitles. **140m/C; DVD, Blu-Ray.** *FR GB CZ* Marion Cotillard; Gerard Depardieu; Emmanuelle Seigner; Pascal Greggory; Sylvie Testud; Clotilde Courau; Jean-Paul Rouve; Catherine Allegret; Jean-Pierre Martins; ***D:*** Olivier Dahan; ***W:*** Olivier Dahan; Isabelle Sobelman; ***C:*** Tetsuo Nagata; ***M:*** Christopher Gunning. Oscars '07: Actress (Cotillard), Makeup; British Acad. '07: Actress (Cotillard), Costume Des., Makeup, Orig. Score; Golden Globes '08: Actress--Mus./Comedy (Cotillard).

La Vie Promise 🦴🦴 1/2 *The Promised Life; Ghost River* **2002** Cold, unmaternal prostitute Sylvia (Huppert) reevaluates her life after meeting 14-year-old Laurence (Forget), the daughter she abandoned years ago. They're forced to go on the lam after Laurence rashly murders Sylvia's abusive pimp. They are joined by the mysterious Joshua (Gerggory) as their journey turns into Sylvia's quest to reunite with her former husband (Marcon) and the young son she also left. In an otherwise mediocre film, Huppert turns in a stunning performance as the whore who must face a past she'd rather forget. Haunting soundtrack and lush French scenery are highlights. French with subtitles. **94m/C; DVD.** *FR* Isabelle Huppert; Pascal Greggory; Maud Forget; Fabienne Babe; Andre Marcon; ***D:*** Olivier Dahan; ***W:*** Agnes Fustier-Dahan; ***C:*** Alex Lamarque.

Labor Day 🦴🦴 1/2 **2013 (PG-13)** Strong performances carry this sometimes melodramatic romantic weepie whose plot wouldn't have been out of place in the 1940s. Adapted from Joyce Maynard's 2009 novel, it's set over a New England Labor Day weekend in 1987 as depressed divorcee Adele (Winslet) and her 13-year-old son, Henry (Griffith), are forced to hide wounded, escaped con, Frank Chambers (Brolin). Intense but gentlemanly, Frank is soon working his sexual charms (note the peach pie scene) on the lonely Adele while offering fatherly advice to the insecure boy. Since the cops are searching for the criminal, it may not be a happy ending. **111m/C; DVD, Blu-Ray.** Kate Winslet; Josh Brolin; Gattlin Griffith; Tobey Maguire; Clark Gregg; ***D:*** Jason Reitman; ***W:*** Jason Reitman; ***C:*** Eric Steelberg; ***M:*** Rolfe Kent.

Labor Pains 🦴🦴 **2009 (PG-13)** ABC Family wound up with this comedy when Lohan's career imploded and it wasn't deemed worthy of a theatrical release. Still, the flick and Lindsay are amusing if you can completely suspend all common sense since the plot is ridiculous. Mouthy publishing assistant Thea needs to keep her job since she's raising her younger sister. About to be fired, she plays the pregnancy card and suddenly everyone in the office is falling for her lie and getting all gooey over her impending single motherhood. Thea even gets the chance to work on a pregnancy book with cutie Nick (Kirby). **89m/C; DVD, Blu-Ray.** Lindsay Lohan; Luke Kirby; Cheryl Hines; Chris Parnell; Janeane Garofalo; Bridgit Mendler; Tracee Ellis Ross; ***D:*** Lara Shapiro; ***W:*** Lara Shapiro; ***C:*** Stacy Kramer; Dan Stoloff; ***M:*** Andrew Hollander. **CABLE**

Labou 🦴🦴 1/2 **2007 (G)** Three kids in Louisiana discover the map to a long lost pirate treasure in the local swamp and in short order have to deal with the pirate's ghost, a strange swamp critter, and a couple of oil barons who want to turn the wilderness into industrial factories. **95m/C; DVD.** Bryan James Kitto; Darnell Hamilton; Marissa Cuevas; Earl Scioneaux; Chris Violette; Kelson Henderson; Barnie Duncan; Ray Nagin; ***V:*** Laura M. Duncan; ***D:*** Greg Aronowitz; ***W:*** Greg Aronowitz; ***C:*** Simon Riera; ***M:*** Christie Yih Chong; Nathan Wang.

Labyrinth 🦴🦴🦴 **1986 (PG)** While babysitting her baby brother Froud, Connelly is so frustrated she asks the goblins to take him away. When the Goblin King, played by Bowie, comes to answer her idle wish, she must try to rescue Froud by solving the fantastic labyrinth. If she does not find him in time, Froud will become one of the goblins forever. During her journey, Connelly is befriended by all sorts of odd creatures created by Henson, and she grows up a little along the way. A fascinating adventure movie for the whole family. **90m/C; VHS, DVD, Blu-Ray.** David Bowie; Jennifer Connelly; Toby Froud; Shelley Thompson; Dave Goetz; Karen Prell; Steve Whitmire; ***D:*** Jim Henson; ***W:*** Jim Henson; Terry Jones; ***C:*** Alex Thomson; ***M:*** David Bowie; Trevor Jones.

Labyrinth 🦴 1/2 **2012** Dull, confusing TV miniseries adapted from Kate Mosse's 2005 novel. Adventurous Alice volunteers at a French archeological site and stumbles over the skeletal remains of two people and a ring engraved with a labyrinth in a cave. She then starts having visions of a young woman--13th-century Alais, who helps her father guard some sacred books that reveal the secret of the Holy Grail from massacring Crusaders. **176m/C; DVD.** *GE UK* Vanessa Kirby; Jessica Brown Findlay; John Hurt; Tony Curran; Sebastian Stan; John Lynch; Tom Felton; Katie McGrath; ***D:*** Christopher Smith; ***W:*** Adrian Hodges; ***C:*** Robert Humphreys; ***M:*** Trevor Jones. **TV**

Labyrinth of Lies 🦴🦴 1/2 *Im Labyrinth des Schweigens* **2014 (R)** In 1958 Germany, discussion of World War II was still uncommon and divisive, even as Germany was financially and internationally putting the conflict behind them. A society that hasn't even discussed the Holocaust comes apart at the seams when a young journalist named Johann (Fehling) investigates German atrocities at the same time a young prosecutor named Thomas (Szymanski) digs into the past himself. The result is the revelation that Germany's government and prominent institutions covered up the very existence of the Nazis and protected them after the fact. It's a well-meaning, if a bit obvious, drama. **124m/C; DVD, Blu-Ray.** *GE* Andre Szymanski; Friederike Becht; Hansi Jochmann; Robert Hunger-Bühler; Gert Voss; ***D:*** Giulio Ricciarelli; ***W:*** Giulio Ricciarelli; Elisabeth Bartel; ***C:*** Martin Langer; Roman Osin; ***M:*** Sebastian Pille; Niki Reiser.

Lace 🦴🦴 **1984** Campy, high-glamour TV miniseries (with equally over-the-top acting) adapted from the Shirley Conran novel. Porno queen turned legit movie star Lili (Cates) gathers three women together (with a particularly notable bit of dialogue) to find out which one is the mother who apparently abandoned her as a baby. Pagan (Adams), Judy (Armstrong), and Maxine (Dombasle) were friends at the same Swiss boarding school and eventually went their separate ways, keeping their secret. The story is told in flashbacks, showing how each of three could possibly be Lili's mother. **300m/C; VHS, DVD.** Phoebe Cates; Brooke Adams; Bess Armstrong; Arielle Dombasle; Anthony (Corlan) Higgins; Angela Lansbury; Francois Guetary; Herbert Lom; Anthony Quayle; Honor Blackman; Nickolas Grace; Leigh Lawson; Trevor Eve; Simon Chandler; ***D:*** William (Billy) Hale; ***W:*** Elliott Baker; ***C:*** Phil Meheux; ***M:*** Nick Bicat. **TV**

Lace 2 🦴 1/2 **1985** The sequel is shorter and not nearly as much fun. Movie star Lili's (Cates) mother heads to Asia to interview the head of a guerilla army and is taken hostage and held for ransom. When Lili can't raise the money herself, she asks her mom's old school friends to help her find her unknown dad, hoping he can help out. According to her mom's roman a clef novel, there are three possibilities (again). **188m/C; DVD.** Phoebe Cates; Arielle Dombasle; Brooke Adams; Deborah Raffin; Anthony (Corlan) Higgins; James Read; Patrick Ryecart; Christopher Cazenove; Walter Gotell; Francois Guetary; Paul Shelley; Ed Wiley; James Faulkner; ***D:*** William (Billy) Hale; ***W:*** Elliott Baker; ***C:*** John Coquillon; ***M:*** Nick Bicat; Tony Bicat. **TV**

Ladder 49 🦴🦴 1/2 **2004 (PG-13)** An old-fashioned homage to firefighters begins when Jack Morrison (Phoenix) is injured and trapped in a burning warehouse. While his chief and mentor, Mike Kennedy (Travolta), coordinates a rescue effort, Jack remembers his first day as a rookie. The movie continues alternating between Jack's career as a firefighter and his current predicament as well as his personal life, which includes his supportive wife Linda (Barrett). That's pretty much it, but the actors are earnest and the action convincing. **115m/C; VHS, DVD, Blu-Ray.** Joaquin Rafael (Leaf) Phoenix; John Travolta; Jacinda Barrett; Robert Patrick; Morris Chestnut; Billy Burke; Balthazar Getty; Tim Guinee; ***D:*** Jay Russell; ***W:*** Lewis Colick; Scott B. Smith; ***C:*** James L. Carter; ***M:*** William Ross.

Ladies and Gentlemen, the Fabulous Stains 🦴 1/2 **1982** Minor price-of-fame drama mainly notable for the beautiful presence of 15-year-old Lane as lead Stain, troubled teen Corinne Burns. She forms an all-girl punk rock band that lacks talent but has a look that can be marketed by their unscrupulous agent Dave (Clennon). They go on the road with a Brit punk quartet and ambitious Corinne steals their songs, leading to public humiliation and a little soul searching. **87m/C; DVD.** Diane Lane; Laura Dern; David Clennon; Ray Winstone; Marin Kanter; Peter Donat; Cynthia Sikes; John Lehne; ***D:*** Lou Adler; ***W:*** Nancy Dowd; ***C:*** Bruce Surtees.

Ladies Crave Excitement 🦴 1/2 **1935** Newsreel cameraman Bob gets involved with wealthy thrill-seeker Wilma, the daughter of a rival company owner. Nevertheless, Wilma helps Don get his scoops, including going after a gang who are fixing horse races. **67m/B; DVD.** Norman Foster; Evalyn Knapp; Gilbert Emery; Esther Ralston; Eric Linden; Purnell Pratt; Emma Dunn; ***D:*** Nick Grinde; ***W:*** Wellyn Totman; ***C:*** William Nobles; Ernest Miller.

Ladies in Lavender 🦴🦴 **2004 (PG-13)** Sisters Janet (Smith) and Ursula (Dench) Widdington have their routine Cornwall cottage life turned about when a handsome, half-drowned young man (Bruhl), who happens to be a Polish violin virtuoso, washes up on their pebbled beach. How, we never find out. Passions and jealousies ignite as the sisters nurse him back to health, intercepting the advances of a pretty young artist attracted to their patient's musical talents. The dames' performances do not disappoint, but the same cannot be said for Bruhl, who lacks depth in comparison. Gallant effort by Dance in reworking William J. Locke's short story, although a bit overreaching. **103m/C; DVD.**

GB Dame Judi Dench; Maggie Smith; Daniel Brühl; Miriam Margolyes; David Warner; ***D:*** Charles Dance; ***W:*** Charles Dance; ***C:*** Peter Biziou; ***M:*** Nigel Hess.

Ladies in Retirement 🦴🦴 **1941** Creepy chiller based on a true story. Ellen is the companion of wealthy retired actress Leonora Fiske. When her two unhinged half-sisters come for a visit they get on Leonora's nerves and she wants them gone. Ellen knows they'll be confined to an asylum so she makes an unexpected decision and must deal with the consequences. **91m/B; DVD.** Ida Lupino; Elsa Lanchester; Louis Hayward; Isobel Elsom; Edith Barrett; Evelyn Keyes; ***D:*** Charles Vidor; ***W:*** Reginald Denham; Garrett Fort; ***C:*** George Barnes; ***M:*** Ernst Toch; Morris Stoloff.

The Ladies' Man 🦴🦴 **1961** Piecemeal Lewis farce, with Jerry playing a clutzy handyman working at a girls' boarding house. Some riotous routines balanced by slow pacing. **106m/C; VHS, DVD.** Jerry Lewis; Helen Traubel; Jack Kruschen; Doodles Weaver; Gloria Jean; ***D:*** Jerry Lewis; ***W:*** Jerry Lewis.

Ladies' Man 🦴🦴 *Lemmy Pour les Dames* **1962** Super agent Lemmy Caution (Constantine) is relaxing on the French Riviera when a woman is murdered. He learns that a Communist government has been blackmailing some married gals whose husbands work for western intelligence agencies and Lemmy comes to their rescue. The sixth time Constantine played the character. Dubbed. **97m/B; DVD.** *FR* Eddie Constantine; Francoise Brion; Yvonne Monlaur; Jacques Berthier; Robert Berri; Claudine Coster; Elaine D'Almeida; Guy Delorme; ***D:*** Bernard Borderie; ***W:*** Bernard Borderie; ***C:*** Armand Thirard; ***M:*** Paul Misraki.

The Ladies Man 🦴 **1/2 2000 (R)** Yet another unsuccessful movie adaptaion of an SNL skit. This time it's Leon Phelps (Meadows), a stuck-in-the-'70s late-night talk show host who dispenses inappropriate romantic advice. Raised by Hugh Hefner but banished for sleeping with the wrong bunny, Leon is then fired from his radio gig. He eases the pain by seducing other men's wives, leading to the formation of an anti-Leon posse. Meanwhile, his faithful ex-producer Julie (Parsons) sticks by him, hoping to tame Leon's wild ways. All comic possibilities of this lame flick are squandered. **84m/C; VHS, DVD.** Tim Meadows; Will Ferrell; Karyn Parsons; Billy Dee Williams; Tiffani(-Amber) Thiessen; Eugene Levy; Lee Evans; John Witherspoon; Julianne Moore; Tamala Jones; ***D:*** Reginald (Reggie) Hudlin; ***W:*** Tim Meadows; Dennis McNicholas; Andrew Steele; ***C:*** Johnny E. Jensen; ***M:*** Marcus Miller.

Ladies of Leisure 🦴🦴 **1930** Adapted from Milton Herbert Gropper's play "Ladies of the Evening," so you know what kind of ladies these gals might be, although the flick refers to them differently. Gold-digging party girl Kay (Stanwyck) sets her marital ambitions on rich young Jerry (Graves) who wants to be an artist. Kay models for him and, though he knows she's after his dough, Jerry falls for her anyway. His parents are horrified and they plead with Kay to leave their boy alone. Stagey and Graves is all wood but Stanwyck has you believing she loves the log. **98m/B; DVD.** Barbara Stanwyck; Ralph Graves; Lowell Sherman; Marie Prevost; Nance O'Neil; George Fawcett; ***D:*** Frank Capra; ***W:*** Jo Swerling; ***C:*** Joseph Walker.

The Ladies of the Bois de Bologne 🦴🦴 *Les Dames du Bois de Bologne; Ladies of the Park* **1944** Beware the woman scorned—as Jean (Bernard) learns. He ends his longtime relationship with Helene (Casares), although they vow to stay friends, but she secretly plots revenge and finds it in the person of Agnes (Labourdette), a former prostitute. Helene introduces Agnes to Jean, hoping they'll be attracted to one another. They are but after the wedding ceremony Helene reveals the truth about Agnes' sordid past. Updated adaptation of a story in Diderot's "Jacques Le Fatalist." French with subtitles. **83m/B; VHS, DVD.** *FR* Maria Casares; Paul Bernard; Elina Labourdette; ***D:*** Robert Bresson; ***W:*** Robert Bresson; Jean Cocteau.

Ladies of the House 🦴🦴 **1/2 2008** Hallmark Channel original. Birdie (Grier), Elizabeth (Mills), and Rose (Henderson) are women of a certain age and wealthy members of the same church. Their pastor asks for help with renovating a donated house he hopes can be resold to fund the church's daycare. The ladies are just supposed to oversee matters but they get very involved and find the changes are being mirrored in their personal lives. **100m/C; DVD.** Pam Grier; Donna Mills; Florence Henderson; Richard Roundtree; Lance Henriksen; Gordon Thomson; Michael Ensign; ***D:*** James A. Contner; ***W:*** Karen Stuck; ***C:*** Brian Shanley; ***M:*** Alex Wilkinson. **CABLE**

Ladies Who Do 🦴🦴 **1/2 1963** A group of cleaning ladies band together against the unscrupulous businessman who wants to tear down their homes in order to build an office tower. Along with a retired colonel, they use the stock market secrets gleaned from the rubbish they toss away to make a killing in the market and save the day. **90m/B; VHS, DVD, Streaming.** *GB* Peggy Mount; Robert Morley; Harry H. Corbett; Miriam Karlin; Avril Elgar; Dandy Nichols; Jon Pertwee; Nigel Davenport; ***D:*** C.M. Pennington-Richards; ***W:*** Michael Pertwee.

Ladrones 🦴🦴 **2015 (PG-13)** A comedy about a pair of modern day Robin Hoods. When a callous businesswoman and her crooked family harms a group of Mexican families by stealing their land deeds and their land, two former thieves are determined to take them back. To complete this mission, Alejandro (Colunga) and Santiago (Yanez) recruit a team of amateurs including a spiritualist, ranch hand, actor, and meteorologist. Together, they try to pull off a caper that puts many wrongs right. Spanish with subtitles. **97m/C; DVD, Streaming, Download.** Fernando Colunga; Eduardo Yanez; Miguel Varoni; Jessica Lindsey; Frank Perozo; ***D:*** Joe Menendez; ***W:*** Jon Molerio; ***C:*** Francis Adamez; ***M:*** Luichy Guzman.

The Lady 🦴🦴 **2011 (R)** Aung San Suu Kyi (Yeoh) returns to Burma as a revolution is unfolding and becomes an icon for her people, even winning the Nobel Peace Prize. The opposing Burmese military keeps her under house arrest and her British family is kept from her. The real story of a woman forced to play a role in history instead of raise her family is fascinating but the film is too conventional for the complex nature of its subject matter. Yeoh and Thewlis (as husband Michael) deliver daring performances in this biopic but it's just not enough. **128m/C; DVD, Blu-Ray.** *FR UK* Michelle Yeoh; David Thewlis; Jonathan Raggett; Jonathan Woodhouse; Htun Lin; ***D:*** Luc Besson; ***W:*** Rebecca Frayn; ***C:*** Thierry Arbogast; ***M:*** Éric Serra.

The Lady and the Duke 🦴🦴 **1/2** *L'Anglaise et le Duc* **2001 (PG-13)** Based on the memoirs of Englishwoman Grace Elliott (Russell), who lived in Paris during the French Revolution and remained a loyal supporter of King Louis XVI. The Duke is her former lover, Philippe, Duc d'Orleans (Dreyfus), a cousin to the King and a moderate revolutionary. Having remained friends, he encourages Grace to return to England, although she refuses. 81-year-old Rohmer commissioned a series of painted backdrops depicting 18th-century France rather than build sets and then superimposed his actors upon the backdrops, offering remarkably effective visuals. French with subtitles. **129m/C; VHS, DVD.** *FR* Lucy Russell; Jean-Claude Dreyfus; Francois Marthouret; Leonard Cobiant; Caroline Morin; Alain Libolt; Marie Riviere; Helena Dubeil; ***D:*** Eric Rohmer; ***W:*** Eric Rohmer; ***C:*** Diane Baratier.

The Lady and the Highwayman 🦴🦴 **1/2 1989** TV adaptation of the Barbara Cartland historical romance finds a rogue falling for the lady he's sworn to protect. Naturally, there's a happy ending. **100m/C; VHS, DVD.** *GB* Hugh Grant; Emma Samms; Oliver Reed; Michael York; Robert Morley; John Mills; Lysette Anthony; ***D:*** John Hough; ***W:*** Terence Feely; ***M:*** Laurie Johnson. **TV**

Lady and the Tramp 🦴🦴🦴🦴 **1955 (G)** The animated Disney classic about two dogs who fall in love. Tramp is wild and carefree; Lady is a spoiled pedigree who runs away from home after her owners have a baby. They just don't make dog romances like this anymore. **76m/C; VHS, DVD, Blu-Ray.** ***V:*** Larry Roberts; Peggy Lee; Barbara Luddy; Stan Freberg; Alan Reed; Bill Thompson; Bill Baucon; Verna Felton; George Givot; Dallas McKennon; Lee Millar; ***D:*** Hamilton Luske; Clyde Geronimi; Wilfred Jackson; ***W:*** Erdman Penner; Ralph Wright; Don DaGradi; ***M:*** Peggy Lee; Sonny Burke.

Lady and the Tramp 🦴🦴 **1/2 2019 (PG)** At Christmas, Jim Dear (Mann) and Darling (Clemons) receive a cocker spaniel puppy they name Lady (Thompson). The couple makes her the center of their world. One day, Lady crosses path with Tramp (Theroux), a scruffy dog who lives on the streets, when he is on the run from a dog catcher (Martinez). Though they don't get along at first, she helps him escape. When Lady's position changes because of a new baby, she leaves and finds Tramp. A passable live action version of the classic Disney animated film that follows the same story, with a few updates. **104m/C; DVD.** Tessa Thompson; Justin Theroux; Sam Elliott; Ashley Jensen; Janelle Monáe; ***D:*** Charlie Bean; ***W:*** Andrew Bujalski; Kari Granlund; ***C:*** Enrique Chediak; ***M:*** Joseph Trapanese. **VIDEO**

Lady Audley's Secret 🦴🦴 **2000** Old-fashioned and rather dull potboiler based on the 1862 novel by Mary Elizabeth Braddon. Governess Lucy (McIntosh) marries her employer, Sir Michael Audley (Cranham). But Lucy has a shady past, including a previous husband, George (Bamber), who turns out to be a friend of Sir Michael's nephew, Robert (Mackintosh). Then George disappears and Robert wonders just how dangerous the new Lady Audley is. **120m/C; VHS, DVD.** *GB* Neve McIntosh; Steven Mackintosh; Kenneth Cranham; Jamie Bamber; Juliette Caton; Melanie Clark Pullen; ***D:*** Betsan Morris-Evans; ***W:*** Donal Hounam; ***C:*** Julian Court; ***M:*** Paul Carr. **TV**

Lady Be Good 🦴🦴 **1/2 1941** Adapted from the 1924 Gershwin Broadway hit although the plot's been revamped. Sothern and Young play a tunesmith duo who excel at musical harmony and marital strife. Applauded for its music (the critics loved Hammerstein's and the Gershwins' tunes), the show's Academy Award-winning song was, ironically, written by Jerome Kern. And if that's not enough, levity man Skelton and hoofer Powell are thrown in for good measure. **111m/B; VHS, DVD.** Eleanor Powell; Ann Sothern; Robert Young; Lionel Barrymore; John Carroll; Red Skelton; Dan Dailey; Virginia O'Brien; Tom Conway; Phil Silvers; Doris Day; ***D:*** Norman Z. McLeod; ***C:*** George J. Folsey; ***M:*** Oscar Hammerstein; Ira Gershwin; Jerome Kern; George Bassman. Oscars '41: Song ("The Last Time I Saw Paris").

Lady Bird 🦴🦴🦴 **2017 (R)** An authentic exploration of the coming-of-age experience and complexities of a mother-daughter relationship packaged in a perfectly balanced comedy-drama. In 2002, 17-year-old Christine (Ronan) has dubbed herself "Lady Bird" and longs to leave Sacramento to attend an East Coast college. Her mother, Marion (Metcalf), works double shifts as a psychiatric nurse to support the family while her husband (Letts) remains unemployed. While Lady Bird and her mother both battle and love each other, the teen also navigates her progressive Catholic school, high school friendships, and boyfriends. With strong casting and multifaceted characters, director/writer Gerwig's semi-autobiographical vision comes fully to life. **94m/C; DVD, Blu-Ray.** Saoirse Ronan; Timothée Chalamet; Odeya Rush; Laurie Metcalf; Kathryn Newton; ***D:*** Greta Gerwig; ***W:*** Greta Gerwig; ***C:*** Sam Levy; ***M:*** Jon Brion. Golden Globes '18: Actress--Mus./Comedy (Ronan), Film--Mus./Comedy; Ind. Spirit '18: Screenplay.

Lady by Choice 🦴🦴 **1/2 1934** Lombard stars as a beautiful young fan dancer who is arrested for a lewd public performance. Taking the advice of her press agent, she hires an old bag lady to pose as her mother on Mother's Day. Robson portrays her "mother" and comes to think of Lombard as her own daughter. Robson encourages Lombard to give up fan dancing and to strive for greater things in life. She also pushes her into romance with a wealthy young man (Pryor). Robson is excellent in her role as "mother" and Lombard shows great comic talent in this charming film. **78m/B; DVD.** Carole Lombard; May Robson; Roger Pryor; Walter Connolly; Raymond Walburn; James Burke; ***D:*** David Burton; ***W:*** Jo Swerling; ***C:*** Ted Tetzlaff.

Lady Chatterley 🦴🦴 **1992** Oh my, Russell takes his provocative ways to D.H. Lawrence's scandalous novel about the adulterous affair between aristocratic Lady Connie Chatterley (Richardson) and her husband's gamekeeper, Oliver Mellors (Bean). Also includes material taken from two early drafts of the book "The First Lady Chatterley" and "John Thomas and Lady Jane." **210m/C; VHS, DVD.** *GB* Joely Richardson; Sean Bean; James Wilby; Shirley Anne Field; Roger Hammond; ***D:*** Ken Russell; ***W:*** Ken Russell; ***C:*** Robin Vidgeon; ***M:*** Jean-Claude Petit. **TV**

Lady Chatterley 🦴🦴🦴 **2010** Lady Chatterley (Hinds) spends her days collecting flowers after her husband (Giradot) is paralyzed in World War I. She encounters gamekeeper Parkin (Coullo'ch) and the two begin an affair that brings about her sexual awakening. Stunningly shot, and director Ferran manages to maintain a high level of eroticism and character development. French adaptation of the second version of the D.H. Lawrence novel. **168m/C; DVD.** *BE FR* Marina Hands; Hippolyte Girardot; Jean-Louis Coulloc'h; Helene Alexandridis; ***D:*** Pascal Ferran; ***W:*** Roger Bohbot; Pierre Trividic; Pascal Ferran; ***C:*** Julien Hirsch; ***M:*** Beatrice Thiriet.

Lady Chatterley's Lover 🦴 **1/2** *L'Amant de Lady Chatterley* **1955** Englishwoman has bad luck to have husband shot up during WWI and sent home paralyzed. In her quest for sexual fulfillment, she takes a new lover, the estate's earthy gamekeeper. Limp adaptation of D.H. Lawrence's novel. In French with English subtitles. **102m/B; VHS, DVD, Streaming.** *FR* Danielle Darrieux; Erno Crisa; Leo Genn; ***D:*** Marc Allegret.

Lady Chatterley's Lover 🦴 **1/2 1981 (R)** Remake of the 1955 film version of D.H. Lawrence's classic novel of an English lady who has an affair with the gamekeeper of her husband's estate. Basically soft-focus soft porn. **107m/C; VHS, DVD, Blu-Ray.** *GB FR* Sylvia Kristel; Nicholas Clay; Shane Briant; ***D:*** Just Jaeckin; ***C:*** Robert Fraisse.

Lady Cocoa 🦴 **1/2 1975 (R)** Routine story of a young woman who gets released from jail for 24 hours and sets out for Las Vegas to find the man who framed her. **93m/C; VHS, DVD, Blu-Ray.** Lola Falana; Joe "Mean Joe" Greene; Gene Washington; Alex Dreier; ***D:*** Matt Cimber.

The Lady Confesses 🦴🦴 **1945** Average mystery that involves Hughes trying to clear her boyfriend of murder. Independently produced. "Leave it to Beaver" fans will want to watch for "Ward Cleaver" Beaumont. **66m/B; VHS, DVD.** Mary Beth Hughes; Hugh Beaumont; Edmund MacDonald; Claudia Drake; Emmett Vogan; Barbara Slater; Edward Howard; Dewey Robinson; Carol Andrews; ***D:*** Sam Newfield; ***W:*** Helen Martin; Irwin H. Franklyn; ***C:*** Jack Greenhalgh; ***M:*** Lee Zahler.

Lady Dragon 🦴🦴 **1992 (R)** A woman and her husband are viciously attacked and only she survives. Found by an old man, she learns a number of martial arts tricks and goes out to get her revenge. **89m/C; VHS, DVD.** Cynthia Rothrock; Richard Norton; Robert Ginty; Bella Esperance; Hengko Tornando; ***D:*** David Worth; ***C:*** David Worth; ***M:*** Jim West.

The Lady Eve 🦴🦴🦴🦴 **1941** Father/daughter (Coburn, Stanwyck) con artists, out to trip up wealthy beer tycoon Charles Pike (Fonda), instead find themselves tripped up when Jean falls in love with the mark. Ridiculous situations, but Sturges manages to keep them believable and funny. With a train scene that's every man's nightmare. Perhaps the best Sturges ever. Based on the story "The Faithful Heart" by Monckton Hoffe. Later remade as "The Birds and the Bees." **93m/B; VHS, DVD.** Barbara Stanwyck; Henry Fonda; Charles Coburn; Eugene Pallette; William Demarest; Eric Blore; Melville Cooper; ***D:*** Preston Sturges; ***W:*** Preston Sturges; ***C:*** Victor Milner. Natl. Film Reg. '94.

Lady for a Day 🦴🦴🦴 **1/2 1933** Delightful telling of the Damon Runyon story, "Madame La Gimp," about an apple peddler (Robson) down on her luck, who is transformed into a lady by a criminal with a heart. "Lady By Choice" is the sequel. **96m/B; VHS, DVD.** May Robson; Warren William; Guy Kibbee; Glenda Farrell; Ned Sparks; Jean Parker; Walter

Connolly; **D:** Frank Capra; **W:** Robert Riskin; **C:** Joseph Walker.

Lady for a Night 🦴🦴 **1942** Jenny Blake (Blondell), the owner of a gambling riverboat, offers to forgive society gentleman Alan Anderson (Middleton) his gambling debts in return for marrying her. His society family is appalled and there's a poisoning plot that goes awry. Wayne's the political boss that sticks by Blondell. **88m/B; DVD, Blu-Ray.** John Wayne; Joan Blondell; Ray Middleton; Philip Merivale; Blanche Yurka; Edith Barrett; Leonid Kinskey; Montagu Love; **D:** Leigh Jason; **W:** Isabel Dawn; Boyce DeGaw; **C:** Norbert Brodine; **M:** David Buttolph.

Lady Frankenstein 🦴 ½ *La Figlia di Frankenstein; The Daughter of Frankenstein; Madame Frankenstein* **1972 (R)** Frankenstein's lovely daughter graduates from medical school and returns home. When she sees what her father's been up to, she gets some ideas of her own. Good fun for fans of the genre. **84m/C; VHS, DVD.** *IT* Joseph Cotten; Rosalba Neri; Mickey Hargitay; Paul Muller; Herbert (Fuchs) Fux; Renate Kasche; Ada Pometti; Lorenzo Terzon; Paul Whiteman; **D:** Mel Welles; **W:** Edward Di Lorenzo; **C:** Riccardo (Pallton) Pallottini.

The Lady From Lisbon 🦴 ½ **1942** While staying at a Lisbon hotel, South American Minghetti agrees to help Nazi spies in return for obtaining the Mona Lisa. But when multiple copies of the priceless work start turning up, a British agent attempts to identify the real deal and Minghetti has a change of heart about working with the bad guys. **75m/B; DVD.** *GB* Francis L. Sullivan; Martita Hunt; Jane Carr; Charles Victor; George Street; Wilfrid Hyde-White; Anthony Holles; **D:** Leslie Hiscott; **W:** Michael Barringer; **C:** Erwin Hillier.

Lady from Louisiana 🦴🦴 **1942** Plodding Republic Pictures programmer that does include an eerie storm scene. Idealistic lawyer John Reynolds (Wayne) comes to New Orleans to clean up a crime syndicate fronting a crooked lottery. He falls for Julie Mirbeau (Munson) but her father (Stephenson) heads the lottery so they have problems even before her General Mirbeau is murdered. **84m/B; DVD, Blu-Ray.** John Wayne; Ona Munson; Dorothy Dandridge; Ray Middleton; Henry Stephenson; Helen Westley; Jack Pennick; **D:** Bernard Vorhaus; **W:** Vera Caspary; Guy Endore; Michael Hogan; **C:** Jack Marta.

The Lady from Shanghai 🦴🦴🦴 ½ **1948** An unsuspecting seaman becomes involved in a web of intrigue when a woman hires him to work on her husband's yacht. Hayworth (a one-time Mrs. Orson Welles), in her only role as a villainess, plays a manipulative, sensual schemer. Wonderful and innovative cinematic techniques from Welles, as usual, including a tense scene in a hall of mirrors. Filmed on a yacht belonging to Errol Flynn. **87m/B; VHS, DVD, Blu-Ray.** Orson Welles; Rita Hayworth; Everett Sloane; Glenn Anders; Ted de Corsia; Erskine Sanford; Gus Schilling; **D:** Orson Welles; **W:** Orson Welles; **C:** Charles Lawton, Jr.; **M:** Heinz Roemheld. Natl. Film Reg. '18.

The Lady Gambles 🦴🦴 **1949** Gets an extra half-bone for Stanwyck's performance because the plot doesn't merit much. Joan (Stanwyck) accompanies her writer husband David (Preston) to Las Vegas and, while he's working, she starts gambling. She loses big, lies, steals, and generally ruins her life until she's suicidal and her estranged hubby comes to her rescue. The psychology given for Joan's destructive behavior is laughable today but probably reasonable enough at the time when less was known about addiction and treatment. **98m/B; DVD.** Barbara Stanwyck; Robert Preston; Stephen McNally; Edith Barrett; John Hoyt; Leif Erickson; **D:** Michael Gordon; **W:** Roy Huggins; Halsted Welles; **C:** Russell Metty; **M:** Frank Skinner.

Lady Godiva 🦴 ½ *Lady Godiva of Coventry* **1955** The lovely O'Hara is wasted in the title role as a Saxon noblewoman married to Leofric (Nader). They're trying to stem Norman influence and Godiva vows to ride naked through the streets of Canterbury to prove the Saxon people's loyalty to King Edward (Franz). Cardboard costumer. Clint Eastwood has a bit as a Saxon soldier. **89m/C; DVD.** Maureen O'Hara; George Nader; Eduard Franz; Leslie Bradley; Victor McLaglen; Torin Thatcher; Rex Reason; **D:** Arthur Lubin; **W:** Oscar Brodney; Harry Ruskin; **C:** Carl Guthrie.

Lady Godiva Rides 🦴 ½ *Lady Godiva Meets Tom Jones* **1968** A bad, campy version of the story of Lady Godiva. Godiva comes to the United States with a bevy of scantily clad maidens and winds up in the Old West. When the town villain threatens to compromise her, Tom Jones comes to the rescue. The film (of course) features Godiva's naked ride on horseback through the town. **88m/C; VHS, DVD.** Marsha Jordan; Forman Shane; Deborah Downey; Elizabeth Knowles; James E. Myers; Jennie Jackson; Liz Renay; Vincent Barbi; **D:** A.C. (Stephen Apostoloff) Stephen; **W:** A.C. (Stephen Apostoloff) Stephen; **C:** R.C. Ruben; **M:** Jay Colonna; Robert E. Lee.

Lady Ice 🦴🦴 **1973 (PG)** Sutherland, as an insurance investigator on the trail of jewel thieves, follows them to Miami Beach and the Bahamas. After stealing a diamond he enters into partnership with a crook's daughter. Worth seeing for the cast. **93m/C; VHS, DVD, Blu-Ray.** Donald Sutherland; Jennifer O'Neill; Robert Duvall; Eric Braeden; **D:** Tom Gries; **W:** Alan R. Trustman; **M:** Perry Botkin.

Lady in a Cage 🦴🦴🦴 **1964** A wealthy widow is trapped in her home elevator during a power failure and becomes desperate when hoodlums break in. Shocking violence ahead of its time probably plays better than when first released. Young Caan is a standout among the star-studded cast. **95m/B; DVD.** Olivia de Havilland; Ann Sothern; James Caan; Jennifer Billingsley; Jeff Corey; Scatman Crothers; Rafael Campos; **D:** Walter Grauman; **W:** Luther Davis; **C:** Lee Garmes; **M:** Paul Glass.

Lady in a Jam 🦴🦴 **1942** Screwball silliness stars Dunne as New York heiress Jane Palmer, who squanders all the money her grandfather left her. Because of her madcap ways, she comes under the supervision of shrink Dr. Enright (Knowles), who poses as her chauffeur when Jane heads to Arizona to convince her tough grandma, Cactus Kate (Vassar), that she deserves a second chance. Kate agrees to let Jane work the family's abandoned gold mine with some unexpected consequences. **83m/B; DVD.** Irene Dunne; Patric Knowles; Queenie Vassar; Ralph Bellamy; Eugene Pallette; Samuel S. Hinds; **D:** Gregory La Cava; **W:** Otho Lovering; **C:** Hal Mohr; **M:** Frank Skinner.

Lady in Cement 🦴 ½ **1968 (R)** The second Tony Rome mystery, in which the seedy Miami dick finds a corpse with cement shoes while swimming. **93m/C; VHS, DVD, Blu-Ray.** Frank Sinatra; Raquel Welch; Richard Conte; Martin Gabel; Lainie Kazan; Pat Henry; Steve Peck; Joe E. Lewis; Dan Blocker; **D:** Gordon Douglas; **C:** Joseph Biroc.

The Lady in Question 🦴 ½ *It Happened in Paris* **1940** A Parisian shopkeeper, played by Aherne, sits on a jury that acquits Hayworth of murder. His interest doesn't end with the trial, however, and matters heat up when his son also becomes involved. Remake of a melodramatic French release. **81m/B; DVD.** Rita Hayworth; Glenn Ford; Brian Aherne; Irene Rich; Lloyd Corrigan; George Coulouris; Evelyn Keyes; Curt Bois; Edward Norris; **D:** Charles Vidor; **W:** Ben Barzman; **C:** Lucien N. Andriot; **M:** Lucien Moraweck.

Lady in Red 🦴🦴 *Guns, Sin and Bathtub Gin* **1979** A story of America in the '30s, and the progress through the underworld of the woman who was Dillinger's last lover. **90m/C; VHS, DVD.** Pamela Sue Martin; Louise Fletcher; Robert Conrad; Christopher Lloyd; Dick Miller; Laurie Heineman; Robert Hogan; Glenn Withrow; Rod Gist; Mary Woronov; **D:** Lewis Teague; **W:** John Sayles; **C:** Daniel Lacambre; **M:** James Horner.

The Lady in the Car with Glasses and a Gun 🦴🦴 ½ *La dame dans l'auto avec des lunettes et un fusil* **2016** A chic psychological thriller based on a novel by Sebastien Japrisot. Seeking a joyride, a enigmatic yet stylish secretary Dany Doremus (Mavor) lifts the sports car owned by her boss (Biolay) after doing an errand for him. Driving the car to a seaside town she has never visited before, she finds that all the residents know her name. She is even more unnerved when a body turns up in her trunk. Her life gets turned upside down when becomes the lead suspect in a murder that she has no memory of. French with subtitles. **93m/C; DVD, Blu-Ray, Streaming, Download.** Freya Mavor; Benjamin Biolay; Elio Germano; Stacy Martin; Thierry Hancisse; **D:** Joann Sfar; **W:** Patrick Godeau; Gilles Marchand; **C:** Manuel Dacosse; **M:** Agnes Olier.

Lady in the Lake 🦴🦴 ½ **1946** Actor Montgomery directs himself in this Philip Marlowe go-round, using a subjective camera style to imitate author Chandler's first person narrative (meaning the only time we see Marlowe/Montgomery's mug is in a mirror). Having decided to give up being a PI, Marlowe turns to the pen to tell the tangled tale of the lady in the lake: once upon a time, a detective was hired to find the wicked wife of a paying client. . .Some find the direction clever but MGM chief Louis B. Mayer made sure this was Montgomery's last project with the studio. **103m/B; VHS, DVD.** Robert Montgomery; Lloyd Nolan; Audrey Totter; Tom Tully; Leon Ames; Jayne Meadows; **D:** Robert Montgomery; **W:** Steve Fisher; **C:** Paul Vogel; **M:** David Snell.

The Lady in the Van 🦴🦴 ½ **2015 (PG-13)** Based on a real event which occurred in London in the 1970s. Smith does her irascible old lady thing again as Miss Shepherd, a woman who lives in a van that finds itself parked in the driveway of Alan Bennett (Jennings). He decides to let her stay there, and the two form a unique friendship over the next 15 years, as he learns that she wasn't always an angry old lady living in a van. Smith is typically enjoyable, and nearly carries the film, but it just doesn't have enough to offer outside of her performance. **104m/C; DVD, Blu-Ray.** Maggie Smith; Jim Broadbent; Alex Jennings; Deborah Findlay; Roger Allam; Dominic Cooper; Frances de la Tour; **D:** Nicholas Hytner; **W:** Alan Bennett; **C:** Andrew Dunn; **M:** George Fenton.

Lady in the Water 🦴🦴 **2006 (PG-13)** This attempt at a modern-day Brothers Grimm fable follows Cleveland Heep (Giamatti), the gloomy superintendent of a gloomy Philadelphia apartment complex, who discovers a translucent creature (Howard) skinny-dipping in the pool. He then tries to rescue the nymph (or "narf" in Shymalan's unoriginal world), the apartment's residents, and himself from a variety of evil forces. More of the same heavy-handed symbolism and convoluted storyline that passed for plot twists. Shyamalan wrote, directed, and gave himself a role in this fairy tale, which he states is based on a bedtime story he told his daughters. **108m/C; DVD, Blu-Ray, HD-DVD.** Bryce Dallas Howard; Paul Giamatti; Jeffrey Wright; Bob Balaban; Freddy Rodriguez; Sarita Choudhury; Jared Harris; Bill Irwin; Mary Beth Hurt; Tovah Feldshuh; M. Night Shyamalan; **Nar:** David Ogden Stiers; **D:** M. Night Shyamalan; **W:** M. Night Shyamalan; **C:** Christopher Doyle; **M:** James Newton Howard. Golden Raspberries '06: Worst Actor (Shyamalan), Worst Director (Shyamalan).

The Lady in White 🦴🦴🦴 **1988 (PG-13)** Small-town ghost story about murder and revenge. When young Haas is locked in school one night, he's visited by the ghost of a little girl who wants his help in discovering who murdered her. Well-developed characters, interesting style, and suspenseful plot make for a sometimes slow but overall exceptional film. **92m/C; VHS, DVD, Blu-Ray.** Lukas Haas; Len Cariou; Alex Rocco; Katherine Helmond; Jason Presson; Renata Vanni; Angelo Bertolini; Jared Rushton; Joelle Jacob; **D:** Frank Laloggia; **W:** Frank Laloggia; **C:** Russell Carpenter; **M:** Frank Laloggia.

The Lady Is a Square 🦴🦴 **1958** Widowed Frances Baring (Neagle) wants to carry on the work of her classical music promoter husband but she doesn't have the money. Singer Johnny Burns (Vaughan) is in love with Frances' daughter Joanna (Scott) but mom doesn't approve of his pop music. When Johnny gets a tune on the charts, he tries to secretly finance Frances' classical concerts. **100m/B; DVD.** *GB* Anna Neagle; Frankie Vaughan; Janette Scott; Anthony Newley; Wilfrid Hyde-White; Christopher Rhodes; **D:** Herbert Wilcox; **W:** Pamela Bower; Harold Purcell; Nicholas Phipps; **C:** Gordon Dines; **M:** Angela Morley.

Lady Jane 🦴🦴🦴 ½ **1985 (PG-13)** An accurate account of the life of 15-year-old Lady Jane Grey, who secured the throne of England for nine days in 1553 as a result of political maneuvering by noblemen and the Church of England. A wonderful film even for non-history buffs. Carter's first film. **140m/C; DVD.** *UK* Helena Bonham Carter; Cary Elwes; Sara Kestelman; Michael Hordern; Joss Ackland; Richard Johnson; Patrick Stewart; **D:** Trevor Nunn; **W:** David Edgar; **C:** Douglas Slocombe; **M:** Stephen Oliver.

Lady Jayne Killer 🦴🦴 *Betrayal* **2003 (R)** Jayne Ferre (Du Page) is an L.A. hitwoman for mobster Frank Bianchi (Mandylor) from whom she has just stolen a million bucks. So she needs to get quietly out of town fast. Emily (Eleniak) and her 16-year-old son Kerry (Lelliott) need money to get to Texas. When Jayne and Emily meet, she offers to foot the bill if she can hitch a ride. Then Kerry discovers the cash, steals it from Jayne, and heads back to L.A. Naturally, Jayne and Emily are soon behind him. And then FBI agent Alex Tyler (Remar) comes into the picture. **90m/C; VHS, DVD.** Julie Du Page; Erika Eleniak; Jeremy Lelliott; James Remar; Louis Mandylor; Adam Baldwin; Damian Chapa; Don Swayze; Peter Dobson; **D:** Mark L. Lester; **W:** C. Courtney Joyner; **C:** Joao Fernandes. **VIDEO**

Lady Killer 🦴🦴🦴 **1933** Racy, pre-Code comedy with mobster Cagney hiding out in Hollywood. He gets discovered and becomes a big star, but his old gang turns up to blackmail him. Lots of movie "in" jokes and Clarke (of "Public Enemy" fame) is great as a wisecracking moll. Based on the story "The Finger Man" by Rosalind Keating Shaffer. **74m/B; VHS, DVD.** James Cagney; Mae Clarke; Leslie Fenton; Margaret Lindsay; Henry O'Neill; Raymond Hatton; George Chandler; **D:** Roy Del Ruth; **W:** Ben Markson; Lillie Hayward.

Lady Killer 🦴🦴 *Ladykiller* **1997 (R)** A serial killer called the Piggyback Murderer is terrorizing a college campus. Police Lt. Jack Lasky (Gazzara) is particularly anxious since his daughter Jennifer (Allman) is a student at the school. When her new boyfriend, aspiring actor Richard Darling (McArthur), keeps turning up at the murder scenes, guess who becomes dad's prime suspect. **80m/C; VHS, DVD.** Ben Gazzara; Alex McArthur; Terri Treas; Renee Allman; **D:** Terence H. Winkless; **W:** Craig J. Nevius; **C:** Christopher Baffa.

Lady L 🦴 ½ **1965** Silly turn-of-the-century farce about a sexy laundress (Loren), married to a French anarchist (Newman!), who also marries the aristocratic Niven (in name only). Elaborate sets and Paris and London backgrounds couldn't overcome the odd casting and weak script. Adapted from the novel by Romain Gary. **107m/C; DVD.** *FR IT* Sophia Loren; Paul Newman; David Niven; Cecil Parker; Claude Dauphin; Marcel Dalio; Philippe Noiret; Michel Piccoli; Daniel Emilfork; Eugene Deckers; **Cameo(s):** Peter Ustinov; **D:** Peter Ustinov; **W:** Peter Ustinov; **C:** Henri Alekan; **M:** Jean Francaix.

Lady Macbeth 🦴🦴🦴 **2017 (R)** A complex period drama based on a novella by Nikolai Leskov that explores the female spirit through one young woman's horrific actions to control her world. In rural 1860s England, young Katherine (Pugh) is sold into a loveless marriage with the far older Alexander (Hilton). The restrictions imposed on her by Alexander and his father Boris (Fairbank) are subverted when they leave on business. Katherine soon starts a passionate affair with a groomsman, Sebastian (Jarvis) and does all she can to retain the pleasures which have set her free. Beautifully shot, the film features a spare soundtrack that adds to the dense tensions. **89m/C; DVD, Blu-Ray.** Florence Pugh; Cosmo Jarvis; Paul Hilton; Naomi Ackie; Christopher Fairbank; **D:** William Oldroyd; **W:** Alice Birch; **C:** Ari Wegner; **M:** Dan Jones.

Lady of Burlesque 🦴🦴 ½ *Striptease Lady* **1943** Burlesque dancer is found dead, strangled with her own G-string. Clever and amusing film based on "The G-String Murders" by Gypsy Rose Lee. **91m/B; VHS, DVD.** Barbara Stanwyck; Michael O'Shea; Janis Carter; Pinky Lee; **D:** William A. Wellman.

A Lady of Chance 🦴🦴 **1928** Tough as nails babe redeemed by true love. Con woman Dolly (Shearer) is forced back into blackmailing wealthy marks when she's recognized by her ex-partners Bradley (Sherman) and Gwen (Lee). Doublecrossing them,

Dolly picks up Steve Crandall (Brown), thinking he's a wealthy southern businessman. When she's really fallen for him, Dolly learns Steve's got lots of charm but not much dough. Although when Bradley and Gwen track Dolly down again, they don't believe her. Shearer's last silent film. **79m/B; Silent; DVD.** Norma Shearer; Johnny Mack Brown; Lowell Sherman; Gwen Lee; Eugenie Besserer; Buddy Messinger; ***D:*** Robert Z. Leonard; ***W:*** Edmund Goulding; A.P. Younger; Ralph Spence; ***C:*** J. Peverell Marley.

Lady of the Evening *Gun Moll; Get Rita; Oopsie Poopsie; La Gangster del Pupa* **1975 (R)** A prostitute and a crook team up to seek revenge against the mob. **110m/C; VHS, DVD.** *IT* Sophia Loren; Marcello Mastroianni; Pierre Brice; Dalia di Lazzaro; Aldo Maccione; ***D:*** Giorgio Capitani; ***W:*** Ernesto Gastaldi; ***C:*** Alberto Spagnoli; ***M:*** Pierro Umiliani.

Lady of the Night **1925** Romantic melodrama with Shearer getting to shine in two showy roles. Orphaned reform school goodtime gal Molly is at the dancehall with her pal Chunky (Arthur) when she's rescued from a lout by aspiring inventor David Page (McGregor). It's Molly, who's fallen for nice guy David, who suggests that he peddle his latest invention to a bank, which is indirectly how he meets refined finishing school grad Florence. David falls for her but then Florence learns of Molly's interest. Notable since neither woman is depicted as a competitive shrew or undeserving of the love of a good man. **86m/B; Silent; DVD.** Norma Shearer; Malcolm McGregor; George K. Arthur; Fred Esmelton; Dale Fuller; Lew Harvey; ***D:*** Monta Bell; ***W:*** Alice Duer Miller; ***C:*** Andre Barlatier.

Lady on a Train **1945** Travelling at Christmas, wealthy young Nicky Collins (Durbin) thinks she sees a murder from her train window but when she arrives in New York she can't get anyone to believe her. Not willing to give up, Nicky turns to Wayne Morgan (Bruce), a mystery writer for help. Recognizing the victim from a newspaper photo, Nicky checks out his family and gets mistaken for a nightclub singer (so Durbin can vamp a torch song). Lots of comedy amidst the mystery and romance, and some surprizes as well. Based on a story by Leslie Charteris. **95m/B; VHS, DVD.** Deanna Durbin; David Bruce; Ralph Bellamy; Dan Duryea; Edward Everett Horton; Allen Jenkins; Elizabeth Patterson; William Frawley; Jacqueline DeWit; George Coulouris; ***D:*** Charles David; ***W:*** Robert O'Brien; Edmund Beloin; ***C:*** Elwood "Woody" Bredell; ***M:*** Miklos Rozsa.

The Lady Refuses **1931** A stuffy Victorian father is disappointed in his wastrel son and decides a poor but honest young woman could be the making of him. Problems arise when the girl falls for the father instead. **70m/B; VHS, DVD, Blu-Ray.** Betty Compson; John Darrow; Margaret Livingston; Gilbert Emery; Ivan Lebedeff; Edgar Norton; Daphne Pollard; Halliwell Hobbes; ***D:*** George Archainbaud; ***W:*** Wallace Smith; ***C:*** Leo Tover.

The Lady Says No **1951** A photographer must photograph an attractive author who has written a book uncomplimentary toward the male sex. **80m/B; VHS, DVD.** Joan Caulfield; David Niven; James Robertson Justice; Frances Bavier; Henry Jones; Jeff York; ***D:*** Frank Ross.

Lady Sings the Blues 1/2 **1972 (R)** Jazz artist Billie Holiday's life becomes a musical drama depicting her struggle against racism and drug addiction in her pursuit of fame and romance. What could be a typical price-of-fame story is saved by Ross' inspired performance as the tragic singer. **144m/C; VHS, DVD.** Diana Ross; Billy Dee Williams; Richard Pryor; James Callahan; Paul Hampton; Sid Melton; ***D:*** Sidney J. Furie; ***C:*** John A. Alonzo.

Lady Snowblood *Shurayukihime; Lady Snowblood: Blizzard from the Nether World; Blood Snow* **1973** A group of thieves break into the house of a rural couple, murder the husband, and rape the wife, who later dies in childbirth after becoming pregnant. A priest raises her daughter to be a skilled swordswoman and sends her out to murder the men who wronged her family when she becomes an adult. Adapted from the comic by Kazuo Koike, who is famous for the Lone Wolf and Cub series, it is the inspiration for much of the film "Kill Bill" by Quentin Tarantino. **67m/C; DVD, Blu-Ray.** *JP* Meiko Kaji; Toshio Kurosawa; Masaki Daimon; Sanae Nakahara; Eiji Okada; Ko Nishimura; Miyoko Akaza; Shinichi Uchida; Takeo Chii; Noboru Nakaya; Yoshiko Nakada; Akemi Negisha; Kaoru Kusuda; Hosei Kimatsu; Makoto Matsuzaki; Hiroshi Hasegawa; Hitoshi Takagi; ***D:*** Toshiya Fujita; ***W:*** Kazuo Koike; Kazuo Kamimura; ***C:*** Masaki Tamura; ***M:*** Masaaki Hirao.

Lady Snowblood: Love Song of Vengeance 1/2 *Shura-yuki-hime: Urami Renga* **1974** After gaining vengeance for her mother in the first film, Lady Snowblood (Kaji) is arrested and offered a way out of prison—become a spy for the secret police and steal a document that will incriminate a political activist while killing him in the process. **89m/C; DVD.** *JP* Meiko Kaji; Juzo Itami; Kazuko Yoshiyuki; Yoshio Harada; Shin Kishida; Toru Abe; Rinichi Yamamoto; Koji Nanbara; Shosuke Hirose; Shunsuke Mizoguchi; Akira Hamada; Hiroshi Ishiya; ***V:*** Mizuho Suzuki; ***D:*** Toshiya Fujita; ***W:*** Kazuo Kamimura; Kazuo Koike; Norio Osada; Kiyohide Ohara; ***C:*** Tatsuo Suzuki; ***M:*** Kenjiro Hirose.

Lady Street Fighter **1986** A well-armed female combat fighter battles an organization of assassins to avenge her sister's murder. **73m/C; VHS, DVD, Blu-Ray.** Renee Harmon; Joel McCrea, Jr.; ***D:*** James Bryan; ***C:*** Max Reed.

Lady Takes a Chance **1943** A romantic comedy about a New York working girl with matrimonial ideas and a rope-shy rodeo rider who yearns for the wide open spaces. Fine fun on the range. **86m/B; VHS, DVD, Blu-Ray.** John Wayne; Jean Arthur; Phil Silvers; Charles Winninger; ***D:*** William A. Seiter.

Lady Terminator *Pembalasan ratu pantai selatan; Nasty Hunter; Revenge of the South Seas Queen; Shooting Star* **1989 (R)** The evil spirit goddess, The South Seas Queen, seduces men and kills them with a magic eel. A would-be suitor steals her eel and transforms it into a knife, so she curses him. Eventually, anthropologist Tania (Constable, also the film's makeup artist), finds the Sea Queen's lair, and becomes possessed and invulnerable. Tania then steals some machine guns and goes on a rampage looking to get her dagger/eel back. Somewhere between a cheesy sexploitation film and a gory "Terminator" ripoff, it's most definitely unique. **82m/C; VHS, DVD.** Barbara Constable; Christopher J. Hart; Joseph McGlynn; Claudia Rademaker; ***D:*** H. Tjut Djalil; Jalil Jackson; ***W:*** Karr Kruinowz; ***C:*** Chuchu Suteja; ***M:*** Ricky Brothers.

The Lady Vanishes **1938** Kindly old lady, Miss Froy (Witty) seemingly disappears from a fast-moving train bound for England. But when her young friend Iris (Lockwood) investigates, she finds no one appears to believe her and she has a spiraling mystery to solve. Of course, Iris has music scholar Gilbert (Redgrave) eager to help her out. Hitchcock's first real winner, a smarmy, wit-drenched British mystery that precipitated his move to Hollywood. Along with "39 Steps," considered an early Hitchcock classic. From the novel "The Wheel Spins," by Ethel Lina White. Remade in 1979. **99m/B; VHS, DVD, Blu-Ray.** *GB* Margaret Lockwood; Paul Lukas; Michael Redgrave; May Whitty; Googie Withers; Basil Radford; Naunton Wayne; Cecil Parker; Linden Travers; Catherine Lacey; Alfred Hitchcock; ***D:*** Alfred Hitchcock; ***W:*** Sidney Gilliat; Frank Launder; ***C:*** Jack Cox; ***M:*** Louis Levy. N.Y. Film Critics '38: Director (Hitchcock).

The Lady Vanishes 1/2 **1979** In this reworking of the '38 Alfred Hitchcock film, a woman on a Swiss bound train awakens from a nap to find that the elderly woman seated next to her was kidnapped. Falls short of the original movie due to the "screwball" nature of the main characters, Gould and Shepherd. Based on Ethel Lina White's novel "The Wheel Spins." **95m/C; DVD.** *UK* Elliott Gould; Cybill Shepherd; Angela Lansbury; Herbert Lom; ***D:*** Anthony Page; ***W:*** George Axelrod; ***C:*** Douglas Slocombe; ***M:*** Richard Hartley.

The Lady Vanishes **2013** BBC/Masterpiece version of the Ethel Lina White novel pales in comparison to Hitchcock's 1938 film although the extremely pretty Middleton is an asset as snobbish, wealthy young Iris Carr. Having made herself disliked by the other English tourists at a Balkan resort, Iris continues her heedless ways on the train trip back to England. After apparently suffering sunstroke, Iris is befriended by English governess Miss Froy (Cadell). However, when that lady vanishes under sinister circumstances, Iris can't get anyone to believe her except, perhaps, besotted engineer Max (Hughes). **82m/C; DVD.** *UK* Tuppence Middleton; Selina Cadell; Tom Hughes; Keeley Hawes; Julian Rhind-Tutt; Alex Jennings; Jesper Christensen; Gemma Jones; ***D:*** Diarmuid Lawrence; ***W:*** Fiona Seres; ***C:*** Peter Greenhalgh; ***M:*** John Lunn. **TV**

Lady Windermere's Fan 1/2 **1925** The silent, Lubitsch adaptation of the Oscar Wilde tale concerning an upper-class couple's marriage being almost destroyed by suspected adultery. **66m/B; Silent; VHS, DVD.** Ronald Colman; May McAvoy; Bert Lytell; ***D:*** Ernst Lubitsch. Natl. Film Reg. '02.

The Lady with the Dog **1959** A bittersweet love story based on the Anton Chekhov story, about two married Russians who meet by chance in a park, fall in love, and realize they are fated to a haphazard, clandestine affair. In Russian with English titles. **86m/B; VHS, DVD.** *RU* Iya Savvina; Alexei Batalov; Ala Chostakova; N. Alisova; ***D:*** Yosif Heifitz.

The Lady With the Lamp 1/2 **1951** In this bio of Florence Nightingale (Neagle), the focus is on the political battles she had to overcome in order to put into place her nursing ideas to improve care for British soldiers during the Crimean War. However, Florence is championed in Parliament by minister of war Sidney Herbert (Wilding). Good contrast between scenes of stately mansions and hospital squalor. **110m/B; DVD.** *GB* Anna Neagle; Michael Wilding; Felix Aylmer; Gladys Young; Julian D'Albie; Arthur Young; Sybil Thorndike; Rosalie Crutchley; ***D:*** Herbert Wilcox; ***W:*** Warren Chetham Strode; ***C:*** Mutz Greenbaum; ***M:*** Anthony Collins.

A Lady Without Passport **1950** Government official Pete (Hodiak) is heading up the effort to stop illegal immigration by posing as a Hungarian making his way to the U.S. through Cuba. So Pete decides to use desperate refugee Marianne (Lamarr), who's in Havana waiting in vain for a passport, to get the goods on human smuggler Palinov (Macready). **72m/B; DVD.** Hedy Lamarr; John Hodiak; George Macready; James Craig; Steven Geray; Bruce Cowling; ***D:*** Joseph H. Lewis; ***W:*** Cyril Hume; Howard Dimsdale; ***C:*** Paul Vogel; ***M:*** David Raskin.

Ladybird, Ladybird **1993 (R)** Loach's emotionally bruising look at working-class life and family in the '90s. Maggie (Rock) is a tough unmarried mother of four who's been battered by her lovers and has come under the over-watchful eye of Britain's social services. She meets Jorge (Vega), a gentle Paraguayan, and just when things are looking up, Jorge gets immigration heat, Maggie's insecurities surface, and her baby daughter is taken into care by child welfare. Rock has a no-nonsense manner and acerbic wit that precludes any hand-wringing for her character, even as you hope she'll win out over circumstance. Based on a true story. **102m/C; VHS, Streaming.** *GB* Crissy Rock; Vladimir Vega; Ray Winstone; Sandie Lavelle; Mauricio Venegas; Clare Perkins; Jason Stracey; Luke Brown; Lily Farrell; ***D:*** Ken Loach; ***W:*** Rona Munro; ***C:*** Barry Ackroyd; ***M:*** George Fenton. Berlin Intl. Film Fest. '94: Actress (Rock).

Ladybugs 1/2 **1992 (PG-13)** Hangdog salesman Dangerfield would like to move up the corporate ladder, but must first turn the company-sponsored girl's soccer team into winners. Routine Dangerfield vehicle exploits nearly everything for laughs, including dressing an athletic boy as a girl so he can play on the team. Obvious fluff. **91m/C; VHS, DVD.** Rodney Dangerfield; Jackee; Jonathan Brandis; Ilene Graff; Vinessa Shaw; Tom Parks; Jeanetta Arnette; Nancy Parsons; Blake Clark; Tommy Lasorda; ***D:*** Sidney J. Furie; ***W:*** Curtis Burch; ***C:*** Dan Burstall; ***M:*** Richard Gibbs.

Ladyhawke 1/2 **1985 (PG-13)** In medieval times, a youthful pickpocket befriends a strange knight who is on a mysterious quest. This unlikely duo, accompanied by a watchful hawk, are enveloped in a magical adventure. **121m/C; VHS, DVD, Blu-Ray.** Matthew Broderick; Rutger Hauer; Michelle Pfeiffer; John Wood; Leo McKern; Alfred Molina; Ken Hutchison; ***D:*** Richard Donner; ***W:*** Edward Khmara; Michael Thomas; Tom Mankiewicz; ***C:*** Vittorio Storaro; ***M:*** Andrew Powell.

Ladykiller **1992 (R)** Rogers stars as a burned-out cop who goes to a dating service to find a man who'll give her the attention she craves. When she meets wealthy professional Shea she thinks he's the one but her cop's curiosity about her lover's past may cost her her life. **92m/C; VHS, DVD.** Mimi Rogers; John Shea; Alice Krige; Tom Irwin; ***D:*** Michael Scott; ***W:*** Shelley Evans.

The Ladykillers 1/2 *The Lady Killers* **1955** A gang of bumbling bank robbers is foiled by a little old lady. Hilarious antics follow, especially on the part of Guinness, who plays the slightly demented-looking leader of the gang. **87m/C; VHS, DVD.** *GB* Alec Guinness; Cecil Parker; Katie Johnson; Herbert Lom; Peter Sellers; Danny Green; Jack Warner; Kenneth Connor; Edie Martin; Jack Melford; ***D:*** Alexander MacKendrick; ***W:*** William Rose; ***C:*** Otto Heller; ***M:*** Tristram Cary. British Acad. '55: Actress (Johnson), Screenplay.

The Ladykillers 1/2 **2004 (R)** Hanks assumes the role of G.H. Dorr with gusto in this quirky remake of the 1955 British pic. The setting shifts to Mississippi, where robbers attempt to burrow from little old lady Mrs. Munson's (Hall) basement to the nearby casino's money room. While Hall is superb and Hanks is often dynamic as he plows through ornate speeches with a wicked laugh, it depends on your tolerance for flowery language and a mannered Southern drawl whether you think he's melodious or annoying. Enjoyable but uneven effort by the Coen brothers that falls short of the original. **104m/C; DVD.** Tom Hanks; Irma P. Hall; Marlon Wayans; J.K. Simmons; Tzi Ma; Ryan Hurst; Diane Delano; George Wallace; John McConnell; Stephen (Steve) Root; Jason Weaver; Greg Grunberg; Blake Clark; Jeremy Suarez; ***D:*** Ethan Coen; Joel Coen; ***W:*** Ethan Coen; Joel Coen; ***C:*** Roger Deakins; ***M:*** Carter Burwell.

The Lady's Not for Burning 1/2 **1987** Romantic comedy, set in a medieval English village, finds ex-soldier Thomas Mendip (Branagh) invading the home of querulous Mayor Hebble Tyson (Hepton), demanding to be hanged. He says he's murdered the local rag and bone merchant but the townspeople insist Jennet Jourdemayne (Lunghi), who's seeking refuge at the mayor's, has turned him into a dog. They demand she be burned as a witch (hence the title, since Thomas, unwillingly but strongly, objects to this action). Adapted by Fry from his play; made for TV. **90m/C; DVD.** *UK* Kenneth Branagh; Cherie Lunghi; Bernard Hepton; Tim Watson; Susannah Harker; Angela Thorne; Shaun Scott; ***D:*** Julian Amyes; ***W:*** Christopher Fry. **TV**

Lafayette Escadrille 1/2 *Hell Bent for Glory* **1958** Action and romance in WWI via the famed flying unit manned by American volunteers. Hunter is banal in the lead role as is his romance with a reformed prostitute (Choreau). Director Wellman actually was a member of the squadron and his son plays him in the film but the director regarded the film as a failure because of studio interference. **92m/B; VHS, DVD.** Tab Hunter; Etchika Choureau; William Wellman, Jr.; Joel McCrea; Dennis Devine; Marcel Dalio; David Janssen; Paul Fix; Will Hutchins; Clint Eastwood; Tom Watson; ***D:*** William A. Wellman; ***W:*** A.S. Fleischman; ***C:*** William Clothier; ***M:*** Leonard Rosenman.

Lagaan: Once upon a Time in India **2001 (PG)** Bollywood musical set in 1893, in the drought-striken village of Champaner. The lagaan is a tax levied by the occupying British on the local rajahs, which the village can't pay. The region's nasty British commander, Captain Russell (Blackthorne), states that if the villagers can beat his soldiers at cricket, the lagaan will be cancelled for three years; if they lose, the lagaan will be tripled. Heroic Bhuvan (Khan) persuades the locals that even if they don't understand the game, they can certainly show those arrogant Brits a thing or two! English, Hindi and Bhojpuri with subtitles. **225m/C; DVD.** *IN* Aamir Khan; Gracy Singh; Rachel Shelley; Paul Blackthorne; Suhasini Mulay; Kulbashan Kharbanda; Raghuvir Yadav; ***D:*** Ashutosh Gowariker; ***W:*** Ashutosh Gowariker; Kumar Dave; Sanjay Dayma; K.P. Saxena; ***C:*** Anil Mehta; ***M:*** A.R. Rahman.

Laggies 1/2 **2013** Megan (Knightley) is a 28-year-old unwilling or just unable to amass the hallmarks of adulthood like a happy marriage and fulfilling job. She basically runs away from home and starts hanging out with a 16-year-old named Annika (Moretz), and meets her charismatic father (Rockwell). The first film directed by Shelton that she didn't write has great turns from Knightley and Rockwell, but they are smothered by predictable quarter-life crisis clichés. **100m/C; DVD, Blu-Ray.** Keira Knightley; Chloë Grace Moretz; Sam Rockwell; Mark Webber; Ellie Kemper; Gretchen Mol; Jeff Garlin; ***D:*** Lynn Shelton; ***W:*** Andrea Seigel; ***C:*** Benjamin Kasulke; ***M:*** Benjamin Gibbard.

Laid to Rest **2009** A blood fest, slasher flick with a relentless, remorseless killer. A young woman wakes up in a coffin with no memory of who she is or how she got there. She escapes and manages to find some help (naturally she's in the middle of nowhere) but then is stalked by ChromeSkull, a serial killer who wears a skull mask made of chrome, uses large serrated knives on his victims, and likes to videotape his actions. Followed by 2011's "ChromeSkull: Laid to Rest 2." **90m/C; DVD.** Bobbi Sue (Bobby Sue) Luther; Kevin Gage; Sean M. Whalen; Thomas Dekker; Nick Principe; Lena Headey; Richard Lynch; Johnathon Schaech; ***D:*** Robert Hall; ***W:*** Robert Hall; ***C:*** Scott Winig. **VIDEO**

Laila **1929** In this silent Norwegian drama, baby Laila is separated from her parents and is found and raised by Laplander Aslag and his family to lead a nomadic life with their reindeer herd. Although she's eventually reunited with her parents, she's torn between two worlds and also the romantic affections of her foster brother Mellet and her cousin Anders. **145m/B; Silent; DVD.** *NO* Mona Martenson; Henry Gleditsch; Harald Schwenzen; Peter Malberg; Tryggve Larssen; ***D:*** George Schneevoigt; ***W:*** George Schneevoigt; ***C:*** Allan Lynge.

The Lair of the White Worm **1988 (R)** Scottish archaeologist uncovers a strange skull, and then a bizarre religion to go with it, and then a very big worm. An unusual look at the effects of Christianity and paganism on each other, colored with sexual innuendo and, of course, giant worms. A cross between a morality play and a horror film. Adapted from Bram Stoker's last writings, done while he was going mad from Bright's disease. Everything you'd expect from Russell. **93m/C; VHS, DVD, Blu-Ray.** *GB* Amanda Donohoe; Sammi Davis; Catherine Oxenberg; Hugh Grant; Peter Capaldi; Stratford Johns; Paul Brooke; Christopher Gable; ***D:*** Ken Russell; ***W:*** Ken Russell; ***C:*** Dick Bush; ***M:*** Stanislas Syrewicz.

Lake City 1/2 **2008 (R)** City boy Billy is on the run from drug dealers after a deal goes bad, and he heads for his mother's farm in Virginia. Mom and son have some emotional baggage to sort out as a long-past family tragedy has kept them apart, but it's all quite uninteresting, convoluted, and remarkably impersonal. A family drama that combines forced, unmatched characters and manufactured, contrived drama with not one but two rookie directors. Spacek is the only positive aspect and script doesn't give her much to work with. **92m/C; On Demand.** Troy Garity; Sissy Spacek; Rebecca Romijn; Dave Matthews; Drea De Matteo; Keith Carradine; Barry Corbin; Colin Ford; ***D:*** Hunter Hill; Perry Moore; ***W:*** Hunter Hill; Perry Moore; ***C:*** Robert Gantz; ***M:*** Aaron Zigman.

Lake Consequence **1992 (R)** Severance plays a suburban housewife who accidentally gets locked in the camper of the tree-trimmer stud (Zane) she's been eyeing while he's been working in her neighborhood. Next thing she knows they wind up at a distant lake where the bored housewife is more than willing to give into her growing sexual fantasies. An unrated version at 90 minutes is also available. **85m/C; VHS, DVD.** Joan Severance; Billy Zane; May Karasun; ***D:*** Rafael Eisenman; ***W:*** Zalman King; Melanie Finn; Henry Cobbold; ***M:*** George S. Clinton.

Lake Dead **2007** Not dead enough. Three sisters learn that the grandfather they never knew has died and left them a motel in the mountains. They promptly get some friends together and decide to check things out. What they find is your basic murderous, inbred family of hillbilly lunatics already occupying the real estate and they're determined that no one is going to leave. At least not alive. **91m/C; DVD.** Kelsey Crane; Tara Gerard; Kelsey Wedeen; James C. Burns; Dan Woods; Jim Devoti; Alex A. Quinn; Malea Richardson; Vanessa Viola; Pat McNeely; Christian Stokes; Trevor Torseth; ***D:*** George Bessudo; ***W:*** Daniel P. Coughlin; ***C:*** Curtis Petersen; ***M:*** Mark Petrie.

Lake Effects 1/2 **2012** Hallmark Channel family drama. Sara (Thomson) returns to her Virginia lakeside hometown for her dad Ray's (Fahey) funeral, which gives her a chance to reunite with her estranged sister Lily (Zima) and mother Vivian (Seymour). While bonding, they find some eccentric locals are searching the lake for a legendary monster. **90m/C; DVD.** Scottie Thompson; Madeline Zima; Jane Seymour; Casper Van Dien; Sean Patrick Flanery; Ben Savage; Jeff Fahey; ***D:*** Michael McKay; ***W:*** Scott Winters; ***C:*** Matthew Boyd; ***M:*** Kaz(imir) Boyle. **CABLE**

The Lake House 1/2 **2006 (PG)** Confusing time-travel romance that appeals because of its leads, who haven't worked together since 1994's "Speed." Chicago doctor Kate (Bullock) leaves a note for the next renter of her glass box lakeside house. Only architect Alex (Reeves) insists that no one has lived in the rundown property for years before him. Hmmm, somehow the attractive twosome communicates with each other despite a two-year time gap. They fall in love, but trying to meet face-to-face is a complicated business. A remake of the 2000 South Korean film "Siworae." **108m/C; DVD, Blu-Ray, HD-DVD.** Keanu Reeves; Sandra Bullock; Shohreh Aghdashloo; Dylan Walsh; Christopher Plummer; Ebon Moss-Bachrach; Willeke Van Ammelrooy; Lynn Collins; ***D:*** Alejandro Agresti; ***W:*** David Auburn; ***C:*** Alar Kivilo; ***M:*** Rachel Portman.

Lake Mungo **2008 (R)** Fake documentary filled with videos, mobile phone images, and interview footage. In 2005, 16-year-old Alice Palmer drowns while swimming in a dam near her small hometown of Ararat, Australia. Strange events occur at the Palmer family's home after her burial and they call in psychic Ray Kemeny. He learns that Alice was living a secret life and that she camped at dry Lake Mungo just before her death. **104m/C; DVD.** *AU* Steve Jodrell; Talia Zucker; Rosie Traynor; David Pledger; Martin Sharpe; Tamara Donnellan; Scott Terrill; ***D:*** Joel Anderson; ***W:*** Joel Anderson; ***C:*** John Brawley; ***M:*** Dai Paterson; Fernando Corona.

Lake Placid 1/2 **1999 (R)** Lame comedy/horror ripoff of "Jaws." Paleontologist Fonda goes to rural Maine to examine a tooth after a grisly death occurs. She discovers that the tooth is prehistoric, but decides to stick around with game warden Pullman, sheriff Gleeson and eccentric professor Platt anyway. You know, just in case the crocodile that escaped through a hole in the plot is still hungry after eating other cast members. Betty White is the lone bright spot as a foul-mouthed old woman who roots for the crocodile. You'll be rooting for it too, but you'll be rooting for it to devour the movie exec who green-lit this crock. **82m/C; VHS, DVD, Blu-Ray.** Bridget Fonda; Bill Pullman; Oliver Platt; Brendan Gleeson; Mariska Hargitay; Meredith Salenger; Betty White; David Lewis; ***D:*** Steve Miner; ***W:*** David E. Kelley; ***C:*** Daryn Okada; ***M:*** John Ottman.

Lake Placid 2 **WOOF! 2007 (R)** A sheriff, a wildlife agent, and a big game hunter track three hungry 30-foot prehistoric crocodiles munching on the local populace. Sci-Fi Channel sequel-in-name-only with really bad CGI and possibly worse acting and script. **84m/C; DVD, Blu-Ray.** John Schneider; Sam McMurray; Cloris Leachman; Sarah Lafleur; Chad Collins; Alicia Ziegler; ***D:*** David Flores; ***W:*** Todd Hurvitz; Howie Miller; ***C:*** Lorenzo Senatore; ***M:*** Nathan Furst. **CABLE**

Lake Placid 3 1/2 **2010 (R)** Typical Syfy Channel creature feature. Nathan Bickerman inherits his mother's house and moves his wife Susan and young son Connor to Lake Placid. Connor takes to secretly feeding some baby crocs, they grow humungous, eat the wildlife, and then move on to humans. **93m/C; DVD.** Colin Ferguson; Kirsty Mitchell; Michael Ironside; Jordan Grehs; Yancy Butler; Mark Evans; Kacey Barnfield; ***D:*** Griff Furst; ***W:*** David Reed; ***C:*** Anton Bakarski. **CABLE**

Lake Placid: The Final Chapter **2012 (R)** Mindless SyFy Channel entertainment with hungry crocs having a buffet of hapless teen. Black Lake has become a crocodile sanctuary but that doesn't stop a high school bus driver mistakenly dropping off his passengers for a field trip that turns into terror. **90m/C; DVD.** Yancy Butler; Elisabeth Rohm; Paul Nicholls; Benedict Smith; Poppy Lee Friar; Robert Englund; ***D:*** Don Michael Paul; ***W:*** David Reed; Mairin Reed; ***C:*** Martin Chichov; ***M:*** Frederik Wiedmann. **CABLE**

Lakeboat 1/2 **2000 (R)** Longtime Mamet collaborator Mantegna makes his directorial debut adapting one of Mamet's earliest, most autobiographical plays. Grad student Dale (Mamet's younger brother Tony) signs on with a Great Lakes ore freighter as the cook. The thrust of the film is Dale's observations and musings from the crew, especially Joe (Forster), who once had artistic and educational ambitions that he gave up for a regular paycheck. Excellent, understated performances by all help mask the film's inability to escape its stage limitations and Mantegna's uneven direction. Dialogue shows the promise, as well as the themes, realized in Mamet's later work. **98m/C; VHS, DVD.** Charles Durning; Peter Falk; Robert Forster; J.J. Johnston; Denis Leary; Jack Wallace; George Wendt; Saul Rubinek; Tony Mamet; Andy Garcia; ***Cameo(s):*** Joe Mantegna; ***D:*** Joe Mantegna; ***W:*** David Mamet; ***C:*** Paul Sarossy; ***M:*** Bob Mamet.

Lakeview Terrace **2008 (PG-13)** Newlyweds Chris and Lisa (Wilson and Washington) move into the posh LA suburb of Lakeview Terrace, and unbeknownst to the interracial couple, they're now next door to a nightmare. Hard-headed neighbor Abel Turner (Jackson) starts off as a pest, but his hatred and brutal racism soon come to a head. They turn to the law, but problem is, Abel's a cop. It's almost disturbing to see Jackson as such a cold-blooded sociopath, with razor-sharp writing letting him go off like a wild dog. An intense study of role-reversed racism with all involved confused about who's to blame. **110m/C; Blu-Ray, UMD, On Demand.** Samuel L. Jackson; Patrick Wilson; Kerry Washington; Regine Nehy; Jay Hernandez; Keith Loneker; Eva LaRue; Mel Rodriguez; Jaishon Fisher; Ron Glass; ***D:*** Neil LaBute; ***W:*** David Loughery; Howard Korder; ***C:*** Rogier Stoffers; ***M:*** Jeff Danna; Mychael Danna.

Lamb **1985** Troubled 10-year-old epileptic Owen Kane (Kane) has been dumped by his abusive mother at a Catholic-run institution for wayward boys in Ireland, run by self-righteous headmaster Brother Benedict (Bannen). Owen becomes Benedict's scapegoat—much to the dismay of Brother Michael Lamb (Neeson). When Lamb claims a small family inheritance, he decides to take Owen and head to London, posing as father and son, where they live in increasingly depressed surroundings while Michael tries painfully to make them into a real family. Based on the novel by MacLaverty, who also wrote the screenplay. **110m/C; VHS, DVD.** *IR* Liam Neeson; Hugh O'Conor; Ian Bannen; Frances Tomelty; ***D:*** Colin Gregg; ***W:*** Bernard MacLaverty; ***C:*** Mike Garfath; ***M:*** Van Morrison.

Lamb 1/2 **2016 (R)** A drama about a life-changing journey, based on a novel by Bonnie Nadzam. David Lamb (Partridge) is at a stressful place in his life after the death of his father and the end of his marriage. Trying to find meaning within himself, he tries to improve the fate of an 11-year-old year who does not seem to fit in, Tommie (Laurence). To better Tommie's view of the world, he takes her on a road trip west from Chicago. While he intends to show her the beauty of the wilderness, the journey comes with unexpected results. **97m/C; DVD, Streaming, Download.** Ross Partridge; Oona Laurence; Jess Weixler; Tom Bower; Scoot McNairy; ***D:*** Ross Partridge; ***W:*** Ross Partridge; ***C:*** Nathan M. Miller; ***M:*** Daniel Belardinelli.

Lambada **1989 (PG)** By day, he's a high school teacher in Beverly Hills; by night, a Latin dirty dancer cum tutor of ghetto teens. The very first of several films based on the short-lived dance craze. **92m/C; VHS, DVD.** J. Eddie Peck; Melora Hardin; Adolfo "Shabba Doo" Quinones; Ricky Paull Goldin; Basil Hoffman; Dennis Burkley; ***D:*** Joel Silberg.

Lamerica **1995** Two Italian hustlers, Fiore (Placido) and his younger partner Gino (Lo Verso), head for poverty-stricken Albania in 1991, the first year after the collapse of the Communist dictatorship. They intend to set up a phony corporation and scam money from government grants but they need an Albanian figurehead. They find simple-minded, elderly Spiro (Di Mazzarelli), who's spent most of his life in prison camps, and stash him in an orphanage for safe keeping. Only when Spiro gets away, Gino heads out to find him and discovers some secrets about Spiro's past and just how the wily Albanians have been surviving. Italian with subtitles. **116m/C; VHS, DVD.** *IT* Enrico Lo Verso; Michele Placido; Carmelo Di Mazzarelli; Piro Milkani; ***D:*** Gianni Amelio; ***W:*** Gianni Amelio; Andrea Porporati; Alessandro Sermoneta; ***C:*** Luca Bigazzi; ***M:*** Franco Piersanti.

Lan Yu **2001** Lan Yu (Ye) is a young architecture student, newly arrived in Beijing in 1988. He's introduced to older businessman Hangdong (Jun) and the two become lovers, though Hangdong is chronically unfaithful and they become estranged. When Lan Yu participates in the demonstrations at Tiananmen Square, Hangdong goes looking for him and the two resume their affair, which continues to be rocky. Based on the anonymous novel "Beijing Story," published only on the Internet in 1997 in order to avoid Chinese censorship. Chinese with subtitles. **86m/C; VHS, DVD.** *CH* Hu Jun; Liu Ye; ***D:*** Stanley Kwan; ***W:*** Jimmy Ngai; ***C:*** Yang Tao; ***M:*** Zhang Yadong.

Lancelot of the Lake *Lancelot du Lac; The Grail; Le Graal* **1974** The Knights of the Round Table return to the court of King Arthur after a long, bloody, and fruitless search for the Holy Grail. Rivalries and jealousies debase the heroes as Lancelot struggles with his feelings for Arthur's Queen Guinevere. Austere acting but the film's rich visuals provide a sensuous air. French with subtitles. **85m/C; VHS, DVD.** *FR* Luc Simon; Laura Duke Condominas; Vladimir Antolek-Oresek; Humbert Balsan; Patrick Bernard; Arthur De Montalembert; ***D:*** Robert Bresson; ***W:*** Robert Bresson; ***C:*** Pasqualino De Santis; ***M:*** Philippe Sarde.

The Land 1/2 **2016 (R)** An inner-city drama set in Cleveland's hip-hop underground. For four teenagers—Cisco (Lendeborg), Junior (Arias), Boobie (Walker), and Patty Cake (Gavron)—believe that skateboarding will take lead to a better life for all of them. They skip school to practice, and even steal cars to get the money needed to finance their efforts. The four find themselves in danger when they become involved with a drug deal and end up crossing a crime leader (Emond). As a result, their friendships and their very lives are on the line. **102m/C; DVD, Streaming, Download.** Jorge Lendeborg, Jr.; Moises Arias; Rafi Gavron; Ezri Walker; Machine Gun Kelly; ***D:*** Steven Caple, Jr.; ***W:*** Steven Caple, Jr.; ***C:*** Steven Holleran; ***M:*** Jongnic Bontemps.

The Land Before Time **1988 (G)** Lushly animated children's film about five orphaned baby dinosaurs who band together and try to find the Great Valley, a paradise where they might live safely. Works same parental separation theme as Bluth's "American Tail." Charming, coy, and shamelessly tearjerking; producers included Steven Spielberg and George Lucas. **67m/C; VHS, DVD, Blu-Ray.** ***V:*** Pat Hingle; Helen Shaver; Gabriel Damon; Candice Houston; Burke Barnes; Judith Barsi; Will Ryan; ***D:*** Don Bluth; ***W:*** Stu Krieger; ***M:*** James Horner.

The Land Before Time 2: The Great Valley Adventure 1/2 **1994 (G)** Sequel to 1988's animated adventure finds dinsosaur pals Littlefoot, Cera, Ducky, Petrie, and Spike happily settled in the Great Valley. But their adventures don't stop as they chase two egg-stealing Struthiomimuses and retrieve an egg of unknown origin from the Mysterious Beyond. **75m/C; VHS, DVD.** ***V:*** Candy Hutson; Jeff Glenn Bennett; Kenneth Mars; Rob Paulsen; Scott McAfee; Heather Hogan; John Ingle; Linda Gary; ***D:*** John Loy; Roy Allen Smith; ***W:*** John Ludin; Dev Ross; ***M:*** Michael Tavera.

The Land Before Time 3: The Time of the Great Giving 🦴🦴 ½ **1995 (G)** Littlefoot and his pals try to find a new source of water when the Great Valley experiences a severe water shortage. **71m/C; VHS, DVD.** ***V:*** Scott McAfee; Candy Hutson; Heather Hogan; Jeff Glenn Bennett; Kenneth Mars; John Ingle; Rob Paulsen; Linda Gary; ***D:*** Roy Allen Smith; ***W:*** John Loy; Dev Ross; John Ludin; ***M:*** Michael Tavera.

The Land Before Time 4: Journey Through the Mists 🦴🦴 ½ **1996** The little dinosaurs travel through the land of the mists in search of a rejuvenation flower that can save the life of Litefoot's sick grandpa. **74m/C; VHS, DVD.** ***V:*** Scott McAfee; Candy Hutson; Heather Hogan; Jeff Glenn Bennett; Kenneth Mars; John Ingle; Rob Paulsen; Linda Gary; ***D:*** Roy Allen Smith; ***W:*** Dev Ross; ***M:*** Michael Tavera.

The Land Before Time 5: The Mysterious Island 🦴🦴 ½ **1997 (G)** When a swarm of insects devour all the plants in the Great Valley, the herds are forced to move. But with the adults fighting, Littlefoot and his pals go off on their own. They cross the Big Water to a mysterious island, which just happens to be the home of their old friend, the baby T-Rex, Chomper. And it's up to Chomper to protect his plant-eating friends from the island's meat-eaters, who look on the little band as dinner. **74m/C; VHS, DVD.** ***V:*** Jeff Glenn Bennett; Kenneth Mars; John Ingle; Rob Paulsen; Thomas Dekker; Aria Noelle Curzon; Miriam Flynn; Anndi McAfee; Brandon Lacroix; ***D:*** Charles Grosvenor; ***W:*** John Loy; ***M:*** Michael Tavera.

The Land Before Time 6: The Secret of Saurus Rock 🦴🦴 ½ **1998 (G)** Children's animated tale takes place in the age of the dinosaurs. In this sequel, Littlefoot and the rest of his dinosaur pals explore the myth of a mysterious lone dinosaur and accidentally set off a series of mishaps in the Great Valley. **77m/C; VHS, DVD.** ***V:*** Jeff Glenn Bennett; Nancy Cartwright; Aria Noelle Curzon; Thomas Dekker; Kris Kristofferson; Miriam Flynn; Kenneth Mars; Anndi McAfee; ***D:*** Charles Grosvenor; ***W:*** John Loy; Libby Hinson; ***M:*** Michael Tavera.

Land Before Time 7: The Stone of Cold Fire 🦴🦴 **2000 (G)** In the seventh installment of the popular kid's series, the young dinosaurs Littlefoot, Cera, Spike, Ducky, and Petrie go off in search of a meteor that only Littlefoot saw. Petrie's disreputable uncle Pterano eggs them on. The moral lessons are simple; the animation is bright; the story moves quickly. In short, the movie delivers exactly what its young fans want to see. The pidgin English dialog will be hard for adults to take. **75m/C; DVD.** ***V:*** Jeff Glenn Bennett; Anndi McAfee; Rob Paulsen; Thomas Dekker; Aria Noelle Curzon; ***D:*** Charles Grosvenor; ***W:*** Len Uhley.

Land Girls 🦴🦴 ½ **2009** Wartime cliches abound but this Brit miniseries has good casting and some juicy moments. The Women's Land Army was formed to place women on farms and in other jobs so men could fight in WWII. Annie, Bea, Joyce, and Nancy are all sent to work for wealthy, arrogant Lady Ellen and her more sympathetic husband, Lord Lawrence Hoxley. There are class clashes, affairs, a pregnancy, and other mischief as the women learn to respect and depend on each other. **223m/C; DVD.** *GB* Christine Bottomley; Jo Woodcock; Becci Gemmell; Summer Strallen; Nathaniel Parker; Sophie Ward; Liam Boyle; Mark Benton; Nicholas Shaw; Danny (Daniel) Webb; Susan Cookson; ***D:*** Paul Gibson; Steve Hughes; ***W:*** Roland Moore; ***C:*** Andy Payne; Chris Preston; ***M:*** Debbie Wiseman. **TV**

Land Ho! 🦴🦴 ½ **2014** Outgoing Mitch (Nelson) convinces his mild-mannered ex-brother-in-law Colin (Eenhorn) that the two gentlemen need a vacation. They head to, of all places, Iceland, hitting some local bars, wandering the hills, and generally enjoying their unique road trip. The men make the journey a worthwhile one through their sheer charisma and one wishes there were more comedies that starred people old enough to be grandparents (in which that wasn't the whole joke). But this one spins its wheels a bit too much after a hysterical opening act. When it's funny, it's very funny, but unfortunately it's also forgettable. **96m/C; DVD, Blu-Ray.** *US IC* Paul Eenhoorn; Earl Lynn Nelson; Karrie Crouse; Elizabeth Mckee; ***D:*** Martha Stephens; Aaron Katz; ***W:*** Martha Stephens; Aaron Katz; ***C:*** Andrew Reed; ***M:*** Keegan DeWitt.

Land of Death 🦴 ½ *Cannibal Ferox 3: Land of Death; Cannibal Holocaust 3: Cannibal vs. Commando; Nella terra dei cannibali* **2003 (R)** A group of commandoes heads out into the jungle to rescue the daughter of a General who has been kidnapped by a cannibal tribe. Fans of 'Predator' and 'Cannibal Holocaust' will have a sense of deja vu as the movie liberally borrows from both movies—even some of the same lines. **93m/C; DVD.** Claudio Morales; Lou Randall; Cindy Jelic Matic; Yadalia Suarez; Silvio Jimenez; Sanit Larrauri; Kenny Krall; ***D:*** Bruno Mattei; ***W:*** Bruno Mattei; Gianni Paolucci; ***C:*** Luis Ciccarese.

Land of Doom 🦴 **1984** An amazon and a warrior struggle for survival in a post-holocaust fantasy setting. **87m/C; VHS, Streaming.** Deborah Rennard; Garrick Dowhen; ***D:*** Peter Maris.

The Land of Faraway 🦴🦴 *Mio in the Land of Faraway* **1987 (G)** A Swedish boy is whisked off to a magical land where he does battle with evil knights and flies on winged horses. Dubbed; based on a novel by Astrid Lindgren. **95m/C; VHS, DVD.** Timothy Bottoms; Christian Bale; Susannah York; Christopher Lee; Nicholas Pickard; ***D:*** Vladimir Grammatikov.

Land of Fury 🦴🦴 *The Seekers* **1955** British naval officer Hawkins steps on New Zealand's shore and into trouble when he accidently walks on sacred Maori burial ground. Very British, very dated colonial saga, based on the novel "The Seekers" by John Guthrie. **90m/C; DVD.** *UK* Jack Hawkins; Glynis Johns; Noel Purcell; Ian Fleming; ***D:*** Ken Annakin.

Land of Mine 🦴🦴 ½ *Under sandet* **2015 (R)** World War II ended in 1945 but much of Europe was not only reduced to rubble rather pockmarked with land mines. In Denmark, the victorious Allies used German POWs to remove an amazing 2.2 million Axis mines from the beaches of the West coast to make them safe again. These young German soldiers are forced to do something terrifying and life-risking, but the soldiers end up befriending them and protecting them from harm. What will happen when the mines are cleared? The symbolism for the damaging, dangerous world that exists after the end of a war is a strong one. **100m/C; DVD.** *DK GE* Roland Moller; Louis Hofmann; Joel Basman; Mikkel Boe Folsgaard; Emil Belton; ***D:*** Martin Zandvliet; ***W:*** Martin Zandvliet; ***C:*** Camilla Hjelm; ***M:*** Sune Martin.

Land of Plenty 🦴🦴 **2004** Director Wenders takes on some post-9/11 angst in this well-meaning digital video feature. Lana (Williams), the daughter of missionaries, arrives in LA after living in the Middle East. She takes a job at a homeless shelter while searching for her long-estranged Uncle Paul (Diehl). Paul, a troubled Vietnam vet, has become a self-appointed homeland security expert—traveling the streets in a van filled with surveillance equipment. The two finally meet, and bond, over their mutual sense of helplessness and confusion. **119m/C; DVD.** Michelle Williams; John Diehl; Shaun Toub; Wendell Pierce; Richard Edson; Burt Young; Gloria Stuart; Bernie (Bernard) White; ***D:*** Wim Wenders; ***W:*** Wim Wenders; Michael Meredith; ***C:*** Franz Lustig; ***M:*** Thomas Hanreich.

Land of Promise 🦴🦴 ½ *Ziemia Obiecana* **1974** At the turn of the century three men build a textile factory in Lodz, Poland. They each represent a particular ethnic group: a Pole (Olbrychski), a German (Seweryn), and a Jew (Pszoniak). Class conflicts threaten to overwhelm as their overworked and underpaid workers plan a revolt. Based on the novel by Wladyslav Reymont. In Polish with English subtitles. **178m/C; VHS, DVD.** *PL* Daniel Olbrychski; Wojciech Pszoniak; Andrzej Seweryn; Anna Nehrebecka; ***D:*** Andrzej Wajda; ***W:*** Andrzej Wajda; ***M:*** Wojciech Kilar.

The Land of Steady Habits 🦴🦴 **2018** Ben Mendelsohn (the actor, not his character) is the only bright spot in a messy, depressing story about midlife and bad choices. He plays Anders Hill, a successful professional who quits his job and leaves his wife and 27-year-old son to pursue happiness on his own terms, which evidently involve drugs, random sex, and condo-living...all of which would be fine if they brought him the happiness he craved. This adaptation of Ted Thompson's novel doesn't feature redemption or character development, just a badly scored bummer of a story. **98m/C; Streaming.** Ben Mendelsohn; Edie Falco; Thomas Mann; Connie Britton; Natalie Gold; ***D:*** Nicole Holofcener; ***W:*** Nicole Holofcener; ***C:*** Alar Kivilo; ***M:*** Marcelo Zarvos. **TV**

Land of the Blind 🦴 **2006 (R)** Failed political satire about a revolution set in an unknown time and a nameless country. Thorne (Sutherland) is a leftist rebel leader who's imprisoned and tortured for his beliefs. But once the dictatorship is overthrown and Thorne assumes power, he becomes just as repressive as the old regime. Former jailer turned second-in-command Joe (Fiennes) realizes what a mistake he's made. Edwards' first feature is also an all-around mistake that even professionals like Fiennes and Sutherland can't salvage. **101m/C; DVD.** *GB* Ralph Fiennes; Donald Sutherland; Tom Hollander; Lara Flynn Boyle; Mark Warren; Camilla Rutherford; Mackenzie Crook; Jodhi May; ***D:*** Robert Edwards; ***W:*** Robert Edwards; ***C:*** Barbara Parkins; ***M:*** Guy Farley; Simon White; Doug Edwards.

Land of the Free 🦴🦴 **1998 (R)** Frank Jennings (Speakman) is the campaign manager for super-patriot Senate hopeful Aidan Carvell (a deliberately hammy Shatner). Then Jennings discovers his boss has big ambitions—he wants to take over the government as the head of a terrorist organization. **96m/C; VHS, DVD.** Jeff Speakman; William Shatner; Chris Lemmon; Charles Robinson; ***D:*** Jerry Jameson; ***W:*** Terry Cunningham; ***C:*** Ken Blakey. **VIDEO**

Land of the Lost 🦴 ½ **2009 (PG-13)** The humor certainly got lost somewhere in this loud, irritating reimaging of the 1970s Sid and Marty Krofft children's TV series. Disgraced paleontologist Rick Marshall's (Ferrell) research involves parallel universes. He manages to find himself in a primeval world, accompanied by winsome Holly (Friel) and goofy tour guide Will (McBride). They encounter the ape-like Chaka (Taccone) as well as the lizard Sleestaks, a very thirsty (and large) mosquito, and a T-Rex that constantly torments Rick. Ferrell is game as usual but his shtick is tired. **93m/C; Blu-Ray, On Demand.** Will Ferrell; Anna Friel; Danny McBride; Jorma Taccone; John Boylan; Matt Laurer; ***D:*** Brad Silberling; ***W:*** Dennis McNicholas; Chris Henchy; ***C:*** Dion Beebe; ***M:*** Michael Giacchino. Golden Raspberries '09: Worst Remake.

Land of the Minotaur 🦴🦴 *The Devil's Men* **1977 (PG)** Small village is the setting for horrifying ritual murders, demons, and disappearances of young terrorists. Fans of Pleasence and Cushing won't want to miss this. **88m/C; VHS, DVD.** *GB* Donald Pleasence; Peter Cushing; Luan Peters; ***D:*** Costa Carayiannis; ***M:*** Brian Eno.

Land of the Pharaohs 🦴🦴 ½ **1955** Epic about the building of Egypt's Great Pyramid. Hawkins is the extremely talkative pharoah and Collins plays his sugary-sweet yet villainous wife. Sort of campy, but worth watching for the great surprise ending. **106m/C; DVD.** Jack Hawkins; Joan Collins; James Robertson Justice; Dewey Martin; Alexis Minotis; Syd Chaplin; ***D:*** Howard Hawks; ***W:*** Harold Jack Bloom; ***C:*** Lee Garmes.

Land Raiders 🦴🦴 **1969** Savalas plays a man who hates Apaches and wants their land, but is distracted when his brother arrives on the scene, igniting an old feud. **101m/C; VHS, DVD.** Telly Savalas; George Maharis; Arlene Dahl; Janet Landgard; ***D:*** Nathan "Jerry" Juran.

The Land That Time Forgot 🦴🦴 **1975 (PG)** A WWI veteran, a beautiful woman, and their German enemies are stranded in a land outside time filled with prehistoric creatures. Based on the 1918 novel by Edgar Rice Burroughs. Followed in 1977 by "The People that Time Forgot." **90m/C; VHS, DVD, Blu-Ray.** *GB* Doug McClure; John McEnery; Susan Penhaligon; Keith Barren; Anthony Ainley; Godfrey James; Bobby Parr; Declan Mulholland; Colin Farrell; Ben Howard; Roy Holder; Andrew McCulloch; Ron Pember; Steve James; ***D:*** Kevin Connor; ***W:*** James Cawthorn; Michael Moorcock; ***C:*** Alan Hume; ***M:*** Douglas Gamley.

The Land That Time Forgot 🦴🦴 **2009** Two newlywed couples are enjoying a charter boat cruise through the Caribbean when they are caught in a bizarre storm. The boat emerges offshore of the island of Caprona, which apparently exists in its own time zone inside the Bermuda Triangle. The charter boat captain and the newlyweds discover they aren't the only ones who have been pulled through time: there's also the crew of a WWII German U-Boat and the island is filled with dinosaurs and other prehistoric creatures. Based on the Edgar Rice Burroughs adventure fantasy. **90m/C; DVD.** C. Thomas Howell; Timothy Bottoms; Lindsey McKeon; Darren Dalton; Anya Benton; Stephen Blackehart; Chris Showerman; Patrick Gorman; Scott Subiono; ***D:*** C. Thomas Howell; ***W:*** Darren Dalton; ***C:*** Mark Atkins; ***M:*** Chris Ridenhour. **VIDEO**

The Land Unknown 🦴🦴 ½ **1957** A Naval helicopter is forced down in a tropical land of prehistoric terror, complete with ferocious creatures from the Mesozoic Era. While trying to make repairs, the crew discovers the sole survivor of a previous expedition who was driven to madness by life in the primordial jungle. Good performances from cast, although monsters aren't that believable. Based on a story by Charles Palmer. **78m/B; VHS, DVD, Blu-Ray.** Jock Mahoney; Shawn Smith; William Reynolds; Henry (Kleinbach) Brandon; Douglas Kennedy; ***D:*** Virgil W. Vogel; ***W:*** Laszlo Gorog; ***M:*** Henry Mancini.

The Landlady 🦴 **1998 (R)** Melanie Leroy (Shire) kills her hubby after discovering him cheating on her. When she becomes the landlady of an apartment house, she decides one of her tenants, nice-guy Patrick (Coleman), would be ideal husband material. And Melanie intends to get rid of any obstacles in her way. **98m/C; VHS, DVD.** Talia Shire; Jack Coleman; Bruce Weitz; Melissa Behr; Susie Singer; Bette Ford; ***D:*** Rob Malenfant; ***W:*** Frank Rehwaldt; George Saunders; ***C:*** Darko Suvak; ***M:*** Eric Lundmark.

Landline 🦴🦴 ½ **2017 (R)** A dramedy about romantic and familial relationships set, for no particular reason, in the 1990s. When younger sister Ali (Quinn) discovers her dad's love poems to an unknown woman, she bonds with her older sister (who's experiencing her own bout of infidelity) to find out what he's up to, all while shielding their mom from their suspicions. Well-acted and funny at times, thanks mostly to the always adorable Slate, but writer/director Robespierre asks us to care about characters that are flawed to the point of unlikeability. **97m/C; DVD.** Jenny Slate; Edie Falco; Abby Quinn; John Turturro; Jay Duplass; ***D:*** Gillian Robespierre; ***W:*** Gillian Robespierre; Elisabeth Holm; ***C:*** Chris Teague; ***M:*** Chris Bordeaux; Jordan Cohen; Clyde Lawrence.

The Landlord 🦴🦴 **1970** Film editor Ashby's first directorial effort is a countercultural satire. Indulged, 29-year-old Elgar Enders (Bridges) decides living on Long Island with his wealthy, conservative parents (Grant, Brooke) is a drag so he buys a Brooklyn tenement. He intends to evict the black tenants and remodel the place into his own swinging bachelor pad, but then he feels some white guilt, gets to see them as—you know—real people, and has a change of heart. Adapted from the Kristin Hunter novel. **112m/C; DVD, Blu-Ray.** Beau Bridges; Lee Grant; Pearl Bailey; Diana Sands; Louis Gossett, Jr.; Marki Bey; Mel Stewart; Douglas Grant; Walter Brooke; Susan Anspach; Robert Klein; ***D:*** Hal Ashby; ***W:*** Bill Gunn; ***C:*** Gordon Willis; ***M:*** Al Kooper.

Landscape After Battle 🦴🦴 *Krajobraz Po Bitwie* **1970** A group of concentration camp survivors are awaiting repatriation in a disused barracks in a German stalag in 1945. Among them are young Poles, Nina and Tadeusz, who fall in love. But tragedy continues when Nina is accidentally killed by an American guard. Based on the stories of Tadeusz Borowski, an Auschwitz survivor who later committed suicide. Polish with subtitles. **101m/C; DVD.** *PL* Daniel Olbrychski; Stanislawa Celinska; Tadeusz Janczar; ***D:*** Andrzej Wajda; ***W:*** Andrzej Wajda; Andrzej Brzozowski; ***C:*** Zygmunt Samosiuk; ***M:*** Zygmunt Konieczny.

Landscape in the Mist *Topio Stin Omichli* **1988** A stark Greek landscape in a rainy winter sets the scene for a tragic search by two children for their unknown father. Relies heavily on symbolism to make its point about unfulfilled desire (including the film's imaginary German-Greek border). In Greek with English subtitles. **126m/C; VHS, DVD.** *GR FR IT* Tania Palaiologou; Michalis Zeke; Stratos Tzortzoglou; Eva Kotamanidou; Aliki Georgouli; ***D:*** Theo Angelopoulos; ***W:*** Thanassis Valtinos; Tonino Guerra; Theo Angelopoulos; ***C:*** Yorgos Arvanitis; ***M:*** Eleni Karaindrou.

Landspeed 1/2 2001 (PG-13) A $50 million prize is offered to any racing team capable of breaking the land speed record of 1,000 miles per hour. Six of the world's top racing drivers and their teams volunteer to race the rocket cars that have been made for the attempt. It's helpful to forget your knowledge of physics. **94m/C; DVD.** Billy Zane; Ray Wise; Pamela Gidley; Scott Wiper; Val Lauren; G.W. Stevens; Simon Rhee; Adam Caine; Dylan Neal; Chad S. Taylor; Robert Zachar; Amanda Reyne; Greg Travis; Paul Butcher; Jamie McShane; Jeanette O'Connor; William Zabka; Stevie Blue Lolan; Amanda Collins; Morgan Lenz; Christian McIntire; Marc McClure; ***D:*** Christian McIntire; ***W:*** Micheal Baldwin; ***C:*** Todd Barron; ***M:*** Rich McHugh.

Language of the Enemy *A House Divided* **2007 (R)** Culture clash doomed love drama has lapsed Jew Romi Meir returning to Jerusalem after learning of his father's death in a terrorist bombing. Reuniting with his tough mother Rebecca, Romi is persuaded to join an Israeli operation to go after Palestinian forces in Ramallah. He runs into trouble and has to rely on young Arab doctor Joleh Kahlid for help. English and Arabic with subtitles. **105m/C; DVD.** Eion Bailey; Linda Hardy; Tovah Feldshuh; F. Murray Abraham; ***D:*** Mitch Davis; ***W:*** Mitch Davis; ***C:*** David Burr; ***M:*** Kevin Kiner.

L'Annee Sainte 1/2 *Pilgrimage to Rome; Holy Year* **1976** In his last film, Gabin is an escaped convict returning to his hidden loot in Rome when his plane is hijacked by international terrorists. Available dubbed. **85m/C; VHS, DVD.** *FR* Jean Gabin; Jean-Claude Brialy; Paul(o) Giusti; Danielle Darrieux; ***D:*** Jean Girault; ***W:*** Louis-Emile Galey; Jacques Vilfrid; ***C:*** Guy Suzuki; ***M:*** Claude Bolling.

Lansdown 1/2 2001 Flat attempt at a neo-noir/crime comedy. Jake (Sheilds) is a bland criminal defense attorney in the fictitious New Jersey title town. His wife Lexi (Carlson) is bored and has been fooling around with roofer Pat (Stewart). When Jake finds out, he decides he wants the lover dead but can't get his former client Gustav (Warren)--who provided the info on the infidelity—to do the hit himself. Instead, Gustav subcontracts to a couple of doofus hit men, who botch it. So Jake is forced to get more personally involved. **80m/C; VHS, DVD.** Adam Fidusiewicz; Paul Shields; Jennifer Carlson; Chris Stewart; D.W. Warren; Patrick Louis; Chris Baran; Marc Krinsky; ***D:*** Tom Zuber; ***W:*** Tom Zuber; ***C:*** Ty Bolia; ***M:*** Atli Ovarsson.

Lansky 1/2 1999 (R) Traces some 70 years in the life of Jewish mobster Meyer Lansky (Dreyfuss), which, surprisingly, doesn't make for exciting drama. Lansky grew up on New York's Lower East Side with Benjamin "Bugsy" Siegel (Roberts) and Charlie "Lucky" Luciano (LaPaglia). Th trio would mastermind a crime syndicate, with Lansky basically serving as the Mob accountant. Story is told in flashbacks as the aged Lansky awaits federal trial in Miami. **120m/C; VHS, DVD.** Richard Dreyfuss; Eric Roberts; Anthony LaPaglia; Illeana Douglas; Beverly D'Angelo; Ryan Merriman; Francis Guinan; Stanley DeSantis; Nick(y) Corello; ***D:*** John McNaughton; ***W:*** David Mamet; ***C:*** John A. Alonzo; ***M:*** George S. Clinton. **CABLE**

Lantana 2001 (R) Impressive Aussie thriller starts off as a seemingly straightforward murder mystery but becomes complicated. Investigating cop Leon (LaPaglia) is cheating on his wife with Jane (Blke), who may know something about the case. His wife is seeing psychiatrist Valerie (Hershey), whose marriage to John (Rush) is damaged by the murder of their young daughter. Jane's neighbors, Nik (Colosimo) and Paula (Farinacci), seem happy, but they're also touched by the mystery. LaPaglia stands out in a brilliant cast, and the deep character studies add dimension to what could have been a standard whodunit. **120m/C; DVD.** *AU* Anthony LaPaglia; Kerry Armstrong; Geoffrey Rush; Barbara Hershey; Rachael Blake; Vince Colosimo; Peter Phelps; Daniela Farinacci; Leah Purcell; Glenn Robbins; ***D:*** Ray Lawrence; ***W:*** Andrew Bovell; ***C:*** Mandy Walker; ***M:*** Paul Kelly. Australian Film Inst. '01: Actor (LaPaglia), Actress (Armstrong), Adapt. Screenplay, Director (Lawrence), Film, Support. Actor (Colosimo), Support. Actress (Blake).

Lap Dancing WOOF! 1995 (R) What hath "Showgirls" wrought? Small town gal Angie Parker moves to Hollywood to become an actress and, when the money runs out, winds up as an exotic dancer. Also available unrated. **90m/C; VHS, DVD.** Lorissa McComas; Tane McClure; C.T. Miller; ***D:*** Mike Sedan; ***W:*** K.C. Martin; ***C:*** Carlos Montaner; ***M:*** Ron Allen; Todd Schroeder. **VIDEO**

L.A.P.D.: To Protect and Serve 2001 Hey, Hopper is actually a good guy in this police corruption drama! He's a captain determined to weed out a group of bad apples in the department. **98m/C; VHS, DVD.** Dennis Hopper; Michael Madsen; Charles Durning; Marc Singer; ***D:*** Ed Anders; ***W:*** Rob Neighbors; ***C:*** Michael Balery. **VIDEO**

L'Appat *Fresh Bait; Live Bait; The Bait* **1994** Deglamourizing look at amoral teens and violence. 18-year-old salesgirl Nathalie (Gillain) supports her boyfriend Eric (Sitruk) and his dim-bulb buddy Bruno (Putzulu). After watching too many gangster videos, the wannabes decide to get rich by dangling Nathalie as sexual bait. She goes to a man's home that Eric and Bruno will then rob, but their plan goes awry when their first victim is killed. What's truly disturbing is the trio's blase attitude that crime is a viable way to live or that anything will happen to them if they're caught. Based on Morgan Sportes book, which recounted the actual 1984 crime. French with subtitles. **117m/C; VHS, DVD.** *FR* Marie Gillain; Olivier Sitruk; Bruno Putzulu; Philippe Duclos; Richard Berry; ***D:*** Bertrand Tavernier; ***W:*** Bertrand Tavernier; Colo Tavernier O'Hagan; ***M:*** Philippe Haim. Berlin Intl. Film Fest. '94: Film.

Lara Croft: Tomb Raider *Tomb Raider* **2001 (PG-13)** Laura Croft (Jolie), the daughter of a British aristocrat/adventurer (Jolie's real-life dad Voight), gives up her upper-crusty life to hunt down ancient treasures that hold the key to controlling time before they fall into the wrong hands. Sounds straightforward enough, right? But too much tinkering results in a muddled story and foggy details that do divert your attention away from the cheesy dialogue and flimsy characters. Stunning sets and visuals, along with Jolie's "let's have some fun" attitude go a long way toward making this disappointment more entertaining than it probably should be. **96m/C; DVD, Blu-Ray, UMD, HD-DVD.** Angelina Jolie; Iain Glen; Daniel Craig; Leslie Phillips; Jon Voight; Noah Taylor; Richard Johnson; Julian Rhind-Tutt; Chris (Christopher) Barrie; ***D:*** Simon West; ***W:*** Patrick Massett; John Zinman; ***C:*** Peter Menzies, Jr.; ***M:*** Graeme Revell.

Lara Croft Tomb Raider: The Cradle of Life 1/2 2003 (PG-13) Arguably better than its predecessor, sequel has Croft (Jolie) searching for Pandora's box: a mythical container allegedly containing unfathomable evils. Lara must outsmart the diabolical Dr. Reiss (Hinds) who wants to use it to wipe out all humanity save the few he would rule over. With her hunky Scottish ex (Butler) in tow, the quest takes the pillow-lipped raider on an undersea adventure in Greece and other exotic locales. Jolie injects Lara with more character, while the plethora of action scenes and special effects are deftly directed by De Bont, though less noisy scenes lack luster. **116m/C; VHS, DVD, Blu-Ray, UMD.** Angelina Jolie; Gerard Butler; Ciaran Hinds; Til Schweiger; Djimon Hounsou; Noah Taylor; ***D:*** Jan De Bont; ***W:*** Dean Georgaris; ***C:*** David Tattersall; ***M:*** Alan Silvestri.

The Laramie Project 2002 (R) A docudrama that explores the 1998 gay-bashing death of Matthew Shepard in Laramie, Wyoming. Shortly after the crime, Moises Kaufman (here played by Carbonell) and members of his New York Tectonic Theater Project arrived in Laramie to interview residents and others associated with the crime. Kaufman then adapted the transcripts into a stage piece, which debuted in Denver. Kaufman himself directs the film adaptation, which includes actual news footage interspersed with actor re-creations. **87m/C; VHS, DVD.** Nestor Carbonell; Peter Fonda; Amy Madigan; Janeane Garofalo; Jeremy Davies; Steve Buscemi; Christina Ricci; Mark Webber; Laura Linney; Terry Kinney; ***D:*** Moises Kaufman; ***W:*** Moises Kaufman; ***C:*** Terry Stacey; ***M:*** Peter Golub. **CABLE**

Larceny in her Heart 1/2 1946 Private eye Michael Shayne (Beaumont) is asked to track down the missing stepdaughter of a local bigwig. Shayne figures out that the stepdaughter has been committed to an asylum, presumably by the bigwig who purports to be searching for her. Then Shayne's client shows up dead and the mystery deepens. **68m/B; DVD.** Hugh Beaumont; Cheryl Walker; Ralph Dunn; Charles C. Wilson; Douglas Fowley; ***D:*** Sam Newfield; ***W:*** Brett Halliday; Raymond L. Schrock; ***C:*** Jack Greenhalgh; ***M:*** Leo Erdody.

Larceny, Inc. 1/2 1942 Maxwell (Robinson) and pal Martin (Crawford) are released from Sing Sing and plan to open a dog track but their partner Davis (Brophy) has lost their bankroll. Maxwell reluctantly agrees to a bank job planned by fellow prisoner Dexter (Quinn) that involves buying the luggage shop next door to the bank and digging a tunnel, but Maxwell is dumbfounded when the store is a success. Thinking his partners are getting cold feet, Dexter escapes to oversee the operation himself. Robinson's last contract film for Warner Bros. **95m/B; DVD.** Edward G. Robinson; Broderick Crawford; Anthony Quinn; Edward Brophy; Jane Wyman; Jack Carson; Harry Davenport; John Qualen; ***D:*** Lloyd Bacon; ***W:*** Everett Freeman; Edwin Gilbert; ***C:*** Gaetano Antonio "Tony" Gaudio; ***M:*** Adolph Deutsch.

L'Argent *Money* **1983** When a young man's parents refuse to lend him any money a friend helps out by giving him a counterfeit 500-franc note. This sets off a chain of events, with every passing of the money leading to another lie, betrayal, and increasingly violent crime. Austere and stylized vision is not for all tastes. In French with English subtitles. **82m/C; VHS, DVD.** *FR* Christian Patey; Sylvie van den Elsen; Michel Briguet; Caroline Lang; ***D:*** Robert Bresson; ***W:*** Robert Bresson; ***C:*** Pasqualino De Santis. Cannes '83: Director (Bresson); Natl. Soc. Film Critics '84: Director (Bresson).

Larger Than Life 1/2 *Nickel and Dime; Large as Life* **1996 (PG)** The pitch for this movie (Murray takes an elephant on a cross-country trip) must have sounded terrific. Murray is his usual smarmy self as cut-rate motivational speaker Jack Corcoran, who inherits the pachyderm and a pile of bills after his circus clown father dies. Following the road movie formula, he encounters wacky characters along the way, including a speed-freak trucker (McConaughey), a sexy animal trainer (Fiorentino) and a strait-laced zookeeper (Garofalo). Elephant Tal previously starred in "Operation Dumbo Drop." **93m/C; VHS, DVD, Blu-Ray.** Bill Murray; Janeane Garofalo; Linda Fiorentino; Matthew McConaughey; Keith David; Pat Hingle; Jeremy Piven; Lois Smith; Anita Gillette; Maureen Mueller; Harve Presnell; Tracey Walter; ***D:*** Howard Franklin; ***W:*** Roy Blount, Jr.; ***C:*** Elliot Davis; ***M:*** Miles Goodman.

The Lark Farm *La Masseria delle Allodole* **2007** Sprawling drama about the 1915-17 Armenian genocide that surprisingly gets away from the usually deft writer/director Taviani brothers. The wealthy Armenian Avakian family ignores the nasty rhetoric coming from Istanbul's Turkish government and heads to their country estate. When a Turkish military detachment arrives, there are shocking acts of violence, a march across the Syrian desert, and some rather unconvincing survival situations. Italian with subtitles. **122m/C; DVD.** *IT* Paz Vega; Arsinee Khanjian; Aram Avakian; Moritz Bleibtreu; Angela Molina; Muhamad (Mohammed) Bakri; Andre Dussollier; Alessandro Preziosi; ***D:*** Paolo Taviani; Vittorio Taviani; ***W:*** Paolo Taviani; Vittorio Taviani; ***C:*** Giuseppe Lanci; ***M:*** Giuliano Taviani.

Larry Crowne 1/2 2011 (PG-13) Hanks offered a triple-threat as he co-wrote and starred in his second directorial effort, but it's an insipid, cutesy pic that wastes its cast in cliches. After being downsized, debt-ridden, affable, middle-aged Larry (Hanks) feels directionless. So he enrolls in community college, bonds with some fellow students, and gets interested in his brittle-but-attractive (and unhappily married) public speech class teacher Mercedes (Roberts). **99m/C; DVD, Blu-Ray.** Tom Hanks; Julia Roberts; Cedric the Entertainer; Bryan Cranston; Taraji P. Henson; George Takei; Peter Scolari; Pam Grier; Ian Gomez; Wilmer Valderrama; Gugu Mbatha-Raw; Rita Wilson; ***D:*** Tom Hanks; ***W:*** Tom Hanks; Nia Vardalos; ***C:*** Philippe Rousselot; ***M:*** James Newton Howard.

Larry McMurtry's Dead Man's Walk 1/2 *Dead Man's Walk* **1996 (PG-13)** McMurtry's prequel to "Lonesome Dove" focuses on the teenaged Gus McCrae (Arquette) and Woodrow Call (Miller) and their first adventures as Texas Rangers in the 1840s. They're involved in the ill-fated Texas-Santa Fe Expedition, led by parrot-owning former seafarer Caleb Cobb (Abraham), to make New Mexico part of the Texas Republic. Instead, a Mexican Army detachment led by Capt. Salazar (Olmos), captures the rag-tag group, which is then forced to march across a deadly stretch of desert that few survive. Likeable leads but the supporting actors, including Carradine and Stanton as scouts, steal the show. **271m/C; VHS, DVD.** Jonny Lee Miller; David Arquette; Keith Carradine; Harry Dean Stanton; F. Murray Abraham; Edward James Olmos; Eric Schweig; Patricia Childress; Jennifer Garner; Haviland (Haylie) Morris; Brian Dennehy; Joaquim de Almeida; Ray McKinnon; Akosua Busia; ***D:*** Yves Simoneau; ***W:*** Larry McMurtry; Diana Ossana; ***C:*** Edward Pei; ***M:*** David Bell. **TV**

Larry McMurtry's Streets of Laredo *Lonesome Dove: Streets of Laredo* **1995** Texas Ranger-turned-bounty hunter Woodrow F. Call (a splendid Garner) is hired by the railroad to track down ruthless Mexican bandit Joey Garza (Cruz), pitting an old man's skills against a young man's daring, and driving both men deep into Mexican territory. Call's old friend Pea Eye Parker (Shepard) reluctantly comes along, with ex-prostitute Lorena (Spacek), now Parker's wife, and Maria (Braga), Joey's tough mom, providing strong support. Casual cruelty and violence are the norm in the sunset days of both Call's life and that of the west itself. Third in the TV sagas, following "Return to Lonesome Dove." **227m/C; VHS, DVD.** James Garner; Alexis Cruz; Sam Shepard; Sissy Spacek; Sonia Braga; Wes Studi; Randy Quaid; Charles Martin Smith; Kevin Conway; George Carlin; Ned Beatty; James Gammon; Tristan Tait; Anjanette Comer; ***D:*** Joseph Sargent; ***W:*** Larry McMurtry; Diana Ossana; ***C:*** Edward Pei; ***M:*** David Shire. **TV**

Larry the Cable Guy: Health Inspector WOOF! 2006 (PG-13) Gross-out comedy appealing to those who like flatulence, vomiting, and other sorts of intestinal distress. Blue-collar comedian Larry the Cable Guy is Larry the Florida health inspector guy, who suspects someone is deliberately causing the food poisoning epidemic that's hitting a number of upscale restaurants. So he goes undercover, along with his uptight partner Amy (Bahr), to find the culprit. Hilarity doesn't ensue. **89m/C; DVD.** Larry the Cable Guy; Joanna Cassidy; David Koechner; Thomas F. Wilson; Joe Pantoliano; Iris Bahr; Bruce Bruce; Brooke Dillman; Tony Hale; Lisa Lampanelli; Megyn Price; ***Cameo(s):*** Jerry Mathers; Kid Rock; ***D:*** Trent Cooper; ***W:*** Jon Bernstein; James Greer; ***C:*** Kim Marks; ***M:*** Steven R. Phillips; Tim P.

Lars and the Real Girl 1/2 2007 (PG-13) Lars (Gosling) is one of those sweetly awkward small-town loonies that movies are so fond of. He's a damaged soul who tries to avoid too much human contact, including from his well-meaning brother Gus (Schneider) and sister-in-law Karin (Mortimer). Then Lars buys a customized life-size sex doll (no, he's not a perv) online and begins introducing her as his girlfriend, Bianca. Family doctor Dagmar (Clarkson) persuades everyone to go along with Lars' delusion for the time being and Bianca is quickly integrated into the community. Fortunately, Gosling et al manage to sell this story without too much ick or schmaltz. **106m/C; Blu-Ray, On Demand.** Ryan Gosling; Paul Schneider; Emily Mortimer; Patricia Clarkson; Kelli Garner; Nancy Beatty; Karen Robinson; ***D:*** Nancy Oliver; ***W:*** Gerri Gillan; ***C:*** Adam Kimmel; ***M:*** David Torn.

Las Vegas Hillbillys 🦴 *Country Music* **1966** A pair of country-singing hillbillies inherit a saloon in Las Vegas and enjoy wine, moonshine, and song. These two make the Clampetts look like high society. Followed, believe it or not, by "Hillbillys in a Haunted House." **85m/C; VHS, DVD.** Mamie Van Doren; Jayne Mansfield; Ferlin Husky; Sonny James; ***D:*** Arthur C. Pierce.

Las Vegas Lady 🦴 **1976 (PG)** Three shrewd casino hostesses plot a multi-million dollar heist in the nation's gambling capital. Non-captivating caper. **90m/C; VHS, DVD.** Stella Stevens; Stuart Whitman; George Dicenzo; Andrew Stevens; Lynne Moody; Linda Scruggs; ***D:*** Noel Nosseck; ***W:*** Walter Dallenbach; ***C:*** Stephen M. Katz; ***M:*** Alan Silvestri.

Las Vegas Nights 🦴🦴 **1941** Three sisters, who have a vaudeville act, inherit a rundown building they decide to turn into a Vegas nightclub. But first they have to find the money to restore the property and outwit a crooked lawyer who has plans of his own. Frank Sinatra makes a brief film debut as the singer for Tommy Dorsey and His Orchestra. **90m/B; DVD.** Constance Moore; Lillian Cornell; Virginia Dale; Bert Wheeler; Phil Regan; Hank Ladd; ***D:*** Ralph Murphy; ***W:*** Ernest Pagano; Harry Clork; ***C:*** William Mellor; ***M:*** Louis Alter.

Las Vegas Serial Killer WOOF! 1986 A serial killer, let out of prison on a technicality, starts killing again. **90m/C; VHS, DVD.** Pierre Agostino; Ron Jason; Tara MacGowran; Kathryn Downey; ***D:*** Ray Dennis Steckler; ***W:*** Ray Dennis Steckler. **VIDEO**

Laser Mission 🦴🦴 ½ **1990** When it is discovered that the Soviets have laser weapon capabilities, an agent is given the task of destroying the weapon and kidnapping the scientist who developed it. **83m/C; VHS, DVD.** Brandon Lee; Debi Monahan; Ernest Borgnine; Werner Pochath; Graham Clarke; Maureen Lahoud; Pierre Knoessen; ***D:*** Beau Davis; ***M:*** David Knopfler.

Laser Moon 🦴🦴 **1992** A serial killer uses a surgical laser beam to kill his beautiful victims, and he strikes at every full moon. When he announces his next attack on a late-night radio talk show the police call in a beautiful rookie cop (Lords) to use as bait. **90m/C; VHS, DVD.** Traci Lords; Crystal Shaw; Harrison Leduke; Bruce Carter; ***D:*** Douglas K. Grimm.

Laserblast WOOF! 1978 (PG) Standard wimp-gets-revenge story in which a frustrated young man finds a powerful and deadly laser which was left near his home by aliens; upon learning of its devastating capabilities, his personality changes and he seeks revenge against all who have taken advantage of him. **87m/C; VHS, DVD, Blu-Ray.** Kim Milford; Cheryl "Rainbeaux" Smith; Keenan Wynn; Roddy McDowall; ***D:*** Michael Raeburn; ***W:*** Frank Ray Perilli; Franne Schacht; ***C:*** Terry Bowen; ***M:*** Richard Band; Joel Goldsmith.

Laserhawk 🦴 ½ **1999 (PG-13)** Now here's an interesting take on the origin of species—millions of years ago carnivorous aliens planted humans as a crop on earth. Now they've returned to harvest their goods and only a band of misfits may have a chance to save humanity if they can find one of the aliens' crashed spacecraft/weapons called a Laserhawk to use against them. **102m/C; VHS, DVD.** Mark Hamill; Jason James Richter; Gordon Currie; Melissa Galianos; ***D:*** Jean Pellerin; ***W:*** John A. Curtis. **VIDEO**

Lassie 🦴🦴 ½ **1994 (PG)** Everyone's favorite collie returns as the Turner family moves to Virginia's Shenandoah Valley to take up sheep ranching. However, because this is the '90s, Dad meets financial disaster, and junior can't stand his stepmom. Can Lassie meet the challenges of dysfunctional family living? "What is it girl? Call a therapist?" This Lassie is a direct descendant of Pal, the original 1943 star. **92m/C; VHS, DVD, Blu-Ray.** Helen Slater; Jon Tenney; Tom Guiry; Brittany Boyd; Richard Farnsworth; Frederic Forrest; Michelle Williams; ***D:*** Daniel Petrie; ***W:*** Matthew Jacobs; Gary Ross; Elizabeth Anderson; ***C:*** Kenneth Macmillan; ***M:*** Basil Poledouris.

Lassie 🦴🦴 ½ **2005 (PG)** Lassie goes back to her British roots (based on Eric Knight's 1938 novel) in this sentimental adventure. Young Joe (Mason) is heartbroken when Lassie must be sold because his miner father has lost his job. Lassie's new owner, the Duke of Rudling (O'Toole), has bought the photogenic collie for his granddaughter Cilla (Odgers), and both dog and girl are soon sent up to Scotland. Lassie's having none of it and escapes to start a 500-mile trek back to Yorkshire, surviving a number of trials along the way. Sweet yet realistic, with great performances throughout. **100m/C; DVD.** *US GB IR FR* Peter O'Toole; Samantha Morton; John Lynch; Peter Dinklage; Jonathan Mason; Steve Pemberton; Jemma Redgrave; Edward Fox; John Standing; Kelly Macdonald; Robert Hardy; Hester Odgers; ***D:*** Charles Sturridge; ***W:*** Charles Sturridge; ***C:*** Howard Atherton; ***M:*** Adrian Johnston.

Lassie, Come Home 🦴🦴 ½ **1943 (G)** In first of the Lassie series, the famed collie is reluctantly sold and makes a treacherous cross-country journey back to her original family. **90m/C; VHS, DVD.** Roddy McDowall; Elizabeth Taylor; Donald Crisp; Edmund Gwenn; May Whitty; Nigel Bruce; Elsa Lanchester; J. Pat O'Malley; ***D:*** Fred M. Wilcox. Natl. Film Reg. '93.

Lassie's Great Adventure 🦴🦴 ½ **1962** Lassie and her master Timmy are swept away from home by a runaway balloon. After they land in the Canadian wilderness, they learn to rely on each other through peril and adventure. **104m/C; VHS, DVD.** June Lockhart; Jon(athan) Provost; Hugh Reilly; ***D:*** William Beaudine; ***W:*** Charles "Blackie" O'Neal. **TV**

Lassiter 🦴🦴 ½ **1984 (R)** Selleck plays a jewel thief who is asked to steal diamonds from the Nazis for the FBI. Supporting cast adds value to what is otherwise a fairly ordinary adventure drama. **100m/C; VHS, DVD.** Tom Selleck; Jane Seymour; Lauren Hutton; Bob Hoskins; Joe Regalbuto; Ed Lauter; Warren Clarke; William Morgan Sheppard; ***D:*** Roger Young.

Last Action Hero 🦴🦴 **1993 (PG-13)** Danny Madigan (O'Brien) finds himself in a movie starring his idol Jack Slater, the kind of guy who never loses a fight and is impervious to gunfire and explosions (and he has a really cool car and a really big gun). Disappointing action/spoof of movies within a movie was critically maimed and never recovered. The concept has been done better before, though Ah-nold possesses his usual self-mocking charm. Look for lots of big stars in small roles and cameos as the script is cluttered with inside Hollywood gags. **131m/C; VHS, DVD, Blu-Ray.** Arnold Schwarzenegger; Austin O'Brien; Mercedes Ruehl; F. Murray Abraham; Charles Dance; Anthony Quinn; Robert Prosky; Tom Noonan; Frank McRae; Art Carney; Bridgette Wilson-Sampras; ***Cameo(s):*** Sharon Stone; Hammer; Chevy Chase; Jean-Claude Van Damme; Tori Spelling; Joan Plowright; Adam Ant; James Belushi; James Cameron; Tony Curtis; Timothy Dalton; Tony Danza; Edward Furlong; Little Richard; Damon Wayans; Robert Patrick; ***D:*** John McTiernan; ***W:*** David Arnott; Shane Black; ***C:*** Dean Semler; ***M:*** Michael Kamen.

The Last Adventure 🦴🦴 ½ *Les Aventuriers* **1967** Two friends find themselves swindled in an insurance scam and set out after the perpetrator who sent them off to Africa in search of a treasure. Available dubbed. **112m/C; VHS, DVD.** *FR* Alain Delon; Lino Ventura; Joanna Shimkus; ***D:*** Robert Enrico; ***W:*** Robert Enrico; ***C:*** Jean Boffety; ***M:*** Francois de Roubaix.

The Last Airbender 🦴 **2010 (PG)** This numbing, awkward fantasy won't break Shyamalan's dismal movie streak, and it's a strong disservice to the popular Nickelodeon anime series. The harmony of the Air Nomads, Water Tribes, and Earth Kingdoms is torn apart when the Fire Nation launches a 100 years war. Twelve-year-old Aang (newcomer Ringer) discovers he's the last of the avatars who can manipulate all four elements once he's had the proper training. The last minute conversion to 3D is negligible as the action is disappointing and the casting is flat. **103m/C; Blu-Ray, On Demand.** Noah Ringer; Nicola Peltz; Jackson Rathbone; Dev Patel; Aasif Mandvi; Clifford Curtis; Shaun Toub; Randall Duk Kim; Seychelle Gabriel; ***D:*** M. Night Shyamalan; ***W:*** M. Night Shyamalan; ***C:*** Andrew Lesnie; ***M:*** James Newton Howard. Golden Raspberries '10: Worst Director (Shyamalan), Worst Picture, Worst Screenplay, Worst Support. Actor (Rathbone).

The Last American Hero 🦴🦴🦴 *Hard Driver* **1973 (PG)** The true story of how former moonshine runner Junior Johnson became one of the fastest race car drivers in the history of the sport. Entertaining slice of life chronicling whiskey running and stock car racing, with Bridges superb in the lead. Based on a series of articles written by Tom Wolfe. **95m/C; VHS, DVD.** Jeff Bridges; Valerie Perrine; Gary Busey; Art Lund; Geraldine Fitzgerald; Ned Beatty; Ed Lauter; Lane Smith; Gregory Walcott; ***D:*** Lamont Johnson; ***W:*** William Roberts; ***M:*** Charles Fox.

Last American Virgin 🦴🦴 **1982 (R)** Usual brainless teen sex comedy about three school buddies who must deal with a plethora of problems in their search for girls who are willing. Music by Blondie, The Cars, The Police, The Waitresses, Devo, U2, Human League, and Quincy Jones. **92m/C; VHS, DVD, Blu-Ray.** Lawrence Monoson; Diane Franklin; Steve Antin; Louisa Moritz; ***D:*** Boaz Davidson; ***W:*** Boaz Davidson.

The Last Assassins 🦴🦴 *Dusting Cliff Seven* **1996 (R)** Ex-CIA agent Anne Bishop (Allen) is persuaded to reunite with former commander McBride (Henriksen) for another mission. Then she discovers he has his own agenda, but when Anne tries to get out, McBride kidnaps her daughter to ensure her cooperation. **90m/C; VHS, DVD.** Lance Henriksen; Nancy Allen; Floyd "Red Crow" Westerman; Dean Scofield; ***D:*** William H. Molina; ***W:*** William H. Molina; Jim Menza; Charles Philip Moore; Justin Stanley; ***C:*** William H. Molina; ***M:*** David Wurst; Eric Wurst. **VIDEO**

The Last Best Sunday 🦴🦴 **1998** Mexican-American Joseph (Spain) kills the two racist thugs who beat him and hides out in the isolated home of religiously brought up classmate Lolly (Bettis), whose parents are away for the weekend. Naturally, the teens bond and then they fall in love. Not quite as obvious as it all sounds. **101m/C; VHS, DVD.** Douglas Spain; Angela Bettis; Kim Darby; William Lucking; Marion Ross; Craig Wasson; Daniel Beer; ***D:*** Donny Most; ***W:*** Karen Kelly; ***C:*** Zoran Hochstatter; ***M:*** Tim Westergren.

The Last Best Year 🦴🦴 ½ **1990 (PG)** Basic TV tearjerker has lonely psychologist Wendy (Moore) befriending patient Jane (Peters), who has a terminal illness. **88m/C; VHS, DVD.** Mary Tyler Moore; Bernadette Peters; Brian Bedford; Dorothy McGuire; Kate Reid; Kenneth Welsh; ***D:*** John Erman; ***W:*** David W. Rintels.

The Last Black Man in San Francisco 🦴🦴🦴 **2019 (R)** Until the age of six, Jimmie (Fails) lived in a Victorian house in San Francisco's Fillmore District until his scheming father (Morgan) lost it. Now an adult, Jimmie lives with his best friend Mont (Majors) and Mont's grandfather (Glover). Jimmie spends his free time repairing the home his family lost, though its wealthy owners resent his trespassing. When the house is emptied again, Jimmie moves in with Mont and tries to retain the place that makes him feel most at home. A love letter to San Francisco, the film explores such topics as gentrification and black masculinity and friendship in moving, sometimes poetic, fashion. **120m/C; DVD, Blu-Ray.** Jimmie Fails; Jonathan Majors; Danny Glover; Tichina Arnold; Rob Morgan; ***D:*** Joe Talbot; ***W:*** Joe Talbot; Rob Richert; ***C:*** Adam Newport-Berra; ***M:*** Emile Mosseri.

The Last Boy Scout 🦴🦴 **1991 (R)** Are you ready for some gunplay? Formula thriller stars Willis as a private eye and Wayans as an ex-quarterback teaming up against a football team owner who will stop at nothing to get political backing for a bill promoting legalized gambling on sports. Another variation of the violent buddy-picture by "Lethal Weapon" screenwriter Black. **105m/C; VHS, DVD, Blu-Ray.** Bruce Willis; Damon Wayans; Halle Berry; Chelsea Field; Noble Willingham; Taylor Negron; Danielle Harris; Chelcie Ross; Bruce McGill; Morris Chestnut; Eddie Griffin; Kim Coates; Joe Santos; Tony Longo; Billy Blanks; Jack Kehler; Michael (Mike) Papajohn; ***D:*** Tony Scott; ***W:*** Shane Black; ***C:*** Ward Russell; ***M:*** Michael Kamen.

Last Breath 🦴🦴 *Lifebreath* **1996 (R)** Martin (Perry) is obsessively devoted to his dying wife, Chrystie (Swift), who needs a double lung transplant to survive. So Martin decides to romance lovely Gail (Carides)?with murder on his mind. Twisted ending. **90m/C; VHS, DVD, Blu-Ray.** Luke Perry; Gia Carides; Francie Swift; David Margulies; Lisa Gay Hamilton; Jack Gilpin; Matt McGrath; Hillary Bailey Smith; ***D:*** P.J. Posner; ***W:*** P.J. Posner; Joel Posner; ***C:*** Oliver Bokelberg; ***M:*** Michael Kessler. **VIDEO**

The Last Brickmaker in America 🦴🦴 ½ **2001 (PG)** For more than 50 years, Henry Cobb (Poitier) has worked in his family's brickyard, hand-making red clay bricks. With the death of his wife, the elderly man doesn't find much passion for his work anymore and feels hopeless until he meets troubled 13-year-old Danny (Potter). Danny's squabbling parents have separated and he needs a refuge and some mentoring, which Henry is willing to supply. **85m/C; DVD.** Sidney Poitier; Cody Newton; Piper Laurie; Bernie Casey; Jay O. Sanders; Wendy Crewson; Mert Hatfield; ***D:*** Gregg Champion; ***W:*** Richard Leder; ***C:*** Gordon C. Lonsdale; ***M:*** Joseph Conlan. **TV**

The Last Broadcast 🦴🦴🦴 **1998** Festival hit predates "The Blair Witch Project" in telling the story of a group of young people who go into the woods with video cameras and meet a grisly fate. But this one is much more complicated and ambitious. Directors Avalos and Weiler play public access cable TV show hosts who take a sound man (Clabbers) and a psychic (Seward) into the Pine Barrens for a live broadcast of their search for the legendary Jersey Devil. Only one comes out. A year later, a documentary filmmaker (Beard) and a video editor (Pulaski) try to find the truth of the matter. **87m/C; DVD.** Stefan Avalos; Lance Weiler; David Beard; Rein Clabbers; Michele Pulaski; ***D:*** Stefan Avalos; Lance Weiler; ***W:*** Stefan Avalos; Lance Weiler; ***C:*** Lance Weiler; ***M:*** Stefan Avalos.

The Last Butterfly 🦴🦴 **1992** Quiet Holocaust movie set in Theresienstadt, the Czechoslovak ghetto city used by the Nazis to persuade the outside world of their humane treatment of the Jews. Noted French mime Antoine Moreau (Courtenay) has fallen under suspicion by the Gestapo. He's "persuaded" to give a performance in Theresienstadt for the benefit of the visiting Red Cross but decides to subvert Nazi propaganda with his own version of "Hansel and Gretel." This time the witch feeds the children into her oven. Muted performances and screenplay (adapted from the Michael Jacot novel) heightened the film's surreal calmness. **106m/C; VHS, DVD.** *CZ* Tom Courtenay; Brigitte Fossey; Freddie Jones; Ingrid Held; Linda Jablonska; ***D:*** Karel Kachyna; ***W:*** Karel Kachyna; Ota Hofman; ***M:*** Alex North.

Last Cab to Darwin 🦴🦴🦴 **2016** A comedy-drama about the end of life set in Australia. Rex (Caton) has never left the mining town of Broken Hill in his life. When he learns he does not have live, the cab driver decides to journey to Darwin where he believes that he can die on his terms. Along the way, he discovers the importance of living before dying and sharing experiences as a key element of life. **123m/C; DVD, Blu-Ray.** Michael Caton; Ningali Lawford; Mark Coles Smith; Emma Hamilton; Jacki Weaver; ***V:*** Jeremy Sims; ***D:*** Jeremy Sims; ***W:*** Reg Cribb; ***C:*** Steve Arnold; ***M:*** Ed Kuepper.

Last Call 1990 (R) Clearly, Joe Sixpack won't rent this bimbo fest for its subtle plot. Katt, a mafiosi-cheated real estate guy, decides to even the score with the assistance of gal pal/playmate of the year Tweed, who's more than willing to compromise her position. Also features the talents of playboy emerita Stevens. Available in rated and unrated versions. **90m/C; VHS, DVD.** William Katt; Shannon Tweed; Joseph Campanella; Stella Stevens; Matt Roe; ***D:*** Jag Mundhra. **VIDEO**

Last Call: The Final Chapter of F. Scott Fitzgerald 1/2 2002 In 1939, aspiring writer Frances Kroll (Campbell) interviews for a secretarial position with F. Scott Fitzgerald (Irons). Alcoholic, in declining health, and haunted by images of his institutionalized wife Zelda (Spacek), Fitzgerald hasn't published in years. She becomes his confidante and Fitzgerald is inspired to stop drinking and begin work on his new novel—a scathing indictment of Hollywood (which will become the unfinished "The Last Tycoon"). Based on the memoir by Kroll Ring. **108m/C; VHS, DVD.** Jeremy Irons; Neve Campbell; Sissy Spacek; Natalie Radford; Shannon Lawson; Paul Hecht; ***D:*** Henry Bromell; ***W:*** Henry Bromell; ***C:*** Jeffrey Jur; ***M:*** Brian Tyler. **CABLE**

The Last Castle 1/2 2001 (R) Irwin (Redford), a legendary army officer, is sent to prison on a charge that isn't clear until well into the film. Prison warden Col. Winter (Gandolfini) clearly admires his new inmate until he begins to resent Irwin's influence over his fellow prisoners. As Winter notices his control slipping away, his punishments grow worse until Irwin leads an insurrection. Although driven by powerhouse performances by Redford and Gandolfini, too much time is spent on their battle of wills while some plotlines are dropped altogether. **133m/C; VHS, DVD.** Robert Redford; James Gandolfini; Mark Ruffalo; Delroy Lindo; Steve (Stephen) Burton; Paul Calderon; Samuel Ball; Clifton (Gonzalez) Collins, Jr.; Frank Military; George W. Scott; Brian Goodman; Michael Irby; Maurice Bullard; Jeremy Childs; Robin Wright; ***D:*** Rod Lurie; ***W:*** Graham Yost; David Scarpa; ***C:*** Shelly Johnson; ***M:*** Jerry Goldsmith.

The Last Challenge 1967 Director Richard Thorpe's final film is a serviceable western that pits a weathered gunslinger against a brash young upstart. Marshal Dan Blaine (Ford) tries to discourage Lot McGuire (Everett) from making his reputation by challenging Blaine to a shootout. Dan's girlfriend Lisa (Dickinson), who owns the saloon, just wants him to stay alive but her interference doesn't matter much in an underwritten role. **96m/C; DVD.** Glenn Ford; Chad Everett; Angie Dickinson; Gary Merrill; Jack Elam; Royal Dano; ***D:*** Richard Thorpe; ***W:*** Albert (John B. Sherry) Maltz; ***C:*** Ellsworth Fredericks; ***M:*** Richard Shores.

The Last Chance 1945 A realistic look at the efforts of three WWII Allied officers to help a group of refugees escape across the Alps from Italy to Switzerland. The officers are played by former pilots who were shot down over Switzerland. In spite of this—or perhaps because of it—the acting is superb. Watch for inspirational scene of refugees singing. **105m/B; VHS, DVD.** E.G. Morrison; John Hoy; Ray Reagan; Odeardo Mosini; Sigfrit Steiner; Emil Gerber; ***D:*** Leopold Lindtberg.

Last Chance 1/2 2007 Hitman Rob gets involved with a beautiful woman who turns out to have close ties to his latest target. Does Rob blow the hit or betray the woman he loves when his own life is on the line? **92m/C; DVD.** Kristof Robinson; Kate Potter; Bob Ferguson; Brandon Michaels; Ben Lawton; ***D:*** Benjamin Todd; ***W:*** Benjamin Todd. **VIDEO**

Last Chance Cafe 2006 Hallie (Vernon) flees L.A. with daughter Kiley (Amlee) after discovering that her retired cop stepfather was murdered for the info he gathered on some crooked cops and her dirty D.A. ex-husband Paul (Novak). She finds a new life and new friends in a rural community as well as a new love with rancher Chance Coulter (Sorbo) but the peaceful times don't last. Adapted from the Linda Lael Miller novel. **90m/C; DVD.** Kate Vernon; Kevin Sorbo; Samantha Ferris; Jessica Amlee; John Novak; Scott Hylands; ***D:*** Jorge Montesi; ***W:*** Pamela Wallace; ***C:*** Gordon Verheul; ***M:*** Hal Beckett. **CABLE**

Last Chance Harvey 1/2 2008 (PG-13) Just before flying to London for his daughter's wedding, Harvey (Hoffman) is canned from his jingle-writing job in NYC. Adding insult, his ex-wife (Baker) breaks the news that he won't be giving away the bride. Meanwhile, Kate (Thompson), an interviewer for a government agency in London, is having a tough time in the dating world. Of course fate brings the two together with Harvey behaving like a complete jerk who later attempts an apology. Poof, the magic begins. An endearing romance ensues as the two pros lift an otherwise forgettable story. **92m/C; Blu-Ray, On Demand.** Dustin Hoffman; Emma Thompson; Kathy Baker; James Brolin; Eileen Atkins; Richard Schiff; Liane Balaban; Michael Landes; ***D:*** Joel Hopkins; ***W:*** Joel Hopkins; ***C:*** John de Borman; ***M:*** Dickon Hinchliffe.

Last Chase 1/2 1981 (PG) Famed race car driver becomes a vocal dissenter against the sterile society that has emerged, in this drama set in the near future. Screenplay written by Christopher Crowe under the pseudonym C.R. O'Cristopher. **106m/C; VHS, DVD.** *CA* Lee Majors; Burgess Meredith; Chris Makepeace; Alexandra Stewart; ***D:*** Martyn Burke; ***W:*** Martyn Burke; Christopher Crowe. **TV**

Last Christmas 2019 (PG-13) Kate (Clarke) has aspirations of a stage career, but she is working at the Christmas-focused shop Yuletide Wonderful on a busy square in London. Though irresponsible Kate is perpetually late and makes bad decisions, the shop's owner, the self-named Santa (Yeoh), expects great things from her as does her immigrant family, including her hovering mother Petra (Thompson), hardworking father Ivan (Isakovic), and secret-keeping sister Marta (Leonard). Kate's perspective on life changes when she meets the mysterious, charming Tom (Golding). The joyless romantic comedy fails at becoming a holiday hit, though there is the George Michael-focused soundtrack. **102m/C; DVD, Blu-Ray.** Emilia Clarke; Henry Golding; Emma Thompson; Michelle Yeoh; Boris Isakovic; ***D:*** Paul Feig; ***W:*** Emma Thompson; Bryony Kimmings; ***C:*** John Schwartzman; ***M:*** Theodore Shapiro.

The Last Circus 1/2 *Balada Triste de Trompeta* 2010 (R) If you're attracted to the grotesque, demented, and blood-splattered, then de la Iglesia's allegorical circus pic is for you. Others will continue to find clowns creepy and perverted. The opening is set during the Spanish Civil War as Republican Army soldiers forcibly conscript circus performers to the Fascist cause. In 1973, revenge-minded Javier (AKA Sad Clown) joins a circus run by violent Sergio (AKA Happy Clown). Javier is enamored by trapeze artist Natalia, a masochist involved with Sergio, and subsequent brutalities occur. Spanish with subtitles. **107m/C; DVD, Blu-Ray.** *SP FR* Carlos Areces; Antonio de la Torre; Carolina Bang; Santiago Segura; Jorge Clemente; ***D:*** Alex de la Iglesia; ***W:*** Alex de la Iglesia; ***C:*** Kiko de la Rica; ***M:*** Roque Baños.

The Last Command 1928 Famous powerful silent film by Sternberg about an expatriate Czarist general forging out a pitiful living as a silent Hollywood extra, where he is hired by his former adversary to reenact the revolution he just left. Next to "The Last Laugh," this is considered Jannings' most acclaimed performance. Deeply ironic, visually compelling film with a new score by Gaylord Carter. **88m/B; Silent; VHS, DVD.** Emil Jannings; William Powell; Evelyn Brent; Nicholas Soussanin; Michael Visaroff; Jack Raymond; Fritz Feld; ***D:*** Josef von Sternberg; ***W:*** Warren Duff; ***M:*** Max Steiner; Gaylord Carter. Oscars '28: Actor (Jannings); Natl. Film Reg. '06.

The Last Confederate: The Story of Robert Adams *Strike the Tent* 2005 (R) Adams portrays his own great-great grandfather Robert, a South Carolina native who becomes a captain in the Confederacy. He falls in love with northern belle Evilyn McCord (Edwards), the sister of best friend Nelson (Lindsey), who also joins the southern cause. When both men are captured and sent to a Union prison camp, Robert plans an escape that will eventually bring him back to Evilyn. **96m/C; DVD.** Amy Redford; Tippi Hedren; Mickey Rooney; Julian Adams; Gwendolyn Edwards; Joshua Lindsey; Eric Holloway; Timmy Sherrill; ***D:*** Julian Adams; A. Blaine Miller; ***W:*** Julian Adams; Gwendolyn Edwards; Joshua Lindsey; ***C:*** Shawn Lewallen; ***M:*** Atli Orvarsson.

The Last Cowboy 1/2 2003 After her grandfather's death, single mom Jacqueline Cooper (Garth) returns to the family's Texas ranch. She not only has to deal with her estranged father but must get the property back on sound financial footing. Made for the Hallmark Channel. **88m/C; DVD.** Jennie Garth; Lance Henriksen; Bradley Cooper; Muse Watson; M.C. Gainey; John Vargas; Dylan Wagner; ***D:*** Joyce Chopra; ***W:*** J.P. Martin; ***C:*** Chris Manley; ***M:*** Richard Friedman; Chris Walden. **CABLE**

Last Dance 1/2 1991 Five scantily clad exotic dancers are ready to compete for the title of Miss Dance-TV, but trouble ensues when the dancers start turning up dead. **86m/C; VHS, DVD.** Cynthia Bassinet; Elaine Hendrix; Kurt T. Williams; Allison Rhea; Erica Ringston; ***D:*** Anthony Markes.

Last Dance 1996 (R) Following closely on the heels of "Dead Man Walking," this death-row drama suffered from bad timing. Convicted murderess Stone's condemned to die in an unnamed Southern state. Rookie attorney Morrow works for the state's clemency office. As a bond grows between the two, he uncovers errors in her trial that his bosses would rather ignore. The movie makes its big mistake by centering on Morrow's callow lawyer instead of Stone's embittered con. Even the clock-ticking countdown to the execution fails to hold attention. **103m/C; VHS, DVD, Blu-Ray.** Sharon Stone; Rob Morrow; Randy Quaid; Peter Gallagher; Jack Thompson; Jayne Brook; Pamela Tyson; Skeet Ulrich; Don Harvey; Diane Sellers; ***D:*** Bruce Beresford; ***W:*** Ron Koslow; ***C:*** Peter James; ***M:*** Mark Isham.

Last Day of Summer 2010 Crude, low-brow comedy wastes a decent performance by Qualls. Misfit Joe cleans restrooms at a fast-food joint and is belittled by his mean boss (Sadler). He tries—and fails—to shoot-up his workplace and winds up with mouthy unwanted hostage Stefanie (Nikki) instead. **105m/C; DVD.** DJ Qualls; Nikki Reed; William Sadler; Adam Scarimbolo; Jason Cruz; Yury Tsykun; ***D:*** Vlad Yudin; ***W:*** Vlad Yudin; ***C:*** Patryk Rebisz; ***M:*** Peter Himmelman; Marc Aaron Jacobs.

The Last Days 1998 (PG-13) Looks at Hitler's final solution in Hungary through eyewitness accounts of five survivors. Though the end of the war was in sight by the time the Germans invaded Hungary in 1944, Hitler still insisted on a roundup of all Hungarian Jews, though it took resources from the military. More than 70 percent of Hungary's one million Jews were killed in a few months. Interviews and archival footage. **87m/C; VHS, DVD.** ***D:*** James Moll. Oscars '98: Feature Doc.

Last Days 1/2 2005 (R) A recluse rock star (Pitt) lives an increasingly bizarre existence, barely interacting with the trail of hangers-on and band members that frequent his stone mansion until he finally takes his own life. Loosely based on the Kurt Cobain tragedy but emphatically denied as any type of biography. **97m/C; DVD.** Michael Pitt; Lukas Haas; Asia Argento; Ricky Jay; Harmony Korine; Scott Green; Nicole Vicius; Ryan Orion; Kim Gordon; Adam Friberg; Andy Friberg; Thadeus A. Thomas; Chip Marks; ***D:*** Gus Van Sant; ***W:*** Gus Van Sant; ***C:*** Harris Savides.

Last Days in the Desert 2016 (PG-13) Rodrigo Garcia's daring drama about Jesus Christ's sojourn to the desert before his crucifixion features a great duel performance by McGregor (as both JC and the devil himself) and stunning cinematography by the legendary Lubezki. Jesus meets a family in the desert, led by a strict father (Hinds) and featuring an increasingly rebellious son (Sheridan). Of course, Jesus is considering his relationship to his father, and how we all deal with parents and God. It's a deeply symbolic film but it has a cumulative and lasting power by refusing to provide simple answers. Even for the non-religious, it's always pretty fascinating. **98m/C; DVD.** Ewan McGregor; Ciaran Hinds; Ayelet Zurer; Tye Sheridan; Susan Gray; ***D:*** Rodrigo Garcia; ***W:*** Rodrigo Garcia; ***C:*** Emmanuel Lubezki; ***M:*** Danny Bensi; Saunder Jurriaans.

Last Days in Vietnam 1/2 2014 Wars do not end easily. And so when the Vietnam War came to an end, there were unimaginable complexities. Allies in South Vietnam feared repercussions from an empowered North Vietnamese Army and the United States still had war intelligence items and personnel in the country. Director Kennedy tells this underreported chapter of controversy and escape from a country before it sank further into wartime drama. The result is a documentary a bit too heavy on talking heads saying the same thing too many times. **98m/C; DVD, Blu-Ray.** ***D:*** Rory Kennedy; ***W:*** Mark Bailey; Keven McAlester; ***C:*** Joan Churchill; ***M:*** Gary Lionelli.

The Last Days of Disco 1998 (R) It's the early 80s and the disco scene is barely alive. Oblivious to this fact are brash Charlotte (Beckinsale) and reserved Alice (Sevigny), recent college grads working as low-level corporate drones by day and partying at a Studio 54-like club by night. The girls mingle with a group of proto-yuppie clones, including hot shot A.D.A. Josh (Keeslar), environmental lawyer Tom (Leonard) and ad man Jimmy (Astin). Also hanging out are assistant manager Des (Eigeman) and shady owner Bernie (Thornton). Lots of sharp, funny dialogue helps ease the fact that the characters are merely poor little rich kids who need to shut up and dance. **113m/C; VHS, DVD, Blu-Ray.** Chloë Sevigny; Kate Beckinsale; Christopher Eigeman; MacKenzie Astin; Robert Sean Leonard; Matt Keeslar; Tara Subkoff; Jennifer Beals; David Thornton; Michael Weatherly; Burr Steers; ***D:*** Whit Stillman; ***W:*** Whit Stillman; ***C:*** John Thomas; ***M:*** Mark Suozzo.

Last Days of Frank & Jesse James 1/2 1986 A tired TV rehash of the well-known western legend in which the famous brothers try to be like others after their personal war against society ends. **100m/C; VHS, DVD.** Johnny Cash; Kris Kristofferson; June Carter Cash; Willie Nelson; Margaret Gibson; Gail Youngs; ***D:*** William A. Graham. **TV**

The Last Days of Frankie the Fly 1996 (R) It's gonna seem familiar because it's yet another criminal low-life story set in L.A. but at least Hopper's presence makes this slightly more than routine. He's Frankie, a semi-pathetic petty thief with big dreams and not much talent. He works for vicious gangster Sal (Madsen) and becomes smitten with ex-junkie Margaret (Hannah), who would like to be a legit actress but is instead working in porn. When Frankie decides to impress Margaret, he naturally gets into trouble. **96m/C; VHS, DVD.** Dennis Hopper; Daryl Hannah; Michael Madsen; Kiefer Sutherland; Dayton Callie; Jack McGee; ***D:*** Peter Markle; ***W:*** Dayton Callie; ***C:*** Phil Parmet; ***M:*** George S. Clinton.

The Last Days of Patton 1/2 1986 Depicts the aging general's autumn years as a controversial ex-Nazi defender and desk-bound WWII historian. Scott reprises his feature-film role. **146m/C; VHS, DVD.** George C. Scott; Ed Lauter; Eva Marie Saint; Richard Dysart; Murray Hamilton; Kathryn Leigh Scott; ***D:*** Delbert Mann. **TV**

Last Days of Pompeii 1/2 1935 Vintage DeMille-style epic based on Lord Lytton's book, where the eruption of Vesuvius threatens noblemen and slaves alike. State-of-the-art special effects still look fantastic today. Remade in 1960; available colorized. **96m/B; VHS, DVD.** Preston Foster; Alan Hale; Basil Rathbone; George L. Baxt; Louis Calhern; David Holt; Dorothy Wilson; Wryley Birch; Gloria Shea; ***D:*** Ernest B. Schoedsack; ***C:*** Jack Cardiff.

The Last Days of Pompeii *Ultimi Giorni di Pompeii* 1960 Superman Reeves plays a gladiator trying to clean up the doomed town of Pompeii in this remake of the 1935 classic. Some spectacular scenes, including the explosive climax when the mountain blows its top. **105m/C; VHS, DVD, Streaming.** *IT* Steve Reeves; Christine Kaufmann; Barbara Carroll; Anne Marie Baumann; Mimmo Palmara; ***D:*** Mario Bonnard; ***W:*** Sergio Leone.

The Last Days of Pompeii 🦴🦴 1/2 **1984** CBS miniseries with a large cast and numerous storylines involving aristocrats, slaves, gladiators, persecuted Christians, pagans, romance, lust, and Mt. Vesuvius about to explode. **144m/C; DVD.** Laurence Olivier; Anthony Quayle; Franco Nero; Lesley-Anne Down; Duncan Regehr; Nicholas Clay; Brian Blessed; Ned Beatty; Linda Purl; Ernest Borgnine; Olivia Hussey; *D:* Peter R. Hunt; *W:* Carmen Culver; *C:* Jack Cardiff; *M:* Trevor Jones. **TV**

The Last Days of Summer 🦴 1/2 **2007** Bland and predictable kiddie comedy. Fifth-grader Luke (Panettiere) doesn't want his summer vacation to be over, especially with the threat of middle school looming. When he has a perfect day at the town's Labor Day carnival, he wishes it would never end and, as fast as you can say "Groundhog Day," it doesn't. But even Luke eventually gets tired of the endless repetition and tries to figure out how to move forward. **88m/C; DVD.** Jessica Tuck; Jackee; Jansen Panettiere; Eli Vargas; Jon Kent Ethridge; Alexandra Krosney; Daniel Samonas; Denyse Tontz; Brendan Miller; Vince Grant; *D:* Blair Treu; *W:* Kent Pierce; *C:* Brian Sullivan; *M:* James L. Venable. **CABLE**

The Last Days on Mars 🦴🦴 **2013 (R)** Derivative but sometimes gripping space thriller. A group of on-edge scientists are counting down the last hours of their tedious, unsuccessful Mars mission. Glory-seeking Petrovich secretly does one last outside exploration after finding a soil sample containing a living organism. This spells doom for everyone when the organism takes over bodies in a zombie-like fashion. Adapted from Sydney J. Bounds' 1975 short story "The Animators." **98m/C; DVD, Blu-Ray.** Liev Schreiber; Olivia Williams; Romola Garai; Elias Koteas; Goran Kostic; Tom Cullen; Johnny Harris; Yusra Warsama; *D:* Ruairi Robinson; *W:* Clive Dawson; *C:* Robbie Ryan; *M:* Max Richter.

The Last Debate 🦴🦴 1/2 **2000** Presidential candidates Richard Meredith (Young) and Paul Greene (Gray) are having only one televised debate in their tight race, which is being moderated by political columnist Mike Howley (Garner) and three fellow journalists (McDonald, Murphy, Sanchez). Just before the debate, Howley is given damaging info about Meredith, which he and the other panelists use without verification. Then investigative journalist Tom Chapman (Gallagher) comes in with a lot of questions about the leak and its source. Based on the novel by Jim Lehrer. **90m/C; VHS, DVD.** James Garner; Peter Gallagher; Audra McDonald; Donna Murphy; Marco Sanchez; Stephen Young; Bruce Gray; Dorian Harewood; *D:* John Badham; *W:* John Maass; *C:* Norayr Kasper. **CABLE**

The Last Descent 🦴🦴 1/2 **2016 (PG)** Based on a true story, this drama explores attempts rescue a man trapped in the Nutty Putty Cave in 2009. That year, John Jones (Hopson) goes exploring in an un-mapped section of the cave and soon found himself in an untenable situation. During his exploration, he gets stuck in a hole that is 1.5 feet wide but he is 150 underground. Rescue crews make heroic efforts to free John as the enormity of the situation envelopes them all. **105m/C; DVD, Blu-Ray.** Chadwick Hopson; Alexis Johnson; Landon Henneman; Jyllian Petrie; Jacob Omer; *D:* Isaac Halasima; *W:* Isaac Halasima; *C:* Isaac Halasima; *M:* Matt Cropper Kalai.

The Last Detail 🦴🦴🦴🦴 **1973 (R)** Two hard-boiled career petty officers (Nicholson and Young) are commissioned to transfer a young sailor facing an eight-year sentence for petty theft from one brig to another. In an act of compassion, they attempt to show the prisoner a final good time. Nicholson shines in both the complexity and completeness of his character. Adapted from a Daryl Ponicsan novel. **104m/C; VHS, DVD, Blu-Ray.** Jack Nicholson; Otis Young; Randy Quaid; Clifton James; Michael Moriarty; Carol Kane; Nancy Allen; Gilda Radner; *D:* Hal Ashby; *W:* Robert Towne; *C:* Michael Chapman; *M:* Johnny Mandel. British Acad. '74: Actor (Nicholson), Screenplay; Cannes '74: Actor (Nicholson); N.Y. Film Critics '74: Actor (Nicholson); Natl. Soc. Film Critics '74: Actor (Nicholson).

The Last Diamond 🦴🦴 1/2 *Le dernier diamant* **2014 (R)** A dramatic crime thriller about a thief on parole who is convinced to do one more job. After being released from prison, diamond thief Simon (Attal) is on parole and with no real interest in going back to his old ways. That is until his friend Albert (Stevenin) convinces him to help with the theft of the famous Florentine diamond in Antwerp. Using all his charm, Simon becomes close with Julia (Bejo), who is in charge of the sale of the Florentine. Becoming involved with Julia, Simon gains the diamond but soon learns that another person involved in the heist wants the gem for a different reason and that gangsters and killers are also in pursuit. Simon is left with a dilemma about continuing with the theft or getting the diamond back for Julia and protecting her. French with subtitles. **108m/C; DVD, Streaming, Download.** Yvan Attal; Berenice Bejo; Jean-Francois Stevenin; Antoine Basler; *D:* Eric Barbier; *W:* Eric Barbier; Marie Eynard; Tran-Minh Nam; *C:* Denis Rouden; *M:* Renaud Barbier. **VIDEO**

The Last Dinosaur 🦴 1/2 **1977** Aging billionaire and big-game hunter Masten Thrust (Boone) leads a scientific team to a newly-discovered lost world located inside a dormant volcano that's populated by prehistoric humans and dinos. Thrust really just wants to kill the ultimate prize—a hungry T-Rex. Japanese/American co-production from Tsuburaya Productions and Rankin/Bass. **95m/C; DVD.** *JP* Richard Boone; Joan Van Ark; Steven Keats; Tetsu Nakamura; Luther Rackley; Masumi Sekiya; *D:* Alexander Grasshoff; Tsugunobu Kotani; *W:* William Overgard; *C:* Shoji Ueda; *M:* Maury Laws.

The Last Don 🦴🦴 1/2 *Mario Puzo's The Last Don* **1997 (R)** Re-edited version of the TV miniseries finds author Puzo sticking to what he knows best. Ruthless Domenico Clericuzio (Aiello) wipes out the rival family his pregnant daughter has married into. Carrying out the Don's orders is nephew Pippi (Mantegna), an enforcer who weds Vegas showgirl Nalene (Miller) and then gets involved in the casino business. The years pass with the Don manipulating the next generation, as bloodthirsty grandson Dante (Cochrane) fights for control against Pippi's cool-headed son Cross (Gedrick). Divided loyalties abound. A complete five-hour version is also available. **150m/C; VHS, DVD.** Danny Aiello; Joe Mantegna; Jason Gedrick; Rory Cochrane; Penelope Ann Miller; Daryl Hannah; Kirstie Alley; Michelle Rene Thomas; David Marciano; Robert Wuhl; k.d. lang; John Colicos; Cliff DeYoung; Michael Massee; *D:* Graeme Clifford; *W:* Joyce Eliason; *C:* Gordon C. Lonsdale; *M:* Roger Bellon; Angelo Badalamenti.

The Last Don 2 🦴🦴 1/2 *Mario Puzo's The Last Don 2* **1998 (R)** Since Don Clericuzio (Aiello) has died there's a power vacuum that forces widower Cross De Lena (Gedrick) back into the family business. The family is besieged by traitors, even as Cross gets involved in a tentative romance with his autistic stepdaughter's teacher, Josie (Kensit). Then there's crazy, vindictive Aunt Rose Marie (Alley) who falls in love with her conflicted priest (Isaacs), problems with the Hollywood studio headed by Cross's sister Claudia (Thomas), and ambitious mobster Billy D'Angelo (Wilder) for Cross to deal with. Unwittingly campy but slower moving than the first installment. **127m/C; VHS, DVD.** Jason Gedrick; Kirstie Alley; Patsy Kensit; James Wilder; David Marciano; Jason Isaacs; Michelle Rene Thomas; Conrad Dunn; Robert Wuhl; Andrew Jackson; Joe Mantegna; *Cameo(s):* Danny Aiello; *D:* Graeme Clifford; *W:* Joyce Eliason; *C:* David Franco; *M:* Roger Bellon. **TV**

The Last Dragon 🦴 1/2 *Berry Gordy's The Last Dragon* **1985 (PG-13)** It's time for a Motown kung fu showdown on the streets of Harlem, for there is scarcely enough room for even one dragon. **108m/C; VHS, DVD, Blu-Ray.** Taimak; Vanity; Christopher Murney; Julius J. Carry, III; Faith Prince; *D:* Michael A. Schultz; *W:* Louis Venosta; *C:* James A. Contner; *M:* Misha Segal.

The Last Drop 🦴🦴 **2005 (R)** Overstuffed WWII adventure that takes place during Operation Market Drop, a failed mission that parachuted British troops into German-occupied Holland. One unit has a separate agenda—they are to rendezvous with Dutch resistance to prevent the Nazis from sending some looted national treasures to Berlin. Only a trio of Nazi deserters are after the same goods. Zane is supposed to be a Canadian pilot and Madsen briefly wanders through as a crusty American officer. **110m/C; DVD.** *GB* Billy Zane; Karel Roden; Michael Madsen; Tommy Flanagan; Alexander Skarsgård; Sean Pertwee; Laurence Fox; Neil Newbon; *D:* Colin Teague; *W:* Colin Teague; Gary Young; *C:* Maxime Alexandre; *M:* David Julyan.

Last Embrace 🦴🦴🦴 **1979 (R)** A feverish thriller in the Hitchcock style dealing with an ex-secret serviceman who is convinced someone is trying to kill him. **102m/C; DVD, Blu-Ray.** Roy Scheider; Janet Margolin; Christopher Walken; John Glover; Charles Napier; Mandy Patinkin; *D:* Jonathan Demme; *M:* Miklos Rozsa.

The Last Emperor 🦴🦴🦴🦴 **1987 (PG-13)** Deeply ironic epic detailing life of Pu Yi, crowned at the age of three as the last emperor of China before the onset of communism. Follows Pu Yi from childhood to manhood (sequestered away in the Forbidden City) to fugitive to puppet-ruler to party proletariat. O'Toole portrays the sympathetic Scot tutor who educates the adult Pu Yi (Lone) in the ways of the western world after Pu Yi abdicates power in 1912. Shot on location inside the People's Republic of China with a cast of thousands. Rich, visually stunning movie. **140m/C; DVD, Blu-Ray.** *IT* John Lone; Peter O'Toole; Joan Chen; Victor Wong; Ryuichi Sakamoto; Dennis Dun; Maggie Han; Ying Ruocheng; Ric Young; *D:* Bernardo Bertolucci; *W:* Mark Peploe; Bernardo Bertolucci; *C:* Vittorio Storaro; *M:* Ryuichi Sakamoto; David Byrne. Oscars '87: Adapt. Screenplay, Art Dir./Set Dec., Cinematog., Costume Des., Director (Bertolucci), Film, Film Editing, Orig. Score, Sound; British Acad. '88: Film; Cesar '88: Foreign Film; Directors Guild '87: Director (Bertolucci); Golden Globes '88: Director (Bertolucci), Film--Drama, Score, Screenplay; L.A. Film Critics '87: Cinematog.; N.Y. Film Critics '87: Cinematog.

The Last Enemy 🦴🦴 **2008** Big brother is watching in this overly-complicated but still fascinating Brit thriller. Introverted mathematician Stephen Ezard (Cumberbatch) returns to London for the funeral of his estranged doctor brother Michael (Beesley), who was supposedly killed in the Middle East while treating refugees killed by a virus despite being inoculated. Stephen's then recruited into helping introduce a controversial national ID program (using his math/computer skills) while getting involved with his brother's widow Yasim (Marinca). But Michael turns up alive, wanting to learn what the government knows about the dead refugees. **310m/C; DVD.** *GB* Benedict Cumberbatch; Max Beesley; Anamaria Marinca; Robert Carlyle; Eva Birthistle; Geraldine James; David Harewood; *D:* Iain B. MacDonald; *W:* Peter Berry; *C:* Nigel Willoughby; *M:* Magnus Fiennes. **TV**

The Last Eve 🦴 **2005** Incredibly bizarre mix of Christian myth, martial arts, and science fiction done as an anthology set in various times and places. Technically it's an avant-garde love story involving Adam and Eve, but theologians will find Biblical accuracy lacking. **88m/C; DVD.** Kelly Hamilton; Bruce Khan; Jourdan Lee; Melanie Jean; Freddie Milligan; Paula LaBaredas; *D:* Young Man Kang; *W:* Young Man Kang; Richard B. Phillips; Tony Young; *C:* Young Man Kang; Cheol Hun Ham; Sang Jin Han; *M:* Mark Crutch; James Hopkins; You Lee Kim. **VIDEO**

Last Exit to Brooklyn 🦴🦴🦴 1/2 **1990 (R)** Hubert Selby Jr.'s shocking book comes to the screen in a vivid film. Leigh gives a stunning performance as a young Brooklyn girl caught between the Mafia, union men, and friends struggling for something better. Set in the 1950s. Fine supporting cast; excellent pacing. **102m/C; VHS, Blu-Ray.** Jennifer Jason Leigh; Burt Young; Stephen Lang; Ricki Lake; Jerry Orbach; Maia Danziger; Stephen Baldwin; Peter Dobson; Sam Rockwell; Jason Andrews; James Lorinz; Mark Boone, Jr.; Alexis Arquette; Rutanya Alda; Frank Vincent; Mike Starr; *D:* Uli Edel; *C:* Stefan Czapsky. N.Y. Film Critics '89: Support. Actress (Leigh).

The Last Exorcism 🦴🦴 1/2 **2010 (PG-13)** Fabian enjoys himself and brings the audience along with him as con man preacher Cotton Marcus, who performs exorcisms for the gullible. Finally disgusted with his fraudulent religious activities, Marcus agrees to let a film crew document his last exorcism, which doesn't go as planned. Filmed in an overly-familiar fake documentary style that doesn't detract too much from the action. **90m/C; Blu-Ray, On Demand.** Patrick Fabian; Louis Herthum; Iris Bahr; Ashley Bell; Tony Bentley; *D:* Daniel Stamm; *W:* Huck Botko; Andrew Gurland; *C:* Zoltan Honti; *M:* Nathan Barr.

The Last Exorcism Part II 🦴 1/2 **2013 (PG-13)** The demon Abalam is back again to torture Nell Sweetzer (Bell), the unassuming woman subjected to violent possession in the 2010 surprise hit. As the insanity reignites, she is quickly shipped to a halfway house in New Orleans, where she's exposed to booze, hard rock, and creepy visits from her dead dad. Dropping the found-footage technique from the original (a la "Blair Witch 2"), this straightforward horror flick relies too much on CGI fireworks and not enough on scares or tension. Reprising her role, naturally-gifted Bell is the only saving grace. **88m/C; DVD, Blu-Ray.** Ashley Bell; Spencer Treat Clark; Muse Watson; Louis Herthum; Andrew Sensenig; *D:* Ed Gass-Donnelly; *W:* Ed Gass-Donnelly; Damien Chazelle; *C:* Brian Steacy; *M:* Michael Wandmacher.

The Last Face 🦴 **2017 (R)** Director Sean Penn does a disservice to his humanitarian causes by showcasing what's truly important: a couple of foreign doctors finding romance amid a backdrop of African war. Relief-aid workers Petersen (Theron, sporting a South African accent that's genuine yet strangely sounds fake) and Leon (Bardem) try to have a relationship in Liberia, but these darned injured and anguished people keep getting in the way. If this was a gift of love between real-life couple Penn and Theron, they should stick with chocolates and flowers. **130m/C; DVD, Blu-Ray.** Charlize Theron; Javier Bardem; Adele Exarchopoulos; Jared Harris; Jean Reno; *D:* Sean Penn; *W:* Erin Dignam; *C:* Barry Ackroyd; *M:* Hans Zimmer.

The Last Five Years 🦴🦴🦴 **2014 (PG-13)** Jason Robert Brown's beloved musical play gets the film adaptation with another performance that proves Kendrick is essentially universally beloved. She steals the show as Cathy, a woman we meet on the final day of her relationship, singing the heartbreaking "Still Hurting." The next scene introduces us to Jamie on the first day of his relationship with Cathy, and the film progresses from there with her arc going back to the beginning of the relationship and his going forward in intercut scenes. The result is a unique way to see the trajectory of love and Kendrick is simply phenomenal, but male co-star Jeremy Jordan can't quite keep up. **94m/C; DVD, Blu-Ray.** Anna Kendrick; Jeremy Jordan; *D:* Richard LaGravenese; *W:* Richard LaGravenese; *C:* Steven Meizler; *M:* Jason Robert Brown.

Last Flag Flying 🦴🦴 1/2 **2017 (R)** A dramedy road movie that explores deep issues of humanity and life. In 2003, Larry "Doc" Shepherd (Carell) lost his wife to cancer and his son died in combat in Iraq. Unable to cope with accompanying his son's body to Arlington alone, he calls on two buddies he served with in Vietnam, Sal Nealon (Cranston) and Richard Mueller (Fishburne). Though Doc has not seen them in decades, they agree to come with him. During the journey, they explore issues of faith, philosophy, and death. Marred by a lack of daring at times, the film is nonetheless moving and features outstanding performances. **125m/C; DVD, Blu-Ray.** Bryan Cranston; Laurence Fishburne; Steve Carell; J. Quinton Johnson; Deanna Reed-Foster; *D:* Richard Linklater; *W:* Richard Linklater; Darryl Ponicsan; *C:* Shane F. Kelly; *M:* Graham Reynolds.

The Last Flight 🦴🦴 **1931** Well-done, downbeat drama explores the postwar 'Lost Generation' of the 1920s. WWI flying ace Cary Lockwood (Barthelmess) can't bring himself to return to his family after his war experiences, so he and some fellow American vets decide to stay in Paris. They meet frantically fun-loving (and wealthy) flapper Nikki (Chandler), who joins their boozing group. Eventually they all drift to Lisbon, looking for excitement and involving themselves in a series of meaningless (mis)adventures. **76m/B; DVD.** Richard Barthelmess; Helen Chandler; Johnny Mack Brown; David Manners; Elliott Nugent; Walter Byron; *D:* William

Dieterle; **W:** John Monk Saunders; **C:** Sidney Hickox.

The Last Flight of Noah's Ark 🦴🦴 1/2 **1980 (G)** Disney adventure concerns a high-living pilot, a prim missionary, and two stowaway orphans who must plot their way off a deserted island following the crash landing of their broken-down plane. **97m/C; VHS, DVD, Blu-Ray.** Elliott Gould; Genevieve Bujold; Rick Schroder; Vincent Gardenia; Tammy Lauren; **D:** Charles Jarrott; **W:** George Arthur Bloom; Steven W. Carabatsos; **C:** Charles F. Wheeler; **M:** Maurice Jarre.

Last Four Days 🦴🦴 **1977 (PG)** A chronicle of the final days of Benito Mussolini. **91m/C; VHS, DVD.** Rod Steiger; Henry Fonda; Franco Nero; **D:** Carlo Lizzani.

Last Frontier 🦴🦴 1/2 **1932** Serial of 12 chapters contains shades of spectacular figures in Western history: Custer, Hickok, and others in a background of grazing buffalo, boom towns, and covered wagon trails. **216m/B; VHS, DVD.** Lon Chaney, Jr.; Yakima Canutt; Francis X. Bushman; **D:** Spencer Gordon Bennet; Thomas L. Story.

The Last Full Measure 🦴🦴 **2019 (R)** Scott Huffman (Stan) is investigating the case for awarding the Medal of Honor to deceased Airman William Pitsenbargar (Irvine), who was killed in combat during the Vietnam War and saved many lives. The airman who sent Pitsenbarger on his last mission, Tulley (Hurt), presses the matter, forcing Scott to learn the truth from Pitsenbargar's peers, including traumatized Jimmy Burr (Fonda). Based on a true story, the drama offers a solid portrayal of war heroism as well as the long-term effects of post-traumatic stress disorder, survivor's guilt, and the treatment of veterans. Despite sometimes clunky dialogue, it's carried by the performances of its seasoned actors. **115m/C; DVD.** Sebastian Stan; William Hurt; Samuel L. Jackson; Ed Harris; Peter Fonda; **D:** Todd Robinson; **W:** Todd Robinson; **C:** Byron Werner; **M:** Philip Klein.

Last Game 🦴🦴 **1980** A college student is torn between his devotion to his blind father and going out for the college's football team. **107m/C; VHS, DVD.** Howard Segal; Ed L. Grady; Terry Alden; **D:** Martin Beck.

The Last Gangster 🦴🦴 **1937** Robinson snarls his way through another gangster role as crime boss Joe Krozac. Joe returns from Europe with young bride Talya (Stradner) but soon winds up in Alcatraz, thanks to a tax evasion conviction. The newspapers hound his wife and young son until nice guy reporter Paul North (Stewart in a cheesy mustache) steps in. With Talya learning what a brute Joe really is, she divorces him and marries Paul. After 10 years, Joe gets out of the slammer vowing to get to know his son (who doesn't know anything about him) but his old gang has other plans for Joe. **81m/B; DVD.** Edward G. Robinson; James Stewart; Rose Stradner; Lionel Stander; Edward Brophy; John Carradine; Douglas Scott; Alan Baxter; Grant Mitchell; **D:** Edward Ludwig; **W:** John Lee Mahin; **C:** William H. Daniels; **M:** Edward Ward.

The Last Godfather 🦴 **2010 (PG-13)** Set in the 1950s. Mob boss Don Carini (Keitel) has decided to retire and appoints his illegitimate Korean son Young-gu (Shim) as his successor. The problem is Young-gu barely knows English and is a clumsy goofball with no experience. The Don's right-hand man Tony V (Rispoli) is supposed to teach his new would-be boss how to be a wiseguy. Maybe this excruciatingly unfunny US/Korean co-production played better in Korea, where Shim is a well-known comedian. **100m/C; DVD.** *NK* Hyung Rae Shim; Harvey Keitel; Michael Rispoli; Jocelin Donahue; Jon Polito; Jason Mewes; **D:** Hyung Rae Shim; **W:** Hyung Rae Shim; **C:** Mark Irwin; **M:** John Lissauer.

The Last Grenade 🦴🦴 1/2 **1970 (R)** Harry Grigsby (Baker) and Kip Thompson (Cord) were friends and fellow soldiers of fortune in the Congo until Kip switched sides in the fighting. Recovering from illness in Britain, Grigsby is asked to travel to Hong Kong and kill his former friend who is causing border disputes with China. **94m/C; DVD.** *GB* Stanley Baker; Alex Cord; Honor Blackman; Richard Attenborough; Andrew Keir; Ray Brooks; Julian Glover; Rafer Johnson; John Thaw; **D:** Gordon Flemyng; **W:** James Mitchell; John Sherlock; Kenneth Ware; **C:** Alan Hume; **M:** John Dankworth.

Last Gun 🦴🦴 **1964** A legendary gunman on the verge of retirement has to save his town from a reign of terror before turning his gun in. **98m/C; VHS, DVD.** *IT* Cameron Mitchell; Carl Mohner; Livio Lorenzon; Celina Cely; Kitty Carver; **D:** Sergio Bergonzelli; **W:** Ambrogio Molteni; **C:** Romolo Garroni; **M:** Marcello Gigante.

The Last Hard Men 🦴🦴 1/2 **1976** Retired sheriff Sam Burgade (Heston) must save his daughter (Hershey) from escaped convict Provo (Coburn) who kidnapped her as revenge for jailing him and accidently killing his wife. Provo and his gang force a showdown with the reluctant former lawman by threatening bodily harm and worse to the daughter if he doesn't show. Solid work by the leads raises this one above the usual genre fare. **103m/C; VHS, Blu-Ray, On Demand.** Charlton Heston; James Coburn; Barbara Hershey; Michael Parks; Jorge (George) Rivero; Larry Wilcox; Thalmus Rasulala; Chris Mitchum; Morgan Paull; John Quade; Robert Donner; **D:** Andrew V. McLaglen; **W:** Guerdon (Gordon) Trueblood; **C:** Duke Callaghan; **M:** Jerry Goldsmith.

The Last Heist 🦴 **2016** What if the hostages in a bank heist included a serial killer? That's the intriguing set-up here, and the serial killer is played by rock icon Henry Rollins. Director Mendez starts his latest thriller with a great concept and casts the perfect person in a pivotal role, but goes absolutely nowhere with it, focusing on the wrong characters and failing to deliver the thrills. Spending more time with the uninteresting bank robbers, Mendez fails to give enough to care about or enough screen time for Rollins. Though the former rocker still finds moments to steal the movie. **84m/C; DVD, Blu-Ray.** Henry Rollins; Torrance Coombs; Victoria Pratt; Mykel Shannon Jenkins; Nick Principe; **D:** Mike Mendez; **W:** Guy Stevenson; **C:** Jan-Michael Losada; **M:** Alexander Bornstein.

The Last Hit Man 🦴🦴 **2008** Aging hitman Harry (Mantegna) botches his latest job (probably because he's dying), but keeps the info from his daughter Racquel (Whitmere) who's been serving as his getaway driver. When younger killer Billy (Orzari) is sent in to fix things, daddy's little girl decides she should take a more active role in the business to protect their interests. **87m/C; DVD.** Joe Mantegna; Romano Orzari; Elizabeth Whitmere; Michael Majeski; **D:** Christopher Warre Smets; **W:** Christopher Warre Smets; **C:** Joe Turner; **M:** Alphonse Lanza. **VIDEO**

Last Holiday 🦴🦴🦴 **1950** A man who is told he has a few weeks to live decides to spend them in a posh resort where people assume he is important. **89m/B; VHS, DVD.** *GB* Alec Guinness; Kay Walsh; Beatrice Campbell; Wilfrid Hyde-White; Bernard Lee; **D:** Henry Cass; **W:** J.B. Priestley.

Last Holiday 🦴🦴 1/2 **2006 (PG-13)** Shy New Orleans salesclerk Georgia Byrd (Queen Latifah) has a passion for gourmet cooking and a habit of setting her dreams aside. This changes when Georgia is (mis-)diagnosed with a fatal disease that gives her only weeks to live. She decides to make the most of her time by giving herself a makeover and a holiday at the ritzy Czech Grandhotel Pupp so she can enjoy the gastronomical delights of her favorite chef, Didier (the charming Depardieu). The Queen is as appealing as ever, even in this warmed-over comedy, which is a remake of the 1950 Alec Guinness comedy. **112m/C; DVD, Blu-Ray.** Queen Latifah; LL Cool J; Timothy Hutton; Giancarlo Esposito; Alicia Witt; Gerard Depardieu; Jane Adams; Susan Kellerman; Jascha Washington; Matt Ross; Ranjit (Chaudry) Chowdhry; Mike Estime; Michael Nouri; Julia Lashae; Richmond Werner; Emeril Lagasse; Shirl Cieutat; **D:** Wayne Wang; **W:** Jeffrey Price; Peter S. Seaman; **C:** Geoffrey Simpson; **M:** George Fenton.

Last Hour WOOF! **2008** Confusing, dumb, dull, and amateurish crime drama. Five criminals (Madsen, D'Amario, DMX, Wong, Caubet) each receive a letter summoning them to a house in Beijing. The guys show up and are trapped in the house (with an assassin no less), which is surrounded by cops who give them an hour to surrender. Remember that mug shot of a drunken, disheveled Nick Nolte? Well, that's what Madsen looks like, and D'Amario died in 2005, so this stinker was moldering somewhere where it should have been left. **95m/C; DVD.** *FR CH* DMX; Michael Madsen; David Carradine; Paul Sorvino; Pascal Caubet; Tony D'Amario; Kwong Leung Wong; Bettina Antoni; Monica Cruz; **D:** Pascal Caubet; **W:** Pascal Caubet; Maxime Lemaitre; **C:** Ting Wo Kwong; **M:** DMX; Alain Mouysset. **VIDEO**

Last House on Dead End Street WOOF! *The Fun House* **1977 (R)** Gore galore as actors die for their art in this splatter flick about snuff films. **90m/C; VHS, DVD.** Steven Morrison; Dennis Crawford; Lawrence Bornman; Janet Sorley; **D:** Victor Janos.

Last House on the Left 🦴🦴 *Krug and Company; Sex Crime of the Century* **1972 (R)** Two girls are kidnapped from a rock concert by a gang of escaped convicts; the girls' parents exact bloody revenge when the guilty parties pay an intended housecall. Controversial and grim low-budget shocker; loosely based on Bergman's "The Virgin Spring." **83m/C; VHS, DVD, Blu-Ray.** David A(lexander) Hess; Lucy Grantham; Sandra Cassel; Mark Sheffler; Fred J. Lincoln; Jeramie Rain; Gaylord St. James; Cynthia Carr; Ada Washington; Martin Kove; **D:** Wes Craven; **W:** Wes Craven; **C:** Victor Hurwitz; **M:** David A(lexander) Hess.

The Last House on the Left 🦴 **2009 (R)** Grisly, graphic remake of Wes Craven's 1972 original. John (Goldwyn), Emma (Potter), and teenaged Mari (Paxton) Collingwood are vacationing in their country home. Mari joins friends Paige (MacIssac) and Justin (Clark) in some pot-induced motel room antics when they are interrupted by Justin's sadistic escaped con daddy Krug (Dillahunt) and a couple of sleazoids. Bad things happen and continue when the creep trio inadvertently seek shelter with the Collingwoods, who only have revenge on their minds. **109m/C; Blu-Ray, On Demand.** Garret Dillahunt; Michael Bowen; Riki Lindhome; Sara Paxton; Monica Potter; Tony Goldwyn; Aaron Paul; Martha MacIsaac; Spencer Treat Clark; Joshua Cox; **D:** Dennis Iliadis; **W:** Carl Ellsworth; Adam Alleca; **C:** Sharone Meir; **M:** John Murphy.

The Last Hunt 🦴🦴 1/2 **1956** Well-performed western starring Taylor as a seedy buffalo hunter who gains his identity from senseless acts of murder. When personalities clash, he seeks revenge on fellow buffalo hunter Granger. Shot in Custer National Park, the buffalo scenes were real-life attempts at keeping the animals controlled. Based on the novel by Milton Lott. **108m/C; VHS, DVD, Blu-Ray.** Robert Taylor; Stewart Granger; Lloyd Nolan; Debra Paget; Russ Tamblyn; Constance Ford; Ainslie Pryor; Ralph Moody; Fred Graham; Dan(iel) White; Bill (William) Phillips; Roy Barcroft; **D:** Richard Brooks; **W:** Richard Brooks; **M:** Daniele Amfitheatrof.

The Last Hunter 🦴 *Hunter of the Apocalypse* **1980 (R)** A soldier fights for his life behind enemy lines during the Vietnam War. **97m/C; VHS, DVD, Blu-Ray.** *IT* Tisa Farrow; David Warbeck; Tony King; Bobby Rhodes; Margit Evelyn Newton; John Steiner; Alan Collins; **D:** Anthony M. Dawson.

The Last Hurrah 🦴🦴 1/2 **1958** An aging Irish-American mayor battles corruption and political backbiting in his effort to get re-elected for the last time. Semi-acclaimed heart warmer, based on the novel by Edwin O'Connor. **121m/B; DVD, Blu-Ray.** Spencer Tracy; Basil Rathbone; John Carradine; Jeffrey Hunter; Dianne Foster; Pat O'Brien; Edward Brophy; James Gleason; Donald Crisp; Ricardo Cortez; Wallace Ford; Frank McHugh; Jane Darwell; Arthur Walsh; **D:** John Ford; **W:** Frank Nugent; **C:** Charles Lawton, Jr. Natl. Bd. of Review '58: Actor (Tracy), Director (Ford).

Last Hurrah for Chivalry 🦴🦴 *Hao xia* **1978** An honorable man cannot defend his family from a ruthless enemy and turns to two swordsmen-for-hire for help. Chinese with subtitles or dubbed. **108m/C; VHS, DVD.** *CH* Damian Lau; Wei Pei; San Lee Hoi; **D:** John Woo; **W:** John Woo; **C:** Ching Yu; Yao Chu Chang.

The Last International Playboy 🦴 *Frost* **2008 (R)** Self-pitying writer Jack Frost is moping around Manhattan because his childhood sweetie Carolina is getting married. Not even the sexual availability of a bevy of models can cheer Jack up. His 11-year-old neighbor, disarmingly sympathetic Sophie, is more mature than Jack whose Peter Pan complex is constantly annoying. **92m/C; DVD.** Jason Behr; Monet Mazur; India Ennenga; Lucy Gordon; Krysten Ritter; Mike Landry; **D:** Steve Clark; **W:** Steve Clark; Thomas Moffett; **C:** Brian Burgoyne.

Last Kind Words 🦴🦴 1/2 **2012** Eli (Daniels) moves into an isolated Kentucky farm with his family to help restore the fields for reclusive owner Waylon (Dourif). He becomes fascinated with a mysterious Amanada (Fast), who makes him promise to never go into the woods. A promise he will quite obviously break for plot purposes and which will make his life a great deal more complicated. **89m/C; DVD.** Spencer Daniels; Alexia Fast; Brad Dourif; **D:** Kevin Barker; **W:** Kevin Barker; **C:** Bill Otto; **M:** Robert A.A. Lowe. **VIDEO**

The Last King of Scotland 🦴🦴🦴 **2006 (R)** Raging biopic recounts the Ugandan dictatorship of Idi Amin, which lasted from 1971-1979 and devastated the country. Whitaker's performance captures the leader's charisma and savagery without flinching. A fictionalized composite character, Scotsman Nicholas Garrigan (McAvoy), enters Amin's camp in 1971 as a doctor determined to help, but slowly finds himself in the unenviable position of being Amin's right-hand man. Title refers to Amin's obsession with British imperialism and his belief that the Scots, whom he admired as fierce fighters, were equally ill-treated. Based on Giles Foden's 1998 novel. **121m/C; DVD.** *GB GE* Forest Whitaker; James McAvoy; Kerry Washington; Gillian Anderson; Simon McBurney; **D:** Kevin MacDonald; **W:** Peter Morgan; Jeremy Brock; **C:** Anthony Dod Mantle; **M:** Alex Heffes. Oscars '06: Actor (Whitaker); British Acad. '06: Actor (Whitaker), Adapt. Screenplay; Golden Globes '07: Actor--Drama (Whitaker); Screen Actors Guild '06: Actor (Whitaker).

The Last Kiss 🦴🦴 1/2 *L'Ultimo Bacio* **2001 (R)** Carlo (Accorsi) lives with his long-time girlfriend Guilia (Mezzogiorno), who tells him she's pregnant. This throws him into a tizzy since he doesn't really want to be a grown-up. Carlo's fading beauty mother, Anna (Sandrelli), also reacts badly since she doesn't want to be a grandma and abruptly decides to leave her boring hubby for new romantic possibilities. Both mother and son use their angst to justify their bad behavior as they decide what they really want from their lives. A generally sophisticated melodrama that doesn't take itself too seriously. Italian with subtitles. **115m/C; DVD.** *IT* Stefano Accorsi; Stefania Sandrelli; Giovanna Mezzogiorno; Martina Stella; Claudio Santamaria; Marco Cocci; Pierfrancesco Favino; Regina Orioli; Giorgio Pasotti; **D:** Gabriele Muccino; **W:** Gabriele Muccino; **C:** Marcello Montarsi; **M:** Paolo Buonino.

The Last Kiss 🦴 1/2 **2006 (R)** Botched remake of the Italian hit "L'Ultimo Bacio," now taking place in Madison, WI. About to hit 30, Michael (Braff, with a constant hangdog expression) finds his life spinning out of control after meeting sexy undergrad Kim (Bilson), while trying to balance the revelation that his live-in girlfriend Jenna (Barrett) is pregnant. Self-conscious dramedy about men unwilling to accept adult responsibility (yawn) and the exasperated women around them. How did Ed Burns not make this? **105m/C; DVD, Blu-Ray.** Zach Braff; Jacinda Barrett; Casey Affleck; Michael Weston; Blythe Danner; Tom Wilkinson; Lauren Lee Smith; Marley Shelton; Rachel Bilson; Eric Christian; Harold Ramis; **D:** Tony Goldwyn; **W:** Paul Haggis; **C:** Tom Stern; **M:** Michael Penn.

Last Knights 🦴🦴 **2015 (R)** A somewhat predictable historical action-adventure exploring themes of vengeance and loyalty. After his master Bartok (Freeman) is dishonored, Raiden (Owen) a fallen warrior with a dark past seeks revenge by organizing a rebellion against Gezza Hott (Hennie), an evil, corrupt man backed by the emporer. Not only has Hott taken Bartok's land and his riches, but Hott is also paranoid and demands Bartok's death. Though Hott lashes out against Raiden and his allies, they put their lives on the line to gain justice and expose the truth about their leaders. **115m/C; DVD, Blu-Ray, Streaming, Download.** Clive Owen; Morgan Freeman; Clifford Curtis; Aksel Hennie; Tsuyoshi Ihara; ***D:*** Kazuaki Kiriya; ***W:*** Michael Konyves; Dove Sussman; ***C:*** Antonio Riestra; ***M:*** Satnam Ramgotra; Martin Tillman.

The Last Laugh 1/2 *Der Letzte Mann* **1924** An elderly man, who as the doorman of a great hotel was looked upon as a symbol of "upper class," is demoted to washroom attendant due to his age. Important due to camera technique and consuming performance by Jannings. Silent with music score. A 91-minute version is also available. **88m/B; Silent; VHS, DVD, Blu-Ray.** *GE* Emil Jannings; Maly Delshaft; Max Hiller; ***D:*** F.W. Murnau; ***W:*** Carl Mayer; ***C:*** Karl Freund; ***M:*** Giuseppe Becce.

The Last Legion **2007 (PG-13)** Barbarians have taken Rome and young Romulus (Sangster), last of the Caesars, flees to Britain under the protection of General Aurelius (Firth), wise-man Ambrosinius (Kingsley), and a rag-tag group of cohorts. Seeking the Roman 9th Legion, they find a group of men who have become farmers and avoid conflict with local warlord Vortygn (Van Gorkum). Bloody battles ensue, although they're reduced to cheap CGI sequences worthy only as a distraction from the unlikeable characters and weak plot. Sangster's adequate as the boy emperor, Firth's desperately miscast as an action hero, and Kingsley chews the scenery. **110m/C; DVD.** *FR GB IT* Colin Firth; Ben Kingsley; Thomas Brodie-Sangster; Kevin McKidd; John Hannah; Iain Glen; Aishwarya Rai; Rupert Friend; Peter Mullan; Alexander Siddig; Harry Van Gorkum; James Cosmo; Owen Teale; ***D:*** Doug Lefler; ***W:*** Jez Butterworth; Tom Butterworth; ***C:*** Marco Pontecorvo; ***M:*** Patrick Doyle.

The Last Letter 1/2 **2004 (R)** A twist ending somewhat redeems the slow pace of this courtroom thriller. Forceful jury foreman Griffith (Forsythe) leads the other jurors in deciding the verdict for a serial killer (writer/director Gannon) accused of 14 gory murders (shown in flashbacks). But their deliberations aren't as clear-cut as you might imagine since the foreman seems determined to raise more than a reasonable doubt that the right man is on trial. **80m/C; DVD.** William Forsythe; Yancy Butler; Grace Zabriskie; Leo Rossi; Russell Gannon; ***D:*** Russell Gannon; ***W:*** Russell Gannon; ***C:*** Sean Dinwoodie; ***M:*** Terry Plumeri. **VIDEO**

The Last Letter **2013** A tense psychological thriller-drama centering on a difficult marriage and a daunting secret. Newlyweds Michael (Hardwick) and Catherine (Leal) seem to have it all. But not only does Michael's mother (Whitfield) disapprove of the marriage, Catherine has something she has kept from Michael. She has a sleep disorder that mixes reality with terrifying nightmares. After a horrible incident from Catherine's past comes back to haunt her, she seeks the help of her foster brother George (Dourdan). Living up to the vow to take care of each other, Catherine attempts to preserve her present by addressing a murderous incident from long ago. **96m/C; DVD, Streaming, Download.** Omari Hardwick; Sharon Leal; Gary Dourdan; Rocsi Diaz; Lynn Whitfield; ***D:*** Paul D. Hannah; ***W:*** Paul D. Hannah; ***C:*** Keith L. Smith; ***M:*** Nima Fakhrara. **VIDEO**

The Last Lieutenant 1/2 *The Second Lieutenant; Secondloitnanten* **1994** Aging Thor Espedal (Skjonberg) is a one-time second lieutenant who has just retired from the Merchant Marines and returned home to his beloved wife, Anna (Tellefsen). But since the year is 1940, his retirement is interrupted by the German Army invading his country. Espedal enlists in the resistance effort but finds the army in complete disarray. Still the old man and a group of volunteers become determined to hold a key mountain pass. Norwegian with subtitles. **102m/C; VHS, DVD.** *NO* Espen Skjonberg; Bjorn Sundquist; Rut Tellefsen; Gard B. Eidsvold; Lars Andreas Larssen; ***D:*** Hans Petter Moland; ***W:*** Hans Petter Moland; Axel Hellstenius; ***C:*** Harald Gunnar Paalgard; ***M:*** Randall Meyers.

Last Light **1993 (R)** A prison guard (Whitaker) on death row forms a tenuous bond with an incorrigible inmate (Sutherland) who's about to be executed. Disturbing, especially the execution scene. Filmed on location at California's Soledad Prison. Sutherland's directorial debut. **95m/C; VHS, DVD.** Kiefer Sutherland; Forest Whitaker; Clancy Brown; Lynne Moody; Kathleen Quinlan; Amanda Plummer; ***D:*** Kiefer Sutherland. **CABLE**

Last Lives **1998 (R)** Confusing parallel universe story has Malakai (Wirth) traveling to an alternate world to search for his lost wife. He discovers Adrienne (Rubin) about to marry Aaron (Howell) and Malakai kidnaps her to take her back to his world. **99m/C; VHS, DVD.** C. Thomas Howell; Jennifer Rubin; Billy Wirth; Judge Reinhold; ***D:*** Worth Keeter; ***W:*** Dan Duling; ***C:*** Kent Wakeford; ***M:*** Greg Edmonson. **VIDEO**

Last Love *Mr. Morgan's Last Love* **2013** Awkward drama finds grief-stricken expat American widower Matthew Morgan (Caine, with a wavering accent) living in Paris. He has some chance meetings with vibrant young dance teacher Pauline (Poesy) and their friendship develops as she urges him to get out and about. But Matthew is suddenly plunged back into despair, leading to a drug overdose that bings his estranged children (Kirk, Anderson) to his hospital bedside, where they squabble and wonder about Pauline. **115m/C; DVD, Blu-Ray.** *GE BE* Michael Caine; Clemence Poesy; Justin Kirk; Gillian Anderson; Jane Alexander; ***D:*** Sandra Nettelbeck; ***W:*** Sandra Nettelbeck; ***C:*** Michael Bertl; ***M:*** Hans Zimmer.

The Last Lovecraft: Relic of Cthulhu 1/2 **2009** Amusing, though uneven, low-budget horror spoof of the Lovecraft mythos. Cubicle-dwelling geek Jeff Phillips learns he's H.P. Lovecraft's last descendent and the only one who can protect an ancient artifact from being used by Cthulhu's cult to release their master from his underwater prison. Jeff and his buds need the help of Captain Olaf, but the film sags while they go a-huntin' before the final battle. **79m/C; DVD.** Kyle Davis; Devin McGuinn; Barak Hardley; Gregg Lawrence; ***D:*** Henry Saine; ***W:*** Devin McGuinn; ***C:*** Cameron Cannon; ***M:*** Michael Tavera. **VIDEO**

The Last Lullaby **2008 (R)** Former hitman Price (Sizemore) finds retirement boring before he unexpectedly gets involved in a kidnapping, which leads him to taking a job offered by millionaire Martin (Smitrovich). Price scopes out his target, small town librarian Sarah (Alexander), develops a soft spot for his mark, and becomes curious as to why Martin wants her whacked. Good performances and some unexpected twists; based on the Max Allan Collins' novel "The Last Quarry." **93m/C; DVD.** Tom Sizemore; Sasha Alexander; Bill Smitrovich; Sprague Grayden; Randall Batinkoff; ***D:*** Jeffrey Goodman; ***W:*** Max Allan Collins; Peter Biegen; ***C:*** Richard Rutkowski; ***M:*** Ben Lovett.

The Last Man **2000 (R)** Overweight, balding, neurotic graduate student Alan (Arnott), who believes he's the last man alive on earth, is thrilled to discover Sarah (Ryan), a babe who would never have even looked at him pre-apocalypse. But a snake appears in Alan's paradise in the form of hitchhiker Raphael (Montgomery), who's as dumb as he is good-looking (and he's very good looking). Naturally, Sarah is attracted to him—much to Alan's jealous dismay. So if you were the last three people alive, just how would you handle the situation? **93m/C; VHS, DVD.** David Arnott; Jeri Ryan; Dan Montgomery, Jr.; ***D:*** Harry Ralston; ***W:*** Harry Ralston; ***C:*** Michael Grady; ***M:*** Woody Jackson; Ivan Knight.

The Last Man 1/2 **2019 (R)** In a chaotic future after environmental and economic disasters, Kurt (Christensen), a veteran with PTSD, struggles to survive and questions what the future holds. Kurt's perspective changes when he hears the prophecy of street preacher Noe (Keitel), who predicts the world will end soon in an electrical storm. To prepare, Kurt builds a bunker and pays for its contents by taking a security job. He also regularly interacts the ghost of Johnny (Kelly), his best friend who died in combat, though it is unclear what reality really is. This dark neo-noir lacks an interesting story, and is further dulled by Kurt's endless narration. **104m/C; DVD.** Hayden Christensen; Harvey Keitel; Marco Leonardi; Liz Solari; Fernan Miras; ***D:*** Rodrigo H. Vila; ***W:*** Rodrigo H. Vila; ***C:*** Daniel Ortega; ***M:*** Emilio Kauderer.

The Last Man on Earth *L'Ultimo Uomo Della Terra* **1964** Price is the sole survivor of a plague which has turned the rest of the world into vampires, who constantly harass him. Uneven U.S./Italian production manages to convey a creepy atmosphere of dismay. **86m/B; VHS, DVD, Blu-Ray.** *IT* Vincent Price; Franca Bettoya; Giacomo "Jack" Rossi-Stuart; Emma Danieli; ***D:*** Ubaldo Ragona; Sidney Salkow; ***W:*** Richard Matheson; William P. Leicester; Furio M. Monetti; ***C:*** Franco Delli Colli; ***M:*** Paul Sawtell; Bert Shefter.

Last Man Standing **1995 (R)** L.A. police officer Wincott discovers corruption after his partner Banks is murdered. **96m/C; VHS, DVD.** Jeff Wincott; Jillian McWhirter; Jonathan Banks; Steve Eastin; Jonathan Fuller; Michael Greene; Ava Fabian; ***D:*** Joseph Merhi; ***W:*** Joseph Merhi; ***M:*** Louis Febre.

Last Man Standing 1/2 *Welcome to Jericho* **1996 (R)** Engaging but unoriginal gangster/western features a plot taken from Sergio Leone's "A Fistful of Dollars" (and Akira Kurosawa's "Yojimbo"). In the small 1930s border town of Jericho Texas, John Smith (Willis) hires himself out to both sides of a bootlegging war in an effort to make some quick cash. Bigger roles for Walken, the flinty trigger man for Irish boss Doyle (Kelly), and Dern, the town sheriff on the mob payroll, could have perked things up more. Willis nicely injects his smirking brand of wit while Hill provides his trademark visually exciting action sequences. **101m/C; DVD, Blu-Ray.** Bruce Willis; Bruce Dern; Christopher Walken; Karina Lombard; William Sanderson; David Patrick Kelly; Alexandra Powers; Leslie Mann; Michael Imperioli; R.D. Call; Ken Jenkins; Ned Eisenberg; ***D:*** Walter Hill; ***W:*** Walter Hill; ***C:*** Lloyd Ahern, II; ***M:*** Ry Cooder.

Last Man Standing *Close Quarters* **2011** Abby Collins has kept her past as a special ops agent a secret and is happy as a suburban wife and mother. Someone in her former unit is murdered and her husband is kidnapped. Abby must use that training to determine why she's now a target and rescue her husband. A Lifetime Original movie. **84m/C; DVD.** Catherine Bell; Mekhi Phifer; Anthony Michael Hall; ***D:*** Ernest R. Dickerson; ***W:*** Jolene Rice; ***C:*** Steven Bernstein; ***M:*** Laura Karpman. **CABLE**

The Last Married Couple in America **1980 (R)** A couple fight to stay happily married amidst the rampant divorce epidemic engulfing their friends. **103m/C; VHS, DVD.** George Segal; Natalie Wood; Richard Benjamin; Valerie Harper; Dom DeLuise; Priscilla Barnes; ***D:*** Gilbert Cates; ***M:*** Charles Fox.

The Last Marshal **1999 (R)** Tough Texas lawman Glenn is mighty riled when some no-account prisoners manage to escape from his jail. So he trails them to Miami to get them back. **102m/C; VHS, DVD.** John Ortiz; Scott Glenn; Constance Marie; Randall Batinkoff; Vincent Castellanos; Raymond Cruz; William Forsythe; Lisa Boyle; ***D:*** Mike Kirton. **VIDEO**

Last Men In Aleppo *De sidste maend i Aleppo* **2017** A documentary look at the Syrian Civil Defence, a group dedicated to rescuing civilians after bombings in Syria's deadly civil war. The documentary's filmmaker, Firas Fayyad, filmed the urban search-and-rescue group, also known as the White Helmets, in 2015 and 2016. Sidestepping the political reasons for the war, Fayyad focuses on members of the White Helmets-normal people taking action in extraordinary circumstances to protect the vulnerable. Fayyad shows them walking the city, listening for attacks, and acting when they hear them. Unflinching and unsentimental, the film lacks a definitive narrative arc but effectively shows how the war impacts average Syrians. **83m/C; DVD, Blu-Ray, Streaming.** *DK SY* ***D:*** Feras Fayyad; Steen Johannessen; ***W:*** Feras Fayyad; ***C:*** Mujahed Abou Al Joud; Fadi Al Halabi; Thaer Mohamed; ***M:*** Karsten Fundal.

The Last Metro *Le Dernier Metro* **1980 (PG)** Truffaut's alternately gripping and touching drama about a theatre company in Nazi-occupied Paris. In 1942, Lucas Steiner (Bennent) is a successful Jewish theatre director who is forced into hiding. He turns the running of the theatre over to his wife, Marion (the always exquisite Deneuve), who must contend with a pro-Nazi theatre critic (Richard) and her growing attraction to the company's leading man (Depardieu), who is secretly working with the Resistance. In French with English subtitles. **135m/C; VHS, DVD, Blu-Ray.** *FR* Catherine Deneuve; Gerard Depardieu; Heinz Bennent; Jean-Louis Richard; Jean Poiret; Andrea Ferreol; Paulette Dubost; Sabine Haudepin; Maurice Risch; Jean-Pierre Klein; Martine Simonet; Franck Pasquier; Jean-Jose Richer; Laszlo Szabo; Jessica Zucman; ***D:*** Francois Truffaut; ***W:*** Francois Truffaut; Suzanne Schiffman; Jean-Claude Grumberg; ***C:*** Nestor Almendros; ***M:*** Georges Delerue. Cesar '81: Actor (Depardieu), Actress (Deneuve), Art Dir./Set Dec., Cinematog., Director (Truffaut), Film, Score, Sound, Writing.

The Last Mile **1932** The staff of a prison prepares for the execution of a celebrated murderer. **70m/B; VHS, DVD.** Preston Foster; Howard Phillips; George E. Stone; ***D:*** Sam Bischoff.

The Last Mile 1/2 **1959** Rooney is surprisingly effective as a vicious prisoner in this remake of the 1932 pic. Death row inmates are constantly abused by sadistic guard Drake (Barry). John 'Killer' Mears (Rooney) leads an uprising, taking the guards and Father O'Connors (Overton) hostage. There's a gun battle, but Warden Stone (Bunce) refuses to negotiate. **81m/B; DVD.** Mickey Rooney; Frank Overton; Michael Constantine; Ford Rainey; Clifford David; John Vari; Harry Millard; John McCurry; Johnny Seven; George Marcy; Donald (Don "Red") Barry; Alan Bunce; Leon Janney; Frank Conroy; ***D:*** Howard W. Koch; ***W:*** Milton Subotsky; Seton I. Miller; ***C:*** Joseph Brun; ***M:*** Van Alexander.

The Last Mimzy **2007 (PG)** Loose adaptation of Lewis Padgett's short story "All Mimzy Were the Borogroves" (yeah, it's from Lewis Carroll's "Jabberwocky"). Noah (O'Neil) and his sister Emma (Wynn) find a box that's filled with odd objects, including a cute stuffed rabbit named Mimzy, who is actually a spokes—uh—rabbit from the future, where things are bad because of pollution and disease. The objects give the kids extraordinary powers that they are expected to use to solve these eco problems. Noah's spiritually-minded science teacher Larry (Wilson) thinks this is very cool, while the kids' parents seem to be fairly oblivious. Overstuffed with ideas but not condescending, which is a plus. **90m/C; DVD.** Joely Richardson; Timothy Hutton; Rainn Wilson; Kathryn Hahn; Noah Wilder; Rhiannon Leigh Wyn; Michael Clarke Duncan; ***D:*** Robert Shaye; ***W:*** Bruce Joel Rubin; Toby Emmerich; ***C:*** J.(James) Michael Muro; ***M:*** Howard Shore.

The Last Minute **2001 (R)** Billy Byrne (Beesley) is the "next big thing" and subjected to an incredible amount of media hype. But when his latest project is considered a dud, he falls just as fast. Jobless, friendless, and hopeless, Billy is taken in by Anna (Corrie), a young ruffian living with a group of adolescents under the thrall of Fagin-like drug dealer Grimshanks (Bell). Billy gets sucked into this new world as easily as he was manipulated in the old one. **104m/C; VHS, DVD.** *GB* Max Beesley; Tom Bell; Emily Corrie; Ciaran McMenamin; Jason Isaacs; Kate Ashfield; Anthony (Corlan) Higgins; Udo Kier; Stephen Dorff; ***D:*** Stephen Norrington; ***W:*** Stephen Norrington; ***C:*** James Welland; ***M:*** Paul Rabjohns.

The Last Movie Star 1/2 *Dog Years* **2017 (R)** A drama about a successful actor who feels that he did not live up to his potential. A 1970s film star, Vic Edwards (Reynolds) is now a lonely old man. Traveling to Nashville to accept an award, he is angered to learn the event was organized by young film geeks and takes place in a bar. He tanks his appearance, and has his indifferent driver, goth Lil (Winter), drive him to Knoxville. As Vic visits places from his past, Lil opens up about her life. Director Rifkin gives Reynolds the creative space to show his talents and the actor does not disappoint. **94m/C; DVD, Blu-Ray, Streaming.** Burt Reynolds; Ariel Winter; Clark Duke; Chevy Chase; Ellar Coltrane; ***D:*** Adam Rifkin; ***W:*** Adam Rifkin; ***C:*** Scott Winig; ***M:*** Austin Wintory.

The Last Musketeer 1/2 **2000** Gifted fencer Steve McTeer (Green) wants to get away from his past and his family's criminal activities. So when he's falsely accused of a crime, he decides to hide out in the Scottish Highlands, taking an instructor position at a girls' boarding school. But he can't really escape. **85m/C; DVD.** *GB* Robson Green; Arkie Whiteley; Maureen Beattie; John McGlynn; ***D:*** Bill Britten; ***W:*** Sebastian Secker Walker; ***C:*** Tony Miller; ***M:*** John Rea. **TV**

The Last New Yorker 1/2 **2007** Stubborn 70-something Lenny (Chianese) is informed by his stockbroker nephew Zach (Hamilton) that he is broke. Hating the changes he sees all around his beloved New York City, Lenny decides to commit suicide but is interrupted by Mimi (Chalfont). Suddenly revitalized, self-deluding Lenny decides to reinvent himself and take another chance on love. **91m/C; DVD.** Dominic Chianese; Dick Latessa; Kathleen Chalfant; Josh Hamilton; Joe Grifasi; Ben Hammer; Sylvia Kauders; Gerry Vichi; ***D:*** Harry Wang; ***W:*** Adam Forgash; ***C:*** Derek McKane; ***M:*** Dario Eskenazi.

Last Night **1998 (R)** It's 6 p.m. in Toronto and the world ends in six hours. And no one's going to save the day. So everyone decides how they're spending their last few hours. Patrick (McKellar) attends a family dinner and then wants to be alone; instead he's drawn into Sandra's (Oh) drama. She's stuck in traffic across town from her husband and Patrick tries to help her get to her rendezvous. Meanwhile, his best friend Craig (Rennie) has a few sexual conquests he still wants to make, including one with their high school French teacher, Mrs. Carlton (Bujold). Mordant humor; appealing performances. **94m/C; VHS, DVD.** *CA* Don McKellar; Sandra Oh; Callum Keith Rennie; Sarah Polley; David Cronenberg; Genevieve Bujold; Tracy Wright; Roberta Maxwell; Robin Gammell; Karen Glave; Jackie Burroughs; ***D:*** Don McKellar; ***W:*** Don McKellar; ***C:*** Douglas Koch; ***M:*** Alexina Louie; Alex Pauk. Genie '98: Actress (Oh), Support. Actor (Rennie).

Last Night **2010 (R)** Attractive marital drama (both the cast and settings) about restlessness vs. fidelity. At a party, Joanna (Knightley) gets green-eyed over the aggressive flirting done by her husband Michael's (Worthington) very attractive coworker Laura (Mendes). This leads to a petty-but-escalating marital quarrel and when Michael leaves on a business trip with Laura, the suggestion is there that some cheating is likely. Joanna just happens to run into her handsome, French ex-lover Alex (Canet) who sees no harm in Joanna doing a little canoodling of her own. **90m/C; DVD, Blu-Ray, On Demand.** *US CA FR* Keira Knightley; Sam Worthington; Eva Mendes; Guillaume Canet; Griffin Dunne; Anson Mount; Stephanie Romanov; Scott Adsit; Justine Cotsonas; ***D:*** Massy Tadjedin; ***W:*** Massy Tadjedin; ***C:*** Peter Deming; ***M:*** Clint Mansell.

The Last of England 1/2 **1987** A furious non-narrative film by avant-garde filmmaker Jarman, depicting the modern British landscape as a funereal, waste-filled rubble-heap—as depleted morally as it is environmentally. **87m/C; VHS, DVD.** *GB* Tilda Swinton; Spencer Leigh; Spring; Gerrard McArthur; ***D:*** Derek Jarman; ***W:*** Derek Jarman; ***C:*** Derek Jarman; Richard Helsop; Christopher Hughes; ***M:*** Simon Fisher Turner.

The Last of His Tribe **1992 (PG-13)** In 1911 an anthropologist befriends an Indian and discovers that Ishi is the last surviving member of California's Yahi tribe. Ishi then becomes a media and scientific society darling, spending the remainder of his remaining life in captivity to academia. A good portrayal of the Native American plight. Based on a true story. **90m/C; VHS, DVD.** Jon Voight; Graham Greene; David Ogden Stiers; Jack Blessing; Anne Archer; Daniel Benzali; ***D:*** Harry Hook. **CABLE**

The Last of Mrs. Cheyney **1929** Stagey early talkie that's still a clever adaptation of the Frederick Lonsdale play. Con artist Mrs. Fay Cheyney (Shearer) is invited to a country estate, but she intends to steal a valuable necklace from her hostess. She's caught in the act by Lord Arthur (Rathbone), who makes a rude proposal, but Fay decides to take her chances that some society blackmail will prevent the police from being called. She has a change of heart when she realizes she's in love with Lord Arthur. **94m/B; DVD.** Norma Shearer; Basil Rathbone; George Barraud; Herbert Bunston; Hedda Hopper; Maude Turner Gordon; ***D:*** Sidney Franklin; ***W:*** Hans Kraly; Claudine West; ***C:*** William H. Daniels.

The Last of Mrs. Cheyney **1937** Remake of Norma Shearer's 1929 hit, based on the play by Frederick Lonsdale, about a sophisticated jewel thief in England. Crawford stars as the jewel thief who poses as a wealthy woman to get into parties hosted by London bluebloods. Dripping with charm, she works her way into Lord Drilling's mansion where she plans a huge heist. The film is handled well, and the cast gives solid performances throughout. This chic comedy of high society proved to be one of Crawford's most popular films of the '30s. **98m/B; DVD.** Joan Crawford; Robert Montgomery; William Powell; Frank Morgan; Nigel Bruce; Jessie Ralph; ***D:*** Richard Boleslawski; George Fitzmaurice; ***C:*** George J. Folsey.

The Last of Mrs. Lincoln 1/2 **1976** Intimate made for TV portrayal of the famous first lady. Film focuses on Mary Todd Lincoln's life from the assassination of her husband, through her autumn years, and her untimely downfall. **118m/C; VHS, DVD.** Julie Harris; Robby Benson; Patrick Duffy; ***D:*** George Schaefer; ***M:*** Lyn Murray. **TV**

The Last of Robin Hood 1/2 **2013 (R)** Based on aged, drunken actor Errol Flynn's (Kline) last affair with teenaged aspiring actress Beverly Aadland (Fanning), enabled by her fame-obsessed mother, Florence (Sarandon). Kline makes a fine, albeit less ravaged-looking, former matinee idol, but the bland onscreen story isn't nearly as outrageous as the real thing. **90m/C; DVD, Blu-Ray.** Kevin Kline; Dakota Fanning; Susan Sarandon; Matt Kane; Bryan Batt; Max Casella; ***D:*** Richard Glatzer; Wash Westmoreland; ***W:*** Richard Glatzer; Wash Westmoreland; ***C:*** Michael Simmonds; ***M:*** Nick Urata.

The Last of Sheila 1/2 **1973 (PG)** A movie producer invites six big-star friends for a cruise aboard his yacht, the "Sheila." He then stages an elaborate "Whodunnit" parlor game to discover which one of them murdered his wife. **119m/C; VHS, DVD.** Richard Benjamin; James Coburn; James Mason; Dyan Cannon; Joan Hackett; Raquel Welch; Ian McShane; Yvonne Romain; Pierre Rosso; Serge Citon; Roberto Rossi; ***D:*** Herbert Ross; ***W:*** Anthony Perkins; Stephen Sondheim; ***C:*** Gerry Turpin; ***M:*** Billy Goldenberg.

The Last of the Blonde Bombshells 1/2 **2000 (PG-13)** Elizabeth (Dench) played sax with the all-girl swing band, The Blonde Bombshells, during WWII. With the urgings of granddaughter Joan (Findlay) and drummer Patrick (Holm)?who played in drag—Elizabeth is encouraged to reunite the band members. If they can find them and get them to agree. Good cast but the charm is on the low-burner and rather than swinging, it's more a sedate fox-trot. **80m/C; VHS, DVD.** Dame Judi Dench; Ian Holm; Olympia Dukakis; Leslie Caron; Cleo Laine; Joan Sims; Billie Whitelaw; June Whitfield; Felicity Dean; Valentine Pelka; Millie Findlay; ***D:*** Gilles Mackinnon; ***W:*** Alan Plater; ***C:*** Richard Greatrex; ***M:*** John Keane. **CABLE**

The Last of the Dogmen 1/2 **1995 (PG)** Cliched modern western with an intriguing premise and good actors. Montana bounty hunter Lewis Gates (Berenger) is recruited to nab three escaped cons but finds them dead and a Cheyenne arrow nearby. Gates does some investigating (in a library no less!) and discovers that maybe some descendants of the 1864 Sand Creek massacre are existing in the woods. He gets anthropologist Lillian Sloan (Hershey) involved, discovers a tribe of modern-day dog soldiers, and finds a very angry sheriff (Smith) on their trail. Alberta, Canada passes for Big Sky country. **117m/C; VHS, DVD.** Tom Berenger; Barbara Hershey; Kurtwood Smith; Steve Reevis; Andrew Miller; Gregory Scott Cummins; ***Nar:*** Wilford Brimley; ***D:*** Tab Murphy; ***W:*** Tab Murphy; ***C:*** Karl Walter Lindenlaub; ***M:*** David Arnold.

The Last of the Finest 1/2 *Street Legal; Blue Heat* **1990 (R)** Overzealous anti-drug task force cops break the rules in trying to put dealer-drug lords in prison; ostensibly a parallel on the Iran-Contra affair. **106m/C; VHS, DVD, Blu-Ray, Streaming.** Brian Dennehy; Joe Pantoliano; Jeff Fahey; Bill Paxton; Deborra-Lee Furness; Guy Boyd; Henry Darrow; Lisa Jane Persky; Michael C. Gwynne; ***D:*** John MacKenzie; ***W:*** George Armitage; Jere P. Cunningham; ***M:*** Jack Nitzsche.

The Last of the High Kings 1/2 *Summer Fling* **1996 (R)** Underachieving Irish Frankie (Leto) decides to forget about his university entrance exams and enjoy his summer (it's 1977) by cutting loose and fantasizing about various girls he knows. What he doesn't realize is that young American Erin (Ricci), who's staying with his crazy family, has fallen for him. Pleasant romance with a talented cast. Based on the novel "The Last of the High Kings" by Ferdia Mac Anna. **103m/C; VHS, DVD.** *IR GB DK* Catherine O'Hara; Jared Leto; Christina Ricci; Gabriel Byrne; Stephen Rea; Colm Meaney; Lorraine Pilkington; Jason Barry; Emily Mortimer; Karl Hayden; Ciaran Fitzgerald; Darren Monks; Peter Keating; Alexandra Haughey; Renee Weldon; Amanda Shun; ***D:*** David Keating; ***W:*** Gabriel Byrne; David Keating; ***C:*** Bernd Heinl; ***M:*** Michael Convertino.

The Last of the Mobile Hotshots **1969** Southern-fried ham adapted from an unsuccessful Tennessee Williams play, "The Seven Descents of Myrtle." Floozy Myrtle (Redgrave) marries dying Jeb (Coburn) during a TV game show. He's inherited the family farm but needs an heir so his despised black half-brother Chicken (Hooks) won't get the property. Myrtle wants the money for herself so she's willing to do whatever's necessary. Title has something to do with Myrtle's previous occupation. **108m/C; DVD.** James Coburn; Lynn Redgrave; Robert Hooks; Perry Hayes; Reggie King; ***D:*** Sidney Lumet; ***W:*** Gore Vidal; ***C:*** James Wong Howe; ***M:*** Quincy Jones.

The Last of the Mohicans **1920** Color tints enhance this silent version of the James Fenimore Cooper rouser. Beery is the villainous Magua, with Bedford memorable as the lovely Cora and Roscoe as the brave Uncas. Fine action sequences, including the Huron massacre at Fort Henry. Director credit was shared when Tourneur suffered an on-set injury and was off for three months. **75m/B; Silent; VHS, DVD.** Wallace Beery; Barbara Bedford; Albert Roscoe; Lillian Hall-Davis; Henry Woodward; James Gordon; George Hackathorne; Harry Lorraine; Nelson McDowell; Theodore Lorch; Boris Karloff; ***D:*** Maurice Tourneur; Clarence Brown; ***W:*** Robert A.(R.A.) Dillon; ***C:*** Charles Van Enger. Natl. Film Reg. '95.

The Last of the Mohicans **1932** Serial based on James Fenimore Cooper's novel of the life-and-death struggle of the Mohican Indians during the French and Indian War. Twelve chapters, 13 minutes each. Remade as a movie in 1936 and 1992 and as a TV movie in 1977. **230m/B; VHS, DVD.** Edwina Booth; Harry Carey, Sr.; Hobart Bosworth; Frank "Junior" Coghlan; ***D:*** Ford Beebe; B. Reeves Eason.

The Last of the Mohicans 1/2 **1936** James Fenimore Cooper's classic about the French and Indian War in colonial America is brought to the screen. Remake of the 1932 serial. **91m/B; VHS, DVD.** Randolph Scott; Binnie Barnes; Bruce Cabot; Henry Wilcoxon; Heather Angel; Hugh Buckler; ***D:*** George B. Seitz.

The Last of the Mohicans **1992 (R)** It's 1757, at the height of the French and English war in the American colonies, with various Native American tribes allied to each side. Hawkeye (Day-Lewis), a white frontiersman raised by the Mohicans, wants nothing to do with either, until he rescues the beautiful Cora (Stowe) from the revenge-minded Huron Magua (Studi in a powerful performance). Graphically violent battle scenes are realistic, but not gratuitous. The real pleasure in this adaptation, which draws from both the James Fenimore Cooper novel and the 1936 film, is in its lush look and attractive stars. Means is terrific in his film debut as Hawkeye's foster-father. **114m/C; VHS, DVD, Blu-Ray.** Daniel Day-Lewis; Madeleine Stowe; Wes Studi; Russell Means; Eric Schweig; Jodhi May; Steven Waddington; Maurice Roeves; Colm Meaney; Patrice Chereau; Pete Postlethwaite; Terry Kinney; Dylan Baker; Dennis Banks; ***D:*** Michael Mann; ***W:*** Michael Mann; Christopher Crowe; ***C:*** Dante Spinotti; ***M:*** Randy Edelman; Trevor Jones. Oscars '92: Sound.

Last of the Red Hot Lovers 1/2 **1972 (PG)** Not so funny adaptation of Neil Simon's Broadway hit. Middle-aged man decides to have a fling and uses his mother's apartment to seduce three very strange women. **98m/C; VHS, DVD.** Alan Arkin; Paula Prentiss; Sally Kellerman; Renee Taylor; ***D:*** Gene Saks; ***W:*** Neil Simon.

The Last of the Unjust *Le Dernier des Injustes* **2013 (PG-13)** Filmmaker Lanzmann held a series of fascinating interviews in 1975 with a man named Benjamin Murmelstein. Nearly 40 years later, Lanzmann returns to his conversations with a man who was there for the formation of the Third Reich and places them in stark context. The result is a fascinating documentary about the eternal impact of World War II on Europe, through the memories of a astounding gentleman, the last President of the Jewish Council in the Theresienstadt ghetto who helps over 100,000 Jews leave Austria during the war. Both a portrait of two men—the filmmaker and the subject—and commentary on memory and war. **220m/C; DVD, Blu-Ray.** *FR AT* ***D:*** Claude Lanzmann; ***W:*** Claude Lanzmann; ***C:*** William Lubtchansky; Caroline Champetier.

Last Orders **2001 (R)** Based on Graham Swift's award-winning 1996 novel, covering some 50 years in the lives of four London friends. Vic (Courtenay), Ray (Hoskins), and Lenny (Hemmings) meet in their favorite East London pub to toast their recently deceased friend Jack (Caine), along with Jack's son, Vince (Winstone). Jack's last request was to have his ashes scattered in the sea at Margate, where he spent his honeymoon with wife Amy (Mirren) in 1939. Amy, however, will not make the trip as she's going to visit their severely handicapped daughter June (Morelli), whom Jack could never accept. Flashbacks fill out the storylines and the cast is stellar. **109m/C; VHS, DVD.** *UK* Michael Caine; Bob Hoskins; Tom Courtenay; David Hemmings; Ray Winstone; Dame Helen Mirren; J.J. Feild; Cameron Fitch; Nolan Hemmings; Anatol Yusef; Kelly Reilly; Laura Morelli; ***D:*** Fred Schepisi; ***W:*** Fred Schepisi; ***C:*** Brian Tufano; ***M:*** Paul Grabowsky.

Last Ounce of Courage **2012 (PG)** A young man connects with his grandfather during their battle to restore Christmas celebrations to their town. **101m/C; DVD, Blu-Ray.** Marshall Teague; Jennifer O'Neill; Rusty Joiner; Fred Williamson; Hunter Gomez; ***D:*** Darrell Campbell; Kevin McAfee; ***W:*** Darrell Campbell; Gina Headrick; Richard Headrick; ***C:*** Jason Cantu; ***M:*** Ron Owen.

Last Outlaw **1936** The last of the famous badmen of the old West is released from jail and returns home to find that times have changed. The action climaxes in an old-time blazing shoot-out. **79m/B; VHS, DVD.** Harry Carey, Sr.; Hoot Gibson; Henry B. Walthall; Tom Tyler; Russell Hopton; Alan Curtis; Harry Woods; Barbara Pepper; ***D:*** Christy Cabanne.

The Last Outlaw 1/2 **1993 (R)** Rourke stars as an ex-Confederate officer who leads a gang of outlaws until his violent excesses leave even them disgusted. The gang shoots Rourke but of course he doesn't die and then he sets out for revenge. **90m/C; VHS, DVD.** Mickey Rourke; Dermot Mulroney; Ted Levine; John C. McGinley; Steve Buscemi; Keith David; ***D:*** Geoff Murphy; ***W:*** Eric Red. **CABLE**

The Last Outpost **1935** During WWI, intelligence agent Stevenson (Rains) rescues British officer Andrews (Grant) from a hostile Kurdish tribe. After being wounded, Andrews is hospitalized in Cairo where he falls for his nurse Rosemary (Michael), who's actually Stevenson's wife. There's a climactic battle at a remote outpost in the Sudan and the two men meet once again. **72m/B; DVD.** Claude Rains; Cary Grant; Gertrude Michael; Akim Tamiroff; Kathleen Burke; Billy Bevan; Colin Tapley; ***D:*** Louis Gasnier; Charles T. Barton; ***W:***

Charles Brackett; Frank Partos; Philip MacDonald; **C:** Theodor Sparkuhl.

Last Passenger 🦴🦴 1/2 **2014 (R)** This hybrid of "Speed" and "Murder on the Orient Express" actually gets points for trying to take a very simple thriller premise – strangers stuck on a moving vehicle – and turning it into something more interesting. A group of sleepy commuters on a late-night London train (led by Scott) slowly realize that their train isn't stopping. Who's behind their runaway train? Director Nooshin wisely spends more time creating tension out of character dynamics rather than special FX, though the third act gets more bombastic and logic-defying than it needed to. **97 minutesm/C; DVD, Blu-Ray.** Dougray Scott; Kara Tointon; Iddo Goldberg; David Schofield; Lindsay Duncan; **D:** Omid Nooshin; **W:** Omid Nooshin; Andy Love; **C:** Angus Hudson; **M:** Liam Bates.

The Last Picture Show 🦴🦴🦴🦴 **1971 (R)** Based on Larry McMurtry's novel and set in Archer City, a backwater Texas town where most of the story plays out at the local hangout run by ex-cowboy Sam the Lion (Johnson). Duane (Bridges) hooks up with spoiled pretty girl Jacy (Shepherd), while sensitive Sonny (Bottoms) has an affair with the coach's neglected wife, Ruth (Leachman). Loss of innocence, disillusionment and confusion are portrayed against the backdrop of a town about to lose its cinema. Shepherd's and Bottoms' film debut. Stunningly photographed by Surtees in B&W (Bogdanovich claimed he didn't want to "prettify" the picture by shooting in color). Followed by a weak sequel, "Texasville." **118m/B; VHS, DVD.** Jeff Bridges; Timothy Bottoms; Ben Johnson; Cloris Leachman; Cybill Shepherd; Ellen Burstyn; Sam Bottoms; Clu Gulager; Sharon Taggart; Randy Quaid; Bill (Billy) Thurman; John Hillerman; **D:** Peter Bogdanovich; **W:** Peter Bogdanovich; Larry McMurtry; **C:** Robert L. Surtees. Oscars '71: Support. Actor (Johnson), Support. Actress (Leachman); British Acad. '72: Screenplay, Support. Actor (Johnson), Support. Actress (Leachman); Golden Globes '72: Support. Actor (Johnson); Natl. Bd. of Review '71: Support. Actor (Johnson), Support. Actress (Leachman); Natl. Film Reg. '98; N.Y. Film Critics '71: Screenplay, Support. Actor (Johnson), Support. Actress (Burstyn); Natl. Soc. Film Critics '71: Support. Actress (Burstyn).

The Last Place on Earth 🦴🦴 1/2 **1985** Saga of bitter hardship and ambition depicting the 1911 race between the British Antarctic Expedition, led by Captain Robert Falcon (Shaw), and his Norwegian rival Roald Amundsen (Ousdal) to conquer the South Pole. On seven cassettes. **385m/C; VHS, DVD.** *CA* Martin Shaw; Sverre Anker Ousdal; Max von Sydow; Susan Wooldridge; **D:** Ferdinand Fairfax; **W:** Trevor Griffiths; **C:** John Coquillon; **M:** Trevor Jones. **TV**

The Last Porno Flick 🦴 **1974 (PG)** A pornographic movie script winds up in the hands of a couple of goofy cab drivers. The twosome sneak the movie's genre past the producers, families, and police. **90m/C; VHS, DVD.** Michael Pataki; Marianna Hill; Carmen Zapata; Mike Kellin; Colleen Camp; Tom Signorelli; Antony Carbone; **D:** Ray Marsh.

The Last Posse 🦴🦴 **1953** Cattle baron Sampson Drune (Bickford) forms a posse, which includes drunken sheriff John Frazier (Crawford), to go after the Romers, who have stolen money from Drune that they believe is rightfully theirs. The posse finally returns to town and flashbacks reveal what happened to the money and the men, who didn't all survive. **82m/B; DVD.** Charles Bickford; Broderick Crawford; John Derek; Wanda Hendrix; Skip Homeier; James Bell; Guy Wilkerson; Warner Anderson; Henry Hull; **D:** Alfred Werker; **W:** Kenneth Gamet; **C:** Burnett Guffey.

Last Rampage 🦴🦴 *Last Rampage: The Escape of Gary Tison* **2017 (R)** A true crime drama centered on a family-driven prison escape. In July 1978, brothers Donny (MacNicoll), Ricky (Moore), and Ray (Brown) smuggle guns into an Arizona prison so their father Gary (Patrick) and fellow inmate Randy (Browning) can escape. Sociopathic Gary is serving a life sentence for killing a prison guard, but he and his guilliable wife Dorothy (Graham) have convinced their sons that Gary is innocent. After the escape, the brothers go on the run with them to Mexico but realize that their father is an unrepentant killer. The well-constructed film is enhanced by strong performances by Patrick and Graham. **93m/C; DVD.** Robert Patrick; Heather Graham; Bruce Davison; Alex MacNicoll; Molly C. Quinn; **D:** Dwight H. Little; **W:** Alvaro Rodriguez; **C:** Rafael Leyva; **M:** Tobias Enhus; Richard Patrick.

The Last Remake of Beau Geste 🦴🦴 **1977 (PG)** A slapstick parody of the familiar Foreign Legion story from the Mel Brooks-ish school of loud genre farce. Gary Cooper makes an appearance by way of inserted footage from the 1939 straight version. **85m/C; VHS, DVD.** Marty Feldman; Ann-Margret; Michael York; Peter Ustinov; James Earl Jones; **D:** Marty Feldman; **W:** Marty Feldman; Chris Allen.

The Last Request 🦴🦴 **2006 (R)** Borscht Belt one-liners find their place in this dark family comedy as dying comedian Pop (Aiello) wants one of his two sons to get married and provide an heir to the family name. Womanizing Tom (Scotti) actually dies trying, which leads to shy seminarian Jeff (Knight) embarking on a disastrous sexual quest. He meets a lot of lunatic prospects while the perfect girl (Lloyd) is right in front of him. **91m/C; DVD.** Danny Aiello; T.R. Knight; Sabrina Lloyd; Nick Scotti; Barbara Feldon; Mario Cantone; Joe Piscopo; Frank Vincent; Vincent Pastore; Tony Lo Bianco; **D:** John DeBellis; **W:** John DeBellis; **C:** Dan Karlok; **M:** Waddy Wachtel. **VIDEO**

Last Resort 🦴🦴 *She Knew No Other Way* **1986 (R)** A married furniture executive unknowingly takes his family on vacation to a sex-saturated, Club Med-type holiday spot, and gets more than he anticipated. **80m/C; VHS, DVD.** Charles Grodin; Robin Pearson Rose; John Aston; Ellen Blake; Megan Mullally; Christopher Ames; Jon Lovitz; Scott Nemes; Gerrit Graham; Mario Van Peebles; Phil Hartman; Mimi Lieber; Steve Levitt; **D:** Zane Buzby; **W:** Jeff Buhai; **C:** Stephen M. Katz; Alex Nepomniaschy; **M:** Steven Nelson; Thom Sharp.

Last Resort 🦴 *Kill Theory* **2009 (R)** Predictable plot, annoying and stupid characters. A group of friends are celebrating their college graduation at a secluded lakeside house. A man just released from a hospital for the criminally insane traps them inside and forces them into a game where they have to kill each other to survive (until only one is left) or they all die. **82m/C; DVD.** Agnes Bruckner; Taryn Manning; Patrick Flueger; Teddy Dunn; Theo Rossi; Daniel Franzee; Kevin Gage; Steffi Wickens; **D:** Chris Moore; **W:** Kelly Palmer; **C:** David A. Armstrong; **M:** Michael Suby. **VIDEO**

The Last Reunion 🦴 1/2 **1980** The only witness to a brutal killing of a Japanese official and his wife during WWII seeks revenge on the guilty American platoon, 33 years later. Violent. **98m/C; VHS, DVD.** Cameron Mitchell; Leo Fong; Chanda Romero; Vic Silayan; Hal Bokar; Philip Baker Hall; **D:** Jay Wertz.

The Last Ride 🦴🦴 *F.T.W.* **1994 (R)** Frank T. Wells (Rourke) is out of prison after 10 years and free to try to recapture his former rodeo glory. Hellcat Scarlett Stuart's on the run from a botched bank job/murder perpetrated by her vicious brother Clem (Berg). Scarlett manages to hook up with Frank and decides to help him out financially by robbing convenience stores. Frank's not too happy when he finds out. Rourke is surprisingly subdued and Singer's properly unsympathetic but they don't seem to be working in the same movie. Nice Montana scenery though. **102m/C; VHS, DVD.** Mickey Rourke; Lori Singer; Brion James; Peter Berg; Rodney A. Grant; Aaron Neville; **D:** Michael Karbelnikoff; **W:** Mari Kornhauser; **C:** James L. Carter; **M:** Gary Chang.

The Last Ride 🦴🦴 **2004** A made-for-TV film designed to sell the newest version of Pontiac's GTO, Dennis Hopper stars as Ronnie Purnell, an ex-con out for revenge on the cop who sent him away 30 years ago. Standing in his way is his own son whom the cop raised, and aiding him is his estranged grandson. Christmas must be fun at their house. **85m/C; DVD.** Dennis Hopper; Will Patton; Fred Ward; **D:** Guy Norman Bee; **W:** Rob Cohen; Ron McGee; **C:** Karl Herrmann; **M:** Frankie Blue. **TV**

Last Ride 🦴🦴 **2009** Kev (Weaving) is a violent ex-con who hits the road with his 10-year-old son Chook (Russell). They move from place to place, heading deeper into the Outback and the reasons for leaving civilization behind are slowly revealed in flashback. The father-son bond is unnerving and the pic is tension-filled yet eerily beautiful. **90m/C; DVD.** *AU* Hugo Weaving; Tom Russell; Anita Hegh; John Brumpton; **D:** Glendyn Ivin; **W:** Mac Gudgeon; **C:** Greig Fraser; **M:** Paul Charlier.

The Last Ride 🦴🦴 1/2 **2012 (PG-13)** An engaging, small-budget indie set in December 1952 as hellraising Hank Williams, ravaged by illness and indulgence, is on a road trip in his powder-blue Cadillac Eldorado. Unhappy young mechanic Silas jumps at the chance to drive 'Mr. Wells" from Montgomery, Alabama to stops in West Virginia and Ohio. He's also supposed to keep the superstar (whom he doesn't recognize) sober, which he is unable to do even as he slowly gains Hank's respect. Based on the last days of Williams, who died in the back seat of his Caddy on January 1, 1953. **106m/C; DVD, Blu-Ray.** Henry Thomas; Jesse James; Fred Dalton Thompson; Kaley Cuoco; Ray McKinnon; Stephen Tobolowsky; **D:** Harry Z. Thomason; **W:** Howard Klausner; **C:** James Roberson.

The Last Ride of the Dalton Gang 🦴🦴 **1979** A long-winded retelling of the wild adventures that made the Dalton gang legendary among outlaws. **146m/C; VHS, DVD.** Larry Wilcox; Jack Palance; Randy Quaid; Cliff (Potter) Potts; Dale Robertson; Don Collier; **D:** Dan Curtis.

The Last Riders 🦴 **1990 (R)** Motorcycle centaur Estrada revs a few motors fleeing from cycle club cronies and crooked cops. Full throttle foolishness. **90m/C; VHS, DVD.** Erik Estrada; William (Bill) Smith; Armando Silvestre; Kathrin Lautner; **D:** Joseph Merhi.

Last Rites 🦴🦴 **1988 (R)** A priest at St. Patrick's Cathedral in New York allows a young Mexican woman to seek sanctuary from the Mob, who soon come after both of them. **103m/C; VHS, DVD.** Tom Berenger; Daphne Zuniga; Chick Vennera; Dane Clark; Carlo Pacchi; Anne Twomey; Paul Dooley; Vassili Lambrinos; **D:** Donald P. Bellisario; **W:** Donald P. Bellisario; **C:** David Watkin; **M:** Bruce Broughton.

The Last Rites of Joe May 🦴 1/2 **2011** After a long hospital stay, aging small-time hustler Joe May (Farina) returns to his Chicago neighborhood to find out everyone assumed he died. His landlord pawned his possessions and rented his apartment to troubled single mom Jenny (Allman), who takes Joe in to pay the rent. Joe takes a shine to her young daughter Angelina (Droeger) and wants to get rid of Jenny's abusive boyfriend (Barford) but not a lot really goes on. **107m/C; DVD.** Dennis Farina; Jamie Anne Allman; Meredith Droeger; Ian Barford; Chelcie Ross; Gary Cole; **D:** Joe Maggio; **W:** Joe Maggio; **C:** Jay Silver; **M:** Lindsay Marcus.

The Last Rites of Ransom Pride 🦴 1/2 **2009 (R)** Odd western set in 1912. Juliette wants to retrieve the remains of her outlaw lover Ransom whose body is being held hostage by revenge-minded Bruja in Mexico. Bruja is willing to trade for Ransom's good brother Champ but their preacher father vetoes the idea and then sends a posse after Juliette and Champ when they ignore his wishes. **83m/C; DVD.** Lizzy Caplan; Cote de Pablo; Jon Foster; Dwight Yoakam; Jason Priestley; Kris Kristofferson; Peter Dinklage; Scott Speedman; **D:** Tiller Russell; **W:** Tiller Russell; Ray Wylie Hubbard; **C:** Roger Vernon; **M:** Jeff Danna. **VIDEO**

The Last Run 🦴 1/2 **1971** Mediocre crime potboiler that's heavy-handed in its symbolism. Chicago mob driver Harry (Scott) has retired to Spain but is called out for one last job. He must drive young escaped con Paul (Musante) and his girlfriend Claudie (Van Devere) into France but they've been double-crossed by the wiseguys who sprung Paul. **95m/C; DVD.** George C. Scott; Trish Van Devere; Tony Musante; Colleen Dewhurst; Aldo Sambrell; **D:** Richard Fleischer; **W:** Alan Sharp; **C:** Sven Nykvist; **M:** Jerry Goldsmith.

Last Run 🦴 1/2 **2001 (R)** Frank (Assante) is a former top-secret op who specialized in rescuing Russian defectors. His last assignment got his lover killed and now Frank is after the assassin who caused his life to go wrong. **98m/C; VHS, DVD.** Armand Assante; Jurgen Prochnow; Ornella Muti; David Lipper; Corey Johnson; **D:** Anthony Hickox; **W:** Anthony Hickox. **VIDEO**

The Last Samurai 🦴🦴🦴 1/2 **2003 (R)** Embittered ex-Army Captain Nathan Algren (Cruise) is hired to train Japanese soldiers in modern warfare in order to quell a rebellion led by samurai Katsumoto (Watanabe). The inexperienced soldiers are forced to go into battle too early and are defeated. Algren is taken prisoner and brought to a remote mountain village where he learns Japanese, swordplay, and the samurai's ancient code of honor. While Cruise is certainly the big name, Watanabe is the one to watch as the magnetic and charismatic samurai leader. A bit over-romanticized, but the intricate battle sequences and spectacular cinematography make up for it. **150m/C; VHS, DVD, Blu-Ray, HD-DVD.** Tom Cruise; Ken(saku) Watanabe; Timothy Spall; Billy Connolly; Tony Goldwyn; Masato Harada; Hiroyuki (Henry) Sanada; Koyuki; William Atherton; Scott Wilson; Togo Igawa; Shun Sugata; Shin Koyamada; Shichinosuke Nakamura; **D:** Edward Zwick; **W:** Edward Zwick; John Logan; Marshall Herskovitz; **C:** John Toll; **M:** Hans Zimmer.

The Last Seduction 🦴🦴🦴🦴 **1994 (R)** Dahl, the master of modern noir, delivers another stylish hit exploring the darker side of urban life. Fiorentino gives the performance of her life as the most evil, rotten femme fatale to ever hit the big screen. Bridget (Fiorentino) rips off the money her husband Clay (Pullman) made in a pharmaceutical drug deal and leaves Manhattan for a small town in Upstate New York. Once there, she takes nice, naive Mike (Berg) as her lover, while Clay tries to ferret her out and get his money back. Lots of dry humor and a wickedly amusing heroine make for a devilishly entertaining film. **110m/C; VHS, DVD, Blu-Ray.** Linda Fiorentino; Peter Berg; J.T. Walsh; Bill Nunn; Bill Pullman; **D:** John Dahl; **W:** Steve Barancik; **C:** Jeffrey Jur; **M:** Joseph Vitarelli. Ind. Spirit '95: Actress (Fiorentino); N.Y. Film Critics '94: Actress (Fiorentino).

The Last Seduction 2 🦴 **1998 (R)** Low-rent sequel finds Bridget Gregory (Severance) enjoying her spoils in Barcelona where she runs a scam on a phone sex service to get even more cash. But a detective, Murphy (Goddard), has been hired to track Bridget down—only the femme fatale has no intention of getting caught. Severance looks sexy but can't match predecessor Fiorentino's cold-blooded wiles. **96m/C; VHS, DVD.** Joan Severance; Beth Goddard; Con O'Neill; Rocky Taylor; Dave Atkins; **D:** Terry Marcel; **W:** David Cummings; **C:** Geza Sinkovics; **M:** Jon Mellor. **VIDEO**

The Last Sentence 🦴🦴 *Dom Over Dod Man* **2012** Based on the real life crusade of Swedish journalist Torgny Segerstedt (Christensen) fighting the Nazis and his country's neutrality with biting editorials. Much of the proceedings focus on the existential analysis of his writings and role in Hitler's demise. Shot in stunning black and white, the look feels right, but what begins as a poignant view into a man's sharp critique of a troubling world war, slowly stretches into a broad melodrama digging up family ghosts and Segerstedt's rocky romances. There comes a time when wartime history is much more interesting than personal history. Swedish with subtitles. **126m/B; DVD.** *SW* Jesper Christensen; Pernilla August; Bjorn Granath; Ulla Skoog; **D:** Jan Troell; **W:** Jan Troell; Klaus Rifberg; **C:** Jan Troell; Mischa Gavrjusjov.

The Last Sentinel 🦴 **2007 (R)** Loner Tallis (Wilson) is a scarred, part bionic super soldier battling cloned drones that have exceeded their protective purpose and are now exterminating humans. Together with an unnamed freedom fighter (Sackhoff), Tallis is out to destroy the drone police command center. If you like either of the leads, you may be able to sit through this crappy Sci-Fi Channel original. **94m/C; DVD.** Don Wilson; Katee Sackhoff; Bokeem Woodbine; Keith David; **D:** Jesse Johnson; **W:** Jesse Johnson; **C:** Robert Hayes; **M:** Marcello De Francisci. **CABLE**

The Last September 🦴🦴 **1999 (R)** Danielstown is an Anglo-Irish estate located in County Cork in 1920—just four years after the Irish rebellion of 1916. Sir Richard (Gambon) and his wife, Lady Myra (Smith), have a houseful of guests, including Richard's overly romantic young niece Lois (Hawes), who's flirting with British officer, Gerald Colthurst (Tennant). But Lois has also taken to frequently visiting an old mill—where Irish guerilla fighter Peter (Lydon) is hiding out. Based on the novel by Elizabeth Bowen; first-time film director Warner is best known for her long career in the theatre. **103m/C; VHS, DVD.** *IR UK FR* Maggie Smith; Michael Gambon; Keeley Hawes; David Tennant; Gary Lydon; Fiona Shaw; Lambert Wilson; Jane Birkin; Jonathan Slinger; Richard Roxburgh; ***D:*** Deborah Warner; ***W:*** John Banville; ***C:*** Slawomir Idziak; ***M:*** Zbigniew Preisner.

The Last Shot ♪♪ **2004 (R)** An exaggeration of a true story about the FBI, mobsters, and an eager beaver filmmaker. Set in 1985, undercover agent Joe Devine (Baldwin) is bent on ensnaring minor mobster Tommy Sanz (Shalhoub) who's taking bribes to keep teamsters in line on film shoots. So Joe poses as a producer and gets a script and director in one package with nebbish Steven Schats (Broderick), who doesn't know the whole thing's a hoax. The fantasy begins to take over as the production rolls along. Joan Cusack has an unbilled cameo as a movie exec. Too-crowded story collapses under its weight after a promising set-up. **93m/C; DVD.** Matthew Broderick; Alec Baldwin; Toni Collette; Tony Shalhoub; Calista Flockhart; Tim Blake Nelson; Ray Liotta; James Rebhorn; Buck Henry; Ian Gomez; Troy Winbush; Evan Jones; Glenn Morshower; Michael (Mike) Papajohn; Jon Polito; Joan Cusack; Sean M. Whalen; ***D:*** Jeff Nathanson; ***W:*** Jeff Nathanson; ***C:*** John Lindley; ***M:*** Rolfe Kent.

The Last Slumber Party WOOF! 1987 A slumber party is beset by a homicidal maniac. Heavy metal soundtrack. **89m/C; VHS, DVD.** Jan Jensen; Nancy Meyer; ***D:*** Stephen Tyler; ***W:*** Stephen Tyler; ***C:*** Georges Cardona; ***M:*** John Brennan.

Last Song ♪ ½ **1980 (PG)** A singer's husband discovers a plot to cover up a fatal toxic-waste accident, and is killed because of it. It's up to her to warn the authorities before becoming the next victim. **96m/C; VHS, DVD.** Lynda Carter; Ronny Cox; Nicholas Pryor; Paul Rudd; Jenny O'Hara; ***D:*** Alan J. Levi.

The Last Song ♪ **2010 (PG)** Yet another soap opera from the pen of Nicholas Sparks. Rebellious teen Veronica Miller (Cyrus) is sent by her divorced mom to Tybee Island, Georgia for the summer to stay with her estranged dad Steve (Kinnear), a former concert pianist. The two eventually bond over their mutual love of music and Veronica finds love and faces tragedy and learns hard lessons, all set to an endless parade of music montages. Kinnear gives this featherweight movie the slightest bit of heft, but Cyrus seems outmatched by the material. **107m/C; Blu-Ray.** Miley Cyrus; Greg Kinnear; Liam Hemsworth; Nick Searcy; Kelly Preston; Bobby Coleman; Hallock Beals; ***D:*** Julie Anne Robinson; ***W:*** Nicholas Sparks; Jeff Van Wie; ***C:*** John Lindley; ***M:*** Aaron Zigman.

Last Stand ♪ **2000** Cheesy race against time flick in which a criminal (dressed a lot like a modern cop) in a post-apocalyptic world gets his hands on a device allowing him control of nuclear weapons. Which of course means he goes completely insane and decides the world must be his. **94m/C; DVD.** Kate Rodger; Josh Barker; Orestes Matacena; Katerina Brozova; David Fisher; Frank Navratil; Borivoj Navratil; Petra Spindler; Michael E. Rodgers; Rudolf Starz; Pavel Cajzl; ***D:*** Lloyd A. Simandl; ***W:*** Chris Hyde; ***C:*** Vladimir Kolar; ***M:*** Peter Allen.

The Last Stand ♪♪ ½ **2013 (R)** Arnold is baaaack...in his first starring role since playing California's governator. The aging sheriff of a sleepy Arizona town, he's surrounded by wacky characters such as gun enthusiast Lewis (Knoxville) and his lazy deputy Mike (Guzman). But the town's shaken up when FBI agents botch a prison escort of a feared drug lord (Noriega). The villain--a part-time racecar driver--eludes authorities in a Corvette, leaving Arnold and his posse to bring him to justice. A fun and harmless B-movie entry with plenty of dusty car chases and tasty gunplay. American debut for respected Korean director Kim. **107m/C; DVD, Blu-Ray.** Arnold Schwarzenegger; Forest Whitaker; Johnny Knoxville; Luis Guzman; Eduardo Noriega; Peter Stormare; Jaimie Alexander; Genesis Rodriguez; ***D:*** Jee-woon Kim; ***W:*** Andrew Knauer; ***C:*** Ji-yong Kim; ***M:*** Mowg.

Last Stand at Saber River ♪♪ ½ **1996** Adaptation of Elmore Leonard's 1959 western finds wounded Confederate Civil War vet Paul Cable (Selleck) coming home to his wife Martha's (Amis) family in Texas. However, Martha was informed he was dead, so imagine her surprise. What Cable wants to do now is return to his pre-war life—a horse ranch in Arizona—but after making the journey, the family discovers their ranch has been taken over by Union sympathizer Duane Kidston (Carradine) and he's not intending to let it go. Selleck was born to ride tall in the saddle. **95m/C; VHS, DVD.** Tom Selleck; Suzy Amis; David Carradine; Keith Carradine; David Dukes; Tracey Needham; Rachel Duncan; Haley Joel Osment; Harry Carey, Jr.; Lumi Cavazos; Patrick Kilpatrick; ***D:*** Dick Lowry; ***W:*** Ronald M. Cohen; ***C:*** Ric Waite; ***M:*** David Shire. **CABLE**

The Last Starfighter ♪♪ **1984 (PG)** A young man who becomes an expert at a video game is recruited to fight in an intergalactic war. Listless adventure which explains where all those video games come from. Watch for O'Herlihy disguised as a lizard. **100m/C; VHS, DVD, Blu-Ray, HD-DVD.** Lance Guest; Robert Preston; Barbara Bosson; Dan O'Herlihy; Catherine Mary Stewart; Cameron Dye; Kimberly Ross; Wil Wheaton; ***D:*** Nick Castle; ***W:*** Jonathan Betuel; ***C:*** King Baggot; ***M:*** Craig Safan.

The Last Station ♪♪ ½ **2009 (R)** In 1910, 82-year-old Russian author Leo Tolstoy (Plummer) still leads an energetic life on his country estate while trying (unsuccessfully) to hold to his various utopian philosophies. His wife, the Countess Sofya (Mirren), is equally passionate, mercurial, and demanding, especially since, considering their long marriage, she feels entitled to inherit Tolstoy's literary estate. This legacy comes into dispute with the writer's pompous, zealous disciple Chertkov (Giamatti), who wants it in the public domain. So he inserts the naive and worshipful Valentin (McAvoy) into the household as his spy. The film, however, belongs to Mirren and Plummer who offer seductive, intelligent performances. Adapted from Jay Parini's 1990 novel. **112m/C; Blu-Ray, On Demand.** *UK GE RU* Christopher Plummer; Dame Helen Mirren; Paul Giamatti; James McAvoy; Anne-Marie Duff; Kerry Condon; John Sessions; Patrick Kennedy; ***D:*** Michael Hoffman; ***W:*** Michael Hoffman; ***C:*** Sebastian Edscmid; ***M:*** Sergey Yevtushenko.

The Last Stop ♪♪ ½ **1999 (R)** Colorado State Trooper Jason (Beach) gets stranded because of a snowstorm at the remote "The Last Stop Cafe and Motel." He greets the other stranded souls who include his ex-girlfriend Nancy (McGowan) and soon finds out that owner Fritz (Prochnow) has stumbled on a murder and a bag of cash that's probably the loot from a recent bank robbery. So just who's guilty? **94m/C; VHS, DVD.** *CA* Adam Beach; Jurgen Prochnow; Rose McGowan; Callum Keith Rennie; Winston Rekert; ***D:*** Mark Malone; ***W:*** Bart Sumner; ***C:*** Tony Westman; ***M:*** Terry Frewer.

Last Stop for Paul ♪♪ **2008 (PG-13)** Writer/director Mandt and cinematographer Carter serve as both cast and crew in this genial road trip/travelogue. Charlie (Mandt) and Cliff (Carter) are L.A. salesmen and cubicle mates. Charlie has been pestering Cliff to join him on one of his international holidays and he finally agrees with a proviso: his best friend Paul has suddenly died and Cliff wants to scatter his ashes along their global trek. So they load the ashes into a thermos and are off on some mild misadventures with an ultimate destination of Thailand. **82m/C; DVD.** Neil Mandt; Marc Carter; Heather Petrone; Eric Wing; ***D:*** Neil Mandt; ***W:*** Neil Mandt; ***C:*** Marc Carter; ***M:*** Doug Spicka.

Last Summer In the Hamptons ♪♪♪ **1996 (R)** In her last film, Lindfors stars as Helena Mora, the matriarch of a charming three generation theatrical clan that gets together one weekend a year at her spacious, slightly run-down estate to participate in drama workshops and perform plays. When Helena is forced to sell the estate, the family reunites for one last weekend of bickering and performing. Featuring fine performances from the entire ensemble (including Lindfors' son and Jaglom's wife), Jaglom's touching and engaging tribute to his family gives nepotism a good name. **105m/C; VHS, DVD.** Victoria Foyt; Viveca Lindfors; Jon Robin Baitz; Andre Gregory; Melissa Leo; Martha Plimpton; Roddy McDowall; Nick Gregory; Savannah Smith Boucher; Roscoe Lee Browne; Ron Rifkin; Diane Salinger; Brooke Smith; Kristopher Tabori; Holland Taylor; Henry Jaglom; ***D:*** Henry Jaglom; ***W:*** Victoria Foyt; Henry Jaglom; ***C:*** Hanania Baer.

The Last Sunset ♪♪ **1961** Fugitive Brendan O'Malley (Douglas) heads to the Mexican ranch of his former love Belle (Malone) and meets her drunken husband John (Cotten) and teenage daughter Missy (Lynley). John hires O'Malley to drive his cattle herd into Texas and O'Malley's joined by lawman Stribling (Hudson) who vows to bring him in when the drive is over. But death, romance, and a secret turn everyone's life into chaos along the way. **112m/C; DVD.** Kirk Douglas; Rock Hudson; Dorothy Malone; Joseph Cotten; Carol Lynley; Neville Brand; Regis Toomey; Jack Elam; ***D:*** Robert Aldrich; ***W:*** Dalton Trumbo; ***C:*** Ernest Laszlo; ***M:*** Ernest Gold.

The Last Supper ♪♪♪ **1976** A repentant Cuban slave-owner in the 18th-century decides to cleanse his soul and convert his slaves to Christianity by having 12 of them reenact the Last Supper. Based on a true story. In Spanish with English subtitles. **110m/C; VHS, DVD.** *CU* Nelson Villagra; Silvano Rey; Lamberto Garcia; Jose Antonio Rodriguez; Samuel Claxton; Mario Balmasada; ***D:*** Tomas Gutierrez Alea.

The Last Supper ♪♪ ½ **1996 (R)** First-time feature director Title dishes out an extremely black comedy about a group of liberal roommates who accidentally kill a racist marine they've invited to dinner. This leads to the devious plan of inviting more right-wingers over, then killing and burying them in a vegetable garden. Somehow manages to avoid excessive preachiness despite taking on all political comers. Performances are good and the victims (led by Perlman's Limbaugh turn) really shine. Too bad their characters aren't on screen very long before they become tomato fertilizer. **91m/C; VHS, DVD, Blu-Ray.** Cameron Diaz; Annabeth Gish; Ron Eldard; Jonathan Penner; Courtney B. Vance; Nora Dunn; Ron Perlman; Jason Alexander; Charles Durning; Mark Harmon; Bill Paxton; ***D:*** Stacy Title; ***W:*** Dan Rosen; ***C:*** Paul Cameron; ***M:*** Mark Mothersbaugh.

Last Tango in Paris ♪♪♪ ½ *L'Ultimo Tango a Parigi; Le Dernier Tango a Paris* **1973 (R)** Brando plays a middle-aged American who meets a French girl and tries to forget his wife's suicide with a short, extremely steamy affair. Bertolucci proves to be a master; Brando gives one of his best performances. Very controversial when made, still quite explicit. Visually stunning. The X-rated version, at 130 minutes, is also available. **126m/C; VHS, DVD.** *FR IT* Marlon Brando; Maria Schneider; Jean-Pierre Leaud; Maria Michi; Massimo Girotti; Catherine Allegret; ***D:*** Bernardo Bertolucci; ***W:*** Bernardo Bertolucci; ***C:*** Vittorio Storaro; ***M:*** Gato Barbieri. N.Y. Film Critics '73: Actor (Brando); Natl. Soc. Film Critics '73: Actor (Brando).

The Last Templar ♪♪ **2009** Overextended quasi-historical adventure based on a novel by Raymond Khoury. Resourceful archeologist Tess Chaykin (Sorvino) is on the trail of a stolen artifact, originally possessed by the titular religious order that disappeared 700 years ago. The theft brings in FBI agent Sean Daley (Foley) and a sinister Vatican representative, Monsignor De Angelis (Garber), as well as a lot of international travel, conspiracy theories, shipwrecks, and a romantic interlude on an idyllic island. **170m/C; DVD.** Mira Sorvino; Scott Foley; Victor Garber; Omar Sharif; ***D:*** Tessa la; ***W:*** Suzette Couture; ***C:*** Thomas Burstyn; ***M:*** Normand Corbeil. **TV**

The Last Temptation of Christ ♪♪♪ ½ **1988 (R)** Scorsese's controversial adaptation of the Nikos Kazantzakis novel, portraying Christ in his last year as an ordinary Israelite tormented by divine doubt, human desires and the voice of God. The controversy engulfing the film, as it was heavily protested and widely banned, tended to divert attention from what is an exceptional statement of religious and artistic vision. Excellent score by Peter Gabriel. **164m/C; VHS, DVD.** *CA* Willem Dafoe; Harvey Keitel; Barbara Hershey; Harry Dean Stanton; Andre Gregory; David Bowie; Verna Bloom; Juliette Caton; John Lurie; Roberts Blossom; Irvin Kershner; Barry Miller; Tomas Arana; Nehemiah Persoff; Paul Herman; Illeana Douglas; ***D:*** Martin Scorsese; ***W:*** Paul Schrader; ***C:*** Michael Ballhaus; ***M:*** Peter Gabriel.

The Last Time ♪♪ **2006 (R)** Ted's (Keaton) a cynical middle-aged salesman in New York who decides to go after new partner Jamie's (Fraser) beautiful fiancee Belisa (Valletta). Belisa is bored with her boyish Midwesterner and ready to move on but the two guys' mental stability seems to short-circuit as they battle in boardroom and bedroom. Keaton's good but Fraser overplays the idiot role; Valletta slinks and pouts convincingly. **97m/C; DVD.** Michael Keaton; Brendan Fraser; Amber Valletta; Daniel Stern; Neal McDonough; Michael Lerner; ***D:*** Michael Caleo; ***W:*** Michael Caleo; ***C:*** Tim Suhrstedt; ***M:*** Randy Edelman.

The Last Time I Committed Suicide ♪♪ **1996 (R)** Based on a Beat-era letter from Neal Cassady to Jack Kerouac and set in the late '40s, this insubstantial pic follows a 20-year-old Cassady (Jane) as he drifts into Denver's bars, and a friendship with poolhall regular Harry (Reeves), in order to escape dealing with girlfriend Joan's (Forlani) attempted suicide. Joan's eventual recovery leads Neal to consider settling down but he blows a job interview thanks to a drunken Harry and decides to take off instead. No background is provided on the characters so their actions are inexplicable although Jane offers some appeal. **93m/C; DVD.** Thomas Jane; Keanu Reeves; Tom Bower; Adrien Brody; Claire Forlani; Marg Helgenberger; Gretchen Mol; ***D:*** Stephen Kay; ***W:*** Stephen Kay; ***C:*** Bobby Bukowski.

The Last Time I Saw Macao ♪♪ ½ *A Ultima Vez Que Vi Macau* **2013** This feature film defies definition as it combines documentary footage, film noir, and a personal travelogue to form a narrative steeped in mystery and detective work. Created by two Portuguese filmmakers, the film opens with a lip-synced version of the Jane Russell song "You Kill Me," performed by the film's hero. His voiceover then unfolds his tale of returning to a city he lived in as a child, Macao, to find Candy, an old friend who may have been kidnapped by a crime syndicate. He searches the underbelly of the city and its streets, without finding Candy. In his search, however, a bigger, more sinister plot comes to light. Portuguese with subtitles. **85m/C; DVD.** Lydie Barbara; Joao Rui Guerra da Mata; Joao Pedro Rodrigues; Cindy Scrash; ***D:*** Joao Rui Guerra da Mata; Joao Pedro Rodrigues; ***W:*** Joao Rui Guerra da Mata; Joao Pedro Rodrigues.

The Last Time I Saw Paris ♪♪ ½ **1954** A successful writer reminisces about his love affair with a wealthy American girl in post-WWII Paris. **116m/C; VHS, DVD, Blu-Ray.** Elizabeth Taylor; Van Johnson; Walter Pidgeon; Roger Moore; Donna Reed; Eva Gabor; ***D:*** Richard Brooks; ***W:*** Richard Brooks; Julius J. Epstein; Philip G. Epstein; ***C:*** Joseph Ruttenberg; ***M:*** Conrad Salinger.

The Last Train ♪♪ **1974** Romance most hopeless in the heart of France during zee beeg war. During the 1940 invasion of Paris a man and woman turn to each other for comfort when separated from their families while trying to escape the city. French, very French. **101m/C; VHS, DVD.** *FR* Romy Schneider; Jean-Louis Trintignant; Maurice Biraud; ***D:*** Pierre Granier-Deferre; ***W:*** Pierre Granier-Deferre; ***C:*** Walter Wottitz; ***M:*** Philippe Sarde.

Last Train from Gun Hill ♪♪♪ **1959** An all-star cast highlights this suspenseful story of a U.S. marshall determined to catch the man who raped and murdered his wife. Excellent action packed western. **94m/C; VHS, DVD.** Kirk Douglas; Anthony Quinn; Carolyn Jones; Earl Holliman; Brad Dexter; Brian Hutton; Ziva Rodann; ***D:*** John Sturges; ***C:*** Charles B(ryant) Lang, Jr.

The Last Tree ♪♪ ½ **2019** Young Femi (Golding) is a boy of Nigerian descent thriving with his foster mother Mary (Black) in rural Lincolnshire, England. Femi's world is turned upside down when his mother, Yinka (Ikumelo), returns to claim him. She takes him to a concrete high rise in south London, shocking and confusing Femi. As a teenager, Femi (Adewunmi) still does not quite fit in. Though a teacher, Mr. Williams (Pinnock), tries to guide his intelligent student, a local hood, Mace (Lapido), offers Femi a different life path. A moving coming-of-age story with impressive visuals and emotional score. **98m/C; DVD.** Nicholas Pinnock; Denise Black; Samuel Adewunmi; Tuwaine Barrett; Gbemisola Ikumelo; ***D:*** Shola Amoo; ***W:*** Shola Amoo; ***C:*** Stil Williams; ***M:*** Segun Akinola.

The Last Trimester ½ **2006** After much disappointment, Eric and Tracy think pregnant Gabby is their chance to adopt a baby. However, shortly after the troubled young woman gives birth, she is murdered and Eric becomes a suspect. Tracy goes to detective Nick for help but he has his own agenda. **90m/C; DVD.** Chandra West; Jim Thorburn; Matthew Harrison; Lara Gilchrist; ***D:*** Mark Cole; ***W:*** Mark Cole; ***C:*** Bill Baxter; ***M:*** Michael Richard Plowman. **CABLE**

The Last Tycoon **1976 (PG)** An adaptation of the unfinished F. Scott Fitzgerald novel about the life and times of a Hollywood movie executive of the 1920s. Confusing and slow moving despite a blockbuster conglomeration of talent. Joan Collins introduces the film. **123m/C; VHS, DVD.** Robert De Niro; Tony Curtis; Ingrid Boulting; Jack Nicholson; Jeanne Moreau; Peter Strauss; Robert Mitchum; Theresa Russell; Donald Pleasence; Ray Milland; Dana Andrews; John Carradine; Anjelica Huston; ***D:*** Elia Kazan; ***W:*** Harold Pinter; ***M:*** Maurice Jarre.

The Last Unicorn ½ **1982 (G)** Peter Beagle's popular tale of a beautiful unicorn who goes in search of her lost, mythical "family." **95m/C; VHS, DVD, Blu-Ray.** ***V:*** Alan Arkin; Jeff Bridges; Tammy Grimes; Angela Lansbury; Mia Farrow; Robert Klein; Christopher Lee; Keenan Wynn; ***D:*** Jules Bass; ***W:*** Peter S. Beagle; ***M:*** Jim Webb.

The Last Valley **1971 (PG)** A scholar tries to protect a pristine 17th century Swiss valley, untouched by the Thirty Years War, from marauding soldiers. Historical action with an intellectual twist. **128m/C; VHS, DVD.** Michael Caine; Omar Sharif; Florinda Bolkan; Nigel Davenport; Per Oscarsson; Arthur O'Connell; ***D:*** James Clavell; ***W:*** James Clavell; ***C:*** John Wilcox; ***M:*** John Barry.

The Last Vampire on Earth **2010 (PG-13)** In the vein of 'Twilight,' a Jehovah's Witness falls for a vampire. **80m/C; DVD.** Michael Bole; Kevin Glaser; McKenzie Grimmet; ***D:*** Vitaliy Versace; ***W:*** Vitaliy Versace; Mandie Abraham; ***C:*** George Anton; ***M:*** David Buker. **VIDEO**

Last Vegas ½ **2013 (PG-13)** The multiple-Oscar-winning cast keeps this riff on "Grown Ups" and "The Hangover" moderately entertaining, but they can't upgrade a script that's built entirely around old-age jokes and non-existent characters. Billy (Douglas) is getting married and his three best friends--Paddy (De Niro), Archie (Freeman), and Sam (Kline)--head to Vegas with the longtime bachelor in an effort to check a party weekend in the city of sin off their bucket lists. These actors are so far above this material it's often embarrassing, but they do their best to keep it light-hearted and entertaining. **105m/C; DVD, Blu-Ray.** Michael Douglas; Robert De Niro; Morgan Freeman; Kevin Kline; Mary Steenburgen; ***D:*** Jon Turteltaub; ***W:*** Dan Fogelman; ***C:*** David Hennings; ***M:*** Mark Mothersbaugh.

The Last Voyage ½ **1960** Suspenseful disaster film in which Stack and Malone play a married couple in jeopardy while on an ocean cruise. To make the film more realistic, the French liner Ile de France was actually used in the sinking scenes. Although a bit farfetched, film is made watchable because of fine performances and excellent camera work. **91m/C; DVD.** Robert Stack; Dorothy Malone; George Sanders; Edmond O'Brien; Woody Strode; Jack Kruschen; ***D:*** Andrew L. Stone; ***W:*** Andrew L. Stone; ***C:*** Hal Mohr; ***M:*** Rudolph (Rudy) Schrager.

The Last Waltz ½ **1978 (PG)** Martin Scorsese filmed this rock documentary featuring the farewell performance of The Band, joined by a host of musical guests that they have been associated with over the years. Songs include: "Up On Cripple Creek," "Don't Do It," "The Night They Drove Old Dixie Down," "Stage Fright" (The Band), "Helpless" (Neil Young), "Coyote" (Joni Mitchell), "Caravan" (Van Morrison), "Further On Up the Road" (Eric Clapton), "Who Do You Love" (Ronnie Hawkins), "Mannish Boy" (Muddy Waters), "Evangeline" (Emmylou Harris), "Baby, Let Me Follow You Down" (Bob Dylan). **117m/C; VHS, DVD, Blu-Ray.** ***D:*** Martin Scorsese; ***C:*** Michael Chapman. Natl. Film Reg. '19.

The Last Warrior ½ *Coastwatcher* **1989 (R)** A good-looking but exploitive "Hell in the Pacific" rip-off, as an American and a Japanese soldier battle it out alone on a remote island during WWII. **94m/C; VHS, DVD; Open Captioned.** Gary (Rand) Graham; Cary-Hiroyuki Tagawa; Maria Holvoe; ***D:*** Martin Wragge.

The Last Warrior **1999 (PG-13)** A devastating earthquake has turned Southern California into an island and Green Beret Nick Preston (Lundgren) takes it upon himself to help a group of survivors finds civilization. Of course there's a villain—a murderer (Mer) who has taken over a maximum security prison and has his own ideas. **95m/C; VHS, DVD.** Dolph Lundgren; Rebecca Cross; Julino Mer; Sherrie Alexander; Joe Michael Burke; ***D:*** Sheldon Lettich; ***W:*** Stephen J. Brackely; Pamela K. Long; ***C:*** David Garfinkel; ***M:*** David Michael Frank. **VIDEO**

The Last Warrior *The Scythian; Skif* **2018** In medieval Eurasia, noble soldier Lutobor (Faddeev) serves a Russian prince but becomes unintentionally drawn into tribal conflicts. When Lutobor's wife and infant are kidnapped by members of the once mighty Scythian tribe, Lutobor embarks on a quest to rescue them and gain revenge. He is added by a former enemy, the charismatic Scythian assassin Weasel (Kuznetsov). Along the way, they become involved in gory acts of violence. This epic historical adventure relies on fantasy cliches and features a story and characters that are not fully realized, but the filmmakers effectively use their Slavic perspective and a unique setting. Russian with subtitles. **105m/C; DVD.** Aleksey Faddeev; Aleksandr Kuznetsov; Yuriy Tsurilo; Izmaylova Vasilisa; Vitaly Kravchenko; ***D:*** Rustam Mosafir; ***W:*** Rustam Mosafir; Vadim Golovanov; ***C:*** Dzmitry Karnachyk. **VIDEO**

The Last Wave **1977 (PG)** An Australian attorney takes on a murder case involving an aborigine and he finds himself becoming distracted by apocalyptic visions concerning tidal waves and drownings that seem to foretell the future. Weir's masterful creation and communication of time and place are marred by a somewhat pat ending. **109m/C; VHS, DVD.** *AU* Richard Chamberlain; Olivia Hamnett; David Gulpilil; Frederick Parslow; Vivean Gray; Nadjiwarra Amagula; Roy Bara; Walter Amagula; Cedric Lalara; Morris Lalara; Peter Carroll; ***D:*** Peter Weir; ***W:*** Peter Weir; Tony Morphett; Petru Popescu; ***C:*** Russell Boyd.

Last Wedding ½ **2001 (R)** Explores the state of contemporary relationships via three couples in their thirties living in Vancouver. Two of the couples are married and happy, while the third is about to enter what will most likely be a disasterous marriage. Ignoring the advice against going foward with the wedding after a brief courtship, the third couple, Noah (Ratner) and Zippora (Betrani), marries. As the honeymoon ends, all three couples feel the strain as issues such as doubt, jealousy, and infidelity surface. All question if they should remain together. **100m/C; DVD.** *CA* Benjamin Ratner; Frida Betrani; Tom Scholte; Nancy Sivak; Vincent Gale; Molly Parker; Marya Delver; Jay Brazeau; Babz Chula; ***D:*** Bruce Sweeney; ***W:*** Bruce Sweeney; ***C:*** David Pelletier; ***M:*** Don MacDonald. **VIDEO**

Last Weekend ½ **2014** Yet another dysfunctional family dramedy with little to recommend but Clarkson's performance. Fussy matriarch Celia asks her sons to spend Memorial Day weekend at their lavish Lake Tahoe vacation home without mentioning that it is going up for sale. The entire family is either self-absorbed or oblivious so you don't actually want to be around them, although the house is spectacular. **94m/C; DVD.** Patricia Clarkson; Chris Mulkey; Joseph Cross; Zachary Booth; Alexia Rasmussen; Devon Graye; Jayma Mays; Rutina Wesley; Fran Kranz; Judith Light; ***D:*** Tom Dolby; Tom Williams; ***W:*** Tom Dolby; ***C:*** Paula Huidobro; ***M:*** Stephen Barton.

The Last Will and Testament of Rosalind Leigh **2012** Antiques dealer Leon has inherited the home of his reclusive, religious, estranged mother, Rosalind, and discovers a shrine to a sort of angel cult. He soons believes his mother's spirit is trying to contact and warn him as Leon begins to suffer from panic attacks and hallucinations. Redgrave is mostly heard (and only seen in video recordings) as she narrates the atmospheric horror tale. **77m/C; DVD.** *CA* Aaron Poole; Vanessa Redgrave; ***D:*** Rodrigo Gudino; ***W:*** Rodrigo Gudino; ***C:*** Samy Inayeh. **VIDEO**

The Last Winter **1984 (R)** An American woman fights to find her Israeli husband who has disappeared in the 1973 Yom Kippur War. Trouble is, an Israeli woman thinks the man she's looking for is really her husband too. **92m/C; Streaming.** *IS* Kathleen Quinlan; Yona Elian; Zipora Peled; Michael Schneider; ***D:*** Riki Shelach.

The Last Winter **2006** Atmospheric eco-disaster pic that uses its locations (in Alaska and Iceland) to tell a disturbing tale. Eco-author James Hoffman (LeGros) and his assistant Elliot (Harrold) have been hired as PR props by North Industries. The company wants to begin oil drilling in the previously protected Arctic National Wildlife Refuge and they are to accompany the first team and say everything is hunky-dory. Team leader Pollack (Perlman) scoffs at Hoffman's global-warming scenarios but the permafrost is melting and releasing who knows what into the air and maybe that's why everyone starts acting hinky. **101m/C; DVD, Blu-Ray.** *IC US* James LeGros; Ron Perlman; Connie Britton; Jamie Harrold; Pato Hoffmann; Kevin Corrigan; Zachary Gifford; Joanne Shenandoah; ***D:*** Larry Fessenden; ***W:*** Larry Fessenden; Robert Leaver; ***C:*** G. Magni Agustsson; ***M:*** Jeff Grace.

The Last Witch Hunter **2015 (PG-13)** Breck Eisner's fantasy action pic is so self-aware in its ridiculousness that it can sometimes be pretty fun if you're in the mood for something mindless. Vin Diesel, King of the Mindless Action Pic, stars as the title character, a sturdy fellow named Kaulder who can live forever. He's been working as a witch hunter since the Middle Ages for an organization called The Axe and Cross, which tries to keep the peace between witches and the human race. It's all just an excuse for crazy magic and illogical action sequences, punctuated by bad dialogue. But Diesel is having enough fun that you might too. **105m/C; DVD, Blu-Ray.** Vin Diesel; Elijah Wood; Rose Leslie; Rena Owen; Olafur Darri Olafsson; ***D:*** Breck Eisner; ***W:*** Cory Goodman; Matt Sazama; Burk Sharpless; ***C:*** Dean Semler; ***M:*** Steve Jablonsky.

The Last Woman on Earth **WOOF!** **1961** Two men vie for the affections of the sole surviving woman after a vague and unexplained disaster of vast proportions. Robert Towne, who appears herein under the pseudonym Edward Wain, wrote the script (his first screenwriting effort). You might want to watch this if it were the last movie on earth, although Corman fans will probably love it. **71m/C; VHS, DVD.** Antony Carbone; Edward (Robert Towne) Wain; Betsy Jones-Moreland; ***D:*** Roger Corman; ***W:*** Robert Towne.

The Last Word **1995 (R)** Journalist Martin (Hutton) writes a newspaper column, often featuring characters based on hometown Detroit mob figures. His info is supplied by his friend, Doc (Pantoliano), who owes the gangsters big bucks. Doc also introduces Martin to his latest column subject—stripper Caprice (Burke)--and then a Hollywood studio gets interested in filming her story. They want more sex and violence, meaning Martin will be betraying Caprice's deepest secrets. Now, he must choose between love, friendship or success. **95m/C; VHS, DVD.** Timothy Hutton; Joe Pantoliano; Michelle Rene Thomas; Chazz Palminteri; Tony Goldwyn; Richard Dreyfuss; Cybill Shepherd; Jimmy Smits; ***D:*** Tony Spiridakis; ***W:*** Tony Spiridakis; ***C:*** Zoltan David; ***M:*** Paul Buckmaster.

The Last Word **2008 (R)** Evan (Bentley) composes epitaphs for people planning suicides. Paying his respects to a late client, Evan meets the man's sister, Charlotte (Ryder), and lies that they were friends in college. Extroverted Charlotte insists upon befriending morose Evan, which has him neglecting his work to placate her. There's a surprise to tidy up the ending. **95m/C; DVD.** Wes Bentley; Winona Ryder; Ray Romano; Allan Rich; Gina Hecht; ***D:*** Geoffrey Haley; ***W:*** Geoffrey Haley; ***C:*** Kees Van Oostrum; ***M:*** John Swihart.

The Last Word **2017 (R)** Harriett Lauler (MacLaine) has controlled almost every aspect of her life, and wants to control how she'll be remembered when she dies. She contacts a young writer at the local newspaper named Anne Sherman (Seyfried) and tells her of her plan to write her own obituary. Her life story will be told the way she wants it to be told. Of course, this all leads to one of those films in which the older woman teaches the younger woman about life and the younger woman teaches the older woman she's not dead yet. Predictable but sometimes sweet. **108m/C; DVD, Blu-Ray.** Shirley MacLaine; Amanda Seyfried; AnnJewel Lee Dixon; Thomas Sadoski; Philip Baker Hall; ***D:*** Mark Pellington; ***W:*** Stuart Ross Fink; ***C:*** Eric Koretz; ***M:*** Nathan Matthew David.

Last Year at Marienbad *L'Anee Derniere a Marienbad* **1961** A young man tries to lure a mysterious woman to run away with him from a hotel in France. Once a hit on the artsy circuit, it's most interesting for its beautiful photography. In French with English subtitles. **93m/B; VHS, DVD, Blu-Ray.** *FR IT* Delphine Seyrig; Giorgio Albertazzi; Sacha (Sascha) Pitoeff; Luce Garcia-Ville; ***D:*** Alain Resnais; ***W:*** Alain Resnais; Alain Robbe-Grillet; ***C:*** Sacha Vierny; ***M:*** Francis Seyrig.

L'Atalante ½ *Le Chaland qui Passe* **1934** Vigo's great masterpiece, a slight story about a husband and wife quarreling, splitting, and reuniting around which has been fashioned one of the cinema's greatest poetic films. In French with English subtitles. **82m/B; VHS, DVD, Blu-Ray.** *FR* Dita Parlo; Jean Daste; Michel Simon; ***D:*** Jean Vigo; ***W:*** Jean Vigo; Jean Guinee; Albert Riera; ***C:*** Boris Kaufman; Louis Berger; ***M:*** Maurice Jaubert.

Late August, Early September ½ *Fin Aout Debut Septembre* **1998** Self-absorbed group of friends and lovers find their relationships in flux and their mortality in question over the course of a year (from August to the following September). Writer Adrien's (Cluzet) work elicits critical but not commercial acclaim. His indecisive friend Gabriel (Amalric) is an editor at a publishing house who has split with long-time love, Jenny (Balibar), for the young Anne (Ledoyen). Meanwhile, Adrien, who's learned he has a terminal illness, plunges into a reckless affair with the teenaged Vera (Hansen-Love). French with subtitles. **112m/C; DVD.** *FR* Mathieu Amalric; Virginie Ledoyen; Francois Cluzet; Jeanne Balibar; Alex Descas; Arsinee Khanjian; Mia Hansen-Love; ***D:*** Olivier Assayas; ***W:*** Olivier Assayas; ***C:*** Denis Lenoir; ***M:*** Ali Sarka Toure.

The Late Bloomer **2016 (R)** A comedy about one man's unexpectedly ate puberty, based on the novel Man Made: A Memoir of My Body. Peter (Simmons) is a doctor who specializes in advising patients on how to divert sexual energy into other areas of their lives. Peter is unusual in that he has no sex drive, but he soon learns that it is because he has never undergone puberty. After he gets the benign tumor that has been resting on his pituitary gland removed, Peter quickly goes through all the ups and downs of puberty in a three-week period. As a result, Peter comes to understand the sexual and romantic urges he once advised his patients to divert. **90m/C; DVD, Streaming, Download.** Johnny Simmons; Blake Cooper; Kumail Nanjiani; Beck Bennett; Lenora Crichlow; ***D:*** Kevin Pollack; ***W:*** Joe Nussbaum; Mark Torgove; Paul A. Kaplan; Kyle Cooper; Austyn Jeffs; ***C:*** Akis Konstantakopoulos; ***M:*** Walter Murphy.

Late Bloomers **1995** Romantic comedy focuses on what happens when two Midwestern women fall in love. Math teacher/basketball coach Dinah (Nelson) is friendly with fellow teacher Rom (Carter) and his wife, Carly (Hennigan), the high school secretary. A misinterpreted note, an impulsive kiss, and Carly's soon out of door and living with Dinah, which leads to a community uproar. The two leads are likeable but the other characters and the situation are heavily cliched. **105m/C; VHS, DVD.** Connie Nelson; Dee Hennigan; Gary Carter; Lisa Peterson; ***D:*** Julia Dyer; ***W:*** Gretchen Dyer; ***C:*** Bill Schwarz; ***M:*** Ted Pine.

Late Bloomers *3 foi 20 ans* **2011** A school teacher entering retirement begins to drive her husband away with obsessions over growing old in this french comedy-drama. **95m/C; DVD, Blu-Ray.** *BE FR UK* William Hurt; Isabella Rossellini; Doreen Mantle; Kate Ashfield; Aidan McArdle; ***D:*** Julie Gavras; ***W:*** Julie Gavras; Olivier Dazat; ***C:*** Nathalie Durand; ***M:*** Sodi Marciszewer. **VIDEO**

Late for Dinner **1991 (PG)** In 1962 Willie, a young, married man, and his best friend Frank are framed by a sleazy land developer. On the run, the two decide to become guinea pigs in a cryonics experiment and wind up frozen for 29 years. It's now 1991 and Willie wants to find his family—only his wife is middle-aged and his daughter is all grown-up. Can he make a life with them again or has time indeed passed him by? **93m/C; VHS, DVD, Blu-Ray.** Brian Wimmer; Peter Berg; Marcia Gay Harden; Peter Gallagher; Ross Malinger; ***D:*** W.D. Richter; ***W:*** Mark Andrus.

Late Last Night **1999 (R)** After a big fight with his wife, Dan (Estevez) hooks up with best pal, Jeff (Weber), who proposes they cut loose for the evening. So they pick up a couple of women and proceed to party, which eventually lands them in the slammer. **90m/C; VHS, DVD.** Emilio Estevez; Steven Weber; Catherine O'Hara; Leah Lail; Lisa Robin Kelly; ***D:*** Steven Brill.

Late Marriage ½ *Hatouna Mehuheret* **2001** Thirty-one-year-old Zaza (Ashkenazi) is an Israeli of Georgian descent who lives in a very close-knit and traditional community. His parents are appalled that he's still single and keep setting him up with virginal likely prospects. They don't know that he's devoted to Judith (Elkabetz), who's not only slightly older (she's 34) but a divorced single mom and Moroccan! When they do find out, they barge into her apartment—humiliating both. But is Zaza strong enough to defy conventions and stay with his true love? In Georgian and Hebrew with subtitles. **100m/C; VHS, DVD.** *IS FR* Lior Ashkenazi; Ronit Elkabetz; Moni Moshonov; Lili Kosashvili; Sapir Kugman; Aya Steinovits Laor; ***D:*** Dover Kosashvili; ***W:*** Dover Kosashvili; ***C:*** Dani Schneor; ***M:*** Joseph Bardanashvili.

Late Night **2019 (R)** When long-time late night show host Katherine Newbury (Thompson) sees her ratings sink and learns she might be replaced by the hyper masculine Daniel Tennant (Barinholtz), she orders a member of her all male staff to hire a woman. Molly Patel (Kaling) lands a job as a writer despite her lack of experience. Though no one in the writer's room wants her there, she uses her experience working in quality control at a chemical plant to challenge expectations about her and women. This comedy skillfully balances the subversive with the humorous as it explores ideas such as diversity, racism, and sexism with sharp wit. **102m/C; DVD.** Emma Thompson; Mindy Kaling; John Lithgow; Hugh Dancy; Reid Scott; ***D:*** Nisha Ganatra; ***W:*** Mindy Kaling; ***C:*** Matthew Clark; ***M:*** Lesley Barber.

A Late Quartet **2012 (R)** A string quartet struggles when they learn that their cellist and founding member (Walken) faces a life-changing diagnosis. The quartet's 25th anniversary concert, as well as their friendships, competing egos and fragile emotional states, hangs in the balance. Their swan song is Beethoven's challenging Opus 131 String Quartet in C-sharp minor, which tests the group's resolve and the cellist's health. Slow, uneven and melodramatic at times, the resolution is somewhat predictable but is a suitable nod to New York culture with an appreciable dose of chamber music. **105m/C; DVD, Blu-Ray.** Christopher Walken; Philip Seymour Hoffman; Catherine Keener; Imogen Poots; Wallace Shawn; Mark Ivanir; Madhur Jaffrey; ***D:*** Yaron Zilberman; ***W:*** Yaron Zilberman; Seth Grossman; ***C:*** Frederick Elmes; ***M:*** Angelo Badalamenti.

The Late Shift ½ **1996 (R)** Cable adaptation of Bill Carter's book chronicling the follies surrounding NBC's "The Tonight Show" succession battle between Jay Leno (Roebuck) and Dave Letterman (Higgins). It's the behind-the-scenes dealmakers that really steal the show, however, including Jay's profane manager Helen Kushnick (Bates) and superagent Michael Ovitz (Williams), who ultimately orchestrated Dave's move to rival CBS. Both Letterman and Leno made the movie/book fodder for their opening monlogues. **96m/C; VHS, DVD.** Daniel Roebuck; John Michael Higgins; Kathy Bates; Treat Williams; Bob Balaban; Ed Begley, Jr.; Rich Little; Sandra Bernhard; Peter Jurasik; Reni Santoni; John Kapelos; John Getz; Lawrence Pressman; ***D:*** Betty Thomas; ***W:*** Bill Carter; George Armitage; ***C:*** Mac Ahlberg; ***M:*** Ira Newborn. **CABLE**

The Late Show **1977 (PG)** A veteran private detective finds his world turned upside down when his ex-partner comes to visit and winds up dead, and a flaky woman whose cat is missing decides to become his sidekick. Carney and Tomlin are fun to watch in this sleeper, a tribute to the classic detective film noirs. **93m/C; VHS, DVD.** Art Carney; Lily Tomlin; Bill Macy; Eugene Roche; Joanna Cassidy; John Considine; ***D:*** Robert Benton; ***W:*** Robert Benton. Natl. Soc. Film Critics '77: Actor (Carney).

Late Spring **1949** An exquisite Ozu masterpiece. A young woman lives with her widowed father for years. He decides to remarry so that she can begin life for herself. Highly acclaimed, in Japanese with English subtitles. Reworked in 1960 as "Late Autumn." **107m/B; VHS, DVD, Blu-Ray.** *JP* Setsuko Hara; Chishu Ryu; Jun Usami; Haruko Sugimura; ***D:*** Yasujiro Ozu.

The Lathe of Heaven ½ **1980** In a late 20th century world suffocating from pollution, George Orr (Davison) visits a dream specialist because he can dream things into being. The specialist wants George to dream of a world free from war, pestilence, and overpopulation, but these dreams have disastrous side effects. Based on the futuristic novel by Ursula K. LeGuin. **100m/C; VHS, DVD.** Bruce Davison; Kevin Conway; Margaret Avery; Peyton E. Park; ***D:*** David Loxton; Fred Barzyk; ***W:*** Roger E. Swaybill; Diane English; ***C:*** Robbie Greenberg; ***M:*** Michael Small. **TV**

The Lathe of Heaven **2002** Remake of the 1980 PBS pic based on the 1971 novel by Ursula LeGuin. George Orr (Haas) refuses to sleep because when he does, his dreams alter reality. Or at least George thinks so, which is why he's forced to see a court-appointed shrink, Dr. William Haber (Caan), after a drug overdose. But when Haber discovers George's ability is real, he uses it for his own purpose. **100m/C; VHS, DVD.** Lukas Haas; James Caan; Lisa Bonet; David Strathairn; Sheila McCarthy; Serge Houde; ***D:*** Philip Haas; ***W:*** Alan Sharp; ***C:*** Pierre Mignot; ***M:*** Angelo Badalamenti. **CABLE**

The Lather Effect **2006** High school friends from the '80s reunite for a wild weekend and find they're older but no wiser. They face the morning after cleaning up after their shindig, reminiscing, and revealing various issues and disappointments. Situations are predictable, but if you lived through the era they'll be familiar (as will the music). **95m/C; DVD.** Connie Britton; Sarah Clarke; Tate Donovan; David Herman; Peter Facinelli; Caitlin Keats; William Mapother; Ione Skye; Eric Stoltz; Kevin Heffernan; Monica Keena; ***D:*** Sarah Kelly; ***W:*** Sarah Kelly; Tim Talbott; ***C:*** Eric Haase; ***M:*** Dominic Kelly.

Latin Dragon ½ **2003 (R)** Home sweet home is in ruins when Danny Silva returns from war duty to find gangs in charge of his L.A. 'hood. Disgusted, he takes it upon himself to hunt down the rotten head honchos behind the chaos. Typical war-hero-turned-vigilante fare. **101m/C; VHS, DVD.** Gary Busey; Lorenzo Lamas; Robert LaSardo; Pepe Serna; Fabian Carrillo; Joyce Giraud; Luis Antonio Ramos; James Hong; ***D:*** Scott Thomas; ***W:*** Fabian Carrillo; James Becket; ***C:*** Mark Eberle; ***M:*** H. Scott Salinas. **VIDEO**

Latino ½ **1985** The self-tortured adventures of a Chicano Green Beret who, while fighting a covert U.S. military action in war-torn Nicaragua, begins to rebel against the senselessness of the war. **108m/C; VHS, DVD, Streaming.** Robert Beltran; Annette Cardona; Tony Plana; James Karen; Ricardo Lopez; Luis Torrentes; Juan Carlos Ortiz; Julio Medina; ***D:*** Haskell Wexler; ***W:*** Haskell Wexler; ***M:*** Diane Louie.

Latitude Zero *Ido Zero Daisakusen; Atragon II; Latitude Zero Military Tactics; Latitude Zero: Big Military Operation* **1969** A quake traps three men in a bathyscaphe, but they're rescued by a 200-year-old man in a high tech submarine who takes them to an underground paradise called Latitude Zero. There, an an evil scientist attempts to destroy them with monsters, James Bond gadgets, and his own super submarine. He even transplants his partner's brain into the body of a lion onto which he's grafted wings. A Japanese and American co-production from the writer of "Them!" and the director of "Godzilla." The effects haven't aged well, but it is considered a classic by many vintage sci-fi fans. **99m/C; DVD.** *JP* Cesar Romero; Akira Takarada; Masumi Okada; Richard Jaeckel; Joseph Cotton; Patricia Medina; Tetsu Nakamura; Linda Haynes; Mari Nakayama; Akihiko Kurata; Hikaru Kuroki; Susumu Kurobe; Haruo Nakajima; ***D:*** Ishio Honda; ***W:*** Warren Lewis; Shinichi Sekizawa; Ted Sherdeman; ***C:*** Taiichi Kankura; ***M:*** Akira Ifukube.

Latter Days ½ **2004** Melodramatic gay romance finds earnest Mormon missionary Aaron (Sandvoss) sent from Idaho to bring the good word to the heathens of West Hollywood. This includes his new neighbor, heedless gay waiter Christian (Ramsey), who sets out to seduce the virgin on a bet. This is a really big religious no-no for Aaron, even as the hot duo find themselves falling in love. Bisset adds some class as surrogate mother figure Lila. Writer/ first-time director Cox is a former Mormon and has some definite issues to air but he manages to offer a certain sweetness along with all the angst. **108m/C; DVD.** Steve Sandross; Wes Ramsey; Rebekah Jordan; Khary Payton; Amber Benson; Jacqueline Bisset; Joseph Gordon-Levitt; Erik Palladino; Mary Kay Place; Rob McElhenney; ***D:*** C. Jay Cox; ***W:*** C. Jay Cox; ***C:*** Carl F. Bartels; ***M:*** Eric Allaman.

L'Auberge Espagnole *The Spanish Apartment; Euro Pudding* **2002 (R)** Exuberant comedy follows French student Xavier (Duris) during an eventful year in Barcelona. He's advised to study Spanish and Spanish economics in order to secure a government job, so he enrolls in an exchange program and bids goodbye to girlfriend Martine (Tantou). Xavier moves into a lively rooming house filled with fellow students and is soon squiring around the shy wife (Godreche) of an obnoxious countryman and crushing on a Belgian exchange student (de France), who sees him only as a friend. Barcelona's baroque charms are another character in Klapisch's light-hearted production. English, French, and Spanish with subtitles. **117m/C; VHS, DVD.** *FR SP* Romain Duris; Audrey Tautou; Judith Godreche; Cecile de France; Kelly Reilly; Kevin Bishop; Xavier De Guillebon; ***D:*** Cedric Klapisch; ***W:*** Cedric Klapisch; ***C:*** Dominique Colin.

Lauderdale **WOOF!** *Spring Fever USA; Spring Break USA* **1989 (R)** Two college schmoes hit the beach looking for beer and babes. Few laughs for the sober and mature. Surf's down in this woofer. **91m/C; VHS, DVD.** Darrel Guilbeau; Michelle Kemp; Jeff Greenman; Lara Belmonte; ***D:*** Bill Milling; ***W:*** Bill Milling.

Laugh, Clown, Laugh **1928** Silent drama finds melancholy Italian circus clown Tito (Chaney Sr.) and his partner Simon (Siegel) adopting a young orphan girl. Naming her Simonetta, she grows up into a beautiful teenager (Young) who catches the eye of wealthy Count Luigi (Asther). Tito has also fallen in love with Simonetta, but knows his feelings are inappropriate and she will only be happy with the younger man. Young was only 14 during filming so the plot seems both creepy and touching. **65m/B; Silent; DVD.** Lon Chaney, Sr.; Bernard Siegel; Loretta Young; Nils Asther; Cissy Fitzgerald; Gwen Lee; ***D:*** Herbert Brenon; ***W:*** Elizabeth Meehan; Joe Farnham; ***C:*** James Wong Howe.

Laughing at Life ½ **1933** A mercenary leaves his family to fight in South America. Years later, when he is the leader of said country, he meets a man who turns out to be his son. Rehashed plot has been done better. **72m/B; VHS, DVD.** Victor McLaglen; William "Stage" Boyd; Lois Wilson; Henry B. Walthall; Regis Toomey; ***D:*** Ford Beebe.

The Laughing Policeman ½ *An Investigation of Murder* **1974 (R)** Two antagonistic cops embark on a vengeful hunt for a mass murderer through the seamy underbelly of San Francisco. Adapted from the Swedish novel by Per Wahloo and Maj Sjowallo. **111m/C; VHS, DVD, Blu-Ray.** Walter Matthau; Bruce Dern; Louis Gossett, Jr.; ***D:*** Stuart Rosenberg; ***M:*** Charles Fox.

Laughing Sinners **1931** Society girl Crawford attempts suicide after Hamilton dumps her and is rescued by Gable—a Salvation Army worker! Predictable drama with some unintentionally funny moments. Gable and Crawford were having an off-screen romance at the time which accounts for the sparks generated on-screen. Based on the play "Torch Song" by Kenyon Nicholson. **71m/B; VHS, DVD.** Joan Crawford; Neil Hamilton; Clark Gable; Marjorie Rambeau; Guy Kibbee; Cliff Edwards; Roscoe Karns; ***D:*** Harry Beaumont; ***C:*** Charles Rosher.

Laughing to the Bank *Laughing to the Bank with Brian Hooks* **2013 (R)** Sometimes you have to make your own luck to be a success! Though Brian Hooks (Hooks) has had some work as an actor in Hollywood, he cannot become truly famous or land the kind of parts that make you a star. After television executives reject his idea for a television show, Brian and his friends decide to raise money for themselves. After they gain the funding, Hooks has to bring all the crazy characters in his head to life so he can become the high-profile actor he has always wanted to be. **87m/C; DVD, Streaming, Download.** Brian Hooks; Steve Turner; Allison Oliver; Tabitha Brown; Laila Odom; ***D:*** Brian Hooks; ***W:*** Roy Hooks; ***C:*** Reggie Brumfield; ***M:*** Phil Thompson.

The Laundromat **2019 (R)** Attorneys Jurgen (Oldman) and Ramon (Banderas) are the masters of shell companies, which enrich the wealthy and negatively impact everyone else. One example is Ellen (Streep), whose settlement check is much smaller than it should have been because the owner's insurance policy is a scam. On the opposite side, wealthy Charles (Anozie) faces a financial crisis but creates imaginary companies and accounts to help himself. Director Soderbergh takes a too-lighthearted view about the topics of wealth, taxation, and corruption, squandering an impressive cast. **95m/C; DVD.** Gary Oldman; Antonio Banderas; Meryl Streep; James Cromwell; Jeff Michalski; ***D:*** Steven Soderbergh; ***W:*** Scott Z. Burns; ***C:*** Steven Soderbergh; ***M:*** David Holmes.

Laura **1944** Detective Mark McPherson (Andrews) assigned to the murder investigation of the late Laura Hunt (Tierney) finds himself falling in love with her painted portrait and discovering some surprising facts. Superb collaboration by excellent cast and fine director. Superior suspense yarn, enhanced by a love story. Based on the novel by Vera Caspary. Rouben Mamoulian was the original director, then Preminger finished the film. **85m/B; DVD, Blu-Ray.** Gene Tierney; Dana Andrews; Clifton Webb; Lane Chandler; Vincent Price; Judith Anderson; Grant Mitchell; Dorothy Adams; Ron Dunn; Clyde Fillmore; James Flavin; ***D:*** Otto Preminger; ***W:*** Elizabeth Reinhardt; Jay Dratler; Samuel Hoffenstein; Ring Lardner, Jr.; ***C:*** Joseph LaShelle; ***M:*** David Raksin. Oscars '44: B&W Cinematog.; Natl. Film Reg. '99.

Laurel Canyon **2002 (R)** Aspiring shrink Sam (Bale) brings fiance and fellow doctor Alex (Beckinsale) home to meet mom Jane (McDormand), a bohemian record producer with very non-maternal views of sex and drugs—she likes 'em, a lot. Sam still resents her, and Jane hasn't changed as she's currently sleeping with Ian (Nivola) whose album she's producing. Then Alex finds herself drawn to their carefree world. Cholodenko falls short by making the story predictable and the characters flat. The only one who comes alive is Jane, due to McDormand's performance, while Nivola has a nice turn as her beau of the month. **101m/C; VHS, DVD.** Frances McDormand; Christian Bale; Kate Beckinsale; Alessandro Nivola; Natascha (Natasha) McElhone; ***D:*** Lisa Cholodenko; ***W:*** Lisa Cholodenko; ***C:*** Wally Pfister; ***M:*** Craig Wedren.

Laurence Anyways 2012 Dolan's too-long, flamboyant melodrama about a transgendered relationship is set throughout the 1990s to a bouncy electro-pop beat. Montreal schoolteacher Laurence is mad for filmmaker Frederique and she for him, except Laurence admits that he doesn't want to be a him anymore. As the situation progresses, both lose their jobs, separate, and Fred tries married life until she reads Laurence's autobiographical novel, which leads to a reconciliation. French with subtitles. **160m/C; DVD, Blu-Ray.** *CA FR* Melvil Poupaud; Suzanne Clément; Nathalie Baye; David Savard; Magalie Lepine-Blondeau; Monia Chokri; ***D:*** Xavier Dolan; ***W:*** Xavier Dolan; ***C:*** Yves Bélanger.

The Lavender Hill Mob 1/2 **1951** A prim and prissy bank clerk schemes to melt the bank's gold down and re-mold it into miniature Eiffel Tower paper-weights for later resale. The foolproof plan appears to succeed, but then develops a snag. An excellent comedy that is still a delight to watch. **78m/B; VHS, DVD, Blu-Ray.** *GB* Alec Guinness; Stanley Holloway; Sidney James; Alfie Bass; Marjorie Fielding; John Gregson; ***Cameo(s):*** Audrey Hepburn; ***D:*** Charles Crichton; ***W:*** T.E.B. Clarke. Oscars '52: Story & Screenplay; British Acad. '51: Film.

L'Avventura 1/2 *The Adventure* **1960** A stark, dry and minimalist exercise in narrative by Antonioni, dealing with the search for a girl on an Italian island by her lethargic socialite friends who eventually forget her in favor of their own preoccupations. A highly acclaimed, innovative film; somewhat less effective now, in the wake of many film treatments of angst and amorality. Subtitled in English. Laser edition features the original trailer, commentary and a collection of still photographs from Antonioni's work. **145m/C; VHS, DVD, Blu-Ray.** *IT* Monica Vitti; Gabriele Ferzetti; Lea Massari; Dominique Blanchar; James Addams; ***D:*** Michelangelo Antonioni; ***W:*** Tonino Guerra; Michelangelo Antonioni; ***C:*** Aldo Scavarda; ***M:*** Giovanni Fusco. Cannes '60: Special Jury Prize.

Law Abiding Citizen 2009 (R) After 10 years, Clyde Shelton (Butler) returns to Philadelphia to get his own justice against A.D.A. Nick Rice (Foxx), the prosecutor who made an expedient deal with one of the suspects in the brutal murder of Shelton's family. Brutally dispatching the perps is only the beginning for Clyde. Starts out as an effective revenge thriller, but the plot holes and increasing absurdity take the whole thing down. **109m/C; Blu-Ray, On Demand.** Gerard Butler; Jamie Foxx; Leslie Bibb; Colm Meaney; Viola Davis; Bruce McGill; Regina Hall; Josh Stewart; Michael Irby; ***D:*** F. Gary Gray; ***W:*** Kurt Wimmer; ***C:*** Jonathan Sela; ***M:*** Brian Tyler.

Law and Disorder 1974 (R) Two average Joes, fed up with the rate of rising crime, start their own auxiliary police group. Alternately funny and serious with good performances from the leads. **103m/C; VHS, DVD.** Carroll O'Connor; Ernest Borgnine; Ann Wedgeworth; Anita Dangler; Leslie Ackerman; Karen Black; Jack Kehoe; ***D:*** Ivan Passer; ***W:*** Ivan Passer; William Richert; Kenneth Harris Fishman; ***C:*** Arthur Ornitz; ***M:*** Angelo Badalamenti.

The Law and Jake Wade 1/2 **1958** Gripping western starring Taylor as a former bank robber turned marshal. His old partner (Widmark) turns up and forces Taylor to lead him to buried loot. **86m/C; VHS, DVD, Blu-Ray.** Robert Taylor; Richard Widmark; Patricia Owens; Robert Middleton; Henry Silva; DeForest Kelley; Burt Douglas; Eddie Firestone; ***D:*** John Sturges.

Law and Order 1/2 1953 Remake of 1932 and 1940 films is a solid B-movie oater with Reagan a competent, if stiff, lead. Frame Johnson (Reagan) is the former marshal of Tombstone, having decided to retire to marry saloon owner Jeannie (Malone) and become a rancher in nearby Cottonwood. Only his new town is under the sway of old nemesis Durling (Foster) and his gang. The townsfolk want Johnson to strap his gunbelt back on and take care of the varmints so they can have a peaceful community and, of course, he does. **80m/C; DVD, Blu-Ray.** Ronald Reagan; Dorothy Malone; Preston Foster; Alex Nicol; Russell Johnson; Barry Kelley; Chubby Johnson; Dennis Weaver; Wally Cassell; Ruth Hampton; ***D:*** Nathan "Jerry" Juran; ***W:*** D.D. Beauchamp; ***C:*** Clifford Stine; ***M:*** Henry Mancini; Milton Rosen; Herman Stein.

The Law and the Lady 1/2 1951 London lady's maid Jane Hoskins decides she wants the good life for herself so she teams up with fellow schemer Nigel Duxbury to fleece the wealthy. Jane passes herself off as a noblewoman and Nigel gets hired as the new butler for San Francisco grand dame Julia Wortin, the owner of a very valuable diamond necklace. However, the larcenous duo's plans are jeopardized when Jane falls for Spanish playboy, Juan. Loose adaptation of the Frederick Lonsdale play "The Last of Mrs. Cheyney." **104m/B; DVD.** Greer Garson; Michael Wilding; Fernando Lamas; Marjorie Main; Hayden Rorke; Margalo Gillmore; ***D:*** Edwin H. Knopf; ***W:*** Karl Tunberg; Leonard Spigelgass; ***C:*** George J. Folsey; ***M:*** Carmen Dragon.

Law of Desire 1/2 *La Ley del Deseo* **1986** A wicked, Almodovarian attack-on-decency farce about a promiscuous gay filmmaker, Pablo (Pancela), who becomes the object of desire for obsessive Antonio (Banderas), whom Pablo treats too casually for his own safety. Also in the mix is Pablo's sister, the transsexual Tina (Maura), and his current lover Juan (Molina). Romantic complications and violence abound. Unlike the work of any other director; Spanish with subtitles. **100m/C; VHS, DVD.** *SP* Carmen Maura; Eusebio Poncela; Antonio Banderas; Bibi Andersson; Miguel Molina; Manuela Valasco; Nacho Martinez; ***D:*** Pedro Almodóvar; ***W:*** Pedro Almodóvar; ***C:*** Angel Luis Fernandez.

Law of the Pampas 1939 Boyd and Hayden ride off to South America to deliver some cattle, but the bad guys intervene. This is Toler's first outing as Hoppy's sidekick, briefly replacing "Gabby" Hayes. **72m/B; VHS, DVD.** William Boyd; Russell Hayden; Steffi Duna; Sidney Toler; Sidney Blackmer; Pedro de Cordoba; Eddie Dean; Glenn Strange; ***D:*** Nate Watt.

Law of the Wild 1934 The search for a magnificent stallion that was hijacked by race racketeers before a big sweepstakes race is shown in this 12 chapter serial. **230m/B; VHS, DVD.** Bob Custer; Ben Turpin; Lucille Browne; Lafe (Lafayette) McKee; ***D:*** B. Reeves Eason; Armand Schaefer.

The Lawless 1950 Mexican-American migrant workers are subjected to prejudice and violence in a northern California town. A dancehall brawl leads to young Paul Rodriguez (Rios) going on the lam after false accusations. Newspaper editor Larry Wilder's (Carey) conscience kicks in and he publicly defends the young man against mob mentality. Mainwaring adapted his own novel. **83m/B; DVD.** MacDonald Carey; Gail Russell; Lalo Rios; Johnny Sands; John Hoyt; Lee Patrick; Argentina Brunetti; ***D:*** Joseph Losey; ***W:*** Daniel Mainwaring; ***C:*** J. Roy Hunt; ***M:*** Mahlon Merrick.

The Lawless 2007 (R) Low-budget thriller made by a crew of five, featuring two undercover police detectives who are outed. Their families are kidnapped by drug cartels, and they are given 24 hours to murder four targets if they wish to see them back. **86m/C; DVD.** Denton Blane Everett; Jason Riley Hoss; Natalie Bell; Luis Caldeira; Eryn Brooke; Marcus Lorenzo; Leroy Castanon; William Burch; Richard Fernandez; ***D:*** Phillip Guzman; ***W:*** Phillip Guzman; ***C:*** Philip Roy; ***M:*** David Frost.

Lawless *The Wettest County in the World* **2012 (R)** Set in Virginia during the Prohibition, Jack (LaBeouf) is the youngest member of a trio of Virginia moonshining brothers, which eventually pits them against an obsessive federal agent (Pearce). Stunning to look at with an amazing ensemble, but the film loses its battle against a muddled script and LaBeouf's being seeming ill-fitted for his role. Based on the Matt Bondurant's--Jack's grandson--true story novel "The Wettest County in the World." A generic story that should have been so much more than an onslaught of violence. **115m/C; DVD, Blu-Ray.** Tom (Thomas) Hardy; Jason Clarke; Shia LaBeouf; Guy Pearce; Jessica Chastain; Mia Wasikowska; Gary Oldman; Noah Taylor; ***D:*** John Hillcoat; ***W:*** Nick Cave; ***C:*** Benoit Delhomme; ***M:*** Nick Cave; Warren Ellis.

The Lawless Breed 1952 Episodic saga based on the autobiography of outlaw John Wesley Hardin, published after his release from prison in 1896. Hardin's (Hudson) life of crime begins with a killing in self-defense that escalates into further bloodshed and flights from the law. Along the way Hardin marries (Adams) and has a son, whom he fears will follow in his violent footsteps. Walsh directs with plenty of brio. **83m/C; VHS, DVD.** Rock Hudson; Julie Adams; John McIntire; Hugh O'Brian; Lee Van Cleef; Dennis Weaver; Glenn Strange; Michael Ansara; ***D:*** Raoul Walsh; ***W:*** Bernard Gordon; ***C:*** Irving Glassberg; ***M:*** Joseph Gershenson.

Lawless Heart 1/2 2001 (R) Divided into three sections, with the characters seen from different perspectives. Resaturant owner Stuart died without a will leaving his sister Judy (Haddington) his unexpected heir and his life/business partner Nick (Hollander) in the lurch. Meanwhile, Judy's husband, Dan (Nighy) has a midlife crisis and starts fliritng with florist, Corinne (Celarie). Nick is also having some unexpected feelings towards Charlie (Smith), a party girl who helps with the loneliness. Finally, there's Tim (Henshall), a feckless boyhood chum of Stuart's who suddenly falls in love with shop owner Leah (Butler). **99m/C; DVD.** *UK* Tom Hollander; Douglas Henshall; Bill Nighy; Clementine Celarie; Josephine Butler; Ellie Haddington; Stuart Laing; Sukie Smith; David Coffey; Dominic Hall; June Barrie; Peter Symonds; ***D:*** Neil Hunter; Tom Hunsinger; ***W:*** Neil Hunter; Tom Hunsinger; ***C:*** Sean Bobbitt; ***M:*** Adrian Johnston. L.A. Film Critics '03: Support. Actor (Nighy).

A Lawless Street 1/2 1955 Scott portrays a sheriff who rides the Colorado Territory cleaning up lawless towns. His dedication to duty has caused his wife to leave him and she won't come back until he lays downs his guns forever, which may come sooner than they think after he rides into the corrupt town of Medicine Bend. Based on the novel "Marshal of Medicine Bend" by Brad Ward. **78m/B; VHS, DVD.** Randolph Scott; Angela Lansbury; Warner Anderson; Jean Parker; Wallace Ford; John Emery; James Bell; Ruth Donnelly; Michael Pate; Don Megowan; Jeannette Nolan; ***D:*** Joseph H. Lewis; ***W:*** Kenneth Gamet; ***C:*** Ray Rennahan.

Lawman 1971 (PG) Brutal western about a fanatical U.S. marshall (Lancaster) who rides into town after Cobb and his six ranch hands. The cowboys have accidentally killed a man and Lancaster is determined to bring them to justice no matter what the cost. Though the entire town is against him that doesn't stop his mission. Brooding and relentless with fine performances, particularly by Ryan as the local marshall living on past glories. **95m/C; VHS, DVD, Blu-Ray.** Burt Lancaster; Robert Ryan; Lee J. Cobb; Sheree North; Joseph Wiseman; Robert Duvall; Albert Salmi; J.D. Cannon; John McGiver; Richard Jordan; John Beck; Ralph Waite; John Hillerman; Richard Bull; ***D:*** Michael Winner; ***W:*** Gerald Wilson; ***C:*** Robert Paynter; ***M:*** Jerry Fielding.

Lawn Dogs 1/2 1996 After moving to a wealthy suburb, Morton (McDonald) and Clare (Quinlan) expect their daughter to mix with the social elite. Instead, Devon (Barton) becomes friends with Trent (Rockwell), an outsider who cuts lawns, bonding over their mutual dislike for the lifeless complex. After a conflict with a couple of dim college boys, events take a turn for the worse and Trent is forced to escape from the community with Devon's help. Interwoven with the Russian fairy tale of Baba Yaga, the climax is visually stunning. Excellent performances from both Rockwell and Barton as the unlikely friends. **101m/C; VHS, DVD.** *GB* Sam Rockwell; Mischa Barton; Kathleen Quinlan; Christopher McDonald; Bruce McGill; David Barry Gray; Eric Mabius; Tom Aldredge; Beth Grant; ***D:*** John Duigan; ***W:*** Naomi Wallace; ***C:*** Elliot Davis; ***M:*** Trevor Jones.

The Lawnmower Man 1992 (R) Brosnan is a scientist who uses Fahey, a dim-witted gardener, as a guinea pig to test his experiments in "virtual reality," an artificial computer environment. With the use of drugs and high-tech equipment, Brosnan is able to increase Fahey's mental powers—but not necessarily for the better. Fantastic special effects and a memorable "virtual reality" sex scene. Available in an unrated version which contains 32 more minutes of footage. So minimally based on a short story by Stephen King that the author sued (and won) to have his name removed from the film. **108m/C; VHS, DVD.** Jeff Fahey; Pierce Brosnan; Jenny Wright; Mark Bringleson; Geoffrey Lewis; Jeremy Slate; Dean Norris; Troy Evans; John Laughlin; ***D:*** Brett Leonard; ***W:*** Brett Leonard; Gimel Everett; ***C:*** Russell Carpenter; ***M:*** Danny Wyman.

Lawnmower Man 2: Beyond Cyberspace *Lawnmower Man 2: Jobe's War* **1995 (PG-13)** Resurrecting Jobe (from the first pic) was easy. So was blowing off his face to explain the new actor (Frewer for Fahey). The hard part was trying to make an original movie with a decent script and believable characters. Corporate baddie Walker (Conway) enlists Jobe to (what else?) take over the world using Virtual Reality. To the rescue comes one burned-out computer expert (Bergin) and a group of VR-addicted kids living in an abandoned subway. Techno-babble abounds but nothing interesting ever happens. **93m/C; VHS, DVD.** Patrick Bergin; Matt Frewer; Austin O'Brien; Kevin Conway; Ely Pouget; Camille (Cami) Cooper; ***D:*** Farhad Mann; ***W:*** Farhad Mann; ***C:*** Ward Russell; ***M:*** Robert Folk.

Lawrence of Arabia 1962 (PG) Exceptional biography of T.E. Lawrence, a British military "observer" who strategically aids the Bedouins battle the Turks during WWI. Lawrence, played masterfully by O'Toole in his first major film, is a hero consumed more by a need to reject British tradition than to save the Arab population. He takes on Arab costume and a larger-than-life persona. Stunning photography of the desert in all its harsh reality. Blacklisted co-writer Wilson had his screen credit restored by the Writers Guild of America in 1995. Laser edition contains 20 minutes of restored footage and a short documentary about the making of the film. Available in letterboxed format. **221m/C; VHS, DVD, Blu-Ray.** *GB* Peter O'Toole; Omar Sharif; Anthony Quinn; Alec Guinness; Jack Hawkins; Claude Rains; Anthony Quayle; Arthur Kennedy; Jose Ferrer; Michel Ray; Norman Rossington; John Ruddock; Donald Wolfit; ***D:*** David Lean; ***W:*** Robert Bolt; Michael Wilson; ***C:*** Frederick A. (Freddie) Young; ***M:*** Maurice Jarre. Oscars '62: Art Dir./Set Dec., Color, Color Cinematog., Director (Lean), Film, Film Editing, Orig. Score, Sound; AFI '98: Top 100; British Acad. '62: Actor (O'Toole), Film, Screenplay; Directors Guild '62: Director (Lean); Golden Globes '63: Director (Lean), Film--Drama, Support. Actor (Sharif); Natl. Bd. of Review '62: Director (Lean); Natl. Film Reg. '91.

Laws of Attraction 2004 (PG-13) Powerhouse New York divorce lawyers Daniel (Brosnan) and Audrey (Moore) fight for their opposing clients and against their growing attraction to each other in this formulaic romantic comedy. Their latest case allows the kind of heated sparring that everyone knows will lead to the bedroom. Their brief, drunken romp leaves them both in emotional denial until one of the disputed assets in the divorce, an Irish castle, forces the two to travel to the quaint country where they proceed to get drunk (again) and married. The two leads provide plenty of chemistry and charm despite the wafer-thin premise. **89m/C; DVD.** Pierce Brosnan; Julianne Moore; Michael Sheen; Parker Posey; Frances Fisher; Nora Dunn; Allan Houston; Vincent Marzello; Mina Badie; ***D:*** Peter Howitt; ***W:*** Aline Brosh McKenna; Robert Harling; ***C:*** Adrian Biddle; ***M:*** Ed Shearmur.

Laws of Gravity 1992 (R) Critically acclaimed debut film from 29-year-old writer/director Gomez is a three day slice of life set in Brooklyn. Hotheaded Jon (Trese) and married friend Jimmy (Greene) channel violent energy into their relationships and illegal activities. Camera follows "cinema verite" style and captures urban tension as it trails them through a gun heist and subsequent arrest. **100m/C; VHS, DVD.** Peter Greene; Edie Falco; Adam Trese; Arabella Field; Paul Schulze; ***D:*** Nick Gomez; ***W:*** Nick Gomez; ***C:*** Jean De Segonzac.

Lawyer Man 1932 Defense attorney Anton Adam (Powell) wins a big case and gets a partnership offer from uptown lawyer Granville Bently (Dinehart). Things don't work out, thanks to Adam taking on a shady breach of promise suit for actress Ginny St. Johns (Dodd) and Adam has to start over with his loyal secretary Olga (Blondell). He decides to get the goods on corrupt political boss John Gilmurry (Landau). **72m/B; DVD.** William Powell; Joan Blondell; David Landau; Claire Dodd; Alan Dinehart; Helen Vinson; Allen Jenkins; Jack La Rue; ***D:*** William Dieterle; ***W:*** Rian James; James Seymour; ***C:*** Robert B. Kurrle.

Lay the Favorite **2012 (R)** Disappointingly broad comedy, adapted from Beth Raymer's memoirs, does boast a standout performance from Hall. Former exotic dancer Beth (Hall) lands in Vegas and is employed by fast-talking pro odds-maker, Dink (Willis). Beth is a natural and Dink thinks of her as his lucky charm, to the jealousy of his wife, Tulip (Zeta-Jones). Beth meets nice guy Jeremy (Jackson), moves to New York, and works for Dink's rival, Rosie (Vaughn), which brings trouble her way. **94m/C; DVD, Blu-Ray.** Rebecca Hall; Bruce Willis; Catherine Zeta-Jones; Joshua Jackson; Vince Vaughn; Laura Prepon; Frank Grillo; ***D:*** Stephen Frears; ***W:*** D.V. DeVincentis; ***C:*** Michael McDonough; ***M:*** James Seymour Brett.

Layer Cake **2005 (R)** The unnamed protagonist (Craig), referred to only as "XXXX" in the closing credits, is a too-cool-for-you cocaine dealer trying to leave the business. But somehow he's convinced to pull "one last job," searching for the daughter of a crime-boss and coordinate the sale of a million stolen tablets of Ecstasy along the way. Of course, a few things go wrong. Vaughn's directorial debut successfully negotiates the cockney-chocked, bass-thumping, and humorously violent British crime genre with pizzazz and twists. **105m/C; DVD, Blu-Ray, UMD, HD-DVD.** *GB* Daniel Craig; Colm Meaney; Kenneth Cranham; George Harris; Jamie Foreman; Michael Gambon; Tamer Hassan; Ben Whishaw; Burn Gorman; Sally Hawkins; Sienna Miller; Stephen Walters; Jason Flemyng; Dragan Micanovic; ***D:*** Matthew Vaughn; ***W:*** J.J. Connolly; ***C:*** Benjamin Davis; ***M:*** Lisa Gerrard; Ilan Eshkeri.

The Layover 1/2 **2017 (R)** A slapstick comedy about friends competing for the same man. Schoolteacher Kate (D'Addario) has job issues, while her best friend Meg (Upton) struggles selling North Korean make-up. To escape, the pair take a holiday trip to the tropics. A hurricane forces the plane to be diverted to St. Louis, where they become interested in the handsome Ryan (Barr), who sat between them on the plane. Kate and Meg go extremes to win Ryan at the hotel, drawing in another guest, Craig (Jones), into the situation. The film's message and fun are undercut by the lack of a believable life-long friendship between the leads. **88m/C; DVD.** Kate Upton; Alexandra Daddario; Matt Barr; Matt Jones; Kal Penn; ***D:*** William H. Macy; ***W:*** David Hornsby; Lance Krall; ***C:*** Mark Irwin; ***M:*** Rob Ellmore; Leah Haywood; Dan Pringle.

The Lazarus Effect **2015 (PG-13)** How do talented people like Duplass and Wilde get involved in such cut-rate nonsense as this should-have-been-straight-to-video horror movie? One will never know. Wilde plays Zoe, one of the lead researchers of a team trying to reverse the inevitability of death. Of course, she dies herself in a lab accident and the rest of the team suddenly has a viable human subject. It's as if they never saw "Flatliners" or "Pet Sematary." A promising start devolves into such clichéd nonsense that the most terrifying thing about it is that anyone thought it was good enough to release. **83m/C; DVD, Blu-Ray.** Olivia Wilde; Mark Duplass; Donald Glover; Evan Peters; Sarah Bolger; Amy Aquino; ***D:*** David Gelb; ***W:*** Luke Dawson; Jeremy T. Slater; ***C:*** Michael Fimognari; ***M:*** Sarah Schachner.

The Lazarus Project 1/2 **2008 (PG-13)** Muddled psycho-drama with an unsatisfying ending. Ex-con Ben Garvey's (Walker) new life is going so well something bad has to happen. First he gets fired and then he makes a really terrible decision to participate in a heist that goes verywrong, and Ben gets the death penalty. He's given a lethal injection and then wakes up a patient in a mental hospital with his previous life just a part of his delusions. Or was it? **99m/C; DVD.** Paul Walker; Piper Perabo; Malcolm Goodwin; Bob Gunton; Tony Curran; Linda Cardellini; Lambert Wilson; Shawn Hatosy; ***D:*** John Glenn; ***W:*** John Glenn; ***C:*** Jerzy Zielinski; ***M:*** Brian Tyler. **VIDEO**

The Lazarus Syndrome **1979** Astute doctor (Gossett Jr.) teams up with an ex-patient of the chief of surgery in an effort to expose the chief's unethical surgical procedures. Served as the pilot for a short-lived TV series. **90m/C; VHS, DVD.** Louis Gossett, Jr.; E.G. Marshall; Ronald Hunter; Sheila Frazier; Lara Parker; ***D:*** Michael Firth; ***W:*** William Blinn; ***C:*** Chuck (Charles G.) Arnold; ***M:*** John Rubenstein. **TV**

Lazer Team 1/2 **2016 (PG-13)** A scifi comedy about four small town guys who must save humanity. When the four unexpectedly find an alien crash site, they discover that the other worldly visitors have left a battle suit behind. Because the suit is genetically tied to them, they are charged with working together to ensure the survival of the human species and planet Earth. Though their quest is affected by the government giving them chase, they must learn to use the alien suit without harming themselves or anyone else to fulfill their unexpected destiny. **102m/C; DVD, Blu-Ray.** Burnie Burns; Gavin Free; Michael Jones; Colton Dunn; Allie DeBerry; ***D:*** Matt Hullum; ***W:*** Burnie Burns; Matt Hullum; Chris Demarais; Josh Flanagan; ***C:*** Philip Roy; ***M:*** Jeff Williams.

Lazybones **1925** Steve (Jones), the lazybones of the title, likes nothing better than to nap, but he steps up when desperate Ruth (Pitts) is forced to give up her daughter Kit (Marsall), and he raises the girl despite small town scandal. After returning from WWI, Steve figures out he's in love with the now-adult Kit (Bellamy) but his mother (Chapman) helps him realize it's not meant to be. **78m/B; Silent; DVD.** Buck Jones; Zasu Pitts; Madge Bellamy; Edythe Chapman; Leslie Fenton; Virginia Marsall; ***D:*** Frank Borzage; ***W:*** Frances Marion; ***C:*** Glen MacWilliams; George Schneiderman.

LBJ 1/2 **2017 (R)** A compelling biographical look at Lyndon Baines Johnson (Harrelson), focusing on the years 1959 to 1963. In this period, Johnson served as the Senate majority leader then became John F. Kennedy's (Donovan) vice president. The film shows Johnson's struggle as he transitioned from being a powerful senator to an unheralded position within the Kennedy administration. After Kennedy's assassination, Johnson's move from background figure to world leader is no less jarring. Emphasizing Johnson's key relationships, including his supportive wife Lady Bird (Leigh), the film also explores how the Civil Rights Act of 1964 came to be. **98m/C; DVD, Blu-Ray.** Woody Harrelson; Jennifer Jason Leigh; C. Thomas Howell; Bill Pullman; Jeffrey Donovan; ***D:*** Rob Reiner; ***W:*** Joey Hartstone; ***C:*** Barry Markowitz; ***M:*** Marc Shaiman.

Le Beau Mariage *A Good Marriage; The Well-Made Marriage* **1982 (R)** An award-winning comedy from the great French director about a zealous woman trying to find a husband and the unsuspecting man she chooses to marry. The second in Rohmer's Comedies and Proverbs series. French with subtitles. **97m/C; VHS, DVD.** *FR* Beatrice Romand; Arielle Dombasle; Andre Dussollier; Feodor Atkine; Pascal Greggory; Sophie Renoir; ***D:*** Eric Rohmer; ***W:*** Eric Rohmer; ***C:*** Bernard Lutic; ***M:*** Ronan Girre; Simon des Innocents. Venice Film Fest. '82: Actress (Romand).

Le Beau Serge *Handsome Serge* **1958** Young theology student Francois returns to his home village and discovers his friend Serge, in despair of ever changing his life, has become a hopeless drunk. So Francois meddles in his life (with the best of intentions) and only causes Serge further disaster. Chabrol's first film, and a major forerunner of the nouvelle vague. In French with English subtitles. **97m/B; VHS, DVD, Blu-Ray.** *FR* Gerard Blain; Jean-Claude Brialy; Michele Meritz; Bernadette LaFont; ***D:*** Claude Chabrol; ***W:*** Claude Chabrol.

Le Bonheur 1/2 *Happiness* **1965** A seemingly happily married carpenter (Drouot) takes a vacation with his wife and children where he meets the local postal clerk and the two begin a passionate affair. Unwilling to leave his family, Drouot believes the two women can share him but when his wife discovers his infidelity she kills herself. His grief does not cause Drouot to stop the affair, instead he moves in with his mistress. An uninvolving, unbelievable tale with a lovely Mozart score. In French with English subtitles. **87m/C; VHS, DVD.** *FR* Jean-Claude Drouot; Claire Drouot; Marie-France Boyer; ***D:*** Agnes Varda; ***W:*** Agnes Varda; ***C:*** Jean Rabier; Claude Beausoleil.

Le Boucher *The Butcher; Il Tagliagole* **1969** In a provincial French town a sophisticated schoolmistress is courted by the shy local butcher—who turns out to be a sex murderer. A well-played thriller that looks at sexual frustration. French with subtitles. **94m/C; VHS, DVD.** *FR* Stephane Audran; Jean Yanne; Antonio Passallia; ***D:*** Claude Chabrol; ***W:*** Claude Chabrol.

Le Cercle Rouge *The Red Circle* **1970** An ex-con, an escaped prisoner, a diamond heist, a police manhunt, and mob vengeance—all set during a wet Paris winter. Ex-con Corey (Delon) is planning to rob a jewelry store; Vogel (Volonte) escapes from his police guard, Mattei (Bourvil), during a train trip; fate brings the two together. They seek the help of ex-con Jansen (Montand) for their heist while Mattei is out to re-capture Vogel to salvage his reputation. It's trench coats and fedoras and the ever-present smoldering cigarette—and it's all very, very cool. French with subtitles. **140m/C; DVD.** *FR* Alain Delon; Gian Marie Volonte; Yves Montand; Andre Bourvil; Francois Perier; ***D:*** Jean-Pierre Melville; ***W:*** Jean-Pierre Melville; ***C:*** Henri Decae; ***M:*** Eric Demarsen.

Le Choc *Shock; Contract in Blood* **1982** Martin (Delon) is a hitman whose boss, Cox (Perrot), refuses to let him retire. His banker Jeanne (Audran) has invested part of Martin's money in a farm managed by Claire (Deneuve) and her alcoholic husband. When Martin goes to check things out, the farm is attacked by some of his enemies and Claire's husband is killed, but she and Martin escape. Martin then finds Jeanne dead and his money gone, but Cox offers him a lot of francs for one last job and the chance to take Claire away to an island paradise. French with subtitles. **100m/C; DVD.** *FR* Alain Delon; Catherine Deneuve; Stephane Audran; Francois Perrot; Philippe Leotard; Etienne Chicot; Jean-Louis Richard; Feodor Atkine; ***D:*** Jean-Louis Richard; ***W:*** Alain Delon; Jean-Louis Richard; Robin Davis; ***C:*** Pierre William Glenn; ***M:*** Philippe Sarde.

Le Corbeau *The Raven* **1943** A great, notorious drama about a small French village whose everyday serenity is ruptured by a series of poison pen letters that lead to suicide and despair. The film was made within Nazi-occupied France, sponsored by the Nazis, and has been subjected to much misdirected malice because of it. In French with English subtitles. **92m/B; VHS, DVD.** *FR* Pierre Fresnay; Noel Roquevert; Ginette LeClerc; Pierre Larquey; Antoine Belpetre; ***D:*** Henri-Georges Clouzot.

Le Dernier Combat *The Last Battle* **1984 (R)** A stark film about life after a devastating nuclear war marks the directorial debut of Besson. The characters fight to survive in a now speechless world by staking territorial claims and forming new relationships with other survivors. An original and expressive film made without dialogue. **93m/B; VHS, DVD.** *FR* Pierre Jolivet; Fritz Wepper; Jean Reno; Jean Bouise; Christiane Kruger; ***D:*** Luc Besson; ***W:*** Luc Besson; ***C:*** Carlo Varini; ***M:*** Éric Serra.

Le Deuxieme Souffle *Second Breath* **1966** An overly-long crime saga that still intrigues. Aging gangster Gustave (Ventura) escapes from prison but doesn't have the money to leave France. He agrees to join in an armored car heist in Paris despite the fact that the job is run by Paul Ricci (Pellegrin), whose brother Jo (Bozzuffi) framed Gustave and sent him to the slammer. The gangster is pursued by the ruthless Commissaire Blot (Meurisse), who isn't afraid of using violence or branding Gustave a stoolie when things don't go as planned. French with subtitles. **144m/B; DVD.** *FR* Lino Ventura; Paul Meurisse; Raymond Pellegrin; Marcel Bozzuffi; Michel Constantin; Paul Frankeur; Christine Fabrega; Pierre Zimmer; Pierre Grasset; ***D:*** Jean-Pierre Melville; ***W:*** Jose Giovanni; ***C:*** Jose Giovanni; ***M:*** Bernard Gerard.

Le Divorce **2003 (PG-13)** Cutie blonde American Isabel Walker (Hudson) heads to Paris to support her equally blonde but depressed pregnant sister Roxeanne (Watts) whose French husband Charles-Henri (Poupard) has walked out because of an obsessive affair. Hubby insists on a quick divorce but Roxy is refusing. Meanwhile, Isabel becomes involved with Charles-Henri's worldly uncle, Edgar (Lhermitte), who knows how to begin and end an affair with aplomb (and gifts). A culture clash comedy of manners that's brittle with artifice. Based on the 1997 novel by Diane Johnson. **115m/C; DVD.** Kate Hudson; Naomi Watts; Thierry Lhermitte; Melvil Poupaud; Leslie Caron; Glenn Close; Stockard Channing; Sam Waterston; Thomas Lennon; Matthew Modine; Rona Hartner; Jean-Marc Barr; Stephen Fry; Bebe Neuwirth; Samuel Labarthe; Nathalie Richard; Romain Duris; Daniel Mesguich; ***D:*** James Ivory; ***W:*** Ruth Prawer Jhabvala; ***C:*** Pierre Lhomme; ***M:*** Richard Robbins.

Le Donk & Scor-Zay-Zee 1/2 **2009** Improvised, brief, and no-budget comedy from Brit Meadows. Le Donk (Considine) is a boastful, angry, longtime music roadie who befriends and decides to boost the career of large and shy young rapper Scor-Zay-Zee (Palinczuk). He promises to get him onstage as the opening slot at an Arctic Monkeys concert but Le Donk nearly sabotages his protege because of his own jealousy. **71m/C; DVD.** *GB* Paddy Considine; Shane Meadows; Olivia Colman; Dean Palinczuk; Richard Graham; Mark Herbert; ***D:*** Shane Meadows; ***W:*** Shane Meadows; ***C:*** Shane Meadows; Dean Rogers.

Le Doulos *Doulos—The Finger Man* **1961** Compelling story of an ex-convict and his buddy, a man who may be a police informant. Chronicles the efforts of the snitch (the "doulos" of the title) to bring the criminal element before the law. Melville blends in several plot twists and breathes a new-French life into the cliche-ridden genre. **108m/B; VHS, DVD, Blu-Ray.** *FR* Serge Reggiani; Jean-Paul Belmondo; Michel Piccoli; ***D:*** Jean-Pierre Melville.

Le Gitan *The Gypsy* **1975** Gypsy Hugo (Delon) steals from the rich to provide for his fellows, who are poverty-stricken outcasts in French society. But no good deed goes unpunished. French with subtitles. **102m/C; DVD.** *FR* Alain Delon; Paul Meurisse; Annie Girardot; Marcel Bozzuffi; Bernard Giraudeau; ***D:*** Jose Giovanni; ***W:*** Jose Giovanni; ***C:*** Jean-Jacques Tarbes; ***M:*** Claude Bolling.

Le Jour Se Leve 1/2 *Daybreak* **1939** The dark, expressionist film about a sordid and destined murder/love triangle that starts with a police stand-off and evolves into a series of flashbacks. The film that put Carne and Gabin on the cinematic map. Highly acclaimed. French with English subtitles. Remade in 1947 as "The Long Night." **89m/B; VHS, DVD.** *FR* Jean Gabin; Jules Berry; Arletty; Jacqueline Laurent; ***D:*** Marcel Carne.

Le Jupon Rouge *Manuela's Loves* **1987** Bacha (Valli) is a human rights activist and concentration camp survivor who is involved with younger fashion designer Manuela (Barrault). But when Manuela becomes drawn to the even younger Claude (Grobon), Bracha's overwhelmed with jealousy and Manuela is torn by her feelings for both women. French with subtitles. **90m/C; VHS, DVD.** *FR* Alida Valli; Marie-Christine Barrault; Guillemette Grobon; ***D:*** Genevieve Lefebvre.

Le Magnifique *The Magnificent One* **1976** Belmondo is a master spy and novelist who mixes fantasy with reality when he chases women and solves cases. **84m/C; VHS, DVD.** *FR* Jean-Paul Belmondo; Jacqueline Bisset; Hans Meyer; Vittorio Caprioli; ***D:*** Philippe de Broca; ***W:*** Francis Veber; Philippe de Broca; ***C:*** Rene Mathelin; ***M:*** Claude Bolling.

Le Mans **1971 (G)** The famous 24-hour sports car race sets the stage for this tale of love and speed. McQueen (who did his own driving) is the leading race driver, a man who battles competition, fear of death by accident, and emotional involvement. Excellent documentary-style race footage almost makes up for weak plot and minimal acting. **106m/C; VHS, DVD.** Steve McQueen; Elga Andersen; Ronald Leigh-Hunt; Luc Merenda; Angelo Infanti; ***D:*** Lee H. Katzin; ***W:*** Harry Kleiner; ***C:*** Robert B. Hauser.

Le Million 1/2 **1931** A comedy/musical masterpiece of the early sound era which centers on an artist's adventures in searching for a winning lottery ticket throughout Paris. Highly acclaimed member of the Clair school of subtle French farce. In French with English subtitles. **89m/B; VHS, DVD.** *FR* Annabella; Rene Lefevre; Paul Olivier; Louis Allibert; ***D:*** Rene Clair.

Le Petit Lieutenant *The Young Lieutenant* **2005** Rookie detective Antoine (Lespert) leaves his wife in Normandy so he can find some action in Paris by working in homicide. His commander is Catherine (Baye), a recovering alcoholic who has just returned to the job, and she takes the new guy under her professional wing. A homeless man is the latest victim of a robbery and murder crew that Antoine investigates with unexpectedly devastating consequences to all. French with subtitles. **110m/C; DVD.** *FR* Nathalie Baye; Jalil Lespert; Roschdy Zem; Antoine Chappey; Jacques Perrin; Berangere Allaux; ***D:*** Xavier Beauvois; ***W:*** Xavier Beauvois; Guillaume Breaud; Jean-Eric Troubat; ***C:*** Caroline Champetier.

Le Petit Soldat **1960** The passage of time has softened the controversy that swirled about Godard's second film (after "Breathless") in the initial release. It's the story of photographer Bruno Forestier (Subor), who joins the French nationalist movement against Algeria. While he tries to decide whether to follow orders to kill one of the opposition, he falls in love with a model (the lovely Karina, in her debut), unaware of her political beliefs. Godard's once-revolutionary on-the-fly filmmaking techniques seem completely contemporary and natural now. **88m/B; VHS, DVD, Blu-Ray.** *FR* Michel Subor; Anna Karina; Henri-Jacques Huet; Paul Beauvais; Georges De Beauregard; Jean-Luc Godard; Laszlo Szabo; ***D:*** Jean-Luc Godard; ***W:*** Jean-Luc Godard; ***C:*** Raoul Coutard; ***M:*** Maurice Leroux.

Le Plaisir 1/2 *House of Pleasure* **1952** An anthology of three Guy de Maupassant stories, "Le Masque," "Le Modele," and "La Maison Teillier," about the search for pleasure. In French with English subtitles. **97m/B; VHS, DVD.** *FR* Claude Dauphin; Simone Simon; Jean Gabin; Danielle Darrieux; Madeleine Renaud; Gaby Morlay; Jean Galland; Ginette LeClerc; Mila Parely; Pierre Brasseur; Daniel Gelin; ***Nar:*** Peter Ustinov; Jean Servais; ***D:*** Max Ophuls; ***W:*** Jacques Matras; ***C:*** Christian Matras; Philippe Agostini; ***M:*** Joe Hajos.

Le Professionnel 1/2 *The Professional* **1981** Assassin Joss Beaumont (Belmondo) was betrayed by his superiors and impirsoned in the African republic of Malagasy. He returns to Paris after two years and his old department is mobilized to eliminate him, but Beaumont is faster and smarter than all of them put together. Fast and clever, the film is a slick package, a spy thriller that relies on brains instead of guns. There's a constant flow of fistfights and combat encounters in the picture, none of which are hyped with cutting or music. Belmondo makes them all credible. French with subtitles. **109m/C; DVD, Blu-Ray.** *FR* Jean-Paul Belmondo; Jean Desailly; Robert Hossein; Michel Beaune; Cyrielle Claire; Jean-Louis Richard; Sidiki Bakaba; ***D:*** Georges Lautner; ***W:*** Georges Lautner; Michel Audiard; ***C:*** Henri Decae; ***M:*** Ennio Morricone.

Le Repos du Guerrier *Warrior's Rest* **1962** Star vehicle for Bardot in which she plays a respectable woman who abandons societal norms to pursue an unbalanced lover. In French with English subtitles. **100m/C; VHS, DVD.** *FR* Brigitte Bardot; Robert Hossein; James Robertson Justice; Jean-Mark Bory; ***D:*** Roger Vadim.

Le Samourai 1/2 *The Samurai; Godson* **1967** Cold, precise professional killer Jef Costello (Delon) lives by his version of the Japanese samurai code. Hired to kill a nightclub owner, he establishes an alibi with the help of his lover Jane (Nathalie Delon, Alain's then-wife) and, unexpectedly, by Valerie (Rosier), the club's black piano-player, which Jef finds suspicious. He's then betrayed by his employers and the subject of a police chase throughout Paris. The icy Delon was perfect for the anti-hero role and Melville's stylized filming heightens the tension and inevitable tragedy. A film much-admired, and copied, by other filmmakers. French with subtitles. **95m/C; VHS, DVD, Blu-Ray.** *FR* Alain Delon; Francois Perier; Cathy Rosier; Nathalie Delon; Jacques Leroy; Jean-Pierre Posier; ***D:*** Jean-Pierre Melville; ***W:*** Jean-Pierre Melville; ***C:*** Henri Decae; ***M:*** Francois de Roubaix.

Le Trou *The Hole; The Night Watch; Il Buco* **1959** Four long-term convicts in a Paris prison cell are planning to escape by tunneling to freedom. Then, a fifth prisoner joins them—is he going to betray them? Or is there already a Judas amongst the men? Based on a true story, the film has no musical score in order to heighten the tension and the actors were all nonprofessionals. Becker died in 1960; this is his final film. French with subtitles. **123m/B; VHS, DVD.** *FR* Phillippe LeRoy; Marc Michel; Catherine Spaak; Andre Bervil; Michel Constantin; Jean-Paul Coquelin; Jean Keraudy; Raymond Meunier; Eddy Rasimi; Dominique Zardi; ***D:*** Jacques Becker; ***W:*** Jacques Becker; Jose Giovanni; Jean Aurel; ***C:*** Ghislan Cloquet.

Le Week-End 1/2 **2014 (R)** Together for decades, Nick (Broadbent) and Meg (Duncan) are looking for a way to rekindle their romance as they head off on a vacation to Paris for the first time since their honeymoon. As the two joke, talk, fight, and reminisce about a life well-lived, they realize there are still many romantic days and nights ahead of them. And the two stars seem to relish playing a pair of roles too rare in modern cinema: Well-written characters beyond retirement age. **93m/C; DVD, Blu-Ray.** *UK* Jim Broadbent; Lindsay Duncan; Jeff Goldblum; Olly Alexander; Judith Davis; ***D:*** Roger Michell; ***W:*** Hanif Kureishi; ***C:*** Nathalie Durand; ***M:*** Jeremy Sams.

Lea **1996** Lea (Vlasakova) becomes mute after witnessing her abusive father kill her mother but writes the dead woman poems and letters to express her motions. However, Lea becomes even more withdrawn from the world when she's given in an arranged marriage to the much-older Herbert (Redl). Herbert marries Lea because she resembles his dead wife but Lea finds he has disturbing similarities to her father. German with subtitles. **100m/C; VHS, DVD.** *GE* Lenka Vlasakov; Christian Redl; Hanna Schygulla; ***D:*** Ivan Fila; ***W:*** Ivan Fila.

Leading Ladies **2010** Sweetly amusing lesbian romance with a ballroom setting. Overbearing stage mother Shari Campari is training daughter Tasi for a competition with older daughter Toni as her stand-in dance partner. Tasi is sidelined by an unexpected pregnancy and Toni is willing to take her place but only if she gets to partner up with lively blonde Mona (and still gets to lead). **102m/C; DVD.** Laurel Vail; Nicole Dionne; Melanie LaPatin; Shannon Lee Smith; Benji Schwimmer; ***D:*** Erika Randall Beahm; Daniel Beahm; ***W:*** Erika Randall Beahm; Jennifer Bechtel; ***C:*** Peter Biagi; ***M:*** Daniel Beahm.

The Leading Man 1/2 **1996 (R)** Bon Jovi's charming in the title role as American movie star Robin Grange. Grange is in London to work in the prestige stage production by playwright Felix Webb (Wilson) and he's become aware of Webb's complex romantic situation. Although married to Elena (Galiena), Felix is having an affair with young leading lady, Hilary Rule (Newton). So the studly Robin proposes that he seduce Elena, thus leaving Felix free to carry on with his own affair. Except Felix gets jealous when Robin succeeds and soon realizes that the actor has his own agenda. **96m/C; VHS, DVD.** *UK* Lambert Wilson; Jon Bon Jovi; Anna Galiena; Thandie Newton; David Warner; Barry Humphries; Patricia Hodge; Diana Quick; Nicole Kidman; ***D:*** John Duigan; ***W:*** John Duigan; ***C:*** Jean-Francois Robin; ***M:*** Ed Shearmur.

The League of Extraordinary Gentlemen **2003 (PG-13)** There's little left from the 1999 comic book by Alan Moore and Kevin O'Neill. Instead, it's overblown action and a lack of heart. In 1899, aging adventurer Allan Quartermain (Connery) is called to defeat a madman bent on starting a world war. He's reluctantly teamed with Captain Nemo (Shah) and his Nautilus submarine, vampiric scientist Mina Harker (Wilson), ageless Dorian Gray (Townsend), invisible man Rodney Skinner (Curran), Dr. Jekyll and his hulkish alter ego Mr. Hyde (Flemyng), and a grown-up Tom Sawyer (West), who's part of the American secret service. Clumsily telegraphs it's plot twists, but the well-read should get a kick out of the literary references. **110m/C; DVD, Blu-Ray, UMD.** Sean Connery; Stuart Townsend; Peta Wilson; Shane West; Tony Curran; Richard Roxburgh; Jason Flemyng; Naseeruddin Shah; David Hemmings; ***D:*** Stephen Norrington; ***W:*** James Robinson; ***C:*** Dan Laustsen; ***M:*** Trevor Jones.

The League of Gentlemen 1/2 **1960** An ex-Army officer plots a daring bank robbery using specially skilled military personnel and irreproachable panache. Hilarious British humor fills the screen. **115m/B; VHS, DVD.** *GB* Jack Hawkins; Nigel Patrick; Richard Attenborough; Roger Livesey; Bryan Forbes; ***D:*** Basil Dearden.

League of Ordinary Gentlemen **2004** Three former Microsoft execs purchased the Pro Bowlers Association for $5 million and hired Steve Miller from Nike to help revive and make it more exciting and media friendly. Film documents the 2003 nationwide tour, which culminated in a tense world championship in Detroit. We witness the tour through the fortunes of four pros, Pete Weber, a flamboyant player, Walter Ray Williams Jr., a low-key guy who can be a bit imposing, Chris Barnes, a clean-cut but moody fellow, and Wayne Webb, who knows after his past broken marriages and bankruptcies this tour will make or break his bowling career. An endearing film touching on American life and the eccentricities and hardships of competition. **100m/C; DVD.** ***D:*** Christopher Browne; ***C:*** Ken Seng.

A League of Their Own **1992 (PG)** Charming look at the Rockford Peaches, one of the teams in the All American Girls Professional Baseball League, formed in the 40s when the men were off at war. Boozy coach Jimmy Dugan (Hanks) reluctantly leads the Peaches and gets credit for the classic "There's no crying in baseball" scene. The focus is on the sibling rivalry between crackerjack catcher Dottie (Davis) and her insecure younger sister, Kit (Petty), the team's pitcher. Great cast of supporting characters, including sarcastic talent scout Ernie (Lovitz), sleay taxi dancer Mae (Madonna), and loud-mouthed Doris (O'Donnell). Lots of baseball for the sports fan. **127m/C; VHS, DVD, Blu-Ray.** Geena Davis; Tom Hanks; Lori Petty; Madonna; Rosie O'Donnell; Megan Cavanagh; Tracy Reiner; Bitty Schram; Jon Lovitz; David Strathairn; Garry Marshall; Bill Pullman; Ann Cusack; Anne Elizabeth Ramsay; Freddie Simpson; Renee Coleman; Tea Leoni; Joey Slotnick; Mark Holton; Gregory Sporleder; David Lander; ***V:*** Harry Shearer; ***D:*** Penny Marshall; ***W:*** Lowell Ganz; Babaloo Mandel; ***C:*** Miroslav Ondricek; ***M:*** Hans Zimmer. Natl. Film Reg. '12.

Lean on Me **1989 (PG-13)** The romanticized version of the career of Joe Clark, a tough New Jersey teacher who became the principal of the state's toughest, worst school and, through controversial hardline tactics, turned it around. **109m/C; VHS, DVD.** Morgan Freeman; Robert Guillaume; Beverly Todd; Alan North; Lynne Thigpen; Robin Bartlett; Michael Beach; Ethan Phillips; Regina Taylor; ***D:*** John G. Avildsen; ***W:*** Michael Schiffer; ***C:*** Victor Hammer; ***M:*** Bill Conti.

Lean on Pete **2017 (R)** A moving coming-of-age adventure drama by gifted filmmaker Andrew Haigh. In the Pacific Northwest, kind, smart 15-year-old Charlie (Plummer) lives in near poverty with his single father. After helping horse trainer Del (Buscemi) with a flat tire, Del hires Charlie to do random jobs. While working at the horse track, Charlie bonds with a race horse named Lean on Pete. When the horse's life is in jeopardy, Charlies acts with his heart, takes him, and goes on a desperate, if not dangerous, extended journey. With a beautiful performance by Plummer and Haigh's lyrical storytelling, the film is mesmerizing. **121m/C; DVD, Blu-Ray.** Charlie Plummer; Amy Seimetz; Travis Fimmel; Steve Buscemi; Chloë Sevigny; ***D:*** Andrew Haigh; ***W:*** Andrew Haigh; ***C:*** Magnus Nordenhof Jønck; ***M:*** James Edward Barker.

Leap! *Ballerina* **2016 (PG)** A charming, if predictable, animated feature about one French orphan girl's desire to become a star in ballet. Felicie (voiced by Fanning) and Victor (voiced by Wolff) run away from their orphanage in rural Brittany, France, to Paris to live out their dreams. While Victor wants to become an inventor, the plucky Felicie longs to dance. To attend the Opera Ballet School, Felicie must pretend to be from a wealthy family and manage her merciless classmates. The target audience will no doubt find this to be inspiring. **89m/C; DVD, Blu-Ray.** Elle Fanning; Nat Wolff; Carly Rae Jepsen; Maddie Ziegler; Julie Khaner; ***D:*** Eric Summer; Eric Warin; ***W:*** Eric Summer; Carol Noble; Laurent Zeitoun; ***C:*** Jerrica Cleland; ***M:*** Klaus Badelt.

Leap of Faith 1/2 **1992 (PG-13)** Jonas Nightengale (Martin) is a traveling evangelist/scam artist whose tour bus is stranded in an impoverished farm town. Nevertheless he sets up his show and goes to work, aided by the technology utilized by accomplice Winger. Both Martin and Winger begin to have a change of heart after experiencing love—Winger with local sheriff Neeson and Martin after befriending a waitress (Davidovich) and her crippled brother (Haas). Martin is in his element as the slick revivalist with the hidden heart but the film is soft-headed as well as soft-hearted. **110m/C; VHS, DVD.** Steve Martin; Debra Winger; Lolita Davidovich; Liam Neeson; Lukas Haas; Meat Loaf Aday; Philip Seymour Hoffman; M.C. Gainey; La Chanze; Delores Hall; John Toles-Bey; Albertina Walker; Ricky Dillard; ***D:*** Richard Pearce; ***W:*** Janus Cercone; ***M:*** Cliff Eidelman.

Leap Year 1/2 **2010 (PG)** Uptight wanna-be bride Anna (Adams) follows her boyfriend Jeremy (Scott) to Dublin after being told of an Irish tradition that says that men must say yes to a proposal made on Leap Year Day. Stranded, Anna must depend on surly (but handsome) innkeeper Declan (Goode) to help her out in this all-too-familiar "opposites attract" romantic comedy. Little wit or charm, but plenty of stock characters and gags you've seen before, set against a scenic Irish backdrop in hopes that the uneven story and unappealing characters aren't noticeable. **100m/C; Blu-Ray.** Amy Adams; Matthew Goode; Adam Scott; John Lithgow; Kaitlin Olson; ***D:*** Anand Tucker; ***W:*** Harry Elfont; Deborah Kaplan; ***C:*** Newton Thomas (Tom) Sigel; ***M:*** Randy Edelman.

The Learning Curve **2001 (R)** Hospital orderly Paul (Giovinazzo) comes to the rescue of Georgia (Mazur) and gets involved in a shady sex scam. These small-timers are in for trouble when they target Marshal (Ventresca) who turns out to be a ruthless L.A. record producer with a lot of clout. Marshal's amused by their chutzpah and decides to bring them into his own shady deals where they are in over their heads. **97m/C; VHS, DVD.** Carmine D. Giovinazzo; Monet Mazur; Vincent Ventresca; Steven Bauer; Majandra Delfino; Richard Erdman; Jack Laufer; ***D:*** Eric Schwab; ***W:*** Eric Schwab; ***C:*** Michael Hofstein; ***M:*** Zoran Boris.

Learning to Drive **2015 (R)** Wendy (Clarkson) has seen her life crumble around her after the dissolution of her marriage. She doesn't even know how to drive. She contacts Darwan, a Sikh driving instructor (Kingsley), who has had some relationship troubles of his own, including a pending arranged marriage. The two form a unique friendship as Darwan gives Wendy more confidence and Wendy shows Darwan how much life has to offer. Obviously, the driving metaphor is a bit on-the-nose, but Clarkson and Kingsley are charming, even if they're above the material at the same time. **105m/C; DVD.** Grace Gummer; Ben Kingsley; Patricia Clarkson; Jake Weber; Sarita Choudhury; ***D:*** Isabel Coixet; ***W:*** Sarah Kernochan; ***C:*** Manel Ruiz; ***M:*** Dhani Harrison; Paul Hicks.

The Learning Tree **1969 (PG)** A beautifully photographed adaptation of Parks' biographical novel about a 14-year-old black boy in the 1920s South, living on the verge of manhood, maturity, love, and wisdom. **107m/C; VHS, DVD.** Kyle Johnson; Alex Clarke; Estelle Evans; Dana Elcar; ***D:*** Gordon Parks; *C:* Burnett Guffey. Natl. Film Reg. '89.

The Least Among You ♪♪ ½ **2009 (PG-13)** Earnest inspirational drama based on a true story. UCLA grad Richard Kelly is wrongly convicted of a crime following the 1965 Watts riots. He's given probation but forced to serve it at an all-white seminary whose president wants to break the color barrier. Richard suffers a lot of racial abuse until janitor Samuel Benton becomes his mentor but there's also more trouble for him back home. **97m/C; DVD.** Cedric Sanders; Louis Gossett, Jr.; Lauren Holly; William Devane; Starletta DuPois; Siena Goines; Cory Hardrict; *D:* Mark Young; *W:* Mark Young; *C:* Zoran Popovic; *M:* Mark Kilian. **VIDEO**

The Least of These ♪♪ **2008** Father Andre James (Washington) returns to his all-male Catholic boarding school to take over from a priest who has gone missing after being transferred. Father James tries to earn the respect of both his fellow priests and his students but when he takes an interest in bullied student Parker (Garrett), rumors abound. **101m/C; DVD.** Isaiah Washington, IV; Jordan Garrett; Robert Loggia; John Billingsley; Bob Gunton; Andrew (Andy) Lawrence; Kirk B.R. Woller; *D:* Nathan Scoggins; *W:* Nathan Scoggins; *C:* Ralph Linhardt; *M:* Mateo Messina.

The Leather Boys ♪♪ *The Leather-boys* **1963** Teenaged Dot (Tushingham) marries mechanic Reggie (Campbell) and soon both begin to look beyond the boundaries of marriage. Dot enjoys her freedom from parental supervision by staying out and coming home drunk while Reggie takes up his friendship with biker pal, Pete (Sutton). Then Dot begins wondering just how close her husband and his best pal really are. Considered very controversial in the '60s, but looks staid now. **110m/B; VHS, DVD.** *GB* Rita Tushingham; Colin Campbell; Dudley Sutton; Gladys Henson; Avice Landon; Betty Marsden; Dandy Nichols; Johnny Briggs; Geoffrey Dunn; Lockwood West; Denholm Elliott; *D:* Sidney J. Furie; *W:* Gillian Freeman; *C:* Gerald Gibbs.

Leather Burners ♪♪ **1943** Hoppy goes under cover to get the goods on a suspected rustler. When his cover is blown, the bad guys frame him for murder. Look for Robert Mitchum in his third bit part in this series. **66m/B; VHS, DVD.** William Boyd; Andy Clyde; Jay Kirby; Victor Jory; George Givot; Bobby Larson; George Reeves; Hal Taliaferro; Forbes Murray; Robert Mitchum; *D:* Joseph Henabery.

Leather Jacket Love Story ♪♪ **1998** Remarkably sweet, campy, and raunchy romance finds 18-year-old Valley boy Kyle (Tataryn) taking a summer rental in bohemian Silver Lake in order to get the proper inspiration for his poetry. The local coffee shop is the preferred hangout and that's where Kyle spots leather-jacketed motorcycle man Mike (Bradley). Some 12 years older than Kyle, easygoing carpenter Mike is not adverse to some sexual fun, but both men are suprised when their feelings for each other start turning serious. **85m/B; VHS, DVD.** Sean Tataryn; Christopher Bradley; Hector Mercado; Geoffrey Moody; ***Cameo(s):*** Mink Stole; *D:* David DeCoteau; *W:* Rondo Mieczkowski; *C:* Howard Wexler; *M:* Jeremy Jordan.

Leather Jackets ♪♪ **1990 (R)** Sweeney plays a nice guy who lets involvement with a childhood pal destroy his life. Elwes is the friend, now gang member, in trouble with both the cops and members of a rival gang, who needs Sweeney's help to escape. Fonda plays Sweeney's girlfriend caught between the two men. Essentially a routine fugitive pic with an attractive cast. **90m/C; VHS, DVD.** D.B. Sweeney; Bridget Fonda; Cary Elwes; Christopher Penn; Marshall Bell; James LeGros; Jon Polito; Craig Ng; Ginger Lynn Allen; *D:* Lee Drysdale; *W:* Lee Drysdale.

Leatherface: The Texas Chainsaw Massacre 3 ♪ *Texas Chainsaw Massacre 3: Leatherface* **1989 (R)** The human-skin-wearing cannibal is at it again in this, the second sequel to the Tobe Hooper protomess. This one sports a bit more humor and is worth seeing for that reason. **81m/C; VHS, DVD, Blu-Ray.** Kate Hodge; William Butler; Ken Foree; Tom Hudson; R.A. Mihailoff; Miriam Byrd-Nethery; Tom Everett; Joe Unger; Viggo Mortensen; David Cloud; Beth de Patie; *D:* Jeff Burr; *W:* David J. Schow; *C:* James L. Carter; *M:* Jim Manzie.

Leatherheads ♪♪ ½ **2008 (PG-13)** The 1925 Duluth Bulldogs, led by charming star player Dodge Connelly (Clooney), are an upstart professional football team during a time when the pros lack the polish and respect of the college game. In a marketing move, Connelly adds well-known war hero Carter "The Bullet" Rutherford (Krasinski) to the roster. Unfortunately, Rutherford's war-hero credentials are suspect, drawing the attention of sassy news hound Lexie Littleton (Zellweger). A kooky romantic triangle ensues. The script's generally a clunker, but there's some chuckles and the period details are spot on. **113m/C; DVD, Blu-Ray.** George Clooney; Renée Zellweger; John Krasinski; Jonathan Pryce; Peter Gerety; Jack Thompson; Stephen (Steve) Root; Wayne Duvall; Keith Loneker; *W:* Duncan Brantley; Rick Reilly; *C:* Newton Thomas (Tom) Sigel; *M:* Randy Newman.

Leave 'Em Laughing ♪♪ **1981** Rooney plays Chicago clown Jack Thum in this based-on-real-life TV movie. Thum takes in orphans even though he cannot find steady work, and then discovers he has cancer. **103m/C; VHS, Streaming.** Mickey Rooney; Anne Jackson; Allen Garfield; Elisha Cook, Jr.; William Windom; Red Buttons; Michael LeClair; *D:* Jackie Cooper.

Leave Her to Heaven ♪♪♪ **1945** Beautiful neurotic Tierney takes drastic measures to keep hubby all to herself and will do anything to get what she wants. Tierney, in a departure from her usual roles, is excellent as this pathologically possessive creature. Oscar-winner Leon Shamroy's photography (in Technicolor) is breathtaking. Based on the novel by Ben Ames Williams. **110m/C; VHS, DVD, Blu-Ray.** Gene Tierney; Cornel Wilde; Jeanne Crain; Vincent Price; Mary (Phillips) Philips; Ray Collins; Darryl Hickman; Gene Lockhart; *D:* John M. Stahl; *W:* Jo Swerling; *C:* Leon Shamroy; *M:* Alfred Newman. Oscars '45: Color Cinematog.; Natl. Film Reg. '18.

Leave It to Beaver ♪♪ **1997 (PG)** Gee, Mrs. Cleaver, that's an awful nice updating of an old TV favorite you have there. Cut the crap, Eddie. The "let's plop a lovable sitcom family into the dysfunctional 90s" bit has had its run. This time the victims are the Cleavers: wise dad Ward (McDonald), perfect mom June (Turner), popular older brother Wally (von Detten). . .and newcomer Cameron Finley as the Beaver. Unlike the Bradys, the modern world has made some impact here. Beav has an African American friend while Mom wears jeans and owns a business. Gosh Wally, do you really think America was anxiously awaiting the return of the impossible-to-live-up-to clan? Don't be such a little dope. **88m/C; VHS, DVD, Blu-Ray.** Christopher McDonald; Janine Turner; Erik von Detten; Cameron Finley; Barbara Billingsley; Ken Osmond; Adam Zolotin; Alan Rachins; *D:* Andy Cadiff; *W:* Brian Levant; *C:* Thomas Del Ruth; *M:* Randy Edelman.

Leave No Trace ♪♪♪ **2018 (PG)** A moving father-daughter drama based on Peter Rock's novel "My Abandonment." In Portland, Will (Foster) and his 13-year-old daughter Tom (McKenzie) live off the grid in a makeshift camp in a park amidst lush greenery. Though their lives are difficult, they share a deep, loving bond. When a jogger spots them, they are taken into custody and split up. The kind actions of a stranger lead the pair to be reunited, but Will chafes at the world that Tom is discovering with wonderment. Writer/director Granik has crafted a insightful film that includes subtle yet effective social and political commentary on modern culture. **109m/C; DVD, Blu-Ray.** Thomasin McKenzie; Ben Foster; Michael Draper; Peter Simpson; Jeff Kober; *D:* Debra Granik; *W:* Debra Granik; Anne Rosellini; *C:* Michael McDonough; *M:* Dickon Hinchliffe.

Leaves from Satan's Book ♪♪ ½ **1921** Impressionistic episodes of Satan's fiddling with man through the ages, from Christ to the Russian Revolution. An early cinematic film by Dreyer, with ample indications of his later brilliance. Silent. **130m/B; Silent; DVD.** *DK* Helge Milsen; Halvart Hoft; Jacob Texiere; *D:* Carl Theodor Dreyer.

Leaves of Grass ♪♪ **2009 (R)** Norton plays very different twin brothers in Nelson's often violent mix of crime comedy and family drama. Popular Brown University classics prof Bill Kincaid goes back to his rural Oklahoma home after being told that his twin Brady has died. It turns out to be ruse because the major pot grower needs Bill to give him a lookalike alibi while Brady takes care of business with Jewish mobster Rothbaum (Dreyfuss). The trip isn't a total waste since Bill finds local poet and teacher Janet (Russell) very appealing. Of course that's before Brady's plans go violently wrong and the plot gets battered as well. **104m/C; Blu-Ray, On Demand.** Edward Norton; Keri Russell; Richard Dreyfuss; Susan Sarandon; Josh Pais; Melanie Lynskey; Tim Blake Nelson; Steve Earle; *D:* Tim Blake Nelson; *W:* Tim Blake Nelson; *C:* Roberto Schaefer; *M:* Jeff Danna.

Leaving Barstow ♪♪ **2008** Andrew wants to leave Barstow, CA but his devotion to his single mom Sandra and his interest in newcomer Jenny hold him back. Eventually Andrew realizes he has to choose whether to put his own dreams first or stay tied to the people he loves. **89m/C; DVD.** Michelle Clunie; Steven Culp; Kevin Sheridan; Ryan Michelle Bathe; Ryan Carnes; *D:* Peter Paige; *W:* Kevin Sheridan; Jayson Crothers; *M:* Kurt Swinghammer.

Leaving Las Vegas ♪♪♪ ½ **1995 (R)** Hopeless alcoholic Ben Sanderson (Cage) goes to Vegas to drink himself to death. He meets Sera (Shue), a lonely hooker who loves him enough not to stop him. Definitely as depressing as it sounds, but still there's a subtle sense of humor and compassion. Cage tops his best work and Shue proves she's his equal. Not for everyone, but worth the effort for people who like to see honest emotion and hate Hollywood's insistence on happy endings. Based on the semi-autobiographical novel by John O'Brien, who committed suicide shortly before production on the film began. **120m/C; VHS, DVD, Blu-Ray.** Nicolas Cage; Elisabeth Shue; Julian Sands; Laurie Metcalf; David Brisbin; Richard Lewis; Valeria Golino; Steven Weber; Mariska Hargitay; Julian Lennon; Carey Lowell; Lucinda Jenney; Ed Lauter; R. Lee Ermey; *D:* Mike Figgis; *W:* Mike Figgis; *C:* Declan Quinn; *M:* Mike Figgis. Oscars '95: Actor (Cage); Golden Globes '96: Actor--Drama (Cage); Ind. Spirit '96: Actress (Shue), Cinematog., Director (Figgis), Film; L.A. Film Critics '95: Actor (Cage), Actress (Shue), Director (Figgis), Film; Natl. Bd. of Review '95: Actor (Cage); N.Y. Film Critics '95: Actor (Cage), Film; Natl. Soc. Film Critics '95: Actor (Cage), Actress (Shue), Director (Figgis); Screen Actors Guild '95: Actor (Cage).

Leaving Metropolis ♪♪ **2002** Hoping to be creatively inspired, successful Winnipeg artist David (Ruptash) rejoins the real world as a waiter for married diner owners Violet (Taylor) and Matt (Corrazza). David keeps his past quiet but is attracted to Matt, who's confused by his own feelings. The two eventually have an affair, with Violet increasingly suspicious of her hubby and David's volatile best gal pal Kryla (Boyd) acting like a jealous spouse herself. The aftermath is messy indeed. Well-played drama that Fraser adapted from his play "Poor Super Man." **89m/C; VHS, DVD.** *CA* Troy Ruptash; Vincent Corazza; Lynda Boyd; Cherilee Taylor; Thom Allison; *D:* Brad Fraser; *W:* Brad Fraser; *C:* Daniel Vincelette; *M:* Dennis Burke.

Leaving Normal ♪ ½ **1992 (R)** Darly (Lahti), a fed-up waitress, and Marianne (Tilly), an abused housewife, meet at a bus stop in Normal, Wyoming and decide to blow town. They travel across the American West, through Canada, and up to Alaska, where Darly's ex-boyfriend has left her a house. Because both women have made bad choices all their lives, they decide to leave their futures to chance, and end up finding their nirvana. Sappy and sentimental to the point of annoyance at times. **110m/C; VHS, DVD.** Christine Lahti; Meg Tilly; Lenny Von Dohlen; Maury Chaykin; James Gammon; Patrika Darbo; Eve Gordon; James Eckhouse; Brett Cullen; Rutanya Alda; *D:* Edward Zwick; *W:* Edward Solomon; *C:* Ralf Bode.

Lebanon ♪♪ **2009 (R)** Covers the first day of the 1982 invasion of Lebanon by Israel. The majority of the film is set inside an Israeli tank as it moves across the border and is told from the viewpoint of the four 20-something soldiers who occupy the vehicle—commander Assi (Tiran), loader Hertzel (Cohen), driver Yigal (Moshonov), and gunner Shmulik (Donat). It's hot, noisy, and claustrophobic and the four conscripts have trouble deciphering civilians from foes. Based on the experiences of writer/director Maoz. English, Hebrew, and Arabic with subtitles. **93m/C; DVD.** *IS FR GE* Itay Tiran; Oshri Cohen; Michael Moshonov; Zohar Strauss; Yoav Donat; *D:* Samuel Maoz; *W:* Samuel Maoz; *C:* Giora Bejach; *M:* Nicolas Becker.

Lebanon, PA ♪ ½ **2010 (PG-13)** Slow-paced, somewhat manipulative indie family drama. Restless Will drives to the title town for his estranged dad's funeral. He unexpectedly develops a bond with his distant second cousin CJ, a 17-year-old who's trying to decide what to do about her unexpected pregnancy. Though he's never been a guy who's able to deal with emotions, Will becomes CJ's uneasy confidante amidst his own mini midlife crisis. **100m/C; DVD.** Josh Hopkins; Rachel Kitson; Ian Merrill Peakes; Samantha Mathis; Hunter Gallagher; Mary Beth Hurt; *D:* Ben Hickernell; *W:* Ben Hickernell; *C:* Jeff Schirmer; *M:* Matt Pond; Chris Hansen.

The Ledge ♪ **2011 (R)** Writer/director Chapman's pic falls apart over eye-rolling stereotypes and excessive melodrama. Troubled Baton Rouge detective Hollis Lucetti (Howard) serves as a framing device as he tries to talk Gavin (Hunnam) out of jumping off a high-rise. Flashbacks depict Gavin's dilemma as he becomes involved with new neighbor Shana (Tyler), who's unhappily married to born-again Christian Joe (Wilson) and what happens when Joe finds out about their romance. **100m/C; DVD, Blu-Ray.** Charlie Hunnam; Liv Tyler; Patrick Wilson; Terrence Howard; Jacqueline Flemming; Christopher Gorham; *D:* Matthew Chapman; *W:* Mathew Chapman; *C:* Bobby Bukowski; *M:* Nathan Barr.

Lee Daniels' The Butler ♪♪ ½ *The Butler* **2013 (PG-13)** Well-intentioned but overly sentimental, director/writer Daniels tells an important story of the progression of race relations over a half-century of American politics. Forest Whitaker stars as the title character, a man who served eight U.S. Presidents over three decades. A star-studded cast portrays the commanders-in-chief and their first ladies while Whitaker adds a much-needed gravity to the episode storytelling. Writer Strong and Daniels play in broad, manipulative emotional strokes but sometimes it works in their favor. Inspired by the true story of Eugene Allen, who served as the White House's butler from 1952 to 1986, written in 2008 by journalist Wil Haygood. **132m/C; DVD, Blu-Ray.** Forest Whitaker; Oprah Winfrey; David Oyelowo; Terrence Howard; Cuba Gooding, Jr.; Lenny Kravitz; Robin Williams; John Cusack; James Marsden; Minka Kelly; Liev Schreiber; Alan Rickman; Jane Fonda; Clarence Williams, III; Mariah Carey; David Banner; Vanessa Redgrave; Alex Pettyfer; *D:* Lee Daniels; *W:* Danny Strong; *C:* Andrew Dunn; *M:* Rodrigo Leao.

The Leech Woman ♪♪ **1959** While in Africa, an older woman (Gray) discovers how to restore her youth through a tribal ritual. The only problem is it requires the pineal gland of males, which causes her to go on a killing spree to keep that youthful look. Based on a story by Ben Pivar and Francis Rosenwald. **77m/B; VHS, DVD, Blu-Ray.** Coleen Gray; Grant Williams; Gloria Talbott; Phillip Terry; *D:* Edward Dein; *W:* David Duncan.

Left Bank ♪♪ *Linkeroever* **2008** Until it descends into predictability in its last half, van Hees' feature debut is a solid Belgian chiller. To get away from her mother, Marie (Kuppens) moves in with new boyfriend Bobby (Schoenaerts) and discovers that the previous female tenant of his apartment disappeared. When Marie investigates, she learns that the complex was built on the site of a village that practiced sinister, possibly satanic rituals, and the building's blocked-up cellar may provide answers that Marie doesn't really want to know. English, Flemish, and French with subtitles. **102m/C; DVD.** *BE* Eline Kuppens; Matthias Schoenaerts; Sien Eggers; Tom de Wispelaere; Marilou Mermans; *D:* Pieter vanHees; *W:* Pieter vanHees; Dimitri Karaktsanis; *C:* Nicols Karakatsanis; *M:* Simon Lenski.

Left Behind ♪ **2014 (PG-13)** A clunky, clumsy mess of a faith-based drama that is never quite sure if it's delivering a religious message or just rallying against common sense. Adulterous commercial airline pilot Rayford Steele (Cage) flies head-first into the Rapture, complete with vanishing passengers, power outages, and general mass hysteria. All of this comes as little surprise to his devout wife (Thompson), who has warned her family for years. A bad remake of a bad film from a popular book series, this unnecessary retelling of the 2000 direct-to-video stinker has all the markings of a fly-by-night cash grab. Destined for cult status, for all the wrong reasons. **110m/C; DVD, Blu-Ray.** Nicolas Cage; Lea Thompson; Nicky Whelan; Chad Michael Murray; Cassi Thomson; Jordin Sparks; ***D:*** Vic Armstrong; ***W:*** Paul LaLonde; John Patus; ***C:*** Jack N. Green; ***M:*** Jack Lenz.

Left Behind: The Movie 🦴 **2000** Ace TV newsman Buck Williams (Cameron) is on hand for a sneak attack on Israel. Right after it, devout Christians and innocent children mysteriously vanish. The film is a dramatization of the novels based on a conservative Christian interpretation of the Book of Revelation. As entertainment, it's heavy handed at every level—plotting, acting, writing, directing. **95m/C; VHS, DVD.** Kirk Cameron; Brad Johnson; Chelsea Noble; Clarence Gilyard, Jr.; Colin Fox; Gordon Currie; Daniel Pilon; Jack Langedijk; ***D:*** Vic Savin; ***W:*** Alan B. McElroy; Joe Goodman; ***C:*** Jiri (George) Tirl.

The Left Hand of God 🦴🦴🦴 **1955** After an American pilot escapes from a Chinese warlord in post-WWII, he disguises himself as a Catholic priest and takes refuge in a missionary hospital. Bogie is great as the flyboy/cleric. **87m/C; VHS, Streaming.** Humphrey Bogart; E.G. Marshall; Lee J. Cobb; Agnes Moorehead; Gene Tierney; ***D:*** Edward Dmytryk.

The Left-Handed Gun 🦴🦴🦴 **1958** An offbeat version of the exploits of Billy the Kid, which portrays him as a 19th-century Wild West juvenile delinquent. Newman's role, which he method-acted, was originally intended for James Dean. Based on a 1955 Philco teleplay by Gore Vidal. **102m/B; VHS, DVD.** Paul Newman; Lita Milan; John Dehner; ***D:*** Arthur Penn.

Left in Darkness 🦴🦴 **1/2 2006** Well-done creepfest. Celia (Keena) goes to a frat party on her 21st birthday and dies after being given a date rape drug. She winds up in an otherworld, battling soul eaters, while her guardian/guide Donovan (Anders) tries to help Celia complete her journey to heaven. **88m/C; DVD.** Monica Keena; Tim Thomerson; David Anders; Chris Engen; ***D:*** Steve Monroe; ***W:*** Philip Daay; ***C:*** Matthew Heckerling; ***M:*** Corey A. Jackson. **VIDEO**

Left Luggage 🦴 **1/2 1998** Sticky family saga set in Antwerp, Belgium in 1972. Non-religious college student Chaja (Fraser) is the daughter of Holocaust survivors (Sagebrecht and Schell), but has never sought to understand their ordeal or her religion. But that doesn't prevent her from taking a job as a nanny to a strict Hasidic family, the Kalmans. Carefree Chaja even manages to coax her mute four-year-old charge into speaking. She learns some lessons, the families learn some lessons (there's the prerequisite tragedy), and it's all so much unfortunate overkill. **100m/C; VHS, DVD.** Laura Fraser; Isabella Rossellini; Jeroen Krabbe; Maximilian Schell; Marianne Saegebrecht; Topol; ***D:*** Jeroen Krabbe; ***W:*** Edwin de Vries; ***C:*** Walther Vanden Ende; ***M:*** Henny Vrienten.

Left to Die: The Sandra and Tammi Chase Story 🦴 **1/2 2012** Typical Lifetime drama based on a true story. Innocent American Sandra Chase (Hershey) is accused of drug smuggling in Ecuador and is immediately imprisoned by a corrupt system. Sandra desperately tries to survive while her daughter Tammi (Cook) tries to rally political support for her mom in D.C. **90m/C; DVD, Blu-Ray.** Barbara Hershey; Rachael Leigh Cook; Nicholas Gonzalez; Vincent Irizarry; Emily Foxler; Derek Ray; ***D:*** Leon Ichaso; ***W:*** Suzette Couture; Agatha Dominik; ***M:*** Laura Karpman. **CABLE**

The Legacy 🦴 **1/2** ***The Legacy of Maggie Walsh*** **1979 (R)** An American couple become privy to the dark secrets of an English family gathering in a creepy mansion to inherit an eccentric millionaire's fortune. Death and demons abound. **100m/C; VHS, DVD.** ***GB*** Katharine Ross; Sam Elliott; John Standing; Roger Daltrey; Ian Hogg; ***D:*** Richard Marquand; ***C:*** Dick Bush.

Legacy 🦴 **2008 (R)** Geeky college freshman Katie tries to rush the most popular sorority on campus and is found murdered during Omega Kappa's big party. Did sorority prez Lana (Duff) and her cohorts do her in to protect their house's exclusivity? Nutso Detective Strasburg (Green) is on the case! **90m/C; DVD.** Haylie Duff; Madeline Zima; Tom Green; Margo Harshman; Monica Lo; Brett Claywell; ***D:*** Irving Rothberg; ***W:*** Jason Dudek; Samantha Silver; ***C:*** Joseph Setele; ***M:*** Jay Israelson. **VIDEO**

Legacy 🦴 **1/2 2010 (R)** Rather overwrought thriller with some serious scenery-chewing. Special operative Malcolm Gray survived capture and torture during a botched mission and is now battling his demons in a rundown Brooklyn motel room. Malcolm suspects his ambitious Republican senator brother Darnell is involved with a weapons dealer and decides to share his story with a journalist, which could destroy Darnell's career and cause political trouble. **95m/C; DVD.** ***GB*** Idris Elba; Eamonn Walker; Clarke Peters; Lara Pulver; Monique Gabriela Curnen; Julian Wadham; Richard Brake; Gerald Kyd; ***D:*** Thomas Ikimi; ***W:*** Thomas Ikimi; ***C:*** Johnathan Harvey; ***M:*** Mark Kilian.

Legacy of Fear 🦴🦴 **2006** As a young girl, Jeanne Joyce survived a serial killer although her mother did not. Thirty years later, Detective Joyce (Polo) is convinced a new series of murders with the same MO have been committed by a copycat but her obsession alienates her colleagues. She gets suspended even as the killer threatens her. Made for Lifetime. **90m/C; DVD.** Teri Polo; Zachary Bennett; Anthony Lemke; Serge Houde; Stephen Spender; Corinne Conley; ***D:*** Don Terry; ***W:*** John Benjamin Martin; ***C:*** Daniel Villeneuve; ***M:*** James Gelfand. **CABLE**

Legacy of Horror WOOF! 1978 (R) A weekend at the family's island mansion with two unfriendly siblings sounds bad enough, but when terror, death, and a few family skeletons pop out of the closets, things go from bad to weird. All-round poor effort with substantial gore. A remake of the director's own "The Ghastly Ones." **83m/C; VHS, DVD.** Elaine Boies; Chris Broderick; Marilee Troncone; Jeannie Cusik; ***D:*** Andy Milligan.

Legacy of Rage 🦴🦴 **1986** Brandon (Lee), a waiter, befriends young mobster Michael (Wong), who turns out to be in love with Brandon's fiancee, May (Kent). In fact, Michael frames Brandon on a murder charge and gets him thrown in prison in order to get the girl. And what's Brandon's first thought when he gets out of the slammer? Revenge. Lee's first feature film. Chinese with subtitles or dubbed. **86m/C; VHS, DVD.** ***CH*** Brandon Lee; Michael Wong; Bolo Yeung; Regina Kent; ***D:*** Ronny Yu.

Legal Eagles 🦴🦴 **1/2 1986 (PG)** An assistant D.A. faces murder, mayhem, and romance while prosecuting a girl accused of stealing a portrait painted by her father. Redford sparkles in this otherwise convoluted tale from Reitman, while Hannah lacks depth as the daffy thief. **116m/C; VHS, DVD, Blu-Ray.** Robert Redford; Debra Winger; Daryl Hannah; Brian Dennehy; Terence Stamp; Steven Hill; David Clennon; Roscoe Lee Browne; John McMartin; Jennifer (Jennie) Dundas Lowe; Ivan Reitman; ***D:*** Ivan Reitman; ***W:*** Jim Cash; Jack Epps, Jr.; ***C:*** Laszlo Kovacs; ***M:*** Elmer Bernstein.

Legalese 🦴🦴 **1/2 1998 (R)** Solid cast provides solid enjoyment in this skewering of tabloid journalists and the legal system. Celeb lawyer Norman Keane (Garner) doesn't take the case of actress Angela Beale (Gershon), who's accused of killing her brother-in-law. But he does recommend new kid attorney, Roy Guyton (Kerr), to take the heat while Keane works behind the scenes. This raises the antennae of tabloid TV anchorwoman Brenda Whitlass (Turner) who winds up with a video of Guyton getting up close and personal with fellow lawyer Rica Martin (Parker). Needless to say, ethics have very little to do with anything. **105m/C; VHS, DVD.** James Garner; Edward Kerr; Kathleen Turner; Mary-Louise Parker; Gina Gershon; ***D:*** Glenn Jordan; ***W:*** Billy Ray; ***C:*** Tobias Schliessler; ***M:*** Stewart Copeland. **CABLE**

Legally Blonde 🦴🦴 **1/2 2001 (PG-13)** Beverly Hills blonde Elle Woods (Witherspoon) is a sorority babe who dresses in pink and has her Chihuahua Bruiser as a constant companion. After getting dumped by frat boyfriend Warner (Davis), Elle wallows in chocolate-fueled misery. But determined to show him that's she more than the sum of her pretty parts, Elle also gets accepted to Harvard Law and shows all those pasty-faced easterners that she has brains as well as blonde roots when she gets involved in a big murder case. Witherspoon is a delight in a very lightweight comedy. **95m/C; VHS, DVD, Blu-Ray.** Reese Witherspoon; Matthew Davis; Selma Blair; Luke Wilson; Ali Larter; Holland Taylor; Victor Garber; Jessica Cauffiel; Jennifer Coolidge; Oz (Osgood) Perkins, II; Raquel Welch; ***D:*** Robert Luketic; ***W:*** Karen McCullah Lutz; Kirsten Smith; ***C:*** Anthony B. Richmond; ***M:*** Rolfe Kent.

Legally Blonde 2: Red White & Blonde 🦴🦴 **2003 (PG-13)** In the sequel to the 2001 surprise hit, Boston lawyer Elle Woods (Witherspoon) heads to D.C. and becomes the aide to congresswoman Rudd (Field) and takes up the cause of animal rights. Witherspoon's zest and charm are the only things to recommend about this mostly unfunny cliche-fest that traps some real talent in ridiculously cardboard roles. Other than Witherspoon, the only bright spots are Coolidge as Elle's manicurist friend, and the dog whose family provides the main plot start. **95m/C; VHS, DVD, Blu-Ray.** Reese Witherspoon; Sally Field; Bob Newhart; Luke Wilson; Jennifer Coolidge; Regina King; Bruce McGill; Dana Ivey; Mary Lynn Rajskub; Jessica Cauffiel; Alanna Ubach; J Barton; ***D:*** Charles Herman-Wurmfeld; ***W:*** Kate Kondell; ***C:*** Elliot Davis; ***M:*** Rolfe Kent.

Legally Blondes 🦴 **1/2 2009 (PG)** In this ABC Family movie, Elle Woods' twin British cousins Annabelle and Isabelle move to Beverly Hills to attends her alma mater Pacific Preparatory. Despite the blonde hair, pink clothing, and tiny dogs, they find themselves ostracized by the popular clique after being exposed as scholarship girls. One of the twins is framed for stealing test answers and is defended in a student court by her sister. **86m/C; DVD.** Camilla Rosso; Rebecca Rosso; Brittany Curran; Christopher Cousins; Lisa Banes; Curtis Armstrong; Bobby Campo; ***D:*** Savage Steve Holland; ***W:*** Chad Gomez Creasy; Dara Resnik Creasey; ***C:*** William Barber; ***M:*** John Coda. **CABLE**

Legend 🦴🦴 **1986 (PG)** A colorful, unabashedly Tolkien-esque fantasy about the struggle to save an innocent waif from the Prince of Darkness. Set in a land packed with unicorns, magic swamps, bumbling dwarves and rainbows. Produced in Great Britain. **89m/C; VHS, DVD, Blu-Ray.** ***GB*** Tom Cruise; Mia Sara; Tim Curry; David Bennent; Billy Barty; Alice Playten; Kiran Shah; Robert Picardo; Cork Hubbert; ***D:*** Ridley Scott; ***C:*** Alex Thomson; ***M:*** Jerry Goldsmith.

Legend 🦴🦴 **2015 (R)** Two performances from Tom Hardy proves to be too many for director Helgeland, a talented filmmaker who has no idea what to do with what his lead actor has given him in this period gangster flick. Hardy plays both Ronnie and Reggie Kray, leaders of the criminal underground in London in the 1960s. Inexplicably, the film is narrated by France (Browning), the doomed wife of Reggie. We see the rise and fall of the Krays and care little about either. To be fair, Hardy is fantastic, providing each Kray twin with a distinct personality, but nothing else about the film is interesting. **132m/C; DVD, Blu-Ray.** Colin Morgan; Tom (Thomas) Hardy; Christopher Eccleston; Joshua Hill; Emily Browning; ***D:*** Brian Helgeland; ***W:*** Brian Helgeland; ***C:*** Dick Pope; ***M:*** Carter Burwell.

Legend of Alfred Packer 🦴 **1/2 1980** The true story of how a guide taking five men searching for gold in Colorado managed to be the sole survivor of a blizzard. **87m/C; VHS, DVD.** Patrick Dray; Ron Haines; Bob Damon; Dave Ellingson; ***D:*** Jim Roberson.

The Legend of Bagger Vance 🦴🦴 **1/2 2000 (PG-13)** Rannulph Junuh (Damon) returns from WWI and the former golf golden boy seems content to squander the rest of his life drinking. His debt-ridden ex-girlfriend Adele (Theron) convinces him to participate in an exhibition against golf giants Bobby Jones (Gretsch) and Walter Hagen (McGill) to showcase her new course. But Rannulph has lost his golf swing until the mysterious Bagger (Smith) appears, offering him guidance about golf and life in Eastern philosophy sound bites. Slow-paced; beautiful scenery. Based on the novel by Steven Pressfield. **127m/C; VHS, DVD.** Matt Damon; Will Smith; Charlize Theron; Joel Gretsch; Jack Lemmon; Bruce McGill; Lane Smith; Harve Presnell; Peter Gerety; Thomas Jay Ryan; J. Michael Moncrief; ***D:*** Robert Redford; ***W:*** Jeremy Leven; ***C:*** Michael Ballhaus; ***M:*** Rachel Portman.

Legend of Billie Jean 🦴🦴 **1985 (PG-13)** Billie Jean believed in justice for all. When the law and its bureaucracy landed hard on her, she took her cause to the masses and inspired a generation. **92m/C; VHS, DVD, Blu-Ray.** Helen Slater; Peter Coyote; Keith Gordon; Christian Slater; Richard Bradford; Yeardley Smith; Dean Stockwell; ***D:*** Matthew Robbins; ***W:*** Mark Rosenthal.

The Legend of Black Thunder Mountain 🦴 **1/2 1979 (G)** A children's adventure in the mold of "Grizzly Adams" and "The Wilderness Family." **90m/C; VHS, DVD.** Holly Beeman; Steve Beeman; Ron Brown; F.A. Milovich; ***D:*** Tom Beeman.

The Legend of Bloody Jack WOOF! 2007 Asylum studio managed to release a completely incompetent and boring slasher pic. Bloody Jack is a campfire urban legend about an Alaskan lumberjack who used his axe for more than chopping wood. However it seems he's resurrected from the dead just in time to go after the usual human camping fodder. **85m/C; DVD.** Craig Bonacorsi; Jonathan Kowalsky; Erica Curtis; Alicia Klein; Josh Evans; Jessica Szabo; Jeremy Flynn; ***D:*** Todd Portugal; ***W:*** Todd Portugal; ***C:*** Daniel Kozman; ***M:*** Patrick Bowsher. **VIDEO**

The Legend of Bloody Mary 🦴🦴 **2008** Long ago some lady named Mary Worth was impregnated by a priest and refused to fess up who the father was. Apparently the standard punishment for Puritan women who get pregnant out of wedlock was to have their face carved off in front of a mirror. Centuries later, partygoers make a game of Mary's plight: write your friends' names on a mirror while chanting her name and she pops out and kills you, all because she's "vengeful." **93m/C; DVD.** Robert Locke; Caitlin Wachs; Rachael Taylor; Dean O'Gorman; Nicole Aiken; Brittany Miller; Inna Costa; Cooper Campbell; Joseph Domingo; Elissa Dowling; Kristen Dalto; Lauren Phillips; ***D:*** John Stecenko; ***W:*** John Stecenko; Dominic R. Domingo; ***C:*** John Stecenko; Joe Hendrick; ***M:*** Steven Keifer. **VIDEO**

Legend of Boggy Creek 🦴 **1/2 1975 (G)** A dramatized version of various Arkansas Bigfoot sightings. **87m/C; VHS, DVD.** Willie E. Smith; John P. Nixon; John W. Gates; Jeff Crabtree; Buddy Crabtree; ***Nar:*** Vern Stierman; ***D:*** Charles B. Pierce; ***W:*** Earl E. Smith; ***C:*** Charles B. Pierce.

The Legend of Butch & Sundance 🦴🦴 **1/2 2004 (PG-13)** This unsold NBC TV pilot is a generally lively western that finds Butch Parker (Rogers) going from easy-going cowboy to bank robber alongside his best friend, gunslinger Harry "Sundance Kid" Longabaugh (Browning). Both become part of Mike Cassidy's (Biehn) "Wild Bunch" gang, targeting banks that are controlled by greedy railroad barons. The two men are also equally attached to schoolteacher Etta Place (Lefevre). When Pinkerton agent Durango (Gibbons) kills Cassidy, Butch takes his last name out of respect and vows vengeance. **120m/C; DVD.** Ryan Browning; Rachelle Lefevre; Michael Biehn; Susan Ruttan; David Clayton Rogers; Blake Gibbons; ***D:*** Sergio Mimica-Gezzan; ***W:*** John Fasano; ***C:*** Igor Maglic; ***M:*** Basil Poledouris. **TV**

The Legend of Cryin' Ryan 🦴🦴 **1998 (PG)** After leveling the tombstone of a long-dead school bully, teenager Kris freaks out when his ghost is set loose. But when the boy, who died at age 13 of unknown causes, tells her about his abusive father she's bent on setting the record straight so that his soul can move along. **90m/C; VHS, DVD.** Harrison Myers; Ernie Lively; Harold Jacob Smith; Dean Tschetter; Rob Lunn; Rhelda Mortensen; ***D:*** Julie St. Claire; ***C:*** Mark Foggetti; ***M:*** Sean Murray. **VIDEO**

The Legend of Drunken Master 🦴🦴🦴 *Drunken Master 2; Jui Kun 2* **1994 (R)** Chan plays legendary Chinese folk hero Wong Fei-hong as a rowdy young man whose martial arts moves get better as he gets drunker. While traveling by train with his father (Lung), he mistakenly takes a package containing a priceless imperial Chinese artifact that is being smuggled out of the country. Evil henchmen are then sent to be pummeled by Fei-hong's inebriated fists. Director Lau Kar-leung performs double duty by playing Fu Min-chi, a grizzled old man also on the trail of the stolen artifact. Released with classic "bad Chinese accent" dubbing. **102m/C; VHS, DVD, Blu-Ray.** *CH* Jackie Chan; Lau Kar Leung; Anita (Yim-Fong) Mui; Ti Lung; Andy Lau; ***D:*** Lau Kar Leung; ***W:*** Edward Tang; ***C:*** Yiu-tsou Cheung; Tong-Leung Cheung; Jingle Ma; Man-Wan Wong; ***M:*** Michael Wandmacher.

The Legend of Frank Woods 🦴🦴 **1977** Gunslinger returns to the land of the free after an extended holiday south of the border. Mistaken for an expected preacher in a small town, he poses as the padre and signs on the dotted line to take out a new lease on life. **88m/C; VHS, DVD.** Troy Donahue; Brad Steward; Kitty Vallacher; Michael Christian; ***D:*** Deno Paoli.

The Legend of Fritton's Gold 🦴🦴 *St. Trinian's 2* **2009** Silly Brit romp set in the all-girls boarding school of St. Trinian's where education is trumped by mischief. The head of a woman-hating secret society learns that headmistress Camilla Fritton is descended from a pirate who hid a fortune in gold. Camilla reveals the secret to niece Annabelle and the girls go on a hunt to get to the treasure first. **106m/C; DVD.** *UK* Rupert Everett; David Tennant; Talulah Riley; Colin Firth; Juno Temple; Tamsin Egerton; Jodie Whittaker; Sarah Harding; ***D:*** Oliver Parker; Barnaby Thompson; ***W:*** Piers Ashworth; Nick Moorcroft; ***C:*** David Higgs; ***M:*** Charlie Mole.

The Legend of Gator Face 🦴 1/2 **1996 (PG)** Hermit Winfield fills three youngsters in on their small community's legend of Gator Face—half-man, half-alligator. Kids being kids, they decide to wade through the swamps in search of the creature, which they find and also realize is harmless. Too bad the local folk don't believe the same thing and call out the national guard to destroy it. **100m/C; VHS, DVD.** Paul Winfield; John White; Dan Warry-Smith; C. David Johnson; Gordon Michael Woolvett; ***D:*** Vic Sarin.

The Legend of Hell House 🦴🦴🦴 **1973 (PG)** A multi-millionaire hires a team of scientists and mediums to investigate his newly acquired haunted mansion. It seems that the creepy house has been the site of a number of deaths and may hold clues to the afterlife. A suspenseful, scary screamfest. Matheson wrote the screenplay from his novel "Hell House." **94m/C; VHS, DVD, Blu-Ray.** Roddy McDowall; Pamela Franklin; Clive Revill; Gayle Hunnicutt; Peter Bowles; Roland Culver; Michael Gough; ***D:*** John Hough; ***W:*** Richard Matheson; ***C:*** Alan Hume; ***M:*** Brian Hodgson; Delia Derbyshire.

The Legend of Hercules WOOF! **2014 (PG-13)** So worthless as to barely stick in the memory before the credits have even finished rolling, this latest swords-and-sandals nonsense only serves as further proof that once A-list director Harlin has no further to sink. This origin story casts the remarkably charisma-less Lutz in the title role as a young Hercules, who is sold into slavery and forced to fight his way back to his rightful place as a ruler of his people. Any excuse for a plot exists merely to support CGI-heavy action scenes, shot in slow-motion, in the rain. **99m/C; DVD, Blu-Ray.** Kellan Lutz; Scott Adkins; Roxanne Mckee; Liam McIntyre; Liam Garrigan; Johnathon Schaech; Gaia Weiss; Rade Serbedzija; ***D:*** Renny Harlin; ***W:*** Sean Hood; Daniel Giat; ***C:*** Sam McCurdy; ***M:*** Tuomas Kantelinen.

The Legend of Johnny Lingo 🦴🦴 **2003 (G)** Orphaned as an infant, Tama winds up on a remote South Pacific island where he is initially revered as a god but ultimately is cast aside. He befriends Mahana, and when he decides to sail away in search of a better life he assures her that he'll come back. Washing up on another island, he meets trader Johnny Lingo, who becomes his mentor and aides him in fulfilling his promise. Drawing from Patricia McGerr's "Johnny Lingo's Eight-Cow Wife" and the 1969 film short "Johnny Lingo" by Wezel O. Whitaker, rookie director Ramirez holds to the tale's feel-good essence but drifts astray in the execution. **95m/C; VHS, DVD.** George Henare; Joe Folau; Rawiri Paratene; Kayte Ferguson; ***D:*** Steve Ramirez; ***W:*** Riwia Brown; ***C:*** Allen Guilford; ***M:*** Kevin Kiner. **VIDEO**

The Legend of Lizzie Borden 🦴🦴🦴 **1975** Shocking ABC TV true crime movie about the 1892 trial of spinster Lizzie Borden for the axe murders of her father and stepmother in their Fall River, Massachusetts home. Montgomery gives an hypnotic lead performance that includes flashbacks as to how the possibly unbalanced Lizzie could have committed the grisly crimes. **96m/C; DVD.** Elizabeth Montgomery; Fionnula Flanagan; Ed Flanders; Fritz Weaver; Katherine Helmond; Don Porter; Bonnie Bartlett; Helen Craig; ***D:*** Paul Wendkos; ***W:*** William Bast; ***C:*** Robert B. Hauser; ***M:*** Billy Goldenberg. **TV**

The Legend of Lucy Keyes 🦴🦴 **2006 (R)** The Cooley family moves into the old Keyes house in Massachusetts, which is reputed to be haunted. In 1755, young Lucy Keyes disappeared while in the nearby woods and her mother Martha went mad searching for her daughter. Now, mom Jeanne (Delpy) begins to have nightmares and fears for her own daughter Lucy (Hinkle), especially when ghostly visions seem to want Jeanne to solve the mystery and let Lucy Keyes finally rest. **93m/C; DVD.** Julie Delpy; Justin Theroux; Brooke Adams; Mark Boone, Jr.; Cassidy Hinkle; Anna Friedman; ***D:*** John Stimpson; ***W:*** John Stimpson; ***C:*** Gary Henoch; ***M:*** Ed Grenga.

The Legend of Lylah Clare 🦴🦴 **1968** Showbiz camp, though that's probably not what director Aldrich intended. Young Chicago actress Elsa (Novak) gets her big break playing the lead in the bio of tragic movie star, German-born Lylah Clare. The film is being directed by Lylah's widower, Lewis (Finch), who becomes romantically interested in Elsa as she becomes more obsessed with Lylah, even apparently channeling the star (hence the gravelly German accent). Jealousy leads to flashbacks of Lylah's life and how she really died. **130m/C; DVD.** Kim Novak; Peter Finch; Ernest Borgnine; Milton Selzer; Rossella Falk; Valentina Cortese; Coral Browne; ***D:*** Robert Aldrich; ***W:*** Hugo Butler; Jean Rouverol; ***C:*** Joseph Biroc; ***M:*** Frank DeVol.

The Legend of 1900 🦴🦴 *The Legend of the Pianist on the Ocean; La Leggenda del Pianista Sull'Oceano* **1998 (R)** Originally released under a different title and at 170 minutes, this re-cut English-language debut feature for Italian director Tornatore still has its problems. An abandoned infant is discovered aboard the luxury liner Virginian in 1900 and reared by the engine crew. As an adult, the nicknamed 1900 (Roth), has become a virtuoso pianist in the ship's orchestra and has superstitiously never set foot off the boat. His best friend is trumpet player Max (Vince), who tells the story in flashback after learning the ship has been condemned. But since 1900 remains an enigma, you won't really care what happens to him. **116m/C; VHS, DVD.** Tim Roth; Pruitt Taylor Vince; Clarence Williams, III; Bill Nunn; Mélanie Thierry; ***D:*** Giuseppe Tornatore; ***W:*** Giuseppe Tornatore; ***C:*** Lajos Koltai; ***M:*** Ennio Morricone. Golden Globes '00: Score.

The Legend of Paul and Paula 🦴🦴 *Die Legende von Paul und Paula* **1973** East German censors tried to ban Carow's film, which focuses on personal freedoms, but it proved to be so popular with audiences that the ban never worked. Paula (Domrose) is a free-spirited unmarried salesclerk with two children while Paul (Glatzeder) is a conservative bureaucrat in a loveless marriage. They met by accident and fall in love while Paula tries to liberate Paul from his dull existence. But Paul finds it difficult to let go'until tragedy beset them. German with subtitles. **106m/C; VHS, DVD.** *GE* Angelica Domrose; Winifried Glatzeder; ***D:*** Heiner Carow; ***W:*** Heiner Carow; Ulrich Plenzdorf; ***C:*** Jurgen Brauer; ***M:*** Peter Gotthardt.

The Legend of Rita 🦴🦴 *Die Stille Nach Dem Schuss; The Silence After the Shot* **1999** Rita (Beglau) is part of a West German left-wing terrorist group in the 1970s. She's caught attempting to enter East Germany by Stasi officer Erwin Hull (Wuttke), who lets her go but slyly offers to come to her aid when needed. After some trouble, Rita agrees to Hull's offer to assume a new identity and live a worker's life in East Germany. Then Rita discovers that her political ideals are at odds with everyday life and people disenchanted by socialism. But she faces a greater change when the Berlin Wall comes down and Rita's terrorist past is exposed. German with subtitles. **101m/C; VHS, DVD.** *GE* Bibiana Beglau; Martin Wuttke; Nadja Uhl; Harald Schrott; Alexander Beyer; Jenny Schily; ***D:*** Volker Schlondorff; ***W:*** Volker Schlondorff; Wolfgang Kohlhaase; ***C:*** Andreas Hofer.

The Legend of Sea Wolf 🦴🦴 *Wolf Larsen* **1975 (PG)** A sadistic sea captain forcefully rules his crew in this weak version of Jack London's novel. **90m/C; VHS, DVD.** *IT* Chuck Connors; Barbara Bach; Joseph Palmer; ***D:*** Giuseppe Vari; ***W:*** Marcello Ciorciolini; ***C:*** Sergio Rubini; ***M:*** Guido de Angelis; Maurizio de Angelis.

The Legend of Suriyothai 🦴🦴 1/2 *Francis Ford Coppola Presents: The Legend of Suriyothai; Suiryothai* **2002 (R)** In Siam (now Thailand) in 1528, the north and south each elected their own kings, and a young girl named Suriyothai (Bhirombhakdi) is forced to leave her true love to marry the man who will become the future king. In 1548 he dies in battle with rival nation Burma, and she must lead her people's army to confront the invaders. Originally 185 minutes long, it has been trimmed to 142 minutes for international release with the help of Francis Ford Coppola. The film was directed and made by Thai royalty. **142m/C; DVD.** *TH* M. L. Piyapas Bhirombakdi; Johnny Anfone; Mai Charoenpura; Sorapong Chatree; Ronrittichai Khanket; Supakorn Kitsuwon; Ampol Lamppon; Chatchai Plengpanich; Sinjai Plengpanit; Saharath Sangkapreecha; ***D:*** Chatrichalerm Yukol; ***W:*** Chatrichalerm Yukol; Sunait Chutintaranond; ***C:*** Anupap Buachand; Stanislav Dorsic; Igor Luther; ***M:*** Richard Harvey.

The Legend of Tarzan 🦴 1/2 **2016 (PG-13)** It's hard to believe that they're still making Tarzan movies this many decades after the peak of the character's film popularity. This time, John Clayton (Skarsgard), the man formerly known as Tarzan, returns to his jungle roots to stop the nefarious efforts of a mining magnate (Waltz), and, eventually, of course, save his Jane (Robbie). The storytelling here is generic at best, and borderline racist at worst, but the cast almost saves it from its own flaws. And it helps greatly that Skarsgard and Robbie have sizzling chemistry. **110m/C; DVD, Blu-Ray.** Alexander Skarsgård; Samuel L. Jackson; Margot Robbie; Djimon Hounsou; Christoph Waltz; ***D:*** David Yates; ***W:*** Adam Cozad; Craig Brewer; ***C:*** Henry Braham; ***M:*** Rupert Gregson-Williams.

Legend of the Bog 🦴 1/2 *Bog Bodies* **2008 (R)** A 2000-year-old mummified murder victim is disturbed from its Irish bog resting place and causes havoc for a group of strangers who turn out to share a disturbing secret. **92m/C; DVD.** Vinnie Jones; Jason Barry; Nora-Jane Noone; Adam Fogerty; Gavin Kelly; ***D:*** Brendan Foley; ***W:*** Brendan Foley; ***C:*** Stephen Murphy; ***M:*** Graham Slack. **VIDEO**

Legend of the Dinosaurs and Monster Birds WOOF! *Legend of the Dinosaurs; Legend of Dinosaurs and Ominous Birds; Kyoryuu: Kaicho no densetsu* **1977** Generally recognized by monster movie fans as one of the worst films of all time. Severe weather changes in the Mount Fuji area awaken a plesiosaur, which immediately begins to perform a bad "Jaws" parody. Meanwhile a gigantic pterodactyl hatches in a nearby cave and adds to the chaos. Eventually they meet in an epic battle. Oddly bloody for an early Japanese monster movie. **92m/C; DVD.** *JP* Mineko Maruhira; Satoru Nabe; ***D:*** Junji Kurata; ***W:*** Masaru Igami; Takeshi Matsumoto; Ichiro Otsu; ***C:*** Shigeru Akatsuka; ***M:*** Masao Yagi.

Legend of the Guardians: The Owls of Ga'Hoole 🦴🦴🦴 **2010 (PG)** Animated 3D fantasy adapted from the first of Kathryn Lasky's three books. Barn owl Soren has grown up listening to the legends of the mythic guardians, the Ga'Hoole, battling the evil owl cult, the Pure Ones. When Soren and his brother Kludd are captured by the Pure Ones, an adventurous journey ensues to seek out the heroic Ga'Hoole to save the day. Director Snyder avoids sap but takes the idea of zombie owls too far at times—too dark and bizarre for little ones and possibly too dopey for the bigger ones. **97m/C; Blu-Ray.** *US AU* ***V:*** Jim Sturgess; Ryan Kwanten; Emily Barclay; David Wenham; Dame Helen Mirren; Richard Roxburgh; Sam Neill; Geoffrey Rush; Hugo Weaving; Abbie Cornish; Essie Davis; Joel Edgerton; Anthony LaPaglia; Miriam Margolyes; Barry Otto; Adrienne DeFaria; ***D:*** Zack Snyder; ***W:*** Emil Stern; John Orloff; ***M:*** David Hirschfelder.

Legend of the Liquid Sword WOOF! *Siu hap Cho Lau Heung; The Liquid Sword; Xiao xia Chu Liu Xiang* **1993** A twisting mess of intrigue where people fight, make friends, fight again, and end up who knows where as well as a weird vampire bad guy named Batman. Even weirder martial arts comedy inspired by a popular Chinese story, and the usual poorly-translated dialogue. Despite Gordon Liu being on the cover, he's only in the film for a scene or two. **82m/C; DVD.** *CH* Julian Cheung; Norman Chu; Aaron Kwok; Chingmy Yau; Anita Yuen; Sharla Cheung; Winnie Lau; Kei Mai; Siu-Lun Wan; Wan-Si Wong; Gloria Yip; Fennie Yuen; ***D:*** Jing Wong; ***W:*** Jing Wong.

Legend of the Lone Ranger 🦴 1/2 **1981 (PG)** The fabled Lone Ranger (whose voice is dubbed throughout the entire movie) and the story of his first meeting with his Indian companion, Tonto, are brought to life in this weak and vapid version of the famous legend. The narration by Merle Haggard leaves something to be desired as do most of the performances. **98m/C; VHS, DVD, Blu-Ray.** Klinton Spilsbury; Michael Horse; Jason Robards, Jr.; Richard Farnsworth; Christopher Lloyd; Matt Clark; ***D:*** William A. Fraker; ***W:*** William Roberts; Ivan Goff; Michael Kane; ***M:*** John Barry. Golden Raspberries '81: Worst Actor (Spilsbury), Worst New Star (Spilsbury).

Legend of the Lost 🦴🦴 **1957** Two men vie for desert treasure and desert women. Interesting only because of Wayne, but certainly not one of his more memorable films. **109m/C; VHS, DVD, Blu-Ray.** John Wayne; Sophia Loren; Rossano Brazzi; Kurt Kasznar; Sonia Moser; ***D:*** Henry Hathaway; ***C:*** Jack Cardiff.

Legend of the Lost Tomb 🦴🦴 1/2 **1997 (PG)** Adventure finds Egyptologist Dr. Leonhardt (Rossovich) discovering half of an ancient papyrus that could lead to the riches of the desert tomb of pharaoh Ramses II. But Leonhardt is ambused by his rival Dr. Bent (Keach), who demands the rest of the document, which just happens to be in the hands of Leonhardt's son (Pierce) and his archaeologist associate Karen (Peterson). **90m/C; VHS, DVD.** Rick Rossovich; Stacy Keach; Kimberlee Peterson; Brock Pierce; ***D:*** Jonathan Winfrey. **CABLE**

Legend of the Northwest 🦴🦴 *Bearheart of the Great Northwest* **1978** Bearheart is a large dog who must take revenge after his owner is shot and killed by a drunken hunter. Due to various mishaps he is labeled a vicious dog wherever he goes and is continually thrown out of town before being adopted elsewhere. Currently only available as part of a collection. **83m/C; DVD.** Denver Pyle; Jeffrey Byron; ***D:*** Rand Brooks; ***W:*** Rand Brooks; Jennings Hobb; ***C:*** Leonard Clairmont; ***M:*** Dean Elliot.

The Legend of the 7 Golden Vampires 🦴 *The Seven Brothers Meet Dracula; Dracula and the Seven Golden Vampires* **1973** It's kung-fu meets horror as Van Helsing pursues Dracula to 19th-century China and is assisted by martial artists. One of the last Hammer coproductions. The Anchor Bay release also contains the 75-minute "Seven Brothers Meet Dracula," which was the U.S. version of the movie. **89m/C; VHS, DVD, Blu-Ray.** *GB* Peter Cushing; David Chang; Robin Stewart; Julie Ege; John Forbes-

Robertson; *D:* Roy Ward Baker; *W:* Don Houghton; *C:* Roy Ford; John Wilcox; *M:* James Bernard.

The Legend of the Shadowless Sword 🦴🦴 1/2 *Muyeong geom; Shadowless Sword; Superfighters* **2008 (R)** It's 10th century Korea, and almost all the members of the Balhae Dynasty have been slain by invaders. The lone surviving Prince Dae Jung-hyun (Seo-jin Lee) lives in self-exile, preferring life as a merchant to that of nobility. A lone female warrior (So-yi Yoon) is dispatched to find him and convince him to return. The invaders have also dispatched their own female killer (Ki-yong Lee) along with a small army to ensure he never returns. Fans of wuxia films (i.e. "Hero", "Crouching Tiger, Hidden Dragon", etc) will love this one. **115m/C; DVD.** *NK* Hyeon-jun Shim; So-yi Yoon; Seo-Jin Lee; Ki-yong Lee; *D:* Young-jun Kim; *W:* Paul Sheen.

The Legend of the Wolf Woman 🦴🦴 1/2 *Daughter of the Werewolf; Werewolf Woman; She-Wolf* **1977 (R)** The beautiful Daniella assumes the personality of the legendary wolfwoman, leaving a trail of gruesome killings across the countryside. Genre fans will find this one surprisingly entertaining. Also on video as "Werewolf Woman." **84m/C; VHS, DVD, Blu-Ray.** *IT* Anne Borel; Frederick Stafford; Tino Carey; Elliot Zamuto; Ollie Reynolds; Andrea Scotti; Karen Carter; Howard Ross; *D:* Rino Di Silvestro; *W:* Rino Di Silvestro; Howard Ross.

Legend of Valentino 🦴🦴 **1975** Docudrama traces the legendary exploits of one of the silver screen's greatest lovers, Rudolph Valentino. Typical TV-movie fare that lacks the power of the legend's life. **96m/C; VHS, DVD.** Franco Nero; Suzanne Pleshette; Lesley Ann Warren; Yvette Mimieux; Judd Hirsch; Milton Berle; Harold J. Stone; *D:* Melville Shavelson. **TV**

The Legend of Wolf Mountain 🦴🦴 1/2 **1992 (PG)** Three children are held hostage by two prison escapees in the Utah mountains. They are aided in their escape by a Native American "wolf spirit." With the criminals on their trail will the three be able to survive in the wilderness until a search party can find them? **91m/C; VHS, DVD.** Mickey Rooney; Bo Hopkins; Don Shanks; Vivian Schilling; Robert Z'Dar; David "Shark" Fralick; Nicole Lund; Natalie Lund; Matthew Lewis; Jonathan Best; *D:* Craig Clyde; *W:* Craig Clyde.

The Legend of Zorro 🦴🦴 1/2 **2005 (PG)** Noisy sequel to "The Mask of Zorro" finds Banderas returning as our swashbuckling masked hero, along with Zeta-Jones as his equally hot-blooded spouse, Elena. They are now the parents of impetuous 10-year-old Joaquin (Alonso), but the marriage has enough cracks that Elena kicks Zorro out on his cape. There's also a couple of bad guys—sneering aristocrat Armand (Sewell) and scurvy McGivens (Chinlund)?and a plot that has to do with California becoming part of the United States. The leads are having a lot of fun and there's enough ridiculous action to make the pic speed by. **129m/C; DVD, Blu-Ray, UMD.** Antonio Banderas; Catherine Zeta-Jones; Rufus Sewell; Nick (Nicholas) Chinlund; Julio Oscar Mechoso; Shuler Hensley; Michael Emerson; Adrian Alonso; *D:* Martin Campbell; *W:* Roberto Orci; Alex Kurtzman; *C:* Phil Meheux; *M:* James Horner.

Legendary 🦴 *In jedem steckt ein Held* **2010 (PG-13)** Puny 15-year-old Cal (Graye) wants to reunite his family, ten years after his father's death, by joining his high school's wrestling team. Cal's hoping that his older brother and one-time team champ Mike (Cena), now a drunk, will return to help Cal train and make peace with the past. Predictable plot with sappy after-school-special dialogue that is only somewhat credible when coming from Clarkson (as the boys' mother) and narrator Glover. Seriously misses the mark for an indie following, as well as bumming out fans of Cena's WWE pyrotechnics. **107m/C; Blu-Ray, On Demand.** Devon Graye; John Cena; Patricia Clarkson; Danny Glover; John Posey; Lara Grice; Kareem Grimes; Tyler Posey; Deneen Tyler; *D:* Mel Damski; *W:* John Posey; *C:* Kenneth Zunder; *M:* James Raymond.

Legendary Weapons of China 🦴🦴 *18 Weapons of Kung-Fu; Shi ba ban wu yi; 18 Legendary Weapons of China; Sap bat ban mo hei* **1982** In one of the Shaw Brothers more hallucinatory films, the Boxer Rebellion is in full swing, and the Empress has dispatched agents to find supernatural martial artists immune to the bullets of Western missionaries. One of these, Lei Kung (Gordon Liu), disbands his school and flees, and is immediately given a death sentence for his apparent treason. Mixes realistic martial arts and Taoist Maoshan folk magic. **110m/C; DVD.** *HK* Sheng Fu; Hou Hsiao; Gordon (Chia Hui) Liu; Chia-Liang Liu; Chia Yung Liu; Kara Hui; *D:* Chia-Liang Liu; *W:* Chia-Liang Liu; Tai-Heng Li; *C:* Chih Chun Ao; *M:* Chin Yung Shing; Chun Hau So.

Legends of Oz: Dorothy's Return 🦴 **2014 (PG)** The latest animated bastardization of the Frank L. Baum classic sees Dorothy, of course, going back to the land of Oz, reuniting with the Scarecrow, Lion, Tin Man, and Glinda, while also introducing a gaggle of new, horrendously designed characters. Dorothy is the only one who can save Oz. You are the only one who can do whatever you can to avoid this movie. It's a boring, stupid mess that even the littlest members of your brood will find annoying and silly. At a reported cost of $70 million, its lackluster box-office draw at least assures no sequel. **92m/C; DVD, Blu-Ray.** *V:* Lea Michele; Martin Short; Hugh Dancy; Dan Aykroyd; James Belushi; Kelsey Grammer; Oliver Platt; Bernadette Peters; Megan Hilty; *D:* Will Finn; Daniel St. Pierre; *W:* Randi Barnes; Adam Balsam; *M:* Toby Chu. Golden Raspberries '14: Worst Support. Actor (Grammer).

Legends of the Fall 🦴🦴 **1994 (R)** Sweeping, melodramatic family saga set in Montana (but filmed in Alberta, Canada). Retired Army colonel William Ludlow (Hopkins) is raising three sons: reserved Alfred (Quinn), idealistic Samuel (Thomas), and wild Tristan (Pitt). In 1913, Samuel returns from Boston with a fiancee, the lovely Susannah (Ormond). Only problem is Alfred and Tristan take one look and also desire her—a passion that will carry them through some 20 years of heartbreak. Film loses the spare toughness of the Jim Harrison novella but is a visual feast (and not just because the camera drools every time Pitt appears on screen.) **134m/C; DVD, Blu-Ray.** Brad Pitt; Aidan Quinn; Julia Ormond; Anthony Hopkins; Henry Thomas; Gordon Tootoosis; Tantoo Cardinal; Karina Lombard; Paul Desmond; Kenneth Welsh; *D:* Edward Zwick; *W:* Susan Shilliday; William D. Wittliff; *C:* John Toll; *M:* James Horner. Oscars '94: Cinematog.

Legends of the Poisonous Seductress 1: Female Demon Ohyaku 🦴🦴 1/2 *Ohyaku: The Female Demon; Yoen dokufuden hannya no ohyaku* **1968** First of a trilogy starring Junko Miyazono that are considered prototypes of the successful Pinky Violence films introduced into Japan in the 1970s (later inspiring "Kill Bill"). Ohyaku (Junko), a female acrobat/prostitute, is sold to the highest bidder after each performance. Rescued by a thief, they settle down to a married life but she is framed and sentenced to years of hell on an island prison. She vows to escape and cut down her tormentors one by one. **90m/B; DVD.** *JP* Tomisaburo Wakayama; Kunio Murai; Junko Miyazono; *D:* Yoshihiro Ishikawa; *W:* Koji Takada; *C:* Nagaki Yamagishi; *M:* Toshiaki Tsushima.

Legends of the Poisonous Seductress 2: Quick Draw Okatsu 🦴🦴 1/2 *Yoen dokufuden: Hitokiri okatsu* **1969** The second film of the series, and the first one in color. Okatsu (Junko Miyazono) is the adopted daughter of a master swordsman who is killed when his son gets too far in debt gambling. It seems the corrupt local magistrate is enamored with Okatsu, and orchestrated the events to make her his concubine. Joined by wild swordswoman Rui (Reiko Oshida), Okatsu carves a bloodstained path of retribution through the local gamblers. **90m/C; DVD.** *JP* Junko Miyazono; Ko Nishimura; Kenji Imai; *D:* Nobuo Nakagawa; *W:* Koji Takada; *C:* Masahiko Iimura; *M:* Koichi Kawabe.

Legends of the Poisonous Seductress 3: Okatsu the Fugitive 🦴🦴 *Yoen dokufuden: Okatsu kyojo tabi* **1969** The only thing the third film in this series has to connect to the others is that the female lead is the same woman (with the same theme of a female swordswoman wanting revenge). This time tomboy Okatsu who's good with a sword, is chasing down a group of corrupt tobacco smugglers who have murdered her parents. There's also many little subplots involving an arranged marriage, a betraying fiance, etc., but they don't detract from the pretty women whacking people with swords. **84m/C; DVD.** *JP* Junko Miyazono; *D:* Nobuo Nakagawa; *W:* Koji Takada; Hideaki Yamamoto; *C:* Yoshikazu Yamisawa; *M:* Koichi Kawabe.

Legion 🦴🦴 **1998 (R)** Major Agatha Doyle (Farrell) is given a group of convicts to lead on a mission to destroy The Legion, a genetically engineered killing machine. But first she has to keep them from killing each other—or her. **97m/C; VHS, DVD.** Terry Farrell; Corey Feldman; Rick Springfield; Parker Stevenson; Audie England; *D:* Jon Hess. **CABLE**

Legion 🦴 **2010 (R)** God loses faith in mankind and sends his angels to begin the apocalypse. A pregnant waitress (Palicki) and the Archangel Michael (Bettany) are humanity's only hope for survival. Unfortunately, they're trapped in a diner with a host of underdeveloped stock characters prone to long, boring speeches. Director Stewart is well-versed in horror movie cliches and uses them to bludgeon the audience. If humanity in this film is as stupid as the characters depicted, it's no wonder God gave up. **100m/C; Blu-Ray, On Demand.** Paul Bettany; Kevin Durand; Dennis Quaid; Tyrese Gibson; Charles S. Dutton; Lucas Black; Kate Walsh; Adrianne Palicki; *D:* Scott Stewart; *W:* Scott Stewart; Peter Schink; *C:* John Lindley; *M:* John (Gianni) Frizzell.

Legion of Iron 🦴 **1990 (R)** Adventures in a computer-run, neo-Roman civilization where men and women battle for supremacy. **85m/C; VHS, Streaming.** Kevin T. Walsh; Erica Nann; Regie De Morton; Camille Carrigan; *D:* Yakov Bentsvi.

Legionnaire 🦴🦴 **1998 (R)** In the 1920s, Alain Lefevre (Van Damme) enlists in the French Foreign Legion and is stationed in Morocco with other new recruits. After rigorous training, the men find themselves being sent into battle at a remote outpost, where they'll learn about war and survival. **99m/C; VHS, DVD.** Jean-Claude Van Damme; Nicholas Farrell; Steven Berkoff; Jim Carter; Adewale Akinnuoye-Agbaje; *D:* Peter Macdonald; *W:* Sheldon Lettich; Rebecca Morrison; *C:* Doug Milsome; *M:* John Altman.

The LEGO Batman Movie 🦴🦴🦴 **2017 (PG)** The team behind the smash-hit "The LEGO Movie" reunite with this spin-off about one of that movie's most popular characters, Batman, voiced by Arnett. This clever flick actually incorporates all versions of Batman, playfully mocking everything from Adam West to Christian Bale. It tells multiple stories, primarily the complex relationship between Batman and The Joker, and his adopting of the boy who would become Robin. It can be a little too hyper for its own good, but it's also very smart and often very funny. This is one of those animated hits that works for both kids and adults. **104m/C; DVD.** Will Arnett; Zach Galifianakis; Michael Cera; Rosario Dawson; Ralph Fiennes; *D:* Chris McKay; *W:* Seth Grahame-Smith; Chris McKenna; Erik Sommers; Jared Stern; John Whittington; *M:* Lorne Balfe.

A Lego Brickumentary 🦴🦴 1/2 **2015 (G)** A feature-length documentary on LEGO toys. This documentary examines the wide impact of more than 400 billion LEGO bricks that have been manufactured since the product debuted in 1958. The LEGO Group's creation has been used for play and creativity by both children and adults, educational purposes, and therapy. The documentary looks at LEGO's wide impact, its worldwide fan base, and the many innovative uses for the simple plastic bricks. **93m/C; DVD, Blu-Ray, Streaming, Download.** Jason Bateman; *D:* Kief Davidson; Daniel Junge; *W:* Kief Davidson; Daniel Junge; Davis Coombe; *C:* Luke Geissbuhler; Robert Muratore; *M:* John Jennings Boyd.

The Lego Movie 🦴🦴🦴 1/2 **2014 (PG)** The popular Lego toys assemble onto the big screen, and their debut product is a spirited, witty, animated romp that is technically astounding. Emmet (Pratt) is a normal guy following all the proper instructions when Wyldstyle (Banks) blasts apart his carefully constructed world by mistakenly thinking she's found in him "The Special" who will save the world from the evil President Business (Ferrell), as was decreed by old wise man Vitruvius (Freeman). Unprepared for such expectations, Emmet is thrown headfirst into the role but is aided by a seemingly endless list of pop culture characters. But this isn't just for kids 8-14 like the box might say. You will laugh, you will cry, and you'll enjoy the action. Because, in the end, "everything is awesome." **100m/C; DVD, Blu-Ray.** *V:* Chris Pratt; Elizabeth Banks; Will Ferrell; Will Arnett; Liam Neeson; Morgan Freeman; Charlie Day; Nick Offerman; Alison Brie; Jonah Hill; Channing Tatum; *D:* Phil Lord; Christopher Miller; *W:* Phil Lord; Christopher Miller; *C:* Pablo Plaisted; *M:* Mark Mothersbaugh. British Acad. '14: Animated Film.

The LEGO Movie 2: The Second Part 🦴🦴 1/2 **2019 (PG)** The sequel to The Lego Movie focuses on the ever optimistic Emmet (Pratt) as he tries, and fails, to impress rebellious Lucy (Banks) with his edginess. These efforts increase when their barren community, Apocalypseburg, is invaded by outer space Lego Duplo creatures who are secretly evil. Led by the shapeshifting alien Queen Watevra Wa'Nabi (Haddish), Emmet, Lucy, Batman (Arnett), and others from Apocalypseburg must survive their journey to the glittery Systar System. Though the film is fun and has a strong cast, some zippy dialogue, and more unforgettable songs, it is not as clever or novel as the original. **107m/C; DVD, Blu-Ray.** *DK NO AU US* Chris Pratt; Elizabeth Banks; Will Arnett; Tiffany Haddish; Stephanie Beatriz; *D:* Mike Mitchell; *W:* Phil Lord; Christopher Miller; *M:* Mark Mothersbaugh.

The LEGO Ninjago Movie 🦴🦴 1/2 **2017 (PG)** A fun animated comedy inspired by the popular Ninjago line of LEGOs. Teenaged Lloyd (Franco) and his outcast pals are secret ninja warriors who, under the training of Master Wu (Chan), band together to defeat Garmadon, Lloyd's own father. The storyline and Vader-Skywalker parallels might be over the heads of younger viewers, but there's plenty of colorful action and silly gags to entertain them. And the live-action cat? One of the greatest things you've ever seen. This third installment isn't the strongest of the LEGO franchise, but it still clicks. **101m/C; DVD, Blu-Ray.** *V:* Jackie Chan; Dave Franco; Justin Theroux; Fred Armisen; Abbi Jacobson; *D:* Charlie Bean; Paul Fisher; Bob Logan; *W:* Paul Fisher; Bob Logan; William Wheeler; Tom Wheeler; Jared Stern; John Whittington; *M:* Mark Mothersbaugh.

Leila 🦴🦴 **1997** Leila, an Iranian woman, finds that she cannot have children shortly after she is married. Although her husband does not mind, Leila's mother-in-law convinces her to let her son take another wife in order to produce an heir. Farsi with subtitles. **129m/C; VHS, DVD.** *IA* Leila Hatami; Ali Mosaffa; Jamileh Sheikhi; *D:* Dariush Mehrjui.

The Leisure Seeker 🦴🦴 1/2 **2017 (R)** A drama about aging and the first English-language film by Paolo Virzi. Former English teacher John Spencer (Sutherland) increasingly feels the effects of dementia. Though married for five decades to the gregarious Ella (Mirren), he often cannot recall her name. Ella does her best to care for him, through struggling her own illness. Despite their health issues, Ella decides that they should take an RV trip from their Massachusetts home to Key West. During the journey, the couple experiences both the expected and the unexpected. The film's veteran actors cannot save the film, including its failed attempts at humor and predictable script. **112m/C; DVD.** Donald Sutherland; Dame Helen Mirren; Kirsty Mitchell; Janel Moloney; Christian McKay; *D:* Paolo Virzi; *W:* Paolo Virzi; Stephen Amidon; Francesca Archibugi; Francesco Piccolo; *C:* Luca Bigazzi; *M:* Carlo Virzi.

Lemming 🦴🦴 **2005** Moll's French puzzler involves the creature of the title—a Scandinavian lemming that somehow finds itself clogging up the French plumbing of computer gadget designer Alain (Lucas) and his wife Benedicte (Gainsbourg). Naturally this happens during a dinner party for Alain's boss, Richard (Dussollier), and his very difficult wife, Alice (Rampling). Alain's life goes from ordinary and pleasant to sinister and unsettled but the flick offers more questions than solutions. French with subtitles. **129m/C; DVD.** *FR* Laurent Lucas; Charlotte Gainsbourg; Charlotte Rampling; Andre Dussollier; Jacques Bonnaffe; Veronique Affholder; ***D:*** Dominik Moll; ***W:*** Dominik Moll; Gilles Marchand; ***C:*** Jean-Marc Fabre; ***M:*** David Whitaker.

Lemon ½ **2017** Sometimes, a movie charms us with its deadpan humor and quirky, even off-putting, characters. This is not that movie. Writer/director Janicza Bravo was too intent on being hip, unconventional, and "indie" to offer anything entertaining, despite a large cast of well-known faces. Brett Gelman (co-writer and Bravo's spouse) plays Isaac, an obnoxious jerk who's failing as an actor and dumped by his blind girlfriend. Anti-Semitism and bathroom humor run rife; even the editing is aggravating, with many scenes feeling either too short or too long. On the plus side, it lives up to its name. **83m/C; DVD.** Brett Gelman; Judy Greer; Michael Cera; Shiri Appleby; Fred Melamed; ***D:*** Janicza Bravo; ***W:*** Brett Gelman; Janicza Bravo; ***C:*** Jason McCormick; ***M:*** Heather Christian.

The Lemon Drop Kid ½ **1951** Second version of the Damon Runyon chestnut about a racetrack bookie who must recover the gangster's money he lost on a bet. As the fast-talking bookie, Hope sparkles. **91m/B; VHS, DVD, Blu-Ray.** Bob Hope; Lloyd Nolan; Fred Clark; Marilyn Maxwell; Jane Darwell; Andrea King; William Frawley; Jay C. Flippen; Harry Bellaver; ***D:*** Sidney Lanfield; ***W:*** Frank Tashlin; Edmund L. Hartmann; Robert O'Brien; ***C:*** Daniel F. Fapp; ***M:*** Ray Evans; Jay Livingston; Victor Young.

The Lemon Sisters **1990 (PG-13)** Three women, friends and performance partners since childhood, struggle to buy their own club. They juggle the men in their lives with less success. Great actresses like these should have done more with this interesting premise, and the excellent male cast has much more potential. **93m/C; VHS, DVD.** Diane Keaton; Carol Kane; Kathryn Grody; Elliott Gould; Ruben Blades; Aidan Quinn; ***D:*** Joyce Chopra; ***W:*** Jeremy Pikser; ***C:*** Bobby Byrne; ***M:*** Dick Hyman.

Lemon Tree *Etz Limon* **2008** Widowed Palestinian Salma (Abbass) has inherited a lemon grove that's right on the Israeli-West Bank border. When Israeli Defense Minister Navon (Tavory) decides to build a new house on the Israeli side, the lemon grove is deemed a security risk and the military fences it off, prior to cutting the trees down. Incensed, Salma hires a young Palestinian lawyer (Suliman) to take on her seemingly hopeless case, which is soon making international headlines. English, Arabic, and Hebrew with subtitles. **106m/C; DVD.** *IS FR GE* Hiam Abbass; Ali Suliman; Rona Lipaz-Michael; Doron Tavory; Tarik Kopty; Amos Lavi; Amnon Wolf; ***D:*** Eran Riklis; ***W:*** Eran Riklis; Suha Arraf; ***C:*** Rainer Klausmann; ***M:*** Habib Shehadeh Hanna.

Lemonade Joe *Limonadovy Joe aneb Konska Opera* **1964** The Czech New Wave does a broad spoof of the American western complete with good guys in white hats, bad guys in black hats, and a saloon gal with a heart of gold. Doug Badman (Kopecky) runs the Trigger Whiskey Saloon, along with his hotsie singer Tornado Lou (Fialova). The hard-drinking bar flies harass sweet temperance worker Winifred (Schoberova) until clean-living soft drink salesman Lemonade Joe (Fiala) shows up to save the day. Czech with subtitles. **87m/B; VHS, DVD.** *CZ* Milos Kopecky; Karel Fiala; Kveta Fialova; Olga Schoberova; ***D:*** Oldrich Lipsky; ***W:*** Oldrich Lipsky; Jiri Brdecka; ***C:*** Vladimir Novotny; ***M:*** Vlastimil Hala; Jan Rychlik.

Lemonade Mouth ½ **2011 (G)** Catchy Disney Channel teen musical, adapted from Mark Peter Hughes' novel, deals with friendship and self-esteem issues without going all talky and boring. Five freshmen meet in detention and are soon forming their own garage band to represent the high school misfits against the elite clique. **107m/C; DVD, Blu-Ray.** Bridgit Mendler; Adam Hicks; Blake Michael; Hayley Kiyoko; Naomi Scott; Tisha Campbell; Christopher McDonald; ***D:*** Patricia Riggen; ***W:*** April Blair; ***C:*** Checco Varese; ***M:*** Christopher Lennertz. **CABLE**

Lemony Snicket's A Series of Unfortunate Events ½ **2004 (PG)** Visually splendid Victorian Gothic adaptation of three books from the series by Snicket (aka Daniel Handler) is playfully gruesome yet not quite subversive enough. Violet (Browning), Klaus (Aiken), and Sunny Baudelaire are wealthy orphans shuttled from one peculiar, distant relative to another. These include sinister Count Olaf (Carrey), who's determined to obtain the family fortune, snake-loving Uncle Monty (Connolly), and phobic Aunt Josephine (Streep). The siblings survive every calamity through pluck, brains, and the fact that toddler Sunny is a ferocious biter. A silhouetted Law (as Snicket himself) supplies ominous narration. **107m/C; VHS, DVD, Blu-Ray, UMD.** Jim Carrey; Liam Aiken; Emily Browning; Kara Hoffman; Shelby Hoffman; Jude Law; Timothy Spall; Catherine O'Hara; Billy Connolly; Meryl Streep; ***D:*** Brad Silberling; ***W:*** Robert Gordon; ***C:*** Emmanuel Lubezki; ***M:*** Thomas Newman. Oscars '04: Makeup.

Lemora, Lady Dracula *The Lady Dracula; The Legendary Curse of Lemora; Lemora: A Child's Tale of the Supernatural* **1973 (PG)** A pretty young church singer is drawn into the lair of the evil Lady Dracula, whose desires include her body as well as her blood. Horror fans will enjoy some excellent atmosphere, particularly in a scene where the girl's church bus is attacked by zombie-like creatures; Smith remains a '70s "B" movie favorite. Perhaps a double feature with "Lady Frankenstein"...? **80m/C; VHS, DVD.** Leslie Gilb; Cheryl "Rainbeaux" Smith; William Whitton; Steve Johnson; Hy Pyke; Maxine Ballantyne; Parker West; ***D:*** Richard Blackburn; ***W:*** Richard Blackburn; Robert Fern; ***C:*** Robert Caramico.

Len & Company ½ **2016** A comedy-drama about a successful music producer who walks away from the business to find himself. Len (Ifans) seems to have it all. He was a punk rock star and became as an in-demand, respected pop music producer. Facing a personal crisis about his place in the world, he quits the industry and retreats to his home in upstate New York. Len's fortress of solitude is undermined when his estranged son Max (Kilmer) and the pop star he has been mentoring, Zoe (Temple), arrive. Looking to Len to solve their problems, he emerges from his stupor in unexpected fashion. **102m/C; DVD, Streaming, Download.** Rhys Ifans; Juno Temple; Jack Kilmer; Keir Gilchrist; Kathryn Hahn; ***D:*** Tim Godsall; ***W:*** Tim Godsall; Katharine Knight; ***C:*** Andre Pienaar; ***M:*** Miles Hankins.

The Lena Baker Story ½ *Hope & Redemption: The Lena Baker Story* **2008 (PG-13)** Lena Baker was the first and only woman to be executed in the electric chair in Georgia in 1945. After succumbing to alcohol and prostitution and being sent to a hard labor camp after an arrest, Lena sobers up and goes straight. Then she's hired as a housekeeper to abusive alcoholic Elliot Arthur, who repeatedly threatens her and her family if she quits. When Lena fights back, there's tragedy, and a trial. **101m/C; DVD.** Tichina Arnold; Peter Coyote; Beverly Todd; Michael Rooker; Chris Burns; ***D:*** Ralph Wilcox; ***W:*** Ralph Wilcox; ***C:*** Shawn Lewallen; ***M:*** Todd Cochran. **VIDEO**

Lena's Holiday **1990 (PG-13)** Fluffy comedy about a winsome East German girl visiting L.A. for the first time, and the culture-shock that ensues. Sharp script and performances. **97m/C; VHS, DVD.** Felicity Waterman; Chris Lemmon; Noriyuki "Pat" Morita; Susan Anton; Michael Sarrazin; Nick Mancuso; Bill Dana; Liz Torres; ***D:*** Michael Keusch; ***W:*** Michael Keusch; Deborah Tilton; ***C:*** Louis DiCesare.

L'Enfer *Jealousy; Torment* **1993** Claustrophobic thriller chronicles the descent into madness of an unstable hotel owner (Cluzet) convinced that his beautiful wife (Beart) is having an affair. Intriguing plot points that blur appearances and reality lead to ambiguous and unsatisfying ending. Clouzot himself began filming his screenplay in 1964, but a heart attack forced him to abandon the project. So this version uses the same script. In French with English subtitles. **103m/C; VHS, DVD.** *FR* Emmanuelle Beart; Francois Cluzet; Nathalie Cardone; Andre Wilms; Marc Lavoine; ***D:*** Claude Chabrol; ***W:*** Claude Chabrol; Henri-Georges Clouzot; Jose-Andre Lacour; ***C:*** Bernard Zitzermann; ***M:*** Matthieu Chabrol.

Lennon Naked **2010** BBC drama covers the period in John Lennon's life from 1964 to 1971—Beatles fame in all its phases, the breakup of both the band and John's first marriage, his meeting and subsequent marriage to Yoko Ono, drugs, art, and Lennon's move from England to New York. Eccleston's fine in the title role but the enigmatic Lennon—while enormously talented—isn't likeable and comes across as a sharp-tongued, insecure, self-absorbed prat. **82m/C; DVD.** *GB* Christopher Eccleston; Naoko Mori; Christopher Fairbank; Claudie Blakely; Rory Kinnear; Allan Corduner; Adrian Bower; Andrew Scott; Craig Cheetham; Jack Morgan; Michael Colgan; ***D:*** Edmund Coulthard; ***W:*** Robert Jones; ***C:*** Matt Gray; ***M:*** Dickon Hinchliffe. **TV**

L'Ennui **1998** Detached rather than titillating look at sexual obsession. Middle-aged, middle-class philosophy prof Martin (Berling) has recently separated from his wife and is dealing (or rather not dealing) with his midlife crisis. Until he meets teenaged artist's model Cecilia (Guillemin) and the two begin a very carnal affair, though Martin thinks his paramour is shallow and stupid. Then he discovers Cecilia also has a lover her own age and she wants to keep them both. In response, Martin turns obsessively jealous. Based on the novel "La Noia" by Alberto Moravia. French with subtitles. **120m/C; VHS, DVD.** *FR* Charles Berling; Sophie Guillemin; Arielle Dombasle; Robert Kramer; Tom Ouedraoge; ***D:*** Cedric Kahn; ***W:*** Cedric Kahn; Laurence Ferreira Barbosa; ***C:*** Pascal Marti.

Lenny **1974 (R)** Smoky nightclubs, drug abuse, and obscenities abound in Hoffman's portrayal of the controversial comedian Lenny Bruce, whose use of street language led to his eventual blacklisting. Perrine is a gem as his stripper wife. Adapted from the Julian Barry play, this is a visually compelling piece that sharply divided critics upon release. **111m/B; VHS, DVD, Blu-Ray.** Dustin Hoffman; Valerie Perrine; Jan Miner; Stanley Beck; ***D:*** Bob Fosse; ***W:*** Julian Barry; ***C:*** Bruce Surtees; ***M:*** Ralph Burns. Cannes '75: Actress (Perrine); Natl. Bd. of Review '74: Support. Actress (Perrine); N.Y. Film Critics '74: Support. Actress (Perrine).

Leo **2002 (R)** Craving love from his dispirited mom who sees him as all that went wrong in her past, Leo connects with incarcerated Stephen during a class writing project. Through their letters they become each other's lifeline and upon his release Stephen is determined to find him. Wants to give an twisty ending and boasts lots of acting talent but payoff doesn't deliver. **103m/C; VHS, DVD.** Mary Stuart Masterson; Joseph Fiennes; Sam Shepard; Elisabeth Shue; Davis Sweat; Dennis Hopper; Deborah Kara Unger; Jake Weber; Justin Chambers; ***D:*** Mehdi Norowzian; ***W:*** Massy Tadjedin; Amir Tadjedin; ***C:*** Zubin Mistry; ***M:*** Mark Adler. **VIDEO**

Leolo **1992** Deeply disturbing black comedy about one of the screen's most dysfunctional families. 12-year-old French-Canadian Leo is determined to remake himself as a Sicilian lad named Leolo, thus escaping from his horrific family into his fantasies (and potential madness). His parents are obsessed with toilet training, his cowardly brother with body-building, his sisters are demented, and his grandfather is a sadistic, dirty old man. Striking cinematography and great soundtrack, but not for the faint of heart (or stomach). French with subtitles. **107m/C; VHS, DVD.** *CA* Maxime Collin; Julien Guiomar; Ginette Reno; Pierre Bourgault; Yves Montmarquette; Roland Blouin; Giuditta del Vecchio; ***D:*** Jean-Claude Lauzon; ***W:*** Jean-Claude Lauzon. Genie '92: Costume Des., Film Editing, Orig. Screenplay.

Leon Morin, Priest ½ **1961** A young priest and a widow, who happens to be a Communist, fall in love during the WWII German occupation of France. Based on the novel by Beatrix Beck. In French with English subtitles. **118m/B; VHS, DVD, Blu-Ray.** *IT FR* Jean-Paul Belmondo; Emmanuelle Riva; ***D:*** Jean-Pierre Melville.

Leon the Pig Farmer ½ **1993** Dry comedic satire about identity. Leon Geller has never quite fitted into his parents' comfortable Jewish society and no wonder—Leon accidentally discovers he is the product of artificial insemination. And what's more, the lab made a mistake and Leon isn't a true Geller after all. His father is actually a genial (and Gentile) Yorkshire pig farmer named Brian Chadwick, who cheerfully welcomes Leon as his long-lost son. All four parents try to cope while Leon moves bewilderedly amongst them. Film tends to be too timid in its satire but still has its witty moments. **98m/C; VHS, Streaming.** *GB* Mark Frankel; Janet Suzman; Brian Glover; Connie Booth; David de Keyser; Maryam D'Abo; Gina Bellman; ***D:*** Vadim Jean; Gary Sinyor; ***W:*** Gary Sinyor; Michael Normand.

Leonard Part 6 **1987 (PG)** A former secret agent comes out of retirement to save the world from a crime queen using animals to kill agents. In the meantime, he tries to patch up his collapsing personal life. Wooden and disappointing; produced and co-written by Cosby, who himself panned the film. **83m/C; VHS, DVD, Blu-Ray.** Bill Cosby; Gloria Foster; Tom Courtenay; Joe Don Baker; ***D:*** Paul Weiland; ***W:*** Bill Cosby; Jonathan Reynolds; ***C:*** Jan De Bont; ***M:*** Elmer Bernstein. Golden Raspberries '87: Worst Actor (Cosby), Worst Picture, Worst Screenplay.

The Leopard ½ *Il Gattopardo* **1963** American Lancaster (allegedly foisted on the movie by the studio to help the box office) holds his own in meeting the style of master director Visconti in this adaptation of Guiseppe di Lampedusa's 1958 bestseller. In the 1860s, Prince Don Fabrizio Salina realizes his privileged way of life is doomed by revolution. Ever practical, he looks to his family's survival by marrying his ambitious nephew Tancredi (Delon) to Angelica (Cardinale), the daughter of a buffoonish, but suddenly powerful, local bureaucrat (Stoppa) . The beautiful ending ballroom sequence lasts some 45 minutes. Italian with subtitles. There are many butchered versions, but the Criterion release was meticulously restored and is the closest available to Visconti's 205 minute original, now lost. **185m/C; DVD, Blu-Ray.** *IT* Burt Lancaster; Alain Delon; Claudia Cardinale; Paolo Stoppa; Rina Morelli; Romolo Valli; Terence Hill; Pierre Clementi; ***D:*** Luchino Visconti; ***W:*** Luchino Visconti; Enrico Medioli; Suso Cecchi D'Amico; Pasquale Festa Companile; ***C:*** Giuseppe Rotunno; ***M:*** Nino Rota.

Leopard in the Snow **1978 (PG)** The romance between a race car driver allegedly killed in a crash and a young woman is the premise of this film. **89m/C; VHS, DVD.** Keir Dullea; Susan Penhaligon; Kenneth More; Billie Whitelaw; ***D:*** Gerry O'Hara.

The Leopard Man ½ **1943** An escaped leopard terrorizes a small town in New Mexico. After a search, the big cat is found dead, but the killings continue. Minor but effective Jacques Tourneur creepie. Based on Cornell Woolrich's novel "Black Alibi." Another Val Lewton Horror production. **66m/B; VHS, DVD, Blu-Ray.** Jean Brooks; Isabel Jewell; James Bell; Margaret Landry; Dennis O'Keefe; Margo; Rita (Paula) Corday; Abner Biberman; ***D:*** Jacques Tourneur; ***W:*** Ardel Wray; ***C:*** Robert De Grasse; ***M:*** Roy Webb.

Lepke ½ **1975 (R)** The life and fast times of Louis "Lepke" Buchalter from his days in reform school to his days as head of Murder, Inc. and his execution in 1944. **110m/C; VHS, DVD.** Tony Curtis; Milton Berle; Gianni Russo; Vic Tayback; Michael Callan; ***D:*** Menahem Golan.

Leprechaun WOOF! **1993 (R)** A sadistic 600-year-old leprechaun wrecks havoc in North Dakota. If this makes no sense, neither does the film, which is basic horror story excess. A man goes to Ireland for his mother's funeral, steals the gold belonging to the leprechaun, locks the creature up, but accidentally takes the evil imp back to the States with him. When the leprechaun gets free, he wants a bloodthirsty revenge—and shoes. One of the so-called humorous bits is the leprechaun's shoe fetish. Irish eyes will not be smiling watching this mess. **92m/C; VHS, DVD, Blu-Ray.** Warwick Davis; Jennifer Aniston; Ken Olandt; Mark Holton; John Sanderford; Robert Gorman; Shay Duffin; John Voldstad; ***D:*** Mark Jones; ***W:*** Mark Jones; ***C:*** Levie Isaacks. **VIDEO**

Leprechaun 2 **1994 (R)** It seems one of the fairy entitlements for the malevolent Irish gnome is possessing any woman he wants if she sneezes three times. Thwarted in his attempt to snare a comely lass 1,000 years earlier, he returns to present-day California to exact revenge on her descendant. Contrary to the popular legend that leprechauns are benign kind-hearted sprites, this nasty combines the treachery of a Gestapo officer with the firepower of Rambo in his attempt to harass the unimpressed gal into his clutches. **85m/C; VHS, DVD, Blu-Ray.** Warwick Davis; Sandy Baron; Adam Biesk; James Lancaster; Clint Howard; Kimmy Robertson; Charlie Heath; Shevonne Durkin; ***D:*** Rodman Flender; ***W:*** Turi Meyer; Al Septien; ***C:*** Jane Castle; ***M:*** Jonathan Elias.

Leprechaun 3 **1995 (R)** A student steals the nasty little beastie's gold and he's off to Las Vegas to get it back and to kill the gamblers, also after his magic money, in decidedly disgusting ways. **93m/C; VHS, DVD, Blu-Ray.** Warwick Davis; John Gatins; Michael Callan; Caroline Williams; Lee Armstrong; ***D:*** Brian Trenchard-Smith; ***W:*** Brian Dubos; ***C:*** David Lewis; ***M:*** Dennis Michael Tenney.

Leprechaun 4: In Space WOOF! 1996 (R) Who knows how the little imp got there but now our old friend the Leprechaun (Davis) is busy terrorizing an alien princess (Carlton) on a distant planet. He wants to marry the babe and rule the universe but its the Marines to the rescue! Yes, an Earth platoon arrives to foil his plans. **98m/C; VHS, DVD, Blu-Ray.** Warwick Davis; Rebekah Carlton; Brent Jasmer; Debbe Dunning; Rebecca Cross; Tim Colceri; ***D:*** Brian Trenchard-Smith; ***W:*** Dennis A. Pratt; ***C:*** David Lewis; ***M:*** Dennis Michael Tenney.

Leprechaun 5: In the Hood WOOF! 1999 (R) This time around the bloodthirsty leprechaun wants revenge on a group of wannabe rap artists who use his magic (and steal his gold) in order to become successful. If you've seen any of the others in this series, you know what to expect. **91m/C; VHS, DVD, Blu-Ray.** Warwick Davis; Ice-T; Coolio; ***D:*** Robert Spera. **VIDEO**

Leprechaun 6: Back 2 Tha Hood WOOF! 2003 (R) This series becomes campier horror with each new installment. Beautician Emily and her friends find the Leprechaun's gold and foolishly spend it, which earns the little imp's wrath. **87m/C; VHS, DVD, Blu-Ray.** Warwick Davis; Tangi Miller; Kirk "Sticky Fingaz" Jones; Shiek Mahmud-Bey; ***D:*** Steven Ayromlooi; ***W:*** Steven Ayromlooi; ***C:*** David Daniel. **VIDEO**

Leroy and Stitch **2006 (G)** In this finale to the television series, Lilo and Stitch have captured and reformed all of the evil alien experiments and earned themselves a place in outer space once again. This gets interrupted by Dr. Hamsterviel escaping prison and attempting yet another galactic takeover via Leroy, a clone of Stitch. **72m/C; DVD.** ***V:*** Daveigh Chase; Tia Carrere; Kevin McDonald; Kevin M. Richardson; David Ogden Stiers; Zoe Caldwell; Liliana Mumy; Jeff Glenn Bennett; Rob Paulsen; Chris (Christopher) Sanders; ***D:*** Tony Craig; Roberts Gannaway; ***W:*** Roberts Gannaway; Jess Winfield; ***M:*** J.A.C. Redford.

Les Biches **1/2** ***The Does; Girlfriends; Bad Girls*** **1968 (R)** An exquisite film that became a landmark in film history with its theme of bisexuality and upper class decadence. A rich socialite picks up a young artist drawing on the streets of Paris, seduces her, and then takes her to St. Tropez. Conflict arises when a suave architect shows up and threatens to come between the two lovers. In French with English subtitles. **95m/C; VHS, DVD.** *FR* Stephane Audran; Jean-Louis Trintignant; Jacqueline Sassard; ***D:*** Claude Chabrol; ***W:*** Claude Chabrol.

Les Bonnes Femmes ***The Good Girls; The Girls; The Good Time Girls; Donne facili*** **1960** Four Paris shopgirls dream of escaping the monotony of their lives and finding romance but instead discover broken dreams and danger. Chabrol's New Wave thriller focuses more on character and irony than suspense. French with subtitles. **105m/B; VHS, DVD.** *FR* Bernadette LaFont; Stephane Audran; Clothilde Joano; Lucile Saint-Simon; ***D:*** Claude Chabrol; ***W:*** Paul Geoauff; ***C:*** Henri Decae; ***M:*** Pierre Jansen; Paul Misraki.

Les Carabiniers ***The Soldiers*** **1963** A cynical, grim anti-war tract, detailing the pathetic adventures of two young bums lured into enlisting with promises of rape, looting, torture and battle without justification. Controversial in its day, and typically elliptical and non-narrative. In French with English subtitles. **80m/B; VHS, DVD.** *GB IT FR* Albert Juross; Marino (Martin) Mase; Catherine Ribeiro; Genevieva Galea; Anna Karina; ***D:*** Jean-Luc Godard; ***W:*** Jean-Luc Godard; ***C:*** Raoul Coutard; ***M:*** Philippe Arthuys.

Les Comperes **1983** A woman suckers two former lovers into finding her wayward son by secretly telling each ex he is the natural father of the punk. Depardieu is a streetwise journalist who teams up with a suicidal hypochondriac/wimp (Richard) to find the little brat. Humorous story full of bumbling misadventures. In French with English subtitles. **92m/C; VHS, DVD.** *FR* Pierre Richard; Gerard Depardieu; Anny (Annie Legras) Duperey; Michel Aumont; ***D:*** Francis Veber; ***W:*** Francis Veber; ***M:*** Vladimir Cosma.

Les Cousins ***Cousins*** **1959** Chabrol's second New Wave feature, a psychological study of youth, privilege and corruption, stars the same two actors as his first film, "Le Beau Serge." Sheltered provincial Charles (Blain) comes to Paris to study law and shares the apartment of his sophisticated, decadent cousin Paul (Brialy). Charles falls for Florence, a friend of Paul's from the same social class, but Paul easily seduces her away. Charles realizes he can't compete in any sphere causing the situation turn grim. French with subtitles. **112m/B; DVD, Blu-Ray.** *FR* Gerard Blain; Jean-Claude Brialy; Juliette Mayniel; Claude Cerval; Genevieve Cluny; Stephane Audran; ***D:*** Claude Chabrol; ***W:*** Claude Chabrol; Paul Gegauff; ***C:*** Henri Decae; ***M:*** Paul Misraki.

Les Destinees **1/2** ***Les Destinees Sentimentales; Sentimental Destinies*** **2000** Sprawling but emotionally flat costume drama follows 40 years in the life of Protestant minister Jean Barnery. When Jean finds that his wife, Nathalie, has been unfaithful, he sends her and their daughter Aline away. Later he meets and falls in love with independent Pauline, but his estranged wife, World War I, the call to return to his family's porcelain business, and the Wall Street crash impose onto their lives. Film is technically and visually impressive, but a lack of any real spark, and the film's length, combine to blunt its impact. Based on the novel by Jacques Chardonne. French with subtitles. **174m/C; VHS, DVD.** *FR SI* Charles Berling; Emmanuelle Beart; Isabelle Huppert; Olivier Perrier; Dominique Reymond; Andre Marcon; Alexandra London; Julie Depardieu; ***D:*** Olivier Assayas; ***W:*** Olivier Assayas; Jacques Fieschi; ***C:*** Eric Gautier; ***M:*** Guillaume Lekeu.

Les Enfants Terrible ***The Strange Ones*** **1950** The classic, lyrical treatment of adolescent deviance adapted by Cocteau from his own play, wherein a brother and sister born into extreme wealth eventually enter into casual crime, self-destruction, and incest. In French with English subtitles. **105m/B; VHS, DVD.** *FR* Edouard Dermithe; Nicole Stephane; ***D:*** Jean-Pierre Melville; ***W:*** Jean Cocteau; Jean-Pierre Melville.

Les Girls **1/2 1957** When one member of a performing troupe writes her memoirs, the other girls sue for libel. Told through a series of flashbacks, this story traces the girls' recollections of their relationships to American dancer Kelly. Cole Porter wrote the score for this enjoyable "Rashomon"-styled musical. **114m/C; VHS, DVD, Blu-Ray.** Gene Kelly; Mitzi Gaynor; Kay Kendall; Taina Elg; Henry Daniell; Patrick Macnee; ***D:*** George Cukor; ***C:*** Robert L. Surtees. Oscars '57: Costume Des.; Golden Globes '58: Actress--Mus./Comedy (Kendall), Film--Mus./Comedy.

Les Miserables **1935** Victor Hugo's classic novel about small-time criminal Jean Valjean and 19th-century France. After facing poverty and prison, escape and torture, Valjean is redeemed by the kindness of a bishop. As he tries to mend his ways, he is continually hounded by the policeman Javert, who is determined to lock him away. The final act is set during a student uprising in the 1830s. This version is the best of many, finely detailed and well-paced with excellent cinematography by Gregg Toland. **108m/B; VHS, DVD.** Fredric March; Charles Laughton; Cedric Hardwicke; Rochelle Hudson; John Beal; Frances Drake; Florence Eldridge; John Carradine; Jessie Ralph; Leonid Kinskey; ***D:*** Richard Boleslawski; ***W:*** W.P. Lipscomb; ***C:*** Gregg Toland; ***M:*** Alfred Newman.

Les Miserables **1/2 1952** Hugo's classic novel done up Italian style with lavish sets and spectacle. Dubbed in English. **119m/B; VHS, DVD, Streaming.** *IT* Gino Cervi; Valentina Cortese; Charlotte Austin; ***D:*** Riccardo Freda; ***C:*** Joseph LaShelle; ***M:*** Alex North.

Les Miserables **1957** An epic French adaptation of the Victor Hugo standard about Valjean, Javert, and injustice. Although this doesn't reach the level of the 1935 classic, it is still worth watching. Dubbed in English. **188m/C; DVD, Blu-Ray.** *FR GE* Jean Gabin; Daniele Delorme; Bernard Blier; Andre Bourvil; Gianni Esposito; Serge Reggiani; ***D:*** Jean-Paul LeChanois; ***W:*** Jean-Paul LeChanois; Michel Audiard; Rene Barjavel; ***C:*** Jacques Natteau; ***M:*** Georges Van Parys.

Les Miserables **1/2 1978** An excellent made-for-TV version of the Victor Hugo classic about the criminal Valjean and the policeman Javert playing cat-and-mouse in 18th-century France. Dauphin's last film role. **150m/C; VHS, DVD.** Richard Jordan; Anthony Perkins; John Gielgud; Cyril Cusack; Flora Robson; Celia Johnson; Claude Dauphin; ***D:*** Glenn Jordan. **TV**

Les Miserables **1997 (PG-13)** Paroled convict Jean Valjean (Neeson) gets chased by police inspector Javert (Rush) while factory worker Fantine (Thurman) turns to prostitution to survive. August begins his adaptation after Valjean's trial and imprisonment for petty theft, and until the final third of the film, doesn't really deal with the political upheaval of the time. Not as sweeping or grand as other versions, but what this lacks in scope, it makes up for with top-notch performances and a more careful study of the characters themselves. **134m/C; DVD, Blu-Ray.** Liam Neeson; Geoffrey Rush; Uma Thurman; Claire Danes; Paris Vaughan; Reine Brynolfsson; Hans Matheson; Mimi Newman; ***D:*** Bille August; ***W:*** Rafael Yglesias; ***C:*** Jorgen Persson; ***M:*** Basil Poledouris.

Les Miserables **1/2 2012 (PG-13)** One of the most successful stage musicals of all time gets its long-awaited film version and the stars align for one of the best movies centered around expression through song in the last two decades. Jackman gets the role of his career as Jean Valjean, a man trying to hide from his past but hunted by the ruthless Javert (Crowe). Revolution, love triangles, and a whole lot of death serve as the foundation of this remarkably accomplished film that unashamedly paints its melodrama in widescreen emotions. It is far from the film that could convince those not into the genre but works for fans of movies where people sing their hearts out. **157m/C; DVD, Blu-Ray.** *UK* Hugh Jackman; Russell Crowe; Anne Hathaway; Amanda Seyfried; Sacha Baron Cohen; Helena Bonham Carter; Eddie Redmayne; Isabelle Allen; ***D:*** Tom Hooper; ***W:*** William Nicholson; ***C:*** Danny Cohen; ***M:*** Claude-Michel Schonberg. Oscars '12: Actress--Supporting (Hathaway), Makeup, Sound; British Acad. '12: Actress--Supporting (Hathaway), Makeup, Production Design, Sound; Golden Globes '13: Actor--Mus./Comedy (Jackman), Actress--Supporting (Hathaway), Film--Mus./Comedy; Screen Actors Guild '12: Actress--Supporting (Hathaway).

Les Misérables 2019 (R) 102m/C. *FR* Damien Bonnard; Alexis Manenti; Djebril Zonga; Issa Perica; Al-Hassan Ly; ***D:*** Ladj Ly; ***W:*** Alexis Manenti; Ladj Ly; Giordano Gederlini; ***C:*** Julien Poupard.

Les Rendez-vous D'Anna ***The Meetings of Anna*** **1978** An independent woman travels through Europe and comes face to face with its post-war modernism. In French with English subtitles. **120m/C; VHS, DVD.** *FR BE GE* Aurore Clement; Helmut Griem; Magali Noel; Hanns Zischler; Lea Massari; Jean-Pierre Cassel; ***D:*** Chantal Akerman; ***W:*** Chantal Akerman.

Les Vampires **1915** Irma Vep (an anagram for vampire) leads a bloodthirsty gang of thieves in Paris. She and her cohorts will use kidnapping, gas, sexual domination, and murder to gain power over the city's elite. Fueillade's 10-part serial has been restored with color-tinting and title cards in English. **420m/B; Silent; VHS, DVD, Blu-Ray.** *FR* Musidora; Jean Ayme; Marcel Levesque; Edouard Mathe; ***D:*** Louis Feuillade; ***W:*** Louis Feuillade.

Les Voleurs ***Thieves*** **1996 (R)** Unexpected romantic triangle among desperate, lonely people, set against a crime backdrop and told from a variety of viewpoints. Edgy cop Alex (Auteuil) is from a family of thieves, including his older brother Ivan (Bezace) who's been murdered. Alex gets involved with sullen Juliette (Cote) without realizing, at first, that her brother Jimmy (Magimel) is a member of Ivan's gang or that she has another lover, her philosophy teacher, Marie (Deneuve). Events finally force a meeting between Marie and Alex over the unstable Juliette (the scenes between Auteuil and Deneuve being the most interesting in the film). French with subtitles. **116m/C; VHS, DVD.** *FR* Catherine Deneuve; Daniel Auteuil; Laurence Cote; Benoît Magimel; Didier Bezace; Fabienne Babe; Ivan Desny; Julien Riviere; ***D:*** Andre Techine; ***W:*** Andre Techine; Gilles Taurand; ***C:*** Jeanne Lapoirie; ***M:*** Philippe Sarde.

Less Than Zero **1987 (R)** An adaptation of Bret Easton Ellis' popular, controversial novel about a group of affluent, drug-abusing youth in Los Angeles. McCarthy and Gertz play friends of Downey who try to get him off his self-destructive path—to no avail. Although it tries, the film fails to inspire any sort of sympathy for this self-absorbed and hedonistic group. Mirrors the shallowness of the characters although Downey manages to rise above this somewhat. Music by the Bangles, David Lee Roth, Poison, Roy Orbison, Aerosmith and more. **98m/C; VHS, DVD.** Andrew McCarthy; Jami Gertz; Robert Downey, Jr.; James Spader; ***D:*** Marek Kanievska; ***W:*** Harley Peyton; ***C:*** Edward Lachman; ***M:*** Thomas Newman.

Lesser Evil **1/2 2006** Fashion designer Karen (Eastwood) is raped by a man who is being protected by the feds until he testifies against his co-conspirators in a terrorism case. She's determined to get justice no matter who stands in her way. **90m/C; DVD.** Alison Eastwood; Nels Lennarson; Thea Gill; Marc Singer; Tahmoh Penikett; Artine Brown; Colin Cunningham; ***D:*** Timothy Bond; ***W:*** James Justice; ***C:*** Mahlon Todd Williams; ***M:*** Peter Allen. **CABLE**

A Lesson Before Dying **1999 (PG-13)** Cheadle's impressive as idealistic teacher Grant Wiggins, who has a one-room school for black children in 1948 Louisiana. He's reluctantly pressed into service by his formidable Aunt Lou (Tyson) and her friend Miss Emma (Hall), who want him to bring some dignity to the life of Jefferson (Phifer). This is no easy task since the young man is awaiting execution for a crime he didn't commit. Based on the 1993 novel by Ernest J. Gaines. **100m/C; VHS, DVD.** Don Cheadle; Cicely Tyson; Mekhi Phifer; Irma P. Hall; Brent Jennings; Lisa Arrindell Anderson; Frank Hoyt Taylor; ***D:*** Joseph Sargent; ***W:*** Ann Peacock; ***C:*** Donald M. Morgan; ***M:*** Ernest Troost. **CABLE**

Let 'Em Have It **1/2** ***False Faces*** **1935** Exciting action saga loosely based on the newly formed FBI and its bouts with John Dillinger. Car chases and tommy guns abound in this fairly ordinary film. **90m/B; VHS, DVD.** Richard Arlen; Virginia Bruce; Bruce Cabot; Harvey Stephens; Eric Linden; Joyce Compton; Gordon Jones; ***D:*** Sam Wood.

Let Freedom Ring **1/2 1939** Sappy, yet enjoyable patriotism that has lawyer Eddy returning to small hometown and fighting corruption. Hokey, but it works largely due to Hecht's fine script. **100m/B; DVD.** Nelson Eddy; Virginia Bruce; Victor McLaglen; Lionel Barrymore; Edward Arnold; Guy Kibbee; Charles Butterworth; H.B. Warner; Raymond Walburn; George "Gabby" Hayes; ***D:*** Jack Conway; ***W:*** Ben Hecht; ***C:*** Sidney Wagner.

Let Go **2011** In this crime comedy, an unhappy parole officer deals with three of his crazier ex-cons: A femme who bilks her boyfriends; a former doctor nailed for insurance fraud; and a 90-year-old holdup man who can't stop backsliding. **95m/C; DVD.** David Denman; Gillian Jacobs; Kevin Hart; Ed Asner; Peggy McKay; Simon Helberg; *D:* Brian Jett; *W:* Brian Jett; *C:* Collin Brink; *M:* Bobby Johnston. **VIDEO**

Let Him Have It 1/2 **1991 (R)** Compelling, controversial film about a miscarriage of justice. In 1952, Christopher Craig, 16, and Derek Bentley, 19, climb onto a warehouse roof in an apparent burglary attempt. The police arrive and capture Bentley; Craig shoots and wounds one policeman and kills another. According to testimony Bentley shouted "Let him have it" but did he mean shoot or give the officer the gun? Bentley, whose IQ was 66, was sentenced to death by the British courts—though he didn't commit the murder. The uproar over the sentence was reignited by this release, leading to a request for a reexamination of evidence and sentencing by the British Home Office. **115m/C; VHS, DVD.** *UK* Christopher Eccleston; Paul Reynolds; Tom Bell; Eileen Atkins; Clare Holman; Michael Elphick; Mark McGann; Tom Courtenay; Ronald Fraser; Michael Gough; Murray Melvin; Clive Revill; Norman Rossington; James Villiers; *D:* Peter Medak; *W:* Robert Wade; Neal Purvis; *C:* Oliver Stapleton; *M:* Michael Kamen.

Let It Be **1970** Documentary look at a Beatles recording session, giving glimpses of the conflicts which led to their breakup. Features appearances by Yoko Ono and Billy Preston. **80m/C; VHS, DVD.** John Lennon; Paul McCartney; George Harrison; Ringo Starr; Billy Preston; Yoko Ono; *D:* Michael Lindsay-Hogg; *M:* John Lennon; Paul McCartney; George Harrison; Ringo Starr. Oscars '70: Orig. Song Score and/or Adapt.

Let It Rain *Parlez-Moi de la Pluie* **2008** Feminist author/politician Agathe (Jaoui) returns to her provincial hometown to help her sister sort through their dead mother's affairs. She agrees to an interview with two family friends, Karim (Debbouze) and Michel (Bacri), who're incompetent journalists putting together a documentary profiling successful women. Along the way, they stumble in and out of neurotic and disastrous romantic interludes. As with her previous work, director/star Jaoui aims for provocative and edgy, dealing with sexism, racism, classism, and a few other isms, but it makes for a lukewarm affair. French with subtitles. **96m/C; DVD.** *FR* Agnes Jaoui; Jamel Debbouze; Frederic Pierrot; Florence Loiret-Caille; Jean-Pierre Bacri; Pascale Arbillot; Guillaume De Tonquedec; Mimouna Hadji; *D:* Agnes Jaoui; *W:* Agnes Jaoui; Jean-Pierre Bacri; *C:* David Quesemand.

Let It Ride **1989 (PG-13)** Dreyfuss is a small-time gambler who finally hits it big at the track. Some funny moments but generally a lame script cripples the cast, although the horses seem unaffected. Garr is okay as his wife who slips further into alcoholism with each race. **91m/C; VHS, DVD.** Richard Dreyfuss; Teri Garr; David Johansen; Jennifer Tilly; Allen Garfield; Ed Walsh; Michelle Phillips; Mary Woronov; Robbie Coltrane; Richard Edson; Cynthia Nixon; *D:* Joe Pytka; *W:* Nancy Dowd; *C:* Curtis J. Wehr; *M:* Giorgio Moroder.

Let It Shine 1/2 **2012** Modern update of "Cyrano de Bergerac" made for the Disney Channel. Cyrus DeBarge (Williams) sings in the Atlanta Baptist church where his father (Vance) is the pastor. Dad doesn't approve of Cyrus' hip hop interest but that doesn't stop him from entering a song in a contest that's being judged by his classmate crush, Roxanna (Jones), who's now a pop star. Only Cyrus' best friend Kris (Jackson) is also singing on the track and Roxxie thinks he's the man with the music. **104m/C; DVD, Blu-Ray.** Tyler James Williams; Coco Jones; Trevor Jackson; Courtney B. Vance; Nicole Sullivan; Dawnn Lewis; *D:* Paul Hoen; *W:* Eric Daniel; *C:* David Makin; *M:* Richard Gibbs. **CABLE**

Let It Snow 1/2 *Snow Days* **1999 (R)** Appealing romantic comedy centers on the emotional insecurity of James Ellis (scripter Marcus, whose brother, Adam, directs), who witnessed his mother Elise's (Peters) post-divorce series of loser boyfriends. His best friend is Sarah (Dylan) and the two dance around the romantic possibilities until a sudden kiss throws their relationship into turmoil. Some mis-communication has Sarah leaving to study in England and James becoming determined to win her love. **90m/C; VHS, DVD.** Kipp Marcus; Alice Dylan; Bernadette Peters; Judith Malina; Henry Simmons; Miriam Shor; Larry Pine; Debra Sullivan; *D:* Adam Marcus; *W:* Kipp Marcus; *C:* Ben Weinstein; *M:* Sean McCourt.

Let It Snow **2019 (PG-13)** On a snowy Christmas Eve, a group of high school seniors faces personal challenges. Introvert Julie (Moner) downplays the time she spends with secretly lonely pop star Stewart (Moore), while neurotic Tobin (Hope) cannot overcome his shyness to admit feelings for his friend and crush The Duke (Shikpa). As Addie (Rush) struggles with her neglectful boyfriend, she pushes away her true friend Dorrie (Hewson). By the time the group reaches a party arranged by DJ Keon (Batalon), each person has reached a breaking point. A routine Christmas-themed romantic comedy, there are too many characters and not enough memorable story to go around. **92m/C; DVD.** Isabela Merced; Shameik Moore; Odeya Rush; Liv Hewson; Mitchell Hope; *D:* Luke Snellin; *W:* Laura Solon; Victoria Strouse; Kay Cannon; *C:* Jeff Cutter; *M:* Keegan DeWitt. **VIDEO**

Let Me In 1/2 **2010 (R)** American remake of the 2008 Swedish chiller "Let the Right One In." Lonely, neglected, and bullied, 12-year-old Owen (Smit-McPhee) finds a best friend and guardian when Abby (Moretz) moves into his apartment building. Abby doesn't attend school, she only comes out at night, and the man acting as her father causes trouble in the neighborhood. Soon enough, Owen realizes she's a vampire. Much respect is given to the original's haunting pace and tone, allowing the tension to build naturally, without flashy gimmicks. The child actors are perfect, capturing the despair and horror of their adolescence. **116m/C; Blu-Ray, On Demand.** Kodi Smit-McPhee; Chloë Grace Moretz; Richard Jenkins; Elias Koteas; Cara Buono; Sasha Barrese; Jimmy Pinchak; *D:* Matt Reeves; *W:* Matt Reeves; *C:* Greig Fraser; *M:* Michael Giacchino.

Let My People Go! **2011** In this busy, silly, camp French comedy, French-Jewish mailman Ruben is living with his blond Nordic lover Teemu in Finland. A lovers' quarrel over money sends Ruben back to Paris just in time for Passover with his dysfunctional family, including a ditzy mother, a dad with a mistress he insists on introducing, a cranky brother, and an unhappy sister getting a divorce. Ruben also discovers an old family friend would like to get to know him better (wink-wink) while both Ruben and Teemu pine over their separation. French and Finnish with subtitles. **87m/C; DVD.** *FR* Nicolas Maury; Carmen Maura; Jean-Francois Stevenin; Jarkko Niemi; Jean-Luc Bideau; *D:* Mikael Buch; *W:* Mikael Buch; Christophe Honore; *C:* Celine Bozon; *M:* Eric Neveux.

Let Sleeping Corpses Lie 1/2 *The Living Dead at Manchester Morgue* **1974** England's answer to "Night of the Living Dead" is more polished and has a more pronounced environmental edge. George (Lovelock) and Edna (Galbo) are the heroes who must confront the cannibalistic animated corpses. If the film lacks the single-mindedness and originality of Romero's work, it's an accurate snapshot of the early 1970s with appropriately gruesome special effects. **93m/C; VHS, DVD, Blu-Ray.** *GB* Ray Lovelock; Christine Galbo; Arthur Kennedy; *D:* Jorge Grau; *W:* Alessandro Continenza; Marcello Coscia; *C:* Francisco Sempere; *M:* Giuliano Sorgini.

Let the Devil Wear Black 1/2 **1999 (R)** A "Hamlet" update gets the noir treatment. Jack (Penner) is suspicious about his dad's murder, especially when his mom (Bisset) suddenly marries his uncle (Sheridan). Jack becomes obsessed with linking his uncle to some shady business dealings also involving dear old dad, while his girlfriend, Julia (Parker), goes a little crazy from Jack's neglect. Cleverly done. **89m/C; VHS, DVD.** Jonathan Penner; Jacqueline Bisset; Jamey Sheridan; Mary-Louise Parker; Philip Baker Hall; Jonathan Banks; Maury Chaykin; Chris Sarandon; Randall Batinkoff; Norman Reedus; *D:* Stacy Title; *W:* Jonathan Penner; Stacy Title; *C:* Jim Whitaker.

Let the Right One In *Lat den Ratte Komma In* **2008 (R)** Freakishly compelling variation of the vampire story. Lonely, neglected 12-year-old Oskar (Hedebrant) is constantly bullied at school and dreams of violent revenge. His new apartment neighbor is seemingly young Eli (Leandersson), whom he sees only at night, and who is cared for by the shifty Hakan (Ragnar). Oskar is unfazed when he realizes that Eli needs fresh blood to live and they become friendly. A vampire is good to know when you are targeted by bullies. Swedish with subtitles. **114m/C; DVD, Blu-Ray.** *SW* Kare Hedebrant; Lina Leandersson; Per Ragnar; Henrik Dahl; Karen Bergquist; Peter Carlberg; *D:* Thomas Alfredson; *W:* John Ajvide Lindqvist; *C:* Hoyte van Hoytema; *M:* Johan Soderqvist.

Let the Sunshine In *Un beau soleil intérieur* **2017** This is one of those films that critics drool over because it's French and...it's French! For everyone else, it's an exercise in patience featuring a clueless, spineless, sex-obsessed divorcée who takes us along on her journey to nowhere. Binoche plays Isabelle, a Parisian painter (how original) who's looking for love while dating a menagerie of cads. Instead of changing her mindset and methods of finding The One, she consults a romance clairvoyant who spouts gibberish about internal sunshine. The movie is in such a hurry to end its own pointlessness that the closing credits roll during -- *during!* -- that final scene. **94m/C; DVD.** Juliette Binoche; Xavier Beauvois; Philippe Katerine; Josiane Balasko; Sandrine Dumas; *D:* Claire Denis; *W:* Claire Denis; Christine Angot; *C:* Agnes Godard; *M:* Stuart A. Staples.

Let There Be Light **2017 (PG-13)** A faith-based film about the transformation of an atheist intellectual to Christian. Dr. Sol Harkens (K. Sorbo) is a popular figure who promotes a hedonistic agenda through his books and appearances. He argues against God because his young son died of cancer and he cannot accept that a benevolent creator would allow such suffering. After a serious car accident, Sol reaches out to his former wife Katy (S. Sorbo), a Christian, who arranges a meeting with her pastor. One conversation convinces Sol to change his life. An uncomplicated morality film intended for believers. **100m/C; DVD, Blu-Ray.** Kevin Sorbo; Sam Sorbo; Daniel Roebuck; Donielle Artese; Gary Grubbs; *D:* Kevin Sorbo; *W:* Dan Gordon; *M:* Marc Vanocur.

Let Us Be Gay **1930** Plain housewife Kitty (Shearer) discovers husband Bob (La Rocque) has been cheating and divorces him. She moves to Paris and, three years later, has become a glamorous flirt. Kitty is befriended by wealthy Mrs. Boucicault (Dressler) who invites Kitty to her Long Island estate. However, Mrs. Boucicault has an ulterior motive: her granddaughter is involved with Bob and she wants Kitty to break up their romance. **82m/B; DVD.** Norma Shearer; Rod La Rocque; Marie Dressler; Sally Eilers; Hedda Hopper; Gilbert Emery; Raymond Hackett; *D:* Robert Z. Leonard; *W:* Frances Marion; *C:* Norbert Brodine.

Let Us Live 1/2 **1939** Brick Tennant (Fonda) and his fiance Mary (O'Sullivan) are planning their wedding and getting Brick's taxi busines started. Their lives are shattered when, thanks to a combination of lousy eyewitness testimony, circumstantial evidence and an aggressive DA, Brick and his friend Joe (Baxter) are convicted of murder and sent to death row. Mary knows they're innocent and gets Lt. Everett (Bellamy) to help her prove it. **70m/B; DVD.** Maureen O'Sullivan; Henry Fonda; Ralph Bellamy; Alan Baxter; Stanley Ridges; *D:* John Brahm; *W:* Anthony Veiller; Allen Rivkin; *C:* Lucien Ballard; *M:* Karol Rathaus.

Lethal WOOF! **2004 (R)** Bounty hunter Sara (Marsden) teams up with an FBI agent (Zagarino) to bring down Russian mobster/weapons smuggler Federov (Lamas, he of the wandering accent). Lethally inept. **90m/C; DVD.** Lorenzo Lamas; Frank Zagarino; Heather Marie Marsden; Mark Mortimer; John Colton; *D:* Dustin Rikert; *W:* Jeff Wright; Robert Yap; *C:* John Muscatine. **VIDEO**

Lethal Dose 1/2 *LD 50 Lethal Dose* **2003 (R)** Extremist animal activist group ditches team member Gary during a botched rescue mission and wants to make it up to him a year later by springing him from the slammer. Instead, a freaky e-mail directs them to a long-deserted lab where grisly torture awaits. **97m/C; VHS, DVD.** Katharine Towne; Melanie (Scary Spice) Brown; Tom (Thomas) Hardy; Ross McCall; Philip Winchester; Stephen Lord; Toby Fisher; Leo Bill; Tania Emery; Alan Talbot; Antony Zaki; Xanthe Elbrick; *D:* Simon DeSelva; *W:* Matthew McGuchan; *C:* Robin Vidgeon; *M:* Michael Price. **VIDEO**

Lethal Force 1/2 *Cottonmouth* **2000** Houston cop Carruth (Tyson) turns vigilante on criminals with the backing of a judge (Vaughn) and some powerful businessmen. Unfortunately, there are innocent victims, including the family of former D.A. Thornton (Owsley), who is persuaded by noisy lawyer Rene (Stafford) to investigate and bring the rogue cop to justice. **95m/C; VHS, DVD.** Richard Tyson; Robert Vaughn; Michelle Stafford; Steven Owsley; *D:* James Dalthorp; *W:* Steven Owsley. **VIDEO**

Lethal Lolita—Amy Fisher: My Story *Amy Fisher: My Story* **1992** The only Amy Fisher story (out of three) whose cast even remotely resemble the real people. This made-for-TV account is Amy's version, portraying her as an incest victim who gets involved with an opportunistic married jerk who drags her into prostitution, leading her to take out her frustration on his wife. If this is true, the obvious question is "why?"...to which she answers, "He loves me. We have great sex. And he fixes my car." Oh. See also: "The Amy Fisher Story" and "Casualties of Love: The 'Long Island Lolita' Story." **93m/C; VHS, DVD.** Noelle Parker; Ed Marinaro; Kathleen Lasky; Boyd Kestner; Mary Ann Pascal; Lawrence Dane; Kate Lynch; *D:* Bradford May. **TV**

Lethal Ninja **1993 (R)** Kickboxers Joe and Pete set out to rescue Joe's wife from some third-world country overrun by ninjas. Hackneyed but lots of action for martial arts fans. **97m/C; VHS, DVD.** Ross Kettle; David Webb; Karyn Hill; Frank Notaro; *D:* Yossi Wein; *W:* Chris Dresser; *C:* Yossi Wein.

Lethal Obsession 1/2 *Der Joker* **1987 (R)** Two cops battle street crime and a powerful drug ring. Filmed in Germany. **100m/C; VHS, DVD.** *GE* Michael York; Elliott Gould; Tahnee Welch; Peter Maffay; Armin Mueller-Stahl; *D:* Peter Patzak; *M:* Tony Carey.

Lethal Seduction 1/2 **1997** Local crime boss Gus Gruman (Estevez) is rapidly losing friends and associates to a sexually oriented serial killer. And there's obsessed cop Trent Jacobson (Mitchum) who's determined to solve the crimes. The one clue is a mystery brunette seen leaving a crime scene. **110m/C; VHS, DVD.** Julie Strain; Chris Mitchum; Joe Estevez; *D:* Frederick P. Watkins; *C:* Robert Dracup.

Lethal Target **1999** A female prisoner is told she can get an early release if she poses as a Marshall while on a visit to a mining colony in space to find out what's going on there. Somewhere between a science fiction horror film like 'Alien' and a typical women in prison sexploitation film, this is sadly not as entertaining as either genre. **92m/C; DVD.** Josh Barker; Kim (Kimberly Dawn) Dawson; David Fisher; Petra Spindler; C.C. Costigan; *D:* Lloyd A. Simandl; *W:* Chris Hyde; *C:* Vladimir Kolar; *M:* Peter Allen.

Lethal Victims *W.A.R., Women Against Rape; Death Blow: A Cry for Justice; I Will Dance on Your Graves: Lethal Victims* **1987** A group of women decide to become vigilantes after their city suffers an epidemic of rapes and the local government seems unwilling to do anything about it. Surprisingly tame considering it's marketed as a sleazy exploitation film. **90m/C; DVD.** Jack Carter; Donna Denton; George "Buck" Flower; Marcia Karr; Martin Landau; Peter Paul Liapis; Lisa London; Henry Moore; Terry Moore; Frank Stallone; Don Swayze; Jerry Van Dyke; Georgette Baker; Wally K. Berns; Leslie Scarborough; *D:* Raphael Nussbaum; *W:* Raphael Nussbaum.

Lethal Weapon **1987 (R)** In Los Angeles, a cop nearing retirement (Glover) unwillingly begins work with a new partner (Gibson), a suicidal, semi-crazed risk-taker who seems determined to get the duo killed. Both Vietnam vets, the pair uncover a vicious heroin smuggling ring run by ruthless ex-Special Forces personnel. Packed with plenty of action, violence, and humorous undertones. Clapton's contributions to the musical score are an added bonus. Gibson and Glover work well together and give this movie extra punch. Followed by three sequels. **110m/C; VHS, DVD, Blu-Ray, HD-DVD.** Mel Gibson; Danny Glover; Gary Busey; Mitchell Ryan; Tom Atkins; Darlene Love; Traci Wolfe; Steve Kahan; Jackie Swanson; Damon Hines; Lycia Naff; Mary Ellen Trainor; Jack Thibeau; Ed O'Ross; Gustav Vintas; Al Leong; Joan Severance; ***D:*** Richard Donner; ***W:*** Shane Black; ***C:*** Stephen Goldblatt; ***M:*** Michael Kamen; Eric Clapton.

Lethal Weapon 2 **1989 (R)** This sequel to the popular cop adventure finds Gibson and Glover taking on a variety of blond South African "diplomats" who try to use their diplomatic immunity status to thwart the duo's efforts to crack their smuggling ring. Gibson finally finds romance, and viewers learn the truth about his late wife's accident. Also features the introduction of obnoxious, fast-talking con artist Leo ("OK, OK") Getz, adeptly played by Pesci, who becomes a third wheel to the crime-fighting team. **114m/C; VHS, DVD, Blu-Ray, HD-DVD.** Mel Gibson; Danny Glover; Joe Pesci; Joss Ackland; Derrick O'Connor; Patsy Kensit; Darlene Love; Traci Wolfe; Steve Kahan; Mary Ellen Trainor; Damon Hines; Jenette Goldstein; Mark Rolston; Dean Norris; Nestor Serrano; Grand L. Bush; ***D:*** Richard Donner; ***W:*** Jeffrey Boam; ***C:*** Stephen Goldblatt; ***M:*** Michael Kamen; Eric Clapton; David Sanborn.

Lethal Weapon 3 **1/2 1992 (R)** Murtaugh and Riggs return for more action in another slam-bang adventure. Murtaugh hopes his last week before retirement will be a peaceful one, but partner Riggs isn't about to let him go quietly. Not many changes from the successful formula with bickering buddies, lots of adventure, exploding buildings, a little comic relief from Pesci, and the addition of Russo as an Internal Affairs cop who proves to be more than a match for Riggs. **118m/C; DVD, Blu-Ray.** Mel Gibson; Danny Glover; Joe Pesci; Rene Russo; Stuart Wilson; Steve Kahan; Darlene Love; Traci Wolfe; Gregory Millar; Jason Meshover-Iorg; Delores Hall; Mary Ellen Trainor; Nick (Nicholas) Chinlund; Damon Hines; Miguel A. Nunez, Jr.; ***D:*** Richard Donner; ***W:*** Jeffrey Boam; Robert Mark Kamen; ***C:*** Jan De Bont; ***M:*** Eric Clapton; David Sanborn; Michael Kamen. MTV Movie Awards '93: Action Seq., On-Screen Duo (Mel Gibson/Danny Glover).

Lethal Weapon 4 **1/2 1998 (R)** It's old home week as Gibson, Glover, Pesci, and Russo reunite for one more escapade. Rock joins the veterans as junior detective Lee Butters, who has some unexpected ties to Murtaugh. They're investigating Asian crimelord Wah Sing Ku (action star Li) who's involved in smuggling and counterfeiting and has no problem with violence, including kicking the bejeezus out of Riggs more than once. Russo had to do her action sequences with a prosthetic belly since Lorna and Riggs are about to become parents. It's the same old-same old but it's still a good time. **125m/C; VHS, DVD, Blu-Ray.** Mel Gibson; Danny Glover; Joe Pesci; Rene Russo; Chris Rock; Jet Li; Steve Kahan; Darlene Love; Mary Ellen Trainor; Jack Kehler; Damon Hines; Traci Wolfe; Richard Libertini; Richard Riehle; ***D:*** Richard Donner; ***W:*** Channing Gibson; ***C:*** Andrzej Bartkowiak; ***M:*** Michael Kamen; Eric Clapton; David Sanborn.

Leto **1/2 2019** In 1980s Leningrad, aspiring musician Viktor Tsoi (Yoo) seeks the advice of a successful band leader, Mike (Zver). Recognizing Viktor's talent, Mike offers him encouragement and includes him in his entourage. At the same time, Mike notices that his wife Natasha (Starshenbaum) has connected with Viktor, a situation that results in a love triangle as their bands create their own sound under the repressive Soviet regime. Based on the life of the USSR band Kino's frontman and including much of his music, the sometimes surreal biopic has many interesting moments but sometimes lags in its pacing. **126m/C; DVD.** Teo Yoo; Irina Starshenbaum; Roman Bilyk; Anton Adasinsky; Semyon Serzin; ***D:*** Kirill Serebrennikov; ***W:*** Kirill Serebrennikov; Mikhail Idov; Lili Idova; Ivan Kapitonov; ***C:*** Vladislav Opelyants; ***M:*** Roman Bilyk.

Let's Be Cops **1/2 2014 (R)** Johnson and Wayans, Jr. make for a talented buddy comedy duo in this surprisingly financially successful hit that nonetheless wastes their ability on a truly awful script. The guys play a pair of struggling Los Angelinos who find new life when they dress up like police officers for a costume party and never take the outfits off. While there's a bit of humor with average dudes finally getting some power through their uniforms, none of director/writer Greenfield's film takes place in the real world. Anything people like about this flick is completely due to its stars. **104m/C; DVD, Blu-Ray.** Jake Johnson; Damon Wayans, Jr.; Nina Dobrev; James D'Arcy; Rob Riggle; Andy Garcia; Keegan Michael Key; ***D:*** Luke Greenfield; ***W:*** Luke Greenfield; Nicholas Thomas; ***C:*** Daryn Okada; ***M:*** Christophe Beck; Jake Monaco.

Let's Dance **1/2 1950** A young widow tries to protect her son from his wealthy, paternal grandmother, while Fred dances his way into her heart. More obscure Astaire vehicle, but as charming as the rest. Needless to say, great dancing. **112m/C; VHS, Streaming.** Betty Hutton; Fred Astaire; Roland Young; Ruth Warrick; Shepperd Strudwick; Lucile Watson; Barton MacLane; Gregory Moffett; Melville Cooper; ***D:*** Norman Z. McLeod.

Let's Do It Again **1/2 1953** Musical remake of 1937's "The Awful Truth." Singer Constance (Wyman) is tired of composer hubby Gary's (Milland) philandering so she tries to get even by allowing him to think she had an affair. The situation escalates and they get a divorce neither of them really wants. They try to make each other jealous with new romances until the inevitable happens. **95m/C; DVD.** Jane Wyman; Ray Milland; Aldo Ray; Karin (Karen, Katharine) Booth; Leon Ames; Valerie Bettis; Tom Helmore; ***D:*** Alexander Hall; ***W:*** Mary Loos; Richard Sale; ***C:*** Charles Lawton, Jr.; ***M:*** George Duning.

Let's Do It Again **1/2 1975 (PG)** Atlanta milkman and his pal, a factory worker, milk two big-time gamblers out of a large sum of money in order to build a meeting hall for their fraternal lodge. Lesser sequel to "Uptown Saturday Night." **113m/C; VHS, DVD.** Sidney Poitier; Bill Cosby; John Amos; Jimmie Walker; Ossie Davis; Denise Nicholas; Calvin Lockhart; ***D:*** Sidney Poitier; ***W:*** Richard Wesley.

Let's Get Harry **1/2** *The Rescue* **1987 (R)** Americans led by mercenaries mix it up with a Columbian cocaine franchise in an attempt to rescue their friend, Harry. Never released theatrically, for good reason. **107m/C; VHS, Streaming, On Demand.** Robert Duvall; Gary Busey; Michael Schoeffling; Thomas F. Wilson; Glenn Frey; Rick Rossovich; Ben Johnson; Matt Clark; Mark Harmon; Gregory Sierra; Elpidia Carrillo; ***D:*** Alan Smithee; ***W:*** Samuel Fuller; Charles Robert Carner; ***M:*** Brad Fiedel.

Let's Get Lost **1988** Absorbing documentary of Chet Baker, the prominent '50s "cool" jazz trumpeter (and occasional vocalist) who succumbed, like many of his peers, to drug addiction. Weber's black-and-white, fashion photography style well suits his subject. Downbeat, but rarely less than worthy. **125m/B; DVD.** Chet Baker; ***D:*** Bruce Weber.

Let's Go to Prison **1/2 2006 (R)** What we have here is a failure to entertain. Bitter ex-con John Lyshitski (Shepard) plots revenge on the judge who sent him up the river three times. John sets up the judge's preppy son Nelson (Arnett), then gets himself thrown back in the pokey so he can give Nelson terrible advice on prison survival. Standard jokes about bad food, soap-dropping and license plates ensue. Eventually, situations involving a psycho white supremacist (Shannon) and an amorous black prisoner (McBride) turn the tables on John. It's not very funny considering the comedy pedigree of director Odenkirk and the majority of the cast. **84m/C; DVD.** Dax Shepard; Will Arnett; Chi McBride; David Koechner; Dylan Baker; Michael Shannon; ***D:*** Bob Odenkirk; ***W:*** Robert Ben Garant; Thomas Lennon; Michael Patrick Jann; ***C:*** Ramsay Nickell; ***M:*** Alan Elliott.

Let's Kill Ward's Wife **1/2 2014** Foley's directorial debut is a sitcomish black comedy about male friendship. No one likes Ward's shrewish wife Stacy and his friends fantasize about getting rid of her. Ward's buddy Tom accidentally does kill Stacy, and the guys try to come up with a plan to dispose of the body and not get caught. **82m/C; DVD, Blu-Ray.** Donald Adeosun Faison; Patrick Wilson; James Carpinello; Greg Grunberg; Amy Acker; Dagmara Dominczyk; Scott Foley; ***D:*** Scott Foley; ***W:*** Scott Foley; ***C:*** Eduardo Barraza; ***M:*** John Spiker. **VIDEO**

Let's Make a Movie **1/2 2011** A film school dropout tired of being treated like a doormat decides to turn her life around by making a film. **102m/C; DVD, Blu-Ray, Streaming.** Hallie York; Johnathan Fernandez; Brian Cheng; Eric James Eastman; Jessica Coles; ***D:*** Elana A. Mugdan; ***W:*** Elana A. Mugdan. **VIDEO**

Let's Make It Legal **1/2 1951** Amusing comedy of a married couple who decide to get a divorce after 20 years of marriage. Colbert stars as the woman who decides to leave her husband, Carey, because he's a chronic gambler. They part as friends, but soon Colbert's old flame, Scott, is back in town and things get rather complicated. A solid cast serves as the main strength in this film. **77m/B; VHS, DVD.** Claudette Colbert; MacDonald Carey; Zachary Scott; Barbara Bates; Robert Wagner; Marilyn Monroe; Frank Cady; Kathleen Freeman; ***D:*** Richard Sale; ***W:*** F. Hugh Herbert; I.A.L. Diamond; ***C:*** Lucien Ballard; ***M:*** Cyril Mockridge.

Let's Make Love **1/2 1960** An urbane millionaire discovers he is to be parodied in an off-Broadway play, and vows to stop it—until he falls in love with the star of the show. He then ends up acting in the play. **118m/C; VHS, DVD, Blu-Ray.** Yves Montand; Marilyn Monroe; Tony Randall; Frankie Vaughan; Bing Crosby; Gene Kelly; Milton Berle; ***D:*** George Cukor; ***W:*** Norman Krasna; ***C:*** Daniel F. Fapp; ***M:*** Lionel Newman.

Let's Make Up *Lilacs in the Spring* **1955** When it comes to giving her heart, Neagle can't decide between two dashing men. **94m/C; VHS, DVD.** *GB* Errol Flynn; Anna Neagle; David Farrar; Kathleen Harrison; Peter Graves; ***D:*** Herbert Wilcox.

Let's Scare Jessica to Death **1971 (PG)** A young woman who was recently released from a mental hospital is subjected to unspeakable happenings at a country home with her friends. She encounters murder, vampires, and corpses coming out of nowhere. A supernatural thriller with quite a few genuine scares. **89m/C; DVD, Blu-Ray.** Zohra Lampert; Barton Heyman; Kevin J. O'Connor; Gretchen Corbett; Alan Manson; ***D:*** John Hancock; ***W:*** John Hancock; Lee Kalcheim; ***C:*** Robert M. "Bob" Baldwin, Jr.; ***M:*** Orville Stoeber.

Let's Sing Again **1936** Eight-year-old singing sensation Bobby Breen made his debut in this dusty musical vehicle, as a runaway orphan who becomes the pal of a washed-up opera star in a traveling show. **70m/B; VHS, DVD.** Bobby Breen; Henry Armetta; George Houston; Vivienne Osborne; Grant Withers; Inez Courtney; Lucien Littlefield; ***D:*** Kurt Neumann.

The Letter **1929** Jeanne Eagels' first talkie is an adaptation of the W. Somerset play. Bored Leslie Crosbie is stuck on a Malay rubber plantation with her older husband Robert (Owen). She has an affair with Geoffrey Hammond (Marshall) but when he leaves her for another woman, she shoots him dead. Still, it looks like Leslie will be acquitted—until a letter she wrote to Geoffrey about their affair suddenly surfaces. The 1940 remake starred Bette Davis. **60m/B; DVD.** Reginald Owen; Herbert Marshall; O.P. Heggie; Jeanne Eagels; Irene Browne; Lady Tsen Mei; Tamaki Yoshiwara; ***D:*** Jean De Limur; ***W:*** Garrett Fort; ***C:*** George J. Folsey.

The Letter **1940** When a man is shot and killed on a Malaysian plantation, the woman who committed the murder pleads self-defense. Her husband and his lawyer attempt to free her, but find more than they expected in this tightly paced film noir. Based on the novel by W. Somerset Maugham. Davis emulated the originator of her role, Jeanne Eagels, in her mannerisms and line readings, although Eagels later went mad from drug abuse and overwork. **96m/B; VHS, DVD, Blu-Ray.** Bette Davis; Herbert Marshall; James Stephenson; Gale Sondergaard; Bruce Lester; Cecil Kellaway; Victor Sen Yung; Frieda Inescort; ***D:*** William Wyler; ***W:*** Howard Koch; ***C:*** Gaetano Antonio "Tony" Gaudio; ***M:*** Max Steiner.

The Letter **2012 (R)** As bewildering and vague as its characters. Playwright/director Martine (Ryder) is in rehearsals for her new work that stars her boyfriend Raymond (Hamilton). Actor Tyrone (Franco) becomes obsessed with her while Martine suddenly has hallucinations and suffers from paranoia. She also starts rewriting her play that now reflects her fragile mental state. **92m/C; DVD.** Winona Ryder; James Franco; Josh Hamilton; Dagmara Dominczyk; Julie Ann Emery; ***D:*** Jay Anania; ***W:*** Jay Anania. **VIDEO**

Letter from an Unknown Woman **1948** In Vienna, Lisa (Fontaine) is seduced by concert pianist Stefan (Jourdan) who goes off on tour. She's pregnant and eventually marries another (Journet) though she remains obsessed with Stefan. Lisa and Stefan meet again years later but the womanizer doesn't remember her until he receives a letter. Told in flashbacks; implausible but madly romantic story of doomed love. **90m/B; DVD, Blu-Ray.** Joan Fontaine; Louis Jourdan; Mady Christians; Marcel Journet; Art Smith; ***D:*** Max Ophuls; ***W:*** Howard Koch; ***C:*** Franz Planer; ***M:*** Daniele Amfitheatrof. Natl. Film Reg. '92.

Letter of Introduction **1/2 1938** A struggling young actress learns that her father is really a well known screen star and agrees not to reveal the news to the public. **104m/B; VHS, DVD.** Adolphe Menjou; Edgar Bergen; George Murphy; Eve Arden; Ann Sheridan; Andrea Leeds; ***D:*** John M. Stahl; ***C:*** Karl Freund.

A Letter to Momo **1/2** *Momo e no tegami* **2011** Seven years in production, director/writer Okiura's delicate variation on using fantasy to deal with grief is a beautiful piece of hand-drawn animation. The title refers to a piece of paper left to Momo by her father that contains only two words—"Dear Momo." What did her father want to write to her before he passed? Forced to move from Tokyo to her mother's small hometown, Momo befriends three supernatural imps who help her process the loss of her father and even provide closure to that incomplete letter. Gentle, sweet, and moving tale that impressively balances fantasy and realism. **120m/C; DVD.** *JP V:* Karen Miyama; Toshiyuki Nishida; Koichi Yamadera; Yuka; ***D:*** Hiroyuki Okiura; ***W:*** Hiroyuki Okiura; ***C:*** Koji Tanada; ***M:*** Mina Kubota.

A Letter to Three Wives **1949** Crain, Darnell, and Sothern star as three friends who, shortly before embarking on a Hudson River boat trip, each receive a letter from Holm (who's never shown), the fourth member in their set. The letter tells them that she has run off with one of their husbands but does not specify his identity. The women spend the rest of the trip reviewing their sometimes shaky unions, which provides some of the funniest and most caustic scenes. Sharp dialogue, moving performances. Based on the novel by John Klempner. Remade for TV in 1985. **103m/B; VHS, DVD.** Jeanne Crain; Linda Darnell; Ann Sothern; Kirk Douglas; Paul Douglas; Jeffrey Lynn; Thelma Ritter; Barbara Lawrence; Connie Gilchrist; Florence Bates; ***V:*** Celeste Holm; ***D:*** Joseph L. Mankiewicz; ***W:*** Joseph L. Mankiewicz; ***C:*** Arthur C. Miller; ***M:*** Alfred Newman. Oscars '49: Director (Mankiewicz), Screenplay; Directors Guild '48: Director (Mankiewicz).

The Letter Writer **1/2 2011** A rebellious teen gets a letter from an unknown author praising her and she sets out to track him down. **86m/C; DVD, Blu-Ray, Streaming.** Aley Underwood; Bernie Diamond; Pam Eichner; Stella McComas; Kylee Thurman; ***D:*** Christian Vuissa; ***W:*** Christian Vuissa; ***C:*** David A. Skousen; ***M:*** Jimmy Schafer. **TV**

The Letters **1/2 2015 (PG)** A biographical fictional film of the life of Mother Theresa (Stevenson). The film tells the Catholic nun's inspirational life story through over five decades of letters with Father Celeste van Exem (von Sydow), her spiritual advisor. From her earliest days to her work in the harsh slums of India to her death, the film also examines her personal struggles, self-doubts, sacrifices, and personal anguish.

104m/C; DVD, Streaming, Download. Juliet Stevenson; Max von Sydow; Rutger Hauer; Priya Darshini; Kranti Redkar; *D:* William Riead; *W:* William Riead; *C:* Jack N. Green; *M:* Ciaran Hope.

Letters from a Killer 🦴🦴 **1998 (R)** Death-row con Race Darnell (Swayze) has been corresponding with four women every since writing a best-seller about his life in prison. After a new trial overturns his conviction and sets him free, Race discovers that one of his correspondents—who believed she was his only love—is framing him for murder in revenge for his "betrayal" of her. **103m/C; VHS, DVD.** Patrick Swayze; Gia Carides; Kim Myers; Olivia Birkelund; Tina Lifford; Elizabeth Ruscio; Roger E. Mosley; Bruce McGill; Mark Rolston; *D:* David Carson; *W:* Nicholas Hicks-Beach; *C:* John A. Alonzo; *M:* Dennis McCarthy.

Letters from Iwo Jima 🦴🦴🦴🦴 **2006 (R)** Recounts the dramatic 36 days of battle on Iwo Jima that began in February 1945, as told from the Japanese viewpoint; serves as a companion to director Eastwood's "Flags of Our Fathers." Facing a completely lopsided confrontation, the 22,000 Japanese military men kept 110,000 American troops in combat far longer than anticipated under the guidance of the gifted Lt. Gen. Tadamichi Kuribayashi (Watanabe), whose letters to his wife provide the story's narrative. Eastwood sets a somber tone, using muted colors to capture the humanity of the Japanese soldiers. First screenplay by Yamashita after being a research assistant on "Flags." Japanese with subtitles. **145m/C; DVD, Blu-Ray, HD-DVD.** Ken(saku) Watanabe; Tsuyoski Ihara; Shido Nakamura; Kazunari Ninomiya; Ryo Kase; *D:* Clint Eastwood; *W:* Iris Yamashita; Paul Haggis; *C:* Tom Stern; *M:* Kyle Eastwood; Michael Stevens. Oscars '06: Sound FX Editing; Golden Globes '07: Foreign Film.

Letters to Juliet 🦴🦴 **1/2 2010 (PG)** Cynics will harp on the cliches and grouse about sappiness. Romantics will give into the beauty of Italy and relax into the story. American Sophie (Seyfried) travels to Italy with her busy fiance Victor (Garcia Bernal). Shes leaves him to visit Verona, the setting for Shakespeare's tragedy "Romeo and Juliet," and meets a group of women who reply to letters found in the lovers' balcony courtyard. Sophie's reply to a lost letter from 1951 inspires Brit Claire (Redgrave) to travel to Italy in search of her former love Lorenzo (Nero) and also gets Sophie involved in an unexpected romance with Claire's grumpy grandson Charlie (Egan). **105m/C; Blu-Ray, On Demand.** Amanda Seyfried; Vanessa Redgrave; Christopher Egan; Franco Nero; Gael Garcia Bernal; *D:* Gary Winick; *W:* Jose Rivera; Tim Sullivan; *C:* Marco Pontecorvo; *M:* Andrea Guerra.

Letting Go 🦴🦴 **1985 (PG)** Comedy-drama about a broken-hearted career woman and a young widower who fall in love. **94m/C; VHS, DVD.** John Ritter; Sharon Gless; Joe Cortese; *D:* Jack Bender. **TV**

Letting Go 🦴🦴 **2012** A romantic about one man's quest for self-discovery and recovery. For Joel Slater (Torem), letting go is extremely difficult even when it negatively impacts his life. When his demanding girlfriend considers leaving him for a new life, Joel begins to examine how own life. He has an employer who is his best friend but has no boundaries, while his biggest client is a sociopath. Just as demanding is Joel's home life which includes three big dogs. For Joel, figuring out the secret to true happiness changes his perspective on everything. **83m/C; DVD, Streaming, Download.** Jake Torem; Shirly Brener; Luca Bercovici; Greg Baker; Christopher Knight; *D:* Jake Torem; *W:* Jake Torem; *C:* David C. Smith. **VIDEO**

The Levenger Tapes 🦴🦴 **2016 (R)** A horror-thriller about a disturbing missing persons case. When three college students go missing, small town detectives only have a very disturbing piece of videotape as evidence. As they go through the footage, they learn that the students had found the bloody dress of a child in the woods and went to look for her. Using all they know from the tape, the detectives try to solve both cases in time to find all four of them alive. **92m/C; DVD, Streaming, Download.** Johanna Braddy; Lili Mirojnick; Morgan Krantz; Chris Mulkey; John Rosenfeld; *D:* Mark Edwin Robinson; *W:* Mark Edwin Robinson; *C:* Magdalena Gorka; *M:* Amber Ojeda. **VIDEO**

Leviathan 🦴🦴 **1989 (R)** A motley crew of ocean-floor miners are trapped when they are accidentally exposed to a failed Soviet experiment that turns humans into insatiable, regenerating fish-creatures. **98m/C; VHS, DVD, Blu-Ray.** Peter Weller; Ernie Hudson; Hector Elizondo; Amanda Pays; Richard Crenna; Daniel Stern; Lisa Eilbacher; Michael Carmine; Meg Foster; *D:* George P. Cosmatos; *W:* David Peoples; Jeb Stuart; *C:* Alex Thomson; *M:* Jerry Goldsmith.

Leviathan 🦴🦴 **1/2 2013** To say this is simply a documentary about the commercial fishing industry would not do it justice. This unique exploration of the New Bedford (Mass.)-based company shows just how savage the process can be, as the directing/writing team of Castaing-Taylor/Paravel uses an abundance of up-close camera angles that put on full display the mass netting and slaughter of their catch. Not for the weak of stomach yet so beautifully captured it's difficult to not get hooked. **87m/C; DVD.** *FR D:* Lucien Castaing-Taylor; Verena Paravel; *W:* Lucien Castaing-Taylor; Verena Paravel; *C:* Lucien Castaing-Taylor; Verena Paravel.

Leviathan 🦴🦴🦴 **2014** Full-time auto mechanic and part-time drunkard, Kolia (Serebriakov) lives a charmless life alongside wife Lilya (Liadova) in a home that sits proudly on a cliffside overlooking the Barents Sea in northern Russia. But when a corrupt mayor (Madyanov) tries to unlawfully snatch the land for himself, Kolia and his slick lawyer must come up with absurd and clever ways to combat the power of the politician's corrupt leverage. Moments of downright depression don't linger too long, as the proceeding are often interrupted with bouts of dark humor. Prized Russian arthouse director Zvyagintsev is at his satirical best. **140m/C; DVD, Blu-Ray.** *RU* Alexey Serebryakov; Elena Lyadova; Roman Madyanov; Vladimir Vdovitchenkov; Sergey Pokhodaev; *D:* Andrey Zvyagintsev; *W:* Andrey Zvyagintsev; Olga Negin; *C:* Mikhail Krichman; *M:* Philip Glass. Golden Globes '15: Foreign Film.

Levitation 🦴 **1/2 1997** Pregnant teenager, Acey (Paulson), decides to leave her unhappy adoptive parents and search for her birth mother. She has an imaginary friend (possibly her guardian angel) she calls Bob (London) and a real friend, DJ Downtime (Hudson), to help her out but her quest doesn't end in happiness. Title refers to Acey's weird uncontrollable ability to levitate, unfortunately the film doesn't—it's a muddled mess. **99m/C; VHS, DVD.** Sarah Paulson; Ernie Hudson; Jeremy London; Ann Magnuson; Brett Cullen; Christopher Boyer; *D:* Scott Goldstein; *W:* Scott Goldstein; *C:* Michael G. Wojciechowski; *M:* Leonard Rosenman.

Levity 🦴🦴 **2003 (R)** Manuel Jordan (Thornton) is released from prison after serving 22 years for killing a clerk during a botched robbery. He returns to his neighborhood, looking for, but not expecting to find redemption. He gets a job at a community center run by a fire-and-brimstone preacher, finds possible romance with the sister (Hunter) of his victim, and tries to protect her and other troubled souls from contrived coincidences and overwrought sentimentality. Soloman was going for mood and atmosphere, but it's moody and crushingly boring instead. **100m/C; VHS, DVD.** Billy Bob Thornton; Morgan Freeman; Holly Hunter; Kirsten Dunst; Dorian Harewood; Geoff Wigdor; Catherine Colvey; Manuel Aranguiz; Luke Robertson; Billoah Greene; *D:* Edward Solomon; *W:* Edward Solomon; *C:* Roger Deakins; *M:* Mark Oliver Everett.

Lewis and Clark and George 🦴🦴 **1997 (R)** Lewis (Xuereb) is a dim-witted killer and Clark (Gunther) is a computer nerd. Both are prison escapees in possession of what is supposed to be a map to a gold mine. Lewis happens to be illiterate and needs Clark, who's afraid of Lewis's trigger-happy ways. George (McGowan) is a sexy mute thief who takes both men for quite a wild ride. Filmed in rural New Mexico. **84m/C; VHS, DVD.** Salvator Xuereb; Dan Gunther; Rose McGowan; Art LaFleur; Aki Aleong; James Brolin; Paul Bartel; *D:* Rod McCall; *W:* Rod McCall; *C:* Mike Mayers; *M:* Ben Vaughn.

L'Homme Blesse 🦴🦴🦴 *The Wounded Man* **1983** A serious erotic film about 18-year-old Henri (Anglade), cloistered by an overbearing family, and his sudden awakening to his own homosexuality. Anglade's film debut. In French with English subtitles. **90m/C; VHS, DVD.** *FR* Jean-Hugues Anglade; Roland Bertin; Vittorio Mezzogiorno; *D:* Patrice Chereau; *C:* Renato Berta. Cesar '84: Writing.

The Liability 🦴 **1/2 2012 (R)** Jarringly-paced Brit crime drama has teenager Adam wrecking the car of his mum's volatile gangster boyfriend, Peter. To make up for it, Peter gives Adam the job of driving hitman Roy around. Over a 24-hour period, it dawns on Adam that he could be one of Roy's next targets. **86m/C; DVD.** *UK* Tim Roth; Peter Mullan; Jack O'Connell; Kierston Wareing; *D:* Craig Viveiros; *W:* John Wrathall; *C:* James Friend.

Liam 🦴🦴 **2000 (R)** Stuttering, 7-year-old Liam (Borrows) is an Irish Catholic living in Liverpool in the 1930s. His hardworking mother is determined that Liam will look presentable for his first Communion no matter what the sacrifice but his family's struggles worsen when his father (Hart) loses his job and becomes increasingly bitter, blaming his woes on others and turning to violence as a solution. **90m/C; VHS, DVD.** *GE GB* Ian Hart; Claire Hackett; David Hart; Anthony Borrows; Megan Burns; Anne Reid; Russell Dixon; Julia Deakin; Andrew Schofield; Bernadette Shortt; David Corey; *D:* Stephen Frears; *W:* Jimmy McGovern; *C:* Andrew Dunn; *M:* John Murphy.

Liane, Jungle Goddess 🦴🦴 **1956** A variation on the Greystoke legend featuring a beautiful (and topless) jungle goddess who is discovered living in the wilds of Africa. Thinking that she may be the lost granddaughter of a wealthy English nobleman, she's brought back to London for a reunion. Will civilization prove to be as dangerous as the jungle? **88m/C; VHS, DVD.** *GE* Marion Michael; Hardy Kruger; Irene Galter; Peter Mosbacher; *D:* Eduard von Borsody; *W:* Ernst von Salomon; *C:* Bruno Timm; *M:* Erwin Halletz.

Lianna 🦴🦴🦴 **1983 (R)** Acclaimed screenwriter/director John Sayles wrote and directed this story of a woman's romantic involvement with another woman. Chronicles an unhappy homemaker's awakening to the feelings of love that she develops for a female professor. Sayles makes an appearance as a family friend. **110m/C; VHS, DVD.** Jon (John) DeVries; Linda Griffiths; Jane Hallaren; Jo Henderson; Jessica Wright MacDonald; ***Cameo(s):*** John Sayles; *D:* John Sayles; *W:* John Sayles; *M:* Mason Daring.

Liar Liar 🦴🦴 **1/2 1997 (PG-13)** Carrey takes on one of his less manic but still appealing personas as compulsive liar and attorney Fletcher Reid. A constant disappointment to his ex-wife Audrey (Tierney) and young son Max (Cooper), Fletcher is forced to tell nothing but the truth for 24 hours, thanks to his son's supernatural birthday wish. This puts a crimp in his legal practice, especially as he tries to defend brazen would-be divorcee Samantha Cole (Tilly). Gets kinda sappy but Carrey can carry almost any situation. **87m/C; DVD, Blu-Ray, HD-DVD.** Jim Carrey; Jennifer Tilly; Maura Tierney; Amanda Donohoe; Swoosie Kurtz; Justin Cooper; Jason Bernard; Mitchell Ryan; Anne Haney; Chip (Christopher) Mayer; Randall "Tex" Cobb; Cary Elwes; Eric Pierpoint; Cheri Oteri; *D:* Tom Shadyac; *W:* Paul Guay; Stephen Mazur; *C:* Russell Boyd; *M:* John Debney. MTV Movie Awards '98: Comedic Perf. (Carrey).

Liar's Moon 🦴🦴 **1982 (PG)** A local boy woos and weds the town's wealthiest young lady, only to be trapped in family intrigue. **106m/C; VHS, DVD.** Cindy Fisher; Matt Dillon; Christopher Connelly; Susan Tyrrell; *D:* David Fisher.

Liar's Poker 🦴 **1/2 1999** Car salesman Jack (Tyson) invests a quarter-million bucks in friend Vic's (Blondell) club and Vic is beginning to resent Jack's not-to-silent partnership. Married Jack is also competing with bud, Niko (Luisi), for the affections of young babe, Rebecca (Heinle) while his own wife, Linda (Gridley), plays around. And fourth buddy Freddie (Flea) enjoys knowing too much about everybody else's business. It finally comes down to a deadly confrontation between the male foursome. Unfortunately, bland acting and a lack of plot details detract from this macho crime drama's twist ending. **93m/C; VHS, DVD.** Richard Tyson; Flea; Jimmy Blondell; Caesar Luisi; Pamela Gidley; Amelia Heinle; Neith Adriana; Colin Patrick Lynch; *D:* Jeff Santo; *W:* Jeff Santo; *C:* Giles M.I. Dunning; *M:* Peter Himmelman.

Libel 🦴🦴 **1959** After Jeffery Buckenham (Massie) sees British peer Sir Mark Lodden (Bogarde) on TV, he recognizes him as a fellow POW from a German WWII camp. Or maybe he's the lookalike actor who was also in the camp. Buckenham accuses Loddon of being an imposter and Mark is urged to sue him in court for libel. Only problem is Mark suffered severe head injuries during the war, has bouts of amnesia, and isn't sure of his own identity when he's questioned. **100m/B; DVD.** *GB* Dirk Bogarde; Olivia de Havilland; Paul Massie; Robert Morley; Wilfrid Hyde-White; Anthony Dawson; Richard Wattis; Martin Miller; Millicent Martin; *D:* Anthony Asquith; *W:* Anatole de Grunwald; Karl Tunberg; *C:* Robert Krasker; *M:* Benjamin Frankel.

Libeled Lady 🦴🦴🦴 **1/2 1936** A fast, complicated screwball masterwork. Newspaper editor Warren Haggerty (Tracy) prints an erroneous story that heiress Connie Allenbury (Loy) is after a married man. Connie sues and in order to defuse the lawsuit, Warren comes up with an elaborate scheme (certain to backfire) that involves his own fiancee Galdys (Harlow) and recently fired reporter Bill (Powell). Remade in 1946 as "Easy to Wed." **98m/B; VHS, DVD.** Myrna Loy; Spencer Tracy; Jean Harlow; William Powell; Walter Connolly; Charley Grapewin; Cora Witherspoon; E.E. Clive; Charles Trowbridge; Dennis O'Keefe; Hattie McDaniel; *D:* Jack Conway; *W:* George Oppenheimer; Howard Emmett Rogers; Maurine Watkins; *C:* Norbert Brodine; *M:* William Axt.

Liberal Arts 🦴🦴 **1/2 2012 (PG-13)** Like so many men in their 30s, Jesse (Radnor, who also wrote and directed) has had trouble finding definition outside of the halls of his liberal arts college. An invitation by a former professor (Jenkins) to speak at his retirement dinner brings Jesse back into a world in which he felt connection and where he may find it again with student Zibby (Olsen). Radnor displays an affinity for his characters and a gift with dialogue that far surpasses his work in the past and hints at potentially great things to come. **97m/C; DVD, Blu-Ray.** Josh Radnor; Elizabeth Olsen; Richard Jenkins; Allison Janney; Elizabeth Reaser; John Magaro; Kate Burton; Robert Desiderio; Zac Efron; *D:* Josh Radnor; *W:* Josh Radnor; *C:* Seamus Tierney; *M:* Ben Toth.

The Liberation of L.B. Jones 🦴🦴 **1970 (R)** A wealthy black undertaker wants a divorce from his wife, who is having an affair with a white policeman. Wyler's final film. **101m/C; VHS, DVD.** Lee J. Cobb; Lola Falana; Barbara Hershey; Anthony Zerbe; Roscoe Lee Browne; *D:* William Wyler; *W:* Stirling Silliphant; *M:* Elmer Bernstein.

The Liberator 🦴🦴 *Libertador* **2013 (R)** The first big-screen adaptation of the life and times of Venezuela's founding father, Simon Bolivar, and his quest for a unified Latin America. Rising from a young, idealistic aristocrat who learns you simply can't buy freedom, Bolivar (Ramirez) became the country's most important general. But Ramirez can't humanize a person who's only allowed to speak in catch phrases and pull-quotes. Almost insultingly romanticized, Bolivar is portrayed not only as cunning on the battlefield, but a stud in the bedroom. Generic to a fault, this admittedly grand biopic can't liberate itself from a bad script. English, Spanish and French with subtitles. **119m/C; DVD, Blu-Ray.** *VZ SP* Edgar Ramirez; Francisco Denis; Manuel Porto; Imanol Arias; Juana Acosta; Danny Huston; *D:* Alberto Arvelo; *W:* Timothy J. Sexton; *C:* Xavi Giminez; *M:* Gustavo Dudamel.

Liberators 🦴 **1969** Kinski stars as a criminal soldier battling with the American authorities, German troops, and his fugitive partner. **91m/C; VHS, DVD.** *IT* Klaus Kinski; George Hilton; Ray Saunders; Betsy Bell; *D:* Tonino Ricci; *W:* Tonino Ricci; *C:* Sandro Mancori; *M:* Riz Ortolani.

The Libertine 🦴🦴 *La Matriarca* **1969** Mimi (Spaak) is a young widow who's just discovered her late husband kept a separate apartment equipped to satisfy his more unusual sexual desires. Intrigued, Mimi decides to keep the apartment and do her own sexual exploring. Dubbed. **90m/C; VHS, DVD.** *IT* Catherine Spaak; Jean-Louis Trintignant; Luigi Pistilli; Luigi Proietti; Renzo Montagnani; ***D:*** Pasquale Festa Campanile; ***C:*** Alfio Contini; ***M:*** Armando Trovajoli.

The Libertine 1/2 **2005 (R)** Covering a portion of the life of the 17th century's famous degenerate the 2nd Earl of Rochester, John Wilmot (Depp). Depp's portrayal is well done, but the story eventually collapses under its own weight. A little taste of Wilmot's naughtiness might be interesting, even fun, but watching him destroy himself with dreadful behavior over and over begins to feel tiresome. Like watching a heavyweight prize fight, eventually you hope the fallen fighter just stays down, relieving everyone's pain. **130m/C; DVD.** Johnny Depp; Samantha Morton; John Malkovich; Rosamund Pike; Tom Hollander; Kelly Reilly; Jack Davenport; Richard Coyle; Francesca Annis; Rupert Friend; Clare Higgins; Johnny Vegas; ***D:*** Laurence Dunmore; ***W:*** Stephen Jeffreys; ***C:*** Alexander Melman; ***M:*** Michael Nyman.

Liberty Heights 1/2 **1999 (R)** Levinson heads back to Baltimore (for the fourth time) for his 1954 coming of age/family drama with his focus on the city's Jewish community and the Kurtzman family in particular. Nate (Mantegna) has a two-bit numbers racket and a failing burlesque house, college son Van (Brody) falls for a shiksa (Murphy), while high schooler Ben (Foster) is captivated by Sylvia (Johnson), the first black student in his class. It may be too early for Bob Dylan but the times were a-changin' indeed and Levinson takes an unsentimental, if heartfelt, look at his past. **127m/C; VHS, DVD.** Adrien Brody; Joe Mantegna; Ben Foster; Bebe Neuwirth; Rebekah Johnson; Orlando Jones; Frania Rubinek; David Krumholtz; Richard Kline; Vincent Guastaferro; Carolyn Murphy; Justin Chambers; James Pickens, Jr.; Anthony Anderson; Kiersten Warren; ***D:*** Barry Levinson; ***W:*** Barry Levinson; ***C:*** Christopher Doyle; ***M:*** Andrea Morricone.

Liberty Stands Still **2002 (R)** Title lends itself to several interpretations, one of which is literal. Liberty Wallace (Fiorentino) is the wife of gun manufacturer Victor (Platt). She takes a cell call while walking in downtown L.A. and is informed if she doesn't handcuff herself to a nearby hotdog cart and keep talking, she will immediately be shot. Joe (Snipes), the sniper/caller, informs Liberty that he has also placed a bomb in the cart itself. His daughter was murdered by a gun and this is his way to bring attention to the situation. Good cast but the points are belabored—guns bad, we get it. **96m/C; VHS, DVD.** Wesley Snipes; Linda Fiorentino; Oliver Platt; Martin Cummins; Hart Bochner; Jonathan Scarfe; Ian Tracey; ***D:*** Keri Skogland; ***W:*** Keri Skogland; ***C:*** Denis Maloney; ***M:*** Michael Convertino.

The Librarian: Curse of the Judas Chalice 1/2 **2008** Flynn Carsen (Wyle) is a little tired as this third adventure begins but he's soon ready to save the world again when he must find the chalice made from Judas' 30 pieces of silver. This time Flynn has a very unusual assistant, New Orleans nightclub singer Simone (Katic) who's also a vampire babe. Seems the chalice is the key to resurrecting a nasty bloodsucker with a desire for world domination. **90m/C; DVD.** Noah Wyle; Bob Newhart; Jane Curtin; Stana Katic; Bruce Davidson; Dirkan Tulane; ***D:*** Jonathan Frakes; ***W:*** Marco Schnabel; ***C:*** David Connell. **CABLE**

The Librarian: Quest for the Spear 1/2 **2004** Cable comic adventure is Indiana Jones-lite. Flynn Carsen (Wyle) is a perpetual student (22 degrees) who finally lands a job as a librarian at the mysterious Metropolitan Public Library, which contains such top-secret and mythic treasures as Excalibur and the Ark of the Covenant. When the Serpent Brotherhood steals the Spear of Destiny, intrepid geek Flynn is paired up with butt-kicking bodyguard Nicole (Walger) to retrieve the spear before it can be used for evil purposes. **92m/C; DVD.** Noah Wyle; Sonya Walger; Bob Newhart; Jane Curtin; Olympia Dukakis; Kyle MacLachlan; Kelly Hu; ***D:*** Peter Winther; ***W:*** David Titcher; ***C:*** Alan Caso; ***M:*** Joseph LoDuca. **CABLE**

The Librarian: Return to King Solomon's Mines 1/2 **2006** In this second adventure, it's up to brainy-not-brawny librarian Flynn (Wyle) to retrieve the stolen map to the legendary King Solomon's Mines. Aided by attractive archeologist Emily Davenport (Anwar), Flynn learns that some miscreants are counting on using the map to gain possession of the Key of Solomon, a powerful book of magic. **92m/C; DVD.** Noah Wyle; Gabrielle Anwar; Bob Newhart; Jane Curtin; Olympia Dukakis; Erik Avari; Hakeem Kae-Kazim; Robert Foxworth; ***D:*** Jonathan Frakes; ***W:*** Marco Schnabel; ***C:*** Walt Lloyd; ***M:*** Joseph LoDuca. **CABLE**

L'Iceberg 1/2 *The Iceberg* **2005** Slight comedy features much physical humor, little dialogue, and is overly cute. Manager Fiona gets locked in the restaurant's walk-in freezer. Barely alive when she's rescued the next day, Fiona returns home to discover her husband and children didn't even notice her missing. She develops an obsession with everything frozen and cold, so she hides out in a frozen food delivery truck and leaves to make a new home for herself on an iceberg. French with subtitles. **84m/C; DVD.** *BE* Fiona Gordon; Dominique Abel; Bruno Romy; Philippe Martz; ***D:*** Fiona Gordon; Dominique Abel; Bruno Romy; ***W:*** Fiona Gordon; Dominique Abel; Bruno Romy; ***C:*** Sebastien Koeppel; ***M:*** Jacques Luley.

License to Drive **1988 (PG-13)** When teen Haim fails the road test for his all-important driver's license, he steals the family car for a hot date with the girl of his dreams. The evening starts out quietly enough, but things soon go awry. If Haim survives the weekend, he'll definitely be able to pass his driving test on Monday morning. Semi-funny in a demolition derby sort of way. **90m/C; VHS, DVD; Open Captioned.** Corey Feldman; Corey Haim; Carol Kane; Richard Masur; Michael Manasseri; Heather Graham; Nina Siemaszko; James Avery; Grant Heslov; Parley Baer; ***D:*** Greg Beeman; ***C:*** Bruce Surtees; ***M:*** Jay Ferguson.

License to Kill **1964** Constantine stars as Agent Nick Carter involved with Oriental spies and a new secret weapon. **100m/C; VHS, DVD.** *FR* Eddie Constantine; Yvonne Monlaur; Paul Frankeur; ***D:*** Henri Decoin.

License to Kill **1984** A young girl is killed by a drunk driver, devastating both families. Offers a strong message against drinking and driving. **96m/C; VHS, DVD.** James Farentino; Don Murray; Penny Fuller; Millie Perkins; Donald Moffat; Denzel Washington; Ari Meyers; ***D:*** Jud Taylor. **TV**

License to Kill **1989 (PG-13)** Dalton's second Bond effort, in which drug lords try to kill 007's best friend and former CIA agent. Disobeying orders for the first time and operating without his infamous "license to kill," Bond goes after the fiends. Fine outing for Dalton (and Bond, too). **133m/C; DVD, Blu-Ray.** *UK* Timothy Dalton; Carey Lowell; Robert Davi; Frank McRae; Talisa Soto; David Hedison; Anthony Zerbe; Everett McGill; Wayne Newton; Benicio Del Toro; Desmond Llewelyn; Priscilla Barnes; Robert Brown; Tom Adams; Caroline Bliss; ***D:*** John Glen; ***W:*** Michael G. Wilson; Richard Maibaum; ***C:*** Alec Mills; ***M:*** Michael Kamen.

License to Wed **2007 (PG-13)** Nothing redeems this dull, obnoxious comedy that mostly serves as a vehicle for Williams to do the same ad-libbed characters he's been doing for years. Newly engaged couple Ben and Sadie (Krasinski and Moore) must undergo Rev. Frank's (Williams) premarital counseling, but what they get is an endless series of laugh-free, sadism-lite tests of endurance. Nothing, from Ben and Sadie's cliche personality mismatch, to Frank's junior sadist sidekick Choir Boy (Flitter), saves this movie from being a big "I don't" for all involved. **91m/C; DVD, Blu-Ray, HD-DVD.** Robin Williams; Mandy Moore; John Krasinski; Eric Christian Olsen; Christine Taylor; Peter Strauss; Rachael Harris; DeRay Davis; Josh Flitter; Mindy Kaling; ***D:*** Ken Kwapis; ***W:*** Kim Barker; Vince DeMeglio; Tim Rasmussen; ***C:*** John Bailey; ***M:*** Christophe Beck.

The Lickerish Quartet **1970 (R)** A bored, aristocratic couple live with their teenaged son in a secluded castle in Italy's Abruzzi mountains. Traveling to a nearby carnival, they think they recognize the female daredevil as the same actress they've just seen in a home-viewed porno film. So they invite her back to the castle for a little family fun—only she may not be the same woman at all. **90m/C; VHS, DVD.** Silvana Venturelli; Frank Wolff; Erika Remberg; Paolo Turco; ***D:*** Radley Metzger; ***W:*** Michael DeForrest; ***C:*** Hans Jura.

L.I.E. **2001 (NC-17)** 15-year-old Howie's (Dano) mother dies in a car accident on the Long Island Expressway (hence the title) and his world falls apart. Howie starts hanging out with troublemaker Gary (Kay), who's both a thief and a hustler. Gary and Howie break into the home of pedophile ex-Marine, Big John Harrigan (Cox), who confronts the boys and takes a purient interest in Howie's charms. At least at first, since the complex Harrigan realizes Howie really needs some friendly guidance and not a sex partner. Cuesta offers no apologies or explanations for the behavior he depicts and Cox is both commanding and subtle. **97m/C; DVD.** Brian Cox; Paul Dano; Billy Kay; Bruce Altman; James Costa; Tony Donnelly; Walter Masterson; Marcia DeBonis; Adam LeFevre; ***D:*** Michael Cuesta; ***W:*** Michael Cuesta; Stephen M. Ryder; Gerald Cuesta; ***C:*** Romeo Tirone; ***M:*** Pierre Foldes. Ind. Spirit '02: Debut Perf. (Dano).

Lie Down with Dogs **1995 (R)** You will wake up with fleas if you watch this dull, very low-budget comedy about young Tommie (White), who heads out of New York for some summer fun in the gay-friendly resort of Provincetown, Massachusetts. There's lots of temporary (discreetly filmed) encounters but no lasting romance and Tommie heads back to the Big Apple at season's end satisfied but no wiser. White's debut film. **85m/C; VHS, DVD.** Wally White; Randy Becker; Darren Dryden; ***D:*** Wally White; ***W:*** Wally White; ***C:*** George Mitas.

Liebestraum **1991 (R)** An architectural expert, his old college friend, and the friend's wife form a dangerous triangle of passion and lust that strangely duplicates a situation that led to a double murder 40 years earlier. The unrated version clocks in at 116 minutes. **109m/C; VHS, DVD.** Kevin Anderson; Bill Pullman; Pamela Gidley; Kim Novak; ***D:*** Mike Figgis; ***W:*** Mike Figgis; ***C:*** Juan Ruiz-Anchia; ***M:*** Mike Figgis.

Lies & Alibis 1/2 *The Alibi* **2006 (R)** Ray Elliot (Coogan) runs a successful L.A. service that offers alibis to cheating spouses. But he doesn't expect Wendell (Marsden), the screw-up son of Ray's best client, tycoon Robert Hatch (Brolin), to accidentally kill his fling Heather (King) during some kinky sex play. So Ray and his new assistant Lola (Romijn), she of the cool head and hot bod, have to really come up with a good alibi, especially when a police detective (Mazar) comes around. Clever crime comedy with Coogan a capable leading man and old pros Brolin and Elliott (as an unhappy Mormon with a cheating wife) obviously enjoying their roles. **90m/C; DVD.** Steve Coogan; Rebecca Romijn; James Brolin; John Leguizamo; James Marsden; Sam Elliott; Debi Mazar; Selma Blair; Deborah Kara Unger; Henry Rollins; Sharon Lawrence; Jaime King; ***D:*** Matt Checkowski; Kurt Mattila; ***W:*** Noah Hawley; ***C:*** Enrique Chediak; ***M:*** Alexandre Desplat.

Lies and Crimes 1/2 **2007** When her undercover cop husband Eddie is killed, Sally moves to his small hometown to regroup. She finds some big city problems there, including a prescription drug ring that stretches back to the life she left behind. When Eddie gets accused of being a dirty cop, Sally decides to find the truth. **90m/C; DVD.** Estella Warren; Art Hindle; J.D Nicholson; James McGowan; Tamara Hope; Richard Fitzpatrick; ***D:*** Mario Azzopardi; ***W:*** Morrie Ruvinsky; ***C:*** John Dyer; ***M:*** Stacey Hersh. **CABLE**

Lies and Illusions **2009 (R)** When his fiancee Samantha (Schultz) disappears, successful self-help author Wes Wilson (Slater) finds himself targeted by her ruthless boss Isaac (Gooding Jr.), who says Samantha stole from him. Suddenly, Wes learns that the woman he was planning to marry is involved in an international smuggling ring but he's clueless as to what's going on. So's the movie, which is implausible and dull. **93m/C; DVD.** Christian Slater; Cuba Gooding, Jr.; Christa Campbell; Sarah Ann Schultz; Robert Giardina; Al Madrigal; ***D:*** Tibor Takacs; ***C:*** Zoran Popovic; ***M:*** Stephen (Steve) Edwards. **VIDEO**

Lies and Whispers *Prague Duet* **1998 (R)** American child psychologist Dr. Lauren Graham (Gershon) is attending a medical convention in Prague, meets dissident Czech writer Jiri Kolmar (Serbedzija), falls instantly in love, and becomes engaged. Lauren decides to explore her own family's ties to the country and discovers grandad was a Nazi war criminal—a very embarassing revelation for Jiri, who's about to be appointed to a government post. **99m/C; VHS, DVD.** Gina Gershon; Rade Serbedzija; Patricia Hodge; Otakar Brousek; Gordon Lovitt; Stuart Milligan; ***D:*** Roger L. Simon; ***W:*** Roger L. Simon; Sheryl Longin; ***C:*** Ivan Slapeta; ***M:*** Boris Zelkin.

Lies Before Kisses **1992 (PG-13)** A woman finds out her loving husband has been spending time with a beautiful call girl. When the call girl is murdered the husband is accused. His wife decides to help him clear his name but she just may have her own type of revenge in mind. **93m/C; VHS, DVD.** Jaclyn Smith; Ben Gazzara; Nick Mancuso; Greg Evigan; Penny Fuller; James Karen; ***D:*** Lou Antonio; ***W:*** Ellen Weston.

Lies I Told My Little Sister **2014** A comedy-drama about a family vacation taken in the wake of a death. When her oldest sister dies, Cory Webber (Walters) agrees to take a family trip to Cape Cod. Cory is now a 30-year-old nature photographer and used to working around the world. Guilted into the vacation, Cory must deal with her younger sister Sarah (Minshew) whom she used to torment and the ingrained patterns of family life. During the trip, the family's tenuous bond is forever changed by secrets, truths, recriminations, and revelations. **98m/C; DVD, Streaming, Download.** Lucy Walters; Alicia Minshew; Ellen Foley; Donovan Patton; Bekka Walker; ***D:*** William J. Stribling; ***W:*** Jonathan Weisbrod; Judy White; ***C:*** Alex Gallitano; ***M:*** Dylan Glatthorn. **VIDEO**

Lies My Mother Told Me **2005** Career con woman/thief Laren Sims (Richardson) decides to make a change and start over again with teenaged daughter Haylei (Panettiere) in Las Vegas. Laren meets and marries wealthy, alcoholic lawyer/rancher Lucas McKenzie (Feore) but she can't help going back to her old ways and gets into more trouble when Lucas finds out about her past. Based on a true crime story. **90m/C; DVD.** Joely Richardson; Hayden Panettiere; Colm Feore; Kailin See; Joe Norman Shaw; Barbara Wilson; ***D:*** Christian Duguay; ***W:*** Matt Dorff; ***C:*** Christian Duguay; ***M:*** Normand Corbeil. **CABLE**

Lt. Robin Crusoe, U.S.N. **1966 (G)** A lighthearted navy pilot crash lands amusingly on a tropical island, falls hard for an island babe and schemes intensely against the local evil ruler. Lackluster Disney debacle. **113m/C; VHS, DVD.** Dick Van Dyke; Nancy Kwan; Akim Tamiroff; ***D:*** Byron Paul; ***M:*** Robert F. Brunner.

Life 1/2 **1999 (R)** New Yorkers Ray (Murphy) and Claude (Lawrence) head south on a moonshine run to pay off a debt to a bootlegger (James). Along the way, ther're framed for murder and sentenced to life on a Mississippi prison farm. Through the years, the two develop a deep, but insult-filled friendship while adjusting to prison life and harboring dreams of freedom. Murphy and Lawrence click well as a comic team, and the movie is best when it stays out of their way. The institutionalized racism of the setting is treated superficially, with the prison appearing to be, despite the slave-like work and gun-toting guards, not an entirely horrible place to live. **108m/C; VHS, DVD, Blu-Ray.** Eddie Murphy; Martin Lawrence; Ned Beatty; Cicely Tyson; Clarence Williams, III; Obba Babatunde; Bernie Mac; Michael "Bear" Taliferro; Miguel A. Nunez, Jr.; Bokeem Woodbine; Barry (Shabaka) Henley; Brent Jennings; Guy Torry; Lisa Nicole Carson; O'Neal Compton; Poppy Montgomery; Ned Vaughn; R. Lee Ermey; Nick Cassavetes; Noah Emmerich; Anthony Anderson; Rick James; ***D:*** Ted (Edward) Demme; ***W:*** Robert Ramsey; Matthew Stone; ***C:*** Geoffrey Simpson; ***M:*** Nelust Wyclef Jean.

Life 🦴🦴🦴 **2015 (R)** A self-conscious biopic about the relationship between iconic actor James Dean (DeHaan) and photographer Dennis Stock (Pattinson). Focusing on the years that Dean was on the verge of Hollywood stardom, Stock is an ambitious young photographer working in Tinsel Town. Recognizing Dean's potential, Stock successfully proposes an in-depth spread featuring the actor to Life magazine. His pictures become some of the best-known images of Dean, but also provide Stock with funds to support his family. As expected from director and former photographer Anton Corbijn, the visuals are stunning though somewhat dull at times despite solid work by the leads. **111m/C; DVD.** Robert Pattinson; Dane DeHaan; Peter J. Lucas; Lauren Gallagher; Alessandra Mastronardi; ***D:*** Anton Corbijn; ***W:*** Luke Davies; ***C:*** Charlotte Bruus Christensen; ***M:*** Owen Pallett.

Life 🦴🦴 **1/2 2017 (R)** Blending elements of sci-fi horror films you've seen before—mostly "Alien" and "Gravity"—the latest proof that we should never go to outer space is well-made but ultimately not extraordinary. The plot is simple enough in that the minute a space station makes the first discovery of life outside of planet Earth, moviegoers know that said life is going to kill them. Can they survive long enough to get back to the safety of Earth without bringing the deadly life force with them? Despite its flaws, it features a strong ensemble with an ending that will keep viewers in suspense. **104m/C; DVD, Blu-Ray.** Jake Gyllenhaal; Rebecca Ferguson; Ryan Reynolds; Hiroyuki (Henry) Sanada; Olga Dihovichnaya; Ariyon Bakare; ***D:*** Daniel Espinosa; ***W:*** Rhett Reese; Paul Wernick; ***C:*** Seamus McGarvey; ***M:*** Jon Ekstrand.

Life, Above All 🦴🦴 **1/2 2010 (PG-13)** Heart-breaking South African drama. Overburdened, 12-year-old Chandra and her family are ostracized in their small township after it's learned that her mother Lillian has AIDS since the townsfolk believe the disease is some kind of divine punishment. Lillian is forced out, but Chandra isn't having any of it and is determined to bring her mother home. Although the film is rated PG13, it's unlikely to be viewed by younger audiences unused to a subtitled, foreign-language (the South African language of Sotho) pic. **100m/C; DVD, Blu-Ray.** *SA GE* Khomotso Manyaka; Lerato Mvelase; Harriet Lenabe; ***D:*** Oliver Schmitz; ***W:*** Dennis Foon; ***C:*** Bernhard Jasper; ***M:*** Ali N. Askin.

Life After Beth 🦴🦴 **2014 (R)** Beth Slocum (Plaza) is dead. Her boyfriend Zach (DeHaan) isn't happy about it. He perks up when Beth comes back from the other side, but she's not quite right in director/writer Baena's zom-rom-com (zombie romantic comedy). The premise offers a unique take on the glutted undead movie genre. But despite being incredibly short, it drags like a zombie moving through the mud. The cast is likable and leads are talented, but they can't save this lifeless affair. **91m/C; DVD, Blu-Ray.** Aubrey Plaza; Dane DeHaan; John C. Reilly; Molly Shannon; Cheryl Hines; Paul Reiser; Matthew Gray Gubler; Anna Kendrick; ***D:*** Jeff Baena; ***W:*** Jeff Baena; ***C:*** Jay Hunter.

The Life and Adventures of Nicholas Nickleby 🦴🦴🦴 **1/2** *Nicholas Nickleby* **1981** Nine-hour performance of the 1838 Dickens' tale by the Royal Shakespeare Company, featuring the work of 39 actors portraying 150 characters. Wonderful performances are characterized by frantic action and smoothly meshing intertwining plots, focusing on the trials and tribulations of the Nickleby family, amidst wealth, poverty, and injustice in Victorian England. Nine cassettes. **540m/C; VHS, DVD.** *GB* Roger Rees; David Thewlis; Emily Richard; John Woodvine; ***D:*** Jim (James) Goddard; ***W:*** David Edgar; ***M:*** Stephen Oliver.

The Life and Death of Colonel Blimp 🦴🦴🦴🦴 *Colonel Blimp* **1943** Chronicles the life of a British soldier who survives three wars (Boer, WWI, and WWII), falls in love with three women (all portrayed by Kerr), and dances a fine waltz. Fine direction and performance abound. **115m/C; VHS, DVD, Blu-Ray.** *GB* Roger Livesey; Deborah Kerr; Anton Walbrook; Ursula Jeans; Albert Lieven; John Varley; ***D:*** Michael Powell; Emeric Pressburger; ***C:*** Georges Perinal.

The Life and Loves of Mozart 🦴🦴 **1/2 1959** Despite the title, this is really about the great composer's later life at the time of the premiere of "Die Zauberfloete" ("The Magic Flute"). This is only partly saved by a stellar performance from Werner, as well as the music. Other than that, it gets bogged down in titillation about W.A.M.'s romantic life. In German with English subtitles. **87m/C; VHS, DVD.** Oskar Werner; Johanna (Hannerl) Matz; Angelika Hauff; ***V:*** Anton Dermota; ***D:*** Karl Hartl.

Life and Nothing But 🦴🦴🦴 **1/2** *La Vie est Rien d'Autre* **1989 (PG)** Two young women search for their lovers at the end of WWI. They're helped by a French officer brutalized by the war and driven to find all of France's casualties. Romantic, evocative, and saddening. In French with English subtitles. **135m/C; VHS, DVD.** *FR* Philippe Noiret; Sabine Azema; Francois Perrot; ***D:*** Bertrand Tavernier; ***W:*** Bertrand Tavernier; ***C:*** Bruno de Keyzer. British Acad. '89: Foreign Film; Cesar '90: Actor (Noiret), Score; L.A. Film Critics '90: Foreign Film.

Life and Nothing More . . . 🦴🦴 *And Life Goes On . . .; Zendegi Va Digar Hich . . .* **1992** Following Iran's devastating 1990 earthquake, a filmmaker and his son search for the young actors who previously worked with him to see if they've survived, meeting various villagers trying to rebuild their lives. Sequel to Kiarostami's film "Where Is My Friend's House?" and followed by "Through the Olive Trees." Farsi with subtitles. **91m/C; VHS, DVD.** *IA* Farhad Kheradmand; Pooya Payvar; ***D:*** Abbas Kiarostami; ***W:*** Abbas Kiarostami; ***C:*** Homayun Payvar.

Life & Nothing More *La vida y nada más* **2017 114m/C.** *SP US* Regina Williams; Andrew Bleechington; ***D:*** Antonio Méndez Esparza; ***W:*** Antonio Méndez Esparza; ***C:*** Barbu Balasoiu.

The Life and Times of Hank Greenberg 🦴🦴🦴🦴 **1999 (PG)** Excellent documentary tells the story of Detroit Tiger Hall of Fame first baseman Hank Greenberg though interviews with sportswriters, teammates, other players of the era, and fans (many of which were young Jewish boys who later became famous themselves), and archival footage from on and off the field. Details Greenberg's struggles as a high-profile Jew in a very anti-Semitic era and as a hero and source of inspiration to the Jewish community. Also does a fine job of exploring the settings (New York and Detroit during the '20s and '30s) in which Greenberg grew up and rose to stardom. **95m/C; VHS, DVD.** ***D:*** Aviva Kempner; ***W:*** Aviva Kempner.

Life & Times of Judge Roy Bean 🦴🦴 **1/2 1972 (PG)** Based on the life of the famed Texas "hanging judge," the film features Newman as the legendary Bean who dispenses frontier justice in the days of the Wild West. Filled with gallows humor. Gardner sparkles as actress Lily Langtry. **124m/C; VHS, DVD, Blu-Ray.** Paul Newman; Stacy Keach; Ava Gardner; Jacqueline Bisset; Anthony Perkins; Roddy McDowall; Victoria Principal; ***D:*** John Huston; ***W:*** John Milius; ***M:*** Maurice Jarre.

Life, Animated 🦴🦴🦴 **2016 (PG)** Roger Ross Williams' documentary adaptation of Ron Suskind's non-fiction book is a beautiful story of how we all use cinema to interpret the world and how film has the power to break down seemingly impenetrable barriers. When he was just a child, Owen Suskind stopped communicating with anybody. He was silent for years, trapped deep in the prison that is autism. His parents and doctors had no idea what to do, but mom and dad knew that Owen liked Disney movies. And then he started using quotes and characters from his favorite animated films to communicate. Try not to cry. **89m/C; DVD.** Owen Suskind; Ron Suskind; Jonathan Freeman; Gilbert Gottfried; ***D:*** Roger Ross Williams; ***W:*** Ron Suskind; ***C:*** Thomas Bergmann; ***M:*** Todd Griffin.

The Life Aquatic with Steve Zissou 🦴🦴 **2004 (R)** Anderson's muddled comedy follows the career of oceanographer Steve Zissou (Murray), famed for his series of pop-culture documentaries. Zissou's latest mission is to take revenge on the shark that ate his longtime partner (Cassel). Besides his motley crew (including Dafoe and Gambon), there is Zissou's business partner/wife Eleanor (Huston), nosy reporter Jane (Blanchett), and amiable newcomer Ned (Wilson), who may be Steve's illegitimate son, as well as his archrival, slick Alistair Hennessey (Goldblum). The detached and melancholy Murray appears to be going through the motions as the rest of cast follows along in his wake. **118m/C; VHS, DVD, Blu-Ray.** Bill Murray; Owen Wilson; Cate Blanchett; Anjelica Huston; Willem Dafoe; Jeff Goldblum; Michael Gambon; Bud Cort; Seymour Cassel; ***D:*** Wes Anderson; ***W:*** Wes Anderson; Noah Baumbach; ***C:*** Robert Yeoman; ***M:*** Mark Mothersbaugh; Randall Poster.

Life as a House 🦴🦴 **1/2 2001 (R)** Architect George (Kline) lives in a rundown shack surrounded by ritzy homes on California's Pacific shore while his ex-wife Robin (Scott Thomas) raises their drugged-out Goth son Sam (Christensen). In quick succession, George is fired from his job and learns he has a fatal disease. He decides to use his remaining time to tear down the old house and build a new one. George forces Sam to help him as a means to repair their relationship while Robin's feelings for George also rekindle. The performances of the excellent ensemble cast save this from sappy symbolism. **124m/C; VHS, DVD.** Kevin Kline; Hayden Christensen; Kristin Scott Thomas; Jena Malone; Mary Steenburgen; Jamey Sheridan; Scott Bakula; Sam Robards; Mike Weinberg; Scotty Leavenworth; Ian Somerhalder; Sandra Nelson; ***D:*** Irwin Winkler; ***W:*** Mark Andrus; ***C:*** Vilmos Zsigmond; ***M:*** Mark Isham. Natl. Bd. of Review '01: Breakthrough Perf. (Christensen).

Life As We Know It 🦴🦴 **2010 (PG-13)** Offers sitcom predictability, two attractive leads playing very familiar roles, and a really cute baby. Uptight caterer Holly (Heigl) and horndog network sports director Eric (Duhamel) have two things in common: mutual best friends and being named the guardians of their friends' infant daughter, Sophie. When the unthinkable happens, these mismatched, work-driven singles must set aside their differences to do what's best, even if it means moving in together. **113m/C; Blu-Ray.** Katherine Heigl; Josh Duhamel; Josh(ua) Lucas; Christina Hendricks; Melissa McCarthy; Hayes Macarthur; Will Sasso; Sarah Burns; ***D:*** Greg Berlanti; ***W:*** Ian Deitchman; Kristin Rusk Robinson; ***C:*** Andrew Dunn; ***M:*** Blake Neely.

The Life Before Her Eyes 🦴🦴 **1/2** *In Bloom* **2007 (R)** Diana (Thurman) attempts to engage in her current life as an educator, wife and mother while wrestling with the devastating memories of a Columbine-like tragedy she survived some 15 years earlier. The story shifts between present and past memories where wild teen Diana (Wood) is inseparable from her strait-laced best friend Maureen (Amurri). As the tragedy's anniversary approaches, Diana's grip on her sanity becomes increasingly strained. Director Perelman uses images from the past filled with life and energy to illustrate the incredible toll of surviving such trauma although the melodrama may be too much for some. **90m/C; Blu-Ray, On Demand.** Uma Thurman; Evan Rachel Wood; Eva Amurri; Jack Gilpin; Oscar Marcus; Gabrielle Brennan; Brett Gilpin; ***D:*** Vadim Perelman; ***W:*** Emil Stern; ***C:*** Pawel Edelman; ***M:*** James Horner.

The Life Before This 🦴🦴 **1999** Complicated tale has six overlapping stories and 44 characters that follow the lives of a group of Torontonians for 12 hours and ends in a casino heist and a related cafe shootout. Film begins and ends with the shooting and takes place in flashbacks that show how each person came to be in the wrong place at the wrong time. Very loosely based on a true incident. **92m/C; VHS, DVD.** *CA* Leslie Hope; David Hewlett; Joel S. Keller; Jacob Tierney; Alberta Watson; Jennifer Dale; Dan Lett; Catherine O'Hara; Martha Burns; Joe Pantoliano; Sarah Polley; Stephen Rea; Callum Keith Rennie; ***D:*** Gerard Ciccoritti; ***W:*** Semi Chellas; ***C:*** Norayr Kasper; ***M:*** Ron Sures. Genie '99: Support. Actress (O'Hara).

Life Begins at Eight-Thirty 🦴🦴 **1942** Curtain going up! At least that's what once-renowned theater actor Madden Thomas (Woolley) wishes. His alcohol problem and acerbic manner has driven everyone away, including his loyal daughter Kathy (Lupino). She does have a new beau, writer Robert (Wilde), who tries to help Madden make a comeback. Upon learning that Kathy and Robert plan to marry and move to L.A., the old man nearly ruins everyone's lives again. Based on the Emlyn Williams play "The Light of the Heart." **85m/B; DVD.** Monty Woolley; Ida Lupino; Cornel Wilde; Sara Allgood; Melville Cooper; J. Edward Bromberg; ***D:*** Irving Pichel; ***W:*** Nunnally Johnson; ***C:*** Edward Cronjager; ***M:*** Alfred Newman.

Life Begins at Forty 🦴🦴 **1/2 1935** Small-town newspaper owner Kenesaw Clark (Rogers) befriends young Lee Austin (Cromwell), who was framed for bank robbery. In retaliation, banker Abercrombie (Barbier) forecloses on the paper, but that doesn't stop Clark's investigation. Meanwhile, he decides to humiliate Abercrombie by cleaning up town bum Meriwether (Summerville) and making him Abercrombie's opposing candidate in a political race. **85m/B; DVD.** Will Rogers; Richard Cromwell; George Barbier; Rochelle Hudson; Jane Darwell; Slim Summerville; Sterling Holloway; Thomas Beck; Roger Imhof; Charles Sellon; ***D:*** George Marshall; ***W:*** Lamar Trotti; ***C:*** Harry Jackson.

Life Begins for Andy Hardy 🦴🦴🦴 **1941** Andy gets a job in New York before entering college and finds the working world to be a sobering experience. Surprisingly downbeat and hard-hitting for an Andy Hardy film. Garland's last appearance in the series. **100m/B; VHS, DVD; Open Captioned.** Mickey Rooney; Judy Garland; Lewis Stone; Ann Rutherford; Fay Holden; Gene Reynolds; Ralph Byrd; ***D:*** George B. Seitz.

Life Blood 🦴 **2009 (R)** Here's one plot that's weird even by trashy, direct-to-video standards. On New Year's Eve in 1968 Brooke confesses to lover Rhea that she did something really bad but it was all for the good of mankind. God appears, doesn't see it that way, and decides to smite Brooke. However, God also decides Rhea's worth saving and wants her to become an evil-fighting angel. Things later go completely cazy as the gals morph into hot lingerie-wearing vamps. **85m/C; DVD.** Sophie Monk; Angela Lindvall; Patrick Renna; Charles Napier; Anya Lahairi; Scout Taylor-Compton; Justin Shilton; ***D:*** Ron Carlson; ***W:*** Ron Carlson; ***C:*** Marc Carter; ***M:*** John D'Andrea. **VIDEO**

Life During Wartime 🦴🦴 **2009 (R)** Setting his story in Miami's Jewish community, Solondz updates (using different actors) the characters and stories from his equally disturbing 1998 film "Happiness." Child molester William (Hinds) wants to reconnect with his sons after being released from prison. Meanwhile, the Jordan sisters—Trish (Janney), Joy (Henderson), and Helen (Sheedy)?endure their own personal crises based on past traumas. **96m/C; Blu-Ray, On Demand.** Shirley Henderson; Allison Janney; Ciaran Hinds; Dylan Riley Snyder; Christopher Marquette; Paul (Pee-wee Herman) Reubens; Michael Lerner; Rich Pecci; Ally Sheedy; Michael K(enneth) Williams; Charlotte Rampling; Gaby Hoffman; Renee Taylor; ***D:*** Todd Solondz; ***W:*** Todd Solondz; ***C:*** Edward Lachman; ***M:*** Doug Bernheim.

Life Happens 🦴 **1/2 2011 (R)** Whiny comedy about irresponsibility. Faced with an unexpected pregnancy, L.A. party girl Kim (Ritter) wants to have her baby. She gets some help from her roommate Deena (Bosworth) but finds managing motherhood, career, and possible romance a challenge. **101m/C; DVD, Blu-Ray.** Krysten Ritter; Kate (Catherine) Bosworth; Rachel Bilson; Geoff Stults; Justin Kirk; ***D:*** Kat Coiro; ***W:*** Krysten Ritter; Kat Coiro; ***C:*** Doug Chamberlain; ***M:*** Mateo Messina. **VIDEO**

Life in the Fast Lane 🦴🦴 **2000 (R)** Mona has accidentally killed her boyfriend. And when his ghost starts to follow her everywhere, Mona realizes how much she still loves him. So just how do you make a romance between a live girl and a dead guy work? **92m/C; VHS, DVD.** Fairuza Balk; Patrick Dempsey; Tea Leoni; Debi Mazar; Noah Taylor; Udo Kier.

A Life in the Theater 🦴🦴 **1/2 1993** Life in the theatre as a hammy stage veteran (Lemmon) shares his experiences (and his dressing room) with a callow newcomer (Broderick). Petty squabbles, missed cues, and rare candor are displayed as the two stage scenes from their various repertory. Gentle, slight Mamet play, written when he was 25. Made for TNT. **78m/C; DVD.** Jack Lemmon; Matthew Broderick; ***D:*** Gregory Mosher; ***W:*** David Mamet; ***C:*** Freddie Francis; ***M:*** David Michael Frank. **CABLE**

A Life Interrupted **2007** In 1989, Debbie Smith (Thompson) is raped and her marriage and entire life are affected. After a six-year wait, a chance DNA match leads to her rapist's arrest but when Debbie learns how many rape kits go untested she makes it her mission to change the situation. **90m/C; DVD.** Lea Thompson; Anthony Lemke; Cindy Busby; Tommy Lioutas; Ralph Prosper; Trevor Hayes; Malcolm Travis; ***D:*** Stefan Pleszczynski; ***W:*** John Wierick; ***C:*** John Ashmore; ***M:*** James Gelford. **CABLE**

Life Is a Bed of Roses *La Vie est un Roman; Life Is a Fairy Tale* **1983** Three intertwined stories from Resnais. Count Forbeck is building a castle in Ardennes, planning to start a utopian society before WWI interferes. After the war, Forbeck tries again, offering his friends a drug that will make them forget the past, although his former love Livia refuses the offer. By the 1980s, the castle has been transformed into a progressive school that allows children's imaginations to roam free, although not all the educators are comfortable with the idea. While the adults fuss over their methods, the children play a fairytale game of knights and dragons. French with subtitles. **110m/C; DVD, Blu-Ray.** *FR* Ruggero Raimondi; Fanny Ardant; Andre Dussollier; Veronique Silver; Robert Manuel; Vittorio Gassman; Sabine Azema; Geraldine Chaplin; Pierre Arditti; ***D:*** Alain Resnais; ***W:*** Jean Gruault; ***C:*** Bruno Nuytten; ***M:*** Michel Philipe-Gerard.

Life Is Beautiful *La Vita E Bella* **1998 (PG-13)** Benigni's stunning epic is not, at its core, a Holocaust movie, but rather a story of family love. Guido's so intent on believing that life is—and should be—beautiful, he goes to great lengths to ensure that vision for his wife and, particularly, his son. The first half is an amusing boy-meets-girl comedy; the second shifts to the concentration camp where Guido and his wife and son are imprisoned. Guido invents an elaborate game to convince his son that the whole ordeal is an endurance test to be won, with prizes forthcoming. If Benigni depicts the concentration camps as less than horrifying, he should be forgiven for his different focus. Italian with subtitles. **122m/C; VHS, DVD, Blu-Ray.** *IT* Roberto Benigni; Nicoletta Braschi; Giustino Durano; Sergio Bustric; Horst Buchholz; Giorgio Cantarini; Marisa Paredes; Lidia Alfonsi; Giuliana Lojodice; ***D:*** Roberto Benigni; ***W:*** Roberto Benigni; Vincenzo Cerami; ***C:*** Tonino Delli Colli; ***M:*** Nicola Piovani. Oscars '98: Actor (Benigni), Foreign Film, Orig. Dramatic Score; Australian Film Inst. '99: Foreign Film; British Acad. '98: Actor (Benigni); Cannes '98: Grand Jury Prize; Cesar '99: Foreign Film; Screen Actors Guild '98: Actor (Benigni); Broadcast Film Critics '98: Foreign Film.

Life is Hot in Cracktown 1/2 **2008 (R)** Ruthlessly downbeat look at crack cocaine addiction based on Giovinazzo's own 1993 short story collection. Unfortunately it also pushes all the usual buttons about being a poor druggie in a big city complete with crime, gangs, prostitution, homelessness, violence, indifference, and child abuse. **99m/C; DVD.** Victor Razuk; Kerry Washington; Desmond Harrington; Evan Ross; Brandon Routh; Shannyn Sossamon; Vondie Curtis-Hall; RZA; Lara Flynn Boyle; Thomas Ian Nicholas; ***D:*** Buddy Giovinazzo; ***W:*** Buddy Giovinazzo; ***C:*** Kat Westergaard; Russell Jaeger; ***M:*** RZA.

Life Is Sweet 1/2 **1990 (R)** The consuming passions of food and drink focus the lives of an oddball English working-class family beset by hopeless dreams and passions. Mother's always fixing family meals—in between helping her friend open a gourmet restaurant featuring revolting dishes. Dad's a chef who buys a snack truck and dreams of life on the road. Grown twins Natalie and Nicola eat their meals in front of the television but Nicola is also a bulimic who binges and purges on chocolate bars behind her bedroom door. An affectionate, if sometimes unattractive, look at a chaotic family. **103m/C; VHS, DVD, Blu-Ray.** *UK* Alison Steadman; Jane Horrocks; Jim Broadbent; Claire Skinner; Timothy Spall; Stephen Rea; David Thewlis; ***D:*** Mike Leigh; ***W:*** Mike Leigh. L.A. Film Critics '91: Support. Actress (Horrocks); Natl. Soc. Film Critics '91: Actress (Steadman), Film, Support. Actress (Horrocks).

Life Itself **2014** Masterful documentarian James adapts his memoir on long-time film critic Roger Ebert in this biographical documentary. James approaches his subject like Ebert would have approached it given his background as a newspaperman. There's a little bit of biography, a little bit of the days before his death, a little bit of this, a little bit of that. And the result becomes a comprehensive look at a man who saw cinema in a new way and taught us how to do the same. **112m/C; DVD, Blu-Ray.** Roger Ebert; ***D:*** Steve James; ***C:*** Dana Kupper; ***M:*** Joshua Abrams.

Life Itself **2018 (R)** This emotionally intense drama tells the interconnected stories of people with ties to New York City. Will (Isaac) is a down-on-his-luck writer who has a daughter he has not yet seen. His daughter, Dylan (Kruse/Cooke), had a sad childhood and never knew her parents, though she wishes she had. In Spain, laborer Javier (Peris-Mencheta) gets promoted to managing the olive orchards of wealthy Mr. Saccione (Banderas). Though there is tension Javier asks for Mr. Saccione's help when his young son Rodrigo (Marrero) needs special treatment. Rodrigo later moves to New York to attend college. The unfortunate events blur together in this cliched, disjointed film. **117m/C; DVD, Blu-Ray.** Oscar Isaac; Olivia Wilde; Annette Bening; Mandy Patinkin; Jean Smart; ***D:*** Dan Fogelman; ***W:*** Dan Fogelman; ***C:*** Brett Pawlak; ***M:*** Federico Jusid.

A Life Less Ordinary 1/2 **1997 (R)** Hapless janitor Robert (McGregor) lose his job, girlfriend, and home. He reacts by kidnapping the boss' daughter, Celine (Diaz), who's more upset at Robert's ineptness than anything else. Meanwhile two angels (Hunter and Lindo) are sent to make these two kids fall in love. Confused? You should be. Hodge's script looks like someone threw "It Happened One Night," "Stairway to Heaven," outtakes from a Tarantino movie, and a Road Runner cartoon into a blender and hit frappe. Some of the surreal set pieces work, and the McGregor/Diaz chemistry clicks sporadically, but the overall effect is overkill. **103m/C; VHS, DVD.** Ewan McGregor; Cameron Diaz; Holly Hunter; Delroy Lindo; Ian Holm; Ian McNeice; Stanley Tucci; Dan Hedaya; Tony Shalhoub; Maury Chaykin; Judith Ivey; K.K. Dodds; ***D:*** Danny Boyle; ***W:*** John Hodge; ***C:*** Brian Tufano; ***M:*** David Arnold.

Life of a King 1/2 **2013 (PG-13)** Inspirational true story plays like a genre cliché but is held together by the strong lead performance of Gooding, Jr. Ex-con Eugene Brown learned how to play chess during his long prison stretch. Now a janitor at his former high school in inner-city D.C., Eugene is called upon to settle down a rowdy group of students in detention. He does so by passing on his chess expertise, eventually turning a foreclosed home into an after-school rec center where the teens can learn how chess can teach them about life as well. **101m/C; DVD, Blu-Ray.** Cuba Gooding, Jr.; Malcolm M. Mays; Lisa Gay Hamilton; Dennis Haysbert; Kevin Hendricks; ***D:*** Jake Goldberger; ***W:*** Jake Goldberger; ***C:*** Mark Schwartzbard; ***M:*** Eric V. Hachikian.

Life of Crime **2013 (R)** Based on a novel by the great Elmore Leonard, Schechter's crime comedy is technically a prequel to "Jackie Brown," the underrated Quentin Tarantino classic. A couple of fumbling criminals (Bey aka Mos Def and Hawkes) kidnap a wealthy socialite (Aniston) but run into a roadblock when her husband (Robbins) decides he'd rather not pay the ransom. It's familiar stuff for Leonard fans and doesn't quite match up to "Get Shorty," but it has moments of similar entertainment value. Set expectations to low and you'll be satisfied as an escapist rental. **98m/C; DVD, Blu-Ray.** John Hawkes; Mos Def; Jennifer Aniston; Tim Robbins; Isla Fisher; Mark Boone, Jr.; Will Forte; Charlie Tahan; ***D:*** Daniel Schechter; ***W:*** Daniel Schechter; ***C:*** Eric Alan Edwards; ***M:*** The Newton Brothers.

The Life of David Gale **2003 (R)** Anti-death penalty activist David Gale (Spacey) awaits his execution after being convicted for the rape and murder of his collegue Constance (Linney). Told in flashback to hard-boiled reporter Bitsey (Winslet), his story plays out from his fall from respected philosophy professor to boorish drunk after an ill-advised dalliance with a student turns into a rape accusation. Pick your poison with this one. If you want social commentary, the heavy-handed diatribes will assault you while you wait for the murder mystery-thriller elements to insult your intelligence with their convoluted, implausible plots and red herrings. **130m/C; VHS, DVD.** Kevin Spacey; Kate Winslet; Laura Linney; Gabriel Mann; Matt Craven; Rhona Mitra; Leon Rippy; Jim Beaver; ***D:*** Alan Parker; ***W:*** Charles Randolph; ***C:*** Michael Seresin; ***M:*** Alex Parker; Jake Parker.

The Life of Emile Zola 1/2 **1937** Writer Emile Zola intervenes in the case of Alfred Dreyfus who was sent to Devil's Island for a crime he did not commit. Well-crafted production featuring a handsome performance from Muni. **117m/B; VHS, DVD.** Paul Muni; Gale Sondergaard; Gloria Holden; Joseph Schildkraut; ***D:*** William Dieterle; ***W:*** Norman Reilly Raine; ***C:*** Gaetano Antonio "Tony" Gaudio; ***M:*** Max Steiner. Oscars '37: Film, Screenplay, Support. Actor (Schildkraut); Natl. Film Reg. '00; N.Y. Film Critics '37: Actor (Muni), Film.

A Life of Her Own 1/2 **1950** Turner stars as a farm girl who takes her dream of becoming a top model to the Big Apple. She signs with an agency and is befriended by Dvorak, an aging model, who acts as her mentor. Turner finds success and is soon the toast of the town until she gets involved with a married man (Milland) and her life starts to crumble. Average soap opera with flimsy script. Turner is good, but Dvorak steals the show in her role as an over-the-hill fashion plate. **108m/B; DVD.** Lana Turner; Ray Milland; Tom Ewell; Louis Calhern; Ann Dvorak; Barry Sullivan; Jean Hagen; Phyllis Kirk; Sara Haden; ***D:*** George Cukor; ***W:*** Isobel Lennart; ***C:*** George J. Folsey.

The Life of Jesus *La Vie de Jesus* **1996** Small town boredom and despair—French style. Twenty-year-old Freddy (Douche) is an unemployed epileptic, who lives with his mother. He spends his time with girlfriend Marie (Cottreel) or riding his moped with his equally disenfranchised buddies. When a young Arab, Kader (Chaatouf), shows an interest in Marie (that's reciprocated), Freddy and his friends beat him up. Apparently the title is a reference to the spiritual suffering Freddy feels, even if he doesn't know exactly how to articulate his emotions. French with subtitles. **96m/C; VHS, DVD, Blu-Ray.** *FR* David Douche; Marjorie Cottreel; Kader Chaatouf; Samuel Boidin; Genevieve Cottreel; ***D:*** Bruno Dumont; ***W:*** Bruno Dumont; ***C:*** Philippe Van Leeuw; ***M:*** Richard Cuvillier.

Life of Lemon 1/2 **2011** Diffident L.A. repairman Lemon vaguely wants more from life but his blue-collar dad Arthur isn't encouraging. Lemon strikes up a friendship with homeless vet Lester who offers him the emotional support to try something new—even if it means failing. **74m/C; DVD.** Barry Kneller; Dan Lauria; Willie C. Carpenter; Rachel Miner; Beth Grant; Mimi Kennedy; ***D:*** Randy Kent; ***W:*** Barry Kneller; ***C:*** Cira Felina Bolla; ***M:*** Don Spangler.

The Life of Lucky Cucumber **WOOF!** **2008** Amateur night drivel. A couple of aspiring filmmakers get a government grant to make a film about local Missouri weirdo Lucky, who's had more than 100 jobs and lives in a cave. **82m/C; DVD.** Dian Bachar; Preston Lacy; Stella Keitel; Sam Maccarone; Patrick O'Hagan; ***D:*** Sam Maccarone; ***W:*** Preston Lacy; Sam Maccarone; ***C:*** Edward Gutentag; ***M:*** Tim Montijo. **VIDEO**

Life of Pi **2012 (PG)** Ang Lee's visually arresting 3D adventure of Yann Martel's 'unfilmable' 2001 bestseller, which finds teenager Piscine Molitor Patel (Sharma) immigrating with his family from India to Canada. The freighter on which they are traveling also contains animals from the family's zoo. It sinks in a storm and Pi spends months adrift in a lifeboat in the Pacific Ocean with a Bengal tiger named Richard Parker. It's as much a meditation on life and religion as a story of survival that's recounted by a middle-aged Pi (Khan). **127m/C; DVD, Blu-Ray.** Suraj Sharma; Irrfan Khan; Tabu; Adil Hussain; Rafe Spall; Ayush Tandon; ***D:*** Ang Lee; ***W:*** David Magee; ***C:*** Claudio Miranda; ***M:*** Mychael Danna. Oscars '12: Cinematog., Director (Lee), Orig. Score, Visual FX; British Acad. '12: Cinematog., Visual FX; Directors Guild '12: Director (Lee); Golden Globes '13: Orig. Score.

Life of the Party **2005 (R)** Michael (Bailey), an ex-golden boy turned alcoholic, goes into a panic when his wife Phoebe (Pompeo) finally leaves him. With Michael in the hospital after a car crash, everyone close to him decides its past time to hold an intervention, which turns into chaos. Refrains from pomposity while showing the consequences alcoholic behavior has on not just the drinker but those around him. **87m/C; DVD.** Eion Bailey; Ellen Pompeo; John Ales; Clifton (Gonzalez) Collins, Jr.; Gabriel Olds; David Clennon; Pamela Reed; Rosalind Chao; Larry Miller; ***D:*** Barra Grant; ***W:*** Barra Grant; ***C:*** Lawrence Sher; ***M:*** Mark Adler.

Life of the Party **2018 (PG-13)** A female-driven comedy about a middle-aged mother who decides to go back to college. When divorcee Deanna "Dee Rock" Miles (McCarthy) faces life alone after daughter Maddie (Gordon) starts college, Dee returns to school with her to finish her degree. Living on campus with goth roomie Leonor (Gardner), Dee faces challenges both social and academic but finds support from Maddie and her friends as well as her new younger boyfriend, Jack (Benward). Though the film echoes the classic comedy Back to School, it does not provide an adequate showcase for McCarthy's many comedic talents. **105m/C; Blu-Ray, Streaming.** Melissa McCarthy; Gillian Jacobs; Maya Rudolph; Julie Bowen; Molly Gordon; ***D:*** Ben Falcone; ***W:*** Melissa McCarthy; Ben Falcone; ***C:*** Julio Macat; ***M:*** Fil Eisler. Golden Raspberries '18: Worst Actress (McCarthy).

Life on a String **1990** Set in the distant past, this is a lyrical story of a young boy searching for a cure for his blindness. His possible cure involves a myth which requires him to devote his life to music and the breaking of 1000 strings on a banjo. Adapted from a story by Shi Tiesheng. In Chinese with English subtitles. **110m/C; VHS, DVD.** *CH* Xu Qing; ***D:*** Chen Kaige; ***W:*** Chen Kaige; ***C:*** Gu Changwei; ***M:*** Xiao-Song Qu.

Life on the Line **2016 (R)** A melodramatic look at the challenges facing electrical lineman, based on true events. After lineman Beau Ginner (Travolta) fails to rig wire correctly during a lightning storm in 1998, his brother and fellow lineman is killed by lightening while trying to fix the mistake. After the incident, Beau raises his orphaned niece Bailey (Bosworth). As an adult, Bailey is involved with bad boy Duncan (Sawa), who straightens his life out and becomes a lineman. As a storm approaches, Beau must face his past in unexpected ways. It's interesting and well-acted, but more sensationalism than suspenseful. **97m/C; DVD.** John Travolta; Kate (Catherine) Bosworth; Devon Sawa; Gil Bellows; Julie Benz; ***D:*** David Hacki; ***W:*** Primo Brown; Marvin Peart; Peter I. Horton; ***C:*** Brian Pearson; ***M:*** Jeff Toyne.

Life or Something Like It 1/2 **2002 (PG-13)** Disappointing fluff bunny blonde role for Jolie, who's best when she's edgy. Shallow Seattle newscaster Lanie Kerigan has a fab life and a fab famous boyfriend in Seattle Mariners player Cal (Kane). Then she interviews street prophet Jack (Shalhoub), who tells Lanie that she's going to die next week—and since all his other predictions have come true, Lanie gets stressed and decides she needs to get in touch with her regular-gal roots again. Of course it doesn't hurt that her cameraman, sexy Pete (Burns), is willing to do all he can to make things better. **104m/C; VHS, DVD.** Angelina Jolie; Edward Burns; Tony Shalhoub; Christian Kane; Melissa Errico; Stockard Channing; James Gammon; Gregory Itzin; ***D:*** Stephen Herek; ***W:*** John Scott Shepherd; Dana Stevens; ***C:*** Stephen Burum; ***M:*** David Newman.

Life Partners 1/2 **2014** Love triangle comedies are common on the indie film circuit but this one is surprisingly effective through the sheer chemistry and comedic talents of its cast. Sasha (Meester) and Paige (Jacobs) are best friends, spending every other night on the couch watching reality TV and lamenting their failed love lives. While lesbian Sasha continues to struggle, Paige meets a guy named Tim (Brody), and her friendship with Sasha is forever altered. Sasha jumps into bad dates, and fights with her former friend. It's familiar but surprisingly funny and heartfelt, thanks mostly to Jacobs. **93m/C; DVD, Blu-Ray.** Leighton Meester; Gillian Jacobs; Adam Brody; Abby Elliot; Gabourney "Gabby" Sidibe; ***D:*** Susanna Fogel; ***W:*** Susanna Fogel; Joni Lefkowitz; ***C:*** Brian Burgoyne; ***M:*** Eric D. Johnson.

Life-Size 1/2 **2000** Twelve-year-old tomboy, Casey (Lohan), desperately misses her recently deceased mother but her dad, Ben (Burns), is dealing with his own grief by becoming a workaholic. Casey tries out a magic spell to resurrect her mom and instead makes her beauty pageant doll, Eve (Banks), come to life. Casey's horrified and wants to send Eve back to her doll world but Eve loves becoming a human and wants to stay. **89m/C; VHS, DVD.** Lindsay Lohan; Tyra Banks; Jere Burns; Anne Marie Loder; Garwin Sanford; Tom Butler; ***D:*** Mark Rosman; ***W:*** Mark Rosman; Stephanie Moore; ***C:*** Philip Linzey; ***M:*** Eric Colvin. **TV**

Life Stinks **1991 (PG-13)** So does the film. A grasping tycoon bets he can spend a month living on the street without money, resulting in cheap laughs, heavy-handed sentiment and one musical number. Those expecting the innovative, hilarious Brooks of "Young Frankenstein" or "Blazing Saddles" will be very disappointed—these jokes are stale and the timing is tedious. Those looking for a Chaplinesque tale for modern times should stick with Chaplin. **93m/C; VHS, DVD, Blu-Ray.** Mel Brooks; Jeffrey Tambor; Lesley Ann Warren; Stuart Pankin; Howard Morris; Teddy Wilson; Michael Ensign; Billy Barty; Carmine Caridi; Rudy DeLuca; ***D:*** Mel Brooks; ***W:*** Mel Brooks; Rudy DeLuca; ***C:*** Steven Poster.

Life Support **2007** Ana Williams (Queen Latifah) is an HIV-positive, recovering junkie, trying to win back the affections of her estranged daughter Kelly (Nicks), who lives with her grandmother (Smith). However, Kelly does ask her mother to help her find her best friend Omari (Ross), who is gay and very sick from AIDS. As the two search the city, talking with Omari's friends and lovers, Ana's heartfelt activism is seen and Kelly's guard begins to come down. Nelson George's portrayal of his sister's real life battle could have come off as sap, but instead it's a solid effort with equally substantial performances. **88m/C; DVD.** Queen Latifah; Anna Deavere Smith; Wendell Pierce; Evan Ross; Rachel Nicks; Gloria Reuben; Tracee Ellis Ross; Darrin Dewitt Henson; Tony Rock; ***D:*** Nelson George; ***W:*** Nelson George; Jim McKay; Hannah Weyer; ***C:*** Uta Briesewitz; ***M:*** Stuart Matthewman. **CABLE**

Life Tastes Good **1999** San Franciscan Harry has been laundering money for the mob and skimming some off the top. He wants to leave a suitcase of cash to his abandoned kids but the wiseguys he stole from want their money back and send a hitman after Harry. Told in beyond-the-grave flashbacks. Gotanda adapted his own play. **88m/C; DVD.** Sab Shimono; Tamlyn Tomita; Julia Nickson-Soul; Kelvin Han Yee; Bob Todd; Tim Lounibos; ***D:*** Sue Upton; ***W:*** Sue Upton; ***C:*** Michael G. Chin; ***M:*** Dan Kuramato.

Life with Father 1/2 **1947** Based on the writings of the late Clarence Day Jr., this is the story of his childhood in NYC during the 1880s. A delightful saga about a stern but loving father and his relationship with his knowing wife and four red-headed sons. **118m/C; VHS, DVD.** William Powell; Irene Dunne; Elizabeth Taylor; Edmund Gwenn; Zasu Pitts; Jimmy Lydon; Martin Milner; ***D:*** Michael Curtiz; ***W:*** Donald Ogden Stewart; ***C:*** William V. Skall; J. Peverell Marley; ***M:*** Max Steiner. Golden Globes '48: Score; N.Y. Film Critics '47: Actor (Powell).

Life with Judy Garland—Me and My Shadows 1/2 **2001 (PG)** Sharp direction, a solid script that goes beyond the cliches, plus excellent performances (especially by Davis and Blanchard) prevent this telling of the tortured life of Judy Garland from slipping into made-for-TV docudrama hell. Garland's life is followed, from her insecure early teens, through the movie success and the many marriages and the drug addiction that brought her downfall. Based on the book "Me and My Shadows: A Family Memoir" by daughter Lorna Luft, who participated in the production. **107m/C; VHS, DVD.** Judy Davis; Victor Garber; Hugh Laurie; Tammy Blanchard; Stewart Bick; John Benjamin Hickey; Sonja Smits; Dwayne Adams; Al Waxman; Jayne (Jane) Eastwood; Marsha Mason; Daniel Kash; Aidan Devine; ***Cameo(s):*** Lorna Luft; ***Nar:*** Cynthia Gibb; ***D:*** Robert Allan Ackerman; ***W:*** Robert Freedman; ***C:*** James Chressanthis; ***M:*** William Ross. **TV**

Life with Mikey 1/2 **1993 (PG-13)** Michael "Mikey" Chapman (Fox) is a washed-up former child star who now half-heartedly runs a minor talent agency for other pint-sized would-be thespians. Ever mindful of his previous glory, he believes he is doomed to obscurity when a 10-year-old Brooklyn pickpocket reanimates his taste for life. Light, sweet comedy is generally predictable, a typical Fox effort. Unbilled cameo from Reuben Blades as Vidal's father. **92m/C; VHS, DVD, Blu-Ray.** Michael J. Fox; Christina Vidal; Cyndi Lauper; Nathan Lane; David Huddleston; Victor Garber; David Krumholtz; Tony Hendra; ***Cameo(s):*** Ruben Blades; ***D:*** James Lapine; ***W:*** Marc Lawrence; ***M:*** Alan Menken.

Life Without Dick 1/2 **2001 (PG-13)** Would-be romantic comedy that's passable on the romance and fails completely at the comedy. Ditzy Colleen (Parker) is devastated when she discovers sleazy boyfriend Dick (Knoxville) is cheating on her. She threatens him with a gun and accidentally kills him. Then Daniel (Connick Jr.) shows up. He works for the Irish mob as a hitman only he can't actually kill anyone. (He really wants to be a professional singer.) Dick was his assignment and he's pleased that everything is already taken care of. Colleen thinks Daniel's just grand and decides she'll help him out by taking on his hitman duties herself. **96m/C; VHS, DVD.** Sarah Jessica Parker; Harry Connick, Jr.; Teri Garr; Johnny Knoxville; Craig Ferguson; Geoffrey Blake; Brigid Brannagh; Ever Carradine; Erik Palladino; Claudia Schiffer; ***D:*** Bix Skahill; ***W:*** Bix Skahill; ***C:*** James Glennon; ***M:*** David Lawrence.

Lifeboat 1/2 **1944** When a German U-boat sinks a freighter during WWII, the eight survivors seek refuge in a tiny lifeboat. Tension peaks after the drifting passengers take in a stranded Nazi. Hitchcock saw a great challenge in having the entire story take place in a lifeboat and pulled it off with his usual flourish. In 1989, the film "Dead Calm" replicated the technique. From a story by John Steinbeck. Bankhead shines. **96m/B; VHS, DVD, Blu-Ray.** Tallulah Bankhead; John Hodiak; William Bendix; Canada Lee; Walter Slezak; Hume Cronyn; Henry Hull; Mary Anderson; Heather Angel; William Yetter, Jr.; ***D:*** Alfred Hitchcock; ***W:*** Jo Swerling; ***C:*** Glen MacWilliams; ***M:*** Hugo Friedhofer. N.Y. Film Critics '44: Actress (Bankhead).

Lifeforce 1/2 **1985 (R)** A beautiful female vampire from outer space drains Londoners and before long the city is filled with disintegrating zombies in this hi-tech thriller. Sex was never stranger. Screenwriters O'Bannon and Jakoby adapted the story from Colin Wilson's novel, "The Space Vampires." **100m/C; VHS, DVD, Blu-Ray.** Steve Railsback; Peter Firth; Frank Finlay; Patrick Stewart; Michael Gothard; Nicholas Ball; Aubrey Morris; Nancy Paul; Mathilda May; John Hallam; ***D:*** Tobe Hooper; ***W:*** Dan O'Bannon; Don Jakoby; ***C:*** Alan Hume; ***M:*** Henry Mancini; Michael Kamen.

Lifeguard **1976 (PG)** The lifeguard lives by the credo that work is for people who cannot surf. But 30ish Rick (Elliott) is wondering if it's time to give up beach life and get a "real" job, especially after his 15th year high school reunion where he hooks up with old flame Cathy (Archer), who's now a divorcee with a young child, and a buddy offers him a job selling Porsches. **96m/C; DVD.** Sam Elliott; Anne Archer; Stephen Young; Parker Stevenson; Kathleen Quinlan; ***D:*** Daniel Petrie; ***W:*** Ron Koslow; ***C:*** Ralph Woolsey; ***M:*** Dale Menten.

The Lifeguard 1/2 **2013 (R)** Unhappy with the way her life is turning out and about to turn 30, former valedictorian Leigh (Bell) returns to the womb of her parents' home in Connecticut and her high school job as an apartment lifeguard. The complex has gone downhill, which must appeal to Leigh's loss of self-esteem as she starts hanging out and smoking weed with a couple of underage teenage punks and then hooks up with one of them. It's all mope and no hope and Bell still comes off as too intelligent to take stupid chances. **98m/C; DVD, Blu-Ray.** Kristen Bell; David Lambert; Martin Starr; Mamie Gummer; Amy Madigan; Adam LeFevre; Alex Shaffer; ***D:*** Liz W. Garcia; ***W:*** Liz W. Garcia; ***C:*** John B. Peters; ***M:*** Fred Avril.

Lifepod 1/2 **1993** Trapped on a ship with a killer—only this time it's a space ship. In the year 2169 an interplanetary liner is sabotaged. Nine people escape in a damaged lifepod emergency craft. The survivors are perilously short of food and water and cannot contact Earth. They also face frightening evidence that the terrorist is among their group and is determined to kill the remaining survivors. Very loose adaptation of Alfred Hitchcock's 1944 film "Lifeboat." **120m/C; VHS, DVD.** Ron Silver; Robert Loggia; CCH Pounder; Stan Shaw; Adam Storke; Jessica Tuck; Kelli Williams; Ed Gate; ***D:*** Ron Silver; ***W:*** M. Jay Roach; Pen Densham. **TV**

Life's a Breeze 1/2 **2014 (R)** Bizarrely sitcomish piece about an old hoarder (Flanagan) who comes home from a trip only to discover that her kids have cleaned up her entire house, including discarding her mattress. Of course, they didn't bother to look in it or realize that grandma didn't believe in banks and kept thousands of Euros in the place she slept. The rest of the film is a wacky adventure to find the fortune once held within the mattress. Tragically thin in terms of character and just not that funny. **88m/C; DVD, Blu-Ray.** ***IR*** Pat Shortt; Fionnula Flanagan; Kelly Thornton; Eva Birthistle; ***D:*** Lance Daly; ***W:*** Lance Daly; ***C:*** Lance Daly; ***M:*** Lance Daly.

Lifespan **1975** A young American scientist visiting Amsterdam discovers experiments involving a drug that halts aging. **85m/C; VHS, DVD.** ***GB*** Klaus Kinski; Hiram Keller; Tina Aumont; ***D:*** Alexander Whitelaw.

Lift 1/2 **2001** Niecy (Washington) is a fashionable designer at a tony Boston store whose second job is as a "booster." She steals jewelry and couture clothes and adds to her own wardrobe while selling some of the merchandise. Her boyfriend Angelo (Byrd) urges Niecy to quit but she's seeking the approval of her embittered mother Elaine (McKee) and decides to boost an expensive necklace her mother has admired. Naturally, this job is the one that goes very wrong. **85m/C; VHS, DVD.** Kerry Washington; Lonette McKee; Eugene Byrd; Todd Williams; Samantha Brown; Kirk "Sticky Fingaz" Jones; Braun Philip; Barbara Montgomery; Annette Miller; Jacqui Parker; Naheem Allah; Susan Alger; ***D:*** DeMane Davis; Khari Streeter; ***W:*** DeMane Davis; ***C:*** David Phillips; ***M:*** Ryan Shore.

Lifted 1/2 **2010 (PG-13)** Alabama middle-schooler Henry Matthews is dealing with a lot: his marine reservist father William has just been deployed to Afghanistan; his mom Lisa is a drug addict; they've lost their home and are forced to move in with Henry's nasty grandfather; and Henry is going to a new school and is targeted by bullies. His one solace is music—a talent he shares with his dad. When Henry learns about a singing competition, he's determined to enter and win. **108m/C; DVD.** Uriah Shelton; Dash Mihok; Nicki Aycox; Trace Adkins; James Handy; Ruben Studdard; ***D:*** Lexi Alexander; ***W:*** Lexi Alexander; ***C:*** David Brower; ***M:*** Kurt Farquhar. **VIDEO**

The Light Ahead 1/2 **1939** Lovers Fishke and Hodel dream of escaping the poverty and prejudices of their shtetl for the possibilities of big city life in Odessa. They're aided in their quest by enlightened bookseller Mendele who turns the town's superstitions to their advantage. Based on the stories of social satirist Mendele Mokher Seforim. In Yiddish with English subtitles. **94m/B; VHS, DVD.** David Opatoshu; Isadore Cashier; Helen Beverly; ***D:*** Edgar G. Ulmer.

Light at the Edge of the World **1971 (PG)** A band of pirates torments a lighthouse keeper near Cape Horn after he sees a shipwreck they caused. **126m/C; VHS, DVD, Blu-Ray.** Kirk Douglas; Yul Brynner; Samantha Eggar; ***D:*** Kevin Billington; ***W:*** Tom Rowe; ***C:*** Henri Decae; ***M:*** Piero Piccioni.

The Light Between Oceans **2016 (R)** Lighthouse keeper Tom Sherbourne (Fassbender) and his wife Isabel (Vikander) are struggling to have a baby. After suffering miscarriages, they feel like God has blessed them when a baby literally washes ashore in a dingy, accompanied by a dead man. They keep the baby, raising her as their own, but drama ensues when Tom crosses paths with the child's real mother Hannah (Weisz). The cast is very good but the melodrama smothers their performances. Based on the 2012 novel by M.L. Stedman. **133m/C; DVD, Blu-Ray.** Michael Fassbender; Alicia Vikander; Rachel Weisz; Florence Clery; Jack Thompson; ***D:*** Derek Cianfrance; ***W:*** Derek Cianfrance; ***C:*** Adam Arkapaw; ***M:*** Alexandre Desplat.

Light from Light **2019** A part-time paranormal researcher investigates the supposed haunting of a Tennessee farmhouse for a widower who achingly needs to believe that his wife never left him. Although there are some low-key ghostly elements, this film is a thoughtful character study and exploration of grief, hope, and love, and the two leads deliver otherworldly performances. **82m/C; DVD.** Marin Ireland; Jim Gaffigan; Josh Wiggins; Atheena Frizzell; David Cale; ***D:*** Paul Harrill; ***W:*** Paul Harrill; ***C:*** Greta Zozula; ***M:*** Adam Granduciel; Jon Natchez.

A Light in the Darkness 1/2 **2002 (R)** Familiar and not-very creepy story that finds Taylor (Terzian) released from a mental hospital after many years. Unfortunately, he's still tormented by hallucinations of his dead shrew of a mom (Black). Given his fragile grip on sanity, Taylor doesn't need the added pressure of his scheming Uncle Stanley (Lewis) or drunken housekeeper Kira (Keyer). **99m/C; DVD.** Karen Black; Geoffrey Lewis; Troy Beyer; Troy Winbush; Matt Terzian; ***D:*** Marshall E. Uzzle; ***W:*** Matt Terzian; Marshall E. Uzzle; ***C:*** Carl F. Bartels; ***M:*** Steve Yeaman.

Light in the Piazza **1961** Margaret Johnson (de Havilland) takes her beautiful daughter Clara (Mimieux) on a European tour and during their stay in Florence she attracts the attention of handsome young Farizio (Hamilton), who's charmed by Clara's naivete. The two are soon engaged, but Margaret feels guilty because Clara is actually mentally disabled because of a childhood accident and has the emotional capacity of a 12-year-old. Margaret finally reveals her secret to Farizio's oh-so-charming father (Brazzi) but he seems unconcerned, and Clara's own father (Sullivan) just wants her out of their lives. Has a rather creepy outcome, until then enjoy the beautiful Italian scenery at least. **101m/C; DVD.** Olivia de Havilland; Yvette Mimieux; George Hamilton; Rossano Brazzi; Barry Sullivan; Nancy Nevinson; Isabel Dean; ***D:*** Guy Green; ***W:*** Julius J. Epstein; ***C:*** Otto Heller; ***M:*** Mario Nascimbene.

Light It Up 1/2 **1999 (R)** Tedious hostage flick. When their favorite high school teacher (Nelson) gets unfairly suspended, a group of fed-up students stage a sit-in. After a confrontational security guard (Whitaker) is shot, the students take him and the crumbling school building hostage. The usual mind games are played until the arrival of a police negotiator (Williams). The youngsters then appeal to the public via the Internet, giving their side of the story and asking for public school reform. The young cast does a good job, but they can't make us believe the wildly inane chain of events. **99m/C; VHS, DVD.** Forest Whitaker; Judd Nelson; Sara Gilbert; Rosario Dawson; Usher Raymond; Robert Ri'chard; Fredro Starr; Glynn Turman; Clifton (Gonzalez) Collins, Jr.; Vic Polizos; Vanessa L(ynne) Williams; ***D:*** Craig Bolotin; ***W:*** Craig Bolotin; ***C:*** Elliot Davis; ***M:*** Harry Gregson-Williams.

Light of My Eyes *Luce Dei Miei Occhi* **2001** Chauffeur Antonio (Lo Cascio) is heading home when he nearly hits a young girl who's wandered into the street. When her mother, Maria (Ceccarelli), comes to rescue the child, Antonio is immediately attracted. He begins to hang around and worms his way into Maria's life but, frankly, it doesn't seem worth the effort. The characters talk a lot (without saying anything worth noting) and, besides Lo Cascio, they're not particularly interesting. Italian with subtitles. **114m/C; DVD.** *IT* Luigi Lo Cascio; Sandra Ceccarelli; Silvio Orlando; *D:* Giuseppe Piccioni; *W:* Giuseppe Piccioni; Umberto Contarello; Linda Ferri; *C:* Arnaldo Catinari; *M:* Ludovico Einaudi.

The Light of the Moon 🦴🦴🦴 **2017** A nuanced, low-budget drama about the ways that rape affects a victim's life. After her boyfriend Matt (Stahl-David) begs off a night out, Bonnie (Beatriz) goes out drinking with friends and is raped in an alley on her short walk home. Saving the evidence of the crime, she reports the incident to police. Through the questioning, she answers truthfully and is judged for her actions. Though Bonnie soon returns to work, her relationship with Matt--and many others in her life--becomes complicated as this trauma is processed. The first film by Jessica Thompson is a thoughtful and sensitive look at its subject. **90m/C; DVD.** Stephanie Beatriz; Michael Stahl-David; Catherine Curtin; Conrad Ricamora; Cindy Cheung; *D:* Jessica M. Thompson; *W:* Jessica M. Thompson; *C:* Autumn Eakin; *M:* David Torn.

The Light of Western Stars 🦴🦴 ½ **1930** Brian plays a young woman from the east who comes to claim her late brother's ranch. She meets her murdered brother's best friend (Arlen) who is a drunken cowboy, and he falls madly in love with her. Wanting to impress her, he quickly sobers up and prevents a gang from taking over the ranch. This was Paramount's first talking adaptation of a Grey novel and the third version of this particular Grey novel; silent versions were made in 1918 and 1925. **70m/B; VHS, DVD.** Richard Arlen; Mary Brian; Regis Toomey; Harry Green; Syd Saylor; George Chandler; *D:* Otto Brower; Edwin H. Knopf.

Light Sleeper 🦴🦴 **1992 (R)** Schrader's moody look at upscale drug dealers in New York. Dafoe is John LaTour, a 40 year-old drug courier to the club scene. Since his boss (Sarandon) is giving up the drug business for the safer world of natural cosmetics, John must look to his own future. His life becomes even more complicated when he runs into a bitter ex-flame (Delany) and finds the attraction is still overpowering. Cynical, contemplative, and menacing. **103m/C; VHS, DVD.** Willem Dafoe; Susan Sarandon; Dana Delany; David Clennon; Mary Beth Hurt; *D:* Paul Schrader; *W:* Paul Schrader; *C:* Edward Lachman; *M:* Michael Been.

The Lighthouse 🦴🦴🦴 **2019 (R)** A contemporary horror film shot in old-timey black and white, the better to emphasize shadows and forlornness. Craggy ol' sea captain (Dafoe), the keeper of a lighthouse in 1890 New England, is forced to share his tight living and work space with an apprentice (Pattinson). Chest butting and cabin fever ensues, with madness and dread not far behind. Unreliable narration pulls the viewer under the hallucinatory spell. The ending may not be perfect, but it shouldn't be overlooked in light of the extraordinary performances by the two leads. The mermaid did an okay job, too. **109m/B; DVD, Blu-Ray.** *US CA* Willem Dafoe; Robert Pattinson; Valeriia Karaman; *D:* Robert Eggers; *W:* Robert Eggers; Max Eggers; *C:* Jarin Blaschke; *M:* Mark Korven. Ind. Spirit '20: Cinematog., Cinematog. (Blaschke), Support. Actor (Dafoe).

Lighthouse Hill 🦴🦴 **2004** When his best friend and business partner Peter dies, Charlie suddenly decides to hit the road and winds up in the mysterious hamlet of Lighthouse Hill, which features a landlocked lighthouse and very welcoming residents. Charlie eventually decides to settle in, especially after getting romantically involved with villager Grace. **94m/C; DVD.** *GB* Jason Flemyng; Kirsty Mitchell; Frank Finlay; Maureen Lipman; John Sessions; *D:* David Fairman; *W:* Sharon Y. Cobb; *C:* Tony Imi; *M:* Christopher Gunning.

Lighting in a Bottle 🦴🦴🦴 ½ **2004 (PG-13)** Smokin' hot concert film documenting the roots and progression of the blues, structured around a 2003 show at New York's Radio City Music Hall. Director Antoine Fuqua and producer Martin Scorsese call on just about every face in the biz, over 50 musicians, to do what they do best—plug in and howl at the moon. The requisite blues legends abound, but it's the more contemporary artists paired with legendary blues songs that really bring down the house. Will undoubtedly generate a new fan base for the genre. **103m/C; DVD.** *D:* Antoine Fuqua; *C:* Lisa Rinzler; *M:* Steve Jordan.

The Lightkeepers 🦴 ½ **2009 (PG)** Predictable and ineptly-told romantic drama with some regrettably hammy acting from Dreyfuss. Curmudgeonly Seth Atkins (Dreyfuss) is a Cape Cod lighthouse keeper with a mysterious young assistant who calls himself John Brown (Wisdom). Both men express their disdain for the fairer sex a little too much. Then, in the summer of 1912, young artist Ruth (Gummer) moves into a nearby cottage with her companion Mrs. Bascomb (Danner) and soon the two men are not-so-reluctantly making their acquaintance. Adams also directed the similarly-themed "The Golden Boys." **96m/C; Blu-Ray, On Demand.** Richard Dreyfuss; Blythe Danner; Tom Wisdom; Bruce Dern; Mamie Gummer; Julie Harris; Stephen Russell; Jason Alan Smith; *D:* Daniel Adams; *W:* Daniel Adams; *C:* Thomas Jewett; *M:* Pinar Toprak.

Lightnin' Bill Carson 🦴🦴 **1936** Marshal Bill Carson chased outlaws Breed Hawkins and the Pecos Kid out of the town of Blue Gap. The Kid witnesses Hawkins kill a deputy during a stage holdup and hides out at his brother Tom's, where Carson arrests him. When the Pecos Kid is lynched, Tom vows revenge on all those involved, including Bill, who learned too late that the Kid wasn't the killer. **75m/B; DVD.** Tim McCoy; Rex Lease; Lois January; Harry Worth; Karl Hackett; John Merton; Jack Rockwell; Edmund Cobb; Lafe (Lafayette) McKee; *D:* Sam Newfield; *W:* Joseph O'Donnell; *C:* Jack Greenhalgh.

Lightning Bolt 🦴 *Operazione Goldman* **1967** Someone is stealing moon rockets from Cape Kennedy, and secret agent Harry Sennet must find out who is doing this devilish deed. It leads him to an evil madman who plots to destroy the world from his underwater hideout. Cheap and unintentionally funny. **96m/C; VHS, DVD.** *IT SP* Anthony Eisley; Wandisa Leigh; Folco Lulli; Diana Lorys; Ursula Parker; *D:* Anthony M. Dawson.

Lightning Bug 🦴🦴 **2004** Drama based loosely on the life of special effects artist Robert Hall. A young man hopes to use his talents to escape his repressive small town to make monster movies in Hollywood. **95m/C; DVD, Blu-Ray, Streaming.** Bret Harrison; Laura Prepon; Kevin Gage; Ashley Laurence; Shannon Eubanks; *D:* Robert Hall; *W:* Robert Hall; *C:* Brandon Trost; *M:* Jason M. Hall. **VIDEO**

Lightning: Fire from the Sky 🦴🦴 **2000** Two large storms are converging on a small Missouri town, and in a twist of fate, every major weather organization has somehow missed it on their radar. Fortunately a young man somehow knows about it (and was promptly ignored by the aforementioned organizations) and has told his estranged father, whom he expects will save everyone. Sounds almost plausible. **94m/C; DVD.** John Schneider; Jesse Eisenberg; Michele Greene; Gary Sandy; Barbara Crampton; Stacy Keach; John James; Miles Chapin; Chase Masterton; Erika Thomas; Tim McKay; Peter L. Beckwith, Sr.; Paul Schnabel; *D:* David Giancola; *W:* David Hunter; *C:* Grosvenor Miles Hafela; *M:* Tim Jones.

Lightning Hutch 🦴 **1926** This is a rare example of the chapter serial genre from the late silent film era. Charles Hutchison battles the bad guys who want to steal the formula for a deadly poisonous gas, while also defending himself from an attempted framing for the theft of valuable bonds. Hutchinson produces an impressive athletic performance including swimming and rock climbing, all in the pursuit of good over evil. **230m/B; Silent; DVD.** Charles (Hutchison) Hutchinson; Edith Thornton; Sheldon Lewis; Eddie (Edward) Phillips; Violet Schram; Virginia Pearson; Gordon Sackville; Leroy Mason; *D:* Charles (Hutchison) Hutchinson; *W:* Jack Natteford.

Lightning Jack 🦴 ½ **1994 (PG-13)** Western comedy about Lightning Jack Kane (Hogan), an aging second-rate outlaw who desperately wants to become a western legend. Mute store clerk Ben (Gooding) winds up as his partner in crime, while barely eluding criticisms of Stepin Fetchitism. Cliches galore, the running gags (including Kane's surreptitious use of his eyeglasses so he can see his shooting targets) fall flat. **93m/C; VHS, DVD.** Paul Hogan; Cuba Gooding, Jr.; Beverly D'Angelo; Kamala Dawson; Pat Hingle; Richard Riehle; Frank McRae; Roger Daltrey; L.Q. Jones; Max Cullen; *D:* Simon Wincer; *W:* Paul Hogan; *C:* David Eggby; *M:* Bruce Rowland.

Lightning Strikes Twice 🦴🦴 **1951** This flick belongs to the dames since Englishman Todd is miscast and stiffer than a board in his role as a husband accused of murdering his wife. He gets off thanks to love-crazed lone jury holdout Liza (McCambridge). Richard goes into hiding since he's still getting suspicious looks until vacationing actress Shelley (Roman), who believes in Richard's innocence, comes along. **91m/B; DVD.** Richard Todd; Ruth Roman; Mercedes McCambridge; Zachary Scott; Frank Conroy; Kathryn Givney; Darryl Hickman; *D:* King Vidor; *W:* Lenore Coffee; *C:* Sidney Hickox; *M:* Max Steiner.

Lightning: The White Stallion 🦴 ½ **1986 (PG)** An old gambler and his two young friends enter a horse race in order to win their beloved white stallion back from thieves. **93m/C; VHS, DVD.** Mickey Rooney; Susan George; Isabel Lorca; *D:* William A. Levey.

Lightning Warrior 🦴🦴 **1931** Western suspense about pioneer life and the unraveling of a baffling mystery. Twelve chapters, 13 minutes each. **156m/B; VHS, DVD.** George Brent; Frankie Darro; *D:* Armand Schaefer; Benjamin (Ben H.) Kline.

Lights in the Dusk 🦴 ½ *Laitakaupungin Valot* **2006** Limp noir finds lonely shopping mall security guard Koiskinen (Hyytiainen) falling for the charms of bombshell Mirja (Jarvenhelmi), who works for sleazy businessman Lindholm (Koviula). Koiskinen becomes the patsy in a jewel robbery and goes to prison, not even ratting out Mirja. Things don't improve from there. Finnish with subtitles. **80m/C; DVD.** *FI* Janne Hyytiainen; Maria Jarvenhelmi; Ilkka Koivula; Maria Heiskanen; *D:* Aki Kaurismaki; *W:* Aki Kaurismaki; *C:* Timo Salminen.

Lights of Old Santa Fe 🦴 ½ **1947** A cowboy rescues a beautiful rodeo owner from bankruptcy. The original, unedited version of the film. **78m/B; VHS, DVD.** Roy Rogers; Dale Evans; George "Gabby" Hayes; Lloyd Corrigan; Tom Keene; Arthur Loft; Roy Barcroft; Lucien Littlefield; Sam Flint; Bob Nolan; *D:* Frank McDonald; *W:* Gordon Kahn; *C:* Reggie Lanning.

Lights Out 🦴🦴 ½ **2016 (PG-13)** David F. Sandberg adapts his 2013 short film into a feature length with surprisingly effective results. Rebecca (Palmer) lives with her depressed mother Sophie (Bello) and younger brother Martin (Gabriel). In a spin on the traditional tale, it's the mother this time who has a reportedly imaginary friend who ends being not so imaginary. Sophie's friend can only be seen in the dark. Very scary and clever. **81m/C; DVD, Blu-Ray.** Teresa Palmer; Gabriel Bateman; Alexander DiPersia; Billy Burke; Maria Bello; *D:* David F. Sandberg; *W:* Eric Heisserer; *C:* Marc Spicer; *M:* Benjamin Wallfisch.

The Lightship 🦴🦴 **1986 (PG-13)** On a stationary lightship off the Carolina coast, the crew rescues three men from a disabled boat, only to find they are murderous criminals. Duvall as a flamboyant homosexual psychopath is memorable, but the tale is pretentious, overdone, and hackneyed. Based on Siegfried Lenz's story. **87m/C; VHS, DVD.** Robert Duvall; Klaus Maria Brandauer; Tom Bower; William Forsythe; Arliss Howard; *D:* Jerzy Skolimowski.

Like a Boss 🦴 ½ *Limited Partners* **2020 (R)** Best friends since middle school, Mia (Haddish) and Mel (Byrne) started a cosmetics company in their garage during college. Two decades later, they have founded their own makeup line, which they sell online and in a store in Atlanta, and share a house. For her own malicious reasons, cosmetics empire founder Claire Luna (Hayek) offers to buy the company from the struggling entrepreneurs. Claire drives a wedge between them because Mia mistrusts Claire but Mel wants to take the money for debt relief. Despite the promising chemistry between Haddish and Byrne, the comedy lacks logic and believability. **83m/C; DVD.** Tiffany Haddish; Rose Byrne; Salma Hayek; Jacob Latimore; Billy Porter; *D:* Miguel Arteta; *W:* Sam Pitman; Adam Cole-Kelly; *C:* Jas Shelton; *M:* Christophe Beck.

Like A Bride 🦴🦴🦴 *Novia Que Te Vea* **1994** Two teenage Jewish girls grapple with their families' expectations and cultural norms during the 1960s in Mexico City when one resists marriage to be an artist while the other falls in love with a Gentile. In Spanish, with subtitles. **115m/C; VHS, DVD.** *MX* Caludette Maille; Maya Michalska; Angelica Aragon; Ernesto Laguardia; Pedro Armendariz, Jr.; *D:* Guita Schyfter; John Gorrie; Christopher Hodson; Tony Wharmby; *W:* Guita Schyfter; Hugo Hiriart; John Gorrie; David Butler; *C:* Toni Kuhn; *M:* Joaquin Gutierrez Heras; Joseph Horovitz. **VIDEO**

Like a Fish Out of Water 🦴🦴 *Comme un Poisson Hors de'Eau* **1999** Muller is an average loveless, middle-aged nobody with a tropical fish hobby. This is how he's set up by a trio of con artists who need his help in stealing a very rare and valuable tropical fish, which they will hold for ransom until the eccentric owner pays up. Belucci's the femme who entices Muller while Karyo is the alleged brains of the operation and Pinon the crazy muscle. French with subtitles. **90m/C; VHS, DVD.** *FR* Michel Muller; Monica Bellucci; Tcheky Karyo; Dominique Pinon; *D:* Herve Hadmar; *W:* Michel Muller; Herve Hadmar; Christopher Bergeronneau; *C:* Jacques Boumendil.

Like a Puppet Out of Strings 🦴 ½ **2005** Brothers Tom and Felipe watch out for each other as they gain more power in the local gangs. Cop Luis, a former gangbanger whose life was turned around by police officer Angelica, goes after the brothers when she's murdered. Tom gets accused although Felipe did the crime, and Felipe does a deal with Luis to save his brother. Eventually, the siblings wind up confronting each other in a situation that calls their loyalty into question. **83m/C; DVD.** *CA* Tom Rodriguez; Ed Casagrande; Leslie Hibberd; Catherine Braund; Felipe Rodriguez; *D:* Felipe Rodriguez; *W:* Felipe Rodriguez; *C:* Felipe Rodriguez; Dylan Harrison; *M:* Louis Marc Vautour.

Like Crazy 🦴🦴🦴 **2011 (PG-13)** American Jacob (Yelchin) and Brit Anna (Jones) fall in love while she's studying stateside but she stays past her student visa's allowance to spend time with him and the decision forces the young lovers into the often-deadly practice of the long-distance relationship. Debut director Doremus focuses on their difficulties--not through melodrama but the small choices that can pull people apart as Jacob and Anna go on with their lives, trying to keep love alive through the phone line. Jones makes a striking debut and Yelchin's strong as well. **89m/C; DVD, Blu-Ray.** Anton Yelchin; Felicity Jones; Jennifer Lawrence; Charlie Bewley; Alex Kingston; Oliver Muirhead; Finola Hughes; Chris Messina; Ben York-Jones; *D:* Drake Doremus; *W:* Ben York-Jones; Drake Doremus; *C:* John Guleserian; *M:* Dustin O'Halloran.

Like Dandelion Dust 🦴 ½ **2009 (PG-13)** When blue-collar Rip Porter goes to prison for alcohol-fueled domestic abuse, pregnant wife Wendy gives their newborn son up for adoption. Joey is raised by the loving, middle-class Campbells but when Rip is released from prison he expects to be reunited with his wife and son. The law's on his side since his name was forged on the adoption papers but the Campbells don't intend to give up their son. Adapted from the Karen Kingsbury novel. **104m/C; DVD.** Mira Sorvino; Barry Pepper; Cole Hauser; Kate Levering; Maxwell Perry Cotton; L. Scott Caldwell; Abby Brammell; Kirk B.R. Woller; *D:* Jon Gunn; *W:* Stephen J. Rivele; Michael Lawrence; *C:* Reynaldo Villalobos; *M:* Nathan Larson.

Like Father 🦴🦴 ½ **2018** Career-driven bride Rachel (Bell) is on business call as her own wedding procession is about to begin. During the ceremony, it becomes clear she will never put work aside and her groom calls off the wedding. Rachel learns that her estranged father Harry (Grammer), whom she has not seen since she was five, witnessed it all. The pair get drunk together, and wake up on the cruise that was to be her honeymoon. During the trip, Rachel bonds with Harry and learns about the value of life outside of work.

The predictable film also seems like an extended commercial for the cruise line. **98m/C; DVD.** Kristen Bell; Danielle Davenport; Kimiko Glenn; Wynter Kullman; Kelsey Grammer; ***D:*** Lauren Miller; ***W:*** Lauren Miller; ***C:*** Seamus Tierney; ***M:*** Roger Neill.

Like Father, Like Son **1987 (PG-13)** First and worst of a barrage of interchangeable switcheroo movies that came out in '87-'88. Moore is in top form, but the plot is contrived. **101m/C; VHS, DVD.** Dudley Moore; Kirk Cameron; Catherine Hicks; Margaret Colin; Sean Astin; ***D:*** Rod Daniel; ***W:*** Steven L. Bloom; Lorne Cameron; ***M:*** Miles Goodman.

Like Father Like Son **½ 2005** When teacher Dominic Milne gets engaged to Dee Stanton, she finally admits that she isn't a widow but that her ex-husband, Paul, is imprisoned as a serial killer. Her 15-year-old son Jamie overhears Dee's confession and demands to see the father he was told was dead and Dee is frightened that Jamie will become fascinated by the manipulative monster. Then Morag, a pupil whom Jamie was accused of stalking, is strangled and he falls under suspicion. Is Jamie following in his father's footsteps or is someone else close to Dee actually the killer? **137m/C; DVD.** *GB* Robson Green; Jemma Redgrave; Somerset Prew; Philip Davis; Tara Fitzgerald; Francesca Fowler; Georgia Moffett; Florence Bell; ***D:*** Nicholas Laughland; ***W:*** Shaun McKenna; ***C:*** Dominic Clemence; ***M:*** John Lunn. **TV**

Like Father, Like Son **½** *Soshite chichi ni naru* **2013** Director/writer Kore-eda has become one of the most observant cultural commentators in his part of the world, particularly as he shows the impact of changes in society upon children in Japan. His latest is a tender, interesting, albeit somewhat thin analysis of nature vs. nurture in a culture that places a strong emphasis on legacy and the accompanying strict parenting required to maintain it. Ryota and Midori Nonomiya (Fukuyama & Ono) learn that their son is not their biological one after a hospital mix-up and are forced to choose between the boy with their DNA or the one they raised. **122m/C; DVD.** *JP* Masaharu Fukuyama; Machiko Ono; Riri Furanki; Yoko Maki; Keita Ninomiya; Sho-gen Hwang; ***D:*** Hirokazu Kore-eda; ***W:*** Hirokazu Kore-eda; ***C:*** Mikiya Takimoto; ***M:*** Takashi Mori.

Like It Is **1998** Craig (Bell) makes his living in illegal bare-knuckles fighting matches in Blackpool. After a win, he heads for a disco, meeting ambitious London record producer, Matt (Rose), who's with his roommate, singer Paula (Behr). Uncertain of his sexual feelings, Craig can't follow through on his attraction, but does soon turn up on Matt's London doorstep. However, not only is jealous Paula a problem for their budding romance but so is Kelvin (Daltry), Matt's manipulative gay boss. Appealing lead performances but vet Daltry steals scenes with smarmy charm. Accents and slang will be a challenge to American ears. **95m/C; DVD.** *UK* Steve Bell; Ian Rose; Dani Behr; Roger Daltrey; ***D:*** Paul Oremland; ***W:*** Robert Cray; ***C:*** Alistair Cameron; ***M:*** Don McGlashan.

Like It Never Was Before *Pensionat Oskar* **1995** Conventional, middleaged marrieds Rune (Falkman) and Gunnel (Ekblad) Runeberg travel to a seaside hotel for their annual vacation with their three children. Ordinary family man Rune, though dissatisfied, is expecting little until he meets, and falls in love with, young handyman Petrus (Norrthon), and suddenly decides to break free. Swedish with subtitles. **108m/B; VHS, DVD.** *SW* Loa Falkman; Stina Ekblad; Simon Norrthon; Philip Zanden; Sif Ruud; Ghita Norby; ***D:*** Suzanne (Susanne) Bier; ***W:*** Jonas Gardell; ***C:*** Kjell Lagerros; ***M:*** Johan Soderqvist.

Like Mike **½ 2002 (PG)** That's "Mike" as in basketball legend Michael Jordan—or at least his basketball shoes. A pair of old shoes, supposedly belonging to Jordan, is donated to an orphanage and end up the property of teen Calvin (Bow Wow). The shoes give him super basketball skills and he wins a chance to play spoiled star Tracey (Chestnutt) during halftime, which impresses the coach (Forster). The hoops story is merely window dressing because most of the story revolves around the efforts of Calvin and fellow orphans Murph (Lipnicki) and Reg (Song) to get adopted. Various NBA players make appearances. **100m/C; DVD, UMD.** Bow Wow; Jonathan Lipnicki; Morris Chestnut; Eugene Levy; Crispin Glover; Robert Forster; Brenda Song; Jesse Plemons; Julius Charles Ritter; Anne Meara; Vanessa Williams; ***D:*** John Schultz; ***W:*** Jordan Moffet; Michael Elliot; ***C:*** Shawn Maurer; ***M:*** Richard Gibbs.

Like Someone in Love **½ 2013** Director/writer Kiarostami offers an elusive reflection on identity, age, and love which may not be his best work but still proves fascinating. Akiko (Takanashi) is an escort assigned to a client on the edge of Tokyo. She reluctantly meets Takashi (Okuno) and discovers he is an elderly, retired professor who just wants to talk. The next day, Akiko's boyfriend (Kase) mistakes the john for Akiko's grandfather and they play along. Well-paced, it lingers long after it ends. **109m/C; DVD, Blu-Ray.** *JP FR* Rin Takanashi; Tadashi Okuno; Ryo Kase; ***D:*** Abbas Kiarostami; ***W:*** Abbas Kiarostami; ***C:*** Katsumi Yanagijima.

Like Water for Chocolate **½** *Como Agua para Chocolate* **1993 (R)** Magical Mexican fairytale set in the early 1900s about family, love, and the power of food. Formidable Mama Elena is left a widow with three daughters. The youngest, Tita, grows up in the kitchen surrounded by all the magic. Nacha, the housekeeper, can impart to her about food. Doomed by tradition to spend her days caring for her mother, Tita escapes by cooking, releasing her sorrows and longings into the food, infecting all who eat it. Wonderfully sensuous and slyly exaggerated. Based on the novel by Esquival, who also wrote the screenplay and whose husband, Arau, directed. In Spanish with English subtitles; also available dubbed. **105m/C; VHS, DVD, Blu-Ray.** *MX* Lumi Cavazos; Marco Leonardi; Regina Torne; Mario Ivan Martinez; Ada Carrasco; Yareli Arizmendi; Caludette Maille; Pilar Aranda; ***D:*** Alfonso Arau; ***W:*** Laura Esquivel; ***C:*** Steven Bernstein; ***M:*** Leo Brouwer.

Li'l Abner **½** *Trouble Chaser* **1940** Al Capp's famed comic strip comes somewhat to life in this low-budget comedy featuring all of the Dogpatch favorites. **78m/C; VHS, DVD.** Cranville Owen; Martha Driscoll; Buster Keaton; ***D:*** Albert Rogell.

Li'l Abner **½ 1959** High color Dogpatch drama adapted from the Broadway play (with most of the original cast) based on the Al Capp comic strip. When Abner's berg is considered as a site for atomic bomb testing, the natives have to come up with a reason why they should be allowed to exist. Choreography by Michael Kidd and Dee Dee Wood. **114m/C; VHS, DVD.** Peter Palmer; Leslie Parrish; Stubby Kaye; Julie Newmar; Howard St. John; Stella Stevens; Billie Hayes; Joe E. Marks; ***D:*** Melvin Frank; ***W:*** Norman Panama; ***C:*** Daniel F. Fapp; ***M:*** Johnny Mercer; Jean De Paul.

Lila & Eve **½ 2015 (R)** A strong performance by the always-great Viola Davis is counterbalanced by a weak one by the often-horrible Jennifer Lopez in this stale, borderline offensive thriller that uses hot button issues manipulatively and grotesquely. The two ladies play a pair of distraught mothers whose children were gunned down in a drive-by shooting. Rather than deal with their grief in resigned silence, they team up to get to the bottom of their son's deaths and kill those responsible. The whole thing looks like a straight-to-Lifetime movie, and the script too often sounds like one too. Davis is way above this material, especially the twist ending. **94m/C; DVD, Blu-Ray, Streaming.** Jennifer Lopez; Viola Davis; Andre Royo; Shea Wigham; Aml Ameen; Chris Chalk; ***D:*** Charles Stone, III; ***W:*** Pat Gilfillan; ***C:*** Wyatt Garfield; ***M:*** Samuel Jones; Alexis Marsh.

Lila Says *Lila Dit Ca* **2004** Chimo (Khouas) is a handsome 19-year-old Arab boy in Marseilles who, rather than further his writing talent, hangs out with his layabout friends and dabbles in petty crime. Along comes Lila (Giocante), a beautiful blond 16-year-old, who ensnares Chimo with her teasing talk. His friends blatantly disapprove of her and as he clings to his chivalrous demeanor, her antics become more annoying. **89m/C; DVD.** *FR GB* Vahina Giocante; Mohammed Khouas; Karim Ben Haddou; Carmen Lebbos; Hamid Dkhissi; Lotfi Chakri; Edmonde Franchi; Stephanie Fatout; ***D:*** Ziad Doueiri; ***W:*** Ziad Doueiri; Joelle Touma; ***C:*** John Daly.

Lili **1953** Delightful musical romance about a 16-year-old orphan who joins a traveling carnival and falls in love with a crippled, embittered puppeteer. Heartwarming and charming, if occasionally cloying. Leslie Caron sings the film's song hit, "Hi-Lili, Hi-Lo." **81m/C; DVD.** Leslie Caron; Jean-Pierre Aumont; Mel Ferrer; Kurt Kasznar; Zsa Zsa Gabor; ***D:*** Charles Walters; ***M:*** Bronislau Kaper. Oscars '53: Orig. Dramatic Score; British Acad. '53: Actress (Caron); Golden Globes '54: Screenplay.

Lilian's Story **½ 1995** Aging Lilian (Cracknell) has just been released after spending 40 years in a mental institution, placed there as an adolescent by her controlling, possessive father. The haunted Lilian is given a room at a residential hotel in Sydney's red-light district where the local prostitutes look out for her and she spends her days wandering the streets. Flashbacks reveal what lead the high-strung young Lilian (Collette) to her incarceration. Based on Kate Greville's 1984 novel, which was a fictional account of real-life Sydney eccentric Bea Miles. **94m/C; VHS, DVD.** *AU* Ruth Cracknell; Barry Otto; Toni Collette; John Flaus; Essie Davis; Susie Lindemann; Anne Louise Lambert; Iris Shand; ***D:*** Jerzy Domaradzki; ***W:*** Steve Wright; ***C:*** Slawomir Idziak; ***M:*** Cezary Skubiszewski. Australian Film Inst. '95: Support. Actress (Collette).

Lilies *Les Feluettes* **1996 (R)** Strange revenge fantasy set in a Quebec men's prison in 1952. A bishop (Sabourin) goes to hear the confession of a dying convict and is taken hostage in the chapel by the prison's homosexual population. There, he's forced to watch a play that recreates a 40-year-old incident in his own life. As the prison walls fade away, the prisoners turn into students Simon (Cadieux) and Vallier (Gilmore), who take the lovers' roles in a pageant about the martyrdom of St. Sebastien too seriously for comfort. The female roles in the flashbacks are played by men. Adapted from Bouchard's play. **95m/C; DVD.** *CA* Marcel Sabourin; Jason Cadieux; Danny Gilmore; Brent Carver; Matthew Ferguson; Alexander Chapman; Aubert Pallascio; ***D:*** John Greyson; ***W:*** Michel Marc Bouchard; ***C:*** Daniel Jobin; ***M:*** Mychael Danna. Genie '96: Art Dir./Set Dec., Costume Des., Film, Sound.

Lilies of the Field **1963** Five former East German nuns, living on a small farm in the Southwest U.S., enlist the aid of a free-spirited Army veteran Homer Smith (Poitier) to build a chapel for them and teach them English. Poitier is excellent as the itinerant laborer, holding the saccharine to an acceptable level, bringing honesty and strength to his role. Actress Skala, as Mother Maria, had been struggling to make ends meet in a variety of day jobs until this opportunity. Poitier was the first African American man to win an Oscar, and the first African American nominated since Hattie MacDaniel in 1939. Followed by "Christmas Lilies of the Field" (1979). **94m/B; VHS, DVD, Blu-Ray.** Sidney Poitier; Lilia Skala; Lisa Mann; Isa Crino; Stanley Adams; Francesca Jarvis; Pamela Branch; Dan Frazer; Ralph Nelson; ***D:*** Ralph Nelson; ***W:*** James Poe; ***C:*** Ernest Haller; ***M:*** Jerry Goldsmith. Oscars '63: Actor (Poitier); Berlin Intl. Film Fest. '63: Actor (Poitier); Golden Globes '64: Actor--Drama (Poitier).

Liliom **½ 1930** Creaky, melodramatic early talkie based on the 1909 play by Ferenc Molnar. Philandering bully Liliom works as an amusement park barker in Budapest along with his girl Julie. She gets pregnant and Liliom agrees to help pal Buzzard with a robbery, but when it goes wrong Liliom kills himself rather than be captured by the cops. He gets a ride on a heaven-bound train and is told he can return to Earth if he spends 10 years in purgatory. After checking in on Julie's life, Liliom decides not to interfere after all. Later adapted as the 1956 musical "Carousel." **89m/B; DVD.** Charles Farrell; Rose Hobart; Lee Tracy; Estelle Taylor; H.B. Warner; Guinn "Big Boy" Williams; Anne Shirley; ***D:*** Frank Borzage; ***W:*** Sonya Levien; S.N. Behrman; ***C:*** Chester Lyons.

Liliom **1935** Boyer goes to heaven and is put on trial to see if he is deserving of his wings. Lang's first film after leaving Nazi Germany is filled with wonderful ethereal imagery, surprising coming from the man responsible for such grim visions as "Metropolis." In French only. **85m/B; VHS, DVD.** *FR* Charles Boyer; Madeleine Ozeray; Florelle; Roland Toutain; ***D:*** Fritz Lang.

Lilith **1964** Therapist-in-training Beatty falls in love with beautiful mental patient Seberg and approaches madness himself. A look at the doctor-patient relationship among the mentally ill and at the nature of madness and love. Doesn't always satisfy, but intrigues. Rossen's swan song. **114m/B; VHS, DVD, Blu-Ray.** Warren Beatty; Jean Seberg; Peter Fonda; Gene Hackman; Kim Hunter; Anne Meacham; Jessica Walter; Robert Reilly; Rene Auberjonois; Olympia Dukakis; James Patterson; ***D:*** Robert Rossen; ***W:*** Robert Rossen; ***C:*** Eugen Shufftan; ***M:*** Kenyon Hopkins.

Lilli Marlene **½ 1950** Mediocre WWII drama takes its title from the popular German song. French singer Lilli is kidnapped and forced to make propaganda broadcasts for the Nazis. After the war is over, she's accused of being a collaborator but American radioman Steve, who loves her, comes to Lilli's aid. **75m/B; DVD.** *GB* Lisa Daniely; Hugh McDermott; Richard Murdoch; Stanley Baker; John Blythe; Arthur Lawrence; Russell Hunter; ***D:*** Arthur Crabtree; ***W:*** Leslie Wood; ***C:*** Jack Asher; Mike Whittaker; ***M:*** Stanley Black.

Lillian Russell **1940** Often draggy biopic of the theatrical legend. In the 1890s, Helen Leonard (Faye) is taking singing lessons when she's heard by impresario Tony Pastor (Carrillo). He changes her name and hires her to sing in his theater, where Lillian becomes the toast of New York and has numerous suitors. She decides to marry musician Edward Solomon (Ameche) and is aided in her continued success by the flattering articles written by old friend Alexander Moore (Fonda). But it wouldn't be showbiz if there wasn't some sorrow to dim the bright lights. **127m/B; DVD.** Alice Faye; Don Ameche; Henry Fonda; Edward Arnold; Leo Carrillo; Warren William; Lynn Bari; Nigel Bruce; Claud Allister; Helen Westley; ***D:*** Irving Cummings, Jr.; ***W:*** William Anthony McGuire; ***C:*** Leon Shamroy; ***M:*** Alfred Newman.

Lillie **1979** The life of Edwardian beauty Lillie Langtry, known as "The Jersey Lily," is portrayed in this British drama. Defying the morals of the times, Lillie was the first publicly acknowledged mistress of the Prince of Wales, only one of her numerous lovers. Shown on "Masterpiece Theatre" on PBS. **690m/C; VHS, DVD.** *GB* Francesca Annis; Cheryl Campbell; John Castle; Dennis (Denis) Lill; Peter Egan; Anton Rodgers; Ann(e) Firbank. **TV**

Lilo & Stitch **2002 (PG)** Entertaining animated tale of Hawaiian problem child Lilo, who's being raised by her sister, who finds an unlikely soulmate when she adopts Stitch, a strange little alien banished from his home planet, from an animal shelter. Stitch is rife with socially unacceptable behavior, creating chaos everywhere they go, which worsens Lilo's situation with a concerned social worker. Kiddies will love the sassy humor and gross-out behavior while parents will love the Elvis references (and songs), and the message of ohana—the Hawaiian word for family. Disney resurrected the appealing hand drawn and watercolored animation, unused since 1942's "Bambi." **85m/C; DVD, Blu-Ray.** ***V:*** Daveigh Chase; Tia Carrere; Jason Scott Lee; David Ogden Stiers; Chris (Christopher) Sanders; Kevin McDonald; Ving Rhames; Zoe Caldwell; Kevin M. Richardson; Amy Hill; Susan Hegarty; ***D:*** Dean DeBlois; Chris (Christopher) Sanders; ***W:*** Dean DeBlois; Chris (Christopher) Sanders; ***M:*** Alan Silvestri.

Lilo & Stitch 2: Stitch Has a Glitch **½ 2005 (PG)** Lilo enters a hula contest and Stitch has a personality shift to evil and even more destructive in this well-done sequel, which will still please the intended audience while amusing teens and adults as well. **68m/C; VHS, DVD, Blu-Ray.** ***V:*** Tia Carrere; Dakota Fanning; Jason Scott Lee; Chris (Christopher) Sanders; Kevin McDonald; David Ogden Stiers; Liliana Mumy; Holliston Coleman; Jillian Henry; ***D:*** Michael LaBash; Anthony Leondis; ***W:*** Michael LaBash; Anthony Leondis; Alexa Junge; Eddie Guzelian. **VIDEO**

Lilting **2014** Small-scale Brit drama (with notable acting) bonds an unlikely pair in mourning, despite their sharing no common language or culture. Aging Cambodian-Chinese widow Junn is unhappily living in the retirement community her son Kai has chosen for her. Kai's recently died and she resents the visits of his "roommate" Richard, whom we learn via flashbacks was actually his long-time lover. Since Junn doesn't speak English, Richard has hired a translator to help them out, but expressions speak louder than words. **86m/C; DVD.** *UK* Ben Whishaw; Pei Pei Cheng; Peter Bowles; Morven Christie; Naomi Christie; Andrew Leung; ***D:*** Hong Khaou; ***W:*** Hong Khaou; ***C:*** Ula Pontikos; ***M:*** Stuart Earl.

Lily & Kat **2015** A beautifully shot comedy-drama about college best friends enjoying their last days together in New York City. After Lily (Rothe) graduates from fashion school, Kat (Murray), her closest friend for the last four years, announces she will be returning home to London in days to join her father's firm. Lily is distraught by the news, but the friends vow to make the most of their last week together. The next night, they attend an art opening on the Lower East Side and meet an intriguing young artist, Henri (Falahee), with whom Lily connects. The trio spend time together, forming a romantic triangle as Lily and Kat test their unbreakable bond. **89m/C; DVD, Streaming, Download.** Jessica Rothe; Hannah Murray; Jack Falahee; Scott Evans; Chris Riggi; ***D:*** Micael Preysler; ***W:*** Micael Preysler; Megan Platts; ***C:*** Todd Antonio Somodevilla; ***M:*** Glowbug.

Lily Dale 1/2 **1996 (PG)** Nineteen-year-old Horace Robedaux (Guinee) is in Houston to visit his estranged mother Corella (Channing) and sister Lily Dale (Masterson) while his taciturn stepfather Pete Davenport (Shepard) is supposed to be away. Pete dislikes Horace and left the boy behind with relatives when he married Corella and they moved away. Self-centered Lily Dale resents Horace taking away attention from herself and matters only get worse when Pete comes home early and Horace becomes so ill that he can't leave. Set in 1910; Foote wrote the play as a memoir to his father, Horace. Made for TV. **95m/C; VHS, DVD.** Tim Guinee; Stockard Channing; Mary Stuart Masterson; Sam Shepard; John Slattery; Jean Stapleton; ***D:*** Peter Masterson; ***W:*** Horton Foote; ***C:*** Don E. Fauntleroy; ***M:*** Peter Melnick.

Lily in Love 1/2 *Playing for Keeps; Jatszani Kell* **1985 (PG-13)** An aging stage star disguises himself as a suave Italian to star in his playwright wife's new play, and woos her to test her fidelity. Charming, warm, and sophisticated. Loosely based on Molnar's "The Guardsman." **100m/C; VHS, DVD, Streaming.** *HU* Maggie Smith; Christopher Plummer; Elke Sommer; Adolph Green; ***D:*** Karoly Makk; ***W:*** Frank Cucci. **TV**

Limbo **1999 (R)** Ambivalent family saga that leaves the viewers deliberately in limbo for good or ill. Alaskan Joe Gastineau (Strathairn) is a former fisherman traumatized by an accident at sea years before. Into his life comes smalltime singer Donna de Angelo (Mastrantonio) and her depressed teen daughter Noelle (Martinez). Joe and Donna start a tentative romance and Joe even goes back to fishing. Then Joe's fast-talking half-brother Bobby (Siemaszko) shows up, precipitating a crisis that leaves Bobby dead and Joe, Donna, and Noelle stranded on a deserted island. **126m/C; VHS, DVD.** David Strathairn; Mary Elizabeth Mastrantonio; Vanessa Martinez; Casey Siemaszko; Kris Kristofferson; Kathryn Grody; Rita Taggart; Leo Burmester; Michael Laskin; ***D:*** John Sayles; ***W:*** John Sayles; ***C:*** Haskell Wexler; ***M:*** Mason Daring.

Lime Salted Love 1/2 **2006** Set in L.A. and told in flashbacks. David Treibel has been released from a mental hospital though he's obviously still got a lot of problems. As does his younger brother Chase, an emotional basket case who can only live in the present. Their guilt from a family tragedy (a third brother's accidental death) consumes them and brings them into contact with fellow lost souls, including Chase's encounter with Ellie, a victim of child abuse. **92m/C; DVD.** David O'Donnell; Kate del Castillo; Kristanna Loken; Billy Drago; Joe Hall; Danielle Agnello; George Castaneda; ***D:*** Joe Hall; Danielle Agnello; ***W:*** Joe Hall; Danielle Agnello; ***C:*** Matthew Rudenberg; ***M:*** John Langdon. **VIDEO**

The Limehouse Golem 1/2 **2017** A Victorian-period mystery, based on Peter Ackroyd's novel. After series of suspicious slayings occur in the squalid Limehouse district of London, Inspector John Kildare (Nighy) becomes obsessed with cracking the case. With the help of his reliable partner, detective George Flood (Mays), Kildare's investigation takes them all over London as John questions various potential suspects, including Karl Marx (Goodman) and an aspiring theater star Lizzie Cree (Cooke), who has been already been arrested for allegedly killing her husband, playwright John Cree (Reid). The lack of character development and depth as well as inconsistent period detail are but two of the film's shortcomings. **109m/C; DVD.** Douglas Booth; Olivia Cooke; Sam Reid; Maria Valverde; Daniel Mays; ***D:*** Juan Carlos Medina; ***W:*** Juan Carlos Medina; ***C:*** Simon Dennis; ***M:*** Johan Soderqvist.

Limelight **1952** A nearly washed-up music hall comedian is stimulated by a young ballerina to a final hour of glory. A subtle if self-indulgent portrait of Chaplin's own life, featuring an historic pairing of Chaplin and Keaton. **120m/B; VHS, DVD, Blu-Ray.** Charlie Chaplin; Claire Bloom; Buster Keaton; Nigel Bruce; Syd Chaplin; ***D:*** Charlie Chaplin; ***W:*** Charlie Chaplin; ***C:*** Karl Struss; ***M:*** Charlie Chaplin.

The Limey **1999 (R)** Sixties icons Stamp and Fonda show that age has not withered their acting chops in Soderbergh's revenge thriller. Cockney career criminal Wilson (Stamp) gets out of a Brit prison and immediately flies to L.A. to investigate the death of his daughter Jenny. She was involved with self-important record producer Valentine (Fonda), who has an obvious fondness for young women. Wilson may be out-of-touch with California culture but he's definitely in control of any situation. Soderbergh's flashback sequences make use of footage from Ken Loach's 1967 film "Poor Cow," which featured Stamp as a young thief named Wilson. **90m/C; VHS, DVD.** Terence Stamp; Peter Fonda; Lesley Ann Warren; Luis Guzman; Barry Newman; Joe Dallesandro; Nicky Katt; Amelia Heinle; Melissa George; Bill Duke; ***D:*** Steven Soderbergh; ***W:*** Lem Dobbs; ***C:*** Edward Lachman; ***M:*** Cliff Martinez.

Limit Up **1989 (PG-13)** An ambitious Chicago Trade Exchange employee makes a deal with the devil to corner the market in soybeans. Turgid attempt at supernatural comedy, featuring Charles as God. Catch Sally Kellerman in a cameo as a nightclub singer. **88m/C; VHS, DVD.** Nancy Allen; Dean Stockwell; Brad Hall; Danitra Vance; Ray Charles; Luana Anders; ***Cameo(s):*** Sally Kellerman; ***D:*** Richard Martini; ***C:*** Peter Lyons Collister.

Limitless **2011 (PG-13)** With no job and no self-esteem, failed writer Eddie (charismatic Cooper) is ready to try an experimental designer smart drug—made to use 100 percent of the human brain—when it's offered. The drug does exactly as promised (with some potentially lethal side effects) and Eddie soon becomes a very successful jerk. His new Wall Street wizardry also draws the attention of mogul Carl Van Loon (De Niro) and a lot of even more sinister types as well. Adapted from Alan Glynn's 2001 novel "The Dark Fields." **105m/C; Blu-Ray, On Demand.** Bradley Cooper; Robert De Niro; Abbie Cornish; Johnny Whitworth; Robert John Burke; Andrew Howard; Anna Friel; Darren Goldstein; Ned Eisenberg; Patricia Kalember; ***D:*** Neil Burger; ***W:*** Leslie Dixon; ***C:*** Jo Willems; ***M:*** Paul Leonard-Morgan.

The Limits of Control **2009 (R)** Jarmusch's self-indulgent travelogue features a nameless, emotionless man who is given a series of cryptic instructions as he makes his way across Spain. **116m/C; DVD, Blu-Ray.** Isaach de Bankole; Paz de la Huerta; Alex Descas; Luis Tosar; John Hurt; Tilda Swinton; Jean-Francois Stevenin; Gael Garcia Bernal; Bill Murray; ***D:*** Jim Jarmusch; ***W:*** Jim Jarmusch; ***C:*** Christopher Doyle; ***M:*** Boris.

The Limping Man **1953** Bridges returns to post-WWII London to renew a wartime romance. On the way, he gets caught up in solving a murder. Unexceptional of-its-era thriller. **76m/B; VHS, DVD.** *GB* Lloyd Bridges; Moira Lister; Leslie Phillips; Helene Cordet; Alan Wheatley; ***D:*** Charles De Latour.

Lincoln **2012 (PG-13)** The intersection of the political machine and heartfelt ideology has never been more deftly captured than it is here by director Spielberg. Day-Lewis perfectly embodies one of history's most iconic Americans in the days near the end of the Civil War, when the freedom of slaves and the safety of his people in wartime were constant pressures. A slew of great performances, perfect technical details, and a stunningly dense screenplay balance writer Kushner's historical acumen with Spielberg's sentimentality resulting in an admittedly talky masterpiece. Based in part on historian Doris Kearns Goodwin's 2006 book "Team of Rivals: The Political Genius of Abraham Lincoln." **150m/C; DVD, Blu-Ray.** Daniel Day-Lewis; Sally Field; David Strathairn; Joseph Gordon-Levitt; Hal Holbrook; Tommy Lee Jones; John Hawkes; Jackie Earle Haley; Bruce McGill; Tim Blake Nelson; Joseph Cross; Jared Harris; Lee Pace; Peter McRobbie; Gulliver McGrath; Gloria Reuben; Jeremy Strong; Michael Stuhlbarg; Stephen Spinella; Walton Goggins; David Oyelowo; Byron Jennings; Julie White; Raynor Scheine; Gregory Itzin; S. Epatha Merkerson; Dakin Matthews; ***D:*** Steven Spielberg; ***W:*** Tony Kushner; ***C:*** Janusz Kaminski; ***M:*** John Williams. Oscars '12: Actor (Day-Lewis), Production Design; British Acad. '12: Actor (Day-Lewis); Golden Globes '13: Actor--Drama (Day-Lewis); Screen Actors Guild '12: Actor (Day-Lewis), Actor--Supporting (Jones).

The Lincoln Lawyer 1/2 **2011 (R)** McConaughey successfully goes back to acting rather than just shirtless posing as street-wise L.A. criminal defense attorney Mick Haller, whose office is the backseat of his chauffeured Lincoln Continental. The venal Mick will take any case if the money is right but gets more than intended when he defends Beverly Hills playboy Louis Roulet (Phillippe) who's accused of assault. The always-watchable and sexy Tomei plays Mickey's smart, prosecuting attorney ex-wife and the rest of the supporting cast are aces as well. Director Furman briskly moves the action along in this adaptation of Michael Connelly's novel. **118m/C; DVD, Blu-Ray.** Matthew McConaughey; Ryan Phillippe; Marisa Tomei; William H. Macy; Josh(ua) Lucas; John Leguizamo; Bryan Cranston; Michaela Conlin; Michael Peña; Frances Fisher; Bob Gunton; Trace Adkins; Shea Whigham; Katherine Moenning; Michael Paré; ***D:*** Brad Furman; ***W:*** John Romano; ***C:*** Lukas Ettlin; ***M:*** Cliff Martinez.

Linda Linda Linda **2005** It's their last annual high school festival, and classmates Nozumi (Shiori Sekine) and Kyoto (Aki Maeda) decide to put together a rock band to play "Linda Linda Linda," a hit punk song in Japan. But their singer and guitarist quit, so they get a Korean girl (who can barely speak Japanese) to sing and a guitarist who usually plays keyboards. They have two days to learn to play together and win the school festival before graduation comes and they must enter the real world. **114m/C; DVD.** *JP* Du-na Bae; Kahori Fujii; Pierre Taki; Shiori Sekine; Aki Maeda; Yu Kashii; Takayo Mimura; ***D:*** Nobuhiro Yamashita; ***W:*** Nobuhiro Yamashita; Wakako Miyashita; Kosuke Mukai; ***C:*** Yoshihiro Ikeuchi; ***M:*** James Iha.

Linda Ronstadt: The Sound of My Voice **2019 (PG-13)** Raised in a musical family in Tucson, singer Linda Ronstadt describes her lifelong interest in multiple genres, the discovery of her singing voice, her love of ballads, and the beginning of her professional career as a teenager. Moving to Los Angeles, she carved a unique path that included finding power in American standards and harmonizing with other musicians. Using her own narration, the documentary provides a wonderful overview of Ronstadt's focus, dedication, and intelligence in her rise to success. Her career was unfortunately cut short due to Parkinson's disease. **95m/C; DVD, Blu-Ray.** Linda Ronstadt; ***D:*** Rob Epstein; Jeffrey Friedman; ***C:*** Ian Coad; Nancy Schreiber; ***M:*** Julian Raymond; Bennett Salvay.

The Lindbergh Kidnapping Case **1976** The famous Lindbergh baby kidnapping in 1932 and the trial and execution of Bruno Hauptmann, convincingly portrayed by Hopkins. DeYoung as Lindbergh is blah, but the script is quite good. Made for TV. **150m/C; DVD.** Anthony Hopkins; Joseph Cotten; Cliff DeYoung; Walter Pidgeon; Dean Jagger; Martin Balsam; Laurence Luckinbill; Tony Roberts; ***D:*** Buzz Kulik; ***W:*** J(ames) P(inckney) Miller; ***M:*** Billy Goldenberg. **TV**

The Line *La Linea* **2008 (R)** A bilingual crime drama with some action, a lot of character study, and some twists to keep things interesting. Salazar (Garcia), the head of a Tijuana cartel, is dying and has already passed on his power to unstable second-in-command Pelon (Morales). Against Salazar's wishes, Pelon makes a deal with Afghani terrorists to trade heroin for U.S. smuggling routes. Shady U.S. authorities secretly hire hitman Shields (Liotta) to off Pelon, but Shields is sidetracked by a guilt complex. English and Spanish with subtitles. **95m/C; DVD.** Andy Garcia; Esai Morales; Ray Liotta; Valerie Cruz; Armand Assante; Danny Trejo; Bruce Davison; Joe Morton; ***D:*** James Cotten; ***W:*** R. Ellis Frazier; ***C:*** Miguel Bunster; ***M:*** David Torn.

The Line of Beauty 1/2 **2006** Middle-class Nick Guest (Stevens) is befriended at Oxford by wealthy Toby Fedden (Coleman), whose father Gerald (McInnerney) is a rising Tory politician in Thatcher's Britain of the 1980s. Guest moves into the family's London home—in part to keep an eye on Toby's trouble-prone sister Catherine (Atwell). The gay Nick also starts exploring his sexuality: first with working-class Leo (Gilet) and then with Wani (Wyndham), the closeted druggie son of a Lebanese tycoon. Scandals eventually catch up with both Nick and the Feddens. Based on the novel by Alan Hollinghurst. **180m/C; DVD.** Tim (McInnerny) McInnery; Alice Krige; Dan Stevens; Oliver Coleman; Hayley Atwell; Alex Wyndham; Don Gilet; ***D:*** Saul Dibb; ***W:*** Andrew Davies; ***C:*** David Odd; ***M:*** Martin Phipps. **TV**

The Lineup **1958** Volatile mob killer Dancer (Wallach) and his mentor Julian (Keith) have to retrieve three packages of heroin that have been planted on unsuspecting travelers to San Francisco. Dancer easily bumps off the first two carriers but the third package was hidden inside a child's doll and the girl mistook the drugs for face powder. Dancer is enraged when his boss accuses him of stealing the drugs and gets more violent even as the cops close in. **85m/B; DVD, Blu-Ray.** Eli Wallach; Robert Keith; Warner Anderson; Richard Jaeckel; William Leslie; Mary Laroche; Emile Meyer; Marshall Reed; Vaughn Taylor; ***D:*** Donald Siegel; ***W:*** Stirling Silliphant; ***C:*** Hal Mohr; ***M:*** Mischa Bakaleinikoff.

Linewatch 1/2 **2008 (R)** Dull story finds Michael Dixon's (Gooding Jr.) past coming back to haunt him. Michael works for the border patrol along the U.S./Mexico divide. Now a family man, he was once part of a violent L.A. gang, and a chance encounter with leader Drake (Hardwick) finds Michael being pressured to help the gang smuggle drugs. **90m/C; DVD.** Cuba Gooding, Jr.; Omari Hardwick; Sharon Leal; Evan Ross; Dean Norris; Chris Browning; ***D:*** Kevin Bray; ***W:*** David Warfield; ***C:*** Paul M. Sommers. **VIDEO**

The Linguini Incident **1992 (R)** An inept escape artist, a pathological liar, a lingerie designer, a deaf restaurant hostess who throws out one-liners in sign language, and two sinister, yet chic, restaurant owners get together in this marginal comedy about magic and adventure. **99m/C; VHS, DVD.** Rosanna Arquette; David Bowie; Eszter Balint; Andre Gregory; Buck Henry; Viveca Lindfors; Marlee Matlin; Lewis Arquette; Andrea King; ***Cameo(s):*** Julian Lennon; Iman; ***D:*** Richard Shepard; ***W:*** Tamar Brott; Richard Shepard; ***C:*** Robert Yeoman; ***M:*** Thomas Newman.

Link WOOF! **1986 (R)** A primatologist and his nubile assistant find their experiment has gone—you guessed it—awry, and their hairy charges are running—yep, that's right—amok. Run for your life! **103m/C; VHS, DVD, Blu-Ray.** *GB* Elisabeth Shue; Terence Stamp; Steven Pinner; Richard Garnett; ***D:*** Richard Franklin; ***W:*** Everett De Roche; ***C:*** Mike Molloy; ***M:*** Jerry Goldsmith.

Linsanity 1/2 **2013 (PG)** A feature-length sports documentary focusing on the life, career, and influence of Jeremy Lin, a gifted Asian-American NBA player who created an unexpected splash in February 2012. Though he was not a scholarship player for a major college program (instead playing for Harvard) nor drafted by any NBA team, the point guard worked hard and was signed by the Golden State Warriors in 2010. By 2012, he was the backup point guard for the struggling New York Knicks and was given a chance to start. He jumpstarted the team by scoring more points in his first five NBA starts than any player in the league's modern era. The documentary explores his rise to fame, work ethic, and the phenomenon known as Linsanity. **88m/C; DVD, Streaming, Download.** Daniel Dae Kim; ***D:*** Evan Leong; ***W:*** Aaron Strongoni; ***C:*** Evan Leong; ***M:*** The Newton Brothers.

Lion 🦴🦴🦴 **2016 (PG-13)** Saroo (Sunny Pawar) is a 5-year-old boy when he's separated from his family near Calcutta, India. He is taken in and adopted by an Australian family, transplanted thousands of miles from his birth home, but he never stops thinking about finding them again. Twenty-five years later, a grown-up Saroo (Patel), with the support of his girlfriend Lucy (Mara), endeavors to find his family, largely through use of Google Maps and his memory of the landscape around his home. This true story is undeniably emotionally effective but also a bit superficial and manipulative. Patel is good but Nicole Kidman, as his adoptive mother, steals the film. **118m/C; DVD, Blu-Ray.** Dev Patel; Rooney Mara; Nicole Kidman; David Wenham; Sunny Pawar; ***D:*** Garth Davis; ***W:*** Luke Davies; ***C:*** Greig Fraser; ***M:*** Volker Bertelmann; Dustin O'Halloran. British Acad. '16: Actor--Supporting (Patel), Adapt. Screenplay.

The Lion Hunters 🦴 ½ **1951** Greedy lion-hunters Forbes (Ankrum) and Martin (Kennedy) have set up camp in the land of the Masai—where lions are sacred—but they've no interest in local customs. Bomba the Jungle Boy (Sheffield) is tasked with setting them straight, saving the lions, and saving kidnapped Jean (Todd) as well. Fifth film in the Monogram series. **75m/B; DVD.** John(ny) Sheffield; Morris Ankrum; Ann E. Todd; Douglas Kennedy; Smoki Whitfield; Davis Roberts; Woody Strode; ***D:*** Ford Beebe; ***W:*** Ford Beebe; ***C:*** William Sickner; ***M:*** Marlin Skiles.

The Lion in Winter 🦴🦴🦴🦴 **1968 (PG)** Medieval monarch Henry II and his wife, Eleanor of Aquitaine, match wits over the succession to the English throne and much else in this fast-paced film version of James Goldman's play. The family, including three grown sons, and visiting royalty are united for the Christmas holidays fraught with tension, rapidly shifting allegiances, and layers of psychological manipulation. Superb dialogue and perfectly realized characterizations. O'Toole and Hepburn are triumphant. Screen debuts for Hopkins and Dalton. Shot on location, this literate costume drama surprised the experts with its boxoffice success. **134m/C; VHS, DVD, Blu-Ray.** Peter O'Toole; Katharine Hepburn; Jane Merrow; Nigel Terry; Timothy Dalton; Anthony Hopkins; John Castle; Nigel Stock; ***D:*** Anthony Harvey; ***W:*** James Goldman; ***M:*** John Barry. Oscars '68: Actress (Hepburn), Adapt. Screenplay, Orig. Score; Directors Guild '68: Director (Harvey); Golden Globes '69: Actor--Drama (O'Toole), Film--Drama; N.Y. Film Critics '68: Film.

The Lion in Winter 🦴🦴🦴 **2003** In this Showtime miniseries remake of the 1968 masterpiece, Close and Stewart gracefully, if not quite as joyously, inhabit the lead roles made classic by Hepburn and O'Toole. Using Goldman's screenplay, Konchalovsky's presentation is admirably true to its source, and the scenery in Hungary and Slovakia splendidly suits the subject. Certainly an excellent effort by a talented cast and crew, but it won't dethrone its predecessor. **167m/C; VHS, DVD.** Patrick Stewart; Glenn Close; John Light; Jonathan Rhys Meyers; Ralph Spall; Yuliya Vysotskaya; Andrew Howard; Clive Wood; ***D:*** Andrei Konchalovsky; ***W:*** James Goldman; ***C:*** Sergei Kozlov; ***M:*** Richard Hartley. **CABLE**

A Lion Is in the Streets 🦴🦴🦴 *A Lion in the Streets* **1953** Cagney stars as a backwoods politician in a southern state who fights on the side of the sharecroppers and wins their support when he exposes the corrupt practices of a powerful businessman. On his way up the political ladder, however, Cagney betrays and exploits the very people who support him. Although this is a familiar storyline, Cagney is riveting as the corrupt politician, and Hale is wonderful as his patient wife. **88m/C; VHS, DVD.** James Cagney; Barbara Hale; Anne Francis; Warner Anderson; John McIntire; Jeanne Cagney; Lon Chaney, Jr.; Frank McHugh; Larry Keating; Onslow Stevens; James Millican; ***D:*** Raoul Walsh; ***W:*** Luther Davis; ***C:*** Harry Stradling, Sr.; ***M:*** Franz Waxman.

The Lion King 🦴🦴🦴🦴 **1994 (G)** A winner for kids and their folks. Like his dad Mufasa (Jones), lion cub Simba (Taylor) is destined to be king, until evil Uncle Scar (Irons) makes him an outcast. Growing up in the jungle, Simba (now Broderick) learns about life and responsibility, before facing his uncle once again. Supporting characters frequently steal the show, including Sabella's warthog, Pumba, and Lane's meerkat, Timon. Disney epic features heartwarming combo of crowd-pleasing songs, a story with depth, and stunning animation. Thirty-second Disney animated feature is the first without human characters. Scenes of violence in the animal kingdom may be too much for younger viewers. **88m/C; DVD, Blu-Ray.** ***V:*** Matthew Broderick; Jeremy Irons; James Earl Jones; Madge Sinclair; Robert Guillaume; Jonathan Taylor Thomas; Richard "Cheech" Marin; Whoopi Goldberg; Rowan Atkinson; Nathan Lane; Ernie Sabella; Niketa Calame; Moira Kelly; Jim (Jonah) Cummings; ***D:*** Rob Minkoff; Roger Allers; ***W:*** Jonathan Roberts; Irene Mecchi; ***M:*** Sir Elton John; Hans Zimmer; ***M:*** Tim Rice. Oscars '94: Orig. Score, Song ("Can You Feel the Love Tonight"); Golden Globes '95: Film--Mus./Comedy, Score, Song ("Can You Feel the Love Tonight?"); Natl. Film Reg. '16; Blockbuster '95: Family Movie, T., Soundtrack.

The Lion King 🦴🦴 ½ **2019 (PG)** On the plains of Africa, Mufasa (Jones) is the king of the lions. His new cub Simba (McCrary) worships his father and is his father's heir. However, his elder brother and former heir Scar (Ejiofor) has plans of his own. Fighting for his rightful place, Scar organizes a battle power that results in Simba's exile. Growing up on his own, adult Simba (Glover) must come to terms and reclaim his rightful place. A live action remake of the animated classic, the realistic-looking film features visuals that are nature documentary quality and memorable voice performances by its star-studded cast. **110m/C; DVD, Blu-Ray.** Chiwetel Ejiofor; John Oliver; James Earl Jones; John Kani; Alfre Woodard; ***D:*** Jon Favreau; ***W:*** Jeff Nathanson; ***C:*** Caleb Deschanel; ***M:*** Hans Zimmer.

The Lion King 1 1/2 🦴🦴🦴 **2004 (G)** Timon and Pumbaa tell the story of the original from their point of view, so we get to see what happened to Simba and how he grew up between the time he ran away and when he returned. Sort of a "Rosencrantz and Guildenstern are Dead" for the pre-teen set. Offers up the original cast (with some new additions), and a new song. Doesn't disappoint fans of the franchise, with plenty of enjoyment for every age group. **77m/C; VHS, DVD, Blu-Ray.** ***V:*** Nathan Lane; Ernie Sabella; Matthew Broderick; Robert Guillaume; Moira Kelly; Whoopi Goldberg; Richard "Cheech" Marin; Julie Kavner; Jerry Stiller; Jim (Jonah) Cummings; Edward Hibbert; Bradley Raymond; Matt Weinberg; Jason Rudofsky; ***W:*** Tom Rogers; ***M:*** Don Harper. **VIDEO**

The Lion King: Simba's Pride 🦴🦴 **1998** Simba's heir comes of age and must be prepared to assume the responsibility of leadership. **75m/C; VHS, DVD, Blu-Ray.** ***V:*** Matthew Broderick; James Earl Jones; Nathan Lane; Ernie Sabella; Robert Guillaume; Andy Dick; Neve Campbell; Suzanne Pleshette; Jason Marsden; ***D:*** Darrell Rooney; Rob LaDuca; ***W:*** Flip Kobler; Cindy Marcus. **VIDEO**

Lion of the Desert 🦴🦴🦴 *Omar Mukhtar* **1981 (PG)** Bedouin horse militias face-off against Mussolini's armored terror in this epic historical drama. Omar Muktar (Quinn as the "Desert Lion") and his Libyan guerrilla patriots kept the Italian troops of Mussolini (Steiger) at bay for 20 years. Outstanding performances enhanced by the desert backdrop. A British-Libyan co-production. **162m/C; VHS, DVD, Blu-Ray.** *GB* Anthony Quinn; Oliver Reed; Irene Papas; Rod Steiger; Raf Vallone; John Gielgud; ***D:*** Moustapha Akkad; ***W:*** H.A.L. Craig; ***C:*** Jack Hildyard; ***M:*** Maurice Jarre.

The Lion of Thebes 🦴🦴🦴 **1964** A muscleman unhesitatingly jumps into the thick of things when Helen of Troy is kidnapped. A superior sword and sandal entry. **87m/C; VHS, DVD.** *IT* Mark Forest; Yvonne Furneaux; Massimo Serato; Pierre Cressoy; Alberto Lupo; Rosalba Neri; ***D:*** Giorgio Ferroni; ***W:*** Giorgio Ferroni; Andrei De Coligny; ***C:*** Angelo Lotti; ***M:*** Francesco De Masi.

Lionheart 🦴 ½ **1987 (PG)** A romantic portrayal of the famous English King Richard the Lionheart's early years. Meant for kids, but no Ninja turtles herein—and this is just as silly, and slow to boot. **105m/C; VHS, DVD.** Eric Stoltz; Talia Shire; Nicola Cowper; Dexter Fletcher; Nicholas Clay; Deborah Maria Moore; Gabriel Byrne; ***D:*** Franklin J. Schaffner; ***W:*** Richard Outten; ***M:*** Jerry Goldsmith.

Lionheart 🦴 ½ *A.W.O.L.; Wrong Bet* **1990 (R)** Van Damme deserts the foreign legion and hits the streets when he learns his brother has been hassled. Many fights ensue, until you fall asleep. **105m/C; VHS, DVD, Blu-Ray.** Jean-Claude Van Damme; Harrison Page; Deborah Rennard; Lisa Pelikan; Brian Thompson; Ashley Johnson; ***D:*** Sheldon Lettich; ***W:*** Jean-Claude Van Damme; Sheldon Lettich; ***C:*** Robert New; ***M:*** John Scott.

Lion's Den 🦴 ½ *Leonera* **2008** Pregnant Julia is accused of murdering her lover and sent to an Argentine prison where she's assigned to a ward for women with kids. Julia gives birth and raises her son in prison as she goes from overwhelmed to confident about her maternal abilities with the help of her fellow inmates. Spanish with subtitles. **113m/C; DVD.** *AR* Martina Gusman; Laura Garcia; Elli Medeiros; Rodrigo Santoro; Leonardo Sauma; Tomas Plotinsky; ***D:*** Pablo Trapero; ***W:*** Pablo Trapero; Alejandro Fadel; Marin Mauregui; Santiago Mitre; ***C:*** Guillermo Nieto.

Lions for Lambs 🦴🦴 **2007 (R)** Interrelated stories of those affected by the Iraq war. Senator Irving (Cruise) pushes a war strategy destined for failure while anti-war Professor Malley (Redford) debates with his students about its validity. Director Redford strives to say something meaningful, but fails to give his characters any depth. Instead, they function as flat representations of different viewpoints, spouting talking points rather than actually interacting. Co-stars Cruise and Streep (as a skeptical journalist) do their best, but a bunch of A-list actors making speeches is less than entertaining. **92m/C; DVD, Blu-Ray.** Robert Redford; Meryl Streep; Tom Cruise; Michael Peña; Peter Berg; Kevin Dunn; Derek Luke; Andrew Garfield; ***D:*** Robert Redford; ***W:*** Matthew Carnahan; ***C:*** Philippe Rousselot; ***M:*** Mark Isham.

LIP Service 🦴 **1999** The L.I.P. Service is an all female detective agency investigating the disappearance of a female porn star. Much like similar films that offer this as an excuse to get pretty women who can't act to simulate softcore lesbian passion. **90m/C; DVD.** Susan Featherly; Elina Madison; Brad Bartram; Zoe Paul; Venessa Blair; Gabriel Shayne; Dave Anderson; ***D:*** Ted Nicolaou; ***W:*** Earl Kenton.

Lip Service 🦴🦴 ½ *Kat and Allison* **2000 (R)** Allison (Temchen) is a conservative, successful, furniture designer with a successful lawyer boyfriend, Stuart (Camargo). She reunites with her old college roommate, Kat (Gertz), a high-strung free spirit who moves into Allison's home. Then Kat discovers that Allison's success is predicated on selling copies of a chair that Kat herself designed and gave to Allison as a gift. So Kat decides to get revenge. **95m/C; VHS, DVD.** Jami Gertz; Sybil Temchen; Jonathan Silverman; Christian Camargo; Adewale Akinnuoye-Agbaje; Jenna Byrne; ***D:*** Shawn Schepps; ***W:*** Shawn Schepps; ***C:*** Feliks Parnell.

Lip Service 🦴🦴 ½ *Out of Synch* **2000** Down-and-out record producer Roger Deacon (Outerbridge) is charged with making a singing star out of Sunni (Wuhrer), an industry bigwig's talentless girlfriend. Roger discovers shy housewife Maggie (O'Grady) has a terrific voice and persuades her to record the vocals while Sunni lip synchs. A VH1 original movie. **91m/C; VHS, DVD.** Gail O'Grady; Kari Wuhrer; Peter Outerbridge; Stewart Bick; ***D:*** Graeme Campbell; ***W:*** Eric Williams; ***C:*** Nikos Evdemon; ***M:*** Jonathan Goldsmith. **CABLE**

Lips of Blood 🦴🦴 ½ *Levres de Sang* **1975** Rollin whips up a typically festive mix of sex, horror, and hallucination in what some have dubbed his best film. A young man (Philippe) has visions of a woman (Briand, AKA Annie Belle) he met as a child in an abandoned castle. When he sees her again, she persuades him to unleash a couple of female vampires. Do not expect anything more in the way of narrative, but it is a well-made low-budget French horror movie. French with subtitles. **88m/C; DVD, Blu-Ray.** *FR* Jean-Loup Philippe; Annie Belle; Nathalie Perrey; Marie Pierre Castel; ***D:*** Jean Rollin.

Lipstick WOOF! **1976 (R)** Fashion model Margaux seeks revenge on the man who brutally attacked and raped her, after he preys on her kid sister (real-life sis Mariel, in her debut). Exquisitely exploitative excuse for entertainment. **90m/C; VHS, DVD.** Margaux Hemingway; Anne Bancroft; Perry King; Chris Sarandon; Mariel Hemingway; ***D:*** Lamont Johnson; ***W:*** David Rayfiel; ***C:*** Bill Butler; William A. Fraker.

Lipstick Camera 🦴🦴 **1993 (R)** Keats wants a career in TV news and seeks out a successful freelance cameraman (Wimmer) to help her out. She also asks to borrow her techno-friend Feldman's mini-camera and then goes after a story on an ex-spy and his sexy companion. Only no one expects what the camera captures. Weak plot but strong cast and high-end production. **93m/C; VHS, DVD.** Ele Keats; Brian Wimmer; Corey Feldman; Sandahl Bergman; Terry O'Quinn; ***D:*** Mike Bonifer; ***W:*** Mike Bonifer; ***C:*** M. David Mullen; ***M:*** Jeff Rona.

Liquid Dreams 🦴🦴 **1992 (R)** In this fast-paced, futuristic thriller, Daly goes undercover as an erotic dancer in a glitzy strip joint to try and solve her sister's murder. She finds that the owner and clientele deal not only in sexual thrills, but also in a strange brain-sucking ritual that provides the ultimate rush. Also available in an unrated version. **92m/C; VHS, DVD.** Richard Steinmetz; Candice Daly; Barry Dennen; Juan Fernandez; Tracey Walter; Frankie Thorn; Paul Bartel; Mink Stole; John Doe; Mark Manos; ***D:*** Mark Manos; ***W:*** Mark Manos; Zach Davis; ***C:*** Ed Tomney; Alexandre Magno.

Liquid Sky 🦴🦴🦴 **1983 (R)** An androgynous bisexual model living in Manhattan is the primary attraction for a UFO, which lands atop her penthouse in search of the chemical nourishment that her sexual encounters provide. Low-budget, highly creative film may not be for everyone, but the audience for which it was made will love it. Look for Carlisle also playing a gay male. **112m/C; VHS, DVD, Blu-Ray.** Anne Carlisle; Paula Sheppard; Bob Brady; Susan Doukas; Otto von Wernherr; Elaine C. Grove; Stanley Knap; Jack Adalist; Lloyd Ziff; ***D:*** Slava Tsukerman; ***W:*** Anne Carlisle; Slava Tsukerman; ***C:*** Yuri Neyman; ***M:*** Slava Tsukerman; Brenda Hutchinson.

The Liquidator 🦴🦴 **1965** Tongue-in-cheek spy action based on the John Gardner novel. Boysie Oakes (Taylor), AKA Agent L, likes the perks of being a London-based spy but is queasy about killing. He hires a hitman to handle the messy stuff thpugh eventually the playboy has to find his inner hero for an assignment. **104m/C; DVD.** *UK* Rod Taylor; Trevor Howard; Jill St. John; Wilfrid Hyde-White; David Tomlinson; Eric Sykes; Akim Tamiroff; ***D:*** Jack Cardiff; ***W:*** Peter Yeldham; ***C:*** Edward (Ted) Scaife; ***M:*** Lalo Schifrin.

Lisa 🦴🦴 *The Inspector* **1962** Slow-paced but effective drama. Young Auschwitz survivor Lisa (Hart) is anxious to emigrate to Palestine but first puts her trust in a man who turns out to be a not-so-former Nazi. She's rescued by guilt-stricken Dutch Inspector Peter Jongman (Boyd) who arranges for them both to be smuggled into Tangiers and on to Palestine with various complications. **112m/C; DVD.** *UK* Stephen Boyd; Dolores Hart; Marius Goring; Leo McKern; Hugh Griffith; Donald Pleasence; Robert Stephens; ***D:*** Philip Dunne; ***W:*** Nelson Gidding; ***C:*** Arthur Ibbetson; ***M:*** Malcolm Arnold.

Lisa and the Devil WOOF! *The House of Exorcism; La Casa Dell'Exorcismo; The Devil and the Dead; The Devil in the House of Exorcism; El Diablo se Lleva a los Muertos; Il Diavolo e i Morti; Lisa e il Diavolo* **1975 (R)** An unfortunate outing for Savalas and Sommer, about devil worship. Poor quality leaves little room for redemption. Just like on the telly, Telly's sucking on a sucker. A shortened version of the director's original 1972 release, re-edited and with additional footage added by producer Alfred Leone. **93m/C; VHS, DVD, Blu-Ray.** *IT SP* Telly Savalas; Elke Sommer; Sylva Koscina; Robert Alda; Alessio Orano; Gabriele Tinti; Eduardo Fajardo; Espartaco (Spartaco) Santoni; Alida Valli; ***D:*** Mario Bava; ***W:*** Mario Bava; Alfred Leone; ***C:*** Cecilio Paniagua; ***M:*** Carlo Savina.

Lisa, Bright and Dark 🦴🦴 ½ **1973** Fans of the John Neufeld novel may be disappointed that this Hallmark Hall of Fame presentation doesn't stick closer to the book but others will be touched by the performances. Teen Lisa (Lenz) is on the verge of a nervous breakdown although her parents are clueless about the severity of their daughter's angst. So three girlfriends come to her rescue by getting involved in some group therapy. **90m/C; DVD.** Kay Lenz; Anne Lockhart; Debralee Scott; Jamie Smith-Jackson; Anne Baxter; John Forsythe; Anson Williams; Erin Moran; ***D:*** Jeannot Szwarc; ***W:*** Lionel E. Siegel; ***C:*** Richard C. Glouner; ***M:*** Rod McKuen. **TV**

Lisa Picard Is Famous 🦴🦴 ½ **2001** Well, New Yorker Lisa (Wolf) would like to be famous but right now, she's best known for a cereal commercial. Neurotic, self-absorbed Lisa just can't catch that one big break—unlike her gay pal Tate (DeWolf) whose one-man confessional show becomes a hit. So Lisa agrees to let a filmmaker (Dunne) document her struggling career in the hopes it will help her would-be career. **87m/C; VHS, DVD.** Laura Kirk; Nat DeWolf; Griffin Dunne; ***Cameo(s):*** Sandra Bullock; Charlie Sheen; Spike Lee; ***D:*** Griffin Dunne; ***W:*** Laura Kirk; Nat DeWolf; ***C:*** William Rexer; ***M:*** Evan Lurie.

Lisboa 🦴🦴 *Lisbon* **1999** Joao (Lopez) is a salesman who travels between Portugal and Spain. One day he picks up Berta (Maura) who is on her way to Lisbon and who refuses to tell him anything about herself. If he knew what was good for him, Joao would have made Berta get out of the car since her nasty husband Jose Luis (Luppi) and psychotic family are soon after them. Spanish with subtitles. **100m/C; VHS, DVD.** *SP* Sergi Lopez; Carmen Maura; Federico Luppi; ***D:*** Antonio Hernandez; ***W:*** Antonio Hernandez; Enrique Braso; ***C:*** Aiter Mantxola; ***M:*** Victor Reyes.

Lisbon Story 🦴🦴 **1994** Director Friedrich Monroe (Bauchau) calls his friend, sound engineer Phillip Winter (Vogler), to come to Lisbon to help him finish his film on the city. By the time Winter arrives in Portugal, Monroe has vanished, leaving the unfinished silent film behind. While waiting for his friend to return, Winter starts work, wandering through the city streets in search of inspiring sounds. English, German, and Portuguese with subtitles. **100m/C; VHS, DVD.** *GE* Ruediger Vogler; Patrick Bauchau; ***D:*** Wim Wenders; ***W:*** Wim Wenders; ***C:*** Lisa Renzler.

The List 🦴🦴 **1999 (R)** When prostitute Gabrielle (Amick) gets herself arrested and tried for solicitation, she attempts to use her client book to barter for her freedom. Judge Miller (O'Neal) has to decide whether to make the list public and embarass many of his wealthy and powerful friends, but when Gabrielle's clients start turning up dead, the judge is forced to take action. **93m/C; VHS, DVD.** Madchen Amick; Ryan O'Neal; Roc Lafortune; Ben Gazzara; ***D:*** Sylvain Guy; ***W:*** Sylvain Guy; ***C:*** Yves Bélanger; ***M:*** Louis Babin. **VIDEO**

The List 🦴🦴 **2007 (PG)** Good vs. evil, but it can't get very intense with a PG rating. After Renny's (Jacobsen) father suddenly dies, he's surprised that the majority of his father's wealth is left to a mysterious trust, the Covenant List. When Renny investigates, he meets Jo Johnston (Burton), whose deceased father was also a member. The current head is malevolent Desmond Larochette (McDowell), who tells them that the List dates back to the end of the Civil War and only male heirs are allowed to assume their father's place. But the more Renny and Jo learn, the less they like what's going on. Based on the novel by Robert Whitlow. **105m/C; DVD.** Hilarie Burton; Malcolm McDowell; Will Patton; Pat Hingle; Chuck Carrington; Mary Beth Peil; ***D:*** Gary Wheeler; ***W:*** Gary Wheeler; ***C:*** Tom Priestley; ***M:*** James Covell. **VIDEO**

The List of Adrian Messenger 🦴🦴🦴 **1963** A crafty murderer resorts to a variety of disguises to eliminate potential heirs to a family fortune. Solid Huston-directed thriller with a twist: you won't recognize any of the name stars. **98m/B; VHS, DVD, Blu-Ray.** Kirk Douglas; George C. Scott; Robert Mitchum; Dana Wynter; Burt Lancaster; Frank Sinatra; ***D:*** John Huston; ***M:*** Jerry Goldsmith.

Listen, Darling 🦴🦴 ½ **1938** Garland is appealing in her first big screen role as Pinky Wingate, who decides to find the perfect husband for her widowed mother (Astor). Pinky and her friend Buzz (Bartholomew) manage to find Pidgeon and have him become the engaging objection of everyone's affections. **70m/C; VHS, DVD.** Judy Garland; Freddie Bartholomew; Mary Astor; Walter Pidgeon; Alan Hale; Scotty Beckett; ***D:*** Edwin L. Marin.

Listen to Your Heart 🦴 ½ **2010** Too many unbelievable situations overwhelm this melodrama. Struggling New York songwriter Danny falls for deaf Ariana whose wealthy controlling mother is determined to keep them apart. When Ariana finally defies her, she finds out Danny is struggling with more than his career. **100m/C; DVD.** Kent Moran; Alexia Rasmussen; Cybill Shepherd; Shirley Knight; Ernie Sabella; Frank Watson; ***D:*** Matt Thompson; ***W:*** Kent Moran; ***C:*** Chase Bowman; ***M:*** Kent Moran. **VIDEO**

Listen Up Philip 🦴🦴 ½ **2014** Schwartzman does the best work of his career as the title character, a pretentious writer named Philip who longs for the recognition he thinks he deserves and an idea for a new book. Philip sabotages almost every relationship in his life, especially that with his girlfriend Ashley (the phenomenal Moss), and his loathsome behavior takes on new dimensions when he finds a kindred soul in the similarly obnoxious writer Ike (Pryce). Perry's dramedy captures the way self-important people feed on each other in fascinating, entertaining ways. **109m/C; Blu-Ray, Streaming.** Jason Schwartzman; Elisabeth Moss; Jonathan Pryce; Krysten Ritter; Jess Weixler; ***Nar:*** Eric Bogosian; ***D:*** Alex Ross Perry; ***W:*** Alex Ross Perry; ***C:*** Sean Price Williams; ***M:*** Keegan DeWitt.

The Listening 🦴 ½ **2006 (R)** Confusing thriller, set in 1999 in Rome, about global audio surveillance and corporate shenanigans. NSA official James (Parks) is after the perps who stole sensitive software. The trail leads to an unwitting Francesca (Sansa), who may become collateral damage if James can't prevent it. **103m/C; DVD.** *GB IT* Michael Parks; Maya Sansa; Andrea Tidona; James Parks; ***D:*** Giacomo Martelli; ***W:*** Giacomo Martelli; Inigo Dominguez; Ricardo Brun; ***C:*** Eric Maddison; ***M:*** Christian Kusche-Tomasini.

Lisztomania **WOOF! 1975 (R)** Russell's excessive vision of what it must have been like to be classical composer/musician Franz Liszt, who is depicted as the first pop star. Rock opera in the tradition of "Tommy" with none of the sense or music. **106m/C; DVD.** *UK* Roger Daltrey; Sara Kestelman; Paul Nicholas; Fiona Lewis; Ringo Starr; Veronica Quilligan; Nell Campbell; John Justin; Andrew Reilly; Anulka Dziubinska; Rick Wakeman; Rikki Howard; Felicity Devonshire; Aubrey Morris; Kenneth Colley; Ken Parry; Otto Diamont; Murray Melvin; Andrew Faulds; Oliver Reed; ***D:*** Ken Russell; ***W:*** Ken Russell; ***C:*** Peter Suschitzky; ***M:*** Rick Wakeman.

Little 🦴🦴 **2019 (PG-13)** After being bullied in middle school, Jordan (Hall) has become a mean adult and a successful, if difficult, software company CEO. Her employees are afraid to stand up to her, including her long-suffering assistant April (Rae). After an encounter with a magician, Jordan wakes up in the body of herself as middle schooler (Martin). Because of the switch, April gets to make corporate decisions on Jordan's behalf while young Jordan is forced to go back to middle school. The comedy hits on common themes found in young/old body switch movies like Big while giving actors like Rae and Martin a chance to shine. **109m/C; DVD, Blu-Ray.** Regina Hall; Issa Rae; Marsai Martin; Justin Hartley; Tracee Ellis Ross; ***D:*** Tina Gordon; ***W:*** Tina Gordon; Tracy Oliver; ***M:*** Germaine Franco.

Little **2019 (PG-13)** A woman is transformed into her younger self at a point in her life when the pressures of adulthood become too much to bear. **109m/C; DVD.** Regina Hall; Issa Rae; Marsai Martin; Justin Hartley; Tracee Ellis Ross; ***D:*** Tina Gordon Chism; ***W:*** Tracy Oliver; Tina Gordon Chism; ***M:*** Germaine Franco.

Little Accidents 🦴🦴 **2014** A sobering look at the moral and legal crises thrust upon a small Appalachian mining town after a mine collapses, killing ten workers. The after-effects rattle high school freshman Owen (Lofland) who's hiding a deadly secret of his own, and put a mining executive's wife (Banks, giving a solid performance) into a marital dilemma with one of the surviving workers (Holbrook). It's one personal predicament after another in an otherwise sleepy community. A slow burning indie drama from confident first-time writer/director Sara Colangelo, working with a strong cast, but runs into predictable plotting territory down the road. **105m/C; DVD.** Boyd Holbrook; Chloë Sevigny; Elizabeth Banks; Josh(ua) Lucas; Jacob Lofland; Travis Tope; ***D:*** Sara Colangelo; ***W:*** Sara Colangelo; ***C:*** Rachel Morrison; ***M:*** Marcelo Zarvos.

The Little American 🦴🦴 ½ **1917** German-American Karl Von Austreim leaves behind sweetheart Angela Moore, returning to Germany to fight in WWI. Angela travels to France to care for her dying aunt and discovers her aunt's chateau has been turned into a hospital. She remains in the face of a German advance and is naturally reunited with her much-changed beau. **80m/B; Silent; VHS, DVD.** Mary Pickford; Jack Holt; Raymond Hatton; Walter Long; Hobart Bosworth; Ben Alexander; DeWitt Jennings; ***D:*** Cecil B. DeMille; ***W:*** Jeanie Macpherson; ***C:*** Alvin Wyckoff.

Little Ashes 🦴 ½ **2009 (R)** Pattinson is miscast (lightweight and with a horrible accent) as young Salvador Dali, the Spanish surrealist as seen in his student days in the early 1920s. Dali goes to Madrid to attend a progressive university and befriends future poet/playwright Federico Garcia Lorca (Beltran) and future filmmaker Luis Bunuel (McNulty). Dali's flamboyance is obvious but his romantic interest in Garcia Lorca is suppressed thanks to his own anxieties, Spain's conservative mores, and Bunuel's homophobic tirades. Bunuel and Dali both travel to Paris in the mid-1920s while Garcia Lorca, who acknowledges his homosexuality, stays in Spain. Director Morrison makes no claims for biopic accuracy, preferring speculations and little analysis for his handsomely-designed and shot film. **112m/C; DVD, Blu-Ray.** *UK SP* Robert Pattinson; Javier Beltran; Matthew McNulty; Marina Gatell; Arly Jover; ***D:*** Paul Morrison; ***W:*** Philippa Goslett; ***C:*** Adam Suschitzky; ***M:*** Miguel Mera.

Little Athens 🦴 **2005 (R)** A day in the life of a multitude of annoying characters who live in Little Athens, Arizona. Drug dealer Jimmy is in hock to a bookie; Heather's paranoid that her boyfriend is cheating on her; self-involved Jessica is worried that her boyfriend will come after her for allegedly giving him an STD; and loopy buds Pedro and Corey are scrambling to pay their overdue rent before they're evicted. All come together at the same party where they'll continue to make bad choices and you won't care. **105m/C; DVD.** John Patrick Amedori; Erica Leerhsen; Eric Szmanda; Rachel Miner; Jill Ritchie; Kenny Morrison; Jorge Garcia; DJ Qualls; Michael Peña; Michelle Horn; ***D:*** Tom Zuber; ***W:*** Tom Zuber; Jeff Zuber; ***C:*** Lisa Wiegand; ***M:*** Barak Moffitt.

Little Big Horn 🦴🦴 ½ *The Fighting Seventh* **1951** Low-budget depiction of Custer et al. at Little Big Horn actually has its gripping moments; solid acting all around helps. **88m/B; VHS, DVD.** Marie Windsor; John Ireland; Lloyd Bridges; Reed Hadley; Hugh O'Brian; Jim Davis; ***D:*** Charles Marquis Warren.

Little Big League 🦴🦴 ½ **1994 (PG)** 12-year-old inherits the Minnesota Twins baseball team from his grandfather, appoints himself manager when everyone else declines, and becomes the youngest owner-manager in history. Nothing new about the premise, but kids and America's favorite pastime add up to good clean family fun. Features real-life baseball players, including the Ken Griffey, Jr. and Paul O'Neill. Screenwriting debut from Pincus, and directorial debut from the executive producer of "Seinfeld," Scheinman. **120m/C; DVD.** Luke Edwards; Jason Robards, Jr.; Kevin Dunn; Dennis Farina; John Ashton; Jonathan Silverman; Wolfgang Bodison; Timothy Busfield; Ashley Crow; Scott Patterson; Billy L. Sullivan; Miles Feulner; ***D:*** Andrew Scheinman; ***W:*** Gregory Pincus; Adam Scheinman; ***C:*** Donald E. Thorin; ***M:*** Stanley Clarke.

Little Big Man 🦴🦴🦴 ½ **1970 (PG)** Based on Thomas Berger's picaresque novel, this is the story of 121-year-old Jack Crabb and his quixotic life as gunslinger, charlatan, Indian, ally to George Custer, and the only white survivor of Little Big Horn. Told mainly through flashbacks. Hoffman provides a classic portrayal of Crabb, as fact and myth are jumbled and reshaped. **135m/C; VHS, DVD, Blu-Ray.** Dustin Hoffman; Faye Dunaway; Chief Dan George; Richard Mulligan; Martin Balsam; Jeff Corey; Aimee (Amy) Eccles; ***D:*** Arthur Penn; ***W:*** Calder Willingham; ***C:*** Harry Stradling, Jr. Natl. Film Reg. '14; N.Y. Film Critics '70: Support. Actor (George); Natl. Soc. Film Critics '70: Support. Actor (George).

Little Bigfoot 🦴🦴 ½ **1996 (PG)** The Shoemaker family are taking a camping vacation when the kids discover a baby bigfoot in the wilderness. They find out the hairy little guy and his mom are threatened by the owner of a logging company, who's hired a group of hunters to get rid of the critters. **99m/C; VHS, DVD.** Ross Malinger; P.J. Soles; Ken Tigar; Kelly Packard; Don Stroud; Matt McCoy; ***D:*** Art Camacho; ***W:*** Richard Preston, Jr.; ***C:*** Ken Blakey; ***M:*** Louis Febre. **VIDEO**

Little Bigfoot 2: The Journey Home 🦴 **1997 (PG)** Dull and saccharine sequel has an unlikeable family on a camping trip finding and protecting the titular critter from hunters and an evil industrialist. **93m/C; VHS, DVD.** Stephen Furst; Steve Eastin; Tom Bosley; Taran Noah Smith; Michael Fishman; Art Camacho; ***D:*** Art Camacho; ***W:*** Art Camacho; ***M:*** Jim Halfpenny.

A Little Bit of Heaven **WOOF! 2011 (PG-13)** Goopy sentiment is the least of this risible dramedy's problems when free-spirited, commitment-phobe Marley (Hudson), who's living the good life in New Orleans, is diagnosed with terminal cancer. She hallucinates that she meets God (Goldberg) who grants her three wishes; falls in love with her doctor, Julian (Garcia Bernal); and gets all squishy with her supportive friends and family. The barfing will be done by the viewer. **106m/C; DVD, Blu-Ray.** Kate Hudson; Gael Garcia Bernal; Whoopi Goldberg; Kathy Bates; Treat Williams; Lucy Punch; Romany Malco; Rosemarie DeWitt; Steven Weber; Peter Dinklage; Alan Dale; Jason Davis; Bailey Bass; Charlotte Bass; ***D:*** Nicole Kassell; ***W:*** Gren Wells; ***C:*** Russell Carpenter; ***M:*** Heitor Pereira; Ivan Neville.

A Little Bit of Soul 🦴🦴 ½ **1997 (R)** Godfrey Usher (Rush) is an ambitious politician whose present position is that of federal treasurer, a job he has no clue about. Usher is married to Grace Michael (Mitchell) the head of a philanthropic foundation. Scientist Richard Shorkinghorm (Wenham) and his ex-lover Kate Haslett (O'Connor) have both applied for funding from the foundation and are invited to the Usher/Michael home for a weekend. Surprises abound for Richard and Kate when they discover their kinky hosts are Satanists. Amusing comedy does falter but its not the fault of the performers. **83m/C; DVD.** *AU* Geoffrey Rush; David Wenham; Frances O'Connor; Heather Mitchell; John Gaden; Kerry Walker; ***D:*** Peter Duncan; ***W:*** Peter Duncan; ***C:*** Martin McGrath; ***M:*** Nigel Westlake.

Little Black Book 🦴 **2004 (PG-13)** Pouty blonde Stacy (Murphy) wants to be a broadcast journalist but is slaving away at a lousy daytime talk show. Maybe things will go better in her romance with sports agent Derek (Livingston). Oops, shouldn't have peeked at his Palm Pilot, which lists his glamorous, maybe-not-so-ex-girlfriends. Since Derek doesn't talk about his past relationships, Stacy sets up "interviews" with three of the gals to check out her possible rivals. Eventually, her snooping and her job converge into one big mess—a fitting description of the movie. **95m/C; DVD.** Brittany Murphy; Holly Hunter; Kathy Bates; Ron Livingston; Julianne Nicholson; Stephen Tobolowsky; Kevin Sussman; Josie Maran; Rashida Jones; Jason Antoon; ***D:*** Nick Hurran; ***W:*** Elisa Bell;

Melissa Carter; ***C:*** Theo van de Sande; ***M:*** Christophe Beck.

Little Boy Blue **1997** Southern Gothic family drama focuses on Jimmy (Phillippe), the son of paranoid, impotent, abusive Vietnam vet Ray West (Savage). Ray runs a bar with his timid wife Kate (Kinski), whom he forces to sleep with Jimmy to satisfy his own twisted sexual kicks. Secrets from the past are dredged up when a mysterious woman (Knight) arrives bringing revenge on Ray for ruining her life and the possibility of freedom for the tormented family. Excellent performances save the twisted ball of loose strings that make up the farfetched plot. **107m/C; DVD.** Ryan Phillippe; John Savage; Nastassja Kinski; Shirley Knight; Jenny Lewis; Tyrin Turner; ***D:*** Antonio Tibaldi; ***W:*** Michael Boston; ***C:*** Ron Hagen; ***M:*** Stewart Copeland.

Little Boy Lost **1978 (G)** The true story of the disappearance of a young boy in Australia. **92m/C; VHS, DVD.** *AU* John Hargreaves; Tony Barry; Lorna Lesley; ***D:*** Alan Spires.

Little Buddha **1993 (PG)** Tibetan Lama Norbu informs the Seattle Konrad family that their 10-year-old son Jesse may be the reincarnation of a respected monk. He wants to take the boy back to Tibet to find out and the family head off on their spiritual quest. In an effort to instruct Jesse in Buddhism, his story is interspersed with that of Prince Siddhartha, who leaves behind his worldly ways to follow the path towards enlightenment and become the Buddha. The two stories are an ill-fit, the acting's awkward, but boy, does the film look good. Filmed on location in Nepal and Bhutan. **123m/C; DVD.** Keanu Reeves; Alex Wiesendanger; Ying Ruocheng; Chris Isaak; Bridget Fonda; ***D:*** Bernardo Bertolucci; ***W:*** Mark Peploe; Rudy Wurlitzer; ***C:*** Vittorio Storaro; ***M:*** Ryuichi Sakamoto.

Little Caesar **1930** A small-time hood rises to become a gangland czar, but his downfall is as rapid as his rise. Still thrilling. The role of Rico made Robinson a star and typecast him as a crook for all time. **80m/B; DVD, Blu-Ray.** Edward G. Robinson; Glenda Farrell; Sidney Blackmer; Douglas Fairbanks, Jr.; ***D:*** Mervyn LeRoy; ***W:*** Francis Edwards Faragoh; ***C:*** Gaetano Antonio "Tony" Gaudio. Natl. Film Reg. '00.

A Little Chaos **1/2 2014 (R)** Rickman's directorial debut features little of the personality he has so often displayed as an actor. It's a particular waste given who Rickman cast in his film. The always-great Winslet stars as Sabine, a landscape designer tasked with building a garden in Versailles for King Louis XIV (Rickman). When Sabine meets the palace's renowned landscape artist Andre Le Notre (Schoenaerts), she falls hard and fast, but class issues keep their romance stifled, of course. This is a surprisingly forgettable historical drama, lacking the passion and character one has come to expect from Rickman and Winslet. **116m/C; DVD, Blu-Ray, Streaming.** *UK* Kate Winslet; Matthias Schoenaerts; Alan Rickman; Stanley Tucci; Helen McCrory; Jennifer Ehle; ***D:*** Alan Rickman; ***W:*** Alan Rickman; Jeremy Brock; Alison Deegan; ***C:*** Ellen Kuras; ***M:*** Peter Gregson.

Little Chenier: A Cajun Story **2006 (R)** Beaux Dupuis (Schaech) looks out for his mentally retarded brother Pemon (Koehler) while scratching out a living on the titular Louisiana bayou. Beaux's reckless enough to have taken up again with Mary-Louise (Braun), an ex-girlfriend who married deputy sheriff Carl Lebauve (Davidson). When Pemon is accused of a crime, jealous Carl works to turn the community against the brothers. The area where the film was shot was destroyed by Hurricane Rita only weeks after shooting was completed. **100m/C; DVD.** Johnathon Schaech; Frederick Koehler; Clifton (Gonzalez) Collins, Jr.; Chris Mulkey; Tamara Braun; Jeremy Davidson; ***D:*** Bethany Ashton Wolf; ***W:*** Tamara Braun; Bethany Ashton Wolf; Jace Johnson; ***C:*** Tanya Koop; ***M:*** Michael Picton.

Little Children **2006 (R)** Adultery in the 'burbs and a vulnerable sex offender on parole collide in Perrotta's adaptation of his 2004 novel. Bored outsider Sarah (Winslet) is with the other moms at the playground where handsome house husband Brad (Wilson) also plays with his son. A brief first meeting slowly leads to an affair, eventually discovered by Brad's successful wife Kathy (Connelly). Meanwhile, Brad's tightly wound, ex-cop buddy Larry (Emmerich) is on a mission to rid the neighborhood of ex-con Ronald (Haley), who's living with his doting mom (Somerville). Field drags things out too long but the performances are strong. **130m/C; DVD.** Kate Winslet; Patrick Wilson; Jennifer Connelly; Jackie Earle Haley; Noah Emmerich; Gregg Edelman; Phyllis Somerville; Sadie Goldstein; ***Nar:*** Will Lyman; ***D:*** Todd Field; ***W:*** Todd Field; Tom Perrotta; ***C:*** Antonio Calvache; ***M:*** Thomas Newman.

Little Church Around the Corner **1/2 1923** Silent small town melodrama about a preacher who falls in love with a mine owner's daughter, but finds he isn't dad's favorite fella when he confronts him about poor mining conditions. When the mine caves in, the preacher man's caught between a rock and hard place when his sweetie's family needs protection from an angry mob. **70m/B; Silent; VHS, DVD.** Kenneth Harlan; Hobart Bosworth; Walter Long; Pauline Starke; Alec B. Francis; Margaret Seddon; George Cooper; ***D:*** William A. Seiter.

Little Cigars **1/2 1973** Cleo witnesses her gangster boyfriend Travis murdering a rival and decides she'd be safer elsewhere. She stumbles across a quintet of hard-living midgets who use a circus act as a cover for their burglary ring. Cleo joins their criminal enterprise but the mobster is still searching for her. Neither as exploitative nor as camp as might be imagined. **92m/C; DVD.** Angel Tompkins; Billy Curtis; Jerry Maren; Felix Silla; Frank Delfino; Emory Souza; Joe De Santis; ***D:*** Chris Christenberry; ***W:*** Frank Ray Perilli; Louis Garfinkle; ***C:*** John Stephens; ***M:*** Harry Betts.

Little City **1/2 1997 (R)** Best friends Kevin (Bon Jovi) and Adam (Charles) discover sex can screw up the best relationship. Adam's current girlfriend Nina (Sciorra) is having an affair with Kevin, while his ex-girlfriend Kate (Going) is having problems with her girlfriend Ann (Williams), who broke up Adam and Kate. Now Kate is having a fling with Rebecca (Miller), who's just flirting with lesbianism, and Rebecca then gets involved with Adam. Meanwhile, Kevin decides he's in love with Nina (she's not reciprocating that emotion) and Kate begins thinking about going back to Adam. San Francisco turns out to be a very small town. **90m/C; VHS, DVD.** Jon Bon Jovi; Penelope Ann Miller; Annabella Sciorra; Josh Charles; Joanna Going; JoBeth Williams; ***D:*** Roberto Benabib; ***W:*** Roberto Benabib; ***C:*** Randall Love.

The Little Colonel **1935 (PG)** After the Civil War, an embittered Southern patriarch turns his back on his family, until his dimple-cheeked granddaughter softens his heart. Hokey and heartwarming. Shirley's first teaming with Bill "Bojangles" Robinson features the famous dance scene. Adapted by William Conselman from the Annie Fellows Johnston best-seller. **80m/B; VHS, DVD.** Shirley Temple; Lionel Barrymore; Evelyn Venable; John Lodge; Hattie McDaniel; Bill Robinson; Sidney Blackmer; ***D:*** David Butler; ***C:*** Arthur C. Miller.

Little Devil **2007** Ten-year-old Oliver knows his parents' marriage is failing. Though they try to keep it from him, they can't stop drinking, fighting, and walking out. Upset that they may get divorced, Ollie first tries to be very, very good but when that doesn't work, he decides to be very, very bad instead. **131m/C; DVD.** *GB* Robson Green; Maggie O'Neill; James Wilby; Emily Joyce; Joseph Friend; ***D:*** David Richards; ***W:*** Tim Loane; ***C:*** Andrew Speller; ***M:*** Hal Lindes. **TV**

Little Dorrit **1/2 2008** Sprawling BBC miniseries based on the sprawling novel by Charles Dickens exposing the 19th-century's harsh class distinctions. Seamstress Amy Dorrit (Foy) has grown up in debtor's prison where her addled father William (Courtenay) has been held for more than 20 years. Employed by Mrs. Clennam (Parfit), Dorrit's plight comes to the attention of Arthur Clennam (Macfadyen), who fears his family is responsible for the Dorrits' misfortune. Romantic impediments keep them apart and there's blackmail, bureaucracy, and shady financial doings besides. **452m/C; DVD.** Matthew Macfadyen; Tom Courtenay; Judy Parfitt; Alun Armstrong; Claire Foy; Andy Serkis; Emma Pierson; Eddie Marsan; Bill Paterson; Sue Johnston; Russell Tovey; Georgia King; James Fleet; ***D:*** Diarmuid Lawrence; Dearbhla Walsh; Adam Smith; ***W:*** Andrew Davies; ***C:*** Owen McPolin; Lukas Strebel; Alan Almond; ***M:*** John Lunn. **TV**

Little Dragons **1980** A grandfather and two young karate students rescue a family held captive by a backwoods gang. **90m/C; VHS, DVD.** Ann Sothern; Joe Spinell; Charles Lane; Chris Petersen; Pat Petersen; Sally Boyden; Rick Lenz; Sharon Weber; Tony Bill; ***D:*** Curtis Hanson; ***W:*** Alan Ormsby.

The Little Drummer Girl **1984 (R)** An Israeli counterintelligence agent recruits an actress sympathetic to the Palestinian cause to trap a fanatical terrorist leader. Solid performances from Keaton as the actress and Kinski as the Israeli counter-intelligence office sustain interest through a puzzling, sometimes boring and frustrating, cinematic maze of espionage. Keaton is at or near her very best. Based on the bestselling novel by John Le Carre. **130m/C; VHS, DVD.** Diane Keaton; Klaus Kinski; Yorgo Voyagis; Sami Frey; Michael Cristofer; Anna Massey; Thorley Walters; ***D:*** George Roy Hill; ***M:*** Dave Grusin.

Little Fish **2005 (R)** As a video store manager in the tough "Little Saigon" suburb of Sydney, Australia, Tracy Heart (a deft Blanchett) has dreams of starting her own business, although the recovering junkie is having trouble securing the funds. Her protective mother Janelle (Hazlehurst) labors to keep her daughter away from the bad influences surrounding her, including the return of her estranged stepfather Lionel (Weaving), a user who Janelle accuses of influencing Tracy's addiction. Vivid storyline focuses on living life post-addiction. **114m/C; DVD.** Cate Blanchett; Sam Neill; Hugo Weaving; Martin Henderson; Noni Hazlehurst; Dustin Nguyen; Joel Tobeck; ***D:*** Rowan Woods; ***W:*** Jacquelin Perske; ***C:*** Danny Ruhlmann; ***M:*** Nathan Larson.

Little Fockers **1/2 2010 (PG-13)** In this third installment in the Fockers franchise, Greg (Stiller) and Pam (Polo) Focker plan a birthday party for their two children (Tahan and Balocchi) at the estate of Pam's uber-wealthy ex-boyfriend Kevin (Wilson). As it happens, Kevin is still obsessed with Pam, which leaves the door open for Pam's father, Jack (DeNiro), to undermine the Fockers' happy marriage. The usual conflict and physical comedy ensues, culminating in an outright maelstrom of absurdity. Hilarious ensemble cast, but don't look for anything new here. **98m/C; Blu-Ray.** Ben Stiller; Robert De Niro; Teri Polo; Blythe Danner; Barbra Streisand; Owen Wilson; Dustin Hoffman; Daisy Tahan; Colin Baiocchi; Sergio Calderon; Jessica Alba; ***D:*** Paul Weitz; ***W:*** Larry Stuckey; John Hamburg; ***C:*** Remi Adefarasin; ***M:*** Stephen Trask. Golden Raspberries '10: Worst Support. Actress (Alba).

The Little Foxes **1/2 1941** A vicious southern woman will destroy everyone around her to satisfy her desire for wealth and power. Filled with corrupt characters who commit numerous revolting deeds. The vicious matriarch is a part made to fit for Davis, and she makes the most of it. Script by Lillian Hellman from her own play. **116m/B; VHS, DVD.** Bette Davis; Herbert Marshall; Dan Duryea; Teresa Wright; Charles Dingle; Richard Carlson; Carl Benton Reid; Patricia Collinge; ***D:*** William Wyler; ***W:*** Lillian Hellman; ***C:*** Gregg Toland; ***M:*** Meredith Willson.

Little Fugitive **1953** Seven-year-old Joey (Andrusco) is convinced by his Brooklyn pals that he's murdered his brother. So the tyke takes off and winds up wandering lost around Coney Island. Independent feature made on a miniscule budget features endearing performances from non-pros. **80m/C; VHS, DVD, Blu-Ray.** Richie Andrusco; Ricky Brewster; Winnifred Cushing; Jay Williams; ***D:*** Morris Engel; Ruth Orkin; Ray Ashley; ***W:*** Ray Ashley; ***C:*** Morris Engel; ***M:*** Eddy Manson. Natl. Film Reg. '97.

Little Fugitive **2006** His dad's in prison and his mom's neglectful, so Lenny must look after his 7-year-old brother Joey. On his 12th birthday, Lenny and his friends intend to go to Coney Island and he tells Joey he must stay behind. When Joey disobeys, Lenny plays a prank that backfires and Joey runs away. A more downbeat remake of the 1953 film. **87m/C; DVD.** Justina Machado; Peter Dinklage; Lois Smith; Brendan Sexton, III; David Castro; Nicolas Marti-Salgado; Austin Talynn Carpenter; ***D:*** Joanna Lipper; ***W:*** Joanna Lipper; ***C:*** Richard Sands; ***M:*** Barrington Pheloung.

The Little Giant **1/2 1933** Gangster spoof finds successful Chicago bootlegger Bugs Ahearn (Robinson) moving to California to live the society life. He falls for Polly (Vinson), a cold-hearted dame with a larcenous family who get Bugs involved in a stock swindle. When it looks like Bugs is going to take the fall, he contacts his Chicago cohorts and uses them as muscle to clear himself. Meanwhile, sweet Ruth (Astor), who's been working as Bugs' social secretary, waits for the lug to realize she's the perfect doll for him. **70m/B; DVD.** Edward G. Robinson; Helen Vinson; Mary Astor; Kenneth Thomson; Russell Hopton; Berton Churchill; Shirley Grey; Donald Dillaway; Louise Mackintosh; ***D:*** Roy Del Ruth; ***W:*** Robert Lord; Wilson Mizner; ***C:*** Sidney Hickox.

Little Giant **1/2 1946** The duo fly separately in this entry, which highlights Costello's comic talents and leaves Abbott in the supporting role. Costello is a country bumpkin come to the big city to get enough money to marry his sweetheart. He's hired to sell vacuum cleaners by Abbott and becomes the butt of everyone's jokes but the joke's on them when Lou becomes the company's top-selling salesman. **92m/B; VHS, DVD.** Bud Abbott; Lou Costello; Brenda Joyce; Jacqueline DeWit; George Cleveland; Elena Verdugo; Mary Gordon; Pierre Watkin; ***D:*** William A. Seiter; ***W:*** Walter DeLeon.

Little Giants **1/2 1994 (PG)** Familiar kids/sport movie about the klutzy coach (Moranis) of an equally woeful pee-wee football team. Coach Danny is up against his overbearing big brother Kevin (O'Neill), former local football hero and the coach of the best team in town. Naturally, there's the big game between the misfit underdogs and the stars. Predictable, of course, but not without some amusing moments. **106m/C; VHS, DVD.** Rick Moranis; Ed O'Neill; Shawna Waldron; Mary Ellen Trainor; Devon Sawa; Susanna Thompson; Todd Bosley; Alexa Vega; Joey Simmrin; Sam Horrigan; Brian Haley; Mathew McCurley; Harry Shearer; Dabbs Greer; ***Cameo(s):*** John Madden; ***D:*** Duwayne Dunham; ***W:*** Tommy Swerdlow; Michael Goldberg; James Ferguson; Robert Shallcross; ***C:*** Janusz Kaminski; ***M:*** John Debney.

Little Girl. . . Big Tease **1975 (R)** Teen society girl is kidnapped and exploited (along with the viewer) by a group which includes her teacher. **86m/C; VHS, DVD.** Jody Ray; Rebecca Brooke; ***D:*** Roberto Mitrotti.

Little Girl Lost: The Delimar Vera Story **1/2 2008** Wrenching true story about a mother's certainty that her infant daughter, Delimar, was not killed in a house fire. Philadelphia mom Luz Cuevas (Reyes) is so convinced that her daughter was taken by her distant cousin Valerie (Ortiz), who then set the fire to cover her tracks, that her marriage breaks up over her obsession. A six-year search ensues with Luz getting help from sympathetic politician Angel Cruz (Martinez). You know where this story is going but it's certainly worth the time. **90m/C; DVD.** Judy Reyes; Ana Ortiz; Marlene Forte; Mark Humphrey; Eli Gabay; A. Martinez; Hector Bustamante; Jillian Bruno; ***D:*** Paul Kaufman; ***W:*** Maria Nation; Christopher Canaan; ***C:*** Mathias Herndl; ***M:*** Joseph Julian Gonzalez. **CABLE**

The Little Girl Who Lives down the Lane **1/2 1976 (PG)** Engrossing, offbeat thriller about a strange 13-year-old girl whose father is never home, and who hides something—we won't say what—in her basement. Very young Foster is excellent, as are her supporters, including Sheen as the child molester who knows what she's hiding. Based on the novel by Koenig, who also penned the script. **90m/C; VHS, DVD, Blu-Ray.** *CA FR* Jodie Foster; Martin Sheen; Alexis Smith; Scott Jacoby; Mort Shuman; Dorothy Davis; Hubert Noel; Jacques Famery; Mary Morter; Judie Wildman; ***D:*** Nicolas Gessner; ***W:*** Laird Koenig; ***C:*** Rene Verzier; ***M:*** Christian Gaubert.

A Little Help **1/2 2011 (R)** It's a few months after 9/11 and stressed Laura's neglectful husband Bobby has dropped dead after recently seeing a doctor. Self-medicating herself with beer and cigarettes, Laura isn't coping with either her angry preteen son Dennis or her intrusive family, who insist she file a malpractice lawsuit. Dennis decides to fit into his new private school by lying that his father was a heroic firefighter who died as a first responder. Hapless Laura goes along, making the situation worse. **109m/C; DVD, Blu-Ray.** Jenna Fischer; Daniel Yelsky; Chris O'Donnell; Kim Coates; Lesley Ann Warren; Ron Leibman; ***D:*** Michael J. Weithorn; ***W:*** Michael J. Weithorn; ***C:*** Tom Harting; ***M:*** Austin Wintory.

Little Heroes 🦴🦴 1/2 **1991 (G)** An impoverished little girl gets through hard times with the aid of her loyal dog (the Hound can relate). A low-budget family tearjerker that nonetheless works, it claims to be based on a true story. **78m/C; VHS, DVD.** Raeanin Simpson; Katherine Willis; Keith Christensen; ***D:*** Craig Clyde; ***W:*** Craig Clyde; ***M:*** Jon McCallum.

The Little Hours 🦴🦴🦴 **2017 (R)** A wicked, hilarious, and raunchy peek behind the veil of a medieval convent. After their abusive insults drive away their laborer, three nuns turn their lusty attention to his replacement (Franco), who finds it increasingly difficult to maintain his cover as a deaf-mute. The setting may be 14th century, but the dialogue and attitude are thoroughly modern. Loosely based on "The Decameron," by Giovanni Boccaccio. **90m/C; DVD, Blu-Ray.** Alison Brie; Dave Franco; Kate Micucci; Aubrey Plaza; John C. Reilly; ***D:*** Jeff Baena; ***W:*** Jeff Baena; ***C:*** Quyen Tran; ***M:*** Dan Romer.

Little House on the Prairie 🦴🦴🦴 **1974** Pilot for the TV series based on the life of Laura Ingalls Wilder and her family's struggles on the American plains in the 1860s. Other episodes are also available on tape, including one in which Patricia Neal guest stars as a terminally ill widow seeking a home for her children. Neal's performance earned her a best actress Emmy in 1975. **98m/C; VHS, DVD.** Michael Landon; Karen Grassle; Victor French; Melissa Gilbert; Melissa Sue Anderson; ***D:*** Michael Landon. **TV**

A Little Inside 🦴🦴 1/2 **2001 (PG)** Ed Mills (King) is a promising minor-league baseball player who quits the game when his wife dies so he can care for their daughter. Five years later, Ed is still struggling with this parenting gig, especially since Abby (Eisenberg) is growing up and getting into girlier things than Ed can cope with. So, since Abby does like baseball, Ed decides to take a second shot at rejoining his old team and regaining Abby's attention. The pint-sized Eisenberg is a scene-stealer par excellence. **95m/C; VHS, DVD.** Benjamin King; Hallie Kate Eisenberg; Kathy Baker; Frankie Faison; Amanda Detmer; Jay Harrington; Sean Michael Arthur; Jared Padalecki; ***D:*** Kara Harshbarger; ***W:*** Kara Harshbarger; ***M:*** James Levine. **VIDEO**

Little Joe 🦴🦴 1/2 **2019** Lead scientist/detached single mom Alice (Beecham) has created happy plants that act as antidepressants. She names them Little Joe after her human son, teen Joe (Connor). Each plant emits a pollen that causes a sneeze and total devotion, but those who inhale the pollen seem emotionally flat rather than happy. When Alice brings Joe one of the plants on the sly, he becomes infected by the plant and the extent of its impact on human interaction comes to light. The science fiction-horror film's unique premise is just creepy enough for genre fans. **100m/C; DVD, Blu-Ray.** Emily Beecham; Ben Whishaw; Kerry Fox; Kit Connor; Phenix Brossard; ***D:*** Jessica Hausner; ***W:*** Jessica Hausner; Geraldine Bajard; ***C:*** Martin Gschlacht.

Little John 🦴🦴 1/2 **2002** Natalie Britain (Reuben) is a Family Court judge with a secret of her own. Twelve years ago, she gave birth to a baby boy that she thought was put up for adoption. Instead, Little John (Bailey Jr.), known as L.J., was raised on a Texas farm by Natalie's estranged father John (Rhames). When John's health begins to fail, it's time for his daughter to learn the truth and for L.J. to get to know his mom. **98m/C; VHS, DVD.** Gloria Reuben; Ving Rhames; Robert Bailey, Jr.; Patty Duke; ***D:*** Dick Lowry. **TV**

The Little Kidnappers 🦴🦴 1/2 **1990 (G)** Embittered man (Heston) is forced to take in his Scottish grandsons when the two boys are orphaned. They settle in with gramps in Nova Scotia but when the duo decide to adopt the abandoned baby they've found, they are accused of being kidnappers. Cable remake of 1953 British film. **100m/C; VHS, Streaming.** *CA* Charlton Heston; Bruce Greenwood; Leah K. Pinsent; Charles Miller; Leo Wheatley; Patricia Gage; ***D:*** Donald Shebib. **CABLE**

Little Ladies of the Night 🦴 *Diamond Alley* **1977** Former pimp tries to save Purl and other teenagers from the world of prostitution. Exploitation posing as "significant drama." **96m/C; VHS, DVD.** Linda Purl; David Soul; Clifton Davis; Carolyn Jones; Louis Gossett, Jr.; ***D:*** Marvin J. Chomsky.

Little Laura & Big John 🦴🦴 **1973** The true-life exploits of the small-time Ashley Gang in the Florida everglades around the turn of the century. Fabian's comeback vehicle, for what it's worth. **82m/C; VHS, DVD.** Fabian; Karen Black; ***D:*** Luke Moberly.

Little Lord Fauntleroy 🦴🦴🦴 1/2 **1936** The vintage Hollywood version of the Frances Hodgson Burnett story of a fatherless American boy who discovers he's heir to a British dukedom. Also available in computer-colorized version. Well cast, charming, remade for TV in 1980. Smith is loveable as the noble tyke's crusty old guardian. **102m/B; VHS, DVD, Blu-Ray.** Freddie Bartholomew; Sir C. Aubrey Smith; Mickey Rooney; Dolores Costello; Jessie Ralph; Guy Kibbee; ***D:*** John Cromwell; ***W:*** Hugh Walpole; ***C:*** Charles Rosher; ***M:*** Max Steiner.

Little Lord Fauntleroy 🦴🦴 1/2 **1995 (G)** British TV adaptation of the Frances Hodgson Burnett classic finds Cedric Erroll's life changing forever when he's discovered to be the only heir to the Earl of Dorincourt. But the Earl turns out to be a bitter miser and it's up to the innocent child to get grandpa to enjoy life. **100m/C; VHS, DVD.** *GB* Michael Benz; Betsy Brantley; George Baker; Bernice Stegers; ***D:*** Andrew Morgan. **TV**

Little Man 🦴 **2006 (PG-13)** Another Wayans family vehicle, probably the worst yet, attempts to make a film about a dwarf jewel thief who poses as a baby in order to retrieve a stolen diamond he stashed with an unsuspecting couple. CGI-manipulation puts Wayans' face on a pint-sized body, while the "humor" seems to have been lifted directly from old Bugs Bunny cartoons and the crotch-shots of "America's Funniest Home Videos," either of which are better than this clunker. Directed by elder Wayans sib, Keenen Ivory. **97m/C; DVD, Blu-Ray.** Marlon Wayans; Shawn Wayans; Kerry Washington; Tracy Morgan; John Witherspoon; Lochlyn Munro; Chazz Palminteri; Linden Porco; Molly Shannon; Gabe Pimental; ***D:*** Keenen Ivory Wayans; ***W:*** Marlon Wayans; Shawn Wayans; Keenen Ivory Wayans; ***C:*** Steven Bernstein; ***M:*** Teddy Castellucci. Golden Raspberries '06: Worst Actor (Wayans), Worst Actor (Wayans), Worst Remake.

Little Man Tate 🦴🦴🦴 **1991 (PG)** A seven-year-old genius is the prize in a tug of war between his mother, who wants him to lead a normal life, and a domineering school director who loves him for his intellect. An acclaimed directorial debut for Foster, with overtones of her own extraordinary life as a child prodigy. **99m/C; VHS, DVD, Blu-Ray.** Jodie Foster; Dianne Wiest; Harry Connick, Jr.; Adam Hann-Byrd; George Plimpton; Debi Mazar; Celia Weston; David Hyde Pierce; Danitra Vance; Josh Mostel; P.J. Ochlan; ***D:*** Jodie Foster; ***W:*** Scott Frank; ***C:*** Mike Southon; ***M:*** Mark Isham.

Little Manhattan 🦴🦴 **2005 (PG)** Puppy love. Average 11-year-old Gabe (Hutcherson) likes to hang out with his pals and play hoops. Then, in karate class, he meets Rosemary (Ray) and Gabe is instantly smitten. But handling all these new emotions makes for some awkward moments. The overly-adult narration by Gabe is jarring but the outlook is sunny. **90m/C; DVD.** Bradley Whitford; Cynthia Nixon; Josh Hutcherson; Willie Garson; Charlie Ray; ***D:*** Marc Levin; ***W:*** Jennifer Flackett; ***C:*** Tim Orr; ***M:*** Chad Fischer.

Little Marines 🦴🦴 **1990** Three young boys journey into the wilderness for three days of fun and instead embark on an incredible adventure. **90m/C; VHS, DVD.** Stephen Baker; Steve Landers, Jr.; Noah Williams; ***D:*** A.J. Hixon.

Little Men 🦴🦴 **1934** Based on the novel by Louisa May Alcott. Jo March and Fritz Bhaer have married and opened a school for homeless boys. Young Nat invites street tough Dan to come to the school and the Bhaers take him in, believing in Dan's innocence even after he's accused of theft. **84m/B; DVD.** Ralph Morgan; Erin O'Brien-Moore; Frankie Darro; David Durand; Dickie Moore; Junior Durkin; Cora Sue Collins; ***D:*** Phil Rosen; ***W:*** Gertrude Orr; Ken Goldsmith; ***C:*** William Nobles; Ernest Miller.

Little Men 🦴 1/2 **1940** A modern version of the classic juvenile story by Louisa May Alcott is too cute for words. **86m/B; VHS, DVD.** Jack Oakie; Jimmy Lydon; Kay Francis; George Bancroft; Anne Howard; ***D:*** Norman Z. McLeod.

Little Men 🦴🦴 1/2 **1998 (PG)** In Louisa May Alcott's sequel to "Little Women," Jo March (Hemingway) has grown up, married Fritz Bhaer (Sarandon), and opened an idyllic, wholesome school for troubled boys. The house is immaculate, the grounds are beautiful, and the boys are little angels. That is, until streetwise 14-year-old Dan (Cook) shows up. He soon has the boys smoking, drinking, and stealing, until they almost burn the place down. Since this is a family movie, with moral lessons to be learned, all's well by the end. Adults may find the syrupy sweetness too much to take, but young kids should enjoy it. **98m/C; Streaming.** Mariel Hemingway; Chris Sarandon; Michael Caloz; Ben Cook; Michael Yarmush; Gabrielle Boni; Ricky Mabe; Julia Garland; B.J. McLellan; Tyler Hines; ***D:*** Rodney Gibbons; ***W:*** Mark Evan Schwartz; ***C:*** Arch Archambault; ***M:*** Milan Kymlicka.

Little Men 🦴🦴🦴 **2016 (PG)** Jake's (Taplitz) grandfather passes away and leaves a building he owned to Jake's father (Kinnear) and mother (Ehle). In that building, Leonor (Garcia) has been running a dress shop at a very low rent for years. Leonor's son Tony (Barbieri) befriends Jake, but the parents squabble over rent increases and the possible sale of the building. How race, class, and family structure play a role in young friendships in major cities has rarely been as delicately handled as it in Sachs' beautiful drama. It helps that the young actors and Kinnear are fantastic. **85m/C; DVD.** Greg Kinnear; Jennifer Ehle; Paulina Garcia; Alfred Molina; Theo Taplitz; Michael Barbieri; ***D:*** Ira Sachs; ***W:*** Ira Sachs; Mauricio Zacharias; ***C:*** Óscar Durán; ***M:*** Dickon Hinchliffe.

The Little Mermaid 🦴🦴 1/2 **1975 (G)** An animated version of Hans Christian Andersen's tale about a little mermaid who rescues a prince whose boat has capsized. She immediately falls in love and wishes that she could become a human girl. Not to be confused with the 1989 Disney version. **71m/C; VHS, DVD.** *JP* ***V:*** Kirsten Bishop; Ian Finley; Thor Bishopric; ***D:*** Tim Reid; ***M:*** Ronald Goodwin.

The Little Mermaid 🦴🦴🦴 1/2 **1989 (G)** Headstrong teenage mermaid falls in love with a human prince and longs to be human too. She makes a pact with the evil Sea Witch to trade her voice for a pair of legs; based on the famous Hans Christian Andersen tale. Charming family musical, which harks back to the days of classic Disney animation, and hails a new era of superb Disney animated musicals. Sebastian the Crab nearly steals the show with his wit and showstopping number "Under the Sea." **82m/C; VHS, DVD, Blu-Ray.** ***V:*** Jodi Benson; Christopher Daniel Barnes; Pat Carroll; Rene Auberjonois; Samuel E. Wright; Buddy Hackett; Jason Marin; Edie McClurg; Kenneth Mars; Nancy Cartwright; ***D:*** John Musker; Ron Clements; ***W:*** John Musker; Ron Clements; ***M:*** Alan Menken; ***M:*** Howard Ashman. Oscars '89: Orig. Score, Song ("Under the Sea"); Golden Globes '90: Score, Song ("Under the Sea").

The Little Mermaid 🦴 1/2 **2018 (PG)** A reporter (Moseley) and his niece discover a real-life mermaid (Drayton) held captive in a 1930s circus by a villainous ringmaster (Gutierrez) who possesses her soul. Drayton is the sole treasure island in a sea of absurd storyline, bad acting, and blatant leveraging of title-association, as this live-action dud has little in common with the famed Disney animated musical or even the original Hans Christian Andersen fairy tale. **85m/C; DVD.** Poppy Drayton; William Moseley; Armando Gutierrez; Shirley MacLaine; Loreto Peralta; ***D:*** Blake Harris; ***W:*** Blake Harris; ***C:*** Neil Oseman; ***M:*** Jeremy Rubolino.

Little Minister 🦴🦴🦴 **1934** An adaptation of the James Barrie novel about a prissy Scottish pastor who falls in love with a free-spirited gypsy...he thinks she is, in fact, the local earl's daughter, played to perfection by the young Hepburn. **101m/B; VHS, DVD.** Katharine Hepburn; John Beal; Alan Hale; Donald Crisp; ***D:*** Richard Wallace; ***W:*** Victor Heerman; ***M:*** Max Steiner.

Little Miss Broadway 🦴🦴 **1938** Orphan Temple brings the residents of a theatrical boarding house together in hopes of getting them into show business. She and Durante give worthwhile performances. Also available in computer-colorized version. **70m/B; VHS, DVD.** Shirley Temple; George Murphy; Jimmy Durante; Phyllis Brooks; Edna May Oliver; George Barbier; Donald Meek; Jane Darwell; ***D:*** Irving Cummings; ***C:*** Arthur C. Miller.

Little Miss Marker 🦴🦴🦴 *Girl in Pawn* **1934** Heartwarming story starring Temple as the title character, who is left with bookie Sorrowful Jones (Menjou) as the IOU for a gambling debt. But when her father doesn't return, it's up to Jones and his racetrack friends to make little Marky a home. Naturally, Temple steals her way into everyone's heart. Based on a story by Damon Runyon; remade three times as "Sorrowful Jones," as "40 Pounds of Trouble," and in 1980 with the original title. **88m/B; VHS, DVD.** Adolphe Menjou; Shirley Temple; Dorothy Dell; Charles Bickford; Lynne Overman; ***D:*** Alexander Hall; ***W:*** Sam Hellman; Gladys Lehman; William R. Lipman; ***M:*** Ralph Rainger. Natl. Film Reg. '98.

Little Miss Marker 🦴 1/2 **1980 (PG)** Mediocre remake of the often retold story of a bookie who accepts a little girl as a security marker for a $10 bet. Disappointing performance from Curtis adds to an already dull film. **103m/C; VHS, DVD.** Walter Matthau; Julie Andrews; Tony Curtis; Bob Newhart; Lee Grant; Sara Stimson; Brian Dennehy; ***D:*** Walter Bernstein; ***W:*** Walter Bernstein; ***M:*** Henry Mancini.

Little Miss Nobody 🦴 1/2 **1936** Spirited young Judy is living in an orphanage when she discovers she's actually the long-lost daughter of a prominent attorney. However, she believes her best friend needs a home more than she does and tries to pass her off as the missing child but the ruse doesnt work for long. **65m/B; DVD.** Jane Withers; Jane Darwell; Ralph Morgan; Sara Haden; Harry Carey, Sr.; ***D:*** John Blystone; ***W:*** Lou Breslow; Paul Berger; Edward Eliscu; ***C:*** Bert Glennon.

Little Miss Sunshine 🦴🦴🦴 **2006 (R)** A quirky, dysfunctional family piles into their VW bus and road trips to California so little sis, Olive (Breslin), can compete (as an alternate from the Albuquerque region) in the titular pre-teen pageant, her young life's ambition. Along for the ride are her hugely unsuccessful motivational speaker dad (Kinnear), ready-to-snap mom (Collette), crass drug-snorting grandpa (Arkin), mute-by-choice Nietzschean brother (Dano), and suicidal despondent uncle (Carrell). Smart script in the hands of top-notch cast results in memorable, off-beat characters and an original, enjoyable movie. **101m/C; DVD, Blu-Ray.** Greg Kinnear; Toni Collette; Abigail Breslin; Steve Carell; Alan Arkin; Paul Dano; Bryan Cranston; Wallace (Wally) Langham; Mary Lynn Rajskub; Beth Grant; ***D:*** Jonathan Dayton; Valerie Faris; ***W:*** Michael Arndt; ***C:*** Tim Suhrstedt; ***M:*** Mychael Danna. Oscars '06: Orig. Screenplay, Support. Actor (Arkin); British Acad. '06: Orig. Screenplay, Support. Actor (Arkin); Ind. Spirit '07: Director (Dayton), Director (Faris), Film, First Screenplay, Support. Actor (Arkin); Screen Actors Guild '06: Cast; Writers Guild '06: Orig. Screenplay.

Little Monsters 🦴🦴 **1989 (PG)** A young boy (Savage) discovers a monster (Mandel) under his bed and eventually befriends it. The pair embark on adventures that land them in trouble. Hardworking, talented cast hurdles the weak script, but can't save the film. **100m/C; VHS, DVD.** Fred Savage; Howie Mandel; Margaret Whitton; Ben Savage;

Daniel Stern; Ric(k) Ducommun; Frank Whaley; ***D:*** Richard Alan Greenberg; ***W:*** Ted Elliott; Terry Rossio; ***C:*** Dick Bush; ***M:*** David Newman.

Little Monsters 1/2 **2019 (R)** After a bad break up, thirtysomething Australian metalhead Dave (England) is enraptured by his nephew Felix's (La Torraca) kindergarten teacher, Miss Caroline (Nyong'o). To impress her, Dave volunteers to chaperone the class field trip to a farm. Dave then realizes that he has no chance with the teacher and the kids are hard to deal with. The situation grows more complicated when zombies appear and the adults must ensure everyone's survival. The zombie comedy is more precious than funny, and its story focuses on Dave instead of the more interesting Miss Caroline and her kindergarteners, thus not fully using Nyong'o's talents. **94m/C; DVD.** Lupita Nyong'o; Alexander England; Josh Gad; Kat Stewart; Diesel La Torraca; ***D:*** Abe Forsythe; ***W:*** Abe Forsythe; ***C:*** Lachlan Milne; ***M:*** Piers Burbrook de Vere.

Little Moon & Jud McGraw 1/2 **1978** A wronged Indian woman and a framed cowpoke take their revenge on a small, corrupt town, razing it overnight. Already-weak plot is disabled by too many flashbacks. **92m/C; VHS, DVD.** James Caan; Sammy Davis, Jr.; Stefanie Powers; Aldo Ray; ***D:*** Bernard Girard.

Little Mother **1971** Metzger's take on Argentina's Eva Peron highlights her sexual powers (of course) as it tells of Eva's climb out of poverty and into the heights of political power. Filmed in Yugoslavia. **95m/C; VHS, DVD.** Christiane Kruger; Ivan Desny; Anton Diffring; ***D:*** Radley Metzger; ***W:*** Brian Phelan; ***C:*** Hans Jura.

Little Murders **1971 (PG)** Black comedy set in NYC. A woman convinces a passive photographer to marry her. Gardenia gives an excellent performance as the woman's father. A shadow of crime, depression, and strife seem to hangs over the funny parts of this film; more often depressing than anything else. Adapted by Jules Feiffer from his own play. **108m/C; VHS, DVD.** Elliott Gould; Marcia Rodd; Vincent Gardenia; Elizabeth Wilson; Jon Korkes; Donald Sutherland; Alan Arkin; Lou Jacobi; ***D:*** Alan Arkin; ***W:*** Jules Feiffer; ***C:*** Gordon Willis.

Little Nellie Kelly 1/2 **1940** Garland plays both mother and daughter in a film based on a musical comedy by George M. Cohan. Garland is married to Irish cop Murphy but dies in childbirth. The film then advances 20 years to daughter Garland who is trying to make good on the stage and have a romance with a young man her father disapproves of. **100m/B; VHS, DVD.** Judy Garland; George Murphy; Charles Winninger; Douglas McPhail; ***D:*** Norman Taurog.

Little Nemo: Adventures in Slumberland 1/2 **1992 (G)** A bland animated tale of a young boy whose dreams take him to Slumberland. There, Nemo unwittingly unleashes a monster from Nightmare Land who kidnaps Slumberland's king. Nemo must then rescue the king—aided by the king's daughter, a comic squirrel sidekick, and a mischievous con-frog. Based on Winsor McCay's 1900 comic strip. Has some cute comic moments for the kiddies and, while the animation is better than Saturday-morning cartoon quality, it's not Disney. **85m/C; VHS, DVD, Blu-Ray.** ***V:*** Gabriel Damon; Mickey Rooney; Rene Auberjonois; Daniel Mann; Laura Mooney; Bernard Erhard; William E. Martin; ***D:*** William T. Hurtz; Masami Hata; ***W:*** Chris Columbus; Richard Outten; ***M:*** Tom Chase; Steve Rucker.

Little Nicky **2000 (PG-13)** Nicky (Sandler), the son of Satan (Keitel) and an angel (Witherspoon), hangs out in a very cartoony hell. When Satan calls his sons together to name his heir, he instead declares that he will rule for another 10,000 years, causing brothers Adrian and Cassius to stage a rebellion by bringing hell to New York City. Nicky and his talking dog sidekick Mr. Beefy (voice of Smigel) are then sent to capture them. Along the way, he gains the standard Hollywood-issued love interest (Arquette). More satirical than most of Sandler's work, it's also the first that has him surrounded by top-line talent (not that it helps any). **93m/C; DVD.** Adam Sandler; Rhys Ifans; Tommy (Tiny) Lister; Harvey Keitel; Patricia Arquette; Reese Witherspoon; Allen Covert; Blake Clark; Rodney Dangerfield; Kevin Nealon; Jon Lovitz; Lewis Arquette; Dana Carvey; Rob Schneider; Michael McKean; ***V:*** Robert Smigel; ***D:*** Steven Brill; ***W:*** Adam Sandler; Steven Brill; Tim Herlihy; ***C:*** Theo van de Sande; ***M:*** Teddy Castellucci.

A Little Night Music 1/2 **1977 (PG)** Features four interwoven, contemporary love stories adapted from the Broadway play, and based loosely on Bergman's "Smiles of a Summer Night." Taylor's pathetic rendition of "Send in the Clowns" should be banned. Filmed on location in Austria. **110m/C; VHS, DVD.** Elizabeth Taylor; Diana Rigg; Hermione Gingold; Len Cariou; Lesley-Anne Down; ***D:*** Harold Prince. Oscars '77: Orig. Song Score and/or Adapt.

Little Nikita **1988 (PG)** A California boy (Phoenix) discovers that his parents are actually Soviet spies planted as American citizens for eventual call to duty. Poitier's performance as the FBI agent tracking the spies is about the only spark in this somewhat incoherent thriller. **98m/C; VHS, DVD, Blu-Ray.** River Phoenix; Sidney Poitier; Richard Bradford; Richard Lynch; Caroline Kava; Lucy Deakins; ***D:*** Richard Benjamin; ***W:*** Bo Goldman; John Hill; ***M:*** Marvin Hamlisch.

Little Odessa 1/2 **1994 (R)** Set in the Russian-Jewish emigre community of Brooklyn's Brighton Beach, Gray's directorial debut explores hitman Joshua's (Roth) relationship with his family—especially kid brother Reuben (Furlong). Not your typical mob opera, this one focuses more on characters than killing. Relationships between family members are explored to the hilt, but the audience is left with too many unanswered questions. Dimly lit and entirely too ambiguous, this family tragedy could cause a serious case of depression. **98m/C; DVD.** Tim Roth; Edward Furlong; Moira Kelly; Vanessa Redgrave; Maximilian Schell; Paul Guilfoyle; Natasha Andreichenko; David Vadim; Mina Bern; Boris McGiver; Mohammed Ghaffari; Michael Khumrov; ***D:*** James Gray; ***W:*** James Gray; ***C:*** Tom Richmond; ***M:*** Dana Sano.

Little Old New York 1/2 **1923** Set in 1806 New York, with Davies starring as a feisty Irish lass who, at her father's (Kerrigan) urging, disguises herself as her late brother so the family can claim an inheritance left to him. Cousin Larry (Ford) would have inherited had the O'Days not shown up but he still befriends young Pat, whom the confused guy eventually realizes is a girl. **106m/B; Silent; DVD.** Marion Davies; Harrison Ford; J.M. Kerrigan; Stephen Carr; Sam Hardy; Riley Hatch; Mahlon Hamilton; Louis Wolheim; George Barraud; Courtenay Foote; Andrew Dillon; Harry Watson; ***D:*** Sidney Olcott; ***W:*** Luther Reed; ***C:*** Ira Morgan; Gilbert Warrenton.

A Little Piece of Sunshine 1/2 **1990** The Caribbean island of Sunshine is about to gain its independence from British rule when the British governor is killed. Scotland Yard's Desmond Hannah is sent in and discovers the island is not a paradise. Hannah meets Miami detective Ernie Favaro, who's trying to find a drug connection between the island and Miami, and someone in the government is plotting with the Cubans. MI-6's Sam McCready is appointed interim governor to help out. Based on a Frederick Forsyth story. **98m/C; DVD.** Larry Lamb; Chris Cooper; Alan Howard; Lauren Bacall; ***D:*** James Cellan Jones; ***W:*** Murray Smith; ***C:*** Cristiano Pogany; ***M:*** Paul Chihara. **TV**

The Little Prince **1974 (G)** Disappointing adaptation of the classic children's story by Antoine de Saint-Exupery, about a little boy from asteroid B-612. Lousy Lerner and Loewe score underscores a general lack of magic or spontaneity. **88m/C; VHS, DVD.** *GB* Richard Kiley; Bob Fosse; Steven Warner; Gene Wilder; Joss Ackland; Clive Revill; Victor Spinetti; Graham Crowden; Donna McKechnie; ***D:*** Stanley Donen; ***W:*** Alan Jay Lerner; ***C:*** Christopher Challis; ***M:*** Frederick Loewe; Alan Jay Lerner. Golden Globes '75: Score.

The Little Prince **2016 (PG)** Mark Osborne uses the beloved children's classic, a story that's been told in nearly every country in the world, as a launching point for a lovely film about the power of friendship and storytelling. A little girl (Mackenzie Foy) moves to a new neighborhood with her anal-retentive, over-planning mother (McAdams), who has her daughter's school life all tracked out for her. Then the girl meets a next-door neighbor, the Aviator (Bridges), who tells her stories of The Little Prince. It's a sweet movie with powerful visuals that captures the imagination of children and adults. **108m/C; DVD.** Jeff Bridges; Rachel McAdams; Paul Rudd; Marion Cotillard; James Franco; Mackenzie Foy; ***D:*** Mark Osborne; ***W:*** Irena Brignull; Bob Persichetti; ***C:*** Kris Kapp; ***M:*** Joann Le Blanc; Richard Harvey; Hans Zimmer; Rebecca Delannet.

The Little Princess 1/2 **1939 (G)** Based on the Frances Hodgson Burnett children's classic; perhaps the best of the moppet's films. Shirley is a young schoolgirl in Victorian London sent to a harsh boarding school when her Army officer father is posted abroad. When her father is declared missing, the penniless girl must work as a servant at the school to pay her keep, all the while haunting the hospitals, never believing her father has died. A classic tearjerker. **91m/B; VHS, DVD.** Shirley Temple; Richard Greene; Anita Louise; Ian Hunter; Cesar Romero; Arthur Treacher; Sybil Jason; Miles Mander; Marcia Mae Jones; E.E. Clive; ***D:*** Walter Lang; ***W:*** Ethel Hill; Walter Ferris; ***C:*** Arthur C. Miller; ***M:*** Walter Bullock.

The Little Princess 1/2 **1987** A three-cassette adaptation of Frances Hodgson Burnett's book. In Victorian England, kind-hearted Sara is forced into poverty when her father suddenly dies. Can his longtime friend find her and restore her happiness? Originally aired on PBS as part of the "Wonderworks" family movie series. **180m/C; VHS, DVD.** *GB* Amelia Shankley; Nigel Havers; Maureen Lipman; ***D:*** Carol Wiseman. **TV**

A Little Princess 1/2 **1995 (G)** Adaptation of the children's book by Frances Hodgson Burnett. Sara's (Matthews) been raised in India by her widowed father (Cunningham). When he's called up to fight in WWI, she's taken to New York to be educated at stern Miss Michin's (Bron) school, where her money makes her a favored boarder. However, Sara suffers a severe reversal of fortune when her father is reported killed and Miss Michin promptly makes her a servant to pay her way. But Sara's made some true friends who become her allies under trying circumstances. Lively script, dazzling visuals, and a welcome lack of sappiness. **97m/C; DVD.** Liesl Matthews; Eleanor Bron; Liam Cunningham; Rusty Schwimmer; Arthur Malet; Vanessa Lee Chester; Errol Sitahal; Heather DeLoach; Taylor Fry; ***D:*** Alfonso Cuarón; ***W:*** Richard LaGravenese; Elizabeth Chandler; ***C:*** Emmanuel Lubezki; ***M:*** Patrick Doyle.

The Little Rascals 1/2 **1994 (PG)** Alfalfa runs afoul of the membership requirements for the "He-Man Womun Haters Club" when he starts to fall for Darla. Charming remake of the short film series, now set in suburban L.A., from Spheeris, who also redid another TV favorite, "The Beverly Hillbillies." **83m/C; VHS, DVD, Blu-Ray.** Daryl Hannah; Courtland Mead; Travis Tedford; Brittany Ashton Holmes; Bug Hall; Zachary Mabry; Kevin Jamal Woods; Ross Bagley; Sam Saletta; Blake Collins; Jordan Warkol; Blake Ewing; Juliette Brewer; Heather Karasek; ***Cameo(s):*** Whoopi Goldberg; ***D:*** Penelope Spheeris; ***W:*** Penelope Spheeris; Paul Guay; Stephen Mazur; ***C:*** Richard Bowen; ***M:*** David Foster; Linda Thompson.

The Little Rascals Save the Day **2014 (PG)** This wannabe reboot of the movie series is an undemanding family flick that can't decide which generation it's supposed to represent. The Rascals make several botched attempts to raise money to save Grandma's bakery. Their last chance is to win the prize money at a local talent show. **98m/C; DVD, Blu-Ray.** Drew Justice; Jet Jurgensmeyer; Isaiah Fredericks; Eden Wood; Doris Roberts; ***D:*** Alex Zamm; ***W:*** Alex Zamm; William Robertson; ***C:*** Levie Isaacks; ***M:*** Chris Hajian. **VIDEO**

Little Richard 1/2 **2000** The struggle between rock 'n' roll and religion is the story behind this biography of the legendary Little Richard Penniman (well-played by Leon). Born in Georgia in 1943, the boy is too much of a sissy for his stern father (Lumbly) although his mother (Lewis) and local minister Preacher Rainey (Morris) encourage his singing in the choir. But soon Little Richard has succumbed to the secular and found success, although he comes to realize the inequities of the music business for a black man. But he also sees signs from God to leave show business for life in the ministry and continues to struggle between the two. **120m/C; DVD.** Leon; Jenifer Lewis; Carl Lumbly; Tamala Jones; Mel Jackson; Garrett Morris; ***D:*** Robert Townsend; ***W:*** Daniel Taplitz; ***C:*** Edward Pei. **TV**

A Little Romance **1979 (PG)** An American girl living in Paris falls in love with a French boy; eventually they run away, to seal their love with a kiss beneath a bridge. Olivier gives a wonderful, if not hammy, performance as the old pickpocket who encourages her. Gentle, agile comedy based on the novel by Patrick Cauvin. **110m/C; VHS, DVD, Blu-Ray.** Laurence Olivier; Diane Lane; Thelonious Bernard; Sally Kellerman; Broderick Crawford; ***D:*** George Roy Hill; ***W:*** Allan Burns; ***M:*** Georges Delerue. Oscars '79: Orig. Score.

Little Secrets 1/2 **2002 (PG)** Fourteen-year-old Emily (Wood) is spending the summer practicing her violin in hopes of auditioning for a place in the local orchestra. As a sideline, she runs a service in her backyard for the neighbor kids, where they can reveal their secrets, which Emily writes down and locks away for safekeeping. The film reassures that it's better to tell the truth than keep secrets and that even big problems are able to be solved if you talk about them. It may not be the real world but it's a nice one to visit. **107m/C; VHS, DVD.** Evan Rachel Wood; David Gallagher; Vivica A. Fox; Michael Angarano; Jan Gardner; ***D:*** Blair Treu; ***W:*** Jessica Barondes; ***C:*** Brian Sullivan; ***M:*** Sam Cardon.

A Little Sex **1982 (R)** Capshaw, in her screen debut, finds herself the wife of womanizer Matheson. Harmless, but pointless, with a TV-style plot. **94m/C; VHS, DVD.** Tim Matheson; Kate Capshaw; Edward Herrmann; Wallace Shawn; John Glover; ***D:*** Bruce Paltrow; ***W:*** Robert De Laurentis; ***C:*** Ralf Bode; ***M:*** Georges Delerue.

Little Shop of Horrors 1/2 **1960** The landmark cheapie classic, which Roger Corman reputedly filmed in three days, about a nebbish working in a city florist shop who unknowingly cultivates an intelligent plant that demands human meat for sustenance. Notable for then-unknown Nicholson's appearance as a masochistic dental patient. Hilarious, unpretentious farce—if you liked this one, check out Corman's "Bucket of Blood" for more of the same. Inspired a musical of the same name; remade as a movie again in 1986. Available colorized. **70m/B; VHS, DVD, Blu-Ray.** Jonathan Haze; Jackie Joseph; Mel Welles; Jack Nicholson; Dick Miller; Myrtle Vail; ***D:*** Roger Corman; ***W:*** Charles B. Griffith; ***C:*** Arch R. Dalzell.

Little Shop of Horrors **1986 (PG-13)** During a solar eclipse, Seymour buys an unusual plant and takes it back to the flower shop where he works. The plant, Audrey 2, grows at an unusual rate, but Seymour learns that he must feed Audrey fresh human blood to keep her growing. Soon, Audrey is giving the orders ("Feed me") and timid Seymour must find "deserving" victims. Martin's performance as the masochistic dentist is alone worth the price. Song, dance, gore, and more prevail in this outrageous musical comedy. Four Tops Levi Stubbs is the commanding voice of Audrey 2. Based on the Off-Broadway play, which was based on Roger Corman's 1960 horror spoof. **94m/C; VHS, DVD, Blu-Ray.** Rick Moranis; Ellen Greene; Vincent Gardenia; Steve Martin; James Belushi; Christopher Guest; Bill Murray; John Candy; Tisha Campbell; Tichina Arnold; ***V:*** Levi Stubbs, Jr.; ***D:*** Frank Oz; ***W:*** Howard Ashman; ***C:*** Robert Paynter; ***M:*** Alan Menken; Miles Goodman; ***M:*** Howard Ashman.

Little Shots of Happiness **1997 (R)** Prim Frances leaves her unstable husband and, unbeknownst to her co-workers, is living out of her office. In the evenings, she creates a wild new identity for herself and hits the Boston nightclubs where she picks up a different man each night. Of course, Frances discovers there's a price to pay for her new liberation. **85m/C; VHS, DVD.** Bonnie Dickenson; Todd Verow; Linda Ekoian; Rita Gavelis; P.J. Marino; Castalia Jason; Leanne Whitney; Bill Dwyer; Eric Sapp; Maureen Picard; Eric Romley; ***D:*** Todd Verow; ***W:*** Todd Verow; Jim Dwyer; ***C:*** Todd Verow.

Little Sister **2016** It really does take all kinds to make the world go around in Zack Clark's clever dramedy, anchored by a great performance by Timlin. Colleen (Timlin) is a young nun who comes home to visit family and try and reconnect with her brother Jacob (Poulson), an Iraq War vet deeply scarred by his time in country. Sheedy plays her mother, confused about how to deal with either extreme of her suddenly religious daughter or hermit son. Clark avoids the pitfalls of the potential clichés in his story, allowing Timlin's character work to be the central focus. She's up to the challenge. **91m/C; DVD, Blu-Ray.** Addison Timlin; Ally Sheedy; Keith Poulson; Peter Hedges; Barbara Crampton; ***D:*** Zach Clark; ***W:*** Zach Clark; Melodie Sisk; ***C:*** Daryl Pittman; ***M:*** Fritz Myers.

The Little Stranger **1/2 2018 (R)** One summer day in 1948, Dr. Faraday (Gleeson) is summoned to Hundreds Hall, where he was raised because his mother worked as a maid there. He is surprised by the manor's faded state and the reason for his visit--to see sick housemaid Betty (Hill). Faraday learns that Betty is faking so she can get sent home because there is evil that affects all who still live there. As Faraday visits more frequently, he finds himself intertwined in these events. Based on a novel by Sarah Wars, the film effectively serves as a meditation on trauma and confinement through an extraordinary ensemble cast. **111m/C; DVD, Blu-Ray.** Domhnall Gleeson; Ruth Wilson; Will Poulter; Charlotte Rampling; Josh Dylan; ***D:*** Lenny Abrahamson; ***W:*** Lucinda Coxon; ***C:*** Ole Bratt Birkeland; ***M:*** Stephen Rennicks.

Little Sweetheart **1/2 1990 (R)** A reworking of "The Bad Seed," with a nine-year-old girl engaging in murder, burglary, and blackmail, ruining the adults around her. Based on "The Naughty Girls" by Arthur Wise. **93m/C; VHS, Streaming; Open Captioned.** John Hurt; Karen Young; Barbara Bosson; John McMartin; Cassie Barasch; ***D:*** Anthony Simmons.

A Little Thing Called Murder **2006** Sicko true crime story. Sante Kimes (Davis) dominates her son Kenny (Jackson) in every possible way, using him in a crime spree that involves cons, murder, and a tabloid dream of a courtroom trial. No holds barred performance by Davis is a beaut in this tawdry tale with lots of oedipal overtones. **90m/C; DVD.** Judy Davis; Jonathan Jackson; Chelcie Ross; Cynthia Stevenson; Brent King; John Furey; Ari Cohen; Garry Chalk; ***D:*** Richard Benjamin; ***W:*** Teena Booth; ***C:*** Robert McLachlan; ***M:*** John (Gianni) Frizzell. **CABLE**

Little Tough Guy *Dead End Kids: Little Tough Guy* **1938** The Little Tough Guys (a.k.a. Dead End Kids) come to the rescue of Halop, a young tough guy gone bad to avenge his father's unjust imprisonment. First of the "Little Tough Guys" series for the former Dead End Kids, who later became the East Side Kids before eventually evolving into the Bowery Boys. **84m/B; VHS, DVD, Streaming.** Helen Parrish; Billy Halop; Leo Gorcey; Marjorie Main; Gabriel Dell; Huntz Hall; ***D:*** Harold Young.

A Little Trip to Heaven **1/2 2005 (R)** Muddled noir wannabe is the first English-language film for Icelandic director Kormakur and something got lost in translation. Insurance agent Abe Holt (Whitaker using a strange accent) is sent to rural Minnesota to investigate the death of a driver in a burned-out car. The alleged corpse was a heavily-insured scam artist and his beneficiary is his hard-luck sister Isold (Stiles) and her drunken husband Fred (Renner), which puts Abe's instincts on red alert. **86m/C; DVD.** *US IC* Forest Whitaker; Julia Stiles; Jeremy Renner; Peter Coyote; Philip Jackson; Anne Reid; Phyllida Law; ***D:*** Baltasar Kormakur; ***W:*** Baltasar Kormakur; Edward Martin Weinman; ***C:*** Ottar Gudnason; ***M:*** Mugison.

The Little Vampire **2000 (PG)** A cluttered storyline and wandering direction help put a stake in the heart of this tale of a lonely boy and a family of vegetarian vampires. Tony (Lipnicki) moves from sunny California to gloomy Scotland for his father's job with crusty Lord Ashton (Wood). Tony's daydreaming about vampires when young vampire Rudolph (Weeks) suddenly appears at his window. They becomes friends and Rudolph introduces Tony to his family, who are trying to become human once again, but need the other half of a magic amulet held by Lord Ashton to complete the spell. Some scenes are visually stunning but the convoluted plot puts this one six feet under. **91m/C; DVD.** Jonathan Lipnicki; Richard E. Grant; Alice Krige; Rollo Weeks; Jim Carter; John Wood; Tommy Hinkley; Pamela Gidley; Anna Popplewell; Ed Stoppard; ***D:*** Uli Edel; ***W:*** Karey Kirkpatrick; Larry Wilson; ***C:*** Bernd Heinl; ***M:*** Nigel Clarke; Michael Csanyi-Wills.

Little Vera *Malenkaya Vera* **1988** Extremely well-done Soviet film chronicles the life of a young working-class woman who loves rock music and who has been profoundly affected by Western civilization. Post-glasnost Soviet production gives Westerners a glimpse into the Russian way of life. A boxoffice bonanza back home. Russian with subtitles. **130m/C; VHS, DVD.** *RU* Natalia (Natalya) Negoda; Andrei Sokolov; Yuri Nazarov; Ludmila Zaisova; Alexander Niegreva; ***D:*** Vassili Pitchul.

Little Voice **1998 (R)** Little Voice (Horrocks) misses her dead father so much that she communicates only by singing along with the records Dad loved. Whether it's Judy Garland, Shirley Bassey, or Edith Piaf, she can match the voice exactly. When her mom's (Blethyn) sleazy talent-agent boyfriend (Caine) hears her, he knows she's his ticket to fame and fortune but she clams up whenever there's an audience. Club owner and weasel Mr. Boo (Broadbent) books her, but everyone wonders if she'll sing. Caine and Broadbent do their best to out-slime each other while Horrocks gives a showcase performance, re-creating her role from the stage play "The Rise and Fall of Little Voice." **97m/C; DVD.** *UK* Jane Horrocks; Michael Caine; Ewan McGregor; Brenda Blethyn; Jim Broadbent; Annette Badland; Philip Jackson; ***D:*** Mark Herman; ***W:*** Mark Herman; ***C:*** Andy Collins; ***M:*** John Altman. Golden Globes '99: Actor--Mus./Comedy (Caine).

Little White Lies *Les Petits Mouhoirs* **2010** Meandering pic is reminiscent of a Gallic "Big Chill" as it features a group of friends reuniting on vacation (after another friend's tragic accident) amidst a '60s and '70s song-filled soundtrack. Everyone's having personal issues they're in denial about and their friends support whatever lies they tell themselves. It's not terribly exciting although it's recognizable behavior. French with subtitles. **154m/C; DVD, Blu-Ray.** *FR* Francois Cluzet; Marion Cotillard; Benoît Magimel; Gilles Lellouche; Laurent Lafitte; Valerie Bonneton; Pascale Arbillot; Jean Dujardin; ***D:*** Guillaume Canet; ***W:*** Guillaume Canet; ***C:*** Christophe Offenstein.

Little Witches **1996 (R)** Rejected group of seniors at Catholic girls' high school are transformed into a witches coven, thanks to a book of spells. A rip-off of "The Craft." **91m/C; VHS, DVD.** Mimi Reichmeister; Jack Nance; Jennifer Rubin; Sheeri Rappaport; Melissa Taub; Zoe Alexander; Zelda Rubinstein; Eric Pierpoint; ***D:*** Jane Simpson; ***W:*** Brian DiMuccio; Dino Vindeni; ***C:*** Ron Turowski; ***M:*** Nicholas Rivera.

Little Women **1933** Louisa May Alcott's Civil War story of the four March sisters—Jo, Beth, Amy, and Meg—who share their loves, their joys, and their sorrows. Everything about this classic film is wonderful, from the lavish period costumes to the excellent script, and particularly the captivating performances by the cast. A must-see for fans of Alcott and Hepburn, and others will find it enjoyable. **107m/B; VHS, DVD.** Katharine Hepburn; Joan Bennett; Paul Lukas; Edna May Oliver; Frances Dee; Spring Byington; Jean Parker; Douglass Montgomery; ***D:*** George Cukor; ***W:*** Victor Heerman; Sarah Y. Mason; ***C:*** Henry W. Gerrard; ***M:*** Max Steiner. Oscars '33: Adapt. Screenplay; Venice Film Fest. '34: Actress (Hepburn).

Little Women **1949** Stylized color remake of the George Cukor 1933 classic. Top-notch if too obvious cast portrays Louisa May Alcott's story of teenage girls growing up against the backdrop of the Civil War. **121m/C; VHS, DVD.** June Allyson; Peter Lawford; Margaret O'Brien; Elizabeth Taylor; Janet Leigh; Mary Astor; ***D:*** Mervyn LeRoy; ***W:*** Andrew Solt; ***M:*** Adolph Deutsch. Oscars '49: Art Dir./Set Dec., Color.

Little Women **1978** The third screen version of Louisa May Alcott's classic story. Lackluster compared to the previous attempts, particularly the sterling 1933 film, but still worthwhile. During the Civil War, four sisters share their lives as they grow up and find romance. Garson's TV debut. Followed by a TV series. **200m/C; VHS, DVD.** Meredith Baxter; Susan Dey; Ann Dusenberry; Eve Plumb; Dorothy McGuire; Robert Young; Greer Garson; Cliff (Potter) Potts; William Shatner; ***D:*** David Lowell Rich; ***M:*** Elmer Bernstein. **TV**

Little Women **1994 (PG)** Beloved story of the March women is beautifully portrayed in a solid production that blends a seamless screenplay with an excellent cast, authentic period costumes, and lovely cinematography and music. Ryder, perfectly cast as the unconventional Jo, is also the strongest of the sisters: domestically inclined Meg (Alvarado), the fragile Beth (Danes), and the youngest, mischevious Amy (the delightful Dunst) who grows up into a sedate young lady (Mathis). Charming adaptation remains faithful to the spirit of the Alcott classic while adding contemporary touches. Fittingly brought to the big screen by producer Denise Di Novi, writer/co-producer Swicord, and director Armstrong. **118m/C; DVD, Blu-Ray.** Winona Ryder; Gabriel Byrne; Trini Alvarado; Samantha Mathis; Kirsten Dunst; Claire Danes; Christian Bale; Eric Stoltz; John Neville; Mary Wickes; Susan Sarandon; ***D:*** Gillian Armstrong; ***W:*** Robin Swicord; ***C:*** Geoffrey Simpson; ***M:*** Thomas Newman.

Little Women **1/2 2018 (PG-13)** A modern retelling on the 150th anniversary of Louisa May Alcott's classic coming of age tale. Four sisters, each with her own ambitions and dreams, revel in good times and endure the bad through their unbreakable family bonds. Thompson charms as a youthful, vibrant Marmee, and the rest of the cast is rounded out by fresh talent that we'll undoubtedly be seeing more of in the future. **112m/C; DVD.** Lea Thompson; Ian Bohen; Sarah Davenport; Lucas Grabeel; Melanie Stone; ***D:*** Clare Niederpruem; ***W:*** Clare Niederpruem; Kristi Shimek; ***C:*** Anka Malatynska; ***M:*** Robert Allen Elliott.

Little Women **2019 (PG)** As Jo (Ronan) writes in New York, her younger sister Amy (Pugh) tours Europe with their wealthy aunt Josephine (Streep) and her elder sister Meg (Watson) raises her own family. Jo is called home to Massachusetts when their youngest sister, shy Beth (Scanlen), becomes seriously ill. Flashbacks to the girls' lives a few years earlier show when they lived with their mother (Dern), became friends with Laurie (Chalamet), and grew into the women they became. Gerwig's fresh adaptation of Alcott's classic novel honors the original while inventively weaving the story together in a way that appeals to contemporary viewers. **135m/C; DVD, Blu-Ray.** Saoirse Ronan; Emma Watson; Florence Pugh; Eliza Scanlen; Laura Dern; ***D:*** Greta Gerwig; ***W:*** Greta Gerwig; ***C:*** Yorick Le Saux; ***M:*** Alexandre Desplat. Oscars '19: Costume Des.; British Acad. '19: Costume Des.

The Littlest Angel **1969** Musical about a shepherd boy who dies falling off a cliff and wants to become an angel. He learns a valuable lesson in the spirit of giving. Made for TV. **77m/C; VHS, DVD.** Johnny Whitaker; Fred Gwynne; E.G. Marshall; Cab Calloway; Connie Stevens; Tony Randall; ***D:*** Joe Layton; ***W:*** Patricia Gray; Lan O'Kun; ***M:*** Joseph Howard. **TV**

The Littlest Horse Thieves **1/2** *Escape from the Dark* **1976 (G)** Good Disney film about three children and their efforts to save some ponies who work in mines. The children take it upon themselves to see that the animals escape the abuse and neglect they are put through. Filmed on location in England with excellent photography. **109m/C; VHS, DVD.** Alastair Sim; Peter Barkworth; Maurice Colbourne; Susan Tebbs; Andrew Harrison; Chloe Franks; ***D:*** Charles Jarrott; ***W:*** Rosemary Anne Sisson; ***C:*** Paul Beeson; ***M:*** Ronald Goodwin.

The Littlest Outlaw **1/2 1954** A Mexican peasant boy steals a beautiful stallion to save it from being destroyed. Together, they ride off on a series of adventures. Disney movie filmed on location in Mexico. **73m/C; VHS, DVD, Streaming.** Pedro Armendariz, Sr.; Joseph Calleia; Andres Velasquez; ***D:*** Roberto Gavaldon.

The Littlest Rebel **1/2 1935 (PG)** Temple stars in this well-done piece set during the Civil War in the Old South. She befriends a Union officer while protecting her father at the same time. She even goes to Washington to talk with President Lincoln. Nice dance sequences by Temple and Robinson. Available in computer-colored version. **70m/B; VHS, DVD.** Shirley Temple; John Boles; Jack Holt; Bill Robinson; Karen Morley; Willie Best; ***D:*** David Butler.

Live! **2007 (R)** Mockumentary on reality TV seems redundant although it's at least deftly done if cynical and disturbing. Programming prez Katy takes an offhand remark about Russian roulette and decides to turn it into the latest TV sensation (despite opposition) and finds would-be suicidal contestants are flooding the casting sessions. **96m/C; DVD.** Eva Mendes; Andre Braugher; David Krumholtz; Katie Cassidy; Rob Brown; Jay Hernandez; Eric Lively; Monet Mazur; Jeffrey Dean Morgan; Missi Pyle; Charlotte Ross; Paul Michael Glaser; ***D:*** Bill Guttentag; ***W:*** Bill Guttentag; ***C:*** Stephen Kazmierski; ***M:*** Phil Marshall.

Live a Little, Love a Little **1968 (PG)** Itinerant photographer Elvis juggles two different jobs by running around a lot. Sexually more frank than earlier King vehicles. **90m/C; VHS, DVD.** Elvis Presley; Michele Carey; Rudy Vallee; Don Porter; Dick Sargent; Sterling Holloway; Eddie Hodges; ***D:*** Norman Taurog.

Live and Let Die **1973 (PG)** Agent 007 (Moore) is out to thwart the villainous Dr. Kananga (Kotto), a black mastermind who plans to control western powers with voodoo and hard drugs. He's aided by psychic tarot-reading virgin Solitaire (Seymour), who falls prey to Bond's charms. Moore's first appearance as Bond in the 8th film in the series. Can't we have the real Bond back? Title song by Paul McCartney and Wings. **131m/C; VHS, DVD, Blu-Ray.** *GB* Roger Moore; Jane Seymour; Yaphet Kotto; Clifton James; Julius W. Harris; Geoffrey Holder; David Hedison; Gloria Hendry; Bernard Lee; Lois Maxwell; Madeleine Smith; ***D:*** Guy Hamilton; ***W:*** Tom Mankiewicz; ***C:*** Ted Moore.

Live by Night **1/2 2016 (R)** Joe Coughlin (Affleck) is a WWI veteran trying to make his name in the Boston crime scene before being shunned all the way to Tampa, where he works with the local Cuban population to make the most of Prohibition-era crime. Rising within the ranks of national crime lords, he makes more than a few enemies. Writer/director Affleck fails to find the pulse of Dennis Lehane's epic Prohibition-era crime saga (published in 2012). A fantastic ensemble is wasted in this bland drama in which the costumes and sets look way too polished and the characters seem nonexistent. **129m/C; DVD, Blu-Ray, Streaming.** Ben Affleck; Elle Fanning; Brendan Gleeson; Chris Messina; Sienna Miller; Zoe Saldana; ***D:*** Ben Affleck; ***W:*** Ben Affleck; ***C:*** Robert Richardson; ***M:*** Harry Gregson-Williams.

Live Flesh **1/2** *Carne Tremula* **1997 (R)** Five lives in Madrid are forever altered when naive Victor (Rabal) accidentally shoots cop David (Bardem) after an argument with one-night stand Elena (Neri). When he gets out of prison, he discovers Elena has transformed from junkie to model wife of the now-paraplegic David. Victor blames Elena and while apparently stalking her, has an affair with Clara (Molina), the wife of David's former partner (Sancho), which dramatically draws all five back together. Complex, noirish drama for director Almodovar, with unexpected twists and a talented, attractive cast. Adapted from a novel by Ruth Rendell. Spanish with subtitles. **100m/C; DVD.** *FR SP* Javier Bardem; Francesca Neri; Angela Molina; Liberto Rabal; Jose Sancho; Penelope Cruz; Pilar Bardem; Alex Angulo; ***D:*** Pedro Almodóvar; ***W:*** Pedro Almodóvar; Ray Loriga; Jorge Guerricaechevarria; ***C:*** Affonso Beato; ***M:*** Alberto Iglesias.

Live Free or Die Hard 1/2 **2007 (PG-13)** The last "Die Hard" was released in 1995 and director Wiseman plays to the fact that times have changed, even if John McClane (Willis) has not. His analog cop in a digital world first thinks he's going to be stuck babysitting smart-mouthed 20-something computer hacker Matt (Long), who's wanted for questioning when the government's computers go wonky. Ah, but it's really supercilious disaffected techie Thomas Gabriel (Olyphant) showing off what happens when you ignore his warnings. Well, you really shouldn't ignore McClane either. Willis acknowledges his years while still kicking badguy butt in some ludicrous but amazing action sequences. **129m/C; DVD, Blu-Ray.** Bruce Willis; Justin Long; Mary Elizabeth Winstead; Timothy Olyphant; Maggie Q; Jeffrey Wright; Kevin Smith; Yancey Arias; Tim Russ; Cyril Raffaelli; Clifford Curtis; Yorgo Constantine; Andrew Friedman; ***D:*** Len Wiseman; ***W:*** Mark Bomback; ***C:*** Simon Duggan; ***M:*** Marco Beltrami.

Live from Baghdad **2003** In 1991, veteran CNN producer Robert Wiener (Keaton) and his longtime producing partner Ingrid Formanek (Bonham Carter) find themselves in Baghdad at the start of the first Gulf War. The other networks have pulled out for safety reasons and CNN is the only game around with Wiener and Formanek risking their lives to get the story. Adapted from the book by Wiener. **108m/C; VHS, DVD.** Michael Keaton; Helena Bonham Carter; Lili Taylor; Bruce McGill; David Suchet; Joshua Leonard; Michael Cudlitz; Matt Keeslar; Robert Wisdom; Michael Murphy; Paul Guilfoyle; John Carroll Lynch; Tom Amandes; Murphy Dunne; ***D:*** Mick Jackson; ***W:*** Richard Chapman; John Patrick Shanley; Timothy J. Sexton; ***C:*** Ivan Strasburg. **CABLE**

Live-In Maid *Cama Adentro* **2004** With Argentina in the midst of an economic meltdown, once-privileged divorcee Beba can't afford to pay her longtime maid Dora and she eventually quits. But after spending nearly 30 years together, despite class and other differences, the women find it tough to let go. Spanish with subtitles. **87m/C; DVD.** *AR SP* Norma Aleandro; Norma Argentina; Marcus Mundstock; Raul Panguinao; ***D:*** Jorge Gaggero; ***W:*** Jorge Gaggero; ***C:*** Javier Julia.

Live Like a Cop, Die Like a Man 1/2 *Uomini Si Nasce Polizziotti Si Muore* **1976** Violent Italian crime action. Alfredo (Porel) and Antonio (Lovelock) are undercover cops in Rome who are part of a special squad targeting organized crime. They are licensed to kill and have no boundaries and no scruples in how they get the job done. Italian with subtitles. **95m/C; DVD.** *IT* Marc Porel; Ray Lovelock; Adolfo Celi; Franco Citti; Silvia Dionisio; Marino (Martin) Mase; ***D:*** Ruggero Deodato; ***W:*** Fernando Di Leo; ***C:*** Guglielmo Mancori; ***M:*** Ubaldo Continiello.

Live, Love and Learn **1937** Okay screwball comedy is helped by the chemistry between the two leads. Rich Julie Stoddard (Russell) marries struggling artist Bob Graham (Montgomery) and discovers she enjoys the bohemian life. Bob unexpectedly becomes successful—and boring—working on commissions, and Julie wants a divorce. Bob finally realizes he can't paint just for money and tries to get Julie back. **78m/B; DVD.** Robert Montgomery; Rosalind Russell; Robert Benchley; Helen Vinson; Monty Woolley; E.E. Clive; Mickey Rooney; ***D:*** George Fitzmaurice; ***W:*** Charles Brackett; Cyril Hume; Richard Maibaum; ***C:*** Ray June.

Live Nude Girls **1995 (R)** Group of 30-something girlfriends get together to throw a bachelorette party for one of their number and sit around gossiping about sex, relationships, family, and friends. Not much plot but nice ensemble work. **92m/C; VHS, DVD, Blu-Ray.** Dana Delany; Kim Cattrall; Cynthia Stevenson; Laila Robins; Olivia D'Abo; Lora Zane; Glenn Quinn; Tim Choate; ***D:*** Julianna Lavin; ***W:*** Julianna Lavin; ***C:*** Christopher Taylor; ***M:*** Anton Sanko.

Live Wire 1/2 **1992 (R)** Brosnan is an FBI bomb expert who needs a new line of work. He's up against a terrorist psychopath who has his greedy hands on a new type of explosive. It's liquid, undetectable, looks as innocent as a glass of water, and is capable of blowing up Washington, D.C. Also available in an unrated version. **85m/C; VHS, DVD.** Pierce Brosnan; Ben Cross; Ron Silver; Lisa Eilbacher; ***D:*** Christian Duguay; ***W:*** Bart Baker. **CABLE**

Live Wire: Human Timebomb 1/2 **1995 (R)** FBI agent Jim Parker is captured by a Cuban general who implants a computer chip into his neck—turning Parker into a human timebomb. **98m/C; VHS, DVD.** Bryan Genesse; Joe Lara; Frantz Dobrowsky; J. Cynthia Brooks; ***D:*** Mark Roper; ***W:*** Jeff Albert; ***C:*** Rod Stewart; ***M:*** Itai Haber.

The Lively Set **1964** Remake of 1954's "Johnny Dark." College dropout Casey (Darren) is more interested in cars than girls as he works on a design for a new gas turbine engine. He changes his mind when he meets Eadie (Tiffin) and they are soon engaged and moving to San Francisco where Casey has been hired to build a new hot rod for millionaire Stanford Rogers (Mann). But Casey can't resist testing the car, which gets him into trouble. **95m/C; DVD.** James Darren; Pamela Tiffin; Doug McClure; Peter Mann; Marilyn Maxwell; Ross Elliott; Charles Drake; Joanie Sommers; ***D:*** Jack Arnold; ***W:*** Mel Goldberg; William Wood; ***C:*** Carl Guthrie; ***M:*** Bobby Darin.

The Lives of a Bengal Lancer **1935** One of Hollywood's greatest rousing adventures. Based in northwest India, Lt. McGregor (Cooper), a seasoned frontier fighter in the Bengals Lancers, befriends new officer Lt. Forsythe (Tone). Also new to the regiment is Donald Stone (Cromwell), the son of the current commanding officer (Standing). All three will soon test their courage when the Brits encounter a vicious local revolution against colonial rule. Swell plot, lotsa action, great comraderie. Based on the novel by Major Francis Yeats-Brown, and remade in 1939 as "Geronimo." **110m/B; VHS, DVD, Blu-Ray.** Gary Cooper; Franchot Tone; Richard Cromwell; Guy Standing; Sir C. Aubrey Smith; Douglass Dumbrille; Kathleen Burke; Noble Johnson; Lumsden Hare; Akim Tamiroff; J. Carrol Naish; Monte Blue; Mischa Auer; George Regas; ***D:*** Henry Hathaway; ***W:*** John Lloyd Balderston; Grover Jones; William Slavens McNutt; Waldemar Young; ***C:*** Charles B(ryant) Lang, Jr.; ***M:*** Milan Roder.

The Lives of Others *Das Leben der Anderen* **2006 (R)** Oscar-winning drama is set in East Berlin in 1984. The population is controlled by the Stasi (the secret police) and its informers. Strict bureaucrat Wiesler (Muehe) doesn't believe that successful playwright Dreyman (Koch) is a true socialist so he wires the man's apartment and becomes intrigued with his life and lover, actress Christa-Maria (Gedeck). Wiesler's loyalty (and belief in the system) is shaken when a superior orders him to pin something on Dreyman; instead, he decides to protect him. Impressive debut for writer/director von Donnersmarck. German with subtitles. **137m/C; DVD, Blu-Ray.** *GE* Martina Gedeck; Ulrich Tukur; Ulrich Muehe; Sebastian Kock; Volkmar Kleinert; ***D:*** Florian Henskel von Donnersmarck; ***W:*** Florian Henskel von Donnersmarck; ***C:*** Hagen Bogdanski; ***M:*** Gabriel Yared; Stephane Moucha. Oscars '06: Foreign Film; British Acad. '07: Foreign Film.

Lives of Performers 1972 90m/B; DVD, Blu-Ray. Yvonne Rainer; ***D:*** Yvonne Rainer; ***W:*** Yvonne Rainer; ***C:*** Babette Mangolte. Natl. Film Reg. '17. **VIDEO**

Livin' Large **1991 (R)** An African-American delivery boy gets the break of his life when a nearby newscaster is shot dead. Grabbing the microphone and continuing the story, he soon finds himself hired by an Atlanta news station as an anchorman, fulfilling a life-long dream. But problems arise when he finds himself losing touch with his friends, his old neighborhood and his roots. Comedy "deals" with the compelling issue of blacks finding success in a white world by trivializing the issue at every turn and resorting to racial stereotypes. **96m/C; VHS, DVD.** Terrence "T.C." Carson; Lisa Arrindell Anderson; Blanche Baker; Nathaniel "Afrika" Hall; Julia Campbell; ***D:*** Michael A. Schultz; ***C:*** Peter Lyons Collister; ***M:*** Herbie Hancock.

Living & Dying **2007 (R)** Supremely stupid crime-doesn't-pay pic. A team of bank robbers become involved in a hostage situation when their job is botched. Unfortunately, among the hostages are a couple of gun-happy killers and outside are a lot of equally trigger-happy cops. **90m/C; DVD.** Edward Furlong; Bai Ling; Jordana Spiro; Michael Madsen; Tom Zembrod; Maurice Ripke; Arnold Vosloo; ***D:*** Jon Keeyes; ***W:*** Jon Keeyes; ***C:*** Sammy Inayeh; ***M:*** David Rosenblad; John Dufilho.

The Living Corpse 1/2 *Zinda Laash; Dracula in Pakistan* **2003** Perhaps the first horror film ever made in Pakistan, it received an X rating on release due to its 'scantily clad' women although their costumes would receive yawns from a Western audience. The dance sequences that were censored then have been restored, making it sort of an awkward musical about a mad scientist looking for eternal life who turns himself into a vampire. Fans of older horror films will notice the plot "borrows" heavily from Hammer Films "Horror of Dracula". **104m/B; DVD.** Ala-Ud-In; Asad Bukhari; Deeba; Rehan; Yasmine; ***D:*** Khwaja Sarfraz; ***W:*** Khwaja Sarfraz; Narseem Rizwani; ***C:*** Nabi Ahmed; Raza Mir; ***M:*** Tassadaque Hussain.

The Living Daylights **1987 (PG)** After being used as a pawn in a fake Russian defector plot, our intrepid spy tracks down an international arms and opium smuggling ring. Fine debut by Dalton, who takes his role as 007 in a more serious vein, in a rousing, refreshing cosmopolitan shoot-em-up. Let's be frank: we were all getting a little fatigued by Roger Moore. The 15th film in the series. **130m/C; DVD, Blu-Ray.** Timothy Dalton; Maryam D'Abo; Jeroen Krabbe; John Rhys-Davies; Robert Brown; Joe Don Baker; Desmond Llewelyn; Art Malik; Geoffrey Keen; Walter Gotell; Andreas Wisniewski; Caroline Bliss; ***D:*** John Glen; ***W:*** Richard Maibaum; Michael G. Wilson; ***C:*** Alec Mills; ***M:*** John Barry.

The Living Dead *The Scotland Yard Mystery* **1933** An English film about a mad, re-animating scientist. **76m/B; VHS, DVD, Streaming.** *GB* Gerald du Maurier; George Curzon; Grete Natzler; Belle Chrystall; Leslie Perrins; ***D:*** Thomas Bentley; ***W:*** Frank Miller; ***C:*** James Wilson.

The Living Dead Girl 1/2 *La Morte Vivante* **1982** Workers illegally trying to dispose of hazardous chemical wastes in a cellar make the mistake of indulging in a bit of grave robbing at the next-door crypt. A 55-gallon drum cracks open; the stuff hits an open coffin and a blonde (Blanchard) with long sharp fingernails and a taste for blood is reanimated. It's another sex-and-gore fest from the prolific Rollin, though this is one of his more polished productions. French with subtitles. **91m/C; DVD, Blu-Ray.** *FR* Marina Pierro; Francoise Blanchard; Mike Marshall; Carina Barone; Fanny Magier; ***D:*** Jean Rollin; ***W:*** Jean Rollin.

Living Doll 1/2 **1990 (R)** A mentally unbalanced med student abducts a cadaver and brings it to his apartment. The beautiful female corpse takes to telling him to seek revenge on those that killed her. **95m/C; DVD.** *GB* Mark Jax; Eartha Kitt; Katie Orgill; ***D:*** George Dugdale; Peter MacKenzie Litten; ***W:*** George Dugdale; Peter MacKenzie Litten; Mark Ezra. **VIDEO**

The Living End **1992** Director Araki's irreverent lovers-on-the-lam story concerns freelance L.A. writer Jon (Gilmore) who has just learned he is H.I.V.-positive. He meets a handsome, violent, hustler named Luke (Dytri) and the two begin a desperate road trip along the California coast which can only end in tragedy. Araki not only wrote and directed the film but also served as cinematographer and editor—all on a $23,000 budget. Stylish, tragic, and filled with black humor and frank homoeroticism. **92m/C; VHS, DVD.** Craig Gilmore; Mike Dytri; Darcy Marta; ***D:*** Gregg Araki; ***W:*** Gregg Araki; ***C:*** Gregg Araki.

Living Free 1/2 **1972 (G)** Sequel to "Born Free," based on the nonfictional books by Joy Adamson. After Elsa's death, Joy and George Adamson are called in to take charge of her three cubs, who are causing havoc on nearby villages. Nice and pleasant, but could you pick up the pace? **91m/C; VHS, DVD.** Susan Hampshire; Nigel Davenport; ***D:*** Jack Couffer; ***W:*** Millard Kaufman; ***C:*** Jack Couffer.

Living In a Big Way **1947** Gene Kelly, a returning vet himself, does a minor MGM musical about GIs in a postwar society. Leo's (Kelly) wartime bride, bratty, rich Margaud (McDonald), is having second thoughts about marriage and wants a divorce. Leo gets a job doing construction on homes for vets, and decides his wife is worth wooing again. Director La Cava's final film; Kelly and Stanley Donen did the choreography. **104m/B; DVD.** Gene Kelly; Marie McDonald; Charles Winninger; Phyllis Thaxter; Spring Byington; Jean Adair; William 'Bill' Phillips; ***D:*** Gregory La Cava; ***W:*** Gregory La Cava; Irving Ravetch; ***C:*** Harold Rosson; ***M:*** Lennie Hayton.

Living in Oblivion **1994 (R)** Humorous tri-part story is an insiders joke on the problems of low-budget filmmaking, including talent, libido, ego, and pervasive chaos. First, director Nick Reve (Buscemi) tries to film an emotional scene with leading lady Nicole (Keener) only to have everything go wrong; then star Chad (LeGros), a dimwit but a "name," arrives to throw his weight around (and seduce Nicole); and finally the leading lady must deal with an overly sensitive dwarf and Nick's mother. A sleeper. **92m/C; DVD, Blu-Ray.** Steve Buscemi; Catherine Keener; James LeGros; Dermot Mulroney; Danielle von Zerneck; Robert Wightman; Rica Martens; Hilary Gilford; Peter Dinklage; Kevin Corrigan; Matthew Grace; Michael Griffiths; ***D:*** Tom DiCillo; ***W:*** Tom DiCillo; ***C:*** Frank Prinzi; ***M:*** Jim Farmer. Sundance '95: Screenplay.

Living in Peril **1997 (R)** Ambitious architect Walter Woods (Lowe) is in L.A. to design a mansion for an eccentric client (Belushi). But a series of accidents threaten to ruin his reputation, if not provoke something more deadly. **95m/C; VHS, DVD.** Rob Lowe; James Belushi; Dean Stockwell; Dana Wheeler-Nicholson; Richard Moll; Alex Meneses; Patrick Ersgard; ***D:*** Joakim (Jack) Ersgard; ***W:*** Joakim (Jack) Ersgard; Patrick Ersgard; ***C:*** Ross Berryman; ***M:*** Randy Miller. **VIDEO**

Living It Up 1/2 **1954** Slow-paced remake of 1937's "Nothing Sacred." Junior railroad man Homer Flagg thinks he's been exposed to radiation at Los Alamos and his quack doctor pal Steve Harris tells him he's dying. Homer's plight is taken up by journalist Wally Cook, who convinces her editor to lay on the sob story by giving Homer and Steve an all-expense paid trip to the Big Apple. Now the guys have to make sure the truth doesn't get out. **94m/C; DVD.** Dean Martin; Jerry Lewis; Janet Leigh; Edward Arnold; Fred Clark; Sig Rumann; ***D:*** Norman Taurog; ***W:*** Jack Rose; Melville Shavelson; ***C:*** Daniel F. Fapp.

Living on Tokyo Time 1/2 **1987** Interesting but often dull, low budget independent comedy about a young Japanese woman who hitches up with a boorish Japanese-American man in order to stay in the United States. An Asian view of Asian-America, filmed on location in San Francisco. **83m/C; VHS, Streaming.** Minako Ohashi; Ken Nakagawa; Kate Connell; Mitzi Abe; Bill Bonham; Brenda Aoki; ***D:*** Steven Okazaki; ***W:*** Steven Okazaki; John McCormick.

Living on Velvet **1935** Amateur pilot Terry Parker (Brent) is at the controls and walks away from the plane crash that kills his parents and sister. Believing he's living on borrowed time, he behaves recklessly but Amy Prentiss (Francis) decides she can change Terry's improvident ways by marrying him. However, when Terry claims his inheritance, he buys another plane and a disgusted Amy decides to leave him. **80m/B; DVD.** Kay Francis; George Brent; Warren William; Helen Lowell; Henry O'Neill; ***D:*** Frank Borzage; ***W:*** Julius J. Epstein; Jerry Wald; ***C:*** Sidney Hickox.

Living Out Loud **1998 (R)** Judith's (Hunter) dumped by her cardiologist husband for a younger woman and spirals into depression., leading (of course) to dramatic self-discovery. She even notices nice-guy elevator operator Pat (DeVito) and they form an unlikely friendship, which teeters on becoming something more. Screenwriter LaGravanese tries his hand at directing but delivers a choppy, hard-to-believe tale of female independence and self-fulfillment. Both leads seem miscast and significant events take place off-screen, leaving the audience to fill in the blanks. **102m/C; DVD.** Holly Hunter; Danny DeVito; Queen Latifah; Martin Donovan; Elias Koteas; Richard Schiff; ***D:*** Richard LaGravenese; ***W:*** Richard LaGravenese; ***C:*** John Bailey; ***M:*** George Fenton.

Living Proof 🦴🦴 1/2 **2008** Sentimental fact-based drama from Lifetime about the work of Dr. Dennis Slamon (Connick Jr.), an oncologist looking to use Herceptin as an experimental drug for breast cancer. Frustrated by his lack of funding, Slamon's work eventually comes to the notice of Lily Tartikoff (Harmon) whose (then-)husband Brandon was the president of NBC Entertainment and had been treated by Slamon. Lily makes fundraising her personal crusade (along with financier Ron Perelman) and raises enough money to have Slamon launch clinical trials. Story is told from multiple viewpoints, including Slamon's patients. **89m/C; DVD.** Harry Connick, Jr.; Angie Harmon; Tammy Blanchard; Amanda Bynes; John Benjamin Hickey; Regina King; Jennifer Coolidge; Swoosie Kurtz; Amy Madigan; Bernadette Peters; Trudie Styler; ***D:*** Dan Ireland; ***W:*** Vivienne Radkoff; ***C:*** James Chressanthis; ***M:*** Halli Cauthery. **CABLE**

Living to Die 🦴 1/2 **1991 (R)** Vegas gumshoe is assigned to investigate a blackmailed official, and discovers a woman believed to be dead is alive and beautiful and living incognito. This mystifies him. **84m/C; VHS, DVD.** Wings Hauser; Darcy Demoss; Asher Brauner; Arnold Vosloo; Jim Williams; ***D:*** Wings Hauser.

The Living Wake 🦴 1/2 **2007 (PG-13)** An alcoholic failed artist and petty swindler, self-important K. Roth Binew (O'Connell) is told that he is dying so he hires Mills (Eisenberg) as his official biographer while he makes his final arrangements. Viewers won't be quite certain whether this is to be taken seriously or as self-conscious silliness. **91m/C; DVD.** Michael O'Connell; Jesse Eisenberg; Ann Dowd; Eddie Pepitone; Jim Gaffigan; Diane Kagan; ***D:*** Sol Tryon; ***W:*** Michael O'Connell; Peter Kine; ***C:*** Scott Miller; ***M:*** Michael O'Connell; Carter Little.

Living Will 🦴 1/2 **2010 (R)** Hard-partying Belcher dies but apparently won't let the bromance between himself and best bud and roomie Will die with him. Belcher comes back as a ghost and is disgusted to find that his cousin Krista has moved in. Fearing Will is becoming domesticated, Belcher vows to break up the lovey-dovey duo. **102m/C; DVD.** Ryan Dunn; Gerard Haitz; April Scott; Chris Ready; ***D:*** Matthew Lauyer; ***W:*** Roy Korikakin; Allan Delikat; ***C:*** Joseph Hennigan. **VIDEO**

Liz & Dick 🦴 **2012** Awful retelling of the Elizabeth Taylor/Richard Burton romance with Lohan badly miscast since she's more petulant than sexy (the costumes and makeup help somewhat) although Bowler does better as the Welsh-born Burton. The married-to-others duo began their torrid affair on the set of the equally-overblown "Cleopatra" and the Lifetime flick goes from there to divorce, marriage, squabbles, drinking, hiding from the paparazzi, etc. as the couple find love isn't enough to keep them together. **88m/C; DVD.** Lindsay Lohan; Grant Bowler; Tanya Franks; Andy Hirsch; Theresa Russell; Charles Shaughnessy; David Eigenberg; ***D:*** Lloyd Kramer; ***W:*** Christopher Monger; ***C:*** Paula Huidobro; ***M:*** Lee Holdridge. **CABLE**

A Lizard in a Woman's Skin 🦴🦴 *Una Lucertola con la Pelle di Donna* **1971** Carol (Bolkan) tells her shrink about dreams in which she kills her party girl neighbor Julia (Strindberg, in her film debut). Of course, Julia winds up dead in exactly the manner Carol has described. Cop Corvin (Baker) thinks Carol is being set up by her two-timing husband Frank (Sorel). Then other people from Carol's dreams begin to die as well. There's some freaky-deaky druggie hippie stuff included, too. Italian with subtitles. **98m/C; DVD, Blu-Ray.** *IT* Florinda Bolkan; Stanley Baker; Jean Sorel; Alberto De Mendoza; Leo Genn; Silvia Monti; Anita Strindberg; ***D:*** Lucio Fulci; ***W:*** Roberto Gianviti; Lucio Fulci; Robert Gianviti; Andre Tranche; ***C:*** Luigi Kuveiller; ***M:*** Ennio Morricone.

Lizzie 🦴🦴 1/2 **2018 (R)** A speculative biography of Lizzie Borden, who was accused, but never convicted, of the violent ax murders of her father and stepmother in 1892 Massachusetts. Sevigny is both sympathetic and chilling as Lizzie, and Stewart captivates as the pretty maid who goes from Lizzie's romantic partner to murderous accomplice. The cinematography is authentic and stylish, and director Macneill doesn't shield the audience from the crime's brutality. The pacing, though, is a frustrating tease to the foregone hatchet conclusion. **105m/C; DVD, Blu-Ray.** Kristen Stewart; Chloë Sevigny; Kim Dickens; Denis O'Hare; Jeff(rey) Perry; ***D:*** Craig William Macneill; ***W:*** Bryce Kass; ***C:*** Noah Greenberg; ***M:*** Jeff Russo.

Lizzie Borden Took an Ax 🦴 1/2 **2014** The grisly murders aren't for those with weak stomachs in this dull Lifetime retelling of the notorious 1892 crime. Spinster Lizzie Borden (Ricci) is living with her sister Emma (Duvall) and their father (McHattie) and stepmother (Botsford) in Fall River, Massachusetts. She allegedly finds the bodies of the latter two, dead from repeated blows from an ax, and quickly is quickly arrested and on trial. Did she do it isn't much in doubt. **90m/C; DVD.** Christina Ricci; Clea DuVall; Billy Campbell; Gregg Henry; Stephen McHattie; Sara Botsford; ***D:*** Nick Gomez; ***W:*** Stephen Kay; ***C:*** Steve Cosens; ***M:*** Tree Adams. **CABLE**

The Lizzie McGuire Movie 🦴🦴 1/2 **2003 (PG)** Tweenie heroine Lizzie (an endearingly klutzy Duff) celebrates her graduation from junior high with a two-week trip to Italy with some classmates. On an outing, Lizzie meets the slightly older Europop star Paolo (Gelman), whose singing partner Isabella has just left him. Lizzie looks like her (Duff plays both roles), and agrees to put on a dark wig and impersonate the Italian diva for an awards show. Some sightseeing and a little romance follow. An adaptation of the Disney Channel series. **90m/C; DVD.** Hilary Duff; Robert Carradine; Hallie Todd; Jake Thomas; Yani Gellman; Adam Lamberg; Brendan Kelly; Ashlie Brillault; Clayton Snyder; Alex Borstein; Carly Schroeder; ***D:*** Jim Fall; ***W:*** Edward Decter; John J. Strauss; Susan Estelle Jansen; ***C:*** Jerzy Zielinski; ***M:*** Cliff Eidelman.

Lloyd 🦴🦴 **2000 (PG)** Goofy 11-year-old Lloyd is the class clown always getting in trouble in school. In fact, he gets demoted to a class of losers where Lloyd gets a crush on pretty Tracy. But how can he compare with junior high rebel Storm for her affections? **72m/C; VHS, DVD.** Todd Bosley; Brendon Ryan Barrett; Mary Mara; Taylor Negron; Tom Arnold; Kristen Parker; ***D:*** Hector Barron; ***W:*** Hector Barron; ***C:*** Michael Orefice; ***M:*** Conrad Pope. **VIDEO**

Lloyds of London 🦴🦴🦴 **1936** If you wonder how the story of a British insurance company can be exciting, just watch this lavish spectacular (which, of course, lacks historical accuracy). Jonathan Blake (Power) has risen in the ranks of the firm, thanks in part to his lifelong friendship with Lord Horatio Nelson (Burton), much to the disgust of haughty Lord Everett Stacy (an ever-supercilious Sanders). As Bonaparte comes to power, Blake travels to France to rescue some friends and saves Elizabeth (Carroll), who turns out to be Stacy's wife. Stacy is also spreading rumors about Lloyds' solvency and Nelson's heroics at Trafalgar and his machinations lead to further trouble with Blake. **115m/B; DVD.** Tyrone Power; George Sanders; Madeleine Carroll; John Burton; Guy Standing; Sir C. Aubrey Smith; Freddie Bartholomew; Virginia Field; Montagu Love; Una O'Connor; Anne Howard; ***D:*** Henry King; ***W:*** Ernest Pascal; Walter Ferris; ***C:*** Bert Glennon.

Lo and Behold: Reveries of the Connected World 🦴🦴🦴 **2016 (PG-13)** Herzog turns his documentarian gaze to nothing smaller than the entire history and future of the Internet. As you might imagine, this is almost too much subject matter for one film but the approach is delightfully inquisitive and episodic. In one moment, he's detailing the first transmission ever sent by a computer, and in another he's speaking with a group of robot designers. By the end, when he's open to the idea that we could one day Tweet thoughts, he's uniquely captured something about the limitless potential of the Internet that few others could. **98m/C; DVD.** Elon Musk; Kevin D. Mitnick; Lawrence Krauss; Sebastian Thrun; Lucianne Walkowicz; ***D:*** Werner Herzog; ***W:*** Werner Herzog; ***C:*** Peter Zeitlinger.

Loaded 🦴🦴 *Bloody Weekend* **1994 (R)** Writer-director Campion (sister of director Jane) follows a group of teens to an abandoned English mansion as they try to film an amateur horror movie. Then they decides to have some fun, with the help of LSD, leading to some therapeutic and angst-ridden discussions about each of their problems, as well as a tragic accident, which changes the lives of all involved. There's some nice character sketches, unfortunately they're more interesting than the loose plot, which leaves too many questions unanswered. Retitled and recut since its original release. **95m/C; DVD.** *NZ UK* Thandie Newton; Catherine McCormack; Oliver Milburn; Nick Patrick; Danny Cunningham; Mathew Eggleton; Biddy Hodson; ***D:*** Anna Campion; ***W:*** Anna Campion; ***C:*** Alan Almond; ***M:*** Simon Fisher Turner.

Loaded 🦴🦴 1/2 **2008 (R)** Tristan Price (Metcalfe) is a handsome young law student from a wealthy family who goes looking for some extra excitement. Then he meets upscale coke dealer Sebastian Cole (Large) and gets more than he bargained for. As Tristan descends deeper into addiction, he's pulled into Sebastian's drug deals, which lead to murder and even more plot twists. **100m/C; DVD.** Jesse Metcalfe; Corey Large; Monica Keena; Nathalie Kelley; Johnny Messner; Jimmy Jean-Louis; Chace Crawford; Vinnie Jones; Erin Gray; John Bennett Perry; ***D:*** Alan Pao; ***W:*** Corey Large; Alan Pao; ***C:*** Roger Chingirian; ***M:*** Ralph Rieckermann. **VIDEO**

Loaded Guns **WOOF!** **1975** Airline stewardess-cum-double agent must totally immobilize a top drug trafficking ring. Pathetic spy tale with plenty of unintended laughs. **90m/C; VHS, DVD.** Ursula Andress; Woody Strode; ***D:*** Fernando Di Leo.

Loaded Pistols 🦴 **1948** Story set in the old West starring Gene Autry. **80m/B; VHS, DVD.** Gene Autry; Jack Holt; Barbara Britton; ***D:*** John English.

Loan Shark 🦴🦴 **1952** An ex-convict gets a job at a tire company, working undercover to expose a loan shark ring. Hackneyed plot moves quickly. **79m/B; DVD.** George Raft; John Hoyt; Dorothy Hart; Paul Stewart; Robert Bice; Russell Johnson; Benny Baker; Lawrence (Larry) Dobkin; Harlan Warde; Margia Dean; William Phipps; ***D:*** Seymour Friedman; ***W:*** Martin Rackin; Eugene Ling; ***C:*** Joseph Biroc; ***M:*** Heinz Roemheld.

The Lobster 🦴🦴 **2016 (R)** Yorgos Lanthimos' festival hit is an undeniably clever film that still kind of wears out its welcome. Farrell plays David, a man forced to a hotel after his wife leaves him. At the hotel, every resident has 45 days to find a partner, or they will be transformed into an animal. David travels with his brother, who is now a dog. He will become a lobster in 45 days if he doesn't find love. Rachel Weisz, Olivia Colman, John C. Reilly, and Ben Whishaw co-star. **118m/C; DVD, Blu-Ray.** Colin Farrell; Rachel Weisz; John C. Reilly; Olivia Colman; Lea Seydoux; ***D:*** Yorgos Lanthimos; ***W:*** Yorgos Lanthimos; Efthymis Filippou; ***C:*** Thimios Bakatakis.

Lobster Man from Mars 🦴🦴 **1989 (PG)** When rich movie producer (Curtis) learns from his accountant that he must produce a flop or be taken to the cleaners by the IRS, he buys a homemade horror movie from a young filmmaker. The film is an ultra-low budget production featuring a kooky lobster man and a screaming damsel. The premise peters out about halfway through, but there are enough yuks to keep you going. **84m/C; VHS, DVD.** Tony Curtis; Deborah Foreman; Patrick Macnee; Tommy Sledge; Billy Barty; Phil(ip) Proctor; Anthony Hickox; Bobby "Boris" Pickett; Stanley Sheff; ***D:*** Stanley Sheff; ***W:*** Bob Greenberg; ***C:*** Gerry Lively; ***M:*** Sasha Matson.

A Lobster Tale 🦴🦴 1/2 **2006** Guess "A Moss Tale" wouldn't have been as good a title. Cody Brewer (Meaney) is a Maine lobsterman suffering hard times, which are also affecting his family. While checking his traps, he discovers an odd green moss that has magical properties. As soon as word gets out, Cody is everyone's best friend so they can get their own piece of the special vegetation. Quirky family fare. **95m/C; DVD.** Colm Meaney; Alberta Watson; Jack Knight; Graham Greene; ***D:*** Adam Massey; ***W:*** Court Crandall; ***C:*** Patrick Mcgowan; ***M:*** Eric Cadesky; Nick Dyer. **VIDEO**

Local Boys 🦴🦴 1/2 **2002 (PG-13)** California surf dude Randy (Olsen) buys his brother Skeet (Sumpter) his first board for his 12th birthday. But Randy gets jealous when Skeet turns to surfing legend Jim Wesley (Harmon) to be his mentor. Things get even more complicated when Wesley begins romancing the boys' widowed mom (Edwards). **103m/C; VHS, DVD.** Mark Harmon; Eric Christian Olsen; Jeremy Sumpter; Stacy Edwards; Giuseppe Andrews; Travis Aaron; Shelby Fenner; Lukas Behnken; ***D:*** Ron Moler; ***C:*** James Glennon. **VIDEO**

Local Color 🦴🦴 **2006 (R)** Sentimental drama turns soft-headed rather than soft-hearted. In 1974, John (Morgan) is a teenager living in Port Chester, New York. He's an admirer of reclusive landscape artist Nicolai Seroff (Mueller Stahl) and pesters the old man until he agrees to tutor John at his Pennsylvania summer home. At first, John is merely household help but Seroff eventually works with him on his paintings amidst various artistic discussions that tend to stop the story cold. **107m/C; DVD.** Trevor Morgan; Samantha Mathis; Ray Liotta; Ron Perlman; Diana Scarwid; Charles Durning; Armin Mueller-Stahl; Julie Lott; ***D:*** George Gallo; ***C:*** Michael Negrin; ***M:*** Chris Boardman.

Local Hero 🦴🦴🦴🦴 **1983 (PG)** Riegert is a yuppie representative of a huge oil company who endeavors to buy a sleepy Scottish fishing village for excavation, and finds himself hypnotized by the place and its crusty denizens. Back in Texas at company headquarters, tycoon Lancaster deals with a psycho therapist and gazes at the stars looking for clues. A low-key, charmingly offbeat Scottish comedy with its own sense of logic and quiet humor, poetic landscapes, and unique characters, epitomizing Forsyth's original style. **112m/C; VHS, DVD, Blu-Ray.** *GB* Peter Riegert; Denis Lawson; Burt Lancaster; Fulton Mackay; Jenny Seagrove; Peter Capaldi; Norman Chancer; ***D:*** Bill Forsyth; ***W:*** Bill Forsyth; ***C:*** Chris Menges; ***M:*** Mark Knopfler. British Acad. '83: Director (Forsyth); N.Y. Film Critics '83: Screenplay; Natl. Soc. Film Critics '83: Screenplay.

The Locator 2: Braxton Returns 🦴 1/2 **2009** Braxton (Bruckner) is a former government hitman who killed the brother of an infamous terrorist who know wants revenge. Which is accomplished by the usual standard of killing everyone he knows. Written, edited, and directed by the man playing the title role, which is usually a bad sign. **90m/C; DVD.** Andre Bruckner; Chris Durant; Cristina Kellog; Lynn MacArthur; ***D:*** Andre Bruckner; ***W:*** Andre Bruckner; ***C:*** Anthony Miles; ***M:*** Donnie Cooley.

Loch Ness 🦴🦴 1/2 **1995 (PG)** American zoologist Jonathan Dempsey (Danson) specializes in hunting legendary animals and his latest assignment is to head for the Scottish highlands and take on the Nessie legend. He gets an assistant (Frain), a potential romance with single mom Laura (Richardson), and a lot of grief from some hostile locals before Laura's young daughter Isabel (Graham) decides to help him out. Jim Henson's Creature Shop takes care of the monster's animatronics. **101m/C; VHS, DVD.** *GB* Ted Danson; Ian Holm; Joely Richardson; Kirsty Graham; James Frain; Harris Yulin; Keith Allen; Nick Brimble; ***D:*** John Henderson; ***W:*** John Fusco; ***C:*** Clive Tickner; ***M:*** Trevor Jones.

Loch Ness Terror 🦴🦴 *Beyond Loch Ness* **2007 (R)** Yeah it's cheap and cheesy and the story is silly but it's surprising B-movie monster fun as well. A Nessie relation has somehow made her way to Lake Superior and she and her bloodthirsty offspring are stomping and chomping locals and vacationers alike. James Murphy (Krause) is the only person to survive an attack and now he's ready to fry some beastie behind. A Sci-Fi Channel original. **91m/C; DVD.** Brian Krause; Don S. Davis; Paul McGillion; Carrie Genzel; Donnelly Rhodes; Niall Matter; Paul Ziller; Jason Bourque; ***W:*** Pinar Toprak; ***C:*** Anthony C. Metchie; ***M:*** Amber Borycki. **CABLE**

Lock, Stock and 2 Smoking Barrels 🦴🦴🦴 **1998 (R)** Plot twist-laden British caper comedy plays like Tarantino and crumpets. Four dim hoods, Bacon (Statham), Soap (Fletcher), Eddy (Moran) and Tom (Flemyng), pool their ill-gotten gains so that Eddy can play in a high stakes card game. The game is fixed and they end up owing gambler Hatchet Harry (Moriarity) 500,000 pounds. The bumbling band plan to rob their drug dealing neighbor Dog (Harper), who's planning on robbing an upper class rival of his own. Throw in a wandering pair of antique shotguns and you have the recipe for a cap-poppin' good time. Rock star Sting appears as the pub-owning father of one of the lads. **105m/C; DVD, Blu-Ray.** *UK* Jason Flemyng; Dexter Fletcher; Nick Moran; Jason Statham; Steven Mackintosh; Vinnie Jones; Sting; Lenny McLean; P. H. Moriarty; Steve Sweeney; Frank Harper; Stephen Marcus; ***D:*** Guy Ritchie; ***W:*** Guy Ritchie; ***C:*** Tim Maurice-Jones; ***M:*** David A. Hughes; John Murphy. MTV Movie Awards '99: New Filmmaker (Ritchie).

Lock Up 🦴 1/2 **1989 (R)** Peaceful con Stallone, with only six months to go, is harassed and tortured by vicious prison warden Sutherland in retribution for an unexplained past conflict. Lackluster and moronic; semicolor; surely Sutherland can find better roles. **115m/C; VHS, DVD, Blu-Ray.** Sylvester Stallone; Donald Sutherland; Sonny Landham; John Amos; Darlanne Fluegel; Frank McRae; ***D:*** John Flynn; ***W:*** Jeb Stuart; ***C:*** Donald E. Thorin; ***M:*** Bill Conti.

Lockdown 🦴 1/2 **1990** Charged with his partner's murder, a detective is forced to ponder the perennial puzzle of life. Not a pretty sight. **90m/C; VHS, DVD.** Joe Estevez; Mike Farrell; Richard Lynch; ***D:*** Frank Harris. **VIDEO**

Lockdown 🦴🦴 1/2 **2000 (R)** Brutal men in the big house pic follows the fortunes of three friends who wind up doing time in New Mexico. Violent drug dealer Cashmere (Casseus) is framed by another player and manages to take two right-living buddies—Avery (Jones) and Dre (Bonds)--down with him. Cashmere joins the in-house crew of black boss Clean Up (Master P) while Avery is lucky enough to be taken under the wing of a self-educated cellmate who passes on wise advice for doing time. Dre is the one who winds up in situations familiar to viewers of the cable series "Oz." Grim watching. **105m/C; DVD.** Richard T. Jones; De'Aundre Bonds; Gabriel Casseus; Master P; Bill Nunn; Clifton Powell; Joe Torry; Anna Maria Horsford; Melissa De Sousa; Kirk "Sticky Fingaz" Jones; ***D:*** John Luessenhop; ***W:*** Preston A. Whitmore, II; ***C:*** Chris Chomyn; ***M:*** John (Gianni) Frizzell.

Locke 🦴🦴 1/2 **2013 (R)** Ivan Locke (Hardy) is going on a road trip and writer/director Knight is going to let you take the journey with him, delivering a film with only one on-screen character in his car. During a nearly real-time road trip, we watch Locke make calls to his wife, employer, colleagues, etc. to reveal his darkest secret. The reason he has to leave them all that night is to attend the birth of his illegitimate child. Hardy is spectacular in the cramped space, even if the story's method is kind of an unfair trick and requires suspension of disbelief. **85m/C; DVD, Blu-Ray.** *UK US* Tom (Thomas) Hardy; Ruth Wilson; Olivia Colman; Tom Holland; Ben Daniels; Andrew Scott; Ben Milner; ***D:*** Steven Knight; ***W:*** Steven Knight; ***C:*** Haris Zambarloukos; ***M:*** Dickon Hinchliffe.

Locked Down 🦴 **2010 (R)** Hits almost all the prison cliches while offering little in return. Set-up and sent to prison, ex-cop Danny is forced to compete in an underground cage fighting ring by gangster Anton Vargas in order to survive. However, with some help from a new mentor, Danny is determined to destroy the fighting circuit. **99m/C; DVD.** Vinnie Jones; Ling Bai; Dwier Brown; Tony Schiena; Dave Fennoy; Rashad Evans; Kevin Ferguson; ***D:*** Daniel Zirilli; ***W:*** Daniel Zirilli; D. Glase Lomond; ***C:*** Christian Herrera; ***M:*** Nicholas Rivera. **VIDEO**

The Locket 🦴 1/2 **1946** Confusing flashback structure needlessly complicates this melodrama that centers around the mental problems of Nancy Blair (Day). Her shrink ex-husband Harry (Aherne) tells her new fiance John (Raymond) about Nancy's sordid past and the stolen gems frequently found in her possession. Nancy's explanation is that as a child she was falsely accused of stealing a valuable locket, which lead to her kleptomania, but there's more to the story. **86m/B; DVD.** Laraine Day; Brian Aherne; Gene Raymond; Robert Mitchum; Katherine Emery; Ricardo Cortez; ***D:*** John Brahm; ***W:*** Sheridan Gibney; Sheridan Gibney; ***C:*** Nicholas Musuraca; ***M:*** Roy Webb.

The Locket 🦴🦴 1/2 **2002** After his mother dies, Michael Keddington (Willett) takes a job at a health-care facility to pay off debts. There he meets Esther Huish (Redgrave), a lonely widow who encourages Michael not to give up his dreams. But when his supportive girlfriend Faye (Moreau) goes off to college and a jealous co-worker (Heuring) accuses Michael of a crime, he needs Esther's strength to see him through. Based on the novel by Richard Paul Evans. **100m/C; VHS, DVD.** Chad Willet; Vanessa Redgrave; Marguerite Moreau; Lori Heuring; Mary (Elizabeth) McDonough; Brock Peters; Terry O'Quinn; ***D:*** Karen Arthur; ***W:*** Ron Raley; ***C:*** Thomas Neuwirth; ***M:*** Bruce Broughton. **TV**

Lockout 🦴 *MS One: Maximum Security* **2012 (PG-13)** In the distant future, prisoners are held on floating space stations guarded by intense space firepower and futuristic technology. The President's daughter (Grace) goes to one on a philanthropic mission to investigate crimes against humanity where she's kidnapped and held hostage. Only a man named Snow (Pearce)--who wants a wrongful conviction overturned--could possibly get her back. It sounds more fun than it actually ends up being as mounting plot holes, a nonsensical climax, and even boring set pieces waste a potentially fun B-movie set-up and a quality performance from its hero. **95m/C; DVD, Blu-Ray, Streaming.** *FR* Guy Pearce; Maggie Grace; Vincent Regan; Joe Gilgun; Lennie James; Peter Stormare; Tim Plester; ***D:*** Stephanie Leger; James Mather; ***W:*** Stephanie Leger; James Mather; Luc Besson; ***C:*** James Mather; ***M:*** Alexandre Azaria.

Loco Love 🦴 1/2 *Mi Casa, Su Casa* **2003 (PG)** Flat and hopelessly dumb romantic comedy. Gardener Miguel (Mejia) wins big in the lottery and makes a deal with former client Donald (Werner): if Donald will make a green card marriage with his sister Catalina (Harring) so she can come to the U.S., Miguel will give Donald a big chunk of change. Donald wants to open a restaurant so he agrees, not realizing that this means Catalina's entire family will be joining them. And (for no apparent reason) Donald's ex-wife Barbara (Scarborough) gets suddenly jealous and decides she wants Donald back. **94m/C; VHS, DVD.** Laura Elena Harring; Gerardo Mejia; Roy Werner; Margaret Scarborough; Barbara Eden; ***D:*** Bryan Lewis; ***W:*** Steven Baer; ***C:*** Thaddeus Wadleigh; ***M:*** Jon McCallum.

The Locusts 🦴 1/2 **1997 (R)** Backwater beefcake Clay Hewitt (Vaughn) swaggers into a small Kansas town where everyone has a lit cigarette and a secret and no one is safe from hopeless cliches and corny dialogue. Clay soon has the women swarming, but he's only interested in helping mentally and emotionally challenged Flyboy (Davies) get out from under his emasculating and abusive mother Delilah (Capshaw), who's also Clay's boss and overly ardent admirer. Judd is barely used as Clay's spunky squeeze in this slow-paced drama by first-time director Kelley. **123m/C; DVD.** Kate Capshaw; Jeremy Davies; Vince Vaughn; Ashley Judd; Paul Rudd; Daniel Meyer; Jessica Capshaw; ***D:*** John Patrick Kelley; ***W:*** John Patrick Kelley; ***C:*** Phedon Papamichael; ***M:*** Carter Burwell.

Locusts: The 8th Plague 🦴 **2005** Too bad a plague of locusts couldn't have attacked this movie and saved the unwary viewer a lot of suffering. Top-secret experiments at an Idaho government lab result in genetically-modified locusts, which escape. The insects turn out to be have a taste for human flesh (because we taste just like chicken). A Sci-Fi Channel original. **88m/C; DVD.** Dan Cortese; Julie Benz; David Keith; Jeff Fahey; Kirk B.R. Woller; ***D:*** Ian Gilmour; ***W:*** D.R. Rosen; ***C:*** Lorenzo Senatore; ***M:*** Pierpaolo Tiano. **CABLE**

The Lodge 🦴🦴 1/2 **2019 (R)** Richard (Armitrage) is going through a divorce, and his children, Aidan (Lieberher) and Mia (McHugh), do not like their father's new girlfriend, Grace (Keough), the only survivor of a doomsday cult that committed mass suicide-.The couple met when he wrote about the cult. To bring Grace and his children together, Richard takes them to the family's remote cabin for Christmas. When Richard has to leave for a few days, Grace and the kids are alone there and strange things begin to occur. The atmospheric horror film features an intense, unsettling story, striking visuals, and sound design that increases the sense of doom. **108m/C; DVD, Blu-Ray.** Riley Keough; Jaeden Martell; Lia McHugh; Alicia Silverstone; Richard Armitage; ***D:*** Severin Fiala; Veronika Franz; ***W:*** Severin Fiala; Veronika Franz; Sergio Casci; ***C:*** Thimios Bakatakis; ***M:*** Danny Bensi; Saunder Jurriaans.

The Lodger 🦴🦴🦴 *The Case of Jonathan Drew; The Lodger: A Case of London Fog* **1926** A mysterious lodger is thought to be a rampaging mass murderer of young women. First Hitchcock film to explore the themes and ideas that would become his trademarks. Silent. Climactic chase is memorable. Remade three times. Look closely for the Master in his first cameo. **91m/B; Silent; VHS, DVD.** *GB* Ivor Novello; Marie Ault; Arthur Chesney; Malcolm Keen; June; ***Cameo(s):*** Alfred Hitchcock; ***D:*** Alfred Hitchcock; ***W:*** Alfred Hitchcock; Eliot Stannard.

The Lodger 🦴 **2009 (R)** Artificial and melodramatic psycho-thriller. Detective Chandler Manning (Molina) is hunting a serial killer who murders prostitutes along Sunset Boulevard. The killer's M.O. is the same as someone Manning previously put away who was also fixated on Jack the Ripper's crimes in Victorian London. Meanwhile, Ellen Burling (Davis) has suspicions about Malcolm (Baker), the mysterious man that has become the Burlings' new lodger. **95m/C; DVD.** Alfred Molina; Simon Baker; Hope Davis; Donal Logue; Shane West; Rachael Leigh Cook; Philip Baker Hall; ***D:*** David Ondaatje; ***W:*** David Ondaatje; ***C:*** David A. Armstrong; ***M:*** John (Gianni) Frizzell.

The Lodgers 🦴🦴 **2017 (R)** A gothic thriller set in 1920s Ireland. Siblings Edward (Milner) and Rachel (Vega) are shut-ins living on their decaying family estate. A family curse forces them to stay there without visitors, and they live in fear of the ghosts that trap them. Though Edward accepts his fate, Rachel wants to challenge them. When Rachel begins a romance with Sean (Simon), a veteran who is returning home after the Irish War of Independence, she becomes bolder, leading to conflict with Edward and their family's traumatic past. Despite an interesting setting, the film suffers from uninspired plotting and one-dimensional characters. **92m/C; DVD, Blu-Ray.** Charlotte Vega; David Bradley; Bill Milner; Eugene Simon; Moe Dunford; ***D:*** Brian O'Malley; ***W:*** David Turpin; ***C:*** Richard Kendrick; ***M:*** David Turpin; Kevin Murphy; Stephen Shannon.

The Loft 🦴🦴 **2014 (R)** Five married businessmen split the cost on a fancy loft in the city as their secret pleasure palace, entertaining mistresses and indulging in amoral weekend getaways. Trouble starts when a beautiful young woman is found dead in the loft, forcing the men to point fingers at each other. A rare remake, allowing the original Belgium director, Erik Van Looy, to translate his 2008 thriller for an American audience. Looy succeeds by filling the sick yuppie fantasy with thick paranoia. Multiple twists elevate a solid murder mystery with a simple premise. **108m/C; DVD, Blu-Ray.** Karl Urban; James Marsden; Wentworth Miller; Eric Stonestreet; Matthias Schoenaerts; Rachael Taylor; Kristin Lehman; Robert Wisdom; ***D:*** Erik van Looy; ***W:*** Wesley Strick; ***C:*** Nicolas Karakatsanis; ***M:*** John (Gianni) Frizzell.

Logan 🦴🦴🦴 1/2 **2017 (R)** Director Mangold reimagines the iconic character of Wolverine as an old-fashioned movie Western hero in this brilliant action movie, one of the best comic book flicks of all time. Jackman also deconstructs his own character, playing Logan/Wolverine as an old man, someone akin to Clint Eastwood in his late genre pics. The X-Men have disbanded and the few remaining mutants have surrendered to their age and ailments. He's got to protect a girl who has similar powers to him, and he realizes this may be his last chance to do something truly heroic. It's a fantastic film that takes its concept seriously without ever feeling pompous and triumphantly uses action to drive storytelling. **137m/C; DVD, Blu-Ray.** Hugh Jackman; Patrick Stewart; Dafne Keen; Boyd Holbrook; Stephen Merchant; ***D:*** James Mangold; ***W:*** James Mangold; Scott Frank; Michael Green; ***C:*** John Mathieson; ***M:*** Marco Beltrami.

Logan Lucky 🦴🦴🦴 **2017 (PG-13)** Marking director Soderbergh's return to filmmaking after a multi-year absence, this heist comedy shares the slick pacing, memorable ensemble, and fun of his "Oceans" trilogy. To address his unlucky family's financial woes, Jimmy (Tatum) enlists his brother Clyde (Driver), sister Mellie (Keough), and others, including imprisoned bomb expert Joe Bang (Craig), to execute an elaborate robbery of millions of dollars at the Charlotte Motor Speedway during a major NASACAR race. Quirky and entertaining as it explores Southern culture, tight father-daughter relationships, and plans that work out somehow in the end. **118m/C; DVD, Blu-Ray.** Channing Tatum; Farrah Mackenzie; Jim O'Heir; Riley Keough; Katie Holmes; ***D:*** Steven Soderbergh; ***W:*** Rebecca Blunt; ***C:*** Steven Soderbergh; ***M:*** David Holmes.

Logan's Run 🦴🦴 1/2 **1976** In the 23rd century, a hedonistic society exists in a huge bubble and people are only allowed to live to the age of 30. Intriguing concepts and great futuristic sets prevail here. Based on the novel by William Nolan and George Clayton Johnson. **120m/C; VHS, DVD, Blu-Ray.** Michael York; Jenny Agutter; Richard Jordan; Roscoe Lee Browne; Farrah Fawcett; Peter Ustinov; Camilla Carr; Ann Ford; ***D:*** Michael Anderson, Sr.; ***W:*** David Zelag Goodman; ***C:*** Ernest Laszlo; ***M:*** Jerry Goldsmith. Oscars '76: Visual FX.

Logan's War: Bound by Honor 🦴🦴 **1998** Logan (Cibrian) sees his family murdered by the Mafia at age 10 and spends 20 years studying martial arts with Chuck Norris before deciding revenge is suddenly necessary. Granted most people would want some training before embarking on a life or death quest for revenge, but 20 years seems like a long time to go obsessing over things. **91m/C; DVD.** Eddie Cibrian; Chuck Norris; Joe Spano; Jeff Kober; R.D. Call; Brendon Ryan Barrett; James Gammon; Vinne Curto; Devon Michael; ***D:*** Michael Preece; ***W:*** Chuck Norris; Aaron Norris; Walter Klenhard; ***C:*** Karl Kases; ***M:*** Christopher L. Stone. **TV**

Loggerheads 🦴🦴🦴 **2005** Families and the ties that bind. Drifter Mark (Pardue) heads to Kure Beach, North Carolina to help rescue the endangered loggerhead turtle. Mark ran away from his adoptive parents, well-meaning religious conservatives Robert (Sarandon) and Elizabeth (Harper), when they learned he was gay. Also living in NC is Mark's birth mother, Grace (Hunt), who's recovering from a breakdown and has decided to find the baby she gave up as a teenager. Meanwhile, Mark is bonding with gentle George (Kelly), whose male lover has died. Enjoyable for fans of the sincere and sentimental with especially strong performances by Harper and Hunt. **93m/C; DVD.** Bonnie Hunt; Kip Pardue; Tess Harper; Chris Sarandon; Michael Learned; Michael Kelly; Robin Weigert; ***D:*** Tim Kirkman; ***W:*** Tim Kirkman; ***C:*** Oliver Bokelberg; ***M:*** Mark Geary.

Lois Gibbs and the Love Canal 🦴🦴 **1982** Mason's TV movie debut as Lois Gibbs, a housewife turned activist, fighting the authorities over chemical-dumping in the Love Canal area of Niagara Falls, New York. The script doesn't convey the seriousness of developments in that region. **100m/C; VHS, Streaming.** Marsha Mason; Bob Gunton; Penny Fuller; Roberta Maxwell; Jeremy Licht; Louise Latham; ***D:*** Glenn Jordan. **TV**

LOL 🦴 **2012 (PG-13)** Azuelos does an American remake of her own 2008 French flick to cliched effect. Lola (Cyrus) is a Chicago teen who spends her waking moments attached to her electronic gadgets and social networking sites. She's angsty over a break-up, wonders if her best male friend could be something more, and ignores her overbearing mother Anne (Moore) whenever possible. Except Lola writes in an actual diary, which her mom reads, and the misunderstandings escalate. Cyrus isn't much of an actress and this pic offers nothing new on teen dynamics. **97m/C; DVD, Blu-Ray.** Miley Cyrus; Demi Moore; Douglas Booth; Ashley Greene; Thomas Jane; Jay Hernandez; Marlo Thomas; Ashley Hinshaw; Adam G. Sevani; ***D:*** Lisa Azuelos; ***W:*** Lisa Azuelos; Kamir Ainouz; ***C:*** Kieran McGuigan; ***M:*** Rob Simonsen. **VIDEO**

Lola 🦴🦴🦴 **1961** A wonderful tale of a nightclub dancer and her amorous adventures. Innovative film that marked the beginning of French New Wave. In French with

English subtitles. **90m/B; VHS, DVD, Blu-Ray.** *FR* Anouk Aimee; Marc Michel; Elina Labourdette; Jacques Harden; ***D:*** Jacques Demy.

Lola 1/2 *The Statutory Affair; Twinky* **1969 (PG)** A teenaged girl links up romantically with a considerably older writer of pornographic books. One would expect more from such a good cast, but the film never follows through. British release was originally 98 minutes. **88m/C; VHS, DVD.** *GB IT* Charles Bronson; Susan George; Trevor Howard; Michael Craig; Honor Blackman; Lionel Jeffries; Robert Morley; Jack Hawkins; Orson Bean; Kay Medford; Paul Ford; ***D:*** Richard Donner.

Lola **1981** In 1957, honest Von Bohm is appointed building commissioner in a German town rife with corruption. Building contractor Schukert has the mayor and city council as his cronies and doesn't want Von Bohm to interfere so his mistress Lola, who's a cabaret singer and part-time whore, seduces Von Bohm, who falls in love with her. If it reminds you of "The Blue Angel," that's a deliberate choice by Fassbinder, although his pic isn't a remake. German with subtitles. **113m/C; DVD, Blu-Ray.** *GE* Barbara Sukowa; Armin Mueller-Stahl; Mario Adorf; Hark Bohm; Matthias Fuchs; Rosel Zech; Helga Feddersen; Ivan Desny; Karin Baal; ***D:*** Rainer Werner Fassbinder; ***W:*** Rainer Werner Fassbinder; Peter Martheseimer; Pia Frohlich; ***C:*** Xaver Schwarzenberger; ***M:*** Peer Raben.

Lola and Billy the Kid *Lola + Bilikid* **1998** Murat (Davrak) is a closeted gay Turkish teenager living in Berlin with his widowed mother and homophobic brother Osman (Mete). Lola (Mukli) is a travestite dancer at a nightclub who lives with hustler Bili (Yildiz). When Lola tries to contact Murat's family, the boy discovers that Lola is his brother, who was thrown out by Osman. Murat meets Lola, who is later killed—apparently by neo-Nazi thugs. Bili vows revenge but Murat learns that the situation isn't as clear as it seems. German and Turkish with subtitles. **95m/C; VHS, DVD.** *GE* Baki Davrak; Gandi Mukli; Erdal Yildiz; Hasan Ali Mete; Michael Gerber; Murat Yilmaz; Inge Keller; ***D:*** Kutlug Ataman; ***W:*** Kutlug Ataman; ***C:*** Chris Squires; ***M:*** Arpad Bondy.

Lola Colt 1/2 *Black Tigress; Lola Colt: Faccia a faccia con El Diablo; Face to Face with El Diablo; Mean and Black* **1967** Lola (Lola Falana) is a saloon dancer who helps a town overrun by a gang of outlaws. Currently only available as part of the 'Westerns Unchained' collection. **85m/C; Blu-Ray.** *IT* Lola Falana; Pietro Martellanza; German Cobos; Tom Felleghy; Evar Maran; ***D:*** Siro Marcellini; ***W:*** Siro Marcellini; Luigi Angelo; Lamberto Antonelli; ***C:*** Giuseppe La Torre; ***M:*** Ubaldo Continiello. **VIDEO**

Lola Montes **1955** Ophuls' final masterpiece (and his only film in color) recounts the life and sins of the famous courtesan, mistress of Franz Liszt and the King of Bavaria. Ignored upon release, but hailed later by the French as a cinematic landmark. Adapted from an unpublished novel by Cecil Saint-Laurent. French with subtitles. The original widescreen release clocked in at 140 minutes. **110m/C; DVD, Blu-Ray.** *FR* Martine Carol; Peter Ustinov; Anton Walbrook; Ivan Desny; Oskar Werner; ***D:*** Max Ophuls; ***W:*** Max Ophuls; ***C:*** Christian Matras; ***M:*** Georges Auric.

Lola Versus 1/2 *Lola gegen den Rest der Welt* **2012 (R)** Lola (a likeable Gerwig) is dumped by her fiancé Luke (Kinnaman) just weeks before their wedding. To add insult to injury, she's about to turn (gasp!) 30. She enlists her pals Henry (Linklater) and Alice (Lister-Jones) to accompany her on adventures to lift her cloud of funk. But Gerwig's best efforts can't lift up this Indie rom-com as it suffers from stereotypical characters and even more stereotypical situations. **87m/C; DVD, Blu-Ray.** Greta Gerwig; Joel Kinnaman; Zoe Lister Jones; Hamish Linklater; Bill Pullman; Debra Winger; ***D:*** Daryl Wein; ***W:*** Zoe Lister Jones; Daryl Wein; ***C:*** Jakob Ihre.

Lolida 2000 1/2 *Lolita 2000* **1997** In the future all sexual activity is prohibited (bummer). Lolita's working for an organization that destroys sexual material but three particular stories arouse feelings in her that she just has to act on. **90m/C; VHS, DVD.** Jacqueline Lovell; Gabriella Hall; Eric Acsell; ***D:*** Cybil (Sybil) Richards.

Lolita **1962** A middle-aged professor is consumed by his lust for a teenage nymphet in this strange film considered daring in its time. Based on Vladimir Nabokov's novel. Watch for Winters' terrific portrayal as Lolita's sex-starved mother. **152m/B; VHS, DVD, Blu-Ray.** *GB* James Mason; Shelley Winters; Peter Sellers; Sue Lyon; Gary Cockrell; Jerry Stovin; Diana Decker; Lois Maxwell; Cec Linder; Bill Greene; Shirley Douglas; Marianne Stone; Marion Mathie; James Dyrenforth; C. Denier Warren; Terence (Terry) Kilburn; John Harrison; ***D:*** Stanley Kubrick; ***W:*** Vladimir Nabokov; ***C:*** Oswald Morris; ***M:*** Nelson Riddle.

Lolita **1997 (R)** Middle-aged college professor Humbert Humbert (Irons) becomes obsessed with nymphet Lolita (Swain), even to the point of marrying her mother Charlotte (Griffith) so he can always be close by. Then Charlotte dies, and the unlikely duo begin an aimless road trip that eventually leads Lolita to a fateful meeting with yet another older man, Quilty (Langella). Director Lyne's no stranger to controversy but his reverential take on the Vladimir Nabokov novel turns out to be much ado about nothing. Then 14-year-old Swain (in a fetchingly flirty performance) debuts as Lolita (along with a body-double). **137m/C; VHS, DVD.** Jeremy Irons; Melanie Griffith; Frank Langella; Dominique Swain; Suzanne Shepherd; Keith Reddin; Erin J. Dean; Ben Silverstone; ***D:*** Adrian Lyne; ***W:*** Stephen Schiff; ***C:*** Howard Atherton; ***M:*** Ennio Morricone.

Lolly-Madonna XXX *The Lolly-Madonna War* **1973** The Feather and Gutshall families have been fussing over a piece of Tennessee meadowland for years. The Feather boys receive a postcard from a mystery woman, signing herself Lolly-Madonna, luring them to a meeting. It's a ruse by the Gutshalls, but the Feathers kidnap the innocent young woman they think wrote the message and the mistake takes the feuding to a new level. Grafton co-scripted from her novel. **105m/C; DVD.** Rod Steiger; Robert Ryan; Jeff Bridges; Season Hubley; Gary Busey; Randy Quaid; Scott Wilson; Ed Lauter; ***D:*** Richard Sarafian; ***W:*** Sue Grafton; Rodney Carr-Smith; ***C:*** Philip H. Lathrop; ***M:*** Fredric Myrow.

Lolo **1992** Outcast Lolo loses his job in Mexico City and then accidentally kills the local moneylender. The only one who will help him is his girlfriend Sonia, who gets the money for them to flee the city by prostituting herself. Spanish with subtitles. **88m/C; VHS, DVD.** *MX* Roberto Sosa; Lucha Villa; ***D:*** Francisco Athie; ***W:*** Francisco Athie; ***C:*** Jorge Medina; ***M:*** Juan Cristobal Perez Grobert.

Lolo **2015** Delpy co-writes, stars, and directs this black comedy about a mother caught between her new beau and her arguably sociopathic son. Violette (Delpy) starts dating Jean-Rene (Boon), and her teenage son Lolo rebels by trying to sabotage the relationship at every turn. Delpy finds some sweetness and cleverness in this unique love triangle. She struggles though when the story's mood shifts and becomes truly vicious, leaving one to wonder if Lolo isn't closer to Norman Bates. It has a few moments here and there (and Boon is great too) but never quite comes together. **99m/B; DVD.** *FR* Julie Delpy; Dany Boon; Vincent Lacoste; Karin Viard; Antoine Longuine; ***D:*** Julie Delpy; ***W:*** Julie Delpy; Eugénie Grandval; ***C:*** Thierry Arbogast; ***M:*** Mathieu Lamboley.

London **2005 (R)** Syd (Evans) is a pathetic drunk and druggie whose girlfriend London (Biel) has unsurprisingly left him for a new guy. She is also leaving New York, and Syd decides to crash her going-away party, accompanied by dealer Bateman (Stratham) from whom Syd has just scored a lot of coke. The two guys spend most of their time in the bathroom doing blow and yapping. They are tiresome and misogynistic and so is the entire enterprise. **92m/C; DVD.** Chris Evans; Jessica Biel; Jason Statham; Isla Fisher; Joy Bryant; Kelli Garner; Dane Cook; ***D:*** Hunter Richards; ***W:*** Hunter Richards; ***C:*** Jo Willems.

London Boulevard **2010 (R)** Superficial, occasionally clever, crime thriller. Ex-con Mitchel (Farrell) wants to go straight and takes a job as a bodyguard for reclusive actress Charlotte (Knightley), who retired after having a breakdown. Mitchel spends too much time with mate Billy (Chaplin), who's working for loan shark Gant (Winstone), and is getting pulled back into his old gangster life. There are a couple more subplots just to make things irritating. Based on the book by Ken Bruen. **103m/C; DVD, Blu-Ray.** *GB US* Colin Farrell; Keira Knightley; Ben Chaplin; Ray Winstone; David Thewlis; Anna Friel; Eddie Marsan; ***D:*** William Monahan; ***W:*** William Monahan; ***C:*** Chris Menges; ***M:*** Sergio Pizzorno.

London Fields 1/2 **2018 (R)** Terminally ill American author Samson Young (Thornton) travels to London in 1999 as part of an apartment swap with a more successful author. Suffering from writer's block, Samson finds his life and work changed by events related to people he meets in a nearby pub. They include Keith Talent (Sturgess), a drunken cab driver/scam artist, and femme fatale clairvoyant Nicola Six (Heard), who can see when people will die and believes she will be killed on her upcoming birthday. This uninspired adaptation of the highly respected 1989 Martin Amis novel fails to capture the depth of the book and its creativity. **118m/C; DVD.** Amber Heard; Theo James; Jim Sturgess; Billy Bob Thornton; Cara Delevingne; ***D:*** Matthew Cullen; ***W:*** Roberta Hanley; Martin Amis; ***C:*** Guillermo Navarro; ***M:*** Adam Barber; Benson Taylor; Toydrum.

London Has Fallen **2016 (R)** Secret Service Agent Mike (Butler) returns for this sequel to "Olympus Has Fallen." Mike is still on POTUS (Eckhart) detail when a trip to London goes horribly awry under terrorist attack. Another action film that exploits terrorism and fear as tools for alleged entertainment. Landmarks explode, Americans save the day. Want to watch thousands of people die in attacks on national landmarks? This is the franchise for you. A waste of a talented cast in this subpar, cliché-riddled, narrow-minded abomination. **?m/C; DVD, Blu-Ray, Streaming.** *BL UK US* Gerard Butler; Charlotte Riley; Morgan Freeman; Jackie Earle Haley; Melissa Leo; ***D:*** Babak Najafi; ***W:*** Creighton Rothenberger; Katrin Benedikt; Chad St. John; Christian Gudegast; ***C:*** Ed Wild; ***M:*** Trevor Morris.

London River **2009** Well-acted but simplistic two-character drama. It's 2005 and widowed, insular Elisabeth travels to London after being unable to reach her daughter Jane following the terrorist bombings. African immigrant Ousmane has been working in France since his estranged son Ali was a child, but he's now in London searching for him. Naturally, Elisabeth and Ousmane not only meet but, after discovering their children were involved, form a bond made up of sympathy and fear. English, French, and Arabic with subtitles. **88m/C; DVD, Blu-Ray.** *UK FR* Brenda Blethyn; Sotigui Kouyate; Sami Bouajila; Roschdy Zem; ***D:*** Rachid Boucharets; ***W:*** Rachid Boucharets; Olivier Lorelle; ***C:*** Jerome Almeras; ***M:*** Armand Amar.

London Town 1/2 *My Heart Goes Crazy* **1946** Aging music hall performer Jerry Sanford (Field) believes he's starring in a new London revue only to learn he's just understudying the lead. His teenaged daughter Peggy (Clark) decides on sabotage to get her dad back in the spotlight. Unfortunately, Britain's first major Technicolor musical was an expensive disaster with Field insisting on only working with an American director who couldn't put over the old-fashioned story. **93m/C; DVD.** *GB* Sid Field; Petula Clark; Greta Gynt; Kay Kendall; Tessie O'Shea; Claude Hulbert; Sonnie Hale; ***D:*** Wesley Ruggles; ***W:*** Sid Herzig; Elliot Paul; ***C:*** Erwin Hillier; ***M:*** James Van Heusen; Johnny Burke.

London Voodoo 1/2 **2004** Workaholic Lincoln (Cockle) and wife Sarah (Stewart) are Yanks in London who, while renovating their new digs, discover a grave in their cellar. It's that of a voodoo priestess who then possesses Sarah. Sex and exorcism are involved. **90m/C; DVD.** *GB* Sara Stewart; Trisha Mortimer; Sven-Bertil Taube; Doug Cockle; Vonda Barnes; Michael Nyqvist; ***D:*** Robert Pratten; ***W:*** Robert Pratten; ***C:*** Patrick Jackson; ***M:*** Steven Severin.

The Lone Defender **1932** A dozen episodes of the western serial starring the canine crusader, Rin Tin Tin. **235m/B; VHS, DVD.** Walter Miller; June Marlowe; Buzz Barton; Josef Swickard; Frank Lanning; Robert F. (Bob) Kortman; ***D:*** Richard Thorpe.

Lone Hero **2002 (R)** You can tell by the video box that Phillips is not the titular hero'in fact, he's Bart (Phillips), a psycho biker gang leader who terrorizes a small town. Flanery is the somewhat goofball hero, John, who plays a gunfighter in the local Wild West show and who is the only one willing to stand up to the violent menace. **91m/C; VHS, DVD, On Demand.** Lou Diamond Phillips; Sean Patrick Flanery; Robert Forster; Tanya Allen; Garry Chalk; ***D:*** Ken Sanzel; ***W:*** Ken Sanzel; ***C:*** David Pelletier; ***M:*** Anthony Marinelli.

Lone Justice 2 1/2 *Ned Blessing: The Story of My Life and Times* **1993 (PG-13)** Laconic hero Ned Blessing (Johnson), along with Mexican sidekick Crecencio (Avalos), return to Blessing's hometown after a six-year absence and find it ruled by six-shooters and fists. The despicable Borgers clan has murdered the local sheriff (who happens to be Blessing's daddy) and rules by intimidation—until Ned gets involved. Cliched but amusing. **93m/C; VHS, DVD.** Brad Johnson; Luis Avalos; Wes Studi; Bill McKinney; Brenda Bakke; Julius Tennon; Richard Riehle; Gregory Scott Cummins; Rob Campbell; Rusty Schwimmer; ***D:*** Jack Bender; ***W:*** William D. Wittliff; ***C:*** Neil Roach; ***M:*** David Bell. **TV**

Lone Justice 3: Showdown at Plum Creek 1/2 **1996 (PG)** Ex-outlaw-turned-sheriff Ned Blessing (Johnson) discovers the body of the previous sheriff has disappeared from its grave, Big Emma has taken over the saloon and wants Blessing out of the way, and Oscar Wilde comes to town. Three re-edited stories from the TV miniseries. **94m/C; VHS, DVD.** Brad Johnson; Wes Studi; Brenda Bakke; William Sanderson; Luis Avalos; Rusty Schwimmer; Stephen Fry; ***D:*** Jack Bender; Dan Lerner; David Hemmings; ***W:*** Stephen Harrigan; ***C:*** Neil Roach. **TV**

The Lone Ranger 1/2 **1938** Western serial about the masked man and his faithful Indian sidekick. From a long-sought print found in Mexico, this program is burdened by a noisy sound track, two completely missing chapters, an abridged episode 15, and Spanish subtitles. **234m/B; VHS, DVD.** Lee Powell; ***D:*** William Witney; John English.

Lone Ranger 1/2 **1956** Tonto and that strange masked man must prevent a war between ranchers and Indians in the first of the "Lone Ranger" series. "Hi-ho Silver!" **87m/C; VHS, DVD.** Clayton Moore; Jay Silverheels; Lyle Bettger; Bonita Granville; ***D:*** Stuart Heisler; ***W:*** Herb Meadow; ***C:*** Edwin DuPar; ***M:*** David Buttolph.

The Lone Ranger **2013 (PG-13)** Trying to find magic like they did with "Pirates of the Caribbean," producer Jerry Bruckheimer, director Verbinski, and star Depp fall flat in this abrasive, bloated update of the classic character and his Native American sidekick. Depp plays Tonto to Hammer's John Reid, aka The Lone Ranger, as the two try to clean up the Old West over the course of some poorly staged action scenes and culturally insensitive jokes. There's enough charisma on display in the two leads that the blame can't really be laid at their feet but legendary production problems made this over-budget mess into more of a chore than a thrill ride. **149m/C; DVD, Blu-Ray.** Johnny Depp; Armie Hammer; Tom Wilkinson; William Fichtner; Helena Bonham Carter; Ruth Wilson; Barry Pepper; James Badge Dale; ***D:*** Gore Verbinski; ***W:*** Ted Elliott; Terry Rossio; Justin Haythe; ***C:*** Bojan Bazelli; ***M:*** Hans Zimmer. Golden Raspberries '13: Worst Remake/Sequel.

Lone Rider 1/2 **2008** Honored Civil War soldier Bobby Hattaway (Phillips) returns to his hometown to find ruthless Stu Croaker (Spano) trying to gain a business monopoly for when the railroad arrives. Bobby discovers his father (Keach) has taken out a mortgage on the family ranch in order to prevent their mercantile business from going under and Croaker is determined to foreclose. The title character is not related to the western movie series. **80m/C; DVD.** Lou Diamond Phillips; Vincent Spano; Stacy Keach; Cynthia (Cyndy, Cindy) Preston; Angela Alvarado; Tom Schanley; Timothy Bottoms; Mike Starr; ***D:*** David S. Cass, Sr.; ***W:*** Frank Sharp; ***C:*** James W. Wrenn; ***M:*** Joe Kraemer. **TV**

The Lone Runner WOOF! **1988 (PG)** An adventurer rescues a beautiful heiress from Arab kidnappers in this dud. **90m/C; VHS, Streaming.** Miles O'Keeffe; Ronald Lacey; Michael J. Aronin; John Steiner; Hal Yamanouchi; ***D:*** Ruggero Deodato.

Lone Star 1/2 **1952** Big stars, big budget western in which Texas fights for independence as good guy Gable and bad-man Crawford fight each other. Gardner plays a fiery newspaper editor as well as Gable's love interest. Script is chock full of holes, but great action scenes make up for it. Based on the story by Borden Chase. **94m/B; VHS, DVD.** Clark Gable; Ava Gardner; Broderick Crawford; Lionel Barrymore; Beulah Bondi; Ed Begley, Sr.; William Farnum; Lowell Gilmore; ***D:*** Vincent Sherman; ***W:*** Howard Estabrook; Borden Chase.

Lone Star 1/2 **1995 (R)** Terrific contemporary western set in the border town Frontera, Texas. Sheriff Sam Deeds (Cooper) still deals with the legacy of his father, legendary lawman Buddy Deeds (McConaughey) who wrestled control of the town from his corrupt predecessor Charlie Wade (Kristofferson) and supposedly sent him packing. But when skeletal remains and a sheriff's badge turn up on an abandoned Army rifle range, guess whose bones they turn out to be? Buddy's friends want Sam to leave the past alone but he can't, and learns some hard home truths. This is only one of the stories that Sayles gracefully tells and, as always, his ensemble cast all offer outstanding performances. **137m/C; DVD.** Chris Cooper; Matthew McConaughey; Kris Kristofferson; Elizabeth Pena; Joe Morton; Ron Canada; Clifton James; Miriam Colon; Frances McDormand; Richard Jones; Gabriel Casseus; ***D:*** John Sayles; ***W:*** John Sayles; ***C:*** Stuart Dryburgh; ***M:*** Mason Daring. Ind. Spirit '97: Support. Actress (Pena).

Lone Star State of Mind 1/2 **2002 (PG-13)** That state seems to be perplexed if not downright idiotic. Good-hearted Earl (Jackson) has promised his ditsy girlfriend Baby (King) that he will take her to L.A. so that she can fulfill her dream of becoming a soap opera actress. Only before they can leave their redneck community, Baby's doofus cousin Junior (Qualls) lands in a whole heap 'o trouble and Earl promises to set things right. **88m/C; VHS, DVD.** Joshua Jackson; Jaime King; DJ Qualls; Matthew Davis; Ryan Hurst; John Cougar Mellencamp; Thomas Haden Church; Sam McMurray; ***D:*** David Semel; ***W:*** Trevor Munson; ***C:*** Michael Barrett; ***M:*** Tyler Bates.

Lone Survivor **2013 (R)** The true story of a failed 2005 mission to capture a Taliban leader, director/writer Berg's harrowing tale recreates the horror of war but it's not much more than a respectable nod to the soldiers who died on that horrible day. Marcus Luttrell (Wahlberg), who wrote the book on which this is based, was one of four soldiers on that Afghani mountain that day they were ambushed by the enemy, pinned down, and fully aware they were unlikely to all make it home. The centerpiece--the actual ambush--is technically effective but the film is more focused on the action. **121m/C; DVD, Blu-Ray.** Mark Wahlberg; Taylor Kitsch; Emile Hirsch; Ben Foster; Eric Bana; ***D:*** Peter Berg; ***W:*** Peter Berg; ***C:*** Tobias Schliessler; ***M:*** Steve Jablonsky.

Lone Tiger *Tiger Mask* **1994** Chuji (Locke) goes to Las Vegas to discover who murdered his father and ends up living as a homeless man till he's taped beating up some bikers. Then he's offered money to compete in illegal underground fighting events and, surprisingly, he accepts. Fans of wrestler 'Tiger Mask' will be bitterly disappointed at this film ripping off his act. **109m/C; DVD.** Bruce Locke; Richard Lynch; Robert Z'Dar; Barbara Niven; Matthias Hues; Timothy Bottoms; Stoney Jackson; John Stuart; Tora Kazama; Lindy Flesher; Greg Paramo; ***D:*** Warren A. Stevens; ***W:*** Hisao Maki; Charles E. Morris; ***C:*** Mark Melville; ***M:*** Marc Bonilla.

Lone Wolf and Cub *Baby Cart 1: Lend a Child. . .Lend an Arm; Lone Wolf and Cub: Sword of Vengeance* **1972** First in a series of six from the sword-wielding samurai genre. Chronicles the events leading up to a samurai warrior's (Wakayama) expulsion from his native village along with his infant son (Tomikawa). Father's intense rivalry with the evil Shogun whom he was ousted by becomes an epic struggle of good vs. evil. The adorable little "Lone Cub" provides an effective counterpoint for Dad's sideline excursion into a local brothel. In Japanese with English subtitles in a letterbox format. **83m/C; VHS, DVD, Blu-Ray.** *JP* Tomisaburo Wakayama; Akihiro Tomikawa; ***D:*** Kenji Misumi.

Lone Wolf and Cub 4 *Lone Wolf and Cub: Baby Cart in Peril* **1972** Fourth in a series of six. A man (Wakayama) pushes his son (Tomikawa) across Japan in a baby cart loaded with deadly accessories including built-in guns and switchblades. Copious amounts of bloodshed. In Japanese with English subtitles in a letterbox format. **80m/C; VHS, DVD.** *JP* Tomisaburo Wakayama; Akihiro Tomikawa; ***D:*** Buichi Sato.

Lone Wolf and Cub: Baby Cart at the River Styx *Baby Cart at the River Styx; Baby Cart 2* **1972** Second of six parts in the "Kozure Ohkami" ("Sword of Vengeance") series about a man who wheels his motherless infant through the Chinese countryside in a baby cart armed with secret weapons, plotting his revenge on the warlord who expelled him. This one features the intro of Sayka and her fellow female assassins. Subtitled in English. **80m/C; VHS, DVD, Blu-Ray.** *JP* Tomisaburo Wakayama; Akihiro Tomikawa; ***D:*** Kenji Misumi.

Lone Wolf and Cub: Baby Cart to Hades *Baby Cart to Hades* **1972** The third "Kozure Ohkami" ("Sword of Vengeance") film once again finds samurai Itto Ogami and his son Diagoro embroiled in a power struggle between a regional landlord and a governor in feudal Japan. Subtitled in English. **88m/C; VHS, DVD, Blu-Ray.** *JP* Tomisaburo Wakayama; Akihiro Tomikawa; ***D:*** Kenji Misumi.

Lone Wolf McQuade 1/2 **1983** Martial arts action abounds in this modern-day Western which pits unorthodox Texas Ranger Norris against a band of gun-running mercenaries led by Carradine. Oh, and there's a conflict-ridden love interest as well. Violent (and not particularly literary) but worthy entry in chop-socky genre. **107m/C; VHS, DVD, Blu-Ray.** Chuck Norris; Leon Isaac Kennedy; David Carradine; L.Q. Jones; Barbara Carrera; ***D:*** Steve Carver; ***W:*** H. Kaye Dyal; ***C:*** Roger Shearman; ***M:*** Francesco De Masi.

The Lone Wolf Meets a Lady 1/2 **1940** The third film in the William Warren series finds supposedly reformed, retired thief Michael Lanyard coming to the aid of Joan Bradley, who's been accused of stealing a diamond necklace belonging to her fiance's family and of murdering her ex, Peter Rennick. Thug Clay Beaudine is involved but Inspector Crane would rather blame Lanyard. Slyly comic valet Jamison backs up his boss. **71m/B; DVD.** Warren William; Jean Muir; Eric Blore; Thurston Hall; Warren Hull; Victor Jory; Roger Pryor; ***D:*** Sidney Salkow; ***W:*** John Larkin; ***C:*** Henry Freulich.

The Loneliest Planet **2012** Viewers are dropped into Loktev's minimalistic drama as experienced travelers Alex (Garcia Bernal) and Nica (Furstenberg) go backpacking through the former Soviet republic of Georgia just months before their wedding. The lovebirds pick up local guide Dato (Gukabidze) for the treacherous mountain portion and something eventually happens, which is never discussed later, that affects the engaged couple's relationship. A little too much of a disconnected feeling but at least the locations are spectacular. Based on the short story "Expensive Trips Nowhere" by Tom Bissell. English and Georgian with subtitles. **113m/C; DVD.** *US GE* Gael Garcia Bernal; Hani Furstenberg; Bidzina Gujabidze; ***D:*** Julia Loktev; ***W:*** Julia Loktev; ***C:*** Inti Briones; ***M:*** Richard Skelton.

The Loneliness of the Long Distance Runner *Rebel with a Cause* **1962** Courtenay, in his film debut, turns in a powerful performance as an angry young man infected by the poverty and hopelessness of the British slums. His first attempt at crime is a bust and lands him in a boys reformatory where he's recruited for the running team. While training for the big event with a rival school, Redgrave's obsession with winning the race and Courtenay's continued indifference to the outcome lock the two in an intriguing power struggle. Though overlooked when first released, it's since been praised as one of the finest teenage angst films of the '60s and a riveting depiction of a boy's rite of passage into manhood. **104m/B; DVD.** *UK* Tom Courtenay; Michael Redgrave; Avis Bunnage; Peter Madden; James Bolam; Julia Foster; Topsy Jane; Frank Finlay; Christopher Parker; ***D:*** Tony Richardson; ***C:*** Walter Lassally; ***M:*** John Addison.

Lonely Are the Brave **1962** A free-spirited cowboy out of sync with the modern age tries to rescue a buddy from a local jail, and in his eventual escape is tracked relentlessly by modern law enforcement. A compelling, sorrowful essay on civilized progress and exploitation of nature. Adapted from the novel "Brave Cowboy" by Edward Abbey. **107m/B; VHS, DVD, Blu-Ray.** Kirk Douglas; Walter Matthau; Gena Rowlands; Carroll O'Connor; George Kennedy; Michael Kane; Karl Swenson; William Schallert; Bill Bixby; ***D:*** David Miller; ***W:*** Dalton Trumbo; ***C:*** Philip H. Lathrop; ***M:*** Jerry Goldsmith.

The Lonely Guy 1/2 **1984 (R)** Romantic comedy with Martin as a jilted writer who writes a best-selling book about being a lonely guy and finds stardom does have its rewards. Based on "The Lonely Guy's Book of Life" by Bruce Jay Friedman. **91m/C; VHS, DVD, Blu-Ray.** Steve Martin; Charles Grodin; Judith Ivey; Steve Lawrence; Robyn Douglass; Merv Griffin; Dr. Joyce Brothers; Tony Giorgio; ***D:*** Arthur Hiller; ***W:*** Stan Daniels; ***C:*** Victor Kemper; ***M:*** Jerry Goldsmith.

Lonely Hearts **1982 (R)** An endearing Australian romantic comedy about a piano tuner, who at 50 finds himself alone after years of caring for his mother, and a sexually insecure spinster, whom he meets through a dating service. Wonderful performances and a good script make this a delightful film that touches the human heart. **95m/C; VHS, DVD.** *AU* Wendy Hughes; Norman Kaye; Jon Finlayson; Julia Blake; Jonathan Hardy; ***D:*** Paul Cox; ***W:*** Paul Cox; John Clarke; ***C:*** Yuri Sokol; ***M:*** Norman Kaye. Australian Film Inst. '82: Film.

Lonely Hearts 1/2 **1991 (R)** A handsome con man works his wiles on a lonely woman in this erotic thriller. Standard plot wastes a good cast. **109m/C; VHS, DVD.** Eric Roberts; Beverly D'Angelo; Joanna Cassidy; ***W:*** R.E. Daniels.

Lonely Hearts **2006 (R)** True crime thriller based on the 1940s Lonely Hearts Killers, previously filmed as "The Honeymoon Killers" (1970). Raymond (Leto) is a smalltime con artist who's overwhelmed by possessive—and homicidal? partner Martha (Hayek), who decides it's best to off their female marks. Morose New York detective Elmer Robinson (Travolta) and partner Hildebrandt (Gandolfini) are assigned to the case. Director Robinson (the grandson of the real-life detective) is matter-of-fact about the violence, which makes it more shocking, and Hayek is the ultimate fatal beauty. **107m/C; DVD.** John Travolta; James Gandolfini; Salma Hayek; Jared Leto; Laura Dern; Scott Caan; Alice Krige; ***D:*** Todd Robinson; ***W:*** Todd Robinson; ***C:*** Peter Levy; ***M:*** Mychael Danna.

The Lonely Man 1/2 **1957** A gunfighter tries to end his career, but is urged into one last battle. Strong performances and tight direction make up for weak plot. **87m/B; DVD.** Jack Palance; Anthony Perkins; Neville Brand; Elaine Aiken; ***D:*** Henry Levin; ***W:*** Harry Essex; ***C:*** Lionel Lindon; ***M:*** Van Cleave.

The Lonely Passion of Judith Hearne **1987 (R)** A self-effacing Dublin spinster meets a man who gives her his attention, but she must overcome her own self-doubt and crisis of faith. Adapted from Brian Moore's 1955 novel. Excellent performances from both Hoskins and Smith. **116m/C; VHS, Streaming.** *GB* Maggie Smith; Bob Hoskins; Wendy Hiller; Marie Kean; Ian McNeice; Alan Devlin; Rudi Davies; Prunella Scales; ***D:*** Jack Clayton; ***W:*** Peter Gill Nelson; ***C:*** Peter Hannan; ***M:*** Georges Delerue. British Acad. '88: Actress (Smith).

A Lonely Place to Die 1/2 **2011** Solid Brit action-thriller. Five climbers in the Scottish Highlands discover Anna, an eight-year-old Serbian child who's been kidnapped. As they try to get her to safety, they are ruthlessly tracked by two of the kidnappers who have no problem with killing the would-be rescuers. **99m/C; DVD, Blu-Ray.** *UK* Melissa George; Alec Newman; Ed Speleers; Kate Magowan; Garry Sweeney; Stephen McCole; Sean Harris; Karel Roden; Eamonn Walker; ***D:*** Julian Gilbey; ***W:*** Julian Gilbey; Will Gilbey; ***C:*** Ali Asad; ***M:*** Michael Richard Plowman.

The Lonely Sex **1959** Creepy and bizarre film in which a maniac kidnaps a young girl and is then harassed by her psychotic housemate. **?m/CVHS, DVD.** Jean Evans; Karl Light; Mary Gonzales; ***D:*** Richard Hilliard; ***W:*** Richard Hilliard; ***C:*** Richard Hilliard.

Lonely Wives **1931** A lawyer hires an entertainer to serve as his double because of his marital problems. **86m/B; VHS, DVD.** Edward Everett Horton; Patsy Ruth Miller; Laura La Plante; Esther Ralston; ***D:*** Russell Mack; ***W:*** Walter DeLeon; ***C:*** Edward Snyder.

Lonesome Dove 1/2 **1989** Classic western saga with Duvall and Jones in outstanding roles as two aging ex-Texas Rangers who decide to leave their quiet lives for a last adventure—a cattle drive from Texas to Montana. Along the way they encounter a new love (Lane), a lost love (Huston), and a savage renegade Indian (well-played by Forrest). Based on Pulitzer prize-winner Larry McMurtry's novel, this handsome TV miniseries is a finely detailed evocation of the Old West, with a wonderful cast and an equally fine production. Followed by "Return to Lonesome Dove." **480m/C; VHS, DVD, Blu-Ray.** Robert Duvall; Tommy Lee Jones; Anjelica Huston; Danny Glover; Diane Lane; Rick Schroder; Robert Urich; D.B. Sweeney; Frederic Forrest; ***D:*** Simon Wincer; ***W:*** William D. Wittliff; ***M:*** Basil Poledouris. **TV**

Lonesome Dove Church **2014 (R)** Based on real events, this western relates the story of the founding of Grapevine, Texas's Lonesome Dove Church in the mid-1840s. Working as a traveling preacher, John Shepherd (Berenger) has one dream: building his own church. Estranged from his son Isaac (Holt), John comes to his son's defense when he is accused of robbery and murder. John risks his future for his son by challenging a cold-blooded killer and seeking redemption for all. **89m/C; DVD, Blu-Ray, Streaming, Download.** Tom Berenger; Greyston Holt; Alex Zahara; Andrea Whitburn; Nicole Oliver; ***D:*** Terry Miles; ***W:*** Bob Thielke; ***C:*** Mahlon Todd Williams; ***M:*** Colin Aguiar.

Lonesome Jim **2006 (R)** Jim (Affleck) is an aimless, melancholic 27-year-old returning to his dull hometown in Indiana after a spirit-crushing stint in New York. Low-key, with mildly eccentric characters, it paints a nice little picture of Midwestern alienation, soaked with dry humor. Buscemi is subtle and meticulous with his direction, working in familiar territory. **91m/C; DVD.** Casey Affleck; Liv Tyler; Mary Kay Place; Seymour Cassel; Kevin Corrigan; Jack Rovello; Mark Boone, Jr.; ***D:*** Steve Buscemi; ***W:*** James C. Strouse; ***C:*** Phil Parmet.

Lonesome Trail 1/2 **1955** Routine Western that differs from the average oater by having the good guys use bows and arrows to fight their battles. **73m/B; VHS, DVD.** John Agar; Margia Dean; Edgar Buchanan; Wayne Morris; Adele Jergens; Douglas Fowley; Earle Lyon; Richard Bartlett; ***D:*** Richard Bartlett; ***W:*** Richard Bartlett; ***M:*** Leo Klatzkin.

The Long Dark Hall 1/2 **1951** Courtroom drama in which an innocent man is brought to trial when his showgirl mistress is found dead. **86m/B; VHS, DVD.** *GB* Rex Harrison; Lilli Palmer; Denis O'Dea; Raymond Huntley; Patricia Wayne; Anthony Dawson; ***D:*** Anthony Bushell; Reginald Beck.

The Long Day Closes **1992 (PG)** It's 1956 Liverpool and 11-year-old Bud (McCormack) is part of a working-class Catholic family who longs to escape from his humdrum life. And how? By going to the movies of course and filling his head with pop songs. Nostalgic view of family life filled with sweet, small everyday moments set in a dreary postwar England. Sequel to Davies's also autobiographical film "Distant Voices, Still Lives." **84m/C; VHS, DVD, Blu-Ray.** *GB*

Leigh McCormack; Marjorie Yates; Anthony Watson; Ayse Owens; ***D:*** Terence Davies; ***W:*** Terence Davies; ***C:*** Michael Coulter.

Long Day's Journey into Night **1962** A brooding, devastating film based on Eugene O'Neill's most powerful and autobiographical play. Depicts a day in the life of a family deteriorating under drug addiction, alcoholism, and imminent death. Hepburn's performance is outstanding. In 1988, the Broadway version was taped and released on video. **174m/B; VHS, DVD, Blu-Ray.** Ralph Richardson; Katharine Hepburn; Dean Stockwell; Jeanne Barr; Jason Robards, Jr.; ***D:*** Sidney Lumet; ***C:*** Boris Kaufman; ***M:*** Andre Previn. Cannes '62: Actress (Hepburn); Natl. Bd. of Review '62: Support. Actor (Robards).

Long Day's Journey into Night **1988** A taped version of the Broadway production of the epic Eugene O'Neill play about a Southern family deteriorating under the weight of terminal illness, alcoholism and drug abuse. In 1962 a movie adaptation of the play was released with outstanding performances from its cast. **169m/C; VHS, DVD.** Jack Lemmon; Bethel Leslie; Peter Gallagher; Kevin Spacey; Jodie Lynne McLintock; ***D:*** Jonathan Miller.

Long Days of Revenge *Long Days of Vengeance; I lunghi giorni della vendetta; Faccia d'angelo; Days of Vengeance; The Deadliest Gunfight; Vendetta* **1967** After years of hard labor, Sheriff Ted Barnett (Giuliano Gemma) escapes prison to get revenge on the men who framed him for the murder of his father. Currently only available as part of the 'Westerns Unchained' collection. **105m/C; Blu-Ray.** *FR IT SP* Giuliano Gemma; Francisco Rabal; Gabriella Giorgella; Conrado San Martin; Franco Cobianchi; ***D:*** Florestano Vancini; ***W:*** Augusto Caminito; Fernando Di Leo; Mahnahen Velasco; ***C:*** Francisco Marin; ***M:*** Ennio Morricone; Armando Travajoli. **VIDEO**

The Long Days of Summer **1980** Set in pre-WWII America, this film portrays a Jewish attorney's struggle against the prejudices of the New England town where he lives. Sequel to "When Every Day Is the Fourth of July." **105m/C; VHS, DVD.** Dean Jones; Joan Hackett; Louanne; Donald Moffat; Andrew Duggan; Michael McGuire; ***D:*** Dan Curtis. **TV**

The Long Dumb Road **1/2** **2019 (R)** Sheltered Nathan (Revolori) takes a road trip from his home in Texas through the Southwest on the way to art school in California. Though he plans on taking pictures of what he calls real America along the way, he lacks knowledge and experience. When Nathan's purple minivan breaks down, eccentric Richard (Mantzoukas), an unemployed mechanic, gets it running again and hitches a ride as he makes his way to Vegas. Along the way, the pair have conversations about life and unexpected adventures. The chemistry between the talented actors drives the loosely constructed yet meaningful and entertaining film. **90m/C; DVD, Blu-Ray.** Tony Revolori; David DeLao; Lora Martinez-Cunningham; Jason Mantzoukas; Derek Blakeney; ***D:*** Hannah Fidell; ***W:*** Hannah Fidell; Carson Mell; ***C:*** Andrew Droz Palermo; ***M:*** Keegan DeWitt.

The Long Good Friday **1/2** **1980** Set in London's dockland, this is a violent story of a crime boss who meets his match. Hoskin's world crumbles over an Easter weekend when his buildings are bombed and his men murdered. He thinks its the work of rival gangsters only to discover an even deadlier threat is behind his troubles. One of the best of the crime genre, with an exquisitely charismatic performance by Hoskins. **109m/C; VHS, DVD.** *GB* Bob Hoskins; Dame Helen Mirren; Dave King; Bryan Marshall; George Coulouris; Pierce Brosnan; Derek Thompson; Eddie Constantine; Brian Hall; Stephen Davies; P. H. Moriarty; Paul Freeman; Charles Cork; Paul Barber; Patti Love; Ruby Head; Dexter Fletcher; Roy Alon; ***D:*** John MacKenzie; ***W:*** Barrie Keefe; ***C:*** Phil Meheux; ***M:*** Francis Monkman.

The Long Goodbye **1973 (R)** Raymond Chandler's penultimate novel with the unmistakable Altman touch—which is to say that some of the changes to the story have pushed purist noses out of joint. Gould is cast as an insouciant anti-Marlowe, the film noir atmosphere has been transmuted into a Hollywood film neon, genre jibing abounds, and the ending has been rewritten. But the revamping serves a purpose, which is to make Marlowe a viable character in a contemporary world. Handsomely photographed by Vilmos Zsigmond. **112m/C; DVD, Blu-Ray.** Elliott Gould; Nina Van Pallandt; Sterling Hayden; Henry Gibson; Mark Rydell; David Arkin; Warren Berlinger; ***Cameo(s):*** Arnold Schwarzenegger; David Carradine; ***D:*** Robert Altman; ***W:*** Leigh Brackett; ***C:*** Vilmos Zsigmond; ***M:*** John Williams. Natl. Soc. Film Critics '73: Cinematog.

The Long Gray Line **1955** Power gives an outstanding performance as Marty Maher, a humble Irish immigrant who became an institution at West Point. This is the inspiring story of his rise from an unruly cadet to one of the academy's most beloved instructors. O'Hara does a fine job of playing his wife, who like her husband, adopts the young cadets as her own. Director Ford gracefully captures the spirit and honor associated with West Point in this affectionate drama. **138m/C; DVD.** Tyrone Power; Maureen O'Hara; Robert Francis; Donald Crisp; Ward Bond; Betsy Palmer; Phil Carey; ***D:*** John Ford; ***W:*** Edward Hope; ***C:*** Charles Lawton, Jr.

The Long Haul **1957** A truck driver becomes involved with crooks as his marriage sours. **88m/C; VHS, DVD, Blu-Ray.** Victor Mature; Diana Dors; Patrick Allen; Gene Anderson; ***D:*** Ken Hughes.

The Long, Hot Summer **1/2** **1958** A tense, well-played adaptation of the William Faulkner story about drifter Ben Quick (Newman), who latches himself onto a tyrannical Mississippi family, the Varners, led by larger-than-life Will Varner (Welles). The first on-screen pairing of Newman and Woodward (who plays spinster daughter Clara), and one of the best. Remade for TV in 1986. **117m/C; VHS, DVD, Blu-Ray.** Paul Newman; Orson Welles; Joanne Woodward; Lee Remick; Anthony (Tony) Franciosa; Angela Lansbury; Richard Anderson; ***D:*** Martin Ritt; ***W:*** Harriet Frank, Jr.; Irving Ravetch; ***C:*** Joseph LaShelle; ***M:*** Alex North. Cannes '58: Actor (Newman).

The Long, Hot Summer **1/2** **1986** TV version of the William Faulkner story, "The Hamlet," about a drifter taken under a Southern patriarch's wing. He's bribed into courting the man's unmarried daughter. Wonderful performances from the entire cast, especially Ivey and surprisingly, Johnson. Remake of the 1958 film with Paul Newman and Joanne Woodward that is on par with the original. **172m/C; VHS, DVD.** Don Johnson; Cybill Shepherd; Judith Ivey; Jason Robards, Jr.; Ava Gardner; William Russ; Wings Hauser; William Forsythe; Albert Hall; ***D:*** Stuart Cooper; ***M:*** Charles Bernstein. **TV**

Long John Silver **1/2** *Long John Silver Returns to Treasure Island* **1954** Famed pirate John Silver plans a return trip to Treasure Island to search for the elusive treasure; unofficial sequel to "Treasure Island" by Disney. **103m/C; VHS, DVD.** *AU* Robert Newton; Connie Gilchrist; Kit Taylor; Grant Taylor; Rod Taylor; ***D:*** Byron Haskin; ***W:*** Martin Rackin; ***C:*** Carl Guthrie; ***M:*** David Buttolph.

The Long Kiss Goodnight **1/2** **1996 (R)** Audience-pleasing, blood-soaked, foul-mouthed, and action-packed. Mild-mannered, brown-haired Samantha Caine's (Davis) a schoolteacher with a daughter, a nice boyfriend, and amnesia. Sam has flashbacks to her past—and what a past it turns out to be. With the help of seedy PI Mitch Henessey (Jackson), she discovers her name is Charly Baltimore and she's a highly trained and very deadly CIA assassin. And the now bleached-blonde, beyond-tough Charly must match her quickly regained lethal abilities with ruthless former nemesis Timothy (Bierko). The body count's high, the blood flows freely, and there's some spectacular stunts. **120m/C; DVD, Blu-Ray.** Geena Davis; Samuel L. Jackson; Craig Bierko; Patrick Malahide; Brian Cox; David Morse; Yvonne Zima; Tom Amandes; Melina Kanakaredes; G.D. Spradlin; ***D:*** Renny Harlin; ***W:*** Shane Black; ***C:*** Guillermo Navarro; ***M:*** Alan Silvestri.

Long Life, Happiness and Prosperity **2002** Set in Vancouver's Chinatown. Twelve-year-old Mindy Lum turns to Taoist magic to fix her overworked single mother Kin's financial and romantic problems. But Mindy's magic charms seem to go astray when the local butcher Bing Lai wins the lottery, elderly security guard Shuck Wong loses his job, and her mother's admirer Alvin becomes interested in someone else. **91m/C; DVD.** *CA* Sandra Oh; Valerie Tian; Russell Yuen; Ric Young; Chang Tseng; Tsai Chin; ***D:*** Mina Shum; ***W:*** Mina Shum; Dennis Foon; ***C:*** Peter Wunstorf; ***M:*** Andrew Lockington.

The Long, Long Trailer **1/2** **1954** A couple on their honeymoon find that trailer life is more than they bargained for. Lots of fun with charming direction from Minelli, and Ball's incredible slapstick style. **97m/C; VHS, DVD.** Desi Arnaz, Sr.; Lucille Ball; Marjorie Main; Keenan Wynn; Gladys Hurlbut; Moroni Olsen; Bert Freed; Madge Blake; Walter Baldwin; ***D:*** Vincente Minnelli; ***W:*** Albert Hackett; Frances Goodrich; ***C:*** Robert L. Surtees; ***M:*** Adolph Deutsch.

Long Lost Son **2006** Just who's the questionable parent may not be so obvious. Kristen's estranged husband Quinn takes their four-year-old son Mark sailing and both are reported lost during a storm. Fourteen years later, Kristen is watching a friend's vacation video when she spots a couple of faces in the background and is convinced they are Quinn and a now 18-year-old Mark prompting her to travel there and investigate. **90m/C; DVD.** Gabrielle Anwar; Craig Sheffer; Chace Crawford; Philip Granger; Ian Robison; Richard Blade; ***D:*** Brian Trenchard-Smith; ***W:*** Richard Blade; ***C:*** Robert Morris; ***M:*** David Reynolds. **CABLE**

The Long Memory **1953** Embittered Philip Davidson (Mills) is released from prison on parole after serving years for a murder he didn't commit. Under police surveillance, he takes refuge on a barge and plots to get even with the witnesses whose lies sent him to the slammer. But a young woman (Bergh) shows Philip love,and he has to decide whether to continue with his revenge or take his second chance for a new life. **93m/B; DVD.** *UK* John Mills; John McCallum; Elizabeth Sellars; Eva Bergh; Geoffrey Keen; John Chandos; John Slater; ***D:*** Robert Hamer; ***W:*** Robert Hamer; Frank Harvey; ***C:*** Harry Waxman; ***M:*** William Alwyn.

The Long Night **1/2** **1947** Remake of Marcel Carne's "Le Journe Se Leve/Daybreak" (1939). WWII vet Joe Adams (Fonda) is having a hard time with civilian life. In fact, he's just killed con man/magician Maximilian (Price) and has barricaded himself from the cops in his apartment. Flashbacks serve to show how Joe got into his present situation (women are involved, naturally). Not too involving. **101m/B; VHS, DVD.** Henry Fonda; Vincent Price; Barbara Bel Geddes; Ann Dvorak; Howard Freeman; Moroni Olsen; Elisha Cook, Jr.; ***D:*** Anatole Litvak; ***W:*** John Wexley; ***C:*** Sol Polito; ***M:*** Dimitri Tiomkin.

A Long Ride From Hell *Vivo per la Tua Morte; I Live for Your Death* **1968 (R)** Reeves stars in (and co-wrote) this spaghetti western that was his last film before his retirement. Rancher Mike Sturges (Reeves) and his brother Roy (Fantasia) are falsely imprisoned for rustling. When his brother dies in the pen, Mike escapes to get revenge on the actual bad guys. Italian with subtitles or dubbed. **104m/C; DVD.** *IT* Steve Reeves; Wayde Preston; Mimmo Palmara; Silvana Venturelli; Nello Pazzafini; Franco Fatasia; Guido Lollobrigida; ***D:*** Camillo Bazzoni; ***W:*** Steve Reeves; Roberto Natale; ***C:*** Enzo Barboni; ***M:*** Carlo Savina.

The Long Ride Home **2001** After being accused of being a gunslinger, Jack Cole (Travis) has spent eight years running from the law and various vigilantes. He finally decides it's time to clear his name and be reunited with his family so he heads home for the final showdown. Plot's more convoluted that it may seem and it's a cliched story to begin with. **?m/CVHS, DVD.** Randy Travis; Eric Roberts; Ernest Borgnine; Stella Stevens; ***D:*** Robert Marcarelli; ***C:*** Gary Graver.

The Long Riders **1980 (R)** Excellent mythic western in which the Jesse James and Cole Younger gangs raid banks, trains, and stagecoaches in post-Civil War Missouri. Stylish, meticulous and a violent look back, with one of the better slow-motion shootouts in Hollywood history. Notable for the portrayal of four sets of outlaw brothers (James, Younger, Miller, Ford) by four Hollywood brother (Keach, Carradine, Quaid, Guest) sets. Complimented by excellent Cooder score. **100m/C; VHS, DVD, Blu-Ray.** Stacy Keach; James Keach; Randy Quaid; Dennis Quaid; David Carradine; Keith Carradine; Robert Carradine; Christopher Guest; Nicholas Guest; Pamela Reed; Savannah Smith; James Whitmore, Jr.; Harry Carey, Jr.; ***D:*** Walter Hill; ***W:*** Stacy Keach; James Keach; Bill Bryden; ***C:*** Ric Waite; ***M:*** Ry Cooder.

Long Shadows **1/2** **1986** An analysis of how the resonating effects of the Civil War can still be felt on society, via interviews with a number of noted writers, historians, civil rights activists and politicians. **88m/C; VHS, DVD.** Robert Penn Warren; Studs Terkel; Jimmy Carter; Robert Coles; Tom Wicker; ***D:*** Ross Spears.

The Long Ships **1964** Silly Viking saga finds brothers Rolfe (Widmark) and Orm (Tamblyn) stealing a ship and heading off in search of a solid-gold bell. Among their trials are a mutinous crew and battling Moorish Prince El Mansuh (Poitier). Something to be left off the resume. **125m/C; VHS, DVD.** Richard Widmark; Russ Tamblyn; Sidney Poitier; Oscar Homolka; Rosanna Schiaffino; Beba Loncar; Lionel Jeffries; Edward Judd; ***D:*** Jack Cardiff; ***W:*** Beverley Cross; Berkely Mather; ***C:*** Christopher Challis; ***M:*** Dusan Radic.

The Long Shot **1/2** **2004** In this Hallmark Channel family drama, single mom Annie Garrett (Benz) has relocated to California with her daughter Taylor (Golightly). Annie finds a job on a stud farm owned by Mary Lou O'Brian (Mason), where she can board her own racehorse, Tolo. Annie hopes to enter Tolo in a riding competition but there's a tragedy and the Garretts have to deal with more hardship. **94m/C; DVD.** Julie Benz; Marsha Mason; Paul LeMat; Gage Golightly; Christopher Cousins; Robert Pine; Laura Johnson; ***D:*** Georg Stanford Brown; ***W:*** David Alexander; ***C:*** Geza Sinkovics; ***M:*** Mark Watters. **CABLE**

Long Shot **1/2** **2019 (R)** When Secretary of State Charlotte Field (Theron) launches a bid for the presidency, she hires Fred Flarsky (Rogen), a disheveled, clumsy speechwriter who fell in love with her when she used to babysit him. Rogen basically plays the same character he always plays, and we love him for it. Theron, however, may surprise viewers with her solid comedy chops. Together they are a delight, and with a supporting cast adding to the fun, this rom-com polls surprisingly well. **125m/C; DVD, Blu-Ray.** Charlize Theron; Seth Rogen; June Diane Raphael; O'Shea Jackson, Jr.; Andy Serkis; ***D:*** Jonathan Levine; ***W:*** Dan Sterling; Liz Hannah; ***C:*** Yves Bélanger; ***M:*** Marco Beltrami; Miles Hankins.

The Long Summer of George Adams **1/2** **1982** Lighthearted NBC TV movie based on the novel by Weldon Hill. It's 1952 in Cushing, Oklahoma and George Adams is a steam-engine expert for a railroad that's switching to diesel. Wife Norma seems not to notice that George is having a midlife crisis. **93m/C; DVD.** James Garner; Joan Hackett; Anjanette Comer; Alex Harvey; ***D:*** Stuart Margolin; ***W:*** John Gay; ***C:*** Andrew Jackson; ***M:*** Stuart Margolin. **TV**

Long-Term Relationship **2006** Glenn's (Montgomery) been a longtime player on L.A.'s gay single scene when he finds his would-be soulmate in the personals—traditional southern charmer Adam (Beach). Only their differences may make a long-term relationship an impossibility. Low-budget romantic comedy (the debut for writer-director Williams) offers a compelling performance from Montgomery but shoves conflicts out of the way to get to a forced happy ending. **97m/C; DVD.** Matthew Montgomery; Windham Beach; Artie O'Daly; Jeremy Lucas; ***D:*** Rob Williams; ***W:*** Rob Williams; ***C:*** Shawn Grice; ***M:*** Ben Holbrook.

Long Time Since **1/2** **1997** A bit too remote and artsy to be involving. On New Year's Eve in 1971, Diane (Porizkova) hit something (or someone) with her car while driving on a remote country road. The repressed Diane has blocked all memories for some 24 years—until she hears "Auld Lang Syne" on the radio and fragments begin to come by. Putting these bits together leads her to the solitary Michael (Sands) whose wife and baby daughter when missing around the same time as Diane's accident. **89m/C; VHS, DVD.** Paulina Porizkova; Julian Sands; Julianne Nicholson; Jeff Webster; ***D:*** Jay Anania; ***W:*** Jay Anania; ***C:*** Oliver Bokelberg; ***M:*** Judy Kuhn.

The Long Voyage Home 🦴🦴🦴 1/2 **1940** A talented cast performs this must-see screen adaptation of Eugene O'Neill's play about crew members aboard a merchant steamer in 1939. Wayne plays a young lad from Sweden who is trying to get home and stay out of trouble as he and the other seaman get shore leave. **105m/B; VHS, DVD.** John Wayne; Thomas Mitchell; Ian Hunter; Barry Fitzgerald; Mildred Natwick; John Qualen; ***D:*** John Ford; ***C:*** Gregg Toland. N.Y. Film Critics '40: Director (Ford).

The Long Walk Home 🦴🦴🦴 **1989 (PG)** In Montgomery Alabama, in the mid 1950s, Martin Luther King Jr. led a bus boycott. Spacek is the affluent wife of a narrow-minded businessman while Goldberg is their struggling maid. When Spacek discovers that Goldberg is supporting the boycott by walking the nine-mile trek to work, she sympathizes and tries to help, antagonizing her husband. The plot marches inevitably toward a white-on-white showdown on racism while quietly exploring gender equality between the women. Outstanding performances by Spacek and Goldberg, and a great 50s feel. **95m/C; DVD.** Sissy Spacek; Whoopi Goldberg; Dwight Schultz; Ving Rhames; Dylan Baker; Dan E. Butler; ***Nar:*** Mary Steenburgen; ***D:*** Richard Pearce; ***W:*** John Cork; ***C:*** Roger Deakins; ***M:*** George Fenton.

A Long Way Down 🦴 1/2 **2014 (R)** Nick Hornby's beloved book gets the maudlin treatment in this over-directed dramedy about four people who form a bond after meeting on a rooftop on New Year's Eve with suicidal intentions. They agree to put off their rooftop leaps and become quasi-celebrities in the process. Of course, each of the four has different personal issues to address, none of which feel real despite the best efforts of Collette and Brosnan. Everything is underlined, highlighted, and bolded for maximum melodramatic impact. They even dance to "I Will Survive" at one point. **96m/C; DVD, Blu-Ray.** *UK GE* Pierce Brosnan; Toni Collette; Imogen Poots; Aaron Paul; Rosamund Pike; Sam Neill; ***D:*** Pascal Chaumeil; ***W:*** Jack Thorne; ***C:*** Ben Davis; ***M:*** Dario Marianelli.

The Long Way Home 🦴🦴 1/2 **1998** Widowed retiree Thomas Gerrin (Lemmon) is tired of his kids treating him like he's helpless. So he decides to leave his Kansas community and look up an old flame in California. Along the way he meets free-spirited college student Leanne (Paulson) and the two decide to travel together. Thomas' children become frantic, wondering where their wayward pop has gone. **96m/C; DVD.** Jack Lemmon; Sarah Paulson; Betty Garrett; Tom Butler; Kristin Griffith; Garwin Sanford; Rosemary Dunsmore; Peter Dvorsky; ***D:*** Glenn Jordan; ***W:*** William Hanley; ***C:*** Tobias Schliessler; ***M:*** Michel Colombier. **TV**

A Long Way Home 🦴 1/2 *Aftermath* **2001** A family is in crisis when teenaged daughter Tess (Waldron) accuses her father Jack (Urich) of sexual abuse. It turns out that both Jack and his wife Carol (Baxter) were themselves victims of child abuse, though Carol has repressed her memories. Jack tries to reconcile with his estranged family after getting help but they aren't certain that he's really changed. **91m/C; DVD.** Robert Urich; Meredith Baxter; Shawna Waldron; Diane Ladd; Chad Michael Murray; ***D:*** Lorraine Senna; ***W:*** David J. Hill; Jayne Martin; Paul Eric Myers; ***C:*** Don E. Fauntleroy; ***M:*** Peter Manning Robinson. **TV**

The Long Weekend WOOF! **2005 (R)** Dismal, crude sex comedy. Ad exec Ed (Fehr) needs to come up with a new campaign to save his job but his sleazy horndog older brother Cooper (Klein) is just interested in getting them laid. Ed is a porn watcher and the (deemed too raunchy for TV) clips actually come from "America's Funniest Home Videos." **85m/C; DVD.** *GB CA* Chris Klein; Brendan Fehr; Chandra West; Craig Fairbrass; Cobie Smulders; Paul Campbell; ***D:*** Pat Holden; ***W:*** Tad Safran; ***C:*** Brian Pearson; ***M:*** David A. Hughes. **VIDEO**

The Longest Day 🦴🦴🦴 1/2 **1962** The complete story of the D-Day landings at Normandy on June 6, 1944, as seen through the eyes of American, French, British, and German participants. Exhaustively accurate details and extremely talented cast make this one of the all-time great Hollywood epic productions. The first of the big budget, all-star war productions; based on the book by Cornelius Ryan. Three directors share credit. Also available in a colorized version. **179m/C; VHS, DVD, Blu-Ray.** John Wayne; Richard Burton; Red Buttons; Robert Mitchum; Henry Fonda; Robert Ryan; Paul Anka; Mel Ferrer; Edmond O'Brien; Fabian; Sean Connery; Roddy McDowall; Arletty; Curt Jurgens; Rod Steiger; Jean-Louis Barrault; Peter Lawford; Robert Wagner; Sal Mineo; Leo Genn; Richard Beymer; Jeffrey Hunter; Stuart Whitman; Eddie Albert; Tom Tryon; Alexander Knox; Ray Danton; Kenneth More; Richard Todd; Gert Frobe; Christopher Lee; John Robinson; ***D:*** Bernhard Wicki; Ken Annakin; Andrew Marton; ***W:*** James Jones; David Pursall; Jack Seddon; Romain Gary; ***C:*** Jean (Yves, Georges) Bourgoin; Pierre Levent; Henri Persin; Walter Wottitz; ***M:*** Maurice Jarre. Oscars '62: B&W Cinematog.

The Longest Drive 🦴🦴 *The Quest* **1976** Two brothers comb the wildest parts of the West for their sister, whom they believe is living with Indians. TV movie originally titled "The Quest," which became a brief television series. Highlights include colorful performances from the veteran actors and a unique horse/camel race. A continuation of the series is available on video as "The Captive: The Longest Drive 2." **92m/C; VHS, DVD.** Kurt Russell; Tim Matheson; Brian Keith; Keenan Wynn; Neville Brand; Cameron Mitchell; Morgan Woodward; Iron Eyes Cody; Luke Askew; ***D:*** Lee H. Katzin. **TV**

The Longest Ride 🦴 **2015 (PG-13)** When will the Nicholas Sparks bandwagon finally come to its last destination? The notable decline in star power in the cast of the latest entry might indicate so. As might the fact that it's awful, even for a Sparks film. Sophia (Robertson) and Luke (Eastwood, son of Clint) are, of course, star-crossed lovers, inspired by the memories of the romance that once was from an old man named Ira (Alda). Of course, the love stories—one flashback and one present day—begin to comment on each other, teaching us again that true love is timeless. Hopefully, Sparks is not. **128m/C; DVD, Blu-Ray.** Britt Robertson; Scott Eastwood; Alan Alda; Jack Huston; Oona Chaplin; ***D:*** George Tillman, Jr.; ***W:*** Craig Bolotin; ***C:*** David Tattersall; ***M:*** Mark Isham.

The Longest Week 🦴 **2014 (PG-13)** If you're going to make a film about one anti-hero who finds love after a long, weird week, he better be a likeable guy. Such is the problem with director Glanz's dull-as-dirt dramedy. Conrad Valmont (Bateman) is a spoiled jerk living at his parents' prestigious Manhattan Hotel. Or he did. Valmont is faced with responsibility and the loss of his cash cow when he's disinherited. Yes, this is actually a film about a rich kid finding his priorities. As you might imagine, you won't care. Even the generally appealing Wilde and Crudup can't make the week end soon enough. **86m/C; Blu-Ray, Streaming.** Jason Bateman; Olivia Wilde; Billy Crudup; Jenny Slate; ***D:*** Peter Glanz; ***W:*** Peter Glanz; ***C:*** Ben Kutchins; ***M:*** Jay Israelson.

The Longest Yard 🦴🦴🦴 **1974 (R)** A one-time pro football quarterback, now an inmate, organizes his fellow convicts into a football team to play against the prison guards. Of course, he's being pressured by the evil warden to throw the game. One of the all-time classic football movies. Filmed on location at Georgia State Prison. **121m/C; VHS, DVD.** Burt Reynolds; Eddie Albert; Bernadette Peters; Ed Lauter; Richard Kiel; Sonny Shroyer; Michael Conrad; James Hampton; Harry Caesar; Charles Tyner; Mike Henry; Anitra Ford; Michael Fox; Joe Kapp; Pepper Martin; Robert Tessier; ***D:*** Robert Aldrich; ***W:*** Tracy Keenan Wynn; ***C:*** Joseph Biroc; ***M:*** Frank DeVol. Golden Globes '75: Film--Mus./Comedy.

The Longest Yard 🦴🦴 **2005 (PG-13)** Does anyone really believe Sandler as a QB? In this remake of the more brutal 1974 original, Sandler is ex-pro Paul 'Wrecking' Crewe, who's stuck in a Texas federal pen that also houses one-time college football legend Nate Scarborough (Reynolds, who formerly played the QB). The football-obsessed warden (Cromwell) okays a televised game that pits the woeful cons against the bone-crunching guards (many cameos by ex-jocks). Motor-mouthed Rock appears as a prison fixer and game day takes up a big part of the movie's running time. The comedy's been amped up, the pace is brisk, and Sandler's tolerable. **113m/C; DVD, UMD.** Adam Sandler; Burt Reynolds; Chris Rock; James Cromwell; Nelly; David Patrick Kelly; Nicholas Turturro; William Fichtner; Tracy Morgan; Brian Bosworth; Ed Lauter; Cloris Leachman; Steve Austin; Bob Sapp; Dalip Singh; Lobo Sebastian; Rob Schneider; Courteney Cox; Edward (Eddie) Bunker; Terry Crews; ***D:*** Peter Segal; ***W:*** Sheldon Turner; ***C:*** Dean Semler; ***M:*** Teddy Castellucci.

Longford 🦴🦴 **2006** In 1967, Lord Frank Aungier Pakenham (Broadbent), 7th Earl of Longford, is the respected leader of the House of Lords and a tireless worker for prison rehabilitation. He stakes his name and career when he befriends notorious convicted child murderess, Myra Hindley (Morton), and campaigns for her parole (over a 30-year period), believing his fellow Catholic convert is truly redemptive. But few share his belief. **90m/C; DVD.** *GB* Jim Broadbent; Samantha Morton; Tam Dean Burn; Lindsay Duncan; Lee Boardman; Andy Serkis; Robert Pugh; Anton Rodgers; Kate Miles; Kika Markham; ***D:*** Tom Hooper; ***W:*** Peter Morgan; ***C:*** Danny Cohen; ***M:*** Robert (Rob) Lane. **TV**

Longitude 🦴🦴🦴 **2000** In 1714, England's Parliament offers a large reward to anyone who can discover a way to accurately measure longitude at sea to prevent nautical disasters. Carpenter John Harrison (Gambon) decides on a mechanical solution in the form of a clock (now known as the marine chronometer) and strives to have his ideas excepted (for 40 years). His story is paralleled with that of shellshocked ex-WWI soldier Rupert Gould (Irons), who discovers Harrison's neglected originals and becomes obsessed with restoring them to working order. The performances carry the somewhat diffuse plot. Based on the book by Dava Sobel. **200m/C; DVD.** *UK* Jeremy Irons; Michael Gambon; Anna Chancellor; Ian Hart; Peter Vaughan; Gemma Jones; John Wood; Stephen Fry; Alec McCowen; Frank Finlay; John Standing; Samuel West; Bill Nighy; Brian Cox; Barbara Leigh-Hunt; Clive Francis; Daragh O'Malley; Tim (McInnerny) McInnery; Nicholas (Nick) Rowe; ***D:*** Charles Sturridge; ***W:*** Charles Sturridge; ***C:*** Peter Hannan; ***M:*** Geoffrey Burgon. **TV**

The Longshot WOOF! **1986 (PG-13)** Four bumblers try to raise cash to put on a sure-bet racetrack tip in this sorry comedy. Mike Nichols is the executive producer. **89m/C; VHS, DVD.** Tim Conway; Harvey Korman; Jack Weston; Ted Wass; Jonathan Winters; Stella Stevens; Anne Meara; ***D:*** Paul Bartel; ***W:*** Tim Conway; John Myhers; ***M:*** Charles Fox.

The Longshots 🦴🦴 1/2 **2008 (PG)** Another based-on-a-true story about a team of misfit athletes has enough trick plays to rise above the typical formula. Director Durst sticks to an authentic feel for the story's hard-luck backdrop of Minton, Illinois, where 11-year-old honor roll student Jasmine's (Palmer) stuck with her unemployed Uncle Curtis (Ice Cube), an ex-jock who discovers she has a surprisingly strong throwing arm. He persuades her to try out for the local football team and she becomes the first girl to play quarterback in Pop Warner. Palmer's performance is honest and highlights a film that skips cliches in favor of a warm vibe. **94m/C; DVD, Blu-Ray.** Ice Cube; Tasha Smith; Keke Palmer; Matt Craven; Jill Marie Jones; Glenn Plummer; Malcolm Goodwin; Dash Mihok; Miles Chandler; ***D:*** Fred Durst; ***W:*** Doug Atchison; Nick Santora; ***C:*** Conrad W. Hall; ***M:*** John Swihart; Teddy Castellucci.

Longtime Companion 🦴🦴🦴 1/2 **1990 (R)** Critically acclaimed film follows a group of gay men and their friends during the 1980s. The closely knit group monitors the progression of the AIDS virus from early news reports until it finally hits home and begins to take the lives of their loved ones. One of the first films to look at the situation in an intelligent and touching manner. Produced by the PBS "American Playhouse" company. **100m/C; VHS, DVD.** Stephen Caffrey; Patrick Cassidy; Brian Cousins; Bruce Davison; John Dossett; Mark Lamos; Dermot Mulroney; Mary-Louise Parker; Michael Schoeffling; Campbell Scott; Robert Joy; Brad O'Hara; Dan E. Butler; ***D:*** Norman Rene; ***W:*** Craig Lucas; ***C:*** Tony Jennelli. Golden Globes '91: Support. Actor (Davison); Ind. Spirit '91: Support. Actor (Davison); N.Y. Film Critics '90: Support. Actor (Davison); Natl. Soc. Film Critics '90: Support. Actor (Davison); Sundance '90: Aud. Award.

Look at Me 🦴🦴🦴 1/2 *Comme une image* **2004 (PG-13)** Unhappy Parisian tale of gigantically egotistical father (Bacri) jet-setting his way around town and his plump daughter (Berry) unsuccessfully vying for his attention. She's a gifted singer, constantly tuning her voice. He's an acclaimed novelist, constantly tuning her out. He's also got a young trophy wife (Desarnauts) who gets nothing from her husband but ridicule and indifference. He wants his wife to look perfect, he wants his daughter to look like her voice sounds. French co-writers and co-stars Agnes Jaoui and Jean-Pierre Bacri craft a poignant, unpredictable film defying stereotypes. **110m/C; DVD.** *FR* Agnes Jaoui; Jean-Pierre Bacri; Laurent Grevill; Marilou Berry; Virginie Desarnauts; Keine Bouhiza; Gregoire Oestermann; ***D:*** Agnes Jaoui; ***W:*** Agnes Jaoui; Jean-Pierre Bacri; ***C:*** Stephane Fontaine; ***M:*** Philippe Rombi.

Look Away 🦴🦴 **2018** Maria (Eisley) is a struggling high school senior. Not only is she bullied at school, her plastic surgeon father (Isaacs) criticizes her appearance and activities. To make herself feel better, depressed Maria often talks to herself in the mirror. One day, her reflection talks back and says all the snarky things Maria has wanted to say to her tormentors. The situation becomes more complicated when the mirror version of Maria takes the place of the real Maria. The psychological horror film suffers from slow pacing and a dark mood that does not match the story. However, it includes an accurate depiction of adolescence's awkwardness. **103m/C; DVD.** India Eisley; Jason Isaacs; Mira Sorvino; Penelope Mitchell; John C. MacDonald; ***D:*** Assaf Bernstein; ***W:*** Assaf Bernstein; ***C:*** Pedro Luque; ***M:*** Mario Grigorov.

Look Back in Anger 🦴🦴🦴 1/2 **1958** Based on John Osbourne's famous play, the first British "angry young man" film, in which a squalor-living lad takes out his anger on the world by seducing his friend's wife. **99m/B; VHS, DVD.** *GB* Richard Burton; Claire Bloom; Mary Ure; Edith Evans; Gary Raymond; Glen Byam Shaw; George Devine; Donald Pleasence; Phyllis Neilson-Terry; ***D:*** Tony Richardson; ***W:*** John Osborne; Nigel Kneale; ***C:*** Oswald Morris; ***M:*** John Addison.

Look Back in Anger 🦴🦴🦴 **1989** There's something about John Osborne's play that brings out the angry young man in British leads. Richard Burton played Osborne's irascible guy in 1958, Malcom McDowell looked back angrily in '80, and now Branagh convincingly vents his spleen on wife and mistress in this made for British TV production. Director Jones earlier filmed "84 Charing Cross Road" and "Jacknife." **114m/C; VHS, DVD.** *GB* Kenneth Branagh; Emma Thompson; Gerard Horan; Siobhan Redmond; ***D:*** David Hugh Jones. **TV**

Look Both Ways 🦴🦴 **2005 (PG-13)** Artist Meryl's (Clarke) constantly imagining disasters (depicted in animated sequences) and then witnesses a real tragedy—a man getting killed by a train. Local photographer Nick (McInnes) takes a picture of the man's anguished widow, which is printed on the newspaper's front page along with reporter Andy's (Hayes) somewhat brutal story. Nick and Meryl make a tentative connection while struggling with fear, loneliness, hope, and forgiveness. The secondary characters and their problems are a distraction but the film's overall quirkiness tends to work well. **100m/C; DVD.** *AU* Justine Clarke; Anthony Hayes; Andrew S. Gilbert; Daniela Farinacci; William McInnes; Lisa Flanagan; Maggie Dence; Sacha Horler; Edwin Hodgeman; ***D:*** Sarah Watt; ***W:*** Sarah Watt; ***C:*** Ray Argall; ***M:*** Amanda Brown.

Look for the Silver Lining 🦴🦴 1/2 **1949** Insipid musical biography of Broadway star Marilyn Miller (Haver). Bolger is the highlight as Miller's mentor from vaudeville to the Great White Way. **100m/C; VHS, DVD.** June Haver; Ray Bolger; Gordon MacRae; Charlie Ruggles; Rosemary DeCamp; S.Z. Sakall; ***D:*** David Butler; ***W:*** Phoebe Ephron; Henry Ephron; Marian Spitzer.

Look in Any Window 𝒥𝒥 **1961** Unhappy teen Craig Fowler (Anka) prowls around his suburban neighborhood peeking in windows--maybe to see if everyone else has secrets too. Craig's dad Jay is a jobless drunk and his frustrated mom Jackie is ready to fool around with local lothario Gareth, while Gareth's wife Betty comes to the conclusion that money doesn't buy happiness. Their daughter Eileen (Perreau) and Craig are simpatico over their lousy parents. Ony directorial credit for producer Alland. **87m/B; DVD.** Paul Anka; Ruth Roman; Alex Nicol; Gigi Perreau; Carol Matthews; Jack Cassidy; ***D:*** William Alland; ***W:*** Laurence E. Mascott; ***C:*** W. Wallace Kelley; ***M:*** Richard Shores.

The Look of Love 𝒥𝒥 **2013** Superficial but flashy biopic set primarily in swinging '60s and decadent '70s London. Brazen Paul Raymond (Coogan) makes a fortune as an impresario by pushing the boundaries of British prudery (and obscenity charges) with his private men's' clubs, soft-core girlie revues and publications, and some judicious real estate buying in Soho. His beloved daughter Debbie (Poots) is a showbiz wannabe who's more eager than talented, and after Daddy funds an expensive revue that flops, Debbie turns to drugs and it doesn't end well. The general tackiness occasionally gives way to gravitas. **101m/C; On Demand.** *UK* Steve Coogan; Anna Friel; Tamsin Egerton; Imogen Poots; Chris Addison; Matthew Beard; James Lance; ***D:*** Michael Winterbottom; ***W:*** Matt Greenhalgh; ***C:*** Hubert Taczanowski; ***M:*** Antony Genn; Martin Slattery.

Look Who's Laughing 𝒥𝒥 **1941** Bergen's plane lands in a town conveniently populated by radio stars. Not much plot here, but it might be worth a look to fans of the stars including Jim and Marion Jordan, better known as Fibber McGee and Molly. Currently only sold as part of a collection. **79m/B; VHS, DVD.** Edgar Bergen; Jim Jordan; Marian Jordan; Lucille Ball; Harold (Hal) Peary; Lee Bonnell; Charles Halton; ***D:*** Allan Dwan.

Look Who's Talking 𝒥𝒥𝒥 **1989 (PG-13)** When Alley bears the child of a married, and quite fickle man, she sets her sights elsewhere in search of the perfect father; Travolta is the cabbie with more on his mind than driving Alley around and babysitting. All the while, the baby gives us his views via the voice of Bruce Willis. A very light comedy with laughs for the whole family. **90m/C; VHS, DVD, Blu-Ray.** John Travolta; Kirstie Alley; Olympia Dukakis; George Segal; Abe Vigoda; ***V:*** Bruce Willis; ***D:*** Amy Heckerling; ***W:*** Amy Heckerling; ***M:*** David Kitay.

Look Who's Talking Now 𝒥 ½ **1993 (PG-13)** Continuing to wring revenue from a tired premise, the family dogs throw in their two cents in the second sequel to "Look Who's Talking." Keaton voices a poodle with an attitude and DeVito's a rough street-smart mutt, who gets thrown into the same household as the bosses' pure-bred. Sparks, Alpo, and butt jokes fly as the dogs mark their territory. Meanwhile, dimwit wife Alley's worried that husband Travolta's having an affair and is determined to get him back. **95m/C; DVD.** John Travolta; Kirstie Alley; Olympia Dukakis; George Segal; Lysette Anthony; ***V:*** Diane Keaton; Danny DeVito; ***D:*** Tom Ropelewski; ***W:*** Tom Ropelewski; Leslie Dixon; ***C:*** Oliver Stapleton; ***M:*** William Ross.

Look Who's Talking, Too 𝒥 **1990 (PG-13)** If Academy Awards for Stupidest Sequel and Lamest Dialogue existed, this diaper doody would have cleaned up. The sequel throws the accountant-cabbie duo into a marital tailspin when Alley's babysitting brother moves in and hubby moves out. Meanwhile, Willis sasses with baby sister Roseanne. A once-clever gimmick now unencumbered by plot and humor. **81m/C; DVD.** Kirstie Alley; John Travolta; Olympia Dukakis; Elias Koteas; ***V:*** Bruce Willis; Mel Brooks; Damon Wayans; Roseanne; ***D:*** Amy Heckerling; ***W:*** Amy Heckerling; Neal Israel; ***C:*** Thomas Del Ruth; ***M:*** David Kitay.

The Lookalike 𝒥𝒥 **2014** Drug suppliers Bobby and Frank want to impress their retiring mob boss by setting him up with his longtime dream woman. Only she dies before than can, so the two scramble for a substitute. Lacey turns out to be a former customer of drug dealer Joe Mulligan and there's a lot more plot, but nothing goes as planned. **100m/C; DVD, Blu-Ray.** John Corbett; Steven Bauer; John Savage; Jerry O'Connell; Justin Long; Gillian Jacobs; Scottie Thompson; Gina Gershon; Luis Guzman; ***D:*** Richard Gray; ***W:*** Michele Davis-Gray; ***C:*** Thomas Scott Stanton; ***M:*** Alies Sluiter. **VIDEO**

Looker 𝒥 ½ **1981 (PG)** Stunning models are made even more beautiful by a plastic surgeon, but one by one they begin to die. Finney plays the Beverly Hills surgeon who decides to investigate when he starts losing all his clients. **94m/C; VHS, DVD, Blu-Ray.** Albert Finney; James Coburn; Susan Dey; Leigh Taylor-Young; ***D:*** Michael Crichton; ***W:*** Michael Crichton.

Lookin' to Get Out 𝒥𝒥 ½ **1982 (R)** Comedy about two gamblers running from their debts. They wind up at the MGM Grand in Las Vegas trying to get out of a mess. **70m/C; VHS, DVD.** Ann-Margret; Jon Voight; Burt Young; Bert Remsen; Clyde Kusatsu; Larry "Flash" Jenkins; Samantha Harper; Angelina Jolie; ***D:*** Hal Ashby; ***M:*** Miles Goodman; John Beal.

Looking for an Echo 𝒥𝒥 ½ **1999 (R)** Widower Vince (Assante), who's pushing 50, had some teen success in a do-wop group and then put his singing aside to marry and raise his kids. His middle son, Anthony (Ballerini), is now bringing up dad's old dreams (and some regrets) by having his own rock band. But Vince's main concerns are for youngest child, Tina (Romano), who's in the hospital battling leukemia. This puts Vince in the flirty orbit of brassy nurse Joanne (Venora), who would like to offer the guy some personal care. Assante supplies lots of charm in a glossy, sentimental tearjerker. **97m/C; DVD.** Armand Assante; Diane Venora; Joe Grifasi; Tom Mason; Anthony John (Tony) Denison; Edoardo Ballerini; David Margulies; Christy Carlson Romano; ***D:*** Martin Davidson; ***W:*** Martin Davidson; Jeffrey Goldenberg; Robert Held; ***C:*** Charles Minsky.

Looking for Comedy in the Muslim World 𝒥 ½ **2006 (PG-13)** Lame conceit has comedian Brooks play himself, more or less. He's asked by the State Department to spend a month traveling in India and Pakistan in order to figure out what Muslims find funny and write a government-sized (500 pages) report. Why this would matter is best left to the bureaucrats. There are some funny moments but not enough to carry the film, and Brooks' mild-mannered neurotic is something of an acquired taste. **98m/C; DVD.** Albert Brooks; Sheetal Sheth; John Carroll Lynch; Jon Tenney; Fred Dalton Thompson; Amy Ryan; Homie Doroodian; Penny Marshall; Duncan Bravo; Emma Lockhart; ***D:*** Albert Brooks; ***W:*** Albert Brooks; ***C:*** Thomas Ackerman; ***M:*** Michael Giacchino.

Looking for Eric 𝒥𝒥 **2009** Good-natured, sometimes touching comedy-drama finds middle-aged Manchester postal worker Eric Bishop's life in increasing chaos. He desperately wants to regain control and also get back together with his first wife (and true love) Lily. A fanatical Manchester United football fan, hapless Eric gets advice from his all-time sports hero Eric Cantona, who magically appears when needed. **116m/C; DVD, Blu-Ray.** *GB FR IT SP BE* Eric Cantona; Gerard Kearns; Steve Evets; Stephanie Bishop; Lucy-Jo Hudson; Stefan Gumbs; John Henshae; ***D:*** Ken Loach; ***W:*** Paul Laverty; ***C:*** Barry Ackroyd; ***M:*** George Fenton.

Looking for Kitty 𝒥𝒥 **2004 (R)** Upstate New York high school baseball coach Abe (Krumholtz in a bad mustache) comes to Manhattan to look for his missing wife Kitty, who supposedly ran off and is now shacked up with a rock star. Abe hires widowed PI Jack (Burns) and decides to tag along as the two lonely guys begin to bond while looking for Abe's missus. Low-key, low-budget. **95m/C; DVD.** David Krumholtz; Edward Burns; Max Baker; Connie Britton; ***D:*** Edward Burns; ***W:*** Edward Burns; ***C:*** William Rexer; ***M:*** Robert Gary; P.T. Walkley.

Looking for Love 𝒥 ½ **1964** Frustrated singer and would-be inventor Libby (Francis) is pursuing promoter Paul (Hutton) for romantic reasons when he gets her on the Johnny Carson show to demonstrate her invention. Johnny also gives her a singing chance and her musical career takes off while Libby realizes Paul may not be the right guy for her after all. **83m/C; DVD.** Connie Francis; Jim Hutton; Susan Oliver; Joby Baker; Barbara Nichols; Jay C. Flippen; Jesse White; Johnny Carson; ***D:*** Don Weis; ***W:*** Ruth Brooks Flippen; ***C:*** Milton Krasner; ***M:*** Georgie Stoll.

Looking for Palladin 𝒥𝒥 **2008** Predictable story worth watching for Gazzara's performance. Disagreeable Hollywood agent Josh (Moscow) goes to Guatemala in search of award-winning retired actor Jake Palladin (Gazzara) to offer him a cameo in a movie remake. The locals are protective of Jake but Josh and Jake turn out to have a past since Jake was once his stepfather and the younger man is still holding onto resentment and some questions. **115m/C; DVD.** Ben Gazzara; David Moscow; Talia Shire; Vincent Pastore; Pedro Armendariz, Jr.; Angelica Aragon; ***D:*** Andrzej Krakowski; ***W:*** Andrzej Krakowski; ***C:*** Giovanni Fabietti; Alberto Chaktoura.

Looking for Richard 𝒥𝒥𝒥 **1996 (PG-13)** Pacino's pic is a semi-documentary dwelling on the filmmaker's struggles to understand the play. Punctuated with comic relief, Pacino makes a pilgrimage to the Globe Theatre, taps Brit theatre heavyweights Gielgud and Redgrave for thoughts on interpreting Shakespeare, and combs New York for candid "man in the street" impressions in a quest to bring his subject to a wider public. Over the course of four years, Pacino plays the deformed usurper with a cast of worthy Americans (Spacey, Kline, Ryder, Baldwin, and Quinn), illustrating key scenes of the play. **108m/C; DVD.** Alec Baldwin; Winona Ryder; Kevin Spacey; Aidan Quinn; F. Murray Abraham; Kenneth Branagh; Kevin Conway; John Gielgud; James Earl Jones; Kevin Kline; Estelle Parsons; Vanessa Redgrave; Harris Yulin; Penelope Allen; Al Pacino; Dominic Chianese; Paul Guilfoyle; ***D:*** Al Pacino; ***C:*** Robert Leacock; ***M:*** Howard Shore. Directors Guild '96: Documentary Director (Pacino).

Looking for Trouble 𝒥 **1996 (PG)** Lame kid-friendly movie finds young Jaime (Butler) befriending a baby circus elephant she names Trouble, who has an abusive owner. When the circus leaves town, worried Jaime follows along. **73m/C; VHS, DVD.** Holly Butler; Shawn McAllister; Art Turk; ***D:*** Peter Tors; Jay Aubrey; ***W:*** Peter Tors; Jay Aubrey.

The Looking Glass 𝒥𝒥 ½ *Swan Song* **2016** A family drama about members of two generations experiencing both disconnection and connection. When her mother dies, 13-year-old Julie (Tarnow) goes to live with her grandmother Karen (Tristan) in Indiana. The troubled teen is stubborn and is conflict with her grandmother. At the same time, Karen keeps the fact that she is in the early stages of Alzheimer's from everyone. As Karen tries to find a way to reach her granddaughter, she soon learns that Julie has a powerful singing voice similar to one Karen once had. Karen hopes to share her legacy with Julie before it is too late for both of them. **110m/C; DVD.** Dorothy Tristan; Grace Tarnow; Trish Basinger; Elizabeth Stenholt; Jeffrey M. Puckett; ***D:*** John D. Hancock; ***W:*** Dorothy Tristan; ***C:*** Misha (Mikhail) Suslov; ***M:*** Orville Stoeber.

The Looking Glass War 𝒥𝒥 **1969 (PG)** Polish defector is sent behind the Iron Curtain on a final mission to photograph a rocket in East Berlin. He's guided by frustrated British security officers Rogers and Richardson, who both offer sly turns. An otherwise slow-moving adaptation of John Le Carre's bestselling spy novel. **108m/C; DVD.** *UK* Christopher Jones; Ralph Richardson; Pia Degermark; Anthony Hopkins; Susan George; Paul Rogers; ***D:*** Frank Pierson; ***W:*** Frank Pierson.

The Lookout 𝒥𝒥𝒥 **2007 (R)** Crime thriller with a stellar performance by Gordon-Levitt as former golden boy jock Chris. After a car accident leaves him with severe brain trauma, Chris struggles with emotional outbursts, memory gaps, and everyday tasks. He lives with sardonic blind roommate Lewis (Daniels) in a small Kansas town and works as a janitor at the bank, giving Chris the perfect in when criminal Gary (Goode) shows up to entice him into a heist to restore some self-esteem. Gary dangles luscious Luvlee (Fisher) as a prize but Chris isn't as dumb as everyone supposes. Screenwriter Frank's neo-noir directorial debut. **99m/C; DVD, Blu-Ray.** Joseph Gordon-Levitt; Jeff Daniels; Matthew Goode; Isla Fisher; Carla Gugino; Bruce McGill; Alberta Watson; Alex Borstein; Sergio Di Zio; Greg Dunham; ***D:*** Scott Frank; ***W:*** Scott Frank; ***C:*** Alar Kivilo; ***M:*** James Newton Howard. Ind. Spirit '08: First Feature.

Looney Looney Looney Bugs Bunny Movie 𝒥𝒥𝒥 *Friz Freleng's Looney Looney Looney Bugs Bunny Movie* **1981 (G)** A feature-length compilation of classic Warner Bros. cartoons tied together with new animation. Cartoon stars featured include Bugs Bunny, Elmer Fudd, Porky Pig, Yosemite Sam, Duffy Duck, and Foghorn Leghorn. **80m/C; VHS, DVD.** ***V:*** Mel Blanc; June Foray; ***D:*** Isadore "Friz" Freleng; Chuck Jones; Bob Clampett.

Looney Tunes: Back in Action 𝒥 **2003 (PG)** Mixing live action with animation, the familiar cast of Looney Toon characters participate in a series of hi-jinx with a selection of normally funny human actors. Sure there's a plot somewhere, as Daffy Duck teams up with human buddy D.J. (Fraser) to find a Blue Monkey Diamond before the bad guys, but that's secondary to pushing out as many pop culture references and corny jokes as possible in a 90 minute span. Since the people who actually knew how to do that best did it right 50 (or so) years ago, your time and money are better spent on seeking out and viewing the original cartoons. **91m/C; VHS, DVD, Blu-Ray.** Brendan Fraser; Jenna Elfman; Steve Martin; Timothy Dalton; Heather Locklear; Joan Cusack; Bill Goldberg; ***V:*** Joe Alaskey; Billy West; Jeff Glenn Bennett; Eric Goldberg; ***D:*** Joe Dante; ***W:*** Larry Doyle; ***C:*** Dean Cundey; ***M:*** Jerry Goldsmith.

Looper 𝒥𝒥𝒥 ½ **2012 (R)** Director Johnson delivers one of the most audacious and inspired science fiction films since "The Matrix" with this time-travelling mind-bender in which a futuristic assassin (an intense Gordon-Levitt) is tasked with chasing down his future self (Willis) to close his own "loop." Along the way he encounters a woman caring for a boy who has special powers. A fascinating look at our future and present day through its examination of responsibility and our need for human connection. Gordon-Levitt wears make-up to convince audiences he will someday look like Willis. **119m/C; DVD, Blu-Ray.** Joseph Gordon-Levitt; Bruce Willis; Emily Blunt; Paul Dano; Piper Perabo; Garret Dillahunt; Tracie Thoms; ***D:*** Rian Johnson; ***W:*** Rian Johnson; ***C:*** Steve Yedlin; ***M:*** Nathan Johnson.

Loophole 𝒥𝒥 **1954** Bank teller Mike Donovan (Sullivan) is robbed—not by the usual masked gunmen, but by a pair of phony bank examiners who've managed to lift $49,900 right from under Donovan's nose. Donovan finds the shortage but doesn't report it right away, and when he does—days later—he's accused of theft and fired, starting a string of lousy luck for him and his wife Ruthie (Malone). Donovan tries to clear his name, but thanks to nasty insurance investigator Gus Slavin (McGraw), he can't get hired anywhere else. **80m/B; DVD.** Barry Sullivan; Dorothy Malone; Charles McGraw; Don Haggerty; Mary Beth Hughes; Don Beddoe; Dayton Lummis; Joanne Jordan; John Eldredge; Richard Reeves; ***D:*** Harold Schuster; ***W:*** Dwight V. Babcock; George Bricker; ***C:*** William Sickner; ***M:*** Paul Dunlap.

Loophole 𝒥𝒥 *Break In* **1983** An out-of-work architect, hard pressed for money, joins forces with an elite team of expert criminals, in a scheme to make off with millions from the most established holding bank's vault. **105m/C; VHS, DVD, Blu-Ray.** *GB* Albert Finney; Martin Sheen; Susannah York; Robert Morley; Colin Blakely; Jonathan Pryce; ***D:*** John Quested.

Loose Ankles 𝒥𝒥 **1930** Risque pre-Hays Code comedy features a teenaged Young as socialite Ann, who's peeved over the terms of her grandmother's will. In order for anyone in the family to inherit, Ann must not be involved in any scandals and she must get marriage approval from her two prudish aunts. Instead, Ann places a newspaper ad for an unsuitable beau and it's answered by would-be gigolo Gil (Fairbanks Jr.). **70m/B;**

DVD. Loretta Young; Douglas Fairbanks, Jr.; Louise Fazenda; Ethel Wales; Otis Harlan; ***D:*** Ted Wilde; ***W:*** Gene Towne; ***C:*** Arthur L. Todd.

Loose Cannons 🦴 **1990 (R)** Yet another mismatched-cop-partner comedy, wherein a mystery is ostensibly solved by a veteran cop and a schizophrenic detective. **95m/C; VHS, DVD.** Gene Hackman; Dan Aykroyd; Dom DeLuise; Ronny Cox; Nancy Travis; David Alan Grier; ***D:*** Bob (Benjamin) Clark; ***W:*** Bob (Benjamin) Clark; Richard Christian Matheson.

Loose Cannons 🦴🦴 *Mine Vaganti* **2010** Vincenzo Cantone wants his family to be together when he announces the merger of their pasta business with that of the Brunettis. Tommaso, who's been studying in Rome, plans to reveal that he's gay so his homophobic dad will freak out and pass the business only to his elder son, Antonio. But his big announcement is trumped when Antonio tells everyone HE's gay, dad has a heart attack, and suddenly Tommaso (who's kept quiet) is expected to take over. With the family in disarray, Tommaso is trying to figure out just what to do next. Italian with subtitles. **110m/C; DVD.** *IT* Riccardo Scamarcio; Ennio Fantastichini; Alessandro Preziosi; Lunetta Savino; Nicole Grimaudo; Carmine Recano; Ilaria Occhini; ***D:*** Ferzan Ozpetek; ***W:*** Ferzan Ozpetek; Ivan Cotroneo; ***C:*** Maurizio Calvesi; ***M:*** Pasquale Catalano.

Loose Screws 🦴 **1985 (R)** Four perverted teenagers are sent to a restrictive academy where they continue their lewd ways in this stupid sequel to "Screwballs." **75m/C; VHS, DVD.** *CA* Bryan Genesse; Karen Wood; Alan Deveau; Jason Warren; ***D:*** Rafal Zielinski; ***W:*** Michael Cory.

Loosies 🦴 **1/2 2011 (PG-13)** A little too-glossy and familiar crime drama. Charming New York pickpocket Bobby is paying off his father's debt to loan shark Jax, but he plans to change his criminal ways when his one-night stand Lucy tells Bobby she's pregnant. This is after he finds himself in big trouble for stealing cop Sullivan's badge to use in a scam and said cop is a very, very unhappy man. **89m/C; DVD.** Peter Facinelli; Jaimie Alexander; Vincent Gallo; Michael Madsen; Joe Pantoliano; William Forsythe; ***D:*** Michael Corrente; ***W:*** Peter Facinelli; ***C:*** Sam Oliver Fleischner; ***M:*** Chad Fischer.

Lord Byron of Broadway 🦴 **1/2 1930** MGM musical about a heel. Songwriter Roy Erskine (Kaley) is willing to use anyone to gain stardom. First he turns old love letters into a hit song (after dumping their author), then he marries loyal vaudeville partner Nancy (Shilling). He neglects her for Broadway star Ardis (Terry), who uses him too, and even exploits the death of best pal Joe (Edwards). Roy's last-minute redemption isn't too believable. Kaley and Terry were stage stars whose inexperience with film was very apparent. **66m/B; DVD.** Marion Shilling; Cliff Edwards; Charles Kaley; Ethelind Terry; Gwen Lee; Benny Rubin; ***D:*** William Nigh; Harry Beaumont; ***W:*** Crane Wilbur; Willard Mack; ***C:*** Henry Sharp; ***M:*** Nacio Herb Brown; Dimitri Tiomkin.

Lord Jim 🦴🦴🦴 **1965** A ship officer (O'Toole) commits an act of cowardice that results in his dismissal and disgrace, which leads him to the Far East in search of self-respect. Excellent supporting cast. Based on Joseph Conrad's novel. **154m/C; DVD.** Peter O'Toole; James Mason; Curt Jurgens; Eli Wallach; Jack Hawkins; Paul Lukas; Akim Tamiroff; Daliah Lavi; Andrew Keir; Jack MacGowran; Walter Gotell; ***D:*** Richard Brooks; ***W:*** Richard Brooks; ***C:*** Frederick A. (Freddie) Young; ***M:*** Bronislau Kaper.

Lord Love a Duck 🦴🦴 **1/2 1966** McDowall plays a high school nerd who grants the wishes of classmate Weld, even as they get increasingly complicated. Excellent '60s satire of society in and around high school. **105m/C; VHS, DVD.** Roddy McDowall; Tuesday Weld; Lola Albright; Martin West; Ruth Gordon; Harvey Korman; Sarah Marshall; Max (Casey Adams) Showalter; Donald Murphy; Joseph Mell; Dan Frazer; Martine Bartlett; ***D:*** George Axelrod; ***W:*** George Axelrod; ***C:*** Daniel F. Fapp; ***M:*** Neal Hefti.

Lord of Illusions 🦴🦴 **1/2** *Clive Barker's Lord of Illusions* **1995 (R)** New York PI Harry D'Amour (Bakula), who has an affinity for the occult, becomes involved with Dorothea (Janssen), the supposed widow of magician Philip Swann (O'Connor). As Harry investigates, he discovers some terrifying secrets, including resurrected cult leader Nix (Von Bargen). Gruesome effects rather than excessive gore but you'll feel like you've been dropped in the middle of a plot without a clear idea of what's happening. Bakula's Harry is intriguing but the attractive Janssen's just around to cower. Barker directs from his own short story "The Last Illusion." **109m/C; DVD, Blu-Ray.** Scott Bakula; Famke Janssen; Kevin J. O'Connor; Daniel von Bargen; Joel Swetow; Barry Sherman; Jordan Marder; Joseph Latimore; Vincent Schiavelli; ***D:*** Clive Barker; ***W:*** Clive Barker; ***C:*** Ronn Schmidt; ***M:*** Simon Boswell.

Lord of the Flies 🦴🦴🦴 **1/2 1963** Proper English schoolboys stranded on a desert island during a nuclear war are transformed into savages. A study in greed, power, and the innate animalistic/survivalistic instincts of human nature. Based on William Golding's novel, which he described as a "journey to the darkness of the human heart." **91m/B; VHS, DVD, Blu-Ray.** *GB* James Aubrey; Tom Chapin; Hugh Edwards; Roger Elwin; Tom Gamen; ***D:*** Peter Brook; ***W:*** Peter Brook; ***C:*** Tom Hollyman; ***M:*** Raymond Leppard.

Lord of the Flies 🦴🦴 **1990 (R)** Inferior second filming of the famed William Golding novel about schoolboys marooned on a desert island who gradually degenerate into savages. Lushly photographed, yet redundant and poorly acted. **90m/C; VHS, DVD, Blu-Ray.** Balthazar Getty; Danuel Pipoly; Chris Furrh; Badgett Dale; Edward Taft; Andrew Taft; ***D:*** Harry Hook; ***W:*** Sara Schiff; ***C:*** Martin Fuhrer; ***M:*** Philippe Sarde.

Lord of the Jungle 🦴 **1955** Sheffield had outgrown the 'jungle boy' several films previously so the 12th and final film put a merciful end to the series. A rogue elephant is on the rampage but because the government hunters don't know which pachyderm it is, they've been hired to slaughter the entire herd. Naturally, Bomba won't let that happen! **70m/B; DVD.** John(ny) Sheffield; Wayne Morris; Leonard Mudie; Nancy Hale; Paul Picerni; William Phipps; ***D:*** Ford Beebe; ***W:*** Ford Beebe; ***C:*** Harry Neumann; ***M:*** Marlin Skiles.

The Lord of the Rings 🦴🦴 **1978 (PG)** An animated interpretation of Tolkien's classic tale of the hobbits, wizards, elves, and dwarfs who inhabit Middle Earth. Animator Ralph Bakshi used live motion animation (roto-scoping) to give his characters more life-like and human motion. Well done in spite of the difficulty of adapting from Tolkien's highly detailed and lengthy works. **128m/C; VHS, DVD.** ***V:*** Christopher Guard; John Hurt; ***D:*** Ralph Bakshi; ***W:*** Peter S. Beagle; J.C. (Chris) Conkling.

Lord of the Rings: The Fellowship of the Ring 🦴🦴🦴 **1/2 2001 (PG-13)** The first in Jackson's trilogy of films based on the books by J.R.R. Tolkein. Young hobbit Frodo Baggins inherits a mysterious ring and leaves home in order to keep it from falling into the hands of its evil creator. Along the way, a fellowship forms to protect the ring-bearer and make sure that the ring arrives at its final destination: Mt. Doom, the only place where it can be destroyed. Jackson's amazing visuals bring the imaginary world and mythology of Tolkein to life. The long pic stays closer to the original novel while still managing to keep a quick enough pace for those unfamiliar with the literary work. **178m/C; DVD, Blu-Ray.** Elijah Wood; Ian McKellen; Liv Tyler; Viggo Mortensen; Sean Astin; Cate Blanchett; John Rhys-Davies; Dominic Monaghan; Billy Boyd; Orlando Bloom; Christopher Lee; Hugo Weaving; Sean Bean; Ian Holm; Andy Serkis; Marton Csokas; ***D:*** Peter Jackson; ***W:*** Peter Jackson; Fran Walsh; Philippa Boyens; ***C:*** Andrew Lesnie; ***M:*** Howard Shore. Oscars '01: Cinematog.; British Acad. '01: Director (Jackson), Film, Visual FX; L.A. Film Critics '01: Score; Natl. Bd. of Review '01: Support. Actress (Blanchett); Screen Actors Guild '01: Support. Actor (McKellen); Broadcast Film Critics '01: Score, Song ("May It Be").

Lord of the Rings: The Two Towers 🦴🦴🦴🦴 **2002 (PG-13)** The second installment of the "Rings" trilogy picks up shortly after the first one left off. Frodo and Samwise are still heading toward Mordor, with Gollum following/abetting their progress. Aragorn, Legolas, and Gimli join together with the denizens of Rohan to fight Saruman's army of Orcs and Gandalf is back with white magic heroics. Plenty of action (the battle scenes are incredible) and plot twists, including Frodo's battle of wills with himself and Gollum, don't disappoint. **179m/C; DVD, Blu-Ray.** Elijah Wood; Sean Astin; Viggo Mortensen; Orlando Bloom; John Rhys-Davies; Ian McKellen; Christopher Lee; Billy Boyd; Dominic Monaghan; Liv Tyler; Bernard Hill; Miranda Otto; David Wenham; Karl Urban; Brad Dourif; Cate Blanchett; Hugo Weaving; ***V:*** John Rhys-Davies; Andy Serkis; ***D:*** Peter Jackson; ***W:*** Peter Jackson; Fran Walsh; Philippa Boyens; Stephen Sinclair; ***C:*** Andrew Lesnie; ***M:*** Howard Shore. Oscars '02: Visual FX; British Acad. '02: Costume Des., Visual FX.

Lord of the Rings: The Return of the King 🦴🦴🦴🦴 **2003 (PG-13)** Jackson's triumphant close to his superb Tolkien trilogy. After the climactic battle for Helm's Deep, Rohan's forces, along with most of the original members of the Fellowship, come to the aid of the capital of Gondor, Minas Tirith, Sauron's next target. They also attempt to distract Sauron from Frodo and Sam, who encounter even worse hardships on their way to Mt. Doom to destroy the ring. Although the two main plots are very different in scope and dynamics, each maintains depth and character development, while keeping the film moving along. As with the first two pics, the photography's breathtaking. **200m/C; DVD, Blu-Ray.** Elijah Wood; Sean Astin; Viggo Mortensen; Orlando Bloom; John Rhys-Davies; Ian McKellen; Billy Boyd; Dominic Monaghan; Liv Tyler; Bernard Hill; Miranda Otto; David Wenham; Karl Urban; Hugo Weaving; Andy Serkis; Cate Blanchett; John Noble; Ian Holm; Sean Bean; Lawrence Makoare; Marton Csokas; ***D:*** Peter Jackson; ***W:*** Peter Jackson; Fran Walsh; Philippa Boyens; ***C:*** Andrew Lesnie; ***M:*** Howard Shore. Oscars '03: Adapt. Screenplay, Art Dir./Set Dec., Costume Des., Director (Jackson), Film, Film Editing, Makeup, Orig. Score, Song ("Into the West"), Sound, Visual FX; British Acad. '03: Adapt. Screenplay, Cinematog., Film, Visual FX; Directors Guild '03: Director (Jackson); Golden Globes '04: Director (Jackson), Film--Drama, Orig. Score, Song ("Into the West"); L.A. Film Critics '03: Director (Jackson); N.Y. Film Critics '03: Film; Screen Actors Guild '03: Cast.

Lord of War 🦴🦴🦴 **2005 (R)** Niccol's look into the dark world of international weapons trade says guns are evil but its vivid imagery suggests something very different. Yuri Orlov (Cage), a Ukrainian immigrant living in Manhattan, would like to put a gun in the hand of every person on the planet. Aided in business by his brother Vitally (Leto) and pursued by Interpol agent Valentine (Hawke), Yuri slickly operates in his frightening underworld of bloody regional conflict. His fabulous life is fueled by profits extracted from the ever-growing stack of dead bodies. **122m/C; DVD, Blu-Ray, UMD.** Nicolas Cage; Jared Leto; Bridget Moynahan; Ian Holm; Ethan Hawke; Eamonn Walker; Sammi Rotibi; Eugene (Yevgeny) Lazarev; ***D:*** Andrew Niccol; ***W:*** Andrew Niccol; ***C:*** Amir M. Mokri; ***M:*** Antonio Pinto.

The Lords of Discipline 🦴🦴 **1/2 1983 (R)** A military academy cadet is given the unenviable task of protecting a black freshman from racist factions at a southern school circa 1964. Based on Pat Conroy's autobiographical novel. **103m/C; VHS, DVD.** David Keith; Robert Prosky; Barbara Babcock; Judge Reinhold; G.D. Spradlin; Rick Rossovich; Michael Biehn; Bill Paxton; Matt Frewer; ***D:*** Franc Roddam; ***C:*** Brian Tufano; ***M:*** Howard Blake.

Lords of Dogtown 🦴🦴 **2005 (PG-13)** A motley crew of surfer-turned-skater kids in 1975's Venice, CA, turn skateboarding into a pop-culture revolution. The skating looks great, but some botched acting and poor pacing confuses everything. Ledger does his best with the clumsy role of Zephyr founder Skip Englom, but others, mostly real life skater kids, aren't as convincing. Starts to click in the second-half, but it's still riddled with bad dialogue and rushed storytelling. A dramatic companion to the documentary "Dogtown and Z-Boys." **107m/C; DVD, Blu-Ray, UMD.** Heath Ledger; Emile Hirsch; Victor Rasuk; John Robinson; Nikki Reed; Michael Angarano; Rebecca De Mornay; Johnny Knoxville; ***D:*** Catherine Hardwicke; ***W:*** Stacy Peralta; ***C:*** Elliot Davis; ***M:*** Mark Mothersbaugh.

The Lords of Flatbush 🦴🦴 **1/2 1974 (PG)** Four street toughs battle against their own maturation and responsibilities in 1950s Brooklyn. Winkler introduces the leather-clad hood he's made a career of and Stallone introduces a character not unlike Rocky. Interesting slice of life. **88m/C; VHS, DVD.** Sylvester Stallone; Perry King; Henry Winkler; Susan Blakely; Armand Assante; Paul Mace; ***D:*** Stephen Verona; Martin Davidson; ***W:*** Sylvester Stallone; Stephen Verona; Martin Davidson; ***M:*** Joseph Brooks.

The Lords of Salem 🦴 **2013 (R)** Rob Zombie continues to carve his own path through the world of the horror genre with mixed results at best. This time, he centers his style on the story of Heidi (Sheri Moon Zombie, who simply cannot act), a DJ in Salem who received a wooden box with a record that causes hallucinatory flashbacks of the violent past of the town best known for burning witches at the stake. Zombie loves atmosphere and produces some nice set-pieces because of it but he can't write dialogue and can't direct actors, especially his wife. **101m/C; DVD, Blu-Ray.** Sheri Moon Zombie; Ken Foree; Jeffrey Daniel Phillips; Maria Conchita Alonso; Bruce Davison; Meg Foster; Dee Wallace; Judy Geeson; Patricia Quinn; Andrew Prine; Michael Berryman; Sid Haig; Brandon Cruz; Barbara Crampton; ***D:*** Rob Zombie; ***W:*** Rob Zombie; ***C:*** Brandon Trost; ***M:*** Griffin Boice; John 5.

Lords of Soaptown: The True Story of Freestyle Walking 🦴🦴 **2016** A documentary about the origins of the sport of freestyle walking and the related business venture. Starting as a prank to get on television, four boys from the suburbs of Chicago claimed that their sport was being banned at schools. Their made-up sport was freestyle walking—essentially skateboarding without the skateboard. As the word spread on their idea via MTV and other sources, a company decided to capitalize on it and invented shoes with a changeable element that would allow freestyle walking. Though the kids helped launch the company and its shoe product, Soaps, they did not see any of the millions made from selling Soaps worldwide and building it into a niche sport. The documentary features interviews with the four boys involved and examines their perspectives on what happened decades after the fact. **97m/C; DVD.** ***D:*** Jason Klamm; ***W:*** Jason Klamm; ***C:*** Ryan Penington; ***M:*** Brian Matteson. **VIDEO**

Lords of the Barrio 🦴 **1/2** *The Impostor* **2002 (R)** Rudy (Perez) is a newly married middle class suburbanite bored with life. Witnessing a mob deal gone bad, he assumes the identity of a dying gun dealer to get rich quick and get out of middle class existence. But when a few local mobsters find out, they decide to cure his boredom by killing him. **90m/C; DVD.** Robert Arevalo; Angie Lucia; Morris Perez; Gustavo Rex; ***D:*** Joe Menendez; ***W:*** Joe Menendez; ***C:*** Nino Neuboeck; David Singh; ***M:*** Lee Sanders.

Lords of the Street 🦴 *Jump Out Boys* **2008 (R)** Mexican drug lord Santiago Rodriguez (Leduc) has escaped from jail with the help of his uncle, who expects compensation. Santiago's girlfriend (Berry) stashed millions away before he was arrested but in a post-Hurricane Katrina New Orleans it won't be easy getting to the money, especially when a determined (and way past retirement-aged) cop (Kritofferson) and his hot-headed partner (DMX) have other ideas. **82m/C; DVD, Blu-Ray.** DMX; Kris Kristofferson; Veronica Berry; Armando Leduc; Sheldon Robins; ***D:*** Amir Valinia; ***W:*** Sheldon Robins; Dan Garcia; ***C:*** Tom Baks; ***M:*** Mary Alice Corton. **VIDEO**

Lore 🦴🦴🦴 **2013** Newcomer Rosendahl delivers a fascinating performance as 14-year-old Lore, a girl whose life is turned upside down when her Nazi parents are arrested at the end of World War II. Left to take care of her younger siblings, Lore comes to terms with not only the roles that her parents must have played in the Third Reich but her own beliefs about her homeland. Director/writer Shortland deftly humanizes people long-ago turned into demons by history and cinema. Lore and her siblings come to symbolize an entire country dealing with its dark past and questionable future. **109m/C; DVD, Blu-Ray.** *GE* Saskia Rosendahl; Nele Trebs; Andre Frid; Mika Seidel; Kai-Peter Malina; *D:* Cate Shortland; *W:* Cate Shortland; Robin Mukherjee; *C:* Adam Arkapaw; *M:* Max Richter.

Lorenzo's Oil **1992 (PG-13)** Based on the true story of Augusto and Michaela Odone's efforts to find a cure for their five-year-old, Lorenzo, diagnosed with the rare and incurable disease ALD (Adrenoleukodystrophy). Confronted by a slow-moving and clinically cold medical community, the Odones embark on their own quest for a cure. Sarandon delivers an outstanding and emotionally charged performance as Lorenzo's determined mother; Nolte's the equally devoted Italian father. They're a powerful presence in a film that's a tribute to what love and hope can accomplish. **135m/C; DVD.** Nick Nolte; Susan Sarandon; Zach O'Malley-Greenberg; Peter Ustinov; Kathleen Wilhoite; Gerry Bamman; Margo Martindale; James Rebhorn; Ann Hearn; Elizabeth Daily; *D:* George Miller; *W:* George Miller; Nick Enright; *C:* John Seale.

Loretta Lynn: Still a Mountain Girl 1/2 **2016** A feature-length documentary about legendary country artist Loretta Lynn. Exploring her life, work, and influence, the documentary features interviews with Lynn, family, friends, and musical peers. Also included are materials from her extensive archives. Topics considered include her musical collaborations, life on the road, songwriting inspirations, and her music's impact on both her fellow musicians and her fans. **113m/C; DVD, Streaming, Download.** Loretta Lynn; *D:* Vikram Jayanti; *W:* Robin Bicknell; *C:* Iris Ng; *M:* Ohad Benchetrit; Justin Small. **VIDEO**

Lorna Doone 1/2 **1922** A young girl of royal descent is kidnapped and raised by the bandit Doone family in the highlands of Scotland. Adapted from the novel by R.D. Blackmore. **79m/B; Silent; VHS, DVD.** Madge Bellamy; John Bowers; *D:* Maurice Tourneur.

Lorna Doone 1/2 **1934** Early version of the R.D. Blackmore novel about an English farmer who falls in love with the daughter of an outlaw family. Set in rural England in the 1600s; remade in 1951 and 1990. **90m/B; VHS, DVD.** *GB* Victoria Hopper; John Loder; Margaret Lockwood; Roy Emerton; Mary Clare; Edward Rigby; Roger Livesey; *D:* Basil Dean; *W:* Miles Malleson.

Lorna Doone 1/2 **1990 (PG)** Classic romance set in 17th-century England based on the novel by R.D. Blackmore. John Ridd (Bean) vows to destroy the land-grabbing Doone family, whom he blames for the death of his parents. Then he meets, and immediately falls in love with, the beautiful and innocent Lorna Doone (Walker). **90m/C; DVD, Streaming.** *UK* Sean Bean; Polly Walker; Clive Owen; Billie Whitelaw; *D:* Andrew Grieve; *W:* Matthew Jacobs. **TV**

Lorna Doone **2001** Based on R.D. Blackmore's novel, which is set in the west country of 17th-century Britain, this swashbuckler is a star-crossed romance with an ultimately happy ending. Farmer John Ridd (Coyle) discovers that Lorna (Warner), the young beauty he loves, is a member of the infamous Doone clan—a once aristocratic family that has turned outlaw. To make things worse for John, Lorna is already betrothed to the violent Carver Doone (Gillen) who will do anything to keep her. **150m/C; DVD.** *UK* Richard Coyle; Amelia Warner; Aidan Gillen; Martin Clunes; Michael Kitchen; Martin Jarvis; Barbara Flynn; Peter Vaughan; Anton Lesser; Jack Shepherd; *D:* Mike Barker; *W:* Adrian Hodges; *C:* Chris Seager; *M:* John Lunn. **TV**

Lorna's Silence *Le Silence de Lorna* **2008 (R)** Albanian immigrant Lorna (Dobroshi) hopes to get her Belgian citizenship papers by agreeing to a green card marriage to junkie Claudy (Renier), which was arranged by lowlife Fabio (Rongione). But Fabio wants Lorna to do something for him in return that will probably result in Claudy's death. Lorna may be desperate but she also turns out to have a (very inconvenient) conscience. Albanian, French, and Russian with subtitles. **95m/C; On Demand.** *BE FR GE IT* Jeremie Renier; Fabrizio Rongione; Morgan Marinne; Olivier Gourmet; Arta Dobroshi; Alban Ukaj; *D:* Jean-Pierre Dardenne; Luc Dardenne; *W:* Jean-Pierre Dardenne; Luc Dardenne; *C:* Alain Marcoen.

Loro **2019** After being removed as prime minister in Italy's 2006 general elections, media mogul Silvio Berlusconi (Servillo) schemes his political comeback with the help of accomplices like billionaire banker Ennio Doris (Servillo). At the same time, the insecure political manipulator indulges in his favorite past time of being close to scantily clad women and disappointing his wife Veronica (Ricci). Released in Italy as a two-part drama, the film is strong as a shorter feature. Though the filmmakers have inserted their fictionalized take on Berlusconi, Servillo's performance gives the film its weight. Italian with subtitles. **151m/C; DVD.** Toni Servillo; Elena Sofia Ricci; Riccardo Scamarcio; Kasia Smutniak; Fabrizio Bentivoglio; *D:* Paolo Sorrentino; *W:* Paolo Sorrentino; Umberto Contarello; *C:* Luca Bigazzi; *M:* Lele Marchitelli.

Los Olvidados 1/2 *The Young and the Damned* **1950** From surrealist Bunuel, a powerful story of the poverty and violence of young people's lives in Mexico's slums. In Spanish with English subtitles. **88m/B; VHS, DVD.** *MX* Alfonso Mejias; Roberto Cobo; *D:* Luis Bunuel. Cannes '51: Director (Bunuel), Film.

Loser 1/2 **1997 (R)** Very low-budget street drama concerns young small-time drug dealer James Dean Ray (Harris) and his self-destruction slide towards oblivion. **90m/C; VHS, DVD.** Kirk Harris; Jonathon Chaus; Peta Wilson; Norman Salect; Jack Rubio; *D:* Kirk Harris; *W:* Kirk Harris; *C:* Kent Wakeford.

Loser **2000 (PG-13)** College comedy finds nerdy midwesterner Biggs branded a loser by his dorm mates at New York University. He's also pining over beauty Suvari, who's having an affair with heartless prof Kinnear. Writer-director Heckerling's trademark sympathy for the adolescent outcast is intact, but this outing is missing the insight, subtlety, and (most importantly) the fun of her earlier efforts. Biggs and Suvari give passable performances, but Kinnear is the bright spot. **95m/C; VHS, DVD.** Jason Biggs; Mena Suvari; Greg Kinnear; Zak Orth; Dan Aykroyd; Tom Sadoski; Jimmi Simpson; Colleen Camp; Robert Miano; Andy Dick; David Spade; Steven Wright; Taylor Negron; Andrea Martin; Scott Thompson; *D:* Amy Heckerling; *W:* Amy Heckerling; *C:* Rob Hahn; *M:* David Kitay.

The Losers 1/2 *Nam's Angels* **1970 (R)** Four motorcyclists are hired by the U.S. Army to rescue a presidential advisor who is being held captive by Asian bad guys. **96m/C; VHS, DVD.** William (Bill) Smith; Bernie Hamilton; Adam Roarke; Houston Savage; Paul Koslo; John Garwood; Jack Starrett; Alan Caillou; *D:* Jack Starrett; *W:* Alan Caillou; *C:* Nonong Rasca; *M:* Stu Phillips.

The Losers 1/2 **2010 (PG-13)** Full-throttle, no-brainer action, adapted from the comic book series. A U.S. black ops unit in Bolivia is betrayed and left for dead by Max (Patric), their ominous boss who's hell-bent on starting a high-tech global war. While trying to escape with no passport and no money, they meet Aisha (Saldana), a beautiful and tough operative sent to kill the group's leader Clay (Morgan), but the two hit it off and team up. A disturbing opening scene leads into a surprisingly tight and effective meat-and-potatoes flick. **97m/C; DVD, Blu-Ray.** Jeffrey Dean Morgan; Idris Elba; Zoe Saldana; Columbus Short; Chris Evans; Oscar Jaenada; Jason Patric; Holt McCallany; *D:* Sylvain White; *W:* Peter Berg; James Vanderbilt; *C:* Scott Kevan; *M:* John Ottman.

Losin' It **1982 (R)** Four teens travel across the Mexican border to Tijuana on a journey to lose their virginity. Cruise meets a married woman who says she is in town for a divorce, while the others become caught up in frenzied undertakings of their own. **104m/C; VHS, DVD, Blu-Ray.** Tom Cruise; John Stockwell; Shelley Long; Jackie Earle Haley; John P. Navin, Jr.; Timothy Brown; Rick Rossovich; *D:* Curtis Hanson; *W:* Bill W.L. Norton; *C:* Gilbert Taylor; *M:* Kenneth Wannberg.

Losing Chase 1/2 **1996 (R)** Bacon makes his directorial debut in this drama that features wife Sedgwick as Elizabeth, mother's helper to Chase (Mirren) and Richard Philips (Bridges) at their summer home on Martha's Vineyard. Chase is still recovering from a mental breakdown, having spent several months in an institution, and she resents Elizabeth's presence, constantly criticizing her. But when the two women are alone together a confusing and emotional bond gradually begins to form between them. **95m/C; VHS, DVD.** Dame Helen Mirren; Kyra Sedgwick; Beau Bridges; *D:* Kevin Bacon; *W:* Anne Meredith; *C:* Dick Quinlan; *M:* Michael Bacon. **CABLE**

Losing Isaiah **1994 (R)** Controversial and emotionally moving story of a social worker (Lange) who adopts the title character, an African American baby abandoned by his drug-addicted mother (Berry). Courtroom battle ensues when four years later mom, now clean and sober, discovers Isaiah is alive. She enlists the aid of a lawyer (Jackson) known for his high-profile, racially charged cases. Lange and Berry lead the parade of fine performances. Taking on some volatile issues, director Gyllenhaal manages (for the most part) to refrain from melodrama. Based on the novel by Seth Margolis. **108m/C; DVD.** Jessica Lange; Halle Berry; David Strathairn; Samuel L. Jackson; Cuba Gooding, Jr.; LaTanya Richardson Jackson; *D:* Stephen Gyllenhaal; *W:* Naomi Foner; *C:* Andrzej Bartkowiak; *M:* Mark Isham.

The Loss of a Teardrop Diamond 1/2 **2008 (PG-13)** Musty attempt at resurrecting an unproduced Tennessee Williams scenario from the 1950s. In 1920s Memphis, heiress Fisher Willow (Howard) behaves too outrageously to be willingly accepted at high-society gatherings. Needing an escort, she hires Jimmy Dobyne (Evans), an impoverished employee of her father's. He's indifferent to her charms and Fisher gets jealous when Jimmy reunites with an ex-flame, so she accuses him of stealing a diamond earring (that she's lost at a party). **102m/C; Blu-Ray, On Demand.** Bryce Dallas Howard; Chris Evans; Ellen Burstyn; Mamie Gummer; Ann-Margret; Will Patton; Peter Gerety; Jessica Collins; *D:* Jodie Markell; *W:* Tennessee Williams; *C:* Giles Nuttgens; *M:* Mark Orton.

The Loss of Sexual Innocence 1/2 **1998 (R)** Figgis' ambitious film follows the fall from grace (literally of Adam and Eve), and the nature of sex, love, jealousy, and violence. Unfortunately, this turns out to be less than scintillating material. Interspersed with scenes from the Garden of Eden story is that of dissatisfied filmmaker Nic (Sands), as he relives his past and ponders his unhappy present. **101m/C; VHS, DVD.** Julian Sands; Saffron Burrows; Stefano Dionisi; Jonathan Rhys Meyers; Kelly Macdonald; Femi Ogumbanjo; Hanne Klintoe; Johanna Torrel; George Moktar; John Cowey; *D:* Mike Figgis; *W:* Mike Figgis; *C:* Benoit Delhomme; *M:* Mike Figgis.

Lost 1/2 **2005** Former L.A. resident Jeremy Stanton (Cain) gets lost on a Mojave highway while driving to meet his family at their new Nevada home. His nightmare journey turns into a maze of detours on flood-closed roads, while he gets bad directions from clueless road-service operator Judy (voiced by Scott). A bank VP, the increasingly panicked Jeremy also has to worry about being tracked by sadistic thug Archer (Trejo) for reasons that are only gradually revealed. A tight thriller in the best B-movie tradition and the debut feature for Lemke. **86m/C; DVD.** Dean Cain; Ashley Scott; Danny Trejo; Irina Bjorklund; Justin Henry; Griffin Armstorff; *D:* Darren Lemke; *W:* Darren Lemke; *C:* Paul Emami; *M:* Russ Landau.

Lost and Delirious **2001** Teen angst, romance, and sexuality taken to extremes. Shy Mouse (Barton) is trying to settle in at her exclusive girls' boarding school with new roomies, wealthy Tory (Pare) and wild Paulie (Perabo). When Mouse realizes that the girls are lovers she takes it in stride but Tory gets anxious and denies the relationship. Mouse watches helplessly as Paulie gets increasingly desperate to win Tory back and matters take a turn for the baroque. Based on the novel "The Wives of Bath" by Susan Swan. **100m/C; VHS, DVD.** *CA* Mischa Barton; Piper Perabo; Jessica Pare; Jackie Burroughs; Graham Greene; Mimi Kuzyk; Luke Kirby; *D:* Lea Pool; *W:* Judith Thompson; *C:* Pierre Gill; *M:* Yves Chamberland. Genie '01: Cinematog.

Lost and Found 1/2 **1979 (PG)** An American professor of English and an English film production secretary fall in love on a skiing vacation. Good cast but Segal and Jackson did romance better in "A Touch of Class." **104m/C; DVD, Streaming.** George Segal; Glenda Jackson; Maureen Stapleton; Hollis McLaren; John Cunningham; Paul Sorvino; John Candy; Martin Short; *D:* Melvin Frank; *W:* Jack Rose.

Lost and Found **1999 (PG-13)** Spade plays Dylan, a sniveling pipsqueak taken with his French neighbor Lila (the lovely Marceau). In a sick attempt to win her love, he kidnaps her dog in order to "find" him a few days later. When the dog swallows an anniversary ring Dylan's holding for a friend, many tasteless dog poo jokes ensue. Spade should stick to the snarky sidekick roles. **97m/C; DVD.** David Spade; Sophie Marceau; Artie Lange; Martin Sheen; Patrick Bruel; Jon Lovitz; Mitchell Whitfield; Carole Cook; Estelle Harris; Marla Gibbs; Natalie Barish; Phil Leeds; Christian Clemenson; Daphne Lynn Duplaix; *D:* Jeff Pollack; *W:* David Spade; J.B. Cook; Marc Meeks; *C:* Paul Elliott; *M:* John Debney.

The Lost & Found Family 1/2 **2009** Faith-based family film. After her husband dies, Ester Hobbes learns she's broke and her only asset is a rundown Georgia home occupied by a foster family. Ester intends to sell the property but slowly becomes involved in the lives of the children and finds a new purpose for her own life. **93m/C; DVD.** Lucas Till; Ellen Bry; Jessica Luza; Jeff Portell; *D:* Barnet Bain; *W:* Terry Collis; Jeff Ross; Anna Waterhouse; *C:* Peter Benison; Brian Gunter; *M:* Nuno Malo. **VIDEO**

Lost Angel 1/2 **1943** Six-year-old orphan Alpha (O'Brien) is an experiment to scientists at the Pickering Institute for Child Psychology who are so busy molding her into a prodigy that she knows nothing about being a child. After she's interviewed by reporter Mike Regan (Craig), Alpha runs away to find him in New York and gets herself involved in both his job and his love life with nightclub singer Katie (Hunt). **92m/B; DVD.** Margaret O'Brien; James Craig; Marsha Hunt; Keenan Wynn; Philip Merivale; Donald Meek; Henry O'Neill; *D:* Roy Rowland; *W:* Isobel Lennart; *C:* Robert L. Surtees; *M:* Daniele Amfitheatrof.

The Lost Angel **2004** Plagued by the memory of her mother's death and facing an internal investigation, a police inspector (Eastwood) must overcome her own demons along with intense media scrutiny to track down a serial killer. **99m/C; VHS, DVD.** Alison Eastwood; Nicholas Celozzi; Judd Nelson; John Rhys-Davies; C. Thomas Howell; Eugene Lipinski; Neville Edwards; *D:* Dimitri Logothetis; *W:* Dimitri Logothetis; *C:* Paul Mitchnick; *M:* Trevor Morris. **VIDEO**

Lost Angels 1/2 **1989 (R)** A glossy "Rebel Without a Cause" '80s reprise providing a no-holds-barred portrait of life in the fast lane. A wealthy, disaffected San Fernando Valley youth immerses himself in sex, drugs and rock 'n' roll. Ultimately he is arrested and sent by his parents to a youth home, where a dedicated therapist assists his tortuous road back to reality. **116m/C; VHS, Streaming.** Donald Sutherland; Adam Horovitz; Amy Locane; Kevin Tighe; John C. McGinley; Graham Beckel; Park Overall; Don Bloomfield; Celia Weston; *D:* Hugh Hudson; *W:* Michael Weller; *M:* Philippe Sarde.

Lost Battalion 1/2 **2001** True story based on the heroism of U.S. Major Charles Whittlesey (Schroder), who won the Congressional Medal of Honor during the closing days of WWI. Part of the Army's 77th Division, Whittlesey and his troops find themselves separated from their allies and surrounded by German forces in the Argonne Forest. Whittlesey led his men on a five-day defensive back to Allied lines despite limited supplies and constant battle. **100m/C; VHS, DVD.** Rick Schroder; Jamie Harris; Phil McKee; Jay Rodan; Adam James; *D:* Russell Mulcahy; *W:* James (Jim) Carabatsos; *C:* Jonathan Freeman; *M:* Richard (Rick) Marvin. **CABLE**

Lost Behind Bars 🦴 1/2 **2006** Documentary filmmaker Lauren Wilde (Brewster) travels to an Oregon prison to research the last two weeks of life for death row inmates. Kevin Reese (Cupo) has been convicted of murdering a local family but Lauren finds the evidence in his case is very hinky and so she starts investigating, unknowingly endangering herself. **90m/C; DVD.** Paget Brewster; Antonio Cupo; Meg Roe; Robert Wisden; Ona Grauer; Diego Klatenhoff; Doron Bell; ***D:*** Scott Williams; ***W:*** Luanne Ensle; ***C:*** George Campbell; ***M:*** Ron Ramin. **CABLE**

The Lost Bladesman 🦴🦴 *Guan Yun Chang* **2016** An epic action/martial arts drama loosely based on Luo Guanzhong's novel Romance of the Three Kingdoms. Set in the warring period of the Three Kingdoms in ancient China, General Cao Cao (Jiang) forces the great warrior Guan Yu (Yen) to help unify the land by kidnapping his beloved Qi Lan (Li) hostage. Guan Yu leads the general's forces to victory and gets Qi Lan released. However Cao Cao now believes he is too much of a threat to live. To survive Guan Yu takes drastic action that becomes the stuff of legends. Mandarin with subtitles. **109m/C; DVD, Blu-Ray, Streaming, Download.** Donnie Yen; Wen Jiang; Li Sun; Bing Shao; Andy On; ***D:*** Felix Chong; Alan Mak; ***W:*** Felix Chong; Alan Mak; ***C:*** Chi Ying Chan; ***M:*** Henry Lai. **VIDEO**

Lost Boundaries 🦴🦴 1/2 **1949** Respected physician Scott Carter (debut role for Ferrer) and his family live and work in a small New Hampshire town, hiding the fact that they are black, passing for white, in their segregated society. But then the truth becomes known. Strong, if slow-moving, and based on a true story; the use of white leads for black roles was common casting. **99m/B; VHS, DVD.** Mel Ferrer; Beatrice Pearson; Richard Hylton; Susan Douglas; Canada Lee; Carleton Carpenter; Seth Arnold; Wendell Holmes; ***D:*** Alfred Werker; ***W:*** Virginia Shaler; Eugene Ling; Charles A. Palmer; Furland de Kay; ***C:*** William J. Miller; ***M:*** Louis Applebaum.

The Lost Boys 🦴🦴🦴 **1978** Holm gives a brilliant performance as writer J.M. Barrie, whose friendship with young George Llewelyn-Davies and his four brothers will lead to the story of Peter Pan. But as the depressed Barrie's marriage falls apart and tragedy strikes the Llewelyn-Davies family, the relationship grows ever more complex. **270m/C; DVD.** *GB* Ian Holm; Tim Pigott-Smith; Anna Cropper; Maureen O'Brien; Ann Bell; ***D:*** Rodney Bennett; ***W:*** Andrew Birkin; ***M:*** Dudley Simpson. **TV**

The Lost Boys 🦴🦴 **1987 (R)** Santa Cruz seems like a dull town when Michael, his younger brother, and their divorced mom move into their eccentric grandfather's home. But when Michael falls for a pretty girl with some hard-living friends he takes on more than he imagines—these partying teens are actually a group of vampires. Some humor, some bloodletting violence, and an attractive cast help out this updated vampire tale. Rock-filled soundtrack. **97m/C; VHS, DVD, Blu-Ray.** Jason Patric; Kiefer Sutherland; Corey Haim; Jami Gertz; Dianne Wiest; Corey Feldman; Barnard Hughes; Edward Herrmann; Billy Wirth; Jamison Newlander; Brooke McCarter; Alex Winter; ***D:*** Joel Schumacher; ***W:*** Jeffrey Boam; Janice Fischer; James Jeremias; ***C:*** Michael Chapman; ***M:*** Thomas Newman.

Lost Boys: The Thirst 🦴 **2010 (R)** Second direct-to-video flick barely seems to be making an effort to be coherent. Embittered vampire hunter Edgar Frog is approached by Gwen to kill alpha vamp DJ X who's pushing a new club drug. Anyone who indulges becomes a bloodsucker, which is how Edgar's brother Alan got turned. If Edgar kills the alpha, Alan will be released from the curse. **81m/C; DVD, Blu-Ray.** Corey Feldman; Tanit Phoenix; Seb Castang; Jamison Newlander; Casey B. Dolan; Steven Van Niekirk; Matthew Dylan Roberts; ***D:*** Dario Piana; ***W:*** Evan Charnov; Hans Rodionoff; ***C:*** Stefano Morcaldo; ***M:*** Elia Cmiral. **VIDEO**

Lost Boys: The Tribe WOOF! 2008 (R) Why bother with this inept mess? Exsurfer Chris (Hilgenbrink) and his teen sister Nicole (Resser) move to seaside Luna Bay, California, to start over after their parents die. The town happens to be populated by bloodsuckers and vamp Shane (Sutherland) goes after Nicole, leaving Chris to wonder why she's acting weird. (Dude, she's a teenaged chick!) Anyway, Frog brother Edgar (Feldman, using the same old shtick) offers his vampire-disposing assistance. Angus Sutherland is the half-brother of Keifer, who starred in the 1987 original; unfortunately, the charisma and acting genes seemed to have passed him by. **94m/C; DVD, Blu-Ray.** Tad Hilgenbrink; Corey Feldman; Gabrielle Rose; Autumn Reeser; Angus Sutherland; ***D:*** P.J. Pesce; ***W:*** Hans Rodionoff; ***C:*** Barry Donlevy; ***M:*** Nathan Barr. **VIDEO**

The Lost Capone 🦴🦴🦴 **1990 (PG-13)** TNT TV version of the story of Al Capone's youngest brother Jimmy, who changes his name to become a clean living small town sheriff who struggles with his sibling's reputation at every turn. **93m/C; DVD.** Ally Sheedy; Eric Roberts; Adrian Pasdar; Titus Welliver; Jimmie F. Skaggs; Maria Pitillo; Anthony Crivello; ***D:*** John Gray; ***W:*** John Gray; ***C:*** Paul Elliott; ***M:*** Mark Snow. **CABLE**

The Lost Child 🦴🦴 1/2 **2000** Rebecca (Ruehl) always knew she was adopted, being raised Jewish in Pennsylvania. After her adoptive parents are both dead, Rebecca searches for her birth parents and discovers she's a full-blooded Navaho taken from her family on the reservation. She immediately takes her children to meet her relatives in Arizona, where they're welcomed into the community. But it isn't so simple for Rebecca's husband, Jack (Sheridan), to deal with his outsider status. Based on the autobiography "Looking for Lost Bird" by Yvette Melanson and Claire Safran. **100m/C; DVD.** Mercedes Ruehl; Jamey Sheridan; Irene Bedard; Dinah Manoff; Ned Romero; Tantoo Cardinal; Michael Greyeyes; Julia McIlvaine; ***D:*** Karen Arthur; ***W:*** Sally Robinson; ***C:*** Thomas Neuwirth; ***M:*** Mark McKenzie. **TV**

The Lost City 🦴🦴 **1934** A feature version of the rollicking vintage movie serial about a lost jungle city, adventurers and mad scientists. **74m/B; VHS, DVD.** William "Stage" Boyd; Kane Richmond; George "Gabby" Hayes; Claudia Dell; ***D:*** Harry Revier.

The Lost City 🦴🦴 **2005 (R)** Garcia's directorial debut is a 20-year, overextended labor of love. Set in 1958 Havana, the old-fashioned saga focuses on the three Fellove brothers and their reactions to the Batista dictatorship and Castro's revolution. Fico (Garcia), the eldest, is an apolitical nightclub owner who wants life to go on as it always has, while his two younger brothers, Luis (Carbonell) and Rico (Murciano), believe in violent change. Politics not only divides the family but soon shatters their comfortable existence, leading Fico into exile from his beloved home (as it did for Garcia's own family). The numerous musical interludes are only in Spanish. **143m/C; DVD, HD-DVD.** Andy Garcia; Nestor Carbonell; Enrique Murciano; Richard Bradford; Steven Bauer; Dustin Hoffman; Julio Oscar Mechoso; Tomas Milian; William Marquez; Bill Murray; Elizabeth Pena; Millie Perkins; Tony Plana; Ines Sastre; Juan Fernandez; Gonzalo Menendez; Jsu Garcia; Ruben Rabasa; ***D:*** Andy Garcia; ***W:*** G. Cabrera Infante; ***C:*** Emmanuel (Manu) Kadosh; ***M:*** Andy Garcia.

Lost City of the Jungle 🦴🦴 1/2 **1945** 13-chapter serial focusing on a crazed Atwill, in his last screen role, believing that he can rule the world from the heart of a deep, dark jungle by utilizing a special mineral. The final Universal serial. **169m/B; VHS, DVD, Blu-Ray.** Russell Hayden; Lionel Atwill; Jane Adams; ***D:*** Ray Taylor; Lewis D. Collins.

The Lost City of Z 🦴🦴🦴 1/2 **2017 (PG-13)** Writer-Director James masterfully adapts David Grann's biography of British explorer Percy Fawcett (Hunnam) and his obsessive search for evidence of an ancient civilization in the Bolivian Amazon. This is a classic epic in the traditional (and best) sense, with beautiful cinematography and smart sequences both in the jungle and at home that belie the film's relatively small budget. Hunnam and Miller, as Fawcett's supportive and formidable wife, show the toll that Fawcett's quest took on their home life. Both the script and Hunnam's portrayal capture the early 20th-Century spirit of adventure and quest for discovery, even as it ignores the colonialism that may have engendered it. **141m/C; DVD, Blu-Ray.** Charlie Hunnam; Robert Pattinson; Sienna Miller; Tom Holland; Edward Ashley; ***D:*** James Gray; ***W:*** James Gray; ***C:*** Darius Khondji; ***M:*** Christopher Spelman.

Lost City Raiders 🦴 1/2 **2008 (PG-13)** Typically cheesy Sci Fi Channel flick. In 2048, the polar ice caps have melted thanks to global warming and flooded most of the planet. John Kubiak and his sons Jack and Thomas salvage treasures from sunken buildings and are hired by the New Vatican to find a relic that could reverse the destruction and save humanity. **90m/C; DVD, Blu-Ray.** James Brolin; Ian Somerhalder; Ben Cross; Jeremy Crutchley; Jamie Thomas King; Bettina Zimmermann; Elodie Frenck; Michael Mendl; ***D:*** Jean De Segonzac; ***W:*** Jean De Segonzac; ***C:*** Giulio Biccari; ***M:*** Gert Wilden. **CABLE**

Lost Colony: The Legend of Roanoke 🦴 1/2 *The Wraiths of Roanoke* **2007 (R)** Low-budget, not terribly scary supernatural horror based on the true story of the first English colony in the U.S. that disappeared without a trace in 1587. Ananias Dare (Paul) is in charge of the colony on Roanoke Island, Virginia. When the colonists start dying in terrible ways, Dare learns from the local tribe that the malevolent Norse spirits of early explorers haunt the island (and apparently want it all to themselves). A Sci-Fi Channel original. **95m/C; DVD.** Adrian Paul; Rhett Giles; Alex McArthur; Frida Show; Michael The; Mari Mascaro; George Calil; ***D:*** Matt Codd; ***W:*** Rafael Jordan; ***C:*** Anton Bakarski; ***M:*** John Dickson. **CABLE**

The Lost Command 🦴🦴 1/2 **1966** A French colonel, relieved of his command, endeavors to regain power by battling a powerful Arab terrorist with his own specially trained platoon of soldiers. Crisp adventure set in post-WWII North Africa. Based on "The Centurions" by Jean Larteguy. **129m/C; DVD.** Anthony Quinn; Michele Morgan; George Segal; Alain Delon; Maurice Ronet; Claudia Cardinale; ***D:*** Mark Robson; ***C:*** Robert L. Surtees.

The Lost Continent 🦴 1/2 **1951** An expedition searching for a lost rocket on a jungle island discovers dinosaurs and other extinct creatures. **82m/B; VHS, DVD.** Cesar Romero; Hillary Brooke; Chick Chandler; John Hoyt; Acquanetta; Sid Melton; Whit Bissell; Hugh Beaumont; ***D:*** Sam Newfield; ***W:*** Richard H. Landau; ***C:*** Jack Greenhalgh; ***M:*** Paul Dunlap.

Lost Dream 🦴 1/2 **2009** Over-privileged college student Perry Roberts hates being in the spotlight because of his father's political career. Questioning where he's going with his life, Perry meets artist Giovanni at a rave and the two begin an unlikely friendship since the self-destructive Gio has been living on the streets since he was a kid. While brooding and whining together, Gio and Perry do drugs and then decide to try out Russian roulette. **90m/C; DVD.** Michael Welch; Sarah Foret; Katie Stuart; Aisha Hinds; Jeremy London; Patricia Richardson; Leonard Wu; Shaun Sipos; ***D:*** Asif Ahmed; ***W:*** Asif Ahmed; ***C:*** Alison Kelly; ***M:*** Nima Fakhrara. **VIDEO**

Lost Embrace 🦴🦴 *El Abrazo Partido* **2004** Aimless Ariel (Hendler), the son of Jewish immigrants, lives in Buenos Aires and helps his mother (Aizenberg) at her lingerie store in a downscale shopping mall. Ariel asks his Polish emigrant grandma (Londner) to help him claim Polish citizenship in order to get a Polish passport so he can move to Europe and start over (he wants to feel "European"). Since grams fled Poland during WWII, she's naturally reluctant and is wise enough to realize that Ariel needs to change his inner self and not merely his outer surroundings. Spanish with subtitles. **99m/C; DVD.** *AR IT SP* Daniel Hendler; Jorge d'Elia; Sergio Boris; Adriana Aizenberg; Rosita Londner; ***D:*** Daniel Burman; ***W:*** Daniel Burman; Marcelo Biromajer; ***C:*** Ramiro Civita; ***M:*** Cesar Lerner.

The Lost Empire 🦴 1/2 **2001** Lavish but muddled (and ultimately dull) story originally broadcast as a four-hour miniseries. American businessman Nicholas Orton (Gibson), who once studied Chinese literature and history, meets cute with a mystery woman who turns out to be Kwan Ying (Ling), the Goddess of Mercy. She tells Nick he has 3 days to save the human world from slavery by saving the classic Chinese manuscript "The Journey to the West" from falling into the wrong hands. Helping Nick are characters from the story, including the anarchic Monkey King (Wong). **134m/C; VHS, DVD.** Thomas Gibson; Bai Ling; Russell Wong; Ric Young; Kabir Bedi; Henry O; ***D:*** Peter Macdonald; ***W:*** David Henry Hwang; ***C:*** David Connell; ***M:*** John Altman. **TV**

The Lost Future 🦴 1/2 **2010** Slow-paced Syfy Channel post-apocalyptic adventure with too many plot threads left dangling by a hasty ending. Nature has reclaimed civilization and, thanks to the usual genetic tinkering gone wrong, an infectious, deadly virus has turned much of the remaining population into zombie-creatures. One band of surviving normal humans is now threatened unless they get the cure from the greedy villain. **91m/C; DVD, Blu-Ray.** Sam Claflin; Corey Sevier; Sean Bean; Annabelle Wallis; Jonathan Pienaar; Eleanor Tomlinson; ***D:*** Mikael Salomon; ***W:*** Bev Doyle; ***C:*** Paul Gilpin; ***M:*** Michael Richard Plowman. **CABLE**

Lost Highway 🦴🦴 **1996 (R)** Welcome once again to Lynch-world—that parallel universe understood only by master David. Jazz musician Fred Madison (Pullman) is on Death Row—supposedly for the murder of his wife Renee (Arquette). Only why does young mechanic Pete Dayton (Getty) wind up in Fred's cell (with Fred missing)? Oh, and why does gangster Mr. Eddy (Loggia) have a girlfriend named Alice (Arquette again) who looks just like Renee? And is she real—or did Fred conjure her up? Who's the Mystery Man (Blake), who literally looks like death warmed over. And....well, you get the idea. Or maybe you're not supposed to. **135m/C; DVD, Blu-Ray.** Bill Pullman; Patricia Arquette; Balthazar Getty; Robert Loggia; Robert (Bobby) Blake; Gary Busey; Jack Nance; Richard Pryor; Natasha Gregson Wagner; Lisa Boyle; Michael Massee; Jack Kehler; Henry Rollins; Gene Ross; Scott Coffey; ***D:*** David Lynch; ***W:*** David Lynch; Barry Gifford; ***C:*** Peter Deming; ***M:*** Angelo Badalamenti.

Lost Holiday: The Jim & Suzanne Shemwell Story 🦴 **2007** The wonder is that these two polar opposite personalities ever got married, not that they're estranged. Suzanne (Gertz) likes to be in control and Jim (Walsh) is devil-may-care. He persuades her to go snowmobiling in the Idaho woods just before Christmas when everything goes horribly wrong and they basically do everything you shouldn't while trying to survive. Based on a true story. **90m/C; DVD.** Dylan Walsh; Jami Gertz; Aaron Pearl; Julia Maxwell; Alexander Arsenault; Judith Buchan; Joe Norman Shaw; ***D:*** Gregory Goodell; ***W:*** Gregory Goodell; ***C:*** Craig Wrobleski; ***M:*** Ron Ramin. **CABLE**

Lost Honeymoon 🦴🦴 **1947** Monkeyshines abound as a soldier marries a girl while in a state of amnesia, and then wakes up to find twin daughters. **70m/B; VHS, DVD.** Franchot Tone; Ann Richards; ***D:*** Leigh Jason.

The Lost Honor of Katharina Blum 🦴🦴🦴 *Die Verlorene Ehre Der Katharina Blum* **1975 (R)** A woman becomes involved with a man who's under police surveillance and finds her life open to public scrutiny and abuse from the media and the government. Based on Heinrich Boll's prize-winning novel. In German with English subtitles. Remade for TV as "The Lost Honor of Kathryn Beck." **97m/C; VHS, DVD.** *GE* Angela Winkler; Mario Adorf; Dieter Laser; Jurgen Prochnow; ***D:*** Volker Schlondorff; Margarethe von Trotta.

Lost Horizon 🦴🦴🦴🦴 **1937** A group of strangers fleeing revolution in China are lost in the Tibetan Himalayas and stumble across the valley of Shangri La. The inhabitants of this Utopian community have lived for hundreds of years in kindness and peace—but what will the intrusion of these strangers bring? The classic romantic role for Colman. Capra's directorial style meshed perfectly with the pacifist theme of James Hilton's classic novel, resulting in one of the most memorable films of the 1930s. This version restores more than 20 minutes of footage which had been cut from the movie through the years. **132m/B; VHS, DVD, Blu-Ray.** Ronald Colman; Jane Wyatt; H.B. Warner; Sam Jaffe; Thomas Mitchell; Edward Everett Horton; Isabel Jewell; John Howard; Margo; ***D:*** Frank Capra; ***W:*** Robert Riskin; ***C:*** Joseph Walker; ***M:***

Dimitri Tiomkin. Oscars '37: Film Editing; Natl. Film Reg. '16.

Lost Horizon 𝒜 **1973 (G)** Disastrous big-budget musical (much of the singing is dubbed) with odd casting, which is a remake of the 1937 film based on the James Hilton novel. Five people escape from 1930s war-torn China but their plane crashes in the Himalayas. They are rescued by monks and taken to the hidden valley of Shangri-La, a Utopian community where the inhabitants don't grow old and live very long lives as long as they remain within the valley. Richard (Finch) finds himself drawn to the peace and serenity but his restless brother George (York) is determined to leave, which has unexpected consequences. **150m/C; DVD, Blu-Ray.** Peter Finch; Michael York; Liv Ullmann; Sally Kellerman; George Kennedy; Bobby Van; John Gielgud; James Shigeta; Charles Boyer; Olivia Hussey; *D:* Charles Jarrott; *W:* Larry Kramer; *C:* Robert L. Surtees; *M:* Burt Bacharach; Hal David.

Lost in a Harem 𝒜𝒜 ½ **1944** Abbott & Costello play magicians in a theatrical troupe stranded in a desert kingdom ruled by an evil sheik. The sheik's nephew (and rightful heir) hires the two to steal some magic rings and the pretty Maxwell to play footsie with his susceptible uncle in an attempt to regain his kingdom. Average comedy with musical numbers by Jimmy Dorsey and His Orchestra. **89m/B; VHS, DVD.** Bud Abbott; Lou Costello; Marilyn Maxwell; John Conte; Douglass Dumbrille; Lottie Harrison; *D:* Charles Reisner.

Lost in Alaska 𝒜𝒜 ½ **1952** Up in the Alaskan wilderness, Abbott & Costello save Ewell from a greedy saloon owner and his cohorts who are trying to get their hands on Ewell's fortune. **87m/B; VHS, DVD.** Bud Abbott; Lou Costello; Tom Ewell; Mitzie Green; Bruce Cabot; Emory Parnell; Jack Ingram; Rex Lease; *D:* Jean Yarbrough; *W:* Martin Ragaway; Leonard Stern; *M:* Henry Mancini.

Lost in America 𝒜𝒜𝒜 **1985 (R)** After deciding that he can't "find himself" at his current job, ad exec David Howard and his wife sell everything they own and buy a Winnebago to travel across the country. This Albert Brooks comedy is a must-see for everyone who thinks that there is more in life than pushing papers at your desk and sitting on "Mercedes leather." **91m/C; VHS, DVD, Blu-Ray.** Albert Brooks; Julie Hagerty; Michael Greene; Tom Tarpey; Garry Marshall; Art Frankel; *D:* Albert Brooks; *W:* Albert Brooks; Monica Johnson; *M:* Arthur B. Rubinstein. Natl. Soc. Film Critics '85: Screenplay.

Lost in Austen 𝒜𝒜 ½ **2008** This sweetly fun and literary romp finds average Londoner Amanda Price (Rooper) yearning for the world depicted by her favorite author. She gets her wish when one of those inexplicable time travel portals suddenly opens up in her bathroom. Amanda's transported to the world of "Pride and Prejudice" while Elizabeth Bennet (Arterton) exchanges places with her. Amanda's strangeness is rather easily accepted but she finds herself unwittingly changing Austen's story and must try to re-establish the proper plot. **177m/C; DVD.** *GB* Jemima Rooper; Gemma Arterton; Elliot Cowan; Alex Kingston; Hugh Bonneville; Daniel Percival; *D:* Dan Zeff; *W:* Guy Andrews; *C:* David Higgs; *M:* Christian Henson. **TV**

Lost in Beijing 𝒜 *Ping Guo* **2007** Tawdry drama of sex and betrayal. Massage parlor worker Ping-guo (Fan) gets drunk at an office party and is raped by her boss Lin (Leung Ka Fai). Her attack just happens to be witnessed by her window cleaner husband An-kun (Tong). When Ping-guo discovers she's pregnant, An-kun thinks it's a great idea to blackmail the married Lin. Only the childless Lin persuades his betrayed wife (Jin) they should adopt the baby, and then An-Kun decides to have a payback affair with Mrs. Lin. Chinese with subtitles. **112m/C; DVD.** *CH* Elaine Jin; Bingbing Fan; Tony Leung Ka Fai; Dawei Tong; *D:* Yu Li; *W:* Yu Li; Fang Li; *C:* Yu Wang; *M:* Peyman Yazdanian.

Lost in La Mancha 𝒜𝒜𝒜 ½ **2003 (R)** Once upon a time, director Terry Gilliam set out to make a film about Don Quixote, called "The Man Who Killed Don Quixote," starring Jean Rochefort and Johnny Depp. In August, 2000, Gilliam arrived in Spain to start filming and watched one disaster (illness, weather, budget problems) after another unfold until the project had to be abandoned (and has yet to be resurrected). Gilliam provided the filmmakers with complete access, even after the misfortunes piled up enough to make the cancellation inevitable. The result is a fascinating inside look at the derailment of the creative process. **93m/C; VHS, DVD.** *GB* *Nar:* Jeff Bridges; *D:* Keith Fulton; Louis Pepe; *W:* Keith Fulton; Louis Pepe; *C:* Louis Pepe; *M:* Miriam Cutler.

Lost in Paris 𝒜𝒜 ½ *Paris pieds nus* **2017** The fourth feature of married directors and stars Dominique Abel and Fiona Gordon highlights their talent for physical comedy and whimsical sense. Librarian Fiona (Gordon) leaves her Canadian home after receiving a concerning letter from her doddering 88-year-old aunt, Martha (Riva), who moved to Paris decades earlier. Once there, Fiona's luggage and identification goes missing but is found by Dom (Abel), a hobo who charms Fiona. Much of the film focuses on the trio narrowly missing each other as they move throughout the city. Though it feels long, its charms and appealing antics make it worth the time. English and French with subtitles. **83m/C; DVD, Blu-Ray.** Fiona Gordon; Dominique Abel; Emmanuelle Riva; Pierre Richard; Frederic Meert; *D:* Fiona Gordon; Dominique Abel; *W:* Fiona Gordon; Dominique Abel; *C:* Claire Childeric; Jean-Christophe Leforestier.

Lost in Space 𝒜𝒜 ½ **1998 (PG-13)** Big-screen remake of the cheesy '60s sci-fi TV show retains the basic plot and premise, but jettisons the camp. In 2058, the Robinsons and pilot Don West (LeBlanc) are chosen to colonize a far-off world because Earth has become nearly uninhabitable. The evil Dr. Smith (Oldman) sabotages the mission but gets stuck on board. Once the family is appropriately lost, the story veers into familiar territory. It's visually impressive, but writer Goldsman can't resist turning the Robinsons into an annoying collection of dysfunction. The occasionally witty inside joke for fans of the show and Oldman's deliciously oily Smith provide some fun. **131m/C; DVD, Blu-Ray.** William Hurt; Mimi Rogers; Gary Oldman; Heather Graham; Matt LeBlanc; Lacey Chabert; Jack Johnson; Lennie James; Jared Harris; Mark Goddard; Edward Fox; Adam Sims; ***Cameo(s):*** June Lockhart; Marta Kristen; Angela Cartwright; *V:* Dick Tufeld; *D:* Stephen Hopkins; *W:* Akiva Goldsman; *C:* Peter Levy; *M:* Bruce Broughton.

Lost in the Barrens 𝒜𝒜 **1991** Two young boys, one a Canadian Indian and the other a rich white boy, get lost in the wilderness of the Canadian north. Out of necessity and common need they become close and form a lifelong friendship. Based on the book by Farley Mowat. **95m/C; VHS, DVD.** *CA* Graham Greene; Nicholas Shields; Evan Adams; Lee J. Campbell; *D:* Michael Scott; *W:* Keith Ross Leckie; *C:* Ina Elkin; *M:* Randolph Peters.

Lost in the Dark 𝒜 ½ **2007** All too predictable thriller. Still adjusting to her recent blindness, 19-year-old Amy is staying at her grandmother's mountain cabin. Naturally, it is the closest habitation when some cons escape and need shelter from a coming blizzard. It takes Amy awhile to realize someone else is in the house with her but she may not be as helpless as the bad guys assume. **90m/C; DVD.** Mae Whitman; Jason Gray-Stanford; Teach Grant; Tom McBeath; Matthew Smalley; Patrick Gilmore; Bonnie Byrnes; *D:* Rob Malenfant; *W:* Devon Lehr; Laura Schultz; *C:* Eric Goldstein; *M:* Zhang Hailin. **CABLE**

Lost in Translation 𝒜𝒜𝒜 ½ **2003 (R)** Coppola's pitch-perfect moody dramedy of loneliness stars Murray as Bob, a washed-up star in Japan to shoot a lucrative commercial. Homesick and jet-lagged, Bob's at the hotel bar where he meets fellow Yank Charlotte (Johansson). Charlotte's accompanying her photographer husband (Ribisi), whose glamorous job she can't understand. Despite their age difference, the two bond over cocktails and karaoke (a memorable scene), discussing the difficulties of marriage and life while steering clear of formulaic romance trappings. Murray's restrained performance conveys a weary acceptance of life while Johansson deftly displays a suitable discontented air. **105m/C; DVD, Blu-Ray, HD-DVD.** Bill Murray; Scarlett Johansson; Giovanni Ribisi; Anna Faris; Yutaka Tadokoro; Catherine Lambert; Fumihiro Hayashi; *D:* Sofia Coppola; *W:* Sofia Coppola; *C:* Lance Acord. Oscars '03: Orig. Screenplay; British Acad. '03: Actor (Murray), Actress (Johansson), Film Editing; Golden Globes '04: Actor--Mus./Comedy (Murray), Film--Mus./Comedy, Screenplay; Ind. Spirit '04: Actor (Murray), Director (Coppola), Film, Screenplay; L.A. Film Critics '03: Actor (Murray); N.Y. Film Critics '03: Actor (Murray), Director (Coppola); Natl. Soc. Film Critics '03: Actor (Murray); Writers Guild '03: Orig. Screenplay.

Lost in Yonkers 𝒜𝒜 ½ *Neil Simon's Lost in Yonkers* **1993 (PG)** Arty and Jay are two teenage brothers who, while their widowed father looks for work, are sent to live with their stern grandmother, small-time gangster uncle, and childlike aunt in 1942 New York. Ruehl reprises her Tony award-winning performance as Aunt Bella, who loses herself in the movies while trying to find a love of her own, out from under the oppressive thumb of her domineering mother (Worth). Performances by the adults are more theatrical than necessary but the teenagers do well in their observer roles. Based on the play by Neil Simon, which again chronicles his boyhood. **114m/C; VHS, DVD.** Mercedes Ruehl; Irene Worth; Richard Dreyfuss; Brad Stoll; Mike Damus; David Strathairn; Robert Miranda; Jack Laufer; Susan Merson; *D:* Martha Coolidge; *W:* Neil Simon; *M:* Elmer Bernstein.

Lost Junction 𝒜𝒜 **2003 (R)** Jimmy bums a ride from Missy not knowing she's got extra cargo in the trunk—her murdered husband. Unsure of her guilt but totally smitten, Jimmy is game to dumping the body for her but the plan gets mucked up when her crazy boyfriend shows up on their tail. **95m/C; VHS, DVD.** Neve Campbell; Billy Burke; Jake Busey; Charles Powell; Michel Perron; David Gow; Norman Mikeal Berketa; Mariah Inger; Dawn Ford; Matt O'Toole; *D:* Peter Masterson; *W:* Jeff Cole; *C:* Thomas Burstyn; *M:* Normand Corbeil. **VIDEO**

The Lost Jungle 𝒜𝒜 **1934** Circus legend Beatty searches for his girl and her dad in the jungle. Animal stunts keep it interesting. Serial in 12 chapters, 13 minutes each. **156m/B; VHS, DVD.** Clyde Beatty; Cecilia Parker; Syd Saylor; Warner Richmond; Wheeler Oakman; *D:* Armand Schaefer; David Howard.

Lost Lagoon 𝒜𝒜 **1958** Unhappily married Charlie Walker is on a fishing trip when he's washed overboard and presumed drowned. Instead, he finds himself on a small island in the Bahamas being cared for by young, pretty Elizabeth. He decides he won't go back to his old life and takes the opportunity to open a small resort hotel with Elizabeth. Everything's swell until an insurance investigator comes poking around. **80m/B; DVD.** Jeffrey Lynn; Leila Barry; Peter Donat; Jane Hartley; Roger Clark; Don Gibson; *D:* John Rawlins; *W:* John Rawlins; *C:* Harry W. Smith; *M:* Terry Brannon; Hubert Smith.

The Lost Language of Cranes 𝒜𝒜𝒜 **1992** David Leavitt's novel is transported from New York to present-day London but the wrenching emotional drama remains the same. A family is in crisis as long-hidden secrets concerning homosexuality and infidelity are finally revealed. The title refers to one character's social worker's thesis on a young boy from a dysfunctional family who imitates the movements of the building cranes he sees. Fine performances by all. Adult sexual situations. **90m/C; VHS, DVD.** *GB* Brian Cox; Eileen Atkins; Angus MacFadyen; Corey Parker; Cathy Tyson; ***Cameo(s):*** John Schlesinger; Rene Auberjonois; *D:* Nigel Finch; *C:* Remi Adefarasin.

Lost, Lonely, and Vicious 𝒜 **1959** Clayton is a suicidal Hollywood actor who spends much of his time indulging his penchant for women, figuring he may as well enjoy what little time he has left. Then he meets Wilson, a drugstore clerk who moves him to reconsider his self-destructive ways. **73m/B; VHS, DVD.** Ken Clayton; Barbara Wilson; Lilyan Chauvin; Richard Gilden; Carole Nugent; Sandra Giles; Allen Fife; Frank Stallworth; Johnny Erben; Clint Quigley; T. Earl Johnson; *D:* Frank Myers; *W:* Norman Graham; *C:* Ted Saizis; Vincent Saizis; *M:* Frederick David.

The Lost Medallion: The Adventures of Billy Stone 𝒜 ½ **2013 (PG)** Fantasy film about kids finding a medallion that allows them to travel in time and help those in need. Focuses on teaching children about having a relationship with god. **98m/C; DVD, Blu-Ray.** Billy Unger; Sammi Hanratty; James Hong; Jansen Panettiere; William Corkery; *D:* Bill Muir; *W:* Bill Muir; *C:* Brian Baugh; *M:* Mark Fantini; Steffan Fantini.

The Lost Missile 𝒜𝒜 **1958** A lost, alien missile circles the Earth, causing overheating and destruction on the planet's surface. A scientist works to find a way to save the planet before it explodes into a gigantic fireball. Director Burke's last film. **70m/B; VHS, DVD.** Robert Loggia; Ellen Parker; Larry Kerr; Phillip Pine; Marilee Earle; *D:* William Berke.

The Lost Moment 𝒜𝒜 **1947** A publisher travels to Italy to search for a valuable collection of a celebrated author's love letters, but finds a neurotic woman in his way. Based on Henry James' "Aspern Papers." **89m/B; DVD, Blu-Ray.** Robert Cummings; Agnes Moorehead; Susan Hayward; *D:* Martin Gabel; *W:* Leonardo Bercovici; *C:* Hal Mohr; *M:* Daniele Amfitheatrof.

The Lost Patrol 𝒜𝒜𝒜 ½ **1934** WWI British soldiers lost in the desert are shot down one by one by Arab marauders as Karloff portrays a religious soldier convinced he's going to die. The usual spiffy Ford exteriors peopled by great characters with a stirring score. Based on the story, "Patrol" by Philip MacDonald. **66m/B; VHS, DVD.** Victor McLaglen; Boris Karloff; Reginald Denny; Wallace Ford; Alan Hale; J.M. Kerrigan; Billy Bevan; Brandon Hurst; Douglas Walton; *D:* John Ford; *W:* Dudley Nichols; Garrett Fort; *C:* Harold Wenstrom; *M:* Max Steiner.

The Lost Princess 𝒜 **2005** Fantasy filmed at a Renaissance Fair, starring Fair regulars Don Juan and Miguel. They team up with a princess to save the Queen's cousin from impending peril. **75m/C; DVD.** Lolly Foy; Dakota Star Granados; Jose Granados; Douglas Kondziolka; *D:* Duncan Pace; *W:* Jose Granados; Douglas Kondziolka; Duncan Pace; *C:* Christopher Gomersall. **VIDEO**

Lost River 𝒜𝒜 **2015 (R)** Gosling's directorial debut was ripped apart at Cannes, but there's some serious potential here in terms of what he does next more than this misfire. Hendricks plays a woman at the edge of poverty in a futuristic variation on Detroit. Her son steals copper from empty houses so they can pay the mortgage, crossing paths with a local tough guy. Meanwhile, she gets a job at an underground club where people pay to watch women pretend to mutilate themselves. Very strong visuals can't disguise a lack of story development. **105m/C; DVD, Blu-Ray.** Christina Hendricks; Iain de Caestecker; Saoirse Ronan; Matt Smith; Ben Mendelsohn; *D:* Ryan Gosling; *W:* Ryan Gosling; *C:* Benoît Debie; *M:* Johnny Jewel.

The Lost Samaritan 𝒜 **2008** Dumb story, bad acting. Accountant William Archer (Somerhalder) stops to assist an injured motorist and finds himself the target of government assassins. **88m/C; DVD.** Ian Somerhalder; Ruta Gedmintas; David Scheller; Anna Fin; Oliver Debuschewitz; *D:* Thomas Jahn; *W:* Chris Artiga-Oliver. **VIDEO**

The Lost Skeleton of Cadavra 𝒜𝒜 **2001 (PG)** Deliberately silly spoof of schlock 1950s horror and sci fi flicks (it's even filmed in black and white). Meteor specialist Dr. Paul Armstrong and his ditzy blonde wife Betty are heading to a remote SoCal location so Paul can find radioactive rocks. His nutso rival, Dr. Fleming, is after the same rocks—only he wants to use them to revive the title cave skeleton. There are also aliens with a disabled spaceship and a mutant. **94m/B; DVD.** Larry Blamire; Fay Masterson; Brian Howe; Jennifer Blaire; Susan McConnell; Andrew Parks; Dan Conroy; *D:* Larry Blamire; *W:* Larry Blamire; *C:* Kevin F. Jones.

The Lost Son 𝒜𝒜 **1998 (R)** Former French narcotics cop Xavier Lombard (Auteuil) has relocated to London where he works as a P.I. An ex-colleague, Carlos (Hinds), asks Lombard to locate his wife Deborah's (Kinski) missing brother Leon, a photographer who has somehow gotten involved with a pedophile ring. Lombard eventually tracks the supposed leader of the ring to Mexico but finds his ultimate answer lies closer to home. A serious topic undone by a one-dimensional script. **102m/C; VHS, DVD.** *GB FR* Daniel Auteuil; Katrin Cartlidge; Ciaran Hinds; Nastassja Kinski; Bruce Greenwood; Marianne (Cuau) Denicourt; Billie Whitelaw; ***D:*** Chris Menges; ***W:*** Eric Leclere; Margaret Leclere; Mark Mills; ***C:*** Barry Ackroyd; ***M:*** Goran Bregovic.

Lost Souls 🦴 1/2 *Nightworld: Lost Souls* **1998** The Robinson family move into a new home in the country and their autistic daughter Meaghan is suddenly able to communicate with the spirits of two children who were the victims of a still-unsolved murder. **90m/C; DVD.** John Savage; Barbara Sukowa; Laura Harling; Nick Deigman; Richard Lintern; Robert Sherman; ***D:*** Jeff Woolnough; ***W:*** Scott Peters; ***C:*** Jon Joffin; ***M:*** Jonathan Goldsmith. **TV**

Lost Souls 🦴 1/2 **2000 (R)** The Devil's back in another second-rate horror flick, trying to take over the world again by possessing the body of atheistic New York crime journalist Peter Kelson (Chaplin). Maya (Ryder), a former possession victim herself, is one of a group of New York exorcists who become aware of the conspiracy. She tries to convince the cynical Peter, but he scoffs at the idea until he begins to experience creepy hallucinations. Directorial debut cinematographer Kaminski, who offers up some beautiful scenes in the midst of an ugly movie. **98m/C; DVD.** Winona Ryder; Ben Chaplin; John Hurt; Elias Koteas; John Diehl; W. Earl Brown; Sarah Wynter; Philip Baker Hall; Brian Reddy; John Beasley; Victor Slezak; Brad Greenquist; ***D:*** Janusz Kaminski; ***W:*** Pierce Gardner; Betsy Stahl; ***C:*** Mauro Fiore; ***M:*** Jan A.P. Kaczmarek.

Lost Stallions:The Journey Home 🦴 1/2 **2008** The story is derivative and the teens' acting is wooden but the horse and the scenery have some appeal. Teenager Jake has been acting out since his dad's death so he and his mom visit the Harmony Ranch family retreat. Owner Chief has Jake work with stallion Troubadour whose mom has died. When Troubadour runs away, Jake and two new friends decide to head into the wilderness to find him. **86m/C; DVD.** Alex Hugh; Mickey Rooney; Rachael Handy; Evan Tilson Stroud; Jan Rooney; Megan Blake; ***D:*** David Rotan; ***W:*** Lovinder Gill; ***C:*** John Rotan; ***M:*** John Baumbach. **VIDEO**

Lost Treasure 🦴 1/2 **2003 (R)** Bryan (Baldwin) and his brother obtain the map to a lost treasure belonging to Christopher Columbus shortly before the brother gets kidnapped. So Bryan hires a pilot to head out into the Panamanian jungle to find the treasure assuming he'll find his brother along the way. **90m/C; DVD.** Stephen Baldwin; Nicolette Sheridan; Hannes Jaenicke; Jerry Doyle; Coby Ryan McLaughlin; Mark Christopher Lawrence; Tami-Adrian George; Scott Schwartz; Bill Monroe; Benny Nieves; Eric James Virgets; Billy "Sly" Williams; Rene Rivera; Joe Sagal; Patrick St. Esprit; ***D:*** Jim Wynorski; ***W:*** Harris Done; Diane Fine; Keoni Waxman; William Monroe; ***C:*** Andrea V. Rossotto; ***M:*** Neal Acree.

The Lost Treasure of Sawtooth Island 🦴 1/2 **1999 (PG)** Danny (Bernard) dreams of the day when he can prove his dead father right and find pirate treasure at the bottom of Lake Michigan. Even his grandfather Ben (Borgnine) doesn't believe him. But when Ben is hospitalized following a diving accident Danny is visited by a pirate ghost who claims he will lead him to the treasure but also warns him there will be competition. **92m/C; DVD.** Ernest Borgnine; Guy Sanville; Seth Bernard; Brennan Hesser; Logan Lipton; Mike Kelly; Randall Godwin; Ashley Bowers; David Montee; Clarence Bailey; John Dew; ***D:*** Richard Brauer; ***W:*** Terry Caszatt; ***C:*** Peter Sensor; ***M:*** Gary Remal Malkin.

The Lost Treasure of the Grand Canyon 🦴 1/2 **2008** Archeologist Susan Jordan (Doherty) leads an expedition to rescue her father (Fraser) who disappeared while searching for a lost city somewhere in the Grand Canyon. A hidden valley reveals evidence of human sacrifice by Aztec warriors, a winged serpent, and lots of treasure. Your generic SciFi Channel feature with mediocre special effects to go along with a mediocre script and acting. **90m/C; DVD.** Shannen Doherty; Michael Shanks; J.R. Bourne; Duncan Fraser; Toby Berner; Heather Doerksen; ***D:*** Farhad Mann; ***W:*** Clay Carmouche; ***C:*** Adam Sliwinski; ***M:*** Michael Neilson. **CABLE**

Lost Treasure of the Maya 🦴 1/2 *No Bad Days* **2008 (PG-13)** Generic action flick with an Indiana Jones-wannabe. Tomb raiders working in the Yucatan discover a trove of Mayan artifacts but run afoul of ex-military man Nico (Protasio, also co-writer and producer) who has been hired to find a missing archeologist by her sister Alexis (Storm). **90m/C; DVD.** Michael Madsen; Keith David; Richard Tyson; Declan Joyce; Heather Storm; Protasio; ***D:*** David Murphy; ***W:*** David Murphy; ***C:*** Eric Felland; ***M:*** Marcello DeFrancisici. **VIDEO**

The Lost Valentine 🦴🦴 1/2 **2011** Hallmark Hall of Fame presentation. Ambitious TV journalist Susan (Hewitt) is tired of being assigned human interest stories until she meets longtime widow Caroline (White). Caroline has kept a 65-year annual pilgrimage to the train station, which is where her husband Neil (Magnussen) left on a WWII troop train. Caroline's grandson Lucas (Faris) is skeptical of Susan's motives, especially when she wants to find out what happened to Naval pilot Neil, who was declared MIA. Adapted from the book by James Michael Pratt. **100m/C; DVD.** Jennifer Love Hewitt; Betty White; Sean Faris; Billy Magnussen; Meghann Fahy; Will Chase; Gil Gerard; ***D:*** Darnell Martin; ***W:*** Maryann Ridini Spencer; Barton Yaney; ***C:*** Frank Prinzi; ***M:*** Mark Adler. **TV**

The Lost Volcano 🦴 1/2 **1950** Young David is kidnapped by two evil hunting guides who want the kid to lead them to a treasure-rich lost city located in a still-active volcano. Bomba rescues David and defeats the bad guys when the volcano erupts. The 3rd pic in the "Bomba" series. **76m/B; DVD.** John(ny) Sheffield; Tommy "T.V." Ivo; John Ridgely; Don C. Harvey; Donald Woods; Marjorie Lord; Elena Verdugo; ***D:*** Ford Beebe; ***W:*** Jack DeWitt; ***C:*** Marcel Le Picard.

Lost Voyage 🦴🦴 **2001 (R)** The cruise ship Corona Queen disappears in the Bermuda Triangle in the early seventies. Aaron Roberts (Nelson) grew up obsessed by the event since his father and stepmother were aboard. Then the ship mysteriously reappears. Roberts, TV reporter Dana Elway (Gunn) and salvager David Shaw (Henriksen) helicopter aboard and unsettling things begin to happen. **95m/C; VHS, DVD.** Judd Nelson; Lance Henriksen; Janet Gunn; Jeff Kober; Mark Sheppard; Robert Pine; Scarlet Chorvat; ***D:*** Christian McIntire; ***W:*** Christian McIntire; ***C:*** Todd Baron; ***M:*** Rich McHugh. **CABLE**

The Lost Weekend 🦴🦴🦴🦴 **1945** The heartrending Hollywood masterpiece about alcoholism, depicting a single weekend in the life of struggling writer Don Birnam (Milland), who cannot believe he's addicted until he finally hits bottom. Except for its pat ending, it is an uncompromising, startlingly harsh treatment, with Milland giving one of the industry's bravest lead performances ever. Acclaimed then and now. **100m/B; VHS, DVD.** Ray Milland; Jane Wyman; Phillip Terry; Howard da Silva; Doris Dowling; Frank Faylen; Mary (Marsden) Young; ***D:*** Billy Wilder; ***W:*** Charles Brackett; Billy Wilder; ***C:*** John Seitz; ***M:*** Miklos Rozsa. Oscars '45: Actor (Milland), Director (Wilder), Film, Screenplay; Cannes '46: Actor (Milland), Film; Golden Globes '46: Actor--Drama (Milland), Director (Wilder), Film--Drama; Natl. Bd. of Review '45: Actor (Milland); Natl. Film Reg. '11; N.Y. Film Critics '45: Actor (Milland), Director (Wilder), Film.

The Lost World 🦴🦴 1/2 **1925** A zoology professor leads a group on a South American expedition in search of the "lost world," where dinosaurs roam in this silent film. Based on a story by Sir Arthur Conan Doyle. A 90-minute version includes the film's original trailer and a re-creation of some of the missing footage (the film was released at 108 minutes). **93m/B; Silent; VHS, DVD, Blu-Ray.** Wallace Beery; Lewis Stone; Bessie Love; Lloyd Hughes; ***D:*** Harry Hoyt; ***W:*** Marion Fairfax; ***C:*** Arthur Edeson. Natl. Film Reg. '98.

The Lost World 🦴 1/2 *Sir Arthur Conan Doyle's The Lost World* **1960** Professor Challenger (Claude Raines) leads an expedition into the Amazon in search of a lost world. Currently only available in a collection with the 1925 version of the film. **97m/C; DVD, Streaming.** Michael Rennie; Jill St. John; David Hedison; Claude Rains; Fernando Lamas; Richard Haydn; ***D:*** Irwin Allen; ***W:*** Irwin Allen; Charles Bennett; ***C:*** Winton C. Hoch; ***M:*** Paul Sawtell; Bert Shefter. **VIDEO**

The Lost World 🦴🦴 1/2 **1992** "Land of the Lost"/"Jurassic Park" themes, based on the story by Sir Arthur Conan Doyle. A scientific team ventures deep into uncharted African jungles where they find themselves confronted by dinosaurs and other dangers. **99m/C; VHS, DVD.** John Rhys-Davies; David Warner; ***D:*** Timothy Bond.

The Lost World 🦴🦴 1/2 **2002** Another version of the Arthur Conan Doyle story about a British expedition to the Amazon in 1912. Eccentric Professor George Challenger (Hoskins) leads a mixed group of characters in search of a remote plateau where he believes dinosaurs still exist. And he turns out to be right. **200m/C; VHS, DVD.** Bob Hoskins; Peter Falk; James Fox; Tom Ward; Matthew Rhys; Elaine Cassidy; ***D:*** Stuart Orme; ***W:*** Adrian Hodges; Tony Mulholland; ***C:*** David Odd; ***M:*** Robert (Rob) Lane. **CABLE**

The Lost World: Jurassic Park 2 🦴🦴 1/2 *Jurassic Park 2* **1997 (PG-13)** Lackluster sequel. Four years later, the surviving dinos have peacefully set up house on a deserted island near Costa Rica. Mathematician Ian Malcolm (Goldblum, reprising his role) reluctantly becomes part of an expedition to monitor the beasts, only because his paleontologist girlfriend (Moore) is so gung-ho. Other characters exist, but are reduced to the role of entrees. More dinos (two T-Rexs, a clan of Raptors, and bite-sized newcomers Compsognathus), thrilling special effects, and more gore make up for thin subplots involving a rich businessman who wants to use the dinosaurs for a new zoo and another who hunts them for sport. **129m/C; DVD, Blu-Ray.** Jeff Goldblum; Julianne Moore; Vince Vaughn; Richard Attenborough; Arliss Howard; Pete Postlethwaite; Peter Stormare; Vanessa Lee Chester; Richard Schiff; Harvey Jason; Thomas F. Duffy; Ariana Richards; Joseph Mazzello; ***D:*** Steven Spielberg; ***W:*** David Koepp; ***C:*** Janusz Kaminski; ***M:*** John Williams.

The Lost Zeppelin 🦴 1/2 **1929** A group of explorers go down in a dirigible in the Antarctic and then must survive the elements as well as a romantic triangle between Commander Hall, his young wife Miriam, and his second-in-command Tom Armstrong. The miniatures used for special effects are good but, because of technical restrictions with voice recordings, this early talkie is also glacially paced whenever it retreats from the action. **73m/B; VHS, DVD.** Conway Tearle; Virginia Valli; Ricardo Cortez; Duke Martin; Kathryn McGuire; Winter Hall; ***D:*** Edward Sloman; ***W:*** Frances Hyland; Charles Kenyon; ***C:*** Jackson Rose.

Lotna 🦴🦴 1/2 **1964** Wadja's first color film serves as a tribute to the Polish calvary who fought against the Germans in WWII. The story is told through the trials of a horse that passes to various military officials until it breaks a leg and must be shot. Wadja himself is the son of a cavalryman killed in the war. Polish with subtitles. **89m/C; VHS, DVD.** *PL* Bozena Kurowska; Jerzy Pichelski; Jerzy Moes; Adam Pawlikowski; ***D:*** Andrzej Wajda; ***W:*** Andrzej Wajda; Wojciech Zukrowski; ***C:*** Jerzy Lipman; ***M:*** Tadeusz Baird.

Lottery Bride 🦴🦴 1/2 **1930** In this charming musical, Jeanette MacDonald is the lottery bride who is won by the brother of the man she really loves. A fine outing for all involved, particularly the supporting cast. **85m/B; VHS, DVD.** Jeanette MacDonald; Joe E. Brown; Zasu Pitts; John Garrick; Carroll Nye; ***D:*** Paul Stein.

The Lottery Ticket 🦴🦴 **2010 (PG-13)** Inconsistent, broadly-told and played comedy still offers some laughs. Kevin Carson (Bow Wow), living in the Atlanta projects with his grandma (Devine), uses fortune cookie numbers to win a $370 million lottery jackpot. But since it's the Fourth of July weekend he can't claim his prize for three days and soon his greedy and threatening neighbors know about Kevin's good fortune. **95m/C; Blu-Ray.** Bow Wow; Brandon T. Jackson; Keith David; Terry Crews; Naturi Naughton; Ice Cube; Bill Bellamy; Mike Epps; Loretta Devine; Charlie (Charles Q.) Murphy; Gbenga Akinnagbe; ***D:*** Erik White; ***W:*** Abdul Williams; ***C:*** Patrick Cady; ***M:*** Teddy Castellucci.

Lotto Land 🦴🦴 1/2 **1995** Looks at the lives of black and Hispanic characters from the same Brooklyn neighborhood. Ambitious high school grad Hank (Gilliard, Jr.) works stocking shelves at the local liquor store for manager Flo (Costallos), who's raised Hank's girlfriend, the college-bound Joy (Gonzalez). The neighborhood's abuzz when someone in their area holds the winning ticket for a $27 million lottery, which was sold from Flo's store, but just who it is and what happens when the money is claimed leads to a dramatic twist. Debut for Rubino, who shows real affection for his characters. **90m/C; DVD.** Larry (Lawrence) Gilliard, Jr.; Barbara Gonzalez; Suzanne Costallos; Paul Calderon; Jamie Tirelli; Luis Guzman; ***D:*** John Rubino; ***W:*** John Rubino; ***C:*** Rufus Standefer; ***M:*** Sherman Holmes.

Louder Than a Bomb 🦴🦴 **2010** Highlights Chicago's 2008 Louder Than a Bomb teen poetry slam festival where soloists and teams from the area's 60 high schools work towards the finals. Included in the showcase are the sometimes unruly participants from Southside's Steinmetz High School (which was a surprise winner in 2007) and their coach James Sloan, Oak Park/River Forest High School, Whitney Young Magnet School, and Northside College Prep. **99m/C; DVD.** ***D:*** Gregory Jacobs; Jon Siskel; ***C:*** Stephen Mazurek.

Louder than Bombs 🦴🦴 **2001** Twenty-one-year-old Marcin is making his father's funeral arrangements, which means he must also deal with his out-of-town relatives who disparage his life as a small-town mechanic. If this wasn't enough stress, Marcin learns his girlfriend Kaska is going to America to attend college. Can he convince her to change her mind by asking him to marry her or should he give her the chance to lead a better life than their small town can offer? Polish with subtitles. **92m/C; VHS, DVD.** *PL* Rafal Mackowiak; Sylwia Juszczak; Magdalena Schejbal; ***D:*** Przemyslaw Wojcieszek; ***W:*** Przemyslaw Wojcieszek; ***C:*** Jolanta Dylewska; ***M:*** Bartek Straburzynski.

Louder Than Bombs 🦴🦴 1/2 **2016 (R)** How do we process grief? And how do we capture it in art? These are the complex questions at the core of Joachim Trier's daring drama. Jonah (Eisenberg) is a young man coming home after the birth of his child sends him emotionally reeling. His younger brother Conrad (Druid) has never recovered from the tragic death of his mother (Huppert), a lauded war photographer, and has grown more distant from dad (Byrne). Far from a traditional family melodrama, Trier's film lingers long after it's over, challenging viewers to think about how art memorializes those we love. **105m/C; DVD.** Gabriel Byrne; Isabelle Huppert; Jesse Eisenberg; Devin Druid; Amy Ryan; ***D:*** Joachim Trier; ***W:*** Joachim Trier; Eskil Vogt; ***C:*** Jakob Ihre; ***M:*** Ola Flottum.

Louder Than Words 🦴🦴 1/2 **2014 (PG-13)** Based on true events, this family drama centers on the impact of an unexpected death. John (Duchovny) and Brenda (Davis) Fareri seem to have it all, including successful careers and four children. When their youngest daughter Maria (Steele Falconer) falls ill and goes to the hospital, the prognosis is initially favorable but she dies suddenly. The death shatters the family. In his grief, John comes up with the idea to supporting the construction of a new children's hospital where healing can take place for all families who visit there. The result keeps his daughter's memory alive and changes how children's hospitals are constructed. **95m/C; DVD, Streaming, Download.** David Duchovny; Hope Davis; Olivia Steele Falconer; Adelaide Kane; Timothy Hutton; ***D:*** Anthony Fabian; ***W:*** Benjamin Chapin; ***C:*** Elliot Davis; ***M:*** Geoff Zanelli.

Louisiana Purchase 🦴🦴 1/2 **1941** Successful screen adaptation of the Broadway musical features several performers from the original cast, lavish costumes, and great musical numbers. As usual, Hope's comedy is extremely funny, especially his famous filibuster scene in Congress. Based on the stage musical by Morrie Ryskind and B. G. DeSylva. **95m/C; VHS, DVD.** Bob Hope; Vera Zorina; Victor Moore; Dona Drake; Irene Bordoni; Raymond Walburn; Maxie "Slapsie" Rosenbloom; Frank Albertson; Barbara Britton; ***D:*** Irving Cummings; ***W:*** Jerome Chodorov; Joseph Fields; ***C:*** Harry Hallenberger; Ray Rennahan.

Louisiana Story 🦴🦴🦴 **1948** The final effort by the master filmmaker, depicting the effects of oil industrialization on the southern

Bayou country as seen through the eyes of a young boy. One of Flaherty's greatest, widely considered a premiere achievement. **77m/B; VHS, DVD.** ***D:*** Robert Flaherty; ***M:*** Virgil Thomson. Natl. Film Reg. '94.

Loulou ☙☙☙½ **1980 (R)** A woman leaves her middle-class husband for a leather-clad, uneducated jock who is more attentive. Romantic and erotic. In French with English subtitles. **110m/C; VHS, DVD, Blu-Ray.** *FR* Isabelle Huppert; Gerard Depardieu; Guy Marchand; ***D:*** Maurice Pialat; ***W:*** Maurice Pialat; Arlette Langmann; ***C:*** Pierre William Glenn; ***M:*** Philippe Sarde.

Love ☙☙☙½ *Szerelem* **1971** Torocsik plays a young woman whose husband has been imprisoned for political crimes. Living in a cramped apartment with her mother-in-law, she keeps the news from the aged and dying woman (Darvas) by reading letters she's fabricated to keep alive the woman's belief that her son is a successful movie director in America. The story is punctuated by the older woman's dreamy remembrances of things past. Exceptional performances by both women, it was Darvas' final film. Based on two novellas by Tibor Dery. Hungarian with subtitles. **92m/B; VHS, DVD.** *HU* Lili Darvas; Mari Torocsik; Ivan Darvas; ***D:*** Karoly Makk; ***W:*** Peter Bacso; ***C:*** Janos Toth; ***M:*** Andras Mihaly.

Love ☙☙ **2005** Dreary thriller set in New York City about Yugoslav hitman Vanya (Trifunovic) who runs into his ex-wife Anna (Lechner) while performing one last job for his old crime boss as repayment for his escape to the United States. Caught in a drug deal gone fatally wrong, Vanya takes Anna as his hostage while her new boyfriend—a police officer—scours the city in search of the pair. Things get mucked up a bit when Anna and Vanya find out that they still have feelings for one another. **90m/C; DVD.** Geno Lechner; Sergej Trifunovic; Didier Flamand; Peter Gevisser; Mario Padula; Al Naz; Eric Frandsen; Liat Glick; Kerry Rossi; Vija Vetra; Mariano Mederos; ***D:*** Vladan Nikolic; ***W:*** Vladan Nikolic; ***C:*** Vladimir Subotic.

Love ☙☙ *Angels & Airwaves Love* **2011** Cerebral scifi movie sponsored by the rock band Angels and Airwaves. Astronaut Lee Miller is stranded on the space station he is sent to repair when Earth tells him he's on his own. What follows are some odd discoveries and a seven year descent into madness. **85m/C; Streaming.** Gunner Wright; Corey Richardson; Bradley Horne; ***D:*** William Eubank; ***W:*** William Eubank; ***C:*** William Eubank. **VIDEO**

Love ☙☙ **2015** A 3D pornographic film from the director of Enter the Void is the kind of movie made for a very specific audience—fans of this groundbreaking filmmaker. Sadly, even they will be disappointed by a movie with a plot about as engaging as the average porno. Murphy (Karl Glusman) is a cinema school student without much purpose. After getting a call that his ex-girlfriend Electra (Aomi Muyock) may have killed herself, Murphy remembers the highlights, including unsimulated sex, of their relationship. Noe is an undeniably creative voice in cinema but this is a misstep, a film designed around 3D images of bodies that feel hollow. **130m/C; DVD, Blu-Ray, Streaming.** *BE FR* Aomi Muyock; Karl Glusman; Klara Kristin; ***D:*** Gaspar Noé; ***W:*** Gaspar Noé; ***C:*** Benoît Debie.

Love Actually ☙☙½ **2003 (R)** One movie, ten love stories, and like any episodic multi-character, intertwining storyline romance, some work and some don't. The most engaging are those involving the bachelor Prime Minister (Grant), his sister (Thompson) with the wandering husband, and the aging rocker Billy Mack (Nighy). Richard Curtis, already established as a worthy romantic comedy writer, crams in absolutely every possible love situation as if he may never direct again. The good is sweet enough to mostly offset the bad, but a less-crowded story would help. **129m/C; VHS, DVD, Blu-Ray.** *GB* Hugh Grant; Martine McCutcheon; Bill Nighy; Emma Thompson; Alan Rickman; Heike Makatsch; Keira Knightley; Chiwetel Ejiofor; Andrew Lincoln; Laura Linney; Rodrigo Santoro; Thomas Brodie-Sangster; Liam Neeson; Kris Marshall; Colin Firth; Lucia Moniz; Joanna Page; Martin Freeman; Billy Bob Thornton; Rowan Atkinson; Claudia Schiffer; Shannon Elizabeth; Denise Richards; Sienna Guillory; Gregor Fisher; ***D:*** Richard Curtis; ***W:*** Richard Curtis; ***C:*** Michael Coulter; ***M:*** Craig Armstrong. British Acad. '03: Support. Actor (Nighy); L.A. Film Critics '03: Support. Actor (Nighy).

Love Affair ☙☙ **1932** Columbia Pictures tested Bogart's leading man potential in this romantic drama. Aircraft engineer Jim Leonard wants to start his own business and wealthy socialite Carol Owen (Mackaill) wants to back him. Carol finds out she's actually broke and her financial advisor Bruce Hardy (Hamilton) has been paying her bills since he wants to marry her. Jim's been neglecting his own dreams for Carol and she has to choose between marrying for money or being poor and in love. **65m/B; DVD.** Dorothy Mackaill; Humphrey Bogart; Hale Hamilton; Astrid Allwyn; Halliwell Hobbes; ***D:*** Thornton Freeland; ***W:*** Dorothy Howell; Jo Swerling; ***C:*** Ted Tetzlaff.

Love Affair ☙☙☙½ **1939** Multi-kleenex weepie inspired countless romantic dreams of true love atop the Empire State Building. Dunn and Boyer fall in love on a ship bound for NYC, but they're both involved. They agree to meet later at, guess where, to see if their feelings hold true, but tragedy intevenes. Excellent comedy-drama is witty at first, more subdued later, with plenty of romance and melodrama. Remade in 1957 (by McCarey) as "An Affair to Remember," a lesser version whose popularity overshadows the original. Remade again in 1994 as "Love Affair." **87m/B; DVD.** Irene Dunne; Charles Boyer; Maria Ouspenskaya; Lee Bowman; Astrid Allwyn; Maurice (Moscovitch) Moscovitch; Scotty Beckett; Joan Leslie; Gerald Mohr; Dell Henderson; Carol Hughes; ***D:*** Leo McCarey; ***W:*** Leo McCarey; Delmer Daves; Donald Ogden Stewart; ***C:*** Rudolph Mate; ***M:*** Roy Webb.

Love Affair ☙☙ **1994 (PG-13)** Second remake has a contemporary look and feel but doesn't justify a new version. The photogenic leads (Beatty, Benning) may meet on a plane, but never fear, the Empire State Building and a tragedy are still the main plot devices. The problem is viewers never feel drawn into their lives. Hepburn has a small but moving role as Beatty's aunt. Superb cinematography makes it easy on the eyes and Morricone's lush romantic score makes it easy on the ears, but ultimately, it's all gloss with little substance. **108m/C; DVD.** Warren Beatty; Annette Bening; Katharine Hepburn; Garry Shandling; Chloe Webb; Pierce Brosnan; Kate Capshaw; Paul Mazursky; Brenda Vaccaro; Glenn Shadix; Barry Miller; Harold Ramis; ***D:*** Glenn Gordon Caron; ***W:*** Warren Beatty; Robert Towne; ***M:*** Ennio Morricone.

The Love Affair, or The Case of the Missing Switchboard Operator ☙☙☙ *Switchboard Operator; Case of the Missing Switchboard Operator; Ljubarni Slucaj; An Affair of the Heart* **1967** Makavejev's second film, a dissertation on the relationship between sex and politics, involving an affair between a switchboard operator and a middle-aged ex-revolutionary, is told in the director's unique, farcically disjointed manner. In Serbian with English subtitles. **73m/B; VHS, DVD.** *YU* Eva Ras; Slobodan Aligrudic; Ruzica Sokic; ***D:*** Dusan Makavejev; ***W:*** Dusan Makavejev.

Love Affair: The Eleanor & Lou Gehrig Story ☙☙☙ **1977** The true story, told from Mrs. Gehrig's point of view, of the love affair between baseball great Lou Gehrig and his wife Eleanor from his glory days as a New York Yankee, to his battle with an incurable disease. Drama supported by Herrmann and Danner's convincing portrayals. **96m/C; VHS, Streaming.** Blythe Danner; Edward Herrmann; Patricia Neal; Ramon Bieri; Lainie Kazan; ***D:*** Fielder Cook. **TV**

Love After Love ☙☙ *Apres l'Amour* **1994** A look at sex and relationships among 30-something professionals in Paris. Lola (Huppert), a successful romance novelist, is suffering a crisis in both her career and, ironically, her love life. She is involved with two men who, in turn, are involved with different women who happen to have borne them children. The movie starts off with so much mate switching and secret sexual rendezvous, that by the second half, you really don't care who Lola ends up with. French with English subtitles. **104m/C; VHS, DVD.** *FR* Isabelle Huppert; Hippolyte Girardot; Lio; ***D:*** Diane Kurys; ***W:*** Diane Kurys; Antoine Lacomblez; ***C:*** Fabio Conversi; ***M:*** Yves Simon; Serge Perathone; Jannick Top.

Love Among Thieves ☙☙½ **1986** A rare acting outing for the mature Hepburn turns out to be a routine TV crime caper although she is charmingly paired up with the shady character played by Wagner. Renowned pianist Caroline DuLac is forced to steal three Faberge eggs from a San Francisco museum as ransom for her kidnapped fiance. She's pursued by some questionable characters, including Mike who travels with Caroline to Mexico where they are captured by bandits who may be in on the plot. **94m/C; DVD.** Audrey Hepburn; Robert Wagner; Patrick Bauchau; Jerry Orbach; Brion James; Samantha Eggar; Christopher Neame; ***D:*** Roger Young; ***W:*** Stephen Black; Henry Stern; ***C:*** Gayne Rescher; ***M:*** Arthur B. Rubinstein. **TV**

Love and a .45 ☙☙ **1994 (R)** Satirical and violent road movie finds petty career criminal Watty Watts (Bellows) living in a Texas trailer park with gal Starlene (Zellweger), for whom he's just purchased an expensive engagement ring. But he's borrowed the money from some crazed gangster types who want the loan repaid in a timely fashion. Soon, the dippy duo are on the run to Mexico with a trail of dead bodies behind them and the media just delighted to make them the next tabloid darlings. **101m/C; DVD.** Renée Zellweger; Rory Cochrane; Ann Wedgeworth; Peter Fonda; Gil Bellows; Jeffrey Combs; Jace Alexander; Charlotte Ross; Michael Bowen; ***D:*** C.M. Talkington; ***W:*** C.M. Talkington; ***C:*** Tom Richmond; ***M:*** Tom Verlaine.

Love and Action in Chicago ☙☙ **1999 (R)** Eddie Jones (Vance) works for the State Department's Eliminator Corps, getting rid of anyone the government doesn't want around. Eddie wants to leave and make a new life with girlfriend Lois (King) but his bosses are pressing him to take one more job. And if he doesn't, he could become number one on the Corps hit parade. Although there's action, this one is of the black comedy variety with Vance particularly good as the reluctant hitman. **97m/C; VHS, DVD.** Courtney B. Vance; Regina King; Jason Alexander; Kathleen Turner; Ed Asner; ***D:*** Dwayne Johnson-Cochran; ***W:*** Dwayne Johnson-Cochran; ***C:*** Phil Parmet; ***M:*** Russ Landau.

Love & Air Sex ☙☙½ *The Bounceback* **2014** Hopeless romantic Stan (Stahl-David) flies from Los Angeles to Austin with the hopes of reuniting with his ex-girlfriend, Kathy (Bell). He crashes with wild man hipster Jeff (Cregger), who's training for an air sex competition (it's like playing air guitar, but down and dirty). Most of the story follows Stan trying to avoid the roadblocks set up by Kathy's friend Kara (Paxton), once she's aware of his plan. A fairly harmless romantic comedy, featuring a cast of newcomers with charisma and quirk. **91m/C; DVD, On Demand.** Ashley Bell; Michael Stahl-David; Sara Paxton; Zach Cregger; Addison Timlin; ***D:*** Brian Poyser; ***W:*** Brian Poyser; Steven Walters; David DeGrow Shotwell; ***C:*** P.J. Raval.

Love and Anarchy ☙☙☙ *Film d'Amore et d'Anarchia* **1973** An oppressed peasant vows to assassinate Mussolini after a close friend is murdered. Powerful drama about the rise of Italian facism. In Italian with English subtitles. **108m/C; VHS, DVD, Blu-Ray.** *IT* Giancarlo Giannini; Mariangela Melato; ***D:*** Lina Wertmuller; ***W:*** Lina Wertmuller; ***C:*** Giuseppe Rotunno; ***M:*** Nino Rota. Cannes '73: Actor (Giannini).

Love and Basketball ☙☙☙ **2000 (R)** Childhood friends and high school sweethearts Monica (Lathan) and Quincy (Epps) pursue their dreams of pro basketball careers and try to sort out their feelings for each other over a 12-year period. First-time director Prince-Bythewood avoids the cliches of most sports movies by removing the Big Game climax and replacing it with thoughtful character study and the understanding of the sacrifices athletes make to excel at their chosen profession. Leads Lathan and Epps are impressive. **124m/C; VHS, DVD, Blu-Ray.** Omar Epps; Sanaa Lathan; Alfre Woodard; Dennis Haysbert; Debbi (Deborah) Morgan; Harry J. Lennix; Kyla Pratt; Glenndon Chatman; ***D:*** Gina Prince-Bythewood; ***W:*** Gina Prince-Bythewood; ***C:*** Reynaldo Villalobos; ***M:*** Terence Blanchard.

Love and Bullets ☙½ **1979 (PG)** An Arizona homicide detective is sent on a special assignment to Switzerland to bring a mobster's girlfriend back to the United States to testify against him in court. **95m/C; VHS, Streaming.** *GB* Charles Bronson; Jill Ireland; Rod Steiger; Strother Martin; Bradford Dillman; Henry Silva; Michael V. Gazzo; ***D:*** Stuart Rosenberg; ***W:*** Wendell Mayes; ***C:*** Fred W. Koenekamp; ***M:*** Lalo Schifrin.

Love and Death ☙☙☙ **1975 (PG)** In 1812 Russia, a condemned man reviews the follies of his life. Woody Allen's satire on "War and Peace," and every other major Russian novel. **89m/C; VHS, DVD, Blu-Ray.** Woody Allen; Diane Keaton; Georges Adel; Despo Diamantidou; Frank Adu; Harold Gould; ***D:*** Woody Allen; ***W:*** Woody Allen; ***C:*** Ghislan Cloquet.

Love and Death on Long Island ☙☙½ **1997 (PG-13)** Stuffy English author Giles De'Ath (Hurt), barely on speaking terms with the 20th century, accidentally encounters a teen exploitation flick and is meserized by star Ronnie Bostock (Priestley). De'Ath's obsession leads to his discovery of fan magazines, TV, and video, as he comes to grips with modern media. It also leads Giles to seek out Bostock at his home on Long Island, where Hurt shines as Giles tries to reconcile his dignity and increasingly irrational behavior. Priestley does a fine job lampooning his own image and the supporting characters are appropriately quirky. Subtle reworking of "Death in Venice," based on Gilbert Adair's novel. **93m/C; DVD.** *UK CA* John Hurt; Jason Priestley; Fiona Loewi; Sheila Hancock; Maury Chaykin; Gawn Grainger; Elizabeth Quinn; Danny (Daniel) Webb; ***D:*** Richard Kwietniowski; ***W:*** Richard Kwietniowski; ***C:*** Oliver Curtis; ***M:*** Richard Grassby-Lewis.

Love and Debate ☙☙ *Thanks to Gravity* **2006** Miami-born Jordan (Philips) is a Jewish-Latina who wins a scholarship to Harvard thanks to her debating skills. She's pursued by a couple of cute guys but, after being raped by a debate opponent at a party, Jordan quits the team. Eventually deciding to pursue her oratory skills again, Jordan makes it to the national finals—only to be confronted by her rapist, who is her debate opponent. **95m/C; DVD.** Gina Philips; Adam Rodriguez; Bryan Greenberg; Austin Nichols; Sean Astin; Shirley Knight; Joaquim de Almeida; Rachel Miner; Chris Mulkey; Azura Skye; Sendhil Ramamurthy; ***D:*** Jessica Kavana; ***W:*** Jessica Kavana; ***C:*** Mauricio Rubinstein; ***M:*** Jeff Cardoni.

Love & Friendship ☙☙☙ **2016 (PG)** It turns out that Jane Austen and Whit Stillman are a perfect match, even though this film is based on Austen's "Lady Susan," not her story that shares a name with it. In the 1790s, Lady Susan Vernon (Beckinsale) intends to find a love match for her daughter Frederica (Clark). What follows is a pretty standard Austen tale of class and relationships, but Stillman has an amazing ability to make the period dialogue and dynamics feel fresh. It helps that Beckinsale and Sevigny do solid work. **92m/C; DVD, Blu-Ray.** Kate Beckinsale; Morfydd Clark; Tom Bennett; Jenn Murray; Lochlann O'Mearain; Eimer Ni Mhaoldomhnaigh; ***D:*** Whit Stillman; ***W:*** Whit Stillman; ***C:*** Richard Van Oosterhout; ***M:*** Benjamin Esdraffo.

Love and Human Remains ☙☙☙ **1993 (R)** Director Arcand's first English-language film features a group of friends trying to come to grips with their place in the world (and their sexuality). Amoral David (Gibson) doesn't believe in love and only manages casual gay relationships while hanging with his pals and their varying sexual natures. Melodramatic framing story about a serial killer who may, or may not, be one of the principal characters proves somewhat of a distraction. Lots of caustically witty dialogue and some fine performances. Adaptation of the play "Unidentified Human Remains and the True Nature of Love" by Fraser, who also did the screenplay. **100m/C; DVD.** *CA* Thomas Gibson; Ruth Marshall; Cameron Bancroft; Mia Kirshner; Joanne Vannicola; Matthew Ferguson; Rick Roberts; ***D:*** Denys Arcand; ***W:*** Brad Fraser; ***C:*** Paul Sarossy. Genie '94: Adapt. Screenplay.

Love and Mary ☙☙ **2007 (PG-13)** Pastry chef Mary (German) is facing eviction from her struggling bakery so she decides to collect on a sizeable engagement gift by hauling her fiance Brent (Mann) home to Houston to meet her eccentric family. When Brent is unable to travel, resourceful Mary bails his n'er-do-well twin brother Jake out of jail to pass him off as her intended. Of course, she just may realize that she's engaged to the wrong brother. **104m/C; DVD.** Lauren German; Gabriel Mann; Whitney Able; Tommy Townsend; Mary Bonner Baker; Bonnie Gallup; Brian Thornton; ***D:*** Elizabeth Harrison; ***W:*** Elizabeth Harrison; ***C:*** Brad Rushing; ***M:*** Tony Tisdale.

Love & Mercy 🦴🦴🦴 **2015 (PG-13)** Jumping back and forth in time, the story of Beach Boys' sad genius Brian Wilson begins in the late 60s with Paul Dano as a floppy-haired perfectionist crafting his masterpiece, "Pet Sounds". Skipping to the '80s, Cusack delivers a world-worn Wilson, medicated and under the thumb of manipulative therapist Eugene Landy (Giamatti). Despite two very different interpretations of the same musical madman, the performances cut to the heart of Wilson's enigmatic practices. Avoids the usual biopic cliches, taking successful risks, while thankfully never attempting to one-up their subjects flair for the experimental. **120m/C; DVD, Blu-Ray, Streaming.** Paul Dano; Elizabeth Banks; Brett Davern; Graham Rogers; John Cusack; Paul Giamatti; ***D:*** Bill Pohlad; ***W:*** Michael Alan Lerner; Oren Moverman; ***C:*** Robert Yeoman; ***M:*** Atticus Ross.

Love and Money 🦴 ½ **1980 (R)** Convoluted thriller, filmed in 1980 but not released until 1982, features the only acting appearance of legendary director King Vidor as the grandfather of bored L.A. investment banker Byron Levin (Sharkey). Byron allows himself to get involved with shady billionaire Frederick Stockheinz (Kinski) who's trying to set-up a mining operation in a silver-rich Latin American country in the midst of a political revolution—and with his sexy wife Catherine (Muti), just to make his life more complicated. **90m/C; DVD.** Ray Sharkey; Klaus Kinski; Ornella Muti; Armand Assante; King Vidor; ***D:*** James Toback; ***W:*** James Toback; ***C:*** Fred Schuler.

Love and Other Disasters 🦴 ½ **2006 (R)** Romantic comedy that will remind you of many other such flicks. Free-spirited Emily "Jacks" Jackson (Murphy, trying a little too hard to be winsome and kooky) lives in London and works for a British fashion mag. She shares a flat with gay best friend Peter (Rhys), a struggling screenwriter, whom she's always trying to set up with Mr. Right. When Jacks meets hot Argentine photo assistant Paolo (Cabrera), she's convinced he's the man for Peter. But that's not who Paolo is actually interested in. Gwyneth Paltrow and Orlando Bloom have last act cameos. **90m/C; DVD.** *GB* Brittany Murphy; Matthew Rhys; Santiago Cabrera; Catherine Tate; Elliot Cowan; Stephanie Beacham; Jamie Sives; Michael Lerner; ***D:*** Alek Keshishian; ***W:*** Alek Keshishian; ***C:*** Pierre Morel; ***M:*** Alexandre Azaria.

Love and Other Drugs 🦴🦴 ½ **2010 (R)** Jaime Randall (Gyllenhaal) is a pharmaceutical rep riding the erectile dysfunction wave right out of Ohio to the Windy City. Through a bizarre series of events, he meets Maggie (Hathaway), a waitress and wannabe artist. The two quickly and frequently hop in the sack, and this would be a fun rom-com if not for Maggie's revelation that she is suffering with the early stages of Parkinson's disease. While there are genuine moments (both funny and sad) and the leads are compelling, the film never really pulls it all together. Based onJamie Reidy's autobiography "Hard Sell: The Evolution of a Viagra Salesman." **113m/C; DVD, Blu-Ray.** Jake Gyllenhaal; Anne Hathaway; Hank Azaria; Oliver Platt; George Segal; Scott Cohen; Josh Gad; Katheryn Winnick; Natalie Gold; ***D:*** Edward Zwick; ***W:*** Edward Zwick; Charles Randolph; Marshall Herskovitz; ***C:*** Steven Fierberg; ***M:*** James Newton Howard.

Love and Other Four Letter Words 🦴🦴 ½ **2007 (R)** Attractive cast, good romance vibes. Stormy LaRue (Miller) sounds like she should be an exotic dancer but she's actually a TV talk show host. She would do anything to please her dying Nana (Wright), including lying about getting married. Soon, Stormy's lie is spinning out of control as she plans for her fake wedding, even auditioning grooms. But when Nana sends her childhood friend Arnold (Alexander), now a pastor, to perform the ceremony, Stormy finds herself truly falling in love and wondering how she can turn her lie into the truth. **87m/C; DVD.** Tangi Miller; Flex Alexander; Marcus Patrick; Aloma Wright; Essence Atkins; Tasha Smith; ***D:*** Steven Ayromlooi; ***W:*** Mandel Holland; ***C:*** Jose Estrada Aguirre; David Daniel; ***M:*** Todd Cochran. **VIDEO**

Love and Pain and the Whole Damn Thing 🦴🦴 **1973** Clumsy middle-aged British spinster Lila (Smith) is on a bus tour in Spain when she is suddenly wooed by insecure young American misfit Walter (Bottom), who's bicycling through the countryside. But their oddball happiness can't last since Lila has a terminal illness. Not quite "Harold and Maude" but eccentrically charming. **110m/C; DVD.** Maggie Smith; Timothy Bottoms; Charles Baxter; Margaret Modlin; Elmer Modling; ***D:*** Alan J. Pakula; ***W:*** Alvin Sargent; ***C:*** Geoffrey Unsworth; ***M:*** Michael Small.

Love and Rage 🦴🦴 **1999 (R)** James Lynchehaun (Craig) turns up on the remote island of Achill in 1896 and soon gets a job looking after the estate of wealthy widow Agnes MacDonnell (Scacchi). He also becomes her lover and the two engage in some unnerving psycho-sexual games that lead to Agnes' being brutalized by James. Based on a true story; adapted from the novel "The Playboy and the Yellow Lady" by James Carney. **100m/C; VHS, DVD.** *IR GE GB* Daniel Craig; Greta Scacchi; Stephen (Dillon) Dillane; Donal Donnelly; Valerie Edmond; ***D:*** Cathal Black; ***W:*** Brian Lynch; ***C:*** Slawomir Idziak; ***M:*** Ralf Wienrich.

Love & Sex 🦴🦴 ½ **2000** Kate's (Janssen) a manic L.A. magazine writer who's almost fired over her inability to write about good relationships because of her own failures. She remembers her romance with doughy artist Adam (Favreau), which is traced from its initial spark to its last gasp and Adam breaking things off. Kate then attempts to make Adam jealous by dating a string of pretty-boy losers, setting the stage for the inevitable happy ending. Good performances and chemistry between the lead actors saves this indie effort from feeling like a really long sitcom episode. **82m/C; VHS, DVD.** Famke Janssen; Jon Favreau; Noah Emmerich; Ann Magnuson; Cheri Oteri; Josh Hopkins; Robert Knepper; Vincent Ventresca; ***D:*** Valerie Breiman; ***W:*** Valerie Breiman; ***C:*** Adam Kane.

Love and the Frenchwoman 🦴🦴🦴 *La Francaise et L'Amour* **1960** A French tale tracing the nature of love through stages. Deals with a story about where babies come from, puppy love, saving sex for marriage, and the way some men treat women. **135m/B; VHS, DVD.** *FR* Jean-Paul Belmondo; Pierre-Jean Vaillard; Marie-Jose Nat; Annie Girardot; ***D:*** Jean Delannoy; ***M:*** Georges Delerue.

Love, Antosha 🦴🦴🦴 **2019 (R)** Actor Anton Yelchin tragically died in a 2016 accident at only 27. The son of Russian figure skaters, Anton was interested in acting from an early age. He worked in film and television, most notably playing Chekov in a revival of Star Trek. Through home videos and interviews with family, friends, and coworkers, his boundless curiosity about the world and his secret battle with cystic fibrosis are revealed. An emotional reflection that beautifully shares the life of a vibrant young man, whose letters to his beloved mother were signed "Love, Antosha." **92m/C; DVD.** Anton Yelchin; ***D:*** Garrett Price; ***C:*** Radan Popovic; ***M:*** Saul Simon MacWilliams.

Love at First Bite 🦴🦴 ½ **1979 (PG)** Intentionally campy spoof of the vampire film. Dracula is forced to leave his Transylvanian home as the Rumanian government has designated his castle a training center for young gymnasts. Once in New York, the Count takes in the night life and falls in love with a woman whose boyfriend embarks on a campaign to warn the city of Dracula's presence. Hamilton of the never-fading tan is appropriately tongue-in-cheek in a role which resurrected his career. **93m/C; VHS, DVD.** George Hamilton; Susan St. James; Richard Benjamin; Dick Shawn; Arte Johnson; Sherman Hemsley; Isabel Sanford; Barry J. Gordon; Michael Pataki; Basil Hoffman; Eric Laneuville; ***D:*** Stan Dragoti; ***W:*** Robert Kaufman; ***M:*** Charles Bernstein.

Love at First Kill 🦴 ½ *The Box Collector* **2008** Crazy mom alert! Artist Henry (Segan) lives with his long-widowed, overprotective mom Beth (Kidder). Beth's paranoia goes into overdrive when sexy divorcee Marie (Renee) and her daughter Kiki (Moffat) move in next door. Henry is soon babysitting Kiki and he and Marie get romantically involved, to Beth's horror. She's determined to keep Henry from leaving her but how far will she go? **94m/C; DVD.** Noah Segan; Margot Kidder; Lyne Renee; Anna Moffat; Victor Low; Michael Bowen; Adriana O'Neil; ***D:*** John Daly; ***W:*** Guy Lee Thys; ***C:*** Jan Kiesser; ***M:*** Stephen Warbeck. **VIDEO**

Love at Large 🦴🦴🦴 **1989 (R)** Hired by a beautiful woman, a private detective accidentally follows the wrong man and winds up being followed himself. He vies with a female detective in solving this case of mistaken identity. **90m/C; VHS, DVD, Blu-Ray.** Tom Berenger; Elizabeth Perkins; Anne Archer; Ann Magnuson; Annette O'Toole; Kate Capshaw; Ted Levine; Kevin J. O'Connor; Ruby Dee; Neil Young; Barry Miller; ***D:*** Alan Rudolph; ***W:*** Alan Rudolph; ***C:*** Elliot Davis.

Love at Stake 🦴🦴 ½ **1987 (R)** It's condo owners versus the witches in this charming parody that features a hilarious cameo by Dr. Joyce Brothers and a very sexy performance from Carrera. **83m/C; VHS, DVD.** Patrick Cassidy; Kelly Preston; Bud Cort; Barbara Carrera; Stuart Pankin; Dave Thomas; Georgia Brown; Annie Golden; ***Cameo(s):*** Dr. Joyce Brothers; ***D:*** John Moffitt; ***M:*** Charles Fox.

Love at the Christmas Table 🦴🦴 **2012** Cute but unremarkable Lifetime movie. Kat and Sam have spent nearly every Christmas Eve together with their families since they sat together at the children's table. Now, Sam's 30 and he's finally ready to admit that Kat's his soulmate--only to fear he's too late telling her. **90m/C; DVD.** Danica McKellar; Dustin Milligan; Alexandra Paul; Lea Thompson; ***D:*** Rachel Goldenberg; ***W:*** Patrick Hobby; ***C:*** Damian Horan; ***M:*** Christian Davis. **CABLE**

Love at the Thanksgiving Day Parade 🦴🦴 **2012** A Hallmark Channel holiday romance. Chicago native Emily Jones is the coordinator of the city's Thanksgiving Day parade. However, this year the director has hired consultant Henry Williams to analyze the parade's finances and increase profits. Emily's afraid Henry will ruin the holiday spirit, but he turns out to be an ally when she has an unexpected setback. **85m/C; DVD.** Autumn Reeser; Antonio Cupo; Ben Cotton; April Telek; ***D:*** Ron Oliver; ***W:*** Nancey Silvers; ***C:*** C. Kim Miles; ***M:*** Peter Allen. **CABLE**

Love Beat the Hell Outta Me 🦴🦴 **2000 (R)** Four friends get together for what's supposed to be a friendly game of dominos, only to find some serious rivalries surfacing. **89m/C; VHS, DVD.** Glenn Plummer; Terrence Howard; Clyde Jones; Charles R. Penland; ***D:*** Kennedy Goldsby; ***W:*** Kennedy Goldsby.

Love Before Breakfast 🦴🦴 ½ **1936** Kay (Lombard) is engaged to ambitious Bill (Romero) who works for mogul Scott (Foster), who wants to marry Kay himself. Scott temporarily sends the competition off to a job in Japan and Kay does fall for Scott. At least until the extent of his machinations is revealed; then she becomes stubbornly determined to resist his he-man charms. Foster's character is rather bullying and Lombard's turn shrill but there's still a screwball charm to the proceedings. **70m/B; DVD.** Carole Lombard; Preston Foster; Cesar Romero; Janet Beecher; Betty Lawford; Richard Carle; Joyce Compton; Mia Ichioka; ***D:*** Walter Lang; ***W:*** Herbert Fields; ***C:*** Ted Tetzlaff; ***M:*** Franz Waxman.

Love Begins 🦴🦴 ½ **2011** Inspired by the "Love Comes Softly" series by Janette Oke and shown on the Hallmark Channel. The Barlow sisters struggle to maintain the family farm after their father's death. Cowboy Clark Davis' brawl causes damages in town and he works off his debt by helping out at the farm though Ellen Barlow tries to stay aloof. This doesn't last long as love finds a way. Followed by "Love's Everlasting Courage." **88m/C; DVD.** Julie Mond; Wes Brown; Jere Burns; Abigail Mavity; Nancy McKeon; David Tom; ***D:*** David S. Cass, Sr.; ***W:*** Michael Moran; ***C:*** Maximo Munzi; ***M:*** Stephen McKeon. **CABLE**

Love Between the Covers 🦴🦴 **2015** This feature-length documentary provides an insightful look into the billion dollar romance fiction industry. Noting that romance novels outsell mystery, science fiction, and fantasy combined, the documentary examines the community of romance writers and readers by focusing on six writers in particular. The film follows them for three years of their lives as they blaze trails and manage upheavals in their lives. **95m/C; DVD, Streaming, Download.** ***D:*** Laurie Kahn; ***W:*** Laurie Kahn; ***C:*** Joseph Friedman. **VIDEO**

The Love Bug 🦴🦴 ½ **1968 (G)** A race car driver (Jones) is followed home by Herbie, a white Volkswagen with a mind of its own. Eventually, Jones follows the "Love Bug" to a life of madcap fun. Followed by several sequels. **110m/C; VHS, DVD, Blu-Ray.** Dean Jones; Michele Lee; Hope Lange; Robert Reed; Bert Convy; ***D:*** Robert Stevenson; ***C:*** Edward Colman; ***M:*** George Bruns.

Love Butcher 🦴 ½ **1982 (R)** A crippled old gardener kills his female employers with his garden tools and cleans up neatly afterward. **84m/C; VHS, DVD, Blu-Ray.** Erik Stern; Kay Neer; Robin Sherwood; ***D:*** Mikel Angel; Donald M. Jones.

Love by Appointment 🦴 **1976** An unlikely romantic comedy with a very unlikely cast has two businessmen meeting up with European prostitutes. **96m/C; VHS, DVD.** *IT* Ernest Borgnine; Robert Alda; Francoise Fabian; Corinne Clery; ***D:*** Armando Nannuzzi; ***M:*** Riz Ortolani. **TV**

Love by the 10th Date 🦴🦴 **2017** A romantic comedy about four women seeking real connections. Best friends Gabrielle (Good), Nell (Stewart), Margot (Rowland), and Billie (Hilson) work at an online magazine. Gabrielle doubts she will have find a real love interest because she has never had 10 dates with a man. Her quest inspires them to have her write an article about getting to the tenth date. At the same time, Gabrielle's friends have their own romantic issues. Margot, for example, finds her celibacy challenged by a musician. While helping Gabrielle, each woman must make a future-defining decision. A sense of sisterhood adds to the predictable movie's appeal. **87m/C; DVD.** Meagan Good; Brandon T. Jackson; Kellee Stewart; Keri Hilson; Kelly Rowland; ***D:*** Nzingha Stewart; ***W:*** Nzingha Stewart; ***C:*** Byron Shah; ***M:*** Laura Karpman; Raphael Saadiq.

Love Camp 🦴 *Divine Emmanuelle* **1981** A woman is invited to a swinger's holiday camp, frolics for a while, then is told she can never leave. Suspenseful hijinks ensue. **100m/C; VHS, DVD.** *GE* Laura Gemser; Christian Anders; Gabriele Tinti; ***D:*** Christian Anders; ***W:*** Christian Anders; ***C:*** Vassilis Christomoglou; ***M:*** Christian Anders.

Love Can Seriously Damage Your Health 🦴🦴 ½ *Amor Perjudica Seriamente la Salud* **1996** At a gala dinner Santi (Puigcorbe) and Diana (Belen) are reunited. Thirty years before, young Beatles fan Diana (Cruz) hides out in John Lennon's room when the group comes to Madrid, reluctantly aided by young hotel bellman Santi (Diego). It's love at first sight and they spend the intervening years falling in and out of a crazy romance. Spanish with subtitles. **118m/C; VHS, DVD.** *SP* Ana Belen; Penelope Cruz; Gabino Diego; Janjo Puigcorbe; Carles Sans; Lola Herrera; ***D:*** Manuel Gomez Pereira; ***W:*** Manuel Gomez Pereira; ***C:*** Juan Amoros.

Love, Cheat & Steal 🦴🦴 **1993 (R)** Convicted murderer Reno Adams (Roberts) breaks out of prison when he hears that his luscious ex (Amick) has just married another man (Lithgow). He turns up on her door, threatening to destroy her new life, but things aren't exactly what they seem. Faux noir. **95m/C; VHS, DVD.** Eric Roberts; Madchen Amick; John Lithgow; Richard Edson; Donald Moffat; David Ackroyd; Dan O'Herlihy; ***D:*** William Curran; ***W:*** William Curran.

Love Child 🦴🦴 **1982 (R)** The story of a young woman in prison who becomes pregnant by a guard and fights to have and keep her baby. **97m/C; VHS, DVD.** Amy Madigan; Beau Bridges; MacKenzie Phillips; Albert Salmi; *D:* Larry Peerce; *M:* Charles Fox.

Love Come Down 2000 (R) Matthew (Cummins) is white; his half-brother Neville (Tate) is black. Their mother is in prison for killing Neville's abusive father but there's a definite question about her guilt. Both boys have been hugely affected by their pasts—Matthew puts his anger into his boxing career while Neville has become a drug addicted stand-up comic. Neville tries to stay clean when he falls for a singer (Cox) with her own family issues but the brothers also have to lay their traumatic past to rest. **102m/C; DVD.** *CA* Larenz Tate; Martin Cummins; Sarah Polley; Deborah Cox; Travis Davis; Jake LeDoux; Rainbow Sun Francks; Barbara Williams; Peter Williams; Clark Johnson; Kenneth Welsh; Jennifer Dale; Naomi Gaskin; *D:* Clement Virgo; *W:* Clement Virgo; *C:* Dylan Mcleod; *M:* Aaron Davis; John Lang. Genie '01: Sound, Support. Actor (Cummins).

Love Comes Lately 2007 Elderly Austrian emigre Max (Tausig) continues to write stories, deliver college lectures, and romance the ladies though his reality is now getting confused with his fictional world. Various mishaps while traveling have Max writing a new story, which he reads at a lecture, which then segues into another of his fictional worlds. This blurring isn't as confusing as it seems because of the sly charm of octogenarian actor Tausig. Based on the stories of Isaac Bashevis Singer. **86m/C; DVD.** Barbara Hershey; Tovah Feldshuh; Rhea Perlman; Elizabeth Pena; Otto Tausig; Caroline Aaron; *D:* Jan Schuette; *W:* Jan Schuette; *C:* Edward Klosinski; Chris Squires; *M:* Henning Lohner.

Love Comes Softly 1/2 2003 Marty Claridge (Heigl) has just moved west with her husband when he suddenly dies. Alone and afraid, she accepts the offer of widowed neighbor Clark Davis (Midkiff) to becomes his housekeeper and look after his tomboy daughter Missie (Bartusiak). Naturally as Marty and Missie slowly bond, Clark and the pretty widow gradually find themselves growing closer. Adapted from the first book in inspirational author Janette Oke's series. **88m/C; DVD.** Katherine Heigl; Dale Midkiff; Skye McCole Bartusiak; Corbin Bernsen; Theresa Russell; *D:* Michael Landon, Jr.; *W:* Michael Landon, Jr.; Cindy Kelley; *C:* James W. Wrenn; *M:* Ken Thorne; William Ashford. **CABLE**

Love Crazy 1/2 1941 Powell and Loy team once again for a non-"Thin Man" romp through a married-people farce. Via a nosy mother-in-law and a series of misunderstandings, Powell and Loy squabble almost to the point of divorce. Not the wry wit the team was known for, but zany, high-action comedy at its best. **99m/B; VHS, DVD.** William Powell; Myrna Loy; Gail Patrick; Jack Carson; Florence Bates; Sidney Blackmer; Sig Ruman; *D:* Jack Conway.

Love Crime *Crime d'Amour* 2010 Psycho-thriller is a corporate and sexual battle between ruthless manager Christine (Scott Thomas) and her one-time protege Isabelle (Sagnier). Christine steals Isabelle's ideas, humiliates her (after being humiliated herself) and blackmails accountant Philippe (Mille), who's involved with both women. Ambitious Isabelle soon plots revenge in more ways than one. Writer/director Corneau's last film. English and French with subtitles. **107m/C; DVD.** *FR* Kristin Scott Thomas; Ludivine Sagnier; Patrick Mille; Marie Guillard; *D:* Alain Corneau; *W:* Alain Corneau; Natalie Carter; *C:* Yves Angelo; *M:* Pharoah Sanders.

A Love Divided 2001 In 1950s Ireland, Protestant Sheila Kelly (Brady) marries Catholic Sean Cloney (Cunningham) and signs an agreement to raise their children Catholic. When it comes time for their daughter Eileen (Bolger) to attend school, however, a battle emerges over religion between the parents and esclates into a situation that divides the village. So Sheila flees with her two daughters to Scotland. Heavy-handed, melodramatic script with one-dimensional characters offering little sympathy for anyone involved. Based on a true story. **98m/C; DVD.** Orla Brady; Liam Cunningham; Brian McGrath; Sarah Bolger; Nicole Bohan; Peter Caffrey; Tony Doyle; Ali White; *D:* Syd Macartney; *W:* Deirdre Dowling; Gerry Gregg; Stuart Hepburn; *C:* Cedric Culliton; *M:* Fiachra Trench.

Love Don't Cost a Thing 1/2 2003 (PG-13) Amusing remake of the 1987 movie "Can't Buy Me Love." Alvin Johnson (Cannon) pays the most popular girl in high school, Paris Morgan (Milian), to pretend to be his girlfriend for two weeks in order to be popular. Charming leads make this one a touch better than the original. **101m/C; VHS, DVD.** Nick Cannon; Christina Milian; Kenan Thompson; Kal Penn; Steve Harvey; Vanessa Bell Calloway; Al Thompson; *D:* Troy Beyer; *W:* Troy Beyer; Michael Swerdlick; *C:* Chuck Cohen; *M:* Richard Gibbs.

Love, etc. 1996 Another messy romantic triangle played for both comedy and tragedy. Shy, thirtysomething bank employee Benoit (Attal) takes out a personal ad, but supplies a picture of his egocentric best friend Pierre (Berling) instead of his own. He meets twentysomething art restorer Marie (Gainsbourg) and, despite the deception and the fact that she's not swept away by romantic passion, Marie marries him. Then Benoit discovers that Pierre thinks he's in love with Marie and has decided to win her away—and she's torn by the attention. Based on the novel "Taking It Over" by Julian Barnes. French with subtitles. **105m/C; VHS, DVD.** *FR* Charlotte Gainsbourg; Yvan Attal; Charles Berling; *D:* Marion Vernoux; *W:* Marion Vernoux; Dodine Herry; *C:* Eric Gautier; *M:* Leonard Cohen; Alexandre Desplat.

Love Field 1/2 1991 (PG-13) Pfeiffer is a Jackie Kennedy-obsessed hairdresser who decides to travel by bus to D.C. when she hears about President Kennedy's assassination. Along the way she gets involved in an interracial friendship with the secretive Haysbert, who's traveling with his young daughter. Pfieffer's Lurene is basically a sweet dim bulb and Haysbert has an unfortunately written one-note character (mainly exasperation). The six-year-old McFadden (in her debut) makes the most impact. **104m/C; VHS, DVD.** Michelle Pfeiffer; Dennis Haysbert; Stephanie McFadden; Brian Kerwin; Louise Latham; Peggy Rea; Beth Grant; Cooper Huckabee; Mark Miller; Johnny Rae McGhee; *D:* Jonathan Kaplan; *W:* Don Roos; *C:* Ralf Bode; *M:* Jerry Goldsmith.

Love Film *Szerelmesfilm; A Film about Love* 1970 A train trip from Budapest, Hungary to Lyon, France leads a young man to recall his past as he journeys to visit a childhood sweetheart. Jancsi and Kata's friendship has been disrupted by the 1956 uprising and Jancsi wonders if the love once developing between them has been broken by distance and time. In Hungarian with English subtitles. **123m/C; VHS, DVD.** *HU* Andras Balint; Judit Halasz; Edit Kelemen; Andras Szamosfalvi; *D:* Istvan Szabo; *W:* Istvan Szabo; *C:* Josef Lorinc.

Love Finds a Home 1/2 2009 A Hallmark Channel movie, the sequel to "Love Finds a Wing," that's based on the novels by Janette Oke. Dr. Belinda Simpson Owens (Jones) is now married to blacksmith Lee (Bridges) and they have adopted the orphaned Lillian (Halverson). However, Belinda is dismayed that she seemingly cannot have children of her own and her feelings are heightened when her pregnant friend Annie (Duff) comes to visit. Belinda suspects there's a health problem but she continually clashes with Annie's mother-in-law Mary (Duke), a midwife who seems set in her ways. **88m/C; DVD.** Sarah Jones; Jordan Bridges; Haylie Duff; Patty Duke; Courtney Halverson; Dahlia Salem; Thomas Kopache; *D:* David S. Cass, Sr.; *W:* Donald Davenport; *C:* Dane Peterson; *M:* Stephen Graziano. **CABLE**

Love Finds Andy Hardy 1938 Young Andy Hardy finds himself torn between three girls before returning to the girl next door. Garland's first appearance in the acclaimed Andy Hardy series features her singing "In Between" and "Meet the Best of my Heart." **90m/B; DVD.** Mickey Rooney; Judy Garland; Lana Turner; Ann Rutherford; Fay Holden; Lewis Stone; Marie Blake; Cecilia Parker; Gene Reynolds; *D:* George B. Seitz; *W:* William Ludwig; *C:* Lester White; *M:* David Snell. Natl. Film Reg. '00.

The Love Flower 1/2 1920 A man kills his second wife's lover and escapes with his daughter to a tropical island, pursued by a detective and a young adventurer. Interesting ending wraps things up nicely. Silent. **70m/B; Silent; VHS, DVD.** Carol Dempster; Richard Barthelmess; George MacQuarrie; Anders Randolph; Florence Short; *D:* D.W. Griffith; *W:* D.W. Griffith.

Love for Lydia 1979 British TV miniseries following wayward beauty Lydia, orphaned heiress to a manufacturing fortune, through the high-spirited 1920s. Set in the industrial Midlands and farming communities of England, Lydia dazzles every man she meets, often to an unhappy end. Based on the novel by H.E. Bates. Available as a boxed set. **657m/C; VHS, DVD.** *GB* Mel Martin; Peter Davison; Jeremy Irons; Michael Aldridge; Rachel Kempson; Beatrix Lehmann; *D:* John Glenister; Simon Langton; Tony Wharmby; *W:* Julian Bond; *C:* Tony Maynard; Jeff Shepherd. **TV**

Love for Rent 1/2 2005 (R) Slight romantic comedy finds Colombian immigrant Sofia's (Cepeda) life falling apart when her green card hubby (Rowe) steals their money. Sofia has big dreams, so rather than return home she becomes a surrogate mother for a wealthy, eccentric couple (Piddock, Dunn). But how will Sofia explain the situation to her new doctor boyfriend Neil (Marino)? **90m/C; DVD.** Ken Marino; Nora Dunn; Jim Piddock; Brad Rowe; Angie Cepeda; Richard Speight, Jr.; Martita Rosa; Max Burkholder; *D:* Shane Edelman; *W:* Andrew Miles; *C:* David Rush Morrison; *M:* Jeff Cardoni.

Love from a Stranger 1937 Thriller about a working woman who wins a lottery. Soon she is charmed by and marries a man whom she later suspects may be trying to kill her. Remade in 1947. **90m/B; VHS, DVD.** *GB* Ann Harding; Basil Rathbone; Binnie Hale; Bruce Seton; Bryan Powley; Jean Cadell; *D:* Rowland V. Lee.

The Love God? 1/2 1970 (PG-13) Very silly comedy finds mild-mannered Abner Peacock (Knotts) trying on Hugh Hefner's mantle. With his bird-watcher's magazine in financial trouble, Abner takes on a couple of shifty partners who change it into a different kind of bird watching magazine (the nude female kind) that gets Abner charged with pornography and finds him becoming a (very) unlikely sex symbol. **103m/C; VHS, DVD.** Don Knotts; Edmond O'Brien; Anne Francis; Maureen Arthur; James Gregory; Margaret (Maggie) Peterson; Marjorie Bennett; *D:* Nat Hiken; *W:* Nat Hiken; *C:* William Margulies; *M:* Vic Mizzy.

The Love Goddesses 1965 A 60-year examination of some of the most beautiful women on the silver screen, reflecting with extraordinary accuracy the customs, manners and mores of the times. Released theatrically in 1972. **83m/B; VHS, DVD.** Marlene Dietrich; Greta Garbo; Jean Harlow; Gloria Swanson; Mae West; Betty Grable; Rita Hayworth; Elizabeth Taylor; Marilyn Monroe; Theda Bara; Claudette Colbert; Dorothy Lamour; Lillian Gish; Sophia Loren; *Nar:* Carl King; *D:* Saul J. Turell; *W:* Saul J. Turell; Graeme Ferguson.

Love Goggles 1999 A low-budget indie that tries to do some interesting things with titles, narration, and monologues to break up the familiar plot before it turns preachy. Nightclub owner and ladies man Topcat (David) is afraid of losing his best friend and fellow player Ollie (Jacoby) to potential new girlfriend Mona (Campbell). However, if he follows Topcat's misogynistic views, Ollie isn't going to have to worry about Mona sticking around. But then those 'love goggles' on his heart are focusing all Ollie's thoughts on romance. **106m/C; DVD.** Trevor David; Ruby Campbell; Steven Peacock Jacoby; Q-Tip; Kirk "Sticky Fingaz" Jones; *D:* Anthony Travis.

The Love Guru 2008 (PG-13) Guru Pitka (Myers), an American raised in an Indian ashram, becomes the world's number two guru, behind real-life romantic mystic and on-screen buddy Deepak Chopra. Things get nutty after the owner (Alba) of the Toronto Maple Leafs hires Pitka to reignite the flame between a hockey star and his estranged wife. Pitka deals with the team's dwarf coach (Troyer), fights off enemies using urine-soaked mops (his specialty, kid you not), and hams it up in lame music video spoofs. Myers spends the entire movie cackling at his own dopey, unfunny wisecracks. **88m/C; Blu-Ray.** Mike Myers; Jessica Alba; Romany Malco; Justin Timberlake; Meagan Good; Verne Troyer; Ben Kingsley; Telma Hopkins; Omid Djalili; Stephen Colbert; Jim Gaffigan; Manu Narayan; John Oliver; *Cameo(s):* Deepak Chopra; *D:* Marco Schnabel; *W:* Mike Myers; Graham Gordy; *C:* Peter Deming; *M:* George S. Clinton. Golden Raspberries '08: Worst Actor (Myers), Worst Picture, Worst Screenplay.

Love Happens *Brand New Day* 2009 (PG-13) Clunky, tear-filled (it's wetter than the Seattle setting) rom com that's not very funny and has a cookie-cutter romance with attractive but mismatched leads. Motivational speaker Burke Ryan (Eckhart) is still devastated after the death of his wife and having a hard time following his own advice. On a speaking trip to Seattle, Burke meets movie cute with goofy, unlucky-in-love florist Eloise (Aniston) when she attends his seminar and decides he might have a second chance at love after all. A parrot is involved—but not in any sort of kinky way that might have been humorous. **109m/C; DVD, Blu-Ray.** Jennifer Aniston; Aaron Eckhart; Martin Sheen; Judy Greer; Dan Fogler; Frances Conroy; John Carroll Lynch; *D:* Brandon Camp; *W:* Brandon Camp; Mike Thompson; *C:* Eric Alan Edwards; *M:* Christopher Young.

Love Happy 1/2 1950 A group of impoverished actors accidentally gain possession of valuable diamonds. Unfortunately for them, detective Grunion is assigned to recover them! **85m/B; VHS, DVD, Blu-Ray.** Groucho Marx; Harpo Marx; Chico Marx; Vera-Ellen; Ilona Massey; Marion Hutton; Raymond Burr; Marilyn Monroe; Eric Blore; *D:* David Miller; *W:* Frank Tashlin; Mac Benoff; *C:* William Mellor; *M:* Ann Ronell.

Love Has Many Faces 1/2 1965 Judith Crist was too kind when she said this was for connoisseurs of truly awful movies. Playgal Turner marries beachboy Robertson and many faces come between them. Much melodrama. Filmed on location. **104m/C; VHS, DVD.** Lana Turner; Cliff Robertson; Hugh O'Brian; Ruth Roman; Stefanie Powers; Virginia Grey; Ron Husmann; *D:* Alexander Singer.

Love, Honour & Obey 2000 Lowlife London bad boys and a karaoke bar. Jonny (Miller) wants his best bud Jude (Law) to get him a job with Jude's gangster uncle, Ray (Winstone), who loves to croon a tune at the local karaoke club. But Jonny loves his new life too much and can't resist stirring up local gangland rivalries—to the grief of everyone. Low-budget, sometime puerile comedy. **95m/C; VHS, DVD.** *GB* Jonny Lee Miller; Jude Law; Ray Winstone; Sadie Frost; Sean Pertwee; Kathy Burke; Rhys Ifans; Laila Morse; Dominic Anciano; Ray Burdis; *D:* Dominic Anciano; Ray Burdis; *W:* Dominic Anciano; Ray Burdis; *C:* John Ward.

Love Hurts 1991 (R) A guy looking for romance finds his hands full with a number of beautiful women. Will he find the love he craves, or will the pain be too much to bear? **110m/C; VHS, DVD.** Jeff Daniels; Judith Ivey; John Mahoney; Cynthia Sikes; Amy Wright; *D:* Bud Yorkin; *W:* Ron Nyswaner.

Love Hurts 2009 (PG-13) Complacent middle-aged doctor Ben Bingham's life is thrown into chaos when Amanda, his wife of 20 years, walks out of their boring marriage after their son Justin leaves for college. Ben sinks into an alcoholic depression while Justin tries a makeover on his dull dad so he can ultimately reunite with Amanda, who's moved on with another man. **94m/C; DVD.** Richard E. Grant; Carrie-Anne Moss; Johnny Pacar; Jenna Elfman; Janeane Garofalo; Camryn Manheim; Jeffrey Nordling; *D:* Barra Grant; *W:* Barra Grant; *C:* Alan Caso; *M:* Mark Adler.

Love in Bloom 1935 Predictable romance, with Burns and Allen providing some much-needed comic relief. Carnival gal Violet Downey (Lee) falls for struggling songwriter Larry Deane (Morrison) but thinks her tawdry background will ruin his chances and takes off. After Larry becomes successful he searches for Violet, still determined to marry her. **75m/B; VHS, DVD.** George Burns; Gracie Allen; Joe Morrison; Dixie Lee; Lee Kohlmar; Richard Carle; *D:* Elliott Nugent; *W:* J.P. McEvoy; Keene Thompson; *C:* Leo Tover.

Love in Pawn 🦴 1/2 **1953** A very silly plot will cause eye-rolling for this cheap Britcom. Struggling artist Roger Fox (Braden) is offered money by an uncle if his work becomes more commercial. The uncle decides to send his attorney to evaluate the worth of Roger and his wife Jean (Kelly) and, to make a good showing, Jean actually pawns Roger to get money to make some improvements. Then she is forced to leave Roger in the pawnshop when she can't meet her payments and becomes a cause celebre. **81m/B; DVD.** *GB* Bernard Braden; Barbara Kelly; Laurence Naismith; John Laurie; Reg Dixon; Jeannie Carson; Walter Crisham; ***D:*** Charles Saunders; ***W:*** Denis Norden; Frank Muir; Guy Morgan; ***C:*** Monty Berman; ***M:*** Temple Abady.

Love in the Afternoon 🦴🦴 1/2 **1957** A Parisian private eye's daughter (Hepburn) decides to investigate a philandering American millionaire (Cooper) and winds up falling in love with him. Cooper's a little old for the Casanova role but Hepburn is always enchanting. **126m/B; DVD, Blu-Ray.** Gary Cooper; Audrey Hepburn; John McGiver; Maurice Chevalier; ***D:*** Billy Wilder; ***W:*** Billy Wilder; I.A.L. Diamond; ***C:*** William Mellor.

Love in the Rough 🦴🦴 **1930** Remake of the 1927 silent "Spring Fever." Working-class clerk Jack Kelly (Montgomery) is his municipal golf links champ—a fact discovered by his golf-loving boss (Nugent) who wants Jack to play in his country club's championship tournament. Once there, Jack neglects his game to romance debutante Marilyn (Jordan), which causes more than one problem. **75m/B; DVD.** Robert Montgomery; Dorothy Jordan; J.C. Nugent; Benny Rubin; Penny Singleton; Tyrell Davis; ***D:*** Charles Riesner; ***W:*** Robert Hopkins; Joe Farnham; ***C:*** Henry Sharp.

Love in the Time of Money 🦴 1/2 **2002 (R)** Overly-familiar story about a group of lonely and/or opportunistic New Yorkers and their various encounters, beginning with hooker Greta (Farmiga), whose client, Eddie (Lombardozzi) won't pay up. From there we go to the dissatisfied drunken wife (Hennessey) of a sexually confused businessman (Gets) who makes a pass at an artist (Buscemi) who's more interest in a gallery assistant (Dawson) who has a boyfriend (Grenier). With a couple of more people on the daisy chain, the bored viewer eventually finds themselves back with Greta. **90m/C; DVD.** Vera Farmiga; Domenick Lombardozzi; Jill(ian) Hennessey; Malcolm Gets; Steve Buscemi; Rosario Dawson; Adrian Grenier; Carol Kane; Michael Imperioli; ***D:*** Peter Mattei; ***W:*** Peter Mattei; ***C:*** Stephen Kazmierski; ***M:*** Theodore Shapiro.

The Love-Ins 🦴 **1967** Hippie protest drama can't escape its dated '60s milieu. Philosophy professor Jonathan Barnett (Todd), who espouses the use of LSD, resigns when his students Larry (MacArthur) and Patricia (Oliver) are expelled over the contents of their underground newspaper. Barnett turns guru, moves in with the duo, and gets more disciples but his actions turn Larry against him. **85m/C; DVD.** Richard Todd; James MacArthur; Susan Oliver; Mark Goddard; Carol Booth; ***D:*** Arthur Dreifuss; ***W:*** Arthur Dreifuss; Hal Collins; ***C:*** John F. Warren; ***M:*** Fred Karger.

Love Is a Ball 🦴🦴 1/2 **1963** Amusing romantic comedy. Matchmaker Etienne Pimm (Boyer) works on the French Riveria pairing up wealthy women with poor-but-titled men. His latest target is tomboy American Millie (Lange) and handsome klutz Grand Duke Gaspard Ducluzeau (Montalban). Etienne has an inside man in rugged chauffeur John (Ford) but Millie is more attracted to the help than Gaspard. **113m/C; DVD.** Charles Boyer; Hope Lange; Glenn Ford; Ricardo Montalban; Telly Savalas; Ulla Jacobsson; Ruth McDevitt; ***D:*** David Swift; ***W:*** David Swift; Tom Waldman; Frank Waldman; ***C:*** Edmond Sechan; ***M:*** Michel Legrand.

Love Is a Gun 🦴 1/2 **1994 (R)** A police photographer (Roberts) begins having violent and erotic hallucinations that begin to affect his fiancee (Garrett). Things get even weirder when a femme fatale model (Preston) enters the picture. **92m/C; VHS, Streaming.** Eric Roberts; Kelly Preston; Eliza (Simons) Garrett; R. Lee Ermey; Jack Kehler; ***D:*** David Hartwell.

Love Is a Many-Splendored Thing 🦴🦴 1/2 **1955** A married American war correspondent and a beautiful Eurasian doctor fall in love in post-WWII Hong Kong. They struggle with racism and unhappiness, until he's sent to Korea to observe the Army's activities there. Based on the novel by Han Suyin. The extensive L.A. Asian acting community got some work out of this film, although the leads are played by Caucasians. Oscar-winning song was a very big popular hit. **102m/C; VHS, DVD, Blu-Ray.** William Holden; Jennifer Jones; Torin Thatcher; Isobel Elsom; Jorja Curtright; Virginia Gregg; Richard Loo; ***D:*** Henry King; ***W:*** John Patrick; ***C:*** Leon Shamroy; ***M:*** Alfred Newman. Oscars '55: Costume Des. (C), Orig. Dramatic Score, Song ("Love Is a Many-Splendored Thing").

Love Is All There Is 🦴🦴 1/2 **1996 (R)** It's a kind of comedic (happy-ending) version of "Romeo and Juliet," set in the Bronx, about rival restaurant families. Beautiful Gina's (Jolie) a finishing-school grad and Rosario's (Marston) the local boy too handsome for his own good. Both sets of parents are crazy. Oddly enough, Sorvino also plays the heroine's dad in the '96 "William Shakespeare's Romeo & Juliet." **98m/C; VHS, DVD.** Angelina Jolie; Nathaniel Marston; Paul Sorvino; Renee Taylor; Joseph Bologna; Lainie Kazan; Barbara Carrera; William Hickey; Abe Vigoda; Dick Van Patten; Connie Stevens; Dominic Chianese; ***D:*** Renee Taylor; Joseph Bologna; ***W:*** Renee Taylor; Joseph Bologna; ***C:*** Alan Jones; ***M:*** Jeff Beal.

Love Is Better Than Ever 🦴🦴 1/2 *The Light Fantastic* **1952** Lightweight romantic-comedy casts Taylor as a dancing instructor who travels to the Big Apple for a convention. Once there, she meets and falls for talent agent Parks. Carefree, bachelor Parks is too busy to be bothered by small town Taylor, but Liz is determined to land her man. Release of this picture was held back because of Parks' blacklisting by the McCarthy committee. **81m/B; VHS, DVD.** Larry Parks; Elizabeth Taylor; Josephine Hutchinson; Tom Tully; Ann Doran; Elinor Donahue; Kathleen Freeman; ***Cameo(s):*** Gene Kelly; ***D:*** Stanley Donen; ***W:*** Ruth Brooks Flippen.

Love Is Blind 🦴🦴 **2019** Lonely Bess (Tarbet) has a disorder in which she cannot see certain people who physically exist. Because of her illness and a long-ago event, she believes that her mother (Sevigny) is dead. Working with autistic therapist Farmer (Walker), Bess falls in love with him. Their therapy sessions are altered when self-destructive construction worker Russell (Turner) comes to town. Farmer tries to help Russell but it is not until Russell sees Bess that he believes he might have something to live for despite her blindness to him. Not particularly well-told comedy drama but pleasant enough. **90m/C; DVD.** Shannon Tarbet; Aidan Turner; Benjamin Walker; Matthew Broderick; Chloë Sevigny; ***D:*** Monty Whitebloom; ***W:*** Jennifer Schuur; ***C:*** Monty Whitebloom.

Love Is Colder Than Death 🦴🦴 *Liebe Ist Kalter Als Der Tod* **1969** Fassbinder's first feature film has a smalltime pimp hooking up with another lowlife to go on a crime spree that ends in a botched bank robbery. German with subtitles. **85m/B; VHS, DVD.** *GE* Ulli Lommel; Hanna Schygulla; Katrin Schaake; Liz Soellner; ***D:*** Rainer Werner Fassbinder; ***W:*** Rainer Werner Fassbinder; ***C:*** Dietrich Lohmann; ***M:*** Peer Raben; Holger Munzer.

Love is in the Air 🦴🦴 1/2 *Amour et Turbulences* **2013** Artsy Julie (Sagnier) boards her flight home from New York to Paris only to find she's been seated next to her womanizing ex Antoine (Bedos). In this French romantic comedy, the couple spends the next six hours hashing out their differences and remembering the good times and bad of their volatile relationship. Sagnier and Bedos are both charming as they shoot accusations and hints of remorse back and forth, but the film occasionally feels as stuck in one place as the two ex-lovers are on their crowded flight. **96m/C; On Demand.** *FR* Ludivine Sagnier; Nicolas Bedos; Jonathan Cohen; Clementine Celarie; Arnaud Ducret; Brigitte Catillon; ***D:*** Alexandre Castagnetti; ***W:*** Vincent Angell; ***C:*** Yannick Ressigeac; ***M:*** Nicolas Wauquiez.

Love Is News 🦴🦴🦴 **1937** Snappy screwball comedy finds madcap heiress Toni Gateson (Young) sick of being hounded by the press. Newsman Steve Layton (Power) tricks Toni into an interview and she's so steamed she tells all the other papers that she and Steve are engaged. Steve protests in vain but of course they do fall in love. Since neither will admit it, many more complications follow until the final clinch. Remade as "Sweet Rosie O'Grady" (1943) and "That Wonderful Urge" (1948). **78m/B; DVD.** Tyrone Power; Loretta Young; Don Ameche; Dudley Digges; George Sanders; Pauline Moore; Slim Summerville; Walter Catlett; Jane Darwell; Stepin Fetchit; Elisha Cook, Jr.; ***D:*** Tay Garnett; ***W:*** Jack Yellen; Harry Tugend; ***C:*** Ernest Palmer; ***M:*** David Buttolph.

Love Is Strange 🦴🦴🦴 **2014 (R)** Director/writer Sachs delivers his best film with this delicate, moving tale of how love reshapes as we get older and deal with the problems of everyday life. Ben (Lithgow) and George (Molina) are getting married after almost four decades together. The romantic union actually separates them after George is fired when the archdiocese finds out he's in a gay marriage, forcing each of them to move in with others. Few films have more deftly captured how being physically separated can redefine people who have become lovingly co-dependent. And Lithgow and Molina have never been better. **94m/C; DVD, Blu-Ray.** John Lithgow; Alfred Molina; Cheyenne Jackson; Manny Perez; Darren E. Burrows; Marisa Tomei; Charlie Tahan; ***D:*** Ira Sachs; ***W:*** Ira Sachs; Mauricio Zacharias; ***C:*** Christos Voudouris.

Love Is the Devil 🦴🦴🦴 1/2 **1998** At the height of his career, British painter Francis Bacon (Jacobi), takes on petty thief George Dyer (Craig) as his model and whipping-boy, exposing his dim lover to a world of high-brow drunks and addicts who entertain themselves by humiliating others. Although the estate refused director/writer Maybury permission to use Bacon's actual paintings, he still captures the painful emotions expressed in Bacon's art. The incredible lead performances by Jacobi and Craig are as brilliant and ferocious as the artist himself. While at times tender and moving, their destructive relationship is difficult to watch, but worth it. **90m/C; DVD, Blu-Ray.** *UK* Derek Jacobi; Daniel Craig; Tilda Swinton; Karl Johnson; Anne Lambton; ***D:*** John Maybury; ***W:*** John Maybury; ***C:*** John Mathieson; ***M:*** Ryuichi Sakamoto.

Love Jones 🦴🦴🦴 **1996 (R)** A contemporary Chicago nightclub, the Sanctuary, is the gathering spot for middle-class black urbanites looking for romance. Would-be writer/poet Darius (Tate) spouts provocative verse to beautiful photographer Nina (Long), who's not too happy with men at the moment (she's just been dumped). But they make a connection, with both protesting a little too much that's it just a "sex thing." Funny what happens when love clearly enters the picture. Witcher's directorial debut features fine lead performances. **105m/C; VHS, DVD.** Larenz Tate; Nia Long; Isaiah Washington, IV; Lisa Nicole Carson; Khalil Kain; Bill Bellamy; Leonard Roberts; Bernardette L. Clarke; ***D:*** Theodore Witcher; ***W:*** Theodore Witcher; ***C:*** Ernest Holzman; ***M:*** Darryl Jones. Sundance '97: Aud. Award.

Love Kills 🦴 1/2 **1998 (R)** Good cast can't hold this messy film together. New Age masseur Poe Finklestein (Van Peebles) arrives at the Beverly Hills estate of wealthy widow Evelyn Heiss (Warren). Also living with Evelyn are her no-account, gay stepson Dominique (Leitch) and her voyeurish sister-in-law Alena (Fletcher). There's shots fired, and drugs, and a cop (Baldwin) and various other hijinks but not much of it makes sense. **97m/C; VHS, DVD.** Mario Van Peebles; Lesley Ann Warren; Daniel Baldwin; Donovan Leitch; Louise Fletcher; Loretta Devine; Melvin Van Peebles; Susan Ruttan; Alexis Arquette; ***D:*** Mario Van Peebles; ***W:*** Mario Van Peebles; ***C:*** George Mooradian.

Love Laughs at Andy Hardy 🦴🦴 **1946** Andy Hardy, college boy, is in love and in trouble. Financial and romantic problems come to a head when Andy is paired with a six-foot tall blind date. One in the series. **93m/B; DVD.** Mickey Rooney; Lewis Stone; Sara Haden; Lina Romay; Bonita Granville; Fay Holden; ***D:*** Willis Goldbeck; ***W:*** Harry Ruskin; William Ludwig; ***C:*** Robert Planck; ***M:*** David Snell.

The Love Letter 🦴🦴 1/2 **1998** Scotty Corrigan (Scott) discovers a love letter in the antique desk he's purchased, written by Lizzie Whitcomb (Leigh) who lived during the Civil War. Haunted, Scotty decides to reply to the missive and, magically, Lizzie receives his letter. Soon, they not only have a regular correspondence but a romance that transcends time. Based on a story by Jack Finney. **99m/C; VHS, DVD.** Campbell Scott; Jennifer Jason Leigh; David Dukes; Estelle Parsons; Daphne Ashbrook; Gerrit Graham; Irma P. Hall; ***D:*** Dan Curtis; ***W:*** James Henerson; ***M:*** Robert Cobert. **TV**

The Love Letter 🦴 1/2 **1999 (PG-13)** Disappointing adaptation of Cathleen Schine's novel takes the focus off the unexpected love story between 40-something Helen (Capshaw) and college student Johnny (Scott) with too many peripheral characters. The love letter in question is an anonymous missive Helen receives at her bookstore, although she's uncertain if it's meant for her or who the secret admirer might be. Then Johnny finds the letter and thinks it's meant for him—or maybe it's for Helen's cynical partner, Janet (DeGeneres). The biggest mystery is why the lovely Danner is playing Capshaw's mother (!) under a ton of rubber makeup. **88m/C; VHS, DVD.** Kate Capshaw; Tom Everett Scott; Tom Selleck; Ellen DeGeneres; Blythe Danner; Gloria Stuart; Geraldine McEwan; Alice Drummond; Jack Black; ***D:*** Peter Chan; ***W:*** Maria Maggenti; ***C:*** Tami Reiker; ***M:*** Luis Bacalov.

Love Letters 🦴🦴 1/2 **1945** Typical '40s weepie finds Victoria (Jones) marrying soldier Roger Morland (Sully) because of the beautiful letters he wrote her. Only he didn't write them, his best bud Alan Quinton (Cotten) did. Roger's actually a wife-beater and winds up dead. Victoria becomes an amnesiac from the shock but when Alan comes to check out the situation he falls immediately in love with her anyway. Based on the novel "Pity My Simplicity" by Chris Massie. **101m/B; DVD.** Jennifer Jones; Joseph Cotten; Robert Sully; Ann Richards; Anita Louise; Cecil Kellaway; Gladys Cooper; Byron Barr; Reginald Denny; ***D:*** William Dieterle; ***W:*** Ayn Rand; ***C:*** Lee Garmes; ***M:*** Victor Young.

Love Letters 🦴🦴🦴 *Passion Play; My Love Letters* **1983 (R)** A young disc jockey falls under the spell of a box of love letters that her mother left behind which detailed her double life. She, in turn, begins an affair with a married man. Thoughtful treatment of the psychology of infidelity. **102m/C; VHS, DVD, Blu-Ray.** Jamie Lee Curtis; Amy Madigan; Bud Cort; Matt Clark; Bonnie Bartlett; Sally Kirkland; James Keach; ***D:*** Amy Holden Jones; ***W:*** Amy Holden Jones; ***C:*** Alec Hirschfeld; ***M:*** Ralph Jones.

Love Letters 🦴🦴🦴 **1999 (PG-13)** Andy (Weber) and Melissa's (Linney) tender friendship began as children and their attraction continued throughout their lives, as Andy recounts after Melissa's death via many years worth of letters between them. Despite the intense feelings, their careers took them in opposite directions as Andy flourished as a lawyer-turned-senator and Melissa toiled as an artist. Directed by the legendary Dohen and based on A.R. Guerney's smash play. **90m/C; VHS, DVD.** Steven Weber; Laura Linney; Emily Hampshire; Chas Lawther; Marcia Diamond; ***D:*** Stanley Donen; ***W:*** A.R. Gurney; ***C:*** Mike Fash; ***M:*** Lee Holdridge. **TV**

Love Lies Bleeding 🦴 1/2 **2007 (R)** Hapless Duke (Geraghty) stumbles across a duffel bag full of money from a drug deal gone bad, grabs it and wife Amber (Dewan), and they head out on the road to start a new life. But they are soon pursued by very ticked-off (and corrupt) DEA agent Pollen (Slater), who wants that money for himself. **91m/C; DVD.** Christian Slater; Jenna Dewan; Brian Geraghty; Craig Sheffer; Jacob Vargas; Tara Summers; ***D:*** Keith Samples; ***W:*** Brian Strasmann. **VIDEO**

The Love Light 🦴🦴 1/2 **1921** Angela (Pickford) is a lighthouse keeper in Italy who's awaiting her soldier brother's return from war. Instead, she learns of his death. When a wounded soldier is washed ashore, Angela rescues him and nurses him back to health, thinking he's an American sailor. They fall in love and marry before she learns that he's really a German spy and may have killed her brother. There's a lot more tragedy before Angela finds happiness. One of Pickford's rare adult roles. **75m/B; Silent; VHS, DVD.** Mary Pickford; Raymond Bloomer; Jean De Briac; Evelyn Dumo; Eddie (Edward) Phillips; Albert Priscoe; George Regas; Fred Thomson; ***D:*** Frances Marion; ***W:*** Frances Marion; ***C:*** Henry Cronjager; Charles Rosher.

Love Liza 2002 (R) An acquired taste of a film that rests firmly on the slumped shoulders of Hoffman. He's Wilson Joel, whose wife Liza has just committed suicide (by carbon-monoxide poisoning in her car). He can't read the note she left him, can't deal with her sympathetic mother Mary Ann (Bates), can't—in fact—do much of anything except mope. Oh, and huff. Yes, Wilson decides to cope with his trauma by inhaling gasoline fumes (the fuel used in his model airplane hobby). Soon, his addiction is all there is to his sad sack existence. **90m/C; VHS, DVD.** Philip Seymour Hoffman; Kathy Bates; Jack Kehler; Stephen Tobolowsky; Sarah Koskoff; Erika Alexander; ***D:*** Todd Louiso; ***W:*** Gordy Hoffman; ***C:*** Lisa Rinzler; ***M:*** Jim O'Rourke. Sundance '02: Screenplay.

Love, Ludlow 2005 (R) Bipolar painter Ludlow (Sexton) has been cared for by his tough older sister Myra (Goranson) since their mother's death. So he feels especially threatened when Myra agrees to date shy co-worker Reggie (Eigenberg) and it turns into something more than casual. Modest romantic comedy that Paterson adapted from his play "Finger Painting in a Murphy Bed." **86m/C; DVD.** Alicia (Lecy) Goranson; Brendan Sexton, III; David Eigenberg; ***D:*** Adrienne J. Weiss; ***W:*** David Paterson; ***C:*** Ruben O'Malley; ***M:*** tomandandy; James Kole.

The Love Machine 1/2 1971 (R) A power-hungry newscaster climbs the corporate ladder by sleeping with many, including the president's wife. An adaptation of Jacqueline Susann's novel. **108m/C; VHS, DVD.** John Phillip Law; Dyan Cannon; Robert Ryan; Jackie Cooper; David Hemmings; Jodi Wexler; William Roerick; Maureen Arthur; Shecky Greene; Clinton Greyn; Sharon Farrell; Alexandra Hay; Eve Bruce; Greg Mullavey; Edith Atwater; Gene Baylos; Claudia Jennings; Mary Collinson; Madeleine Collinson; Ann Ford; Gayle Hunnicutt; ***D:*** Jack Haley, Jr.; ***W:*** Samuel A. Taylor; ***C:*** Charles B(ryant) Lang, Jr.; ***M:*** Artie Butler.

Love Me 1/2 2012 (PG-13) Sylvia (Lindsey Shaw) has a crush on the new kid in chool until the police think he's responsible for a missing girl. **97m/B; Silent; DVD, Blu-Ray, Streaming.** *US CA* Lindsey Shaw; Jamie Johnston; Jean-Luc Bilodeau; Kaitlyn Leeb; Mikaela Cochrane; ***D:*** Rick Bota; ***W:*** Kat Candler; ***C:*** Paul Slatter; ***M:*** Mike Shields. **CABLE**

Love Me Deadly 1973 (R) A young woman tries to get her husband interested in her new hobby—necrophilia. **95m/C; VHS, DVD, Blu-Ray.** Mary Wilcox; Lyle Waggoner; Christopher Stone; Timothy Scott; ***D:*** Jacques Lacerte; ***W:*** Jacques Lacerte; ***C:*** David Aaron; ***M:*** Phil Moody.

Love Me if You Dare *Jeux D'Enfants; Child's Play* 2003 (R) Overwrought romance-French style. Julien (Canet) and Sophie (Cotillard) have played a game of dare since childhood-no matter how embarrassing or dangerous the challenge. Obsessed with each other, they are unable to admit their devotion in any conventional way and perpetuate their play for the excitement it brings them even as they risk self-destruction. Unfortunately for the viewer, the duo are mainly exasperating. French with subtitles. **95m/C; DVD.** *FR BE* Guillaume Canet; Marion Cotillard; Thibault Verhaeghe; Josephine Lebas Joly; Emmanuelle Gronvold; Gerard Watkins; ***D:*** Yann Samuell; ***W:*** Yann Samuell; Jacky Cuckier; ***C:*** Antoine Roch; ***M:*** Philippe Rombi.

Love Me or Leave Me 1955 A hard-hitting biography of '20s torch singer Ruth Etting and her rise and fall at the hand of her abusive, gangster husband, a part just made for Cagney. Day emotes and sings expressively in one of the best performances of her career. **122m/C; VHS, DVD, Blu-Ray.** Doris Day; James Cagney; Cameron Mitchell; Robert Keith; Tom Tully; Veda Ann Borg; ***D:*** Charles Vidor. Oscars '55: Story.

Love Me Tender 1956 A Civil War-torn family is divided by in-fighting between two brothers who both seek the affections of the same woman. Presley's first film. Songs include "Poor Boy," "We're Gonna Move," and the title tune. **89m/B; VHS, DVD, Blu-Ray.** Richard Egan; Debra Paget; Elvis Presley; Neville Brand; Mildred Dunnock; James Drury; Barry Coe; Robert Middleton; William Campbell; Russ Conway; L.Q. Jones; ***D:*** Robert D. Webb; ***W:*** Robert Buckner; ***C:*** Leo Tover; ***M:*** Lionel Newman.

Love Me Tonight 1932 Effervescent early Paramount musical with a score by Richard Rodgers and Lorenz Hart. Paris tailor Maurice (Chevalier) is owed a fortune by playboy Vicomte Gilbert de Vareze (Ruggles). Maurice goes to the family's chateau to collect and Gilbert begs him for more time and passes the tailor off to his family as a visiting baron. Maurice charms everyone, including young widow Princess Jeanette (MacDonald) who returns his affections—at least until his real identity is revealed. **104m/B; DVD.** Maurice Chevalier; Jeanette MacDonald; Charlie Ruggles; Myrna Loy; Charles Butterworth; Sir C. Aubrey Smith; ***D:*** Rouben Mamoulian; ***W:*** George Marion, Jr.; Waldemar Young; Samuel Hoffenstein; ***C:*** Victor Milner.

Love Meetings *Comizi d'Amore* 1964 Pasolini acts as director and interviewer to query a wide-range of individuals on their experiences at love, including homosexuality, prostitution, marital and non-marital interludes. In Italian with English subtitles. **90m/B; VHS, DVD.** *IT* ***D:*** Pier Paolo Pasolini; ***W:*** Pier Paolo Pasolini; ***C:*** Tonino Delli Colli; Mario Bernardo.

Love N' Dancing 1/2 2009 (PG-13) Cliches abound in this dance flick with hearing-challenged motivational speaker Jake Mitchell (Malloy) involved in swing-dancing with his squabbling fiancee Corinne (Royston). After breaking off their engagement, Tom finds a new partner in schoolteacher Jessica (Smart) who has her own romantic problems. There is, of course, a big dance competition for the finale. **93m/C; DVD.** Tom Malloy; Amy Smart; Billy Zane; Nicola Royston; Caroline Rhea; Betty White; Rachel Dratch; Leila Arcieri; ***D:*** Robert Iscove; ***W:*** Tom Malloy; ***C:*** Frank Byers; ***M:*** Bruce Robb; David Iscove.

Love Nest 1951 Lundigan stars as Jim Scott, the landlord of an apartment building brimming with wacky tenants, including Monroe, Paar, and Fay. He dreams of becoming a famous writer, but his time is always filled with fixing up the building and trying to pay the mortgage. When one of the tenants ends up in jail because he was living off wealthy widows, Scott's luck changes. This moderately funny film is a good look at the early careers of Monroe and Paar. **84m/B; VHS, DVD.** William Lundigan; June Haver; Frank Fay; Marilyn Monroe; Jack Paar; ***D:*** Joseph M. Newman; ***W:*** I.A.L. Diamond; ***M:*** Cyril Mockridge.

Love Notes 2007 An unexpected pregnancy changes the life of classical music critic Nora (Leighton) after she has a one-night stand with country music star Jamie (Cupo). She needs his consent to put the baby up for adoption but Jamie has other ideas about his offspring and Nora. **90m/C; DVD.** Laura Leighton; Antonio Cupo; Ellie Harvie; Lorena Gale; Aaron Pearl; ***D:*** David Weaver; ***W:*** Rachel Feldman; ***M:*** Hal Beckett. **CABLE**

The Love of Jeanne Ney 1/2 1927 Wildly convoluted silent film begins in Russia where Jeanne's (Jehanne) Bolshevik lover (Henning) kills her father for betraying the cause, and then shifts to Paris where the pair face even more daunting obstacles. The new score by Timothy Brock is engaging and effective. **113m/B; Silent; VHS, DVD, Blu-Ray.** *GE* Edith Jehanne; Brigitte Helm; Uno Henning; Eugen Jenson; Fritz Rasp; ***D:*** G.W. Pabst; ***W:*** Ilya Ehrenburg; Ladislaus Vayda.

Love on a Bet 1/2 1936 Would-be theatrical producer Michael MacCreigh (Raymond) makes a bet with his wealthy Uncle Carlton (Collier) that he can leave New York without money or clothes and arrive in L.A. with both--plus a fiancee. If he wins, he gets the dough for his play; if he loses, Michael has to join the family business. He thumbs it in his skivvies and gets a ride from madcap Paula (Barrie) and her aunt (Broderick). **77m/B; DVD.** Gene Raymond; Wendy Barrie; Helen Broderick; William Collier, Sr.; ***D:*** Leigh Jason; ***W:*** P.J. Wolfson; ***C:*** Robert De Grasse.

Love on a Pillow 1/2 *Les Repos du Guerrier; The Rest of the Warrior* 1962 Beautiful Genevieve (Bardot) accidentally prevents the suicide of alcoholic Renaud (Hossein) and decides she must redeem him. They fall in love but Genevieve finally tires of his cynical abuse and leaves, which serves as a wake-up call to Renaud. Bardot's a looker but the film is very sloooooow and her character is a masochist for sticking with such a loser. French with subtitles. **102m/C; DVD.** *FR IT* Brigitte Bardot; Robert Hossein; Jean-Mark Bory; Michel Serrault; ***D:*** Roger Vadim; ***W:*** Roger Vadim; Claude Choublier; ***C:*** Armand Thirard; Edmond Sechan; ***M:*** Michel Magne.

Love on the Dole 1941 In a gloomy industrial section of England during the early '30s a family struggles to survive and maintain dignity. Grim Depression drama salvaged by great acting. **89m/B; VHS, DVD.** *GB* Deborah Kerr; Clifford Evans; George Carney; ***D:*** John Baxter.

Love on the Run 1/2 1936 Enjoyable romantic comedy starring Crawford as a rich American heiress and Gable and Tone (Crawford's real husband at the time) as journalists stationed in Europe. Gable and Tone are assigned to cover an international aviator, who turns out to be an evil spy, as well as the upcoming wedding of flighty Crawford. When Crawford asks for help in getting out of her marriage, Gable and Tone steal a plane and the trio are chased across Europe by spies. Wild and farfetched plot, but the stars make it worthwhile. Based on the story "Beauty and the Beast" by Alan Green and Julian Brodie. **80m/B; DVD.** Joan Crawford; Clark Gable; Franchot Tone; Reginald Owen; Mona Maris; Ivan Lebedeff; Charles (Judel, Judells) Judels; William Demarest; ***D:*** W.S. Van Dyke; ***W:*** John Lee Mahin; Manuel Seff; Gladys Hurlbut.

Love on the Run *L'Amour en Fuite* 1978 (PG) The further amorous adventures of Antoine Doinel, hero of "The 400 Blows," "Stolen Kisses," and "Bed and Board." Doinel is now in his 30s and newly divorced. He renews affairs with several women from his past but, after his mother's death, must contend with his emotional immaturity and his inability to sustain a relationship. In French with English subtitles. **95m/C; VHS, DVD.** *FR* Jean-Pierre Leaud; Marie-France Pisier; Claude Jade; ***D:*** Francois Truffaut; ***C:*** Nestor Almendros; ***M:*** Georges Delerue. Cesar '80: Score.

Love on the Side *Deluxe Combo Platter* 2004 (R) Quirky small town comedy. When tall, blonde, gorgeous Linda (Schnarre) suddenly turns up in Squamish, British Columbia, she brings trouble to the would-be romance of waitress Eve (Sokoloff), who has big self-esteem issues, and local dumb hunk Jeff (Watson). But Linda is keeping secrets—such as the fact that she's romantically attracted to Eve and has some interest in the local real estate too. **102m/C; DVD.** *CA* Monica Schnarre; Marla Sokoloff; Barry Watson; Dave Thomas; Jennifer Tilly; ***D:*** Vic Sarin; ***W:*** Brigitte Talevski; ***C:*** Vic Sarin; ***M:*** Daryl Bennett.

Love or Money 2001 Daniel (Duffy) and Samantha (Cunniffe) are strangers to each other when they become contestants on a reality TV show where they are chosen by the audience to get married. If they can form a relationship and stay together for six months, they win $1 million. But between media scrutiny, family interference, and personal difficulties, the pressure may be too much. **90m/C; DVD.** *GB* Emma Cunniffe; George Costigan; Sheila Hancock; David Calder; Steven Duffy; Nicky Henson; Pippa Heywood; Toby Jones; ***D:*** Martyn Friend; ***W:*** Elizabeth (Lizzie) Mickery; ***C:*** Sean Van Hales; ***M:*** Nigel Hess. **TV**

The Love Parade 1/2 1929 Lubitsch's first sound film takes place in Sylvania, one of those mythic, musical, mitt-European countries with a royal ruler. In this case, it's unmarried and lonely Queen Louise (MacDonald in her film debut). Recalling her randy ambassador, Count Alfred Renard (Chevalier), from Paris for his indiscretions, Louise is nonetheless entranced by his charms and they quickly marry. But Count Alfred soon discovers that being a royal consort is not to his liking. **107m/B; DVD.** Jeanette MacDonald; Maurice Chevalier; Lupino Lane; Lillian Roth; Edgar Norton; Lionel Belmore; Eugene Pallette; E.H. Calvert; ***D:*** Ernst Lubitsch; ***W:*** Ernest Vajda; Guy Bolton; ***C:*** Victor Milner; ***M:*** Victor Schertzinger.

Love Potion #9 1/2 1992 (PG-13) Two nerdy biochemists procure a love potion that they test on animals. Meeting with success they agree to test it on themselves. Predictably, the scientists are transformed and fall in love with each other. Features a talented young cast, with an amusing cameo by Bancroft, but the script is a real disappointment because of its shallow characters and lame gags. Inspired by the song by Jerry Leiber and Mike Stoller. **96m/C; VHS, DVD.** Tate Donovan; Sandra Bullock; Mary Mara; Dale Midkiff; Hillary Bailey Smith; Dylan Baker; Anne Bancroft; Rebecca Staab; ***D:*** Dale Launer; ***W:*** Dale Launer; ***C:*** William Wages; ***M:*** Jed Leiber.

The Love Punch 1/2 2013 (PG-13) Once-married, Richard (Brosnan) and Kate (Thompson), are now happily divorced, playfully takes jabs whenever they run into each other. For whatever reason, their grown children, friends, even strangers, want them back together. When a greedy French tycoon swindles them out of their pensions, the two must join forces to con the money back. Inevitably, they start to remember why they fell in the love in the first place. As charming as it may sound, this absolute waste of talent, pitting two seasoned professionals against one another in a lame-brained rom-com caper, is as bland as its title. **94m/C; DVD.** *UK FR* Pierce Brosnan; Emma Thompson; Timothy Spall; Celia Imrie; Laurent Lafitte; Louise Bourgoin; ***D:*** Joel Hopkins; ***W:*** Joel Hopkins; ***C:*** Jerome Almeras; ***M:*** Jean-Michel Bernard.

Love Ranch 1/2 2010 (R) Loosely based on the true story of Sally and Joe Conforte (here called Grace and Charlie Bontempo) who opened the Mustang Ranch, the first legal brothel in Reno, Nevada, in 1971. Here, Charlie (Pesci) is a swaggering hothead and chronically unfaithful to his tolerant, business savvy madam wife Grace (Mirren). Charlie's latest ambition is to manage hunky Argentinian boxer Armando (Peris-Mencheta) with whom Grace (who has cancer) decides to have a romance. The best thing is Mirren's performance (as usual). **117m/C; Blu-Ray.** Dame Helen Mirren; Joe Pesci; Scout Taylor-Compton; Taryn Manning; Gil Birmingham; Sergio Peris-Mencheta; Gina Gershon; Bai Ling; ***D:*** Taylor Hackford; ***W:*** Mark Jacobson; ***C:*** Kieran McGuigan; ***M:*** Chris P. Bacon.

Love Serenade 1996 (R) Former big-time Brisbane DJ Ken Sherry (Shevtsov) arrives in a backwater town, setting off a rivalry between bored sisters, Dimity (Otto) and Vicki-Ann (Frith). Fishing's one of their hobbies and metaphorically, Ken's the big fish in a very little pond. To them, his pretentious schmooze comes off as sophistication, mostly because he uses Barry White lyrics and his pillow-talk DJ voice to sell it. Critically speaking, director/writer Barrett's debut demonstrates an ear for dialogue and some comic timing, but it's also boring and very strange. **101m/C; DVD.** *AU* Miranda Otto; Rebecca Frith; George Shevtsov; John Alansu; Jessica Napier; ***D:*** Shirley Barrett; ***W:*** Shirley Barrett; ***C:*** Mandy Walker.

Love Sick Love 2012 (R) A woman desperate for love kidnaps her loathsome boyfriend, and takes him to her family of insane rednecks in the country. The plan being for him to meet her kids and force him to live though a year's worth of holidays in one weekend to prove how they are meant for each other. **84m/C; DVD, Streaming.** Katia Winter; Matthew Settle; Charlotte Rae; Michael E. Walsh; Jim Gaffigan; ***D:*** Christian Charles; ***W:*** Ryan Oxford; ***C:*** J.P. Lipa; ***M:*** John Swihart. **VIDEO**

Love, Simon 2018 (PG-13) An empowering, entertaining romantic comedy about a teenage boy's coming out. Simon

(Robinson) knows he has great family and friends but has hesitated to tell them he is gay because he believes everything will change when he does so. Connecting with someone posting as "Blue" on a message board about being afraid to come out, Simon's romantic feelings for Blue grow as he tries to learn Blue's identity. When Martin (Miller) learns of Simon's correspondence with Blue, Martin blackmails Simon and launches a cycle of manipulation that harms his friendships and personal happiness. Smart dialogue adds to the film's realistic depiction of teens. **110m/C; DVD, Blu-Ray.** Nick Robinson; Jennifer Garner; Josh Duhamel; Katherine Langford; Alexandra Shipp; ***D:*** Greg Berlanti; ***W:*** Elizabeth Berger; Isaac Aptaker; ***C:*** John Guleserian; ***M:*** Rob Simonsen.

A Love Song for Bobby Long 🦴🦴 **2004 (R)** Bobby Long (Travolta) and protege Lawson Pines (Macht) are alcoholic literary has-beens who escape a shady past by relocating to a notorious singer's house in New Orleans. When the singer dies, her 18-year-old daughter (Johansson) shows up to claim the house, but must share it with the shabby twosome. Misunderstandings and bonding moments ensue. Very over-the-top story is saved by the relaxed performances of the cast although neither Travolta nor Johansson ever master a believable southern accent. But Travolta does get to sing again. **119m/C; VHS, DVD.** John Travolta; Scarlett Johansson; Gabriel Macht; Deborah Kara Unger; Sonny Shroyer; Dane Rhodes; ***D:*** Shainee Gabel; ***W:*** Shainee Gabel; ***C:*** Elliot Davis; ***M:*** Nathan Larson.

Love Songs 🦴🦴 *Paroles et Musique* **1984** Margaux's (Deneuve) husband is on an extended trip to New York to write a book, leaving her with their two kids and a demanding job as a recording company exec. She's being pressured to find and sign new talent and discovers the duo of Michel (Anconina) and Jeremy (Lambert). Complications arise when Jeremy becomes more interested in Margaux than his music, but he needs to makes a decision when Michel goes alone to an ultimately successful audition. French with subtitles. **107m/C; DVD.** *FR* Catherine Deneuve; Christopher Lambert; Richard Anconina; Jacques Perrin; Nick Mancuso; Charlotte Gainsbourg; ***D:*** Elie Chouraqui; ***W:*** Elie Chouraqui; ***C:*** Robert Alazraki; ***M:*** Michel Legrand.

Love Songs 🦴🦴 ½ **1999** Trilogy of stories all set in the same black neighborhood. "A Love Song for a Champ" concerns boxer Townsend who agrees to throw a fight. "A Love Song for Jean and Ellis" concerns the would-be romance between grocer Braugher and the haughty Whitfield. "A Love Song for Dad" follows bartender Grossett who comes to the aid of his abused sister-in-law. **101m/C; VHS, DVD.** Robert Townsend; Andre Braugher; Louis Gossett, Jr.; Rachael Crawford; Carl Gordon; Lynn Whitfield; Brent Jennings; Dulé Hill; Sandra Caldwell; ***D:*** Robert Townsend; Andre Braugher; Louis Gossett, Jr.; ***W:*** Charles Fuller; ***C:*** James R. Bagdonas; ***M:*** Pete Anthony; Ronnie Laws. **CABLE**

Love Songs 🦴🦴 *Les Chansons d'Amour* **2007** Ismael (Garel) lives with longtime girlfriend Julie (Sagnier) and has just persuaded her (reluctantly) into a three-way with his co-worker Alice (Hesme). Julie's sudden death plunges the immature Ismael into a series of complicated emotional situations involving Julie's sister Jeanne (Mastroiani), Alice's new beau Gwendal (Renier), and Gwendal's teenaged brother Erwann (Leprince-Riguet), who develops a serious crush on Ismael. And every so often the cast bursts out singing, which sometimes works (and sometimes doesn't). French with subtitles. **95m/C; DVD.** *FR* Ludivine Sagnier; Chiara Mastroianni; Gregoire Leprince-Ringuet; Yannick Renier; Louis Garrel; Brigitte Rouan; ***D:*** Christophe Honore; ***W:*** Christophe Honore; ***C:*** Remy Chevrin; ***M:*** Alexandre Beaupain.

Love Stinks 🦴 ½ **1999 (R)** In this joyless "unromantic" comedy, witer Seth Winnick (Stewart) meets Chelsea (Wilson) at the wedding of his pals Larry (Bellamy) and Holly (Banks). After he's lured into her clutches, she begins to take over his life while dropping hints that he should pop the big question. When he doesn't follow through, Chelsea sues him for palimony. The non-couple then inexplicably live together until the trial, but this situation is humor-free as well. Stewart attempts to rise above the material with his excellent comedic timing, but he's unable to escape this misogynistic mess. **94m/C; DVD.** French Stewart; Bridgette Wilson-Sampras; Tyra Banks; Bill Bellamy; Tiffani(-Amber) Thiessen; Steve Hytner; Jason Bateman; ***D:*** Jeff Franklin; ***W:*** Jeff Franklin; ***C:*** Uta Briesewitz; ***M:*** Bennett Salvay.

Love Story 🦴🦴 ½ *The Lady Surrenders* **1944** Wartime Brit tearjerker. Concert pianist Lissa (Lockwood) is dying from a heart ailment and decides to have a last fling. She travels to Cornwall and meets ex-RAF pilot Kit Firth (Granger), who is going blind. Neither confides in the other until Lissa learns from Kit's jealous would-be girlfriend Judy (Roc) that she has talked him out of a dangerous operation that could restore his sight. **108m/B; DVD.** *GB* Margaret Lockwood; Stewart Granger; Patricia Roc; Tom Walls; Moira Lister; Reginald Purdell; ***D:*** Leslie Arliss; ***W:*** Leslie Arliss; Doreen Montgomery; ***C:*** Bernard Knowles; ***M:*** John Bath.

Love Story 🦴🦴🦴 **1970 (PG)** Melodrama had enormous popular appeal. O'Neal is the son of Boston's upper crust at Harvard; McGraw's the daughter of a poor Italian on scholarship to study music at Radcliffe. They find happiness, but only for a brief period. Timeless story, simply told, with artful direction from Hiller pulling exceptional performances from the young duo (who have never done as well since). The end result is perhaps better than Segal's simplistic novel, which was produced after he sold the screenplay and became a best-seller before the picture's release—great publicity for any film. Remember: "Love means never having to say you're sorry." **100m/C; VHS, DVD, Blu-Ray.** Ryan O'Neal; Ali MacGraw; Ray Milland; John Marley; Tommy Lee Jones; ***D:*** Arthur Hiller; ***W:*** Erich Segal; ***C:*** Richard Kratina; ***M:*** Francis Lai. Oscars '70: Orig. Score; Golden Globes '71: Actress--Drama (MacGraw), Director (Hiller), Film--Drama, Score, Screenplay.

Love Takes Wing 🦴🦴 ½ **2009** Usual sentimental story is the seventh film based on Janette Oke's novels. After her husband dies, grieving Dr. Belinda Simpson (Jones) accepts a job in rural Sikeston, Missouri. A cholera epidemic, which apparently started at the orphanage run by Hattie Clarence (Leachman), has the townspeople fearful and determined to shut the place down. Belinda must win everyone's trust, relying on her faith and the friendships of Annie (Duff) and blacksmith Lee (Bridges) to help her. **88m/C; DVD.** Sarah Jones; Haylie Duff; Cloris Leachman; Jordan Bridges; Patrick Duffy; John Bishop; Erin Cottrell; Lou Diamond Phillips; Annalise Basso; ***D:*** Lou Diamond Phillips; ***W:*** Rachel Stuhler; ***C:*** Dane Peterson; ***M:*** Terry Plumeri. **CABLE**

Love That Brute 🦴🦴 **1950** Gangster comedy set in 1928. Bored Chicago racketeer Big Ed takes a shine to Ruth and hires her as his children's governess so he can pitch woo. Since he doesn't have kids, Big Ed decides to hire a pint-size tough. Ruth soon gets wise and then Hanley comes up with a convoluted plot to frame his rival, Pretty Willie, so he can go straight and be with the babe. **86m/B; DVD.** Paul Douglas; Jean Peters; Cesar Romero; Keenan Wynn; Joan Davis; Peter Price; Arthur Treacher; ***D:*** Alexander Hall; ***W:*** Karl Tunberg; Darrell Ware; ***C:*** Lloyd Ahern; ***M:*** Cyril Mockridge.

Love the Coopers 🦴 **2015 (PG-13)** Another year, another mediocre holiday family comedy. The 2015 version features four generations of Coopers descending on the same family table for their annual Christmas Eve celebration. Of course, nothing goes as planned, secrets are revealed, emotions are manipulated, and wacky hijinks ensue. This year's ensemble of "People Too Good For This" includes Diane Keaton, John Goodman, Alan Arkin, Marisa Tomei, and more actors clearly in it for the paycheck. If you've seen one movie about a family getting together for Christmas, you've seen one movie about a family getting together for Christmas that's better than this one. **107m/C; DVD, Blu-Ray.** Diane Keaton; John Goodman; Ed Helms; Alex Borstein; Timothée Chalamet; Amanda Seyfried; Alan Arkin; Marisa Tomei; Olivia Wilde; June Squibb; Anthony Mackie; Jon Tenney; ***V:*** Steve Martin; ***D:*** Jessie Nelson; ***W:*** Steven Rogers; ***C:*** Elliot Davis; ***M:*** Nick Urata.

Love the Hard Way 🦴🦴 **2001** Would-be hipster writer Jack Grace (Brody) runs smalltime scams with his friend Charlie (Seda). Grad student Claire (Ayanna) falls for the romeo, even though she can see he's a loser. Though Jack cheats on her, Claire hangs around, even deciding that the best way to keep him is to join in Jack's con games. The characters are tedious as is the story; Grier shows up to give the film some spark in the small role of a cop out to bust Jack. "Inspired" by the Chinese novel "Fire and Ice" by Wang Shuo. **104m/C; VHS, DVD.** Adrien Brody; Charlotte Ayanna; Jon Seda; Pam Grier; August Diehl; David W. Ross; ***D:*** Peter Sehr; ***W:*** Peter Sehr; Marie Noelle; ***C:*** Guy Dufaux; ***M:*** Darien Dahoud.

Love Thy Neighbor 🦴 ½ **2002** Two married neighbors, Jack (Gwaltney) and Molly (Overbey), decide to hook up, and the simple affair leads to potentially disastrous fallout when Molly's husband admits to Jack that he might have AIDS. The resulting juxtaposition of emotions—marital boredom, betrayal among friends, and threat of disease—is awkward at best and ultimately forgettable. **87m/C; VHS, DVD.** Jack Gwaltney; Kellie Overbey; John Enos; Jennifer Bransford; Roy Scheider; Wallace Shawn; Jake Weber; ***D:*** Nick Gregory; ***W:*** Nick Gregory; Kirk Aanes; ***C:*** Dejan Georgevich; ***M:*** Stephen Coleman. **VIDEO**

A Love to Keep 🦴🦴 *Electroshock* **2007** Teachers Pilar and Elvira fall in love during the waning days of the Franco dictatorship in the 1970s. Pilar's domineering mother is so appalled that she has her daughter committed to an asylum, where Pilar undergoes brutal electroshock and other therapy. Eventually she's released to her parents' house where the ever-faithful Elvira tries to contact her. Pilar makes her escape but the women's reunion is overshadowed by the physical and mental effects of Pilar's ordeal. Spanish with subtitles. **98m/C; DVD.** *SP* Carmen Elias; Julieta Serrano; Juan Fernandez; Susi Sanchez; Juli Mira; Sergio Caballero; ***D:*** Juan Carlos Claver; ***W:*** Juan Carlos Claver; Agustin Madariaga; ***C:*** Javier Quintanilla; ***M:*** Alejandro Roman.

Love to Kill 🦴🦴 *The Girl Gets Moe* **1997 (R)** Moe (Danza) is a low-level arms dealer who falls for Elizabeth (Barondes), a gal who happens to like guns. But things go wrong thanks to dead bodies, double-crosses, and dirty cops. **102m/C; VHS, DVD.** Tony Danza; Michael Madsen; James Russo; Elizabeth Barondes; Louise Fletcher; Amy Locane; Richmond Arquette; Rustam Branaman; ***D:*** James Bruce; ***W:*** Rustam Branaman; Monica Clemens; ***C:*** Keith L. Smith; ***M:*** Barry Coffing. **CABLE**

The Love Trap 🦴🦴 ½ **1929** Early partial talkie (the film starts off as a silent with captions) is your basic Cinderella story. Chorus girl Laura Todd (La Plante) loses her job and gets booted out of her apartment. Cabbie Peter Cadwallader (Hamilton) offers his taxi as shelter and the two fall in love and marry—much to the displeasure of his snooty (and wealthy) family. The DVD includes the documentary "Directed by William Wyler." **71m/B; VHS, DVD.** Laura La Plante; Neil Hamilton; Robert Ellis; Rita La Roy; Jocelyn Lee; Norman Trevor; Clarissa Selwynne; ***D:*** William Wyler; ***W:*** Clarence Marks; John B. Clymer; Albert DeMond; Clarence Thompson; ***C:*** Gilbert Warrenton.

Love Unto Death 🦴🦴 *L'Amour a Mort* **1984** Simon (Arditi) and Elisabeth (Azema) are still working out their romantic relationship when he suddenly dies—and is quickly revived. His near-death experience has Simon becoming obsessed with mortality and he starts to withdraw from daily life. Friends Judith (Ardant) and Jerome (Dussollier), who are also Protestant ministers, offer their guidance but the idea of a love beyond death is all Simon can think about. French with subtitles. **92m/C; DVD, Blu-Ray.** *FR* Jean Daste; Pierre Arditti; Sabine Azema; Fanny Ardant; Andre Dussollier; Alain Resnais; ***W:*** Jean Gruault; ***C:*** Sacha Vierny; ***M:*** Hans Werner Henze.

Love! Valour! Compassion! 🦴🦴 ½ **1996 (R)** Follows eight gay men, longtime friends, who spend summer holiday weekends together at a beach house. The cast features Alexander as Buzz, who has a severe show tune fixation, and Glover playing a pair of twins with very different personalities (and they're actually named Jeckyll). Together they wander through the turmoil of AIDS, infidelity, rage and impromptu ballet practice. Excellent cast only occasionally swerves from humor and genuine pathos into the maudlin. Intermittent periods of stagy claustrophobia betray pic's Broadway origin. Based on the play by Terrence McNally. **120m/C; DVD.** Jason Alexander; John Glover; Randy Becker; John Benjamin Hickey; Stephen Bogardus; Stephen Spinella; Justin Kirk; ***D:*** Joe Mantello; ***W:*** Terrance McNally; ***C:*** Alik Sakharov; ***M:*** Harold Wheeler.

Love Walked In 🦴🦴 *The Bitter End* **1997 (R)** Hardly an original story but this B-movie has a standout performance from the edgy Leary. He's Jack Hanaway, a lounge piano player with a sultry singer/wife, Vicky (Sanchez-Gijon). Jack's old P.I. friend Eddie (Badalucco) shows up with a scheme to make them all rich. He's been hired by a wealthy woman (Dusay) who suspects her husband Fred (Stamp) of infidelity. Fred's faithful (he likes his wife's money) but he's a patron of Jack's and is naturally appreciative of Vicky's charms. So they try to set Fred up. Scenes of would-be writer Jack's pulp novel intrude into the action and provide an unneeded distraction. Adapted from the novel by Jose Pable Feinmann. **90m/C; DVD.** Denis Leary; Aitana Sanchez-Gijon; Terence Stamp; Michael Badalucco; Marj Dusay; Danny Nucci; Moira Kelly; Neal Huff; J.K. Simmons; ***D:*** Juan J. Campanella; ***W:*** Larry Golin; Juan J. Campanella; ***C:*** Daniel Shulman; ***M:*** Wendy Blackstone.

Love, Wedding, Marriage 🦴 ½ **2011 (PG-13)** Bride Eva (Moore) and bridegroom Charlie (Lutz) look like they belong on top of a wedding cake but the marriage therapist and her vintner hubby are going to experience some bumps in their newly-wedded bliss. Eva is shocked when her long-married parents (Seymour, Brolin) announce they're divorcing and she risks her own marriage to meddle and keep them together. There's much over-acting in an effort to keep the formulaic yet dumb plot moving in Mulroney's inconsequential directorial debut. **90m/C; DVD, Blu-Ray.** Mandy Moore; Kellan Lutz; James Brolin; Jane Seymour; Jessica Szohr; Michael Weston; ***D:*** Dermot Mulroney; ***W:*** Anouska Chydzik; Caprice Crane; ***C:*** Ottar Gudnason; ***M:*** Blake Neely.

The Lovebirds 🦴🦴 **2020 (R)** After their first night together, documentary filmmaker Jibran (Nanjiani) and advertising exec Leilani (Rae) click so well that they believe becoming romantically involved will be easy. Four years later, they are still together but the magic is gone as the differences in their personalities become points of tension. A planner, Jibran schedules everything, while Leilani is more spontaneous and likes taking risks. This impasse is challenged when the pair become entangled in a criminal conspiracy. To avoid getting killed, they have to work together as detectives. A satisfying comedy thanks to the stars' skills and chemistry. **96m/C; DVD.** Issa Rae; Kumail Nanjiani; Paul Sparks; Anna Camp; Nicholas X. Parsons; ***D:*** Michael Showalter; ***W:*** Brendan Gall; Aaron Abrams; ***C:*** Brian Burgoyne; ***M:*** Michael Andrews.

The Loved One 🦴🦴 ½ **1965** A famously outlandish, death-mocking farce based on Evelyn Waugh's satire about a particularly horrendous California funeral parlor/cemetery and how its denizens do business. A shrill, protracted spearing of American capitalism. **118m/B; VHS, DVD, Blu-Ray.** Robert Morse; John Gielgud; Rod Steiger; Liberace; Anjanette Comer; Jonathan Winters; James Coburn; Dana Andrews; Milton Berle; Tab Hunter; Robert Morley; Lionel Stander; Margaret Leighton; Roddy McDowall; Bernie Kopell; Alan Napier; Paul Williams; Barbara Nichols; Jamie Farr; ***D:*** Tony Richardson; ***W:*** Terry Southern; Christopher Isherwood; ***C:*** Haskell Wexler; ***M:*** John Addison.

Lovelace 🦴 ½ **2013 (R)** Another cautionary tale about the pitfalls of working in the sex industry, although this one features one of the most recognizable names in the history of adult film, Linda Lovelace. This flaccid, predictable biopic stars Seyfried as Lovelace, the naïve girl from a strict religious family who became an icon of the sexual revolution when she starred in the smash 1972 hit "Deep Throat." At the time of her fame, Lovelace presented the world of adult film as one of freedom and exploration but directors Epstein and Friedman illustrate the darker side of it all. Seyfried is solid though not quite right for the role. **93m/C; DVD, Blu-Ray.** Amanda Seyfried; Peter Sarsgaard; Sharon Stone; Robert Patrick; Hank Azaria; Chris Noth; Bobby Cannavale; Adam Brody; Juno Temple; James Franco; Eric Roberts; ***D:*** Robert Epstein; Jeffrey Friedman; ***W:*** Andy Bellin; ***C:*** Eric Alan Edwards; ***M:*** Stephen Trask.

Loveless **1983 (R)** A menacing glance into the exploits of an outcast motorcycle gang. In the 50s, a group of bikers on their way to the Florida Cycle Races stop for lunch in a small-town diner. While repairs are being made on their motorcycles, they decide to take full advantage of their situation. **85m/C; VHS, DVD, Blu-Ray.** Robert Gordon; Willem Dafoe; J. Don Ferguson; ***D:*** Kathryn Bigelow; ***W:*** Kathryn Bigelow.

Loveless *Nelyubov* **2018 (R)** An intense drama about a divorcing couple and their son. The loveless marriage between Boris (Rozin) and Zhenya (Spivak) has already fallen apart, and the couple is trying to sell their apartment where Zhenya still lives with their 12-year-old son, the emotionally distraught Alyosha (Novikov). Neither of his parents want him, and they have found other partners. When Alyosha is reported missing, authorities and volunteers look for the lost boy. Though his parents play a role in the search, they remained estranged and self-absorbed in their own worlds and new lives. A powerful film that considers big issues in society in intimate fashion. Russian with subtitles. **127m/C; DVD, Blu-Ray.** Maryana Spivak; Aleksey Rozin; Matvey Novikov; Vladimir Vdovichenkov; Varvara Shmykova; ***D:*** Andrey Zvyagintsev; ***W:*** Andrey Zvyagintsev; Oleg Negin; ***C:*** Mikhail Krichman; ***M:*** Evgueni Galperine; Sacha Galperine.

Loveless in Los Angeles **2007 (R)** Dave (Mihok) has a good job producing a reality TV dating show but he strenuously avoids commitment. That is until he bumps into now-divorced Kelly (Daniel), the girl he crushed on in college. But Dave's sleazy womanizing drives Kelly up the wall and he needs her to find his inner nice guy once again. Standard romance isn't really worth the effort. **95m/C; DVD.** Dash Mihok; Brittany Daniel; James Lesure; Navi Rawat; Christopher Coppola; Stephen Tobolowsky; Geoffrey Arend; ***D:*** Archie Gip; ***W:*** Archie Gip; ***C:*** Michael Marius Passah; ***M:*** Gregg Lehrman. **VIDEO**

Lovelife **1/2 1997 (R)** Yet another romantic saga about a group of disenchanted boomer friends who can't seem to make that love connection work. Maybe they should stop serial dating within their same small circle and take advantage of the outside world. **97m/C; VHS, DVD.** Sherilyn Fenn; Bruce Davison; Saffron Burrows; Jon Tenney; Carla Gugino; Matt Letscher; Tushka Bergen; Peter Krause; ***D:*** John Harmon Feldman; ***W:*** John Harmon Feldman; ***C:*** Anthony C. "Tony" Jannelli; ***M:*** Adam Fields. **VIDEO**

Lovelines **1984 (R)** Two rock singers from rival high schools meet and fall in love during a panty raid. Laughs uncounted ensue. **93m/C; VHS, DVD.** Greg Bradford; Michael Winslow; Mary Beth Evans; Don Michael Paul; Tammy Taylor; Stacey Toten; Miguel Ferrer; Shecky Greene; Aimee (Amy) Eccles; Sherri Stoner; ***D:*** Rod Amateau.

Lovely & Amazing **2002 (R)** Mom (Blethyn) watches over her three dysfunctional daughters: bored, married Michelle (Keener), insecure wannabe actress Elizabeth (Mortimer), and adopted eight-year-old African-American Annie (Goodwin), who's preoccupied with her looks. Unstable Michelle begins a hopeless affair with a teenager (Gyllenhaal), while a post-coital scene between Elizabeth and her lover (Mulroney) shows the extent of her body image problem. Annie just wants to look like everyone else in the family. The cast expertly embody their complicated, quirky characters in this skillfully written and directed character study by Holofcener. **91m/C; DVD.** Brenda Blethyn; Catherine Keener; Emily Mortimer; Raven Goodwin; Dermot Mulroney; Jake Gyllenhaal; Aunjanue Ellis; Clark Gregg; James LeGros; Michael Nouri; ***D:*** Nicole Holofcener; ***W:*** Nicole Holofcener; ***C:*** Harlan Bosmajian; ***M:*** Craig Richey. Ind. Spirit '03: Support. Actress (Mortimer).

The Lovely Bones **2009 (PG-13)** Just before Christmas 1973, 14-year-old Susie Salmon (Ronan) encounters neighbor George Harvey (Tucci) and is never seen alive again. Susie narrates from beyond the grave as she watches her mother (Weisz) and father (Wahlberg), her killer, and the police investigation. Eventually, Susie must decide whether to move on or continue observing what she can't change. Director Jackson chooses to give the Alice Sebold novel a fantasized, effects-heavy approach but in doing so drowns much of the quiet intimacy and nuance of the book. The end result is a movie that's shallow with too much style despite fine performances by the leads. **139m/C; DVD, Blu-Ray.** Saoirse Ronan; Mark Wahlberg; Rachel Weisz; Stanley Tucci; Susan Sarandon; Michael Imperioli; Rose McIver; Carolyn Dando; ***D:*** Peter Jackson; ***W:*** Peter Jackson; Fran Walsh; Philippa Boyens; ***C:*** Andrew Lesnie; ***M:*** Brian Eno.

Lovely by Surprise **2007** Quirky, low-budget indie. Novelist Marian (Preston) has severe writer's block and can't figure out what to do with the two brothers—Humkin (Chernus) and Mopekey (Roberts)?in her latest work. She decides to take the advice of mentor (and ex-lover) Jackson (Pendleton) and kill off one brother to add some drama. Marian decides on Humpkin, only he actually survives the threat and takes off—into the real world. When Marian realizes what's happened, her own grip on reality begins to loosen. **99m/C; DVD.** Carrie Preston; Michael Chernus; Dallas Roberts; Austin Pendleton; Reg Rogers; Kate Burton; Richard Masur; ***D:*** Kirt Gunn; ***W:*** Kirt Gunn; ***C:*** Steve Yedlin; ***M:*** Shelby Bryant.

Lovely, Still **2008 (PG)** Orderly, elderly, and in fragile health, Robert Malone (Landau) is nonetheless eager for a last romance with new neighbor Mary (Burstyn). Then Robert becomes anxious as he's convinced he knows Mary from sometime in his past. Even feature film debuting writer/director Fackler's rather logic-defying twist can't damage the strong performances of Landau and Burstyn. **90m/C; DVD.** Martin Landau; Ellen Burstyn; Elizabeth Banks; Adam Scott; ***D:*** Nicholas Fackler; ***W:*** Nicholas Fackler; ***C:*** Sean Kirby; ***M:*** Nate Wolcott; Mike Mogis.

Lovely to Look At **1952** Three wanna-be Broadway producers (Skelton, Keel, Champion) go to gay Paree to peddle Skelton's half interest in Madame Roberta's, a chi chi dress shop. There, they meet the shop's other half interest, two sisters (Champion and Miller), and together they stage a fashion show to finance the floundering hospice of haute couture. Lavish production, light plot. Filmed in Technicolor based on Kern's 1933 Broadway hit (inspired by Alice Duer Miller's "Gowns by Roberta"). Vincent Minnelli staged the fashion show, with gowns by Adrian. **105m/C; DVD.** Kathryn Grayson; Red Skelton; Howard Keel; Gower Champion; Marge Champion; Ann Miller; Zsa Zsa Gabor; Kurt Kasznar; Marcel Dalio; Diane Cassidy; ***D:*** Mervyn LeRoy; ***C:*** George J. Folsey.

A Lovely Way to Die **1/2 1968** Snoozy crime melodrama. Tough New York detective Jim Schuyler (Douglas) turns in his badge to go private and is hired as a bodyguard for Rena Westabrook (Koscina). She's accused of murdering her wealthy husband but Jim soon realizes it's all a set-up. **104m/C; DVD.** Kirk Douglas; Sylva Koscina; Eli Wallach; Kenneth Haigh; Martyn Green; Sharon Farrell; Dana Elcar; Ralph Waite; ***D:*** David Lowell Rich; ***W:*** A.J. Russell; ***C:*** Morris Hartzband; ***M:*** Kenyon Hopkins.

The Lovemaster **1997 (R)** A concert film with filmed vignettes about a comedian's life and influences. Stand-up comedian Craig Shoemaker explains how he came to be The Lovemaster in his major concert film. The stories and situations he describes are also discussed in filmed bits such as therapy sessions and episodes from his life, including be raised by his pot-smoking grandmother and belly-dancing mother as well his many failed relationships. **84m/C; DVD.** Craig Shoemaker; George Wendt; Esther Auerbach; Courtney Thorne-Smith; Harley Jane Kozak; ***D:*** Michael Goldberg; ***W:*** Craig Shoemaker; Michael Goldberg; ***C:*** Phil Parmet; Jeff Zimmerman; ***M:*** Giorgio Bertuccelli; Michael Skloff. **VIDEO**

The Lover *L'Amant* **1992 (R)** Portrays the sexual awakening of a French teenager and her older Chinese lover in Indochina in 1929. The characters, who remain nameless, meet on a ferry where the man is smitten by the girl's beauty. Detached and unromantic (the opposite of her indolent lover), she allows herself to be seduced for the experience, and money, he offers. The film is equally detached, including the beautifully photographed but uninvolving sex scenes. Moreau narrates as an adult looking back on her life. March's debut; filmed on location in Vietnam. Based on the semi-autobiographical novel by Marguerite Duras. **103m/C; DVD.** *FR* Jane March; Tony Leung Ka-Fai; Frederique Meininger; Arnaud Giovanietti; Melvil Poupaud; Lisa Faulkner; Xiem Mang; ***Nar:*** Jeanne Moreau; ***D:*** Jean-Jacques Annaud; ***W:*** Gerard Brach; Jean-Jacques Annaud; ***C:*** Robert Fraisse; ***M:*** Gabriel Yared. Cesar '93: Score.

Lover Come Back **1/2 1961** More Day-Hudson antics in which an advertising executive falls in love with his competitor but that doesn't stop him from stealing her clients. Is there no shame? **107m/C; VHS, DVD, Blu-Ray.** Rock Hudson; Doris Day; Tony Randall; Edie Adams; Joe Flynn; Ann B. Davis; Jack Oakie; Jack Albertson; Jack Kruschen; Howard St. John; ***D:*** Delbert Mann.

Loverboy **1989 (PG-13)** A college schnook takes a summer job as a Beverly Hills pizza delivery boy and is preyed upon by many rich and sex-hungry housewives. **105m/C; VHS, DVD.** Patrick Dempsey; Kate Jackson; Barbara Carrera; Kirstie Alley; Carrie Fisher; Robert Ginty; Elizabeth Daily; ***D:*** Joan Micklin Silver; ***W:*** Tom Ropelewski; Leslie Dixon; ***M:*** Michel Colombier.

Loverboy **2005 (R)** Obsessive mom love. Bacon directs wife Sedgwick in this adaptation of Victoria Redel's novel. Young Emily (played by daughter Sosie Bacon) always felt like an outsider because her parents (Tomei, Bacon) were so wrapped up in each other. So when she's an adult, Emily ruthlessly decides to become a single mom and give son Paul all the love she missed out on. But Emily freaks out at the slightest hint of independence from the growing Paul (Kay), who she still insists on calling "Loverboy." Really creepy pic is spent waiting for Emily to go completely off the rails. **86m/C; DVD.** Kyra Sedgwick; Kevin Bacon; Blair Brown; Matt Dillon; Oliver Platt; Campbell Scott; Marisa Tomei; John Lafayette; Dominic Scott Kay; Sosie Bacon; Jessica Stone; Melissa Errico; Nancy Giles; Sandra Bullock; ***D:*** Kevin Bacon; ***W:*** Hannah Shakespeare; ***C:*** Nancy Schreiber; ***M:*** Michael Bacon.

The Lovers **1959** Chic tale of French adultery with Moreau starring as a provincial wife whose shallow life changes overnight when she meets a young man. Had a controversial American debut because of the film's tender eroticism and innocent view of adultery. In French with English subtitles. **90m/B; VHS, DVD.** *FR* Jeanne Moreau; Alain Cuny; Jose-Luis De Villalonga; Jean-Mark Bory; ***D:*** Louis Malle; ***W:*** Louis Malle. Venice Film Fest. '59: Special Jury Prize.

The Lovers **2017 (R)** Middle-aged couple Mary (Winger) and Michael (Letts) are in the middle of a loveless marriage and separate affairs. They both decide to end the marriage and acknowledge their outside relationships (both of which seem headed toward the same malaise as their current one) when they unexpectedly rekindle feelings for each other and begin cheating on their respective flings with each other. The mood swings between quirky relationship comedy and brutal emotional drama, but the mesmerizing leads manage to hold it all together, despite the fact that you don't know if you should even like them, let alone root for a happy ending. **97m/C; DVD, Blu-Ray.** Debra Winger; Tracy Letts; Melora Walters; Aidan Gillen; Jessica Sula; ***D:*** Azazel Jacobs; ***W:*** Azazel Jacobs; ***C:*** Tobias Datum; ***M:*** Mandy Hoffman.

Lovers and Liars *Travels with Anita; A Trip with Anita* **1981 (R)** A romantic adventure in Rome turns into a symphony of zany mishaps when the man forgets to tell the woman that he is married!! **93m/C; VHS, DVD.** *IT* Goldie Hawn; Giancarlo Giannini; Laura Betti; ***D:*** Mario Monicelli; ***W:*** Mario Monicelli; Paul Zimmerman; ***C:*** Tonino Delli Colli; ***M:*** Ennio Morricone.

Lovers and Other Strangers **1970 (R)** Two young people decide to marry after living together for a year and a half. Various tensions surface between them and among their families as the wedding day approaches. Good comedy features some charming performances. Keaton's first film. **106m/C; VHS, DVD, Blu-Ray.** Gig Young; Bea Arthur; Bonnie Bedelia; Anne Jackson; Harry Guardino; Michael Brandon; Richard S. Castellano; Bob (Robert) Dishy; Marian Hailey; Cloris Leachman; Anne Meara; Diane Keaton; ***D:*** Cy Howard; ***W:*** Renee Taylor; Joseph Bologna; David Zelag Goodman. Oscars '70: Song ("For All We Know").

The Lovers and the Despot **2016** Two of the most famous South Korean film personalities—divorced couple actress Choi Eun-hee and director Shin Sang-ok—were kidnapped by Kim Jong-Il's men in the 1970s and forced to develop propaganda films for the notorious dictator. Meanwhile, these estranged lovers collected evidence of Kim's crimes and plotted their escape. Ross Adam and Robert Cannan's documentary is so fascinating that it's been optioned for a feature, fiction film. However, this telling of the tale doesn't really work. It's too in love with the oddity of its story that it loses sight of these victims. **98m/C; DVD.** Shin Sang-ok; Choi Eun-hee; ***D:*** Ross Adam; Robert Cannan; ***W:*** Ross Adam; Robert Cannan; ***M:*** Nathan Halpern.

Lovers Courageous **1/2 1932** Working-class Willie Smith (Montgomery) travels the world taking odd jobs as he tries to become a playwright. He and admiral's daughter Mary Blayne (Evans) fall in love but she's already engaged to dopey British aristocrat Lord Jimmy (Owen). It's not until Willie writes about his romance with a wealthy woman that he finds success, which makes him more socially acceptable to Mary's father (Kerr). Despite its staginess, this is not based on a play by Frederick Lonsdale but on his original screenplay. **77m/B; DVD.** Robert Montgomery; Madge Evans; Frederick Kerr; Reginald Owen; Evelyn Hall; Beryl Mercer; Halliwell Hobbes; ***D:*** Robert Z. Leonard; ***W:*** Frederick Lonsdale; ***C:*** William H. Daniels.

Lovers Like Us **1/2** *Le Sauvage; The Savage* **1975** Two people each leave their spouses, meet one another, and fall in love. **103m/C; VHS, DVD.** *FR* Catherine Deneuve; Yves Montand; Luigi Vannucchi; Tony Roberts; Dana Wynter; ***D:*** Jean-Paul Rappeneau; ***W:*** Jean-Paul Rappeneau.

Lovers of Hate **1/2 2010** Pic gets a little more interesting when it moves from its opening Austin, Texas, setting to a luxury Park City, Utah, ski lodge as it follows the rivalry between brothers Paul and Rudy over Rudy's wife Diana, who's left him. Rudy is a slob/loser (and wannabe writer) while Paul is the successful author of silly fantasy novels, so it's easy for Paul to persuade bored Diana to join him on vacation. Rudy knows Paul's scheming and sneaks along to play some gotcha surprises on his bro. **93m/C; DVD.** Heather Kafka; Chris Doubek; Alex Karpovsky; Zach Green; ***D:*** Bryan Poyser; ***W:*** Bryan Poyser; ***C:*** David Lowery; ***M:*** Kevin Bewersdorf. **VIDEO**

Lovers of the Arctic Circle *Los Amantes del Circulo Polar* **1998 (R)** Complex romantic drama set in Spain and Finland. Otto and Ana meet as children and instantly recognize each other as soul mates—their first kiss occuring over a geography book describing the Arctic Circle. When Otto's divorced father takes up with Ana's widowed mother, the now-adolescent pair wind up sharing the same house, and secretly become lovers. When Otto's mother dies, he blames himself for abandoning her and leaves Ana. She, in turn, becomes obsessed with being where the Arctic sun never sets and fate brings the adult duo together in Finland. Spanish with subtitles. **112m/C; DVD.** *SP* Fele Martinez; Najwa Nimri; Nancho Novo; Maru Valdivielso; Beate Jensen; ***D:*** Julio Medem; ***W:*** Julio Medem; ***C:*** Gonzalo F. Berridi; ***M:*** Alberto Iglesias.

The Lovers on the Bridge *Les Amants du Pont-Neuf* **1991 (R)** Overblown, extravagant romantic drama about two homeless lovers who live on Paris' Pont-Neuf bridge, which is closed for repairs. Michele (Binoche), a disoriented artist losing her eyesight, has left her home and stumbles upon the bridge squatters who include Alex (Lavant), a disturbed and alcoholic street performer. Alex rescues her and becomes Michele's protector and lover. He also becomes obsessive—fearing Michele will leave him and desperate to stop her. Set in 1989, the bicentennial of the French Revolution. The Alex character also appears in the Carax films "Boy Meets Girl" (1984) and "Bad Blood" (1986). French with subtitles. **125m/C; DVD, Blu-Ray.** *FR* Juliette Binoche; Denis Lavant; Klaus-Michael Gruber; Marion Stalens; ***D:*** Leos Carax; ***W:*** Leos Carax; ***C:*** Jean-Yves Escoffier.

Lover's Prayer 🦴🦴 1/2 *All Forgotten* **1999 (PG-13)** Wealthy, innocent young man (Stahl) becomes infatuated with a mysterious young woman (Dunst) who has moved next door for the summer. Then he learns that romance isn't what he had fantasized it to be. **106m/C; VHS, DVD.** Nick Stahl; Kirsten Dunst; Julie Walters; Geraldine James; Nathaniel Parker; James Fox; ***D:*** Reverge Anselmo; ***W:*** Reverge Anselmo; ***C:*** David Watkin; ***M:*** Joel McNeely.

Love's Abiding Joy 🦴🦴 1/2 **2006 (PG)** The fourth in the series, following "Love's Long Journey." Missie (Cottrell) and Willie (Bartholomew) are struck by tragedy when their baby daughter dies and a lingering drought devastates their cattle ranch. Willie reluctantly agrees to an offer from Mayor Doros (Laughlin) to become the new sheriff to earn some extra money but finds his job involves evicting neighbors who have fallen behind on loans made by Doros, who wants to control the community. Based on the novel by Janette Oke. **87m/C; DVD.** Erin Cottrell; Logan Bartholomew; John Laughlin; Dale Midkiff; Drew Tyler Bell; Mae Whitman; William Morgan Sheppard; James Tupper; ***D:*** Michael Landon, Jr.; ***W:*** Michael Landon, Jr.; Douglas Lloyd McIntosh; Bridget Terry; ***C:*** Brian Shanley; ***M:*** Kevin Kiner.

Loves & Times of Scaramouche 🦴 1/2 *Scaramouche* **1976** Eighteenth-century rogue becomes involved in a plot to assassinate Napoleon and winds up seducing Josephine in the process. Dubbed. **92m/C; VHS, DVD.** *IT* Michael Sarrazin; Ursula Andress; Aldo Maccione; ***D:*** Enzo G. Castellari.

Love's Christmas Journey 🦴🦴 1/2 **2011** A Hallmark Channel family drama based on the book series by Janette Oke. Recently widowed Ellie King goes to visit her brother Aaron Davis and his children for Christmas. Aaron goes out of town on a business trip but the holiday is threatened when he goes missing. **172m/C; DVD.** Natalie Hall; Greg Vaughan; Dylan Bruce; JoBeth Williams; Sean Astin; Charles Shaughnessy; Ernest Borgnine; Bobby Campo; Ryan Wynott; Jada Facer; ***D:*** David S. Cass, Sr.; ***W:*** George Tierne; ***C:*** Maximo Munzi; ***M:*** Nathan Furst. **CABLE**

Love's Enduring Promise 🦴🦴 1/2 **2004** In this follow-up to "Love Comes Softly," it's 10 years later and Marty and Clark are happily married and raising their young children while the now-grown Missie (Jones) has become a teacher. She is also being courted by both the wealthy Grant (Astin) and poor but hard-working Willie (Bartholomew). But romance will have to wait when Clark has an accident and Missie must help out on the farm. From the novel by Janette Oke. **88m/C; DVD.** Katherine Heigl; Dale Midkiff; January Jones; MacKenzie Astin; Logan Bartholomew; Cliff De Young; ***D:*** Michael Landon, Jr.; ***W:*** Michael Landon, Jr.; Cindy Kelley; ***C:*** Maximo Munzi; ***M:*** Kevin Kiner. **CABLE**

Love's Everlasting Courage 🦴🦴 1/2 **2011** Hallmark Channel sequel to "Love Begins," inspired by Janette Oke's "Love Comes Softly" series. Clark Davis and his wife Ellen are facing hard times on the family farm. Tragedy strikes when Ellen suddenly dies and Clark and their young daughter Missie must learn to live without her. **88m/C; DVD.** Wes Brown; Julie Mond; Morgan Lily; Cheryl Ladd; Bruce Boxleitner; Kirk B.R. Woller; James Eckhouse; ***D:*** Bradford May; ***W:*** Kevin Bocarde; ***C:*** Maximo Munzi; ***M:*** Brian Byrne. **CABLE**

Love's Kitchen 🦴 **2011** Generally unappetizing Brit rom com that suffers from blandness and some bad taste. Recently widowed dad Rob Haley (Scott) is a chef who needs a change of scenery and something to occupy him. His friends encourage him to get out of London and turn a rundown country pub into a gourmet restaurant. Food critic Kate (Forlani) happens to be visiting her dad (Bowles) in the same village, samples Rob's wares, and the two become an item more complicated than anything on the menu. **90m/C; DVD.** *GB* Dougray Scott; Claire Forlani; Peter Bowles; Michelle Ryan; Simon Callow; Joshua Bowman; Cherie Lunghi; ***Cameo(s):*** Gordon Ramsay; ***D:*** James Hacking; ***W:*** James Hacking; ***C:*** Jordan Cushing; ***M:*** Tom Howe. **VIDEO**

Love's Labour's Lost 🦴🦴 **2000 (PG)** Branagh dips into the Bard again with a setting in the 1930s and the music of Cole Porter, the Gershwins, and Jerome Kern. Just as four men vow to swear off women and concentrate on their studies along comes a French princess and her three companions. Guess what happens. As with the 1996 Woody Allen film, "Everyone Says I Love You," the actors try their best to be singing/dancing fools but just end up looking foolish. As for Shakespeare, well about two-thirds of the text is actually gone and even lesser Will shouldn't be treated like that. **93m/C; DVD.** *GB* Kenneth Branagh; Alicia Silverstone; Natascha (Natasha) McElhone; Alessandro Nivola; Matthew Lillard; Nathan Lane; Timothy Spall; Geraldine McEwan; Carmen Ejogo; Adrian Lester; Emily Mortimer; Richard Briers; Stefania Rocca; Jimmy Yuill; ***D:*** Kenneth Branagh; ***W:*** Kenneth Branagh; ***C:*** Alex Thomson; ***M:*** Patrick Doyle.

Love's Long Journey 🦴🦴 1/2 **2005** The third in the series, following "Love's Enduring Promise." Missie (Cottrell) has married Willie LaHaye (Bartholomew) and the two have left their families and community to begin a new life together on a cattle ranch. A pregnant Missie befriends their Native American neighbor Miriam (Bedard) but there's trouble when three strangers show up, looking for money that's supposedly hidden on the property. From the novel by Janette Oke. **88m/C; DVD.** Irene Bedard; William Morgan Sheppard; Richard Lee Jackson; Erin Cottrell; Logan Bartholomew; James Tupper; Cindy Kelley; ***D:*** Michael Landon, Jr.; ***W:*** Michael Landon, Jr.; Douglas Lloyd McIntosh; ***C:*** Brian Shanley; ***M:*** Kevin Kiner. **CABLE**

Loves of a Blonde 🦴🦴🦴 1/2 *A Blonde in Love; Lasky Jedne Plavovlasky* **1965** A shy teenage factory girl falls in love with a visiting piano player when the reservist army comes to her small town. But when she goes to visit his family, she discovers things aren't as she imagined. Touching look at the complications of love and our expectations. Czech with subtitles. **88m/B; VHS, DVD.** *CZ* Hana Brejchova; Josef Sebanek; Vladimir Pucholt; Milada Jezkova; ***D:*** Milos Forman; ***W:*** Milos Forman; Vaclav Sasek; Ivan Passer; Jaroslav Papousek; ***C:*** Miroslav Ondricek; ***M:*** Evsen Illin.

The Loves of Carmen 🦴🦴 1/2 **1948** Film version of the classic Prosper Merrimee novel about a tempestuous Spanish gypsy and the soldier who loves her. Hayworth is great to look at and the film's main selling point. **98m/C; VHS, DVD.** Rita Hayworth; Glenn Ford; Ron Randell; Victor Jory; Arnold Moss; Luther Adler; Joseph Buloff; ***D:*** Charles Vidor; ***W:*** Helen Deutsch; ***C:*** William E. Snyder; ***M:*** Mario Castelnuovo-Tedesco.

The Loves of Hercules WOOF! *Hercules and the Hydra; Hercules vs. the Hydra; Gli Amori di Ercole* **1960** The mythic mesomorph finds a mate with equiponderant chest measurements, and must save her from an evil queen. Somehow it eludes him that both queen and maiden are Miss Jayne in red and black wigs. Kudos for worst dubbing and special effects; a must see for connoisseurs of kitsch. **94m/C; VHS, DVD.** *IT FR* Jayne Mansfield; Mickey Hargitay; ***D:*** Carlo L. Bragaglia; ***W:*** Alessandro Continenza.

Loves of Three Queens 🦴 *Eternal Woman; L'Amante di Paride* **1954** In this silly costume drama, Hedy asks the advice of three male friends on what historical figure she should portray at a costume ball. One suggests Helen of Troy, another says Empress Josephine, and the third, Genevieve of Brabant, a wronged wife of medieval legend. Hedy then images herself in their lives. **97m/C; DVD.** *IT* Hedy Lamarr; Massimo Serato; Robert Beatty; Gerard Oury; Cesare Danova; ***D:*** Marc Allegret; Edgar G. Ulmer; ***W:*** Marc Allegret; Salka Viertel; ***C:*** Desmond Dickinson; ***M:*** Nino Rota.

Love's Unending Legacy 🦴🦴 1/2 **2007** The fifth film in author Janette Oke's bestselling series. After Willie LeHaye's death, Missie (Cottrell) returns to her father's (Midkiff) ranch and eventually adopts a troubled teenaged girl. As Missie becomes romantically interested in town sheriff Zach Tyler (Browne), she discovers that her new daughter's brother is being mistreated by the family who adopted him. **84m/C; DVD.** Erin Cottrell; Dale Midkiff; Victor Browne; Samantha Smith; Holliston Coleman; Brett Coker; Hank Stratton; Braeden Lemasters; ***D:*** Mark Griffiths; ***W:*** Pamela Wallace; ***C:*** Brian Stanley; ***M:*** Kevin Kiner. **CABLE**

Love's Unfolding Dream 🦴🦴 1/2 **2007** Belinda Tyler (Taylor-Compton), Missie's (Cottrell) adopted daughter, is determined to become a doctor—not something done by a woman in the 19th-century. But she proves her worth to Dr. Jackson (Pine) and he grudgingly agrees to help her. Then young lawyer Drew Simpson (Levis) comes to town to sell the farm he's inherited. As soon as that's done, he intends to return to New York—until he meets Belinda, that is. But she has her dream and Drew expects a traditional marriage. Based on the sixth novel in the series by Janette Oke. **88m/C; DVD.** Scout Taylor-Compton; Patrick Levis; Erin Cottrell; Victor Browne; Dale Midkiff; Robert Pine; Samantha Smith; ***D:*** Harry Frost; ***W:*** Michael Landon, Jr.; Cindy Kelley; ***C:*** Brian Shanley; ***M:*** Stephen Graziano. **CABLE**

Lovesick 🦴🦴 **1983 (PG)** A very-married New York psychiatrist goes against his own best judgment when he falls in love with one of his patients. **98m/C; DVD.** Dudley Moore; Elizabeth McGovern; Alec Guinness; John Huston; Ron Silver; ***D:*** Marshall Brickman; ***W:*** Marshall Brickman; ***C:*** Gerry Fisher; ***M:*** Philippe Sarde.

Lovesick 🦴🦴 **2014** A comedy about a man whose love life is nonexistent because of a most unusual personal glitch. Charles Darby (LeBlanc) seems to have it all. He has a great job as an elementary school principal, friends, and family. However, he lacks romance in his life because he whenever he gets close to a woman, he goes clinically insane. When Charles meets a new woman, Molly Kingston (Larter) who could be a romantic partner, he faces his mental health issue head with the help of friends so he finally find love. **85m/C; DVD, Streaming.** Matt LeBlanc; Ali Larter; Adam Rodriguez; Ashley Williams; Rebecca Naomi Jones; ***D:*** Luke Matheny; ***W:*** Dean Young; ***C:*** Bobby Webster; ***M:*** Sasha Gordon.

Lovesong 🦴🦴 **2017** Sarah (Keough) is generally ignored by her husband, and so to get a little companionship she goes on a road trip with her daughter and old friend Mindy (Malone). The friendship turns into something more as the trip progresses, and the two get physical, but part when it ends. Years later, Sarah sees Mindy again in the days before Mindy's wedding. This is a character-driven, moving drama, about regret, friendship, and love with two fantastic performances at its center. It's a delicate, unrequited love story. **84m/C; DVD.** Jena Malone; Riley Keough; Brooklyn Decker; Ryan Eggold; Rosanna Arquette; ***D:*** So Yong Kim; ***W:*** So Yong Kim; Bradley Rust Gray; ***C:*** Guy Godfree; Kat Westergaard; ***M:*** Johann Johannsson.

Lovespell 🦴 *Tristan and Isolde* **1979** A retelling of the legend of Isolde and Tristan. Stilted direction and writing, but another chance to reminisce on Richard Burton. **91m/C; VHS, DVD.** Richard Burton; Kate Mulgrew; Nicholas Clay; Cyril Cusack; Geraldine Fitzgerald; Niall Toibin; Diana Van Der Vlis; Niall O'Brien; ***D:*** Tom Donovan.

Loving 🦴🦴 **1970 (R)** Nondescript dramedy has Segal as a commercial artist whose midlife crisis comes to a head when his wife, mistress, and neighborhood witness his drunken tryst with a neighbor's wife via closed-circuit TV. Saint is very good as the wronged wife, but the whole thing is much duller than it should be. **89m/C; DVD.** George Segal; Eva Marie Saint; Sterling Hayden; Keenan Wynn; David Doyle; Paul Sparer; Andrew Duncan; Roland Winters; Edgar Stehli; Diana Douglas; Roy Scheider; Sab Shimono; Janis Young; Nancie Phillips; Sherry Lansing; ***D:*** Irvin Kershner; ***W:*** Don Devlin; ***C:*** Gordon Willis; ***M:*** Bernardo Segall.

Loving 🦴🦴🦴 **2016 (PG-13)** Richard and Mildred Loving never wanted to change the world. And yet it was their love that would finally put an end in 1967 to anti-miscegenation laws in the United States. After being arrested in Virginia just for being married at a time when races couldn't mix in the country, the pair was forcibly separated. They were told not only could they not be married but couldn't be in the same state at the same time. The ACLU took up the case. Negga and Edgerton are phenomenal here, both delivering subtle, graceful, respectful performances as two very private people. **123m/C; DVD, Blu-Ray.** Joel Edgerton; Ruth Negga; Michael Shannon; Marton Csokas; Nick Kroll; ***D:*** Jeff Nichols; ***W:*** Jeff Nichols; ***C:*** Adam Stone; ***M:*** David Wingo.

Loving Annabelle 🦴🦴 **2006** Senator's daughter Annabelle (Kelly) attends St. Theresa's, a strict Catholic boarding school where her rebelliousness gives the Mother Superior (Graff) fits. So she instructs Annabelle's favorite teacher, Simone Bradley (Gaidry), to help the girl cope. But what teacher and student soon realize is that there's a romantic attraction between them, which Annabelle is determined to pursue. A modern update of the 1931 German film "Maedchen in Uniform." **79m/C; DVD.** Ilene Graff; Kevin McCarthy; Michelle Horn; Marla Maples; Diane Gaidry; Erin Kelly; Wendy Schaal; ***D:*** Katherine Brooks; ***W:*** Katherine Brooks; ***C:*** Cynthia Pusheck.

Loving Couples 🦴🦴 **1980 (PG)** Two happily married couples meet at a weekend resort...and switch partners. Tired and predictable but it has its moments. **120m/C; VHS, DVD.** Shirley MacLaine; James Coburn; Susan Sarandon; Stephen Collins; Sally Kellerman; ***D:*** Jack Smight.

Loving Evangeline 🦴 1/2 **1998** Robert (Mancuso) is convinced that the boating mishap that killed his brother was no accident. And his suspicions are echoed by marina owner Evie Shaw (Rowan). From the Harlequin Romance Series; adapted from the Lisa Howard novel. **95m/C; DVD.** *CA* Nick Mancuso; Kelly Rowan; Shari Belafonte; Winston Rekert; Eugene Robert Glazer; ***D:*** Timothy Bond; ***W:*** Charles Lazar; ***C:*** Peter Benison; ***M:*** Ian Thomas. **TV**

A Loving Father 🦴 1/2 *Aime Ton Pere; Honor They Father* **2002** After famed French writer Leo Shepherd wins the Nobel Prize for Literature, he decides to ride his motorcycle to the Stockholm ceremony. His estranged son Paul has been trying to contact him and decides to follow, causing a freak accident that has the police thinking Leo is dead. Instead, Paul has kidnapped Leo and is forcing him to confront the problems of their past. Writer/director Berger used his own relationship with his father, writer John Berger, as the basis for this odd concoction, but pere and fils Depardieu, renowned for their own familial battles, must have found circumstances hitting very close to home. French with subtitles. **100m/C; DVD.** *FR* Gerard Depardieu; Guillaume Depardieu; Sylvie Testud; Julien Boisselier; ***D:*** Jacob Berger; ***W:*** Jacob Berger; Edward A. Radtke; Pascal Bavollier; ***C:*** Pascal Martin; ***M:*** Jean-Claude Petit.

Loving Jezebel 🦴🦴 **1999 (R)** If anything, writer/director Kwyn Bader's "Loving Jezebel" proves that Hill Harper ("The Skulls," "In Too Deep," etc.) is a terrific talent. The problem is, even at a mere 88 minutes, Bader's film seems long and even Harper can't act his way out of a weak and contrived script. The gist of the story is that he, Hill Harper, has a track record for falling in love with his friends' and other men's girlfriends—the theme of many a sit-com—with consistently bad results. Of course you have to give Harper credit for one thing, he has excellent taste in women as all of his "girlfriends" are "eye-candy" super models. **88m/C; DVD.** Hill Harper; Laurel Holloman; Nicole Ari Parker; Sandrine Holt; David Moscow; Elisa Donovan; Phylicia Rashad; *D:* Kwyn Bader; *W:* Kwyn Bader; *C:* Horacio Marquinez; *M:* Tony Prendatt.

Loving Leah ½ **2009** A gently sentimental and romantic Hallmark Hall of Fame production. According to a tenet of Orthodox Judaism, a man should marry his brother's childless widow to carry on the brother's name. Secular cardiologist Jake Lever (Kaufman) was estranged from his rabbi brother but he still feels obligated to his pretty widow Leah (Ambrose). He impulsively agrees to a marriage of convenience and invites Leah to move to his home in D.C., which allows her to pursue her college dreams. But the changes from Brooklyn nearly overwhelm Leah and Jake is having trouble coping with his new situation as well. Goldstein adapted from her play. **90m/C; DVD.** Lauren Ambrose; Adam Kaufman; Susie Essman; Mercedes Ruehl; Harris Yulin; Natasha Lyonne; Ricki Lake; *D:* Jeff Bleckner; *W:* P'nenah Goldstein; *C:* Charles Minsky; *M:* Jeff Beal. **TV**

Loving Vincent ½ **2017 (PG-13)** An animated look at the end of the life of tragic painter Vincent Van Gogh in the form of the first fully painted feature film. Featuring 65,000 oil-painted frames that incorporate about 120 of Van Gogh's paintings, the film is a visual masterpiece full of energy and color. Interspersed with hand-painted live action footage of actors, it explores whether Van Gogh committed suicide or was shot by another person through an investigation and interviews conducted by its narrator, Armand Roulin (Booth). Unfortunately the story and performances disappoint. **94m/C; DVD, Blu-Ray.** Douglas Booth; Josh Burdett; Holly Earl; Robin Hodges; Chris O'Dowd; *D:* Dorota Kobiela; Hugh Welchman; Justyna Wierszynska; *W:* Dorota Kobiela; Hugh Welchman; Jacek Dehnel; *C:* Tristan Oliver; Lukasz Zal; *M:* Clint Mansell.

Loving You **1957** A small town boy with a musical style all his own becomes a big success thanks to the help of a female press agent. Features many early Elvis hits. **101m/C; VHS, DVD.** Elvis Presley; Wendell Corey; Lizabeth Scott; Dolores Hart; James Gleason; Paul Smith; Jana Lund; Grace Hayle; *D:* Hal Kanter; *W:* Hal Kanter; *C:* Charles B(ryant) Lang, Jr.; *M:* Walter Scharf.

A Low Down Dirty Shame **1994 (R)** Shame (Wayans) is a down-on-his-luck private eye, with the obligatory wisecracking secretary, Peaches (Pinkett), who's hired by an old friend to find a vicious drug lord, a sultry ex-girlfriend, and $20 million. Lots of fun stunts and one liners can't make up for major plot holes. **100m/C; VHS, DVD.** Keenen Ivory Wayans; Jada Pinkett Smith; Salli Richardson-Whitfield; Charles S. Dutton; Andrew Divoff; Corwin Hawkins; *D:* Keenen Ivory Wayans; *W:* Keenen Ivory Wayans.

Low Heights ½ *Ertefa-e Past; Low Altitude* **2002** Based on a true story, a darkly humorous action film about one man's quest to protect his family. Ghassem (Farrokhnezhad) has one goal: get his family out of Iran and to the West. Desperate and at his wit's end, he and his pregnant wife Nargess (Hatami) hijack a plane to make their escape to Dubai where they hope to be granted asylum. They also pack the plane with family and friends to ensure their success. However, there are undercover police officers aboard the flight, their friends and family don't necessarily want to escape, and the highjacking does not go anywhere near as planned. Persian with subtitles. **115m/C; DVD.** Hamid Farokhnezhad; Leila Hatami; Gohar Kheirandish; Mohammad Ali Inanloo; Reza Shafi' Jam; *D:* Ebrahim Hatamikia; *W:* Ebrahim Hatamikia; Asghar Farhadi; *C:* Hassan Pooya. **VIDEO**

The Low Life ½ **1995 (R)** A "day in the life" sort of story about aspiring writer John (Cochrane) who comes to L.A. with high hopes but instead gets stuck in the low life of awful temp jobs, a lousy landlord (LeGros), and now, his newly arrived loser cousin Andrew (Astin). He tries to cozy up to looker Sedgwick but she doesn't seem too interested—so what's a would-be cool guy to do? **96m/C; VHS, DVD.** Rory Cochrane; Kyra Sedgwick; Sean Astin; James LeGros; Christian Meoli; Shawnee Smith; J.T. Walsh; Renée Zellweger; *D:* George Hickenlooper; *W:* George Hickenlooper; John Enbom; *C:* Richard Crudo; *M:* Bill Boll.

Low Tide **2019 (R)** Bored working class kids Alan (Johnson), Red (Neustaedter), and Smitty (Zolghardri) live by the Jersey shore and break into McMansions to steal items to better their lives. When Smitty gets seriously injured during a robbery, Alan and Red need a new lookout and bring in Alan's brother Peter (Martell).When they find a real treasure, cracks in their relationship begin to appear. While Red is territorial and a fighter, Alan is a lover and becomes intrigued by Mary (Froseth), who hangs out with a wealthier group. The coming-of-age thriller is predictable but capably told. **86m/C; DVD.** Jaeden Martell; Keean Johnson; Shea Whigham; Alex Neustaedter; Daniel Zolghadri; *D:* Kevin McMullin; *W:* Kevin McMullin; *C:* Andrew Ellmaker; *M:* Brooke Blair; Will Blair.

The Lower Depths ½ *Les Bas Fonds; Underground* **1936** Renoir's adaptation of the Maxim Gorky play about a thief and a financially ruined baron learning about life from one another. In French with English subtitles. **92m/B; VHS, DVD.** *FR* Jean Gabin; Louis Jouvet; Vladimir Sokoloff; Robert Le Vigan; Suzy Prim; *D:* Jean Renoir; *W:* Jean Renoir; Charles Spaak; *C:* Jean Bachelet; *M:* Jean Wiener.

The Lower Depths ½ *Donzoko* **1957** Kurosawa sets the Maxim Gorky play in Edo during the final Tokugawa period, using Noh theatre elements in depicting the lowly denizens of a low-rent hovel. In Japanese with English subtitles. **125m/B; VHS, DVD.** *JP* Toshiro Mifune; Isuzu Yamada; Ganjiro Nakamura; Kyoko Kagawa; Bokuzen Hidari; *D:* Akira Kurosawa; *W:* Akira Kurosawa; Hideo Oguni; *C:* Kazuo Yamazaki; *M:* Masaru Sato.

Lower Learning ½ **2008 (R)** The Geraldine Ferraro Elementary School will be closed unless hapless vice-principal Tom (Biggs) can convince district inspector Rebecca (Longoria Parker) to help him rally the lazy teachers, expose Principal Billings' (Corddry) corruption, and get those test scores up! **97m/C; DVD.** Jason Biggs; Eva Longoria; Rob Corddry; Ryan Newman; Monica Potter; Will Sasso; *D:* Mark Lafferty; *W:* Mark Lafferty; *C:* David Robert Jones; *M:* Ryan Shore. **VIDEO**

Lower Level **1991 (R)** While working late, an attractive business woman becomes trapped in an office building by her psychotic secret admirer. **88m/C; VHS, DVD.** David Bradley; Elizabeth (Ward) Gracen; Jeff Yagher; *D:* Kristine Peterson; *W:* Joel Soisson; *C:* Wally Pfister; *M:* Terry Plumeri.

Lowlife ½ **2018** One fateful day in one city, a group of low-life characters end up in the same motel room. They include underworld big wig Teddy (Burnham), who runs a fish taco stand, a human organ harvesting operation, and an underage prostitution ring. El Monstruo (Zarate) is a violent, local wrestler who is obsessed by the idea of legacy. Crystal (Micheaux) hires Teddy to get a kidney for her seriously ill husband (Cardenas), but becomes horrified when she learns someone she knows will be the donor. The unoriginal indie tries to create memorable characters and an interesting, non-chronological story but it just doesn't work. **96m/C; DVD.** Nicki Micheaux; Ricardo Adam Zarate; Jon Oswald; Mark Burnham; Clayton Cardenas; *D:* Ryan Prows; *W:* Ryan Prows; Jake Gibson; Shaye Ogbonna; Maxwell Michael Towson; *C:* Benjamin Kitchens; *M:* Pepijn Caudron.

Lowriders **2017 (PG-13)** An intergenerational family drama set in the Mexican-American car culture of Los Angeles. Patriarch Miguel (Bichir) runs an auto body shop by day, but his life is defined by his hobby of fixing up cars for lowrider competitions. Miguel is painfully aware of the mistakes he has made in his life and his tense relationship with his sons. Francisco (Rossi) has just been released from prison while Danny (Chavarria) is a graffiti artist who ignores danger to share his art with the world. Though the themes and conflicts are familiar, the strong performances, especially Bichir's soulful turn, give this scrappy film its appeal. **98m/C; DVD.** Gabriel Chavarria; Demian Bichir; Theo Rossi; Tony Revolori; Melissa Benoist; *D:* Ricardo de Montreuil; *W:* Elgin James; Cheo Hodari Coker; *C:* Andres Sanchez; *M:* Bryan Senti.

Lucas **1986 (PG-13)** A high school brain falls in love with the new girl in town, and tries to win her by trying out for the football team. Genuine film about the perils of coming of age. Thoughtful, non-condescending, and humorous. **100m/C; VHS, DVD, Blu-Ray.** Corey Haim; Kerri Green; Charlie Sheen; Winona Ryder; Courtney Thorne-Smith; Tom (Thomas E.) Hodges; *D:* David Seltzer; *W:* David Seltzer; *M:* Dave Grusin.

Luce **2019 (R)** Star high school student Luce (Harrison) excels in academics and sports. Formerly a child soldier in Africa, he was adopted by two white parents Peter (Tim Roth) and Amy (Watts), and overcame his past with therapy. Luce's early life becomes a point of contention when he writes a paper that considers the topic of necessary violence for Harriet Wilson's (Spencer) class. Convinced he will act out, Harriet takes actions that affect Luce, the school, and the Edgars' marriage. The thriller touches on topical issues related to race and privilege -- but perhaps not quite enough -- and Harrison and Spencer give strong performances. **109m/C; DVD.** Naomi Watts; Octavia Spencer; Kelvin Harrison, Jr.; Tim Roth; Norbert Leo Butz; *D:* Julius Onah; *W:* Julius Onah; J. C. Lee; *C:* Larkin Seiple; *M:* Geoff Barrow; Ben Salisbury.

Lucia, Lucia *La Hija del Canibal; The Cannibal's Daughter* **2003 (R)** Middle-aged Lucia (Roth) is the unreliable narrator of this Mexican fable. Lucia's husband, Ramon (Moreno), disappears in the Mexico City airport--maybe he abandoned her or maybe Ramon was kidnapped. Since the police are no help, Lucia turns to two neighbors for help—Felix (Alvarez-Novoa), an elderly Spanish Civil War veteran, and young, handsome Adrian (Becker). There's a botched ransom drop, Ramon's exposure as an embezzler, Lucia's tryst with Adrian, and many, many red herrings. Although it doesn't matter much. Spanish with subtitles. **113m/C; VHS, DVD.** *MX SP* Cecilia (Celia) Roth; Carlos Alvarez-Novoa; Kuno Becker; Jose Elias Moreno, Jr.; Margarita Isabel; Javier Diaz Duenas; Hector Ortega; *D:* Antonio Serrano; *W:* Antonio Serrano; *C:* Xavier Perez Grobet; *M:* Nacho Mastretta.

The Lucifer Complex **1978** Nazi doctors are cloning exact duplicates of such world leaders as the Pope and the President of the United States on a remote South American island in the year 1996. **91m/C; VHS, DVD.** Robert Vaughn; Merrie Lynn Ross; Keenan Wynn; Aldo Ray; *D:* David L. Hewitt; Kenneth Hartford.

Luck of the Draw **2000 (R)** Ex-con Marshall, who finds going straight to be very dull, finds some unexpected excitement when a couple of counterfeit printing plates come into his possession. He soon realizes that a lot of unsavory types are after the plates, including mob boss Hopper. Run-of-the-mill. **108m/C; VHS, DVD.** James Marshall; Michael Madsen; Ice-T; Frank Gorshin; Eric Roberts; Dennis Hopper; Wendy Benson; William Forsythe; Sasha Mitchell; Richard Ruccolo; *D:* Luca Bercovici; *W:* Namon Ami; Rick Bloggs; Kandice King; *C:* Keith L. Smith; *M:* Stephen (Steve) Edwards. **VIDEO**

The Luck of the Irish ½ **1948** A comedy that forgoes being twinkly despite the presence of a leprechaun. Hard-boiled reporter Stephen Fitzgerald (Power) takes a trip to Ireland and is stuck at a rural inn where owner Nora (Baxter) tells him about leprechauns and their pot o' gold. When he spots a strange man (Kellaway), he follows him and jokingly demands his treasure. When the gold appears, Stephen's so surprised, he refuses it, so the leprechaun then owes him a favor. Back in New York, Stephen's new job with right-wing publisher Auger (Cobb) gets him an apartment and a valet, but Stephen's shocked when Horace the valet looks exactly like his leprechaun. **99m/B; DVD.** Tyrone Power; Anne Baxter; Cecil Kellaway; Lee J. Cobb; Jayne Meadows; James Todd; *D:* Henry Koster; *W:* Philip Dunne; *C:* Joseph LaShelle; *M:* Cyril Mockridge.

Lucky ½ **2011 (R)** Unsuccessful black comedy has mama's boy Ben (Hanks) turning out to be a serial killer of young blonde women who resemble the childhood crush who always rejected him. That would be manipulative Lucy (Graynor) who isn't so dismissive when Ben wins millions in the lottery (thanks to a victim's ticket). She hustles him to the altar, finds about his deadly hobby, and keeps quiet until she can get the dough. There's nothing particularly compelling about either the characters or the plot. **103m/C; DVD.** Colin Hanks; Ari Graynor; Ann-Margret; Jeffrey Tambor; Mimi Rogers; Tom Amandes; *D:* Gil Cates, Jr.; *W:* Ken Sublette; *C:* Darren Genet; *M:* John Swihart.

Lucky **2017** A meaningful dramatic exploration of life, death, health, and loneliness through a 90-year-old man (Stanton). Living in a small Arizona desert town, Lucky is a retired veteran whose days are filled with visits to a local coffee shop and a bar, and doing yoga and smoking cigarettes. Through all of Lucky's interactions with quirky locals, topics like philosophy, morality, religion, and popular culture are discussed and argued. As Lucky struggles with end of his life issues, he remains defiantly atheistic but reaches out to others in realistic fashion. Stanton's performance is memorable. **98m/C; DVD.** Harry Dean Stanton; David Lynch; Ron Livingston; Ed Begley, Jr.; Tom Skerritt; *D:* John Carroll Lynch; *W:* Logan Sparks; Drago Sumonja; *C:* Tim Suhrstedt; *M:* Elvis Kuehn.

Lucky Break **2001 (PG-13)** Small-time crooks Jimmy (Nesbitt) and Rudy (James) wind up in the same prison after a bank job gone wrong. Eccentric prison governor Mortimer (Plummer) loves musicals and has written one of his own. Jimmy encourages Mortimer to let the prisoners stage his opus and plans an escape attempt during the performance. Film gets schzoid with comic rehearsals, a tentative romance between Jimmy and support worker Annabel (Williams), a suicide, and the confusing prison break. **109m/C; VHS, DVD.** *GB* James Nesbitt; Lennie James; Christopher Plummer; Olivia Williams; Timothy Spall; Bill Nighy; Ron Cook; Frank Harper; Peter Wight; Celia Imrie; Raymond Waring; Julian Barratt; *D:* Peter Cattaneo; *W:* Ronan Bennett; *C:* Alwin Kuchler; *M:* Anne Dudley.

Lucky Christmas ½ **2011** Hallmark Channel movie. Unlucky single mom Holly (Berkley) buys a lottery ticket, puts it in the glove box of her car, and hopes for a happier holiday. Her car goes missing, and the winning ticket along with it. Struggling Mike (Gray-Stanford) has Holly's car--and the ticket--but will he do the right thing and return both without trying to get some of the money for himself? **87m/C; DVD.** Elizabeth Berkley; Jason Gray-Stanford; Mitchell Kummen; Mike Bell; *D:* Gary Yates; *W:* Sheri Davenport; *C:* Brenton Spencer; *M:* Shawn Pierce. **CABLE**

Lucky Day **1991** Artist Kari (Madigan) has been caring for her mentally-challenged younger sister Allison (Webb) for years since their alcoholic mother Katherine (Dukakis) abandoned her children. But when Allison wins the lottery, their mother reappears and wants to reconcile. **95m/C; DVD.** Amy Madigan; Chloe Webb; Olympia Dukakis; Terence Knox; John Beasley; Allen Hamilton; *D:* Donald Wrye; *W:* John Axness; Jennifer Miller; *C:* Jon Kranhouse; *M:* David Bell. **TV**

Lucky Days ½ **2008** Dowdy Virginia tries to be the rock for everyone around her while ignoring her own needs—and the fact that she's been involved with Vincent for 18 years and his mother still hates her. Her childhood boyfriend Zeth comes back into her life and Virginia finally decides to let loose, which includes the last weekend of fun before the Coney Island Amusement Park falls to developers. **103m/C; DVD.** Angelica Torn; Luke Zarzecki; Federico Castelluccio; Rip Torn; Will Patton; Anne Jackson; Marilyn Sokol; Tina Benko; Tony Torn; *D:* Angelica Torn; Tony Torn; *W:* Angelica Torn; *C:* Nils Kenaston; *M:* Christopher North.

Lucky Grandma ½ **2020** Chain-smoking, 80-year-old widow Grandma Wong (Chin) spent much of her life working hard only to be destitute and in danger of losing her beloved apartment. Believing luck is on her side after a visit with a fortune teller, she takes her fate into her own hands by gambling at a casino and stealing money from a dead man that belongs to the Chinese mafia. When Grandma begins enjoying her funds, the gang claiming the money shows up, compelling her to hire a cut-rate bodyguard, Big Pong (Ha). The comedic debut feature of Sealy features a unique heroine in Wong and Chin's memorable performance. Mandarin and Cantonese with subtitles. **97m/C; DVD.** Tsai Chin; Hsiao-Yuan Ha; Michael Tow; Woody

Fu; Yan Xi; ***D:*** Sasie Sealy; ***W:*** Sasie Sealy; Angela Cheng; ***C:*** Eduardo Enrique Mayen; ***M:*** Andrew Orkin.

Lucky in Love 🦴 ½ **2014** Not so lucky in this predictable Hallmark Channel rom com. Mira feels like she's being pranked when she gets a big promotion on April Fool's Day as well as meeting the seemingly perfect guy. But her new opportunity turns out to have lots of strings attached and the new guy may not be the man she's meant to be with. So Mira has to figure out just what 'perfect' really means. **90m/C; DVD.** Jessica Szohr; Ben Hollingsworth; Deidre Hall; Ryan Kennedy; ***D:*** Kevin Fair; ***W:*** Talia Green; Nina Weinman; ***C:*** Kamal Derkaoui; ***M:*** Michael Richard Plowman. **CABLE**

Lucky Jim 🦴🦴 ½ **1958** A junior lecturer in history at a small university tries to get himself in good graces with the head of his department, but is doomed from the start by doing the wrong things at the worst possible times. Minus the social satire of the Kingsley Amis novel on which it was based; what's left is a cheerful comedy. **91m/B; VHS, DVD.** *GB* Ian Carmichael; Terry-Thomas; Hugh Griffith; Sharon Acker; Jean Anderson; Maureen Connell; Clive Morton; John Welsh; Reginald Beckwith; Kenneth Griffith; Jeremy Hawk; Harry Fowler; ***D:*** John Boulting; Roy Boulting; ***W:*** Jeffrey Dell; Patrick Campbell; ***C:*** Mutz Greenbaum; ***M:*** John Addison.

Lucky Luciano 🦴🦴 *A Proposito Luciano; RE: Lucky Luciano* **1974 (R)** A violent depiction of the final years of Lucky Luciano, gangster kingpin. **108m/C; VHS, DVD.** *IT FR* Edmond O'Brien; Rod Steiger; Vincent Gardenia; Gian Marie Volonte; ***D:*** Francesco Rosi; ***C:*** Pasqualino De Santis.

Lucky Luke 🦴🦴 ½ **1994 (PG)** Fastest gun in the west brings the law to Daisy Town, aided by his horse, Jolly Jumper—who can talk. Not exactly John Wayne material but amusing. **91m/C; VHS, DVD.** Terence Hill; Nancy Morgan; Ron Carey; ***V:*** Roger Miller; ***D:*** Terence Hill; ***W:*** Rene Goscinny; ***C:*** Carlo Tafani; Gianfranco Transunto; ***M:*** David Grover; Aaron Schroeder.

Lucky Me 🦴🦴 **1954** A group of theatre entertainers are stranded in Miami and are forced to work in a hotel kitchen. They soon acquire the support of a wealthy oilman (Goodwin) who invests in their show, but not before his spoiled daughter tries to thwart all plans. **100m/C; DVD.** Doris Day; Robert Cummings; Phil Silvers; Eddie Foy, Jr.; Nancy Walker; Martha Hyer; Bill Goodwin; Marcel Dalio; James Burke; Dolores Dorn; William "Billy" Bakewell; ***D:*** Jack Donohue.

Lucky Number Slevin 🦴🦴 **2006 (R)** Too-twisty thriller owes a lot to the wicked gravitas of Freeman and Kingsley as rival New York mobsters (known respectively as "The Boss" and "The Rabbi"), who both mistake sweet-faced Slevin (Hartnett) for his missing friend Nick, who owes big money to both men. The Boss will forgive the debt if Slevin will kill someone for him, while the Rabbi just wants the cash. Meanwhile, sexy neighbor Lindsey (Liu), who's a coroner, is romancing the hunk and trying to help him avoid certain death—maybe at the hands of hitman Mr. Goodkat (Willis). Except, nothing is really as it appears to be. **110m/C; DVD, HD-DVD.** Josh Hartnett; Morgan Freeman; Ben Kingsley; Lucy Liu; Stanley Tucci; Bruce Willis; Peter Outerbridge; Mykelti Williamson; Danny Aiello; Robert Forster; Dorian Missick; Jennifer Miller; Kevin Chamberlin; Oliver Davis; Michael Rubenfeld; ***D:*** Paul McGuigan; ***W:*** Jason Smilovic; ***C:*** Peter Sova; ***M:*** J. Ralph.

Lucky Numbers 🦴 ½ **2000 (R)** In this unfortunate comedy, TV weatherman Russ (Travolta) is caught up in a lavish lifestyle he can't afford. He schemes with the station's morally lax lotto ball girl Crystal (Kudrow) to fix a jackpot lottery, with her oafish cousin Walter (Moore) as the front man with the ticket. Their plan slips out, so they're hounded by a host of greedy dimwits hoping to get in on the action. Resnick, who hails from Harrisburg, where the movie is set, apparently has no qualms painting his fellow townspeople as amoral losers. Loosely based on a 1980 attempt to fix the Pennsylvania State Lottery. **105m/C; DVD.** John Travolta; Lisa Kudrow; Tim Roth; Ed O'Neill; Michael Rapaport; Daryl (Chill) Mitchell; Bill Pullman; Richard Schiff; Michael Moore; Michael Weston; Sam McMurray; ***D:*** Nora Ephron; ***W:*** Adam Resnick; ***C:*** John Lindley; ***M:*** George Fenton.

The Lucky One 🦴 **2012 (PG-13)** During Marine Logan Thibault's (Efron) service in Iraq, he is inspired by a photo of a girl he never met. When he makes it back from his time in country, he seeks out the girl, assuming that her soldier beau is dead, and finds himself connected to her. This routine romantic drama tries to manipulatively pull at the heartstrings but fails even as a cheesy diversion. But Efron makes for great eye candy. Based on the 2010 Nicholas Sparks novel that plays like a greatest hits collection of his clichés. **101m/C; DVD, Blu-Ray, Streaming.** Zac Efron; Taylor Schilling; Blythe Danner; Riley Thomas Stewart; Jay Ferguson; ***D:*** Scott Hicks; ***W:*** Will Fetters; ***C:*** Alar Kivilo; ***M:*** Mark Isham; Hal Lindes.

The Lucky Ones 🦴🦴 **2008 (R)** Collee (McAdams), T.K. (Pena), and Cheever (Robbins) are three Iraq War vets who find their homecomings delayed when their flights out of a NYC airport are cancelled. So they road-trip it across the country, meeting a bevy of fellow-citizen stereotypes along the way, all with strong opinions, good and bad, about the war and vets. Stacked with too many trite coincidences and too much melodrama, but the performances of the three leads salvage an otherwise sappy road trip. Tries to be too many things and ends up being nothing special. **115m/C; On Demand.** Rachel McAdams; Tim Robbins; Michael Peña; Molly Hagan; Mark L. Young; Annie Corley; John Diehl; John Heard; ***D:*** Neil Burger; ***W:*** Neil Burger; Dirk Wittenborn; ***C:*** Declan Quinn; ***M:*** Rolfe Kent.

Lucky Partners 🦴🦴 **1940** When an artist and an errand girl share a winning lottery ticket, funny complications arise as they embark on a fantasy honeymoon. Although Rogers' innocence and Coleman's savoir faire provide an interesting contrast, the script isn't equal to the status of its stars. **101m/B; VHS, DVD.** Ronald Colman; Ginger Rogers; Jack Carson; Spring Byington; Harry Davenport; Cecilia Loftus; ***D:*** Lewis Milestone; ***W:*** Lewis Milestone; Allan Scott; John Van Druten; ***C:*** Robert De Grasse; ***M:*** Dimitri Tiomkin.

Lucky Seven 🦴🦴 ½ **2003 (PG-13)** Amy's dying mother (O'Grady) informs her seven-year-old daughter that she has drawn a timeline for her life, including the fact that Amy will marry her seventh boyfriend. Amy (Williams) has always followed her mother's advice, but the successfull lawyer now has a problem—she's fallen for boyfriend #6, Peter (Dempsey). So should she follow her heart or wait for #7, who's the equally handsome and charming Daniel (Rowe). Amusing romantic comedy with a very attractive cast. **90m/C; VHS, DVD.** Kimberly Williams; Patrick Dempsey; Brad Rowe; Gail O'Grady; ***D:*** Harry Winer; ***W:*** Jessica Barondes; ***C:*** Jon Joffin; ***M:*** Danny Lux. **CABLE**

Lucky Star 🦴🦴 **1929** Poverty-stricken Mary (Gaynor) lives in a shack with her widowed mother (Reicher), who wants her daughter to marry Martin (Williams), an ex-soldier with good prospects. However, Mary's already in love with Timothy (Farrell), who's been looking out for her, but he's crippled from war wounds and is doing menial work so he doesn't fit in with her mother's plans. Miraculously, Timothy regains his strength before the wedding and fights his rival for the girl. **85m/B; Silent; DVD.** Janet Gaynor; Charles Farrell; Guinn "Big Boy" Williams; Paul Fix; Hedwig Reicher; ***D:*** Frank Borzage; ***W:*** Sonya Levien; John Hunter Booth; ***C:*** Chester Lyons; William Cooper Smith.

Lucky Stiff 🦴🦴 **1988 (PG)** A fat, unpopular dweeb has the shock of his life when a radiant woman falls in love with him, the strangeness of which becomes evident when he meets her very weird family. **93m/C; VHS, DVD.** Donna Dixon; Joe Alaskey; Jeff Kober; Elizabeth Arlen; Charles Frank; Barbara Howard; ***D:*** Anthony Perkins; ***W:*** Pat Proft.

Lucky Them 🦴🦴 ½ **2013 (R)** Griffiths low-key road tripper succeeds thanks to the performances of Collette and Church. Seattle-based music critic Ellie Klug is warned her job is on the line if she can't write the big story suggested by her editor. What happened to rock legend Matthew Smith, Klug's ex-lover, who disappeared 10 years before and is thought to have committed suicide. In the midst of a midlife crisis, the cynical Ellie takes to the road with dilettante and would-be documentary filmmaker Charlie, but it's the (emotional) journey and not its results that becomes important. **97m/C; Streaming.** Toni Collette; Thomas Haden Church; Ryan Eggold; Ahna O'Reilly; Nina Arianda; Oliver Platt; ***Cameo(s):*** Johnny Depp; ***D:*** Megan Griffiths; ***W:*** Huck Botko; Emily Wachtel; ***C:*** Ben Kutchins; ***M:*** Craig Wedren.

Lucky You 🦴🦴 **2007 (PG-13)** Talented poker player Huck Cheever (Bana) makes his living fleecing tourists in Las Vegas and dreaming of making it big in the World Championship (Series) of Poker. Unfortunately, his emotions usually get in the way, especially when dealing with his deadbeat father, L.C. (Duvall), who becomes his poker arch-nemesis. On his way to a showdown with Dad, Huck alternately romances and rips off struggling lounge singer Billie (Barrymore). Hansen obviously loves his characters, poker, and the eccentrics that make up Las Vegas's underbelly, but it's not enough to help this movie's desperate identity crisis. **123m/C; DVD.** Eric Bana; Robert Duvall; Drew Barrymore; Debra Messing; Horatio Sanz; Jean Smart; Charles Martin Smith; Robert Downey, Jr.; Kelvin Han Yee; Evan Jones; Michael Shannon; ***D:*** Curtis Hanson; ***W:*** Curtis Hanson; Eric Roth; ***C:*** Peter Deming; ***M:*** Christopher Young.

Luckytown 🦴 ½ **2000 (R)** Part road movie, part Vegas movie, part family ties, and none of the parts turn out to fit together. Oklahoman Lidda (Dusnt) gets a check on her 18th birthday from her long-gone dad, gambler Charlie (Caan), so she decides to track him down in Vegas. Along for the ride is store clerk and potential beau Colonel (Kartheiser), who happens to know his way around the cards himself. Only it turns out dad is in big trouble with club owner Tony (Miano) and the kids are soon caught in the middle. **101m/C; VHS, DVD.** Kirsten Dunst; Vincent Kartheiser; James Caan; Robert Miano; Luis Guzman; Jennifer Gareis; Theresa Russell; ***D:*** Paul Nicholas; ***W:*** Brendon Beseth; ***C:*** Denis Maloney; ***M:*** Greg Edmonson.

Lucy 🦴🦴 ½ **2014 (R)** Besson's gleeful action flick stars Johansson as the revenge-minded Lucy, who's turned into an unwilling drug mule by Korean mobsters. When the packet sewn into her body ruptures, Lucy's nervous system is flooded by a super-drug that turns her super-smart, super-dangerous, and with a limited time to live. Lucy intends to make the most of it and the pic moves deliriously along, speedily ignoring any plot issues and weirdness, anchored by the actress's ferocious performance. **89m/C; DVD, Blu-Ray.** *FR* Scarlett Johansson; Morgan Freeman; Min-Sik Choi; Amr Waked; ***D:*** Luc Besson; ***W:*** Luc Besson; ***C:*** Thierry Arbogast; ***M:*** Éric Serra.

Lucy in the Sky 🦴 **2019 (R)** This disappointing drama never quite finds its footing and wanders aimlessly as a tangential drama, despite a better than the film deserves performance from Portman, who stars as Lucy Cola, a dedicated and driven astronaut who, after returning home from a deeply spiritual space mission, finds that her personal life and connection to reality has begun to fall apart. Loosely based on the weird-but-true story of astronaut Lisa Novak. **124m/C; DVD.** Natalie Portman; Jon Hamm; Dan Stevens; Zazie Beetz; Pearl Amanda Dickson; ***D:*** Noah Hawley; ***W:*** Noah Hawley; Elliott DiGuiseppi; Brian C. Brown; ***C:*** Polly Morgan; ***M:*** Jeff Russo.

Ludwig 🦴🦴 **1972 (PG)** Lavish-but-slow epic bio of Bavaria's mad monarch, Ludwig II (Berger), who built extravagent fantasy castles and sponsored composer Richard Wagner (Howard), whom the king became obsessed with. Italian with subtitles. **231m/C; VHS, DVD, Blu-Ray.** *IT GE* Helmut Berger; Trevor Howard; Romy Schneider; Silvana Mangano; Helmut Griem; Gert Frobe; ***D:*** Luchino Visconti; ***W:*** Luchino Visconti; ***C:*** Armando Nannuzzi.

Luka Chuppi 🦴🦴 **2019** After highly respected cable news anchor Guddu (Aaryan) meets journalism intern Rashmi (Sanon) in her small town in northern India, they fall in love. Though marriage would normally be the next step in her community, Rashmi wants to try living with Guddu for a time before they tie the knot. However, their community does not support such relationships because of protests led by Rashmi's own conservative politician father (Pathak). The entertaining romantic comedy features quirky characters and social commentary. Though the leads have chemistry, their appearance seems out of step with their characters. Hindi with subtitles. **126m/C; DVD.** Kartik Aaryan; Kriti Sanon; Aparshakti Khurana; Pankaj Tripathi; Vinay Pathak; ***D:*** Laxman Utekar; ***W:*** Rohan Shankar; ***C:*** Milind Jog; ***M:*** Tanishk Bagchi; White Noise; Ketan Sodha; Abhijit Vaghani.

Lullaby 🦴 ½ **2008** American Stephanie travels to Johannesburg after being notified that her drug addict son has been kidnapped and is being held for ransom. When the ransom meet doesn't go as planned, Stephanie's only chance is to work with her son's pregnant girlfriend Tina against the drug lord holding Kyle hostage. **96m/C; DVD.** Melissa Leo; Russel Savadier; Joey Dedio; Lisa-Marie Schneider; Kyle Siebert; ***D:*** Darrell Roodt; ***W:*** Michael D. Sellers; Donald A. Barton; ***M:*** Alun Richards. **VIDEO**

Lullaby 🦴🦴 ½ **2014 (R)** This comedy-drama explores a dysfunctional family dynamic as its patriarch reaches the end of his life. Though Jonathan Lowenstein (Hedlund) has been estranged from his wealthy family for years, he has been informed that his father Robert (Jenkins) will die within a few days. Robert has been seriously ill for a decade with lung cancer and is making the choice to take himself off life support within 48 hours. Agreeing to visit, Jonathan travels from his Los Angeles home to his family in New York. His appearance sets off a family conflict as complicated emotions and resentments surface. Yet all involved experience the unexpected, including reconnection, transformation, and the power of life. **117m/C; DVD, Streaming, Download.** Garrett Hedlund; Richard Jenkins; Anne Archer; Jessica Brown Findlay; Amy Adams; ***D:*** Andrew Levitas; ***W:*** Andrew Levitas; ***C:*** Florian Ballhaus.

Lullaby of Broadway 🦴🦴 ½ **1951** Many songs highlight this flimsy musical about a girl (Day) who ventures from England to the Big Apple in search of an acting career. She soon discovers that her mom has become a has-been actress now performing in a Greenwich Village dive. Day struggles to gain her own success while coping with her mother's downfall. **93m/C; DVD.** Doris Day; Gene Nelson; S.Z. Sakall; Billy DeWolfe; Gladys George; Florence Bates; ***D:*** David Butler.

Lulu 🦴 ½ **2002** Transsexual Lulu, an ex-prostitute who runs a bar in a seaside town, becomes the prime suspect when pimp/extortionist Fabio is murdered. A local drunk claims he saw Lulu commit the crime but detective Samuel decides to run his own investigation. French with subtitles. **90m/C; DVD.** *FR* Elli Medeiros; Jean-Pierre Kalfon; Gerard Meylan; Bruno Putzulu; Tony Gatlif; Robert Guediguian; Thomas Fourneau; Ariane Ascaride; ***D:*** Jean-Henri Roger; ***W:*** Jean-Henri Roger; Jean-Francois Goyet; Claude Vesperini; ***C:*** Renato Berta; ***M:*** Jacno.

Lulu Belle 🦴🦴 **1948** We follow the life and misadventures of Lulu Belle (Dorothy Lamour), a nightclub singer who can't seem to choose just one man. Even worse, her taste in men is somewhat questionable, as are her increasingly convoluted relationships with bad people. **87m/B; DVD, Blu-Ray.** Dorothy Lamour; George Montgomery; Albert Dekker; Otto Kruger; Glenda Farrell; ***D:*** Leslie Fenton; ***W:*** Everett Freeman; Karl Kamb; ***C:*** Ernest Laszlo; ***M:*** Henry Russell.

Lulu on the Bridge 🦴🦴 ½ **1998 (PG-13)** Jazz saxman Izzy Maurer (Keitel) sinks into depression when he can no longer perform. Walking one night, Izzy stumbles across a dead body and finds no ID—only a phone number and a mysterious stone that emits a blue light. Izzy calls the number, which belongs to actress/waitress Celia (Sorvino), and their first meeting finds them instantly in love (or some variation). Meanwhile, the mysterious Dr. Van Horn (Dafoe) questions Izzy about finding the stone. And things don't get much clearer. First solo directorial effort for Auster, who co-directed Keitel in "Blue in the Face," the spinoff to his screenplay "Smoke." **104m/C; DVD.** Harvey

Keitel; Mira Sorvino; Willem Dafoe; Gina Gershon; Mandy Patinkin; Vanessa Redgrave; Victor Argo; Kevin Corrigan; Richard Edson; *D:* Paul Auster; *W:* Paul Auster; *C:* Alik Sakharov; *M:* Graeme Revell.

Luminarias 🦴🦴 **1999 (R)** Four Hispanic friends, looking for love in East L.A., meet to console each other at the Luminarias restaurant. Lawyer Andrea (Fernandez), finds herself attracted to anglo Joseph (Bakula); therapist Sofia's (DuBois) surprised by her feelings for cute Mexican waiter Pablo (Lopez); artist Lilly (Moya) hopes to change her luck with Korean Lu (Lim) only to run into prejudice from his parents; and designer Irene (Ortelli) has sworn off sex for Lent while trying to accept her cross-dressing gay brother (Rivas). The friendships are believable even if there's too much going on with the plot. **101m/C; DVD.** Evelina Fernandez; Marta DuBois; Dyana Ortelli; Angela Moya; Scott Bakula; Robert Beltran; Sal Lopez; Andrew C. Lim; Geoffrey Rivas; Richard "Cheech" Marin; *D:* Jose Luis Valenzuela; *W:* Evelina Fernandez; *C:* Alex Phillips, Jr.; *M:* Eric Allaman.

Luminous Motion 🦴🦴 **2000** Phillip (Lloyd) is an introspective 10-year-old who spends his life on the road travelling in a red Impala with his mother (Unger), a beautiful, depressed lush who drifts from man to man. But the only male she's really close to is her son—until Phillip's father (Sheridan) finds them and wants to reclaim his family. Except the boundaries between Phillip's reality and his imagination aren't very clear at all. Based on Bradfield's novel "The History of Luminous Motion." **94m/C; VHS, DVD, Blu-Ray.** Eric Lloyd; Deborah Kara Unger; Jamey Sheridan; Terry Kinney; Paz de la Huerta; James Berland; *D:* Bette Gordon; *W:* Scott Bradfield; Robert Roth; *C:* Teodoro Maniaci; *M:* Lesley Barber.

Lumumba 🦴🦴🦴½ **2001** Powerful biopic of Patrice Lumumba, the first elected Prime Minister of the Congo, who was assassinated mere months after the country gained its independence from Belgium. Director-writer Peck uses flashbacks to show Lumumba's ascent from beer salesman to his eventual rise to, and violent removal from, power. French actor Ebouanay gives a masterful performance, finding the humanity behind the icon. Filmed in Zimbabwe and Mozambique because the Congo was suffering through yet another civil war. English, French, and Lingala with subtitles. **115m/C; DVD.** *FR BE GE* Eriq Ebouaney; Alex Descas; Theophile Moussa Sowie; Maka Kotto; Dieudonne Kabongo; Pascal Nzonzi; Mariam Kaba; *D:* Raoul Peck; *W:* Raoul Peck; Pascal Bonitzer; *C:* Bernard Lutic; *M:* Jean-Claude Petit.

Luna: Spirit of the Whale 🦴🦴½ **2007 (PG)** A young orphaned killer whale has taken up residence in a small Canadian coastal town bay and government official Priestley has been hired to capture the whale and try to return it to its pod. Only the local native peoples would rather that the whale was left alone. Based on a true story. **93m/C; DVD.** *CA* Jason Priestley; Adam Beach; Graham Greene; Tantoo Cardinal; Michelle Harrison; Aaron Miko; *D:* Don McBrearty; *W:* Elizabeth Stewart; *C:* Jan Kiesser. **TV**

The Lunatic 🦴🦴 **1992 (R)** A robust, oversexed, and scheming German tourist travels to Jamaica where she meets the village idiot, a man who regularly holds conversations with the local plants. The two hook up with a butcher, and the three live happily in the hills, that is until the money is gone. The Jamaican scenery, a few bawdy laughs, and a great reggae soundtrack make this one worthwhile. **93m/C; VHS, Streaming.** *GB* Julie Wallace; Paul Campbell; Reggie Carter; Carl Bradshaw; *D:* Lol Creme; *M:* Wally Badarou.

The Lunchbox 🦴🦴½ *Dabba* **2013 (PG)** Writer/director Batra's debut is enjoyable and sweet even if it's a little slight at the same time. Ila (Kaur) plans to spice up her marriage by placing notes in her husband's lunchboxes every day. The lunchbox is delivered to another man named Saajan (Khan) and the two form a unique friendship, exchanging notes with every day's meal. In an era in which complete strangers form bonds all the time over social media, it's refreshing to see a movie about the power of the old-fashioned written word to connect people. English and Hindi with subtitles. **104m/C; DVD, Blu-Ray.** *IN GE FR* Irrfan Khan; Nimrat Kaur; Nawazuddin Siddiqui; Nakul Vaid; *D:* Ritesh Batra; *W:* Ritesh Batra; *C:* Michael Simmonds; *M:* Max Richter.

Lure of the Wilderness 🦴🦴 **1952** Remake of 1941's "Swamp Water" with Brennan reprising his role as Jim Harper, who's unjustly accused of murder. In 1910, Jim takes his daughter Laurie (Peters) to hide out in the Georgia swamps until they are accidentally discovered by Ben Tyler (Hunter). Jim claims he couldn't get a fair trial and Ben agrees to help him, but the real killers don't want Jim to make it out of the swamps alive. **90m/C; DVD.** Walter Brennan; Jean Peters; Jeffrey Hunter; Tom Tully; Constance Smith; Jack Elam; Pat Hogan; *D:* Jean Negulesco; *W:* Louis Lantz; *C:* Edward Cronjager; *M:* Franz Waxman.

Lured 🦴🦴½ **1947** Ball gives a fine dramatic performance in Sirk's glossy thriller. Sandra (Ball) is an American dancer in London whose friend falls victim to a lonelyhearts killer. She agrees to act as a decoy for Scotland Yard even while getting involved with nightclub owner Robert Fleming (Sanders), who turns out to be one of the suspects. **103m/B; VHS, DVD.** Lucille Ball; George Sanders; Charles Coburn; Cedric Hardwicke; Boris Karloff; Alan Mowbray; George Zucco; Joseph Calleia; Tanis Chandler; Alan Napier; Robert Coote; *D:* Douglas Sirk; *W:* Leo Rosten; *C:* William H. Daniels; *M:* Michel Michelet.

Lured Innocence 🦴🦴 **1997 (R)** Steamy romance in a small town leads to murderous impulses. Elsie (Shelton) is having an affair with older, married Rick (Hopper). Then his ailing wife (Shire) finds out and threatens the twosome. The lovers aren't pleased and there's an eventual murder trial where one of the key witnesses is a newspaper reporter (Gummersall), who was also Elsie's lover. **97m/C; VHS, DVD.** Dennis Hopper; Marley Shelton; Devon Gummersall; Talia Shire; *D:* Kikuo Kawasaki; *W:* Kikuo Kawasaki; *C:* Irek Hartowicz.

Lurkers WOOF! **1988 (R)** An unappealing metaphysical morass about a woman who has been haunted throughout her life by...something. **90m/C; VHS, DVD, Blu-Ray.** Christine Moore; Gary Warner; Marina Taylor; Carissa Channing; Tom Billett; *D:* Roberta Findlay; *W:* Ed Kelleher; Hariette Vidal; *C:* Roberta Findlay.

Lurking Fear 🦴🦴 **1994 (R)** The town of Lefferts Corner has suffered from generations of horror thanks to man-eating ghouls that dwell beneath the local graveyard and arise whenever a storm breaks out. The inhabitants prepare to fight back but their plan is hindered by the arrival of a group of criminals who are after a fortune supposedly hidden in one of the graves. Based on a story by H.P. Lovecraft. Part of the 'Full Moon Classics, Vol. 2' collection. **78m/C; VHS, DVD, Blu-Ray.** Jon Finch; Blake Bailey; Ashley Laurence; Jeffrey Combs; Paul Mantee; Allison Mackie; Joe Leavengood; Vincent Schiavelli; *D:* C. Courtney Joyner; *W:* C. Courtney Joyner; *M:* Jim Manzie.

Luscious 🦴½ *Vivid* **1997 (R)** It's about sex. Cole (Shellan) is a painter having inspiration problems. Then he splashes girlfriend Billie (Wuhrer) with paint and they have sex on the canvas. Suddenly his art is selling like hotcakes but Billie gets a little tired being a literal paint brush. An unrated version has three more minutes of sex and nudity. **83m/C; VHS, DVD.** Stephen Shellen; Kari Wuhrer; *D:* Evan Georgiades. **VIDEO**

Lush 🦴🦴 **2001 (R)** The New Orleans setting is the best thing about this limp drama. Alcoholic golf pro Lionel Exley (Scott) is friends with alcoholic lawyer Carter (Harris), who names his buddy his beneficiary in an insurance policy. The lawyer promptly gets murdered and Exley decides to go on the lam from the suspicious cops, winding up taking refuge with two upper-crusty sisters Ahley (Holloman) and Rachel (Linney). **94m/C; VHS, DVD.** Campbell Scott; Laura Linney; Jared Harris; Laurel Holloman; *D:* Mark Gibson; *W:* Mark Gibson; *C:* Caroline Champetier; *M:* Barrett Martin.

Lust, Caution 🦴🦴 *Se, Jie* **2007 (NC-17)** A broad epic of intrigue and lust in Japanese-occupied China during WWII. Chinese patriot Wong (Wei) is involved in a plot to assassinate Mr. Yee (Leung), a collaborator with the Japanese. Once she seduces him, however, she realizes that she's in way over her head. Wei and Leung are both excellent, but Lee's adaptation goes far beyond Eileen Chang's original short story and much of the early portion of the film seems unfocused; the heart of the story is in the second half. Earned an NC-17 rating and a great deal of attention because of its extremely erotic and explicit sex scenes. **158m/C; DVD, Blu-Ray.** *US CH CH* Tony Leung Chiu-Wai; Tang Wei; Joan Chen; Wang Leehom; Chu Tsz-ying; *D:* Ang Lee; *W:* James Schamus; Wang Hui-ling; *C:* Rodrigo Prieto; *M:* Alexandre Desplat.

Lust for a Vampire 🦴🦴 *To Love a Vampire* **1971 (R)** The sanguine tale of a deadly vampire who indiscriminately preys on pupils and teachers when she enrolls at a British finishing school. Moody and erotically charged, with an impressive ending. Quasi-sequel to "The Vampire Lovers." **95m/C; VHS, DVD, Blu-Ray.** *GB* Ralph Bates; Barbara Jefford; Suzanna Leigh; Michael Johnson; Yutte Stensgaard; Pippa Steele; Helen Christie; David Healy; Mike Raven; *D:* Jimmy Sangster; *W:* Tudor Gates; *C:* David Muir.

Lust for Dracula WOOF! **2004 (R)** Softcore Dracula story has Mina Harker (Mundae) kept in a drugged stupor by husband Jonathan (Wells)?so drugged that she apparently doesn't realize her husband is a woman. But then, so is Dracula (Caine) and all the vamp minions. Mina's sister Abigail (Shelly Jones) wants to destroy Dracula and get Jonathan for herself. Let's face it, no one's watching this for the plot but for skin and girl-on-girl action. **90m/C; DVD.** Darian Caine; Misty Mundae; Shelly Jones; Julian Wells; Andrea Davis; *D:* Anthony Marsiglia; *W:* Anthony Marsiglia; *C:* Dang Lenawea; *M:* Don Mike. **VIDEO**

Lust for Freedom 🦴 **1987** An undercover cop decides to hit the road after she sees her partner gunned down. She winds up near the California-Mexico border, where she is wrongly imprisoned with a number of other young women in a white slavery business. This low-budget film includes lots of steamy women-behind-bars sex scenes. **92m/C; VHS, DVD.** Melanie Coll; William J. Kulzer; *D:* Eric Louzil.

Lust for Gold 🦴🦴 **1949** Ford battles against greedy former lover Lupino and her husband for control of the Lost Dutchman gold mine. **90m/B; VHS, DVD.** Ida Lupino; Glenn Ford; Gig Young; William Prince; Edgar Buchanan; Will Geer; Paul Ford; Jay Silverheels; *D:* S. Sylvan Simon; *M:* George Duning.

Lust for Life 🦴🦴🦴½ **1956** Absorbing, serious biography of Vincent Van Gogh, from his first paintings to his death. Remarkable for Douglas' furiously convincing portrayal. Featuring dozens of actual Van Gogh works from private collections. Based on an Irving Stone novel, produced by John Houseman. **122m/C; VHS, DVD, Blu-Ray; Open Captioned.** Kirk Douglas; Anthony Quinn; James Donald; Pamela Brown; Everett Sloane; Henry Daniell; Niall MacGinnis; Noel Purcell; Lionel Jeffries; Jill Bennett; *D:* Vincente Minnelli; *M:* Miklos Rozsa. Oscars '56: Support. Actor (Quinn); Golden Globes '57: Actor--Drama (Douglas); N.Y. Film Critics '56: Actor (Douglas).

Lust in the Dust 🦴🦴🦴 **1985 (R)** When part of a treasure map is found on the derriere of none other than Divine, the hunt is on for the other half. This comedy western travels to a sleepy town called Chile Verde (green chili for those who don't speak Spanish) and the utterly ridiculous turns comically corrupt. Deliciously distasteful fun. Features Divine singing a bawdy love song in his/her break from John Waters. **85m/C; VHS, DVD, Blu-Ray.** Tab Hunter; Divine; Lainie Kazan; Geoffrey Lewis; Henry Silva; Cesar Romero; Gina Gallego; Courtney Gains; Woody Strode; Pedro Gonzalez-Gonzalez; *D:* Paul Bartel; *W:* Philip John Taylor; *C:* Paul Lohmann; *M:* Peter Matz.

Luster 🦴🦴½ **2002** Looks at the L.A. gay/punk scene while coasting on its own oddball charms. Skateboarding, blue-haired Jackson (Herwick) works at a record store while aspiring to be a poet. After too many drunken, druggy sexual encounters, he decides he needs a real romance—maybe with crush Billy (Blechman) who'd rather just be friends. Meanwhile, preppie customer Derek (Thibodeau) thinks Jackson is swell. Add to the mix naive newcomer Jed (Wyatt), closeted rock star Sonny Spike (Garson), and Jackson's chic lesbian pals, Alyssa (Gidley) and Sandra (Melvoin). **90m/C; DVD.** Justin Herwick; Shane Powers; B. Wyatt; Jonah Blechman; Pamela Gidley; Sean Thibodeau; Willie Garson; Susannah Melvoin; *D:* Everet Lewis; *W:* Everet Lewis; *C:* Humberto DeLuna; *M:* Michael Leon.

The Lusty Men 🦴🦴🦴 **1952** Two rival rodeo champions, both in love with the same woman, work the rodeo circuit until a tragic accident occurs. Mitchum turns in a fine performance as the has-been rodeo star trying to make it big again. **113m/B; DVD.** Robert Mitchum; Susan Hayward; Arthur Kennedy; Arthur Hunnicutt; *D:* Nicholas Ray; *W:* Horace McCoy; *C:* Lee Garmes; *M:* Roy Webb.

Luther 🦴🦴½ **1974 (G)** A well-acted characterization of Martin Luther's development from a young seminarian to his leadership of the Reformation Movement. **112m/C; VHS, DVD, Blu-Ray.** Stacy Keach; Patrick Magee; Hugh Griffith; Robert Stephens; Alan Badel; Julian Glover; Dame Judi Dench; Leonard Rossiter; Maurice Denham; Peter Cellier; Thomas Heathcote; Malcolm Stoddard; Bruce Carstairs; *D:* Guy Green; *W:* Edward Anhalt; John Osborne; *C:* Frederick A. (Freddie) Young; *M:* John Addison.

Luther 🦴🦴½ **2003 (PG-13)** Tame religious biopic follows the 16th century law student turned young monk who started the Protestant religious movement. Despite depicting a plethora of the remarkable moments that made up Luther's life, pic lacks focus that might have illuminated this important historical figure. Refusing to recant his beliefs, including the famous 95 Theses questioning Catholic Church practices, Luther was excommunicated, which sparked the Reformation and Protestantism. Fiennes gives an able but diluted performance in the title role while Ustinov as Prince Frederick is at his scene-stealing best. **112m/C; VHS, DVD.** *GE* Joseph Fiennes; Alfred Molina; Jonathan Firth; Claire Cox; Peter Ustinov; Bruno Ganz; Uwe Ochsenknecht; Matthieu Carriere; Jochen Horst; *D:* Eric Till; *W:* Camille Thomasson; Bart Gavigan; *C:* Robert Fraisse; *M:* Richard Harvey.

Luther the Geek WOOF! **1990** Little Luther's visit to the circus is dramatically changed when he sees the geek, a sideshow freak. Since then Luther has taken to biting off chicken's heads and drinking their blood in his small Illinois town; the town will never be the same. (And neither will you if you watch this stupid film.) **90m/C; VHS, DVD, Blu-Ray.** Edward Terry; Joan Roth; J. Jerome Clarke; Tom Mills; Stacy Haiduk; *D:* Carlton J. Albright; *W:* Whitey Styles; *C:* David Knox.

Luv 🦴½ **1967 (PG)** Although good cast tries hard, they can't do much with this comic farce. Three intellectuals, including one that's suicidal, discuss the trials and tribulations of their middle-class New York existence. **95m/C; VHS, DVD.** Jack Lemmon; Peter Falk; Elaine May; *D:* Clive Donner; *W:* Murray Schisgal; *C:* Ernest Laszlo.

LUV 🦴🦴 **2013 (R)** Woody (Rainey Jr.) adores his Uncle Vincent (Common) and spends a day with him, getting lessons in thug life and street justice in a series of episodic encounters that never amount to what director/writer Candis wishes they would. The charismatic Common deserves better material than this cliched coming-of-age story about a day-in-the-life of a Baltimore pre-teen and the uncle he once idolized. The film purports to condemn Common's character but never does so in a dramatically engaging way. Common and great co-stars like Haysbert, Glover, Dutton, and Good put in an admirable effort. **94m/C; DVD.** Common; Michael Rainey Jr.; Dennis Haysbert; Danny Glover; Charles S. Dutton; Meagan Good; Lonette McKee; Michael K(enneth) Williams; Russell Hornsby; *D:* Sheldon Candis; *W:* Sheldon Candis; *C:* Gavin Kelly; *M:* Nuno Malo.

Luxury Liner 🦴🦴½ **1948** Typical MGM musical fare although Brent also played the same role in the 1933 non-musical version. Polly (Powell), the daughter of widowed captain Jeremy Bradford (Brent), wants to go on his next cruise to Rio but he insists she stay at boarding school. So Polly stows away and then decides the best thing would be for her dad to remarry so she picks a likely passenger in the bewildered Laura (Gifford). **98m/C; DVD.** George Brent; Jane Powell; Frances Gifford; Lauritz Melchior; Thomas E. Breen; Xavier Cugat; ***D:*** Richard Whorf; ***W:*** Karl Kamb; Gladys Lehman; Richard Connell; ***C:*** Robert Planck; ***M:*** Georgie Stoll.

The Luzhin Defence 🦴🦴 **2000 (PG-13)** Luzhin (Turturro) is an eccentric Russian chess genius who is staying at an Italian lakeside resort in 1929 preparing for an important match. Also preparing for a match—the marital kind—is Russian emigre Natalia (Watson) and her aristocratic mother Vera (James). And Luzhin is not the man Vera has in mind for her daughter, no matter what Natalia thinks. But as the stress of the match takes its toll on Luzhin, he believes he cannot have both love and the game. Based on the 1930 novel by Vladimir Nabokov. **106m/C; VHS, DVD.** *FR GB* John Turturro; Emily Watson; Geraldine James; Stuart Wilson; Christopher Thompson; Peter Blythe; Orla Brady; Fabio Sartor; ***D:*** Marleen Gorris; ***W:*** Peter Berry; ***C:*** Bernard Lutic; ***M:*** Alexandre Desplat.

Lymelife 🦴🦴 **2008 (R)** Wood-tick fearing Long Islanders give the film its odd title in this vividly-acted black comedy. Timid teen Scott (Rory Culkin) exists to be bullied; his brother Jim (Kieran Culkin) is off to serve in the military; their mother Brenda (Hennessy) is over-anxious about Lyme disease; and workaholic dad Mickey (Baldwin) is having an affair. Scott is crushing on Adrianna (Roberts) with an awkward first time sex scene between the teens and a lot of marital squabbling between various adults. **95m/C; DVD.** Rory Culkin; Alec Baldwin; Jill Hennessy; Kieran Culkin; Emma Roberts; Timothy Hutton; Cynthia Nixon; ***D:*** Derick Martini; ***W:*** Derick Martini; Steven Martini; ***C:*** Frank Goodwin; ***M:*** Steven Martini.

M 🦴🦴🦴🦴 **1931** The great Lang dissection of criminal deviance, following the tortured last days of a child murderer, and the efforts of both the police and the underground to bring him to justice. Poetic, compassionate, and chilling. Inspired by real-life serial killer Peter Kurten, known as "Vampire of Dusseldorf," Lang also borrowed story elements from Jack the Ripper's killing spree. Lorre's screen debut. Lang's personal favorite among his own films. In German with English subtitles. Remade in 1951. **111m/B; VHS, DVD, Blu-Ray.** *GE* Peter Lorre; Ellen Widmann; Inge Landgut; Gustav Grundgens; Otto Wernicke; Ernest Stahl-Nachbaur; Franz Stein; Theodore Loos; Fritz Gnass; Fritz Odemar; Paul Kemp; Theo Lingen; Georg John; Karl Platen; Rosa Valetti; Hertha von Walther; Rudolf Blumner; ***D:*** Fritz Lang; ***W:*** Fritz Lang; Thea von Harbou; ***C:*** Fritz Arno Wagner; Gustav Rathje; ***M:*** Edvard Grieg.

M. Butterfly 🦴🦴 **1993 (R)** Disappointing adaptation of Hwang's award-winning play, which was based on a true story. Rene Gallimard's (Irons) a minor French diplomat sent to China in 1964. Taken in by the exoticism of the mysterious east, he falls for a Chinese opera performer, Song Liling (Lone). Only she's no lady and the oblivious diplomat turns out to be a patsy as Song Liling uses him to gather information. The story only works if the passion, however deceptive, between the two is believable, passion which it isn't. Irons comes across as too intelligent to be gullibile and the usually excellent Lone does not make his role believable. **101m/C; DVD.** Jeremy Irons; John Lone; Ian Richardson; Barbara Sukowa; Vernon Dobtcheff; Annabel Leventon; Shizuko Hoshi; Richard McMillan; ***D:*** David Cronenberg; ***W:*** David Henry Hwang; ***M:*** Howard Shore.

The M Word 🦴🦴 **2014 (R)** Jaglom's disorderly, gabby comedy-drama has Moxie Landon, the star of a children's show at a struggling L.A. TV station, filming a documentary on menopause that features family members and co-workers. When a cost-cutting TV exec shows up to start layoffs, Moxie stages an unlikely sit-in to save their jobs, but Charlie turns out to be more interested in turning Moxie's documentary into a reality TV show. **111m/C; DVD.** Tanna Frederick; Michael Imperioli; Frances Fisher; Gregory Harrison; Corey Feldman; Mary Crosby; Eliza Roberts; ***D:*** Henry Jaglom; ***W:*** Henry Jaglom; Ron Vignone; ***C:*** Hanania Baer.

Ma 🦴🦴 **1/2 2019 (R)** High schooler Maggie (Silvers) has moved back to her mother Erica's (Lewis) small Ohio hometown. While hanging with new friends outside a liquor store, Maggie asks a passing woman, Sue Ann (Spencer), to buy them alcohol. Sue Ann agrees and goes drinking with them at a rock quarry. The teens start partying in Sue Ann's basement, and they give her the name "Ma" as she waits on them. The situation takes a dark turn as Ma begins to show up unexpectedly and demands their attention. The horror film has an interesting premise and Spencer gives an enthusiastic performance but it is ultimately comes up short. **99m/C; DVD, Blu-Ray.** Octavia Spencer; Diana Silvers; Juliette Lewis; McKaley Miller; Corey Fogelmanis; ***D:*** Tate Taylor; ***W:*** Scotty Landes; ***C:*** Christina Voros; ***M:*** Gregory Tripi.

Ma and Pa Kettle 🦴🦴 **1/2** *The Further Adventures of Ma and Pa Kettle* **1949** The hillbilly couple were supporting characters in "The Egg and I" but their popularity found them spun off into their own cornpone series. This first feature finds the couple and their 15 children about to be evicted only to have Pa win a tobacco slogan contest. The prize is a brand-new fully automated house whose futuristic contraptions get the better of Pa. **76m/B; VHS, DVD.** Marjorie Main; Percy Kilbride; Richard Long; Meg Randall; Esther Dale; Barry Kelley; Patricia Alphin; ***D:*** Charles Lamont; ***W:*** Al Lewis; Herbert Margolis; Louis Morheim.

Ma and Pa Kettle at Home 🦴🦴 **1/2 1954** Elwin, one of the Kettle's 15 children, is a finalist in an essay contest that could win him a college scholarship. Then Pa Kettle hears the two judges plan to visit each of the finalists' homes so he tries to spruce-up the family's tumbled-down farm. **80m/B; VHS, DVD.** Marjorie Main; Percy Kilbride; Alan Mowbray; Ross Elliott; Brett Halsey; Mary Wickes; Irving Bacon; Emory Parnell; ***D:*** Charles Lamont; ***W:*** Kay Lenard.

Ma and Pa Kettle at the Fair 🦴🦴 **1/2 1952** The Kettle's eldest daughter Rosie wants to go to college so Ma enters the county fair baking contest to win some money and Pa buys a decrepit old nag to enter in the fair's horse race. Somehow things just have a way of working out for the Kettles. **79m/B; VHS, DVD.** Marjorie Main; Percy Kilbride; Lori Nelson; James Best; Esther Dale; Russell Simpson; Emory Parnell; ***D:*** Charles T. Barton; ***W:*** John Grant; Richard Morris.

Ma and Pa Kettle at Waikiki 🦴🦴 **1/2 1955** Ma (Main) and Pa (Kilbride), as well as oldest daughter Rosie (Nelson), head for Hawaii to help out cousin Rodney's (Smith) pineapple factory. Seems he's ill and about to go bankrupt and he thinks Pa is some kind of financial whiz who can bail him out. Pa accidentally does help the business and then gets kidnapped by some sleazy competitors. But it's Ma to the rescue (and the bad guys don't stand a chance). Kilbride retired after his seventh take as Pa in the comedy series. **79m/B; VHS, DVD.** Marjorie Main; Percy Kilbride; Lori Nelson; Loring Smith; Russell Johnson; Byron Palmer; Mabel Albertson; Hilo Hattie; Fay Roope; Oliver Blake; Lowell Gilmore; Teddy Hart; ***D:*** Lee Sholem; ***W:*** Jack Henley; Harry Clork; Elwood Ullman.

Ma and Pa Kettle Back On the Farm 🦴🦴 **1/2 1951** First-time grandparents, the Kettles have to deal with their daughter-in-law's snobby Bostonian parents and their parenting ideas. The family's also moved back to their ramshackle farm where Pa thinks he's found uranium, leading to all sorts of problems. **81m/B; VHS, DVD.** Marjorie Main; Percy Kilbride; Richard Long; Meg Randall; Ray Collins; Barbara Brown; Emory Parnell; ***D:*** Edward Sedgwick; ***W:*** Jack Henley.

Ma and Pa Kettle Go to Town 🦴🦴 **1/2 1950** Ma and Pa head off for New York City when Pa wins a jingle-writing contest, unknowingly leaving their brood in the care of on the lam mobster Mike, who asks the Kettles to deliver a package to his brother. This gets both the crooks and the cops trailing the hillbilly couple, whose backwoods ways are more than a match for any city slicker. **80m/B; VHS, DVD.** Marjorie Main; Percy Kilbride; Richard Long; Meg Randall; Charles McGraw; Ray Collins; Esther Dale; Ellen Corby; Barbara Brown; ***D:*** Charles Lamont; ***W:*** Martin Ragaway; Leonard Stern.

Ma and Pa Kettle on Vacation 🦴🦴 **1/2** *Ma and Pa Kettle Go to Paris* **1953** Ma and Pa visit Paris as guests of their son's wealthy in-laws and Pa unwittingly gets involved with spies and shady ladies. **79m/B; VHS, DVD.** Marjorie Main; Percy Kilbride; Ray Collins; Sig Rumann; Bodil Miller; Barbara Brown; Peter Brocco; Jay Novello; ***D:*** Charles Lamont; ***W:*** Jack Henley.

Ma Barker's Killer Brood 🦴🦴 **1960** Biography of the infamous American criminal and her four sons, edited together from a TV serial. The shoot-'em-up scenes and Tuttle's performance keep the pace from slackening. **82m/B; VHS, DVD.** Lurene Tuttle; Tristram Coffin; Paul Dubov; Nelson Leigh; Myrna Dell; Vic Lundin; Donald Spruance; ***D:*** Bill Karn.

Ma Saison Preferee 🦴🦴🦴 *My Favorite Season* **1993** Focuses on the intense relationship between a middleaged brother (Auteuil) and sister (Deneuve). When the elderly Berthe (Villalonga) collapses, she stays with daughter Emilie and her family, which provides Emilie with an excuse to invite her estranged brother Antoine for Christmas. It's a disaster that leads Emilie to declare her marriage over and to an eventual reaproachmont with Antoine. Film is divided into four parts, to coincide with the four seasons, beginning with autumn and ending with summer. French with subtitles. **124m/C; DVD.** *FR* Daniel Auteuil; Catherine Deneuve; Marthe Villalonga; Jean-Pierre Bouvier; Chiara Mastroianni; Anthony Prada; Carmen Chaplin; ***D:*** Andre Techine; ***W:*** Andre Techine; ***C:*** Thierry Arbogast; ***M:*** Philippe Sarde.

Ma Vie en Rose 🦴🦴🦴 *My Life in Pink* **1997 (R)** Berliner's debut portrays seven-year-old misfit Ludovic (Du Fresne), who's convinced he's really a girl and dresses in girls' clothes. His close-knit family merely regards this as a childhood eccentricity until Ludovic decides he's going to marry Jerome (Rivere), the boy next door, and stages a mock wedding ceremony. Jerome's father, straitlaced Albert (Hanssens), isn't nearly so understanding (neither are the other neighbors in the conservative Parisian suburb). Poignant and funny look at a child's search for identity. Convincing turn by pre-pubescent performer Du Fresne. French with subtitles. **90m/C; DVD.** *BE FR UK* Georges DuFresne; Jean-Philippe Ecoffey; Michele Laroque; Daniel Hanssens; Julien Riviere; Helene Vincent; Laurence Bibot; Jean-Francois Galotte; Caroline Baehr; Marie Bunel; ***D:*** Alain Berliner; ***W:*** Alain Berliner; Chris Vander Stappen; ***C:*** Yves Cape; ***M:*** Dominique Dalcan. Golden Globes '98: Foreign Film.

Maborosi 🦴🦴🦴 *Mirage; Maboroshi no Hikari* **1995** Yumiko (Esumi) has a contented life in Osaka with her husband Ikuo (Asano) and their newborn son. Yet, inexplicably, her husband commits suicide one night. Later, a neighbor of Yumiko's helps her with an arranged marriage to prosperous widower Tamio (Naitoh), who lives in a remote fishing village, and once again things seem to be happy. But her first husband's death still haunts her and Yumiko seeks an explanation that will allow her to have some peace in her life. Adapted from a story by Teru Miyamoto. Japanese with subtitles. **110m/C; DVD, Blu-Ray.** *JP* Makiko Esumi; Takashi Naito; Tadanobu Asano; Gohki Kashiyama; ***D:*** Hirokazu Kore-eda; ***W:*** Yoshihisa Ogita; ***C:*** Masao Nakabori; ***M:*** Chen Ming-Chang.

Mac 🦴🦴🦴 **1993 (R)** It's a family affair. Immigrant carpenter's funeral is the starting point for the story of his three sons, construction workers who live in Queens, New York in the 1950s. The passionate bros battle, bitch, and build, with Turturro as the eldest summing up the prevailing philosophy: "It's the doing, that's the thing." Turturro's directorial debut is a labor of love and a tribute to his own dad. Filmed on location in New York City. Fine performances from newcomers Badalucco and Capotorto are complemented by smaller roles from Amos, Barkin, and Turturro's real-life wife Borowitz and brother Nick. **118m/C; VHS, DVD.** John Turturro; Carl Capotorto; Michael Badalucco; Katherine Borowitz; John Amos; Olek Krupa; Ellen Barkin; Joe Paparone; Nicholas Turturro; Dennis Farina; Steven Randazzo; ***D:*** John Turturro; ***W:*** John Turturro; Brandon Cole; ***C:*** Ron Fortunato; ***M:*** Richard Termini; Vin Tese.

Mac and Me 🦴 **1988 (PG)** Lost E.T.-like alien stranded on Earth befriends a wheelchair-bound boy. Aimed at young kids, it's full of continual product plugs, most notably for McDonald's. Make the kids happy and stick to the real thing. **94m/C; VHS, DVD, Blu-Ray.** Christine Ebersole; Jonathan Ward; Katrina Caspary; Lauren Stanley; Jade Calegory; ***D:*** Stewart Raffill; ***W:*** Stewart Raffill; ***M:*** Alan Silvestri. Golden Raspberries '88: Worst Director (Raffill).

Macabre 🦴 **1/2 1958** A rather weak Castle horror flick that finds widowed small town doctor Rodney Barrett's young daughter kidnapped and buried alive. He has just five hours to find her coffin before she suffocates. But there's a twist to the tale, of course. **72m/B; DVD.** William Prince; Jim Backus; Christine White; Jacqueline Scott; Susan Morrow; Dorothy Morris; Philip Tonge; ***D:*** William Castle; ***W:*** Robb White; ***C:*** Carl Guthrie; ***M:*** Les Baxter.

Macabre 🦴 *Frozen Terror* **1980** A madman resembling both Jack Frost and Jack the Ripper claims victims at random. **90m/C; VHS, DVD.** Bernice Stegers; Stanko Molnar; Veronica Zinny; Roberto Posse; ***D:*** Lamberto Bava; ***W:*** Lamberto Bava; Antonio Avati; ***C:*** Franco Delli Colli.

Macao 🦴🦴🦴 **1952** On the lam for a crime he didn't commit, an adventurer sails to the exotic Far East, meets a buxom cafe singer, and helps Interpol catch a notorious crime boss. A strong film noir entry. Russell sneers, Mitchum wise cracks. Director von Sternberg's last film for RKO. **81m/B; VHS, DVD.** Robert Mitchum; Jane Russell; William Bendix; Gloria Grahame; ***D:*** Josef von Sternberg.

Macaroni 🦴 **1/2** *Maccheroni* **1985 (PG)** An uptight American businessman returns to Naples 40 years after being stationed there in WWII. Comedic situations abound when he is reunited with his Italian war buddy, brother of his lover. Pleasant acting can't save irritating script. **104m/C; VHS, Streaming.** *IT* Jack Lemmon; Marcello Mastroianni; Daria Nicolodi; Isa Danieli; ***D:*** Ettore Scola; ***W:*** Ettore Scola.

MacArthur 🦴🦴 **1977 (PG)** General Douglas MacArthur's life from Corregidor in 1942 to his dismissal a decade later in the midst of the Korean conflict. Episodic saga with forceful Peck but weak supporting characters. Fourteen minutes were cut from the original version; intended to be Peck's "Patton," it falls short of the mark. **130m/C; VHS, DVD, Blu-Ray.** Gregory Peck; Ivan Bonar; Ward (Edward) Costello; Nicolas Coster; Dan O'Herlihy; John McKee; ***D:*** Joseph Sargent; ***W:*** Matthew Robbins; Hal Barwood; ***C:*** Mario Tosi; ***M:*** Jerry Goldsmith.

MacArthur Park 🦴🦴 **1/2 2001 (R)** A group of L.A. crack addicts try to escape the despair of their lives by duping a celebrity junkie. Cody (Byrd), a middle-aged former musician, is the de facto leader of the group, whose estranged son brings news that his ex-wife has died. Actor-turned-director Wirth turns in a fine film which includes excellent performances and a rare insight into the inner lives of the "crackheads" that are often just part of the periphery of most urban dramas. **86m/C; DVD.** Thomas Jefferson Byrd; Louis Freese; Ellen Cleghorne; Brandon Adams; Lori Petty; Julie Delpy; Balthazar Getty; David Faustino; Rachel Hunter; Glenn Plummer; Miguel A. Nunez, Jr.; Sydney Tamiia Poitier; Sydney Walsh; Cynda Williams; Kirk "Sticky Fingaz" Jones; Bad Azz; ***D:*** Billy Wirth; ***W:*** Billy Wirth; Tyrone Atkins; Aaron Courseault; Sheri Sussman; ***C:*** Kristian Bernier; ***M:*** Stephen Perkins. **VIDEO**

Macbeth 🦴🦴🦴 **1/2 1948** Shakespeare's classic tragedy is performed with a celebrated lead performance by Welles, who plays the tragic king as a demonic leader of a barbaric society. A low budget adaptation with cheap sets, a three-week shooting schedule, lots of mood, and an attempt at Scottish accents. After making this film, Welles took a 10-year break from Hollywood. **111m/B; DVD, Blu-Ray.** Orson Welles; Jeannette Nolan; Dan O'Herlihy; Roddy McDowall; Robert Coote; ***D:*** Orson Welles.

Macbeth *Play of the Month: MacBeth* **1970** An extraordinary version of Shakespeare's "Macbeth" in which all the fire, ambition and doom of his text come brilliantly to life. **137m/C; DVD.** Eric Porter; Janet Suzman; John Alderton; Michael Goodliffe; John Thaw; Daphne Heard; Hilary Mason; ***D:*** John Gorrie. **TV**

Macbeth **1971 (R)** Polanski's notorious adaptation of the Shakespearean classic, marked by realistic design, unflinching violence, and fatalistic atmosphere. Finch and Annis star as Macbeth and his equally murderous lady (who appears nude in the sleepwalking scene). Polanski's first film following the grisly murder of his pregnant wife, actress Sharon Tate, was torn apart by critics but it contains stunning fight scenes and fine acting. It is in fact a worthy continuation of his work in the horror genre. Very well made. First film made by Playboy Enterprises. Originally rated X. **139m/C; VHS, DVD, Blu-Ray.** Jon Finch; Nicholas Selby; Martin Shaw; Francesca Annis; Terence Baylor; John Stride; Stephan Chase; Noelle Rimmington; Maisie Farquhar; Elsie Taylor; ***D:*** Roman Polanski; ***W:*** Roman Polanski; Kenneth Tynan; ***C:*** Gilbert Taylor.

Macbeth **½ 2006** MacBeth as gangster tale? Interesting idea but it loses much in translation. Director Wright moves the action to modern day Melbourne, where MacBeth (Worthington) whacks his boss Duncan (Sweet), as well as anyone he thinks is a threat. Lacking in subtlety, too dark, too gloomy, too stylish, and occasionally too campy for its own good. But other than that, it's fine. Weak rip-off of better gangster movies with a slightly more ambitious pedigree. **109m/C; DVD.** *AU* Sam Worthington; Victoria Hill; Lachy Hulme; Gary Sweet; Steve Bastoni; ***D:*** Geoffrey Wright; ***W:*** Victoria Hill; Geoffrey Wright; ***C:*** William Gibson; ***M:*** John Clifford White.

Macbeth **½ 2015 (R)** The incredible ability of two talented actors carries the latest adaptation of one of the Bard's most famous plays over some questionable decisions by its director. The story is largely the same, although the focus is on brutality and capturing a Macbeth who fights for what he believes fate owes him no matter the cost. Fassbender captures Macbeth as a near-crazed maniac while Cotillard is perfectly cast as the devil on his shoulder, pushing him on to take the throne. The umpteenth version of Shakespeare's classic play doesn't offer much new outside of the two performances, but that will be enough for some people. **113m/C; DVD, Blu-Ray.** Michael Fassbender; Marion Cotillard; Paddy Considine; Lochlann Harris; Lynn Kennedy; ***D:*** Justin Kurzel; ***W:*** Jacob Koskoff; Michael Lesslie; Todd Louiso; ***C:*** Adam Arkapaw; ***M:*** Jed Kurzel.

MacGruber **2010 (R)** Will SNL never learn that you can't make a movie from a one-joke skit? Here they attempt to sustain their MacGyver TV parody into a full-length feature. Clueless MacGruber (Forte) searches for enemy Dieter Von Cunth (Kilmer) after he steals a nuclear warhead. Typical potty humor ensues. The movie can't decide whether to be an 80s action film or a parody, and only occasionally succeeds at either. **90m/C; Blu-Ray.** Will Forte; Kristen Wiig; Val Kilmer; Ryan Phillippe; ***D:*** Jorma Taccone; ***W:*** Will Forte; Jorma Taccone; John Solomon; ***C:*** Brandon Trost.

Mach 2 **½ 2000 (R)** A senator, who's running for president, has gotten hold of a computer disk that reveals treachery by the current vice president. White House Secret Service agents are sent to retrieve the disk from the Senator (who's boarded the Concorde) and set it up so that the plane will be destroyed. Bosworth is the Air Force hero who won't let that happen. **94m/C; VHS, DVD.** Brian Bosworth; Michael Dorn; Shannon Whirry; Cliff Robertson; Lance Guest; Bruce Weitz; ***D:*** Fred Olen Ray; ***W:*** Steve Latshaw; ***C:*** Thomas Callaway; ***M:*** Eric Wurst; David Wurst. **VIDEO**

Machete **2010 (R)** Rodriguez based his exuberant exploitation feature on the fake trailer filmed for 2007's "Grindhouse." The perfectly cast Trejo plays the title character, a former Mexican Federale, who is double-crossed over a staged assassination attempt on corrupt, anti-immigration Senator McLaughlin (De Niro). So Machete wields his blades, and any other convenient weapon, in revenge. **105m/C; Blu-Ray.** Danny Trejo; Jeff Fahey; Robert De Niro; Steven Seagal; Michelle Rodriguez; Richard "Cheech" Marin; Lindsay Lohan; Jessica Alba; Don Johnson; Daryl Sabara; Tom Savini; Michael Parks; Tito Larriva; Rose McGowan; Gilbert Trejo; Shea Whigham; ***D:*** Robert Rodriguez; Ethan Maniquis; ***W:*** Robert Rodriguez; Alvaro Rodriguez; ***C:*** Jimmy Lindsey; ***M:*** John Debney. Golden Raspberries '10: Worst Support. Actress (Alba).

Machete Kills **½ 2013 (R)** Rodriguez's follow-up to his action B-movie extravaganza that itself was based on a fake trailer in the movie "Grindhouse." The thin basis for the first film is stretched far past its breaking point in this annoying pic, a B-movie without the interesting cast of the first movie and one in which the joke of the Machete character has worn out his welcome. Trejo returns as the tough guy in a story about the President (Sheen) stopping an arms dealer (Gibson) that's purely an excuse for blood, guts, and intentionally cheesy dialogue. **107m/C; DVD, Blu-Ray.** Danny Trejo; Mel Gibson; Demian Bichir; Michelle Rodriguez; Charlie Sheen; Sofia Vergara; Alexa Vega; Vanessa Anne Hudgens; Amber Heard; Lady Gaga; Cuba Gooding, Jr.; Walton Goggins; William Sadler; Antonio Banderas; Jessica Alba; ***D:*** Robert Rodriguez; ***W:*** Kyle Ward; ***C:*** Robert Rodriguez; ***M:*** Robert Rodriguez.

The Machine **½ 2013 (R)** This under-the-radar British sci-fi thriller has an identity crisis. It wants to be a treatise on the thin line between humanity and technology but also wants to have high-octane robot smackdowns. Director James almost gets the balance right, in this story of a dystopian future where genius scientist Vincent (Stephens) turns his slain programmer pal Ava (Lotz) into the world's first android with a soul. But while Vincent wants Ava to heal wounded soldiers, his bosses want her to be their own personal Terminatrix. The angst/action equilibrium is off, but it's well-crafted and stylish. **91 minutesm/C; DVD, Blu-Ray.** Toby Stephens; Caity Lotz; Sam Hazeldine; Denis Lawson; ***D:*** Caradog W. James; ***W:*** Caradog W. James; ***C:*** Nicolai Bruel; ***M:*** Tom Raybould.

The Machine Girl *Kataude mashin garu* **2007** If played as pure comedy, or as pure horror, this pic might have worked. As it stands, with the deliberately bad (and over-the-top gory) effects, campy acting, and just plain weirdness (the lead female baddie sports a pair of lethal drills on her, um, chest), it amounts to little more than dumb fun. Includes a bloody, knife-wielding schoolgirl, ninjas, vengeful parents in football uniforms, chainsaws, yakuza, and throwing stars in cgi (how hard is it to find actors who can throw the real thing?). **96m/C; DVD, Blu-Ray.** *JP* Kentaro Shimizu; Taro Suwa; Minase Yoshiro; Asami; Honoka; Nobuhiro Nishihara; Yuya Ishikawa; Ryosuke Kawamura; Demo Tanaka; Nahana; ***D:*** Noboru Iguchi; ***W:*** Noboru Iguchi; ***C:*** Yasatako Nagano; ***M:*** Takashi Nakagawa.

Machine Gun McCain **½ 1969** Cheap and violent Italian crime flick filmed in Las Vegas. Hank McCain (Cassavetes) owes his prison release to the influence of West Coast mob boss Charlie Adamo (Falk) who wants Hank to rob a casino. When Adamo learns it's owned by his East Coast counterparts, he tries to call McCain off but things go from bad to worse when McCain and his new bride Irene (Ekland) decide to play by their own rules. **96m/C; DVD.** *IT* John Cassavetes; Peter Falk; Britt Ekland; Gena Rowlands; Gabriele Ferzetti; Tony Kendall; Pierluigi Apra; ***D:*** Guiliano Montaldo; ***W:*** Guiliano Montaldo; Mino Rolli; ***C:*** Erico Menczer; ***M:*** Ennio Morricone.

Machine Gun Preacher **2011 (R)** Violent ex-con Sam Childers (Butler) finds Jesus and tries to turn his life around after his wife Lynn (Monaghan) becomes a Christian. Sam becomes a missionary, travels to Uganda on a relief trip, but finds his true calling when he enters neighboring Sudan. After witnessing the atrocities, he opens an orphanage, which puts him at odds with the warlords. This true story is simplistic and violent but Butler certainly has the action man status to keep it interesting. **129m/C; DVD, Blu-Ray.** Gerard Butler; Michelle Monaghan; Michael Shannon; Kathy Baker; Souleymane Sy Savane; Madeline Carroll; Peter Carey; ***D:*** Marc Forster; ***W:*** Jason Keller; ***C:*** Roberto Schaefer; ***M:*** Thad Spencer.

Machined **WOOF! 2006 (R)** Sicko Motor Man Dan accidentally runs over Ryan, so he takes him back to his shack to "fix" him. Which means Dan robocops him into a half-man/half-machine, all serial killer freak. Then the two go on a murder spree. As nasty as it sounds. **92m/C; DVD.** David C. Hayes; Jose Rosette; Patti Tindall; ***D:*** Craig McMahon; ***W:*** Craig McMahon; ***M:*** Craig McMahon. **VIDEO**

The Machinist *El Maquinista* **2004 (R)** Bale dropped more than 60 pounds to portray Trevor, a lonely, disturbed insomniac whose inattention causes a co-worker (Ironside) to lose an arm. Trevor believes his fellow workers now want revenge and, in his paranoid imagination, his hooker girlfriend Stevie (Leigh) is playing him false, he's the victim of a conspiracy and bedeviled by unseen tormentors, and his only solace is kindly waitress Marie (Sanchez-Gijon). It's creepy and stylistic (there's a cold blue tinge to the photography) and Anderson provides a quasi-believable conclusion as a payoff for all the misery endured. **102m/C; DVD, Blu-Ray.** Christian Bale; Jennifer Jason Leigh; Michael Ironside; Reg E. Cathey; Anna Massey; Aitana Sanchez-Gijon; John Sharian; Larry (Lawrence) Gilliard, Jr.; Matthew Romero Moore; ***D:*** Brad Anderson; ***W:*** Scott Kosar; ***C:*** Xavi Gimenez; ***M:*** Roque Baños.

Maciste in Hell **½** *Witch's Curse* **1960** Inexplicably living in 17th century Scotland, Italian hero Maciste pursues a witch into the depths of Hell. She's placed a curse on the world and he wants her to remove it. **78m/C; VHS, DVD.** *IT* Kirk Morris; Helene Chanel; Vira (Vera) Silenti; Andrea Bosic; Angelo Zanolli; John Karlsen; ***D:*** Riccardo Freda.

The Mack **½ 1973 (R)** The Mack is a pimp who comes out of retirement to reclaim a piece of the action in Oakland, California. Violent blaxploitation flick was boxoffice dynamite at time of release. Early Pryor appearance. **110m/C; VHS, DVD.** Max Julien; Richard Pryor; Don Gordon; Roger E. Mosley; Carol Speed; ***D:*** Michael Campus.

MacKenna's Gold **½ 1969 (PG)** Grim desperados trek through Apache territory to uncover legendary cache of gold in this somewhat inflated epic. Subdued stars Peck and Shariff vie for attention here with such overactors as Cobb, Meredith, and Wallach. Meanwhile, Newmar (Catwoman of TV's Batman) swims nude. A must for all earthquake buffs. **128m/C; VHS, DVD.** Gregory Peck; Omar Sharif; Telly Savalas; Julie Newmar; Edward G. Robinson; Keenan Wynn; Ted Cassidy; Eduardo Ciannelli; Eli Wallach; Raymond Massey; Lee J. Cobb; Burgess Meredith; Anthony Quayle; John David Garfield; Robert Phillips; ***D:*** J. Lee Thompson; ***W:*** Carl Foreman; ***C:*** Joe MacDonald; ***M:*** Quincy Jones.

Mackintosh Man **½ 1973 (PG)** An intelligence agent must undo a communist who has infiltrated the free world's network in this solid but somewhat subdued thriller. Good cast keeps narrative rolling, but don't look here for nudity-profanity-violence fix. **100m/C; VHS, DVD.** Paul Newman; Dominique Sanda; James Mason; Ian Bannen; Nigel Patrick; Harry Andrews; Leo Genn; Peter Vaughan; Michael Hordern; ***D:*** John Huston; ***W:*** Walter Hill; ***M:*** Maurice Jarre.

Macon County Line **½ 1974 (R)** A series of deadly mistakes and misfortunes lead to a sudden turn-around in the lives of three young people when they enter a small Georgia town and find themselves accused of brutally slaying the sheriff's wife. Sequelled by "Return to Macon County" in 1975, starring Don Johnson and Nick Nolte. **89m/C; VHS, DVD.** Alan Vint; Jesse Vint; Cheryl Waters; Geoffrey Lewis; Joan Blackman; Max Baer, Jr.; ***D:*** Richard Compton.

Mad About Men **½ 1954** In this slight sequel to 1948's "Miranda," the flirtatious mermaid (Johns) once again decides she wants to be land-bound. When she discovers distant cousin Caroline, a prim schoolteacher, is vacationing nearby, she persuades Caroline to allow Miranda to impersonate her. She uses her wheelchair ruse and accommodating nurse Cary (Rutherford) to pull off the deception, but the first thing Miranda does is to dump Caroline's stuffy fiancé in order to find someone who's more fun. **82m/C; DVD.** *UK* Glynis Johns; Donald Sinden; Margaret Rutherford; Anne Crawford; Dora Bryan; Peter Martyn; ***D:*** Ralph Thomas; ***W:*** Peter Blackmore; ***C:*** Ernest Steward; ***M:*** Benjamin Frankel.

Mad About Money *He Loved an Actress; Stardust* **1937** Comedy about a bespectacled mild-mannered fellow who runs up against a Mexican spitfire. **80m/B; VHS, DVD.** *GB* Lupe Velez; Wallace Ford; Ben Lyon; Harry Langdon; Jean Colin; ***D:*** Melville Brown.

Mad About Music **1938** On the advice of her publicist, film star Gwen Taylor (Patrick) sends her teenaged daughter Gloria (Durbin) off to a Swiss boarding school and keeps her identity a secret. So Gloria invents an exciting world-traveler father that envious schoolmate Felice (Parrish) insists upon meeting. Gloria manages to persuade a complete stranger, composer Richard Todd (Marshall), into playing the role (he's charmed by her singing). Naturally, there's lots of confusion, especially when mother and "father" finally meet. **92m/B; VHS, DVD.** Deanna Durbin; Herbert Marshall; Gail Patrick; Arthur Treacher; Helen Parrish; William Frawley; Marcia Mae Jones; Jackie Moran; ***D:*** Norman Taurog; ***W:*** Bruce Manning; Felix Jackson; ***C:*** Joseph Valentine.

The Mad Adventures of Rabbi Jacob *Les Adventures de Rabbi Jacob* **1973 (G)** In order to hide out from Arab revolutionaries and the police, bigoted businessman Victor Pivert borrows the identity of a beloved Rabbi returning to France after 30 years. Much French slapstick hilarity and some musings on racism and tolerance ensues. One of the most popular comedies of all time in France (even though Jerry Lewis is nowhere to be seen!), it's also one of the most-requested video releases here in the States. Suitable for children, it might serve as a good way to introduce them to foreign films. **100m/C; VHS, DVD, Blu-Ray.** *FR* Louis de Funes; Suzy Delair; Marcel Dalio; Claude Giraud; Renzo Montagnani; Andre Falcon; Henri Guybet; Miou-Miou; ***W:*** Josy Eisenberg; ***M:*** Vladimir Cosma.

Mad Bad **½ 2007 (R)** Justin DeMeer (Everett) just got out of prison after 10 years and is trying to reconnect with his angry younger sister Haydon (Dunning). She's got a promising music career but no money for recording sessions so Justin teams up with buddy Ethan (Gamble) to boost cars to sell to chop shops. He then puts his ill-gotten gains into Haydon's music. Justin steals a car filled with heroin and dealer Gino (Riverside) will do anything to get his merchandise back. **93m/C; DVD.** Maurice Ripke; Denton Blane Everett; Landon Dunning; Vince Riverside; Anna Zelinski; Terry Gamble; Russell Fuentes; ***D:*** Jon Keeyes; ***W:*** Jason Kabolati; Chip Joslin; ***C:*** Jason Todd Hampton; ***M:*** David Rosenblad. **VIDEO**

The Mad Bomber **WOOF!** *Police Connection; Detective Geronimo* **1972** Grim lawman Edwards tracks deranged bomber Connors, who is determined to blow up anyone who ever offended him. A must for all connoisseurs of acting that is simultaneously overblown and flat. **80m/C; VHS, DVD, Blu-Ray.** Vince Edwards; Chuck Connors; Neville Brand; ***D:*** Bert I. Gordon.

Mad Bull **1977** Sensitive wrestler finds meaning in life when he falls in love. If you ever cared about Karras, then you probably already saw this. If you never cared about Karras, then you probably never heard of this. If you ever cared about Anspach, rent "Five Easy Pieces" instead. **96m/C; VHS, Streaming.** Alex Karras; Susan Anspach; Nicholas Colasanto; Tracey Walter; ***D:*** Walter Doniger.

The Mad Butcher *The Mad Butcher of Vienna; The Strangler of Vienna; The Vienna Strangler; Der Wurger kommt auf leisen Socken; Lo Strangolatore di Vienna; Meat Is Meat* **1972 (R)** Typically unhinged mental patient seeks teenage flesh for his various instruments of torture and death. Buono has never been more imposing. **82m/C; VHS, DVD.** *IT* Victor Buono; Karin (Karen) Field; Brad Harris; ***D:*** Guido Zurli.

Mad City **½ 1997 (PG-13)** Out-of-work security guard Sam Baily (Travolta) goes postal, taking hostages in a museum while has-been journalist Max Brackett (Hoffman) manages to exploit Baily and hype the situation into a massive broadcast news event. The media circus that ensues provides social commentary on the questionable state of journalism. Relationship between Max and Sam carries the most interest in Costa-Gravas' intense drama, while uneven tone and script inadequacies hold back satisfying story development. Talented supporting cast (Alda, Danner, Kirshner, Prosky) have little to do. **114m/C; DVD.** John Travolta; Dustin Hoffman; Mia Kirshner; Alan Alda; Blythe Danner; Robert Prosky; William Atherton; Ted Levine; Bill Nunn; ***D:*** Constantin Costa-Gavras; ***W:*** Tom Mathews; ***C:*** Patrick Blossier; ***M:*** Thomas Newman.

Mad Cowgirl ✓✓ **2006** Probably the first mad cow disease movie. Meat inspector Therese (Lassez) goes off the rails when she's diagnosed with brain cancer, possibly caused by tainted beef. She revels in various surreal sex and splatter scenarios, including assuming the identity of her favorite kung-fu TV heroine and having a torrid liaison with her brother (Duval). Designed to turn watchers into vegetarians, if not vegans. **89m/C; DVD.** Sarah Lassez; James Duval; Devon Odessa; Walter Koenig; Vic Chao; Chris Dimassis; ***D:*** Gregory Hatanka; ***W:*** Gregory Hatanka; North Soth; ***C:*** Gregory Hatanka.

Mad Doctor of Blood Island
WOOF! *Tomb of the Living Dead; Blood Doctor* **1968** Dull band of travelers arrive on mysterious tropical island and encounter bloodthirsty creature. Warning: This film is not recognized for outstanding achievements in acting, dialogue, or cinematography. **110m/C; VHS, DVD, Blu-Ray.** *PH* John Ashley; Angelique Pettyjohn; Ronald Remy; Alicia Alonzo; Alfonso Carvajal; Johnny Long; Nadja; Bruno Punzalan; ***D:*** Gerardo (Gerry) De Leon; Eddie Romero; ***W:*** Reuben Candy; ***C:*** Justo Paulino; ***M:*** Tito Arevalo.

Mad Dog **WOOF!** **1984** An escaped convict seeks revenge on the cop responsible for his imprisonment. **90m/C; VHS, DVD.** Helmut Berger; Marisa Mell; ***D:*** Sergio Grieco.

Mad Dog and Glory ✓✓✓ **1993 (R)** Cast against type, Murray and De Niro play each other's straight man in this dark romantic comedy. Meek "Mad Dog" (De Niro) is an off-duty police photographer who happens upon a convenience store robbery and saves the life of Frank (Murray), obnoxious gangster by day, obnoxious stand-up comic by night. To settle up, Frank offers him Glory (Thurman), for a week. Eventually, Frank wants Glory back, forcing wimpy Mad Dog to either confront or surrender. Uneven and not of the knee-slapper ilk, but the performances are tight, including Caruso as a cop buddy of De Niro's. **97m/C; DVD, Blu-Ray.** Robert De Niro; Uma Thurman; Bill Murray; David Caruso; Mike Starr; Tom Towler; Kathy Baker; Derek Anunciation; J.J. Johnston; Richard Belzer; ***D:*** John McNaughton; ***W:*** Richard Price; ***C:*** Robby Muller; ***M:*** Elmer Bernstein.

Mad Dog Coll ✓ **1961** Distorted, violent bio of psycho 1920s killer Vincent Coll (Chandler), who gets into a gang war with mobster Dutch Schultz (Gardenia). Coll was machine-gunned to death in 1932 at the age of 23, although not under the circumstances depicted in the flick. **86m/B; DVD.** John Davis Chandler; Vincent Gardenia; Brooke Hayward; Jerry Orbach; Telly Savalas; Neil Nephew; ***D:*** Burt Balaban; ***W:*** Edward Schreiber; ***C:*** Gayne Rescher; ***M:*** Stu Phillips.

Mad Dog Killer ✓✓ *La Belva Col Mitra; Beast with a Gun* **1977** Sleazy Eurotrash of the type that seems especially suited to the 1970s. Rabidly violent Nanni Vitali (Berger) busts out of the slammer with several cohorts and proceeds to go on a revenge and crime spree, starting with the gruesome execution of the snitch who put him behind bars. The snitch's girlfriend Giuliana (Mell) is an unfortunate witness so Nanni kidnaps and brutalizes her, even forcing her to help plan his next heist. She eventually escapes and exposes Nanni's plan to cop Santini (Harrison). So the heist is botched and the psycho is royally ticked off. Last film for director/writer Grieco. Italian with subtitles. **91m/C; DVD.** *IT* Helmut Berger; Marisa Mell; Richard Harrison; Maria Angela Giordano; Vittorio Duse; Luigi Bonos; ***D:*** Sergio Grieco; ***W:*** Sergio Grieco; ***C:*** Vittorio Bernini; ***M:*** Umberto Smaila.

Mad Dog Morgan ✓✓ 1/2 *Mad Dog* **1976 (R)** Hopper delivers as engaging outlaw roaming outlands of 19th-century Australia. Quirky and violent G'day man. Based on a true story. **93m/C; VHS, DVD.** *AU* Dennis Hopper; David Gulpilil; ***D:*** Philippe Mora.

The Mad Executioners ✓✓ *Der Henker Von London* **1965** Scotland Yard inspector searches for a sex maniac who decapitates women. In the meantime, a group of vigilantes capture criminals and sentence them without a trial. Confusing film with a predictable ending. Based on the book "White Carpet" by Bryan Edgar Wallace. **92m/B; VHS, DVD.** *GE* Hansjorg Felmy; Maria Perschy; Dieter Borsche; Rudolph Forster; Chris Howland; Wolfgang Preiss; ***D:*** Edwin Zbonek.

Mad Hot Ballroom ✓✓✓ **2005 (PG)** Sweet documentary about ballroom dancing. Only the participants are New York City fifth graders participating in a 10-week program organized by the American Ballroom Theater. The doc follows students from Bensonhurst, Tribeca, and Washington Heights (a mixture of races, ethnicities, and incomes) as they learn the fox trot, meringue, rumba, swing, and tango (and how to deal with the opposite sex) in order to take part in an annual city-wide competition. **105m/C; DVD.** ***D:*** Marilyn Agrelo; ***W:*** Amy Sewell; ***C:*** Claudia Raschke; ***M:*** Steven Lutvak; Joseph Baker.

Mad Love ✓✓✓ *The Hands of Orlac* **1935** Brilliant surgeon Gogol (Lorre) falls madly in love with actress Yvonne Orlac (Drake), but she rebuffs him. When her pianist husband Stephen's (Clive) hands are cut off in a train accident, Gogol agrees to attach new hands, using those of a recently executed knife-wielding murderer, Reagan (Brophy). Gogol then kills Stephen's stepfather and uses psychological terror to make the pianist think he killed him. There's also an appearance by the supposedly dead murderer who shows up to reclaim his hands. A real chiller about obsessive love and psychological fear. The only downfall to this one is the unnecessary comic relief by Healy. Lorre's first American film. **70m/B; DVD.** Peter Lorre; Colin Clive; Frances Drake; Ted Healy; Edward Brophy; Sara Haden; Henry Kolker; Keye Luke; May (Mae) Beatty; ***D:*** Karl Freund; ***W:*** P.J. Wolfson; John Lloyd Balderston; Guy Endore; ***C:*** Gregg Toland; Chester Lyons; ***M:*** Dimitri Tiomkin.

Mad Love ✓ 1/2 **1995 (PG-13)** Teen love has rarely been so insipid. Impulsive and annoyingly melodramatic Casey (Barrymore) bewitches responsible, straightlaced Matt (O'Donnell) with her kewpie-doll charm and penchant for mischief. When Casey's bipolar ways land her in a mental hospital, Matt breaks her out and the unconvincing duo hit the road, where their supposedly free-spirited, passion-filled escapades grow increasingly silly, eventually halted by Casey's clinical crash. Slightly redeemed by a cool soundtrack and decent acting, but otherwise dull and insignificant, with an ending that may induce involuntary eyerolling. **95m/C; DVD, Blu-Ray.** Chris O'Donnell; Drew Barrymore; Joan Allen; Kevin Dunn; Jude Ciccolella; Amy Sakasitz; T.J. Lowther; ***D:*** Antonia Bird; ***W:*** Paula Milne; ***C:*** Fred Tammes.

Mad Love ✓✓ 1/2 *Madness of Love; Juana la Loca; Joan the Mad* **2001 (R)** Peculiar costume drama based on the life of Spanish queen Joan (known as "Joan the Mad"), daughter of King Ferdinand and Queen Isabella. In 1496, she's sent to marry Prince Philip of Flanders ("Philip the Handsome"). Although the marriage is arranged, the two are instantly smitten, but as the passion wears thin for Philip, he begins fooling around, and her intense love is enhanced by jealousy. Philip uses this to gain the throne by having Joan declared insane after Isabella dies. Pic does well with its subtle attention to detail and the standout performance of Lopez de Ayala as the lusty queen. Spanish with subtitles. **117m/C; DVD.** *SP IT PT* Pilar Lopez de Ayala; Daniele Liotti; Manuela Arcuri; Eloy Azorin; Rosana Pastor; Giuliano Gemma; ***D:*** Vicente Aranda; ***W:*** Vicente Aranda; ***C:*** Paco Femenia; ***M:*** Jose Nieto.

The Mad Magician ✓✓ **1954** Don Gallico (Price) designs magic illusions for his boss Ormond (Randolph) who sells them to other magicians. Gallico longs to perform himself but his chance is stopped by Ormond who legally owns the illusions and wants rival magician Rinaldi (Emery) to perform Gallico's 'lady and the buzzsaw' act. This sends Gallico over the edge and his illusions become deadly reality as he gets his revenge (which involves a severed head and disguises). Originally released in 3D. **73m/B; DVD, Blu-Ray.** Vincent Price; Donald Randolph; John Emery; Eva Gabor; Patrick O'Neal; Jay Novello; Mary Murphy; Lenita Lane; ***D:*** John Brahm; ***W:*** Crane Wilbur; ***C:*** Bert Glennon; ***M:*** Arthur Lange; Emil Newman.

Mad Max ✓✓✓ 1/2 **1980 (R)** Set on the stark highways of the post-nuclear future, an ex-cop seeks personal revenge against a rovin' band of vicious outlaw bikers who killed his wife and child. Futuristic scenery and excellent stunt work make for an exceptionally entertaining action-packed adventure. Followed by "The Road Warrior" (also known as "Mad Max 2") in 1981 and "Mad Max Beyond Thunderdome" in 1985. **93m/C; VHS, DVD, Blu-Ray, UMD.** *AU* Mel Gibson; Joanne Samuel; Hugh Keays-Byrne; Steve Bisley; Tim Burns; Roger Ward; Vincent (Vince Gill) Gil; ***D:*** George Miller; ***W:*** George Miller; ***C:*** David Eggby; ***M:*** Brian May.

Mad Max: Beyond Thunderdome ✓✓ 1/2 **1985 (PG-13)** Max drifts into evil town ruled by Turner and becomes gladiator, then gets dumped in desert and is rescued by band of feral orphans. Third in a bleak, extremely violent, often exhilarating series. **107m/C; VHS, DVD, Blu-Ray.** *AU* Mel Gibson; Tina Turner; Helen Buday; Frank Thring, Jr.; Bruce Spence; Robert Grubb; Angelo Rossitto; Angry Anderson; George Spartels; Rod Zuanic; ***D:*** George Miller; George Ogilvie; ***W:*** George Miller; Terry Hayes; ***C:*** Dean Semler; ***M:*** Maurice Jarre.

Mad Max: Fury Road ✓✓✓ **2015 (R)** George Miller's action masterpiece proves that there's still a market for stunt work and auteur-driven filmmaking, even in the world of summer blockbusters. Max (Hardy) has been reimagined as a haunted shell of a man, going through the motions of survival before death takes him. He is captured by the War Boys of brutal dictator Immortan Joe and sent on a mission to recapture Joe's fleeing warrior Furiosa (Theron). The bulk of the film is non-stop action but Miller manages to inject character and even social commentary into his blockbuster set-pieces. It's remarkable on every level. **120m/C; DVD, Blu-Ray.** Tom (Thomas) Hardy; Charlize Theron; Nicholas Hoult; Hugh Keays-Byrne; Josh Helman; ***D:*** George Miller; ***W:*** George Miller; Brendan McCarthy; Nico Lathouris; ***C:*** John Seale; ***M:*** Junkie XL. Oscars '15: Costume Des., Film Editing, Makeup, Production Design, Sound, Sound FX Editing; British Acad. '15: Costume Des., Film Editing, Makeup, Production Design.

Mad Miss Manton ✓✓ **1938** A socialite turns detective to solve murder. Pleasant comedy-mystery provides occasional laughs and suspense. **80m/B; VHS, DVD.** Barbara Stanwyck; Henry Fonda; Hattie McDaniel; Sam Levene; Miles Mander; Charles Halton; ***D:*** Leigh Jason.

Mad Mission 3 ✓ 1/2 *Aces Go Places 3: Our Man From Bond Street* **1984** Chinese man vacationing in Paris becomes involved in plot to recover precious jewels stolen from England's royal crown. Has there already been "Mad Mission" and "Mad Mission 2"? **81m/C; VHS, DVD.** *CH* Richard Kiel; Sam Hui; Peter Graves; Sylvia Chang; ***Cameo(s):*** Tsui Hark; ***D:*** Tsui Hark; ***W:*** Raymond Wong; ***C:*** Henry Chan; ***M:*** Lynsey De Paul; Terry Britten.

Mad Money ✓ 1/2 **2008 (PG-13)** Bridget's (Keaton) middleclass lifestyle is threatened when her husband's (Danson) downsized. The only job she can find is as a janitor at the Federal Reserve Bank, where she forges unlikely friendships with single mom Nina (Queen Latifah) and young dreamer Jackie (Holmes). Of course, the women aren't content in their menial positions and find an opportunity to even the score by deciding to "recycle" (i.e., steal) old, out-of-circulation bills that are about to be destroyed anyway. Bridget gets greedy and the plan starts to fall apart as does the fizzling silliness in this caper flick. **104m/C; DVD, Blu-Ray, On Demand.** *US UK* Diane Keaton; Queen Latifah; Katie Holmes; Ted Danson; Stephen (Steve) Root; Christopher McDonald; Adam Rothenberg; Barry; ***D:*** Callie Khouri; ***W:*** Glen Gers; ***C:*** John Bailey; ***M:*** Martin Davich; James Newton Howard.

The Mad Monster ✓ 1/2 **1942** This "Wolf Man"-inspired cheapie looks like a misty relic today. A mad scientist furthers the war effort by injecting wolf's blood into a handyman, who becomes hairy and anti-social. **77m/B; VHS, DVD.** Johnny Downs; George Zucco; Anne Nagel; Sarah Padden; Glenn Strange; Gordon DeMain; Mae Busch; ***D:*** Sam Newfield.

Mad Monster Party ✓✓ 1/2 **1968** Frankenstein is getting older and wants to retire from the responsibilities of being senior monster, so he calls a convention of creepy creatures to decide who should take his place—The Wolfman, Dracula, the Mummy, the Creature, It, the Invisible Man, or Dr. Jekyll and Mr. Hyde. Animated feature using the process of "Animagic." **94m/C; VHS, DVD, Blu-Ray.** ***V:*** Boris Karloff; Ethel Ennis; Phyllis Diller; ***D:*** Jules Bass.

The Mad Room ✓ 1/2 **1969** Ellen learns her teenaged brother and sister, who were institutionalized after being suspected of murdering their parents, are being released. She asks her employer, wealthy Mrs. Armstrong, if they can stay and the kids are reluctantly taken in, which doesn't end well for her in this crazy plot. **92m/C; DVD.** Stella Stevens; Shelley Winters; Skip Ward; Carol Cole; Severn Darden; Beverly Garland; ***D:*** Bernard Girard; ***W:*** Bernard Girard; A.Z. Martin; ***C:*** Harry Stradling, Sr.; ***M:*** Dave Grusin.

Madagascar ✓✓ 1/2 **2005 (PG)** Marty the Zebra (Rock) wants to escape the comfortable confines of New York's Central Park Zoo and head off into "the wild" (okay, Connecticut). Aided by a group of sassy penguins, he makes his break, but his zoo buddies—Alex the Lion (Stiller), Gloria the Hippo (Pinkett Smith), and Melman the Giraffe (Schwimmer)--escape to stop him. Things go awry and the authorities ship them off to a Kenyan animal reserve. Things go more awry and the group ends up on the shores of Madagascar. A romp for the kids with lots of pizzazz but not much substance. **80m/C; DVD, Blu-Ray.** ***V:*** Ben Stiller; Chris Rock; Jada Pinkett Smith; David Schwimmer; Cedric the Entertainer; Andy Richter; Sacha Baron Cohen; ***D:*** Eric Darnell; Tom McGrath; ***W:*** Eric Darnell; Tom McGrath; Billy Frolick; Mark Burton; ***M:*** Hans Zimmer.

Madagascar: Escape 2 Africa ✓✓ 1/2 **2008 (PG)** The strong cast is all back for the animated sequel and the top-notch computer animation is super sharp. Former zoo inhabitants Alex, Marty, Melman, and Gloria—along with King Julien, Maurice, and the penguins—have been stranded in Madagascar and attempt to escape to Africa. They end up in an African preserve where Alex (Stiller) is reunited with his father (Mac) and mother (Shepherd). Baron Cohen's King Julien the Lemur serves up some of the best laughs and makes the whole thing worth sitting through while the kids will fully appreciate the sophomoric gag fest. **89m/C; DVD, Blu-Ray, On Demand.** ***V:*** Ben Stiller; David Schwimmer; Chris Rock; Jada Pinkett Smith; Sacha Baron Cohen; Cedric the Entertainer; Bernie Mac; Andy Richter; Alec Baldwin; Sherri Shepherd; Christopher Knight; Conrad Vernon; will.i.am; Chris Miller; Elisa Gabrielli; ***D:*** Eric Darnell; Tom McGrath; ***W:*** Eric Darnell; Tom McGrath; ***M:*** Hans Zimmer; will.i.am.

Madagascar 3: Europe's Most Wanted ✓✓ 1/2 **2012 (PG)** In this latest DreamWorks animated adventure, Alex, Marty, Gloria, and Melman are still trying to get back home to Manhattan. This time they join a European traveling circus with the penguins and King Julien along for the trip. Surprisingly robust, it's a sweet well-paced movie that mostly works for adults and serves up more than enough eye candy for the wee ones. Pretty good for a threequel. **93m/C; DVD, Blu-Ray, Streaming.** ***V:*** Ben Stiller; Chris Rock; David Schwimmer; Jada Pinkett Smith; Sacha Baron Cohen; Cedric the Entertainer; Andy Richter; Frances McDormand; ***D:*** Eric Darnell; Tom McGrath; Conrad Vernon; ***W:*** Eric Darnell; Noah Baumbach; ***M:*** Hans Zimmer.

Madagascar Skin ✓✓ **1995 (R)** Harry (Hannah) is a young gay man who's disfigured by a large port-wine birthmark on one side of his face (in the shape of Madagascar). Suicidally depressed he drives to a deserted beach on the Welsh coast but before making any final decisions, he picks up an overturned bucket lying on the sand. To his shock, it's covering the head of the very much alive middle-aged Flint (Hill), who's been buried up to his neck in sand and left to drown by some fellow crooks. Flint knows of a deserted beach shack, the oddly matched duo move in, and Harry falls in love. Deliberately dreamlike in some respects, the leads provide a bittersweet, adult romance. **95m/C; VHS, DVD.** *GB* John Hannah; Bernard Hill; ***D:*** Chris Newby; ***W:*** Chris Newby; ***C:*** Oliver Curtis.

Madam Satan 1/2 **1930** Extremely bizarre DeMille film highlighted by lavish musical numbers and outrageous costumes. Wealthy socialite realizes she's losing her husband to a young showgirl, so she disguises herself as a sultry French tramp and entices her husband at a masquerade party aboard a zeppelin—surely one of the wildest party scenes ever captured on film. Chorus girls perform several exotic dance numbers inside the airship that are nothing short of fantastic. A storm breaks out and the floating dirigible is struck by lightning—leading viewers to wonder if the mad party-goers will make it to safety or crash and burn like this pic did at the boxoffice. **115m/B; DVD.** Kay Johnson; Reginald Denny; Lillian Roth; Roland Young; Boyd Irwin; Elsa Peterson; ***D:*** Cecil B. DeMille.

Madame Bovary **1949** Young adultress with delusions of romantic love finds only despair, even in this Hollywood version of Flaubert's classic. Mason/Flaubert is put on trial for indecency following publication of the novel, with the story told from the witness stand. While this device occasionally slows the narrative, astute direction helps the plot along. Minnelli's handling of the celebrated ball sequence is superb. **115m/B; VHS, DVD.** Jennifer Jones; Van Heflin; Louis Jourdan; James Mason; Gene Lockhart; Gladys Cooper; George Zucco; ***D:*** Vincente Minnelli; ***M:*** Miklos Rozsa.

Madame Bovary 1/2 **1991 (PG-13)** Provincial 19th-century France is the setting for the tragedy of a romantic woman based on the Gustave Flaubert novel. Emma Bovary is bored by her marriage to an unsuccessful country doctor and longs for passion and excitement. She allows herself to be seduced (and abandoned) by a local aristocrat and herself seduces a young banker. She also struggles with an increasing burden of debt as she continues her quest for luxury. Never finding the passion she desires, Emma takes drastic measures. Sumptuous-looking film, with an extraordinary performance by Huppert. In French with subtitles. **130m/C; DVD.** *FR* Isabelle Huppert; Jean-Francois Balmer; Christophe MaLavoy; Jean Yanne; ***D:*** Claude Chabrol; ***W:*** Claude Chabrol; ***M:*** Matthieu Chabrol.

Madame Bovary **2015 (R)** Gustave Flaubert's timeless literary creation, Madame Bovary, has been reinterpreted dozens of times in dozens of languages, and yet most of them pale in comparison to the source material. Despite strong casting and high production values, this adds another flat version of Bovary to the cinematic list. The well-cast Wasikowska stars as the title character, a farmer's wife in Normandy, France who is bored with her standing in life. She cheats on her husband, trying to find love, but finds no satisfaction, even in the arms of others. This version misses the passion of the original, coming off as too bland for its talented ensemble. **118m/C; DVD, Blu-Ray, Streaming.** *BE GE US* Mia Wasikowska; Ezra Miller; Rhys Ifans; Paul Giamatti; Laura Carmichael; Logan Marshall-Green; ***D:*** Sophie Barthes; ***W:*** Sophie Barthes; Felipe Marino; ***C:*** Andrij Parekh; ***M:*** Evgueni Galperine; Sacha Galperine.

Madame Butterfly **1995** A French production, filmed in Tunisia, with a Chinese soprano, and Italian subtitles. Mitterrand takes on Puccini's opera, setting it in 1904 Nagasaki, but playing most of the story straight (he adds some documentary footage of old Japan between the acts). 15-year-old Butterfly (Huang) is a geisha who makes the mistake of falling in love and marrying deceitful American naval officer Pinkerton (Troxell). She's disowned by her family, he eventually sails away, and when he does return, it's with an American bride. Tragedy ensues. Newcomer Huang's fine but the handsome Troxell's a little stiff. **129m/C; VHS, DVD.** *FR* Ying Huang; Richard Troxell; Ning Liang; Richard Cowan; ***D:*** Frederic Mitterrand; ***W:*** Frederic Mitterrand; ***C:*** Philippe Welt.

Madame Claude *The French Woman* **1977** Based vaguely on the true story of the real Madame Clause who provided prostitutes for dignitaries and politicians. A photographer attempts to escape prosecution for his own crimes by providing the police with photographs of Claude's clients in compromising positions. **105m/C; DVD, Streaming.** *FR* Murray Head; Klaus Kinski; Francoise Fabian; Dayle Haddon; Vibeke Knudsen; ***D:*** Just Jaeckin; ***W:*** Andre G. Brunelin; ***C:*** Robert Fraisse; ***M:*** Serge Gainsbourg.

Madame Curie **1943** The film biography of Madame Marie Curie, the woman who discovered Radium. A deft portrayal by Garson, who is reteamed with her "Mrs. Miniver" co-star, Pidgeon. Certainly better than most biographies from this time period and more truthful as well. **124m/B; VHS, DVD.** Greer Garson; Walter Pidgeon; Robert Walker; May Whitty; Henry Travers; Sir C. Aubrey Smith; Albert Bassermann; Victor Francen; Reginald Owen; Van Johnson; ***D:*** Mervyn LeRoy; ***C:*** Joseph Ruttenberg.

Madame O 1/2 *Zoku akutokui: Joi-hen* **1967** Sequel to a film unreleased in the States, provides generous flashbacks telling the story of its main character. Seiko (Michiko Aoyama) is raped at 16 and suffers not only impregnation and syphilis, but also an uncontrollable sexual desire and hatred of men whom she believes are all evil. Now one of the country's most successful doctors by day, she prowls the street at night looking for evil men to infect. Falling in love with another doctor she decides to call it quits until she starts getting blackmailed by a former victim. **81m/B; DVD.** *JP* Michiko Sakyo; Naomi Tani; ***D:*** Seiichi Fukuda; ***W:*** Tomomi Tsukasa; ***C:*** Jiro Ooyama.

Madame Sans-Gene *Madame* **1962** Bawdy laundress Catherine (Loren) falls for Lefevre (Hossein), a soldier in Napoleon's (Berthea) army. While the French battle the Austrians, Catherine seeks her new husband on the battlefield and they both become accidental heroes. When Napoleon becomes emperor, he rewards them with a title but his sisters think Catherine is too uncouth and try to force the couple apart. But they don't know who they're dealing with. French and Italian with subtitles. **104m/C; DVD.** *FR IT* Sophia Loren; Robert Hossein; Julien Bertheau; Marina Berti; Analia Gade; Laura Valenzuela; Mary Renaud; ***D:*** Christian-Jaque; ***W:*** Christian-Jaque; ***C:*** Roberto Gerardi; ***M:*** Angelo Francesco Lavagnino.

Madame Sata **2002** First feature for director Karim Ainouz is a stylized portrait of Joao Francisco dos Santos, who became a legend in the slums and prisons of Brazil as both a criminal and the cabaret performer Madame Sata. The film covers a period in 1930s Rio showcasing Joao's (Ramos) life at the Blue Danube club and the boarding-house where he lives with his ready-made family—hooker Laurita (Cartaxo) and her baby daughter and flamboyant hustler Taboo (Bauraqui). Ramos gives a compelling performance of a sometimes violent character who lives his life without apologies. Portuguese with subtitles. **105m/C; DVD.** *BR FR* Lazaro Ramos; Marcella Cartaxo; Flavio Bauraqui; Felippe Marques; ***D:*** Karim Ainouz; ***W:*** Karim Ainouz; ***C:*** Walter Carvalho; ***M:*** Marcos Suzano; Sacha Ambak.

Madame Sin 1/2 **1971** Aspiring world dominator enlists former CIA agent in scheme to obtain nuclear submarine. Davis is appealing as evil personified, in her first TV movie. **91m/C; VHS, Streaming.** Bette Davis; Robert Wagner; ***D:*** David Greene; ***M:*** Michael Gibbs. **TV**

Madame Sousatzka **1988 (PG-13)** Eccentric, extroverted piano teacher helps students develop spiritually as well as musically. When she engages a teenage Indian student, however, she finds herself considerably challenged. MacLaine is perfectly cast in this powerful, winning film. **113m/C; VHS, DVD; Open Captioned.** Shirley MacLaine; Peggy Ashcroft; Shabana Azmi; Twiggy; Leigh Lawson; Geoffrey Bayldon; Navin Chowdhry; Lee Montague; ***D:*** John Schlesinger; ***W:*** Ruth Prawer Jhabvala; John Schlesinger; ***M:*** Gerald Gouriet. Golden Globes '89: Actress—Drama (MacLaine); Venice Film Fest. '88: Actress (MacLaine).

Madame X **1929** The first sound version of the Alexandre Bisson play suffers from stagey acting as the cast transitions from silents to talkies and somewhat static direction but is still worth a look-see. Jacqueline Floriot (Chatterton) is forced to leave her family after her husband Louis (Stone) discovers she's having an affair. Deserted by her lover, Jacqueline hits the skids and, years later ends up in trouble with the law. Put on trial, the mysterious Madame X is defended by the son (Hackett) who doesn't know who she is. **95m/B; DVD.** Ruth Chatterton; Lewis Stone; Raymond Hackett; Holmes Herbert; Eugenie Besserer; Sidney Toler; ***D:*** Lionel Barrymore; ***W:*** Willard Mack; ***C:*** Arthur Reed.

Madame X 1/2 **1937** Fourth version of this classic tearjerker finds diplomat's wife George having a fling with a playboy. There's a murder and she turns to her nasty mother-in-law for aid. She arranges for daughter-in-law-dearest's "death" in order to prevent a scandal. Then George is on the slippery path to alcoholism and prostitution. Adapted from the play by Alexandre Bisson. Run-of-the-mill; Lana Turner's 1966 version is still the one to watch. **96m/B; VHS, DVD.** Gladys George; John Beal; Warren William; Reginald Owen; William Henry; Henry Daniell; Phillip Reed; Lynne Carver; Emma Dunn; Ruth Hussey; ***D:*** Sam Wood; ***W:*** John Meehan.

Madame X 1/2 *Absinthe* **1966** Lonely diplomat's wife Holly (Turner) has a fling with playboy Phil (Montalban) who dies in her presence. Her nasty mother-in-law (Bennett in her last role) advises her to skedaddle or ruin hubby Clay's (Forsythe) career. She leaves her young son and eventually winds up a prostitute in Mexico where she falls in with slimy crook Sullivan (Meredith). Holly winds up killing him and goes on trial as Madame X. Oft-filmed melodrama works because of Turner's heartfelt and affecting performance. **100m/C; VHS, DVD, Blu-Ray.** Lana Turner; John Forsythe; Ricardo Montalban; Burgess Meredith; Virginia Grey; Constance Bennett; Keir Dullea; ***D:*** David Lowell Rich; ***W:*** Jean Holloway; ***C:*** Russell Metty; ***M:*** Frank Skinner.

Made 1/2 **2001 (R)** Favreau, who also wrote and directed, teams up again with "Swingers" buddy Vaughn in this tale of two wannabes. Bobby (Favreau), a past-his-prime boxer, chauffeurs his stripper girlfriend Jessica (Janssen) to her gigs. Ricky (Vaughn), his motor-mouthed friend, wants to get mobbed up with crime boss Max (Falk). Max sends them to New York with cryptic instructions to follow the orders of slick gangsta Ruiz (Combs) but Ricky's rash behavior lands them in constant trouble. Vaughn's comic riffing occasionally crosses into excess, but the chemistry between the two leads is excellent and the laughs are plentiful. **94m/C; DVD, Blu-Ray.** Jon Favreau; Vince Vaughn; Famke Janssen; Faizon Love; David O'Hara; Vincent Pastore; Peter Falk; Sean (Puffy, Puff Daddy, P. Diddy) Combs; Drea De Matteo; ***D:*** Jon Favreau; ***W:*** Jon Favreau; ***C:*** Christopher Doyle; ***M:*** John O'Brien; Lyle Workman.

Made for Each Other **1939** Newlyweds John (Stewart) and Jane (Lombard) Mason must overcome meddlesome in-laws, poverty, and even the arrival of a baby in this classic melodrama. Things become so serious, they decide to separate but their child's serious illness brings them together for a second chance. Dated but appealing. **94m/B; VHS, DVD, Blu-Ray.** James Stewart; Carole Lombard; Charles Coburn; Lucile Watson; ***D:*** John Cromwell; ***W:*** Jo Swerling; ***C:*** Leon Shamroy; ***M:*** Louis Forbes.

Made in America **1993 (PG-13)** High-energy, lightweight comedy stars Whoopi as a single mom whose daughter Long discovers her birth was the result of artifical insemination. More surprising is her biological dad: white, obnoxious, country-western car dealer Danson. Overwrought with obvious gags, basically a one-joke movie. Nonetheless, Goldberg and Danson chemically connect onscreen while supporting actor Smith grabs comedic attention as Teacake, Long's best friend. But both Goldberg and Danson deserve better material. **111m/C; DVD.** Whoopi Goldberg; Ted Danson; Will Smith; Nia Long; Paul Rodriguez; Jennifer Tilly; Peggy Rea; Clyde Kusatsu; ***D:*** Richard Benjamin; ***W:*** Holly Goldberg Sloan; ***C:*** Ralf Bode; ***M:*** Mark Isham.

Made in Dagenham **2010 (R)** Dramatization of the 1968 labor strike at the Ford Dagenham car plant in England where 850 female workers walked out to protest sexual discrimination on their job performance reviews from a company with antifeminist attitudes and policies. Rita O'Grady (Hawkins) and her female colleagues challenge their bosses, their community, and their government to fight for the respect they deserve. Apt and inspirational—though a tad schmaltzy—depiction of the intelligence, humor, and bravery that the women drew upon to change the system. **113m/C; DVD, Blu-Ray.** Rosamund Pike; Miranda Richardson; Sally Hawkins; Geraldine James; Bob Hoskins; Richard Schiff; Daniel Mays; John Sessions; ***D:*** Nigel Cole; ***W:*** Billy Ivory; ***C:*** John de Borman; ***M:*** David Arnold.

Made in Heaven **1952** Arid comedy in which British newlyweds try to sustain honeymoon for entire year. The bride, however, eventually suspects her husband of shenanigans with the maid. If this sounds good, then you may like it. **90m/C; VHS, DVD.** *GB* Petula Clark; David Tomlinson; Sonja Ziemann; A.E. Matthews; Charles Victor; Sophie Stewart; John Stainton; Ferdinand "Ferdy" Mayne; Richard Wattis; Alfie Bass; Dora Bryan; ***D:*** Jack Paddy Carstairs; ***W:*** George H. Brown; William Douglas-Home; ***C:*** Geoffrey Unsworth.

Made in Heaven 1/2 **1987 (PG)** Two souls in heaven fall in love and must find each other after being reborn on Earth if they are to remain eternal lovers. Contains ethereal interpretations of heaven and several cameo appearances by famous actors and musicians. **105m/C; VHS, DVD.** Timothy Hutton; Kelly McGillis; Maureen Stapleton; Mare Winningham; Ann Wedgeworth; Don Murray; Amanda Plummer; Timothy Daly; Marj Dusay; ***Cameo(s):*** Ellen Barkin; Neil Young; Tom Petty; Ric Ocasek; Tom Robbins; Debra Winger; Gary Larsen; David Rasche; ***D:*** Alan Rudolph; ***W:*** Raynold Gideon; Bruce A. Evans; ***M:*** Mark Isham.

Made in Paris 1/2 **1965** Maggie (Ann-Margaret), Barclay Department Store's assistant fashion buyer, is sent to Paris when her boss Irene (Adams) decides to get married. Maggie is wooed by ladies' man designer Marc Fontaine (Jourdan) and newspaperman Herb Stone (Crenna), who is actually supposed to keep an eye on her for Ted Barclay (Everett), the store owner's son who is in love with her. When it looks like Maggie has cost the store the Fontaine account, Ted comes to Paris on the pretext of straightening things out. Ann-Margaret has little to do beyond exploiting her sex-kitten persona. **103m/C; DVD.** Ann-Margret; Louis Jourdan; Richard Crenna; Chad Everett; John McGiver; Edie Adams; ***D:*** Boris Sagal; ***W:*** Stanley Roberts; ***C:*** Milton Krasner; ***M:*** Georgie Stoll.

Made in Romania 1/2 **2010** Behind-the-scenes showbiz comedy. Sebastian, a producer of low-budget genre flicks, finally gets a chance to film his dream project but only if he accepts a shady tax deal to shoot in Romania. Economic, language, and cultural barriers soon wreck havoc with the hapless production. **95m/C; DVD.** *GB* Joe Norman Shaw; Jennifer Tilly; Jason Flemyng; Elizabeth Hurley; Joey Slotnick; Gareth Thomas; Nicholas Le Prevost; Bobbi Sue (Bobby Sue) Luther; ***D:*** Guy J. Louthan; ***W:*** Guy J. Louthan; ***C:*** Gabriel Kosuth; ***M:*** Trevor Gilchrist.

Made Men **1999 (R)** Former hitman, now in the witness protection program, gets caught stealing 12 million from the mob. If he wants to save his life, he's got to outwit four mobsters sent to get the money. **90m/C; VHS, DVD.** James Belushi; Michael Beach; Timothy Dalton; Vanessa Angel; Steve Railsback; ***D:*** Louis Morneau; ***C:*** George Mooradian; ***M:*** Stewart Copeland. **VIDEO**

Made of Honor 1/2 **2008 (PG-13)** Swinging single Tom (Dempsey) brags to his buddies that he lives a perfect life: he bags a new babe almost every night and still has the companionship of his lovely long-time best friend Hannah (Monaghan) for balance. But when Hannah returns from a Scotland vacation with the ultimate souvenir—a fiance—Tom quickly realizes he's missed his chance at true love. He accepts her offer to be the "maid" of honor, hoping to sabotage the wedding from the inside. Little more than a bland gender-reversed version of "My Best Friend's Wedding" with paper-thin characters that bomb the chemistry test. **101m/C; DVD, Blu-Ray, Streaming.** Patrick Dempsey; Michelle Monaghan; Kevin McKidd; Kathleen Quinlan; Sydney Pollack; Kadeem Hardison; Chris Messina; Busy Philipps; Kelly Carlson; James B. Sikking; Richmond Arquette; Beau Garrett; Whitney Cummings; Emily Nelson; Kevin Sussman; Selma Stern; ***D:*** Paul Weiland; ***W:*** Deborah Kaplan; Adam Sztykiel; Harry Elfont; ***C:*** Tony Pierce-Roberts; ***M:*** Rupert Gregson-Williams.

Made On Broadway 🦴🦴 **1933** In this sophisticated rom com, New York press agent and fixer Jeff Bidwell (Montgomery) has a society and political clientele and a sympathetic ex-wife, Claire (Evans). He's not too smart about women after rescuing down-and-out Minnie (Eilers) from suicide and giving her a makeover and a new name--Mona Martine. Jeff thinks he's in love but ambitious Mona plugs her amorous dance instructor and uses Jeff to spin the truth during her murder trial. **68m/B; DVD.** Robert Montgomery; Madge Evans; Sally Eilers; Eugene Pallette; C. Henry Gordon; Ivan Lebedeff; Jean Parker; ***D:*** Harry Beaumont; ***W:*** Courtney Terrett; ***C:*** Norbert Brodine.

A Madea Family Funeral 🦴 1/2 *Tyler Perry's A Madea Family Funeral* **2019 (PG-13)** After the death of Vianne's (Harper) husband Anthony (Morgan), Madea has only two days to put his funeral together. Though the family objects to the quick burial, unfaithful Anthony had a heart attack while having sex with Vianne's best friend in a hotel. This event was overheard and witnessed by A.J. (Burrell) and Gia (Miranda), who were cheating on their partners in the same hotel. More of Anthony's secrets, the effects of his actions, and related family issues are revealed. Perhaps the last film by Perry featuring Madea, it's the usual bawdy humor that will appeal its fans. **109m/C; DVD, Blu-Ray.** Tyler Perry; Cassi Davis; Patrice Lovely; Mike Tyson; Ciera Payton; ***D:*** Tyler Perry; ***W:*** Tyler Perry; ***M:*** Philip White.

Madea Goes to Jail 🦴🦴 *Tyler Perry's Madea Goes to Jail* **2009 (PG-13)** Formulaic dramedy that makes outlaw grandma Medea (Perry) even more obnoxious than usual. This time Medea's law-breaking antics takes second place to the story of up-from-the-ghetto assistant DA Joshua Hardaway (Luke) who's shocked by the arrest of childhood friend Candace (Knight Pulliam), now a druggie hooker. Joshua's upscale fiancee Linda (Overman) is naturally upset by Joshua's persistence in trying to help Candace (which isn't selfless). Medea comes in when she winds up in the joint with Candace as a fellow inmate, thus allowing Medea to offer her own brand of trash-talking inspiration. **103m/C; Blu-Ray, On Demand.** Keisha Knight Pulliam; Tyler Perry; Derek Luke; Vanessa Ferlito; RonReaco Lee; Ion Overman; Viola Davis; David Mann; Tamela Mann; ***D:*** Tyler Perry; ***W:*** Tyler Perry; ***C:*** Alexander Grusynski; ***M:*** Aaron Zigman.

Madea's Big Happy Family 🦴🦴 *Tyler Perry's Madea's Big Happy Family* **2011 (PG-13)** Perry returns to his classic character Madea, who teams up with the unruly Aunt Bam (Davis) to reunite the family after Madea's niece Shirley (Devine) discovers that she has serious health problems. But arranging the reunion is an uphill battle when Shirley's selfish adult children (Desselle, Kane, and Bow Wow) are too preoccupied with their own troubles to support their mother. An absurd, comedic flick that showcases a vivacious ensemble cast. Based on Perry's stage play. **105m/C; DVD, Blu-Ray, On Demand.** Tyler Perry; Loretta Devine; Bow Wow; Shannon Kane; Natalie Desselle; Cassi Davis; Tamela Mann; Maury Povich; ***D:*** Tyler Perry; ***W:*** Tyler Perry; ***C:*** Toyomichi Kurita; ***M:*** Aaron Zigman.

Madea's Family Reunion 🦴 1/2 **2006 (PG-13)** Director/writer/actor Perry dresses in drag again to fill grandmamma's shoes in this sequel to his popular "Diary of a Mad Black Woman." Madea now must use her sassy tongue to help her nieces deal with their messed-up love lives while keeping her new foster child on the right track. The witty banter stumbles when mixed with serious social issues. **107m/C; DVD.** Tyler Perry; Blair Underwood; Lynn Whitfield; Boris Kodjoe; Henry Simmons; Lisa Arrindell Anderson; Maya Angelou; Rochelle Aytes; Jenifer Lewis; Cicely Tyson; Keke Palmer; ***D:*** Tyler Perry; ***W:*** Tyler Perry; ***C:*** Toyomichi Kurita; ***M:*** Tyler Perry; Elvin D. Ross.

Madea's Witness Protection 🦴 1/2 *Tyler Perry's Madea's Witness Protection* **2012 (PG-13)** New Yorker George Needleman (Levy) is a financial exec who's set up as the fall guy for a mob-backed Ponzi scheme that bilked charities. To protect George and his dysfunctional family, D.A. Bryan (Perry) sends them to his Aunt Madea's in Georgia. Madea and Uncle Joe are going to practice some tough love on the brood while George and Madea team up to recover the money from the bad guys. Rowdy and predictable but less preachy than usual. **115m/C; DVD, Blu-Ray; Closed Captioned.** Tyler Perry; Eugene Levy; Denise Richards; Doris Roberts; Danielle Campbell; Devan Leos; Romeo Miller; Tom Arnold; John Amos; Marla Gibbs; ***D:*** Tyler Perry; ***W:*** Tyler Perry; ***C:*** Alexander Gruszynski; ***M:*** Aaron Zigman.

Madeleine 🦴🦴 1/2 *The Strange Case of Madeleine* **1950** Courtroom drama of woman charged with poisoning her French lover in 1850s Scotland. Directed by the same David Lean who made "Bridge on the River Kwai" and "Lawrence of Arabia." Here, though, he was merely trying to provide a vehicle for his wife, actress Todd. Intrigued? **114m/B; VHS, DVD.** Ann Todd; Leslie Banks; Ivan Desny; Norman Wooland; Barbara Everest; Susan Stranks; Patricia Raine; Elizabeth Sellars; Edward Chapman; Jean Cadell; Eugene Deckers; Amy Veness; John Laurie; Henry Edwards; Ivor Barnard; Barry Jones; David Morne; Andre Morell; ***D:*** David Lean; ***W:*** Nicholas Phipps; Stanley Haynes; ***C:*** Guy Green; ***M:*** William Alwyn.

Madeline 🦴🦴 **1998 (PG)** Adaptation of Ludwig Bemelmans' classic 1939 children's books about the trouble-finding orphan Madeline (Jones), her schoolmates, and their patient teacher Miss Clavel (McDormand). Travelling through the plots of four of the six Madeline books, the acting seems a little flat, even for kids. McDormand and Hawthorne as Lord "Cucuface" Covington are unable to act to their fullest, and the child actors are mostly forgettable. If you liked the books as a kid, you may be disappointed; but it's a good way to introduce your own children to the series. **90m/C; DVD.** Hatty Jones; Frances McDormand; Nigel Hawthorne; Ben Daniels; Arturo Venegas; Stephane Audran; Katia Caballero; ***D:*** Daisy von Scherler Mayer; ***W:*** Marc Levin; Jennifer Flackett; Chris Weitz; Paul Weitz; ***C:*** Pierre Aim; ***M:*** Michel Legrand.

Madeline's Madeline 🦴🦴 1/2 **2018** Madeline (Howard) is a biracial teen suffering from mental illness on top of the expected adolescent issues, and she often acts out against her overprotective mother Regina (July). Madeline has a supportive outlet in her acting class, but her sympathetic instructor Evangeline (Parker) has allowed her pregnancy to distract her from completing a new work for the troupe. Evangeline uses Madeline's mental illness and other difficulties as the basis of the production, leaving Madeline adrift and confused. Howard's inspired performance provides insight into Madeline, otherwise this drama sells its message short. **93m/C; DVD, Blu-Ray.** Helena Howard; Miranda July; Molly Parker; Okwui Okpokwasili; Sunita Mani; ***D:*** Josephine Decker; ***W:*** Josephine Decker; ***C:*** Ashley Connor; ***M:*** Caroline Shaw.

Mademoiselle 🦴🦴 **1966** Moreau is a psychotic, sexually repressed schoolteacher in a small village who manages to keep herself under control until studly woodcutter Manni and his son take up residence. The locals distrust the stranger but Moreau can't wait to get her hands on him. Suddenly, the village is battered by a rash of poisonings, fires, and floods, all of which are blamed on Manni, leading the locals to exact a terrible vengeance. In French with English subtitles. **105m/B; VHS, DVD.** *FR GB* Jeanne Moreau; Ettore Manni; Umberto Orsini; Keith Skinner; Jane Berretta; Mony Rey; ***D:*** Tony Richardson; ***W:*** Jean Genet; ***C:*** David Watkin.

Mademoiselle C 🦴🦴 1/2 **2013 (R)** An insightful documentary about former Vogue Paris editor Carine Rotfield, as she moves to New York City and starts her own new magazine, CR Fashion Book. Looking at both her professional and personal life, the film includes appearances from numerous models, actors, actresses, fashionistas, and other well-known members of the world of fashion. Rotfield's family also is included as she prepares to become a grandmother. **93m/C; DVD, Blu-Ray.** Carine Roitfeld; Anna Wintour; Marion Cotillard; James Franco; Kirsten Dunst; Linda Evangelista; Liv Tyler; Jean-Paul Gaultier; ***D:*** Fabien Constant; ***C:*** Raphael Laski; Matt Elkind; ***M:*** The Shoes. **VIDEO**

Mademoiselle Chambon 🦴🦴 1/2 **2009** Married housing contractor Jean meets his son's beautiful teacher Veronique and there is an immediate attraction between them. He begins doing repair work to stay close to her but they are both reluctant to have it turn into an affair even as the passion between them grows. Adapted from the Eric Holder novel. French with subtitles. **101m/C; DVD.** *FR* Vincent Lindon; Sandrine Kiberlain; Aure Atika; Jean-Marc Thibault; Arthur Le Houerou; ***D:*** Stephane Brize; ***W:*** Stephane Brize; Florence Vignon; ***C:*** Antoine Heberle; ***M:*** Ange Ghinozzi.

Madeo 🦴🦴 *Mother* **2009 (R)** Tough widow Hye-ja (Kim) runs a shop in a rural Korean town and tries to watch out for her mentally-challenged 27-year-old son Do-joon (Bin) who lives with her. Unfortunately, his best friend is local troublemaker Jin-tae (Jin). Do-joon becomes an easy target for the lazy local cops when a teenaged girl is the victim of a brutal sexual murder and they get a confession from the confused man. His mother knows better and she is on a one-woman crusade, determined to prove his innocence. Bong tends to throw in plot curves and he likes his small towns to have dark secrets but Kim gives an engrossing performance about maternal love. Korean with subtitles. **128m/C; DVD, Blu-Ray, On Demand.** *NK* Hye-ja Kim; Bin Won; Ku Jin; ***D:*** Joon-ho Bong; ***W:*** Joon-ho Bong; Eun-kyo Park; ***C:*** Kyung-Pyo Hong; ***M:*** Byeong-woo Lee.

Madhouse 🦴🦴 **1974** A troubled horror film star tries to bring his "Dr. Death" character to TV, but during production people begin dying in ways remarkably similar to the script. A strong genre cast should hold the fans' attention during this mild adaptation of Angus Hall's novel "Devilday." **92m/C; VHS, DVD, Blu-Ray.** *GB* Vincent Price; Peter Cushing; Robert Quarry; Adrienne Corri; Natasha Pyne; Linda Hayden; Michael Parkinson; ***D:*** Jim Clark.

Madhouse 🦴🦴 **2004 (R)** Clark Stevens (Leonard) accepts a psychiatric internship at a dilapidated asylum where murders begin to occur, and he's haunted by the figure of a young boy. He teams up with sympathetic nurse Sara (Ladd) to find out what's going on. **91m/C; DVD.** Joshua Leonard; Jordan Ladd; Natasha Lyonne; Lance Henriksen; Leslie Jordan; Patrika Darbo; Christian Leffler; Dendrie Taylor; Aaron Strongoni; ***D:*** William Butler; ***W:*** William Butler; Aaron Strongoni; ***C:*** Viorel Sergovici, Jr.; ***M:*** Alberto Caruso.

Madigan 🦴🦴🦴 **1968** Realistic and exciting and among the best of the behind-the-scenes urban police thrillers. Hardened NYC detectives (Widmark and Guardino) lose their guns to a sadistic killer and are given 72 hours to track him down. Fonda is the police chief none too pleased with their performance. Adapted by Howard Rodman, Abraham Polonsky, and Harry Kleiner from Richard Dougherty's "The Commissioner." **101m/C; VHS, DVD, Blu-Ray.** Richard Widmark; Henry Fonda; Inger Stevens; Harry Guardino; James Whitmore; Susan Clark; Michael Dunn; Don Stroud; ***D:*** Donald Siegel; ***W:*** Abraham Polonsky; ***C:*** Russell Metty; ***M:*** Don Costa.

Madigan's Millions WOOF! **1967 (G)** Incompetent Treasury agent treks to Italy to recover funds swiped from deceased gangster. This is Hoffman's first film, and is to his career what "The Last Chalice" was to Paul Newman's and "Studs and Kitty" was Sylvester Stallone. Recommended only to the terminally foolhardy. **89m/C; VHS, DVD.** Dustin Hoffman; Elsa Martinelli; Cesar Romero; ***D:*** Stanley Prager.

Madison 🦴🦴 1/2 **2001 (PG)** Predictably cliched sports drama based on a true story. Title refers to Madison IN, a hard-luck community that, by 1971, has little going for it but a tradition of hydroplane racing and a chance to host the Gold Cup tournament. It also has all-around great guy Jim McCormick (Caviezel), a former pilot of the community-owned race boat, the Miss Madison. Both McCormick and Miss Madison have seen better days but golly, Jim just has to make his son Mike (Lloyd) proud. There's nothing actually wrong with the film but, boy, have you seen this story before. **94m/C; DVD.** James (Jim) Caviezel; Jake Lloyd; Mary McCormack; Bruce Dern; Brent Briscoe; Paul Dooley; Reed Edward Diamond; Chelcie Ross; Frank Knapp; Byrne Piven; William Shockley; Matt Letscher; Richard Lee Jackson; Kristina Anapau; Vincent Ventresca; Cody McMains; ***D:*** William Bindley; ***W:*** William Bindley; Scott Bindley; ***C:*** James Glennon; ***M:*** Kevin Kiner.

Madman 🦴 **1979 (R)** Deranged Soviet Jew joins Israeli army to more effectively fulfill his desire to kill loathsome Soviets. Good date movie for those nights when you're home alone. Weaver's first starring role. **95m/C; VHS, DVD.** *IS* Sigourney Weaver; Michael Beck; F. Murray Abraham; ***D:*** Dan Cohen.

Madman 🦴 **1982 (R)** Camp leader prompts terror when he revives legend regarding ax murderer. Seems that when you call his name, he appears. Buffoon does not believe story and calls out madman's name. Madman hears the call and emerges from forest, says hi, and hacks everyone to death. Lesson learned, case closed. Filmed on Long Island. **89m/C; VHS, DVD, Blu-Ray.** Alexis Dubin; Tony Fish; Paul Ehlers; Carl Fredericks; ***D:*** Joe Giannone; ***W:*** Joe Giannone; Gary Sales; ***C:*** James (Momel) Lemmo; ***M:*** Gary Sales; Stephen Horelick.

Madness in the Method 🦴🦴 **2019** Though Jay (Mewes) has always played stoner buddy roles in films, he longs to not be typecast. After reading a recommended Method acting book, he wants to prove he can play grittier roles by showing up at a casting director's house late one night unannounced. The aftermath of the incident is blamed on his sobriety buddy, actor Vinnie Jones (Jones), and Jay receives an unexpected career boost that has ripple effects for himself and those in his circle. An uneven satiric Hollywood comedy that both is based on and mocks filmmakers Mewes' career. **99m/C; DVD.** Jason Mewes; Kevin Smith; Gina Carano; Jaime Camil; Vinnie Jones; ***D:*** Jason Mewes; ***W:*** Dominic Burns; Chris Anastasi; ***C:*** Vince Knight; ***M:*** Si Begg.

The Madness of King George 🦴🦴🦴 1/2 **1994 (R)** Poor King George is a monarch with problems—his 30 years of royal authority are being usurped by Parliament, his American colonies have been lost, and, in 1788, he's begun to periodically lose his mind. So what do you do when a ruler becomes irrational? The royal physicians are baffled, his loving Queen Charlotte (Mirren) is in despair, but the noxious Prince of Wales (Everett) can barely contain his glee at finally having a chance at the throne. Brilliant performance by Hawthorne (who originated the stage role in Bennett's 1991 play "The Madness of George III"). Tony Award-winning Hytner makes his feature-film directing debut. **110m/C; DVD, Blu-Ray.** *UK* Nigel Hawthorne; Dame Helen Mirren; Ian Holm; Rupert Everett; Amanda Donohoe; Rupert Graves; Julian Wadham; John Wood; Julian Rhind-Tutt; Jim Carter; ***D:*** Nicholas Hytner; ***W:*** Alan Bennett; ***C:*** Andrew Dunn; ***M:*** George Fenton. Oscars '94: Art Dir./Set Dec.; British Acad. '95: Actor (Hawthorne); Cannes '95: Actress (Mirren).

Mado 🦴🦴🦴 **1976** A middle-aged businessman's life is undone when he falls for a mysterious woman. Piccoli and Schneider are, as usual, convincing. Another of underrated director Sautet's effective, low-key works. In French with subtitles. **130m/C; VHS, DVD.** Romy Schneider; Michel Piccoli; Charles Denner; ***D:*** Claude Sautet. Cesar '77: Sound.

Madonna of the Seven Moons 🦴 1/2 **1945** All-around unbelievable Brit romantic drama. Maddalena (Calvert) develops a split personality after being raped as a girl. She lives in Rome as the wife of wealthy wine merchant Giuseppe

(Stuart) and mother of teenager Angela (Roc), but sometimes Maddalena disappears and winds up in the slums of Florence as Rosanna, the lover of gypsy thief Nino (Granger). **88m/B; DVD.** *UK* Phyllis Calvert; Stewart Granger; Patricia Roc; Peter Glenville; John Stuart; Nancy Price; Reginald Tate; ***D:*** Arthur Crabtree; ***W:*** Roland Pertwee; ***C:*** Jack Cox; ***M:*** Hans May.

Madron 🦴 ½ **1970 (PG)** Road western filmed in the Israel desert, complete with menacing Apaches, wagon train massacre, a nun and a gunslinger. **93m/C; VHS, DVD.** Richard Boone; Leslie Caron; Paul Smith; ***D:*** Jerry Hopper; ***W:*** Edward Chappell; Lee McMahon; ***C:*** Marcel Grignon; Adam Greenberg; ***M:*** Riz Ortolani.

The Madwoman of Chaillot 🦴 ½ **1969 (G)** Four men conspire to drill for oil which they believe lurks under Paris. Hepburn finds out about their plot and tells each man that oil is bubbling up through her basement. Before the men can arrive at her house to confirm this, she and her three cronies hold a mock trial and sentence the men to death. Features a stellar cast, but this modern-day adaptation of Jean Giraudoux's play "La Folle de Chaillot" falls flat. **142m/C; VHS, DVD, Streaming.** Katharine Hepburn; Charles Boyer; Claude Dauphin; Edith Evans; John Gavin; Paul Henreid; Oscar Homolka; Margaret Leighton; Giulietta Masina; Nanette Newman; Richard Chamberlain; Yul Brynner; Donald Pleasence; Danny Kaye; Fernand Gravey; ***D:*** Bryan Forbes; ***W:*** Edward Anhalt.

Maelstrom 🦴🦴 **2000** Offbeat mixture of the surreal, the whimsical, and the melodramatic. A drunken Bibliane (Croze) commits a hit-and-run and reads in the next day's newspaper that the man, a fishmonger, has died. Guilt-stricken, she meets the man's son, a deep sea diver named Evian (Verrault), at the funeral home and he mistakes her for a concerned neighbor. Bibliane's friendship with Evian leads to an affair but she becomes compelled to tell him the truth and accept whatever punishment he decrees. There's lots of water and fish imagery. French with subtitles. **86m/C; VHS, DVD.** *CA* Marie Josee Croze; Jean-Nicholas Verreault; Stephanie Morgenstern; Bobby Beshro; ***D:*** Denis Villenueve; ***W:*** Denis Villenueve; ***C:*** Andre Turpin; ***M:*** Pierre Desrochers. Genie '00: Actress (Croze), Cinematog., Director (Villenueve), Film, Screenplay.

Mafia! 🦴🦴 *Jane Austen's Mafia!* **1998 (PG-13)** Director Abrahams returns to the "Airplane" well once again as he takes aim at the Mafia movies of Coppola and Scorsese. The results are hit and miss, with the joke machine gun set on full automatic. Plot follows that of the Godfather trilogy most closely, with Bridges (in his last film) as klutzy patriarch Vincenzo Cortino. His sons, sensitive war hero Anthony (Mohr) and hot tempered Joey (Burke), wrestle for control after pop takes the dirt nap. Basically, the actors' jobs are to remain deadpan while all manner of shenanigans and hijinks take place and hilarity allegedly ensues. **87m/C; DVD, Blu-Ray.** Lloyd Bridges; Jay Mohr; Billy Burke; Olympia Dukakis; Christina Applegate; Pamela Gidley; Tony LoBianco; Joe (Johnny) Viterelli; Vincent Pastore; Jason Fuchs; Gregory Sierra; Louis Mandylor; ***D:*** Jim Abrahams; ***W:*** Jim Abrahams; Michael McManus; Greg Norberg; ***C:*** Pierre Letarte; ***M:*** John (Gianni) Frizzell.

Mafia 🦴 **2011 (R)** Tired, cliched crime drama set in New York in the 1970s. Crime boss Renzo Wes (Rhames) is taking out the local drug dealers in a turf war, Detective Womack (Grier) is the cop obsessed with bringing him down while her new partner, Dupree (Patrick), has his own agenda. **81m/C; DVD.** Ving Rhames; Pam Grier; Robert Patrick; Persia White; Sean Derry; ***D:*** Ryan Combs; ***W:*** Ryan Combs; ***C:*** Mario Signore. **VIDEO**

Mafioso 🦴🦴 ½ **1962** Black comedy from Lattuada that was revolutionary for its depiction of everyday Mafia life in Sicily. Nino (Sordi) is a longtime foreman at the Fiat plant in Milan. He decides to use his vacation time and take his wife (Conti) and daughters to visit his small hometown of Calamo. It's Nino's first visit home in years (and quite a culture shock for his wife) but that doesn't mean he's forgotten where to pay his respects. But town boss Don Vincenzo (Attanasio) is quick to remind Nino that he still owes him a favor and the Don now wants to collect. Italian with subtitles. **108m/B; DVD.** *IT* Alberto Sordi; Norma Bengell; Cinzia Bruno; Ugo Attanasio; Gabriella Conti; Armando Tine; Francesco Lo Briglio; Katiusca Piretti; ***D:*** Alberto Lattuada; ***W:*** Rafael Azcona; Marco Ferreri; Agenore Incrocci; Furio Scarpelli; ***C:*** Armando Nannuzzi; ***M:*** Piero Piccioni.

The Magdalene Sisters 🦴🦴🦴 ½ **2002 (R)** Semi-fictionalized stories of four young Irish women sentenced to life in a religious labor camp run by the Sisters of the Magdalene Order from 1964 to 1969. Their "crimes" include overt flirtatiousness, having been raped, bearing a child out of wedlock, and other perceived sexual offenses. They're treated cruelly by the ogre in authority, Sister Bridget (McEwan) and any attempt at escape is met with more brutality. Grim, powerful film captures the atrocities of 1960s-era Irish Catholicism with frightful clarity. **119m/C; VHS, DVD.** *GB IR* Geraldine McEwan; Anne-Marie Duff; Nora-Jane Noone; Dorothy Duffy; Eileen Walsh; Mary Murray; Britta Smith; Frances Healy; Eithne McGuinness; Daniel Costello; ***D:*** Peter Mullan; ***W:*** Peter Mullan; ***C:*** Nigel Willoughby; ***M:*** Craig Armstrong. Venice Film Fest. '02: Film.

Maggie 🦴🦴 **2015 (PG-13)** Schwarzenegger's most interesting film choice post-Governator is also a film that most people, sadly, didn't see, largely because it was very difficult to market. On one hand, Henry Hobson's film is a traditional zombie story, so horror fans should enjoy it, but it's also something much deeper about how far a father will go for his child. Arnie plays Wade Vogel, an old-fashioned Midwestern farmer who lives through a nightmare when a new disease turns people into brain-eating zombies, including his daughter Maggie (Breslin). Hobson kind of fumbles his ending but Arnold is really good here in a challenging role. **95m/C; DVD, Blu-Ray.** Arnold Schwarzenegger; Abigail Breslin; Joely Richardson; Douglas M. Griffin; J.D. Evermore; ***D:*** Henry Hobson; ***W:*** John Scott 3; ***C:*** Lukas Ettlin; ***M:*** David Wingo.

Maggie's Plan 🦴🦴 **2016 (R)** Rebecca Miller's dramedy has its moments but feels ultimately unsatisfying. Gerwig plays Maggie, a headstrong New Yorker who wants to become a single mother through insemination by a former friend (Fimmel). Of course, right around then, Maggie falls for a man named John (Hawke), who happens to be married to Georgette (Moore). After successfully prying John away from Georgette, Maggie realizes she doesn't love him as much and works to get his former marriage back together. Having control over motherhood and marriage is an interesting theme but Miller can't keep a grip on it. **98m/C; DVD, Blu-Ray.** Travis Fimmel; Ethan Hawke; Julianne Moore; Maya Rudolph; Greta Gerwig; ***D:*** Rebecca Miller; ***W:*** Rebecca Miller; ***C:*** Sam Levy; ***M:*** Michael Rohatyn.

Magic 🦴🦴 ½ **1978 (R)** Ventriloquist Hopkins and his dummy, an all-too-human counterpart, get involved with a beautiful but impressionable woman lost between reality and the irresistible world of illusion. Spine-chilling psycho-drama with a less-than-believable premise. Screenplay by Goldman from his novel. **106m/C; VHS, DVD.** Anthony Hopkins; Ann-Margret; Burgess Meredith; Ed Lauter; Jerry Houser; David Ogden Stiers; Lillian Randolph; ***D:*** Richard Attenborough; ***W:*** William Goldman; ***C:*** Victor Kemper; ***M:*** Jerry Goldsmith.

Magic Beyond Words: The JK Rowling Story 🦴🦴 ½ **2011** This Lifetime movie is an unauthorized biopic of the Harry Potter creator. Montgomery charms as the struggling welfare mom decides to focus on her writing and get her fantasy novel published. Script also includes looks at Rowling's childhood and troubled marriage and her subsequent success. Special effects illustrate some of Rowling's ideas for Harry. **90m/C; DVD.** Poppy Montgomery; Emily Holmes; Antonio Cupo; Janet Kidder; Andy Maton; Paul McGillion; ***D:*** Paul A. Kaufman; ***W:*** Jeffrey Berman; Tony Caballero; ***C:*** Mathias Herndl; ***M:*** Jeff Toyne. **CABLE**

The Magic Blade 🦴🦴 ½ *Tien ya ming yue dao; The Moonlight Blade; Tin ngai ming yuet do* **2008** The Shaw Brothers abandon their standard martial arts film for a fantasy wuxia style film more popular in the '60s. Ti Lung (Fu Hung Hsieh) is a superhuman swordsman out to kill rival Lieh Lo (Yen Fan Fei), but ends up joining forces with him when he finds out Lord Yu is out to kill them both and steal a supernatural weapon, thus giving him dominion over the martial arts world. Along the way to find the weapon themselves they encounter many mystical assassins, including the Devil's Grandma. They get a thumbs up for that name alone. **101m/C; DVD.** *CH* Lung Ti; Lieh Lo; Li Ching; Ni Tien; Lily Li; Feng Ku; Ching Tang; Szu Chia Chen; Hui-Ling Liu; Mei Sheng Fan; Theresa Hsia Ping; ***D:*** Yuen Chor; ***W:*** Lung Ku; Kuang Ni; On Szeto.

The Magic Bow 🦴 ½ **1947** Typically ridiculous musical bio'this time of violinist Nicolo Paganini (Granger). He's the talented poor boy who falls for the wealthy Jeanne (Calvert) but his one true love is for his Stradivarius. Yehudi Menuhim plays the solos. Based on the novel by Manuel Komroff. **105m/B; VHS, DVD.** *GB* Stewart Granger; Phyllis Calvert; Jean Kent; Dennis Price; Cecil Parker; Felix Aylmer; Frank Cellier; Marie Lohr; ***D:*** Bernard Knowles; ***W:*** Roland Pertwee; Norman Ginsburg; ***C:*** Jack Asher; Jack Cox.

The Magic Bubble 🦴🦴 ½ **1993 (PG-13)** On her 40th birthday, Julia Cole finds the fountain of youth...inside a bottle of enchanted bubbles. Ageless and timeless, she begins to know the meaning of true happiness. **90m/C; VHS, DVD.** Diane Salinger; John Calvin; Priscilla Pointer; Colleen Camp; Tony Peck; Wallace Shawn; George Clooney; ***D:*** Alfredo Ringel; Deborah Taper Ringel; ***W:*** Meridith Baer; Geof Pryssir.

The Magic Carpet 🦴 ½ **1951** Mediocre, low-budget fantasy stars a wooden Agar and a miscast Ball. Grand Vizier Boreg (Burr), sultry Princess Narah (Ball), and her father Ali (Gay) kill the royal family to usurp the kingdom although not before the heir, baby Ramoth, is spirited away to safety on a magic carpet. He grows up to be the scourge of the bad guys, taking on the heroic dual identity of royal physician and the Scarlet Falcon (Agar). Medina is his equally wooden love interest Lida. **84m/C; DVD.** Lucille Ball; Raymond Burr; John Agar; Patricia Medina; Gregory Gay; George Tobias; Rick Vallin; ***D:*** Lew Landers; ***W:*** David Matthews; ***C:*** Ellis W. Carter; ***M:*** Arthur Morton.

The Magic Christian 🦴🦴🦴 **1969 (PG)** A series of related skits about a rich man (Sellers) and his son (Starr) who try to prove that anyone can be bought. Raucous, now somewhat dated comedy; music by Badfinger, including Paul McCartney's "Come and Get It." **101m/C; VHS, DVD, Blu-Ray.** *GB* Peter Sellers; Ringo Starr; Isabel Jeans; Wilfrid Hyde-White; Graham Chapman; John Cleese; Peter Graves; John Lennon; Yoko Ono; Richard Attenborough; Leonard Frey; Laurence Harvey; Christopher Lee; Spike Milligan; Yul Brynner; Roman Polanski; Raquel Welch; Caroline Blakiston; Ferdinand "Ferdy" Mayne; ***D:*** Joseph McGrath; ***W:*** Peter Sellers; Graham Chapman; John Cleese; Terry Southern; ***C:*** Geoffrey Unsworth; ***M:*** Ken Thorne.

The Magic Flute 🦴🦴🦴 ½ **1973 (G)** Bergman's acclaimed version of Mozart's famous comic opera, universally considered one of the greatest adaptations of opera to film ever made. Staged before a live audience for Swedish TV. Subtitled. **134m/C; VHS, DVD, Blu-Ray.** *SW* Josef Kostlinger; Irma Urrila; Hakan Hagegard; Elisabeth Erikson; ***D:*** Ingmar Bergman.

Magic in the Moonlight 🦴 ½ **2014 (PG-13)** Allen is back with his annual dramedy and continues his pattern of following a critical smash (Oscar winner "Blue Jasmine") with a lesser effort. This time, Firth stars as a magician who's also a debunker of magic, who's asked to prove that the clairvoyant Sophie (Stone) is, in fact, a fraud. So light on its feet as to drift away, the always-charming Firth and Stone have more than a few chances to prove why they're movie stars. Viewers may pay more attention to the French setting, costumes, and the 1920s time period than anything the characters are doing. **97m/C; DVD, Blu-Ray.** Colin Firth; Emma Stone; Eileen Atkins; Hamish Linklater; Simon McBurney; Jacki Weaver; Marcia Gay Harden; Jeremy Shamos; Erica Leerhsen; ***D:*** Woody Allen; ***W:*** Woody Allen; ***C:*** Darius Khondji.

Magic in the Water 🦴 ½ **1995 (PG)** Divorced, obnoxious radio shrink and neglectful dad Dr. Jack Black (Harmon) takes the kiddies on a summer jaunt to a Canadian lake, where they explore the legend of Orky, Canada's answer to the Loch Ness monster. Dad becomes a believer when Orky possesses his body and releases his inner child. Harmless fun for the kids, but parents will gag at the attempt to provide a meaningful and symbolic message. Beautiful cinematography showcasing the British Columbia landscape helps, but not enough. **100m/C; DVD.** Mark Harmon; Joshua Jackson; Harley Jane Kozak; Sarah Wayne; Willie Nark-Orn; Frank S. Salsedo; ***D:*** Rick Stevenson; ***W:*** Icel Dobell Massey; Rick Stevenson; ***C:*** Thomas Burstyn; ***M:*** David Schwartz. Genie '95: Cinematog., Sound.

Magic Kid 🦴🦴 ½ *Ninja Dragons* **1992 (PG)** Thirteen-year-old martial-arts champ Kevin and his older sister vacation in L.A., staying with their shady Uncle Bob, a second-rate talent agent. Kevin wants to meet his martial arts movie idol and his sister her favorite soap opera hunk. But they wind up being chased by the mobsters Uncle Bob owes money to. **91m/C; VHS, DVD.** Ted Jan Roberts; Shonda Whipple; Stephen Furst; Joseph Campanella; Billy Hufsey; Sondra Kerns; Pamela Dixon; Lauren Tewes; Don "The Dragon" Wilson; ***D:*** Joseph Merhi; ***W:*** Stephen Smoke; ***M:*** Jim Halfpenny.

Magic Kid 2 🦴🦴 ½ **1994 (PG)** The young star of a popular martial arts program wants to quit and go to high school like a normal teenager. But the studio execs have other ideas. **90m/C; VHS, DVD, On Demand.** Ted Jan Roberts; Stephen Furst; Donald Gibb; Jennifer Savidge; ***D:*** Stephen Furst.

Magic Magic 🦴 ½ **2013 (R)** Psychodrama has emotionally fragile Alicia joining her cousin Sarah, an exchange student in Chile, on a road trip tto Patagonia with Sarah's boyfriend Augustin and his sister Barbara, and oddball American Brink. They travel to a remote island where Alicia starts acting bizarrely, not helped by the irritating antics of the antisocial Brink. Suffering from insomnia and paranoia, Alicia's actions finally cause alarm but Silva's pic is a lot of atmosphere with little payoff. **97m/C; DVD.** *CL US* Juno Temple; Michael Cera; Emily Browning; Augustin Silva; Catalina Sandino Moreno; ***D:*** Sebastian Silva; ***W:*** Sebastian Silva; ***C:*** Christopher Doyle; ***M:*** Danny Bensi.

Magic Man 🦴 ½ **2010** Aspiring magician Tatiana heads to Las Vegas with a couple of gal pals to see her idol Krell Darius. Tatiana's mother was a magician's assistant who died a maybe-not-accidental death onstage and Darius may know more than he's saying. Tatiana's friends wind up dead and the cops become very interested in the magician's tricks. **85m/C; DVD.** Billy Zane; Estelle Raskin; Robert Davi; Armand Assante; Bai Ling; Richard Tyson; Alexander Nevsky; Christina Vidal; Sarah Jayne Jensen; Andrew Divoff; ***D:*** Roscoe Lever; ***W:*** George Saunders; Brent Huff; ***C:*** Curtis Petersen. **VIDEO**

Magic Mike 🦴🦴 ½ **2012 (R)** Based loosely on the actual history of star Channing Tatum, director Soderbergh's drama lifts the curtain on the life of a male stripper with mixed results. Magic Mike (Tatum), the veteran at a Tampa all-male revue, brings rookie stripper "The Kid" (Pettyfer) into the fold only to realize that he's possibly reached the end of the line in this profession. Tatum and McConaughey are more than eye-catching and Soderbergh has undeniable technical skills, but ultimately it lacks the depth it needs and a few supporting performances are rather ho-hum. But the Hound hears it's popular with the ladies. **110m/C; DVD, Blu-Ray, Streaming.** Matthew McConaughey; Channing Tatum; Olivia Munn; Alex Pettyfer; Cody Horn; Joe Manganiello; Matt Bomer; ***D:*** Steven Soderbergh; ***W:*** Reid Carolin; ***C:*** Steven Soderbergh. Ind. Spirit '13: Actor--Supporting (McConaughey).

Magic Mike XXL 🦴🦴 ½ **2015 (R)** The loose, free-form, sometimes plot-free structure of Jacobs follow-up to the Steven Soderbergh hit is admirable, but it's still too difficult to shake the feeling that this is a sequel that never really justifies its existence. It's been three years since Mike (Tatum) hung up his man-thong, but he gets the "band" back together for one more big show in Myrtle Beach. Co-stars like Bomer and Manganiello are having fun—as is newcomer Jada Pinkett Smith—but McConaughey's absence is notable. The whole piece feels like a lark—fun at times, but lacking the weight of the first film. **115m/C; DVD, Blu-Ray, Streaming.** Channing Tatum; Joe Manganiello; Kevin Nash; Matt Bomer; Adam Rodriguez; *D:* Gregory Jacobs; *W:* Reid Carolin; *C:* Steven Soderbergh.

The Magic of Belle Isle ♪♪ 1/2 **2012 (PG)** Slow-paced sentimental story that's not without its charms, especially Freeman's performance. He's curmudgeonly, widowed, wheelchair-bound one-time writer Monte Wildhorn, who indulges in regrets and alcohol. He's spending the summer dog-sitting for his nephew at his lakeside cabin, which is next-door to the home of Charlotte O'Neil (Madsen) and her three daughters. He grumpily agrees to mentor middle-child Finnegan, which leads Monte to re-engage in life. **109m/C; DVD, Blu-Ray.** Morgan Freeman; Virginia Madsen; Madeline Carroll; Emma Fuhrmann; Nicolette Pierini; Kenan Thompson; Fred Willard; Kevin Pollak; Ash Christian; *D:* Rob Reiner; *W:* Guy Thomas; *C:* Reed Morano; *M:* Marc Shaiman.

The Magic Stone ♪♪ 1/2 *Kilian's Chronicle* **1995** Kilian is the 10th-century Irish slave of brutish Viking Ivar, who decides to sacrifice him to the Norse god Thor when the Vikings become lost while sailing off the North American coast. Kilian manages to escape and make it to shore where he's rescued by a Native American tribe and falls in love with local beauty, Turtle. But Ivar goes after Kilian to steal his magic stone, which can navigate a ship through the worst weather, and begins a Viking war with the tribe. **95m/C; VHS, DVD.** Christopher Johnson; Robert McDonough; Eva Kim; Jonah Ming Lee; *D:* Pamela Berger; *W:* Pamela Berger; *C:* John Hoover; *M:* R. Carlos Nakai; Bevan Manson.

The Magic Sword ♪♪ *St. George and the Seven Curses; St. George and the Dragon* **1962** A family-oriented adventure film about a young knight who sets out to rescue a beautiful princess who is being held captive by an evil sorcerer and his dragon. **80m/C; VHS, DVD, Blu-Ray.** Basil Rathbone; Estelle Winwood; Gary Lockwood; *D:* Bert I. Gordon.

Magic Town ♪♪ 1/2 **1947** An opinion pollster investigates a small town which exactly reflects the views of the entire nation, making his job a cinch. The publicity causes much ado in the town with ensuing laughs. Uneven but entertaining. **103m/B; DVD, Blu-Ray.** Jane Wyman; James Stewart; Kent Smith; Regis Toomey; Donald Meek; *D:* William A. Wellman; *W:* Robert Riskin; *C:* Joseph Biroc; *M:* Roy Webb.

Magic Trip: Ken Kesey's Search for a Kool Place ♪ 1/2 **2011 (R)** Gibney and Ellwood culled more than 40 hours of archival footage to reconstruct the LSD-fueled 1964 California to New York road trip of Ken Kesey and his Merry Pranksters. Since no one on the bus knew how to synchronize sound to the 16-millimeter film, the directors used commentary provided by some of the participants after they viewed the raw footage 10 years later. The results are generally sloppy, silly, and sad. **107m/C; DVD.** Ken Kesey; Neal Cassady; *Nar:* Stanley Tucci; *D:* Alex Gibney; Alison Ellwood; *W:* Alex Gibney; Alison Ellwood; *C:* Alison Ellwood; *M:* David Kahne.

The Magic Voyage ♪♪ 1/2 **1993 (G)** Animated tale of a friendly woodworm named Pico who voyages with Columbus to the new world and convinces him that the world is indeed round. He then comes to the aid of a magical firefly named Marilyn who helps Columbus find gold to bring back to Spain. **82m/C; VHS, DVD.** *V:* Dom DeLuise; Mickey Rooney; Corey Feldman; Irene Cara; Dan Haggerty; Samantha Eggar; *D:* Michael Schoemann.

The Magic Voyage of Sinbad ♪♪ *Sadko* **1952** Sinbad embarks on a fantastic journey after promising the people of his Covasian home that he will find the elusive Phoenix, the bird of happiness. Unreleased in the U.S. until 1962; rewritten for the American screen by a young Coppola. **79m/C; VHS, DVD.** *RU* Sergey Stolyarov; Alla Larionova; Mark Troyanovsky; *D:* Alexander Ptushko; *W:* Francis Ford Coppola.

Magical Girl ♪♪♪ **2014** A dramatic thriller centered the unexpected consequences of trying to fulfill a dying girl's last wish. An out-of-work literature teacher, Luis (Bermejo) is devoted to Alicia (Pollan), his 12-year-old daughter. Alicia is suffering from terminal leukemia and her only desire is to own a dress of anime star Magical Girl Yukiro. Though the price is far more than he can pay, Luis does everything he can—include abuse and blackmail—to grant his Alicia her dying wish. Though he gets her the dress, the impact of his choices is far-reaching and costs him dearly. Spanish with subtitles. **127m/C; DVD.** Luis Bermejo; Lucia Pollan; Jose Sacristan; Bárbara Lennie; Alberto Chaves; *D:* Carlos Vermut; *W:* Carlos Vermut; *C:* Santiago Racaj. **VIDEO**

The Magical Legend of the Leprechauns ♪ 1/2 **1999** Goofy fantasy finds American businessman Jack Woods (Quaid) sent to a remote part of Ireland where he happens to save the life of leprechaun, Seamus Muldoon (Meaney), which puts the "little person" in his debt. While Jack tries to romance neighbor Kathleen (Brady), the leprechauns are getting into a fracas with their enemies, the Trooping Fairies, leading to a battle and Jack's involvement. **139m/C; VHS, DVD.** Randy Quaid; Colm Meaney; Orla Brady; Whoopi Goldberg; Roger Daltrey; Daniel Betts; Zoe Wanamaker; Caroline Carver; Kieran Culkin; Frank Finlay; Phyllida Law; *D:* John Henderson; *W:* Peter Barnes; *C:* Clive Tickner; *M:* Richard Harvey. **TV**

The Magician ♪♪ 1/2 **1926** Deranged surgeon and would-be alchemist Oliver Haddo learns from an ancient text that the heart's blood of a virgin is needed to reanimate a corpse. So Dr. Haddo hypnotizes beautiful sculptress Margaret Dauncey and spirits her off to his crumbling castle laboratory with evil intent. Based on the 1908 novel by W. Somerset Maugham. Some of the visual effects will be familiar to later 1931 "Frankenstein" fans. **88m/B; Silent; DVD.** Paul Wegener; Alice Terry; Ivan Petrovich; Gladys Hamer; *D:* Rex Ingram; *W:* Rex Ingram; *C:* John Seitz.

The Magician ♪♪♪ **1958** A master magician in 19th century Sweden (von Sydow) wreaks ill in this darkly comical, supernatural parable. Dark, well photographed early Bergman effort. In Swedish with English subtitles. **101m/B; VHS, DVD, Blu-Ray.** *SW* Max von Sydow; Ingrid Thulin; Gunnar Bjornstrand; Bibi Andersson; Naima Wifstrand; *D:* Ingmar Bergman; *W:* Ingmar Bergman. Venice Film Fest. '59: Special Jury Prize.

The Magician ♪♪ 1/2 **1993** In the early 1980s, Scotland Yard detective George Byrne (Owen) partners with shady American businessman David Katz (Acovone) to bring down a counterfeiting ring. Katz goes undercover to try and meet the mysterious head of the ring (the title character) but risks his family by getting too involved. Meanwhile, the IRA also wants the counterfeiter so they can destabilize the British economy by flooding the country with fake currency. Based on a true story. **99m/C; DVD.** *GB* Jay Acovone; Clive Owen; Jeremy Kemp; Peter Howitt; Jennifer Calvert; *D:* Terry Winsor; *W:* Jeff Pope. **TV**

Magma: Volcanic Disaster ♪ **2006 (PG-13)** Silly cable disaster flick with cheesy CGI. Dr. Peter Shepard (Berkley) believes that volcanic eruptions in Iceland are the precursor to global catastrophe. Naturally, the bureaucrats don't believe him until there's more explosions. Now it's up to Peter to test out his theory that deep sea ventilation will relieve the pressure build-up and save the planet! **87m/C; DVD.** Xander Berkeley; Amy Jo Johnson; Michael Durrell; Reiko Aylesworth; Doug Dearth; David O'Donnell; *D:* Ian Gilmore; *W:* Rebecca Rian; *M:* Nathan Furst. **CABLE**

The Magnet ♪ 1/2 **1950** Young Johnny Brent (Fox) finds a horseshoe-shaped magnet he believes will bring him good luck but the possession becomes a coveted object in the schoolyard, causing all sorts of problems. **79m/B; DVD.** *GB* James Fox; Stephen Murray; Kay Walsh; Meredith Edwards; Gladys Henson; Wylie Watson; *D:* Charles Friend; *W:* T.E.B. Clarke; *C:* Lionel Banes; *M:* William Alwyn.

The Magnetic Monster ♪ 1/2 **1953** A local scientist finds a new element and bombards it with radiation, causing it to convert matter into itself. Agents must work furiously as they have 24 hours before it grows big enough to throw the earth out of orbit. **80m/B; DVD, Blu-Ray.** Richard Carlson; King Donovan; Jean Byron; Harry Ellerbe; Leo Britt; *D:* Curt Siodmak; Herbert L. Strock; *W:* Curt Siodmak; Ivan Tors; *C:* Charles Van Enger; *M:* Blaine Sanford. **VIDEO**

The Magnificent Ambersons ♪♪♪♪ **1942** Welles's second film. A fascinating, inventive translation of the Booth Tarkington novel about a wealthy turn of the century family collapsing under the changing currents of progress. Pure Welles, except the glaringly bad tacked-on ending that the studio shot (under the direction of the great Robert Wise and Fred Fleck), after taking the film from him. It seems they wanted the proverbial happy ending. **88m/B; VHS, Blu-Ray.** Joseph Cotten; Anne Baxter; Tim Holt; Richard Bennett; Dolores Costello; Erskine Sanford; Ray Collins; Agnes Moorehead; *D:* Freddie Fleck; Robert Wise; Orson Welles; *W:* Orson Welles; *M:* Bernard Herrmann; Roy Webb. Natl. Film Reg. '91; N.Y. Film Critics '42: Actress (Moorehead).

The Magnificent Ambersons ♪♪ 1/2 **2002** George Amberson (Rhys Meyers) is the spoiled son of an upper-class, turn-of-the-century Midwestern family. When his widowed mother Isabel (Stowe) is reunited with old flame Eugene Morgan (Greenwood), George becomes obsessively jealous and schemes to break up the match even as he romances Eugene's daughter, Lucy (Mol). Stowe looks beautiful but Rhys Meyers over-emphasizes George's less-than-filial response to his mother. Adaptation of Booth Tarkington's novel that reportedly used Orson Welles original script for his 1942 film. **139m/C; VHS, DVD.** Madeleine Stowe; Bruce Greenwood; Jonathan Rhys Meyers; Jennifer Tilly; Gretchen Mol; James Cromwell; William Hootkins; *D:* Alfonso Arau. **CABLE**

Magnificent Doll ♪♪ **1946** Boring Hollywood bio of first lady Dolly Madison (Rogers) who is wooed by dynamic Aaron Burr (Niven) before she decides on marrying quiet James Madison (Meredith) and pushing his political career to the office of the presidency. **93m/B; DVD, Blu-Ray.** Ginger Rogers; David Niven; Burgess Meredith; Stephen McNally; Peggy Wood; Grandon Rhodes; Arthur Space; Robert Barrat; *D:* Frank Borzage; *W:* Irving Stone; *C:* Joseph Valentine; *M:* Hans J. Salter.

Magnificent Obsession ♪♪ 1/2 **1935** Drunken playboy Bob Merrick (Taylor) indirectly causes the death of Helen Hudson's (Dunne) beloved and dedicated doctor husband. Then Bob's later apology causes Helen to flee, get hit by a car, and blinded. This double whammy to Bob's conscience leads him to resume his medical studies in an effort to become a brain surgeon. He also secretly befriends Helen and falls in love with her until she finds out about their past connection. But you know his medical skills will later come in handy. Shameless but well-done weepy based on the 1929 novel by Lloyd C. Douglas. Remade in Technicolor in 1954. **112m/B; DVD.** Irene Dunne; Robert Taylor; Charles Butterworth; Ralph Morgan; Betty Furness; Sara Haden; Arthur Treacher; *D:* John M. Stahl; *W:* Sarah Y. Mason; Victor Heerman; George O'Neil; *C:* John Mescall.

Magnificent Obsession ♪♪ 1/2 **1954** A drunken playboy (Hudson) kills a man and blinds his wife in an automobile accident. Plagued by guilt, he devotes his life to studying medicine in order to restore the widow's sight. Well-acted melodrama lifted Hudson to stardom. Faithful to the 1935 original, based on a novel by Lloyd C. Douglas. **108m/C; VHS, DVD, Blu-Ray.** Jane Wyman; Rock Hudson; Barbara Rush; Agnes Moorehead; *D:* Douglas Sirk; *W:* Robert Blees; *C:* Russell Metty.

The Magnificent Seven ♪♪♪♪ **1960** Western remake of Akira Kurosawa's classic "The Seven Samurai." Mexican villagers hire gunmen to protect them from the bandits who are destroying their town. Most of the actors were relative unknowns, though not for long. Sequelled by "Return of the Seven" in 1966, "Guns of the Magnificent Seven" in 1969, and "The Magnificent Seven Ride" in 1972. Excellent score. Uncredited writing by Walter Newman and Walter Bernstein. **126m/C; VHS, DVD, Blu-Ray.** Yul Brynner; Steve McQueen; Robert Vaughn; James Coburn; Charles Bronson; Horst Buchholz; Eli Wallach; Brad Dexter; *D:* John Sturges; *W:* William Roberts; *C:* Charles B(ryant) Lang, Jr.; *M:* Elmer Bernstein. Natl. Film Reg. '13.

The Magnificent Seven ♪♪ 1/2 **1998** Pilot movie for the brief TV series that was loosely based on the 1960 film. An indian chief hires seven gunslingers to help defend tribal land from a gang of greedy outlaws who want the tribe's gold mine. **90m/C; VHS, DVD.** Michael Biehn; Ron Perlman; Dale Midkiff; Eric Close; Anthony Starke; Laurie Holden; Andrew Kavovit; Rick Worthy; Kurtwood Smith; Ned Romero; Daragh O'Malley; Michael Greyeyes; Tony Burton; *D:* Geoff Murphy; *W:* Frank Q. Dobbs; Chris Black; *C:* Jack Conroy; *M:* Don Harper. **TV**

The Magnificent Seven ♪♪ **2016 (PG-13)** In a remake of the 1960 classic, which in turn was a remake of a 1954 Japanese classic, seven mercenary cowboys join forces to protect a small town from an evil industrialist (Sarsgaard). A star-studded cast and workmanlike director can't salvage this flat remake of the Akira Kurosawa and Western classics. Washington steps into Yul Brynner's shoes as the strong and silent Man in Black, joined by an international array of cohorts, including Hawke, Pratt, D'Onofrio, and others. Predictability in the Western is common but this one is too by-the-numbers given the talents involved. **133m/C; DVD, Blu-Ray.** Denzel Washington; Chris Pratt; Ethan Hawke; Vincent D'Onofrio; Byung-hun Lee; Manuel Garcia-Rulfo; Martin Sensmeier; *D:* Antoine Fuqua; *W:* Richard Wenk; Nic Pizzolatto; *C:* Mauro Fiore; *M:* Simon Franglen; James Horner.

The Magnificent Trio ♪♪ *Bian cheng san xia; Three Heroes of Border Town* **1966** In this classic Shaw Brothers swordplay film, peasants have kidnapped the daughter of a corrupt magistrate, and have asked a soldier for help in dealing with him. He turns the daughter over in exchange for the magistrate leaving the town alone, but the magistrate goes back on his word (duh!) and throws him in jail. Unfortunately for our villain his daughter has fallen in love with the man who gets two of his sword-fighting buddies to help when she lets him go. It's notable mostly for being one of the first films to team director Chang Cheh and the actors of the "Five Deadly Venoms". **105m/C; DVD.** *CH* Ping Chin; Margaret Tu Chuan; Yu Wang; Fanny Fan; Lieh Lo; Lei Cheng; *D:* Cheh Chang; *W:* Cheh Chang; *C:* Yung-lung Wang; *M:* Fu-ling Wang.

The Magnificent Two ♪ 1/2 **1967** The comedy team of Morecambe and Wise did better on the telly than in their movie appearances, particularly this lame foreign adventure comedy. Eric and Ernie are traveling toy salesman who arrive in Parazuelia, South America, in the midst of a revolution. Since Eric looks like the son of a dead revolutionary hero, he's forced to pose as the man at official events. A lingerie-clad female army finally solves the crisis. **92m/C; DVD.** *GB* Margit Saad; Virgilio Teixeira; Eric Morecambe; Ernie Wise; *D:* Cliff Owen; *W:* Peter Blackmore; S.C. Green; R.M. Hills; *C:* Ernest Steward; *M:* Ronald Goodwin.

The Magnificent Yankee ♪♪♪ *The Man with Thirty Sons* **1950** Adaptation of Emmet Lavery's Broadway play on the life of Supreme Court Justice Oliver Wendell Holmes, starring Calhern (who also did the stage version). America's foremost legal mind was well-served by Calhern, with Harding as his ever-patient wife. **80m/B; VHS, DVD.** Louis Calhern; Ann Harding; Eduard Franz; Philip Ober; Ian Wolfe; Edith Evanson; Richard Anderson; Jimmy Lydon; Robert Sherwood; Hugh Sanders; *D:* John Sturges; *W:* Emmet Lavery.

Magnolia ♪♪♪ **1999 (R)** It's a really long, frantic, and surreal look into a 24-hour series of interlocking stories, with a fine ensemble cast. Bad dads Jimmy Gator (Hall) and Earl Partridge (Robards) are both dying and estranged from their children—Jimmy's coke-addicted daughter, Claudia (Walters), and Earl's flashy motivational speaker son, Frank (Cruise). Earl's trophy wife Linda (Moore) is having a breakdown but he's being cared for by kind-hearted nurse Phil (Hoffman). And then there's a popular game show (of which Jimmy is the host) and its current and past quiz kids, and a rain of frogs, and everyone suddenly breaks into song, and, well, just watch it. **188m/C; DVD.** Jason Robards, Jr.; Julianne Moore; Tom Cruise; Philip Seymour Hoffman; Philip Baker Hall; Melora Walters; John C. Reilly; Melinda Dillon; William H. Macy; Michael Bowen; Jeremy Blackman; Emmanuel Johnson; ***D:*** Paul Thomas Anderson; ***W:*** Paul Thomas Anderson; ***C:*** Robert Elswit; ***M:*** Jon Brion; Aimee Mann. Golden Globes '00: Support. Actor (Cruise); Natl. Bd. of Review '99: Support. Actor (Hoffman), Support. Actress (Moore).

Magnum Force 🦴🦴 ½ **1973 (R)** Eastwood's second "Dirty Harry" movie. Harry finds a trail leading from a series of gangland killings straight back to the P.D. Less gripping than "Dirty Harry" (1971), but still effective. Holbrook is cast intriguingly against type. **124m/C; DVD, Blu-Ray.** Clint Eastwood; Hal Holbrook; Mitchell Ryan; David Soul; Tim Matheson; Robert Urich; Kip Niven; Felton Perry; Margaret Avery; ***D:*** Ted Post; ***W:*** John Milius; Michael Cimino; ***C:*** Frank Stanley; ***M:*** Lalo Schifrin.

Magnum P.I.: Don't Eat the Snow in Hawaii 🦴🦴 ½ **1980** Series pilot finds Vietnam-vet-turned-private-eye Thomas Sullivan Magnum (Selleck) living in Hawaii (in the guest house of never-seen mystery writer Robin Masters) and investigating the death of a wartime buddy. Hillerman excels as autocratic major domo Higgins. **99m/C; VHS, DVD.** Tom Selleck; John Hillerman; Roger E. Mosley; Larry Manetti; ***D:*** Roger Young; ***W:*** Donald P. Bellisario; Glen Larson. **TV**

Mahler 🦴🦴🦴 **1974 (PG)** Strange Russell effort on the life of the great composer Gustav Mahler. Imperfect script is rescued by fine acting. **110m/C; VHS, DVD.** Robert Powell; Georgina Hale; Richard Morant; Lee Montague; Terry O'Quinn; ***D:*** Ken Russell; ***W:*** Ken Russell; ***C:*** Dick Bush.

Mahogany 🦴 ½ **1975 (PG)** Poor girl becomes world-famous high fashion model and designer, ditches boyfriend in the old neighborhood, gets a career boost when she daringly appears in a dress of her own creation at a Roman fashion show, and still yearns for the boy back home. Motown attempt to make mainstream hit that's glossy and predictable. **109m/C; VHS, DVD.** Diana Ross; Billy Dee Williams; Jean-Pierre Aumont; Anthony Perkins; Nina Foch; ***D:*** Berry Gordy; ***W:*** John Byrum; ***C:*** David Watkin.

The Maid 🦴🦴 ½ *Kimyo na sakasu* **2005** Rosa has traveled from the Philippines to Singapore seeking work as a maid to provide money for her ill brother back home. But she has arrived during the seventh month of the Chinese Lunar Calendar, known as the Hungry Ghost Festival. For 30 days the gates of hell are opened, and the dead are allowed to walk among the living. To avoid repercussions one must follow several rules, among them: don't swim, never turn your head at night when someone calls your name, and don't speak to strangers on a deserted road. But Rosa doesn't know the rules. And her employers don't seem especially sympathetic to her plight. **93m/C; DVD.** Allesandra de Rossi; Huifang Hong; Benny Soh; Zhenwei Guan; Mohd Haizad Bin Imram; Griffin Chan; Shucheng Chen; Celine Chia; Tan Ooh Chye; Christina Goh; Cecilia Heng; Li Rong Heng; Chua Swee Hwang; Nur Awal'liyah Ja'afar; Zen Law; ***D:*** Kelvin Tong; ***W:*** Kelvin Tong; ***C:*** Lucas Jodogne; ***M:*** Joe Ng; Alex Oh.

The Maid 🦴🦴🦴 ½ *La Nana* **2009** After 23 years of unappreciated live-in maid service, Raquel hears her Chilean family employer may hire another maid to pick up her slack. Infuriated with the insulting decision, she sets out to run off all applicants with fierce passive aggression until her cheerful polar opposite, Lucy, plays against her every move. An incredible performance from Catalina Saavedra carries the emotional arch, with almost haunting results. A Sundance favorite, honoring first time director Sebastian Silva. Spanish with subtitles. **96m/C; On Demand.** *CL* Catalina Saavedra; Cladia Celedon; Mariana Loyola; Alejandro Goic; Delfina Guzman; Andrea Garcia-Huidobro; Agustin Silva; Anita Reeves; ***D:*** Sebastian Silva; ***W:*** Sebastian Silva; Pedro Peirano; ***C:*** Sergio Armstrong.

Maid in Manhattan 🦴🦴 ½ **2002 (PG-13)** Ralph Fiennes smiles! Okay, so the serious-minded Brit isn't known for romantic comedies—in fact, this bit of fluff is his first. He's wealthy political scion Christopher Marshall, who's running for the New York Senate when he meets cute with Marisa (Lopez), the ambitious Latina single mom who's working as a maid in a posh NYC hotel. He mistakes her for a guest and there's much angst (and tabloid gossip) until the prerequisite happy ending. Lopez is tenacious but her best scenes are with cutie newcomer Posey, who plays her 10-year-old son, and loud-mouthed best friend Matrone. **105m/C; DVD, Blu-Ray.** Jennifer Lopez; Ralph Fiennes; Natasha Richardson; Stanley Tucci; Tyler Garcia Posey; Marissa Matrone; Bob Hoskins; Frances Conroy; Christopher Eigeman; Priscilla Lopez; Amy Sedaris; ***D:*** Wayne Wang; ***W:*** Kevin Wade; ***C:*** Karl Walter Lindenlaub; ***M:*** Alan Silvestri.

Maid of Salem 🦴 ½ **1937** Colbert does her best but MacMurray is miscast in this grim story about the Salem witch trials. In 1692 Salem, troublemaking Anne Goode (Granville) starts a witch hysteria that puts innocent Barbara (Colbert) on trial and nearly costs her life. Can romantic interest Roger (MacMurray) rescue her in time? The dark subject matter did no one any favors during the Depression and was a boxoffice failure. **85m/B; DVD.** Fred MacMurray; Bonita Granville; Harvey Stephens; Gale Sondergaard; Louise Dresser; Edward Ellis; Beulah Bondi; Benny Barlett; Donald Meek; ***D:*** Frank Lloyd; ***W:*** Bradley King; ***C:*** Leo Tover; ***M:*** Victor Young.

Maid to Order 🦴 ½ **1987 (PG)** Rich girl Sheedy's fairy godmother puts her in her place by turning her into a maid for a snooty Malibu couple. Good-natured and well-acted if rather mindless Cinderella story. **92m/C; VHS, DVD.** Ally Sheedy; Beverly D'Angelo; Michael Ontkean; Dick Shawn; Tom Skerritt; Valerie Perrine; Rigg Kennedy; ***D:*** Amy Holden Jones; ***W:*** Perry Howze; ***M:*** Georges Delerue.

Maiden 🦴🦴🦴 **2018 (PG)** In the late 1980s, British sailor Tracy Edwards wanted to enter the difficult Whitbred Around the World Challenge. Women had not been allowed to serve as captains during the race, but could only serve as cooks on the few ships that welcomed them. After serving as a cook, Tracy entered the race in 1989. She put together an all-female crew and restoring a boat, dubbed Maiden. After finding sponsorship to gain entry, Tracy and her team faced other challenges including pushback from other crews and the race itself. The documentary captures the women's fighting spirit while telling a dramatic sports story. **97m/C; DVD, Blu-Ray.** ***D:*** Alex Holmes; ***C:*** Chris Openshaw; ***M:*** Rob Manning; Samuel Sim.

The Maiden Heist 🦴🦴 *The Lonely Maiden* **2008 (PG-13)** Best seen for the three leads because the heist story is rather a letdown. Three longtime museum security guards (Walken, Freeman, Macy) plot to steal their three favorite artworks rather than let them be sold and taken out of the country when the museum is undergoing renovations. Despite meticulous planning, their heist (naturally) faces complications. **89m/C; DVD.** Morgan Freeman; Christopher Walken; William H. Macy; Marcia Gay Harden; ***D:*** Peter Hewitt; ***W:*** Michael LeSieur; ***C:*** Ueli Steiger; ***M:*** Rupert Gregson-Williams. **VIDEO**

Maiden Voyage: Ocean Hijack 🦴 ½ **2004** Former Special Forces officer Kyle Considine (square-jawed Van Dien) brings his son Zach along when he gets a job evaluating security on a cruise ship. Too bad Kyle didn't start sooner because the ship is hijacked shortly out of port, with the terrorists threatening to blow up the liner unless the ransom is paid. Zach and ship's officer Lynn Fabrizio (Cormack) team up to distract the terrorists so Kyle can diffuse the bombs. **90m/C; DVD.** Casper Van Dien; Danielle Cormack; Angela Dotchin; Peter Anthony Elliott; Christopher Stollery; Anton Tennet; John Sumner; ***D:*** Colin Budds; ***W:*** James Makichuk; Ron McGee; ***C:*** Renaud Maire; ***M:*** Peter Blake; Tom McLeod. **CABLE**

Maids of Wilko 🦴🦴 *The Young Ladies of Wilko; Panny z Wilka; The Young Girls of Wilko* **1979** Wajda's adaptation of Jaroslav Iwaszkiewicz's memoirs set in the late '20s. Viktor Ruben (Olbrychski) reexamines his life following the death of a friend. He returns to the home of his aunt and uncle in Wilko where he renews friendships with five sisters on a neighboring estate in an attempt to resurrect a happier past. Lots of fruitless romantic yearning. In French and Polish with English subtitles. **118m/C; VHS, DVD.** *PL FR* Daniel Olbrychski; Christine Pascal; Maja Komorowska; Anna Seniuk; Krystyna Zachwatowicz; Stanislawa Celinska; Zofia Jaroszewska; Tadeusz Bialoszczynski; ***D:*** Andrzej Wajda; ***W:*** Zbigniew Kaminski.

Mail Order Bride 🦴 ½ **1963** Silly western comedy. Aging cowpoke Will (Ebsen) inherits the ranch of a friend and the duty of shaping up the man's troublesome son Lee (Dullea). Will thinks Lee will settle down if he marries so he finds him a mail order bride in Annie (Nettleton), a widow with a young son. Lee agrees to the marriage to get the ranch back but it's not smooth going. **83m/C; DVD.** Buddy Ebsen; Keir Dullea; Lois Nettleton; Warren Oates; Barbara Luna; Paul Fix; Marie Windsor; William (Bill) Smith; Denver Pyle; ***D:*** Burt Kennedy; ***W:*** Burt Kennedy; ***C:*** Paul Vogel; ***M:*** George Bassman.

Mail Order Bride 🦴🦴 ½ **2008** Hallmark Channel movie set in the 1880s. Con woman Diana McQueen (Zuniga) is working for Tom Rourke (Evigan) in Boston but wants out from under his control. She appears to get her chance when a dying friend, who was about to become the mail order bride of Wyoming rancher Beau (Bancroft), asks Diana to take her place. But can Diana really change her ways? A sassy woman, a handsome cowboy, and a shoot-out—what more could you ask for? **88m/C; DVD, Blu-Ray.** Daphne Zuniga; Cameron Bancroft; Greg Evigan; Tom Heaton; Vincent Gale; Ted Whittall; Katharine Isabelle; William Macdonald; ***D:*** Anne Wheeler; ***W:*** Tippi Dobrofsky; Neal Dobrofsky; ***C:*** David Pelletier. **CABLE**

Mail Order Wife 🦴🦴 **2004 (R)** Making a documentary parody really only works if the subject is funny and the characters are caricatures. Abusive men who order wives through the mail doesn't quite have the same comic appeal. Director Andrew Gurland, playing himself, is a documentary filmmaker getting wrapped up in a mail-order marriage gone bad, who then offers the overseas newlywed a place to stay (i.e. his bed) and helps her find a job. The camera bobs and weaves, trying to focus the entire time. It's almost like it doesn't want to watch, either, especially with such an unlikable cast. **92m/C; DVD, Blu-Ray.** Andrew Gurland; Eugenia Yuan; Adrian Martinez; Deborah Teng; ***D:*** Huck Botko; Andrew Gurland; ***W:*** Huck Botko; Andrew Gurland; ***C:*** Luke Geissbuhler.

Mail to the Chief 🦴🦴 **2000** Junior high schooler Kenny has a school assignment on the upcoming presidential election. So he goes to a chat room and starts dissing the incumbent's gaffes, only to discover his online chat buddy is actually the President himself. The eighth-grader gives the prez some advice and when he starts to follow it, the President's popularity starts to rise in the polls. **89m/C; VHS, DVD.** Randy Quaid; Holland Taylor; Bill Switzer; Ashley Gorrell; Martin Doyle; ***D:*** Eric Champnella; ***W:*** Eric Champnella; ***C:*** Albert J. Dunk; ***M:*** Peter Bernstein. **VIDEO**

The Main Event 🦴🦴 **1979 (PG)** Streisand plays a wacky—and bankrupt—cosmetic executive who must depend on the career of washed-up boxer O'Neal to rebuild her fortune. Desperate (and more than a little smitten), she badgers and bullies him back into the ring. Lame, derivative screwball comedy desperate to suggest chemistry of Streisand and O'Neal's "What's Up, Doc?" (1972). Streisand sings the title song. **109m/C; VHS, DVD.** Barbra Streisand; Ryan O'Neal; ***D:*** Howard Zieff.

Main Street 🦴 ½ **2010 (PG)** Uneven ensemble drama about the fading North Carolina town of Durham was the final screenplay of Foote, who died in 2009. Georgiana Carr (Burstyn), the aging heiress of a once-wealthy tobacco-manufacturing family, is stuck with a number of empty tobacco warehouses. Too-smooth Texan Gus Leroy (Firth) wants to rent the properties, but Georgiana learns he intends to store hazardous waste containers and wants niece Willa (Clarkson) to advise her. In one of many narrative lapses, Willa starts a romance with Gus instead. A couple of subplots are also underdeveloped. **92m/C; DVD, Blu-Ray, On Demand.** Colin Firth; Ellen Burstyn; Patricia Clarkson; Amber Tamblyn; Orlando Bloom; Andrew McCarthy; Margo Martindale; Isiah Whitlock, Jr.; Tom Wopat; ***D:*** John Doyle; ***W:*** Horton Foote; ***C:*** Donald McAlpine; ***M:*** Patrick Doyle.

Mainline Run 🦴 ½ **1998** Smalltime drug runner Taro (Speer) gets out of prison and immediately goes back to work for crime boss Mr. Fletcher (Ward). Taro sets up a deal, which goes bad, the drugs are lost, and one of his men is killed. Now Taro and his buddy Sean (Joseph) are looking to get out, but Mr. Fletcher has something else in mind. **96m/C; VHS, DVD.** Hugo Speer; Andrew Joseph; Nelson E. Ward; Kelly Marcel; ***D:*** Howard Ford; ***C:*** Jonathan Ford.

Maisie 🦴🦴 ½ **1939** After being stranded, New York burlesque dancer Maisie Ravier (Sothern) gets work as a maid on a Wyoming ranch. Foreman Slim Martin (Young) isn't happy but Maisie proves herself when Slim is accused of murdering ranch owner Clifford Ames (Hunter). Based on the novel "Dark Dame" by Wilson Collison; the first of 10 films in MGM's "Maisie" series. **72m/B; DVD.** Ann Sothern; Robert Young; Ian Hunter; Ruth Hussey; John Hubbard; Richard Carle; Cliff Edwards; ***D:*** Edwin L. Marin; ***W:*** Mary C. McCall; ***C:*** Leonard Smith; ***M:*** Edward Ward.

Maisie Gets Her Man 🦴🦴 ½ **1942** Maisie (Sothern) meets comedian Hap Hixby (Skelton), who can't do his act because of severe stage fright. Instead, Hap gets a job as a building manager and hires Maisie as his assistant. Since Maisie's life never goes smoothly, she and Hap are soon in trouble with the law after unwittingly getting mixed up in a con game. Sixth in the MGM series. **85m/B; DVD.** Ann Sothern; Red Skelton; Allen Jenkins; Leo Gorcey; Donald Meek; Lloyd Corrigan; Fritz Feld; Rags Ragland; ***D:*** Roy Del Ruth; ***W:*** Elizabeth Reinhardt; Mary C. McCall; ***C:*** Harry Stradling, Sr.; ***M:*** Lennie Hayton.

Maisie Goes to Reno 🦴🦴 **1944** Wartime riveter Maisie (Sothern) uses her vacation to take a nightclub gig in Reno. She agrees to take Sgt. Bill Fullerton's (Drake) letter to his wife Gloria (Gardner) asking her to stop their divorce. But after doing her duty, Maisie gets suspicious and stumbles upon an elaborate con. Hodiak plays a casino worker who helps Maisie out. Eighth in the MGM series. **90m/B; DVD.** Ann Sothern; John Hodiak; Tom Drake; Ava Gardner; Marta Linden; Bernard Nedell; Paul Cavanagh; Donald Meek; Chick Chandler; ***D:*** Harry Beaumont; ***W:*** Mary C. McCall; ***C:*** Robert Planck; ***M:*** David Snell.

Maisie Was a Lady 🦴🦴 ½ **1941** Wealthy drunk Robert Rawlston (Ayres) gets Maisie (Sothern) fired from the carnival so he gets her a job as a maid at his family's mansion. Bob's sister Abby (O'Sullivan) is engaged to Link Phillips (Ashley), but is too innocent to realize he's just a fortune hunter. Maisie takes the family in hand by giving patriarch Cap Rawlston (Cavanagh) some tough advice about neglecting his children. Fourth in the MGM series. **79m/B; DVD.** Ann Sothern; Lew Ayres; Maureen O'Sullivan; Edward Ashley; Paul Cavanagh; Joan Perry; Sir C. Aubrey Smith; ***D:*** Edwin L. Marin; ***W:*** Mary C. McCall; Elizabeth Reinhardt; ***C:*** Charles Lawton, Jr.; ***M:*** David Snell.

Maitresse 🦴🦴 ½ **1976** An examination of the sexual underworld in the same vein as "Blue Velvet" and "Crimes of Passion" as a man falls for a high-priced dominatrix. Director Scroeder also created "Reversal of Fortune." In French with English subtitles. **112m/C; VHS, DVD.** *FR* Gerard Depardieu; Bulle Ogier; ***D:*** Barbet Schroeder; ***C:*** Nestor Almendros.

The Majestic 🦴🦴 ½ **2001 (PG)** Carrey is a blacklisted writer who suffers from amnesia after a car crash. He winds up in a small town where he's mistaken for a presumed MIA soldier, who was the son of Landau, the local movie theatre owner. Darabont's self-admitted ode to Frank Capra evokes the All-American innocence and decency that Capra's films revelled in, but doesn't quite match the charm. Cynics will think it's too sentimental and tries too hard, romantics and others not quick to sneer at nostalgia should enjoy themselves. Carrey does a fine job with the lead role. **152m/C; DVD, Blu-Ray.** Jim Carrey; Martin Landau; Laurie Holden; David Ogden Stiers; James Whitmore; Jeffrey DeMunn; Ron Rifkin; Hal Holbrook; Bob Balaban; Brent Briscoe; Gerry Black; Susan Willis; Catherine Dent; Chelcie Ross; Amanda Detmer; Allen Garfield; Daniel von Bargen; Shawn Doyle; Bruce Campbell; Clifford Curtis; ***D:*** Frank Darabont; ***W:*** Michael Sloane; ***C:*** David Tattersall; ***M:*** Mark Isham.

The Major and the Minor ♪♪♪ 1/2 **1942** Very funny comedy that marked Wilder's directorial debut. Susan Applegate (Rogers) decides she's had it with New York and wants to head home to Iowa, but she only has enough money for a child's half-price train ticket. So she passes herself off as a 12-year-old (!) and then runs into problems when Army major Kirby (Milland), who's traveling to a boys military school, decides to take the child under his protective wing. Soon he's insisting Susan stay at the school until her mother (played by Rogers' mother Lela) can collect her. Potentially risque situations never cross the line into sleaze but remain bright and breezy. **101m/B; VHS, DVD, Blu-Ray.** Ginger Rogers; Ray Milland; Rita Johnson; Robert Benchley; Diana Lynn; Frankie Thomas, Jr.; ***D:*** Billy Wilder; ***W:*** Billy Wilder; Charles Brackett; ***C:*** Leo Tover; ***M:*** Robert Emmett Dolan.

Major Barbara ♪♪♪ 1/2 **1941** A wealthy, idealistic girl joins the Salvation Army against her father's wishes. Based on the play by George Bernard Shaw. The excellent adaptation of the original and the cast make this film a winner. Deborah Kerr's film debut. **90m/B; VHS, DVD.** *GB* Wendy Hiller; Rex Harrison; Robert Morley; Sybil Thorndike; Deborah Kerr; ***D:*** Gabriel Pascal.

Major Dundee ♪♪ 1/2 **1965** A Union army officer (Heston) chases Apaches into Mexico with a motley collection of prisoner volunteers. Too long and flawed; would have been better had Peckinpah been allowed to finish the project. Excellent cast. **124m/C; DVD, Blu-Ray.** Charlton Heston; Richard Harris; James Coburn; Jim Hutton; Ben Johnson; Slim Pickens; ***D:*** Sam Peckinpah; ***W:*** Sam Peckinpah; Oscar Saul; Harry Julian Fink; ***C:*** Sam Leavitt; ***M:*** Daniele Amfitheatrof.

Major League ♪♪ 1/2 **1989 (R)** The Cleveland Indians are a pathetic major league baseball team with new owner, ex-showgirl Rachel (Wilton), scheming to lose the season and relocate the team to Miami. Sheen's okay as pitcher Ricky "Wild Thing" Vaughan, who suffers with control problems (both on and off the field). Predictable sports spoof is good for a few laughs, particularly those scenes involving Haysbert as slugger Pedro Cerrano with voodoo on his mind (and in his locker) and Snipes as base stealer Willie Mays Hayes, whose only problem is getting on base. Followed by two sequels. **107m/C; DVD, Blu-Ray.** Tom Berenger; Charlie Sheen; Corbin Bernsen; James Gammon; Margaret Whitton; Bob Uecker; Rene Russo; Wesley Snipes; Dennis Haysbert; Charles Cyphers; Chelcie Ross; ***D:*** David S. Ward; ***W:*** David S. Ward; ***C:*** Reynaldo Villalobos; ***M:*** James Newton Howard.

Major League 2 ♪ 1/2 **1994 (PG)** It's been five years since they won the series, and this plodding sequel finds the wacky championship Cleveland Indians ruined by success and once again struggling in last place. Limited charm of original is lost; dull and filled with so many lame jokes that you won't care if they manage to make it to the top again. Cast returns, with the exception of Wesley Snipes as Willie Mays Hays (now played by Epps). **105m/C; VHS, DVD, Blu-Ray.** Charlie Sheen; Tom Berenger; Corbin Bernsen; James Gammon; Dennis Haysbert; Omar Epps; David Keith; Bob Uecker; Alison Doody; Michelle Rene Thomas; Margaret Whitton; Eric Bruskotter; Takaaki Ishibashi; Randy Quaid; ***D:*** David S. Ward; ***W:*** R.J. Stewart; ***C:*** Victor Hammer; ***M:*** Michel Colombier.

Major League 3: Back to the Minors ♪ 1/2 **1998 (PG-13)** Three strikes and this franchise is out. Gus Cantrell (Bakula) is a burned-out pitcher who's offered the chance to manage the Minnesota Twins' Triple A team and finds a bunch of central casting misfits. Just when you thought they'd run out of baseball cliches, in comes a young prospect who won't take advice (Goggins), an arrogant manager (McGinley), and the "big game" showdown (twice!). We've seen this stuff done (not much better) in the first two "Major Leagues" and (very much better) elsewhere. Bakula's always solid, but it's not enough to get the save. Take an intentional pass on this one. **90m/C; DVD, Blu-Ray.** Scott Bakula; Corbin Bernsen; Dennis Haysbert; Takaaki Ishibashi; Jensen (Jennifer) Daggett; Eric Bruskotter; Walton Goggins; Ted McGinley; Kenneth Johnson; Judson Mills; Bob Uecker; Steve Yeager; ***D:*** John Warren; ***W:*** John Warren; ***C:*** Tim Suhrstedt; ***M:*** Robert Folk.

Major Payne ♪ **1995 (PG-13)** When the marines have no more use for killing-machine Major Payne (Wayans), he reluctantly agrees to train the inept junior ROTC cadets at academically challenged Madison Academy. The misfit brigade contains the usual assortment of stock loser-types who follow the predictable "outcasts get even" plot to the letter. Wayans shows flashes of comic genius, but not nearly enough to make up for the one-dimensional characters and indifferent writing. Sub-moronic remake of 1955's "The Private War of Major Benson." **97m/C; DVD, Blu-Ray.** Damon Wayans; Karyn Parsons; William Hickey; Albert Hall; Steven Martini; Andrew Harrison Leeds; Scott "Bam Bam" Bigelow; ***D:*** Nick Castle; ***W:*** Damon Wayans; Dean Lorey; Gary Rosen; ***C:*** Richard Bowen; ***M:*** Craig Safan.

The Majorettes ♪ **1987 (R)** Eek! Someone is lurking around a high school murdering the majorettes with their own batons. A bare-bones plot lurks within this otherwise worthless pic. **93m/C; VHS, DVD, Blu-Ray.** Kevin Kindlin; Terrie Godfrey; Mark V. Jevicky; Sueanne Seamans; John A. Russo; Bill (William Heinzman) Hinzman; Russell Streiner; ***D:*** Bill (William Heinzman) Hinzman; ***W:*** John A. Russo.

A Majority of One ♪♪ 1/2 **1956** Dated comedy about late-in-life romance and prejudice. Russell stars as Jewish Brooklyn widow Mrs. Jacoby, who tags along with her daughter and diplomat son-in-law on their shipboard trip to Japan. She meets the charming Koichi Asano (a surprisingly effective Guinness), who's with the Japanese diplomatic corp, runs into problems with her family, and decides she must give up her chance at romance. Adapted from the play by Leonard Spigelgass. **149m/C; VHS, DVD.** Rosalind Russell; Alec Guinness; Ray Danton; Madlyn Rhue; Mae Questel; Frank Wilcox; Alan Mowbray; ***D:*** Mervyn LeRoy; ***W:*** Leonard Spigelgass.

Make a Million ♪♪ **1935** The Depression is played (successfully) for yuks in this tale of an economics professor fired from his post for advocating radical income redistribution. He doesn't get mad, he gets even: he makes a million by advertising for money. **66m/B; VHS, DVD.** Charles Starrett; Pauline Brooks; George E. Stone; James Burke; Guy Usher; Norman Houston; ***D:*** Lewis D. Collins; ***W:*** Charles Logue; ***C:*** Milton Krasner.

Make a Wish ♪♪ **1937** A noted composer goes stale in this colorful musical about backstage life. The comic relief provides the films best moments. **80m/B; VHS, DVD.** Basil Rathbone; Leon Errol; Bobby Breen; Ralph Forbes; ***D:*** Kurt Neumann; ***M:*** Oscar Straus.

Make It Happen ♪ 1/2 **2008 (PG-13)** Harmless, cliched dance flick. Smalltown Lauryn heads to Chicago to audition for dance school but is rejected. Not wanting to go back home, Lauryn accepts help from fellow dancer Dana in landing a bookkeeping job at a dance club. Soon Lauryn is moving from the office to the stage in order to regain her confidence. **90m/C; DVD.** Mary Elizabeth Winstead; Tessa Thompson; John Reardon; Riley Smith; Julissa Bermudez; ***D:*** Darren Grant; ***W:*** Duane Adler; Nicole Avril; ***C:*** David Claessen; ***M:*** Paul Haslinger. **VIDEO**

Make Me a Star ♪♪ 1/2 **1932** Erwin stars as a small town hick with big Hollywood dreams of becoming a serious cowboy star. Merton Gill talks his way into a Hollywood studio and movie extra Flips (Blondell) takes pity and gets him a part in a western. However, he's horrified after realizing he was filmed as the comic foil. Director Beaudine took full advantage of working on the Paramount lot, including sets, buildings, and cameos by a variety of the studio's actors. Based on the novel and play "Merton of the Movies" and remade, starring Red Skelton, in 1947. **70m/B; DVD.** Stuart Erwin; Joan Blondell; Zasu Pitts; Ben Turpin; Charles Sellon; Florence Roberts; Helen Jerome Eddy; ***D:*** William Beaudine; ***W:*** Arthur Kober; Sam Mintz; Walter DeLeon; ***C:*** Allen Siegler.

Make Mine Mink ♪♪♪ **1960** Oft-hilarious British comedy about guests at an elegant but run-down mansion who become unlikely thieves, stealing furs for charity. Good cast headed by Terry-Thomas. **100m/C; VHS, DVD.** *GB* Terry-Thomas; Billie Whitelaw; Hattie Jacques; ***D:*** Robert Asher.

Make the Yuletide Gay ♪ 1/2 **2009** Out at college, Gunn lives with his sweetie Nathan. The boys go their separate ways at Christmas break but when Nathan's parents desert him for a trip to Israel, he decides to surprise Gunn by showing up at his parental home in Wisconsin. Nathan's surprised too since Gunn is in the closet at home, his dad's a stoner, and his mom is a holiday freak who wants to fix up her boy with his ex-girlfriend. Now Gunn needs to decide whether to tell the truth before Nathan decides to leave. **89m/C; DVD.** Keith Jordan; Adamo Ruggiero; Hallee Hirsh; Kelly Keaton; Derek Long; Alison Arngrim; Gates (Cheryl) McFadden; Ian Buchanan; ***D:*** Rob Williams; ***W:*** Rob Williams; ***C:*** Ian Mcglocklin; ***M:*** Austin Wintory. **VIDEO**

Make Way for Tomorrow ♪♪ 1/2 **1937** Multi-hankie family drama about loving elderly couple Barkley and Lucy Cooper. They lose their home to foreclosure during the Depression and the couple must separate since none of their children are willing to care for both parents. Eventually, feeling unwanted and realizing they will probably be apart the rest of their lives, Barkley and Lucy spend one last day together revisiting their honeymoon spot. **91m/B; DVD, Blu-Ray.** Victor Moore; Beulah Bondi; Thomas Mitchell; Fay Bainter; Barbara Read; Elisabeth Risdon; Porter Hall; Minna Gombell; Ralph Remley; ***W:*** Vina Delmar; ***C:*** William Mellor; ***M:*** Victor Young; George Antheil. Natl. Film Reg. '10.

Make Your Bets Ladies ♪ 1/2 *Faites Vous Jeux, Mesdames* **1965** Secret agent Mike Warner (Constantine) is searching for a missing NATO scientist, which leads him to a Russian agent and a female gang. They are lead by gypsy Soledad (Benedetti) and their ransom demands for said scientist are diamonds and fur coats! Dubbed. **90m/B; DVD.** *FR SP* Eddie Constantine; Nelly Benedetti; Daniel Ceccaldi; Laura Valenzuela; Luis Davila; Dieter Kollesch; ***D:*** Marcel Ophuls; ***W:*** Jacques Robert; ***C:*** Alain Boisnard; ***M:*** Ward Swingle.

Make Your Move ♪ 1/2 **2013 (PG-13)** Donny (Hough) falls for Aya (Korean pop star BoA), the leader of a hip-hop dance crew in New York. It's another Romeo & Juliet riff with a bumping beat. What's the one thing that can bring people together? Dancing, of course. Relatively stale with lackluster storytelling that can't get viewers from step to step. Though a few of the 3D dance sequences do sparkle, and the cast is likable enough to make it forgivable, in the end it's mostly just for those who enjoy a good dance sequence. **110m/C; DVD, Blu-Ray.** Derek Hough; BoA; Wesley Jonathan; Will Yun Lee; Jefferson Brown; ***D:*** Duane Adler; ***W:*** Duane Adler; ***C:*** Gregory Middleton; ***M:*** Michael Corcoran; Eric Goldman.

The Makeover ♪♪ 1/2 **2013** Satisfying Hallmark Hall of Fame presentation that's a gender reversal of "My Fair Lady" (or "Pygmalion"). Bright but prickly Hannah Higgins (Stiles) loses a congressional campaign, and she and her colleague Colleen (Manheim) decide to groom their own candidate. She and language-mangling Boston beer vendor Elliot Doolittle (Walton) meet-cute and he cleans up real well. Their professional association turns personal but neither transition goes smoothly. **90m/C; DVD.** Julia Stiles; David Walton; Camryn Manheim; Frances Fisher; Jay Dunigan; ***D:*** John Gray; ***W:*** C. Jay Cox; ***C:*** James Chressanthis; ***M:*** Michael A. Levine. **TV**

The Maker ♪♪ 1/2 **1998 (R)** Restless SoCal high-schooler Josh (Rhys Myers) indulges in petty crime with lesbian friend Bella (Balk) but isn't really in trouble until his long-missing older brother Walter (Modine) hits town. Walter soon pulls Josh into his shady schemes that turn into some very dangerous games. **98m/C; VHS, DVD.** Jonathan Rhys Meyers; Matthew Modine; Mary-Louise Parker; Fairuza Balk; Michael Madsen; Jesse Borrego; Kate McGregor-Stewart; Lawrence Pressman; Jeff Kober; ***D:*** Tim Hunter; ***W:*** Rand Ravich; ***C:*** Hubert Taczanowski; ***M:*** Paul Buckmaster.

Makin' Baby ♪ **2002 (R)** Newlyweds Michael and Alicia are having a tough time coping with the married life itself, when Alicia suddenly raises the stakes, deciding she wants a baby. If that isn't enough to push hip-hop-hopeful Michael over the edge, the temptation of a slimy music exec (Mystikal, in his feature debut) offering to take him under his wing and transform him into a full-time rhymin' thug puts the sweethearts in danger. Mean-spirited jokes fall flat and come at the worst times. Fans of Mystikal will be severely dissed by his limited screen time. And, nope, he doesn't even rap. **94m/C; VHS, DVD.** Portia Realer; Aaron Spears; Mystikal; Sheila Lussier; Kim Hill; ***D:*** Paul Wynne; ***W:*** Brennon Jones. **VIDEO**

Making Babies ♪♪ **2019** Married couple Katie (Coupe) and John (Howey) have unsuccessfully tried for years to have a child. Compounding the situation, each of them has professional frustrations. To address the fertility issue, they consult a fertility specialist (Begley) with a quirky personality. The couple also take other steps, including visits to a New Age healer (Daly), despite the objections of Kate's religious mother (Headly). Though the comedy explores a sensitive topic, it features a predictable, stereotypical plot that challenges the ability of the actors to make it funny. The film also marks the last on-screen appearance by respected actor Headly. **86m/C; DVD.** Eliza Coupe; Steve Howey; Ed James Begley, Jr.; Glenne Headly; Bob Stephenson; ***D:*** Josh F. Huber; ***W:*** Josh F. Huber; ***C:*** Matt Edwards; ***M:*** Keegan DeWitt.

Making Contact ♪ 1/2 **1986 (PG)** A small boy's telekinetic powers enable him to bring to life his favorite toys. The ridicule he endures because of this leads him to set off on terrifying adventures with only his toys and a friend for company. **83m/C; VHS, DVD, Blu-Ray.** Joshua Morrell; Eve Kryll; ***D:*** Roland Emmerich.

Making Love ♪♪ **1982 (R)** A closet homosexual risks his eight-year marriage by getting involved with a carefree writer. What could be a powerful subject gets only bland treatment. **112m/C; VHS, DVD.** Kate Jackson; Harry Hamlin; Michael Ontkean; Wendy Hiller; Arthur Hill; Nancy Olson; Terry Kiser; Camilla Carr; Michael Dudikoff; ***D:*** Arthur Hiller; ***W:*** Barry Sandler.

Making Mr. Right ♪♪ 1/2 **1986 (PG-13)** Under-rated satire about a high-powered marketing and image consultant who falls in love with the android that she's supposed to be promoting. Unbelievable comedy is shaky at times, but Magnuson and Malkovich create some magic. **95m/C; VHS, DVD, Blu-Ray.** John Malkovich; Ann Magnuson; Glenne Headly; Ben Masters; Laurie Metcalf; Polly Bergen; Hart Bochner; Polly Draper; Susan Anton; ***D:*** Susan Seidelman; ***W:*** Floyd Byars; Laurie Frank.

Making Mr. Right ♪♪ **2008** Lifetime channel rom com finds New York magazine features editor Hallie Galloway (Cox) betting a fellow employee that she can makeover hairy street con man Eddie (Cain) into a suitable eligible bachelor for a cover story. If she wins, she gets a promotion but Eddie thinks Hallie needs more than work in her life. **85m/C; DVD.** Christina Cox; Dean Cain; David Lewis; Michael Karl Richards; Jocelyne Loewen; Greg Rogers; Tom Butler; Michael Daingerfield; ***D:*** Paul Fox; ***W:*** Dan Beckerman; Julie L. Saunders; Guy Mann; ***C:*** Michael Balfry; ***M:*** Peter Allen; John Sereda. **CABLE**

The Making of a Lady ♪♪ 1/2 **2012** Educated but penniless, Emily (Wilson) takes a job as companion to Lady Maria (Lumley). She meets her employer's widowed heir, Lord Walderhurst (Roache), and agrees to his practical marriage proposal since he needs his own heir to the estate. Now pregnant, Emily's left alone on the family's isolated country estate when her husband's sinister nephew (D'Arcy) and his wife (Haque) come to stay. British TV movie based on a novel by Frances Hodgson Burnett. **96m/C; DVD, Blu-Ray.** *UK* Lydia Wilson; Linus Roache; James D'Arcy; Hasina Haque; Joanna Lumley; ***D:*** Richard Curson Smith; ***W:*** Kate Brooke; ***C:*** Tony Slater-Ling; ***M:*** Rob Lane. **TV**

Making of a Male Model 🦴🦴 **1983** Campy ABC TV movie has Manhattan modeling agent/owner Kay Dillon salivating over hunky Nevada ranch hand Tyler, whom she persuades into a new career and a romance. Despite his success, Tyler is really a country boy at heart, especially after getting caught up in the booze, drugs, and glitz, realizing its change or die. **94m/C; DVD.** Joan Collins; Jon-Erik Hexum; Jeff Conaway; Kevin McCarthy; Arte Johnson; Ted McGinley; Roxie Roker; ***D:*** Irving J. Moore; ***W:*** A.J. Carothers; ***C:*** Richard L. Rawlings; ***M:*** Artie Butler. **TV**

Making Plans for Lena 🦴🦴 **2009** Unsentimental family drama with a self-destructive, infuriating central character. A divorced mother of two, Lena is subjected to the well-meaning but annoying criticism of her family during a summer holiday. She has a tense relationship with everyone, including her ex-husband, who bails Lena out of one of her self-made crises. As the story heads from Brittany to Paris, Lena continues to lose her sanity and the viewer's patience. French with subtitles. **107m/C; DVD.** *FR* Chiara Mastroianni; Marina Fois; Jean-Marc Barr; Marie-Christine Barrault; Fred Ulysse; Louis Garrel; ***D:*** Christophe Honore; ***W:*** Christophe Honore; ***C:*** Laurent Brunet; ***M:*** Alexandre Beaupain.

Making the Grade 🦴🦴 *Preppies* **1984 (PG)** Jersey tough kid owes the mob; attends prep school in place of a rich kid who can't be bothered. Better than similar '80s teen flicks, but not by much. **105m/C; VHS, DVD, Blu-Ray.** Judd Nelson; Joanna Lee; Dana Olsen; Ronald Lacey; Scott McGinnis; Gordon Jump; Carey Scott; Andrew Silverstein; ***D:*** Dorian Walker; ***W:*** Gene Quintano; ***C:*** Jacques Haitkin; ***M:*** Basil Poledouris.

Making the Rules 🦴 1/2 **2014 (R)** When workaholic sous chef Abby suffers a severe hand cut, she's forced to take off work for the summer. While trying to adjust to having leisure time, Abby realizes that she and her husband have grown apart and she's tempted to start something with an ex-beau. **78m/C; DVD, Blu-Ray.** Jaime Pressly; Robin Thicke; Tygh Runyan; Joey Lauren Adams; Frances Conroy; ***D:*** Jimbo Lee; ***W:*** Jimbo Lee; ***C:*** Mark Putnam; ***M:*** Kasiemba Okeyo. **VIDEO**

The Makioka Sisters 🦴🦴🦴 **1983** Much praised drama centering around the lives of four Japanese sisters who are heiresses to the family fortune and, hence, must be found proper husbands. The efforts of the older sisters to "match" their younger siblings are entwined with a gradual realization on the part of the elders that the quiet way of life representative of their own formative years is passing away with the advent of WWII. The movie is as visually stunning as it is poignant. In Japanese with English subtitles. **140m/C; VHS, Blu-Ray.** *JP* Keiko Kishi; Yoshiko Sakuma; Sayuri Yoshinaga; Juzo Itami; Ittoku Kishibe; Jun Hamamura; Yuko Kotegawa; Koji Ishizaka; Toshiyuki Hosokawa; ***D:*** Kon Ichikawa; ***W:*** Kon Ichikawa; Shinya Hidaka; ***C:*** Kiyoshi Hasegawa.

Maladies 🦴 **2013** Pretentious and dull conceptual piece, allegedly set in 1960s New York but deliberately filled with anachronisms. Video artist Carter's drama stars Franco as a mentally unstable former soap opera star who goes to live with his equally unstable sister, Patricia (Goodson), and begin a new career as a writer. He's vaguely looked after by cross-dressing, artist girlfriend, Catherine (Keener), and doted on by fan/neighbor, Delmar (Strathairn). Pic at least looks good. **97m/C; On Demand.** James Franco; Catherine Keener; Fallon Goodson; David Strathairn; ***D:*** Carter; ***W:*** Carter; ***C:*** Doug Chamberlain; ***M:*** J. Ralph.

Malarek 🦴🦴 **1989 (R)** Tough Montreal journalist Victor Malarek exposed abuse in that city's teen detention center in his book "Hey, Malarek." Compelling lead performance from Koteas in decent though not great screen adaptation. **95m/C; VHS, DVD.** Michael Sarrazin; Elias Koteas; Al Waxman; Kerrie Keane; ***D:*** Roger Cardinal.

Malay Nights 🦴 **1932** Wealthy pearl merchant Jim Wilson marries unwed mother Eve so the courts won't take her baby away. He intends to return to the South Seas, thinking everything with Eve is okay, but then Eve unexpectedly abandons the tyke and Jim must take custody. **63m/B; DVD.** Johnny Mack Brown; Dorothy Burgess; Ralph Ince; Raymond Hatton; ***D:*** E. Mason Hopper; ***W:*** John Thomas "Jack" Neville; ***C:*** Jules Cronjager.

Malaya 🦴🦴 1/2 *East of the Rising Sun* **1949** Hokey adventure tale set in WWII that's based on a true story. Stewart and Tracy are hired to smuggle a huge shipment of rubber out of Malaya to waiting U.S. ships without the Japanese finding out. Greenstreet does his usual shifty role. **98m/B; VHS, DVD.** Spencer Tracy; James Stewart; Sydney Greenstreet; Valentina Cortese; John Hodiak; Lionel Barrymore; Gilbert Roland; Richard Loo; Roland Winters; ***D:*** Richard Thorpe; ***W:*** Frank Fenton; ***C:*** George J. Folsey; ***M:*** Bronislau Kaper.

Malcolm 🦴🦴 1/2 **1986 (PG-13)** An offbeat comedy about a slightly retarded young man who is mechanically inclined and his unusual entry into a life of crime. Directorial debut for actress Tass, whose husband Parker wrote the screenplay (and designed the Tinkertoys). Music score performed by The Penguin Cafe Orchestra. **86m/C; VHS, DVD.** *AU* Colin Friels; John Hargreaves; Lindy Davies; Chris Haywood; Charles "Bud" Tingwell; Beverly Phillips; Judith Stratford; ***D:*** Nadia Tass; ***W:*** David Parker; ***C:*** David Parker; ***M:*** Simon Jeffes. Australian Film Inst. '86: Actor (Friels), Film.

Malcolm X 🦴🦴🦴 **1992 (PG-13)** Stirring tribute to the controversial black activist, a leader in the struggle for black liberation. Hitting bottom during his imprisonment in the '50s, he became a Black Muslim and then a leader in the Nation of Islam. His assassination in 1965 left a legacy of black nationalism, self-determination, and racial pride. Marked by strong direction from Lee and good performances (notably Freeman Jr. as Elijah Muhammad), it is Washington's convincing performance in the title role that truly brings the film alive. Based on "The Autobiography of Malcolm X" by Malcolm X and Alex Haley. **201m/C; DVD.** Denzel Washington; Angela Bassett; Albert Hall; Al Freeman, Jr.; Delroy Lindo; Spike Lee; Theresa Randle; Kate Vernon; Lonette McKee; Tommy Hollis; James McDaniel; Ernest Thompson; Jean LaMarre; Giancarlo Esposito; Craig Wasson; John Ottavino; David Patrick Kelly; Shirley Stoler; ***Cameo(s):*** Christopher Plummer; Karen Allen; Peter Boyle; William Kunstler; Bobby Seale; Al Sharpton; ***D:*** Spike Lee; ***W:*** Spike Lee; Arnold Perl; James Baldwin; ***M:*** Terence Blanchard. MTV Movie Awards '93: Male Perf. (Washington); Natl. Film Reg. '10; N.Y. Film Critics '92: Actor (Washington).

The Maldonado Miracle 🦴🦴 1/2 **2003 (PG)** The small desert border town of San Ramos is slowly dying until the church's Jesus statue is found to be crying tears of blood. This development brings pilgrims, media, and curiosity seekers at the same time a Mexican boy arrives looking for his father and on the run from Immigration. Hayek's directorial debut is uplifting and earnest, if a bit predictable, and she gets solid performances from an excellent cast. **100m/C; DVD.** Peter Fonda; Mare Winningham; Ruben Blades; Bill Sage; Eddy Martin; Soledad St. Hilaire; Scott Michael Campbell; Jesse Borrego; Christina Cabot; ***D:*** Salma Hayek; ***W:*** Paul Cooper; ***C:*** Claudio Rocha; ***M:*** Leonardo Heiblum; Jacob Lieberman. **CABLE**

Male and Female 🦴🦴🦴🦴 **1919** A group of British aristocrats is shipwrecked on an island and must allow their efficient butler (Meighan) to take command for their survival. Swanson is the spoiled rich girl who falls for her social inferior. Their rescue provides a return to the rigid British class system. Based on the play "The Admirable Crichton" by James M. Barrie. **110m/B; Silent; VHS, DVD.** Gloria Swanson; Thomas Meighan; Lila Lee; Raymond Hatton; Bebe Daniels; ***D:*** Cecil B. DeMille; ***W:*** Jeanie Macpherson; ***C:*** Alvin Wyckoff.

The Male Animal 🦴🦴 1/2 **1942** Fonda uses his penchant for playing principled men to uneven comedic effect as stuffy English professor Tommy Turner. He gets into trouble with university trustees over his views about free speech and it threatens his job, which worries wife Ellen (de Havilland). Tommy gets jealous when Ellen's college beau, ex-football star Joe Ferguson (Carson), suddenly shows up on campus and seems to want to rekindle the flame. The men behave like idiots while Ellen deals with their male posturing. Based on the play by James Thurber and director Nugent. Fonda later played the same role in a Broadway revival. **101m/B; DVD.** Henry Fonda; Olivia de Havilland; Jack Carson; Joan Leslie; Eugene Pallette; Herbert Anderson; Hattie McDaniel; Don DeFore; ***D:*** Elliott Nugent; ***W:*** Julius J. Epstein; Philip G. Epstein; Stephen Morehouse Avery; ***C:*** Arthur Edeson; ***M:*** Heinz Roemheld.

Maleficent 🦴🦴 1/2 **2014 (PG)** Cinema's need to repurpose and reboot its most iconic characters continues in this origin story for the legendary villainess of Disney's classic Sleeping Beauty. What elevates this one from the standard children's fare is a layering of women's issues into a children's fantasy. The title character, played perfectly by Jolie, is betrayed and places a curse on her betrayer's infant daughter, Aurora. Of course, vengeance doesn't satisfy and Maleficent is torn when it seems Aurora could be the key to peace in her kingdom and her own happiness. The CGI is sloppy, but the performances and narrative are much stronger than average. **97m/C; DVD, Blu-Ray.** Angelina Jolie; Elle Fanning; Sharlto Copley; Lesley Manville; Imelda Staunton; Juno Temple; Brenton Thwaites; Sam Riley; ***D:*** Robert Stromberg; ***W:*** Linda Woolverton; ***C:*** Dean Semler; ***M:*** James Newton Howard.

Maleficent: Mistress of Evil 🦴🦴 1/2 **2019 (PG)** The human goddaughter Aurora (Fanning) of bad queen Maleficent (Jolie) is engaged to another human, Prince Phillip (Dickinson), and the couple hopes to bring together humans and magical creatures. However, Phillip's mother, Queen Ingrith (Pfeiffer) is a genocidal bigot. During the couple's engagement dinner, Ingrith takes action to incite Maleficent, which works as planned and leads to wider warfare between the two worlds. The sequel to the popular 2014 fantasy is not as entertaining despite the potential of the on-screen clash between Jolie and Pfeiffer and some of striking visuals. **118m/C; DVD, Blu-Ray.** Angelina Jolie; Elle Fanning; Harris Dickinson; Michelle Pfeiffer; Sam Riley; ***D:*** Joachim Ronning; ***W:*** Linda Woolverton; Micah Fitzerman-Blue; Noah Harpster; ***C:*** Henry Braham; ***M:*** Geoff Zanelli.

Malena 🦴🦴 **2000** Nostalgic coming of age story centered on a fantasy woman. The beautiful Malena (Bellucci) inspires lust in the men and jealousy in the women of her Sicilian village in 1940. Her husband is away fighting and, because of unjustified gossip, Malena loses her teaching job and eventually turns to prostitution to support herself. Only puberty-struck 13-year-old Renato (Sulfaro) shows any interest in her plight, which becomes worse as the war drags on. Italian with subtitles. **106m/C; VHS, DVD.** *IT* Monica Bellucci; Giuseppe Sulfaro; Luciano Federico; Matilde Piana; Pietro Notarianni; Gaetano Aronica; ***D:*** Giuseppe Tornatore; ***W:*** Giuseppe Tornatore; ***C:*** Lajos Koltai; ***M:*** Ennio Morricone.

Malevolence 🦴 **2004 (R)** Debut for writer/director Mena is a basic slasher film. There's something about a serial killer, an abducted single mom, a bank heist gone wrong, and lots of blood. Mena had to start somewhere but this effort is unmemorable at best. **90m/C; Blu-Ray, On Demand.** Samantha Dark; Brandon Johnson; Heather Magee; Richard Glover; Courtney Bertolone; John Richard Ingram; ***D:*** Stevan Mena; ***W:*** Stevan Mena; ***C:*** Tsuyashi Kimoto; ***M:*** Stevan Mena.

Malibu Beach 🦴 1/2 **1978 (R)** The California beach scene is the setting for this movie filled with bikini clad girls, tanned young men, and instant romances. For connoisseurs of the empty-headed teen beach movie. **93m/C; VHS, DVD.** Kim Lankford; James Daughton; ***D:*** Robert J. Rosenthal; ***C:*** Jamie Anderson.

The Malibu Beach Vampires **WOOF! 1991 (R)** Three unscrupulous yuppies, Congressman Teri Upstart, Col. Ollie West and Rev. Timmy Fakker, keep beautiful mistresses in their Malibu beach house. What they don't know is, the girls are all really vampires who have injected them with a serum that compels them to tell the truth! Will our "heroes" continue to dupe the American Public, or will the sexy blood suckers cause their downfall? **90m/C; VHS, DVD.** Angelyne; Becky LeBeau; Joan Rudelstein; Marcus A. Frishman; Rod Sweitzer; Francis Creighton; Anet Anatelle; Yvette Buchanan; Cherie Romaors; Kelly Galindo; ***D:*** Francis Creighton.

Malibu Express 🦴 **1985 (R)** Mystery/adventure plot about a P.I. is the excuse; babes in swimsuits is the reason for this waste of time. **101m/C; VHS, DVD, Blu-Ray.** Darby Hinton; Sybil Danning; Art Metrano; Shelley Taylor Morgan; Niki Dantine; Barbara (Lee) Edwards; ***D:*** Andy Sidaris.

Malibu High 🦴 **1979 (R)** The accidental death of a young prostitute's client leads her to a new series of illegal activities of the "sex and hit" variety. Dark, sleazy, and antisocial; belies Beach Boys-esque title. **92m/C; VHS, DVD, Blu-Ray.** Jill Lansing; Stuart Taylor; ***D:*** Irvin Berwick.

Malibu Shark Attack **WOOF! 2009** Cheap, dull, and totally stupid fare from the Syfy Channel. A tsunami hits Malibu and with it comes a pack of hungry deep-sea goblin sharks (the only unexpected bit to the flick). Lifeguards beware! **86m/C; DVD.** Evert McQueen; Chelan Simmons; Sonya Salomaa; Remi Broadway; Peta Wilson; ***D:*** David Lister; ***W:*** Keith Shaw; ***C:*** Brian J. Breheny; ***M:*** Michael Neilson. **CABLE**

Malibu's Most Wanted 🦴🦴 **2003 (PG-13)** Brad "B-Rad" Gluckman's (Kennedy) a rich white wannabe rapper from Malibu, whose dad (O'Neal) is running for governor. When he embarrasses pop at a campaign stop, dad takes drastic action. He hires black actors Sean (Diggs) and PJ (Anderson) to kidnap Brad to South Central for a little "Scared White" therapy. Since the middle class actors have no idea how to be "gangsta," they enlist the help of Sean's cousin Shondra (Hall), who promptly falls for Brad, angering her ex-boyfriend Tec (Wayans), who lives the thug life. Minimally amusing. **86m/C; DVD.** Jamie Kennedy; Taye Diggs; Anthony Anderson; Blair Underwood; Regina Hall; Ryan O'Neal; Bo Derek; Damien Dante Wayans; Jeffrey Tambor; Kal Penn; ***V:*** Snoop Dogg; ***D:*** John Whitesell; ***W:*** Jamie Kennedy; Fax Bahr; Adam Small; Nick Swardson; ***C:*** Mark Irwin; ***M:*** John Van Tongeren; Damon Elliott.

Malice 🦴🦴 1/2 **1993 (R)** In a sleepy little college town, strange things sure do happen. Too bad rumpled college dean Andy Safian (Pullman) didn't see "Pacific Heights." If he did, he would know that sometimes roommates are more trouble than they're worth, even if renovation on that old Victorian is getting expensive. Routine thriller throws out an inventive twist to keep things moving, but manages to be fairly predictable anyway. **107m/C; VHS, DVD, Blu-Ray.** Alec Baldwin; Nicole Kidman; Bill Pullman; Bebe Neuwirth; Anne Bancroft; George C. Scott; Peter Gallagher; Josef Sommer; Gwyneth Paltrow; ***D:*** Harold Becker; ***W:*** Aaron Sorkin; Scott Frank; ***C:*** Gordon Willis; ***M:*** Jerry Goldsmith.

Malice in Wonderland 🦴🦴 **2009 (R)** Down the rabbit hole indeed in this modern update of Lewis Carroll's "Alice in Wonderland" set in a nighttime London. American Alice (Grace) gets knocked down by always-late Whitey's (Dyer) cab and finds herself with amnesia. Whitey's got a job to do for gangster Harry Hunt (Parker) so he doesn't have time to worry about helping Alice out until he discovers her wealthy family is offering money for her return. They have some adventures with underworld types who sort of correspond to Carroll's characters. **87m/C; DVD.** *UK* Maggie Grace; Danny Dyer; Matt King; Nathaniel Parker; Bronagh Gallagher; Anthony (Corlan) Higgins; ***D:*** Simon Fellows; ***W:*** Jayson Rothwell; ***C:*** Christopher Ross; ***M:*** Christian Henson.

Malicious Intent 🦴 1/2 *Civility* **1999** Young man returns home for his father's funeral and learns that he was murdered. So he gets together with some of his father's buddies on a plan for revenge—and money. **86m/C; VHS, DVD.** Zack (Zach) Ward; Tom Arnold; William Forsythe; Rachel Ticotin; Clarence Williams, III; Ed Lauter; Liam Waite; Christopher Atkins; *D:* Caesar Cavaricci; *W:* Caesar Cavaricci. **VIDEO**

Mallrats 1/2 **1995 (R)** Smith's better-financed follow-up to the legendary "Clerks" follows Jersey slackers T.S. (London) and Brodie (Lee) to the mall, where they intend to wallow in food-court cookies and reclaim their girlfriends, who recently dumped them. While wandering the mall in low-key and confused pursuit of their women and self respect, they encounter the usual band of bizarre inhabitants, including Silent Bob (Smith) and stoner Jay (Mewes). Dialogue and sight gags are director/writer Smith's strong point; moving the plot forward is not high on the priority list. **95m/C; DVD, Blu-Ray, HD-DVD.** Jeremy London; Jason Lee; Shannen Doherty; Claire Forlani; Kevin Smith; Michael Rooker; Priscilla Barnes; Renee Humphrey; Ben Affleck; Joey Lauren Adams; Jason Mewes; Brian O'Halloran; David Brinkley; Art James; Ethan Suplee; Sven-Ole Thorsen; *Cameo(s):* Stan Lee; *D:* Kevin Smith; *W:* Kevin Smith; *C:* David Klein; *M:* Ira Newborn.

Malone 1/2 **1987 (R)** A burnt-out secret agent stumbles into a real-estate swindle/murder plot in Oregon and sets out to stop it. Film tries hard but doesn't succeed in being believable. **92m/C; VHS, DVD, Blu-Ray.** Burt Reynolds; Lauren Hutton; Cliff Robertson; Kenneth McMillan; Scott Wilson; Cynthia Gibb; *D:* Harley Cokliss; *M:* David Newman.

Malta Story 1/2 **1953** A British WWII flier (Guiness) becomes involved with the defense of Malta, as well as a Maltese lovely. The romance is shoehorned into the ultra-patriotic action, not always smoothly. **103m/B; VHS, DVD.** Alec Guinness; Jack Hawkins; Anthony Steel; Flora Robson; Muriel Pavlow; *D:* Brian Desmond Hurst.

The Maltese Falcon *Dangerous Female* **1931** A good first screen version of the Dashiell Hammett story about private detective Sam Spade's search for the elusive Black Bird. Remade five years later as "Satan Met a Lady" with Bette Davis. Its most famous remake, however, occurred in 1941 with Humphrey Bogart in the lead. **80m/B; VHS, DVD.** Bebe Daniels; Ricardo Cortez; Dudley Digges; Thelma Todd; Una Merkel; Dwight Frye; Robert Elliott; *D:* Roy Del Ruth.

The Maltese Falcon **1941** After the death of his partner, detective Sam Spade (Bogart) finds himself enmeshed in a complicated, intriguing search for a priceless statuette. "It's the stuff dreams are made of," says Bogart of the Falcon. Excellent, fast-paced film noir with outstanding performances, great dialogue, and concentrated attention to details. Director Huston's first film and Greenstreet's talky debut. First of several films starring Bogart and Astor. Based on the novel by Dashiell Hammett. Also available colorized. **101m/B; VHS, DVD, Blu-Ray.** Humphrey Bogart; Mary Astor; Peter Lorre; Sydney Greenstreet; Ward Bond; Barton MacLane; Gladys George; Lee Patrick; Elisha Cook, Jr.; Jerome Cowan; Walter Huston; *D:* John Huston; *W:* John Huston; *C:* Arthur Edeson; *M:* Adolph Deutsch. AFI '98: Top 100; Natl. Film Reg. '89.

Mama **2013 (PG-13)** Two young girls have been abandoned in a forest cabin and living on their own. Or have they? Annabel (Chastain) and Lucas (Coster-Waldau) find his nieces and take them home to care for them. But they bring back something malevolent that is trying to protect its daughters. Some of the plot twists are contrived and clichéd but the scares are real, thanks in no small part to another great turn by Chastain. The Guillermo Del Toro-produced horror flick proves that PG-13 horror is not dead if a talented director can work with atmosphere instead of just gore. **100m/C; DVD, Blu-Ray.** Jessica Chastain; Nikolaj Coster-Waldau; Megan Charpentier; Isabelle Nelisse; Daniel Kash; Javier Botet; Jane Moffat; *D:* Andres Muschietti; *W:* Andres Muschietti; Neil Cross; Barbara Muschietti; *C:* Antonio Riestra; *M:* Fernando Velazquez.

Mama Africa 1/2 **2002** Three segments, directed by three different African filmmakers, with authoritative introductions by Queen Latifah. All three tales involve young, poverty-stricken Africans facing difficult moral choices. In two, young, single mothers Raya and Uno take up with questionable men for love or money and find themselves tempted to enter their criminal worlds. In director Onwurah's modern-day fable, young Nigerian Kwame desperately needs $100 to buy a pair of basketball sneakers for a tryout with an American scout and is enticed by a slimy gangster to get what he needs. Fine performances and a refreshing lack of melodrama or moralizing. **89m/C; DVD.** Rehane Abrahams; Damien Chamley; Ivan Lucas; Oscar Petersen; Denise Newman; Hyppolite Ouangrawa; Alima Salouka; Cindy Sampson; Graham Weir; *D:* Fanta Regina Nacro; Zulfar Otto-Sallies; Ingrid Sinclair.

Mama Dracula WOOF! **1980** Fletcher stars in this poor satire of the horror genre. She's a vampire who needs the blood of virgins to stay young. Her son helps out—what good son wouldn't? **90m/C; VHS, DVD.** *FR* Louise Fletcher; Bonnie Schneider; Maria Schneider; Marc-Henri Wajnberg; Alexander Wajnberg; Jess Hahn; *D:* Boris Szulzinger.

Mama Flora's Family 1/2 **1998** Based on the novel by Alex Haley, which was finished by co-author Stevens after Haley's 1992 death. Loosely based on Haley's mother, Mama Flora (Tyson) endures one tragedy after another while raising her family. First, as a teenaged servant, Flora gets pregnant and is forced to give the child up. Then when she does marry, her husband is killed and their property burned. Meanwhile, her other children and grandchildren struggle with discrimination and grow up angry and resentful. Holds together because of the force of Tyson's portrayal. **175m/C; VHS, DVD.** Cicely Tyson; Mario Van Peebles; Blair Underwood; Queen Latifah; Hill Harper; Shemar Moore; Della Reese; *D:* Peter Werner; *W:* David Stevens; Carol Schreder; *C:* Neil Roach. **TV**

Mama's Boy WOOF! **2007 (PG-13)** Jeffrey (Heder) is a 29-year-old slacker who's happy living with his mom Jan (Keaton). But his free ride is threatened when mom announces she's marrying her boyfriend Mert (Daniels). So Jeffrey enlists aspiring singer Nora (Faris) to help him dislodge Mert from his mom's life and—horrors!?grows up in the process. Heder's indifferent portrayal of his irredeemably shelfish character is only the most obvious of many problems with this unfunny mess. Watch it with "Step Brothers" and weep for the future—and the present. **93m/C; DVD.** Jon Heder; Diane Keaton; Jeff Daniels; Anna Faris; Dorian Missick; Sarah Chalke; Eli Wallach; Mary Kay Place; Laura Kightlinger; Simon Helberg; *D:* Tim Hamilton; *W:* Hank Nelken; *C:* Jonathan Brown; *M:* Mark Mothersbaugh.

Mambo 1/2 **1955** A poor young dancer inspires patronage and lust by dancing the Mambo. Although attracted to Gassman, she marries Rennie for his money. Technically weak but artistically interesting, though Rennie and Mangano have done their roles somewhat better elsewhere. **94m/B; VHS, DVD.** Silvana Mangano; Michael Rennie; Vittorio Gassman; Shelley Winters; Katherine Dunham; Mary Clare; Eduardo Ciannelli; *D:* Robert Rossen; *M:* Nino Rota.

Mambo Cafe **2000 (PG-13)** Low-budget mob comedy with a quirky premise. The Mambo Cafe is a Spanish Harlem restaurant in dire need of some business. So the owners invite a local mobster to dine at their establishment in hopes he'll be murdered and they'll get a boost from the publicity. He is, business improves, but the restaurant and the family also draw unwelcome Mob scrutiny. **98m/C; VHS, DVD.** Paul Rodriguez; Rosanna Desoto; Danny Aiello; Thalia; Kamar De Los Reyes; *D:* Reuben Gonzalez; *W:* Reuben Gonzalez. **VIDEO**

Mambo Italiano **2003 (R)** Broad, ethnic romantic comedy that could be titled "My Big Gay Italian/Canadian Wedding." Angelo Barberini's (Kirby) a 30-year-old nice Italian boy still living with his parents in Montreal's version of Little Italy> He he falls for childhood bully Nino (Miller), now a cop and secretly also gay. The two begin a clandestine relationship and move in together while both families unsuccessfully begin a whirlwind of last-ditch matchmaking activities. A pleasant turn by lead Kirby highlights this good-natured yet technically simple comedy where most of the performances, and accents, are uneven. **99m/C; DVD.** *CA* Luke Kirby; Ginette Reno; Paul Sorvino; Claudia Ferri; Peter Miller; Mary Walsh; Sophie Lorain; Tim Post; Lisa Bronwyn Moore; *D:* Emile Gaudreault; *W:* Emile Gaudreault; Steve Galluccio; *C:* Serge Ladouceur.

The Mambo Kings **1992 (R)** Armand and Banderas (in his first English speaking role) are Cesar and Nestor Castillo, two brothers who flee Cuba for New York City with dreams of hitting it big with their mambo music. Desi Arnaz Jr. gets to play his own dad in a funny and technical scene that leads to a climactic confrontation between the brothers. Good cast and great music make this one worthwhile. Based on the Pulitzer prizewinning novel "The Mambo Kings Play Songs of Love" by Oscar Hijuelos. **100m/C; VHS, DVD.** Armand Assante; Antonio Banderas; Cathy Moriarty; Maruschka Detmers; Desi Arnaz, Jr.; Celia Cruz; Roscoe Lee Browne; Vondie Curtis-Hall; Tito Puente; Talisa Soto; *D:* Arne Glimcher; *W:* Cynthia Cidre; *C:* Michael Ballhaus; *M:* Robert Kraft; Carlos Franzetti.

Mame **1974 (PG)** In an adaptation of the Broadway musical "Auntie Mame" by Jerry Herman, Ball plays a dynamic woman who takes it upon herself to teach a group of eccentrics how to live life to the fullest. Arthur plays Mame's friend just as splendidly as she did in the Broadway version, but Ball in her last feature film is a lame Mame. Overly ambitious production avoids reaching goal. **132m/C; VHS, DVD, Blu-Ray.** Lucille Ball; Bea Arthur; Robert Preston; Joyce Van Patten; Bruce Davison; Jane Connell; Doria Cook; Don Porter; Audrey Christie; John McGiver; Patrick Labyorteaux; Lucille Benson; Burt Mustin; Barbara Bosson; *D:* Gene Saks; *W:* Paul Zindel; *C:* Philip H. Lathrop; *M:* Jerry Herman.

Mamma Mia! 1/2 **2008 (PG-13)** Tunes from Swedish '70s popsters ABBA provide the backdrop for this harmless romp, a 2001 Broadway-musical-turned-film. Sophie (Seyfried) and mom Donna (Streep) run an inn on a gorgeous Greek island and are preparing for Sophie's wedding. Sophie wants her dad, whom she's never known, to show, so she invites three of Donna's long-ago summer flings (Firth, Brosnan, and Skarsgard), which throws mom for a loop and makes for all sorts of romance, hijinks, and lavish musical numbers over the wedding weekend. Baranski steals scenes as Donna's friend, Tanya. **108m/C; Blu-Ray, On Demand.** *US GB* Meryl Streep; Pierce Brosnan; Colin Firth; Amanda Seyfried; Stellan Skarsgard; Julie Walters; Christine Baranski; Dominic Cooper; *D:* Phyllida Lloyd; *W:* Catherine Johnson; *C:* Haris Zambarloukos; *M:* Benny Andersson; Bjorn Ulvaes; Stig Anderson. Golden Raspberries '08: Worst Support. Actor (Brosnan).

Mamma Mia! Here We Go Again 1/2 **2018 (PG-13)** In this sequel to Mamma Mia!, a pregnant Sophie learns about her mother's past through flashbacks. More of the same folks singing ABBA songs, which will undoubtedly bring joy to fans of the original. But, beware, Streep is but a shadow in this one...though Cher makes a grand entrance later in the movie. **114m/C; Blu-Ray.** *US UK GE* Meryl Streep; Pierce Brosnan; Colin Firth; Stellan Skarsgard; Amanda Seyfried; *D:* Ol Parker; *W:* Ol Parker; Richard Curtis; Catherine Johnson; *C:* Robert Yeoman; *M:* Benny Andersson; Anne Dudley; Björn Ulvaeus.

Mamma Roma 1/2 **1962** Pasolini's second film is a heartbreaking story of family ties, escaping the past, and dreams of the future. The title character (Magnani) is a former prostitute who attempts respectability for herself and her teenaged son (Garofolo). But her ex-pimp (Citti) threatens her new life and Rome's big-city temptations prove to be a pathway to crime and tragedy for the boy. Magnani gives one of her finest performances. Italian with subtitles. **110m/B; VHS, DVD.** *IT* Anna Magnani; Ettore Garofolo; Franco Citti; Silvana Corsini; Luisa Loiano; *D:* Pier Paolo Pasolini; *W:* Pier Paolo Pasolini; *C:* Tonino Delli Colli.

Mammoth **2006** Frank Abernathy (Ventresca) is the curator of a natural history museum in Blackwood, Louisiana. When a meteor hits the building, it thaws the ice-encased star attraction. That would be a mammoth that can suck the life out of people with its trunk when it's not stomping on 'em. Unfortunately, the pic's tone varies from goofy to banal to gross, which diminishes it's cheese factor. A Sci-Fi Channel original. **90m/C; DVD.** Vincent Ventresca; Summer Glau; Leila Arcieri; Tom Skerritt; Cole Williams; Marcus Lyle Brown; Charles Carroll; *D:* Tim Cox; *W:* Sean Keller; Tim Cox; Brook Durham; *C:* Bing Sokolsky; *M:* John Dickson. **CABLE**

Mammoth 1/2 **2009** First English-language film from Moodysson is a repetitive narrative about three sets of working parents. Naturally the Americans, Ellen (Williams) and Leo (Garcia Bernal), are wealthy and shallow (yawn) whose daughter is cared for by their live-in Filipino nanny, Gloria (Necesito). Gloria's own young sons (who live in Manila) lay a guilt trip on mom for being away. Then, when Leo travels to Thailand for business, he meets bargirl Cookie (Srinikornchot), who's another working mom using the sex industry to support her own baby. Title refers to a very expensive pen made from woolly mammoth ivory. **125m/C; DVD, On Demand.** *DK GE SW* Gael Garcia Bernal; Michelle Williams; Thomas (Tom) McCarthy; Maria del Carmen; Marife Necesito; Sophie Nyweide; Run Srinikornchot; Jan Nicdao; Martin Delos Santos; *D:* Lukas Moodysson; *W:* Lukas Moodysson; *C:* Marcel Zyskind; *M:* Jesper Kurlandsky; Linus Gierta; Erik Holmquist.

Mammuth **2010** Absurd French satire with Depardieu resembling a hairy mammoth although the title refers to a 1973 Munch Mammut motorcycle. Newly-retired, working-class Serge learns he won't get his full pension benefits because former employers didn't do the required paperwork. He hits the road on his motorcycle to get things straightened out. Serge also has a sometime companion on his journey—his dead-but-chatty first love Yasmine, who died in a motorcycle accident. French with subtitles. **91m/C; DVD.** *FR* Gerard Depardieu; Isabelle Adjani; Yolande Moreau; *D:* Benoit Delepine; Gustave Kervern; *W:* Benoit Delepine; Gustave Kervern; *C:* Hughes Poulain; *M:* Gaetan Roussel.

The Man **2005 (PG-13)** Andy Fiddler (Levy) an eccentrically nerdy dental-supply salesman from Milwaukee, travels to Detroit for a convention where some illegal arms-dealing crooks mistake him for hard-boiled ATF agent, Derrick Vann (Jackson). Andy gets drawn into the crime-busting plot. Jackson and Levy deliver exactly what you expect in this old school kooky crime buster, but nothing more in this seen-it-done-better-elsewhere attempt at mismatched buddy comedy. **79m/C; DVD.** Samuel L. Jackson; Eugene Levy; Luke Goss; Miguel Ferrer; Anthony Mackie; Horatio Sanz; Rachael Crawford; Susie Essman; Tomorrow Baldwin; *D:* Les Mayfield; *W:* Jim Piddock; Margaret Grieco Oberman; Stephen Carpenter; *C:* Adam Kane; *M:* John Murphy; Dana Sano.

A Man, a Woman, and a Bank 1/2 *A Very Big Weekend* **1979 (PG)** Two con-men plan to rob a bank by posing as workers during the bank's construction. An advertising agency woman snaps their picture for a billboard to show how nice the builders have been, then becomes romantically involved with one of the would-be thieves. Nice performances, but wacky touches aren't plentiful enough or well timed to sustain comedy. **100m/C; VHS, DVD, Blu-Ray.** *CA* Donald Sutherland; Brooke Adams; Paul Mazursky; *D:* Noel Black; *W:* Bruce A. Evans; Raynold Gideon; *C:* Jack Cardiff; *M:* Bill Conti.

A Man About the House 1/2 **1947** Two unmarried English sisters move into the Italian villa they have inherited. There, one marries the caretaker, who secretly plans to regain the property that once belonged to his family. When the newly married sister is found dead, her sibling sets out to solve the murder. **83m/B; VHS, DVD, Streaming.** *GB* Kieron Moore; Margaret Johnston; Dulcie Gray; Guy Middleton; Felix Aylmer; *D:* Leslie Arliss.

A Man and a Woman *Un Homme et Un Femme* **1966** When a man and a woman, both widowed, meet and become interested in one another but experience difficulties in putting their past loves behind them. Intelligently handled emotional conflicts within a well-acted romantic drama, acclaimed for excellent visual detail. Remade in 1977 as "Another Man, Another Chance." Followed in 1986 with "A Man and A Woman:

20 Years Later." Dubbed. **102m/C; VHS, DVD.** *FR* Anouk Aimee; Jean-Louis Trintignant; Pierre Barouh; Valerie Lagrange; ***D:*** Claude Lelouch; ***W:*** Claude Lelouch; Pierre Uytterhoeven; ***C:*** Claude Lelouch; ***M:*** Francis Lai. Oscars '66: Foreign Film, Story & Screenplay; British Acad. '67: Actress (Aimee); Cannes '66: Film; Golden Globes '67: Actress--Drama (Aimee), Foreign Film.

A Man and a Woman: 20 Years Later 🦴 1/2 *Un Homme et Une Femme: Vingt Ans Deja* **1986 (PG)** Slouchy sequel to the highly praised "A Man and a Woman" that catches up with a couple after a long separation. The sad romantic complications of the original are more mundane in this sequel, which is burdened by a film-within-a-film script as well as shots from the original. In French with English subtitles. **112m/C; VHS, DVD.** *FR* Jean-Louis Trintignant; Anouk Aimee; Richard Berry; ***D:*** Claude Lelouch; ***W:*** Claude Lelouch.

Man & Boy 🦴🦴 *Ride a Dark Horse* **1971 (G)** A black Civil War veteran, played by Bill Cosby, encounters bigotry and prejudice when he tries to set up a homestead in Arizona. An acceptable family film, some might be disappointed that Cosby is not playing this one for laughs. **98m/C; VHS, DVD.** Bill Cosby; Gloria Foster; George Spell; Henry Silva; Yaphet Kotto; ***D:*** E.W. Swackhamer; ***M:*** Quincy Jones.

The Man and the Monster 🦴 1/2 **1965** When a concert pianist sells his soul to the devil, he fails to realize that part of the deal has him turning into a hideous beast every time he hears a certain piece of music. Maybe it was "Stairway to Heaven." **78m/B; VHS, DVD.** *MX* Enrique Rambal; Abel Salazar; Martha Roth; ***D:*** Rafael Baledon, Sr.

A Man Apart 🦴🦴 **2003 (R)** DEA agent Sean Vetter (Diesel) and his partner Hicks (Tate) close a seven-year case by busting cartel head Lucero (Silva). Then Vetter's wife is killed on the orders of the supposedly-defunct cartel's new ruler, El Diablo. Vetter goes into full revenge mode, and all semblence of restraint is eliminated with no cliche (or pyrotechic equipment) unused as Vetter and Diablo careen toward the inevitable showdown. As you might expect, it all looks really cool and stuff gets blowed up real good. **114m/C; DVD, Blu-Ray.** Vin Diesel; Larenz Tate; Timothy Olyphant; Geno Silva; Jacqueline Obradors; Steve Eastin; Juan Fernandez; Jeff Kober; George Shaperson; ***D:*** F. Gary Gray; ***W:*** Christian Gudegast; Paul Scheuring; ***C:*** Jack N. Green; ***M:*** Anne Dudley.

Man Bait 🦴🦴 1/2 *The Last Page* **1952** A complex web of intrigue and mystery surrounds a blackmailed book dealer when he allows a blonde woman to catch his eye. A competently made film. **78m/B; DVD.** *UK* George Brent; Marguerite Chapman; Diana Dors; Raymond Huntley; ***D:*** Terence Fisher; ***W:*** Frederick Knott; ***C:*** Walter J. (Jimmy W.) Harvey; ***M:*** Frank Spencer.

Man Bites Dog 🦴🦴 *C'est Arrive pres de Chez Vous* **1991 (NC-17)** A pseudo-documentary about a serial killer, filled with ever-mounting violence. Ben is the killer being followed by a two-man camera/sound crew (which he's hired), who record his casual carnage without lifting a finger to stop him. Indeed his continued killing and robbing is to pay for financing the documentary about himself. This satire on film violence, as well as reality-based TV shows, is both appalling and humorous in a sick way. French with English subtitles. Also available in an unrated edited version. **95m/B; VHS, DVD.** *BE* Benoit Poelvoorde; Remy Belvaux; Andre Bonzel; Vincent Tavier; Jean-Marc Chenut; ***D:*** Benoit Poelvoorde; Remy Belvaux; Andre Bonzel; ***W:*** Benoit Poelvoorde; Remy Belvaux; Andre Bonzel; Vincent Tavier; ***C:*** Andre Bonzel; ***M:*** Jean-Marc Chenut; Laurence Dufrene.

A Man Called Adam 🦴 1/2 **1966** A jazz musician is tortured by prejudice and the guilt created by his having accidentally killed his wife and baby years before. Davis is appropriately haunted, but the film is poorly produced. **103m/B; VHS, DVD.** Sammy Davis, Jr.; Louis Armstrong; Ossie Davis; Cicely Tyson; Frank Sinatra, Jr.; Lola Falana; Mel Torme; Peter Lawford; ***D:*** Leo Penn; ***C:*** Jack Priestley.

A Man Called Horse 🦴🦴🦴 **1970 (PG)** After a wealthy Britisher is captured and tortured by the Sioux Indians in the Dakotas, he abandons his formal ways and discovers his own strength. As he passes their torture tests, he is embraced by the tribe. In this very realistic and gripping portrayal of American Indian life, Harris provides a strong performance. Sequelled by "Return of a Man Called Horse" (1976) and "Triumphs of a Man Called Horse" (1983). **114m/C; VHS, DVD, Blu-Ray.** Richard Harris; Judith Anderson; Jean Gascon; Stanford Howard; Manu Tupou; Dub Taylor; ***D:*** Elliot Silverstein; ***W:*** Jack DeWitt; ***C:*** Robert B. Hauser.

A Man Called Ove 🦴🦴🦴 *En man som heter Ove* **2015 (PG-13)** Ove (Rolf Lassgard) is a bitter old man who has all but decided to end his life. His beloved wife is dead, he's been deposed as president of his condo association, and the new neighbors have crushed his mailbox. His plucky new neighbor, however, may convince him to renew his interest in life. Based on the best selling novel by Fredrik Backman. **116m/C; DVD, Blu-Ray, Streaming.** *SW* Rolf Lassgard; Bahar Pars; ***D:*** Hannes Holm; ***W:*** Hannes Holm; ***C:*** Goran Hallberg; ***M:*** Gaute Storaas.

A Man Called Peter 🦴🦴🦴 **1955** A biographical epic about Peter Marshall, a Scottish chaplain who served the U.S. Senate. Todd does his subject justice by sensitively showing all that was human in Marshall, and a talented supporting cast makes for a thoroughly watchable film. **119m/C; VHS, DVD, Blu-Ray.** Richard Todd; Jean Peters; Marjorie Rambeau; Jill Esmond; Les Tremayne; Robert Burton; ***D:*** Henry Koster.

A Man Called Sarge 🦴 1/2 **1990 (PG-13)** Sophomoric comedy about a daffy WWII sergeant leading his squad against the Germans at Tobruk. **88m/C; VHS, Streaming.** Gary Kroeger; Marc Singer; Gretchen German; Jennifer Runyon; Bobby DiCicco; ***D:*** Stuart Gillard.

A Man Called Sledge 🦴🦴 **1971** Garner fans might be surprised to see the star play a villain in this violent story of a gang of outlaws who wind up fighting each over a cache of gold. This is mainstream Western entertainment. **93m/C; VHS, DVD.** James Garner; Dennis Weaver; Claude Akins; John Marley; Laura Antonelli; Angelo Infanti; ***D:*** Vic Morrow.

Man Down 🦴 1/2 **2016 (R)** U.S. Marine Gabriel (LaBeouf) returns home from Afghanistan a shattered man. Flanked by his buddy Devin (Courtney), they travel across a wasteland of post-apocalyptic America, in search of his estranged son and wife. The film jumps back and forth to the soldier's time in basic training, in combat, and back at home, revealing piece by piece what happened to him and the country. Writer/director Montiel's drama is a cheap exploitation device that uses PTSD for a twisty mystery and totally wastes a solid performance from LaBeouf. It's a defiantly silly piece of nonsense. **92m/C; DVD, Blu-Ray.** Shia LaBeouf; Jai Courtney; Gary Oldman; Kate Mara; Tory Kittles; ***D:*** Dito Montiel; ***W:*** Dito Montiel; Adam G. Simon; ***C:*** Shelly Johnson; ***M:*** Clint Mansell.

A Man Escaped 🦴🦴🦴 1/2 *Un Condamne a Mort s'est Echappe, Ou le Vent Souffle ou il Vent; A Man Escaped, or the Wind Bloweth Where It Listeth; A Condemned Man Has Escaped* **1957** There's an excruciating realism about Bresson's account of a WWII Resistance fighter's escape from a Nazi prison just before he's to be executed by the Gestapo. It's the sounds and lingering camera shots, not the wham bam variety of action, that create and sustain the film's suspense. Bresson, who had been a Nazi prisoner, solicited the supervision of Andre Devigny, whose true story the film tells. Contributing to the realistic feel is the use of non-professional actors. French with subtitles. **102m/B; DVD, Blu-Ray.** Francois Leterrier; Charles Le Clainche; Roland Monod; Maurice Beerblock; Jacques Ertaud; Jean-Paul Delhumeau; Roger Treherne; Jean-Philippe Delamarre; Cesar Gattegno; Jacques Oerlemans; Klaus Detlef Grevenhorst; Leonard Schmidt; ***D:*** Robert Bresson; ***W:*** Robert Bresson; ***C:*** Leonce-Henri Burel. Cannes '57: Director (Bresson).

A Man for All Seasons 🦴🦴🦴🦴 **1966 (G)** Sterling, heavily Oscar-honored biographical drama concerning the life and subsequent martyrdom of 16th-century Chancellor of England, Sir Thomas More (Scofield). Story revolves around his personal conflict when King Henry VIII (Shaw) seeks a divorce from his wife, Catherine of Aragon, so he can wed his mistress, Anne Boleyn—events that ultimately lead the King to bolt from the Pope and declare himself head of the Church of England. Remade for TV in 1988 with Charlton Heston in the lead role. **120m/C; VHS, DVD, Blu-Ray.** *GB* Paul Scofield; Robert Shaw; Orson Welles; Wendy Hiller; Susannah York; John Hurt; Nigel Davenport; Vanessa Redgrave; ***D:*** Fred Zinnemann; ***W:*** Constance Willis; Robert Bolt; ***C:*** Ted Moore; ***M:*** Georges Delerue. Oscars '66: Actor (Scofield), Adapt. Screenplay, Color Cinematog., Costume Des. (C), Director (Zinnemann), Film; British Acad. '67: Actor (Scofield), Film, Screenplay; Directors Guild '66: Director (Zinnemann); Golden Globes '67: Actor--Drama (Scofield), Director (Zinnemann), Film--Drama, Screenplay; Natl. Bd. of Review '66: Actor (Scofield), Director (Zinnemann), Support. Actor (Shaw); N.Y. Film Critics '66: Actor (Scofield), Director (Zinnemann), Film, Screenplay.

A Man for All Seasons 🦴🦴🦴 **1988** Fresh from the London stage, Heston directs and stars in this version of Robert Bolt's play depicting the conflict between Henry VIII and his chief advisor, Sir Thomas More. Strong supporting cast. **150m/C; VHS, DVD.** Charlton Heston; Vanessa Redgrave; John Gielgud; Richard Johnson; Roy Kinnear; Martin Chamberlain; ***D:*** Charlton Heston. **CABLE**

Man Friday 🦴🦴 **1975 (PG)** Stranded on a deserted island, a man forces a native from a neighboring island to be his slave. Based on the classic story "Robinson Crusoe" by Daniel Defoe, this adaptation charts the often-brutal treatment the native receives as his captor tries to civilize him. Through his intelligence, the enslaved man regains his freedom and returns home with his former captor, who then seeks acceptance from the native's tribe. A sometimes confusing storyline and excessive blood and guts detract from this message-laden effort. **115m/C; VHS, DVD, Blu-Ray.** *GB* Peter O'Toole; Richard Roundtree; Peter Cellier; Christopher Cabot; Joel Fluellen; ***D:*** Jack Gold; ***M:*** Carl Davis.

Man from Button Willow 🦴🦴 **1965 (G)** Classic animated adventure is the story of Justin Eagle, a man who leads a double life. He is a respected rancher and a shrewd secret agent for the government, but in 1869 he suddenly finds himself the guardian of a four-year-old Oriental girl, leading him into a whole new series of adventures. Strictly for younger audiences. **79m/C; VHS, DVD.** ***V:*** Dale Robertson; Edgar Buchanan; Barbara Jean Wong; Howard Keel; ***M:*** George Bruns.

Man from Cairo 🦴🦴 **1954** An American in Algiers is mistaken for a detective in search of gold lost during WWII and decides to play along. **82m/B; VHS, DVD.** *IT* George Raft; Gianna Maria Canale; ***D:*** Ray Enright.

Man from Colorado 🦴🦴 1/2 **1949** An odd Technicolor western about two Civil War vets at odds, one an honest marshall, the other a sadistic judge. Solid Western fare with a quirky performance by Ford. **99m/C; VHS, DVD.** William Holden; Glenn Ford; Ellen Drew; Ray Collins; Edgar Buchanan; Jerome Courtland; James Millican; Jim Bannon; ***D:*** Henry Levin; ***M:*** George Duning.

Man from Del Rio 🦴🦴 **1956** Mexican gunfighter Robles (Quinn) is proud to be hired as the new sheriff until he learns it's because he's quick on the trigger. Shifty saloon owner Bannister (Whitney) thinks he can use Robles to take over the town but the new lawman actually wants to do a good job. **82m/B; DVD.** Anthony Quinn; Peter Whitney; Katy Jurado; Douglas Fowley; John Larch; Whit Bissell; Guinn "Big Boy" Williams; ***D:*** Harry Horner; ***W:*** Richard Carr; ***C:*** Stanley Cortez; ***M:*** Fred Steiner.

The Man from Earth 🦴🦴 1/2 *Jerome Bixby's Man from Earth* **2007** College professor John Oldman (Smith) gathers his most trusted colleagues at a remote cabin to inform them that he's actual an immortal who has been evolving since the Cro-Magnon age. So is he telling the truth or just nuts? Low-key, speculative fiction from classic sci-fi writer Bixby. Falls apart at the end but until then it's an interesting look at belief. **90m/C; DVD, Blu-Ray.** David Lee Smith; John Billingsley; Richard Riehle; Tony Todd; William Katt; Ellen Crawford; Annika Peterson; Alexis Thorpe; ***D:*** Richard Schenkman; ***W:*** Jerome Bixby; ***C:*** Afshin Shahidi. **VIDEO**

The Man from Elysian Fields 🦴🦴🦴 **2001 (R)** Failing novelist Byron's (Garcia) having trouble supporting his family. At his lowest, Byron meets dapper escort service operator Luther (Jagger), who offers him work as a highly paid gigolo. Hiding his new job from his wife (Margulies), Byron begins seeing Andrea (Williams), the wife of his literary hero Tobias Alcott (Coburn). The agreeable Tobias soon begins asking Byron for help on his novel, which he believes will be his swan song. Meanwhile, Luther is having his own complications with a client (Huston) with whom he has fallen in love. An offbeat look at seduction, betrayal and forgiveness. **106m/C; DVD.** Andy Garcia; Mick Jagger; Julianna Margulies; Olivia Williams; James Coburn; Anjelica Huston; Michael Des Barres; Richard Bradford; ***D:*** George Hickenlooper; ***W:*** Jayson Philip Lasker; ***C:*** Kramer Morgenthau; ***M:*** Anthony Marinelli.

Man From God's Country 🦴 1/2 **1958** Uninvolving western. Gunslinging ex-sheriff Dan Beattie (Montgomery) heads to lawless Sundown to join his friend Curt (Peters) but is mistaken for a railroad agent after he arrives. Businessman Beau Santee (Wilcox) wants to keep the railroad out and has his thugs try to get rid of Beattie. **72m/C; DVD.** George Montgomery; Randy Stuart; House Peters, Jr.; Frank Wilcox; Gregg Barton; Kim Charney; Susan Cummings; James J. Griffith; ***D:*** Paul Landres; ***W:*** George Waggner; ***C:*** Harry Neumann; ***M:*** Marlin Skiles.

The Man from Laramie 🦴🦴🦴 1/2 **1955** Aging ranch baron Alec Waggoman (Crisp), who is going blind, worries about which of his two sons he will leave the ranch to. Into this tension-filled familial atmosphere rides Lockhart (Stewart), a cow-herder obsessed with hunting down the men who sold guns to the Indians that killed his brother. Needless to say, the tension increases. Tough, surprisingly brutal western, the best of the classic Stewart-Mann films. **104m/B; VHS, DVD, Blu-Ray.** James Stewart; Arthur Kennedy; Donald Crisp; Alex Nicol; Cathy O'Donnell; Aline MacMahon; Wallace Ford; Jack Elam; ***D:*** Anthony Mann; ***W:*** Philip Yordan; ***C:*** Charles B(ryant) Lang, Jr.; ***M:*** George Duning.

The Man from Left Field 🦴 1/2 **1993** Homeless man winds up coaching a little league baseball team, inspiring the kids, and turning his life around. Made for TV. **96m/C; VHS, DVD.** Burt Reynolds; Reba McEntire; ***D:*** Burt Reynolds; ***M:*** Bobby Goldsboro. **TV**

The Man from Planet X 🦴🦴 **1951** Making a belated arrival on home video is this prototypical low-budget first-contact tale. All the elements are there—reporter, aging scientist, his nubile daughter, crafty associate—but the setting is Scotland. Not that it matters, because virtually all of the action takes place on sets. **71m/B; DVD, Blu-Ray.** Robert Clarke; Margaret Field; William Schallert; ***D:*** Edgar G. Ulmer; ***W:*** Aubrey Wisberg; Jack Pollexfen; ***C:*** John L. "Jack" Russell; ***M:*** Charles Koff.

The Man from Snowy River 🦴🦴 1/2 **1982 (PG)** Stunning cinematography highlights this otherwise fairly ordinary adventure story set in 1880s Australia. Jim Craig (Burlinson) is an orphaned young man coming of age in the mountains while seeking a life of his own and falling in love with the well-brought up Jessica (Thornton). In a dual role, Douglas portrays battling brothers, one a rich landowner and the other a one-legged prospector. A wild horse roundup is a stunning highlight. Based on the epic poem by A.B. "Banjo" Paterson and followed by "Return to Snowy River." A big hit in Australia and not directed by "Mad Max's" Miller, but another Miller named George. **104m/C; VHS, DVD.** *AU* Kirk Douglas; Tom Burlinson; Sigrid Thornton; Terence Donovan; Tommy Dysart; Jack Thompson; Bruce Kerr; ***D:*** George Miller; ***W:*** Fred Cullen; John Dixon; ***C:*** Keith Wagstaff; ***M:*** Bruce Rowland.

Man from the Alamo 🦴🦴🦴 **1953** A soldier sent from the Alamo during its last hours to get help is branded as a deserter, and struggles to clear his name. Well acted, this film will satisfy those with a taste for action. **79m/C; VHS, DVD, Blu-Ray.** Glenn Ford; Julie Adams; Chill Wills; Victor Jory; Hugh O'Brian; ***D:*** Budd Boetticher.

The Man From Toronto **1932** Brit rom com. Leila and Fergus are bequeathed a fortune but on the condition that they marry to each other within a year. Since they are strangers, Leila poses as a maid in Fergus' home to see what's he's like and they begin to fall in love. Then Fergus discovers her deception and he's not happy. **77m/B; DVD.** *UK* Jessie Matthews; Ian Hunter; Frederick Kerr; Ben Field; Margaret Yarde; ***D:*** Sinclair Hill; ***W:*** W.P. Lipscomb; ***C:*** Leslie Rowson.

The Man from U.N.C.L.E. **2015 (PG-13)** Ritchie adapts the '60s hit TV show in a way that's so self-aware and smug that it nearly turns its own coolness into an art form. Napoleon Solo (Cavill) helps Russian spy Gaby Teller (Vikander) defect and battles an agent named Illya Kuryakin (Hammer). Before they know it, the trio is actually working together to stop a deadly criminal organization. No one ever breaks a sweat or wrinkles a suit in this uber-cool take on the spy game. **116m/C; DVD, Blu-Ray.** Henry Cavill; Armie Hammer; Alicia Vikander; Hugh Grant; Jared Harris; ***D:*** Guy Ritchie; ***W:*** Guy Ritchie; Lionel Wigram; ***C:*** John Mathieson; ***M:*** Daniel Pemberton.

The Man From Yesterday **1932** Melodramatic romantic triangle begins in WWI when nurse Sylvia Suffolk (Colbert) marries Capt. Tony Clyde (Brook). She receives word that he's been killed and Army surgeon Rene Goudin (Boyer) offers to help the pregnant widow, with love following in time. Of course if Tony were really dead, it wouldn't be much of a triangle, would it? **71m/B; DVD.** Claudette Colbert; Clive Brook; Charles Boyer; Andy Devine; Alan Mowbray; ***D:*** Berthold Viertel; ***W:*** Oliver H.P. Garrett; ***C:*** Karl Struss.

Man Hunt **1941** Atmospheric wartime thriller from Lang finds English big-game hunter Thorndike (Pidgeon) making his way to Bavaria with a chance to assassinate Hitler. He's captured and tortured by the Gestapo (Sanders), escapes, and is pursued while returning to England aboard a Danish steamer. Aboard the ship Thorndike discovers his identity has been usurped by the mysterious Mr. Jones (Carradine). Befriended by a cockney prostitute (Bennett), Thorndike's plight comes down to a confrontation in a London subway tunnel. **105m/B; DVD, Blu-Ray.** Walter Pidgeon; Joan Bennett; George Sanders; John Carradine; Roddy McDowall; ***D:*** Fritz Lang; ***W:*** Dudley Nichols; ***C:*** Arthur C. Miller; ***M:*** Alfred Newman.

The Man I Love **1946** Slick drama about nightclub singer Lupino falling for no-good mobster Alda. Enjoyable and well-acted, although script doesn't make sense. Great selection of tunes. This film inspired Scorsese's "New York, New York." Based on the novel "Night Shift" by Maritta Wolff. **96m/B; DVD.** Ida Lupino; Robert Alda; Andrea King; Martha Vickers; Bruce Bennett; Alan Hale; Dolores Moran; John Ridgely; Don McGuire; Warren Douglas; Craig Stevens; ***D:*** Raoul Walsh; ***W:*** Catherine Turney; Jo Pagano; W.R. Burnett; ***M:*** Max Steiner.

The Man I Love *L'Homme Qui J'aime* **1997** Heart-on-its-sleeve romance originally made for French TV. Martin (Di Fonzo Bo) is hired to work at a Marseilles municipal swimming pool and falls immediately for golden boy lifeguard Lucas (Portal), who has a live-in girlfriend, Lise (Seigner). Lise thinks Lucas's new buddy is lots of fun—never suspecting that exuberant Martin is after the hunk. Of course, Lucas isn't as straight as he seems and eventually switches partners. But there's another problem, Martin, who's HIV-positive, decides to take a break from his onerous treatment, despite the consequences. French with subtitles. **87m/C; DVD.** *FR* Marcial Di Fonzo Bo; Jean-Michel Portal; Mathilde Seigner; Vittoria Scognamiglio; Jacques Hansen; ***D:*** Stephane Giusti; ***W:*** Stephane Giusti; ***C:*** Jacques Bouquin; ***M:*** Lazare Boghossian. **TV**

The Man I Married **1940** Propaganda piece, intercut with newsreel footage for authenticity. In 1938, American Carol Hoffman (Bennett) and her German-born husband Eric (Lederer) leave New York to visit his father Heinrich (Kruger) in Germany. Eric is immediately impressed by the Nazis, thanks in part to attractive party member Frieda (Sten). He asks Carol for a divorce and insists on custody of their son. Carol is horrified and her father-in-law, who's disgusted by his son's new politics, comes to her aid. **77m/B; DVD.** Joan Bennett; Francis Lederer; Anna Sten; Otto Kruger; Lloyd Nolan; ***D:*** Irving Pichel; ***W:*** Oliver H.P. Garrett; ***C:*** J. Peverell Marley; ***M:*** David Buttolph.

The Man in 3B **2016 (R)** A murder mystery centered on a former gang member who charms his neighbors. After Daryl Graham (Rucker) moves into an apartment building in Jamaica, Queens, New York, he charms all his neighbors. For example, Daryl helps unhappily married Connie (Evans) lose weight, and lost teen Benny (Ri'chard) finds a role model in him. Though some questions bubble under the surface, all seems find until a murder takes place and everyone is suspected of the crime. **90m/C; DVD, Streaming, Download.** Lamman Rucker; Christian Keyes; Brely Evans; DB Woodside; Robert Ri'chard; ***D:*** Trey Haley; ***W:*** Carl Weber; ***C:*** Eric Wycoff; ***M:*** Matthew Head.

The Man in Grey **1943** In a story of romantic intrigue set in 19th-century England, a Marquis's wife is betrayed by her vile husband and the schoolmate she once befriended who has an affair with him. Stunning costumes and fine performances compensate for the overly extravagant production values in a work that helped bring stardom to Mason. **93m/B; DVD.** *UK* James Mason; Margaret Lockwood; Stewart Granger; Phyllis Calvert; ***D:*** Leslie Arliss; ***W:*** Leslie Arliss; Margaret Kennedy; Doreen Montgomery; ***C:*** Arthur Crabtree.

A Man in Love *Un Homme Amoureux* **1987 (R)** An international romantic melodrama set during the Italian filming of a biography of suicidal author Cesar Pavese. The self-important lead actor and a beautiful supporting actress (Coyote and Scacchi) become immersed in the roles and fall madly in love, oblivious to the fact that Coyote is married and Scacchi's engaged. The two make a steamy pair, to the detriment of friends, family, and the movie they're making. Kurys' first English-language film is visually appealing with a lush, romantic score, seamlessly weaving the storylines among vivid characters. **110m/C; VHS, Streaming.** *FR* Peter Coyote; Greta Scacchi; Jamie Lee Curtis; Peter Riegert; Jean Pigozzi; John Berry; Claudia Cardinale; Vincent Lindon; ***D:*** Diane Kurys; ***W:*** Diane Kurys; Olivier Schatzky; Israel Horovitz; ***M:*** Georges Delerue.

The Man in Possession **1931** Pre-Hays Code romantic comedy gets pretty steamy as black sheep Raymond Dabney (Montgomery) and former kept woman Crystal Wetherby (Purcell) hit the sheets before falling in love. Crystal now has big debts and the local law serves a writ on her property. Raymond is hired to keep an eye on things and doesn't know that his brother Claude (Owen) wants to marry Crystal for her supposed fortune. Raymond finds out in a farcical situation when he poses as Crystal's butler for a dinner party for his family. **84m/B; DVD.** Robert Montgomery; Irene Purcell; Charlotte Greenwood; Reginald Owen; Alan Mowbray; Sir C. Aubrey Smith; Beryl Mercer; ***D:*** Sam Wood; ***W:*** Sarah Y. Mason; P.G. Wodehouse; ***C:*** Oliver Marsh.

Man in the Attic 1/2 **1953** Mild but creepy pathologist Slade (Palance) rents an attic room from Mrs. Harley and moons over her actress daughter Lily (Smith) in late 1880s London. About the same time Lily starts finding Slade attractive and interesting, Mrs. Harvey starts suspecting him of being Jack the Ripper. Satisfying suspenser keeps the audience guessing thanks largely to Palance's ambiguous performance. **82m/B; VHS, DVD.** Jack Palance; Constance Smith; Byron Palmer; Frances Bavier; Rhys Williams; Sean McClory; Leslie Bradley; Lester Matthews; Harry Cording; Lillian Bond; Isabel Jewell; ***D:*** Hugo Fregonese; ***W:*** Barre Lyndon; Robert Presnell, Jr.; ***C:*** Leo Tover; ***M:*** Hugo Friedhofer.

The Man in the Glass Booth **1975 (PG)** In this adaptation of a play written by actor Robert Shaw, a successful Jewish businessman is suspected of being a Nazi war criminal. Loosely based on the life of death camp commandant Otto Adolf Eichmann, the film depicts the arrest and subsequent trial of the former Nazi by the Israelis. The film's title is derived from the fact that Eichmann sat in a glass booth during his trial. Schell's performance is outstanding. **117m/C; VHS, DVD, Blu-Ray.** Maximilian Schell; Lois Nettleton; Luther Adler; Lawrence Pressman; Henry Brown; Richard Rasof; ***D:*** Arthur Hiller; ***W:*** Edward Anhalt; ***C:*** Sam Leavitt.

The Man in the Gray Flannel Suit 1/2 **1956** A very long and serious adaptation of the Sloan Wilson novel about a Madison Avenue advertising exec trying to balance his life between work and family. The Hollywood treatment falls short of the adaptation potential of the original story. **152m/C; VHS, DVD.** Gregory Peck; Fredric March; Jennifer Jones; Ann Harding; Arthur O'Connell; Henry Daniell; Lee J. Cobb; Marisa Pavan; Gene Lockhart; Keenan Wynn; Gigi Perreau; Joseph Sweeney; Kenneth Tobey; DeForest Kelley; ***D:*** Nunnally Johnson.

The Man in the Iron Mask **1939** Swashbuckling tale about twin brothers (played by Hayward) separated at birth. One turns out to be King Louis XIV of France, and the other is imprisoned and forced to wear an iron mask that hides his identity. Philippe is eventually rescued by musketeer D'Artagnan (William) and the musketeers join forces for action-packed adventure and royal revenge. Remake of the "The Iron Mask" (1929) with Douglas Fairbanks and subsequently remade several times for both TV and the big screen. **110m/B; VHS, DVD.** Louis Hayward; Alan Hale; Joan Bennett; Warren William; Joseph Schildkraut; Walter Kingsford; Marion Martin; ***D:*** James Whale; ***W:*** George Bruce; ***C:*** Robert Planck; ***M:*** Lucien Moraweck.

The Man in the Iron Mask **1977** A tyrannical French king kidnaps his twin brother and imprisons him on a remote island. Chamberlain, the king of the miniseries, is excellent in a dual role in this big production swashbuckler. Adapted from the Dumas classic. **105m/C; VHS, Blu-Ray, Streaming.** Richard Chamberlain; Patrick McGoohan; Louis Jourdan; Jenny Agutter; Ian Holm; Ralph Richardson; ***D:*** Mike Newell. **TV**

The Man in the Iron Mask 1/2 **1997** Low-budget, personalized version of the Dumas swashbuckler from director Richert, which he filmed at the historic Mission Inn in Riverside, CA. Prologue establishes the birth of twin royals to the French Queen (Foster) and the fate of Philippe (Richert's son Nick) as the man in the iron mask. A deathbed confession to Count Aramis (the director himself) alerts the Musketeers, who decide to set things right. Well-intentioned but not a lot of fun. **85m/C; VHS, DVD.** William Richert; Edward Albert; Rex Ryon; Timothy Bottoms; Dennis Hayden; Nick Richert; Meg Foster; James Gammon; Dana Barron; Brigid Brannagh; Fannie Brett; ***D:*** William Richert; ***W:*** William Richert; ***C:*** William Barber; ***M:*** Jim Ervin.

The Man in the Iron Mask **1998 (PG-13)** Lavish retelling of Alexandre Dumas's classic story. Snotty tyrant King Louis XIV's (DiCaprio) lust for women leads to the reunion of the retired Musketeers, bent on replacing cold Louis with his more sensitive twin brother Phillippe, an inmate of the Bastille who's hidden behind a ghastly mask. Irons, Malkovich, Depardieu, and Byrne bring a welcome seriousness and style as the older, jaded Musketeers, while DiCaprio holds his own in the presence of such formidable company. The high gloss production provides old-fashioned escapist entertainment from first-time director Wallace. **132m/C; DVD, Blu-Ray.** Leonardo DiCaprio; Gabriel Byrne; Jeremy Irons; John Malkovich; Gerard Depardieu; Anne Parillaud; Judith Godreche; Edward Atterton; Peter Sarsgaard; Hugh Laurie; ***D:*** Randall Wallace; ***W:*** Randall Wallace; ***C:*** Peter Suschitzky; ***M:*** Nick Glennie-Smith.

Man in the Mirror: The Michael Jackson Story **2004 (PG-13)** Like rubber-necking at a car wreck. Poorly-dramatized showbiz bio of the pop star (Alexander) in all his legendary weirdness. It takes us from Jackson's musical success to his career slide, unnerving marriages, and the scandals that plagued him. Listen to the music instead. **87m/C; DVD.** Flex Alexander; Eugene Clark; Jason Griffith; April Telek; Krista Rae; ***D:*** Allan Moyle; ***W:*** Claudia Salter; ***C:*** David (Robert) A. Greene; ***M:*** Bruce Leitl. **CABLE**

The Man in the Moon 1/2 **1991 (PG-13)** Beautifully rendered coming-of-age tale. On a farm outside a small Louisiana town in the 1950s, 14-year-old Dani wonders if she will ever be as pretty and popular as her 17-year-old sister Maureen. This becomes especially important as Dani is beginning to notice boys, particularly Court, the 17-year-old young man she meets when swimming. Although Dani and Maureen have always been especially close, a rift develops between the sisters after Court meets Maureen. Intelligently written, excellent direction, lovely cinematography, and exceptional acting make this a particularly worthwhile and entertaining film. **100m/C; VHS, DVD, Blu-Ray.** Reese Witherspoon; Emily Warfield; Jason London; Tess Harper; Sam Waterston; Gail Strickland; ***D:*** Robert Mulligan.

The Man in the Net 1/2 **1959** Melodramatic, nonsensical crime mystery. John Hamilton (Ladd) leaves NYC with his crazy, drunken wife Linda (Jones) and moves to a small Connecticut town to work on his art career. Linda hates the place and fools around with a local to pass the time, meanwhile accusing John of being abusive. She suddenly disappears and the townsfolk suddenly turn vigilante on John believing he's a murderer. Ladd seems to take little interest in his role and neither will the viewer. **97m/B; DVD.** Alan Ladd; Carolyn Jones; Diane Brewster; John Lupton; Charles McGraw; Tom Helmore; Betty Lou Holland; ***D:*** Michael Curtiz; ***W:*** Reginald Rose; ***C:*** John Seitz; ***M:*** Hans J. Salter.

Man in the Saddle 1/2 *The Outcast* **1951** Western star Scott gets roped in a romantic triangle out on the range, leading to some exciting gunplay. As usual, justice triumphs in this above average oater. Based on the novel by Ernest Haycox. **87m/C; VHS, DVD.** Randolph Scott; Joan Leslie; Ellen Drew; Alexander Knox; Richard Rober; John Russell; ***D:*** Andre de Toth; ***W:*** Kenneth Gamet.

Man in the Shadow 1/2 *Pay the Devil; Seeds of Wrath* **1957** Sheriff Ben Sadler (Chandler) is the only man in the county willing to stand up to wealthy Texas rancher Virgil Renchler (Welles). Sadler suspects Renchler is behind the brutal death of a Mexican laborer but gets no support when he tries to find justice. **80m/C; VHS, DVD, Blu-Ray.** Jeff Chandler; Orson Welles; Ben Alexander; Colleen Miller; John Larch; James Gleason; Barbara Lawrence; Royal Dano; Paul Fix; William Schallert; ***D:*** Jack Arnold; ***W:*** Gene L. Coon; ***C:*** Arthur E. Arling; ***M:*** Joseph Gershenson.

Man in the Vault **1956** Low-budget crime noir from John Wayne's Batjac production company. Locksmith Tommy Dancer (Campbell) is hired by hood Willis Trent (Kroeger) for a simple job and then is invited to a party at Trent's where he meets wealthy Betty (Sharpe). She's on the rebound from her cheating lawyer beau Farraday (Keys), but is out of Tommy's pay scale. At least until Trent offers Tommy a lot of dough to make keys to open a safety deposit box that happens to belong to crime boss DeCamp (Seay), which is just asking for trouble. **72m/C; DVD.** William Campbell; Berry Kroeger; Anita Ekberg; James Seay; Paul Fix; Mike Mazurki; Karen Sharpe; Robert Keys; ***D:*** Andrew V. McLaglen; ***W:*** Burt Kennedy; ***C:*** William Clothier; ***M:*** Henry Vars.

The Man in the White Suit 1/2 **1951** A humble laboratory assistant in a textile mill invents a white cloth that won't stain, tear, or wear out, and can't be dyed. The panicked garment industry sets out to destroy him and the fabric, resulting in some sublimely comic situations and a variety of inventive chases. **82m/B; VHS, DVD, Blu-Ray.** *GB* Alec Guinness; Joan Greenwood; ***D:*** Alexander MacKendrick.

Man in the Wilderness 1/2 **1971 (PG)** Harris is part of an expedition traveling through the Northwest Territory. He's mauled by a grizzly and left for dead by leader Huston. While Harris fights for survival, he also plots revenge. Blood and violence is somewhat offset by good lead performances.

108m/C; VHS, DVD, Blu-Ray. Richard Harris; John Huston; Henry Wilcoxon; Percy Herbert; Dennis Waterman; Prunella Ransome; Norman Rossington; James Doohan; *D:* Richard Sarafian; *W:* Jack DeWitt; *M:* Johnny Harris.

A Man in Uniform 𝄞𝄞 *I Love a Man in Uniform* **1993 (R)** A look at the making of a sociopath. Henry (McCamus) is a quiet bank employee who moonlights as an actor. Then he gets his big break in the role of a self-righteous cop in a TV series. Only the lines between his make-believe cop and the real world begin to blur and Henry's intensity turns to violence. Fine performances lead to an unsatisfying film conclusion. **99m/C; VHS, DVD.** *CA* Tom McCamus; Brigitte Bako; Kevin Tighe; David Hemblen; Alex Karzis; Graham McPherson; Richard Blackburn; *D:* David Wellington; *W:* David Wellington; *C:* David Franco; *M:* Ron Sures. Genie '93: Actor (McCamus), Support. Actor (Tighe).

Man Is Not a Bird 𝄞𝄞 ½ *Covek Nije Tica* **1965** Follows the destructive love of a factory engineer and a hairdresser in a small Yugoslavian mining town. In Serbian with English subtitles. **80m/B; VHS, DVD.** *YU* Eva Ras; Milena Dravic; Janez Urhovec; *D:* Dusan Makavejev; *W:* Dusan Makavejev; *C:* Aleksandar Petkovic; *M:* Petar Bergamo.

A Man Named Rocca 𝄞𝄞 *Un Nomme La Rocca* **1961** Smalltime gangster La Rocca comes to Marseille to help his friend Xavier who's been framed and thrown in prison. After getting revenge, there's another subplot about racketeers and La Rocca eventually winds up in the joint alongside Xavier until the two men volunteer to clear land mines to get a pardon. French with subtitles. **106m/B; DVD.** *FR* Jean-Paul Belmondo; Pierre Vaneck; Christine Kaufmann; Nico; Beatrice Altariba; Henri Virlojeux; *D:* Jean Becker; *W:* Jean Becker; *C:* Ghislan Cloquet; *M:* Claude Normand.

Man of a Thousand Faces 𝄞𝄞𝄞 ½ **1957** A tasteful and touching portrayal of Lon Chaney, from his childhood with his deaf and mute parents to his success as a screen star. Recreates some of Chaney's most famous roles, including the Phantom of the Opera and Quasimodo in "Notre Dame." Cagney is magnificent as the long-suffering film star who was a genius with makeup and mime. **122m/B; VHS, DVD, Blu-Ray.** James Cagney; Dorothy Malone; Jane Greer; Marjorie Rambeau; Jim Backus; Roger Smith; Robert Evans; *D:* Joseph Pevney; *W:* Ivan Goff; *C:* Russell Metty; *M:* Frank Skinner.

Man of Aran 𝄞𝄞𝄞 **1934** Celebrated account of a fisherman's struggle for survival on a barren island near the west coast of Ireland, featuring amateur actors. Three years in the making, it's the last word in man against nature cinema, and a visual marvel. A former explorer, Flaherty became an influential documentarian. Having first gained fame with "Nanook of the North," he compiled an opus of documentaries made for commercial release. **132m/B; VHS, DVD.** *D:* Robert Flaherty. **TV**

Man of Evil 𝄞𝄞 *Fanny by Gaslight* **1948** The hard times of the illegitimate daughter of a member of the British Parliament in the early 1900s, told with an astonishing number of plot twists and a plodding melodramtic style. Based on the novel "Fanny by Gaslight." **108m/B; VHS, DVD, Streaming.** *GB* Phyllis Calvert; James Mason; Wilfred Lawson; Stewart Granger; Margaretta Scott; Jean Kent; John Laurie; Stuart Lindsell; Nora Swinburne; Amy Veness; Ann Wilton; Helen Haye; Cathleen Nesbitt; Guy Le Feuvre; John Turnbull; Peter Jones; *D:* Anthony Asquith.

Man of Flowers 𝄞𝄞 ½ **1984** Because of his puritan upbringing, a reclusive art collector has trouble coping with his feelings of sexuality. He pays a woman to disrobe in front of him, but is never able to bring himself to see her naked. A moody piece with overtones of black humor, this work has limited audience appeal. **91m/C; VHS, DVD.** *AU* Norman Kaye; Alyson Best; Chris Haywood; Sarah Walker; Julia Blake; Bob Ellis; Werner Herzog; *D:* Paul Cox; *W:* Bob Ellis; Paul Cox; *C:* Yuri Sokol; *M:* Gaetano Donizetti. Australian Film Inst. '83: Actor (Kaye).

Man of Iron 𝄞𝄞𝄞 *Wajda: Czlowiek Z Zelaza* **1981 (PG)** Director Wajda's follow-up to "Man of Marble" deals with a reporter (Odania) who is expected to tow the government line when writing about the Gdansk shipyard strike of 1980. He meets the harassed laborer son (Radziwilowicz) of worker-hero Birkut, against whom Odania is expected to conduct a smear campaign, and finds his loyalties tested. In Polish with English subtitles. **116m/C; VHS, DVD.** *PL* Jerzy Radziwilowicz; Marian Opania; Krystyna Janda; *D:* Andrzej Wajda; *W:* Aleksander Scibor-Rylski; *C:* Edward Klosinski; *M:* Andrzej Korzynski. Cannes '81: Film.

Man of La Mancha 𝄞 ½ **1972 (PG)** Arrested by the Inquisition and thrown into prison, Miguel de Cervantes relates the story of Don Quixote. Not nearly as good as the Broadway musical it is based on. **129m/C; VHS, DVD, Blu-Ray.** Peter O'Toole; Sophia Loren; James Coco; Harry Andrews; John Castle; Brian Blessed; *D:* Arthur Hiller. Natl. Bd. of Review '72: Actor (O'Toole).

Man of Legend 𝄞𝄞 **1971 (PG)** An adventure-romance filmed in Morocco; a WWI German soldier flees to the Foreign Legion and fights with nomadic rebels, ultimately falling in love with their chief's beautiful daughter. An unoriginal desert saga. **95m/C; VHS, DVD.** *IT SP* Peter Strauss; Tina Aumont; Pier Paolo Capponi; *D:* Sergio Grieco.

Man of Marble 𝄞𝄞𝄞 **1976** A satire on life in post-WWII Poland. A young filmmaker sets out to tell the story of a bricklayer who, because of his exceptional skill, once gained popularity with other workers. He became a champion for worker rights, only to then find himself being persecuted by the government. The conclusion was censored by the Polish government. Highly acclaimed and followed by "Man of Iron" in 1981. In Polish with English subtitles. **160m/C; VHS, DVD.** *PL* Krystyna Janda; Jerzy Radziwilowicz; Tadeusz Lomnicki; Jacek Lomnicki; Krystyna Zachwatowicz; *D:* Andrzej Wajda; *W:* Aleksander Scibor-Rylski; *M:* Andrzej Korzynski.

The Man of My Life 𝄞𝄞 *L'Homme de Sa Vie* **2006** Frederic (Campan) is on holiday with his wife (Drucker) at his family's home in the Provencale countryside. They invite their new neighbor, cynical gay Hugo (Berling), to a party and he and Frederic wind up talking for hours. An unexpected bond develops between the two middle-aged men and starts disrupting Frederic's marriage. French with subtitles. **111m/C; DVD.** *FR IT* Bernard Campan; Charles Berling; Lea Drucker; *D:* Zabou Breitman; *W:* Zabou Breitman; Agnes de Sacy; *C:* Michel Amathieu; *M:* Liviu Badiu; Laurent Korcia.

A Man of Passion 𝄞𝄞 **1988 (R)** Quinn plays an aging artist living pleasurably on a Mediterranean isle. His summer guest is his uptight grandson, a classical pianist. Naturally, Gramps is about to teach the kid to loosen up, including appreciating one of his lovely artist's models. Another variation for Quinn on his "Zorba" personality but it works. **90m/C; VHS, Streaming.** Anthony Quinn; Ramon Sheen; Maud Adams; Elizabeth Ashley; R.J. Williams; Ray Walston; Victoria Vera; *D:* Jose Antonio De La Loma; *W:* Jose Antonio De La Loma.

Man of Steel 𝄞 ½ **2013 (PG-13)** CGI overload invades the DC Universe in this truly disappointing take on the legend of Superman courtesy of director Snyder. Cavill steps into the notorious tights as Superman's origin story is told yet again with Crowe as his Kryptonian father and Costner his Earthbound one. Adams is Lois Lane while Shannon steals the film as the notorious Emperor Zod. Snyder's take is all noise and fury, draining the story of any semblance of humanity in favor of a self-seriousness tone that only be described as joyless. There is no comparison to 1978's classic "Superman: The Movie." **148m/C; DVD, Blu-Ray.** Henry Cavill; Michael Shannon; Kevin Costner; Russell Crowe; Amy Adams; Diane Lane; Laurence Fishburne; Ayelet Zurer; Harry J. Lennix; Christopher Meloni; Richard Schiff; *D:* Zack Snyder; *W:* David S. Goyer; *C:* Amir M. Mokri; *M:* Hans Zimmer.

Man of Tai Chi 𝄞 ½ **2013 (R)** Reeve's workmanlike directorial debut is a simplistc martial arts tale that's best seen for Tiger Chen's action skills. Beijing Tai Chi student Chen is offered the chance to make some money by fighting, but deems it unworthy of his training until money is needed to save the temple where he practices. Chen travels to Hong Kong and learns crime boss Donaka Mark (a particularly blank-faced Reeves) runs a series of lucrative-but-illegal underground fight clubs the cops want to bust. English, Mandarin, and Cantonese with subtitles. **105m/C; Blu-Ray, On Demand.** *CH US* Tiger Chen; Keanu Reeves; Karen Mok; Simon Yam; *D:* Keanu Reeves; *W:* Michael Cooney; *C:* Elliot Davis; *M:* Kwong Wing Chan.

Man of the Century 𝄞 ½ **1999 (R)** Journalist Johnny Twennies (Frazier) is an anachronism living in 1990s Manhattan. He dresses, talks, and acts as if it were the 1920s. But Johnny doesn't seem to find anything strange in this, nor does anyone else. **77m/C; VHS, DVD.** Gibson Frazier; Susan Egan; Anthony Rapp; Cara Buono; Dwight Ewell; Brian Davies; Frank Gorshin; *D:* Adam Abramham; *W:* Gibson Frazier; Adam Abramham; *C:* Matthew Jensen; *M:* Michael Weiner.

Man of the House 𝄞𝄞 **1995 (PG)** Kids' comedy about a boy's plan to sabotage his mother's new love interest. Ben (Thomas) joins the YMCA Indian Guides to discourage daddy wanna-be Jack (Chase), while mom (Fawcett) stands idly by tolerating her son's bratty behavior. Subplot involves a screwy gangster theme that deteriorates into a "Home Alone"-ish ending. Film attempts to play off of Chase's knack for physical comedy, but falls short. Will probably appeal more to younger crowds as Thomas's schemer upstages Chase's deadpan dad-to-be. **97m/C; DVD.** Chevy Chase; Farrah Fawcett; Jonathan Taylor Thomas; George Wendt; David Shiner; Art LaFleur; Richard Portnow; Richard Foronjy; Spencer Vrooman; John Disanti; Chief Leonard George; Peter Appel; George Greif; Chris Miranda; Ron Canada; Zachary Browne; Nicholas Garrett; *D:* James Orr; *W:* James Orr; Jim Cruickshank; *C:* Jamie Anderson; *M:* Mark Mancina.

Man of the House 𝄞𝄞 **2005 (PG-13)** Jones, with his weathered face and deadpan grumpiness, goes slumming in this silly comedy about cheerleaders who witness a murder. Stoic Texas Ranger Roland Sharp's assigned to protect five (Milian, Keena, Garces, Ferlito, Garner) giggy (and jiggly) members of the University of Texas Longhorns' cheerleading squad. He moves into their sorority house and offers fatherly advice while trying to awkwardly woo an age-appropriate professor (Archer) and find the bad guy. For some reason Cedric the Entertainer turns up briefly as an ex-con preacher with his own pep squad moves. **99m/C; DVD, UMD.** Tommy Lee Jones; Cedric the Entertainer; Christina Milian; Paula Garces; Monica Keena; Vanessa Ferlito; Kelli Garner; Anne Archer; Brian Van Holt; Shea Whigham; R. Lee Ermey; Paget Brewster; Liz Vassey; Curtis Armstrong; Terry Parks; Marie Woodward; *Cameo(s):* James Richard Perry; *D:* Stephen Herek; *W:* Robert Ramsey; Matthew Stone; John McLaughlin; *C:* Peter Menzies, Jr.; *M:* David Newman.

Man of the West 𝄞𝄞 ½ **1958** Reformed bad guy Cooper is asked to deliver a tidy hunk of cash to another city to recruit a school marm. Ambushed en route by his former partners in crime (who are led by his wacko uncle) he's forced to revert to his wanton ways in order to survive and save innocent hostages. There's a raging debate among Cooper fans whether this late effort has been unduly overlooked or duly ignored. A number of things conspire to give it a bad rap: Cooper does little but look mournful until the very end; there's no hiding the fact that he's older than Cobb, who plays his uncle; and the acting is in general more befitting of a B-grade slice and dicer. You be the judge. **100m/C; DVD, Blu-Ray.** Gary Cooper; Julie London; Lee J. Cobb; Arthur O'Connell; Jack Lord; John Dehner; Royal Dano; Guy Wilkerson; Emory Parnell; *D:* Anthony Mann; *W:* Reginald Rose.

Man of the World 𝄞𝄞 **1931** Outcast journalist Michael Trevor (Powell) lives in Paris and blackmails wealthy Americans, aided by girlfriend Irene (Gibson). He wants to go straight when he falls for debutante Mary Kendall (Lombard) but tables are turned when Irene threatens to expose Michael's schemes. Pre-Production Code flick says crime may not pay but you still can get away. **74m/B; VHS, DVD.** William Powell; Carole Lombard; Wynne Gibson; Guy Kibbee; Lawrence Gray; *D:* Richard Wallace; Edward Goodman; *W:* Herbert J. Mankiewicz; *C:* Victor Milner.

Man of the Year 𝄞 **2006 (PG-13)** Schizoid blend of comedy and political thriller that features a subdued Williams as Tom Dobbs, a late-night talk show host whose joke about running for president turns into the real thing. But when he wins, it's thanks to a voting machine glitch that computer nerd Eleanor (Linney) warned her company about. When Eleanor tries to turn whistleblower, things really turn ridiculous, with the lady on the run from corporate hit men. Levinson should have stuck with a political satire about a well-intentioned guy taking on the biggest job in the land, which he is totally unequipped to handle. **108m/C; DVD.** Robin Williams; Laura Linney; Christopher Walken; Lewis Black; Jeff Goldblum; Rick Roberts; *D:* Barry Levinson; *W:* Barry Levinson; *C:* Dick Pope; *M:* Graeme Revell.

Man on a Ledge 𝄞𝄞 **2012 (PG-13)** More afraid of depth than heights, this revenge thriller follows Nick (Worthington), an escaped fugitive who threatens to jump off the ledge of a Manhattan hotel while NYPD hostage negotiator Lydia (Banks) tries to talk him down. The balancing act is actually a diversion for quarrelling robbers Joey (Bell) and Angie (Rodriguez) to find the diamond that Nick was convicted of stealing from an oily tycoon (Harris). The heist is so convoluted that your suspension of disbelief may actually end up expelled, but the action moves along at a brisk pace. **102m/C; DVD, Blu-Ray.** Sam Worthington; Elizabeth Banks; Jamie Bell; Anthony Mackie; Genesis Rodriguez; Ed Harris; Ed Burns; Titus Welliver; Kyra Sedgwick; *D:* Asger Leth; *W:* Pablo F. Fenjves; *C:* Paul Cameron; *M:* Henry Jackman.

Man On a String 𝄞 ½ **1960** Russian-born movie producer Boris Mitrov (Borgnine) emigrates to the U.S. and gets caught doing some Soviet spying for the sake of his family. The CIA make it clear that he needs to become a double agent and convince the KGB in East Berlin that he's useful with the goal of working in Moscow. Dull Cold War anti-communist propaganda based on actual events. **92m/B; DVD, Blu-Ray.** Ernest Borgnine; Kerwin Mathews; Colleen Dewhurst; Alexander Scourby; Glenn Corbett; Richard Kendrick; Ed Prentiss; *Nar:* Clete Roberts; *D:* Andre de Toth; *W:* John Kafka; Virginia Shaler; *C:* Charles Lawton, Jr.; *M:* George Duning.

Man on a Swing 𝄞 ½ **1974** Grey works overtime to keep this crime drama interesting. Staid small town police chief Lee Tucker (Robertson) is at a dead end in a murder investigation when he's contacted by alleged psychic Franklin Wills (Grey). Wills' information is eerily accurate, and Tucker looks on him as a suspect, especially since his behavior is increasingly unpredictable. **108m/C; DVD, Blu-Ray.** Cliff Robertson; Joel Grey; Dorothy Tristan; Peter Masterson; Ron Weyand; *D:* Frank Perry; *W:* David Zelag Goodman; *C:* Adam Holender; *M:* Lalo Schifrin.

Man on a Tightrope 𝄞𝄞 ½ **1953** Good depiction of life under communist rule and the desire for escape. When the communists take over Czechoslovakia, Karel Cernik's (March) family-owned circus comes under government control, much to his disgust. Karel secretly plots to have everyone flee across the border into West Germany during a tour but discovers there's a state spy in their midst. **105m/B; DVD.** Terry Moore; Fredric March; Cameron Mitchell; Adolphe Menjou; Richard Boone; Alexander D'Arcy; Robert Beatty; Gloria Grahame; *D:* Elia Kazan; *W:* Robert Sherwood; *C:* Georg Krause; *M:* Franz Waxman.

Man on Fire 𝄞𝄞 ½ **2004 (R)** Slick actioner deploys Washington as a world-weary anti-hero whose mission is to find a kidnapped young girl in Mexico City. Problem is, Creasy, a former government assassin who drinks too much, was hired as the bodyguard for Pita (Fanning), her Mexican businessman father Samuel (Anthony), and American mother Lisa (Mitchell). Creasy's investigation reveals Mexican police involvement and government ties while a botched ransom drop sets Creasy off on a rage-fueled rampage. Walken shows up to goose the plot as an old military buddy. Pic is full of non-stop action and gritty style, highlighted by an excellent Washington. **145m/C; DVD, Blu-**

Ray, UMD. Denzel Washington; Christopher Walken; Dakota Fanning; Radha Mitchell; Marc Anthony; Giancarlo Giannini; Rachel Ticotin; Mickey Rourke; Jesus Ochoa; *D:* Tony Scott; *W:* Brian Helgeland; *C:* Paul Cameron; *M:* Harry Gregson-Williams.

Man on the Eiffel Tower ✓✓✓ **1948** Laughton plays Inspector Maigret, the detective created by novelist Georges Simenon, in a highly suspenseful and cerebral mystery about a crazed killer who defies the police to discover his identity. This is the first film Meredith directed. **82m/C; VHS, DVD.** Charles Laughton; Burgess Meredith; Franchot Tone; Patricia Roc; *D:* Burgess Meredith.

The Man On the Flying Trapeze ✓✓ **1935** Frustrated, henpecked Ambrose Wolfinger (Fields) is beset by an overbearing family (except for daughter Hope) as two drunken burglars are the start of a series of unfortunate events. Ambrose gets fired after lying to his boss and into a series of scrapes with the police--even landing in jail--while trying to be rebellious. **65m/B; DVD.** W.C. Fields; Mary Brian; Kathleen Howard; Grady Sutton; Vera Lewis; Lucien Littlefield; Walter Brennan; Tammany Young; *D:* Clyde Bruckman; *W:* Ray Harris; Sam Hardy; *C:* Alfred Gilks.

Man on the Moon ✓✓ **1999 (R)** Clunky bio of bizarro comedian Andy Kaufman (Carrey) who died of cancer at age 35 in 1984. The problem is that Kaufman is opaque—he doesn't seem to have a true personality but assumes bizarre alter-egos, including obnoxious lounge singer Tony Clifton. Kaufman turned out to be most appealing as innocent Latka on the sitcom "Taxi," which he professes to despise. For all Carrey's expertise, you won't care too much about what's onscreen. Title comes from R.E.M.'s song about Kaufman; they also supplied the film's music. **118m/C; VHS, DVD, Blu-Ray.** Jim Carrey; Courtney Love; Danny DeVito; Paul Giamatti; Vincent Schiavelli; Peter Bonerz; Marilu Henner; Judd Hirsch; *D:* Milos Forman; *W:* Scott M. Alexander; Larry Karaszewski; *C:* Terry Michos. Golden Globes '00: Actor--Mus./Comedy (Carrey).

The Man on the Train ✓✓✓ *L'Homme du Train* **2002 (R)** A chance encounter offers viewers subtle pleasures. Elderly retired teacher Manesquier (Rochefort) is intrigued when leather-jacketed stranger Milan (Hallyday) turns up in his small provincial town. The bored Manesquier offers Milan hospitality and shows little concern after realizing Milan is a thief waiting for his partner so that they can rob the local bank. Manesquier's led a proper dull life while Milan's done the opposite and they develop an odd friendship. Old-pro Rochefort, in his seventh film with Leconte, is engaging while French pop icon Hallyday offers a surprisingly strong performance that's a mixture of machismo and sensitivity. French with subtitles. **90m/C; DVD.** *FR* Jean Rochefort; Johnny Hallyday; Jean-Francois Stevenin; Charlie Nelson; Isabelle Petit-Jacques; Edith Scob; Pascal Parmentier; *D:* Patrice Leconte; *W:* Claude Klotz; *C:* Jean-Marie Dreujou; *M:* Pascal Esteve. L.A. Film Critics '03: Foreign Film.

The Man on the Train ✓ ½ **2011** Slow-paced English-language remake of the 2002 French drama about a retired poetry professor (Sutherland) who wants to trade lives with a thief (Mullen Jr.) who shows up in town to rob the local bank. The ill older man invites the thief to stay at his home, intrigued by his polar opposite lifestyle, and conversations lead to an unlikely bond. Mullen Jr., the drummer for the band U2, makes his acting debut. **100m/C; DVD.** *CA IR* Donald Sutherland; Larry Mullen, Jr.; *D:* Mary McGuckian; *W:* Mary McGuckian; *C:* Stefan von Bjorn.

Man on Wire ✓✓ ½ **2008 (PG-13)** On August 7, 1974, French aerialist Philippe Petit and his team entered the not-yet-completed World Trade Center and strung a high-wire between the two towers, which Petit proceeded to illegally cross. A documentary hybrid of actual and restaged footage shows Petit training for his walk (across the towers of Notre Dame and the Sydney Bridge) as well as the extensive preparations for the New York walk. Petit is a charming raconteur and his feat still astonishes; based on his memoir "To Reach the Clouds." (Director Marsh does not mention the 9/11 destruction of the World Trade Center.) **94m/C; DVD.** *GB D:* James Marsh; *C:* Igor Martinovic; *M:* Michael Nyman. Oscars '08: Feature Doc.

Man or Gun ✓ ½ **1958** Standard western yarn involving a drifter who rides into a town operated by a powerful family and liberates the cowardly townsfolk. **79m/B; VHS, Streaming.** MacDonald Carey; Audrey Totter; James Craig; James Gleason; Warren Stevens; Harry Shannon; *D:* Albert C. Gannaway; *W:* Vance Skarstedt; James C. Cassity.

The Man Outside ✓✓ **1968 (R)** After a CIA agent is fired for allegedly assisting another agent in defecting to the East, he becomes involved in further intrigue. A Russian spy is looking to defect. In the process, the ex-agent is framed for murder. Straightforward espionage tale taken from Gene Stackleborg's novel "Double Agent." **98m/C; VHS, DVD.** *GB* Van Heflin; Heidelinde Weis; Pinkas Braun; Peter Vaughan; Charles Gray; Ronnie Barker; *D:* Samuel Gallu.

Man Outside ✓ **1988 (PG-13)** Logan is an ex-lawyer who takes to the Arkansas outback after his wife dies. Anthropologist/teacher Quinlan takes a shine to him. He seems like an okay guy, but bad guy Dillman has made it look like he's a child snatcher. Slick on the outside but empty inside independent effort. Look for former members of The Band in supporting roles. **109m/C; VHS, DVD.** Robert F. Logan; Kathleen Quinlan; Bradford Dillman; Rick Danko; Levon Helm; *D:* Mark Stouffer.

Man, Pride and Vengeance ✓✓ *With Django Comes Death; L'uomo, L'orgoglio, la vendetta* **1967** Odd spaghetti western with the plot taken from the same Prosper Merimee novella that also inspired Bizet's opera "Carmen." Spanish soldier Jose is lured into a life of crime after being seduced by gypsy femme fatale Carmen. Filmed in Andalucía, Spain although the West German co-produced version changes the location to Mexico and the characters' names. Italian with subtitles or dubbed. **100m/C; DVD, Blu-Ray.** *IT GE* Franco Nero; Tina Aumont; Klaus Kinski; Guido Lollobrigida; *D:* Luigi Bazzoni; *W:* Luigi Bazzoni; Suso Cecchi D'Amico; *C:* Camillo Bazzoni.

The Man They Could Not Hang ✓✓ ½ **1939** A good doctor tinkering with artificial hearts is caught by police while experimenting on a willing student. When the doctor is convicted and hanged for a murder, his assistant uses the heart to bring him back to life. No longer a nice guy, he vows revenge against the jurors that sentenced him. Karloff repeated the same story line in several films, and this one is representative of the type. **70m/B; VHS, DVD.** Boris Karloff; Adrian Booth; Roger Pryor; Robert Wilcox; *D:* Nick Grinde.

A Man to Remember ✓✓ ½ **1938** Remake of 1933's "One Man's Journey" begins with Dr. Abbott's (Ellis) funeral and then uses a series of flashbacks to show the life of the kindly country doc. Again his selflessness precludes wealth and professional notice although a polio epidemic figures in. Kanin's directorial debut. **79m/B; DVD.** Edward Ellis; Anne Shirley; Lee Bowman; John Wray; William Henry; Granville Bates; Frank M. Thomas, Sr.; Harlan Briggs; *D:* Garson Kanin; *W:* Dalton Trumbo; *C:* J. Roy Hunt; *M:* Roy Webb.

Man-Trap ✓ ½ **1961** Implausible crime drama adapted from the John D. MacDonald novel "Taint of the Tiger." Matt (Hunter) saves Vince's (Janssen) life in Korea and he vows to repay him. It takes eight years for Vince to show up with a crazy scheme involving a dictator, illegal funds, and reward money but Matt's stuck in a bad marriage to boozer Nina (Stevens) and is willing to listen. Predictably, Vince's plan goes wrong in more ways than one. **93m/B; DVD, Blu-Ray.** Jeffrey Hunter; David Janssen; Stella Stevens; Elaine Devry; Virginia Gregg; *D:* Edmond O'Brien; *W:* Ed Waters; *C:* Loyal Griggs; *M:* Leith Stevens.

Man Trouble ✓✓ **1992 (PG-13)** A divorcing opera singer (Barkin) seeks the help of a sleazy attack-dog trainer (Nicholson) when she becomes the victim of a stalker. Nicholson hits on her, first because that's one of his habits, and then because he is being paid to by a billionaire who wants him to steal the manuscript of a tell-all book written by Barkin's sister. Although both Nicholson and Barkin are excellent actors, they lack the electricity to make the romance credible. Supporting cast, including D'Angelo, Stanton, and McKean, provide the funny parts in this otherwise dull film. **100m/C; DVD.** Jack Nicholson; Ellen Barkin; Harry Dean Stanton; Beverly D'Angelo; Michael McKean; Saul Rubinek; Viveka Davis; Veronica Cartwright; David Clennon; John Kapelos; Paul Mazursky; *D:* Bob Rafelson; *W:* Adrien (Carole Eastman) Joyce; *C:* Stephen Burum; *M:* Georges Delerue.

The Man Who Came Back ✓ ½ **2008 (R)** When a former Confederate army officer defends black plantation workers in 1876, he's framed for murder and his family is killed. So he comes back for revenge. **112m/C; DVD.** Eric Braeden; Billy Zane; George Kennedy; Armand Assante; Carol Alt; Sean Young; James Patrick Stuart; Peter Jason; Ken Norton; *D:* Glen Pitre; *W:* Glen Pitre; Chuck Walker; *C:* Stops Langensteiner; *M:* Phil Marsell. **VIDEO**

The Man Who Came to Dinner ✓✓✓ ½ **1941** Based on the Moss Hart-George S. Kaufman play, this comedy is about a bitter radio celebrity (Woolley) on a lecture tour (a character based on Alexander Woolcott). He breaks his hip and must stay in a quiet suburban home for the winter. While there, he occupies his time by barking orders, being obnoxious and generally just driving the other residents nuts. Woolley reprises his Broadway role in this film that succeeds at every turn, loaded with plenty of satiric jabs at the Algonquin Hotel Roundtable regulars. **112m/B; VHS, DVD.** Monty Woolley; Bette Davis; Ann Sheridan; Jimmy Durante; Reginald Gardiner; Richard Travis; Billie Burke; Grant Mitchell; Mary Wickes; George Barbier; Ruth Vivian; Elisabeth Fraser; *D:* William Keighley; *W:* Julius J. Epstein; Philip G. Epstein; *C:* Gaetano Antonio "Tony" Gaudio.

The Man Who Captured Eichmann ✓✓ ½ **1996** In 1960 Israeli Mossad agents prepare to capture Adolf Eichmann (Duvall), who organized the transport of millions of Jews to the concentration camps, from his home in Argentina. Peter Malkin (Howard), the agent responsible for the kidnapping, holds Eichmann in a Buenos Aires safe house before smuggling him into Israel as Eichmann tries to ingratiate himself with Malkin, refusing to accept responsiblity and constantly maintaining his innocence. Based on the book "Eichmann In My Hands" by Peter Z. Malkin and Harry Stein. Made for TNT. **96m/C; DVD.** Robert Duvall; Arliss Howard; Jeffrey Tambor; Jack Laufer; Nicolas Surovy; Joel Brooks; Sam Robards; Michael Tucci; *D:* William A. Graham; *W:* Lionel Chetwynd; *C:* Robert Steadman; *M:* Laurence Rosenthal. **CABLE**

The Man Who Cheated Himself ✓✓ **1950** Efficient film noir although Dall's character is remarkably annoying. Longtime San Francisco police detective Ed Cullen (Cobb) is in love with married socialite Lois Frazer (Wyatt). Lois suspects her fortune-hunting husband Howard (Warde) is going to kill her after she finds his gun and winds up plugging her spouse in Ed's presence. Ed figures he can cover up the crime but his rookie detective brother Andy (Dall) is assigned to the case and is determined to solve it. **75m/B; DVD, Blu-Ray.** Lee J. Cobb; Jane Wyatt; John Dall; Harlan Warde; Lisa Howard; *D:* Felix Feist; *W:* Seton I. Miller; Philip MacDonald; *M:* Russell Harlan.

The Man Who Could Cheat Death ✓ ½ **1959** Excessively talky Hammer horror set in Paris in 1890. Dr. Georges Bonnet appears to be in his 30s but he's actually over 100. He uses an elixir to remain youthful but it's made from the thyroid glands of the women he murders and he becomes increasingly unstable as the time nears for another shot of his rejuvenating formula. Remake of 1945's "The Man in Half Moon Street." **82m/C; DVD, Blu-Ray.** *GB* Anton Diffring; Christopher Lee; Hazel Court; Arnold Marle; Francis De Wolff; Delphi Lawrence; *D:* Terence Fisher; *W:* Jimmy Sangster; *C:* Jack Asher; *M:* Richard Rodney Bennett.

The Man Who Could Work Miracles ✓✓✓ ½ **1937** A mild-mannered draper's assistant becomes suddenly endowed with supernatural powers to perform any feat he wishes. Great special effects (for an early film) and fine performances result in a classic piece of science fiction. **82m/B; VHS, DVD.** Ralph Richardson; Joan Gardner; Roland Young; *D:* Lothar Mendes.

The Man Who Cried ✓✓ **2000 (R)** In 1927 Russia, young Jewish Fegele is separated from her father (who emigrates to America) and ends up in England instead, where she's adopted and renamed Suzie. An adult Suzie (Ricci) heads to Paris in the late '30s and finds bit work in an opera company, sharing a garret with gold-digging Russian Lola (a lively Blanchett) and a romance with gypsy Cesar (Depp). Lola has set her sights on hammy opera singer, Dante (Turturro). Then the Nazis invade Paris. The film's surprisingly plodding and the characters either stereotypical and/or underwritten. **97m/C; DVD.** *UK FR* Christina Ricci; Johnny Depp; Cate Blanchett; John Turturro; Harry Dean Stanton; Oleg Yankovsky; *D:* Sally Potter; *W:* Sally Potter; *C:* Sacha Vierny; *M:* Osvaldo Golijov. Natl. Bd. of Review '01: Support. Actress (Blanchett).

The Man Who Fell to Earth ✓✓✓ ½ **1976 (R)** Entertaining and technically adept cult classic about a man from another planet (Bowie, in a bit of typecasting) who ventures to earth in hopes of finding water to save his family and drought-stricken planet. Instead he becomes a successful inventor and businessman, along the way discovering the human vices of booze, sex, and television. Also available in a restored version at 138 minutes. Remade for TV in 1987 and based on Walter Tevis's novel. **118m/C; VHS, DVD, Blu-Ray.** *GB* David Bowie; Candy Clark; Rip Torn; Buck Henry; Bernie Casey; Jackson D. Kane; Rick Riccardo; Tony Mascia; *D:* Nicolas Roeg; *W:* Paul Mayersberg; *C:* Anthony B. Richmond; *M:* John Phillips.

The Man Who Had Everything ✓ ½ **1920** Thoughtless millionaire's son Harry Bullway (Pickford) nearly runs over blind beggar Matt Sills (Francis) who puts an unusual curse on Harry so he'll get everything he wants. Even the over-indulged Harry soon tires of this and realizes he won't appreciate anything unless he can earn it himself. **66m/B; Silent; DVD.** Jack Pickford; Lionel Belmore; Priscilla Bonner; Alec B. Francis; Shannon Day; *D:* Alfred E. Green; *W:* Arthur F. Statter; *C:* Clyde Cook.

The Man Who Haunted Himself ✓✓ **1970** While a man lies in critical condition on the operating table after a car accident, his alter-ego emerges and turns his ideal life into a nightmare until the man recovers and moves toward a fateful encounter. An expanded version of an episode of the TV series "Alfred Hitchcock Presents," this was Moore's first movie after having starred in the TV series "The Saint," and it was Dearden's last film; he died in a car accident the following year. Appeals primarily to those fascinated by "Hitchcock" or "The Twilight Zone"?where mystery matters most. Filmed in London. **94m/C; VHS, DVD, Blu-Ray.** *GB* Roger Moore; Hildegard(e) Neil; Olga Georges-Picot; *D:* Basil Dearden; *W:* Bryan Forbes; *C:* Tony Spratling; *M:* Michael Lewis.

The Man Who Invented Christmas ✓✓ ½ **2017 (PG)** An essentially effective look at the origins of the modern celebration of Christmas based on the nonfiction book by Les Standiford. In 1843, famous author Charles Dickens (Stevens) has reached an impasse in his career and needs income to support his wife (Clark) and children. Inspired by a comment made by the family's new maid (Murphy), Dickens quickly writes "A Christmas Carol" to take advantage of the forthcoming Christmas holiday. Despite challenges such as the chaotic nature of his home life, Dickens finds inspiration in various people and events he observes in London. A familiar story told in broad fashion. **104m/C; DVD, Blu-Ray.** Dan Stevens; Christopher Plummer; Jonathan Pryce; Simon Callow; Miriam Margolyes; *D:* Bharat Nalluri; *W:* Susan Coyne; *C:* Ben Smithard; *M:* Mychael Danna.

The Man Who Killed Don Quixote ✓✓ **2018** When director Toby Grisoni (Driver) visits Spain, he comes across a DVD of a short student film he made about the Miguel de Cervantes character Don Quixote. Inspired, he locates two actors from the film, an old man named Javier (Pryce) and a younger woman named Angelica (Ribeiro). Toby learns that Javier believes he is Don Quixote and Toby is his sidekick, Sancho Panza. As the line between fantasy and blur, the pair embarks upon an unexpected journey. Imaginative though muddled, it features memorable performances by Driver and Pryce. **132m/C; DVD, Blu-Ray.** *BE SP FR UK PT* Adam Driver; William Miller; Will Keen; Jason Watkins; Paloma Bloyd; ***D:*** Terry Gilliam; ***W:*** Terry Gilliam; Tony Grisoni; ***C:*** Nicola Pecorini; ***M:*** Roque Baños.

The Man Who Killed Hitler and Then the Bigfoot 🦴🦴 **2019** The aged Calvin Barr (Elliott) lives a relatively normal life in a small town. When hassled by would-be muggers, he easily dispatches them. Calvin has an impressive history as the man who killed Adolf Hitler. However, he does not believe he did anything heroic, and his service indirectly led to a loss of someone he loved. Calvin's life changes when he is recruited by the U.S. government to kill Bigfoot, which carries a virus to which he is immune. Though the film has a stellar production team and cast, the directorial debut of Krzykowski has an overly sincere revisionist plot. **98m/C; DVD.** Sam Elliott; Aidan Turner; Sean Bridgers; Ron Livingston; Caitlin FitzGerald; ***D:*** Robert D. Krzykowski; ***W:*** Robert D. Krzykowski; ***C:*** Alex Vendler; ***M:*** Joe Kraemer.

The Man Who Knew Infinity 🦴🦴 **2016 (PG-13)** There's nothing particularly wrong with this well-intentioned biopic, but if you close your eyes you can picture the whole movie. Dev Patel plays Srinivasa Ramanujan Iyengar, a poor young man in Madras, India, who earns his way into Cambridge University during World War I. With the assistance of a professor named G.H. Hardy (Irons), Sri becomes a pioneer in the field of mathematical theories. Patel and Irons do their best to inject their clichéd characters with a bit of reality. **108m/C; DVD, Blu-Ray.** Jeremy Irons; Dev Patel; Malcolm Sinclair; Dhritiman Chatterjee; Stephen Fry; ***D:*** Matthew Brown; ***W:*** Matthew Brown; ***C:*** Larry Smith.

The Man Who Knew Too Little 🦴🦴 ½ *Watch That Man* **1997 (PG)** Wallace (Murray) travels to London to surprise his yuppie brother James (Gallagher) on his birthday. James is hosting an important dinner party, so he sends his less than upper-crusty brother to the Theater of Life, where the patrons take part in scenes with actors in real-life settings. Wallace is then unwittingly thrown into a plot to rekindle the Cold War. Totally oblivious to the danger, he treats every threat with a sly smile and a smart-aleck remark. Whalley's the call girl/spy who turns into the sidekick/love interest. Mainly a stretched out one-joke premise even with comic maestro Murray. **94m/C; DVD, Blu-Ray.** Bill Murray; Peter Gallagher; Joanne Whalley; Alfred Molina; Richard Wilson; Geraldine James; John Standing; Anna Chancellor; Nicholas Woodeson; Simon Chandler; ***D:*** Jon Amiel; ***W:*** Howard Franklin; Robert Harrar; ***C:*** Robert M. Stevens; ***M:*** Chris Young.

The Man Who Knew Too Much 🦴🦴🦴 **1934** Hitchcock's first international success. A British family man on vacation in Switzerland is told of an assassination plot by a dying agent. His daughter is kidnapped to force his silence. In typical Hitchcock fashion, the innocent person becomes caught in a web of intrigue; the sticky situation culminates with surprising events during the famous shootout in the final scenes. Remade by Hitchcock in 1956. **75m/B; VHS, DVD, Blu-Ray.** *GB* Leslie Banks; Edna Best; Peter Lorre; Nova Pilbeam; Pierre Fresnay; Frank Vosper; Hugh Wakefield; Cicely Oates; D. A. Clarke-Smith; George Curzon; Henry Oscar; Wilfrid Hyde-White; ***D:*** Alfred Hitchcock; ***W:*** Emlyn Williams; Charles Bennett; A.R. Rawlinson; Edwin Greenwood; D. B. Wyndham-Lewis; ***C:*** Curt Courant.

The Man Who Knew Too Much 🦴🦴 ½ **1956 (PG)** Hitchcock's remake of his 1934 film, this time about an American doctor and his family vacationing in Marrakech. They become involved in a complicated international plot involving kidnapping and murder. While Doris tries to save the day by singing "Que Sera, Sera," Stewart tries to locate his abducted son. More lavish settings and forms of intrigue make this a less focused and, to some, inferior version. **120m/C; VHS, DVD, Blu-Ray.** James Stewart; Doris Day; Brenda de Banzie; Bernard Miles; Ralph Truman; Daniel Gelin; Alan Mowbray; Carolyn Jones; Hillary Brooke; ***D:*** Alfred Hitchcock; ***W:*** John Michael Hayes; ***C:*** Robert Burks; ***M:*** Bernard Herrmann. Oscars '56: Song ("Que Sera, Sera").

The Man Who Laughs 🦴🦴🦴 ½ **1927** Veidt's sensitive performance highlights this silent classic. He plays a young man whose features are surgically altered into a permanent smile because his family are political enemies of the current ruler. The man is befriended by the owner of a sideshow who first exhibits him as a freak but later finds Veidt gaining fame as a clown. A beautiful blind girl in the show loves Veidt for who he is and the two find happiness. **110m/B; Silent; VHS, DVD, Blu-Ray.** Conrad Veidt; Mary Philbin; Olga Baclanova; Josephine Crowell; George Siegmann; Brandon Hurst; ***D:*** Paul Leni.

The Man Who Lies 🦴🦴 *L'Homme qui Ment* **1968** Arty melodrama with an untrustworthy narrator. Boris is a WWII refugee escaping from German soldiers. He comes to a French village, claiming to be a resistance fighter and a comrade of their local (and supposedly dead) hero. Boris continues to tell his tall tales, but then a man arrives claiming to be said hero. French with subtitles. **95m/B; DVD, Blu-Ray.** *FR* Jean-Louis Trintignant; Ivan Mistrik; ***D:*** Alain Robbe-Grillet; ***W:*** Alain Robbe-Grillet; ***C:*** Igor Luther; ***M:*** Michel Fano.

The Man Who Lived at the Ritz 🦴🦴 **1991** TV miniseries based on the A.E. Hotchner novel. American artist Philip Weber (King) is a longtime resident of the Ritz Hotel in Paris. When the Germans overrun France, Nazi Hermann Goering (Ackland) makes the hotel his headquarters and wants Philip to help him 'acquire' valuable art. Philip wanted to remain neutral during the war but now has to decide which side he's on. **200m/C; DVD.** Perry King; Joss Ackland; Leslie Caron; David McCallum; Cherie Lunghi; David Robb; Mylene Demongeot; ***D:*** Desmond Davis; ***W:*** Gordon Cotler; ***C:*** Claude Robin; ***M:*** Richard Rodney Bennett. **TV**

Man Who Loved Cat Dancing 🦴🦴 **1973 (PG)** Reynolds is an outlaw on the run after avenging his wife's murder and robbing a safe with pals Hopkins and Warden, and Miles has recently escaped from her abusive husband. It's love on the run as Burt and Sarah are pursued by bounty hunters and their tragic pasts—coming close to making us care, but close doesn't mean as much in movies as it does in dancing. Based on Marilyn Durham's novel. **114m/C; VHS, DVD.** Burt Reynolds; Sarah Miles; Jack Warden; Lee J. Cobb; Jay Silverheels; Robert Donner; Bo Hopkins; Nancy Malone; ***D:*** Richard Sarafian; ***W:*** Eleanor Perry; ***C:*** Harry Stradling, Jr.; ***M:*** John Williams.

The Man Who Loved Women 🦴🦴🦴 *L'Homme Qui Aimait les Femmes* **1977** An intelligent, sensitive bachelor writes his memoirs and recalls the many, many, many women he has loved. Truffaut couples sophistication and lightheartedness, the thrill of the chase and, when it leads to an accidental death, the wondering what-it's-all-about in the mourning after. In French with English subtitles. Remade in 1983. **119m/C; VHS, DVD.** *FR* Charles Denner; Brigitte Fossey; Leslie Caron; Nelly Borgeaud; Genevieve Fontanel; Nathalie Baye; Sabine Glaser; ***D:*** Francois Truffaut; ***W:*** Francois Truffaut; Suzanne Schiffman; Michel Fermaud; ***C:*** Nestor Almendros; ***M:*** Maurice Jaubert.

The Man Who Loved Women 🦴🦴 **1983 (R)** A remake of the 1977 French film, this is slower, tries to be funnier, and is less subtle than the original. Reynolds is a Los Angeles sculptor whose reputation as a playboy leads him to a psychoanalyst's couch, where a lot of talk slows the action—though Burt & Julie (the shrink) do share the couch. **110m/C; VHS, DVD.** Burt Reynolds; Julie Andrews; Kim Basinger; Marilu Henner; Cynthia Sikes; Jennifer Edwards; ***D:*** Blake Edwards; ***W:*** Blake Edwards; ***C:*** Haskell Wexler; ***M:*** Henry Mancini.

The Man Who Never Was 🦴🦴🦴 **1955** Tense true story (with melodramatic embroidery) from WWII shows in step-by-step detail how Britain duped the Axis by letting them find an Allied corpse bearing phony invasion plans. Based on the book by the scheme's mastermind Ewen Montagu, played by Webb; Peter Sellers provides the voice of an offscreen Winston Churchill. **102m/C; VHS, DVD.** *GB* Clifton Webb; Gloria Grahame; Robert Flemyng; Josephine Griffin; Stephen Boyd; Andre Morell; Laurence Naismith; Geoffrey Keen; Michael Hordern; ***D:*** Ronald Neame; ***C:*** Oswald Morris. British Acad. '56: Screenplay.

The Man Who Played God 🦴🦴 **1932** After losing his hearing, concert pianist Montgomery Royale becomes an embittered recluse in his New York apartment before learning to read lips. He then spies on couples in Central Park via his binoculars, eavesdropping on conversations and helping those in financial trouble. Davis has an early role as the loyal-but-torn fiancé. Arliss played the same role in a 1922 silent; remade as 1955's "Sincerely Yours." **81m/B; DVD.** George Arliss; Bette Davis; Violet Heming; Donald Cook; Ivan Simpson; Louise Closser Hale; ***D:*** John G. Adolfi; ***W:*** Julien Josephson; Maude Howell; ***C:*** James Van Trees.

The Man Who Shook the Hand of Vicente Fernandez 🦴🦴🦴 **2012** Rex Page (Ernest Borgnine in his last starring role) is a bitter radio DJ who finds a sort of fame among the Latino staff of a nursing home. Rex has always wanted to be the hero in a spaghetti western film, and now finds himself in the real life position of being a hero for the oppressed staff. **99m/C; DVD, Blu-Ray, Streaming.** Ernest Borgnine; Barry Corbin; Carla Ortiz; Arturo del Puerto; Tony Plana; ***D:*** Elia Petridis; ***W:*** Elia Petridis; ***C:*** Eric Leach; ***M:*** Ruy Folguera. **VIDEO**

The Man Who Shot Liberty Valance 🦴🦴🦴 ½ **1962** Tough cowboy Wayne and idealistic lawyer Stewart join forces against dreaded gunfighter Liberty Valance, played leatherly by Marvin. While Stewart rides to Senatorial success on his reputation as the man who shot the villain, he suffers moral crises about the act, but is toughened up by Wayne. Wayne's use of the word "pilgrim" became a standard for his impersonators. Strong character acting, great Western scenes, and value judgments to ponder over make this last of Ford's black-and-white westerns among his best. **123m/B; VHS, DVD, Blu-Ray.** James Stewart; John Wayne; Vera Miles; Lee Marvin; Edmond O'Brien; Andy Devine; Woody Strode; Ken Murray; Jeannette Nolan; John Qualen; Strother Martin; Lee Van Cleef; John Carradine; Denver Pyle; Willis Bouchey; ***D:*** John Ford; ***W:*** James Warner Bellah; Willis Goldbeck; ***C:*** William Clothier; ***M:*** Cyril Mockridge; Alfred Newman. Natl. Film Reg. '07.

The Man Who Sued God 🦴🦴 **2001** In this comedy, lawyer Steve Myers (Connolly) is disillusioned with his career as a lawyer and quits. Buying a boat to become a fisherman, the vessel is struck by lightning with Myers aboard and destroyed. Because Myers' insurance company denies his claim as an "Act of God," he sues God and names certain prominent clergy members as God's representatives. Catching the attention of the media, God and His existence is put on trial. As a result of the lawsuit, Myers also strikes up a friendship with journalist Anna Redmond (Davis). **97m/C; DVD.** Billy Connolly; Judy Davis; Colin Friels; Wendy Hughes; Bille Brown; ***D:*** Mark Joffe; ***W:*** John Clarke; Don Watson; ***C:*** Peter James; ***M:*** David Bridie. **VIDEO**

The Man Who Turned to Stone 🦴 ½ **1957** A group of 18th-century scientists harnessed the electrical energy of young women to make themselves immortal and if they don't keep up with their experiments, the men literally turn to stone. Then they start using the women prisoners from a reformatory but the prison doctor gets suspicious by the sudden rise of inmate deaths. **71m/B; DVD.** Victor Jory; Ann Doran; Charlotte Austin; William (Bill) Hudson; Paul Cavanagh; Victor Varconi; George Lynn; ***D:*** Laszlo Kardos; ***W:*** Bernard Gordon; ***C:*** Benjamin (Ben H.) Kline.

The Man Who Wasn't There 🦴 **1983 (R)** A member of the State department receives a formula from a dying spy that can render him invisible, see? He has to use the formula to protect himself from the police and other spies, becoming a comic "Invisible Man," see? Generally chaotic tale that's bad, but not so bad that it's worth seeing, though you might want to see what invisibility looks like in 3-D. **111m/C; VHS, Streaming.** Steve Guttenberg; Jeffrey Tambor; Art Hindle; Lisa Langlois; Victor Rendina; ***D:*** Bruce Malmuth; ***M:*** Miles Goodman.

The Man Who Wasn't There 🦴🦴🦴 **2001 (R)** Ed Crane (Thornton, in a masterfully underplayed performance) is a small-town barber who goes unnoticed by many. He suspects that his wife Doris (McDormand) is cheating on him with Dave (Gandolfini), who owns the store where she works. When Ed decides that he wants to invest in the new "dry cleaning" process that a stranger tells him about, he decides to try blackmail. What follows is a series of stately paced twists and complications. **116m/B; VHS, DVD.** Billy Bob Thornton; Frances McDormand; Michael Badalucco; James Gandolfini; Katherine Borowitz; Jon Polito; Scarlett Johansson; Richard Jenkins; Tony Shalhoub; ***D:*** Joel Coen; ***W:*** Joel Coen; Ethan Coen; ***C:*** Roger Deakins; ***M:*** Carter Burwell. L.A. Film Critics '01: Cinematog.; Natl. Bd. of Review '01: Actor (Thornton).

The Man Who Would Be King 🦴🦴🦴🦴 **1975 (PG)** A grand, old-fashioned adventure based on the classic story by Rudyard Kipling about two mercenary soldiers who travel from India to Kafiristan in order to conquer it and set themselves up as kings. Splendid characterizations by Connery and Caine, and Huston's royal directorial treatment provides it with adventure, majestic sweep, and well-developed characters. **129m/C; VHS, DVD, Blu-Ray.** Sean Connery; Michael Caine; Christopher Plummer; Saeed Jaffrey; Shakira Caine; ***D:*** John Huston; ***W:*** Gladys Hill; John Huston; ***C:*** Oswald Morris; ***M:*** Maurice Jarre.

The Man With a Cloak 🦴 ½ **1951** Overstuffed and pretentious period piece with Stanwyck appearing as a would-be murderous housekeeper. In 1848, Madeline arrives in New York from France to persuade dying Charles Thevenet to reinstate his estranged grandson (and her lover) in his will. This upsets the plans of his housekeeper and butler who intend to inherit themselves. The revised will is hidden by Thevenet's pet raven and Madeline must rely on her new friend—the poetry-spouting drunk of the title—for help. Adapted from a John Dickson Carr story. **81m/B; DVD.** Leslie Caron; Louis Calhern; Joseph Cotten; Barbara Stanwyck; Joe De Santis; Jim Backus; Margaret Wycherly; Richard Hale; ***D:*** Fletcher Markle; ***W:*** Frank Fenton; ***C:*** George J. Folsey; ***M:*** David Raksin.

Man with a Gun 🦴🦴 ½ **1995 (R)** Hitman John Hardin (Madsen) is asked by mobster employer Jack Rushton (Busey) to kill his ex-girlfriend Rena (Tilly) and get a CD-ROM filled with info he doesn't want to get out. Rena now happens to be John's gal pal but isn't too upset since she figures they'll substitute Rena's goody two-shoes twin sister Kathy for the needed corpse. Too bad John starts to fall for the intended victim, leaving the plan to unravel. It's a connect-the-dots plot with a creditable cast. Based on the novel "The Shroud Society" by Hugh C. Rae. **100m/C; VHS, DVD.** Michael Madsen; Jennifer Tilly; Gary Busey; Robert Loggia; Ian Tracey; Bill Cobbs; ***D:*** David Wyles; ***W:*** Laurie Finstad-Knizhik; ***C:*** Jan Kiesser; ***M:*** George Blondheim.

A Man with a Maid 🦴 *The Groove Room; What the Swedish Butler Saw; Swedish Wildcats* **1973** A bizarre British exploitation pic mixes spookhouse cliches and sex, as a young man finds his new bachelor pad haunted by Jack the Ripper. Originally shot in 3-D. **83m/C; VHS, DVD.** Sue Longhurst; Martin Long; Diana Dors; ***D:*** Vernon Becker.

The Man with Bogart's Face 🦴🦴 *Sam Marlowe, Private Eye* **1980 (PG)** Sacchi is no Bogart, but he does imitate him well. Bogart fans will enjoy this fond tribute to the late great actor, but the story uncertainly wavers between genuine detective story and detective spoof. **106m/C; VHS, DVD.** Robert Sacchi; Misty Rowe; Sybil Danning; Franco Nero; Herbert Lom; Victor Buono; Olivia Hussey; ***D:*** Robert Day; ***W:*** Andrew J. Fenady; ***M:*** John Beal; George Duning. Golden Raspberries '80: Worst Song ("The Man with Bogart's Face").

The Man with One Red Shoe
1985 (PG) Hanks is a lovable clod of a violinist who ensnares himself in a web of intrigue when CIA agents, both good and evil, mistake him for a contact by his wearing one red shoe. Sporadically funny remake of the French "The Tall Blond Man with One Black Shoe." **92m/C; VHS, DVD.** Tom Hanks; Dabney Coleman; Lori Singer; Carrie Fisher; James Belushi; Charles Durning; Edward Herrmann; Tom Noonan; Gerrit Graham; David Lander; David Ogden Stiers; ***D:*** Stan Dragoti; ***M:*** Thomas Newman.

The Man with the Golden Arm **1955** A gripping film version of the Nelson Algren junkie melodrama, about an ex-addict who returns to town only to get mixed up with drugs again. Crooked card dealer Frankie Machine (Sinatra in a standout performance) returns after a stint in rehab, hoping to pursue new dreams. But his crippled wife Zosch (Parker) wants him to stick with what he knows while drug dealer Louie (McGavin) makes Frankie offers he finds harder and harder to refuse, even with blonde beauty Molly (Novak) to offer Frankie comfort. Considered controversial in its depiction of addiction when released. **119m/B; VHS, DVD.** Frank Sinatra; Kim Novak; Eleanor Parker; Arnold Stang; Darren McGavin; Robert Strauss; George Mathews; John Conte; Doro Merande; ***D:*** Otto Preminger; ***W:*** Lewis Meltzer; Walter Newman; ***C:*** Sam Leavitt; ***M:*** Elmer Bernstein.

The Man with the Golden Gun 1/2 **1974 (PG)** Roger Moore is the debonair secret agent 007 in this ninth James Bond flick. Assigned to recover a small piece of equipment which can be utilized to harness the sun's energy, Bond engages the usual bevy of villains and beauties. **134m/C; VHS, DVD, Blu-Ray.** *GB* Roger Moore; Christopher Lee; Britt Ekland; Maud Adams; Herve Villechaize; Clifton James; Soon-Teck Oh; Richard Loo; Marc Lawrence; Bernard Lee; Lois Maxwell; Desmond Llewelyn; ***D:*** Guy Hamilton; ***W:*** Tom Mankiewicz; ***C:*** Ted Moore; ***M:*** John Barry.

The Man with the Iron Fists 1/2
2012 (R) Essentially a messy vanity project (with a certain manic excitement) for rapper RZA who stars, co-writes, and makes his directorial debut. RZA is a nameless blacksmith in a 19th-century Chinese village who gets caught up in martial arts mayhem having to do with a treasure. The blacksmith really just wants to be happy with his girl (Chung) but he has obligations. To reinforce the craziness, Crowe appears as a smirking British knife-toting associate. **95m/C; DVD, Blu-Ray.** RZA; Russell Crowe; Lucy Liu; Rick Yune; Jamie Chung; Daniel Wu; Dave Bautista; Cung Le; ***D:*** RZA; ***W:*** RZA; Eli Roth; ***C:*** Chi Ying Chan; ***M:*** RZA; Howard Drossin.

The Man with the Movie Camera 1/2 *Chelovek s Kinoapparatom* **1929** A plotless, experimental view of Moscow through the creative eye of the cameraman Dziga Vertov, founder of the Kino Eye. The editing methods and camera techniques used in this silent film were very influential and still stand up to scrutiny today. **69m/B; Silent; VHS, DVD.** *RU* ***D:*** Dziga Vertov; ***W:*** Dziga Vertov; ***C:*** Mikhail Kaufman; ***M:*** Pierre Henry.

The Man with Two Brains
1983 (R) Did you hear the one about the brilliant neurosurgeon who falls in love with a woman's disembodied brain in his laboratory? Dr. Michael Hfuhruhurr (Martin) only has two problems: dealing with his frigid, covetous wife (Turner) and finding a body for his cerebral lover. Isn't it nice that a serial killer is on the loose? Plenty of laughs in this spoof of mad scientist movies that is redeemed from potential idiocy by the cast's titillating performances. Listen closely and you'll recognize the voice of Spacek as the brain-in-the-jar of Martin's dreams. **91m/C; DVD, Blu-Ray.** Steve Martin; Kathleen Turner; David Warner; Paul Benedict; James Cromwell; Francis X. (Frank) McCarthy; George Furth; Randi Brooks; Bernard Behrens; Stephanie Kramer; ***Cameo(s):*** Merv Griffin; ***V:*** Sissy Spacek; ***D:*** Carl Reiner; ***W:*** Steve Martin; Carl Reiner; George Gipe; ***C:*** Michael Chapman; ***M:*** Joel Goldsmith.

The Man with Two Faces **1934** Flamboyant stage actor-manager Dawson Wells (Robinson) plots revenge on his evil brother-in-law Stanley Vance (Calhern) for ruining the life of his actress sister Jessica (Astor). Vance is visited by European producer Jules Chautard (you might guess from the title who that really is) and a murder occurs. Based on the comic-mystery play "The Dark Tower" by Alexander Woollcott and George S. Kaufman. Filmed with two endings: one that adhered to the stage version and one more ambiguous. **72m/B; DVD.** Edward G. Robinson; Louis Calhern; Mary Astor; Ricardo Cortez; Mae Clarke; David Landau; Margaret Dale; ***D:*** Archie Mayo; ***W:*** Niven Busch; Tom Reed; ***C:*** Gaetano Antonio "Tony" Gaudio.

The Man with Two Lives 1/2
1942 Well done horror thriller about a wealthy young man who's killed in a car accident, then brought back to life by a mad scientist. At precisely the moment his life is restored, a murderous gangster is executed and his soul enters the young man's body. **65m/B; VHS, DVD.** Edward Norris; Addison Richards; Marlo Dwyer; Eleanor Lawson; ***D:*** Phil Rosen; ***W:*** Joseph Hoffman; ***C:*** Harry Neumann.

The Man Without a Face 1/2
1993 (PG-13) Gibson plays a badly scarred recluse in Maine who develops a mentor relationship with a lonely, fatherless boy. Chuck (Stahl) wants to go away to military school, but flunks the extrance exam, and enlists former teacher McLeod as a tutor. First foray for Gibson into the director's chair tends to be overly melodramatic. Adapted from a novel by Isabelle Holland. **115m/C; VHS, DVD.** Mel Gibson; Nick Stahl; Margaret Whitton; Fay Masterson; Richard Masur; Gaby Hoffman; Geoffrey Lewis; Jack DeMave; ***D:*** Mel Gibson; ***W:*** Malcolm MacRury; ***M:*** James Horner.

The Man Without a Past *Mies Vailla Menneisyytta* **2002** Deadpan comedy/drama takes place on the outskirts of Helsinki and the fringes of society. A man (Peltola) is robbed and left for dead; he stumbles out of the hospital with amnesia and is found by two young brothers who take him home to their parents and a shantytown existence in a shipping container. He gets housing in his own container, does odd jobs to make some money, and finds romance with Salvation Army worker Irma (Outinen). When his identity is finally discovered, it doesn't matter. Finnish with subtitles. **97m/C; DVD.** *FI GE FR* Markku Peltola; Kati Outinen; Juhani Nielmela; Kaija Pakarinen; Sakari Kuosmanen; ***D:*** Aki Kaurismaki; ***W:*** Aki Kaurismaki; ***C:*** Timo Salminen. Natl. Soc. Film Critics '03: Foreign Film.

Man Without a Star **1955** A cowboy helps ranchers stop a ruthless cattle owner from taking over their land. The conflict between freedom in the wild west and the need for order and settlements is powerfully internalized in Douglas, whose fight for justice will tame the cowboy code he lives by. You'll shed a tear for the fading frontier. **89m/B; VHS, DVD, Blu-Ray.** Kirk Douglas; Jeanne Crain; Claire Trevor; William Campbell; ***D:*** King Vidor.

Man, Woman & Child **1983 (PG)** A close, upscale California family is shocked when a child from the husband's long-ago affair with a Frenchwoman appears at their door. Pure sentimentalism, as the family confronts this unexpected development. Two hankies—one each for fine performances by Sheen and Danner. Based on a sentimental novel by Erich Segal of "Love Story" fame, who co-wrote the script. **99m/C; VHS, DVD.** Martin Sheen; Blythe Danner; Craig T. Nelson; David Hemmings; ***D:*** Dick Richards; ***W:*** Erich Segal; ***M:*** Georges Delerue.

Management **2009 (R)** Upwardly-mobile sales rep Sue (Aniston) spends lots of time on the road in no-name motels, such as the one in Arizona that is owned by night manager Mike's (Zahn) folks. Mike is a nice, aimless guy and, after he admires her butt, he and Sue have an afternoon quickie resulting in the smitten stoner following Sue back to Baltimore. Rather than think him a freaky stalker, Sue lets him hang around. Mike is still determined to win Sue's love even when her ex-boyfriend, yogurt mogul Jango (Harrelson), gets back into the picture. Harmless rom-com that offers nothing much new, especially for Aniston. **93m/C; DVD.** Jennifer Aniston; Steve Zahn; Woody Harrelson; Fred Ward; Margo Martindale; James Hiroyuki Liao; ***D:*** Stephen Belber; ***W:*** Stephen Belber; ***C:*** Eric Alan Edwards; ***M:*** Mychael Danna; Rob Simonsen.

Manborg 1/2 **2011** In this over the top tribute to 80s schlockfests, humanity must fight an army of demonic vampire nazis to surivive and their only hope is the cheesily named Manborg. **72m/C; DVD, Streaming.** *CA* Matthew Kennedy; Adam Brooks; Meredith Sweeney; Conor Sweeney; Jeremy Gillespie; ***D:*** Steven Kostanski; ***W:*** Steven Kostanski; ***C:*** Jeremy Gillespie; ***M:*** Brian Wiacek. **VIDEO**

Manchester by the Sea 1/2
2016 (R) Writer/director Lonergan's multiple award winner is one of the best films ever made about grief. Lee Chandler (Affleck) is a shell of a man after an unimaginable tragedy. He is forced to return home to take care of his nephew Patrick (Hedges) after the death of Lee's brother (Chandler), and he has to confront the ghosts of his past. Lonergan's script is character-driven, never once feeling manipulative but producing raw emotion from the viewer. This is a film not about overcoming grief but learning to live with it and every element—performance, script, tech—works perfectly to form an unforgettable film. **137m/C; DVD, Blu-Ray.** Casey Affleck; Michelle Williams; Kyle Chandler; Lucas Hedges; Gretchen Mol; ***D:*** Kenneth Lonergan; ***W:*** Kenneth Lonergan; ***C:*** Jody Lee Lipes; ***M:*** Lesley Barber. Oscars '16: Actor (Affleck), Orig. Screenplay; British Acad. '16: Actor (Affleck), Orig. Screenplay; Golden Globes '17: Actor--Drama (Affleck); Ind. Spirit '17: Actor (Affleck).

The Manchurian Candidate **1962** Political thriller about an American Korean War vet who suspects that he and his platoon may have been brainwashed during the war, with his highly decorated, heroic friend programmed by commies to be an operational assassin. Loaded with shocks, conspiracy, inventive visual imagery, and bitter political satire of naivete and machinations of the left and right. Excellent performances by an all-star cast, with Lansbury and Gregory particularly frightening. Based on the Richard Condon novel. **126m/B; VHS, DVD, Blu-Ray.** Frank Sinatra; Laurence Harvey; Angela Lansbury; Janet Leigh; James Gregory; Leslie Parrish; John McGiver; Henry Silva; Khigh Deigh; James Edwards; Barry Kelley; Albert Paulsen; ***D:*** John Frankenheimer; ***W:*** John Frankenheimer; George Axelrod; ***C:*** Lionel Lindon; ***M:*** David Amram. AFI '98: Top 100; Golden Globes '63: Support. Actress (Lansbury); Natl. Bd. of Review '62: Support. Actress (Lansbury); Natl. Film Reg. '94.

The Manchurian Candidate
2004 (R) Political cynicism at its most sinister in this updated take on the 1962 John Frankenheimer classic. Ben Marco (Washington) and Raymond Shaw (Schreiber) are now Gulf War I vets. New York congressman Shaw has mom, Sen. Eleanor Shaw (Streep), pulling his strings. Marco believes his men were brainwashed by mega-corporation Manchurian Global who, with Eleanor's aid, are positioning Shaw to be a vice-presidential candidate they can control via microchip. Washington is properly heroic and tormented while Schreiber is tormented and forlorn. Streep has fun with her power-hungry, mother-knows-best viper. Based on the novel by Richard Condon. **130m/C; DVD, Blu-Ray, UMD, HD-DVD.** Denzel Washington; Liev Schreiber; Meryl Streep; Kimberly Elise; Vera Farmiga; Jon Voight; Jeffrey Wright; Miguel Ferrer; Simon McBurney; Pablo Schreiber; Ted Levine; Bruno Ganz; Dean Stockwell; Zeljko Ivanek; ***D:*** Jonathan Demme; ***W:*** Dean Georgaris; Daniel Pyne; ***C:*** Tak Fujimoto; ***M:*** Nelust Wyclef Jean; Rachel Portman.

Mandabi 1/2 *The Money Order; Le Mandat* **1968** Unlocking, perhaps for the first time onscreen, the complex daily world of modern Africa, Senegalese filmmaker Ousmane Sembene's second feature is a deceptively simple story of a man who receives a money order and runs straight into a barrage of bureaucracy—Third World bureaucracy, but bureaucracy nevertheless—when he attempts to cash it. Gradually but unmistakably gaining deeper and more far-reaching meaning as it progresses, Sembene's moving, witty, masterful storytelling is also a sharply etched portrait of a civilization in the throes of change. Thirty years after its initial release, it remains fresh, exciting, warm, subtle, and heartbreaking. **90m/C; DVD.** *SE* Christoph Colomb; Makhouredia Gueye; Isseu Niang; Mustapha Ture; ***D:*** Ousmane Sembene.

The Mandarin Mystery 1/2 **1937** In the process of trying to retrieve a stolen Mandarin stamp, detective Ellery Queen uncovers a counterfeiting ring. Some fine performances, but a muddled script creates a mystery as to whether or not the action is played for laughs. **65m/B; VHS, DVD.** Eddie Quillan; Charlotte Henry; Rita La Roy; Wade Boteler; Franklin Pangborn; George Irving; Kay Hughes; William "Billy" Newell; ***D:*** Ralph Staub.

Mandela **1987** A gripping, powerful drama about human rights and dignity, tracing the real-life trials of Nelson and Winnie Mandela. The story focuses on the couple's early opposition to South African apartheid, as well as the events leading up to Nelson's life-imprisonment sentencing in 1964. Excellent, restrained performances from Glover and Woodard. **135m/C; VHS, DVD.** Danny Glover; Alfre Woodard; John Matshikiza; Warren Clarke; Allan Corduner; Julian Glover; ***D:*** Philip Saville. **CABLE**

Mandela and de Klerk 1/2 **1997 (PG)** Docudrama about the two men who changed South Africa. White Afrikaaner president F.W. de Klerk (Caine) declared an end to apartheid in 1992 and two years later was succeeded as the country's president by Nelson Mandela (Poitier), a black activist imprisioned on treason charges for 27 years before his release. Both men shared the Nobel Peace Prize for their efforts to unite South Africa. **114m/C; DVD.** Sidney Poitier; Michael Caine; Tina Lifford; Ian Roberts; Gerry Maritz; Jerry Mofokeng; ***D:*** Joseph Sargent; ***W:*** Richard Wesley; ***C:*** Tobias Schliessler; ***M:*** Cedric Gradus-Samson. **CABLE**

Mandela: Long Walk to Freedom 1/2 **2013 (PG-13)** Straightforward, sprawling bio of the late South African leader, based on Mandela's autobiography. Elba does an intense job in the title role as the film traces Mandela's rural roots, his work as a lawyer, his rise in the African National Congress, and his arrest and conviction on charges of sabotage and conspiracy that lead to a 27 year imprisonment. Second wife Winnie is played with strength and grace by Harris although the couple's eventual divisions aren't ignored when Mandela is finally released. Director Chadwick finishes--appropriately enough--with the official end to apartheid in 1994. English, Afrikaans and Xhosa with subtitles. **139m/C; DVD, Blu-Ray.** *SA UK* Idris Elba; Naomie Harris; Tony Kgoroge; Terry Pheto; ***D:*** Justin Chadwick; ***W:*** William Nicholson; ***C:*** Lol Crawley; ***M:*** Alex Heffes. Golden Globes '14: Song ("Ordinary Love").

Manderlay **2005** Yet another tiresome screed from Danish director Von Trier, following 2003's "Dogville." In 1933, Grace (now played by Howard instead of Nicole Kidman) comes across the titular Alabama plantation where slavery still exists. Grace self-righteously decides to meddle, against her gangster father's (Dafoe) warnings, and finds out that, despite appearances, everyone else is okay with the status quo and it's Grace who must change. Deliberately artificial and of interest only to the director's devotees. **139m/C; DVD.** Bryce Dallas Howard; Isaach de Bankole; Danny Glover; Willem Dafoe; Lauren Bacall; Jean-Marc Barr; Geoffrey Bateman; Jeremy Davies; Michael Abiteboul; Virgile Bramly; Ruben Brinkman; Dona Croll; Udo Kier; Zeljko Ivanek; ***Nar:*** John Hurt; ***D:*** Lars von Trier; ***W:*** Lars von Trier; ***C:*** Anthony Dod Mantle.

Mandingo **1975 (R)** Overheated Southern-fried tale of slavery in the Deep South, circa 1840, dealing with the tangled loves and hates of a family and their slaves. Heavyweight boxer Norton made his screen debut in the title role as the slave who makes his master money with his boxing prowess. King is the wastrel son who makes Norton's wife, another slave, his mistress. Followed by 1975's "Drum." Based on the novel by Kyle Onstott. **127m/C; VHS, DVD, Blu-Ray.** James Mason; Susan George; Perry King; Richard Ward; Ken Norton; Ben Masters; Brenda Sykes; Paul Benedict; Ji-Tu Cumbuka; Debbi (Deborah) Morgan; ***D:*** Richard Fleischer; ***W:*** Richard H. Kline; Norman Wexler; ***M:*** Maurice Jarre.

Mandragora 1997 Marek (Caslavka) is a 16-year-old small town boy who takes off for the bright lights of post-Communist Prague. He's soon selling his body on the streets and makes friends with fellow hustler, David (Svec), but the duo sink into the usual morass of drugs and self-destruction. Czech with subtitles. **133m/C; VHS, DVD.** *CZ* Miroslav Caslavka; David Svec; Miroslav Breu; Pavel Skripaz; ***D:*** Wiktor Grodecki; ***W:*** Wiktor Grodecki; David Svec; ***C:*** Vladimir Holomek; ***M:*** Wolfgang Hammerschmid.

Mandrake *Unearthed* **2010** Formulaic monster movie from the Syfy Channel. Wealthy creep Harry Vargas (Martinez) funds a treasure-hunting expedition led by Darren McCall (Martini) to find a bejeweled conquistador's dagger in a jungle burial ground. Taking the dagger releases the not-so-fearsome killer plant that is thirsty for human blood. **89m/C; DVD.** Maximillian Martini; Benito Martinez; Betsy Russell; Nick Gomez; Jon Mack; Wayne Pere; ***D:*** Tripp Reed; ***W:*** David Ray; ***C:*** Ken Blakey; ***M:*** Jermaine Stegall. **CABLE**

Mandroid 1/2 **1993 (R)** Two scientists design a high-tech robot, Mandroid, to handle a powerful new element they've discovered. Dr. Zimmer and daughter Zanna want to use their creation to help mankind while mad scientist Dr. Drago wants the power Mandroid can give him. When a laboratory accident leaves Drago horribly disfigured it also gives him the chance to steal Mandroid and put his evil plan into action. Filmed on location in Romania. **81m/C; VHS, DVD.** Brian Cousins; Jane Caldwell; Michael DellaFemina; Curt Lowens; Patrick Ersgard; Robert Symonds; ***D:*** Joakim (Jack) Ersgard; ***W:*** Jackson Barr; Earl Kenton.

Mandy 1/2 **2018** In 1983, a quiet life in the woods led by lumberjack Red Miller (Cage) and his girlfriend Mandy (Riseborough) is disrupted when she unintentionally attracts the attention of cult leader Jeremiah Sand (Roache). Determined to have her, Jeremiah hires a demonic motorcycle gang to kidnap her for him. Though Red is tortured and nearly loses his life when she is taken, his personal trauma and deep grief briefly becomes all consuming but ultimately fuel his plans for bloody vengeance. Cage excels in this surreal, nontraditional horror/thriller. **121m/C; DVD, Blu-Ray.** Nicolas Cage; Andrea Riseborough; Linus Roache; Ned Dennehy; Olwen Fourere; ***D:*** Panos Cosmatos; ***W:*** Panos Cosmatos; Aaron Stewart-Ahn; ***C:*** Benjamin Loeb; ***M:*** Johann Johannsson.

Maneater 1/2 **2007** Here, big stripey puddy-cat! A dismembered body turns up on the Appalachian Trail near Mount Raven, Georgia. A print proves the predator is a Bengal tiger that's escaped from a traveling carnival. Big-game hunter Graham (Clark) arrives to track the cat but the story has hit the national headlines, bringing TV reporters, the National Guard, and thrill-seekers into the area, making things a lot more difficult. **88m/C; DVD.** Gary Busey; Ian D. Clark; Ty Wood; Marina Stephenson Kerr; Sarah Constible; Diana Reis; Blake Taylor; ***D:*** Gary Yates; ***W:*** Phil Morton; ***C:*** Peter Benison; ***M:*** Glenn Burr. **TV**

Maneater **2009** In this Lifetime two-parter, based on the novel by Gigi Levangie Grazer, 32-year-old party girl Clarissa (Chalke) is horrified at the thought of having to support herself when her dad Teddy (Harrison) pushes her off the gravy train. Naturally she decides to marry rich and weds hot producer Aaron Mason (Winchester) but they don't live happily ever after. Probably because, even in Hollywood, Clarissa stands out for her snarky shallowness. **176m/C; DVD.** Sarah Chalke; Philip Winchester; Gregory Harrison; Judy Greer; Paul Leyden; Maria Conchita Alonso; Marla Sokoloff; Garcelle Beauvais; ***D:*** Timothy Busfield; ***W:*** Suzanne Martin; ***C:*** Kenneth Zunder; ***M:*** Daniel Licht. **CABLE**

Manfish 1/2 **1956** Two men venture out in a boat, the Manfish, to hunt for sunken treasure in the Caribbean. Only one survives the trip, as his greed destroys the other. The scenes off the Jamaican coast are lovely, but the story fails to take hold. Though there is a star aboard in Chaney, you'll look astern and bow out with a sinking feeling. Derived from two Edgar Allan Poe stories, "The Gold Bug" and "The Tell-Tale Heart." **76m/C; VHS, DVD.** John Bromfield; Lon Chaney, Jr.; Victor Jory; Barbara Nichols; ***D:*** W. Lee Wilder.

Manglehorn 1/2 **2015 (PG-13)** Pacino plays the title character, a locksmith with an estranged son (Messina), sick cat, and little more to enjoy in life than his flirtation with a local bank teller (Hunter). Director Green's episodic film follows Manglehorn over a few important events in his average life but doesn't create an emotional connection. A shambling, boring character study that again captures an old man striving for happiness before he dies. Worst of all, we never care what happens to him. **97m/C; DVD, Blu-Ray, Streaming.** Al Pacino; Holly Hunter; Harmony Korine; Chris Messina; Natalie Wilemon; ***D:*** David Gordon Green; ***W:*** Paul Logan; ***C:*** Tim Orr; ***M:*** David Wingo; Explosions in the Sky.

The Mangler **1994 (R)** Laundry machines munch workers in a small-town Maine industrial plant. Boss Englund's only concern is keeping the machines well-fed. Weak attempt at horror by veteran Hooper that tries to capitalize on the popularity of story originator Stephen King. Offers little in plot or scare, but fans of gore will enjoy the overuse of chunky-style blood and guts spewed from the monstrous steam ironer and folder that is apparently possesed by the devil. About 45 minutes too long for anybody to suspend their disbelief. **106m/C; DVD, Blu-Ray.** Robert Englund; Ted Levine; Daniel Matmor; Vanessa Pike; Demetre Phillips; Lisa Morris; Ashley Hayden; Vera Blacker; ***D:*** Tobe Hooper; ***W:*** Tobe Hooper; Harry Alan Towers; Stephen Brooks; ***C:*** Amnon Salomon; ***M:*** Barrington Pheloung.

Mango Yellow *Amarelo Manga* **2002** A volatile brew of conniving characters in a sweltering, poor Brazilian neighborhood. A slaughterhouse butcher delivers meat to a rickety hotel with a kitchen run by the flamboyantly gay cook with whom he is having an affair while a sultry barkeep pours her sexuality into the glass of every customer while fighting off their dirtbag advances. As expected, things get sticky in this steambath of a dramedy. Dirty hodgepodge character piece is sometimes an entertaining glimpse into a very deranged subculture, but too often feels cheap and easy. Portuguese with subtitles. **100m/C; DVD.** Leona Cavalli; Chico Diaz; Dira Paes; Matheus Nachtergaele; ***D:*** Claudio Assis; ***W:*** Hilton Lacerda; ***C:*** Walter Carvalho.

Manhattan **1979 (R)** Successful TV writer Isaac Davis (Allen) yearns to be a serious writer. He struggles through a series of ill-fated romances, including one with high school senior Tracy (Hemingway) and another with Mary (Keaton), who's also having an on-again, off-again affair with Yale (Murphy), Isaac's best friend. Streep does very well with her role of Jill, Isaac's ex-wife who's come out as a lesbian and written a withering (and successful) account of their marriage. Scathingly serious and comic view of modern relationships in urban America and of the modern intellectual neuroses. Shot in black-and-white to capture the mood of Manhattan and mated with an excellent Gershwin soundtrack. **96m/B; VHS, DVD.** Woody Allen; Diane Keaton; Meryl Streep; Mariel Hemingway; Michael Murphy; Wallace Shawn; Anne Byrne; Tisa Farrow; Mark Linn-Baker; David Rasche; Karen Allen; ***D:*** Woody Allen; ***W:*** Woody Allen; Marshall Brickman; ***C:*** Gordon Willis. British Acad. '79: Film, Screenplay; Cesar '80: Foreign Film; L.A. Film Critics '79: Support. Actress (Streep); Natl. Film Reg. '01; N.Y. Film Critics '79: Director (Allen), Support. Actress (Streep); Natl. Soc. Film Critics '79: Director (Allen), Support. Actress (Streep).

Manhattan Baby **1982** Unscary horror film about an archaeologist who digs up a relic that draws evil into the world and infects an American girl with powers that lead to many deaths. Advice to you that might have saved the archaelogist: don't dig this. **90m/C; VHS, DVD, Blu-Ray.** *IT* Christopher Connelly; Martha Taylor; Brigitta Boccoli; Giovanni Frezza; Lucio Fulci; ***D:*** Lucio Fulci; ***W:*** Elisa Briganti; Dardano Sacchetti; ***C:*** Guglielmo Mancori; ***M:*** Fabio Frizzi.

Manhattan Love Song 1/2 **1934** Socialite sisters Jerry and Carol Stewart are swindled out of their money. In order to save their home, they become the household help for their former chauffeur Williams and maid Annette, who have both saved their wages. It's not so bad for Jerry when she realizes that Williams is quite a guy. Based on the Cornell Woolrich novel. **72m/B; DVD.** Robert Armstrong; Dixie Lee; Helen Flint; Nydia Westman; Franklin Pangborn; Harold Waldbridge; ***D:*** Leonard Fields; Carl Pierson; ***W:*** Leonard Fields; Dave Silverstein; ***C:*** Robert Planck.

Manhattan Melodrama 1/2 **1934** Powell and Gable are best friends from childhood, growing up together in an orphanage. Their adult lives take different paths as Powell becomes a respected prosecuting attorney while Gable becomes a notorious gambler/racketeer. Lovely Loy is Gable's girl who comes between the two. Eventually, Powell must prosecute his life-long friend in order to win the governorship. One of Gable's toughest roles; Powell's character, however, is a bit unbelievable as his ethics seem to extend beyond love and friendship. This is the first film to team Powell and Loy, who would go on to make 13 more films together, including the "Thin Man" series. **93m/B; DVD.** Clark Gable; William Powell; Myrna Loy; Leo Carrillo; Nat Pendleton; George Sidney; Isabel Jewell; Muriel Evans; Claudelle Kaye; Frank Conroy; Jimmy Butler; Mickey Rooney; Edward Van Sloan; ***D:*** W.S. Van Dyke; ***W:*** Joseph L. Mankiewicz; Oliver H.P. Garrett; ***C:*** James Wong Howe. Oscars '34: Story.

Manhattan Merenque! 1/2 *Rice, Beans and Ketchup* **1995 (R)** Young mambo dancer Miguel (Perez) has been unable to get a visa to come to the U.S. from the Dominican Republic so he stows away and eventually makes it to New York with new friend Carmello (Leonardi), who's searching for an old girlfriend and their son. While Miguel tries for dance work on Broadway, he makes a friend in dance instructor Susan (Reed) and locates long-lost girlfriend Rosita (Cavazos). Too bad Carmello's luck isn't as good. Sweetly cornball and romantic. **100m/C; VHS, DVD.** George Perez; Lumi Cavazos; Marco Leonardi; Alyson Reed; ***D:*** Joseph B. Vasquez; ***W:*** Joseph B. Vasquez; Rue Kent Wildman; ***C:*** David Castillo; ***M:*** Lalo Schifrin.

Manhattan Merry-Go-Round **1937** One of the movies where a corrupt boss—in this case a record producer—threatens a bunch of good people as a pretense for a plot when the movie simply serves as a showcase for stars. Features many singing stars of the '30s ("where have you gone Cab Calloway?") plus Joltin' Joe, who ended up having a hit-streak in another genre. **89m/B; VHS, DVD.** Cab Calloway; Louis Prima; Ted Lewis; Ann Dvorak; Phil Regan; Kay Thompson; Gene Autry; Joe DiMaggio; ***D:*** Charles Reisner.

Manhattan Murder Mystery **1993 (PG)** Keaton and Allen team up again as two New Yorkers who get involved in a mystery when their neighbor dies under strange circumstances. Light, entertaining comedy steers clear of some of Allen's heavier themes and should keep audiences laughing till the end. Allen, writing with Brickman for the first time since "Annie Hall" and "Manhattan," makes viewers fall in love with the magic of NYC all over again. **105m/C; VHS, DVD, Blu-Ray.** Woody Allen; Diane Keaton; Anjelica Huston; Alan Alda; Jerry Adler; Ron Rifkin; Joy Behar; Lynn Cohen; Melanie Norris; Zach Braff; ***D:*** Woody Allen; ***W:*** Woody Allen; Marshall Brickman; ***C:*** Carlo Di Palma.

The Manhattan Project *Manhattan Project: The Deadly Game* **1986 (PG-13)** An exceptionally bright teenager decides to build a nuclear bomb for his project at the New York City science fair. He's out to prove how dangerously easy it is to build big bombs. When he steals plutonium from a local government installation, the feds attempt to nab the precocious youngster. Light moral overtones abound. Director Brickman co-wrote similarly titled "Manhattan." **112m/C; VHS, DVD, Blu-Ray.** John Lithgow; Christopher Collet; Cynthia Nixon; Jill Eikenberry; John Mahoney; Richard Council; Robert Schenkkan; Paul Austin; Dan E. Butler; Robert Sean Leonard; John David (J.D.) Cullum; Richard Jenkins; Timothy Carhart; Sully Boyar; Jimmie Ray Weeks; ***D:*** Marshall Brickman; ***W:*** Marshall Brickman; Thomas Baum; ***C:*** Billy Williams.

Manhunt *The Italian Connection; La Mala Ordina* **1973 (R)** A man marked for execution by the mob launches his own assault on the organization's headquarters. Action and Italian food, but not much else. Dubbed. **93m/C; VHS, DVD.** *IT* Henry Silva; Mario Adorf; Woody Strode; Luciana Paluzzi; ***D:*** Fernando Di Leo.

The Manhunt **1986** A framed cowhand escapes from prison to prove his innocence. De Angelis used the pseudonym Larry Ludman. **89m/C; VHS, DVD.** Ernest Borgnine; Bo Svenson; John Ethan Wayne; ***D:*** Fabrizio de Angelis. **TV**

Manhunt *Caceria* **2001** Daniel used to work for a gangster named Lucas but he betrayed him and now Lucas wants revenge. Daniel has returned to his hometown of Redemption and re-establishes his friendship with boyhood chum Miguel and long-lost love Elisa, even though he knows his chance of happiness is fleeting. And soon enough Lucas and his men show up to hunt Daniel down. Spanish with subtitles. **90m/C; VHS, DVD.** *AR* Luis Luque; Claribel Medina; Juan Palomino; Matias Sansone; Carlos Leyes; ***D:*** Ezio Massa; ***W:*** Ezio Massa; Jorge Bechara; ***C:*** Mariano Cuneo; Ada Frontini; ***M:*** Mariano Nunez West.

Manhunter *Red Dragon* **1986 (R)** Will Graham (Petersen) retired from the FBI's Behavioral Science Unit after a harrowing pursuit of a serial killer, but he's called back to find a psychotic family murderer. His technique is to match the thought processes of the killer and thus anticipate their moves. Intense thriller, based on the Thomas Harris novel "Red Dragon." Harris also wrote "The Silence of the Lambs," whose most notorious character Hannibal ("The Cannibal") Lecter, appears here as well as Graham visits the prisoner to get fresh insights and Lektor (Cox) plays his usual nasty mind games. Director Mann creates a quiet, moody intensity broken by sudden onslaughts of violence. **100m/C; VHS, DVD, Blu-Ray.** William L. Petersen; Kim Greist; Joan Allen; Brian Cox; Dennis Farina; Stephen Lang; Tom Noonan; Benjamin Hendrickson; David Seaman; Dan E. Butler; Norman Snow; Frankie Faison; Garcelle Beauvais; Patricia Charbonneau; ***D:*** Michael Mann; ***W:*** Michael Mann; ***C:*** Dante Spinotti; ***M:*** Michel Rubini.

Maniac WOOF! **1934** A scientist has designs on raising the dead and searches for victims on which to experiment. Bizarre "adults only" exploitation feature was considered very risque for its time, and includes eaten eyeballs, a cat fight with syringes, and a rapist who thinks he's an orangutan. A must for genre aficionados. **67m/B; VHS, DVD.** Bill Woods; Horace Carpenter; Ted Edwards; Thea Ramsey; Jennie Dark; Marcel Andre; Celia McGann; ***D:*** Dwain Esper; ***W:*** Hildegarde Stadie; ***C:*** William C. Thompson.

Maniac **1963** An American artist living in France becomes involved with the daughter of a cafe owner, not suspecting that murder will follow. Seems that her old man is locked up in an insane asylum for torching the daughter's rapist several years earlier. Part of the 'The Icons of Suspense Collection: Hammer Films' collection. **86m/B; VHS, DVD, Blu-Ray.** *GB* Kerwin Mathews; Nadia Gray; Donald Houston; Liliane Brousse; ***D:*** Michael Carreras; ***W:*** Jimmy Sangster; ***C:*** Wilkie Cooper; ***M:*** Stanley Black.

Maniac *Ransom; Assault on Paradise; The Town That Cried Terror* **1977 (PG)** A New York cop hunts down an arrow-shooting and obviously crazed Vietnam veteran who endeavors to hold an entire Arizona town for ransom. Which is entirely appropriate, since the cast is in it only for the money. **87m/C; VHS, DVD.** Oliver Reed; Deborah Raffin; Stuart Whitman; Jim Mitchum; Edward Brett; John Ireland; Paul Koslo; Bill Allen; ***D:*** Richard Compton.

Maniac WOOF! **1980** A psycho murderer slaughters and scalps his victims, adding the "trophies" to his collection. Carries a self-imposed equivalent "X" rating due to its highly graphic gore quotient. For extremely strong stomachs only. **91m/C; VHS, DVD, Blu-Ray.** Joe Spinell; Caroline Munro; Gail Lawrence; Kelly Piper; Tom Savini; Rita Montone; Hyla Marrow; William Lustig; Sharon Mitchell; ***D:*** William Lustig; ***W:*** Joe Spinell; C.A. Rosenberg; ***C:*** Robert Lindsay; ***M:*** Jay Chattaway.

Maniac 🦴 ½ **2012** This psychological thriller of a Jack Ripper-esque story in modern day Los Angeles is a remake of a Joe Spinell film from 1980 of the same name. Frank (Wood) is socially withdrawn, eccentric owner of a mannequin store who kills anyone woman who gets too close to him. Frank's psyche is challenged by the appearance of Anna (Arnezeder), an artist who approaches him seeking help with her new exhibit. Frank becomes obsessed with her and even more maniac, taking to the streets to stalk and kill. **90m/C; DVD, Blu-Ray, Streaming.** *FR US* Elijah Wood; Nora Arnezeder; Megan Duffy; Genevieve Alexandra; Jan Broberg; America Olivo; ***D:*** Franck Khalfoun; ***W:*** Alexandre Aja; Gregory Levasseur; ***C:*** Maxime Alexandre; ***M:*** Robin Coudert.

Maniac Cop 🦴 **1988 (R)** In New York city, a cop goes beyond the realm of sanity and turns vigilante. Low-budget slasher/thriller that too often sags. **92m/C; VHS, DVD, Blu-Ray.** Tom Atkins; Bruce Campbell; Laurene Landon; Richard Roundtree; William (Bill) Smith; Robert Z'Dar; Sheree North; Sam Raimi; ***D:*** William Lustig; ***W:*** Larry Cohen; ***C:*** Vincent Rabe; James (Momel) Lemmo; ***M:*** Jay Chattaway.

Maniac Cop 2 🦴 **1990 (R)** Everyone thought he was dead but you can't keep a bad guy down so this grossly disfigured policeman forms a one-man vigilante squad, seeking revenge (why never matters—just the body count). Blood and guts fly as any plot shortcomings are cleverly disguised by an array of violent video deaths. Sequel to "Maniac Cop." **90m/C; VHS, DVD, Blu-Ray.** Robert Davi; Claudia Christian; Michael Lerner; Bruce Campbell; Laurene Landon; Robert Z'Dar; Clarence Williams, III; Leo Rossi; James Dixon; Robert Earl Jones; ***D:*** William Lustig; ***W:*** Larry Cohen; ***C:*** James (Momel) Lemmo.

Maniac Cop 3: Badge of Silence 🦴 **1993 (R)** The grossly disfigured policeman returns yet again to exact gory vengeance as the good guys try to get rid of him once and for all. **85m/C; VHS, DVD, Blu-Ray.** Robert Z'Dar; Robert Davi; Gretchen Becker; Paul Gleason; Doug Savant; Caitlin Dulany; Jackie Earle Haley; Robert Forster; Bobby DiCicco; ***D:*** William Lustig; Joel Soisson; ***W:*** Larry Cohen; ***M:*** Jerry Goldsmith.

Maniac Nurses Find Ecstasy WOOF! 1994 Even by Troma standards, this one's scraping the bottom of the barrel. The nearly non-existent plot is an excuse to present several young women dressed in nurse uniforms and underwear while holding various weapons. The sense of energy that's needed for good exploitation is lacking. **80m/C; VHS, DVD.** Susanna Makay; Hajni Brown; Nicole A. Gyony; Csilia Farago; ***D:*** Harry M. (Leon P. Howard) Love; ***W:*** Harry M. (Leon P. Howard) Love.

Manic 🦴🦴 ½ **2001 (R)** Lyle (Gordon-Levitt), prone to fits of violent rage, is sent to a juvenile psychiatric hospital to control his temper. There he meets a variety of other mentally and emotionally troubled teens. Led by patient counselor David (Cheadle), they endure group sessions that introduce the audience to the varied, if stereotypical, problems of the other patients. Lyle is eventually drawn to shy Tracy, who suffers from crushingly low self-esteem. Excellent performances and script keep the situations and emotions mostly avoiding cliche, but the affected jittery hand-held digital camera work is a distraction. **100m/C; DVD.** Joseph Gordon-Levitt; Don Cheadle; Zooey Deschanel; Cody Lightning; Sara Rivas; Michael Bacall; William Richert; Elden (Ratliff) Henson; Blayne Weaver; ***D:*** Jordan Melamed; ***W:*** Michael Bacall; Blayne Weaver; ***C:*** Nick Hay.

The Manions of America 🦴🦴 ½ **1981** The long and sometimes interesting rags-to-riches tale of Rory O'Manion, a feisty Irish patriot who leaves his native land during the potato famine of 1845 to settle in America. Originally a TV miniseries. **290m/C; VHS, DVD.** Pierce Brosnan; Kate Mulgrew; Linda Purl; David Soul; Kathleen Beller; Simon MacCorkindale; ***D:*** Joseph Sargent; Charles S. Dubin. **TV**

Manipulator 🦴 **1971 (R)** A deranged ex-movie makeup man (Rooney, playing to type) kidnaps a young actress and holds her prisoner in a deserted Hollywood sound stage. **91m/C; VHS, DVD, Streaming.** Mickey Rooney; Luana Anders; Keenan Wynn; ***D:*** Yabo Yablonsky.

Manito 🦴🦴🦴 **2003** Slice of life family drama set in New York City's largely Hispanic Washington Heights neighborhood. Manny Moreno (Minaya) is about to graduate from high school and has been accepted to college on a full scholarship. His older brother, Junior (Franky G), is an ex-con who was busted for working with their drug-dealer dad (Cabral). Junior is trying to go straight and keep Manny away from trouble as well by refusing to allow their father any contact with the family. But it's just not that simple. Debut film for Eason is somewhat limited by being shot on digital video, but the performances are powerful. **77m/C; DVD.** Franky G.; Leo Minaya; Manuel Cabral; Hector Gonzalez; Julissa Lopez; Jessica Morales; ***D:*** Eric Eason; ***W:*** Eric Eason; ***C:*** Didier Gertsch; ***M:*** Saundi Wilson.

The Manitou 🦴🦴 **1978 (PG)** A San Francisco woman suffers from a rapidly growing neck tumor which eventually grows into a 400-year-old Indian witch doctor. (I hate when that happens.) Redeemed only by good special effects, especially those that kept Curtis, Strasberg, and Meredith from laughing. **104m/C; VHS, DVD, Blu-Ray.** Susan Strasberg; Tony Curtis; Stella Stevens; Ann Sothern; Burgess Meredith; Michael Ansara; Jon Cedar; Paul Mantee; Lurene Tuttle; Jeannette Nolan; ***D:*** William Girdler; ***W:*** William Girdler; Jon Cedar; Tom Pope; ***C:*** Michel Hugo; ***M:*** Lalo Schifrin.

Manna from Heaven 🦴🦴 **2002 (PG)** A cash-strapped extended family, living in a working-class Buffalo neighborhood, receive an unexpected windfall when a passing truck with a faulty door dumps a load of $20 bills. A pious young girl thinks the money is a gift from God but, 30 years later, Sister Teresa (Burton) has now decided the money was just a loan and God must be repaid. However, the money's long spent and the rest of those involved are reluctant (at first) to go along with the nun's fund-raising efforts. **119m/C; DVD.** Shirley Jones; Cloris Leachman; Harry Groener; Jill Eikenberry; Ursula Burton; Faye Grant; Wendie Malick; Seymour Cassel; ***D:*** Gabrielle C. Burton; Maria Burton; ***W:*** Gabrielle B. Burton; ***C:*** Ed Slattery.

Mannaja: A Man Called Blade 🦴 ½ *A Man Called Blade* **1977** Spaghetti western ("Mannaja" is knife in Italian). Hatchet-wielding bounty hunter Blade's hired by Suttonville's wheelchair-bound mayor McGowan to find his missing daughter Deborah. The mayor's corrupt partner Valler is involved, there's a silver shipment to steal, and Blade also has a revenge agenda of his own. **101m/C; DVD.** *IT* Maurizio Merli; Philippe Leroy; John Steiner; Sonja Jeannine; Donald O'Brien; ***D:*** Sergio Martino; ***W:*** Sergio Martino; ***C:*** Federico Zanni; ***M:*** Guido de Angelis; Maurizio de Angelis.

Mannequin 🦴🦴 ½ **1937** Tracy and Crawford star in this romantic story of a poor girl who finds temporary happiness by marrying a wealthy man after ditching her con-artist husband. Somewhat predictable, the movie reads like a "People" magazine story on The Donald and Ivana. Tracy and Crawford keep the story afloat (in their only film together), with an able assist from Curtis. **95m/B; VHS, DVD.** Joan Crawford; Spencer Tracy; Alan Curtis; Ralph Morgan; Leo Gorcey; Elisabeth Risdon; Paul Fix; ***D:*** Frank Borzage; ***W:*** Lawrence Hazard; ***C:*** George J. Folsey.

Mannequin 🦴🦴 **1987 (PG)** A young artist creates a store window display using various mannequins, one of which contains the spirit of an ancient Egyptian woman. She comes to life when he is around, and naturally none of his co-workers believe him. Very light comedy, featuring two pretty stars and music by Jefferson Starship. **90m/C; DVD, Blu-Ray.** Andrew McCarthy; Kim Cattrall; Estelle Getty; James Spader; Meshach Taylor; Carole (Raphaelle) Davis; G.W. Bailey; ***D:*** Michael Gottlieb; ***W:*** Ed Rugoff; ***C:*** Tim Suhrstedt; ***M:*** Sylvester Levay.

Mannequin 2: On the Move WOOF! 1991 (PG) Less of a sequel, more of a lame rehash proving that the first "Mannequin" could have been even dumber. At this rate part three will be off the scale. Now it's a lovesick Teutonic princess frozen for 1,000 years who revives in a department store. Taylor reprises his grotesque gay role. **95m/C; VHS, DVD.** Kristy Swanson; William Ragsdale; Meshach Taylor; Terry Kiser; Stuart Pankin; ***D:*** Stewart Raffill; ***W:*** Ed Rugoff.

Manny & Lo 🦴🦴🦴 **1996 (R)** Krueger's directorial debut features fine performances in a story about three misfits forming a unique family bond. Surly 16-year-old Lo (Palladino) and her serious 11-year-old sister Manny (Johansson) have run away from their foster homes and hit the road together. Living hand-to-mouth, it's Manny who persuades her irresponsible pregnant sister that they need a home and they settle into an isolated cabin. When the sisters visit a baby store, eccentric clerk Elaine (Place) seems such a font of wisdom that the girls kidnap her and hold her as a hostage to help with the pregnancy. But Elaine's not trying to escape and has an agenda of her own. **90m/C; DVD.** Mary Kay Place; Scarlett Johansson; Aleksa Palladino; Paul Guilfoyle; Glenn Fitzgerald; Cameron Boyd; Novella Nelson; Angie Phillips; ***D:*** Lisa Krueger; ***W:*** Lisa Krueger; ***C:*** Tom Krueger; ***M:*** John Lurie.

Manon 🦴🦴 *Manon 70* **1968** Updated version of the 18th-century novel "Manon Lescaut." Prostitute Manon (Deneuve) caters to a rich clientele but falls for poor reporter Des Grieux (Frey). Since she has expensive tastes, Manon keeps her job and sees her lover on the side although he's unhappy about the situation. French with subtitles. **105m/C; DVD.** *FR* Catherine Deneuve; Sami Frey; Jean-Claude Brialy; Elsa Martinelli; Robert Webber; Paul (Christian) Hubschmid; ***D:*** Jean-Claude Brialy; Jean Aurel; Cecil Saint-Laurent; ***W:*** Jean-Claude Brialy; Jean Aurel; Cecil Saint-Laurent; ***C:*** Edmond Richard; ***M:*** Serge Gainsbourg.

Manon of the Spring 🦴🦴🦴 ½ *Manon des Sources; Jean de Florette 2* **1987 (PG)** In this excellent sequel to "Jean de Florette," the adult daughter of the dead hunchback, Jean, discovers who blocked up the spring on her father's land. She plots her revenge, which proves greater than she could ever imagine. Montand is astonishing. Based on a Marcel Pagnol novel. In French with English subtitles. **113m/C; VHS, DVD, Blu-Ray.** *FR* Yves Montand; Daniel Auteuil; Emmanuelle Beart; Hippolyte Girardot; Margarita Lozano; Elisabeth Depardieu; Yvonne Gamy; Armand Meffre; Gabriel Bacquier; ***D:*** Claude Berri; ***W:*** Claude Berri; Gerard Brach; ***C:*** Bruno Nuytten; ***M:*** Jean-Claude Petit; Roger Legrand. Cesar '87: Support. Actress (Beart).

Manos sucias 🦴🦴🦴 **2015** A pair of unlikely drug traffickers journey up Colombia's coast with millions of dollars in cocaine, and must face conflict between them and within the region they are traversing. Spanish with subtitles. **84m/C; DVD.** Cristian James Abvincula; Jarlin Javier Martinez; Hadder Blandon; Andres Reina Ruiz; Maria Perlaza; ***D:*** Josef Kubota Wladyka; ***W:*** Josef Kubota Wladyka; Alan Blanco; ***C:*** Alan Blanco; ***M:*** Scott Thorough.

Manos, the Hands of Fate WOOF! 1966 Horrible acting and laughable special effects elevate this story of a family ensnared by a satanic cult a notch above your average bad horror film. Highlights include a Satan-like character who can't stop laughing; the dreaded "hounds of hell" (or are those mangy dogs with big ears glued on?); and Torgo the monstrous henchman, who you know is evil because he has giant kneecaps (a sure sign of the devil's work). **74m/C; VHS, DVD, Blu-Ray.** Tom Nayman; Diane Mahree; Hal P. Warren; John Reynolds; ***D:*** Hal P. Warren; ***W:*** Hal P. Warren.

Manpower 🦴🦴 **1941** A dame comes between pals and it doesn't end well. Linemen Hank (Robinson) and Johnny (Marshall) compete for the attention of L.A. nightclub floozy Fay (Dietrich) but Fay accepts Hank's marriage proposal since he's the more stable guy. Still, Fay tells Johnny she loves him but he rejects her out of loyalty to Hank, who finds out his new missus doesn't plan to hang around—and why. **105m/B; DVD.** Edward G. Robinson; George Raft; Marlene Dietrich; Alan Hale; Frank McHugh; Eve Arden; Barton MacLane; Ward Bond; Walter Catlett; Joyce Compton; ***D:*** Raoul Walsh; ***W:*** Jerry Wald; Richard Macaulay; ***C:*** Ernest Haller; ***M:*** Adolph Deutsch.

Man's Best Friend 🦴 ½ **1993 (R)** A guard dog is the object of a genetic experiment that has given him the agressiveness of other creatures, including a cobra and a leopard. Since Max is an enormous Tibetan mastiff this means big trouble for everyone but the reporter (Sheedy) who rescued him—and even she better watch out. **87m/C; VHS, DVD, Blu-Ray.** Ally Sheedy; Lance Henriksen; Frederic Lehne; Robert Costanzo; John Cassini; J.D. Daniels; ***D:*** John Lafia; ***W:*** John Lafia; ***M:*** Joel Goldsmith.

Man's Favorite Sport? 🦴🦴 ½ **1963** A slapstick comedy about a renowned fishing expert author who actually hates fishing, but is forced to compete in a major tournament by a romantically inclined publicity agent. Very funny in spots. **121m/C; VHS, DVD, Blu-Ray.** Rock Hudson; Paula Prentiss; Charlene Holt; Maria Perschy; John McGiver; ***D:*** Howard Hawks; ***M:*** Henry Mancini.

Mansfield Park 🦴🦴 ½ **1985** Fanny is an impoverished young woman, snubbed by society, who earns the respect and love of her cousin in a BBC miniseries adaptation of the Jane Austen classic set in 19th-century England. **261m/C; VHS, DVD.** *GB* Sylvestria Le Touzel; Bernard Hepton; Anna Massey; Donald Pleasence; ***D:*** David Giles. **TV**

Mansfield Park 🦴🦴 ½ **1999 (PG-13)** Poor relation Fanny Price (O'Connor) has grown up with her wealthy cousins at their elegant home, Mansfield Park. While some of the Bertrams have been civil, others have treated Fanny as little better than a servant. However, cousin Edmund (Miller) has been very kind indeed and Fanny develops very warm feelings towards him. Then the entire family is thrown into chaos by the arrival of Henry Crawford (Nivola) and his sister Mary (Davidtz) and scandal seems about to break. Jane Austen's 3rd novel has been given a feminist slant and some belabored relevancy by Rozema. **110m/C; DVD.** Frances O'Connor; Jonny Lee Miller; Alessandro Nivola; Embeth Davidtz; Harold Pinter; Lindsay Duncan; Sheila Gish; Justine Waddell; Victoria Hamilton; James Purefoy; Hugh Bonneville; ***D:*** Patricia Rozema; ***W:*** Patricia Rozema; ***C:*** Michael Coulter; ***M:*** Lesley Barber.

Mansfield Park 🦴🦴 ½ **2007** As a child, Fanny Price (Piper) was sent to grow up with her rich relatives, the Bertrams, at Mansfield Park. As the poor relation, plucky Fanny is subjected to much belittling by everyone except handsome cousin Edmund (Ritson). But their new and flirtatious neighbors the Crawfords cause trouble: Mary (Atwell) sets her eyes on Edmund while her brother Henry (Beattie) flirts with both Fanny and her cousin Maria (Ryan). Only Fanny seems to realize their insincerity and her insight does her no good (at first). Based on the novel by Jane Austen. **90m/C; DVD.** *GB* Billie Piper; Blake Ritson; Hayley Atwell; James D'Arcy; Joseph Beattie; Michelle Ryan; Jemma Redgrave; Douglas Hodge; Rory Kinnear; Catherine Steadman; Maggie O'Neill; ***D:*** Iain B. MacDonald; ***W:*** Maggie Wadey; ***C:*** Nick Dance; ***M:*** John Keane. **TV**

Mansion of the Doomed 🦴 *House of Blood; Eyes of Dr. Chaney* **1976 (R)** A mad scientist overwhelmed with guilt from accidentally blinding his daughter decides to make amends by purposefully blinding all visitors in the hopes of performing an eye transplant to save her. Post Office and Census Bureau employees should take note of his address. **99m/C; DVD, Streaming.** Richard Basehart; Lance Henriksen; Al Ferrara; Vic Tayback; Gloria Grahame; Trish Stewart; ***D:*** Michael Pataki; ***W:*** Frank Ray Perilli; ***C:*** Andrew Davis; ***M:*** Robert O. Ragland.

The Manson Family 🦴 ½ **2004** A graphic depiction of Charlie (Games), his followers, and their crimes, which took director Van Bebber something like 15 years to finance and complete. You can admire his dedication without admiring the results, which intentionally look like exploitation schlock. A framing device has a TV reporter (Day) working on a documentary of the Family that leads to flashbacks of the sex, drugs, and violence that consume them. **95m/C; DVD, Blu-Ray.** ***D:*** Jim Van Bebber; ***C:*** Mike King.

The Manster *The Manster—Half Man, Half Monster; The Split; The Two-Headed Monster* **1959** Another masterpiece from the director who brought us "Monster from Green Hell." Womanizing, whiskey swilling American journalist receives mysterious injection from crazed scientist and sprouts unsightly hair and extra head. Although shot in the land of the rising sun, lips move in sync with dialogue. **72m/B; VHS, DVD, Blu-Ray.** *JP* Peter Dyneley; Jane Hylton; Satoshi Nakamura; Terri Zimmern; Tetsu Nakamura; Jerry Ito; Toyoko Takechi; ***D:*** Kenneth Crane; George Breakston; ***W:*** William J. Sheldon; ***C:*** David Mason; ***M:*** Hirooki Ogawa.

Manticore **2005** Usual low-budget cheesefest from the Sci-Fi Channel. American soldiers patrolling an Iraqi town check a bombed-out museum and are attacked by insurgents. An ancient medallion was stolen from the museum and megalomaniac Umari wants to use it to unleash the power of the manticore, only to figure out too late that he can't control it. **88m/C; DVD.** Robert Beltran; Jeff Fahey; Chase Masterson; Faran Tahir; Heather Donahue; A.J. Buckley; ***D:*** Tripp Reed; ***W:*** John Werner; ***C:*** Lorenzo Senatore; ***M:*** David Williams. **CABLE**

Mantis in Lace ½ *Lila* **1968 (R)** A go-go dancer slaughters men while tripping on LSD. Watch it for the "hep" dialogue. **68m/C; VHS, DVD.** Susan Stewart; Steve Vincent; M.K. Evans; Vic Lance; Pat Barrington; Janu Wine; Stuart Lancaster; John Carrol; Judith Crane; Cheryl Trepton; ***D:*** William Rotsler; ***W:*** Sanford White; ***C:*** Laszlo Kovacs; ***M:*** Frank A. Coe.

The Manxman ½ **1929** Hitchcock's last silent film, a romantic melodrama about ambition and infidelity on the Isle of Man. **129m/B; Silent; VHS, DVD, Blu-Ray.** *GB* Carl Brisson; Anny Ondra; Malcolm Keen; Randle Ayrton; ***D:*** Alfred Hitchcock; ***W:*** Hall Caine; Eliot Stannard; ***C:*** Jack Cox.

The Many Adventures of Winnie the Pooh ½ **1977 (G)** Disney's 22nd animated feature offers A.A. Milne's beloved characters and their adventures in the Hundred Acre Wood. Includes a behind-the-scenes featurette with the original creators, animators, and voices. **83m/C; VHS, DVD, Blu-Ray.** ***V:*** Sterling Holloway; Paul Winchell; John Fiedler; Junius Matthews; Howard Morris; ***Nar:*** Sebastian Cabot; ***D:*** John Lounsbery; Wolfgang Reitherman.

Many Rivers to Cross **1955** Western comedy finds Kentucky frontiersman Bushrod Gentry (Taylor) setting his traps for furs, not a wife. But this doesn't stop feisty spinster Mary (Parker) from setting her sights on becoming Mrs. Gentry. And her pappy's (McLaglen) shotgun is mighty persuasive. **92m/C; DVD.** Robert Taylor; Eleanor Parker; Russ Tamblyn; James Arness; Alan Hale; Rosemary DeCamp; Russell Johnson; Victor McLaglen; ***D:*** Roy Rowland; ***W:*** Harry Brown; Guy Trosper; ***C:*** John Seitz; ***M:*** Cyril Mockridge.

Mao's Last Dancer **2009 (PG)** Graceful though conventional and melodramatic biopic of Chinese ballet star Li Cunxin, who defected in 1981 after living in Houston as a cultural exchange student. Flashbacks depict Li's rural childhood and training in Beijing and the restrictions Communism forces on his art. Adapted from the dancer's autobiography. Lead dancer/actor Chi is himself a graduate of the Beijing Dance Academy. English and Mandarin with subtitles. **117m/C; Blu-Ray.** *AU* Bruce Greenwood; Kyle MacLachlan; Joan Chen; Amanda Schull; Ferdinand Hoang; Penne Hackforth-Jones; Aden Young; Jack Thompson; Chi Cao; Camilla Vergotis; ***D:*** Bruce Beresford; ***W:*** Jan Sardi; ***C:*** Peter James; ***M:*** Christopher Gordon.

Map of the Human Heart **1993 (R)** Thirty-year saga told in flashback. Young Eskimo Avik (Lee) and his Metis love interest Albertine (Parillaud) struggle with racism in a white world. They meet and become friends as children and years later meet again in Dresden during WWII, but now Albertine is married to Avik's once close friend, denying her heritage and living in the white world that he has been fighting for so long. Mediocre movie with extraordinary Arctic scenery. Cusack has a small role as a mapmaker. **109m/C; VHS, DVD.** Jason Scott Lee; Anne Parillaud; Patrick Bergin; Robert Joamie; Annie Galipeau; John Cusack; Jeanne Moreau; ***D:*** Vincent Ward; ***W:*** Vincent Ward; Louis Nowra.

A Map of the World **1999 (R)** Excellent cast; tough story, based on the novel by Jane Hamilton. Flinty farm wife/mom Alice Goodwin (Weaver) hasn't endeared herself to her Wisconsin community. But she's a good deal more vulnerable than anyone suspects as Alice finds her life falling apart. Her neighbor Theresa's (Moore) daughter accidentally drowns while in Alice's care and soon after Alice is shockingly accused of sexual abuse in her role as school nurse, which lands her in jail. Uneven script is part family, part prison, part courtroom, and part melodrama, which doesn't necessarily make for a coherent movie. **125m/C; DVD, On Demand.** Sigourney Weaver; David Strathairn; Julianne Moore; Ron Lea; Arliss Howard; Chloë Sevigny; Louise Fletcher; ***D:*** Scott Elliott; ***W:*** Peter Hedges; Polly Platt; ***C:*** Seamus McGarvey; ***M:*** Pat Metheny. Natl. Bd. of Review '99: Support. Actress (Moore).

The Mapmaker ½ **2001** Engineer Richard Markey is hired to map out some land in a rural border town in Northern Ireland. Only he uncovers the body of an alleged informer tied to the IRA and puts his own life in danger when old hostilities surface. **89m/C; DVD.** *GB IR* Brian F. O'Byrne; Susan Lynch; Brendan Coyle; Ian McElhinney; Oisin Kearney; ***D:*** Johnny Gogan; ***W:*** Johnny Gogan; ***C:*** Owen McPolin; ***M:*** Cathal Coughlan. **TV**

Maps to the Stars ½ **2014 (R)** Cronenberg travels to L.A. for the first time in his illustrious career, working with Wagner to tell a sordid tale of celebrity excess. Moore rocks as Havana Sagrand, an over-the-hill and over-the-top actress willing to do anything to get the right part, especially when she hears they're remaking the film that made her actress mother's breakthrough film. She hires a personal assistant (Wasikowska) with a secret of her own, and the track is laid for tragedy. Rarely has the dynamic of a celebrity culture that eats itself been more fully realized, even if the follow-through doesn't quite pay off the great set-up. **111m/C; DVD, Blu-Ray.** *CA GE* Julianne Moore; Mia Wasikowska; Sarah Gadon; John Cusack; Evan Bird; Olivia Williams; Robert Pattinson; ***D:*** David Cronenberg; ***W:*** Bruce Wagner; ***C:*** Peter Suschitzky; ***M:*** Howard Shore.

Mara Maru ½ **1952** The aging Flynn does what he can with this sea-going adventure. Salvage diver Gregory Mason's (Flynn) partner Andy (Webb) is murdered after boasting that they've discovered where a sunken treasure is located. When Mason's ship is burned, sinister collector Benedict (Burr) offers his own yacht in return for a cut of the loot but Mason is well-aware that he's planning a doublecross. **98m/B; DVD.** Errol Flynn; Raymond Burr; Ruth Roman; Paul Picerni; Richard Webb; Georges Renavent; ***D:*** Gordon Douglas; ***W:*** N. Richard Nash; ***C:*** Robert Burks; ***M:*** Max Steiner.

Mararia **1998** Romantic triangle set amidst the heat and beauty of 1940s island life on Lanzarote in the Canary Islands. The newly arrived Dr. Fermin (Gomez) falls under the spell of enticing local beauty Mararia (Toledo), who returns his affections. At least until British surveyor Bertrand (Glen) comes to the island and she changes her mind. This might be a woman's perogative but in Mararia's case, it leads to tragedy for all. Spanish with subtitles. **109m/C; VHS, DVD.** *SP* Goya Toledo; Carmelo Gomez; Iain Glen; Mirta Ibarra; ***D:*** Antonio J. Betancor; ***W:*** Antonio J. Betancor; Carlos Alvarez; ***C:*** Juan Ruiz-Anchia; ***M:*** Pedro Guerra.

Marathon **1980** When a middle-aged jogger's ego gets a boost through the attention of a beautiful young woman, he takes up marathon running. Light comedy. **100m/C; VHS, DVD.** Bob Newhart; Leigh Taylor-Young; Herb Edelman; Dick Gautier; Anita Gillette; John Hillerman; ***D:*** Jackie Cooper. **TV**

Marathon **2009** American Poet Laureate William Meredith suffers a stroke in 1983 and his longtime lover, fellow poet Richard Harteis (who's also a marathon runner), is determined to nurse Meredith back to health. This is despite the opposition of Meredith's family who don't acknowledge their decades-long relationship, a lack of legal recognition, and an arduous therapy routine. Based on a book by Harteis. **84m/C; DVD.** Alec Danna; Roy Pomeroy; Beth Campbell; Donna Del Bueno; Giovanni Capitello; ***D:*** Biju Viswanath; ***W:*** Biju Viswanath; Celia de Freine; ***C:*** Biju Viswanath.

Marathon Man **1976 (R)** Nightmarish chase-thriller in which a graduate student becomes entangled in a plot involving a murderous Nazi fugitive. As student Hoffman is preparing for the Olympic marathon, he is reunited with his secret-agent brother, setting the intricate plot in motion. Courtesy of his brother, Hoffman becomes involved with Olivier, an old crazed Nazi seeking jewels taken from concentration camp victims. Non-stop action throughout, including a torture scene sure to set your teeth on edge. Goldman adapted the screenplay from his novel. **125m/C; VHS, DVD, Blu-Ray.** Dustin Hoffman; Laurence Olivier; Marthe Keller; Roy Scheider; William Devane; Fritz Weaver; Richard Bright; Marc Lawrence; ***D:*** John Schlesinger; ***W:*** William Goldman; ***C:*** Conrad L. Hall; ***M:*** Michael Small. Golden Globes '77: Support. Actor (Olivier).

Marauders **2016 (R)** Bank robbers are targeting safety deposit boxes of the rich and powerful, and all at establishments owned by a financial king, played with half-asleep commitment by Willis. Meloni is the cop investigating the series of crimes and Grenier a new FBI agent assigned to the case. Everyone involved with this ugly and forgettable action-conspiracy flick phones it in, including the new king of the VOD movie, Bruce Willis, and the consistently awful Grenier. The action is poorly choreographed and the final act contains senseless twists and turns. **107m/C; DVD, Blu-Ray.** Christopher Meloni; Bruce Willis; Dave Bautista; Adrian Grenier; Johnathon Schaech; ***D:*** Steven C. Miller; ***W:*** Michael Cody; Chris Sivertson; ***C:*** Brandon Cox; ***M:*** Ryan Dodson.

The Marc Pease Experience ½ **2009 (PG-13)** Stale showbiz comedy. Marc Pease (Schwartzman) is a limo-driving wannabe singer who can't get over a high-school debacle in which he humiliated himself and infuriated his arrogant director Gribble (Stiller) during a production of "The Wiz." Still, Marc naively believes that Gribble will actually produce his a cappella group's demo album if he can find the financing. **84m/C; DVD.** Jason Schwartzman; Ben Stiller; Anna Kendrick; Ebon Moss-Bachrach; Gabrielle Dennis; Jay Paulson; ***D:*** Todd Louiso; ***W:*** Todd Louiso; Jacob Koskoff; ***C:*** Tim Suhrstedt; ***M:*** Christophe Beck. **VIDEO**

March of the Penguins **2005 (G)** Oscar winner proves that animals can be movie stars even if they aren't animated. Director Jacquet traveled to Antarctica to film the mating rituals of the Emperor penguin and walked away with pure film gold. You'll marvel at how ridiculously far the penguins will go to propagate their species—endless marching over frozen wastelands, working daily to escape predators, cutely ignoring the French camera crew, all brought together by the smooth vocal stylings of narrator Morgan Freeman. Tries a bit too hard to imbue the birds with human personalities, but the astounding footage wins in the end. **80m/C; DVD, Blu-Ray, HD-DVD.** ***Nar:*** Morgan Freeman; ***D:*** Luc Jacquet; ***W:*** Jordan Roberts; ***C:*** Laurent Chalet; Jerome Maison. Oscars '05: Feature Doc.; Natl. Bd. of Review '05: Feature Doc.; Broadcast Film Critics '05: Feature Doc.

March of the Wooden Soldiers *Babes in Toyland* **1934** The classic Mother Goose tale about the secret life of Christmas toys, with Laurel and Hardy as Santa's helpers who must save Toyland from the wicked Barnaby. A Yuletide "must see." Also available in a colorized version. **73m/B; VHS, DVD, Blu-Ray.** Stan Laurel; Oliver Hardy; Charlotte Henry; Henry (Kleinbach) Brandon; Felix Knight; Jean Darling; Johnny Downs; Marie Wilson; ***D:*** Charles R. Rogers; Gus Meins; ***W:*** Frank Butler; Nick Grinde; ***C:*** Art Lloyd; Francis Corby.

March or Die ½ **1977 (PG)** Great potential, unrealized. An American joins the French Foreign Legion during WWI after his dismissal from West Point. Following the brutality of training, he is assigned to guard an archeological expedition in Morocco, where he pulls together a rag-tag outfit for the mission. Hackman proves once again the wide range of his acting abilities, surmounting the cliched and fairly sadistic plot. Shot on location in the Sahara Desert. **104m/C; VHS, DVD.** *GB* Gene Hackman; Terence Hill; Max von Sydow; Catherine Deneuve; Ian Holm; ***D:*** Dick Richards; ***W:*** David Zelag Goodman; ***M:*** Maurice Jarre.

The March Sisters at Christmas ½ **2012** An unnecessary modern update of the Louisa May Alcott characters from Lifetime. The March girls are shocked when their parents inform them that their family home needs extensive repairs they can't afford so, after Christmas, it's going up for sale. With their parents away, Jo talks her sisters in doing the work themselves in hopes they can afford to stay. Frustrations grow, including some romantic issues, as the siblings try to meet a Christmas deadline. **96m/C; Streaming.** Julie Marie Berman; Kaitlin Doubleday; Melissa Farman; Molly Kunz; John Shea; Justin Bruening; Mark Famiglietti; Charlie Hofheimer; ***D:*** John Stimpson; ***W:*** Jennifer Maisel; ***C:*** Brian Crane; ***M:*** Ed Grenga. **CABLE**

Marci X **2003 (R)** Ill-begotten social satire stars Kudrow as the title character, who takes over for dad Ben (director Benjamin) at his record company after he suffers a heart attack. When the the lyrics of Dr. S (Wayans), the label's top rapper, provoke conservative U.S. Senator Spinkle (Baranski) to attempt to ban the rapper's songs, the uptown, Jewish Marci tries to smooth things over and ends up falling for the Dr.'s downtown charms. Culture clash comedy has its moments, but is ultimately too predictable and the characters too one-dimensional to care about. **97m/C; DVD.** Lisa Kudrow; Damon Wayans; Richard Benjamin; Christine Baranski; Paula Garces; Jane Krakowski; Veanne Cox; ***D:*** Richard Benjamin; ***W:*** Paul Rudnick; ***C:*** Robbie Greenberg; ***M:*** Mervyn Warren.

Marco **1973** Entertaining musical adventure of Marco Polo's life casts Arnaz as Marco Polo and Mostel as Kublai Khan. A couple of cut-ups, right? One of the first films to combine animation with live action. Shot partially on location in the Orient. **109m/C; VHS, DVD.** Desi Arnaz, Jr.; Zero Mostel; Jack Weston; Cie Cie Win; ***D:*** Seymour Robbie.

Marco Polo ½ **2007** Thirteenth-century explorer Marco Polo (Somerhalder) reminisces about his travels from his home in Venice, recalling his time in China and his meeting with leader Kublai Khan (uh, Dennehy? Who cast this thing?). Cheesy, but the scenery's pretty. **176m/C; DVD.** Ian Somerhalder; Brian Dennehy; B.D. Wong; Desiree Slahaan; ***D:*** Kevin Connor; ***W:*** Ron Hutchinson; ***C:*** Thomas Burstyn. **CABLE**

Marco Polo, Jr. *Marco Polo Junior Versus the Red Dragon* **1972** Marco Polo Jr., the daring descendant of the legendary explorer, travels the world in search of his destiny in this song-filled, feature-length, but poorly animated, fantasy. **82m/C; VHS, DVD.** *AU* ***V:*** Bobby Rydell; Arnold Stang; Kevin Golsby; Corie Sims; ***D:*** Eric Porter; ***W:*** Sheldon Moldoff.

Mardi Gras for the Devil *Night Trap* **1993 (R)** Black magic and the occult combine as a New Orleans cop tries to catch a killer who strikes only at Mardi Gras. The cop's got his work cut out for him since the killer is no mere mortal but a demon who believes in human sacrifice. **95m/C; VHS, DVD.** Robert Davi; Michael Ironside; Lesley-Anne Down; Lydie Denier; Mike Starr; Margaret Avery; John Amos; ***D:*** David A. Prior; ***W:*** David A. Prior.

Mardi Gras Massacre **WOOF!** *Crypt of Dark Secrets* **1978** Aztec priest arrives in New Orleans during Mardi Gras to revive the blood ritual of human sacrifice to an Aztec god. A police detective relentlessly pursues him. Much gore and gut-slicing, with no redeeming social value. **92m/C; VHS, DVD.** Curt Dawson; Gwen Arment; Wayne Mack; Laura Misch; ***D:*** Jack Weis.

Mardi Gras: Spring Break WOOF! 2011 (R) Lowest-common denominator gross-out comedy. It's college senior year but three buddies are mostly talk and not much co-ed experience. They head to New Orleans for some drunken revelry that somehow includes breaking into Carmen Electra's hotel room. **88m/C; DVD.** Josh Gad; Bret Harrison; Nicholas D'Agosto; Danneel Harris; Arielle Kebbel; Regina Hall; Charles Shaughnessy; Carmen Electra; ***D:*** Phil Dornfeld; ***W:*** Josh Heald; ***C:*** Thomas Ackerman; ***M:*** Marcus Miller. **VIDEO**

Margaret **2011 (R)** Writer/director Lonergan's over-long, overambitious drama was filmed in 2005 and was in legal limbo until a brief 2011 release. Shrill, frustrating, and heavy-handed, it follows the story of entitled Upper West Side high schooler Lisa (Paquin) who inadvertently causes a bus accident and pedestrian death when she distracts the driver (Ruffalo). Lisa then makes the tragedy all about her and takes out her traumatic guilt and anger on those around her, but her hysterics become wearying. The title is a poetry reference from Gerard Manley Hopkins' "Spring and Fall." **150m/C; DVD, Blu-Ray.** Anna Pacquin; Mark Ruffalo; J. Smith-Cameron; Jean Reno; Jeannie Berlin; Kieran Culkin; Matt Damon; Allison Janney; Matthew Broderick; ***D:*** Kenneth Lonergan; ***W:*** Kenneth Lonergan; ***C:*** Ryszard Lenczewski; ***M:*** Nico Muhly.

Margaret's Museum **½ 1995 (R)** The museum of the title is the bizarre shrine Margaret (Bonham Carter) dedicates to the family members who have been killed in the coal mines that dominate her small (1940s) Cape Breton, Nova Scotia town. Both Margaret and her mother, Catherine (Nelligan), are embittered by their tragedies and when Margaret finds romance with eccentric bagpiper Neil (Russell), she makes him promise he'll never return to mine work. But with a bad economy, Neil is forced back to the pits and inevitable disaster. It's Bonham Carter's picture all the way and she shows a wide (and welcome) range of emotions and strength. Adapted from a story by Sheldon Currie. **114m/C; VHS, DVD.** *CA GB* Helena Bonham Carter; Clive Russell; Kate Nelligan; Kenneth Welsh; Craig Olejnik; ***D:*** Mort Ransen; ***W:*** Mort Ransen; Gerald Wexler; ***C:*** Vic Sarin; ***M:*** Milan Kymlicka. Genie '95: Actress (Bonham Carter), Adapt. Screenplay, Costume Des., Score, Support. Actor (Welsh), Support. Actress (Nelligan).

Margarita Happy Hour **2001** Zelda (Hutchins) is a hard-partying New York single mom who makes a living (barely) as an illustrator and lives with her toddler daughter's unemployed, passive father Max (Fessenden), who has a drinking problem. Zelda's support group are her single mom friends whom she regularly meets at a local bar for happy hour. Zelda's life gets more complicated when her recovering junkie friend Natali (Ramos) moves in, needing to get her act together although she hasn't a clue how to do it. She's in good company. **98m/C; DVD.** Eleanor Hutchins; Larry Fessenden; Holly Ramos; Barbara Sicuranza; Amanda Vogel; Macha Ross; Kristen Dispaltro; Will Keenan; ***D:*** Ilya Chaiken; ***W:*** Ilya Chaiken; ***C:*** Gordon Chou; ***M:*** Max Lichtenstein.

Margin Call **2011 (R)** A Wall Street investment bank right on the verge of the bursting of the financial bubble in 2008 is the setting for this well-acted and tense drama featuring strong ensemble performances from veterans Bettany, Irons, and Spacey. Over a span of 36 hours, these canaries in the coal mine of the coming depression face moral corporate decisions that would be echoed for years to come. Director Chandor's debut film is nearly perfect as it tackles large, complex issues without dumbing them down. **107m/C; DVD, Blu-Ray.** Zachary Quinto; Jeremy Irons; Kevin Spacey; Penn Badgley; Paul Bettany; Simon Baker; Demi Moore; Stanley Tucci; Mary McDonnell; Aasif Mandvi; Ashley Williams; ***D:*** J.C. Chandor; ***W:*** J.C. Chandor; ***C:*** Frank DeMarco; ***M:*** Nathan Larson. Ind. Spirit '12: Cast, First Feature.

Margin for Error **½ 1943** Nazi-leaning Karl Braumer (Preminger) is embezzling funds while working for the German consulate in New York. When he's murdered (by multiple methods), Jewish policeman Moe Finkelstein (Berle) is reluctantly on the case. Preminger hams it up and directs with a heavy hand; adapted from the play by Clare Booth Luce. **74m/B; DVD.** Joan Bennett; Milton Berle; Carl Esmond; Howard Freeman; Poldi Dur; Otto Preminger; ***D:*** Otto Preminger; ***W:*** Lillie Hayward; ***C:*** Edward Cronjager; ***M:*** Leigh Harline.

Margot **½ 2009** Excellent bio pic of the latter-day life and career of prima ballerina Dame Margot Fonteyn. Over 40, Fonteyn is expected to retire from the Royal Ballet by its director Ninette de Valois. Instead, after charismatic Rudolf Nureyev defects from Russia in 1961, she begins a legendary partnership with the dancer despite a nearly 20-year age difference. The TV film also shows Margot coping with her less-than-ideal marriage to Panamanian diplomat Roberto de Arias. **213m/C; DVD.** *GB* Anne-Marie Duff; Michiel Huisman; Con O'Neill; Lindsay Duncan; Derek Jacobi; Penelope Wilton; ***D:*** Otto Bathurst; ***W:*** Amanda Coe; ***C:*** Florian Hoffmeister. **TV**

Margot at the Wedding **2007 (R)** Writer Margot (Kidman) returns to her family's home for her sister Pauline's (Leigh) wedding to "artist" Malcolm (Black), but years of contempt, ego, and neuroses boil over among the sisters, their children, and anyone else who happens to be around. Writer/director Baumbach specializes in finding biting humor and poignancy in the struggles of flawed, overly educated East Coasters, but the nasty, petty characters he's created here are so hard to relate to that anything funny or moving is buried under an avalanche of meanness. **92m/C; On Demand.** Nicole Kidman; Jennifer Jason Leigh; Jack Black; John Turturro; Ciaran Hinds; Flora Cross; Halley Feiffer; Zane Pais; ***D:*** Noah Baumbach; ***W:*** Noah Baumbach; ***C:*** Harris Savides.

Marguerite **½ 2016 (R)** A drama based on the life of Marguerite Dumont. In 1920s Paris, wealthy socialite Dumont (Frot) loves music, especially the opera. She greatly enjoys singing in front of family and friends, who let her believe that she is a talented singer through she sings completely out of tune. When she holds real performances at her castle for carefully curated audiences of friends and supportive music lovers, they indulge her and let her believe she has a gift. The situation grows out of control when a journalist publishes a reave review of one of her performances. Ignoring her husband's concerns, Marguerite decides to pursue her dream of holding her first recital in front of strangers. **129m/C; DVD, Blu-Ray, Streaming, Download.** Catherine Frot; Andre Marcon; Michel Fau; Christa Theret; Denis Mpunga; ***D:*** Xavier Giannoli; ***W:*** Xavier Giannoli; ***C:*** Glynn Speeckaert; ***M:*** Ronan Maillard.

Maria Full of Grace *Maria, llena eres de gracia* **2004 (R)** Moreno (in her film debut) gives a graceful performance in the title role of also-debuting director Marston's look at desperation and heroin trafficking. Pregnant teenager Maria impulsively quits her job and is ripe for the sweet talk of Franklin (Toro), who tells Maria about all the money to be made if she'll become a drug mule. After swallowing heroin-filled pellets, Maria boards a plane for New York along with her friend Blanca (Vega) and fellow courier Lucy (Lopez). Problems arise when Lucy becomes ill and thugs threaten the girls, so Maria flees into the city's Colombian immigrant community for safety. Spanish with subtitles. **101m/C; VHS, DVD.** Catalina Sandino Moreno; Yenny Paola Vega; Giulied Lopez; John Alex Toro; Patricia Rae; Wilson Guerrero; Jaime Osorio Gomez; Johanna Andrea Mora; Orlando Tobon; Fernando Velasquez; ***D:*** Joshua Marston; ***W:*** Joshua Marston; ***C:*** Jim Denault; ***M:*** Jacob Lieberman; Leonardo Heiblum. Ind. Spirit '05: Actress (Moreno), First Screenplay.

Marianne & Leonard: Words of Love **½ 2019 (R)** Musician Leonard Cohen and one-time muse Marianne Ihlen met on the Greek island Hydra, where she fell in love with him, followed him to New York, and inspired several songs. Through interviews and footage, it offers a personal glimpse into their relationship, Cohen's career, including financial and drug woes, as well the effect the relationship had on Ihlen's life. The nature of life on Hydra in the 1960s is also given context, as it was a center of the dark side of the counterculture. Director Broomfield is a friend of Marianne, which provides both some insights into her and Leonard's romance but also inhibits perhaps difficult details being put on display. **102m/C; DVD.** Nick Broomfield; ***D:*** Nick Broomfield; ***C:*** Barney Broomfield; ***M:*** Nick Laird-Clowes.

Maria's Lovers **½ 1984 (R)** The wife (Kinski) of an impotent WWII veteran (Savage) succumbs to the charms of a rakish lady-killer (Spano). Savage turns to the charms of an older woman, finds love again with Kinski, but is still impotent; she gets pregnant by a wandering minstrel (Carradine) and on we go to film climax. Offbeat and uneven, representing Russian director Konchalovsky's first American film and one of Kinski's better roles. **103m/C; VHS, DVD.** Nastassja Kinski; John Savage; Robert Mitchum; Keith Carradine; Anita Morris; Bud Cort; Karen Young; Tracy Nelson; John Goodman; Vincent Spano; ***D:*** Andrei Konchalovsky; ***W:*** Andrei Konchalovsky; Marjorie David; Gerard Brach; Paul Zindel; ***C:*** Juan Ruiz-Anchia; ***M:*** Gary S. Remal.

Marie **1985 (PG-13)** In this true story, a divorced (and battered) mother works her way through school and the system to become the first woman to head the Parole Board in Tennessee. Finding rampant corruption, she blows the whistle on her bosses, who put her life in jeopardy. Spacek gives a powerful performance, as does first-time actor Thompson, portraying himself as the abused woman's attorney. Based on the book by Peter Maas. **113m/C; VHS, DVD.** Sissy Spacek; Jeff Daniels; Keith Szarabajka; John Cullum; Morgan Freeman; Fred Dalton Thompson; Don Hood; Lisa Banes; Vincent Irizarry; ***D:*** Roger Donaldson; ***W:*** John Briley; ***C:*** Chris Menges; ***M:*** Francis Lai.

Marie and Bruce **½ 2004 (R)** It doesn't make for a very interesting evening, watching a dysfunctional marriage disintegrate. Shrill Marie is determined to leave her plodding husband Bruce. Marie has several surreal experiences before meeting Bruce at a party, where she's irked by the chatter and Bruce's sociability. They finally have a disastrous dinner where Marie springs her news and Bruce gets drunk. Adaptation of Wallace Shawn's 1979 play. **90m/C; DVD.** Julianne Moore; Matthew Broderick; Bob Balaban; ***D:*** Tom Cairns; ***W:*** Tom Cairns; Wallace Shawn; ***C:*** Patrick Cady; ***M:*** Mark De Gli Antoni.

Marie Antoinette **½ 1938** An elephantine costume drama chronicling the French queen's life from princesshood to her final days before the Revolution. A Shearer festival all the way, and a late example of MGM's overstuffed period style and star-power. Overlong, but engrossing for the wrong reasons. Morley, in his first film, plays Louis XVI. Power's only MGM loan-out casts him as a Swedish count and Marie's romantic dalliance. Based on a book by Stephan Zweig, with script assistance from (among others) F. Scott Fitzgerald. **160m/B; DVD.** Norma Shearer; Tyrone Power; John Barrymore; Robert Morley; Gladys George; Anita Louise; Joseph Schildkraut; Henry Stephenson; Reginald Gardiner; Peter Bull; Albert Dekker; Joseph Calleia; George Zucco; Cora Witherspoon; Barry Fitzgerald; Mae Busch; Harry Davenport; Scotty Beckett; ***D:*** W.S. Van Dyke; ***W:*** F. Scott Fitzgerald; ***C:*** William H. Daniels.

Marie Antoinette **2006 (PG-13)** Coppola goes her own anachronistic way in this revisionist biopic. Pink-and-white Dunst dimples her way through as the teenaged Marie Antoinette, an Austrian princess who is married off at 14 to bumptious French prince (and eventual king) Louis (Schwartzman), who can't even bed her properly. So what's a bored and lonely young woman, stuck in a hostile royal court, to do? Why, party, party, party (extravagantly) of course. It's all pop tunes and lavish costumes and splendid isolation at Versailles while the rabble rouses. Fortunately, Coppola ends her confection before tragedy befalls the delectable Marie. **123m/C; DVD, Blu-Ray.** Kirsten Dunst; Jason Schwartzman; Judy Davis; Rip Torn; Rose Byrne; Asia Argento; Molly Shannon; Shirley Henderson; Danny Huston; Marianne Faithfull; Jamie Dornan; Mary Nighy; Steve Coogan; Lauriane Mascaro; Florrie Betts; ***D:*** Sofia Coppola; ***W:*** Sofia Coppola; ***C:*** Lance Acord. Oscars '06: Costume Des.

Marie Galante **1934** Fine spy drama has Tracy running into Gallian in Panama (years earlier she had been left there after a kidnapping). He finds her most helpful in his attempt to thwart the bombing of the Panama Canal. It's the performances that raise this otherwise standard thriller up a few notches. **88m/B; VHS, DVD.** Spencer Tracy; Ketti Gallian; Ned Sparks; Helen Morgan; Sig Rumann; Leslie Fenton; Jay C. Flippen; ***D:*** Henry King.

Marigold **2007 (PG-13)** Cultural clash romance that's Westernized Bollywood. Marigold Lexton (Larter) is a first-class diva and a third-rate actress. She heads to Goa, India, for a low-budget film and then is stranded when it falls through. Stumbling across a local movie production, she convinces the director she knows how to dance (she doesn't) and falls for handsome choreographer Prem (Khan). Getting interested in him means Marigold also gets interested in the culture before Prem reveals he's betrothed in an arranged marriage. **107m/C; DVD.** *US IN* Ali Larter; Salman Khan; Ian Bohen; Nandana Sen; Helen Khan; ***D:*** Willard Carroll; ***W:*** Willard Carroll; ***C:*** Anil Mehta; ***M:*** Graeme Revell.

Marilyn Hotchkiss' Ballroom Dancing & Charm School **½ 2006 (PG-13)** When he was only eight, Steve promised his sweetheart Lisa that in 40 years they would meet again at their dance school's class reunion. Now here we are, trying to believe that this is happening and that Steve is still passionately fixated on this historic moment. Everything goes wrong and Steve wonders if he'll ever get to see his long-lost love again. Silly story, which somehow snagged an incredible cast, takes itself too seriously, gushing its own bittersweet sentiment all over. Based on the director's own short film made 15 years earlier. **103m/C; DVD.** Robert Carlyle; Marisa Tomei; Mary Steenburgen; John Goodman; Donnie Wahlberg; Sonia Braga; Sean Astin; Danny DeVito; David Paymer; Camryn Manheim; Adam Arkin; Elden (Ratliff) Henson; Ernie Hudson; Miguel (Michael) Sandoval; Ian Abercrombie; Mary Pat Gleason; ***D:*** Randall Miller; ***W:*** Randall Miller; Jody Savin; ***C:*** Jonathan Sela; ***M:*** Mark Adler.

Marina Abramovic the Artist Is Present **2012** Although Akers' documentary offers a celebratory look at Abramovic's work, it's best appreciated by her overwhelmed fans. The title refers to the Serbian performance artist's 2010 retrospective at New York's Museum of Modern Art. Her art is intended to raise issues of sex, violence, and identity, and interviews help explain the experiences that formed her. Includes archival footage. **106m/C; DVD.** ***D:*** Matthew Akers; ***C:*** Matthew Akers; ***M:*** Nathan Halpern.

The Marine **½ 2006 (PG-13)** A frozen slab of grade-A beef, wrestler Cena makes his movie debut (as does director Bonito) in this slam-bang actioner. When John Triton is shipped back to South Carolina from Iraq, he decides to take his hottie wife Kate (Carlson) on vacation. But they wind up in the wrong place just when a violent gang of jewel thieves need a hostage and take Kate. This pisses off John and you don't want anybody that big angry at you. Cartoonish mayhem follows (it's PG-13, remember). Patrick has fun with his villainous ringleader role but you know he's slumming. **93m/C; DVD, Blu-Ray.** Robert Patrick; Kelly Carlson; Anthony Ray Parker; Jerome Ehlers; John Cena; Abigail Bianca; ***D:*** John Bonito; ***W:*** Alan B. McElroy; Michelle Gallagher; ***C:*** David Eggby; ***M:*** Don Davis.

The Marine 2 **½ 2009 (R)** A competent in-name-only action sequel has recon sniper Joe Linwood and his wife vacationing at a Thailand resort that's suddenly besieged by a separatist group. With the terrorists taking hostages, it's up to Joe to come up with a plan to save the day. **95m/C; DVD, Blu-Ray.** Ted DiBiase, Jr.; Michael Rooker; Temuera Morrison; Lara Cox; ***D:*** Roel Reine; ***W:*** Christopher Borrelli; John Chapin Morgan; ***M:*** Trevor Morris. **VIDEO**

The Marine 3: Homefront **½ 2011 (R)** Low-budget action from WWE Studios. Sgt. Jake Carter comes home on leave and discovers his sister Lilly has witnessed a crime and was kidnapped by the perps--a violent extremist group planning a terrorist act. That means it's time for big bro to come to the rescue. **90m/C; DVD, Blu-Ray.** Mike Mizanin; Neal McDonough; Ashley Bell; Jeff(rey) Ballard; Jared Keeso; Camille Sullivan; Michael Eklund; ***D:*** Scott Wiper; ***W:*** Scott Wiper; Declan O'Brien; ***C:*** Ron Stannett. **VIDEO**

A Marine Story 🦴🦴 **2010** Self-assured Marine major Alexandra Everett is forced to leave the service after running afoul of the 'don't ask, don't tell' policy. She returns to her desert California hometown but doesn't know what to do without her military career until the sheriff, who's dealing with a crystal meth epidemic, asks Alexandra to help prepare shoplifter Saffron for boot camp rather than prison. A mentor-protege (only) relationship develops but Alexandra's toughness sets her up against some vindictive locals. **93m/C; DVD.** Dreya Weber; Paris Pickard; Anthony Michael Jones; Christine Mourad; Gregg Daniel; Troy Ruptash; Deacon Conroy; Jeff Sugarman; ***D:*** Ned Farr; ***W:*** Ned Farr; ***C:*** Alexandre Naufel; ***M:*** Craig Richey.

Marines, Let's Go 🦴 ½ **1961** Unexceptional military comedy turns serious at the end. A Marine platoon gets R&R in Tokyo--drinking and chasing girls--before being redeployed to combat in Korea. Hard to believe it was directed by Walsh, although it was at the end at his 50-plus years career. **103m/C; DVD.** Tom Tryon; David Hedison; Tom Reese; William Tyler; Barbara Stuart; Linda Hutchings; ***D:*** Raoul Walsh; ***W:*** John Twist; ***C:*** Lucien Ballard; ***M:*** Irving Gertz.

Marion Bridge 🦴🦴 **2002** Chain-smoking alcoholic Rose (McNeil) is dying, which brings her three daughters back together with all their past family traumas unresolved. Former wild child Agnes (Parker) was sexually abused by their father, which resulted in the birth of a child whom she gave up. Now that child is a sullen teen living nearby with her adoptive mother and Agnes would like to befriend her. Eldest sister Theresa (Jenkins) is a bitter divorcee who can't let go of her ex and middle sister Louise (Smith) is a couch potato who is slowly working up the courage to admit she's a lesbian. Much angst ensues for all. Screenwriter McIvor adapted from his play. **90m/C; DVD.** *CA* Molly Parker; Rebecca Jenkins; Stacy Smith; Marguerite McNeill; ***D:*** Wiebke von Carolsfeld; ***W:*** Daniel MacIvor; ***C:*** Stefan Ivanov; ***M:*** Lesley Barber.

Marius 🦴🦴🦴🦴 **1931** This is the first of Marcel Pagnol's trilogy ("Fanny" and "Cesar" followed), about the lives and adventures of the people of Provence, France. Marius is a young man who dreams of going away to sea. When he acts on those dreams, he leaves behind his girlfriend, Fanny. Realistic dialogue and vivid characterizations. Adapted by Pagnol from his play. The musical play and film "Fanny" (1961) were adapted from this trilogy. **125m/B; VHS, DVD, Blu-Ray.** *FR* Raimu; Pierre Fresnay; Charpin; Orane Demazis; ***D:*** Alexander Korda; ***W:*** Marcel Pagnol; ***M:*** Francis Gromon.

Marius and Jeannette 🦴🦴 ½ *Marius et Jeannette: Un Conte de L'Estaque* **1997** Single mother Jeannette (Ascaride) works as a checkout clerk in a poor Marseilles neighborhood. Marius (Meylan) works as a security guard at a closed cement factory and meets Jeannette when he catches her stealing paint cans from the property. He offers to help her paint her apartment and the two begin a tentative romance. But something spooks Marius and he begins to drink heavily, abandoning Jeannette. Two of Jeannette's male neighbors decide to find out what Marius' problem is and get the twosome back together. Very sweet and sentimental. French with subtitles. **101m/C; DVD.** *FR* Ariane Ascaride; Gerard Meylan; Pascale Roberts; Jacques Boudet; Jean-Pierre Darroussin; Frederique Bonnal; ***D:*** Robert Guediguian; ***W:*** Robert Guediguian; Jean-Louis Milesi; ***C:*** Bernard Cavile. Cesar '98: Actress (Ascaride).

Marjoe 🦴🦴 **1972 (PG)** Documentary follows the career of rock-style evangelist Marjoe Gortner, who spent 25 years of his life touring the country as a professional preacher. Marjoe later went on to become an actor and professional fundraiser. **88m/C; VHS, DVD.** Marjoe Gortner; ***D:*** Howard Smith; Sarah Kernochan. Oscars '72: Feature Doc.

Marjorie Morningstar 🦴🦴 **1958** A temperate Hollywood adaptation of the Herman Wouk story of a young actress who fails to achieve stardom and settles on being a housewife. Wood slipped a bit in this story. **123m/C; VHS, DVD, Blu-Ray.** Natalie Wood; Gene Kelly; Martin Balsam; Claire Trevor; Ed Wynn; Everett Sloane; Carolyn Jones; ***D:*** Irving Rapper; ***C:*** Harry Stradling, Sr.; ***M:*** Max Steiner.

Marjorie Prime 🦴🦴 ½ **2017** A subtle drama with science fiction bones, this philosophical film considers the human condition through an artificial intelligence technology. In her Long Island home, elderly Marjorie (Smith) remembers her past through long discussions with a therapeutic hologram of her late husband Walter (Hamm) from when he was in his forties. Marjorie lives with daughter Tess (Davis) and son-in-law Jon (Robbins). Though Jon is enthusiastic about the hologram's value, Tess does not share his feelings because of her past and Walter. Adapted from a Jordan Harrison play, the graceful film explores memory and identity with an engrossing story and unexpected plot twists. **99m/C; DVD.** Hannah Gross; Jon Hamm; Geena Davis; Tim Robbins; Lois Smith; ***D:*** Michael Almereyda; ***W:*** Michael Almereyda; ***C:*** Sean Price Williams; ***M:*** Mica Levi.

The Mark 🦴🦴🦴 ½ **1961** Story of a convicted child molester who cannot escape his past upon his release from prison. Whitman gives a riveting performance as the convict. **127m/B; VHS, DVD.** *GB* Stuart Whitman; Maria Schell; Rod Steiger; Brenda de Banzie; Maurice Denham; Donald Wolfit; Paul Rogers; Donald Houston; Amanda Black; Russell Napier; Marie Devereux; ***D:*** Guy Green; ***W:*** Sidney Buchman; Raymond Stross; ***C:*** Dudley Lovell; ***M:*** Richard Rodney Bennett.

The Mark 🦴 **2012** So the world is on the verge of economic collapse and ex-soldier Chad Turner is the unexpected guinea pig who's implanted with a biometric chip that's supposed to be explained at the G-20 summit. Naturally, there are bad guys who want the chip and they hijack the plane Chad is on, fighting and stuff follows. Pretty reporter Dao says the chip is evil because there are strange faith-based elements mixed in with the action, but the plot doesn't make that much sense anyway. **98m/C; DVD.** Craig Sheffer; Eric Roberts; Gary Daniels; Ivan Kamaras; Sonia Couling; ***D:*** James Chankin; ***W:*** Leland Jourdan; ***C:*** Wych Kaos; ***M:*** Edwin Wendler. **VIDEO**

The Mark 2: Redemption 🦴 *The Mark: Redemption* **2013** The bad guys are out to control the world via a microchip implanted in a U.S. Marine. **94m/C; DVD, Blu-Ray.** Craig Sheffer; Sonia Couling; Eric Roberts; Gary Daniels; Ivan Kamaras; ***D:*** James Chankin; ***W:*** Paul Duran; Leland Jourdan; John Patus; Michael Scott; David A.R. White; Russell Wolfe; ***C:*** Wych Kaos; ***M:*** Edwin Wendler. **VIDEO**

Mark Felt: The Man Who Brought Down the White House 🦴🦴 ½ **2017 (PG-13)** The true story of the man known as Deep Throat. Focusing on his time at the FBI during the Nixon administration, Mark Felt (Neeson) is an able, prepared deputy director who initially promises to keep the adminstration's secrets and destroys FBI director J. Edgar Hoover's private files upon his death. After Nixon aide L. Patrick Gray (Csokas) replaces Hoover, Felt is dismayed that he was not chosen and takes action to keep the Watergate investigation open by leaking information to journalists. Focusing on Felt's loyalties and motivations, the film offers a complex portrait of Felt that leaves viewers wanting to know more. **103m/C; DVD, Blu-Ray.** Liam Neeson; Diane Lane; Marton Csokas; Tony Goldwyn; Ike Barinholtz; ***D:*** Peter Landesman; ***W:*** Peter Landesman; ***C:*** Adam Kimmel; ***M:*** Daniel Pemberton.

Mark of the Astro-Zombies 🦴 **2002** Director Mikels re-imagines his older film "The Astro-Zombies." Aliens are kidnapping people and turning them into cyborg-zombie-killing machines before arming them with machetes and sending them to invade earth. **86m/C; DVD.** Sean Morelli; Anton Funtek; Scott Blacksher; Gene Ellison-Jones; Robert J. Southerland; Ted V. Mikels; Tura Satana; Liz Renay; Brinke Stevens; ***D:*** Ted V. Mikels; ***W:*** Ted V. Mikels; ***C:*** Siria Tena. **VIDEO**

Mark of the Devil 🦴 *Burn, Witch, Burn; Brenn, Hexe, Brenn; Austria 1700; Satan; Hexen bis aufs Blut Gequaelt* **1969 (R)** Witchcraft and romance don't mix, as a Medieval witch hunter and a sexy girl accused of witchery discover. Notoriously graphic torture scenes add to the mayhem but the weird part is that this is based on true stories. **96m/C; VHS, DVD, Blu-Ray.** *GB GE* Herbert Lom; Olivera Vuco; Udo Kier; Reggie Nalder; Herbert (Fuchs) Fux; Michael Maien; Ingeborg (Inge) Schoener; Johannes Buzalski; Gaby Fuchs; Adrian Hoven; ***D:*** Michael Armstrong; ***W:*** Adrian Hoven; Sergio Casstner; ***C:*** Ernst W. Kalinke; ***M:*** Michael Holm.

Mark of the Devil 2 🦴 **1972 (R)** Sadistic witchhunters torture satan's servants and torch sisters of mercy, whilst trying to horn in on a nobleman's fortune. It's just not as gross without the vomit bags. **90m/C; VHS, DVD.** *GB GE* Erika Blanc; Anton Diffring; Reggie Nalder; ***D:*** Adrian Hoven.

Mark of the Gorilla 🦴 **1958** Princess Nyobi (Dalbert) and Jungle Jim (Weissmuller) search for tribal gold stolen by the Nazis and buried in the jungle. A gang, masquerading in gorilla suits to scare the natives, is searching as well. Third in the Jungle Jim series. **68m/B; DVD.** Johnny Weissmuller; Trudy Marshall; Onslow Stevens; Suzanne Dalbert; Selmer Jackson; Pierce Lyden; Robert H. Purcell; ***D:*** William Berke; ***W:*** Carroll Young; ***C:*** Ira Morgan.

The Mark of the Hawk 🦴🦴🦴 *The Accused* **1957** A uniquely told story of African nations struggling to achieve racial equality after gaining independence. Songs include "This Man Is Mine," sung by Kitt. **83m/C; VHS, DVD.** *GB* Sidney Poitier; Eartha Kitt; Juano Hernandez; John McIntire; ***D:*** Michael Audley.

Mark of the Witch 🦴 **1970** Walsh is a looker but this talky, low-budget horror flick is deservedly obscure. While taking a class on the occult, college coed Jill (Walsh) is possessed by the spirit of a 17th-century witch who wants revenge on the descendents of the men who condemned her. **84m/C; DVD.** Anitra Walsh; Robert Elston; Darryl Wells; Jack Gardner; Marie Santell; ***D:*** Tom Moore; ***W:*** Mary Davis; ***C:*** Robert Bethard.

Mark of Zorro 🦴🦴🦴 **1920** Fairbanks plays a dual role as the hapless Don Diego and his dashing counterpart, Zorro, the hero of the oppressed. Silent film. **80m/B; Silent; VHS, DVD.** Douglas Fairbanks, Sr.; Marguerite de la Motte; Noah Beery, Sr.; Mary Astor; Noah Beery, Jr.; Milton Berle; Charles Stevens; ***D:*** Fred Niblo; ***W:*** Douglas Fairbanks, Sr.; ***C:*** William McGann; Harris (Harry) Thorpe. Natl. Film Reg. '15.

The Mark of Zorro 🦴🦴🦴 ½ **1940** The dashing Power swashbuckles his way through this wonderfully acted and directed romp. He's the foppish son of a 19th-century California aristocrat who is secretly the masked avenger of the oppressed peons. Bromberg plays the wicked governor, with the beautiful niece (Darnell) beloved by Power, and Rathbone is supremely evil as his cruel minion. Lots of swordplay with a particularly exciting duel to the death between Rathbone and Power. Based on the novel "The Curse of Capistrano" by Johnston McCulley. Remake of the 1921 silent film and followed by a number of other Zorro incarnations. **93m/B; DVD, Blu-Ray.** Tyrone Power; Linda Darnell; Basil Rathbone; Gale Sondergaard; Eugene Pallette; J. Edward Bromberg; Montagu Love; Janet Beecher; ***D:*** Rouben Mamoulian; ***W:*** John Taintor Foote; ***C:*** Arthur C. Miller; ***M:*** Alfred Newman. Natl. Film Reg. '09.

Marked 🦴 **2007** Low-budget and dull horror. Diella becomes obsessed with the paranormal after her father is killed. Now she leads a research team searching for evidence of life after death and discovers that evil is stronger when the team investigate a haunted house. **85m/C; DVD.** Tara Carroll; Samuel Child; Tony Suraci; Mark Colson; ***D:*** Dustin Voight; ***W:*** Dustin Voight; ***C:*** Adam Biddle; ***M:*** Mel Lewis. **VIDEO**

Marked for Death 🦴 ½ *Screwface* **1990 (R)** Having killed a prostitute, DEA agent Seagal decides it's time to roll out the white picket fence in the 'burbs with the little woman and brood. Trouble is, a bunch of guys with dreadlocks don't approve of his early retirement, and the Jamaican gangsters plan to send him and his family to the great Rasta playground in the sky. Whereupon the Stevester kicks and punches and wags his ponytail. Much blood flows, mon. Tunes by Jimmy Cliff. **93m/C; VHS, DVD.** Steven Seagal; Joanna Pacula; Basil Wallace; Keith David; Danielle Harris; Arlen Dean Snyder; Teri Weigel; ***D:*** Dwight Little; ***W:*** Mark Victor; Michael Grais; ***C:*** Ric Waite; ***M:*** James Newton Howard.

The Marked One 🦴 ½ **1963** Blackmailer demands the plates for making forged banknotes, believing recently released con Don Mason knows where they are. When his young daughter is kidnapped to make him cooperate, Don figures out the getaway vehicle has counterfeit license plates and helps the police crack the case. **65m/B; DVD.** *GB* William Lucas; Zena Walker; Patrick Jordan; David Gregory; Laurie Leigh; Edward Ogden; ***D:*** Francis Searle; ***W:*** Paul Erickson; ***C:*** Frank Kingston; ***M:*** Bernie Fenton; Frank Patten.

Marked Woman 🦴🦴🦴 **1937** Gangster drama about crusading District Attorney who persuades a group of clipjoint hostesses to testify against their gangster boss. A gritty studio melodrama loosely based on a true story. **97m/B; VHS, DVD.** Bette Davis; Humphrey Bogart; Eduardo Ciannelli; Isabel Jewell; Jane Bryan; Mayo Methot; Allen Jenkins; Lola Lane; ***D:*** Lloyd Bacon; ***C:*** George Barnes. Venice Film Fest. '37: Actress (Davis).

Marker 🦴 **2005** A young woman in a small Pacific northwestern town is persecuted when a virus causes an unusual condition. **93m/C; DVD.** *CA* Iris Graham; Jonathan Cherry; Philip Granger; Eric Johnson; Sonja Bennett; ***D:*** John Paizs; ***W:*** Anthony Grieco; ***C:*** Danny Nowak; ***M:*** Patric Caird. **VIDEO**

Marking Time 🦴🦴 **2003** Coming-of-age first romance that starts off with hope and ends in disillusionment. In 2000, the small Australian town of Brackley is excited by the Sydney Olympics and the fact that former Olympian Geoff Fleming (Morrell) is part of their community. Meanwhile, his teenaged son Hal (Forsythe) is falling in love with Afghani refugee Randa (Novakovic) despite the disapproval of his no-account friends. Then a new election brings in an anti-immigration government and, after 9/11, Hal has to find a way to protect Randa from racist insults and violence as well as the threat of deportation. **206m/C; DVD.** *AU* Geoff Morrell; Abbie Cornish; Katie Wall; Graeme Blundell; Abe Forsythe; Bojana Novakovic; Elena Carapetis; Lech Mackiewicz; Matt LeNevez; ***D:*** Cherie Nowlan; ***W:*** John (Roy Slaven) Doyle; ***C:*** Anna Howard; ***M:*** Martin Armiger; John Butler. **TV**

Marley & Me 🦴🦴 ½ **2008 (PG)** Based on John Grogan's 2005 memoir that follows his (Wilson) and wife Jenny's (Aniston) lives as reporters in Florida. John's unhappy when his newspaper editor (Arkin) gives him a column-writing assignment while also tentative about Jenny's desire to have a baby. Enter Marley, a loveable but highly energetic and destructive yellow lab John dubs "the world's worst dog," who manages to win their hearts as he eats their furniture and becomes their constant companion. Appealing to youngsters but parents should beware a major tearjerker at the end. Wilson and Aniston get along well enough, but it plays more like a sitcom than a major film. **116m/C; DVD, Blu-Ray, On Demand.** Owen Wilson; Jennifer Aniston; Haley Bennett; Eric Dane; Alan Arkin; Kathleen Turner; Nathan Gamble; Ann Dowd; ***D:*** David Frankel; ***W:*** Scott Frank; Don Roos; ***C:*** Florian Ballhaus; ***M:*** Theodore Shapiro.

Marley & Me: The Puppy Years 🦴 ½ **2011 (PG)** Direct-to-video prequel to 2008's "Marley & Me." Troublemaking pup Marley is being looked after by tween Bodi while his owners are away. The kid wants a pet of his own but his mom refuses unless Bodi can prove he can handle the responsibility. Naturally, Marley makes this difficult until Bodi comes up with the idea of training the pup and his two friends for the Ultimate Puppy Championships. Marley and his pals are shown talking thanks to some rather creepy CGI. **86m/C; DVD, Blu-Ray.** Travis Turner; Chelah Horsdal; Donnelly Rhodes; Sydney Imbeau; ***V:*** Grayson Russell; Ryan Grantham; Lauren Lavoie; ***D:*** Michael Damian; ***W:*** Michael Damian; Janeen Damian; ***C:*** Ron Stannett; ***M:*** Mark Thomas. **VIDEO**

Marlowe ½ **1969 (PG)** Updated telling by Stirling Silliphant of Chandler's "The Little Sister" sports retro guy Garner as Philip Marlowe, gumshoe. Hired by a mystery blonde to find her misplaced brother, rumpled sleuth Marlowe encounters kicking Bruce Lee in his first film. Slick looking, but the story's a bit slippery. **95m/C; VHS, Blu-Ray.** James Garner; Gayle Hunnicutt; Carroll O'Connor; Rita Moreno; Sharon Farrell; William Daniels; Bruce Lee; ***D:*** Paul Bogart; ***W:*** Stirling Silliphant; ***C:*** William H. Daniels.

Marmaduke ½ **2010 (PG)** Bland, generally family-friendly talking animals comedy based on Brad Anderson's comic strip that began in 1954. The Winslows, and their trouble-prone, klutzy Great Dane (drawlingly voiced by Wilson), move from Kansas to Orange County, California and get to upset a whole new neighborhood. Marmaduke makes some scruffy new pals but wants to hang with the purebreds at the dog park until he learns a lesson in true friendship. **88m/C; DVD, Blu-Ray.** Judy Greer; Lee Pace; William H. Macy; Finley Jacobsen; Caroline Sunshine; ***V:*** Owen Wilson; Emma Stone; Christopher Mintz-Plasse; Ron Perlman; Steve Coogan; George Lopez; Damon Wayans, Jr.; Jeremy Piven; Stacy "Fergie" Ferguson; ***D:*** Tom Dey; ***W:*** Vince Di Meglio; Tim Rasmussen; ***C:*** Greg Gardiner; ***M:*** Christopher Lennertz.

Marnie ½ **1964** A lovely blonde with a mysterious past robs her employers and then changes her identity. When her current boss catches her in the act and forces her to marry him, he soon learns the puzzling aspects of Marnie's background. Criticized at the time of its release, the movie has since been accepted as a Hitchcock classic. **130m/C; VHS, DVD, Blu-Ray.** Tippi Hedren; Sean Connery; Diane Baker; Bruce Dern; Louise Latham; Martin Gabel; Henry Beckman; Mariette Hartley; Alan Napier; ***D:*** Alfred Hitchcock; ***W:*** Jay Presson Allen; ***C:*** Robert Burks; ***M:*** Bernard Herrmann.

Maroc 7 **1967** Slow story of a secret agent after a thief suffering from a split personality. **92m/C; VHS, DVD.** Gene Barry; Elsa Martinelli; Cyd Charisse; Leslie Phillips; ***D:*** Gerry O'Hara.

Marooned ½ *Space Travellers* **1969 (G)** Tense thriller casts Crenna, Hackman, and Franciscus as astronauts stranded in space after a retro-rocket misfires and their craft is unable to return to earth. Amazingly inept despite an Academy Award for effects and an excellent cast. Story bears a striking resemblance to 1995's "Apollo 13." **134m/C; VHS, DVD.** Gregory Peck; David Janssen; Richard Crenna; James Franciscus; Gene Hackman; Lee Grant; ***D:*** John Sturges; ***C:*** Daniel F. Fapp. Oscars '69: Visual FX.

Marooned in Iraq *The Songs of My Homeland; Avazhaye Sarzamine Madariyam* **2002** Set between 1989 and 1991. Victimized by Suddam Hussein, Iraqi Kurds fled to Iran and an uncertain future in refugee camps. One such family is led by the aged Mirza (Ebrahimi), a locally famous singer who has summoned his sons, Barat (Mohammadi) and Audeh (Rashtiani), to accompany him back to Iraq in order to find his ex-wife, Hanareh (Ghobadi), whom he has learned is in trouble. Robbers steal all their possessions and they are forced to walk, eventually coming to other camps of displaced people. Folk music and comic bits help break up the admittedly bleak story. Kurdish with subtitles. **97m/C; VHS, DVD.** *IA* Shahab Ebrahimi; Fa-eq Mohammadi; Alah-Morad Rashtian; Iran Ghobadi; ***D:*** Bahman Ghobadi; ***W:*** Bahman Ghobadi; ***C:*** Saed Nikzat; Shahriar Asadi; ***M:*** Arsalan Komkar.

Marquis de Sade ½ *Dark Prince: Intimate Tales of Marquis de Sade* **1996 (R)** Justine searches for her sister Juliette in 17th-century Paris and is drawn into the sexually deviant world of the Marquis de Sade. Also available unrated. **88m/C; VHS, DVD.** Nick Mancuso; Janet Gunn; John Rhys-Davies; ***D:*** Gwyneth Gibby; ***W:*** Craig J. Nevius; ***C:*** Eugeny Guslinsky. **CABLE**

The Marquise of O *Die Marquise Von O* **1976 (PG)** In the early 18th century, the Russian army is invading Lombardy. The widowed Marquise (Clever) is drugged and raped by Count F (Ganz), an officer with the Russians. When the Marquise discovers she's pregnant, she forces the Count to marry her, although they separate immediately after the ceremony. Adaptation of Heinrich Von Kleist's novella. German with subtitles. **102m/C; VHS, DVD, Blu-Ray.** *FR GE* Edith Clever; Bruno Ganz; Peter Luhr; Edda Seipel; Otto Sander; Ruth Drexel; ***D:*** Eric Rohmer; ***W:*** Eric Rohmer; ***C:*** Nestor Almendros.

The Marriage Circle **1924** A pivotal silent comedy depicting the infidelity of several married couples in Vienna. Director Lubitsch's first American comedy. Remade as a musical, "One Hour With You," in 1932. Silent. **90m/B; Silent; VHS, DVD.** Florence Vidor; Monte Blue; Marie Prevost; Creighton Hale; Adolphe Menjou; Harry C. (Henry) Myers; Dale Fuller; ***D:*** Ernst Lubitsch; ***W:*** Paul Bern; ***C:*** Charles Van Enger.

The Marriage-Go-Round ½ **1961** Newmar reprises her Broadway role in Leslie Steven's watered-down, generally dull adaptation of his stage comedy. Swedish beauty Katrin searches for a brainy man to father her child so the combo of brains and beauty will make a 'perfect' child. She sets her sights on a family acquaintance, anthropology professor Paul Delville (Mason), but Paul's wife, Content (Hayward), is not content with the idea. **98m/C; DVD.** James Mason; Susan Hayward; Julie Newmar; Robert Paige; ***D:*** Walter Lang; ***W:*** Leslie Stevens; ***C:*** Leo Tover; ***M:*** Dominic Frontiere.

Marriage Is Alive and Well **1980** A wedding photographer reflects on the institution of marriage from his unique perspective. **100m/C; DVD.** Joe Namath; Jack Albertson; Melinda Dillon; Judd Hirsch; Susan Sullivan; Fred McCarren; Swoosie Kurtz; ***D:*** Russ Mayberry. **TV**

Marriage Italian Style **1964** When an engaged man hears that his mistress is on her death bed, he goes to her side and, in an emotional gesture, promises to marry her if she survives. She does, and holds him to his promise. After they're married, however, she gives him a big surprise—three grown sons. A silly film, but DeSica's direction keeps it from being too fluffy. Lots of fun. Based on the play "Filumena Marturano" by Eduardo De Filippo. **102m/C; VHS, DVD, Blu-Ray.** *IT* Sophia Loren; Marcello Mastroianni; Aldo Puglisi; Tecla Scarano; Marilu Tolo; ***D:*** Vittorio De Sica. Golden Globes '65: Foreign Film.

The Marriage of Maria Braun *Die Ehe Der Maria Braun* **1979 (R)** In post-WWII Germany, a young woman uses guile and sexuality to survive as the nation rebuilds itself into an industrial power. The first movie in Fassbinder's trilogy about German women in Germany during the post war years, it is considered one of the director's finest films, and an indispensable example of the New German Cinema. In German with English subtitles. **120m/C; VHS, DVD, Blu-Ray.** *GE* Hanna Schygulla; Klaus Lowitsch; Ivan Desny; Gottfried John; Gisela Uhlen; ***D:*** Rainer Werner Fassbinder; ***W:*** Rainer Werner Fassbinder; Peter Marthesheimer; Pea Frolich; ***C:*** Michael Ballhaus; ***M:*** Peer Raben. Berlin Intl. Film Fest. '79: Actress (Schygulla).

Marriage on the Rocks **1965** Mildly amusing marital comedy finds Valerie (Kerr) bored by her 20-year marriage to Dan (Sinatra) so she decides to divorce him. The family lawyer (McGiver) persuades them to take a would-be second honeymoon to Mexico instead, which is cut short for Dan by business. Meanwhile, a mix-up with Mexican lawyer Santos (Romero) actually has the couple divorced. Then, when Dan's womanizing best buddy Ernie (Martin) shows up, he accidentally marries Valerie. More complications ensue but not much comes of all the havoc. **109m/C; VHS, DVD.** Frank Sinatra; Deborah Kerr; Dean Martin; Cesar Romero; John McGiver; Hermione Baddeley; Tony Bill; Nancy Sinatra; ***D:*** Jack Donohue; ***W:*** Cy Howard; ***C:*** William H. Daniels; ***M:*** Nelson Riddle.

Marriage Story **2019 (R)** After separating and reconciling several times, Nicole (Johansson) and Charlie (Driver) are finally getting divorced. Actress Nicole moves from New York to Los Angeles with their young son Henry (Robertson) to film a pilot, while talented theater director Charlie is staging an important play in New York. As they go through the process, their conflict greatly increases, leading to unexpected fractures and changes in how they view themselves. Director Baumbach's revealing domestic drama compassionately depicts the subtle way divorce painfully changes everyone involved with outstanding direction, a memorable story, and poignant performances by Driver and Johansson. **136m/C; DVD.** Adam Driver; Scarlett Johansson; Azhy Robertson; Laura Dern; Ray Liotta; ***D:*** Noah Baumbach; ***W:*** Noah Baumbach; ***C:*** Robbie Ryan; ***M:*** Randy Newman. Oscars '19: Actress--Supporting (Dern); British Acad. '19: Actress--Supporting (Dern); Golden Globes '20: Actress--Supporting (Dern); Ind. Spirit '20: Screenplay; Screen Actors Guild '19: Actress--Supporting (Dern).

Married Life **2007 (PG-13)** Set in 1949 and steeped in the style, mood, and sensibilities of the time. Buttoned-down married man Harry Allen (Cooper) falls for young, gorgeous widow Kay (McAdams). Burdened with guilt and hoping for understanding, Harry confides in his womanizing pal Richard (Brosnan), who also becomes fascinated with Kay. Harry decides to end his marriage but is so duty bound to wife Pat (Clarkson) that he plans to murder her rather than subject her to the pain of a divorce (hmm, wonder if that's the option she'd pick). Several big surprises hold together this intriguing, smart drama. **90m/C; DVD, Blu-Ray.** Chris Cooper; Patricia Clarkson; Rachel McAdams; Pierce Brosnan; David Wenham; ***D:*** Ira Sachs; ***W:*** Ira Sachs; Oren Moverman; ***C:*** Peter Deming; ***M:*** Dickon Hinchliffe.

A Married Man **1984** Story focusing on a bored British lawyer who begins cheating on his wife. Amid the affair, someone gets murdered. **200m/C; VHS, DVD.** *GB* Anthony Hopkins; Ciaran Madden; Lise Hilboldt; Yvonne Coulette; John Le Mesurier; Sophie Ashton; ***D:*** John Davies. **TV**

Married People, Single Sex ½ **1993 (R)** Three couples decide to spread their sexual wings. Shelly takes a new lover; Artie makes obscene phone calls; and Beth and Mike, who end their relationship, still can't keep out of bed. An unrated version is also available. **110m/C; VHS, DVD.** Chase Masterson; Joe Pilato; Darla Haun; Shelley Michelle; Wendi Westbrook; Robert Zachar; Samuel Mongiello; Teri Thompson; ***D:*** Mike Sedan; ***W:*** Catherine Tavel.

Married to It **1993 (R)** Three vastly different couples work together to plan a pageant at a private school. The oil and water group includes struggling hippie leftovers Bridges and Channing, '80s-era corporate cutthroats Shepherd and Silver, and starry-eyed newlyweds Masterson and Leonard. Contrived plot offers few humourous moments, with the main focus revolving around coping rather than comedy. And the coping is slow business, done by characters you don't really care about with problems that don't really matter. **112m/C; VHS, DVD.** Beau Bridges; Stockard Channing; Robert Sean Leonard; Mary Stuart Masterson; Cybill Shepherd; Ron Silver; ***D:*** Arthur Hiller; ***W:*** Janet Kovalcik; ***M:*** Henry Mancini.

Married to the Mob **1988 (R)** After the murder of her husband, an attractive Mafia widow tries to escape "mob" life, but ends up fighting off amorous advances from the current mob boss while being wooed by an undercover cop. A snappy script and a spry performance by Pfeiffer pepper this easy-to-watch film. **102m/C; VHS, DVD, Blu-Ray.** Michelle Pfeiffer; Dean Stockwell; Alec Baldwin; Matthew Modine; Mercedes Ruehl; Anthony J. Nici; Joan Cusack; Ellen Foley; Chris Isaak; Trey Wilson; Charles Napier; Tracey Walter; Al Lewis; Nancy Travis; David Johansen; Jonathan Demme; ***D:*** Jonathan Demme; ***W:*** Mark Burns; Barry Strugatz; ***C:*** Tak Fujimoto; ***M:*** David Byrne. N.Y. Film Critics '88: Support. Actor (Stockwell); Natl. Soc. Film Critics '88: Support. Actor (Stockwell), Support. Actress (Ruehl).

The Married Virgin **1918** One of the earliest films in which Valentino appeared in a featured role prior to "The Four Horsemen of the Apocalypse" and "The Sheik." Count Roberto di Fraccini (Valentino) is a fortune hunter having an affair with Ethel Spencer McMillan (Kirkham), wife of wealthy older businessman Fiske McMillan (Jobson). After the couple unsuccessfully plot to blackmail McMillan, the Count tells his lover's daughter, Mary (Sisson), that in return for her hand in marriage (and her dowry), he will save her father from a life in prison. **71m/B; Silent; DVD.** Rudolph Valentino; Kathleen Kirkham; Edward Jobson; Vera Sisson; Frank Newburg; ***D:*** Joe Maxwell; ***W:*** Hayden Talbott.

A Married Woman *La Femme Mariee* **1965** Dramatizes a day in the life of a woman who has both a husband and a lover. One of Godard's more mainstream efforts. **94m/B; VHS, DVD, Blu-Ray.** *FR* Macha Meril; Phillippe LeRoy; Bernard Noel; ***D:*** Jean-Luc Godard; ***W:*** Jean-Luc Godard; ***C:*** Raoul Coutard.

Marry Me ½ **2010** The likeable Liu stars in this Lifetime miniseries as the not-always-likeable Rae Ann, a wannabe artist-turned-social worker who believes in a fairytale romance. Instead of a marriage proposal, her boyfriend Adam (Cannavale) wants a time out because of his career. Friends introduce Rae Ann to nice guy Luke (Pasquale) setting off a whirlwind romance until she meets his wealthy friend Harry (Murciano), who's also interested. Oh, and Adam re-enters her life as well, so a confused and indecisive Rae Ann now has three men ready to propose. **170m/C; DVD.** Lucy Liu; Steven Pasquale; Bobby Cannavale; Enrique Murciano; Annie Potts; David Andrews; ***D:*** James Hayman; ***W:*** Barbara Hall; ***C:*** Neil Roach; ***M:*** Jonathan Grossman. **CABLE**

The Marrying Kind ½ **1952** Marrieds Florence (Holliday) and Chet (Ray) Keefer are in the chambers of Judge Carroll (Kennedy) talking about why they want a divorce. They flashback to their courtship and marriage and the bumps they've endured along the way, and then realize they still love each other. Holliday reunited with Cukor and scriptwriters Gordon and Kanin after their triumph with "Born Yesterday." **92m/B; VHS, DVD.** Judy Holliday; Aldo Ray; Madge Kennedy; Sheila Bond; John Alexander; Peggy Cass; Rex Williams; ***D:*** George Cukor; ***W:*** Ruth Gordon; Garson Kanin; ***C:*** Joseph Walker; ***M:*** Hugo Friedhofer.

The Marrying Man ½ **1991 (R)** Charley's (Baldwin) buddies take him to Vegas for his bachelor party and he falls for singer Vicki (Basinger), not knowing she belongs to crime boss Bugsy Siegel (Assante), who catches them together and forces them to marry. They immediately divorce, can't forget each other and re-marry, again and again and again. Silly story supposedly based on the lives of Harry Karl and Marie MacDonald. Basinger and Baldwin's offstage romance created quite a stir but their chemistry onscreen is zilch. Ineffective, poorly paced and acted, it's a good example of what happens when egotistical stars get their way. **116m/C; DVD, Blu-Ray.** Alec Baldwin; Kim Basinger; Robert Loggia; Armand Assante; Elisabeth Shue; Paul Reiser; Fisher Stevens; Peter Dobson; Gretchen Wyler; ***D:*** Jerry Rees; ***W:*** Neil Simon; ***M:*** David Newman.

Mars ½ **1996** Fast-paced space western finds independent lawman Caution Templar (Gruner) receiving a frantic message from his brother to return to the wild mining town of Alpha City, Mars. Only by the time he arrives his brother is dead and Templar is determined to find out what happened. **92m/C; VHS, DVD.** Olivier Gruner; Shari Belafonte; Scott Valentine; Amber Smith; Alex Hyde-White; Lee DeBroux; Gabriel Dell; ***D:*** Jon Hess; ***W:*** Patrick Highsmith; Steven Hartov. **VIDEO**

Mars Attacks! ½ **1996 (PG-13)** Only director Burton could make a movie based on a series of 1960s trading cards. Intentionally tacky, this huge scale epic spoof of monster, sci-fi, and disaster flicks finds moronic President Dale (Nicholson), his frigid wife (Close) and a cast of thousands battling the green-skinned invaders. Plot zig-zags wildly throughout, but the gist is that the aliens are bent on destroying the population, and have little trouble battling the bumbling humans. Brosnan is the hilariously deluded alien-hugger, Professor Kessler. Pic goes all out for the camp laugh, but its big budget effects, way over-the-top style and all-star cast can't conquer the audience. **106m/C; DVD, Blu-Ray.** Jack Nicholson; Glenn Close; Martin Short; Pierce Brosnan; Lukas Haas; Sarah Jessica Parker; Michael J. Fox; Natalie Portman;

Rod Steiger; Paul Winfield; Annette Bening; Sylvia Sidney; Danny DeVito; Joe Don Baker; Pam Grier; Jim Brown; Lisa Marie; Jack Black; ***Cameo(s):*** Tom Jones; ***D:*** Tim Burton; ***W:*** Jonathan Gems; ***C:*** Peter Suschitzky; ***M:*** Danny Elfman.

Mars Needs Moms ½ **2011 (PG)** Moms need a better movie but it should still hold the kids' attention. In this animated 3D comedy, 9-year-old Milo (Green) stows away on a Martian spaceship when the aliens kidnap his mom (Cusack) to use her DNA to look after their own youngsters. The Martians are ruled by an ancient, grumpy female supervisor (Sterling) who wants to download Mom's maternal instincts into femme-robot nannies. The performance-capture is much less creepy than usual but since Seth Green didn't sound like a young boy, it's his motion and Seth Dusky's voice that combine for Milo. Based on the children's book by Berkeley Breathed. **88m/C; DVD, Blu-Ray, On Demand.** ***V:*** Seth Green; Joan Cusack; Dan Fogler; Elisabeth Harnois; Mindy Sterling; Kevin Cahoon; Tom Everett Scott; ***D:*** Simon Wells; ***W:*** Simon Wells; Wendy Wells; ***C:*** Robert Presley; ***M:*** John Powell.

Mars Needs Women **1966** When the Martian singles scene starts to drag, Mars boys cross the galaxy in search of fertile earth babes to help them repopulate the planet. Seems Batgirl Craig, the go-go dancing lady scientist, is at the top of their dance cards. **80m/C; VHS, DVD.** Tommy Kirk; Yvonne Craig; Warren Hammack; Tony Houston; Larry Tanner; Cal Duggan; ***D:*** Larry Buchanan; ***W:*** Larry Buchanan; ***C:*** Robert C. Jessup.

Marshall ½ **2017 (PG-13)** Legal thriller on a case argued by future U.S. Supreme Court justice Thurgood Marshall (Boseman). In the 1940s, then-NAACP attorney Marshall is sent to defend Joseph Spell (Brown) on charges of rape and attempted murder of white society woman Eleanor Strubing (Hudson). Spell can find no local lawyers to represent him because the local community already believes he is guilty. Muted by the white judge (Cromwell) in court, Marshall defends Spell through his inexperienced co-counsel Sam Friedman (Gad). Buoyed by the stellar performances of the leads, it entertains while effectively exploring issues of race, religion, and gender. **118m/C; DVD, Blu-Ray, Streaming.** Chadwick Boseman; Josh Gad; Kate Hudson; Sterling K. Brown; Dan Stevens; James Cromwell; Michael Koskoff; ***D:*** Reginald Hudlin; ***W:*** Jacob Koskoff; ***C:*** Newton Thomas (Tom) Sigel; ***M:*** Marcus Miller.

The Marshal's Daughter ½ **1953** A father and daughter team up to outwit an outlaw. Features many cowboy songs, including the title track by Tex Ritter. **71m/B; VHS, DVD.** Tex Ritter; Ken Murray; Laurie Anders; Preston Foster; Hoot Gibson; ***D:*** William Berke.

Martha Marcy May Marlene **2011 (R)** A young woman named Martha (Olsen, in an impressive debut) is caught between worlds after escaping a cult led by the charismatic sociopath Patrick (Hawkes). Returning to normal life proves challenging when she moves in with her distant sister (Paulson) and her husband (Dancy). Plays not unlike a dream as Martha's memories of her time away reveal exactly what happened to her, while her paranoia that cult members may be coming after her increases the tension of her return and makes for a mesmerizing thriller. **101m/C; DVD, Blu-Ray.** Elizabeth Olsen; Sarah Paulson; Hugh Dancy; John Hawkes; Brady Corbet; ***D:*** Sean Durkin; ***W:*** Sean Durkin; ***C:*** Jody Lee Lipes; ***M:*** Saunder Jurriaans; Danny Bensi.

Martial Outlaw **1993 (R)** DEA man Kevin White (Wincott) has been following a drug-dealing ex-KGB kingpin from Moscow to San Francisco. The Russian's latest move takes him to Los Angeles where Kevin meets up with his older brother Jack (Hudson), a maverick LA cop. Jack persuades Kevin to let him in on the action but Kevin begins to suspect Jack is playing both sides and their sibling rivalry could lead to death. **89m/C; VHS, Streaming.** Jeff Wincott; Gary Hudson; Richard Jaeckel; Krista Errickson; Vladimir Skomarovsky; Liliana Komorowska; Gary Wood; ***D:*** Kurt Anderson; ***W:*** Thomas Ritz; John Bryant.

The Martian ½ **2015 (PG-13)** Science is made cool again in Scott's fantastic adaptation of Andy Weir's hit book. Astronaut Mark Watney (Damon) is stranded on the red planet after a manned mission has to quickly vacate with the rest of his crew mistakenly thinking he's dead. It's not long before Earth discovers Watney is still alive, but it will take so long to get back and retrieve him that the only man on Mars has to use his ingenuity to stay alive. Tense, funny, and incredibly well-cast down to the smallest roles, it's old-fashioned blockbuster entertainment, the kind that inspires wonder across the generations. **134m/C; DVD, Blu-Ray.** Matt Damon; Jessica Chastain; Kristen Wiig; Kate Mara; Sebastian Stan; ***D:*** Ridley Scott; ***W:*** Drew Goddard; ***C:*** Dariusz Wolski; ***M:*** Harry Gregson-Williams. Golden Globes '15: Film--Mus./Comedy; Golden Globes '16: Actor--Mus./Comedy (Damon).

Martian Child ½ **2007 (PG)** Who better to adopt orphan Dennis (Coleman), who believes he is from Mars, than a successful science fiction writer? Widower David's (Cusack) life revolves around his dog, a frenetic agent who's pressuring him to write the sequel to his successful novel, the cute friend (Peet) of his dead wife, and his harried sister (real-life sibling Joan Cusack). David's drawn to Dennis, the kid at the orphanage who lives in a cardboard box. The mild tale of love and patience and identity never packs much of a punch, but this suitable-for-the-entire-family film is relatively charming and generally unoffending. **106m/C; DVD.** John Cusack; Bobby Coleman; Amanda Peet; Sophie Okonedo; Oliver Platt; Joan Cusack; Anjelica Huston; ***D:*** Menno Meyjes; ***W:*** Seth Bass; Jonathan Tolins; ***C:*** Robert Yeoman; ***M:*** Aaron Zigman.

The Martian Chronicles: Part 1 ½ **1979** Series episode "The Explorers." Adapted from Ray Bradbury's critically acclaimed novel. Futuristic explorations of the planet Mars. Strange fates of the discovery teams make everything more curious. **120m/C; VHS, DVD.** Rock Hudson; Bernie Casey; Nicholas Hammond; Darren McGavin; ***D:*** Michael Anderson, Sr. **TV**

The Martian Chronicles: Part 2 ½ **1979** Episode following the television movie. This part is called "The Settlers." The planet Mars meets with its first colonization and the settlers watch the Earth explode. **97m/C; VHS, DVD.** Rock Hudson; Fritz Weaver; Roddy McDowall; Bernie Casey; Darren McGavin; Gayle Hunnicutt; Barry Morse; Bernadette Peters; ***D:*** Michael Anderson, Sr. **TV**

The Martian Chronicles: Part 3 ½ **1979** In the final chapter of this space saga, the Martian's secrets become known and will forever change man's destiny. Adapted from Ray Bradbury's classic novel. **97m/C; VHS, DVD.** Rock Hudson; Bernadette Peters; Christopher Connelly; Fritz Weaver; Roddy McDowall; Bernie Casey; Nicholas Hammond; Darren McGavin; Gayle Hunnicutt; Barry Morse; ***D:*** Michael Anderson, Sr. **TV**

Martin **1977 (R)** Martin is a charming young man, though slightly mad. He freely admits the need to drink blood. Contemporary vampire has found a new abhorrent means of killing his victims. **96m/C; VHS, DVD.** John Amplas; Lincoln Maazel; Christine Forrest; Elyane Nadeau; Tom Savini; Sarah Venable; George A. Romero; Fran Middleton; ***D:*** George A. Romero; ***W:*** George A. Romero; ***C:*** Michael Gornick; ***M:*** Donald Rubinstein.

Martin Chuzzlewit ½ **1994** Martin Chuzzlewit (Scofield) is a rich and elderly man with a lot of greedy relatives just waiting for him to die so they can get their hands on his money. The only exceptions being his already disinherited namesake grandson and his young orphaned nurse, Mary Graham. Adapted from the Charles Dickens novel. On three cassettes. **288m/C; VHS, DVD.** Paul Scofield; John Mills; Pete Postlethwaite; Tom Wilkinson; Julia Sawalha; David Bradley; ***D:*** Pedr James. **TV**

Martin (Hache) **1997** "Hache" means Junior, and 19-year-old Martin is named after his estranged film director father. When the teenager accidentally overdoses after a bad break-up, his remarried mother insists her ex finally take responsibility and sends Martin to live with his dad in Madrid. Alicia, his dad's lover, and flamboyant best friend Dante try to make the boy feel welcome, but Martin Sr. is not doing his part. Spanish with subtitles. **123m/C; DVD.** *AR SP* Federico Luppi; Juan Diego Botto; Cecilia (Celia) Roth; Eusebio Poncela; ***D:*** Adolfo Aristarain; ***W:*** Adolfo Aristarain; Kathy Saavedra; ***C:*** Porfirio Enriquez; ***M:*** Fito Paez.

Martin Luther ½ **1953** French-made biography of the 16th century reformer who began the Protestant Reformation. **105m/B; VHS, DVD.** *FR* Niall MacGinnis; John Ruddock; Pierre Leeavre; Guy Verney; ***D:*** Irving Pichel; ***W:*** Allan Sloane; Lothar Wolff; ***C:*** Joseph Brun; ***M:*** Mark Lothar.

Marty ½ **1955** Marty is a painfully shy bachelor who feels trapped in a pointless life of family squabbles. When he finds love, he also finds the strength to break out of what he feels is a meaningless existence. A sensitive and poignant film from the writer of "Altered States." Remake of a TV version that originally aired in 1953. Notable for Borgnine's sensitive portrayal, one of his last quality jobs before sinking into the B-movie sludge pit. **91m/B; VHS, DVD, Blu-Ray.** Ernest Borgnine; Betsy Blair; Joe Mantell; Esther Minciotti; Jerry Paris; Karen Steele; Augusta Ciolli; Frank Sutton; Walter Kelley; Robin Morse; ***D:*** Delbert Mann; ***W:*** Paddy Chayefsky; ***C:*** Joseph LaShelle; ***M:*** Roy Webb; Harry Warren. Oscars '55: Actor (Borgnine), Director (Mann), Film, Screenplay; British Acad. '55: Actor (Borgnine), Actress (Blair); Directors Guild '55: Director (Mann); Golden Globes '56: Actor--Drama (Borgnine); Natl. Bd. of Review '55: Actor (Borgnine); Natl. Film Reg. '94; N.Y. Film Critics '55: Actor (Borgnine), Film.

Martyrs **2016** The original 2008 French horror flick earned a reputation in genre circles for its intensity and unapologetic lack of morality. There is zero reason to remake it other than all foreign hits eventually get their English language treatment. Lucie (Bellisario) escapes a warehouse in which she was held prisoner and tortured, but is unable to escape the nightmarish visions. She befriends another girl named Anna (Noble), and the pair decides to track down Lucie's torturers. It's a grisly affair that has no reason to exist, especially if you've seen the superior original. **86m/C; DVD, Blu-Ray.** Troian Bellisario; Bailey Noble; Kate Burton; Caitlin Carmichael; Melissa Tracy; ***D:*** Kevin Goetz; Michael Goetz; ***W:*** Mark L. Smith; ***C:*** Sean O'Dea; ***M:*** Evan Goldman.

Marvin's Room ½ **1996 (PG-13)** Guaranteed sobfest with a gifted set of performers. Sensitive spinster Bessie (Keaton) is living in Orlando where she's been caring for her bedridden father, Marvin (Cronyn), who's been dying for the last 20 years, and her eccentric aunt Ruth (Verdon). When she's stricken with leukemia and needs a bone marrow donor, Bessie must rely on tough, estranged sister Lee (Streep) to help out. But divorcee Lee's got her hands full with rebellious teenaged son Hank (DiCaprio) and his geeky younger bro Charlie (Scardino) and is none too eager to renew the family ties. Based on Scott McPherson's 1991 Off-Broadway play. **98m/C; DVD, Blu-Ray.** Diane Keaton; Meryl Streep; Leonardo DiCaprio; Hume Cronyn; Gwen Verdon; Hal Scardino; Robert De Niro; Dan Hedaya; Margo Martindale; Cynthia Nixon; ***D:*** Jerry Zaks; ***W:*** Scott McPherson; ***C:*** Piotr Sobocinski; ***M:*** Rachel Portman.

Marwencol ½ **2010** Documentary following the life of Mark Hogancamp, who suffers amnesia after nearly being beaten to death. To cope he makes photos of an imaginary WWII town using 1/6th scale dolls, and finds himself conflicted when an art magazine picks them up for display. **83m/C; DVD, Blu-Ray.**

Mary ½ **2019 (R)** When David (Oldman) buys an old yacht to fix up, his wife Sarah (Mortimer) is annoyed but gets caught up in his enthusiasm. After completing repairs, the couple, their two daughters, teen Lindsey (Scott) and young Mary (Perrin), and two others sail from Florida to Bermuda, through the Bermuda Triangle. Strange things begin to occur, such as wet footprints with no one around, which grow more dire. A supernatural nautical thriller that fails to terrify. **84m/C; DVD.** Gary Oldman; Emily Mortimer; Manuel Garcia-Rulfo; Stefanie Scott; Chloe Perrin; ***D:*** Michael Goi; ***W:*** Anthony Jaswinski; ***C:*** Michael Goi; ***M:*** The Newton Brothers.

Mary and Martha **2013** Well-intentioned but stiff HBO drama. American Mary (Swank) decides to take her young son on an extended trip to Africa where he's bitten by a malaria-carrying mosquito and dies. She soon meets Britisher Martha (Blethyn) whose son also died of malaria while working in an African orphanage. The women soon learn that hundreds of thousands die from the preventable disease each year, most of them African children, so they work to bring attention to fighting the disease. **95m/C; DVD.** *UK US* Hilary Swank; Brenda Blethyn; Sam Claflin; Frank Grillo; James Woods; ***D:*** Phillip Noyce; ***W:*** Richard Curtis; ***C:*** Roberto De Angelis; ***M:*** Philip Miller. **CABLE**

Mary and Max ½ **2009** Claymation feature from Australia about a couple of pen pals. Mary (Collette) lives in Melbourne; an unloved, lonely child, she randomly picks a name from a New York phone book, writes a letter, and receives a reply from elderly Jewish Max (Hoffman). They bond over their mutual love of candy and their dismal social status (and way too many scatological references). The two remain friends as Max eventually reveals his emotional problems while Mary outgrows her awkwardness. The story becomes repetitive although the detailed visuals hold the eye. **92m/C; DVD, Blu-Ray.** *AU* Toni Collette; Philip Seymour Hoffman; Eric Bana; Barry Humphries; ***Nar:*** Barry Humphries; ***C:*** Gerald Thompson.

Mary Higgins Clark: Lucky Day ½ *Lucky Day* **2002 (PG-13)** Aspiring actress Nora Barkin supports herself by working for a courier service. After coworker Bill Reagan tells Nora he has a winning lottery ticket worth millions, he's murdered. Despite being discouraged by Det. Marinello, Nora decides to do her own sleuthing. **95m/C; DVD.** Amanda Donohoe; Tony LoBianco; Gregor Torzs; Guylaine St. Onge; Gino Marrocco; ***D:*** Penelope Buitenhuis; ***W:*** Peter Mohan; ***C:*** Richard Wincenty; ***M:*** Domenic Troiano. **TV**

Mary Magdalene **2019 (R)** A woman of faith, Mary Magdalene (Mara) wants to do more with her life than be married and have children. Because she is not welcome in the same spaces of worship as men, her father and brothers subject her to a forced exorcism and nearly kill her in the process. When healer Jesus (Phoenix) comes to her town, she becomes a devoted follower and shares his message of love. As one of his apostles, Mary witnesses his miracles, his growing following, and the fear that comes with being called the messiah. This extraordinary re-telling of Mary's life features an empathetic, moving performance by Rooney. **120m/C; DVD, Blu-Ray.** Rooney Mara; Joaquin Rafael (Leaf) Phoenix; Chiwetel Ejiofor; Tahar Rahim; Ariane Labed; ***D:*** Garth Davis; ***W:*** Helen Edmundson; Philippa Goslett; ***C:*** Greig Fraser; ***M:*** Hildur Guonadottir; Johann Johannsson.

Mary, Mary **1963** Overlong comedy (with quippy dialogue) based on the play by Jean Kerr. Separated and finalizing divorce details, New York publisher Bob (Reynolds) is in trouble with the IRS and has to ask his nearly-ex wife Mary (Reynolds) to help him explain some expenses. Bob is already seeing Tiffany (McBain) and when the two go out of town, Mary winds up staying at Bob's apartment where his actor friend Dirk (Rennie) makes a play for her. Bob's unexpected return leads to surprising results. **126m/C; DVD.** Debbie Reynolds; Barry Nelson; Diane McBain; Michael Rennie; Hiram Sherman; ***D:*** Mervyn LeRoy; ***W:*** Richard L. Breen; ***C:*** Harry Stradling, Sr.; ***M:*** Frank Perkins.

Mary, Mary, Bloody Mary **1976 (R)** Young beautiful artist ravages Mexico with her penchant for drinking blood. Turns out she's a bisexual vampire. When even her friends become victims, her father steps in to end the bloodbath. **85m/C; VHS, DVD, Blu-Ray.** Christina Ferrare; David Young; Helena Rojo; John Carradine; ***D:*** Juan Lopez Moctezuma; ***W:*** Malcolm Marmorstein; ***M:*** Tom Bahler.

Mary, Mother of Jesus ½ **1999** The life of Jesus (Bale) is retold through the eyes of his mother (August), as her faith is tested by her son's ultimate sacrifice. The production stays close to the Biblical scripts of Matthew, Mark, Luke, and John and the characters are pretty much reverential cardboard. **94m/C; VHS, DVD.** Christian Bale; Pernilla August; Geraldine Chaplin; David Threlfall; Hywel Bennett; Christopher Lawford; ***D:*** Kevin Connor; ***W:*** Albert Ross; ***C:*** Elemer Ragalyi; ***M:*** Mario Klemens. **TV**

Mary of Scotland **1936** The historical tragedy of Mary, Queen of Scots and her cousin, Queen Elizabeth I of England is enacted in this classic film. Traces Mary's claims to the throne of England which ultimately led to her execution. Based on the Maxwell Anderson play. **123m/B; VHS, DVD.** Katharine Hepburn; Fredric March; Florence Eldridge; Douglas Walton; John Carradine; Robert Barrat; Gavin Muir; Ian Keith; Moroni Olsen; William Stack; Alan Mowbray; ***D:*** John Ford.

Mary Poppins **½ 1964** Magical English nanny arrives one day on the East Wind and takes over the household of a very proper London banker. She introduces her two charges to her friends and family, including Bert, the chimney sweep (Van Dyke), and eccentric Uncle Albert (Wynn). She also changes the lives of everyone in the family. From her they learn that life can always be happy and joyous if you take the proper perspective. Film debut of Andrews. Based on the books by P.L. Travers. A Disney classic that hasn't lost any of its magic. Look for the wonderful sequence where Van Dyke dances with animated penguins. **139m/C; VHS, DVD, Blu-Ray.** Julie Andrews; Dick Van Dyke; Ed Wynn; Hermione Baddeley; David Tomlinson; Glynis Johns; Karen Dotrice; Matthew Garber; ***D:*** Robert Stevenson; ***W:*** Bill Walsh; Whip Wilson; ***C:*** Edward Colman; ***M:*** Richard M. Sherman; Robert B. Sherman. Oscars '64: Actress (Andrews), Film Editing, Orig. Score, Song ("Chim Chim Cher-ee"), Visual FX; Golden Globes '65: Actress--Mus./Comedy (Andrews); Natl. Film Reg. '13.

Mary Poppins Returns **½ 2018 (PG)** Set two decades after the original (1964) classic, this sequel heralds the return of the magical nanny to care for the next generation of Banks children. The filmmakers, aware that they were treading on sacred ground, remained faithful to the tone and spirit of the original. Blunt captures the magic, kindness, and slight smugness of Andrews' iconic Poppins. The songs and their accompanying animation have that 1960s' feel, even if they are apropos of nothing, plot-wise. It may not be "practically perfect in every way," but it's a perfectly fine family musical. **130m/C; Blu-Ray, Streaming.** Emily Blunt; Lin-Manuel Miranda; Ben Whishaw; Emily Mortimer; Julie Walters; ***D:*** Rob Marshall; ***W:*** Rob Marshall; David Magee; John DeLuca; ***C:*** Dion Beebe; ***M:*** Marc Shaiman.

Mary, Queen of Scots **½ 1971 (PG-13)** Redgrave does a spirited job in the title role as the headstrong and romantic queen who came to an unfortunate end. Mary is raised in France by her mother's Catholic family, from whom she inherits the Scottish title after her mother's death. She claims the throne much to the dismay of her Protestant half-brother James Stuart (McGoohan) and England's equally Protestant Queen Elizabeth (Jackson), who does not want her own Catholic subjects to get any ideas. Mary makes two unfortunate marriages and winds up being betrayed, eventually forcing Elizabeth to eliminate her dangerous cousin. **128m/C; VHS, DVD.** Vanessa Redgrave; Glenda Jackson; Patrick McGoohan; Timothy Dalton; Nigel Davenport; Trevor Howard; Daniel Massey; Ian Holm; ***D:*** Charles Jarrott; ***W:*** John Hale; ***C:*** Christopher Challis; ***M:*** John Barry.

Mary Queen of Scots **½ 2018 (R)** Mary Stuart (Ronan), Queen of France, returns to Scotland in 1561 at the ripe old age of 18 to reclaim her rightful crown as the Scottish queen. Still not satisfied, she makes the moves on the English throne, scheming to overthrow her cousin Elizabeth I (Robbie), a move that ultimately gets her executed. As with most period pieces, the costumes and scenery are gorgeous. The historical inaccuracies are more troubling, however, and are obvious even to viewers who aren't hep to 16th-century European politics. Based on John Guy's book, "Queen of Scots: The True Life of Mary Stuart." **124m/C; DVD, Blu-Ray, Streaming.** *UK* Saoirse Ronan; Margot Robbie; Jack Lowden; Joe Alwyn; David Tennant; ***D:*** Josie Rourke; ***W:*** Beau Willimon; ***C:*** John Mathieson; ***M:*** Max Richter.

Mary Reilly **1995 (R)** Mary (Roberts) is an innocent maid whose employer happens to be the infamous Dr. Jekyll (Malkovich). They both seem to be employed by Dr. Freud in this dank, dreary psychosexual thriller. Mary is torn between the repressed affection of the doctor and the oily sexuality of his alter ego, who conjures up images of her abusive father. Most of the gloomy sets will make you wish you were wearing galoshes. The ending of the film was reshot (more than once) but it didn't help. Based on the novel by Valerie Martin. **108m/C; DVD, Blu-Ray.** Julia Roberts; John Malkovich; George Cole; Michael Gambon; Kathy Staff; Glenn Close; Michael Sheen; Bronagh Gallagher; Linda Bassett; Henry Goodman; Ciaran Hinds; Sasha Hanau; David Ross; ***D:*** Stephen Frears; ***W:*** Christopher Hampton; ***C:*** Philippe Rousselot; ***M:*** George Fenton.

Mary Shelley **½ 2017 (PG-13)** A biopic of the Frankenstein author as a young woman. Sixteen-year-old Mary (Fanning) aspires to be an author, just like her parents. Especially fond of ghost stories, she begins to write and her supportive father (Dillane) sends her to Scotland to help her find her voice. There, she meets poet Percy Bysshe Shelley (Booth), and the pair soon elope. After Mary learns about Percy's unfaithfulness, she puts her complex emotions into a story she writes while at the Swiss home of poet Lord Byron (Sturridge). More soap opera than inspiring story, still Fanning shines. **120m/C; DVD, Blu-Ray, Streaming.** *LU UK US* Elle Fanning; Douglas Booth; Joanne Froggatt; Maisie Williams; Stephen (Dillon) Dillane; ***D:*** Haifaa Al-Mansour; ***W:*** Haifaa Al-Mansour; Emma Jensen; ***C:*** David Ungaro; ***M:*** Amelia Warner.

Mary Shelley's Frankenstein **½ *Frankenstein* 1994 (R)** Branagh turns from Shakespeare to another form of literary classic with his operatic (and loose) adaptation of the Shelley novel. He also plays Victor, the overwrought medical student who decides that death can be vanquished and sets out to prove his theories by making a man. De Niro is sufficiently grisly (though lacking in pathos) as the reanimated corpse with Bonham Carter alternately suffering and excitable as Victor's fiancee Elizabeth. Visually arresting—particularly the Creature's birth scene—pic doesn't engender audience sympathy for the characters' trials and final fates. **123m/C; DVD.** Kenneth Branagh; Robert De Niro; Helena Bonham Carter; Tom Hulce; Aidan Quinn; John Cleese; Ian Holm; Richard Briers; Robert Hardy; Cherie Lunghi; Celia Imrie; Trevyn McDowell; ***D:*** Kenneth Branagh; ***W:*** Frank Darabont; Steph Lady; ***C:*** Roger Pratt; ***M:*** Patrick Doyle.

Mary White **1977** The true story of Mary White, the 16-year-old daughter of a newspaper editor who rejects her life of wealth and sets out to find her own identity. **102m/C; VHS, DVD.** Ed Flanders; Kathleen Beller; Tim Matheson; Donald Moffat; Fionnula Flanagan; ***D:*** Jud Taylor; ***C:*** Bill Butler.

Maryam **½ 2000** High school senior Maryam (Parris) considers herself a typical New Jersey teen, circa 1979. She doesn't think much about her Iranian or Muslim heritage and works her way around some of her father's cultural strictures. But then the Iran hostage crisis provokes knee-jerk hostility from her classmates and Maryam's fundamentalist cousin Ali (Ackert) arrives from Tehran to pursue his college studies. Maryam's father feels compelled to take in the orphaned Ali, but it causes tensions to rise within while the family must also cope with the tensions they experience in their community as the hostage crisis continues. **90m/C; VHS, DVD.** Marriam Parris; David Ackert; Shaun Toub; Shohreh Aghdashloo; ***D:*** Ramin Serry; ***W:*** Ramin Serry; ***C:*** Harlan Bosmajian; ***M:*** Ahrin Mishram.

Masada **1981** Based on Ernest K. Gann's novel "The Antagonists," this dramatization re-creates the 1st-century A.D. Roman siege of the fortress Masada, headquarters for a group of Jewish freedom fighters. Abridged from the original TV presentation. **131m/C; VHS, DVD.** Peter O'Toole; Peter Strauss; Barbara Carrera; Anthony Quayle; Giulia Pagano; David Warner; ***D:*** Boris Sagal; ***M:*** Jerry Goldsmith.

Masala **1991** An experiment in a variety of genres, including glitzy musical-comedy numbers, erotic fantasy sequences, and all manner of kitsch. Krishna (who both stars and directs in his feature film debut) is a violence-prone, ex-junkie still trying to recover from the deaths of his family in a plane crash as they travelled from their home in Toronto to a vacation in India. Jaffrey has multi-roles as Krishna's unscrupulous uncle and cousin as well as the blue-skinned Indian deity, Lord Krishna, who appears to an Indian grandmother on her TV set. Multicultural confusion. **105m/C; VHS, DVD.** *CA* Srinivas Krishna; Saeed Jaffrey; Zohra Sehgal; Sakina Jaffrey; ***D:*** Srinivas Krishna; ***W:*** Srinivas Krishna.

Mascots **2016** Christopher Guest's lifetime love affair with the goofy and obsessed portions of the human race finds a natural subject in people who dress up like animals and other sports mascots as a part of their profession. He assembles much of his improv-trained cast for this mockumentary, including Jane Lynch, Parker Posey, Fred Willard, and Jennifer Coolidge, to tell the story of the World Mascot Association's championship for the Gold Fluffy Award. The movie has its moments but too often feels like he's going for the easy joke, or, worse, a joke he's told before. **89m/C; DVD.** Jane Lynch; Parker Posey; Fred Willard; Ed Begley, Jr.; Christopher Guest; Chris O'Dowd; ***D:*** Christopher Guest; ***W:*** Christopher Guest; Jim Piddock; ***C:*** Kris Kachikis; ***M:*** C.J. Vanston.

Masculine Feminine **½ *Masculin Feminin* 1966** A young Parisian just out of the Army engages in some anarchistic activities when he has an affair with a radical woman singer. Hailed as one of the best French New Wave films. In French with English subtitles. **103m/B; VHS, DVD.** *FR* Jean-Pierre Leaud; Chantal Goya; Marlene Jobert; ***D:*** Jean-Luc Godard. Berlin Intl. Film Fest. '66: Actor (Leaud).

M*A*S*H **1970 (R)** Hilarious, irreverent, and well-cast black comedy about a group of surgeons and nurses at a Mobile Army Surgical Hospital in Korea. The horror of war is set in counterpoint to their need to create havoc with episodic late-night parties, practical jokes, and sexual antics. An all-out anti-war festival, highlighted by scenes that starkly uncover the chaos and irony of war, and establish Altman's influential style. Watch for real-life football players Fran Tarkenton, Ben Davidson, and Buck Buchanan in the game. Loosely adapted from the novel by the pseudonymous Richard Hooker (Dr. H. Richard Hornberger and William Heinz). Subsequent hit TV series moved even further from the source novel. **116m/C; VHS, DVD, Blu-Ray.** Donald Sutherland; Elliott Gould; Tom Skerritt; Sally Kellerman; JoAnn Pflug; Robert Duvall; Rene Auberjonois; Roger Bowen; Gary Burghoff; Fred Williamson; John Schuck; Bud Cort; G(eorge) Wood; David Arkin; Michael Murphy; Indus Arthur; Ken Prymus; Bobby Troup; Kim Atwood; Timothy Brown; Carl Gottlieb; ***V:*** Sal Viscuso; ***D:*** Robert Altman; ***W:*** Ring Lardner, Jr.; ***C:*** Harold E. Stine; ***M:*** Johnny Mandel. Oscars '70: Adapt. Screenplay; AFI '98: Top 100; Cannes '70: Film; Golden Globes '71: Film--Mus./Comedy; Natl. Film Reg. '96; Natl. Soc. Film Critics '70: Film; Writers Guild '70: Adapt. Screenplay.

M*A*S*H: Goodbye, Farewell & Amen **½ 1983** The final two-hour special episode of the TV series "M*A*S*H" follows Hawkeye, B.J., Colonel Potter, Charles, Margaret, Klinger, Father Mulcahy, and the rest of the men and women of the 4077th through the last days of the Korean War, the declaration of peace, the dismantling of the camp, and the fond and tearful farewells. **120m/C; VHS, DVD.** Alan Alda; Mike Farrell; Harry (Henry) Morgan; David Ogden Stiers; Loretta Swit; Jamie Farr; William (Bill) Christopher; Allan Arbus; G.W. Bailey; Rosalind Chao; ***D:*** Alan Alda; ***W:*** Alan Alda. **TV**

The Mask ***Eyes of Hell; The Spooky Movie Show* 1961** A deservedly obscure gory horror film about a masked killer, filmed mostly in 3-D. With special 3-D packaging and limited edition 3-D glasses. **85m/B; VHS, DVD, Blu-Ray.** *CA* Paul Stevens; Claudette Nevins; Bill (William) Walker; Anne Collings; Martin Lavut; Leo Leyden; Bill Bryden; Eleanor Beecroft; Steven Appleby; ***D:*** Julian Roffman; ***W:*** Slavko Vorkapich; Franklin Delessert; Sandy Haver; Frank Taubes; ***C:*** Herbert S. Alpert; ***M:*** Louis Applebaum.

Mask **1985 (PG-13)** A dramatization of the true story of a young boy afflicted with craniodiaphyseal dysplasia (elephantiasis). The boy overcomes his appearance and revels in the joys of life in the California bikers' community. Well acted, particularly the performances of Stoltz and Cher. A touching film, well-directed by Bogdanovich, that only occasionally slips into maudlin territory. **120m/C; VHS, DVD.** Cher; Sam Elliott; Eric Stoltz; Estelle Getty; Richard Dysart; Laura Dern; Harry Carey, Jr.; Lawrence Monoson; Marsha Warfield; Barry Tubb; Andrew (Andy) Robinson; Alexandra Powers; ***D:*** Peter Bogdanovich; ***W:*** Anna Hamilton Phelan; ***C:*** Laszlo Kovacs. Oscars '85: Makeup; Cannes '85: Actress (Cher).

The Mask **1994 (PG-13)** Mild-mannered bank clerk Carrey discovers an ancient mask that has supernatural powers. Upon putting on the mask, he turns into one truly animated guy. He falls for a dame (Diaz) mixed up with gangsters and from there on, our hero deals not only with the incredible powers of the mask, but with hormones and bad guys as well. Based on the Dark Horse comic book series and originally conceived as a horror flick, director Russell recast this one as a hellzapoppin' cartoon-action black comedy. Carrey's rubber face is an asset magnified by the breakthrough special effects courtesy of Industrial Light and Magic. **100m/C; VHS, DVD.** Jim Carrey; Cameron Diaz; Peter Greene; Peter Riegert; Amy Yasbeck; Orestes Matacena; Richard Jeni; Ben Stein; ***D:*** Chuck Russell; ***W:*** Mike Werb; ***C:*** John R. Leonetti; ***M:*** Randy Edelman. Blockbuster '95: Comedy Actor, T. (Carrey), Female Newcomer, T. (Diaz); Blockbuster '96: Comedy Actor, V. (Carrey).

Mask Maker **WOOF!** *Maskerade* **2010 (R)** Nasty slasher flick has Jennifer and Evan get a too-good-to-be-true deal on an old Louisiana plantation house. Soon their friends show up to help with renovations and they discover why the place was so cheap when they encounter a previous owner—a deformed killer who skins off the faces of his victims. **94m/C; DVD, Blu-Ray.** Nikki Deloach; Stephen Colletti; Terry Kiser; Anabella Casanova; Treat Williams; Michael Berryman; Ross Britz; ***D:*** Griff Furst; ***W:*** Eric Miller; ***C:*** Andrew Strahorn; ***M:*** Nathan Furst. **VIDEO**

Mask of Death **1997 (R)** Detective Dan McKenna's (Lamas) wife is killed by Frank Dallio (Dunn) during the criminal's escape from the FBI and he's shot in the face by Dallio's buddy Mason, who happens to be a ringer for McKenna and conveniently dies in a car crash. Since the FBI want Dallio, Agent Jeffries (Williams) persuades McKenna to pose as Mason, which he does in order to get revenge. **125m/C; VHS, DVD.** Lorenzo Lamas; Billy Dee Williams; Rae Dawn Chong; Conrad Dunn; ***D:*** David Mitchell; ***C:*** David Pelletier; ***M:*** Norman Orenstein.

The Mask of Diijon **½ 1946** A mad magician suspects that his wife is cheating on him and tries to hypnotize her into killing her supposed paramour. Von Stroheim's performance makes it worthwhile. **73m/B; VHS, DVD.** Erich von Stroheim; Jeanne Bates; William Wright; Edward Van Sloan; Denise Vernac; ***D:*** Lew Landers; ***W:*** Griffin Jay; Arthur St. Claire; ***C:*** Jack Greenhalgh; ***M:*** Lee Zahler.

The Mask of Dimitrios **1944** Dutch mystery writer Leyden (Lorre) is vacationing in Instanbul, where he meets a fan, Col. Haki (Katch), at a party. Haki, the head of the secret police, informs Leyden that the body of arch criminal Dimitrios Makropoulous (Scott) has washed ashore and the man was stabbed to death. Leyden decides to write a novel about the criminal and delves into a dark world of intrigue and danger. Adapted from Eric Ambler's novel "A Coffin for Dimitrios." **96m/B; DVD.** Peter Lorre; Kurt Katch; Zachary Scott; Sydney Greenstreet; Faye Emerson; George Tobias; Victor Francen; Steven Geray; Florence Bates; Eduardo Ciannelli; George Metaxa; Monte Blue; ***D:*** Jean Negulesco; ***W:*** Frank Gruber; ***C:*** Arthur Edeson; ***M:*** Adolph Deutsch.

The Mask of Fu Manchu **½ 1932** The evil Dr. Fu Manchu and his equally evil daughter set out to capture the scimitar and golden mask of Genghis Khan. With them, they will be able to destroy all white men and rule the world. Although a detective from Scotland Yard tries to stop them, the pair obtain the treasures and begin sadistically torturing their victims to death. Can they be stopped before they destroy the earth? One of the creepiest entries in the Fu Manchu series, and Loy's last oriental role. Based on the novel by Sam Rohmer. **72m/B; VHS, DVD.** Boris Karloff; Lewis Stone; Karen Morley; Charles Starrett; Myrna Loy; Jean Hersholt; Lawrence Grant; David Torrence; ***D:*** Charles Brabin; ***C:*** Gaetano Antonio "Tony" Gaudio.

The Mask of Zorro 🦴🦴🦴 *Zorro* **1998 (PG-13)** The dashing masked swordsman, who first made an appearance in a 1919 newspaper comic, returns to the big screen. Aging Zorro (Hopkins) escapes from 20 years in prison when he discovers his mortal enemy Montero (Wilson) is looking to establish an independent republic of California. But he needs some help and picks bandit Alejandro (Banderas), who needs a lot of training. Caught in the middle is Elena (Zeta Jones), a spirited beauty who was raised by Montero (Wilson) and doesn't know she's really Zorro's daughter. She wields quite a mean sword herself as Alejandro learns before any romancing can begin. A little long but offering swashbuckling fun. **136m/C; DVD, Blu-Ray, UMD.** Antonio Banderas; Anthony Hopkins; Catherine Zeta-Jones; Stuart Wilson; Matt Letscher; Maury Chaykin; Tony Amendola; Pedro Armendariz, Jr.; L.Q. Jones; ***D:*** Martin Campbell; ***W:*** Ted Elliott; Terry Rossio; John Eskow; ***C:*** Phil Meheux; ***M:*** James Horner.

Masked and Anonymous 🦴 **2003 (PG-13)** For hard-core Dylan fans only, the pic has abundant, muddled meanderings about fame, life, politics and the like. Co-written and starring the enigmatic folk legend, the tenuous threads of a plot have Dylan as a has-been musical legend who's been sprung from jail by rock promoter Uncle Sweetheart (Goodman) and partner Nina Veronica (Lange) for a dubious benefit concert in a post-revolutionary, America-like country. Dylan is then given a chance to croon, and his "Dixie" alone may be enough to satisfy fans. A host of big-names drop in for walk-ons and seeming improv performances. **113m/C; DVD, Blu-Ray.** *US UK* Bob Dylan; Jeff Bridges; Penelope Cruz; John Goodman; Jessica Lange; Luke Wilson; Angela Bassett; Bruce Dern; Ed Harris; ***D:*** Larry Charles; ***W:*** Rene Fontaine; Sergei Petrovich Antonov; ***C:*** Rogier Stoffers; ***M:*** Bob Dylan.

Masked Rider—The First 🦴🦴 *Kamen Rider First; Kamen Raida: The First* **2005** Next to Godzilla, Ultraman, and possibly Astro Boy, few old school Japanese fantasy series are as immediately recognizable to longtime fans as Kamen Rider. It started as a manga, then became several television live action series, and even had a movie or two. This attempted reboot falls a little flat, and keeps only some of the original story. Takeshi Hongo (Kikawada) is turned into a monstrous bug-eyed cyborg by the terrorist organization Shocker, but escapes before his brainwashing can commence and uses his newfound powers to hunt them down. **90m/C; DVD.** *JP* Masaya Kikawada; Hassei Takano; Rena Komine; Hiroshi Miyauchi; Eisei Amamoto; ***D:*** Takao Ngaishi; ***W:*** Toshiki Inoue; Shotaro Ishinomori; ***C:*** Kazunari Tanaka; ***M:*** Goro Yasukawa.

The Masked Saint 🦴 ½ **2016 (PG-13)** Sonoda's faith-based drama is based on the true story from the 2009 book by Chris Whaley. Granstaff plays Chris Samuels, a former professional wrestler who lives in a small town and became a pastor. Of course, as in all religious films, the protagonist sees heathens and evil around him, and this time he transforms to a masked vigilante to stop them. How can this religious batman keep his secret and his new life of violence with his calling? It means well, but it's poorly made and poorly acted, and confuses its own message by essentially promoting vigilantism as a way to salvation. **111m/C; DVD.** Brett Granstaff; Lara Jean Chorostecki; T.J. McGibbon; Diahann Carroll; Roddy Piper; ***D:*** Warren Sonoda; ***W:*** Scott Crowell; ***C:*** James Griffith; ***M:*** Roger St-Denis.

Maslin Beach WOOF! 1997 Hmmm, if this flick was intended as some sort of romantic comedy, it failed. Of course, probably having a coherent script and a cast who could do more than appear comfortable nude (or in minimal beach attire) would have helped too. Yep, the titular beach is a real nudist beach in South Australia where these characters bare their bodies as they look for love or sex or friendship or something. The Hound hopes they used lots of sunscreen. **80m/C; VHS, DVD.** *AU* Garry Waddell; Bonnie-Jaye Lawrence; Michael Allen; Eliza Lovell; ***D:*** Wayne Groom; ***W:*** Wayne Groom; ***C:*** Rodney Bolton; ***M:*** Robert Kral.

Masque of the Red Death 🦴🦴🦴 **1965** An integral selection in the famous Edgar Allan Poe/Roger Corman canon, it deals with an evil prince who traffics with the devil and playfully murders any of his subjects not already dead of the plague. Remade in 1989 with Corman as producer. **88m/C; VHS, DVD, Blu-Ray.** *GB* Vincent Price; Hazel Court; Jane Asher; Patrick Magee; David Weston; Nigel Green; Julian Burton; Skip Martin; Gaye Brown; John Westbrook; ***D:*** Roger Corman; ***W:*** Charles Beaumont; Robert W(right) Campbell; ***C:*** Nicolas Roeg; ***M:*** David Lee.

Masquerade 🦴🦴🦴 **1988 (R)** A lonely young heiress meets a handsome "nobody" with a mysterious background and it is love at first sight. The romance distresses everyone in the circle of the elite because they assume that he is after her money and not her love. At first it seems decidedly so, then definitely not, and then nothing is certain. A real romantic thriller, with wonderful scenes of the Hamptons. **91m/C; VHS, DVD.** Rob Lowe; Meg Tilly; John Glover; Kim Cattrall; Doug Savant; Dana Delany; Eric Holland; ***D:*** Bob Swaim; ***W:*** Dick Wolf; ***C:*** David Watkin; ***M:*** John Barry.

Mass Appeal 🦴🦴 **1984 (PG)** An adaptation of the Bill C. Davis play about the ideological debate between a young seminarian and a complacent but successful parish pastor. Lemmon has had better roles and done better acting. **99m/C; VHS, DVD.** Jack Lemmon; Zeljko Ivanek; Charles Durning; Louise Latham; James Ray; Sharee Gregory; Talia Balsam; ***D:*** Glenn Jordan; ***W:*** Bill Davis; ***M:*** Bill Conti.

Mass Effect: Paragon Lost 🦴 ½ **2012** Prequel to the video game Mass Effect 3 set several months after the end of Mass Effect 2. An Alliance Marine must protect a distant colony from an alien threat known as The Collectors. **84m/C; DVD, Blu-Ray, Streaming.** *US CA JP SK* ***V:*** Laura Bailey; Bruce Carey; Freddie Prinze, Jr.; Jason Douglas; Todd Haberkorn; ***D:*** Atsushi Takeuchi; ***W:*** Henry Gilroy; ***M:*** David S. Kates; Joshua Mosley. **VIDEO**

Massacre 🦴 ½ **1934** That would be what the cavalry frequently did to the Indians. Joe Thunder Horse (miscast Barthelmess) is a Sioux who has been appearing in a Wild West show. He learns his father is dying and returns to the reservation, only to see how his people have been mistreated by the corrupt agents of the Bureau of Indian Affairs. So he goes to Washington to protest. **70m/B; DVD.** Richard Barthelmess; Ann Dvorak; Dudley Digges; Sidney Toler; Claire Dodd; Henry O'Neill; Robert Barrat; Arthur Hohl; ***D:*** Alan Crosland; ***W:*** Sheridan Gibney; Ralph Block; Sheridan Gibney; ***C:*** George Barnes.

Massacre 🦴🦴 **1956** Mexican Federales Ramon (Clark) and Ezparza (Craig) suspect trading post owner Miguel Chavez (Torruco) and his wife Angelica (Roth) of selling guns to the Yaqui Indians. Chavez gets away but the two arrest Angelica hoping she will decide to lead them to her husband. Instead, Angelica uses her feminine wiles to pit the two partners against each other. Lives up to its title but not in the way you might expect. **76m/C; DVD.** Dane Clark; James Craig; Martha Roth; Jaime Fernandez; Miguel Torruco; ***D:*** Louis King; ***W:*** D.D. Beauchamp; ***C:*** Gilbert Warrenton; ***M:*** Gonzalo Curiel.

Massacre at Central High 🦴🦴 ½ *Blackboard Massacre* **1976 (R)** A new student takes matters into his own hands when gang members harass other students at a local high school. Other than some silly dialogue, this low-budget production is above average. **85m/C; VHS, DVD.** Derrel Maury; Andrew Stevens; Kimberly Beck; Robert Carradine; Roy Underwood; Steve Bond; Steve Sikes; Lani O'Grady; Damon Douglas; Cheryl "Rainbeaux" Smith; ***D:*** Renee Daalder; ***W:*** Renee Daalder; ***C:*** Bert Van Munster.

Massacre in Dinosaur Valley 🦴 ½ **1985** A dashing young paleontologist and his fellow explorers go on a perilous journey down the Amazon in search of the Valley of the Dinosaur. **98m/C; VHS, DVD.** *IT* Michael Sopkiw; Suzanne Carvall; Milton Morris; Marta Anderson; ***D:*** Michael Tarantini; ***W:*** Michael Tarantini; ***C:*** Edson Batista.

Massacre in Rome 🦴🦴 ½ **1973 (PG)** A priest opposes a Nazi colonel's plan to execute Italian civilians in retaliation for the deaths of 33 German soldiers. Strong drama based on a real event. **110m/C; VHS, DVD.** Richard Burton; Marcello Mastroianni; Leo McKern; John Steiner; Anthony Steel; ***D:*** George P. Cosmatos; ***W:*** George P. Cosmatos; ***M:*** Ennio Morricone.

Massacre River 🦴 ½ **1949** Buddy western not as exciting as the title implies. Army soldiers Larry (Madison) and Phil (Calhoun) are stationed near the Wachupi River, the site of bloody confrontations between white settlers and Indians defending their land. But the two men are more interested in their romantic rivalry over their commander's daughter, Kitty (Downs), at least until Phil finds himself another gal, saloon owner Laura (Mathews). **78m/B; DVD.** Guy Madison; Rory Calhoun; Carole Mathews; Cathy Downs; Iron Eyes Cody; Art Baker; ***D:*** John Rawlins; ***W:*** Louis Stevens; ***C:*** Jack MacKenzie; ***M:*** Lucien Moraweck.

Massage Parlor Murders 🦴 ½ *Massage Parlor Hookers* **1973 (R)** In 1970s New York City a serial killer is on the loose, this time targeting 'massage parlor' women. **110m/C; DVD, Blu-Ray.** Chris Jordan; John Moser; Sandra Peabody; George Spencer; Brother Theodore; ***D:*** Chester Fox; Alex Stevens. **VIDEO**

Masseuse 🦴 **1995 (R)** Kristy (Drew) decides to get back at cheating fiance Jack (Abell), who's out of town on a business trip, by turning their house into a massage parlor. **90m/C; VHS, DVD.** Griffin (Griffen) Drew; Monique Parent; Tim Abell; Brinke Stevens; ***D:*** Daniel Peters; ***W:*** Steve Armogida; ***C:*** Gary Graver; ***M:*** Paul Di Franco.

Massive Retaliation 🦴 **1985** Hordes of pesky villagers seek refuge within the secluded safety of a family's country house as WWIII approaches. **90m/C; VHS, DVD.** Tom Bower; Peter Donat; Karlene Crockett; Jason Gedrick; Michael Pritchard; ***D:*** Thomas A. Cohen.

The Master 🦴🦴 *Three Evil Masters; Bui bun si mun* **1980** An aging kung fu master is attacked and gravely injured by three evil rivals called (appropriately enough) the Three Devils. He is returned to health by a young orphan boy named Gao Jian (Tak Yuan) who wants to be a kung fu master himself, but his skills are pitiful. Eventually the master agrees to teach Gao all his secrets, and he must return the favor and defend his teacher when the Three Devils return. A bit cheesy but the fight scenes make up for it. **92m/C; DVD.** *CH* Kuan Tai Chen; Tak Yuen; Hsueh-erh Wen; Lung Wei Wang; ***D:*** Chin-Ku Lu; ***W:*** Kuang Ni; ***C:*** Lu Ying Ho; ***M:*** Eddie Wang.

The Master 🦴🦴🦴 **2012 (R)** Director Anderson's sweeping portrait of misguided, drunken Naval seaman Freddie Quell (Phoenix). After WWII, he aimlessly takes odd jobs until stowing away on a cruise ship heading from California to New York owned by eccentric cult leader Lancaster Dodd, referred to as "The Master" (a superb Hoffman). Freddie quickly becomes Dodd's short-tempered right-hand man and favorite guinea pig, the subject of endless psychological experiments. Despite Anderson's reluctance to admit, his epic tragedy at times appears to criticize Scientology. Still, a fascinating portrait of a disturbed sociopath created by Phoenix's startling, anticlimactic (in more ways than one) performance. **138m/C; DVD, Blu-Ray.** Philip Seymour Hoffman; Joaquin Rafael (Leaf) Phoenix; Amy Adams; Jesse Plemons; Laura Dern; ***D:*** Paul Thomas Anderson; ***W:*** Paul Thomas Anderson; ***C:*** Mihai Malaimare, Jr.; ***M:*** Jonny Greenwood.

Master 🦴🦴 *Ma-seu-teo* **2016** Ui-seok Jo has created two movies in one, neither of which really works when put together, even with the film's gigantic running time (143 minutes). The first half consists of an investigator trying to catch the popular head of a Korean business that is basically a pyramid scheme, ripping off his employers and investors. When he finally gets the goods on the bad guy, the villain flees, turning the second half into more of a chase movie. The final act features some rock-solid action but it takes forever to get there, and you'll likely be bored long before you do. **143m/C; Blu-Ray.** *SK* Dong-won Gang; Woo-bin Kim; ***D:*** Ui-seok Jo.

Master and Commander: The Far Side of the World 🦴🦴🦴 **2003 (PG-13)** Captain Jack Aubrey (Crowe) is the relentless commander of the HMS Surprise of the British navy, whose mission is to capture and destroy the Acheron, a much larger French ship. Among the crew is ship's surgeon Maturin (Bettany), who serves as a quiet balance to Aubrey's fiery man of action. Epic contains some spectacular naval battles, but pays close attention to the relationships and respect that are forged in such extreme living conditions. Crowe does a brilliant job showcasing Aubrey's leadership and Bettany is his equal in poise. Based on the first and 10th books of the nautical series by Patrick O'Brien. **139m/C; VHS, DVD, Blu-Ray.** Russell Crowe; Paul Bettany; Billy Boyd; Max Pirkis; James D'Arcy; Mark Lewis Jones; Chris Larkin; Richard McCabe; Robert Pugh; Lee Ingleby; George Innes; David Threlfall; Edward Woodall; Ian Mercer; Max Benitz; ***D:*** Peter Weir; ***W:*** Peter Weir; John Collee; ***C:*** Russell Boyd; ***M:*** Christopher Gordon; Iva Davies; Richard Tognetti. Oscars '03: Cinematog., Sound FX Editing; British Acad. '03: Costume Des., Director (Weir), Sound; Natl. Soc. Film Critics '03: Cinematog.

Master Key 🦴 ½ **1944** Federal agents battle Nazis in this action-packed 12-chapter serial. **169m/B; VHS, DVD.** Jan Wiley; Milburn Stone; Lash LaRue; Dennis Moore; ***D:*** Ray Taylor; Lewis D. Collins.

The Master of Ballantrae 🦴🦴 **1953** Flynn plays James Durrisdear, the heir to a Scottish title, who gets involved in a rebellion with Bonnie Prince Charlie against the English crown. When the rebellion fails, Flynn heads for the West Indies where he and his partner amass quite a fortune through piracy. Flynn eventually returns to Scotland where he finds that his brother has taken over his title as well as his longtime love. Based on the novel by Robert Louis Stevenson. Flynn's riotous life had put him long past his peak swashbuckling days, as this film unfortunately demonstrates. **89m/C; VHS, DVD.** Errol Flynn; Roger Livesey; Anthony Steel; Beatrice Campbell; Yvonne Furneaux; Jacques Berthier; Felix Aylmer; Mervyn Johns; ***D:*** William Keighley; ***C:*** Jack Cardiff.

Master of Disguise 🦴 ½ **2002 (PG)** This disjointed patchwork of lame comedy routines tries to masquerade as "family friendly" entertainment, but is revealed to be a mess that kids may tolerate and parents will hate. Pistachio Disguisey (Carvey) is a waiter at his father Fabbrizio's (Brolin) restaurant, where he displays a talent for mimicking all the customers. Turns out this is a family legacy, coveted by flatulent criminal Devlin Bowman (Spiner) who kidnaps Fabbrizio. So Pistachio has to get his act together, rescue dad, and defeat Devlin. There is no saving the movie, however. Running time is actually padded with 15 minutes of credits and outtakes. **80m/C; DVD.** Dana Carvey; Jennifer Esposito; Brent Spiner; James Brolin; Edie McClurg; Harold Gould; Maria Canals; Austin Wolff; ***D:*** Perry Andelin Blake; ***W:*** Dana Carvey; Harris Goldberg; ***C:*** Peter Lyons Collister; ***M:*** Marc Ellis.

Master of Dragonard Hill 🦴 ½ **1989** A low-rent swashbuckling romance-novel pastiche. **92m/C; VHS, Streaming.** Oliver Reed; Eartha Kitt; ***W:*** R.J. Marx.

Master of the Flying Guillotine 🦴🦴 ½ *Du bi quan wang da po xue di zi; One Armed Boxer II; One Armed Boxer vs. the Flying Guillotine; Duk bei kuen wong daai poh huet dik ji* **1975** One of the most famously over-the-top Kung-Fu films, this is actually a sequel to "The One-Armed Boxer." The Manchu Dynasty wishes to quell rebellion in the recently acquired Han province, and sends the Master of the Flying Guillotine (Kang Chin) to murder as many people as are necessary to get the job done. A local fighting tournament is announced not long after he arrives, and the One-Armed Boxer is said to be participating. Since he killed several of the Master's disciples, the Master decides to participate, beginning a series of ever-more bizarre fights between ever-more bizarre martial artists. **83m/C; DVD.** *CH* Yu Wang; Kang Chin; Chung-erh Lung; Chia Yung Liu; Lung-Wai Wang; Tsim Po Sham; Fei Lung; Pai Cheng Hau; ***D:*** Yu Wang; ***W:*** Yu Wang; ***C:*** Yao Hu Chiu; ***M:*** Hsun Chi Chen.

Master of the House *Thou Shalt Honour Thy Wife* **1925** Story of a spoiled husband, a type extinct in this country but still in existence abroad. Silent with titles in English. **118m/B; Silent; DVD, Blu-Ray.** *CZ* Johannes Meyer; Astrid Holm; Mathilde Nielsen; Karin Nellemose; ***D:*** Carl Theodor Dreyer; ***W:*** Carl Theodor Dreyer; ***C:*** George Schneevoigt.

Master of the World 1/2 **1961** Visionary tale of a fanatical 19th century inventor who uses his wonderous flying fortress as an antiwar weapon. Adapted from "Robur, the Conqueror" and "Master of the World," both by Jules Verne. **95m/C; VHS, DVD, Blu-Ray.** Vincent Price; Charles Bronson; Henry Hull; ***D:*** William Witney; ***W:*** Richard Matheson; ***M:*** Les Baxter.

The Master Plan **1955** Dull red scare flick. Communist spies plot to set-up an American Army officer, who's working in postwar Germany. Major Thomas Brent (Morris) is suffering from blackouts so the spies plan to steal classified documents and make him look like a traitor. **78m/B; DVD.** Wayne Morris; Tilda Thamar; Norman Woodland; Arnold Bell; Marjorie Stewart; Mary MacKenzie; ***D:*** Cy Endfield; ***W:*** Cy Endfield; ***C:*** Jonah Jones.

The Master Race **1944** Propaganda film, released in September of 1944, meant as a warning that the Nazi threat still remained. Zealous Nazi officer Von Beck (Coulouris) poses as a guerilla fighter to infiltrate a small bombed-out Belgian village that has been liberated by the Allies. He's there to sow dissent amongst the war-weary townspeople and intimates that the 'master race' will rise again although his own identity is threatened by the presence of German POWs. **96m/B; DVD.** George Coulouris; Stanley Ridges; Carl Esmond; Osa Massen; Nancy Gates; Lloyd Bridges; Helen Beverly; ***D:*** Herbert Biberman; ***W:*** Herbert Biberman; Rowland Leigh; Anne Froelich; ***C:*** Russell Metty; ***M:*** Roy Webb.

Master Spy: The Robert Hanssen Story **2002 (R)** Drawn-out drama that finds FBI agent Robert Hanssen (Hurt), deeply in debt and frustrated by his lack of career advancement, selling documents to the KGB. Hanssen's so low-key he would be completely uninteresting if not for a couple of personal quirks: he likes to take naughty photos of his deeply devoted wife Bonnie (Parker) and pass them along to best buddy Jack (Strathairn) and he has a platonic relationship with stripper Priscilla (Pace), who becomes Hanssen's confidante. **122m/C; VHS, DVD.** William Hurt; Mary-Louise Parker; David Strathairn; Hilit Pace; Ron Silver; Wayne Knight; Peter Boyle; ***D:*** Lawrence Schiller; ***W:*** Norman Mailer; ***C:*** Alan Caso; ***M:*** Laurence Rosenthal. **TV**

Master Touch 1/2 *Hearts and Minds; Un Uomo da Rispettare* **1974 (PG)** When a legendary safecracker is released from prison, he attempts one last heist at a Hamburg insurance company. **96m/C; VHS, DVD.** *GE IT* Kirk Douglas; Florinda Bolkan; Giuliano Gemma; ***D:*** Michele Lupo; ***M:*** Ennio Morricone.

Master with Cracked Fingers *Snake Fist Fighter* **1971 (R)** In one of the highest-grossing martial arts movies of all time, Jackie Chan uses the deadly "snake fist" technique against the bad guys. Chan's first feature is an abominable low-budget flick which, reportedly, sat on a shelf until he became a star. Then it was re-edited and footage of a double was inserted. **83m/C; VHS, DVD.** *CH* Jackie Chan; ***D:*** Chin Hsin.

Masterminds 1/2 **2016 (PG-13)** After sitting on the shelf for years, Jared Hess' comedy limped into theaters without much laughter or success. David Ghantt (Galifianakis) is an armored truck driver looking for a better life. His crush, Kelly (Wiig), convinces him to abscond with $17 million from the truck he drives every day. While the script never quite comes together, the incredible likability of the cast goes a long way to making it tolerable (Kate McKinnon, Jason Sudeikis, Leslie Jones, and Owen Wilson). Inspired by the events of the 1997 Loomis Fargo robbery in Charlotte, North Carolina. **95m/C; DVD, Blu-Ray.** Zach Galifianakis; Owen Wilson; Kristen Wiig; Kate McKinnon; Leslie Jones; Jason Sudeikis; ***D:*** Jared Hess; ***W:*** Chris Bowman; Hubbel Palmer; Emily Spivey; ***C:*** Erik Alexander Wilson; ***M:*** Geoff Zanelli.

Masters of Horror: Dream Cruise 1/2 **2007** An American businessman working in Japan is having an affair with Yuri, the lovely wife of one of his clients, Eiji Saito. When the three embark on a cruise together it turns into terror on the high seas. **87m/C; DVD.** Daniel Gillies; Ryo Ishibashi; Yoshino Kimura; ***D:*** Norio Tsurata.

Masters of the Universe **1987 (PG)** A big-budget live-action version of the cartoon character's adventures, with He-Man battling Skeletor for the sake of the universe. **109m/C; VHS, DVD, Blu-Ray.** Dolph Lundgren; Frank Langella; Billy Barty; Courteney Cox; Meg Foster; ***D:*** Gary Goddard; ***W:*** David Odell; ***C:*** Hanania Baer; ***M:*** Bill Conti.

Mata Hari **1932** During WWI, a lovely German spy steals secrets from the French through her involvement with two military officers. Lavish production and exquisite direction truly make this one of Garbo's best. Watch for her exotic pseudo-strip tease. **90m/B; VHS, DVD.** Greta Garbo; Ramon Novarro; Lionel Barrymore; Lewis Stone; C. Henry Gordon; Karen Morley; Alec B. Francis; ***D:*** George Fitzmaurice; ***C:*** William H. Daniels.

Mata Hari **1985 (R)** Racy, adventure-prone story of WWI's most notorious spy, Mata Hari, who uses her seductive beauty to seduce the leaders of Europe. Stars "Emmanuelle" Kristel. **105m/C; VHS, DVD.** Sylvia Kristel; Christopher Cazenove; Oliver Tobias; Gaye Brown; Gottfried John; ***D:*** Curtis Cunningham.

Matador 1/2 **1986** Bizarre, entertaining black comedy about a retired matador who finds a new way to satiate his desire to kill. He meets his match in an equally deadly woman and the two are drawn closer together by a young bullfighting student who confesses to a series of murders. Not for all tastes, but fine for those who like the outrageous. In Spanish with English subtitles. **90m/C; VHS, DVD.** *SP* Assumpta Serna; Antonio Banderas; Nacho Martinez; Eva Cobo; Carmen Maura; Julieta Serrano; Chus (Maria Jesus) Lampreave; Eusebio Poncela; ***D:*** Pedro Almodóvar; ***W:*** Pedro Almodóvar; Jesus Ferrere; ***C:*** Angel Luis Fernandez; ***M:*** Bernardo Bonezzi.

The Matador **2006 (R)** Quirky black comedy stars Brosnan as a veteran hitman with a case of the yips. Boorish, drunken Julian Noble meets desperate businessman Danny Wright (Kinnear) in a Mexico City bar and the unlikely duo become increasingly simpatico. After botching two assignments, Julian needs his only friend Danny's help in fulfilling his last-chance contract. The men are complemented by Davis' portrayal of Danny's devoted wife, Carolyn, who's titillated by Julian's fatal attractions. **96m/C; DVD, HD-DVD.** Pierce Brosnan; Greg Kinnear; Hope Davis; Philip Baker Hall; Dylan Baker; Adam Scott; ***D:*** Richard Shepard; ***W:*** Richard Shepard; ***C:*** David Tattersall; ***M:*** Rolfe Kent.

A Matador's Mistress 1/2 *Monolete* **2008** Inaccurate and corny romantic bio of famed Spanish matador Manolete. In the Franco-ruled Spain of 1947, Manolete (Brody) is preparing for a bullfight as flashbacks reveal his life. This includes his hot-blooded romance with tempestuous actress Lupe Sino (Cruz) whose leftist sympathies win her no friends. **92m/C; DVD, Blu-Ray.** *SP GB* Adrien Brody; Penelope Cruz; Santiago Segura; Juan Echanove; Ann Mitchell; Josep Lineusa; Nacho Aldeguer; ***D:*** Menno Meyjes; ***W:*** Menno Meyjes; ***C:*** Robert Yeoman; ***M:*** Dan (Daniel) Jones; Javier Limon.

Matango 1/2 *Attack of the Mushroom People; Matango the Fungus of Terror; Curse of the Mushroom People; Fungus of Terror* **1963 (PG)** Directed by Ishiro Honda (director of most of the classic "Godzilla" films), this is the story of an asylum inmate being interviewed by doctors. He, along with six other men and two women get lost on a yacht in foggy waters, and stop on an uncharted isle because of the damage their boat has taken in a night storm. While searching for food and water they notice that large mushrooms seem to be everywhere, and eventually they find a wrecked research ship. And then something finds them. **70m/B; VHS, DVD.** *JP* Akira Kubo; Kumi Mizuno; Hiroshi Koizumi; Yoshio Tsuchiya; Kenji Sahara; Hiroshi Tachikawa; Miki Yashiro; Eisei Amamoto; Haruo Nakajima; Jiro Kumagai; ***D:*** Inoshiro Honda; ***W:*** Takeshi Kimura; ***C:*** Hajime Koizumi; ***M:*** Sadao Bekku.

The Match Factory Girl *Tulitikkutehtaan Tytto* **1990** Kaurismak's final segment of his "working class" trilogy. Iris, a plain, shy outsider shares a drab dwelling with her one-dimensional mother and stepfather, works in a match factory, and hopes desperately for romantic love. Her world is transformed when the extraordinary occurs—she spots a brightly colored party dress in a shop window, buys it, wears it to a bar, and meets the Scandinavian creep who will soon get her pregnant and dump her. Angry at the world, Iris seeks revenge, and in so doing the audience learns that she has become very real and human. Kaurismaki makes his point that beauty can exist in ugly places. In Finnish with English subtitles. **70m/C; VHS, DVD.** *SW FI* Kati Outinen; Elina Salo; Esko Nikkari; Vesa Vierikko; ***D:*** Aki Kaurismaki; ***W:*** Aki Kaurismaki.

Match Point 1/2 **2005 (R)** Brilliantly Allen-esque—full of layers and complexities—but with a new setting, new scenery, and some new players too. Allen ventures all the way to London, where gorgeous, tortured social-climbers find themselves torn apart by lust, morality, and class divisions. Chris Wilton (Rhys-Meyers), a former tennis pro of modest means, is introduced to high society through the wealthy family of his pal Tom Hewett (Goode). He soon hooks up with Tom's sister Chloe (Mortimer), but Chris' tryst with Tom's smoldering American girlfriend (Johannson) sets the scene for good old-fashioned murder. **124m/C; DVD.** Scarlett Johansson; Jonathan Rhys Meyers; Emily Mortimer; Matthew Goode; Brian Cox; Penelope Wilton; Ewen Bremner; James Nesbitt; Rupert Penry-Jones; Margaret Tyzack; ***D:*** Woody Allen; ***W:*** Woody Allen; ***C:*** Remi Adefarasin.

The Matchmaker **1958** An adaptation of the Thornton Wilder play concerning two young men in search of romance in 1884 New York. Later adapted as "Hello Dolly." An amusing diversion. **101m/B; DVD.** Shirley Booth; Anthony Perkins; Shirley MacLaine; Paul Ford; Robert Morse; Perry Wilson; Wallace Ford; Russell Collins; Rex Evans; Gavin Gordon; Torben Meyer; ***D:*** Joseph Anthony; ***W:*** John Michael Hayes; ***C:*** Charles B(ryant) Lang, Jr.

The Matchmaker 1/2 **1997 (R)** Cynical American Marcy (Garofalo) heads to a wee quaint Ireland burgh where she finds love and humanity amid the blarney-slinging locals. Aide to a politico spin doctor (Leary), Marcy is there to track down some Irish relatives of an American senator up for reelection but hits town during the annual matchmaking festival. She then becomes the target of an Irish marriage broker (O'Shea) who matches her with laconic local Sean (O'Hara). Entertaining enough, this rom com flirts heavily with cliche. Filmed in the village of Roundstone, Ireland. **97m/C; DVD.** Janeane Garofalo; Milo O'Shea; David O'Hara; Denis Leary; Jay O. Sanders; Rosaleen Linehan; Maria Doyle Kennedy; Saffron Burrows; Paul Hickey; Jimmy Keogh; ***D:*** Mark Joffe; ***W:*** Karen Janszen; Louis Nowra; Graham Linehan; ***C:*** Ellery Ryan; ***M:*** John Altman.

Matchstick Men 1/2 **2003 (PG-13)** Smalltime con man Roy (Cage) suffers from a host of psychological ticks, including OCD, but he's urged by his longtime partner (Rockwell) into a "really big score." Enter a teenage daughter, Angela (Lohman), he never knew. While Roy occasionally displays a kind of smug pride in his work, being with Angela causes Roy to admit that he actually has little to be truly proud of. Cage is at the top of his game, and he and Rockwell play off each other perfectly, while Lohman proves a worthy co-star. Director Scott mixes just the right amounts of comedy, drama, and suspense. Adapted from the novel by Eric Garcia. **120m/C; VHS, DVD, Blu-Ray.** Nicolas Cage; Alison Lohman; Sam Rockwell; Bruce Altman; Bruce McGill; Sheila Kelley; Beth Grant; Steve Eastin; ***D:*** Ridley Scott; ***W:*** Ted Griffin; Nicholas Griffin; ***C:*** John Mathieson; ***M:*** Hans Zimmer.

Material Girls WOOF! **2006 (PG)** And we are living in a material world, which explains why movies like this get made. Two snotty, vapid cosmetic-heir sisters (Hilary and Haylie Duff) find themselves suddenly penniless when their company faces scandal. They spend much of the running time yelling at each other as they primp and mug and fuss over the indignities of being poor. By the time they make their obligatory transformation to girls with hearts of gold, they're so unlikable it's impossible to care. And the Duffs' limp cover of the title song sounds like it was performed by automatons on karaoke night. **100m/C; DVD.** Haylie Duff; Hilary Duff; Anjelica Huston; Brent Spiner; Lukas Haas; Judy Tenuta; Maria Conchita Alonso; Obba Babatunde; Marcus Coloma; ***D:*** Martha Coolidge; ***W:*** Amy Rardin; John Quaintance; Jessica O'Toole; ***C:*** Johnny E. Jensen; ***M:*** Jennie Muskett.

Matewan 1/2 **1987 (PG-13)** An acclaimed dramatization of the famous Matewan massacre in the 1920s, in which coal miners in West Virginia, reluctantly influenced by union organizer Joe Kenehan (Cooper), rebelled against terrible working conditions. Complex and imbued with myth, the film is a gritty, moving, and powerful drama with typically superb Sayles dialogue and Haskell Wexler's beautiful and poetic cinematography. Jones delivers an economical yet intense portrayal of the black leader of the miners. Sayles makes his usual onscreen appearance, this time as an establishment-backed reactionary minister. Partially based on the Sayles novel "Union Dues." **130m/C; VHS, DVD, Blu-Ray.** Chris Cooper; James Earl Jones; Mary McDonnell; William Oldham; Kevin Tighe; David Strathairn; John Sayles; Jace Alexander; Gordon Clapp; Mason Daring; Joe Grifasi; Bob Gunton; Jo Henderson; Jason Jenkins; Ken Jenkins; Nancy Mette; Josh Mostel; Michael B. Preston; Maggie Renzi; Frank Hoyt Taylor; ***D:*** John Sayles; ***W:*** John Sayles; ***C:*** Haskell Wexler; ***M:*** Mason Daring. Ind. Spirit '88: Cinematog.

Matilda **1996 (PG)** Intelligent child Matilda Wormwood (Wilson) is oppressed by both her monstrous parents (DeVito and Perlman) and awful school principal, Trunchbull (Ferris). However, her first grade teacher, appropriately named Miss Honey (Davidtz), believes in her, which is enough to make Matilda plot an appropriate fate for the miserable people in her life. Excellent adaptation of a typically subversive book by Roald Dahl. Director DeVito, who wanted to create the illusion of a live-action cartoon, built among other things a "Carrot-cam" to capture the flying food of a food fight. **93m/C; DVD, Blu-Ray.** Mara Wilson; Danny DeVito; Rhea Perlman; Embeth Davidtz; Pam Ferris; Paul (Pee-wee Herman) Reubens; Tracey Walter; ***D:*** Danny DeVito; ***W:*** Robin Swicord; Nicholas Kazan; ***C:*** Stefan Czapsky; ***M:*** David Newman.

Matinee 1/2 **1992 (PG)** "MANT: Half-man, Half-ant, All Terror!" screams from the movie marquee after Lawrence Woolsey, promoter extraordinare, and Ruth Corday, his leading lady, roll into Key West circa 1962. Meanwhile, teen Gene Loomis listens to his health teacher push the benefits of red meat and his girlfriend question life, while worrying about his dad, stationed in Cuba. Builds sly parallels between real life and movie horror by juxtaposing Woolsey (modeled after B-movie king William Castle) hyping his schlock, shown in "Atomo-Vision," against JFK solemnly announcing the Russian's approach. Fun, nostalgic look at days gone by—and the matinees that died with them. **98m/C; DVD, Blu-Ray.** John Goodman; Cathy Moriarty; Omri Katz; Lisa Jakub; Lucinda Jenney; James Villemaire; Robert Picardo; Dick Miller; John Sayles; Charles S. Haas; Mark McCracken; Simon Fenton; Kellie Martin; Jesse Lee; Jesse White; David Clennon; Luke Halpin; Robert Cornthwaite; Kevin McCarthy; William Schallert; ***D:*** Joe Dante; ***W:*** Charles S. Haas; Jerico Stone; ***C:*** John Hora; ***M:*** Jerry Goldsmith.

Matinee Idol 1/2 **1933** When a famous actor is murdered, actress Sonia (Horn) turns amateur sleuth because her sister Christine

(Allan) has been accused of the crime. **75m/B; DVD, Blu-Ray.** *GB* Camilla Horn; Miles Mander; Anthony Hankey; Marguerite Allan; Viola Keats; ***D:*** George King; ***W:*** Charles Bennett; ***C:*** Eric Cross; ***M:*** Arthur Dulay.

Mating Dance 🦴 **2008** Pam keeps setting up her cop husband's best friend on blind dates. Then one of her coworkers seems to be the perfect match but she's got a furry supernatural secret. **102m/C; DVD.** Shawn Christian; Lauren German; Susan Blakely; Lisa Rotondi; Roberto Sanchez; Eric Lange; ***D:*** Cate Caplin; ***W:*** Cate Caplin; ***C:*** Eric MacIver. **VIDEO**

The Mating Game 🦴🦴🦴 **1959** A fast-paced comedy about a tax collector, a beautiful girl, and a wily farm couple. Randall is the straitlaced IRS agent who finds out that the farming Larkins have never paid taxes and use a complicated barter system to get along. Randall falls for farm daughter Reynolds, gets drunk with her Pa, and decides to help the family out of their government dilemma—to the dismay of his superiors. Randall has a terrific drunk scene among his many comedic capers and Reynolds is a highlight. **96m/C; VHS, DVD.** Tony Randall; Debbie Reynolds; Paul Douglas; Una Merkel; Fred Clark; Philip Ober; Charles Lane; ***D:*** George Marshall; ***W:*** William Roberts.

The Mating Habits of the Earthbound Human 🦴 ½ **1999 (R)** One-joke premise has an alien narrator (Pierce) making a nature doumentary about humans, focusing on the mating habits of nebbishy accountant Bill (Astin) and babe Jenny (Electra). The actors do what they can but the humor and situations are predictable. **90m/C; VHS, DVD.** MacKenzie Astin; Carmen Electra; Markus Redmond; Lucy Liu; Jack Kehler; ***Nar:*** David Hyde Pierce; ***D:*** Jeff Abugov; ***W:*** Jeff Abugov; ***C:*** Michael Bucher; ***M:*** Michel McCarty.

The Matrimonial Bed 🦴🦴 **1930** Racy pre-Code comedy. Juliet Corton (Eldridge) discovers that Paris society hairdresser Leopold (Fay) is actually her amnesiac husband Adolphe, who was presumed killed in a train crash five years earlier. Since both Juliet and Adolphe are now married-with-kids, this news causes complications. Dr. Friedland (Carewe) hypnotizes Adolphe, but that erases the past five years and causes even more trouble. **70m/B; DVD.** Florence Eldridge; Frank Fay; James Gleason; Vivien Oakland; Arthur Edmund Carewe; Lilyan Tashman; Beryl Mercer; ***D:*** Michael Curtiz; ***W:*** Harvey Thew; ***C:*** Devereaux Jennings.

Matrimonium 🦴 **2005** Shallow and painfully unfunny gay comedy. Aspiring actor Malcolm Caulfield needs money and becomes a contestant on a reality TV show where the prize is a million dollars. The only problem is it revolves around a gay wedding and allegedly straight Malcolm has to convince everyone that he's about to marry country boy Spencer Finch. **88m/C; DVD.** Rick Federman; Sandon Berg; ***D:*** Michael D. Akers; ***W:*** Sandon Berg; Michael D. Akers; ***C:*** Alexander Yellin; ***M:*** Aram Mandossian. **VIDEO**

The Matrix 🦴🦴🦴 ½ **1999 (R)** Visually wild ride (and rather complicated plot). Mild-mannered computer programmer Thomas Anderson (Reeves) turns into hacker Neo by night. Neo thinks something is off about his world and he's right. Seems everything around him is just a computer-generated illusion, fostered by machines who use human beings as an electrical energy source. Neo is shown the truth by the mysterious Morpheus (Fishburne) and his renegade team, including capable and beautiful Trinity (Moss). Is Neo the chosen one, who'll make the world safe for humanity once again? Spectacular action sequences, a hissably evil villain (Weaving), a magisterial mentor, and a reluctant hero. What more could you ask for? **136m/C; DVD, Blu-Ray, UMD.** Keanu Reeves; Carrie-Anne Moss; Laurence Fishburne; Joe Pantoliano; Hugo Weaving; Gloria Foster; Marcus Chong; Paul Goddard; Robert Taylor; Julian (Sonny) Arahanga; Matt Doran; Belinda McClory; Anthony Ray Parker; ***D:*** Lilly Wachowski; Lana Wachowski; ***W:*** Lilly Wachowski; Lana Wachowski; ***C:*** Bill Pope; ***M:*** Don Davis. Oscars '99: Film Editing, Sound, Visual FX; British Acad. '99: Sound, Visual FX; MTV Movie Awards '00: Fight (Keanu Reeves/Laurence Fishburne), Film, Male Perf. (Reeves); Natl. Film Reg. '12.

The Matrix Reloaded 🦴🦴 ½ **2003 (R)** Neo, Morpheus, Trinity, and the denizens of Zion brace for the machines' attempt to find and destroy the last human stronghold. Neo also discovers more about his destiny as he deals with the ubiquitous and even more powerful Agent Smith. The Wachowskis went all-out to top the original, and at least visually, they have succeeded. But this one suffers from mixing navel-gazing ponderings with the visceral thrills, all while trying to move the story forward. A daunting task, the pic provides a complicated twist, but doesn't mix it as smoothly with the show-stopping action set-pieces. Not a failure, but not an overwhelming success either. **138m/C; DVD, Blu-Ray.** Keanu Reeves; Carrie-Anne Moss; Laurence Fishburne; Hugo Weaving; Jada Pinkett Smith; Monica Bellucci; Gloria Foster; Nona Gaye; Lambert Wilson; Randall Duk Kim; Anthony Zerbe; Helmut Bakaitis; Harold Perrineau, Jr.; Gina Torres; Harry J. Lennix; Daniel Bernhardt; Matt McColm; ***D:*** Lilly Wachowski; Lana Wachowski; ***W:*** Lilly Wachowski; Lana Wachowski; ***C:*** Bill Pope; ***M:*** Don Davis.

The Matrix Revolutions 🦴🦴🦴 **2003 (R)** The battle for the last human stronghold continues, as Zion itself comes under attack. Meanwhile Neo battles with Agent Smith and the machines in his own way, in and out of the Matrix. Better blending of action (there's plenty), philosophy, and narrative helps this one surpass the somewhat disappointing sequel. It also helps that the effects are more smoothly integrated and less obvious. Add a half-bone if you think the Wachhowskis can do no wrong, subtract one if you thought the whole thing was ridiculous to begin with. You must choose. **130m/C; DVD, Blu-Ray.** Keanu Reeves; Laurence Fishburne; Carrie-Anne Moss; Hugo Weaving; Mary Alice; Monica Bellucci; Jada Pinkett Smith; Harold Perrineau, Jr.; Nona Gaye; Anthony Zerbe; Lambert Wilson; Harry J. Lennix; Collin Chou; Ian Bliss; Bruce Spence; Gina Torres; Helmut Bakaitis; Lachy Hulme; Robyn Nevin; Essie Davis; Anthony Wong; Kevin M. Richardson; ***D:*** Lilly Wachowski; Lana Wachowski; ***W:*** Lilly Wachowski; Lana Wachowski; ***C:*** Bill Pope; ***M:*** Don Davis.

A Matter of Dignity 🦴🦴 *To Telefteo Psemma* **1957** Chloe (Lambetti), whose family is on the brink of financial ruin, agrees to marriage with an incredibly boring millionaire to try and save them. She has to make a painful journey of self-discovery in order to escape the shallowness of how she was raised and the life she doesn't want to lead. Greek with subtitles. **104m/B; VHS, DVD.** *GR* Georges Pappas; Ellie Lambetti; Athena Michaelidou; Eleni Zafirou; ***D:*** Michael Cacoyannis; ***W:*** Michael Cacoyannis; ***C:*** Walter Lassally; ***M:*** Manos Hadjidakis.

A Matter of Time WOOF! **1976 (PG)** Maid is taught to enjoy life by an eccentric, flamboyant contessa, then finds the determination to become an aspiring actress. Often depressing and uneven, arguably Minnelli's worst directing job and his last film. Also Boyer's last appearance and first bit for Bergman's daughter Rosellini, in a small part as a nun. **97m/C; VHS, DVD.** Liza Minnelli; Ingrid Bergman; Charles Boyer; Tina Aumont; Spiros Andros; Anna Proclemer; Isabella Rossellini; ***D:*** Vincente Minnelli; ***C:*** Geoffrey Unsworth.

Matter of Trust 🦴🦴 **1998 (R)** Mike D'Angelo (Howell) is an alcoholic L.A. cop barely hanging onto his job. The woman he loves, Theresa (Severance), is not only an Assistant D.A. but is married to a prominent doctor, Peter (Mancuso). But their paths aren't as separate as Mike might believe. **90m/C; VHS, DVD.** C. Thomas Howell; Joan Severance; Nick Mancuso; Robert Miano; Jennifer Leigh Warren; Randee Heller; ***D:*** Joey Travolta; ***W:*** John Penney; ***C:*** Dan Heigh; ***M:*** Jeff Lass. **VIDEO**

A Matter of WHO 🦴🦴 **1962** A detective for the World Health Organization, or WHO, investigates the disease related deaths of several oil men. Travelling to the Middle East, he uncovers a plot by an unscrupulous businessman to control the oil industry by killing off its most powerful members. Although intended as a comedy, the subject matter is too grim to be taken lightly. **92m/B; VHS, DVD, Streaming.** *GB* Terry-Thomas; Alex Nicol; Sonja Ziemann; Richard Briers; Clive Morton; Vincent Ball; Honor Blackman; Carol White; Martin Benson; Geoffrey Keen; ***D:*** Don Chaffey; ***M:*** Edwin Astley.

Matthew Shepard Is a Friend of Mine 🦴🦴 ½ **2014** A personal documentary attempts to humanize a young man whose death became a symbol for the gay rights movement and turned him into something of a martyr. And yet Matt Shepard was just a boy, a friend, and a son. This honest and intimate portrait captures not just his horrible death but the life before it through interviews with those who knew Shepard. It also, of course, gets into his murder and the impact it had around the world. It's an emotional, confidently made documentary about a story that doesn't get the headlines it once did but should never be forgotten. **89m/C; DVD.** ***Nar:*** Michele Josue; ***D:*** Michele Josue; ***W:*** Michele Josue; ***C:*** Craig Trudeau.

Maudie 🦴🦴🦴 **2017 (PG-13)** A moving biopic about the life of celebrated Canadian folk artist Maud (Dowley) Lewis, focusing on her complex relationship with the reclusive Everett Lewis (Hawk). To escape the oppressive home of her Aunt Ida (Rose), Maud (Hawkins) takes a job as a live-in maid with Everett. Though he treats her cruelly, they marry at her insistence. Limited by debilitating arthritis, Maud gets permission from him to paint everything she can, including their small shack, postcards, and pieces of wood. Their lives change forever when Maud's joyful work is discovered by an outsider and shared with the world. A beautiful film defined by Hawkins' spectacular performance. **115m/C; DVD.** Ethan Hawke; Sally Hawkins; Kari Matchett; Zachary Bennett; Gabrielle Rose; ***D:*** Aisling Walsh; ***W:*** Sherry White; ***C:*** Guy Godfree; ***M:*** Michael Timmins.

Maurice 🦴🦴🦴 **1987 (R)** Based on E.M. Forster's novel about a pair of Edwardian-era Cambridge undergraduates who fall in love, but must deny their attraction and abide by British society's strict norms regarding homosexuality. Maurice finds, however, that he cannot deny his nature, and must come to a decision regarding family, friends, and social structures. A beautiful and stately film of struggle and courage. **139m/C; DVD, Blu-Ray.** *UK* James Wilby; Hugh Grant; Rupert Graves; Mark Tandy; Ben Kingsley; Denholm Elliott; Simon Callow; Judy Parfitt; Helena Bonham Carter; Billie Whitelaw; Phoebe Nicholls; Barry Foster; ***D:*** James Ivory; ***W:*** James Ivory; Kit Hesketh-Harvey; ***C:*** Pierre Lhomme; ***M:*** Richard Robbins.

Mausoleum 🦴🦴 **1983 (R)** Only one man can save a woman from eternal damnation. **96m/C; VHS, DVD, Blu-Ray.** Marjoe Gortner; Bobbie Bresee; Norman Burton; LaWanda Page; Shari Mann; Julie Christy Murray; Laura Hippe; Maurice Sherbanee; ***D:*** Michael Dugan; ***W:*** Robert Madero; Robert Barich; ***C:*** Robert Barich.

Mauvais Sang 🦴🦴 *Bad Blood* **1986** Carax's second film tells the story of rival gangsters who are searching for a serum that cures a devastating disease. Streetwise Alex (Lavant) from "Boy Meets Girl" (1984) also returns as the thief who is supposed to steal the serum (his character is again seen in 1991's "The Lovers on the Bridge."). French with subtitles. **125m/C; VHS, DVD, Blu-Ray.** *FR* Michel Piccoli; Denis Lavant; Juliette Binoche; Hans Meyer; Julie Delpy; Carroll Brooks; Serge Reggiani; Hugo Pratt; Mireille Perrier; ***D:*** Leos Carax; ***W:*** Leos Carax; ***C:*** Jean-Yves Escoffier; ***M:*** Serge Reggiani; Charles Aznavour.

Mauvaise Graine 🦴🦴 *Bad Seed* **1933** Wilder (in his debut) filmed this comedy-drama (along with Esway) before heading off to Hollywood. Parisian wastrel Henri Pasquier (Mingand) impulsively steals a car when his disgusted wealthy father cuts him off. This lands Henri in with a professional gang of thieves, headed by Jean (Galle), who uses his pretty teenaged sister Jeannette (Darrieux) as a decoy. Henri enjoys his new career (and Jeannette) until jealousy gets in the way. French with subtitles. **76m/B; VHS, DVD.** *FR* Pierre Mingand; Danielle Darrieux; Raymond Galle; Jean Wall; ***D:*** Billy Wilder; Alexander Esway; ***W:*** Billy Wilder; Alexander Esway; ***C:*** Paul Cotteret; Maurice Delattre; ***M:*** Franz Waxman; Walter Gray.

Maverick 🦴🦴 ½ **1994 (PG)** Entertaining remake of the popular ABC series is fresh and funny, with sharp dialogue and a good cast. Everybody looks like they're having a great time, not difficult for the charming Gibson, but a refreshing change of pace for the usually serious Foster and Greene. In a fun bit of casting, Garner, the original Maverick, shows up as Marshal Zane Cooper. Lightweight, fast-paced comedy was reportedly highly improvised, though Donner retained enough control to keep it coherent. Keep your eyes peeled for cameos from country stars, old time Western actors, and an unbilled appearance from Glover. **127m/C; DVD.** Mel Gibson; Jodie Foster; James Garner; Graham Greene; James Coburn; Alfred Molina; Paul Smith; Geoffrey Lewis; Max Perlich; ***Cameo(s):*** Dub Taylor; Dan Hedaya; Robert Fuller; Doug McClure; Bert Remsen; Denver Pyle; Will Hutchins; Kathy Mattea; Waylon Jennings; Danny Glover; Clint Black; ***D:*** Richard Donner; ***W:*** William Goldman; ***C:*** Vilmos Zsigmond; ***M:*** Randy Newman. Blockbuster '95: Comedy Actress, T. (Foster).

Max 🦴🦴 **2002 (R)** Historical fantasy has an interesting premise: what would have happened if Adolf Hitler had been successful as an artist? In 1919, Hitler (Taylor) is a starving, embittered (but ambitious) war veteran in Munich who is befriended by Max Rothman (Cusack), a Jewish art dealer and fellow veteran who has just opened his own avant-garde gallery. Hitler's art is kitsch but Max encourages him anyway and shrugs off his rantings, which draw more attention from fellow Army officer Mayr (Thomsen). Mayr thinks Adolf would make a good political spokesman. Guess who was proved right? Rothman is a fictional character, Mayr is not, and the film drew a lot of protest for "humanizing" Hitler. The movie is flawed but not for that reason. **106m/C; VHS, DVD.** *HU CA GB* John Cusack; Noah Taylor; Leelee Sobieski; Molly Parker; David Horovitch; Janet Suzman; Peter Capaldi; Kevin McKidd; John Grillo; Ulrich Thomsen; ***D:*** Menno Meyjes; ***W:*** Menno Meyjes; ***C:*** Lajos Koltai; ***M:*** Dan (Daniel) Jones.

Max 🦴 ½ **2015 (PG)** Faux patriotism comes to the animal adventure movie in this nauseatingly manipulative and melodramatic "family film". Kyle Wincott (Arnell) has a loyal, intelligent war dog named Max who serves by his side in country. When Kyle is killed, his dog becomes a bit unhinged, unable to listen to any new owners. It's only when Max meets Kyle's brother Justin (Wiggins) that he comes back to normalcy, especially after he's adopted by Justin. Of course, then Max gets a chance to save Justin too because, well, America. Surprisingly dark for a PG movie and predictably thin as a patriotic one. **111m/C; DVD, Blu-Ray, Streaming.** Josh Wiggins; Lauren Graham; Thomas Haden Church; Jay Hernandez; Luke Kleintank; Robbie Amell; ***D:*** Boaz Yakin; ***W:*** Boaz Yakin; Sheldon Lettich; ***C:*** Stefan Czapsky; ***M:*** Trevor Rabin.

Max Dugan Returns 🦴🦴 **1983 (PG)** A Simon comedy about an ex-con trying to make up with his daughter by showering her with presents bought with stolen money. Sweet and light, with a good cast. **98m/C; VHS, DVD.** Jason Robards, Jr.; Marsha Mason; Donald Sutherland; Matthew Broderick; Kiefer Sutherland; ***D:*** Herbert Ross; ***W:*** Neil Simon; ***M:*** David Shire.

Max Keeble's Big Move 🦴🦴 **2001 (PG)** Max (Linz), about to enter 7th grade, decides he must become cooler, much to the dismay of his pals Megan (Grey) and Robe (Peck). But on the first day of school, he's confronted with two bullies, a fussy principal (Miller) who wants to tear down an animal shelter that Max loves, and a renegade ice cream man. When Max's dad comes home and announces they're moving to Chicago, Max hatches numerous messy plots to get back at everyone who's tormenting him. Except Max can't escape the consequences of his actions after all. Not very original, but the kids should still enjoy it. **101m/C; DVD.** Alex D. Linz; Larry Miller; Jamie Kennedy; Zena Grey; Josh Peck; Orlando Brown; Noel Fisher; Nora Dunn; Robert Carradine; Clifton Davis; Amy Hill; Amber Valletta; Justin Berfield; ***D:*** Timothy Hill; ***W:*** Jon Bernstein; Mark Blackwell; James Greer; ***C:*** Arthur Albert; ***M:*** Michael Wandmacher.

Max Manus: Man of War 🦴🦴 ½ **2008** Adventure biopic based on the WWII exploits of Norwegian resistance fighter Max Manus. When the Germans invade Norway in 1940, Max joins up with other like-minded young men to resist the Nazi occupation. Eventually, Max and his friends receive special saboteur training and their success leads to fierce reprisals from the Gestapo. English, German, and Norwegian with subtitles. **113m/C; DVD.** *NO* Aksel Hennie; Nicolai Cleve Broch; Ken Duken; Christian Rubeck; Knut Joner; Mats Eldoen; Kyrre Haugen Sydness; Agnes Kittelsen; *D:* Espen Sandberg; Joachim Roenning; *W:* Thomas Nordseth-Tiller; *C:* Geir Hartly Andreassen; *M:* Trond Bjerknaes.

Max, Mon Amour 🦴🦴 *Max, My Love* **1986** A very refined British diplomat in Paris discovers his bored wife has become involved with Max, who happens to be a chimpanzee. Instead of being upset, the husband decides Max should live with them. Very strange menage a trois manages to avoid the obvious vulgarities. In French with English subtitles. **97m/C; VHS, DVD.** *FR* Anthony (Corlan) Higgins; Charlotte Rampling; Victoria Abril; Christopher Hovik; Anne-Marie Besse; Pierre Etaix; *D:* Nagisa Oshima; *W:* Jean-Claude Carriere; Nagisa Oshima; *C:* Raoul Coutard; *M:* Michel Portal.

Max Payne 🦴 1/2 **2008 (PG-13)** Another cold, dreary, emotionless videogame unnecessarily brought to the big screen. DEA agent Max Payne (Wahlberg), and assassin Mona Sax (Kunis), come together to solve a series of murders sweeping New York City. These vigilantes, fighting to avenge the deaths of family members, are being hunted not only by the mob, but also by the police and a major corporation as well. Aimless plot stays true to its roots, with stilted dialogue and stone-faced performances lifted straight from the game. Little more than an excuse for slow-mo gun firing and mindless action—neither of which is much fun without a joystick. **99m/C; DVD, Blu-Ray, On Demand.** Mark Wahlberg; Mila Kunis; Beau Bridges; Chris Bridges; Donal Logue; Chris O'Donnell; Kate Burton; Ted Atherton; Jamie Hector; Olga Kurylenko; Amaury Nolasco; *D:* John Moore; *W:* Beau Thorne; *C:* Jonathan Sela; *M:* Marco Beltrami; Buck Sanders.

Max Rules 🦴🦴 1/2 **2005** Young Max and his friends Jessica and Scott like to play spy games and stage elaborate pranks. Thanks to Max's scientist uncle, who works for the government, the kid has access to some high-tech gizmos. But when the trio discovers the whereabouts of a stolen microchip, the junior spies put all their know-how to work. Amusing kid fare. **80m/C; DVD.** William B. Davis; Jason Dittmer; Andrew C. Maier; Jennifer Lancheros; Spencer Esau; Paul Eenhoorn; *D:* Robert Burke; *W:* Robert Burke; *C:* John Jeffcoat; *M:* Matthew Bennett. **VIDEO**

Max Steel 🦴 **2016 (PG-13)** A movie based on a toy line that has no energy or creativity of its own, this sci-fi adventure lacks even the creativity of most basic cable kids shows. Max McGrath (Winchell) is just your average teenager, until he encounters an alien companion named Steel (Brener). The two work together to form a superhero named, you guessed it, Max Steel. They are forced to fight mysterious forces that threaten our world in this Mighty Morphin Power Rangers riff that just about nobody on Earth except for the Mattel company asked for. **92m/C; DVD, Blu-Ray.** Ben Winchell; Josh Brener; Maria Bello; Andy Garcia; Ana Villafane; *D:* Stewart Hendler; *W:* Christopher Yost; *C:* Brett Pawlak; *M:* Nathan Lanier.

Maxed Out: Hard Times, Easy Credit and the Era of Predatory Lenders 🦴🦴 1/2 **2006** Scurlock tries to explain the wheeling and dealing of the financial community by focusing on the worst case scenarios of the consumer-lending industry, involving massive consumer debt, too easy credit, ill-advised loans, and bankruptcy and foreclosures. Basically most people are dumb about money and even dumber when it comes to borrowing and getting into (and less likely out of) debt. **86m/C; DVD.** *D:* James D. Scurlock; *W:* James D. Scurlock; *C:* Jon Aaron Aaseng; *M:* Benoit Vharest.

Maxie 🦴🦴 **1985 (PG)** Highly predictable, and forgettable, comedy where a ghost of a flamboyant flapper inhabits the body of a modern-day secretary, and her husband is both delighted and befuddled with the transformations in his spouse. Close is okay, but the film is pretty flaky. **98m/C; VHS, DVD.** Glenn Close; Ruth Gordon; Mandy Patinkin; Barnard Hughes; Valerie Curtin; Harry Hamlin; *D:* Paul Aaron; *W:* Patricia Resnick; *M:* Georges Delerue.

Maximum Conviction 🦴🦴 **2012 (R)** Simple--if nonsensical--plot and lots of action. Former black ops Cross (Seagal) and his partner Manning (Austin) are overseeing the arrival of two mysterious female prisoners at a decommissioned facility. Before long a mercenary force arrives looking for the women who have info that's wanted by the CIA. **98m/C; DVD, Blu-Ray.** Steven Seagal; Steve Austin; Michael Paré; Aliya O'Brien; Steph Song; *D:* Keoni Waxman; *W:* Richard Beattie; *C:* Nathan Wilson; *M:* Michael Richard Plowman. **VIDEO**

Maximum Force 🦴 1/2 **1992 (R)** Three renegade cops join together to infiltrate the underworld and bring to justice both the city's leading crime king and their own corrupt chief of police. **90m/C; VHS, Streaming.** Sam Jones; Sherrie Rose; Jason Lively; John Saxon; Richard Lynch; Mickey Rooney; Jeff Langton; *D:* Joseph Merhi.

Maximum Impact 🦴 **2018** To improve relations, the U.S. Secretary of State (Roberts) travels to Moscow for a secret summit with the Russian head of state. This goal is put in jeopardy by a deal between a shady American businessman (Baldwin) and the Germans to create a terrorist attack that will look like the Russians initiated. To stop the terrorists, U.S intelligence interests, including Secret Service officer Kate (Hu), must work with the Russian FSB, including agent Maxim (Nevsky). This Russian-American co-production is a B-movie quality action comedy full of familiar actors. **110m/C; DVD, Blu-Ray.** Alexander Nevsky; Danny Trejo; Tom Arnold; Kelly Hu; Mark Dacascos; *D:* Andrzej Bartkowiak; *W:* Ross LaManna; *C:* Vern Nobles; *M:* Sean Murray.

Maximum Overdrive 🦴 **1986 (R)** Based upon King's story "Trucks," recounts what happens when a meteor hits Earth and machines run by themselves, wanting only to kill people. Score by AC/DC. King shows that as a director, he's an excellent horror writer. **97m/C; VHS, DVD, Blu-Ray.** Emilio Estevez; Pat Hingle; Laura Harrington; Christopher Murney; Yeardley Smith; Stephen King; *D:* Stephen King; *W:* Stephen King; *C:* Armando Nannuzzi; *M:* AC/DC.

Maximum Risk 🦴🦴 1/2 **1996 (R)** Like we need two of them? Van Damme plays identical twins—a good French guy and a bad Russian guy—and when the bad guy gets killed, his brother takes over his life to find out whodunit. Risk and danger aside, the ruse is not all bad, what with Henstridge as his sib's squeeze, unaware that the man she has in a lip lock is not her beloved. Has all the action you'd expect with guns, fists, and car chases. Hong Kong action auteur Lam's stateside debut ensures that fast-paced chases and full-throttle combat are well done and visually appealing. **100m/C; DVD, Blu-Ray.** Jean-Claude Van Damme; Natasha Henstridge; Jean-Hugues Anglade; Stephane Audran; Paul Ben-Victor; Zach Grenier; Frank Senger; *D:* Ringo Lam; *W:* Larry Ferguson; *C:* Alexander Grusynski; *M:* Robert Folk.

Maximum Security 🦴 **1987** A small-budget prison film detailing the tribulations of a model prisoner struggling to resist mental collapse. **113m/C; VHS, DVD.** Geoffrey Lewis; Jean Smart; Robert Desiderio; *D:* Bill Duke.

Maximum Thrust WOOF! *Waldo Warren: Private Dick Without a Brain* **1988** A few white men confront a deadly Caribbean voodoo tribe. **80m/C; VHS, DVD.** Rick Gianasi; Joe Derrig; Jennifer Kanter; Mizan Nunes; *D:* Tim Kincaid.

May 🦴🦴 **2002 (R)** May's (Bettis) motto is "If you can't find a friend, make one." Thanks to a disturbed childhood (where her only companion was a doll), May is one messed-up chick. She works at an animal hospital with lesbian Polly (Faris), sews as a hobby, and falls for Adam (Sisto), who thinks he likes weird girls. He doesn't know from weird. When Adam finally rejects May, she looks around and decides to make her own best friend—using only the choicest body parts. **95m/C; VHS, DVD.** Angela Bettis; Jeremy Sisto; Anna Faris; James Duval; Nichole Hiltz; Kevin Gage; Merle Kennedy; *D:* Lucky McKee; *W:* Lucky McKee; *C:* Steve Yedlin; *M:* Jaye Barnes-Luckett.

May in Summer 🦴🦴 **2013 (R)** In this drama, newly successful author May Brennan (Dabis) seems to have a perfect life. Returning to Amman, she must deal with her difficult family situation. Though she is engaged to her stable scholarly fiance Ziad (Siddig), her born-again Christian mother Nadine (Abbass) is boycotting the wedding because he is Muslim. Her father, Edward (Pullman), has been estranged since his divorce from his mother, but seems interested in making amends. The closer her wedding day gets, the more May must deal with the fallout from the divorce and her increasingly out of control life. **99m/C; DVD, Blu-Ray, Streaming, Download.** Hiam Abbass; Cherien Dabis; Nadine Malouf; Bill Pullman; Alia Shawkat; Alexander Siddig; *D:* Cherien Dabis; *W:* Cherien Dabis; *C:* Brian Rigney Hubbard; *M:* Kareem Roustom. **VIDEO**

May in the Summer 🦴🦴 **2013 (R)** Successful author May returns home to Jordan to wed her fiancée Ziad, only to find her family squabbling and in disarray. Her born-again mother objects to her marrying a Muslim, her estranged father suddenly wants to be friends, and her sisters are out of control. Not exactly what you want the man marrying you to see about his potential in-laws. English and Arabic with subtitles. **99m/C; DVD, Blu-Ray, Streaming.** *JD QA US* Cherien Dabis; Hiam Abbass; Nadine Malouf; Bill Pullman; Alia Shawkat; Alexander Siddig; *D:* Cherien Dabis; *W:* Cherien Dabis; *C:* Brian Rigney Hubbard; *M:* Kareem Roustom.

Maya Dardel 🦴🦴 1/2 **2017** A biographical portrait of acclaimed poet Maya Dardel (Olin), focusing on her last years. Calmly announcing on NPR that she intends to commit suicide, Maya also tells listeners that she needs a young male writer to act as her literary estate's executor. After interviews with and testing of candidates, Maya narrows the field to two finalists. Gentle Ansel (Keyes) is horrified that Maya is going to kill herself, while arrogant Paul (Koch) meets Maya on her level. The two men then compete for the ultimate prize in the increasingly difficult contest. Though passionate, the film does not match Olin's unfettered performance. **104m/C; DVD.** Lena Olin; Rosanna Arquette; Nathan Keyes; Alexander Koch; Jordan Gavaris; *D:* Zachary Cotler; Magdalena Zyzak; *W:* Zachary Cotler; Magdalena Zyzak; *C:* Patrick Scola; *M:* Zachary Cotler.

Maybe Baby 🦴🦴 1/2 **1999 (R)** Sam (Laurie) and Lucy (Richardson) Bell are a happily married couple trying to have a baby. She's a talent agent and he works for the BBC. Dissatisfied at work, Sam tries his hand at scriptwriting and decides his subject will be a comic look at the couple's infertility problems. Naturally, he keeps this a secret from Lucy, although she finds out when his script is accepted and walks out on Sam. Tends towards the smug and the leads don't particularly click as a couple, which makes the supporting players the most interesting to watch onscreen. **93m/C; VHS, DVD.** *GB FR* Hugh Laurie; Joely Richardson; Adrian Lester; James Purefoy; Tom Hollander; Joanna Lumley; Rowan Atkinson; Dawn French; Emma Thompson; Rachael Stirling; *D:* Ben Elton; *W:* Ben Elton; *C:* Roger Lanser; *M:* Colin Towns.

Maybe I'll Come Home in the Spring 🦴🦴 *Maybe I'll Be Home in the Spring; Deadly Desire* **1971** Originally shown as an ABC movie of the week. Teenager Denise (Field) runs away from her middle-class suburban life to live on a hippie commune with boyfriend Flack (Carradine). When she comes home you see how dysfunctional her family is and although she's changed, nothing else has. Denise tries to warn younger sister Susie (Bradbury) away from drugs and following in her footsteps, but she won't listen. **75m/C; VHS, DVD.** Sally Field; Eleanor Parker; Jackie Cooper; David Carradine; Lane Bradbury; *D:* Joseph Sargent; *W:* Bruce Feldman; *C:* Russell Metty; *M:* Earl Robinson. **TV**

Mayday at 40,000 Feet 🦴 1/2 **1976** Typically ridiculous '70s TV disaster flick finds the pilot of a 747 dealing with engine trouble, a violent snowstorm, and a madman with a gun. **97m/C; DVD.** David Janssen; Jane Powell; Ray Milland; Don Meredith; Christopher George; Lynda Day George; Marjoe Gortner; Broderick Croawford; Hari Rhodes; *D:* Robert Butler; *W:* Dick Nelson; Andrew J. Fenady; *C:* William B. Jurgensen; *M:* Richard Markowitz. **TV**

Mayerling 🦴🦴🦴 1/2 **1936** Considered one of the greatest films about doomed love. Story of the tragic and hopeless affair between Crown Prince Rudolf of Hapsburg and young Baroness Marie Vetsera. Heart wrenching and beautiful, with stupendous acting. Remade in 1968. In French with English subtitles. **95m/B; VHS, DVD.** Charles Boyer; Danielle Darrieux; *D:* Anatole Litvak. N.Y. Film Critics '37: Foreign Film.

Mayerling 🦴 1/2 **1968 (PG-13)** Based on the tragic romance between Crown Prince Rudolf of Hapsburg (Sharif) and the teenaged Baroness Maria Vetsera (Deneuve). Set in 1888, the royal Rudolf defies his father, the Emperor Franz Josef (Mason), to take part in a student revolt for the liberation of Hungary and to fall for the common-born Maria (despite his political marriage). No doubt meant to be a sweeping combo of politics and love ala "Doctor Zhivago," it's mostly tedious; see the 1936 version instead. **140m/C; VHS, DVD.** *GB FR* Omar Sharif; Catherine Deneuve; James Mason; Ava Gardner; James Robertson Justice; Genevieve Page; Ivan Desny; Fabienne Dali; *D:* Terence Young; *W:* Terence Young; *C:* Henri Alekan; *M:* Francis Lai.

Mayflower Madam 🦴🦴 **1987 (R)** Fairly unsexy and uninteresting TV movie recounting the business dealings and court battles of the real-life Sydney Biddle Barrows. Barrows/Bergen is a prominent New York socialite and madam of an exclusive escort service whose clientele includes businessmen and dignitaries. **93m/C; VHS, DVD.** Candice Bergen; Chris Sarandon; Chita Rivera; *D:* Lou Antonio; *M:* David Shire. **TV**

Mayhem 🦴🦴 1/2 **2017** A brutal action horror film set in corporate America. A new airborne disease, Red Eye, causes the infected to lose all sense of morality and societal norms. After a law firm successfully creates a Red Eye defense for a murderer, the money-driven members become unhinged when infected themselves. Boss John Towers (Brand) seeks protection, and finds it in underling Derek (Yeun). Derek and firm client Melanie (Weaving) fearlessly go after all those above him with a hammer and a nail gun, but find those in power will make any excuse to survive. A stylish, smart gory film that reflects contemporary society's anger. **86m/C; DVD, Blu-Ray.** Steven Yeun; Samara Weaving; Steven Brand; Caroline Chikezie; Kerry Fox; *D:* Joe Lynch; *W:* Matias Caruso; *C:* Steve Gainer; *M:* Steve Moore.

Mayor Cupcake 🦴🦴 1/2 **2011 (PG)** Thompson stars with her real-life daughters in this modest family comedy. Mary Maroni's daughters nominate her to run for mayor but an accident to the incumbent sends the unprepared cupcake baker straight into the office. Mary might not know politics but she does know how to run a business (and a family), so she puts her skills to use to straighten out her debt-ridden community. **86m/C; DVD.** Lea Thompson; Judd Nelson; Zoey Deutch; Madelyn Deutch; Frankie Faison; Dorian Harewood; Thomas (Tom) McCarthy; *D:* Alex Pires; *W:* Alex Pires; Art D'Alessandro; *C:* Neil Roach; *M:* Kays Al-Atrakchi. **VIDEO**

The Mayor of Casterbridge 🦴🦴 1/2 **2003** Appropriately brooding adaptation of Thomas Hardy's dark novel of regret. Farm worker Michael Henchard (Hinds) gets drunk and sells his wife Susan (Aubrey) and their baby daughter at a country fair. Since her husband is an abusive drunk and the buyer (Russell) is a good-natured sailor, Susan decides to take her chances. Suffering from a drunkard's remorse, Henchard searches fruitlessly for his family. He eventually settles in Casterbridge where, through sobriety and hard work, Henchard becomes the town's mayor. Then his past returns to haunt him when Susan and his now-grown daughter, Elizabeth-Jane (May), seek him out. **200m/C; DVD.** *GB* Ciaran Hinds; James Purefoy; Jodhi May; Juliet Aubrey; Polly Walker; Clive Russell; *D:* David Thacker; *W:* Ted Whitehead; *C:* Ivan Strasburg; *M:* Adrian Johnston. **CABLE**

The Mayor of 44th Street 🦴 **1942** Mean-spirited drama finds Broadway agent Joe Jonathan (Murphy) attempting to help a paroled racketeer and kid who's part of a street gang go straight, but both try to take over his agency for nefarious purposes. Last film for Barthelmess, who then retired. **86m/B; DVD.** George Murphy; Richard Barthelmess; Anne Shirley; William Gargan; Rex Downing; ***D:*** Alfred E. Green; ***W:*** Lewis R. Foster; Frank Ryan; ***C:*** Robert De Grasse; ***M:*** Harry Revel.

The Mayor of Hell 🦴🦴 ½ **1933** Gangster Patsy Gargan (Cagney) has his political cronies appoint him the titular head of a state reformatory. But when he sees the brutal conditions, Gargan makes improvements and tries to get the teenaged criminal inmates to see the error of their ways. However, when Gargan is forced into hiding after killing a rival, things get bad again until he finally decides to step up. Remade as 1938's "Crime School." **85m/B; DVD.** James Cagney; Madge Evans; Allen Jenkins; Dudley Digges; Frankie Darro; Carolyn Farina; ***D:*** Archie Mayo; ***W:*** Edward Chodorov; ***C:*** Barney McGill.

Mayor of the Sunset Strip 🦴🦴🦴 **2003 (R)** As a popular Los Angeles disc jockey, Rodney Bingenheimer pushed new musical acts into the limelight—including the Sex Pistols, Blondie, and Nirvana—meanwhile living as the greatest groupie, befriending The Beatles, Elton John, Elvis, and the Doors. But in his documentary, director-writer Hickenlooper poignantly reveals how this man rose up from a lonely childhood to unexpectedly become the "get to know me" guy on the music scene, only to learn that life inside all of the glittering lights can be just as harsh and emotionally isolating as was his youth. Music industry cameos and interviews abound. **94m/C; VHS, DVD.** ***D:*** George Hickenlooper; ***W:*** George Hickenlooper; ***C:*** Kramer Morgenthau; Igor Meglic; ***M:*** Anthony Marinelli.

Maytime 🦴🦴🦴 **1937** Lovely story of an opera star (MacDonald) and penniless singer (Eddy) who fall in love in Paris, but her husband/teacher (Barrymore) interferes. One of the best films the singing duo ever made. **132m/B; VHS, DVD.** Jeanette MacDonald; Nelson Eddy; John Barrymore; Herman Bing; Tom Brown; Lynne Carver; ***D:*** Robert Z. Leonard; ***W:*** Noel Langley.

Maze 🦴🦴 ½ **2001 (R)** Introverted New York artist Lyle Maze (Morrow) is a sculptor afflicted with Tourette's syndrome, which makes him romantically hesitant. Lyle's best friend is a doctor named Mike (Sheffer), whose devotion is to his career rather than his girlfriend Callie (Linney). Mike leaves Callie for a months-long tour with Doctors Without Borders in Africa and when Callie discovers she is pregnant, she turns to Lyle for emotional support. Unsurprisingly, the needy duo fall in love before they have to explain what's happened on Mike's return. **98m/C; VHS, DVD.** Rob Morrow; Laura Linney; Craig Sheffer; Gia Carides; Rose Gregorio; Robert Hogan; ***D:*** Rob Morrow; ***W:*** Rob Morrow; Bradley White; ***C:*** Wolfgang Held; ***M:*** Bobby Previte.

The Maze Runner 🦴🦴 ½ **2014 (PG-13)** After waking up in a group of young boys with no memory of how he got there, Thomas (charismatic newcomer O'Brien) comes to discover that they're trapped in a maze that is also occupied by deadly creatures should they dare attempt escape. As he settles into his new community, he finds most have accepted this life. But flashbacks and the arrival of Teresa (Scodelario)--the first girl ever--leave Thomas wanting answers. It's a pretty superficial lesson (the "maze" of life), but director Ball maintains tension and the action is well-done. Based on the first book of the James Dashner trilogy. **113m/C; DVD, Blu-Ray.** Dylan O'Brien; Will Poulter; Kaya Scodelario; Thomas Brodie-Sangster; Patricia Clarkson; ***D:*** Wes Ball; ***W:*** Noah Oppenheim; Grant Pierce Myers; T.S. Nowlin; ***C:*** Enrique Chediak; ***M:*** John Paesano.

Maze Runner: The Death Cure 🦴🦴 ½ **2018 (PG-13)** In this satisfying conclusion to the trilogy, Thomas and his fellow escapees from the Maze work to take down the WCKD agency and halt its experimentation in curing "The Flare" zombie-virus. Unlike other drawn-out YA franchises, each Maze Runner installment is at least as good as its predecessor. A bit long, but fans of the series will receive the answers they've wanted. You'd never know it from watching O'Brien literally throw himself into the action, but only days into filming he suffered a stunt-related head injury so severe that production was shut down for months. **141m/C; DVD, Blu-Ray.** Dylan O'Brien; Ki Hong Lee; Kaya Scodelario; Thomas Brodie-Sangster; Dexter Darden; ***D:*** Wes Ball; ***W:*** T.S. Nowlin; ***C:*** Gyula Pados; ***M:*** John Paesano.

Maze Runner: The Scorch Trials 🦴🦴 **2015 (PG-13)** The second entry into the Maze Runner series based on the books by James Dashner, the Gladers finds life outside the Maze as challenging as within. As they traverse the Scorch (a devastated part of their world filled with obstacles), the truth about the goals of the WCKD (Wicked) are slowly revealed. As in all YA fiction, they band together to take down the authority figures trying to keep them under control. Thrilling action scenes try to compensate for the gaps in the storytelling. **120m/C; DVD, Blu-Ray.** Dylan O'Brien; Thomas Brodie-Sangster; Aidan Gillen; Kaya Scodelario; Ki Hong Lee; ***D:*** Wes Ball; ***W:*** T.S. Nowlin; ***C:*** Gyula Pados; ***M:*** John Paesano.

Mazes and Monsters 🦴🦴 ½ *Rona Jaffe's Mazes and Monsters; Dungeons and Dragons* **1982** A group of university students becomes obsessed with playing a real life version of the fantasy role-playing game, Dungeons and Dragons (known in the film as Mazes & Monsters since D&D is trademarked). Early Hanks appearance is among the film's assets. Adapted from the book by Rona Jaffe. **100m/C; VHS, DVD.** *CA* Tom Hanks; Wendy Crewson; David Wallace; Chris Makepeace; Lloyd Bochner; Peter Donat; Murray Hamilton; Vera Miles; Louise Sorel; Susan Strasberg; Anne Francis; ***D:*** Steven Hilliard Stern; ***M:*** Hagood Hardy. **TV**

McCabe & Mrs. Miller 🦴🦴🦴🦴 **1971 (R)** Altman's characteristically quirky take on the Western casts Beatty as a self-inflated entrepreneur who opens a brothel in the Great North. Christie is the madame who helps stabilize the haphazard operation. Unfortunately, success comes at a high price, and when gunmen arrive to enforce a business proposition, Beatty must become the man he has, presumably, merely pretended to be. A poetic, moving work, and a likely classic of the genre. Based on the novel by Edmund Naughton. **121m/C; VHS, DVD, Blu-Ray.** Warren Beatty; Julie Christie; William Devane; Keith Carradine; John Schuck; Rene Auberjonois; Shelley Duvall; Bert Remsen; Michael Murphy; Hugh Millais; Jack Riley; ***D:*** Robert Altman; ***W:*** Robert Altman; ***C:*** Vilmos Zsigmond; ***M:*** Leonard Cohen. Natl. Film Reg. '10.

McCanick 🦴 ½ **2014 (R)** Derivative cop drama. Gruff veteran Philly detective Eugene 'Mack' McCanick (Morse) is enraged to learn that Simon Weeks (Monteith), whom he put in prison, has been released early on parole. Over the course of one day, Mack pursues Weeks as flashbacks reveal why the dirty cop wants the ex-street hustler to keep quiet--preferably by being dead. **96m/C; DVD, Blu-Ray.** David Morse; Cory Monteith; Mike Vogel; Ciaran Hinds; ***D:*** Josh C. Waller; ***W:*** Daniel Noah; ***C:*** Martin Ahlgren; ***M:*** Johann Johannsson.

The McConnell Story 🦴🦴 ½ *Tiger in the Sky* **1955** True story of ace flyer McConnell, his heroism during WWII and the Korean conflict, and his postwar aviation pioneer efforts. Fine acting from Allyson and Ladd, with good support from Whitmore and Faylen. **107m/C; VHS, DVD.** Alan Ladd; June Allyson; James Whitmore; Frank Faylen; ***D:*** Gordon Douglas; ***M:*** Max Steiner.

The McCullochs 🦴 ½ *The Wild McCullochs* **1975 (PG)** Texas millionaire J.J. McCulloch (Tucker) is the kind of domineering patriarch whose kids wind up hating him and destroying their own lives. Stereotypical family saga set in 1949. **93m/C; VHS, DVD.** Forrest Tucker; Julie Adams; Janice Heiden; Max Baer, Jr.; Don Grady; Chip Hand; Dennis Redfield; William Demarest; Harold J. Stone; Vito Scotti; James Gammon; Mike Mazurki; ***D:*** Max Baer, Jr.; ***W:*** Max Baer, Jr.; ***C:*** Fred W. Koenekamp; ***M:*** Ernest Gold.

McFarland USA 🦴🦴 ½ **2015 (PG)** A surprisingly moving and subtle family sports from the company that does this kind of thing better than anyone: Disney. A cross country track coach named Jim White (a great Costner) finds himself in a small California town without much focus or potential until he notices that a number of locals, including a number of migrant Hispanic workers, are a little faster than average. Director Caro takes the true sports story template that Disney has mined before and provides honest insight into the immigrant story in modern America. **128m/C; DVD, Blu-Ray.** Kevin Costner; Maria Bello; Carlos Pratts; Ramiro Rodriguez; Johnny Ortiz; Rafael Martinez; Hector Duran; Diana Maria Riva; ***D:*** Niki Caro; ***W:*** Christopher Cleveland; Bettina Gilois; Grant Thompson; ***C:*** Adam Arkapaw; ***M:*** Antonio Pinto.

McHale's Navy 🦴🦴 ½ **1964** The TV sitcom came to the big screen with its silly humor intact as Lt. Commander Quinton McHale (Borgnine) and the reprobate crew of PT-73 get into debt gambling with a bunch of marines, which they try to get out of in a variety of unorthodox ways. **93m/C; VHS, DVD.** Ernest Borgnine; Tim Conway; Joe Flynn; Bob Hastings; Billy (Billie) Sands; Gavin MacLeod; George Kennedy; ***D:*** Edward Montagne; ***W:*** Frank Gill, Jr.; George Carleton Brown; ***C:*** William Margulies.

McHale's Navy 🦴 ½ **1997 (PG)** Yet another (unsuccessful) attempt to take a TV series and let it loose on the big screen. Retired Navy skipper McHale (Arnold) has set up his scheming ways on the Caribbean island of San Ysidro, where he can be a thorn in the side of Capt. Binghampton (Stockwell), the newly transferred commanding officer of the island's sleepy naval base. McHale's former cronies aid their leader when he's reluctantly reunited with the Navy in order to prevent the terrorist threats of his former Soviet nemesis Vladakov (Curry). TV's original McHale, Borgnine, has a cameo (and gets a promotion to admiral). **108m/C; DVD.** Tom Arnold; Tim Curry; Dean Stockwell; David Alan Grier; Debra Messing; Thomas Chong; Bruce Campbell; French Stewart; Brian Haley; Danton Stone; ***Cameo(s):*** Ernest Borgnine; ***D:*** Bryan Spicer; ***W:*** Peter Crabbe; ***C:*** Buzz Feitshans, IV; ***M:*** Dennis McCarthy.

McKenzie Break 🦴🦴🦴 **1970** Irish intelligence agent John Connor (Keith) is sent to Scotland to Camp McKenzie, a prison for German POWs during WWII. Captured U-boat commander Schluetter (Griem) is suspected of planning a mass escape and Connor is supposed to stop the action. The battle of wills between the hard-headed Connor and wily Schluetter provides taut, suspenseful drama. Adapted from "The Bowmanville Break" by Sidney Shelley. **106m/C; VHS, DVD, Blu-Ray.** Brian Keith; Helmut Griem; Ian Hendry; Jack Watson; Horst Janson; Patrick O'Connell; ***D:*** Lamont Johnson; ***W:*** William W. Norton, Sr.; ***C:*** Michael Reed; ***M:*** Riz Ortolani.

McLintock! 🦴🦴🦴 **1963** Rowdy western starring Wayne as a tough cattle baron whose refined wife (O'Hara) returns from the east after a two-year separation. She wants a divorce and custody of their 17-year-old daughter (Powers), who's been away at school. In the meantime, he's hired a housekeeper (De Carlo), whose teenage son (real-life son Patrick) promptly falls for Powers. It's a battle royal between the feisty wife and cantankerous husband but no one out-dukes the Duke. Other Wayne family members involved in the production include daughter Aissa (as the housekeeper's daughter) and son Michael who produced the film. **127m/C; VHS, DVD, Blu-Ray.** John Wayne; Maureen O'Hara; Yvonne De Carlo; Patrick Wayne; Stefanie Powers; Jack Kruschen; Chill Wills; Jerry Van Dyke; Edgar Buchanan; Bruce Cabot; Perry Lopez; Michael Pate; Strother Martin; Gordon Jones; ***D:*** Andrew V. McLaglen; ***W:*** James Edward Grant; ***C:*** William Clothier.

The McMasters 🦴🦴 *The Blood Crowd; The McMasters. . .Tougher Than the West Itself* **1970 (PG)** Set shortly after the Civil War, the film tells the story of the prejudice faced by a black soldier who returns to the southern ranch on which he was raised. Once there, the rancher gives him half of the property, but the ex-soldier has difficulty finding men who will work for him. When a group of Native Americans assist him, a band of bigoted men do their best to stop it. The movie was released in two versions with different endings: in one, prejudice prevails; in the other, bigotry is defeated. **89m/C; VHS, DVD.** Burl Ives; Brock Peters; David Carradine; Nancy Kwan; Jack Palance; Dane Clark; L.Q. Jones; Alan Vint; John Carradine; ***D:*** Alf Kjellin.

McQ 🦴🦴 ½ **1974 (PG)** After several big dope dealers kill two police officers, a lieutenant resigns to track them down. Dirty Harry done with an aging Big Duke. **116m/C; VHS, DVD, Blu-Ray.** John Wayne; Eddie Albert; Diana Muldaur; Clu Gulager; Colleen Dewhurst; Al Lettieri; Julie Adams; David Huddleston; ***D:*** John Sturges; ***C:*** Harry Stradling, Jr.; ***M:*** Elmer Bernstein.

McQueen 🦴🦴🦴 **2018 (R)** A documentary on Alexander McQueen (1969-2010), a British fashion designer who translated the violent influences in his life into outrageous, disturbing, and newsworthy creations. A solid and moving portrait, and a must-see for anyone interested in fashion. **111m/C; DVD, Blu-Ray.** Alexander McQueen; Gary James McQueen; Janet McQueen; ***D:*** Ian Bonhôte; Peter Ettedgui; ***W:*** Peter Ettedgui; ***C:*** Alexander Alexandrov; Will Pugh; ***M:*** Michael Nyman.

MDMA 🦴🦴 *Angie X* **2018** Chinese American Angie (Q.) leaves the tough streets of Newark, New Jersey to attend a renowned Bay Area college in the mid '80s. Taking a bus to get there, Angie receives guidance from her frugal father (Yuan). She lives it up with roommate Jeanine (Eastwood) until she loses her funding. Desperate, she delves into the drug world by producing and selling Ecstasy. As she encounters local criminal elements, she still attends classes. But nothing good can come from living this kind of life. Based on writer/director Wang's true story, it's stylish with solid performances but we never feel connected to the lead. **98m/C; DVD.** Annie Q.; Francesca Ruth Eastwood; Elisa Donovan; Yetide Badaki; Pierson Fode; ***D:*** Angie Wang; ***W:*** Angie Wang; ***C:*** Brett Pawlak; ***M:*** Pei Pei Chung.

Me and Earl and the Dying Girl 🦴🦴🦴 **2015 (PG-13)** An indie hit that brings a fresh take on the tired coming-on-age story, in a way that big studios can't. Greg (Mann), a high school senior just barely hiding his geeky tendencies, makes silly parodies of classic films with equally closeted-geek Earl (Cycler). A Sockwork Orange, Senior Citizen Cane, and the like take inspiration from Earl's dad's (Offerman) eclectic movie colleciton. Forced by his overbearing mom to visit Rachel (Cooke), a girl with leukemia, Greg slowly realizes that she may be his biggest fan. Quick-witted and unconventional in all the best ways, this funny and heartbreaking take on young love feels like a homemade Valentine's Day card crafted by Cupid himself. **104m/C; DVD, Blu-Ray, Streaming.** Thomas Mann; R.J. Cyler; Olivia Cooke; Nick Offerman; Connie Britton; ***D:*** Alfonso Gomez-Rejon; ***W:*** Jesse Andrews; ***C:*** Chung-hoon Chung; ***M:*** Brian Eno; Nico Muhly.

Me & Mrs. Jones 🦴🦴 ½ **2002** Unhappy divorced tabloid reporter Liam Marple (Green) writes a gossip column under the nom de plume "Mrs. Jones." He knows nothing about politics but his ex-wife Jane (Hawes), who's also his boss, wants dirt on female prime minister Laura Bowden (Goodall), who is in the middle of an election campaign. Liam manages to worm his way into Laura's confidence (naturally, she doesn't know who he really is) but he finds himself with unwanted pangs of conscience when they unexpectedly fall in love. **100m/C; VHS, DVD.** *GB* Robson Green; Caroline Goodall; Philip Quast; Keeley Hawes; Michael Maloney; Peter Firth; Aisling O'Sullivan; ***D:*** Catherine Morshead; ***W:*** Caleb Ranson; ***C:*** John Daly; ***M:*** Simon Lacey. **TV**

Me and My Gal 🦴 ½ **1932** Pic doesn't know what it wants to be--a wisecracking crime comedy, drama, romance--so it ends up as nothing much. New York Irish copper Danny Dolan (Tracy) is in love with waitress Helen (Joan), whose sister Kate (Burns) is trying to get away from gangster boyfriend Duke (Walsh), despite her still loving the creep. There's a marriage, prison escape, bank robbery, a crippled old man, and somewhere in the mix, Danny is supposed to be bringing Duke to justice. **79m/B; DVD.** Spencer Tracy; Joan Bennett; Marion Burns; George Walsh; George Chandler; Noel Madison; Henry B. Walthall; ***D:*** Raoul Walsh; ***W:*** Arthur Kober; ***C:*** Arthur C. Miller.

Me and Orson Welles 🦴🦴 ½ **2009 (PG-13)** In 1937, 17-year-old theater lover Richard Samuels (Efron) has a chance encounter with 22-year-old Orson Welles (McKay), who offers him a small role in his upcoming Mercury Theater production of "Julius Caesar" (with Welles playing Brutus). This gives Richard a behind-the-scenes look at the genius' charm, confidence, abrasiveness, and manipulations as well as the egos, insecurities, and squabbles that envelop the company. The experience for the cocky Richard is exhilarating and disillusioning with Efron overshadowed by the larger-than-life performance of McKay. Adapted from the 2003 novel by Robert Kaplow. **114m/C; DVD, Blu-Ray, On Demand.** *UK* Christian McKay; Zac Efron; Claire Danes; Zoe Kazan; James Tupper; Leo Bill; Eddie Marsan; Ben Chaplin; Kelly Reilly; Patrick Kennedy; ***D:*** Richard Linklater; ***W:*** Holly Gent Palmo; Vince Palmo; ***C:*** Richard Pope; ***M:*** Michael J. McEvoy.

Me and the Kid 1/2 **1993 (PG)** Minor career criminals Aiello and Pantoliano try a robbery on a ruthless financier's (Dukes) home and wind up kidnapping his 10-year-old son instead. But dad doesn't want to pay the ransom and Aiello dumps his partner (who wants to kill the kid) and heads out on the road with the boy. **97m/C; VHS, DVD.** Danny Aiello; Joe Pantoliano; Alex Zuckerman; Cathy Moriarty; David Dukes; Anita Morris; ***D:*** Dan Curtis.

Me and the Mob 1/2 *Wo Do I Gotta Kill?* **1994 (R)** Writer Jimmy Corona (Lorinz) thinks the way to get some colorful stories is to join up with his mobster uncle (Darrow). But Jimmy's no tough guy and the feds coerce him into wearing a wire to bust the local godfather. Low-budget comedy is a lesson in tedium. **85m/C; VHS, DVD.** James Lorinz; Tony Darrow; John A. Costelloe; Sandra Bullock; Anthony Michael Hall; Stephen Lee; Ted (Theodore) Sorel; ***Cameo(s):*** Steve Buscemi; ***D:*** Frank Rainone; ***W:*** James Lorinz; Frank Rainone.

Me & Will 1/2 **1999 (R)** Babes on bikes take to the road. Aspiring writer Jane (Rose) and artist Will (Behr) both have bad luck with men and drug problems, as well as a liking for chopper-riding. They meet in rehab and decide a road trip in search of the cycle ridden by Peter Fonda in "Easy Rider" is just the kind of quest they need. Uneven quality but a lot of recognizable faces in supporting roles. **93m/C; VHS, DVD.** Sherrie Rose; Melissa Behr; Patrick Dempsey; Seymour Cassel; Grace Zabriskie; M. Emmet Walsh; Steve Railsback; Traci Lords; Billy Wirth; ***D:*** Sherrie Rose; Melissa Behr; ***W:*** Sherrie Rose; Melissa Behr; ***C:*** Joey Forsyte. **VIDEO**

Me and You 1/2 *Io e Te* **2012** A 14-year-old named Lorenzo (Antinori) tells his parents that he's going on a ski trip when he's actually hiding out in his basement. His sister (Falco) finds him, leading to an emotional series of confrontations and conversations in this very-talky film. The confined setting likely made the production possible due to director Bertolucci's back problems but the result is a sometimes-bland affair. His first film in a decade should be a major event for the film-going world but seems like an afterthought compared to the rest of his remarkable resume. **103m/C; DVD.** *IT* Jacopo Olmo Antinori; Tea Falco; Sonia Bergamasco; ***D:*** Bernardo Bertolucci; ***W:*** Bernardo Bertolucci; Niccolo Ammaniti; ***C:*** Fabio Cianchetti; ***M:*** Franco Piersanti.

Me and You and Everyone We Know **2005 (R)** Debut feature from conceptual artist July finds her playing wistful, struggling video artist Christine, who's unexpectedly involved with Richard (Hawkes), a shoe salesmen with a raw heart from his recent divorce and two precocious sons with their own problems. Seven-year-old Robby (Ratcliff) unwittingly visits an online sex chat room, where he's mistaken for an adult with kinky sexual ideas, while his older brother Peter (Thompson) is tormented by two classmates who want to practice their oral sex techniques on him. Saves itself from just being quirky and precious with winning performances. **95m/C; DVD, Blu-Ray.** *US GB* John Hawkes; Carlie Westerman; Miranda July; Miles Thompson; Brandon Ratcliff; Natasha Slayton; Najarra Townsend; ***D:*** Miranda July; ***W:*** Miranda July; ***C:*** Chuy Chavez; ***M:*** Michael Andrews.

Me Before You **2016 (PG-13)** This adaptation of Jojo Moyes' hit book features a star-making turn by Emilia Clarke ("Game of Thrones" star), but she's really the only thing keeping this from descending into "Nicholas Sparks Adaptation" fodder. She plays Lou Clark, a young woman who ends up falling in love with Will Traynor (Claflin), despite the fact that he's paralyzed. Of course, Lou and Will are going to teach other about the sacrifice of love and the meaning of life, but Clarke sells the emotional gravity of her character's dilemma, making it feel more believable than cliché. The rest of the movie, not so much. **110m/C; DVD, Blu-Ray.** Sam Claflin; Emilia Clarke; Vanessa Kirby; Samantha Spiro; Brendan Coyle; ***D:*** Thea Sharrock; ***W:*** Jojo Moyes; ***C:*** Remi Adefarasin; ***M:*** Craig Armstrong.

Me, Myself and Her 1/2 *Io e lei* **2016** A comedy about the difficulties of being in a long-term relationship, the temptations that challenge couples, and the complexities of sexual attraction. Marina (Ferilli) and Federica (Buy) seem to have the perfect private life. Together for five years, they share an apartment in Rome. Independent Marina is a former actress, current health food restaurant operator, and certain of her sexuality. Federica is an architect who was once married to a man and has son. Unlike Marina, Federica has never stated that she is a lesbian and keeps here relationship with Marina discrete. The relationship faces serious challenges when Federica runs into a man she once had a crush on and begins to question what she wants out of life and love. Italian with subtitles. **102m/C; DVD, Streaming.** Margherita Buy; Sabrina Ferilli; Fausto Maria Sciarappa; Alessia Barela; Domenico Diele; ***D:*** Maria Sole Tognazzi; ***W:*** Maria Sole Tognazzi; Ivan Cotroneo; Francesca Marciano; ***C:*** Arnaldo Catinari; ***M:*** Gabriele Roberto. **VIDEO**

Me, Myself, and Irene **2000 (R)** Charlie's (Carrey) a Rhode Island state trooper whose split personality (one meek, the other a sociopath) is controlled by medication, which he loses when transporting crime suspect Irene (Zellweger). Both sides fall for the girl and declare war on each other. Carrey's verbal and physical acrobatics, along with the Farrellys' patented gross-out scenes are as joyfully disgusting as you'd imagine. The romance between Charlie and Irene can't keep up with the energy of the comedic scenes, especially the ones involving Charlie's three Mensa-candidate, African-American sons, who almost steal the movie right out from under him. **117m/C; DVD, Blu-Ray.** Jim Carrey; Renée Zellweger; Robert Forster; Chris Cooper; Richard Jenkins; Traylor Howard; Daniel Greene; Zen Gesner; Tony Cox; Anthony Anderson; Lenny Clarke; Shannon Whirry; Rob Moran; Mongo Brownlee; Jerod Mixon; Michael Bowman; Mike Cerrone; ***Cameo(s):*** Anna Kournikova; Cam Neely; Brendan Shanahan; ***V:*** Rex Allen; ***D:*** Bobby Farrelly; Peter Farrelly; ***W:*** Bobby Farrelly; Peter Farrelly; Mike Cerrone; ***C:*** Mark Irwin; ***M:*** Peter Yorn; Lee Scott.

Me Myself I **1999 (R)** Pamela Drury (Griffiths) is a successful Sydney journalist who's also single, in her late 30s, and depressed by both situations. She moans about not marrying her long-ago beau Robert Dickson (Roberts) and, lo and behold, Pam's whisked into the life she could have had—marriage and mother of three in the suburbs. Of course, this Pam doesn't have a clue as to how her new life runs, which makes for some comic mileage. But it's the appealing Griffiths that holds all the unlikely yet cliched situations together. **104m/C; VHS, DVD.** *AU* Rachel Griffiths; David Roberts; Sandy Winton; ***D:*** Pip Karmel; ***W:*** Pip Karmel; ***C:*** Graeme Lind; ***M:*** Charlie Sook Kim Chan.

Me Without You **2001 (R)** Marina (Friel) and Holly (Williams) are adolescent friends in London in 1974, whose changing relationship is seen over a 20-year period. Holly fancies Marina's brother Nat (Milburn) but Marina's jealousy prevents anything serious from developing. In college, Holly studies, Marina parties, and both become rivals for American lecturer Daniel (MacLachlan). Holly becomes increasingly dissatisfied with Marina's selfishness and eventually decides to pursue a relationship with Nat after all. Friel plays a brat whose vulnerability is occasionally revealed, while Williams works on her English accent as the idealistic nice girl. **107m/C; VHS, DVD.** *UK* Anna Friel; Michelle Williams; Oliver Milburn; Kyle MacLachlan; Trudie Styler; Nicky Henson; Allan Corduner; Deborah Findlay; Marianne (Cuau) Denicourt; Steve John Shepherd; ***D:*** Sandra Goldbacher; ***W:*** Sandra Goldbacher; Laurence Coriat; ***C:*** Denis Crossan; ***M:*** Adrian Johnston.

Me You Them *Eu Tu Eles* **2000 (PG-13)** Hard-working Darlene (Case) returns to her dusty Brazilian village with a young son (and no husband). She marries elderly Osias (Duarte), basically because he has a new house, and has another son, whose father is probably not Osias. Then Osias's younger cousin Zezinho (Garcia) moves in. Yep, there's another baby. Finally, Darlene meets younger Ciro (Vasconcelos), a migrant worker, and invites him to stay around. You can guess what happens next. There's a little squabbling but soon everyone settles into a big, contented family. Portuguese with subtitles. **107m/C; VHS, DVD.** *BR PT* Regina Case; Lima Duarte; Stenio Garcia; Luiz Carlos Vasconcelos; Nilda Spencer; ***D:*** Andrucha Waddington; ***W:*** Elena Soarez; ***C:*** Breno Silveira; ***M:*** Gilberto Gil.

Mea Maxima Culpa: Silence in the House of God **2012** Deeply disturbing documentary on the practice and concealment of sexual abuse of children within the Catholic Church. Director Gibney focuses on the allegations against Fr. Lawrence Murphy, who taught at St. John's School for the Deaf in Milwaukee, Wisconsin, from 1950-74. He interviews journalists, Catholic clergy and lay peiople as well as some of the priest's deaf victims (Lawrence died in 1998) before addressing the Vatican's 'conspiracy of silence' to the longstanding problem. **106m/C; DVD.** ***D:*** Alex Gibney; ***W:*** Alex Gibney; ***C:*** Lisa Rinzler; ***M:*** Ivor Guest.

Meadowland **2015 (R)** Sarah (Wilde) and Phil (Wilson) have suffered something unimaginable—the disappearance of their only child. A year after his kidnapping from a gas station, and with no sign of his return or discovery of his body, they are in total limbo. Sarah becomes obsessed with an autistic kid at the school at which she works while Phil looks dazed and confused in group meetings and befriends another man (Leguizamo) who has dealt with loss. Wilde and Wilson are both excellent here and cinematographer-turned-director Morano shows confidence, but too much of the melodrama is less than subtle. **95m/C; DVD, Streaming.** Olivia Wilde; Elisabeth Moss; Giovanni Ribisi; John Leguizamo; Luke Wilson; Ty Simpkins; ***D:*** Reed Morano; ***W:*** Chris Rossi; Adam Taylor; ***C:*** Reed Morano. **VIDEO**

Mean Creek **2004 (R)** Shy, slight 13-year-old Sam (Culkin) is the favorite target of school bully George (Peck). Tough older bro Rocky (Morgan) decides to get even by inviting George on a boat trip and then humiliating and stranding him. Along for the ride are two of Rocky's friends as well as Sam's potential girlfriend. Of course, the plan goes awry as the characters prove to be multi-dimensional: the bully is lonely and vulnerable; the macho kid hides deep insecurities. Unexpected consequences reveal that the taste of revenge isn't sweet at all. The rating is primarily for language but isn't likely to shock the film's peer group. **89m/C; DVD.** Rory Culkin; Ryan Kelley; Scott Mechlowicz; Trevor Morgan; Josh Peck; Carly Schroeder; ***D:*** Jacob Aaron Estes; ***W:*** Jacob Aaron Estes; ***C:*** Sharone Meir; ***M:*** tomandandy.

Mean Dreams 1/2 **2017 (R)** A small town thriller centered on two young lovers. When teen Casey (Nelisse) moves to a small community with her corrupt police officer father Wayne Caraway (Paxton), her life is changed forever when she meets the farm boy next door, Jonas (Wiggins). Though the possessive Wayne tries to stop the romance, Jonas sees the depth of his abuse of his daughter. The teens go on the run together after Jonas is an inadvertent witness to Wayne's deadly illegal activity. The script is weak, but its visuals somewhat make up for it. The film also features one of Paxton's last performances before his death. **108m/C; DVD.** Josh Wiggins; Sophie Nelisse; Joe Cobden; Bill Paxton; Vickie Papavs; ***D:*** Nathan Morlando; ***W:*** Kevin Coughlin; Ryan Grassby; ***C:*** Steve Cosens; ***M:*** Son Lux.

Mean Frank and Crazy Tony **1975 (R)** A mobster and the man who idolizes him attempt a prison breakout in this fun, action-packed production. **92m/C; VHS, DVD.** *IT* Lee Van Cleef; Tony LoBianco; Jean Rochefort; Jess Hahn; ***D:*** Michele Lupo.

Mean Girls **2004 (PG-13)** Fey successfully takes her sassy wit from TV to the big screen with this clever teen comedy. At 16, Cady (Lohan) is a home-schooled kid, raised in Africa, who uses jungle animals as her frame of reference. The popular girls are The Plastics, Barbie-esque divas led by Regina (McAdams), who take in the brainy Cady for sport. When Cady stupidly reveals her crush on Regina's ex, she quickly becomes a target. Familiar but updated, edgy portrayal of the high school social caste system is probably the smartest teen comedy since the heyday of John Hughes. Based on the non-fiction book "Queen Bees and Wannabees" by Rosalind Wiseman. **97m/C; DVD, Blu-Ray.** Lindsay Lohan; Rachel McAdams; Lacey Chabert; Amanda Seyfried; Tina Fey; Lizzy Caplan; Tim Meadows; Amy Poehler; Ana Gasteyer; Daniel Franzese; Courtney Chase; Neil Flynn; Jonathan Bennett; ***D:*** Mark S. Waters; ***W:*** Tina Fey; ***C:*** Daryn Okada; ***M:*** Rolfe Kent.

Mean Girls 2 **2011 (PG-13)** Embarrassingly clueless ABC Family sequel to the 2004 pic. Newcomer Jo quickly runs afoul of the Mandi-led high school clique The Plastics. She befriends belittled Abby and the duo decides to take down the mean girls. The big climax is a girls' football face-off between Mandi's Plastics and Jo's Anti-Plastics. Football? **95m/C; DVD.** Meaghan Martin; Maiara Walsh; Jennifer Stone; Nicole Gale Anderson; Diego Boneta; Linden Ashby; Rhoda Griffis; Donn Lamkin; Tim Meadows; ***D:*** Melanie Mayron; ***W:*** Allison Schroeder; Elana Lesser; David Steven Cohen; ***C:*** Levie Isaacks; ***M:*** Transcenders. **CABLE**

Mean Guns 1/2 **1997 (R)** Lots of mayhem will redeem this silly plot for the action fan. Moon (Ice-T) lures 100 assassins to an abandoned prison with the promise of $10 million for the last three men standing. Lou (Lambert) and Marcus (Halsey) are Moon's rivals. **90m/C; VHS, DVD.** Ice-T; Christopher Lambert; Michael Halsey; Deborah Van Valkenburgh; Tina Cote; Yuji Okumoto; ***D:*** Albert Pyun; ***W:*** Andrew Witham; Nat Whitcomb; ***C:*** George Mooradian; ***M:*** Tony Riparetti. **VIDEO**

Mean Johnny Barrows 1/2 **1975** When Johnny Barrows returns to his home town after being dishonorably discharged from the Army he is offered a job as a gang hitman. **83m/C; VHS, DVD.** Fred Williamson; Roddy McDowall; Stuart Whitman; Luther Adler; Jenny Sherman; Elliott Gould; ***D:*** Fred Williamson.

Mean Machine *Un Tipo con Una Faccia Strana ti Cerca per Ucciderti; Cauldron of Death; Gangland; The Dirty Mob; Ricco* **1973 (R)** A man and his beautiful cohort plot revenge on organized crime for the murder of his father. **89m/C; VHS, DVD.** *IT SP* Chris Mitchum; Barbara Bouchet; Arthur Kennedy; Eduardo Fajardo; Paola Senatore; ***D:*** Tulio Demicheli; ***W:*** Mario di Nardo; Santiago Moncada; ***C:*** Francisco Fraile; ***M:*** Nando De Luca.

Mean Machine **2001 (R)** British remake of Robert Aldrich's 1974 film, "The Longest Yard," that stresses comedy and crazies. Danny Meechan (former soccer star Jones) is a disgraced pro player who winds up in prison on assault charges. The warden (Hemmings) wants Danny to coach the guards' soccer team instead of chief guard Burton (Brown), who will make Danny's life very difficult if he accepts. So Danny proposes a compromise—he'll train and coach an inmate team in a match against the guards. You can guess where this one is going but Jones and Statham (who plays a violent con) are worth watching. **98m/C; DVD.** *US UK* Vinnie Jones; Jason Statham; David Hemmings; Ralph Brown; David Kelly; Jason Flemyng; Danny Dyer; Vas Blackwood; John Forgeham; Robbie Gee; ***D:*** Barry Skolnick; ***W:*** Charlie Fletcher; Chris Baker; Andrew Day; ***C:*** John Murphy; ***M:*** Alex Barber.

Mean Season **1985 (R)** A vicious mass murderer makes a Miami crime reporter his confidante in his quest for publicity during his killing spree. In time, the madman's intentions become clear as the tensions and headlines grow with each gruesome slaying. Then the reporter must come to terms with the idea that he is letting himself be used due to the success that the association is bringing him. Suspenseful story with a tense ending. Good performance from Russell as the reporter. Screenplay written by Christopher Crowe under the pseudonym Leon Piedmont. **106m/C; VHS, DVD, Blu-Ray.** Kurt Russell; Mariel Hemingway; Richard Jordan; Richard Masur; Andy Garcia; Joe Pantoliano; Richard Bradford; William (Bill) Smith; ***D:*** Phillip Borsos; ***W:*** Christopher Crowe; ***M:*** Lalo Schifrin.

Mean Streets **1973 (R)** A grimy slice of street life in Little Italy among lower echelon Mafiosos, unbalanced punks, and petty criminals. Charlie (Keitel), the nephew of mob boss Giovanni (Danova), struggles to keep his crazy friend Johnny Boy (De Niro) out of serious trouble. A riveting, free-form feature film, marking the formal debut by Scorsese (five years earlier he had completed a student film, "Who's That Knocking At My Door?"). Unorthodox camera movement and gritty performances by De Niro and Keitel, with underlying Catholic guilt providing the moral conflict. Excellent early '60s soundtrack. **112m/C; VHS, DVD, Blu-Ray.** Harvey Keitel; Robert De Niro; David Proval; Amy Robinson; Richard Romanus; David Carradine; Robert Carradine; Cesare Danova; George Memmoli; Victor Argo; ***D:*** Martin Scorsese; ***W:*** Martin Scorsese; Mardik Martin; ***C:*** Kent Wakeford. Natl. Film Reg. '97; Natl. Soc. Film Critics '73: Support. Actor (De Niro).

The Meanest Man in Texas **2019** In 1920s Texas, Clyde Thompson (Ward), a minister's son, is set up for multiple murders by his girlfriend's brothers, convicted, and sentenced to death. Unexpectedly paroled to prison, he is hardened by the experience. In the harsh environment, he survives by acting violently and gaining a reputation for toughness. Clyde even gets a prison guard fired for not killing him when threatened. Clyde's life is profoundly changed when meets Julia Perryman (Bard), finds God, and becomes a Christian. This faith-based film, adapted from a novel about the real Thompson, is a bit too amateurish in its execution. **105m/C; DVD.** Mateus Ward; Jamie McShane; Alexandra Bard; Casey Bond; Ben Reed; ***D:*** Justin Ward; ***W:*** Justin Ward; Don Umphrey; ***C:*** Will Barratt; ***M:*** Steve Dorff.

The Meanest Men in the West **1967 (PG)** Two criminal half-brothers battle frontier law and each other. **92m/C; VHS, DVD.** Charles Bronson; Lee Marvin; Lee J. Cobb; James Drury; Albert Salmi; Charles Grodin; ***D:*** Samuel Fuller; ***W:*** Charles S. Dubin; ***C:*** Lionel Lindon; Alric Edens; ***M:*** Hal Mooney. **TV**

Meant to Be 1/2 **2012** The story of a young man searching for the mother who gave him up. **90m/C; DVD, Blu-Ray, Streaming.** Bradley Dorsey; Erika Eleniak; Eric Sossamon; Della Reese; Dean Cain; Michael Gross; ***D:*** Bradley Dorsey; ***W:*** Bradley Dorsey; Lori Marett; Marshal Younger; ***C:*** Roger Lindley; ***M:*** Will Musser. **VIDEO**

Meantime **1981** British TV comedy/drama about the working class finds brothers Mark (Daniels) and Colin (Roth) living with their unemployed dad in a depressing East London flat. Colin, who's looking to escape his dreary life, befriends skinhead Coxy (Oldman) to the dismay of the rest of the family. **90m/C; VHS, DVD, Blu-Ray.** *GB* Tim Roth; Gary Oldman; Phil Daniels; Alfred Molina; Pam Ferris; ***D:*** Mike Leigh; ***C:*** Roger Pratt; ***M:*** Andrew Dickson.

Meatballs **1979 (PG)** The Activities Director at a summer camp who is supposed to organize fun for everyone prefers his own style of "fun." If you enjoy watching Murray blow through a movie, you'll like this one even as it lapses into boxoffice sentimentality. **92m/C; VHS, DVD, Blu-Ray.** *CA* Bill Murray; Harvey Atkin; Kate Lynch; ***D:*** Ivan Reitman; ***W:*** Len Blum; Harold Ramis; Janis Allen; ***C:*** Donald Wilder; ***M:*** Elmer Bernstein. Genie '80: Actress (Lynch).

Meatballs 2 1/2 **1984 (PG)** The future of Camp Sasquatch is in danger unless the camp's best fighter can beat Camp Patton's champ in a boxing match. The saving grace of Bill Murray is absent in this one. **87m/C; VHS, DVD, Streaming.** Archie Hahn; John Mengatti; Tammy Taylor; Kim Richards; Ralph Seymour; Richard Mulligan; Hamilton Camp; John Larroquette; Paul (Pee-wee Herman) Reubens; Misty Rowe; Elayne Boosler; ***D:*** Ken Wiederhorn.

Meatballs 4 1/2 **1992 (R)** Feldman stars as a water skier hired to serve as recreation director of Lakeside Water Ski Camp. His enemy is Monica (Douglas) of a nearby rival camp who wants to buy out Lakeside's owner and use the land for real estate development. Lame plot only serves to showcase some good water skiing stunts. **87m/C; VHS, DVD.** Corey Feldman; Jack Nance; Sarah Douglas; Bojesse Christopher; ***D:*** Bob Logan.

The Mechanic 1/2 *Killer of Killers* **1972 (R)** Bronson stars as Arthur Bishop, a wealthy professional killer for a powerful organization. When old friend "Big Harry" comes to him for help against the organization, he becomes Bishop's next job. Harry's son then shows up, wanting Bishop to mentor him in the ways of a hit man. A little slow but well done. One of Bronson's better action outings. **100m/C; VHS, DVD, Blu-Ray.** Charles Bronson; Jan-Michael Vincent; Keenan Wynn; Jill Ireland; Linda Ridgeway; ***D:*** Michael Winner; ***W:*** Lewis John Carlino; ***C:*** Richard H. Kline; ***M:*** Jerry Fielding.

The Mechanic 1/2 **2011 (R)** Arthur Bishop (Statham) is a mechanic—an elite, emotionally-detached hitman, perfectly skilled to assassinate any target. When his mentor, Harry (Sutherland) is murdered, Harry's volatile son Steve (Foster) demands that Bishop teach him the business so he can get vengeance for his father's death. Accustomed to working alone, Bishop reluctantly takes Steve into his work—but no one can be trusted completely and the uneasy partnership threatens to explode. Strong performances, but the story and action sequences are movie cliches. Remake of the 1972 Charles Bronson flick. **100m/C; DVD, Blu-Ray, On Demand.** Jason Statham; Ben Foster; Donald Sutherland; Christa Campbell; Tony Goldwyn; Jeffrey Chase; Mini Anden; ***D:*** Simon West; ***W:*** Richard Wenk; Lewis John Carlino; ***C:*** Eric Schmidt; ***M:*** Mark Isham.

Mechanic: Resurrection **2016 (R)** This sequel nobody asked for opens with Statham's hit man Arthur Bishop in retirement in Rio de Janeiro. He's pulled out for another job when a woman finds him and says that her employer has three targets for him to kill. He refuses, but is attacked and basically forced to fight the man who claimed he wanted to hire him. Jones can't even pretend to care in a supporting role and Alba continues a career that seems designed to never be in a good movie. **98m/C; DVD, Blu-Ray.** Jason Statham; Jessica Alba; Tommy Lee Jones; Michelle Yeoh; Sam Hazeldine; ***D:*** Dennis Gansel; ***W:*** Philip Shelby; Tony Mosher; ***C:*** Daniel Gottschalk; ***M:*** Mark Isham.

The Medallion *Highbinders* **2003 (PG-13)** So-so actioner has Hong Kong cop Eddie (Chan) transformed into an immortal warrior with superhuman powers thanks to a mysterious medallion. Eddie teams up with British Interpol agents Watson (Evans) and the beautiful Nicole (Forlani) and travels to Dublin to learn the medallion's secrets, rescue a kidnapped holy child, and fight the evil Snakehead (Sands). Pic is watchable due to Chan's usual skills and considerable charm, but his signature brand of gymnastic-style martial-arts is undercut by digital enhancement and an unnecessary array of special effect, fast-motion sequences. **90m/C; VHS, DVD.** *US CH* Jackie Chan; Claire Forlani; Julian Sands; Lee Evans; John Rhys-Davies; Anthony Wong; Christy Chung; Johann Myers; ***D:*** Gordon Chan; ***W:*** Gordon Chan; Bey Logan; ***C:*** Arthur Wong Ngok Tai; ***M:*** Adrian Lee.

The Meddler **2015 (PG-13)** Writer/director Scafaria tells the deeply personal story of how she and her mother dealt with her father's death in this dramedy about something Hollywood typically avoids: grief. As writer Lori (Byrne) is retreating from her social circles, Marnie (Sarandon, her best performance in years) can't figure out what to do with herself. She has more money than she will ever need, throwing it at anyone who will ask, and she catches the eye of retired cop Zipper (Simmons). Scafaria's film is a gentle, sweet, and, most of all, heartfelt examination of mothers, daughters, and loss. **100m/C; DVD, Blu-Ray.** Susan Sarandon; Rose Byrne; J.K. Simmons; Jerrod Carmichael; Cecily Strong; ***D:*** Lorene Scafaria; ***W:*** Lorene Scafaria; ***C:*** Brett Pawlak; ***M:*** Jonathan Sadoff.

Meddling Mom **2013** Typical Hallmark Channel fluff. Widowed Carmen vega can't stop butting into the lives of grown daughters Yolanda and Ally. They try to set their mom up with ballroom dance teacher Luis so she'll have someone else to concentrate on but Carmen still manages to cause problems for Ally's boyfriend, Ben. And this time Carmen may have gone too far. **90m/C; DVD.** Sonia Braga; Mercedes Renard; Ana Ayora; Tony Plana; Rob Mayes; Saundra Santiago; ***D:*** Patricia Cardoso; ***W:*** Nina Weinman; ***C:*** Jens Piotrowski; ***M:*** Joseph Julian Gonzalez. **CABLE**

Medea 1/2 **1970** Cinema poet Pasolini directs opera diva Callas in this straightforward adaptation of Euripides's classic about a sorceress whose escapades range from assisting in the theft of the Golden Fleece to murdering her own children. Not Pasolini at his best, but still better than most if what you're looking for is something arty. In Italian with English subtitles. **118m/C; VHS, DVD, Blu-Ray.** *IT* Maria Callas; Guiseppi Gentile; Laurent Terzieff; ***D:*** Pier Paolo Pasolini.

Medea **1988** Director von Trier's adaptation of the classic Greek play by Euripides was filmed for Danish TV from a script originally co-written by Carl-Theodor Dreyer. Jason (Kier) betrays his lover Medea (Olesen) and their two sons when he agrees to a marriage with the daughter (Glinska) of King Creon (Jensen). Medea enacts a very bloody revenge. Danish with subtitles. **76m/C; VHS, DVD.** *DK* Udo Kier; Kirsten Olesen; Henning Jensen; Ludmilla Glinska; Baard Owe; ***D:*** Lars von Trier; ***W:*** Lars von Trier; Carl Theodor Dreyer; Preben Thomsen; ***C:*** Sejr Brockmann; ***M:*** Joachim Holbek. **TV**

Medicine for Melancholy **2008** Jenkins' feature debut offers stylish if momentary pleasures. After a drunken-party sexual encounter, upscale San Franciscan Joanne (Heggins) and downscale Micah (Cenac) share a cab, with Joanne making it clear that she's not interested in continuing their acquaintance. But when Micah returns her forgotten wallet, Joanne agrees to hang out although not much more happens than a contemplation of the city's housing woes and small African-American population. **88m/C; DVD.** Wyatt Cenac; Tracey Heggins; ***D:*** Barry Jenkins; ***W:*** Barry Jenkins; ***C:*** James Laxton.

Medicine Man **1992 (PG-13)** Connery's usual commanding presence and the beautiful scenery are the only things worth recommending. Dr. Robert Campbell (Connery) is a biochemist working in the Amazon rain forest on a cancer cure. Dr. Rae Crane's (Bracco) been sent by the institute sponsoring Campbell to see how things are going. Although Crane is uptight and Campbell is gruff, they fall in love (supposedly), but they're sorely lacking in chemistry. And the cancer cure is made from a rare flower being eradicated by the destruction of the rain forest. This politically correct cause meets romance falls short of ever being truly entertaining. **105m/C; VHS, DVD.** Sean Connery; Lorraine Bracco; Jose Wilker; Rodolfo de Alexandra; Francisco Tsirene Tsere Rereme; Elias Monteiro da Silva; ***D:*** John McTiernan; ***W:*** Tom Schulman; ***C:*** Donald McAlpine; ***M:*** Jerry Goldsmith.

The Medicine Show 1/2 **2001 (R)** Dark comedy in which sarcastic cartoon writer Taylor (Silverman) is diagnosed with colon cancer. As the disease, and treatment, progress, he views the reactions of co-workers and family, the absurdity of the hospital experience, and impending surgery with sardonic wit. (A welcome departure from the usual treacly, disease-of-the week approach.) The proceedings begin to lose their edge, however, when Taylor meets and romances cute, quirky leukemia patient Lynn. Silverman does an excellent job in the lead role. Based on the experiences of writer-director Morris. **100m/C; DVD.** Jonathan Silverman; Natasha Gregson Wagner; Greg Grunberg; Kari Wuhrer; Annabelle Gurwitch; Maz Jobrani; Dennis Libscomb; ***D:*** Wendell Morris; ***W:*** Wendell Morris; ***C:*** Ramsay Nickell. **CABLE**

Mediterranea **2015** Based on a true story, considers the dangerous struggles faced by refugees through the lives of two men from Africa seeking a better life in Europe. **107m/C; DVD.** Koudous Seihon; Alassane Sy; Pio Amato; Mary Elizabeth Innocence; Paolo Sciarretta; ***D:*** Jonas Carpignano; ***W:*** Jonas Carpignano; ***C:*** Wyatt Garfield; ***M:*** Dan Romer; Benh Zeitlin.

The Mediterranean in Flames 1/2 **1972** In Nazi-occupied Greece, a small but brave resistance is formed to fight its captors. One of the women within the group is forced to seduce a Nazi officer in an attempt to learn enemy secrets. **85m/C; VHS, DVD.** *GR* Costas Karras; Costas Precas; ***D:*** Dimis Dadiras.

The Medium **1951** A phony medium is done in by her own trickery in this filmed version of the Menotti opera. **80m/B; VHS, DVD.** Marie Powers; Anna Maria Alberghetti; Leo Coleman; ***D:*** Gian-Carlo Menotti; ***W:*** Gian-Carlo Menotti.

Medium Cool 1/2 **1969** Commentary on life in the '60s focuses on a TV news cameraman and his growing apathy with the events around him. His involvement with a Appalachian woman and her young son reawakens his conscience, leading to the three getting caught up in the turbulence of the 1968 Chicago Democratic convention. A frightening depiction of detachment in modern society. **111m/C; VHS, DVD, Blu-Ray.** Robert Forster; Verna Bloom; Peter Bonerz; Marianna Hill; Peter Boyle; Harold Blankenship; Charles Geary; Sid McCoy; Christine Bergstrom; William Sickingen; ***D:*** Haskell Wexler; ***W:*** Haskell Wexler; ***C:*** Haskell Wexler; ***M:*** Michael Bloomfield. Natl. Film Reg. '03.

Medium Raw: Night of the Wolf 1/2 **2010** Sometimes laughable dialogue doesn't badly hinder indie horror. Serial killer The Wolf (think Little Red Riding Hood) murdered Johnny Morgan's sister. After the killer is finally captured, Det. Carbon and cop Johnny get to see him incarcerated in an asylum for the criminally insane, where Johnny's wife Jamie happens to work. A power outage opens the cell doors for all freaks to do what they do best. **100m/C; DVD.** John Rhys-Davies; William B. Davis; Andrew Cymek; Brigitte Kingsley; Mercedes McNab; Andrew Martin; Jason Reso; ***D:*** Andrew Cymek; ***W:*** Andrew Cymek; ***C:*** Brad Smith; ***M:*** Emir Isilay. **VIDEO**

Medusa *Twisted* **1974** A bizarre series of events occur when an abandoned yacht containing two lifeless bodies is found on the Aegean Sea. **103m/C; VHS, DVD.** George Hamilton; Cameron Mitchell; Luciana Paluzzi; Theodore Roubanis; ***D:*** Gordon Hessler.

Medusa Against the Son of Hercules *Perseus the Invincible; Perseo l'Invincibile; Medusa vs. the Son of Hercules* **1962** This time the strongman takes on the evil Medusa and her deadly army of rock men. **90m/C; VHS, DVD.** *IT* Richard Harrison; Elisa Cegani; Anna Ranalli; Angel Jordan; ***D:*** Alberto De Martino; ***W:*** Mario Caiano; ***C:*** Eloy Mella; ***M:*** Carlo Franci.

The Medusa Touch **1978 (R)** A man is struck over the head and is admitted to a hospital. Meanwhile, strange disasters befall the surrounding city. It seems that despite his unconscious state, the man is using his telekinetic powers to will things to happen.... **110m/C; VHS, Blu-Ray, Streaming.** *GB* Richard Burton; Lino Ventura; Lee Remick; Harry Andrews; Alan Badel; Marie-Christine Barrault; Michael Hordern; Derek Jacobi; Jeremy Brett; ***D:*** Jack Gold; ***W:*** Jack Gold; John Briley.

Meek's Cutoff **2010 (PG)** Based on the true story of three families trudging through Oregon's Cascades Mountains during 1845, led by hired guide Stephen Meek (Greenwood). He guarantees them safety, loudly boasting detailed knowledge of the landscape. The would-be settlers push through an unmarked cutoff but suspect they are lost, uncertain of their guide's intentions. The journey's tensions compound once Meek captures a lone Indian (Rondeaux) and insists on killing him, though the others object. Director Reichardt's fascination with the day-to-day chores of these pioneers give a realistic feel and it's devoid of any typical

Western action. **101m/C; DVD, Blu-Ray.** Bruce Greenwood; Michelle Williams; Will Patton; Zoe Kazan; Paul Dano; Shirley Henderson; Neal Huff; Tommy Nelson; Rod Rondeaux; *D:* Kelly Reichardt; *W:* Jonathan Raymond; *C:* Christopher Blauvelt; *M:* Jeff Grace.

Meet Bill ♪♪ *Bill* **2007 (R)** Bill (Eckhart) is a pudgy, nice guy doormat. He works a dead-end job for his father-in-law, and his indifferent wife Jess (Banks) is having an affair with a sleazy local TV anchorman (Olyphant). Then he becomes a reluctant mentor to a self-assured prep student (Lerman) who encourages Bill to confront his mid-life crisis and go after what he wants—which happens to be a donut franchise. Alba pops up in the thankless role of a lingerie saleswoman who gives Bill fashion advice. About as memorable as its title, pic just never engages the viewer enough to care if Bill becomes his own man or not. **97m/C; DVD.** Aaron Eckhart; Jessica Alba; Elizabeth Banks; Logan Lerman; Timothy Olyphant; Holmes Osborne; Kristen Wiig; Jason Sudeikis; *D:* Bernie Goldman; Melisa Wallack; *W:* Melisa Wallack; *C:* Peter Lyons Collister; *M:* Ed Shearmur.

Meet Dave ♪ **2008 (PG)** Alien Commander Dave (Murphy) and his equally tiny crew land on Earth in their human-form spaceship, which looks just like Commander Dave. They're tasked with making Spaceship Dave move and act just like a human while searching for an orb that landed in Manhattan. The aliens are snobs, but eventually warm to the humans and make friends that help in their quest. The real laughs happen as Spaceship Dave wanders the city with the crew desperately pulling levers and pressing buttons, trying to figure out how to make Dave work. The physical comedy is funny, but the rest falls flat. **90m/C; DVD, Blu-Ray, On Demand.** Eddie Murphy; Elizabeth Banks; Gabrielle Union; Ed Helms; Judah Friedlander; Shawn Christian; Scott Caan; Marc Blucas; Pat Kilbane; Michael O'Malley; Kevin Hart; Austin Lind Myers; *D:* Brian Robbins; *W:* Bill Corbett; Rob Greenberg; *C:* Clark Mathis; *M:* John Debney.

Meet Dr. Christian ♪ ½ **1939** The good old doctor settles some problems. Part of a series. **72m/B; VHS, DVD.** Jean Hersholt; Robert Baldwin; Paul Harvey; *D:* Bernard Vorhaus.

Meet Him and Die ♪ ½ *Pronto ad Uccidere* **1976** Crazy Italian crime flick where the plot is secondary to the action. Cop Massimo Torlani (Lovelock) goes undercover in prison to get close to gangster leader Giulianelli (Balsam) in a revenge plot. He stages a breakout, which gets him a job with the boss, and then goes after rival Mafioso Perrone (Manni) by seducing his beautiful (and nameless) secretary (Sommer) who may not be trustworthy. Italian with subtitles. **94m/C; DVD, Blu-Ray.** *IT* Ray Lovelock; Elke Sommer; Martin Balsam; Ettore Manni; *D:* Franco Prosperi; *W:* Claudio Fragasso; *C:* Roberto D'Ettorre Piazzoli; *M:* Ubaldo Continiello.

Meet Joe Black ♪♪ **1998 (PG-13)** It's too long. And it's unremittingly hokey. But it does have the savvy Hopkins and Pitt in full desirable object mode. In this reworking of 1934's "Death Takes a Holiday," Pitt plays a not-so-Grim Reaper who decides to see what living is all about by inhabiting the body of a recently deceased man. He grants some extra time to wealthy businessman William Parrish (Hopkins), if he'll serve as Death's guide. Now named Joe Black, Death takes to his new life but causes problems in Parrish's household, especially when he falls in love with Parrish's doctor daughter, Susan (a weak Forlani). **180m/C; DVD, Blu-Ray, HD-DVD.** Brad Pitt; Anthony Hopkins; Claire Forlani; Marcia Gay Harden; Jeffrey Tambor; Jake Weber; *D:* Martin Brest; *W:* Ron Osborn; Jeff Reno; Kevin Wade; Bo Goldman; *C:* Emmanuel Lubezki; *M:* Thomas Newman.

Meet John Doe ♪♪♪ **1941** A social commentary about an unemployed, down-and-out man selected to be the face of a political goodwill campaign. Honest and trusting, he eventually realizes that he is being used to further the careers of corrupt politicians. Available in colorized version. **123m/B; VHS, DVD.** Gary Cooper; Barbara Stanwyck; Edward Arnold; James Gleason; Walter Brennan; Spring Byington; Gene Lockhart; Regis Toomey; Ann Doran; Rod La Rocque; *D:* Frank Capra; *W:* Robert Riskin; Robert Presnell, Sr.; *C:* George Barnes; *M:* Dimitri Tiomkin.

Meet Market ♪ ½ **2008 (R)** Obvious comedy about the dating scene. L.A. singles hang out at the local grocery store on Saturday nights hoping to meet like-minded shoppers. Oblivious soap star Hutch (McMahon), dweeby screenwriter Danny (Tudyk), kooky Jane (Tyler) and her best friend, cynic Lucinda (Allen), and would-be actress Linda (Berkley) are among the selections. Squeeze at your own risk. **80m/C; DVD.** Julian McMahon; Alan Tudyk; Krista Allen; Aisha Tyler; Elizabeth Berkley; Missi Pyle; Laurie Holden; Susan Egan; Jennifer Sky; *D:* Charles Loventhal; *W:* Charles Loventhal; *C:* David Robbins; Steven Fierberg. **VIDEO**

Meet Me After the Show ♪♪ ½ **1951** Musical comedy has Broadway star Delilah (Grable) realizing her producer husband Jeff (Carey) is fooling around, so she quits his show. Feigning amnesia, she returns to Miami where she strated out and begins a romance with local playboy David (Calhoun). Jeff tracks her down, is jealous, but Delilah takes a lot of wooing to win back. **86m/C; DVD.** Betty Grable; MacDonald Carey; Rory Calhoun; Eddie Albert; Fred Clark; Lois Andrews; Irene Ryan; *D:* Richard Sale; *W:* Richard Sale; Mary Loos; *C:* Arthur E. Arling; *M:* Ken Darby.

Meet Me in St. Louis ♪♪♪ ½ **1944** Wonderful music in this charming tale of a St. Louis family during the 1903 World's Fair. One of Garland's better musical performances. **113m/C; VHS, DVD, Blu-Ray.** Judy Garland; Margaret O'Brien; Mary Astor; Lucille Bremer; Tom Drake; June Lockhart; Harry Davenport; *D:* Vincente Minnelli; *C:* George J. Folsey. Natl. Film Reg. '94.

Meet Mr. Callaghan ♪ ½ **1954** Cynthia (Johns) gets suspicious when she learns that her wealthy, elderly uncle suddenly changed his will in her favor so she hires hard-boiled PI Slim Callaghan (de Marney) to investigate. He discovers that the uncle is already dead, so who rewrote the will? Based on the novel by Peter Cheyney. **88m/B; DVD.** *GB* Derrick DeMarney; Harriette Johns; Peter Neil; Adrienne Corri; Trevor Reid; *D:* Charles Saunders; *W:* Brock Williams; *C:* Harry Waxman; *M:* Eric Spear.

Meet Monica Velour ♪♪ ½ **2010 (R)** Cartoonish fantasy about awkward teen Tobe (Ingram), who heads to his nearby Indiana strip club to meet his '80s porn idol, Monica Velour (Cattrall), dead set on losing his virginity to the aging star. His aspirations are slightly tainted when the two meet and Tobe gets a glimpse of the real life of a woman pushing 50, living in a trailer, and in the middle of an ugly custody battle. Cattrall owns the screen, projecting an indefinable sexuality both as an outdated sex goddess and single mother. Surprisingly sweet and innocent, avoiding cheap teen sex cliches. **97m/C; DVD, Blu-Ray.** Kim Cattrall; Dustin Ingram; Brian Dennehy; Keith David; Jee Young Han; Daniel Yelsky; Jamie Tisdale; *D:* Keith Bearden; *W:* Keith Bearden; *C:* Masanobu Takayanagi; *M:* Andrew Hollander.

Meet Nero Wolfe ♪♪ **1936** Rex Stout's sleuth makes his first screen appearance (adapted from Stout's novel "Fer de Lance") and your enjoyment will depend on how believable you find Arnold in the title role, with Stander as his assistant Archie Goodwin. The corpulent, orchid-growing, beer-drinking detective works to discover if the deaths of a college dean and a mechanic are related. Rita Hayworth has a small role, originally billed under her real name—Rita Cansino. **73m/B; DVD.** Edward Arnold; Lionel Stander; Dennie Moore; Victor Jory; Nana Bryant; Joan Perry; Russell Hardie; Boyd Irwin; *D:* Herbert Biberman; *W:* Joseph Anthony; Howard J. Green; Bruce Manning; *C:* Henry Freulich; *M:* Howard Jackson.

Meet the Blacks ♪♪ **2016 (R)** An African American-focused parody of the Purge series of films. When Carl Black (Epps), the patriarch of his family, comes into a large sum of money, he decides that his family should move from inner city Chicago to a well-to-do neighborhood in Beverly Hills to live a better life. Soon after they move in, the Blacks soon find themselves caught up the city's annual purge during which all crime is legal for 12 hours. **94m/C; DVD, Blu-Ray, Streaming, Download.** Mike Epps; Gary Owen; Zulay Henao; Bresha Webb; Lil Duval; *D:* Deon Taylor; *W:* Deon Taylor; Nicole DeMasi; *C:* John T. Connor; *M:* RZA.

Meet the Deedles ♪ ½ **1998 (PG)** Phil and Stew Deedle (Walker and Van Wormer) are two rich surfer airheads who just wanna have fun, dude. The twins are forced to attend the bogus Camp Broken Spirit where they fall on a plot device and wake up in the hospital, mistaken for rookie Yellowstone park rangers there to fight a prairie dog problem. It seems that bitter ex-ranger Slater (Hopper, phoning in his patented mondo-weirdo) has enslaved the rodents and is trying to redirect the geyser Old Faithful. Features heinous dialogue and stunts lifted from Mountain Dew commercials. **94m/C; DVD, Streaming.** Steve Van Wormer; Paul Walker; A.J. (Allison Joy) Langer; John Ashton; Dennis Hopper; Eric Braeden; Richard Lineback; Robert Englund; Ana Gasteyer; Megan Cavanagh; *D:* Steve Boyum; *W:* Jim Herzfeld; Dale Pollock; *C:* David Hennings; *M:* Steve Bartek.

Meet the Feebles ♪♪ **1989** Sex and violence gorefest perpetuated by puppets—and the dementia of director Jackson. A TV variety show, populated by animal puppets and humans in costume, is the setting for backstage mayhem, including sex, drugs, and a shooting spree. Among the characters are a sleazy walrus producer, his slinky Siamese cat mistress, a junkie frog, and a manic-depressive elephant. There's also several musical production numbers, if things aren't strange enough for you already. **94m/C; VHS, DVD.** *NZ V:* Peter Vere-Jones; Mark Hadlow; Stuart Devine; Donna Atkinson; Mark Wright; Brian Sergent; *D:* Peter Jackson; *W:* Peter Jackson; Danny Mulheron; Fran Walsh; Stephen Sinclair; *C:* Murray Milne; *M:* Peter Dasent.

Meet the Fockers ♪♪ ½ **2004 (PG-13)** Free-spirited Jews meet uptight WASPs in this sequel to 2000's "Meet the Parents." Nervous Greg Focker (Stiller) and fiancee Pam (Polo) take Dina (Danner) and Jack (De Niro) to finally meet his folks: lawyer turned house hubby Bernie (Hoffman) and senior citizen sex therapist Roz (Streisand). The duo extravagantly adores each other, much to Greg's embarrassment, and of course, there's more cat issues and a baby to create more problems for poor Greg. Culture clashes follow predictably and everyone seems to be coasting comfortably on their talent. **116m/C; VHS, DVD, Blu-Ray, HD-DVD.** Robert De Niro; Ben Stiller; Dustin Hoffman; Barbra Streisand; Blythe Danner; Teri Polo; Tim Blake Nelson; Alanna Ubach; Ray Santiago; Kali Rocha; Shelley Berman; Owen Wilson; Spencer Pickren; Bradley Pickren; *D:* Jay Roach; *W:* Jim Herzfeld; John Hamburg; *C:* John Schwartzman; *M:* Randy Newman.

Meet the Guilbys ♪♪ *Paris Willouby* **2015** A comedy-drama about a family road trip full of unexpected humor. When Claire's (Carre) father dies, she and her husband Maurice (De Groodt) take their blended family on a road trip to the funeral. Clair's son Alex (Lacourt) is a vegetarian and fond of Maurice's teenage rebel daughter Lucie (Japy). Prune (Audiard), Claire and Maurice's daughter, becomes obsessed with the cows she sees in the country. Though the family is close knit, the trip itself proves hilariously challenging. French with subtitles. **83m/C; DVD.** Isabelle Carre; Stephane De Groodt; Alex Lutz; Josephine Japy; Aminthe Audiard; *D:* Arthur Delaire; Quentin Reynaud; *W:* Arthur Delaire; Quentin Reynaud; *C:* Yannick Ressigeac; *M:* Gush. **VIDEO**

Meet the Hollowheads ♪ ½ **1989 (PG-13)** Family situation comedy set in a futuristic society. **89m/C; VHS, DVD.** John Glover; Nancy Mette; Richard Portnow; Matt Shakman; Juliette Lewis; Anne Ramsey; *D:* Tom Burman; *W:* Tom Burman.

Meet the Navy ♪♪ **1946** Post-war musical revue about a pianist and a dancer. **81m/B; VHS, DVD.** Lionel Murton; Margaret Hurst; John Pratt; Robert Goodier; *D:* Alfred Travers; *W:* Lester Cooper; *C:* Ernest Palmer; Geoffrey Unsworth; *M:* Louis Silvers.

Meet the Parents ♪♪♪ **2000 (PG-13)** If you have any empathy at all, you'll be squirming uncomfortably for Greg (Stiller), a nice Jewish boy who suffers an extended brainlock when he meets his girlfriend Pam's (Polo) WASPy parents during her sister's wedding weekend. It doesn't help that her father Jack (De Niro) is an ex-CIA profiler who takes an immediate dislike to his prospective son-in-law. Greg starts off on the wrong foot by accidentally smashing the urn holding the ashes of Jack's mother, and his luck goes down from there. The rest of the cast perform well, especially Danner as Pam's mother, and De Niro plays off of his tough guy image for a brilliant comedic performance. **108m/C; VHS, DVD, Blu-Ray, HD-DVD.** Ben Stiller; Robert De Niro; Teri Polo; Blythe Danner; James Rebhorn; Jon Abrahams; Owen Wilson; Phyllis George; Kali Rocha; Thomas (Tom) McCarthy; Nicole DeHuff; *D:* Jay Roach; *W:* Jim Herzfeld; John Hamburg; *C:* Peter James; *M:* Randy Newman.

Meet the People ♪♪ **1944** Patriotic propaganda in a musical setting. Shipyard welder William Swanson (Powell) writes a patriotic play and it's optioned by Broadway star Julie Hampton (Ball) who wants to make it into a musical. Hearing this, Swanson withdraws his consent and she is left to prove to him that she's just folks and can make his play work. **100m/B; DVD.** Lucille Ball; Dick Powell; Virginia O'Brien; Bert Lahr; Rags Ragland; June Allyson; Steven Geray; *D:* Charles Riesner; *W:* Sid Herzig; Fred Saidy; *C:* Robert L. Surtees.

Meet the Robinsons ♪♪ ½ **2007 (G)** Based on William Joyce's book "A Day With Wilbur Robinson," which finds young science geek Lewis despairing of ever being adopted. But his luck changes thanks to teenager Wilbur Robinson and his time machine. Wilbur takes Lewis into the future to meet his eccentric family, but everyone's dreams are threatened by the sinister man in the bowler hat, who's got it out for Lewis. The jovial T-Rex, who's meant to aid the bad guy, is a scene-stealer. Hyperactive animated comedy is the first release by Disney in its Digital 3-D process. **102m/C; DVD, Blu-Ray.** *V:* Jordan Fry; Angela Bassett; Tom Selleck; Harland Williams; Daniel Hansen; Wesley Singerman; Laurie Metcalf; Adam West; Nicole Sullivan; Stephen John Anderson; *D:* Stephen John Anderson; *W:* Jon Bernstein; Donald Hall; Stephen John Anderson; Michelle Spitz; Nathan Greno; Aurian Redson; Joe Mateo; *M:* Danny Elfman.

Meet the Spartans WOOF! **2008 (PG-13)** Brain-dead spoof of the hardly cerebral but ripe for parody "300" swords-and-sandals epic hangs on the story of Leonidas (Maguire) leading his fierce army of 13 into battle against the invading hordes of Xerxes (Davitian), supported by his Queen Margo (Electra). But plot hardly matters as Seltzer and Friedberg once again scrape the bottom of the pop-culture barrel for a make-it-stop string of lazy swipes at movies and celebs buoyed by body-function gags and gay jokes that barely bother to be funny, let alone subversive. Way too long and way too dumb. **83m/C; DVD, Blu-Ray.** Carmen Electra; Ken Davitian; Kevin Sorbo; Diedrich Bader; Sean Maguire; Method Man; Phil Morris; Travis Van Winkle; Jareb Dauplaise; *D:* Aaron Seltzer; Jason Friedberg; *W:* Aaron Seltzer; Jason Friedberg.

Meet the Stewarts ♪♪ ½ **1942** Modest rom com with a familiar plot. Young lawyer Michael Stewart (Holden) and wealthy daddy's girl Candace Goodwin (Dee) get married after Candy insists she can live on Mike's modest means. She can't, hides the truth, and the newlyweds have issues. **74m/B; DVD.** William Holden; Frances Dee; Grant Mitchell; Marjorie Gateson; Anne Revere; Margaret Hamilton; *D:* Alfred E. Green; *W:* Karen DeWolf; *C:* Henry Freulich; *M:* Leo Shuken.

Meet Wally Sparks ♪♪ **1997 (R)** No-brow "Man Who Came to Dinner." Smutty TV shock-talk host Sparks (Dangerfield) is given one week to save his failing show. Opportunity knocks when he's invited to a party at the governor's mansion to interview the conservative head honcho (Stiers). Once there, a freak accident with a drunken horse prevents Sparks from leaving and the new guest makes himself at home by turning the fancy digs into a broadcast studio. Dangerfield's machine gun spray of one liners occasionally hits, as do his sometimes lengthy and elaborately set up jokes, but not much beyond Rodney makes lackluster "Sparks" fly.

107m/C; VHS, DVD. Rodney Dangerfield; David Ogden Stiers; Burt Reynolds; Debi Mazar; Cindy Williams; Alan Rachins; ***D:*** Peter Baldwin; ***W:*** Rodney Dangerfield; Harry Basil; ***C:*** Richard H. Kline; ***M:*** Michel Colombier.

Meeting at Midnight 🦴🦴 **1944** Charlie Chan is invited to a seance to solve a perplexing mystery. Chan discovers that they use mechanical figures and from there on solving the murder is easy. **67m/B; VHS, DVD.** Sidney Toler; Joseph Crehan; Mantan Moreland; Frances Chan; Ralph Peters; Helen Beverly; ***D:*** Phil Rosen.

Meeting Daddy 🦴🦴 **1/2 1998 (R)** Neurotic New Yorker Peter (Charles) falls in love with Georgia peach Melanie (Wentworth) and then he travels to Savannah to meet her southern-fried family, including her eccentric, irascible father, The Colonel (Bridges). **91m/C; VHS, DVD.** Lloyd Bridges; Josh Charles; Alexandra Wentworth; Beau Bridges; Walter Olkewicz; Kristy Swanson; ***D:*** Peter Gould; ***W:*** Peter Gould; ***C:*** Mike Mayers; ***M:*** Adam Fields. **VIDEO**

Meeting Evil 🦴 **2012 (R)** Nonsensical psycho-thriller, based on the 1992 Thomas Berger novel, which wastes a good cast. Financially troubled failed family man John (Wilson) meets charismatic stranger Richie (Jackson) who brings the clueless man along on what turns out to be a crime spree. Naturally, the cops believe John is the criminal and he can't seem to find his backbone to prove his innocence. **89m/C; DVD.** Luke Wilson; Samuel L. Jackson; Leslie Bibb; Peyton List; Tracie Thoms; Muse Watson; ***D:*** Chris Fisher; ***W:*** Chris Fisher; ***C:*** Marvin V. Rush; ***M:*** Ryan Beveridge. **VIDEO**

Meeting Spencer 🦴 **1/2 2011 (R)** Single set, real time showbiz comedy is helped along by Tambor's performance as a Broadway director who failed in Hollywood. Harry Chappell (Tambor) sweeps into a famed New York restaurant with a chance to resurrect his career with a new play. He's meeting various people, including struggling actor Spencer (Plemons), and becomes the center of attention as everyone wants to know what's going on. **88m/C; DVD, Blu-Ray.** Jeffrey Tambor; Melinda McGraw; Jesse Plemons; Yvonne Zima; Jill Marie Jones; Caroline Aaron; William Morgan Sheppard; Julian Bailey; ***D:*** Malcolm Mowbray; ***W:*** Andrew Kole; Andrew Delaplaine; Scott Kasdin; ***C:*** Paula Huidobro; ***M:*** Stephen Coates.

Meeting Venus 🦴🦴 **1/2 1991 (PG-13)** Backstage drama featuring Close as Karin Anderson, a world-famous Swedish opera diva. An international cast of characters adds to this sophisticated film of romance, rivalry and political confrontation set amidst a newly unified Europe. **121m/C; VHS, DVD.** Glenn Close; Niels Arestrup; Erland Josephson; Johanna Ter Steege; Maria De Medeiros; Ildiko Bansagi; Macha Meril; Dorottya Udvaros; Jay O. Sanders; Victor Poletti; ***V:*** Kiri Te Kanawa; ***D:*** Istvan Szabo; ***W:*** Istvan Szabo; Michael Hirst; ***C:*** Lajos Koltai.

The Meg 🦴🦴 **2018 (PG-13)** Jonas Taylor (Statham) was once the world's best deep sea rescue diver until a failed rescue, which included an encounter with a mysterious creature, led him to spend years living low in Thailand. When Jonas's ex-wife (McNamee) is trapped in a research sub far below the sea and seems to have been attacked in the same way, Jonas agrees to help save her. Traveling to a underwater research facility near Shanghai, Jonas learns that a megalodon, a massive shark believed to be extinct, is behind both events. This adaptation of Steven Alten's best-selling novel is no Jaws but a predictable, yet escapist, thriller. **113m/C; DVD, Blu-Ray.** Jason Statham; Li Bingbing; Rainn Wilson; Clifford Curtis; Winston Chao; ***D:*** Jon Turteltaub; ***W:*** Dean Georgaris; Jon Hoeber; Erich Hoeber; ***C:*** Tom Stern; ***M:*** Harry Gregson-Williams.

Mega Piranha 🦴 **1/2 2010** Energetically bad creature feature (from the Syfy channel) has apparently incompetent scientist Sarah Monroe (Tiffany) genetically experimenting with Venezuelan piranha so they'll grow larger and become a viable food source. They grow into giant mutant killers, escape, and start swimming and eating their way towards Miami even as covert action man Fitch (Logan) is sent to South America to check things out. **90m/C; DVD.** Tiffany; Paul Logan; Barry Williams; David Labiosa; Jude Gerard Prest; Jesse Daly; ***D:*** Eric Forsberg; ***W:*** Eric Forsberg; ***C:*** Brian Olinger; ***M:*** Chris Ridenhour. **CABLE**

Mega Python Vs. Gatoroid 🦴 **2011** The most fun fight isn't between the giant pythons threatening the alligators of the Florida Everglades but between eco-activist and snake expert Nikki Riley (Gibson) and Parks and Rec officer Terry O'Hara (Tiffany). Both ladies are totally incompetent at their jobs, but this is a Syfy original so you expect that and much worse, which also happens. **91m/C; DVD.** Tiffany; Deborah Gibson; A. Martinez; Kathryn Joosten; Kevin M. Horton; Carey Van Dyke; ***Cameo(s):*** Mickey Dolenz; ***D:*** Mary Lambert; ***W:*** Naomi L. Selfman; ***C:*** Troy Smith; ***M:*** Chris Ridenhour. **CABLE**

Mega Shark vs. Crocosaurus 🦴 **1/2 2010 (R)** The scientifically impossible shark from the first film has apparently survived his fight with the Giant Octopus, so the military comes up with the brilliant idea to fight it by using newly awakened 1500' crocodile. **89m/C; DVD, Blu-Ray, Streaming.** Gary Stretch; Jaleel White; Sarah Lieving; Robert Picardo; Gerald Webb; ***D:*** Christopher Ray; ***W:*** Micho Rutare; Naomi L. Selfman; ***C:*** Alexander Yellen; ***M:*** Chris Ridenhour. **VIDEO**

Mega Shark Vs. Giant Octopus 🦴 **1/2 2009 (R)** Well, doesn't the title just say it all. Two Ice Age sea critters get thawed out and the octopus attacks Tokyo while the shark goes after San Francisco. It takes international cooperation (via submarine) to end the madness by getting the two together for a mega-confrontation. Sushi and calamari for everyone! **90m/C; DVD, Blu-Ray.** Lorenzo Lamas; Deborah Gibson; Vic Chao; Sean Lawlor; Jonathan Nation; ***D:*** Jack Perez; ***W:*** Jack Perez; ***C:*** Alexander Yellen; ***M:*** Chris Ridenhour. **VIDEO**

Megafault WOOF! 2009 So whose fault is it that this Syfy original is so lame? Seismologist Amy Lane (Murphy) is giving a lecture on earthquakes when one hits a mining community in West Virginia. A massive new fault line is opened and continues cracking its way westward, leading Amy to come up with various ridiculous-sounding plans to apparently prevent the U.S. from breaking in two. **90m/C; DVD, Blu-Ray.** Brittany Murphy; Eriq La Salle; Bruce Davison; Paul Logan; Justin Hartley; ***D:*** David Michael Latt; ***W:*** Paul Bales; ***C:*** Adam Silver; ***M:*** Ralph Rieckermann. **CABLE**

Megalodon 🦴🦴 **2003 (PG-13)** Prehistoric 11-ton shark, Carchardodon Megalodon, is rudely awakened by unsuspecting deep-sea oil diggers and he's not in the mood to make nice with the trespassers. **91m/C; VHS, DVD.** Robin Sachs; Al Sapienza; Leighanne Littrell; Mark Sheppard; Jennifer Sommerfield; Evan Mirand; Steve Scionti; Gary J. Tunnicliffe; Fred Belford; Yasmine Delawari; Stanley Isaacs; Will Boroers; John Michael Mauer; ***D:*** Pat Corbitt; ***W:*** Gary J. Tunnicliffe; Stanley Isaacs; ***C:*** Timothy Housel; ***M:*** Tony Fennell; Billy T. James; Brian Randazzo. **VIDEO**

Megamind 🦴🦴🦴 **2010 (PG)** Animated spoof of the super hero flick finds a clever spark, thanks to a great cast, in a genre that is quickly running out of energy. Super villain Megamind (Ferrell) is continuously thwarted from taking over Metro City by insufferably smug hero Metro Man (Pitt). When he accidentally kills his rival, Megamind gets bored and decides to create a new foe. He uses his big blue brain to convert a dorky cameraman named Hal (Hill) into a new archenemy. Hal would rather be a bad guy than a good guy, however, so Megamind switches sides. The two battle each other for control of the city and the hand of perky reporter Roxanne (Fey). **96m/C; Blu-Ray.** ***V:*** Will Ferrell; Brad Pitt; Tina Fey; Jonah Hill; David Cross; Ben Stiller; Justin Theroux; ***D:*** Tom McGrath; ***W:*** Alan Schoolcraft; Brent Simons; ***M:*** Lorne Balfe; Hans Zimmer.

Megan Is Missing 🦴 **2011** Nasty exploitation in the guise of warning about online sexual predators. Mixes various electronic footage (news reports, webcam, videos) with the banal online chats of best friends Megan and Amy. Popular 14-year-old Megan is a party girl while 13-year-old Amy is socially awkward. Megan starts an internet relationship with allegedly 17-year-old Josh, agrees to meet him, and disappears. Three weeks later, Amy goes missing as well. **86m/C; DVD.** Rachel Quinn; Amber Perkins; Dean Waite; April Stewart; John Fraizer; Tammy Klein; ***D:*** Michael Goi; ***W:*** Michael Goi; ***C:*** Keith Eisberg; Josh Harrison. **VIDEO**

Megan Leavey 🦴🦴 **1/2 2017 (PG-13)** The true story of a marine (Mara) and her bomb-sniffing partner, Rex. Cowperthwaite's feature directorial debut pays due respect to both the sacrifice of soldiers and the canine-human bond, and gives us a hero that you'll want to salute as well as scratch behind the ears. Have a tissue handy. **116m/C; DVD, Blu-Ray.** Kate Mara; Tom Felton; Ramon Rodriguez; Bradley Whitford; Edie Falco; ***D:*** Gabriela Cowperthwaite; ***W:*** Pamela Gray; Annie Mumolo; Tim Lovestedt; ***C:*** Lorenzo Senatore; ***M:*** Mark Isham.

Megasnake 🦴 **1/2** ***Mega Snake*** **2007 (R)** Ah yes, another Sci-Fi Channel original (with some decent CGI). In a backwater town filled with snakes and snake handlers, dimwit Duff steals a very rare snake to add to his collection. It must be super-snake because, given the chance, it grows and grows and grows until it can swallow a man in a single gulp. Having escaped Duff, Megasnake heads off to have some fun at the county fair (and we don't mean elephant ears and ring toss). **90m/C; DVD, On Demand.** Michael Shanks; Siri Baruc; Mick Harvey; Ben Cardinal; John T. Woods; Matthew Atherton; ***D:*** Tibor Takacs; ***W:*** Rob Robinson; Alexander Volz; ***C:*** Emil Topuzov; ***M:*** Guy Zerafa; Dave Klotz. **CABLE**

Melancholia 🦴🦴🦴 **2011 (R)** Director Von Trier's most notable accomplishment since "Breaking the Waves" features a career-best performance from Dunst as Justine, a woman woefully afflicted by depression, much like the controversial writer/director. Turning his own emotional disorder into art, Von Trier crafts a sci-fi melodrama about a planet called Melancholia that's about to crash into Earth. Told in two equal halves, the first act of the film centers on Justine's doomed wedding to Michael (Skarsgard) and the second on her family's reaction and sister's (Gainsbourg) denial of their eventual annihilation. **135m/C; DVD, Blu-Ray.** ***DK FR GE SW*** Kirsten Dunst; Charlotte Gainsbourg; Alexander Skarsgård; Brady Corbet; John Hurt; Charlotte Rampling; Stellan Skarsgard; Kiefer Sutherland; Jesper Christensen; Udo Kier; ***D:*** Lars von Trier; ***W:*** Lars von Trier; ***C:*** Manuel Alberto Claro.

Melinda and Melinda 🦴🦴 **2005 (PG-13)** Allen sticks to the familiar in a talky tale of Manhattanites chattering over dinner. Comedic playwright Sy (Shawn) and tragedienne Max (Pine) entertain themselves with an urban anecdote about an unhappy, neurotic woman named Melinda (Mitchell). In both stories she crashes the dinner party of friends with her tale of disaster, causing marital misunderstandings. The leading males in the story are both ineffectual, unemployed actors (Miller, Ferrell) while their wives (Sevigny, Peet) are successful. Despite the talent involved, it's all rather too precious and rarefied an atmosphere to take much interest. **99m/C; DVD.** Radha Mitchell; Chloë Sevigny; Jonny Lee Miller; Will Ferrell; Amanda Peet; Chiwetel Ejiofor; Wallace Shawn; ***D:*** Woody Allen; ***W:*** Woody Allen; ***C:*** Vilmos Zsigmond.

Melissa 🦴🦴 **1997** Unemployed reporter Guy Foster (Dutton) is trying to make a new career as a novelist. But when his wife Melissa (Ehle) is murdered, all the evidence points to Guy and he has to find the real killer to prove his innocence. Based on the novel by Francis Durbridge. **150m/C; DVD.** ***GB*** Tim Dutton; Jennifer Ehle; Adrian Dunbar; Julie Walters; Faith Edwards; Hugh Quarshie; Diana Weston; ***D:*** Bill Anderson; ***W:*** Alan Bleasdale; ***C:*** Dick Dodd; ***M:*** Richard Harvey. **TV**

Melo 🦴🦴 **1986** The title is short for "melodrama" so you know exactly when sort of story you're in for. Discontented Romaine begins an affair with womanizing concert violinist Marcel, an old friend of her boring husband Pierre's. While Marcel is away on tour, Pierre becomes seriously (and suspiciously) ill. When Romaine's perfidy is discovered, she commits suicide. However, years later, Pierre demands the truth from Marcel. French with subtitles. **112m/C; DVD, Blu-Ray.** ***FR*** Sabine Azema; Pierre Arditti; Andre Dussollier; Fanny Ardant; Jacques Dacqmine; ***D:*** Alain Resnais; ***W:*** Alain Resnais; ***C:*** Charlie Van Damme; Michel Philippe-Gerard.

Melody 🦴🦴 **1971 (G)** Sensitive but slow study of a special friendship which enables two pre-teens to survive in a regimented and impersonal world. Features music by the Bee Gees. **106m/C; VHS, DVD.** ***GB*** Tracy Hyde; Jack Wild; Mark Lester; Colin Barrie; Roy Kinnear; ***D:*** Waris Hussein; ***W:*** Alan Parker.

Melody for Three 🦴🦴 **1941** In the tradition of matchmaker, Doctor Christian aids in the reuniting of music-teacher mother and great-conductor father, who have been divorced for years, in order to help the couple's son, a violin prodigy. **69m/B; VHS, DVD.** Jean Hersholt; Fay Wray; ***D:*** Erle C. Kenton.

Melody Master 🦴🦴 ***New Wine*** **1941** Romanticized biography of composer Franz Schubert, chronicling his personal life and loves, along with performances of his compositions. If you just have to know what drove the composer of "Ave Maria" it may hold your interest, but otherwise not very compelling. **80m/B; VHS, DVD.** Alan Curtis; Ilona Massey; Binnie Barnes; Albert Bassermann; Billy Gilbert; Sterling Holloway; ***M:*** Miklos Rozsa.

Melody Ranch 🦴 **1/2 1940** Gene returns to his home town as an honored guest and appointed sheriff. But gangster MacLane is determined to drive him out of town. **84m/C; VHS, DVD.** Gene Autry; Jimmy Durante; George "Gabby" Hayes; Ann Miller; Barton MacLane; Joseph (Joe) Sawyer; Horace McMahon; Veda Ann Borg; ***D:*** Joseph Santley. Natl. Film Reg. '02.

Melody Time 🦴🦴🦴 **1948** Seven animated/musical tales from the Disney studios, including "Blame It On the Samba" with Donald Duck; "Once Upon a Wintertime;" "Bumble Boogie;" "Johnny Appleseed;" "Little Toot" with musical narration provided by the Andrews Sisters; Fred Waring and the Pennsylvanians singing "Trees," the Joyce Kilmer poem; and Roy Rogers narrating the story of "Pecos Bill." **75m/C; VHS, DVD.** Roy Rogers; ***V:*** Dennis Day; Ethel Smith; Buddy Clark; Bob Nolan; Andrews Sisters; Frances Langford; ***D:*** Clyde Geronimi; Wilfred Jackson; Jack Kinney; Hamilton Luske; ***C:*** Winton C. Hoch.

Meltdown 🦴🦴 ***High Risk; Shu Dan Long Wei*** **1995** This action/comedy revolves around drunken action star Frankie (Cheung) who claims to do all of his own stunts but uses a team of stuntmen, including former cop Kit Li (Li), whose wife and son were killed (in a particularly ridiculous opening sequence) by an evil criminal mastermind (Wong). Who, with his gang, turns up to steal the Russian crown jewels that are being exhibited in a Hong Kong hotel. Think slapstick "Die Hard," although it's virtually impossible for western audiences to figure out where the action ends and the comedy begins. **100m/C; DVD.** ***CH*** Jet Li; Jacky Cheung; Chingmy Yau; Valerie Chow; Charlie Yoeh; Kelvin Wong; ***D:*** Wong Jing; ***W:*** Wong Jing.

Meltdown WOOF! 2006 Which is what you'll want to do to the DVD after you've wasted your time on this lame "Armageddon-is-a-comin'" flick. Scientist blows up an asteroid endangering earth, but the fragments push our planet's orbit closer to the sun, causing intense global warming and evacuations to the Arctic. Uh, isn't all that ice supposed to melt? What do these people have—an ark? Maybe the hungry polar bears will get to them first. **93m/C; DVD.** Casper Van Dien; Stefanie von Pfetten; Venus Terzo; Amanda Crew; Vincent Gale; Ryan McDonell; ***D:*** J.P. Howell; ***W:*** Rick Drew; ***C:*** Adam Sliwinski; ***M:*** Ron Ramin. **CABLE**

Melvin and Howard 🦴🦴🦴 **1/2 1980 (R)** Story of Melvin Dummar, who once gave Howard Hughes a ride. Dummar later claimed a share of Hughes's will. Significant for Demme's direction and fine acting from Steenburgen/LeMat, and Robards in a small role as Hughes. Offbeat and very funny. **95m/C; VHS, DVD, Blu-Ray.** Paul LeMat; Jason Robards, Jr.; Mary Steenburgen; Michael J. Pollard; Dabney Coleman; Elizabeth Cheshire; Pamela Reed; Cheryl "Rainbeaux" Smith; ***D:*** Jonathan Demme; ***W:*** Bo Goldman; ***C:*** Tak Fujimoto; **M:** Bruce Langhorne. Oscars '80: Orig. Screenplay, Support. Actress (Steenburgen); Golden Globes '81: Support. Actress (Steenburgen); L.A. Film Critics '80: Support. Actress (Steenburgen); N.Y. Film Critics '80: Director (Demme), Screenplay, Support. Actress (Steenburgen); Natl. Soc. Film Critics '80: Film, Screenplay, Support. Actress (Steenburgen); Writers Guild '80: Orig. Screenplay.

Melvin Goes to Dinner ♪♪ **2003 (R)** Joey (Price) invites Melvin (Blieden) and Alex (Courtney) to dinner as a way of catching up; they are also unexpectedly joined by Alex's friend Sarah (Gurwitch). Since each person is a stranger to at least one other person at the table, there's a certain awkwardness at first, but then the conversation (often confessional) starts to flow. Oh, and despite the title, the characters are not actually shown dining, so at least you won't get hungry, although all the talking may make you sleepy. **83m/C; VHS, DVD.** Michael Blieden; Stephanie Courtney; Matt Price; Annabelle Gurwitch; Maura Tierney; **D:** Bob Odenkirk; **W:** Michael Blieden; **C:** Alex Vendler; **M:** Michael Penn.

Melvin Purvis: G-Man ♪♪ *The Legend of Machine Gun Kelly; Kansas City Massacre* **1974** Mediocre action film has dedicated federal agent tracking killer Machine Gun Kelly across American Midwest during Depression. **78m/C; VHS, Streaming.** Dale Robertson; Harris Yulin; Margaret Blye; Matt Clark; Elliot Street; Dick Sargent; John Karlen; David Canary; **D:** Dan Curtis. **TV**

The Member of the Wedding ♪♪♪ **1952** While struggling through her adolescence, 12-year-old tomboy Frankie (played by 26-year-old Harris) is growing up in 1945 Georgia and seeking solace from her family's cook, Berenice (Waters) and her cousin, John Henry (de Wilde). Based on Carson McCullers's play, this story of family, belonging, and growth is well acted and touching. **90m/C; VHS, DVD, Blu-Ray.** Ethel Waters; Julie Harris; Brandon de Wilde; Arthur Franz; William Hansen; Nancy Gates; James Edwards; Harry Bolden; **D:** Fred Zinnemann; **W:** Edward Anhalt; **C:** Hal Mohr; **M:** Alex North.

Memento ♪♪♪ 1/2 **2000 (R)** Twisty and engaging noir thriller of a man searching for his wife's killer in LA. Only problem is, Leonard Shelby (Pearce) lost his short-term memory after the attack and forgets all current events every 15 minutes, or so. Problem solved as Shelby tattoos the most vital info all over his body and leaves other clues for himself on Post-Its and Polaroids of his suspects. Ingeniously constructed story is told backwards, from Shelby's shooting of the killer to his puzzle-like construction of events and renders the audience as clueless as the impaired hero, but it's worth the effort. Director Nolan adapted the film from short story by brother Jonathan. **116m/C; DVD, Blu-Ray.** Guy Pearce; Carrie-Anne Moss; Joe Pantoliano; Mark Boone, Jr.; Stephen Tobolowsky; Callum Keith Rennie; Harriet Sansom Harris; Jorja Fox; **D:** Christopher Nolan; **W:** Christopher Nolan; **C:** Wally Pfister; **M:** David Julyan. Ind. Spirit '02: Director (Nolan), Film, Screenplay, Support. Actress (Moss); L.A. Film Critics '01: Screenplay; Natl. Film Reg. '17; Broadcast Film Critics '01: Screenplay.

Memento Mori ♪♪ *Yeogo Goedam 2* **2000 (R)** The second film in the Ghost School trilogy. The central story has Min-Ah discovering a diary detailing a torrid lesbian affair between two of her classmates, Shi-eun and Hyo-Shin. The strange diary has many hidden passages and, eventually, Min-Ah starts calling off sick to go through it all. When Hyo-Shin appears to commit suicide, Min-Ah shows the diary to friends and they try to find out what really happened. It's then that the hallucinations and unusual occurrences start, and Min-Ah suddenly realizes the diary is more than it seems. **94m/C; DVD.** *NK* Ji-yeon Park; Min-sun Kim; Yeh-jin Park; Young-jin Lee; Jong-hak Baek; Jae-in Kim; Hyo-jin Kong; Min Han; Seung-Yeon Han; Hye-mi Lee; Seong-Eon Lim; **D:** Tae-Yong Kim; Kyu-Dong Min; **W:** Tae-Yong Kim; Kyu-Dong Min; **C:** Yoon-soo Kim; **M:** Sun-woo Jo.

Memoirs of a Geisha ♪♪ **2005 (PG-13)** This look into the world of Japan's "Geisha" escorts in the 1930s flounders thanks to Marshall's bizarre decision to cast the film with Chinese actors and shoot it in the U.S. Sayuri (Zhang) is sold into a geisha household, where her companionship skills are refined by Mameha (Yeoh), the chief rival of the household's "Mother" (Momoi). Sayuri begins relishing her role as a renowned geisha, and the predictable plot grows in both heft and velocity, straining audience patience with it's long running time and melodrama. **137m/C; DVD, Blu-Ray, UMD.** Ken(saku) Watanabe; Michelle Yeoh; Koji Yakusho; Youki Kudoh; Tsai Chin; Cary-Hiroyuki Tagawa; Gong Li; Randall Duk Kim; Mako; Kenneth Tsang; Shizuko Hoshi; Ziyi Zhang; Kaori Momoi; Suzuka Ohgo; Thomas Ikeda; Zoe Weizenbaum; **D:** Rob Marshall; **W:** Robin Swicord; **C:** Dion Beebe; **M:** John Williams. Oscars '05: Art Dir./Set Dec., Cinematog., Costume Des.; British Acad. '05: Cinematog., Costume Des., Orig. Score; Golden Globes '06: Orig. Score; Natl. Bd. of Review '05: Support. Actress (Li); Broadcast Film Critics '05: Orig. Score.

Memoirs of an Invisible Man ♪ 1/2 **1992 (PG-13)** Nick Halloway, a slick and shallow stock analyst, is rendered invisible by a freak accident. When he is pursued by a CIA agent-hit man who wants to exploit him, Nick turns for help to Alice, a documentary filmmaker he has just met. Naturally, they fall in love along the way. Effective sight gags, hardworking cast can't overcome pitfalls in script, which indecisively meanders between comedy and thrills. **99m/C; DVD, Blu-Ray.** Chevy Chase; Daryl Hannah; Sam Neill; Michael McKean; Stephen Tobolowsky; Jim Norton; Patricia Heaton; Rosalind Chao; **D:** John Carpenter; **W:** Robert Collector.

Memorial Day ♪♪ 1/2 **2012 (R)** Earnest indie drama deals with two generations of military men amidst a coming of age story and numerous flashbacks. In 2005, while recovering from wounds suffered in Iraq, Sgt. Kyle Vogel (Bennett) remembers a 1993 Memorial Day he spent with his grandfather, Bud (a stellar James Cromwell), as the old man reluctantly described some of his WWII combat experiences as a young soldier (John Cromwell). Rather drawn-out ending leaves some ambiguity as to both men's subsequent feelings about doing their military duty. **104m/C; DVD, Blu-Ray.** Jonathan Bennett; James Cromwell; John Cromwell; Jackson Bond; Emily Fradenburgh; **D:** Samuel Fischer; **W:** Marc Conklin; **C:** Bo Hakala; **M:** Paul Hartwig. **VIDEO**

Memorial Valley Massacre ♪ **1988 (R)** When campers settle for a weekend in a new, unfinished campground, they're slaughtered in turn by a nutty hermit. **93m/C; VHS, DVD.** Cameron Mitchell; William (Bill) Smith; John Kerry; Mark Mears; Lesa Lee; John Caso; **D:** Robert C. Hughes.

Memories of Me ♪♪ **1988 (PG-13)** A distraught doctor travels to L.A. to see his ailing father and make up for lost time. Both the doctor and his father learn about themselves and each other. Story of child/parent relationships attempts to pull at the heartstrings but only gets as far as the liver. Co-written and co-produced by Crystal, this film never quite reaches the potential of its cast. **103m/C; VHS, DVD, Blu-Ray.** Billy Crystal; Alan King; JoBeth Williams; David Ackroyd; Sean Connery; Janet Carroll; Angela Clarke; **D:** Henry Winkler; **W:** Billy Crystal; Eric Roth; **M:** Georges Delerue.

Memories of Murder ♪♪ *Salinui chueok* **2003** Effective South Korean thriller based on a true incident. In 1986, the body of a young woman is found raped and murdered in a backwater town near Seoul. The two local detectives, Park (Song) and Jo (Rwe-ha Kim), are ill-equipped to deal with what turns into bizarre serial killings in a country where multiple homicides are a rarity. An experienced big city cop, Seo (Sang-kyung Kim), shows up and clashes with the others. Frustration mounts as bodies continue to be found (until 1991, in fact) and the investigation drags on. A coda is set in 2003. Korean with subtitles. **132m/C; DVD.** *NK* Song Kang-ho; Kim Sang-gyeong; Kim Roi-ha; Song Jae-ho; Byeon Heui-bong; Ryu Tae-ho; Park Noh-shik; Park Hae-il; **D:** Bong Joon-ho; **W:** Bong Joon-ho; Shim Seong-bo; **C:** Kim Hyeong-gu; **M:** Taro Iwashiro.

Memory ♪ **2006 (R)** Nonsensical story with Zane chewing scenery. While in Brazil, Dr. Taylor Briggs (Zane) accidentally ingests a hallucinogen that a local tribe uses in rituals that bestow memories of the user's ancestors. But Taylor has visions of little girls being kidnapped and killed and hopes to discover who's behind the crimes. Hmmmm, could it be someone close to him? **98m/C; DVD, Blu-Ray.** Billy Zane; Tricia Helfer; Ann-Margret; Dennis Hopper; Terry Chen; **D:** Bennett Davlin; **W:** Bennett Davlin; Anthony Badalucco; **C:** Peter Benison; **M:** Anthony Marinelli; Clint Bennett.

A Memory In My Heart ♪ 1/2 **1999** An implausible TV movie about amnesia that depends too much on silly coincidences and unbelievable situations. Rebecca's (Seymour) marriage to Joe (Martinez) has always been marred by her amnesia. When she starts having panic attacks, a chance meeting leads her to a nearby town where her abusive ex Chase (Davison) lives as well as the three kids who were told she was dead. Chase would really like to make that happen. **91m/C; DVD.** Jane Seymour; Bruce Davison; A. Martinez; Amanda Barfield; Colton James; Mika Boreem; David Keith; Cathy Lee Crosby; **D:** Harry Winer; **W:** Lindsay Harrison; Renee Longstreet; **C:** Donald M. Morgan; **M:** Mark Snow. **TV**

The Memory Keeper's Daughter ♪♪ **2008** Lifetime cable drama based on the best-selling novel by Kim Edwards. Dr. David Henry (Mulroney) is horrified when he sees that one of the twins his wife Norah (Mol) has just delivered has Down's Syndrome. Afraid of the toll the care of a special needs child will take, David tells his wife their daughter was stillborn and arranges for attending nurse Caroline (Watson) to take the baby to an institution. Horrified by the conditions she finds, Caroline decides to keep the child and immediately moves away to begin a new life. But the circumstances will haunt everyone for more than 20 years. **90m/C; DVD.** Dermot Mulroney; Gretchen Mol; Emily Watson; Hugh Thompson; Hope Nausbaum; Paul Henry; **D:** Mick Jackson; **W:** John Pielmeier; **M:** Daniel Licht. **CABLE**

The Memory of a Killer ♪♪ *The Alzheimer Affair; De Zaak Alzheimer* **2003 (R)** Kinky crime thriller takes places in 1995 when tough, aging hitman Angelo (Declair) travels to Antwerp for a job. But when he won't fulfill his contract, his employers turn on him. Angelo may be in the early stages of Alzheimer's (which he realizes) but he's still not a guy you mess with. There's a nasty tie-in to a child prostitution ring and blackmail that has local cop Vincke (De Bouw) working the case and he and Angelo soon cross paths. In Flemish and French with English subtitles. **120m/C; DVD.** Jan Decleir; Werner De Smedt; Gene Bervoets; Koen de Bouw; Jo de Meyere; Tom Van Dyck; **D:** Erik van Looy; **W:** Erik van Looy; **C:** Danny Elsen; Carl Joos; **M:** Stephen Warbeck.

Memphis Belle ♪♪♪ **1990 (PG-13)** Satisfying Hollywood version of the same-titled documentary captures the true story of the final mission of a WWII bomber crew stationed in England. The Memphis Belle B-17 crewmen were the first to complete a 25 mission tour—no small feat in an air war that claimed many lives. Good ensemble cast of young actors; Lithgow has a nice turn as an army PR guy determined to exploit their charms on the homefront. Caton-Jones effectively uses 1940s film techniques and some original footage, making up for a rather hokey script. Produced by Catherine Wyler, whose father, Wlliam Wyler, made the original. **107m/C; DVD, Blu-Ray.** Matthew Modine; John Lithgow; Eric Stoltz; Sean Astin; Harry Connick, Jr.; Reed Edward Diamond; Tate Donovan; D.B. Sweeney; Billy Zane; David Strathairn; Jane Horrocks; Courtney Gains; Neil Giuntoli; **D:** Michael Caton-Jones; **W:** Monte Merrick; **C:** David Watkin; **M:** George Fenton.

Memron WOOF! **2004** Thoroughly unfunny attempt at a mockumentary of the Enron scandal. The bankrupt company's CEO (McShane) is locked away at a country club prison where he spends his time practicing his golf swing. Meanwhile, his greedy wife (Forlani) spends what cash is left, and the company's former employees (all of whom seem to be mentally challenged) scramble to find new jobs. **79m/C; DVD.** Michael McShane; Claire Forlani; Mary Pat Gleason; Tim Bagley; John Lehr; David Wiater; Joey Slotnik; **D:** Nancy Hower; **W:** Nancy Hower; Robert Stark Hickey; **C:** Nancy Hower; **M:** Steven Argila. **CABLE**

The Men ♪♪♪ 1/2 *Battle Stripe* **1950** A paraplegic WWII veteran sinks into depression until his former girlfriend manages to bring him out of it. Marlon Brando's first film. A thoughtful story that relies on subtle acting and direction. **85m/B; DVD, Blu-Ray.** Marlon Brando; Teresa Wright; Everett Sloane; Jack Webb; **D:** Fred Zinnemann; **W:** Carl Foreman; **C:** Robert De Grasse; **M:** Dimitri Tiomkin.

Men ♪♪ *Some Girl* **1997 (R)** Aspiring chef Stella James (Young) is encouraged by best friend Teo (Dylan Walsh) to move from New York to L.A. in search of romance. Stella promptly lands a job and gets involved with George (Heard), the restaurant's owner. However, a new man, photographer Frank (Hillman), comes onto the scene and Stella decides she likes him too. But what she thinks will be another casual encounter becomes unexpectedly serious. Based on the novel by Margaret Diehl. **93m/C; VHS, DVD.** Sean Young; John Heard; Dylan Walsh; Richard Hillman; Karen Black; **D:** Zoe Clarke-Williams; **W:** Zoe Clarke-Williams; Karen Black; **C:** Susan Emerson; **M:** Mark Mothersbaugh.

Men Against the Sky ♪ 1/2 **1940** Pilot Phil Mercedes (Dix) loses his license and reputation due to his drinking. When his sister, Kay (Barrie), gets a job at failing McLean Aircraft, Phil helps her re-work some of his old designs to use for the company's experimental plane and then hopes to redeem his reputation by test flying the new aircraft. Lots of aerial camerawork make this RKO programmer mildly interesting. **75m/B; DVD.** Richard Dix; Wendy Barrie; Kent Taylor; Edmund Lowe; **D:** Leslie Goodwins; **W:** Nathanael West; **C:** Frank Redman.

Men & Chicken ♪♪ 1/2 *Maend & hons* **2015** A dark, eccentric comedy-drama about unexpected family relationships and deep secrets. After their father dies, brothers Gabriel (Dencik) and Elias (Mikkelsen) learn from his will that they are really adopted half-brothers. The socially awkward brothers decide to find their biological father. Locating him on a self-contained island, the duo learns they have three more half-brothers with their own issues. As Gabriel and Elias become part of this new family, they stumble onto a family secret that draws them all together. Danish with subtitles. **104m/C; Blu-Ray, Streaming, Download.** David Dencik; Mads Mikkelsen; Nikolaj Lie Kaas; Soren Malling; Nicolas Bro; **D:** Anders Thomas Jensen; **W:** Anders Thomas Jensen; **C:** Sebastian Blenkov; **M:** Frans Bak; Jeppe Kaas.

Men at Work ♪♪ **1990 (PG-13)** Garbage collectors Sheen and Estevez may not love their work, but at least it's consistent from day to day. That is, until they get wrapped up in a very dirty politically motivated murder. And who will clean up the mess when the politicians are through trashing each other? A semi-thrilling semi-comedy that may leave you semi-satisfied. **98m/C; VHS, DVD, Blu-Ray.** Charlie Sheen; Emilio Estevez; Leslie Hope; Keith David; **D:** Emilio Estevez; **W:** Emilio Estevez; **C:** Tim Suhrstedt; **M:** Stewart Copeland.

Men Don't Leave ♪♪ 1/2 **1989 (PG-13)** A recent widow tries to raise her kids single-handedly, suffers big city life, and takes a chance at a second love. Good performances by all, especially Cusack as the sweet seducer of teenaged O'Donnell. By the director of "Risky Business." **115m/C; VHS, DVD.** Jessica Lange; Arliss Howard; Joan Cusack; Kathy Bates; Charlie Korsmo; Corey Carrier; Chris O'Donnell; Tom Mason; Jim Haynie; **D:** Paul Brickman; **W:** Barbara Benedek; Paul Brickman; **C:** Bruce Surtees; **M:** Thomas Newman.

Men in Black ♪♪♪ *MIB* **1997 (PG-13)** Charm, wit and some outrageous insect-type aliens make a winning cosmic combination. K (Jones) and J (Smith) are top-secret government operatives, investigating alien visitations on Earth, who must stop a terrorist extraterrestrial from causing a galactic disaster. Excellent chemistry between deadpan leads strengthened by a very funny script. Director Sonnenfeld tops it off with just enough detail and human element to keep the special effects from stealing the show, and with Rick Baker around, that's not easy to do. Adapted from the Marvel comic book. **98m/C; DVD, Blu-Ray.** Tommy Lee Jones; Will Smith; Linda Fiorentino; Rip Torn; Vincent

D'Onofrio; Tony Shalhoub; Carel Struycken; Sergio Calderon; Siobhan Fallon Hogan; *D:* Barry Sonnenfeld; *W:* Edward Solomon; *C:* Don Peterman; *M:* Danny Elfman. Oscars '97: Makeup; MTV Movie Awards '98: Fight (Will Smith/alien), Song ("Men in Black").

Men in Black 2 2002 (PG-13) K (Jones) had returned to civilian life at the end of the first film (with no memory of his past life), while J (Smith) went on with the men in black. When evil alien Serleena (Boyle) takes the entire MiB hostage, lone escapee J must convince K to help him save the galaxy. So-so effort suffers from lackluster script and doesn't have the spark of the original, but is helped along by solid performances all around. There are plenty of amusing scenes, mostly provided by the supporting players (especially the talking dog). **88m/C; DVD, Blu-Ray.** Tommy Lee Jones; Will Smith; Lara Flynn Boyle; Johnny Knoxville; Rosario Dawson; Rip Torn; Tony Shalhoub; Patrick Warburton; Jack Kehler; David Cross; Colombe Jacobsen; Peter Spellos; Lenny Venito; ***Cameo(s):*** Michael Jackson; Martha Stewart; Peter Graves; *V:* Tim Blaney; *D:* Barry Sonnenfeld; *W:* Robert Gordon; Barry Fanaro; *C:* Greg Gardiner; *M:* Danny Elfman.

Men in Black 3 1/2 2012 (PG-13) It took 10 years to get another sequel but the government agents are back in black (and in 3D). When Agent K's (Jones in 2012, Brolin in 1969) life is in danger from a notorious interstellar maniac (Clement), his longtime partner Agent J (Smith) must learn his partner's secrets and travel back to the 1960s to team up with a young Agent K to save the future. A fun third installment for fans of the series, though probably not enough for a fourth. Newcomer Brolin breathes life into the flick with his impersonation of co-star Jones from two other films. **106m/C; DVD, Blu-Ray, Streaming.** Will Smith; Tommy Lee Jones; Josh Brolin; Jemaine Clement; Emma Thompson; Alice Eve; David Rasche; Michael Stuhlbarg; *D:* Barry Sonnenfeld; *W:* Etan Cohen; David Koepp; *C:* Bill Pope; *M:* Danny Elfman.

Men in Black: International 1/2 2019 (PG-13) After a childhood encounter with an alien and the Men in Black, adult Molly (Thompson) seeks out the agency, gets hired by Agent O (Thompson), dubbed Agent M, and sent to London. There, M meets the rogueish Agent H (Hemsworth). M and H are charged with protecting an important alien, the party-friendly Vungus the Ugly (Novak), who possesses a highly destructive weapon, but fail and must find the weapon and save their agency. The film has a poorly written script that ignores the rules of the franchise and lacks surprises. Though Thompson and Hemsworth's have some chemistry, their characters are a bit drab. **114m/C; DVD, Blu-Ray.** Chris Hemsworth; Tessa Thompson; Kumail Nanjiani; Rebecca Ferguson; Rafe Spall; *D:* F. Gary Gray; *W:* Matt Holloway; Art Marcum; *C:* Stuart Dryburgh; *M:* Chris Bacon; Danny Elfman.

Men in War 1/2 1957 Korean War drama about a small platoon trying to take an enemy hill by themselves. A worthwhile effort with some good action sequences. **100m/B; VHS, DVD, Blu-Ray.** Robert Ryan; Robert Keith; Aldo Ray; Vic Morrow; Phillip Pine; Nehemiah Persoff; James Edwards; L.Q. Jones; Scott Marlowe; Adam Kennedy; Race Gentry; Walter Kelley; Anthony Ray; Robert Normand; Michael Miller; Victor Sen Yung; *D:* Anthony Mann; *W:* Philip Yordan; Ben Maddow; *C:* Ernest Haller; *M:* Elmer Bernstein.

Men in White 1934 Dedicated physician George Ferguson (Gable) is engaged to wealthy Laura Hudson (Loy) who wants him to spend more time with her by taking up a society practice. While on the outs with Laura, George has a fling with nurse Barbara (Allan), who gets pregnant. She has a back-alley abortion and dies, which makes George and Laura both realize that he needs to do more serious work. Adapted from the Sidney Kingsley play. The first of several pairings for Gable and Loy. **73m/B; DVD.** Clark Gable; Myrna Loy; Jean Hersholt; Elizabeth Allan; Otto Kruger; C. Henry Gordon; Henry B. Walthall; *D:* Richard Boleslawski; *W:* Waldemar Young; *C:* George J. Folsey; *M:* William Axt.

Men Men Men *Uomini Uomini Uomini* 1995 Quartet of gay friends are permanent Peter Pans. Never having grown up, they extend their adolescence in a series of increasingly vicious pranks at the expense of both strangers and friends. But eventually they're forced to re-examine their behavior. Very funny, if certainly non-pc, comedy. Italian with subtitles. **84m/C; VHS, DVD.** *IT* Christian de Sica; Massimo Ghini; Leo Gullotta; Alessandro Haber; Monica Scattini; Paco Reconti; *D:* Christian de Sica; *W:* Christian de Sica; *C:* Gianlorenzo Battaglia; *M:* Manuel De Sica.

The Men Next Door 1/2 2012 Low-budget, light-hearted rom com. Gay Pilates instructor Doug (Dean) isn't happy about turning 40, until he meets two very different men. Fifty-year-old Jacob (Nicklin) came out later in life and 30-year-old Colton (Lutz) is literally the guy next door. What Doug doesn't know is that the two have a relationship that puts him in the middle of an oddball romantic triangle. **84m/C; DVD.** Eric Dean; Michael Nicklin; Benjamin Lutz; Heidi Rhodes; *D:* Rob Williams; *W:* Rob Williams; *C:* Paul D. Hart; *M:* Jake Monaco. **VIDEO**

Men of Boys Town 1/2 1941 Sequel to 1938's "Boys Town" has the same sentimentality, even more if that's possible. Father Flanagan's reformatory faces closure, while the kids reach out to an embittered new inmate. Worth seeing for the ace cast reprising their roles. **106m/B; VHS, DVD.** Spencer Tracy; Mickey Rooney; Darryl Hickman; Henry O'Neill; Lee J. Cobb; Sidney Miller; *D:* Norman Taurog.

Men of Honor 1/2 *Navy Diver* 2000 (R) Based on the true story of Carl Brashear, the first African-American to break the color barrier in the U.S. Navy's diving program. A straightforward no-frills tribute with Brashear (Gooding) the very embodiment of perseverence, as shown in his rise from sharecropper's son to military man. De Niro plays Billy Sunday (a composite character), a racist training officer whose discrimination nearly kills Brashear before he earns Sunday's respect. As Brashear's career advances, Sunday's declines due to drunkenness and insubordination. When Brashear loses his leg in the line of duty, the now-recovered Sunday helps him retrain using a prosthetic leg. **129m/C; DVD, Blu-Ray.** Cuba Gooding, Jr.; Robert De Niro; Charlize Theron; David Keith; Michael Rapaport; Hal Holbrook; Powers Boothe; Aunjanue Ellis; Joshua Leonard; David Conrad; Glynn Turman; Holt McCallany; Lonette McKee; Carl Lumbly; *D:* George Tillman, Jr.; *W:* Scott Marshall Smith; *C:* Anthony B. Richmond; *M:* Mark Isham.

Men of Respect 1991 (R) Shakespeare meets the mafia in this misbegotten gangster yarn. Turturro, a gangster MacBeth, is prodded by wife and psychic to butcher his way to the top o' the mob. Well acted but ill conceived, causing Bard's partial roll over in grave. **113m/C; VHS, DVD.** John Turturro; Katherine Borowitz; Peter Boyle; Dennis Farina; Chris Stein; Steven Wright; Stanley Tucci; *D:* William Reilly; *W:* William Reilly; *C:* Bobby Bukowski.

Men of the Fighting Lady 1/2 *Panther Squadron* 1954 Action-adventure offers plenty of exciting battle footage. Features the stories of selected pilots stationed on a U.S. aircraft carrier in the Pacific during the Korean War. The stories, told to Calhern as writer James A. Michener, center around the lead pilot Johnson. Dramatic airflights include a scene in which Johnson helps a blinded Martin land his plane safely on the carrier deck. Gene Ruggerio's editing of the war footage was so expertly done that he was questioned by the Pentagon when they had a hard time believing the scenes were achieved by skillful editing and painted backdrops. Look for "Beaver" Mathers as one of Wynn's sons. **81m/C; DVD.** Van Johnson; Walter Pidgeon; Louis Calhern; Dewey Martin; Keenan Wynn; Frank Lovejoy; Robert Horton; Bert Freed; Lewis Martin; Dick Simmons; *D:* Andrew Marton; *W:* Art Cohn; *C:* George J. Folsey; *M:* Miklos Rozsa.

Men of the Sea 1/2 *Midshipman Easy* 1935 Low-budget Brit swashbuckler, set in the 18th-century, finds teenager Jack Easy joining the British Navy aboard the HMS Harpy and having lots of adventures, including rescuing a young woman from pirates and finding a treasure-laden Spanish ship. **70m/B; DVD.** *GB* Margaret Lockwood; Roger Livesey; Hughie Green; Dennis Wyndham; Harry Tate; *D:* Carol Reed; *W:* Anthony Kimmins; Peggy Thompson; *C:* John Boyle; *M:* Ernest Irving; Frederic Austin.

Men of War 1/2 1994 (R) Ex-Special Forces mercenaries decide to defend, rather than destroy, the inhabitants of an exotic island, whose land is wanted by a suspicious company interested in mining rights. **102m/C; VHS, DVD, Blu-Ray.** Dolph Lundgren; Charlotte Lewis; B.D. Wong; Anthony John (Tony) Denison; Tim Guinee; Don Harvey; Tommy (Tiny) Lister; Trevor Goddard; Kevin Tighe; *D:* Perry Lang; *W:* John Sayles; Ethan Reiff; Cyrus Voris; *C:* Ronn Schmidt; *M:* Gerald Gouriet.

Men On Her Mind 1/2 1944 Lily has always wanted success as a singer and when she leaves the orphanage she pursues her career as well as romance although her love life doesn't work out. When she becomes a star, Lily has the opportunity to choose between her three previous suitors. **67m/B; DVD.** Mary Beth Hughes; Edward Norris; Alan Edwards; Ted North; Luis Alberni; Kay Linaker; Lyle Latell; *D:* Wallace Fox; *W:* Raymond L. Schrock; *C:* Robert E. Cline; *M:* Lee Zahler.

The Men Who Stare at Goats 2009 (R) The sort of film that proves 'military intelligence' is an oxymoron. Journalist Bob Wilton (McGregor) goes to Kuwait City in 2003 looking for a war story. He's been told about a secret government op to utilize psychic abilities and that the lead loon is named Cassady (Clooney)--who does stare at goats. Wilton persuades Cassady to take him along on his secret mission to Iraq to find the missing founder (Bridges) of the New Age psychic soldiers. A strong cast almost makes this meandering film watchable. Based on events in journalist Jon Ronson's 2004 nonfiction work of the same name. **94m/C; DVD.** George Clooney; Ewan McGregor; Jeff Bridges; Kevin Spacey; Rebecca Mader; Robert Patrick; Stephen Lang; Stephen (Steve) Root; Glenn Morshower; *D:* Grant Heslov; *W:* Peter Straughan; *C:* Robert Elswit; *M:* Rolfe Kent.

Men with Brooms 1/2 2002 Goofy Canadian comedy about curling. In the small mining town of Long Bay, curling player/coach Donald Foley (Douglas) has just died (although his narration continues throughout the pic). At his funeral, members of his last team reunite and decide to reform the team and compete for the Golden Broom curling championship trophy in Foley's honor. Among them are oil roughneck Chris (Gross), who convinces his eccentric dad Gordon (Nielsen) to coach the team. **102m/C; DVD.** *CA* Paul Gross; Molly Parker; Peter Outerbridge; Leslie Nielsen; James Allodi; James B. Douglas; Polly Shannon; Jed Rees; Michelle Nolden; Barbara Gordon; Kari Matchett; Jane Spidell; *D:* Paul Gross; *W:* Paul Gross; John Krizanc; *C:* Thom Best; *M:* Paul Gross; Jack Lenz.

Men with Wings 1/2 1938 Aviation ace Wellman does a Technicolor drama for flyboys. Daredevil barnstormer Pat marries childhood sweetie Peggy, who's also loved by their mutual pal, airplane designer Scott. After his aerial battles in WWI, Pat can't settle to civilian life, takes off for China, and leaves Peggy behind. Scott's there to comfort her. **102m/C; DVD.** Fred MacMurray; Ray Milland; Louise Campbell; Andy Devine; Lynne Overman; *D:* William A. Wellman; *W:* Robert Carson; *C:* Theodor Sparkuhl.

Men, Women & Children 1/2 2014 (R) Wearing its heart boldly on its sleeve, this desperate plea to break free from social media and the technology that disconnects us from one another means well, but is almost too silly to be taken seriously. A talented ensemble cast ranging from Thompson to Garner to the likes of Sandler attempt to navigate the new information superhighway and raise their children properly. From Internet porn addiction to mothers who police cyberspace with an iron fist, director Reitman employs cute graphics to ease the intensity of his patronizing melodrama. Occasionally funny and light, but ultimately a weak antisocial take on social media. **119m/C; DVD, Blu-Ray.** Adam Sandler; Rosemarie DeWitt; Travis Tope; Olivia Crocicchia; Judy Greer; Jennifer Garner; Kaitlyn Dever; Ansel Elgort; Dean Norris; Elena Kampouris; *D:* Jason Reitman; *W:* Jason Reitman; Erin Cressida Wilson; *C:* Eric Steelberg.

Menace on the Mountain 1970 (G) Family-oriented drama about a father and son who battle carpetbagging Confederate deserters during the Civil War. **89m/C; VHS, DVD.** Pat(ricia) Crowley; Albert Salmi; Charles Aidman; Jodie Foster; Dub Taylor; Richard Anderson; Mitch Vogel; *D:* Vincent McEveety.

Menace II Society 1/2 1993 (R) Portrayal of black teens lost in inner-city hell is realistically captured by 21-year-old twin directors, in their big-screen debut. Caine (Turner) lives with his grandparents and peddles drugs for spending money, from the eve of his high school graduation to his decision to escape south-central LA for Atlanta. Bleak and haunting, with some of the most unsettling, bloodiest violence ever shown in a commercial film. Disturbing to watch, but critcally acclaimed. The Hughes' make their mark on contemporary black cinema with intensity, enhanced by an action-comics visual flair. **104m/C; DVD.** Tyrin Turner; Larenz Tate; Samuel L. Jackson; Glenn Plummer; Julian Roy Doster; Bill Duke; Charles S. Dutton; Jada Pinkett Smith; Vonte Sweet; Ryan Williams; *D:* Allen Hughes; Albert Hughes; *W:* Tyger Williams; *C:* Lisa Rinzler. Ind. Spirit '94: Cinematog.; MTV Movie Awards '94: Film.

Menage *Tenue de Soiree* 1986 Depardieu is the homosexual crook who breaks into the home of an impoverished couple—the dominating Miou-Miou and her submissive husband, Blanc. An unrepentant thief, he begins to take over their lives, introducing them to the wonderful world of crime, among other, more kinky, pastimes. Gender-bending farce that doesn't hold up to the end but is worth watching for sheer outrageousness. In French with English subtitles. **84m/C; VHS, DVD.** *FR* Gerard Depardieu; Michel Blanc; Miou-Miou; Bruno Cremer; Jean-Pierre Marielle; *D:* Bertrand Blier; *W:* Bertrand Blier; *M:* Serge Gainsbourg. Cannes '86: Actor (Blanc).

Menashe 1/2 2017 (PG) In his Hasidic Jewish community, Menashe is a bit of an oddball. While still a highly orthodox man of faith, he doesn't completely conform to his community, so he resists a new marriage after his wife dies, a decision that costs him custody of his son in accordance with Jewish law. Heartbroken, Menashe is granted a week to prove his worth in fatherhood and faith. Weinstein utilizes his documentary style by employing the Yiddish tongue, shunning a musical score and fancy camera work, and casting non-actors in many roles, culminating in an intimate portrayal of universal themes. **82m/C; DVD.** Menashe Lustig; Ruben Niborski; Yoel Weisshaus; Meyer Schwartz; *D:* Joshua Z Weinstein; *W:* Joshua Z Weinstein; Alex Lipschultz; Musa Syeed; *C:* Joshua Z Weinstein; Yoni Brook; *M:* Aaron Martin; Dag Rosenqvist.

The Mend 2015 Two brothers who regularly estranged from each other must share a Harlem apartment for a time and explore their dysfunctional family dynamic through words. **111m/C; DVD.** Josh(ua) Lucas; Stephen Plunkett; Lucy Owen; Cory Nichols; Mickey Sumner; *D:* John Magary; *W:* John Magary; *C:* Chris Teague; *M:* Judd Greenstein; Michi Wiancko.

Menno's Mind 1/2 1996 Rebel leader Bruce Campbell downloads his brain into a computer before being killed. Now his associates force computer techie Menno (Bill Campbell) to upload the material into his own mind in order to thwart presidential candidate Bernsen, who wants to use his online skills to influence the outcome of the election. **95m/C; VHS, DVD.** Billy Campbell; Corbin Bernsen; Bruce Campbell; Michael Dorn; Robert Picardo; Robert Vaughn; Richard Speight, Jr.; *D:* Jon Kroll; *W:* Mark Valenti; *C:* Gary Tieche; *M:* Christopher Franke. **CABLE**

The Men's Club 1/2 1986 (R) Seven middle-aged buddies get together for a single night, and bare their respective souls and personal traumas, talking about women and eating and drinking. Banal. Based on novel by Leonard Michael. **100m/C; VHS, Blu-Ray, Streaming.** Harvey Keitel; Roy Scheider; Craig Wasson; Frank Langella; David Dukes; Richard Jordan; Treat Williams; Stockard Channing; Jennifer Jason Leigh; Ann Dusenberry; Cindy Pickett; Gwen Welles; *D:* Peter Medak.

Mephisto ½ **1981** Egomaniacal stage actor Hendrik Hofgren (compellingly played by Brandauer) sides with the Nazis to further his career, with disastrous results. An updated version of the Faust legend and the first of three brilliant films by Szabo and Brandauer exploring the price of power and personal sublimation in German history. Klaus Mann based his 1936 novel on the career of German stage actor Gustaf Grundgens who became the director and star of Berlin's Prussian State Theater during WWII. German with subtitles. Followed by "Colonel Redl" and "Hanussen." **144m/C; VHS, DVD.** *HU* Klaus Maria Brandauer; Krystyna Janda; Ildiko Bansagi; Karin Boyd; Rolf Hoppe; Christine Harbort; Gyorgy Cserhalmi; Christiane Graskoff; Peter Andorai; Ildiko Kishonti; *D:* Istvan Szabo; *W:* Istvan Szabo; Peter Dobai; *C:* Lajos Koltai; *M:* Zdenko Tamassy. Oscars '81: Foreign Film.

The Mephisto Waltz **1971 (R)** Journalist gets more than a story when he is granted an interview with a dying pianist. It turns out that he is a satanist and the cult he is a part of wants the journalist. Chilling adaptation of the Fred Mustard Stewart novel features a haunting musical score. **108m/C; VHS, DVD, Blu-Ray.** Alan Alda; Jacqueline Bisset; Barbara Parkins; Curt Jurgens; Bradford Dillman; William Windom; Kathleen Widdoes; *D:* Paul Wendkos; *M:* Jerry Goldsmith.

The Mercenaries ½ *I Masnadieri* **1962** Romantic warrior fights to save the lives and honor of his people who are under attack from mercenaries murdering and raping their way across Europe. **98m/C; VHS, DVD.** *IT* Daniela Rocca; Antonio Cifariello; Folco Lulli; Debra Paget; Salvo Randone; *D:* Mario Bonnard; *W:* Mario Bonnard; Nino Minuto; *C:* Marco Scarpelli; *M:* Giulio Bonnard.

The Mercenaries *Cuba Crossing; Kill Castro; Assignment: Kill Castro; Key West Crossing; Sweet Dirty Tony* **1980** A tough guy, given the assignment to kill Fidel Castro, encounters all sorts of adversity along the way. Key West scenery is the only thing of interest. **92m/C; VHS, DVD.** Stuart Whitman; Robert Vaughn; Caren Kaye; Raymond St. Jacques; Woody Strode; Sybil Danning; Albert Salmi; Michael V. Gazzo; *D:* Chuck Workman.

Mercenaries ½ **2011 (R)** Mediocre, low-budget Brit action. The Prime Minister of Serbia is assassinated and the U.S. ambassador is kidnapped, Colonel Torida (Zane) hires former S.A.S. soldier-turned-mercenary Andy Marlow (Fucilla) to reunite with some of his pals and go on a black ops rescue mission. **97m/C; DVD.** *UK* Robert Fucilla; Geoff Bell; Vas Blackwood; Rob James-Collier; Kirsty Mitchell; Billy Zane; *D:* Paris Leonti; *W:* Paris Leonti; *C:* Roger Bonnici; *M:* Haim Frank Ilfman. **VIDEO**

Mercenary **1996** Ex-Commando-turned-mercenary Alex Hawks (Gruner) is hired by wealthy businessman Jonas Ambler (Ritter) to avenge his wife's death at the hands of terrorists. Only Ambler's desk jockey doesn't want to stay on the sidelines and watch—he wants to do. So, Hawks is forced to take him along to Iraq when he goes after the bad guys. **97m/C; VHS, DVD.** Olivier Gruner; John Ritter; Robert Culp; Ed Lauter; Martin Kove; *D:* Avi Nesher; *W:* Avi Nesher; Steven Hartov; *C:* Irek Hartowicz; *M:* Roger Neill.

Mercenary: Absolution *Absolution* **2015 (R)** An action-adventure crime drama about an assassin facing a serious dilemma. Contract killer John Alexander (Seagal) has been hired by a government agency to take out an Afghani drug and weapons dealer. During the course of the job, he comes in contact with Nadia (Stetcu), a young woman trying to escape a mob leader known as The Boss (Jones), with powerful political connections and links to the Afghani. He also learns that both men might also be involved with human trafficking. Because of the circumstances, John must chose between protecting Nadia and the other women and loyalty to his old employer, the U.S. government. **96m/C; DVD, Blu-Ray, Streaming, Download.** Steven Seagal; Byron Mann; Howard Dell; Adina Stetcu; Vinnie Jones; *D:* Keoni Waxman; *W:* Keoni Waxman; Richard Beattie; *M:* Michael Richard Plowman.

The Merchant of Four Seasons **1971** Story focuses on the depression and unfulfilled dreams of an average street merchant. Direction from Fassbinder is slow, deliberate, and mesmerizing. In German with English subtitles. **88m/C; VHS, DVD, Blu-Ray.** Hans Hirschmuller; Irm Hermann; Hanna Schygulla; Andrea Schober; Gusti Kreissl; *D:* Rainer Werner Fassbinder; *W:* Rainer Werner Fassbinder.

The Merchant of Venice **1973** Shakespeare's tragedy of prejudice, vengeance, and sacrifice stars Olivier as the persecuted money lender Shylock, who demands his payment of a pound of flesh for a defaulted loan. **131m/C; VHS, Streaming.** *GB* Laurence Olivier; Joan Plowright; Jeremy Brett; Michael Jayston; Anthony Nicholls; *D:* John Sichel.

The Merchant of Venice *William Shakespeare's The Merchant of Venice* **2004 (R)** Antonio (Irons) makes a deal with calculating money-lender Shylock (Pacino) to help his friend Bassanio (Fiennes) gain the hand of fair Portia (Collins). When the deal goes south, Shylock demands a pound of flesh from Antonio's breast and it's up to Portia, disguised as a young lawyer, to save him. Lavish, but subtle, take on Shakespeare's classic comedy. Pacino takes care to make Shylock as sympathetic as possible; and director Radford places the play's overt racism in historical context, making the play feel less viciously anti-semitic than usual. **138m/C; DVD.** Al Pacino; Jeremy Irons; Joseph Fiennes; Zuleikha Robinson; Kris Marshall; Heather Goldenhersch; John Sessions; Mackenzie Crook; Gregor Fisher; Ron Cook; Allan Corduner; Anton Rodgers; Lynn Collins; Charlie Cox; *D:* Michael Radford; *W:* Michael Radford; *C:* Benoit Delhomme; *M:* Jocelyn Pook.

Merchants of War **1990 (R)** Sent out by the CIA on a mission, two best friends are soon the target of one of the most dangerous terrorists in the world. The fanatical Islamic terrorist soon casts his wrath upon the two men. **100m/C; VHS, DVD.** Asher Brauner; Jesse Vint; Bonnie Beck; *D:* Peter M. MacKenzie.

Merci Docteur Rey **2004 (R)** Odd choice for a Merchant-Ivory production. Enjoyable French farce mixes questionable sexual orientation, mistaken identity, murder, and an estranged father for a rousing ride. Wiest's opera diva visits her closeted gay son, who witnesses a murder on a blind date with a chat room hook-up. Complimented by an eclectic soundtrack ranging from pop to opera. **91m/C; DVD.** *FR* Dianne Wiest; Jane Birkin; Stanislas Merhar; Bulle Ogier; Jerry Hall; Simon Callow; *Cameo(s):* Vanessa Redgrave; *D:* Andrew Litvack; *W:* Andrew Litvack; *C:* Laurent Machuel; *M:* Geoff(rey) Alexander. **VIDEO**

Merci pour le Chocolat *Nightcap* **2000** This is Huppert's movie all the way. She's Mika Muller, a chocolate company manager in Switzerland who has just re-married widowed concert pianist Andre (Dutronc) after 18 years. In the meantime, Andre married and had son Guillaume (Pauly), who was nearly switched at birth for Jeanne (Mouglalis), an 18-year-old with musical talent (unlike Guillaume). Jeanne impulsively decides to meet Andre and they bond over music, which causes the polite but pathologically jealous Mika to pour hot chocolate and plot. Based on the novel "The Chocolate Cobweb" by Charlotte Armstrong. French with subtitles. **99m/C; DVD, Blu-Ray.** *FR SI* Isabelle Huppert; Jacques Dutronc; Anna Mouglalis; Rodolphe Pauly; Michel Robin; Brigitte Catillon; Mathieu Simonet; *D:* Claude Chabrol; *W:* Claude Chabrol; Caroline Eliacheff; *C:* Renato Berta; *M:* Matthieu Chabrol.

Mercury Man ½ *Ma noot lhek lai* **2006 (R)** Pretty but heavily flawed superhero film obviously heavily influenced by both 'Spider Man' and 'The X-Men'. A fire fighter has a medallion embedded in his chest that gives him super powers which he must use to defend he country against religious extremists. At times the film feels like nationalist propaganda more than a superhero movie. **106m/C; DVD.** *TH* Parinya Jaroenphon; Wasan Khantaau; Jivipa Kheawkunya; Parinya Kiatbusaba; Matinee Kingpoyom; Erik Markus Schuetz; Anon Saisangcharn; Attakorn Suwannaraj; *D:* Bhandit Thongdee; *W:* Bhandit Thongdee; *M:* Traithep Wongpaiboon.

Mercury Plains **2016 (R)** An action-thriller about a lost young adult who finds himself and trouble in the Mexican desert. Bored and eager escape his life issues, a down on his luck Mitch Davis (Eastwood) runs away from Texas to Mexico. There, he finds purpose when he is recruited for a paramilitary group of teens who fight drug cartels. Alone with the vigilante group in the desert, Mitch proves himself to be an ideal fighter and soon becomes the top soldier for the group's leader, The Captain (Chinlund). When Mitch learns the true focus of the group, he realizes he must outwit his leader and return to America before being arrested by the Mexican police. **102m/C; DVD, Streaming, Download.** Scott Eastwood; Angela Sarafyan; Nick (Nicholas) Chinlund; Justin Arnold; Mark Hanson; *D:* Charles Burmeister; *W:* Charles Burmeister; *C:* Philip Roy; *M:* Austin Wintory. **VIDEO**

Mercury Rising ½ **1998 (R)** Renegade FBI agent Art Jeffries (Willis) must protect an orphaned autistic child who has inadvertently cracked a secret government code. Together, they dodge bullets from evil government forces headed by Nicholas Kudrow (Baldwin), who insists on having the innocent boy killed rather than change the code. That glaring logic aside, Willis shows some tenderness as he bonds with the boy in between nailing bad guys. Baldwin is effective as the snake who truly believes killing a child will benefit national security. Film generally rises above tepid to provide thrills. **112m/C; DVD.** Bruce Willis; Alec Baldwin; Miko Hughes; Kim Dickens; Chi McBride; Robert Stanton; Peter Stormare; Kevin Conway; *D:* Harold Becker; *W:* Larry Konner; Mark Rosenthal; *C:* Michael Seresin; *M:* John Barry. Golden Raspberries '98: Worst Actor (Willis).

Mercy **1996 (R)** When New York lawyer Frank Kramer's (Rubenstein) daughter is kidnapped he comes to realize it wasn't for ransom but for revenge. **82m/C; VHS, DVD.** John Rubinstein; Sam Rockwell; Phil Brock; Novella Nelson; Amber Kain; Jane Lanier; *D:* Richard Shepard; *W:* Richard Shepard; *C:* Sarah Cawley.

Mercy **2000 (R)** Glossy sleaze based on the book by David L. Lindsey. Catherine Barker (Barkin) is a hard-drinking homicide detective investigating a serial killer with sexual kinks. Bombshell Vickie Kittrie (Wilson) reveals that each female victim belonged to an exclusive club that liked to experiment with the wilder side of life. All the victims also turn out to be patients of psychotherapist Dominick Broussard (Sands), who may be more psycho than anyone knows. **94m/C; VHS, DVD.** Ellen Barkin; Peta Wilson; Julian Sands; Wendy Crewson; Karen Young; Marshall Bell; Stephen Baldwin; Beau Starr; Bill MacDonald; Stewart Bick; *D:* Damian Harris; *W:* Damian Harris; *C:* Manuel Teran; *M:* B.C. Smith.

Mercy **2009** Time-shifting indie, which stumbles somewhat over its cliches, features Caan pere and fils as cynical, yet surprisingly vulnerable romantics. Slick, womanizing John Ryan is a bestselling writer whose latest book is savaged by beautiful literary critic Mercy for being shallow. Naturally, John finds her a challenge but neither of them expects to fall in love. **87m/C; DVD.** Scott Caan; Troy Garity; James Caan; Erika Christensen; Alexie Gilmore; Dylan McDermott; Whitney Able; Wendy Glenn; John Boyd; *D:* Patrick Hoelck; *W:* Scott Caan; *C:* Phil Parmet; *M:* Mader.

The Mercy ½ **2019** Though entrepreneur Donald Crowhurst (Firth) is only a day trip sailer, he enters the Golden Globe Race in 1968. The race is a competition to be the first person to go around the globe on a boat alone without going ashore. Though his family gives him support reluctantly, he designs his own boat, gains sponsors, and hires a press agent. Determined Donald faces difficult challenges including his boat not being ready in time and the threat of financial ruin if he does not finish. It's an interesting, true story with a strong performance by Firth, demonstrating Donald's energy and conviction. **101m/C; DVD.** Rachel Weisz; Colin Firth; David Thewlis; Mark Gatiss; Genevieve Gaunt; *D:* James Marsh; *W:* Scott Z. Burns; *C:* Eric Gautier; *M:* Johann Johannsson.

Mercy Black **2019** Fifteen years ago, Maria (Pineda) and a friend lured a girl into a ravine and killed her as a sacrifice to Mercy Black. In return, they hoped the force would take away their sadness. Instead, Marina was locked up. As she leaves psychiatric care to stay with her sister Alice (LaMont) and Alice's young son Bryce (Emmons), Mercy Black continues to live and has gone viral. Haunted by her crime, Marina is further disturbed by strange events at Alice's house that affect both Marina and Bryce. Though the horror film features some spookiness and dread, its monster is not as disturbing as it could be. **88m/C; DVD.** Daniella Pineda; Austin Amelio; Elle LaMont; Lee Eddy; Miles Emmons; *D:* Owen Egerton; *W:* Owen Egerton; *C:* Ellie Ann Fenton; *M:* Kaz(imir) Boyle. **VIDEO**

Mercy Mission ½ **1993** Young pilot Bakula runs into trouble over the Pacific with his small plane and it's upto Air New Zealand airline pilot Loggia, who risks the lives of his passengers and crew, to come to his rescue. **92m/C; VHS, DVD.** Scott Bakula; Robert Loggia; *D:* Roger Young.

Mercy Streets ½ **2000 (PG-13)** Neo-noir, spiritually-themed crime drama about brotherly redemption. Con man John plans to go straight after getting out of prison but falls right back into a counterfeiting scheme with mentor Rome. This soon involves John's estranged twin brother Jeremiah, an Episcopal priest, after John tries double-crossing Rome and Jeremiah is mistaken for John and held hostage. **106m/C; DVD.** Eric Roberts; Cynthia Watros; Shiek Mahmud-Bey; Robert LaSardo; Stacy Keach; Lawrence Taylor; David A.R. White; *D:* Jon Gunn; *W:* Jon Gunn; John Mann; *C:* Chris Magee; *M:* Staffan Fantini. **VIDEO**

Merlin **1998** Legend of Camelot and Arthur's mentor is brought to the small screen with fine performances and equally impressive special effects. Merlin is conceived through the magic of evil Queen Mab (Richardson) to bring Britain back to its pagan roots. But Merlin doesn't really like magic and grows up to be (in the commanding persona of Neill) a most reluctant sorcerer. Still, he mentors Arthur (Curran) and continues to battle Mab, who works with Arthur's half sister Morgan Le Fey (Bonham Carter) to destroy Camelot. Merlin also pursues a long-time romance with Nimue (Rossellini), who falls victim to Mab's treachery. **140m/C; DVD.** Sam Neill; Miranda Richardson; Isabella Rossellini; Martin Short; Helena Bonham Carter; Rutger Hauer; Paul Curran; Billie Whitelaw; Lena Headey; Jason Done; Mark Jax; John McEnery; Nicholas Clay; Sebastien Roche; Jeremy Sheffield; *Cameo(s):* John Gielgud; *V:* James Earl Jones; *D:* Steven Barron; *W:* David Stevens; Edward Khmara; *C:* Sergei Kozlov; *M:* Trevor Jones. **TV**

Merlin and the Book of Beasts *Book of Beasts* **2009** Bad CGI and a dull narrative doom this SciFi saga about the dark side of Camelot. Arthur is gone and the Round Table has been destroyed. Terror reigns from evil sorcerer Arkadian (Thorburn) and his equally evil creatures so Camelot's remaining knights must look to a bitter Merlin (Callis) to save them. **92m/C; DVD.** James Callis; Laura Harris; Jim Thorburn; Patrick Sabongui; Donald Adams; Jesse Moss; Megan Vincent; Maja Stace-Smith; *D:* Warren Sonoda; *W:* Brook Durham; *C:* Mathias Herndl; Adam Sliwinski; *M:* Craig McConnell. **CABLE**

Merlin and the War of the Dragons ½ **2008 (PG)** Apprentice wizard Merlin must confront an army of dragons in the English countryside as he battles his former friend Hengest, who has teamed up with a Saxon warlord trying to conquer Britain. Filmed on location in Wales. **90m/C; DVD.** Simon Lloyd-Roberts; Jurgen Prochnow; Iago McGuire; Joseph Stacey; Dylan Jones; Hefin Wyn; Gary Twomey; William Huw; Carys Eleri; Nia Ann; Iona Thonger; *D:* Mark Atkins; *W:* Jon Macy; *C:* Mark Atkins; *M:* Chris Ridenhour. **VIDEO**

Merlin's Apprentice ½ **2006** Disappointingly cheesy sort of sequel to the 1998 miniseries "Merlin." Merlin (Neill again) takes a 50-year nap and awakens to find Arthur dead, the Holy Grail missing, and Camelot under siege. When a young thief, Jack (Reardon), tries to steal his wand, Merlin discovers he has magical abilities and takes Jack on as his apprentice to help save Camelot. Richardson is back too, but this time she plays the Lady of the Lake. **185m/C; DVD.** *US CA* Sam Neill; John Reardon; Miranda Richardson; Duncan Fraser; Christopher Jacot; Andrew Jackson; Garwin Sanford; Meaghan Ory; Alexander Kalugin; ***D:*** David Wu; ***W:*** Christian Ford; Roger Soffer; ***C:*** John Spooner; ***M:*** Lawrence Shragge. **CABLE**

Mermaid 1/2 **2000** Young Desi is mourning her father's death. She writes a letter to him and ties it to a balloon, hoping that it will fly to heaven so he can read it. Instead, the winds blow the balloon to Canada's St. Edward's Island and the small town of Mermaid. When the letter is found, the islanders decide to respond to Desi's message. **94m/C; VHS, DVD.** Samantha Mathis; Ellen Burstyn; David Kaye; Jodelle Ferland; Blu Mankuma; Tom Heaton; ***D:*** Peter Masterson; ***W:*** Todd Robinson; ***C:*** Jon Joffin; ***M:*** Peter Melnick. **CABLE**

The Mermaid *Mei Ren Yu* **2016 (R)** A mermaid-centered fantasy comedy-drama. Because the ecosystem of the mermaids may be under duress because of developer Liu Xuan (Deng), mermaid Shan (Lin) is chosen to kill him to save her species. Xuan's plan includes reclaiming the sea. However, during the course of her assignment, Shan and Xuan fall in love with each other. Though Xuan plans to stop the project because of Shan, a secret organization begins to hunt the mermaids and Xuan must take action before Shan and her friends lose their lives. **94m/C; DVD, Blu-Ray, Streaming, Download.** Jelly Lin; Chao Deng; Zhixiang Luo; Yuqi Zhang; Hark Tsui; ***D:*** Stephen (Chiau) Chow; ***W:*** Stephen (Chiau) Chow; Hing-Ka Chan; Chi Keung Fung; Miu-Kei Ho; Ivy Kong; Si-Cheun Lee; Zhengyu Lu; Kan-Cheung (Sammy) Tsang; ***C:*** Sung Fai Choi; ***M:*** Fuhua Huang; Wendy Zheng.

The Mermaid Chair 1/2 **2006** Married artist Jessie (Basinger), suffering from ennui, must return to her hometown in Egret Island, SC when her mother inexplicably begins mutilating herself. Still haunted by the death of her father, Jessie discovers the truth about her past, rediscovers her passion for art, and then her passion for love when she falls for very hunky Benedictine monk Brother Thomas (Carter). Based on the bestselling novel by Sue Monk Kidd. **90m/C; DVD.** Kim Basinger; Alex Carter; Bruce Greenwood; Roberta Maxwell; Lorena Gale; Ken Pogue; Debra Mooney; Ellie Harvie; ***D:*** Steven Schachter; ***W:*** Suzette Couture; ***C:*** Mike Southon; ***M:*** Rolf LevLand. **CABLE**

Mermaids **1990 (PG-13)** Mrs. Flax (Cher) is the flamboyant mother of two who hightails out of town every time a relationship threatens to turn serious. Having moved some 18 times, her daughters, Charlotte (Ryder), 15, and Kate (Ricci), 8, are a little worse for the wear, psychologically speaking. One aspires to be a nun though not Catholic, and the other holds her breath under water. Now living in Massachusetts, Mrs. Flax starts having those "I got you, babe" feelings for Hoskins, a shoestore owner. Amusing, well-acted multi-generational coming of ager based on a novel by Patty Dann. **110m/C; VHS, DVD, Blu-Ray.** Cher; Winona Ryder; Bob Hoskins; Christina Ricci; Michael Schoeffling; Caroline McWilliams; Jan Miner; ***D:*** Richard Benjamin; ***W:*** June Roberts; ***C:*** Howard Atherton; ***M:*** Jack Nitzsche. Natl. Bd. of Review '90: Support. Actress (Ryder).

The Mermaids of Tiburon *The Aqua Sex* **1962** A marine biologist and a criminal travel to a remote island off Mexico in search of elusive, expensive "fire pearls." There they encounter a kingdom of lovely mermaids who promptly liven things up. Filmed in "Aquascope" for your viewing pleasure. **77m/C; VHS, DVD.** Diane Webber; George Rowe; Timothy Carey; Jose Gonzales-Gonzales; John (Jack) Mylong; Gil Baretto; Vicki Kantenwine; Nani Morrissey; Judy Edwards; Jean Carroll; Diana Cook; Karen Goodman; Nancy Burns; ***D:*** John Lamb; ***W:*** John Lamb.

Merrill's Marauders 1/2 **1962** Chandler is the commander of a battle-hardened regiment fighting in the jungles of Burma in 1944. The exhausted unit gains their latest objective and expects to be relieved, only to be continuously pushed into more fighting down the line. Director Fuller excels at showing the confusion of battle; Chandler's last film role (he died before the film was released). **98m/C; VHS, DVD, Blu-Ray.** Jeff Chandler; Ty Hardin; Peter Brown; Andrew Duggan; Will Hutchins; Claude Akins; John Hoyt; Chuck Hicks; Charles Briggs; Vaughan Wilson; Pancho Magalona; ***D:*** Samuel Fuller; ***W:*** Samuel Fuller; Milton Sperling; Charlton Ogburn, Jr.; ***C:*** William Clothier; ***M:*** Howard Jackson.

Merrily We Go to Hell **1932** Jerry Corbett (March) is a frequently drunk reporter and an aspiring playwright. He misses his engagement party to status-conscious heiress Joan (Sidney) by going on a bender and continues drinking even after they marry. When Joan finds out Jerry has been flirting with an old flame (Allen) as well, she goes back home to dad (Irving) only to discover she's pregnant. Complications arise and Jerry eventually finds out his missus is in the hospital and he begs for a second chance. **78m/B; DVD.** Fredric March; Sylvia Sidney; George Irving; Richard "Skeets" Gallagher; Cary Grant; Adrienne Allen; ***D:*** Dorothy Arzner; ***W:*** Edwin Justus Mayer; ***C:*** David Abel.

Merrily We Live **1938** In this delightful screwball comedy, wealthy, daffy Emily Kilbourne (Burke) is obsessed by good works and hires various down-and-outers as the family help (it is the Depression). No one is surprised by yet another stranger showing up at their door, although when writer Rawling (Aherne) is mistaken for Emily's latest project, he decides to stick around after getting a good look at Emily's daughter Jerry (Bennett). **90m/B; DVD, Blu-Ray.** Brian Aherne; Constance Bennett; Billie Burke; Tom Brown; Clarence (C. William) Kolb; Bonita Granville; Ann Dvorak; Phillip Reed; Alan Mowbray; Patsy Kelly; ***D:*** Norman Z. McLeod; ***W:*** Eddie Moran; Jack Jevne; ***C:*** Norbert Brodine.

Merry Andrew 1/2 **1958** Kaye is a little less manic than usual but this circus romance is still amusing. Andrew Larabee (Kaye) teaches at a stuffy British boys' school, but his real love is archeology. He spends the summer on a dig in Italy where he meets lovely acrobat Selena (Angeli), whose family has a small traveling circus. Convoluted circumstances have Andrew joining the circus as a clown, ringmaster, and reluctant lion-tamer and finding himself engaged to two women while still pursuing his archeological adventures. Adaptation of a Paul Gallico story. **103m/C; DVD.** Danny Kaye; Pier Angeli; Salvatore Baccaloni; Patricia Cutts; Robert Coote; Noel Purcell; ***D:*** Michael Kidd; ***W:*** I.A.L. Diamond; Isobel Lennart; ***C:*** Robert L. Surtees; ***M:*** Saul Chaplin.

Merry Christmas, Mr. Lawrence **1983 (R)** An often overlooked drama about a WWII Japanese POW camp. Taut psychological drama about clashing cultures and physical and emotional survival focusing on the tensions between Bowie as a British POW and camp commander Sakamato, who also composed the outstanding score. A haunting and intense film about the horrors of war. Based on the novel by Laurens van der Post. **124m/C; VHS, DVD, Blu-Ray.** *JP GB* David Bowie; Tom Conti; Ryuichi Sakamoto; Takeshi "Beat" Kitano; Jack Thompson; Takashi Naito; Alistair Browning; Johnny Okura; Yuya Uchida; Ryunosuke Kaneda; Kan Mikami; Yuji Honma; Diasuke Iijima; ***D:*** Nagisa Oshima; ***W:*** Nagisa Oshima; Paul Mayersberg; ***C:*** Toichiro Narushima. Natl. Bd. of Review '83: Actor (Conti).

The Merry Frinks **1934** The Frinks aren't merry, they're nuts and downright unpleasant. Mom Hattie (MacMahon) is the only somewhat sane and responsible member of her bickering family. When Uncle Newt (Kibbee) dies and leaves her a half-million dollar inheritance it's with the proviso that she leaves the family. **67m/B; DVD.** Aline MacMahon; Guy Kibbee; Hugh Herbert; Allen Jenkins; Helen Howell; Joan Wheeler; Frankie Darro; Ivan Lebedeff; Louise Beavers; ***D:*** Alfred E. Green; ***W:*** Kathryn Scola; Gene Markey; ***C:*** Arthur Edeson.

The Merry Gentleman 1/2 **2008 (R)** Frank Logan (Keaton) is a gentlemanly Chicago hitman who is apparently depressed by his job since he tries to commit suicide after his latest killing. Kate (Macdonald, a particularly lovely presence) spots Frank as he is about to jump, screams, and inadvertently saves his life. But Frank also realizes she may be able to identify him so he has to make her acquaintance. Since Kate is a fellow bruised and lonely soul (having fled an abusive marriage) the two seem made for each other as long as Frank doesn't decide to kill her. Keaton, in his directorial debut, refrains from most cliches. **110m/C; DVD.** Michael Keaton; Kelly Macdonald; Tom Bastounes; Bobby Cannavale; Darlene Hunt; Guy Van Swearingen; William Dick; ***D:*** Michael Keaton; ***W:*** Ron Lazzeretti; ***C:*** Chris Seager; ***M:*** Jonathan Sadoff; Sean Douglas.

Merry-Go-Round **1923** A handsome Austrian count is engaged to a woman of his class when he meets the beautiful Agnes, who works as an organ grinder for the local merry-go-round. He disguises himself to woo her but finally decides to marry his fiance, although Agnes continues to love him. But the story doesn't end for the two lovers who are destined to be together. Producer Thalberg and director von Stroheim battled over the expense and length of the film until Thalberg had the director replaced. However, much of the film still shows the von Stroheim brillance and attention to lavish detail. **110m/B; Silent; VHS, DVD.** Norman Kerry; Mary Philbin; Cesare Gravina; Edith Yorke; George Hackathorne; ***D:*** Rupert Julian; Erich von Stroheim.

Merry In-Laws **2012** Peter hasn't told fiance Alex one important fact about his parents when they come for a pre-Christmas visit--they're Santa and Mrs. Claus! Alex's young son Max is excited (especially by the reindeer parked in the garage) but the lovebirds experience some relationship trouble with folks who are more bah humbug than jolly. **90m/C; DVD.** Lucas Bryant; Kassia Warshawski; George Wendt; Shelley Long; Jacob Thurmeier; Greg Lawson; ***D:*** Leslie Hope; ***W:*** Barbara Kymlicka; ***C:*** Courtenay Forster; ***M:*** John McCarthy. **VIDEO**

A Merry War *Keep the Aspidistra Flying* **1997** Gordon Comstock (Grant) is a frustrated ad-man in London, circa 1935. He believes that his comfortable middle-class lifestyle is stifling his creativity so he quits his job and moves into a shabby little apartment to augment his misery, despite the doubts of girlfriend Rosemary (Bonham Carter). Based on George Orwell's only comedy, which fictionalized his own experience. A funny film with solid performances that still has that Orwellian feel of political commentary and, naturally, makes a statement on social classes. Very British pic will appeal to fans of '30s era dialogue. **101m/C; DVD.** Richard E. Grant; Helena Bonham Carter; Julian Wadham; Jim Carter; Harriet Walter; Liz Smith; Barbara Leigh-Hunt; ***D:*** Robert Bierman; ***W:*** Alan Plater; ***C:*** Giles Nuttgens; ***M:*** Mike Batt.

The Merry Widow **1925** Von Stroheim makes a success of his silent MGM version of the operetta though he uses little of the original story. Womanizing European royals Prince Danilo (Gilbert) and Crown Prince Mirko (D'Arcy) compete for the favors of American dancer Sally O'Hara (Murray), who's also courted by wealthy Baron Sadoja (Marshall). Sally eventually marries one but fate brings the others back into her life. **137m/B; Silent; DVD.** John Gilbert; Roy D'Arcy; Mae Murray; Tully Marshall; George Fawcett; Josephine Crowell; Edward Connelly; ***D:*** Erich von Stroheim; ***W:*** Erich von Stroheim; Benjamin Glazer; ***C:*** Oliver Marsh.

The Merry Widow 1/2 *The Lady Dances* **1934** The first sound version of the famous Franz Lehar operetta, dealing with a playboy from a bankrupt kingdom who must woo and marry the land's wealthy widow or be tried for treason. A delightful musical comedy, with a sterling cast and patented Lubitschian gaiety. Made as a silent in 1912 and 1925; remade in color in 1952. **99m/B; DVD.** Maurice Chevalier; Jeanette MacDonald; Edward Everett Horton; Una Merkel; George Barbier; Minna Gombell; Ruth Channing; Sterling Holloway; Henry Armetta; Barbara Leanard; Donald Meek; Akim Tamiroff; Herman Bing; ***D:*** Ernst Lubitsch; ***M:*** Franz Lehar; ***M:*** Lorenz Hart.

Merton of the Movies 1/2 **1947** Skelton stars as star-struck, small town theatre usher Merton Gill who wins a trip to Hollywood. He's befriended by stunt double Phyllis (O'Brien) who recognizes his comedic talents and works to get him that big break. Based on the play by George S. Kaufman and Marc Connelly and previously filmed in 1924 and 1932 (as "Make Me a Star"). **82m/B; VHS, DVD.** Red Skelton; Virginia O'Brien; Gloria Grahame; Leon Ames; Alan Mowbray; Charles D. Brown; Hugo Haas; Harry Hayden; ***D:*** Robert Alton; ***W:*** George Wells; Lou Breslow.

Mesa of Lost Women **WOOF!** *Lost Women; Lost Women of Zarpa* **1952** Mad scientist creates brave new race of vicious women with long fingernails. So bad it's a wanna-B. Addams Family buffs will spot the Fester in Coogan. **70m/B; VHS, DVD.** Jackie Coogan; Richard Travis; Allan Nixon; Mary Hill; Robert Knapp; Tandra Quinn; Lyle Talbot; Katherine Victor; Angelo Rossitto; Dolores Fuller; ***D:*** Ron Ormond; Herbert Tevos; ***W:*** Herbert Tevos; ***C:*** Gilbert Warrenton; Karl Struss; ***M:*** Hoyt Curtin.

Meskada 1/2 **2010 (R)** Colorless, slow-paced crime drama. A botched home robbery in the wealthy community of Hillard leaves a child dead. His well-connected mother Allison (Benanti) puts pressure on detective Noah Cordin (Stahl) and his state police partner Leslie Spencer (Nichols) to quickly find the perps. The only clue leads Noah back to his working-class hometown, where the locals may be keeping quiet because of their resentment of their wealthier neighbors. **88m/C; DVD.** Nick Stahl; Rachel Nichols; Norman Reedus; Laura Benanti; Kellan Lutz; Jonathan Tucker; James McCaffrey; Grace Gummer; ***D:*** Josh Sternfeld; ***W:*** Josh Sternfeld; ***C:*** Daniel Sariano; ***M:*** Steve Weisberg.

Mesmer **1994** Rickman gives a bravura performance in the title role of controversial 18th-century Austrian doctor Franz Anton Mesmer, who put the term "mesmerize" in the dictionary. This court (in Vienna and Paris) physician's unorthodox healing practices were concerned with filtering out negative magnetism through hypnotism and positive thinking. Was he a charlatan or merely a man ahead of his time? **107m/C; VHS, DVD, On Demand.** *GB* Alan Rickman; Donal Donnelly; Peter Dvorsky; David Hemblen; Simon McBurney; Gillian Barge; Jan Rubes; ***D:*** Roger Spottiswoode; ***W:*** Dennis Potter; ***C:*** Elemer Ragalyi; ***M:*** Michael Nyman.

Mesmerized *Shocked* **1984** Based on the work by Jerzy Skolimowski, the film is a dramatization of the Victoria Thompson murder case in 1880s New Zealand. A teenaged orphaned girl marries an older man and decides after years of abuse to kill him through hypnosis. An unengaging drama, though the lovely New Zealand landscape serves as a fitting contrast to the film's ominous tone. **90m/C; VHS, DVD.** *GB NZ AU* John Lithgow; Jodie Foster; Michael Murphy; Dan Shor; Harry Andrews; ***D:*** Michael Laughlin; ***W:*** Michael Laughlin; ***C:*** Louis Horvath; ***M:*** Georges Delerue.

Mesrine: Part 1—Killer Instinct *L'Instinct de Mort* **2008 (R)** Brutal crime drama based on the true story of French criminal Jacques Mesrine (Cassel), who was killed in 1979. Flashbacks depict the beginnings of his activities over the 20 previous years, including a move to Quebec (after trouble in Paris) and time in prison (from which he escapes). As played by Cassel, Mesrine is violent, intelligent, and charismatic—a dangerous combination for both the cops and his fellow criminals. Partially adapted from Mesrine's memoir. French with subtitles. **114m/C; Blu-Ray.** *FR CA IT* Vincent Cassel; Cecile de France; Gerard Depardieu; Roy Dupuis; Gilles Lellouche; Elena Anaya; Florence Thomassin; Michel Duchaussoy; Myriam Boyer; ***D:*** Jean-Francois Richet; ***W:*** Jean-Francois Richet; Abdel Raouf Dafri; ***C:*** Robert Gantz; ***M:*** Marco Beltrami.

Mesrine: Part 2—Public Enemy Number 1 *L'Ennemi Public No. 1* **2008 (R)** Part 2 follows the later years of Mesrine (Cassel) after he returns to France and becomes bloated, both physically and on his own notoriety. He seals his own fate with his publicity-seeking and taunting of the cops who'll bring Mesrine down by any means necessary. French with subtitles. **134m/C; Blu-Ray.** *FR* Vincent Cassel; Ludivine Sagnier; Mathieu Amalric; Samuel Le Bihan; Gerard Lanvin; Olivier Gourmet; Anne Consigny; George Wilson; Michel Duchaussoy; *D:* Jean-Francois Richet; *W:* Jean-Francois Richet; Abdel Raouf Dafri; *C:* Robert Gantz; *M:* Marco Beltrami; Marcus Trump.

The Message 🦴🦴 *Mohammad: Messenger of God; Al-Ris-Alah* **1977 (PG)** Sprawling saga of the genesis of the religion of Islam, with Quinn portraying Mohammad's uncle, Hamza, an honored warrior. The story behind the movie might prove much more successful as a sequel than did the movie itself. The filming itself created a religious controversy. **220m/C; VHS, DVD, Blu-Ray.** *GB* Damien Thomas; Anthony Quinn; Irene Papas; Michael Ansara; Johnny Sekka; Michael Forest; Neville Jason; *D:* Moustapha Akkad; *W:* H.A.L. Craig; *C:* Jack Hildyard; *M:* Maurice Jarre.

Message from Space 🦴 ½ *Uchu kara no messeji; Return to Jelucia* **1978 (PG)** A sometimes unintentionally hilarious Japanese space opera often referred to as being 'inspired' by 'Star Wars.' An evil empire is attacking the planet of Jillucia and theys send out eight holy seeds that track down the eight people who will be chosen to rescue the planet from a race of steel plated aliens. **105m/C; DVD, Blu-Ray.** *JP* Sonny Chiba; Vic Morrow; Philip Casnoff; Etsuko (Sue) Shihomi; Peggy Lee Brennan; *D:* Kinji Fukasaku; *W:* Kinji Fukasaku; Shotaro Ishinomori; Hiro Matsuda; Masahiro Noda; *C:* Toru Nakajima; *M:* Ken-Ichiro Morioka. **VIDEO**

Message in a Bottle 🦴🦴 **1998 (PG-13)** Romantic drama that's paced slower than the method of mail delivery in the title. Divorced mother Theresa (Wright) finds a love note written to a lost love floating in the Atlantic. She tracks the note to strong silent guy Garrett (Costner), still grieving for his dead wife. She tries to get him to open up and move on with his life (with her preferably), but this takes a mind-numbingly long time. The sole reason to watch this movie is to see old pro Paul Newman steal every scene he's in as Costner's father. **132m/C; DVD.** Kevin Costner; Robin Wright; Paul Newman; John Savage; Illeana Douglas; Robbie Coltrane; Jesse James; Bethel Leslie; Tom Aldredge; Viveka Davis; Raphael Sbarge; Richard Hamilton; Rosemary Murphy; Steven Eckholdt; *D:* Luis Mandoki; *W:* Gerald Di Pego; *C:* Caleb Deschanel; *M:* Gabriel Yared.

A Message to Garcia 🦴 ½ **1936** Hollywood version of a true story. During the Spanish-American War, President McKinley tasks soldier Andrew Rowan (Boles) with delivering a message of support to Cuban general Garcia (Acosta). Rowan teams up with Marine deserter Dory (Beery) to get to the rebel's mountain hideout but there's danger and betrayal all around. Stanwyck, attempting a Spanish accent, is patriot Raphaelita. **77m/B; DVD.** John Boles; Wallace Beery; Barbara Stanwyck; Alan Hale; Enrique Acosta; *D:* George Marshall; *W:* Sam Hellman; Gladys Lehman; *C:* Rudolph Mate.

The Messenger 🦴🦴🦴 **2009 (R)** Realistic look at a soldier's difficulties readjusting to life back home. Iraq War vet Will Montgomery (Foster) is assigned to the Casualty Notification Office, which informs next of kin of a soldier's death. His own wounds cause post-traumatic stress and his job only intensifies his problems even as Will falls for widowed Olivia (Morton) and struggles with his recovering alcoholic commanding officer Anthony Stone (Harrelson). First-time director Moverman takes on one of the darkest and most unseen aspects of war and treats it with skillful respect and dignity, thanks largely to outstanding performances by the leads. **112m/C; DVD, Blu-Ray.** Ben Foster; Woody Harrelson; Samantha Morton; Eamonn Walker; Jena Malone; Steve Buscemi; *D:* Oren Moverman; *W:* Oren Moverman; Alessandro Camon; *C:* Bobby Bukowski; *M:* Nathan Larson. Ind. Spirit '10: Support. Actor (Harrelson).

Messenger of Death 🦴🦴 ½ **1988 (R)** A tough detective investigates the slaughter of a Mormon family, and uncovers a conspiracy centering around oil-rich real estate. **90m/C; VHS, DVD, Blu-Ray.** Charles Bronson; Trish Van Devere; Laurence Luckinbill; Daniel Benzali; Marilyn Hassett; Jeff Corey; John Ireland; Penny Peyser; Gene Davis; *D:* J. Lee Thompson; *W:* Paul Jarrico; *M:* Robert O. Ragland.

The Messenger: The Story of Joan of Arc 🦴🦴 **1999 (R)** Besson's take on the legendary 15th-century French teen martyr Joan of Arc (Jovovich) leans heavily on gory battle scenes, stilted dialogue, and spectacle. Joan hears heavenly voices that tell her that she must free her country from the English invaders. After a visit with the Dauphin, several bloody battles ensue, and Joan is eventually captured and put on trial for sorcery and heresy. Awaiting her fate, she has internal conversations that bring up questions as to whether she was divinely inspired or crazy. Jovovich's pop-eyed, semi-intelligible performance helps this poor effort go up in flames. **148m/C; DVD.** Milla Jovovich; John Malkovich; Faye Dunaway; Dustin Hoffman; Pascal Greggory; Vincent Cassel; Tcheky Karyo; Richard Ridings; Desmond Harrington; *D:* Luc Besson; *W:* Luc Besson; Andrew Birkin; *C:* Thierry Arbogast; *M:* Éric Serra.

The Messengers 🦴 ½ **2007 (PG-13)** Hong Kong filmmakers, the Pang brothers, go Americana with a derivative haunted farmhouse tale. The Solomon family moves onto a dilapidated North Dakota farm (the previous owners were slaughtered) in a last-ditch effort to forestall personal and economic ruin. No one believes sullen teenager Jess (Stewart), who thinks the place has some bad juju, and only toddler Ben (the Turner twins) can see the ghosts skittering around. Dull rather than ominous. **84m/C; DVD, Blu-Ray, HD-DVD.** Kristen Stewart; Dylan McDermott; Penelope Ann Miller; John Corbett; Evan Turner; Theodore Turner; Dustin Milligan; *D:* Danny Pang; Oxide Pang; *W:* Mark Wheaton; *C:* David Geddes; *M:* Joseph LoDuca.

Messengers 2: The Scarecrow 🦴 **2009 (R)** In a prequel to the first flick, farmer John Rollins (Reedus) places a mysterious scarecrow in his fields and finds his bad luck changing for the better. Of course it doesn't last. **94m/C; DVD.** Norman Reedus; Claire Holt; Richard Riehle; Darcy Fowers; Matthew McNulty; Heather Stephens; *D:* Martin Barnewitz; *W:* Todd Farmer; *C:* Lorenzo Senatore; *M:* Joseph LoDuca. **VIDEO**

Messiah of Evil 🦴 *Dead People; Return of the Living Dead; Revenge of the Screaming Dead; The Second Coming* **1974 (R)** California coastal town is invaded by zombies. Confusing low-rent production from the writers of "American Graffiti." **90m/C; VHS, DVD, Blu-Ray.** Marianna Hill; Joy Bang; Royal Dano; Elisha Cook, Jr.; Michael Greer; *D:* Gloria Katz; Willard Huyck; *W:* Gloria Katz; Willard Huyck.

Metal Shifters 🦴 ½ *Iron Invader* **2011 (PG-13)** Nonsensical Syfy Channel pic at least has decent CGI for its gigantor metal killer. Brothers Jake and Ethan find a satellite that crashed in rural Redeemer, Idaho. They sell the metal to scrap dealer Earl who's building a robot/monster for the town's parade. Only alien bacteria were hitching a ride and the green goo feasts on metal, allowing it to become animated--and savage. **90m/C; DVD, Blu-Ray.** Kavan Smith; Nicole de Boer; Donnelly Rhodes; Colby Johannson; Chris Gauthier; Paul McGillion; Chelah Horsdal; *D:* Paul Ziller; *W:* Paul Ziller; Gary Hawes; *C:* Anthony C. Metchie; *M:* Christopher Nickel. **CABLE**

Metal Skin 🦴 ½ **1994** Nilhilistic nightmare, set in Melbourne, plays like an unintentional parody of '50s "B" juvenile delinquent movies. Aimless Joe (Young) has been taken under the wing of local Romeo Dazey (Mendelsohn), who's been romancing Roslyn (Garner) and Savina (Morice), two girls Joe is also interested in. Dazey also has Joe involved in illegal drag racing, leading, after much interim angst, to a racing battle between the two. Director Wright has shown his way with violent characters living on the fringes of society (see "Romper Stomper") but this is too much of a bad thing. **115m/C; DVD.** *AU* Aden Young; Ben Mendelsohn; Tara Morice; Nadine Garner; *D:* Geoffrey Wright; *W:* Geoffrey Wright.

Metal Tornado 🦴 ½ **2011 (PG)** Syfy Channel disaster movie. Ambitious CEO Jonathan Smith's (Evigan) pressing his scientists to find a way to turn solar flares into clean energy. Naturally the experiment goes wrong and some of the energy has turned into a magnetic field that captures anything metallic in its path. **90m/C; DVD.** Lou Diamond Phillips; Nicole de Boer; Greg Evigan; John Maclaren; Sophie Gendron; *D:* Gordon Yang; *W:* Jason Bourque; *C:* Bill St. John; *M:* Richard Bowers. **CABLE**

Metallica: Some Kind of Monster 🦴🦴🦴 **2004** Headbangers' "Let It Be" is a story of celebrity confession and, possibly, redemption. No Metallica career overview, concert showcases, or archival clips included. What you'll see is the psychoanalytically-assisted recording misadventure of St. Anger, a warts and all portrait exposing artist insecurity. Originally Elektra Records commissioned a film promoting the making of an album, but when talk of turning the footage into a half-hour reality series ensued, Metallica reimbursed the label's money and added another $2.3 to have it completed. **140m/C; DVD, Blu-Ray.** James Hetfield; Lars Ulrich; Kirk Hammett; Robert Trujillo; Jason Newsted; Dave Mustaine; Bob Rock; Phil Towle; *D:* Joe Berlinger; Bruce Sinofsky; *C:* Robert Richman. Ind. Spirit '05: Feature Doc.

Metallica Through the Never 🦴🦴 ½ **2013 (R)** Decades of head-banging have done nothing to diminish the rock-and-roll spirit of James Hetfield and the rest of the gang in Metallica, who get their first concert film in this 3D extravaganza. Features intense concert footage intercut with a weak story about a roadie named Trip (Dehaan) dealing with an urban nightmare as he tries to get gas to a stranded band vehicle nearby. Director Antal's camera work makes the viewer not feel like they're in the audience but on stage with the band. **93m/C; DVD, Blu-Ray.** Dane DeHaan; *D:* Nimrod Antal; *W:* Nimrod Antal; *C:* Gyula Pados.

Metalstorm: The Destruction of Jared Syn 🦴 **1983 (PG)** It's the science fiction battle of the ages with giant cyclopes and intergalactic magicians on the desert planet of Lemuria. **84m/C; VHS, DVD, Blu-Ray.** Jeffrey Byron; Mike (Michael) Preston; Tim Thomerson; Kelly Preston; Richard Moll; *D:* Charles Band; *W:* Alan J. Adler; *C:* Mac Ahlberg; *M:* Richard Band.

Metamorphosis 🦴 **1990 (R)** Novice scientist foolishly uses himself as the guinea pig for his anti-aging experiments. He quickly loses control of the project. **90m/C; VHS, DVD, Blu-Ray.** Gene Le Brock; Catherine Baranov; Stephen Brown; Harry Cason; Jason Arnold; *D:* G.L. Eastman.

Metamorphosis 🦴 ½ **2007 (R)** Writer Keith and two friends travel through Hungary so Keith can research the life of 16th-century countess Elizabeth Bathory, who may have been a serial killer, vampire or both. When the trio gets into trouble, they are rescued by another Elizabeth who leads them to a medieval castle, but there's no safety there either. **105m/C; DVD.** *GB GE HU* Corey Sevier; Irena A. Hoffman; Christopher Lambert; Jennifer Higham; Charlie Hollway; Adel Kovats; *D:* Jeno Hodi; *W:* Jeno Hodi; Tibor Fonyodi; Allan Katz; *C:* Geza Sinkovics; Martin Szecsanov; *M:* Gabor Presser. **VIDEO**

Metamorphosis: The Alien Factor 🦴🦴 ½ **1993 (R)** Gerard is a genetic engineer who is bitten by a frog injected with a mutation sample from outer space. He turns into a slimy virus that infects everything he touches. **92m/C; VHS, DVD.** George Gerard; Tony Gigante; Katharine Romaine; *D:* Glen Takakjian.

Meteor **WOOF!** **1979 (PG)** American and Soviet scientists attempt to save the Earth from a fast-approaching barrage of meteors from space in this disaster dud. Destruction ravages parts of Hong Kong and the Big Apple. **107m/C; VHS, DVD, Blu-Ray.** Sean Connery; Natalie Wood; Karl Malden; Brian Keith; Martin Landau; Trevor Howard; Henry Fonda; Joseph Campanella; Richard Dysart; *D:* Ronald Neame; *W:* Stanley Mann; *C:* Paul Lohmann; *M:* Laurence Rosenthal.

Meteor 🦴 **2009** Unintentionally campy TV miniseries about a chunk of space rock destined to annihilate the planet. Unless, of course, a couple of unlikely scientists can save the day. There are various side plots but it's all so silly that they don't matter. **180m/C; DVD.** Jason Alexander; Marla Sokoloff; Billy Campbell; Michael Rooker; Stacy Keach; Ernie Hudson; Christopher Lloyd; Mimi Michaels; *D:* Ernie Barbarash; *W:* Alexander Greenfield; *C:* Maximo Munzi; *M:* Jonathan Snipes. **TV**

Meteor Apocalypse 🦴 ½ **2010** A giant meteor enters Earth's atmosphere and the President decides to nuke the sucker except the meteor debris hits California and Nevada, destroying L.A. and Vegas. Big oops! Naturally, the government starts trying to control a panicking populace. **90m/C; DVD.** Joe Lando; Claudia Christian; Cooper Harris; Sueann Han; Cecile Johnson; *D:* Micho Rutare; *W:* Micho Rutare; Brian Brinkman; *C:* Adam Silver; *M:* Douglas Edward. **VIDEO**

The Meteor Man 🦴🦴 ½ **1993 (PG)** Townsend is a school teacher who reluctantly becomes a hero when he acquires semi-super powers after being hit by a meteor. Meteor Man flies only four feet off the ground (because he's afraid of heights) and wears costumes fashioned by his mother. Funny premise satires "superhero" movies, but is inconsistent with some hilarious gags and others that fall flat. Includes interesting cameos by Cosby, Sinbad, Vandross, and Page. **100m/C; VHS, DVD, Blu-Ray.** Robert Townsend; Robert Guillaume; Marla Gibbs; James Earl Jones; Frank Gorshin; Bill Cosby; Sinbad; Luther Vandross; LaWanda Page; Louis Freese; *D:* Robert Townsend; *W:* Robert Townsend; *C:* John A. Alonzo.

Meteor Storm 🦴 **2010** Silly Syfy Channel disaster flick has meteors breaking off from a comet and crashing through Earth's atmosphere to strike San Francisco. Naturally, the Golden Gate Bridge gets it. Hero Tom (Trucco) is married to astrophysicist Michelle (Matchett) and they squabble about what to do while the military just wants to nuke something. **90m/C; DVD.** Michael Trucco; Kari Matchett; Kirsten Prout; Brett Dier; Eric Johnson; Kevin McNulty; *D:* Tibor Takacs; *W:* Peter Mohan; *C:* Barry Gravelle; *M:* Jim Guttridge. **CABLE**

The Method 🦴🦴🦴 *El Metodo* **2005** Seven job applicants for a high-end position at a corporation in Madrid participate in the Gronholm method of selection. Individuals play games using the monitor and keyboard provided them, setting out to destroy the competition while proving their own credibility. After each round the monitor shuts down on the candidate being eliminated and an electronic voice announces "It's over." Humorous, dark, and engaging view of business culture. English and Spanish with subtitles. **115m/C; DVD.** *AR IT SP* Eduardo Noriega; Najwa Nimri; Eduardo Fernandez; Pablo Echarvi; Ernesto Alterio; Natalia Verbeke; Adriana Ozores; Carmelo Gomez; *D:* Marcelo Pineyro; *W:* Marcelo Pineyro; *C:* Alfredo Mayo; *M:* Frederic Begin.

Metro 🦴 ½ **1996 (R)** Murphy has now officially made this exact movie one kajillion times. He plays fast-talking, fast-shooting cop Axel Fo... er... Scott Roper, who's forced to accept a partner that he doesn't want, played by Nick... um... Judge... uh... Michael Rapaport! When a villain kills his best friend, he vows revenge. He and his sidekick are involved in car chases, shoot-outs and a tense situation where his girlfriend is taken hostage. Any of this ring a bell? Maybe it was in that "Another 48 Beverly Hills Cop Movies." **117m/C; VHS, DVD.** Eddie Murphy; Michael Rapaport; Michael Wincott; Carmen Ejogo; Denis Arndt; Art Evans; Donal Logue; Paul Ben-Victor; Kim Miyori; David Michael Silverman; *D:* Thomas Carter; *W:* Randy Feldman; *C:* Fred Murphy; *M:* Steve Porcaro.

Metro Manila 🦴🦴 **2013** British writer-director Ellis visits the Philippines and (eventually) comes back with a movie. Farmer Oscar Ramirez and his family flee poverty in the countryside hoping for a better life in the big city. Instead, their naivete leads to their constantly being taken advantage of. Wife Mai is forced to work in a sleazy club while Oscar thinks his luck has changed when he's hired at an armored truck company. He even makes friends with senior officer Ong. But the work is dangerous, corruption is rampant, and Oscar's luck may just be all bad. Tagalog with subtitles. **115m/C; DVD.** *UK PH* Jack Macapagal; Althea Vega; John Arcilla; *D:* Sean Ellis; *W:* Sean Ellis; Frank E. Flowers; *C:* Sean Ellis; *M:* Robin Foster.

Metroland 🦴🦴 **1997 (R)** Marital ennui and male friendship is explored in this adaptation of Julian Barnes' 1980 novel. In 1977, advertising exec Chris Lloyd (Bale) is settled in a London suburb with his wife, Marion (Watson), and their baby. His predictable existence is blasted when old chum, Toni (Ross), arrives. The duo once shared a dream of living a bohemian life and Chris is reminded of a time he spent in Paris in the late-'60s and his wild French lover. Toni increasingly tries to undermine Chris' marriage as he struggles to decide what he expects from life. **105m/C; VHS, DVD.** *GB FR* Christian Bale; Emily Watson; Lee Ross; Elsa Zylberstein; Ifan Meredith; Rufus; Amanda Ryan; ***D:*** Philip Saville; ***W:*** Adrian Hodges; ***C:*** Jean-Francois Robin; ***M:*** Mark Knopfler.

Metropolis **1926** Now a classic meditation on futurist technology and mass mentality, this fantasy concerns mechanized society. Original set design and special effects made this an innovative and influential film in its day. Is now considered one of the hippest films of the sci-fi genre. Silent, with musical score. The 1984 re-release features some color tinting, reconstruction, and a digital score with songs by Pat Benatar, Bonnie Tyler, Giorgio Moroder, and Queen. **115m/B; Silent; VHS, DVD, Blu-Ray.** *GE* Brigitte Helm; Alfred Abel; Gustav Froehlich; Rudolf Klein-Rogge; Fritz Rasp; Heinrich George; Theodore Loos; Erwin Biswanger; Olaf Storm; Hans Leo Reich; Heinrich Gotho; Fritz Alberti; Max Dietze; ***D:*** Fritz Lang; ***W:*** Fritz Lang; Thea von Harbou; ***C:*** Karl Freund; Gunther Rittau; Eugen Shufftan; ***M:*** Gottfried Huppertz.

Metropolitan **1990 (PG-13)** The Izod set comes of age on Park Avenue during Christmas break. Tom Townsend (Clements), a member of the middle class, finds himself drawn into a circle of self-proclaimed urban haute bourgeoisie types. They're embarrassingly short on male escorts for the holiday season's parties so he stands in and gets an inside look at life with the brat pack. Intelligently written and carefully made, it transcends the flirting-with-adulthood genre. **98m/C; VHS, DVD, Blu-Ray.** Carolyn Farina; Edward Clements; Taylor Nichols; Christopher Eigeman; Allison Rutledge-Parisi; Dylan Hundley; Isabel Gillies; Bryan Leder; Will Kempe; Elizabeth Thompson; ***D:*** Whit Stillman; ***W:*** Whit Stillman; ***C:*** John Thomas; ***M:*** Mark Suozzo. Ind. Spirit '91: First Feature; N.Y. Film Critics '90: Director (Stillman).

The Mexican **2001 (R)** South-of-the-border snorer has Jerry (Pitt), an inept go-fer for mobster Margolese (Hackman), on a mission for a priceless antique gun with a name which gives the movie its title. Jerry's quirky girlfriend Samantha (Roberts) wants him to go straight and, when he refuses, heads to Vegas to pursue her dreams of becoming a croupier. Sam's dreams are temporarily sidetracked when she's kidnapped as leverage for the supposedly cursed gun by homosexual hitman Leroy (Gandolfini). Gandolfini is far-and-away the standout as the sensitive hood with whom Samantha bonds during her captivity. Screwball romantic comedy is neither, as the few but much-anticipated scenes with Pitt and Roberts are easily outshone by Roberts' chemistry with Gandolfini. Pitt does his part, providing some comic moments in Mexico but can't save cliched tale. **123m/C; VHS, DVD.** Brad Pitt; Julia Roberts; James Gandolfini; Bob Balaban; Gene Hackman; J.K. Simmons; David Krumholtz; Michael Ceveris; ***D:*** Gore Verbinski; ***W:*** J.H. (Joel Howard) Wyman; ***C:*** Dariusz Wolski; ***M:*** Alan Silvestri.

Mexican Blow *Warrior* **2002 (R)** Dangerous drug lords invade the deepest jungles of South America to build their drug manufacturing and distribution headquarters. Dreadmon (Klyn) watches the marauders kill his adopted father and then scares them away with his supernatural powers, but they're not happy to go. Dreadmon must fight inner battles and overcome both his own demons and the drug lords. Shot in the jungles of Costa Azul and the urban setting of Puerto Vallarta, it's a truly bizarre and pointless mix of action, adventure and fantasy. **97m/C; VHS, DVD.** Vincent Klyn; Ron Joseph; Yukmouth; ***D:*** Will Harper; ***W:*** William Lawlor; ***C:*** Rick Lamb; ***M:*** Peter Meisner. **VIDEO**

Mexican Bus Ride 1/2 *Ascent to Heaven; Subida Al Cielo* **1951** A good-natured Bunuel effort about a newlywed peasant who travels to the big city to attend to his mother's will. While en route, he encounters a diversity of people on the bus and some temptation. In Spanish with English subtitles. **85m/B; VHS, DVD.** *MX* Lilia Prado; Esteban Marquez; Carmelita Gonzalez; ***D:*** Luis Bunuel.

Mexican Gangster **2008** Orphaned Johnny Sunshine has always lived the life of a barrio thug but he wants something better for his younger brother than a life of smuggling and drug dealing. But his protectiveness is seen as a weakness by other gangsters who want Johnny's business. **96m/C; DVD.** Damian Chapa; Joe Loretto; Christine Manoukian; Stanley Griego; Augustine Torres; Tom Druilhet; ***D:*** Damian Chapa; ***W:*** Damian Chapa; ***C:*** Pierre Chemaly; ***M:*** Don Bodin. **VIDEO**

Mexican Hayride **1948** Bud heads a gang of swindlers and Lou is the fall guy. When things up north get too hot, the boys head south of the border to cool off and start a mining scam. Watch for the hilarious bullfighting scene. Believe it or not, this is based on a Cole Porter musical—minus the music. **77m/B; VHS, DVD.** Bud Abbott; Lou Costello; Virginia Grey; Luba Malina; John Hubbard; Pedro de Cordoba; Fritz Feld; Tom Powers; Pat Costello; Frank Fenton; ***D:*** Charles T. Barton; ***W:*** Oscar Brodney.

Mexican Spitfire **1940** Velez is typecast as the title character—newlywed Carmelita who has some problems to deal with in her brand-new marriage to Dennis (Woods). There's her fiery temper, a meddling aunt, and an ex-fiancee who's determined to wreck the twosome. First in the series. **67m/B; VHS, DVD.** Lupe Velez; Leon Errol; Donald Woods; Linda Hayes; Elisabeth Risdon; Cecil Kellaway; ***D:*** Leslie Goodwins; ***W:*** Joseph Fields; Charles E. Roberts; ***C:*** Jack MacKenzie.

Mexican Spitfire at Sea 1/2 **1942** The feisty wife from South of the Border heads for Hawaii to close a deal for her husband. He goes along to help her, impersonating nobility. The thin storyline keeps it from being quite as good as the first "Mexican Spitfire" film. Most of the action takes place aboard ship. **73m/B; DVD.** Lupe Velez; Leon Errol; Charles "Buddy" Rogers; Zasu Pitts; Elisabeth Risdon; Florence Bates; Marion Martin; Eddie Dunn; Harry Holman; ***D:*** Leslie Goodwins.

The Mexican Spitfire Out West 1/2 **1940** The third comedy in the series finds Carmelita furious because she thinks hubby Dennis is two-timing her. So she impulsively heads to Reno to start divorce proceedings. Dennis and Uncle Matt follow but Matt has his own troubles since he's been impersonating Lord Epping, Dennis' boss, when the real Lord Epping shows up. **76m/B; DVD.** Lupe Velez; Leon Errol; Donald Woods; Elisabeth Risdon; Cecil Kellaway; Linda Hayes; Lydia Bilbrook; ***D:*** Leslie Goodwins; ***W:*** Charles E. Roberts; ***C:*** Jack MacKenzie; ***M:*** Roy Webb.

The Mexican Spitfire Sees a Ghost 1/2 **1942** Errol takes the lead in his dual roles of Uncle Matt and Lord Epping. His Lordship needs Matt to impersonate him since he'll be on a hunting trip when he's supposed to impress some clients visiting his estate. To add to the confusion, the Lindsays think the place is haunted. Sixth in the series. **70m/B; DVD.** Lupe Velez; Leon Errol; Charles "Buddy" Rogers; Elisabeth Risdon; Donald MacBride; Minna Gombell; Don Barclay; Mantan Moreland; Lillian Randolph; ***D:*** Leslie Goodwins; ***W:*** Charles E. Roberts; Monte Brice; ***C:*** Russell Metty.

The Mexican Spitfire's Baby 1/2 **1941** Carmelita and Dennis are having marital problems so Uncle Matt thinks they should adopt a war orphan to help them settle down. He contacts Lord Epping in England but there's a misunderstanding and his Lordship sends beautiful Frenchwoman Fifi, who's a WWI war orphan in her 20s. Uncle Matt's efforts to rectify the situation only cause more trouble. The fourth in the series. **69m/B; DVD.** Lupe Velez; Leon Errol; Charles "Buddy" Rogers; Elisabeth Risdon; Marion Martin; Fritz Feld; Zasu Pitts; Lydia Bilbrook; Lloyd Corrigan; ***D:*** Leslie Goodwins; ***W:*** Jerome Cady; Charles E. Roberts; ***C:*** Jack MacKenzie.

Mexico City 1/2 **2000 (R)** This one gets points for having a strong heroine in Edwards. She plays Mitch who takes a holiday in Mexico with photographer brother Sam (Zander). Only Sam disappears and Mitch enlists the help of a local taxi driver (Robles) to help her find him. Shows the seedy underworld side of Mexico City—not exactly a tourist mecca. **88m/C; VHS, DVD.** Stacy Edwards; Jorge Robles; Johnny Zander; Robert Patrick; Alexander Gould; ***D:*** Richard Shepard; ***W:*** Richard Shepard; Jonathan Stern. **VIDEO**

The Meyerowitz Stories (New and Selected) **2017 (PG-13)** Ensemble-driven, humane comedy-drama centering on the rippling generation impact of a family's self-absorbed patriarch, Harold Meyerowitz (Hoffman). Because of charming Harold's dark self-righteousness, his three children, Jean (Marvel), Matthew (Stiller), and Danny (Sandler), have their own issues. Through the vignettes that provide the film's structure, the audience learns much about each character's life, including Harold's somewhat successful sculpting career, Jean's sidelined status as only daughter, Matthew's limiting neuroses, and Danny's failed songwriting career and positive relationship with his daughter Eliza (Van Patten). Outstanding performances-especially by Sandler, an effective naturalistic style, and warm exploration of family dysfunction add value to the film. **112m/C; DVD.** Adam Sandler; Grace Van Patten; Dustin Hoffman; Elizabeth Marvel; Emma Thompson; ***D:*** Noah Baumbach; ***W:*** Noah Baumbach; ***C:*** Robbie Ryan; ***M:*** Randy Newman. **TV**

MI-5 1/2 *Spooks: The Greater Good* **2015 (R)** A stylish thriller adapted from the British television series Spooks. During what should be a routine handover between the MI-5 and the CIA, the CIA's most wanted terrorist escapes from the custody of British intelligence agency. In the wake of this incident, MI-5 Intelligence Chief Harry Pearce (Firth) is disgraced and goes missing. Former MI-5 Will Holloway (Harington) is recalled by the agency and is charged with finding his former mentor Pearce. Holloway ultimately must work with Pearce to find the traitor his mentor believes is in the ranks of MI-5 and the terrorist before London is attacked. **104m/C; DVD, Blu-Ray, Streaming, Download.** Peter Firth; Kit Harington; Tuppence Middleton; Elliot Levey; Elyes Gabel; ***D:*** Bharat Nalluri; ***W:*** Jonathan Brackley; Sam Vincent; ***C:*** Hubert Taczanowski; ***M:*** Dominic Lewis.

Mi Vida Loca *My Crazy Life* **1994 (R)** Looks at the lives of Latina gang members from L.A.'s Echo Park. The women talk about their romantic dreams, friendships, families, and raising children amidst the pervasive violence and despair of their tough neighborhood. Small budget and some unpolished performances don't lessen film's impact—about the stupidity of violence and how "average" the hopes and dreams of these women are. **92m/C; VHS, DVD.** Angel Aviles; Jacob Vargas; Jesse Borrego; Seidy Lopez; Marlo Marron; Neilida Lopez; Bertila Damas; Art Esquer; Christina Solis; Salma Hayek; Magali Alvarado; Julian Reyes; Panchito Gomez; ***D:*** Allison Anders; ***W:*** Allison Anders; ***M:*** John Taylor.

Mia Madre 1/2 **2016 (R)** Filmmaker Margherita (Buy) is directing her latest project while her mother is dying and her daughter is growing more distant. The process is made more difficult by her American leading man Barry (Turturro), who is an egocentric child. Writer/co-star/director Moretti has made a dramedy that's far too self-aware, especially in how the director within the film is constantly wondering whether her movie is a truthful reflection of the world. The result is a surprisingly flat and boring film, even if Buy and Turturro nearly save it. **106m/C; DVD, Blu-Ray.** Margherita Buy; John Turturro; Giulia Lazzarini; Nanni Moretti; Beatrice Mancini; ***D:*** Nanni Moretti; ***W:*** Nanni Moretti; Francesco Piccolo; Valia Santella; ***C:*** Arnaldo Catinari.

Miami Beach Cops 1/2 **1993** Two vets return home expecting life to be routine when they become sheriff's deputies. But when bad guys murder a local merchant things heat up fast. **97m/C; VHS, DVD.** Frank Maldonatti; Salvatore Rendino; William Childers; Joyce Geier; Raff Baker; Dan Preston; Deborah Daniels; ***D:*** James R. Winburn.

Miami Blues 1/2 **1990 (R)** Cold-blooded killer plays cat-and-mouse with bleary cop while diddling with an unflappable prostitute. Violent and cynical, with appropriate performances from three leads. Based on the novel by Charles Willeford. **97m/C; VHS, DVD, Blu-Ray.** Fred Ward; Alec Baldwin; Jennifer Jason Leigh; Nora Dunn; Charles Napier; Jose Perez; Paul Gleason; Obba Babatunde; Martine Beswick; Shirley Stoler; ***D:*** George Armitage; ***W:*** George Armitage; ***C:*** Tak Fujimoto; ***M:*** Gary Chang. N.Y. Film Critics '90: Support. Actress (Leigh).

Miami Connection **WOOF!** *American Streetfighters* **1987** In 1980s Florida a gang of motorcycle ninjas arrives to take over the local drug trade and beat down the hometown martial arts rock band. **87m/C; DVD, Blu-Ray, Streaming.** *US CH* Y. K. Kim; Vincent Hirsch; Joseph Diamand; Maurice Smith; Angelo Janotti; ***D:*** Y. K. Kim; Woo-sang Park; ***W:*** Y. K. Kim; Joseph Diamand; Woo-sang Park; ***C:*** Maximo Munzi; ***M:*** Jon McCallum. **VIDEO**

Miami Hustle 1/2 **1995 (R)** Con artist Marsha (Ireland) is forced by a sleazy lawyer to impersonate a bar waitress (England) who's about to inherit a fortune. But when things turn sour, she gets a computer mogul (Enos) to figure out who's setting her up. **81m/C; VHS, DVD.** Kathy Ireland; John Enos; Audie England; Richard Sarafian; ***D:*** Lawrence Lanoff. **CABLE**

Miami Magma *Swamp Volcano* **2011** Scifi original about a disreputable oil drilling company trying to conceal the fact that they've drilled into a chain of underground super volcanoes in the Gulf of Mexico and may destroy Miami. **97m/C; Blu-Ray.** Cleavant Derricks; Rachel Hunter; Melissa Ordway; ***D:*** Todor Chapkanov; ***W:*** Declan O'Brien; ***C:*** Lorenzo Senatore; ***M:*** Andrew Morgan Smith. **CABLE**

Miami Rhapsody **1995 (PG-13)** Rom com finds young, neurotic, newly-enaged copywriter Gwyn (Parker) unsure about marrying after becoming disillusioned as she discovers every member of her family is having an affair. Most of the characters come across as annoying, self-absorbed whiners, except for Banderas, who charms as a sexy Cuban nurse. Film moves along with its light-hearted narrative, but director/writer Frankel is Woody Allen lite. Filmed on location in Miami. **95m/C; DVD, Blu-Ray.** Sarah Jessica Parker; Gil Bellows; Antonio Banderas; Mia Farrow; Paul Mazursky; Kevin Pollak; Barbara Garrick; Carla Gugino; Bo Eason; Naomi Campbell; Jeremy Piven; Kelly Bishop; Ben Stein; ***D:*** David Frankel; ***W:*** David Frankel; ***C:*** Jack Wallner; ***M:*** Mark Isham.

The Miami Story **1954** Gritty crime melodrama filmed in documentary style. A surge in gang violence prompts the feds and the Miami police to hire former Chicago gangster Mick Flagg (Sullivan) to get the goods on crime boss Tony Brill (Adler). Flagg then poses as the head of a Cuban syndicate who threatens Brill's gambling action. **75m/B; DVD, Blu-Ray.** Barry Sullivan; Luther Adler; John Baer; Beverly Garland; Adele Jergens; ***D:*** Fred F. Sears; ***W:*** Robert E. Kent; ***C:*** Henry Freulich; ***M:*** Mischa Bakaleinikoff.

Miami Vice 1/2 **1984** Pilot for the popular TV series paired Crockett and Tubbs for the first time on the trail of a killer in Miami's sleazy underground. Music by Jan Hammer and other pop notables. **99m/C; VHS, DVD.** Don Johnson; Philip Michael Thomas; Saundra Santiago; Michael Talbott; John Diehl; Gregory Sierra; ***D:*** Thomas Carter. **TV**

Miami Vice 1/2 **2006 (R)** Writer/director Mann gives his Miami cop story the big-screen treatment in this update of his popular '80s TV series. Today's Crockett (Farrell) and Tubbs (Foxx) find themselves dangerously deep undercover with the same curious access to super-fast, super-expensive cars and boats as their small-screen predecessors, essential, no doubt, to catching the multicultural, drug-dealing bad guys and attracting their multicultural, multi-talented girlfriends. The actors come across as stiff, while the story's overly-complicated and ultimately secondary to film's style, which really is everything. **132m/C; DVD, Blu-Ray, HD-DVD.** John Ortiz; Colin Farrell; Jamie Foxx; Gong Li; Naomie Harris; Luis Tosar; Barry (Shabaka) Henley; Ciaran Hinds; Justin Theroux; Elizabeth Rodriguez; John Hawkes; ***D:*** Michael

Mann; ***W:*** Michael Mann; ***C:*** Dion Beebe; ***M:*** John Murphy.

Michael 🦴🦴 1/2 **1996 (PG)** Travolta tries on the giant, molting wings of Michael, an atypical archangel with an amazing joie de vive and an appetite for alcohol, women, and sugar. Residing in Iowa with the elderly Pansy (Stapleton), Michael's being tracked by a cynical tabloid reporter (Hurt) and an angel expert (MacDowell), so he figures he might as well play cupid. A dance sequence takes place in a bar to the tune of "Chain of Fools" and is one of the movie's highlights. While Travolta gives a stellar performance, Hurt and MacDowell have little to do but play out their tired romantic subplot in a script that could've used some inspiration from its lead. **105m/C; DVD.** John Travolta; William Hurt; Andie MacDowell; Bob Hoskins; Robert Pastorelli; Jean Stapleton; Teri Garr; ***D:*** Nora Ephron; ***W:*** Nora Ephron; Delia Ephron; Pete Dexter; ***C:*** John Lindley; ***M:*** Randy Newman.

Michael 🦴 1/2 **2011** Michael, single and middle-aged, prefers to keep to himself with good reason. He's a pedophile who has kidnapped 10-year-old Wolfgang and keeps him locked in the basement of his suburban home. Since the boy is dependent on Michael, he goes through with the mundane routines of their everyday life. The film isn't graphic but the implications are unsettling. German with subtitles. **96m/C; DVD.** *AT* Michael Fuith; David Rauchenberger; ***D:*** Marcus Schleinzer; ***W:*** Marcus Schleinzer; ***C:*** Gerald Kerkletz.

Michael Clayton 🦴🦴🦴 1/2 **2007 (R)** The titular Clayton (Clooney) is a ruthless, conflicted "fixer" for a giant law firm—the guy you bring in to do whatever it takes to secure a win. When Clayton's friend and top-notch litigator Arthur (Wilkinson) suffers a breakdown over a pollution case, Clayton's boss (Pollack) tells him to fix the problem despite Clayton's seeing just how wrong his firm truly is. Unfortunately, he's too good, and in too deep, to give it all up. The ending's in doubt right up until the final, powerful scene. A heady, fascinating exploration of a world where people spend so much time inhabiting grey areas, they've forgotten what black and white look like. **119m/C; DVD.** George Clooney; Tom Wilkinson; Tilda Swinton; Sydney Pollack; Michael O'Keefe; Jennifer Van Dyck; Ken Howard; Robert Prescott; ***D:*** Tony Gilroy; ***W:*** Tony Gilroy; ***C:*** Robert Elswit; ***M:*** James Newton Howard. Oscars '07: Support. Actress (Swinton); British Acad. '07: Support. Actress (Swinton).

Michael Collins 🦴🦴🦴 **1996 (R)** Collins (Neeson) was a revolutionary leader with the Irish Volunteers, a guerilla force (an early version of the IRA) dedicated to freeing Ireland from British rule by any means necessary. After a number of successful moves against British intelligence, Collins is unwillingly drawn into a statesman's role as negotiations for an Anglo-Irish Treaty begin in 1921, ultimately dividing the country in two and leading to Collins' own assassination. Controversy surrounded the film as historians, politicians, and the media took potshots at director Jordan's admittedly personal look at the complexities of Irish life and one of its equally complicated heroes. **117m/C; DVD, Blu-Ray.** Liam Neeson; Aidan Quinn; Alan Rickman; Stephen Rea; Julia Roberts; Ian Hart; Sean McGinley; Gerard McSorley; Stuart Graham; Brendan Gleeson; Charles Dance; Jonathan Rhys Meyers; ***D:*** Neil Jordan; ***W:*** Neil Jordan; ***C:*** Chris Menges; ***M:*** Elliot Goldenthal. L.A. Film Critics '96: Cinematog.; Venice Film Fest. '96: Actor (Neeson), Golden Lion.

Michael Jackson's This Is It 🦴🦴 1/2 *This Is It* **2009 (PG)** In more ways than one. Hastily compiled homage taken from some 120 hours of rehearsal footage recorded between March and June at L.A.'s Staples Center for Jackson's comeback London concerts before his death on June 25, 2009. Jackson is very much in work mode—generally holding back as he tries out dance moves, arrangements, etc. Interest will probably vary between those who are true fans and those who are morbidly curious to see how the singer/dancer looked and acted given the mass media hysteria surrounding his sudden demise. Includes numerous dance numbers as well as conversations between Jackson, director Ortega, the dancers and musicians, and others. **112m/C; Blu-Ray, UMD, On Demand.** Michael Jackson; ***D:*** Kenny Ortega; ***C:*** Sandrine Orabona; ***M:*** Michael Bearden.

Michael Shayne: Private Detective 🦴🦴 1/2 **1940** Brett Halliday's shamus made it to the big screen in a seven-film series starring Nolan. Shayne is a wisecracking, usually broke PI with ethics, which is why he first refuses the suspicious job offer made by wealthy Hiram Brighton (Kolb). Hiram wants him to keep an eye on Phyllis (Weaver), his gambling-addicted daughter, who's been betting on the ponies. When a shady money lender is murdered, Shayne is set up to take the fall but he learns the suspect list is long. First in the series. **77m/B; DVD.** Lloyd Nolan; Clarence (C. William) Kolb; Marjorie Weaver; Douglass Dumbrille; George Meeker; Walter Abel; Joan Valerie; Donald MacBride; Elizabeth Patterson; Charles Coleman; ***D:*** Eugene Forde; ***W:*** Stanley Rauh; Manning O'Connor; ***C:*** George Schneiderman; ***M:*** Cyril Mockridge.

Mickey 🦴🦴 **1917** Spoof on high society as a penniless young woman moves in with relatives and works as the family's maid. Silent film. **105m/B; Silent; VHS, DVD.** Mabel Normand; Lew Cody; Minta Durfee; ***D:*** Mack Sennett.

Mickey 🦴 **1948** A tomboy becomes a woman even as she plays matchmaker for her own father and sings a few songs. Not too exciting; you may fall alseep if you're slipped this "Mickey." Based on the novel "Clementine," by Peggy Goodin. **87m/C; VHS, DVD.** Lois Butler; Bill Goodwin; Irene Hervey; John Sutton; Hattie McDaniel; ***D:*** Ralph Murphy.

Mickey Blue Eyes 🦴🦴 1/2 **1999 (PG-13)** Grant reprises his role as the maddeningly polite, apologetic British guy for about the bazillionth time. This time he plays Michael Felgate, an art auctioneer who proposes to schoolteacher Gina (Tripplehorn). Her father Frank (Caan) turns out to be a mobster, whose boss wants to use his auction house as a front for money laundering. After Michael tells a string of lies to hide his involvement from Gina, a series of wild events and misunderstandings leads to Michael posing as mobster Little Big Mickey Blue Eyes from Kansas City. Listening to tea-and-crumpety Grant trying to pronounce "fuhgeddaboudit" briefly brings the movie to life, but the premise is quickly abandoned and he sinks back into his droopy British bit again. All is wrapped up in your standard issue romantic comedy ending. **103m/C; DVD.** Hugh Grant; Jeanne Tripplehorn; James Caan; Burt Young; Gerry Becker; James Fox; Joe (Johnny) Viterelli; ***D:*** Kelly Makin; ***W:*** Robert Kuhn; Adam Scheinman; ***C:*** Donald E. Thorin; ***M:*** Wolfgang Hammerschmid.

Mickey, Donald, Goofy: The Three Musketeers 🦴 1/2 *The Three Musketeers* **2004 (G)** The titular cartoon characters star as janitors at Musketeer Headquarters and get promoted to guard the Princess as part of a plot by the head of the Musketeers who believes they are incompetent and wishes to kidnap the Princess to gain control of the kingdom. Not one of Disney's best. **75m/C; DVD, Blu-Ray.** ***V:*** Wayne Allwine; Tony Anselmo; Bill Farmer; ***D:*** Donovan Cook; ***W:*** David Mickey Evans; ***M:*** Bruce Broughton.

Mickey One 🦴🦴 1/2 **1965** Nightclub comic Mickey (Beatty) gets into trouble when he can't pay his gambling debts. So he hides out in Chicago under an assumed name, working as a janitor, but can't live without the applause. His agent finds him a club job but Mickey panics, thinking the place is under mob control, and spends a lot of time running around, trying to clear his debts. Finally, returning to the club, Mickey resigns himself to a bleak fate. Beatty's jumpy character is an acquired taste—as is the film. **93m/B; VHS, DVD.** Warren Beatty; Hurd Hatfield; Alexandra Stewart; Franchot Tone; Teddy Hart; Jeff Corey; ***D:*** Arthur Penn; ***W:*** Alan M. Surgal; ***C:*** Ghislan Cloquet; ***M:*** Jack Shaindlin; Eddie Sauter.

Mickey the Great 🦴🦴 1/2 **1939** Stitched together from several late '20s Mickey McGuire shorts, starring 10-year-old Rooney. **70m/B; VHS, DVD.** Mickey Rooney; Billy Barty.

Micki & Maude 🦴🦴 **1984 (PG-13)** When a man longs for a baby, he finds that his wife, Micki, is too busy for motherhood. Out of frustration, he has an affair with Maude that leads to her pregnancy. Still shocked by the news of his upcoming fatherhood, the man learns that his wife is also expecting. **117m/C; VHS, DVD.** Dudley Moore; Amy Irving; Ann Reinking; Richard Mulligan; Wallace Shawn; George Gaynes; Andre the Giant; ***D:*** Blake Edwards; ***W:*** Jonathan Reynolds; ***C:*** Harry Stradling, Jr. Golden Globes '85: Actor--Mus./Comedy (Moore).

Micmacs 🦴🦴 *Micmac a Tire-Larigot* **2009 (R)** Surreal, slapstick, good-vs.-evil French comedy set in Paris. Bazil's (Boon) dad was killed by a roadside bomb while serving in the military and later Bazil is hit by a stray bullet from a drive-by shooting. It's lodged in his brain and the doctors fear to remove it, so he leaves the hospital with various physical and behavioral issues. Bazil hooks up with some junkyard-dwelling misfits and persuades them to assist him in a revenge plot against the two armament manufacturers he blames for his troubles. French title is slang for 'non-stop madness' or 'shenanigans.' French with subtitles. **105m/C; DVD, Blu-Ray.** *FR* Dany Boon; Andre Dussollier; Jean-Pierre Marielle; Yolande Moreau; Nicolas Marie; Dominique Pinon; Julie Ferrier; Marie-Julie Baup; ***D:*** Jean-Pierre Jeunet; ***W:*** Jean-Pierre Jeunet; Guillaume Laurant; ***C:*** Tetsuo Nagata; ***M:*** Raphael Beau.

Microcosmos 🦴🦴🦴 **1996 (G)** Warning: Do not attempt to smash the bugs on the screen with your shoe. They're supposed to be there. This French documentary uses special cameras and sound recording devices to explore the world of insects like never before. The editing and score also add a human dimension to the creepy-crawly world under the lawn, making amorous snails and workaholic beetles seem like people you know (well, if they had an extra set of legs and a shell-like carapace). Of course, if you don't like bugs, then this is just a 77-minute gross out. Cameo appearances by some birds and frogs. **77m/C; DVD, Blu-Ray.** *FR* ***D:*** Claude Nuridsany; Marie Perennou; ***C:*** Claude Nuridsany; Marie Perennou; Hughes Ryffel; Thierry Machado; ***M:*** Bruno Coulais. Cesar '97: Art Dir./Set Dec., Cinematog., Film Editing, Score, Sound.

Microwave Massacre 🦴 **1983 (R)** Killer kitchen appliances strike again as late lounge comic Vernon murders nagging wife and 'waves her. Overcome by that Betty Crocker feeling, he goes on a microwave murdering/feeding spree of the local ladies. Lots of Roger Corman copying. **80m/C; VHS, DVD, Blu-Ray.** Jackie Vernon; Loren Schein; Al Troupe; Claire Ginsberg; Lou Ann Webber; Sarah Alt; ***D:*** Wayne Berwick; ***W:*** Thomas Singer; ***C:*** Karen Grossman; ***M:*** Leif Horvath.

Midaq Alley 🦴🦴🦴 *The Alley of Miracles; El Callejon de los Milagros* **1995** Amusing melodrama based on the 1947 novel by Egyptian Naguib Mahfouz and transported from Cairo's backstreets to those of a rundown, modern-day Mexico City neighborhood known as "The Alley of Miracles." Four segments all begin on the same Sunday afternoon and follow a variety of the Alley's inhabitants, including a married man who becomes attracted to a young male clerk, a beauty who falls prey to a suave pimp, and a homely woman looking for love and finding Mr. Wrong. Spanish with subtitles. **140m/C; VHS, DVD, Blu-Ray.** *MX* Ernesto Cruz; Maria Rojo; Salma Hayek; Bruno Bichir; Claudio Obregon; Delia Casanova; Margarita Sanz; Juan Manuel Bernal; Luis Felipe Tovar; Daniel Gimenez Cacho; ***D:*** Jorge Fons; ***W:*** Vicente Lenero; ***C:*** Carlos Marcovich; ***M:*** Lucia Alvarez.

Middle Men 🦴 1/2 **2010 (R)** Deliberately grubby and vulgar depiction of online porn distribution and organized crime. Jack Harris (Wilson) is a calculating Texas businessman who knows his way around the internet and credit card transactions, which gets him unexpectedly involved in the online porn industry in the late 1990s. His sleazy and not-too-bright partners (Macht, Ribisi) then lead to Jack's involvement in drugs, Vegas glitz, and Russian mobsters. **99m/C; Blu-Ray.** Luke Wilson; Giovanni Ribisi; Gabriel Macht; Jacinda Barrett; Laura Ramsey; Terry Crews; Rade Serbedzija; Kevin Pollak; James Caan; Robert Forster; ***D:*** George Gallo; ***W:*** George Gallo; Andy Weiss; ***C:*** Lukas Ettlin; ***M:*** Brian Tyler.

Middle of Nowhere 🦴🦴 1/2 **2012 (R)** Ruby (Corinealdi) is a woman stuck between Derek (Hardwick), who grows increasingly distant as he does a stint behind bars, and new suitor Brian (Oyelowo), who seems like he could give her a bright future. At times too much like a soap opera, director/writer DuVernay's Sundance Award-winning film more often spotlights the honesty of average people stuck at crucial crossroads of their lives. Corinealdi gives a striking performance, presenting a complex character in a genre in which they're too rare. **97m/C; DVD.** Emayatzy Corinealdi; Omari Hardwick; David Oyelowo; Sharon Lawrence; Dondre T. Whitfield; Lorraine Toussaint; Maya Gilbert; ***D:*** Ava DuVernay; ***W:*** Ava DuVernay; ***C:*** Bradford Young; ***M:*** Kathryn Bostic.

Middle of the Night 🦴🦴 **1959** Talky Paddy Chayefsky drama adapted from his play. Wealthy Jewish widower/businessman Jerry Kingsley (March) falls in love with his much-younger divorced receptionist Betty (Novak). Jerry is lonely and Betty is needy so they get engaged, but the disapproval of both families finds them with cold feet. **118m/B; DVD.** Fredric March; Kim Novak; Glenda Farrell; Jan Norris; Albert Dekker; Joan Copeland; Edith Meisner; Lee Phillips; Lee Grant; Martin Balsam; ***D:*** Delbert Mann; ***W:*** Paddy Chayefsky; ***C:*** Joseph Brun; ***M:*** George Bassman.

Middle School: The Worst Years of My Life 🦴🦴 1/2 **2016 (PG)** Rafe Khatchadorian (Gluck) is an average middle school student with a passion for art who transfers to a new school called Hills Village and crosses paths with a horrendous man known as Principal Dwight (Daly). His new Principal rules with an iron fist and tries to squash all artistic expression. He even goes as far as destroying Rafe's sketchbook, leading the student to plan to break every single one of the Principal's rules in creative ways. This mostly clever John Hughes-esque comedy has its moments, but is also pretty forgettable. You could do worse though. **92m/C; DVD, Blu-Ray.** Griffin Gluck; Lauren Graham; Alexa Nisenson; Andrew Daly; Thomas Barbusca; ***D:*** Steve Carr; ***W:*** Chris Bowman; Hubbel Palmer; Kara Holden; ***C:*** Julio Macat; ***M:*** Jeff Cardoni.

Middlemarch 🦴🦴🦴 **1993** Stylish British TV costume drama, adapted from George Eliot's 1872 novel, finds idealistic Dorothea Brooke (Aubrey) determined to be a helpmate to the older scholar, the Rev. Edward Casaubon (Malahide), whom she marries. Too bad that he takes so little interest in her ability (or in Dorothea herself). This leads Casaubon's distant cousin, young and handsome Will Ladislaw (Sewell), to discreetly make his interest clear. Naturally, Eliot has a number of other plots (some dealing with the impact of the Industrial Revolution on 19th-century life) and romances worked into the mix. Filmed in Stamford, England. **360m/C; DVD.** *UK* Juliet Aubrey; Patrick Malahide; Rufus Sewell; Douglas Hodge; Trevyn McDowell; Michael Hordern; Robert Hardy; John Savident; Jonathan Firth; Peter Jeffrey; Simon Chandler; Julian Wadham; ***D:*** Anthony Page; ***W:*** Andrew Davies; Stanley Myers; ***C:*** Brian Tufano.

Middletown 🦴 **2006** Story goes off the rails as does its lead character. After serving as a missionary in Africa, Reverend Gabriel Hunter (Macfayden) returns to his small Irish hometown to take up his new pastoral duties. He's shocked to find various vices are prevalent and that his black sheep brother Jim (Mays) and Jim's pregnant wife Caroline (Birthistle) are no exceptions. The fanatical Gabriel becomes even more zealous, determined to save the souls of the town's inhabitants whether they want him to or not. **89m/C; DVD.** *GB IR* Matthew Macfadyen; Daniel Mays; Eva Birthistle; Gerard McSorley; Richard Dormer; Sorcha Cusack; David Wilmot; ***D:*** Brian Kirk; ***W:*** Daragh Carville; ***C:*** Adam Suschitzky; ***M:*** Debbie Wiseman.

Midnight 🦴🦴 1/2 *Call It Murder* **1934** A jury foreman's daughter is romantically involved with a gangster who is interested in a particular case before it appears in court. The foreman, who sentenced a girl to death, faces a dilemma when his own daughter is arrested for the same crime. An early Bogart appearance in a supporting role led to a re-release of the film as "Call it Murder" after Bogart made it big. Weak melodrama. **74m/B; VHS, DVD.** Humphrey Bogart; Sidney (Sydney) Fox; O.P. Heggie; Henry Hull; Richard Whorf; Margaret Wycherly; Lynne Overman; ***D:*** Chester Erskine; ***W:*** Chester Erskine.

Midnight 1/2 **1939** Struggling showgirl Colbert masquerades as Hungarian countess in sophisticated comedy of marital conflicts. Near-classic film scripted by Wilder and Brackett. Based on a story by Edwin Justus Mayer and Franz Schulz. Remade as "Masquerade in Mexico." **94m/B; VHS, DVD.** Claudette Colbert; Don Ameche; John Barrymore; Francis Lederer; Mary Astor; Hedda Hopper; Rex O'Malley; ***D:*** Mitchell Leisen; ***W:*** Billy Wilder; Charles Brackett; ***C:*** Charles B(ryant) Lang, Jr. Natl. Film Reg. '13.

Midnight *Backwoods Massacre* **1981 (R)** Russo, who cowrote the original "Night of the Living Dead," wrote and directed this film about a runaway girl who is driven out of her home by a lecherous stepfather and meets two young thieves and then a family of cultists. Russo adapted his own novel. He also attains some of "Night of the Living Dead's" low-budget ambience. **88m/C; VHS, DVD.** Lawrence Tierney; Melanie Verliin; John Hall; John Amplas; ***D:*** John A. Russo.

Midnight 2: Sex, Death, and Videotape **1993** Sequel to "Midnight" finds the sole surviving member of the crazed family stalking a beautiful unsuspecting teller with a video camera. Only she's teamed up with a detective to solve the murder of her best friend—even if it means she's bait for a psycho. **70m/C; VHS, DVD, Streaming.** Matthew Jason Walsh; Jo Norcia; ***D:*** John A. Russo.

Midnight Bayou **2009** Lawyer Declan Fitzpatrick (O'Connell) impulsively buys Manet Hall, a newly-restored plantation house near New Orleans that's reputed to be haunted. Declan begins having visions of life in the house more than 100 years ago that are linked to present-day Cajun beauty Lena (Stamile) and murder. Romantic suspense from Lifetime that's based on the book by Nora Roberts. **90m/C; DVD.** Jerry O'Connell; Lauren Stamile; Faye Dunaway; Isabella Hofmann; ***D:*** Ralph Hemecker; ***W:*** Stephen Tolkin; ***C:*** Anghel Decca; ***M:*** Chris P. Bacon; Stuart M. Thomas. **CABLE**

A Midnight Clear **1992 (PG)** Sensitive war drama that takes place in the Ardennes Forest, near the French-German border in December 1944. It's Christmastime and six of the remaining members of a 12-member squad are sent on a dangerous mission to an abandoned house to locate the enemy. Filmed in a dreamy surreal style, the setting is somewhat reminiscent of a fairytale, although a sense of anguish filtrates throughout the picture. A solid script, excellent direction, and a good cast make this a worthwhile film that pits the message of peace against the stupidity of war. Adapted from the novel by William Wharton. **107m/C; DVD, Blu-Ray.** Peter Berg; Kevin Dillon; Arye Gross; Ethan Hawke; Gary Sinise; Frank Whaley; John C. McGinley; Larry Joshua; Curt Lowens; David Jensen; Rachel Griffin; Tim Shoemaker; ***D:*** Keith Gordon; ***W:*** Keith Gordon; ***C:*** Tom Richmond; ***M:*** Mark Isham.

Midnight Clear **2006 (PG-13)** Five strangers, battling misfortune and loneliness, cross paths on Christmas Eve and find their lives changed by acts of kindness. Keeps its Christian themes low-key. Jenkins directs from an adaptation of his father Jerry's short story. **102m/C; DVD.** Stephen Baldwin; K. Callan; Kirk B.R. Woller; Victoria Jackson; Richard Riehle; Richard Fancy; Mary Thornton; Mitchell Jarvis; ***D:*** Dallas Jenkins; ***W:*** Wes Halula; ***C:*** Randall Walker Gregg; ***M:*** Jeehun Hwang.

Midnight Confessions **1995 (R)** Provocative night-time DJ Vannesse (Hoyt) lures her listeners into revealing their sexual fantasies. But when an obsessed fan begins killing women just how deeply is she involved? **98m/C; VHS, DVD.** Carol Hoyt; Julie Strain; Monique Parent; Richard Lynch; ***D:*** Allan Shustak; ***W:*** Jake Jacobs; Allan Shustak; Marc Cushman; Timothy O'Rawe; ***C:*** Tom Frazier; ***M:*** Scott Singer.

Midnight Cop **1988 (R)** A young woman gets tangled up in a web of murder, intrigue, prostitution and drugs, and she enlists the aid of a cop to help get her out of it. **100m/C; VHS, DVD.** Michael York; Morgan Fairchild; Frank Stallone; Armin Mueller-Stahl; ***D:*** Peter Patzak.

Midnight Cowboy 1/2 **1969 (R)** Drama about the relationship between a naive Texan hustler and a seedy derelict, set in the underbelly of NYC. Graphic and emotional character study is brilliantly acted and engaging. Shocking and considered quite risque at the time of its release, this film now carries an "R" rating. It was the only "X"-rated film ever ever to win the Best Picture Oscar. From James Leo Herlihy's novel. **113m/C; VHS, DVD, Blu-Ray.** Dustin Hoffman; Jon Voight; Sylvia Miles; Brenda Vaccaro; John McGiver; Bob Balaban; Barnard Hughes; ***D:*** John Schlesinger; ***W:*** Waldo Salt; ***C:*** Adam Holender; ***M:*** John Barry. Oscars '69: Adapt. Screenplay, Director (Schlesinger), Film; AFI '98: Top 100; British Acad. '69: Actor (Hoffman), Director (Schlesinger), Film, Screenplay; Directors Guild '69: Director (Schlesinger); Natl. Film Reg. '94; N.Y. Film Critics '69: Actor (Voight); Natl. Soc. Film Critics '69: Actor (Voight); Writers Guild '69: Adapt. Screenplay.

Midnight Crossing **1987 (R)** Two married couples are subjected to jealousy, betrayal and uncloseted-skeletons as their pleasure cruise on a yacht turns into a ruthless search for sunken treasure. **96m/C; VHS, DVD.** Faye Dunaway; Daniel J. Travanti; Kim Cattrall; John Laughlin; Ned Beatty; ***D:*** Roger Holzberg.

Midnight Dancers **1994** Seamy look at Manila's gay subculture and male prostitution. Sonny and his older brothers Dennis and Joel work as dancers at a sleazy club whose upstairs apartments are used for prostitution. The boys need the money to help their impoverished family survive in the slums but the emotional wear and tear (not to mention police raids and assorted brutalities) provide lots of melodrama. Filipino with subtitles. **115m/C; VHS, DVD.** *PH* Alex Del Rosario; Gandong Cervantes; Laurence David; Perla Bautista; Soxy Topacio; ***D:*** Mel Chionglo; ***W:*** Ricardo Lee; ***C:*** George Tutanes; ***M:*** Nonong Buenoamino.

Midnight Episode **1950** Shakespeare-spouting hobo Professor Prince (Holloway) makes spare change by opening car doors for theatergoers. A dead body falls out of limosine, the body disappears, but the Professor finds the dead man's cash-filled wallet. He keeps the wallet and gets trouble from the killer. Based on the Georges Simenon novel "Monsieur La Souris." **78m/B; DVD.** *UK* Sterling Holloway; Leslie Dwyer; Reginald Tate; Meredith Edwards; Wilfrid Hyde-White; Sebastian Cabot; ***D:*** Gordon Perry; ***W:*** William Templeton; David Evans; ***C:*** Hone Glendinning; ***M:*** Mischa Spoliansky.

Midnight Express **1978 (R)** Gripping and powerful film based on the true story of Billy Hayes (Davis), a young American busted in Turkey wfor trying to smuggle hashish. He is sentenced to a brutal and nightmarish prison for life as an example to other potential smugglers. After enduring tremendous mental and physical torture, Billy seeks the "Midnight Express," his chance at escape. Not always easy to watch, but the overall effect is riveting and unforgettable. Adapted from the book by Hayes and William Hoffer. **120m/C; VHS, DVD.** John Hurt; Randy Quaid; Brad Davis; Paul Smith; Bo Hopkins; Oliver Stone; ***D:*** Alan Parker; ***W:*** Oliver Stone; ***C:*** Michael Seresin; ***M:*** Giorgio Moroder. Oscars '78: Adapt. Screenplay, Orig. Score; British Acad. '78: Director (Parker), Support. Actor (Hurt); Golden Globes '79: Film--Drama, Score, Screenplay, Support. Actor (Hurt); Writers Guild '78: Adapt. Screenplay.

Midnight Faces **1926** Mysterious doings abound in a house in the Florida bayous, recently inherited by Bushman. Silent, with original organ music. **72m/B; Silent; VHS, DVD.** Francis X. Bushman; Jack Perrin; Kathryn McGuire; ***D:*** Bennett Cohen; ***W:*** Bennett Cohen; ***C:*** King Gray.

Midnight Girl 1/2 **1925** A fading opera impresario plots to steal a family's fortune. Lugosi before he became Dracula. Silent. Currently only sold as part of a collection. **84m/B; Silent; VHS, DVD.** Bela Lugosi; Lila Lee; Charlotte Walker; Gareth Hughes; Dolores Cassinelli; ***D:*** Wilfred Noy; ***W:*** Jean Conover; Wilfred Noy; ***C:*** Frank Zucker; G.W. Blitzer.

Midnight Heat 1/2 *Black Out* **1995 (R)** Football player is the prime suspect when his lover's husband (who happens to be the team owner) is murdered. **97m/C; VHS, DVD.** Tim Matheson; Stephen Mendel; Mimi (Meyer) Craven; ***D:*** Harvey Frost.

The Midnight Hour 1/2 **1986** A group of high schoolers stumbles upon a vintage curse that wakes up the dead. More humor than horror. **97m/C; VHS, DVD.** Shari Belafonte; LeVar Burton; Lee Montgomery; Dick Van Patten; Kevin McCarthy; Jonelle Allen; Peter DeLuise; Dedee Pfeiffer; Mark Blankfield; ***D:*** Jack Bender; ***C:*** Rexford Metz; ***M:*** Brad Fiedel. **TV**

Midnight in Paris **2011 (PG-13)** Fabulous romantic comedy follows a young engaged couple, Gil (Wilson) and Inez (McAdams), who are part of a family contingent in Paris on business. The glamorous city brings life-changing experiences, and naive Gil imagines himself beginning a brand new and improved life there. And along the way he just happens to run into some famous folks from past times during his nightly travels. Allen's 41st film is magical and clever, with his typically amusing observations about life. Wilson shines in the lead role. Like Gil, you'll be seduced by Paris and the promises it offers. **100m/C; DVD, Blu-Ray.** Owen Wilson; Rachel McAdams; Kathy Bates; Adrien Brody; Marion Cotillard; Michael Sheen; Alison Pill; Tom Hiddleston; Corey Stoll; Kurt Fuller; Mimi Kennedy; Nina Arianda; Carla Bruni; ***D:*** Woody Allen; ***W:*** Woody Allen; ***C:*** Darius Khondji; Johanne Debas. Oscars '11: Orig. Screenplay; Golden Globes '12: Screenplay; Writers Guild '11: Orig. Screenplay.

Midnight in the Garden of Good and Evil **1997 (R)** An all-star cast can't save Eastwood's grossly mishandled adaptation of John Berendt's best-selling novel on the eccentric citizens and lush scenery of Savannah. New York journalist John Kelso (Cusack) is sent to report on the glamourous Christmas parties of famed citizen and ham Jim Williams (Spacey, oozing his usual silky charm), only to be detoured by Williams shooting his male, live-in companion. Was it cold-blooded murder or self defense? With Eastwood's clumsy direction, a dragging running time, and an overabundance of characters, the rich subject matter is all but lost and the answer to the above question moot. **155m/C; DVD, Blu-Ray.** Kevin Spacey; John Cusack; Jack Thompson; Alison Eastwood; Lady Chablis; Irma P. Hall; Paul Hipp; Jude Law; Dorothy Loudon; Anne Haney; Kim Hunter; Geoffrey Lewis; ***D:*** Clint Eastwood; ***W:*** John Lee Hancock; ***C:*** Jack N. Green; ***M:*** Lennie Niehaus.

Midnight Kiss 1/2 **1993 (R)** When a woman police detective investigates a mysterious series of deaths—women whose blood has been drained—she gets more than she bargains for. She's attacked by a vampire and is herself turned into a reluctant bloodsucker. Quick moving and some gross special effects. Also available in an unrated version. **85m/C; VHS, DVD.** Michelle Owens; Gregory A. Greer; Celeste Yarnall; ***D:*** Joel Bender; ***W:*** John Weidner; Ken Lamplugh.

The Midnight Lady 1/2 **1932** Speakeasy owner Nita St. George (Padden) decides to take the rap when her long-lost daughter Jean (Dell) is accused of murdering her louse of a boyfriend. But Jean actually didn't do the crime so Nita's going to the slammer for nothing unless someone finds out the truth. A low-rent "Madame X." **65m/B; DVD.** Sarah Padden; Claudia Dell; John Darrow; Montagu Love; Theodore von Eltz; Lena Basquette; Brandon Hurst; ***D:*** Richard Thorpe; ***W:*** Edward T. Lowe; ***C:*** M(ilton) A(rthur) Anderson.

Midnight Madness **1980 (PG)** Five teams of college stereotypes search LA for clues as part of a wacky scavenger hunt designed by a fellow student. Features the big-screen debut of Michael J. Fox as the little brother of David "I'm a Pepper" Naughton (look closely to see the former Pepper pitchman drinking a bottle of the stuff; it's the only near-witty moment). Also casts Stephen "Flounder" Dorf, making this flick somewhat of an "It's a Mad, Mad, Mad, Mad Animal House," but to say that is an insult to both of those films. Even the presence of arch-geek Eddie Deezen can't save the outing. **110m/C; VHS, DVD.** David Naughton; Stephen Furst; Debra Clinger; Eddie Deezen; Michael J. Fox; Maggie Roswell; ***D:*** David Wechter; ***W:*** David Wechter; ***C:*** Frank V. Phillips; ***M:*** Julius Wechter.

Midnight Mary **1933** Orphaned Mary (Young) gets involved with a gang of thieves and becomes gangster Leo's (Cortez) moll. She falls for wealthy playboy Tom (Tone) and tries to go straight but her past catches up with her. We see Mary's life in flashbacks as she awaits trial for murder. It may be a pre-Hays Code film but that doesn't mean there can't be a (somewhat unlikely) happy ending. **71m/B; DVD.** Loretta Young; Ricardo Cortez; Andy Devine; Una Merkel; Warren Hymer; Frank Conroy; Franchot Tone; ***D:*** William A. Wellman; ***W:*** Kathryn Scola; Gene Markey; ***C:*** James Van Trees; ***M:*** William Axt.

The Midnight Meat Train **2008 (R)** Photographer Leon Kaufman (Cooper) is encouraged by gallery owner Susan Hoff (Shields) to dig more deeply into the darkest, most disturbing aspects of grim human potential, which draws him into the frightening world of a serial killer/mutilator known as Mahogany (Jones), who searches the subway for victims. Kaufman falls further into the killer's inhuman world, pulling his innocent, vegan girlfriend Maya (Bibb) along with him. Based on a short story by Clive Barker, this Ryuhei Kitamura directed film is an artful slasher in the J-Horror tradition but offers nothing particularly original. **100m/C; DVD, Blu-Ray, On Demand.** Bradley Cooper; Leslie Bibb; Vinnie Jones; Brooke Shields; Roger Bart; Tony Curran; Barbara Harris; Theodore (Ted) Raimi; ***D:*** Ryuhei Kitamura; ***W:*** Jeff Buhler; ***C:*** Jonathan Sela; ***M:*** Robert Williamson; Johannes Kobilke.

Midnight Run **1988 (R)** An ex-cop, bounty hunter must bring in an ex-mob accountant who has embezzled big bucks from his former boss. After he catches up with the thief, the hunter finds that bringing his prisoner from New York to Los Angeles will be very trying, especially when it is apparent that the Mafia and FBI are out to stop them. The friction between the two leads—De Niro and Grodin—is fun to watch, while the action and comic moments are enjoyable. **125m/C; VHS, DVD, Blu-Ray, HD-DVD.** Robert De Niro; Charles Grodin; Yaphet Kotto; John Ashton; Dennis Farina; Joe Pantoliano; Richard Foronjy; Wendy Phillips; ***D:*** Martin Brest; ***W:*** George Gallo; ***C:*** Donald E. Thorin; ***M:*** Danny Elfman.

Midnight Special **2016 (PG-13)** Shannon stars as a man willing to do anything to get his "special" son to a predetermined place at a specific time. The journey sends all manner of authorities after him because the son happens to have some sort of supernatural powers. It's all very loosely defined so as to serve as an allegory for the loss of a sick child. It's powerful, amazing moviemaking. Nichols has created a beautiful meld of "Starman" and "Lorenzo's Oil"--a film about fatherhood and faith. **112m/C; DVD, Blu-Ray.** Adam Driver; Joel Edgerton; Kirsten Dunst; Michael Shannon; Sam Shepard; ***D:*** Jeff Nichols; ***W:*** Jeff Nichols; ***C:*** Adam Stone; ***M:*** David Wingo.

Midnight Sun **2018 (PG-13)** A teen romantic drama based on a 2006 Japanese film. For nearly her whole life, bright 17-year-old Katie (Thorne) has spent most of her daytime hours inside because she suffers from a rare condition which makes the sun's rays potentially deadly. Her widower father (Riggle) has taken every precaution to protect Katie. On the night she graduates from home school, she finally meets Charlie (Schwarzenegger), a graduating senior. As the pair begin dating, they push each other to grow in unexpected ways. Though targeted at teens, the film is refreshingly wholesome and reminiscent of Love Story. **91m/C; DVD, Blu-Ray.** Bella Thorne; Patrick Schwarzenegger; Rob Riggle; Quinn Shephard; Ken Tremblett; ***D:*** Scott Speer; ***W:*** Kenji Bando; Eric Kirsten; ***C:*** Karsten Gopinath; ***M:*** Ethan Dorr; Morgan Dorr; Nate Walcott.

Midnight Tease 1/2 **1994** Strip bar, the Club Fugazi, is having trouble with its help—the dancers keep getting murdered. Dancer Samantha (Leigh) actually dreams about the murders before they occur, so naturally she becomes the prime suspect. Leigh can actually do more than look fetching but plot is barely apparent. **87m/C; VHS, DVD.** Cassandra Leigh; Rachel Reed; Edmund

Halley; Ashlie Rhey; Todd Joseph; ***D:*** Scott Levy; ***W:*** Daniella Purcell; ***C:*** Dan E. Toback; ***M:*** Christopher Lennertz.

Midnight Tease 2 **1995 (R)** Jen Brennan (Kelly) goes undercover at an L.A. strip club to find out who's been murdering the dancers, including her sister. **93m/C; VHS, DVD.** Kimberly Kelley; Tane McClure; Ross Hagen; ***D:*** Richard Styles; ***W:*** Richard Styles; ***C:*** Gary Graver.

Midnight Warrior **1989** A reporter strikes it big when he investigates the underside of L.A. nightlife, but things go terribly wrong when he becomes wrapped up in the sleaze. **90m/C; VHS, DVD.** Bernie Angel; Michelle Berger; Kevin Bernhardt; Lilly Melgar; ***D:*** Joseph Merhi.

Midnight Witness **1/2 1993 (R)** Guy finds himself on the run when after he videotapes the beating of a young drug dealer by corrupt cops. Plot bears more than a little resemblance to the Rodney King incident, but according to writer Foldy it was written before it took place. Low-budget thriller went direct to video. **90m/C; VHS, DVD.** Maxwell Caulfield; Jan-Michael Vincent; Paul Johansson; Karen Moncrieff; Mark Pellegrino; Virginia Mayo; ***D:*** Peter Foldy; ***W:*** Peter Foldy; ***M:*** Graydon Hillock. **VIDEO**

Midnight's Child **1/2 1993** Another Nanny-from-Hell story, only this time it's literal. D'Abo is the Nanny in question, who belongs to a Satanic cult. Her mission is to select the young daughter in her care as a bride for the devil, even if the girl's parents don't approve of the match. **89m/C; VHS, DVD.** Olivia D'Abo; Marcy Walker; Cotter Smith; Elisabeth Moss; Jim Norton; Judy Parfitt; Roxann Biggs-Dawson; Mary Larkin; ***D:*** Colin Bucksey; ***W:*** David Chaskin.

Mid90s **1/2 2018 (R)** Actor turned writer/director Jonah Hill delivers a poignant, authentic coming-of-age tale about a 13-year-old growing up in 1990s Los Angeles. Young Stevie has a pretty rotten time both at home and at school, but he discovers kinship and hope when he's befriended by a crew of skateboarding, similarly struggling lost boys. **85m/C; DVD, Blu-Ray.** Sunny Suljic; Katherine Waterston; Lucas Hedges; Na-kel Smith; Olan Prenatt; ***D:*** Jonah Hill; ***W:*** Jonah Hill; ***C:*** Christopher Blauvelt; ***M:*** Atticus Ross.

Midsommar **1/2 2019 (R)** Graduate student Dani (Pugh) is emotionally traumatized after the death of a family member, and tags along on a trip to Sweden with other young academics including longtime boyfriend Christian (Reynor). Among them is Josh (Harper), who is attending a festival held once every 90 years for academic research. Once they arrive, the situation is not what they expected. They are given hallucinatory drugs in tea and find themselves trapped in rituals that are not what they seem. The second film from writer/director Aster, the horror film has a tense sense of dread. **147m/C; DVD, Blu-Ray.** Florence Pugh; Jack Reynor; William Jackson Harper; Vilhelm Blomgren; Will Poulter; ***D:*** Ari Aster; ***W:*** Ari Aster; ***C:*** Pawel Pogorzelski; ***M:*** The Haxan Cloak.

Midsummer Madness **1/2** *Janu Nakts; St. John's Night* **2007** Young American Curt arrives in Riga, Latvia in search of an unknown half-sister just as the country is about to celebrate St. John's night. The summer solstice brings out the crazy in everyone as Curt gets an eye-opening ride from an eccentric cabbie and various folk take friendship, sex, and romance to another level. **90m/C; DVD.** *AT GB* Dominique Pinon; Maria De Medeiros; Chulpan Khamatova; Orlando Wells; Victor McGuire; Gundars Abolins; Birgit Minichmayr; James-William Watts; ***D:*** Alexander Hahn; ***W:*** Norman Hudis; Alexander Hahn; Alexander Mahler; ***C:*** Jerzy Palacz; ***M:*** Boris Resnik.

A Midsummer Night's Dream **1935** Famed Reinhardt version of the Shakespeare classic, featuring nearly every star on the Warner Bros. lot. The plot revolves around the amorous battle between the king (Jory) and queen (Louise) of a fairy kingdom, and the humans who are drawn into their sport. Features de Havilland's first film role (as Hermia), althogh Rooney, as the fairy Puck, seems to be having the most fun. Classic credit line: Dialogue by William Shakespeare. **117m/B; VHS, DVD.** James Cagney; Dick Powell; Joe E. Brown; Hugh Herbert; Olivia de Havilland; Ian Hunter; Mickey Rooney; Victor Jory; Arthur Treacher; Billy Barty; Ross Alexander; ***D:*** Max Reinhardt; William Dieterle; ***W:*** Mary C. McCall; Charles Kenyon; ***C:*** Hal Mohr. Oscars '35: Cinematog., Film Editing.

A Midsummer Night's Dream **1/2 1968** Fine acting from the Royal Shakespeare Company cast in this filmed version of the play. Makes very little use of the Athens, Greece scenery. **124m/C; VHS, DVD.** *GB* David Warner; Diana Rigg; Ian Richardson; Dame Judi Dench; Ian Holm; Barbara Jefford; Nicholas Selby; Dame Helen Mirren; Michael Jayston; Derek Godfrey; Hugh Sullivan; Paul Rogers; Sebastian Shaw; Bill Travers; ***D:*** Peter Hall.

A Midsummer Night's Dream **1/2 1996 (PG-13)** The Royal Shakespeare Company offers their version of the Shakespeare classic in which a spat between Oberon and Titania, the king and queen of the fairies, leads to a romantic and comedic woodland fantasy for a quartet of would-be lovers who get caught up in their spells, as well as a group of rustics rehearsing their own play. **103m/C; VHS, DVD.** *GB* Lindsay Duncan; Alex Jennings; Desmond Barrit; Barry Lynch; Monica Dolan; Emily Raymond; ***D:*** Adrian Noble; ***C:*** Ian Wilson; ***M:*** Howard Blake.

A Midsummer Night's Sex Comedy **1/2 1982 (PG)** Allen's homage to Shakespeare, Renoir, Chekhov, Bergman, and who knows who else is an engaging ensemble piece about hijinks among friends and acquaintances gathered at a country house at the turn of the century. Standouts include Ferrer as pompous professor and Steenburgen as Allen's sexually repressed wife. Mia's first for the Woodman. **88m/C; VHS, DVD, Blu-Ray.** Woody Allen; Mia Farrow; Mary Steenburgen; Tony Roberts; Julie Hagerty; Jose Ferrer; Kate McGregor-Stewart; ***D:*** Woody Allen; ***W:*** Woody Allen; ***C:*** Gordon Willis.

Midway **1976 (PG)** The epic WWII battle of Midway, the turning point in the war, is retold through Allied and Japanese viewpoints by a big all-star cast saddled with dumpy dialogue and enough weaponry to seize Hollywood on any given Wednesday. **132m/C; VHS, DVD, Blu-Ray.** Charlton Heston; Henry Fonda; James Coburn; Glenn Ford; Hal Holbrook; Robert Mitchum; Cliff Robertson; Robert Wagner; Kevin Dobson; Christopher George; Toshiro Mifune; Tom Selleck; Sab Shimono; Robert Webber; Ed Nelson; James Shigeta; Monte Markham; Biff McGuire; Glenn Corbett; Gregory Walcott; Noriyuki "Pat" Morita; John Fujioka; Dale Ishimoto; Dabney Coleman; Erik Estrada; Clyde Kusatsu; Robert Ito; Steve Kanaly; Kip Niven; Mitchell Ryan; Susan Sullivan; ***D:*** Jack Smight; ***W:*** Donald S. Sanford; ***C:*** Harry Stradling, Jr.; ***M:*** John Williams.

Midway **2019 (PG-13)** In 1937, intelligence officer Edwin T. Layton (Wilson) warns that Japan may attack the United States, while Japanese Admiral Isoroku Yamamoto (Toyokawa) wants to avoid such conflict. After the Japanese bomb Pearl Harbor and bring the U.S. into World War II, Japanese naval leaders, including Yamamoto, try to disable U.S. forces in the Pacific. Americans such as daredevil fighter pilot Dick Best (Skrein) prepare for battle as Layton helps design strategies. Excellent sound mixing brings the World War II battles to life, but it struggles from the excessive use of CGI and subpar storytelling. **138m/C; DVD, Blu-Ray.** Ed Skrein; Patrick Wilson; Woody Harrelson; Luke Evans; Mandy Moore; ***D:*** Roland Emmerich; ***W:*** Wes Tooke; ***C:*** Robby Baumgartner; ***M:*** Harald Kloser; Thomas Wanker.

The Midwife *Sage femme* **2017** An affecting character-driven drama featuring two esteemed actresses of French cinema. Claire (Frot) is an excellent midwife whose maternity clinic is closing but hesitates to take a position at a more impersonal hospital. Her staid life is changed by her late father's mistress, Beatrice (Deneuve). The free-spirited Beatrice has brain cancer and turns to Claire to make amends for abandoning her father and to not be alone as she deals with her illness. Centering on the common idea that life should be lived to its fullest, the multi-layered performances by Deneuve and Frot make it worthy. French with subtitles. **117m/C; DVD.** Catherine Deneuve; Catherine Frot; Olivier Gourmet; Quentin Dolmaire; Mylene Demongeot; ***D:*** Martin Provost; ***W:*** Martin Provost; ***C:*** Yves Cape; ***M:*** Gregoire Hetzel.

A Midwinter's Tale **1/2** *In the Bleak Midwinter* **1995 (R)** Branagh assembles a largely unknown cast in this low-budget backstage saga about an out-of-work thesp, Joe Harper (Maloney), who assembles a shaggy crew of actors to stage an alternative "Hamlet" in a small English country church. The diverse cast squabble, stumble, and emote their way through rehearsals, finally pulling together for the big show. Funny and interesting performances manage to show through the dense and somewhat cliched script with Maloney and Sessions as a camp queen playing the Queen (Gertrude, that is) standing out. **98m/B; DVD.** *UK* Michael Maloney; Richard Briers; Mark Hadfield; Nicholas Farrell; Gerard Horan; John Sessions; Celia Imrie; Hetta Charnley; Julia Sawalha; Joan Collins; Jennifer Saunders; ***D:*** Kenneth Branagh; ***W:*** Kenneth Branagh; ***C:*** Roger Lanser; ***M:*** Jimmy Yuill.

Mifune *Mifunes Sidste Sang; Mifune's Last Song* **1999 (R)** Third release for the Danish film collective Dogma 95 (following "The Idiots" and "The Celebration") is a comedy/romance with a couple of twists. Yuppie Kresten (Berthelsen) travels to the family's run-down farm to check on his mentally handicapped brother, Rud (Asholt), after their father's death. Kresten needs a housekeeper and winds up with attractive Livia (Hjeljle), who neglects to tell him she is a hooker on the lam from her threatening pimp and also shows up with her younger brother (Tarding). Kresten and Livia soon share a mutual attraction and lots of obstacles. Title refers to Rud's hero worship of actor Toshiro Mifune. Danish with subtitles. **102m/C; VHS, DVD.** *DK* Iben Hjejle; Anders W. Berthelsen; Jesper Asholt; Emil Tarding; Anders (Tofting) Hove; Sofie Gråbol; Paprika Steen; Mette Bratlann; ***D:*** Soeren Kragh-Jacobsen; ***W:*** Soeren Kragh-Jacobsen; Anders Thomas Jensen; ***C:*** Anthony Dod Mantle; ***M:*** Karl Bille; Christian Sievert.

The Mighty **1998 (PG-13)** Kevin's (Culkin) smart and brave despite suffering from Morquio's syndrome. His new neighbor, Max (Henson), is just the opposite: large in size, not too bright, and afraid of everything. When Kevin becomes Max's reading tutor, he brings along a book on the legend of King Arthur. Kevin rides Max's shoulders and, dubbing themselves "Freak the Mighty" (the title of Rodman Philbrick's novel, on which the film is based), the inspired boys embark on knightly neighborhood quests. Henson's amazing as the at-first introverted Max and Culkin does an equally good job. Stone's understated performance as Kevin's mom shows she's more than a sexpot. **100m/C; DVD.** Kieran Culkin; Elden (Ratliff) Henson; Sharon Stone; Gillian Anderson; Harry Dean Stanton; Gena Rowlands; James Gandolfini; Joe Perrino; Meat Loaf Aday; Jenifer Lewis; ***D:*** Peter Chelsom; ***W:*** Charles Leavitt; ***C:*** John de Borman; ***M:*** Trevor Jones.

Mighty Aphrodite **1/2 1995 (R)** Neurotic New York sportswriter Lenny Weinrib (Allen) is trapped in an unhappy marriage to art dealer Amanda (Bonham Carter), who talks him into adopting a child. Film comes alive when Lenny tracks down his son's biological mother, consummate dumb blond and hooker/porno actress Linda, played with over-the-top gusto by Sorvino. Lenny attempts to reform his son's bio mom while a Greek chorus provide a running commentary on the tragedy/comedy of Lenny's predicaments. Allen's 31st film treads into familiar Woodman waters but falls short of his past comic genius. **95m/C; DVD.** Woody Allen; Helena Bonham Carter; Mira Sorvino; F. Murray Abraham; Michael Rapaport; Jack Warden; Olympia Dukakis; Peter Weller; Claire Bloom; David Ogden Stiers; ***D:*** Woody Allen; ***W:*** Woody Allen; ***C:*** Carlo Di Palma; ***M:*** Dick Hyman. Oscars '95: Support. Actress (Sorvino); Golden Globes '96: Support. Actress (Sorvino); Natl. Bd. of Review '95: Support. Actress (Sorvino); N.Y. Film Critics '95: Support. Actress (Sorvino); Broadcast Film Critics '95: Support. Actress (Sorvino).

The Mighty Celt **1/2 2005** Donal (McKenna) is 14 and lives in Belfast with his hard-pressed single mum Kate (Anderson). Donal is crazy about greyhound racing and he works for trainer Good Joe (Stott), who's far from good since he drowns the greyhounds who lose a race. The teen has been training an unlikely dog he's named the Mighty Celt, and Joe promises him ownership if the dog wins three races in a row. Of course, Joe's a liar and a problem for ex-IRA man O (Carlyle), who returns from exile and has ties with Joe he'd sooner forget. What he hasn't forgotten is Kate. **82m/C; DVD.** *GB IR* Gillian Anderson; Robert Carlyle; Ken Stott; Tyrone McKenna; ***D:*** Pearse Elliott; ***W:*** Pearse Elliott; ***C:*** Seamus Deasy; ***M:*** Adrian Johnston.

The Mighty Ducks **1/2 1992 (PG)** Bad News Bears on skates. Selfish yuppie lawyer is arrested for drunk driving and as part of his community service sentence, he is forced to coach an inner-city hockey team full of the usual misfits and underachievers. Although sarcastic and skeptical, Coach Gordon Bombay (Estevez) eventually bonds with the Ducks and learns to treat them with respect. Dual themes of teamwork and redemption are repeated constantly, and it gets a bit hokey at times, but the kids won't mind with this fun Disney film, while adults will appreciate the sarcasm. Followed by "D2: The Mighty Ducks." **114m/C; DVD, Blu-Ray.** Emilio Estevez; Joss Ackland; Lane Smith; Heidi Kling; Josef Sommer; Matt Doherty; Steven Brill; Joshua Jackson; Elden (Ratliff) Henson; Shaun Weiss; ***D:*** Stephen Herek; ***W:*** Steven Brill; Brian Hohlfeld; ***C:*** Thomas Del Ruth; ***M:*** David Newman.

Mighty Fine **1/2 2012 (R)** Joe Fine (Chazz Palminsteri) uproots his Brooklyn family to New Orleans and begins living a life of extravagance despite his business crumbling around him. **79m/C; DVD, Streaming.** Chazz Palminteri; Andie MacDowell; Jodelle Ferland; Rainey Qualley; Paul Ben-Victor; ***D:*** Debbie Goodstein; ***W:*** Debbie Goodstein; ***C:*** Bobby Bukowski; ***M:*** Max Lichtenstein. **VIDEO**

A Mighty Heart **2007 (R)** Based on Mariane Pearl's memoir about the kidnapping and execution of her husband, Wall Street Journal reporter Daniel, when he was on assignment in Karachi, Pakistan in 2002. His beheading by Islamic extremists was videotaped for broadcast on the Internet while the pregnant Mariane (a journalist herself) worked her way through bureaucrats and false leads to get answers. Brit director Winterbottom has done films on the complexities of the Mideast before, and he treats his harrowing story matter-of-factly. Jolie (a somewhat controversial choice for the role) does a fine, low-key job with Futterman, as Daniel, in flashbacks during happier times. **103m/C; DVD, Blu-Ray, HD-DVD.** Angelina Jolie; Dan Futterman; Will Patton; Archie Panjabi; Irfan Khan; Denis O'Hare; Sajid Hasan; Gary Wilmes; ***D:*** Michael Winterbottom; ***W:*** Michael Winterbottom; Laurence Coriat; John Orloff; ***C:*** Marcel Zyskind; ***M:*** Molly Nyman; Harry Escott.

Mighty Joe Young **1/2 1949** Tongue-in-cheek King Kong variation features giant ape brought to civilization and exploited in a nightclub act, whereupon things get darned ugly. Bullied and given the key to the liquor cabinet, mild-mannered Joe goes on a drunken rampage, but eventually redeems himself by rescuing orphans from a fire. Special effects (courtesy of Willis O'Brien and the great Ray Harryhausen) are probably the film's greatest asset. Also available colorized. **94m/B; DVD, Blu-Ray.** Terry Moore; Ben Johnson; Robert Armstrong; Frank McHugh; ***D:*** Ernest B. Schoedsack; ***W:*** Ruth Rose; ***C:*** J. Roy Hunt; ***M:*** Roy Webb.

Mighty Joe Young **1998 (PG)** Loose adaptation of the 1949 film has special effects wizard Rick Baker creating a very life-like model of the 15-foot, 2,000-lb. gorilla. With his elaborate features, including a pair of huge brown eyes, this Joe has more personality than his human allies Jill (Theron) and O'Hara (Paxton) who, in between saving Joe from evil South African poachers, spend most of the film giving each other the googoo eyes. Wholesome, harmless, lightweight (the movie, not the gorilla) family entertainment. **114m/C; VHS, DVD, Blu-Ray.** Bill Paxton; Charlize Theron; David Paymer; Regina King; Rade Serbedzija; Peter Firth; Lawrence Pressman; Linda Purl; Ray Harryhausen; ***D:*** Ron Underwood; ***W:*** Mark Rosenthal; Larry Konner; ***C:*** Don Peterman; Oliver Wood; ***M:*** James Horner.

The Mighty Macs 1/2 **2009 (G)** Inspirational true sports drama sat on the shelf for two years until its brief onscreen release in 2011. In 1971, Cathy Rush (Gugino) is hired as the basketball coach at tiny Catholic all-girls Immaculata College in Pennsylvania. The program has no money, no gym, and can barely put together a team but there is a lot of faith. The coach's feisty, unwavering belief helps turn the early defeatist attitude of her players around but you always know where the story is going. **102m/C; DVD.** Carla Gugino; David Boreanaz; Marley Shelton; Ellen Burstyn; Lauren Bittner; Phyllis Somerville; Kimberly Blair; Katie Hayek; Margaret Anne Florence; Kate Nowlin; Jesse Draper; ***D:*** Tim Chamber; ***W:*** Tim Chamber; ***C:*** Chuck Cohen; ***M:*** William Ross.

Mighty Morphin Power Rangers: The Movie **1995 (PG)** From the living room onto the big screen, these six surburban teenagers with super powers battle the evil Ivan Ooze to save Earth. Offers more special effects, new Zord animals, more ooze and more growth to the retail toy industry than the small screen could provide. A child's dream come true, but a parent's nightmare. **93m/C; VHS, DVD.** Paul Freeman; Jason Harold Yost; Amy Jo Johnson; Jason David Frank; John Yong Bosch; Stephen Antonio Cardenas; ***D:*** Bryan Spicer; ***W:*** Arne Olsen; John Kamps; ***C:*** Paul Murphy; ***M:*** Graeme Revell.

The Mighty Peking Man WOOF! *Goliathon* **1977 (PG-13)** A ten-story-tall gorilla resides in the jungle and is sought by a group of Hong Kong businessman who want to display the creature. Johnny, the hunter hired to find the beast, discovers both the gorilla and a beautiful jungle goddess. Incredibly campy, with badly dubbed and hilariously awful dialogue. **91m/C; VHS, DVD.** *CH* Evelyn Kraft; Danny Lee; Chen Cheng-Fen; ***D:*** Meng Hua Ho; ***W:*** Yi Kuang; ***C:*** Tsao Hui-Chi; Wu Cho-Hua; ***M:*** Chuen Yung-Yu.

The Mighty Quinn 1/2 **1989 (R)** While investigating the local murder of a rich white guy, the black Jamaican head of police becomes convinced that the prime suspect, a childhood friend, is innocent. As the police chief, Denzel is good in this off-beat comedy mystery. **98m/C; VHS, DVD; Open Captioned.** Denzel Washington; Robert Townsend; James Fox; Mimi Rogers; M. Emmet Walsh; Sheryl Lee Ralph; Esther Rolle; Art Evans; Norman Beaton; Keye Luke; ***D:*** Carl Schenkel; ***W:*** Hampton Fancher; ***C:*** Jacques Steyn; ***M:*** Anne Dudley.

The Mighty Ursus 1/2 *Ursus* **1961** Euro muscleman flick finds soldier Ursus returning home and learning his fiancé Attea has been kidnapped by a religious cult and is now controlled by the high priest. Ursus is aided by blind slave girl Doreide. A bullfight provides some decent action. Italian with subtitles. **92m/C; DVD.** *IT SP* Ed Fury; Moira Orfei; Maria Luisa Merlo; Luis Prendes; Mario Scaccia; Cristina Gaioni; ***D:*** Carlo Campogalliani; ***W:*** Giuliano Carnimeo; Giuseppe Mangione; ***C:*** Eloy Mela; ***M:*** Roman Vlad.

A Mighty Wind **2003 (PG-13)** Folk music and its aging practitioners are the targets for Guest and company's observant eye and sharp wit. When legendary folk music producer/promoter Irving Sheinbloom dies, his neurotic son Jonathan organizes a tribute concert of his father's favorite acts. They include the earnest, WASPy trio The Folksmen; nine-member, terminally perky cult/troupe New Main Street Singers; and former marrieds Mitch and Mickey. While the dead-on satire is still present, it's muted and more subtle, maybe because the characters are more fully-realized and engaging, maybe because Guest knows this particular genre may be running out of air. **92m/C; DVD, Blu-Ray.** Bob Balaban; Christopher Guest; John Michael Higgins; Jane Lynch; Eugene Levy; Catherine O'Hara; Michael McKean; Parker Posey; Harry Shearer; Fred Willard; Ed Begley, Jr.; Larry Miller; Jennifer Coolidge; Michael Hitchcock; ***D:*** Christopher Guest; ***W:*** Christopher Guest; Eugene Levy; ***C:*** Arlene Donnelly Nelson; ***M:*** John Michael Higgins; Eugene Levy; Catherine O'Hara; Michael McKean; Harry Shearer; Annette O'Toole; C.J. Vanston. N.Y. Film Critics '03: Support. Actor (Levy).

Migrating Forms **2000** An intense experimental film about sexuality by respected avant-garde filmmaker James Fotopoulos. Shot in 16 mm black and white, the film explores the concept of sexual dysfunction and its consequences in minimalist fashion. At the heart of the film is a man (Baty) and a blonde woman (Lewis) meeting for passionless sex in a nearly empty room joined only by the man's cat. Imagery underscores the movies themes, such as a growth on the woman's back moving to the man. **80m/B; DVD.** Preston Baty; Rebecca Lewis; Kiele Sanchez; Edward Flynn; Mimi Marks; ***D:*** James Fotopoulos; ***W:*** James Fotopoulos; ***C:*** John Wagner; ***M:*** Tom Nicholl.

Mike and Dave Need Wedding Dates **2016 (R)** Based on a true story, this raunchy comedy turns the tables on traditional gender roles in the genre, making the women the sex-crazed troublemakers. Efron and DeVine play brothers Mike and Dave Stangle, a pair of ne'er-do-wells who have made such idiots of themselves at past weddings that their family demands they bring dates to their sister's nuptials. They take out an ad on Craigslist, and best friends Tatiana and Alice (Plaza & Kendrick) answer, looking for a free vacation and place to get into trouble. It gets old before it's over but the cast is fun. **98m/C; DVD, Blu-Ray.** Zac Efron; Anna Kendrick; Adam Devine; Aubrey Plaza; Stephen (Steve) Root; ***D:*** Jake Szymanski; ***W:*** Andrew Jay Cohen; Brendan O'Brien; ***C:*** Matthew Clark; ***M:*** Jeff Cardoni.

Mike Wallace Is Here **2019 (PG-13)** Documentary covering influential television journalist Mike Wallace's career. Consisting of archival footage primarily of Wallace, who died in 2012, it spans the whole of his career, including his early years as a pitchman and actor on 1950s television with a heavy focus on his years in investigative journalism for programs such as 60 Minutes. Though Wallace's principled perspective is praised, the sensationalistic aspects of his confrontational interview style are not ignored. Gives an overview of his complicated personal life, including the early death of a son. A balanced look at Wallace while noting his impact on today's news cycle. **90m/C; DVD.** Mike Wallace; ***D:*** Avi Belkin; ***M:*** John Piscitello.

Mike's Murder 1/2 **1984 (R)** Disjointed drama about a shy bank teller who falls for a slick tennis player. When he is murdered, she investigates the circumstances, placing herself in dangerously close contact with his seedy, drug-involved buddies. The twists and confused plot leave the viewer bewildered. **109m/C; VHS, DVD.** Debra Winger; Mark Keyloun; Paul Winfield; Darrell Larson; Dan Shor; William Ostrander; ***D:*** James Bridges; ***W:*** James Bridges; ***M:*** John Barry.

Mikey 1/2 **1992 (R)** Mikey seems like such a sweet little boy—but these awful things keep happening all around him. At every foster home and every school people have such dreadful, and deadly, accidents. But innocent Mikey couldn't be to blame—or could he. **92m/C; VHS, DVD.** Brian Bonsall; John Diehl; Lyman Ward; Josie Bissett; Ashley Laurence; Mimi (Meyer) Craven; Whitby Hertford; ***D:*** Dennis Dimster-Denk; ***W:*** Jonathan Glassner; ***C:*** Thomas Jewett; ***M:*** Tim Truman.

Mikey & Nicky 1/2 **1976 (R)** Quirky, uneven film about longtime friends dodging a hit man during one long night. Bears little evidence of time and money invested. Cassavetes and Falk, however, provide some salvation. **105m/C; VHS, DVD, Blu-Ray.** John Cassavetes; Peter Falk; Ned Beatty; Oliver Clark; William Hickey; ***D:*** Elaine May; ***W:*** Elaine May.

The Milagro Beanfield War 1/2 **1988 (R)** Redford's endearing adaptation of John Nichols's novel about New Mexican townfolk opposing development. Seemingly simple tale provides plenty of insight into human spirit. Fine cast, with especially stellar turns from Blades, Braga, and Vennera. **118m/C; VHS, DVD.** Chick Vennera; John Heard; Ruben Blades; Sonia Braga; Daniel Stern; Julie Carmen; Christopher Walken; Richard Bradford; Carlos Riqueline; James Gammon; Melanie Griffith; Freddy Fender; M. Emmet Walsh; ***D:*** Robert Redford; ***W:*** David S. Ward; ***C:*** Robbie Greenberg; ***M:*** Dave Grusin. Oscars '88: Orig. Score.

Mildred Pierce 1/2 **1945** Gripping melodrama features Crawford as hard-working divorcee rivaling daughter for man's love. Things, one might say, eventually get ugly. Adaptation of James M. Cain novel is classic of its kind. **113m/B; VHS, DVD, Blu-Ray.** Joan Crawford; Jack Carson; Zachary Scott; Eve Arden; Ann Blyth; Bruce Bennett; ***D:*** Michael Curtiz; ***W:*** Ranald MacDougall; ***M:*** Max Steiner. Oscars '45: Actress (Crawford); Natl. Film Reg. '96.

Mildred Pierce 1/2 **2011** Excessive miniseries version (previously filmed in 1945) sticks closer to James M. Cain's 1941 novel and has a cast that can back up all that melodrama. Depression-era, Southern California divorcee Mildred (Winslet) has to support herself and her daughter, so she moves from waitressing to opening her own restaurant. Along the way, she has various affairs, including one with Pasadena playboy Monty (Pearce), and heartbrokenly dotes on her snobby daughter Veda (Wood), who disdains her mother's low-class origins and hard work. **345m/C; DVD, Blu-Ray.** Kate Winslet; Evan Rachel Wood; Guy Pearce; Melissa Leo; Mare Winningham; James LeGros; Brian F. O'Byrne; Hope Davis; Morgan Turner; ***D:*** Todd Haynes; ***W:*** Todd Haynes; Jon Raymond; ***C:*** Edward Lachman; ***M:*** Carter Burwell. **CABLE**

Mile a Minute Love **1937** Very familiar plot does this cheapie no favors. An idealistic inventor develops a high-powered boat engine but crooks are more interested in using it to win a speedboat race. **70m/B; DVD.** William "Billy" Bakewell; Arletta Duncan; Duncan Renaldo; Vivien Oakland; Wilfred Lucas; Earl Douglas; Etta McDaniel; ***D:*** Elmer Clifton; ***W:*** Edwin Anthony; ***C:*** Arthur Martinelli.

Mile 22 1/2 **2018 (R)** High-strung CIA paramilitary operative Silva (Wahlberg) heads up a covert team in SE Asia along a 22-mile route (hence, the title) to retrieve someone willing to exchange top-secret info for safe transport out of the country. This military thriller spills a lot of blood and makes a lot of noise as it tries to drown out the senselessness of the story. Marks the fourth pairing of director Berg and Wahlberg. **90m/C; DVD, Blu-Ray, Streaming.** *US CH* Mark Wahlberg; Lauren Cohan; Iko Uwais; Ronda Rousey; Terry Kinney; ***D:*** Peter Berg; ***W:*** Lea Carpenter; Graham Roland; ***C:*** Jacques Joffret; ***M:*** Jeff Russo.

Miles **2017** An inspirational true story about a gay teenager's quest to get a sports scholarship. After the death of his father, small-town high schooler Miles (Boardman) learns that his father had spent all of Miles' college money during an affair. Desperate to attend school in Chicago, Miles wants a men's volleyball scholarship to Loyola University but has to play on his school's girls' team because there is no boys' team. As Miles tries to impress the Loyola coach, his team faces forfeits because of the competitive imbalance. **90m/C; DVD.** Tim Boardman; Missi Pyle; Paul Reiser; Molly Shannon; Stephen (Steve) Root; ***D:*** Nathan Adloff; ***W:*** Nathan Adloff; Justin D.M. Palmer; ***C:*** Hunter Baker; ***M:*** Justin Bell; Jonathan Levi Shanes.

Miles Ahead **2016 (R)** A nontraditional, jazz-like biopic of the great jazz legend Miles Davis (Cheadle). During the period in which Davis disappeared from public view in the late 1970s, he focused on drugs and pain medications. When music reporter Dave Braden (McGregor) works his way into Davis's life, he spends several wild days helping Davis recover stolen tapes which feature Davis's latest competitions. Also exploring Davis's past and inner life, the film reveals the role his art plays in his sense of self and his future. **100m/C; DVD, Blu-Ray, Download.** Don Cheadle; Ewan McGregor; Emayatzy Corinealdi; Lakeith Stanfield; Brian Bowman; ***D:*** Don Cheadle; ***W:*** Don Cheadle; Steven Baigelman; ***C:*** Roberto Schaefer; ***M:*** Robert Glasper.

Miles from Nowhere 1/2 *Chasing a Dream* **2009** Hallmark Channel original finds teenager Cameron Stiles (Lawrence) up for a college football scholarship that's going to make his demanding coach father Gary (Williams) proud. That's before Cam's best friend, track star John Van Horn (McLaughlin), is killed in a car crash that Cam feels guilty about. To honor John, Cam ignores everyone's advice and expectations and decides to follow John's dream of running a sub-four-minute mile. **89m/C; DVD.** Andrew (Andy) Lawrence; Treat Williams; Joanna Going; Jake McLaughlin; Kevin Kilner; Jarrod Bailey; ***D:*** David Burton Morris; ***W:*** Bryce Zabel; Jackie Zabel; ***C:*** Brian Shanley; ***M:*** Stephen Graziano. **CABLE**

Miles to Go 1/2 **1986** A successful businesswoman tries to enjoy her last days after learning she has terminal cancer. **88m/C; VHS, DVD.** Mimi Kuzyk; Tom Skerritt; Jill Clayburgh; ***D:*** David Greene.

Military Intelligence and You! **2006** At times this spoof of WWII newsreels, propaganda, and training films is a fairly heavy-handed allegory on 9/11 and the invasion of Iraq but it's also generally funny. Military analyst Major Nick Reed (Muldoon) is the subject of a training film that has him working with former flame Lt. Monica Tasty (Bennett). Reed's efforts to locate a hidden German airbase are stymied by the lack of accurate intelligence and those darn foreigners (who aren't necessarily enemy agents but should be looked upon with suspicion anyway). **78m/B; DVD.** Patrick Muldoon; Elizabeth Bennett; MacKenzie Astin; John Moore; Eric Jungmann; ***D:*** Dale Kutzera; ***W:*** Dale Kutzera; ***C:*** Mark Parry.

Militia **1999 (R)** ATF agents Ethan Carter (Cain) and Julie Sanders (Beals) must enlist the help of William Fain (Forrest), an imprisoned member of a radical militia group, in order to stop the deployment of three stolen missiles and an assassination attempt on the President. **97m/C; VHS, DVD.** Dean Cain; Jennifer Beals; Frederic Forrest; Stacy Keach; John Beck; Jeff Kober; Brett Butler; ***D:*** Jim Wynorski; ***W:*** Steve Latshaw; William Carson; ***C:*** Mario D'Ayala; ***M:*** Neal Acree. **VIDEO**

Milk 1/2 **2008 (R)** After moving to San Francisco with lover Scott Smith (Franco), businessman and political activist Harvey Milk (Penn) becomes the first openly gay man to be elected to public office. But Milk is soon clashing with fellow city supervisor Dan White, who eventually assassinates Milk and Mayor George Mascone after losing his job. Penn delivers another top-notch turn as he immerses himself into the role with enough skill and talent to honor Milk without portraying merely a characterization. Both Penn's performance and the film as a whole seem rooted in genuine passion and admiration for the man and his legacy. **127m/C; DVD, Blu-Ray.** Sean Penn; Josh Brolin; Emile Hirsch; James Franco; Diego Luna; Brandon Boyce; Lucas Grabeel; Victor Garber; Alison Pill; Denis O'Hare; Stephen Spinella; Kelvin Yu; Joseph Cross; Zvi Howard Rosenman; Jeff Koons; ***D:*** Gus Van Sant; ***W:*** Dustin Lance Black; ***C:*** Harris Savides; ***M:*** Danny Elfman. Oscars '08: Actor (Penn), Orig. Screenplay; Ind. Spirit '09: First Screenplay, Support. Actor (Franco); Screen Actors Guild '08: Actor (Penn); Writers Guild '08: Orig. Screenplay.

Milk and Honey **2003** Manhattan stockbroker Rick Johnson (Jordan) goes on a midlife freak-out touched off by his suspicion that his wife Joyce (Russell) is cheating on him. What ensues is a string of events that spirals downward, ensnaring people along the way in the most incredibly absurd ways. The digital video filming suits the frenzied nature of this off the wall romp, but the characters are utterly unsympathetic and the string of events falls just outside of the realm of believability. **91m/C; DVD.** Clint Jordan; Kirsten Russell; Eleanor Hutchins; Dudley Findlay, Jr.; Anthony Howard; Greg Amici; ***D:*** Joe Maggio; ***W:*** Joe Maggio; ***C:*** Gordon Chou; ***M:*** Hal Hartley; Yo La Tengo.

Milk Money 1/2 **1994 (PG-13)** Twelve year-old Frank (Carter) talks his pals into pooling their milk money and heading to the big city so they can get a look at a naked woman. They find a prostitute (Griffith) for the job, whom Frank decides would be perfect to bring home to his widower dad (Harris). Although Griffith is generally adorable and the movie is actually less salacious than the premise might suggest, overall, it's sappy and another in the long line of cute-hooker/Cinderella fairytales. **110m/C; VHS, DVD.** Michael Patrick Carter; Melanie Griffith; Ed Harris; Malcolm McDowell; Casey Siemaszko; Anne Heche; Philip Bosco; ***D:*** Richard Benjamin; ***W:*** John Mattson; ***M:*** Michael Convertino.

The Milk of Sorrow *La Teta Asustada* **2009** Title refers to the trauma (including rape and torture) suffered by women during the violent Peruvian regime in the 1980s, which they are alleged to have passed onto their daughters through breast-feeding. (The literal translation of the title is "the frightened breast.") Young Lima maid-servant Fausta suffers from paralyzing fear and her only solace is in her improvised songs, but when her mother dies, Fausta is determined to return her body to her native village. Spanish and Quechua with subtitles. **95m/C; DVD, Blu-Ray.** *PV* Susi Sanchez; Magaly Solier; Marino Ballon; Efrain Solis; Barbara Lazon; ***D:*** Claudia Llosa; ***W:*** Claudia Llosa; ***C:*** Natasha Braier; ***M:*** Selma Mutal Vermeulen.

Milky Way 1/2 **1936** Loopy comedy about milkman who finds unhappiness after accidentally knocking out champion boxer. Adequate, but not equal to Lloyd's fine silent productions. **89m/B; VHS, DVD.** Harold Lloyd; Adolphe Menjou; Verree Teasdale; Helen Mack; William Gargan; ***D:*** Leo McCarey.

The Milky Way **1968** Wicked anti-clerical farce. Two bums team on religious pilgrimage and encounter seemingly all manner of strangeness and sacrilege in this typically peculiar Bunuel work. Perhaps the only film in which Jesus is encouraged to shave. In French with English subtitles. **102m/C; VHS, DVD, Blu-Ray.** *FR* Laurent Terzieff; Paul Frankeur; Delphine Seyrig; Alain Cuny; Bernard Verley; Michel Piccoli; Edith Scob; ***D:*** Luis Bunuel; ***W:*** Jean-Claude Carriere.

The Mill and the Cross 1/2 **2011** Religious allegory and political protest with the title referring to Flemish painter Pieter Bruegels' 1564 work "The Procession to Calvary." It depicts the crucifixion amidst the brutal occupation of his country by Spanish invaders, including members of the Inquisition. Bluescreen technology allows the actors to exist inside the artistic tableau but the English dialogue clanks. **92m/C; DVD, Blu-Ray.** *PL SW* Rutger Hauer; Charlotte Rampling; Michael York; Joanna Litwin; Marian Makula; Dorota Lis; ***D:*** Lech Majewski; ***W:*** Lech Majewski; ***C:*** Adam Sikora; ***M:*** Jozef Skrzek.

Mill of the Stone Women 1/2 *Il Mulino delle Donne di Pietra; Horror of the Stone Women; The Horrible Mill Women; Drops of Blood* **1960** Sculpture-studying art student encounters strange carousel with beautiful babes rather than horsies, and soon finds out that the statues contain shocking secrets. Filmed in Holland, it's offbeat and creepy. **94m/C; VHS, DVD.** *FR IT* Pierre Brice; Scilla Gabel; Dany Carrel; Wolfgang Preiss; Herbert Boenne; Liana Orfei; Marco Guglielmi; Olga Solbelli; ***D:*** Giorgio Ferroni; ***W:*** Giorgio Ferroni; Giorgio Stegani; Remigio del Grosso; Ugo Liberatore; ***C:*** Pier Ludovico Pavoni; ***M:*** Carlo Innocenzi.

The Mill on the Floss **1939** Based on George Eliot's classic novel, this film follows the course of an ill-fated romance and family hatred in rural England. Underwhelming, considering the source. **77m/B; DVD.** *UK* James Mason; Geraldine Fitzgerald; Frank Lawton; Victoria Hopper; Fay Compton; Griffith Jones; Mary Clare; ***D:*** Tim Whelan; ***W:*** Tim Whelan; John Drinkwater; ***C:*** John Stumar.

The Mill on the Floss 1/2 **1997** Maggie Tulliver (Watson) is a smart, emotional young woman painfully at odds with her conventional times. She adores her intolerant older brother Tom (Meredith) but when Maggie becomes involved with Philip Wakeum (Frain), the son of their father's greatest enemy, she reluctantly acquieses when Tom forbids the romance. When Stephen Guest (Weber-Brown), the fiance of Maggie's cousin, falls in love with her, his attentions bring scandal and tragedy to both Maggie and Tom. Watson is fine as the harried heroine but Meredith seems too young for his role, upsetting the sibling balance between the two. Based on the novel by George Eliot. **90m/C; DVD.** *UK* Emily Watson; Ifan Meredith; James Frain; Bernard Hill; James Weber-Brown; Lucy Whybrow; Nicholas Gecks; Cheryl Campbell; ***D:*** Graham Theakston; ***W:*** Hugh Stoddart; ***C:*** David C(lark) Johnson; ***M:*** John Scott.

Millennium 1/2 **1989 (PG-13)** The Earth of the future is running out of time. The people are sterile and the air is terrible. To keep the planet viable, Ladd and company must go back in time and yank people off planes that are doomed to crash. Great special effects and well-thought out script make this a ball of fun. **108m/C; VHS, DVD, Blu-Ray.** Kris Kristofferson; Cheryl Ladd; Daniel J. Travanti; Lloyd Bochner; Robert Joy; Brent Carver; Maury Chaykin; David McIlwraith; Al Waxman; ***D:*** Michael Anderson, Sr.; ***W:*** John Varley; ***C:*** Rene Ohashi; ***M:*** Eric N. Robertson.

Miller's Crossing 1/2 **1990 (R)** From the Coen brothers comes this extremely dark entry in the gangster movie sweepstakes of 1990. Jewish, Italian, and Irish mobsters spin webs of deceit, protection, and revenge over themselves and their families. Byrne is the protagonist, but no hero, being as deeply flawed as the men he battles. Harden stuns as the woman who sleeps with Byrne and his boss, Finney, in hopes of a better life and protection for her small-time crook brother. Visually exhilarating, excellently acted and perfectly paced. **115m/C; VHS, DVD.** Albert Finney; Gabriel Byrne; Marcia Gay Harden; John Turturro; Jon Polito; J.E. Freeman; ***D:*** Joel Coen; ***W:*** Ethan Coen; Joel Coen; ***M:*** Carter Burwell.

The Millerson Case 1/2 *The Crime Doctor's Vacation* **1947** Dr. Ordway (Baxter) takes a much-needed vacation in the Blue Ridge Mountains. Instead of hunting, fishing and relaxing, he's pressed into service by the county health department to help with a typhoid breakout. But during an autopsy of one of the victims, the doc finds no trace of typhoid—this guy was poisoned. Now Ordway has to help solve a murder mystery and rid the town of infection. **72m/B; DVD.** Warner Baxter; Nancy Saunders; Clem Bevans; Griff Barnett; Paul Guilfoyle; James Bell; Addison Richards; Mark Dennis; Robert Kellard; ***D:*** George Archainbaud; ***C:*** Philip Tannura; ***M:*** Mischa Bakaleinikoff.

Millie 1/2 **1931** Creaky melodrama about a divorcee who wants every man but one. He pursues her teenage daughter instead, leading to tragedy and courtroom hand-wringing. Twelvetrees still stands out in this hokum, based on a Donald Henderson novel considered daring in its day. **85m/B; VHS, DVD, Blu-Ray.** Helen Twelvetrees; Robert Ames; Lilyan Tashman; Joan Blondell; John Halliday; James Hall; Anita Louise; Frank McHugh; ***D:*** John Francis Dillon.

Million Dollar Arm **2014 (PG)** Jon Hamm seeks to make the jump from TV star to movie star in this mediocre, melodramatic sports drama about a slimy sports agent who finds a potential MLB goldmine in a group of Indian cricket players. Bernstein (Hamm) finds two young Indian athletes and works with them to transition from a cricket-playing culture to major league baseball stars. Foreign misunderstandings, commerce over humanity, and general sports melodrama—it has all of the usual trappings but Hamm's Bernstein is never likable, creating a serious lack of a hero to root. **124m/C; DVD, Blu-Ray.** Jon Hamm; Aasif Mandvi; Suraj Sharma; Madhur Mittal; Alan Arkin; Bill Paxton; Lake Bell; ***D:*** Craig Gillespie; ***W:*** Thomas (Tom) McCarthy; ***C:*** Gyula Pados; ***M:*** A.R. Rahman.

Million Dollar Baby 1/2 **2004 (PG-13)** Multi-Oscar winning flick finds old school boxing trainer Frankie Dunn (Eastwood) managing a rundown LA gym, aided by his best friend, former boxer Scrap (Freeman, who also narrates). Abrasive Frankie, long estranged from his own daughter, thinks 30-ish, uneducated waitress Maggie (Swank) is too old to train. But Maggie fiercely bets that boxing can change her life—and it does, although not in a way anyone could have expected. Downer ending doesn't negate the heart-tugging vulnerability of its characters or its emotional power. A knockout. Based upon "Rope Burns: Stories from the Corner" by Jerry Boyd, under the pen name F.X. Toole. **133m/C; VHS, DVD, Blu-Ray, HD-DVD.** Clint Eastwood; Hilary Swank; Morgan Freeman; Anthony Mackie; Jay Baruchel; Mike Colter; Lucia Rijker; Brian F. O'Byrne; Margo Martindale; Riki Lindhome; ***D:*** Clint Eastwood; ***W:*** Paul Haggis; ***C:*** Tom Stern; ***M:*** Clint Eastwood. Oscars '04: Actress (Swank), Director (Eastwood), Film, Support. Actor (Freeman); Directors Guild '04: Director (Eastwood); Golden Globes '05: Actress--Drama (Swank), Director (Eastwood); Screen Actors Guild '04: Actress (Swank), Support. Actor (Freeman).

Million Dollar Duck 1/2 **1971 (G)** A family duck is doused with radiation and begins to lay gold eggs. Okay Disney family fare, especially for youngsters. **92m/C; VHS, DVD.** Dean Jones; Sandy Duncan; Joe Flynn; Tony Roberts; ***D:*** Vincent McEveety; ***M:*** Buddy (Norman Dale) Baker.

The Million Dollar Hotel **1999 (R)** Director Wenders displays his obsession with disposable Americana in this tale of the murder of an entertainment mogul's son in a sleazy, rundown hotel. FBI special agent Skinner (Gibson) is sent to investigate and discovers a group of oddballs and losers inhabit the hotel, including mildly retarded narrator Tom Tom (Davies). Skinner carries on the investigation by spying on the tenants and making life even more miserable for them. The scattered storyline is countered somewhat by Wenders always brilliant visual style, but the acting is mixed, with Gibson giving the only notable performance. **122m/C; DVD.** Mel Gibson; Jeremy Davies; Milla Jovovich; Jimmy Smits; Peter Stormare; Amanda Plummer; Gloria Stuart; Tom Bower; Donal Logue; Bud Cort; Julian Sands; Tim Roth; Richard Edson; Harris Yulin; Charlaine Woodard; Conrad Roberts; ***D:*** Wim Wenders; ***W:*** Nicholas Klein; ***C:*** Phedon Papamichael; ***M:*** Brian Eno; Bono; Daniel Lanois; John Hassell.

The Million Dollar Kid 1/2 *Fortune Hunters* **1999 (PG)** A $50 million lottery jackpot is up for grabs when the winning ticket goes missing. Now Shane and his family must find their lost prize before someone else does. **92m/C; VHS, DVD.** Richard Thomas; Maureen McCormick; John Ritter; C. Thomas Howell; Corey Feldman; Clint Howard; Randy Travis; Andrew Sandler; ***D:*** Neil Mandt. **VIDEO**

Million Dollar Mermaid **1952** The prototypical Williams aquashow, with the requisite awesome Berkeley dance numbers. As a biography of swimmer Annette Kellerman it isn't much, but as an MGM extravaganza, it fits the bill. **115m/C; VHS, DVD.** Esther Williams; Victor Mature; Walter Pidgeon; Jesse White; David Brian; Maria Tallchief; Howard Freeman; Busby Berkeley; ***D:*** Mervyn LeRoy; ***C:*** George J. Folsey.

Million Dollar Mystery 1/2 **1987 (PG)** A dying man's last words indicate that several million dollars have been stashed near a diner. Chaos breaks out as nearly everyone in town tries to dig up the loot. **95m/C; VHS, DVD.** Eddie Deezen; Penny Baker; Tom Bosley; Rich Hall; Wendy Sherman; Rick Overton; Mona Lyden; ***D:*** Richard Fleischer; ***W:*** Rudy DeLuca; Tim Metcalfe; ***C:*** Jack Cardiff.

The Million Dollar Rip-Off 1/2 **1976** NBC TV movie stars Prinze as ex-con Muff Kovak, an electronics whiz who gets fired from the Chicago Transit Authority. Muff uses his insider knowledge to ripoff the subway collection centers with the help of four beautiful women in some really bad disguises. There's trouble from the local crime boss and Muff's associates don't prove to be so loyal. **73m/C; DVD.** Freddie Prinze; Allen Garfield; Christine Belford; Linda Scruggs; Joanna Kerns; Brooke Mills; James Sloyan; ***D:*** Alexander Singer; ***W:*** Andrew Peter Marin; ***C:*** Jules Brenner; ***M:*** Vic Mizzy. **TV**

A Million to Juan 1/2 **1994 (PG)** Familiar rags-to-riches tale, this time set in a L.A. barrio, centers on Juan Lopez (Rodriguez), an uneducated good guy struggling to raise his son. Juan gets his lucky break when a stranger hands him a check for $1 million, explains it's a loan, and if Juan can use the money properly for a month, he'll get a reward. Juan remains incredibly noble; the movie remains mushy. Loose adaptation of the Mark Twain story "The Million Pound Bank Note." Directorial debut for Rodriguez. **97m/C; VHS, DVD.** Paul Rodriguez; Polly Draper; Pepe Serna; Bert Rosario; Jonathan Hernandez; Gerardo Mejia; Victor Rivers; Edward James Olmos; Paul Williams; ***Cameo(s):*** Tony Plana; Ruben Blades; Richard "Cheech" Marin; David Rasche; Liz Torres; ***D:*** Paul Rodriguez; ***W:*** Francisca Matos; Robert Grasmere.

A Million Ways to Die In the West **2014 (R)** MacFarlane indulges his worst tendencies in cashing the blank check handed to him after the massive success of Ted. The result is an absolute disaster—an obscene, misogynistic, bloated comedy that merely plays as an ego project for its star and proof of his limited abilities as a filmmaker. The charmless MacFarlane stars as Albert, a sheep herder who is dumped by Louise (Seyfried) and then wooed by the new girl in town (Theron), who happens to be the wife of a legendary gunslinger (Neeson). A film made by and for people who think the word poop is inherently funny. **116m/C; DVD, Blu-Ray.** Seth MacFarlane; Charlize Theron; Neil Patrick Harris; Amanda Seyfried; Liam Neeson; Giovanni Ribisi; Sarah Silverman; Wes Studi; ***D:*** Seth MacFarlane; ***W:*** Seth MacFarlane; Alec Sulkin; Wellesley Wild; ***C:*** Michael Barrett; ***M:*** Joel McNeely.

The Millionaire's Express *Shanghai Express; Fu Gui Lie Che* **1986** Hung returns to his village with a plan to derail the local train, which carries a number of wealthy passengers, in hopes of saving his poor hometown. Chinese with subtitles or dubbed. **107m/C; VHS, DVD.** *CH* Sammo Hung; Yuen Biao; Cynthia Rothrock; Richard Norton; Yukari Oshima; ***D:*** Sammo Hung; ***W:*** Sammo Hung.

The Millionairess 1/2 **1960** Loren is an incredibly rich woman who has ended a bad marriage, and feels that the only thing she still needs to fulfill her life is a good husband. She meets a humble doctor from India, in the person of Sellers, and finds he evades her every effort to snare him. In the process she learns that money can't buy everything. From a play by George Bernard Shaw. **90m/C; VHS, DVD.** *GB* Sophia Loren; Peter Sellers; Alastair Sim; Vittorio De Sica; Dennis Price; ***D:*** Anthony Asquith; ***C:*** Jack Hildyard.

Millions 1/2 **1990 (R)** To a family of millionaires, money is everything, and the heir to the family fortune is willing to do anything to get his hands on all that money. Even if it means sleeping with his sister-in-law and cousin! Lucky for him they happen to be beautiful models. **118m/C; VHS, DVD.** *IT* Billy Zane; Lauren Hutton; Carol Alt; Alexandra Paul; Catherine Hickland; Donald Pleasence; ***D:*** Carlo Vanzina.

Millions **2005 (PG)** Boyle shows he can do sweet family entertainment with the same ease he does violent and creepy. Just before Christmas, practical 9-year-old Anthony (McGibbon) and his dreamer 7-year-old brother Damian (Etel) are living with their recently widowed father Ronnie (Nesbitt) outside Liverpool. Damian is hanging out near the rail line when a bag filled with (stolen) English pound notes literally comes flying through the air. Damian wants to use the money to help the poor while Anthony would prefer to keep it for themselves. In any case, the boys have only a few days to use the loot since the currency will become scrap paper as Britain makes an (imagined) switch to the euro. **97m/C; DVD.** James Nesbitt; Christopher Fulford; Alun Armstrong; Kathryn Pogson; Alex(ander Nathan) Etel; Lewis Owen McGibbon; Daisy Donovan; Pearce Quigley; Jane Hogarth; Enzo Cilenti; Nasser Memarzia; Harry Kirkham; Cornelius Macarthy; Kolade Agboke; ***Cameo(s):*** Leslie Phillips; ***D:*** Danny Boyle; ***W:*** Frank Cottrell Boyce; ***C:*** Anthony Dod Mantle; ***M:*** John Murphy.

Milo **1998 (R)** Four young girls are lured to the home of creepy kid Milo where they witness the murder of one of their friends. Sixteen years later, the girls are reunited for a wedding and Milo returns as well. **94m/C; VHS, DVD.** Jennifer Jostyn; Maya McLaughlin; Asher Metchik; Paula Cale; Vincent Schiavelli; Antonio Fargas; Rae'ven (Alyia Larrymore) Kelly; Walter Olkewicz; ***D:*** Pascal Franchot; ***W:*** Craig Mitchell; ***C:*** Yuri Neyman; ***M:*** Kevin Manthei. **VIDEO**

Milo & Otis 1/2 **1989 (G)** Charming tale of a kitten named Milo and his best friend, a puppy named Otis. The two live on a farm and, when exploring the countryside, Milo is swept down a rushing river. Otis goes after to rescue his friend and the two begin a series of adventures as they try to return home. **76m/C; VHS, DVD.** ***Nar:*** Dudley Moore; ***D:*** Masanori Hata; ***W:*** Mark Saltzman; ***C:*** Hideo Fujii; Shinji Tomita; ***M:*** Michael Boddicker.

The Milpitas Monster **1975 (PG)** Creature spawned in a Milpitas, California, waste dump terrorizes the town residents. **80m/C; VHS, DVD.** Doug Hagdahl; Scott A. Henderson; Scott Parker; ***Nar:*** Paul Frees; ***D:*** Robert L. Burrill.

Milton's Secret 🦴🦴 1/2 **2016 (PG)** A family drama about a boy coming to terms with his anxiety. Milton Adams (Ainscough) is 11 years old and deals with many daily stressors. His parents are continually anxious about money and their careers. Milton also must deal with being the preferred target of the neighborhood bully. Milton's feelings of constantly living in a crisis are soothed by a visit from his Grandpa Howard (Sutherland), who shows him that worrying makes him miss the true happiness found in living in the moment. **88m/C; DVD, Streaming, Download.** William Ainscough; Donald Sutherland; Graham Abbey; Ella Ballentine; Jessica Greco; ***D:*** Barnet Bain; ***W:*** Barnet Bain; Sara B. Cooper; Donald Martin; ***C:*** Ray Dumas.

Milwaukee, Minnesota 🦴🦴 **2003 (R)** Chaotic comedy features a number of oddballs who inhabit a weird Midwestern world. Albert (Garity in a strong performance) is a champion ice fisherman looked after by his overprotective mother Edna (Monks) since he's a bit slow and overly eager-to-please. When mom dies suddenly, Albert is left at the mercy of various con artists who want a piece of his inheritance and fishing prize money. Dern plays a kindly protector to Albert, who has more on the ball than people suspect. Mindel's feature debut. **95m/C; DVD.** Troy Garity; Alison Folland; Randy Quaid; Bruce Dern; Hank Harris; Debra Monk; Josh Brolin; Holly Woodlawn; ***D:*** Allan Mindel; ***W:*** Richard D. (R.D.) Murphy; ***C:*** Bernd Heinl.

Mimesis 🦴 1/2 *Mimesis: Play Dead; Mimesis: Night of the Living Dead* **2011 (R)** Horror fans attending a party at a lonely farm house awaken to find themselves unwilling participants in a re-enactment of the classic Romero film "Night of the Living Dead" led by a group of psychopathic zombies. **95m/C; DVD, Blu-Ray, Streaming.** Allen Maldonado; Sid Haig; Lauren Mae Shafer; Courtney Gains; Taylor Piedmonte; ***D:*** Douglas Schulze; ***W:*** Douglas Schulze; Joshua Wagner; ***C:*** Lon Stratton; ***M:*** Diego Navarro Abella. **VIDEO**

Mimic 🦴🦴 1/2 **1997 (R)** Married biotech scientists Sorvino and Northam upset the balance of nature when they cure a plague only to have their insectoid concoction unleashed in the New York subways. This causes giant cockroaches to mimic—and kill—humans. Far-fetched story is forgiven with a unique script (both John Sayles and Steven Soderbergh made additions) and original kills and thrills. Plenty of gore also makes it a worthy addition to the horror genre. **105m/C; VHS, DVD, Blu-Ray.** Jeremy Northam; Mira Sorvino; Josh Brolin; Charles S. Dutton; Giancarlo Giannini; F. Murray Abraham; Alexander Goodwin; ***D:*** Guillermo del Toro; ***W:*** John Sayles; Steven Soderbergh; Matthew Robbins; ***C:*** Dan Laustsen; ***M:*** Marco Beltrami.

Mimic 2 🦴🦴 1/2 **2001 (R)** If you like squishy giant bug movies, this direct-to-video sequel is for you. New York detective Campos and entomologist Koromzay discover that a mutant six-foot cockroach is responsible for three murders where the victims' face has been ripped off. And now it wants to mate. **82m/C; VHS, DVD, Blu-Ray.** Alix Koromzay; Bruno Campos; Will Estes; Edward Albert; Jon Polito; Gaven Eugene Lucas; ***D:*** Jean De Segonzac; ***W:*** Joel Soisson; ***C:*** Nathan Hope. **VIDEO**

Mimic 3: Sentinel 🦴🦴 **2003 (R)** Those gigantic humanoid cockroaches are back and badder than ever in this second sequel. Severely asthmatic Marvin (Geary), who's confined to his apartment, thinks he and his sister Rosy (Dziena) are witnesses to a murder. Then they realize that it's just giant bugs invading the neighborhood and they must put up a defense or become victims. **76m/C; VHS, DVD, Blu-Ray.** Karl Geary; Lance Henriksen; Alexis Dziena; Rebecca Mader; John Kapelos; Amanda Plummer; ***D:*** J.T. Petty; ***W:*** J.T. Petty; ***C:*** Alexandru Sterian; ***M:*** Henning Lohner. **VIDEO**

Min & Bill 🦴🦴 **1930** Patchy early talkie about two houseboat dwellers fighting to preserve their waterfront lifestyle and keep their daughter from being taken to a "proper" home. **66m/B; VHS, DVD.** Marie Dressler; Wallace Beery; Marjorie Rambeau; Dorothy Jordan; ***D:*** George W. Hill. Oscars '31: Actress (Dressler).

The Mind Benders 🦴🦴 1/2 **1963** Bogarde is a scientist who volunteers to undergo an experimental sensory deprivation/brainwashing technique after the suicide of a colleague. Why would he do something that may have caused one death already? He's trying to convince an agent that there was no traitorous activity going on, but the price of clearing his name may be the love of his family. Sharp execution of an interesting idea. **99m/C; DVD, Blu-Ray.** Dirk Bogarde; Mary Ure; John Clements; Michael Bryant; Wendy Craig; Harold Goldblatt; Geoffrey Keen; Norman Bird; Roger Delgado; Edward Fox; Terence Alexander; ***D:*** Basil Dearden; ***W:*** James Kennaway; ***C:*** Denys Coop; ***M:*** Georges Auric.

Mind, Body & Soul 🦴🦴 **1992 (R)** When a woman witnesses a human sacrifice performed by her boyfriend's satanic cult, she goes to the police. The cops, however, believe she is part of the cult, so she is forced to rely on the public defender to protect her from angry cult members. Pretty dull, but Hauser and Allen add some spice to this hokey thriller. **93m/C; VHS, DVD.** Wings Hauser; Ginger Lynn Allen; Jay Richardson; Ken Hill; Jesse Kaye; Tami Bakke; ***D:*** Rick Sloane; ***W:*** Rick Sloane; ***C:*** Robert Hayes; ***M:*** Alan Der Marderosian.

The Mind of Mr. Soames 🦴🦴 **1970** Thirty-year-old John Soames (Stamp) has been in a coma since birth until American neurosurgeon Bergen (Vaughn) restores his consciousness. However, Soames has the mental capacity of a child and his educational progress is taped for a TV special. He becomes a media star but Bergen and Dr. Maitland (Davenport) clash over how Soames should be brought up. Exploited and confused, Soames runs away but the outside world is bewildering and hostile. Adapted from Charles Eric Maine's 1961 novel. **96m/C; DVD.** *GB* Terence Stamp; Robert Vaughn; Nigel Davenport; Donal Donnelly; Christian Roberts; Scott Forbes; Judy Parfitt; ***D:*** Alan Cooke; ***W:*** Edward Simpson; John Hale; ***C:*** Billy Williams; ***M:*** Michael Dress.

The Mind Reader 🦴 1/2 **1933** Carnival grifter Chandler (William) comes up with a phony clairvoyant act but falls for mark Sylvia (Cummings), marries her, and tries going straight. His legit job doesn't work out, and Chandler is easily persuaded back to his old racket--this time as an upmarket spiritualist who can detect cheating spouses. However, his scams lead to tragedy. **70m/B; DVD.** Warren William; Constance Cummings; Allen Jenkins; Clarence Muse; Mayo Methot; Natalie Moorhead; ***D:*** Roy Del Ruth; ***W:*** Robert Lord; Wilson Mizner; ***C:*** Sol Polito.

Mind Snatchers 🦴🦴 1/2 **1972 (PG)** An American G.I. becomes involved in U.S. Army experimental psychological brain operations when he is brought into a western European hospital for treatment. Also know as "The Happiness Cage." **94m/C; VHS, DVD.** Christopher Walken; Ronny Cox; Ralph Meeker; Joss Ackland; ***D:*** Bernard Girard.

Mind the Gap 🦴🦴 **2004 (R)** Fate brings five lonely people together in New York City to deal with past guilt and unhappiness in an effort to make a fresh start. Cranky senior citizen Herb (King in his last role) plans to fulfill a promise to his late wife; single dad Sam (Schaeffer) suspects he's terminally ill; introverted folkie busker Jody (singer-songwriter Sobule) has heart trouble; John's (Parnell) a suicidal yuppie; and Malissa's (Reaser) an eccentric country gal saddled with a nasty dying mom. Film is less indulgent than Schaeffer's usual oeuvre but it's also less than noteworthy. **130m/C; DVD.** Eric Schaeffer; Alan King; John Heard; Mina Badie; Elizabeth Reaser; Jill Sobule; Charles Parnell; Christopher Kovaleski; Kim Raver; Todd Weeks; Deirdre Kingsbury; ***D:*** Eric Schaeffer; ***W:*** Eric Schaeffer; ***C:*** Marc Blandori; ***M:*** Veigar Margeirsson.

A Mind to Murder 🦴🦴 1/2 *P.D. James: A Mind to Murder* **1996** Scotland Yard Commander Adam Dalgliesh (Marsden) is still depressed over the murder of a colleague some months earlier when he's discreetly called in to investigate the stabbing death of the administrator of the Steen Clinic, located in East Anglia. The exclusive psychiatric facility is home to some politically sensitive patients and Dalgleish is under pressure to solve the crime quickly and quietly. His work would go a lot easier if people cooperated, but naturally the investigation doesn't go smoothly at all. Based on the 1963 novel by P.D. James and updated for the TV movie. **100m/C; VHS, DVD.** *GB* Roy Marsden; Sean Scanlan; Robert Pugh; Mairead Carty; Frank Finlay; Cal Macaninch; Ann-Gisel Glass; Sian Thomas; Jerome Flynn; Suzanne Burden; Donald Douglas; Christopher Ravenscroft; ***Cameo(s):*** David Hemmings; ***D:*** Gareth Davies; ***C:*** Bill Broomfield. **TV**

Mind Warp 🦴 1/2 *Grey Matter; The Brain Machine* **1972 (R)** A future society exercises mental control and torture over its citizens. **92m/C; VHS, DVD.** James Best; Barbara Burgess; Gil Peterson; Gerald McRaney; Marcus J. Grapes; Doug Collins; Anne Latham; ***D:*** Joy Houck, Jr.

Mindhunters WOOF! **2005 (R)** A group of FBI profilers-in-training are sent to a deserted island for their final test but end up victims of a real serial killer through a gamut of enormously complicated, special-effect-laden murders. Disappointing execution of an interesting premise. **106m/C; DVD.** *US GB NL FI* Val Kilmer; Christian Slater; LL Cool J; Eion Bailey; Clifton (Gonzalez) Collins, Jr.; Wil-l(iam) Kemp; Jonny Lee Miller; Kathryn Morris; Patricia Velasquez; ***D:*** Renny Harlin; ***W:*** Wayne Kramer; Kevin Brodbin; ***C:*** Robert Gantz; ***M:*** Tuomas Kantelinen.

Minding the Gap 🦴🦴🦴 **2018** A documentary look at a group of lower middle class male friends on the verge of adulthood and the struggles they experience living in the economically depressed Rockford, Illinois. Filmmaker Biu uses his camera to explore the complicated lives of him and his skateboarding friends, Keire and Zack, and their loved ones. Though major life events occur, including Zack becoming a father unexpectedly, Biu's film subtly reveals how each person sees themselves and struggles to change. Insightful and engrossing, it adeptly portrays class and gender issues. **93m/C; DVD.** ***D:*** Bing Liu; ***C:*** Bing Liu; ***M:*** Nathan Halpern; Chris Ruggiero.

The Mind's Eye 🦴🦴 **2016** An action-filled science fiction/horror exploration of power and control. Unlike most children, Zack Connors (Skipper) and Rachel Meadows (Carter) were born with amazing psychokinetic capabilities. As knowledge about their talents spread, a maniac doctor, Michael Slovak (Speredakos) imprisoned them so he could control and use their powers for his own purposes. Though they manage to escape from his institution, they face great danger as he does all he can to find them and their gifts. **87m/C; DVD, Blu-Ray, Streaming, Download.** Graham Skipper; Lauren Ashley Carter; John Speredakos; Larry Fessenden; Noah Segan; ***D:*** Joe Begos; ***W:*** Joe Begos; ***C:*** Joe Begos; ***M:*** Steve Moore.

Mindstorm 🦴🦴 1/2 **2001 (R)** The plot has holes big enough to fly a helicopter through but the action keeps things from being boring. Psychic private eye Tracy Wellman (Vaugier) is hired to free Senator Armitage's (Ironside) daughter from the clutches of cult leader David Mendez (a prototypically evil Roberts) and is aided by FBI hunk Dan Oliver (Sabato). Turns out that Mendez and Wellman have a past together—they're both telepaths as the result of a government mind control experiment when they were children—a project headed by Armitage. **106m/C; VHS, DVD.** *CA* Emmanuelle Vaugier; Antonio Sabato, Jr.; Eric Roberts; Michael Ironside; Clarence Williams, III; Michael Moriarty; Ed O'Ross; William B. Davis; James Kirk; ***D:*** Richard Pepin; ***W:*** Paul A. Berkitt; ***C:*** Adam Sliwinski; ***M:*** John Sereda. **CABLE**

Mindwarp 🦴🦴 **1991 (R)** After an ecological disaster, residents of Earth move to a sterile haven known as "Inworld." When survivor Judy (Alicia) seeks answers about her missing father (accidentally killing her mother in the process), she is cast from "Inworld" into Earth's wasteland, where she and human compatriot Stover (Campbell) are left to fight the elements and learn the awful truth about Judy's father. **91m/C; VHS, Blu-Ray, Streaming.** Marta Alicia; Bruce Campbell; Angus Scrimm; Elizabeth Kent; Mary Becker; ***D:*** Steve Barnett; ***W:*** John Brancato; Michael Ferris.

Mine Own Executioner 🦴🦴🦴 **1947** Determined but unstable psychologist in postwar London struggles to treat schizophrenic who suffered torture by Japanese while wartime prisoner. Strong, visually engrossing fare. **102m/B; VHS, DVD.** *GB* Burgess Meredith; Kieron Moore; Dulcie Gray; Christine Norden; Barbara White; John Laurie; Michael Shepley; ***D:*** Anthony Kimmins.

The Minion 🦴🦴 *Fallen Knight* **1998 (R)** Lucas (Lundgren) is a modern-day Knights Templar, the emissary of an ancient religious order that guards a temple door, which is the gateway to the antichrist. When the key to the door is discovered, Lucas must battle an ancient demon who has risen from hell to claim possession. But since the demon can inhabit anyone, how's Lucas going to know who to fight? **97m/C; VHS, DVD, Blu-Ray.** *CA* Dolph Lundgren; Francoise Robertson; Roc Lafortune; Michael Greyeyes; David Nerman; Karen Goodleaf; ***D:*** Jean-Marc Piche; ***W:*** Matt Roe; Ripley Highsmith; ***C:*** Barry Parrell.

Minions 🦴🦴 **2015 (PG)** Animated feature follows the Minions through history as they serve a series of evil masters, including Scarlet Overkill (Bullock), and ultimately prevent all the minions from being made extinct. An unnecessary spin-off of the hit Despicable Me animated franchise allows the supporting, gibberish-speaking sidekicks of those films their own time in the spotlight. Heavy on physical humor, it should make those under 8 in your family giggle more often than those old enough to drive. As with most incidences of supporting characters made lead ones, you'll probably think less is more. **91m/C; DVD, Blu-Ray, Streaming.** ***V:*** Sandra Bullock; Jon Hamm; Jennifer Saunders; Katy Mixon; Geoffrey Rush; Pierre Coffin; ***D:*** Pierre Coffin; Kyle Balda; ***W:*** Brian Lynch; ***C:*** Heitor Pereira; ***M:*** Heitor Pereira.

The Ministers 🦴 **2009 (R)** Implausible and overly-familiar crime drama. After witnessing the murder of her detective dad as a teenager, Celeste has grown up to join the NYPD and bring his killers to justice. It's no secret (to the viewer) that they are a pair of biblically-inspired and revenge-minded brothers who turn out to have another tie to Celeste besides homicide. **90m/C; DVD.** Florencia Lozano; John Leguizamo; Harvey Keitel; Diane Venora; Wanda De Jesus; Manny Perez; ***D:*** Franc Reyes; ***W:*** Franc Reyes; ***C:*** Frank Byers; ***M:*** George Acogny. **VIDEO**

Ministry of Fear 🦴🦴🦴 **1944** Creepy noir based on the novel by Graham Greene. Stephen Neale (Milland) has just been released from two years in an insane asylum. As he waits for a train, he decides to visit a nearby carnival that turns out to be fronted by a Nazi organization, where Neale's mistaken for an agent. After finally reaching London, he's later accused of murder, escapes the police, and is aided by the sympathetic Carla (Reynolds). No one and nothing is as it seems, however, and soon the unwitting Neale is deeply involved in espionage. Since the viewer sees only what Neale does, it's just as puzzling for the audience as it is for the character. **85m/B; DVD, Blu-Ray.** Ray Milland; Marjorie Reynolds; Percy Waram; Dan Duryea; Carl Esmond; Hillary Brooke; Alan Napier; Erskine Sanford; ***D:*** Fritz Lang; ***W:*** Seton I. Miller; ***C:*** Henry Sharp; ***M:*** Victor Young.

Ministry of Vengeance 🦴 **1989 (R)** A psychotic murderer who hates grapes of any kind finds the woman of his dreams—she's a psychotic murderer who hates grapes! Together they find bliss—until the plumber discovers their secret! **90m/C; VHS, DVD; Open Captioned.** John Schneider; Ned Beatty; George Kennedy; Yaphet Kotto; James Tolkan; Apollonia; ***D:*** Peter Maris; ***W:*** Mervyn Emeryys; ***C:*** Mark Harris; ***M:*** Scott Roewe.

The Miniver Story 🦴🦴 **1950** Weepy sequel to "Mrs. Miniver" reunites the family in post-WWII England, but clearly lacks the inspiration of the original. Garson is again Mrs. Miniver and she's secretly suffering from a never-named fatal disease. She decides to straighten out the family troubles before her time is up, including her daughter's love life and her husband's plan to move to Brazil. Depressing and glum. **104m/B; VHS, DVD.** *GB* Greer Garson; Walter Pidgeon; John Hodiak; Leo Genn; Cathy O'Donnell; Reginald Owen; Anthony Bushell; ***D:*** H.C. Potter; ***W:*** Ronald Millar; George Froeschel; ***C:*** Joseph Ruttenberg; ***M:*** Miklos Rozsa.

Minnesota Clay 🦴 1/2 *L'Homme du Minnesota* **1965** A blind gunman, who aims by sound and smell, is marked by two rival gangs and a tempestuous tramp. **89m/C; VHS, DVD.** *FR IT* Cameron Mitchell; Diana Martin; ***D:*** Sergio Corbucci.

Minnie and Moskowitz 🦴🦴 1/2 **1971** Minnie's (Rowlands) about to turn 40 and wants out of her affair with married man, Jim (Cassavetes). She accepts a blind date with Zelmo (Avery) and when he turns out to be a nut, Minnie's rescued by parking attendant Moskowitz (Cassel). Through the opposites attract ploy, Minnie and Moskowitz start dating and soon decide to get married. It's basically a Cassavetes home movie, featuring a number of family and friends who probably had a better time making it than you'll have watching it. **114m/C; VHS, DVD.** Gena Rowlands; Seymour Cassel; Val Avery; Timothy Carey; Holly Near; Katherine Cassavetes; Mary Allen "Lady" Rowlands; David Rowlands; Elizabeth Deering; Elsie Adams; John Cassavetes; ***D:*** John Cassavetes; ***W:*** John Cassavetes; ***C:*** Arthur Ornitz.

Minority Report 🦴🦴🦴 1/2 **2002 (PG-13)** In 2054 D.C., a law enforcement agency employs seers called Pre-Cogs to anticipate homicides. John Anderton (Cruise) is chief of the Pre-Crime unit, created to go after potential perps before they can commit the crime. When one of the Pre-Cogs names Anderton as a suspect, however, he's forced to go on the run. Engaging story and interesting characters help pic race along, figuratively and literally, along with the visual sophistication and technical wizardry that Spielberg does so well. Based on a 1956 short story by Philip K. Dick. **145m/C; DVD, Blu-Ray.** Tom Cruise; Samantha Morton; Colin Farrell; Max von Sydow; Neal McDonough; Lois Smith; Peter Stormare; Tim Blake Nelson; Steve Harris; Kathryn Morris; Mike Binder; Daniel London; Spencer Treat Clark; Jessica Capshaw; Patrick Kilpatrick; Jessica Harper; Ashley Crow; Arye Gross; ***D:*** Steven Spielberg; ***W:*** Scott Frank; Jon Cohen; ***C:*** Janusz Kaminski; ***M:*** John Williams.

The Minus Man 🦴🦴 **1999 (R)** Vann Siegert (Wilson) is the blandest, nicest serial killer you are ever likely to meet. A drifter, Vann has settled into a small California town where he boards with a troubled married couple, Doug (Cox) and Jane (Ruehl), who come to think of ever-smiling Vann as a surrogate son. Vann gets a job at the post office (!), befriends lonely co-worker Ferrin (Garofalo), and calmly proceeds to off the locals. Eerie thriller offers no explanations for Vann's behavior, which makes it all the creepier. Adapted from the 1990 novel by Lew McCreary, who has a cameo as a victim. **112m/C; VHS, DVD.** Owen Wilson; Brian Cox; Mercedes Ruehl; Janeane Garofalo; Dwight Yoakam; Dennis Haysbert; Eric Mabius; Sheryl Crow; Larry Miller; ***D:*** Hampton Fancher; ***W:*** Hampton Fancher; ***C:*** Bobby Bukowski; ***M:*** Marco Beltrami.

A Minute to Pray, a Second to Die 🦴🦴 *Un Minuto Per Pregare, Un Istante Per Morire; Dead or Alive; Outlaw Gun* **1967** A notorious, wanted-dead-or-alive gunman retreats to the amnesty of the New Mexico Territory, but finds he cannot shake his past. **100m/C; VHS, DVD, Blu-Ray.** *IT* Robert Ryan; Arthur Kennedy; Alex Cord; ***D:*** Franco Giraldi.

Minutemen 🦴🦴 1/2 **2008 (G)** Social outcasts Virgil (Dolley) and genius Charlie (Benward) are high school seniors who team up with metal-shop loner Zeke (Braun) to build a time machine so they can right various high-school injustices. But when the trio's adventures are noticed by the FBI, they learn that fooling with the timeline has made the whole space-time continuum shaky, leading to a wormhole forming that could swallow the planet! A Disney Channel original. **92m/C; DVD.** Jason Dolley; Luke Benward; Nicholas Braun; Chelsea Staub; Steve McQueen; J.P. Manoux; ***D:*** Lev L. Spiro; ***W:*** John Killoran; ***C:*** Bruce Douglas Johnson; ***M:*** Nathan Wang. **CABLE**

Miracle 🦴🦴🦴 **2004 (PG)** Russell stars as coach Herb Brooks, who led the upstart 1980 U.S. Olympic hockey team to victory against the Russians and a gold medal. Brooks uses aggressive mind-games and innovative strategy to take a squad of college hotshots and turn them into a single unit capable of defeating the Russian powerhouse. Russell is excellent as Minnesotan Brooks, down to his clipped accent and bad pants. Director O'Connor manages to push all the right buttons while mostly avoiding heavy-handed cliches. The end result is a solid sports movie. Brooks served as an advisor but died during post-production. **135m/C; VHS, DVD.** Kurt Russell; Patricia Clarkson; Noah Emmerich; Sean McCann; Kenneth Welsh; Nathan West; Kenneth Mitchell; Eddie Cahill; Patrick O'Brien Demsey; Michael Mantenuto; Eric Peter-Kaiser; Bobby Hanson; Joseph Cure; Billy Schneider; Nate Miller; ***D:*** Gavin O'Connor; ***W:*** Eric Guggenheim; ***C:*** Dan Stoloff; ***M:*** Mark Isham.

Miracle at Midnight 🦴🦴 1/2 **1998** Having occupied Denmark for several years, the Nazis decide to round up all Danish Jews on October 1, 1943. Word is leaked and a number of citizens risk their lives to warn and hide the Jews, spiriting more than 7,000 to safety in Sweden. This Disney version focuses on the non-Jewish Kloster family and how each of them become involved in the rescue. **89m/C; VHS, DVD.** Sam Waterston; Mia Farrow; Justin Whalin; Nicola Mycroft; Barry McGovern; Patrick Malahide; ***D:*** Ken Cameron; ***W:*** Chris Bryant; Monte Merrick. **TV**

Miracle at Sage Creek 🦴🦴 1/2 **2005 (PG)** Uplifting drama begins in 1888 Wyoming. Crusty rancher Ike (Carradine) is still enraged by the murder of his wife by a Sioux war party 10 years earlier. This turns him against his neighbor John (Abell), whose wife Sunny (Bedard) is Sioux, although she and Ike's married daughter Mary (Aldrich) are close friends. Ike tries to take their ranch until a tragedy and a Christmas miracle occur. **85m/C; DVD.** David Carradine; Tim Abell; Irene Bedard; Wes Studi; Sarah Aldrich; Daniel Quinn; Fred Griffith; ***D:*** James Intveld; ***W:*** Thadd Turner; ***C:*** Virgil Harper; ***M:*** James Intveld. **VIDEO**

Miracle at St. Anna 🦴🦴 1/2 **2008 (R)** After complaining about the lack of African-American representation in previous WWII dramas, Lee steps up and directs his own. His version focuses on four American soldiers from the all-black 92nd Buffalo Solider Division who get separated from their unit and are trapped behind enemy lines in a small Tuscan village in 1944. Lee goes for epic with a long runtime, but it backfires, resulting in a scattered, tedious, meandering patchwork of takes on history, war, race, religion, and sentimentality. Pic has its moments, but a heavy dose of editing and focus would have meant a much stronger finished product. McBride adapted his own 2002 novel. **160m/C; DVD, Blu-Ray.** *US IT* Derek Luke; Michael Ealy; Laz Alonso; Omar Benson Miller; Pierfrancesco Favino; Valentina Cervi; John Turturro; Joseph Gordon-Levitt; Matteo Sciabordi; John Leguizamo; Kerry Washington; D.B. Sweeney; Robert John Burke; Malcolm Goodwin; James Gandolfini; Walton Goggins; Omari Hardwick; ***D:*** Spike Lee; ***W:*** James McBride; ***C:*** Matthew Libatique; ***M:*** Terence Blanchard.

Miracle Beach 🦴 1/2 **1992 (PG-13)** Scotty McKay has lost his job, his apartment, and his girl. Then he gets rejected by Dana, the super model he's secretly adored. Can things get any worse? Scotty decides to take a walk along the beach and sort things out when he stumbles across a girl genie, named Jeanie, who has been sent to Earth on a good will mission. Scotty gets Jeanie to grant his every material wish in order to dazzle model Dana. But when Jeanie falls in love with Scotty can she get him to recognize the difference between true love and fantasy? **88m/C; VHS, Blu-Ray, Streaming.** Dean Cameron; Felicity Waterman; Ami Dolenz; Alexis Arquette; Martin Mull; Noriyuki "Pat" Morita; Vincent Schiavelli; ***D:*** Skott Snider.

Miracle Dogs 🦴🦴 1/2 **2003** After accidentally running over a stray springer spaniel, the Logans (Jackson, Shackelford) discover that the dog has cancer and must have a foreleg amputated. Son Charlie (Hutcherson) cares for the dog in the basement of the hospital where his folks work. When dog Annie recovers, she takes to visiting patients and miraculously starts making them feel better too. **105m/C; DVD.** Josh Hutcherson; Kate Jackson; Ted Shackleford; Rue McClanahan; Stacy Keach; Alana Austin; Wayne Rogers; ***D:*** Craig Clyde; ***W:*** Craig Clyde; ***C:*** Neal Brown; ***M:*** Joseph Conlan. **CABLE**

Miracle Dogs Too 🦴🦴 1/2 **2006** When 10-year-old Zack (Evans) discovers two stolen cocker spaniels caged and abandoned in the woods, he frees the dogs and takes them home. Turns out Sissy and Buddy have healing powers that change those around them. When the crooks discover that, they want the dogs back. **90m/C; DVD.** Dustin Hunter Evans; Casey Evans; Patrick Muldoon; Janine Turner; Lesley Ann Warren; Jaleel White; Alana Austin; Charles Durning; David Keith; ***D:*** Richard Gabai; ***W:*** Leland Douglas; ***C:*** Hank Baumert, Jr.; ***M:*** Boris Zelkin; Deeji Mincey. **CABLE**

Miracle in Harlem 🦴🦴 **1948** A gang tries to take over a candy shop and when the gang leader is killed, the evidence points to the foster daughter of the shop owner. The script suffers from cliched dialog and less-than-believable situations, but the all-black cast turns in good performances. **69m/B; VHS, DVD.** Sheila Guyse; Stepin Fetchit; Hilda Offley; Lawrence Criner; Monte Hawley; ***D:*** Jack Kemp.

Miracle in Lane Two 🦴🦴 **2000** Based on the true story of 12-year-old Justin Yoder (Muniz) who's confined to a wheelchair but still wins a national soap box derby championship. **89m/C; VHS, DVD.** Frankie Muniz; Roger Aaron Brown; Molly Hagan; Rick Rossovich; Tuc Watkins; ***D:*** Greg Beeman. **CABLE**

Miracle in Milan 🦴🦴🦴 *Miracolo a Milano* **1951** An innocent, child-like fantasy about heavenly intervention driving capitalists out of a Milanese ghetto and helping the poor to fly to a new Utopia. Happy mixture of whimsy and neo-realism. In Italian with English subtitles. **95m/B; VHS, DVD.** *IT* Francesco Golisano; Brunella Bovo; Emma Gramatica; Paolo Stoppa; ***D:*** Vittorio De Sica; ***W:*** Cesare Zavattini. Cannes '51: Film; N.Y. Film Critics '51: Foreign Film.

Miracle in the Wilderness 🦴🦴 1/2 **1991** A Christmas western based on Paul Gallico's novella, "The Snow Goose." Kristofferson stars as Jericho Adams, a former Indian fighter, who turns to farming to support his wife and child. When they are captured by a raiding party of Blackfeet, Adams discovers they have never heard the story of the Nativity. **88m/C; DVD.** Kris Kristofferson; Kim Cattrall; John Dennis Johnston; Joanelle Romero; Dennis Olvers; Sheldon Peters Wolfchild; David Oliver; ***D:*** Kevin James Dobson; ***W:*** Jim Byrnes.

The Miracle Maker: The Story of Jesus 🦴🦴 1/2 **2000** Elaborate 3-D claymation is surprisingly effective in telling the story of Jesus, based on the Gospel of St. Luke. Christ's ministry is seen through the eyes of sickly child, Tamar, who is healed by one of his miracles. **87m/C; VHS, DVD.** ***V:*** Ralph Fiennes; Rebecca Callard; Michael Bryant; Julie Christie; James Frain; Richard E. Grant; Ian Holm; William Hurt; Daniel Massey; Alfred Molina; Bob Peck; Miranda Richardson; Anthony Sher; Ken Stott; David Thewlis; ***D:*** Derek Hayes; Stanislav Sokolov; ***W:*** Murray Watts; ***M:*** Anne Dudley. **TV**

Miracle Mile 🦴🦴🦴 **1989 (R)** A riveting, apocalyptic thriller about a mild-mannered misfit who, while inadvertently standing on a street corner at 2 a.m., answers a ringing pay phone. The caller is a panicked missile-silo worker who announces that the bombs have been launched for an all-out nuclear war. With about an hour left before the end, he decides to head into the city and rendezvous with his new girlfriend. A surreal, wicked farce sadly overlooked in theatrical release. Music by Tangerine Dream. **87m/C; VHS, DVD, Blu-Ray.** Anthony Edwards; Mare Winningham; John Agar; Denise Crosby; Lou Hancock; Mykelti Williamson; Kelly Jo Minter; Kurt Fuller; Robert DoQui; Danny De La Paz; O-lan Jones; Alan Rosenberg; Claude Earl Jones; Edward (Eddie) Bunker; ***D:*** Steve DeJarnatt; ***W:*** Steve DeJarnatt; ***C:*** Theo van de Sande; ***M:*** Tangerine Dream.

The Miracle of Marcelino 🦴🦴 1/2 *Marcelino, Pan y Vino; Marcelino* **1955** Marcelino (Calvo) was left at birth on a monastery doorstep and raised by the Franciscan friars. The high-spirited young boy finds a life-sized crucifix in the church attic and, believing the figure of Christ to be real, befriends the image, bringing it food and wine. Then, one day, the image of Jesus comes to life. Spanish with subtitles. **88m/B; VHS, DVD.** *SP* Pablito Calvo; Fernando Rey; Rafael Rivelles; ***D:*** Ladislao Vajda; ***W:*** Ladislao Vajda; ***C:*** Enrique Guerner; ***M:*** Pablo Sarozabal.

Miracle of Morgan's Creek 🦴🦴🦴🦴 **1944** Sturges's breakneck comedy details the misadventures of wartime floozy Trudy Kockenlocker (Hutton) who gets drunk at a party, thinks she marries a soldier on leave, gets pregnant, forgets the whole thing, and then tries to evade scandal by getting local schnook and sometimes boyfriend Norval (Bracken) to take responsibility. Oh yeah, and it turns out Trudy's expecting sextuplets. Hilarious, out-to-make-trouble farce that shouldn't have, by all rights, made it past the censors of the time. The director's most scathing assault on American values. Loosely remade as 1958's "Rock-A-Bye Baby" starring Jerry Lewis. **98m/B; DVD.** Eddie Bracken; Betty Hutton; Diana Lynn; Brian Donlevy; Akim Tamiroff; Porter Hall; Emory Parnell; Alan Bridge; Julius Tannen; Victor Potel; Almira Sessions; Chester Conklin; William Demarest; Jimmy Conlin; ***D:*** Preston Sturges; ***W:*** Preston Sturges; ***M:*** Leo Shuken; Charles Bradshaw. Natl. Film Reg. '01.

Miracle of Our Lady of Fatima 🦴🦴 *The Miracle of Fatima* **1952** Slick cold-war version of the supposedly true events surrounding the sighting of a holy vision by three children in Portugal during WWI. **102m/C; VHS, DVD.** Gilbert Roland; Susan Whitney; Sherry Jackson; Sammy Ogg; Angela (Clark) Clarke; Frank Silvera; Jay Novello; ***D:*** John Brahm; ***M:*** Max Steiner.

The Miracle of the Bells 🦴🦴 **1948** A miracle occurs after a dead movie star is buried in the cemetary of her modest hometown. Given the premise, the casting is all the more peculiar. Adapted by Ben Hecht from Russell Janney's novel. **120m/B; DVD, Blu-Ray.** Fred MacMurray; Alida Valli; Frank Sinatra; Lee J. Cobb; ***D:*** Irving Pichel; ***W:*** Ben Hecht; Quentin Reynolds; ***C:*** Robert De Grasse; ***M:*** Leigh Harline.

Miracle of the Heart: A Boys Town Story 🦴🦴 **1986** Based on the story of Boys Town, and an old priest who sticks up for Boys Town's principles in the face of a younger priest with rigid ideas. **100m/C; VHS, DVD.** Art Carney; Casey Siemaszko; Jack Bannon; ***D:*** Georg Stanford Brown. **TV**

The Miracle of the White Stallions 🦴 1/2 *The Flight of the White Stallions* **1963** A disappointing Disney adventure about the director of a Viennese riding academy who guides his prized Lipizzan stallions to safety when the Nazis occupy Austria in WWII. **92m/C; VHS, DVD.** Robert Taylor; Lilli Palmer; Eddie Albert; Curt Jurgens; ***D:*** Arthur Hiller; ***W:*** A.J. Carothers.

Miracle on Ice 🦴🦴 1/2 **1981** Occasionally stirring TV film recounts the surprise triumph of the American hockey team over the touted Soviet squad during the 1980 Winter Olympics at Lake Placid. **150m/C; VHS, Streaming.** Karl Malden; Steve Guttenberg; Andrew Stevens; Lucinda Dooling; Jessica Walter; ***D:*** Steven Hilliard Stern. **TV**

Miracle on 34th Street 🦴🦴🦴🦴 *The Big Heart* **1947** The actual Kris Kringle is hired as Santa Claus for the Macy's Thanksgiving parade but finds difficulty in proving himself to the cynical parade sponsor. When the boss's daughter also refuses to acknowledge Kringle, he goes to extraordinary lengths to convince her. Holiday classic equal to "It's a Wonderful Life," with Gwenn and Wood particularly engaging. Also available colorized. **97m/B; VHS, DVD, Blu-Ray.** Maureen O'Hara; John Payne; Edmund Gwenn; Natalie Wood; William Frawley; Porter Hall; Gene Lockhart; Thelma Ritter; Jack Albertson; ***D:*** George Seaton; ***W:*** George Seaton; ***C:*** Lloyd Ahern; Charles G. Clarke; ***M:*** Cyril Mockridge. Oscars '47: Screenplay, Story, Support. Actor (Gwenn); Golden Globes '48: Screenplay, Support. Actor (Gwenn); Natl. Film Reg. '05.

Miracle on 34th Street 🦴🦴 1/2 **1994 (PG)** Updated remake of the 1947 Christmas classic in which a jolly, bearded gent (Attenborough) claiming to be Santa Claus brings happiness to a doubting girl (Wilson) and her jaded mother (Perkins). Before he can prove himself to the precocious child, he must prove himself in a court of law with the help of Perkins's impossibly perfect neighbor (McDermott), a lawyer with a heart of gold (talk about your Christmas miracles!). This version can't compete with the original's "classic" status, but Attenborough and Wilson bring soul and substance to this otherwise average adaptation. **114m/C; VHS, DVD, Blu-Ray.** Richard Attenborough; Elizabeth Perkins; Dylan McDermott; J.T. Walsh; Mara Wilson; Joss Ackland; James Remar; Jane Leeves; Simon Jones; Robert Prosky; William Windom; *D:* Les Mayfield; *W:* John Hughes; George Seaton; *M:* Bruce Broughton.

The Miracle Rider 𝒥𝒥 **1935** A 15-chapter serial finds the bad guys trying to run the Indians off their lands in this saga of the old west. **295m/B; VHS, DVD.** Tom Mix; Joan Gale; Charles Middleton; Jason Robards, Sr.; Pat O'Malley; Robert Frazer; Wally Wales; Tom London; George Chesebro; Lafe (Lafayette) McKee; *D:* B. Reeves Eason; Armand Schaefer.

Miracle Run 𝒥𝒥 ½ **2004** Based on a true story. When single mom Corinne Morgan's (Parker) twin sons are finally diagnosed as autistic she is advised to put them up for adoption or have them institutionalized. Instead, Corinne starts a long fight to mainstream Steven and Phillip and offer them as normal a life as she can provide and they can handle. **90m/C; DVD.** Mary-Louise Parker; Aidan Quinn; Zac Efron; Bubba Lewis; Jake Cherry; Jeremy Shada; *D:* Gregg Champion; *W:* Mike Maples; *C:* Gordon C. Lonsdale; *M:* Joseph Conlan. **CABLE**

The Miracle Season 𝒥𝒥 ½ **2018 (PG)** A drama about how a high school volleyball team handles a tragedy, based on a true story. Kelly (Moriarty) and Caroline (Yarosh) have been best friends since they were small, and continue to be close in high school where they are members of the volleyball team. Lively Caroline pushes Kelly out of her comfort zone. When Caroline dies suddenly in a car accident just as the season is getting underway, the team and her family must figure out how to move forward. Solid, genuine performances uplift the middling story. **101m/C; DVD.** Helen Hunt; Erin Moriarty; Tiera Skovbye; William Hurt; Danika Yarosh; *D:* Sean McNamara; *W:* David Aaron Cohen; Elissa Matsueda; *C:* Brian Pearson; *M:* Roque Baños.

The Miracle Woman 𝒥𝒥 ½ **1931** Stanwyck's particularly fine as evangelist Florence "Faith" Fallon, who becomes very successful thanks to her way with words, some fake miracles, and the talents of shady promoter Hornsby (Hardy). After blind ex-pilot John Carson (Manners) hears her on the radio, he decides Faith might be able to cure him. Florence winds up falling in love with John but Hornsby starts to worry she's going soft and will end their scam. Even Capra apparently thought this film was corny but it still works. Based on the play "Bless You Sister" by John Meehan and Robert Riskin. **90m/B; DVD.** Barbara Stanwyck; David Manners; Sam Hardy; Beryl Mercer; Russell Hopton; Charles Middleton; Eddie Boland; *D:* Frank Capra; *W:* Dorothy Howell; Jo Swerling; *C:* Joseph Walker.

The Miracle Worker 𝒥𝒥𝒥 ½ **1962** Depicts the unconventional methods that teacher Anne Sullivan used to help the deaf and blind Helen Keller adjust to the world around her and shows the relationship that built between the two courageous women. An intense, moving experience. William Gibson adapted his own play for the screen. **107m/B; VHS, DVD, Blu-Ray.** Anne Bancroft; Patty Duke; Victor Jory; Inga Swenson; Andrew Prine; Beah Richards; *D:* Arthur Penn; *W:* William Gibson; *C:* Ernesto Caparros; *M:* Laurence Rosenthal. Oscars '62: Actress (Bancroft), Support. Actress (Duke); British Acad. '62: Actress (Bancroft); Natl. Bd. of Review '62: Actress (Bancroft).

The Miracle Worker 𝒥𝒥𝒥 **1979** Remade for TV story of blind, deaf and mute Helen Keller and her teacher, Annie Sullivan, whose patience and perseverance finally enable Helen to learn to communicate with the world. Duke was Keller in the 1962 original, but plays the teacher in this version. **98m/C; VHS, DVD, Blu-Ray.** Patty Duke; Melissa Gilbert; *D:* Paul Aaron; *M:* Billy Goldenberg. **TV**

The Miracle Worker 𝒥𝒥 ½ **2000** Yet another remake of William Gibson's Tony award-winning play, following the 1962 movie and the 1979 TV version. This time around precocious Eisenberg is young Helen Keller and Elliott (particularly good) is her dedicated teacher Annie Sullivan. Rather a genteel retelling although Annie's breakthrough with Helen still carries a strong emotional power. **90m/C; VHS, DVD.** Hallie Kate Eisenberg; Alison Elliott; David Strathairn; Lucas Black; Kate Greenhouse; *D:* Nadia Tass; *W:* Monte Merrick; *C:* David Parker; *M:* William Goldstein. **TV**

Miracles 𝒥𝒥 ½ *Qiji; Black Dragon* **1989 (PG-13)** Chan stars (and writes and directs) as a bumpkin who saves the life of a mob boss and is thrust into the world of crime in 1930s Hong Kong. He gets some social help from a mysterious woman that gives him the confidence to romance nightclub singer Mui. But when his mob patron is murdered, Chan decides he has to show his loyalty by seeking justice. Humor and action turn out to be a winning combo. **106m/C; VHS, DVD.** *CH* Jackie Chan; Anita (Yim-Fong) Mui; Richard Ng; Yuen Biao; *D:* Jackie Chan; *W:* Jackie Chan.

Miracles for Sale 𝒥𝒥 **1939** New York illusionist Michael Morgan (Young) likes to expose fake psychics and magicians who prey on the public's gullibility. When Judy Barclay (Rice) gets caught up in murder, Morgan vows to help her and a lot of trickery is involved. Browning's last film as a director. **71m/B; DVD.** Robert Young; Florence Rice; Frank Craven; Henry Hull; Lee Bowman; Astrid Allwyn; Cliff Clark; Frederick Worlock; Gloria Holden; Walter Kingsford; William Demarest; *D:* Tod Browning; *W:* Harry Ruskin; Marion Parsonnet; James Edward Grant; *C:* Charles Lawton, Jr.

Miracles From Heaven 𝒥𝒥 **2016 (PG)** Director Riggen's faith-based film--while designed to literally preach to the choir--is better than some in this trendy genre simply because of a committed performance by Garner as Christy Beam, mother to a sick girl named Anna (Rogers). Anna falls out of a tree and nearly dies, triggering a "miracle" that cures her debilitating disease. She tells people that she went to Heaven after the fall and God sent her back cured. It may be predictably manipulative and melodramatic but the always-underrated Garner gives it more than it deserves. **109m/C; DVD, Blu-Ray, Streaming.** Jennifer Garner; Kylie Rogers; Martin Henderson; Brighton Sharbino; Courtney Fansler; *D:* Patricia Riggen; *W:* Randy Brown; *C:* Checco Varese; *M:* Carlo Siliotto.

Miraculous Journey 𝒥 ½ **1948** Minor jungle adventure. After a plane crashes in an African jungle, pilot Larry Burke (Calhoun) takes charge in order to led the survivors to safety. They're unexpectedly aided by the survivor (Cleveland) or an earlier crash. **83m/C; DVD.** Rory Calhoun; Audrey Long; Virginia Grey; Thurston Hall; Jim Bannon; George Cleveland; *D:* Sam Newfield; *W:* Fred Myton; *C:* Jack Greenhalgh.

Mirage 𝒥𝒥𝒥 **1966** An amnesiac finds himself the target of a dangerous manhunt in New York City in this offbeat thriller. Peck is particularly sympathetic in the lead, and McCarthy, Matthau, and Kennedy all shine in supporting roles. Worth it just to hear thug Kennedy grunt, "I owe this man some pain!" **108m/B; VHS, DVD, Blu-Ray.** Gregory Peck; Diane Baker; Walter Matthau; Jack Weston; Kevin McCarthy; Walter Abel; George Kennedy; *D:* Edward Dmytryk; *M:* Quincy Jones.

Mirai 𝒥𝒥𝒥 *Mirai no Mirai* **2018 (PG)** Young Kun (Waldman) feels pushed aside when his adorable newborn sister Mirai (Hondo) becomes part of the family. Used to being the center of attention, he throws tantrums to get his overwhelmed mother's (Hall) attention. His mother convinces the children's clueless father (Cho) to help with parenting, though Kun's demands do not cease. The uneven animated Japanese feature offers insight into Kun's innermost thoughts and feelings by bringing his fantasies to life in literal, colorful fashion. **98m/C; DVD.** Jaden Waldman; Victoria Grace; John Cho; Rebecca Hall; Crispin Freeman; *D:* Mamoru Hosoda; *W:* Mamoru Hosoda; *M:* Masakatsu Takagi.

Miral 𝒥𝒥 **2010 (PG-13)** Schnabel's well-intentioned but muddled and fragmented historical drama about three generations of women living under Israeli occupation. The opening finds Hind Husseini (Abbass) establishing an orphanage for Palestinian girls after the 1948 creation of Israel. In the 1960s, Nadia (El Masri) and Fatima (Blal) meet in prison and Nadia later marries a devout Muslim, Jamal (Siddig). She gives birth to Miral, who grows up in war-torn Jerusalem and become a teacher (Pinto) in a refugee camp where she falls for PLO activist Hani (Metwally). Screenwriter Jabreal adapted her own semi-autobiographical novel. **106m/C; DVD, Blu-Ray.** *FR IS IT IN* Freida Pinto; Hiam Abbass; Omar Metwally; Willem Dafoe; Alexander Siddig; Yolanda El Karam; Yasmine El Masri; Roba Blal; Vanessa Redgrave; Stella Schnabel; *D:* Julian Schnabel; *W:* Rula Jebreal; *C:* Eric Gautier.

Miranda 𝒥𝒥 ½ **1948** Amusing Brit fantasy. Mermaid Miranda (Johns) rescues Dr. Paul Marton (Jones) from drowning and insists he thank her by showing her London. She becomes a patient at his clinic, using a wheelchair and hiding her tail under a blanket. Paul's wife Claire (Withers) is jealous since Miranda attracts every man within reach, including a couple of clueless bachelors (McCallum, Tomlinson). Johns returned in the 1954 sequel "Mad About Men." **80m/B; DVD.** *GB* Glynis Johns; Griffith Jones; Googie Withers; Margaret Rutherford; John McCallum; David Tomlinson; *D:* Ken Annakin; *W:* Peter Blackmore; Denis Waldock; *C:* Ray Elton; *M:* Temple Abady.

Miranda 𝒥 ½ **2001 (R)** A romantic fantasy that takes too many complicated turns for its own good. Naive librarian Frank (Simm) is instantly smitten by the oh-so-experienced Miranda (Ricci), who is working on a real estate scam. She heads to London after one night with Frank for a new target, twisted tycoon Nailor (MacLachlan), with her foolish lover trailing behind. Miranda tries to get Frank to leave and instead he gets overly involved in her business. Ricci gets to play dress-up as Miranda goes through a lot of disguises and she's intriguing—the movie's not. **92m/C; VHS, DVD, On Demand.** *GB* Christina Ricci; John Simm; Kyle MacLachlan; John Hurt; Julian Rhind-Tutt; Matthew Marsh; *D:* Marc Munden; *W:* Rob Young; *C:* Benjamin Davis; *M:* Murray Gold.

The Mirror 𝒥𝒥𝒥 *Zerkalo; A White White Boy* **1975** Wonderful child's view of life in Russia during WWII. Black and white flashbacks of important events in the country's history are interspersed with scenes of day-to-day family life. In Russian with English subtitles. **106m/C; VHS, DVD.** *RU* Margarita Terekhova; Philip Yankovsky; Ignat Daniltsev; Oleg (Yankovsky) Jankowsky; *D:* Andrei Tarkovsky; *W:* Andrei Tarkovsky; *C:* Georgy Rerberg; *M:* Eduard Artemyev.

The Mirror Crack'd 𝒥𝒥 **1980 (PG)** While filming a movie in the English countryside, an American actress is murdered and Miss Marple must discover who the killer is. Based on the substantially better Agatha Christie novel. **105m/C; VHS, DVD.** *GB* Angela Lansbury; Wendy Morgan; Margaret Courtenay; Charles Gray; Maureen Bennett; Carolyn Pickles; Elizabeth Taylor; Rock Hudson; Kim Novak; Tony Curtis; Edward Fox; Geraldine Chaplin; Pierce Brosnan; *D:* Guy Hamilton; *W:* Barry Sandler; *C:* Christopher Challis; *M:* John Cameron.

The Mirror Has Two Faces 𝒥𝒥 **1996 (PG-13)** Gregory (Bridges) is a hunky, but flustered, professor looking for romance without all that complicated sex, which leads him to ugly duckling Rose (Streisand). Rose's mother (Bacall) is happier with Rose's much-married sister (Rogers), who is headed down the aisle again with gorgeous Alex (Brosnan). Rose decides it's her turn, despite Gregory's protests, and she weds the bow-tied educator anyway. When Gregory leaves on a book tour, frumpy Rose decides a big makeover is in order. Her newfound outer beauty, however, becomes the beast on the inside. Bacall gives a memorable, Oscar-nominated performance. Remake of a 1959 French film. **127m/C; DVD.** Barbra Streisand; Jeff Bridges; Pierce Brosnan; Mimi Rogers; Lauren Bacall; Brenda Vaccaro; Austin Pendleton; George Segal; Elle Macpherson; *D:* Barbra Streisand; *W:* Richard LaGravenese; *C:* Dante Spinotti; Andrzej Bartkowiak; *M:* Barbra Streisand; Marvin Hamlisch. Golden Globes '97: Support. Actress (Bacall); Screen Actors Guild '96: Support. Actress (Bacall).

Mirror Images 𝒥 ½ **1991 (R)** Although sexy twins Kaitlin and Shauna may look alike, they couldn't have more diverse personalities. Yet the gorgeous twins find their lives thrown together in a mad tornado of passion and danger when they each encounter a handsome, mysterious stranger. Could it be that this guy has something more on his mind than love, something like... murder? Also available in an even steamier unrated version. **94m/C; VHS, DVD.** Delia Sheppard; Jeff Conaway; Richard Arbolino; John O'Hurley; Korey Mall; Julie Strain; Nels Van Patten; *D:* Alexander Gregory (Gregory Dark) Hippolyte.

Mirror, Mirror 𝒥𝒥 **1990 (R)** The prolific Ms. Black turns on the ol' black magic when her daughter's classmates decide it's open season for taunting shrinking violets. Thanks to a magical mirror on the wall, the cheerleading classmates are willed to the great pep rally in the sky. **105m/C; VHS, DVD, Blu-Ray.** Karen Black; Rainbow Harvest; Kristin Dattilo-Hayward; Ricky Paull Goldin; Yvonne De Carlo; William Sanderson; Charlie Spradling; Ann Hearn; Stephen Tobolowsky; *D:* Marina Sargenti; *W:* Marina Sargenti; *C:* Robert Brinkmann; *M:* Jimmy Lifton.

Mirror Mirror 𝒥𝒥 ½ *Snow White* **2012** A retelling of the classic Grimm Brothers fairytale that finds the Evil Queen usurping the throne and Snow White banished to the forest to face certain death. Only she's rescued by the seven dwarves, who are now highway robbers, and is determined to win back her kingdom. **106m/C; DVD, Blu-Ray.** Lily Collins; Julia Roberts; Armie Hammer; Nathan Lane; Sean Bean; Mare Winningham; *D:* Tarsem Singh; *W:* Melisa Wallack; Jason Keller; *C:* Brendan Galvin; *M:* Alan Menken.

Mirror, Mirror 2: Raven Dance 𝒥 ½ **1994 (R)** Teenaged Marlee (Wells) and her brother are temporarily housed in a convent after the death of their parents. The mystery mirror is discovered and looking into it causes Marlee to become partially blind. Meanwhile, her inheritance is threatened and a mysterious stranger, living in the convent's basement, may be Marlee's only hope. **91m/C; VHS, DVD, Blu-Ray.** Tracy Wells; Roddy McDowall; Sally Kellerman; Veronica Cartwright; William Sanderson; Lois Nettleton; *D:* Jimmy Lifton; *W:* Jimmy Lifton; Virginia Perfili; *C:* Troy Cook; *M:* Jimmy Lifton.

Mirror, Mirror 3: The Voyeur 𝒥 ½ **1996** Artist discovers a mirror in an abandoned mansion and sees that it reflects the presence of his lost lover, who is now able to manipulate his dreams. **91m/C; VHS, DVD.** Billy Drago; Monique Parent; David Naughton; Mark Ruffalo; Elizabeth Baldwin; Richard Cansino; *D:* Rachel Gordon; Virginia Perfili; *W:* Steve Tymon; *C:* Nils Erickson.

Mirror of Death 𝒥 *Dead of Night* **1987** A woman subject to physical abuse gets more than she bargains for when she seeks revenge by unleashing the gruesome Queen of Hell. Watch this if you dare! **85m/C; VHS, DVD.** Julie Merrill; Kuri Browne; John Reno; Deryn Warren; *W:* Jerry Daly; *M:* David Michael Frank.

Mirror Wars: Reflection One **WOOF! 2005** Something obviously got lost in translation with the Russian portion of the cast and crew since this minor actioner is a muddled mess. A terrorist wants to steal a new Russian stealth-fighter prototype and provoke a war between Russia and the USA, but the plane's young pilot proves uncooperative. The "names" in the cast apparently were just picking up a paycheck. **109m/C; DVD.** Malcolm McDowell; Armand Assante; Rutger Hauer; Alexander Efimov; Olga Yakovtseva; *D:* Vasili Chiginsky; *W:* Alex Kustanovich; *M:* David Robbins.

MirrorMask 𝒥𝒥 **2005 (PG)** McKean teams with "Sandman" author Neil Gaiman in this otherworldly escapade from the Jim Henson Company. Helena (Leonidas) is the teenaged daughter of circus performers who longs for a "normal" life. But when her mom (McKee) lapses into a coma, Helena has to travel into a fantasy world to recover the MirrorMask from the Queen of Shadows. McKean's trippy CGI landscapes (rendered on a bare-bones budget) produce some of the most exciting film visuals in years, but you'll be so bored waiting for the story to kick in that the sugar rush from the eye candy wears off way too fast. **101m/C; DVD, UMD.** Jason Barry; Stephanie Leonidas; Gina McKee; Rob Brydon; Dora Bryan; Stephen Fry; *D:* David McKean; *W:* Neil Gaiman; David McKean; *C:* Antony Shearn; *M:* Ian Ballamy.

Mirrors 🦴 **2008 (R)** Ben Carson (Sutherland) takes a job as night watchman at a burned-out department store while suspended from the NYPD, estranged from his family,and struggling with his alcoholism. So is it any surprise that no one wants to believe his story of haunted mirrors? The malevolent spirits go after Carson's wife and kids, rendering some of the most disturbing scenes. Director Aja manages to mix in a little psychological thriller with the ample gore in this remake of the 2003 Korean flick, "Into the Mirror," but it follows an expected track. Genre fans only here. **110m/C; DVD, Blu-Ray, On Demand.** Kiefer Sutherland; Paula Patton; Amy Smart; Cameron Boyce; Mary Beth Peil; Julian Glover; John Shrapnel; Erica Gluck; ***D:*** Alexandre Aja; ***W:*** Alexandre Aja; Gregory Levasseur; ***C:*** Maxime Alexandre; ***M:*** Javier Navarrete.

Mirrors 2 🦴 ½ **2010 (R)** Max takes a job as a night security guard at the Mayflower Department Store in New Orleans and soon sees visions of a young woman who was murdered and wants her revenge. Then Max sees mirror reflections of his coworkers being killed but the police regard him as a suspect. **86m/C; DVD.** Nick Stahl; Emmanuelle Vaugier; William Katt; Evan Jones; Christy Carlson Romano; Lawrence Turner; Wayne Pere; Lance E. Nichols; Stephanie Honore; ***D:*** Victor Garcia; ***W:*** Matt Venne; ***C:*** Lorenzo Senatore; ***M:*** Frederik Wiedmann. **VIDEO**

The Misadventures of Merlin Jones 🦴 ½ **1963 (G)** A pair of college sweethearts become embroiled in a rollicking chimp-napping scandal. Disney pap done appropriately. A sequel, "The Monkey's Uncle," followed. **90m/C; VHS, DVD.** Tommy Kirk; Annette Funicello; Leon Ames; Stuart Erwin; Connie Gilchrist; Kelly Thordsen; ***D:*** Robert Stevenson; ***W:*** Alfred Lewis Levitt; Helen Levitt; ***C:*** Edward Colman; ***M:*** Buddy (Norman Dale) Baker.

Misbegotten 🦴🦴 **1998 (R)** Infertile couple Paul (Mancuso) and Caitlin (Anthony) are able to have their bundle of joy thanks to artifical insemination. Only psycho donor daddy Billy Crapshoot (Dillon) finds out who they are and decides to come for his soon-to-be-born offspring. **97m/C; VHS, DVD.** Kevin Dillon; Nick Mancuso; Lysette Anthony; Robert Lewis; Matthew (Matt) Walker; Stefan Arngrim; ***D:*** Mark L. Lester; ***W:*** Larry Cohen; ***C:*** Mark Irwin. **CABLE**

Mischief 🦴🦴 **1985 (R)** Alienated youths form a friendship during James Dean's heyday. Warning: this film offers a fairly convincing recreation of the 1950s. **97m/C; VHS, DVD.** Doug McKeon; Catherine Mary Stewart; Kelly Preston; Chris Nash; D.W. Brown; Jami Gertz; Margaret Blye; Graham Jarvis; Terry O'Quinn; ***D:*** Mel Damski; ***W:*** Noel Black.

Mischief Night 🦴🦴 ½ **2013** A dramatic horror thriller centering on one brave young woman's quest to save herself and her family from a mysterious intruder. After her mother died in a car accident, Emily Watson (Coet) developed psychosomatic blindness. The night before Halloween, she faces an unexpected challenge when a murderous stranger breaks into their home. Emily draws on all her instincts to make sure she and her family survive. **87m/C; DVD, Streaming, Download.** Noell Coet; Adam C. Edwards; Stephanie Erb; Daniel Hugh Kelly; Charlie O'Connell; ***D:*** Richard Schenkman; ***W:*** Richard Schenkman; ***C:*** Richard J. Vialet; ***M:*** Anastasia Devana.

Misconceptions 🦴 ½ **2008** Southern Christian conservative Miranda sees a TV news item about gay Boston doctor Sandy and his husband Terry who want to be parents. She decides to become their surrogate because Sandy is working to find a cure for the disease that killed Miranda's own child. But there's a sexual and cultural clash in store when African-American Terry actually shows up at her door—much to Miranda's shock. **95m/C; DVD.** A.J. Cook; Orlando Jones; David Moscow; David Sutcliffe; Sarah Carter; Samuel Ball; ***D:*** Ron Satlof; ***W:*** Ron Satlof; Ira Pearlstein; ***C:*** Curtis Graham; ***M:*** Michael A. Levine. **VIDEO**

Misconduct 🦴🦴 **2016 (R)** A legal dramatic thriller with big name stars and unexpected twists but little tension. Ben Cahill (Duhamel) is a determined young lawyer trying to make a name for himself. Ben agrees to take on a major case targeting a ruthless executive of a major pharmaceutical company, Arthur Denning (Hopkins). Because of the case, Ben becomes caught up in blackmail and corruption as his life is turned upside down. **105m/C; DVD, Blu-Ray, Streaming, Download.** Josh Duhamel; Anthony Hopkins; Al Pacino; Alice Eve; Malin Akerman; ***D:*** Shintaro Shimosawa; ***W:*** Simon Boyes; Adam Mason; ***C:*** Michael Fimognari; ***M:*** Federico Jusid.

The Miseducation of Cameron Post 🦴🦴 ½ **2018** In small town Pennsylvania in 1993, Cameron Post (Moretz) is a self-assured teen orphan who is a lesbian. After being caught passionately kissing prom queen Coley Taylor (Shephard), Cameron is forcibly sent to a Christian gay conversion therapy camp to "cure" her same-sex attraction. Though she knows nothing is wrong with her and bonds with like-minded campers, her sense of self is challenged by the emotionally abusive Dr. Lydia Marsh (Ehle) and the doctor's formerly gay brother Reverend Rick (Gallagher). This moving coming of age drama won Sundance's Grand Jury Prize and features a strong performance by Moretz along with an affirming message. **90m/C; DVD, Blu-Ray.** Chloë Grace Moretz; Quinn Shephard; Jennifer Ehle; John Gallagher, Jr.; Kerry Butler; ***D:*** Desiree Akhavan; ***W:*** Desiree Akhavan; Cecilia Frugiuele; ***C:*** Ashley Connor; ***M:*** Julian Wass.

Misery 🦴🦴🦴 **1990 (R)** Author Caan decides to chuck his lucrative but unfulfilling pulp novels and write seriously by finishing off his most popular character, Misery Chastain. However, fate intervenes when he crashes his car near the home of Bates, his "biggest fan ever," who saves his life, but then tortures him into resurrecting her favorite character. Bates is chillingly glib and calmly brutal—watch your ankles. Based on the novel by Stephen King. **107m/C; VHS, DVD, Blu-Ray.** James Caan; Kathy Bates; Lauren Bacall; Richard Farnsworth; Frances Sternhagen; Graham Jarvis; ***D:*** Rob Reiner; ***W:*** William Goldman; ***C:*** Barry Sonnenfeld; ***M:*** Marc Shaiman. Oscars '90: Actress (Bates); Golden Globes '91: Actress--Drama (Bates).

Misfire 🦴🦴 **2014** An action-crime drama focused on a DEA agent's personal quest to crush drug cartels on the border between the United States and Mexico. The bold DEA agent, Cole (Daniels) is is on a one-man crusade to bring down the drug cartels. His commitment to this cause becomes personal when his ex-wife is kidnapped and his brother is framed for the crime. Assisted by Gracie (Vasquez), a local reporter, he searches the Tijuana underworld looking for the drug kingpin Raul Montenegro (Gatica) whom he believes has kidnapped his ex-wife. Though Montenegro wants to hold public office, Cole wants a showdown for justice. **90m/C; DVD, Blu-Ray, Streaming, Download.** Gary Daniels; Vannessa Vasquez; Michael Greco; Luis Gatica; Geoffrey Ross; ***D:*** R. Ellis Frazier; ***W:*** Benjamin Budd; ***C:*** Anthony J. Rickert-Epstein; Jorge Roman; ***M:*** Larry Groupe. **VIDEO**

The Misfits 🦴🦴🦴 **1961** A cynical floozy befriends grim cowboys in this downbeat drama. Compelling performances from leads Clift, Monroe (screenwriter Miller's wife), and Gable. Last film for the latter two performers, and nearly the end for Clift. **124m/B; VHS, DVD, Blu-Ray.** Clark Gable; Marilyn Monroe; Montgomery Clift; Thelma Ritter; Eli Wallach; James Barton; Estelle Winwood; ***D:*** John Huston; ***W:*** Arthur Miller; ***C:*** Russell Metty; ***M:*** Alex North.

Mishima: A Life in Four Chapters 🦴🦴🦴 **1985 (R)** Somewhat detached account and indulgent portrayal of the narcissistic Japanese author (and actor, filmmaker, and militarist) alternates between stylized interpretations of his books and a straightforward account of his life. Culminates in a pseudo-military operation that, in turn, resulted in Mishima's ritualistic suicide. A U.S./Japanese production. Innovative design by Eiko Ishioka. In Japanese with English subtitles. **121m/C; VHS, DVD, Blu-Ray.** Ken Ogata; Kenji Sawada; Yasosuke Bando; ***Nar:*** Roy Scheider; ***D:*** Paul Schrader; ***W:*** Leonard Schrader; Paul Schrader; ***C:*** John Bailey; ***M:*** Philip Glass.

Miss All-American Beauty 🦴 ½ **1982** A behind-the-scenes look at a small-time Texas beauty pageant. Lane stars as a contestant who comes to realize her self-respect is more important than winning an award. Meadows's mean pageant director adds an ironic edge that the movie as a whole lacks. **96m/C; VHS, DVD.** Diane Lane; Cloris Leachman; David Dukes; Jayne Meadows; Alice Hirson; Brian Kerwin; ***D:*** Gus Trikonis. **TV**

Miss Austen Regrets 🦴🦴 ½ **2007** A "what-if" biography of the writer. Jane Austen (Williams) receives a proposal from a wealthy suitor but changes her mind when she realizes that a wife's duties will prevent her from writing. So she and her unmarried older sister Cassandra (Scacchi) live with their waspish mother (Law) under strained financial circumstances. Jane wonders about her choices when her favorite niece, Fanny (Poots), insists on asking Jane's opinion of her own potential suitors. Included with the DVD of the 2008 BBC production of "Sense and Sensibility." **90m/C; DVD.** *GB* Olivia Williams; Greta Scacchi; Phyllida Law; Pip Torrens; Adrian Edmondson; Hugh Bonneville; Imogen Poots; Jack Huston; Tom Hiddleston; ***D:*** Jeremy Lovering; ***W:*** Gwyneth Hughes; ***C:*** Michas Kotz; ***M:*** Luke Dunkley. **TV**

Miss Bala 🦴🦴 ½ **2012 (R)** In Tijuana, Mexico, Laura (Sigman) is a young working-class woman with ambitions that begin with entering a beauty pageant. Going to a disco with a friend one night, drug dealers break in and start killing people. Though Laura escapes, she does not know what happened to her friend and ends up in the hands of a drug lord, Lino (Hernandez), after asking a police officer for help. As she tries to escape, fearful Laura is forced to do tasks that often result in people dying. A violent look at how the drug trade in Mexico affects everything, the film entertains while telling hard truths. **113m/C; DVD.** Stephanie Sigman; Juan Carlos Galvan; Noe Hernandez; Irene Azuela; Javier Zaragoza; ***D:*** Gerardo Naranjo; ***W:*** Gerardo Naranjo; Mauricio Katz; ***C:*** Mátyás Erdély; ***M:*** Emilio Kauderer.

Miss Bala 🦴🦴 **2019 (PG-13)** Gloria (Rodriguez) is a Mexican-born, U.S.-raised makeup artist. Visiting her close friend Sizu (Rodlo) in Tijuana, the pair go to a nightclub where a drug cartel-linked shooting takes place. Separated from Sizu, Gloria tries to find out what happened to her but becomes captured by the cartel in the process. Gloria's attempts to get help from the U.S. authorities fails, and she finds herself exploited by the cartel as she tries to escape. A remake of the 2012 Mexican film of the same name, this action-oriented film is a sanitized version of the original. **104m/C; DVD.** Gina Rodriguez; Ricardo Abarca; Ismael Cruz Cordova; Matt Lauria; Anthony Mackie; ***D:*** Catherine Hardwicke; ***W:*** Gareth Dunnet-Alcocer; ***C:*** Patrick Murguia; ***M:*** Alex Heffes.

Miss Cast Away 🦴🦴 *Miss Castaway and the Island Girls* **2004** Absurd antics abound in this wide-ranging parody of big-budget flicks such as "The Perfect Storm" and "The Lord of the Rings." An airplane filled with beauty-pageant contestants crash-lands on a deserted island on its way to Japan and its two pilots (Roberts and Schlatter) must protect the ladies by fending off all manner of strange inhabitants including ape people. Features cameo by the former King of Pop himself, Michael Jackson, as Special Agent M. Surely you can't be serious if you think this ranks anywhere near the Zucker/Abrahams/Zucker ouvre. **91m/C; DVD.** Eric Roberts; Charlie Schlatter; Joyce Giraud; Stuart Pankin; Evan Marriott; ***D:*** Bryan Michael Stoller; ***W:*** Bryan Michael Stoller. **VIDEO**

Miss Conception 🦴 ½ **2008 (R)** A misconceived comedy for sure. Thirty-something Londoner Georgina (Graham) has just waved bye-bye to boyfriend Zak (Ellis), who's off to Ireland on business. Desperately wanting a baby (despite Zak's protests), Georgina checks in with a fertility doctor and is horrified to learn that she's on the verge of early menopause and her next ovulation cycle is her last chance. With Zak a no-hoper, Georgina goes on a misguided search for a shag who'll get her pregnant. Although she's blonde and beautiful, this isn't as easy as you might think. **94m/C; DVD.** Heather Graham; Mia Kirshner; Nicholas Le Prevost; Vivienne Moore; Orlando Seale; Ruta Gedmintas; Tom Ellis; Will Mellor; ***D:*** Eric Styles; ***W:*** Camilla Leslie; ***C:*** Ed Mash; ***M:*** Christian Henson.

Miss Congeniality 🦴🦴 **2000 (PG-13)** Tough FBI agent Gracie Hart (Bullock) must go undercover at the Miss USA Pageant after the event is threatened by terrorists. Eric (Bratt) is a helpful fellow agent (and potential beau) while down-on-his-luck consultant Victor Melling (Caine) is hired to girly-up Gracie and make her pageant material. Predictable comedy shows flashes of witty satire but lives up to its name by easing up on intended targets at the moment of truth. Bullock, as always, is game and both Bergen as a former beauty queen turned pageant manager and Shatner as unctuous pageant host add a spark to the proceedings. **111m/C; DVD.** Sandra Bullock; Benjamin Bratt; Michael Caine; William Shatner; Ernie Hudson; Candice Bergen; Heather Burns; Melissa De Sousa; Steve Monroe; John DiResta; Jennifer Gareis; Wendy Raquel Robinson; ***D:*** Donald Petrie; ***W:*** Donald Petrie; Marc Lawrence; ***C:*** Laszlo Kovacs; ***M:*** Ed Shearmur.

Miss Congeniality 2: Armed and Fabulous 🦴 ½ **2005 (PG-13)** Contrived sequel, set a few weeks after the first flick. Gracie Hart's (Bullock) now a celebrity and can't work undercover, so she's reassigned to be the Bureau's public face. Accompanied by her flamboyant personal stylist Joel (Bader) and her angry FBI bodyguard, Sam Fuller (King), Gracie heads to Vegas when the current Miss United States, Heather (Burns), and pageant director Stan (Shatner) are kidnapped. Many slapstick shenanigans follow in this trifling female buddy comedy. **115m/C; DVD.** Sandra Bullock; Regina King; Enrique Murciano; William Shatner; Ernie Hudson; Heather Burns; Diedrich Bader; Treat Williams; Abraham Benrubi; Nick Offerman; Elisabeth Rohm; ***D:*** John Pasquin; ***W:*** Marc Lawrence; ***C:*** Peter Menzies, Jr.

Miss Evers' Boys 🦴🦴 ½ **1997 (PG)** Wrenching docudrama covers a 40-year U.S. Public Health Service study in which black men suffering from syphillis were monitored but not treated for the disease. Eunice Evers (Woodard) is a nurse at Alabama's Tuskegee Hospital in 1932, assisting Dr. Brodus (Morton) in the care of the afflicted men. When Dr. Douglas' (Sheffer) treatment funding is cut, he's offered funding only to study whether the disease affects blacks and whites differently. Brodus and Evers both lie to their patients as they realize that only the men's deaths will provide the final information for the study. Based on the play by David Feldshuh. **120m/C; DVD.** Alfre Woodard; Laurence Fishburne; Joe Morton; Craig Sheffer; Obba Babatunde; Ossie Davis; E.G. Marshall; ***D:*** Joseph Sargent; ***W:*** Walter Bernstein; ***C:*** Donald M. Morgan; ***M:*** Charles Bernstein. **CABLE**

Miss Firecracker 🦴🦴🦴 **1989 (PG)** Hunter, longing for love and self-respect, decides to change her promiscuous image by entering the local beauty pageant in her conservative southern hometown. The somewhat drippy premise is transformed by a super script and cast into an engaging and upbeat film. Henley's script was adapted from her own Off-Broadway play where Hunter created the role. Actress Lahti, wife of director Schlamme, makes a brief appearance. **102m/C; VHS, DVD; Open Captioned.** Holly Hunter; Scott Glenn; Mary Steenburgen; Tim Robbins; Alfre Woodard; Trey Wilson; Bert Remsen; Ann Wedgeworth; Christine Lahti; Amy Wright; ***D:*** Thomas Schlamme; ***W:*** Beth Henley; ***C:*** Arthur Albert; ***M:*** David Mansfield.

Ms. 45 🦴🦴🦴 *Angel of Vengeance* **1981 (R)** Rough, bristling cult favorite about a mute girl who, in response to being raped and beaten twice in one night, goes on a man-killing murder spree. Wild ending. **84m/C; VHS, DVD, Blu-Ray.** Zoe Tamerlis; Steve Singer; Jack Thibeau; Peter Yellen; Darlene Stuto; Editta Sherman; Albert Sinkys; Abel Ferrara; ***D:*** Abel Ferrara; ***W:*** Nicholas St. John; ***C:*** James (Momel) Lemmo; ***M:*** Joe Delia.

Miss Grant Takes Richmond 🦴🦴 *Innocence is Bliss* **1949** Zipperhead secretary finds herself in hot water a la Lucy when she finds out the company she's been working for is really the front for a gambling getup. Only Lucy fans need apply. **87m/B; VHS, DVD.** Lucille Ball;

William Holden; Janis Carter; James Gleason; Gloria Henry; Frank McHugh; George Cleveland; Arthur Space; Will Wright; Jimmy Lloyd; *D:* Lloyd Bacon.

Miss Hokusai 🦴🦴 *Sarusuberi: Miss Hokusai* **2016 (PG-13)** Keiichi Hara's anime adaptation of the hit manga series is a unique biopic in that the "famous" person at its center, world-renowned artist Hokusai is something of a supporting character. Instead, we see the history of his art and the role of the artist in his era through the eyes of his daughter O-Ei, herself an accomplished artist stifled by gender roles and the large shadow of her father. There are some very interesting sequences in Hara's film but it's defiantly episodic and never quite becomes as memorable as a whole. **93m/C; DVD.** Anne Watanabe; Yutaka Matsushige; Gaku Hamada; Shion Shimizu; Michitaka Tsutsui; *D:* Keiichi Hara; *W:* Miho Maruo; *C:* Koji Tanaka; *M:* Harumi Fuki.

Miss Julie 🦴🦴 *Froken Julie* **1950** Melodramatic stew adapted from from the August Strindberg play about a confused noblewoman who disgraces herself when she allows a servant to seduce her. In Swedish with English subtitles. **90m/B; VHS, DVD.** *SW* Anita Bjork; Ulf Palme; Anders Henrikson; Max von Sydow; *D:* Alf Sjoberg; *W:* Alf Sjoberg; *C:* Goran Strindberg; *M:* Dag Wiren. Cannes '51: Film.

Miss Julie 🦴🦴 **1999 (R)** Dry adaptation of August Strindberg's 1889 banned-in-Sweden play about the turbulent relationship between an imperious young noblewoman and an ambitious servant. Neurotic Miss Julie (Burrows), restless and bored, strides into the servants' kitchen and begin ordering about her father's footman, Jean (Mullan). Their upstairs/downstairs division deteriorates into a series of psycho/sexual clashes over an evening where mutual loathing, humiliation, and self-destruction are the only means of communication. **101m/C; VHS, DVD.** *GB* Saffron Burrows; Peter Mullan; Maria Doyle Kennedy; *D:* Mike Figgis; *W:* Helen Cooper; *C:* Benoit Delhomme; *M:* Mike Figgis.

Miss Julie 🦴🦴 **2014** Based on the August Strindberg play, director Ullmann puts on a well-staged but ultimately flat chamber piece. It is 1890 in Fermanagh, and Julie (Chastain), a daughter of the Court, is trying to seduce her father's valet Jean (Farrell), even though his fiancé (Morton) is in the house. As in the source, Ullmann is playing with issues of power, class, and sexuality. The three actors are uniformly strong, especially the always phenomenal Chastain, but it doesn't quite justify its existence. No one asked why it should be told again. **129m/C; DVD.** *NO UK* Jessica Chastain; Colin Farrell; Samantha Morton; *D:* Liv Ullmann; *W:* Liv Ullmann; *C:* Mikhail Krichman.

Miss Juneteenth 🦴🦴 ½ **2020** Former beauty queen and Miss Juneteenth Turquoise Jones (Beharie) is proud of her past. Still something of a local celebrity, she now works at a dive barbeque restaurant in Fort Worth, Texas. Turquoise is also a single mom raising a headstrong teenager, Kai (Chikaeze), whom she wishes would follow in her footsteps. Kai is more interested in practicing for her school dance team tryout than preparing for the Miss Juneteenth pageant, despite her mother's actions. Hardworking Turquoise also lacks support from her ex Ronnie (Sampson) and her judgy mother (Hayes). It's an authentic melodrama with a heart of gold. **99m/C; DVD.** Nicole Beharie; Kendrick Sampson; Alexis Chikaeze; Lori Hayes; Marcus M. Mauldin; *D:* Channing Godfrey Peoples; *W:* Channing Godfrey Peoples; *C:* Daniel Patterson; *M:* Emily Rice.

Miss London Ltd. 🦴🦴 **1943** Wartime musical/comedy with some risque elements. American Terry (Dall) arrives in London to claim her half-share of a failing escort agency. Forced to find new offices, the Miss London agency settles into the Hotel Splendide but they run into trouble because it's owned by unhappy client Capt. Rory O'More (Graves), who fell for—and was rejected by—one of their new hires. **99m/B; DVD.** *GB* Evelyn Dall; Arthur Askey; Peter Graves; Anne Shelton; Richard Hearne; Max Bacon; Jack Train; *D:* Val Guest; *W:* Val Guest; Marriott Edgar; *C:* Basil Emmott; *M:* Bob Busby.

Miss March **WOOF!** **2009 (R)** You don't expect much from your typical raunchy sex comedy, but it should at least attempt to be funny. This is just ragged and moronic. Goody two-shoes virgin Eugene (Cregger) is pressed by girlfriend Cindi (Alessi) to have sex after their prom. Instead, Eugene has an accident and goes into a coma for four years. When he wakes up, his horn-dog best bud Tucker (Moore) informs Eugene that Cindi has become a Playboy Playmate, so they take off for the Chicago Playboy Mansion so Eugene and Cindi can be reunited. Hugh Hefner (who looks like a wax effigy) cameos. **89m/C; DVD, Blu-Ray, On Demand.** Zach Cregger; Trevor Moore; Raquel Alessi; Craig Robinson; Molly Stanton; Geoff Meed; ***Cameo(s):*** Hugh Hefner; *D:* Zach Cregger; Trevor Moore; *W:* Zach Cregger; Trevor Moore; *C:* Anthony B. Richmond; *M:* Jeff Cardoni.

Miss Meadows 🦴 ½ **2014** Minor black comedy that's a bit too prim for its own good. Mary Meadows (Holmes) is the proper new substitute elementary teacher who punishes bad adult behavior in a permanent way. Turns out she's an unhinged vigilante with a gun. Her romantic interest, who's the local sheriff (Dale), begins to suspect all is not well and it gets worse when child molester Skylar (Mulvey) is paroled and returns to the area. **88m/C; DVD.** Katie Holmes; James Badge Dale; Callan Mulvey; Mary Kay Place; Jean Smart; *D:* Karen Leigh Hopkins; *W:* Karen Leigh Hopkins; *C:* Barry Markowitz; *M:* Jeff Cardoni.

Miss Minoes 🦴🦴 ½ **2001 (PG)** Dubbed Dutch whimsy is kid friendly, especially for any cat fanciers. Miss Minoes (Van Housten) is a cat-turned-human who moves in with timid reporter Tibbe (Maassen) and gets room and board in exchange for news scoops. Minoes rallies her fellow cats to help Tibbe investigate a local factory owner/philanthropist who's actually a bad guy. **86m/C; DVD.** *NL* Carice van Houten; Theo Maassen; Sarah Bannier; Pierre Bokma; *D:* Vincent Bal; *W:* Vincent Bal; *C:* Walther van den Ende; *M:* Peter Vermeersch.

Miss Monday 🦴🦴 **1998 (R)** A blocked writer turns voyeur and begins watching a young woman in order to get material for his work. **90m/C; DVD.** Andrea Hart; James Hicks; Nick Moran; Michael Coles; Alex Giannini; John Woolvett; *D:* Benson Lee; *W:* Benson Lee; Richard Morel; *M:* Woody Pak.

Miss Nobody 🦴 ½ **2010 (R)** Lowly secretary Sarah Jane believes in signs and karma, so maybe she shouldn't be surprised that the promotion she lied to get is given instead to newcomer Milo. Sarah accidentally kills Milo, successfully conceals the crime, and starts moving up the corporate ladder, one murder at a time. But remember, karma can be a—well, you know. **87m/C; DVD.** Brandon Routh; Leslie Bibb; Adam Goldberg; Kathy Baker; Missi Pyle; Vivica A. Fox; Geoffrey Lewis; David Anthony Higgins; *D:* Tim Cox; *W:* Douglas Steinberg; *C:* Mateo Londono; *M:* John Dickson. **VIDEO**

Miss Peregrine's Home for Peculiar Children 🦴🦴 **2016 (PG-13)** Tim Burton's take on Ransom Riggs' hit book is one of those Young Adult flicks in which everything should work on paper, but lacks the imagination or creative spark needed to make it memorable. Jacob (Butterfield) is a young man who discovers clues to an ancient mystery that leads him to the title location, run by the eccentric Miss Peregrine (Green). Of course, Jacob learns he's a little "peculiar" too. It looks incredible but it's peculiarly hollow. **127m/C; DVD, Blu-Ray.** Eva Green; Asa Butterfield; Samuel L. Jackson; Chris O'Dowd; Allison Janney; Rupert Everett; *D:* Tim Burton; *W:* Jane Goldman; *C:* Bruno Delbonnel; *M:* Michael Higham; Matthew Margeson.

Miss Pettigrew Lives for a Day 🦴🦴🦴 **2008 (PG-13)** Middle-aged governess Miss Guinevere Pettigrew (McDormand) is unemployed yet again in 1939 London. Flat broke, she pushes her way into working as the social secretary for American actress/singer Delysia Lafosse (Adams) and her glamorous high society life. Delysia's love interests are as dizzying as her busy career, but Miss Pettigrew might just find love of her own in dashing and kind fashion designer Joe (Hinds). It doesn't matter one bit that we know exactly where this film is going—the journey is so fun and the characters so charming, we happily jaunt right along. **92m/C; DVD.** *GB US* Frances McDormand; Amy Adams; Lee Pace; Ciaran Hinds; Mark Strong; Shirley Henderson; Christina Cole; Tom Payne; *D:* Bharat Nalluri; *W:* David Magee; Simon Beaufoy; *C:* John de Borman; *M:* Paul Englishby.

Miss Pinkerton 🦴 ½ **1932** Bored Nurse Adams (Blondell) is looking after elderly Juliet Mitchell (Patterson) whose nephew has died under suspicious circumstances in their creepy old house. The dead man was heavily insured, and Police Inspector Patten (Brent) thinks Adams is in the perfect position to snoop around (hence the title). **70m/B; DVD.** Joan Blondell; George Brent; Elizabeth Patterson; Ruth Hall; John Wray; *D:* Lloyd Bacon; *W:* Niven Busch; Lillie Hayward; *C:* Barney McGill.

Miss Potter 🦴🦴 ½ **2006 (PG)** Charming, though staid, bio of the creator of Peter Rabbit. Beatrix Potter (Zellweger) was a genteel spinster from a nouveau riche family (the film covers 1902-06). Her talents were generally dismissed until the elder editors at the Warne family publishing firm decide the project will keep youngest brother Norman (McGregor) busy. He turns out to be enthusiastic for not only the book but for Beatrix herself, and she is soon friendly with both Norman and his unmarried sister, Millie (Watson). Noonan has Potter's drawings come to life when she talks to them, otherwise this is standard fare. Watson and McGregor make a lively, charming duo while Zellweger seems rather too restrained. **92m/C; DVD.** *GB US* Renée Zellweger; Ewan McGregor; Emily Watson; Barbara Flynn; Bill Paterson; Matyclock Gibbs; Anton Lesser; David Bamber; Phyllida Law; Lloyd Owen; *D:* Chris Noonan; *W:* Richard Maltby, Jr.; *C:* Andrew Dunn; *M:* Nigel Westlake.

Miss Right 🦴 **1981 (R)** A young man determines to find the ideal woman for himself and casts aside his other romantic interests. Sputtering lightweight comedy. **98m/C; VHS, DVD.** William Tepper; Karen Black; Virna Lisi; Margot Kidder; Marie-France Pisier; *D:* Paul Williams.

Miss Sadie Thompson 🦴🦴🦴 **1953** Based on the novel "Rain" by W. Somerset Maugham. Promiscuous tart Sadie (Hayworth) arrives on a Pacific island occupied by a unit of Marines and sanctimonious preacher Alfred (Ferrer). While Sadie parties and becomes involved with Sgt. O'Hara (Ray), Alfred moralizes and insists she return to the mainland to face moral charges. Quasi-musical with a scattering of dubbed songs; Hayworth includes a memorable erotic dance scene complete with tight dress and dripping sweat. Her strong performance carries the picture with Ferrer and Ray turning in cardboard versions of their Maugham characters. Originally filmed in 3-D. **91m/C; DVD, Blu-Ray.** Rita Hayworth; Jose Ferrer; Aldo Ray; Charles Bronson; Russell Collins; *D:* Curtis Bernhardt; *W:* Harry Kleiner; *C:* Charles Lawton, Jr.

Miss Sloane 🦴🦴 ½ **2016 (R)** It takes quite an actor to make us care about a cutthroat, high-stakes D.C. lobbyist, but Chastain is that actor. Elizabeth Sloane (Chastain) really doesn't like to lose and has gone to any and all lengths necessary on her way to the top. But when the case for less gun regulation comes along, she jeopardizes her career but jumping ship. While director Madden hasn't broken any political thriller mold with this, it's definitely a thrilling ride. Thanks mostly to Chastain's amazing and complex performance, the movie's flaws can be mostly overlooked. **132m/C; DVD, Blu-Ray.** Jessica Chastain; Gugu Mbatha-Raw; Michael Stuhlbarg; John Lithgow; Mark Strong; *D:* John Madden; *W:* Jonathan Perera; *C:* Sebastian Blenkov; *M:* Max Richter.

Miss Stevens 🦴🦴 ½ **2016** One weekend, high school English teacher Rachel Stevens (Rabe) drives three of her drama students--intelligent Margo (Reinhart), openly gay Sam (Quintal), and troubled yet talented Billy (Chalamet)--to an off-campus drama competition in which they perform monologues for prizes and school arts funding. Though Margot is critical of Rachel's taste in music, Billy tries to connect with Rachel, especially after she discusses an emotional incident with him, but she ensures that he understands they are teacher-student. The smart indie comedy-drama explores the tensions between Miss Stevens's difficulties with her life and her calling as a teacher, while serving as an understated tribute to teachers. **86m/C; DVD.** Lily Rabe; Timothée Chalamet; Lili Reinhart; Anthony Quintal; Oscar Nunez; *D:* Julia Hart; *W:* Julia Hart; Jordan Horowitz; *C:* Sebastian Wintero; *M:* Rob Simonsen.

Miss Tatlock's Millions 🦴🦴 ½ **1948** In this amusing screwball comedy, caretaker Denno (Fitzgerald) doesn't want to admit that crazy Schuyler Tatlock is missing just when he's needed to attend the reading of a family will. So he hires Hollywood stuntman Burke (Lund) to impersonate the man (who's lived for years in Hawaii, estranged from his family) so his sister Nan (Hendrix) can get her inheritance. Too bad that Burke is soon having inappropriate feelings for his 'sister.' **101m/B; DVD.** John Lund; Wanda Hendrix; Barry Fitzgerald; Monty Woolley; Ilka Chase; Robert Stack; Dorothy Stickney; Leif Erickson; *D:* Richard Haydn; *W:* Charles Brackett; Richard L. Breen; *C:* Charles B(ryant) Lang, Jr.; *M:* Victor Young.

Miss You Already 🦴🦴 **2015 (PG-13)** If you think every generation needs a new "Beaches," this maudlin drama might work for you. Jess (Barrymore) and Milly (Collette) have been friends for most of their lives, but that bond is about to be challenged. Jess and her boyfriend are having trouble having a baby, which is hard enough on anyone, but her life is really turned upside down when Milly is diagnosed with breast cancer. To say that Barrymore and Collette really elevate the material would be an understatement. The script is unoriginal and manipulative, but the actresses nearly rescue it. **112m/C; DVD, Blu-Ray.** Drew Barrymore; Toni Collette; Dominic Cooper; Paddy Considine; Tyson Ritter; *D:* Catherine Hardwicke; *W:* Morwenna Banks; *C:* Elliot Davis; *M:* Harry Gregson-Williams.

Missile to the Moon 🦴 ½ **1959** First expedition to the moon encounters not acres of dead rock but a race of gorgeous women in lingerie and high heels. A bad but entertaining remake of "Cat Women of the Moon," featuring a bevy of beauty contest winners from New Hampshire to Yugoslavia. Who says truth is stranger than fiction. **78m/B; VHS, DVD.** Gary Clarke; Cathy Downs; K.T. Stevens; Laurie Mitchell; Michael Whalen; Nina Bara; Richard Travis; Tommy Cook; Marjorie Hellen; *D:* Richard Cunha; *W:* Vincent Fotre; H.E. Barrie; *C:* Meredith Nicholson; *M:* Nicholas Carras.

Missiles from Hell 🦴 ½ *Battle of the V-1* **1958** Very stiff-upper-lip WWII drama. In 1943, Stefan (Rennie) and his friend Tadek (Knight) are members of the Polish resistance. They allow themselves to be captured and taken to a labor camp in order to find out about the Nazis' V-1 rocket program. They manage to get word to the allies, who destroy the camp, but the Nazis regroup and the next move is to get a completed V-1 rocket, smuggle it out of the country, and send it to Britain. Utilizes footage of actual air raids. **80m/B; DVD.** *GB* Michael Rennie; David Knight; Peter Madden; Christopher Lee; Patricia Medina; Milly Vitale; Esmond Knight; *D:* Vernon Sewell; *W:* Jack Hanley; Eryk Wlodek; *C:* Basil Emmott; *M:* Robert Sharples.

Missiles of October 🦴🦴🦴 **1974** Telling the story of the October 1962 Cuban Missile crisis, this TV drama keeps you on the edge of your seat while unfolding the sequence of events within the U.S. government. Well written, with a strong cast including Devane, who turns in a convincing performance as—guess who'J.F.K. **155m/C; VHS, DVD.** William Devane; Ralph Bellamy; Martin Sheen; Howard da Silva; James Hong; James Callahan; Keene Curtis; John Dehner; Peter Donat; Andrew Duggan; Charles Cyphers; Dana Elcar; Arthur Franz; Larry Gates; Richard Karlan; Michael Lerner; Stacy Keach, Sr.; Wright King; Will Kuluva; Paul Lambert; Doreen Lang; Byron Morrow; Stewart Moss; James Olson; Dennis Patrick; Albert Paulsen; Nehemiah Persoff; William Prince; John Randolph; Kenneth Tobey; Harris Yulin; George Wyner; *D:* Anthony Page; *M:* Laurence Rosenthal. **TV**

Missing 🦴🦴🦴 ½ **1982 (PG)** At the height of a military coup in Chile (never named in the movie), a young American writer (Shea) disappears. His right-wing father Lemmon tries to get to the bottom of his disappearance while bickering with Shea's wife, played by Spacek, a bohemian who is the political opposite of her father-in-law. Outstanding performances by Spacek and Lemmon along with excellent writing and direction result in a gripping and thought-provoking thriller. Based on the book by Thomas Hauser from the true story of Charles Horman. **122m/C; VHS, DVD.** Jack Lemmon; Sissy Spacek; John Shea; Melanie Mayron; David Clennon; Charles Cioffi; Joe Regalbuto; Richard Venture; Janice Rule; ***D:*** Constantin Costa-Gavras; ***W:*** Constantin Costa-Gavras; Donald Stewart; ***M:*** Vangelis. Oscars '82: Adapt. Screenplay; British Acad. '82: Screenplay; Cannes '82: Actor (Lemmon), Film; Writers Guild '82: Adapt. Screenplay.

The Missing **2003 (R)** Director Howard successfully tries his hand at a gritty western. Maggie Gilkeson (Blanchett), a mother of two daughters, supports her family by working the ranch and serving as a healer to the community. Maggie is estranged from her father Samuel Jones (the perfectly craggy-faced Jones) who left her and her mother years ago to live with the Apaches. But she seeks his help after her oldest daughter Lilly (Wood) is kidnapped by an evil Native American shaman (Schweig). Blanchett and Jones both have the acting chops to keep this story interesting and well worth watching. Based on the Thomas Eidson novel "The Last Ride." **135m/C; DVD.** Tommy Lee Jones; Cate Blanchett; Eric Schweig; Jenna Boyd; Evan Rachel Wood; Steve Reevis; Ray McKinnon; Val Kilmer; Aaron Eckhart; Simon Baker; Jay Tavare; Sergio Calderon; Clint Howard; Elisabeth Moss; Max Perlich; ***D:*** Ron Howard; ***W:*** Ken Kaufman; ***C:*** Salvatore Totino; ***M:*** James Horner.

Missing Brendan **1/2** **2003** After three painful decades, George Calden (Asner) goes to Vietnam with his two sons and grandson upon learning that his MIA-son Brendan's crashed plane has been found. Desperate to fulfill his wife's dying wish to bring his remains home, the family grapples with many more challenges including lack of cooperation by the Vietnamese government, a father-son clash when his grandson dates a local girl, and George's hidden terminal illness. **100m/C; VHS, DVD.** Ed Asner; Robin Thomas; Illeana Douglas; Richard Cox; Adam Brody; Harold Sylvester; Kathleen Luong; Aki Aleong; Dale Dye; Brenda Strong; ***D:*** Eugene Brady; ***W:*** Christopher White; ***C:*** Jeffrey Smith. **VIDEO**

Missing Girls **1/2** **1936** Runaway Ann Jason takes refuge at New York's Traveler's Aid Society and is befriended by socialite Dorothy Benson. Dorothy's senator father is murdered by gangsters for trying to get gambling legalized and reporter Jimmie Dugan starts nosing around. Then Ann and Dorothy are kidnapped and Jimmie must come to their rescue. **66m/B; DVD.** Roger Pryor; Ann Doran; Muriel Evans; Noel Madison; Sidney Blackmer; Wallis (Clarke) Clark; Dewey Robinson; Vera Lewis; ***D:*** Phil Rosen; ***W:*** John Krafft; ***C:*** M(ilton) A(rthur) Anderson.

The Missing Gun **1/2** *Xun qiang* **2002 (PG-13)** Detective Ma Shen (Wen Jiang) loses his gun after getting stone drunk at his sister's wedding reception. This is bad for him because the gun is government issued, and its loss means the possible end of his job, especially if it ends up involved in a crime. Obligingly, his old girlfriend soon ends up dead in her new lover's residence, and tests confirm the bullets are from Ma's gun. Now not only must he find the gun, he has to clear himself of any possible charges in his old flame's death. **90m/C; DVD.** *CH* Wen Jiang; Nina Huang; Shi Liang; Jing Ning; ***D:*** Chuan Lu; ***W:*** Chuan Lu; ***C:*** Zhengyu Xie.

Missing in Action **1/2** **1984 (R)** An army colonel returns to the Vietnam jungle to settle some old scores and rescue some POWs while on an MIA fact-finding mission. Box office smash. **101m/C; VHS, DVD, Blu-Ray.** Chuck Norris; M. Emmet Walsh; ***D:*** Joseph Zito; ***W:*** James Bruner; ***C:*** Joao Fernandes; ***M:*** Jay Chattaway.

Missing in Action 2: The Beginning **1985 (R)** Set in Vietnam, this prequel to the original "Missing in Action" provides some interesting background on Norris's rocky relationship with communism. Packed with violence, bloodshed and torture. **96m/C; VHS, DVD, Blu-Ray.** Chuck Norris; Soon-Teck Oh; Cosie Costa; Steven Williams; ***D:*** Lance Hool; ***W:*** Steve Bing.

Missing Link **1/2** **2019 (PG)** Nineteenth century British explorer Sir Lionel Frost (Jackman) travels around the world searching for myths and monsters. After receiving a letter, Lionel finds a hairy giant first called Mr. Link and later Susan (Galifianakis) in the Pacific Northwest. The creature wrote the letter after learning English by observation. Susan encourages Lionel to travel to the Himalayas to find a city of Yeti. The pair embarks on the long journey together, joined by adventurer Adelina Fortnight (Saldana) and followed by evil explorer/assassin Willard Stenk (Olyphant). This animated adventure/buddy film features interesting characters, beautiful visuals, and, at its heart, an effective, funny comedy duo. **94m/C; DVD, Blu-Ray.** *CA US* Hugh Jackman; David Walliams; Stephen Fry; Matt Lucas; Zach Galifianakis; ***D:*** Chris Butler; ***W:*** Chris Butler; ***C:*** Chris Peterson; ***M:*** Carter Burwell. Golden Globes '20: Animated Film.

The Missing Person **1/2** **2009** Self-conscious contemporary noir with depressed, hard-drinking PI John Roscow (Shannon) hired to pursue mystery man Harold Fullmer (Wood) on a train trip to L.A. Then Rostow gets to follow Fullmer to a Mexican orphanage and eventually get him back to New York. It's washed-out and generally dull. **95m/C; DVD.** Michael Shannon; Frank Wood; Amy Ryan; Linda Edmond; John Ventimiglia; Margaret Colin; ***D:*** Noah Buschel; ***W:*** Noah Buschel; ***C:*** Ryan Samul.

The Missing Picture *L'image manquante* **2013** A mixed-media documentary that finds writer-director Panh using clay figures, propaganda newsreel footage, and narration to recall his teenage years from 1975 to 1979 under the Cambodian dictatorship of Pol Pot. His family is forced from the city by the Khmer Rouge into agricultural labor camps for reeducation where conditions are so harsh that many die from starvation and others are murdered for ideological reasons. An agonizingly emotional telling of an appalling period in history. French with subtitles. **92m/C; DVD.** *CB FR* ***D:*** Rithy Panh; ***W:*** Rithy Panh; Christophe Bataille; ***C:*** Prum Mesar; ***M:*** Marc Marder.

The Mission **1986 (PG)** Sweeping, cinematically beautiful historical drama about an 18th-century Jesuit mission in the Brazilian jungle. The missionaries struggle against the legalized slave trade of Portugal and political factions within the church. Written by Bolt (of "A Man for All Seasons" fame), its visual intensity is marred by length and so much overt symbolism that an emotional coolness surfaces when the action slows. Nonetheless, epic in ambition and nearly in quality. Magnificent musical score. **125m/C; DVD.** Robert De Niro; Jeremy Irons; Ray McAnally; Aidan Quinn; Liam Neeson; Cherie Lunghi; Rev. Daniel Berrigan; Ronald Pickup; ***D:*** Roland Joffé; ***W:*** Robert Bolt; ***C:*** Chris Menges; ***M:*** Ennio Morricone. Oscars '86: Cinematog.; British Acad. '86: Support. Actor (McAnally); Cannes '86: Film; Golden Globes '87: Score, Screenplay; L.A. Film Critics '86: Cinematog.

The Mission **1/2** *Cheung Fo* **1999** A Hong Kong mobster hires five gunmen to be his bodyguards. Everything's cool until one of them has an affair with the boss's wife. Director To revisits Tarantino-Woo territory. Most of the guys have bad haircuts and all of them have big pistols. **84m/C; DVD.** *CH* Anthony Wong; Frances Ng; Roy Cheung; Simon Yam; Jackie Lui; Lam Suet; ***D:*** Johnny To; ***W:*** Nai-Hoi Yau.

Mission **2000** New York native Marvin (Coburn) moves to the Mission District of San Francisco to write a novel. He rooms with wannabe musician Jay (Leonard) and falls for beauty Ima (Holt), who tells him that he's too uptight to be a good writer. Well, if the Mission District can't loosen Marvin up, he's doomed. **87m/C; VHS, DVD.** Chris Coburn; Joshua Leonard; Sandrine Holt; Bellamy Young; Adam Arkin; ***D:*** Loren Marsh; ***W:*** Loren Marsh; ***C:*** Matthew Uhry.

Mission: Impossible **1996 (PG-13)** Blockbuster based on the popular '60s TV series. Ethan Hunt (Cruise) is point-man extraordinaire of the IMF team headed by Jim Phelps (Voight). Their team is sent to recover a computer disk with devastating information from a mercenary Russian spy. Smelling a doublecross, Hunt confronts his conniving agency boss Kitteridge (Czerny) and creates his own team of crack agents to get to the truth. The plotline may have self-destructed two-thirds into the movie, but with solid acting talent, tight pacing, alluring European locales, and tension-inducing special effects, who has time to notice? **110m/C; DVD, Blu-Ray, HD-DVD.** Tom Cruise; Jon Voight; Emmanuelle Beart; Ving Rhames; Henry Czerny; Emilio Estevez; Vanessa Redgrave; Jean Reno; Dale Dye; ***D:*** Brian De Palma; ***W:*** Robert Towne; David Koepp; ***C:*** Stephen Burum; ***M:*** Danny Elfman.

Mission: Impossible 2 *M:I 2* **2000 (PG-13)** In this visually stunning sequel, Ethan Hunt (Cruise) tracks rogue IMF agent Ambrose (Scott), who threatens to release a deadly virus on Sydney, Australia and corner the market on the cure. Ambrose's ex-girlfriend Nyah (Newton), a jewel thief, is recruited by Hunt to spy on Ambrose from inside. Of course, Nyah and Hunt fall in love (the weakest element of the movie). Director Woo brings his trademark balletic style to the action, and the stunts and fights, while completely preposterous, are beautifully done. The plot is also a lot less convoluted than the first pic. **125m/C; DVD, Blu-Ray, HD-DVD.** Tom Cruise; Anthony Hopkins; Dougray Scott; Thandie Newton; Ving Rhames; Brendan Gleeson; John Polson; Richard Roxburgh; Rade Serbedzija; ***D:*** John Woo; ***W:*** Robert Towne; ***C:*** Jeffrey L. Kimball; ***M:*** Hans Zimmer.

Mission: Impossible 3 **2006 (PG-13)** This third MI chapter is a cracking good yarn with Abrams, in his feature debut, grounding the film by bringing back the cool gadgets and teamwork that everyone loved about the original TV show. Ethan Hunt (Cruise) is ready to retire from the IMF, when evil arms dealer Davian (a scene-stealing Hoffman) kills Hunt's protege and kidnaps his wife (Monaghan). Hunt goes into rescue/revenge mode and the non-stop action... well... never stops. Great example of a summer blockbuster that works. **126m/C; DVD, Blu-Ray, HD-DVD.** Tom Cruise; Ving Rhames; Keri Russell; Philip Seymour Hoffman; Michelle Monaghan; Laurence Fishburne; Billy Crudup; Simon Pegg; Jonathan Rhys Meyers; Sasha Alexander; Greg Grunberg; Carla Gallo; Eddie Marsan; Jose Zuniga; Maggie Q; ***D:*** J.J. (Jeffrey) Abrams; ***W:*** J.J. (Jeffrey) Abrams; Alex Kurtzman; Roberto Orci; ***C:*** Dan(iel) Mindel; ***M:*** Michael Giacchino.

Mission: Impossible Rogue Nation **2015 (PG-13)** An international rogue organization known as the Syndicate is doing their best to eliminate Ethan Hunt (Cruise) and the rest of IMF (including returning stars Renner and Pegg) in this fifth installment of the franchise. Of course, Hunt has to save the day with the help of franchise staples like nifty gadgets and imperceptible disguises. McQuarrie picks up the baton passed by Brad Bird from the last film and runs with it, producing one of the most purely entertaining summer blockbusters of 2015. The plot can seem a bit ludicrous, but it's too much fun to care while you're watching it. **131m/C; DVD, Blu-Ray, Streaming.** Tom Cruise; Jeremy Renner; Ving Rhames; Simon Pegg; Rebecca Ferguson; ***D:*** Christopher McQuarrie; ***W:*** Christopher McQuarrie; ***C:*** Robert Elswit; ***M:*** Joe Kraemer.

Mission: Impossible—Fallout **1/2** *M:I 6—Mission Impossible* **2018 (PG-13)** This sixth installment demonstrates that the franchise shows no sign of slowing down. Thank goodness. Continuing the story from *Rogue Nation*, Ethan Hunt (Cruise, who at 56 miraculously refuses to age), his IMF team, and a few new allies trek the globe to reacquire three plutonium cores stolen by the Apostles, a nefarious group led by fundamentalist John Lark. The action is relentless, the stunts are mind-blowing, the set-pieces are magnificent, and the story holds together throughout. A near-perfect summer blockbuster. **147m/C; DVD, Blu-Ray.** Tom Cruise; Henry Cavill; Ving Rhames; Simon Pegg; Rebecca Ferguson; ***D:*** Christopher McQuarrie; ***W:*** Christopher McQuarrie; ***C:*** Rob Hardy; ***M:*** Lorne Balfe.

Mission: Impossible—Ghost Protocol **2011 (PG-13)** Director Bird makes a stunning live-action debut after his years as a Pixar genius and delivers the best Mission: Impossible film to date. Ethan Hunt (Cruise) and his IMF team are disavowed after the Kremlin is destroyed and they are implicated but, of course, they may be the only ones who can stop World War III. With spectacular action set-pieces, excellent sound design, and some amazing camera work (especially in IMAX), it's pure blockbuster entertainment of the highest caliber. It actually makes one long for another sequel. **133m/C; DVD, Blu-Ray.** Tom Cruise; Jeremy Renner; Simon Pegg; Paula Patton; Josh Holloway; Ving Rhames; Michael Nyqvist; Vladimir Mashkov; Lea Seydoux; Anil Kapoor; Tom Wilkinson; ***D:*** Brad Bird; ***W:*** Josh Applebaum; André Nemec; ***C:*** Robert Elswit; ***M:*** Michael Giacchino.

Mission. . . Kill **1/2** **1985 (R)** An American demolitions expert (Ginty) joins a Latin American guerrilla force in battling tyrannical junta force. Fast-paced thriller is big on revenge and violence but not much else. **97m/C; VHS, DVD.** Robert Ginty; Olivia D'Abo; Cameron Mitchell; ***D:*** David Winters.

Mission Mangal **2019** Working for the Indian space agency, scientist Rakesh Dhawan (Kumar) takes responsibility for the miscalculation of project director Tara Shinde (Balan) that results in the abortion of an unmanned space launch. Demoted to an underfunded project focused on launching on a satellite to Mars, Rakesh believes it will never take off but Tara comes up with a novel solution that pushes the project forward. Though Rakesh gets approval to keep going, his mostly female crew relies on more improvised shortcuts to ensure it has a chance to succeed. The feel-good, "Hidden Figures"-type film is based on real events and has an exceptional cast. Hindi with subtitles. **130m/C; DVD.** Akshaya Kumar; Vidya Balan; Nithya Menon; Taapsee Pannu; Sonakshi Sinha; ***D:*** Jagan Shakti; ***W:*** R. Balki; ***C:*** S. Ravi Varman; ***M:*** Tanishk Bagchi; Amit Trivedi.

Mission Manila **1987 (R)** An ex-CIA operative and Manila-based drug addict is called by his ex-lover to return to Manila to help his brother, who has gotten in much the same trouble he had. **98m/C; VHS, DVD.** Larry Wilcox; Tetchie Agbayani; Sam Hennings; Al Mancini; James Wainwright; Robin Eisenman; ***D:*** Peter M. MacKenzie; ***W:*** Peter M. MacKenzie; ***C:*** Les Parrott; ***M:*** Nicholas Pike.

Mission of Death *Merchant of Death* **1997 (R)** Cop Jim Randall (Pare) has been accused of murder and suspended from the force. Something in his past offers the clue to proving his innocence but Randall doesn't want to remember. **96m/C; VHS, DVD.** Michael Paré; Linda Hoffman; John Simon Jones; Anthony Fridjhon; Justin Illusion; ***D:*** Yossi Wein; ***W:*** Dan Lerner; David Sparling; ***C:*** Peter Belcher; ***M:*** Serge Colbert. **VIDEO**

Mission of the Shark **1991** A top secret naval mission leads to a scandal-ridden court martial in this true WWII saga, based on the worst sea disaster in naval history. The USS Indianapolis has just completed a secret mission when it is torpedoed by enemy subs. The survivors spend five days in shark-infested waters awaiting rescue and, when the Navy points fingers, the ship's highly decorated and well-respected Captain McVay accepts responsibility for the good of the service. Contains some harrowing scenes of sailors versus sharks. **92m/C; DVD.** Stacy Keach; Richard Thomas; Steve Landesberg; Carrie Snodgress; Bob Gunton; Andrew Prine; Stacy Keach, Sr.; Don Harvey; ***D:*** Robert Iscove; ***W:*** Alan Sharp. **TV**

Mission Stardust **1/2** *4...3...2...1...Morte* **1968** An internationally produced but thoroughly unambitious adaptation of the once-popular Perry Rhodan sci-fi serial, in which Rhodan and his team bring ill aliens back to Earth and defend them against evil spies. Dubbed. **90m/C; VHS, DVD.** *GE IT SP* Essy Persson; Gianni Rizzo; Lang Jeffries; Pinkas Braun; ***D:*** Primo Zeglio.

Mission to Death **1966** Small American patrol during WWII is beset by numerous attacks on their way to their final destination and each time more members of the unit are wounded or killed. **71m/C; VHS, DVD.** Jim Brewer; James E. McLarty; Jim Westerbrook; Robert Stolper; Dudley Hafner; Jerry

Lasater; *D:* Kenneth W. Richardson; *C:* Ronald Perryman; *M:* Emil Cadkin; William Loose.

Mission to Glory *The Father Kino Story* **1980 (PG)** This dozer tells the story of Father Francisco "Kino" Kin, a tough, 17th-century priest in California who took on the Apaches and murderous Conquistadors in defense of his people. **100m/C; VHS, DVD.** Richard Egan; John Ireland; Cesar Romero; Ricardo Montalban; Rory Calhoun; Michael Ansara; Keenan Wynn; Aldo Ray; *D:* Ken Kennedy.

Mission to Mars ½ **2000 (PG)** When the first manned flight to Mars ends in disaster, leaving Commander Luke Graham (Cheadle) as the only survivor, NASA sends a rescue mission consisting of Graham's best friend Jim (Sinise), married astronauts Woody (Robbins) and Terri (Nielsen), and generic tech guy Phil (O'Connell). On the way to Mars they encounter problems you've seen in other, better-done sci-fi flicks. Once on Mars, they find the New Age-y, touchy-feely secrets of creation. DePalma is known for his visual wizardry, and on that element he doesn't disappoint, but the horrible script and indifferent performances undermine whatever it was he was trying to accomplish. **112m/C; VHS, DVD.** Tim Robbins; Gary Sinise; Don Cheadle; Connie Nielsen; Jerry O'Connell; Kim Delaney; Elise Neal; Peter Outerbridge; Jill Teed; Kavan Smith; *D:* Brian De Palma; *W:* Jim Thomas; John Thomas; Graham Yost; *C:* Stephen Burum; *M:* Ennio Morricone.

Mission to Moscow ½ **1943** Blatant propaganda piece made at the time the Soviet Union was allied with the U.S. against Hitler (whose troops had invaded the USSR). Based on the book by U.S. Ambassador Joseph E. Davies (Huston) who comes across as remarkably naive and accommodating as he arrives in Moscow. (Gee, that Stalin—what a great guy!) **123m/B; DVD.** Walter Huston; Ann Harding; Oscar Homolka; Gene Lockhart; George Tobias; Eleanor Parker; Helmut Dantine; Henry Daniell; Dudley Field Malone; Manart Kippen; *D:* Michael Curtiz; *W:* Howard Koch; *C:* Bert Glennon; *M:* Max Steiner.

Mission to Venice **1963** Flynn plays a sleuth attempting to find a missing husband when he accidentally stumbles upon a ring of spies. **88m/C; VHS, DVD.** Sean Flynn; Madeleine Robinson.

The Missionary ½ **1982 (R)** A mild-mannered English missionary returns to London from his work in Africa and is recruited into saving the souls of a group of prostitutes. Aspiring to gentle comedy status, it's often formulaic and flat, with Palin and Smith fighting gamely to stay above script level. Still, good for some laughs, particularly during the near classic walking butler sequence. **86m/C; VHS, DVD.** *GB* Michael Palin; Maggie Smith; Trevor Howard; Denholm Elliott; Michael Hordern; *D:* Richard Loncraine; *W:* Michael Palin.

Missionary Man **2007 (R)** Ryder comes into town on his hog and learns that a friend was murdered because he got in the way of John Reno's plans to build a casino on an Indian reservation. So Ryder decides to bring some of that old-time, eye-for-an-eye religion and a case of whup-ass on those evildoers. **92m/C; DVD.** Dolph Lundgren; Mathew Tompkins; John Enos; August Schellenberg; James Chalke; Morgana Shaw; Charles Solomon, Jr.; *D:* Dolph Lundgren; *W:* Dolph Lundgren; Frank Valdez; *C:* Xiaobing Rao; *M:* Elia Cmiral. **VIDEO**

Mississippi **1935** In this uneven musical comedy, Philadelphia Yankee Tom Grayson (Crosby) is engaged to southern belle Elvira Rumford (Patrick). But when he refuses to duel one of her other suitors, the engagement is off and he's branded a coward. Tom gets a job singing aboard a riverboat piloted by Commodore Orlando Jackson (Fields) and eventually realizes that his true love is actually Elvira's younger and more sympathetic sister Lucy (Bennett). Fields steals everything that's not nailed down, leaving ostensible star Bing in the dust. Based on the play "Magnolia" by Booth Tarkington. **80m/B; DVD.** Bing Crosby; W.C. Fields; Joan Bennett; Gail Patrick; Fred Kohler, Sr.; Claude Gillingwater; Queenie Smith; John Miljan; *D:* Edward Sutherland; *W:* Francis Martin; Jack Cunningham; Herbert Fields; Claude Binyon; *C:* Charles Lang.

Mississippi Burning **1988 (R)** Hard-edged social drama centers around the civil rights movement in Mississippi in 1964. When three activists turn up missing, FBI agents Anderson (Hackman) and Ward (Dafoe) are sent to head up the investigation. Unfortunately, this is another example of a "serious" film about racial conflict in which white characters predominate and blacks provide background. **127m/C; DVD, Blu-Ray.** Gene Hackman; Willem Dafoe; Frances McDormand; Brad Dourif; R. Lee Ermey; Gailard Sartain; Stephen Tobolowsky; Michael Rooker; Pruitt Taylor Vince; Badja (Medu) Djola; Kevin Dunn; Frankie Faison; Tom Mason; Park Overall; *D:* Alan Parker; *W:* Chris Gerolmo; *C:* Peter Biziou; *M:* Trevor Jones. Oscars '88: Cinematog.; Berlin Intl. Film Fest. '88: Actor (Hackman); Natl. Bd. of Review '88: Actor (Hackman), Director (Parker), Support. Actress (McDormand).

The Mississippi Gambler **1953** Dashing gambler Mark Fallon decides to leave riverboats behind to become a New Orleans casino owner. He gets treated like dirt by society belle Angelique though he saves her weak-willed brother Laurent from financial ruin. Still, Angelique becomes insanely jealous when Mark becomes the protector of impoverished Ann. More trouble follows. **99m/C; DVD.** Tyrone Power; Piper Laurie; Julie Adams; John McIntire; John Baer; Paul Cavanagh; Ron Randell; *D:* Rudolph Mate; *W:* Seton I. Miller; *C:* Irving Glassberg; *M:* Frank Skinner.

Mississippi Grind **2015 (R)** Mendelsohn embodies the lovable loser, the kind of gambling addict who we know will eventually lose but we root to win anyway. The great character shines as Gerry, a long-time loser who goes on a winning streak after meeting the suave Curtis (Reynolds) at a poker game. Convinced that this new friendship has turned their luck around, the pair head on a road trip to hit every casino along the Mississippi on their way to a legendary poker game. Of course, things don't go as planned. Mendelsohn and Reynolds are fantastic here, overcoming the script's relative clichés. **96m/C; DVD, Blu-Ray, Streaming.** Ben Mendelsohn; Ryan Reynolds; Sienna Miller; Robin Weigert; Alfre Woodard; Analeigh Tipton; *D:* Anna Boden; Ryan Fleck; *W:* Anna Boden; Ryan Fleck; *C:* Andrij Parekh; *M:* Scott Bomar.

Mississippi Masala **1992 (R)** "Masala" is an Indian seasoning blending different-colored spices, as this film is a blend of romance, comedy, and social conscience. An interracial romance sets off a cultural collision and escalates racial tensions in a small Southern town when Mina, a sheltered young Indian woman, falls in love with Demetrius, an ambitious black man with his own carpet-cleaning business. Washington and Choudhury are engaging as the lovers with Seth, as Mina's unhappy father, especially watchable. **118m/C; VHS, DVD.** Denzel Washington; Sarita Choudhury; Roshan Seth; Sharmila Tagore; Charles S. Dutton; Joe Seneca; Ranjit (Chaudry) Chowdhry; *Cameo(s):* Mira Nair; *D:* Mira Nair; *W:* Sooni Taraporevala; *M:* L. Subramaniam.

Mississippi Mermaid *Le Sirene du Mississippi* **1969 (PG)** Truffaut generally succeeds in merging his own directorial style with Hitchcockian suspense. Millionaire tobacco planter Louis (Belmondo) looks for a bride in the personals and finds Julie (Deneuve). Louis feels lucky landing this beauty until she leaves him and takes his money with her. After a breakdown, he finds his wife working in a dancehall under another name. Louis agrees to a reconciliation, which proves to be a mistake. Look for numerous references to the movies, including Bogart, Balzac and Cocteau. Based on the Cornell Woolrich novel "Waltz into Darkness." French with subtitles. **110m/C; DVD, Blu-Ray.** *FR IT* Jean-Paul Belmondo; Catherine Deneuve; Michel Bouquet; Nelly Borgeaud; Marcel Berbert; Martine Ferriere; *D:* Francois Truffaut; *W:* Francois Truffaut; *C:* Denys Clerval; *M:* Antoine Duhamel.

Missouri Breaks **1976 (PG)** Thomas McGuane wrote the screenplay for this offbeat tale of Montana ranchers and rustlers fighting over land and livestock in the 1880s. Promising combination of script, cast and director unfortunately yields rather disappointing results, though both Brando and Nicholson chew up scenery to their hearts' content. **126m/C; VHS, DVD, Blu-Ray.** Jack Nicholson; Marlon Brando; Randy Quaid; Kathleen Lloyd; Frederic Forrest; Harry Dean Stanton; *D:* Arthur Penn; *W:* Thomas McGuane; *M:* John Williams.

Missouri Traveler **1958** An orphan boy struggles to get his own farm in Missouri. Family fare based on John Buress' novel. **103m/C; VHS, DVD.** Lee Marvin; Gary Merrill; Brandon de Wilde; Paul Ford; *D:* Jerry Hopper; *W:* Norman S. Hall; *C:* Winton C. Hoch; *M:* Jack Marshall.

Mrs. Brown *Her Majesty Mrs. Brown* **1997 (PG)** Unusual drama finds Queen Victoria (Dench), bereft by the death of Prince Albert, withdrawing from public life to her Scottish retreat at Balmoral. There she's looked after by coarse highlander John Brown (Connolly), who encourages her to take an interest in life. As he rises in the Queen's esteem, the brash commoner begins to become overly protective; leading to unsavory whispers. The Prince of Wales (Westhead) and Prime Minister Disraeli (Sher) must persuade Brown to withdraw from Victoria's company in order to preserve her reputation. Stunning performances by the leads make this well worth watching. **103m/C; DVD.** *UK* Dame Judi Dench; Billy Connolly; Geoffrey Palmer; Anthony Sher; Richard Pasco; Gerard Butler; David Westhead; *D:* John Madden; *W:* Jeremy Brock; *C:* Richard Greatrex; *M:* Stephen Warbeck. British Acad. '97: Actress (Dench), Costume Des.; Golden Globes '98: Actress--Drama (Dench).

Mrs. Brown, You've Got a Lovely Daughter ½ **1968 (G)** The Herman's Hermits gang inherits a greyhound and attempts to make a racer out of him while singing their songs. For the Brit group's die-hard fans only. **95m/C; VHS, DVD.** Peter Noone; Stanley Holloway; Mona Washbourne; *D:* Saul Swimmer.

Mrs. Dalloway ½ **1997 (PG-13)** Mannered retelling of the Virginia Woolf novel has a radiant performance by Redgrave in the title role. Wealthy, middle-aged, and long-married to boring politician Richard (Standing), Clarissa Dalloway is making preparations for her latest soiree in 1923 London. But the past rudely intrudes when old flame Peter Walsh (Kitchen) suddenly appears, causing Clarissa to reflect on her youth and the choices she's made. She's also shaken out of her social ennui by the unexpected sight of a shell-shocked WWI veteran (Graves) whose tragic plight disturbs her placid life. Director Gorris' English-language debut. **97m/C; DVD.** *UK* Vanessa Redgrave; Michael Kitchen; John Standing; Rupert Graves; Natascha (Natasha) McElhone; Alan Cox; Sarah Badel; Lena Headey; Robert Portal; Amelia Bullmore; Margaret Tyzack; Robert Hardy; *D:* Marleen Gorris; *W:* Eileen Atkins; *C:* Sue Gibson; *M:* Ilona Sekacz.

Mrs. Doubtfire ½ **1993 (PG-13)** Williams is an unemployed voiceover actor going through a messy divorce. When his wife gets custody, the distraught father decides to dress up as a woman and become a nanny to his own children. He also has to deal with the old flame who re-enters his ex-wife's life. Williams schtick extraordinaire with more than a little sugary sentimentality. Based on the British children's book "Madame Doubtfire" by Anne Fine. **120m/C; VHS, DVD, Blu-Ray.** Robin Williams; Matthew Lawrence; Sally Field; Pierce Brosnan; Harvey Fierstein; Robert Prosky; Mara Wilson; Paul Guilfoyle; Lisa Jakub; Martin Mull; Polly Holliday; *D:* Chris Columbus; *W:* Randi Mayem Singer; Leslie Dixon; *C:* Donald McAlpine; *M:* Howard Shore. Oscars '93: Makeup; Golden Globes '94: Actor--Mus./Comedy (Williams), Film--Mus./Comedy; MTV Movie Awards '94: Comedic Perf. (Williams).

Mrs. Harris **2005** Jean Harris (Bening) is the head of a posh girls' school and the longtime mistress of Scarsdale diet doctor Herman Tarnower (Kingsley), a chronic womanizer. The depressed, pill-popping Jean gets fed up and kills her lover and then endures a sensational trial, which Nagy revisits from both Jean's point of view (a suicide attempt gone wrong) or that she committed cold-blooded murder. The cast is fine but the goings-on get tedious. True crime from the 1980s. **94m/C; DVD.** Annette Bening; Ben Kingsley; Frances Fisher; Frank Whaley; Cloris Leachman; Chloë Sevigny; Bill Smitrovich; Michael Gross; *Cameo(s):* Ellen Burstyn; *D:* Phyllis Nagy; *W:* Phyllis Nagy; *C:* Steven Poster; *M:* John (Gianni) Frizzell. **CABLE**

Mrs. Henderson Presents **2005 (R)** The recently widowed Mrs. Henderson (Dench), in an attempt to relieve her own boredom, purchases the rundown and struggling Windmill Theatre in 1930s-40s London. Working her way through the theatre's revitalization, she hires Vivian Van Damm (Hoskins) as the theatre's manager. The two come up with the idea of staging all-nude revues, which are suitably tasteful but still a bit racy for the time. Once World War II breaks out, the story becomes one of British determination to cling to fragile everyday life in the face of the difficulties of war. All told, an interesting look at homefront England. **102m/C; DVD.** *UK* Dame Judi Dench; Bob Hoskins; Christopher Guest; Kelly Reilly; Will Young; Thelma Barlow; *D:* Stephen Frears; *W:* Martin Sherman; *C:* Andrew Dunn; *M:* George Fenton. Natl. Bd. of Review '05: Cast.

Mrs. Miniver **1942** A moving tale of a courageous, gentle middle-class British family and its struggle to survive during WWII. A classic that garnered six Academy Awards, it's recognized for contributions to the Allied effort. Contains one of the most powerful orations in the film history, delivered by Wilcoxon, who portrayed the vicar. Followed by "The Miniver Story." Adapted from Jan Struther's book. **134m/B; VHS, DVD, Blu-Ray.** Greer Garson; Walter Pidgeon; Teresa Wright; May Whitty; Richard Ney; Henry Travers; Reginald Owen; Henry Wilcoxon; Helmut Dantine; Aubrey Mather; Rhys Williams; Tom Conway; Peter Lawford; Christopher Severn; Clare Sandars; Marie De Becker; Connie Leon; Brenda Forbes; John Abbott; Billy Bevan; John Burton; Mary Field; Forrester Harvey; Arthur Wimperis; Ian Wolfe; *D:* William Wyler; *W:* George Froeschel; James Hilton; Claudine West; Arthur Wimperis; *C:* Joseph Ruttenberg; *M:* Herbert Stothart. Oscars '42: Actress (Garson), B&W Cinematog., Director (Wyler), Film, Screenplay, Support. Actress (Wright); Natl. Film Reg. '09.

Mrs. Miracle ½ **2009** There may be a little too much Christmas mush in this Hallmark Channel movie (based on the Debbie Macomber novel) but 'tis the season for—uh—miracles. Widower Seth Webster (Van Der Beek) is overwhelmed by his high-spirited six-year-old twin sons until he hires the magical Mrs. Merkle (Roberts) as his new housekeeper/nanny. Not only does she take control of the Webster family but she decides to play matchmaker for Seth as well. **92m/C; DVD.** Doris Roberts; James Van Der Beek; Erin Karpluk; Valin Shinyei; Michael Strusievici; Chelah Horsdal; *D:* Michael Scott; *W:* David Golden; *C:* Adam Sliwinski. **CABLE**

Mrs. Palfrey at the Claremont ½ **2005** Charming, gentle and somewhat melancholy comedy about the unlikely friendship between a 70-something widow and a 20-something writer. Mrs. Palfrey (Plowright) lives in a London residential hotel for the elderly. She literally stumbles into young Ludovic Meyer (Friend), an equally lonely soul, and a bond begins that extends to Ludovic passing himself off as her absent grandson, Desmond (O'Toole), to maintain Mrs. Palfrey's pride. An adaptation of the Elizabeth Taylor novel, which was set in the 1950s. This film's budget couldn't stretch to such a re-creation so it was updated to the present, with some awkwardness. **108m/C; DVD.** *GB* Joan Plowright; Rupert Friend; Zoe Tapper; Anna Massey; Robert Lang; Marcia Warren; Millicent Martin; Lorcan O'Toole; Anna Carteret; *D:* Dan Ireland; *W:* Ruth Sacks; *C:* Claudio Rocha; *M:* Stephen Barton.

Mrs. Parker and the Vicious Circle ½ *Mrs. Parker and the Round Table* **1994 (R)** Bio of witty, suicidal writer Dorothy Parker and her equally witty friends, including theatre critics, playwrights, and novelists, who lunched together at New York's Algonquin Hotel for most of the 1920s. An irreverant band known as the Algonquin Round Table, their numerous bon mots were regularly reported in the papers. Their private lives were often less than happy with alcohol, drug addiction and depression prominent factors. Parker's downward spiral is depressing though compelling to watch, thanks to Leigh's performance (in spite of much criticism for her lockjawed accent) but many of the characters come and go so quickly they make little impression. **124m/C; DVD.** Jennifer Jason Leigh; Matthew Broderick; Andrew McCarthy; Campbell Scott; Jennifer Beals; Tom McGowan; Nick Cassavetes; Sam Robards; Rebecca Miller; Wallace Shawn; Martha Plimpton; Gwyneth Paltrow; Peter Gallagher; Lili Taylor; Mina Badie; Natalie Strong; ***D:*** Alan Rudolph; ***W:*** Rudolph Coburn; Randy Sue Coburn; ***C:*** Jan Kiesser; ***M:*** Mark Isham. Natl. Soc. Film Critics '94: Actress (Leigh).

Mrs. Parkington 1/2 **1944** Overblown epic drama spanning six decades tells the story of the rise and fall of an American dynasty made on easy money. Garson plays the woman who goes from working as a maid in a boarding house to living a life of luxury when she marries a multimillionaire. This was the fifth pairing of Garson and Pidgeon and although it's not one of their best, it proved to be a big hit with audiences. Lavish costumes and good performances by Garson and Moorehead. Based on the novel by Louis Bromfield. **124m/B; VHS, DVD.** Greer Garson; Walter Pidgeon; Edward Arnold; Frances Rafferty; Agnes Moorehead; Selena Royle; Gladys Cooper; Lee Patrick; ***D:*** Tay Garnett; ***W:*** Robert Thoeren; Polly James; ***C:*** Joseph Ruttenberg. Golden Globes '45: Support. Actress (Moorehead).

Mrs. Santa Claus 1/2 **1996 (G)** Who better than Lansbury to star as the title character in this sweet TV musical set in 1910. Vivacious Mrs. C is tired of being left home during Santa's (Durning) annual trip and decides to borrow the sleigh for a test drive just before the big day. But bad weather and an injured reindeer force an emergency landing in New York City where she befriends the young sweatshop workers at villainous toy-maker A.P. Tavish's (Mann) factory and does a little matchmaking too. But Mrs. Claus still must make it back to the North Pole by Christmas Eve. **90m/C; VHS, DVD.** Angela Lansbury; Charles Durning; Terrence Mann; David Norona; Debra Wiseman; Rosalind Harris; Bryan Murray; Lynsey Bartilson; Michael Jeter; ***D:*** Terry Hughes; ***W:*** Mark Saltzman; ***C:*** Stephen M. Katz; ***M:*** Jerry Herman.

Mrs. Soffel 1/2 **1984 (PG-13)** Falling in love with a convicted murderer and helping him flee confinement occupies the time of the prison warden's wife. Effectively captures the 1901 setting, yet a dark pall fairly strangles any emotion. Based on a true story. **110m/C; VHS, DVD.** Diane Keaton; Mel Gibson; Matthew Modine; Edward Herrmann; Trini Alvarado; Terry O'Quinn; Jennifer (Jennie) Dundas Lowe; Danny Corkill; Maury Chaykin; Dana Wheeler-Nicholson; ***D:*** Gillian Armstrong; ***W:*** Ron Nyswaner; ***C:*** Russell Boyd; ***M:*** Mark Isham.

Mrs. Washington Goes to Smith 1/2 **2009** Cliche-ridden Hallmark Channel melodrama. Recently divorced, Alice Washington (Shepherd) decides it's time to finish her degree at Smith College. Roommate Zoe (English) has mommy issues, Alice feels out-of-place and then finds herself attracted to her poetry professor (Nordling), and the rest is so much filler. **89m/C; DVD.** Cybill Shepherd; Jeffrey Nordling; Lee Garlington; Al Sapienza; Corri English; ***D:*** Armand Mastroianni; ***W:*** Susan Rice; ***C:*** Patrick McGinley; ***M:*** Harry Manfredini. **CABLE**

Mrs. Wiggs of the Cabbage Patch 1/2 **1934** A warm, funny, and altogether overdone story of a mother whose husband abandons her, leaving the woman to raise their four children alone. It's Thanksgiving, so the rich visit the poor household to deliver a turkey dinner, and in the end all live happily ever after. Not one of Fields' larger roles; he doesn't even make an appearance until midway through the schmaltz. **80m/B; Silent; DVD.** Pauline Lord; Zasu Pitts; W.C. Fields; Evelyn Venable; Kent Taylor; Donald Meek; Charles Middleton; Jimmy Butler; George Breakston; Virginia Weidler; ***D:*** Norman Taurog; ***W:*** William Slavens McNutt; ***C:*** Charles B(ryant) Lang, Jr.

Mrs. Winterbourne **1996 (PG-13)** Pregnant loser Connie Doyle (Lake) is whisked into the lap of luxury when she's assumed to be the widowed Patricia Winterbourne after a train wreck. The grieving family (who had never met the bride) accept her and her baby as part of the household. Since her life is now going well, Connie decides to keep her true identity a secret while she falls for faux-brother-in-law Bill (Fraser). MacLaine is brilliant as the spirited matriarch of the family. Retooled as a comedy, the story is actually based on the noirish novel "I Married a Dead Man" by Cornell Woolrich and a remake of 1950's equally dark "No Man of Her Own." **106m/C; DVD.** Ricki Lake; Brendan Fraser; Shirley MacLaine; Miguel (Michael) Sandoval; Loren Dean; Susan Haskell; Paula Prentiss; ***D:*** Richard Benjamin; ***W:*** Phoef Sutton; Lisa-Marie Rodano; ***C:*** Alex Nepomniaschy; ***M:*** Patrick Doyle.

The Mist **2007 (R)** Writer/director Derabant adapts Stephen King's short story into what only appears to be a typical horror film. Locals and tourists are trapped in a grocery store by a thick, malevolent fog that follows after a freak storm in a small Maine town. Commercial artist David Drayton (Jane) and Mrs. Carmody (Harden), a bible-thumping kook, both try to lead the others through the crisis as people begin to crack under the pressure. Ultimately the inhumanity they direct at each other proves to be as great a threat as whatever is in the mist. The ending may be mildly disappointing but the movie is otherwise well done. **125m/C; DVD, Blu-Ray.** Thomas Jane; Marcia Gay Harden; Laurie Holden; Andre Braugher; Nathan Gamble; Toby Jones; William Sadler; Jeffrey DeMunn; Alexa Davalos; ***D:*** Frank Darabont; ***W:*** Frank Darabont; ***C:*** Ronn Schmidt; ***M:*** Mark Isham.

The Mistake *Die Verfehlung* **1991** In 1988, Jacob (who's from Hamburg in West Germany) falls in love with Elisabeth, who lives in an East German village. They secretly meet in East Berlin, but the Stasi are informed of the affair by someone in Elisabeth's village and Jacob is deported. Elisabeth knows who done her wrong and plans her revenge. German with subtitles. **100m/C; DVD.** *GE* Angelica Domrose; Gottfried John; Jorg Gudzuhn; Dagmar Manzel; Katja Paryla; ***D:*** Heiner Carow; ***W:*** Wolfram Witt; ***C:*** Martin Schlesinger; ***M:*** Stefan Carow.

Mistaken Identity 1/2 **1936** A swank hotel is the setting for this so-so comedy about three con men who wind up conning each other as much as their supposed victims. A couple of light romances are also thrown in for good measure. **75m/B; VHS, Streaming.** Chick Chandler; Evalyn Knapp; Berton Churchill; Patricia Farr; Richard Carle; Bradley Page; Lew Kelly; ***D:*** Phil Rosen.

Mr. Accident 1/2 **1999 (PG-13)** Australian comedian Serious returns as star/writer/director/producer. Accident-prone Roger Crumpkin (Serious) finds out his egg-processing factory boss (Fiels) is planning to produce eggs that are filled with nicotine so that people will become addicted. No, not to eggs!?to cigarettes! A lame attempt at comedy. **89m/C; VHS, DVD.** *AU* Yahoo Serious; David Field; Helen Dallimore; Grant Piro; Jeanette Cronin; ***D:*** Yahoo Serious; ***W:*** Yahoo Serious; ***C:*** Steve Arnold; ***M:*** Nerida Tyson-Chew.

Mr. Ace 1/2 **1946** A congresswoman decides to run for governor without the approval of the loyal political kingpin, Mr. Ace. **85m/B; VHS, DVD.** George Raft; Sylvia Sidney; Sara Haden; Stanley Ridges; ***D:*** Edwin L. Marin; ***W:*** Fred Finklehoffe; ***C:*** Karl Struss; ***M:*** Heinz Roemheld.

Mister America 1/2 **2019 (R)** After power hungry Tim (Heidecker) has a personal legal victory, he runs for district attorney of San Bernardino and has a documentary crew follow his campaign. His opponent, current D.A. Vincent Rosetti (Pecchia), once tried to put Tim in prison. Narcissistic Tim has no idea what he is doing and is setting himself up for failure. At the same time, Tim is in perpetual conflict with television movie review series co-host Greg (Turkington). An extension of the cult parody web series "On Cinema at the Cinema," the fake documentary is an effective dry political comedy with appeal to fans and newcomers. **86m/C; DVD.** Tim Heidecker; Gregg Turkington; Terri Parks; Curtis Webster; Don Pecchia; ***D:*** Eric Notarnicola; ***W:*** Tim Heidecker; Gregg Turkington; Eric Notarnicola; ***C:*** Gabriel Patay.

Mr. & Mrs. Bridge **1990 (PG-13)** Set in the '30s and '40s in Kansas City, Ivory's adaptation of Evan S. Connell's novels painstakingly portrays an upper middle-class family struggling to survive within an emotional vacuum. Newman and Woodward, together for the first time in many years as Walter and Ivory Bridge, bring a wealth of experience and insight to their characterizations. Many consider this to be Newman's best, most subtle and nuanced performance. **127m/C; VHS, DVD.** Joanne Woodward; Paul Newman; Kyra Sedgwick; Blythe Danner; Simon Callow; Diane Kagan; Robert Sean Leonard; Saundra McClain; Margaret Welsh; Austin Pendleton; Gale Garnett; Remak Ramsay; ***D:*** James Ivory; ***W:*** Ruth Prawer Jhabvala; ***C:*** Tony Pierce-Roberts; ***M:*** Richard Robbins. N.Y. Film Critics '90: Actress (Woodward), Screenplay.

Mr. & Mrs. Loving **1996 (PG-13)** Fact-based movie, set in the 1960s, follows the romance, marriage, and struggle of Richard Loving (Hutton) and Mildred "Bean" Jeter (Rochon). Growing up in rural Virginia, their interracial relationship isn't considered uncommon. But when Bean gets pregnant, they aren't allowed to marry because of Virginia's racial laws. Instead, the Lovings start a life in Washington, D.C., but desperately homesick and increasingly aware of the civil rights movement, Bean writes a letter to the Attorney General's office. What results is young ACLU lawyer Bernie Cohen (Parker) taking on their case—which eventually leads to a landmark Supreme Court decision about miscegenation laws. **95m/C; DVD.** Timothy Hutton; Lela Rochon; Corey Parker; Ruby Dee; Isaiah Washington, IV; Bill Nunn; Charles Gray; ***D:*** Richard Friedenberg; ***W:*** Richard Friedenberg; ***C:*** Kenneth Macmillan; ***M:*** Branford Marsalis. **CABLE**

Mr. & Mrs. Smith 1/2 **1941** Hitchcock's only screwball comedy, an underrated, endearing farce about a bickering but happy modern couple who discover their marriage isn't legitimate and go through courtship all over again. Vintage of its kind, with inspired performances and crackling dialogue. **95m/B; DVD.** Carole Lombard; Robert Montgomery; Gene Raymond; Jack Carson; Lucile Watson; Charles Halton; ***D:*** Alfred Hitchcock; ***W:*** Norman Krasna.

Mr. & Mrs. Smith **2005 (PG-13)** Who knew that pretty people shooting at each other could be so much fun? Director Liman offers a stylish tale of hitman love-gone-wrong. Suburban couple John (Pitt) and Jane (Jolie) are getting bored with their marriage, but they're both hiding a big secret—they're the world's top assassins who unwittingly fell in love and got hitched. When they're assigned to kill each other, every ounce of their simmering martial tensions finds expression through shotguns and dropkicks. The plot wanes and bad guys are ridiculously disposable, but the leads have palpable on-screen chemistry. **119m/C; DVD, Blu-Ray, On Demand.** Brad Pitt; Angelina Jolie; Adam Brody; Vince Vaughn; Kerry Washington; Chris Weitz; Keith David; Rachael Huntley; Michael Kaplan; Michelle Monaghan; Stephanie March; Jennifer (Jenny) Morrison; ***V:*** Angela Bassett; William Fichtner; ***D:*** Doug Liman; ***W:*** Simon Kinberg; ***C:*** Bojan Bazelli; ***M:*** John Powell.

Mr. Arkadin *Confidential Report* **1955** Screenwriter, director, star Welles, adapting from his own novel, gave this plot a dry run on radio during early 1950s. Welles examines the life of yet another ruthless millionaire, but this one can't seem to remember the sordid source of all that cash. Investigator Arden follows the intriguing and descending trail to a surprise ending. As in "Citizen Kane," oblique camera angles and layered dialogue prevail, but this time only serve to confuse the story. Shot over two years around Europe, required seven years of post production before finding distribution in 1962. **99m/B; VHS, DVD.** *GB* Orson Welles; Akim Tamiroff; Michael Redgrave; Patricia Medina; Robert Arden; Mischa Auer; ***D:*** Orson Welles; ***W:*** Orson Welles; ***C:*** Jean (Yves, Georges) Bourgoin.

Mr. Art Critic 1/2 **2007 (PG-13)** Caustic Chicago art critic M.J. Clayton (Pinchot) gets a reaming from his boss over his brutal reviews and goes to lick his wounds at his Mackinac Island cottage. He runs into one of the artists he's criticized and makes a drunken bet that anyone can make art. So he decides to enter the local art festival. **90m/C; DVD.** Toni Trucks; John Lepard; ***D:*** Richard Brauer; ***W:*** Richard Brauer. **VIDEO**

Mr. Average *Comme Tout le Monde* **2006** Jalil (Maadour) wins big on a game show that's a front for a market research company looking for test subjects. Jalil is so adept at agreeing with survey questions that the firm secretly tracks his every move and even hires a would-be girlfriend, actress Claire (Dhavernas), to move in and funnel products to Jalil that they want tested. But then Claire develops a conscience. French with subtitles. **90m/C; DVD.** *FR* Caroline Dhavernas; Thierry Lhermitte; Amina Annabi; Gilbert Melki; Delphine Rich; Khalid Madour; Chantal Lauby; ***D:*** Pierre-Paul Renderss; Pierre-Paul Renders; ***W:*** Pierre-Paul Renderss; Pierre-Paul Renders; Denis Lapiere; ***C:*** Virginie Saint-Martin.

Mr. Barrington 1/2 **2003** Agoraphobic poet Lila (Porter) is at first charmed and then menaced by mysterious neighbor, Mr. Barrington (McArdie). Is this some reflection of her tragic past at St. Agatha's orphanage? Mr. Barrington certain wants to settle some old score and Samuel (Schweig), Lila's supportive husband, decides to investigate so they can overcome the danger. Filmed in Maine. **100m/C; DVD.** Eric Schweig; Jonelle Allen; Jennifer Nicole Porter; Brian McArdie; ***D:*** Dana Packard; ***C:*** Eric Goldstein.

Mr. Baseball **1992 (PG-13)** Washed-up American baseball player tries to revive his career by playing in Japan and experiences cultures clashing under the ballpark lights. Semi-charmer swings and misses often enough to warrant return to minors. Film drew controversy during production when Universal was bought by the Japanese Matsushita organization and claims of both Japan- and America-bashing were thrown about. **109m/C; VHS, DVD, Blu-Ray.** Tom Selleck; Ken Takakura; Toshi Shioya; Dennis Haysbert; Aya Takanashi; ***D:*** Fred Schepisi; ***W:*** Gary Ross; Kevin Wade; Monte Merrick; ***C:*** Ian Baker; ***M:*** Jerry Goldsmith.

Mr. Bean's Holiday **2007 (PG)** Love him or hate him, Mr. Bean (Atkinson) has returned for yet another round of low-brow slapstick. On his way to France for vacation, Mr. Bean manages to lose his wallet and gain a lost child (Baldry), and spends much of the rest of the movie in awkward situations trying to reunite the boy and his father. Plenty of Atkinson's physical gags and base jokes, but there's not much here for non-Bean fans. Title is an homage to Jacques Tati's 1953 comedy "M Hulot's Holiday." **90m/C; DVD, Blu-Ray, HD-DVD.** *GB US* Rowan Atkinson; Emma de Caunes; Willem Dafoe; Jean Rochefort; Max Baldry; Karel Roden; Steve Pemberton; ***D:*** Steve Bendelack; ***W:*** Robin Driscoll; Hamish McColl; ***C:*** Baz Irvine; ***M:*** Howard Goodall.

Mr. Belvedere Rings the Bell **1951** Mr. Belvedere (Webb) is on a lecture tour for his bestselling book about staying young. He tests some of his theories on a church-run old folks home with a lot of grumpy residents. He passes himself off as a new resident, much to the consternation of his business agent (Mostel). The third and final time Webb played the character. Adapted from the play "The Silver Whistle" by Robert E. McEnroe. **87m/B; DVD.** Clifton Webb; Joanne Dru; Hugh Marlowe; Zero Mostel; William Lynn; Doro Merande; ***D:*** Henry Koster; ***W:*** Ranald MacDougall; ***C:*** Joseph LaShelle; ***M:*** Cyril Mockridge.

Mr. Billion **1977 (PG)** Engaging chase adventure comedy about an Italian mechanic who stands to inherit a billion dollar fortune if he can travel from Italy to San Francisco in 20 days. Of course, things get in his way. Hill made his American debut in this film. **89m/C; VHS, DVD.** Jackie Gleason; Terence Hill; Valerie Perrine; Slim Pickens; Chill Wills; ***D:*** Jonathan Kaplan; ***W:*** Jonathan Kaplan; Ken Friedman; ***M:*** Dave Grusin.

Mr. Blandings Builds His Dream House 1/2 **1948** Jim Blandings (Grant), wife Muriel (Loy), and their two daughters must give up their Manhattan apartment for new digs. City boy Jim wants to become a suburbanite and the Blandings decide to build their dream house—with many complications. Timely at its release because of the post-WWII housing shortage and building boom, this classic comedy is still a humorous treat with Grant at his funniest. Loy and Douglas provide strong backup. A must for all homeowners. Based on the novel by Eric Hodgins. **93m/B; VHS, DVD.** Cary Grant; Myrna Loy; Melvyn Douglas; Lex Barker; Reginald Denny; Louise Beavers; Jason Robards, Sr.; ***D:*** H.C. Potter; ***W:*** Norman Panama; Melvin Frank; ***C:*** James Wong Howe; ***M:*** Leigh Harline.

Mr. Brooks **2007 (R)** Costner goes the bad guy route in this suspense thriller about a serial killer who's the family man next door (if more tightly wound). Earl Brooks is a loving father and husband, a successful businessman, and a philanthropist. If he just didn't have that pesky alter-ego, Marshall (Hurt), constantly telling him it's time to kill again. But Brooks makes an uncharacteristic mistake and is seen by Mr. Smith (Cook), who blackmails him into coming along on his next bloody excursion. It's really the Brooks/Marshall show and if you're interested in either/both Costner and Hurt, you'll enjoy yourself. **120m/C; DVD, Blu-Ray.** Kevin Costner; William Hurt; Marg Helgenberger; Demi Moore; Dane Cook; Danielle Panabaker; Ruben Santiago-Hudson; Lindsay Crouse; Jason Lewis; Reiko Aylesworth; Aisha Hinds; Matt Schulze; Michael Cole; ***D:*** Bruce A. Evans; ***W:*** Bruce A. Evans; Raynold Gideon; ***C:*** John Lindley; ***M:*** Ramin Djawadi.

Mister Buddwing 1/2 **1966** Charming Garner is miscast as a man who wakes up on a bench in Central Park with amnesia. Based on the few things in his pockets, he tries to figure out who he is and what's happened. Encounters with various women help rekindle his memories but his crisis doesn't add up to much. Adapted from a novel by Evan Hunter. **99m/B; DVD.** James Garner; Angela Lansbury; Katharine Ross; Suzanne Pleshette; Jean Simmons; Jack Gilford; Raymond St. Jacques; ***D:*** Delbert Mann; ***W:*** Dale Wasserman; ***C:*** Ellsworth Fredericks; ***M:*** Kenyon Hopkins.

Mr. Church **2016 (PG-13)** In 1965, Mr. Church (Murphy) begins working as a household cook for Charlotte (Robertson) and her dying mother Marie (McElhone), and over time weaves a lasting family bond with Charlotte. Oddly misdated and even insulting, director Beresford's flat tale can't seem to figure out what story it's telling. The racial issues of a black servant are largely ignored, as is the odd implication that Mr. Church goes to gay clubs and lives a closeted life. **104m/C; DVD, Blu-Ray.** Eddie Murphy; Britt Robertson; Natascha (Natasha) McElhone; Xavier Samuel; Lucy Fry; ***D:*** Bruce Beresford; ***W:*** Susan McMartin; ***C:*** Sharone Meir; ***M:*** Mark Isham.

Mister Cinderella **1936** Slapstick comedy in which celebrity-obsessed barber Joe Jenkins (Haley) is willing to pass himself off as a millionaire for a weekend adventure. Only there are complications, including Joe falling for society dame Patricia (Furness). **75m/B; DVD.** Jack Haley; Betty Furness; Monroe Owsley; Rosina Lawrence; Arthur Treacher; Tom Dugan; Raymond Walburn; Edward Brophy; ***D:*** Edward Sedgwick; ***W:*** Richard Flournoy; Arthur V. Jones; ***C:*** Milton Krasner.

Mr. Deeds 1/2 **2002 (PG-13)** With chutzpah and schtick, Sandler plays the must-miss Deeds of this joyless remake. Longfellow Deeds is an owner of a New Hampshire pizza joint and aspiring greeting card poet (gag) before learning of a multi-billion dollar inheritance that gives him control of a mammoth media company. Gallagher is the slimy CEO who secretly wants hayseed Deeds to disappear back to the boonies, while Ryder is tabloid reporter/love interest Babe Bennett, out to dupe man-child Deeds for a sensational story. Turturro, as Deeds' sneaky butler, is the sole comic relief. **97m/C; DVD, Blu-Ray.** Adam Sandler; Winona Ryder; John Turturro; Peter Gallagher; Steve Buscemi; Jared Harris; Allen Covert; Erik Avari; Peter Dante; Conchata Ferrell; Harve Presnell; Blake Clark; J.B. Smoove; Rob Schneider; ***Cameo(s):*** John McEnroe; ***D:*** Steven Brill; ***W:*** Tim Herlihy; ***C:*** Peter Lyons Collister; ***M:*** Teddy Castellucci.

Mr. Deeds Goes to Town 1/2 **1936** Typical Capra fare offers Cooper as small town Vermonter and philanthropic fellow Longfellow Deeds, who inherits $20 million and promptly donates it to the needy, which leads to a courtroom hearing on his sanity. He also manages to find time to fall in love with beautiful reporter and tough cookie, Babe Bennett (Arthur), who's determined to fathom the good guy's motivation. Superior entertainment. Based on Clarence Budington Kelland's story "Opera Hat." **118m/B; VHS, DVD, Blu-Ray.** Gary Cooper; Jean Arthur; Raymond Walburn; Walter Catlett; Lionel Stander; George Bancroft; H.B. Warner; Ruth Donnelly; Douglass Dumbrille; Margaret Seddon; Margaret McWade; ***D:*** Frank Capra; ***W:*** Robert Riskin; ***C:*** Joseph Walker. Oscars '36: Director (Capra); N.Y. Film Critics '36: Film.

Mr. Destiny **1990 (PG-13)** Mid-level businessman Belushi has a mid-life crisis of sorts when his car dies. Wandering into an empty bar, he encounters bartender Caine who serves cocktails and acts omniscient before taking him on the ten-cent tour of life as it would've been if he hadn't struck out in a high school baseball game. Less than wonderful rehash of "It's a Wonderful Life." **110m/C; VHS, DVD, Blu-Ray.** James Belushi; Michael Caine; Linda Hamilton; Jon Lovitz; Bill McCutcheon; Hart Bochner; Rene Russo; Jay O. Sanders; Maury Chaykin; Pat Corley; Douglas Seale; Courteney Cox; Kathy Ireland; ***D:*** James Orr; ***W:*** James Orr; Jim Cruickshank.

Mr. District Attorney **1941** Minor low-budget noir adapted from the radio series. Fresh out of law school, Jones (O'Keefe) botches a case so he's shuffled off into investigating the whereabouts of politician Hyde (Lorre), who disappeared after a big payoff. Newspaper dame Terry (Rice) helps Jones out. **69m/B; DVD.** Dennis O'Keefe; Florence Rice; Peter Lorre; Minor Watson; Stanley Ridges; Joan Blair; ***D:*** William M. Morgan; ***W:*** Malcolm Stuart Boylan; Karl Brown; ***C:*** Reggie Lanning; ***M:*** Cy Feuer.

Mister 880 1/2 **1950** Elderly Skipper Miller (Gwenn) is a longtime counterfeiter who prints dollar bills to support himself. Federal agents have been after him for years but newcomer Steve Buchanan (Lancaster) traces some money to Ann Winslow (McGuire) and figures the crook must live in Ann's apartment building. Even the hard-nosed fed finds Skipper charming and wants to help him out. **90m/B; DVD.** Burt Lancaster; Dorothy McGuire; Edmund Gwenn; Millard Mitchell; Minor Watson; ***D:*** Edmund Goulding; ***W:*** Robert Riskin; ***C:*** Joseph LaShelle; ***M:*** Sol Kaplan.

Mr. Fix It 1/2 **2006 (R)** Charming romantic comedy. Lance Valenteen (Boreanaz) is a relationship fixer. Lovelorn guys who want to get back the gal who dumped them come to Lance and he makes like Casanova with said ex. But he breaks their heart and, suddenly, that former boyfriend is the greatest guy in the world. Then Lance gets hired by Bob (Healy), who got dumped for lying to beautiful Sophia (de la Garza). Too bad Lance actually falls for Sophia and then has to figure out how to come clean without her dumping him too. **93m/C; DVD.** David Boreanaz; Patricia Healy; Paul Sorvino; Terrence Evans; Alana de la Garza; Herschel Bleefeld; ***D:*** Darin Ferriola; ***W:*** Darin Ferriola; ***C:*** Irek Hartowicz; ***M:*** Kevin Saunders Hayes.

Mister Foe *Hallam Foe* **2007** A surprisingly sweet tale about voyeurism. Troubled teen Hallam Foe (Bell) blames his new stepmother (Forlani) for his mother's death and retreats into a semi-fantasy world where he spies on people from his treehouse. Moving to Edinburgh for a fresh start, Hallam is instantly smitten by attractive Kate (Myles), a ringer for his late mom, and gets a job at the hotel where she works. He also takes to the roofs to spy on her and when he gets caught peeping, she's titillated instead of outraged. Especially good performances by Bell and Myles. **95m/C; DVD.** *UK* Jamie Bell; Sophia Myles; Ciaran Hinds; Jamie Sives; Claire Forlani; Maurice Roeves; Ewen Bremner; ***D:*** David Mackenzie; ***W:*** David Mackenzie; Ed Whitmore; ***C:*** Giles Nuttgens.

Mr. Hobbs Takes a Vacation **1962** Good-natured comedy in which beleaguered parents try to resolve family squabbles while the entire brood is on a seaside vacation. Stewart and O'Hara are especially fine and funny as the well-meaning parents. **116m/C; VHS, DVD, Blu-Ray.** James Stewart; Maureen O'Hara; Fabian; John Saxon; Marie Wilson; John McGiver; Reginald Gardiner; ***D:*** Henry Koster; ***W:*** Nunnally Johnson; ***M:*** Henry Mancini. Berlin Intl. Film Fest. '62: Actor (Stewart).

Mr. Hockey: The Gordie Howe Story 1/2 **2013 (PG)** In 1973, hockey legend Gordie Howe (Michael Shanks) emerged from retirement to join his sons on the Houston Aeros hockey team at the ripe old age of 44. This film follows the life of his family during that period of time. **90m/C; DVD, Blu-Ray, Streaming.** Michael Shanks; Kathleen Robertson; Martin Cummins; Dylan Playfair; Andrew Herr; ***D:*** Andy Mikita; ***W:*** Malcolm MacRury; ***C:*** James Alfred Menard; ***M:*** James Jandrisch. **CABLE**

Mr. Holland's Opus **1995 (PG)** Well-done Disney tearjerker begins in 1965 as musician Glenn Holland (Dreyfuss) takes a teaching job to get himself off the wedding reception circuit and help support his wife, Iris (Headly), and their deaf son. Spanning three decades, with actual newsreel footage thrown in to highlight time passing, Holland sets aside his dream of composing a great symphony and finds his true calling—mentoring and inspiring young minds. Holland's son being deaf might have proved corny, but their rocky relationship is deeply rooted to the storyline. Dreyfuss turns in a vibrant performance and, while sentimental buttons are definitely pushed, director Herek avoids falling into sappiness. **142m/C; DVD.** Richard Dreyfuss; Glenne Headly; Jay Thomas; Olympia Dukakis; William H. Macy; Alicia Witt; Jean Louisa Kelly; Anthony Natale; ***D:*** Stephen Herek; ***W:*** Patrick Sheane Duncan; ***C:*** Oliver Wood; ***M:*** Michael Kamen.

Mr. Holmes **2015 (PG)** Sherlock Holmes is resurrected yet again in another take on the legendary creation of Sir Arthur Conan Doyle, but this one doesn't really work for anyone other than the most diehard fans of the literary icon or the actor who plays him. One couldn't really cast an aged Holmes better than McKellen, who plays the irascible genius in retirement, forced to come out of it to finally solve the one case that has haunted him for over three decades. McKellen is typically fantastic, but the film is surprisingly dull and flat, like a PBS Masterpiece variation on the tale. **104m/C; DVD, Blu-Ray, Streaming.** *UK US* Ian McKellen; Laura Linney; Milo Parker; Patrick Kennedy; Hattie Morahan; Hiroyuki (Henry) Sanada; ***D:*** Bill Condon; ***W:*** Jeffrey Hatcher; ***C:*** Tobias A. Schliessler; ***M:*** Carter Burwell.

Mr. Hulot's Holiday 1/2 *Les Vacances de Monsieur Hulot; Monsieur Hulot's Holiday* **1953** Superior slapstick details the misadventures of an oblivious bachelor's seaside holiday, where disaster follows his every move. Inventive French comedian Tati at his best. Light-hearted and natural, with magical mime sequences. Followed by "Mon Oncle." French with subtitles. **86m/B; VHS, DVD, Blu-Ray.** *FR* Jacques Tati; Natalie Pascaud; Michelle Rolia; ***D:*** Jacques Tati; ***W:*** Jacques Tati; Henri Marquet; Jacques Lagrange; Pierre Aubert; ***C:*** Jacques Mercanton; ***M:*** Alain Romans.

Mr. Imperium 1/2 **1951** Lousy title, trite story, and there's no romantic chemistry between the leads although Turner looks great and Pinza sings. A playboy prince falls for a nightclub singer but must leave her when he becomes king. Years later, when she's a Hollywood star, they briefly resume their romance until duty calls him home again. **87m/C; DVD.** Ezio Pinza; Lana Turner; Marjorie Main; Debbie Reynolds; Cedric Hardwicke; Barry Sullivan; ***D:*** Don Hartman; ***W:*** Don Hartman; Edwin H. Knopf; ***C:*** George J. Folsey; ***M:*** Bronislau Kaper.

Mr. Jealousy 1/2 **1998 (R)** When Lester Grimm (Stoltz) was 15, he chickened out on a good night kiss with his girl, and later spied her necking with another boy. Ever since then, he's had this thing about infidelity and he trashes every relationship because of his suspicions. It's no different when he meets the vivacious Ramona (Sciorra), who has recently broken up with arrogant author Dashiell (Eigemann). Lester joins Dashiell's therapy group to spy on his possible competition. Writer-director Baumbach stretches this thin material by making the characters interesting and the dialogue funny. Fonda's role is a cameo as Dashiell's stuttering girlfriend. **105m/C; VHS, DVD.** Eric Stoltz; Annabella Sciorra; Christopher Eigeman; Carlos Jacott; Marianne Jean-Baptiste; Brian Kerwin; Peter Bogdanovich; ***Cameo(s):*** Bridget Fonda; ***D:*** Noah Baumbach; ***W:*** Noah Baumbach; ***C:*** Steven Bernstein; ***M:*** Robert Een; Luna.

Mr. Jingles **WOOF!** *2 S.I.C.K.* **2006 (R)** Angie has been in a psych ward for years, ever since the murder of her parents by Mr. Jingles. Finally released into the care of her aunt and cousins, Angie's nightmare comes back when the clown also returns to finish off his only witness. No wonder clowns have such bad reps, with flicks like these. **80m/C; DVD.** Kelli Jensen; Jessica Hall; John Anton; Nathaniel Ketcham; Heather Doba; Nicole Majdali; ***D:*** Tommy Brunswick; ***W:*** Todd Brunswick; ***C:*** Todd Brunswick; ***M:*** James Souva.

Mister Johnson **1991 (PG-13)** In 1923 Africa, an educated black man working for the British magistrate constantly finds himself in trouble, thanks to backfiring schemes. This highly enjoyable film from the director of "Driving Miss Daisy" suffers only from the underdevelopment of the intriguing lead character. Based on the novel by Joyce Cary. **105m/C; VHS, DVD.** Pierce Brosnan; Edward Woodward; Maynard Eziashi; Beatie Edney; Denis Quilley; Nick Reding; ***D:*** Bruce Beresford; ***W:*** Bruce Beresford; William Boyd; ***C:*** Peter James; ***M:*** Georges Delerue.

Mr. Jones 1/2 **1993 (R)** Psychiatrist (Olin) falls in love with her manic-depressive patient (Gere). Head case Mr. Jones (Gere) is a charmer who gets a rush from tightrope walking a high beam on a construction site, yet is prone to bad moods when he fails to remember his own name. He can't resist flirting with the seductive Dr. Bowen, who eagerly leaps past professional boundaries while trying to coax him out of his illness. Wastes the talents of its stars with Gere showy, Olin brittle, and the whole story as contrived as their prefunctory love affair. Psychiatrists are getting as bad a rep professionally as lawyers in their recent film appearances. **110m/C; VHS, DVD.** Richard Gere; Lena Olin; Anne Bancroft; Tom Irwin; Delroy Lindo; Bruce Altman; Lauren Tom; ***D:*** Mike Figgis; ***W:*** Michael Cristofer; Eric Roth; ***C:*** Juan Ruiz-Anchia; ***M:*** Maurice Jarre.

Mr. Jones 1/2 **2014 (PG-13)** When two artists move to a remote cabin to improve their lives and their creativity, their reclusive neighbor proves to become their biggest nightmare. Seeking a less pressure-filled life outside of the city, Scott (Foster) and Penny (Jones) seem to have found peace in a cabin near the woods. They soon learn their neighbor is well-known artist, Mr. Jones. He only comes out at night to bring his odd, scary sculptures into the woods. With growing curiosity, they push too close to Mr. Jones for his taste and soon learn the many terror- and mayhem-filled ways he can ruin their new lives. **84m/C; DVD, Blu-Ray, Download.** Jon Foster; Sarah Jones; Mark Steger; Faran Tahir; Stanley B. Herman; ***D:*** Karl Mueller; ***W:*** Karl Mueller; ***C:*** Mathew Rudenberg; ***M:*** Herwig Maurer.

Mr. Klein **1976 (PG)** Cleverly plotted script and fine direction in this dark and intense film about French-Catholic art dealer Robert Klein (Delon), who buys valuables from Jews trying to escape Nazi occupied France in 1942, paying far less than what the treasures are worth. Ironically, he is mistaken for another Robert Klein, a Jew who's wanted for anti-Nazi activities. French with subtitles. **122m/C; VHS, DVD.** *FR* Alain Delon; Jeanne Moreau; Suzanne Flon; Michael (Michel) Lonsdale; Juliet Berto; Louis Seigner; Francine Racette; Massimo Girotti; ***D:*** Joseph Losey; ***W:*** Franco Solinas; ***C:*** Gerry Fisher; ***M:*** Egisto Macchi. Cesar '77: Film.

Mister Lonely 1/2 **2007** Former enfant terrible Korine foists this self-conscious cult item about celebrity impersonators on an uncaring public. It begins with a Michael Jackson impersonator (Luna) meeting a Marilyn Monroe impersonator (Morton) who lives with a bunch of other oddballs in a commune in the Scottish Highlands. Michael joins them but there's trouble a-brewing. There's also a bunch of weird scenes involving Herzog as a priest who's running a jungle mission with some nuns. Nah, we didn't get it either. **112m/C; DVD.** Diego Luna; Samantha Morton; Denis Lavant; James Fox; Esme Creed-Miles;

Anita Pallenberg; Werner Herzog; Melita Morgan; Jason Pennycooke; Richard Strange; ***D:*** Harmony Korine; ***W:*** Harmony Korine; Avi Korine; ***C:*** Marcel Zyskind; ***M:*** Jason Spaceman.

Mr. Lucky **1943** Likeable wartime drama about a gambler who hopes to swindle a philanthropic organization, but then falls in love and determines to help the group in a fundraising effort. Grant is, no surprise, excellent as the seemingly cynical con artist who actually has a heart of gold. Cliched, but nonetheless worthwhile. Later developed into a TV series. **99m/B; VHS, DVD.** Cary Grant; Laraine Day; Charles Bickford; Gladys Cooper; Paul Stewart; Henry Stephenson; Florence Bates; ***D:*** H.C. Potter; ***C:*** George Barnes.

Mr. Magoo **1997 (PG)** Live-action version of the cartoon character popular in the '50s and '60s. Elderly myopic millionaire Quincy Magoo (Nielsen) unwittingly comes into possession of a stolen gem that he gives to his bulldog Angus as a toy. Bumbling government agents and evil arch-criminals are after the gem and Magoo, but he avoids them through luck and bad plot devices. Meanwhile, Magoo mistakes a mummy's sarcophagus for a phone booth, a riverboat paddle wheel for an escalator and...well, you get the idea. Opening and closing sequences include animated Magoo bits. **87m/C; DVD.** Leslie Nielsen; Kelly Lynch; Matt Keeslar; Nick (Nicholas) Chinlund; Ernie Hudson; Malcolm McDowell; Stephen Tobolowsky; Jennifer Garner; Miguel Ferrer; ***D:*** Stanley Tong; ***W:*** Pat Proft; Tom Sherohman; ***C:*** Jingle Ma; ***M:*** Michael Tavera.

Mr. Magorium's Wonder Emporium **2007 (G)** Mr. Magorium (Hoffman) is the ageless owner of a magic toy store who's gearing up to retire and wants to turn the store over to his manager Mahoney (Portman), who dreams of being a classical pianist. In the meantime, he hires uptight accountant Henry (Bateman) to assess the value of the store (and perhaps find a little magic in himself). An unapologetically whimsical family movie, it has occasional charming moments but mostly leans on its far superior influences ("Pee-Wee's Big Adventure" and "Willie Wonka and the Chocolate Factory," to name a few) for inspiration, and much of the fairy-tale feel seems forced and unoriginal. **94m/C; Blu-Ray, On Demand.** Dustin Hoffman; Natalie Portman; Jason Bateman; Zach Mills; ***D:*** Zach Helm; ***W:*** Zach Helm; ***C:*** Roman Osin; ***M:*** Aaron Zigman; Alexandre Desplat.

Mr. Majestyk 1/2 **1974 (PG)** When a Vietnam veteran's attempt to start an honest business is thwarted by Mafia hitmen and the police, he goes after them with a vengeance. Based on Leonard's novel (he also did the screenplay). **103m/C; VHS, DVD, Blu-Ray.** Charles Bronson; Al Lettieri; Linda Cristal; Lee Purcell; ***D:*** Richard Fleischer; ***W:*** Elmore Leonard; ***M:*** Charles Bernstein.

Mr. Mike's Mondo Video **1979 (R)** A bizarre, outrageous comedy special declared too wild for TV and conceived by the "Saturday Night Live" alumnus Mr. Mike. **75m/C; VHS, DVD.** Michael O'Donoghue; Dan Aykroyd; Jane Curtin; Carrie Fisher; Teri Garr; Joan Haskett; Deborah Harry; Margot Kidder; Bill Murray; Laraine Newman; Gilda Radner; Julius LaRosa; Paul Shaffer; Sid Vicious; ***W:*** Mitch Glazer.

Mr. Mom **1983 (PG)** Tireless auto exec Jack (Keaton) loses his job and stays home with the kids while his wife Caroline (Garr) becomes the breadwinner. He's forced to cope with the rigors of housework and child care, resorting to drugs, alcohol and soap operas. Keaton's hilarious as the homebound dad chased by killer appliances and poker buddy to the ladies in the neighborhood. **92m/C; VHS, DVD, Blu-Ray.** Michael Keaton; Teri Garr; Christopher Lloyd; Martin Mull; Ann Jillian; Edie McClurg; Valri Bromfield; Jeffrey Tambor; ***D:*** Stan Dragoti; ***W:*** John Hughes; ***C:*** Victor Kemper; ***M:*** Lee Holdridge.

Mr. Moto in Danger Island **1939** Mr. Moto (Lorre) is after diamond smugglers (this sounds familiar) in Puerto Rico and is aided by wrestler Twister McGurk (Hymer). 7th in the series. **80m/B; DVD.** Peter Lorre; Warren Hymer; Jean Hersholt; Richard Lane; Amanda Duff; Leon Ames; Douglass Dumbrille; Charles D. Brown; ***D:*** Peter Milne; ***W:*** Herbert I. Leeds; ***C:*** Lucien N. Andriot; ***M:*** Samuel Kaylin.

Mr. Moto's Gamble **1938** Mr. Moto (Lorre) is teaching a class for would-be sleuths and one of his students is Charlie Chan's son, Lee (Luke), who helps out when Moto investigates the murder of a boxer during a fight. Originally intended as a Charlie Chan film that was already in production, the script was rewritten because of Warner Oland's health problems and doesn't quite fit the other Moto adventures. 3rd in the series. **72m/B; DVD.** Peter Lorre; Keye Luke; Maxie "Slapsie" Rosenbloom; Lynn Bari; Dick Baldwin; Douglas Fowley; Jayne Regan; Harold Huber; Ward Bond; Lon Chaney, Jr.; ***D:*** James Tinling; ***W:*** Charles Belden; Jerome Cady; ***C:*** Lucien N. Andriot; ***M:*** Samuel Kaylin.

Mr. Moto's Last Warning **1939** One of the better in the series of Mr. Moto, the wily detective! Lorre is convincing in the title role and gets good support from character villains Carradine and Sanders in this story of saboteurs converging on the Suez Canal plotting to blow up the French Fleet. **71m/B; VHS, DVD.** Peter Lorre; George Sanders; Ricardo Cortez; John Carradine; Virginia Field; Robert Coote; ***D:*** Norman Foster.

Mr. Nanny **1993 (PG)** For those who fear change, this predictable plot should serve as comforting assurance that Hollywood will still sacrifice substance for the quick buck. Basic storyline has the child-hating Hulkster playing nanny/bodyguard to a couple of bratty kids. Meanwhile, his arch rival (Johansen) hatches a scheme to gain world dominance by kidnapping the kids for the ransom of their father's top secret computer chip. Never fear—in this world, the good guys kick butt, naturally, and everyone learns a lesson. **85m/C; DVD.** Hulk Hogan; Sherman Hemsley; Austin Pendleton; Robert Gorman; Madeline Zima; Mother Love; David Johansen; ***D:*** Michael Gottlieb; ***W:*** Michael Gottlieb; Ed Rugoff; ***C:*** Peter Stein; ***M:*** David Johansen; Brian Koonin.

Mr. Nice **2010** A fact-is-stranger-than-fiction biopic based on the 1996 autobiography of Howard Marks, a Welshman who controlled much of the hashish trade in the 1970s and '80s. Resourceful and unrepentant, Marks (Ifans, a real-life friend of Marks) serves as a genial narrator, highlighting his life from his time at Oxford University to his profitable international smuggling operation, his recruitment by MI-5 as a freelance spy, and his time as a fugitive after a London arrest. Title refers to one of Marks' many aliases. **120m/C; DVD, Blu-Ray.** *GB* Rhys Ifans; Chloë Sevigny; David Thewlis; Luis Tosar; Elsa Pataky; Andrew Tiernan; Omid Djalili; Crispin Glover; Christian McKay; Jack Huston; Jamie Harris; Ken Russell; ***D:*** Bernard Rose; ***W:*** Bernard Rose; ***C:*** Bernard Rose; ***M:*** Philip Glass.

Mr. Nice Guy 1/2 *Yatgo Ho Yan* **1998 (PG-13)** Chan plays a TV cooking show host who gets into boiling water when he saves a female reporter (Fitzpatrick) who has videotaped a drug deal. He ends up with the videotape, so reptilian bad guy Giancarlo (Norton) sends his lackeys out to chop-suey Jackie, though they turn out to be boneless chickens. The high action/low talk meter is cranked up in this outing, due to the fact that it's Chan's first movie filmed primarily in English (although still produced in Hong Kong). The plot seems to have been chopped up a bit too, but Chan fans know that the whirling dervish stunts are more important anyway. **90m/C; DVD, Blu-Ray.** *CH* Jackie Chan; Richard Norton; Gabrielle Fitzpatrick; Miki Lee; Karen McLymont; Vince Poletto; Barry Otto; Sammo Hung; ***D:*** Sammo Hung; ***W:*** Edward Tang; Fibe Ma; ***C:*** Raymond Lam; ***M:*** J. Peter Robinson.

Mr. Nobody **2013 (R)** Long sci-fi/fantasy filmed in 2009. Nemo (Leto) is shown at various stages of his life: 9, 15 and 118 (in 2092) when he is the last mortal, aging human in a world of quasi-immortals. He can apparently time travel as well as exist in multiple incarnations although this may be an unreliable memory he's relating to the journalist who's interviewing him. Pic's not as confusing as expected but cineastes will enjoy it more than the casual viewer. **141m/C; DVD, Blu-Ray.** *FR* Jared Leto; Diane Kruger; Sarah Polley; Linh Dan Pham; Daniel Mays; Thomas Byrne; Tony Regbo; Juno Temple; Rhys Ifans; Natasha Little; ***D:*** Jaco Van Dormael; ***W:*** Jaco Van Dormael; ***C:*** Christophe Beaucarne; ***M:*** Pierre Van Dormael.

Mr. North 1/2 **1988 (PG)** Capra-corn fable about a charming, bright Yale graduate who encounters admiration and disdain from upper-crust Rhode Island residents when news of his miraculous "cures" spreads. Marks the directorial debut of Danny Huston, son of John Huston, who co-wrote the script and served as executive producer before dying several weeks into shooting. Set in the 1920s and adapted from Thornton Wilder's "Theophilus North." **90m/C; VHS, DVD.** Anthony Edwards; Robert Mitchum; Lauren Bacall; Harry Dean Stanton; Anjelica Huston; Mary Stuart Masterson; Virginia Madsen; Tammy Grimes; David Warner; Hunter Carson; Christopher Durang; Mark Metcalf; Katharine Houghton; Christopher Lawford; ***D:*** Danny Huston; ***W:*** John Huston; Janet Roach; James Costigan; ***C:*** Robin Vidgeon; ***M:*** David McHugh.

Mr. Peabody & Sherman 1/2 **2014 (PG)** A good-natured, zippy animated adventure based on the Jay Ward characters from 1960s TV "The Rocky and Bullwinkle Show." Mr. Peabody--the smartest (and punloving) dog in the world--must rescue his adopted boy, Sherman, after he borrows the time-travelling WABAC machine and his adventures could change history. There's flashbacks to how Mr. Peabody and Sherman became a family and a potential problem when some folk think Mr. Sherman isn't the proper sort of dad for a human boy, but all the social commentary is low-key. **92m/C; DVD, Blu-Ray.** ***V:*** Ty Burrell; Max Charles; Ariel Winter; Stephen Colbert; Leslie Mann; Allison Janney; Patrick Warburton; Stanley Tucci; Lake Bell; Guillaume Aretos; Mel Brooks; ***D:*** Rob Minkoff; ***W:*** Craig Wright; ***M:*** Danny Elfman.

Mr. Popper's Penguins 1/2 **2011 (PG)** Modern adaptation of the 1938 children's book by Richard and Florence Atwater. Carrey resumes his physical comedic shtick in ridiculous situations to generally amusing effect. New York real-estate developer Tom Popper (Carrey) inherits six penguins from his deceased adventurer dad and then turns his upscale apartment into an arctic wonderland to house them. Naturally the situation goes out of control. The penguins' performance is a mixture of live-action and CGI shots. **94m/C; DVD, Blu-Ray.** Jim Carrey; Carla Gugino; Angela Lansbury; Madeline Carroll; Maxwell Perry Cotton; ***D:*** Mark S. Waters; ***W:*** Sean Anders; John Morris; Jared Stern; ***C:*** Florian Ballhaus; ***M:*** Rolfe Kent.

Mr. Ricco 1/2 **1975** Lackluster crime drama with a miscast Martin barely going through the motions. San Francisco defense attorney Joe Ricco (Martin) gets black militant Frankie Steele (Rasulala) acquitted. He manages to get caught up in the conspiracy surrounding some cop killings. Did Steele do the crimes or is it a set-up? **98m/C; DVD.** Dean Martin; Thalmus Rasulala; Eugene Roche; Denise Nicholas; Philip Michael Thomas; Cindy Williams; Geraldine Brooks; ***D:*** Paul Bogart; ***W:*** Robert Hoban; ***C:*** Frank Stanley; ***M:*** Chico Hamilton.

Mr. Rice's Secret **2000 (PG)** Mysterious Englishman Mr. Rice (Bowie) lives next door to 13-year-old Owen (Switzer), who has cancer. He's struggling but Mr. Rice offers words of wisdom (that come from the fact he's lived hundreds of years). When Mr. Rice suddenly does die, it's not before letting Owen in on some posthumous life-saving secrets. **113m/C; VHS, DVD.** *CA* David Bowie; Garwin Sanford; Bill Switzer; Teryl Rothery; ***D:*** Nicholas (Nick) Kendall; ***W:*** J.H. (Joel Howard) Wyman; ***C:*** Gregory Middleton; ***M:*** Simon Kendall; Al Rodger.

Mr. Right **2006** Gay rom com that finds Louise (Zaris) narrating the love problems of three London couples. Her best friend Alex (de Woolfson) is a working-class actor/caterer who has found security with upper-class reality TV producer Harry (Lance). Art dealer William (Marshall) is falling for soap actor Lawrence (Ockenden) while professionally queer artist Tom (screenwriter Morris) is trying to hold on to hustler Lars (Hart). A disaster of a dinner party forces the couples out of their usual habitues to which they can either comfortably return or break free. **94m/C; DVD.** *GB* Luke De Woolfson; James Lance; Rocky Marshall; Leon Ockenden; Benjamin Hart; Georgia Zaris; Maddie Planer; David Morris; ***D:*** David Morris; Jacqui Morris; ***W:*** David Morris; Jacqui Morris; ***C:*** Michael Wood; ***M:*** Jacqueline Kroft.

Mr. Right **2016 (R)** Landis pulls the typically-great Rockwell and Kendrick into this black hole of non-talent with his latest script for this horrendous black comedy. Francis (Rockwell) is a smart-assed professional assassin who actually only kills the people who hire him as some sort of moral justice crusader. He runs into Martha (Kendrick) in a convenience store. Martha has had a very bad week, including catching her boyfriend with another man. Will this killer be Mr. Right? You won't care. Not even for a second. And, more importantly, you won't laugh either. **90m/C; DVD, Blu-Ray.** Sam Rockwell; Anna Kendrick; Tim Roth; James Ransone; Anson Mount; ***D:*** Paco Cabezas; ***W:*** Max Landis; ***C:*** Daniel Aranyo; ***M:*** Aaron Zigman.

Mister Roberts **1955** Crew of a WWII Navy cargo freighter in the South Pacific relieves the boredom with a series of elaborate practical jokes, mostly at the expense of their long-suffering, slightly crazy captain (Cagney), who then determines that he will get even. The ship's cargo officer, Mr. Roberts (Fonda) , longs to be transferred to a fighting vessel and see some action. Originally a hit Broadway play (based on the novel by Thomas Heggen) that also featured Fonda in the title role. Great performance from Lemmon as Ensign Pulver. Powell's last film. Sequelled in 1964 by "Ensign Pulver," and later a short-lived TV series as well as a live TV special. **120m/C; VHS, DVD.** Henry Fonda; James Cagney; Jack Lemmon; William Powell; Betsy Palmer; Ward Bond; Harry Carey, Jr.; Nick Adams; Phil Carey; Ken Curtis; Martin Milner; Jack Pennick; Perry Lopez; Patrick Wayne; Tige Andrews; William Henry; ***D:*** John Ford; Mervyn LeRoy; ***W:*** Frank Nugent; Joshua Logan; Thomas Heggen; ***C:*** Winton C. Hoch; ***M:*** Franz Waxman. Oscars '55: Support. Actor (Lemmon).

Mr. Robinson Crusoe 1/2 **1932** Rollicking adventure in the South Seas as Fairbanks makes a bet that he can live on a desert island for a year without being left any refinements of civilization. Lucky for him, a woman arrives. Also written by Fairbanks. **76m/B; VHS, DVD.** Douglas Fairbanks, Sr.; William Farnum; Maria Alba; Earle Brown; ***D:*** Edward Sutherland; ***W:*** Douglas Fairbanks, Sr.; ***M:*** Alfred Newman.

Mr. Rock 'n' Roll: The Alan Freed Story 1/2 **1999** In the early 1950s, Cleveland disc jockey Alan Freed (Nelson) decides to play the newfangled rock 'n' roll on his station, where it becomes an immediate hit and an immediate controversy. Freed's success takes him to New York and further celebrity but career missteps lead to the payola scandal and his eventual disgrace. Original recordings are used and they turn out to be the most exciting thing about this TV movie. Based on the book by John A. Jackson. **91m/C; VHS, DVD.** Judd Nelson; Madchen Amick; Leon; Paula Abdul; ***Cameo(s):*** Bobby Rydell; Fabian; ***D:*** Andy Wolk; ***W:*** Matt Dorff; ***C:*** Derick Underschultz. **TV**

Mr. Roosevelt 1/2 **2017** An indie comedy about a comedic actress grappling with her messy life. Working to make it big in LA, Emily Martin (Wells) doesn't hesitate to return home to Austin, Texas, when her ex-boyfriend Eric (Thune) tells her that her beloved cat, Mr. Roosevelt, has died. Arriving without a plan, she assumes she can stay with Eric and his new girlfriend Celeste (Lower). Emily is appalled by Austin's home upgrades, Eric's life changes, and the formidable Celeste, but also connects with a new friend Jen (Pineda). Observant and honest, the characters are complex and the story funny. **90m/C; DVD.** Noel Wells; Nick Thune; Britt Lower; Daniella Pineda; Andre Hyland; ***D:*** Noel Wells; ***W:*** Noel Wells; ***C:*** Dagmar Weaver-Madsen; ***M:*** Ryan Miller.

Mr. St. Nick 1/2 **2002** Agreeable Christmas comedy with a little twist. It seems that being Santa is a family business—each St. Nick gets 100 years on the job. The current Santa (Durning) should be settling into retirement and leaving things to Santa Jr. (Grammer) soon, but Junior's been waiting so long that he's more bah-humbug than ho-ho-ho. So, it's about time that he learned the true meaning of the holiday. **100m/C; DVD.** Kelsey Grammer; Charles Durning; Katherine Helmond; Brian Bedford; Elaine Hendrix; Lupe Ontiveros; Wallace Shawn; Ana Ortiz; *D:* Craig Zisk; *W:* Maryedith Burrell; Steve Hayes; Debra Frank; *C:* David Franco; *M:* John Altman. **TV**

Mr. Sardonicus *Sardonicus* **1961** Tidy little horror film finds the title character's (Rolfe) face frozen in a hideous grin after being cursed for stealing a winning lottery ticket from his father's corpse. Sardonicus has been experimenting with solutions to his problem (each more disgusting than the last) and finally forces neurosurgeon, Sir Robert Cargrave (Lewis), to assist him with his dilemma. **89m/B; VHS, DVD, Blu-Ray.** Guy Rolfe; Ronald Lewis; Oscar Homolka; Audrey Dalton; Vladimir Sokoloff; *D:* William Castle; *W:* Ray Russell; *C:* Burnett Guffey; *M:* Von Dexter.

Mr. Saturday Night ½ **1992 (R)** Crystal, in his directorial debut, stars as Buddy Young Jr., a self-destructive comedian whose career spans five decades. His nasty one-liners and witty jokes combine with poignancy in this satisfying comedy/drama. Paymer is excellent as Young's long-suffering, faithful brother and manager. Watch for Lewis in a cameo role. Expectations were very high and the boxoffice results were disappointing, but fans of Crystal shouldn't miss this one. **118m/C; VHS, DVD, Blu-Ray.** Billy Crystal; David Paymer; Julie Warner; Helen Hunt; Mary Mara; Jerry Orbach; Ron Silver; Sage Allen; Jackie Gayle; Carl Ballantine; Slappy (Melvin) White; Conrad Janis; Jerry Lewis; *D:* Billy Crystal; *W:* Billy Crystal; Babaloo Mandel; Lowell Ganz; *C:* Don Peterman; *M:* Marc Shaiman.

Mr. Scoutmaster ½ **1953** Stuffy TV host Robert Jordan (Webb) faces cancellation unless he can attract younger viewers. His minister asks him to become the church troop's new scoutmaster, and Jordan agrees even though he doesn't really like children. He struggles to control the unruly youngsters although neglected Cub Scout Mike (Winslow) thinks Jordan is just swell. Various outdoor misadventures follow. **87m/B; DVD.** Clifton Webb; Frances Dee; George Winslow; Edmund Gwenn; Veda Ann Borg; *D:* Henry Levin; *W:* Leonard Praskins; Barney Slater; *C:* Joseph LaShelle; *M:* Cyril Mockridge.

Mr. Skeffington **1944** A super-grade soap opera spanning 26 years in the life of a ravishing, spoiled New York socialite. The beauty with a fondness for bedrooms marries for convenience, abuses her husband, then enjoys a highly equitable divorce settlement. Years later when diphtheria leaves her totally deformed and no man will have her, she is saved by her former husband. Based on the novel by "Elizabeth" (Mary Annette Beauchamp Russell) and adapted by "Casablanca's" Julius and Philip Epstein. **147m/B; VHS, DVD.** Bette Davis; Claude Rains; Walter Abel; Richard Waring; George Coulouris; John Alexander; *D:* Vincent Sherman.

Mr. Skitch **1933** Weak Rogers offering. Couple loses their farm and begins cross country jaunt with mishaps at every turn. All ends well when their daughter meets an Army cadet, but few laughs and lots of loose ends. **70m/B; VHS, DVD.** Will Rogers; Zasu Pitts; Rochelle Hudson; Charles Starrett; *D:* James Cruze.

Mr. Smith Goes to Washington **1939** Another classic from Hollywood's golden year of 1939. Jimmy Stewart is an idealistic and naive young man selected to fill in for an ailing Senator. Upon his arrival in the Capitol, he is inundated by a multitude of corrupt politicians. He takes a stand for his beliefs and tries to denounce many of those he feels are unfit for their positions, meeting with opposition from all sides. Great cast is highlighted by Stewart in one of his most endearing performances. Quintessential Capra tale sharply adapted from Lewis Foster's story. Outstanding in every regard. **130m/B; VHS, DVD, Blu-Ray.** James Stewart; Jean Arthur; Edward Arnold; Claude Rains; Thomas Mitchell; Beulah Bondi; Eugene Pallette; Guy Kibbee; Harry Carey, Sr.; H.B. Warner; Porter Hall; Jack Carson; Charles Lane; *D:* Frank Capra; *W:* Sidney Buchman; *M:* Dimitri Tiomkin. Oscars '39: Story; AFI '98: Top 100; Natl. Film Reg. '89; N.Y. Film Critics '39: Actor (Stewart).

Mr. Soft Touch **1949** Returning vet Joe Miracle (Ford) discovers gangster Barney Teener (Bohnen) has taken over his nightclub. After stealing the money he thinks he's owed, Joe hides out in a settlement house run by Jenny Jones (Keyes) but Teener wants revenge. It ends with Miracle dressing up as Santa Claus. Thanks to having two directors, who were apparently making two different films, the pic is uneven at best as it travels from would-be noir to Christmas mush. **93m/B; DVD.** Glenn Ford; Evelyn Keyes; Roman Bohnen; John Ireland; Ted de Corsia; Beulah Bondi; Percy Kilbride; *D:* Gordon Douglas; Henry Levin; *W:* Orin Jannings; *C:* Charles Lawton, Jr.; Joseph Walker; *M:* Heinz Roemheld.

Mr. Superinvisible *Mr. Invisible; L'Inafferrabile Invincibile* **1973 (G)** Searching to cure the common cold, a bumbling scientist invents a bizarre virus, then strives with his loyal (of course) sheepdog to keep it from falling into the wrong hands. The Disney-like plot, featuring enemy agents and invisibility, may appeal to youngsters. **90m/C; VHS, DVD.** *IT GE SP* Dean Jones; Ingeborg (Inge) Schoener; Gastone Moschin; *D:* Anthony M. Dawson.

Mr. 3000 ½ **2004 (PG-13)** Lackluster sports comedy follows egotistical Milwaukee Brewers star Stan Ross (Mac), who abruptly quit the team as soon as he got his 3,000 hit. His comfy retirement of 10 years is interrupted when an old record-keeping error is corrected, revealing that Stan only has 2,997 career hits. So, the 47-year-old decides to come back long enough to get those missing hits. He must contend with resentful younger teammates, numerous strikeouts, the accompanying ridicule, and Mo, his beautiful former flame who's now a reporter for ESPN covering his comeback. Mac and Bassett have a lot of charm together but much of the film is predictable, and the on-field action lacks any urgency. **104m/C; VHS, DVD.** Bernie Mac; Angela Bassett; Michael Rispoli; Evan Jones; Dondre T. Whitfield; Paul Sorvino; Earl Billings; Chris Noth; Brian White; Ian Anthony Dale; Amaury Nolasco; ***Cameo(s):*** Tom Arnold; John Salley; *D:* Charles Stone, III; *W:* Eric Champnella; Keith Mitchell; *C:* Shane Hurlbut; *M:* John Powell.

Mr. Toad's Wild Ride *The Wind in the Willows* **1996 (PG)** Kenneth Grahame's 1908 children's book, set in Edwardian England, has a modern slant with Jones' adaptation removing much of the gentle whimsy and replacing it with skits. Mole (Coogan) wakes up one day to find his home being bulldozed by the industrialist weasels who have purchased the property from the motor-car-infatuated Mr. Toad (Jones). Mole, along with friends Rat (Idle) and Badger (Williamson), must eventually help Toad escape from jail and reclaim his land. Grahame's fable railing against modern industralism's encroachment on the countryside becomes a satire on '90s consumerism and corporate greed. **88m/C; DVD.** *UK* Terry Jones; Steve Coogan; Eric Idle; Anthony Sher; Nicol Williamson; John Cleese; Stephen Fry; Bernard Hill; Michael Palin; Nigel Planer; Julia Sawalha; Victoria Wood; Richard James; *D:* Terry Jones; *W:* Terry Jones; *C:* David Tattersall; *M:* Terry Jones; John Du Prez.

Mr. Troop Mom ½ **2009 (G)** In this Nickelodeon family comedy, widowed lawyer Eddie wants to spend more time with his nine-year-old daughter Naomi so they can bond. When a mom drops out of chaperone duty, Eddie agrees to step in at the Go Girls Jamboree at Running Pines Camp without realizing just what he's letting himself in for. **84m/C; DVD, Blu-Ray.** George Lopez; Daniela Bobadilla; Jane Lynch; Julia Anderson; Elizabeth Thai; *D:* William Dear; *W:* Thomas Ian Griffith; *C:* Ron Stannett; *M:* David Kitay. **CABLE**

Mr. Turner **2014 (R)** Director Leigh delivers a period piece with a personal connection in the story of J.M.W. Turner (Spall), a wildly influential painter with, well, a few rough edges. Turner was an amazing artist, who generally failed when it came to the rest of his life. The idea that someone who has been described as prickly in the real world would make a film that really dissects the difference between art and artist makes perfect sense. How does someone who doesn't seem to like the world find so much beauty in it to paint? Spall is phenomenal here. **150m/C; DVD, Blu-Ray.** *UK* Timothy Spall; Marion Bailey; Joshua McGuire; Dorothy Atkinson; Ruth Sheen; Paul Jesson; *D:* Mike Leigh; *W:* Mike Leigh; *C:* Dick Pope; *M:* Gary Yershon.

Mr. Vampire **1986** Undertaker Uncle Kau (Ying) is also a master vampire hunter—necessary when your town is under siege from a vampire army who can make new converts with a single bite. Vampire movie with a Chinese twist combines elements of both comedy and horror, presenting a vampire who comes closer to resembling a corpse, who, when not levitating, hops like a bunny. Chinese with subtitles or dubbed. **99m/C; VHS, DVD.** *CH* Ching-Ying Lam; Ricky Hui; Pauline Wong; Moon Lee; *D:* Ricky Lau; *W:* Roy Szeto; *C:* Peter Ngor.

Mr. Winkle Goes to War *Arms and the Woman* **1944** A weak, nerdy former banker is drafted for service during WWII and proves himself a hero by bulldozing a Japanese foxhole. Bits of genuine war footage add a measure of realism to an otherwise banal flag-waving comedy that is based on a novel by Theodore Pratt. **80m/B; VHS, DVD.** Edward G. Robinson; Ruth Warrick; Richard Lane; Robert Armstrong; Ted Donaldson; Richard Gaines; Bob Haymes; Hugh Beaumont; Walter Baldwin; Howard Freeman; *D:* Alfred E. Green; *W:* Waldo Salt; Louis Solomon; *C:* Joseph Walker; *M:* Paul Sawtell; Carmen Dragon.

Mr. Wise Guy **1942** The East Side Kids break out of reform school to clear one of the Kids' brother of a murder charge. Typical pre-Bowery Boys vehicle. **70m/B; VHS, DVD.** Leo Gorcey; Huntz Hall; Billy Gilbert; Guinn "Big Boy" Williams; Benny Rubin; Douglas Fowley; Ann Doran; Jack Mulhall; Warren Hymer; David Gorcey; *D:* William Nigh.

Mr. Wonderful ½ **1993 (PG-13)** Bittersweet (rather than purely romantic) look at love and romance. Divorced Con Ed worker Gus (Dillon) is hard up for cash and tries to marry off ex-wife Lee (Sciorra) so he can use her alimony to invest in a bowling alley with his buddies. Routine flick's saved by the cast, who manage to bring a small measure of believability to a transparent plot. This was director Minghella's sophomore effort, between "Truly, Madly, Deeply" and "The English Patient." **99m/C; VHS, DVD.** Matt Dillon; Annabella Sciorra; William Hurt; Mary-Louise Parker; Luis Guzman; Dan Hedaya; Vincent D'Onofrio; James Gandolfini; Bruce Kirby; Jessica Harper; Bruce Altman; Paul Bates; *D:* Anthony Minghella; *W:* Amy Schor; Vicki Polon; *C:* Geoffrey Simpson; *M:* Michael Gore.

Mr. Wong, Detective **1938** The first in the Mr. Wong series, the cunning detective traps a killer who feigns guilt to throw suspicion away from himself. The plot is loaded with the usual twists and villains. However, Karloff is a standout. **69m/B; VHS, DVD.** Boris Karloff; Grant Withers; *D:* William Nigh; *W:* Houston Branch; *C:* Harry Neumann.

Mr. Wong in Chinatown ½ **1939** Third of the Mr. Wong series finds James Lee Wong investigating the murder of a wealthy Chinese woman. She had been helping to fund the purchase of airplanes to equip China in its 1930s' struggle with Japan. **70m/B; DVD.** Boris Karloff; Grant Withers; William Royle; Marjorie Reynolds; Peter George Lynn; Lotus Long; Richard Loo; *D:* William Nigh.

Mr. Woodcock ½ **2007 (PG-13)** Mr. Woodcock (Thornton) is the world's nastiest (and most unfortunately named) gym teacher. Former student John (Scott) has turned his childhood trauma at Woodcock's hands into a self-help book, and he returns home to discover that his nemesis is now dating his mother Beverly (Sarandon). Vulgar jokes, slapstick, and cruel antics ensue. Thornton phones in a character he's played a million times before, while Scott serves up a meltdown of epic proportions, all leading up to a contrived happy ending that makes any legitimate bite the movie had ring false. **87m/C; DVD, Blu-Ray.** Billy Bob Thornton; Seann William Scott; Susan Sarandon; Kyley Baldridge; Melissa Sagemiller; Amy Poehler; Melissa Leo; Bill Macy; Ethan Suplett; *D:* Craig Gillespie; *W:* Michael Carnes; Josh Gilbert; *C:* Tami Reiker; *M:* Theodore Shapiro.

Mr. Write **1992 (PG-13)** Modest advertising satire mixed with romance. Aspiring writer Charlie (Reiser) decides to make some money by acting in commercials. He falls for ad exec Nicole (Tuck) but there are some complications to be overcome first, including her dim bulb boyfriend and obnoxious father. Adapted from the play by Howard J. Morris. **89m/C; VHS, DVD.** Paul Reiser; Jessica Tuck; Doug Davidson; Martin Mull; Wendie Jo Sperber; Eddie Barth; Darryl M. Bell; Thomas F. Wilson; Jane Leeves; Calvert Deforest; Ben Stein; *D:* Charles Loventhal; *W:* Howard J. Morris; *C:* Elliot Davis.

Mr. Wrong **1995 (PG-13)** In her feature film debut, DeGeneres plays Martha, a 30-something single woman with wacky friends who's being pressured by parents toward marriage while having little luck in the dating scene. Pullman plays Whitman, her dreamboat who quickly turns into the Titanic. Along the relationship road to ruin she is forced to deal with bad poetry, charades and...gum in her hair!! The usually entertaining DeGeneres is given little to do but react lamely to the wild events going on around her. **97m/C; DVD, Blu-Ray.** Ellen DeGeneres; Bill Pullman; Joan Cusack; Dean Stockwell; Joan Plowright; John Livingston; Robert Goulet; Ellen Cleghorne; Brad William Henke; Polly Holliday; Briant Wells; *D:* Nick Castle; *W:* Chris Matheson; Kerry Ehrin; Craig Munson; *C:* John Schwartzman; *M:* Craig Safan.

Mr. Wu **1927** Grim silent drama has Chaney playing the dual roles of a ruthless Chinese aristocrat and his grandfather. Mr. Wu is obsessed with his beautiful daughter Nang Ping's honor. When she is seduced by wealthy visiting Briton Basil Gregory, Wu enacts a cruel ritual on Nang Ping and then turns his vengeance on Basil and his family. **90m/B; Silent; DVD.** Lon Chaney, Sr.; Renee Adoree; Ralph Forbes; Louise Dresser; Gertrude (Olmstead) Olmsted; Holmes Herbert; Anna May Wong; *D:* William Nigh; *W:* Lorna Moon; *C:* John Arnold.

Mr. X: Leos Carax **2014** The internationally renowned French director, Leos Carax, has remained something of an enigma, shying away from interviews or examinations of his process, and Louise-Salome's documentary about him parallels the subject matter. Most interestingly, regular collaborators of Carax's, particularly the great Denis Levant, offer anecdotal insight into Carax's unique process. Louise-Salome's rare visual style gives a poetic, visionary filmmaker a poetic, visionary tribute. **72m/C; DVD.** *FR* *D:* Tessa-Louise Salome; *W:* Tessa-Louise Salome; Chantal Perrin; Adrien Walter; *C:* Kaname Onoyama; *M:* Gael Rakotondrabe.

Mistletoe Over Manhattan **2011** Rebecca Claus, Santa's missus, is worried that workaholic Santa is more bah-humbug than ho-ho-ho. She heads to Manhattan, which is where Rebecca and Nick fell in love, and befriends cop Joe, who's still in love with his wife Lucy, even though they're in the middle of a divorce. Rebecca hopes by getting Joe and Lucy to embrace the Christmas spirit, she can get Nick to do the same in this Hallmark Channel drama. **88m/C; DVD.** Tedde Moore; Greg Bryk; Tricia Helfer; Mairtin O'Carrigan; Ken Hall; *D:* John Bradshaw; *W:* Rickie Castaneda; *C:* Russ Goozee; *M:* Gary Koftinoff. **CABLE**

Mistral's Daughter ½ **1984** Frothy miniseries, based on the Judith Krantz novel, about a French artist and his relationship with three beautiful women. Formulaic TV melodrama offers sexual scenes and revealing glimpses. Produced, like other Krantz miniseries, by author's hubby, Steve. **390m/C; VHS, DVD.** Stefanie Powers; Lee Remick; Stacy Keach; Robert Urich; Timothy Dalton; *D:* Douglas Hickox; *M:* Vladimir Cosma. **TV**

Mistress **1991 (R)** A weak script does in a formidable cast in a behind-the-scenes look at movie making. Wuhl plays Marvin Landisman, a failed director/screenwriter, who's approached by has-been producer Jack Roth (Landau) who says he's found a backer to finance a movie from one of Marvin's old scripts. It turns out Roth has three men (De Niro, Aiello, and Wallach) ready to finance the film as long as each of their mistresses, who all have acting ambitions, gets the starring role. Double-dealing at a bargain basement level sets up the rest of this lifeless comedy. **100m/C; VHS, DVD.** Robert Wuhl; Martin Landau; Robert De Niro; Eli Wallach; Danny Aiello; Sheryl Lee Ralph; Jean

Smart; Tuesday Weld; Jace Alexander; Laurie Metcalf; Christopher Walken; Ernest Borgnine; *D:* Barry Primus; *W:* J.F. Lawton; Barry Primus; *C:* Sven Kirsten; *M:* Galt MacDermot.

Mistress America 🦴🦴 **2015 (R)** Baumbach and Gerwig reteam for this comedy that almost plays like two distinctly different movies, and neither of them really work. Tracy (Kirke) is a lonely college freshman in New York, encouraged by her mother (Erbe) to contact the woman who will be her new stepsister. Enter Brooke (Gerwig), an outgoing socialite with some issues of her own. For an hour, Brooke and Tracy flit around NYC, becoming friends, and then the piece becomes a really awkward physical comedy as the final act all takes place in one upstate home. Both movies are mediocre. **86m/C; DVD, Blu-Ray.** Greta Gerwig; Heather Lind; Michael Chernus; Lola Kirke; Charlie Gillette; *D:* Noah Baumbach; *W:* Greta Gerwig; Noah Baumbach; *C:* Sam Levy; *M:* Britta Phillips; Dean Wareham.

The Mistress of Atlantis 🦴 ½ *The Lost Atlantis* **1932** A remake of an earlier silent film based on the French novel "L'Atlantide." A French Foreign Legion officer discovers the lost kingdom of Atlantis underground in the Sahara Desert. Taken captive by its possibly divine Queen, he quickly discovers that her youth comes at a price he may have to pay. Plot was noticeably shortened from the original lengthy book. **87m/B; DVD.** *GE FR* Brigitte Helm; John Stuart; Gustav Diesl; Gibb McLaughlin; Matthias Wieman; Florelle; Tela Tchai; Georges Tourreil; *D:* G.W. Pabst; *W:* Miles Mander; Ladislao Vajda; Pierre Benoit; Herman Oberlander; *C:* Joseph Barth; Ernest Korner; Eugen Shufftan; *M:* Wolfgang Zeller.

The Mistress of Spices 🦴 ½ **2005** Beautiful but remarkably inert attempt at magical realism. Tilo (Rai) has been taught to use the magic of various spices to help others. She emigrates from India and opens a spice shop in Oakland, but there are three severe restrictions she must follow: she can't use the spices for personal gain; she can't touch the skin of another human being; and she can't ever leave the shop. Tilo seems okay with all this until studly Doug (McDermott) has an accident right outside. She helps him, he helps her, and the spices turn on Tilo (and her clients). Although it hardly seems fair that anyone as luscious as Rai should be held hostage by saffron (which attracts love by the way). **96m/C; DVD.** *US GB* Aishwarya Rai; Dylan McDermott; Ayesha Dharker; Nitin Ganatra; Anupam Kher; Adewale Akinnuoye-Agbaje; Sonny Gill Dulay; Padma Lakshmi; *D:* Paul Mayeda Berges; *W:* Paul Mayeda Berges; Gurinder Chadha; *C:* Santosh Sivan; *M:* Craig Pruess.

Mistresses 🦴🦴 *Lyubovnitsky* **2019** In a bar in present-day Russia, three women from very different backgrounds, Alisa (Boritch), Ira (Andreeva), and Masha (Aleksandrova), unexpected meet and all into conversation. During their talk, they discover that each of them has recently broken up with her boyfriend because she was deceived. All their lovers were married men. They trio decides to get revenge on their former lovers. After each of them has received her due justice, they form a secret society and use all that they have learned to help other women who have been wronged by their faithless lovers. Russian with subtitles. **98m/C; DVD.** Yuliya Aleksandrova; Paulina Andreeva; Elizaveta Arzamasova; Aleksandra Bortich; Evgenia Brik; *D:* Elena Hazanov; *W:* Elena Hazanov; Denis Kuryshev; Artyom Vitkin; *C:* Mark Ziselson; *M:* Diana Arbenina.

Mistrial 🦴🦴 **1996 (R)** NYC cop Steve Donohue (Pullman) is incensed when accused cop killer Eddie Rios (Seda) is acquited and Donohue himself is about to be charged in the wrongful deaths of the suspect's wife and brother, which occurred during his pursuit. So he takes the entire courtroom hostage. **90m/C; VHS, DVD.** Bill Pullman; Robert Loggia; Jon Seda; Blair Underwood; Casey Siemaszko; Josef Sommer; Roberta Maxwell; James Rebhorn; Leo Burmester; Roma Maffia; Kate Burton; *D:* Heywood Gould; *W:* Heywood Gould; *C:* Paul Sarossy; *M:* Brad Fiedel. **CABLE**

Mists of Avalon 🦴🦴🦴 **2001** A woman-centric version of the story of Camelot based on Marion Zimmer Bradley's 1982 bestseller. Morgaine (Margulies) is the niece of the Lady of the Lake, Viviane (Huston), who raises her in the mother/goddess religion even as Christianity takes hold of the land. Morgaine is reunited with her half-brother Arthur (Atterton), who is betrothed to the Christian Gwenhwyfer (Mathis), who falls for Arthur's best friend and knight, Lancelot (Vartan). But as the years pass, Viking invasions and familial circumstances threaten to tear Arthur's kingdom apart and Morgaine can only watch as the vision of Avalon disappears as well. **180m/C; VHS, DVD.** Julianna Margulies; Anjelica Huston; Samantha Mathis; Edward Atterton; Joan Allen; Michael Vartan; Hans Matheson; Caroline Goodall; Michael Byrne; Clive Russell; Mark Lewis Jones; *D:* Uli Edel; *W:* Gavin Scott; *C:* Vilmos Zsigmond; *M:* Lee Holdridge. **CABLE**

Misty 🦴🦴 ½ **1961** Based on the Marguerite Henry novel "Misty of Chincoteague." Every year some of the wild ponies who live on the islands off the Virginia coast are rounded up and auctioned off to thin out the herd. Young Paul and Maureen Beebe want to help capture the elusive Phantom so they can buy her, but they discover the mare has had a foal and they name her Misty. Only when the duo comes up for sale, they are bought by someone else. **91m/C; DVD.** David Ladd; Pam Smith; Arthur O'Connell; Anne Seymour; Duke Farley; *D:* James B. Clark; *W:* Ted Sherdeman; *C:* Lee Garmes; Leo Tover; *M:* Paul Sawtell; Bert Shefter.

Mitch Albom's Have a Little Faith 🦴🦴 *Have a Little Faith* **2011** Hallmark Hall of Fame presentation based on the true story novel by Albom. The columnist, author, and non-practicing Jew (Whitford), is asked by his childhood rabbi, Albert Lewis (Landau), to deliver his eulogy, which gives Mitch a chance to examine what faith means. He meets Henry Covington (Fishburne) in Detroit and learns of his drug addiction and criminal past that he turned around when he asked God for help. Henry becomes the founder/minister of "I Am My Brother's Keeper," working in a dilapidated church to help stop others from following a dead-end road of violence. Darker than the usual Hallmark pic. **90m/C; DVD.** Bradley Whitford; Martin Landau; Laurence Fishburne; Anika Noni Rose; Mykelti Williamson; Melinda McGraw; Deanna Dunagan; *D:* Jon Avnet; *W:* Mitch Albom; *C:* Denis Lenoir; *M:* Edward Shearmur. **TV**

Mitchell 🦴 **1975 (R)** Tough cop battles drug traffic and insipid script. Big screen release with that certain TV look. **90m/C; DVD.** Joe Don Baker; Linda Evans; Martin Balsam; John Saxon; Merlin Olsen; Harold J. Stone; Robert Phillips; *D:* Andrew V. McLaglen; *W:* Ian Kennedy Martin; *C:* Harry Stradling, Jr.; *M:* Jerry Styner.

Mitt 🦴🦴 **2014** Whiteley and his team were given unprecedented access to the Romney campaign against John McCain in 2008 and then for President in 2012. Sadly, they didn't find much there. A lot of effort has been expended in the name of "humanizing" Romney. He is often shown with his wife and kids, typically going through standard routines like practicing for a speech or walking the hall to an event. The revelation that Romney loves his family and puts his pants on one leg at a time isn't enough in today's political doc world. **94m/C; On Demand.** Mitt Romney; *D:* Greg Whiteley; *C:* Greg Whiteley; Rod Santiano; Gabriel Patay; Erik Olsen; *M:* Perrin Cloutier.

Mixed Blood 🦴🦴 ½ **1984 (R)** From the renowned underground film-maker, a dark comedy that examines the seedy drug subculture in New York. Violent, fast, and funny. **98m/C; VHS, DVD.** Marilia Pera; Richard Ulacia; Linda Kerridge; Geraldine Smith; Angel David; *D:* Paul Morrissey; *W:* Paul Morrissey.

Mixed Nuts 🦴 *Lifesavers* **1994 (PG-13)** Misfits man a suicide hotline on Christmas Eve in this unfunny, pathetic comedy. Director/writer Ephron (along with her co-writer sister Delia) try way too hard to fashion a hip, racy, madcap farce but the film never finds its style and the storyline is very weak. Most of the performances are over the top, although Martin, Shandling, and Kahn are good for a few amusing scenes. It's a shame that the taletns of Ephron and the cast are virtually wasted here. Adapted from the French film "Le Pere Noel Est une Ordure." **97m/C; DVD.** Steve Martin; Madeline Kahn; Robert Klein; Anthony LaPaglia; Juliette Lewis; Rob Reiner; Adam Sandler; Rita Wilson; Garry Shandling; Liev Schreiber; *D:* Nora Ephron; *W:* Nora Ephron; Delia Ephron; *M:* George Fenton.

Mixing Nia 🦴🦴 ½ **1998 (R)** Biracial ad exec Nia (Parsons) becomes upset when she is asked to head a new beer campaign aimed at black youth. She quits, and decides to write a novel about the black experience and then realizes that she's lost touch with that part of her heritage. So, Nia decides to regain her roots and finds a real culture clash. **93m/C; VHS, DVD.** Karyn Parsons; Isaiah Washington, IV; Eric Thal; Diego Serrano; Heidi Schanz; Rosalyn Coleman; *D:* Alison Swan.

Mo' Better Blues 🦴🦴 ½ **1990 (R)** Not one of his more cohesive or compelling works, Lee's fourth feature is on the surface a backstage jazz biopic. Bleek Gilliam (Washington) is a handsome, accomplished jazz trumpeter who divides his extra-curricular time between Clarke (Williams) and Indigo (Lee sibling Joie). What's interesting is not so much the story of self-interested musician and ladies' man Gilliam, but the subtle racial issues his life draws into focus. The Branford Marsalis Quartet provides the music for Bleek's group, scored by Lee's dad Bill (on whose life the script is loosely based). **129m/C; DVD.** Denzel Washington; Spike Lee; Joie Lee; Wesley Snipes; Cynda Williams; Giancarlo Esposito; Robin Harris; Bill Nunn; John Turturro; Dick Anthony Williams; Ruben Blades; Nicholas Turturro; Samuel L. Jackson; Abbey Lincoln; Tracy C. Johns; Joe Seneca; *D:* Spike Lee; *W:* Spike Lee; *C:* Ernest R. Dickerson; *M:* Bill Lee; Branford Marsalis.

Mo' Money 🦴🦴 ½ **1992 (R)** Damon Wayans is a small-time con-artist who is inspired to go straight by a beautiful woman (Dash). He lands a job at the credit card company she works for, but temptation overcomes him, he swipes some plastic, and the scamming begins anew. With the help of his younger brother (played by real-life younger brother Marlon), they get involved in an even bigger, more dangerous scam being operated by the credit card company's head of security. Crude formula comedy driven by energetic, inventive performances by the brothers Wayans. **97m/C; DVD, Blu-Ray.** Damon Wayans; Marlon Wayans; Stacey Dash; Joe Santos; John Diehl; Harry J. Lennix; Mark Beltzman; Quincy Wong; Larry Brandenburg; Almayvonne; *D:* Peter Macdonald; *W:* Damon Wayans; *C:* Don Burgess; *M:* Jay Gruska.

Moana 🦴🦴🦴 **2016 (PG)** Disney may have gone to the Princess Narrative a few too many times but this trip to the well includes great voice work by Dwayne Johnson and songs by Lin-Manuel Miranda, so it can be forgiven. Auli'I Cravalho voices the title character, the young lady who must try to save her Polynesian people, with the help of an immortal hero named Maui (Johnson). The relatively familiar and unfocused plot, based on actual stories from Polynesian mythology, is just an excuse for the gorgeous animation and fantastic songs by Miranda. It's not Disney's most memorable film, but it's an enjoyable one. **107m/C; DVD, Blu-Ray.** Auli'i Cravalho; Dwayne "The Rock" Johnson; Rachel House; Temuera Morrison; Jemaine Clement; *D:* Ron Clements; *W:* Jared Bush; *M:* Opetaia Foa'i; Mark Mancina; Lin-Manuel Miranda.

The Mob 🦴🦴 **1951** Brutally efficient film noir where the 'good' guys are just as ruthless as the criminals. Cop Johnny Damico (Crawford) goes undercover as an easily corruptible dock worker who wants to become part of the mob running the wharf. He gets in with the gangsters and discovers another cop (Kiley) is already on the inside trying to find out who the big boss is. **87m/B; DVD.** Broderick Crawford; Richard Kiley; Matt Crowley; Neville Brand; Ernest Borgnine; *D:* Robert Parrish; *W:* William Bowers; *C:* Joseph Walker; *M:* George Duning.

Mob Rules 🦴 ½ *Tic* **2010 (R)** Derivative crime drama. Years after a heist gone wrong, London gangsters Anton and Tyrone have carefully planned their revenge against ex-partner C-Note. He stole their loot and fled to America and now they've decided to come and get what's theirs. **97m/C; DVD.** Lennie James; Treva Etienne; Gary McDonald; Tina Casciani; Courtney Hope; Daniele Favilli; *D:* Keith Palmer; *W:* Keith Palmer; *C:* Jon Myers; *M:* Tree Adams.

Mob Story 🦴 ½ **1990 (R)** Vernon stars as a big-wig mob boss on the run from the government and a few of his "closest" friends. He plans to disappear into Canada, but if his girl (Kidder) and best friend (Waxman) find him first he'll be traveling in a body-bag. Very silly, but fun. **98m/C; VHS, DVD.** John Vernon; Margot Kidder; Al Waxman; Kate Vernon; *D:* Gabriel Markiw; Jancarlo Markiw.

Mob War 🦴 ½ **1988 (R)** A war breaks out between the head of New York's underworld and a media genius. After deciding to become partners, the "family" tries to take over. For fun, count how many times the word "respect" pops up in the script. Tries hard but fails. **96m/C; VHS, DVD.** John Christian; David Henry Keller; Jake LaMotta; Johnny Stumper; *D:* J. Christian Ingvordsen; *W:* J. Christian Ingvordsen; John Weiner; *C:* Steven Kaman.

Mobile Homes 🦴🦴 **2019** Worn down Ali (Poots), her scheming boyfriend Evan (Turner), and their son Bone (Oulton) live a life of functional poverty, residing partly in their van and supporting themselves by selling various items and animals. They train a chicken for cockfighting, but after the event, the family falls apart because Evan convinces Bone to sell drugs. Ali and Bone leave Evan and find a purpose with the help of Robert (Rennie), a mobile home contractor. As Ali builds mobile homes, she envisions a new life. Though the indie film poetically dramatizes the trio's unpredictable lives, the characters lack full development despite Poots' memorable performance. **105m/C; DVD.** Imogen Poots; Callum Turner; Callum Keith Rennie; Karen LeBlanc; Cyndy Day; *D:* Vladimir de Fontenay; *W:* Vladimir de Fontenay; *C:* Benoit Soler; *M:* Matthew Otto.

Mobius 🦴 ½ **2013 (R)** Monotonous crime drama briefly enlivened by De France's sensuality. American banker Alice, now living in Russia, is the key to bringing down a money laundering operation run by oligarch Ivan. This means FSB agent Moise needs to get close to Alice, but maybe not as close as he does. **108m/C; DVD, Blu-Ray.** Jean Dujardin; Cecile de France; Tim Roth; Emilie Dequenne; John Lynch; *D:* Eric Rochant; *W:* Eric Rochant; *C:* Pierre Novion; *M:* Jonathan Morali. **VIDEO**

Mobsters 🦴 ½ **1991 (R)** It sounded like a great idea, casting the hottest young actors of the '90s as youthful racketeers "Lucky" Luciano, Meyer Lansky, Bugsy Siegel, and Frank Costello. But it would take an FBI probe to straighten out the blood-choked plot, as the pals' loyalties get tested the hard way in a dismembered narrative. Sicker than the violence is a seeming endorsement of the glamorous hoods. **104m/C; VHS, DVD, Blu-Ray, HD-DVD.** Christian Slater; Patrick Dempsey; Richard Grieco; Costas Mandylor; Anthony Quinn; F. Murray Abraham; Lara Flynn Boyle; Michael Gambon; Christopher Penn; Joe (Johnny) Viterelli; *D:* Michael Karbelnikoff; *W:* Nicholas Kazan; *C:* Lajos Koltai.

Moby Dick 🦴🦴🦴 **1956** This adaptation of Herman Melville's high seas saga features Peck as Captain Ahab. His obsession with revenge upon the great white whale, Moby Dick, isn't always believable, but the moments that click make the film more than worthwhile. **116m/C; VHS, DVD, Blu-Ray.** Gregory Peck; Richard Basehart; Orson Welles; Leo Genn; Harry Andrews; Friedrich Ledebur; *D:* John Huston; *W:* Ray Bradbury; John Huston; *C:* Oswald Morris. Natl. Bd. of Review '56: Director (Huston); N.Y. Film Critics '56: Director (Huston).

Moby Dick 🦴🦴 ½ **1998 (PG)** TV adaptation of Herman Melville's 1851 novel, starring a mesmerizing Stewart as the obsessive peg-legged Captain Ahab. Novice seaman Ishmael (Thomas) signs aboard the whaling ship Pequod, making friends with Polynesian native, harpooner Queequeg (Waretini). Soon enough Ishmael learns about the great white whale who claimed the captain's leg and Ahab's determination to seek revenge on the beast, no matter what the cost to himself, his crew, or the ship. Peck, who starred as Ahab in the 1956 movie version, takes on the role of Jonah-and-the-whale sermonizing Father Mapple. **145m/C; DVD.** Patrick Stewart; Henry Thomas; Ted Levine; Piripi Waretini; Gregory Peck; Bill Hunter; Hugh Keays-Byrne; Norman D. Golden, II; Bruce Spence; *D:* Franc Roddam; *W:* Franc Roddam; Anton Diether; *C:* David Connell; *M:* Christopher Gordon. **TV**

Moby Dick ½ **2011** Nigel Williams' script takes a lot of liberties in this cable version of Herman Melville's 1851 novel. The basic story is recognizable as Captain Ahab (a hammy Hurt) is still obsessed with killing the great (CGI) white whale Moby Dick, which results in disaster for the crew of the Pequod. **184m/C; DVD, Blu-Ray.** William Hurt; Ethan Hawke; Charlie Cox; Eddie Marsan; Gillian Anderson; Billy Boyd; Raoul Trujillo; James Gilbert; *D:* Mike Barker; *W:* Nigel Williams; *C:* Richard Greatrex; *M:* Richard G. Mitchell. **CABLE**

Mockery ½ **1927** Chaney plays a peasant working for a Russian countess. He becomes involved in a peasant revolution against the rich and threatens the countess but eventually saves her from the mob. **75m/B; Silent; VHS, DVD.** Lon Chaney, Sr.; Barbara Bedford; Ricardo Cortez; Emily Fitzroy; *D:* Benjamin Christiansen.

Mockingbird Don't Sing **2001** Based on the true story of Katie, which came to light in 1970. She is rescued from some 12 years of abuse and isolation imposed by her mentally unbalanced parents. Unable to speak and with no social skills, Katie is little more than a lab rat to a variety of psychologists and doctors who see her more as a case study than a person. Even her caring social worker Sandra (Errico) is unable to beat a system that just offers a different type of abuse to the young girl. **98m/C; VHS, DVD.** Tarra Steele; Melissa Errico; Sean Young; Joe Regalbuto; Michael Lerner; *D:* Harry Bromley-Davenport; *W:* Daryl Haney; *C:* Jeff Baustert; *M:* Mark Hart.

The Mod Squad **1999 (R)** Tangled rehash of the '60s TV series tries very hard to be cool, but ends up as hip as a $2 haircut. Unbelievable teen criminals-turned-cops Pete (Ribisi), Linc (Epps), and Julie (Danes) all glower sullenly as they try to crack a convoluted case involving drugs, prostitution and their dead boss Capt. Greer (Farina). Director Silver manages to crush what little dramatic tension was left in the stale script into a bland pulp. **94m/C; DVD.** Claire Danes; Giovanni Ribisi; Omar Epps; Dennis Farina; Josh Brolin; Richard Jenkins; Larry Brandenburg; Steve Harris; Sam McMurray; Michael Lerner; Bodhi (Pine) Elfman; Holmes Osborne; Dey Young; Eddie Griffin; Carmen (Lee) Llywelyn; *D:* Scott Silver; *W:* Scott Silver; Stephen Kay; Kate Lanier; *C:* Ellen Kuras; *M:* B.C. Smith.

The Model and the Marriage Broker ½ **1951** Ritter steals the movie as nobody's fool marriage broker Mae Swazey, whose clientele is generally less-attractive than beautiful model Kitty Bennett (Crain). However, Kitty's involved with a married man so Mae introduces her to eligible Matt (Brady) and hopes romance follows. **103m/B; DVD.** Jeanne Crain; Thelma Ritter; Scott Brady; Zero Mostel; Michael O'Shea; Frank Fontaine; *D:* George Cukor; *W:* Richard L. Breen; Walter Reisch; Charles Brackett; *C:* Milton Krasner; *M:* Cyril Mockridge.

A Model Employee **2002** A modest thriller. Francois Maurey is the owner of a small software company who refuses to sell his latest products to a large American firm. Then Florence is hired and becomes a model employee and the middle-aged Francois is smitten, but Florence is a femme who's definitely fatale. French with subtitles. **88m/C; DVD.** *FR* Francois Berleand; Bruno Todeschini; Nicole Calfan; Francois Morel; Delphine Rollin; *D:* Jacques Otmezguine; *W:* Jacques Otmezguine; *C:* Alain Marcoen; *M:* Philippe Rombi.

Model Shop ½ **1969** American film from French director Demy is filled with talky angst and ennui. L.A. architect George (a dull Lockwood), who's about to be drafted, spots beautiful Lola (Aimee) and becomes very interested. The world-weary Frenchwoman is working as a nude pin-up model after being stranded when her husband ran out. **90m/C; DVD, Blu-Ray.** Gary Lockwood; Anouk Aimee; Alexandra Hay; Tom Holland; Carol Cole; Neil Elliot; *D:* Jacques Demy; *W:* Jacques Demy; Adrien (Carole Eastman) Joyce; *C:* Michel Hugo.

The Modern Adventures of Tom Sawyer **1999 (PG)** Title sums it up. Mark Twain's mischevious hero is still getting into trouble only this time in the present-day. Harmless, but insubstantial time-waster tries to capitalize on the enduring popularity of the character. **92m/C; VHS, DVD.** Laraine Newman; Erik Estrada; David Lander; Phillip Van Dyke; Bethany Richards; Adam Dior; *D:* Adam Weissman; *W:* Adam Weissman; *C:* Howard Wexler; *M:* Kristopher Carter. **VIDEO**

A Modern Affair ½ *Mr. 247* **1994 (R)** Single executive Grace Rhodes' (Eichorn) biological clock is ringing and without Mr. Right in sight, she decides to visit a sperm bank. Grace gets pregnant and also very curious about her anonymous donor—who of course doesn't stay anonymous. Grace even manages to fall for photographer Peter Kessler (Tucci) but how does she tell him she's carrying his baby when they haven't even had sex yet? **91m/C; VHS, DVD.** Lisa Eichhorn; Stanley Tucci; Caroline Aaron; Tammy Grimes; Robert Joy; Wesley Addy; Cynthia Martells; Mary Jo Salerno; *D:* Vern Oakley; *W:* Paul Zimmerman; *C:* Rex Nicholson; *M:* Jan Hammer.

Modern Girls ½ **1986 (PG-13)** Teen comedy about three bubble-headed LA rock groupies and their various wild adventures during a single night on the town. Surprising in that the three lead actresses waste their talents in this lesson in exploitation. Bruce Springsteen's younger sister portrays a drug user. **82m/C; DVD, Blu-Ray, Streaming.** Cynthia Gibb; Daphne Zuniga; Virginia Madsen; *D:* Jerry Kramer; *W:* Laurie Craig; *M:* Eddie Arkin.

Modern Love **1990 (R)** An average slob realizes that marriage, fatherhood and in-law-ship isn't quite what he expected. Benson stars, directs and produces as well as co-starring with real-life wife DeVito. A plotless hodgepodge of bits that were more successful in "Look Who's Talking" and "Parenthood." **89m/C; VHS, DVD.** Robby Benson; Karla DeVito; Rue McClanahan; Kaye Ballard; Frankie Valli; Cliff Bemis; Louise Lasser; Burt Reynolds; Lyric Benson; *D:* Robby Benson; *W:* Robby Benson.

Modern Love **2007** Disquieting Australian psycho-horror. Middle-aged businessman John has inherited his Uncle Tom's farm, which is located in a weird coastal community. John, his unhappy wife Emily, and their young son Edward come for what they think will be a quick visit, but John soon undergoes a radical personality change. John starts hearing voices telling him his uncle was murdered and things gets even stranger from that point on. **95m/C; DVD.** *AU* Mark Constable; Victoria Hill; William Traegar; Craig Behenna; *D:* Alex Frayne; *W:* Nick Remy Matthews; *C:* Nick Remy Matthews; *M:* Tom Heuzenroeder.

Modern Problems **1981 (PG)** A man involved in a nuclear accident discovers he has acquired telekinetic powers, which he uses to turn the tables on his professional and romantic rivals. A fine cast but an unsuccessful fission trip. **93m/C; VHS, DVD.** Chevy Chase; Patti D'Arbanville; Mary Kay Place; Brian Doyle-Murray; Nell Carter; Dabney Coleman; *D:* Ken Shapiro.

Modern Romance **1981 (R)** The romantic misadventures of a neurotic film editor who is hopelessly in love with his girlfriend but can't seem to maintain a normal relationship with her. Smart and hilarious at times and always simmering with anxiety. Offers an honest look at relationships as well as an accurate portrait of filmmaking. **102m/C; VHS, DVD, Blu-Ray.** Albert Brooks; Kathryn Harrold; Bruno Kirby; George Kennedy; James L. Brooks; Bob Einstein; *D:* Albert Brooks; *W:* Albert Brooks; Monica Johnson.

Modern Times **1936** This "mostly" silent film finds Chaplin playing a factory worker who goes crazy from his repetitious job on an assembly line and his boss's demands for greater speed and efficiency. Ultimately encompassing the tyranny of machine over man, this cinematic masterpiece has more relevance today than ever. Chaplin wrote the musical score which incorporates the tune "Smile." Look for a young Gloria De Haven as one of Goddard's sisters; she's the real-life daughter of Chaplin's assistant director. **87m/B; Silent; VHS, DVD, Blu-Ray.** Charlie Chaplin; Paulette Goddard; Henry Bergman; Stanley Sandford; Gloria De Haven; Chester Conklin; *D:* Charlie Chaplin; *W:* Charlie Chaplin; *C:* Ira Morgan; Roland H. Totheroh; *M:* Charlie Chaplin. AFI '98: Top 100; Natl. Film Reg. '89.

Modern Vampires ½ *Revenant* **1998 (R)** Think vampire-lite. A community of European vamps have moved to L.A., where the beautiful Nico (Wagner) is threatening their anonymity by her bloody kills. Dallas (Van Dien), Nico's vampire boyfriend, tries to protect her from Dracula (Pastorelli), who wants her destroyed. Meanwhile, vampire hunter Van Helsing (Steiger) seeks to get rid of the entire community. **95m/C; VHS, DVD.** Casper Van Dien; Natasha Gregson Wagner; Rod Steiger; Robert Pastorelli; Kim Cattrall; Natasha Andreichenko; Gabriel Casseus; Udo Kier; Natasha Lyonne; *D:* Richard Elfman; *W:* Matthew Bright; *M:* Danny Elfman; Michael Wandmacher.

The Moderns **1988 (R)** One of the quirkier directors around, this time Rudolph tries a comedic period piece about the avant-garde art society of 1920s Paris. Fleshed out with some familiar characters (Ernest Hemingway, Gertrude Stein) and some strange art-world types. The tone is not consistently funny but, instead, romantic as the main characters clash over art and love. **126m/C; VHS, DVD, Blu-Ray.** Keith Carradine; Linda Fiorentino; John Lone; Genevieve Bujold; Geraldine Chaplin; Wallace Shawn; Kevin J. O'Connor; *D:* Alan Rudolph; *W:* Alan Rudolph; *M:* Mark Isham. L.A. Film Critics '88: Support. Actress (Bujold).

Modesty Blaise ½ **1966** Adaptation of Peter O'Donnell's comic strip finds his tough British babe spy embodied by Italian beauty Vitti, aided by her right-hand man Willie Garvin (Stamp). The secret agent is watching out for a diamond shipment, which is the target of her archrival Gabriel (Bogarde). Very campy and '60s pop-arty, with everyone having fun and not taking any situation seriously. O'Donnell retired himself and Modesty in 2001. **118m/C; VHS, DVD, Blu-Ray.** *GB* Monica Vitti; Terence Stamp; Dirk Bogarde; Harry Andrews; Michael Craig; Clive Revill; Alexander Knox; Rossella Falk; *D:* Joseph Losey; *W:* Evan Jones; *C:* Jack Hildyard; *M:* John Dankworth.

Modigliani **2004 (R)** Garcia is miscast as debauched Italian Jewish artist Amedeo Modgliani, who's living it up in Paris, circa 1919, and having a tragic love affair with his beautiful Catholic mistress, Jeanne (Zylberstein), who leaves her family for him. Writer/director Davis invents a feud between Modigliani and a glowering Picasso (Djalili) to further liven up the action. It doesn't work and neither does the film, which is almost a melodramatic parody of screen bios about the art world. **128m/C; DVD.** *FR IT RO GE GB US* Andy Garcia; Elsa Zylberstein; Omid Djalili; Hippolyte Girardot; Udo Kier; Peter Capaldi; Miriam Margolyes; Susie Amy; Dan Astileanu; Theodor Danetti; Eva Herzigova; Ion Siminie; *D:* Mick Davis; *W:* Mick Davis; *C:* Emmanuel (Manu) Kadosh; *M:* Guy Farley.

Moebius **2013** As twisted as cinema can get, director/writer Ki-duk's latest experiment is not for the faint of heart or easily queasy. It's a film about incest, castration, sexual perversion, and murder that's conveyed without a single word of dialogue. There's plenty of grunting, screaming, and moaning in this tale of a mother who castrates her son after learning that her husband is cheating on her, but not an actual spoken line. Kim's film, believe it or not, is really a pitch-black comedy, a modern spin on themes of Greek tragedy. **89m/C; DVD, Blu-Ray.** *SK* Jae-hyeon Jo; Eun-woo Lee; Young-ju Seo; *D:* Ki-Duk Kim; *W:* Ki-Duk Kim; *C:* Ki-Duk Kim; *M:* In-young Park.

Mogambo **1953** Remake of "Red Dust," this is the steamy story of a love triangle between an African game hunter, a proper British lady, and an American showgirl in the jungles of Kenya. **115m/C; VHS, DVD.** Clark Gable; Ava Gardner; Grace Kelly; Donald Sinden; Philip Stainton; Eric Pohlmann; Denis O'Dea; *D:* John Ford; *W:* John Lee Mahin; *C:* Robert L. Surtees. Golden Globes '54: Support. Actress (Kelly).

The Moguls *The Amateurs* **2005 (R)** Good cast is wasted in a lame comedy about middle-aged small-town guys who decide to make their own porn flick. Genial loser Andy (Bridges) comes up with the initial idea and gets local video store clerk Emmett (Fugit) to operate the camera while closeted Moose (Danson) offers to be the on-camera stud, and the appropriately nicknamed Some Idiot (Pantoliano) is writer-director. Other pals fill in as needed. One-note joke with equally one-note roles for the women involved. **100m/C; DVD, Blu-Ray, HD-DVD.** *GB US* Jeff Bridges; Ted Danson; William Fichtner; Patrick Fugit; Tim Blake Nelson; Joe Pantoliano; Glenne Headly; Lauren Graham; Jeanne Tripplehorn; Valerie Perrine; Isaiah Washington, IV; *D:* Michael Traeger; *W:* Michael Traeger; *C:* Denis Maloney; *M:* Nicolas Tenbroek.

Mohawk ½ **1956** A cowboy and his Indian maiden try to stop a war between Indian tribes and fanatical landowners. **80m/C; VHS, DVD.** Rita Gam; Neville Brand; Scott Brady; Lori Nelson; *D:* Kurt Neumann; *W:* Maurice Geraghty; Milton Krims; *C:* Karl Struss; *M:* Edward L. Alperson, Jr.

Mojave **2015 (R)** An intense, Hitchcock-like thriller with unexpected twists and turns. Los Angeles-based Thomas (Hedlund) is a suicidal artist in search of himself or, at least, a sense of peace, heads to the desert. There, he meets Jack (Isaac). Thomas soon realizes that Jack is not what he seems. Unlike Thomas's sensitive soul, Jack is a drifter and a murderer with a homicidal bent. Jack's true intent soon emerges, and the pair engage in a game of cat and mouse that moves from the desert back to Thomas's privileged world. Jack tries to use his knowledge of a secret of Thomas's to destroy his life, but Thomas does all he can to rise to the challenge to protect himself and his family. **93m/C; DVD, Blu-Ray, Streaming, Download.** Garrett Hedlund; Oscar Isaac; Louise Bourgoin; Walton Goggins; Fran Kranz; *D:* William Monahan; *W:* William Monahan; *C:* Don Davis; *M:* Andrew Hewitt.

Mojave Moon ½ **1996 (R)** Middle-aged car dealer Al (Aiello) is asked by nymphet Ellie (Jolie) to drive her home—a trailer in the desert where Al meets her perky-yet-kinky mom Julie (Archer) and Julie's violent boyfriend Boyd (Biehn). A series of strange happenings finds Al tied to the trio and discovering both adventure and romance. **95m/C; VHS, DVD.** Danny Aiello; Anne Archer; Angelina Jolie; Michael Biehn; Alfred Molina; *D:* Kevin Dowling; *W:* Leonard Glasser; *C:* James Glennon.

Mokey ½ **1942** Dated family drama with a lot of questionable parenting. When his busy, widowed dad remarries, lonely 8-year-old Mokey wants his new stepmom to love him. She's completely inexperienced and thrown by the demands of a child and, after a series of misunderstandings, the kid runs away. Helped by an equally young friend, Mokey finds a surrogate mom and is gone for months until things with his 'real' family are set right. **88m/B; DVD.** Dan Dailey; Donna Reed; Robert (Bobby) Blake; Billie "Buckwheat" Thomas; Cordell Hickman; Etta McDaniel; Cleo Desmond; *D:* Wells Root; *W:* Wells Root; Jan Fortune; *C:* Charles Rosher; *M:* Lennie Hayton.

Mole Men Against the Son of Hercules **1961** Italian muscleman Maciste battles the pale-skinned denizens of an underground city. **99m/C; VHS, DVD.** *IT* Mark Forest; Moira Orfei; Raffaella Carra; Paul Wynter; Enrico Glori; Roberto Miali; *D:* Antonio Leonviola; *W:* Marcello Baldi; Giuseppe Mangione; *C:* Alvaro Mancori; *M:* Armando Trovajoli.

The Mole People **1956** A really bad '50s creature feature which finds two archeologists accidentally discovering an underground civilization of albinos who shun all forms of light. They've also enslaved the local populace of half-human, half-mole creatures who decide to help the good guys escape by rising up in a revolt against their evil masters. When the weapon of choice is a flashlight you know not to expect much. **78m/B; VHS, DVD, Blu-Ray.** John Agar; Cynthia Patrick; Hugh Beaumont; Alan Napier; Nestor Paiva; Phil Chambers; *D:* Virgil W. Vogel; *W:* Laszlo Gorog.

Moliere **2007** Bittersweet costume farce that explores the lost months in 1644 between the French satirist's release from prison and his return to Paris. In order to avoid his creditors, Moliere (Duris) agrees to board at the home of wealthy bourgeois Jourdain (Luchini) who wants acting lessons so he can perform in a play he has written to impress the marquise Celimere (Sagnier). Meanwhile, Moliere flirts with Jourdain's wife Elmire (Morante) and she returns his interest, although she thinks his name is Tartuffe. French with subtitles. **120m/C; DVD.** *FR* Romain Duris; Laura Morante; Fabrice Luchini; Ludivine Sagnier; Edouard Baer; Fanny Valette; Gilian Petrovsky; Gonzague Requillart; ***D:*** Laurent Tirard; ***W:*** Gregoire Vigneron; ***C:*** Gilles Henry; ***M:*** Frederic Talgorn.

Moll Flanders 1/2 *The Fortunes and Misfortunes of Moll Flanders* **1996** Rousing, bawdy TV retelling of Daniel Defoe's 1722 novel about the wickedly seductive Moll (Kingston). Born in London's Newgate prison, Moll becomes a house servant, embarks on her first marriage, is soon widowed, and decides to make her own way (and fortune). She becomes a thief, a whore, marries several more times, and eventually winds up back in prison and a likely candidate for the gallows. But the ever-enterprising Moll always finds her way. **210m/C; DVD.** *UK* Alex Kingston; Daniel Craig; Diana Rigg; Colin Buchanan; Christopher Fulford; James Fleet; Ian Driver; Tom Ward; ***D:*** David Attwood; ***W:*** Andrew Davies; ***C:*** Ivan Strasburg; ***M:*** Jim Parker. **TV**

Moll Flanders 1/2 **1996 (PG-13)** Writer/director Densham takes only the title character and the 18th-century London setting from Daniel Defoe's 1722 novel in telling of spirited heroine Moll Flanders' (Wright) life. Orphaned Moll finds herself working at the brothel of greedy, scheming Mrs. Allworthy (Channing). Her life as a prostitute leads her to drink and near suicide until she falls for an impoverished artist (Lynch) and briefly finds happiness. Wright's heartfelt performance holds everything together (with help from a talented supporting cast) but things get dreary. **120m/C; DVD.** Robin Wright; Morgan Freeman; Stockard Channing; John Lynch; Brenda Fricker; Aisling Corcoran; Geraldine James; Jim Sheridan; Jeremy Brett; Britta Smith; Ger Ryan; ***D:*** Pen Densham; ***W:*** Pen Densham; ***C:*** David Tattersall; ***M:*** Mark Mancina.

Molly **1999 (PG-13)** Sounds like a ripoff of 1968's "Charly," which was more successful and sensitive. Molly (Shue) is a mentally challenged woman who undergoes experimental surgery that leaves her functionally normal—temporarily. She begins an affair with fellow patient Sam (Jane) but, as her brain rejects the operation, she sinks back into the fog of her previous illness. Her brother/guardian Buck (Eckhart) also goes from apathetic to overprotective seemingly overnight. While Shue's performance is fairly good, the horrible editing and ill-conceived storyline doom this would-be drama. **87m/C; DVD.** Elisabeth Shue; Aaron Eckhart; Jill(ian) Hennessey; Thomas Jane; D.W. Moffett; Elizabeth Mitchell; Robert Harper; Elaine Hendrix; Michael Paul Chan; Lucy Liu; ***D:*** John Duigan; ***W:*** Dick Christie; ***C:*** Gabriel Beristain; ***M:*** Trevor Jones.

Molly & Lawless John **1972** Average western, with Miles the wife of a sadistic sheriff who helps a prisoner escape the gallows so they can run away together. Enough cliches for the whole family to enjoy. **90m/C; VHS, DVD.** Sam Elliott; Vera Miles; ***D:*** Gary Nelson.

The Molly Maguires 1/2 **1970 (PG)** Dramatization based on a true story, concerns a group of miners called the Molly Maguires who resort to using terrorist tactics in their fight for better working conditions during the Pennsylvania Irish coal mining rebellion in the 1870s. During their reign of terror, the Mollies are infiltrated by a Pinkerton detective who they mistakenly believe is a new recruit. It has its moments but never fully succeeds. Returned less than 15% of its initial $11 million investment. **123m/C; DVD.** Sean Connery; Richard Harris; Samantha Eggar; Frank Finlay; ***D:*** Martin Ritt; ***W:*** Walter Bernstein; ***C:*** James Wong Howe; ***M:*** Henry Mancini.

Molly Moon and The Incredible Book of Hypnotism 1/2 **2015 (PG)** Based on the best-selling novel by Georgia Byng, this family film focuses on a young girl who finds an extraordinary book that changes her life. While at her local library, the rule-breaking Molly Moon (Cassidy) sees an interesting book by a master hypnotist. She uses to hypnotize people, that takes her far from the orphanage. Traveling to London, she even uses it to hypnotize her way onto a show there, and gains wealth and fame. However, Molly is not the only person who wants her book. A man, Nockman (Monaghan), follows her to London, steals her dog Petula, and uses the dog to force Molly to help him become rich. She is forced to assist him as he steals what robbers have taken during their robbery of all the jewels found in a major bank. **98m/C; DVD, Streaming, Download.** Raffey Cassidy; Anne-Marie Duff; Dominic Monaghan; Emily Watson; Joan Collins; ***D:*** Christopher N. Rowley; ***W:*** Christopher N. Rowley; Tom Butterworth; Georgia Byng; Chris Hurford; ***C:*** Remi Adefarasin; ***M:*** Peter Raeburn.

Molly's Game 1/2 **2017 (R)** Based on the true story of Molly Bloom (Chastain), this drama marks the directorial debut of acclaimed screenwriter Aaron Sorkin. Molly was an Olympic-class skier who moves to Los Angeles after her career is cut short. There, she becomes involved in organizing a weekly underground poker game with Dean Keith (Strong). After learning the ropes, she makes the game her own, begins hosting games in ritzy hotel suites, and earns a fortune. When the FBI arrests her for running an illegal gambling operation, she convinces lawyer Charlie Jaffey (Elba) to represent her. Brisk pacing and Chastain's dazzling performance make the film engaging. **140m/C; DVD, Blu-Ray.** Jessica Chastain; Idris Elba; Kevin Costner; Michael Cera; Jeremy Strong; ***D:*** Aaron Sorkin; ***W:*** Aaron Sorkin; ***C:*** Charlotte Bruus Christensen; ***M:*** Daniel Pemberton.

Molokai: The Story of Father Damien 1/2 **1999** In the 19th century, the government sent suspected lepers to the island of Molokai in an effort to stop the spread of infection. The inhabitants were dependant on the efforts of the church to ease their suffering. Father Damien (Wenham) volunteers to go to the island to provide spiritual and physical comfort and care, even at the risk of contracting the disease himself. Based on a true story. **112m/C; VHS, DVD.** David Wenham; Derek Jacobi; Alice Krige; Kris Kristofferson; Peter O'Toole; Sam Neill; Leo McKern; Tom Wilkinson; Jan Decleir; ***D:*** Paul Cox; ***W:*** John Briley; ***M:*** Wim Mertens. **VIDEO**

Mom **WOOF! 1989 (R)** When his mother is bitten by a flesh-eater, Clay Dwyer is at a loss as to what to do. How do you tell your own mother that she must be destroyed, lest she continue to devour human flesh? A campy horror/comedy. **95m/C; VHS, Streaming.** Mark Thomas Miller; Art Evans; Mary (Elizabeth) McDonough; Jeanne Bates; Brion James; Stella Stevens; Claudia Christian; ***D:*** Patrick Rand.

Mom & Dad **1947** An innocent young girl's one night of passion leads to an unwanted pregnancy. Stock footage of childbirth and a lecture on the evils of syphilis concludes this campy schlock that features the national anthem. Banned or denied release for years, this movie is now a cult favorite for its time-capsule glimpse at conventional 1940s sexual attitudes. **97m/B; VHS, DVD, Blu-Ray.** Hardie Albright; Sarah Blake; George Eldredge; June Carlson; Jimmy Clark; Bob Lowell; ***D:*** William Beaudine; ***W:*** Mildred Horn; ***C:*** Barney A. Sarecky.

Mom and Dad Save the World 1/2 **1992 (PG)** A suburban housewife (Garr) is transported along with her husband in the family station wagon to the planet Spengo, ruled by King Tod Spengo (Lovitz), who has fallen in love with her and wants to save her from his plans to blow up Earth. While trying to prevent the king from marrying her and killing him, Garr and Jones wind up in many goofy situations and wind up saving the Earth from its imminent doom. Uninspired comedy just isn't funny, and the excellent cast is misused, especially Idle and Shawn. Save this one for the kiddies. **87m/C; VHS, DVD.** Teri Garr; Jeffrey Jones; Jon Lovitz; Eric Idle; Wallace Shawn; Dwier Brown; Kathy Ireland; Thalmus Rasulala; ***D:*** Greg Beeman; ***M:*** Jerry Goldsmith.

Mom at Sixteen **2005** When teenaged Jacey (Panabaker) gets pregnant, mom Terry (Ruehl) insists she keep it a secret and put the baby up for adoption. Jacey decides to keep her son but Terry has them move and then claims the baby is her own child. Jacey's confusion leads to her confiding in guidance counselor Donna Cooper (Krakowski) and making another life-changing decision. **90m/C; DVD.** Danielle Panabaker; Mercedes Ruehl; Jane Krakowski; Colin Ferguson; Clare Stone; ***D:*** Peter Werner; ***W:*** Nancey Silvers; ***C:*** Neil Roach; ***M:*** Richard (Rick) Marvin. **CABLE**

Mom, Can I Keep Her? 1/2 **1998 (PG)** Goofy family film features 12-year-old Timmy who's having problems at school and at home with a too-busy father and a new stepmom. But that's nothing compared to the new friend that follows Timmy home—a 500 lb. gorilla. **90m/C; VHS, DVD.** Gil Gerard; Kevin Dobson; Terry Funk; Justin Berfield; Alana Stewart; Henry Darrow; Don Mcleod; ***D:*** Fred Olen Ray; ***W:*** Sean O'Bannon; ***C:*** Jesse Weathington. **VIDEO**

Mom, Dad and Her **2008** Volatile teen Sydney is sent to spend the summer in the country with her dad Ben and unwelcome stepmom Emma when her own mom can't cope. Emma is pregnant with her first child and even self-absorbed Sydney can't help getting a little interested in the coming arrival of her half-sibling. **90m/C; DVD.** Melora Hardin; Brittney Wilson; Paul McGillion; Kyla Hazelwood; Sarah Deakins; Tantoo Cardinal; Jesse Moss; ***D:*** Anne Wheeler; ***W:*** Anna Sandor; ***C:*** Paul Mitchnick; ***M:*** Graeme Coleman. **CABLE**

The Moment **2013** War photographer Lee (Leigh) must go down a rabbit hole of family secrets after stopping by her ex-boyfriend John's (Henderson) house and discovering he's missing. Jarringly out of sequence, her search leads to a psychiatrist (Jean-Baptiste) who helps Lee piece together a disturbing puzzle involving John and her estranged daughter (Shawkat). As straightforward as the story should be, the flashbacks inside of flashbacks destroy any coherence, and the stretch five minutes of one good moment into a 90 minutes of way too many dull moments. A psychological thriller without the thrills. **90m/C; DVD.** Jennifer Jason Leigh; Martin Henderson; Marianne Jean-Baptiste; Alia Shawkat; Meat Loaf Aday; ***D:*** Jane Weinstock; ***W:*** Jane Weinstock; Gloria Norris; ***C:*** James Laxton; ***M:*** Nathan Larson.

Momentum **2003** Although reluctant to use his unwanted telekinetic powers, physics professor Zach Shefford (McCouch) agrees to help FBI agent Raymond Addison (Gossett Jr.) by going undercover in a gang of telekinetic troublemakers. But things get a little blurry when he learns that the group's leader Adrian Greer (Massee) was once part of a government project that went fatally awry at the hands of Addison. Meanwhile another agent (a wickedly fun Hatcher) tails both Shefford and Addison. Created for cable's Sci-Fi Channel. **97m/C; VHS, DVD.** Louis Gossett, Jr.; Teri Hatcher; Grayson McCouch; Michael Massee; Nicki Aycox; Daniel Dae Kim; ***D:*** James Seale; ***W:*** Deverin Karol; ***C:*** Maximo Munzi; ***M:*** Joseph Williams. **CABLE**

Momentum **2015** A crime action-thriller about one last heist that turns out to be something entirely more sinister. Thief Alex Farraday (Kurylenko) is contacted by a former partner about doing one more job together, stealing diamonds. As the heist takes place, Alex realizes the job was just a set-up. Instead, she finds herself in deadly game with an assassin intent on her demise. As she tries to stay alive, she must find out the truth about her situation and those responsible for it. **96m/C; DVD, Blu-Ray, Streaming, Download.** Olga Kurylenko; Morgan Freeman; James Purefoy; Jenna Saras; Lee-Anne Summers; ***D:*** Stephen S. Campanelli; ***W:*** Adam Marcus; Debra Sullivan; ***C:*** Glen MacPherson; ***M:*** Laurent Eyquem.

Mommie Dearest **1981 (PG)** Film based on Christina Crawford's memoirs of her incredibly abusive and violent childhood at the hands of her adoptive mother, actress Joan Crawford. The story is controversial and sometimes trashy, but fairly well done nevertheless. However, it is also so campy and the immortal Crawford/Dunaway screech "No wire hangers—ever!" became so associated with Dunaway's over-the-top performance that it was thought by some to have damaged the actress's career. **129m/C; VHS, DVD.** Faye Dunaway; Diana Scarwid; Steve Forrest; Mara Hobel; Rutanya Alda; Harry Goz; Howard da Silva; ***D:*** Frank Perry; ***W:*** Frank Perry; Robert Getchell; Frank Yablans; ***C:*** Paul Lohmann; ***M:*** Henry Mancini. Golden Raspberries '81: Worst Actress (Dunaway), Worst Picture, Worst Screenplay, Worst Support. Actor (Forrest), Worst Support. Actress (Scarwid).

Mommy 1/2 **1995** Schoolteacher is stalked by murderous mom who'll do anything for her daughter. Mommy McCormack was the original "Bad Seed" child. Filmed in Muscatine, Iowa. **89m/C; VHS, DVD, Blu-Ray.** Patty McCormack; Majel Barrett; Jason Miller; Brinke Stevens; Rachel Lemieux; Mickey Spillane; Michael Cornelison; Sarah Jane Miller; ***D:*** Max Allan Collins; ***W:*** Max Allan Collins; ***C:*** Phillip W. Dingeldein; ***M:*** Richard Lowry.

Mommy **2014** Boozing, fun-loving widow Diane (Dorval) is running out of ways to keep her 15-year-old son Steve (Pilon) out of trouble. His violent and borderline-schizophrenic behavior has forced him out of schools, gotten attention from the police, and put Diane in legal trouble. Neighbor Kyla (Clement) takes an odd liking to Steve and soon begins to relieve some of the mounting tension between mother and son. Shot in a square frame, this challenging arthouse drama from Quebec's wunderkind Xavier Dolan, featuring incredibly tortured performances, is just as unhinged as its subject. In French with subtitles. **139m/C; DVD, Blu-Ray.** *CA* Anne Dorval; Antoine-Olivier Pilon; Suzanne Clément; Patrick Huard; ***D:*** Xavier Dolan; ***W:*** Xavier Dolan; ***C:*** Andre Turpin.

Mommy 2: Mommy's Day 1/2 **1996** Murderous Mommy (McCormack) returns as does her beloved daughter (now rebellious teenager), Jessica Ann (Lemieux). Mommy's on Death Row, awaiting execution after her murder spree but the Mommy-style killings continue. Shot on location in Iowa. **89m/C; VHS, DVD, Blu-Ray.** Patty McCormack; Rachel Lemieux; Brinke Stevens; Michael Cornelison; Sarah Jane Miller; Mickey Spillane; Gary Sandy; Paul Petersen; Arlen Dean Snyder; Todd Eastland; Del Close; ***D:*** Max Allan Collins; ***W:*** Max Allan Collins; ***C:*** Phillip W. Dingeldein; ***M:*** Richard Lowry.

Moms' Night Out **2014 (PG)** Like a Christian Conservative version of "The Hangover," this cultural oddity targets religious, stay-at-home moms with its flat, boring, insulting brand of humor. Allyson (Drew) just wants a night out, away from her husband and kids. She gets a bunch of friends to go out and not-so-wacky hijinks ensue. Sean Astin and Trace Adkins show up for no good reason. Buying into archaic gender roles—dads can't take care of kids!—it attempts to target those who think most modern comedies are amoral and dangerous. And those without a sense of humor. **98m/C; DVD, Blu-Ray.** Sarah Drew; Logan White; Patricia Heaton; Sean Astin; Robert Amaya; Abbie Cobb; Trace Adkins; ***D:*** Andrew Erwin; Jon Erwin; ***W:*** Jon Erwin; ***C:*** Kristopher S. Kimlin; ***M:*** Marc Fantini; Steffan Fantini.

Mom's Outta Sight **2001 (PG)** Substandard kiddie SF comedy exudes cheapness. Special effects and props are bargain-basement material. The story has something to do with a matter transmission machine that turns a sexy woman into a mincing man and makes another (Williamson) invisible. The only redeeming feature is an all-too-brief cameo by Brinke Stevens. **89m/C; VHS, DVD.** Hannes Jaenicke; Melissa Williamson; Steve Scionti; Ariauna Albright; Brinke Stevens; ***D:*** Fred Olen Ray; ***W:*** Sean O'Bannon; ***C:*** Theo Angell; ***M:*** Jay Bolton. **VIDEO**

Mon Oncle *My Uncle; My Uncle, Mr. Hulot* **1958** Tati's celebrated comedy contrasts the simple life of Monsieur Hulot with the technologically complicated life of his family when he aids his nephew in war against his parents' ultramodern, push-button home. An easygoing, delightful comedy, this is the director's first piece in color. Sequel to "Mr. Hulot's Holiday," followed by "Playtime." In French with English subtitles. **110m/C; VHS, DVD, Blu-Ray.** *FR* Jacques Tati; Jean-Pierre Zola; Adrienne Serrantie; Alain Bacourt; ***D:*** Jacques Tati; ***W:*** Jacques Tati; Jacques Lagrange; ***C:*** Jean (Yves, Georges) Bourgoin; ***M:*** Alain Romans; AMG. Oscars '58: Foreign Film; Cannes '58: Grand Jury Prize; N.Y. Film Critics '58: Foreign Film.

Mon Oncle Antoine 1/2 **1971** A splendid tale of young Benoit, who learns about life from a surprisingly compassionate uncle, who works as everything from undertaker to grocer in the depressed area where they live. **104m/C; VHS, DVD.** *CA* Jean Duceppe; Olivette Thibault; ***D:*** Claude Jutra.

Mon Oncle d'Amerique 1/2 *Les Somnambules* **1980 (PG)** Three French characters are followed as they try to find success of varying kinds in Paris, interspersed with ironic lectures by Prof. Henri Laborit about the biology that impels human behavior. Their disappointments lead them to dream of a legendary American uncle, who could make their desires come true. An acclaimed, witty comedy by former Nouvelle Vague filmmaker, dubbed into English. **123m/C; VHS, DVD.** *FR* Gerard Depardieu; Nicole Garcia; Roger-Pierre; Marie DuBois; ***D:*** Alain Resnais; ***W:*** Jean Gruault; ***C:*** Sacha Vierny; ***M:*** Arie Dzierlatka. Cannes '80: Grand Jury Prize; N.Y. Film Critics '80: Foreign Film.

Mona Lisa 1/2 **1986 (R)** Jordan's wonderful, sad, sensitive story of a romantic, small-time hood who gets personally involved with the welfare and bad company of the high-priced whore he's been hired to chauffeur. Hoskins is especially touching and Caine is chilling as a suave gangster. Fine film debut for Tyson. Brilliantly filmed and critically lauded. **104m/C; VHS, DVD.** *GB* Bob Hoskins; Cathy Tyson; Michael Caine; Clarke Peters; Kate Hardie; Robbie Coltrane; Zoe Nathenson; Sammi Davis; Rod Bedall; Joe Brown; Pauline Melville; ***D:*** Neil Jordan; ***W:*** Neil Jordan; David Leland; ***C:*** Roger Pratt; ***M:*** Michael Kamen. British Acad. '86: Actor (Hoskins); Cannes '86: Actor (Hoskins); Golden Globes '87: Actor--Drama (Hoskins); L.A. Film Critics '86: Actor (Hoskins), Support. Actress (Tyson); N.Y. Film Critics '86: Actor (Hoskins); Natl. Soc. Film Critics '86: Actor (Hoskins).

Mona Lisa Smile 1/2 **2003 (PG-13)** Katherine Watson's (Roberts) an art history professor from California who takes a position at Wellesley, an all-girl college of impeccable standing. Watson, of course, wants to enlighten her students to the possibilities that lay outside of their safe, WASPish upbringing and expectations. You've seen the "Maverick-teacher-tries-to-inspire-the-complacent" plot before and really there's nothing new here but the gender. Strong ensemble cast doesn't have much to work with. **117m/C; DVD.** Julia Roberts; Kirsten Dunst; Julia Stiles; Maggie Gyllenhaal; Ginnifer Goodwin; Juliet Stevenson; Dominic West; Topher Grace; John Slattery; Marcia Gay Harden; Jordan Bridges; Marian Seldes; Donna Mitchell; Terence Rigby; ***D:*** Mike Newell; ***W:*** Larry Konner; Mark Rosenthal; ***C:*** Anastas Michos; ***M:*** Rachel Portman.

Monarch of the Moon **2005** Homage to old hero serials like 'Flash Gordon' set in WWII. American superhero Yellow Jacket (Wheatley) is leading the charge against an Axis supervillainess when they learn of a worse evil living on the moon. **98m/B; DVD, Streaming.** Blane Wheatley; Monica Himmel; Brent Moss; Kimberly Page; Will MacMillan; Penny Drake; David Boller; Richard Patton; ***D:*** Richard Lowry; ***W:*** Richard Lowry; Chris Patton; ***C:*** Gregory Marquette; ***M:*** Richard Lowry. **VIDEO**

Monday Night Mayhem 1/2 **2002** Behind-the-scenes look at "Monday Night Football," the unexpectedly sucessful televised game sanctioned by the NFL in 1969 and produced for ABC by Roone Arledge (Heard). TV broadcaster Howard Cosell (John Turturro) makes his mark but comes to resent players-turned-commentators Frank Gifford (Anderson) and Don Meredith (Beyer) who join him. **98m/C; VHS, DVD.** John Turturro; John Heard; Kevin Anderson; Nicholas Turturro; Brad Beyer; Patti LuPone; Eli Wallach; ***D:*** Ernest R. Dickerson; ***W:*** Bill Carter; ***C:*** Jonathan Freeman; ***M:*** Van Dyke Parks. **CABLE**

Mondays in the Sun *Los Lunes al Sol* **2002 (R)** Hard times and no easy answers in this biting drama—often filled with corrosive humor—about unemployment and its consequences. The shipyard where Santa (Bardem) and his friends work has been shut down after being sold to a Korean company. Rico (Climent), the only one to accept a management severance package, opens a waterfront bar where the others hang out drinking, brooding, and unable to find work in a tight job market. Spanish with subtitles. **113m/C; DVD.** *SP* Javier Bardem; Luis Tosar; Jose Angel Egido; Joaquin Climent; Nieve De Medina; Enrique Villen; Celso Bugallo; ***D:*** Fernando Leon de Aranoa; ***W:*** Fernando Leon de Aranoa; Ignacio del Moral; ***C:*** Alfredo Mayo; ***M:*** Lucio Godoy.

Mondo Cane *A Dog's Life* **1963 (R)** A documentary showcasing the eccentricities of human behavior around the world, including cannibalism, pig killing and more. Dubbed in English. Inspired a rash of "shockumentaries" over the next several years. The song "More" made its debut in this film. **105m/C; VHS, DVD.** *IT* ***Nar:*** Stefano Sibaldi; ***D:*** Gualtiero Jacopetti; ***W:*** Gualtiero Jacopetti; ***C:*** Antonio Climati; Benito Frattari; ***M:*** Riz Ortolani; Nino Oliviero.

Mondo Cane 2 *Mondo Pazzo; Mondo Insanity; Crazy World; Insane World* **1964 (R)** More documentary-like views of the oddities of mankind and ethnic rituals around the world. Enough, already. **94m/C; VHS, DVD.** *IT* ***D:*** Gualtiero Jacopetti; Franco Prosperi.

Mondovino 1/2 **2004 (PG-13)** French/American documentary looks at the wine industry in the context of the rise of globalization, marketing, and corporate groupthink vs. craftsmanship, independent thought, and tradition. Thought-provoking, if somewhat meandering and bloated piece also explores issues such as relations between the U.S and France, and America's perceived economic imperialism. **131m/C; DVD.** ***D:*** Jonathan Nossiter; ***C:*** Jonathan Nossiter; Stephanie Pommez.

The Money **1975 (R)** The quest for money drives a young man to kidnap the child that his girlfriend is baby-sitting. Average but Workman's direction is right on the money. **88m/C; VHS, DVD.** Laurence Luckinbill; Elizabeth Richards; Danny DeVito; Graham Beckel; ***D:*** Chuck Workman.

Money Buys Happiness 1/2 **1999** Money (Weatherford) and Georgia (Murphy) are on the verge of divorce when a friend commits suicide and leaves them an upright piano. Their problems crystallize as they attempt to transport the instrument 50 blocks across town. That's a curious premise for a comedy but this one manages to generate some genuine wit. **104m/C; DVD.** Megan Murphy; Jeff Weatherford; Michael Chick; Cynthia Whalen; Caveh Zahedi; ***D:*** Gregg Lachow; ***W:*** Gregg Lachow; ***C:*** Jamie Hook; ***M:*** Jim Ragland.

Money for Nothing **1993 (R)** $1.2 million falls off a truck in the warehouse district of Philadelphia where a simple-minded unemployed longshoreman (Cusack) finds the chance of a lifetime. Indiscreetly leaving behind a trail of spending, he soon has a detective (Madsen) snooping around dangerously close. But he only digs himself deeper by enlisting the assistance of the mob to help him launder the money. At this point the film disintegrates into a limp diatribe on the injustice of capitalism on society's downtrodden. Mazar plays Joey's ex-girlfriend who double-times it back to the fold after his find. Based on a true story. **100m/C; VHS, DVD, Blu-Ray.** John Cusack; Michael Madsen; Benicio Del Toro; Michael Rapaport; Debi Mazar; Fionnula Flanagan; Maury Chaykin; James Gandolfini; Elizabeth Bracco; Ashleigh Dejon; Lenny Venito; ***D:*** Ramon Menendez; ***W:*** Ramon Menendez; Carol Sobieski; Tom Musca; ***M:*** Craig Safan.

Money for Nothing: Inside the Federal Reserve **2013** What is the Federal Reserve? What do they do and how do they do it? Narrated by Schreiber, director/writer Bruce's documentary tries to pull back the curtain on the international impact of an institution about which most viewers know absolutely nothing. Current and former officials from the Federal Reserve debate their critics, detail their history, and offer insight as to how to make sure the financial collapse of 2008 doesn't happen again. While the subject matter is important and the warnings presented should be heeded, the film plays too much like something to be watched in a classroom. **104m/C; DVD.** ***Nar:*** Liev Schreiber; ***D:*** Jim Bruce; ***W:*** Jim Bruce; ***C:*** Robert Richman; Antonio Rossi; ***M:*** Nora Kroll-Rosenbaum.

Money from Home 1/2 **1953** Typical Martin-Lewis musical comedy, their first to be filmed in color. Gambler Herman "Honey Talk" Nelson (Martin) is being pressured by tough guy Jumbo (Leonard) to pay up. So he promises to fix a horse race by using his cousin Virgil (Lewis), a vet's apprentice. But Herman falls for the horse's owner (Millar), while Virgil gets mixed up with a horse-owning sheik (Vincent) and ends up impersonating a famous jockey. Based on a story by Damon Runyon. **100m/C; DVD, Blu-Ray.** Dean Martin; Jerry Lewis; Sheldon Leonard; Marjie Millar; Pat Crowley; Richard Haydn; Robert Strauss; Gerald Mohr; Jack Kruschen; Romo Vincent; ***D:*** George Marshall; ***W:*** James Allardice; Hal Kanter; ***C:*** Daniel F. Fapp; ***M:*** Leigh Harline.

Money Kings 1/2 *Vig* **1998 (R)** Slow-starter is worth the time it takes to get the story moving. Soft-hearted Vinnie Glenn (Falk) runs a Boston bar and serves as a small-time bookie for some backroom gambling. Then the local mob decide Vinnie needs an assistant to help him collect on the bad debts and send in a young hothead, Anthony (Prinze). Vinnie would like to restore the status quo before he heads to a Florida vacation with loyal wife Ellen (Daly), if only Anthony will listen. **96m/C; VHS, DVD.** Peter Falk; Freddie Prinze, Jr.; Lauren Holly; Timothy Hutton; Tyne Daly; ***D:*** Graham Theakston.

Money Madness **1947** Beaumont (Ward Cleaver) plays a taxi driver turned thief in this curiosity. **73m/C; VHS, DVD.** Hugh Beaumont; Frances Rafferty; Harlan Warde; Cecil Weston; Ida Moore; Danny Morton; Joel Friedkin; Lane Chandler; ***D:*** Sam Newfield; ***W:*** Al Martin; ***C:*** Jack Greenhalgh.

Money Monster **2016 (R)** Foster's action-drama is a well-intentioned thriller laden with social commentary, but it fails to come together, partially due to a weak script but also because the often-talented Foster can't quite figure out which story she's trying to tell. Clooney stars as Lee Gates, a financial TV network personality, who is taken hostage on live television by Kyle Budwell (O'Connell), a dangerous young man bankrupted after following one of Gates' tips. Roberts plays the producer of the show, forced to keep it on the air or risk the murder of her number one star. **98m/C; DVD, Blu-Ray.** George Clooney; Julia Roberts; Jack O'Connell; Dominic West; Caitriona Balfe; ***D:*** Jodie Foster; ***W:*** Jamie Linden; Alan DiFiore; Jim Kouf; ***C:*** Matthew Libatique; ***M:*** Dominic Lewis.

The Money Pit **1986 (PG)** A young yuppie couple encounter sundry problems when they attempt to renovate their newly purchased, seemingly self-destructive, Long Island home. However, the collapse of their home leads directly to the collapse of their relationship as well. Somewhat modeled after "Mr. Blandings Builds His Dream House." Hanks and Long fail to jell as partners and the many sight gags are on the predictable side. A Spielberg production. **91m/C; VHS, DVD, Blu-Ray.** Tom Hanks; Shelley Long; Alexander Godunov; Maureen Stapleton; Philip Bosco; Joe Mantegna; Josh Mostel; Yakov Smirnoff; Carmine Caridi; Brian Backer; Wendell Pierce; Mike Starr; Frankie Faison; Nestor Serrano; Michael Jeter; ***D:*** Richard Benjamin; ***W:*** David Giler; ***C:*** Gordon Willis; ***M:*** Michel Colombier.

Money Talks **1997 (R)** Hustler Franklin Hatchett (Tucker) is falsely accused of orchestrating a violent jail break. Ratings-hungry TV reporter James Russell (Sheen) agrees to help Franklin clear his name in return for exclusive rights to his story. The mismatched pair search for stolen jewels, dodge bullets and endure explosive escapes, but this being an action-comedy, there needs to be some laughs. These are provided (intermittently) by the frenzied comic style of Tucker, who easily eclipses Sheen's straight man demeanor. **92m/C; DVD.** Chris Tucker; Charlie Sheen; Heather Locklear; Paul Sorvino; Veronica Cartwright; Elise Neal; Paul Gleason; Larry Hankin; Daniel Roebuck; David Warner; Michael Wright; Gerard Ismael; ***D:*** Brett Ratner; ***W:*** Joel Cohen; Alec Sokolow; ***C:*** Russell Carpenter; Robert Primes; ***M:*** Lalo Schifrin.

Money Train 1/2 **1995 (R)** Snipes and Harrelson are New York City transit cops (and foster brothers) who decide to rob the money train—a subway car that collects all the cash accrued from the transit system each day. To complicate matters, they're both in love with their new Latina partner (Lopez). Lame actioner neglects to have a competent script and the movie is almost over before the train actually becomes part of the plot. Film came under criticism when it was blamed for a series of "copycat" arsons in which a New York City subway clerk was killed. **110m/C; DVD.** Woody Harrelson; Wesley Snipes; Jennifer Lopez; Robert (Bobby) Blake; Chris Cooper; Joe Grifasi; Skipp (Robert L.) Sudduth; Vincent Laresca; Aida Turturro; Vincent Pastore; Enrico Colantoni; Jose Zuniga; Bill Nunn; Larry (Lawrence) Gilliard, Jr.; Michael Artura; ***D:*** Joseph Ruben; ***W:*** Doug Richardson; David Loughery; ***C:*** John Lindley; ***M:*** Mark Mancina.

The Money Trap 1/2 **1965** New York police detective Joe Baron (Ford) lives large because wife Lisa (Sommer) inherited a stock portfolio. When the dividends stop, the Barons are in deep financial trouble just as Joe discovers wealthy physician Van Tilden (Cotten) is a pusher to the Park Avenue crowd. He also learns the doc keeps dough and heroin in his safe so he and partner Peter (Montalban) decide on a rip-off and things go from bad to worse. **92m/B; DVD.** Glenn Ford; Elke Sommer; Joseph Cotten; Ricardo Montalban; Rita Hayworth; Tom Reese; James Mitchum; ***D:*** Burt Kennedy; ***W:*** Walter Bernstein; ***C:*** Pavel Vogel; ***M:*** Hal Schaefer.

Moneyball 1/2 **2011 (PG-13)** Pitt does career-best work in this true story of Oakland A's General Manager Billy Beane, a man tasked with putting together a competitive baseball team with very limited payroll. With the assistance of a new number-centric staff member (Hill), Beane redefines how to assemble a winning organization. Director Miller's film crackles with energy (due to a smart script by Zaillian and Sorkin) in a unique, contemplative way. It's smart, engaging, and fun for baseball fans—and non-fans—alike. Based on the 2003 book "Moneyball: The Art of Winning an Unfair Game" by Michael Lewis. **133m/C; DVD, Blu-Ray.** Brad Pitt; Jonah Hill; Philip Seymour Hoffman; Kerris Dorsey; Robin Wright; Kathryn Morris; Chris Pratt; Tammy Blanchard; Glenn Morshower; Stephen Bishop; Brent Jennings; ***D:*** Bennett Miller; ***W:*** Aaron Sorkin; Steven Zaillian; ***C:*** Wally Pfister; ***M:*** Mychael Danna.

Mongol **2007 (R)** Russian director Bodrov develops a beautiful, sweeping epic, intended as the first of a trilogy covering the life of the infamous Genghis Khan. The story begins in 1192 with the nine-year-old Temudgin (Odsuren) and his father (Ba Sen) and then moves into the brutal and tragedy-laden years that see the mature Temudgin (Asano) develop into the powerful leader capable of uniting the Mongol clans framed by the enduring romance between he and his wife and advisor, Borte (Chuluun). The Mongol leader is treated as a complicated, conflicted and ultimately sympathetic character in spite of the relentless bloody scenes of warring factions. **120m/C; DVD, Blu-Ray.** *KZ* Tadanobu Asano; Honglei Sun; Khulan Chuluun; Odnyam Odsuren; Amarbold Tuvinbayar; Bayartsetseg Erdenasbat; Ba Sen; ***D:*** Sergei Bodrov; ***W:*** Sergei Bodrov; Arif Aliyev; ***C:*** Sergei Trofimov; Rogier Stoffers; ***M:*** Tuomas Kantelinen.

Mongolian Death Worm **2010** Blah Syfy Channel creature feature. An American oil company is pumping superheated water into their Mongolian desert rig site. This revives bloodthirsty death worms that promptly breed and then eat anyone unlucky enough to get in their way. Treasure hunter Daniel (Flannery) and doctor Alicia (Pratt) are around because someone has to try and stop those worms. **90m/C; DVD.** Sean Patrick Flanery; Victoria Pratt; Drew Waters; George Kee Cheung; Nate Rubin; Cheryl Chin; ***D:*** Steven R. Monroe; ***W:*** Steven R. Monroe; Kevin Leeson; Neil Elman; ***C:*** Neil Lisk; ***M:*** Emir Isilay; Pinar Toprak. **CABLE**

The Mongols 1/2 *Les Mongols* **1960** Splashy Italian production has Genghis Khan's son repelling invading hordes while courting buxom princess. Pairing of Palance and Ekberg makes this one worthy of consideration. **105m/C; VHS, DVD.** *IT FR* Jack Palance; Anita Ekberg; Antonella Lualdi; Franco Silva; Gianni "John" Garko; Roldano Lupi; Gabriella Pallotta; ***D:*** Andre de Toth; Leopoldo Savona; Riccardo Freda.

Mongo's Back In Town 🦴🦴 **1971** In this ABC "Movie of the Week," contract killer Mongo Nash (Baker) is called home by his brother Mike (Cioffi), who's being investigated for counterfeiting. After Mike is murdered, Mongo's got gangsters and relentless Lt. Tolstad (Savalas) both looking his way. Field plays the naive woman who falls for the criminal. **73m/C; DVD.** Joe Don Baker; Telly Savalas; Sally Field; Anne Francis; Martin Sheen; Charles Cioffi; ***D:*** Marvin J. Chomsky; ***W:*** Herman Miller; ***C:*** Archie Dalzell; ***M:*** Michael Melvoin. **TV**

Monika 🦴🦴 ½ *Summer with Monika* **1952** Two teenagers who run away together for the summer find the winter brings more responsibility than they can handle when the girl becomes pregnant and gives birth. Lesser, early Bergman, sensitively directed, but dull. Adapted by Bergman from a Per Anders Fogelstrom novel. In Swedish with English subtitles. Currently sold under the title 'Summer with Monika'. **96m/B; VHS, DVD, Blu-Ray.** *SW* Harriet Andersson; Lars Ekborg; John Harryson; Georg Skarstedt; Dagmar Ebbesen; Ake Gronberg; ***D:*** Ingmar Bergman; ***W:*** Ingmar Bergman; ***M:*** Les Baxter.

Monkey Business 🦴🦴🦴 ½ **1931** Marx Brothers run amok as stowaways on ocean liner. Fast-paced comedy provides seemingly endless amount of gags, quips, and pratfalls, including the fab four imitating Maurice Chevalier at Immigration. This film, incidentally, was the group's first to be written—by noted humorist Perelman—directly for the screen. **77m/B; VHS, DVD, Blu-Ray.** Groucho Marx; Harpo Marx; Chico Marx; Zeppo Marx; Thelma Todd; Ruth Hall; Harry Woods; Tom Kennedy; Rockliffe Fellowes; Maxine Castle; ***D:*** Norman Z. McLeod; ***W:*** S.J. Perelman; Arthur Sheekman; ***C:*** Arthur L. Todd.

Monkey Business 🦴🦴🦴 **1952** A scientist invents a fountain-of-youth potion, a lab chimpanzee mistakenly dumps it into a water cooler, and then grown-ups start turning into adolescents. Top-flight crew occasionally labors in this screwball comedy, though comic moments shine. Monroe is the secretary sans skills, while absent-minded Grant and sexy wife Rogers race hormonally as teens. **97m/B; VHS, DVD.** Cary Grant; Ginger Rogers; Charles Coburn; Marilyn Monroe; Hugh Marlowe; Larry Keating; George Winslow; Charlotte Austin; ***D:*** Howard Hawks; ***W:*** Ben Hecht; Charles Lederer; I.A.L. Diamond; ***C:*** Milton Krasner; ***M:*** Leigh Harline.

Monkey Hustle 🦴 **1977 (PG)** Vintage blaxploitation has trouble hustling laffs. The Man plans a super freeway through the ghetto, and law abiding do gooders join forces with territorial lords of vice to fight the project. Shot in the Windy City. **90m/C; VHS, DVD.** Yaphet Kotto; Rudy Ray Moore; Rosalind Cash; Debbi (Deborah) Morgan; Thomas Carter; ***D:*** Arthur Marks.

Monkey Kingdom 🦴🦴🦴 **2015 (G)** A Disney nature documentary that adds a clumsy dramatic storyline to its impressive footage of macaques in Sri Lanka. Narrated with comedic flair by actress Tina Fey, the film focuses on a macaque mother dubbed Maya and her band of mischievous monkeys. The story centers on Maya's lowly position in her band and her rise in the ranks to the top. While the film of the macaques being themselves in their daily activities provides insights and natural laughs, the focus on Maya detracts from the documentary's overall effect. **81m/C; DVD.** Tina Fey; ***D:*** Mark Linfield; Alastair Fothergill; ***C:*** Gavin Thurston; ***M:*** Harry Gregson-Williams.

Monkey Shines 🦴🦴 *Monkey Shines: An Experiment in Fear; Ella* **1988 (R)** Based on the novel by Michael Stuart, this is a sick, scary yarn about a quadriplegic who is given a specially trained capuchin monkey as a helpmate. However, he soon finds that the beast is assuming and acting on his subconscious rages. **108m/C; VHS, DVD, Blu-Ray.** Jason Beghe; John Pankow; Kate McNeil; Christine Forrest; Stephen (Steve) Root; Joyce Van Patten; Stanley Tucci; Janine Turner; ***D:*** George A. Romero; ***W:*** George A. Romero; ***C:*** James A. Contner; ***M:*** David Shire.

Monkey Trouble 🦴🦴 ½ **1994 (PG)** Lonely schoolgirl Birch is feeling abandoned when mom and stepdad shower attention on her new baby brother. Then a monkey trained as a pickpocket enters her life. Keitel is the organ grinder turned bad who must answer to the mob when the monkey scampers off to suburbia. Stakes a lot of its entertainment wallop on the considerable talents of the slippery-fingered monkey, who steals the show. Birch is amusing as the youngster caught in all sorts of uncomfortable situations. Formula abounds, but the milk and cookies set won't notice; fine family fare. **95m/C; VHS, DVD.** Thora Birch; Harvey Keitel; Mimi Rogers; Christopher McDonald; ***D:*** Franco Amurri; ***W:*** Franco Amurri; Stu Krieger; ***M:*** Mark Mancina.

Monkeybone 🦴🦴 **2001 (PG-13)** Weird comedy about comatose cartoonist Stu Miley (Fraser), who must escape from his own comic fantasy world in order to return to consciousness after an accident. Monkeybone, a chimp embodiment of a teenager's libido from his "Show Me the Monkey" animated pilot is the focus of the rest of the film as he escapes from the underworld and "steals" Stu's body to romance his awaiting girlfriend (Fonda). Turturro puts his considerable talent to voicing a monkey, but one-note libidinous simian humor makes flimsy material for a film. Based on the graphic novel "Dark Town" by Kaja Blackley. **92m/C; DVD.** Brendan Fraser; Bridget Fonda; Whoopi Goldberg; Chris Kattan; Dave Foley; Giancarlo Esposito; Rose McGowan; Megan Mullally; Lisa Zane; ***V:*** John Turturro; ***D:*** Henry Selick; ***W:*** Sam Hamm; ***C:*** Andrew Dunn; ***M:*** Anne Dudley.

Monkeys, Go Home! 🦴 ½ **1966** Dumb Disney yarn about young American who inherits a badly neglected French olive farm. When he brings in four chimpanzees to pick the olives, the local townspeople go on strike. People can be so sensitive. Based on "The Monkeys" by G. K. Wilkinson. Chevalier's last film appearance. **89m/C; VHS, DVD, Blu-Ray.** Dean Jones; Yvette Mimieux; Maurice Chevalier; Clement Harari; Yvonne Constant; ***D:*** Andrew V. McLaglen; ***M:*** Robert F. Brunner.

The Monkey's Mask 🦴🦴 **2000** Lesbian private detective Jill Fitzpatrick (Porter) is hired by the parents of missing student Mickey Norris (Cornish). Jill meets Mickey's married poetry professor Diana (McGillis) and the two soon embark on a torrid affair. Then Mickey is found strangled and Jill searches (rather ineptly) for the killer and nearly becomes a victim herself. Who knew poetry could be so dangerous? Based on the 1994 nonrhyming verse thriller by Dorothy Porter. **94m/C; VHS, DVD.** *AU* Susie Porter; Kelly McGillis; Marton Csokas; Francoise Verley; Caroline Gillmer; Jean-Pierre Mignon; Jim Holt; John Noble; Linden Wilkinson; ***D:*** Samantha Lang; ***W:*** Anne Kennedy; ***C:*** Garry Phillips.

Monkey's Uncle 🦴 ½ **1965** A sequel to Disney's "The Misadventures of Merlin Jones" and featuring more bizarre antics and scientific hoopla, including chimps and a flying machine. **90m/C; VHS, DVD.** Tommy Kirk; Annette Funicello; Leon Ames; Arthur O'Connell; ***D:*** Robert Stevenson; ***W:*** Alfred Lewis Levitt; Helen Levitt; ***C:*** Edward Colman; ***M:*** Buddy (Norman Dale) Baker.

The Monocle 🦴🦴 **1964** Steele plays a seductive villainess in this rare, spy/comedy thriller. **100m/C; VHS, DVD.** *FR* Paul Meurisse; Barbara Steele; Marcel Dalio; ***D:*** Georges Lautner; ***W:*** Jacques Robert; ***C:*** Maurice Fellous; ***M:*** Michel Magne.

Monogamy 🦴 ½ **2010** Narrative feature debut from documentarian Shapiro. Bored photographer Theo (Messina) goes into a voyeuristic sideline he calls 'Gumshoot' by taking surveillance-type photos of paying clients. He becomes obsessed with an adventurous blonde, known only as Subgirl (Dohan), who plays to Theo's camera to the dismay of Theo's fiance Nat (Jones) and their comfortable relationship. Since Theo is just another New York guy having an existential crisis, Shapiro's flick isn't anything special. **96m/C; On Demand.** Chris Messina; Meital Dohan; Rashida Jones; Zak Orth; Ivan Martin; Neal Huff; ***D:*** Dana Adam Shapiro; ***W:*** Dana Adam Shapiro; Evan M. Wiener; ***C:*** Doug Emmett; ***M:*** Jamie Saft.

The Monolith Monsters 🦴🦴 **1957** A geologist investigates a meteor shower in Arizona and discovers strange crystals. The crystals attack humans and absorb their silicone, causing them to grow into monsters. Good "B" movie fun. **76m/B; VHS, DVD, Blu-Ray.** Grant Williams; Lola Albright; Les Tremayne; Trevor Bardette; ***D:*** John Sherwood; ***W:*** Norman Jolley; Robert M. Fresco; Jack Arnold; ***M:*** Joseph Gershenson.

Monos 🦴🦴🦴 **2019 (R)** On an isolated mountaintop, a squadron of teen commandos, known as Monos, are part of a bigger rebel army, The Organization. Their brutal superior shows up at random times to put them through drills and bring supplies. The members of Monos spend most of their time guarding a prisoner, an American engineer called Doctora (Nicholson), and have been instructed to not harm her nor their milk cow. As the unpredictable teens engage in dangerous play, the Doctora fights to stay alive. Though familiar, it's a powerful drama with extraordinary cinematography and a tense score. Spanish with subtitles. **102m/C; DVD, Blu-Ray.** Julianne Nicholson; Moises Arias; Sofia Buenaventura; Deiby Rueda; Karen Quintero; ***D:*** Alejandro Landes; ***W:*** Alejandro Landes; Alexis Dos Santos; ***C:*** Jasper Wolf; ***M:*** Mica Levi.

Monsieur Beaucaire 🦴 ½ **1924** The Duke of Chartres ditches France posing as a barber, and once in Britain, becomes a lawman. Not a classic Valentino vehicle. **100m/B; Silent; VHS, DVD.** Rudolph Valentino; Bebe Daniels; Lois Wilson; Doris Kenyon; Lowell Sherman; John Davidson; ***D:*** Sidney Olcott.

Monsieur Beaucaire 🦴🦴🦴 **1946** Entertaining Hope vehicle that casts him as a barber impersonating a French nobleman in the court of Louis XV. He's set to wed a Spanish princess in order to prevent a full-scale war from taking place. However, he really wants to marry social-climber chambermaid Caulfield. Director Marshall was at his best here. Based on the novel by Booth Tarkington. **93m/B; VHS, DVD.** Bob Hope; Joan Caulfield; Patric Knowles; Marjorie Reynolds; Cecil Kellaway; Joseph Schildkraut; Reginald Owen; Constance Collier; ***D:*** George Marshall; ***W:*** Melvin Frank; Norman Panama; ***C:*** Lionel Lindon.

Monsieur Gangster 🦴🦴 *Les Tontons Flingueurs* **1963** Slapstick crime comedy has a dying mob boss asking an old friend to come out of retirement to take over his business and protect his daughter. Rival families don't like the idea and try to take Naudin (Ventura) out, but he declares war on them. French with subtitles. **105m/B; DVD, Blu-Ray.** *FR* Lino Ventura; Bernard Blier; Francis Blanche; Sabine Sinjen; Claude Rich; ***D:*** Georges Lautner; ***W:*** Michel Audiard; ***C:*** Maurice Fellous; ***M:*** Michel Magne.

Monsieur Hire 🦴🦴🦴 ½ *M. Hire* **1989 (PG-13)** The usual tale of sexual obsesssion and suspense. Mr. Hire spends much of his time trying to spy on his beautiful young neighbor woman, alternately alienated and engaged by her love affairs. The voyeur soon finds his secret desires have entangled him in a vicious intrigue. Political rally set-piece is brilliant. Excellent acting, intense pace, elegant photography. Based on "Les Fiancailles de M. Hire" by Georges Simenone and adapted by Leconte and Patrick Dewolf. In French with English subtitles. **81m/C; VHS, DVD.** *FR* Michel Blanc; Sandrine Bonnaire; Luc Thuillier; Eric Berenger; Andre Wilms; ***D:*** Patrice Leconte; ***W:*** Patrice Leconte. Cesar '90: Sound.

Monsieur Ibrahim 🦴🦴🦴 *Monsieur Ibrahim and the Flowers of the Koran; Monsieur Ibrahim et les Fleurs du Coran* **2003 (R)** Coming-of-age story set in the low-rent district of 1960s Paris. Momo (Boulanger) is a Jewish street youth burdened with a chronically depressed father (Melki) and a mother who deserted him. Ibrahim (Sharif) is a philosophy-spouting Turkish Muslim shopkeeper who befriends and adopts Momo after his father kills himself. Ibrahim tends to Momo's spiritual development while the local prostitutes and the girl next door teach him about sex and romance. Duperyon creates a lighthearted, sentimental fairytale about tolerance and spirituality. Adapted from writer Schmitt's semi-autobiographical book and play. **94m/C; DVD.** *FR* Omar Sharif; Pierre Boulanger; Gilbert Melki; Lola Naymark; Anne Suarez; Isabelle Renauld; Isabelle Adjani; ***D:*** Francois Dupeyron; ***W:*** Francois Dupeyron; ***C:*** Remy Chevrin.

Monsieur Lazhar 🦴🦴 ½ *Bachir Lazhar* **2011 (PG-13)** Well-done Canadian melodrama. Montreal elementary school pupils Simon and Alice witness the suicide of their teacher, who hangs herself in her classroom. A desperate administrator then hires recent Algerian immigrant Bachir (Fellag) to take over the traumatized class. Though experienced professionally, Monsieur Lazhar has a lot to learn culturally about a Francophone Canada. He is also dealing with his own grief. An excellent examination of how adults deal with tragedy and children who are forced to grow up too soon. Nominated for a 2011 Oscar for Best Foreign Language Film. English, French and Arabic with subtitles. **94m/C; DVD, Blu-Ray, Streaming.** *CA* Mohamed Fellag; Sophie Nelisse; Emilien Neron; Danielle Proulx; Brigitte Poupart; ***D:*** Philippe Falardeau; ***W:*** Philippe Falardeau; ***C:*** Ronald Plante; ***M:*** Martin Leon.

Monsieur N. 🦴🦴🦴 **2003** An engaging work of historical speculation that wonders if the body believed to belong to Napoleon Bonaparte truly is the corpse of the legendary French emperor. Opening in 1840, when Napoleon's remains were returned to Paris, the narrative shifts back in time to the emperor's exile on the island of St. Helena after 1815. Basil Heathcoate (Rodan) is the liaison between Napoleon's (Torreton) plotting retinue and fuming Sir Hudson Lowe (Grant), the British governor of the island. Caunes deftly keeps the mystery brisk, while Torreton delivers a hypnotic portrayal. **127m/C; DVD.** Philippe Torreton; Richard E. Grant; Jay Rodan; Elsa Zylberstein; Bruno Putzulu; Stephane Freiss; Frederic Pierrot; Roschdy Zem; Siobhan Hewlett; ***D:*** Antoine de Caunes; ***W:*** Rene Manzor; ***C:*** Pierre Aim; ***M:*** Stephan Eicher.

Monsieur Verdoux 🦴🦴🦴 **1947** A thorough Chaplin effort, as he produced, directed, wrote, scored and starred. A prim and proper bank cashier in Paris marries and murders rich women in order to support his real wife and family. A mild scandal in its day, though second-thought pacifism and stale humor date it. A bomb upon release (leading Chaplin to shelve it for 17 years) and a cult item today, admired for both its flaws and complexity. Raye fearlessly chews scenery and croissants. Initially based upon a suggestion from Orson Welles. **123m/B; DVD, Blu-Ray.** Charlie Chaplin; Martha Raye; Isobel Elsom; Mady Correll; Marilyn Nash; Irving Bacon; William Frawley; Allison Roddan; Robert Lewis; ***D:*** Charlie Chaplin; ***W:*** Charlie Chaplin; ***C:*** Curt Courant; Roland H. Totheroh; ***M:*** Charlie Chaplin.

Monsieur Vincent 🦴🦴🦴 **1947** True story of 17th century French priest who became St. Vincent de Paul (Fresnay). He forsakes worldly possessions and convinces members of the aristocracy to finance his charities for the less fortunate. Inspirational. French with subtitles. **112m/B; VHS, DVD.** *FR* Pierre Fresnay; Lisa (Lise) Delamare; Aime Clariond; Jean Debucourt; Pierre Dux; Gabrielle Dorziat; Jean Carmet; Michel Bouquet; ***D:*** Maurice Cloche; ***W:*** Jean Anouilh; Jean-Bernard Luc; ***C:*** Claude Renoir; ***M:*** Jean Jacques Grunenwald. Oscars '48: Foreign Film.

Monsignor WOOF! **1982 (R)** Callow, ambitious priest befriends mobsters and even seduces a nun while managing Vatican's business affairs. No sparks generated by Reeve and Bujold (who appears nude in one scene), and no real conviction related by most other performers. Absurd, ludicrous melodrama best enjoyed as unintentional comedy. Based on Jack Alain Leger's book. **121m/C; VHS, DVD.** Christopher Reeve; Fernando Rey; Genevieve Bujold; Jason Miller; ***D:*** Frank Perry; ***W:*** Abraham Polonsky; Wendell Mayes; ***C:*** Billy Williams; ***M:*** John Williams.

Monsoon 🦴🦴 **1997** Ambitious project from director Mundhra (known best for his erotic thrillers) is set in Goa, India. That's where Kenneth Blake (Tyson) and his fiancee Sally Stephens (McShane) go to visit his friend (McCoy). But in a previous incarnation Kenneth was a lover of Leela (Brodie), who's now married to the local drug lord Miranda (Grover). Their centuries-spanning affair causes the usual complications. Local color is actually much more interesting and the film looks very sharp. **96m/C; DVD.** Richard Tyson; Matt McCoy; Gulshan Grover; Jenny (Jennifer) McShane; Doug Jeffery; Helen Brodie; ***D:*** Jag Mundhra; ***C:*** Blain Brown; ***M:*** Alan Dermot Derosian.

Monsoon Wedding 🦴🦴🦴 **2001 (R)** Outlines the clash of India's traditional culture with the modern sensibilities of the new

Delhi. Aditi Vermas (Das) is promised in marriage to Hemant (Dabas) an Indian computer programmer living in Houston. The problem is, Aditi has a life of her own, including a married TV host boyfriend. When Aditi and Hemant finally meet, tensions and attraction arise as a bevy of romantic subplots swirl like the title's monsoon around them. Nair's engaging storylines, fresh premise and lush cinematography succeed in depicting the turbulent modern life in Delhi. English, and Hindi and Punjabi with subtitles. **113m/C; DVD, Blu-Ray.** *IN US* Naseeruddin Shah; Lillete Dubey; Shefali Shetty; Vasundhara Das; Parvin Dabas; Vijay Raaz; Tilotama Shome; Rajat Kapoor; ***D:*** Mira Nair; ***W:*** Sabrina Dhawan; ***C:*** Declan Quinn; ***M:*** Mychael Danna.

The Monster **1925** This silent horror film has all the elements that would become genre standards. Mad scientist Dr. Ziska (Chaney), working in an asylum filled with lunatics, abducts strangers to use in his fiendish experiments to bring the dead back to life. There's the obligatory dungeon and even a lovely heroine (Olmsted) that needs rescuing. Great atmosphere and Chaney's usual spine-tingling performance. Based on the play by Crane Wilbur. **86m/B; Silent; VHS, DVD.** Lon Chaney, Sr.; Gertrude (Olmstead) Olmsted; Johnny Arthur; Charles Sellon; Walter James; Hallam Cooley; ***D:*** Roland West; ***W:*** Albert Kenyon; Willard Mack; ***C:*** Hal Mohr.

Monster **1978 (R)** Bloodthirsty alien indiscriminately preys on gaggle of teens in wilds of civilization. Performers struggle with dialogue and their own self-esteem. **98m/C; VHS, DVD.** Jim Mitchum; Diane McBain; Roger Clark; John Carradine; Phil Carey; Anthony Eisley; Keenan Wynn; ***D:*** Herbert L. Strock.

The Monster 1/2 *Il Monstro* **1996 (R)** Italian impresario Benigni co-wrote, directed and starred in this broad comedy of errors with Loris as a criminal Clouseau, an incompetent petty thief whom police mistake for a serial murderer on the loose. Cops install an attractive female detective (Braschi) in the sexually strained shyster's apartment to tempt him into striking again. Sight gags aplenty populate Benigni's highly physical performance. French director and actor Blanc is great as the loony police psychiatrist. Italian with subtitles. **110m/C; DVD, Blu-Ray.** *IT* Roberto Benigni; Nicoletta Braschi; Michel Blanc; Dominique Lavanant; Jean-Claude Brialy; Ivano Marescotti; Laurent Spielvogel; Massimo Girotti; Franco Mescolini; ***D:*** Roberto Benigni; ***W:*** Roberto Benigni; Vincenzo Cerami; ***C:*** Carlo Di Palma; ***M:*** Evan Lurie.

Monster **2003 (R)** Charlize Theron plays Aileen Wuornos, the first woman serial killer executed in the U.S., who murdered seven men on the highways of Florida in the 1980s. Focuses on the love affair between Selby Wall (Ricci) and Wuornos. While the film itself has some flaws, not the least of which is portraying Wournos as a victim whose motive was self-defense, Theron's complete transformation for and commitment to the role is fascinating to watch. Her performance alone is worth the rental. **111m/C; DVD.** Charlize Theron; Christina Ricci; Bruce Dern; Scott Wilson; Pruitt Taylor Vince; Lee Tergesen; Annie Corley; ***D:*** Patty Jenkins; ***W:*** Patty Jenkins; ***C:*** Steven Bernstein; ***M:*** BT (Brian Transeau). Oscars '03: Actress (Theron); Golden Globes '04: Actress--Drama (Theron); Ind. Spirit '04: Actress (Theron), First Feature; Natl. Soc. Film Critics '03: Actress (Theron); Screen Actors Guild '03: Actress (Theron).

Monster WOOF! **2008** American filmmakers Erin and Sarah are in Tokyo working on a documentary when the city experiences a major earthquake. Except their video footage shows the disaster was actually caused by some kind of monster (hence the title) but the film budget is so low that only bits (looks like tentacles) of the creature are ever seen. The gals spend their time running, crawling, hiding out, and it's all incredibly boring and silly. **90m/C; DVD, Blu-Ray.** Sarah Lynch; Erin Evans; Justin L. Jones; Kazuyuki Okada; Yoshi Ando; Jennifer Kim; ***D:*** Erik Estenberg; ***W:*** Erik Estenberg; David Michael Latt. **VIDEO**

The Monster **2016 (R)** Kazan gives a fantastic performance as a horrible mother in Bryan Bertino's allegory of addiction. Kazan's mother is taking her daughter on a night road trip to essentially give her up to her birth father forever after addiction has broken their union forever. Into this already-difficult dynamic, Bertino throws a literal monster, as the pair stumbles upon a literal horror on a lonely road. Of course, the black, Alien-esque monster that hunts the pair is a symbol for the addiction that Kazan's mother has to overcome, but she sells it the believability of the moment, making it a simple but powerful horror flick. **91m/C; DVD, Blu-Ray.** Zoe Kazan; Scott Speedman; Ella Ballentine; Aaron Douglas; Christine Ebadi; ***D:*** Bryan Bertino; ***W:*** Bryan Bertino; ***C:*** Julie Kirkwood; ***M:*** tomandandy.

Monster a Go-Go! WOOF! **1965** Team of go-go dancers battle a ten-foot monster from outerspace whose mass is due to a radiation mishap. He can't dance, either. **70m/B; VHS, DVD.** Phil Morton; June Travis; Bill Rebane; Herschell Gordon Lewis; Lois Brooks; George Perry; ***D:*** Bill Rebane; Herschell Gordon Lewis; ***W:*** Herschell Gordon Lewis.

A Monster Calls **2017 (PG-13)** Bayona adapts Patrick Ness' fantasy novel about a tree that comes to life, becomes a monster, and tells a young boy stories as a way to guide him through the emotional minefield surrounding his mother's imminent death from cancer. Neeson voices the monster, who comes to 12-year-old Conor O'Malley (MacDougall) one night while he's trying to fall asleep. Of course, each story is a parable about grief and loss, but Ness' screenplay and Bayona's approach too often tell viewers what to feel instead of allowing them to interpret and feel for themselves. It's well-meaning but a missed opportunity. **108m/C; DVD, Blu-Ray.** Sigourney Weaver; Felicity Jones; Lewis MacDougall; Liam Neeson; Toby Kebbell; ***D:*** Juan Antonio Bayona; ***W:*** Patrick Ness; ***C:*** Oscar Faura; ***M:*** Fernando Velazquez.

The Monster Club **1985** Price and Carradine star in this music-horror compilation, featuring songs by Night, B.A. Robertson, The Pretty Things and The Viewers. Soundtrack music by John Williams, UB 40 and The Expressos. **104m/C; VHS, DVD, Blu-Ray.** *GB* Vincent Price; Donald Pleasence; John Carradine; Stuart Whitman; Britt Ekland; Simon Ward; Patrick Magee; ***D:*** Roy Ward Baker.

Monster Dog WOOF! **1982** A rock band is mauled, threatened, and drooled upon by an untrainable mutant canine. Rock star Cooper plays the leader of the band. No plot, but the German shepherd is worth watching. **88m/C; VHS, DVD, Blu-Ray.** Alice Cooper; Victoria Vera; ***D:*** Claudio Fragasso.

Monster from Green Hell **1958** An experimental rocket containing radiation-contaminated wasps crashes in Africa, making giant killer wasps that run amok. Stinging big bug horror. **71m/B; VHS, DVD.** Jim Davis; Robert E. (Bob) Griffin; Barbara Turner; Eduardo Ciannelli; ***D:*** Kenneth Crane; ***W:*** Endre Bohem; Louis Vittes; ***C:*** Ray Flin; ***M:*** Albert Glasser.

Monster from the Ocean Floor *It Stalked the Ocean Floor; Monster Maker* **1954** An oceanographer in a deep-sea diving bell is threatened by a multi-tentacled creature. Roger Corman's first production. **66m/C; VHS, DVD.** Anne Kimball; Stuart Wade; Jonathan Haze; Wyott Ordung; David Garcia; Dick Pinner; ***D:*** Wyott Ordung; ***W:*** William Danch; ***C:*** Floyd Crosby; ***M:*** Andre Brummer.

Monster High **1989 (R)** Bloodthirsty alien indiscriminately preys on gaggle of teens in wilds of civilization. Even the people who made this one may not have seen it all the way through. **89m/C; VHS, DVD.** David Marriott; Dean Iandoli; Diana Frank; D.J. Kerzner; ***D:*** Rudiger Poe.

Monster House **2006 (PG)** Artistically and effectively creepy outing from executive producers Zemeckis and Spielberg is just the second film to utilize stop-motion animation (their "Polar Express" was the first). Halloween-worthy story follows a trio of kids who investigate the neighborhood haunted house, which devours anything or anyone who gets too close. State-of-the-art technique allows animated characters, including the house, to show emotion and expression while excellent voice work from the likes of Buscemi and Gyllenhaal lend real human talent to the eye-popping visual technology. **91m/C; DVD, Blu-Ray.** ***V:*** Sam Lerner; Steve Buscemi; Maggie Gyllenhaal; Jon Heder; Mitchel Musso; Spencer Locke; Nick Cannon; Kevin James; Jason Lee; Catherine O'Hara; Kathleen Turner; Fred Willard; ***D:*** Gil Kenan; ***W:*** Pamela Pettler; Dan Harmon; Rob Schrab; ***C:*** Xavier Perez Grobet; ***M:*** Douglas Pipes.

Monster in a Box **1992 (PG-13)** Master storyteller Gray spins a wonderful tale about his life, including stories about his adventures at a Moscow film festival, a trip to Nicaragua, and his first experience with California earthquakes. Filled with wit, satire, and hilarity. Filmed before an audience, this is based on Gray's Broadway show of the same title. By the way, the monster in the box is a 1,900-page manuscript of his autobiography and the box in which he lugs it around. **88m/C; VHS, DVD.** Spalding Gray; ***D:*** Nick Broomfield; ***W:*** Spalding Gray; ***C:*** Michael Coulter; ***M:*** Laurie Anderson.

Monster-in-Law **2005 (PG-13)** Awfully nice girl from Venice Beach (Lopez) has a whirlwind courtship and romance with an Adonis-like surgeon (Vartan) but meets with great resistance from his has-been television reporter mother (Fonda) upon the announcement of their engagement. A bevy of battles to put-down or one-up one another ensues. Lopez's character is nothing new, Vartan shows no personality, and although Fonda makes the atrocious behavior of her character palatable, one still wonders why she choose this one-dimensional and craven comedy for a comeback. **100m/C; VHS, DVD.** Jane Fonda; Jennifer Lopez; Michael Vartan; Wanda Sykes; Will Arnett; Adam Scott; Annie Parisse; Monet Mazur; Elaine Stritch; Stephen Dunham; ***D:*** Robert Luketic; ***W:*** Anya Kochoff; Scott Hill; ***C:*** Russell Carpenter; ***M:*** David Newman; Dana Sano.

A Monster in Paris 1/2 *Un Monstre a Paris* **2011** Animated comedy set in 1910s Paris, in which a scientist looking to create super farms tries to find a mysterious creature created by two men fooling around in his lab. It has obvious ties to 'Frankenstein,' 'King Kong,' and 'Phantom of the Opera' as an odd conglomerate of people (and 1 monkey) work to save the poor creature from the local citizenry. **87m/C; DVD, Blu-Ray.** *FR* Vanessa Paradis; Gad Elmaleh; Ludivine Sagnier; Sebastian Desjours; ***V:*** Mathieu Chedid; ***D:*** Bibo Bergeron; ***W:*** Bibo Bergeron; Stephane Kazandjian; ***M:*** Mathieu Chedid. **VIDEO**

Monster in the Closet **1986 (PG)** A gory horror spoof about a rash of San Francisco murders that all take place inside closets. A news reporter and his scientist friend decide they will be the ones to protect California from the evil but shy creatures. From the producers of "The Toxic Avenger." **87m/C; VHS, DVD.** Donald Grant; Claude Akins; Denise DuBarry; Stella Stevens; Howard Duff; Henry Gibson; Jesse White; John Carradine; Paul Dooley; ***D:*** Bob Dahlin; ***W:*** Bob Dahlin; ***C:*** Ronald W. McLeish; ***M:*** Barrie Guard.

The Monster Maker **1944** Low-budget gland fest in which deranged scientist develops serum that inflates heads, feet, and hands. He recklessly inflicts others with this potion, then must contend with deformed victims while courting a comely gal. **65m/B; VHS, DVD.** J. Carrol Naish; Ralph Morgan; Wanda McKay; Terry Frost; ***D:*** Sam Newfield; ***W:*** Martin Mooney; Pierre Gendron; ***C:*** Robert E. Cline; ***M:*** Albert Glasser.

Monster Man **2003 (R)** Horror flick rule number one: don't be the idiots who rile up the disfigured, ill-tempered guy with the big truck. College buddies Adam and Harley, road tripping to reach the girl they both love to prevent her impending nuptials, are just such idiots. Could be enjoyable genre fun if you're in the mood. **95m/C; VHS, DVD.** Eric Jungmann; Justin Urich; Aimee Brooks; Michael Bailey Smith; Robert (Bobby Ray) Shafer; Joe Goodrich; ***D:*** Michael Davis; ***W:*** Michael Davis; ***C:*** Matthew Irving; ***M:*** John Coda. **VIDEO**

The Monster of Phantom Lake 1/2 **2006** Faithful homage to 50s era sci-fi that finds Professor Jackson (Craig) and a group of partying teens and a soldier mutated by toxic waste dumped into the local lake. **97m/B; DVD, Blu-Ray, Streaming.** Josh Craig; Leigha Horton; Deanne McDonald; Justen Overlander; Rachel Grubb; Michael Cook; M. Scott Taulman; Michael G. Kaiser; Mike Mason; ***D:*** Christopher R. Mihm; ***W:*** Christopher R. Mihm; ***C:*** Christopher R. Mihm; ***M:*** Christopher R. Mihm. **VIDEO**

Monster on the Campus 1/2 *Monster in the Night; Stranger on the Campus* **1959** Science-fiction thriller about the blood of a prehistoric fish turning college professor into murderous beast. Will the halls of Dunsfield University ever be safe again? **76m/B; VHS, DVD, Blu-Ray.** Arthur Franz; Joanna Moore; Judson Pratt; Nancy Walters; Troy Donahue; ***D:*** Jack Arnold; ***W:*** David Duncan.

Monster Party **2018** Friends Dodge (Hall), Casper (Strike), and Iris (Gardner) also work as a small-time burglary ring. They decide to hit a bigger mark when Casper's father is detained by a loan shark because he owes $10,000. Iris uses her part-time gig at a catering company to get them in the house of a wealthy family during a dinner party. Their plan to burglarize the house during the party goes off track when the event and the guests turns out to be disturbing and dark. This horror revels in its goriness but does so with a sense of humor and entertaining style. **89m/C; DVD.** Sam Strike; Virginia Gardner; Brandon Micheal Hall; Kian Lawley; Erin Moriarty; ***D:*** Chris von Hoffmann; ***W:*** Chris von Hoffmann; ***C:*** Tobias Deml; ***M:*** Felix Erskine; Nao Sato.

The Monster Squad 1/2 **1987 (PG-13)** Youthful monster enthusiasts find their community inundated by Dracula, Frankenstein creature, Wolf Man, Mummy, and Gill Man(!?!), who are all searching for a life-sustaining amulet. Somewhat different, but still somewhat mediocre. **82m/C; VHS, DVD, Blu-Ray.** Andre Gower; Stephen Macht; Tom Noonan; Duncan Regehr; Mary Ellen Trainor; ***D:*** Fred Dekker; ***W:*** Fred Dekker; Shane Black; ***M:*** Bruce Broughton.

The Monster That Challenged the World 1/2 **1957** Huge, ancient eggs are discovered in the Salton Sea and eventually hatch into killer, crustaceous caterpillars. Superior monster action. **83m/B; VHS, DVD, Blu-Ray.** Tim Holt; Audrey Dalton; Hans Conried; Harlen Ward; Max (Casey Adams) Showalter; Mimi Gibson; Gordon Jones; ***D:*** Arnold Laven; ***W:*** Pat Fielder; ***C:*** Lester White; ***M:*** Heinz Roemheld.

Monster Trucks 1/2 **2016 (PG)** No, this is not a film about rallies with giant vehicles with wheels bigger than your house. It's more literal that that as a monster is unearthed from a dig site that likes to feed on oil, basically taking home in the engine of a truck and, well, turning it into a "monster truck." Tripp Coley (Till) is a high school senior who befriends the monster in this retro flick. Jane Levy, Amy Ryan, and Danny Glover are too talented for the supporting cast. **104m/C; DVD, Blu-Ray, Streaming.** Lucas Till; Jane Levy; Thomas Lennon; Barry Pepper; Rob Lowe; ***D:*** Chris Wedge; ***W:*** Derek Connolly; Matthew Robinson; Jonathan Aibel; Glenn Berger; ***C:*** Don Burgess; ***M:*** David Sardy.

A Monster with a Thousand Heads *Un monstruo de mil cabezas* **2015** Premiering at the Venice Film Festival, Rodrigo Pla's politically-charged thriller speaks to a world increasingly frustrated by the growing divides between the haves and the have-nots. Sonia Bonet (Raluy) is a woman at the end of her rope after an insurance company denies the health coverage that her husband needs to live. What would you do when bureaucracy essentially hands your loved one a death sentence? She takes drastic, violent action, and Pla's film effectively mixes thriller/action structure with social commentary. Nominated for seven Ariel Awards, the Mexican equivalent of the Oscar, including Best Picture (won Best Adapted Screenplay). **74m/C; DVD.** Jana Raluy; Sebastian Aguirre; Hugo Albores; Emilio Echevarria; Ursula Pruneda; ***D:*** Rodrigo Pla; ***W:*** Laura Santullo; ***C:*** Odei Zabaleta; ***M:*** Leonardo Heiblum; Jacobo Lieberman.

Monsters **2010 (R)** Not an alien monster movie for fanboys expecting terrifying creatures and bloodshed since the menace remains mostly unseen in Edwards' allegorical road movie (his feature debut). A

NASA probe bringing back alien life forms crashes and scatters its contents over Mexico. Six years later, the area between northern Mexico and the U.S. has been quarantined as an infected zone as the aliens evolved so Andrew (McNairy) is not happy about escorting his boss' stranded daughter Samantha (Able) through the zone to safety at the border. **97m/C; DVD.** *GB* Scoot McNairy; Whitney Able; ***D:*** Gareth Edwards; ***W:*** Gareth Edwards; ***C:*** Gareth Edwards; ***M:*** Jon Hopkins.

Monsters and Men ☙☙ 1/2 **2018 (R)** When Darius Larson (Edwards) is killed outside a bodega by a police officer, it profoundly affects the lives of others. His friend Manny (Ramos) films the incident and deciding what to do with the video weighs on him, especially after being threatened by the police about it. At the same time, Dennis (Washington), a black cop, is conflicted about his role as an officer and a witness to Larson's unnecessary death. Young baseball prospect Zyric (Harrison) experiences his own incident of police racism that links him to Darius. A sensitive and compelling exploration of race and police authority with excellent performances by the leads. **96m/C; DVD, Blu-Ray.** John David Washington; Anthony Ramos; Kelvin Harrison, Jr.; Chanté Adams; Rob Morgan; ***D:*** Reinaldo Marcus Green; ***W:*** Reinaldo Marcus Green; ***C:*** Patrick Scola; ***M:*** Kris Bowers.

Monster's Ball ☙☙☙☙ **2001 (R)** Georgia death-row prison guard Hank (Thornton) is following in his father Buck's (Boyle) footsteps as both a guard and bigot. His son (Ledger) doesn't have the heart or stomach for the same job and throws up during the execution of Lawrence Musgrove (Combs). Hank flies into a rage that makes him reexamine his life. Soon after, he helps out waitres Leticia (Berry) who, unbeknownst to Hank, is Musgrove's widow. The two begin a desperate sexual relationship that changes both of them. Director Forster and scripters Addica and Rokos provide a well-done, raw, and unflinching story that the excellent cast, especially Berry and Thornton, inhabit perfectly. **111m/C; DVD, Blu-Ray.** Billy Bob Thornton; Halle Berry; Heath Ledger; Peter Boyle; Sean (Puffy, Puff Daddy, P. Diddy) Combs; Coronji Calhoun; Mos Def; Will Rokos; Milo Addica; ***D:*** Marc Forster; ***W:*** Will Rokos; Milo Addica; ***C:*** Roberto Schaefer. Oscars '01: Actress (Berry); Natl. Bd. of Review '01: Actor (Thornton), Actress (Berry); Screen Actors Guild '01: Actress (Berry).

Monsters: Dark Continent ☙☙ **2015 (R)** The sequel to "Monsters" finds American troops in the Middle East fighting a new breed of aliens. A decade after the events of "Monsters," there are more Infected Zones worldwide. When a different type of alien appears in monster territory in the Middle Eastern desert, an American platoon goes on a mission to find them and fight them. When they reach their goal, they learn the real monsters may not be alien. **119m/C; DVD, Blu-Ray, Streaming, Download.** Johnny Harris; Sam Keeley; Joe Dempsie; Kyle Soller; Nicholas Pinnock; ***D:*** Tom Green; ***W:*** Tom Green; ***C:*** Christopher Ross; ***M:*** Neil Davidge.

Monsters, Inc. ☙☙☙ 1/2 **2001 (G)** Sweet-natured animated film from Pixar. Monstropolis is a town that is powered by the screams of human children, which are captured in tanks thanks to "scarers" who invade the kids' bedrooms via their closet doors. Sully (Goodman) is the best there is, with the help of buddy Mike (Crystal), but he has a problem when human toddler Boo (Gibbs) accidentally gets loose in monster town, which is a big no-no, and Sully has to get her safely home. Very colorful and more silly than scary (what's scary is the familiar toddler behavior). **92m/C; DVD, Blu-Ray.** ***V:*** John Goodman; Billy Crystal; Steve Buscemi; Mary Gibbs; James Coburn; Jennifer Tilly; John Ratzenberger; Frank Oz; Bob Peterson; Bonnie Hunt; ***D:*** Pete Docter; ***W:*** Andrew Stanton; Daniel Gerson; ***M:*** Randy Newman. Oscars '01: Song ("If I Didn't Have You").

Monsters University ☙☙ 1/2 **2013 (G)** Not quite as joyful as its predecessor, this Pixar prequel has a smart script, strong voice cast, and its heart in the right place. Iconic monsters Mike (Crystal) and Sully (Goodman) return in this telling of their early days in college, when they first started honing their skills at hiding under the bed and jumping out of closets. They didn't get along in their Monsters U dorm but are thrown together and forced to become friends. And the rest, as they say, is history. It's not the breakthrough work we've come to expect but it's fun for the whole gang. **104m/C; DVD, Blu-Ray.** ***V:*** Billy Crystal; John Goodman; Steve Buscemi; Dame Helen Mirren; Sean P. Hayes; Dave Foley; Peter Sohn; Alfred Molina; Nathan Fillion; Aubrey Plaza; ***D:*** Dan Scanlon; ***W:*** Dan Scanlon; Daniel Gerson; Robert L. Baird; ***M:*** Randy Newman.

Monsters vs. Aliens ☙☙ 1/2 **2009 (PG)** Susan (Witherspoon) is struck by a meteorite, causing her to suddenly grow to nearly 50-feet tall. The army immediately sweeps her off to a top-secret military silo. Susan, renamed Ginormica, meets four other misfit monsters confined to the prison-like conditions—a dimwitted blob (Rogan), a cockroach humanoid mad scientist (Laurie), a courageous fishman creature (Arnett), and a giant snot-shooting caterpillar. They are soon released into society so they can stop the invasion of Earth by evil alien Gallaxhar (Wilson). Smart animated Dreamworks feature disguised as a '50s B-movie, loaded with quick sci-fi references and outrageous sight gags. **94m/C; DVD, Blu-Ray, On Demand.** ***V:*** Reese Witherspoon; Seth Rogen; Kiefer Sutherland; Paul Rudd; Hugh Laurie; Rainn Wilson; Will Arnett; Stephen Colbert; John Krasinski; Renée Zellweger; Jeffrey Tambor; Ed Helms; Amy Poehler; Julie White; ***D:*** Rob Letterman; Conrad Vernon; ***W:*** Rob Letterman; Maya Forbes; Wally Wolodarsky; Jonathan Aibel; Glenn Berger; ***M:*** Henry Jackman.

Monsterwolf ☙ 1/2 **2010 (R)** Syfy Channel horror. An oil company starts illegally blasting in a sacred burial ground in Louisiana in preparation for drilling, releasing an indestructible spirit wolf that seeks an indiscriminate bloody revenge. **90m/C; DVD.** Robert Picardo; Leonor Varela; Jason London; Marc Macaulay; Steve Reevis; John Eyez; Griff Furst; Ricky Wayne; ***D:*** Todor Chapkonov; ***W:*** Charles Bolon; ***C:*** Lorenzo Senatore; ***M:*** Miles Hankins. **CABLE**

Montana ☙☙ **1950** Miniscule-budgeted western filmed at Warner's studio-owned Calabasas Ranch in the San Fernando Valley. Australian sheep man Morgan Lane (Flynn) comes to Montana cattle country looking for government-owned grazing space for his woolies. He hides his profession from cattle owner Maria Singleton (Smith) because he's smitten but a range war nearly breaks out when she discovers the truth. Cuddly Sakall provides his usual comic relief. **76m/C; DVD.** Errol Flynn; Alexis Smith; S.Z. Sakall; Douglas Kennedy; James Brown; Charles Irwin; Ian MacDonald; ***D:*** Ray Enright; ***W:*** Ian MacDonald; Borden Chase; James R. Webb; Charles "Blackie" O'Neal; ***C:*** Karl Freund; ***M:*** David Buttolph.

Montana Moon ☙☙ **1930** Joan is a wealthy, headstrong type who prefers New York society to the family's Montana ranch. Still, she heads west after some man trouble and falls for cowpoke, Larry. They immediately get married, but Larry's the jealous type and thinks his bride is too friendly with a former beau. When Joan leaves in a huff, Larry has a unique idea to retrieve his wife. **89m/B; DVD.** Joan Crawford; Johnny Mack Brown; Dorothy Sebastian; Ricardo Cortez; Lloyd Ingraham; Cliff Edwards; Malcolm St. Clair; ***W:*** Frank Butler; Sylvia Thalberg; Joe Farnham; ***C:*** William H. Daniels.

Montana Sky ☙☙ 1/2 **2007** Jack Mercy's will is very clear—his three daughters must live on his Montana ranch for one year in order to claim their inheritance. But the women, who are half-sisters, are strangers to each other and they anticipate trouble with their forced family reunion. What they get is a saboteur who is determined to drive them from the ranch before they can claim dad's fortune. A Lifetime original movie based on the novel by Nora Roberts. **95m/C; DVD.** Charlotte Ross; John Corbett; Diane Ladd; Nathaniel Arcand; Ashley Williams; Laura Mennell; Aaron Pearl; ***D:*** Mike Robe; ***W:*** April Smith; ***C:*** Eric Van Haren Noman; ***M:*** Steve Porcaro. **CABLE**

Monte Carlo ☙☙ 1/2 **1930** Poor Countess Vera (MacDonald) dumps her boring rich fiance, Prince Otto (Allister), and heads to Monte Carlo, hoping to win big. Shy Count Rudolph (Buchanan) thinks Vera will bring him good luck and asks to stroke her blonde curls. When Vera wins instead, she decides to hire Rudolph, whom she mistakenly believes is a hairdresser. When her fortunes reverse, Vera contemplates marrying the boring prince again without realizing that Rudolph is in love with her (and that he has loads of cash). **90m/B; DVD.** Jeanette MacDonald; Jack Buchanan; Zasu Pitts; Claud Allister; Lionel Belmore; Tyler Brooke; John Roche; ***D:*** Ernst Lubitsch; ***W:*** Ernest Vajda; ***C:*** Victor Milner; ***M:*** W. Franke Harling.

Monte Carlo ☙☙ **1986** A sexy Russian woman aids the Allies by relaying important messages during WWII. Fun TV production featuring Collins at her seductive best. **200m/C; VHS, DVD.** Joan Collins; George Hamilton; Lisa Eilbacher; Lauren Hutton; Robert Carradine; Malcolm McDowell; ***D:*** Anthony Page. **TV**

Monte Carlo ☙☙ 1/2 **2011 (PG)** Bubbly, girly comedy. Grace (Gomez) and her best friend Emma (Cassidy) are forced by her parents to take her uptight older stepsister Meg (Meester) along on their long-planned graduation trip to Paris. While there, Grace is mistaken for a spoiled British heiress and, when she decides to play along, the trio is suddenly whisked away to a luxury time in Monte Carlo. Many complications follow. **109m/C; DVD, Blu-Ray, On Demand.** Selena Gomez; Leighton Meester; Katie Cassidy; Catherine Tate; Cory Monteith; Brett Cullen; Luke Bracey; Andie MacDowell; Pierre Boulanger; ***D:*** Thomas Bezucha; ***W:*** Thomas Bezucha; Maria Maggenti; April Blair; ***C:*** Jonathan Brown; ***M:*** Michael Giacchino.

Monte Cristo ☙☙ **1922** Adaptation of the Alexandre Dumas novel with Gilbert starring as the unjustly imprisoned Edmond Dantes. Escaping after 20 years, Edmond finds the vast treasure promised to him by crazy fellow prisoner, the Abbe Faria, and sets out to wreak revenge on those who wronged him. **100m/B; Silent; DVD.** John Gilbert; Estelle Taylor; Robert McKim; Spottiswoode Aitken; Virginia Brown Faire; Ralph Clonlinger; ***D:*** Emmett j. Flynn; ***W:*** Bernard McConville; ***C:*** Lucien N. Andriot.

Monte Walsh ☙☙☙ **1970 (PG)** Aging cowboy sees declining of Old West, embarks on mission to avenge best friend's death. Subdued, moving western worthy of genre greats Marvin and Palance. Cinematographer Fraker proves himself a proficient director in this, his first venture. Based on Jack Schaefer's novel. **100m/C; VHS, DVD, Blu-Ray.** Lee Marvin; Jack Palance; Jeanne Moreau; Jim Davis; Mitchell Ryan; John McKee; ***D:*** William A. Fraker; ***W:*** David Zelag Goodman; ***M:*** John Barry.

Monte Walsh ☙☙ 1/2 **2003** Tried-and-true horse opera adapted from the novel by Jack Schaefer and a remake of the 1970 film. Aging cowpoke Monte Walsh (Selleck) realizes that life in 1892 Wyoming's Antelope Junction is changing. An eastern company is taking over the western free-range society and fewer cowboys are making a living. Monte has his loyal love Martine (Rossellini) to sustain him, but pal Chet (Carradine) needs a way to support his family and hotheaded Shorty (Eads) has turned to crime. Selleck has become a comfortable old hand at these roles; the pleasures may be undemanding but they're still present. **120m/C; DVD.** Tom Selleck; Isabella Rossellini; Keith Carradine; George Eads; William Devane; Barry Corbin; James Gammon; William Sanderson; Wallace Shawn; Joanna Miles; ***D:*** Simon Wincer; ***W:*** Robert B. Parker; Michael Brandman; David Zelag Goodman; Lukas Heller; ***C:*** David Eggby; ***M:*** Eric Colvin. **CABLE**

Montenegro ☙☙☙ 1/2 *Montenegro'Or Pigs and Pearls* **1981** Offbeat, bawdy comedy details experiences of bored, possibly mad housewife who lands in a coarse, uninhibited ethnic community. To its credit, this film remains unpredictable to the end. And Anspach, an intriguing, resourceful—and attractive—actress, delivers what is perhaps her greatest performance. **97m/C; VHS, DVD.** *SW* Susan Anspach; Erland Josephson; ***D:*** Dusan Makavejev; ***W:*** Dusan Makavejev; ***C:*** Tomislav Pinter; ***M:*** Kornell Kovac.

Monterey Pop ☙☙☙ 1/2 **1968** This pre-Woodstock rock 'n' roll festival in Monterey, California, features landmark performances by some of the most popular '60s rockers. Compelling for the performances, and historically important as the first significant rock concert film. Appearances by Jefferson Airplane, Janis Joplin, Jimi Hendrix, Simon and Garfunkel, The Who, and Otis Redding. **72m/C; VHS, DVD, Blu-Ray.** ***D:*** James Desmond; Richard Leacock; D.A. Pennebaker. Natl. Film Reg. '18.

A Month by the Lake ☙☙ 1/2 **1995 (PG)** Redgrave takes the plunge into romantic comedy of the Proper English sort and glides effortlessly through this slow-moving but often charming adaptation of an H. E. Bates short story. Set in pre-WWII northern Italy, Miss Bentley (Redgrave) sets her spinster's eye on the somewhat wooden, but gradually warming, Major Wilshaw (Fox). Petulant American nanny Miss Beaumont (Thurman) arrives to provide an arresting diversion for Wilshaw, while young Vittorio (Gassman) proves an unwitting pawn for Miss Bentley's romantic game. Lighthearted performances are complemented by glorious cinematography. **92m/C; DVD.** Vanessa Redgrave; Edward Fox; Uma Thurman; Alida Valli; Alessandro Gassman; Carlo Cartier; ***D:*** John Irvin; ***W:*** Trevor Bentham; ***C:*** Pasqualino De Santis; ***M:*** Nicola Piovani.

A Month in the Country ☙☙☙ **1987** The reverently quiet story of two British WWI veterans, one an archaeologist and the other a church painting restorer, who are working in a tiny village while trying to heal their emotional wounds. Based on the novel by J.L. Carr. **92m/C; VHS, DVD, Blu-Ray.** *GB* Colin Firth; Natasha Richardson; Kenneth Branagh; Patrick Malahide; Tony Haygarth; Jim Carter; ***D:*** Pat O'Connor; ***W:*** Simon Gray; ***C:*** Kenneth Macmillan; ***M:*** Howard Blake.

Monty Python and the Holy Grail ☙☙☙ 1/2 **1975 (PG)** Britain's famed comedy band assaults the Arthurian legend in a cult classic replete with a Trojan rabbit and an utterly dismembered, but inevitably pugnacious, knight. Fans of manic comedy—and graphic violence—should get more than their fill here. **90m/C; VHS, DVD, Blu-Ray, UMD.** *GB* Graham Chapman; John Cleese; Terry Gilliam; Eric Idle; Terry Jones; Michael Palin; Carol Cleveland; Connie Booth; Neil Innes; Patsy Kensit; ***D:*** Terry Gilliam; Terry Jones; ***W:*** Graham Chapman; John Cleese; Terry Gilliam; Eric Idle; Terry Jones; Michael Palin; ***C:*** Terry Bedford; ***M:*** Neil Innes; De Wolfe.

Monty Python's Life of Brian ☙☙☙ 1/2 *Life of Brian* **1979 (R)** Often riotous spoof of Christianity tracks hapless peasant mistaken for the messiah in A.D. 32. Film reels from routine to routine, and only the most pious will remain unmoved by a chorus of crucifixion victims. Probably the group's most daring, controversial venture. **94m/C; VHS, DVD.** *GB* Graham Chapman; John Cleese; Terry Gilliam; Eric Idle; Michael Palin; George Harrison; Terry Jones; Kenneth Colley; Spike Milligan; Carol Cleveland; Neil Innes; Andrew MacLachlan; ***D:*** Terry Jones; ***W:*** Graham Chapman; John Cleese; Terry Gilliam; Eric Idle; Michael Palin; Terry Jones; ***C:*** Peter Biziou; ***M:*** Geoffrey Burgon.

Monty Python's The Meaning of Life ☙☙☙ **1983 (R)** Funny, technically impressive film conducts various inquiries into the most profound questions confronting humanity. Notable among the sketches here are a live sex enactment performed before bored schoolboys, a student-faculty rugby game that turns quite violent, and an encounter between a physician and a reluctant, untimely organ donor. Another sketch provides a memorable portrait of a glutton prone to nausea. And at film's end, the meaning of life is actually revealed. **107m/C; VHS, DVD, Blu-Ray, HD-DVD.** *GB* Graham Chapman; John Cleese; Terry Gilliam; Eric Idle; Terry Jones; Michael Palin; Carol Cleveland; Matt Frewer; Simon Jones; Patricia Quinn; Andrew MacLachlan; ***D:*** Terry Gilliam; Terry Jones; ***W:*** Graham Chapman; John Cleese; Terry Gilliam; Eric Idle; Terry Jones; Michael Palin; ***C:*** Peter Hannan; ***M:*** Graham Chapman; John Cleese; Eric Idle; Terry Jones; Michael Palin; John Du Prez. Cannes '83: Grand Jury Prize.

Monument Ave. ☙☙ 1/2 *Snitch* **1998 (R)** Irish-American version of Martin Scorsese's "Mean Streets" focuses on a group of petty thieves from Boston's mostly

Irish Charleston neighborhood. The hoods, lead by Bobby O'Grady (Leary), pass time stealing cars, snorting cocaine, and waxing poetic about their dead-end lives. But when a member of their gang is murdered by neighborhood kingpin Jackie O' (Meaney), Bobby must decide to either uphold the code of silence or avenge his pal's death. Excellent performances, especially from Leary who grew up in this neighborhood. Originality, however, is not the film's strong suit although it's a worthy effort. **90m/C; DVD.** Denis Leary; Billy Crudup; Famke Janssen; Colm Meaney; Martin Sheen; Jeanne Tripplehorn; Ian Hart; Jason Barry; John Diehl; Noah Emmerich; Greg Dulli; ***D:*** Ted (Edward) Demme; ***W:*** Mike Armstrong; ***C:*** Adam Kimmel; ***M:*** Amanda Scheer-Demme.

The Monuments Men **2013 (PG-13)** Convincing the president that recovering stolen works of art from the Nazis is a top priority, Frank Stokes (Clooney) recruits a "Dirty Dozen"-type platoon of scholars to help out, including a sculptor, a museum curator, and an architect. They're given a quick military briefing and a Cliff's Notes-style boot camp, then shipped overseas. The outcome is as confusing and uneven and it sounds. The all-star cast, including Damon, Goodman, Murray, and Blanchett is simply playing make-believe in WWII costumes at the request of their good buddy actor/director Clooney. **118m/C; DVD, Blu-Ray.** *US GE* George Clooney; Matt Damon; Bill Murray; John Goodman; Bob Balaban; Cate Blanchett; Hugh Bonneville; Jean Dujardin; Dimitri Leonidas; ***D:*** George Clooney; ***W:*** George Clooney; Grant Heslov; ***C:*** Phedon Papamichael; ***M:*** Alexandre Desplat.

Mood Indigo ½ *L'Ecume des Jours* **2013** Director/writer Gondry's quirky love story finds the talented filmmaker playing with romance and his unique visual talents in a sci-fi fantasy of sorts. Colin (Duris) makes pianocktails (cocktails that are formed by a piano piece) and lives the good life. When he meets the delightful Chloe (Tautou), he falls deeply in love, before learning that she has a deadly condition caused by a flower growing in her heart. The only cure? Surrounding her with a constant supply of fresh flowers. As you can imagine, the romantic dramedy can be oppressively whimsical and sweet but Gondry pulls it off. **94m/C; DVD.** *FR* Romain Duris; Audrey Tautou; Omar Sy; Gad Elmaleh; Aïssa Maïga; Philippe Torreton; ***D:*** Michel Gondry; ***W:*** Michel Gondry; Luc Bossi; ***C:*** Christophe Beaucarne; ***M:*** Etienne Charry.

Moola ½ **2007 (PG-13)** A truth-is-stranger-than-fiction comedy that's nothing special but amusing enough for a look-see. Best pals and business partners Steve (Mapother) and Harry (Baldwin) both have crumbling marriages and a business making chemical light sticks that's about to go under. Then they learn that dairy farmers are using their glow-sticks to determine a cow's fertility cycle. Soon slimy businessman Montgomery (Hutchison) is offering to buy them out and the guys start spending money they don't actually have, which gets them into further trouble. **110m/C; DVD.** William Mapother; Daniel Baldwin; Doug Hutchison; Curtis Armstrong; Treat Williams; Efren Ramirez; Charlotte Ross; Annabelle Gurwitch; ***D:*** Donny Most; ***W:*** Jeffrey Allen Arbaugh; ***M:*** Rick Marotta; Roberto Blasini. **VIDEO**

Moolaade *Protection* **2004** Eighty-one-year-old Senegalese filmmaker/activist Sembene focuses on the practice of female genital mutilation that still occurs in a number of African countries. In a small village, Colle (Coulibaly), the fearless second wife of a village elder, refuses to allow her daughter Amasatou (Traore) to undergo the purification ceremony that has caused her own lifelong pain. She then offers sanctuary to four young girls also fleeing the ceremony. To defend the girls, Colle invokes the traditional protective spirit of the title so the girls cannot be removed from her care and discovers her resistance is considered a threat to the social order of village life. Bambara and French with subtitles. **124m/C; DVD.** Fatoumata Coulibaly; Maimouna Helene Diarra; Salimata Traore; Dominique T. Zeida; Mah Compaore; Aminata Dao; ***D:*** Ousmane Sembene; ***W:*** Ousmane Sembene; ***C:*** Dominique Gentil; ***M:*** Boncana Maiga.

Moon **2009 (R)** First feature for director Duncan Jones, son of David Bowie, was filmed on the soundstages of England's Shepperton Studios. Sam Bell (Rockwell) is a lonely corporate astronaut completing a solo three-year stint on the Moon for a mining company. His only companion is the snarky voice of his robot Gerty (Spacey) and long-distance contact with his wife and daughter. Then Sam suddenly becomes ill and starts having hallucinations (or are they?) of a cloned Sam. Space Oddity indeed. **97m/C; Blu-Ray, On Demand.** *US GB* Sam Rockwell; Kaya Scodelario; Matt Berry; Robin Chalk; Benedict Wong; Dominique McElligott; ***V:*** Kevin Spacey; ***D:*** Duncan Jones; ***W:*** Nathan Parker; ***C:*** Gary Shaw; ***M:*** Clint Mansell.

The Moon and Sixpence **1943** Stockbroker turns ambitious painter in this adaptation of W. Somerset Maugham's novel that was, in turn, inspired by the life of artist Paul Gauguin. Fine performance from Sanders. Filmed mainly in black and white, but uses color sparingly to great advantage. Compare this one to "Wolf at the Door," in which Gauguin is played by Donald Sutherland. **89m/B; VHS, DVD.** George Sanders; Herbert Marshall; Steven Geray; Doris Dudley; Eric Blore; Elena Verdugo; Florence Bates; Albert Bassermann; Heather Thatcher; ***D:*** Albert Lewin.

The Moon & the Stars **2007** Davide (Molina) is a gay, Jewish film producer trying to get a non-operatic version of "Tosca" made in 1939 as the fascists come power in Italy. Money problems plague the production being filmed at Rome's Cinecitta Studio where Davide needs a fascist patron to make things legit and there are tensions on and off the set. **90m/C; DVD.** *GB HU IT* Alfred Molina; Jonathan Pryce; Catherine McCormack; Andras Balint; Rupert Friend; Roberto Purvis; Ivano Marescotti; Surama DeCastro; Niccolo Senni; ***D:*** John Irvin; ***W:*** Peter Barnes; ***C:*** Elemer Ragalyi; ***M:*** Adriano Maria Vitali.

Moon 44 ½ **1990 (R)** A space prison is overrun by thugs who terrorize their fellow inmates. Fine cast, taut pacing. Filmed in Germany. **102m/C; VHS, DVD.** *GE* Malcolm McDowell; Lisa Eichhorn; Michael Paré; Stephen Geoffreys; Roscoe Lee Browne; Brian Thompson; Dean Devlin; Mechmed Yilmaz; Leon Rippy; ***D:*** Roland Emmerich.

Moon in the Gutter ½ *La Lune Dans le Caniveau* **1983 (R)** In a ramshackle harbor town, a man searches despondently for the person who killed his sister years before. Various sexual liaisons and stevedore fights intermittently spice up the action. Nasty story that doesn't make much sense on film; adapted from a book by American pulp writer David Goodis. In French with English subtitles. **109m/C; VHS, DVD, Blu-Ray.** *IT FR* Gerard Depardieu; Nastassja Kinski; Victoria Abril; Vittorio Mezzogiorno; Dominique Pinon; ***D:*** Jean-Jacques Beineix; ***W:*** Jean-Jacques Beineix; ***C:*** Philippe Rousselot; ***M:*** Gabriel Yared. Cesar '84: Art Dir./Set Dec.

The Moon Is Blue ½ **1953** A young woman flaunts her virginity in this stilted adaptation of F. Hugh Herbert's play. Hard to believe that this film was once considered risque. Good performances, though, from Holden and Niven. **100m/B; DVD.** William Holden; David Niven; Maggie McNamara; Tom Tully; ***D:*** Otto Preminger; ***C:*** Ernest Laszlo. Golden Globes '54: Actor--Mus./Comedy (Niven).

The Moon is Down **1943** Ther German army occupies a small coastal town in Norway, and as winter settles in the occupiers realize that maintaining a hold on a captive population of angry people is not so easy as their superiors told them it would be. **90m/B; DVD.** Cedric Hardwicke; Henry Travers; Lee J. Cobb; Dorris Bowdon; Margaret Wycherly; ***D:*** Irving Pichel; ***W:*** Nunnally Johnson; ***C:*** Arthur C. Miller; ***M:*** Alfred Newman. **VIDEO**

Moon of the Wolf **1972** A small town in bayou country is terrorized by a modern-day werewolf that rips its victims to shreds. **74m/C; VHS, DVD.** David Janssen; Barbara Rush; Bradford Dillman; John Beradino; Geoffrey Lewis; Royal Dano; ***D:*** Daniel Petrie; ***W:*** Alvin Sapinsley; ***C:*** Richard C. Glouner; ***M:*** Bernardo Segall. **TV**

Moon over Broadway **1998** Filmmakers (and spouses) Pennebaker and Hegedus follow the Broadway-bound comedy "Moon over Buffalo" in its evolution from pen to premierel. Along the way we see how professionals try to fine-tune a very average script into a funny comedy, and all the rewrites, conflicts, and jealousies that entails. As the celebrity of the cast, Burnett is at first resented, but winds up being the life of the party, injecting most of the humor, and shows herself to be the real trouper among them. All in all an interestingly tense, and sometimes funny, backstage documentary. **92m/C; VHS, DVD.** Carol Burnett; Philip Bosco; ***D:*** D.A. Pennebaker; Chris Hegedus; ***C:*** D.A. Pennebaker; James Desmond.

Moon over Harlem ½ **1939** A musical melodrama about a widow who unwittingly marries a fast-talking gangster involved in the numbers racket. The film features 20 chorus girls, a choir, and a 60-piece orchestra. **67m/B; VHS, DVD.** Bud Harris; Cora Green; Alec Lovejoy; Sidney Bechet; ***D:*** Edgar G. Ulmer.

Moon over Miami **1941** Man-hunting trio meet their match in this engaging musical. A remake of 1938's "Three Blind Mice," this was later remade in 1946 as "Three Little Girls in Blue." **91m/C; VHS, DVD.** Don Ameche; Betty Grable; Robert Cummings; Carole Landis; Charlotte Greenwood; Jack Haley; ***D:*** Walter Lang; ***W:*** Mitch Glazer; ***C:*** Leon Shamroy.

Moon over Parador ½ **1988 (PG-13)** An uneven comedy about a reluctant American actor who gets the role of his life when he gets the chance to pass himself off as the recently deceased dictator of a Latin American country. A political strongman wants to continue the charade until he can take over, but the actor begins to enjoy the benefits of dictatorship. Look for a cameo by director/writer Mazursky in drag. **103m/C; VHS, DVD.** Richard Dreyfuss; Sonia Braga; Raul Julia; Jonathan Winters; Fernando Rey; Ed Asner; Dick Cavett; Michael Greene; Sammy Davis, Jr.; Polly Holliday; Charo; Marianne Saegebrecht; Dana Delany; Ike Pappas; Paul Mazursky; ***D:*** Paul Mazursky; ***W:*** Paul Mazursky; Leon Capetanos; ***M:*** Maurice Jarre.

Moon over Tao **1997** In 16th-century Japan, a samurai (Abe) and a sorcerer (Nagashima) are dispatched to discover the origins of a strange sword that can cut through solid stone. They learn that the sword was forged from a meteorite, which also housed a strange orb that contains the power to destroy the world. Meanwhile, three mysterious alien females are dispatched to Earth to retrieve the orb, which has fallen into the hands of an evil tyrant (Enoki) who wants to use its powers to rule the planet. Successfully mixes sword & sorcery action with a science fiction slant. Director Amemiya evokes an interesting narrative and impressive fight scenes. **96m/C; DVD.** *JP* Toshiyuki Nagashima; Hiroshi Abe; Takaaki Enoki; ***D:*** Keito Amamiya.

Moon Pilot **1962** An astronaut on his way to the moon encounters a mysterious alien woman who claims to know his future. **98m/C; VHS, Streaming.** Tom Tryon; Brian Keith; Edmond O'Brien; Dany Saval; Tommy Kirk; ***D:*** James Neilson.

The Moon-Spinners ½ **1964 (PG)** Lightweight Disney drama featuring Mills as a young tourist traveling through Crete who meets up with a young man, accused of being a jewel thief, and the two work together to find the real jewel thieves. Watch for silent film star Pola Negri. **118m/C; VHS, DVD.** Hayley Mills; Peter McEnery; Eli Wallach; Pola Negri; Joan Greenwood; Irene Papas; Sheila Hancock; ***D:*** James Neilson; ***W:*** Michael Dyne; ***M:*** Ron Grainer.

Moon Zero Two **1970** Underwhelming Hammer studios space western. William Kemp, the first man to step foot on Mars, is now piloting a scavenger ship and taking various odd jobs. He gets another chance for adventure when he agrees to find Clementine's missing brother, a miner on the Moon who's become a victim of a corporate scheme involving a crashed asteroid. **100m/C; DVD.** *GB* James Olson; Catherine Schell; Warren Mitchell; Adrienne Corri; Ori Levy; Dudley Foster; ***D:*** Roy Ward Baker; ***W:*** Michael Carreras; ***C:*** Paul Beeson; ***M:*** Don Ellis.

Moondance **1995 (R)** When lovely young German tourist Anya (Brendler) comes to an Irish fishing village on a summer holiday, two young brothers, Patrick (Shaw) and Dominic (Conroy), vie for her affections causing a family rift. Adapted from the novel "The White Hare" by Francis Stuart. **96m/C; VHS, DVD.** *GB* Ruaidhri Conroy; Ian Shaw; Julia Brendler; Marianne Faithfull; Gerard McSorley; Kate Flynn; Brendan Grace; ***D:*** Dagmar Hirtz; ***W:*** Burt Weinshanker; Matt Watters; ***C:*** Steven Bernstein; ***M:*** Van Morrison; Fiachra Trench.

Moondance Alexander ½ **2007 (G)** Appealing family film. Awkward 15-year-old Moondance (Panabaker) lives with her eccentric mom Gelsey (Loughlin) and expects to have an uneventful summer. Then she finds pinto pony Checkers has jumped his paddock fence, so she returns him to ranch owner Dante Longpre (Johnson). Convinced that Checkers is a champion jumper just waiting for his chance, Moondance then convinces Dante to train her and Checkers for an upcoming competition. **94m/C; DVD.** Kay Panabaker; Don Johnson; Lori Loughlin; James Best; Sasha Cohen; Whitney Sloan; Joe Norman Shaw; ***D:*** Michael Damian; ***W:*** Michael Damian; Janeen Damian; ***C:*** Julien Eudes; ***M:*** Mark Thomas. **VIDEO**

Moonfleet ½ **1955** Follows the adventures of an 18th century buccaneer who tries to swindle a young lad in his charge of a valuable diamond. From J. Meade Falkner's novel. **89m/C; VHS, DVD, Blu-Ray.** Stewart Granger; Jon Whiteley; George Sanders; Viveca Lindfors; Joan Greenwood; Ian Wolfe; ***D:*** Fritz Lang; ***M:*** Miklos Rozsa.

Moonlight ½ **2016 (R)** Barry Jenkins delivers one of the best dramas in years in this tone poem about a young Florida man's search for identity as a black, gay male. Jenkins story is divided into three chapters, all taking different names used by its protagonist, Chiron, played by three different actors. Chiron is a quiet, young man, teased at school and left adrift by an addict mother (Harris). He finds a father figure in a local drug dealer and comfort in the arms of a male friend. Years later, he's lost and confused about his role in society. Jenkins' film is an elegant masterpiece. **111m/C; DVD, Blu-Ray.** Mahershala Ali; Shariff Earp; Alex Hibbert; Ashton Sanders; Trevante Rhodes; Naomie Harris; ***D:*** Barry Jenkins; ***W:*** Barry Jenkins; ***C:*** James Laxton; ***M:*** Nicholas Britell. Oscars '16: Actor--Supporting (Ali), Adapt. Screenplay, Film; Golden Globes '17: Film--Drama; Ind. Spirit '17: Cinematog., Director (Jenkins), Film, Film Editing, Screenplay; Screen Actors Guild '16: Actor--Supporting (Ali); Writers Guild '16: Orig. Screenplay.

Moonlight & Mistletoe **2008** Passable holiday fare from the Hallmark Channel finds Nick's (Arnold) business about to go bankrupt. He runs a year-round Christmas attraction called Santaville and his troubling news brings daughter Holly (Cameron-Bure) back to try and help her dad save not only his livelihood but the holiday spirit. Arnold is a little grating but Cameron-Bure is sweet. **90m/C; DVD.** Tom Arnold; Candace Cameron Bure; Christopher Wiehl; Barbara Niven; Matt Walton; ***D:*** Karen Arthur; ***W:*** Duane Poole; Joany Kane; ***C:*** Thomas Neuwirth; ***M:*** Lawrence Shragge. **CABLE**

Moonlight and Valentino **1995 (R)** To help her recover from the death of her husband, Rebecca (Perkins)turns to the comfort of flaky neighbor Sylvie (Goldberg), self-destructive sis Lucy (Paltrow), and overbearing ex-stepmother Alberta (Turner). Together they sit around and talk some of the more contrived and cliched "women talk" in recent film history. The finale, a hokey ritual in a cemetery, will have you pulling out hair rather than hankies. Rock star Bon Jovi makes his screen debut as the beefcake (discussion of his butt takes up about two-thirds of the dialogue) who puts the fire back into Rebecca's life. Not for the estrogen impaired. **104m/C; DVD, Blu-Ray.** Elizabeth Perkins; Whoopi Goldberg; Gwyneth Paltrow; Kathleen Turner; Jon Bon Jovi; Jeremy Sisto; Josef Sommer; Peter Coyote; ***D:*** David Anspaugh; ***W:*** Ellen Simon; ***C:*** Julio Macat; ***M:*** Howard Shore.

Moonlight Mile **2002 (PG-13)** Quirky look at dealing with grief in the aftermath of tragedy. Circa 1973, Joe Nast (Gyllenhaal) has attended the funeral of his fiancee Diana Floss at the home of her parents

Ben (Hoffman) and JoJo (Sarandon). Literally at a loss, Joe moves in to the Floss home and forms an unusual bond with these virtual strangers. Joe is eventually aided in his grief when he meets attractive postal worker Bertie (Pompeo) who has experienced similar loss. Great performances all around. Loosely based on director Silberling's experience as the boyfriend of murdered actress Rebecca Schaffer. **112m/C; VHS, DVD.** Jake Gyllenhaal; Dustin Hoffman; Susan Sarandon; Holly Hunter; Ellen Pompeo; Richard T. Jones; Allan Corduner; Dabney Coleman; Akelsia Landeau; Roxanne Hart; *D:* Brad Silberling; *W:* Brad Silberling; *C:* Phedon Papamichael; *M:* Mark Isham.

Moonlight Serenade 🦴🦴 **2009 (PG-13)** Successful financial manager Nate (Newman) is a closet piano player who hears an exceptional voice singing outside his apartment window. The tuneful sparrow is coat check girl Chloe (Adams) who works at a jazz club. Soon the two decide to perform together and their beautiful music extends offstage as well. **91m/C; DVD.** Alec Newman; Amy Adams; Harriet Sansom Harris; Moon Bloodgood; Scott Cohen; *D:* Giacarlo Tallarico; *W:* Jonathan Abrahams; *C:* Eric William Larson; *M:* Joey DeFrancesco. **VIDEO**

Moonlight Sonata 🦴🦴 1/2 **1938** Professional concert pianist Paderewski performs his way through a confusing soap-opera of a film. Includes performances of Franz Liszt's "Second Hungarian Rhapsody" and Frederic Chopin's "Polonaise." **80m/B; VHS, DVD.** *GB* Ignace Jan Paderewski; Charles Farrell; Marie Tempest; Barbara Greene; Eric Portman; *D:* Lothar Mendes.

Moonlight Whispers 🦴🦴 1/2 *Gekko no sasayaki; Sasayaki* **1999 (R)** In this unusual teen romance, a young woman discovers her boyfriend has been collecting her used socks and undies and he breaks down and admits he wants to be her dog. She freaks out and dumps him, but he continues to vie for her affections anyway, and she soon realizes she actually enjoys tormenting him and that they both share a common fetish. So she must either choose a conventional relationship with her new boyfriend or return to a decidedly unusual one with her former lover. Despite what could be disturbing subject matter the film is a romantic drama as opposed to an exploitation film. Japanese with subtitles. **100m/C; DVD.** *JP* Kenji Mizuhashi; Tsugumi; Kouta Kisano; Harumi Inoue; *D:* Akihiko Shiota; *W:* Masahiko Kikuni; Yoichi Nishiyama; Skihiko Shiota; *C:* Shigeru Kumatsubara; *M:* Shinsuke Honda.

The Moonlighter 🦴🦴 **1953** Title refers to MacMurray's jailed character Wes Anderson who herds cows by day and rustles 'em by night. When a lynch mob attacks the jail, Wes escapes but an innocent man is hanged in his place. Wes vows revenge and turns bank robber and his ex-gal Rela (Stanwyck), obviously a match for any man, is deputized to bring him in. Disjointed western story; watch the film noir pairing of MacMurray and Stanwyck in 1944's "Double Indemnity" instead. **77m/B; DVD.** Barbara Stanwyck; Fred MacMurray; Ward Bond; William Ching; John Dierkes; Jack Elam; *D:* Roy Rowland; *W:* Niven Busch; *C:* Heinz Roemheld; *M:* Bert Glennon.

Moonlighting 🦴🦴🦴 1/2 **1982 (PG)** Compelling drama about Polish laborers illegally hired to renovate London flat. When their country falls under martial law, the foreman conceals the event and pushes workers to complete project. Unlikely casting of Irons as foreman is utterly successful. **97m/C; VHS, DVD, Blu-Ray.** *PL GB* Jeremy Irons; Eugene Lipinski; Jiri Stanislay; Eugeniusz Haczkiewicz; *D:* Jerzy Skolimowski; *C:* Tony Pierce-Roberts; *M:* Hans Zimmer.

Moonlighting 🦴🦴 1/2 **1985** Pilot for the popular detective show, where Maddie and David, the daffy pair of impetuous private eyes, meet for the first time and solve an irrationally complex case. **93m/C; VHS, DVD.** Cybill Shepherd; Bruce Willis; Allyce Beasley; *D:* Robert Butler; *W:* Glenn Gordon Caron; *C:* Michael D. Margulies; *M:* Lee Holdridge. **TV**

Moonraker 🦴🦴 **1979 (PG)** Uninspired Bond fare has 007 unraveling intergalactic hijinks. Bond is aided by a female CIA agent, assaulted by a giant with jaws of steel, and captured by Amazons when he sets out to protect the human race. Moore, Chiles, and Lonsdale all seem to be going through the motions only. **136m/C; VHS, DVD, Blu-Ray.** *GB* Roger Moore; Lois Chiles; Richard Kiel; Michael (Michel) Lonsdale; Corinne Clery; Geoffrey Keen; Emily Bolton; Walter Gotell; Bernard Lee; Lois Maxwell; Desmond Llewelyn; *D:* Lewis Gilbert; *W:* Christopher Wood; *C:* Jean Tournier; *M:* John Barry.

Moonrise Kingdom 🦴🦴🦴 1/2 **2012 (PG-13)** Twelve-year-olds Sam (Gilman) and Suzy (Hayward) have found young love and decide to run off into the woods together. This sends their parents and the local authorities (Willis, as the local sheriff) into a frenzy since a storm is approaching little their island off the coast of New England. Set in the summer of 1965, writer/director Anderson returns to form, delivering a truly sweet ode to the adventuresome days of pre-teen life when romance was often as important as life and death. A stellar cast highlights this imaginative script that was co-written by Coppola. **94m/C; DVD, Blu-Ray, Streaming.** Bruce Willis; Edward Norton; Bill Murray; Frances McDormand; Tilda Swinton; Jared Gilman; Kara Hayward; Jason Schwartzman; *D:* Wes Anderson; *W:* Wes Anderson; Roman Coppola; *C:* Robert Yeoman; *M:* Alexandre Desplat.

The Moon's Our Home 🦴🦴 1/2 **1936** A fast-paced, breezy, screwball comedy about an actress and adventurer impulsively marrying and then bickering through the honeymoon. Silliness at its height. Fonda and Sullavan were both married and then divorced before filming this movie. **80m/B; DVD.** Margaret Sullavan; Henry Fonda; Beulah Bondi; Charles Butterworth; Margaret Hamilton; Walter Brennan; Grace Hayle; Lucien Littlefield; Spencer Charters; Henrietta Crosman; Margaret Fielding; *D:* William A. Seiter; *W:* Alan Campbell; Isabel Dawn; Dorothy Parker; *C:* Joseph Valentine.

Moonshine Mountain WOOF! *White Trash on Moonshine Mountain* **1964** A country-western star travels with his girlfriend to the singer's home in backwoods Carolina. When the girl is killed by a lusting resident, all hell breaks loose. One of gore-meister Lewis' excursions into the dramatic. **90m/C; VHS, DVD.** Chuck Scott; Adam Sorg; Jeffrey Allen; Bonnie Hinson; Carmen Sotir; Ben Moore; Pat Patterson; Mark Douglas; *D:* Herschell Gordon Lewis; *W:* Herschell Gordon Lewis; *C:* Herschell Gordon Lewis; *M:* Herschell Gordon Lewis.

The Moonshine War 🦴 1/2 **1970** Before Prohibition is repealed, U.S. Revenue Agent Frank Long (McGoohan) wants to get ahold of Son Martin's (Alda) stash of corn liquor so he can sell the 'shine himself. Only the two ex-cons Long hires to get Martin to do his bidding doublecross the revenuer with some violent plans of their own. Leonard adapted from his own novel but the direction is weak and Alda is hardly convincing as a Kentucky moonshiner. **100m/C; DVD.** Patrick McGoohan; Richard Widmark; Alan Alda; Lee Hazlewood; Will Geer; Melodie Johnson; Harry Carey, Jr.; *D:* Richard Quine; *W:* Elmore Leonard; *C:* Richard H. Kline; *M:* Fred Karger.

The Moonstone 🦴🦴 1/2 **1972** The moonstone is a fabulous jewel from India that lovely Rachel Verinder (Heilbron) receives on her birthday. However, the gem is stolen property and is now stolen from Rachel, which brings Sgt. Cuff (Welsh) of Scotland Yard in to solve the crime. Adaptation of the 1868 Wilkie Collins novel. **221m/C; DVD.** *GB* Vivien Heilbron; John Welsh; Robin Ellis; Martin Jarvis; Basil Dignam; Colin Baker; Anna Cropper; Kathleen Byron; *D:* Paddy Russell; *W:* Hugh Leonard. **TV**

The Moonstone 🦴🦴🦴 **1997** In the mid-19th century, the Moonstone, a sacred Hindu diamond, is stolen from a shrine in India. The jewel, which carries a curse, winds up in the hands of heiress Rachel Verinder (Hawes), thanks to her suitor Franklin Blake (Wise). But when the diamond is stolen from Rachel, police Sergeant Cuff (Sher) investigates and uncovers deception and a variety of villains. Based on the novel by Wilkie Collins and considered the first detective story, some 20 years before Conan Doyle's Sherlock Holmes. **120m/C; VHS, DVD.** Greg Wise; Anthony Sher; Keeley Hawes; Patricia Hodge; *D:* Robert Bierman. **TV**

Moonstruck 🦴🦴🦴 1/2 **1987 (PG-13)** Winning romantic comedy about widow engaged to one man but falling in love with his younger brother in Little Italy. Excellent performances all around, with Cher particularly fetching as attractive, hapless widow. Unlikely casting of usually dominating Aiello, as unassuming mama's boy also works well, and Cage is at his best as a tormented one-handed opera lover/baker. **103m/C; VHS, DVD, Blu-Ray.** Cher; Nicolas Cage; Olympia Dukakis; Danny Aiello; Vincent Gardenia; Julie Bovasso; Louis Guss; Anita Gillette; Feodor Chaliapin, Jr.; John Mahoney; *D:* Norman Jewison; *W:* John Patrick Shanley; *C:* David Watkin; *M:* Dick Hyman. Oscars '87: Actress (Cher), Orig. Screenplay, Support. Actress (Dukakis); Berlin Intl. Film Fest. '87: Director (Jewison); Golden Globes '88: Actress--Mus./Comedy (Cher), Support. Actress (Dukakis); L.A. Film Critics '87: Support. Actress (Dukakis); Natl. Bd. of Review '87: Support. Actress (Dukakis); Writers Guild '87: Orig. Screenplay.

Moontide 🦴🦴 **1942** French star Gabin made his American debut in a routine melodrama about a drunken longshoreman accused of murder. Awakening from his latest drunken spree, Bobo can't remember committing any crime but he decides to lay low on a bait boat with his derelict friend Tiny (Mitchell) who promises to keep quiet. Then Bobo saves waitress Anna (Lupino) from a suicide attempt, invites her onboard, and three's a crowd. Especially when Anna is able to figure out who really committed the crime. **94m/B; DVD.** Jean Gabin; Thomas Mitchell; Ida Lupino; Claude Rains; Jerome Cowan; Ralph Byrd; Victor Sen Yung; *D:* Archie Mayo; *W:* John O'Hara; *C:* Charles G. Clarke.

Moonwalkers 🦴 1/2 **2016 (R)** There are still a surprising number of people convinced that the United States faked the moon landing, possibly even with the help of filmmaker Stanley Kubrick. This comedy uses that conspiracy theory as a jumping off point for a character piece centering on CIA agent Kidman (Perlman) and a rock band manager named Jonny (Grint) who work together to stage the moon landing. To be blunt, the result is a comedy that's just not funny enough. There's a shocking degree of violence too, especially in the climax, and the whole thing just needs to be sent into a black hole. **107m/C; DVD, Blu-Ray.** Rupert Grint; Ron Perlman; Robert Sheehan; Stephen Campbell Moore; Kevin Bishop; *D:* Antoine Bardou-Jacquet; *W:* Dean Craig; *C:* Glynn Speeckaert.

Mooz-Lum 🦴🦴 **2010 (PG-13)** Melodramatic indie with an impressive performance by Ross. African-American Tariq was raised by his devout Muslim father Hassan, whose fundamentalism has alienated his family. Tariq reinvents himself as a college freshman and wants to have a secular identity but he becomes a victim of anti-Muslim rage as 9/11 unfolds. **95m/C; DVD.** Evan Ross; Roger Guenveur; Nia Long; Kimberley Drummond; Danny Glover; Dorian Missick; Summer Bishil; *D:* Qasim Basir; *W:* Qasim Basir; *C:* Ian Dudley; *M:* Misha Segal.

Mope 🦴 1/2 **2019** Steven Clancy Hill (Stewart-Jarrett) is an extra in porn films under the name Steven Driver. He lives and works with his best friend/fellow porn extra Hebert Hin Wong, known in porn as Tom Dong (Sry). Though both Steven and Herbert are not great actors, Steven believes he will be the biggest adult film actor in history while Herbert is more aware of his shortcomings. Steven's delusions ultimately lead to acts of violence. Based on true events, it does not shy away from the facts of the real story. But it's lackluster and not worth viewing all the distastefulness. **105m/C; DVD.** Nathan Stewart-Jarrett; Kelly Sry; Brian Huskey; Max Adler; David Arquette; *D:* Lucas Heyne; *W:* Lucas Heyne; Zack Newkirk; *C:* Bryan Koss; *M:* Jonathan Snipes.

Moran of the Lady Letty 🦴🦴 1/2 **1922** Seaweed saga of Ramon Laredo (Valentino), a high society guy who's shanghaied aboard a pirate barge. When the salty dogs capture Moran (Dalton) from the floundering Lady Letty, Ramon is smitten with the pretty tomboy and battles courageously to prevent the pirates from selling her as a slave. Excellent fight scenes with much hotstepping over gangplanks and swinging from masts, with a 60-foot death dive from above. Little-known Dalton was a celluloid fave in the 'teens and twenties and Valentino is atypically cast as a man's man. **71m/B; Silent; DVD.** Dorothy Dalton; Rudolph Valentino; Charles Brinley; Walter Long; Emil Jorgenson; *D:* George Melford; *W:* Monte Katterjohn; *C:* William Marshall.

More 🦴🦴 1/2 **1969** Smells like teen angst in the '60s when a German college grad falls for an American in Paris, to the tune of sex, drugs, and Pink Floyd. Schroeder's first effort as director, it's definitely a '60s pic. In French with English subtitles. **110m/C; VHS, DVD.** Mimsy Farmer; Klaus Grunberg; Heinz Engelmann; Michel Chanderli; *D:* Barbet Schroeder; *C:* Nestor Almendros.

More American Graffiti 🦴 1/2 **1979 (PG)** Sequel to 1973's acclaimed '50s homage "American Graffiti" charts various characters' experiences in the more radical '60s. George Lucas didn't direct, Richard Dreyfuss didn't reprise. Ron Howard doesn't direct, he acts. B.W.L. Norton doesn't direct either, though he's credited. Pass on this one and have that root canal done instead. **111m/C; VHS, DVD, Blu-Ray.** Candy Clark; Bo Hopkins; Ron Howard; Paul LeMat; MacKenzie Phillips; Charles Martin Smith; Anna Bjorn; Richard Bradford; Cindy Williams; Scott Glenn; Delroy Lindo; James Houghton; John Lansing; Mary Kay Place; Rosanna Arquette; Jon(athan) Gries; Naomi Judd; Harrison Ford; *D:* Bill W.L. Norton; *W:* Gloria Katz; Willard Huyck; *C:* Caleb Deschanel.

More Dead Than Alive 🦴🦴 1/2 **1968** Gunslinger Cain (Walker) is released from an 18-year prison stint and is soon taking his sharpshooter credentials to a cheap wild west show run by Ruffalo (Price). But Cain's presence upsets former headliner, hot-headed young shooter Billy (Hampton). Surprise ending. **101m/C; DVD, Blu-Ray.** Clint Walker; Vincent Price; Anne Francis; Paul Hampton; Mike Henry; Craig Littler; *D:* Robert Sparr; *W:* George Schenck; *C:* Jacques "Jack" Marquette; *M:* Philip Springer.

More Dogs Than Bones 🦴 **2000 (R)** Crook Victoria (Ruehl) is on the lam, so she decides to hide $1 million in the luggage of Indian tourist Raj (Girafi), who's on his way to L.A. When she sends her boys (Mantegna, Hipp) to retrieve the loot, they discover Raj is staying at his nephew Andy's (Naidu) apartment and Andy's dog has buried the bag—only no one knows where. Too bad the pooch couldn't have buried this movie as well. **92m/C; VHS, DVD.** Mercedes Ruehl; Joe Mantegna; Paul Hipp; Peter Coyote; Chaim Girafi; Ajay Naidu; Debi Mazar; Louise Fletcher; DB Woodside; Whoopi Goldberg; Kevin Weisman; Eddie Kaye Thomas; *D:* Michael Browning; *W:* Michael Browning.

More Money More Family 🦴🦴 **2015 (R)** Two cousins trick their family into getting back together through a false promise of money in this comedy. After their uncle dies and no one comes to his funeral, cousins Rudy (Lil Duval) and Shawn (Silkk Tha Shocker) take action to bring their estranged mothers back together. The formulate a scheme that involves telling their whole family that they won the lottery and are throwing a party to give out the money. While they hope their mothers will come and make peace, they know plan could backfire and further tear the family apart. **90m/C; DVD, Streaming, Download.** Michael Blackson; Bob Brusco; Lil Duval; Johnathan Martin, Jr.; silkk the Shocker; *D:* Michael Ryan; *W:* silkk the Shocker; Jeff Farley; *C:* Christy Koch. **VIDEO**

More of Me 🦴🦴 **2007** In this domestic comedy, overwhelmed wife and mom Alice (Shannon) splits into three personalities while trying to take care of her husband (Weber), kids, and be an environmental activist. But when Alice realizes that her alter egos are doing things she doesn't approve of, she decides one of her is all that's needed. **90m/C; DVD.** Molly Shannon; Steven Weber; Jake Beale; Abigail Falle; *D:* Daisy von Scherler Mayer; *W:* Kelli Pryor; *C:* Rhett Morita; *M:* Jeff Cardoni. **CABLE**

More Sex and the Single Mom 🦴🦴 **2005** In this sequel to 2003's "Sex and the Single Mom," Jess is engaged to lawyer Steve and raising the young son fathered by Alex Lofton, who's just come back into her life without knowing they had a child together. Her 18-year-old college-bound daughter Sara is still worrying about her own sex life as Jess struggles to impart some parental wisdom based on experience.

89m/C; DVD. Gail O'Grady; Chelsea Hobbs; Grant Show; Rick Roberts; Barbara Gordon; Lucas Bryant; Larissa Laskin; ***D:*** Don McBrearty; ***W:*** Judith Paige Mitchell; ***C:*** Rhett Morita; ***M:*** James Levine. **CABLE**

More Than a Game ½ **2008 (PG)** Would anyone really be interested in Belman's familiar basketball documentary (no matter how well-done) if LeBron James wasn't an NBA superstar? The true story focuses on five basketball players at St. Vincent-St. Mary High School in Akron, Ohio, who played for coach Dru Joyce II since grade school. Over a six-year period James becomes a teen superstar with solid NBA prospects who, along with his teammates Romeo Travis, Sian Cotton, Dru Joyce III, and Willie McGee, bulldozed their competition to the 2003 High School National Championship amidst various personal and professional dramas. **105m/C; DVD.** LeBron James; Dru Joyce; Romeo Travis; Sian Cotton; Willie McGee; ***D:*** Kristopher Belman; ***W:*** Kristopher Belman; Brad Hogan; ***C:*** Kristopher Belman; ***M:*** Harvey W. Mason.

More Than a Miracle ½ **1967** Slow-moving Cinderella fantasy. Spanish prince Rodrigo (Sharif) is expected to marry one of the princesses his mother (Del Rio) has chosen for him. Instead, he winds up at a monastery, taking advice about true love from Brother Joseph (French), who gives him some magical hokum about his ideal woman. Of course, this turns out to be beautiful, lusty peasant Isabella (Loren) and there's more nonsense with witches and a spell that turns out wrong. Beautiful scenery and we're not just talking about Loren. Italian with subtitles. **110m/C; DVD.** *IT* Sophia Loren; Omar Sharif; Dolores Del Rio; Leslie French; Georges Wilson; ***D:*** Francesco Rosi; ***W:*** Francesco Rosi; Giuseppe Patroni-Griffi; Raffaele La Capria; Tonino Guerra; ***C:*** Pasqualino De Santis; ***M:*** Piero Piccioni.

More Than A Secretary **1936** Arthur shines through the dated premise. Secretarial agency co-owner Carol (Arthur) heads to the offices of health magazine publisher Fred Gilbert (Brent) to see why he can't keep an assistant (because he's pompous and obsessive). She's mistaken for his latest hire and takes the job when she's suddenly smitten. The magazine is in trouble because it's boring and Carol manages to liven that up too. **77m/B; DVD.** Jean Arthur; George Brent; Lionel Stander; Ruth Donnelly; Reginald Denny; Dorothea Kent; ***D:*** Alfred E. Green; ***W:*** Lynn Starling; Dale Van Every; ***C:*** Henry Freulich.

More Than Friends **1978** An ABC TV movie. Alan (Reiner) and Matty (Marshall) grew up together in the Bronx in the late 1950s, sharing many awkward moments. Alan stays in New York to become a writer while Matty heads to Hollywood to become an actress. They keep in touch and, over the years, begin an on-and-off romance but can never seem to get their feelings in sync. Reiner and Marshall were married at the time the pic was filmed. **96m/C; DVD.** Rob Reiner; Penny Marshall; Dabney Coleman; Howard Hesseman; Kay Medford; Claudette Nevins; Michael McKean; Joe Pantoliano; ***D:*** James Burrows; ***W:*** Rob Reiner; Phil Mishkin; ***C:*** Sol Negrin; ***M:*** Fred Karlin. **TV**

The More the Merrier **1943** Likeable romantic comedy in which working girl must share apartment with two bachelors in Washington, D.C., during WWII. Arthur is especially endearing as a young woman in male company. **104m/B; VHS, DVD; Open Captioned.** Joel McCrea; Jean Arthur; Charles Coburn; Richard Gaines; Bruce Bennett; Ann Savage; Ann Doran; Frank Tully; Grady Sutton; ***D:*** George Stevens. Oscars '43: Support. Actor (Coburn); N.Y. Film Critics '43: Director (Stevens).

More Wild, Wild West **1980** Another feature-length continuation of the satirical TV western series, with Winters taking on Conrad and Martin. **94m/C; VHS, DVD.** Robert Conrad; Ross Martin; Jonathan Winters; Victor Buono; ***D:*** Burt Kennedy. **TV**

Morgan **2012** A predictable romance wrapped around a complex story of disability. Morgan Oliver (Minaya) is paralyzed in a bicycle accident while training for a race. He meets sports fan Dan (Kesy), who helps him start training again. Morgan gets obsessive, feeling he has something to prove in-and-out of the bedroom, and the new lovers find their relationship in trouble. **89m/C; DVD.** Leo Minaya; Jack Kesy; Benjamin Budd; Madalyn McKay; ***D:*** Michael D. Akers; ***W:*** Michael D. Akers; Sandon Berg; ***C:*** Chris Brown; ***M:*** Ryan Rapsys. **VIDEO**

Morgan ½ **2016 (R)** A science fiction "what if" centering on the viability of humanoids in a not-so-distant future. Morgan (Taylor-Joy) is an artificially created humanoid who has grown into a teenager. Created and owned by company who keeps her at a remote research facility, Morgan looks and acts human with her caretakers but her future is called into question when she stabs one of them in anger. The company sends risk management consultant Lee Weathers (Mara) to decide Morgan's fate. What she learns there makes termination a difficult decision, and the experience has a profound impact on Lee's career and future. **92m/C; DVD, Blu-Ray, Streaming, Download.** Kate Mara; Anya Taylor-Joy; Rose Leslie; Michael Yare; Toby Jones; ***D:*** Luke Scott; ***W:*** Seth W. Owen; ***C:*** Mark Patten; ***M:*** Max Richter.

Morgan: A Suitable Case for Treatment ½ *Morgan!; A Suitable Case for Treatment* **1966** Offbeat comedy in which deranged artist copes with divorce by donning ape suit. Some laughs ensue. Based on David Mercer's play. **93m/B; VHS, DVD.** *GB* Vanessa Redgrave; David Warner; Robert Stephens; Irene Handl; Bernard Bresslaw; Arthur Mullard; Newton Blick; Nan Munro; Graham Crowden; John Rae; Peter Collingwood; Edward Fox; ***D:*** Karel Reisz; ***W:*** David Mercer; ***C:*** Larry Pizer; ***M:*** John Dankworth. British Acad. '66: Screenplay; Cannes '66: Actress (Redgrave).

Morgan Stewart's Coming Home *Home Front* **1987 (PG-13)** When Dad needs a good family image in his political race, he brings Morgan home from boarding school. Fortunately, Morgan can see how his parents are using him and he doesn't approve at all. He decides to turn his family's life upside down while pursuing the love of his life. **96m/C; VHS, DVD.** Jon Cryer; Lynn Redgrave; Nicholas Pryor; Viveka Davis; Paul Gleason; Andrew Duncan; Savely Kramorov; John David (J.D.) Cullum; Robert Sedgwick; Waweru Njenga; Sudhir Rad; ***D:*** Alan Smithee; ***M:*** Peter Bernstein.

Morgan's Ferry **1999 (PG-13)** Kinder, gentler "Desperate Hours" has three escaped cons, Sam (Zane), Monroe (Rollins), and Darcy (Galecki) happen upon the modest cottage of spinster Vonee (McGillis) and hold her hostage. Not only is she not afraid of the trio, but she falls in love with charming, sensitive Sam and hides him when his buddies decide to split. Interesting cast and nice twist on the escaped-cons-take-hostage story make this one better than it should be. **91m/C; VHS, DVD.** Billy Zane; Kelly McGillis; Henry Rollins; Johnny Galecki; Roscoe Lee Browne; Muse Watson; ***D:*** Sam Pillsbury; ***C:*** Johnny E. Jensen; ***M:*** Mader.

The Morgue ½ **2007 (R)** Margo's job involves vacuuming the local morgue and handing the night watchman his nightly whiskey ration. A family stops by and asks to use the bathroom (yes, morgues have bathrooms), and following close behind is a group of heavily injured men. Then the power goes out as they all get stalked and killed by a shadowy figure. For poor Margo, it's all in a day's work. **84m/C; DVD.** Bill Cobbs; Heather Donahue; Googy Gress; Michael Raye; Lisa Crilley; Chris Devlin; Taylor Lipman; Brady Matthews; Fred Ochs; Brandon Quinn; Sammy Sheik; Chris Torres; ***D:*** Halder Gomes; Gerson Sanginitte; ***W:*** Najla Ann Al-Doori; Andrew Pletcher; ***C:*** Jack Anderson; ***M:*** Perry La Marca. **VIDEO**

Morituri *Saboteur: Code Name Morituri; The Saboteur* **1965** Gripping wartime drama in which an Allied spy tries to persuade German gunboat captain to surrender his vessel. Brando is—no surprise—excellent. **123m/C; VHS, DVD, Blu-Ray.** Marlon Brando; Yul Brynner; Trevor Howard; Janet Margolin; Wally Cox; William Redfield; ***D:*** Bernhard Wicki; ***W:*** Daniel Taradash; ***C:*** Conrad L. Hall; ***M:*** Jerry Goldsmith.

A Mormon Maid ½ **1917** Young woman and her family, after being saved from an Indian attack by a Mormon group, come to live among them without converting to their beliefs. Considered a shocking expose of controversial Mormon practices, including polygamy. **78m/B; Silent; DVD.** Mae Murray; Frank Borzage; Hobart Bosworth; Noah Beery, Sr.; ***D:*** Robert Z. Leonard.

Morning **2010 (R)** Minimalist and raw exploration of parental grief is the first feature for Orser, who stars with wife Tripplehorn as upper-middle-class Californians, Mark and Alice. After their only child drowns in the family pool , Mark drinks, eats junk food, and demolishes vases of flowers with a golf club. The equally anguished Alice flees to a hotel, unable to eat or sleep and delusional. The supporting players are effective in their brief screen time but the fim is ultimately exhausting. **95m/C; DVD.** Leland Orser; Jeanne Tripplehorn; Laura Linney; Elliott Gould; Julie White; Kyle Chandler; Jason Ritter; Charlie McDermott; ***D:*** Leland Orser; ***W:*** Leland Orser; ***C:*** Paula Huidobro; ***M:*** Chris Douridas.

The Morning After **1986 (R)** A predictable suspense-thriller about an alcoholic actress who wakes up one morning with a corpse in bed next to her, but cannot remember anything about the night before. She evades the police, accidentally meets up with an ex-cop, and works with him to unravel an increasingly complicated mystery. **103m/C; VHS, DVD.** Jane Fonda; Jeff Bridges; Raul Julia; Diane Salinger; Richard Foronjy; Geoffrey Scott; Kathleen Wilhoite; Frances Bergen; Rick Rossovich; Kathy Bates; ***D:*** Sidney Lumet; ***W:*** James Cresson; ***C:*** Andrzej Bartkowiak.

Morning Departure ½ **1950** Suspenseful disaster story. During a postwar mission a British submarine hits a forgotten electric mine and sinks to the sea-bed with 12 survivors. Eight men use the only working snorkel equipment to get to safety while the sub's captain, Armstrong (Mills), tries to keep a stiff upper lip and keep the remaining three sailors calm while they await rescue. **102m/B; DVD.** *GB* John Mills; Richard Attenborough; James Hayter; Nigel Patrick; Bernard Lee; Kenneth More; ***D:*** Roy Ward Baker; ***W:*** William Fairchild; ***C:*** Desmond Dickinson.

Morning Glory ½ **1933** Small-town girl finds love and fame in the big city. Predictable fare nonetheless boasts fine performances from Hepburn and Fairbanks. Adapted from Zoe Atkins' stage play. **74m/B; VHS, DVD.** Katharine Hepburn; Douglas Fairbanks, Jr.; Adolphe Menjou; Mary Duncan; ***D:*** Lowell Sherman; ***M:*** Max Steiner. Oscars '33: Actress (Hepburn).

Morning Glory ½ **1993 (PG-13)** Sappy romance, set during the Depression, about a pregnant widow (Raffin) trying to survive on her hardscrabble farm in Georgia. Elly Dinsmore advertises for a husband, not for romance but to help with the work, and is answered by Will Parker (Reeve), an ex-con trying to live down his past. When a local floozy who's been eyeing Will is killed, the sheriff (Walsh) is only too happy to go after the stranger in town. Light-weight with some unbelievable plot twists. Based on the novel "Morning Glory" by LaVyrle Spencer. **90m/C; VHS, DVD.** Deborah Raffin; Christopher Reeve; Lloyd Bochner; Nina Foch; Helen Shaver; J.T. Walsh; ***D:*** Steven Hilliard Stern; ***W:*** Deborah Raffin; Charles Jarrott; ***M:*** Jonathan Elias.

Morning Glory ½ **2010 (PG-13)** It's as if your morning coffee turned out to be weak, cold, and decaffeinated. Young TV producer Becky Fuller (McAdams) has the unenviable job of trying to save a failing morning show by controlling its veteran feuding anchors Mike Pomeroy (Ford) and Colleen Peck (Keaton). Mike is a pompous grouch who refuses to do the happy talk and silly segments that diva Colleen has long smiled through, but Becky is going to get him to cooperate. McAdams tries to overcome the predictable fluff through sheer force of will but it's an unworthy task. **107m/C; DVD, Blu-Ray.** Harrison Ford; Diane Keaton; Rachel McAdams; Jeff Goldblum; Patrick Wilson; John Pankow; Ty Burrell; Matt Malloy; Patti D'Arbanville; ***D:*** Roger Michell; ***W:*** Aline Brosh McKenna; ***C:*** Alwin Kuchler; ***M:*** David Arnold.

Morning Light ½ **2008 (PG)** Squeaky-clean Disney-made documentary following fifteen young sailors as they embark on the 2500 mile TransPac race from Los Angeles to Hawaii. The ships' crews are obviously aware that they're on camera, which leads to very few spontaneous moments, as well as a few seemingly rigged scenes. Aware of the small audience that actually follows this kind of elite sailing competition, Disney sets it up like a lame reality show, complete with a climactic elimination. Too bad Fox wasn't involved. They could've at least brought in some bikini babes and a keg. **98m/C; Blu-Ray.** ***D:*** Paul Crowder; Mark Monroe; ***C:*** Josef Nalevansky; Richard Deppe.

Morocco ½ **1930** A foreign legion soldier falls for a world-weary chanteuse along the desert sands. Cooper has never been more earnest, and Dietrich has never been more blase and exotic. In her American film debut, Dietrich sings "What Am I Bid?" A must for anyone drawn to improbable, gloriously well-done kitsch. Based on Benno Vigny's novel, "Amy Jolly." **92m/B; VHS, DVD, Blu-Ray.** Marlene Dietrich; Gary Cooper; Adolphe Menjou; Ullrich Haupt; Francis McDonald; Eve Southern; Paul Porcasi; ***D:*** Josef von Sternberg; ***C:*** Lee Garmes. Natl. Film Reg. '92.

Morons from Outer Space **1985 (PG)** Slow-witted aliens from elsewhere in the universe crash onto Earth, but unlike other sci-fis, these morons become internationally famous, despite them acting like intergalactic stooges. Plenty of sight gags. **87m/C; VHS, DVD.** *GB* Griff Rhys Jones; Mel Smith; James B. Sikking; Dinsdale Landen; Jimmy Nail; Joanne Pearce; Paul Bown; ***D:*** Mike Hodges; ***W:*** Griff Rhys Jones; Mel Smith; ***C:*** Phil Meheux; ***M:*** Peter Brewis.

Morris from America **2016 (R)** This Sundance award winner from writer/director Hartigan is a delightful look at a fish very far from his traditional water. Markees Christmas plays Morris, an African-American teenager living in Germany, where his single father (Robinson) works. As he deals with the traditional issues of adolescence—including a serious crush on an older girl at his school who strings him along—his problems are compounded by cultural and social differences. It never feels manipulative or melodramatic, rather allowing an emotional final act, carried by a great turn from Robinson, to really hit home. **91m/C; DVD, Blu-Ray.** Markees Christmas; Craig Robinson; Carla Juri; Patrick Güldenberg; Lina Keller; ***D:*** Chad Hartigan; ***W:*** Chad Hartigan; ***C:*** Sean McElwee; ***M:*** Keegan DeWitt.

The Morrison Murders **1996** Based on the murders of the Culverhouse family. A man, his wife, and his youngest son are found dead. Their two older sons stand to inherit the trucking company, but surprise comes when it's revealed the younger of the two is the sole beneficiary of a large life insurance policy making him a top suspect. **92m/C; DVD.** John Corbett; Jonathan Scarfe; Maya McLaughlin; Tanya Allen; Alex Carter; Patricia Gage; Gordon Clapp; Barry Flatman; Marc Donato; Hayley Lochner; ***D:*** Chris Thomson; ***W:*** Keith Ross Leckie; ***C:*** Robert Saad; ***M:*** Micky Erbe; Maribeth Solomon. **TV**

Mortal Challenge ½ **1997 (R)** A corrupt police force, known as the Centurions, guard a futuristic L.A., which is divided into rich and poor sectors. When wealthy Tori is captured visiting her wrong-side-of-the-sectors boyfriend, the Centurions decide to have some fun by matching her with a cyborg in a death game. **77m/C; VHS, DVD.** Timothy Bottoms; David McCallum; Evan Lurie; Nick (Nicholas, Niko) Hill; ***D:*** Randolph Cheveldare. **VIDEO**

Mortal Engines **2018 (PG-13)** After a brief yet devastating war nearly wipes out humanity, cities become mobile fortresses that roam the planet, gobbling up smaller towns to claim their resources. Based on the first book of Philip Reeve's young-adult quartet, this post-apocalyptic, sci-fi adventure follows three young rebels, led by Hester Shaw (Hilmar), who defy the odds in trying to stop Thaddeus Valentine (Weaving) and his imperialistic London-on-wheels. The graphics are impressive, but despite some pathos injected into backstories, there's not much to the characters. And by the time this flick rolled into theaters, the steampunk aesthetic was passé. **128m/C; DVD, Blu-Ray, Streaming.** *NZ US* Hera Hilmar; Robert Sheehan; Hugo Weaving; Jihae; Ronan Raftery; ***D:*** Christian Rivers; ***W:*** Peter

Jackson; Fran Walsh; Philippa Boyens; ***C:*** Simon Raby; ***M:*** Junkie XL.

The Mortal Instruments: City of Bones **2013 (PG-13)** The never-ending stream of Young Adult films vainly trying to replicate the success of the "Twilight" saga continues with this inane fantasy film based on Cassandra Clare's novel. NYC girl Clary (Collins) discovers she's from a long line of demon slayers with supernatural skills previously unbeknownst to her (and that the writers can't coherently explain). After hooking up with three other kids of her kind (Campbell Bower, West, and Zegers)--what timing!--she goes about rescuing her mother (Headey) from "bad demon slayer" Valentine (Rhys Meyers). Lacking its own identity, the result plays like a genre parody, producing more laughs than intended. **130m/C; DVD, Blu-Ray.** *CA GE* Lily Collins; Jamie Campbell Bower; Kevin Zegers; Jemima West; Jonathan Rhys Meyers; Robert Sheehan; Lena Headey; Godfrey Gao; CCH Pounder; Jared Harris; Aidan Turner; Kevin Durand; ***D:*** Harald Zwart; ***W:*** Jessica Postigo Paquette; ***C:*** Geir Hartly Andreassen; ***M:*** Atli Orvarsson.

Mortal Kombat 1: The Movie **1995 (PG-13)** Inevitable film version of mega popular arcade game intended to cash in fast on the game's popularity. Shameless nirvana for youngin's with permanent joystick scars on their hands. Grown-ups forced to sit through it may get into some of the eye-popping special effects and nifty martial arts sequences if they can block out the contrived plot, lame acting, and Lambert's presence as Thunder God. **101m/C; VHS, DVD, Blu-Ray.** Christopher Lambert; Talisa Soto; Cary-Hiroyuki Tagawa; Bridgette Wilson-Sampras; ***D:*** Paul W.S. Anderson; ***W:*** Kevin Droney; ***C:*** John R. Leonetti; ***M:*** George S. Clinton.

Mortal Kombat 2: Annihilation **1/2 1997 (PG-13)** The treacherous Shao-Khan brings his evil horde of videogame villians through a portal ripped in the universe and threatens to destroy the Earth in this highly unneccesary sequel. Liu Kang and his buds are on the scene to once again do battle to save humanity. Moves from one badly staged fight scene to another with little story or acting. However, kids and gamers should enjoy the new characters, the same-sounding pulse-pounding techno music, and the non-stop, but fairly bloodless, violence. **98m/C; DVD, Blu-Ray.** James Remar; Robin Shou; Talisa Soto; Daron McBee; Sandra Hess; Brian Thompson; Reiner Schone; Musetta Vander; Marjean Holden; Litefoot; Lynn Red Williams; Irina Pantaeva; ***D:*** John R. Leonetti; ***W:*** Brent Friedman; Bruce Zabel; ***C:*** Matthew F. Leonetti; ***M:*** George S. Clinton.

The Mortal Storm **1/2 1940** Phyllis Bottome's famous novel comes to life in this extremely well acted film about the rise of the Nazi regime. Stewart and Sullavan are young lovers who risk everything to escape the country after their families are torn apart by the Nazi takeover. Although Germany is never identified as the country, it is obvious in this story about the early days of WWII. Hitler took one look at this and promptly banned all MGM movies in Nazi Germany. **100m/B; VHS, DVD.** Margaret Sullavan; James Stewart; Robert Young; Frank Morgan; Robert Stack; Bonita Granville; Irene Rich; ***D:*** Frank Borzage; ***W:*** Claudine West; George Froeschel; Anderson Ellis; ***C:*** William H. Daniels.

Mortal Thoughts **1/2 1991 (R)** Best friends find their relationship tested when the brutal husband of one of them is murdered. Moore and Headly are exceptional, capturing the perfect inflections and attitudes of the hard-working New Jersey beauticians sure of their friendship. Excellent pacing, fine supporting cast, with Keitel and Willis stand-outs. **104m/C; VHS, DVD.** Demi Moore; Bruce Willis; Glenne Headly; Harvey Keitel; John Pankow; Billie Neal; ***D:*** Alan Rudolph; ***W:*** William Reilly; Claude Kerven; ***C:*** Elliot Davis; ***M:*** Mark Isham. Natl. Soc. Film Critics '91: Support. Actor (Keitel).

Mortal Transfer **2001** Comic mystery finds Paris shrink Michel Durand (Anglade) in trouble after getting a call from police inspector Chapireau (Podalydes). Klepto Olga (De Fougerolles) claims she was in Durand's office after she's accused of shoplifting and he covers for her because he falls asleep during her sessions. Only the next time it happens, Durand wakes up to find a tragedy has occurred. Rather than fessing up, Durand opts for a cover-up. French with subtitles. **122m/C; DVD.** *FR GE* Jean-Hugues Anglade; Helene de Fougerolles; Denis Podalydes; Miki (Predrag) Manojlovic; Yves Renier; Robert Hirsch; Valentina Sauca; ***D:*** Jean-Jacques Beineix; ***C:*** Benoit Delhomme; ***M:*** Reinhardt Wagner.

Mortdecai WOOF! **2015 (R)** There are bad movies, really bad movies, and then there's Mortdecai. Director Koepp's comedy is fascinating only in the sense that train wrecks involving formerly interesting A-list stars are always fascinating. Depp gives a grating, horrendous performance as the title character, an eccentric art dealer with a curly mustache and a penchant for puns. McGregor, Paltrow, Bettany, and more talented actors get sucked into the gravity of this horrendous comic adventure that almost feels like the performance art answer to the question "How blatantly unfunny can a film possibly be before audiences demand their money back?" **107m/C; DVD, Blu-Ray.** Johnny Depp; Gwyneth Paltrow; Paul Bettany; Ewan McGregor; Jeff Goldblum; Olivia Munn; Michael Culkin; Ulrich Thomsen; ***D:*** David Koepp; ***W:*** Eric Aronson; ***C:*** Florian Hoffmeister; ***M:*** Geoff Zanelli; Mark Ronson.

The Mortician **2011 (R)** This U.S./U.K. co-production is dull urban noir (with some filmmaking tricks) and not a horror flick. A lonely, nameless mortician (Method Man) with mother issues works in a violent, blight-ridden city. The body of a tattooed woman ends up on his table and he is forced to reconnect when frightened street kid Kane (Santiago) insists on seeing his mom who was killed by his thug dad Carver (Mihok), who wants the boy dead as well. **89m/C; DVD.** *UK US* Method Man; Cruz Santiago; Dash Mihok; Wendell Pierce; Edward Furlong; ***D:*** Gareth Maxwell Roberts; ***W:*** Gareth Maxwell Roberts; ***C:*** Michael McDonough; ***M:*** Mike Benn. **VIDEO**

Mortuary *Funeral Home* **1981 (R)** Young woman's nightmares come startlingly close to reality. **91m/C; VHS, DVD, Blu-Ray.** Christopher George; Lynda Day George; Paul Smith; ***D:*** Howard (Hikmet) Avedis; ***W:*** Howard (Hikmet) Avedis.

Mortuary WOOF! **2005 (R)** The Doyle family (widowed mom and two kids) move to a small California town where mom (Crosby) thinks it's a great idea to reopen the long-abandoned funeral home that has a cemetery in the yard. According to townspeople, the mortuary is built on haunted property and soon some sort of toxic killer fungus that's oozing around is raising the corpses. Ick in more ways than one. **94m/C; DVD, Blu-Ray.** Denise Crosby; Dan Byrd; Courtney Peldon; Bug Hall; Stephanie Patton; ***D:*** Tobe Hooper; ***W:*** Jace Anderson; Adam Gierasch; ***C:*** Jaron Presant; ***M:*** Joseph Conlan. **VIDEO**

Mortuary Academy **1991 (R)** To win an inheritance two brothers must attend the family mortician school, a situation paving the way for aggressively tasteless jokes on necrophilia. An attempt to recapture the successful black humor of the earlier Bartel/Woronov teaming "Eating Raoul," this one's dead on arrival. **86m/C; VHS, DVD.** Christopher Atkins; Perry Lang; Paul Bartel; Mary Woronov; Tracey Walter; Lynn Danielson-Rosenthal; Cesar Romero; Wolfman Jack; ***D:*** Michael Schroeder; ***W:*** William Kelman; ***C:*** Roy Wagner; Ronald Vidor; ***M:*** David Spear.

Morvern Callar **1/2 2002** Morvern (Morton) wakes on Christmas morning to find her boyfriend's body, wrists slashed, beside her bed. His legacy is a personalized compilation tape, his cash card, and a novel he's written for her. After she dismembers and disposes of his body, replaces his name on the manuscript with her own and sends it off to a publisher (who buys it), she goes off on a holiday to Spain with her sex and drug crazed girlfriend (McDermott). Morvern's emotions are revealed through the lyrics of the compilation tape constantly pounding through her headphones. Ramsey's second film, based on a novel by Alan Warner, is a moody beauty that's not altogether gratifying. **97m/C; DVD.** *UK CA* Samantha Morton; Kathleen McDermott; ***D:*** Lynne Ramsay; ***W:*** Lynne Ramsay; Liana Dognini; ***C:*** Alwin Kuchler.

Moscow, Belgium *Aanrijding in Moscou* **2008** Working-class comedy-drama with a compellingly world-weary performance by Sarafian. Tough 40-something postal worker Matty (Sarafian) has three kids with art teacher hubby Werner (Hildenbergh) whose midlife crisis results in his leaving his family for a student. Matty gets into a fender-bender with younger truck driver Johnny (Delnaet) and decides to indulge her sexual curiosity. And then Werner decides to return. As if Matty didn't have enough to deal with. Flemish with subtitles. **106m/C; DVD.** *BE* Barbara Sarafian; Jurgen Delnaet; Johan Hildenbergh; Anemone Valcke; Sofia Ferri; Julian Borsani; ***D:*** Christophe van Rompaey; ***W:*** Jean-Claude van Rijkeghem; Pat van Biers; ***C:*** Ruben Impens.

Moscow Does Not Believe in Tears *Moscow Distrusts Tears; Moskwa Sljesam Nje Jerit* **1980** Three provincial girls—Lyuda (Muravyova), Tonya (Ryazanova), and Katya (Alentova)?realize very different fates when they pursue their dreams in 1958 Moscow. The film picks up 20 years later to see what became of the women. Bittersweet, moving fare that seems a somewhat surprising production from pre-Glasnost USSR. In Russian with English subtitles. A 150-minute version has also been released. **115m/C; VHS, DVD.** *RU* Vera Alentova; Irina Muravyova; Raisa Ryazanova; Natalie Vavilova; Alexei Batalov; Alexander Fatyushin; Yuri Vasilyev; ***D:*** Vladimir Menshov; ***W:*** Valentin Chernykh; ***C:*** Igor Slabnevich; ***M:*** Sergei Nikitin. Oscars '80: Foreign Film.

Moscow Heat **1/2 2004 (R)** In a possible homage to 'Red Heat,' a cop is murdered and his father and partner track the arms dealer responsible to Moscow. Subsequently arrested, a Russian cop is assigned to ensure they're deported but ends up helping them when the bad guys try to whack him as well. Decent though original action fare. **90m/C; DVD.** Michael York; Richard Tyson; Rob Madrid; Andrew Divoff; Joanna Pacula; Adrian Paul; Maria Golubkina; Jeff Celentano; Alexander Nevsky; Alexander Izotov; Sergey Gorobchenko; Gennadi Vengerov; Stanislov Eventov; Evgeniy Berezovskiy; Grigoriy Levakov; Ekaterina Rydenkova; Yuriy Sherstnyov; Viktoriya Talyshinskaya; ***D:*** Jeff Celentano; ***W:*** Rob Madrid; Alexander Nevsky; ***C:*** John Aronson; ***M:*** Richard John Baker.

Moscow on the Hudson **1984 (R)** Good-natured comedy has Williams as Soviet defector trying to cope with new life of freedom in fast-paced, freewheeling melting pot of New York City. Williams is particularly winning as naive jazzman, though Alonso also scores as his Hispanic love interest. Be warned though, it's not just played for laughs. **115m/C; VHS, DVD, Blu-Ray.** Robin Williams; Maria Conchita Alonso; Cleavant Derricks; Alejandro Rey; Elya Baskin; ***D:*** Paul Mazursky; ***W:*** Paul Mazursky; Leon Capetanos; ***C:*** Donald McAlpine; ***M:*** David McHugh.

Moscow Zero WOOF! **2006 (R)** Incoherent and laughably bad. After an anthropologist vanishes in the catacombs beneath the streets of Moscow, a rescue team is sent searching for him and discovers a strange occult society that believes in demons and a gateway to Hell. **82m/C; DVD.** *SP* Vincent Gallo; Rade Serbedzija; Joss Ackland; Val Kilmer; Joaquim de Almeida; Sage Stallone; ***D:*** Maria Lidon; ***W:*** Adela Ibanez; ***C:*** Ricardo Aronovich; ***M:*** Javier Navarrete.

Moses WOOF! **1976 (PG)** Lancaster goes biblical as Moses, the man with the tablets. Edited from the 360-minute British TV series, with no improvement obvious from the economy, except that the bad parts are shorter. Poor chatter and scattered bouts of acting are surpassed in inadequacy only by special effects. **141m/C; VHS, DVD.** Burt Lancaster; Anthony Quayle; Ingrid Thulin; Irene Papas; William Lancaster; ***D:*** Gianfranco DeBosio; ***W:*** Anthony Burgess; Vittorio Bonicelli; ***M:*** Ennio Morricone.

Moses **1/2 1996** Another entry in TNT's series of Bible stories finds a humble Moses (Kingsley), raised in the Egyptian court, finding his way to his own people, the Israelites. Chosen by God to be his messenger and lead his people out of bondage, Moses must unleash a series of plagues upon Egypt before pharaoh Mernefta (Langella) will let them go. If you want action, look to "The Ten Commandments," since this is a faithful but tedious retelling. Filmed on location in Morocco; on two cassettes. **185m/C; VHS, DVD.** Ben Kingsley; Frank Langella; David Suchet; Christopher Lee; Anna Galiena; Enrico Lo Verso; Geraldine McEwan; Maurice Roeves; Anthony (Corlan) Higgins; Anton Lesser; ***D:*** Roger Young; ***W:*** Lionel Chetwynd; ***C:*** Raffaele Mertes; ***M:*** Marco Frisina.

Mosquito **1995 (R)** Alien forces transform the annoying insects into monstrous mutants. Schlocky special effects are good for laughs. **92m/C; VHS, DVD, Blu-Ray.** Gunnar Hansen; Ron Asheton; Steve Dixon; Rachel Loiselle; Tim Loveface; ***D:*** Gary Jones; ***W:*** Gary Jones; Steve Hodge; Tom Chaney; ***C:*** Tom Chaney; ***M:*** Allen Lynch; Randall Lynch.

The Mosquito Coast **1/2 1986 (PG)** Ambitious adaptation of Paul Theroux's novel about an asocial inventor who transplants his family to a rainforest to realize his utopian dream. A nightmare ensues. Ford tries hard, but supporters Mirren and Phoenix are main appeal of only intermittently successful drama. **119m/C; VHS, DVD.** Harrison Ford; Dame Helen Mirren; River Phoenix; Andre Gregory; Martha Plimpton; Conrad Roberts; Butterfly McQueen; Jadrien Steele; Hilary Gordon; Rebecca Gordon; Dick O'Neill; Jason Alexander; ***D:*** Peter Weir; ***W:*** Paul Schrader; ***C:*** John Seale; ***M:*** Maurice Jarre.

Mosquito Man **1/2** *Mansquito* **2005** Break out the giant can of mosquito repellent for this genre cheese of '50s big bug flicks. A death row convict (Jordan) is used for scientific experiments and exposed to a DNA-altering concoction that turns him into the blood-slurping creature of the title. Cop Tom Randall (Nemec) tracks the blood trail while scientist babe Jennifer Allen (Vander) tries to prevent the change from happening again—to her. Originally shown on the Sci-Fi Channel. **92m/C; DVD.** Corin "Corky" Nemec; Musetta Vander; Jay Benedict; Patrick Dreikauss; Austin Jordan; ***D:*** Tibor Takas; ***W:*** Michael Hurst; ***C:*** Emil Topuzov; ***M:*** Joseph Conlan; Sophia Morizet. **CABLE**

Mosquito Squadron **1/2 1970** Quint Monroe (McCallum) is an RAF pilot in WWII who has the sad news of telling his best friend's wife her husband is dead. They eventually begin a romance as he is tapped to head a bombing run on France where the Nazis are secretly building rockets to attack Britain. Plans are made to destroy it when Quint makes an incredible discovery that might threaten the mission—or lives. **90m/B; DVD.** *GB* David McCallum; Suzanne Neve; Charles Gray; David Buck; Dinsdale Landen; David Dundas; Nicky Henson; Bryan Marshall; Michael Anthony; Peter Copley; Vladek Sheybal; Michael McGovern; ***D:*** Boris Sagal; ***W:*** Donald S. Sanford; Joyce Perry; ***C:*** Paul Beeson; ***M:*** Frank Cordell.

Most Beautiful Island **2017** A slow-building horror thriller that explores the immigrant experience. Spanish native Luciana (Asensio) struggles to get by in New York City. She has two jobs: working as a chicken restaurant's mascot and babysitting two bratty children. A short-term solution presents itself when Olga (Romanova), another chicken mascot, invites her to a one-time job at a party. Paid to stand and look attractive in a creepy basement, Luciana finds that the party guests are experiencing something horrific. Though Luciana is a sympathetic character, the film takes too long to get down to business. **80m/C; DVD.** Ana Asensio; Natasha Romanova; David Little; Nicholas Tucci; Larry Fessenden; ***D:*** Ana Asensio; ***W:*** Ana Asensio; ***C:*** Noah Greenberg; ***M:*** Jeffery Alan Jones.

The Most Dangerous Game *The Hounds of Zaroff* **1932** Shipwrecked McRae washed ashore on the island of Banks's Count Zaroff, a deranged sportsman with a flair for tracking humans. Guess who becomes the mad count's next target. Oft-told tale is compellingly related in this, the first of many using Richard Connell's famous short story. If deja vu sets in, don't worry. This production uses most of the scenery, staff, and cast from its studio cousin, "King Kong." Remade in 1945 as "A Game of Death" and in 1956 as "Run for the Sun." **78m/B; VHS, DVD, Blu-Ray.** Joel McCrea; Fay Wray; Leslie Banks; Robert Armstrong; Noble Johnson; ***D:*** Ernest B. Schoedsack; Irving Pichel; **W:** James A. Creelman; **C:** Henry W. Gerrard; **M:** Max Steiner.

Most Dangerous Man Alive ♪ 1/2 **1961** Framed mob boss Eddie Candell escapes while being transported to prison and accidentally wanders into an atomic testing range. He's bombarded by a newly-discovered radioactive element that literally transforms him into a man of steel. Nearly invincible, Eddie's determined to get revenge on everyone who betrayed him. **82m/B; DVD.** Ron Randell; Elaine Stewart; Anthony Caruso; Debra Paget; Gregg (Hunter) Palmer; Morris Ankrum; Tudor Owen; **D:** Allan Dwan; **W:** James Leicester; Michael Pate; **C:** Carl Carvahal; **M:** Louis Forbes.

A Most Violent Year ♪♪♪ **2014 (R)** A gritty crime drama set in 1981 snow-covered New York, during statistically one of the city's most violent years. The mobster-in-law saga follows immigrant Abel Morales (Isaac), the hard-working owner of a heating-oil company, through an abnormally tense 30 days. With the help of his Brooklyn-born, mob-connected wife (Chastain), the squeaky clean businessman concocts a plan to pay off a large loan on time, while battling high jackers who continue to swipe his trucks. Troubling and moody throughout, director J.C. Chandor never plays it easy, showing the darkest parts of the American dream gone way wrong. **125m/C; DVD, Blu-Ray.** Oscar Isaac; Jessica Chastain; David Oyelowo; Elyes Gabel; Albert Brooks; Alessandro Nivola; Jerry Adler; **D:** J.C. Chandor; **W:** J.C. Chandor; **C:** Bradford Young; **M:** Alex Ebert.

Most Wanted ♪♪ 1/2 **1997 (R)** Marine Sgt. James Dunn (Wayans), framed for the assassination of the first lady, is on the run from the various agencies and the covert team he was working with, which is led by a gung-ho general (Voight) who set up the whole scam. Screenwriter Wayans seems convinced that an action hero must be of the strong-silent-superhero mold, and appears at a loss without a joke to crack. Voight, however, is right at home in the bad-guy role, employing an overdone but effective southern drawl. Plenty of elaborate stunts, oversized fireballs, shootings, and chases provide the expected wild ride. **99m/C; DVD.** Keenen Ivory Wayans; Jon Voight; Jill(ian) Hennessey; Eric Roberts; Paul Sorvino; Robert Culp; Wolfgang Bodison; Simon Baker; **D:** David Glenn Hogan; **W:** Keenen Ivory Wayans; **C:** Marc Reshovsky; **M:** Paul Bruckmaster.

A Most Wanted Man ♪♪ 1/2 **2014 (R)** Adapted from John le Carré's blue-collar spy novel, this thriller is a subdued interpretation from high-art director Corbijn. The jigsaw-puzzle plot follows German counterterrorism agent Gunther Bachmann (Hoffman) as he tracks Russian refugee (Dobrygin) through Hamburg's Muslim villages. Chain-smoking his way into double crosses at every corner, the weathered agent forms unlikely alliances with a slew of questionable characters, including a compassionate attorney (McAdams) and a sly bank CEO (Dafoe). Intricate to a note, emotionally exhausting, and never easy. Fans of crossword puzzles with feel right at home. **122m/C; DVD, Blu-Ray.** *GE US* Philip Seymour Hoffman; Rachel McAdams; Willem Dafoe; Rainer Bock; Grigory Dobrygin; Homayon Ershadi; Robin Wright; **D:** Anton Corbijn; **W:** Andrew Bovell; **C:** Benoit Delhomme; **M:** Herbert Gronemeyer.

The Most Wonderful Time of the Year ♪♪ 1/2 **2008** Optimistic Uncle Ralph (Winkler), a retired cop, thinks his bah-humbug niece Jen (Burns) needs some Christmas spirit. And what better way than to introduce her to a great guy named Morgan (Christie) that even her six-year-old son Brian (Levins) likes. It's meddling for such a good reason. **87m/C; DVD, Blu-Ray.** Henry Winkler; Brooke Burns; Connor Christopher Levins; Warren Christie; Rosalind Ivan; Paul Cavanagh; Morton Lowry; **D:** Henry Winkler; Don Siegel; **W:** Peter Milne; **C:** Ernest Haller; Frederick "Friedrich" Hollander; **M:** Frederick "Friedrich" Hollander. **CABLE**

Mostly Martha ♪♪♪ *Drei Sterne; Bella Martha* **2001 (PG)** Martha, a top chef at a fancy French restaurant in Hamburg, is so obsessed with her job that she really only connects with life through food. Things get stirred up when two new ingredients are added. First, a new sous-chef (Castellitto), scruffy and care-free as opposed to Martha's icy professionalism, enters her kitchen. Then, she takes in her 8-year-old neice (Foerste) after the death of the child's mother (Martha's sister). Appealing romantic comedy benefits form excellent performances by the leads, as well director Nettlebeck's assured style. German with subtitles. **107m/C; VHS, DVD.** *GE AT SI IT* Martina Gedeck; Sergio Castellitto; Ulrich Thomsen; Maxime Foerste; Sibylle Canonica; August Zirner; **D:** Sandra Nettelbeck; **W:** Sandra Nettelbeck; **C:** Michael Bertl.

Motel Blue ♪ 1/2 **1998 (R)** Kyle Rivers (Frye) is an agent with the Department of Defense, who's doing a security clearance check on scientist Lana Hawking (Young). Lana maintains an expensive lifestyle that suggests she may be selling government secrets. But when Lana finds out about Kyle's suspicions, Kyle gets framed and suspended. Kyle decides to continue the investigation on her own terms. No particular surprises but there are a number of sleazy sex scenes. **96m/C; VHS, DVD.** Sean Young; Soleil Moon Frye; Seymour Cassel; Robert Vaughn; Rob Stewart; Lou Rawls; Spencer Rochfort; **D:** Sam Firstenberg; **W:** Marianne S. Wibberley; Cormac Wibberley; **C:** Moshe Levin. **VIDEO**

Motel Hell ♪ 1/2 **1980 (R)** A completely tongue-in-cheek gore-fest about a farmer who kidnaps tourists, buries them in his garden, and reaps a human harvest to grind into his distinctive brand of smoked, preservative-free sausage. **102m/C; VHS, DVD, Blu-Ray.** Rory Calhoun; Nancy Parsons; Paul (Link) Linke; Nina Axelrod; Wolfman Jack; Elaine Joyce; Dick Curtis; Rosanne Katon; Monique St. Pierre; John Ratzenberger; **D:** Kevin Connor; **W:** Robert Jaffe; Steven-Charles Jaffe; **C:** Thomas Del Ruth; **M:** Lance Rubin.

The Motel Life ♪♪ **2012 (R)** Family drama, set in 1990, has too many flashbacks and animated sequences detailing the characters' stories to be effective despite some strong performances. Hard-scrabble brothers Jerry Lee (Dorff) and Frank (Hirsch) are headed from Reno to Elmo, Nevada where Frank hopes to reunite with lost love Annie (Fanning), but the law is right behind them. **85m/C; DVD, Blu-Ray.** Emile Hirsch; Stephen Dorff; Kris Kristofferson; Dakota Fanning; Dayton Callie; **D:** Alan Polsky; Gabe Polsky; **W:** Noah Harpster; Micah Fitzerman-Blue; **C:** Roman Vasyanov; **M:** David Holmes.

The Moth Diaries ♪ 1/2 **2011 (R)** Director Harron has proven skills with horror but the blend of adolescent angst with supernatural elements falls short in this inert bore-fest. When Ernessa (Cole), the mysterious new student at an all-girls boarding school, gets in the middle of a close friendship between Lucy (Gadon) and Rebecca (Bolger), the latter begins to suspect that this goth girl may be more than she appears. Maybe even a vampire. The story is clearly designed as a parable about the body and love issues that face an adolescent girl but the material falls flat. **82m/C; DVD, Blu-Ray.** *CA IR* Sarah Bolger; Lily Cole; Sarah Gadon; Scott Speedman; Judy Parfitt; **D:** Mary Harron; **W:** Mary Harron; **C:** Declan Quinn; **M:** Lesley Barber.

Mother ♪♪♪ 1/2 **1926** Pudovkin's innovative classic about a Russian family shattered by the uprising in 1905. A masterpiece of Russian cinema that established Pudovkin, and rivaled only Eisenstein for supremacy in montage, poetic imagery, and propagandistic ideals. Based on Maxim Gorky's great novel, it's one of cinematic history's seminal works. Striking cinematography, stunning use of montage make this one important. Silent with English subtitles. **70m/B; Silent; VHS, DVD, Blu-Ray.** *RU* Vera Baranovskaya; Nikolai Batalov; **D:** Vsevolod Pudovkin.

Mother ♪♪ 1/2 **1994 (R)** Olivia Hendrix (Ladd) is a very over-protective mom—even though son Tom (Weisser) is nineteen and anxious to untie the apron strings. But Mom thinks she knows best and she's willing to kill to make certain Tom stays home where he belongs. **90m/C; VHS, DVD.** Diane Ladd; Olympia Dukakis; Morgan Weisser; Ele Keats; **D:** Frank Laloggia.

Mother ♪♪ 1/2 **1996 (PG-13)** Yes, you will shake your head in recognition of that parent-child bond. Twice-divorced writer John Henderson (Brooks) decides it's all Mom's fault he has problems with women, so he decides to move back home and figure out what went wrong. Mom Beatrice (Reynolds) is exasperated and married younger brother Jeff (Morrow) winds up jealous of mom's attentions to his sibling. Reynolds' first feature film in 25 years. **104m/C; VHS, DVD.** Albert Brooks; Debbie Reynolds; Rob Morrow; Lisa Kudrow; John C. McGinley; Isabel Glasser; Peter White; Vanessa Williams; **D:** Albert Brooks; **W:** Albert Brooks; Monica Johnson; **C:** Lajos Koltai; **M:** Marc Shaiman. N.Y. Film Critics '96: Screenplay; Natl. Soc. Film Critics '96: Screenplay.

The Mother ♪♪♪ **2003 (R)** Reid gives a ferociously honest performance as the 60-ish May, a lifelong suburban wife and mother left bereft of purpose when her husband (Vaughn) suddenly dies. She moves to London to live with her preoccupied son Bobby (Mackintosh) and tries to straighten out the life of her self-pitying divorcee daughter, Paula (Bradshaw), who's involved in a messy relationship with rugged married builder, Darren (Craig). May finds herself attracted to the younger man's unexpected kindness and also begins an affair with the weak-willed Darren—the revelation of which causes no end of drama. An angry late scene between May and Paula is the only false note. **111m/C; VHS, DVD.** *GB* Anne Reid; Daniel Craig; Steven Mackintosh; Cathryn Bradshaw; Oliver Ford Davies; Peter Vaughan; Anna Wilson Jones; **D:** Roger Michell; **W:** Hanif Kureishi; **C:** Alwin Kuchler; **M:** Jeremy Sams.

Mother ♪ *Social Nightmare* **2013** The ridiculous cover art makes it look like a bad horror flick but it's actually a contrived Lifetime teen drama. Overachieving high school student Catherine Hardy suddenly becomes the target of a vicious smear campaign on her social media site. Her page now contains questionable messages and photos that ruin her reputation and threaten her college chances. Now she has to figure out who's behind the hate (with some sympathy from her mom). **90m/C; DVD, Blu-Ray.** Kirsten Prout; Daryl Hannah; Chloe Bridges; Brandon Smith; Rachel True; Tim Russ; Keith Allan; **D:** Mark Quod; **W:** Keith Allan; Delondra Williams; **C:** Richard J. Vialet; **M:** Chris Ridenhour. **CABLE**

mother! ♪♪ 1/2 **2017 (R)** The most divisive film of the year. In an isolated farmhouse, Bardem plays a poet with writer's block, seeking distraction and admiration. To the dismay of his meek partner (Lawrence), he invites a stranger to stay the night. The next day, the man's wife turns up, followed by more and more strangers. These guests become increasingly rude and aggressive, and Lawrence (who gives a universally acclaimed performance) receives the brunt of their intense abuse. Deeper meaning(s) can be found in biblical allegory, indictments of the patriarchy and the artist's ego, and writer/director Aronofsky's statement on climate change, but the brutality is so disturbing, especially because its target is a box-office darling (Aronofsky's own girlfriend), that audiences overwhelmingly cried uncle on "mother!" **121m/C; DVD, Blu-Ray.** Jennifer Lawrence; Javier Bardem; Ed Harris; Michelle Pfeiffer; Domhnall Gleeson; **D:** Darren Aronofsky; **W:** Darren Aronofsky; **C:** Matthew Libatique.

Mother and Child ♪♪ **2009 (R)** Exceptionally well-acted ensemble drama. Fifty-year-old Karen (Bening) is still regretful over the daughter she gave up 35 years before after a teen pregnancy. It takes the death of her own mother (Ryan) to get Karen to move on and tentatively get involved witht co-worker Paco (Smits). Karen's daughter, Elizabeth's (Watts) a frighteningly self-possessed lawyer who initiates a no-strings affair with her boss Paul (Jackson) until she gets pregnant. Meanwhile, married, anxiety-ridden Lucy (Washington) discovers she's infertile and is determined to adopt the child of unmarried young Ray (Epps), who isn't sure that Lucy is the right choice. **125m/C; DVD, Blu-Ray, On Demand.** Annette Bening; Naomi Watts; Kerry Washington; Samuel L. Jackson; Jimmy Smits; Shareeka Epps; Amy Brenneman; David Morse; David Ramsey; Cherry Jones; Marc Blucas; Ahmed Best; S. Epatha Merkerson; Lisa Gay Hamilton; Tatyana Ali; **D:** Rodrigo Garcia; **W:** Rodrigo Garcia; **C:** Xavier Perez Grobet; **M:** Ed Shearmur.

Mother and Son ♪♪ *Mat i Syn; Mutter und Sohn* **1997** Slow-paced, dreamlike story about a dedicated son's (Ananishnov) caring for his dying mother (Geyer) in their old house in the country. She wishes to go outside—he carries her along a path in the woods and they recall his childhood. She eventually goes back to her bed where they discuss death and she falls asleep, never to waken. Russian with subtitles. **73m/C; VHS, DVD.** *RU GE* Gudrun Geyer; Alexi Ananishnov; **D:** Alexander Sokurov; **W:** Yuri Arabov; **C:** Aleksei Federov; **M:** Otmar Nussio.

Mother Didn't Tell Me ♪♪ 1/2 **1950** Routine comedy. A head cold turns to love when Jane (McGuire) marries her doctor (Lundigan). An interfering mother-in-law (Landis), demanding patients, and William's partnership wih his attractive colleague (Mackenzie) prove challenging to the new missus. **88m/B; DVD.** Dorothy McGuire; William Lundigan; Joyce MacKenzie; Jessie Royce Landis; Gary Merrill; June Havoc; Leif Erickson; **D:** Claude Binyon; **W:** Claude Binyon; **C:** Joseph LaShelle; **M:** Cyril Mockridge.

Mother Is a Freshman ♪♪ 1/2 **1949** Lighthearted comedy. Beautiful widow Abigail Abbott (Young) is paying daughter Susan's (Lynn) college tuition from a family trust. Because of some stipulations, Abigail must also enroll in school. She joins Susan on campus where she catches the eye of English professor Richards Michaels (Johnson), whom Susan has a crush on. **80m/C; DVD.** Loretta Young; Van Johnson; Betty Lynn; Robert Arthur; Rudy Vallee; **D:** Lloyd Bacon; **W:** Mary Loos; Richard Sale; **C:** Arthur E. Arling; **M:** Alfred Newman.

Mother Joan of the Angels ♪♪♪ *The Devil and the Nun; Matka Joanna Od Aniolow* **1960** A priest investigating demonic possession among nuns in a 17th-century Polish convent becomes involved in a mutual attraction with the Mother Superior. A powerful allegory complemented by the stylized narrative and performances. Polish with subtitles. Based on actual events at Loudun and also the subject of a play by John Whiting, an opera by Krzysztof Penderecki, "The Devils of Loudon" novel by Aldous Huxley, and Ken Russell's movie "The Devils." **108m/B; VHS, DVD.** *PL* Lucyna Winnicka; Mieczyslaw Voit; Anna Ciepielewska; Maria Chwalibog; **D:** Jerzy Kawalerowicz; **W:** Jerzy Kawalerowicz; Tadeusz Konwicki; **M:** Adam Walacinski. Cannes '61: Grand Jury Prize.

Mother, Jugs and Speed ♪ 1/2 **1976 (PG)** Black comedy about the day-to-day tragedies encountered by a group of ambulance drivers. Interesting mix of stars. **95m/C; VHS, DVD.** Bill Cosby; Raquel Welch; Harvey Keitel; Allen Garfield; Larry Hagman; Bruce Davison; Dick Butkus; L.Q. Jones; Toni Basil; **D:** Peter Yates; **W:** Tom Mankiewicz.

Mother Kusters Goes to Heaven ♪♪♪ *Mutter Kusters Fahrt Zum Himmel* **1976** Mrs. Kusters's husband is a frustrated factory worker who goes over the edge and kills the factory owner's son and himself. Left alone, she learns that everyone is using her husband's death to further their own needs, including her daughter, who uses the publicity to enhance her singing career. A statement that you should trust no one, not even your family and friends. This film was banned from the Berlin Film Festival because of its political overtones. German with subtitles. **108m/C; DVD.** *GE* Brigitte Mira; Ingrid Caven; Armin Meier; Irm Hermann; Gottfried John; Margit Carstensen; Karl-Heinz Boehm; **D:** Rainer Werner Fassbinder; **W:** Rainer Werner Fassbinder; **C:** Michael Ballhaus.

Mother Lode ♪ 1/2 *Search for the Mother Lode; The Last Great Treasure* **1982 (PG)** The violent conflict between twin brothers (played by Heston) is intensified by greed, near madness, and the all-consuming lust for gold in this action-adventure. Heston's son, Fraser Clarke Heston, wrote as well as produced the film. **101m/C; VHS, DVD.** Charlton Heston; Nick Mancuso; Kim Basinger; **D:** Charlton Heston.

Mother, May I Sleep With Danger? ♪ **1996** Gets its bones rating for being an indulgently bad, cheesefest classic of the TV movie genre. Laurel (wannabe actress Spelling) finally realizes her too-attentive boyfriend Kevin (overacting Sergei) is actually an aggressive obsessive. Laurel's mother Jessica (Baines) is sure he's a nut job but neither of them knows just how crazy Kevin is—until he kidnaps Laurel and she discovers his dangerous past. **93m/C; DVD.** Tori Spelling; Ivan Sergei; Lisa Baines; Suzy Joachim; Bryn Erin; Todd Caldecott; Lochlyn Munro; ***D:*** Jorge Montesi; ***W:*** Edmond Stevens; ***C:*** Philip Linzey; ***M:*** Irwin Fisch. **TV**

Mother Night **1996 (R)** American writer Howard Campbell (Nolte) is recruited as a spy in pre-WWII Germany in this black comedy adaptation of Kurt Vonnegut's 1962 novel. He poses as a Nazi sympathizer in broadcasts to American troops, but his anti-semitic diatribes are actually coded information crucial to the Allies. After the war, Campbell's life unravels when the U.S. government refuses to acknowledge his efforts. He is captured by Israeli Nazi-hunters and imprisoned in Israel where he converses with fellow prisoner Adolf Eichmann (Gibson). **113m/C; VHS, DVD.** Nick Nolte; Sheryl Lee; Alan Arkin; John Goodman; Kirsten Dunst; David Strathairn; Arye Gross; Frankie Faison; Bernard Behrens; Henry Gibson; ***D:*** Keith Gordon; ***W:*** Robert B. Weide; ***C:*** Tom Richmond; ***M:*** Michael Convertino.

Mother of George **2013 (R)** A beautifully shot and gently presented story of immigrants facing challenges in the United States. Adenike (Gurira) and Ayodele (De Bankole) are a Nigerian couple, living in Brooklyn, who are struggling with their difficulty in conceiving a child that Ayodele's mother insists they call George after his father. Adenike faces such grief and turmoil over the situation that she turns to a seemingly awful solution, allowing another man to be the father. The cultural issues at play ring true for those forced to deal with expectations of male and female roles even in a new country. **107m/C; DVD, Blu-Ray.** Danai Gurira; Isaach de Bankole; Yaya DaCosta; ***D:*** Andrew Dosunmu; ***W:*** Darci Picoult; ***C:*** Bradford Young.

Mother of Mine *Aideista Parhain* **2005** During WWII, when conflict breaks out between Finland and Russia, 9-year-old Eero (Majaniemi) is sent to live with a neutral family in Sweden by his mother (Maijala), who believes he will be safer. Eero adapts quickly although his foster father (Nygvist) takes a shine to him immediately, his foster mother (Lundqvist) takes some time. When he finally returns home there's more trauma until the adult Eero can finally reconcile his feelings after attending his surrogate mother's funeral and then visiting his own elderly mother. Visually pleasing, emotionally engaging, and with a fabulous score. Finnish and Swedish with subtitles. **111m/C; DVD.** *FI* Michael Nyqvist; Topi Majaniemi; Maria Lundqvist; Kari-Pekka Toivonen; ***D:*** Klaus Haro; ***W:*** Jimmy Karlsson; Kirsi Vikman; ***C:*** Jarkko T. Laine; ***M:*** Tuomas Kantelinen.

Mother of Tears *La Terza Madre; The Third Mother* **2008** The third and final installment in Argento's loosely formed "mother witches" trilogy is a hallucinogenic tale of a horde of lesbian witches rampaging through Rome, encountering psychic girls, zombies, deranged priests, and a resurrected witch who may signal the end of the world. Completely bonkers, yet visually compelling. **102m/C; DVD.** Asia Argento; Cristian Solimeno; Adam James; Valeria Cavalli; Moran Atias; Phillippe LeRoy; Daria Nicolodi; Coralina Cataldi-Tassoni; Udo Kier; Jun Ichikawa; Clive Riche; Robert Madison; Tommaso Banfi; Paolo Stella; Barbara Mautino; Franco Leo; Silvia Rubino; Luca Pescatore; Alessandro Zeme; Simonetta Solder; ***D:*** Dario Argento; ***W:*** Dario Argento; Jace Anderson; Adam Gierasch; Walter Fasano; Simona Simonetti; ***C:*** Frederic Fasano; ***M:*** Claudio Simonetti. **VIDEO**

Mother Teresa: In the Name of God's Poor **1997** Bio of the missionary begins when the 36-year-old cloistered nun (Chaplin) starts her work in the Calcutta slums and founds the Missionaries of Charity, and culminates with her 1979 Nobel Peace Prize acceptance speech. This drama was unauthorized and reportedly did not receive the approval of Mother Teresa when she learned of the project. **93m/C; VHS, DVD.** Geraldine Chaplin; Keene Curtis; William Katt; Alan Shearman; Cornelia Hayes O'Herlihy; ***D:*** Kevin Connor; ***W:*** Dominique Lapierre; Carol Kaplan. **CABLE**

Mother Wore Tights **1947** Colorful nostalgic musical stars Grable as married turn-of-the-century vaudevillian Myrtle McKinley Burt, who leaves the stage to raise her two daughters. Once they're grown, Myrtle decides to rejoin husband Frank (Dailey) in the theatre again, thus embarassing daughter Iris (Freeman) who's at a snotty finishing school. Of course, Iris learns what's really important in life. **107m/C; DVD, Blu-Ray.** Betty Grable; Dan Dailey; Mona Freeman; Connie Marshall; Vanessa Brown; Robert Arthur; Sara Allgood; William Frawley; ***D:*** Walter Lang; ***W:*** Lamar Trotti; ***C:*** Harry Jackson; ***M:*** Josef Myrow; Alfred Newman; ***M:*** Mack Gordon. Oscars '47: Scoring/Musical.

Motherhood ½ **2009 (PG-13)** Messy and self-conscious comedy, taking place over a single day, about harried (and annoying) Manhattan mom and children's blog writer Eliza Welch (Thurman with dark brown hair and nerd glasses). Nothing much happens as Eliza checks her to-do list and schleps through her domestic and childcare routines, including gossiping on the playground with other moms and preparing for her 6-year-old daughter's birthday party. **90m/C; Blu-Ray.** Uma Thurman; Minnie Driver; Anthony Edwards; Stephanie Szostak; ***Cameo(s):*** Jodie Foster; ***D:*** Katherine Dieckmann; ***W:*** Katherine Dieckmann; ***C:*** Nancy Schreiber; ***M:*** Joe Henry.

Motherland *Bayang Ina Mo* **2017 94m/C; DVD, Blu-Ray, Streaming.** *PH US* ***D:*** Ramona S. Diaz; ***C:*** Clarissa delos Reyes; Nadia Hallgren.

Motherless Brooklyn ½ **2019 (R)** For two decades, Edward Norton wanted to adapt Jonathan Lethem's 1999 novel for the big screen. Taking the reins as director, screenplay writer, and lead actor, he finally succeeded. He plays Lionel Essrog, a lonely private eye plagued by Tourette's Syndrome in 1950s New York City who doggedly investigates the murder of his mentor (Willis). The film noir vibe is furthered by a mysterious yet captivating woman (Mbatha-Raw) and a corrupt big-city leader (Baldwin) that appears untouchable. It's all nice looking and capably done, but coming in at 2-1/2 hours, it may leave viewers feeling more nostalgic about intermissions than gumshoe flicks. **?m/C; DVD, Blu-Ray.** Edward Norton; Gugu Mbatha-Raw; Alec Baldwin; Bobby Cannavale; Willem Dafoe; Bruce Willis; ***D:*** Edward Norton; ***W:*** Edward Norton; ***C:*** Dick Pope; ***M:*** Daniel Pemberton.

Mother's Boys **1994 (R)** Estranged mother Curtis attempts to reunite with the family she abandoned only to be snubbed, inspiring in her a ruthless effort to win back the children and oust father Gallagher's new live-in girlfriend Whalley-Kilmer. With an almost psychotic devotion, she terrorizes everyone in the family, including enticing her 12-year-old son Edwards into a nude bathtub game of peek-a-boo. Film lacks the tension necessary to carry suspense. Based on the novel by Bernard Taylor. **96m/C; VHS, DVD, Blu-Ray.** Jamie Lee Curtis; Peter Gallagher; Joanne Whalley; Luke Edwards; Vanessa Redgrave; Colin Ward; Joss Ackland; Paul Guilfoyle; John C. McGinley; J.E. Freeman; Ken Lerner; Lorraine Toussaint; Joey Zimmerman; Jill Freedman; ***D:*** Yves Simoneau; ***W:*** Richard Hawley; Barry Schneider; ***C:*** Elliot Davis; ***M:*** George S. Clinton.

Mothers Cry **1930** Obscure, rather creepy tearjerking talkie. Widow Mary Williams (Petersen) struggles to provide for her four children. Her eldest son Danny (Woods) is a bad seed who has a perverse fixation on his sister, Beattie (Chandler). **73m/B; DVD.** Dorothy Peterson; Edward (Eddie) Woods; Helen Chandler; David Manners; Evalyn Knapp; Jean Laverty; Sidney Blackmer; Pat O'Malley; ***D:*** Hobart Henley; ***W:*** Lenore Coffee; ***C:*** Gilbert Warrenton.

Mother's Day ½ **1980** Three women who were former college roommates plan a reunion together in the wilderness. All goes well until they are dragged into an isolated house by two insane boys who constantly watch TV, ardently consume the products advertised, and then terrorize and torture people to please their mom. Sanitized gore with black satiric intentions. **98m/C; VHS, DVD, Blu-Ray.** Tiana Pierce; Nancy Hendrickson; Deborah Luce; Holden McGuire; Billy Ray McQuade; Rose Ross; ***D:*** Charles Kaufman; ***W:*** Charles Kaufman; Warren Leight; ***C:*** Joseph Mangine; ***M:*** Phil Gallo; Clem Vicari, Jr.

Mother's Day ½ **2010 (R)** Uneven horror/crime flick, which boasts a creepy title performance by De Mornay, is a loose remake of the 1980 Troma film. Beth and Daniel are hosting a party in their new house when the three Koffin brothers barge in. It's their childhood home and they don't realize that their mother lost it to foreclosure. The brothers are on the lam from a botched robbery and waiting for their controlling mama to tell them what to do. The soft-spoken psycho eventually shows up and doesn't disappoint. **112m/C; DVD, Blu-Ray.** Rebecca De Mornay; Patrick Flueger; Warren Kole; Matt O'Leary; Jaime King; Frank Grillo; Deborah Ann Woll; Shawn Ashmore; ***D:*** Darren Lynn Bousman; ***W:*** Scott Milam; ***C:*** Joseph White; ***M:*** Bobby Johnston. **VIDEO**

Mother's Day **WOOF!** **2016 (PG-13)** Sandy (Aniston) is a divorced mother of two; Roberts plays Miranda, a writer who gave up her only child (later played by Robertson); and Hudson plays Jesse, a woman surprised by a visit from her parents. Sudeikis, Olyphant, and, of course, Hector Elizondo join the cast of people who should know better than to star in this lifeless, unfunny, insulting holiday ensemble "comedy." Garry Marshall's last directorial credit prior to his passing in July 2016. **118m/C; DVD.** Jennifer Aniston; Timothy Olyphant; Shay Mitchell; Caleb Brown; Brandon Spink; Julia Roberts; Kate Hudson; ***D:*** Garry Marshall; ***W:*** Anya Kochoff; Matthew Walker; Tom Hines; ***C:*** Charles Minsky; ***M:*** John Debney.

A Mother's Gift **1995** CBS TV movie adapted from the Bess Streeter Aldrich novel "A Lantern in Her Hand." Margaret chooses to marry William Deal and her mother gives her daughter her pearls as a wedding gift. The newlyweds leave their hometown to become western pioneers but find life is a struggle that eventually threatens their family. **97m/C; DVD.** Nancy McKeon; Adrian Pasdar; Adam Storke; Lucy Deakins; Jeremy London; Judith Hoag; ***D:*** Jerry London; ***W:*** Earl Hamner; ***C:*** Dennis C. Lewiston; ***M:*** Lee Holdridge. **TV**

Mothman **2010** Underdeveloped Syfy Channel monster flick with the usual dumb protagonists. Four friends covered up an accidental drowning but are still haunted by their crime 10 years later. That's when reporter Katharine returns to her Point Pleasant hometown to cover the annual local legend Mothman Festival. This year the Mothman returns as well—to get revenge on the stupid foursome. **88m/C; DVD.** Jewel Staite; Connor Fox; Susie Abromeit; Michael Aills; Jerry Leggio; ***D:*** Sheldon Wilson; ***W:*** Sonny Lee; Patrick Walsh; ***C:*** John Tarver; ***M:*** Steve London. **CABLE**

The Mothman Prophecies **2002 (PG-13)** Supernatural thriller based on true events occurring in Point Pleasant, WV, in the mid-1960s. John and Mary Klein (Gere, Messing) are in a car crash with a moth-like creature only seen by Mary. She later dies, but not before making some sketches of the insect-like beast. Reporter John ends up in Point Pleasant, where things get weird. Cop Connie's (Linney) the sole voice of reason in the superstitious bunch of locals as she and John team up to solve the Mothman mystery. Gere and Linney are fine actors wasted in this ho-hum story although the movie does have an aptly creepy tone. **119m/C; DVD.** Richard Gere; Laura Linney; Will Patton; Debra Messing; Lucinda Jenney; Alan Bates; David Eigenberg; Nesbitt Blaisdell; ***D:*** Mark Pellington; ***W:*** Richard Hatem; ***C:*** Fred Murphy; ***M:*** tomandandy.

Mothra *Mosura; Daikaiju Masura* **1962** Classic Japanese monster shenanigans about an enraged giant caterpillar that invades Tokyo while searching for the Alilenas, a set of very tiny, twin princesses who've been kidnapped by an evil nightclub owner in the pursuit of big profits. After tiring of crushing buildings and wreaking incidental havoc, the enormous crawly thing zips up into a cocoon and emerges as Mothra, a moth distinguished by both its size and bad attitude. Mothra and the wee babes make appearances in later Godzilla epics. **101m/C; VHS, DVD, Blu-Ray.** *JP* Frankie Sakai; Hiroshi Koizumi; Kyoko Kagawa; Yumi Ito; Emi Ito; Lee Kresel; Ken Uehara; Akihiko Hirata; Kenji Sahara; Takashi Shimura; ***D:*** Inoshiro Honda; ***W:*** Shinichi Sekizawa; ***C:*** Hajime Koizumi; ***M:*** Yuji Koseki.

The Motive ½ *El autor* **2018** Fortysomething aspiring author Alvaro (Gutierrez) works as a notary and is annoyed that his wife Amanda (Leon) is a successful award-winning writer. When Alvaro witnesses Amanda's infidelity, he moves into his own apartment and plans to write his own meaningful literature. However, Alvaro cannot come up with an original idea alone and takes the advice of his writing teacher (de la Torre) to find inspiration in his own life too literally by manipulating his new neighbors' live. This adaptation of the Javier Cercas novella fails to make the good use of the story's inherent black comedy and suspense. Spanish with subtitles. **112m/C; DVD.** Javier Gutierrez; Maria Leon; Adelfa Calvo; Adriana Paz; Tenoch Huerta; ***D:*** Manuel Martin Cuenca; ***W:*** Manuel Martin Cuenca; Alejandro Hernandez; ***C:*** Pau Esteve Birba; ***M:*** Pablo Perales Carrasco; Jose Luis Perales.

Motives **2003 (R)** Handsome, successful, and married businessman Emery Simms (Moore) indulges in a dangerous fling with free-spirited Allanah (Brooks) and winds up involved in murder. **87m/C; VHS, DVD.** Shemar Moore; Vivica A. Fox; Keisha Knight Pulliam; Golden Brooks; Victoria Rowell; Mel Jackson; Joe Torry; Sean Blakemore; ***D:*** Craig Ross, Jr.; ***W:*** Kelsey Scott; ***C:*** Ken Stipe. **VIDEO**

Motives 2—Retribution ½ **2007 (R)** In the first film, Emery Simms was convicted of a crime he didn't commit, and in the second he dies in prison after his best friend has married his ex-wife and achieved success. Emery's brother Donovan (White) arrives to find out what happened, and before long finds out if he keeps pressing for the truth he may end up sharing a grave with his brother. **94m/C; DVD.** Brian White; Vivica A. Fox; Sean Blakemore; ***D:*** Aaron Courseault; ***W:*** Kelsey Scott; ***C:*** Ken Stipe; ***M:*** Steve Gutheinz.

Motor Home Massacre **2005 (R)** Typical low-budget slasher that has the good sense not to take itself seriously. Seven friends set out for a woodland adventure in a vintage RV and come under attack from a power-tool wielding psycho. **91m/C; DVD.** Shan Holleman; Nelson Bonilla; Justin Geer; Tanya Fraser; Breanne Ashley; Greg Corbett; ***D:*** Allen Wilbanks; ***W:*** Allen Wilbanks; ***C:*** Allen Wilbanks. **CABLE**

Motor Psycho **WOOF!** *Motor Rods and Rockers; Rio Vengeance* **1965** When a motorcycle gang rapes a woman, she and her husband pursue them into the desert to seek their brutal revenge. **73m/B; VHS, DVD.** Haji; Alex Rocco; Stephen Oliver; Holle K. Winters; Joseph Cellini; Thomas Scott; Coleman Francis; Sharon Lee; Russ Meyer; ***D:*** Russ Meyer; ***W:*** Russ Meyer; William E. Sprague; ***C:*** Russ Meyer.

Motorama **1991 (R)** A 10-year-old juvenile delinquent becomes obsessed with winning a gas station contest which involves collecting game cards. So he steals a car and hits the road where he gets his first tattoo and encounters a beautiful "older" woman (Barrymore) and lots of trouble. **89m/C; VHS, DVD.** Jordan Christopher Michael; Martha Quinn; Flea; Michael J. Pollard; Meat Loaf Aday; Drew Barrymore; Garrett Morris; Robin Duke; Sandy Baron; Mary Woronov; Susan Tyrrell; John Laughlin; John Diehl; Robert Picardo; Jack Nance; Vince Edwards; Dick Miller; Allyce Beasley; Shelley Berman; ***D:*** Barry Shils; ***W:*** Joe Minion; ***C:*** Joseph Yacoe; ***M:*** Andy Summers.

The Motorcycle Diaries *Diarios de motocicleta* **2004 (R)** Unadorned narrative about the life of a pre-revolutionary Che Guevara, based on his diaries and a memoir from his best friend. In 1952, 23-year-old medical student Ernesto Guevara (Garcia Bernal) and his rowdy, older compadre, Alberto Granado (de la Serna) spend a few months on Ernesto's motorcycle traveling from Buenos Aires to Venezuela. Ernesto is dismayed by the poverty and injustice he sees around him; an extended stay caring for the sick in the San Pablo leper colony provides an emotional turning point. The film avoids being either a travelogue or a political polemic, thanks to the skill of both director Salles and his two leads. Spanish with subtitles. **128m/C; DVD, Blu-Ray.** *CL US AR PV* Gael Garcia Bernal; Rodrigo de la Serna; Mia Maestro; Gustavo Bueno; Jorge Chiarella; ***D:*** Walter Salles; ***W:*** Jose Rivera; ***C:*** Eric Gautier; ***M:*** Gustavo Santaolalla. Oscars '04: Song ("Al Otro Lado Del Rio"); British Acad. '04: Foreign Film, Orig. Score; Ind. Spirit '05: Cinematog., Debut Perf. (de la Serna).

Mouchette 🦴🦴🦴 1/2 **1967** A lonely 14-year-old French girl, daughter of a drunk father and dying mother, eventually finds spiritual release by committing suicide. Typically somber, spiritual fare from unique master filmmaker Bresson. Perhaps the most complete expression of Bresson's austere, Catholic vision. In French with English subtitles. **80m/B; VHS, DVD.** *FR* Nadine Nortier; Maria Cardinal; Paul Hebert; ***D:*** Robert Bresson; ***C:*** Ghislan Cloquet.

Moulin Rouge 🦴🦴🦴 1/2 **1952** Colorful, entertaining portrait of acclaimed Impressionist painter Toulouse-Lautrec, more famous for his production stories than on-screen drama, Ferrer delivers one of his most impressive performances as the physically stunted, cynical artist who basked in the seamy Montmartre nightlife. **119m/C; VHS, DVD; Open Captioned.** Jose Ferrer; Zsa Zsa Gabor; Christopher Lee; Peter Cushing; Colette Marchand; Katherine Kath; Michael Balfour; Eric Pohlmann; Suzanne Flon; Claude Nollier; Muriel Smith; Mary Clare; Walter Crisham; Harold Kasket; Jim Gerald; George Lannes; Lee Montague; Maureen Swanson; Tutte Lemkow; Jill Bennett; Theodore Bikel; ***D:*** John Huston; ***W:*** John Huston; Anthony Veiller; ***C:*** Oswald Morris. Oscars '52: Art Dir./Set Dec., Color, Costume Des. (C).

Moulin Rouge 🦴🦴🦴 **2001 (PG-13)** Luhrmann resurrects the famed Parisian/Montmartre nightclub decadence in his surreal quasi 1899-set movie musical that stars Kidman as the club's star singer/dancer/courtesan Satine, who entrances naive poet, Christian (McGregor). Naturally, their love is doomed—in part because she has this nasty cough. Luhrmann likes to shake up staid genres and in this case he uneasily married pop music with extraordinary elaborate visuals. This doesn't always work but the director deserves points for sheer chutzpah and Kidman has never looked more stunning. **126m/C; DVD, Blu-Ray.** *AU US* Nicole Kidman; Ewan McGregor; John Leguizamo; Jim Broadbent; Garry McDonald; Kylie Minogue; Richard Roxburgh; David Wenham; Natalie Mendoza; ***D:*** Baz Luhrmann; ***W:*** Baz Luhrmann; Craig Pearce; ***C:*** Donald McAlpine; ***M:*** Craig Armstrong. Oscars '01: Art Dir./Set Dec., Costume Des.; Australian Film Inst. '01: Cinematog., Costume Des., Film Editing, Sound; British Acad. '01: Score, Sound, Support. Actor (Broadbent); Golden Globes '02: Actor--Mus./Comedy, Actress--Mus./Comedy (Kidman), Film--Mus./Comedy, Score; L.A. Film Critics '01: Support. Actor (Broadbent); Natl. Bd. of Review '01: Film, Support. Actor (Broadbent).

The Mountain 🦴🦴 **1956** A man and his shady younger brother set out to inspect a Paris-routed plane that crashed in the French Alps. After some harrowing experiences in climbing the peak, it becomes evident that one brother has designs to save whatever he can, while the other intends to loot it. Many real, as well as staged, climbing scenes. Based on Henri Troyat's novel. **105m/C; VHS, DVD.** Spencer Tracy; Robert Wagner; Claire Trevor; William Demarest; Richard Arlen; E.G. Marshall; ***D:*** Edward Dmytryk.

The Mountain 🦴🦴 **2019** Brooding teenager Andy (Sheridan) works at an ice rink where his strict German figure skating father (Kier) trains young girls. Andy struggles with the absence of his mother, who was institutionalized years ago, and his lack of knowledge about her fate. After his father dies, Dr. Wallace Fiennes (Goldblum), who once treated Andy's mother, invites Andy to be his photographer on a road trip to mental institutions where he performs lobotomies on patients. Loosely based on Walter Jackson Freeman II, the developer of the transorbital lobotomy, it's somber mood emphasizes the dark side of humanity. **106m/C; DVD, Blu-Ray.** Tye Sheridan; Jeff Goldblum; Hannah Gross; Denis Lavant; Udo Kier; ***D:*** Rick Alverson; ***W:*** Rick Alverson; Dustin Guy Defa; Colm O'Leary; ***C:*** Lorenzo Hagerman; ***M:*** Robert Donne.

The Mountain Between Us 🦴 1/2 **2017 (PG-13)** A doctor (Elba), photojournalist (Winslet), and a dog (uncredited) survive the crash of their charter plane in the remote, snowy mountains of Utah. What begins as a mission of survival devolves into a romance so cheesy that you'll root for the mountain to prevail over these two talented yet sorely miscast leads. Based on the novel by Charles Martin. **100m/C; DVD, Blu-Ray.** Idris Elba; Kate Winslet; Beau Bridges; Dermot Mulroney; Linda Sorensen; ***D:*** Harry Abu-Assad; ***W:*** J. Mills Goodloe; Chris Weitz; ***C:*** Mandy Walker; ***M:*** Ramin Djawadi.

Mountain Family Robinson 🦴🦴 **1979 (G)** An urban family, seeking escape from the hassles of city life, moves to the Rockies, determined to get back to nature. They soon find that nature may be more harsh than rush-hour traffic and nasty bosses when a bear comes calling. More "Wilderness Family"-type adventures. **102m/C; VHS, DVD.** Robert F. Logan; Susan Damante-Shaw; Heather Rattray; Ham Larsen; William (Bill) Bryant; George "Buck" Flower; ***D:*** John Cotter.

The Mountain Men 🦴 1/2 **1980 (R)** Dull adventure drama set in the American West of the 1880s. Two trappers argue about life and have trouble with Indians. **102m/C; VHS, DVD.** Charlton Heston; Brian Keith; John Glover; Seymour Cassel; Victor Jory; ***D:*** Richard Lang; ***W:*** Fraser Heston; ***C:*** Michel Hugo; ***M:*** Michel Legrand.

Mountain of the Cannibal God WOOF! *Il Montagna di Dio Cannibale; Slave of the Cannibal God* **1979** Beautiful Andress is captured by "native" cannibals; Keach must save her. **103m/C; VHS, DVD, Blu-Ray.** *IT* Stacy Keach; Ursula Andress; Claudio Cassinelli; Franco Fantasia; ***D:*** Sergio Martino; ***M:*** Guido de Angelis; Maurizio de Angelis.

Mountains May Depart 🦴🦴🦴 *Shan he gu ren* **2016** The excellent Chinese director Jia Zhangke delivers arguably his most ambitious effort but also, ultimately, one of his most flawed in this time-spanning epic about the changes the filmmaker has seen in his country over the years and what he expects to come. This trio of stories opens in 1999 as a young woman has two suitors on different ends of the economic spectrum. In 2014, her son Dollar has become estranged from his mother. Even further in the future, Dollar (whose name is not coincidental) becomes a symbol for the Americanization of the East. It's interesting, but the final act really doesn't work. **131m/C; DVD, Blu-Ray.** Tao Zhao; Yi Zhang; Jing Dong Liang; Zijian Dong; Sylvia Chang; ***D:*** Zhangke Jia; ***W:*** Zhangke Jia; ***C:*** Nelson Lik-wai Yu; ***M:*** Yoshihiro Hanno.

Mountains of the Moon 🦴🦴🦴 1/2 **1990 (R)** Sprawling adventure detailing the obsessive search for the source of the Nile conducted by famed Victorian rogue/explorer Sir Richard Burton and cohort John Hanning Speke in the late 1800s. Spectacular scenery and images. Director Rafelson, better known for overtly personal films such as "Five Easy Pieces" and "The King of Marvin Gardens," shows considerable skill with this epic. From William Harrison's novel "Burton and Speke." **140m/C; VHS, DVD.** Patrick Bergin; Iain Glen; Fiona Shaw; Richard E. Grant; Peter Vaughan; Roger Rees; Bernard Hill; Anna Massey; Leslie Phillips; John Savident; James Villiers; Delroy Lindo; Roshan Seth; ***D:*** Bob Rafelson; ***W:*** Bob Rafelson; ***C:*** Roger Deakins; ***M:*** Michael Small.

Mountaintop Motel Massacre WOOF! **1986 (R)** A resort motel's hostess is a raving lunatic who regularly slaughters her guests. **95m/C; VHS, DVD.** Bill (Billy) Thurman; Anna Chappell; Will Mitchell; ***D:*** Jim McCullough, Sr.; ***W:*** Jim McCullough, Jr.; ***C:*** Joseph M. Wilcots; ***M:*** Ron Di Lulio.

Mountbatten: The Last Viceroy 🦴🦴 1/2 *Lord Mountbatten: The Last Viceroy* **1986** Originally a British TV miniseries detailing English viceroy Lord Mountbatten's (Williamson) turning over ruling power from Great Britain to India in 1947 and the birth of Pakistan. **107m/C; VHS, DVD.** *GB* Nicol Williamson; Janet Suzman; Sam Dastor; Nigel Davenport; Wendy Hiller; Ian Richardson; Julian Wadham; ***D:*** Tom Clegg; ***W:*** David Butler; ***C:*** Peter Jessop; ***M:*** John Scott.

Mouse Hunt 🦴🦴🦴 **1997 (PG)** The Smuntz brothers (Lane, Evans) inherit a rundown mansion from their wealthy string magnate father (Hickey, in his last role). Since the boys are estranged, they're happy to accept an offer from a preservation society. They try to fix up the house, only to be foiled by the mouse who's been its occupant. There are plenty of new mouse traps and tricks thanks to the 65 trained mice (along with 3D animation) who play the hero. The plucky rodent must also battle a psychotic cat and an obsessed exterminator (Walken). If you've ever laughed at a cartoon character taking an anvil to the head, you'll like this. Directorial debut of Verbinski. **97m/C; DVD.** Nathan Lane; Lee Evans; Christopher Walken; William Hickey; Vicki Lewis; Maury Chaykin; Eric Christmas; Michael Jeter; Debra Christofferson; Camilla Soeberg; ***D:*** Gore Verbinski; ***W:*** Adam Rifkin; ***C:*** Phedon Papamichael; ***M:*** Alan Silvestri.

The Mouse on the Moon 🦴🦴🦴 **1962** Sort-of sequel to "The Mouse That Roared" lacks the presence of Peter Sellers but maintains the whimsical tone of the original. The prime minister (Moody) of the Duchy of Grand Fenwick asks for American aid in setting up a space program. (Actually, he wants the money for indoor plumbing.) When it turns out that the local wine is actually rocket fuel, his amiable goof of a son (Cribbins) fulfills his lifelong dream of becoming an astronaut. The mild spoof of cold war politics lacks the anarchic spirit that director Lester has brought to "Help!" and his "Musketeer" films. **85m/C; DVD.** *GB* Margaret Rutherford; Ron Moody; Bernard Cribbins; Terry-Thomas; June Ritchie; David Kossoff; ***D:*** Richard Lester; ***W:*** Michael Pertwee; ***C:*** Wilkie Cooper; ***M:*** Ron Grainer.

The Mouse That Roared 🦴🦴🦴 **1959** With its wine export business going down the drain, a tiny, desperate country decides to declare war on the United States in hopes that the U.S., after its inevitable triumph, will revive the conquered nation. So off to New York go 20 chain-mail clad warriors armed with bow and arrow. Featured in three roles, Sellers is great as the duchess, less effective (though still funny) as the prime minister, and a military leader. A must for Sellers' fans; maintains a sharp satiric edge throughout. Based on the novel by Leonard Wibberley. **83m/C; VHS, DVD.** *GB* Peter Sellers; Jean Seberg; Leo McKern; David Kossoff; William Hartnell; Timothy Bateson; MacDonald Parke; Monte Landis; ***D:*** Jack Arnold; ***W:*** Roger MacDougall; Stanley Mann; ***M:*** Edwin Astley.

Mouth to Mouth 🦴🦴 *Boca a Boca* **1995 (R)** Budding actor Victor (Bardem) is working in Madrid as a phone sex operator while waiting to hear about his big break on an American picture. Victor's regularly called by repressed gay surgeon Ricardo (Flotats) and Amanda (Sanchez-Gijon), who says she's Ricardo's wife. Naive Victor falls for Amanda—who of course isn't Ricardo's wife but seems to be involved in a plot to kill Ricardo masterminded by his real wife Angela (Barranco) and her lover David (Gutierrez Caba). The plot's a little tangled but there's lots of visual gags and bedroom farce and the virile Bardem turns out to be a gifted comedian. Spanish with subtitles. **97m/C; DVD.** *SP* Javier Bardem; Aitana Sanchez-Gijon; Josep Maria Flotats; Maria Barranco; Emilio Gutierrez-Caba; Fernando Guillen; Myriam Meziere; ***D:*** Manuel Gomez Pereira; ***W:*** Manuel Gomez Pereira; Joaquin Oristrell; Naomi Wise; Juan Luis Iborra; ***C:*** Juan Amoros; ***M:*** Bernardo Bonezzi.

Move Over, Darling 🦴🦴 1/2 *Something's Gotta Give* **1963** Remake of 1938's "My Favorite Wife" has widower Garner having his wife Ellen (Day) declared legally dead five years after a plane crash. He remarries, only to have Ellen turn up on his mother's doorstep. Turns out she was stranded on a desert island for those years, and she wasn't alone. Fluffy but enjoyable Day vehicle is the second attempt to remake "Wife," after the ill-fated "Something's Gotta Give," the film Marilyn Monroe was working on when she died. Garner and Day are fine, but are often upstaged by the excellent supporting cast. **103m/C; VHS, DVD.** Doris Day; James Garner; Polly Bergen; Thelma Ritter; Chuck Connors; Fred Clark; Don Knotts; Edgar Buchanan; Elliott Reid; John Astin; Pat Harrington, Jr.; Eddie Quillan; Max (Casey Adams) Showalter; Alvy Moore; ***D:*** Michael Gordon; ***W:*** Hal Kanter; Leo McCarey; Jack Sher; ***C:*** Daniel F. Fapp; ***M:*** Lionel Newman. Golden Globes '63: Actress--Mus./Comedy (Day).

Movers and Shakers 🦴 1/2 **1985 (PG)** An irreverent spoof of Hollywood depicting a filmmaker's attempt to render a best-selling sex manual into a blockbuster film. Fails to live up to its potential and wastes a star-studded cast. **100m/C; VHS, Streaming.** Walter Matthau; Charles Grodin; Gilda Radner; Vincent Gardenia; Bill Macy; Tyne Daly; Steve Martin; Penny Marshall; Luana Anders; ***D:*** William Asher; ***W:*** Charles Grodin.

Movie Crazy 🦴 1/2 **1932** Movie crazy Kansas hayseed Harold Hall (Lloyd) is mistakenly offered a Hollywood screen test but the accident-prone fella causes havoc in the studio. The studio bosses finally decide he'd be perfect for comic roles and sign Harold to a contract. Silent star Lloyd's familiar antics were becoming obsolete in the talkie era and this comedy falls flat. **81m/B; DVD.** Harold Lloyd; Constance Cummings; Kenneth Thomson; Sydney Jarvis; Eddie Fetherston; Robert McWade; Louise Closser Hale; Spencer Charters; ***D:*** Clyde Bruckman; ***W:*** Vincent Lawrence; ***C:*** Walter Lundin.

Movie 43 WOOF! **2013 (R)** Shot piecemeal over the course of several years, the Peter Farrelly-produced anthology comedy proves that the only thing worse than one bad idea is a bunch of bad ideas. With 14 different storylines featuring an all-star cast, all of these comedy short films are presented as the brainchild of a project being pitched by a mad screenwriter (Quaid). Shockingly unfunny, the film feels like it was produced in conjunction with some sort of Hollywood community service. Commit a crime, be forced to do a segment in Movie 43. Interestingly, upon its release, none of its stars would promote it. **94m/C; DVD, Blu-Ray.** Dennis Quaid; Greg Kinnear; Hugh Jackman; Kate Winslet; Seth MacFarlane; Naomi Watts; Anna Faris; Chris Pratt; Kieran Culkin; Emma Stone; Richard Gere; Kate (Catherine) Bosworth; Jack McBrayer; Justin Long; Jason Sudeikis; Uma Thurman; Patrick Warburton; Gerard Butler; Johnny Knoxville; Halle Berry; Stephen Merchant; Terrence Howard; Elizabeth Banks; Josh Duhamel; ***D:*** Elizabeth Banks; Bob Odenkirk; Steven Brill; Steve Carr; Rusty Cundieff; James Duffy; Griffin Dunne; Peter Farrelly; Patrik Forsberg; Will Graham; James Dunn; Brett Ratner; Jonathan Van Tulleken; ***W:*** Patrik Forsberg; Steve Baker; Rocky Russo; Jeremy Sosenko; ***C:*** William Rexer; Matthew F. Leonetti; Daryn Okada; ***M:*** Tyler Bates; Christophe Beck; William Goodrum; Dave Hodge. Golden Raspberries '13: Worst Director (Brill), Worst Director (Carr), Worst Director (Cundieff), Worst Director (Duffy), Worst Director (Dunn), Worst Director (Dunne), Worst Director (Forsberg), Worst Director (Graham), Worst Director (Odenkirk), Worst Director (Ratner), Worst Director (Van Tulleken), Worst Picture, Worst Screenplay.

The Movie House Massacre 🦴 **1978** A psychopath runs rampant in a theatre killing and maiming moviegoers. No refunds are given. **80m/C; VHS, DVD.** Mary Woronov; Jenny Cunningham; Jonathan Blakely; Andrew Cofrin; ***D:*** Rick Sloane; ***W:*** Rick Sloane; ***C:*** Bill Fishman; ***M:*** Rick Sloane.

Movie, Movie 🦴🦴 1/2 **1978 (PG)** Acceptable spoof of 1930s films features Scott in twin-bill of black and white "Dynamite Hands," which lampoons boxing dramas, and "Baxter's Beauties," a color send-up of Busby Berkeley musicals. There's even a parody of coming attractions. Wholesome, mildly entertaining. **107m/B; VHS, Blu-Ray, Streaming.** Stanley Donen; George C. Scott; Trish Van Devere; Eli Wallach; Red Buttons; Barbara Harris; Barry Bostwick; Harry Hamlin; Art Carney; ***D:*** Stanley Donen; ***W:*** Larry Gelbart; ***M:*** Ralph Burns. Writers Guild '78: Orig. Screenplay.

Moving 🦴 **1988 (R)** An engineer must relocate his family from New Jersey to Idaho in order to get his dream job. Predictable calamities ensue. Not apt to move you. **89m/C; VHS, DVD.** Richard Pryor; Randy

Quaid; Dana Carvey; Dave Thomas; Rodney Dangerfield; Stacey Dash; *D:* Alan Metter; *W:* Andy Breckman; *M:* Howard Shore.

Moving Malcolm **2003** Feature directorial debut of screenwriter and star Ratner. Gene Maxwell was dumped at the altar by B-movie actress Liz Woodward (Berkley). He's surprised when Liz suddenly shows up at his door, but all she wants is a favor: help move her eccentric elderly father Malcolm (Neville) into a new apartment. Still smitten, Gene agrees, hoping it will rekindle their romance. Instead, Liz heads off to Prague for a movie shoot and he and Malcolm become kindred spirits. **83m/C; DVD.** *CA* Benjamin Ratner; Elizabeth Berkley; John Neville; Jay Brazeau; Babz Chula; Nicholas Lea; Rebecca Harker; *C:* Gregory Middleton; *M:* Chris Ainscough.

Moving McAllister ½ **2007 (PG-13)** Rick Robinson (Gourley) is a lowly intern at a Miami law firm. Desperate to score points with his boss, Maxwell McAllister (Hauer), he agrees to move McAllister's seductive niece Michelle (Kunis), her pet pig Dorothy, and various possessions cross-country. They pick up quirky hitchhiker Orlick Prescott Hope (Heder), and Rick finds his adventures just beginning. Unfortunately, they're boring and predictable and so's the movie. **90m/C; DVD.** Mila Kunis; Jon Heder; Rutger Hauer; Ben Gourley; *D:* Andrew Black; *W:* Ben Gourley; *C:* Douglas Chamberlain; *M:* Didier Rachou.

Moving Out **1983** Adolescent migrant Italian boy finds it difficult to adjust to his new surroundings in Melbourne, Australia. **91m/C; VHS, DVD.** Vince Colosimo; Sally Cooper; Maurice Devincentis; Tibor Gyapjas; *D:* Michael Pattinson.

Moving Target ½ **1989 (R)** A young woman witnesses the brutal murder of her boyfriend by mobsters and flees to Florida. Unbeknownst to her, the thugs are still after her. Although top-billed, Blair's role is actually a supporting one. **85m/C; VHS, DVD.** *IT* Linda Blair; Ernest Borgnine; Stuart Whitman; Charles Pitt; Jainine Linde; Kurt Woodruff; *D:* Marius Mattei.

Moving Target **1996 (R)** Sonny McClean (Dudikoff) is a bounty hunter. But his latest job has him framed for murder and caught up in the middle of mob rivalries. So in order to clear his name, Sonny has to avoid getting killed by violent gangs and quick-draw cops. **106m/C; VHS, DVD.** *CA* Michael Dudikoff; Billy Dee Williams; Michelle Johnson; Ardon Bess; Tom Harvey; Len Doncheff; Noam Jenkins; *D:* Damian Lee; *W:* Mark Sevi; Kevin McCarthy; *C:* David Pelletier; *M:* David Lawrence.

Moving Target **2000 (R)** Martial arts expert Wilson is framed for murder and must battle the mob to clear his name. **86m/C; VHS, DVD.** Don "The Dragon" Wilson; Bill Murphy; Hilary Kavanagh; Terry McMahon; Eileen McCloskey; Lisa Duane; *D:* Paul Ziller; *W:* Paul Ziller; *C:* Yoram Astrakhan; *M:* Derek Gleason. **VIDEO**

Moving Targets **1987** A young girl and her mother find themselves tracked by a homicidal maniac. **95m/C; VHS, DVD.** *AU* Michael Aitkens; Carmen Duncan; Annie Jones; Shane Briant; *D:* Chris Langman.

Moving Violation **1976 (PG)** Crooked cops chase two young drifters who have witnessed the local sheriff commit a murder. Corman car chase epic. **91m/C; VHS, DVD.** Eddie Albert; Kay Lenz; Stephen McHattie; Will Geer; Lonny (Lonnie) Chapman; *D:* Charles S. Dubin; *W:* William W. Norton, Sr.

Moving Violations **1985 (PG-13)** This could be entitled "Adventures in Traffic Violations School." A wise-cracking tree planter is sent to traffic school after accumulating several moving violations issued to him by a morose traffic cop. Bill Murray's little brother in feature role. **90m/C; VHS, DVD, Blu-Ray.** John Murray; Jennifer Tilly; James Keach; Brian Backer; Sally Kellerman; Fred Willard; Clara Peller; Wendie Jo Sperber; *D:* Neal Israel; *W:* Pat Proft; *C:* Robert Elswit; *M:* Ralph Burns.

Mowgli: Legend of the Jungle *Mowgli* **2018 (PG-13)** Human boy Mowgli (Chan) is orphaned as an infant after tiger Shere Khan (Cumberbatch) kills his mother. Mowgli is rescued and raised by wolves including Akela (Mullan), with the help of black panther Bagheera (Bale) and Baloo the bear (Serkis). Though the animals train young Mowgli in survival skills, his journey takes an unexpected turn when human hunter Lockwood (Rhys) captures Mowgli and he faces a choice about his future. Based on stories by Rudyard Kipling, the dark film includes realistic violence and brutality. The life-like computer-generated animals add an unexpected dimension to the film, but ultimately it doesn't improve the story. **104m/C; DVD.** Christian Bale; Cate Blanchett; Benedict Cumberbatch; Naomie Harris; Andy Serkis; *D:* Andy Serkis; *W:* Callie Kloves; *C:* Michael Seresin; *M:* Nitin Sawhney.

Mozart and the Whale ½ **2005 (PG-13)** Based on a true story. Donald (Hartnett) and Isabelle (Mitchell) both have Asperger's Syndrome (a form of autism), which results in problems dealing with the outside world or other people. Donald has assembled a support group, which Isabelle decides to join. Since Donald is so shy, she makes the first romantic move at a Halloween party where she's dressed as Mozart and Donald hides inside a whale costume. The relationship grows stronger but has a lot of pitfalls as Donald gains self-confidence while Isabelle grows more uncertain. Filmed on location in Spokane, Washington. **93m/C; DVD.** Josh Hartnett; Radha Mitchell; Gary Cole; Sheila Kelley; John Carroll Lynch; Rusty Schwimmer; Robert Wisdom; *D:* Petter Naess; *W:* Ronald Bass; *C:* Svein Krovel; *M:* Deborah Lurie.

Mozart's Sister ½ *Nannerl, Mozart's Sister; Nannerl, la Soeur de Mozart* **2010** Refreshing, though ultimately sad, historical costumer. Maria Anna 'Nannerl' Mozart, five years older than her brother Wolfgang, is the first prodigy in the family, an accomplished composer, singer, and musician in her own right. As the family travels to Europe's royal courts, her talent is soon overshadowed by that of her brother and the social mores of the times. Her father Leopold soon limits teenager Nannerl to merely accompanying Wolfgang and she worries about her prospects, especially after meeting Louise de France, the young convent-cloistered daughter of Louis XV, and Louise's widowed brother, the Dauphin. French with subtitles. **120m/C; DVD, Blu-Ray.** *FR* Marc Barbe; Delphine Chuillot; Marie Feret; David Moreau; Clovis Fouin; Lisa Feret; *D:* Rene Feret; *W:* Rene Feret; *C:* Benjamin Echazarreta; *M:* Marie-Jeanne Serrero.

Mrs. Lowry & Son ½ **2019** A dramatic portrait of L.S. Lowry, an English painter known for industrial scenes with distinctive "matchstick men," and his fraught relationship with his bedridden, hypercritical mother. The cinematography is unique, with Lowry imagining himself inside his landscape subjects before taking brush to canvas. Spall and Redgrave are masterclass actors who overcome the limitations of the screenplay, which retains the shadow of its origin as a stage and radio play. **91m/C; DVD.** Vanessa Redgrave; Timothy Spall; Stephen Lord; David Schaal; Michael Keogh; *D:* Adrian Noble; *W:* Martyn Hesford; *C:* Josep Civit; *M:* Craig Armstrong.

Ms. Purple ½ **2019** Kasie (Chu) works as a hostess in a private karaoke room to pay for a home nurse to care for her dying father (Kang). When the nurse quits, she begs Kasie to call a hospice. Refusing to do so, Kasie contacts her brother Carey (Lee), who ran away at 15. Though Carey has been estranged from his family, he has nothing better to do. Though there is wariness at first, the siblings come together as their past traumas surface. A moving exploration of family ties and obligations in Los Angeles's Koreatown, it's beautifully shot and features an engaging performance by Chu. **87m/C; DVD, Blu-Ray.** Crystal Lee; Jake Choi; Alma Martinez; Tiffany Chu; Teddy Lee; *D:* Justin Chon; *W:* Justin Chon; *C:* Ante Cheng; *M:* Roger Suen.

MTV's Wuthering Heights ½ *Wuthering Heights* **2003 (PG-13)** MTV pop-rock version, set in California, of Emily Bronte's classic romantic tragedy. The star-crossed lovers are blonde beauty Cate (Christensen) and a motorcyle-riding, up-and-coming rocker named Heath (Vogel). Cate's brother Hendrix (Whitworth) is suspicious and jealous and Cate, who's scared of her feelings, impulsively decides to marry nice guy Edward (Masterton). Certainly not for purists—or anyone out of their teen years. **88m/C; VHS, DVD.** Erika Christensen; Mike Vogel; Christopher K. Masterson; Katherine Heigl; Johnny Whitworth; John Doe; *D:* Suri Krishnamma; *W:* Max Enscoe; Annie de Young; *C:* Claudio Chea; *M:* Stephen Trask. **CABLE**

Much Ado about Nothing ½ **1993 (PG-13)** Shakespeare for the masses details romance between two sets of would-be lovers—the battling Beatrice and Benedick (Thompson, Branagh) and the ingenuous Hero and Claudio (Beckinsale, Leonard). Washington is the noble warrior leader, Reeves his evil half-dressed half-brother, and Keaton serves comic relief as the officious, bumbling Dogberry. Sunlit, lusty, and revealing about all the vagaries of love, Branagh brings passion to his quest of making Shakespeare more approachable. His second attempt after "Henry V" at breaking the stuffy Shakespearean tradition. Filmed on location in Tuscany, Italy. **110m/C; DVD.** *UK* Kenneth Branagh; Emma Thompson; Robert Sean Leonard; Kate Beckinsale; Denzel Washington; Keanu Reeves; Michael Keaton; Brian Blessed; Phyllida Law; Imelda Staunton; Gerard Horan; Jimmy Yuill; Richard Clifford; Ben Elton; Richard Briers; *D:* Kenneth Branagh; *W:* Kenneth Branagh; *C:* Roger Lanser; *M:* Patrick Doyle.

Much Ado About Nothing ½ **2005** BBC TV production is a contemporary update of the Shakespeare play set behind the scenes at a TV station. After her co-host is fired, presenter Beatrice must work with Benedict with whom she shares an unhappy past. The two trade sharp retorts while denying romantic feelings unlike weather girl Hero who's in love with reporter Claudio. Unfortunately, their romance isn't running any smoother. **90m/C; DVD.** *UK* Sarah Parish; Damian Lewis; Billie Piper; Tom Ellis; Derek Riddell; Martin Jarvis; Olivia Colman; *D:* Brian Percival; *W:* David Nicholls; *C:* Peter Greenhalgh; *M:* Tim Atack. **TV**

Much Ado About Nothing **2013 (PG-13)** Whedon's surprisingly faithful and entertaining modern take on Shakespeare's classic rom com was shot in black and white during a handful of weekends at the director's house in Santa Monica. Sworn bachelor Benedick (Denisof) is in full comic delight, tripping over his every step to find out whether the tough-talking, hardened single-lady Beatrice (Acker) may actually be falling for him. The entire thread, even down to the fouled wedding between Claudio and Hero remain true to the text. Unconventional enough to distance itself from earlier versions, while still maintaining the Bard's fine touches. Whedon is clearly a fan. **109m/B; DVD, Blu-Ray.** Amy Acker; Alexis Denisof; Fran Kranz; Jillian Morgese; Clark Gregg; Reed Edward Diamond; Sean Maher; Nathan Fillion; *D:* Joss Whedon; *W:* Joss Whedon; *C:* Jay Hunter; *M:* Joss Whedon.

Muck ½ **2015** An indie horror homage to the genre's late twentieth century heyday. On St. Patrick's Day, a group of friends feel lucky to have escaped from evil from an ancient burial ground that emerged from the marshes of Cape Cod. Though two of their friends have been lost and presumed dead, they feel lucky to find refuge in an empty vacation home on the Cape. After one friend leaves to locate help, the rest find that the evil from the marsh has followed them and a more savage force in the house also wants them dead. The friends must figure out how to escape both with their lives. **99m/C; DVD, Blu-Ray, Streaming, Download.** Lachlan Buchanan; Puja Mohindra; Bryce Draper; Laura Jacobs; Grant Alan Ouzts; *D:* Steve Wolsh; *W:* Steve Wolsh; *C:* Michael Solidum; *M:* Dan Marschak; Miles Senzaki.

Mud ½ **2012 (PG-13)** Writer/director Nichols weaves this accomplished, old-fashioned tale of a drifter named Mud (McConaughey), the girl Juniper he's come to rescue (Witherspoon), and the boy Ellis (Sheridan) caught in the middle. While Ellis' family life is falling apart (his parents are teetering on divorce), he finds Mud living in a boat in the middle of the woods. Mud says he's come to win back Juniper despite his run-ins with the law and her family. A relatively standard--yet impressive--character study by Nichols that symbolizes how a teen boy looks at divorce. McConaughey gives arguably the best performance of this career. **130m/C; DVD, Blu-Ray.** Matthew McConaughey; Tye Sheridan; Reese Witherspoon; Jacob Lofland; Sam Shepard; Michael Shannon; Sarah Paulson; *D:* Jeff Nichols; *W:* Jeff Nichols; *C:* Adam Stone; *M:* David Wingo. Ind. Spirit '14: Cast.

Mudbloods: A Movie About Quidditch ½ **2014** A documentary about the collegiate club sport quidditch, based on the fictional competition described by JK Rowling in her Harry Potter novels. In this documentary, the growing popularity of quidditch as a real sport is explored. To show the seriousness of the competitions, the filmmakers follow the underdog quidditch team from the University of California Los Angeles as they prepare for and compete in the Fifth Annual Quidditch World Cup in New York City. **89m/C; DVD, Streaming, Download.** *D:* Farzad Sangari; *W:* Farzad Sangari; Eric Martin; *C:* Jason Knutzen; *M:* Kevin Matley.

The Mudge Boy ½ **2003 (R)** Duncan Mudge (Hirsch) is not your average teenage boy. Wearing his dead mother's clothing, he bikes around town with his pet chicken in tow. Not surprisingly, he's picked on by the other boys and scorned by his own father (Jenkins). But one boy is drawn to Duncan, a tough kid named Perry (Guiry). Perry's confused sexuality leads him to abuse and then reject Duncan, with gruesome results. Explores the pain of loss and youth well. Cast is uniformly good, particularly Hirsch and Jenkins. And hey, who knew you could calm a chicken by sticking its head in your mouth? **94m/C; DVD.** Emile Hirsch; Tom Guiry; Richard Jenkins; Pablo Schreiber; Zachery Knighton; Ryan Donowho; Meredith Handerhan; Beckie King; *D:* Michael Burke; *W:* Michael Burke; *C:* Vanja Cernjul; *M:* Marcelo Zarvos.

Mudbound **2017 (R)** Thoughtful period melodrama that contrasts black and white families in post-World War II America. White supremacist Henry McAllan (Clarke) feels humiliated that he shares a piece of land with the black Jackson family after a bad business deal. In contrast, Jackson family patriarch Hap (Morgan) sees owning the land as a step up and enjoys farming. Henry's brother Jamie (Hedlund) and Florence Jackson's son Ronsel (Mitchell) bond over their service in World War II, where their perspectives on race and social mores evolved. Despite strong ties between some members of the families, violence eventually erupts. Superb performances abound in this well-crafted film. **134m/C; DVD.** Garrett Hedlund; Carey Mulligan; Jason Clarke; Rob Morgan; Jonathan Banks; Mary J. Blige; *D:* Dee Rees; *W:* Dee Rees; Virgil Williams; *C:* Rachel Morrison; *M:* Tamar-kali.

The Mudlark ½ **1950** Heartwarming historical drama. Orphaned urchin Wheeler (Ray) finds a cameo of Queen Victoria in the mudflats beside the Thames. Told she is Britain's 'mother,' the lad thinks that means she's his mother too and manages to slip into Windsor Castle to look for her. The Queen (Dunne) has been in seclusion for years following the death of Prince Albert, much to the dismay of Prime Minister Disraeli (Guinness). Can innocent Wheeler make a difference? **99m/B; DVD.** *UK* Irene Dunne; Alec Guinness; Andrew Ray; Beatrice Campbell; Finlay Currie; Anthony Steel; *D:* Jean Negulesco; *W:* Nunnally Johnson; *C:* Georges Perinal; *M:* William Alwyn.

The Mugger ½ **1958** Based on the second book in Ed McBain's 87th Precinct series, although it dispenses with the precinct cops to focus on cop/shrink Peter Graham. He's called in to help find a mugger who cuts women on one cheek after stealing their purses. The 12th victim is murdered but when the mugger is caught, he denies being the killer and Graham finds the actual criminal closer than he realizes. **74m/B; DVD.** Kent Smith; Nan Martin; James Franciscus; Dolores Sutton; George Maharis; Stefan Schnabel; *D:* William Berke; *W:* Henry Kane; *C:* J. Burgi Contner; *M:* Albert Glasser.

Muhammad Ali's Greatest Fight ½ **2013** HBO drama follows the court case of boxer Muhammad Ali, who was convicted of draft evasion, stripped of his world heavyweight title, and banned from boxing. In 1971, his appeal is heard by the Supreme Court, which is lead by Nixon-appointed conservative Chief Justice Warren Burger (Langella). Justice John Harlan II (Plummer) is chosen to write the opinion (against Ali) but the findings of his anti-war law clerk Kevin Connolly (Walker) that Ali is entitled to conscientious objector status causes Harlan to reconsider the decision. Ali is only seen in archival footage. **92m/C; DVD.** Christopher Plummer; Benjamin Walker; Frank Langella; Ed Begley, Jr.; Peter Gerety; Barry Levinson; Danny Glover; Harris Yulin; John Bedford Lloyd; Fritz Weaver; ***D:*** Stephen Frears; ***W:*** Shawn Slovo; ***C:*** Jim Denault. **CABLE**

Mulan 🦴🦴 ½ **1998 (G)** Disney's 36th animated tale is taken from a Chinese fable. The Emperor (Morita) sends out an order that one man from every family must become a soldier in order to repel the advances of Shan-Yu (Ferrer) and his army. Mulan (Wen) decides to take her ill father's place and disguises herself as a warrior. The family's ancestral spirits enlist pint-sized dragon, Mushu (Murphy), as Mulan's guardian. However, the two mainstays of Disney animated features—the songs and the comedy-relief sidekicks—turn out to be the weak links in this story. Impressive visuals and careful voice characterization make up for any formulaic missteps. **87m/C; DVD, Blu-Ray.** ***V:*** Ming Na; Eddie Murphy; B.D. Wong; Miguel Ferrer; Soon-Teck Oh; Noriyuki "Pat" Morita; Harvey Fierstein; Gedde Watanabe; James Hong; Freda Foh Shen; Matthew Wilder; June Foray; Marni Nixon; George Takei; Miriam Margolyes; James Shigeta; Frank Welker; Lea Salonga; Donny Osmond; Jerry S. Tondo; ***D:*** Barry Cook; Tony Bancroft; ***W:*** Philip LaZebnik; Raymond Singer; Rita Hsiao; Chris (Christopher) Sanders; Eugenia Bostwick-Singer; ***M:*** Matthew Wilder; Jerry Goldsmith; ***M:*** David Zippel.

Mulan 2 🦴🦴 ½ **2004 (G)** A more comic Disney continuation of the animated adventure. Heroine Mulan becomes engaged to General Shang but the wedding is delayed when the Emperor asks them to escort his three daughters across China to their arranged marriages. Guardian dragon Mushu realizes he'll be out of work if Mulan marries, so he's determined to break the couple up. **79m/C; DVD, Blu-Ray.** ***V:*** Ming Na; B.D. Wong; Mark Moseley; Lucy Liu; Sandra Oh; Lauren Tom; Harvey Fierstein; Gedde Watanabe; Pat Morita; June Foray; George Takei; ***D:*** Darrell Rooney; Lynne Sutherland; ***W:*** Michael Lucker; Chris Parker; Roger S.H. Schulman; ***M:*** Joel McNeely. **VIDEO**

Mulberry Street 🦴🦴 **2006 (R)** Everyone knows that there's lots of rats in New York City. Only this time the rodents are infected with a virus that has them attacking humans. The humans are then transformed into rat/human, flesh-eating zombies. Former boxer Clutch (Damici) looks out for his Mulberry Street neighbors but he really has him work cut out for him now. Low-budget but surprisingly scary. **84m/C; DVD.** Nick Damici; Kimberly Blair; Ron Brice; Larry Fleishman; Bo Corre; Larry Medich; Javier Picyo; ***D:*** Jim Mickle; ***W:*** Nick Damici; Jim Mickle; ***C:*** Ryan Samul; ***M:*** Andreas Kapsalis.

The Mule 🦴🦴🦴 **2018 (R)** The true story of Earl Stone, an 87-year-old drug courier for the Mexican cartel. This is classic Eastwood: a serious, gravely, flawed man making questionable choices and regretting his past, particularly where his family is concerned. As his cargo and his wealth increases, so does his exposure, and soon DEA agent Colin Bates (Cooper) has Stone in his sights. Inspired by the *New York Times Magazine* article "The Sinaloa Cartel's 90-Year Old Drug Mule," by Nick Schenk. Sam Dolnick (inspired by the New York Times Magazine Article "The Sinaloa Cartel's 90-Year Old Drug Mule" by) **116m/C; DVD, Blu-Ray.** Clint Eastwood; Bradley Cooper; Michael Peña; Taissa Farmiga; Jill Flint; ***D:*** Clint Eastwood; ***W:*** Nick Schenk; ***C:*** Yves Bélanger; ***M:*** Arturo Sandoval.

Mulholland Drive 🦴🦴🦴 **2001 (R)** Lynch is up to his old trippy surrealistic tricks with lush visuals and atmospheric Badalamenti music the key ingredients in this hypnotic look at Hollywood through a kaleidoscope. Betty (Watts), an aspiring actress staying at her aunt's vacant apartment, comes home to find Rita (Harring) taking a shower. Rita has amnesia and Betty tries to help her piece her life together. Meanwhile, successful director Adam (Theroux) is threatened with death unless he casts a certain actress favored by a wheelchair-bound dwarf who issues orders over a cell phone. Then things get even weirder. Originally conceived as a pilot for ABC TV, but reshot as a feature. **146m/C; DVD, Blu-Ray.** Naomi Watts; Laura Elena Harring; Justin Theroux; Ann Miller; Dan Hedaya; Lafayette Montgomery; Michael J. Anderson; Scott Coffey; Chad Everett; Melissa George; James Karen; Katharine Towne; Billy Ray Cyrus; Angelo Badalamenti; Mark Pellegrino; Lee Grant; Kathrine (Kate) Forster; Missy (Melissa) Crider; Brent Briscoe; Marcus Graham; Vincent Castellanos; Michael Des Barres; Robert Forster; ***D:*** David Lynch; ***W:*** David Lynch; ***C:*** Peter Deming; ***M:*** Angelo Badalamenti. Cesar '01: Foreign Film; Ind. Spirit '02: Cinematog.; L.A. Film Critics '01: Director (Lynch); Natl. Bd. of Review '01: Breakthrough Perf. (Watts); N.Y. Film Critics '01: Film; Natl. Soc. Film Critics '01: Actress (Watts), Film.

Mulholland Falls 🦴🦴 ½ **1995 (R)** Noir meets the nuclear age in this stylish period piece from New Zealand director Tamahori. Nolte plays the leader of the Hat Squad, a vicious group of fedora-sporting detectives assigned to bust organized crime in '50s L.A. at all costs. While investigating the murder of his ex-mistress, Nolte and cohorts Madsen, Palminteri and Penn discover evidence linking the murder to a general (Malkovich) in charge of the top secret nuclear program. Although the cast is dripping with big name stars, the best performance is put in by the glossy set design of Richard Sylbert, who probably had a strong case of deja vu, having previously done "Chinatown." **107m/C; VHS, DVD, Blu-Ray.** Nick Nolte; Melanie Griffith; Chazz Palminteri; Michael Madsen; Christopher Penn; Treat Williams; Jennifer Connelly; Andrew McCarthy; John Malkovich; Daniel Baldwin; Bruce Dern; Ed Lauter; ***Cameo(s):*** William L. Petersen; Rob Lowe; ***D:*** Lee Tamahori; ***W:*** Pete Dexter; ***C:*** Haskell Wexler; ***M:*** Dave Grusin. Golden Raspberries '96: Worst Support. Actress (Griffith).

Mulligan 🦴 ½ **2000** Amateurish indie buddy comedy. Jordan hates his job and his girlfriend has left him so he plays golf with his three equally messed-up buddies. They all need a do-over (and not just in their golf game). **86m/C; DVD.** Cedric Yarbrough; Steve Lattery; Joshua Will; Trei Michaels; Bill Borea; ***D:*** Tim Vandesteeg; ***W:*** Kevin Ross; Joshua Will; Bill Borea; Tim Vandesteeg; ***C:*** Afshin Shahidi; ***M:*** Michael Whalen.

Mulligans 🦴🦴 ½ **2008** Tyler Davidson brings gay college buddy Chase home to quaint Prospect Lake and they both get summer jobs at the golf course. Tyler's parents got married right after high school and his dad Nathan has been repressing some long-held feelings. The situation gets worse when Chase realizes he's attracted to Nathan. Well-told family drama that never descends into bathos. **90m/C; DVD.** *CA* Dan Payne; Thea Gill; Charlie David; Derek Baynham; Grace Vukovic; ***D:*** Chip Hale; ***W:*** Charlie David; ***C:*** Alice Brooks; ***M:*** Robert (Bob) Buckley.

Multiple Sarcasms 🦴 ½ **2010 (R)** Flaking out on his job and family, New York architect Gabriel (Hutton) undergoes a generic midlife crisis and focuses on writing a play about his existential dilemma. If that weren't bad enough, he turns to alcohol for inspiration and slowly convinces himself that he's in love with his childhood friend, Cari (Sorvino). Nearly obsessive detail is spent crafting a perfect 1979 decor, but unfortunately Gabriel is an annoyingly self-centered bore with zero of the charisma writer/director Branch intended. Self-indulgent rather than a witty, self-aware drama. **97m/C; Blu-Ray, On Demand.** Timothy Hutton; Mira Sorvino; Dana Delaney; India Ennenga; Mario Van Peebles; Stockard Channing; Laila Robins; ***D:*** Brooks Branch; ***W:*** Brooks Branch; Linda Morris; ***C:*** Jacek Laskus; ***M:*** George J. Fontenette.

Multiplicity 🦴🦴 ½ **1996 (PG-13)** With too many business and personal responsibilities, construction supervisor Doug Kinney (Keaton) is a prime candidate for the cloning experiments of Dr. Leeds (Yulin). Since the cloning process isn't exactly perfect, each clone (Doug winds up with three) has a different dominant personality trait—a hard-charger, a "Mister Mom," and a dopey slacker. Confusion reigns as wife Laura (MacDowell) deals with separation anxiety on a grand scale. Pleasant comedy shows Keaton can still be funny given the chance. **117m/C; VHS, DVD, Blu-Ray.** Michael Keaton; Andie MacDowell; Harris Yulin; Richard Masur; Eugene Levy; Obba Babatunde; Ann Cusack; Brian Doyle-Murray; Julie Bowen; ***D:*** Harold Ramis; ***W:*** Harold Ramis; Chris Miller; Lowell Ganz; Babaloo Mandel; Mary Hale; ***C:*** Laszlo Kovacs; ***M:*** George Fenton.

Mumford 🦴🦴🦴 **1999 (R)** Writer/director Kasdan creates another ensemble gem in this story of small town psychologist Mumford (Dean), who uses unusual methods to help the quirky townsfolk deal with their problems. His ability to actually listen to people helps out a young skateboarding millionaire (Lee), a shopaholic wife (McDonnell), her loutish husband (Danson), and nearly everyone else--except a slimy lawyer (Short) who the good doctor fires as a patient. He begins to dig up facts that may prove that Mumford isn't even a doctor. Since there's no big plot payoff or mind-boggling twists, some viewers may find it a bit boring. **112m/C; VHS, DVD, Blu-Ray.** Loren Dean; Alfre Woodard; Hope Davis; Jason Lee; Mary McDonnell; Pruitt Taylor Vince; Zooey Deschanel; Martin Short; David Paymer; Jane Adams; Dana Ivey; Kevin Tighe; Ted Danson; Jason Ritter; Elisabeth Moss; Robert Stack; ***D:*** Lawrence Kasdan; ***W:*** Lawrence Kasdan; ***C:*** Ericson Core; ***M:*** James Newton Howard.

The Mummy 🦴🦴🦴 ½ **1932** Scientists examine a sarcophagus taken from an unmarked grave at an archeological dig in 1921 Egypt. There is a warning that it should not be opened. Does this stop anyone? Of course not! So Im-Ho-Tep (Karloff), a 4000-year-old priest who was buried alive is now revived. His objective—heroine Helen (Johann) whom the wrapped one believes is the reincarnation of his long-gone love. Eerie chills mark this classic horror tale that found Karloff undergoing eight hours of extraordinary makeup (by Jack Pierce) to transform him into the macabre mummy. The directing debut of famed German cinematographer Freund. The first in the Universal series. **72m/B; DVD, Blu-Ray.** Boris Karloff; Zita Johann; David Manners; Edward Van Sloan; Arthur Byron; Bramwell Fletcher; Noble Johnson; Leonard Mudie; Henry Victor; ***D:*** Karl Freund; ***W:*** John Lloyd Balderston; ***C:*** Charles Stumar.

The Mummy 🦴🦴🦴 **1959** A group of British archaeologists discover they have made a grave mistake when a mummy kills off those who have violated his princess' tomb. A summation of all the previous "mummy" films, this one has a more frightening mummy (6'4" Lee) who is on screen much of the time. Additionally, there is pathos in this monster, not merely murder and revenge. An effective remake of the 1932 classic. **88m/C; VHS, DVD, Blu-Ray.** *GB* Peter Cushing; Christopher Lee; Felix Aylmer; Yvonne Furneaux; Eddie Byrne; Raymond Huntley; George Pastell; Michael Ripper; John Stuart; ***D:*** Terence Fisher; ***W:*** Jimmy Sangster; ***C:*** Jack Asher.

The Mummy 🦴🦴 ½ **1999 (PG-13)** Cheesy fun in the Saturday matinee tradition, this horror tale is a loose remake of the 1932 Boris Karloff-starrer. In the 1920s, American adventurer Rick O'Connell (Fraser) is hired by British librarian Evelyn (Weisz) and her Egyptologist brother Jonathan (Hannah) to escort them to the ancient Egyptian city of the dead. Unfortunately, their meddling results in the release of cursed mummified priest Imhotep (Vosloo), who manages to regenerate into living flesh and who wants to use Evelyn to resurrect his dead girlfriend. Lots of zombies, mummies, skeletons, and flesh-eating beetles as well as spooky tombs. **124m/C; VHS, DVD, Blu-Ray, HD-DVD.** Brendan Fraser; Rachel Weisz; Arnold Vosloo; John Hannah; Kevin J. O'Connor; Jonathan Hyde; Oded Fehr; Erik Avari; Tuc Watkins; Stephen Dunham; Corey Johnson; Bernard Fox; Aharon Ipale; Omid Djalili; Patricia Velasquez; ***D:*** Stephen Sommers; ***W:*** Stephen Sommers; ***C:*** Adrian Biddle; ***M:*** Jerry Goldsmith.

The Mummy 🦴🦴 **2017 (PG-13)** The Mummy is the first of Universal's classic horror characters to be dug up and rereleased under its Dark Universe banner, but the reboot lacks any understanding of what made those monsters classic in the first place. A couple of soldiers (Cruise and Johnson) stumble into the crypt of Ahmanet, an Egyptian princess who was long ago done wrong and turned evil, and now she wants to take over the modern world, starting with London. The Hound thinks this snore should cruise back to the vault. **120m/C; DVD, Blu-Ray.** Tom Cruise; Russell Crowe; Annabelle Wallis; Sofia Boutella; Jake Johnson; ***D:*** Alex Kurtzman; ***W:*** David Koepp; Christopher McQuarrie; Dylan Kussman; ***C:*** Ben Seresin; ***M:*** Brian Tyler. Golden Raspberries '17: Worst Actor (Cruise).

The Mummy Lives 🦴🦴 **1993 (PG-13)** Vegeance-minded mummy goes on a murderous rampage against the defilers of his tomb and becomes obsessed with a woman he believes is his reincarnated lost love. **97m/C; VHS, DVD.** Tony Curtis; Greg Wrangler; Muhamad (Mohammed) Bakri; Leslie Hardy; ***D:*** Gerry O'Hara; ***W:*** Nelson Gidding; ***C:*** Avi Koren; ***M:*** Dov Seltzer.

The Mummy Returns 🦴🦴 ½ **2001 (PG-13)** Bombastic sequel to the 1999 hit is set a decade later and finds marrieds Rick (Fraser) and Evelyn (Weisz) living in London with their young son, Alex (Boath). Unfortunately, a reincarnated Anck-Su-Namun (Velasquez) manages to bring crispy Inhotep (Vosloo) back again to rule the world. Fehr returns as desert warrior Ardeth Bay, as does Hannah as Evelyn's ne'er-do-well brother. Wrestler Dwayne "The Rock" Johnson briefly shows up as a new villain—The Scorpion King, who's going to have his own film. But there's too much going on—it's loud and crowded, sacrificing the original's unexpected charm for visual overkill. **129m/C; VHS, DVD, Blu-Ray, HD-DVD.** Brendan Fraser; Rachel Weisz; Oded Fehr; John Hannah; Patricia Velasquez; Dwayne "The Rock" Johnson; Arnold Vosloo; Flip Kobler; Adewale Akinnuoye-Agbaje; Shaun Parkes; Alun Armstrong; ***D:*** Stephen Sommers; ***W:*** Stephen Sommers; ***C:*** Adrian Biddle; ***M:*** Alan Silvestri.

The Mummy: Tomb of the Dragon Emperor 🦴🦴 **2008 (PG-13)** Third time around for overly-experienced mummy battler Rick O'Connell (Fraser), joined by his wife Evelyn (Bello) in aiding their son Alex (Ford), who has accidentally awakened the evil Dragon Emperor (Li). The emperor resurrects an undead army of 10,000 to conquer the world, but luckily the emperor's archenemy, the fierce sorceress Zi Juan (Yeoh), doesn't approve, bringing her own CGI soldiers into the mix. Little more than a poor man's Indiana Jones flick on steroids. **114m/C; DVD, Blu-Ray, On Demand.** Brendan Fraser; Jet Li; Maria Bello; Luke Ford; John Hannah; Michelle Yeoh; Isabella Leong; Anthony Wong; Liam Cunningham; Russell Wong; ***D:*** Rob Cohen; ***W:*** Alfred Gough; Miles Millar; ***C:*** Simon Duggan; ***M:*** Randy Edelman.

Mummy's Boys 🦴 **1936** Static would-be horror/slapstick comedy from Wheeler & Woolsey lacks the budget to make for a memorable mummy. Ditch-diggers Stanley and Aloyius take a job on an archeological expedition in Egypt. So far nine of the 10 archeologists at the site have been murdered, allegedly for tomb desecration, but the killer is as obvious as the jokes. **68m/B; DVD.** Bert Wheeler; Robert Woolsey; Moroni Olsen; Barbara Pepper; Frank M. Thomas, Sr.; ***D:*** Fred Guiol; ***W:*** Jack Townley; Philip G. Epstein; Charles E. Roberts; ***C:*** Jack MacKenzie; ***M:*** Roy Webb.

The Mummy's Hand 🦴🦴 ½ **1940** Although this is the followup to 1932's "The Mummy," it actually has little to do with the original film. Archaeologists Steve Banning (Foran) and Babe Jensen (Ford) are searching for the tomb of ancient Egyptian Princess Ananka. Crazy high priest Andoheb (Zucco) sends mummy Kharis (Tyler), who is the tomb's guardian, to kill anyone who defiles her rest. So Kharis shuffles off but finds Marta (Moran) instead. And being a guy, albeit a long-dead guy, wants to make the beauty his bride. Low-budget but the mix of scares and comedy make this worth watching. **70m/B; VHS, DVD, Blu-Ray.** Dick Foran; Wallace Ford; Peggy Moran; Cecil Kellaway; George Zucco; Tom Tyler; Eduardo Ciannelli; Charles Trowbridge; ***D:*** Christy Cabanne; ***W:*** Griffin Jay; Maxwell Shane; ***C:*** Elwood "Woody" Bredell; ***M:*** Hans J. Salter.

The Mummy's Shroud 🦴🦴 **1967** Hammer's next-to-last Mummy horror is a handsomely produced but tepid affair. The plot trots out the familiar elements—British archeological dig led by Sr. Basil Walden (Morell) discovers the remains of Pharaoh Kah-to-Bey; hieroglyphics from the shroud are read aloud...you know the drill. Lots of talk, comparatively little action. **90m/C; DVD, Blu-Ray.** *GB* Andre Morrell; John Phillips; David Buck; Elizabeth Sellars; ***D:*** John Gilling; ***W:*** John Gilling; ***C:*** Arthur Grant; ***M:*** Don Banks.

The Mummy's Tomb **1942** Chaney Jr. is in wraps for the first time in this sequel to "The Mummy's Hand." Kharis is transported to America by a crazed Egyptian high priest to kill off surviving members of the expedition. Weakened by a lame script and too much stock footage. Based on a story by Neil P. Varnick. **71m/B; VHS, DVD, Blu-Ray.** Lon Chaney, Jr.; Dick Foran; John Hubbard; Elyse Knox; George Zucco; Wallace Ford; Turhan Bey; Jack Arnold; ***D:*** Harold Young; ***W:*** Griffin Jay; Henry Sucher; ***C:*** George Robinson.

Munchie **1/2 1992 (PG)** A forgotten alien critter is discovered in a mine shaft by young Gage. Munchie turns out to be a good friend, protecting Gage from bullies and granting other wishes. Frequent sight gags help keep the film moving but it's still awfully slow. Sequel to "Munchies" (1987). **80m/C; VHS, DVD, Blu-Ray.** Loni Anderson; Andrew Stevens; Arte Johnson; Jamie McEnnan; ***V:*** Dom DeLuise; ***D:*** Jim Wynorski.

Munchies **1987 (PG)** "Gremlins" rip-off about tiny aliens who love beer and fast food, and invade a small town. Lewd and ribald. **83m/C; VHS, DVD, Blu-Ray.** Harvey Korman; Charles (Charlie) Stratton; Nadine Van Der Velde; Alix Elias; Jon Stafford; Charlie Phillips; Hardy Rawls; Robert Picardo; Wendy Schaal; Paul Bartel; ***D:*** Bettina Hirsch; ***W:*** Lance Smith; ***C:*** Jonathan West.

Munich **1/2 2005 (R)** Spielberg explores in horrifying magnification the politics and far-reaching aftermath of the real-life shocking murders of 11 Israeli athletes at the 1972 Munich Olympics. However, the film is primarily about a team of Israeli agents (Bana, Craig, Hinds, Kassovitz) hired to exact revenge on the Palestinian assassins. Gold standard screenwriters Kushner and Roth draw liberally from George Jonas's nonfiction tome "Vengeance," and, like his other fact-based dramas, Spielberg delivers a thought-provoking and intense experience, making us cringe at the transforming power of revenge. **164m/C; DVD, Blu-Ray.** Eric Bana; Daniel Craig; Ciaran Hinds; Mathieu Kassovitz; Hanns Zischler; Geoffrey Rush; Michael (Michel) Lonsdale; Mathieu Amalric; Lynn Cohen; Marie Josee Croze; Makram Khoury; Moritz Bleibtreu; Gila Almagor; Moshe Ivgi; Yvan Attal; Hiam Abbass; Valeria Bruni-Tedeschi; Meret Becker; Ayelet Zurer; Igal Naor; Omar Metwally; Mostefa Djadjam; ***D:*** Steven Spielberg; ***W:*** Tony Kushner; Eric Roth; ***C:*** Janusz Kaminski; ***M:*** John Williams.

Munster, Go Home! **1/2 1966** Herman learns he's inherited the stately manor Munster Hall so he and the family head for jolly old England to claim their family history. Will the Brits ever recover? **96m/C; VHS, DVD, Blu-Ray.** Fred Gwynne; Yvonne De Carlo; Al Lewis; Butch Patrick; Debbie Watson; Terry-Thomas; Hermione Gingold; Robert Pine; John Carradine; Bernard Fox; Richard Dawson; Arthur Malet; ***D:*** Earl Bellamy; ***W:*** Joe Connelly; Bob Mosher; George Tibbles; ***C:*** Benjamin (Ben H.) Kline; ***M:*** Jack Marshall.

The Munsters' Revenge **1981** Based on the continuing adventures of the 1960s comedy series characters. Herman, Lily, and Grandpa have to contend with robot replicas of themselves that were created by a flaky scientist. **96m/C; VHS, DVD.** Fred Gwynne; Yvonne De Carlo; Al Lewis; Jo McDonnell; Sid Caesar; Ezra Stone; Howard Morris; Bob Hastings; K.C. Martel; ***D:*** Don Weis; ***M:*** Vic Mizzy. **TV**

The Muppet Christmas Carol **1/2 1992 (G)** Christmas classic features all the muppet favorites together and in Victorian garb. Storyline is more or less faithful to Dickens original, with pleasant special effects. Gonzo the Great as Dickens narrates the tale as Scrooge (Caine) takes his legendary Christmas Eve journey escorted by three (flannel) spirits. The Cratchits are led by Kermit and Miss Piggy. Directed by Brian Henson, Jim's son, the film is as heartwarming as the Cratchit's crackling fire, but doesn't quite achieve the former muppet magic. Also features some sappy songs by Williams, including "Love is Like a Heatwave" and "Island in the Sun." **120m/C; VHS, DVD, Blu-Ray.** Michael Caine; ***V:*** Dave Goetz; Steve Whitmire; Jerry Nelson; Frank Oz; ***D:*** Brian Henson; ***C:*** John Fenner; ***M:*** Paul Williams; Miles Goodman.

The Muppet Movie **1/2 1979 (G)** Seeking fame and footlights, Kermit the Frog and his pal Fozzie Bear travel to Hollywood, and along the way are joined by sundry human and muppet characters, including the lovely Miss Piggy. A delightful cult favorite filled with entertaining cameos, memorable (though somewhat pedestrian) songs and crafty special effects—Kermit rides a bike and rows a boat! A success for the late Jim Henson. **94m/C; VHS, DVD, Blu-Ray.** *GB* ***Cameo(s):*** Edgar Bergen; Milton Berle; Mel Brooks; Madeline Kahn; Steve Martin; Carol Kane; Paul Williams; Charles Durning; Bob Hope; James Coburn; Dom DeLuise; Elliott Gould; Cloris Leachman; Telly Savalas; Orson Welles; ***V:*** Jim Henson; Frank Oz; Jerry Nelson; Richard Hunt; Dave Goetz; ***D:*** James Frawley; ***W:*** Jack Burns; Jerry Juhl; ***C:*** Isidore Mankofsky; ***M:*** Paul Williams. Natl. Film Reg. '09.

Muppet Treasure Island **1/2 1996 (G)** Literary classic gets its first coat of felt as Kermit the Frog, Miss Piggy and the entire Muppet gang hit the high seas in an adaptation of Robert Louis Stevenson's 1883 well-worn adventure tale. Delightful settings, from an old English tavern to an exotic south sea island, frame the journey of young Jim Hawkins (flesh and blood Bishop), who along with tavern owners Rizzo the Rat (Whitmire) and the Great Gonzo (Goelz) search for buried treasure. Long John Silver is played to the hilt by Curry, master of the over-the-top villain. Helmer Henson steers a steady ship, with over 400 Muppet critters making an appearance. **99m/C; VHS, DVD, Blu-Ray; Closed Captioned.** Tim Curry; Kevin Bishop; Billy Connolly; Jennifer Saunders; ***V:*** Steve Whitmire; Frank Oz; Dave Goetz; ***D:*** Brian Henson; ***W:*** Jerry Juhl; James V. Hart; Kirk R. Thatcher; ***C:*** John Fenner; ***M:*** Hans Zimmer.

The Muppets **2011 (PG)** Part nostalgia piece, part kid's movie, and part old-fashioned vaudeville show, this reboot of the legendary Jim Henson creation is a success for all ages. Segel co-wrote and stars as Gary, older brother to Walter (a new puppet) and boyfriend of Mary (Adams). The three end up at the center of a telethon to save their beloved Muppets. With numerous nods to the original show and films, director Bobin's comedy plays as well for parents who fondly remember Kermit & Fozzie as it does for their kids who may not yet know about the Rainbow Connection. **98m/C; DVD, Blu-Ray.** Jason Segel; Amy Adams; Chris Cooper; Rashida Jones; ***V:*** Steve Whitmire; Eric Jacobson; Dave Goelz; Bill Barretta; David Rudman; ***D:*** James Bobin; ***W:*** Jason Segel; Nicholas Stoller; ***C:*** Don Burgess; ***M:*** Christophe Beck. Oscars '11: Song ("Man or Muppet").

Muppets from Space **1/2 1999 (G)** The sixth full-length movie featuring Jim Henson's uberpuppets centers on Gonzo and his search for his real family. He discovers that he is an alien from a distant planet and announces his findings on Miss Piggy's talk show. Soon, government bad guy K. Edgar Singer (Tambor) is after him. After escaping Singer, Gonzo must decide whether to stay on earth with his friends or leave on the family spaceship. Features cameos by Ray Liotta, F. Murray Abraham, Andie MacDowell, and Hulk Hogan. Perfect for the sippy-cup set. **88m/C; VHS, DVD.** Jeffrey Tambor; F. Murray Abraham; David Arquette; Ray Liotta; Andie MacDowell; Rob Schneider; Josh Charles; Kathy Griffin; Pat Hingle; ***V:*** Frank Oz; Dave Goetz; Steve Whitmire; ***D:*** Timothy Hill; ***W:*** Jerry Juhl; Joseph Mazzarino; ***C:*** Alan Caso.

Muppets Most Wanted **2014 (PG)** The Muppets do a Euro-caper film as they head off on a world tour, thanks to their renewed popularity and slick new promoter, Dominic Badguy (Gervais). However, the pic is more slapdash than slapstick with too many human cameos and not enough Muppet interaction. Badguy is just a henchman for Russian criminal frog, Constantine, who's Kermit's double. With our hero frog kidnapped and thrown into a Siberian gulag, Constantine romances Miss Piggy and goes on a crime spree that's to end with stealing the Crown Jewels in the Tower of London. Our furry friends are always a welcome sight, but this sequel is too safe. **112m/C; DVD, Blu-Ray.** Ricky Gervais; Ty Burrell; Tina Fey; ***V:*** Steve Whitmire; Eric Jacobson; Matt Vogel; ***D:*** James Bobin; ***W:*** James Bobin; Nicholas Stoller; ***C:*** Don Burgess; ***M:*** Christophe Beck.

The Muppets Take Manhattan **1984 (G)** Following a smashing success with a college musical, the Muppets take their show and talents to Broadway, only to face misfortune in the form of an unscrupulous producer. A less imaginative script than the first two Muppet movies, yet an enjoyable experience with numerous major stars making cameo appearances. **94m/C; VHS, DVD.** ***Cameo(s):*** Dabney Coleman; James Coco; Art Carney; Joan Rivers; Gregory Hines; Linda Lavin; Liza Minnelli; Brooke Shields; John Landis; ***V:*** Jim Henson; Frank Oz; Tom Patchett; ***D:*** Frank Oz; ***W:*** Frank Oz; ***C:*** Robert Paynter; ***M:*** Ralph Burns.

The Muppets' Wizard of Oz **2005 (PG)** The sock-puppets that made the world fall in love with the "Rainbow Connection" find themselves somewhere over the rainbow in this made-for-TV feature. Granted, the Muppets have been much, much funnier in the past, but after the likes of "Muppets Christmas Carol" and "Muppets Treasure Island," it's nice to see the folks at the Henson Company trying to return their creations to their comedic roots. Sure, Ashanti is a pretty dull lead as Dorothy, but the supporting cast is strong and the humor is surprisingly adult. (Quentin Tarantino cameos!) **100m/C; DVD.** Ashanti; Queen Latifah; David Alan Grier; Jeffrey Tambor; ***Cameo(s):*** Quentin Tarantino; ***V:*** Steve Whitmire; Dave Goelz; Bill Barretta; Eric Jacobson; ***D:*** Kirk R. Thatcher; ***W:*** Debra Frank; Steve Hayes; Adam F. Goldberg; Tom Martin; ***C:*** Tony Westman. **VIDEO**

Murda Muzik **1/2 2003** Up-and-coming rapper Fresh can't keep the hard life on the mean Queens' streets behind him, risking more than just his big recording contract. Music from popular hip-hop and rap stars, including 50 Cent, Snoop Dogg, and Mobb Deep, are the main draw. **72m/C; VHS, DVD.** Nasir Jones; Big Noyd; Havoc; Cormega; Chinky; Prodigy; ***D:*** Lawrence Page; ***W:*** Prodigy. **VIDEO**

Murder **1930** Believing in a young woman's innocence, one jurist begins to organize the pieces of the crime in order to save her. Fine early effort by Hitchcock based on play "Enter Sir John," by Clemense Dane and Helen Simpson. **92m/B; VHS, DVD.** *GB* Herbert Marshall; Nora Baring; Phyllis Konstam; Miles Mander; ***D:*** Alfred Hitchcock; ***W:*** Alfred Hitchcock; ***C:*** Jack Cox; ***M:*** John Reynders.

Murder Ahoy **1/2 1964** Miss Marple looks perplexed when dead bodies surface on a naval cadet training ship. Dame Marge is the dottie detective in the final, and least appealing, of her four Agatha Christie films of the '60s (although it was released in the States prior to "Murder Most Foul"). **74m/B; VHS, DVD.** Margaret Rutherford; Lionel Jeffries; Charles "Bud" Tingwell; William Mervyn; Francis Matthews; ***D:*** George Pollock.

Murder at Devil's Glen **1/2** ***What We Did That Night*** **1999** Henry (Schroder) is a manipulative ex-con who returns to his hometown with a proposition for three of his former college buddies, who have all become successful. They all share a secret—during a frat party hazing incident a young woman accidentally died and the foursome buried her body in the woods. Now Henry wants to develop that particular piece of property, so they have to go back and dig up the evidence of their crime. Ah, if only it were that easy. The sweet-faced Schroder makes a remarkably capable and creepy bad guy. **90m/C; VHS, DVD.** Rick Schroder; Jack Noseworthy; Michael Easton; Jayce Bartok; Jennifer Jostyn; Tara Reid; ***D:*** Paul Shapiro; ***W:*** Eric Harlacher; ***C:*** Brian Reynolds; ***M:*** Dana Kaproff. **TV**

Murder at 45 R.P.M. ***Meurtre en 45 Tours*** **1965** A singer and her lover suspect each other of her husband's murder. Things become sticky when she receives a recorded message from her dead husband. Average. **98m/C; DVD.** *FR* Danielle Darrieux; Michel Auclair; Jean Servais; Henri Guisol; ***D:*** Etienne Perier.

Murder at Midnight **1931** The killings begin with a game of charades in which the gun wasn't supposed to be loaded, and continue as members of English high society die one by one. "Blondie" director Strayer still working on his change of pace. **69m/B; VHS, DVD.** Alice White; Leslie Fenton; Aileen Pringle; Hale Hamilton; Robert Elliott; Clara Blandick; Brandon Hurst; ***D:*** Frank Strayer.

Murder at 1600 **1997 (R)** Jaded D.C. detective Harlan Regis (Snipes) is called to investigate the murder of Carla Town (Moore), a secretary found dead in a White House bathroom. He's reluctantly assisted by hard-boiled Secret Service agent Chance (Lane), while head of security Nick Spikings (Benzali) wants the whole matter wrapped up quickly and quietly. Cliche-fest script gives stereotypical characters a little more development than you may be used to, but doesn't give them anything new or interesting. Snipes and Lane make a good team and Miller, as Snipes' police partner, is an effortless, wisecracking sidekick. **107m/C; DVD.** Wesley Snipes; Diane Lane; Daniel Benzali; Dennis Miller; Alan Alda; Ronny Cox; Tate Donovan; Diane Baker; Mary Moore; Harris Yulin; Richard Blackburn; ***D:*** Dwight Little; ***W:*** Wayne Beach; David Hodgin; ***C:*** Steven Bernstein; ***M:*** Christopher Young.

Murder at the Baskervilles ***Silver Blaze; Sherlock Holmes: The Silver Blaze*** **1937** Sherlock Holmes is invited to visit Sir Henry Baskerville at his estate, but then finds that Baskerville's daughter's fiance is accused of stealing a race horse and murdering its keeper. Based on Sir Arthur Conan Doyle's story "Silver Blaze." Remade in 1977. **67m/B; VHS, DVD.** *GB* Arthur Wontner; Ian Fleming; Lyn Harding; ***D:*** Thomas Bentley.

Murder at the Gallop **1/2 1963** Snooping Miss Marple doesn't believe a filthy rich old-timer died of natural causes, despite the dissenting police point of view. Wheedling her way into the police investigation, she discovers the secret of the Gallop club, a place where people bounce up and down on top of horses. Much mugging between Dame Margaret and Morley. Marple's assistant, Mr. Stringer, is the real life Mr. Dame Margaret. Based on Christie's Poirot mystery "After the Funeral." **81m/B; VHS, DVD.** Margaret Rutherford; Robert Morley; Flora Robson; Charles "Bud" Tingwell; Duncan Lamont; Stringer Davis; ***D:*** George Pollock; ***W:*** James P. Cavanagh; ***C:*** Arthur Ibbetson; ***M:*** Ronald Goodwin.

Murder at the Vanities **1/2 1934** Vintage murder mystery set against a musical revue format, in which a tough detective must find a killer before the Earl Carroll-based cabaret ends and he or she will escape with the exiting crowd. Also featured is a mind-boggling production number based on the song "Marijuana." **91m/B; VHS, DVD.** Victor McLaglen; Kitty Carlisle Hart; Jack Oakie; Duke Ellington; Carl Brisson; Dorothy Stickney; Gertrude Michael; Jessie Ralph; Charles Middleton; Gail Patrick; Donald Meek; Toby Wing; Lucille Ball; Ann Sheridan; ***D:*** Mitchell Leisen; ***W:*** Sam Hellman; ***C:*** Leo Tover; ***M:*** Arthur Johnston.

Murder by Contract **1958** Cold-blooded hitman Claude (Edwards) goes to L.A. to take out ex-moll Billie (Toriel) who's going to testify against his never-seen boss Mr. Brink in a federal trial. Billie is heavily guarded and Claude blows two attempts. Realizing his boss won't forgive and forget even if he finally succeeds, Claude does the unexpected. **81m/B; DVD.** Vince Edwards; Phillip Pine; Michael Granger; Herschel Bernardi; Caprice Toriel; ***D:*** Irving Lerner; ***W:*** Benjamin Simcoe; ***C:*** Lucien Ballard; ***M:*** Perry Botkin.

Murder by Death **1/2 1976 (PG)** Capote is an eccentric millionaire who invites the world's greatest detectives to dinner, offering $1 million to the one who can solve the evening's murder. Entertaining and hammy spoof of Agatha Christie's "And Then There Were None" and the earlier "Ten Little Indians." **95m/C; VHS, DVD, Blu-Ray.** Peter Falk; Alec Guinness; David Niven; Maggie Smith;

Peter Sellers; Eileen Brennan; Elsa Lanchester; Nancy Walker; Estelle Winwood; Truman Capote; James Coco; *D:* Robert Moore; *W:* Neil Simon; *C:* David M. Walsh; *M:* Dave Grusin.

Murder by Decree 🦴🦴🦴 **1979 (PG)** Realistic and convincing version of the Jack the Ripper story. Sherlock Holmes and Dr. Watson find a vast web of conspiracy when they investigate the murders of Whitechapel prostitutes. Based partially on facts, it's a highly detailed suspenser with interesting camera work and fine performances. **120m/C; VHS, DVD.** *CA* Christopher Plummer; James Mason; Donald Sutherland; Genevieve Bujold; Susan Clark; David Hemmings; Frank Finlay; John Gielgud; Anthony Quayle; *D:* Bob (Benjamin) Clark; *W:* John Hopkins. Genie '80: Actor (Plummer), Director (Clark), Support. Actress (Bujold).

Murder by Invitation 🦴🦴 *Murder at Midnight* **1941** Comic mystery of the old dark house variety. Upset when her greedy relatives try to declare her incompetent, eccentric Aunt Cassie invites them to her mansion so she can decide who will inherit. Wisecracking reporter Bob White and his secretary Nora are also along and start investigating when one murder occurs at midnight and more follow. **67m/B; DVD, Blu-Ray.** Wallace Ford; Marian Marsh; Sarah Padden; Herb Vigran; George Guhl; Wallis (Clarke) Clark; Gavin Gordon; Minerva Urecal; Hazel Keener; *D:* Phil Rosen; *W:* George Bricker; *C:* Marcel Le Picard.

Murder by Numbers 🦴🦴 ½ **2002 (R)** Homicide detective Cassie Mayweather (Bullock) is a crime scene specialist saddled with a by-the-book new partner, Sam Kennedy (Chaplin). This isn't good since she has to prove that two wealthy young men (Gosling, Pitt) have committed what they think is the perfect murder (shades of Leopold and Loeb and with nods to Hitchcock). Naturally, Cassie has baggage and must come to terms with her past in order to solve the crime. Gosling's downright scary while Pitt well-plays his weaker partner; Bullock works against being likeable as a loner toughie. **120m/C; VHS, DVD.** Sandra Bullock; Ben Chaplin; Ryan Gosling; Michael Pitt; Christopher Penn; R.D. Call; Agnes Bruckner; *D:* Barbet Schroeder; *W:* Tony Gayton; *C:* Luciano Tovoli; *M:* Clint Mansell.

Murder By Two 🦴 ½ *Ladies Man; L—Homme a Femmes* **1960** The murder of a blackmailer comes back to haunt married Gabrielle and her niece Catherine but, as the police investigate, several more suspects come to light. French with subtitles. **95m/B; DVD.** *FR* Danielle Darrieux; Catherine Deneuve; Mel Ferrer; Claude Rich; Pierre Brice; Alan Randolph Scott; *D:* Jacques-Gerard Cornu; *W:* Maurice Clavel; *C:* Jean Tournier; *M:* Claude Bolling.

Murder C.O.D. 🦴🦴 **1990** Alex Brandt (Devane) is a serial killer with a novel way of making money off his mental disability: find someone who has bitter disagreements with someone else who has money and off him. Then bill the rival 100 grand as a fee for services rendered backed up with the threat of framing them for the murder if they say no. Eventually a cop figures out what he's up to and gets billed for Brandt's services to hush him up. **100m/C; DVD.** Patrick Duffy; Chelsea Field; Alex Hyde-White; Janet Margolin; Allan Miller; Charles Robinson; Mariette Hartley; William Devane; Harris Laskawy; *D:* Alan Metzger; *W:* Barbara Paul; Andrew Peter Marin; *C:* Bernd Heinl; *M:* Fred Karlin. **TV**

Murder, He Says 🦴🦴 ½ **1945** Sinister comedy finds insurance salesman Peter Marshall (MacMurray) sent to gather statistics in the Ozarks and encountering the murderous hillbilly Fleagle family and various other looney characters. Naturally, the prettiest girl in the area, Claire (Walker), also happens to be the only sane person, which is lucky for Peter. **91m/B; DVD, Blu-Ray.** Fred MacMurray; Helen Walker; Marjorie Main; Peter Whitney; Barbara Pepper; Jean Heather; Mabel Paige; Porter Hall; *D:* George Marshall; *W:* Lou Breslow; *C:* Theodor Sparkuhl; *M:* Robert Emmett Dolan.

Murder in a Small Town 🦴🦴 ½ **1999** It's the 1930s and Broadway director Wilder has moved to Connecticut after his wife's murder and runs the community theatre. But soon he finds himself surrounded by dead bodies and, with the aid of an opera-loving cop (Starr), Wilder decides to do some detecting. **100m/C; VHS, DVD.** Gene Wilder; Mike Starr; Cherry Jones; Frances Conroy; Deirdre O'Connell; Terry O'Quinn; *D:* Joyce Chopra; *W:* Gene Wilder; *C:* Bruce Surtees; *M:* John Morris. **CABLE**

Murder in Coweta County 🦴🦴 ½ **1983** Griffith and Cash are strong in this true-crime drama based on the book by Margaret Anne Barnes. Griffith is a Georgia businessman who thinks he's gotten away with murder; Cash is the lawman who tenaciously pursues him. Based on an actual 1948 case. **100m/C; VHS, DVD.** Johnny Cash; Andy Griffith; Earl Hindman; June Carter Cash; Cindi Knight; Ed Van Nuys; *D:* Gary Nelson; *W:* Dennis Nemec; *C:* Larry Pizer; *M:* Brad Fiedel. **TV**

Murder in Greenwich 🦴🦴 *Dominick Dunne Presents Murder in Greenwich* **2002 (R)** Based on former LAPD detective Mark Fuhrman's book. Fuhrman (Meloni) investigates the unsolved 25-year-old murder of 15-year-old Martha Moxley (Grace), which happened in Greenwich, CT in the 1970's. This is the case that eventually led to the arrest and conviction of Kennedy nephew Michael Sakal for the crime. **88m/C; VHS, DVD.** Christopher Meloni; Robert Forster; Maggie Grace; Toby Moore; Jon Foster; Andrew Mitchell; *D:* Tom McLoughlin; *W:* Dave Erickson; *C:* Mark Wareham; *M:* Don Davis. **CABLE**

Murder in New Hampshire: The Pamela Smart Story 🦴🦴 ½ **1991 (PG-13)** A sleazy true story about a young high school teacher who seduces an impressionable student into murdering her husband. Hunt's fine as the seductress but this TV fare is just average. **93m/C; VHS, DVD.** Helen Hunt; Chad Allen; Larry Drake; Howard Hesseman; Ken Howard; Michael Learned; *D:* Joyce Chopra; *M:* Gary Chang. **TV**

Murder in the First 🦴🦴 ½ **1995 (R)** Hours after leaving a three-year stint in solitary confinement at Alcatraz, petty thief Henri Young (Bacon) kills the inmate he thinks ratted him out. Young, eager-puppy lawyer James Stamphill (Slater) defends Young by claiming that inhumane and brutal prison treatment turned him into a murderer. Heavy-handed and uneven despite excellent performances by top-notch cast. Oldman does his usual fine job with yet another unsympathetic character, the sadistic warden. Loosely based on a true story that led to the closing of Alcatraz. **123m/C; DVD, Blu-Ray.** Christian Slater; Kevin Bacon; Gary Oldman; Embeth Davidtz; William H. Macy; Stephen Tobolowsky; Brad Dourif; R. Lee Ermey; Mia Kirshner; Stefan Gierasch; Kyra Sedgwick; *D:* Marc Rocco; *W:* Dan Gordon; *C:* Fred Murphy; *M:* Christopher Young. Broadcast Film Critics '95: Actor (Bacon).

Murder in the Hamptons 🦴🦴 ½ **2005** True crime story covers the 2001 murder of multi-millionaire investment banker Ted Ammon (Sutcliffe), which sends shockwaves through the tony Hamptons. Though Ted, wife Generosa Rand (Montgomery), and their two adopted children appear to have it all, flashbacks reveal that Generosa is succumbing to the crazies and her paranoia leads to divorce proceedings and a new man in her life, working-class Danny Pelosi (Christian). **90m/C; DVD.** Poppy Montgomery; Shawn Christian; David Sutcliffe; Peter Outerbridge; Donna Goodhand; Helene Joy; Gabriel Hogan; Maxim Roy; *D:* Jerry Ciccoritti; *W:* Robert Freedman; *C:* Michael Storey; *M:* Robert Carli. **CABLE**

Murder in the Old Red Barn 🦴 *Maria Marten* **1936** Based on the real murder of an unassuming girl by a randy squire. Stiff, melodramatic performances are bad enough, but the play-style production, unfamiliar to modern viewers, is the last nail in this one's coffin. **67m/B; VHS, DVD.** *GB* Tod Slaughter; Sophie Stewart; D.J. Williams; Eric Portman; *D:* Milton Rosmer.

Murder, Inc. 🦴🦴 **1960** Brisk (if familiar) crime drama based on the killers-for-hire crime syndicate that operated out of Brooklyn in the 1930s. Crusading DA Turkus (Morgan) is after racketeer Louis "Lepke" Buchalter (Stewart). Killer Abe "Kid Twist" Reles (Falk) sucks Joey Collins (Whitman) and his wife Eadie (Britt) into the gang and forces them to hide an on-the-lam Lepke, who gets ratted out by his own men. Both Collins and Reles turn up as witnesses for the state (although Reles managed to "fall" out of a window before the trial). **103m/B; DVD.** Peter Falk; Stuart Whitman; Harry (Henry) Morgan; David J. Stewart; May Britt; Simon Oakland; Morey Amsterdam; *D:* Stuart Rosenberg; Burt Balaban; *W:* Mel Barr; Irve Tunick; *C:* Gayne Rescher; *M:* Frank DeVol.

Murder Is My Beat 🦴 ½ **1955** Convoluted crime drama. Eden Lane (Payton) is wrongfully convicted of murdering her boyfriend and is escorted to the slammer via train. She claims the dead man is still alive and there's a blackmail scheme as smitten cop Ray Patrick (Langton) tries to find the truth. **77m/B; DVD.** Barbara Payton; Paul Langton; Robert Shayne; Tracey Roberts; Roy Gordon; *D:* Edgar G. Ulmer; *W:* Aubrey Wisberg; *C:* Harold E. Wellman; *M:* Albert Glasser.

The Murder Man 🦴🦴 **1935** Tracy's first MGM pic is a routine, but entertaining, crime programmer. Hard-drinking New York reporter Steve Grey's (Tracy) latest scoop lands shady financier Mander (Stephens) on Sing Sing's Death Row. Grey's editor wants him to do Mander's last interview before he gets the chair, but it seems the newshound has a guilty conscience. Stewart makes his feature film debut as cub reporter Shorty. **70m/B; DVD.** Spencer Tracy; Virginia Bruce; Lionel Atwill; Harvey Stephens; Robert Barrat; James Stewart; *D:* Tim Whelan; *W:* Tim Whelan; John C. Higgins; *C:* Lester White; *M:* William Axt.

Murder Mansion 🦴 ½ **1970** Some decent scares ensue when a group of travelers is stranded in an old haunted mansion. **84m/C; VHS, DVD.** *SP* Evelyn Stewart; Analia Gade; *D:* Francisco Lara Polop.

Murder Most Foul 🦴🦴🦴 **1965** Erstwhile school marm Dame Margaret is excellent as the only jury member to believe in the accused's innocence. Posing as a wealthy actress to insinuate herself into the local acting troupe, she sniffs out the true culprit. Based on the Poirot mystery "Mr. McGinty's Dead." **90m/B; VHS, DVD.** Margaret Rutherford; Ron Moody; Charles "Bud" Tingwell; Megs Jenkins; Dennis Price; Ralph Michael; Francesca Annis; *D:* George Pollock.

Murder, My Sweet 🦴🦴🦴 ½ *Farewell, My Love* **1944** Down-on-his-luck private detective Philip Marlowe (Powell) searches for an ex-convict's missing girlfriend through a dark world of murder, mayhem, and ever-twisting directions. Classic film noir screen version of Raymond Chandler's tense novel "Farewell, My Lovely," which employs flashback fashion using that crisp Chandler narrative. A breakthrough dramatically for singer Powell; Chandler's favorite version. Remade using the novel's title in 1975. **95m/B; DVD.** Dick Powell; Claire Trevor; Mike Mazurki; Otto Kruger; Anne Shirley; Miles Mander; Douglas Walton; Esther Howard; Donald "Don" Douglas; *D:* Edward Dmytryk; *W:* John Paxton; *C:* Harry Wild; *M:* Roy Webb.

Murder of a Cat 🦴🦴 **2014** An offbeat comedy crime caper involving the murder of a beloved pet cat. A man-child living in a small suburban town, Clinton (Kranz) is beside himself when someone kills his aging cat. When his demands for justice are not managed in way he wants, the intensely sad Clinton decides to solve the case himself. To solve the case, he finds an unlikely partner in Greta (Reed). The pair begin to investigate to find out the truth, and Clinton finds a conspiracy that goes far deeper than he could have ever guessed. **101m/C; DVD, Streaming, Download.** Fran Kranz; Nikki Reed; J.K. Simmons; Blythe Danner; Greg Kinnear; *D:* Gillian Greene; *W:* Christian Magalhaes; Robert Snow; *C:* Christophe Lanzenberg; *M:* Deborah Lurie.

A Murder of Crows 🦴🦴 ½ **1999 (R)** Alcoholic, disbarred New Orleans attorney Lawson Russell (Gooding Jr.) decides to write a book. He happens to meet an elderly man who lets him read his own murder mystery manuscript and when the man unexpectedly dies, Lawson gets the book published as his own. It's a success—only it seems the the story about five lawyers being murdered is real and a detective (Berenger) thinks that since Russell knows so much about the crimes, he must be the killer. **102m/C; VHS, DVD.** Cuba Gooding, Jr.; Tom Berenger; Marianne Jean-Baptiste; Eric Stoltz; *D:* Rowdy Herrington; *W:* Rowdy Herrington.

The Murder of Mary Phagan 🦴🦴🦴 ½ **1987 (PG)** Lemmon stars as John Slaton, governor of Georgia during one of America's most notorious miscarriages of justice. In 1913, timid, Jewish factory manager Leo Frank is accused of the brutal murder of a female worker. Prejudice and a power hungry prosecuting attorney conspire to seal the man's fate at the end of the hangman's noose. Sensing the injustice, Slaton re-opens the case, causing riots in Atlanta. Top-notch TV drama, featuring a superb re-creation of turn-of-the-century atmosphere and a compelling, true story which was not finally resolved until the 1970s. **251m/C; DVD, Streaming.** Jack Lemmon; Peter Gallagher; Richard Jordan; Robert Prosky; Paul Dooley; Rebecca Miller; Kathryn Walker; Charles S. Dutton; Kevin Spacey; Wendy J. Cooke; *D:* William (Billy) Hale; *M:* Maurice Jarre. **TV**

A Murder of Quality 🦴🦴 ½ **1990** Spymaster George Smiley (Elliott) comes to aid of colleague Ailsa Brimley (Jackson) when he agrees to investigate the nefarious goings-on at the Carne School for boys. It seems a schoolmaster's wife predicted her murder and named her husband as the killer. Now she's dead but her husband has a very solid alibi. Based on the novel by John Le Carre. **103m/C; VHS, DVD.** *GB* Denholm Elliott; Glenda Jackson; Joss Ackland; Billie Whitelaw; David Threlfall; Ronald Pickup; Christian Bale; Matthew Scurfield; *D:* Gavin Millar; *C:* Denis Crossan; *M:* Stanley Myers. **TV**

Murder On a Bridle Path 🦴🦴 **1936** The sophisticated Broderick does a one-shot in the 4th film in RKO's Hildegarde Withers series and the quality is sliding. Amateur sleuth Withers gets involved when a young society dame is found dead on the bridle path in Central Park. The brief mystery is hampered by two directors and four writers! Followed by "The Plot Thickens." **63m/B; DVD.** Helen Broderick; James Gleason; Louise Latimer; Owen Davis, Jr.; Leslie Fenton; John Arledge; *D:* William Hamilton; Edward Killy; *W:* James Gow; Dorothy Yost; Thomas Lennon; Edmund H. North; *C:* Nicholas Musuraca.

Murder On a Honeymoon 🦴🦴 ½ **1935** Nosy schoolteacher Hildegarde Withers (Oliver) finds dead bodies even on vacation. This time it's one of the passengers abaord the seaplane taking them to Catalina Island. When the dead man turns out to be the witness in a New York mob case, Hildegarde calls Inspector Piper (Gleason) to come to sunny California and lend a hand. 3rd in the RKO series and the last for Oliver who left the studio for MGM. Followed by "Murder On a Bridle Path." **74m/B; DVD.** Edna May Oliver; James Gleason; Lola Lane; Leo G. Carroll; Dorothy Libaire; Harry Ellerbe; Chick Chandler; George Meeker; *D:* Lloyd Corrigan; *W:* Seton I. Miller; Robert Benchley; *C:* Nicholas Musuraca.

Murder on Approval 🦴 *Barbados Quest* **1956** Conway is a carbon-copy Sherlock Holmes, called in to verify the authenticity of a stamp and finds himself involved in murder. Slow-paced, weak and transparent. **70m/B; VHS, DVD.** Tom Conway; Delphi Lawrence; Brian Worth; Michael Balfour; John Colicos; *D:* Bernard Knowles.

Murder on Flight 502 🦴🦴 **1975** A crisis arises on a 747 flight from New York to London when a terrorist runs amuck. Big cast of TV stars and Stack as the pilot keep this stale flick from getting lost in the ozone. **97m/C; VHS, DVD.** Farrah Fawcett; Sonny Bono; Ralph Bellamy; Theodore Bikel; Dane Clark; Polly Bergen; Laraine Day; Fernando Lamas; George Maharis; Hugh O'Brian; Molly Picon; Walter Pidgeon; Robert Stack; *D:* George McCowan. **TV**

Murder on Pleasant Drive 🦴🦴 **2006** After Fran Smith (Hogan) disappears, her daughter Deanna (Williams) and sister Sherrie (Madigan) become convinced that her weird-acting husband John (Arkin) has murdered her. But without a body they have trouble proving a crime has been committed so Deanna starts an 11-year investigation that eventually uncovers the mysterious disappearance of John's first wife as well.

90m/C; DVD. Kelli Williams; Amy Madigan; Adam Arkin; Susan Hogan; Bill Marchant; Vincent Gale; Eric Keenleyside; Brian Markinson; *D:* Michael Scott; *W:* Walter Klenhard; *C:* Adam Sliwinski; *M:* Philip Griffin. **CABLE**

Murder on the Bayou ♪♪♪ *A Gathering of Old Men* **1991 (PG)** Down on the L'siana bayou, a white guy who thinks civil rights are color coded is murdered, and an elderly black man is accused of the crime. Made for TV, well performed, engaging. From the novel by Ernest J. Gaines. **91m/C; VHS, DVD.** Louis Gossett, Jr.; Richard Widmark; Holly Hunter; Woody Strode; Joe Seneca; Papa John Creach; Julius W. Harris; Will Patton; *D:* Volker Schlondorff. **TV**

Murder On the Blackboard ♪♪ ½ **1934** Teacher Hildegarde Withers (Oliver) discovers the body of the school's music teacher in her classroom but the body has disappeared by the time Inspector Oscar Piper (Gleason) arrives. However, the amateur sleuth realizes that music notes scribbled on the blackboard are a clue to the murderer. 2nd in the RKO series; followed by "Murder On a Honeymoon." **71m/B; DVD.** Edna May Oliver; James Gleason; Bruce Cabot; Edgar Kennedy; Gertrude Michael; Regis Toomey; *D:* George Archainbaud; *W:* Willis Goldbeck; *C:* Nicholas Musuraca.

Murder On the Home Front ♪ ½ **2013** Dreary British mystery set in London during the 1940 Blitz. Criminals are using the bombings to try and cover their crimes, but pathologist Lennox Collins (Kennedy) and his eager secretary, Molly (Merchant), discover a serial killer is on the loose. **90m/C; DVD, Blu-Ray.** *UK* Patrick Kennedy; Tamzin Merchant; Ryan Gage; John Heffernan; John Bowe; David Sturzaker; *D:* Geoffrey Sax; *W:* David Kane; *C:* David Higgs; *M:* Rob Lane. **TV**

Murder on the Midnight Express ♪ ½ *Night is the Time for Killing* **1974** Mystery about spies, thieves, honeymooners, and a corpse aboard an all-night train. All aboard. **70m/C; VHS, DVD.** Judy Geeson; James Smilie; Charles Gray; Alister Williamson; *W:* Brian Clemens. **TV**

Murder on the Orient Express ♪♪♪ **1974 (PG)** An Agatha Christie mystery lavishly produced with an all-star cast. In 1934, a trainful of suspects and one murder victim make the trip from Istanbul to Calais especially interesting. Super-sleuth Hercule Poirot sets out to solve the mystery. An entertaining whodunit, ably supported by the remarkable cast. Followed by "Death on the Nile." **128m/C; VHS, DVD.** *GB* Albert Finney; Martin Balsam; Ingrid Bergman; Lauren Bacall; Sean Connery; Richard Widmark; Anthony Perkins; John Gielgud; Jacqueline Bisset; Jean-Pierre Cassel; Wendy Hiller; Rachel Roberts; Vanessa Redgrave; Michael York; Colin Blakely; George Coulouris; Denis Quilley; Vernon Dobtcheff; Jeremy Lloyd; *D:* Sidney Lumet; *W:* Paul Dehn; *C:* Geoffrey Unsworth; *M:* Richard Rodney Bennett. Oscars '74: Support. Actress (Bergman); British Acad. '74: Support. Actor (Gielgud), Support. Actress (Bergman).

Murder on the Orient Express ♪♪ **2001** Purists certainly won't care for this modern update of the 1934 Agatha Christie mystery with Molina taking on the role of Hercule Poirot. The crime is still the same, involving the murder of the despised Samuel Ratchett (Strauss), aboard the stranded (by a landslide) train and the killer being among the passengers. This time Poirot doesn't just have to rely on his brains, he's got his laptop as well (which isn't nearly so exciting). **100m/C; DVD.** Alfred Molina; Peter Strauss; Meredith Baxter; Leslie Caron; Amira Casar; Kai Wiesinger; Tasha De Vasconcelos; David Hunt; Adam James; Dylan Smith; Natasha Wightman; Fritz Wepper; *D:* Carl Schenkel; *W:* Stephen Harrigan; *C:* Rex Maidment; *M:* Christopher Franke. **TV**

Murder on the Orient Express ♪♪♪ **2010** Much darker than the previous 1974 and 2001 versions of the Agatha Christie mystery. Detective Hercule Poirot (Suchet) is returning to London and is offered the chance to travel from Istanbul to Calais on the famed Orient Express train. A snow drift strands the train and obnoxious American Samuel Ratchett (Jones) is brutally murdered. Poirot knows that the culprit must be one of the 12 other passengers, but even the great detective is vexed by the case's contradictions. **90m/C; DVD.** *GB* David Suchet; Toby Jones; Brian J. Smith; David Morrissey; Jessica Chastain; Eileen Atkins; Susanne Lothar; Denis Menochet; Barbara Hershey; Hugh Bonneville; Marie Josee Croze; Samuel West; Joseph Mawle; Stanley Weber; Elena Satine; Serge Hazanavicius; *D:* Philip Martin; *W:* Stewart Harcourt; *C:* Alan Almond; *M:* Christian Henson. **TV**

Murder on the Orient Express ♪♪♪ **2017 (PG-13)** A mystery thriller based on the popular Agatha Christie novel that does not quite live up to the source material. After an engaging introduction to fastidious, well-mustached detective Hercule Poirot (Branagh, who also directs), the film reveals the rest of the characters/suspects who will share the train traveling to Istanbul to Calais with less panache. Though the cast is stellar, they are not given many opportunities to shine amidst clever camera trickery and standard plotting. Overall, nothing that properly conveys Christie's masterwork to modern audiences. **114m/C; DVD, Blu-Ray.** Kenneth Branagh; Daisy Ridley; Leslie Odom, Jr.; Manuel Garcia-Rulfo; Penelope Cruz; *D:* Kenneth Branagh; *W:* Michael Green; *C:* Haris Zambarloukos; *M:* Patrick Doyle.

Murder Once Removed ♪ ½ **1971** A private eye discovers that a respectable doctor has a bedside manner that women are dying for. **74m/C; VHS, DVD.** John Forsythe; Richard Kiley; Barbara Bain; Joseph Campanella; *D:* Charles S. Dubin; *M:* Robert Drasnin. **TV**

Murder One ♪ **1988 (R)** Two half-brothers escape from a Maryland prison and go on a killing spree, dragging their younger brother with them. Low-budget and it shows. Based on a true story. **83m/C; VHS, DVD.** Henry Thomas; James Wilder; Stephen Shellen; Errol Slue; *D:* Graeme Campbell.

Murder 101 ♪♪ **1991 (PG-13)** Brosnan plays Charles Lattimore, an author and English professor who specializes in murder mysteries. He gives his students a rather unique assignment of planning the perfect murder. When a student is killed right before his eyes and a fellow teacher turns up dead, Lattimore realizes he's being framed for murder. Surprising twists abound in this stylish thriller. **93m/C; VHS, DVD.** Pierce Brosnan; Dey Young; Raphael Sbarge; Kim Thomson; *D:* Bill Condon; *W:* Bill Condon.

Murder over New York ♪♪ **1940** Episode in the Charlie Chan mystery series. Chan visits New York City and becomes involved in an investigation at the airport. With the aid of his klutzy son, he sleuths his way through a slew of suspects until the mystery is solved. Standard fare for the Chan fan. **65m/B; VHS, DVD.** Sidney Toler; Marjorie Weaver; Robert Lowery; Ricardo Cortez; Donald MacBride; Melville Cooper; Victor Sen Yung; *D:* Harry Lachman.

Murder Rap ♪ **1987** An aspiring musician/sound technologist becomes involved with a mysterious woman and her plot to kill her husband. Complications galore, especially for the viewer. **90m/C; VHS, DVD.** John Hawkes; Seita Kathleen Feigny; *D:* Kliff Keuhl.

Murder She Said ♪♪ ½ *Meet Miss Marple* **1961** Dame Margaret, playing the benign Miss M for the first time, witnesses a murder on board a train, but the authorities don't seem inclined to believe her. Posing as a maid at an estate near where she thought the body was dropped, she solves the murder and lands three more Miss Marple movies. Based on Christy's "4:50 From Paddington," it features Marple-to-be Hickson as the cook. **87m/B; DVD.** *UK* Margaret Rutherford; Arthur Kennedy; Muriel Pavlow; James Robertson Justice; Thorley Walters; Charles "Bud" Tingwell; Conrad Phillips; *D:* George Pollock; *W:* David Pursall; Jack Seddon; *C:* Geoffrey Faithfull; *M:* Ronald Goodwin.

Murder Story ♪♪ ½ **1989 (PG)** An aspiring mystery writer finds himself mixed up in a real murder and winds up involving his mentor as well. An overdone story, but a reasonably enjoyable film. **90m/C; VHS, DVD.** Christopher Lee; Bruce Boa; *D:* Eddie Arno; Markus Innocenti; *W:* Eddie Arno.

Murder With Pictures ♪♪ **1936** Crime boss Nate Girard (Stevens) gets off on a murder rap but his mouthpiece Redfield (Cossart) is murdered soon after. Snappy newspaper photog Murdock (Ayres) is on the story, especially when a mystery dame (Patrick) begs for his help. A photo holds the key to the increasingly convoluted plot. **69m/B; DVD.** Lew Ayres; Gail Patrick; Onslow Stevens; Joyce Compton; Benny Baker; Paul Kelly; Ernest Cossart; Joseph (Joe) Sawyer; *D:* Charles T. Barton; *W:* Sidney Salkow; John Moffitt; *C:* Ted Tetzlaff.

Murder Without Conviction ♪♪ ½ **2004** When ex-nun Christine Bennett (Ward) visits her cousin in a mental facility, she meets savant James Talley (Proval). He and his twin, Edward, have been separated for 30 years, ever since they were accused, but not convicted, of their mother's murder on Good Friday, 1974, and a judge sent them to separate hospitals. Christine becomes suspicious and teams up with handsome detective Jack Brooks (Weisser) to have the case re-opened. But someone is deadly serious about wanting Christine to mind her own business. **90m/C; DVD.** Megan Ward; Morgan Weisser; David Proval; Rutanya Alda; Matt Lutz; Patty Duke; *D:* Kevin Connor; *W:* Bruce Franklin Singer; *C:* Dane Peterson; *M:* Roger Bellon. **CABLE**

Murder Without Motive ♪♪ ½ **1992** When two African American teenagers harrass an undercover cop, a struggle ensues and one teen ends up dead. Was the struggle racially motivated, or did the police act justifiably? **93m/C; VHS, DVD.** Curtis McClarin; Anna Maria Horsford; Carla Gugino; Christopher Daniel Barnes; Cuba Gooding, Jr.; Georg Stanford Brown; *D:* Kevin Hooks.

Murderball ♪♪♪♪ **2005 (R)** Fast-paced doc catches the warriors of Quad Rugby on and off the court. Quadriplegics candidly answer the questions people are afraid to ask them and boast about sexual escapades. Joe Soares has been a fierce American team leader until being cut from the roster due to his age. His revenge is to coach the Canadian team to their first victory over the U.S. in 12 years. Mark Zupan is the best U.S. player. We also witness breakthroughs for motorcross champ Keith Cavill as he returns home after months of rehabilitation. Attending a quad rugby demonstration, the thought of learning a new sport recharges Cavill. Powerful, must see film. **85m/C; DVD.** *D:* Henry Alex Rubin; Dana Adam Shapiro; *C:* Henry Alex Rubin; *M:* Jamie Saft.

Murder.com ♪ ½ **2008 (R)** Miami lawyer Stacy (Paul) returns to her Florida hometown when she's informed that her estranged sister Kate (Daniels) has been murdered. Bobby (Chokachi), the local law, has no leads, but when Stacy checks out Kate's computer she discovers her sister had a profile set up on a kinky sex website. Stacy joins, hoping to meet the same guys that Kate did and find her killer. **85m/C; DVD.** Alexandra Paul; Robin (Robyn) Lively; David Chokachi; Bart Johnson; David Moretti; Ellyn Daniels; *D:* Rex Piano; *W:* Tom Nelson; Jake Gerhardt; *C:* Mark Melville; *M:* Chris Anderson. **VIDEO**

Murdercycle ♪ **1999 (PG-13)** A meteorite falls to Earth near a CIA installation, taking over a motorcycle and it's rider. Combined they begin a spree of laser-induced terror. **90m/C; DVD.** Charles Wesley; Cassandra Ellis; Robert Donavan; Michael Vachetti; Robert Staccardo; *D:* Tom Callaway; *W:* Benjamin Carr; Daniel Eliot; *C:* Thomas Callaway; *M:* David Arkenstone. **VIDEO**

The Murderer Lives at Number 21 ♪ ½ *L'Assassin Habite Au 21* **1942** In this awkward French crime comedy, a serial killer is on the loose in Paris, leaving a calling card at every crime scene. The address on the card is a seedy boardinghouse so detective Wenscelas Vorobechik (Fresnay) goes undercover as a minister to see if he can figure out which one of the inhabitants is the criminal. Although co-screenwriter Steeman's novel is set in London, writer/director Clouzot couldn't leave Paris because of the Nazi occupation. French with subtitles. **79m/B; DVD.** *FR* Pierre Fresnay; Suzy Delair; Jean Tissier; Pierre Larquey; Noel Roquevert; Odette Talazac; Rene Genin; *D:* Henri-Georges Clouzot; *W:* Henri-Georges Clouzot; Stanislas-Andre Steeman; *C:* Armand Thirard; *M:* Maurice Yvain.

The Murderers Are Among Us ♪♪ *Die Morder Sind Unter Uns* **1946** In post WWII Germany, Suzanne Wallner (Knef) returns from a concentration camp to her apartment in Berlin only to find it occupied by Dr. Hans Mertens (Borchert). Haunted by his wartime experiences, Mertens has turned to women and alcohol. Suzanne refuses to give up her claim and moves in with Hans, eventually falling in love with him. In turn, Hans decides to face his demons by going after his former superior, Colonel Otto Bruckner (Paulsen), who's living an untroubled life despite the war crimes he committed. German with subtitles. **84m/B; VHS, DVD.** *GE* Hildegarde Knef; Ernst Borchert; Arno Paulsen; *D:* Wolfgang Staudte; *W:* Wolfgang Staudte; *C:* Friedl Behn-Grund; Eugen Klagemann; *M:* Ernst Roters.

Murderer's Keep **WOOF!** *Maxie; The Butchers* **1970** Secret ingredients used in the Central Meat Market's hamburger are discovered by a young, deaf girl. Beware of filler, she learns, particularly if it's someone you know. **89m/C; VHS, DVD.** Vic Tayback; Talia Shire; Robert Walden; *D:* Paulmichel Miekhe.

Murderers' Row ♪ ½ **1966** Daredevil bachelor and former counter-espionage agent Matt Helm is summoned from his life of leisure to ensure the safety of an important scientist. Martin's attempt as a super-spy doesn't wash, and Margret is implausible as the kidnapped scientist's daughter. Unless you want to hear Martin sing "I'm Not the Marrying Kind," don't bother. Second in the "Matt Helm" series. **108m/C; VHS, DVD.** Dean Martin; Ann-Margret; Karl Malden; Beverly Adams; James Gregory; Camilla Sparv; *D:* Henry Levin; *W:* Herbert Baker; *C:* Sam Leavitt; *M:* Lalo Schifrin.

Murderland ♪♪ ½ **2009** Three-part Brit crime drama about a traumatic murder that still resonates 15 years later. In 1994, prostitute Sally is found dead by her young daughter Carrie. Detective Hain fails to find the killer and some shaky police work leads to his early retirement. Carrie—now Carol—is still obsessed and pressures Hain to help her find closure when some new info is revealed, even if it means risking her own life. **138m/C; DVD.** *GB* Robbie Coltrane; Bel Powley; Amanda Hale; Sharon Small; Nicholas Greaves; Andrew Tiernan; Lorraine Ashbourne; David Westhead; Steven Robertson; Lucy Cohu; *D:* Catherine Morshead; *W:* David Pirie; *C:* Erik Wilson; *M:* Richard Hartley. **TV**

Murderous Intent ♪♪♪ ½ *Like Minds* **2006** Psychotic thriller set in an all-boys' prep school includes a great mix of twists, flashbacks, investigative details and touches of the occult topped off with a totally unanticipated ending. Alex (Redmayne), the headmaster's son, gets Nigel (Sturridge) as his new roommate despite major objections. The newcomer is obsessed with history and necrophilia, leading to a series of ritual-influenced deaths. Although Alex is sickened, he's also oddly fascinated. Then Nigel ends up dead. From script to score, acting to set design, this Australian/British creation is a fine piece of film art. **110m/C; DVD.** *GB AU* Toni Collette; Eddie Redmayne; Thomas Sturridge; Richard Roxburgh; Patrick Malahide; Kate Maberly; *D:* Gregory J. Read; *W:* Gregory J. Read; *C:* Nigel Bluck; *M:* Carlo Giacco.

Murderous Maids ♪♪ *Les Blessures Assassines* **2000** Based on the 1933 true crime story of domestics Christine and Lea Papin, who brutally murder their employer and her daughter. Christine is obsessive and obstinate while Lea is pliable and naive and Christine extends her love for her younger sibling into the sexual. When their employer suspects something's amiss and confronts Christine, the violence occurs. Director Denis can't come up with a better motive than insanity but, unlike in other versions, he doesn't stress the lurid. French with subtitles. **94m/C; DVD.** *FR* Sylvie Testud; Julie-Marie Parmentier; Isabelle Renauld; Dominique Labourier; Francois Levantal; Jean-Gabriel Nordmann; Mane Donnio; *D:* Jean-Pierre Denis; *W:* Jean-

Pierre Denis; Michele Halberstadt; ***C:*** Jean-Marc Fabre.

Murders in the Rue Morgue 🦴🦴 1/2 **1971 (PG)** A young woman has frightening dreams inspired by a play that her father is producing in Paris at the turn of the century. After many people associated with the production become murder victims, the girl becomes involved with one of her father's former associates, a man who killed her mother years ago and then faked his own suicide. The fourth film based on Edgar Allan Poe's classic horror story. **87m/C; VHS, DVD, Blu-Ray.** Jason Robards, Jr.; Lilli Palmer; Herbert Lom; Michael Dunn; Christine Kaufmann; Adolfo Celi; ***D:*** Gordon Hessler.

The Murders in the Rue Morgue 🦴🦴🦴 **1986 (PG)** The fifth filmed version of the Edgar Allan Poe story. Set in 19th-century Paris; actors in a mystery play find their roles coming to life. Scott is terrific, with good supporting help. **92m/C; VHS, DVD.** George C. Scott; Rebecca De Mornay; Val Kilmer; Ian McShane; Neil Dickson; ***D:*** Jeannot Szwarc; ***C:*** Bruno de Keyzer. **TV**

Muriel 🦴🦴🦴 1/2 *Muriel, Ou le Temps d'Un Retour; The Time of Return; Muriel, Or the Time of Return* **1963** A complex, mosaic drama about a middle-aged woman who meets an old lover at Boulogne, and her stepson who cannot forget the needless suffering he caused a young woman named Muriel while he was a soldier at war. Throughout, director Alain Resnais plumbs the essential meanings of memory, age, and the anxieties created from the tension between personal and public actions. Acclaimed; in French with subtitles. **115m/C; VHS, DVD, Blu-Ray.** *FR IT* Delphine Seyrig; Jean-Pierre Kerien; Nita Klein; Jean-Baptiste Thierree; ***D:*** Alain Resnais; ***W:*** Jean Cayrol; ***C:*** Sacha Vierny; ***M:*** Georges Delerue. Venice Film Fest. '63: Actress (Seyrig).

Muriel's Wedding 🦴🦴🦴 **1994 (R)** Muriel (Collette) can catch a bridal bouquet, but can she catch a husband? Her blonde, bitch-goddess friends don't think so. But dowdy, overweight Muriel dreams of a fairy tale wedding anyway. How she fulfills her obsessive fantasy is the basis for this quirky, hilarious, and often touchingly poignant ugly duckling tale with the occasional over-the-top satiric moment. Strong cast is led by sympathetic and engaging performances from Collette (who gained 40-plus pounds for the role) and Griffiths as her best friend, Rhonda. '70s pop supergroup ABBA lends its kitschy but catchy tunes to the plot and soundtrack. **105m/C; DVD.** *AU* Toni Collette; Bill Hunter; Rachel Griffiths; Jeanie Drynan; Gennie Nevinson Brice; Matt(hew) Day; Daniel Lapaine; Sophie Lee; Rosalind Hammond; Belinda Jarrett; ***D:*** P.J. Hogan; ***W:*** P.J. Hogan; ***C:*** Martin McGrath; ***M:*** Peter Best. Australian Film Inst. '94: Actress (Collette), Film, Sound, Support. Actress (Griffiths).

Murmur of the Heart 🦴🦴🦴 1/2 *Dearest Love; La Souffle au Coeur* **1971 (R)** Honest treatment of a 14-year-old's coming of age. After his older brothers take him to a prostitute for his first sexual experience, he comes down with scarlet fever. He then travels to a health spa with his mom to recover. There they find that their mother-son bond is stronger than most. Music by Charlie Parker is featured in the score. In French with English subtitles. **118m/C; VHS, DVD.** *FR* Benoit Ferreux; Daniel Gelin; Lea Massari; Corinne Kersten; Jacqueline Chauveau; Marc Wincourt; Michael (Michel) Lonsdale; ***D:*** Louis Malle; ***W:*** Louis Malle; ***C:*** Ricardo Aronovich; ***M:*** Charlie Parker.

Murph the Surf 🦴🦴 1/2 *Live a Little, Steal a Lot; You Can't Steal Love* **1975 (PG)** Fact-based, engrossing story of two beach bums turned burglars who grow bored with small-time robbery and plan a trip to New York City to steal the Star of Africa sapphire. Notable among the many action scenes is a boat chase through the inland waterways of Miami, Florida. **102m/C; VHS, DVD.** Robert Conrad; Don Stroud; Donna Mills; Luther Adler; Robyn Millan; Paul Stewart; ***D:*** Marvin J. Chomsky.

Murphy's Law 🦴 **1986 (R)** A hard-headed cop gets framed for his ex-wife's murder and embarks on a mission to find the actual killer. He is slowed down by a smart-mouthed prostitute who is handcuffed to him during his search. Casting a female in the role of a psycho-killer is unique to the genre. **101m/C; VHS, DVD, Blu-Ray.** Charles Bronson; Carrie Snodgress; Kathleen Wilhoite; Robert F. Lyons; Richard Romanus; Angel Tompkins; Bill Henderson; James Luisi; Janet MacLachlan; Lawrence Tierney; ***D:*** J. Lee Thompson; ***C:*** Alex Phillips, Jr.; ***M:*** Marc Donahue.

Murphy's Romance 🦴🦴🦴 **1985 (PG-13)** A young divorced mother with an urge to train horses pulls up the stakes and heads for Arizona with her son. There she meets a pharmacist who may be just what the doctor ordered to help her build a new life. **107m/C; VHS, DVD.** James Garner; Sally Field; Brian Kerwin; Corey Haim; Dennis Burkley; Charles Lane; Georgann Johnson; ***D:*** Martin Ritt; ***W:*** Harriet Frank, Jr.; Irving Ravetch; ***M:*** Carole King.

Murphy's War 🦴🦴 **1971 (PG)** In WWII, the Germans sink an English ship and gun down most of its crew. An Irishman, however, survives and returns to health with the help of a nurse. He then seeks revenge on those who killed his crewmates, even after he learns the war has ended. O'Toole is interesting as the revenge-minded seaman though saddled with a mediocre script. **106m/C; VHS, DVD.** *GB* Peter O'Toole; Sian Phillips; Philippe Noiret; ***D:*** Peter Yates; ***W:*** Stirling Silliphant; ***M:*** John Barry.

Musa: The Warrior 🦴🦴🦴 *Wu Shi; Musa; The Warrior Princess* **2001 (R)** Set in 1375, the Ming Dynasty is beginning to settle into power, and Korea sends an envoy to make start diplomatic relations with China's new rulers. Upon arrival, the lead diplomat is jailed and the rest are exiled for spying. The survivors attempt to get back to Korea, and incidentally rescue a Ming Princess who has been kidnapped by a deposed Chinese faction. Deciding that protecting her may be their best option for survival, they make for a lonely military outpost in the hopes they can get help. **157m/C; DVD.** *CH NK* Ziyi Zhang; Woo-sung Jung; Sung-kee Ahn; Jin-mo Ju; Yong-woo Park; Jeong-hak Park; Hye-jin Yu; Seok-yong Jeong; Du-il Lee; Yeong-mak Han; ***D:*** Sung-su Kim; ***W:*** Sung-su Kim; ***C:*** Hyung-ku Kim; ***M:*** Shiroh Sagisu.

Muscle Beach Party 🦴🦴 **1964** Sequel to "Beach Party" finds Frankie and Annette romping in the sand again. Trouble invades teen nirvana when a new gym opens and the hardbodies try to muscle in on surfer turf. Meanwhile, Paluzzi tries to muscle in on Funicello's turf. Good clean corny fun, with the usual lack of script and plot. Lorre appeals in a cameo, his final screen appearance. Watch for "Little" Stevie Wonder in his debut. Rickles' first appearance in the "BP" series; Lupus was credited as Rock Stevens. Followed by "Bikini Beach." **94m/C; VHS, DVD, Blu-Ray.** Frankie Avalon; Annette Funicello; Buddy Hackett; Luciana Paluzzi; Don Rickles; John Ashley; Jody McCrea; Morey Amsterdam; Peter Lupus; Candy Johnson; Dolores Wells; Peter Lorre; Stevie Wonder; Donna Loren; Amadee Chabot; Dick Dale; ***D:*** William Asher; ***W:*** William Asher; Robert Dillon; ***C:*** Harold E. Wellman; ***M:*** Les Baxter.

Muscle Shoals 🦴🦴🦴 **2013 (PG)** Rick Hall founded a little recording studio on the shores of a small town in Alabama and the rest is rock 'n' roll history. Dozens of music luminaries passed through those doors and recorded smash hits in that little room, looking for that "Muscle Shoals" sound. Legends like Aretha Franklin, Bono, Keith Richards, and dozens more return to discuss their recording sessions but director Greg Camalier wisely focuses on the place and the people who stayed there, including the studio musicians who played on dozens of hits and rarely got their deserved recognition, instead of those who came and went. **111m/C; DVD, Blu-Ray.** ***D:*** Greg Camalier; ***C:*** Anthony Arendt.

The Muse 🦴🦴 1/2 **1999 (PG-13)** Creatively bereft screenwriter Steven (Brooks) can't get a job until fellow scribe Jack (Bridges) introduces him to Sarah (Stone), who may actually be one of the Greek goddesses of inspiration. Of course, she may be a total lunatic too. After he discovers that some big Hollywood names swear by her mojo, Steven is thrilled when he's deemed worthy of her service. Unfortunately, Sarah's inspiration comes with a big price tag, which draws the suspicion of his wife Laura (MacDowell). As he begins writing, Steven discovers that Sarah has also inspired Laura to start a career of her own and kick him out of bed. Lots of movie in-jokes and cameos. **97m/C; VHS, DVD, Blu-Ray.** Albert Brooks; Sharon Stone; Jeff Bridges; Andie MacDowell; Steven Wright; Mark Feuerstein; Bradley Whitford; Dakin Matthews; Concetta Tomei; Stacey Travis; ***Cameo(s):*** James Cameron; Rob Reiner; Martin Scorsese; Jennifer Tilly; Lorenzo Lamas; ***D:*** Albert Brooks; ***W:*** Albert Brooks; Monica Johnson; ***C:*** Thomas Ackerman; ***M:*** Sir Elton John.

Museum Hours 🦴🦴🦴 **2013** A Canadian woman named Anne forms a lovely friendship with a security guard at the Kunsthistorisches Art Museum in Vienna in writer/director Cohen's beautiful drama. Anne knows no one in this European town that she's been forced to visit when a loved one is hospitalized there, and so she responds openly when Johann helps her navigate the gorgeous city. Cohen alternates long scenes of dialogue between the two and beautiful cinematography showcasing Vienna. Ultimately, the lines begin to blur as one can see art in architecture and the simplest of human friendships. English and German with subtitles. **107m/C; DVD, Blu-Ray.** *AT* Mary Margaret O'Hara; Bobby Sommer; ***D:*** Jem Cohen; ***W:*** Jem Cohen; ***C:*** Jem Cohen; Peter Roehsler; ***M:*** Mary Margaret O'Hara.

Music & Lyrics 🦴🦴 1/2 **2007 (PG-13)** The somewhat smarmy, frequently self-deprecating charm of Grant is on full display, opposite Barrymore as his sunny romantic foil. Alex (Grant) is the less-successful half (he wrote the music) of a long-disbanded '80s pop duo. Making a decent living on the nostalgia circuit, Alex gets another chance at a hit when current teen queen Cora (newcomer Bennett) wants her one-time crush to write a duet for them. Alex then stumbles onto insecure, would-be lyricist Sophie (Barrymore) and puts her to work. Grant and Barrymore don't make the most convincing romantic couple (she's too young and ditsy) but it's light-hearted fluff, and the pseudo-80s music videos are hysterical. **106m/C; DVD, Blu-Ray, HD-DVD.** Hugh Grant; Drew Barrymore; Brad Garrett; Kristen Johnston; Aasif Mandvi; Campbell Scott; Haley Bennett; ***D:*** Marc Lawrence; ***W:*** Marc Lawrence; ***C:*** Xavier Perez Grobet; ***M:*** Adam Schlesinger.

Music Box 🦴🦴 1/2 **1989 (R)** An attorney defends her father against accusations that he has committed inhumane Nazi war crimes. If she loses, her father faces deportation. As the case progresses, she must struggle to remain objective in the courtroom and come to terms with the possibility that her father is guilty. Lange's portrayal of an ethnic character is highly convincing. **126m/C; VHS, DVD; Open Captioned.** Jessica Lange; Frederic Forrest; Lukas Haas; Armin Mueller-Stahl; Michael Rooker; Donald Moffat; Cheryl Lynn Bruce; ***D:*** Constantin Costa-Gavras; ***W:*** Joe Eszterhas; ***C:*** Patrick Blossier; ***M:*** Philippe Sarde.

Music For Millions 🦴🦴 1/2 **1944** In this wartime MGM musical, pregnant Barbara (Allyson) plays in a touring orchestra, where she's joined by her spunky young sister Mike (O'Brien). All her friends keep the news that her husband is MIA a secret but she notices how oddly they're acting. It's mainly an excuse for musical numbers and some comedy from Durante. **117m/B; DVD.** June Allyson; Jimmy Durante; Margaret O'Brien; Marsha Hunt; Marie Wilson; Jose Iturbi; ***D:*** Henry Koster; ***W:*** Myles Connolly; ***C:*** Robert L. Surtees.

Music from Another Room 🦴🦴 1/2 **1997 (PG-13)** Danny (Law) is a hopeless romantic who decided, at five, to marry Anna, whose birth he assisted. But the icy adult Anna (Mol) doesn't seem to be Danny's ideal when he happens to meet her again—and she's got a fiance. **104m/C; VHS, DVD.** Jude Law; Gretchen Mol; Brenda Blethyn; Jennifer Tilly; Martha Plimpton; Jon Tenney; Jeremy Piven; Vincent Laresca; Jane Adams; Kevin Kilner; Jan Rubes; Judith Malina; Jon Polito; ***D:*** Charlie Peters; ***W:*** Charlie Peters; ***C:*** Richard Crudo; ***M:*** Richard Gibbs.

Music in My Heart 🦴 1/2 **1940** Two taxi cabs crash and spur the love of Martin and Hayworth. She proceeds to break off her engagement to save Martin from deportation. Hayworth's last low-budget film before becoming a Hollywood goddess. **69m/B; VHS, DVD.** Rita Hayworth; Tony Martin; Edith Fellows; Alan Mowbray; Eric Blore; George Tobias; Joseph Crehan; George Humbert; Phil Tead; ***D:*** Joseph Santley; ***M:*** Robert Wright; Chet Forrest.

The Music Man 🦴🦴🦴🦴 **1962 (G)** Con man (Preston) in the guise of a traveling salesman gets off the train in River City, Iowa. After hearing about plans to build a pool hall, he argues it would be the gateway to hell for the young, impressionable males of the town. He then convinces the citizens to instead finance a wholesome children's marching band. Although the huckster plans to take their money and run, his feelings for the town librarian (Jones) cause him to think twice about fleecing the town. This isn't just a slice of Americana; it's a whole pie. Acting and singing are terrific with a capital 'T' and that rhymes with 'P' and that stands for" Preston, who epitomizes the charismatic pitchman. **151m/C; VHS, DVD.** Robert Preston; Shirley Jones; Buddy Hackett; Hermione Gingold; Paul Ford; Pert Kelton; Ron Howard; ***D:*** Morton DaCosta; ***W:*** Marion Hargrove; ***C:*** Robert Burks; ***M:*** Meredith Willson; Ray Heindorf. Oscars '62: Adapt. Score; Golden Globes '63: Film—Mus./Comedy; Natl. Film Reg. '05.

The Music Never Stopped 🦴🦴 **2011 (PG)** Male weepie loosely based on a case study by neurologist Oliver Sacks. The removal of 36-year-old Gabriel Sawyer's (Pucci) brain tumor saves him but the damage erases 20 years of his life. He thinks he's still a 19-year-old hippie in the 1960s who is estranged from his bourgeois parents. Gabriel responds best to music therapy so therapist Dianne (Ormond) encourages his grumpy, conservative, but willing father Henry (Simmons) to learn to love rock 'n' roll. **105m/C; DVD.** Lou Taylor Pucci; J.K. Simmons; Cara Seymour; Julia Ormond; Mia Maestro; Tammy Blanchard; Scott Adsit; Kelly AuCoin; ***D:*** Jim Kohlberg; ***W:*** Gwyn Lurie; Gary Marks; ***C:*** Stephen Kazmierski; ***M:*** Paul Cantelon.

The Music of Chance 🦴🦴 1/2 **1993 (R)** Convoluted story about a smalltime gambler (Spader) and a drifter (Patinkin) who wind up involved in a bizarre high stakes poker game with a Laurel and Hardyish pair (Durning, Grey) who live in an isolated mansion. When Spader and Patinkin lose, their debt forces them into an indentured servitude where they must construct a brick wall around their new masters' estate. Bloated with symbolism, this adaptation from cult fave novelist Auster (who has a small part), loses its eclectic significance in the translation to the big screen. Nonetheless, valiant effort by rookie director Haas. **98m/C; VHS, DVD.** James Spader; Mandy Patinkin; Joel Grey; Charles Durning; M. Emmet Walsh; Samantha Mathis; Christopher Penn; Pearl Jones; Paul Auster; ***D:*** Philip Haas; ***W:*** Philip Haas; Belinda Haas; ***C:*** Bernard Zitzermann; ***M:*** Philip Johnston.

Music of the Heart 🦴🦴 1/2 *50 Violins* **1999 (PG)** Based on the true story of violin teacher Roberta Guaspari, who was also the subject of the 1996 documentary, "Small Wonders." A divorced Guaspari (Streep) leaves suburbia with her two young sons and a dream to teach music to children, using the 50 violins she had purchased. Roberta finds herself working with a group of Harlem students on what will become the landmark East Harlem Violin Program. Despite numerous obstacles, their determination eventually leads to a performance at Carnegie Hall. Streep gives her usual professionally winning performance in this sentimental heart-tugger. **124m/C; VHS, DVD.** Meryl Streep; Angela Bassett; Aidan Quinn; Gloria Estefan; Cloris Leachman; Kieran Culkin; Charlie Hofheimer; Jay O. Sanders; Josh Pais; ***D:*** Wes Craven; ***W:*** Pamela Gray; ***C:*** Peter Deming; ***M:*** Mason Daring.

The Music Teacher 🦴🦴 1/2 *Le Maitre de Musique* **1988 (PG)** A Belgian costume drama dealing with a famed singer who retires to devote himself to teaching two students exclusively. In time, he sees his prized pupils lured into an international competition by an old rival of his. Although the singing is sharp, the story is flat. In French with yellow English subtitles. **95m/C; VHS, DVD.** *BE* Patrick Bauchau; Sylvie Fennec; Philippe Volter; Jose Van Dam; Johan Leysen; Anne Roussel; ***D:*** Gerard Corbiau.

Music Within 🦴🦴 ½ **2007 (R)** True story plays like an inspirational movie of the week but is not without its appeal. Richard Pimentel (Livingston) has always wanted to be a public speaker; instead he winds up fighting in Vietnam where he loses most of his hearing in a bomb blast. He returns home, goes to college, and makes an unlikely connection with acerbic Art Honeyman (Sheen), who's wheelchair-bound because of cerebral palsy. Both are discriminated against and ostracized because of their disabilities, which leads Richard to his work as a motivational speaker and one of the leading advocates for what will become the Americans With Disabilities Act. **94m/C; DVD.** Ron Livingston; Michael Sheen; Melissa George; Yul Vazquez; Rebecca De Mornay; Hector Elizondo; ***D:*** Steven Sawalich; ***W:*** Brett McKinney; Mar Andrew Olsen; Kelly Kennemer; ***C:*** Irek Hartowicz; ***M:*** James T. Sale.

The Musketeer 🦴🦴 **2001 (PG-13)** Very loose adaptation of Dumas' "The Three Musketeers." D'Artagnan (Chambers) is motivated to join the famed battalion to avenge the murder of his parents by the evil Febre (Roth). He's disappointed that the musketeers have been disbanded by the scheming Cardinal Richelieu (Rea), so he forms an alliance with Athos (Gregor), Porthos (Speirs) and Aramis (Moran) to set things right. Along the way he falls for Francesca (Suvari), a close confidant of the queen (Deneuve). Despite murky direction, the scenic French countryside is filmed beautifully and the actors do their best with the garbled material. **105m/C; DVD.** Justin Chambers; Mena Suvari; Tim Roth; Catherine Deneuve; Stephen Rea; Daniel Mesguich; David Schofield; Nick Moran; Jeremy Clyde; Michael Byrne; Steve Spiers; Jan Gregor Kremp; Jean-Pierre Castaldi; ***D:*** Peter Hyams; ***W:*** Gene Quintano; ***C:*** Peter Hyams; ***M:*** David Arnold.

Mussolini & I 🦴🦴 ½ *Mussolini: The Decline and Fall of Il Duce* **1985** Docudramatization of the struggle for power between Italy's Benito Mussolini and his son-in-law, Galeazzo Ciano. Narrated by Sarandon in the role of Il Duce's daughter. **130m/C; VHS, DVD.** Bob Hoskins; Anthony Hopkins; Susan Sarandon; Annie Girardot; Barbara DeRossi; Fabio Testi; Kurt Raab; ***D:*** Alberto Negrin. **CABLE**

Must Love Dogs 🦴🦴 **2005 (PG-13)** Recently-divorced Sarah (Lane), a 40ish preschool teacher, is thrown into the online dating world by her family, a large group of cackling Irish Americans. But first Sarah meets Bob (Mulroney), the separated father of one of her students, and later Jake (superwitty Cusack), a romantic who builds wooden boats by hand, and the triangle ensues. Former TV director Goldberg and a star-loaded cast don't quite make a love connection, but a passable date movie is in here somewhere. The title is a good motto to live by, though. **98m/C; DVD.** Diane Lane; John Cusack; Dermot Mulroney; Christopher Plummer; Stockard Channing; Elizabeth Perkins; Ben Shenkman; Julie Gonzalo; Brad Hall; Brad William Henke; Ali Hillis; Steve Schirripa; Laura Kightlinger; Jordana Spiro; ***D:*** Gary David Goldberg; ***W:*** Gary David Goldberg; ***C:*** John Bailey; ***M:*** Craig Armstrong.

Must Read After My Death 🦴🦴 **2009** Writer/director Dews' discovered more than 200 hours of home movies, 50 hours of Dictaphone and tape recordings, and 300 pages of transcripts after the death of his maternal grandmother Allis in 2001. They reveal a family history of an unhappy 'open' marriage between Allis and alcoholic husband Charley and Allis' dissatisfaction with her lot as a 1950s housewife, which had her turning to therapy for help. It eventually ensnares their four children, who also come under some dubious psychiatric care. Dews' POV is generally limited to that of his grandmother, which protects the identity of his other family members but makes you wonder what they thought of Allis' revelations. **73m/C; DVD.** ***D:*** Morgan Dews; Peter Dews; ***W:*** Morgan Dews; Peter Dews; ***M:*** Paul Damian Hogan; Paul Hogan.

Mustang 🦴🦴🦴 **2015 (PG-13)** Coming-of-age stories don't get much more delightful than Deniz Gamze Erguven's festival hit about five Turkish sisters, the French selection for the Oscar for Best Foreign Language Film. The tale of five siblings is really through the eyes of the youngest, Lale (Sensoy), who watches her four older sisters age in a society that isn't kind to female independence. After local townspeople see the girls flirting with some boys, they're basically locked in their family home until it's time to marry. Some conform, others rebel—all of them are fascinating, well-rounded characters. Turkish with subtitles. **97m/C; DVD, Blu-Ray.** Gunes Sensoy; Doga Zeynap Doguslu; Tugba Sunguroglu; Elit Iscan; Ilayda Akdogan; ***D:*** Deniz Gamze Erguven; ***W:*** Deniz Gamze Erguven; Alice Winocour; ***C:*** David Chizallet; Ersin Gok; ***M:*** Warren Ellis.

The Mustang 🦴🦴🦴 **2019 (R)** Imprisoned for a domestic violence incident, reserved Roman (Schoenaerts) struggles with anger issues. Though he receives therapy in his rural Nevada prison, he is broken and struggling. Roman's life changes when he is forced to take part in a prison program, which involves him taming a wild mustang that will be later sold at auction. With the help of trainer Myles (Dern), Roman and the horse slowly build trust and tame each other. In the process, Roman grows closer to his pregnant daughter Martha (Adlon). The moving, powerful film effectively explores ideas like forgiveness and second chances and features a masterful performance by Schoenaerts. **96m/C; DVD, Blu-Ray.** Matthias Schoenaerts; Jason Mitchell; Bruce Dern; Gideon Adlon; Connie Britton; ***D:*** Laure de Clermont-Tonnerre; ***W:*** Laure de Clermont-Tonnerre; Brock Norman Brock; ***C:*** Ruben Impens; ***M:*** Jed Kurzel.

Mutant 🦴 ½ *Night Shadows* **1983 (R)** Another argument for the proper disposal of toxic waste. Hazardous materials transform the people of a southern town into monsters. **100m/C; VHS, DVD, Blu-Ray.** Wings Hauser; Bo Hopkins; Jennifer Warren; Lee Montgomery; ***D:*** John Cardos; ***W:*** Michael Jones; ***C:*** Alfred Taylor; ***M:*** Richard Band.

Mutant Chronicles 🦴 ½ **2008 (R)** In the year 2707 Earth's resources are dwindling with four giant corporations picking over the pieces. Amidst the combat an ancient seal is shattered, releasing a mutant army that carries a plague that threatens humanity with extinction. But a religious order keeps a chronicle that tells how to defeat the threat. You'll root for the mutants because the humans tend to be boring and/or dumb. **100m/C; DVD.** Thomas Jane; Ron Perlman; Devon Aoki; Sean Pertwee; Benno Furmann; John Malkovich; ***D:*** Simon Hunter; ***W:*** Philip Eisner; ***C:*** Geoff Boyle; ***M:*** Richard Wells.

Mutant Hunt **WOOF!** *Matt Riker* **1987** Story of a battle between robots gone haywire and an all-American hero. The detective cyborgs are set free while high on a sexual stimulant called Euphoron to wreak their technological havoc on a rampage in Manhattan. **90m/C; VHS, DVD, Streaming.** Rick Gianasi; Mary-Anne Fahey; ***D:*** Tim Kincaid; ***W:*** Tim Kincaid. **VIDEO**

Mutants **WOOF!** **2008 (R)** If a flick is going to be called "Mutants" then it should show lots of mutants and this lame talky tale apparently couldn't stretch its low-budget that far. A corporate conspiracy adds chemical enhancements to common sugar to make it more addictive but instead turns consumers into zombies. **84m/C; DVD.** Michael Ironside; Steven Bauer; Louis Herthum; Tony Senzamici; ***D:*** Amir Valinia; ***W:*** Jodie Jones; ***C:*** Barry Strickland; ***M:*** Sammy Huen. **VIDEO**

Mute Witness 🦴🦴 ½ **1995 (R)** Low-budget British thriller, lensed in a Moscow film studio, about U.S. filmers making a cheap thriller in a Moscow film studio. Billy (Sudina) is the mute make-up artist of the title who, returning to the studio for a forgotten item, witnesses some of the crew shooting a snuff film with a real-life stabbing. First-timer Waller mocks both thriller genre and film biz, sometimes relying on, rather than spoofing, cliched elements. Highlight is 20-minute long chase scene with the killers pursuing Billy in the cavernous studio. Guinness makes a surprise appearance in a cameo. **100m/C; DVD.** *UK* Marina Sudina; Fay Ripley; Evan Richards; Oleg (Yankovsky) Jankowsky; Igor Volkow; Sergei Karlenkov; ***Cameo(s):*** Alec Guinness; ***D:*** Anthony Waller; ***W:*** Anthony Waller; ***C:*** Egon Werdin; ***M:*** Wilbert Hirsch.

The Muthers 🦴🦴 **1976 (R)** Women prisoners escape from their confinement in a South American jungle. **101m/C; VHS, DVD.** Jeannie Bell; Rosanne Katon; Jayne Kennedy; Trina Parks; ***D:*** Cirio H. Santiago.

Mutiny 🦴🦴 **1952** In the War of 1812, the crew of an American ship carrying $10 million in gold fight among themselves for a part of France's donation to the war effort. The beautiful photography doesn't make up for the predictability of the storyline. **76m/C; VHS, DVD.** Mark Stevens; Gene Evans; Angela Lansbury; Patric Knowles; ***D:*** Edward Dmytryk; ***W:*** Philip Yordan.

Mutiny Ahead 🦴 ½ **1935** Kent (Hamilton) is a rich playboy now destitute and unable to pay off his gambling debts. In desperation he gets involved in a jewel heist and later a treasure hunt that leads to death and misfortune. **65m/B; DVD.** Neil Hamilton; Kathleen Burke; Leon Ames; Reginald Barlow; Noel Francis; Paul Fix; Dick Curtis; Ray Turner; Katherine Jackson; Roger Moore; Edward Earle; Matthew Betz; Maidel Turner; ***D:*** Thomas Atkins; ***W:*** Stuart Anthony; ***C:*** Herbert Kirkpatrick; ***M:*** Chris Ridenhour.

Mutiny in the Big House 🦴🦴 ½ **1939** A man is sent to prison for writing a bad $10 check and must choose between seeking salvation with the prison chaplain or toughing it out with a hardened convict. Suprisingly good low-budget programmer. **83m/B; VHS, DVD.** Charles Bickford; Barton MacLane; Pat Moriarity; Dennis Moore; William Royle; Charles Foy; George Cleveland; ***D:*** William Nigh.

The Mutiny of the Elsinore 🦴 **1939** A writer on board an old sailing ship fights mutineers and wins back both the helm and the captain's daughter. Tedious British flotsam that made hash of an oft-filmed Jack London tale, and made news even in 1939 for its use of modern-day slang and clothing in the period setting. **74m/B; VHS, DVD.** Paul Lukas; Lyn Harding; Kathleen Kelly; Clifford Evans; Ben Soutten; Jiro Soneya; ***D:*** Roy Lockwood.

Mutiny on the Bounty 🦴🦴🦴🦴 **1935** Compelling adaptation of the true story of sadistic Captain Bligh, Fletcher Christian and their turbulent journey aboard the HMS Bounty and the subsequent mutiny in 1788. No gray here: Laughton's Bligh is truly a despicable character and extremely memorable in this MGM extravaganza. Remade twice, in 1962 and again in 1984 as "The Bounty." Much, much better than the 1962 remake. **132m/B; VHS, DVD, Blu-Ray.** Clark Gable; Franchot Tone; Charles Laughton; Donald Crisp; Dudley Digges; Spring Byington; Henry Stephenson; Eddie Quillan; Herbert Mundin; Movita; Ian Wolfe; ***D:*** Frank Lloyd; ***W:*** Talbot Jennings; Jules Furthman; Carey Wilson; ***M:*** Herbert Stothart. Oscars '35: Film; AFI '98: Top 100; N.Y. Film Critics '35: Actor (Laughton).

Mutiny on the Bounty 🦴🦴 ½ **1962** This account of the 1789 mutiny led by Fletcher Christian against Captain Bligh of the Bounty is highlighted by lavish photography and an eccentric, though interesting, portrayal of the mutiny leader by Brando. Though overshadowed by Laughton's compelling performance in the original 1935 masterpiece, Howard's Bligh is ship-shape as the cold-hearted, single-minded captain. Brando is all knickers and attitude as the peeved Mr. Christian, who finally can take no more of Bligh's social criticism. The other actors, especially Harris, join in the slightly over the top spirit of things. **177m/C; DVD, Blu-Ray, HD-DVD.** Marlon Brando; Trevor Howard; Richard Harris; Hugh Griffith; Richard Haydn; Percy Herbert; Noel Purcell; ***D:*** Lewis Milestone; ***W:*** Charles Lederer; ***C:*** Robert L. Surtees.

MVP: Most Valuable Primate 🦴 ½ **2000 (PG)** Predictable and lackluster tale about a hockey-playing chimp and the team of lovable losers that he helps to the inevitable "big game." After animal behaviorist Dr. Kendall dies, his chimp Jack mistakenly ends up in Nelson, British Columbia. He then makes contact with Tara, a deaf girl picked on by her classmates, and her older brother Steven, a hockey player on the worst team in the league. They discover that Jack has natural hockey skills and recruit him for Steven's team. Unfortunately, evil Dr. Peabody wants Jack back in the lab, setting up a showdown. **91m/C; VHS, DVD.** Kevin Zegers; Ric(k) Ducommun; Oliver Muirhead; Jamie Renee Smith; Lomax Study; ***D:*** Robert Vince; ***W:*** Robert Vince; Anne Vince; ***C:*** Glen Winter; ***M:*** Brahm Wenger.

MVP2: Most Vertical Primate 🦴 ½ **2001** Takes up where those "Air Bud" movies left off. In this equally dumb sequel, Jack the chimp is thrown out of the ZHL hockey league and goes on the lam from authorities. He meets homeless boy Ben (Goodman), who introduces the hairy one to amateur skateboarding. Of course, the chimp is a natural and many monkeyshines ensue. **97m/C; VHS, DVD.** Richard Karn; Cameron Bancroft; Scott Goodman; Bob Burnquist; ***D:*** Robert Vince; ***W:*** Robert Vince; Anne Vince; Elan Mastai. **VIDEO**

MXP: Most Xtreme Primate 🦴🦴 *MVP 3* **2003 (G)** Jack the chimp is at it again. This time he finds himself in Colorado, befriending lonely kid Pete, who's having trouble adjusting to a new town. Of course, Pete is an avid snowboarder, and teaches Jack some moves (Why wouldn't you?). They team up for a tournament while trying to avoid kidnappers. Third in the series again proves the comedy axiom "Monkeys are funny." Plot isn't great, but Jack's monkeyshines will keep the whole family amused anyway. **71m/C; VHS, DVD.** *CA* Robby Benson; Devin Douglas Drewitz; Gwynyth Walsh; Trevor Wright; Nicole McKay; Ian Bagg; ***D:*** Robert Vince; ***W:*** Robert Vince; Anne Vince; Anna McRoberts; ***C:*** Mike Southon; ***M:*** Brahm Wenger. **VIDEO**

My Afternoons with Marguerite 🦴🦴🦴 *La Tete en Friche* **2010 (R)** Fifty-something and practically illiterate, laborer Germain (Depardieu) sits on a park bench and has a chance encounter with elegant 95-year-old Marguerite (Casadeus), who is reading aloud from her novel. They continue to meet every afternoon, quickly and unexpectedly forming a heartfelt friendship that alters the way they think about themselves. A hopeful, feel-good film that is just the right amount of maudlin as it reaffirms the important roles of reading and friendship in revitalizing one's life. French with subtitles. **82m/C; DVD, Blu-Ray.** *FR* Gerard Depardieu; Gisele Casadesus; Claire Maurier; Jean-Francois Stevenin; Patrick Bouchitey; Sophie Guillemin; Maurane; Francois-Xavier Demaison; ***D:*** Jean Becker; ***W:*** Jean Becker; Jean-Loup Debadie; ***C:*** Arthur Cloquet; ***M:*** Laurent Voulzy.

My All American 🦴🦴 **2015 (PG)** Overly sentimental true life sports story featuring too much schmaltz. Set in the late 1960s, talented yet undersized quarterback Freddie Steinmark (Wittrock) plays college football at the University of Texas for legendary coach Darrell Royal (Eckhart). Freddie leads and plays with intense heart but is struck down in his prime. Much of the film focuses on his courtship with his girlfriend, leaving the story a bit fuzzy. **118m/C; DVD, Blu-Ray.** Finn Wittrock; Sarah Bolger; Robin Tunney; Aaron Eckhart; Alex MacNicoll; ***D:*** Angelo Pizzo; ***W:*** Angelo Pizzo; ***C:*** Frank G. DeMarco; ***M:*** John Paesano.

My American Cousin 🦴🦴🦴 **1985 (PG)** Award-winning autobiographical Canadian coming-of-age comedy set in 1959 on a British Columbia farm. 12-year-old Sandy (Langrick) exasperates her parents and has just discovered the appeal of boys when her rebellious, fun-loving, runaway 17-year-old American cousin Butch (Wildman) shows up (in a red Cadillac convertible) over summer vacation. Followed by "American Boyfriends" (1989) **94m/C; VHS, Streaming.** *CA* Margaret Langrick; John Wildman; Richard Donat; Jane Mortifee; ***D:*** Sandy Wilson; ***W:*** Sandy Wilson. Genie '86: Actor (Wildman), Actress (Langrick), Director (Wilson), Film.

My Amityville Horror 🦴🦴🦴 **2012** Daniel Lutz recounts his experiences in the most infamous haunted house in American history in this surprisingly moving and fascinating documentary. Did Lutz and his family really experience the supernatural in that house in Amityville? Director Eric Walter offers no simple answers, presenting an honest portrait of a man dealing with deep psychological scars whether one believes his stories of possession or thinks, as the movie somewhat implies, that an abusive stepfather interested in the occult could explain a lot of Lutz's dark past. Whatever happened in Amityville, Walter's film adds an interesting new chapter. **89m/C; Streaming.** ***D:*** Eric Walter; ***W:*** Eric Walter; ***C:*** Charlie Anderson; ***M:*** Herman Witkam.

My Architect: A Son's Journey 1/2 **2003** Slow but moving documentary about the life of famed architect Louis Kahn, written and directed by his son, Nathaniel. The movie begins with Kahn's death in 1974, when Nathaniel discovers in the obituary that his father had children by two other women. From there, he tries to uncover the mystery of Kahn's secretive life while highlighting his public achievements. What results is a film as much about a son trying to find his place in his father's life as Kahn's life itself. A depressing, poignant film only occasionally marred by Nathaniel's focus on his personal relationship, he still creates a bittersweet but empathetic portrait of his complex father. **116m/C; VHS, DVD.** ***Nar:*** Nathaniel Kahn; ***D:*** Nathaniel Kahn; ***W:*** Nathaniel Kahn; ***C:*** Robert Richman; ***M:*** Joseph Vitarelli. Directors Guild '03: Documentary Director (Kahn).

My Baby Is Missing 1/2 **2007** Pregnant Jenna is being monitored at home by a nurse when she suddenly wakes up in the hospital and is told that her baby girl was stillborn. The hospital knows nothing about her nurse, the baby's body has been cremated, and Jenna is absolutely sure that her own baby is still alive. The cops suspect Jenna killed her child while she believes the baby is being put up for a black-market adoption. **90m/C; DVD.** Gina Phillips; Ellie Harvie; Warren Christie; Peter Bryant; ***D:*** Neill Fearnley; ***W:*** Don Nelson; ***C:*** Larry Lynn; ***M:*** Chris Ainscough. **CABLE**

My Baby's Daddy **2004 (PG-13)** Three irresponsible doofuses end up fathers in this hip-hop rehash of an old formula. Lonnie (Griffin) and his buddies G (Anderson) and Dominic (Imperioli) struggle with how new fatherhood will affect their lives as South Philly small-time players with big dreams. Sweet attitude, but the laughs are intermittent in this bland, dumb story that's basically "Three Playaz and Some Shorties." **86m/C; VHS, DVD.** Eddie Griffin; Anthony Anderson; Michael Imperioli; John Amos; Method Man; Bai Ling; Marsha Thomason; Paula Jai Parker; Amy Sedaris; Tommy (Tiny) Lister; Denis Akayama; Scott Thompson; Joanna Bacalso; Dee Freeman; ***D:*** Cheryl Dunye; ***W:*** Eddie Griffin; Brent Goldberg; David T. Wagner; Damon "Coke" Daniels; ***C:*** Glen MacPherson; ***M:*** Richard Gibbs.

My Beautiful Laundrette **1985 (R)** Omar (Warnecke), the nephew of a Pakistani businessman, is given the opportunity to better himself by turning his uncle's rundown laundry into a profitable business. He reunites with Johnny (Day Lewis), a childhood friend and a working-class street punk, and they go into the business together. They find themselves battling the prejudice of each other's families and friends in order to succeed. An intelligent look at the sexuality, race relations and economic problems of Thatcher's London. Great performances by a relatively unknown cast (for contrast, note Day Lewis' performance in "Room with a View," released in the same year.) **93m/C; VHS, DVD, Blu-Ray.** Gordon Warnecke; Daniel Day-Lewis; Saeed Jaffrey; Roshan Seth; Shirley Anne Field; Derrick Branche; Rita Wolf; Souad Faress; Richard Graham; ***D:*** Stephen Frears; ***W:*** Hanif Kureishi; ***C:*** Oliver Stapleton; ***M:*** Stanley Myers; Ludus Tonalis. Natl. Bd. of Review '86: Support. Actor (Day-Lewis); N.Y. Film Critics '86: Screenplay, Support. Actor (Day-Lewis); Natl. Soc. Film Critics '86: Screenplay.

My Best Friend 1/2 ***Mon Meilleur Ami*** **2006 (PG-13)** Arrogant loner art dealer Francois (Auteuil) bets his business partner (Gayet) that he has a friend, and he is willing to do anything to win. He recruits taxi driver Bruno (Boon) to help him find a friend, only to discover that friendship isn't as easy to pin down (or buy) as he thought. Director Leconte thoughtfully takes the buddy comedy premise and turns it into an examination of friendship and loneliness in a world of consumerism. **94m/C; DVD.** ***FR*** Daniel Auteuil; Dany Boon; Julie Gayet; Julie Durand; ***D:*** Patrice Leconte; ***W:*** Patrice Leconte; Jerome Tonnerre; ***C:*** Jean-Marie Dreujou; ***M:*** Xavier Demerliac.

My Best Friend Is a Vampire **1988 (PG)** Another teenage vampire story, about trying to cope with certain changes that adolescence and bloodsucking bring. Good supporting cast. **90m/C; VHS, DVD.** Robert Sean Leonard; Evan Mirand; Cheryl Pollak; Rene Auberjonois; Cecilia Peck; Fannie Flagg; Kenneth Kimmins; David Warner; Paul Willson; Kathy Bates; ***D:*** Jimmy Huston; ***W:*** Tab Murphy; ***C:*** James Bartle; ***M:*** Steve Dorff.

My Best Friend's Girl **2008 (R)** Supposed rom com that's misogynistic and plays like a practical joke. Tank's (Cook) a professional "rebound guy" hired by men to date their ex-girlfriends and show them such a terrible time that they go running back to their former lover. Right. Things get ugly when Tank's roommate Dustin (Biggs) hires him to disgust Alexis (Hudson), Dustin's "just wants to be friends" co-worker. Somehow Tank's sleazy tactics do not repulse her and the two hit it off. A mean-spirited script filled with unlikable characters sets off a chain reaction of poor judgments by director Deutch. **101m/C; DVD, Blu-Ray, On Demand.** Kate Hudson; Dane Cook; Jason Biggs; Lizzy Caplan; Alec Baldwin; Nate Torrence; Diora Baird; Jenny Mollen; Riki Lindhome; Taram Killam; Kate Albrecht; Amanda Brooks; Mini Anden; Faye Grant; ***D:*** Howard Deutch; ***W:*** Jordan Cahan; ***C:*** Jack N. Green; ***M:*** John Debney.

My Best Friend's Wedding 1/2 **1997 (PG-13)** Best friends Julianne (Roberts) and Michael (Mulroney) have a pact that they'll marry each other if neither has found someone else by the age of 28. Michael finds sweet, wealthy Kimmy (Diaz) and invites Julianne to his nuptials. Naturally, Julianne realizes she's in love with Michael and she'll stop at nothing to break up the wedding, even enlisting gay friend George (Everett) to pose as her new beau. Roberts extends her range of physical comedy; Diaz gets to be nice; Everett steals every scene he's in; and Mulroney gets to be the lucky object of two lovely women's affections. Shot on location in Chicago. **105m/C; VHS, DVD, Blu-Ray.** Julia Roberts; Dermot Mulroney; Cameron Diaz; Rupert Everett; Philip Bosco; M. Emmet Walsh; Rachel Griffiths; Susan Sullivan; Paul Giamatti; ***D:*** P.J. Hogan; ***W:*** Ronald Bass; ***C:*** Laszlo Kovacs; ***M:*** James Newton Howard.

My Best Girl **1927** Plucky Maggie (Pickford) is a store clerk who is the main support for her eccentric family. She falls in love with the store owner's son (future hubby Rogers) but his father is skeptical of the match. A gentle satire on middle-American life in the 1920s. **88m/B; Silent; VHS, DVD.** Mary Pickford; Charles "Buddy" Rogers; Lucien Littlefield; Carmelita Geraghty; Sunshine Hart; Hobart Bosworth; ***D:*** Sam Taylor; ***W:*** Hope Loring; Tim Whelan; Allen McNeil; ***C:*** Charles Rosher; David Keeson.

My Big Fat Greek Wedding 1/2 **2002 (PG)** Toula (Vardalos) is a frumpy 30-year-old waitress at her Greek parents' Chicago restaurant. They expect her to marry a Greek boy, have babies, and feed everyone. Then she undegoes a makeover, meets handsome Ian Miller (Corbett), a non-Greek vegetarian schoolteacher who really, really likes her. Enough to want to marry her—if Toula's family can ever recover from the shock of her marrying outside their heritage. Every cliche imaginable is trotted out and you won't care as you'll laugh and groan at the too-recognizable family behavior (no matter what your ethnicity). Based on Vardalos' stage monologue. **95m/C; DVD, Blu-Ray.** Nia Vardalos; John Corbett; Lainie Kazan; Michael Constantine; Gia Carides; Louis Mandylor; Andrea Martin; Joey Fatone; Bruce Gray; Fiona Reid; Bess Meisler; Ian Gomez; ***D:*** Joel Zwick; ***W:*** Nia Vardalos; ***C:*** Jeffrey Jur; ***M:*** Chris Wilson; Alexander Janko. Ind. Spirit '03: Debut Perf. (Vardalos).

My Big Fat Greek Wedding 2 **2016 (PG-13)** At least a decade too late, this unfortunate follow-up to the 2002 sleeper hit catches up with Toula Portokalos Miller (Vardalos), who is still working in her family's Greek restaurant, of course. Her daughter Paris is getting ready to graduate from high school (don't do the math) and she's having marriage difficulties with her husband Ian (Corbett). Toula's parents find out they were never officially married, which means only one thing...wedding! Of course, it's one of those '80s sitcom style affairs in which everyone's problems are solved by the end of it. **94m/C; DVD, Blu-Ray, Streaming.** ***CA US*** Nia Vardalos; John Corbett; Louis Mandylor; Rita Wilson; Mark Margolis; ***D:*** Kirk Jones; ***W:*** Nia Vardalos; ***C:*** Jim Denault; ***M:*** Christopher Lennertz.

My Blind Brother **2016 (R)** Bill's (Kroll) brother Robbie (Scott) may be the toast of the town, especially after running a marathon despite the fact that he's blind, but he's also kind of a jerk. Enter Rose (Slate), who first sleeps with Bill before ending up in a dissatisfying relationship with Robbie, creating a unique love triangle. Kroll does career-best work here as a man who at least partially blames himself for his brother's blindness, and Slate matches him as someone equally driven by self-blame who realizes that these two were made for each other. It's funny, sweet and just acerbic enough to stand out. **85m/C; DVD, Blu-Ray.** Adam Scott; Nick Kroll; Jenny Slate; Zoe Kazan; Talia Tabin; ***D:*** Sophie Goodhart; ***W:*** Sophie Goodhart; ***C:*** Eric Lin; ***M:*** Ian Hultquist.

My Blood Runs Cold **1965** Your blood will be frozen stiff from boredom by the blonde blandness of the leads. Julie (Heatherton) gives motorcyclist Ben Gunther (Donahue) a lift but is puzzled when he insists on calling her 'Barbara.' Julie's Aunt Sarah (Nolan) says an ancestral Barbara had an affair with a Ben Gunther. Ben insists that he and Julie are reincarnations of the past lovers and Julie decides to elope with him. Ben is a psycho and Julie doesn't have two working brain cells. **103m/B; DVD.** Troy Donahue; Joey Heatherton; Barry Sullivan; Nicolas Coster; Jeannette Nolan; Russ Thorson; ***D:*** William Conrad; ***W:*** John Mantley; ***C:*** Sam Leavitt; ***M:*** George Duning.

My Bloody Banjo 1/2 **2015** A comedic fantasy-horror film centered on one young man's quest for revenge. In his office job, Peltzer Arbuckle (Hamer-Morton) is bullied and humiliated by his co-workers. The meek man has an egomanical boss and colleagues who regularly tease him. Even in his private life, he is degraded as his partner is cheating on him. After gossip about his sexual accident travels through his workplace, Peter takes action and conjures up his imaginary childhood friend Ronnie (Morter). Unexpectedly, Ronnie tries to talk Peter into taking revenge by the gruesome tormenting of his co-workers. At first, Peter follows Ronnie's guidance, but after more people die, Peter must decide who will control his future. **82m/C; DVD, Streaming, Download.** James Hamer-Morton; Damian Morter; Dani Thompson; Vito Trigo; Clay von Carlowitz; ***D:*** Liam Regan; ***W:*** Liam Regan; ***C:*** Damian Morter; ***M:*** Kurt Dirt.

My Bloody Valentine **1981 (R)** Psychotic coal miner visits the peaceful little town of Valentine Bluffs on the night of the yearly Valentine Ball. Many of the townspeople have their hearts removed with a pick axe and sent to the sheriff in candy boxes. The bloodiest scenes were cut out to avoid an X-rating. **91m/C; VHS, DVD, Blu-Ray.** ***CA*** Paul Kelman; Lori Hallier; Neil Affleck; Keith Knight; Alf Humphreys; Cynthia Dale; Terry Waterland; Peter Cowper; Don Francks; Jack Van Evera; ***D:*** George Mihalka; ***W:*** John Beaird; ***C:*** Rodney Gibbons.

My Bloody Valentine 3D **2009 (R)** Tom returns to his hometown of Harmony on the 10th anniversary of the Valentine's Day slaughter of 22 people, which ended with the killer's death. Then Tom becomes the prime suspect when the killing starts again. An unnecessary remake of the 1981 original that follows the same old horny-teens-systematically-slaughtered-mid-coitus-formula, complete with gratuitous nudity, sex and violence. The halfway decent use of the 3-D technology is the only thing that makes this stinker worth a mention, but how many flying eyeballs and projectile streams of blood can one endure? **101m/C; DVD, Blu-Ray.** Jensen Ackles; Jaime King; Kerr Smith; Edi Gathegi; Kevin Tighe; Rich Walters; Betsy Rue; Tom Atkins; Megan Boone; Karen Baum; ***D:*** Patrick Lussier; ***W:*** Todd Farmer; Zane Smith; ***C:*** Brian Pearson; ***M:*** Michael Wandmacher.

My Blue Heaven 1/2 **1950** Sentimental musical comedy-drama has successful husband and wife showbiz team Grable and Dailey try to start a family. When pregnant Molly (Grable) loses her baby in a car accident, she and husband/partner Jack (Dailey) decide to adopt, as they also try to make the transition from a popular radio show to TV. Some dialogue considered risque at the time of release wouldn't raise an eyebrow today. **96m/C; DVD.** Betty Grable; Dan Dailey; David Wayne; Jane Wyatt; Mitzi Gaynor; Una Merkel; Dan Hicks; Louise Beavers; Mae Marsh; Elinor Donahue; ***D:*** Henry Koster; ***W:*** Claude Binyon; Lamar Trotti; ***C:*** Arthur E. Arling.

My Blue Heaven **1990 (PG-13)** After agreeing to rat on the Mafia, Martin is dropped into suburbia as part of the witness protection program. Moranis plays the FBI agent assigned to help the former mobster become an upstanding citizen. Adjusting to life in the slow lane isn't easy for an ex con who has grown accustomed to the big time. Not the typical role for Martin, who plays a brunette with a New York accent and is handcuffed by bad writing. **96m/C; DVD, Blu-Ray.** Steve Martin; Rick Moranis; Joan Cusack; Melanie Mayron; Carol Kane; Bill Irwin; William Hickey; Daniel Stern; ***D:*** Herbert Ross; ***W:*** Nora Ephron; ***C:*** John Bailey; ***M:*** Ira Newborn.

My Blueberry Nights **2007 (PG-13)** Director Wong's first English-language feature sets up as a bit of a road movie. New Yorker Elizabeth (Jones), in the wake of an ugly breakup, happens into a Manhattan cafe where she orders a piece of blueberry pie and meets waiter/cook Jeremy (Law). Elizabeth is headed out of town and, while on the road, she works various jobs and encounters other wandering souls. Finally she heads back to New York, perhaps hungry for another slice of blueberry pie. Don't look for any real plot here—Wong has just artfully strung together a series of vignettes, which works if that's your thing. **90m/C; DVD.** ***FR CH*** Jude Law; David Strathairn; Rachel Weisz; Natalie Portman; Norah Jones; Chan Marshall; ***D:*** Wong Kar-Wai; ***W:*** Larry Block; Wong Kar-Wai; ***C:*** Darius Khondji; ***M:*** Ry Cooder.

My Bodyguard **1980 (PG)** An undersized high school student fends off attacking bullies by hiring a king-sized, withdrawn lad as his bodyguard. Their "business" relationship, however, develops into true friendship. An adolescent coming of age with more intelligence and sensitivity than most of its ilk, and a pack of up and coming stars as well as old stand-bys Houseman and Gordon. **96m/C; VHS, DVD, Blu-Ray.** Chris Makepeace; Adam Baldwin; Martin Mull; Ruth Gordon; Matt Dillon; John Houseman; Joan Cusack; Craig Richard Nelson; Tim Kazurinsky; George Wendt; Jennifer Beals; ***D:*** Tony Bill; ***W:*** Alan Ormsby; ***C:*** Michael D. Margulies; ***M:*** Dave Grusin.

My Boss's Daughter **2003 (PG-13)** Kutcher and Reid are at the center of a gaggle of tasteless and largely unfunny mishaps and gags. Tom's (Kutcher) a clueless schlub who works for Jack (Stamp), a tough-as-nails publishing exec. Wanting to further his career and get in good with Jack's party-hearty but pretty daughter Lisa (Reid), Tom takes a job house-sitting for his cantankerous, and very particular, boss. Despite a solid supporting cast, this one's just a predictable whirlwind of destructive disaster and Kutcher's deer-in-the-headlights routine runs thin. **84m/C; DVD.** Ashton Kutcher; Tara Reid; Terence Stamp; Jeffrey Tambor; Andy Richter; Michael Madsen; Jon Abrahams; David Koechner; Carmen Electra; Molly Shannon; Kenan Thompson; ***D:*** David Zucker; ***W:*** David Dorfman; ***C:*** Martin McGrath; ***M:*** Teddy Castellucci.

My Boy Jack 1/2 **2007** British author Rudyard Kipling (Haig, who also wrote the 1997 play the TV movie is based on) pulls strings that allow his only son, teenager Jack (Radcliffe), to enlist in the army in WWI in spite of the boy's bad eyesight. This is done over the objections of his American wife Caroline (Cattrall). When Jack is reported missing in 1915 in his first battle, the patriotic Kipling is overwhelmed by guilt and grief and spends years searching for answers before Jack's death is confirmed. **120m/C; DVD.** ***GB*** David Haig; Daniel Radcliffe; Kim Cattrall; Carey Mulligan; Julian Wadham; Martin McCann; Richard Dormer; ***D:*** Brian Kirk; ***W:*** David Haig; ***C:*** David Odd; ***M:*** Adrian Johnston. **TV**

My Boyfriend's Back ***Johnny Zombie*** **1993 (PG-13)** Embarassingly dumb flick about a teenage boy who wants to take the prettiest girl in the school to the prom. The only problem is that he's become a zombie. Bits of him keep falling off (his girl thoughtfully glues them back on) and if he wants to stay "alive" long enough to get to the dance he has to munch on human flesh. Yuck. **85m/C; VHS, DVD, Blu-Ray.** Andrew Lowery; Traci Lind; Edward Herrmann; Mary Beth Hurt; Danny Zorn; Austin Pendleton; Jay O. Sanders; Paul Dooley; Bob (Robert) Dishy; Cloris Leachman; Matthew Fox; Paxton Whitehead; ***D:*** Bob Balaban; ***W:*** Dean Lorey; ***C:*** Mac Ahlberg.

My Boys Are Good Boys ♪ **1978 (PG)** A young foursome steal from an armored car and have to face the consequences. Quirky with an implausible storyline. **90m/C; VHS, DVD.** Ralph Meeker; Ida Lupino; Lloyd Nolan; David Doyle; ***D:*** Bethel Buckalew.

My Brilliant Career ♪♪♪ **1/2 1979 (G)** Sybella (Davis) is a poor, headstrong young woman who spurns the social expectations of turn-of-the-century Australia and pursues opportunities to broaden her intellect and preserve her independence. This despite the fact that she loves Harry (Neill), a handsome, wealthy farmer. Davis is energetic and charismatic, especially in the scenes transforming her from a tomboy to a "lady." Has an excellent supporting cast. Based on an autobiographical novel by Miles Franklin which has been marvelously transferred to the screen. Armstrong deserves credit for her fine direction. **101m/C; VHS, DVD, Blu-Ray.** *AU* Judy Davis; Sam Neill; Wendy Hughes; Robert Grubb; Patricia Kennedy; Aileen Britton; Peter Whitford; Alan Hopgood; Julia Blake; ***D:*** Gillian Armstrong; ***W:*** Eleanor Witcombe; ***C:*** Donald McAlpine; ***M:*** Nathan Waks. Australian Film Inst. '79: Film; British Acad. '80: Actress (Davis).

My Brother ♪♪ **2006 (PG-13)** Moving family drama about the love of a mother and the bond of brothers. Living in poverty in the inner city, L'Tisha Morton (Williams) is terminally ill with tuberculosis and worried about her young sons aged 8 and 11. One is developmentally disabled, and her efforts to get them adopted together fail. To help them survive, she works on ensuring they have a deep bond of love and feel like they share one soul. As adults, Isaiah (Kerse) resents lacking independence because of James (Scott) and his needs. After Isaiah tries and fails to spread his wings by becoming a stand-up comedian, he finds himself facing danger with his brother over a package he was to deliver and realizes the importance of his relationship with James. **100m/C; DVD.** Vanessa Williams; Tatum O'Neal; Nashawn Kearse; Christopher Scott; Fredro Starr; ***D:*** Anthony Lover; ***W:*** Anthony Lover; ***C:*** John Sawyer; ***M:*** John Califra.

My Brother ♪♪ **2006 (PG-13)** Dying mom L'Tisha is desperate to have her two sons, Isaiah and developmentally disabled James, adopted together. Though that doesn't happen, the brothers' unshakeable bond stays with them into adulthood even when Isaiah gets involved with some hoods in a rather obvious subplot. **90m/C; DVD.** Vanessa L(ynne) Williams; Fredro Starr; Tatum O'Neal; Nashawn Kearse; Rodney Henry; Christopher Scott; Donovan Jennings; ***D:*** Anthony Lover; ***W:*** Anthony Lover; ***C:*** John Sawyer; ***M:*** John Califra. **VIDEO**

My Brother Is an Only Child ♪♪ *Mio Fratello e Figlio Unico* **2007** Sibling rivalry mixes with social and political upheaval in the 1960s. Manrico (Scamarcio) follows his father into factory work and communism while his skeptical younger brother Accio (Germano) heads towards fascism. Both also become rivals for the affections of Francesca (Fleri), who leaves her bourgeoisie family for left-wing radicalism. Italian with subtitles. **104m/C; DVD.** *FR IT* Elio Germano; Angela Finocchiaro; Riccardo Scarmarcio; Diane Fleri; Alba Rohrwacher; Massimo Popolizio; ***D:*** Daniele Luchetti; ***W:*** Daniele Luchetti; Sandro Petraglia; Stefano Rulli; ***C:*** Claudio Collepiccolo; ***M:*** Franco Piersanti.

My Brother Jonathan ♪♪ **1/2 1985** BBC TV miniseries adapted from the novel by Francis Brett Young. Ungainly Jonathan Dakers is neglected by his parents in favor of his handsome, athletic younger sibling, Harold. Their father dies and Jonathan gives up his dream of becoming a surgeon to work for a small practice, support his widowed mother, and further Harold's education. The brothers remain close but the family drama continues. **248m/C; DVD.** *UK* Daniel Day-Lewis; Benedict Taylor; Helen Ryan; Mark Kingston; Barbara Kellerman; Caroline Bliss; ***D:*** Anthony Garner; ***W:*** James Andrew Hall; ***C:*** Garth Tucker; ***M:*** Stanley Myers. **TV**

My Brother Talks to Horses ♪♪ **1/2 1947** Amusing family comedy. In turn-of-the-century Baltimore, young Lewie Penrose lives with his widowed mother, who takes in boarders to make ends meet, and his much-older brother John, a bank clerk who tries to be the voice of reason. Lewie has the ability to communicate with all sorts of animals, including racehorses who give him tips for the track. Lewie's ability to pick winners brings him to the notice of a local gambler and John must protect his young brother. The big race takes place at the Preakness. **92m/B; DVD.** Peter Lawford; Jackie "Butch" Jenkins; Beverly Tyler; Spring Byington; O.Z. Whitehead; Edward Arnold; Charlie Ruggles; ***D:*** Fred Zinnemann; ***C:*** Harold Rosson; ***M:*** Rudolph Kopp.

My Brother the Devil ♪♪ **2012** Heavy Brit accents and street vernacular are a challenge in El Hosaini's compelling feature film debut. Teenager Mo is growing up in a traditional Egyptian household although it's in the Hackney area of East London. His charismatic older brother Rashid belongs to the local gang and deals drugs to get money for Mo's education. But Mo wants to emulate his brother and gets pulled into gang life just as Rashid is trying to get out, aided by the friendship of French photographer Sayyid who offers him a chance at another life. Mo's resentful and it leads to problems. **112m/C; DVD.** *UK* James Floyd; Fady Elsayed; Said Taghmaoui; Anthony Welsh; ***D:*** Sally El Hosaini; ***W:*** Sally El Hosaini; ***C:*** David Raedeker; ***M:*** Stuart Earl.

My Brothers ♪♪ **1/2 2010** Noel (Timmy Creed) accidentally breaks his dying father's prized watch and quickly drags his younger brothers into a spontaneous road trip to find a replacement. **92m/C; DVD, Blu-Ray.** *IR* Timmy Creed; Paul Courtney; Tj Griffin; Don Wycherley; Kate Ashfield; ***D:*** Paul Fraser; ***W:*** William Collins; ***C:*** P. J. Dillon; ***M:*** Richard James. **VIDEO**

My Brother's Keeper ♪♪♪ **1995** Twin brothers, Bob and Tom Bradley, fight for an experimental procedure when Tom is declared HIV positive. **94m/C; DVD.** John Lithgow; Annette O'Toole; Veronica Cartwright; Ellen Burstyn; Richard Masur; Zeljko Ivanek; Brian Doyle-Murray; Amy Aquino; Julie Fulton; Mark Harelik; ***D:*** Glenn Jordan; ***W:*** Gregory Goodell.

My Brother's War ♪♪ **1/2 1997 (R)** Brothers Gerry (Foy) and Liam (Xuereb) find themselves on opposite sides of the troubles in Ireland. Then, CIA operative Hall (Brolin) arrives to prevent Liam kidnapping three politicians who are trying to reach a peace accord. Some plot twists help out this standard actioner. **85m/C; VHS, DVD.** Salvator Xuereb; Patrick Foy; James Brolin; Josh Brolin; Jennie Garth; Cristi Conaway; ***D:*** James Brolin; ***W:*** Alex Simon; ***C:*** Michael Bucher; ***M:*** John Graham.

My Brother's Wife ♪♪ **1/2 1989 (PG)** Barney (Ritter), the black sheep of a wealthy family, spends two decades pursuing Eleanor (Harris), the woman of his dreams. Unfortunately, she's already married—to the brother he despises. Adapted from the play "The Middle Ages" by A.R. Gurney. **94m/C; VHS, DVD.** John Ritter; Mel Harris; Polly Bergen; Dakin Matthews; David Byron; Lee Weaver; ***D:*** Jack Bender; ***W:*** Percy Granger. **TV**

My Chauffeur ♪♪ **1/2 1986 (R)** When a wise-cracking female is hired on as a chauffeur at an all-male chauffeur service, sparks fly. And when the owner takes a definite liking to her work, things take a turn for the worse. As these sort of sexploitation flicks go, this is one of the better ones. **94m/C; VHS, DVD, Blu-Ray.** Deborah Foreman; Sam Jones; Howard Hesseman; E.G. Marshall; Sean McClory; ***D:*** David Beaird; ***W:*** David Beaird.

My Childhood ♪♪♪ *Childhood of Maxim Gorky* **1938** The first of director Donskoi's trilogy on the life of Maxim Gorky, based on Gorky's autobiographical stories. In this first film, Donskoi depicts Gorky's childhood of abuse and poverty with his grandparents in the 1870s. Eventually, Gorky is forced into the streets and he becomes a wandering beggar. In Russian with English subtitles. Followed by "My Apprenticeship" and "My Universities." **100m/C; VHS, DVD, Streaming.** *RU* Varvara O. Massalitinova; Aleksei Lyarsky; Mikhail Troyanovsky; Yelizaveta Alekseyeva; ***D:*** Mark Donskoi; ***W:*** Ilya Gruzdev; ***C:*** Pyotr Yermolov; ***M:*** Lev Shvarts.

My Cousin Rachel ♪♪ **1/2 1952** Multi-Oscar nominated Gothic romance based on the Daphne Du Maurier bestseller. Philip Ashley (Burton, in his first American film) is suspicious when he hears of his cousin Ambrose's death in Italy. Ambrose wrote him letters suggesting that his younger wife Rachel (de Havilland) was poisoning him. Philip is the sole heir to Ambrose's estate, which includes the Cornish seaside home where Philip lives. Rachel comes to stay and Philip is quickly obsessed with her but then his own doubts surface. The ending is somewhat unsatisfying, but until then the atmosphere and lead performances are riveting. **98m/B; DVD.** Olivia de Havilland; Richard Burton; George Dolenz; Audrey Dalton; Ronald Squire; John Sutton; Tudor Owen; J.M. Kerrigan; ***D:*** Henry Koster; ***W:*** Nunnally Johnson; ***C:*** Joseph LaShelle; ***M:*** Franz Waxman.

My Cousin Rachel ♪♪ **1/2 2017 (PG-13)** Cousins everywhere, and they're either falling in love with or trying to kill each other. Young Philip (Claflin) is adopted by his cousin Ambrose, who eventually dies but not before implicating his wife Rachel (Weisz), his half-Italian cousin, as his murderer. Philip's plans for revenge are complicated by his newfound love for her, setting the stage for another death, but by whose hands? Gorgeous atmosphere and a beguiling performance by Weisz pay homage to Daphne du Maurier's classic novel. **106m/C; DVD, Blu-Ray.** Rachel Weisz; Sam Claflin; Holliday Grainger; Iain Glen; Simon Russell Beale; ***D:*** Roger Michell; ***W:*** Roger Michell; ***C:*** Mike Eley; ***M:*** Rael Jones.

My Cousin Vinny ♪♪♪ **1992 (R)** Vinny Gambini (Pesci), a lawyer who took the bar exam six times before passing, goes to Wahzoo City, Alabama to get his cousin and a friend off the hook when they're accused of killing a store clerk. Leather jackets, gold chains, Brooklyn accents, and his fiancee Mona Lisa's (Tomei) penchant for big hair and bold clothing don't go over well with conservative Judge Haller (Gwynne), causing plenty of misunderstandings. Surprising hit with simplistic story reaches popular heights via entertaining performances by the entire cast, especially by Tomei who got an Oscar to prove it. **120m/C; DVD, Blu-Ray.** Joe Pesci; Ralph Macchio; Marisa Tomei; Mitchell Whitfield; Fred Gwynne; Lane Smith; Austin Pendleton; Bruce McGill; ***D:*** Jonathan Lynn; ***W:*** Dale Launer; ***C:*** Peter Deming; ***M:*** Randy Edelman. Oscars '92: Support. Actress (Tomei); MTV Movie Awards '93: Breakthrough Perf. (Tomei).

My Darling Clementine ♪♪♪ **1/2 1946** One of the best Hollywood westerns ever made, this recounts the precise events leading up to and including the gunfight at the O.K. Corral. Fonda's the lawman, with Bond, Holt, and Garner as his brothers, and Mature co-stars as best friend, Doc Holliday. Schoolteacher Clementine (Downs) is Earp's gal, but the real revelation should be Brennan as old man Clanton—he's chilling not folksy. Ford allegedly knew Wyatt Earp and used his stories to recount the details vividly, though not always accurately. Remake of 1939's "Frontier Marshal." **97m/B; VHS, DVD, Blu-Ray.** Henry Fonda; Victor Mature; Walter Brennan; Linda Darnell; Tim Holt; Ward Bond; John Ireland; Cathy Downs; Alan Mowbray; Don Garner; Jane Darwell; Grant Withers; ***D:*** John Ford; ***W:*** Sam Hellman; Winston Miller; Samuel G. Engel; ***C:*** Joe MacDonald; ***M:*** David Buttolph; Cyril Mockridge. Natl. Film Reg. '91.

My Date With Drew ♪♪♪ **2005 (PG)** That would be actress Drew Barrymore, whom struggling filmmaker Herzlinger idolizes. He gives himself 30 days (since Herzlinger must return his video camera to the electronics store in that time in order to get a refund—yes, it's really low-budget). He must also attract her attention and not have her think he's a crazed stalker (he's actually kind of funny in an insecure way). And in the case of this documentary, it's all about the quest and not the outcome, which will not be revealed. **90m/C; DVD.** Brian Herzlinger; ***D:*** Jon Gunn; Brian Herzlinger; Brett Winn; ***C:*** Jon Gunn; Brian Herzlinger; Brett Winn; ***M:*** Steven Stern; Stuart Hart.

My Dear Secretary ♪♪ **1/2 1949** After she marries her boss, a woman grows jealous of the secretary that replaces her. Comedic dialogue and antics result. **94m/B; VHS, DVD.** Kirk Douglas; Laraine Day; Keenan Wynn; Rudy Vallee; Florence Bates; Alan Mowbray; Charles Halton; ***D:*** Charles Martin; ***W:*** Charles Martin.

My Demon Lover ♪♪ **1987 (PG-13)** This sex comedy is complicated by the hero's transformation into a demon whenever he is aroused. Saved from complete mediocrity by Family Ties's Valentine in a likable performance. **90m/C; DVD.** Scott Valentine; Michelle Little; Arnold Johnson; Gina Gallego; ***D:*** Charles Loventhal; ***M:*** David Newman; Ed Alton.

My Dinner with Andre ♪♪♪ **1/2 1981** Two friends talk about their lives and philosophies for two hours over dinner one night. A wonderful exploration into storytelling, the conversation juxtaposes the experiences and philosophies of nerdish, bumbling Shawn and the globe-trotting spiritual pilgrimage of Gregory, in this sometimes poignant, sometimes comic little movie that starts you thinking. **110m/C; VHS, DVD, Blu-Ray.** Andre Gregory; Wallace Shawn; Roy Butler; Jean Lenauer; ***D:*** Louis Malle; ***W:*** Andre Gregory; Wallace Shawn; ***C:*** Jeri Sopanen; ***M:*** Allen Shawn.

My Dog Shep ♪ **1/2 1946** An orphan and his dog run away and are pursued diligently when it is discovered that he is a wealthy heir. **71m/B; VHS, DVD.** Tom Neal; William Farnum; Lannie Rees; Russell Simpson; Sarah Padden; Al "Fuzzy" St. John; Helen Chapman; Douglas Evans; Reed Howes; Grady Sutton; ***D:*** Ford Beebe; ***W:*** Ford Beebe; ***C:*** Fred Mandl.

My Dog Skip ♪♪♪ **1999 (PG)** In 1940s Mississippi, awkward only child Willie (Muniz) sees his life change when, over the protests of his overprotective father (Bacon), he gets a puppy, Skip, for his ninth birthday. Amid much nostalgia and sentiment, Willie learns to be more outgoing and has many coming-of-age moments. Even if some of the plot elements are weak, the look and feel of the period is captured well, and Muniz does a fine job, although no human is likely to compete with the pooch. Kids will love the antics of Skip, and adults will enjoy having their hearts, and memories, tugged. Based on the book by Willie Morris. **95m/C; DVD.** Frankie Muniz; Diane Lane; Kevin Bacon; Luke Wilson; Caitlin Wachs; Bradley Coryell; Daylan Honeycutt; Cody Linley; ***Nar:*** Harry Connick, Jr.; ***D:*** Jay Russell; ***W:*** Gail Gilchriest; ***C:*** James L. Carter; ***M:*** William Ross.

My Dog the Champion ♪♪ **1/2** *Champion* **2014 (G)** A family film about finding new bonds and the true meaning of family in an unexpected place. Living with her mom in a big city, 16-year-old Madison (Burge) is self-centered with a typical teenage social life. However, when her mom is sent overseas for three months, Madison is sent to live with her hard-nosed grandfather Billy (Henrikson) at his cattle ranch in the country. Living without Wi-Fi and other city comforts is difficult for Madison, but she meets an attractive 17-year-old dog trainer, Eli (Linley), finds there is more to her grandfather than meets the eye, and bonds with a cattle dog that may be a champion. **87m/C; DVD, Download.** Dora Madison Burge; Lance Henriksen; Cody Linley; Reis Myers McCormick; Farah White; ***D:*** Kevin Nations; Robin Nations; ***W:*** Robin Nations; Richard Dane Scott; ***C:*** Darren Abate; ***M:*** Jonathan Franklin. **VIDEO**

My Dog, the Thief ♪ **1969** A helicopter weatherman is unaware that the lovable St. Bernard he has adopted is a kleptomaniac. When the dog steals a valuable necklace from a team of professional jewel thieves, the fun begins. **88m/C; VHS, DVD.** Joe Flynn; Elsa Lanchester; Roger C. Carmel; Mickey Shaughnessy; Dwayne Hickman; Mary Ann Mobley; ***D:*** Robert Stevenson.

My Dog Tulip ♪♪♪ **2009** Animated film about an author's bittersweet relationship with the German Shepherd who becomes his greatest friend. Based on the memoirs of J.R. Ackerley. **82m/C; DVD, Blu-Ray, Streaming.** ***V:*** Christopher Plummer; Lynn Redgrave; Isabella Rossellini; Peter Gerety; Brian Murray; ***D:*** Paul Fierlinger; Sandra Fierlinger; ***W:*** Paul Fierlinger; Sandra Fierlinger; ***M:*** John Avarese.

My Dream Is Yours 1/2 **1949** Day plays an up-and-coming radio star in this Warner Bros. musical comedy with a cameo from Bugs Bunny in a dream sequence. This fresh, fun remake of "Twenty Million Sweethearts" is often underrated, but is well worth a look. **101m/C; VHS, DVD.** Jack Carson; Doris Day; Lee Bowman; Adolphe Menjou; Eve Arden; S.Z. Sakall; Selena Royle; Edgar Kennedy; ***D:*** Michael Curtiz.

My Effortless Brilliance 1/2 **2008** If you like improvised dialogue and situations that basically go nowhere, then Shelton's mumblecore effort may be for you. Narcissistic writer Eric Lambert Jones and his childhood friend Dylan have inevitably drifted apart because of differing personalities and choices. Eric still isn't willing to let go and when he's on a book tour, he decides to intrude on Dylan's manly cabin-in-the-woods lifestyle for a drunken weekend with Dylan and his new best bud Jim. **79m/C; DVD.** Sean Nelson; Basil Harris; Calvin Reeder; Jeanette Maus; ***D:*** Lynn Shelton; ***W:*** Sean Nelson; Lynn Shelton; Basil Harris; Calvin Reeder; Jeanette Maus; ***C:*** Benjamin Kasulke; ***M:*** Ted Speaker.

My Entire High School Sinking Into the Sea 1/2 **2017 (PG-13)** A minimalist-looking animated feature with a chaotic storyline. High school sophomores Dash (Schwartzmann) and Assaf (Watts) are best friends until the genial Assaf begins a romantic relationship with Verti (Rudolph). The angry Dash learns that the school is not up to earthquake code and will collapse into the sea when the new auditorium is open. Dash's warnings are not heeded and the worst happens, which forces everyone to come together and devise an escape from the doomed building. Complex with appealing visuals, nonetheless the story is wishy-washy. **75m/C; DVD.** Jason Schwartzman; Lena Dunham; Reggie Watts; Maya Rudolph; Susan Sarandon; ***D:*** Dash Shaw; ***W:*** Dash Shaw; ***M:*** Rani Sharone.

My Fair Lady 1/2 **1964 (G)** Colorful production of Lerner and Loewe's musical version of "Pygmalion," about ill-mannered cockney Eliza (Hepburn) who is plucked from her job as a flower girl by Professor Henry Higgins (Harrison). Higgins makes a bet with a colleague that he can turn this rough diamond into a "lady." Winner of eight Academy Awards. Hepburn's singing voice is dubbed by Marni Nixon, who was also responsible for the singing in "The King and I" and "West Side Story"; the dubbing may have undermined Hepburn's chance at an Oscar nomination. Typecasting role for Harrison as the crusty, egocentric Higgins. A timeless classic. **170m/C; VHS, DVD, Blu-Ray.** Audrey Hepburn; Rex Harrison; Stanley Holloway; Wilfrid Hyde-White; Theodore Bikel; Mona Washbourne; Jeremy Brett; Robert Coote; Gladys Cooper; ***D:*** George Cukor; ***W:*** Alan Jay Lerner; ***C:*** Harry Stradling, Sr.; ***M:*** Frederick Loewe; Alan Jay Lerner. Oscars '64: Actor (Harrison), Adapt. Score, Art Dir./Set Dec., Color, Color Cinematog., Costume Des. (C), Director (Cukor), Film, Sound; AFI '98: Top 100; British Acad. '65: Film; Directors Guild '64: Director (Cukor); Golden Globes '65: Actor--Mus./Comedy (Harrison), Director (Cukor), Film--Mus./Comedy; Natl. Film Reg. '18; N.Y. Film Critics '64: Actor (Harrison), Film.

My Fake Fiance **2009** Creaky romantic comedy from ABC Family. Cynical Jennifer (Hart) is seated next to debt-ridden gambler Vince (Lawrence) at a wedding and hostilities ensue. Through various contrivances the duo agrees to a fake engagement because they need the gifts for monetary reasons. Of course unless they go through with the wedding, etiquette demands that the presents be returned. Naturally their feelings towards one another change just in time. **95m/C; DVD.** Melissa Joan Hart; Joseph Lawrence; Steve Schirripa; Diane Neal; Nicole Tubiola; ***D:*** Gil Junger; ***W:*** Howard March; ***C:*** Greg Gardiner; ***M:*** Danny Lux. **CABLE**

My Family 1/2 *Mi Familia* **1994 (R)** Patriarch Jose Sanchez (Rojas) comes to America in the early 1900s from Mexico and soon finds that the grass is not always greener. Thus begins the multigenerational saga of the Sanchez family in L.A., which chronicles their struggles and hopes over a time span of 60 years. Features soulful performances from the ensemble cast, especially Smits and Morales as troubled men from separate generations. Their deep-seated need to assimilate, matched by a disdain for authority, provide most of the family's heartaches. English and Spanish dialogue. **126m/C; DVD.** Jimmy Smits; Esai Morales; Eduardo Lopez Rojas; Jenny Gago; Elpidia Carrillo; Lupe Ontiveros; Jacob Vargas; Jennifer Lopez; Scott Bakula; Edward James Olmos; Michael Delorenzo; Maria Canals; Leon Singer; Jonathan Hernandez; Constance Marie; Enrique Castillo; Mary Steenburgen; ***Nar:*** Edward James Olmos; ***D:*** Gregory Nava; ***W:*** Gregory Nava; Anna Thomas; ***C:*** Edward Lachman; ***M:*** Pepe Avila; Mark McKenzie.

My Faraway Bride *My Bollywood Bride* **2006** Genial cross-cultural rom com with a leading man who's handsome but is easily shown up by his co-stars. Adventure novelist Alex (Lewis) spends several days in L.A. with Indian tourist Reena (Shah), who cuts her trip short and heads back home without any explanation. Desperate to reunite with his love, Alex flies to Mumbai to track Reena down, finally learning she's a Bollywood star about to marry a powerful producer (Grover). Reena fobs Alex off on fellow actor Bobby (Suri) while she tries to figure out what's best. **95m/C; DVD.** *US IN* Kashmira Shah; Jason Lewis; Gulshan Grover; Sanjay Suri; Neha Debey; ***D:*** Rajeev Manoj; Brad Listermann; ***W:*** Richard Martini; ***C:*** John Drake; ***M:*** Anu Malik.

My Father, My Mother, My Brothers and My Sisters *Mon Pere, Ma Mere, Mes Freres et Mes Soeurs* **1999** Free-spirit Anne (Abril) has three children by three different men and has never bothered to inform any of them about their offspring. She's surprised when her young son Victor expresses an interest in meeting his dad, which just happens to be possible since Anne and her brood are vacationing at the same Mexican resort where all three of her ex-lovers happen to also be staying with their significant others. French with subtitles. **95m/C; VHS, DVD.** *FR* Victoria Abril; Alain Bashung; Pierre-Jean Cherit; Charlotte de Turckheim; ***D:*** Charlotte de Turckheim; ***W:*** Charlotte de Turckheim; Philippe Giangreco; ***C:*** Javier Salmones; ***M:*** Cyril de Turckheim.

My Father the Hero **1993 (PG)** Another adaptation of a French film ("Mon Pere, Ce Heroes") finds 14-year-old Heigl on an island paradise with divorced dad Depardieu, passing him off as her boyfriend (without his knowledge) to impress a cute boy, causing obvious misunderstandings. Depardieu shows a flair for physical comedy, but his talent is wasted in a role that's vaguely disturbing; one of the few funny moments finds him unwittingly singing "Thank Heaven For Little Girls" to a horrified audience. Topnotch actress Thompson's surprising (uncredited) cameo is due to her friendship with Depardieu. **90m/C; VHS, DVD, Blu-Ray.** Gerard Depardieu; Katherine Heigl; Dalton James; Lauren Hutton; Faith Prince; ***Cameo(s):*** Emma Thompson; ***D:*** Steve Miner; ***W:*** Francis Veber; Charlie Peters; ***M:*** David Newman.

My Father's Glory *La Gloire de Mon Pere* **1991 (G)** Based on Marcel Pagnol's tales of his childhood, this is a sweet, beautiful memory of a young boy's favorite summer in the French countryside of the early 1900s. Not much happens, yet the film is such a perfect evocation of the milieu that one is carried swiftly into the dreams and thoughts of all the characters. One half of a duo, followed by "My Mother's Castle." In French with English subtitles. **110m/C; VHS, DVD.** *FR* Julien Ciamaca; Philippe Caubere; Nathalie Roussel; Therese Liotard; Didier Pain; ***D:*** Yves Robert; ***W:*** Lucette Andrei; ***C:*** Robert Alazraki; ***M:*** Vladimir Cosma.

My Favorite Blonde **1942** Beautiful British spy Carroll convinces Hope to aid her in carrying out a secret mission. Lots of fun as Hope and his trained penguin, along with Carroll, embark on a cross-country chase to elude the Nazis. Hope's behavior is hilarious and the pacing of the film is excellent. Based on a story by Melvin Frank and Norman Panama. **78m/B; VHS, DVD.** Bob Hope; Madeleine Carroll; Gale Sondergaard; George Zucco; Lionel Royce; Walter Kingsford; Victor Varconi; Bing Crosby; ***D:*** Sidney Lanfield; ***W:*** Frank Butler; Don Hartman; ***C:*** William Mellor; ***M:*** David Buttolph.

My Favorite Brunette 1/2 **1947** Detective parody starring Hope as a photographer turned grumbling private eye. He becomes involved with a murder, a spy caper, and a dangerous brunette (Lamour). **85m/B; VHS, DVD, Blu-Ray.** Bob Hope; Dorothy Lamour; Peter Lorre; Lon Chaney, Jr.; Alan Ladd; Reginald Denny; Bing Crosby; ***D:*** Elliott Nugent; ***W:*** Edmund Beloin; Jack Rose; ***C:*** Lionel Lindon; ***M:*** Robert Emmett Dolan.

My Favorite Martian 1/2 **1998 (PG)** A less-than-mediocre retread of the semi-successful '60s TV sitcom. Tim (Daniels) is a TV producer cajoled into hiding his "Uncle Martin." Martin (Lloyd) is actually an alien whose spaceship has crashed and he's on the run from a government agency and the prying press. Tim must also throw a racy reporter (Hurley) off the trail, although he has a crush on her. Numerous animated and computer morphed sight gags, including a horny wise-cracking spacesuit named Zoot (who brings new meaning to the term "skirt chasing"), take the place of a plot. **93m/C; VHS, DVD.** Jeff Daniels; Christopher Lloyd; Elizabeth Hurley; Daryl Hannah; Wallace Shawn; Christine Ebersole; Ray Walston; Michael Lerner; ***D:*** Donald Petrie; ***W:*** Sherri Stoner; Deanna Oliver; ***C:*** Thomas Ackerman; ***M:*** John Debney.

My Favorite Spy 1/2 **1951** Spy spoof from Hope. Burlesque comic Peanuts White (Hope) is recruited by the government to take the place of captured spy Eric Augustine and pick up some microfilm in Tangiers. Peanuts gets some questionable assistance from Eric's girlfriend Lily (Lamarr), who's working for spymaster Karl (Sullivan). To complicate matters, Eric escapes and the double's got trouble. **93m/B; DVD, Blu-Ray.** Bob Hope; Hedy Lamarr; Francis L. Sullivan; Arnold Moss; John Archer; Morris Ankrum; Stephan Chase; Luis van Rooten; ***D:*** Norman Z. McLeod; ***W:*** Jack Sher; Edmund L. Hartmann; ***C:*** Victor Milner; ***M:*** Victor Young.

My Favorite Wife **1940** Handsome widower Nick (Grant) has just married Bianca (Patrick) only to discover that first wife Ellen (Dunne), shipwrecked seven years earlier and presumed dead, has reappeared. Ellen wants Nick back and makes him jealous by revealing that she spent her island sojourn with fellow survivor, Stephen (Scott). Eventually, a judge must decide what to do about their most unusual situation. Farcical and hilarious story filled with a clever cast. The 1963 remake "Move Over Darling" lacks the style and wit of this presentation. **88m/B; VHS, DVD.** Irene Dunne; Cary Grant; Randolph Scott; Gail Patrick; Scotty Beckett; Ann Shoemaker; Granville Bates; ***D:*** Garson Kanin; ***W:*** Samuel Spewack; Bella Spewack; Leo McCarey; ***C:*** Rudolph Mate; ***M:*** Roy Webb.

My Favorite Year *My Favourite Year* **1982 (PG)** A young writer on a popular live TV show in the 1950s is asked to keep a watchful eye on the week's guest star—his favorite swashbuckling movie hero. Through a series of misadventures, he discovers his matinee idol is actually a drunkard and womanizer who has trouble living up to his cinematic standards. Sterling performance from O'Toole, with memorable portrayal from Bologna as the show's host, King Kaiser (a take-off of Sid Caesar from "Your Show of Shows"). **92m/C; VHS, DVD, Blu-Ray.** Peter O'Toole; Mark Linn-Baker; Joseph Bologna; Jessica Harper; Lainie Kazan; Bill Macy; Anne DeSalvo; Lou Jacobi; Adolph Green; Cameron Mitchell; Gloria Stuart; ***D:*** Richard Benjamin; ***W:*** Norman Steinberg; ***M:*** Ralph Burns.

My Fellow Americans **1996 (PG-13)** Political "Odd Couple" pits cantankerous conservative Kramer (Lemmon) against womanizing liberal Douglas (Garner) when the current President (Aykroyd) frames his two predecessors for a White House scandal. The age-old adversaries must set aside their differences long enough to clear their names by reaching Kramer's presidential library, where he has vindicating papers. Along the way, they encounter adventure, danger and the average Americans they used to work for. Lemmon is plenty cranky while Garner's charisma is a suitable foil. Supporting characters aren't as well served as the two leads. **96m/C; DVD.** Dan Aykroyd; James Garner; Jack Lemmon; John Heard; Sela Ward; Wilford Brimley; Everett McGill; Bradley Whitford; Lauren Bacall; James Rebhorn; Esther Rolle; Conchata Ferrell; Jack Kehler; Tom Everett; Jeff Yagher; ***D:*** Peter Segal; ***W:*** E. Jack Kaplan; Richard Chapman; Peter Tolan; ***C:*** Julio Macat; ***M:*** William Ross.

My First Mister 1/2 **2001 (R)** Explores the delicate friendship between two lost and lonely souls. Teenaged Jennifer (Sobieski) is a goth girl whose look and attitude alienates both school and family members. Looking for a job, she is unexpectedly hired as a stock clerk by men's clothing salesman, Randall (Brooks), a middle-aged conservative in both dress and manner. They discover they have a number of feelings in common, although Randall is careful never to let their relationship get out of control. Film does take an unfortunate turn towards the maudlin when we learn that Randall is dying but the leads keep sentimentality fairly well-checked. **109m/C; VHS, DVD.** Albert Brooks; Leelee Sobieski; Desmond Harrington; Carol Kane; Michael McKean; Mary Kay Place; John Goodman; Lisa Jane Persky; ***D:*** Christine Lahti; ***W:*** Jill Franklyn; ***C:*** Jeffrey Jur; ***M:*** Steve Porcaro.

My First Wedding **WOOF! 2004 (PG-13)** Disastrous and raunchy would-be romcom with unlikable characters and ridiculous situations. Bride-to-be Vanessa (Cook) is having sex fantasies about other men just days before her wedding and heads to confession. Horndog carpenter Nick (Doughty) happens to be fixing the confessional booth and is mistaken for the priest. Vanessa pleads with the faker to save her from sin. Of course Nick wants to sin big time and does his best to persuade Vanessa to call off the nuptials. **100m/C; DVD.** Rachael Leigh Cook; Kenny Doughty; Paul Hopkins; Valerie Mahaffey; ***D:*** Laurent Firode; ***W:*** Joan Carr-Wiggin; ***C:*** Vernon Layton; ***M:*** Michel Cusson.

My 5 Wives **2000 (R)** Dangerfield is a thrice-divorced real estate tycoon who discovers the Utah land he's invested in comes complete with five wives. **100m/C; VHS, DVD.** Rodney Dangerfield; Andrew Silverstein; John Byner; Molly Shannon; Jerry Stiller; John Pinette; Emmanuelle Vaugier; Fred Keating; Kate Luyben; Judy Tylor; Angelika Baran; Anita Brown; ***D:*** Sidney J. Furie; ***W:*** Rodney Dangerfield; Harry Basil; ***C:*** Curtis Petersen; ***M:*** Robert Carli. **VIDEO**

My Forbidden Past 1/2 **1951** Melodrama set in 1890 New Orleans centers on a young woman (Gardner) with an unsavory past who unexpectedly inherits a fortune and vows to break up the marriage of the man (Mitchum) she loves. His wife is murdered and he is charged with doing the deed until Gardner, exposing her past, wins his love and helps to extricate him. **81m/B; VHS, DVD.** Ava Gardner; Melvyn Douglas; Robert Mitchum; Lucile Watson; Janis Carter; ***D:*** Robert Stevenson; ***W:*** Marion Parsonnet; ***C:*** Harry Wild; ***M:*** Frederick "Friedrich" Hollander.

My Friend Dahmer 1/2 **2017 (R)** Based on John Beckderf's graphic novel, a look into the life of serial killer Jeffrey Dahmer (Lynch) as a teen before he began killing. Informed by Beckderf's personal knowledge of young Dahmer, the film explores Dahmer's experiences, including being a social outcast and his tumultuous home life. Focusing especially on Dahmer's senior year, Beckderf (Wolff) and his friends encourage Dahmer's extreme actions for laughs until they realize the extent of his emotional disturbance. It becomes clearer that Dahmer wants to seriously hurt someone. Well-crafted with strong performances, Dahmer's alienation and later disturbing acts are better understood. **107m/C; DVD, Blu-Ray.** Ross Lynch; Alex Wolff; Vincent Kartheiser; Anne Heche; Dallas Roberts; ***D:*** Marc Meyers; ***W:*** Marc Meyers; ***C:*** Daniel Katz; ***M:*** Andrew Hollander.

My Friend Flicka **1943** Boy makes friends with four-legged beast. Dad thinks the horse is full of wild oats, but young Roddy trains it to be the best gosh darned horse in pre-Disney family faredom. Based on Mary O'Hara book, followed by "Thunderhead, Son of Flicka," and TV series. **89m/C; VHS, DVD.** Roddy McDowall; Preston Foster;

Rita Johnson; James Bell; Jeff Corey; *D:* Harold Schuster.

My Friend from India 1/2 **1927** Multiple-identity silent comedy. Charlie wants to keep sponging off his wealthy, status-conscious Aunt Bedelia so he convinces his friend Tommy to pose as an East Indian prince whose visit will add to her social cachet. **74m/B; Silent; DVD.** Franklin Pangborn; Ben Hendricks, Jr.; Ethel Wales; Elinor Fair; Jeanette Loff; Tom Ricketts; *D:* E. Mason Hopper; *W:* Rex Taylor; *C:* Dewey Wrigley.

My Friend Irma 1/2 **1949** An adaptation of the radio series, featuring Wilson as the dumb blonde with boyfriend trouble and Lynn as her sensible pal. The film debut of Martin (singing) and Lewis (mugging) as juice-bar operators. Followed by a sequel, "My Friend Irma Goes West," and later by a TV series. **103m/B; DVD.** Marie Wilson; Diana Lynn; John Lund; Don DeFore; Dean Martin; Jerry Lewis; Hans Conried; *D:* George Marshall; *W:* Cy Howard; *C:* Leo Tover; *M:* Roy Webb.

My Friend Irma Goes West **1950** The sequel has Martin & Lewis taking over with crooning and slapstick. A producer offers Steve a chance in Hollywood so the gang hop a train bound for L.A. only to discover the producer is actually an escapee from a mental hospital. Various mishaps eventually land them in Las Vegas instead. Based on the radio show. **90m/B; DVD.** Dean Martin; Jerry Lewis; John Lund; Marie Wilson; Diana Lynn; Charles Evans; Corinne Calvet; *D:* Hal Walker; *W:* Cy Howard; *C:* Lee Garmes; *M:* Leigh Harline.

My Future Boyfriend 1/2 **2011** ABC Family rom com about anthropologist Pax (Watson), who lives in the 32nd century. He finds a romance novel written by 21st century author Elizabeth Barrett (Rue) and travels back in time to meet her in New Orleans. He doesn't understand the idea of love but, of course, Elizabeth thinks the socially awkward Pax is just crazy. **76m/C; DVD.** Barry Watson; Sara Rue; Fred Willard; Valerie Harper; *D:* Michael Lange; *W:* James Orr; Jim Cruickshank; *C:* Mark Irwin; *M:* Kenneth Burgomaster. **CABLE**

My Gal Sal **1942** Largely fictional showbiz musical about 1890s Tin Pan Alley songwriter Paul Dresser (Mature), loosely based on the memoirs of his younger brother, author Theodore Dreiser. After leaving Indiana and working in a medicine show, Paul is a Broadway success but has a love/hate relationship with musical star Sally Elliott (Hayworth). **103m/C; DVD, Blu-Ray.** Victor Mature; Rita Hayworth; Carole Landis; James Gleason; Phil Silvers; John Sutton; Walter Catlett; *D:* Irving Cummings; *W:* Seton I. Miller; Karl Tunberg; Darrell Ware; *C:* Ernest Palmer; *M:* Alfred Newman. Oscars '42: Art Dir./Set Dec., Color.

My Gal Sunday **2014** Hallmark Channel crime/romance where nothing much works, including most of the acting, pace, and plot. Lawyer Sandra 'Sunday' O'Brien has married former politico Henry Parker and the two are using their contacts to become private investigators. It gets personal when Sunday's Secret Service agent dad and Henry's mom are kidnapped by the revenge-seeking brother of a convicted killer, who's convinced his sibling is innocent and wants him released. Based on a novel by Mary Higgins Clark. **90m/C; DVD.** Rachel Blanchard; Cameron Mathison; Jack Wagner; Janet-Laine Green; *D:* Kristopher Tabori; *W:* Howard Burkons; *M:* Claude Foisy. **CABLE**

My Geisha 1/2 **1962** MacLaine and husband experience bad karma because she wants to be in his new film. In pancake makeup and funny shoes, she poses as a geisha girl and is cast as Madame Butterfly. Her husband, however, is one sharp cookie. Filmed in Japan. **120m/C; DVD.** Shirley MacLaine; Yves Montand; Edward G. Robinson; Robert Cummings; Yoko Tani; Tatsuo Saito; *D:* Jack Cardiff; *W:* Norman Krasna; *C:* Shunichiro Nakao; *M:* Franz Waxman.

My Giant **1998 (PG)** Billy Crystal plays a short, Hollywood-type guy and Romanian-born NBA player Gheorghe Muresan plays a really tall Romanian guy, so you know there's no originality happening here. Brutish showbiz agent Sammy accidently stumbles onto monestery-dwelling Max. Sammy, being an agent, quickly finds a way to make money off of him. Max is talked into a movie career so he can be reunited with his childhood crush Lillianna (Pacula). The odd couple schtick is milked until bone dry and then the sentimentality floodgates open when it's discovered that Max has a serious medical condition. **103m/C; VHS, DVD.** Billy Crystal; Gheorghe Muresan; Kathleen Quinlan; Joanna Pacula; Rider Strong; Harold Gould; Doris Roberts; Philip Sterling; Heather Thomas; Zane Carney; Michael (Mike) Papajohn; *Cameo(s):* Steven Seagal; *D:* Michael Lehmann; *W:* David Seltzer; *C:* Michael Coulter; *M:* Marc Shaiman.

My Girl 1/2 **1991 (PG)** Chlumsky is delightful in her film debut as an 11-year-old tomboy who must come to grips with the realities of life. Culkin plays her best friend Thomas, who understands her better than anyone else, including her father, a mortician, and his girlfriend, the makeup artist at the funeral parlor. Some reviewers questioned whether young children would be able to deal with some unhappy occurrences in the film, but most seemed to classify it as a movie the whole family would enjoy. **102m/C; VHS, DVD, Blu-Ray.** Dan Aykroyd; Jamie Lee Curtis; Macaulay Culkin; Anna Chlumsky; Griffin Dunne; Raymond Buktenica; Richard Masur; Ann Nelson; Peter Michael Goetz; Tom Villard; *D:* Howard Zieff; *W:* Laurice Elehwany; *C:* Paul Elliott; *M:* James Newton Howard. MTV Movie Awards '92: Kiss (Macaulay Culkin/Anna Chlumsky).

My Girl 2 1/2 **1994 (PG)** It's 1974 and Chlumsky is back as Vada (this time without Culkin, given the killer bee attack in MG1) in this innocent coming-of-ager. Portly Aykroyd and flaky Curtis return as parental window dressing who encourage Vada's search for information on her long-dead mother. She tracks down old friends of her mom's who are having difficulties with their obnoxious adolescent son (O'Brien). Predictable, but enjoyable. Certain to fail the credibility test of viewers who may wonder why the only thing Aykroyd can remember of his first wife is that she left behind a paper bag with a date scribbled on it. **99m/C; DVD, Blu-Ray.** Anna Chlumsky; Dan Aykroyd; Jamie Lee Curtis; Austin O'Brien; Richard Masur; Christine Ebersole; Ben Stein; *D:* Howard Zieff; *W:* Janet Kovalcik; *C:* Paul Elliott; *M:* Cliff Eidelman.

My Girlfriend's Back 1/2 **2010 (PG-13)** Attorney Derek has just become—somewhat unwillingly—engaged to Becca, a beautiful but domineering, rich daddy's girl. Then Derek's equally fine but hard-working, free-spirited ex-girlfriend Nicki comes back into his life and starts him rethinking his personal and professional lives. **81m/C; DVD.** Malik Yoba; Tangi Miller; Victoria Platt; CCH Pounder; Brent Jennings; DeRay Davis; *D:* Steven Ayromlooi; *W:* Mandel Holland; *C:* David Daniel. **VIDEO**

My Girlfriend's Boyfriend 1/2 **2010 (PG-13)** Unlucky-in-love waitress Jessie is searching for true romance and then meets apparently two perfect prospects. Troy is a self-confident ad exec and sweet Ethan is an unpublished writer. While she's deciding, Jessie tries to keep her two suitors from finding out about each other. **84m/C; DVD.** Alyssa Milano; Christopher Gorham; Michael Landes; Beau Bridges; Tom Lenk; Carol Kane; *D:* Darryn Tufts; *W:* Darryn Tufts; *C:* Brandon Christensen; *M:* Sam Carden. **VIDEO**

My Golden Days *Trois souvenirs de ma jeunesse* **2015 (R)** Desplechin's coming-of-age story is also one of his most personal dramas. It echoes developments in Europe over the last 20 years. Paul (Amalric) is preparing to leave Tajikistan when he is forced to remember his adolescent years, including young love, a troublesome mother, and even a trip to the USSR. Dolmaire plays Paul as a young man and Desplechin's style captures the hazy days of growing up with unique flair and intelligence. It finds ways to make Paul's story universal without feeling it's trying to do so. **123m/C; DVD.** *FR* Quentin Dolmaire; Lou Roy-Lecollinet; Mathieu Amalric; Dinara Drukarova; Cecile Garcia-Fogel; *D:* Arnaud Desplechin; *W:* Arnaud Desplechin; Julie Peyr; *C:* Irina Lubtchansky; *M:* Gregoire Hetzel; Mike Kourtzer.

My Guardian Angel **2016** A thriller centering on an autistic girl who fears her deceased twin is demanding she takes revenge for her twin's death. Raised by abusive parents, eleven-year-old Hannah (Jacobson) is mute and autistic. Her twin Angel (Jacobson) died but her parents refused to allow Hannah to grieve or find any solace in her sister's possessions. Finally taken to a new school by her parents, she fears her life will soon end because of them. Her perspective on the world changes when a knife starts appearing under her pillow and she begins to hear a persistent voice which she comes to believe might be Angel. Hannah must decide if she should let herself be guided by the voice and do the bad things the voice demands. **100m/C; DVD, Blu-Ray.** Holly Jacobson; Maria Figgins; Petra Bryant; Adrian Annis; Tova Leigh; *D:* Mumtaz Yildirimlar; *W:* Mumtaz Yildirimlar; Deanna Dewey; Jane Alexandra Foster; *C:* Ben Jacobson; *M:* Mumtaz Yildirimlar. **VIDEO**

My Gun Is Quick 1/2 **1957** Enter the brutal L.A world of Mickey Spillane's PI Mike Hammer (Bray) as he investigates the murder of a young prostitute he briefly befriended in a diner. Mike finds links to a diamond ring the girl was wearing and stolen jewels from WWII. **90m/B; DVD, Blu-Ray.** Robert Bray; Whitney Blake; Donald Randolph; Pamela Duncan; Patricia Donahue; Jan Chaney; Booth Colman; Peter Mamakos; *D:* George White; Phil Victor; *W:* Richard Powell; Richard Collins; *C:* Harry Neumann; *M:* Marlin Skiles.

My House in Umbria **2003** Scenic, quality HBO production adapted from the novella by William Trevor. Emily Delahunty (Smith) is aboard a Milan-bound train when her peace is shattered by a bomb. Emily invites the other survivors from her train car to recuperate at her house in Umbria, including young American Aimee (Clarke), whose parents were killed in the explosion. Aimee begins to lean on Emily and then her frosty Uncle Thomas (Cooper) shows up to collect his niece. Emily's voiceover ramblings are sometimes distracting but Smith finds the pathos in her character without going overboard. The versatile Cooper also offers excellent support in an unsympathetic role. **103m/C; VHS, DVD.** Maggie Smith; Chris Cooper; Timothy Spall; Emmy Clarke; Benno Furmann; Ronnie Barker; Giancarlo Giannini; Libero De Rienzo; *D:* Richard Loncraine; *W:* Hugh Whitemore; *C:* Marco Pontecorvo; *M:* Claudio Capponi. **CABLE**

My Husband's Double Life 1/2 *The Familiar Stranger* **2001** Men are scum. Cable drama based on a true story finds Elizabeth Welsh (Sanders) trying to cope with the apparent suicide of her embezzling husband Patrick (Sanders). She has to sell the house and get a job to support their kids. Then, 10 years later, the Social Security Department informs Elizabeth that the weasel is alive and living in Maine. Naturally, Elizabeth heads off to confront the two-timer. **96m/C; VHS, DVD.** Margaret Colin; Jay O. Sanders; Will Estes; Aaron Ashmore; Gary Hudson; Victoria Snow; *D:* Alan Metzger; *W:* Alan Hines. **CABLE**

My Left Foot **1989 (R)** A gritty, unsentimental drama based on the life and autobiography of cerebral-palsy victim Christy Brown. Considered an imbecile by everyone but his mother (Fricker, in a stunning award-winning performance) until he teaches himself to write. He survives his impoverished Irish roots to become a painter and writer using his left foot, the only appendage over which he has control. He also falls in love and finds some heartaches along the way. Day-Lewis is astounding; the supporting cast, especially Shaw and Cusack, match him measure for measure. **103m/C; VHS, DVD, Blu-Ray.** *IR* Daniel Day-Lewis; Brenda Fricker; Ray McAnally; Cyril Cusack; Fiona Shaw; Hugh O'Conor; Adrian Dunbar; Ruth McCabe; Alison Whelan; *D:* Jim Sheridan; *W:* Shane Connaughton; Jim Sheridan; *C:* Jack Conroy; *M:* Elmer Bernstein. Oscars '89: Actor (Day-Lewis), Support. Actress (Fricker); British Acad. '89: Actor (Day-Lewis), Support. Actor (McAnally); Ind. Spirit '90: Foreign Film; L.A. Film Critics '89: Actor (Day-Lewis), Support. Actress (Fricker); Montreal World Film Fest. '89: Actor (Day-Lewis); N.Y. Film Critics '89: Actor (Day-Lewis), Film; Natl. Soc. Film Critics '89: Actor (Day-Lewis).

My Life 1/2 **1993 (PG-13)** Maudlin, sometimes depressing production preaches the power of a well-examined life. Public relations exec Keaton is diagnosed with cancer and the doctors predict he will most likely die before the birth of his first child. Film follows his transition from uncommunicative and angry to acceptance, a role to which Keaton brings a sentimental strength. Kidman is window dressing as the ever-patient, nobly suffering wife, a cardboard character notable mainly for her beauty. **114m/C; VHS, DVD.** Michael Keaton; Nicole Kidman; Haing S. Ngor; Bradley Whitford; Queen Latifah; Michael Constantine; Toni Sawyer; Rebecca Schull; Lee Garlington; *D:* Bruce Joel Rubin; *W:* Bruce Joel Rubin; *C:* Peter James; *M:* John Barry.

My Life and Times with Antonin Artaud *En Compagnie d'Antonin Artaud; Artaud* **1993** Postwar Parisian bohemia is depicted in the obsessive friendship between ambitious young poet Jacques Prevel (Barbe) and famed intellectual/poet/impressario Antonin Artaud (Frey), who founded the Theatre of Cruelty. Artaud has returned to Paris after spending nine years in an asylum and is suffering from terminal cancer, the misery of which is partially alleviated by the opiates that Prevel can provide. Delusional and paranoid, Artaud makes his self-destruction into genius while Prevel documents Artaud's last two years in diaries, hoping to gain some measure of fame for himself. French with subtitles. Based on Prevel's "En Compagnie d'Antonin Artaud." **93m/B; VHS, DVD.** *FR* Sami Frey; Marc Barbe; Valerie Jeannet; Julie Jezequel; Charlotte Valandrey; *D:* Gerard Mordillat; *W:* Gerard Mordillat; Jerome Prieur; *C:* Francois Catonne; *M:* Jean-Claude Petit.

My Life As a Dog *Mitt Liv Som Hund* **1985** A troublesome boy is separated from his brother and is sent to live with relatives in the country when his mother is taken ill. Unhappy and confused, he struggles to understand sexuality and love and tries to find security and acceptance. Remarkable Swedish film available with English subtitles or dubbed. **101m/C; VHS, DVD, Blu-Ray.** *SW* Anton Glanzelius; Tomas von Bromssen; Anki Liden; Melinda Kinnaman; Kicki Rundgren; Ing-mari Carlsson; *D:* Lasse Hallstrom; *W:* Lasse Hallstrom; Per (Pelle) Berglund; Brasse Brannstrom; *C:* Jorgen Persson; Rolf Lindstrom; *M:* Bjorn Isfalt. Golden Globes '88: Foreign Film; Ind. Spirit '88: Foreign Film; N.Y. Film Critics '87: Foreign Film.

My Life as a Zucchini *Ma vie de Courgette* **2016 (PG-13)** Clauda Barras' beautiful, Oscar-nominated, stop-motion animated film is more for pre-teens and older than the little ones, although this is the kind of lovely movie that offers a little something different for everyone. Courgette is an awkward boy who is forced to go to an orphanage after the accidental death of his mother (for which he is somewhat to blame), and what follows is a series of encounters with the other young people of the establishment, who bring the boy nicknamed "Zucchini" out of his shell. This is a funny, moving, sweet little tale that has remarkable power. **70m/C; DVD, Blu-Ray.** *FR SI V:* Will Forte; Nick Offerman; Ellen Page; Amy Sedaris; Erick Abbate; *D:* Claude Barras; *W:* Claude Barras; Céline Sciamma; Germano Zullo; Morgan Navarro; *C:* David Toutevoix; *M:* Sophie Hunger.

My Life in Ruins **2009 (PG-13)** Moderately amusing comedy relies on too many tourist cliches with a slimmed-down, glammed-up Vardalos not particularly believable as a romantically-challenged tour guide who's lost her zest for life. Greek-American Georgia, a would-be classics professor, is not a particularly popular guide in Athens. She gets stuck with the dilapidated bus, the sullen driver (Georgoulis), and the most stereotypical tourists because she provides pedantic lectures rather than shopping excursions. Her latest week's tour offers gorgeous Greek scenery, bonding situations, a chance at romance, and too much that's tired and obvious. **95m/C; DVD, Blu-Ray, On Demand.** Nia Vardalos; Richard Dreyfuss; Rachel Dratch; Maria Botto; Harland Williams; Alexis Georgoulis; Sheila Bernette; Ralph Nossek; Bernice Stegers; Maria Adanez; *D:* Donald Petrie; *W:* Mike Reiss; *C:* Jose Luis Alcaine; *M:* David Newman.

My Life on Ice *The True Story of My Life in Rouen; Ma Vraie Vie a Rouen* **2002** Sixteen-year-old Etienne (Tavares) has two obsessions: figure skating and filming everything that happens around him with the video camera he got for his birthday. He films his mom, Caroline (Ascaride), and her new boyfriend Laurent (Zaccai), his grandmother (Surgere), and his best friend Ludovic (Bonnifait)--few of whom are happy to constantly be in the camera's eye. The viewer also becomes aware (although those around him seem oblivious) to the virginal Etienne's sexuality—he has a crush on both Laurent, who happens to be his history teacher, and pal Ludovic, who can't deal with any sexual revelations. French with subtitles. **100m/C; VHS, DVD.** *FR* Jimmy Tavares; Ariane Ascaride; Helene Surgere; Jonathan Zaccai; Lucas Bonnifait; ***D:*** Olivier Ducastel; Jacques Martineau; ***W:*** Olivier Ducastel; Jacques Martineau; ***C:*** Mathieu Poirot-Delpech; Pierre Milon; ***M:*** Philippe Miller.

My Life So Far 1/2 **1998 (PG-13)** In the 1920s, the Pettigrews live on the family estate of Gamma Macintosh (Harris) in the Scottish Highlands. Eccentric would-be inventor Edward (Firth) ineffectually manages the property, with wife Moira (Mastrantonio) and his children, including mischievious 10-year-old Fraser (Norman). Fraser's safe world is rocked by the arrival of his businessman Uncle Morris (McDowell) and his uncle's seductive French fiancee, Heloise (Jacob), who draws the immediate and overly attentive gaze of Edward. Based on the autobiographical book "Son of Adam" by Sir Denis Forman. **93m/C; VHS, DVD.** *GB* Colin Firth; Mary Elizabeth Mastrantonio; Irene Jacob; Malcolm McDowell; Rosemary Harris; Tcheky Karyo; Robert Norman; Kelly Macdonald; ***D:*** Hugh Hudson; ***W:*** Simon Donald; ***C:*** Bernard Lutic; ***M:*** Howard Blake.

My Life to Live *Vivre Sa Vie; It's My Life* **1962** A woman turns to prostitution in this probing examination of sexual, and social, relations. Idiosyncratic Godard has never been more starstruck than in this vehicle for the endearing Karina, his wife at the time. A classic. In French with English subtitles. **85m/B; VHS, DVD, Blu-Ray.** *FR* Anna Karina; Sady Rebbot; Andre S. Labarthe; Guylaine Schlumberger; ***D:*** Jean-Luc Godard; ***W:*** Jean-Luc Godard; ***C:*** Raoul Coutard; ***M:*** Michel Legrand. Venice Film Fest. '62: Special Jury Prize.

My Life Without Me 1/2 **2003 (R)** Writer/director Coixet delivers a weepy drama about a woman who keeps her impending death a secret from her family. Diagnosed with inoperable ovarian cancer, married 23-year-old Ann (Polley) decides against telling husband Don (Speedman) and their children about her condition. With only a few months to live, Ann draws up a bucket list, including falling in love with another man. She finds a cooperative lover in Lee (Ruffalo) while also trying to set up Don with a replacement wife (Watling). Despite the far-fetched, soap operatic script and less than sympathetic main character, earnest performances ratchet up the believability factor. **106m/C; VHS, DVD.** *CA SP* Sarah Polley; Scott Speedman; Mark Ruffalo; Deborah Harry; Alfred Molina; Leonor Watling; Amanda Plummer; Julian Richings; Maria De Medeiros; ***D:*** Isabel Coixet; ***W:*** Isabel Coixet; ***C:*** Jean-Claude Larrieu; ***M:*** Alfonso de Villalonga.

My Life's in Turnaround **1994 (R)** Amusing low-budget comedy takes a behind-the-scenes, semi-autobiographical look at the lives of two would-be filmmakers. They try for cool but manage only goofy. **84m/C; VHS, DVD.** Eric Schaeffer; Donal Lardner Ward; Lisa Gerstein; Dana Wheeler-Nicholson; Debra Clein; Sheila Jaffe; ***Cameo(s):*** Casey Siemaszko; John Sayles; Martha Plimpton; Phoebe Cates; ***D:*** Eric Schaeffer; Donal Lardner Ward; ***W:*** Eric Schaeffer; Donal Lardner Ward; ***M:*** Reed Hays.

My Little Assassin **1999** In 1959, idealistic 19-year-old Marita Lorenz (Anwar) is in Cuba with her CIA operative mother (Clayburgh), when she falls for revolutionary leader Fidel Castro (Mantegna). She winds up pregnant and alone in New York, where the CIA tries to convince her that Fidel's a bad guy. So, she decides to return to Cuba and assassinate him. In 1993, Lorenz wrote a book detailing her affair, the birth of their daughter, and Lorenz's involved in a failed plot to poison the dictator in 1960. If you can suspend your credulity, you'll discover a watchable potboiler with Mantegna as a charismatic Cuban leader. **90m/C; VHS, DVD.** Joe Mantegna; Gabrielle Anwar; Jill Clayburgh; Robert Davi; Scott Paulin; Tony Plana; Reiner Schone; Mike Moroff; Glenn Morshower; Dean Norris; ***D:*** Jack Bender; ***W:*** Howard Korder; ***M:*** David Schwartz. **CABLE**

My Little Chickadee **1940** Classic comedy about a gambler and a fallen woman who marry for convenience so they can respectably enter an unsuspecting town. Sparks fly in their adventures together. Fields and West are both at their best playing their larger-than-life selves. **91m/B; VHS, DVD.** W.C. Fields; Mae West; Joseph Calleia; Dick Foran; Margaret Hamilton; Donald Meek; Ruth Donnelly; Fuzzy Knight; ***D:*** Edward F. (Eddie) Cline; ***W:*** W.C. Fields; Mae West; ***C:*** Joseph Valentine; ***M:*** Frank Skinner.

My Little Pony: The Movie **2017 (PG)** An animated feature based on the popular 1980s cartoon and toys that emphasizes friendship and kindness. Twilight Sparkle (Strong), the leader of a pony group, finds her plans for a friendship festival undermined by a sinister force who kidnaps pony princesses to harness their power. With the help of six pony friends, Twilight Sparkle takes a journey to save the kidnapped and their home. During the quest, the ponies must outmaneuver a sulky unicorn (Blunt) and accept help from those who may not have good intentions. The target age will be more enthralled than adults, even those on a nostalgia trip. **99m/C; DVD.** Uzo Aduba; Ashleigh Ball; Emily Blunt; Kristin Chenoweth; Taye Diggs; ***D:*** Jayson Thiessen; ***W:*** Meghan McCarthy; Rita Hsiao; Michael Vogel; ***C:*** Anthony Di Ninno; ***M:*** Daniel Ingram.

My Louisiana Sky 1/2 **2002** Twelve-year-old Tiger Ann (Keel) lives with her grandma Jewel (Knight) and her "slow" parents in Saitler, Louisiana. She's looking forward to the summer when her glamorous aunt, Dorie Kay (Lewis), will visit but Jewel's unexpected death has Tiger Ann re-thinking what matters to her after she goes to live with her aunt in the city. Based on the book by Kimberly Willis Holt. **99m/C; VHS, DVD.** Kelsey Keel; Shirley Knight; Juliette Lewis; Karen Robinson; Amelia Campbell; Chris Owens; Michael Cera; ***D:*** Adam Arkin; ***W:*** Anna Sandor; ***C:*** Gavin Smith; ***M:*** Mader. **CABLE**

My Love Came Back 1/2 **1940** Poor violin student Amelia (de Havilland), who can't afford her music academy, suddenly gets a scholarship from flirtatious music publishing company owner Julius Malette (Winniger). His children assume the worst but Amelia's friends Dusty (Albert) and Joy (Wyman) are thrilled since they persuade Amelia to use the money to help them form a swing band. More complications follow when Amelia falls for Tony (Lynn), the manager of Malette's company. **81m/B; DVD.** Olivia de Havilland; Charles Winninger; Jeffrey Lynn; Eddie Albert; Jane Wyman; William Orr; Ann Gillis; Spring Byington; S.Z. Sakall; Grant Mitchell; ***D:*** Curtis Bernhardt; ***W:*** Ivan Goff; Earl Baldwin; Robert Buckner; ***C:*** Charles Rosher; ***M:*** Heinz Roemheld.

My Love For Yours 1/2 *Honeymoon in Bali* **1939** The romantic tale of a young man hoping to win the love of a beautiful but icy girl. A tad silly in parts, but the clever dialogue moves the story along. **99m/B; VHS, DVD.** Fred MacMurray; Madeleine Carroll; ***D:*** Edward H. Griffith.

My Lucky Elephant **2013 (PG)** An orphan boy finds a friend and purpose with an elephant. Raised in the jungle, Boy Mahout (Khunchan) is an orphan without friends, ties, or connections, until he finds an abandoned elephant named Lucky. Bonding as friends, they have several adventures including finding an art school where elephants learn to paint. Lucky proves to be a natural at painting, and soon gains fame for his works. Because of Lucky's paintings, the pair have money and food. Mahout faces a new life challenge when Lucky falls in love with a female elephant named Candy and they have babies together, but Mahout's life has already been changed for the better. **91m/C; DVD, Streaming, Download.** First Khunchan; Thanyarat Praditthaen; Charlie Sungkawess; Wallop Terathong; Georges Levillain; ***D:*** Eric Schwab; ***W:*** Eric Schwab; ***C:*** Scott Galinsky; ***M:*** Patrick Schmitz. **VIDEO**

My Lucky Star 1/2 **1938** Skating star Henie plays a department store clerk that gets sent off to college to model clothes from the store's sports line. She somehow manages to convince school officials to stage their winter ice show in the department store, where she gets to show off her stuff. Don't miss the grand finale, a performance of "Alice in Wonderland Ice Ballet." Based on the story "They Met in Chicago" by Karl Tunberg and Don Ettlinger. **81m/B; DVD.** Sonja Henie; Richard Greene; Joan Davis; Cesar Romero; Buddy Ebsen; Arthur Treacher; George Barbier; Gypsy Rose Lee; ***D:*** Roy Del Ruth; ***W:*** Harry Tugend; Jack Yellen.

My Magic Dog 1/2 **1997** Lucky is eight-year-old Toby's dog. Lucky happens to be invisible. Which turns out to be a good thing when evil Aunt Violet tries to steal Toby's inheritance. **98m/C; VHS, DVD.** Leo Millbrook; Russ Tamblyn; John Phillip Law; ***D:*** John Putch. **VIDEO**

My Man and I **1952** Endlessly hard-working and noble Mexican-born migrant farmer Chu Chu Ramirez (Montalban) is proud to have become a new American citizen. He's unjustly thrown in jail when racist San Joaquin farmer Ansel Ames (Corey) and his jealous wife (Trevor) lie about an accidental shooting, but Chu Chu's hard-luck girlfriend Nancy (Winters) and his friends are going to prove his innocence. **99m/B; DVD.** Ricardo Montalban; Wendell Corey; Claire Trevor; Shelley Winters; Robert Burton; Jack Elam; ***D:*** William A. Wellman; ***W:*** John Fante; Jack Leonard; ***C:*** William Mellor; ***M:*** David Buttolph.

My Man Godfrey **1936** Spoiled rich girl Irene Bullock (Lombard) picks up someone she assumes is a bum (Powell) as part of a scavenger hunt and decides to keep him on as her family's butler. In the process, Godfrey teaches her about life, money, and happiness—and that everything is not as it seems. Top-notch screwball comedy defines the genre. Lombard is a stunner alongside the equally charming Powell. Watch for Jane Wyman as an extra in the party scene. From the novel by Eric Hatch. Remade in 1957 with June Allyson and David Niven. **95m/B; VHS, DVD, Blu-Ray.** William Powell; Carole Lombard; Gail Patrick; Alice Brady; Mischa Auer; Eugene Pallette; Alan Mowbray; Franklin Pangborn; Jane Wyman; ***D:*** Gregory La Cava; ***W:*** Gregory La Cava; Morrie Ryskind; ***C:*** Ted Tetzlaff; ***M:*** Charles Previn. Natl. Film Reg. '99.

My Man Godfrey 1/2 **1957** Inferior remake of the sophisticated screwball comedy of the '30s about a butler who brings a touch of the common man to the filthy rich. Niven stars as the butler and Allyson plays the rich girl, but nothing compares to the original roles created by Powell and Lombard. **92m/C; VHS, DVD.** June Allyson; David Niven; Martha Hyer; Jessie Royce Landis; Robert Keith; Eva Gabor; Jay Robinson; Jeff Donnell; ***D:*** Henry Koster; ***W:*** Everett Freeman; Peter Berneis; William Bowers; ***C:*** William H. Daniels.

My Man Is a Loser 1/2 **2014 (R)** Sexist raunch about two hapless guys whose marriages are floundering, so they ask their womanizing bud to give them advice. But their frustrated wives aren't buying it. Not a complete waste thanks to some amusing performances, but not a high pick for date night. **95m/C; DVD.** Michael Rapaport; Bryan Callen; John Stamos; Tika Sumpter; Kathy Searle; Heidi Armbruster; ***D:*** Mike Young; ***W:*** Mike Young; ***C:*** Harlan Bosmajian; ***M:*** Brian Kim. **VIDEO**

My Mom's a Werewolf 1/2 **1989 (PG)** An average suburban mother gets involved with a dashing stranger and soon, to her terror, begins to turn into a werewolf. Her daughter and companion must come up with a plan to regain dear, sweet mom. **90m/C; VHS, DVD.** Susan Blakely; John Saxon; John Schuck; Katrina Caspary; Ruth Buzzi; Marilyn McCoo; Marcia Wallace; Diana Barrows; ***D:*** Michael Fischa; ***W:*** Mark Pirro; ***C:*** Bryan England; ***M:*** Dana Walden; Barry Fasman.

My Mom's New Boyfriend **2008 (PG-13)** Oh Meg, how embarrassing. Widowed Martha (Ryan) had been fat and depressed when her uptight FBI son Henry (Hanks) left for an undercover assignment. Returning to Shreveport three years later with his fiancee Emily (Blair) in tow, Henry discovers Martha—now Marty—has transformed herself into a high-spirited hottie. She also has a suave but suspicious boyfriend, Tommy (Banderas), whom Henry learns is an international art thief. The Bureau wants Henry to set up surveillance and stop Tommy's latest heist, which means spying on his mom and learning way more than any son should about her personal life. **97m/C; DVD.** Meg Ryan; Antonio Banderas; Colin Hanks; Selma Blair; Eli Danker; Enrico Colantoni; ***D:*** George Gallo; ***W:*** George Gallo; ***C:*** Michael Negrin; ***M:*** Chris Boardman. **VIDEO**

My Mother Likes Women *A mi madre le gustan las mujeres* **2002** Screwy, somewhat strained, Spanish comedy has successful, middle-aged classical pianist Sofia (Sarda) introducing her younger, female lover Eliska (Sirova), a shy Czech immigrant, to her three shocked daughters. Conservative, married Jimena (Pujalte) is the eldest, would-be writer Elvira (Watling) is the neurotic middle child, and the youngest, Sol (Abascal), is a breezy pop singer willing to follow her sisters' opinion. Which is that Eliska is a gold-digger and has to be gotten rid of. Czech and Spanish with subtitles. **96m/C; DVD.** *SP* Leonor Watling; Rosa Maria Sarda; Silvia Abascal; Chisco Amado; Alex Angulo; Maria Pujalte; Eliska Sirova; Xabier Elorriaga; Aitor Mazo; Sergio Otegui; ***D:*** Ines Paris; Daniela Fejerman; ***W:*** Ines Paris; Daniela Fejerman; ***C:*** David Omedes; ***M:*** Juan Bardem.

My Mother's Castle 1/2 *Le Chateau de Ma Mere* **1991 (PG)** The second half of the two part film series based on the autobiography of Marcel Pagnol. Picking up where "My Father's Glory" left off, the family begins a series of vacations in a beautiful country home. Dynamically acted and tenderly directed, charming and suitable for the entire family. In French with English subtitles. **98m/C; VHS, DVD.** *FR* Philippe Caubere; Nathalie Roussel; Didier Pain; Therese Liotard; Julien Ciamaca; Victorien Delmare; ***D:*** Yves Robert; ***M:*** Vladimir Cosma.

My Mother's Courage *Mutters Courage* **1995** Based on writer George Tabori's memoir of his Jewish mother, Elsa (Collins), who managed to escape deportation from Budapest in 1944. Her husband is in prison, her sons have left the country, but an unwavering Elsa remains to care for her asthmatic sister. Finally, she is detained and sent to the railyard to be deported—until she confronts a Nazi official and manages to obtain her release. German with subtitles. **88m/C; VHS, DVD.** *GE GB* Pauline Collins; Ulrich Tukur; Natalie Morse; ***D:*** Michael Verhoeven; ***W:*** Michael Verhoeven; ***C:*** Michael Epp; Theo Bierkes; ***M:*** Julian Nott; Simon Verhoeven.

My Mother's Smile *L'ora di religione; Il sorriso di mia madre* **2002** Controversial drama about religion and family. Artist—and atheist—Ernesto (Castellitto) is disdainful when he learns from a church emissary that his deceased mother (Conti) is a candidate for canonization. Ernesto loathed his pious, cold mother, who was murdered by his mentally unstable brother, and his attitude deepens the rift with his family, who are looking at monetary and social gains should the beatification take place. Both melodramatic and mystical, the narrative is also sometimes puzzling. Italian with subtitles. **103m/C; DVD.** *IT* Sergio Castellitto; Jacqueline Lustig; Chiara Conti; Alberto Mondini; Gianni Schicchi; Maurizio Donadoni; Gigio Alberti; ***D:*** Marco Bellocchio; ***W:*** Marco Bellocchio; ***C:*** Pasquale Mari; ***M:*** Riccardo Giagni.

My Name Is Bill W. **1989** Woods gave an Emmy-winning performance as Bill Wilson, a successful stockbroker who loses everything in the 1929 crash. Bill turns to alcohol for solace and, after realizing his life is in a downward spiral, forms a support group with Dr. Bob (Garner), which will become Alcoholics Anonymous. **100m/C; DVD.** James Woods; James Garner; JoBeth Williams; Gary Sinise; Fritz Weaver; ***D:*** Daniel Petrie; ***W:*** William G. Borchert; ***C:*** Neil Roach; ***M:*** Laurence Rosenthal. **TV**

My Name Is Bruce 1/2 **2008 (R)** Cult movie fave Bruce Campbell mocks his career and B-movie hero status in this stupid horror comedy (which he also directed). The deadbeat drunk and womanizer (who's living in a trailer) is kidnapped by teen fan Jeff, who believes all those movie heroics. Seems while desecrating a cemetery, Jeff and his buds released a Chinese demon that's now terrorizing the mining town of Gold Lick, Oregon. Campbell thinks it's some prank until he comes face-to-demon. **86m/C; DVD.** Bruce Campbell; Theodore (Ted) Raimi; Taylor Sharpe; Grace Thorsen; James J. Peck; ***D:*** Bruce Campbell; ***W:*** Mark Verheiden; ***C:*** Kurt Rauf; ***M:*** Joseph LoDuca.

My Name Is Ivan 🦴🦴🦴 1/2 *Ivan's Childhood; The Youngest Spy* **1962** Tarkovsky's first feature film is a vivid, wrenching portrait of a young Soviet boy surviving as a spy behind enemy lines during WWII. Technically stunning, heralding the coming of modern cinema's greatest formalist. In Russian with English subtitles. **84m/B; VHS, DVD, Blu-Ray.** *RU* Kolya Burlyayev; Valentin Zubkov; Ye Zharikov; S. Krylov; ***D:*** Andrei Tarkovsky. Venice Film Fest. '62: Film.

My Name Is Joe 🦴🦴 **1998 (R)** Set in Glasgow, the Scots accents prove a distinct challenge in this story of working-class romance. Unemployed alcoholic Joe Kavanagh (Mullan) is 10 months sober and does odd jobs to get by, while coaching the local no-hoper football team. By chance he meets community health worker Sarah (Goodall) and the two are drawn together by their similar outlooks on life and begin a cautious romance. But Joe's loyalty to his mates and his efforts to get his friend Liam (McKay) out of trouble, helps to put a strain on the relationship. **105m/C; VHS, Streaming.** *GB* Peter Mullan; Louise Goodall; David McKay; Annemarie Kennedy; David Hayman; Gary Lewis; Lorraine McIntosh; ***D:*** Ken Loach; ***W:*** Paul Laverty; ***C:*** Barry Ackroyd; ***M:*** George Fenton. Cannes '98: Actor (Mullan).

My Name is Modesty: A Modesty Blaise Adventure 🦴 *Modesty Blaise: The Beginning* **2004 (R)** Based on the comic strip/novels by Peter O'Donnell, this cheap quickie (filmed in Romania) was turned out by Miramax so it could retain its rights to the potential franchise. So what we get is mighty Modesty's backstory as an orphan learning to survive in the war-torn Balkans, who winds up working at a small casino in Tangiers. Her criminal boss Louche is killed by bad guy Miklos, who wants what's in Louche's safe and doesn't care how he gets it. There's little action and Staden is a mannequin in a role that calls for beauty, brains, and butt-kicking. **77m/C; DVD.** Alexandra Staden; Nikolaj Coster-Waldau; Raymond Cruz; ***D:*** Scott Spiegel; ***W:*** Lee Batchler; Janet Scott Batchler; ***C:*** Vivi Dragan Vasile; ***M:*** Deborah Lurie.

My Name Is Nobody 🦴🦴 1/2 *Il Mio Nome e Nessuno* **1974 (PG)** Fast-paced spaghetti-western wherein a cocky, soft-hearted gunfighter is sent to kill the famous, retired outlaw he reveres, but instead they band together. **115m/C; VHS, DVD, Blu-Ray.** *IT* Henry Fonda; Terence Hill; R.G. Armstrong; ***D:*** Tonino Valerii; ***M:*** Ennio Morricone.

My Name Is Sarah 🦴🦴 **2007** Sarah (Beals) has isolated herself socially with her cold attitude, which changes when she notices a group gathering in the church across the street. It turns out to be an AA meeting and when Sarah looks in out of curiosity, she is drawn to recovering alcoholic Charlie (Outerbridge). Sarah feels guilty when she's embraced by the group who have mistaken her for someone in the program and has to make a decision about revealing the truth about herself. **90m/C; DVD.** Jennifer Beals; Peter Outerbridge; Nolan Gerard Funk; Crystal Buble; Sarah Edmondson; ***D:*** Paul A. Kaufman; ***W:*** Julie Brazier; ***C:*** Robert Aschmann; ***M:*** James McVay. **CABLE**

My Nanny's Secret 🦴 1/2 **2009** Live-in nanny Claudia (Duff) suspects her troubled brother Carter (Casey) may be responsible for the home invasion that left a member of the wealthy Tyrell family dead. But the more Claudia snoops, the more danger she finds. **90m/C; DVD.** Haylie Duff; Dillon Casey; Tyrone Benskin; Paul Jean Hixson; Stewart Bick; Sophie Gendron; Eric Johnson; Allison Graham; ***D:*** Douglas Jackson; ***W:*** Christine Conradt; ***C:*** Bert Tougas; ***M:*** Joseph Conlan. **CABLE**

My Neighbor Totoro 🦴🦴 1/2 **1988 (G)** Rather gooey Japanese animated movie about Satsuki and her younger sister Lucy, whose new house in the country is filled with magic, including a friendly creature named Totoro. Totoro is a cuddly, if weird, mix of bear, owl, and seal, with whiskers and a gentle roar. He can fly, has a magic bus, and can only be seen by children. Naturally, every time the two girls get into mischief Totoro is there to rescue them. Dubbed into English. **76m/C; VHS, DVD, Blu-Ray.** *JP* ***V:*** Frank Welker; Lea Salonga; Timothy Daly; Paul Butcher; Pat Carroll; ***D:*** Hayao Miyazaki; ***W:*** Hayao Miyazaki.

My Neighbor's Keeper 🦴 1/2 **2007** Kate Powell is desperate to have a family but would she actually kill her best friend to do so? When Ann Harding is murdered on Halloween, her not-so-good husband Mike is willing to let Kate take on the role of surrogate mom to their two kids. But when suspicions turn towards Kate being involved in Ann's death, she sets out to exonerate herself. **90m/C; DVD.** Laura Elena Harring; Linden Ashby; Ken Tremblett; Brenda Campbell; Nathaniel DeVeaux; ***D:*** Walter Klenhard; ***W:*** Lindsay MacAdam; ***C:*** Anthony C. Metchie; ***M:*** Ron Ramin. **CABLE**

My Neighbor's Secret 🦴 1/2 **2009** Obvious creepfest. Widower Brent Cavanaugh (Brendon) befriends Jason (Ventresca) and Casey (West), the new couple next door. It's soon apparent that Brent is spying on them because he's hidden cameras all through their house. He isn't just some weirdo voyeur, he's a weirdo with a revenge plan that has something to do with his late wife. **90m/C; DVD.** Nicholas Brendon; Chandra West; Vincent Ventresca; Dakota Goyo; Natalie Lisinska; Nick Baillie; Mark Camacho; ***D:*** Leslie Hope; ***W:*** Michael J. Murray; ***C:*** Bert Tougas; ***M:*** Zack Ryan. **CABLE**

My New Gun 🦴🦴 1/2 **1992 (R)** Uneven, restless dark comedy about Debbie and Gerald Bender, yuppified suburban couple whose lives are disrupted by a gun. When their newly engaged friends get a gun, Gerry decides they need a gun as well. Debbie is very uncomfortable about having a weapon in the house and doesn't want anything to do with it. When mysterious neighbor LeGros steals the gun, it sets off a bizarre chain of events that culminate at the wedding of their friends. Impressive first effort for writer/director Cochran. **99m/C; VHS, DVD.** Diane Lane; Stephen Collins; James LeGros; Tess Harper; Bill Raymond; Bruce Altman; Maddie Corman; ***D:*** Stacy Cochran; ***W:*** Stacy Cochran; ***M:*** Pat Irwin. Cannes '92: Film.

My Night at Maud's 🦴🦴🦴 *My Night with Maud; Ma Nuit Chez Maud* **1969** Typically subtle Rohmer entry concerns quandary of upright fellow who finds himself drawn to comparatively carefree woman. Talky, somewhat arid film is one of director's Six Moral Tales. You'll either find it fascinating or wish you were watching "Rocky XXIV" instead. In French with English subtitles. **111m/B; VHS, DVD, Blu-Ray.** *FR* Jean-Louis Trintignant; Francoise Fabian; Marie-Christine Barrault; Antoine Vitez; ***D:*** Eric Rohmer; ***W:*** Eric Rohmer; ***C:*** Nestor Almendros. N.Y. Film Critics '70: Screenplay; Natl. Soc. Film Critics '70: Cinematog., Screenplay.

My Old Lady 🦴🦴 **2014 (PG-13)** Mathias (Kline) is a down-and-out New Yorker who inherits a Parisian apartment from his estranged father. When he travels to the city of lights to liquidate the estate, he finds an old woman named Mathilde (Smith) living there with her daughter (Scott Thomas). It turns out that Mathilde has some rights to the location and that Mathias can't sell the place until she dies. The two decide to share the apartment, and learn a thing or two from each other. While it's nice to see Kline play a real character, this is standard, manipulative, rather boring stuff for everyone but diehard fans of its stars. **105m/C; DVD, Blu-Ray.** Kevin Kline; Maggie Smith; Kristin Scott Thomas; Dominique Pinon; ***D:*** Israel Horowitz; ***W:*** Israel Horowitz; ***C:*** Michel Amathieu; ***M:*** Mark Orton.

My Old Man 🦴🦴 1/2 **1979** Plucky teen and her seedy horsetrainer father come together over important horse race. Oates makes this one worth watching on a slow evening. Based on a Hemingway story. **102m/C; VHS, DVD.** Kristy McNichol; Warren Oates; Eileen Brennan; ***D:*** John Erman. **TV**

My One and Only 🦴🦴 1/2 **2009 (PG-13)** Well-tanned actor George Hamilton offers an affectionate memoir of his aging southern belle mother Ann (Zellweger) in Loncraine's sweetly indulgent 1950s-set family comedy. When Ann finds her husband Dan (Bacon) indulging in yet another infidelity she decides on divorce, packs ups teenaged sons George (Lerman) and Robbie (Rendall), and buys a baby blue Cadillac Eldorado convertible. The three head west, with stops along the way as Ann decides she needs a wealthy new husband but her quest increasingly frustrates George who wants some stability in his life. **108m/C; DVD, Streaming.** Renée Zellweger; Logan Lerman; Kevin Bacon; Troy Garity; Mark Rendall; David Koechner; Eric McCormack; Chris Noth; Nick Stahl; Steven Weber; Robin Weigert; Molly C. Quinn; ***D:*** Richard Loncraine; ***W:*** Charlie Peters; ***C:*** Marco Pontecorvo; ***M:*** Mark Isham.

My Outlaw Brother 🦴🦴 *My Brother, the Outlaw* **1951** A man travelling West to visit his brother in Mexico meets a Texas Ranger on the train. The man discovers that his brother is an outlaw, and teams up with the Ranger to capture him. Based on the novel "South of the Rio Grande" by Max Brand. **82m/B; VHS, DVD.** Mickey Rooney; Wanda Hendrix; Robert Preston; Robert Stack; Jose Torvay; ***D:*** Elliott Nugent; ***W:*** Gene Fowler, Jr.; ***C:*** Jose Ortiz Ramos.

My Own Country 🦴🦴 1/2 **1998 (R)** Abraham Verghese (Andrews) is an Indian immigrant who becomes the head of infectious diseases at the rural Johnson City, Tennessee hospital, where he had interned, in 1985. Considered an outsider, the doctor also finds himself dealing with the area's first AIDS cases, and his patients who are discriminated against. In fact, Verghese becomes so obsessed with their care that he neglects his own wife and children. Based on Verghese's memoirs. **106m/C; VHS, DVD.** Naveen Andrews; Glenne Headly; Marisa Tomei; Hal Holbrook; Swoosie Kurtz; Sean Hewitt; William Webster; ***D:*** Mira Nair; ***W:*** Sooni Taraporevala; Jim Leonard, Jr. **CABLE**

My Own Love Song 🦴 1/2 **2010** Tiresome road pic turns cloying with cliches and unbelievable characters. Folksinger Jane (Zellweger) was left paralyzed after a car accident that also killed her husband and put her son in foster care. Her best friend Joey (Whitaker) is so traumatized by the fire that killed his family he talks to angels. Joey also talks Jane into heading to New Orleans, encountering various crazy Southerners and problems along the way. Best feature is the Bob Dylan soundtrack. **102m/C; DVD.** Renée Zellweger; Forest Whitaker; Madeline Zima; Elias Koteas; Nick Nolte; Chandler Frantz; Annie Parisse; ***D:*** Olivier Dahan; ***W:*** Olivier Dahan; ***C:*** Matthew Libatique; ***M:*** Bob Dylan.

My Own Private Idaho 🦴🦴🦴 **1991 (R)** Director Van Sant examines another group of outsiders--young, male hustlers. On the streets of Seattle, narcoleptic Mike (Phoenix) meets slumming rich boy Scott (Reeves), and together they begin a search for Mike's lost mother, which leads them to Idaho and Italy. Stunning visuals, an elliptical plot, and a terrific performance by Phoenix highlight this search for love, the meaning of life, and power. Van Sant couples these activities with scenes from Shakespeare's "Henry IV" for a sometimes inscrutable, but always memorable film. Look for director Richert's Falstaff role as an aging chickenhawk. **105m/C; VHS, DVD, Blu-Ray.** River Phoenix; Keanu Reeves; James Russo; William Richert; Rodney Harvey; Michael Parker; Flea; Chiara Caselli; Udo Kier; Grace Zabriskie; Tom Troupe; ***D:*** Gus Van Sant; ***W:*** Gus Van Sant; ***C:*** John J. Campbell; Eric Alan Edwards. Ind. Spirit '92: Actor (Phoenix), Screenplay; Natl. Soc. Film Critics '91: Actor (Phoenix).

My Pal Trigger 🦴🦴 **1946** Roy is unjustly imprisoned in this high adventure on the plains. Better than usual script and direction makes this one of the more entertaining of the singing cowboy's films. **79m/B; VHS, DVD.** Roy Rogers; George "Gabby" Hayes; Dale Evans; Jack Holt; ***D:*** Frank McDonald.

My Piece of the Pie 🦴 1/2 *Ma Part du Gateau* **2011** Rather heavy-handed class warfare satire. Volatile, 40-something single mom France (Viard) loses her longtime factory job when the work is outsourced to China. She moves to Paris and gets work as a housekeeper to rich, borish financial manager Steve (Lellouche), who uses her as a nanny and occasional public girfriend. Since neither are terribly likeable, what happens is only occassionally diverting. **109m/C; DVD.** *FR* Karin Viard; Gilles Lellouche; ***D:*** Cedric Klapisch; ***W:*** Cedric Klapisch; ***C:*** Christophe Beaucarne; ***M:*** Loik Dury.

My Reputation 🦴🦴 **1946** Dated melodrama actually filmned in 1944. Jessica Drummond (Stanwyck) is an attractive young widow who's lonely and chafing under the restrictions of her overbearing long-widowed mother (Watson). While vacationing with friends, Jess meets Maj. Scott Landis (Brent) and sparks are struck, though Landis makes it clear he's not interested in marriage. Nevertheless, Jess sees him back in Chicago and gossip follows, thanks to some busybodies, though nothing has actually happened. Jess sets the record straight, Landis has a change of heart, and the ending is rather abrupt and sappy even for the times. **94m/B; DVD.** Barbara Stanwyck; George Brent; Warner Anderson; Lucile Watson; Eve Arden; John Ridgely; Jerome Cowan; ***D:*** Curtis Bernhardt; ***W:*** Catherine Turney; ***C:*** James Wong Howe; ***M:*** Max Steiner.

My Sassy Girl 🦴 1/2 **2008 (PG-13)** This remake of the 2001 Korean hit isn't sassy at all. Hapless Midwestern Charlie (Bradford) has his life planned out until he falls in love with free-spirited beauty Jordan (Cuthbert), who's going to break his heart. Jordan's keeping secrets and Charlie has to convince her not only to trust him but to believe that it's their destiny to be together. **95m/C; DVD.** Jesse Bradford; Elisha Cuthbert; Joanna Gleason; Austin Basis; William Abadie; ***D:*** Yann Samuell; ***W:*** Victor Levin; ***C:*** Eric Schmidt; ***M:*** David Kitay.

My Science Project 🦴 1/2 **1985 (PG)** Teenager Stockwell stumbles across a crystal sphere with a funky light. Unaware that it is an alien time-travel device, he takes it to school to use as a science project in a last-ditch effort to avoid failing his class. Chaos follows and Stockwell and his chums find themselves battling gladiators, mutants, and dinosaurs. Plenty of special effects and a likeable enough, dumb teenage flick. **94m/C; VHS, DVD, Blu-Ray.** John Stockwell; Danielle von Zerneck; Fisher Stevens; Raphael Sbarge; Richard Masur; Barry Corbin; Ann Wedgeworth; Dennis Hopper; Candace Silvers; Beau Dremann; Pat Simmons; Pamela Springsteen; ***D:*** Jonathan Betuel; ***W:*** Jonathan Betuel; ***C:*** David M. Walsh; ***M:*** Peter Bernstein.

My Sex Life. . . Or How I Got into an Argument 🦴🦴 *Ma Vie Sexuelle...Comment Je Me Suis Dispute* **1996** Paul (Amalric) is unhappy personally and professionally. He's a bored grad student/assistant professor of philosophy and breaking up with lover of ten years, Esther (Devos). Soon Paul's romancing other women, one of whom, Sylvia (Denicourt), is already involved with Paul's best friend Nathan (Salinger). Very talky and Frenchly intellectual. French with subtitles. **178m/C; VHS, DVD.** *FR* Mathieu Amalric; Marianne (Cuau) Denicourt; Emmanuelle Devos; Emmanuel Salinger; Jeanne Balibar; Michel Vuillermoz; ***D:*** Arnaud Desplechin; ***W:*** Arnaud Desplechin; Emmanuel Bourdieu; ***C:*** Eric Gautier; ***M:*** Krishna Levy.

My Side of the Mountain 🦴🦴 1/2 **1969 (G)** A 13-year-old boy decides to emulate his idol, Henry David Thoreau, and gives up his home and his family to live in the Canadian mountains. **100m/C; VHS, DVD.** *CA* Teddy Eccles; Theodore Bikel; ***D:*** James B. Clark.

My Side Piece 🦴🦴 **2016 (PG-13)** A drama about the consequences of betrayal, greed, and lust. When Susan (Redd) was married to wealthy attorney Dillard (Allen), she had a life of luxury. The marriage ended, however, and Susan found love again with police officer Mike (Mystikal). While Susan misses the lifestyle Dillard provided, he is facing the loss of it himself because of a scam artist. For all involved, temptations prove formidable. **134m/C; DVD.** Mando Allen; Adriane Conrad; Mystikal; Karlie Redd; Diamonique Richard; ***D:*** Dewey Allen; ***W:*** Dewey Allen; Terrie Todd. **VIDEO**

My Silent Partner 1/2 **2006** San Francisco cop Phyllis Webber is in a bitter custody battle with her ex over their son when a mobbed-up lawyer offers his services in exchange for certain privileged information. A desperate Phyllis agrees, which only leads to more requests from the shyster's crime boss and threats if she doesn't comply. **90m/C; DVD.** Joanna Going; Greg Evigan; Tim Conlon; Nelson Wong; Shawn Reis; Josh Hayden; ***D:*** Ron Oliver; ***W:*** Michael Gleason; ***C:*** George Campbell; ***M:*** Michael Richard Plowman. **CABLE**

My Sister Eileen 1/2 **1942** Sisters Ruth (Russell) and Eileen (Blair) leave small-town Ohio for a basement apartment in Greenwich Village with a shady landlord and crazy neighbors. Aspiring writer Ruth tries to sell stories to magazine editor Baker (Aherne) while ditzy aspiring actress Eileen just attracts every man in sight. Based on a series of autobiographical magazine articles by Ruth McKenney, adapted into a Broadway play. The Three Stooges have cameos as subway drillers. **96m/B; DVD.** Rosalind Russell; Janet Blair; Brian Aherne; George Tobias; Allyn Joslyn; Elizabeth Patterson; Grant Mitchell; June Havoc; Richard Quine; Clyde Fillmore; Gordon Jones; ***D:*** Alexander Hall; ***W:*** Jerome Chodorov; Joseph Fields; ***C:*** Joseph Walker.

My Sister Eileen **1955** Ruth and Eileen are two small-town Ohio sisters who move to Manhattan seeking excitement. They live in a basement apartment in Greenwich Village with an assortment of oddball tenants as they pursue success and romance. Everyone is daffy and charming, as is the film. Fun, but unmemorable songs; however, the terrific choreography is by Fosse, who also appears as one sister's suitor. Remake of a 1942 film, which was based on a Broadway play, which was based on a series of autobiographical stories published in the New Yorker. **108m/C; VHS, DVD, Blu-Ray.** Janet Leigh; Betty Garrett; Jack Lemmon; Bob Fosse; Kurt Kasznar; Dick York; Lucy Marlow; Tommy (Thomas) Rall; Barbara Brown; Horace McMahon; ***D:*** Richard Quine; ***W:*** Blake Edwards; Richard Quine; ***M:*** Jule Styne.

My Sister, My Love 1/2 *The Cage; The Mafu Cage* **1978 (R)** Odd tale of two sisters' incestuous relationship and what happens when one of them takes another lover. The cage of the alternate titles refers to the place where their pet apes are kept and seems to symbolize the confining nature of their life together. **102m/C; VHS, DVD, Blu-Ray.** Lee Grant; Carol Kane; Will Geer; James Olson; ***D:*** Karen Arthur.

My Sister's Keeper 1/2 **2002** Christina (Bates) and her sister Judy (Perkins) couldn't have more different lives. Christina struggles to cope with her schizophrenia and her dependence on others while Judy is a work-obsessed art editor in New York. When their mother Helen (Redgrave) dies, Judy is suddenly responsible for Christina's care and they must struggle to accept and support one another. Based on the memoir by Margaret Moorman. **98m/C; VHS, DVD.** Kathy Bates; Elizabeth Perkins; Lynn Redgrave; Bobby Harwell; Kimberly J. Brown; Hallee Hirsh; Kathleen Wilhoite; Jascha Washington; ***D:*** Ron Lagomarsino; ***W:*** Susan Tarr; ***C:*** Lloyd Ahern, II; ***M:*** Lawrence Shragge. **TV**

My Sister's Keeper 1/2 **2009 (PG-13)** Anna (Breslin) was conceived as a genetic match to save her leukemia-stricken older sister Kate (Vassileva). Having undergone countless medical procedures through the years, she now wants to become medically emancipated and make her own decisions about her body to the distress of their relentless mother Sara (Diaz). Fans of the Jodi Picoult novel probably won't be happy about the plot changes and, despite the good performances, the weepie premise is disturbing rather than uplifting. **109m/C; DVD, Blu-Ray.** Cameron Diaz; Abigail Breslin; Sofia Vassilieva; Jason Patric; Alec Baldwin; Evan Ellingson; Thomas Dekker; Joan Cusack; David Thornton; ***D:*** Nick Cassavetes; ***W:*** Nick Cassavetes; Jeremy Leven; ***C:*** Caleb Deschanel; ***M:*** Aaron Zigman.

My Son John **1952** Obvious, overwrought red scare propaganda. John (Walker) sneers at his family's patriotism but his mother, Lucille (Hayes), can't believe it when FBI agent Stedman (Van Heflin) tells her John is a communist spy. She goes to see him in DC and things take a turn for the earnestly tragic. Walker died during production and some are his scenes are patched together using doubles. **122m/B; DVD, Blu-Ray.** Robert Walker; Helen Hayes; Van Heflin; Dean Jagger; Richard Jaeckel; Minor Watson; Frank McHugh; ***D:*** Leo McCarey; ***W:*** Leo McCarey; Myles Connolly; John Lee Mahin; ***C:*** Harry Stradling, Sr.; ***M:*** Robert Emmett Dolan.

My Son, My Son, What Have Ye Done 1/2 **2009** Oddball David Lynch serves as executive producer and presenter of weirdo Herzog's bizarre crime drama that's inspired by a true story. San Diego homicide detective Hank Havenhurst (Dafoe) has a slam-dunk case with the murder of Mrs. McCullum (Zabriskie) since her son Brad (Shannon) did the crime and there are witnesses. However, crazy Brad has locked himself in at home with a couple of hostages. It's probably not intended to make much sense (ostriches, flamingos, and a little person are also involved) but it's too surreal for enjoyment unless you're a Herzog fan. **87m/C; DVD, On Demand.** Willem Dafoe; Michael Shannon; Chloë Sevigny; Michael Peña; Udo Kier; Brad Dourif; Grace Zabriskie; Irma P. Hall; Loretta Devine; Verne Troyer; ***D:*** Werner Herzog; ***W:*** Werner Herzog; Herbert Golder; ***C:*** Peter Zeitlinger; ***M:*** Ernst Reijseger.

My Son the Fanatic **1997 (R)** Pakistani immigrant Parvez (Puri) has been driving a cab in Bradford, England and trying to fit in his new country for 25 years. He ekes out a living driving prostitutes around town, which leads to a relationship with hooker Bettina (Griffiths). His working-class life is disrupted when Parvez realizes his son, Farid (Kurtha) is exploring his cultural roots by turning to Islamic fundamentalism. Moral and religious tensions lead to a climactic conflict between father and son. **86m/C; VHS, DVD.** *GB* Om Puri; Rachel Griffiths; Stellan Skarsgard; Akbar Kurtha; ***D:*** Udayan Prasad; ***W:*** Hanif Kureishi; ***C:*** Alan Almond; ***M:*** Stephen Warbeck.

My Son, the Vampire 1/2 *Old Mother Riley Meets the Vampire; The Vampire and the Robot; Vampire Over London; Mother Riley Meets the Vampire* **1952** Last of Britain's Old Mother Riley series in which Lucan plays the Irish housekeeper in drag. Lugosi is a crazed scientist who thinks he's a vampire and wants to take over the world with his giant robot. Mother Riley interferes. Theme song by Alan Sherman. **72m/B; DVD.** *UK* Bela Lugosi; Arthur Lucan; Dora Bryan; Richard Wattis; ***D:*** John Gilling; ***W:*** Val Valentine; ***C:*** Stanley Pavey.

My Soul to Take **2010 (R)** Sleepy Riverton has a past—a serial killer who, legend tells, vows to return to slay the seven kids born the night he died (or did he?). Sixteen years later and Riverton residents are mysteriously disappearing. Is the Riverton Ripper back? Or could it be he's reincarnated as one of the 'Riverton Seven'? Horror guru Wes Craven delivers a formulaic teen slasher that even the use of 3D gimmicks can't improve. **107m/C; Blu-Ray.** Max Thieriot; Emily Meade; Nick Lashaway; Denzel Whitaker; Shareeka Epps; Raul Esparza; Frank Grillo; Zena Grey; John Magaro; Paulina Olszynski; Jessica Hecht; Dennis Boutsikaris; ***D:*** Wes Craven; ***W:*** Wes Craven; ***C:*** Petra Korner; ***M:*** Marco Beltrami.

My Spy **2019 (PG-13)** After years of work as a CIA operative, agent JJ (Bautista) is temporarily demoted after a mission goes bad. JJ and his tech support Bobbi (Schaal) are then assigned to a surveillance job. They are charged with spying on nurse Kate (Fitz-Henley) and her young daughter Sophie (Coleman) because Sophie's uncle is involved in criminal activity. Sophie catches on to what they are doing and blackmails JJ to be her personal driver and teach her about the spy game. The family friendly comedy is not particularly funny or believable, despite the best efforts of Coleman and Bautista. **99m/C; DVD.** Dave Bautista; Kristen Schaal; Parisa Fitz-Henley; Chloe Coleman; Ken Jeong; ***D:*** Peter Segal; ***W:*** Erich Hoeber; Jon Hoeber; ***C:*** Larry Blanford; ***M:*** Dominic Lewis.

My Stepmother Is an Alien **1988 (PG-13)** When eccentric physicist Aykroyd sends a message beam to another galaxy on a stormy night, the last thing he expects is a visit from beautiful alien Basinger. Unfortunately, he does not realize that this gorgeous blonde is an alien and he continues to court her despite her rather odd habits. Only the daughter seems to notice the strange goings on, and her dad ignores her warnings, enabling Basinger's evil sidekick to continue in its plot to take over the Earth. **108m/C; VHS, DVD.** Dan Aykroyd; Kim Basinger; Jon Lovitz; Alyson Hannigan; Joseph Maher; Seth Green; Wesley Mann; Adrian Sparks; Juliette Lewis; Tanya Fenmore; ***D:*** Richard Benjamin; ***W:*** Herschel Weingrod; Timothy Harris; Jonathan Reynolds; Jerico Stone; ***C:*** Richard H. Kline; ***M:*** Alan Silvestri.

My Summer of Love 1/2 **2005 (R)** Teenaged Mona (Press) lives with her ex-con brother, Phil (Considine), over the closed family pub in a dull Yorkshire village. Phil has become a born-again Christian, much to Mona's confusion, and she turns for companionship to wealthy Tamsin (Blunt), who's summering at the family mansion. They soon indulge in a hothouse romance that's part crush, part loneliness, and part boredom. The young women have certain secrets and Tamsin has a streak of cruelty. A dangerous and unsettling atmosphere prevails, along with satisfying performances. Based on the novel by Helen Cross. **85m/C; DVD.** *GB* Emily Blunt; Paddy Considine; Nathalie Press; Dean Andrews; Michelle Byrne; Paul Antony-Barber; Lynette Edwards; Kathryn Sumner; ***D:*** Pawel Pawlikowski; ***W:*** Pawel Pawlikowski; Michael Wynne; ***C:*** Ryszard Lenczewski; ***M:*** Alison Goldfrapp; Will Gregory.

My Summer Story 1/2 *It Runs in the Family* **1994 (PG)** Humorist Shepherd and director Clark re-team for another period family comedy in the tradition of their first collaboration, "A Christmas Story." This time the Parkers find themselves battling their crazy new neighbors, the Bumpus family; Ralphie (Kieran Culkin) has troubles with a neighborhood bully and tries to bond with his dad (Grodin) while fishing; and mom (Steenburgen) goes loopy over gravy boats. Charming family fun. Based on Shepherd's novels "In God We Trust, All Others Pay Cash" and "Wanda Hickey's Night of Golden Memories and Other Disasters." **85m/C; VHS, DVD, Blu-Ray.** Charles Grodin; Mary Steenburgen; Kieran Culkin; Chris Culkin; Al Mancini; Troy Evans; Glenn Shadix; Dick O'Neill; Wayne Grace; ***Nar:*** Jean Shepherd; ***D:*** Bob (Benjamin) Clark; ***W:*** Jean Shepherd; Bob (Benjamin) Clark; Leigh Brown; ***C:*** Stephen M. Katz; ***M:*** Paul Zaza.

My Super Ex-Girlfriend **2006 (PG-13)** "Fatal Attraction" meets "Wonder Woman" in this weak effort from veteran director Ivan Reitman. Uma Thurman plays the dual role of Jenny Johnson, Manhattan art curator by day, and G-Girl, crime-fighting superheroine at night, who, unfortunately for her unsuspecting new boyfriend, Matt (Luke Wilson), is super-insecure as well. When Matt makes the mistake of dumping the possessive Jenny, she unleashes the fury of her powers on him. Reitman doesn't know what he wants—comedy, girl-power statement, relationship/date movie—and fails on all fronts as a result. **96m/C; DVD, Blu-Ray.** Uma Thurman; Luke Wilson; Anna Faris; Rainn Wilson; Eddie Izzard; Wanda Sykes; Mark Consuelos; ***D:*** Ivan Reitman; ***W:*** Don Payne; ***C:*** Don Burgess; ***M:*** Teddy Castellucci.

My Sweet Suicide **1998** Very low-budget comedy about staging the perfect suicide. Depressed Kevin (Aldrich) can't even manage to kill himself. He confides his dilemma to eccentric bookstore clerk Thompson, who agrees to help him out. **78m/C; VHS, DVD.** Matthew Aldrich; Michelle Leigh Thompson; Eric Wheeler; ***D:*** David Michael Flanagan; ***W:*** David Michael Flanagan.

Dean Spanley 1/2 *My Talks with Dean Spanley* **2008 (PG)** In Edwardian England, Fisk Junior (Northam) is obligated to visit his difficult father, Fisk Senior (O'Toole), each week. Fisk Junior dreads the time with his father, who has not dealt with family tragedies. On one occasion, they attend a lecture on reincarnation, which marks the first meeting with mysterious Dean (Neill). Invited to dinner by Fisk Junior, Dean enthusiastically shares his belief that he lived as a dog in a previous life and an unexpected connection with Fisk Senior. An appealing slice of life focus with an impressive cast. **?m/C; DVD.** Jeremy Northam; Sam Neill; Bryan Brown; Peter O'Toole; Judy Parfitt; ***D:*** Toa Fraser; ***W:*** Alan Sharp; ***C:*** Leon Narbey; ***M:*** Don McGlashan.

My Teacher Ate My Homework *Shadow Zone: My Teacher Ate My Homework* **1998 (PG)** Jesse is convinced that his teacher Mrs. Fink has it in for him. When he finds a doll that looks just like her, Jesse can live out all his revenge fantasies but bad things start happening when the doll takes on an attitude of its own. Based on J.R. Black's "Shadowzone" books. **91m/C; VHS, DVD.** *CA* MacKenzie Gray; Gregory Edward Smith; Shelley Duvall; Dara Perlmutter; Tim Progosh; Sheila McCarthy; Edwin Hodge; Dan Warry-Smith; Diana Theodore; John Neville; Karen Robinson; Margot Kidder; Damon D'Oliveira; ***D:*** Stephen Williams; ***W:*** Garfield Reeves-Stevens; Judith Reeves-Stevens; ***C:*** Curtis Petersen; ***M:*** John McCarthy. **VIDEO**

My Teacher's Wife 1/2 **1995 (R)** High-schooler London has big college plans, which won't get anywhere if he doesn't pass math. So he asks Carrere to tutor him, only the problems they study become more personal. **90m/C; VHS, DVD.** Tia Carrere; Jason London; Christopher McDonald; Leslie Lyles; Zak Orth; Jeffrey Tambor; ***D:*** Bruce Leddy; ***W:*** Bruce Leddy; Seth Greenland; ***C:*** Zoltan David; ***M:*** Kevin Gilbert. **VIDEO**

My Tutor 1/2 **1982 (R)** When a high school student is in danger of flunking French, his parents hire a private tutor to help him learn the lessons. It becomes clear that his studies will involve many more subjects, however. Standard teen sex comedy. **97m/C; VHS, DVD, Blu-Ray.** Caren Kaye; Matt Lattanzi; Kevin McCarthy; Clark Brandon; Bruce Bauer; Arlene Golonka; Crispin Glover; Shelley Taylor Morgan; Amber Denyse Austin; Francesca "Kitten" Natividad; Jewel Shepard; Marilyn Tokuda; ***D:*** George Bowers; ***W:*** Joe Roberts; ***C:*** Mac Ahlberg; ***M:*** Webster Lewis.

My Uncle Silas **2001** Finney certainly has fun in the title role as an aging reprobate (with an eye for the ladies) who teaches his 10-year-old grandnephew Edward (Prospero) how to enjoy life. Based on five short stories by H.E. Bates and set during a rural English summer in the early 1900s. **120m/C; VHS, DVD.** *GB* Albert Finney; Charlotte Rampling; Joe Prospero; Annabelle Apsion; ***D:*** Philip Saville; ***C:*** John Kenway. **TV**

My Uncle: The Alien 1/2 **1996 (PG)** Kelly, President Sullivan's teenaged daughter, travels to L.A. to visit a children's shelter at Christmas. When she finds out the shelter needs money to stay open, she eludes the Secret Service and hatches a plan to raise the funds. But she does have someone watching out for her—no, not a guardian angel, a guardian alien! **90m/C; VHS, DVD, On Demand.** Hailey Foster; ***D:*** Henri Charr.

My Week With Marilyn **2011 (R)** Strong supporting performances almost make up for a black hole of a male lead and a script that never gets beneath the surface of its legendary characters. The story is told through the eyes of Colin Clark (Redmayne), a young man working on "The Prince and the Showgirl" with Marilyn Monroe (Williams) and Sir Laurence Olivier (Branagh) in the summer of 1956. Clark falls in love, Monroe battles her demons, and Olivier tries to get his movie made in a script that's surprisingly prosaic. Williams finds the pathos beneath the beauty but the pic doesn't give her much subtle characterization with which to work. **99m/C; DVD, Blu-Ray.** Michelle Williams; Eddie Redmayne; Kenneth Branagh; Dougray Scott; Dominic Cooper; Dame Judi Dench; Julia Ormond; Emma Watson; Derek Jacobi; Zoe Wanamaker; ***D:*** Simon Curtis; ***W:*** Adrian Hodges; ***C:*** Ben Smithard; ***M:*** Conrad Pope. British Acad. '11: Actress (Williams), Support. Actor (Branagh); Golden Globes '12: Actress--Mus./Comedy (Williams); Ind. Spirit '12: Actress (Williams).

My Wife is an Actress 1/2 *Ma Femme est une Actrice* **2001 (R)** Yvan (Attal) is a TV sports journalist married to famous actress Charlotte (Gainsbourg). He's irritated by the public demands celebrity makes on their relationship and jealous of her co-stars when she films sex scenes. Charlotte's off to London for her latest project, with a courtly and seductive older leading man, John (Stamp). Charlotte can't understand her husband's neuroses and Yvan's fretting increases. Self-mocking and frequently charming although the sub-plot concerning Yvan's pregnant sister is an annoying distraction. French with subtitles. **93m/C; VHS, DVD.** *FR* Yvan Attal; Charlotte Gainsbourg; Terence Stamp; Noemie Lvovsky; Ludivine Sagnier; Keith Allen; Lionel Abelanski; Laurent Bateau; Jo McInnes; ***D:*** Yvan Attal; ***W:*** Yvan Attal; ***C:*** Remy Chevrin.

My Wife's Best Friend **1952** Virginia (Baxter) and George (Carey) are en route to their vacation when their plane develops serious engine trouble. Thinking they are going to die, George confesses to having an almost-affair with Virginia's best friend Jane (McLeod). They land safely and Virginia is furious--fantasizing various punishments for her contrite hubby. Their minister (Kellaway) tries to get Virginia to forgive George but she isn't quite ready. **87m/B; DVD.** Anne Baxter; MacDonald Carey; Cecil Kellaway; Catherine McLeod; Max (Casey Adams) Showalter; Leif Erickson; Frances Bavier; Martin Milner; ***D:*** Richard Sale; ***W:*** Isobel Lennart; ***C:*** Leo Tover; ***M:*** Leigh Harline.

My Wild Irish Rose **1/2 1947** Morgan stars in this Technicolor Warner Bros. musical biopic of tenor Chauncey Olcott. The Irish immigrant went from tugboat skipper to minstrel shows and composer of sentimental ballads, including "When Irish Eyes Are Smiling," "Mother Machree," and the title tune. Famed vaudeville star Lillian Russell (King) gives Olcott his big break, which causes jealousy in his relationship with true love Rose (Dahl). **101m/C; DVD.** Dennis Morgan; Andrea King; Arlene Dahl; Alan Hale; George Tobias; Ben Blue; William Frawley; George O'Brien; Sara Allgood; George Cleveland; ***D:*** David Butler; ***W:*** Peter Milne; ***C:*** Arthur Edeson; William V. Skall; ***M:*** Ray Heindorf; Max Steiner.

My Worst Nightmare **1/2** *Mon Pire Cauchemar* **2011** Icy Parisian art gallery owner Agathe is living in a long-term (and long-cooled) relationship with older publisher Francois. Francois hires vulgar, drunken Patrick to work on their apartment, where he stays in the maid's quarters and continually offends Agathe with his boorish behavior. Meanwhile, Francois meets Patrick's pretty young social worker, Julie, impulsively leaves Agathe for her, and you can imagine the cliches that follow. French with subtitles. **100m/C; DVD.** *FR* Isabelle Huppert; Benoit Poelvoorde; Andre Dussollier; Virginie Efira; ***D:*** Anne Fontaine; ***W:*** Anne Fontaine; Nicolas Mercier; ***C:*** Jean-Marc Fabre; ***M:*** Bruno Coulais.

My Year Without Sex **2009** Melbourne mom Natalie (Horler) survives a brain aneurysm with impaired motor skills and doctor's orders to abstain from sex while she recovers. The normal stresses of marriage and family get amplified until anxiety takes over and the lack of a sex life just adds to Natalie's insecurity and re-evaluation of her life. **96m/C; DVD.** *AU* Sacha Horler; Matt(hew) Day; Jonathan Segat; Portia Bradley; Maude Davey; Katie Wall; Sonya Suares; Fred Whitlock; ***D:*** Sarah Watt; ***W:*** Sarah Watt; ***C:*** Graeme Wood.

My Zinc Bed **2008** Three-character piece adapted by David Hare from his play. Recovering alcoholic Paul (Considine) is unexpectedly befriended by wealthy Victor (Pryce), who offers him a job. Elsa (Thurman), Victor's younger wife, is also a drinker but resists admitting it and going to AA as Paul does. Over the summer, a romantic triangle develops, leading to examinations of friendship and fidelity. **75m/C; DVD.** *GB* Jonathan Pryce; Uma Thurman; Paddy Considine; ***D:*** Anthony Page; ***W:*** David Hare; ***C:*** Brian Tufano; ***M:*** Simon Boswell. **CABLE**

Myra Breckinridge **WOOF! 1970 (R)** A tasteless version of the Gore Vidal novel. An alleged satire of a film critic who undergoes a sex change operation and then plots the destruction of the American male movie star stereotype. Created an outcry from all sides, and hung out to dry by studio where it's reportedly still blowing in the wind. **94m/C; VHS, DVD.** Mae West; John Huston; Raquel Welch; Rex Reed; Farrah Fawcett; Jim Backus; John Carradine; Andy Devine; Tom Selleck; ***D:*** Michael Sarne; ***W:*** Michael Sarne; David Giler; ***C:*** Richard Moore; ***M:*** Lionel Newman.

Mysteria **1/2** **2011** Drunken, washed-up screenwriter Aleister Bain (Miano) has a last chance but his script and life are interacting when his characters turn out to be real--and murdered. A couple of cops investigate but Bain is the prime suspect in this tepid thriller. **90m/C; DVD.** Robert Miano; Michael Rooker; Danny Glover; Martin Landau; Billy Zane; Peter Mark Richman; ***D:*** Lucius C. Kuert; ***W:*** Lucius C. Kuert; ***C:*** Keith L. Smith. **VIDEO**

The Mysterians **1/2** *Earth Defense Forces; Chikyu Boelgun* **1958** A race of gigantic scientific intellects from a doomed planet attempts to conquer Earth. They want to rebuild their race by reproducing with earth women. Earth fights back. From the director of "Godzilla." Dubbed in English from Japanese. **85m/C; VHS, DVD.** *JP* Kenji Sahara; Yumi Shirakawa; Takashi Shimura; ***D:*** Inoshiro Honda.

Mysteries **1/2 1984** A rich tourist becomes obsessed by a beautiful local girl. As his obsession grows, his behavior becomes stranger. Interesting and well-acted. The film is an adaptation of the famous love story by Nobel-laureate Knut Hamsun. Suffers from poor dubbing. **100m/C; VHS, DVD.** Rutger Hauer; Sylvia Kristel; David Rappaport; Rita Tushingham; ***D:*** Paul de Lussanet.

Mysteries of Lisbon *Misterios de Lisboa* **2010** A long period drama with a number of characters and digressions based on the book by Camilo Castelo Branco. The illegitimate Joao grows up in a religious boarding school in Lisbon, discovers his mother is a Countess and his father was murdered by her husband's hired killer. There's a kindly priest, more nobility, and lots of detours into France, Spain, Italy, and Brazil. Director Ruiz manages to hold his story together despite the numerous twists. Portuguese and French with subtitles. **257m/C; DVD, Blu-Ray.** *PT FR* Joao Luis Arrais; Alfonso Pimentel; Adriano Luz; Maria Joao Bastos; Albano Jeronimo; Lea Seydoux; Clotilde Hesme; ***D:*** Raul Ruiz; ***W:*** Carlos Saboga; ***C:*** Andre Szankowski; ***M:*** Jorge Arriagada.

The Mysteries of Pittsburgh **2008 (R)** Poor adaptation of Michael Chabon's 1988 debut novel that takes considerable liberties with the story, making it conventional and dull. Wishy-washy Art Bechstein (Foster) doesn't want to work for his mobster father Joe (Nolte), so he remains in Pittsburgh after college graduation in order to study for his stockbroker's exam (film is set in the '80s). He gets a job working at a bookstore, where his manager Phlox (Suvari) uses Art for sex, and then meets aspiring musician Jane (Miller). She is already involved with bad boy Cleveland (Sarsgaard), who befriends Art who then gets drawn into Cleveland's gambling problems and criminal activities. **95m/C; DVD.** Jon Foster; Sienna Miller; Peter Sarsgaard; Mena Suvari; Nick Nolte; Omid Abtahi; ***D:*** Rawson Marshall Thurber; ***W:*** Rawson Marshall Thurber; ***C:*** Michael Barrett; ***M:*** Theodore Shapiro.

Mysterious Island **1/2 1961** Exhilirating sci-fi classic adapted from Jules Verne's novel about escaping Civil War soldiers who go up in Verne balloon and come down on a Pacific island populated by giant animals. They also encounter two shipwrecked English ladies, pirates, and Captain Nemo (and his sub). Top-rate special effects by master Ray Harryhausen. **101m/C; VHS, DVD, Blu-Ray.** *GB* Michael Craig; Joan Greenwood; Michael Callan; Gary Merrill; Herbert Lom; Beth Rogan; Percy Herbert; Dan Jackson; Nigel Green; ***D:*** Cy Endfield; ***W:*** John Prebble; Daniel Ullman; Crane Wilbur; ***C:*** Wilkie Cooper; ***M:*** Bernard Herrmann.

Mysterious Island **1/2** *Jules Verne's Mysterious Island* **2005** Based very, very loosely on the novel by Verne and starring the always-wooden Kyle McLachlan. Five prisoners of war escape in a balloon and end up on an island of giant monsters and pirates. **170m/B; DVD.** Kyle MacLachlan; Gabrielle Anwar; Jason Durr; Patrick Stewart; Omar Gooding; Vinnie Jones; Roy Marsden; Chris Larkin; Dom Hetrakul; Danielle Calvert; Tom Mison; Nate Harrison; Geoffrey Giuliano; ***D:*** Russell Mulcahy; ***W:*** Nora Kay Foster; Jules Verne; Adam Amus; ***C:*** James Chressanthis; ***M:*** Roger Bellon.

Mysterious Island of Beautiful Women **1979** A male sextet is stranded on a South Sea island, where they must endure the trials of an angry tribe of conveniently bikini-clad women. **100m/C; VHS, DVD.** Jamie Lyn Bauer; Jayne Kennedy; Kathryn Davis; Deborah Shelton; Susie Coelho; Peter Lawford; Steven Keats; Clint Walker; ***D:*** Joseph Pevney.

The Mysterious Lady **1/2 1928** Pre-Ninotchka Garbo plays Russian spy who betrays her mother country because she does not want to be alone. **99m/B; Silent; VHS, DVD.** Greta Garbo; Conrad Nagel; Gustav von Seyffertitz; Richard Alexander; Albert Pollet; Edward Connelly; ***C:*** William H. Daniels.

The Mysterious Magician **1/2 1965** Entertaining suspense story of the mad murderer known as "The Wizard," who was thought by Scotland Yard to be dead, but the current murderwave in London suggests otherwise. Based on an Edgar Wallace story. **95m/C; VHS, DVD.** *GE* Joachim Fuchsberger; Eddi Arent; Sophie Hardy; Karl John; Heinz Drache; ***D:*** Alfred Vohrer.

Mysterious Mr. Nicholson **1/2 1947** A burglar (Hulme) is suspected of murder and discovers he has a doppelganger who's actually committed the crime. So he teams up with messenger Peggy (Osmond) to prove his innocence. **78m/B; DVD.** *GB* Anthony Hulme; Andy Laurence; Douglas Day Stewart; Lesley Osmond; Frank Hawkins; ***D:*** Oswald Mitchell; ***W:*** Oswald Mitchell; Frances Miller; ***C:*** S.D. Onions; ***M:*** Isaac Snoek.

Mysterious Museum *Search for the Jewel of Polaris: Mysterious Museum; Night at the Magic Museum* **1999 (PG)** Two siblings are sucked into a medieval world in a museum painting and must acquire a magical jewel to return. **80m/C; DVD.** *RO US* A.J. Trauth; Brianna Brown; Megan Lusk; Michael Lee Gogin; John Duerler; ***D:*** David Schmoeller; ***W:*** Adam Wohl; ***C:*** Gabriel Kosuth; ***M:*** Carl Dante. **CABLE**

Mysterious Skin **2004 (NC-17)** As kids in 1981, Brian and Neil both play Little League--and both are sexually abused by their Coach (Sage). By 1991, Neil (Gordon-Levitt) has become a reckless hustler and Brian (Corbet) is an awkward misfit who (having suppressed the abuse) believes he was abducted and experimented upon by aliens. He has a vague memory of Neil and tracks him down to find out what really happened—a confrontation that takes place in a challenging scene set on Christmas Eve. Araki displays a fearless candor in showing the damage without exploiting his inflammatory subject matter. Both leads give strong, gut-wrenching performances. Based on the 1995 novel by Scott Heims. **103m/C; DVD.** Brady Corbet; Joseph Gordon-Levitt; Michelle Trachtenberg; Elisabeth Shue; Jeff(rey) Licon; Mary Lynn Rajskub; Chris Mulkey; Richard Riehle; Lisa Long; Billy Drago; William Sage; George Webster; Chase Ellison; ***D:*** Gregg Araki; ***W:*** Gregg Araki; ***C:*** Steve Gainer; ***M:*** Harold Budd; Robin Guthrie.

Mysterious Two **1/2 1982** Two aliens visit the Earth in an effort to enlist converts to travel the universe with them. **100m/C; VHS, DVD.** John Forsythe; Priscilla Pointer; Noah Beery, Jr.; Vic Tayback; James Stephens; Karen Werner; Robert Englund; Robert Pine; ***D:*** Gary Sherman.

Mysterious Ways **2015** A drama centered on a mother's loss and her search for peace. When her young son died at the hands of a hit-and-run driver, Marilyn (Robinson) lost a piece of herself. Though she had strong relationships at home and in her work as a church choir director, she could not find inner calm. However, when she meets a homeless man named Mozart (Dourdan), her perspective changes and she understands that forgiveness can help see her life differently. **80m/C; DVD, Streaming, Download.** Wendy Raquel Robinson; Gary Dourdan; Tiara Ashleigh; Jerome Ro Brooks; David Terrell; ***D:*** Dan Garcia; ***W:*** Robert Irvin; ***C:*** Tony Aaron, II. **VIDEO**

Mystery, Alaska **1/2 1999 (R)** Amiable sports comedy that plays like a TV movie (with a little more sex and language). Journalist and ex-local Charles Danner (Azaria) does a Sports Illustrated feature on his hometown's weekly cutthroat hockey game. Danner's story draws NHL interest and, for a publicity stunt, the New York Rangers fly in for an exhibition game. This leads to hurt feelings since aging team captain (and local sheriff) John Biebe (Crowe) is asked to step aside for young phenom Stevie Weeks (Northcott). Expect cliches. **118m/C; VHS, DVD.** Russell Crowe; Hank Azaria; Mary McCormack; Burt Reynolds; Ron Eldard; Lolita Davidovich; Colm Meaney; Maury Chaykin; Ryan Northcott; Scott Grimes; Judith Ivey; Rachel Wilson; Mike Myers; ***Cameo(s):*** Little Richard; ***D:*** Jay Roach; ***W:*** David E. Kelley; Sean O'Byrne; ***C:*** Peter Deming; ***M:*** Carter Burwell.

Mystery Date **1991 (PG-13)** A sort of teen version of "After Hours," in which a shy college guy gets a date with the girl of his dreams, only to be mistaken for a master criminal and pursued by gangsters, police and a crazed florist. Not terrible, but if you're old enough to drive you're probably too old to watch with amusement. **98m/C; VHS, DVD, Blu-Ray.** Ethan Hawke; Teri Polo; Brian McNamara; Fisher Stevens; B.D. Wong; ***D:*** Jonathan Wacks; ***W:*** Terry Runte; Parker Bennett; ***M:*** John Du Prez.

Mystery Kids **1/2** *Finding Kelly* **1999 (PG)** Preteens Herford and Baltes spend their summer snooping into the disappearance of high school girl Lakin in order to claim a reward. They first think her boyfriend killed her but then discover Lakin has just run away and is working as a singer in a local bar. So the kids decide to try and reconcile the troubled teen with her family. Innocuous family fare but the two would-be sleuths are good. **88m/C; VHS, DVD.** Brighton Hertford; Jameson Baltes; Christine Lakin; ***D:*** Lynn Hamrick. **VIDEO**

Mystery Mansion **1983 (PG)** Fortune in gold and a hundred-year-old mystery lead three children into an exciting treasure hunt. Family fare. **95m/C; VHS, DVD.** Dallas McKennon; Greg Wynne; Jane Ferguson; Barry Hostetler; ***D:*** David S. Jackson; ***W:*** David S. Jackson; ***C:*** Milas C. Hinshaw; ***M:*** William Loose.

Mystery Men **1/2 1999 (PG-13)** A cast of quirky comedy all-stars, including Garafalo, Stiller and Macy, help deflate the superhero genre by playing a team of bush league crimefighters. The superhero washouts use their dubious powers to save Champion City from party monster villain Casanova Frankenstein (Rush), who has kidnapped real superhero Captain Amazing (Kinnear). Great concept and dialogue are stretched a bit thin over the long running time. Based on the Dark Horse comic book. **120m/C; DVD, Blu-Ray, HD-DVD.** Ben Stiller; Hank Azaria; William H. Macy; Paul (Pee-wee Herman) Reubens; Claire Forlani; Wes Studi; Janeane Garofalo; Kel Mitchell; Geoffrey Rush; Lena Olin; Greg Kinnear; Tom Waits; Eddie Izzard; Ricky Jay; Louise Lasser; ***D:*** Kinka Usher; ***W:*** Neil Cuthbert; ***C:*** Stephen Burum; ***M:*** Stephen Warbeck.

Mystery Mountain **1/2 1934** Twelve episodes depict the villain known as the "Rattler" attempting to stop the construction of a railroad over Mystery Mountain. **156m/B; VHS, DVD.** Ken Maynard; Gene Autry; Smiley Burnette; ***D:*** Otto Brower; B. Reeves Eason.

The Mystery of a Hansom Cab **1/2 2012** Set in Melbourne in 1886, this Victorian murder mystery is based on the Fergus Hume novel. A drunken man takes a hansom cab ride, but is murdered before he reaches his destination. Flashbacks show that Oliver Whyte had a number a questionable habits, including blackmail, so the detective on the case has numerous possible suspects. **100m/C; DVD.** *AU* Brett Climo; John Waters; Jessica De Gouw; Oliver Ackland; Shane Jacobson; Marco Chiappi; Helen Morse; ***D:*** Shawn Seet; ***W:*** Glen Dolman; ***C:*** Jaems Grant; ***M:*** Cezary Skubiszewski. **TV**

The Mystery of Edwin Drood **1/2 1935** Nicely creepy gothic atmosphere highlights this version of Charles Dickens' final novel, which was unfinished at the time of his death. English choirmaster and opium addict John Jasper (Rains) is visited by his nephew Edwin Drood (Manners), who's soon to enter into an arranged marriage with Rosa (Angel). Unbeknownst to anyone, Jasper has long desired Rosa for himself and kills his nephew in a jealous rage. Now that Drood's disappeared, will Jasper have Rosa to himself? **85m/B; DVD.** Claude Rains; Heather Angel; Douglass Montgomery; Valerie Hobson; David Manners; Francis L. Sullivan; Ethel Griffies; E.E. Clive; ***D:*** Stuart Walker; ***W:*** John Lloyd Balderston; Gladys Unger; ***C:*** George Robinson; ***M:*** Edward Ward.

The Mystery of Edwin Drood 🦴🦴 ½ **2012** Dickens died before completing this 1870 novel; writer Hughes offers as reasonable a solution as any in this BBC adaptation. Edwin Drood (Fox) is engaged to reluctant teenager Rosa (Merchant). He's unaware that his brooding, opium-taking uncle, John Jasper (Rhys), obsessively desires Rosa and has hallucinations of murdering Edwin. Edwin goes missing, and Jasper assumes the worst. The Landless twins, who hold a grudge against the Drood family, also have secrets to reveal. **120m/C; DVD, Blu-Ray.** *UK* Matthew Rhys; Freddie Fox; Tamzin Merchant; Rory Kinnear; Amber Rose Revah; Sacha Dhawan; Ian McNeice; Alun Armstrong; Julia McKenzie; Rob Dixon; ***D:*** Diarmuid Lawrence; ***W:*** Gwyneth Hughes; ***C:*** Alan Almond; ***M:*** John Lunn. **TV**

The Mystery of Marie Roget 🦴 ½ **1942** Based on the Poe story about a true unsolved New York murder. Parisian actress Marie Roget plots to kill her younger sister, Camille. When Marie goes missing instead and a woman's mutilated corpse is found, detective Dupin investigates. **91m/B; DVD.** Patric Knowles; Maria Montez; Nell O'Day; Lloyd Corrigan; John Litel; Maria Ouspenskaya; ***D:*** Phil Rosen; ***W:*** Michael Jacoby; ***C:*** Elwood "Woody" Bredell.

Mystery of Mr. Wong 🦴 ½ **1939** The largest star sapphire in the world, the "Eye of the Daughter of the Moon," is stolen from a museum in its home country of China. Mr. Wong becomes involved in trying to trace its trail and the perpetrator of the murders that follow in its wake. One in the series of detective films. **67m/B; VHS, DVD.** Boris Karloff; Grant Withers; Dorothy Tree; Lotus Long; ***D:*** William Nigh.

Mystery of Picasso 🦴🦴🦴 *The Picasso Mystery* **1956** Famous, rarely seen documentary chronicles 15 paintings-in-progress by the modern master. He and Clouzot agreed to subsequently destroy the paintings, leaving the film as their only record. Highly acclaimed. In French with English subtitles. **85m/C; VHS, DVD.** *FR* ***D:*** Henri-Georges Clouzot.

The Mystery of Rampo 🦴🦴🦴 **1994 (R)** Visually dazzling fantasy that propels mystery writer Edogawa Rampo (Takenaka) into his own stories. Set just before WWII, Rampo is despondent when his latest novel (about a woman suffocating her husband in a trunk) is censored and then amazed when a newspaper story reveals a similar crime. Rampo meets widow Shizuko (Hada) and discovers she's a double for his fictional character. He writes a sequel and again finds reality and fiction colliding. Rampo was the pseudonym for renowned writer Hirai Taro, regarded as the Japanese Edgar Allan Poe. The film had its own complications when the version directed by director Rentaro Mayusumi was rejected by producer Okuyama, who then reshot much of the film himself. Japanese with subtitles. **96m/C; VHS, DVD.** *JP* Naoto Takenaka; Michiko Hada; Masahiro Motoki; Teruyuki Kagawa; Mikijiro Hira; ***D:*** Kazuyoshi Okuyama; ***W:*** Kazuyoshi Okuyama; Yuhei Enoki; ***C:*** Yasushi Sasakibara; ***M:*** Akira Senju.

Mystery of the Wax Museum 🦴🦴🦴 **1933** Rarely seen, vintage horror classic about a wax-dummy maker who, after a disfiguring fire, resorts to murder and installs the wax-covered bodies of his victims in his museum. Famous for its pioneering use of two-strip Technicolor. Remade in 1953 in 3-D as "House of Wax." **77m/C; VHS, DVD, Blu-Ray.** Lionel Atwill; Fay Wray; Glenda Farrell; Frank McHugh; Allen Vincent; Holmes Herbert; ***D:*** Michael Curtiz; ***W:*** Carl Erickson; Don Mullaly; ***C:*** Ray Rennahan.

Mystery Science Theater 3000: The Movie 🦴🦴 ½ **1996 (PG-13)** Mad scientist Dr. Clayton Forrester maroons Mike Nelson on the Satellite of Love, forces him to watch bad movies, and monitors his reactions. Mike and his robotic pals, Tom Servo and Crow T. Robot, save their sanity by wisecracking their way through the movies. Today's experiment is "This Island Earth," an uncharacteristically semi-respectable flick. As regular viewers know, the jokes and snide remarks come fast and in bunches. Not all of them work, but the ones that do will be remembered and repeated often. **73m/C; DVD, Blu-Ray.** Trace Beaulieu; Jim Mallon; Michael J. Nelson; Kevin Murphy; John Brady; ***D:*** Jim Mallon; ***W:*** Trace Beaulieu; Jim Mallon; Michael J. Nelson; Kevin Murphy; Mary Jo Pehl; Paul Chaplin; Bridget Jones; ***C:*** Jeff Stonehouse; ***M:*** Billy Barber.

Mystery Squadron 🦴🦴 **1933** Twelve chapters, 13 minutes each. Daredevil air action in flight against the masked pilots of the Black Ace. **240m/B; VHS, DVD.** Bob Steele; Guinn "Big Boy" Williams; Lucille Browne; Jack Mulhall; J. Carrol Naish; Jack Mower; ***D:*** Colbert Clark.

Mystery Street 🦴🦴 **1950** Unusual for two reasons: an immigrant detective who ignores race baiting for a shot at his first big case and the use of forensics (then a new science) to solve it. Bar girl Vivian (Sterling) gets the brush-off from her married lover and decides to confront him. She persuades drunken Henry (Thompson) to loan her his car so she can meet the louse. Months later a skeleton turns up on a Cape Cod beach and Portuguese-American detective Peter Morales (Montalban) gets his chance to move up the cop ladder. He enlists the aid of Harvard forensic expert Dr. McAdoo (Bennett) to identity the bones. Then the car turns up, putting foolish Henry (who reported it stolen) in the hot seat. McAdoo insists forensics show Henry is the wrong guy but Morales is skeptical. **93m/B; DVD.** Ricardo Montalban; Bruce Bennett; Marshall Thompson; Jan Sterling; Elsa Lanchester; Edmon Ryan; Sally Forrest; Wally Maher; ***D:*** John Sturges; ***W:*** Richard Brooks; Sydney (Sidney) Boehm; ***C:*** John Alton; ***M:*** Rudolph Kopp.

Mystery Train 🦴🦴🦴 **1989 (R)** A run down hotel in Memphis is the scene for three vignettes concerning the visit of foreigners to the U.S. Themes of mythic Americana, Elvis, and life on the fringe pervade this hip and quirky film. The three vignettes all tie together in clever and funny overlaps. Waits fans should listen for his performance as a DJ. **110m/C; VHS, DVD.** Masatoshi Nagase; Youki Kudoh; Screamin' Jay Hawkins; Cinque Lee; Joe Strummer; Nicoletta Braschi; Elizabeth Bracco; Steve Buscemi; Tom Noonan; Rockets Redglare; Rick Aviles; Rufus Thomas; Vondie Curtis-Hall; ***V:*** Tom Waits; ***D:*** Jim Jarmusch; ***W:*** Jim Jarmusch; ***C:*** Robby Muller; ***M:*** John Lurie.

Mystery Woman: Mystery Weekend 🦴🦴 ½ **2005** Samantha Kinsey (Martin) inherits a struggling mystery bookstore and tries to boost business by inviting three successful authors to speak as part of a mystery weekend. Only the mystery really begins when one of the writers is murdered. Originally shown on the Hallmark Channel. **87m/C; DVD.** Kellie Martin; Clarence Williams, III; Nina Siemaszko; Colleen Camp; Casey Sander; Deborah Van Valkenburgh; Paul Satterfield; Beth Broderick; ***D:*** Mark Griffiths; ***W:*** Joyce Burdett; ***C:*** Maximo Munzi; ***M:*** Joe Kraemer. **CABLE**

Mystic Circle Murder 🦴 *Religious Racketeers* **1939** Reporter sets out to uncover phony mediums, particularly the Great La Gagge, whose fake apparitions are so convincing that it caused one of his clients to have a heart attack. Cheaply made, and it's obvious. Watch for a cameo by Harry Houdini's wife, who talks about life after death. Based on a story by director O'Connor. **69m/B; VHS, DVD.** Betty Compson; Robert (Fisk) Fiske; Helene Le Berthon; Arthur Gardner; ***D:*** Frank O'Connor.

The Mystic Masseur 🦴🦴 ½ **2001 (PG)** Ganesh (Mandvi), a disgruntled schoolteacher, is part of the Indian community of Trinidad. He longs to become a writer and is inspired when he returns to his rural village for the funeral of his father, a famed masseur and healer. Ganesh discovers he also has a talent for healing, finds success as a writer, and even tries his hand at politics before finding a private contentment. Based on a novel by V.S. Naipaul. **117m/C; VHS, DVD.** *GB IN* Aasif Mandvi; Om Puri; Ayesha Dharker; Jimi Mistry; Zohra Sehgal; James Fox; ***D:*** Ismail Merchant; ***W:*** Caryl Phillips; ***C:*** Ernest Vincze; ***M:*** Richard Robbins; Zakir Hussain.

Mystic Pizza 🦴🦴🦴 **1988 (R)** Intelligent coming of age drama centers on two sisters and their best friend as they struggle with their hopes, loves, and family rivalries in the small town of Mystic, Connecticut. At times predictable, there are enough unexpected moments to keep interest high; definite appeal to young women, but others may not relate. The relatively unknown Roberts got most of the attention, but is the weakest of the three leads, so watch this one for the strong performances from Gish and Taylor. **101m/C; VHS, DVD.** Annabeth Gish; Julia Roberts; Lili Taylor; Vincent D'Onofrio; William R. Moses; Adam Storke; Conchata Ferrell; Joanna Merlin; Matt Damon; Arthur Walsh; ***D:*** Donald Petrie; ***W:*** Amy Holden Jones; Perry Howze; Alfred Uhry; ***C:*** Tim Suhrstedt; ***M:*** David McHugh. Ind. Spirit '89: First Feature.

Mystic River 🦴🦴🦴 ½ **2003 (R)** Complex drama is Eastwood's 24th directorial effort. Jimmy (Penn), Dave (Robbins), and Sean (Bacon) have grown up together in a working-class Boston Irish neighborhood. As a child, Dave was kidnapped as his buddies looked on helplessly and he's never completely recovered. Decades later, Sean is a homicide detective; Dave, a subdued loser; and Jimmy, an ex-con who manages a local market. Tragedy brings the guys back together when Jimmy's beloved 19-year-old daughter Katie (Rossum) is murdered and he wants to get the killer before the cops do. Some strange circumstances have suspicion falling on Dave, leading to a climax filled with regret, loss, and the perils of vigilante justice. Based on the novel by Dennis Lehane. **137m/C; VHS, DVD, Blu-Ray.** Sean Penn; Tim Robbins; Kevin Bacon; Laurence Fishburne; Marcia Gay Harden; Laura Linney; Tom Guiry; Kevin Chapman; Emmy Rossum; Spencer Treat Clark; Adam Nelson; Jenny O'Hara; Andrew Mackin; Robert Wahlberg; ***D:*** Clint Eastwood; ***W:*** Brian Helgeland; ***C:*** Tom Stern; ***M:*** Clint Eastwood. Oscars '03: Actor (Penn), Support. Actor (Robbins); Golden Globes '04: Actor--Drama (Penn), Support. Actor (Robbins); Natl. Bd. of Review '03: Actor (Penn), Film; Natl. Soc. Film Critics '03: Director (Eastwood); Screen Actors Guild '03: Support. Actor (Robbins).

The Myth of Fingerprints 🦴🦴 ½ **1997 (R)** Adult siblings return to their New England home to spend Thanksgiving with their parents. As with most movie families, old resentments and issues abound. Dad (Scheider), a sullen, misanthropic near-recluse, isn't thrilled about the reunion. Son Warren (Wyle) hopes to reconcile with his high school sweetheart. Older sister Mia (Moore) is sharp-tongued and tomboy sister Leigh (Holloman) does the sibling rivalry dance with her. Subdued and interesting, Freundlich's debut doesn't go for a grand conclusion or startling revelation, which could be its greatest weakness or asset. Excellent performances by the cast should have a bearing on the decision. **91m/C; VHS, DVD.** Blythe Danner; Roy Scheider; Julianne Moore; Noah Wyle; Michael Vartan; Laurel Holloman; Hope Davis; Brian Kerwin; James LeGros; ***D:*** Bart Freundlich; ***W:*** Bart Freundlich; ***C:*** Stephen Kazmierski; ***M:*** David Bridie; John Phillips.

The Myth of the American Sleepover 🦴🦴 **2010** Writer/director David Robert Mitchell's debut covers very familiar territory in his up-all-night teen comedy-drama, set in the Detroit suburbs. Maggie and her friend Beth decide to leave the last of summer, Saturday night, all-girl sleepover for more adventurous opportunities and older boys. Scott pursues the Abbey twins and Rob tries to find the hot blonde he saw in a supermarket. Parents are nowhere to be found but cigarettes, pot, and alcohol are. **96m/C; DVD.** Claire Sloma; Annette DeNoyer; Amanda Bauer; Brett Jacobsen; Marlon Morton; Nikita Ramsey; Jade Ramsey; ***D:*** David Robert Mitchell; ***W:*** David Robert Mitchell; ***C:*** James Laxton; ***M:*** Kyle Newmaster.

Mythica 2: The Darkspore 🦴🦴 **2015** The second installment of the Mythica fantasy series centers on a quest to regain the Darkspore. Still working with her team, aspiring wizard Marek (Stone) faces a new challenge when the Darkspor, a powerful ancient relic, is stolen and broken into pieces. As Marek and her cohorts begin to search for the relic, she learns she has a rival in a mystic who seeks the Darkspore for his master, Szorlok (Mercer). The rivals must travel through lands brimming with deadly creatures on their way to an abandoned underground city. Though Marek faces personal danger from the bounty hunters who are pursuing her, she knows she must find the Darkspore in time to save the world. **107m/C; DVD, Blu-Ray, Streaming, Download.** Melanie Stone; Adam Johnson; Jake Stormoen; Nicola Posener; Matthew Mercer; ***D:*** Anne K. Black; ***W:*** Anne K. Black; Jason Faller; Kynan Griffin; Liska Ostojic; Justin Partridge; ***C:*** A. Todd Smith; ***M:*** Nathaniel Drew. **VIDEO**

Mythica: A Quest for Heroes 🦴🦴 **2015** The first Mythica fantasy movie introduces young aspiring wizard and her first great adventure. Though Marek (Stone) is an indentured servant, she believes she can be a wizard some day. Her life changes when she meets Teela (Posener), a priestess in distress because her sister is being held prisoner by orcs and ogres. After escaping her master, Teela puts together a team to help. On their quest to free Teela's sister and others who are imprisioned, the team must raid an orc camp, take a journey through hellhounds and dragons, and work together to defeat the man-eating ogre in the mountains. **93m/C; DVD, Streaming, Download.** Melanie Stone; Adam Johnson; Jake Stormoen; Nicola Posener; Kevin Sorbo; ***D:*** Anne K. Black; ***W:*** Anne K. Black; Jason Faller; Kynan Griffin; ***C:*** A. Todd Smith; ***M:*** Nathaniel Drew. **VIDEO**

Mythica: The Iron Crown 🦴 ½ **2016** This entry in the Mythica fantasy series centers on a young wizard's efforts to save the world from the undead. Young wizard Marek (Stone) manages to steal the last piece of the Darkspore as her heroic team commandeers a steam-powered battle wagon. Though Marek intends to take it to the gods so that the cursed item will be safe, she and her team find themselves trapped in a race to the death with mercenaries and demons. Before an of her allies die, Marek has to take charge and ensure that pieces of the Darkspore are not united because of the devastating consequences that would result. **93m/C; DVD, Streaming, Download.** Melanie Stone; Kevin Sorbo; Jasen Wade; Maclain Nelson; Eve Mauro; ***D:*** John Lyde; ***W:*** Jason Faller; ***M:*** James Schafer.

Mythica: The Necroromancer 🦴🦴 **2015** The third entry in the Mythica fantasy series finds Marek (Stone) facing her greatest challenge. Marek and her team agree to serve the Thieves Guild to rescue her closest friend Thane (Johnson), who has been taken prisoner by the evil master of the guild. Unexpectedly, this quest takes into the arms of their biggest enemy, Szorlok (Mercer), Marek must decide how much she will sacrifice to save the lives of her friends and prevent Szorlok from gaining his most valued prize, the Darkspore. **93m/C; DVD.** Melanie Stone; Adam Johnson; Jake Stormoen; Nicola Posener; Matthew Mercer; ***D:*** A. Todd Smith; ***W:*** Jason Faller; Liska Ostojic; Justin Partridge; ***C:*** Casey Wilson; ***M:*** Nathaniel Drew. **VIDEO**

Nabonga 🦴🦴 *Gorilla; Jungle Woman* **1944** The daughter of an embezzler, whose plane crashes in the jungle, befriends a gorilla who protects her. Soon a young man comes looking for the embezzler's cash, meets the woman and the ape, and together they go on a wonderful journey. **72m/B; VHS, DVD.** Buster Crabbe; Fifi d'Orsay; Barton MacLane; Julie London; Herbert Rawlinson; ***D:*** Sam Newfield.

Nacho Libre 🦴 ½ **2006 (PG)** Surprising misfire offers a few chuckles and the chance to see Black in spandex and a cape but not much else. Ignacio is a cook at a Mexican orphanage who assumes the alter ego of masked wrestler Nacho Libre in order to help out the tykes. He now has a tag-team buddy, skinny Esqueleto (Jimemez), and they somewhat resemble a cheap version of Laurel and Hardy. It's also not nearly as outrageous as the actual Lucha Libre wrestling it features. **91m/C; DVD, Blu-Ray, HD-DVD.** Jack Black; Peter Stormare; Ana de la Reguera; Hector Jimenez; Richard Montoya; Darius A. Rose; Moises Arias; Diego Eduardo Gomez; Carlos Maycotte;

Cesar Gonzalez; *D:* Jared Hess; *W:* Jared Hess; Jerusha Hess; Mike White; *C:* Xavier Perez Grobet; *M:* Danny Elfman.

Nadia 1/2 **1984** Entertaining account of the life of Nadia Comaneci, the Romanian gymnast who earned six perfect tens with her stunning performance at the 1976 Olympic Games. **100m/C; VHS, DVD.** Talia Balsam; Jonathan Banks; Simone Blue; Johann Carlo; Carrie Snodgress; *D:* Alan Cooke; *M:* Christopher L. Stone. **TV**

Nadine 1/2 **1987 (PG)** In Austin circa 1954, an almost divorced beautician witnesses a murder and goes undercover with her estranged husband to track down the murderer, before he finds her. Plenty of low-key humor. Well-paced fun; Basinger is terrific. **83m/C; VHS, DVD.** Jeff Bridges; Kim Basinger; Rip Torn; Gwen Verdon; Glenne Headly; Jerry Stiller; Jay Patterson; *D:* Robert Benton; *W:* Robert Benton; *C:* Nestor Almendros; *M:* Howard Shore.

Nadja **1995 (R)** Modern comic take on the vampire tale. Tired of nightly bloodletting, Nadja (Lowensohn), lives in New York's East Village and wants to change her life. She seduces and falls in love with Lucy (Craze), whose husband is the nephew of old family nemesis Van Helsing (Fonda, in a surprisingly comedic role). Meanwhile, Nadja finds her long lost twin brother (Harris) and Lucy discovers sex with Nadja is draining. Innovative camera work (vampire point-of-view scenes shot with a toy Pixelvision camera and blown up to 35mm for a moody, grainy look) and a great score keep "Nadja" watchable despite some plot missteps. **92m/B; DVD.** Elina Lowensohn; Suzy Amis; Galaxy Craze; Martin Donovan; Peter Fonda; Karl Geary; Jared Harris; ***Cameo(s):*** David Lynch; *D:* Michael Almereyda; *W:* Michael Almereyda; *C:* Jim Denault; *M:* Simon Fisher Turner.

Nail Gun Massacre WOOF! 1986 A crazed killer with a penchant for nailing bodies to just about anything goes on a hammering spree. In horrific, vivid color. **90m/C; VHS, DVD, Blu-Ray.** Rocky Patterson; Ron Queen; Beau Leland; Michelle Meyer; *D:* Bill Lesley.

Naked *Mike Leigh's Naked* **1993 (R)** Existential angst in a '90s London filled with Leigh's usual eccentrics. The unemployed Johnny (Thewlis) comes to London and bunks with former girlfriend Louise (Sharp). After seducing her flatmate Sophie (Cartlidge), Johnny leaves to wander the streets, exchanging philosophical, if foul-mouthed, dialogues with a variety of odd characters. Thewlis gives an explosive performance as the calculatingly brutal and desolate Johnny. Chaotic shifts in mood from comedy to violence to love prove a challenge and the pervasive abuse of all the women characters is very disturbing. Critically acclaimed; see it as a reflection on the mess of modern England. **131m/C; DVD.** *UK* David Thewlis; Lesley Sharp; Katrin Cartlidge; Greg Cruttwell; Claire Skinner; Peter Wight; Ewen Bremner; Susan Vidler; Deborah MacLaren; Gina McKee; *D:* Mike Leigh; *W:* Mike Leigh; *C:* Dick Pope; *M:* Andrew Dickson. Cannes '93: Actor (Thewlis), Director (Leigh); N.Y. Film Critics '93: Actor (Thewlis); Natl. Soc. Film Critics '93: Actor (Thewlis).

The Naked Angels **1969 (R)** Rape, mayhem, beatings, and road-hogging street-bikes highlight this biker film, acted, in part, by actual bikers, and in part by others who were actually (almost) actors. The gang war rages from Los Angeles to Las Vegas. Roger Corman was the executive producer. **83m/C; VHS, DVD.** Michael Greene; Richard Rust; Felicia Guy; *D:* Bruce (B.D.) Clark; *W:* Bruce (B.D.) Clark.

The Naked City 1/2 **1948** Film noir classic makes spectacular use of its NYC locations. Beautiful playgirl is murdered and police detectives Fitzgerald and Taylor are left without clues. They spend most of their time running down weak leads and interviewing various suspects and witnesses. When they finally get a break, it leads to playboy Duff. Spectacular ending on the Williamsburg Bridge between cops and killer. Producer Hellinger provided the hard-boiled narration, patterned after the tabloid newspaper stories he once wrote. Served as the impetus for the TV show of the same name, where Hellinger's film postscript also became the show's noted tagline: "There are eight million stories in the naked city, this has been one of them." **96m/B; VHS, DVD.** Barry Fitzgerald; Don Taylor; Howard Duff; Ted de Corsia; Dorothy Hart; *Nar:* Mark Hellinger; *D:* Jules Dassin; *W:* Albert (John B. Sherry) Maltz; *C:* William H. Daniels; *M:* Miklos Rozsa. Oscars '48: B&W Cinematog., Film Editing; Natl. Film Reg. '07.

The Naked Civil Servant 1/2 **1975** Remarkable film, based on the life of flamboyant homosexual Quentin Crisp, who came out of the closet in his native England, long before his lifestyle would be tolerated by Britains. For mature audiences. **80m/C; VHS, DVD.** John Hurt; *D:* Jack Gold; *M:* Carl Davis.

Naked Evil 1/2 **1966** Two rival West Indian street gangs are causing problems in their Midlands community and one of them has turned to Jamaican voodoo to release a demon. Violent deaths follow. **85m/B; DVD.** *GB* Basil Dignam; Olaf Pooley; Anthony Ainley; Suzanne Neve; Richard Coleman; John Ashley Hamilton; Brylo Forde; *D:* Stanley Goulder; *W:* Stanley Goulder; *C:* Geoffrey Faithfull; *M:* Bernard Ebbinghouse.

The Naked Face **1984 (R)** A psychiatrist tries to find out why his patients are being killed. He gets no help from police, who suspect he is the murderer. A dull affair featuring unusual casting of Moore, while Steiger's suspicious police captain character provides spark. From the novel by Sidney Sheldon. **105m/C; DVD, Blu-Ray.** Roger Moore; Rod Steiger; Elliott Gould; Art Carney; Anne Archer; David Hedison; *D:* Bryan Forbes; *W:* Bryan Forbes.

The Naked Flame WOOF! 1968 (R) O'Keefe plays an investigator in a strange town inhabited by weird, religious fanatics. After he arrives, the womenfolk shed their clothes in this pitiful, pathetic hilarity. **90m/C; VHS, DVD.** *CA* Dennis O'Keefe; Kasey Rogers; Al Ruscio; Linda Bennett; Tracey Roberts; Barton Heyman; Robert Howay; *D:* Larry Matanski; *W:* Al Everett Dennis; *C:* Paul Ivano.

The Naked Gun: From the Files of Police Squad **1988 (PG-13)** More hysterical satire from the creators of "Airplane!" The short-lived TV cop spoof "Police Squad" moves to the big screen and has Lt. Drebin uncover a plot to assassinate Queen Elizabeth while she is visiting Los Angeles. Nearly nonstop gags and pratfalls provide lots of laughs. Nielsen is perfect as Drebin and the supporting cast is strong; cameos abound. **85m/C; VHS, DVD, Blu-Ray.** Leslie Nielsen; Ricardo Montalban; Priscilla Presley; George Kennedy; O.J. Simpson; Nancy Marchand; John Houseman; Mark Holton; ***Cameo(s):*** Weird Al Yankovic; Reggie Jackson; Dr. Joyce Brothers; *D:* David Zucker; *W:* Jerry Zucker; Jim Abrahams; Pat Proft; David Zucker; *M:* Ira Newborn.

Naked Gun 33 1/3: The Final Insult **1994 (PG-13)** Ever dumb, crass, and crude, Lt. Drebin returns to the force from retirement to lead an investigation into terrorist activities in Hollywood. Lots of current events jokes—dated as soon as they hit the screen. Sure to satisfy genre fans with a taste for bad puns. Watch for the cameos, especially at the "Oscars." **90m/C; VHS, DVD, Blu-Ray.** Leslie Nielsen; Priscilla Presley; O.J. Simpson; Fred Ward; George Kennedy; Ed Williams; Kathleen Freeman; Raquel Welch; Anna Nicole Smith; Ellen Greene; Randall "Tex" Cobb; R. Lee Ermey; Joe Grifasi; Julie Strain; ***Cameo(s):*** Pia Zadora; James Earl Jones; Weird Al Yankovic; Ann B. Davis; *D:* Peter Segal; *W:* Pat Proft; Robert Locash; David Zucker; *M:* Ira Newborn. Golden Raspberries '94: Worst New Star (Smith), Worst Support. Actor (Simpson).

Naked Gun 2 1/2: The Smell of Fear 1/2 **1991 (PG-13)** Lt. Drebin returns to rescue the world from a faulty energy policy devised by the White House and oil-lords. A notch down from the previous entry but still hilarious cop parody. Nielsen has this character down to a tee, and there's a laugh every minute. **85m/C; VHS, DVD, Blu-Ray.** Leslie Nielsen; Priscilla Presley; George Kennedy; O.J. Simpson; Robert Goulet; Richard Griffiths; Jacqueline Brookes; Lloyd Bochner; Tim O'Connor; Peter Mark Richman; ***Cameo(s):*** Mel Torme; Eva Gabor; Weird Al Yankovic; *D:* David Zucker; *W:* David Zucker; Pat Proft; *M:* Ira Newborn.

Naked Hills 1/2 **1956** Meandering tale about a man (Wayne) who, suffering from gold fever, searches for 40 years in 19th Century California and ends up out of luck, losing his wife and family. **72m/C; VHS, DVD.** David Wayne; Keenan Wynn; James Barton; Marcia Henderson; Jim Backus; Denver Pyle; Myrna Dell; Frank Fenton; Fuzzy Knight; *D:* Josef Shaftel; *W:* Josef Shaftel.

Naked in New York 1/2 **1993 (R)** Aspiring New York playwright Jake Briggs (Stoltz) and his girlfriend Joanne (Parker), an aspiring photographer, find their relationship in jeopardy when their respective careers start to take off. Offspring of the "Annie Hall" school of neurotic romance examines a number of issues, including ambition, commitment, and the societal dynamics of theatre and art. Directorial debut of Scorsese protege Algrant is uneven but charming. Parker is particularly strong, and Turner's a riot as a sexpot soap star on the prowl for Jake. **89m/C; DVD.** Eric Stoltz; Mary-Louise Parker; Ralph Macchio; Jill Clayburgh; Tony Curtis; Kathleen Turner; Timothy Dalton; Lynne Thigpen; Roscoe Lee Browne; ***Cameo(s):*** Whoopi Goldberg; William Styron; Eric Bogosian; Quentin Crisp; *V:* David Johansen; *D:* Daniel Algrant; *W:* Daniel Algrant; John Warren; *M:* Angelo Badalamenti.

Naked Jungle **1954** Suspenseful, well-done jungle adventure of a plantation owner (Heston) in South America and his North American mail-order bride (Parker), who do battle with a deadly, miles-long siege of red army ants. Realistic and worth watching. Produced by George Pal, shot by Ernest Laszlo and based on the story "Leiningen vs. the Ants" by Carl Stephenson. **95m/C; DVD.** Charlton Heston; Eleanor Parker; Abraham Sofaer; William Conrad; *D:* Byron Haskin; *W:* Philip Yordan; *C:* Ernest Laszlo; *M:* Daniele Amfitheatrof.

Naked Kiss 1/2 *The Iron Kiss* **1964** Fuller's most savage, hysterical film noir. A brutalized prostitute escapes her pimp and tries to enter respectable small-town society. She finds even more perversion and sickness there. **92m/B; VHS, DVD.** Constance Towers; Anthony Eisley; Michael Dante; Virginia Grey; Patsy Kelly; Betty Bronson; Edy Williams; Marie Devereux; Karen Conrad; Linda Francis; Barbara Perry; Walter Matthews; Betty Robinson; *D:* Samuel Fuller; *W:* Samuel Fuller; *C:* Stanley Cortez; *M:* Paul Dunlap.

Naked Lie **1989** A District Attorney and a judge engage in an ultra-steamy affair and inevitably clash when she is assigned as a prosecutor on the politically explosive case over which he is presiding. **89m/C; VHS, DVD.** Victoria Principal; James Farentino; Glenn Withrow; William Lucking; Dakin Matthews; *D:* Richard A. Colla; *M:* Robert Alcivar.

Naked Lies **1998 (R)** FBI agent Cara Landry (Tweed) gets transferred to treasury after a drug bust goes bad and is assigned to work an undercover operation that reunites Cara with ex-lover Mitch Kendall (Baker). Kendall has been trying to bust international counterfeiter Damian Medina (Allende) and sends Cara in to work one of Medina's casinos. But Cara finds herself drawn to the bad guy, putting both her career and her life in jeopardy. **93m/C; VHS, DVD.** Shannon Tweed; Jay Baker; Fernando Allende; Steven Bauer; Hugo Stiglitz; *D:* Ralph Portillo. **VIDEO**

Naked Lunch **1991 (R)** Whacked-out movie based on William S. Burroughs's autobiographical account of drug abuse, homosexuality, violence, and weirdness set in the drug-inspired land called Interzone. Hallucinogenic images are carried to the extreme: typewriters metamorphose into beetles, bloblike creatures with sex organs scurry about, and characters mainline insecticide. Some of the characters are clearly based on writers of the Beat generation, including Jane and Paul Bowles, Allen Ginsberg, and Jack Kerouac. **117m/C; VHS, DVD, Blu-Ray.** *CA GB* Peter Weller; Judy Davis; Ian Holm; Julian Sands; Roy Scheider; Monique Mercure; Nicholas (Nick) Campbell; Michael Zelniker; Robert A. Silverman; Joseph Scorsiani; *D:* David Cronenberg; *W:* David Cronenberg; *C:* Peter Suschitzky; *M:* Howard Shore. Genie '92: Adapt. Screenplay, Art Dir./Set Dec., Cinematog., Director (Cronenberg), Film, Sound, Support. Actress (Mercure); N.Y. Film Critics '91: Screenplay, Support. Actress (Davis); Natl. Soc. Film Critics '91: Director (Cronenberg), Screenplay.

The Naked Prey **1966** Unnerving African adventure which contains some unforgettably brutal scenes. A safari guide (Wilde), leading a hunting party, must watch as an indigenous tribe murders all his companions, and according to their customs, allows him to be set free, sans clothes or weapons, to be hunted by the best of the tribe. **96m/C; VHS, DVD, Blu-Ray.** Cornel Wilde; Gertrude Van Der Berger; Ken Gampu; *D:* Cornel Wilde.

Naked Souls **1995 (R)** Artist Brit Clark (Anderson) must save scientist fiance Edward (Krause) from the evil experiments of murderous scientist Longstreet (Warner). Like you'll care as long as the Anderson bod is on display. **90m/C; VHS, DVD.** Pamela Anderson; Brian Krause; Clayton Rohner; Justina Vail; David Warner; Michael (Mike) Papajohn; ***Cameo(s):*** Dean Stockwell; *D:* Lyndon Chubbuck; *W:* Frank Dietz; *C:* Eric Goldstein; *M:* Nigel Holton.

The Naked Spur 1/2 **1953** A compulsive bounty hunter tracks down a vicious outlaw and his beautiful girlfriend. An exciting film from the Mann-Stewart team and considered one of their best, infusing the traditional western with psychological confusion. Wonderful use of Rockies locations. **93m/C; VHS, DVD.** James Stewart; Robert Ryan; Janet Leigh; Millard Mitchell; Ralph Meeker; *D:* Anthony Mann; *W:* Sam Rolfe; Harold Jack Bloom; *C:* William Mellor; *M:* Bronislau Kaper. Natl. Film Reg. '97.

The Naked Truth 1/2 *Your Past is Showing* **1958** A greedy publisher tries to get rich quick by publishing a scandal magazine about the "lurid" lives of prominent citizens. Well-drawn characters in an appealing offbeat comedy. **92m/C; VHS, DVD.** *GB* Peter Sellers; Terry-Thomas; Shirley Eaton; Dennis Price; *D:* Mario Zampi.

Naked Venus 1/2 **1958** Ulmer's last film is a slow-paced tale about an American artist, married to a model who poses in the nude and belongs to a nudist camp, whose wealthy mother tries to tear the marriage apart. Discrimination and intolerance of nudist camps is explored. **80m/B; VHS, DVD.** Patricia Conelle; *D:* Edgar G. Ulmer.

Naked Weapon *Chek law dak gung* **2003 (R)** A one-of-a-kind female assassin is slain, and her employer decides the easiest way to replace her is to kidnap 40 middle school girls and spend six years training them. Eventually they will all fight each other to the death to determine who will succeed to their predecessor's job. One of the most improbable exploitation films of all time. **92m/C; DVD.** *CH* Daniel Wu; Maggie Q; Pei Pei Cheng; Dennis Chan; Martt Thoresen; Almen Wong Piu-Ha; Anya; Jewel Lee; Hoi Lin; *D:* Siu-Tung Ching; *W:* Jing Wong; *C:* Sung Fai Choi; *M:* Ken Chan; Kwong Wing Chan.

Naked Youth WOOF! *Wild Youth* **1959** Seedy drive-in cheapie about two punks breaking out of juvenile prison and heading south of the border on a trail filled with crime, drugs, and loose women. **80m/B; VHS, DVD.** Robert Hutton; John Goddard; Carol Ohmart; Jan Brooks; Robert Arthur; Steve Rowland; Clancy Cooper; *D:* John F. Schreyer.

Nam Angels **1988 (R)** Hell's Angels enter Southeast Asia and rescue POWs. **91m/C; VHS, DVD.** *PH* Brad Johnson; Vernon Wells; Kevin Duffis; Fred Bailey; Archie Adamos; Rick Dean; Jeff Griffith; Eric Hahn; Ken Metcalfe; Tonichi Fructuoso; Leah Navarro; Ruben Ramos; *D:* Cirio H. Santiago; *C:* Ricardo Remias; Chris Squires; *M:* Jaime Fabregas.

A Name for Evil **1970 (R)** Having grown tired of city living, a couple moves to an old family estate out in the country near the Great Lakes. Strange sounds in the night are the first signs of the terror to come.

74m/C; VHS, DVD. Robert Culp; Samantha Eggar; Sheila Sullivan; Mike Lane; ***D:*** Bernard Girard.

The Name of the Rose 🦴🦴 ½ **1986 (R)** An exhaustive, off-center adaptation of the bestselling Umberto Eco novel about violent murders in a 14th-century Italian abbey. An English monk struggles against religious fervor in his quest to uncover the truth. **128m/C; VHS, DVD, Blu-Ray.** *IT GE FR* Sean Connery; F. Murray Abraham; Christian Slater; Ron Perlman; William Hickey; Feodor Chaliapin, Jr.; Elya Baskin; Michael (Michel) Lonsdale; ***D:*** Jean-Jacques Annaud; ***W:*** Andrew Birkin; Gerard Brach; Howard Franklin; ***C:*** Tonino Delli Colli; ***M:*** James Horner. British Acad. '87: Actor (Connery); Cesar '87: Foreign Film.

The Nameless 🦴🦴 *Los sin nombre* **1999 (R)** Five years after being told her daughter is dead, Claudia (Emma Vilarasau) receives a phone call from someone claiming to be her daughter asking for help before she is killed. Tapping a burned out ex-cop and a parapsychology reporter she quickly finds out her daughter is alive and in danger from a sadistic cult. **102m/C; DVD, Blu-Ray.** *SP* Emma Vilarasau; Karra Elejalde; Tristan Ulloa; Brendan Price; Pep Tosar; ***D:*** Jaume Balaguero; ***W:*** Jaume Balaguero; ***C:*** Xavi Gimenez; ***M:*** Carles Cases. **VIDEO**

The Names of Love 🦴🦴 *Le Nom des Gens* **2010 (R)** Racy French comedy about politics and sex. Young Bahia, the daughter of an Arab refugee whose family fled the Algerian War for safety in France, uses sex to convert right-wing believers to her leftist views. A radio show provides an introduction to middle-aged, Jewish Arthur, whose own family suffered under the Vichy regime. Arthur is a fervent socialist but Bahia has sex with him anyway and the two bond into an improbable romantic couple. French with subtitles. **102m/C; DVD, Blu-Ray.** *FR* Sara Forestier; Jacques Gamblin; Zinedine Soualem; Carole Franck; Jacques Boudet; Michele Moretti; ***D:*** Michel Leclerc; ***W:*** Michel Leclerc; Baya Kasmi; ***C:*** Vincent Mathias; ***M:*** Jerome Bensoussan; David Euverte.

The Namesake 🦴🦴🦴 **2006 (PG-13)** Nair's thoughtful adaptation of Jhumpa Lahiri's novel about two generations of a Bengali family living in the U.S. Ashoke (Khan) enters into an arranged marriage with Ashima (Tabu) and they move to New York, settling uneasily into their new lives. The couple's first child, Nikhil, is nicknamed Gogol after Ashoke's favorite writer. The name confusion will continue as the boy accepts and then rejects his various monikers, growing into a young man (Penn) torn between tradition and pursuing his own life. Penn has true dramatic presence to go along with his more familiar comic gifts. **122m/C; DVD.** Kal Penn; Tabu; Irfan Khan; Jacinda Barrett; Zuleikha Robinson; ***D:*** Mira Nair; ***W:*** Sooni Taraporevala; ***C:*** Frederick Elmes; ***M:*** Nitin Sawhney.

Namu, the Killer Whale 🦴🦴 ½ *Namu, My Best Friend* **1966** Based on the true story of a marine biologist (Lansing) who gets the perfect opportunity to study killer whales when one is confined to a small cove. The local fisherman want to kill the creature because it feeds on the salmon they catch but they are persuaded against their baser instincts. Filmed on location in the San Juan Islands of Puget Sound. The real Namu lived at the Seattle Public Aquarium. **89m/C; VHS, DVD.** Robert Lansing; John Anderson; Robin Mattson; Richard Erdman; Lee Meriwether; Joe Higgins; ***D:*** Laszlo Benedek.

Nana 🦴🦴🦴 **1955** French version of Emile Zola's novel about an actress-prostitute who seduces the high society of Paris in the late 1880s, and suffers a heart-breaking downfall and death. Film has three remakes of the original 1926 version. **118m/C; VHS, DVD.** *FR* Charles Boyer; Martine Carol; Jacques Castelot; Paul Frankeur; Noel Roquevert; Walter Chiari; Jean Debucourt; Elisa Cegani; ***D:*** Christian-Jaque; ***W:*** Christian-Jaque; Jean Ferry; Henri Jeanson; ***C:*** Christian Matras; ***M:*** Georges Van Parys.

Nancy 🦴🦴 ½ **2018** Though thirtysomething Nancy (Riseborough) is an aspiring, determined writer with an active imagination, the reality of her life is more desperate. She lives in a dirty hotel with her mother Betty (Dowd), who suffers from Parkinson's disease, and works in a local dentistry mill. After the death of her mother, Nancy tries to convince Ellen (Cameron) and Leo (Buscemi) that she could be Brooke, the daughter they lost 30 years earlier when she disappeared at the age of five. A challenging feature debut of filmmaker Choe, its appeal turns on the intense yet balanced performance of Riseborough. **85m/C; DVD.** Andrea Riseborough; Steve Buscemi; Ann Dowd; John Leguizamo; J. Smith-Cameron; ***D:*** Christina Choe; ***W:*** Christina Choe; ***C:*** Zoe White; ***M:*** Peter Raeburn.

Nancy Drew 🦴 ½ **2007 (PG)** Poor Nancy! this effort to modernize the teen sleuth is awkward and dull. Nancy (Roberts) accompanies her lawyer dad Carson (Donovan) to L.A. She discovers that their rented home was the scene of movie star Dehlia Draycott's (Harring) murder, an unsolved case that Nancy can't resist. However, the story really falls apart with Nancy in high school, where her anachronisms make her an object of popular girl scorn. But Nancy's sheer perky tenaciousness can overcome any obstacle (okay, except this script). Based on the Carolyn Keene character. **98m/C; DVD.** Emma Roberts; Tate Donovan; Josh Flitter; Max Thieriot; Rachael Leigh Cook; Amy Bruckner; Kay Panabaker; Laura Elena Harring; Kelly Vitz; Marshall Bell; Caroline Aaron; David Doty; Daniella Monet; Barry Bostwick; ***D:*** Andrew Fleming; ***W:*** Andrew Fleming; Tiffany Paulsen; ***C:*** Alexander Grusynski; ***M:*** Ralph Sall.

Nancy Drew and the Hidden Staircase 🦴🦴 **2019 (PG)** Precocious high schooler Nancy Drew (Lillis) solves mysteries in her community using her intelligence and logic. Her detective work impresses her best friends Bess (Graham) and George (Renee). When Bess is bullied at school, Nancy take action to even the score. Though this action leads to a sentence of community service, Nancy uses it to help shut-in Flora (Lavin). Nancy then uses her skills to solve the mystery related to the haunting of Flora's historical mansion, Twin Elms. Based on the classic 1939 young adult novel, it's a clever update of the intelligent heroine detective. **89m/C; DVD.** Sophia Lillis; Zoe Renee; Mackenzie Graham; Andrea Anders; Laura Wiggins; ***D:*** Katt Shea; ***W:*** Nina Fiore; John Herrera; ***C:*** Edd Lukas; ***M:*** Sherri Chung.

Nancy Drew, Reporter 🦴🦴 **1939** The young sleuth gets to play reporter after winning a newspaper contest. In no time at all, she's involved in a murder mystery. **68m/B; VHS, DVD.** Bonita Granville; John Litel; Frankie Thomas, Jr.; Mary Lee; Sheila Mannors; Betty Amann; Dick(ie) Jones; Olin Howlin; Charles Halton; ***D:*** William Clemens.

Nancy Drew—Detective 🦴🦴 **1938** Nancy Drew (Granville) and Ted Nickerson (Thomas) are on the case of a kidnapping, or, well-to-do elderly lady napping. Ted fakes it as a nurse and Nancy plays the part of a widow to find both the nappee and the nappers. **66m/B; VHS, DVD.** Bonita Granville; John Litel; James Stephenson; Frankie Thomas, Jr.; Frank Orth; Helena Phillips Evans; Renie Riano; ***D:*** William Clemens; ***W:*** Kenneth Gamet; Mildred Wirt Benson.

Nancy Drew—Trouble Shooter 🦴🦴 **1939** Nancy Drew's (Granville) uncle Matt gets slapped with a murder charge, only he's no murderer and it takes Nancy and Ted Nickerson (Thomas) to clear him. They have to find the real murderer, and they're stuck in some perilous situations in order to do just that. **66m/B; VHS, DVD.** Bonita Granville; Frankie Thomas, Jr.; John Litel; Aldrich Bowker; Charlotte Wynters; Renie Riano; Edgar Edwards; ***D:*** William Clemens; ***W:*** Kenneth Gamet; Mildred Wirt Benson.

Nancy Goes to Rio 🦴🦴 ½ **1950** Actresses Powell and Sothern compete for the same part in a play and for the same man. Catch is, they're mother and daughter. Zany consequences ensue. Sothern's last film for MGM. **99m/C; VHS, DVD.** Ann Sothern; Jane Powell; Barry Sullivan; Carmen Miranda; Louis Calhern; Scotty Beckett; Hans Conried; Glenn Anders; ***D:*** Robert Z. Leonard; ***W:*** Sidney Sheldon.

Nancy Steele Is Missing 🦴🦴 **1937** To protest America's entry into WWI, political activist Dannie O'Neill (McLaglen) kidnaps the baby daugher of munitions manufacturer Michael Steele (Connolly). The baby grows up with friends as Dannie spends years in prison on other charges. When released, Dannie wants to make it up to his "daughter" (Lang) only his sleazy ex-cellmate Sturm (Lorre) knows about the kidnapping and has his own ideas. **85m/B; DVD.** Victor McLaglen; Peter Lorre; Walter Connolly; June Lang; John Carradine; Jane Darwell; Granville Bates; ***D:*** George Marshall; ***W:*** Hal Long; Gene Fowler, Sr.; ***C:*** Barney McGill.

The Nanny 🦴🦴 ½ **1965** Creepfest stars Davis as a seemingly proper nameless nanny who's been accused by her young charge Joey (Dix) of drowning his sister in the bathtub. But it's Joey who's sent away to a home for disturbed children and when he returns two years later (and just why is the nanny still around a childless home?) it's a battle of wills between the duo over who's responsible for some evil goings-on. Based on a novel by Evelyn Piper. **93m/B; VHS, DVD.** *GB* Bette Davis; William Dix; Wendy Craig; Jill Bennett; James Villiers; Pamela Franklin; Jack Watling; Alfred Burke; Maurice Denham; ***D:*** Seth Holt; ***W:*** Jimmy Sangster; ***C:*** Henry Waxman; ***M:*** Richard Rodney Bennett.

The Nanny Diaries 🦴🦴 **2007 (PG-13)** Recent NYU graduate Annie (Johansson), unsure of herself after bombing a job interview, accepts a nanny job from Manhattan power-mommy extraordinaire Mrs. X (Linney), whose number one priority is herself, and her husband, uptight jerk Mr. X (Giamatti). Meanwhile, she's got the hots for a Harvard man (Adams), the neighbor upstairs. Johansson somehow manages not to give Annie any depth or humor, which is sorely missed amid the other superficial stereotypes. Aspires to satire, but the result is weak social commentary about the class divide between insanely rich Manhattanites and white, college educated upwardly mobile wannabes. Based on a novel fictionalizing its authors' real life Manhattan nanny experiences. **105m/C; DVD.** Scarlett Johansson; Laura Linney; Paul Giamatti; Chris Evans; Nicholas Reese Art; Alicia Keys; Donna Murphy; Judith Anna Roberts; Nathan (Nate) Corddry; ***D:*** Shari Springer Berman; ***W:*** Shari Springer Berman; ***C:*** Terry Stacey; ***M:*** Mark Suozzo.

The Nanny Express 🦴🦴 ½ **2008** In this Hallmark Channel original, Kate (Marcil) needs a job since she's caring for her sick dad (Stockwell) and working on her teaching degree. So she's not about to let the two terrors of depressed widower David Chandler (Elliott) scare her off. Young Ben (Shelton) is easily handled but bitter teen Emily (Dreyfus) is determined to oust Kate, especially when her dad takes too much of an interest in the new nanny. **100m/C; DVD.** Vanessa Marcil; Brennan Elliott; Dean Stockwell; Stacy Keach; Peter Dobson; Natalie Dreyfus; Uriah Shelton; Jennifer Seibel; ***D:*** Bradford May; ***W:*** Stephen Langford; Riley Weston; Judith Kriegsman; ***C:*** Yaron Levy. **CABLE**

A Nanny for Christmas 🦴🦴 ½ **2010** Ally (Vaugier) needs a job but when she interviews with Beverly Hills exec Samantha Ryland (Gibbs) it turns out Samantha needs a nanny and not someone for her advertising firm. Ally takes it anyway and brings some much-needed fun into the Ryland kids? lives. She also finds out that Danny (Cain), the owner of a chocolate company, wants a new advertising campaign. So Ally tells some little white lies...but Santa knows if you—re naughty. **88m/C; DVD.** Emmanuelle Vaugier; Cynthia Gibb; Sierra McCormick; Jared Gilmore; Dean Cain; Richard Ruccolo; Sarah Thompson; ***D:*** Michael Feifer; ***W:*** Michael Ciminiera; Richard Gnolfo; ***M:*** Chad Rehmann. **VIDEO**

Nanny Insanity 🦴 ½ *Domestic Import* **2006 (PG-13)** Over-the-top sitcom situations. Overwhelmed marrieds David (Dorf) and Marsha (Preston) decide to hire an experienced housekeeper/nanny since they're about to have their first child. But somehow they wind up with crazy Ukrainian immigrant Sophia (Korot), who's soon inviting her equally wacky family to move in as well. **94m/C; DVD.** Cynthia (Cyndy, Cindy) Preston; Mindy Sterling; Howard Hesseman; Stephanie Patton; Larry Dorf; Alla Korot; Lauri Johnson; ***D:*** Kevin Connor; ***W:*** Andrea Malamut; ***C:*** Barry M. Wilson; ***M:*** Adam Malamut. **VIDEO**

Nanny McPhee 🦴🦴 ½ **2006 (PG)** Thompson wrote the screenplay and stars as the spectacularly ugly title character, who comes complete with magical abilities and a no-nonsense manner destined to overcome the horrors wrought by the seven motherless Brown children. Their clueless father, Cedric (Firth), counts on a stipend from Aunt Adelaide (Lansbury) to support the unruly brood but she has now demanded that he marry in 30 days or lose the money. Cedric is in love with unsuitable scullery maid Evangeline (Macdonald) but decides on garish, greedy widow Mrs. Quickly (Imrie) instead. Naturally, Nanny will put everything right. Loosely based on Christianna Brand's 1960s "Nurse Matilda" series. **97m/C; DVD, Blu-Ray.** *US GB* Emma Thompson; Colin Firth; Kelly Macdonald; Derek Jacobi; Pat Barlow; Celia Imrie; Imelda Staunton; Thomas Brodie-Sangster; Angela Lansbury; Jenny Daykin; Eliza Bennett; Raphael Coleman; Samuel Honywood; Holly Gibbs; Hebe Barnes; Zinnia Barnes; ***D:*** Kirk Jones; ***W:*** Emma Thompson; Matt Robinson; ***C:*** Henry Braham; ***M:*** Patrick Doyle.

Nanny McPhee Returns 🦴🦴 ½ *Nanny McPhee and the Big Bang* **2010 (PG)** The grotesque-looking Nanny McPhee (Thompson) appears at the door of harried mom Isabel Green (Gyllenhaal) who's trying to run the family farm while her husband is away at war. However, Nanny discovers the Green children have their own war going on with their spoiled city cousins who have moved in because of the London Blitz. Nanny doesn't tolerate ill-mannered behavior and proceeds to teach the children five meaningful lessons (which parents will appreciate). **109m/C; Blu-Ray.** Emma Thompson; Maggie Gyllenhaal; Rhys Ifans; Ralph Fiennes; Maggie Smith; Asa Butterfield; Lil Woods; Oscar Steer; Eros Vlahos; Rosie Taylor-Ritson; Ewan McGregor; Sam Kelly; Sinead Matthews; Katy Brand; Daniel Mays; ***D:*** Susanna White; ***W:*** Emma Thompson; ***C:*** Mike Eley; ***M:*** James Newton Howard.

Nanook of the North 🦴🦴🦴 ½ **1922** This landmark documentary, the first of its kind, is about an Eskimo and his family's struggle for survival in the Arctic wastelands. Flaherty's first full-length film, and a true pioneer in form as well as authentic cinema verite. Silent, with music soundtrack. **70m/B; Silent; VHS, DVD, Blu-Ray.** ***D:*** Robert Flaherty; ***M:*** Stanley Silverman. Natl. Film Reg. '89.

Napoleon 🦴🦴 **1955** Depicts life story of Napoleon from his days as a soldier in the French army to his exile on the Island of Elba. Falls short of the fantastic 1927 silent classic as it attempts to delve into Napoleon the man, as opposed to his conquests. Some might find it too slow for their tastes. **123m/C; VHS, DVD.** *FR* Raymond Pellegrin; Orson Welles; Maria Schell; Yves Montand; Erich von Stroheim; Jean Gabin; Jean-Pierre Aumont; ***D:*** Sacha Guitry.

Napoleon 🦴🦴 ½ **1996 (G)** Cute pic for young kiddies who like animals. A very curious golden retriever puppy named Muffin manages to slip into a balloon-covered basket and finds himself airborne across Australia. Deciding he likes the idea of adventuring, Muffin renames himself Napoleon because it sounds braver. He lands unexpectedly near Sydney Harbor and is befriended by Birdo, who becomes his guide when Napoleon decides he wants to meet his wild dog cousins, the dingoes. And it's off into the bush, with kangaroos, koalas, snakes, and lizards to help or hinder along the way. **81m/C; VHS, DVD.** *AU JP* ***V:*** Jamie Croft; Philip Quast; Carole Skinner; Anne Louise Lambert; David Argue; Joan Rivers; Steven Vidler; Susan Lyons; ***D:*** Mario Andreacchio; ***W:*** Mario Andreacchio; Mark Saltzman; ***C:*** Roger Dowling; ***M:*** Bill Conti.

Napoleon 🦴🦴 ½ **2003** Epic miniseries starts off with a bedraggled general Napoleon Bonaparte (Clavier) managing to make both personal and professional marks in 1794 Paris: he thwarts a royalist riot at the end of the French Revolution and he meets Josephine (Rossellini). Soon, Napoleon is rising through the military ranks, winning the loyalty of the people, and proclaiming himself Emperor. But since Josephine can't give him a child, he has to make some dynastic decisions and begins to lose control. A lavish spectacle and a charismatic titular performance by Clavier. Based on the biography by Max Gallo. **360m/C; VHS, DVD.** Christian Clavier; Isabella Rossellini; Gerard Depardieu; John Malkovich; Anouk Aimee; Heino Ferch;

Ennio Fantastichini; Guillaume Depardieu; Sebastian Koch; Julian Sands; Toby Stephens; John Wood; Mavie Horbiger; Yves Jacques; ***D:*** Yves Simoneau; ***W:*** Didier Decoin; ***C:*** Guy Dufaux; ***M:*** Richard Gregoire. **CABLE**

Napoleon and Josephine: A Love Story **1987** ABC miniseries focuses on the romantic drama between ambitious Corsican conqueror Napoleon Bonaparte (Assante) and older, sophisticated widow Josephine(Bisset). Strains are put on their marriage amidst constant military campaigns, infidelities, and the fact that Josephine cannot give the declared Emperor of France an heir. **275m/C; DVD.** Armand Assante; Jacqueline Bisset; Leigh Taylor-Young; Anthony Perkins; Patrick Cassidy; Ione Skye; Anthony (Corlan) Higgins; Nickolas Grace; ***D:*** Richard T. Heffron; ***W:*** James H. Lee; ***C:*** Jean Tournier; ***M:*** Gerald Fried. **TV**

Napoleon and Samantha **1972** Disney adventure about Napoleon, an orphan (Whitaker), who is befriended by Danny, a college student (Douglas). After the death of his grandfather, Napoleon decides to take Major, his elderly pet lion, and follow Danny, who is herding goats for the summer, across the American northwest mountains and they are joined by Samantha (Foster in her film debut). Worth watching. **91m/C; VHS, DVD.** Jodie Foster; Johnny Whitaker; Michael Douglas; Will Geer; Henry Jones; ***D:*** Bernard McEveety; ***W:*** Stewart Raffill; ***C:*** Monroe Askins; ***M:*** Buddy (Norman Dale) Baker.

Napoleon Dynamite **2004 (PG)** Filmed in Preston, Idaho, the debut of director Hess is a small-budget, small-scale, overreaching effort about the unfortunately named title character (Heder), an awkward, frizzy-haired, high school uber-nerd whose life is one exasperation after another. His only friend is a shy Mexican immigrant, Pedro (Ramirez), whom Napoleon assists in his campaign for class president against popular blonde goddess, Summer (Duff). His home life isn't muh better with creepily macho Uncle Rico (Gries) looking after the family. You should want to root for the underdog but you may become just as exasperated as Napoleon watching this flick. **86m/C; VHS, DVD, Blu-Ray, UMD.** Jon(athan) Gries; Tina Majorino; Diedrich Bader; Jon Heder; Aaron Ruell; Efren Ramirez; Haylie Duff; Trevor Snarr; Shondrella Avery; ***D:*** Jared Hess; ***W:*** Jared Hess; Jerusha Hess; ***C:*** Munn Powell; ***M:*** John Swihart.

Narc ½ **2002 (R)** Nick Tellis (Patric) is an undercover narcotics cop on suspension for a bust that went tragically wrong. But now the suits want him to investigate the murder of another undercover cop, teaming him with the deceased's partner, Henry Oak (Liotta), who's out to nail the killers although his motives may be more than just revenge. As the investigation continues, the tension and suspense become palpable. Carnahan's tale is brutal, dark, and full of dread, but it is always gripping, and he uses cop drama conventions to great effect with both Patric and Liotta taking well to their roles. **105m/C; DVD.** John Ortiz; Ray Liotta; Jason Patric; Chi McBride; Busta Rhymes; Richard Chevolleau; Alan Van Sprang; Krista Bridges; Anne Openshaw; ***D:*** Joe Carnahan; ***W:*** Joe Carnahan; ***C:*** Alex Nepomniaschy; ***M:*** Cliff Martinez.

Narco Cultura **2013 (R)** There is a growing movement of music from the Mexico-U.S. border that both glamorizes and thrives from the drug trafficking that takes place in crime-fueled towns like the deadly Juarez. Director Schwarz parallels the fortunes being made in this drug-inspired music scene with an investigator named Richi Soto who tries to do something about the rampant crime on his beat. The film is a harrowing expose into both the drug/violence scene in Mexico and the way it's influenced not just life on the streets but the very culture of what's coming out of that part of the world. **103m/C; DVD, Blu-Ray.** *US MX* ***D:*** Shaul Schwarz; ***C:*** Shaul Schwarz; ***M:*** Jeremy Turner.

The Narcotics Story **WOOF!** *The Dreaded Persuasion* **1958** Bad film on the same vein as "Reefer Madness." Originally intended as a police training film, this shows the evils and destruction of heroin addiction. Portrayals of drug addicts are hilarious. **75m/C; VHS, DVD.** Sharon Strand; Darlene Hendricks; Herbert Crisp; Fred Marratto; ***Nar:*** Art Gilmore; ***D:*** Robert W. Larsen.

The Narrow Margin **1952** Well-made, harrowing adventure about a cop who is in charge of transporting a gangster's widow to a trial where she is to testify. On the train he must try to keep her safe from the hit-men who would murder her. A real cat and mouse game—one of the best suspense movies of the '50s. **71m/B; DVD.** Charles McGraw; Marie Windsor; Jacqueline White; Queenie Leonard; Gordon Gebert; Don Beddoe; Harry Harvey; ***D:*** Richard Fleischer.

Narrow Margin **1990 (R)** Archer reluctantly agrees to testify against the mob after witnessing a murder, and Los Angeles D.A. Hackman is assigned to protect her on the train through the Rockies back to L.A. Bad idea, she finds out. No match for its '52 predecessor. **99m/C; VHS, DVD.** Gene Hackman; Anne Archer; James B. Sikking; J.T. Walsh; M. Emmet Walsh; ***D:*** Peter Hyams; ***W:*** Peter Hyams; ***M:*** Bruce Broughton.

The Narrows ½ **2008 (R)** Overly-familiar story finds Brooklyn-born Mike Manadoro (Zegers) needing money for college so his numbers-running dad Vinny (D'Onofrio) arranges some work with his mobster bosses. However, Mike runs into problems with a girl (Bush) and an old friend (Cahill) who'll get him into trouble. Adapted from Tim McLoughlin's novel "The Heart of the Old Country." **106m/C; DVD.** Kevin Zegers; Vincent D'Onofrio; Sophia Bush; Eddie Cahill; Titus Welliver; Monica Keena; Roger Rees; ***D:*** Francois Velle; ***W:*** Tatiana Blackington; ***C:*** Seamus Tierney; ***M:*** Richard (Rick) Marvin.

Nashville **1975 (R)** Altman's stunning, brilliant film tapestry that follows the lives of 24 people during a political campaign/music festival in Nashville. Seemingly extemporaneous vignettes, actors playing themselves (Elliott Gould and Julie Christie), funny, touching, poignant character studies concerning affairs of the heart and despairs of the mind. Repeatedly blurs reality and fantasy. **159m/C; VHS, DVD, Blu-Ray.** Keith Carradine; Lily Tomlin; Henry Gibson; Ronee Blakley; Keenan Wynn; David Arkin; Geraldine Chaplin; Lauren Hutton; Shelley Duvall; Barbara Harris; Allen Garfield; Karen Black; Christina Raines; Michael Murphy; Ned Beatty; Barbara Baxley; Scott Glenn; Jeff Goldblum; Gwen Welles; Bert Remsen; Robert DoQui; Elliott Gould; Julie Christie; Allan Nicholls; ***D:*** Robert Altman; ***W:*** Joan Tewkesbury; ***C:*** Paul Lohmann; ***M:*** Richard Baskin. Oscars '75: Song ("I'm Easy"); Golden Globes '76: Song ("I'm Easy"); Natl. Bd. of Review '75: Director (Altman), Support. Actress (Blakley); Natl. Film Reg. '92; N.Y. Film Critics '75: Director (Altman), Film, Support. Actress (Tomlin); Natl. Soc. Film Critics '75: Director (Altman), Film, Support. Actor (Gibson), Support. Actress (Tomlin).

Nasty Baby *Gaugua Cochina* **2015 (R)** Few films have ever survived a tonal shift as drastic as the one at the end of the second act of Sebastian Silva's dramedy and the controversial writer/director can't quite pull it off either. Silva plays Freddy, a filmmaker who wants to have a baby with his partner Mo (Tunde Adebimpe of TV on the Radio). They ask friend Polly (Kristen Wiig) to be the surrogate, and the majority of the film comically captures this impending, modern family. Then something tragic happens involving an aggressive man named The Bishop (Reg E. Cathey) on their block, and the film takes a hard left and never recovers. **101m/C; DVD, Streaming.** *CL US* Sebastian Silva; Kristen Wiig; Tunde Adebimpe; Reg E. Cathey; Mark Margolis; Alia Shawkat; ***D:*** Sebastian Silva; ***W:*** Sebastian Silva; ***C:*** Sergio Armstrong; ***M:*** Danny Bensi; Saunder Jurriaans.

The Nasty Girl ½ *Das Schreckliche Madchen* **1990 (PG-13)** A bright young German model plans to enter a national essay contest on the topic of her hometown's history during the Third Reich. While researching the paper, she's harassed and even brutalized, but refuses to cease her sleuthing. Excellent performances, tight direction, with comedic touches that charmingly imparts an important message. Based on a true story. In German with English subtitles. **93m/C; VHS, DVD.** *GE* Lena Stolze; Monika Baumgartner; Michael Gahr; ***D:*** Michael Verhoeven; ***W:*** Michael Verhoeven; ***C:*** Axel de Roche. British Acad. '91: Foreign Film; N.Y. Film Critics '90: Foreign Film.

Nasty Habits **1977 (PG)** Broad farce depicting a corrupt Philadelphia convent as a satiric parallel to Watergate, with nuns modeled on Nixon, Dean and Mitchell. Includes cameo appearances by various media personalities. Based on the British novel "The Abbess of Crewe" by Muriel Spark. **92m/C; DVD.** *UK* Glenda Jackson; Geraldine Page; Anne Jackson; Melina Mercouri; Sandy Dennis; Susan Penhaligon; Anne Meara; Edith Evans; Rip Torn; Eli Wallach; Jerry Stiller; ***D:*** Michael Lindsay-Hogg; ***W:*** Robert Enders; ***C:*** Douglas Slocombe; ***M:*** John Cameron.

Nasty Rabbit *Spies-A-Go-Go* **1964** Ridiculous spoof about Soviet spies intent on releasing a rabbit with a hideous Communist disease into the U.S. Everyone gets in on the chase: Nazi forces, cowboys and Indians, sideshow freaks, banditos—what is the point? **88m/C; VHS, DVD.** Arch Hall, Jr.; Micha(el) Terr; Liz Renay; John Akana; ***D:*** James Landis.

The Natalee Holloway Story **2009** Lifetime movie about the 2005 disappearance of Alabama teenager Natalee Holloway while on spring break in Aruba. Her mother Beth and her stepfather Jug Twitty head to the island when the case drags on and remains unsolved (Natalee's body is not found), suspects change their stories, and it seems that the police are involved in a cover-up to hide their incompetence. **96m/C; DVD.** Tracy Pollan; Grant Show; Catherine Dent; Amy Gumenick; Jacques Strydom; Sean Higgs; Sean Cameron Michael; ***D:*** Mikael Salomon; ***W:*** Teena Booth; ***C:*** Paul Gilpin; ***M:*** Christopher Ward. **CABLE**

Nate and Hayes ½ **1983 (PG)** Set during the mid-1800s in the South Pacific, the notorious real-life swashbuckler Captain "Bully" Hayes ("good pirate") helps young missionary Nate recapture his fiancee from a cutthroat gang of evil slave traders. Entertaining "jolly rogers" film. **100m/C; VHS, DVD.** *NZ* Tommy Lee Jones; Michael O'Keefe; Max Phipps; Jenny Seagrove; ***D:*** Ferdinand Fairfax; ***M:*** Trevor Jones.

Nathalie ½ **2003** Remarkably dull psycho-sexual tease finds Catherine (Ardant) distressed to learn that Bernard (Depardieu), her husband of 25 years, has been cheating. So Catherine hires a beautician/prostitute named Marlene (Beart) to become Bernard's sex partner and report back to her. In great detail. Oh, and Marlene should call herself Nathalie. French with subtitles. **105m/C; DVD.** *FR* Fanny Ardant; Emmanuelle Beart; Gerard Depardieu; ***D:*** Anne Fontaine; ***W:*** Anne Fontaine; Jacques Fieschi; ***C:*** Jean-Marc Fabre; ***M:*** Michael Nyman.

Nathalie Granger ½ **1972** Maybe Duras was trying to bore her audience to death with this experimental drama. Isabelle (Bose) and her nameless friend (Moreau) go through their dull daily housekeeping rituals moderately worried about getting Isabelle's apparently troubled young daughter Nathalie (Mascolo) into a new school. Depardieu shows up as a door-to-door salesman. French with subtitles. **79m/B; DVD.** *FR* Lucia Bose; Jeanne Moreau; Gerard Depardieu; Luce Garcia-Ville; Valerie Mascolo; ***D:*** Marguerite Duras; ***W:*** Marguerite Duras; ***C:*** Ghislan Cloquet.

The National Health **1973** Hit-and-miss satire of the British National Health System set in a rundown London hospital that's filled with equally crazy patients and staff. A number of actors play dual roles as there's also a send-up of a hospital-set TV soap opera called 'Nurse Norton's Affair.' Nichols adapted his own play. **97m/C; DVD.** *GB* Lynn Redgrave; Sheila Scott-Wilkinson; Eleanor Bron; Donald Sinden; Jim Dale; Neville Aurelius; Colin Blakely; ***D:*** Jack Gold; ***W:*** Peter Nichols; ***C:*** John Coquillon; ***M:*** Carl Davis.

National Lampoon Goes to the Movies **1981** Parodies of popular Hollywood genres, including cop thrillers, melodramas, and inspirational biographies, done in goofy "Lampoon" style. **89m/C; VHS, DVD.** Robby Benson; Candy Clark; Diane Lane; Christopher Lloyd; Peter Riegert; Richard Widmark; Henny Youngman; Bobby DiCicco; ***D:*** Henry Jaglom.

National Lampoon Presents Cattle Call **WOOF!** *Cattle Call* **2006 (R)** Like having a root canal without anesthetic. Losers Sherman, Glenn, and Richie live in L.A. so what better way to meet chicks than to pretend to be casting agents for an indie film and taking their pick from the actresses who show up? After a number of raunchy auditions, the guys each find their special someone, but when the ladies in question discover it was all a scam they are out for male body parts. **87m/C; DVD.** Diedrich Bader; Thomas Ian Nicholas; Jenny Mollen; Nicole Eggert; Andrew Kates; Jonathan Winters; Paul Mazursky; Chelsea Handler; ***D:*** Martin Guigui; ***W:*** Martin Guigui; ***C:*** Massimo Zeri; ***M:*** Cody Westheimer. **VIDEO**

National Lampoon Presents: Endless Bummer **2009 (R)** Another lackluster National Lampoon offering. A kid buys a custom made surfboard, gets it stolen, and goes looking for revenge. Various things happen and it becomes apparent his life is not destined for greatness. **105m/C; DVD.** Khan Chittenden; Colton James; Ray Santiago; Jane Leeves; Caitlin Wachs; Matthew Lillard; Jules Bruff; James Thomas; Joan Jett; Andy Fischer-Price; Michael Siebert; Jack Siebert; Andrew Carillo; Richmond Arquette; Kathleen Wilhoite; Allison Scagliotti; ***D:*** Sam Pillsbury; ***W:*** Affion Crockett; John J.D. Drury; Kevin Lyman; John F. Sullivan; The Greg Wilson; ***C:*** Chris Moseley; ***M:*** Jay Ferguson.

National Lampoon Presents RoboDoc *RoboDoc* **2008 (R)** Another lame effort from the franchise. Jason Dockery (Faustino) is hired by a healthcare company to build a robot doctor that can never make a misdiagnosis or medical mistake, all to thwart obnoxious lawyer Jake Gorman (Babel), who specializes in medical malpractice. But Jake thinks he can find a way to sue even a mechanical man. **90m/C; DVD.** David Faustino; Alan Thicke; Corin "Corky" Nemec; David DeLuise; Michael Winslow; Kenny Babel; William Haze; ***D:*** Stephen Maddocks; ***W:*** Doug Gordon; ***C:*** Stephen Campbell. **VIDEO**

National Lampoon's Adam & Eve *Adam & Eve* **2005 (R)** Raunchy, gross, yet amusing and occasionally intelligent sex comedy. Adam (Douglas) falls for virginal sorority babe Eve (Chriqui), who doesn't believe in putting out to keep some horny frat dude around. She's after true love and Adam waits . . . and waits. But both are pressured by their so-called friends (not to mention hormonal urges) to either consummate the relationship or break up. **91m/C; DVD.** Cameron Douglas; Emmanuelle Chriqui; Chad Lindberg; Courtney Peldon; Jake Hoffman; George Dzundza; Lisa Wilhoit; ***D:*** Jeff Kanew; ***W:*** Justin Kanew; ***C:*** John Darbonne. **VIDEO**

National Lampoon's Animal House ½ *Animal House* **1978 (R)** Classic Belushi vehicle running amuck. Set in 1962 and responsible for launching Otis Day and the Knights and defining cinematic food fights. Every college tradition from fraternity rush week to the homecoming pageant is irreverently and relentlessly mocked in this wild comedy about Delta House, a fraternity on the edge. Climaxes with the homecoming parade from hell. Sophomoric, but very funny, with a host of young stars who went on to more serious work. Remember: "Knowledge is good." **109m/C; VHS, DVD, Blu-Ray, UMD, HD-DVD.** John Belushi; Tim Matheson; John Vernon; Donald Sutherland; Peter Riegert; Stephen Furst; Bruce McGill; Mark Metcalf; Verna Bloom; Karen Allen; Tom Hulce; Mary Louise Weller; James Widdoes; Kevin Bacon; Doug Kenney; Martha Smith; Cesare Danova; Stephen Bishop; Sarah Holcomb; ***D:*** John Landis; ***W:*** Doug Kenney; Harold Ramis; Chris Miller; ***C:*** Charles Correll; ***M:*** Elmer Bernstein. Natl. Film Reg. '01.

National Lampoon's Christmas Vacation ½ *Christmas Vacation* **1989 (PG-13)** The third vacation for the Griswold family finds them hosting repulsive relatives for Yuletide. The sight gags, although predictable, are sometimes on the mark. Quaid is a standout as the slovenly cousin. **93m/C; VHS, DVD, Blu-Ray.** Chevy Chase; Beverly D'Angelo; Randy Quaid; Diane Ladd; John Randolph; E.G. Marshall; Doris Roberts; Julia Louis-Dreyfus; Mae Questel; William Hickey; Brian Doyle-Murray; Juliette Lewis; Johnny Galecki; Nicholas Guest; Miriam Flynn; ***D:*** Jeremiah S. Chechik; ***W:*** John Hughes; ***C:*** Thomas Ackerman; ***M:*** Angelo Badalamenti.

National Lampoon's Christmas Vacation 2: Cousin Eddie's Big Island Adventure 🦴🦴 *National Lampoon's Cousin Eddie's Christmas Vacation Lost; Christmas Vacation 2: Cousin Eddie; Christmas Vacation 2: Cousin Eddie's Island Adventure* **2003** Quaid is back as boorish Cousin Eddie. This time his nutty gaggle gets to spend the holidays on a South Pacific island as a payoff from his old boss for a monkey mishap. But their fateful trip instead ends up on an uncharted desert isle. Again, the lessons of "Caddyshack 2" and "Blues Brothers 2000" go tragically unheeded. **83m/C; VHS, DVD.** Randy Quaid; Miriam Flynn; Dana Barron; Jake Thomas; Beverly Garland; Stephen Furst; Eric Idle; Fred Willard; Ed Asner; Sung Hi Lee; Julian Stone; Kate Bradley; ***D:*** Nick Marck; ***W:*** Matty Simmons; ***M:*** Nathan Furst. **TV**

National Lampoon's Class Reunion **WOOF!** *Class Reunion* **1982 (R)** Class reunion with some very wacky guests and a decided lack of plot or purpose. Things go from bad to worse when a crazed killer decides to join in on the festivities. Disappointing with very few laughs. **85m/C; VHS, DVD, Blu-Ray.** Shelley Smith; Gerrit Graham; Michael Lerner; ***D:*** Michael Miller; ***W:*** John Hughes; ***C:*** Philip H. Lathrop; ***M:*** Peter Bernstein.

National Lampoon's Dad's Week Off 🦴🦴 *Dad's Week Off* **1997 (R)** Jack (Winkler) is a stressed-out salesman who decides he needs time away from both his job and his family. His wife agrees to take their kids camping while Jack spends a week peacefully at home. But before he knows it, Jack's bud (Jeni) has introduced him to kooky Cherice (d'Abo) and it's party-time at Jack's place. **92m/C; VHS, Streaming.** Henry Winkler; Olivia D'Abo; Richard Jeni; Justin Louis; Ken Pogue; Wendel Meldrum; ***D:*** Neal Israel; ***W:*** Neal Israel; ***C:*** Jan Kiesser; ***M:*** Marc Bonilla. **CABLE**

National Lampoon's Dirty Movie **WOOF!** *Dirty Movie* **2011 (R)** A series of dirty jokes are strung together with a flimsy plot about a low-budget producer who wants to make a movie about the filthiest jokes every told. You may hear a few new dirty jokes to share with your friends but if you want to see a good movie about a dirty joke, watch the 2005 documentary "The Aristocrats" and not this drivel. **91m/C; DVD.** Christopher Meloni; Robert Klein; Mario Cantone; Adam Ferrara; ***D:*** Christopher Meloni; Jerry Daigle; ***W:*** Tanner Colby; Alan Donnes; ***C:*** George Gibson; ***M:*** Joe Delia. **VIDEO**

National Lampoon's European Vacation 🦴 ½ *European Vacation* **1985 (PG-13)** Sappy sequel to "Vacation" that has witless Chase and his family bumbling around in the land "across the pond." The Griswolds nearly redefine the term "ugly American." Stonehenge will never be the same. **94m/C; VHS, DVD, Blu-Ray.** Chevy Chase; Beverly D'Angelo; Dana Hill; Jason Lively; Victor Lanoux; John Astin; William Zabka; Robbie Coltrane; Mel Smith; ***Cameo(s):*** Eric Idle; ***D:*** Amy Heckerling; ***W:*** John Hughes; Robert Klane; Eric Idle; ***M:*** Charles Fox.

National Lampoon's Gold Diggers **WOOF!** *Lady Killers* **2004 (PG-13)** Why does anyone bother releasing this tripe on the big screen when it barely qualifies for basic cable or direct-to-video? The gold diggers of the title are a couple of inept twenty-something con men (Friedle, Owen) who plot to marry two elderly sisters (Taylor, Lasser) who are supposed to be wealthy Beverly Hills heiresses. Only the gals (who are, of course, broke) have their own insurance scam in mind. Can't even be enjoyed as trash. **82m/C; DVD.** Will Friedle; Chris Owen; Louise Lasser; Renee Taylor; Nikki Ziering; ***D:*** Gary Preisler; ***W:*** Gary Preisler; ***C:*** Thomas Callaway.

National Lampoon's Golf Punks 🦴 ½ **1999 (PG-13)** Innocuous comedy finds luckless former golf pro Al Oliver (Arnold) in desperate need of cash to pay off his gambling debts. So, he becomes an instructor to a bunch of teen misfits and decides to enter the uncoordinated group in a prestigious tournament. **95m/C; VHS, DVD.** *CA* Tom Arnold; James Kirk; Rene Tardif; ***D:*** Harvey Frost; ***W:*** Jill Mazursky; ***C:*** Patrick Williams; ***M:*** Richard Bronskill. **VIDEO**

National Lampoon's Holiday Reunion 🦴 *Thanksgiving Family Reunion* **2003 (PG-13)** Think "Christmas Vacation" but without the Griswolds, or the funny. Thanksgiving stands in for Wally World, Europe, Christmas, and Vegas. Cousin Woodward—you, sir, are no Cousin Eddie! **90m/C; VHS, DVD.** Bryan Cranston; Judge Reinhold; Reece Thompson; Penelope Ann Miller; Hallie Todd; Brittney Irvin; Antony Holland; Noel Fisher; David Paetkau; ***D:*** Neal Israel; ***W:*** Marc Warren; ***M:*** Robert Folk; Brad Segal. **TV**

National Lampoon's Last Resort 🦴 *Last Resort* **1994 (PG-13)** Retired film actor finds his long-time movie nemesis can't separate screen life from the real thing anymore and is planning an invasion of the actor's private island. So, he calls on his nephew (who brings along a friend) to help him out. **91m/C; DVD.** Corey Feldman; Corey Haim; Geoffrey Lewis; Robert Mandan; ***D:*** Rafal Zielinski; ***W:*** Patrick Labyorteaux; ***C:*** Peter Benison; ***M:*** Ronald J. Weiss.

National Lampoon's Loaded Weapon 1 🦴 ½ *Loaded Weapon 1* **1993 (PG-13)** Cop Jack Colt (Estevez) and partner Wes Luger (Jackson) attempt to recover a microfilm which contains a formula for turning cocaine into cookies. Essentially a sendup of the popular "Lethal Weapon" series, although other movies and themes make an appearance, well sort of. Short on plot and long on slapstick, but that's the whole point. Tired formula creates nostalgia for the granddaddy of them all, "Airplane." Lots of cameos, including one from sibling spoof star Sheen. The magazine folded while the movie was in production, an ominous sign. **83m/C; DVD.** Emilio Estevez; Samuel L. Jackson; Jon Lovitz; Tim Curry; Kathy Ireland; William Shatner; Dr. Joyce Brothers; James Doohan; Richard Moll; F. Murray Abraham; Denis Leary; Corey Feldman; Phil Hartman; J.T. Walsh; Erik Estrada; Larry Wilcox; Allyce Beasley; Charlie Sheen; Frank McRae; Bill Nunn; Denise Richards; Paul Gleason; Beverly Johnson; Whoopi Goldberg; Bruce Willis; ***D:*** Gene Quintano; ***W:*** Don Holley; Gene Quintano; ***C:*** Peter Deming; ***M:*** Robert Folk.

National Lampoon's Ratko: The Dictator's Son 🦴 *Ratko: The Dictator's Son* **2009 (R)** Raunchy, stupid, copycat college comedy. Freshman foreign exchange student Ratko (Ramirez) throws his dictator dad's money around, transforming the dormitory into his own private palace. He falls for political activist Holly (Bowden) who informs the uninformed Ratko that his dad is a bad guy. So the sheltered son vows to make some changes—if he can stop indulging himself long enough to try. **82m/C; DVD.** Efren Ramirez; Katrina Bowden; Jeff(rey) Ballard; Adam West; Curtis Armstrong; Dennis Haskins; Charlie Fleischer; ***D:*** Savage Steve Holland; ***W:*** Robert Mittenthal; Mike Rubiner; ***C:*** William Barber. **VIDEO**

National Lampoon's Senior Trip 🦴 *Senior Trip* **1995 (R)** According to the promotion, "they came, they saw, they passed out." Good dumb fun is hard to come by, particularly here. Lesser "Lampoon" effort is about midwestern high school seniors who take a bus trip to Washington to meet the President. Along the way they have hijinks, including manipulation by a stereotypically corrupt senator out to embarrass his politcal opponent. Frewer is the inept principal who leads the hopelessly cliched group of misfits through the dopey corridors of power. **91m/C; DVD.** Matt Frewer; Valerie Mahaffey; Lawrence Dane; Thomas Chong; Kevin McDonald; ***D:*** Kelly Makin; ***W:*** I. Marlene King; Roger Kumble.

National Lampoon's The Don's Analyst 🦴🦴 *The Don's Analyst* **1997 (R)** Don Vito (Loggia) has lots of problems—his wife has left him, his sons are too stupid to take over the business, and his mob rival wants both his business and his wife. The Don's so upset he's thinking of going legit. Instead, his sons kidnap therapist Dr. Riceputo (Pollak) to straighten the Don out. **103m/C; Streaming.** Robert Loggia; Kevin Pollak; Joseph Bologna; Angie Dickinson; Sherilyn Fenn; ***D:*** David Jablin; ***W:*** David Hurwitz; ***C:*** Levie Isaacks. **CABLE**

National Lampoon's The Legend of Awesomest Maximus **WOOF!** *The Legend of Awesomest Maximus* **2011** Snickering, crude spoof of sword-and-sandal flicks. Lazy general Maximus and King Looney's not-so-manly son Orlando are sent from Troy to Greece to make nice with King Erotic. After Orlando and his new BFF, the king's wife Ellen, return to Troy together, it turns into a war with Maximus having to fight Greek warrior Testiclees. **91m/C; DVD.** Will Sasso; Rip Torn; Sophie Monk; Ian Ziering; Khary Payton; Gary Lundy; Kristanna Loken; ***D:*** Jeff Kanew; ***W:*** Jason Burinescu; ***C:*** John Darbonne; ***M:*** Scott Glasgow.

National Lampoon's The Stoned Aged **WOOF!** *Homo Erectus* **2007 (R)** No one actually expects a watchable film from anything slapped with this franchise label anymore, and this is no exception. Meek caveman Ishbo (Rifkin) tries to persuade his tribe to evolve (using tools and stuff) but they're not big on his radical ideas. And while Ishbo is angsting over his dream cavegirl Fardart (Larter), his big, dumb older brother Thudnik (MacArthur) just clubs the chick on the head and drags her back to the cave. **88m/C; DVD.** Adam Rifkin; Ali Larter; Hayes Macarthur; David Carradine; ***D:*** Adam Rifkin; ***W:*** Adam Rifkin; ***C:*** Scott Billups; ***M:*** Alex Wurman. **VIDEO**

National Lampoon's Vacation 🦴🦴🦴 *Vacation* **1983 (R)** The Clark Griswold (Chase) family of suburban Chicago embarks on a westward cross-country vacation via car to the renowned "Wally World." Ridiculous and hysterical misadventures, including a falling asleep at the wheel sequence and the untimely death of Aunt Edna. **98m/C; VHS, DVD, Blu-Ray, HD-DVD.** Chevy Chase; Beverly D'Angelo; Imogene Coca; Randy Quaid; Christie Brinkley; James Keach; Anthony Michael Hall; John Candy; Eddie Bracken; Brian Doyle-Murray; Eugene Levy; Dana Barron; Jane Krakowski; Miriam Flynn; Frank McRae; John Diehl; Mickey Jones; ***D:*** Harold Ramis; ***W:*** John Hughes; Harold Ramis; ***C:*** Victor Kemper; ***M:*** Ralph Burns.

National Lampoon's Van Wilder 🦴 *Van Wilder* **2002 (R)** Cliched and crass college comedy of suave coed Van Wilder (Reynolds) who gets cut off by his dad (Matheson), who realizes his son's seven college years have not yielded a degree. The universally adored, high-profile, frat house toastmaster then uses his charm to helps fund his education by helping the underprivileged undergrads meet women and have fun—for a price, of course. A circus of gross-out jokes and sight gags ensue. Reid is typically vapid as the lackluster Lois Lane college reporter and love interest. **92m/C; DVD, Blu-Ray, UMD.** Ryan Reynolds; Tara Reid; Tim Matheson; Kal Penn; Teck Holmes; Daniel Cosgrove; Deon Richmond; Alex Burns; Paul Gleason; Tom Everett Scott; Chris Owen; Curtis Armstrong; Kim Smith; Erik Estrada; Michelle Rene Thomas; ***D:*** Walt Becker; ***W:*** Brent Goldberg; David T. Wagner; ***C:*** James R. Bagdonas; ***M:*** David Lawrence.

National Lampoon's Van Wilder 2: The Rise of Taj **WOOF!** *Van Wilder 2: The Rise of Taj* **2006 (R)** Despite the title, Ryan Reynolds' Van Wilder is completely—and smartly—MIA as his former underling Taj Mahal Badalandabad (Penn) is all grown up and ready to tackle the countless and pointless sexual innuendo jokes that make up this aimless sequel. Taj goes off to Camford University in England as a student-teacher and gets his own crew of flunkies to whip into shape. They must prove themselves to the school's elite in order to win the coveted Camford Cup. Shamelessly—and poorly—rips off scenes from too many other movies to keep track of. So bad it makes the original look good. **95m/C; DVD.** Lauren Cohan; Daniel Percival; Glen Barry; Kal Penn; Anthony Cozens; Steven Rathman; Holly Davidson; ***D:*** Mort Nathan; ***W:*** David Gallagher; ***C:*** Hubert Taczanowski; ***M:*** Robert Folk.

National Security 🦴 ½ **2003 (PG-13)** Earl Montgomery (Lawrence, seeming surprisingly bored) is a police academy reject and Hank Rafferty (Zahn) is a disgraced cop. Working as security guards, they uncover a smuggling operation in standard buddy-cop fashion. What the problem is? Car chases and Lawrence's rapid-fire "comic" rantings replace any semblance of plot or direction to make a mess that wastes the time of all involved. But at least it has spiteful racial politics played for laughs. **90m/C; VHS, DVD.** Martin Lawrence; Steve Zahn; Eric Roberts; Bill Duke; Colm Feore; Timothy Busfield; Robine Lee; Matt McCoy; Brett Cullen; Stephen Tobolowsky; Joe Flaherty; ***D:*** Dennis Dugan; ***W:*** Jay Scherick; David Ronn; ***C:*** Oliver Wood; ***M:*** Randy Edelman.

National Treasure 🦴🦴 **2004 (PG)** Old-fashioned and underwhelming adventure tale. The legendary treasure of King Solomon supposedly made its way to colonial-era America where the Freemasons protected it. The treasure is a longtime obsession for Benjamin Franklin Gates (Cage), who thinks his best clue is concealed on the reverse side of the Declaration of Independence. When his sinister benefactor Howe (Bean) plots to steal the document, patriotic Ben and his techie sidekick Riley (Bartha) alert the authorities, including hottie conservator Abigail (Kruger). Many uninvolving twists and less-than-exciting action sequences follow. **130m/C; DVD, Blu-Ray, UMD.** Nicolas Cage; Diane Kruger; Justin Bartha; Sean Bean; Jon Voight; Harvey Keitel; Christopher Plummer; ***D:*** Jon Turteltaub; ***W:*** Jim Kouf; Marianne S. Wibberley; Cormac Wibberley; ***C:*** Caleb Deschanel; ***M:*** Trevor Rabin.

National Treasure: Book of Secrets 🦴🦴 ½ **2007 (PG)** Equally old-fashioned sequel to the 2004 treasure hunt. Ben Gates (Cage) and dad Patrick (Voight) defend the family honor from dastardly southerner Mitch Wilkinson (Harris), who insists a Gates ancestor was actually behind Lincoln's assassination. Interesting historical clues combine with a presidential book of secrets and a global hunt for missing gold to create an enjoyable adventure. Includes all the players from the original, along with new addition, Gates matriarch Emily (an admirably game Mirren). **124m/C; Blu-Ray.** Nicolas Cage; Jon Voight; Diane Kruger; Justin Bartha; Dame Helen Mirren; Harvey Keitel; Ed Harris; Bruce Greenwood; Alicia Coppola; Michael Maize; Timothy Murphy; Joel Gretsch; ***D:*** Jon Turteltaub; ***W:*** Cormac Wibberley; Marianne S. Wibberley; ***C:*** John Schwartzman; Amir M. Mokri; ***M:*** Trevor Rabin.

The National Tree 🦴🦴 ½ **2009** In this Hallmark Channel holiday drama, widower Corey Burdock plants a tree in honor of his late wife. When Corey decides to sell his Oregon property years later, the tree is to be bulldozed until it's chosen to be the official White House Christmas tree. Corey and his sullen teenaged son Rock are driving a big rig to deliver the tree in person accompanied by Faith, whose company bought Corey's land and is reaping the publicity, and Katie, Rock's video chat room friend who's blogging about their trip. **88m/C; DVD.** Andrew McCarthy; Evan Williams; Kari Matchett; Paula Brancati; ***D:*** Graeme Campbell; ***W:*** J.B. White; ***C:*** Francois Dagenais; ***M:*** Ian Thomas. **CABLE**

National Velvet 🦴🦴🦴🦴 **1944 (G)** Velvet Brown (Taylor) wins a horse in a raffle and is determined to train it to compete in the famed Grand National race with the help of her best friend, Mi (Rooney). Taylor, only 12 at the time, is superb in her first starring role. Rooney also gives a fine performance. Filmed with a loving eye on lushly decorated sets, this is a masterpiece version of the story of affection between a girl and her pet. Based on the novel by Enid Bagnold and followed by the dismal "International Velvet" in 1978. **124m/C; VHS, DVD.** Elizabeth Taylor; Mickey Rooney; Arthur Treacher; Donald Crisp; Anne Revere; Angela Lansbury; Reginald Owen; Norma Varden; Jackie "Butch" Jenkins; Terence (Terry) Kilburn; ***D:*** Clarence Brown; ***W:*** Helen Deutsch; Theodore Reeves; ***C:*** Leonard Smith; ***M:*** Herbert Stothart. Oscars '45: Film Editing, Support. Actress (Revere); Natl. Film Reg. '03.

Native Son 🦴🦴 **2019** Bigger Tom (an impressive Sanders) is a young African-American living in Chicago without a sense of direction. He works as a bike messenger and spends time with his family and girlfriend Bessie (Layne). His life changes when he is offered a job as a driver for the family of wealthy real estate developer Mr. Dalton (Camp). Most of his job involves watching over Dalton's spoiled college-age daughter Mary (Qualley), who convinces Bigger to let her stay out late. One night, events go wrong, impacting both their lives. An updated adaptation of the 1940 Richard Wright novel, the film looks good but the story is messy. **84m/C; DVD.** Ashton Sanders; Margaret Qualley; Nick Robinson; KiKi Layne; Bill Camp; *D:* Rashid Johnson; *W:* Suzan-Lori Parks; *C:* Matthew Libatique; *M:* Kyle Dixon; Michael Stein. **VIDEO**

The Nativity Story 1/2 **2006 (PG)** Faithful retelling of the events leading to the birth of Jesus, from the arrangement of Mary's (Castle-Hughes) marriage to Joseph (Isaac) to the Immaculate Conception to their journey to Bethlehem. A sort of kinder, gentler companion to Mel Gibson's "The Passion of the Christ," it conveys the hope that Jesus' arrival brings amid the mayhem caused by King Herod (Hinds). Though it plays mostly as a Sunday school lesson, director Hardwicke uses her skills as a former production designer to make the scenery gorgeous and detailed, and the teenage Castle-Hughes' performance is solid and mature. **102m/C; DVD, Blu-Ray.** Keisha Castle-Hughes; Shohreh Aghdashloo; Hiam Abbass; Shaun Toub; Oscar Isaac; Stanley Townsend; Ciaran Hinds; Alexander Siddig; Alessandro Giuggioli; Nadim Sawalha; Eriq Ebouaney; *D:* Catherine Hardwicke; *W:* Mike Rich; *C:* Elliot Davis; *M:* Mychael Danna.

The Natural **1984 (PG)** A beautifully filmed movie about baseball as myth. A young man, whose gift for baseball sets him apart, finds that trouble dogs him, particularly with a woman. In time, as an aging rookie, he must fight against his past to lead his team to the World Series, and win the woman who is meant for him. From the Bernard Malamud story. **134m/C; VHS, DVD, Blu-Ray.** Robert Redford; Glenn Close; Robert Duvall; Kim Basinger; Wilford Brimley; Barbara Hershey; Richard Farnsworth; Robert Prosky; Darren McGavin; Joe Don Baker; Michael Madsen; *D:* Barry Levinson; *W:* Roger Towne; Phil Dusenberry; *C:* Caleb Deschanel; *M:* Randy Newman.

Natural Born Killers **1994 (R)** An old script by Tarantino is resurrected by Stone and invested with its own unique subtle nuance and style. Controversial (natch, considering the director and writer) look at the way the media portrays criminals. Harrelson and Lewis are the lovestruck, white-trash serial killers who become tabloid-TV darlings, thanks to a sensationalistic press led by Downey Jr. Stone's dark and manic comment on America's fascination and revulsion with violence is strictly of the love it or leave it variety. Bloodshed galore, dazzling photography, and a dynamite soundtrack (with over 75 selections) add up to sensory overload. **119m/C; DVD, Blu-Ray.** Woody Harrelson; Robert Downey, Jr.; Juliette Lewis; Tommy Lee Jones; Richard Lineback; Tom Sizemore; Rodney Dangerfield; Rachel Ticotin; Arliss Howard; Russell Means; Denis Leary; Steven Wright; Pruitt Taylor Vince; *D:* Oliver Stone; *W:* Oliver Stone; *C:* Robert Richardson; *M:* Trent Reznor.

Natural Born Pranksters **2016 (R)** Prank-focused comedy from three YouTube stars. Each of the three stars organize and take part in numerous, epic pranks intended for the big screen. Focusing on social experiments, they involve bystanders in such pranks as framing people for crimes while playing on common stereotypes. **90m/C; DVD, Streaming, Download.** Roman Atwood; Vitaly Zdorovetskiy; Dennis Roady; Dave England; Tim Scanlon; *D:* Roman Atwood; Ben Pluimer; *W:* Roman Atwood; Vitaly Zdorovetskiy; Dennis Roady; *C:* Donny Anderson.

Natural City *Mo* **2003 (R)** It's now 2080, and the world has been painfully rebuilt after a devastating war. Humans are now served by cyborgs, but they are beginning to want rights of their own and are rebelling, so an elite military squad has been tasked with squashing them. But the squad's leader R (Ji-tae Yu) has fallen in love with his own cyborg, and is using AI chips stolen from dead cyborgs to save her life without the knowledge of his employers. **113m/C; DVD.** *NK* Ji-tae Yu; Jae-un Lee; Rin Seo; *D:* Byung-chun Min; *W:* Byung-chun Min; *C:* Byung-chun Min; *M:* Jun-kyu Lee.

Natural Enemy **1996 (R)** Unsuspecting married couple become the target of a disturbed man with a big secret. **88m/C; VHS, DVD.** Donald Sutherland; William McNamara; Lesley Ann Warren; Joe Pantoliano; Tia Carrere; *D:* Douglas Jackson; *W:* Kevin Bernhardt; *C:* Rodney Gibbons; *M:* Alan Reeves. **CABLE**

Natural Selection **2011 (R)** Long-married Linda White and her husband Abe are devout conservative Christians living in Houston. They are childless and when Abe has a stroke, Linda is shocked to learn he has been donating to a sperm bank for more than 20 years. Linda tracks down one of Abe's biological offspring in Tampa but Raymond is an antisocial lowlife with a criminal past (and present). Their road trip back to Texas provides revelations as the ever-chipper Linda tries to be welcoming to Raymond, who doesn't understand and can't quite believe she's sincere. **89m/C; DVD, Blu-Ray.** Matt O'Leary; Rachael Harris; John Diehl; Gayland Williams; Jon(athan) Gries; *D:* Robbie Pickering; *W:* Robbie Pickering; *C:* Steve Capitano Calitri; *M:* Curt Schneider.

Natural Selection 1/2 **2012 (R)** A comedy-drama about finding redemption and unexpectedly coming to terms with the past. Living in suburban Texas, Linda White (Harris) is a childless Christian with a dying husband, Abe (Diehl). Before his death, she learns that her husband has an illegitimate 23-year-old son Raymond (O'Leary) living in Florida. Though her world has been upended, she takes the journey to find Raymond and bring him home before her husband's death. Bringing Raymond back to Texas provides Linda with an interesting new perspective on the world and more self understanding. **90m/C; DVD, Blu-Ray, Streaming, Download.** Matt O'Leary; Rachael Harris; John Diehl; Gayland Williams; Jon(athan) Gries; *D:* Robbie Pickering; *W:* Robbie Pickering; *C:* Steven Capitano Calitri; *M:* Izler; Curt Schneider.

Nature Calls **2012 (R)** Randy (Patton Oswalt) and Kirk (Johnny Knoxville) are bitter rivals despite being brothers. This emotional rift leads Randy to kidnap Kirk's son (and his friends) and take him on a disastrous camping trip. **79m/C; DVD, Blu-Ray, Streaming.** Johnny Knoxville; Maura Tierney; Patton Oswalt; Rob Riggle; Patrice O'Neal; *D:* Todd Rohal; *W:* Todd Rohal; *C:* Steve Gainer; *M:* Ryan Miller; Joseph Stevens.

Nature of the Beast **1994 (R)** A businessman and a drifter are both hiding deadly secrets as police search for both a serial killer and the $1 million missing in a Vegas casino robbery. Just which man is involved in which crime? **91m/C; VHS, DVD.** Eric Roberts; Lance Henriksen; Brion James; *D:* Victor Salva; *W:* Victor Salva.

Nature of the Beast 1/2 **2007 (PG)** Silly ABC Family Channel flick about a young man with a hairy secret. Rich works for Animal Control but once a month—at the full moon—he retires to his cabin in the woods so he can turn into a werewolf in seclusion. Rich has managed to keep his secret from his overly-understanding fiance Julia but there's a problem since their wedding date is too close to his next transformation for comfort. **90m/C; DVD.** Eddie Kaye Thomas; Autumn Reeser; Eric Mabius; *D:* Rodman Flender; *W:* Bob Young; David Kendall; *C:* Kim Derko; *M:* Charles Sydnor. **CABLE**

Nature's Grave 1/2 *Long Weekend* **2008 (R)** Aussie horror/thriller is a misguided, overly-respectful remake of the far more terrifying 1978 film "Long Weekend." Sniping marrieds Peter (Caviezel) and Carla (Karvan) go camping on a holiday weekend. Their isolated beach campsite proves treacherous when their carelessness causes the local wildlife to go all eco-vengeance on their human butts. **88m/C; DVD.** *AU* James (Jim) Caviezel; Claudia Karvan; *D:* Jamie Blanks; *W:* Everett De Roche; *C:* Karl Von Moller; *M:* Jamie Blanks.

Naughty Marietta 1/2 **1935** A French princess switches identities with a mail-order bride to escape from her arranged marriage, and is captured by pirates. When she's saved by a dashing Indian scout, it's love at first sight. The first MacDonald-Eddy match-up and very popular in its day. **106m/B; VHS, DVD.** Jeanette MacDonald; Nelson Eddy; Frank Morgan; Elsa Lanchester; Douglass Dumbrille; Cecilia Parker; *D:* W.S. Van Dyke; *C:* William H. Daniels. Oscars '35: Sound; Natl. Film Reg. '03.

The Naughty Nineties **1945** Bud and Lou help a showboat owner fend off crooks in the 1890s. Usual slapstick shenanigans, but highlighted by verbal banter. Includes the first on-screen rendition of the classic "Who's on First?" routine. **72m/B; VHS, DVD.** Bud Abbott; Lou Costello; Henry Travers; Alan Curtis; Joseph (Joe) Sawyer; Rita Johnson; Joe (Joseph) Kirk; Lois Collier; *D:* Jean Yarbrough.

Nautilus **1999 (R)** In the year 2100, the planet has been destroyed by a series of cataclysisms caused by a scientific experiment, so a scientist decides to go back in time aboard a futuristic submarine in order to change the past and save the future. **90m/C; VHS, DVD.** Richard Norton; Hannes Jaenicke; Miranda Wolfe; *D:* Rodney McDonald; *W:* C. Courtney Joyner; *M:* David Wurst; Eric Wurst. **VIDEO**

Navajo Blues **1997 (R)** Police detective Nicholas Epps is installed in the federal witness protection program after seeing a mob hit on his partner. He's sent to a Native American reservation to hide out until the trial but can't resist investigating a series of local murders. **99m/C; VHS, DVD.** Steven Bauer; Irene Bedard; Charlotte Lewis; Ed O'Ross; Michael Horse; Tom Fridley; *D:* Joey Travolta; *C:* Dan Heigh.

Navajo Joe 1/2 **1967** The sole survivor of a massacre single-handedly kills each person involved in the atrocity, and aids a terrorized, though unappreciative, town in the process. Low-budget Spanish-Italian western only worth watching because of Reynolds. Filmed in Spain. **89m/C; VHS, DVD, Blu-Ray.** *IT SP* Burt Reynolds; Aldo Sambrell; Tanya Lopert; Fernando Rey; *D:* Sergio Corbucci; *M:* Ennio Morricone.

The Navigator **1988 (PG)** A creative time-travel story of a 14th-century boy with visionary powers who leads the residents of his medieval English village away from a plague by burrowing through the earth's core and into late-20th-century New Zealand. Quite original and refreshing. **92m/C; VHS, DVD.** *NZ* Hamish McFarlane; Bruce Lyons; Chris Haywood; Marshall Napier; Noel Appleby; Paul Livingston; Sarah Pierse; *D:* Vincent Ward; *W:* Vincent Ward. Australian Film Inst. '88: Cinematog., Director (Ward), Film.

The Navigators **2001 (R)** In 1995, British Rail is privatized and a portion of the South Yorkshire line is now serviced by two competing companies. The new owners break up the union system—some of the former workers decide to retire while others, including four friends, have to stick it out. Since fewer men are employed in maintaining the railway depot and lines, accidents increase and the increased stress just isn't professional but personal as well. **92m/C; VHS, DVD.** *GB GE SP* Steve Huison; Dean Andrews; Tom Craig; Joe Duttine; Venn Tracey; *D:* Ken Loach; *W:* Rob Dawber; *C:* Barry Ackroyd; Mike Eley; *M:* George Fenton.

Navy Blue and Gold 1/2 **1937** Three football-playing midshipmen (Young, Stewart, and Brown) at Annapolis share a friendship. Stewart has registered under a false name since his dad was unfairly cashiered from the service. When he hears some slander about his old man he stands up and tells the truth and gets suspended, just before the big game with Army. Naturally, he's reinstated just in time to make the big play and carry the team to victory. Well-done, old-fashioned hokum. **94m/B; VHS, DVD.** James Stewart; Robert Young; Tom Brown; Lionel Barrymore; Florence Rice; Billie Burke; Samuel S. Hinds; Paul Kelly; Frank Albertson; Minor Watson; *D:* Sam Wood; *W:* George Bruce.

Navy Blues 1/2 **1929** Haines successfully transitioned into sound with his first talkie but he played a familiar caddish role in this more drama-than-comedy tearjerker. Bad boy sailor Jack Kelly (Haines) gets shore leave and promptly romances Alice Brown (Page) whose family is extremely opposed to her seeing Jack. She leaves with him but gets dumped when Jack says he's not the marrying kind. When he finally comes to his senses he finds Alice's life has taken an unfortunate turn. **75m/B; DVD.** William Haines; Karl (Daen) Dane; Anita Page; Edythe Chapman; Wade Boteler; J.C. Nugent; *D:* Clarence Brown; *W:* W.L. River; Elliott Nugent; Dale Van Every; *C:* Merritt B. Gerstad.

Navy Blues 1/2 *Manners of the Sky* **1937** Bland military comedy. Sailor Rusty (Purcell) pretends to be in the Naval Academy to impress librarian Doris (Brian) but she knows he's lying. He lies again and tells her he's in naval intelligence, which gets them kidnapped by spies involved in an assassination plot. **77m/B; DVD.** Dick Purcell; Mary Brian; Warren Hymer; Joe Sawyer; Edward (Eddie) Woods; Horace McMahon; *D:* Ralph Staub; *W:* Eric Taylor; Gordon Kahn; *C:* Jack Marta.

Navy SEALS 1/2 **1990 (R)** A group of macho Navy commandos, whose regular work is to rescue hostages from Middle Eastern underground organizations, finds a stash of deadly weapons. They spend the balance of the movie attempting to destroy the arsenal. Sheen chews the scenery as a crazy member of the commando team. Lots of action and violence, but simplistic good guys-bad guys philosophy and plot weaknesses keep this from being more than below average. **113m/C; VHS, DVD.** Charlie Sheen; Michael Biehn; Joanne Whalley; Rick Rossovich; Cyril O'Reilly; Bill Paxton; Dennis Haysbert; Paul Sanchez; Ron Joseph; Nicholas Kadi; *D:* Lewis Teague; *W:* Gary Goldman; *C:* John A. Alonzo; *M:* Sylvester Levay.

Navy Seals vs. Zombies 1/2 **2015** An action-horror zombie film set in Baton Rouge, Louisiana. During a political campaign, the vice president (Fox) makes a stop in Baton Rouge, but the U.S. government loses contact with him. To find and rescue the vice president, a SEAL team that has recently returned from Afghanistan is sent into the city. They find that the Louisiana city is under siege by hordes of flesh-eating zombies and the infection that creates them is spreading fast. The SEALs must quickly complete their mission and make it out of the city alive, if they can. **97m/C; DVD, Blu-Ray, Streaming, Download.** Ed Quinn; Michael Dudikoff; Rick Fox; Molly Hagan; Kevin Kent; *D:* Stanton Barrett; *W:* Matthew Carpenter; *C:* Don E. Fauntleroy; *M:* Patrick De Caumette; Brian Jackson Harris; Drew Jordan; Justin Raines; Michael Wickstrom. **VIDEO**

Navy vs. the Night Monsters
WOOF! *Monsters of the Night* **1966** When horrifying, acid-secreting plant monsters try to take over the world, Van Doren and the Navy must come to the rescue, with the action taking place in a tropical South Pole setting. Amazing deployment of talents. **87m/C; VHS, DVD.** Mamie Van Doren; Anthony Eisley; Pamela Mason; Bobby Van; Russ Bender; *D:* Michael Hoey; *W:* Michael Hoey.

Navy Way **1944** Hurriedly produced war propaganda film in which a boxer gets inducted into the Navy just before his title shot. **74m/B; VHS, DVD.** Robert Lowery; Jean Parker; Roscoe Karns; William Henry; Robert Armstrong; Tom Keene; *D:* William Berke; *W:* Maxwell Shane; *C:* Fred H. Jackman, Jr.; *M:* Willy Stahl.

Ne Zha 1/2 *Ne Zha zhi mo tong jiang shi* **2019** At birth, Ne Zha (Yanting) was infused by the spirit gods with the evil spirit of Demon Pearl and is fated to be killed by a lightning bolt at the age of three. Since birth, Ne Zha has been an amoral, destructive superkid. To protect him, his wealthy parents have tried to keep him locked up in their compound. Though Ne Zha does not know his fate, he struggles with his destiny and his desire to be normal. The highest grossing non-U.S. film in history, the animated feature has a lush, shiny visual style and has a high-spirited energy. Mandarin with subtitles. **110m/C; DVD, Blu-Ray.** Yanting Lu; Jiongsensefu; Mo Han; Hao Chen; Qi Lu; *D:* Yu Yang; *W:* Yu Yang; *M:* Wan Pin Chu.

Nea 1/2 **1978 (R)** Comic drama about a young girl from a privileged home who writes a best selling pornographic novel anonymously. When her book writing talents are made public through betrayal, she gets even in a most unique way. Subtitled "A Young Emmanuelle." Kaplan also performs. Appealing and sophisticated. **101m/C; VHS, DVD.** Sami Frey; Ann Zacharias; Heinz Bennent; *D:* Nelly Kaplan.

Neapolitan Carousel *Carosello Napoletano* **1954** Musical structured after the Commedia del 'Arte, featuring ballet, opera, mime, and popular songs and dances. A family of street musicians travels to various towns where patriarch Salvatore (Stoppa) introduces the different pieces. These include Loren as a model of naughty postcards who falls in love with a soldier in WWI and a ballet starring Massine. Italian with subtitles. **124m/C; DVD.** *FR* Paolo Stoppa; Clelia Matania; Sophia Loren; Leonide Massine; Maria Fiore; Giacomo Rondinella; ***D:*** Ettore Giannini; ***W:*** Ettore Giannini; Remigio del Grosso; Guiseppe Marotta; ***C:*** Piero Portalupi; ***M:*** Raffaele Gervasio.

Near Dark **1987 (R)** Southwestern farm boy Caleb (Pasdar) is attracted to the pretty Mae (Wright) and falls in unwillingly with a family of thirsty, outlaw-fringe vampires who roam the West in a van. The first mainstream effort by Bigelow, and a rollicking, blood-saturated, slaughterhouse of a movie, with enough laughs and stunning imagery to revive the genre. **95m/C; VHS, DVD, UMD.** Adrian Pasdar; Jenny Wright; Bill Paxton; Jenette Goldstein; Lance Henriksen; Tim Thomerson; Joshua John Miller; ***D:*** Kathryn Bigelow; ***W:*** Kathryn Bigelow; Eric Red; ***C:*** Adam Greenberg; ***M:*** Tangerine Dream.

A Near-Death Experience 1/2 **2008** Ellie Daly can see and speak with the dead after a near-death experience. She's haunted by the angry ghost of Taylor Nicholson, who claims her husband Daniel murdered her in a custody battle over their son. Since the husband and kid are living in Ellie's apartment building, Taylor wants Ellie to bring Daniel to justice. Only maybe he's not guilty after all. A Lifetime Original movie. **96m/C; DVD.** Amy Acker; Steve Cumyn; Bronwen Booth; Robert Naylor; John Ralston; ***D:*** Don Terry; ***W:*** Helen Frost; Don MacLeod; ***C:*** Daniel Villeneuve; ***M:*** Claude Minot. **CABLE**

Nearing Grace **2005 (R)** In 1978, responsible high school senior Henry Nearing (Smith) is trying to cope with the death of his mother, while his dad (Morse) and older brother (Moscow) take to drinking, drugs, and reckless behavior. Henry can't see that his gal pal Merna (Johnson) is perfect for him and instead he pants after sexy tease Grace (Brewster), until he learns better. Smith and Johnson are a cute twosome but the story's familiar. Based on Scott Sommers' 1979 novel. **105m/C; DVD.** Gregory Edward Smith; Jordana Brewster; Ashley Johnson; David Moscow; David Morse; Chad Faust; Brian Murray; Logan Bartholomew; ***D:*** Rick Rosenthal; ***W:*** Jacob Aaron Estes; ***C:*** David Geddes; ***M:*** John E. Nordstrom.

Nearlyweds **2013** Hallmark Channel rom com finds newlyweds Erin, Casey, and Stella learning that a clerical error by the pastor who married them has annulled all their marriages. The three friends contemplate married life as Erin competes with mother-in-law Renee over husband Dave; Casey isn't sure about Nick's commitment; and career-minded Stella realizes Mark wants a stay-at-home wife. Should they marry again or take their situation as a sign to call it quits? **90m/C; DVD.** Danielle Panabaker; Jessica Parker Kennedy; Brittney Irvin; Ryan Kennedy; Travis Milne; Steve Bacic; Naomi Judd; ***D:*** Mark Griffiths; ***W:*** Aury Wallington; ***C:*** Eric Goldstein; ***M:*** Billy Lincoln. **CABLE**

Nebraska 1/2 **2013 (R)** Bitter alcoholic Woody (Dern, in a career-best performance), near the end of his life, finds purpose when he receives a sweepstakes lottery advising him that he may have won a million dollars. He travels to Lincoln, Nebraska to claim it, despite advice from son David (Forte) and wife Kate (Squibb) that such letters usually only lead to heartbreak. Along the way, addled dad and estranged son stop to reminisce in the town in which Woody was born and director Payne's film becomes a wistful love letter to small town life in the heartland. It's beautiful and bittersweet. **115m/B; DVD, Blu-Ray.** Bruce Dern; Will Forte; June Squibb; Bob Odenkirk; Stacy Keach; ***D:*** Alexander Payne; ***W:*** Bob Nelson; ***C:*** Phedon Papamichael; ***M:*** Mark Orton. Ind. Spirit '14: First Screenplay.

Necessary Parties **1988** Based on Barbara Dana's book that has a 15-year-old boy filing a lawsuit to stop his parents' divorce. Originally aired on PBS as part of the "Wonderworks" family movie series. **120m/C; VHS, DVD.** Alan Arkin; Mark-Paul Gosselaar; Barbara Dana; Adam Arkin; Donald Moffat; Julie Hagerty; Geoffrey Pierson; Taylor Fry; ***D:*** Gwen Arner.

Necessary Roughness **1991 (PG-13)** After losing their NCAA standing, the Texas Southern University (passing for the real Texas State) Armadillos football team looks like it's headed for disaster. The once proud football factory is now composed of assorted goofballs instead of stud players. But hope arrives in the form of a 34-year-old farmer with a golden arm, ready to recapture some lost dreams as quarterback. Can this unlikey team rise above itself and win a game, or will their hopes be squashed all over the field? **108m/C; VHS, DVD.** Scott Bakula; Robert Loggia; Harley Jane Kozak; Sinbad; Hector Elizondo; Kathy Ireland; Jason Bateman; ***D:*** Stan Dragoti; ***W:*** Rick Natkin; David Fuller; ***C:*** Peter Stein; ***M:*** Bill Conti.

Necessity 1/2 **1988** Lauren LaSalle (Anderson) is a model-turned-wife who discovers her wealthy husband is rich because he sells drugs. So she steals $2 million of his money, kidnaps their daughter, and for some reason assumes the repercussions will not be death by assassin. **93m/C; DVD.** Loni Anderson; Hank Baumert; John Heard; Sherman Howard; Kathryn Howell; Harris Laskawy; James Naughton; Deborah Pryor; ***D:*** Michael Miller; ***W:*** Brian Garfield; Michael Ahnemann; ***C:*** Rexford Metz; ***M:*** Johnny Harris. **TV**

Necromancer: Satan's Servant **1988 (R)** After a woman is brutally raped, she contacts a sorceress and makes a pact with the devil to ensure her successful revenge. Plenty of graphic violence and nudity. **90m/C; VHS, DVD.** Elizabeth Kaitan; Russ Tamblyn; Rhonda Dorton; ***D:*** Dusty Nelson; ***W:*** William T. Naud; ***C:*** Eric Cayla; Richard Clabaugh; ***M:*** Kevin Klinger; Bob Mamet; Gary Stockdale.

Necromentia 1/2 **2009** Disturbing set of seemingly unconnected tales about a vengeful demon, a professional torturer, and an obsessed lunatic hoping to ressurect his girlfriend. **85m/C; DVD, Blu-Ray, Streaming.** Layton Matthews; Chad Grimes; Santiago Craig; Zelieann Rivera; Cole Braxton; ***D:*** Pearry Reginald Teo; ***W:*** Pearry Reginald Teo; Stephanie Joyce; ***C:*** Darin Meyer; ***M:*** Timothy Andrew Edwards. **VIDEO**

Necropolis **1987 (R)** A witch burned at the stake 300 years ago is brought back to life as a motorcycle punkette in New York searching for a sacrificial virgin (in New York?). New wave horror should have been watchable. **77m/C; VHS, DVD.** Leeanne Baker; Michael Conte; Jacquie Fritz; William Reed; Paul Ruben; ***D:*** Tim Kincaid.

Ned Kelly 1/2 *Ned Kelly, Outlaw* **1970 (PG)** Dramatizes the life of Australia's most notorious outlaw. Kelly (Jagger) and his family start off as horse thieves and proceed from there. A manhunt results in death and the eventual capture and execution of Kelly. The very contemporary British Jagger was miscast as a period Australian and British director Richardson seems to have lacked an empathy for the material, given his lethargic direction. **100m/C; VHS, DVD, Blu-Ray.** *GB* Mick Jagger; Allen Bickford; Geoff Gilmour; Mark McManus; Serge Lazareff; Peter Sumner; Ken Shorter; James Elliott; Diane Craig; Sue Lloyd; Clarissa Kaye; ***D:*** Tony Richardson; ***W:*** Ian Jones; Tony Richardson; ***M:*** Shel Silverstein.

Ned Kelly 1/2 **2003 (R)** Another telling of the legend of Australian outlaw Ned Kelly (Ledger), based on the novel "Our Sunshine" by Robert Drewe. Kelly was falsely imprisoned for three years and faced such harassment from corrupt law officers that he took up bank robbery with a gang of four others and became a folk hero for the lower class. Ledger fits the role well but Orlando Bloom (as Kelly's Gang member Joe Byrne) is a true scene-stealer. Very genuine, well-made effort with a brutal final showdown between the police and the gang, but the presentation doesn't always flow well. **109m/C; DVD, Blu-Ray.** *AU* Heath Ledger; Orlando Bloom; Geoffrey Rush; Naomi Watts; Joel Edgerton; Laurence Kinlan; Kris McQuade; Emily Browning; Kiri Paramore; Rachel Griffiths; Charles "Bud" Tingwell; Peter Phelps; Russell Dykstra; ***D:*** Gregor Jordan; ***W:*** John Michael McDonagh; ***C:*** Oliver Stapleton; ***M:*** Klaus Badelt.

Need for Speed 1/2 **2014 (PG-13)** Too long, mindless crime drama adapted from Electronic Arts' racing videogame franchise. Mechanic Tobey Marshall (Paul) did time after being framed by ex-NASCAR driver Dino Brewster (Cooper). Tobey wants revenge by taking Dino down in a high-stakes underground race but this means a cross-country ride with a bounty on his head when Dino finds out. Tobey gets his old crew together, gets a sweet Shelby Mustang, some British babe (Poots) to ride with him, and it's time to burn some rubber. **130m/C; DVD, Blu-Ray.** Aaron Paul; Dominic Cooper; Imogen Poots; Michael Keaton; Rami Malek; Ramon Rodriguez; Scott Mescudi; Dakota Johnson; ***D:*** Scott Waugh; ***W:*** John Gatins; George Gatins; ***C:*** Shane Hurlbut; ***M:*** Nathan Furst.

Needful Things 1/2 **1993 (R)** Stephen King film adaptations are becoming as prolific as his novels, though few seem to improve in the transition from page to screen. This time a scheming Maine shopkeeper (Von Sydow) sells unsuspecting small towners peculiar items that, not surprisingly, begin to cause horror and mayhem. Harris is the town sheriff who tries to warn everyone that he's the devil in disguise. Big screen directorial debut for Heston (yes, Charlton's son). **120m/C; VHS, DVD, Blu-Ray.** Ed Harris; Bonnie Bedelia; Max von Sydow; Amanda Plummer; J.T. Walsh; William Morgan Sheppard; ***D:*** Fraser Heston; ***W:*** W.D. Richter; ***C:*** Tony Westman; ***M:*** Patrick Doyle.

Needle **2010 (R)** Ben Rutherford inherits a strange 18th-century wooden box that contains a mechanical device reputed to have voodoo powers. After the contraption is stolen, Ben's college friends start dying in grisly ways. He reunites with his estranged brother Marcus to figure out who has the box and how to stop the murders. **89m/C; DVD.** *AU* Michael Dorman; Travis Fimmel; Jane Badler; Ben Mendelsohn; John Jarratt; ***D:*** John V. Soto; ***W:*** John V. Soto; ***C:*** Stephen F. Windon; ***M:*** Jamie Blanks.

Nefertiti, Queen of the Nile **1964** Woman, married against her will, turns into Nefertiti. For fans of Italo-Biblical epics only. **97m/C; VHS, DVD.** *IT* Jeanne Crain; Vincent Price; Edmund Purdom; Amedeo Nazzari; Liana Orfei; ***D:*** Fernando Cerchio.

Negadon: The Monster from Mars 1/2 *Wakusei daikaiju Negadon* **2005** In 2025 a Japanese expedition to Mars returns with a rock formation that hatches into a giant crustacean of some sort that begins destroying Tokyo. The city's only hope is a robotics constructor devastated by an accident that cost him his daughter and his left eye. An homage to classic Japanese science fiction and giant robot films, containing many nods to films from the 1950s (especially "Godzilla"). The creators even take pains to make the animated film (one of the first films done completely in cgi) look like a grainy film from that era. Too bad it's so darn short. **70m/C; DVD.** *JP* Masafumi Kishi; Takuma Sasahara; Dai Shimizu; Akane Yumoto; ***D:*** Jun Awazu; ***W:*** Jun Awazu; ***C:*** Jun Awazu; ***M:*** Shingo Terasawa.

Negative Happy Chainsaw Edge 1/2 *Negatibu happi chenso ejji* **2008** Yosuke (Ichihara) is mourning his friend when he meets Eri (Seki) who is mourning her family. He falls in love, only to find out each night a monster called the Chainsaw Man falls down from the moon and tries to kill Eri who defends herself with supernatural martial arts skills. Blinded by love he decides to help her defeat the monster. **109m/C; DVD.** *JP* Hayato Ichihara; Itsuji Itao; Haruma Miura; Megumi Seki; Yosuke Asari; ***D:*** Takuji Kitamura; ***W:*** Tatsuhiko Takimoto; Hiroshi Kobayashi; ***C:*** Gen Kobayashi; ***M:*** Soulja; Tetsuya Takahashi.

The Negotiator 1/2 **1998 (R)** Police hostage negotiator Danny Roman (Jackson) has had his life destroyed by false accusations of theft and murder. So he decides to go after his accusers by taking the Chicago Internal Affairs Bureau staff (what else?) hostage. Chris Sabian (Spacey), a negotiator from another precinct, is Roman's only hope to save himself and find the real culprits. Jackson and Spacey are excellent in their scenes together, and the supporting cast does a fine job. Nice action sequences and suspenseful storyline make for a thrilling ride, as long as you don't contemplate the details for too long. **115m/C; VHS, DVD, Blu-Ray.** Samuel L. Jackson; Kevin Spacey; David Morse; Ron Rifkin; John Spencer; Regina Taylor; J.T. Walsh; Siobhan Fallon Hogan; Paul Giamatti; Paul Guilfoyle; Carlos Gomez; Nestor Serrano; ***D:*** F. Gary Gray; ***W:*** James DeMonaco; Kevin Fox; ***C:*** Russell Carpenter; ***M:*** Graeme Revell.

The Neighbor 1/2 **1993 (R)** See nice city couple John and Mary move to small town Vermont. See their nice retired obstetrician neighbor Myron welcome them. See Mary get pregnant and Myron take an obsessional interest. See John arrested for murder. See Mary left alone—except for Myron's tender care. **93m/C; VHS, DVD.** Linda Kozlowski; Ron Lea; Rod Steiger; Frances Bay; Bruce Boa; Jane Wheeler; ***D:*** Rodney Gibbons; ***W:*** Kurt Wimmer.

The Neighbor 1/2 **2007 (PG-13)** Jeff's (Modine) life starts unraveling when he learns his ex-wife is marrying his best friend and his apartment neighbor, real estate developer Christine (Laroque), is determined to drive him out so she can combine their spaces. Jeff finally agrees to move if Christine will attend the wedding with him and pretend to be his new girlfriend, but the festivities just happen to change their opinion of each other. **98m/C; DVD.** Matthew Modine; Michele Laroque; Edward Quinn; Gina Mantegna; Ann Cusack; Richard Kind; Krysten Leigh Jones; ***D:*** Eddie O'Flaherty; ***W:*** Eddie O'Flaherty; J.P. Davis; ***C:*** Michael Fimognari; ***M:*** Stephen (Steve) Edwards.

Neighboring Sounds *O Som ao Redor; Neighbouring Sounds* **2012** A middle class neighborhood in Brazil is sent into paroxysms of fear by a few petty crimes and hires a private security force to set themselves at ease. Instead it only seems to increase their anxiety as the film explores modern class divisions. **131m/C; DVD, Blu-Ray.** *BR* Ana Rita Gurgel; Caio Almeida; Maeve Jinkings; Dida Maia; Felipe Bandeira; ***D:*** Kleber Mendonca Filho; ***W:*** Kleber Mendonca Filho; ***C:*** Pedro Sotero; Fabricio Tadeu; ***M:*** DJ Dolores.

Neighbors **1981 (R)** The Keeses (Belushi and Walker) live in a quiet, middle-class suburban neighborhood where life is calm and sweet. But their new neighbors, Ramona and Vic (Aykroyd and Moriarty), prove to be loud, obnoxious, crazy, and free-loading. Will Earl and Enid Keese mind their manners as their neighborhood disintegrates? Some funny moments, but as the script fades, so do the laughs. Belushi's last waltz is based on Thomas Berger's novel. **90m/C; VHS, DVD, Blu-Ray, Streaming.** John Belushi; Dan Aykroyd; Kathryn Walker; Cathy Moriarty; ***D:*** John G. Avildsen; ***W:*** Larry Gelbart; ***M:*** Bill Conti.

Neighbors 1/2 **2014 (R)** A simple concept—family life vs. frat life—gets an injection of successful comedy energy from a great cast, led by Rogen as a family man who watches as a fraternity sprouts up next to him. Mac (Rogen) has to confront the frat, headed up by the rambunctious Teddy Sanders (Efron), as wild parties are thrown and the neighborhood's level of maturity takes a dive. The film smartly doesn't overplay the differences between the two leads, rather highlighting their similarities. Mac secretly wants to party all night more than deal with a crying baby. It's a bit juvenile, but in a good way. **97m/C; DVD, Blu-Ray.** Seth Rogen; Rose Byrne; Zac Efron; Dave Franco; Christopher Mintz-Plasse; Lisa Kudrow; ***D:*** Nicholas Stoller; ***W:*** Andrew J. Cohen; Brendan O'Brien; ***C:*** Brandon Trost; ***M:*** Michael Andrews.

Neighbors 2: Sorority Rising **2016 (R)** What's less funny than the same joke told again? We don't laugh if we know the punchline, and this follow-up to the 2014 comedy hit features too many of the same punchlines, even if the gender dynamic has been cleverly switched up. Mac (Rogen) and Kelly (Byrne) are trying to sell their home when a sorority moves in next door (led by Moretz) and causes havoc yet again. The dynamic of "old vs. young" is played for laughs yet again, and the film gets a bunch of 'em, but you won't shake the feeling that you've seen this before. **92m/C; DVD, Blu-Ray.** Kiersey Clemons; Beanie Feldstein; Seth Rogen; Zac Efron; Rose Byrne; Chloë Grace Moretz; Ike Barinholtz; *D:* Nicholas Stoller; *W:* Seth Rogen; Nicholas Stoller; Andrew Jay Cohen; Brendan O'Brien; Evan Goldberg; *C:* Brandon Trost; *M:* Michael Andrews.

Neil Gaiman's NeverWhere 🦴🦴 1/2 *NeverWhere* **1996** Ordinary Londoner Richard Mayhew never before realized there's an extraordinary world beneath his feet. Until he helps an injured mystery woman named Door. The next morning Richard's world is turned upside down—no one he knows remembers him and he's now jobless and homeless. When Richard finds his way into London Below, he sees Door again and discovers a feudal society and much strangeness as he tries to get back to his old reality. **180m/C; DVD.** *GB* Gary Bakewell; Laura Fraser; Hywel Bennett; Clive Russell; Paterson Joseph; Trevor Peacock; Freddie Jones; Peter Capaldi; Stratford Johns; *D:* Dewi Humphreys; *W:* Neil Gaiman; Lenny Henry; *C:* Steve Murray; Steve Saunderson; *M:* Brian Eno. **TV**

Neil Young: Heart of Gold 🦴🦴🦴 **2006 (R)** Demme shot two acoustic concert performances by Young at Nashville's fabled Ryman Auditorium on August 18 and 19, 2005, where Young featured songs from his new album "Prairie Wind" as well as some old favorites. In April of that year, Young had been diagnosed with a life-threatening brain aneurysm and wrote and recorded the album before his surgery. The concerts were the first after his recovery. **103m/C; DVD.** *D:* Jonathan Demme; *C:* Ellen Kuras; *M:* Neil Young.

Neither Heaven Nor Earth 🦴🦴 1/2 *Ni le ciel ni la terre* **2016** War as Hell is something certainly seen before but this latest effort reimagines the end of conflict as a supernatural Purgatory. The excellent Renier plays Antares Bonassieu, a French captain in Afghanistan in the final days of a mission there. Hardly anything happens for days at a time. A shepherd entering the neutral zone is the highlight of a week. But then Antares' men start disappearing. Have the enemies taken them? Or is there something more insidious at play? Cogitore's thriller builds great tension through simple framing, but ends with more of a fizzle than a bang. **100m/C; DVD.** Jeremie Renier; Swann Arlaud; Marc Robert; Kévin Azaïs; Finnegan Oldfield; *D:* Clément Cogitore; *W:* Clément Cogitore; *C:* Sylvain Verdet; *M:* Eric Bentz; Francoise-Eudes Chanfrault.

Neither the Sea Nor the Sand 🦴 1/2 **1973** Unhappily married Anna takes a holiday on the Isle of Jersey where she falls in love with the local lighthouse keeper. He suddenly dies, but returns to haunt Anna. Or maybe she's just crazy. **116m/C; DVD.** *GB* Susan Hampshire; Frank Finlay; Jack Lambert; Michael Petrovitch; *D:* Fred Burnley; *W:* Gordon Honeycombe; *C:* David Muir; *M:* Nachum Heiman.

Nekromantik 🦴🦴 **1987** How much can we say—not to everyone's taste? How's this: a romantic story of necrophilia. Followed by "Nekromantik 2." In German with English subtitles. **74m/C; VHS, DVD, Blu-Ray.** *GE* Daktari Lorenz; Harald Lundt; Henri Boeck; Clemens Schwenter; Holger Suhr; Jorg Buttgereit; Monika M.; *D:* Jorg Buttgereit; *W:* Jorg Buttgereit; Franz Rodenkirchen; *C:* Uwe Bohrer; *M:* Herman Kopp.

Nekromantik 2 🦴🦴 1/2 **1991** Includes highlights from the first "Nekro"; the sequel picks up with a new nekro-chick who obtains the head of Rob, the jilted necrophile of the previous movie. Slicker than its predecessor, with less non-stop shock and a little more plot. In German with English subtitles. **100m/C; VHS, DVD, Blu-Ray.** *GE* Monika M.; Mark Reeder; Simone Sporl; Wolfgang Muller; *D:* Jorg Buttgereit; *W:* Jorg Buttgereit; Franz Rodenkirchen; *C:* Manfred O. Jelinski; *M:* Herman Kopp; Daktari Lorenz.

Nell 🦴🦴 1/2 **1994 (R)** "Wild child" story—adult version. When illiterate, barely verbal backwoods Nell (Foster) is discovered after her stroke-afflicted mother's death, she's placed in the care of a doctor (Neeson) and psychologist (Richardson) who have different ideas about how to bring her into society. Unfairly dismissed by some as self-indulgent, Foster's raw, physical performance is truly mesmerizing; dull script, unconvincingly tidy ending, and gross over-sentimentality are what disappoint. From the play "Idioglossia" by Mark Handley. **114m/C; VHS, DVD.** Jodie Foster; Liam Neeson; Natasha Richardson; Richard Libertini; *D:* Michael Apted; *W:* William Nicholson. Screen Actors Guild '94: Actress (Foster).

Nelly et Monsieur Arnaud 🦴🦴🦴 *Nelly and Mr. Arnaud* **1995** Chatty adult May/December would-be romance between 25-year-old secretary Nelly (Beart) and Pierre Arnaud (Serrault), the mid-60s retired magistrate for whom she's working. The arrogant divorced Arnaud is intrigued by the independent Nelly, whom he finds he can't control, while she comes to appreciate their emotional ties (altogether different from the selfishness of the younger men she knows). Conclusion avoids a neat resolution to a situation beset by bad timing. French with subtitles. **105m/C; VHS, DVD, Blu-Ray.** *IT GE FR* Emmanuelle Beart; Michel Serrault; Jean-Hugues Anglade; Francoise Brion; Claire Nadeau; Michael (Michel) Lonsdale; Charles Berling; Michele Laroque; *D:* Claude Sautet; *W:* Jacques Fieschi; Claude Sautet; *C:* Jean-Francois Robin; *M:* Philippe Sarde. Cesar '96: Actor (Serrault), Director (Sautet).

Nelson Algren: The End Is Nothing, the Road Is All 🦴🦴 **2015** A feature-length biographical documentary on American mid-twentieth century writer Nelson Algren. The author of The Man with the Golden Arm, Algren is widely considered a unique literary voice but one that is often misunderstood. The documentary examines his life, work, and impact, including his love affair with Simone de Beauvoir. Also featured are interviews with such authors as Kurt Vonnegut and Studs Terkel, rare archival footage, and the voice of the author himself. **86m/C; DVD.** *D:* Mark Blottner; Ilko Davidov; Denis Mueller; *W:* Mark Blottner; Ilko Davidov; Denis Mueller; *C:* Mark Blottner; Denis Mueller; Judy Hoffman; *M:* Richard Biethan; Warren Leming; David Maddox. **VIDEO**

Nemesis 🦴 1/2 **1993 (R)** Futuristic thriller that combines cybernetics and cyborgs in post-nuclear Los Angeles. Gruner plays a human (although he's mostly composed of mechanical replacement parts) in a world overwrought with system cowboys, information terrorists, bio-enhanced gangsters, and cyborg outlaws. Film's biggest flaw is the extremely confusing script that makes no attempt at logic whatsoever. Special visual effects are good despite the obviously low f/x budget. **95m/C; VHS, DVD, Blu-Ray.** Olivier Gruner; Tim Thomerson; Cary-Hiroyuki Tagawa; Merle Kennedy; Yuji Okumoto; Marjorie Monaghan; Nicholas Guest; Vincent Klyn; *D:* Albert Pyun; *W:* Rebecca Charles; *C:* George Mooradian; *M:* Michel Rubini.

Nemesis 4: Cry of Angels 🦴 **1997 (R)** Alex (Price) is an assassin in the year 2082. When she mistakenly kills the son of crimelord Bernardo (Divoff), a bounty is placed on her head. Cartoonish dreck. **80m/C; VHS, DVD, Blu-Ray.** Sue Price; Norbert Weisser; Andrew Divoff; Simon Poland; Nicholas Guest; *D:* Albert Pyun; *W:* Albert Pyun; *C:* George Mooradian. **VIDEO**

Nemesis Game 🦴🦴 1/2 **2003 (R)** Vern (Paul) is a comic-book store owner who introduces introverted college student Sara (Pope) to a mysterious game that involves finding various riddles located in out-of-the-way places and answering them to move on to the next clue. But then Sara notices when she solves a riddle, people start to die. **91m/C; VHS, DVD.** *CA* Adrian Paul; Carly Pope; Brendan Fehr; Jay Baruchel; Ian McShane; Rena Owen; Vanessa Guy; Brian Rhodes; *D:* Jesse Warn; *W:* Jesse Warn; *C:* Aaron Morton; *M:* Matthew Fletcher. **VIDEO**

Nenette and Boni 🦴🦴🦴 **1996** Boni (Colin) is a 19-year-old pizza chef in Marseilles who likes to have sexual fantasies about the local baker's sensuous wife (Bruni-Tedeschi). His life is basically carefree until his pregnant, rebellious 15-year-old sister Nenette (Houri) shows up at his door, having run away from school. Nenette really doesn't want to deal with the pregnancy until Boni forces her to do so and, just to make the teens lives more complicated, their estranged small-time gangster dad (Nolot) has learned about Nenette's condition and wants to help her out. Fine performances. French with subtitles. **103m/C; DVD.** *FR* Gregoire Colin; Alice Houri; Valeria Bruni-Tedeschi; Jacques Nolot; Vincent Gallo; Gerard Meylan; Alex Descas; Jamila Farah; Christine Gaya; *D:* Claire Denis; *W:* Claire Denis; Jean-Pol Fargeau; *C:* Agnes Godard.

Neo Ned 🦴🦴 **2005** Unusual romantic drama that involves mental hospitals and the Aryan Brotherhood. Ned (Renner) is a lost soul without a stable family life as a child. He joins the Aryan Brotherhood, becomes involved in a racially motivated murder, and is committed to a mental institution. Struggling to control his emotions, Ned's world is turned upside down when Rachael (Union) is admitted to the same institution. A young black woman, she believes she is possessed by Adolf Hitler's spirit. Ned initially makes fun of Rachael, but the pair soon find common ground. **97m/C; DVD.** Jeremy Renner; Gabrielle Union; David E. Allen; Michael Shamus Wiles; Sally Kirkland; Tim Boughn; *D:* Van Fischer; *C:* Chris Manley; *M:* Manish Raval; Tom Wolfe. **VIDEO**

The Neon Bible 🦴🦴 **1995** Beautifully crafted, yet thin telling of the struggles of a rural family in 1940s Georgia. Unfolding in a series of flashbacks as a 15-year-old boy travels alone on a train, reflecting on his dysfunctional early adolescence. An abusive father (Leary) who dies in the war, suicidal mom (Scarwid), and ex-showgirl visiting aunt (Rowlands) provide plenty of opportunities for familial angst. Starts out strong, but director Davies never ventures far from the narrative territory he's covered thoroughly in his other films. Adapted from the novel by Pulitzer Prize winning author John Kennedy Toole. **92m/C; DVD.** Gena Rowlands; Jacob Tierney; Diana Scarwid; Drake Bell; Denis Leary; Leo Burmester; Frances Conroy; Peter McRobbie; Joan Glover; Dana Dick; Virgil Graham Hopkins; *D:* Terence Davies; *W:* Terence Davies; *C:* Michael Coulter.

The Neon Demon 🦴🦴 1/2 **2016 (R)** Nicolas Winding Refn takes no prisoners and offers no concessions to standard moviemaking in his bold, daring look at the fashion industry. Jesse (Fanning) is a naturally beautiful girl thrust into the world of models who will do anything to get ahead (captured by Malone, Heathcote, and Lee). As men fawn over Jesse, the women around her grow increasingly jealous. And as Jesse begins to realize the power her beauty gives her, true danger closes in. Refn's film is violent, twisted, and pretentious. Your enjoyment comes down to how much pretension you can forgive. **118m/C; DVD, Blu-Ray.** Elle Fanning; Karl Glusman; Jena Malone; Bella Heathcote; Abbey Lee; Keanu Reeves; Christina Hendricks; *D:* Nicolas Winding Refn; *W:* Nicolas Winding Refn; Mary Laws; Polly Stenham; *C:* Natasha Braier; *M:* Cliff Martinez.

Neon Maniacs WOOF! **1986 (R)** An even half-dozen fetish-ridden zombies stalk the streets at night, tearing their victims into teensy weensy bits. Brave teenagers try to stop the killing. Brave viewers will stop the tape. **90m/C; VHS, DVD, Blu-Ray.** Allan Hayes; Leilani Sarelle Ferrer; Bo Sabato; Donna Locke; Victor Elliot Brandt; *D:* Joseph Mangine.

Neon Signs 🦴 1/2 **1996** Otis (Ashley) was abandoned as a child at a rundown motel in the Arizona desert. As a teen he dreams of Los Vegas and sets off to find it, only to be picked up by two aging female criminals on their way to hook up with a con man who intends to swindle a high stakes poker game. *CNT **91m/C; DVD.** William (Bill) Smith; Carol Lynley; Barbara McNair; *D:* Marc Kolbe; *W:* Lazar Saric; *C:* Howard Wexler; *M:* Tim May.

The Nephew 🦴🦴 **1997** Part culture clash, part melodrama. Teenager Chad (Harper) heads to Inis Dora, a small island off the Irish coast, in order to fulfill his mother Karen's last request—that her ashes be scattered in her homeland. Karen was long estranged from her family and they're shocked to discover that Chad's father is black. Everyone tries to make the best of the situation but Chad's would-be romance with Aislin (McGuckin), whose father Joe (Brosnan) once loved Karen, causes a lot of friction. **104m/C; VHS, Streaming.** *IR* Hill Harper; Aislin McGuckin; Pierce Brosnan; Donal McCann; Sinead Cusack; Lorraine Pilkington; *D:* Eugene Brady; *W:* Jacqueline O'Neill; Sean P. Steele; *C:* Jack Conroy; *M:* Stephen McKeon.

Neptune Factor 🦴 *The Neptune Disaster; An Underwater Odyssey* **1973 (G)** Scientists board a special new deep-sea sub to search for their colleagues lost in an undersea earthquake. Diving ever deeper into the abyss that swallowed their friend's Ocean Lab II, they end up trapped themselves. The plot's many holes sink it. **94m/C; VHS, DVD, Blu-Ray.** Ben Gazzara; Yvette Mimieux; Walter Pidgeon; Ernest Borgnine; *D:* Daniel Petrie; *W:* Jack DeWitt.

Neptune's Daughter 🦴🦴 **1949** A swim-happy bathing suit designer finds romance and deep pools of studio water to dive into. Typically lavish and ridiculous Williams aqua-parade. **92m/C; VHS, DVD.** Esther Williams; Red Skelton; Ricardo Montalban; Betty Garrett; Keenan Wynn; Xavier Cugat; Ted de Corsia; Mike Mazurki; Mel Blanc; Juan Duvall; George Mann; Joi Lansing; *D:* Edward Buzzell; *C:* Charles Rosher. Oscars '49: Song ("Baby It's Cold Outside").

Nerolio 🦴🦴 **1996** Three imagined episodes depicting the final months of an unnamed poet/director (Cavicchioli), who is actually based on homosexual writer/filmmaker Pier Paolo Pasolini. The contradictory, hypocritical, aging Poet is shown buying sex, while extolling the virtues of male beauty in voiceover, and as the maker of his own doom (Pasolini was murdered in 1975). "Nerolio" is a contraction of "nero" (black) and "Petrolio" (oil), which refers to Pasolini's posthumous novel "Petrolio." Italian with subtitles. **82m/B; VHS, DVD.** *IT* Marco Cavicchioli; Vincenzo Crivello; Salvatore Lazzaro; *D:* Aurelio Grimaldi; *W:* Aurelio Grimaldi; *C:* Maurizio Calvesi; *M:* Maria Soldatini.

Neruda 🦴🦴 1/2 **2016 (R)** Pablo Larrain's other 2016 biopic (besides "Jackie") is an equally unusual approach to a legendary figure with slightly less successful results. Famous Chilean politician/poet/Communist Pablo Neruda (Gnecco) is in hiding in 1948 and hunted by Chief of Police Oscar Peluchonneau (Bernal) after criticizing President Gabriel Gonzalez Videla (Castro). Sort of hunted. It turns out the detective is actually a lyrical creation of Neruda's in a film that blends history and poetry in a unique, engaging way. It meanders for about an hour, but the end is so interesting that it justifies the patience to get there. **107m/C; DVD.** Gael Garcia Bernal; Luis Gnecco; Mercedes Morán; Emilio Gutierrez-Caba; Diego Muñoz; *D:* Pablo Larrain; *W:* Guillermo Calderon; *C:* Sergio Armstrong; *M:* Federico Jusid.

Nerve 🦴🦴 1/2 **2016 (PG-13)** High school senior Vee (Roberts) gets drawn into an online game called Nerve. In the game, one can be a "player" or a "watcher." The latter basically gives dares to the former, winning cash and fame for doing more and more extreme stunts around New York City. As the insecure Vee comes out of her shell, the true danger of Nerve becomes clear, and Vee meets a charismatic male player named Ian (Franco) with whom she'll have to work to survive the ultimate challenges. The concept of young people pushing boundaries isn't new but this is more engaging than most. **96m/C; DVD, Blu-Ray.** Emma Roberts; Dave Franco; Emily Meade; Miles Heizer; Juliette Lewis; *D:* Henry Joost; Ariel Schulman; *W:* Jessica Sharzer; *C:* Michael Simmonds; *M:* Rob Simonsen.

Nervous Ticks 🦴🦴 1/2 **1993 (R)** Ninety minutes in the life of airline employee York Daley. All he needs to do is get off work, go home, grab his luggage, pick up his married girfriend, and get back to the airport for a flight to Rio De Janeiro. Simple, right? Not in this movie. **95m/C; VHS, Streaming.** Bill Pullman; Julie Brown; Peter Boyle; James LeGros; Brent Jennings; *D:* Rocky Lang; *W:* David Frankel.

The Nest 🦴🦴 1/2 **1988 (R)** A small island is overcome by giant cockroaches created by, you guessed it, a scientific experiment gone wrong. Special effects make it watchable. **89m/C; VHS, DVD, Blu-Ray.** Robert Lansing; Lisa Langlois; Franc Luz; Terri Treas; Stephen Davies; Diana Bellamy; Nancy Morgan; *D:* Terence H. Winkless; *W:* Robert King; *C:* Ricardo Jacques Gale; *M:* Rick Conrad.

The Nest *Nid de guepes; Wasps' Nest* **2002 (R)** A French Special Forces officer is assigned to escort an Albanian crime lord to trial when his men attack the convoy holding him. She decides they will hide out in a warehouse, which is unfortunate, as a group of thieves have picked that night to rob it. Pretty soon both thieves and cops are teaming up to fight for their lives. **105m/C; DVD.** *FR* Samy Naceri; Benoît Magimel; Nadia Fares; Pascal Greggory; Sami Bouajila; Anisia Uzeyman; Richard Sammel; Valerio Mastandrea; Martial Odone; Alexandre Hamidi; Angelo Infanti; Martin Amic; ***D:*** Florent Emilio Siri; ***W:*** Florent Emilio Siri; Jean-Francois Tarnowski; ***C:*** Giovanni Fiore Coltellacci; ***M:*** Alexandre Desplat.

The Nesting ½ **1980 (R)** Too-long tale of a neurotic author who rents a haunted Victorian manor and finds herself a pawn in a ghostly plan for revenge. Features Grahame's last performance. **104m/C; VHS, DVD, Blu-Ray.** Robin Groves; John Carradine; Gloria Grahame; Christopher Loomis; Michael David Lally; ***D:*** Armand Weston; ***C:*** Joao Fernandes.

The Net ½ **1995 (PG-13)** The ever-spunky Bullock gets stuck behind a computer screen rather than the wheel of a bus as reclusive computer systems analyst Angela Bennett. She's puzzled by a mysterious Internet program, which Angela finds can easily access highly classified databases. It's soon apparent that someone knows she knows because every record of her identity has been erased and the conspirators decide to take care of one last detail by eliminating her as well. Miller's the ex she turns to for help and Northam's a seductive British hacker. Techno paranoia. **114m/C; VHS, DVD, Blu-Ray.** Sandra Bullock; Jeremy Northam; Dennis Miller; Diane Baker; Ken Howard; Wendy Gazelle; Ray McKinnon; ***D:*** Irwin Winkler; ***W:*** John Brancato; Michael Ferris; ***C:*** Jack N. Green; ***M:*** Mark Isham.

The Net 2.0 **2006 (R)** Computer systems analyst Hope (DeLoach) takes a job in Istanbul where her identity is stolen and she's framed for criminal activities that land her in prison. But no, it's not a babes-behind-bars flick (more's the pity), it's a lame go-on-the-run-and-prove-you're-innocent adventure. **93m/C; DVD.** Nikki Deloach; Keegan Connor Tracy; Demet Akbag; Neil Hopkins; ***D:*** Charles Winkler; ***W:*** Rob Cowan; ***C:*** S. Douglas Smith; ***M:*** Stephen Endelman. **VIDEO**

Net Games **2003 (R)** Married Adam (Howell) is just looking for a little fantasy fun when he logs on to a website called cyber-chat. He thinks it's all eye candy and no risk—especially when he meets seductive Angel (Sloatman). Too bad she's your basic psycho-babe, who soon has Adam involved in blackmail and murder. **97m/C; VHS, DVD.** C. Thomas Howell; Lala Sloatman; Ed Begley, Jr.; Marina Sirtis; Samuel Ball; Lochlyn Munro; Maeve Quinlan; Monique Demers; Joan Van Ark; ***D:*** Andrew Van Slee; ***W:*** Andrew Van Slee; ***C:*** Kristian Bernier; ***M:*** William Richter. **VIDEO**

Netherbeast Incorporated **2007** A horror comedy set in the corporate world. Berm-Tech Industries is run by vampires who have kept their secret for more than 100 years. But when the head of the firm falls ill, he decides to hire some humans, who are soon wondering about their co-workers (the stake through the heart may be a give-away). **93m/C; DVD.** Dave Foley; Jason Mewes; Darrell Hammond; Judd Nelson; Steven Burns; Amy Davidson; Robert Wagner; ***D:*** Dean Ronalds; ***W:*** Bruce Dellis; ***C:*** Stefan von Bjorn; ***M:*** Tim Clark. **VIDEO**

Netherworld ½ **1990 (R)** A young man investigating his mysterious, dead father travels to his ancestral plantation in the bayou. To his horror, he discovers that his father was involved in the black arts. Now two beautiful young witches are after him. Can he possibly survive this madness? **87m/C; VHS, DVD.** Michael C. Bendetti; Denise Gentile; Anjanette Comer; Holly Floria; Robert Burr; Robert Sampson; ***D:*** David Schmoeller; ***W:*** Billy Chicago; ***C:*** Adolfo Bartoli; ***M:*** Edgar Winter.

Network ½ **1976 (R)** As timely now as it was then; a scathing indictment of the TV industry and its propensity towards self-prostitution. A television newscaster's mental breakdown turns him into a celebrity when the network tries to profit from his illness. The individual characters are startlingly realistic and the acting is excellent. **121m/C; VHS, DVD.** Faye Dunaway; Peter Finch; William Holden; Robert Duvall; Wesley Addy; Ned Beatty; Beatrice Straight; Lane Smith; Conchata Ferrell; William Prince; Ted (Theodore) Sorel; Lance Henriksen; Marlene Warfield; ***D:*** Sidney Lumet; ***W:*** Paddy Chayefsky; ***C:*** Owen Roizman. Oscars '76: Actor (Finch), Actress (Dunaway), Orig. Screenplay, Support. Actress (Straight); AFI '98: Top 100; British Acad. '77: Actor (Finch); Golden Globes '77: Actor--Drama (Finch), Actress--Drama (Dunaway), Director (Lumet), Screenplay; L.A. Film Critics '76: Director (Lumet), Film; Natl. Film Reg. '00; N.Y. Film Critics '76: Screenplay; Writers Guild '76: Orig. Screenplay.

Nevada Smith **1966** The half-breed Nevada Smith (previously introduced in Harold Robbins' story "The Carpetbaggers" and film of same name) seeks the outlaws who killed his parents. Standard western plot, characters. Later remade as a TV movie. **135m/C; VHS, DVD.** Steve McQueen; Karl Malden; Brian Keith; Arthur Kennedy; Raf Vallone; Suzanne Pleshette; Paul Fix; Pat Hingle; Janet Margolin; Howard da Silva; John Doucette; Gene Evans; Val Avery; Lyle Bettger; ***D:*** Henry Hathaway; ***W:*** John Michael Hayes; ***C:*** Lucien Ballard; ***M:*** Alfred Newman.

The Nevadan ½ *The Man From Nevada* **1950** A marshal goes in search of an outlaw's gold cache, only to be opposed by a crooked rancher. Good scenery and action, but not one of Scott's best. **81m/C; VHS, DVD.** Randolph Scott; Dorothy Malone; Forrest Tucker; Frank Faylen; George Macready; Charles Kemper; Jeff Corey; Tom Powers; Jock Mahoney; ***D:*** Gordon Douglas; ***W:*** Rowland Brown; George W. George; ***C:*** Charles Lawton, Jr.; ***M:*** Arthur Morton.

Never a Dull Moment **1968 (G)** Mobsters mistake an actor for an assassin in this gag-filled adventure. They threaten the thespian into thievery, before the trouble really starts when Ace, the actual assassin, arrives. **90m/C; VHS, DVD.** Dick Van Dyke; Edward G. Robinson; Dorothy Provine; Henry Silva; Joanna Moore; Tony Bill; Slim Pickens; Jack Elam; ***D:*** Jerry Paris; ***W:*** A.J. Carothers; ***M:*** Robert F. Brunner.

Never Again **2001 (R)** The best thing is seeing a radiant fiftysomething Clayburgh back on the big screen. Divorcee Grace (Clayburgh) winds up meeting cute with exterminator/jazz musician Christopher (Tambor). Both vow to maintain a no-strings relationship, no matter how great the sex is, though they can't help becoming emotionally involved. Unfortunately, the film is often more contrived and crude than romantic. **97m/C; VHS, DVD.** Jill Clayburgh; Jeffrey Tambor; Michael McKean; Caroline Aaron; Sandy Duncan; Bill Duke; ***D:*** Eric Schaeffer; ***W:*** Eric Schaeffer; ***C:*** Tom Ostrowski; ***M:*** Amanda Kravat.

Never Back Down **2008 (PG-13)** Mild-mannered teen Jake Tyler (Faris) is set off by the school bully's trash talk, exploding into an ugly fist fight. Soon after, boxing trainer Jean (Honsou) takes Jake under his wing, teaching him the ways of the sport and the meaning of self-respect, eventually leading to an inevitable rematch with the bully. And, yes, he wins the girl, rehashing "The Karate Kid" and countless other underdog sports dramas. Oddly preaches a message of non-violence while cheering on Jake's bloody bare-knuckle beat-downs. **110m/C; DVD.** Sean Faris; Amber Heard; Djimon Hounsou; Leslie Hope; Cam Gigandet; Evan Peters; Wyatt Smith; ***D:*** Jeff Wadlow; ***W:*** Chris Hauty; ***C:*** Lukas Ettlin; ***M:*** Michael Wandmacher.

Never Back Down 2: The Beatdown ½ **2011 (R)** Four fighters train together under ex-con and former mixed martial arts star Case Walker (White) but ultimately have to fight each other to succeed in an underground, pay-per-view tournament. White is the only one with any acting ability as the others seem to have been chosen for their fighting skills and looking decent while shirtless and sweaty. **104m/C; DVD.** Michael Jai White; Dean Geyer; Alex Meraz; Scottie Epstein; Evan Peters; Todd Duffee; ***D:*** Michael Jai White; ***W:*** Chris Hauty; ***C:*** Yaron Levy; ***M:*** David Wittman. **VIDEO**

Never Back Down: No Surrender **2016 (R)** The follow-up to Never Back Down 2 focuses on a former champion seeking glory once again. After a new, powerful MMA league forms that wants its fighters to use performance-enhancing drugs, former MMA champion Case Walker (White) focuses on small regional matches and continues his winning ways. An old friend and gifted fighter, Brody James (Barnett) is training in Thailand for a big fight against the undefeated Caesar Braga (Jones). Case goes to Thailand to help him train, but Brody is injured and the promoter (Morales) successfully pressures Case into fighting in his place on his own terms. **101m/C; DVD, Streaming, Download.** Michael Jai White; Josh Barnett; Gillian White; Esai Morales; Nathan Jones; ***D:*** Michael Jai White; ***W:*** Michael Jai White; ***C:*** Ross W. Clarkson. **VIDEO**

Never Been Kissed **1999 (PG-13)** Lightweight and logic-defying, Barrymore's producing debut hypothesizes that the people who were unpopular in high school want another chance at it. Not. Still-nerdy newspaper copyeditor Josie is assigned to go undercover as a student and write about high school life. She see it as a chance to now be one of the "cool kids." When it turns out that not much has changed for her, she enlists the help of her brother (Arquette) and a coworker (Shannon), and eventually falls for sensitive teacher Sam (Vartan). Barrymore is sweet, but it might be more enjoyable if you're actually high school age. **107m/C; DVD, Blu-Ray.** Drew Barrymore; David Arquette; Leelee Sobieski; Michael Vartan; Molly Shannon; John C. Reilly; Garry Marshall; Sean M. Whalen; Jeremy Jordan; Marley Shelton; Jordan Ladd; Jessica Alba; Carmen (Lee) Llywelyn; ***D:*** Raja Gosnell; ***W:*** Abby Kohn; Marc Silverstein; ***C:*** Alex Nepomniaschy; ***M:*** David Newman.

Never Been Thawed **2005** Mockumentary follows the obsessions of the members of the Mesa Frozen Entree Enthusiasts' Club (frozen food addicts) and their leader, Shawn Anderson (Anders). Besides his obsession with frozen entrees, Shawn has converted to Christianity and fronts a once hardcore punk band that has turned into a Christian rock group so they can increase their music sales. Easy targets, lame humor. **87m/C; DVD.** John Morris; Sean Anders; ***W:*** John Morris; Sean Anders; Le Vinus Chuck; ***C:*** Sean Anders; ***M:*** Sean Anders; Thomas Laufenberg.

Never Cry Werewolf **2008** List how many other movies this flick reminds you of (it'll keep you from nodding off from boredom). Sixteen-year-old Loren becomes obsessed with spying on her new neighbor Jared, especially when it seems all his dates go missing. Suspecting Jared turns furry at the full moon, Loren goes to Redd Tucker, the host of a cheesy local TV hunting show, for help in tracking Jared. **87m/C; DVD.** Kevin Sorbo; Peter Stebbings; Nina Dobrev; Spence Van Wyck; Sean O'Neill; Melanie Leishmann; ***D:*** Brenton Spencer; ***W:*** David Benullo; ***C:*** Curtis Petersen; ***M:*** Michael Richard Plowman. **VIDEO**

Never Cry Wolf ½ **1983 (PG)** A young biologist is sent to the Arctic to study the behavior and habitation of wolves, then becomes deeply involved with their sub-society. Based on Farley Mowat's book. Beautifully photographed. **105m/C; VHS, DVD.** Charles Martin Smith; Brian Dennehy; Samson Jorah; ***D:*** Carroll Ballard; ***W:*** Curtis Hanson; Sam Hamm; ***C:*** Hiro Narita; ***M:*** Mark Isham. Natl. Soc. Film Critics '83: Cinematog.

Never Die Alone ½ **2004 (R)** Vicious drug dealer King David (DMX) pays the price for his deeds when he is fatally stabbed. Struggling writer Paul (Arquette) inherits King David's possessions, including a stack of audiotapes detailing the events of his wretched life (which provide the at-times tedious narrative), but Paul doesn't realize how dangerous a predicament this is. Director Dickerson presents some powerful images and purposefully avoids garnering sympathy for his lead while DMX is engrossing as the suave seducer/violent hoodlum. Based on the 1974 novel by ex-con Donald Goines. **88m/C; DVD, UMD.** DMX; Michael Ealy; Antwon Tanner; David Arquette; Clifton Powell; Tommy (Tiny) Lister; Aisha Tyler; Michele Shay; Reagan Gomez-Preston; Damion Poitier; Jennifer Sky; Drew Sidora; ***D:*** Ernest R. Dickerson; ***W:*** James Gibson; ***C:*** Matthew Libatique; ***M:*** DMX; George Duke.

Never Down **2006** Latino con Rico (LaSardo) is fresh out of the joint after a five-year stint. He's hoping his ex-wife will allow him access to their young daughter but new forces conspire to send him back down that criminal path. Vonnegut (in his last role) makes a brief appearance as a benefactor. **82m/C; DVD.** Robert LaSardo; Mary Kelsey; ***Cameo(s):*** Kurt Vonnegut, Jr.; James Toback; ***D:*** Robert Oppel. **VIDEO**

Never Forever ½ **2007 (R)** New York housewife Sophie (Farmiga) is married to Korean-American lawyer Andrew (McInnis), though there has always been tension within his family over their mixed-marriage and the pressure for them to have a child. Andrew is probably sterile and, after his father dies, he attempts suicide. A desperate Sophie meets poor illegal immigrant Jihah (Ha) and impulsively says she'll pay him for sex until she conceives. Jihah resents Sophie's businesslike attitude but she can't really suppress her emotional needs for long. Lots of nudity but writer/director Kim never makes her story salacious. English and Korean with subtitles. **104m/C; DVD.** *NK* Vera Farmiga; Jung-woo Ha; David L. McInnis; ***D:*** Gina Kim; ***W:*** Gina Kim; ***C:*** Matthew Clark; ***M:*** Michael Nyman.

Never Forget **1991** True story of California resident Mel Mermelstein (played by Nimoy), a survivor of Hitler's death camps who accepted a pro-Nazi group's challenge to prove in court that the Holocaust of six million Jews really happened. A sincere, well-meaning courtroom drama that just can't surmount the uncinematic nature of the source material. Made for TNT. **94m/C; DVD.** Leonard Nimoy; Blythe Danner; Dabney Coleman; ***D:*** Joseph Sargent; ***W:*** Ronald Rubin; ***C:*** Kees Van Oostrum; ***M:*** Henry Mancini. **CABLE**

Never Forget ½ **2008 (R)** But Frank (Phillips) already did, which is the problem. He wakes up alone and bloodied in the woods without any idea of how he got there. But when his best friend Andy (Holden-Ried) accuses him of a vicious murder, Frank better find the answers. **83m/C; DVD.** Lou Diamond Phillips; Kris Holden-Ried; Sarah Manninen; Jonathan Whittaker; James Byron; ***D:*** Leo Scherman; ***W:*** Mark Steinberg; ***C:*** Marcus Elliott; ***M:*** Eric Cadesky; Nick Dyer. **VIDEO**

Never Give a Sucker an Even Break ½ *What a Man* **1941** An almost plotless comedy, based on an idea reputedly written on a napkin by Fields (he took screenplay credit as Otis Criblecoblis), and features Fields at his most unleashed. It's something of a cult favorite, but not for all tastes. Classic chase scene ends it. Fields' last role in a feature-length film. **71m/B; VHS, DVD.** W.C. Fields; Gloria Jean; Franklin Pangborn; Leon Errol; Margaret Dumont; Susan Miller; ***D:*** Edward F. (Eddie) Cline; ***W:*** W.C. Fields; John Thomas "Jack" Neville; Prescott Chaplin; ***C:*** Charles Van Enger; ***M:*** Frank Skinner.

Never Goin' Back **2018 (R)** A week in the life of two teen girls from the wrong side of the tracks in Fort Worth, Texas. Angela (Mitchell) takes best friend Jessie (Morrone) to the beach to celebrate her 17th birthday. The pair works at a diner and lives with several deadbeat male housemates. Angela's plan is challenged when she and Jessie are thrown in jail after their home is robbed and they lose their jobs. As Angela schemes desperately to pay for the trip, they cannot even pay their rent. This appealing indie and its leads celebrate female friendship in ways that are both outrageous and sweet. **85m/C; DVD, Blu-Ray.** Maia Mitchell; Camila Morrone; Kyle Mooney; Joel Allen; Kendal Smith; ***D:*** Augustine Frizzell; ***W:*** Augustine Frizzell; ***C:*** Greta Zozula; ***M:*** Sarah Jaffe.

Never Grow Old ½ **2019 (R)** Undertaker/carpenter/Irish immigrant Patrick Tate (Hirsch) lives with his family in a grim but peaceful town on the California Trail called Garlow. The town's way of life is disrupted when outlaw Dutch Albert (Cusack) moves in. Ignoring the local ban on liquor, Dutch opens a saloon, then turns it into a brothel. Dutch also kills people, which leads to more business for Patrick. As Dutch takes an interest in Patrick, the pair forms an unlikely alliance that has far-reaching consequences for them both. A revisionist Western, it's nothing to write home about, though a different take on the genre as it considers the role of the Irish in the West. **100m/C; DVD, Blu-Ray.** Emile Hirsch; Antonia Campbell-Hughes; Danny (Daniel) Webb; Deborah Francois; ***D:*** Ivan Kavanagh; ***W:*** Ivan Kavanagh; ***C:*** John Cusack; Piers McGrail; ***M:*** Aza Hand; William Slattery; Gast Waltzing.

Never Let Go 🦴🦴 **1960** A man unwittingly tracks down the mastermind of a gang of racketeers. Sellers sheds his comedic image to play the ruthless and brutal gang boss, something he shouldn't have done. **91m/C; VHS, DVD.** *GB* Peter Sellers; Richard Todd; Elizabeth Sellars; Carol White; ***D:*** John Guillermin; ***M:*** John Barry.

Never Let Me Go 🦴🦴 **1/2 1953** Implausible yet entertaining account of American newsman Gable trying to smuggle ballerina wife Tierney out of Russia. Hard to believe Gable as a one-man assault force infiltrating Russia, but enjoyable nonetheless. Based on the novel "Came the Dawn" by Roger Bax. **94m/B; DVD.** Clark Gable; Gene Tierney; Richard Haydn; Bernard Miles; Kenneth More; Karel Stepanek; Theodore Bikel; ***D:*** Delmer Daves; ***W:*** Ronald Millar; George Froeschel; ***C:*** Robert Krasker; ***M:*** Hans May.

Never Let Me Go 🦴🦴 **2010 (R)** Ambitious and dour alternate reality drama adapted from the Kazuo Ishiguro novel. Kathy, Tommy, and Ruth grow up in an isolated British boarding school where it's quickly known that they are cloned children raised for the sole purpose of organ donation. They are shown at three different stages in their lives (beginning in 1978) with a romantic triangle developing between the young adult Kathy (Mulligan), Tommy (Garfield), and Ruth (Knightley). **103m/C; Blu-Ray.** *GB* Carey Mulligan; Andrew Garfield; Keira Knightley; Charlotte Rampling; Sally Hawkins; Kate Bowes Renna; Oliver Parsons; David Sterne; Isobel Meikle-Small; Ella Purnell; Charlie Rowe; ***D:*** Mark Romanek; ***W:*** Alex Garland; ***C:*** Adam Kimmel; ***M:*** Rachel Portman.

Never Look Away 🦴🦴🦴 *Werk ohne Autor* **2018 (R)** In 1930s Germany, young Kurt (Cohrs) is greatly impacted when he is taken to a Nazi exhibition of "degenerate art." Unable to study art until after the war, adult Kurt (Schilling) finds that the Communist rulers of East Germany are also limiting study to Socialist Realism. As Kurt finds his own artistic voice over the years, he grapples with the limitations placed on him and his family. Based loosely on German artist Gerhard Richter, it's overly long but offers insight into an artist discovering his voice and vision and the wider effects of oppression on people and society. **189m/C; DVD.** Tom Schilling; Sebastian Koch; Paula Beer; Saskia Rosendahl; Oliver Masucci; ***D:*** Florian Henckel von Donnersmarck; ***W:*** Florian Henckel von Donnersmarck; ***C:*** Caleb Deschanel; ***M:*** Max Richter.

Never Love a Stranger 🦴🦴 **1958** A young man becomes a numbers runner for a mobster and ultimately winds up heading his own racket. Later he finds himself in conflict with his old boss and the district attorney. No surprises here. Based on the Harold Robbins' novel. **93m/B; VHS, DVD.** John Drew (Blythe) Barrymore, Jr.; Steve McQueen; Lita Milan; Robert Bray; ***D:*** Robert M. Stevens.

Never Met Picasso 🦴🦴 **1/2 1996** Thirty-year-old artist Andrew (Arquette) lives with self-absorbed actress/mom Genna (Kidder) in Boston, struggling with both his lack of work and romantic prospects. Andrew's one consolation is gay Uncle Alfred (Epstein), who serves as a role model. Until, unexpectedly, Andrew meets confident Jerry (McKellar) at his mother's dreadful opening night bash. After Alfred dies suddenly, Andrew discovers some hidden photos of his uncle's lover and seeks to make connections between the past and the present. **97m/C; VHS, DVD.** Alexis Arquette; Margot Kidder; Don McKellar; Alvin Epstein; Georgia Ringsdale; ***D:*** Stephen Kijak; ***W:*** Stephen Kijak; ***C:*** David Tames; ***M:*** Kristen Hersh.

Never on Sunday 🦴🦴🦴 **1960** An American intellectual tries to turn a Greek prostitute into a refined woman. Fine performances and exhilarating Greek photography. Fun all around. **91m/B; VHS, DVD.** *GR* Melina Mercouri; Titos Vandis; Jules Dassin; Mitsos Liguisos; ***D:*** Jules Dassin; ***W:*** Jules Dassin; ***M:*** Manos Hadjidakis. Oscars '60: Song ("Never on Sunday"); Cannes '60: Actress (Mercouri).

Never on Tuesday 🦴 **1/2 1988 (R)** Two jerks from Ohio head to California and find themselves stuck midway in the desert with a beautiful girl, who has plans of her own. **90m/C; VHS, Streaming.** Claudia Christian; Andrew Lauer; Peter Berg; ***Cameo(s):*** Charlie Sheen; Emilio Estevez; ***D:*** Adam Rifkin; ***W:*** Adam Rifkin.

Never Rarely Sometimes Always 🦴🦴🦴 **2020 (PG)** Quiet 17-year-old Autumn (Flanigan) is pregnant. Though she is a talented singer, she is full of melancholy and her only friend is her cousin, Skylar (Ryder). When Autumn decides to get an abortion, she travels from her home state of Pennsylvania, which requires parental consent, to New York, which does not. Though she does not have much money, she convinces Skylar to take the bus with her to New York City where they encounter unexpected setbacks as Autumn seeks to get the procedure. Writer-director Hittman's powerful, realistic drama is highlighted by genuine performances by the leads. **101m/C; DVD.** Talia Ryder; Sidney Flanigan; Sharon Van Etten; Ryan Eggold; Mia Dillon; ***D:*** Eliza Hittman; ***W:*** Eliza Hittman; ***C:*** Helene Louvart; ***M:*** Julia Holter.

Never Say Die 🦴🦴 **1/2 1939** Wealthy John Kidley (Hope) is at the Swiss spa of Bad Gasswasser, thinking he only has a few weeks to live. So he marries Mickey Hawkins (Raye) to save her from a crazy Russian, Prince Smirnov (Mowbray), and ends up fighting a duel! Oh, and Mickey thinks she's in love with bus driver Henry Munch (Devine), who accompanies the duo on their honeymoon. Much silliness. Based on the play by William H. Post. **82m/B; VHS, DVD.** Bob Hope; Martha Raye; Alan Mowbray; Andy Devine; Gale Sondergaard; Monty Woolley; Sig Rumann; ***D:*** Elliott Nugent; ***W:*** Preston Sturges; Don Hartman; Frank Butler; ***C:*** Leo Tover.

Never Say Die 🦴🦴 **1994 (R)** Ex-Special Forces soldier John Blake (Zagarino), ambushed and left to die, returns to seek vengeance on the renegade commander who betrayed him. And he has the perfect opportunity when his nemesis kidnaps a general's daughter. **99m/C; VHS, DVD.** Frank Zagarino; Billy Drago; Todd Jensen; Jenny (Jennifer) McShane; Robin Smith; ***D:*** Yossi Wein; ***W:*** Jeff Albert; ***M:*** Wendy Oldfield; Adrian Levy.

Never Say Goodbye 🦴🦴 **1946** Cliche-ridden story about a man trying to win back his divorce-bound wife. Flynn tries hard, but the material just isn't up to par. Based on the story "Don't Ever Leave Me" by Ben and Norma Barzman. Co-screenwriter Diamond later became famous when he teamed up with Billy Wilder to script "Some Like it Hot" and "The Apartment." **97m/B; VHS, DVD.** Errol Flynn; Eleanor Parker; Lucile Watson; S.Z. Sakall; Forrest Tucker; Donald Woods; Peggy Knudsen; Tom D'Andrea; Hattie McDaniel; ***D:*** James V. Kern; ***W:*** James V. Kern; I.A.L. Diamond; Lewis R. Foster.

Never Say Macbeth 🦴🦴 **1/2 2007** Actors believe that saying the name of Shakespeare's Scottish play will bring about bad luck and nebbish science teacher Danny (Gold) doesn't need any more of that. Lovelorn, he heads to L.A. to reunite with his ex-girlfriend, actress Ruth (Turner), who's been cast as Lady Macbeth. Eccentric director Jason (Enberg) thinks Danny is auditioning for a role and hires him, but Danny has already doomed the production by uttering the "M" word. Oh, and he can suddenly see that the theater is haunted by the ghosts of actors who died in a fire when—you guessed it—that play was last performed. It may sound dopey but it's actually charming and funny. **87m/C; DVD.** Joe Tyler Gold; Ilana Turner; Tania Getty; Alexander Enberg; Tammy Caplan; Mark Deklin; ***D:*** Christopher J. Prouty; ***W:*** Joe Tyler Gold; ***C:*** Michael Millikan; ***M:*** Tim Labor. **VIDEO**

Never Say Never Again 🦴🦴 **1/2 1983 (PG)** James Bond matches wits with a charming but sinister tycoon who is holding the world nuclear hostage as part of a diabolical plot by SPECTRE. Connery's return to the world of Bond after 12 years is smooth in this remake of "Thunderball" hampered by an atrocious musical score. Carrera is stunning as Fatima Blush. Although Connery is back, purists will have qualms considering this part of the "official" Bond series since longtime Bond producer, Albert "Cubby" Broccoli, had nothing to do with this endeavor. **134m/C; VHS, DVD.** Sean Connery; Klaus Maria Brandauer; Max von Sydow; Barbara Carrera; Kim Basinger; Edward Fox; Bernie Casey; Pamela Salem; Rowan Atkinson; Valerie Leon; Prunella Gee; Saskia Cohen Tanugi; ***D:*** Irvin Kershner; ***W:*** Lorenzo Semple, Jr.; ***C:*** Douglas Slocombe; ***M:*** Michel Legrand.

Never So Few 🦴🦴 **1/2 1959** A military commander and his outnumbered troops overcome incredible odds against the Japanese. There is a lot of focus on romance, but the script and acting make a strong impression nonetheless. Based on the novel by Tom T. Chamales. **124m/C; VHS, DVD, Blu-Ray.** Frank Sinatra; Gina Lollobrigida; Peter Lawford; Steve McQueen; Richard Johnson; Paul Henreid; Charles Bronson; ***D:*** John Sturges; ***C:*** William H. Daniels.

Never Surrender 🦴 **2009 (R)** Marketed as the first time some of the world's top MMA fighters appear in one movie, this film is a disaster. The appearances by Georges St. Pierre and the other fighters are cameos, and the rest of the time is filled with bad soft-core porn, unlikely choreographed fights, and horrible dubbing (even for the English-speaking actors). An MMA champ is lured into underground cage-fighting and once in realizes the fights are to the death. **88m/C; DVD.** Hector Echavarria; Patrick Kilpatrick; James Russo; Silvia Koys; Georges St. Pierre; ***D:*** Hector Echavarria; ***W:*** Hector Echavarria; David Storey; ***C:*** Curtis Petersen; ***M:*** Evan Evans.

Never Take Candy From a Stranger 🦴🦴 *Never Take Sweets From a Stranger* **1960** Child molestation drama was not the typical fare for Hammer studios, which may be one reason it wasn't a boxoffice success. The Carters move from England to smalltown Canada for Peter's (Allen) new job. Elderly founding father Clarence Olderberry, Sr. (Aylmer) likes to persuade little girls to dance for him naked in exchange for candy. The townsfolk cover up his sick predilections but when the Carters discover that their 9-year-old daughter Jean (Faye) and her friend Lucille (Green) are victims, they go to court. The outcome is nasty but the aftermath is worse. **81m/B; VHS, DVD, Blu-Ray.** *UK GB* Patrick Allen; Felix Aylmer; Gwen Watford; Janina Faye; Frances Green; Bill Nagy; Niall MacGinnis; Alison Leggatt; MacDonald Parke; Michael Gwynn; James Dyrenforth; Robert Arden; Vera Cook; Bud Knapp; Frances Green; Estelle Brody; ***D:*** Cyril Frankel; ***W:*** John Hunter; ***C:*** Freddie Francis; ***M:*** Elisabeth Lutyens; Elizabeth Luytens.

Never Talk to Strangers 🦴🦴 **1995 (R)** Sarah Taylor (DeMornay) is an uptight criminal psychologist who gets involved with handsome stranger Tony Ramirez (Banderas) while working on the case of a serial killer (Stanton). Then Sarah finds herself the target of an increasingly malevolent stalker—and she has lots of suspects to choose from. Typical woman-in-peril film with equally standard frights but the leads certainly look good (and Banderas is a fine sex object in a bit of role reversal). Filmed in Toronto. **86m/C; VHS, DVD.** Rebecca De Mornay; Antonio Banderas; Harry Dean Stanton; Dennis Miller; Len Cariou; Beau Starr; ***D:*** Peter Hall; ***W:*** Lewis Green; Jordan Rush; ***C:*** Elemer Ragalyi; ***M:*** Pino Donaggio.

Never Too Late 🦴 **1/2 1965** Very silly comedy has middle-aged Edith (O'Sullivan) delighted to discover she's pregnant. Her grumbling husband Harry (Ford) and married daughter Kate (Stevens) don't share her happy mood, especially since Kate and her hubby Charlie (Hutton) have infertility issues hampering their own baby plans. A fed-up Edith eventually leaves until everyone can accept the situation and behave sensibly. **105m/C; DVD.** Maureen Sullivan; Paul Ford; Connie Stevens; Jim Hutton; Jane Wyatt; Henry Jones; Lloyd Nolan; ***D:*** Bud Yorkin; ***W:*** Sumner Arthur Long; ***C:*** Philip H. Lathrop; ***M:*** David Rose.

Never 2 Big 🦴🦴 **1998 (R)** A young record company exec wants to prove that someone at the company murdered his singer sister in order to prevent her from leaving and signing with another label. Only he's been framed for the crime and has to stay out of jail and prove his own innocence. **100m/C; VHS, DVD.** Ernie Hudson; Nia Long; Tony Todd; Donnie Wahlberg; Terrence Howard; Donald Adeosun Faison; Tommy (Tiny) Lister; Salli Richardson-Whitfield; Shemar Moore; ***D:*** Peter Gathings Bunche; ***W:*** Peter Gathings Bunche; ***C:*** Nancy Schreiber; ***M:*** Joseph Williams. **VIDEO**

Never Wave at a WAC 🦴🦴 **1/2** *The Private Wore Skirts* **1952** A Washington socialite joins the Women's Army Corps hoping for a commission that never comes. She has to tough it out as an ordinary private. A reasonably fun ancestor of "Private Benjamin," with a cameo by Gen. Omar Bradley as himself. **87m/B; VHS, DVD.** Rosalind Russell; Paul Douglas; Marie Wilson; William Ching; Arleen Whelan; Leif Erickson; Hillary Brooke; Regis Toomey; ***Cameo(s):*** Omar Bradley; ***D:*** Norman Z. McLeod; ***M:*** Elmer Bernstein.

The NeverEnding Story 🦴🦴🦴 **1/2 1984 (PG)** A lonely young boy helps a warrior save the fantasy world in his book from destruction by the Nothing. A wonderful, intelligent family movie about imagination, with swell effects and a sweet but not overly sentimental script. Petersen's first English-language film, based on the novel by Michael Ende. **94m/C; VHS, DVD, Blu-Ray.** Barret Oliver; Noah Hathaway; Gerald McRaney; Moses Gunn; Tami Stronach; Patricia Hayes; Sydney Bromley; Thomas Hill; ***D:*** Wolfgang Petersen; ***W:*** Wolfgang Petersen; Herman(n) Weigel; ***C:*** Jost Vacano; ***M:*** Klaus Doldinger; Giorgio Moroder.

NeverEnding Story 2: The Next Chapter 🦴🦴 **1991 (PG)** Disappointing sequel to the first story that didn't end. Bastian (Brandis) must again save Fantasia, this time from the evil sorceress Xayride (Burt). So dull, the kids may wander away. But wait: contains the first Bugs Bunny theatrical cartoon in 26 years, "Box Office Bunny." **90m/C; VHS, DVD, Blu-Ray.** Jonathan Brandis; Kenny Morrison; Clarissa Burt; John Wesley Shipp; Martin Umbach; ***D:*** George Miller; ***W:*** Karin Howard; ***C:*** David Connell; ***M:*** Robert Folk.

The NeverEnding Story 3: Escape from Fantasia 🦴🦴 **1994 (G)** The third time was not the charm in this case. Bastian, on the edge of puberty, is being bullied by a group at school called the Nasties. He seeks refuge in the library and enters the world of Fantasia through the "Neverending Story" tome. When the book is stolen by the Nasties, it is up to Bastian to return it. Unfortunately, the story does not have the charm of the original, trying to incorporate too much reality and not enough of dreamland. **95m/C; VHS, DVD.** Jason James Richter; Melody Kay; Freddie Jones; Jack Black; Ryan Bollman; Tracey Ellis; Kevin McNulty; ***D:*** Peter Macdonald; ***C:*** Robin Vidgeon; ***M:*** Peter Wolf.

Neverland 🦴🦴 **1/2 2011** Syfy Channel miniseries' revisionist twist (there's no Wendy or the Darling family) on the story of Peter Pan and Captain Hook. Teenage Peter (Rowe) is the leader of a gang of young London thieves who work for Jimmy Hook (Ifans). They steal a magical orb at Hook's behest and are transported to Neverland, which is now a planet filled with pirates, giant crocs and spiders, tree sprites (that would be Tinker Bell), the Kaw Indian tribe (who are battling the pirates). **169m/C; DVD, Blu-Ray.** Charlie Rowe; Rhys Ifans; Anna Friel; Bob Hoskins; Q'orianka Kilcher; Charles Dance; Cas Anvar; Raoul Trujillo; ***V:*** Keira Knightley; ***D:*** Nick Willing; ***W:*** Nick Willing; ***C:*** Seamus Deasy; ***M:*** Ronan Hardiman. **CABLE**

Nevermore 🦴🦴 **2007** Well it certainly sounds like someone has been looking through those Poe stories for a plot. Wealthy Jonathan Usher (Nelson) isolates himself in his childhood home, living on the brink of sanity. Having forced his trophy wife Lydia (O'Dell) to give up her social pleasures, he's now convinced she wants to drive him over the edge to get his money. So Jonathan asks his friend Devin Bayliss (Spano) to visit and confirm or deny his suspicions. Of course paranoid Jonathan is soon questioning Devin's loyalty. **95m/C; DVD.** Judd Nelson; Jennifer O'Dell; Vincent Spano; Sidi Henderson;

D: Thomas Zambeck; *W:* Thomas Zambeck; *C:* Oren Goldenberg; *M:* Mark Krench. **VIDEO**

Nevil Shute's The Far Country 1/2 *The Far Country* **1985** Carl Zlintner (York), once a doctor in Hitler's army, escapes to Australia from post-war Europe to begin a new life with a new identity. Falling in love with the beautiful Jennifer Morton (Thornton), Carl hopes he's left his past behind. But nothing is every that simple. Adaptation of the Shute novel. **200m/C; VHS, DVD.** *AU* Michael York; Sigrid Thornton; Fred Steele; *D:* George Miller. **TV**

The New Adventures of Pippi Longstocking 1/2 **1988 (G)** Decent cast is trapped in another musical rehashing of the Astrid Lindgren children's books about a precocious red-headed girl and her fantastic adventures with horses, criminals, and pirates. **101m/C; VHS, DVD.** Tami Erin; Eileen Brennan; Dennis Dugan; Dianne Hull; George DiCenzo; John Schuck; Dick Van Patten; *D:* Ken Annakin; *W:* Ken Annakin; *C:* Roland Smith; *M:* Misha Segal.

The New Adventures of Tarzan *Tarzan and the Green Goddess* **1935** Twelve episodes, each 22 minutes long, depict the adventures of Edgar Rice Burrough's tree-swinging character—Tarzan. **260m/B; VHS, DVD.** Bruce Bennett; Ula Holt; Frank Baker; Dale Walsh; Lewis Sargent; *D:* Edward Kull.

The New Age **1994 (R)** Illusions in L.A. centering on talent agent Peter (Weller) and art designer Katherine (Davis) Witner. Katherine loses her job the same day Peter decides to quit his and suddenly the caustic duo are dependent upon each other. The trendy couple decide to open a boutique and quickly find themselves in a fiscal sinkhole and on a downhill slide. The acting is fine but the story is empty. **106m/C; VHS, Blu-Ray, Streaming.** Peter Weller; Judy Davis; Adam West; Patrick Bauchau; Corbin Bernsen; Jonathan Hadary; Samuel L. Jackson; Patricia Heaton; Audra Lindley; Paula Marshall; Maureen Mueller; Bruce Ramsay; Sandra Seacat; Susan Traylor; *D:* Michael Tolkin; *W:* Michael Tolkin; Mark Mothersbaugh.

New Best Friend 1/2 *Depraved Indifference; Mary Jane's Last Dance* **2002 (R)** Obvious and sleazy whodunit wastes its cast. Alicia (Kirshner) is in a cocaine-induced coma after getting in with the wrong college crowd. Working-class mom Connie (O'Connor) raises a stink with new sheriff Bonner (Diggs) to investigate, though the school wants all the sordid details swept under the rug since it involves some wild partying by rich and vapid students. **91m/C; VHS, DVD.** Mia Kirshner; Dominique Swain; Rachel True; Meredith Monroe; Scott Bairstow; Taye Diggs; Glynnis O'Connor; Eric Michael Cole; Oliver Hudson; *D:* Zoe Clarke-Williams; *W:* Victoria Strouse; *C:* Tom Priestley; *M:* David A. Hughes; John Murphy.

New Blood **1999 (R)** Violent thriller that has a few nifty twists. After seven years, Danny White (Moran) turns up on the doorstep of his estranged father, Alan (Hurt). Danny is bleeding from a gunshot wound and makes the devil's own deal with dad: Danny's twin sister needs a heart transplant and Danny offers his own organ if dad will participate in a mob ordered kidnapping that's gone wrong once already. Solid performances are an asset. **92m/C; VHS, DVD.** *GB* Nick Moran; John Hurt; Carrie-Anne Moss; Shawn Wayans; Joe Pantoliano; Eugene Robert Glazer; Richard Fitzpatrick; Rob Freeman; *D:* Michael Hurst; *W:* Michael Hurst; *C:* David Pelletier; *M:* Jeff Danna.

The New Centurions 1/2 **1972 (R)** Rookies training for the Los Angeles Police Department get the inside info from retiring cops. Gritty and realistic drama based on the novel by former cop Joseph Wambaugh. Tends to be disjointed at times, but overall is a good adaptation of the bestseller. Scott, excellent as the retiring beat-walker, is supported well by the other performers. **103m/C; VHS, DVD, Blu-Ray.** George C. Scott; Stacy Keach; Jane Alexander; Scott Wilson; Erik Estrada; James B. Sikking; *D:* Richard Fleischer; *W:* Stirling Silliphant; *M:* Quincy Jones.

New Crime City: Los Angeles 2020 1/2 **1994 (R)** Prisoner Tony Ricks (Rossovich) is executed and then revived thanks to technology. But there's a price to pay for his life and freedom—he must retrieve a biowarfare weapon from a prison gang and he only has 24 hours to do it. **95m/C; VHS, DVD.** Rick Rossovich; Stacy Keach; Sherrie Rose; *W:* Rick Rossovich.

The New Daughter 1/2 **2010 (PG-13)** Cliched supernatural thriller that really falls apart in the third act. When his unfaithful wife walks out, bewildered John James (Costner) packs up preteen daughter Louisa (Banquero) and 8-year-old son Sam (Griffith) and moves them to a creepy house in rural South Carolina that has an apparent Indian burial mound on the property. Soon Louisa becomes withdrawn and starts sleepwalking, showing up mud-covered and scarred. Daddy can't deal as the situation becomes increasingly ominous. **109m/C; DVD, Blu-Ray.** Kevin Costner; Ivana Banquero; Gattlin Griffith; Samantha Mathis; Noah Taylor; James Gammon; Erik Palladino; *D:* Luis Berdejo; *W:* John Travis; *C:* Checco Varese. **VIDEO**

The New Eve *La Nouvelle Eve* **1998 (R)** Camille (Viard in an astonishing performance) is a hard-partying Parisienne whose hedonistic life is changed when she meets Alexis (Rajot). He's a political activist, married with a couple of kids—not at all the sort of drugged-up playboy she is used to. Their rocky relationship is both sexual and emotional. French with subtitles. **90m/C; VHS, DVD.** *FR* Karin Viard; Pierre-Loup Rajot; Catherine Frot; Sergi Lopez; Mireille Roussel; Nozha Khouadra; *D:* Catherine Corsini; *W:* Catherine Corsini; Marc Syrigas; *C:* Agnes Godard.

New Faces of 1937 1/2 **1937** Typical showbiz musical comedy from RKO. Broadway producer Robert Hunt deliberately goes after flops so he can pocket his backers' money. He skips town after leaving comedian/manager Wellington Wedge in charge of a show built around unknowns, but it turns into a hit. **100m/B; DVD.** Jerome Cowan; Milton Berle; Harriet Hilliard Nelson; Joe Penner; Parkyakarkus (Harry Einstein); *D:* Leigh Jason; *W:* Nat Perrin; Philip G. Epstein; Irving Brecher; *C:* J. Roy Hunt.

New Faces of 1952 1/2 **1954** Based on the hit Broadway revue. The plot revolves around a Broadway show that is about to be closed down, and the performers who fight to keep it open. Lots of hit songs. Mel Brooks is credited as a writer, under the name Melvin Brooks. **98m/C; VHS, DVD.** Ronny Graham; Eartha Kitt; Robert Clary; Alice Ghostley; June Carroll; Carol Lawrence; Paul Lynde; *D:* Harry Horner.

New Fist of Fury *Xin Ching-wu Men* **1976** During WWII, a former pickpocket becomes a martial arts whiz with the assistance of his fiancee, and fights the entire Imperial Army. **120m/C; VHS, DVD.** Jackie Chan; *D:* Lo Wei; *W:* Lo Wei.

The New Girlfriend 1/2 *Une nouvelle amie* **2014 (R)** Claire's (Demoustier) best friend Laura (Le Besco) has recently died, and Francois Ozon tricks viewers at the beginning of his effective dramedy by leading them to believe it will be about the unique friendship between these two and how one deals with the grief of loss. The tone shifts drastically (something Ozon likes to do) when Claire discovers that Laura's husband David (Duris) is a cross-dresser. Her new girlfriend is her dead girlfriend's husband. Ozon is having some playful fun here, and Duris is great, even if the final product feels less than the sum of its parts. **108m/C; DVD, Blu-Ray.** *FR* Romain Duris; Anais Demoustier; Raphael Personnaz; Aurore Clement; Jean-Claude Bolle-Reddat; Isild Le Besco; *D:* Francois Ozon; *W:* Francois Ozon; *C:* Pascal Marti; *M:* Philippe Rombi.

The New Gladiators **WOOF!** **1983** In the future, criminals try to kill each other on TV for public entertainment. Two such gladiators discover that the network's computer is using the games in order to take over mankind, and they attempt to stop it. Even if the special effects were any good, they couldn't save this one. **90m/C; VHS, DVD.** *IT* Jared Martin; Fred Williamson; Eleanor Gold; Howard Ross; Claudio Cassinelli; *D:* Lucio Fulci; *W:* Elisa Briganti; Dardano Sacchetti; *C:* Guiseppe Pinori; *M:* Riz Ortolani.

The New Guy 1/2 **2002 (PG-13)** Dorky high school senior Dizzy (Qualls) wants to transform himself into a cool guy—by getting expelled and transferring to another school. Instead, he winds up in prison where he meets Luther (Griffin), who gives him an attitude makeover. Once he hits the new school, his newfound popularity has him winning a hottie cheerleader (Dushku) and uniting the school. High school flick shows a certain lack of effort on most everyone's part, most notably the director, writer, and cinematographer. Qualls is likable, Deschanel is better than pic deserves, and Dushku supplies the expected sexual spark. **88m/C; DVD.** DJ Qualls; Eddie Griffin; Eliza Dushku; Zooey Deschanel; Lyle Lovett; Illeana Douglas; Kurt Fuller; Matt Gogin; Sunny Mabrey; Parry Shen; *Cameo(s):* Tommy Lee; Henry Rollins; Gene Simmons; *D:* Edward Decter; *W:* David Kendall; *C:* Michael D. O'Shea; *M:* Ralph Sall.

New in Town *Chilled in Miami* **2009 (PG-13)** Corporate exec Lucy Hill (Zellweger) is sent from Miami to rural New Ulm, Minnesota to oversee the downsizing of her company's processing plant, a cornerstone of employment in the community. She gives the locals lots to laugh about with her big city ways but Lucy's career aspirations are soon at odds with her unexpected fondness for her new north country friends, particularly hunky widower dad Ted (Connick), the plant union rep and town's sole eligible bachelor. A fish-out-of-water formula flick with all the cliched Minnesota practical jokes, don'tcha know! **96m/C; DVD, Blu-Ray, On Demand.** Renée Zellweger; Harry Connick, Jr.; Siobhan Fallon Hogan; J.K. Simmons; Rashida Jones; Frances Conroy; *D:* Jonas Elmer; *W:* C. Jay Cox; Kenneth Rance; *C:* Chris Seager; *M:* John Swihart.

New Jack City 1/2 **1991 (R)** Just say no ghetto-melodrama. Powerful performance by Snipes as wealthy Harlem drug lord sought by rebel cops Ice-T and Nelson. Music by Johnny Gill, 2 Live Crew, Ice-T and others. **101m/C; VHS, DVD, Blu-Ray.** Wesley Snipes; Ice-T; Mario Van Peebles; Chris Rock; Judd Nelson; Tracy C. Johns; Allen Payne; Kim Park; Vanessa Williams; Nick Ashford; Thalmus Rasulala; Michael Michele; Bill Nunn; Russell Wong; *D:* Mario Van Peebles; *W:* Keith Critchlow; Barry Michael Cooper; *C:* Francis Kenny; *M:* Roger Bourland; Michel Colombier.

New Jersey Drive 1/2 **1995 (R)** Jason (Corley) has dreams of life outside the mean streets of Newark, but he jeopardizes his future by stealing cars and joyriding around the neighborhood with his friends. Unblinking realism, provided by credible actors (especially Corley, a former gang member), dialogue, and filming in the projects of Brooklyn and Queens, is neutralized by stereotypical characters (especially the lily-white, sadistically brutal cops) and lack of a sympathetic point of view. Loosely based on a series of articles by Michel Mariott, a reporter for the "New York Times." **98m/C; VHS, DVD.** Sharron Corley; Gabriel Casseus; Saul Stein; Andre Moore; Donald Adeosun Faison; Conrad Meertin, Jr.; Deven Eggleston; Gwen McGee; Koran C. Thomas; Samantha Brown; Christine Baranski; Robert Jason Jackson; Roscoe Orman; Dwight Errington Myers; Gary DeWitt Marshall; *D:* Nick Gomez; *W:* Nick Gomez; Michel Marriott; *C:* Adam Kimmel; *M:* Wendy Blackstone.

The New Kids **1985 (R)** An orphaned brother and sister find out the limitations of the good neighbor policy. A sadistic gang terrorizes them after their move to a relatives' home in Florida. They go after expected revenge. **90m/C; VHS, DVD, Blu-Ray.** Shannon Presby; Lori Loughlin; James Spader; Eric Stoltz; *D:* Sean S. Cunningham; *W:* Brian Taggert; Stephen Gyllenhaal.

A New Kind of Love 1/2 **1963** Romantic fluff starring real-life couple Newman and Woodward who meet en route to Paris and end up falling in love. Newman plays a reporter and Woodward is a fashion designer in this light comedy set amidst the sights of Paris. **110m/C; VHS, DVD.** Paul Newman; Joanne Woodward; Thelma Ritter; Eva Gabor; Maurice Chevalier; George Tobias; *D:* Melville Shavelson; *W:* Melville Shavelson; *C:* Daniel F. Fapp.

The New Land *Nybyggarna* **1972 (PG)** Sequel to "The Emigrants" follows Von Sydow and his family as they struggle to make their new home in the new world. Hardships include severe weather which devastates the farm, a Sioux indian uprising, and a disastrous trek to the Southwest to search for gold. Sensitive performances and direction. Based on the novels by Vilhelm Moberg. Dubbed into English. **161m/C; VHS, Streaming.** *SW* Max von Sydow; Liv Ullmann; Allan Edwall; Eddie Axberg; Hans Alfredson; Halvar Bjork; Peter Lindgren; Monica Zetterlund; Pierre Lindstedt; Per Oscarsson; *D:* Jan Troell; *W:* Jan Troell; Bengt Forslund; *C:* Jan Troell; *M:* Bengt Ernryd; George Oddner. Natl. Bd. of Review '73: Actress (Ullmann); Natl. Soc. Film Critics '73: Actress (Ullmann).

A New Leaf 1/2 **1971 (G)** A playboy who has depleted his financial resources tries to win the hand of a clumsy heiress. May was the first woman to write, direct and star in a movie. She was unhappy with the cuts that were made by the studio, but that didn't seem to affect its impact with the public. Even with the cuts, the film is still funny and May's performance is worth watching. **102m/C; DVD, Blu-Ray, Streaming.** Walter Matthau; Elaine May; Jack Weston; George Rose; William Redfield; James Coco; *D:* Elaine May; *W:* Elaine May. Natl. Film Reg. '19.

New Mafia Boss 1/2 *Crime Boss* **1972 (PG)** Italian-made plodder has Savalas taking over a huge Mafia family and all hell breaking loose. **90m/C; VHS, DVD.** *IT* Telly Savalas; Lee Van Cleef; Antonio (Tony) Sabato; Paola Tedesco; *D:* Alberto De Martino.

New Moon 1/2 **1940** An adaptation of the operetta by Sigmund Romberg and Oscar Hammerstein II. A French heiress traveling on a boat that is captured by pirates falls in love with their leader. Remake of the 1930 film. Includes the 1935 Robert Benchley MGM short "How to Sleep." **106m/B; DVD.** Jeanette MacDonald; Nelson Eddy; Buster Keaton; Joe Yule; Jack Perrin; Mary Boland; *D:* Robert Z. Leonard.

New Morals for Old **1932** Neither Ralph (Young) nor his sister Phyllis (Perry) wants to follow in the footsteps of their fuddy-duddy parents. Ralph goes off to Paris to study art, has a romance with neighbor Myra (Loy), but soon realizes he has no artistic talent. Meanwhile, Phyllis has an affair with a married man who finally gets a divorce to marry her. Their new morality leads to some very old-fashioned outcomes. Adaptation of John Van Druten's play "After All." **75m/B; DVD.** Robert Young; Margaret Perry; Lewis Stone; Laura Hope Crews; Myrna Loy; David Newell; Jean Hersholt; *D:* Charles Brabin; *W:* Zelda Sears; Wanda Tuchock; *C:* John Mescall.

New Orleans 1/2 **1947** The great legends of jazz re-enact its birth in this song-filled tribute to the town where it all began. When the proprietor (de Cordova) of a Bourbon Street gambling joint (and haven for musicians) falls for an opera-singing socialite, he realizes that only through music will he gain responsibility. He begins a campaign to bring jazz to the highbrow American stage. **90m/B; VHS, DVD.** Arturo de Cordova; Dorothy Patrick; Louis Armstrong; Billie Holiday; Woody Herman; Richard Hageman; *D:* Arthur Lubin; *W:* Elliot Paul; Dick Irving Hyland; *C:* Lucien N. Andriot.

New Orleans Uncensored 1/2 **1955** Filmed in a semi-documentary fashion meant to emphasize the flick's take on corruption. Navy vet Dan Corbett (Franz) gets a job as a longshoreman in New Orleans and quickly discovers the docks are mob-controlled. When a friend gets killed, Dan goes to the cops and persuades them to let him work undercover to get the goods on the gangsters. **76m/B; DVD, Blu-Ray.** Arthur Franz; Michael Ansara; Beverly Garland; William Henry; Ed Nelson; Mike Mazurki; Helene Stanton; Stacy Harris; *D:* William Castle; *W:* Orville H. Hampton; Lewis Meltzer; *C:* Henry Freulich; *M:* Mischa Bakaleinikoff.

New Police Story 1/2 *San Ging Chaat Goo Si* **2004 (R)** Of course it's the action that carries these pics and 19 years after the 1985 original, star Chan still made it work. Inspector Wing hits the bottle after his team is killed in a shootout with evil Joe (Wu) and his gang. But rookie Frank (Tse) dries Wing out so he can return to the force and finally settle the score. Chinese with subtitles. **123m/C; DVD.** *CH* Jackie Chan; Nicholas Tse; Daniel Wu; Charlene (Cheuk-Yin) Choi; Charlie Yeung; *D:* Benny Chan; *W:* Alan Yuen; *C:* Anthony Pun; *M:* Tommy Wai.

The New Romantic **2018** College newspaper sex columnist Blake (Barden) longs for the romance in relationships that she believes is dead. After she writes a column in which she wonders if the main characters in "If Harry Met Sally" would just be casual sex partners today, she is fired. Running with an idea that will give her a story to use as a writer, Blake looks for and finds a sugar daddy. Fortysomething Ian (Sharp) gives her valuable gifts in exchange for dates, compelling her to both embrace and question this lifestyle. A mediocre rom-com despite Barden's spirited efforts. **82m/C; DVD.** Hayley Law; Brett Dier; Camila Mendes; Timm Sharp; ***D:*** Carly Stone; ***W:*** Carly Stone; ***C:*** Michael Robert McLaughlin; ***M:*** Matthew O'Halloran.

New Rose Hotel 1/2 **1998 (R)** Corporate raider Fox (Walken) and his assistant X (Dafoe) are hired to get scientific genius Hiroshi (Amano) into working for another company. Slinky Sandii (Argento) is the lure. She succeeds but double-crosses her employers who now expect to be killed for not fulfilling their contract. (Industrial espionage is apparently quite hazardous.) Frustrating as director Ferrara repeats scenes with minor variations, leaving viewers bewildered if nothing else. Based on a story by William Gibson. **92m/C; VHS, DVD.** Christopher Walken; Willem Dafoe; Asia Argento; Yoshitaka Amano; Annabella Sciorra; Gretchen Mol; John Lurie; Ryuichi Sakamoto; ***D:*** Abel Ferrara; ***W:*** Abel Ferrara; Chris Zois; ***C:*** Ken Kelsch.

The New Twenty **2008** Rather ruthlessly unsentimental ensemble piece about the lives of five college pals several years after graduation. Mainly there's the romantic/business triangle between investment banker Andrew (Locke), who's engaged to Julie (Bilderback), and Louie (Serpico), the obnoxious venture capitalist who's repressing his attraction to Andrew. Other players include Julie's brother Tony (Wei Lin), lonely Ben (Fickes), and druggie Felix (Sadoski), although their stories remain sketchy. **92m/C; DVD.** Ryan Locke; Nicole Bilderback; Andrew Lin; Colin Fickes; Terry Serpico; Tom Sadoski; Bill Sage; ***D:*** Chris Mason Johnson; ***W:*** Chris Mason Johnson; Ishmael Chawla; ***C:*** David Tumblety; ***M:*** Jeff Toyne.

New Waterford Girl 1/2 **1999** Mooney Pottie (Balaban) is a 15-year-old stuck in a small coal-mining community in Nova Scotia in the 1970s. Mooney has won a scholarship to a prestigious arts school and is desperate to attend but her parents refuse to let her. But careful observation has shown Mooney that girls who get themselves into "trouble" leave the community to have their babies in secret and she decides to transform herself into a slut (while keeping her virginity) and get out of town. Sweetly amusing with a compelling debut performance from Balaban. **97m/C; VHS, DVD.** *CA* Liane Balaban; Tara Spencer-Nairn; Andrew McCarthy; Nicholas (Nick) Campbell; Mary Walsh; Cathy Moriarty; ***D:*** Allan Moyle; ***W:*** Tricia Fish; ***C:*** Derek Rogers.

A New Wave **2007 (R)** Bank teller Desmond (Keegan) hates his job and allows his movie-obsessed pal Rupert (Krasinski) to talk him into being the inside man in a heist he's lifted from the plots of favorite flicks. Surprise! Things start to go wrong when Desmond begins having second thoughts and the heist is botched. **94m/C; DVD.** Andrew Keegan; Lacey Chabert; John Krasinski; William Sadler; Dean Edwards; ***D:*** Jason Carvey; ***W:*** Jason Carvey; ***C:*** Kambui Olujimi; ***M:*** Chris Blackburn. **VIDEO**

New World 1/2 *Le Nouveau Monde* **1995 (R)** Unflattering portrait of American soldiers in postwar France in the 1950s. Their presence is resented by most of the locals, who are still suffering the depredations caused by WWII unlike their American counterparts, who won't even learn a little French to get by. Young Patrick (Chatel), however, is smitten with American culture, thanks to his meeting with soldier Will (Gandolfini) and All-American girl Trudy (Silverstone). President DeGaul would eventually force the American bases to close. English and French dialogue with subtitles. **117m/C; VHS, DVD.** *FR* Nicolas Chatel; James Gandolfini; Alicia Silverstone; Sarah Grappin; Guy Marchand; ***D:*** Alain Corneau; ***C:*** William Lubtchansky.

The New World **2005 (PG-13)** Malick's vision offers the story of Pocahontas (Kilcher), stripped of its revisionist history and cartoon-fantasy world and elevated to a mythic retelling of the establishment of an American colony by the London based Virginia Co., which brought Captain John Smith (Ferrell) in contact with the Powhatan Indians. As the story surrounding Fort James unfolds, Malick brings into question the motives and desires of Pocahontas, Smith, and later John Rolfe (Bale), the tobacco farmer who eventually marries Pocahontas and brings her back home to England. Ends up as a beautifully crafted metaphor for the effect Europe had on the new world and vice versa. **160m/C; DVD, Blu-Ray.** Colin Farrell; Christopher Plummer; Christian Bale; August Schellenberg; Wes Studi; David Thewlis; Yorick Van Wageningen; Ben Mendelsohn; Raoul Trujillo; Brian F. O'Byrne; Irene Bedard; John Savage; Jamie Harris; Alex Rice; Michael Greyeyes; Noah Taylor; Jonathan Pryce; Q'orianka Kilcher; Kalani Queypo; Alexandra Malick; ***D:*** Terrence Malick; ***W:*** Terrence Malick; ***C:*** Emmanuel Lubezki; ***M:*** James Horner. Natl. Bd. of Review '05: Breakthrough Perf. (Kilcher).

New World Disorder **1999 (R)** Action thriller combines familiar elements of the formula with high-tech computer jargon. A gang of thieves led by the bestudded Bishop (McCarthy) blasts into a computer chip company and steals the Rosetta encryption program. Young computer-savvy FBI agent Paddock (Fitzgerald) winds up working with old-fashioned local cop Marx (Hauer) to catch the bad guys. The action scenes are fairly ambitious for a video premiere. **94m/C; VHS, DVD.** Rutger Hauer; Andrew McCarthy; Tara Fitzgerald; ***D:*** Richard Spence; ***W:*** Ehren Kruger; Jeffrey Smith; ***C:*** Ivan Strasburg; ***M:*** Gast Waltzing. **VIDEO**

New Year's Day **1989 (R)** Jaglom continues his look at modern relationships in this story of a man reclaiming his house from three female tenants. Introspective character study lightened by humor and insight. **90m/C; VHS, DVD.** Maggie Jakobson; Gwen Welles; Melanie Winter; Milos Forman; Michael Emil; David Duchovny; Tracy Reiner; Henry Jaglom; ***D:*** Henry Jaglom; ***W:*** Henry Jaglom.

New Year's Eve **WOOF!** **2011 (PG-13)** Like getting drunk before the ball drops on the last night of the year, director Marshall's follow-up to the mega-hit "Valentine's Day" is most notable for the amount of high-powered actors and actresses who wasted their time making it. Roughly a dozen plot arcs—including a singer trying to get back the one who got away, a couple stuck in an elevator and a dying man trying to make it to one more year—are intertwined into one romantic comedy that is neither romantic nor funny. The film proves that just casting A-list actors does not a movie make. **118m/C; DVD, Blu-Ray.** Robert De Niro; Ashton Kutcher; Michelle Pfeiffer; Hilary Swank; Lea Michele; Katherine Heigl; Josh Duhamel; Sofia Vergara; Jessica Biel; Zac Efron; Sarah Jessica Parker; Jon Bon Jovi; Abigail Breslin; Hector Elizondo; Chris Bridges; Seth Meyers; Til Schweiger; Halle Berry; ***D:*** Garry Marshall; ***W:*** Katherine Fugate; ***C:*** Charles Minsky; ***M:*** John Debney.

New York Cop 1/2 **1994 (R)** Japanese martial arts expert Toshi (Nakamura) joins the NYPD and is given an undercover assignment to infiltrate a gun-running gang that supplies both drug lords and Japanese mobsters. But internal rivalries force Toshi to bond with gang leader Hawk (McQueen) and the duo to do battle together. **88m/C; VHS, DVD.** Toru Nakamura; Chad McQueen; Mira Sorvino; ***D:*** Toru Murakawa.

New York Doll **2005 (PG-13)** Arthur "Killer" Kane was the bassist for the 1970s glam-rock band the New York Dolls, going from the excesses of rock 'n' roll (the Dolls broke up in 1975) to obscurity and battling a variety of demons (chemical and otherwise) until a belated recovery and his adoption of the Mormon faith. In 2004, die-hard fan Morrissey persuaded Kane to reunite with his two remaining bandmates for a London music festival. Whiteley follows Kane from his settled life in LA to the Dolls' bitter-sweet reunion. Kane died of leukemia shortly after the concert. **73m/C; DVD.** ***D:*** Greg Whiteley; ***C:*** Rod Santiano; Seth Gordon.

New York, I Love You 1/2 **2009 (R)** An American follow-up to 2006's "Paris, Je T'Aime" with 10 filmmakers directing vignettes about love in New York's five boroughs. The stories don't intersect, and each director was only given two days to shoot and one week to edit. Some have ironic twist endings, others are small slices of life with a classic New York vibe. As expected, the results are uneven, but with a maximum eight-minute runtime per story, there's always something new coming shortly. **103m/C; DVD, Blu-Ray, On Demand.** Natalie Portman; Shia LaBeouf; Cloris Leachman; Blake Lively; Hayden Christensen; Christina Ricci; Anton Yelchin; Orlando Bloom; Rachel Bilson; Robin Wright; Ethan Hawke; Drea De Matteo; James Caan; Julie Christie; Bradley Cooper; John Hurt; Maggie Q; Olivia Thirlby; Andy Garcia; Chris Cooper; Eli Wallach; ***D:*** Natalie Portman; Fatih Akin; Yvan Attal; Shunji Iwai; Joshua Marston; Allen Hughes; Shekhar Kapur; Mira Nair; Brett Ratner; Wen Jiang; ***W:*** Natalie Portman; Fatih Akin; Yvan Attal; Shunji Iwai; Joshua Marston; Anthony Minghella; Alexandra Cassavetes; Jeff Nathanson; Scarlett Johansson; Hu Hong; Olivier Lecot; Suketu Mehta; Yao Meng; Stephen Winter; ***C:*** Benoît Debie; Pawel Edelman; Declan Quinn; Mauricio Rubinstein; ***M:*** Paul Cantelon; Mychael Danna; Mark Mothersbaugh; Atticus Ross; Leopold Ross; Claudia Sarne; Marcelo Zarvos; Tonino Baliardo; Nicholas Britell; Ilhan Ersahin; Shoji Mitsui.

New York Minute 1/2 **2004 (PG)** Sporting different hair color, way too much make-up, and a sheen only multi-millions from straight-to-video hits can bring, the Olsen twins take New York City in this dumb semi-screwball, wanna-be action comedy. Blonde do-gooder Jane (Ashley) and dark-haired rebel Roxy (Mary-Kate) have recently lost their mom and live with their dad (Pinsky) in the Long Island suburbs. The couldn't-be-more-different twins share a ride into The City in search of their respective dreams (Jane's is an Oxford fellowship; Roxy's a career in rock) when things go awry and they end up running amok to marginal comic effect, while being tailed by truant officer Levy. The twins' TV dad Saget shows up in an amusing cameo. **91m/C; VHS, DVD.** Ashley (Fuller) Olsen; Mary-Kate Olsen; Eugene Levy; Andy Richter; Riley Smith; Jared Padalecki; Darrell Hammond; Andrea Martin; Alannah Ong; ***Cameo(s):*** Bob Saget; ***D:*** Dennie Gordon; ***W:*** Emily Fox; Adam Cooper; Bill Collage; ***C:*** Greg Gardiner; ***M:*** George S. Clinton.

New York, New York **1977 (PG)** Tragic romance evolves between a saxophonist and an aspiring singer/actress in this salute to the big-band era. A love of music isn't enough to hold them together through career rivalries and life on the road. Fine performances by De Niro and Minnelli and the supporting cast. Re-released in 1981 with the "Happy Endings" number, which was cut from the original. Look for "Big Man" Clarence Clemons on sax. **163m/C; VHS, DVD, Blu-Ray.** Robert De Niro; Liza Minnelli; Lionel Stander; Barry Primus; Mary Kay Place; Dick Miller; Diahnne Abbott; ***D:*** Martin Scorsese; ***W:*** Mardik Martin; ***M:*** Ralph Burns.

New York Ripper **WOOF!** *Lo Squartatore de New York; The Ripper* **1982** A New York cop tracks down a rampaging murderer in this dull, mindless slasher flick. **88m/C; VHS, DVD, Blu-Ray.** *IT* Jack Hedley; Antonella Interlenghi; Howard Ross; Andrea Occhipinti; Alessandra Delli Colli; Paolo Malco; ***D:*** Lucio Fulci; ***W:*** Lucio Fulci; Gianfranco Clerici; Vincenzo Mannino; Dardano Sacchetti; ***C:*** Luigi Kuveiller; ***M:*** Francesco De Masi.

New York Stories **1989 (PG)** Entertaining anthology of three separate short films by three esteemed directors, all set in New York. In "Life Lessons" by Scorsese, an impulsive artist tries to prevent his live-in girlfriend from leaving him. "Life Without Zoe" by Coppola involves a youngster's fantasy about a wealthy 12-year-old who lives mostly without her parents. Allen's "Oedipus Wrecks," generally considered the best short, is about a 50-year-old man who is tormented by the specter of his mother. **124m/C; VHS, DVD, Blu-Ray; Open Captioned.** Nick Nolte; Rosanna Arquette; Woody Allen; Mia Farrow; Mae Questel; Julie Kavner; Talia Shire; Giancarlo Giannini; Don Novello; Patrick O'Neal; Peter Gabriel; Paul Herman; Deborah Harry; Steve Buscemi; Heather McComb; Chris Elliott; Carole Bouquet; Edward I. Koch; ***D:*** Woody Allen; Martin Scorsese; Francis Ford Coppola; ***W:*** Woody Allen; Francis Ford Coppola; Richard Price; Sofia Coppola; ***C:*** Sven Nykvist; Nestor Almendros; ***M:*** Carmine Coppola.

The New Yorker **1998** Frenchman Alfred (Demy) fell for American Alice (Phillips) while she was vacationing in Paris. So he impulsively flies to New York after her, only to be told to go away. Thinking he can win Grace back, Alfred decides to stick around and gets a job with a thug (Elliott) to tide him over, which turns out to be a problem. English and French with subtitles. **75m/C; DVD.** *FR* Mathieu Demy; Grace Phillips; Shawn Elliott; Gretchen Cleevely; ***D:*** Benoit Graffin; ***W:*** Benoit Graffin; David Block; ***C:*** Antoine Herberte.

Newcastle **2008** Seventeen-year-old Jesse and his brothers live in the small town of Newcastle, Australia where Jesse is a rising surf star. Jesse fights with resentful older brother Victor and plans a weekend off with his mates that is crashed by his trouble-bringing sibling. Meanwhile, Jesse's twin brother Fergus is battling his attraction to Jesse's best pal, Andy. **107m/C; DVD.** *AU* Anthony Hayes; Barry Otto; Gigi Edgley; Lachlan Buchanan; Xavier Samuel; Reshad Strik; Kirk Jenkins; Shane Jacobson; ***D:*** Dan Castle; ***W:*** Dan Castle; ***C:*** Richard Michalak; ***M:*** Michael Yezerski.

The Newlydeads 1/2 **1987** An uptight, conservative, honeymoon resort owner murders one of his guests and finds out that "she" is really a he. Fifteen years later, on his wedding night, all of his guests are violently murdered by the transvestite's vengeful ghost. Oddball twist to the usual slasher nonsense. **84m/C; VHS, DVD.** Scott Kaske; Jim Williams; Jean Levine; Jay Richardson; ***D:*** Joseph Merhi; ***W:*** Joseph Merhi; Sean Dash; ***C:*** Richard Pepin; ***M:*** John Gonzalez.

Newlyweds 1/2 **2011** New York newlyweds Buzzy (Burns) and Katie (Fitzgerlad) figure they are experienced and old enough to make their marriage work, despite their impulsive elopement. Their bliss is quickly tested by miscommunication and resentment precipitated by family angst. Katie's older sister Marsha (Dietlein) is bitterly observing her own longtime marriage disintegrate when Buzzy's flaky half-sister Linda (Bishe), newly arrived from L.A., overstays her welcome with her erratic behavior. Maybe if everyone would just relax, the newlyweds could figure out what to do. **95m/C; DVD.** Edward Burns; Caitlin FitzGerald; Marsha Dietlein; Kerry Bishe; Max Baker; Johnny Solo; ***D:*** Edward Burns; ***W:*** Edward Burns; ***C:*** William Rexer; ***M:*** P.T. Walkley.

News at Eleven **1986** A fading news anchorman is pressured by his ambitious young boss to expose a touchy local sex scandal, forcing him to consider the public's right to know versus the rights of the individual. About average for TV drama. **95m/C; VHS, DVD.** Martin Sheen; Peter Riegert; Barbara Babcock; Sheree J. Wilson; Sydney Penny; David S. Sheiner; Christopher Allport; ***D:*** Mike Robe. **TV**

News from Home **1976** Scenes of life in New York are juxtaposed with voiceover from the letters of a mother to her young daughter. Plotless narrative deals with the small details of life. **85m/C; VHS, DVD.** ***Nar:*** Chantal Akerman; ***D:*** Chantal Akerman; ***W:*** Chantal Akerman.

Newsbreak **2000 (R)** Reckless and arrogant reporter John McNamara (Rooker) has made a lot of enemies. When he decides to investigate the disappearance of a fellow journalist, John uncovers citywide corruption that involves the president of a construction company (Reinhold) and his own father (Culp), a judge with a sterling reputation. **95m/C; VHS, DVD.** Michael Rooker; Judge Reinhold; Robert Culp; Kelly Miller; Kim Darby; Noelle Parker; ***D:*** Serge Rodnunsky; ***W:*** Serge Rodnunsky; Paul Tarantino; ***C:*** Howard Wexler; ***M:*** Evan Evans. **VIDEO**

Newsfront **1978** A story about two brothers, both newsreel filmmakers, and their differing approaches to life and their craft in the 1940s and '50s. Tribute to the days of newsreel film combines real stories and fictionalized accounts with color and black and white photography. Noyce's feature film debut. **110m/C; VHS, DVD.** *AU* Bill Hunter; Gerard Kennedy; Angela Punch McGregor; Wendy Hughes; Chris Haywood; John Ewart; Bryan Brown; *D:* Phillip Noyce. Australian Film Inst. '78: Actor (Hunter), Film.

Newsies 🦴 1/2 **1992 (PG)** An unfortunate attempt at an old-fashioned musical with a lot of cute kids and cardboard characters and settings. The plot, such as it is, concerns the 1899 New York newsboys strike against penny-pinching publisher Joseph Pulitzer. Bale plays the newsboy's leader and at least shows some charisma in a strictly cartoon setting. The songs are mediocre but the dancing is lively. However, none of it moves the story along. Add a bone for viewers under 12. Choreographer Ortega's feature-film directorial debut. **121m/C; VHS, DVD, Blu-Ray.** Christian Bale; Bill Pullman; Robert Duvall; Ann-Margret; Michael Lerner; Kevin Tighe; Charles Cioffi; Luke Edwards; Max Casella; David Moscow; *D:* Kenny Ortega; *W:* Bob Tzudiker; *C:* Noni White; *M:* Alan Menken; *M:* Jack Feldman. Golden Raspberries '92: Worst Song ("High Times, Hard Times").

The Newton Boys 🦴🦴 1/2 **1997 (PG-13)** Fact-based drama chronicling the careers and loves of the Newton brothers, who robbed their way from Texas to Toronto during the '20s and '30s. They lived and worked by a romantic credo: no killing, stealing from women or children, and no ratting each other out. Willis (McConaughey) and Joe (Ulrich) lead the group and both actors prove likeable gangsters. Highlight is the great train robbery, which garnered the outlaws $3 million and eventually landed them in court. Though well-acted with interesting material, Linklater doesn't keep the story humming. Stealing the pic is the real-life footage of a 1980 "Tonight Show" where Johnny Carson interviews the personable Joe. **122m/C; DVD, Blu-Ray.** Matthew McConaughey; Skeet Ulrich; Ethan Hawke; Vincent D'Onofrio; Julianna Margulies; Dwight Yoakam; Gail Cronauer; Chloe Webb; Charles Gunning; Becket Gremmels; Richard Jones; *D:* Richard Linklater; *W:* Claude Stanush; Clark Lee Walker; *C:* Peter James; *M:* Edward D. Barnes.

Newtown 🦴🦴🦴 **2016** Kim Snyder's documentary is devastating but essential, especially in the way it captures the resilience and healing that came in the aftermath of unimaginable horror. The subject here, of course, is the shooting at Sandy Hook Elementary School in Newtown, Connecticut on December 14, 2012. Snyder respectfully interviews several of the parents who lost children on that horrible day. But rather than deliver a memorial, she captures a community that came together to survive. They might not have made it if they didn't. This is a very difficult watch, especially for parents, but know that it's more about survival than murder. **85m/C; DVD.** David Wheeler; *D:* Kim A. Snyder; *C:* Derek Wiesehahn; *M:* Fil Eisler.

Next 🦴🦴 **2007 (PG-13)** Struggling Vegas magician Cris (Cage) has the ability to see two minutes into the future. Somehow, FBI agent Ferris (Moore) becomes aware of his ability and wants him to help them find a nuclear weapon that's been smuggled into L.A. Cris would rather focus on meeting his dream girl, Liz (Biel), but the two plot points soon cross paths. Cage stays low-key, Biel is beautiful and bewildered, and director Tamahori handles the action well, but it's ultimately a forgettable gimmick. Adapted from a story by Philip K. Dick. **96m/C; DVD, Blu-Ray, HD-DVD.** Nicolas Cage; Jessica Biel; Julianne Moore; Thomas Kretschmann; Tory Kittles; Peter Falk; Jose Zuniga; Jim Beaver; Michael Trucco; Jason Butler Harner; *D:* Lee Tamahori; *W:* Gary Goldman; Jonathan Hensleigh; Paul Bernbaum; *C:* David Tattersall; *M:* Mark Isham.

The Next Best Thing 🦴 1/2 **2000 (PG-13)** L.A. yoga instructor Abbie (Madonna) manages to get preggers thanks to a drunken one-nighter with gay best friend, Robert (Everett). She has the kid, they decide to live together and share parental responsibilities and for six years things just go along swimmingly. Then Abbie meets the perfect guy—investment banker Ben (Bratt). But Ben is planning to relocate to New York and suddenly sole custody is all that matters to Abbie—even it means a court case. Sappy, predictable story falls prey to Madonna's limited acting ability though both Everett and Bratt supply charm galore. **108m/C; DVD.** Madonna; Rupert Everett; Benjamin Bratt; Michael Vartan; Josef Sommer; Lynn Redgrave; Malcolm Stumpf; Neil Patrick Harris; Illeana Douglas; Mark Valley; Stacy Edwards; *D:* John Schlesinger; *W:* Tom Ropelewski; *C:* Elliot Davis; *M:* Gabriel Yared. Golden Raspberries '00: Worst Actress (Madonna).

The Next Big Thing 🦴 1/2 **2002 (R)** Gus Bishop (Eigeman) is a struggling New York artist who meets con man Deech Scumble (Harris) when Deech steals his wallet and, later, a painting. Deech sells the painting, signed "GB," to art gallery owner Arthur (Granger) by inventing a tragic background for the artist he's renamed Geoff Buonardi. Deech manages to convince Gus to continue the scam since his new artistic persona is making them a lot of money. But soon more and more people become aware of the deception. **85m/C; VHS, DVD.** Christopher Eigeman; Jamie Harris; Connie Britton; Janet Zarish; Farley Granger; Mike Starr; Marin Hinkle; *D:* P.J. Posner; *W:* P.J. Posner; Joel Posner; *C:* Oliver Bokelberg; *M:* Ferdinand Jay Smith.

Next Day Air 🦴 1/2 **2009 (R)** Stoned deliveryman Leo (Faison) drops off a package at the wrong apartment where inept criminals Brody (Epps) and Guch (Harris) discover it contains 10 kilos of cocaine. They immediately decide to sell their unexpected bounty but the merchandise was intended for their hot-headed neighbor (Reyes) and was sent by his drug kingpin boss (Rivera) and neither are happy it's gone astray. Offers a few streetwise yuks, and has cult hit potential. **90m/C; On Demand.** Mike Epps; Wood Harris; Emilio Rivera; Donald Adeosun Faison; Omari Hardwick; Darius McCrary; Mos Def; Debbie Allen; Cisco Reyes; Yasmin Deliz; *D:* Beeny Boom; *W:* Blair Cobbs; *C:* David A. Armstrong; *M:* The Elements.

Next Friday 🦴🦴 **2000 (R)** Amiable, meandering sequel to 1995's surprise hit "Friday" finds Craig (Ice Cube) fleeing to the suburbs to escape Debo (Lister), who's out of prison and looking for payback. Uncle Elroy (Curry) has hit the lotto and moved to the 'burbs, giving Craig, and a whole new bunch of central casting characters a new place to hang out and cause some mischief. The original's biggest success came on home video and cable, and this one's likely to duplicate that pattern. **93m/C; VHS, DVD, Blu-Ray.** Ice Cube; Tommy (Tiny) Lister; John Witherspoon; Justin Pierce; Jacob Vargas; Lobo Sebastian; Rolando Molina; Tamala Jones; Mike Epps; Don "DC" Curry; Lisa Rodriguez; Kym E. Whitley; Amy Hill; Robin Allen; Kirk "Sticky Fingaz" Jones; *D:* Steve Carr; *W:* Ice Cube; *C:* Christopher Baffa; *M:* Terence Blanchard.

The Next Hit 🦴 1/2 **2008 (R)** A recording company specializing in rap artists has fallen on hard times and concocts an unorthodox plan to make money by putting hits on its own musicians in order to make them posthumously famous. A little too reminiscent of Tupac Shakur's life. **98m/C; DVD.** Shaneequa Cannon; Vanessa Cruz; Alex Livinalli; Flo Rida; Rick Ross; Della Savoury; Fredro Starr; *D:* Antwan Smith; *W:* David Garvin; *C:* Lenny Gonzalez; *M:* Gorilla Tek.

The Next Karate Kid 🦴🦴 1/2 **1994 (PG)** Fourth installment in the "Kid" series finds martial arts expert Miyagi (Morita) training Julie Pierce (Swank), the orphaned tomboy daughter of an old war buddy who saved his life 50 years earlier. He even teaches her the waltz, just in time for the prom, but she's still tough enough to scrap with a guy. A must-see for "Karate Kid" fans, if there are any left. **107m/C; VHS, DVD, Blu-Ray.** Noriyuki "Pat" Morita; Hilary Swank; *D:* Christopher Cain; *W:* Mark Lee; *M:* Bill Conti.

The Next of Kin 🦴 1/2 **1942** Brit wartime propaganda. Nazi agent Davis (Johns) is working in Britain to discover details of a planned raid on a French port. He fits together bits of information gathered from indiscreet conversations and British casualties are heavy because the enemy was prepared. Loose lips and all that. Davis is free to gather more intel. Title refers to notification of relatives after the death of a soldier. **83m/B; DVD.** *UK* Mervyn Johns; John Chandos; Nova Pilbeam; Reginald Tate; *D:* Thorold Dickinson; *W:* Thorold Dickinson; Basil Bartlett; John Dighton; Angus MacPhail; *C:* Ernest Palmer; *M:* William Walton.

Next of Kin 🦴🦴 **1984** A young man experiencing familial difficulties undergoes experimental video therapy where he views a videotape of an Armenian family who gave their son up for adoption. When he discovers the actual family he insinuates himself into their life, determined to be their long-lost son. **72m/C; VHS, DVD.** *CA* Patrick Tierney; *D:* Atom Egoyan; *W:* Atom Egoyan.

Next of Kin 🦴🦴 **1989 (R)** A Chicago cop returns to his Kentucky home to avenge his brother's brutal murder. Swayze's return to action films after his success in "Dirty Dancing" is unimpressive. **108m/C; VHS, DVD, Blu-Ray.** Patrick Swayze; Adam Baldwin; Bill Paxton; Helen Hunt; Andreas Katsulas; Ben Stiller; Michael J. Pollard; Liam Neeson; *D:* John Irvin; *C:* Steven Poster; *M:* Jack Nitzsche.

Next One 🦴 1/2 **1984** Mysterious visitor from another time winds up on an isolated Greek island as the result of a magnetic storm. The local inhabitants are amazed when the visitor displays some Christ-like characteristics. **105m/C; VHS, DVD.** Keir Dullea; Adrienne Barbeau; Jeremy Licht; Peter Hobbs; *D:* Nico Mastorakis.

The Next Step 🦴🦴 1/2 **1995** Nick Mendez (Negron) is a 35-year-old Broadway dancer who's feeling the wear and tear of his profession. A practiced seducer, Nick does have a devoted girlfriend in ex-dancer turned physical therapist, Amy (Moreu). Amy gets a job offer in Connecticut just as Nick's confidence is shaken when he's rejected for a dance role he originated in favor of a younger performer. Amy wants Nick to retire and move away with her but life away from Broadway leaves Nick wondering what he'd do. Negron is a former Broadway dancer and offers a compelling performance in a film that's ripe with showbiz cliches. **97m/C; VHS, DVD.** Rick Negron; Kristin Moreu; Denise Faye; Taylor Nichols; *D:* Christian Faber; *W:* Aaron Reed; *C:* Zack Winestine; *M:* Mio Morales; Brian Otto; Roni Skies.

Next Stop, Greenwich Village 🦴🦴🦴 **1976 (R)** An affectionate, autobiographical look by Mazursky at a Brooklyn boy with acting aspirations, who moves to Greenwich Village in 1953. Good performances, especially by Winters as the overbearing mother. **109m/C; VHS, DVD, Blu-Ray.** Lenny Baker; Christopher Walken; Ellen Greene; Shelley Winters; Lou Jacobi; Mike Kellin; *D:* Paul Mazursky; *W:* Paul Mazursky; *M:* Bill Conti.

Next Stop, Wonderland 🦴🦴 1/2 **1998 (R)** Charming romance, set in Boston, about a couple of odd ducks who are totally right for each other. Waifish Eric (Davis) is a nurse whose boyfriend Sean (Hoffman) has just left her. So her meddling mom Piper (Taylor) secretly places a personal ad to get her daughter some dates. They're a bunch of losers but plumber/marine-biology student Alan (Gelfant), whom Erin keeps seeing on the subway is Mr. Right. If only the duo could get together. Intelligent characters and a terrific bossa nova soundtrack. Title refers to the name of an actual subway stop. **96m/C; DVD.** Hope Davis; Alan Gelfant; Holland Taylor; Robert Klein; Cara Buono; Jose Zuniga; Phil Hoffman; Lyn Vaus; Larry (Lawrence) Gilliard, Jr.; Victor Argo; Roger Rees; Robert Stanton; Pamela Hart; *D:* Brad Anderson; *W:* Brad Anderson; Lyn Vaus; *C:* Uta Briesewitz; *M:* Claudio Ragazzi.

The Next Three Days 🦴🦴 **2010 (PG-13)** Remake of the 2008 French film "Pour Elle." College professor John Brennan's (Crowe) wife, Lara (Banks), is arrested and imprisoned for a murder she says she didn't commit. When Lara's final appeal is rejected in court, John's only hope is breaking her out of prison. Against insurmountable odds he designs an escape plan and embarks on a dangerous journey to free the woman he loves. Crowe and Banks are bold but the excitement of the farfetched story doesn't always translate. **122m/C; Blu-Ray.** Russell Crowe; Elizabeth Banks; Liam Neeson; Brian Dennehy; Olivia Wilde; Jonathan Tucker; RZA; Lennie James; Jason Beghe; Moran Atias; Nazanin Boniadi; Ty(rone) Giordano; Ty Simpkins; Helen Carey; Daniel Stern; *D:* Paul Haggis; *W:* Paul Haggis; Fred Cavaye; Guillaume Lemans; *C:* Stephane Fontaine; *M:* Alberto Iglesias; Danny Elfman.

Next Time 🦴🦴 1/2 **1999** Offbeat romance tells the story of the relationship between Matt (Campbell), a young white guy, and Evelyn (Allen), a 39-year-old black woman, who meet at a laundrette. **97m/C; DVD.** Jonelle Allen; Christian Campbell; Ishtar Robert Harper; Iona Morris; *D:* L. Alan Fraser; *W:* L. Alan Fraser; *C:* William Hooke; *M:* James S. Mulhollan, Jr.

Next Time I Marry 🦴 1/2 **1938** Lucy fraternizes with ditch digger Ellison because she needs to hitch a Yankee in order to inherit $20 mill. Seems she really loves a foreigner, though. Not much to bobaloo about. Director Kanin's second effort. CUrrently only sold as part of a collection. **65m/B; VHS, DVD.** Lucille Ball; James Ellison; Lee Bowman; Granville Bates; Mantan Moreland; Florence Lake; *D:* Garson Kanin.

Next Time We Love 🦴🦴 1/2 **1936** Ambitious reporter Chris Tyler (Stewart) and actress Cicely (Sullavan) impulsively marry. Best friend Tommy (Milland) gets Cicely a shot on Broadway while Chris is assigned to his paper's Rome bureau. Cecily learns she's pregnant and Chris comes back to New York, losing his job. Tommy pulls some strings but Chris' new position is overseas again and Cecily basically raises their son alone while becoming a Broadway star. Eventually, Tommy admits he loves her and Cecily goes to Europe to settle things with Chris. Romantic melodrama also suffers because Cecily isn't a particularly likeable character. **87m/B; DVD.** James Stewart; Margaret Sullavan; Ray Milland; Grant Mitchell; Robert McWade; Anna Demetrio; *D:* Edward H. Griffith; *W:* Melville Baker; *C:* Joseph Valentine; *M:* Franz Waxman.

The Next Voice You Hear 🦴🦴 1/2 **1950** Lives are changed forever when a group of people hear the voice of God on the radio. Interesting premise presented seriously. **84m/B; VHS, DVD.** James Whitmore; Nancy Davis; Gary Gray; Lillian Bronson; Art Smith; Tom D'Andrea; Jeff Corey; George Chandler; *D:* William A. Wellman.

Next Year in Jerusalem 🦴🦴 **1998** Charlie is openly gay—but what he's hiding is his Orthodox Jewish background. Pressured by his mother, Charlie shows up at the family Passover seder, where he meets Manny. Devout Manny is supposed to marry the Rabbi's daughter, only he's got a secret too. The duo soon begin a relationship they keep from their families but it becomes clear that Charlie and Manny need to be honest about who they truly are. **103m/C; VHS, DVD.** Peter J. Byrnes; Reed McGowan; Georgina Spelvin; Louis Edmonds; *D:* David Nahmod; *W:* David Nahmod; *C:* Kelvin Walker; *M:* Richard Barone.

Nezulla the Rat Monster 🦴 1/2 **2002** A small town is being overrun by plague, which a defunct local chemical company fesses up to causing when infected rats escaped during experiments for the American military. But a giant rubber rat monster may have the cure locked within its DNA. So a joint team of Japanese and American Special Forces (all of whom look Japanese) storm the company's facility and get locked inside, and a self-destruct countdown begins. While backstabbing each other the troops find out rat monsters only laugh it off when you shoot them. **90m/C; DVD.** *JP* Daisuke Ryu; Mika Katsumura; Yoshiyuki Kubota; Ayumi Tokitou; *D:* Kanta Tagawa; *W:* Kanta Tagawa; *C:* Gen Kobayashi; *M:* Takashi Nakagawa.

Niagara 🦴🦴 1/2 **1952** During their honeymoon in Niagara Falls, a scheming wife (Monroe) plans to kill her crazed war-vet husband (Cotten). Little does she know that he is plotting to double-cross her. Steamy, quasi-Hitchcockian mystery ably directed, with interesting performances. Monroes sings "Kiss." **89m/B; VHS, DVD, Blu-Ray.** Joseph Cotten; Jean Peters; Marilyn Monroe; Max (Casey Adams) Showalter; Don Wilson; Denis O'Dea; Lurene Tuttle; Harry Carey, Jr.; Russell Collins; Minerva Urecal; *D:* Henry Hathaway; *W:* Charles Brackett; Walter Reisch; *C:* Joe MacDonald; *M:* Sol Kaplan.

Niagara Motel 🦴🦴 **2006** A run-down motel in Niagara Falls houses the usual malcontents and oddballs, beginning with its drunken Scottish manager, Phillie (Ferguson). Lily (Crewson) is thinking about turning tricks since her husband can't find a job; waitress and wannabe actress Caroline (Dhavernas) is being pushed into filming porn by her sleazy agent Michael (Pollak); and drug addict Denise (Friel) wants to reclaim her daughter from foster care. **88m/C; DVD.** *CA* Craig Ferguson; Anna Friel; Wendy Crewson; Caroline Dhavernas; Kevin Pollak; Peter Keleghan; Kris Holden-Ried; Tom Barnett; Gary Yates; Dani Romain; ***W:*** George F. Walker; ***C:*** Ian Wilson; ***M:*** Guy Fletcher.

Niagara, Niagara **1997 (R)** Marcy (Tunney) is a victim of Tourette's Syndrome, which causes the sufferer to twitch and unleash strings of profanity that would make a longshoreman blush. She meets shy, introverted Seth (Thomas) while they're both shoplifting, and it's love at first sight. They hit the road, but when Seth is injured in a botched robbery, they're taken in by fellow oddball Walter, a tow truck driver who dotes on a pet chicken named after his dead wife. These lost characters go nowhere and are pulled apart by Marcy's bourbon-fueled tics and tantrums. A compelling performance by Tunney carries this dull, flat movie. **96m/C; DVD.** Robin Tunney; Henry Thomas; Michael Parks; Stephen Lang; John MacKay; ***D:*** Bob Gosse; ***W:*** Matthew Weiss; ***C:*** Michael Spiller; ***M:*** Michael Timmins; Jeff Bird.

Nice Guy Johnny 1/2 **2010** Familiar indie rom com from Burns with a wimpy lead. Smalltime Oakland sports radio host Johnny (Bush) is engaged to marry his more-ambitious college sweetheart Claire (Wood). She sends Johnny off to New York for a job interview and he meets up with his womanizing Uncle Terry (Burns), who proposes a weekend of debauchery in the Hamptons to his pushover nephew. Johnny meets the gorgeous Brooke (Bishe), who also thinks he needs to man up and actually decide what he wants instead of just going along. **92m/C; DVD.** Edward Burns; Matthew Bush; Kerry Bishe; Anna Wood; Callie (Calliope) Thorne; Jay Paterson; ***D:*** Edward Burns; ***W:*** Edward Burns; ***C:*** William Rexer; ***M:*** P.T. Walkley.

The Nice Guys **2016 (R)** Shane Black's spiritual sequel to "Kiss Kiss Bang Bang" is another rollicking buddy action/comedy. This one takes place in 1977 Los Angeles—and Black's film is at least somewhat about the end of Camelot and free love and the start of cynicism—and stars Gosling and Crowe as a pair of bumbling private dicks who stumble upon a conspiracy involving the auto industry, porn industry and local politicians. The two leads are spectacularly cast, and the film works because of their chemistry and comic timing. **116m/C; DVD, Blu-Ray.** Ryan Gosling; Russell Crowe; Angourie Rice; Matt Bomer; Margaret Qualley; ***D:*** Shane Black; ***W:*** Shane Black; Anthony Bagarozzi; ***C:*** Philippe Rousselot; ***M:*** David Buckley; John Ottman.

Nice Guys Sleep Alone **1999 (R)** Overachieving independent rom com finds nice guy Carter (O'Bryan) hearing those three dreaded words "let's be friends" at the end of each date. He has resolved to take a new approach when he meets Maggie (Temchen), a vet recently arrived in Louisville from New York. The complications that keep the plot moving are familiar and Carter's rival Robert (Murray) is such a swine that it's impossible any intelligent woman would pay attention to him, no matter how rich he is. But most characters are engaging, especially Carter's stepsister Erin (Marcil), and the film has its heart in the right place. **92m/C; DVD.** Sean O'Bryan; Sybil Temchen; Vanessa Marcil; Blake Steury; Christopher Murray; Morgan Fairchild; William Sanderson; ***D:*** Stu Pollard; ***W:*** Stu Pollard; ***C:*** Nathan Hope.

Nicholas and Alexandra 1/2 **1971 (PG)** Epic chronicling the final years of Tsar Nicholas II, Empress Alexandra, and their children. Their lavish royal lifestyle gives way to imprisonment and eventual execution under the new Lenin government. Beautiful, but overlong costume epic that loses steam in the second half. Based on the biography by Robert Massie. **183m/C; VHS, DVD, Blu-Ray.** Michael Jayston; Janet Suzman; Tom Baker; Laurence Olivier; Michael Redgrave; Harry Andrews; Jack Hawkins; Alexander Knox; Curt Jurgens; ***D:*** Franklin J. Schaffner; ***W:*** James Goldman; ***C:*** Frederick A. (Freddie) Young; ***M:*** Richard Rodney Bennett. Oscars '71: Art Dir./Set Dec., Costume Des.

Nicholas Nickleby *The Life and Adventures of Nicholas Nickleby* **1946** An ensemble cast works hard to bring to life Charles Dickens' novel about an impoverished family dependent on their wealthy but villainous uncle. Young Nicholas is an apprentice at a school for boys, and he and a student run away to a series of exciting adventures. An enjoyable film, though it is hard to tell the entire story in such a small amount of time. **108m/B; VHS, DVD, Streaming.** *GB* Cedric Hardwicke; Stanley Holloway; Derek Bond; Alfred Drayton; Sybil Thorndike; Sally Ann Howes; Bernard Miles; Mary Merrall; Cathleen Nesbitt; ***D:*** Alberto Cavalcanti; ***C:*** Georges Perinal.

Nicholas Nickleby **2002 (PG)** Director McGrath reliably takes on another period piece with this sprawling Dickens classic, which he nicely condenses for mass consumption. Nicholas (Hunnam) is a 19 year-old in England forced to grow up quickly when his father dies and he takes over as head of the family. Well acted, with Hunnam able but not outstanding in an overall lighthearted and lively production. **130m/C; VHS, DVD, Blu-Ray.** Charlie Hunnam; Christopher Plummer; Jamie Bell; Jim Broadbent; Juliet Stevenson; Tom Courtenay; Alan Cumming; Edward Fox; Romola Garai; Anne Hathaway; Timothy Spall; Nathan Lane; Barry Humphries; Gerard Horan; Stella Gonet; ***D:*** Douglas McGrath; ***W:*** Douglas McGrath; ***C:*** Dick Pope; ***M:*** Rachel Portman.

Nick & Norah's Infinite Playlist **2008 (PG-13)** Recently dumped Jersey kid Nick (Cera) tries to woo back his ex, mean girl Tris (Dziena), with one mix CD after another, but she's oblivious to his geeky-cool charm. Nora (Dennings) bumps into Nick in Manhattan for Nick's alt-rock band's gig and, eventually, they embark on a search for an indie band playing a show so secret that they have to criss-cross the city in Nick's yellow Yugo, picking up clues about the location. What they really find is that they were looking for each other. Director Sollett tosses in enough updated twists to keep the teen rom com fresh. **90m/C; DVD, Blu-Ray, On Demand.** Michael Cera; Kat Dennings; Alexis Dziena; Aaron Yoo; Rafi Gavron; Ari Graynor; Jay Baruchel; Zachary Booth; ***D:*** Peter Sollett; ***W:*** Lorene Scafaria; ***C:*** Tom Richmond; ***M:*** Mark Mothersbaugh.

Nick Carter, Master Detective **1939** Detectve Nick Carter originally began as a series of stories in Pulp magazines before making the move to radio shows and subsequently three films. In this first movie set just before WWII, the detective is asked to help foil spies at a local aircraft factory working on an experimental new fighter plane. **65m/B; DVD.** Walter Pidgeon; Rita Johnson; Henry Hull; Stanley Ridges; Donald Meek; ***D:*** Jacques Tourneur; ***W:*** Bertram Millhauser; ***C:*** Charles Lawton, Jr.; ***M:*** Edward Ward; Daniele Amfitheatrof. **VIDEO**

Nick Knight **1989** An L.A. cop on the night beat is really a good-guy vampire, who quaffs cattle blood as he tracks down another killer who's draining humans of their plasma. A gimmicky pilot for a would-be TV series that eventually morphed into "Forever Knight." **92m/C; VHS, DVD.** Rick Springfield; Michael Nader; Laura Johnson; John Kapelos; ***D:*** Farhad Mann; ***W:*** James D. Parriott; ***C:*** Frank Beasoechea; ***M:*** Joseph Conlan. **TV**

Nick of Time 1/2 **1995 (R)** A malicious stranger (Walken) and his cohort give ordinary accountant Gene Watson (Depp) 90 minutes to assassinate the governor of California (Mason) or his little girl will be killed. Walken as an evil psycho. . .now there's a stretch. On the other hand, Depp as a button-down, conservative widower is a bit of a switch after his usually quirky roles. Illogical scenarios (even for an action flick) and curiously uneven pacing do this one in. Shot almost entirely in L.A's Bonaventure Hotel in real time with a handheld camera. **98m/C; DVD.** Johnny Depp; Christopher Walken; Charles S. Dutton; Peter Strauss; Roma Maffia; Gloria Reuben; Marsha Mason; Courtney Chase; Bill Smitrovich; G.D. Spradlin; ***D:*** John Badham; ***W:*** Patrick Duncan; ***C:*** Roy Wagner; ***M:*** Arthur B. Rubinstein.

The Nickel Children **2005** Two 14-year-old runaways become prostitutes to survive in L.A. The story focuses more on street-savvy Cat, who only softens her attitude around the puppyish Nolan, who has a shy romantic interest in her. When Cat finds out she's pregnant, and after the murder of a hooker friend, she makes a decision to return home. **95m/C; DVD.** Tamara Hope; Tom Sizemore; Jeremy Sisto; Marsha Thomason; John Billingsley; Maeve Quinlan; ***D:*** Glenn Klinker; ***W:*** Eric Litra; ***C:*** John Bartley; ***M:*** Rich Ragsdale.

The Nickel Ride **1974** Loose contemporary film noir finds low-level L.A. mobster Cooper (Miller) in trouble with his boss Carl (Hillerman) when he can't close an important real estate deal that's necessary to their hijacking business. Cooper realizes his days are numbered when Carl sends apparent yokel Turner (Hopkins) to keep an eye on him. Crime never seemed so banal. **98m/C; DVD.** Jason Miller; John Hillerman; Bo Hopkins; Victor French; Linda Haynes; Lou Frizzell; ***D:*** Robert Mulligan; ***W:*** Eric Roth; ***C:*** Jordan Cronenweth; ***M:*** Dave Grusin.

Nickelodeon 1/2 **1976** Bogdanovich tries unsuccessfully to capture his love for the movies in this underwhelming comedy about the early—and often violent days—of the industry. Bumbling lawyer Leo Harrigan (O'Neal) finds himself directing a slapstick silent western in California with cowboy Buck Greenway (Reynolds), who was hired by another company to stop the production, as his reluctant star. **121m/C; DVD.** Ryan O'Neal; Burt Reynolds; Jane Hitchcock; Tatum O'Neal; John Ritter; Brian Keith; Stella Stevens; Harry Carey, Jr.; M. Emmet Walsh; ***D:*** Peter Bogdanovich; ***W:*** Peter Bogdanovich; W.D. Richter; ***C:*** Laszlo Kovacs; ***M:*** Richard Hazard.

Nicky's Family **2013** Documentary focusing on well-off British stockbroker Nicholas Winton who saw the horrors of the Nazi occupation first hand during a ski trip to WWII Prague, as Jewish children sat held up waiting for death. Normally complacent, the jet setter sets up an underground railroad to bring these children to safety in his homeland. A rare uplifting account of a horrific period, unfortunately falls flat when turning to wishy-washy re-enactments that give off a made-for-TV vibe. The most thunder is felt when the camera turns on the still living 103-year-old Winton for his version of the story. **96m/C; DVD.** *SV* Nicholas Winton; Michal Slany; ***D:*** Matej Minac; ***W:*** Matej Minac; Patrik Pass; ***C:*** Dodo Simoncic; ***M:*** Janusz Stoklosa.

Nico and Dani 1/2 *Krampack* **2000** Best buddies Nico (Vilches) and Dani (Ramallo) are 17-year-old virgins who hope to change that situation while on a Spanish beach vacation. Nico has the hots for pretty Elena (Orozco), who returns his interest, which leaves her cousin Berta (Nubiola) pining for Dani. Too bad Dani realizes that he not only loves Nico, he's IN love with him and that Nico doesn't share his sexual feelings. Dani finds a mentor in an older gay man (Amado) but the situation remains tangled in an all-too realistic (if somewhat overly sunny) way. Based on the play "Krampack" by Jordi Sanchez. Spanish with subtitles. **90m/C; DVD.** *SP* Fernando Ramallo; Jordi Vilches; Marieta Orozco; Esther Nubiola; Chisco Amado; Ana Gracia; ***D:*** Cesc Gay; ***W:*** Cesc Gay; Tomas Aragay; ***C:*** Andreu Rebes; ***M:*** Riqui Sabates; Joan Diaz; Jordi Prats.

Nico Icon **1995 (R)** Documentary probes the life of Velvet Underground sensation and Warhol superstar Nico. A pastiche showing V.U. concert footage and movie clips from Nico's most famous film appearances: Fellini's "La Dolce Vita" and Warhol's "The Chelsea Girls." Also features interviews from Warhol's Factory inhabitants, band members, and Nico's grown son Ari. Visually as interesting as the subject herself, film manages to bring the viewer closer to the untouchable Teutonic figure without being sensational or overly flashy. Some French and German with subtitles. **75m/C; VHS, DVD.** *GE* ***D:*** Susanne Ofteringer; ***W:*** Susanne Ofteringer; ***C:*** Judith Kaufmann.

Nico the Unicorn **1998** Fantasy family adventure based on the Frank Sacks children's novel. Julie Hastings and her 11-year-old son Billy move to a new town to start over after a bad accident left Billy with a permanent leg injury. They visit a ragtag local circus and find a neglected mare they arrange to take home only to find the pony is pregnant—with a unicorn. **90m/C; DVD.** *CA* Kevin Zegers; Anne Archer; Elisha Cuthbert; Michael Ontkean; Johnny Morina; ***D:*** Graeme Campbell; ***W:*** Frank Sacks; ***C:*** Walter Bal; ***M:*** Alan Reeves.

Nicole *Crazed* **1972 (R)** The downfall of a wealthy woman who is able to buy everything she wants except love. Currently sold under the title 'Crazed'. **91m/C; VHS, DVD.** Leslie Caron; Catherine Bach; Ramon Bieri; ***D:*** Itsvan Ventilla.

Nicotina 1/2 **2003 (R)** Hacker Lolo is commissioned to get Swiss account info for a Russian mobster. But Lolo is a voyeur who has been using spy cams to watch neighbor Andrea and his obsession leads to his supplying the wrong discs to the Russian, causing all sorts of complications. Plot takes place over one night in Mexico City and features debates about smoking and frustrated smokers (hence the title). Spanish with subtitles. **90m/C; DVD.** *MX* Diego Luna; Lucas Crespi; Jesus Ochoa; Norman Sotolongo; Marta Belaustegui; Rafael Inclan; Daniel Gimenez Cacho; Rosa Maria Bianchi; Carmen Madrid; Jose Maria Yazpik; ***D:*** Hugo Rodriguez; ***W:*** Martin Salinas; ***C:*** Marcelo Iacarino; ***M:*** Fernando Corona.

Night Across the Street 1/2 *La noche de enfrente* **2012** A drama about the intersections of dreams, memories, and reality, based on short stories by Hernan del Solar. As Don Celso (Hernandez) nears his forced retirement from his position in an office, he starts to remember memories from his life. Though his remembrances are both real and imagined, they are all rich with imagery such as a time when he went to the movies as a child with Beethoven and stayed for a time in a haunted hotel. Ideas of fiction, history, and life are mixed together to create an elegy to his existence. Spanish and French with subtitles. **110m/C; DVD.** Christian Vadim; Sergio Hernandez; Santiago Figueroa; Valentina Vargas; Chamila Rodriguez; ***D:*** Raoul Ruiz; ***W:*** Raoul Ruiz; ***C:*** Inti Briones; ***M:*** Jorge Arriagada.

The Night After Halloween *Snapshot* **1979 (R)** A young woman gets the shock of her life when she discovers that her boyfriend is a crazed killer. **90m/C; VHS, DVD.** *AU* Chantal Contouri; Robert Bruning; Sigrid Thornton; ***D:*** Simon Wincer; ***W:*** Everett De Roche; Chris De Roche; ***C:*** Vincent Monton; ***M:*** Brian May.

Night After Night 1/2 **1932** West's screen debut finds her in an unaccustomed secondary role, although a prime scene-stealer. In Raft's first starring role, he's a monied low-life who opens a fancy nightclub and becomes infatuated with Park Avenue beauty Cummings. His problems are compounded by the arrival of raucous ex-flames West and Gleason. When a hatcheck girl cries "Goodness!" over West's diamonds, she replies, in suggestive West-style, "Goodness had nothing to do with it, dearie." Adapted from the novel "Single Night" by Louis Bromfield. **73m/B; DVD.** George Raft; Constance Cummings; Mae West; Wynne Gibson; Alison Skipworth; Roscoe Karns; Louis Calhern; ***D:*** Archie Mayo; ***W:*** Mae West; Kathryn Scola; Vincent Lawrence.

Night Alarm 1/2 **1934** Newshound Hal Ashby wants to leave his gardening column behind for investigative journalism but he objects when the column is given over to Helen Smith, the daughter of a wealthy but shady industrialist who's in with city officials. After popping off about Helen's dad, Hall starts investigating a series of arson fires at Smith's factories and even rescues Helen from danger. **65m/B; DVD.** Bruce Cabot; Judith Allen; H.B. Warner; Sam Hardy; Harry Holman; ***D:*** Spencer Gordon Bennett; ***W:*** Earle Snell; ***C:*** James S. Brown, Jr.

Night Ambush 1/2 *Ill Met by Moonlight* **1957** A Nazi general is kidnapped on Crete by British agents, who embark on a dangerous trip to the coast where a ship awaits to take them to Cairo. The general tries to thwart their plans, but they outwit him at every turn. Based on a novel by W. Stanley Moss that details a similar real-life event. **100m/B; VHS, DVD.** *GB* Dirk Bogarde; Marius Goring; David Oxley; Cyril Cusack; Christopher Lee; ***D:*** Michael Powell; Emeric Pressburger.

Night and Day 1/2 **1946** Sentimental musical about the life of bon-vivant composer-extraordinaire Cole Porter. His intensity and the motivations for his music are dramatized, but this film succeeds best as a fabulous showcase for Porter's songs. **128m/C; VHS, DVD.** Cary Grant; Alexis Smith; Jane Wyman; Eve Arden; Mary Martin; Alan Hale; Monty Woolley; Ginny Simms; Dorothy Malone; ***D:*** Michael Curtiz; ***M:*** Max Steiner.

Night and the City 1/2 **1950** A film noir classic about a hustler's money-making schemes. Harry Fabian 's (Widmark) a small-time promoter working for slimy nightclub owner Philip (Sullivan), whose job is to hustle the marks into the club where his girlfriend Mary (Tierney) sings. Harry also happens to be romancing Phillips's wife, Helen (Withers), and wants her to back his latest con. But his schemes go awry and Fabian's on the run for his life. Widmark gives a riveting performance of a lowlife whose brains don't match his ambitions. Filmed in London with appropriate brooding tawdriness. Adapted from the novel by Gerald Kersh; remade in 1992. **95m/B; VHS, DVD, Blu-Ray.** *GB* Richard Widmark; Gene Tierney; Googie Withers; Francis L. Sullivan; Hugh Marlowe; Herbert Lom; Mike Mazurki; Charles Farrell; ***D:*** Jules Dassin; ***W:*** Jo Eisinger; ***M:*** Franz Waxman.

Night and the City **1992 (R)** Harry Fabian (De Niro), a con-artist/ambulance-chaser, concocts a scheme to make it big, and approaches an old boxing great (Warden) to come out of retirement and revive a local boxing night. Problem is, although Harry has energy and ambition, he also has a talent for making enemies out of the wrong people, like the boxer's brother (King), a neighborhood mobster. Filled with details more interesting than the plot; more about fast-living, fast-talking New Yorkers, a fine showcase for De Niro's talent. Winkler's remake of the 1950 Jules Dassin film. **98m/C; VHS, DVD.** Robert De Niro; Jessica Lange; Cliff Gorman; Alan King; Jack Warden; Eli Wallach; Barry Primus; Gene Kirkwood; Pedro Sanchez; Joseph (Joe) D'Onofrio; Michael Badalucco; Michael Rispoli; ***Cameo(s):*** Regis Philbin; Joy Philbin; Richard Price; ***D:*** Irwin Winkler; ***W:*** Richard Price; ***C:*** Tak Fujimoto; ***M:*** James Newton Howard.

The Night and the Moment 1/2 **1994 (R)** Dull, mishmashy costume drama (set in the 17th century) about an imprisoned author (Dafoe) who became intrigued with the mystery woman who had occupied the next cell. They exchanged notes, and he vows to find her when he's released from prison. But first he spends a seductive night, exchanging stories about past conquests, at the chateau of the Marquise (Olin), who, of course, turns out to be the mystery lady. Based on the novel "La Nuit er le Moment" by Claude-Prosper de Jolyot Crebillon. **89m/C; VHS, DVD.** *GB FR IT* Willem Dafoe; Lena Olin; Miranda Richardson; Jean-Claude Carriere; Carole Richert; ***D:*** Anna Maria Tato; ***W:*** Jean-Claude Carriere; Anna Maria Tato; ***C:*** Giuseppe Rotunno; ***M:*** Ennio Morricone.

Night at the Golden Eagle **2002 (R)** As bleak as the Tom Waits song on the soundtrack. Tommy's (Montemarno) an aging small-time crook fresh out of a seven year prison stint. He meets up with old partner Mic (Agiro) and is dismayed to find out that Mic has gone legit and wants them to move from L.A. to Vegas to work in a casino. Mic takes his pal back to the sleazy Golden Eagle hotel where he's been living. Unfortunately, their plans are soon derailed by a dead hooker (Lyonne) who works for vicious pimp Rodan (Jones). Paralelling the Tommy/Mic friendship is that of veteran whore Sally (Magnuson) to whom Rodan gives runaway teenager Lori Ann (Jacobs) for training. **87m/C; VHS, DVD.** Donnie Montemarano; Vinny Argiro; Ann Magnuson; Vinnie Jones; Nicole Jacobs; Natasha Lyonne; Fayard Nicholas; Sam Moore; Francesca "Kitten" Natividad; ***Cameo(s):*** James Caan; ***D:*** Adam Rifkin; ***W:*** Adam Rifkin; ***C:*** Checco Varese; ***M:*** Tyler Bates.

Night at the Museum **2006 (PG)** Wanting to impress his 10-year-old son (Cherry) when his ex-wife's (Raver) new fiance (Rudd) proves to be a better role model, Larry (Stiller) decides to change his flighty ways and takes a night guard job at NYC's Museum of Natural History. He gets more than he bargained for when the displays come alive at night, a minor detail left unrevealed by his predecessors (the comic-legend trio of Rooney, Van Dyke, and Cobbs). But it's not as fun as it sounds—the hyper CGI effects, combined with the weak tale of Larry's life woes, chase away the charm of Milan Trenc's original children's book. **108m/C; DVD, Blu-Ray.** Ben Stiller; Carla Gugino; Dick Van Dyke; Mickey Rooney; Bill Cobbs; Kim Raver; Ricky Gervais; Robin Williams; Jake Cherry; Owen Wilson; Steve Coogan; Patrick Gallagher; Mizuo Peck; Paul Rudd; Anne Meara; Rami Malek; ***D:*** Shawn Levy; ***W:*** Robert Ben Garant; Thomas Lennon; ***C:*** Guillermo Navarro; ***M:*** Alan Silvestri.

Night at the Museum: Battle of the Smithsonian 1/2 **2009 (PG)** Follow-up (and more of the same) to the successful 2006 film finds Larry Daley (Stiller) is now an ex-security guard turned entrepreneur. While visiting the Natural History Museum, Larry learns that the old exhibits have been packed up and shipped to the Smithsonian's federal archives. In an effort to secure the Egyptian tablet that brings the exhibits to life, Larry finagles his way into the Smithsonian to stop lisping pharaoh Kahmunrah (Azaria) and his cohorts from committing evil. Adams plays helpful Amelia Earhart as a brash screwball comedy dame. **105m/C; DVD, Blu-Ray, On Demand.** Ben Stiller; Owen Wilson; Steve Coogan; Amy Adams; Bill Hader; Ricky Gervais; Dick Van Dyke; Hank Azaria; Christopher Guest; Eugene Levy; Jake Cherry; Jon Bernthal; Robin Williams; Jonah Hill; Alain Chabat; ***D:*** Shawn Levy; ***W:*** Robert Ben Garant; Thomas Lennon; Scott Frank; ***C:*** John Schwartzman; ***M:*** Alan Silvestri.

Night at the Museum: Secret of the Tomb 1/2 **2014 (PG)** Can a movie work through sheer will of its all-star cast alone? This noisy, star-packed family film sequel sure tries. Bringing back most of the cast from the previous two films (including one of the final roles for Williams), this international hit works from a more-is-more place of family filmmaking. The louder and crazier the better. And so we get Stiller working with his come-to-life museum characters to learn the history of the tablet that animated them by travelling to the British Museum. The journey allows for new characters like King Arthur and Sir Lancelot but it's really just a lot more of the same. **97m/C; DVD, Blu-Ray.** Ben Stiller; Skyler Gisondo; Robin Williams; Dan Stevens; Rebel Wilson; Owen Wilson; Steve Coogan; Ben Kingsley; Anjali Jay; Mickey Rooney; Dick Van Dyke; ***D:*** Shawn Levy; ***W:*** David Guion; Michael Handelman; ***C:*** Guillermo Navarro; ***M:*** Alan Silvestri.

A Night at the Opera **1935** The Marx Brothers get mixed up with grand opera in their first MGM-produced epic and their first without Zeppo. Jones, as a budding opera singer warbles "Alone" and "Cosi Cosa." One of their best films, blessed with a big budget—used to reach epic anarchic heights. Some scenes were tested on live audiences before inclusion, including the Groucho/Chico paper-tearing contract negotiation and the celebrated stateroom scene, in which the boys are joined in a small closet by two maids, the ship's engineer, his assistant, a manicurist, a young woman, a cleaning lady, and four food-laden waiters. **92m/B; DVD.** Groucho Marx; Chico Marx; Harpo Marx; Allan Jones; Kitty Carlisle Hart; Sig Rumann; Margaret Dumont; Walter Woolf King; Edward (Ed Kean, Keene) Keane; Robert Emmett O'Connor; ***D:*** Sam Wood; ***W:*** George S. Kaufman; Morrie Ryskind; Bert Kalmar; Harry Ruby; Al Boasberg; ***C:*** Merritt B. Gerstad; ***M:*** Herbert Stothart. Natl. Film Reg. '93.

A Night at the Roxbury 1/2 **1998 (PG-13)** The Bubati brothers, like so many Saturday Night Live veterans before them, make the leap to the big screen with limited success. Steve and Doug (Ferrell and Kattan) continue their fruitless quest to gain entrance into the hallowed Roxbury night club. Their luck changes when they get into a fender bender with former "21 Jump Street" star Richard Grieco (playing himself), who gets them in. Typical of the SNL skits-to-big-screen formula, the bit works as a three-minute sketch but isn't funny or interesting enough to sustain even its meager 82 minute running time. **83m/C; VHS, DVD.** Will Ferrell; Chris Kattan; Molly Shannon; Dan Hedaya; Loni Anderson; Richard Grieco; Elisa Donovan; Lochlyn Munro; Dwayne Hickman; Mark McKinney; ***D:*** John Fortenberry; ***W:*** Will Ferrell; Chris Kattan; Steve Koren; ***C:*** Francis Kenny; ***M:*** David Kitay.

Night Beast **1983** Alien creature lands his spaceship near a small town and begins a bloody killing spree. Recycled plot. **90m/C; VHS, DVD, Blu-Ray.** Tom Griffith; Richard Dyszel; Jaimie Zemarel; George Stover; ***D:*** Donald M. Dohler.

The Night Before 1/2 **1988 (PG-13)** Snobby high school beauty Loughlin loses a bet and has to go to the prom with the school geek Reeves. On the way, they get lost on the wrong side of the tracks, and become involved with pimps, crime, and the police. A drunken Reeves loses Loughlin as well as his father's car. Typical teen farce. **90m/C; VHS, DVD.** Keanu Reeves; Lori Loughlin; Trinidad Silva; Michael Greene; Theresa Saldana; Suzanne Snyder; Morgan Lofting; Gwil Richards; ***D:*** Thom Eberhardt; ***W:*** Gregory Scherick; Thom Eberhardt.

The Night Before **2015 (R)** Rogen's arrested development schtick blends well with the holiday-themed comedy even if the law of diminishing returns is somewhat in effect here. We've seen Rogen do this thing before. This time, he plays Isaac, best friend to Ethan (Gordon-Levitt) and Chris (Mackie). The trio has been getting into trouble every Christmas Eve since Ethan lost his parents in a car accident. As Isaac approaches fatherhood himself, this year's debauchery promises to be the last. Some of the resultant hijinks are very funny, but a few jokes fall flat, and we can't help but feel this is nothing new. **101m/C; DVD, Blu-Ray.** Joseph Gordon-Levitt; Seth Rogen; Anthony Mackie; Jillian Bell; Lizzy Caplan; ***D:*** Jonathan Levine; ***W:*** Jonathan Levine; Kyle Hunter; Ariel Shaffir; Evan Goldberg; ***C:*** Brandon Trost; ***M:*** Marco Beltrami; Miles Hankins.

The Night Before the Night Before Christmas 1/2 **2010** In this Hallmark Channel movie, a confused Santa starts his deliveries on the 23rd, a big mistake since he crashes into the home of workaholic Angela and Wayne Fox. He has amnesia and the parents and their neglected kids, along with elf Nigel, have to figure out a way to save Christmas (and for the Fox clan to put their own fractured family into the holiday spirit). **90m/C; DVD.** Jennifer Beals; Rick Roberts; Gage Munroe; Rebecca Williams; R.D. Reid; Jordan Prentice; Marcia Bennett; ***D:*** James Orr; ***W:*** James Orr; Jim Cruickshank; ***C:*** Peter Benison; ***M:*** James Gelfand. **CABLE**

Night Birds **1931** Early British thriller about a notorious crook named "Flash Jack," who heads a gang of top-hatted criminals that rob the wealthy. Poor production quality and Raine's standoffish screen presence contribute to this below-average film. **76m/B; VHS, DVD.** *GB* Jameson Thomas; Jack Raine; Muriel Angelus; Eve Gray; ***D:*** Richard Eichberg; ***W:*** Miles Malleson.

Night Call Nurses *Young L.A. Nurses 2* **1972 (R)** Three gorgeous nurses find danger and intrigue on the night shift at a psychiatric hospital. Third in the "nurse" quintet is back on target, shrugging off the previous film's attempts at "serious" social commentary. Miller provides comic relief. Preceded by "The Student Nurses" and "Private Duty Nurses," and followed by "The Young Nurses" and "Candy Stripe Nurses." **85m/C; VHS, DVD.** Patricia T. Byrne; Alana Collins; Mittie Lawrence; Clinton Kimbrough; Felton Perry; Stack Pierce; Richard Young; Dennis Dugan; Dick Miller; ***D:*** Jonathan Kaplan; ***W:*** George Armitage.

The Night Caller **1997 (R)** Radio psychologist attracts the attentions of a deranged listener. **94m/C; VHS, DVD.** Shanna Reed; Tracy Nelson; Mary Crosby; Cyndi Pass; ***D:*** Rob Malenfant; ***W:*** Frank Rehwaldt; ***C:*** M. David Mullen.

Night Caller from Outer Space 1/2 *Blood Beast from Outer Space; The Night Caller* **1966** When a woman-hunting alien arrives in London, women begin to disappear. At first, incredibly, no one makes the connection, but then the horrible truth comes to light. **84m/B; VHS, DVD.** *GB* John Saxon; Maurice Denham; Patricia Haines; Alfred Burke; Jack Watson; Aubrey Morris; ***D:*** John Gilling; ***W:*** James O'Connolly; ***C:*** Stephen Dade; ***M:*** Johnny Gregory.

Night Cargo 1/2 **1936** Shady Singapore businessman Shark Moran (Miller) makes wealthy Bruce Donaldson (Hughes) his partner. Bruce is looking for lost showgirl love Claire (Bishop), who happens to be dancing at one of Shark's waterfront dives. Shark wants her, she rejects him, and there's trouble. **66m/B; DVD.** Julie Bishop; Lloyd Hughes; Walter Miller; Charlotte (Carlotta) Monti; Jimmy Aubrey; Lloyd Whitlock; ***D:*** Charles (Hutchison) Hutchinson; ***W:*** Sherman Lowe; ***C:*** Walter Lundin.

Night Catches Us 1/2 **2010 (R)** It's the summer of 1976 and Marcus returns to his Philadelphia 'hood for the funeral of his minister father. He left under suspicious circumstances—a member of the Black Panthers/Black Power movement, Marcus was suspected of betraying comrade Neil, who was killed in a police shootout, because of his love for Neil's wife Patricia. She's still there, and an activist lawyer, but they're both older and wiser. Unlike Patricia's frustrated young cousin Jimmy who wants to replay the radicalism, and various inhabitants believing they have scores to settle. Hamilton's debut feature. **88m/C; DVD.** Anthony Mackie; Kerry Washington; Jamie Hector; Wendell Pierce; Tariq Trotter; Jamara Griffin; Amari Cheatom; ***D:*** Tanya Hamilton; ***W:*** Tanya Hamilton; ***C:*** David Tumblety.

Night Comes On **2018** Though Angel (Fishback) remembers what it was like when her parents were alive and together, she was put into foster care with her younger sister Abby (Hall) after her father murdered their mother. Angel turned to crime, and eventually served time in prison on firearms possession charges. After her release, she immediately plots revenge for her mother's death. Angel returns to her problematic foster family, where the sisters are aware they are essentially on their own. As Angel's plan becomes reality, her personal pain become more acute as Fishback achingly expresses her character's hopelessness. **90m/C; DVD.** Dominique Fishback; Tatum Marilyn Hall; Natashia Fuller; Max Casella; Erin Drake; ***D:*** Jordana Spiro; ***W:*** Jordana Spiro; Angelica Nwandu; ***C:*** Hatuey Viveros Lavielle; ***M:*** Matthew Robert Cooper.

Night Creature *Out of the Darkness; Fear* **1979 (PG)** A tough, Hemingway-type writer is determined to destroy the man-eating black leopard which nearly killed him once before. Filmed in Thailand. **83m/C; VHS, DVD.** Donald Pleasence; Nancy Kwan; Ross Hagen; ***D:*** Lee Madden.

Night Crossing 1/2 **1981 (PG)** The fact-based story of two East German families who launch a daring escape to the West in a homemade hot air balloon. Exciting action for the whole family. **106m/C; VHS, DVD.** John Hurt; Jane Alexander; Glynnis O'Connor; Doug McKeon; Beau Bridges; ***D:*** Delbert Mann; ***W:*** John McGreevey; ***M:*** Jerry Goldsmith.

The Night Digger 1/2 *The Road Builder* **1971** Middle-aged Maura (Neal) has spent her dreary life looking after her blind mother (Brown). Handsome Billy (Clay) shows up offering handyman services and Maura is willing to overlook a lot, including the fact that Billy is being pursued by the police as a suspected rapist and serial killer. Undeveloped story and a silly ending from a screenplay by Neal's then-husband Roald Dahl. **110m/C; DVD.** *GB* Patricia Neal; Nicholas Clay; Pamela Brown; Jean Anderson; Graham Crowden; Sebastian Breaks; ***D:*** Alastair Reid; ***W:*** Roald Dahl; ***C:*** Alex Thomson; ***M:*** Bernard Herrmann.

Night Divides the Day **2001** A serial killer is stalking the students at Hollow Pointe University. The exceptionally low-budget film is more of a serious independent effort than exploitation. **125m/C; DVD.** Tiffany Richards; John Stump; David Strowell; Jeff Burton; Michael McCallum; Lynn Wolfbrandt; ***D:*** Jeff Burton; ***W:*** Jeff Burton; Alex Hencken; Joe Cottonmouth; ***M:*** Jeff Burton.

Night Editor 1/2 **1946** Story is told in flashbacks by newspaper night editor Stewart (Brown) as a cautionary tale about a once-honest cop who gets involved with a very bad dame. Married New York detective Tony Cochrane (Gargan) is carrying on with equally married socialite Jill (Carter). They witness a murder while on a rendezvous but keep quiet. Then Tony is guilt-stricken when an innocent man takes the fall and tries to convince Jill to tell the truth but she is one cold-hearted femme. Story is based on the radio program of the same title. **65m/B; DVD.** William Gargan; Janis Carter; Jeff Donnell; Charles D. Brown; Frank Wilcox; Roy Gordon; Paul E. Burns; Coulter Irwin; ***D:*** Henry Levin; ***W:*** Hal Smith; ***C:*** Philip Tannura; Burnett Guffey; ***M:*** Mischa Bakaleinikoff.

The Night Evelyn Came Out of the Grave 🦴 1/2 *La Notte Che Evelyn Usca Dalla Tomba* **1971 (R)** A wealthy Italian playboy, obsessed with his dead, flame-haired wife, lures living redheads into his castle, where he tortures and kills them. Standard '70s Euro/horror/sex stuff enlivened by the presence of the incredible Erika Blanc as a stripper who works out of a coffin. **99m/C; VHS, DVD, Blu-Ray.** *IT* Anthony Steffen; Marina Malfatti; Rod Murdock; Erika Blanc; Giacomo "Jack" Rossi-Stuart; Umberto Raho; ***D:*** Emilio P. Miraglio.

Night Falls on Manhattan 🦴🦴🦴 **1996 (R)** Adaptation of "Tainted Evidence" by Robert Daley. Ex-cop turned junior DA, Sean Casey (Garcia), leads the prosecution in a sensational NY trial involving a drug dealer/cop killer, who also seriously wounded Sean's cop father, Liam (Holm). He wins but allegations of police corruption dog the trial, thanks to liberal defense lawyer Vigoda (Dreyfuss). When Sean unexpectedly becomes the new DA, the issue becomes a full-blown scandal, leading the naive Sean very close to home. Veteran director Lumet knows this crime territory very well and is aided by fine performances from his leads. **114m/C; VHS, DVD.** Andy Garcia; Ian Holm; Richard Dreyfuss; Lena Olin; James Gandolfini; Ron Leibman; Colm Feore; Shiek Mahmud-Bey; Paul Guilfoyle; Dominic Chianese; ***D:*** Sidney Lumet; ***W:*** Sidney Lumet; ***C:*** David Watkin; ***M:*** Mark Isham.

Night Fire 🦴 1/2 **1994 (R)** Barry wants wife Lydia to try to rekindle the passion in their marriage by getting away for the weekend at their remote ranch. But they're interrupted in their leisure by the stranded Cal and Gwen. Only it turns out Barry has hired the duo, who like kinky games, to peak Lydia's interest. She's merely disgusted and Barry gets nasty. Also available unrated. **93m/C; VHS, DVD.** Shannon Tweed; John Laughlin; Martin Hewitt; Rochelle Swanson; ***D:*** Mike Sedan; ***W:*** Catherine Tavel; Helen Haxton; ***C:*** Zoran Hochstatter; ***M:*** Miriam Cutler.

Night Flight 🦴🦴 1/2 **1933** Riviere (John Barrymore) is obsessively devoted to his air delivery service, Trans Andean European Air Mail, putting prompt delivery over the safety of his own men. His best pilot, Jules (Gable), tries to satisfy Riviere's schedule, which includes dangerous night flights over the Andes Mountains. Based on the novel by Antoine de Saint-Exupery. Lionel Barrymore manages to steal scenes from his brother as an airline mechanic. **84m/B; VHS, DVD.** John Barrymore; Clark Gable; Helen Hayes; Lionel Barrymore; Robert Montgomery; Myrna Loy; William Gargan; ***D:*** Clarence Brown; ***W:*** Oliver H.P. Garrett; ***C:*** Elmer Dyer; Oliver Marsh; Charles A. Marshall; ***M:*** Herbert Stothart.

Night Flight from Moscow 🦴🦴 1/2 *The Serpent* **1973 (PG)** A Soviet spy defects with a fistful of secret documents that implicate every free government. Then the CIA must decide if he's telling the truth. Complex espionage thriller. **113m/C; VHS, DVD.** *FR IT GE* Yul Brynner; Henry Fonda; Dirk Bogarde; Virna Lisi; Philippe Noiret; Farley Granger; Robert Alda; Marie DuBois; Elga Andersen; ***D:*** Henri Verneuil; ***M:*** Ennio Morricone.

A Night for Dying Tigers 🦴🦴 **2010** Family secrets get revealed during a drunken dinner party. Jack (Bellows) is about to start a five-year prison sentence, so he gets together with the relatives at the family home. His wife Melanie (Beals)doesn't want to spend time with the in-laws but that's only the beginning of the troubled evening. Beals' fragile, frazzled spouse is the one to watch. **90m/C; DVD.** *CA* Gil Bellows; Jennifer Beals; Lauren Lee Smith; John Pyper-Ferguson; Tygh Runyan; Kathleen Robertson; Leah Gibson; ***D:*** Terry Miles; ***W:*** Terry Miles; ***C:*** Lindsay George; ***M:*** Eiko Ishiwata.

Night Fright 🦴 1/2 **1967** An ape sent into space to test the effects of cosmic radiation on animals crashlands and returns as a mutant killing machine. **75m/C; DVD.** John Agar; Carol Gilley; Ralph Baker, Jr.; Dorothy Davis; Bill (Billy) Thurman; ***D:*** James A. Sullivan; ***W:*** Russ Marker; ***C:*** Robert C. Jessup; ***M:*** Christopher Trussell. **VIDEO**

A Night Full of Rain 🦴 1/2 *End of the World* **1978 (R)** Italian communist tries unsuccessfully to seduce vacationing American feminist. They meet again in San Francisco and wedding bells chime. They argue. They argue more. They put all but rabid Wertmuller fans to sleep. The director's first English-language film. **104m/C; VHS, DVD.** *IT* Giancarlo Giannini; Candice Bergen; Anne Byrne; Flora Carabella; ***D:*** Lina Wertmuller; ***W:*** Lina Wertmuller.

Night Gallery 🦴🦴🦴 **1969** Serling is the tour guide through an unusual art gallery consisting of portraits that reflect people's greed, desire, and guilt. Pilot for the 1969-1973 TV series. Three stories, including "Eyes," which saw novice Spielberg directing veteran Crawford. **95m/C; VHS, DVD.** Joan Crawford; Roddy McDowall; Tom Bosley; Barry Sullivan; Ossie Davis; Sam Jaffe; Kate Greenfield; Richard Kiley; George Macready; Norma Crane; Barry Atwater; ***D:*** Steven Spielberg; Boris Sagal; Boris Shear; ***W:*** Rod Serling; ***C:*** Richard Batcheller; ***M:*** Billy Goldenberg. **TV**

The Night Has Eyes 🦴🦴 1/2 *Terror House* **1942** Tense melodrama concerns a young teacher who disappears on the Yorkshire moors at the same spot where her girlfriend had vanished the previous year. Early film appearance for Mason. **79m/B; VHS, DVD.** *GB* James Mason; Joyce Howard; Wilfred Lawson; Mary Clare; ***D:*** Leslie Arliss.

Night Has Settled 🦴🦴 **2014** An award-winning coming-of-age drama about a 13-year-old boy's complex introduction to adolescence. In 1983 New York City, Oliver Nicholas (List) is on the brink of having his first teen introduction to sex, alcohol, and love. His world is turned upside down when the housekeeper who raised him, Aida (Barraza), suffers a debilitating stroke. Family instability adds to his turmoil. Through all this emotional turmoil, Oliver experiences mania, depression, drunkenness, betrayal, death, and romantic/sexual complexities. **90m/C; DVD, Streaming, Download.** Spencer List; Pilar Lopez de Ayala; Adriana Barraza; Eric Nelsen; Courtney Baxter; ***D:*** Steve Clark; ***W:*** Steve Clark; ***C:*** Adolfo Doring; ***M:*** Tony Morales. **VIDEO**

The Night Heaven Fell 🦴🦴 1/2 *Les Bijoutiers du Clair de Lune* **1957** Ursula (Bardot) returns from the convent to the Spanish town where her Aunt Florentine (Valli) lives unhappily with Count Ribera (Nieto), a macho brute and womanizer. A local malcontent, Lambert (Boyd) has returned from political exile to find his sister dead by suicide over the Count and a deadly feud is reignited. Complicating matters is Aunt Florentine's unwillingness to admit her love for Lambert and virgin Ursula's attraction to him. It's serious, overheated melodrama in a commercial package that reveals Vadim to be basically the sex merchant everyone accuses him of being. **95m/C; DVD.** *FR IT* Brigitte Bardot; Stephen Boyd; Alida Valli; Pepe Nieto; ***D:*** Roger Vadim; ***W:*** Roger Vadim; Peter Viertel; Jacques Remy; ***C:*** Armand Thirard; ***M:*** Georges Auric.

The Night Holds Terror 🦴 1/2 **1955** Low-budget thriller based on actual events. Family man Gene (Kelly) is driving home when he makes the mistake of picking up hitchhiking psycho Victor (Edwards), who holds a gun on Gene while they pick up his two accomplices Robert (Cassavetes) and Luther (Cross). The escaped cons hide out in Gene's house overnight, holding his family hostage until Gene can get them some dough. When the trio takes Gene with them the next day, the FBI gets involved. **86m/B; DVD, Blu-Ray.** Jack Kelly; Vince Edwards; John Cassavetes; David Cross; Hildy Parks; Eddie Marr; Jack Kruschen; ***D:*** Andrew L. Stone; ***W:*** Andrew L. Stone; ***C:*** Fred H. Jackman, Jr.; ***M:*** Lucien Cailliet.

Night Hunter 🦴🦴 **1995 (R)** Jack Cutter's (Wilson) vampire-hunting parents were killed by a group of bloodsuckers so he teams up with a tabloid reporter (Smith) to eliminate the last nine vampires who have gathered together in Los Angeles and plan to multiply. **86m/C; VHS, DVD.** Don "The Dragon" Wilson; Melanie Smith; Nicholas Guest; Maria Ford; ***D:*** Rick Jacobson.

Night Hunter 🦴 1/2 *Nomis* **2019 (R)** After suspected serial killer Simon (Fletcher) is arrested by local cops, he refuses to give up information about his horrific crimes. Simon shows signs of paranoid schizophrenia and speaks nonsense as a distraction. Cop Marshall (Cavill) and profiler Rachel (Daddario) try to profile him despite his evasiveness because of Simon's booby-trapped basement sex dungeon. They believe other victims are out there, sparking the interest of vigilantes Michael (Kingsley), a former judge, and Lara (Jones), a teen who Michael uses to lure sexual predators for punishment. A predictable thriller with an unbelievable central character in Simon and an unbelievable story designed to displease viewers. **96m/C; DVD.** Henry Cavill; Ben Kingsley; Alexandra Daddario; Stanley Tucci; Brendan Fletcher; ***D:*** David Raymond; ***W:*** David Raymond; ***C:*** Michael Barrett; ***M:*** Alex Lu; Benjamin Wallfisch.

A Night in Casablanca 🦴🦴🦴 **1946** Groucho, Harpo and Chico find themselves in the luxurious Hotel Casablanca, going after some leftover Nazis searching for treasure. One of the later Marx Brothers' films, but still loaded with the familiar wisecracks and mayhem. **85m/B; VHS, DVD.** Groucho Marx; Harpo Marx; Chico Marx; Charles Drake; Dan Seymour; Sig Rumann; Lisette Verea; Lois Collier; Paul Harvey; Lewis L. Russell; ***D:*** Archie Mayo; ***W:*** Roland Kibbee; Frank Tashlin; Joseph Fields; ***C:*** James Van Trees; ***M:*** Werner Janssen.

A Night in Heaven WOOF! **1983 (R)** A college teacher gets involved with one of her students, who moonlights as a male stripper. Will he earn that extra credit he needs to pass? Uninspired, overly explicit. Look for Denny Terrio of "Dance Fever" fame. **85m/C; VHS, DVD.** Christopher Atkins; Lesley Ann Warren; Carrie Snodgress; Andy Garcia; ***D:*** John G. Avildsen; ***W:*** Joan Tewkesbury. Golden Raspberries '83: Worst Actor (Atkins).

A Night in Old Mexico 🦴 **2014** Duvall seriously slums in this manipulative drama, playing a variation on roles he's starred in for decades but without the depth of the best versions of the crotchety old man he's practically trademarked. The living legend plays Red Bovie, a cantankerous Texas rancher forced to give up his land who takes one last trip south of the border with his grandson before heading off to the great cattle stampede in the sky. If you can imagine a grumpy old caricature of Robert Duvall roaming the streets of Mexico with a naïve young actor in over his head, then you can imagine the entire movie. **104m/C; DVD, Blu-Ray.** *SP US* Robert Duvall; Jeremy Irvine; Angie Cepeda; Joaquin Cosio; Luis Tosar; ***D:*** Emilio Aragon; ***W:*** Bill Wittliff; ***C:*** David Omedes; ***M:*** Emilio Aragon.

A Night in the Life of Jimmy Reardon 🦴 1/2 **1988 (R)** A high school Casanova watches his friends leave for expensive schools while he contemplates a trip to Hawaii with his rich girlfriend, a ruse to avoid the dull business school his father has picked out. Well photographed, but acting leaves something to be desired. Based on Richert's novel "Aren't You Even Going to Kiss Me Good-bye?" **95m/C; VHS, DVD.** River Phoenix; Meredith Salenger; Matthew Perry; Louanne; Ione Skye; Ann Magnuson; Paul Koslo; Jane Hallaren; Jason Court; ***D:*** William Richert; ***W:*** William Richert; ***C:*** John J. Connor; ***M:*** Elmer Bernstein; Bill Conti.

Night Is My Future 🦴🦴 1/2 *Music in Darkness* **1947** A young musician, blinded in an accident, meets a girl who tries to bring him happiness. Usual somber Bergman, but unimportant story. In Swedish with English subtitles. **89m/B; VHS, DVD.** *SW* Mai Zetterling; Birger Malmsten; Naima Wifstrand; Olof Winnerstrand; Hilda Borgstrom; ***D:*** Ingmar Bergman.

Night Junkies 🦴🦴 **2007 (R)** Twist on the familiar vampire genre makes this one worth watching. Exotic dancer Ruby is turned by her philosophical vampire lover Vincent and the two hunt for victims along London's seedy waterfront while dealing with their blood addiction. **90m/C; DVD.** *GB* Katia Winter; Giles Anderson; Jonathan Coyne; Sasha Jackson; ***D:*** Lawrence Pearce; ***W:*** Lawrence Pearce; ***C:*** Sadik Ahmed; ***M:*** Michael England. **VIDEO**

The Night Listener 🦴🦴 1/2 **2006** Williams does drama in this adaptation of Maupin's novel. New York radio show host Gabriel Noone is distracted by his break-up with longtime lover, Jess (Cannavale), which is affecting his work. His outlook changes when a friend gives him a memoir purportedly written by dying teenaged fan, Pete. Gabriel begins a telephone relationship with Pete (Culkin) and his foster mother, Donna (Collette), but becomes suspicious about Pete's actual existence when Donna won't let them meet. **90m/C; DVD, Blu-Ray.** Robin Williams; Toni Collette; Bobby Cannavale; Joe Morton; Rory Culkin; Sandra Oh; John Cullum; ***D:*** Patrick Stettner; ***W:*** Patrick Stettner; Armistead Maupin; Terry Anderson; ***C:*** Lisa Rinzler; ***M:*** Peter Nashel.

Night Master 🦴 **1987** A handful of karate students practice their homework with much higher stakes away from the classroom. For them, deadly Ninja games are the only way to study. **87m/C; VHS, DVD.** Tom Jennings; Nicole Kidman; Vince Martin; ***D:*** Mark Joffe.

Night Monster 🦴🦴 1/2 *House of Mystery* **1942** A maniac wears artifical limbs to hunt down and murder the doctors responsible for amputating his legs. Picture was shot in 11 days. Fire scene was stock footage from "The Ghost of Frankenstein." **80m/B; DVD, Blu-Ray.** Bela Lugosi; Ralph Morgan; Lionel Atwill; Leif Erickson; Don Porter; Irene Hervey; Nils Asther; ***D:*** Ford Beebe; ***W:*** Clarence Upson Young; ***C:*** Charles Van Enger.

'night, Mother 🦴🦴 1/2 **1986 (PG-13)** A depressed woman, living with her mother, announces one evening that she is going to kill herself. Her mother spends the evening reliving their lives and trying to talk her out of it, but the outcome seems inevitable. Well acted, though depressing. Based on Marsha Norman's Pulitzer Prize-winning novel. **97m/C; VHS, DVD.** Sissy Spacek; Anne Bancroft; Ed Berke; Carol Robbins; Jennifer Roosendahl; ***D:*** Tom (Thomas R.) Moore; ***W:*** Marsha Norman; ***M:*** David Shire.

Night Moves 🦴🦴🦴 1/2 **1975 (R)** Small-time L.A. detective Harry Moseby (Hackman) is hired by fading actress Arlene Iverson (Ward) to find her wild teenaged daughter Delly (Griffith) who has taken off for the Florida Keys. Delly winds up dead and Harry uncovers a bizarre smuggling ring. Hackman is realistic as the detective whose own life is unraveling and Penn and screenwriter Sharp tweaked the detective convention with Harry being an ultimately ineffectual hero. Underrated when released and worth a view. **100m/C; VHS, DVD, Blu-Ray.** Gene Hackman; Susan Clark; Jennifer Warren; Melanie Griffith; Harris Yulin; Edward Binns; Kenneth Mars; James Woods; Dennis Dugan; Max Gail; Janet Ward; ***D:*** Arthur Penn; ***W:*** Alan Sharp; ***C:*** Bruce Surtees; ***M:*** Michael Small.

Night Moves 🦴🦴 1/2 **2013 (R)** Renown director Reichardt's thriller about a trio of environmental extremists (Eisenberg, Fanning, Sarsgaard) who plot to blow up a hydroelectric dam. The first half focuses on the tension-filled planning of the explosion; the second half details the inevitable fallout. Reichardt is more interested in the human frailties that make planning difficult and recovery from tragedy near impossible. Eisenberg is sometimes a bit too muted but there is an air of dread that most films like it do not have, accompanied by a gorgeously ambiguous ending. **112m/C; DVD, Blu-Ray.** Jesse Eisenberg; Dakota Fanning; Peter Sarsgaard; ***D:*** Kelly Reichardt; ***W:*** Kelly Reichardt; Jonathan Raymond; ***C:*** Christopher Blauvelt; ***M:*** Jeff Grace.

Night Must Fall 🦴🦴🦴 **1937** Effective thriller based on the play by Emlyn Williams. Wheelchair-bound grand dame Mrs. Branson (Whitty) hires personable Danny (Montgomery) as a handyman for the cottage she lives in with niece, Olivia (Russell). Danny is, of course, too good to be true. He's a creepy killer after moolah, which Olivia discerns but does nothing about until he strikes again. Oh yeah, he also keeps a suspicious hatbox in his room. Remade in 1964 with Albert Finney as the killer. **101m/B; VHS, DVD.** Robert Montgomery; May Whitty; Rosalind Russell; Merle Tottenham; Alan Marshal; Kathleen Harrison; Matthew Boulton; *D:* Richard Thorpe; *W:* John Van Druten; *C:* Ray June; *M:* Edward Ward.

Night Must Fall 🦴 1/2 **1964** Based on the play by Emlyn Williams and previously filmed in 1937. Psychopath Danny charms his way into the home of wealthy, wheelchair-bound widow Mrs. Bramson and her susceptible daughter Olivia. Atmospheric, but not as chilling as the earlier version as Danny's psychosis is a lot more evident. **101m/B; DVD.** *UK* Albert Finney; Mona Washbourne; Susan Hampshire; Sheila Hancock; *D:* Karel Reisz; *W:* Clive Exton; *C:* Freddie Francis; *M:* Ron Grainer.

Night Nurse 🦴🦴🦴 **1931** Stanwyck is a nurse who uncovers a sordid plot involving the murder of two young children for an inheritance. An entertaining, overlooked crime-drama, initially notorious for Stanwyck and roommate Blondell's continual onscreen dressings and undressings. Gable is compelling in an early, villainous role. **72m/B; VHS, DVD.** Barbara Stanwyck; Ben Lyon; Joan Blondell; Charles Winninger; Charlotte Merriam; Eddie Nugent; Blanche Frederici; Allan "Rocky" Lane; Walter McGrail; Ralf Harolde; Clark Gable; *D:* William A. Wellman.

Night Nurse 🦴 **1977** Young nurse signs on to care for an aging, wheelchair-ridden opera star, only to find that the house is haunted. **80m/C; VHS, DVD.** Davina Whitehouse; Kay Taylor; Gary Day; Kate Fitzpatrick; *D:* Igor Auzins.

Night of a Thousand Cats 🦴🦴 *La Noche de los Mil Gatos; Blood Feast; Cats* **1972 (R)** A reclusive playboy cruises Mexico City in his helicopter, searching for beautiful women. It seems he needs their bodies for his cats who, for some reason, eat only human flesh. He keeps the heads, for some reason, for his private collection. A really odd '70s cannibal cat entry, but it moves along nicely and features some truly groovy fashions (floppy hats, translucent blouses, etc.). Not to be confused with the 1963 film of the same name. From the director of "Night of the Bloody Apes" and "Survive!" **83m/C; VHS, DVD.** *MX* Anjanette Comer; Zulma Faiad; Hugo Stiglitz; Christa Linder; Teresa Velazquez; Barbara Ange; *D:* Rene Cardona, Jr.

Night of Bloody Horror 🦴 1/2 **1969 (R)** Tale of a former mental patient who is believed to be responsible for the brutal murders of his ex-girlfriends. A night of bloody horror indeed, as the gore is liberally spread. **89m/C; VHS, DVD.** Gaye Yellen; Evelyn Hendricks; Gerald McRaney; Michael Anthony; *D:* Joy Houck, Jr.; *W:* Joy Houck, Jr.; Robert A. Weaver; *C:* Robert A. Weaver.

Night of Dark Shadows 🦴🦴🦴 *Curse of Dark Shadows* **1971 (PG)** Underrated, atmospheric follow-up to "House of Dark Shadows." When newlyweds Quentin (Selby) and Tracy Collins (Jackson) move into the family mansion, they find the place haunted by a ghostly woman named Angelique (Parker). As Quentin is disturbed by visions of the past, he finds himself possessed by the spirit of Angelique's lover (also Selby) and Tracy's life in danger from the vengeful specter. Though occasionally muddled due to last-minute cuts ordered by the studio, the film still delivers a surplus of chills and is beautifully photographed. **94m/C; DVD, Blu-Ray.** David Selby; Kate Jackson; Lara Parker; Grayson Hall; John Karlen; Nancy Barrett; James Storm; Thayer David; *D:* Dan Curtis; *W:* Sam Hall; *C:* Richard Shore. **TV**

Night of Evil 🦴 1/2 **1962** Girl is released from reform school and promptly wins a beauty contest. Her bid to win the Miss America title is blown to smithereens however, when it is discovered that she has been secretly married all along. From there she resorts to working in strip joints and attempts to pull off an armed robbery. As exploitation fare goes, a winner. **88m/B; VHS, DVD.** Lisa Gaye; William Campbell; *Nar:* Earl Wilson; *D:* Richard Galbreath.

Night of Terror WOOF! **1987** A bizarre family conducts brain experiments on themselves and then begins to kill each other. Bloodshed for the whole family. **105m/C; Streaming.** Renee Harmon; Henry Lewis; *D:* Felix Girard; *W:* Renee Harmon; *C:* Richard Simonton, Jr.; *M:* Rick Vartian.

Night of the Assassin 🦴 *Rendezvous with Dishonour; Appuntamento col Disonore* **1970** Priest leaves his pulpit to become a terrorist. He plans a surprise for a U.N. secretary visiting Greece that would put the U.S. and Greek governments in the palm of his hand. Hard to believe. **98m/C; DVD.** *IT* Klaus Kinski; Michael Craig; Eva Renzi; Adolfo Celi; George Sanders; *D:* Adriano Bolzoni; *W:* Adriano Bolzoni; *C:* Guglielmo Garroni; *M:* Gianni Ferrio.

Night of the Bloody Apes WOOF! *Gomar the Human Gorilla; La Horriplante Bestia Humana* **1968 (R)** When a doctor transplants an ape's heart into his dying son's body, the son goes berserk. Gory Mexican-made horror at its finest. **84m/C; VHS, DVD.** *MX* Jose Elias Moreno; Armando Silvestre; Norma Lazarendo; Augustin Martinez Solares; Gina Moret; Noelia Noel; Gerard Zepeda; Carlos Lopez Moctezuma; *D:* Rene Cardona, Jr.; *W:* Rene Cardona, Jr.; *C:* Raul Martinez Solares; *M:* Antonio Diaz Conde.

Night of the Comet 🦴🦴 1/2 **1984 (PG-13)** After surviving the explosion of a deadly comet, two California girls discover that they are the last people on Earth. When zombies begin to chase them, things begin to lose their charm. Cute and funny, but the script runs out before the movie does. **90m/C; VHS, DVD, Blu-Ray.** Catherine Mary Stewart; Kelli Maroney; Robert Beltran; Geoffrey Lewis; Mary Woronov; Sharon Farrell; Michael Bowen; *D:* Thom Eberhardt; *W:* Thom Eberhardt; *C:* Arthur Albert.

Night of the Creeps 🦴🦴 1/2 *Creeps; Homecoming Night* **1986 (R)** In 1958 an alien organism lands on earth and infects a person who is then frozen. Thirty years later he is accidentally unfrozen and starts spreading the infection throughout a college town. B-movie homage contains every horror cliche there is. Director Dekker's first film. **89m/C; VHS, DVD, Blu-Ray.** Jason Lively; Jill Whitlow; Tom Atkins; Steve Marshall; Wally Taylor; Bruce Solomon; Kenneth Tobey; Dick Miller; David Oliver; *D:* Fred Dekker; *W:* Fred Dekker; *C:* Robert New; *M:* Barry DeVorzon.

Night of the Death Cult 🦴🦴 *Night of the Seagulls* **1975** After moving to a quiet seaside community, a young couple is plagued by cult practising human sacrifice in order to appease the Templars, a zombie-like pack of ancient clergymen who rise from the dead and torture the living. Last in a four film series about the Templars. **90m/C; VHS, DVD, Blu-Ray.** *SP* Victor Petit; Julie James; Maria Kosti; Sandra Mozarowsky; *D:* Armando de Ossorio.

Night of the Demon WOOF! **1980** Anthropology students are attacked by the legendary Bigfoot. Later they discover that he has raped and impregnated a young woman. Gore and sex prevail. **97m/C; VHS, DVD.** Jay Allen; Michael J. Cutt; Bob Collins; Jodi Lazarus; *D:* James C. Watson.

Night of the Demons 🦴🦴 **1988 (R)** A gory, special-effects-laden horror farce about teenagers calling up demons in a haunted mortuary. On Halloween, of course. **92m/C; VHS, DVD, Blu-Ray.** Linnea Quigley; Cathy Podewell; Alvin Alexis; William Gallo; Mimi Kinkade; Lance Fenton; *D:* Kevin S. Tenney; *W:* Joe Augustyn.

Night of the Demons 🦴🦴 **2009 (R)** Gierasch's deliberately one-dimensional and somewhat campy, though fast-paced, horror remake of the 1988 Halloween-set flick. Friends party in a haunted New Orleans mansion until they discover they can't leave. Seven demons need to possess their bodies by daybreak in order to break free of a curse and become flesh again. **93m/C; Blu-Ray.** Shannon Elizabeth; Monica Keena; Diora Baird; Bobbi Sue (Bobby Sue) Luther; Edward Furlong; John Beach; Michael Copon; *D:* Adam Gierasch; *W:* Adam Gierasch; Jace Anderson; *C:* Yaron Levy; *M:* Joseph Bishara.

Night of the Demons 2 🦴🦴 **1994 (R)** Some humor and reasonable special effects help this rise above the usual teen-slasher horror sequels. The demonic Angela (complete with her skull-shaped lollipops) lives on in legend, handily haunting her creepy old house where a group of dumb teens end up on Halloween (and soon wind up dead). With each casualty, a new victim also joins the ranks of the undead. Funniest parts come with heroic rescuer, yardstick-wielding Sister Gloria, who's not about to let any of Satan's helpers get the better of her. **96m/C; VHS, DVD, Blu-Ray.** Amelia Kinkade; Jennifer Rhodes; Merle Kennedy; Bobby Jacoby; Rod McCary; Zoe Trilling; Cristi Harris; Johnny Moran; Rick Peters; Christine Taylor; Ladd York; Darin Heames; *D:* Brian Trenchard-Smith; *W:* Joe Augustyn; *M:* Jim Manzie.

Night of the Demons 3 WOOF! *Demon House* **1997 (R)** Yet another bunch of moronic teenagers take refuge in Hull House funeral home on Halloween. Don't they know the mansion houses a bloodthirsty demon by now? May the demon win. **85m/C; VHS, DVD.** Amelia Kinkade; Kris Holden-Ried; Vlasta Vrana; *D:* Jim Kaufman.

The Night of the Devils 🦴🦴 *La notte dei diavoli; La noche de los diablos* **1972** A young man whose car breaks down encounters a family whose members are turned into vampires by a vengeful witch. Based on a story by Leo Tolstoy titled "The Wurdalak." **95m/C; Blu-Ray.** *IT SP* Gianni "John" Garko; Agostina Belli; Roberto Maldera; Cinzia de Carolis; Teresa Gimpera; *D:* Giorgio Ferroni; *W:* Eduardo Brochero; Romano Migliorini; Gianbattista Mussetto; *C:* Manuel Berenguer; *M:* Giorgio Gaslini. **VIDEO**

The Night of the Following Day 🦴🦴 **1969 (R)** Four professional criminals kidnap a young girl at France's Orly airport, demanding a large ransom from her wealthy father. Each kidnapper turns out to be beset by personal demons, hindering their plans and leading to a bloody climax. Then, there's a final twist to the entire story. Brando and Boone are properly chilling but the plot is muddled and melodramatic. From the novel "The Snatchers" by Lionel White. **93m/C; VHS, DVD.** Marlon Brando; Richard Boone; Rita Moreno; Pamela Franklin; Jess Hahn; Jacques Marin; Gerard Buhr; Hughes Wanner; *D:* Hubert Cornfield; *W:* Robert Phippeny; Hubert Cornfield.

Night of the Fox 🦴🦴 **1990 (R)** An American officer with top secret knowledge is captured by Germans on the brink of D-Day. His home team plans to kill him if he cannot be rescued before spilling the beans. On-location filming adds much. **95m/C; VHS, DVD.** Michael York; Deborah Raffin; George Peppard; *D:* Charles Jarrott. **CABLE**

Night of the Generals 🦴🦴🦴 *La Nuit de Generaux* **1967 (R)** A Nazi intelligence officer is pursuing three Nazi generals who may be involved in the brutal murder of a Warsaw prostitute. Dark and sinister, may be too slow for some tastes. Based on Hans Helmut Kirst's novel. **148m/C; VHS, DVD, Blu-Ray, Streaming.** Peter O'Toole; Omar Sharif; Tom Courtenay; Joanna Pettet; Donald Pleasence; Christopher Plummer; Philippe Noiret; John Gregson; Charles Gray; *D:* Anatole Litvak; *M:* Maurice Jarre.

Night of the Ghouls WOOF! *Revenge of the Dead* **1959** Second to last in Wood's celebrated series of inept horror films that began with "Bride of the Monster" and "Plan 9 from Outer Space." This one tells of a phony spiritualist who swindles the grieving by pretending to raise the dead. To his great surprise he actually does enliven some cadavers, who then go after him. Unreleased for over 20 years because Wood couldn't pay the film lab. Not quite as classically bad as his other films, but still a laugh riot. **69m/B; VHS, DVD.** Paul Marco; Tor Johnson; Duke Moore; Kenne Duncan; John Carpenter; Criswell; Bud Osborne; Anthony Cardoza; Vampira; Valda Hansen; Karl Johnson; *D:* Edward D. Wood, Jr.; *W:* Edward D. Wood, Jr.; *C:* William C. Thompson.

Night of the Grizzly 🦴🦴 **1966** An ex-lawman's peaceful life as a rancher is threatened when a killer grizzly bear goes on a murderous rampage terrorizing the residents of the Wyoming countryside. **99m/C; VHS, DVD, Blu-Ray.** Clint Walker; Martha Hyer; *D:* Joseph Pevney.

Night of the Hunted 🦴 1/2 *La nuit des traquees* **1980** A man picks up a young woman running at night who claims to have trouble forming memories. The moment he leaves for work she's nabbed by 'psychiatrists' and returned to an ominous building full of people with the same problems. **87m/C; DVD, Blu-Ray.** *FR* Brigitte Lahaie; Dominique Journet; Bernard Papineau; Rachel Mhas; Cathy Stewart; *D:* Jean Rollin; *W:* Jean Rollin; *C:* Jean-Cloude Couty; *M:* Philippe Brejean. **VIDEO**

The Night of the Hunter 🦴🦴🦴🦴 **1955** The nightmarish story of psychotic bogus preacher Harry Powell (Mitchum) who has the words H-A-T-E tattooed on the knuckles of his left hand and L-O-V-E on his right. He marries lonely widow Willa Harper (Winters), who has two children, in the hopes of finding the cache of money her thieving husband (Graves) had stashed. Gish plays Rachel, the shotgun-wielding, Bible-reading old lady who defends the kids when Harry threatens them. A dark, terrifying tale, completely unique in Hollywood's history. Mitchum is terrific. From novel by Davis Grubb and, sadly, Laughton's only directorial effort. **93m/B; VHS, DVD, Blu-Ray.** Robert Mitchum; Shelley Winters; Lillian Gish; Don Beddoe; Evelyn Varden; Peter Graves; James Gleason; Billy Chapin; Sally Jane Bruce; Gloria Castillo; Mary Ellen Clemons; Cheryl Callaway; Corey Allen; Paul Bryar; *D:* Charles Laughton; *W:* James Agee; *C:* Stanley Cortez; *M:* Walter Schumann. Natl. Film Reg. '92.

The Night of the Iguana 🦴🦴🦴 **1964** An alcoholic ex-minister acts as a tour guide in Mexico, becoming involved with a spinster and a hotel owner. Based on Tennessee Williams' play. Excellent performances from Burton and Gardner. **125m/B; VHS, DVD.** Richard Burton; Deborah Kerr; Ava Gardner; Grayson Hall; Sue Lyon; Emilio Fernandez; Cyril Delevanti; *D:* John Huston; *W:* John Huston; Anthony Veiller; *C:* Gabriel Figueroa; *M:* Benjamin Frankel. Oscars '64: Costume Des. (B&W).

Night of the Lepus 🦴🦴 **1972 (PG)** Giant mutant bunny wabbits lay waste to the countryside after a failed hormone experiment goes horribly awry. Where's Elmer Fudd when you need him? Debate still rages about whether this is an incompetent B-movie horror flick, or an intentionally campy spoof of giant critter flicks. Watch it as the latter to get maximum enjoyment out of it. **88m/C; DVD, Blu-Ray.** Stuart Whitman; Janet Leigh; Rory Calhoun; DeForest Kelley; Paul Fix; William (Bill) Elliott; *D:* William Claxton; *W:* Don Holliday; Gene R. Kearney; *C:* Ted Voightlander; *M:* Jimmie Haskell.

Night of the Living Dead 🦴🦴🦴 1/2 *Night of the Flesh Eaters; Night of the Anubis* **1968** Cult favorite is low budget but powerfully frightening. Space experiments set off a high level of radiation that makes the newly dead return to life, with a taste for human flesh. Handful of holdouts find shelter in a farmhouse. Claustrophobic, terrifying, gruesome, extreme, and, yes, humorous. Followed by "Dawn of the Dead" (1979) and "Day of the Dead" (1985). Romero's directorial debut. Available in a colorized version. **90m/B; VHS, DVD, Blu-Ray.** Judith O'Dea; Duane Jones; Karl Hardman; Marilyn Eastman; Keith Wayne; Judith Ridley; Russell Streiner; Bill "Chilly Billy" Cardille; John A. Russo; Kyra Schon; Bill (William Heinzman) Hinzman; John Simpson; Vincent Survinski; George A. Romero; *D:* George A. Romero; *W:* John A. Russo; George A. Romero; *C:* George A. Romero. Natl. Film Reg. '99.

Night of the Living Dead 🦴🦴 **1990 (R)** A bunch of people are trapped in a farmhouse and attacked by ghouls with eating disorders. Remake of the '68 classic substitutes high tech blood 'n' guts for bona fide frights. **92m/C; VHS, DVD, Blu-Ray.** Tony Todd; Patricia Tallman; Tom Towler; William Butler; Bill Moseley; McKee Anderson; Kate Finneran; Bill "Chilly Billy" Cardille; *D:* Tom Savini; *W:* George A. Romero; John A. Russo; *C:* Frank Prinzi; *M:* Paul McCollough.

Night of the Living Deb 🦴🦴 1/2 **2014** A comedy horror about a one-night stand turned fight for survival against zombies. When quirky Deb (Thayer) goes on a girls' night out in Portland, Minnesota, she ends up meeting and spending the night with the hottest guy in town, Ryan (Cassidy). In the morning, she cannot remember how she got there but is happy about the situation, while Ryan realizes he made a mistake. He tries to send her home but a full-blown zombie apocalypse is going on outside. Instead of walking home, the pair must fight for their lives and learn to trust each other. **85m/C; DVD, Blu-Ray, Streaming, Download.** Maria Thayer; Michael Cassidy; Christopher Marquette; Ray Wise; Syd Wilder; ***D:*** Kyle Rankin; ***W:*** Andy Selsor; ***C:*** Thomas E. Ackerman; ***M:*** Steven Gutheinz.

Night of the Running Man 🦴 ½ **1994 (R)** Las Vegas cab driver McCarthy finds $1 million stolen from a casino and goes on the run from hit man Glenn, who's been hired to recover the loot. **93m/C; VHS, Streaming.** Scott Glenn; Andrew McCarthy; John Glover; ***D:*** Mark L. Lester.

Night of the Scarecrow 🦴🦴 ½ **1995 (R)** Hundreds of years before a small town makes a pact with a warlock (Lazar) to ensure prosperity. After regretting the deal, the townspeople kill him and bury the body in a field where it's eventually uncovered. Now the warlock's ghost inhabits the frame of a scarecrow and is off on a murderous rampage. Formula horror with some decent production values. Based on a comic book. **90m/C; VHS, Blu-Ray, Streaming.** Elizabeth Barondes; John Mese; Stephen (Steve) Root; Bruce Glover; Dirk Blocker; Howard Swain; Gary Lockwood; John Lazar; John Hawkes; Martine Beswick; ***D:*** Jeff Burr; ***W:*** Reed Steiner; Dan Mazur; ***C:*** Thomas Callaway; ***M:*** Jim Manzie.

Night of the Sharks WOOF! 1987 Mercenaries in a downed plane go after a jewel-ridden shipwreck despite a plethora of sharks. **87m/C; VHS, DVD.** Treat Williams; Christopher Connelly; Antonio Fargas; Janet Agren; ***D:*** Anthony Richmond.

The Night of the Shooting Stars 🦴🦴🦴🦴 *The Night of San Lorenzo; La Notte di San Lorenzo* **1982 (R)** Set in an Italian village during the last days of WWII, this film highlights the schism in the village between those who support the fascists and those who sympathize with the Allies. This division comes to a head in the stunning final scene. A poignant, deeply moving film. **106m/C; VHS, DVD.** *IT* Omero Antonutti; Margarita Lozano; Claudio Bigagli; Massimo Bonetti; Norma Martel; ***D:*** Paolo Taviani; Vittorio Taviani; ***W:*** Tonino Guerra; Giuliani G. De Negri; Paolo Taviani; Vittorio Taviani; ***C:*** Franco Di Giacomo; ***M:*** Nicola Piovani. Cannes '82: Grand Jury Prize; Natl. Soc. Film Critics '83: Director (Taviani), Director (Taviani), Film.

Night of the Sorcerers WOOF! 1970 An expedition to the Congo uncovers a bizarre tribe of vampire leopard women who lure young girls to their deaths. **85m/C; VHS, DVD.** Jack Taylor; Simon Andreu; Kali Hansa; ***D:*** Armando de Ossorio.

Night of the Strangler 🦴🦴 **1973 (R)** A love affair between a white society girl and a young black man causes a chain of events that end with brutal murders in New Orleans. **88m/C; VHS, DVD.** Mickey Dolenz; James Ralston; Susan McCullough; ***D:*** Joy Houck, Jr.

Night of the Twisters 🦴🦴 ½ **1995** Teenager Dan (Sawa) and his new stepfather Jack (Schneider) must work together to protect the family when tornadoes rip through their small Nebraska town. Based on the book by Ivy Ruckman. **91m/C; VHS, DVD.** John Schneider; Devon Sawa; Lori Hallier; Helen Hughes; ***D:*** Timothy Bond; ***M:*** Lawrence Shragge. **CABLE**

Night of the Warrior 🦴 **1991 (R)** Music videos and martial arts don't mix...not here, anyway. A hunky exotic-dance-club owner pays his disco bills by fighting in illegal, underground blood matches, but not enough to make it exciting. Lamas stars with real life wife Kinmont and mom Dahl. **96m/C; VHS, DVD.** Lorenzo Lamas; Anthony Geary; Kathleen Kinmont; Arlene Dahl; Wilhelm von Homburg; ***D:*** Rafal Zielinski; ***W:*** Thomas Ian Griffith; ***C:*** Edward Pei; ***M:*** Ed Tomney.

The Night of the White Pants 🦴 ½ **2006 (R)** Takes family dysfunction to a not terribly exciting level. Dallas good ole boy Max Hagan (Wilkinson) and his brood are left in the cold one night when his nearly-ex trophy wife Barbara (Turner) claims the property and kicks everyone out. Max (in his white pants) tags along with daughter Beth (Blair) and her punk rocker boyfriend Raff (Stahl) on a round of drugs and debauchery until some semblance of family values reasserts itself when the Hagans finally reunite at the same hotel. **87m/C; DVD.** Tom Wilkinson; Nick Stahl; Selma Blair; Frances Fisher; Geri Jewell; Fran Kranz; Janine Turner; Laura Jordan; ***D:*** Amy Talkington; ***W:*** Amy Talkington; ***C:*** Jim Denault; David Daniel; ***M:*** Tony Tisdale.

Night of the Wilding 🦴 **1990** Very, very loosely based on the story of the female jogger who was gang-raped and left for dead in New York's Central Park. Made soon after the actual incident occurred. **90m/C; VHS, DVD.** Erik Estrada; Kathrin Lautner; ***D:*** Joseph Merhi. **TV**

Night of the Zombies 🦴 *Gamma 693; Night of the Wehrmacht Zombies* **1981 (R)** WWII soldiers with eating disorders shuffle through 88 minutes of gratuitous gore, while pursued by porn star cum intelligence agent. From the director of "Bloodsucking Freaks." **88m/C; VHS, DVD.** James Gillis; Ryan Hilliard; Samantha Grey; Joel M. Reed; ***D:*** Joel M. Reed; ***W:*** Joel M. Reed.

Night on Earth 🦴🦴🦴 **1991 (R)** Jarmusch's "road" movie comprises five different stories taking place on the same night in five different cities—Los Angeles, New York, Paris, Rome, and Helsinki—between cabbies and their passengers. As with any anthology some stories work better than others but all have their moments in this ambitious film with its outstanding international cast. Subtitled in English for the three foreign segments. **125m/C; VHS, DVD, Blu-Ray.** Winona Ryder; Gena Rowlands; Giancarlo Esposito; Armin Mueller-Stahl; Rosie Perez; Beatrice Dalle; Roberto Benigni; Paolo Bonacelli; Matti Pellonpaa; Kari Vaananen; Sakari Kuosmanen; Tomi Salmela; Lisanne Falk; Isaach de Bankole; Alan Randolph Scott; Anthony Portillo; Richard Boes; Pascal Nzonzi; Emile Abossolo-M'Bo; ***D:*** Jim Jarmusch; ***W:*** Jim Jarmusch; ***C:*** Frederick Elmes; ***M:*** Tom Waits; Kathleen Brennan. Ind. Spirit '93: Cinematog.

Night Orchid 🦴🦴🦴 **1997 (R)** Filmmaker Mark Atkins heads for Stephen King territory with the story of a young psychic (Paris) who arrives in a rural hamlet and has visions of murders. For a low-budget video premiere, this one looks very good. It's made with a degree of style and originality. Fans have seen worse. **93m/C; DVD.** Dale Paris; Alyssa Simon; Mary Ellen O'Brien; ***D:*** Mark Atkins; ***C:*** Paul Atkins; ***M:*** C.C. Adcock.

Night Owls 🦴🦴 **2015 (R)** Workaholic Kevin (Pally) goes home for a one-night stand with a beautiful woman named Madeline (Salazar). Caught up in the heat of passion, he doesn't notice until he wakes up that he happens to be in his boss's house. And he's even more shocked when Madeline takes an overdose of pills in a suicide attempt. It turns out Madeline is Kevin's boss's ex-mistress, and she's going to cause problems. The slapstick is refined but the misogyny is a little thick, and it's hard to shake the "seen this before" feeling. **90m/C; DVD.** Adam Pally; Rosa Salazar; Rob Huebel; Tony Hale; Peter Krause; ***D:*** Charles Hood; ***W:*** Charles Hood; Seth Goldsmith; ***C:*** Adrian Correia; ***M:*** Kevin Blumenfeld.

Night Passage 🦴🦴 ½ **1957** Grant McLaine's (Stewart) an ex-lawman hired to protect a railroad payroll from a band of outlaws who've heisted previous funds. Unbeknownst to Grant, the gang is led by his brother (Murphy), who's known as the "Utica Kid." Eventually Grant and the Kid will have to have a showdown, unless Grant can convince him to go straight. Anthony Mann was set to direct at Stewart's request, but declined, damaging his relationship with the actor. Fans of the stars and the genre will enjoy this solid outing. Stewart plays accordian and sings two songs. **90m/C; DVD, Blu-Ray.** James Stewart; Audie Murphy; Dan Duryea; Dianne Foster; Elaine Stewart; Brandon de Wilde; Jay C. Flippen; Herbert Anderson; Robert J. Wilke; Hugh Beaumont; Jack Elam; Tommy Cook; Paul Fix; Olive Carey; James Flavin; Donald Curtis; Ellen Corby; ***D:*** James Neilson; ***W:*** Borden Chase; ***C:*** William H. Daniels; ***M:*** Dimitri Tiomkin.

Night Patrol WOOF! 1985 (R) The streets of Hollywood will never be the same after the night patrol runs amuck in the town. Crude imitation of "Police Academy." **87m/C; VHS, DVD, Blu-Ray.** Linda Blair; Pat Paulsen; Jaye P. Morgan; Jack Riley; Murray Langston; Billy Barty; Noriyuki "Pat" Morita; Sydney Lassick; Andrew Silverstein; ***D:*** Jackie Kong; ***C:*** Hanania Baer. Golden Raspberries '85: Worst Actress (Blair).

Night People 🦴🦴 **1954** In this taut Cold War drama intelligence officer Steve Van Dyke (Peck) learns that an Army corpsman was kidnapped by the Soviets and is being held in Berlin's Russian zone.The kid's politically powerful dad (Crawford) wants him back no matter what, but the trade gets complicated. Johnson's first directorial effort. **93m/C; DVD.** Gregory Peck; Broderick Crawford; Anita Bjork; Rita Gam; Walter Abel; Buddy Ebsen; Max (Casey Adams) Showalter; ***D:*** Nunnally Johnson; ***W:*** Nunnally Johnson; ***C:*** Charles G. Clarke; ***M:*** Cyril Mockridge.

The Night Porter 🦴🦴 *Il Portiere de Notte* **1974 (R)** Max, an ex-SS concentration camp officer, unexpectedly meets his former lover-victim at the Viennese hotel where he works as the night porter. After they get reacquainted, the couple must hide from the porter's ex-Nazi friends who want the women dead because they fear she will disclose their past. A sado-masochistic voyage not for the faint-hearted. **115m/C; VHS, DVD, Blu-Ray.** *IT* Dirk Bogarde; Charlotte Rampling; Phillippe LeRoy; Gabriele Ferzetti; Isa Miranda; ***D:*** Liliana Cavani; ***W:*** Liliana Cavani; ***C:*** Alfio Contini; ***M:*** Daniele Paris.

Night School 🦴 *Terror Eyes* **1981 (R)** A police detective must find out who has been decapitating the women attending night school at Wendell College. Ward's first film. **89m/C; VHS, DVD, Blu-Ray, Streaming.** Leonard Mann; Rachel Ward; Drew Snyder; Joseph R. Sicari; Nicholas Cairis; Bill McCann; Margo Skinner; ***D:*** Ken Hughes; ***W:*** Ruth Avergon; ***C:*** Mark Irwin; ***M:*** Brad Fiedel.

Night School 🦴🦴 **2018 (PG-13)** When high school dropout Teddy Walker (Hart) must get his GED to get a new job to support his spendthrift lifestyle, he takes night school classes taught by no-nonsense yet inspiring Carrie (Haddish). These classes are held at the same high school Teddy dropped out of years ago, and the principal is his former tormenter Stewart (Killam). As Stewart renews his conflict with Teddy, Teddy and the rest of his misfit night school classmates look for shortcuts to graduation. This goofy comedy is light on plot but Hart's performance and chemistry with the rest of the cast adds to the film's appeal. **111m/C; DVD, Blu-Ray.** Tiffany Haddish; Kevin Hart; Keith David; Mary Lynn Rajskub; Anne Winters; ***D:*** Malcolm Lee; ***W:*** Kevin Hart; Harry Ratchford; Joey Wells; Matthew Kellard; Nicholas Stoller; John Hamburg; ***C:*** Greg Gardiner; ***M:*** David Newman.

Night Screams 🦴 **1987** Violent scaremonger about two escaped convicts who crash a high school house party. Kids and convicts start getting killed, one by one. **85m/C; VHS, DVD.** Joe Manno; Ron Thomas; Randy Lundsford; Megan Wyss; ***D:*** Allen Plone.

Night Shadow 🦴 **1990 (R)** A woman, returning home after being away for years, picks up a hitchhiker. Soon after her arrival, terrible serial killings begin, and only she has the nerve to track down the killer. **90m/C; VHS, DVD.** Brenda Vance; Dana Chan; Tom Boylan; ***D:*** Randolph Cohlan; ***W:*** Randolph Cohlan.

Night Shift 🦴🦴 **1982 (R)** Two morgue attendants, dull Winkler and manic Keaton, decide to spice up their latenight shift by running a call-girl service on the side. Keaton turns in a fine performance in his film debut, and Howard's sure-handed direction almost overcomes the silly premise. Watch closely for Costner in the morgue frat party scene. **106m/C; VHS, DVD.** Henry Winkler; Michael Keaton; Shelley Long; Kevin Costner; Pat Corley; Bobby DiCicco; Nita Talbot; Richard Belzer; Shannen Doherty; Clint Howard; Joe Spinell; ***V:*** Vincent Schiavelli; ***D:*** Ron Howard; ***W:*** Babaloo Mandel; Lowell Ganz; ***C:*** James A. Crabe; ***M:*** Burt Bacharach.

Night Siege Project: Shadowchaser 2 🦴🦴 ½ *Project Shadowchaser 2* **1994 (R)** Smooth actioner finds a terrorist android taking over a nuclear arsenal and threatening to make Washington, D.C. a mushroom cloud. Naturally, there's a hero (and a heroine) to take care of the evildoers. **97m/C; VHS, DVD.** Bryan Genesse; Frank Zagarino; Beth Toussaint; ***D:*** John Eyres; ***W:*** Nick Davis; ***M:*** Stephen (Steve) Edwards.

Night Skies 🦴 **2007 (R)** Allegedly based on a UFO incident reported in Arizona in 1997, this silly low-budget sci-fier is a yawn. Friends in an RV get in a wreck after staring at strange lights in the sky, which then leads to alien abductions. **84m/C; DVD.** Jason Connery; A.J. Cook; Gwendoline Yeo; Ashley Peldon; George Stults; Joe Sikora; Michael Dorn; ***D:*** Roy Knyrim; ***W:*** Eric Miller; ***C:*** Steve Adcock; ***M:*** Paul D'Amou; Brad Laner.

Night Song 🦴🦴 ½ **1947** RKO tearjerker. Socialite Cathy Mallory (Oberon) goes slumming and encounters embittered, blind pianist Dan (Andrews) playing in a jazz joint. Instantly smitten, Cathy gets Dan to give her piano lessons by pretending to also be blind and broke as well. She becomes a patroness by sponsoring a classical music composition contest to get Dan some recognition, but what will happen to their romance when he discovers the truth? **102m/B; DVD.** Merle Oberon; Dana Andrews; Ethel Barrymore; Hoagy Carmichael; Jacqueline White; ***D:*** John Cromwell; ***W:*** Dick Irving Hyland; Frank Fenton; DeWitt Bodeen; ***C:*** Lucien Ballard; ***M:*** Leith Stevens.

The Night Stalker 🦴🦴 ½ **1971** Pilot movie for the TV series finds veteran reporter Carl Kolchak (McGavin) investigating a series of murders that lead him to believe a modern-day vampire is stalking the streets of Vegas. **73m/C; VHS, DVD, Blu-Ray.** Darren McGavin; Carol Lynley; Simon Oakland; Ralph Meeker; Claude Akins; Kent Smith; Larry Linville; Barry Atwater; ***D:*** John Llewellyn Moxey; ***W:*** Richard Matheson; ***M:*** Robert Cobert. **TV**

Night Stalker 🦴🦴 **1987 (R)** A bloodthirsty serial killer is tracked by a detective through the streets in New York. The usual rigamarole of fisticuffes, gunplay, and car chases ensure. Impressive acting from Napier raises the film from the run-of-the-mill. **91m/C; VHS, DVD.** Charles Napier; John Goff; Robert Viharo; Robert Z'Dar; Joseph Gian; Gary Crosby; Joan Chen; Michelle Reese; ***D:*** Max Cleven; ***C:*** Don Burgess.

Night Stalker WOOF! 2009 (R) Lommel's fixation on serial killers continues as does his totally ignoring all but the most basic true crime facts. Richard Ramirez moved to L.A. from Texas, got into drugs and devil worship, and went on a women-killing spree in 1984, becoming known as 'The Night Stalker.' About as worthless as you can imagine. **85m/C; DVD.** Elissa Dowling; Jamie Bernadette; Jeff Dylan Graham; Adolph Cortez; ***D:*** Ulli Lommel; ***W:*** Ulli Lommel; ***C:*** Ulli Lommel. **VIDEO**

The Night Strangler 🦴🦴 ½ **1972** Still creepy sequel to 1971's "The Night Stalker" finds reporter Carl Kolchak (McGavin) investigating of series of murders with female victims. He discovers that similar crimes have been committed in Seattle every 21 years for more than a century and the killer's description is always the same. **90m/C; VHS, DVD, Blu-Ray.** Darren McGavin; Richard Anderson; Simon Oakland; Wally Cox; Margaret Hamilton; John Carradine; Al Lewis; ***D:*** Dan Curtis; ***W:*** Richard Matheson; ***M:*** Robert Cobert. **TV**

Night Sun 🦴🦴 ½ *Il Sole Anche di Notte; Sunshine Even by Night* **1990** Sergio (Sands) is an 18th-century nobleman who discovers his fiance was once the king's mistress. He abandons worldly pursuits to become a monk and find some peace but temptation follow him. Based on the Tolstoy story "Father Sergius." Sands' voice was dubbed by Italian actor Giancarlo Giannini. Italian with subtitles. **112m/C; VHS, DVD.** *IT* Julian Sands; Charlotte Gainsbourg; Massimo Bonetti; Margarita Lozano; Ruediger Vogler; ***D:*** Paolo Taviani; Vittorio Taviani; ***W:*** Tonino Guerra; Paolo Taviani; Vittorio Taviani; ***C:*** Giuseppe Lanci; ***M:*** Nicola Piovani.

The Night the Bridge Fell Down 🦴 ½ **1983** TV disaster movie from producer Irwin Allen. The Madison

Bridge partially gives way, stranding nine people as it continues to collapse. However, a gun-wielding bank robber, using the bridge as his escape route, panics and refuses to let rescuers come to their aid. **194m/C; DVD.** James MacArthur; Eve Plumb; Desi Arnaz, Jr.; Char Fontane; Leslie Nielsen; Barbara Rush; Richard Gilliland; Howard Culver; Gregory Sierra; Philip Baker Hall; ***D:*** Georg Fenady; ***W:*** Alvin Boretz; Ray Goldstone; ***C:*** John M. Nickolaus, Jr.; ***M:*** Richard LaSalle. **TV**

The Night the Lights Went Out in Georgia **1981 (PG)** Loosely based on the popular hit song, the film follows a brother and sister as they try to cash in on the country music scene in Nashville. McNichol is engaging. **112m/C; VHS, DVD.** Kristy McNichol; Dennis Quaid; Mark Hamill; Don Stroud; ***D:*** Ronald F. Maxwell; ***W:*** Bob Bonney; ***C:*** Bill Butler; ***M:*** David Shire.

The Night They Raided Minsky's *The Night They Invented Striptease* **1969 (PG)** Chaotic but interesting period comedy about a young Amish girl who leaves her tyrannical father to come to New York City in the 1920s. She winds up at Minsky's Burlesque and accidentally invents the striptease. Lahr's last performance—he died during filming. **97m/C; VHS, DVD, Blu-Ray.** Jason Robards, Jr.; Britt Ekland; Elliott Gould; Bert Lahr; Norman Wisdom; Denholm Elliott; ***D:*** William Friedkin; ***W:*** Norman Lear; Arnold Schulman.

Night Tide **1/2 1961** Hopper in another off the wall character study, this time as a lonely sailor. He falls for a mermaid (Lawson) who works at the dock. She may be a descendent of the man-killing Sirens. Interesting and different little love story, sometimes advertised as horror, which it is not. **84m/B; DVD, Blu-Ray.** Dennis Hopper; Gavin Muir; Linda Lawson; Luana Anders; Marjorie Eaton; Tom Dillon; ***D:*** Curtis Harrington; ***W:*** Curtis Harrington; ***C:*** Vilis Lapenieks; ***M:*** David Raksin.

A Night to Remember **1942** A murder-mystery writer's wife convinces him to move to a new apartment because she thinks the change might help him finish a novel he started long ago. When they find a dead body behind their new building, they try their hands at sleuthing. A clever and witty mystery, indeed, supported by likeable performances. **91m/B; DVD.** Loretta Young; Brian Aherne; Sidney Toler; Gale Sondergaard; William Wright; Donald MacBride; Blanche Yurka; ***D:*** Richard Wallace; ***W:*** Richard Flournoy; ***C:*** Joseph Walker; ***M:*** Werner R. Heymann.

A Night to Remember **1958** Gripping tale of the voyage of the Titanic with an interesting account of action in the face of danger and courage amid despair. Large cast is effectively used. Adapted by Eric Ambler from the book by Walter Lord. **119m/B; VHS, DVD.** Kenneth More; David McCallum; Anthony Bushell; Honor Blackman; Michael Goodliffe; George Rose; Laurence Naismith; Frank Lawton; Alec McCowen; Jill Dixon; John Cairney; Joseph Tomelty; Jack Watling; Richard Clarke; Ralph Michael; Kenneth Griffith; ***D:*** Roy Ward Baker; ***W:*** Eric Ambler; ***C:*** Geoffrey Unsworth. Golden Globes '59: Foreign Film.

Night Train **1/2 2009 (R)** On Christmas Eve, travelers Chloe and Peter discover a dead body in a train compartment and also find a fortune in diamonds in a wooden box. They convince conductor Miles that they should dump the body and split the gems three ways—until greed gets the better of them. A supernatural element about the mysterious nature of the box itself prove problematic in what seems to be a more straightforward suspenser. (And why is O'Brien in drag?) **91m/C; DVD.** Danny Glover; Leelee Sobieski; Steve Zahn; Richard O'Brien; ***D:*** Brian King; ***W:*** Brian King; ***C:*** Christopher Popp; ***M:*** Henning Lohner. **VIDEO**

Night Train Murders **WOOF!** *L'Ultimo Treno della Notte; The Last Train of the Night* **1975** If you're a fan of the Italian giallo genre then this is the horror for you—if you're not, then ick, ick, ick, ick, ick. Lisa (D'Angelo) and Margaret (Miracle) are taking the train from Germany to Italy to visit Lisa's family. On board, they encounter a sicko trio (DeGrassi, Bucci, Meril) who torture, rape, and eventually kill the girls. The sickos then wind up at the home of Lisa's parents, who enact an equally violent revenge when they discover who their visitors are. The only comic relief is the completely ridiculous English dubbing of the Italian dialogue. **94m/C; DVD, Blu-Ray.** *IT* Flavio Bucci; Macha Meril; Irene Miracle; Enrico Maria Salerno; Marina Berti; Gianfranco de Grassi; Laura D'Angelo; ***D:*** Aldo Lado; ***W:*** Aldo Lado; Renato Izzo; ***C:*** Gabor Pogany; ***M:*** Ennio Morricone.

Night Train to Lisbon **1/2 2013 (R)** Old-fashioned, dully genteel mystery. Boring Swiss philosophy professor Raimund Gregorius (Irons) has his routine shaken when he stops a young woman from jumping off a bridge. She leaves behind her coat, a train ticket, and a 40-yar-old book in Portuguese. Raimund uses the ticket to travel to Lisbon and find out about the deceased author's troubled life (shown in flashbacks) as a revolutionary caught up in a romantic triangle, but it doesn't add much excitement to the story. **111m/C; DVD.** *GE SI* Jeremy Irons; Jack Huston; Melanie Laurent; August Diehl; Lena Olin; Bruno Ganz; Tom Courtenay; Charlotte Rampling; Christopher Lee; ***D:*** Bille August; ***W:*** Greg Latter; Ulrich Herrmann; ***C:*** Filip Zumbrunn; ***M:*** Annette Focks.

Night Train to Munich *Night Train; Gestapo* **1940** There's Nazi intrigue galore aboard a big train when a scientist's daughter joins allied intelligence agents in retrieving some secret documents. From the book "Report on a Fugitive" by Gordon Wellesley. **93m/B; VHS, DVD, Blu-Ray.** *GB* Margaret Lockwood; Rex Harrison; Paul Henreid; Basil Radford; Naunton Wayne; James Harcourt; Felix Aylmer; Roland Culver; Raymond Huntley; Austin Trevor; Keneth Kent; C.V. France; Frederick Valk; Morland Graham; Wally Patch; Irene Handl; Albert Lieven; David Horne; ***D:*** Carol Reed; ***W:*** Frank Launder; Sidney Gilliat; ***C:*** Otto Kanturek.

Night Train to Terror **WOOF!** *Shiver* **1984 (R)** Strange things start happening on the train where a rock band makes its last appearance. Clips from other horror flicks were pieced together to make this film that's so bad it's almost good. **98m/C; VHS, DVD, Blu-Ray.** John Phillip Law; Cameron Mitchell; Marc Lawrence; Charles Moll; Ferdinand "Ferdy" Mayne; ***D:*** Jay Schlossberg-Cohen; ***W:*** Philip Yordan.

Night Train to Venice **1993 (R)** Martin (Grant) is aboard the Orient Express on his way to Venice to deliver his book about the rise of neo-Nazism. He meets a mystery man (McDowell) and an actress (Welch) with ties to a neo-Nazi group, who also happen to be aboard the train and anxious to stop Martin from delivering his expose. Extended dream sequences and flashbacks tend to stop the story cold but Grant is a draw (and probably the only reason this mishmash has been released to video). **98m/C; VHS, Streaming.** Hugh Grant; Malcolm McDowell; Tahnee Welch; Kristina Soderbaum; ***D:*** Carlo U. Quinterio; ***W:*** Leo Tichat; Toni Hirtreiter; ***M:*** Alexander Bubenheim.

Night Unto Night **1/2 1949** John Galen (Reagan) rents a Florida beach house from widow Ann Gracy (Lindfors) after he's diagnosed with epilepsy. Ann thinks the house is haunted by her husband but it's just her grief and she has other things to concentrate on when John turns suicidal after a violent seizure. Filmed in 1947, Warner Bros. was disappointed in the result and shelved the drama for two years. **84m/B; DVD.** Ronald Reagan; Viveca Lindfors; Broderick Crawford; Rosemary DeCamp; Craig Stevens; Osa Massen; Art Baker; ***D:*** Donald Siegel; ***W:*** Kathryn Scola; ***C:*** J. Peverell Marley; ***M:*** Franz Waxman.

Night Vision **1997 (R)** Burned-out detective Dak Smith (Williamson) has been demoted to motorcycle cop on the graveyard shift. But he unexpectedly becomes involved with the case of a serial killer who likes to stalk and videotape his victims. Now Dak and his new partner Kristen O'Conner (Rothrock) are working to capture this psychopath. **95m/C; VHS, DVD.** Fred Williamson; Cynthia Rothrock; Robert Forster; Frank Pesce; Willie Gault; Amanda Welles; Nina Richardson; ***D:*** Gil Bettman; ***W:*** Michael Thomas Montgomery; ***C:*** Trey Smith. **VIDEO**

The Night Visitor **1/2 1970 (PG)** A man in a prison for the criminally insane seeks violent vengeance on those he believes have set him up. Heavily detailed, slow moving. Ullman and von Sydow can do better. **106m/C; VHS, DVD, Blu-Ray.** *GB DK* Max von Sydow; Liv Ullmann; Trevor Howard; Per Oscarsson; Andrew Keir; ***D:*** Laszlo Benedek; ***M:*** Henry Mancini.

Night Visitor *Never Cry Devil* **1989 (R)** A retired police detective teams up with a teenage peeping tom to disclose the identity of a satanic serial killer. The killer, of course, is one of the youth's teachers. **95m/C; VHS, DVD.** Derek Rydall; Shannon Tweed; Elliott Gould; Allen Garfield; Michael J. Pollard; Richard Roundtree; Henry Gibson; ***D:*** Rupert Hitzig; ***W:*** Randal Viscovich.

Night Watch **1/2** *Le Trou; Il Buco* **1972** A woman recovering from a nervous breakdown witnesses a murder, but no one will believe her. **100m/C; VHS, DVD.** *GB* Elizabeth Taylor; Laurence Harvey; Billie Whitelaw; ***D:*** Brian G. Hutton; ***C:*** Billy Williams.

Night Watch *Nochnoi Dozor* **2004 (R)** Russian take on the battle between the forces of good and evil, set in present-day Moscow. A prologue establishes that a diplomatic truce exists between the two: the Night Watch keeps a check on the dark side and the Day Watch on the light. But after centuries, a prophecy about the Great Other, who will tip the balance, seems about to come true. Somewhat chaotic and convoluted but still intense. The first in a trilogy based on the novels of co-writer Lukyanenko. Russian with subtitles. **114m/C; DVD, Blu-Ray.** *RU* Vladimir Menshov; Viktor Verzhbitsky; Konstantin Khabensky; Maria Poroshina; Galina Tyunina; Gosha Kytsenko; Alexsei Chadov; Zhanna Friske; Ilya Lagutenko; Rimma Markova; Maria Mironova; Alexei Maklakov; Anna Dubrovskaya; Aleksandr Samojlenko; Anna Slyusaryova; Dmitry Martynov; ***D:*** Timur Bekmambetov; ***W:*** Timur Bekmambetov; Sergey Lukyanenko; ***C:*** Sergei Trofimov; ***M:*** Yuri Potyeyenko; Valera Viktorov; Mukstar Mirzakeev.

Night Watcher **WOOF!** **2008 (R)** Following her mother's suicide, Angela joins a survivors' support group and meets Brian, whose father died. Then they both receive tapes that chronicle their loved ones last days. Angela comes to believe that a rash of local suicides were actually murders but she and Brian don't call the cops. No, they decide to turn amateur sleuths even as the killer stalks them. **93m/C; DVD.** Christopher Kadish; Allison Tyler; Zack Stewart; Daniel Vincent Gordh; Robert Petrarca; ***D:*** Will Gordh; ***W:*** Daniel Vincent Gordh; David Murray; ***C:*** Chris Tonkovich; ***M:*** Nicholas Bonardi. **VIDEO**

The Night We Called It a Day **1/2** *All the Way* **2003** Taken-from-reality tale finds Frank Sinatra (Hopper) in Australia doing a tour in 1974 with struggling producer Rod Blue (Edgerton). Ol' Blue Eyes barely gets off the airplane before mouthing off at reporter Hilary Hunter (de Rossi) when asked some too-personal questions. The resulting countrywide brouhaha keeps him captive in his hotel as unions protest outside and demand that he apologize. Hopper is a natural at doing Sinatra, though Tom Burlinson—often a Sinatra impersonator—performed the vocals. **97m/C; VHS, DVD.** *AU US* Dennis Hopper; Melanie Griffith; Portia de Rossi; Joel Edgerton; Rose Byrne; David Hemmings; David Field; Nicholas Hope; ***D:*** Paul Goldman; ***W:*** Peter Clifton; Michael Thomas; ***C:*** Danny Ruhlmann; ***M:*** Rupert Gregson-Williams. **VIDEO**

The Night We Never Met **1/2 1993 (R)** Three yuppies bring different visions of romance and a case of mistaken identity to a time-share apartment in New York's Greenwich Village. Sam (Broderick) needs a quiet space to get over being dumped by a flaky performance artist (Tripplehorn). Ellen (Sciorra) is looking for space to paint away from the confines of her thick-headed spouse (Mantell) and slob. Brian (Anderson) wants a space where he can be one of the boys and escape from his cloying fiancee (Bateman). Fairly predictable but enjoyable romantic comedy. **98m/C; DVD.** Matthew Broderick; Annabella Sciorra; Kevin Anderson; Justine Bateman; Jeanne Tripplehorn; Michael Mantell; Doris Roberts; Tim Guinee; Christine Baranski; Dana Wheeler-Nicholson; Dominic Chianese; Greg Germann; ***D:*** Warren Leight; ***W:*** Warren Leight; ***C:*** John Thomas; ***M:*** Evan Lurie.

Nightbreed **1/2 1990 (R)** A teenager flees a chaotic past to slowly become a member of a bizarre race of demons that live in a huge, abandoned Canadian graveyard; a place where every sin is forgiven. Based on Barker's novel "Cabal," and appropriately gross, nonsensical and strange. Good special effects almost save this one. **102m/C; VHS, DVD, Blu-Ray.** *CA* Craig Sheffer; Anne Bobby; David Cronenberg; Charles Haid; ***D:*** Clive Barker; ***W:*** Clive Barker; ***C:*** Robin Vidgeon; ***M:*** Danny Elfman.

The Nightcomers **1972 (R)** A pretend "prequel" to Henry James's "The Turn of the Screw," wherein an Irish gardener trysts with the nanny of two watchful children who believe that lovers unite in death. Don't be fooled: stick to the original. **96m/C; VHS, DVD, Blu-Ray.** *GB* Marlon Brando; Stephanie Beacham; Thora Hird; Harry Andrews; Christopher Ellis; Verna Harvey; Anna Palk; ***D:*** Michael Winner; ***W:*** Michael Hastings; ***C:*** Robert Paynter; ***M:*** Jerry Fielding.

Nightcrawler **2014 (R)** Louis Bloom (Gyllenhaal) is a sociopath who discovers that the best place for his specific kind of insanity is in evening news. After years scraping the bottom of the moral barrel, Lou buys a video camera and a police scanner and becomes a "stringer," the guys who get the breaking news footage that sells. It's not long before Lou isn't just reporting on the biggest stories of the L.A. night but assisting in their creation. Gyllenhaal does his best work in this fascinating piece about a creature of the night who finds his purpose behind a news camera. **117m/C; DVD, Blu-Ray.** Jake Gyllenhaal; Rene Russo; Bill Paxton; Riz Ahmed; ***D:*** Dan Gilroy; ***W:*** Dan Gilroy; ***C:*** Robert Elswit; ***M:*** James Newton Howard. Ind. Spirit '15: First Feature, Screenplay.

Nightfall **1956** Ray, accused of a crime he didn't commit, is forced to flee from both the law and the underworld. Classic example of film noir, brilliantly filmed by Tourneur. **78m/B; VHS, DVD.** Aldo Ray; Brian Keith; Anne Bancroft; Jocelyn Brando; James Gregory; Frank Albertson; ***D:*** Jacques Tourneur; ***W:*** Stirling Silliphant.

Nightfall **1988 (PG-13)** Adaptation of the classic Isaac Asimov short story. A planet that has two suns (and therefore no night) experiences an eclipse and its inhabitants go mad. **87m/C; VHS, DVD, Blu-Ray.** David Birney; Sarah Douglas; Alexis Kanner; Andra Millian; ***D:*** Paul Mayersberg; ***C:*** Dariusz Wolski. **TV**

Nighthawks **1978** Jim (Robertson) is a geography teacher in London who lives a closeted life. His quiet daily routine is separate from his cruising of the city's gay pleasure spots until his two worlds converge when he's confronted by his students. **113m/C; VHS, DVD.** *GB* Ken Robertson; ***D:*** Ron Peck; ***W:*** Ron Peck; Paul Hallam; ***C:*** Johanna Davis; ***M:*** David Graham Ellis.

Nighthawks **1/2 1981 (R)** NYC cops scour Manhattan to hunt down an international terrorist on the loose. They race from disco to subway to an airborne tramway. Exciting and well paced. Hauer's American film debut. **100m/C; VHS, DVD, Blu-Ray.** Sylvester Stallone; Billy Dee Williams; Rutger Hauer; Lindsay Wagner; Nigel Davenport; Persis Khambatta; Catherine Mary Stewart; Joe Spinell; Robert Pugh; ***D:*** Bruce Malmuth; ***W:*** David Shaber; ***C:*** James A. Contner; ***M:*** Keith Emerson.

The Nightingale **2018 (R)** In early nineteenth century colonial Australia, Clare (Franciosi) is an Irish convict imprisoned by a British officer, Lieutenant Hawkins (Claflin). Though Clare should have been released three years earlier, he refuses to and instead forces her to sing for his soldiers. The British troops are putting down rebellions, subduing the locals, and committing genocide on the Aboriginal peoples. When some soldiers commit a horrifying act, Clare wants revenge. Though the performances are outstanding, the indie drama-thriller is brutal and violent, with a repetitive story that makes it feel longer than it really is. **136m/C; DVD, Blu-Ray.** Aisling Franciosi; Sam Claflin; Michael Sheasby; Claire Jones; Damon Herriman; Ewen Leslie; *D:* Jennifer Kent; *W:* Jennifer Kent; *C:* Radek Ladczuk; *M:* Jed Kurzel.

Nightjohn 1/2 **1996 (PG-13)** Nightjohn (Lumbly) is the new slave purchased by Southern plantation owner Clel Walker (Bridges). He moves into the cabin shared by 12-year-old Sarny (Jones) and Delie (Toussaint). When Sarny finds out that Nightjohn can read and write (illegal for slaves), she's determined to learn from him. And with her new knowledge, Sarny looks for ways to help her fellow slaves. Based on Gary Paulsen's 1993 novel; filmed on location at Rip Raps Plantation in Sumter, South Carolina. **96m/C; VHS, DVD.** Carl Lumbly; Allison Jones; Beau Bridges; Lorraine Toussaint; Bill Cobbs; Kathleen York; Gabriel Casseus; Tom Nowicki; Monica Ford; Joel Thomas Traywick; *D:* Charles Burnett; *W:* Bill Cain; *C:* Elliot Davis; *M:* Stephen James Taylor. **CABLE**

The Nightman **1993 (R)** Ex-soldier Marcoux becomes the night manager of a failing southern resort, run by sexy, and lonely, Kerns. They begin an affair, which turns sour when Robertson, Kerns's teenaged daughter, also falls for the stud. Then mom is murdered and Marcoux goes to prison. But 18 years later Robertson's past comes back to haunt her. Just what did happen all those years ago? Made-for-TV thriller with additional footage. **96m/C; VHS, DVD.** Ted Marcoux; Jenny Robertson; Joanna Kerns; *D:* Charles Haid; *W:* James Poe; *M:* Gary Chang. **TV**

Nightmare 1/2 **1963** As a child, Janet sees her insane mother stab her father to death. Left in the care of two guardians, the now-grown Janet has recurring nightmares and fears she's inherited her mother's madness. Routine, with red herrings galore. **83m/B; VHS, DVD, Blu-Ray.** *GB* Jennie Linden; David Knight; Moira Redmond; Brenda Bruce; *D:* Freddie Francis; *W:* Jimmy Sangster; *C:* John Wilcox; *M:* Don Banks.

Nightmare **1991 (PG-13)** Single mom Linda Hemmings (Principal) takes matters into her own hands when her daughter Dana (Harris) is kidnapped. Though Dana escapes and her assailant, Edward Ryter (Banks), is arrested, he's soon released and threatening Dana to prevent her testifying. So mom teams up with police detective Jake Wilman (Sorvino) to get the goods on the psycho before he can do further harm. **84m/C; VHS, DVD.** Victoria Principal; Jonathan Banks; Paul Sorvino; Danielle Harris; *D:* John Pasquin; *W:* Rick Husky; *C:* Denis Lewiston; *M:* Dana Kaproff.

Nightmare 1/2 **2007** Mediocre supernatural horror. Molly Duggan (Duff) is doing graduate studies on sleep disorders, including the sleep paralysis that took her mother's life. When Molly starts suffering herself she feels an evil presence and it seems science must take a backseat to legend and the mystery of Molly's family. **90m/C; DVD.** Haylie Duff; Bruce Ramsay; Gwynyth Walsh; Jesse Hutch; Meaghan Ory; Cassandra Sawtell; Teach Grant; Anna Williams; *D:* Terry Ingram; *W:* David Golden; *M:* Michael Richard Plowman. **CABLE**

Nightmare Alley 1/2 **1947** Dark and disturbing noir has Power, in one of his best roles, as con man/carny who learns the secrets of a mentalist act and turns it into fame and fortune. When a femme fatale shrink persuades him to join a scheme to bilk the rich, it leads to a fascinating and precipitous downfall. Power fought to get the film made, and for the chance to play against his matinee idol type. **111m/B; DVD.** Tyrone Power; Joan Blondell; Coleen Gray; Helen Walker; Taylor Holmes; Ian Keith; Mike Mazurki; *D:* Edmund Goulding; *W:* Jules Furthman; *C:* Lee Garmes; *M:* Cyril Mockridge.

Nightmare at Bittercreek **1991 (PG-13)** Four babes and a tour guide are pursued by psycho gang in the Sierra mountains. Made for TV nightmare in your living room. **92m/C; VHS, DVD.** Tom Skerritt; Joanna Cassidy; Lindsay Wagner; Constance McCashin; Janne Mortil; *D:* Tim Burstall. **TV**

Nightmare at 43 Hillcrest 1/2 **1974** A family's life becomes a living hell when the police mistakenly raid their house. Based on a true story. Currently only available as part of a collection. **72m/C; VHS, Streaming.** Jim Hutton; Mariette Hartley; *D:* Dan Curtis; *W:* William Katz; *M:* Robert Cobert.

Nightmare at Noon **1987 (R)** Watered-down thriller about a small desert town beset by violent terrorists (who are really locals gone mad from a chemical experiment dumped into the water system). Only the sheriff's small staff is there to stop them. **96m/C; VHS, DVD, Blu-Ray.** Wings Hauser; George Kennedy; Bo Hopkins; Brion James; Kimberly Beck; Kimberly Ross; *D:* Nico Mastorakis.

Nightmare at the End of the Hall **2008** Courtney Snow (Rue) takes a job teaching at the prep school she once attended—the same school where her best friend committed suicide. She befriends student Laurel (MacInnes-Wood), who appears to be a reincarnation of her friend Jane. Is Jane now trying to communicate because she didn't kill herself after all? **90m/C; DVD.** Sara Rue; Jacqueline MacInnes-Wood; Duncan Regehr; Kavan Smith; Amber Borycki; Sebastian Gacki; *D:* George Mendeluk; *W:* Nora Zuckerman; *C:* Anthony C. Metchie; *M:* Clinton Shorter. **CABLE**

The Nightmare Before Christmas *Tim Burton's The Nightmare Before Christmas* **1993 (PG)** Back when he was a animator trainee at Disney, Burton came up with this adventurous idea but couldn't get it made; subsequent directorial success brought more clout. Relies on a painstaking stop-motion technique that took more than two years to film and is justifiably amazing. The story revolves around Jack Skellington, the Pumpkin King of the dangerously weird Halloweentown. Suffering from ennui, he accidentally discovers the wonders of Christmastown and decides to kidnap Santa and rule over this peaceable holiday. Fast pace is maintained by the equally breathless score. Not cuddly, best appreciated by those with a feel for the macabre. **75m/C; VHS, DVD, Blu-Ray, UMD.** *V:* Danny Elfman; Chris Sarandon; Catherine O'Hara; William Hickey; Ken Page; Ed Ivory; Paul (Pee-wee Herman) Reubens; Glenn Shadix; Greg Proops; *D:* Henry Selick; *W:* Caroline Thompson; Tim Burton; Michael McDowell; *C:* Pete Kozachik; *M:* Danny Elfman.

Nightmare Castle *Amanti d'Oltretomba; Night of the Doomed; The Faceless Monsters; Lovers from Beyond the Tomb* **1965** Jealous mad scientist murders his wife and her lover. Then he conducts a bizarre experiment, using the dead couple's blood to rejuvenate an old servant. Not quite satisfied with his revenge, he then seeks to marry his late wife's sister after realizing that she has been left the inheritance. In time, the perturbed ghosts of the late lovers appear and seek revenge. A real nightmare. **90m/B; VHS, DVD, Blu-Ray.** *IT* Barbara Steele; Paul Muller; Helga Line; *D:* Allan Grunewald; *M:* Ennio Morricone.

Nightmare Cinema **2019 (R)** A horror anthology, the film is organized around the recurring segment "The Projectionist" in which a projectionist (Rourke) shows people's deepest fears on the screen of an old movie theater. The twisted "The Thing in the Woods" centers on a woman covered in blood being pursued by the weapons-heavy Welder, while "Mirare" explores the effects of a plastic surgery gone wrong. Other segments consider mental illness and someone who can see the dead. The unfocused anthology has much promise because of its premise and the filmmakers involved. While some segments are entertaining, the film as a whole is uneven. **119m/C; DVD, Blu-Ray.** Mickey Rourke; Richard Chamberlain; Adam Godley; Orson Chaplin; Eric Nelsen; *D:* Alejandro Brugues; Joe Dante; Mick Garris; Ryuhei Kitamura; David Slade; *W:* Alejandro Brugues; Mick Garris; David Slade; Sandra Becerril; Lawrence C. Connolly; Richard Christian Matheson; *C:* Andrew Russo; Matthias Schubert; Jo Willems; *M:* Richard Band; Kyle Newmaster; Aldo Shllaku; J.G. Thirlwell.

A Nightmare Come True 1/2 *A Dream of Murder* **1997** A young woman moves home after her apartment burns down, only to be told by her stepfather days later that his wife left him without saying a word. Needless to say she doesn't believe him, the police don't believe her, and she starts having paranoid dreams about murder. One could only dream there was something new—or well done—here. **120m/C; DVD.** Gerald McRaney; Shelley Fabares; Katy Boyer; Joel Bissonnette; Jeremy Renner; Dann Florek; Judith Scott; Mark Benninghoffen; William Utay; Claire Malis; Jocko Marcellino; Steven Marcus Gibbs; *D:* Christopher Leitch; *W:* Gerald Di Pego; Nevin Schreiner; *C:* Stephen McNutt; *M:* Jeff Eden Fair; Star Parodi. **TV**

Nightmare Detective *Akumu Tantei* **2006** An older man sitting in a creepy apartment learns from a younger man named Kagenuma that he's being haunted by the soul of an aborted daughter his wife never told him about. The older man thanks Kagenuma, who leaves what turns out to be a dream for the real world, where the older man is on life support. Eventually he is drawn into a police case where an unknown person appears to be causing sleeping people to kill themselves. A surpringly mainstream film from director Tsukamato who's also the writer, cinematographer, and main bad guy. **106m/C; DVD.** *JP* Ryuhei Matsuda; Mansanobu Ando; Shinya Tsukamoto; Hitomi; *D:* Shinya Tsukamoto; *W:* Shinya Tsukamoto; *C:* Shinya Tsukamoto; *M:* Chu Ishikawa; Tadashi Ishikawa.

Nightmare Honeymoon 1/2 **1973** Newlyweds David and Jill Webb are on their way to New Orleans for their honeymoon when they witness a murder. When psycho killer Lee realizes he's been seen, he knocks David unconcious and rapes Jill. After learning of his bride's assault, David wants revenge. Based on the novel by Lawrence Block. **95m/C; DVD.** Dack Rambo; Rebecca Dianna Smith; John Beck; Pat Hingle; Roy Cameron Jenson; David Huddleston; *D:* Elliot Silverstein; *W:* S. Lee Pogostin; *C:* Harry Stradling, Jr.; *M:* Elmer Bernstein.

Nightmare in Blood 1/2 *Horror Convention* **1975** Vampires lurk in San Francisco and wreak havoc on the night life. **90m/C; VHS, DVD.** Kerwin Mathews; Jerry Walter; Barrie Youngfellow; *D:* John Stanley.

Nightmare in Wax 1/2 *Crimes in the Wax Museum* **1969** After suffering disfigurement in a fight with a studio boss, a former make-up man starts a wax museum. For fun, he injects movie stars with a formula that turns them into statues. **91m/C; VHS, DVD.** Cameron Mitchell; Anne Helm; *D:* Bud Townsend.

Nightmare Man **2006 (R)** Ellen (Metz) is being haunted by the title character, which resembles an exotic fertility mask she recently purchased. Husband Bill (Szafir) just thinks she's crazy and needs a little stay in the loony bin. As he's driving through the woods, the car runs out of gas, and Bill leaves Ellen alone. Sure enough, she gets attacked by her nightmare demon. Ellen escapes to a nearby cabin where the occupants should never have let a bloody, screaming woman inside. The women seem to spend a lot of time topless or in their underwear and there is a twist ending, but it's still bad. **90m/C; DVD.** Tiffany Shepis; Blythe Metz; Hanna Putnam; James Ferris; Jack Sway; Luciano Szafir; Aaron Sherry; *D:* Rolfe Kanesky; *W:* Rolfe Kanesky; *C:* Paul Deng; *M:* Christopher Farrell.

A Nightmare on Elm Street 1/2 **1984 (R)** Feverish, genuinely frightening horror film about Freddy Krueger (Englund), a scarred maniac in a fedora and razor-fingered gloves who kills neighborhood teens in their dreams and, subsequently, in reality. Of the children-fight-back genre, in which the lead victim (Langenkamp) ingeniously goes to great lengths to destroy Freddy. In the tradition of "Friday the 13th's" Jason and "Halloween's" Michael Myers, "Elm Street" spawned a "Freddy" phenomenon: multiple sequels, a TV series, and an army of razor-clawed trick or treaters at Halloween. **92m/C; DVD, Blu-Ray.** John Saxon; Heather Langenkamp; Ronee Blakley; Robert Englund; Amanda Wyss; Jsu Garcia; Johnny Depp; Charles Fleischer; *D:* Wes Craven; *W:* Wes Craven; *C:* Jacques Haitkin; *M:* Charles Bernstein.

A Nightmare on Elm Street 1/2 **2010 (R)** Ineffective, creepy, not particularly scary (but slickly made) relaunch of the venerable horror series with Haley taking on the role of serial killer Freddy Krueger. Dead Fred was a child molester working at a preschool, and his present-day victims are the teens who are recovering their repressed memories of the trauma. Dean (Lutz) is the first to go but his friends quickly realize that death follows them into their nightmares, so they can't fall asleep if they want to live. If you're familiar with the 1984 original, you'll recognize some recreated scenes. **95m/C; DVD, Blu-Ray.** Jackie Earle Haley; Rooney Mara; Kyle Gallner; Thomas Dekker; Kellan Lutz; Katie Cassidy; Connie Britton; Clancy Brown; *D:* Samuel Bayer; *W:* Wesley Strick; Eric Heisserer; *C:* Jeff Cutter; *M:* Steve Jablonsky.

A Nightmare on Elm Street 2: Freddy's Revenge 1/2 **1985 (R)** Mediocre sequel to the popular horror film. Freddy, the dream-haunting psychopath with the ginsu knife hands, returns to possess a teenager's body in order to kill again. Nothing new here, however praise is due for the stunning high-tech dream sequence. **87m/C; DVD, Blu-Ray.** Mark Patton; Hope Lange; Clu Gulager; Robert Englund; Kim Myers; Robert Rusler; Marshall Bell; Sydney Walsh; *D:* Jack Sholder; *W:* David Chaskin; *C:* Jacques Haitkin.

A Nightmare on Elm Street 3: Dream Warriors **1987 (R)** Chapter three in this slice and dice series. Freddy Krueger is at it again, haunting the dreams of unsuspecting suburban teens. Langenkamp, the nightmare-freaked heroine from the first film, returns to counsel the latest victims of Freddy-infested dreams. Noted for the special effects wizardry but little else. Followed by "A Nightmare on Elm Street 4: Dream Master." **96m/C; DVD, Blu-Ray.** Patricia Arquette; Robert Englund; Heather Langenkamp; Craig Wasson; Laurence Fishburne; Priscilla Pointer; John Saxon; Brooke Bundy; Jennifer Rubin; Rodney Eastman; Nan Martin; Dick Cavett; Zsa Zsa Gabor; *D:* Chuck Russell; *W:* Chuck Russell; Bruce Wagner; Wes Craven; Frank Darabont; *C:* Roy Wagner; *M:* Angelo Badalamenti.

A Nightmare on Elm Street 4: Dream Master 1/2 **1988 (R)** Freddy Krueger is still preying on people in their dreams, but he may have met his match as he battles for supremacy with a telepathically talented girl. What Part 4 lacks in substance, it makes up for in visual verve, including scenes of a kid drowning in his waterbed, and a pizza covered with pepperoni-like faces of Freddy's previous victims. Followed by "A Nightmare on Elm Street 5: Dream Child." **99m/C; DVD, Blu-Ray.** Robert Englund; Rodney Eastman; Danny Hassel; Andras Jones; Tuesday Knight; Lisa Wilcox; Ken Sagoes; Toy Newkirk; Brooke Theiss; Brooke Bundy; *D:* Renny Harlin; *W:* Brian Helgeland; Scott Pierce; *C:* Steven Fierberg; *M:* Craig Safan.

A Nightmare on Elm Street 5: Dream Child **1989 (R)** The fifth installment of Freddy Krueger's never-ending adventures. Here, America's favorite knife-wielding burn victim, unable to best the Dream Master from the previous film, haunts the dreams of her unborn fetus. Gore fans may be disappointed to discover that much of the blood and guts ended up on the cutting room floor. **90m/C; DVD, Blu-Ray.** Robert Englund; Lisa Wilcox; Kelly Jo Minter; Danny Hassel; Erika Anderson; Nicholas Mele; Beatrice Boepple; *D:* Stephen Hopkins; *W:* Leslie Bohem; *C:* Peter Levy; *M:* Jay Ferguson. Golden Raspberries '89: Worst Song ("Bring Your Daughter to the Slaughter").

Nightmare Sisters **WOOF! 1987 (R)** Three sorority sisters become possessed by a demon and then sexually ravage a nearby fraternity. **83m/C; VHS, DVD, Blu-Ray.** Brinke Stevens; Michelle (McClellan) Bauer; Linnea Quigley; *D:* David DeCoteau.

Nightmare Weekend **1986 (R)** A professor's evil assistant lures three young women into his lab and performs cruel and vicious experiments that transform the girls and their dates into crazed zombies. **86m/C; VHS, DVD.** Dale Midkiff; Debbie Laster; Debra Hunter; Lori Lewis; *D:* Henry Sala.

Nightmares **1983 (PG)** A less-than-thrilling horror anthology featuring four tales in which common, everyday occurrences take on the ingredients of a nightmare. In the same vein as "Twilight Zone" and "Creepshow." **99m/C; VHS, DVD, Blu-Ray.** Christina Raines; Emilio Estevez; Moon

Zappa; Lance Henriksen; Richard Masur; Veronica Cartwright; ***D:*** Joseph Sargent; ***W:*** Jeffrey Bloom; Christopher Crowe; ***C:*** Mario DiLeo; Gerald Perry Finnerman; ***M:*** Craig Safan.

Nights and Days 🦴🦴 ½ **1976** Adaptation of writer Maria Dabrowska's tale about a Polish family chronicles the persecution, expulsions, and land grabbing that occurred after the unsuccessful Uprising of 1864. In Polish with English subtitles. **255m/C; VHS, DVD.** *PL* Jadwiga Baranska; Jerzy Binczycki; ***D:*** Jerzy Antczak.

Nights and Weekends 🦴 **2008** Honestly, does anybody really want to watch a couple of dullards break up their long-distance relationship? Writer/director/stars Gerwig and Swanberg do their improvisational mumblecore indie thing as Mattie lives in New York and James lives in Chicago. They yak a lot on the phone and get together sometimes for graphic but decidedly uninteresting sex until they realize absence does not make the heart grow fonder. **80m/C; DVD.** Greta Gerwig; Joe Swanberg; ***D:*** Greta Gerwig; Joe Swanberg; ***W:*** Greta Gerwig; Joe Swanberg; ***C:*** Matthias Grunsky; Benjamin Kasulke.

Nights in Rodanthe 🦴🦴 **2008 (PG-13)** Adrienne Willis (Lane) needs some peace and quiet to ponder her chaotic personal life, so she decides to spend a weekend at a friend's coastal North Carolina inn. A major storm is forecast so the only guest is Dr. Paul Flanner (Gere), who's trying to reconcile with his estranged son Mark (Franco). Naturally, the unhappy (but impossibly attractive) pair turns to each other for advice, and soon they're cooing and wooing against the swoony Outer Banks setting. The completely predictable and contrived story feels engineered simply to jerk tears. Based on the 2002 Nicholas Sparks novel. **96m/C; DVD, Blu-Ray.** Diane Lane; Richard Gere; James Franco; Scott Glenn; Christopher Meloni; Mae Whitman; Viola Davis; Pablo Schreiber; Charlie Tahan; Betty Ann Baker; ***D:*** George C. Wolfe; ***W:*** Ann Peacock; John Romano; ***C:*** Affonso Beato; ***M:*** Jeanine Tesori.

Nights of Cabiria 🦴🦴🦴 ½ *Le Notti de Cabiria; Cabiria* **1957** Fellini classic which details the personal decline of a naive prostitute who thinks she's found true love. In Italian with English subtitles or dubbed. Basis for the musical "Sweet Charity." **117m/B; VHS, DVD.** *IT* Giulietta Masina; Amedeo Nazzari; Francois Perier; Franca Marzi; Dorian Gray; Aldo Silvani; Ennio Girolami; ***D:*** Federico Fellini; ***W:*** Federico Fellini; Tullio Pinelli; Ennio Flaiano; ***C:*** Aldo Tonti; ***M:*** Nino Rota. Oscars '57: Foreign Film; Cannes '57: Actress (Masina).

Nightscare 🦴🦴 *Night Scare; Beyond Bedlam* **1993 (R)** When Dr. Stephanie Lyell's (Hurley) drug behavior-modification experiment goes wrong it allows serial killer Marc Gilmour (Allen) to get to his victims through their dreams. The doc tries to prove to Detective Inspector Terry Hamilton (Fairbrass) that the drug is safe by injecting them both but things get out of hand. Adapted from the novel by Harry Adam Knight. **89m/C; VHS, Streaming.** *GB* Craig Fairbrass; Elizabeth Hurley; Keith Allen; Jesse Birdsall; Craig Kelly; ***D:*** Vadim Jean; ***W:*** Vadim Jean.

NightScreams 🦴 ½ **1997** Cameron is having terrible nightmares and also sees the ghost of a young woman—the same woman involved in the unexplained murder/suicide that caused the death of Cameron's boyfriend. **90m/C; VHS, DVD.** Casper Van Dien; Teri Garr; Candace Cameron Bure; ***D:*** Noel Nosseck; ***W:*** Raymond Singer; Eugenia Singer; ***C:*** Paul Maibaum; ***M:*** Garry Schyman. **VIDEO**

Nightstalker WOOF! *Don't Go Near the Park* **1981** A brother and sister who were condemned to eternal death 12,000 years ago must eat virgins to keep their bodies from rotting. Trouble is, while they search for dinner, the movie decomposes. For mature audiences with no fantasies of celluloid nirvana. **90m/C; VHS, DVD.** Aldo Ray; Meeno Peluce; Tamara Taylor; Linnea Quigley; ***D:*** Lawrence Foldes; ***W:*** Lawrence Foldes; ***C:*** William de Diego.

Nightstalker 🦴🦴 **2002 (R)** Based on the '80s true crime saga of L.A. serial killer Robert Ramirez, aka the Nightstalker. Cop Gabriella Martinez (Sanchez), who discovered some of the victims, is offered a promotion to the task force investigating the murders. But she makes a judgement error when she leaks info to reporter Adrianne Deloia (Emma) and is suspended. However, Gabriela's old partner Frank Luis (Trejo) has some info of his own and Gabriela learns that she's become one of the Nightstalker's targets. **95m/C; VHS, DVD, Blu-Ray.** Roselyn Sanchez; Danny Trejo; Evan Dexter Parke; Bret Roberts; Derek Hamilton; Douglas Spain; Brandi Emma; ***D:*** Chris Fisher; ***W:*** Chris Fisher; ***C:*** Eliot Rockett; ***M:*** Ryan Beveridge.

Nightwatch 🦴🦴 **1996 (R)** Law student Martin (McGregor) takes a job as a night watchman in a morgue at the same time a serial killer is killing prostitutes and gouging out their eyes. He also has to deal with a cop (Nolte) who suspects him, a sadistic best friend (Brolin) who likes to scare him on the job, and a creepy boss (Dourif) who doesn't like him. Adapted by director Bornedal from his Danish film "Nattevagten," this one's effectively creepy, but disjointed. Excellent cast is misused, as hardly any of the characters are developed beyond simple types. **101m/C; DVD.** Ewan McGregor; Nick Nolte; Patricia Arquette; Josh Brolin; John C. Reilly; Brad Dourif; Lonny (Lonnie) Chapman; Alix Koromzay; Lauren Graham; ***D:*** Ole Bornedal; ***W:*** Ole Bornedal; Steven Soderbergh; ***C:*** Dan Laustsen; ***M:*** Joachim Holbek.

Nightwatching 🦴🦴 **2007 (R)** Not much more than the sum of its visually striking parts. Needing money when his wife becomes pregnant, Dutch artist Rembrandt reluctantly accepts a commission to paint the members of the Amsterdam Civil Guard. The murder of a guardsman leads Rembrandt to realize that they are power-mad and covering up some nasty sexual secrets. So he uses painterly codes within "The Night Watch" to expose the men. **134m/C; DVD.** *GB NL* Martin Freeman; Eva Birthistle; Jodhi May; Natalie Press; Adam Kotz; Adrian Lukis; Toby Jones; Emily Holmes; ***D:*** Peter Greenaway; ***W:*** Peter Greenaway; ***C:*** Reinier van Brummeten; ***M:*** Giovanni Solamar; Wlodek Pawlik.

Nightwaves 🦴🦴 **2003 (PG-13)** A car accident cripples and widows Shelby, who battles pain and boredom by picking up the sorted details of her rich, married neighbors' lives via their phone calls on her police scanner. But when a woman winds up in a body bag Shelby is shoved into a mess that is more than what it seems and makes her a target. **99m/C; VHS, DVD.** Sherilyn Fenn; David Nerman; Bruce Dinsmore; Francis X. (Frank) McCarthy; Joanna Noyes; Frank Fontaine; Emma Campbell; Jennifer Morehouse; Kevin Jubinville; ***D:*** Jim Kaufman; ***W:*** Melissa Jo Peltier; ***C:*** Georges Archambault; ***M:*** Simon Carpentier. **TV**

Nightwing 🦴 ½ **1979 (PG)** Suspense drama about three people who risk their lives to exterminate a colony of plague-carrying vampire bats in New Mexican Indian community. From the novel by Martin Cruz Smith and adapted by Smith, Steve Shagan, and Bud Shrake. O.K. viewing for those who aren't choosy about their rabid bat movies. **103m/C; VHS, DVD, Blu-Ray.** Nick Mancuso; David Warner; Kathryn Harrold; Strother Martin; Stephen Macht; Pat Corley; Charles Hallahan; Ben Piazza; George Clutesi; ***D:*** Arthur Hiller; ***W:*** Steve Shagan; Bud Shrake; Martin Cruz Smith; ***C:*** Charles Rosher, Jr.; ***M:*** Henry Mancini.

Nightwish 🦴 ½ **1989 (R)** Students do more than homework when a professor leads them into their own horrifying dreams. Soon it becomes impossible to distinguish dreams from reality. **96m/C; VHS, Blu-Ray, Streaming.** Jack Starrett; Robert Tessier; Clayton Rohner; Elizabeth Kaitan; Alisha Das; Tom Dugan; Brian Thompson; Artur Cybulski; ***D:*** Bruce Cook, Jr.; ***W:*** Bruce Cook, Jr.

Nijinsky 🦴🦴 **1980 (R)** An opulent biography of the famous ballet dancer. His exciting and innovative choreography gets little attention. The film concentrates on his infamous homosexual lifestyle and his relationship with impresario Sergei Diaghilev (Bates, in a tour-de-force performance). Lovely to look at, but slow and unconvincing. **125m/C; VHS, DVD, Streaming.** Alan Bates; George de la Pena; Leslie Browne; Alan Badel; Carla Fracci; Colin Blakely; Ronald Pickup; Ronald Lacey; Vernon Dobtcheff; Jeremy Irons; Frederick Jaeger; Janet Suzman; Sian Phillips; ***D:*** Herbert Ross.

Nikki, the Wild Dog of the North 🦴 ½ **1961 (G)** When a Malemute pup is separated from his Canadian trapper master, he teams up with a bear cub for a series of adventures. Later the pup is reunited with his former master for still more adventures. Adapted from a novel by James Oliver Curwood for Disney. **73m/C; VHS, DVD.** *CA* Jean Coutu; Emile Genest; Uriel Luft; Robert Rivard; ***D:*** Jack Couffer; Don Haldane; ***W:*** Winston Hibler; Ralph Wright; ***C:*** Lloyd Beebe; ***M:*** Oliver Wallace.

Nil by Mouth 🦴🦴 **1996 (R)** Oldman draws on his own dysfunctional working-class London background for his impressive writer/director debut, which casually puts you into the middle of one Cockney family's life. There's brutal Ray (Winstone), husband to Val (Burke) and brother-in-law to young addict Billy (Creed-Miles), as well as his tough mother-in-law Janet (Morse) and her mother, Kath (Dore). Billy gets kicked out of the house while a drunken Ray beats the pregnant Val, prompting a display of female solidarity. Formless pic drops into characters' lives at random, showcasing family loyalty and generosity amidst the violence. **128m/C; DVD.** *UK* Ray Winstone; Kathy Burke; Charlie Creed-Miles; Laila Morse; Edna Dore; Steve Sweeney; Chrissie Cotterill; Jon Morrison; Jamie Foreman; ***D:*** Gary Oldman; ***W:*** Gary Oldman; ***C:*** Ron Fortunato; ***M:*** Eric Clapton. British Acad. '97: Film, Orig. Screenplay; Cannes '97: Actress (Burke).

Nim's Island 🦴🦴 ½ **2008 (PG)** A sweet fantasy adventure featuring some excellent special effects. Nim (Breslin) lives on a tropical isle with her scientist dad Jack (Butler). They have a dreamy life with the friendly wildlife and Nim's beloved books, especially those by Alex Rover (Foster), who in real life is a hermit. Then Jack leaves on an ocean journey but doesn't return, leaving poor Nim to fend for herself. Through an unlikely series of events, Alex learns of her plight and musters the courage to save Nim, who's afraid she'll lose her island to developers. It's a little dizzying, but there is enough charm to satisfy young viewers. **95m/C; DVD.** Abigail Breslin; Jodie Foster; Gerard Butler; ***D:*** Marc Levin; Jennifer Flackett; ***W:*** Marc Levin; Jennifer Flackett; Joseph Kwong; Paula Mazur; ***C:*** Stuart Dryburgh; ***M:*** Patrick Doyle.

Nina 🦴 **2016** Director Cynthia Mort's biopic of multitalented artist, Grammy nominee, and political activist Nina Simone is so horrendously misguided and clichéd that the Simone estate even spoke out against it. Rather than focusing on her prime, Mort decides to capture Simone in the late '80s when she was dealing with alcoholism and mental instability. Light-skinned actress Zoe Saldana is actually covered in make-up to darken her skin to make her more believable. When a film sits on the shelves for four years, there's usually a valid reason for why it should stay there. **90m/C; DVD, Blu-Ray.** Zoe Saldana; David Oyelowo; Kevin Mambo; Ronald Guttman; Chuma Gault; ***D:*** Cynthia Mort; ***W:*** Cynthia Mort; ***C:*** Mihai Malaimare, Jr.; ***M:*** Ruy Folguera.

Nina Takes a Lover 🦴🦴 **1994 (R)** Romantic comedy finds Nina (San Giacomo) deciding that the passion is gone from her three-year marriage so, while her husband is out of town, she picks up a nameless Welsh photographer (Rhys) and begins an affair. The affair is over as the movie begins but Nina tells her story to a tabloid journalist (O'Keefe) who's writing about adultery. Gimmicky, with shallow if attractive characters and an equally attractive San Francisco setting. **100m/C; VHS, DVD.** Laura San Giacomo; Paul Rhys; Michael O'Keefe; Cristi Conaway; Fisher Stevens; ***D:*** Alan Jacobs; ***W:*** Alan Jacobs; ***C:*** Phil Parmet; ***M:*** Todd Boekelheide.

Nina's Heavenly Delights 🦴 ½ **2006 (PG-13)** Nina Shah (Conn) is an Indo-Scot who left her Glasgow home after an argument with her father. She returns for his funeral, intending to stay to help run the family's curry restaurant, only to learn that it may have to be sold because of her dad's gambling debts. Nina decides to brush up on her culinary skills, with the help of pretty chef Lisa (Fraser), and enter the televised "Best of the West" curry competition. Not very spicy romance with some embarrassingly amateurish scenes. **94m/C; DVD.** *GB* Laura Fraser; Art Malik; Ronny Jhutti; Raji James; Veena Sood; Atta Yaqub; Pratibha Parmar; ***W:*** Andrea Gibb; ***C:*** Simon Dennis; ***M:*** Steve Isles.

Nine 🦴🦴 ½ **2009 (PG-13)** Adaptation of the 1982 Broadway musical, which was itself inspired by Fellini's 1963 film, "8 1/2." Famous film director Guido Contini (Day-Lewis) is in the midst of working on his latest movie while struggling with his complicated personal life, which includes a number of women. The music that needs to be onstage is, instead, playing over and over inside his head. A massive challenge to bring to the screen and that collapses under its own grandeur. Devoid of Felliniesque surrealism and even fails to deliver a single show-stopping number. Disappointing follow-up for "Chicago" director Rob Marshall. **110m/C; DVD, Blu-Ray, On Demand.** Daniel Day-Lewis; Nicole Kidman; Kate Hudson; Penelope Cruz; Dame Judi Dench; Marion Cotillard; Sophia Loren; Stacy "Fergie" Ferguson; ***D:*** Rob Marshall; ***W:*** Anthony Minghella; Michael Tolkin; ***C:*** Dion Beebe; ***M:*** Andrea Guerra.

9 🦴🦴🦴 ½ **2009 (PG-13)** In this spectacularly animated post-apocalyptic, post-human world, nine numbered doll creatures (known by the number stitched into their backs) must battle for survival against machines intent on the annihilation of any remaining life. 9 (Wood), the youngest and most brave of the group is also the inspirational hero of the film's story. Director Acker uses the small band of survivors as a proxy for the range of characteristics found in humankind, from the most heroic and caring to the basest and most destructive, to hold a mirror up to current human condition. The dialogue and story development are both a little light but the detailed animated action more than compensates for it. **79m/C; DVD, Blu-Ray, On Demand.** ***V:*** Elijah Wood; Jennifer Connelly; Crispin Glover; Martin Landau; Christopher Plummer; John C. Reilly; ***D:*** Shane Acker; ***W:*** Pamela Pettler; Shane Acker; ***M:*** Deborah Lurie.

Nine Ages of Nakedness 🦴 **1969** The story of a man whose ancestors have been plagued by a strange problem: beautiful, naked women who create carnal chaos. **88m/C; VHS, DVD.** George Harrison Marks; ***Nar:*** Charles Gray; ***D:*** George Harrison Marks; ***W:*** George Harrison Marks.

9 1/2 Ninjas 🦴🦴 ½ **1990 (R)** A cautious and disciplined martial artist trains a young and flirtatious woman in the ways of the ninja. His life becomes exciting in more ways than one, when he realizes she's being followed by ninjas with more on their minds than her training—they want to assassinate her! Crazy mixture of sex, kung fu and humor make this film one surprise after another. **88m/C; VHS, Streaming.** Michael Phenicie; Andee Gray; Tommy (Tiny) Lister; ***D:*** Aaron Worth; ***W:*** Bill Crounse.

9 1/2 Weeks 🦴🦴 ½ **1986 (R)** Chance meeting between a Wall Street exec and an art gallery employee evolves into an experimental sexual relationship bordering on sado-masochism. Video version is more explicit than the theatrical release, but not by much. Strong characterizations by both actors prevent this from being strictly pornography. Well-written, with strength of male and female personalities nicely balanced. Intriguing, but not for all tastes. **114m/C; VHS, DVD.** Mickey Rourke; Kim Basinger; Margaret Whitton; Karen Young; David Margulies; Christine Baranski; Roderick Cook; Dwight Weist; ***D:*** Adrian Lyne; ***W:*** Patricia Louisianna Knop; Zalman King; ***C:*** Peter Biziou; ***M:*** Jack Nitzsche.

Nine Days a Queen 🦴🦴🦴 *Lady Jane Grey; Tudor Rose* **1936** An historical drama based on the life of Lady Jane Grey, proclaimed Queen of England after the death of Henry VIII of England and summarily executed for treason by Mary Tudor after a nine-day reign. An obscure tragedy with good performances and absorbing story line. Remade as "Lady Jane" (1985). **80m/B; VHS, DVD.** *GB* John Mills; Cedric Hardwicke; Nova Pilbeam; Sybil Thorndike; Leslie Perrins; Felix Aylmer; Miles Malleson; Frank Cellier; Desmond Tester; Gwen Francon-Davies; Martita Hunt; John Laurie; Roy Emerton; John Turnbull; J.H. Roberts; ***D:*** Robert Stevenson; ***W:*** Miles

Malleson; Robert Stevenson; *C:* Mutz Greenbaum.

Nine Dead **2010 (R)** There's a joke somewhere in this psycho-horror flick but it's mostly on the audience. A lawyer (Hart), a priest (Macaulay), a bartender (Cates), and six other apparent strangers are drugged and wake up in a room, handcuffed all around a pole. The usual masked nutburger shows up and announces that they must figure out what they have in common and why they've being held. Oh, and see that 10-minute timer on the wall Every time it counts down to zero and they don't have the answer, he kills one hostage. Less bloody than "Saw" and less interesting if that's your thing. **98m/C; DVD.** Melissa Joan Hart; Marc Macaulay; William Lee Scott; John Terry; Lucille Soong; Daniel Baldwin; John Cates; Chip Bent; Lawrence Turner; James C. Victor; Edrick Browne; *D:* Chris Shadley; *W:* Patrick Wehe Mahoney; *C:* Mark Vargo; *M:* Danny Lux. **VIDEO**

Nine Deaths of the Ninja WOOF! **1985 (R)** Faceless ninja warrior Kosugi leads a team of commandos on a mission to rescue a group of political prisoners held captive in the Philippine jungles. Features Ozone-depleted plot, incongruous performances, and inane dialogue, not to mention two main villains—a neurotic Nazi in a wheelchair and a black lesbian amazon—who chew jungle and bring bad art to a new level of appreciation. Amazing in its total badness. Produced by Cannon. **93m/C; VHS, DVD.** Sho Kosugi; Brent Huff; Emelia Lesniak; Regina Richardson; Kane (Takeshi) Kosugi; Vijay Amritraj; Blackie Dammett; Sonny Erang; Bruce Fanger; *D:* Emmett Alston; *W:* Emmett Alston; *M:* Cecile Calayco.

9/11 ½ **2017 (R)** Adapted from a play entitled "Elevator," this film tells the fictional tale of five people trapped in an elevator in the North Tower of New York's World Trade Center on that fateful date. A shoestring budget and occasionally trite dialog give it a made-for-TV feel, and a release date near the 16th anniversary of the tragedy seems exploitative. Still, it taps into emotions of reliving that day by cutting to real-life news coverage and by paying homage to a point of view largely unexplored on the big screen. **90m/C; DVD.** Charlie Sheen; Whoopi Goldberg; Gina Gershon; Luis Guzman; Wood Harris; Olga Fonda; *D:* Martin Guigui; *W:* Martin Guigui; Steven James Golebiowski; *C:* Massimo Zeri; *M:* Jeff Toyne.

Nine Lives **2005 (R)** Character study that captures brief but intense moments in the lives of nine women, ranging from a pregnant married woman (Wright) running into a former lover (Isaacs) at a supermarket to a teenager's (Seyfried) attentiveness to her disabled father (McShane), to cancer, romance, adultery, divorce, death, and mothers and daughters. Writer/director Garcia (the son of famed writer Gabriel Garcia Marquez) showcases his leading ladies while not forgetting to support his equally talented supporting males. **115m/C; DVD.** Kathy Baker; Amy Brenneman; Elpidia Carrillo; Glenn Close; Stephen (Dillon) Dillane; Dakota Fanning; William Fichtner; Lisa Gay Hamilton; Holly Hunter; Jason Isaacs; Joe Mantegna; Ian McShane; Molly Parker; Mary Kay Place; Sydney Tamiia Poitier; Aidan Quinn; Miguel (Michael) Sandoval; Amanda Seyfried; Sissy Spacek; Robin Wright; *W:* Rodrigo Garcia; *C:* Xavier Perez Grobet; *M:* Ed Shearmur.

Nine Lives WOOF! **2016 (PG)** Why?!?! In 2016, it's hard to believe that anyone is still making movies with talking cats, but it's even harder to believe that such a movie could gather enough money to hire an Oscar winner to voice the feline in question. And yet here we are, with a horrible movie about a spoiled businessman (Spacey) who ends up transplanted into the body of a house cat, and, of course, learns lessons about what's really important in life while parents lose their will to live in the audience. This is garbage through and through. It used all nine lives at once. **87m/C; DVD, Blu-Ray.** Kevin Spacey; Jennifer Garner; Robbie Amell; Malina Weissman; Christopher Walken; Mark Consuelos; *D:* Barry Sonnenfeld; *W:* Gwyn Lurie; Matt Allen; Caleb Wilson; Dan Antoniazzi; Ben Shiffrin; *C:* Karl Walter Lindenlaub; *M:* Evgueni Galperine; Sacha Galperine.

Nine Lives of Fritz the Cat **1974** Fritz feels that life's too square in the '70s, so he takes off into some of his other lives for more adventure. Cleaner but still naughty sequel to the X-rated "Fritz the Cat," featuring neither the original's writer/director Ralph Bakshi nor cartoonist Robert Crumb. Tame and lame. Animated. **77m/C; VHS, DVD.** *V:* Skip Hinnant; *D:* Robert Taylor; *W:* Robert Taylor; Eric Monte.

Nine Months ½ **1995 (PG-13)** Happily single Samuel (Grant) gets girlfriend Rebecca (Moore) pregnant and promptly wigs out. He makes amends, they marry, and true to writer/director Columbus' style, live happily ever after. Bachelor pal Sean (Goldblum) and an expectant couple (Arnold, Cusack) with three kids round out the cast. Williams offeris his usual manic flair as a Russian obstetrician, improvising his scenes with glee. Grant's knack for clumsy befuddlement fits well with the warm, fuzzy style of Columbus. Pic doesn't go out on any limbs, but is a pleasant diversion anyway. Remake of the French film "Neuf Mois." **103m/C; DVD.** Hugh Grant; Julianne Moore; Tom Arnold; Joan Cusack; Jeff Goldblum; Robin Williams; Alexa Vega; Ashley Johnson; Mia Cottet; Kristin Davis; Joey Simmrin; *D:* Chris Columbus; *W:* Chris Columbus; *C:* Donald McAlpine; *M:* Hans Zimmer.

$9.99 **2008 (R)** Clay nudity and sex! That'll draw in the crowds! Yep this oddball Australian/Israeli co-production is done in a deliberately crude stop-motion animation style with an adult story. Title refers to the price of a self-help, mail-order booklet that purports to reveal the meaning of life. The denizens of a Sydney apartment building find meaning in entirely different ways, including a homeless man—a suicide—who returns as a surly guardian angel. **78m/C; Blu-Ray.** *AU IS V:* Geoffrey Rush; Anthony LaPaglia; Samuel Johnson; Ben Mendelsohn; Joel Edgerton; Claudia Karvan; Barry Otto; Jamie Katsamatsas; Leanna (Leeanna) Walsman; *D:* Tatia Rosenthal; *W:* Tatia Rosenthal; Etgar Keret; *C:* Susan Stitt; James Lewis; Richard Bradshaw.

Nine Queens *Nueve Reinas* **2000 (R)** Juan (Pauls), a rookie con man in Buenos Aries, is taken under the wing of the more-experienced Marcos (Darin). Marcos stumbles across an opportunity to fence the Nine Queens, a famous set of defectively printed stamps from Weimar Germany. Actually, Marcos' ruse is to peddle a counterfeit set to a stamp-collecting patsy named Gandolfo (Abadal). Things get complicated when Marcos needs his angry sister Valeria's (Bredice) help, the stamps are stolen, and even Argentina's economic woes come to play a significant role. Spanish with subtitles. **115m/C; DVD.** *AR* Ricardo Darin; Gaston Pauls; Leticia Bredice; Ignasi Abadal; Tomas Fonzi; *D:* Fabian Bielinsky; *W:* Fabian Bielinsky; *C:* Marcelo Camorino; *M:* Cesar Lerner.

9 Souls ½ *Nine Souls* **2003** Surreal film begins as a slapstick comedy and ends up as a brutally depressing nightmare drama. Nine prisoners escape from lockup because they know of the location of hidden loot that they hope will give them all a second chance at life so they can start over. Lots of symbolism and metaphor that might be lost on native audiences let alone American ones, so it's definitely not for everyone. But it has prison midgets; can't go wrong with that. **120m/C; DVD.** *JP* Yoshio Harada; Ryuhei Matsuda; Kiyohiko Shibukawa; Mame Yamada; Asami Imajuku; Onimaru; *D:* Toshiyaki Toyoda; *W:* Toshiyaki Toyôda; *C:* Junichi Fujisawa.

9 to 5 ½ **1980 (PG)** In this caricature of large corporations and women in the working world, Coleman plays the male chauvinist boss who calls the shots and keeps his employees, all female, under his thumb. Three of the office secretaries daydream of Coleman's disposal and rashly kidnap him after a silly set of occurrences threaten their jobs. While they have him under lock and key, the trio take office matters into their own hands and take a stab at running things their own way, with amusing results. Basis for a TV series. **111m/C; VHS, DVD, Blu-Ray.** Jane Fonda; Lily Tomlin; Dolly Parton; Dabney Coleman; Sterling Hayden; Norma Donaldson; *D:* Colin Higgins; *W:* Patricia Resnick; *C:* Reynaldo Villalobos; *M:* Charles Fox.

976-EVIL **1988 (R)** Englund (the infamous Freddy from the Nightmare on Elm Street epics) directs this horror movie where a lonely teenager dials direct to demons from hell. **102m/C; VHS, DVD, Blu-Ray.** Stephen Geoffreys; Jim Metzler; Maria Rubell; Sandy Dennis; Robert Picardo; Lezlie (Dean) Deane; Pat O'Bryan; J.J. (Jeffrey Jay) Cohen; *D:* Robert Englund; *W:* Brian Helgeland; Rhet Topham; *C:* Paul Elliott; *M:* Tom Chase; Steve Rucker.

976-EVIL 2: The Astral Factor ½ **1991 (R)** Satan returns the call in this supernatural thriller that sequels the original film. **93m/C; VHS, Streaming.** Pat O'Bryan; Rene Assa; Debbie James; *D:* Jim Wynorski; *W:* Erik Anjou.

The Nines **2007 (R)** Three stars play three roles in three different, interconnected stories in this ambitious puzzle of a movie whose twists and turns mostly succeed. Each story features Reynolds, McCarthy, and Davis dealing with conflicts internal and external that all seem to come back to "the nines," whatever that may be. Each story connects to the other while the actors' relationships change from episode to episode. Keeps you guessing throughout the build-up but the resolution doesn't entirely pay off. **99m/C; DVD, Blu-Ray.** Ryan Reynolds; Hope Davis; Melissa McCarthy; *D:* John August; *W:* John August; *C:* Nancy Schreiber; *M:* Alex Wurman.

1945 **2017** A gorgeously shot Holocaust film that explores post-World War II tensions when two Orthodox Jews return to the Hungarian village from which Jews were deported. Arriving by train with trunks that may or may not contain perfume or cosmetics, Istvan Szentes (Angelus) and his son Arpad (Nagy) walk down a dusty road from the train station to the village. Ahead of their arrival, the villagers express concern about the men and the purpose of their visit while revealing their fears, guilts, actions, and resentments. Though well directed and captivating, the closure does not match the power of the setup. Hungarian with subtitles. **91m/B; DVD, Blu-Ray.** Peter Rudolf; Bence Tasnadi; Tamas Szabo Kimmel; Dora Sztarenki; Agi Szirtes; *D:* Ferenc Torok; *W:* Ferenc Torok; Gabor Szanto; *C:* Elemer Ragalyi; *M:* Tibor Szèmzo.

1917 ½ **2019 (R)** During World War I, two British soldiers, Blake (Chapman) and Schofield (MacKay), are selected for an important assignment – deliver a message to prevent a catastrophic attack. The dangerous journey takes them through no-man's land to the front lines, where Blake's brother is part of a company scheduled to blitz the Germans in a few hours. British intelligence has learned that the recent German retreat is a ruse, and the British company will be ambushed. Co-writer/director Mendes' single-shot drama is a powerful, taut story inspired by his grandfather's real-life experiences. **110m/C; DVD, Blu-Ray.** Dean-Charles Chapman; George MacKay; Daniel Mays; Colin Firth; Pip Carter; *D:* Sam Mendes; *W:* Sam Mendes; Krysty Wilson-Cairns; *C:* Roger Deakins; *M:* Thomas Newman. Oscars '19: Cinematog., Sound, Visual FX; British Acad. '19: Cinematog., Director (Mendes), Film, Production Design, Sound, Visual FX; Directors Guild '19: Director (Mendes); Golden Globes '20: Director (Mendes), Film--Drama.

1922 ½ **2017** A horror drama about a murdering husband, based on a novella by Stephen King. Though Wilfred James (Jane) is content with his life on his Nebraska farm, his wife Arlette (Parker) wants to move to the city. Their teenage son Henry (Schmid) also does not want to leave because of his interest in neighbor Shannon Cotterie (Bernard). Arlette's desire irks Wilfred so much that he rationalizes his plan to kill her and convinces Henry to help commit the crime. After her death, Wilfred begins to lose his grip on reality. Though the source material is stretched thin, there are moments of inspired dark comedy. **102m/C; DVD.** Thomas Jane; Molly Parker; Dylan Schmid; Kaitlyn Bernard; Neal McDonough; *D:* Zak Hilditch; *W:* Zak Hilditch; *C:* Ben Richardson; *M:* Mike Patton.

1900 *Novecento* **1976 (R)** Bertolucci's impassioned epic about two Italian families, one land-owning, the other, peasant. Shows the sweeping changes of the 20th century begun by the trauma of WWI and the onslaught of Italian socialism. Edited down from its original 360-minute length and dubbed in English from three other languages, the film suffers somewhat from editing and from its nebulous lack of commitment to any genre. **255m/C; VHS, DVD, Blu-Ray.** *FR IT GE* Robert De Niro; Gerard Depardieu; Burt Lancaster; Donald Sutherland; Dominique Sanda; Sterling Hayden; Laura Betti; Francesca Bertini; Werner Bruhns; Stefania Sandrelli; Anna Henkel; Alida Valli; *D:* Bernardo Bertolucci; *W:* Giuseppe Bertolucci; Bernardo Bertolucci; *C:* Vittorio Storaro.

1911 *Xinhai Geming* **2011 (R)** War epic (a China-Hong Kong coproduction) is an expensive propaganda piece commissioned to honor the centenary of the revolution led by Sun Yat-Sen and his deputy Huang Xing that ends the Qing dynasty. Speeches and battles fill the screen but it won't mean anything to those unfamiliar with Chinese history. Mandarin with subtitles. **120m/C; DVD, Blu-Ray.** *CH CH* Winston Chao; Jackie Chan; Li Bingbing; Joan Chen; Chun Sun; *D:* Li Zhang; *W:* Xingdong Wang; *C:* Wei Huang; *M:* Wei Ding.

1915 **1982** Aussie mates Billy and Walter decide to leave their country homes and enlist in the army, dreaming of heroics in WWI, only to be shocked by the realities of war. Based on the novel by Roger MacDonald. **352m/C; DVD.** *AU* Scott Burgess; Bill Hunter; Sigrid Thornton; Bill Kerr; Scott McGregor; Lorraine Bayly; Jackie Woodburne; *D:* Di Drew; Chris Thomson; *W:* Peter Yeldham; *C:* Peter Hendry; *M:* Bruce Smeaton. **TV**

1918 ½ **1985** An adaptation of the Horton Foote play about the effects of WWI and an influenza epidemic on a small Texas town. Slow-moving but satisfying. Score by Willie Nelson. Originally produced for PBS's "American Playhouse." Prequelled by "On Valentine's Day." **89m/C; VHS, DVD.** Mathew Broderick; Hallie Foote; William Converse-Roberts; Rochelle Oliver; Michael Higgins; Horton Foote, Jr.; William (Bill) McGhee; Jeannie McCarthy; Charles Solomon, Jr.; *D:* Ken Harrison; *W:* Horton Foote; *M:* Willie Nelson.

1931: Once Upon a Time in New York **1972** Prohibition-era gangsters war, beat each other up, make headlines, and drink bathtub gin. **90m/C; VHS, DVD.** *IT* Richard Conte; Adolfo Celi; Lionel Stander; Irene Papas; Tony Anthony; *D:* Luigi Vanzi; *W:* Tony Anthony; *C:* Riccardo (Pallton) Pallottini.

1941 ½ **1979 (PG)** Proved to be the most expensive comedy of all time with a budget exceeding $35 million when originally produced, the film was considered a flop when put up against Spielberg's other films. The depiction of Los Angeles in the chaotic days after the bombing of Pearl Harbor combines elements of fantasy and black humor—sometimes effectively. **120m/C; DVD, Blu-Ray.** John Belushi; Dan Aykroyd; Ned Beatty; Slim Pickens; Murray Hamilton; Christopher Lee; Tim Matheson; Toshiro Mifune; Warren Oates; Robert Stack; Nancy Allen; Elisha Cook, Jr.; Lorraine Gary; Treat Williams; Mickey Rourke; John Candy; Wendie Jo Sperber; Walter Olkewicz; *D:* Steven Spielberg; *W:* Bob Gale; Robert Zemeckis; John Milius; *C:* William A. Fraker; *M:* John Williams.

1969 ½ **1989 (R)** Three teenage friends during the 1960s become radicalized by the return of one of their friends from Vietnam in a coffin. Critically lambasted directorial debut for "On Golden Pond" author Ernest Thompson. **96m/C; VHS, DVD, Blu-Ray.** Kiefer Sutherland; Robert Downey, Jr.; Winona Ryder; Bruce Dern; Joanna Cassidy; Mariette Hartley; Christopher Wynne; *D:* Ernest Thompson; *W:* Ernest Thompson; *C:* Jules Brenner; *M:* Michael Small.

1982 ½ **2016 (R)** A Philadelphia-set period drama about family and the power of a father's love. Hard-working Tim Brown (Harper) is devoted to his wife Shenae (Leal) and daughter Maya (Zee). This happy household is undermined when Shenae's former boyfriend/dealer Alonzo (Brady) is released from prison, convinces her to join him in his illegal drug enterprises, and leave her family. Despite this blow, the ever-hopeful Tim does all he can to reunite his family. **90m/C; DVD, Streaming, Download.** Hill Harper; Sharon Leal; Troi Zee; Wayne Brady; Omar Benson Miller; *D:* Tommy Oliver; *W:* Tommy Oliver; *C:* Daniel Vecchione; *M:* John Jennings Boyd. **VIDEO**

1984 🦴🦴🦴 **1956** Winston Smith and Julia struggle to find happiness through forbidden love in a dystopian totalitarian future ruled by omnipresent dictator Big Brother. Excellently dreary adaptation of the George Orwell novel was made only seven years after the novel's debut, and at the height of the noir age and Cold War, making it that much scarier to contemporary audiences. Seen today, it still captures the dread and paranoia of the novel. **90m/B; VHS, DVD.** *GB* Edmond O'Brien; Jan Sterling; Michael Redgrave; David Kossoff; Mervyn Johns; Donald Pleasence; Carol Wolveridge; Ernest Clark; Ronan O'Casey; Kenneth Griffith; ***D:*** Michael Anderson, Sr.; ***W:*** William Templeton; Ralph Gilbert Bettinson; ***C:*** N. Peter Rathvon.

1984 🦴🦴🦴 1/2 **1984 (R)** A very fine adaptation of George Orwell's infamous novel, this version differs from the overly simplistic and cautionary 1954 film because of fine casting and production design. The illegal love affair of a government official becomes his attempt to defy the crushing inhumanity and lack of simple pleasures of an omniscient government. Filmed in London, it skillfully visualizes our time's most central prophetic nightmare. **117m/C; VHS, DVD, Blu-Ray.** *GB* John Hurt; Richard Burton; Suzanna Hamilton; Cyril Cusack; Gregor Fisher; Andrew Wilde; Rupert Baderman; ***D:*** Michael Radford; ***C:*** Roger Deakins.

1990: The Bronx Warriors WOOF! *1990 I Guerrieri del Bronx; Bronx Warriors* **1983 (R)** Good street gang members combat evil corporate powers in a semi-futuristic South Bronx. Lame copy of "Escape from New York." **86m/C; VHS, DVD, Blu-Ray.** *IT* Vic Morrow; Christopher Connelly; Fred Williamson; ***D:*** Enzo G. Castellari.

1991: The Year Punk Broke 🦴🦴 1/2 **1992** Documents a grunge rock tour of European festivals in 1991 when the alternative bands were largely unknown to all but hardcore fans. Follows Sonic Youth, Nirvana, Dinosaur Jr., Babes in Toyland, Gumball, and grandaddy punk idols, The Ramones, behind-the-scenes and through their performances. **95m/C; VHS, DVD.** ***D:*** David Markey.

1999 🦴🦴 **1998 (R)** On New Year's Eve, Rufus King (Futterman) is partying like it's 1999 (which it is), deciding it's the perfect opportunity to make some life-changing decisions. Like dumping his sweet girlfriend for the office sexpot (Peet). **93m/C; VHS, DVD.** Dan Futterman; Jennifer Garner; Matt McGrath; Amanda Peet; Steven Wright; Sandrine Holt; Buck Henry; Margaret Devine; Daniel Lapaine; David Gelb; Nick Davis; ***D:*** Nick Davis; ***W:*** Nick Davis; ***C:*** Howard Krupa; ***M:*** Sue Jacobs; Lynne Geller.

The 19th Wife 🦴 1/2 **2010** Dull Lifetime drama about a polygamous sect (both in the present-day and the 19th-century) and a murder. BeckyLynn is in prison, accused of murdering her husband. Queenie doesn't believe it and calls in BeckyLynn's excommunicated son Jordan to find the truth. The parallel story has Ann Eliza finding it difficult to adjust to being the latest of Brigham Young's many wives. Based on David Ebershoff's novel. **86m/C; DVD.** Chyler Leigh; Matt Czuchry; Patricia Wettig; Lara Jean Chorostecki; Patrick Garrow; John Bourgeois; Karl Pruner; Jeff Hephner; Alexia Fast; ***D:*** Rod Holcomb; ***W:*** Richard Friedenberg; ***C:*** Peter Benison; ***M:*** Steve Porcaro. **CABLE**

90 Minutes in Heaven 🦴 **2015 (PG-13)** The latest pandering attempt at faith-based cinema should be an insult to the very audience it so blatantly targets. "Based on a true story," of course, this drama tells the saga of a man in a car crash who reportedly died for an hour and a half, visiting heaven in his time away. The film takes as fact that he was in heaven, more chronicling the man's frustration at being returned to Earth and dealing with pain and recovery. Why would God do that to him? Why should you care? Acting, production, writing—everything here is cheesy. **122m/C; DVD, Blu-Ray, Streaming.** Kate (Catherine) Bosworth; Hayden Christensen; Dwight Yoakam; Hudson Meek; Bobby Batson; ***D:*** Michael Polish; ***W:*** Michael Polish; ***C:*** M. David Mullen; ***M:*** Michael W. Smith.

99 Pieces 🦴 **2007** Low budget, incoherent torture experience in which a man wakes up to find his wife missing while a serial killer orders him to trap himself in his own house to save his spouse. **94m/C; DVD, Streaming.** Anthony C. Falcon; Marcus D. Shelby; April Potter; Lauren DeLong; Leslie Goodman; ***D:*** Anthony C. Falcon; ***W:*** Anthony C. Falcon; ***C:*** Anthony C. Falcon; ***M:*** Anthony C. Falcon. **VIDEO**

96 Minutes 🦴🦴 **2011 (R)** In this dramatic thriller inspired by true events and told in real time, four lives are changed forever after a carjacking. The film follows the four kids—Carley (Snow), Dre (Ross), Lena (Serratos), and Kevin (Trautmann)—from the beginning of the day. While exploring their backgrounds, the film shows the decisions that brought them into the car that was carjacked that night and the consequences that impact their survival. **96m/C; DVD, Blu-Ray.** Brittany Snow; Christian Serratos; Evan Ross; J. Michael Trautmann; David Oyelowo; ***D:*** Aimee Lagos; ***W:*** Aimee Lagos; ***C:*** Michael Fimognari; ***M:*** Kurt Farquhar.

92 in the Shade 🦴🦴🦴 **1976 (R)** Based upon McGuane's novel, the film deals with a bored, wealthy rogue who becomes a fishing guide in the Florida Keys, and battles against the competition of two crusty, half-mad codgers. Sloppy, irreverent comedy as only a first-time writer-turned-director can fashion. **91m/C; VHS, Streaming.** Peter Fonda; Warren Oates; Margot Kidder; Burgess Meredith; Harry Dean Stanton; ***D:*** Thomas McGuane; ***W:*** Thomas McGuane.

99 & 44/100 Dead 🦴 *Call Harry Crown* **1974 (PG)** Frankenheimer falters with this silly gangster flick. Harris is hired to kill Dillman, by local godfather O'Brien. Originally written as a satirical look at gangster movies, but it doesn't stick to satire, and as a result is disappointing. **98m/C; VHS, DVD.** Richard Harris; Chuck Connors; Edmond O'Brien; Bradford Dillman; Ann Turkel; ***D:*** John Frankenheimer; ***W:*** Robert Dillon; ***M:*** Henry Mancini.

99 Homes 🦴🦴🦴 **2014 (R)** Dennis Nash (Andrew Garfield) has been evicted from his home, forced to move to a hotel with his mother (Dern) and son (Lomax). Through happenstance, the best way for Dennis to make the money to buy back his home comes in working for Rick Carver (Shannon), the real estate shark who guided the Nash eviction in the first place. Will Dennis get his home back or fall victim to the housing bust? Writer/director Bahrani expands his scope and his budget, producing his slickest and most crowd-pleasing effort to date without losing any of his precise cultural commentary. The cast is uniformly fantastic here. **112m/C; DVD, Blu-Ray.** Andrew Garfield; Michael Shannon; Laura Dern; Noah Lomax; Tim Guinee; Cullen Moss; ***D:*** Ramin Bahrani; ***W:*** Ramin Bahrani; Amir Naderi; Bahareh Azimi; ***C:*** Bobby Bukowski; ***M:*** Antony Partos; Matteo Zingales.

99 River Street 🦴🦴 **1953** Pulp noir revenge. Failed boxer Ernie Driscoll (Payne) is now driving a cab to the ridicule of his bitter wife Pauline (Castle). He's enraged when she takes up with diamond thief Victor Rawlins (Dexter) but Ernie is the prime suspect when a dead Pauline is found in the back of his cab. He has to track down Victor and prove his innocence. There's a secondary plotline with Keyes that just gets in the way. **83m/B; DVD, Blu-Ray.** John Payne; Peggy Castle; Brad Dexter; Evelyn Keyes; Frank Faylen; Jay Adler; Jack Lambert; ***D:*** Phil Karlson; ***W:*** Robert Smith; ***C:*** Franz Planer; ***M:*** Emil Newman; Arthur Lange.

99 Women 🦴 1/2 *Isle of Lost Women* **1969 (R)** Sympathetic prison warden attempts to investigate conditions at a women's prison camp. Thin and exploitative view of lesbianism behind bars that sensationalizes the subject. **90m/C; VHS, DVD, Blu-Ray.** *GB SP GE IT* Maria Schell; Herbert Lom; Mercedes McCambridge; Luciana Paluzzi; ***D:*** Jess (Jesus) Franco.

Ninja Academy 🦴 1/2 **1990 (R)** Seven wimps, losers, and spoiled brats come to the Ninja Academy to learn the art. Will they make it? **93m/C; VHS, DVD.** Will Egan; Kelly Randall; Gerald Okomura; Michael David; Robert Factor; Jeff Robinson; ***D:*** Nico Mastorakis.

Ninja Assassin 🦴🦴 **2009 (R)** The vicious Ozunu Clan adopts the orphaned Raizo (Rain) and raises him to be the most deadly, wicked ninja of all time. But after the clan executes his sweetheart, he flees seeking revenge, eventually joining up with Interpol agent Mika Coretti (Harris). Connecting a money-for-political-murders scheme to Far East assassins, Mika defies orders to discontinue her investigation making her a target to be saved by Raizo. Its thin plot is nothing more than an excuse to repeatedly show off sweet gore effects and carefully choreographed ninja fight scenes. Made specifically for its target audience, nothing more, nothing less. **99m/C; DVD, Blu-Ray, On Demand.** Rain; Naomie Harris; Rick Yune; Ben Miles; Sho Kosugi; ***D:*** James McTeigue; ***W:*** Matthew Sand; J. Michael Straczynski; ***C:*** Karl Walter Lindenlaub; ***M:*** Ilan Eshkeri.

Ninja Connection 🦴 **1990** Ninja terrorism is employed as a scare tactic to deter a group who wants to break up an international drug ring. **90m/C; VHS, DVD.** Patricia Greenford; Jane Kingsly; Joe Nelson; Louis Roth; Henry Steele; Stuart Steen; ***D:*** York Lam.

Ninja in the U.S.A. 🦴 1/2 **1988** Evil drug kingpin Tyger McFerson (Albergo) is acquitted of murder charges because all witnesses against him have been killed by his ninja army. Cops Rodney Kuen and Jerry Wong (Lou) give McFerson the benefit of the doubt because he saved their lives in Viet Nam. But when Jerry's reporter wife is kidnapped by Tyger's ninjas to suppress evidence against him, Jerry suits up with all his ninja gear and storms McFerson's compound. Despite the video release title, there's no reason to believe any of this takes place anywhere in the United States. **93m/C; VHS, DVD.** *TW* Alexander Lou; George Nicholas Albergo; Eugene Thomas; Alex Yip; ***D:*** Dennis Wu; ***W:*** Ed Jones; ***C:*** Owen Casey; ***M:*** Sherman Chow.

Ninja the Battalion 🦴 **1990** Agents from America, the Soviet Union, and China try to recover germ warfare secrets stolen by the Japanese secret service. **90m/C; VHS, DVD.** Roger Crawford; Sam Huxley; Alexander Lou; Dickson Warn; ***D:*** Victor Sears.

Ninja's Creed 🦴 *Royal Kill* **2009 (PG-13)** A female assassin is sent to the United States to murder the last living heir to the Himalayan throne. The Himalayan government sends a soldier to protect her. One soldier. Farfetched, to say the least. Mostly notable as Pat Morita's last film. **90m/C; DVD.** Pat Morita; Eric Roberts; Lalaine; Alexander Wraith; Gail Kim; Nicole Brown; ***D:*** Babar Ahmed; ***W:*** Babar Ahmed; ***C:*** Jonathan Belinski; ***M:*** Kenneth Lampl.

Ninotchka 🦴🦴🦴 1/2 **1939** Delightful romantic comedy. Garbo is a cold Russian agent sent to Paris to check up on her comrades, who are being seduced by capitalism. She inadvertently falls in love with a playboy, who melts her communist heart. Garbo talks and laughs. Satirical, energetic, and witty. Later a Broadway musical called "Silk Stockings." **110m/B; VHS, DVD.** Greta Garbo; Melvyn Douglas; Ina Claire; Sig Rumann; Felix Bressart; Bela Lugosi; ***D:*** Ernst Lubitsch; ***W:*** Billy Wilder; ***C:*** William H. Daniels. Natl. Film Reg. '90.

The Ninth Configuration 🦴🦴🦴 *Twinkle, Twinkle, Killer Kane* **1979 (R)** Based on Blatty's novel "Twinkle, Twinkle, Killer Kane" (also the film's alternate title), this is a weird and surreal tale of a mock rebellion of high-ranking military men held in a secret base hospital for the mentally ill. Keach is good as the commander who is just as insane as the patients. Available in many different lengths, this is generally considered to be the best. **115m/C; VHS, DVD, Blu-Ray.** Stacy Keach; Scott Wilson; Jason Miller; Ed Flanders; Neville Brand; Alejandro Rey; Robert Loggia; George DiCenzo; ***D:*** William Peter Blatty; ***W:*** William Peter Blatty. Golden Globes '81: Screenplay.

The Ninth Day 🦴🦴🦴 *Der Neunte Tag* **2004** Examines Nazism from the side of its victims through the plight of Rev. Henri Kremer, a Roman Catholic priest imprisoned at Dachau. A cruel plot is devised to use Kremer to coerce his bishop into declaring that Nazism is compatible with church doctrine, upon which they will 'grant' him a nine-day furlough. Failure will result in the execution of 18 priests in his Dachau block and will also bring harm to his family. Performances are stellar as Scholondorff lays out the theological and ethical debates without over-dramatizing them. German with subtitles. **90m/C; DVD.** *GE* Ulrich Matthes; August Diehl; Germain Wagner; Bibiana Beglau; Jean-Paul Raths; Ivan Jirik; Karel Hromadka; Miroslav Sichman; Adolf Filip; Vladimir Fiser; Petr Varga; Petr Janis; Zdenek Pechacek; Karel Dobry; Goetz Burger; Hilmar Thate; ***D:*** Volker Schlondorff; ***W:*** Eberhard Goerner; Andreas Pflueger; ***C:*** Tomas Erhart; ***M:*** Alfred Schnittke.

The Ninth Gate 🦴🦴 **1999 (R)** Less-than-scrupulous rare-book dealer Dean Corso (Depp) is hired by wealthy publishing mogul Balkan (Langella) to find and authenticate three copies of a 17th-century book that supposedly holds the secrets to conjuring up the devil. Naturally, he encounters many spooky and deadly people along the way. Depp is perfectly cast as the sleazy bookworm and every scene is appropriately atmospheric, but Polanski's glacial pace and lack of any dramatic tension keeps this flick from getting its due. **127m/C; VHS, DVD, Blu-Ray.** *FR SP* Johnny Depp; Frank Langella; Lena Olin; Emmanuelle Seigner; Barbara Jefford; Jack Taylor; James Russo; Jose Lopez Rodero; ***D:*** Roman Polanski; ***W:*** Roman Polanski; John Brownjohn; Enrique Urbizu; ***C:*** Darius Khondji; ***M:*** Wojciech Kilar.

The 9th Life of Louis Drax 🦴 1/2 **2016 (R)** When a nine-year-old boy named Louis Drax (Longworth) falls off a cliff after a lifetime of odd incidents, people look to blame his father (Paul) but Dr. Allan Pascal (Dornan) is convinced there's something more unusual going on in this boy's life. Directed by horror auteur Alexandre Aja, this odd thriller has supernatural elements and a twist worthy of M. Night Shyamalan but they don't quite mesh with the family drama. Part of the problem is that Dornan's flat acting style doesn't work as the protagonist. **108m/C; DVD, Blu-Ray.** Jamie Dornan; Sarah Gadon; Aaron Paul; Aiden Longworth; Oliver Platt; Molly Parker; Barbara Hershey; ***D:*** Alexandre Aja; ***W:*** Max Minghella; ***C:*** Maxime Alexandre; ***M:*** Patrick Watson.

Nirvana 🦴🦴 **1997 (R)** Jimi Dini (Lambert) is a computer game designer whose latest creation, Nirvana, has a lead character called Solo (Abatantuono). But when Jimi plays the game, he finds out that a computer virus has imparted self-awareness to Solo who pleads to be deleted from his virtual world. Jimi's agreeable but this doesn't turn out to be so easy. **108m/C; VHS, DVD.** *FR IT* Christopher Lambert; Diego Abatantuono; Emmanuelle Seigner; Sergio Rubini; ***D:*** Gabriele Salvatores; ***W:*** Gabriele Salvatores.

Nitti: The Enforcer 🦴🦴 **1988 (PG-13)** Made-for-TV saga about Al Capone's brutal enforcer and right-hand man, Frank Nitti. Diversified cast (Moriarty in particular) do their best to keep things moving along, and the atmosphere is consistently and appropriately violent. Made to capitalize on the success of 1987's "The Untouchables." **94m/C; VHS, DVD.** Anthony LaPaglia; Vincent Guastaferro; Trini Alvarado; Michael Moriarty; Michael Russo; Louis Guss; Bruno Kirby; ***D:*** Michael Switzer.

The Nitwits 🦴🦴 **1935** Grable has an early film role in this extended Wheeler & Woolsey slapstick comedy. She plays Mary Roberts, secretary to the president of a music publishing company and the girlfriend of would-be songwriter Johnny, who runs a cigar stand along with partner Newton. Johnny thinks Mary shot and killed her boss after he made a pass, so he takes the blame although it was really the work of the notorious "Black Widow." **81m/B; DVD.** Bert Wheeler; Robert Woolsey; Betty Grable; Fred Keating; Evelyn Brent; Hale Hamilton; ***D:*** George Stevens; ***W:*** Al Boasberg; Fred Guiol; ***C:*** Edward Cronjager; ***M:*** Roy Webb.

Nixon 🦴🦴🦴 **1995 (R)** Stone again "interprets" historical events of the '60s and '70s with a sprawling, bold bio of Richard Nixon. Covering all the highlights of Nixon's public life, and speculating on his private one, Hopkins convincingly portrays "Tricky Dick" as an embattled, lonely political genius. Gigantic all-star cast is lead by Oscar-caliber performance of Allen as Pat Nixon. As usual, Stone has taken some creative license, which lead to the Nixon daughters publicly trashing the film. **192m/C; DVD.** Anthony Hopkins; Joan Allen; Ed Harris; Bob Hoskins; David Paymer;

Paul Sorvino; J.T. Walsh; James Woods; Madeline Kahn; Brian Bedford; Mary Steenburgen; Powers Boothe; E.G. Marshall; David Hyde Pierce; Kevin Dunn; Annabeth Gish; Tony Goldwyn; Larry Hagman; Edward Herrmann; Saul Rubinek; Tony LoBianco; Kamar De Los Reyes; Michelle Krusiec; *D:* Oliver Stone; *W:* Oliver Stone; Christopher Wilkinson; Stephen J. Rivele; *C:* Robert Richardson; *M:* John Williams. L.A. Film Critics '95: Support. Actress (Allen); Natl. Soc. Film Critics '95: Support. Actress (Allen).

No ½ **2012 (R)** The last in Chilean director Larrain's loose trilogy on the Pinochet dictatorship (1973-90), following 2008's "Tony Manero" and 2010's "Post Mortem." In 1988, the government decides to hold a plebiscite and advertising whiz Rene Saavedra (Bernal), the son of an exiled dissident, is hired by the opposition to craft a campaign to encourage people to vote 'no' against the military dictatorship. The leftists believe the referendum will be rigged but the coalition hopes Rene's ridiculously cheery message can swing the election. A stark look at a pivotal time in history. Spanish with subtitles. **118m/C; DVD, Blu-Ray.** *CL* Gael Garcia Bernal; Luis Gnecco; Alfredo Castro; Antonia Zegers; *D:* Pablo Larrain; *W:* Pedro Peirano; *C:* Sergio Armstrong; *M:* Carlos Cabezas.

No Alibi ½ **2000 (R)** Upstanding businessman Bob Valenz (Cain) becomes involved with beautiful Camille (Doig), who also has something kinky going on with Bob's smalltime crook brother, Phil (Stebbings). Phil gets dead and it leads back not only to Camille but to the third man in her life, criminal slickster Vic (Roberts). But by then Bob and Camille are married and she's pregnant. But Bob won't stop investigating his brother's death and he's not going to like what he finds out. **94m/C; VHS, DVD.** *CA* Dean Cain; Eric Roberts; Lexa Doig; Peter Stebbings; Richard Chevolleau; Frank Schorpion; Melissa Di Marco; *D:* Bruce Pittman; *W:* Ivan Kane; John Schafer; *C:* Michael Storey; *M:* Marty Simon. **VIDEO**

No Big Deal ½ **1983 (PG-13)** Dillon is a streetwise teenager who makes friends at his new school. Blah promise; bad acting makes this no big deal. **86m/C; VHS, DVD.** Kevin Dillon; Sylvia Miles; Tammy Grimes; Jane Krakowski; Christopher Gartin; Mary Joan Negro; *D:* Robert Charlton.

No Blade of Grass **1970** An environmental catastrophe has left millions dead and resources polluted or used up. The Custance family, led by John and Ann, leave London for a safer haven in Scotland, but they have to turn to violence to survive. **97m/C; DVD.** *GB* Nigel Davenport; Jean Wallace; Anthony May; John Hamill; Lynne Frederick; Patrick Holt; *D:* Cornel Wilde; *W:* Cornel Wilde; Sean Forestal; *C:* H.A.R. Thomson; *M:* Burnell Whibley.

No Blood No Tears *Pido nunmuldo eobshi* **2002** Gyeong-seon (Lee Hye-eun) is a tough butt-kicking female cab driver who worries about how she will pay her deadbeat ex husband's debts to the local mob. Her cab is hit by Su-Jin (Jeon Doyeon), who is the unwilling bed partner of a local gangster named Bulldog. Together they concoct a scheme to rob him. It's sort of a Korean version of "Lock, Stock, and Two Smoking Barrels," but with more martial arts chicks. **120m/C; DVD.** *NK* Do-yeon Jeon; Hye-yeong Lee; Jae-yeong Jong; Goo Shin; Doohong Jung; *D:* Seung-wan Ryoo; *W:* Seung-wan Ryoo; Jin-wan Jeong; *C:* Yeong-hwon Choi; *M:* Jawe-kwon Han.

No Boundaries **2009 (R)** Emotional, low-budget debut drama from Mendoza. Illegal immigrant Isabel moves to Philadelphia to stay with her cousin Martin so she can earn more money to support her ailing mother. She falls in love with Christopher Fox, but doesn't know he's an Immigration and Customs Enforcement agent. Martin gets arrested and deported and Isabel starts worrying about Christopher and her own choices. **109m/C; DVD.** Dani Garza; Mark McGraw; Victor Velez; Tatiana St.Phard; Tyrone Holt; John D'Alonzo; *D:* Violet Mendoz; *W:* Violet Mendoz; *C:* Jake Willing; *M:* Pete Tramo. **VIDEO**

No Brother of Mine ½ **2007** In this Lifetime family drama Nina's (Martin) had to hide from her psycho brother Drew (MacDonald) who's always been extremely over-protective of her. She makes a visit to their dying grandmother and Drew tracks Nina back to Chicago and is so ingratiating that her husband Stuart (Neal) and their friends are happy to get to know him. But Drew learns that Stuart's cheating on Nina and decides his sister needs his help again. **96m/C; DVD.** Kellie Martin; Dylan Neal; Marianne Farley; Adam MacDonald; Zara Taylor; Conrad Pla; Franc Viens; *D:* Philippe Gagnon; *W:* Valerie West; *C:* Denis Villenueve; *M:* Carl Bastien; Martin Roy. **CABLE**

No Code of Conduct **1998 (R)** Veteran cop Bill Peterson (Sheen) is working with the DEA on a sting operation to recover millions in heroin but when things go wrong, Bill suspects corruption within his own department. So he calls on hot-headed cop son Jake (Charlie Sheen) for help. **90m/C; VHS, DVD, Blu-Ray.** Mark Dacascos; Joe Estevez; Charlie Sheen; Martin Sheen; Courtney Gains; Paul Gleason; Joe Lando; Meredith Salenger; Bret Michaels; *D:* Bret Michaels; *W:* Charlie Sheen; Bret Michaels; Bill Gucwa; Ed Masterson; *C:* Adam Kane; *M:* Bret Michaels. **VIDEO**

No Contest **1994 (R)** International terrorists, lead by Oz (Clay), hold the TV host (Tweed) and contestants of the Ms. Galaxy beauty pageant hostage with a $10 million ransom demand. **98m/C; VHS, DVD.** Andrew Silverstein; Shannon Tweed; Robert Davi; Roddy Piper; Nicholas (Nick) Campbell; *D:* Paul Lynch; *W:* Robert Cooper.

No Country for Old Men **2007 (R)** When cowboy Llewelyn Moss (Brolin) happens upon a drug deal gone bad in the West Texas wilderness and grabs a case holding more than $2 million, it's up to world-weary sheriff Ed Tom Bell (Jones) to track him down. However, both men find themselves tangled up with cold-blooded killer Anton Chigurh (Bardem), who's determined to track down the missing money and willing to kill anyone in his way. Expertly adapted from the Cormac McCarthy novel, writers/directors/producers Joel and Ethan Coen have crafted a masterpiece: a painstakingly intense, dark thriller that doubles as a meditation on the role of violence in American society. **122m/C; Blu-Ray.** Tommy Lee Jones; Javier Bardem; Josh Brolin; Woody Harrelson; Kelly Macdonald; Tess Harper; Garret Dillahunt; Barry Corbin; *D:* Joel Coen; Ethan Coen; *W:* Joel Coen; Ethan Coen; *C:* Roger Deakins; *M:* Carter Burwell. Oscars '07: Adapt. Screenplay, Director (Coen), Director (Coen), Film, Support. Actor (Bardem); British Acad. '07: Cinematog., Director (Coen), Director (Coen), Support. Actor (Bardem); Directors Guild '07: Director (Coen), Director (Coen); Golden Globes '08: Screenplay, Support. Actor (Bardem); Screen Actors Guild '07: Cast, Support. Actor (Bardem); Writers Guild '07: Adapt. Screenplay.

No Dead Heroes **1987** Green Beret Vietnam war hero succumbs to Soviet scheming when they plant a computer chip in his brain. Unoriginal and unworthy. **86m/C; VHS, Streaming.** Max (Michael) Thayer; John Dresden; Toni Nero; *D:* J.C. Miller.

No Deposit, No Return *Double Trouble* **1976 (G)** Tedious, silly, pointless Disney action comedy. Rich brats persuade bumbling crooks to kidnap them, offer them for ransom to millionaire grandfather. **115m/C; VHS, DVD.** David Niven; Don Knotts; Darren McGavin; Barbara Feldon; Charles Martin Smith; *D:* Norman Tokar; *W:* Arthur Alsberg; *M:* Buddy (Norman Dale) Baker.

No Dessert Dad, 'Til You Mow the Lawn ½ **1994 (PG)** Suburban parents Ken and Carol Cochran (Robert Hays and Joanna Kerns) are harassed at home by their annoying offspring, Justin, Monica, and Tyler. When they try hypnosis tapes to quit smoking, the kids discover by doctoring the tapes, they can plant suggestions resulting in parental perks. **80m/C; VHS, DVD.** Robert Hays; Joanna Kerns; Joshua Schaefer; Allison Meek; Jimmy Marsden; Richard Moll; Larry Linville; *D:* Howard McCain.

No Down Payment **1957** Highlights the problems of four couples in a cookie-cutter Southern California suburb amidst a consumer culture, easy credit, and increasing debt. Though everyone seems to know their neighbors' business there are secrets behind the locked doors. **102m/B; DVD.** Jeffrey Hunter; Patricia Owens; Pat Hingle; Barbara Rush; Cameron Mitchell; Joanne Woodward; Tony Randall; Sheree North; *D:* Martin Ritt; *W:* Ben Maddow; *C:* Joseph LaShelle; *M:* Leigh Harline.

No End *Bez Konca* **1984** The ghost of a dead lawyer watches as his wife and young son struggle to survive without him, including the widow getting involved in her husband's last case about a worker arrested for organizing a strike. Well-acted but overly solemn and slow; set during Poland's martial law in 1982. In Polish with English subtitles. **108m/C; VHS, DVD.** *PL* Grazyna Szapolowska; Jerzy Radziwilowicz; Maria Pakulnis; Aleksander Bardini; Artur Barcis; Michal Bajor; *D:* Krzysztof Kieslowski; *W:* Krzysztof Piesiewicz; Krzysztof Kieslowski.

No End in Sight ½ **2007** Brookings Institute scholar and political science PhD Charles Ferguson's documentary of the war in Iraq is a powerful, compelling analysis and critique of U.S. policy. Rather than criticize the war as a whole, Ferguson focuses in on the period immediately following the overthrow of Saddam and the Bush Administration's lack of a plan to rebuild Iraq. Offers compelling interviews with individuals whos efforts were hindered by disorganization and ideological agendas. By focusing on experts involved in the war rather than outside critics, Ferguson skips partisanship to create a sharp, hard to ignore film. **102m/C; DVD.** *D:* Charles Ferguson; *W:* Charles Ferguson; *C:* Antonio Rossi; *M:* Peter Nashel.

No Escape ½ *City on the Hunt* **1953** Lackluster crime thriller with an ending you can see a mile away. San Francisco artist Peter Hayden is murdered and suspicion falls on good-time gal Pat Peterson. Her sleazy detective boyfriend Simon Shayne wants to pin the rap on loser piano player John Tracy but Pat tells John and tries to get him out of town. With every cop looking for Tracy, Pat and John hide out in Hayden's apartment with Simon not about to give up on his plan. **76m/B; DVD.** Marjorie Steele; Lew Ayres; Sonny Tufts; Lewis Martin; James J. Griffith; *D:* Charles Bennett; *W:* Charles Bennett; *C:* Benjamin (Ben H.) Kline; *M:* Bert Shefter.

No Escape ½ **1994 (R)** In 2022, Captain Robbins (Liotta) has been banished to a prison colony island inhabited by the most dangerous criminals. With no walls and no guards, the prisoners are left to kill each other. Then Robbins discovers a relatively peaceful community of prisoners who help each other. But this group is soon bedeviled by the evil nasties on the other side of the island. Attempts at escape define the plot, so the film is filled with superhuman feats of sheer courage, determination, and guts. Adapted from the book "The Penal Colony" by Richard Herley. **118m/C; DVD.** Ray Liotta; Lance Henriksen; Stuart Wilson; Kevin Dillon; Kevin J. O'Connor; Michael Lerner; Ernie Hudson; Ian McNeice; Jack Shepherd; *D:* Martin Campbell; *W:* Joel Gross; *C:* Phil Meheux; *M:* Graeme Revell.

No Escape **2015 (R)** Jack (Wilson) and his family move to an unnamed Southeast Asian country when he gets a job heading a water manufacturing plant. At first, Jack and his brood simply struggle with the inferior civilization (running water, electricity problems, etc.) but things get really intense when an uprising engulfs Jack on a trip to the market. Can he even get back to the hotel and get his family to safety? A mysterious British tourist (Brosnan) is there to help. Xenophobic to an extreme, this is an ugly, boring movie that paints an entire part of the world in broad strokes and redefines Ugly American. **101m/C; DVD, Blu-Ray.** Lake Bell; Pierce Brosnan; Owen Wilson; Sterling Jerins; Spencer Garrett; *D:* John Erick Dowdle; *W:* John Erick Dowdle; Drew Dowdle; *C:* Leo Hinstin; *M:* Marco Beltrami; Buck Sanders.

No Escape, No Return ½ **1993 (R)** An FBI agent (Nouri) and a police captain (Saxon) force three renegade cops (Nguyen, Caulfield, and Loveday) to infiltrate a drug syndicate. But things go from bad to worse when a war breaks out between rival drug gangs, leaving a lot of bodies, and a large chunk of money gone missing. Now the trio is sought by both the cops and the crooks. **93m/C; VHS, DVD, On Demand.** Maxwell Caulfield; Dustin Nguyen; Denise Loveday; John Saxon; Michael Nouri; Kevin Benton; *D:* Charles Kanganis; *W:* Charles Kanganis; *M:* Jim Halfpenny.

No God, No Master ½ **2012 (PG-13)** Clunky historical drama based on a true story. A series of package bombs are delivered to prominent politicians and businessmen in the summer of 1919. Agent William Flynn (Straithairn) investigates and discovers an anarchist plot and civil unrest in an anti-immigrant America. **94m/C; DVD.** David Strathairn; Ray Wise; Sam Witwer; Alessandro Mario; James Madio; Edoardo Ballerini; *D:* Terry Green; *W:* Terry Green; *C:* Paul Sanchez; *M:* Nuno Malo.

No Good Deed ½ *The House on Turk Street* **2002 (R)** Mild thriller adapted from the Dashiell Hammett story, "The House on Turk Street." Diabetic, cello-playing cop Jack Friar (Jackson) postpones his vacation to look for a neighbor's runaway daughter. While checking around Turk Street, he comes to the aid of elderly Mrs. Quarre (Zabriskie) and winds up the hostage of a gang planning a bank robbery: mastermind Tyrone (Skarsgard), hothead Hoop (Hutchinson), inside man David (Higgins), and Tyrone's sexy and duplicitious girlfriend Erin (Jovovich), who's given the job of guarding Jack. Naturally, Jack's diabetes and his cello-playing will both come into play. **97m/C; VHS, DVD.** Samuel L. Jackson; Milla Jovovich; Stellan Skarsgard; Doug Hutchison; Grace Zabriskie; Joss Ackland; Jonathan Higgins; *D:* Bob Rafelson; *W:* Christopher Canaan; Steve Barancik; *C:* Juan Ruiz-Anchia; *M:* Jeff Beal.

No Good Deed **2014 (PG-13)** Lonely, single mother Terri (Henson), who has dealt with domestic abuse in her life before, makes a tragic mistake when she politely invites a charming man named Colin (Elba) into her home after a car accident. Colin refuses to leave, terrorizing our poor heroine until a twist ending casts everything in a new light (which doesn't really make much sense). An implausible, silly, melodramatic thriller that you catch on cable in the middle of the night and wonder how it ever got made let alone released in theaters. **84m/C; DVD, Blu-Ray.** Idris Elba; Taraji P. Henson; Leslie Bibb; Henry Simmons; Kate del Castillo; *D:* Sam Miller; *W:* Aimee Lagos; *C:* Michael Barrett; *M:* Paul Haslinger.

No Greater Glory **1934** Anti-war allegory based on Ferenc Molnar's autobiographical novel "The Paul Street Boys." Frail Nemecsek longs to belong to a military-run gang led by Boka (Butler). They literally go to war against an older group of boys who have captured their flag, with Nemecsek proving himself useful at great personal cost. **117m/B; DVD.** George Breakston; Jimmy Butler; Frankie Darro; Jackie Searl; Donald Haines; *D:* Frank Borzage; *W:* Jo Swerling; *C:* Joseph August.

No Hands on the Clock ½ **1941** Wisecracking PI Humphrey Campbell (Morris) and his bride, heiress Louise (Parker), are honeymooning in Reno when they get involved in a bank robbery and a missing persons case. The plot gets more complicated when murder and mistaken identity are added in but it's fast-paced and Morris and Parker are a delightful duo. Based on the novel by Daniel Mainwaring. **76m/B; DVD.** Chester Morris; Jean Parker; Rose Hobart; Dick Purcell; Astrid Allwyn; Rod Cameron; *D:* Frank McDonald; *W:* Maxwell Shane; *C:* Fred H. Jackman, Jr.; *M:* Paul Sawtell.

No Highway in the Sky **1951** Eccentric scientist Theodore Honey (Stewart) works for the Royal Aircraft Establishment, which has just produced a new plane, the Reindeer. But Honey tells his boss Dennis Scott (Hawkins) that the plane has a serious defect. While flying to examine a Reindeer crash site, Honey befriends Monica (Dietrich), a musical star, and stewardess Marjorie (Johns), who support him when his company accuses him of maliciously damaging the aircraft's reputation. Dietrich steals every scene with her Christian Dior wardrobe and star attitude. Based on the novel "No Highway" by Nevil Shute. **98m/B; DVD, Streaming.** *UK* James Stewart; Marlene Dietrich; Glynis Johns; Jack Hawkins; Ronald Squire; Niall MacGinnis; Elizabeth Allan; Kenneth

More; David Hutcheson; *D:* Henry Koster; *W:* R.C. Sherriff; Oscar Millard; *M:* Malcolm Arnold.

No Holds Barred 🦴 1/2 **1989 (PG-13)** Cheesy, campy remake of cheesy, campy 1952 wrestling movie. Hulk Hogan on the big screen, at last. **98m/C; VHS, DVD, Blu-Ray.** Hulk Hogan; Kurt Fuller; Joan Severance; Tommy (Tiny) Lister; *D:* Thomas J. Wright.

No Home Movie 🦴🦴 **2015** The last film created by Chantal Akerman, this documentary explores her relationship with her mother before both women died. The feature-length documentary an in-depth portrait of Natalia Ackerman, who was confined to her apartment in Brussels, Belgium. The film explores Natalia's Polish-Jewish heritage, how she survived Auschwitz, and the chronic anxiety she suffered from her whole life. The film primarily consists of conversations between mother and daughter as Chantal discusses her own creativity, thematic focuses, and film work. **115m/C; DVD, Streaming, Download.** Chantal Akerman; Natalia Akerman; *D:* Chantal Akerman; *W:* Chantal Akerman; *C:* Chantal Akerman.

No Kidding 🦴 1/2 *Beware of Children* **1960** Weak Brit com. David (Phillips) and Catherine (McEwan) Robinson inherit a large country home and, needing money for upkeep, decide to turn it into a summer camp for rich kids neglected by their parents. Naturally, most of the youngsters are little horrors or hormonal teens, the help is drunk and/or inept, and busy-body alderwoman Mrs. Spicer (Handl) wants to take the property for a community center. **83m/B; DVD.** *GB* Leslie Phillips; Geraldine McEwan; Irene Handl; Joan Hickson; Noel Purcell; Julia Lockwood; June Jago; *D:* Gerald Thomas; *W:* Norman Hudis; Robin Estridge; *C:* Alan Hume; *M:* Bruce Montgomery.

No Looking Back 🦴🦴 *Long Time, Nothing New* **1998 (R)** Smalltown waitress Claudia (Holly) is about to settle for a boring life with dull Michael (Bon Jovi) when her ne'er-do-well ex-boyfriend Charlie (Burns) comes home looking to relive the glory days. With themes that cover economic hopelessness and a yearning to escape, Burns tries for a cinematic distillation of Bruce Springsteen's music and many Springsteen songs are used to set scenes. Burns knows the working class vernacular, and uses it well, but all traces of sublety are gone, and the story plays out pretty much as expected. Holly doesn't help much, barely registering in the crucial role. **96m/C; DVD.** Lauren Holly; Edward Burns; Jon Bon Jovi; Blythe Danner; Connie Britton; *D:* Edward Burns; *W:* Edward Burns; *C:* Frank Prinzi; *M:* Joe Delia.

No Man Is an Island 🦴🦴 1/2 **1962** Wartime adventure based on the exploits (Hollywoodized) of U.S. Naval radio operator George R. Tweed (Hunter), who is stationed on Guam when the Japanese invade. He hides out in the jungle to avoid capture and is aided by the natives for nearly three years until he's able to contact some American warships. Thanks to Tweed's info, the Americans are able to recapture the island. **114m/C; VHS, DVD.** Jeffrey Hunter; Marshall Thompson; Ronald Remy; Rolf Bayer; Barbara Perez; Joseph de Cordova; *D:* John Monks, Jr.; Richard Goldstone; *W:* John Monks, Jr.; Richard Goldstone; *C:* Carl Kayser; *M:* Restie Umali.

No Man of Her Own 🦴🦴 1/2 **1932** Gable and Lombard in their only screen pairing. Gambler Babe Stewart (Gable) marries small town librarian (Lombard) on a bet and attempts to hide his secret life from her. Neither star's best film. **81m/B; VHS, DVD.** Carole Lombard; Clark Gable; Grant Mitchell; Elizabeth Patterson; Dorothy Mackaill; George Barbier; J. Farrell MacDonald; Walter Walker; Paul Ellis; *D:* Wesley Ruggles; *W:* Benjamin Glazer; Edmund Goulding; Maurine Watkins; *C:* Leo Tover; *M:* W. Franke Harling.

No Man's Land 🦴🦴 **1987 (R)** Undercover cop Sweeney tails playboy car thief Sheen but is seduced by wealth and glamour. Flashy surfaces, shiny cars, little substance. **107m/C; VHS, DVD.** Charlie Sheen; D.B. Sweeney; Lara Harris; Randy Quaid; *D:* Peter Werner; *W:* Dick Wolf; *M:* Basil Poledouris.

No Man's Land 🦴🦴 1/2 **2001 (R)** Let's talk about the futility and stupidity of war. In Bosnia in 1993, Croatian soldier Ciki (Branko Djuric) and Serbian Nino (Rene Bitorajac) wind up sharing the same trench between enemy lines, which is booby-trapped by a land mine. Laying on the mine is injured Croat Cera (Filip Sovagovic) and if he moves, they all die. Reluctantly brought into the already tense situation is ineffectual U.N. officer Col. Soft (Callow) and then journalist Jane (Cartlidge) also shows up. Bosnian with subtitles. **98m/C; VHS, DVD.** *BS FR IT BE GB* Branko Djuric; Rene Bitorajac; Filip Sovagovic; Georges Siatidis; Serge-Henri Valcke; Simon Callow; Katrin Cartlidge; *D:* Danis Tanovic; *W:* Danis Tanovic; *C:* Walther Vanden Ende; *M:* Danis Tanovic. Oscars '01: Foreign Film; Cannes '01: Screenplay; L.A. Film Critics '01: Foreign Film.

No Man's Law 1927 Hardy plays the depraved villian desperate to get the goldmine owned by an old prospector and his beautiful daughter. But the mine is protected by Rex the Wonder Horse! **?m/B; Silent; VHS, DVD.** Oliver Hardy; Barbara Kent; James Finlayson; Theodore von Eltz; *D:* Fred W. Jackman.

No Men Beyond This Point 🦴🦴 1/2 **2015** A sci-fi comedy mockumentary about procreation. In an alternate version of reality, women have been able to have children without men since 1953. It's now 2003, and women have stopped giving birth to men. The mockumentary follows the youngest man still alive at 37 years old. While working as a housekeeper for a household of women, he is unexpectedly at the center of the movement to keep the male gender from becoming extinct. **80m/C; DVD, Streaming, Download.** Ali Skovbye; Rekha Sharma; Andrea Brooks; David Lewis; Ben Cotton; *D:* Mark Sawers; *W:* Mark Sawers; *C:* Christopher Charles Kempinski; Thomas Billingsley; *M:* Don MacDonald. **VIDEO**

No Mercy 🦴🦴 **1986 (R)** A Chicago cop (Gere) plunges into the Cajun bayou in order to avenge the murder of his partner. He falls for a beautiful girl enslaved by the killer, but that doesn't stop him from using her to flush out the powerful swamp-inhabiting crime lord. Absurd story without much plot. **108m/C; VHS, DVD.** Richard Gere; Kim Basinger; Jeroen Krabbe; George Dzundza; William Atherton; Ray Sharkey; Bruce McGill; *D:* Richard Pearce; *W:* James (Jim) Carabatsos; *C:* Michel Brault; *M:* Alan Silvestri.

No Money Down 🦴🦴 *The Definite Maybe* **1997 (R)** When Eric (Lucas) needs a new place to live, his best pal Ziggy (Beuhl) takes him to the Hamptons for the weekend to look at houses and enjoy the cocktails parties and other amenities—such as fraud, adultery, and attempted murder. **90m/C; DVD.** Josh(ua) Lucas; Bob Balaban; Jeffrey Beuhl; Claudia Rocafort; *D:* Sam Sokolow; Rob Rollins Lobl; *W:* Sam Sokolow; Rob Rollins Lobl; *C:* Elia Lyssy; *M:* Tree Adams; Billy Jay Stein.

No More Ladies 🦴🦴 1/2 **1935** Glamorous fare (costumes, settings, plot) designed to take Depression-era audiences away from their worries. Cafe society denizen Marcia (Crawford) decides to marry (and reform) playboy Sheridan 'Sherry' Warren (Montgomery). Despite some good intentions, Sherry doesn't give up his philandering ways so Marcia sets out to make him jealous with would-be flame James Salston (Tone). George Cukor took over direction halfway through the pic but went uncredited. **81m/B; DVD.** Joan Crawford; Robert Montgomery; Edna May Oliver; Franchot Tone; Charlie Ruggles; Gail Patrick; Joan Fontaine; Vivienne Osborne; Arthur Treacher; Reginald Denny; *D:* Edward H. Griffith; *W:* Horace Jackson; Donald Ogden Stewart; *C:* Oliver Marsh; *M:* Edward Ward.

No More Orchids 🦴🦴 1/2 **1932** In this routine melodrama--enlivened by Lombard's performance--wealthy New Yorker Anne Holt falls for poor lawyer Tony Gage (Talbot). Her father Bill's (Connolly) bank runs into financial trouble, and she agrees to her snob grandfather's (Smith) plans for an arranged marriage to a prince (Thomas) since this is the only way the old man will bail Bill out. Bill takes drastic action to ensure his little girl only marries for love. **71m/B; DVD.** Carole Lombard; Lyle Talbot; Walter Connolly; Sir C. Aubrey Smith; Jameson Thomas; Louise Closser Hale; *D:* Walter Lang; *W:* Keene Thompson; Gertrude Purcell; *C:* Joseph August.

No Name on the Bullet 🦴🦴🦴 **1959** Aloof gunman John Gant (Murphy) is seeking revenge from someone in the town of Lordsburg, only none of the inhabitants know who the intended victim is. And slowly the town's citizens begin to panic. Great final showdown. **77m/C; VHS, DVD.** Audie Murphy; Charles Drake; Joan Evans; Edgar Stehli; Warren Stevens; R.G. Armstrong; Whit Bissell; Karl Swenson; *D:* Jack Arnold; *W:* Gene L. Coon; *C:* Harold Lipstein.

No News from God 🦴🦴 *Sin Noticias de Dios; Don't Tempt Me!* **2001 (R)** Angel Lola (Abril) is a nightclub singer in heaven who is sent by her boss Marina (Ardant) to Earth to save the soul of boxer Many (Bechir). But when Jack (Garcia Bernal), Marina's counterpart in hell, hears the news, he sents devil waitress Carmen (Cruz) to do the deed first. To Many, Lola appears to be his ex, while Carmen is a cousin. Naturally, Lola tries to get Many to be good and Carmen wants him to be bad—and Many is well on his way to the latter. Starts out offbeat but then goes conventional. Spanish, French, and English dialogue. **115m/C; DVD.** *SP FR IT MX* Victoria Abril; Penelope Cruz; Demian Bechir; Fanny Ardant; Gael Garcia Bernal; Juan Echanove; Bruno Bichir; Emilio Gutierrez-Caba; *D:* Agustin Diaz Yanes; *W:* Agustin Diaz Yanes; *C:* Paco Femenia; *M:* Bernardo Bonezzi.

Free Fall 🦴🦴 *Freier Fall* **2013** A romantic drama about the outfall when a police officer falls in love with a fellow member of law enforcement. Marc (Reimelt) seems to have it all, with a child on the way and a promising career. His life changes forever when he meets Kay (Koffler), another officer. The free-spirited Kay is gay. As the pair begin to spend time together, Marc finds his perspective on life changing and soon finds himself developing feelings for a man for the first time. Personally divided between his stable life and they exhilaration he feels with Kay, Marc soon finds himself unable to manage the disruption to his life and the lives of those around him. German with subtitles. **100m/C; DVD, Blu-Ray, Streaming, Download.** Hanno Koffler; Max Riemelt; Attila Borlan; Katharina Schuttler; Stephanie Schonfeld; *D:* Stephan Lacant; *W:* Stephan Lacant; Karsten Dahlem; *C:* Sten Mende; *M:* Durbeck & Dohmen. **VIDEO**

No, No Nanette 🦴 1/2 **1940** Lackluster filming of the Broadway production which fared better on the stage. Stock story of a young woman (Neagle) who rescues her uncle from financial ruin and finds romance in the process. **96m/B; VHS, DVD.** Anna Neagle; Richard Carlson; Victor Mature; Roland Young; Zasu Pitts; Eve Arden; Billy Gilbert; Keye Luke; *D:* Herbert Wilcox; *C:* Russell Metty.

No One Cries Forever WOOF! **1985** When a prostitute breaks away from a gangster-madam after finding love, she is tracked down and disfigured. Swedish; dubbed. **96m/C; DVD.** Elke Sommer; Howard Carpendale; Zoli Marks; *D:* Jans Rautenbach.

No One Sleeps 🦴🦴 **2001** Berlin medical researcher Stefan Hein (Wlaschiha) is attending an AIDS conference in San Francisco just as a serial killer is targeting men who are HIV positive. Stefan also wants to investigate his late father's theory that U.S. researchers used prisoners to test a virus that created HIV by trying to find an alleged list of the injected prisoners. Along the way Stefan meets detective Louise Tolliver (Levi) and discovers the two investigations may be linked. **108m/C; VHS, DVD.** Tom Wlashchiha; Irit Levi; Jim Thalman; Kalene Parker; *D:* Jochen Hick; *W:* Jochen Hick; *C:* Thomas M. (Tom) Harting; Michael Maley; *M:* James Hardway.

No Orchids for Miss Blandish 🦴🦴 **1948** Controversial (because of the story's amorality and violence) Brit noir attempt to emulate a hard-boiled American crime drama. Three hoods kill the fiance of Miss Blandish (Travers) during a robbery gone wrong and then kidnap the heiress. Soon they're dead and the sheltered beauty is in the hands of ruthless gangster Slim Grisson (LaRue). But Slim and the heiress fall hard for each other, much to his gang's disgust since all they want is the ransom money and no witnesses. Based on the James Hadley Chase novel. **104m/B; DVD, Blu-Ray.** *UK* Jack LaRue; Linden Travers; Hugh McDermott; Lilli Molnar; Walter Crisham; MacDonald Parke; *D:* St. John Legh Clowes; *W:* St. John Legh Clowes; *C:* Gerald Gibbs; *M:* George Melachrino.

No Pay, Nudity 🦴🦴 1/2 **2016 (R)** Lawrence (Gabriel Byrne) is an aging actor who feels he has lost his way with his career, and his home life. He embarks on some soul searching with friends (also aging actors) to find his place in the world once again. Fans of comedy drama will be happy with this, but it's not for you if you want something snappy or quickly paced. **92m/C; DVD, Blu-Ray, Streaming.**

No Place on Earth 🦴🦴 1/2 **2012 (PG-13)** In 1993, New York spelunker Chris Nicola is exploring the gypsum caves in western Ukraine when he finds modern artifacts. After questioning reluctant locals, Nicola pieces together the story behind this Holocaust documentary. In 1942, members of the Jewish Stermer and Wexler families took refuge in the caves until the Soviet liberation in 1944. Writer-director Tobias uses actors to recreate actions from their ordeal and also interviews survivors, but the overlapping narration sometimes confuses. English, German, and Yiddish with subtitles. **83m/C; On Demand.** *D:* Janet Tobias; *W:* Janet Tobias; Paul Laikin; *C:* Cesar Charlone; Eduard Grau; Sean Kirby; Peter Simonite; *M:* John Piscitello.

No Regrets for Our Youth 🦴🦴🦴 **1946** A feminist saga depicting the spiritual growth of a foolish Japanese girl during the tumultuous years of WWII. In Japanese with English subtitles. **110m/B; VHS, DVD.** *JP* Setsuko Hara; Susumu Fujita; Denjiro Okochi; Haruko Sugimura; Eiko Miyoshi; *D:* Akira Kurosawa; *W:* Akira Kurosawa; *C:* Asakazu Nakai; *M:* Tadashi Hattori.

No Reservations 🦴 1/2 **2007 (PG)** Uptight, temperamental chef Kate (Zeta-Jones) meets her match romantically and professionally in laid back sous chef Nick (Eckhart). He's perfect, but she's too neurotic to recognize it, and just for a touch of extra conflict she's saddled with an orphaned pre-teen niece (Breslin). Aspires to be the romantic comedy version of fine dining but the end result is a bland and uninspired dish. Remake of popular German film "Mostly Martha." **105m/C; DVD, Blu-Ray, HD-DVD.** Catherine Zeta-Jones; Aaron Eckhart; Abigail Breslin; Patricia Clarkson; Jenny Wade; Bob Balaban; Brian F. O'Byrne; Lily Rabe; Celia Weston; John McMartin; Stephanie Barry; *D:* Scott Hicks; *W:* Carol Fuchs; *C:* Stuart Dryburgh; *M:* Philip Glass.

No Room for the Groom 🦴 1/2 **1952** Mild domestic comedy seems an unlikely project for director Sirk. Vineyard owner Alvah (Curtis) elopes to Vegas with Lee (Laurie) before he's shipped out to Korea. When he gets leave, he discovers his bride has moved a lot of obnoxious relatives into the house and she hasn't told her meddling mama (Byington) about the marriage. Also, Alvah is being pressured by wealthy cement plant owner Strouple (DeFore) to sell his property and the guy is also the one Mama wants Lee to marry! **82m/B; DVD.** Tony Curtis; Piper Laurie; Don DeFore; Spring Byington; Lillian Bronson; Jack Kelly; *D:* Douglas Sirk; *W:* Joseph Hoffman; *C:* Clifford Stine; *M:* Frank Skinner.

No Sad Songs For Me 🦴🦴 1/2 **1950** Well-played women's weepie about a topic not then discussed in films—dying from cancer. Mary Scott (Sullavan in her last film role) keeps the news of her terminal illness from her husband Brad (Corey) and young daughter Polly (Wood). Mary's upset to see Brad flirting with his co-worker Chris (Lindfors) but then decides to befriend the woman so Brad and Polly will have someone to lean on after she dies. Yes, the depiction of her last months is unrealistic and the medical ethics reflect the times but Sullavan sells the melodrama. **88m/B; DVD.** Margaret Sullavan; Wendell Corey; Viveca Lindfors; Natalie Wood; John McIntire; Jeannette Nolan; Ann Doran; *D:* Rudolph Mate; *W:* Howard Koch; *C:* Joseph Walker; *M:* George Duning.

No Safe Haven 🦴 **1987 (R)** A government agent seeks revenge for his family's death. **92m/C; VHS, DVD.** Wings Hauser; Marina Rice; Robert Tessier; *D:* Ronnie Rondell;

W: Wings Hauser; Nancy Locke; *C:* Steve McWilliams; *M:* Joel Goldsmith.

No Sex Please—We're British 🦴 1/2 **1973** Silly—and now dated—sex farce finds a postman accidentally delivering a parcel of pornography to a conservative bank. The contents inflame the bank's stuffy employees and suddenly it's a sexual free-for-all! Based on the play by Anthony Marriott and Alistair Foot. **90m/C; VHS, DVD.** *GB* Ronnie Corbett; Beryl Reid; Arthur Lowe; Ian Ogilvy; Susan Penhaligon; Michael Bates; Gerald Sim; David Swift; *D:* Cliff Owen; *W:* John Mortimer; Anthony Marriott; Brian Cooke; *C:* Ken Hodges; *M:* Eric Rogers.

No Sleep 'Til Madison 🦴🦴 1/2 **2002** Thirty-something Owen (Gaffigan) rounds up his old high school buddies for their yearly trek back to sweet home Wisconsin for their alma mater's hockey tournament. Along the way, he discovers that growing up is hard to do as his chums desert him when adulthood beckons. The message in this lighthearted flick is as subtle as a crosscheck to the face, but the likeable Gaffigan won't be sent to the penalty box for his efforts. **89m/C; VHS, DVD.** Jim Gaffigan; Rebekah Louise Smith; Ian Brennan; T.J. Jagodowski; Michael Gilio; Jed Resnik; Molly Glynn; Jason Wells; David Fleer; Erik Moe; *D:* David Fleer; Erik Moe; Peter Rudy; *W:* David Fleer; Erik Moe; Peter Rudy; *C:* Bradley W. Milsap; *M:* Stephen (Steve) Edwards. **VIDEO**

No Small Affair 🦴🦴 **1984 (R)** A 16-year-old aspiring photographer becomes romantically involved with a sultry 22-year-old rock star. **102m/C; VHS, DVD.** Jon Cryer; Demi Moore; George Wendt; Peter Frechette; Elizabeth Daily; Tim Robbins; Jennifer Tilly; Ric(k) Ducommun; Ann Wedgeworth; *D:* Jerry Schatzberg; *C:* John A. Alonzo; *M:* Rupert Holmes.

No Smoking 🦴 1/2 **1955** Scientist Reg Bates (Dixon) discovers a successful formula to cure nicotine addiction. Of course when he tries to manufacture and distribute his new pill, he runs into serious opposition from the tobacco industry. **72m/B; DVD.** *GB* Reg Dixon; Peter Martyn; Belinda Lee; Lionel Jeffries; Myrtle Rowe; Ruth Trouncer; Alexander Gauge; *D:* Lionel Jeffries; Henry Cass; *C:* Monty Berman; *M:* Ivor Slaney.

No Stone Unturned 2017 111m/C; Streaming. *UK US D:* Alex Gibney; *W:* Alex Gibney; *C:* Stan Harlow; Ross McDonnell; *M:* Ivor Guest.

No Strings Attached 🦴🦴 **1998 (R)** Mark Demetrius (Spano) is a reporter working on a story about women's sexual fantasies. To the distress of his fiancee, he enters a relationship with a mysterious woman he knows only through telephone conversations. To nobody's surprise, murder ensues. **97m/C; VHS, DVD.** Vincent Spano; Cheryl Pollak; Traci Lind; David Packer; Michael McKean; *D:* Josef Rusnak; *W:* Nicholas Bogner; Michael Holden; *C:* Wedigo von Schultzendorff; *M:* Eric Lundmark.

No Strings Attached 🦴🦴 **2011 (R)** Long-lost childhood friends Adam (Kutcher) and Emma (Portman) rediscover one another as adults at a dinner party. Adam was recently dumped and nursing student Emma is too busy for emotional commitments, so the two discuss the possibility of a purely sexual relationship but soon struggle to stick to their game plan. Portman is great, Kutcher is dopey, and what could have been a sharp, smart rom com comes off as too gooey sweet for its inaccurate R-rating. **110m/C; DVD, Blu-Ray, On Demand.** Ashton Kutcher; Natalie Portman; Kevin Kline; Greta Gerwig; Cary Elwes; Lake Bell; Olivia Thirlby; Talia Balsam; Chris Bridges; *D:* Ivan Reitman; *W:* Elizabeth Meriwether; *C:* Rogier Stoffers; *M:* John Debney.

No Such Thing 🦴🦴 **2001 (R)** This "Beauty and the Beast" fairytale for grownups doesn't always work but it's at least intriguing. Burke stars as an ill-tempered, drunken, ageless, nameless monster who has been terrorizing the remote areas of Iceland. When timid Beatrice (Polley) learns that her fiance, part of a news crew, has been slaughtered by the beast, she persuades her ratings-driven TV news show boss (Mirren) to send her to follow up on the story. Monster and Beatrice develop an unexpected rapport and she brings him back to New York where he's exploited, not unknowingly, as the lastest celeb. **103m/C; DVD.** Sarah Polley; Robert John Burke; Dame Helen Mirren; Julie Christie; Baltasar Kormakur; *D:* Hal Hartley; *W:* Hal Hartley; *C:* Michael Spiller; *M:* Hal Hartley.

No Surrender 🦴🦴🦴 **1986 (R)** An unpredictable, darkly charming comedy about a Liverpool nightclub newly managed by Angelis. On New Year's Eve, a small drunken war is triggered when two groups of irate senior citizens are booked into the club and clash over their beliefs. The group is made up of Protestants and Catholics and the fight resembles the ongoing conflicts in modern-day Northern Ireland, although most of the action takes place in the loo. Watch for Costello as an inept magician. **100m/C; VHS, DVD.** *GB* Ray McAnally; Michael Angelis; Avis Bunnage; James Ellis; Tom Georgeson; Mark Mulholland; Joanne Whalley; Elvis Costello; Bernard Hill; Michael Ripper; *D:* Peter Smith; *W:* Alan Bleasdale; *C:* Michael Coulter; *M:* Daryl Runswick.

No Time For Comedy 🦴🦴 1/2 **1940** Newsman Gaylord Esterbrook (Stewart) comes to New York to do rewrites on his first Broadway play and is soon married to star Linda Paige (Russell). After collaborating on four successful comedies, Gaylord gets arrogant and is persuaded by married manhunter Amanda Swift (Tobin) to write something serious, but his drama is a big stinkeroo and his antics nearly ruin his career and marriage. Adapted from the S.N. Behrman play. The only cinematic pairing of Stewart and the delightful Russell. **92m/B; DVD.** James Stewart; Rosalind Russell; Genevieve Tobin; Charlie Ruggles; Allyn Joslyn; Louise Beavers; *D:* William Keighley; *W:* Julius J. Epstein; Philip G. Epstein; *C:* Ernest Haller; *M:* Heinz Roemheld.

No Time For Love 🦴🦴🦴 **1943** Sparkling screwball comedy. Snooty New York fashion photographer Katherine Grant battles with her editor and winds up with an assignment to go underground and shoot tunnel sandhogs. She meets tough guy Jim and, after getting him into trouble and suspended, Katherine hires him to be her assistant. They've been bickering (i.e. falling in love) but she mistakenly thinks he's too low-class (she's wrong) so he flirts with chorus girl Darlene and Katherine gets jealous. **83m/B; DVD.** Claudette Colbert; Fred MacMurray; June Havoc; Ilka Chase; Richard Haydn; Paul McGrath; Marjorie Gateson; *D:* Mitchell Leisen; *W:* Warren Duff; Claude Binyon; *C:* Charles Lang; *M:* Victor Young.

No Time for Sergeants 🦴🦴🦴 **1958** Hilarious film version of the Broadway play by Ira Levin, which was based on the novel by Mac Hyman. Griffith is excellent as Georgia farm boy Will Stockdale, who gets drafted into the service and creates mayhem among his superiors and colleagues. Of course, Griffith had already played the role both on stage and in a TV version. McCormick was also repeating his Broadway role of Sgt. King. Note Don Knotts in a small role along with Jameel Farah who went on to star in TV's "M*A*S*H" after changing his name to Jamie Farr. **119m/B; DVD.** Andy Griffith; Nick Adams; Murray Hamilton; Myron McCormick; Howard Smith; Will Hutchins; Sydney Smith; Don Knotts; Jamie Farr; *D:* Mervyn LeRoy; *W:* John Lee Mahin; *C:* Harold Rosson; *M:* Ray Heindorf.

No Time to Be Young 🦴 1/2 **1957** Draft-dodging dropout Buddy (Vaughn) enlists a couple of other losers in a robbery that goes wrong. Buddy decides to try to outrun the cops and the chase is the best part of the flick. **82m/B; DVD.** Robert Vaughn; Roger Smith; Tom Pittman; Merry Anders; Kathleen Nolan; Sarah Selby; Dorothy Green; *D:* David Lowell Rich; *W:* John McPartland; *C:* Henry Freulich; *M:* Mischa Bakaleinikoff.

No Tomorrow 🦴 1/2 **1999 (R)** Criminal Busey works with shipping-company employee Daniels to broker a multimillion-dollar arms deal. As word of the deal spreads, both a gangster (Master P) and an FBI agent (Grier) get involved as well. Lots of shootouts and explosions cover the threadbare plot. **99m/C; VHS, DVD.** Gary Busey; Gary Daniels; Pam Grier; Jeff Fahey; Master P; *D:* Master P. **VIDEO**

No Trace 🦴🦴 **1950** A writer who broadcasts his crime stories as part of a radio show is the victim of blackmail. It seems a former associate is aware that the stories are all based in fact. A Scotland Yard detective investigates when murder rears its ugly head. **76m/B; VHS, DVD.** *GB* Hugh Sinclair; Dinah Sheridan; John Laurie; Barry Morse; Michael Brennan; Dora Bryan; *D:* John Gilling.

No Turning Back 🦴🦴 1/2 **2001 (R)** Intriguing based-on-real-events story of Pablo Hernandez (Nebot), an illegal immigrant who came to southern California after losing everything except his six-year-old daughter, Cristina (Rendon), during 1998's Hurricane Mitch in Honduras. After Pablo unintentionally mows down a well-to-do young girl with a borrowed truck, the pair is on the run with Soid (Price), a struggling journalist who agrees to aid the desperate man in exchange for filming the getaway. Along with playing the lead role, Nebot also co-wrote and makes his debut as co-director. **98m/C; VHS, DVD.** Jesus Nebot; Lindsay Price; Vernee Watson-Johnson; Susan Haskell; Chelsea Rendon; Joe Estevez; Niki Botelho; Kenya Moore; Gage Hunter Bebank; *D:* Jesus Nebot; Julia Montejo; *W:* Jesus Nebot; Julia Montejo; *C:* Ian Fox; *M:* Steven Chesne. **VIDEO**

No Vacancy 🦴🦴 1/2 **1999 (R)** LA's Pink Motel may be a dump but it feels like home to the kooky folks who are hanging out there, such as Lillian (Ricci), who's shook up to see that the man in her bed isn't her fiance. Also, there's two druggies who stiff their working girls andhave to deal with the gals' super-slick pimp (Wagner). **83m/C; VHS, DVD.** Olek Krupa; Lolita Davidovich; Timothy Olyphant; Christina Ricci; Ryan Bollman; Steven Schub; Tracy Tutor; Joaquim de Almeida; Patricia Velasquez; Graham Beckel; Gabriel Mann; Robert Wagner; Rhona Bennett; June Velar; Tracey Minner; Micaela Lockridge; Irina Gasanova; Tom Todoroff; *D:* Marius Balchunas; *W:* Marius Balchunas; *C:* Denis Maloney; *M:* Jeff Marsh; Alex Wurman. **VIDEO**

No Way Back 🦴🦴 **1974 (R)** Way. Writer, director, and producer Williamson portrays Jess Crowder, a man-for-hire who is an expert with guns, fists, and martial arts. An angry look at the white establishment. **92m/C; VHS, DVD.** Fred Williamson; Charles Woolf; Tracy Reed; Virginia Gregg; Don Cornelius; *D:* Fred Williamson.

No Way Back WOOF! *Ain't No Way Back* **1990 (R)** Two men find themselves in a trashy mess when they come to the aid of a damsel in distress while hunting the backwoods. One man dies and the other, Fletcher (Scott), must stop a family feud if he hopes to survive. Actually filmed in 1989, this terrible terror movie sat on the shelf for 16 years before our good friends at Troma decided to rescue it. **90m/C; DVD.** Campbell Scott; Virginia Lantry; Bernie (Bernard) White; John Durbin; Sean McGuirk; Dennis Ott; *D:* Michael Borden; *W:* Morgan Sloane; *C:* Nastaran Dibai; *M:* Murielle Hamilton. **VIDEO**

No Way Back 🦴🦴 **1996 (R)** FBI agent Zack Grant (Crowe) has never dealt with the death of his wife in childbirth and his career has suffered. His last professional chance is a sting operation involving the Mafia and the Yakuza. But when the operation goes wrong, Grant has a vendetta on his hands. Mafia boss Serlano (Lerner) kidnaps Zack's young son so Zack will turn over his prisoner—Yuji (Toyokawa), a Yakuza whom Serlano believes is responsible for his own son's death. Zack's only interest is to rescue his son and he doesn't care who gets in his way, including his fellow feds and the gangsters. **92m/C; DVD.** Russell Crowe; Helen Slater; Michael Lerner; Etsushi Toyokawa; Ian Ziering; Kelly Hu; *D:* Frank Cappello; *W:* Frank Cappello; *C:* Richard Clabaugh; *M:* David Williams.

No Way Home 🦴🦴 **1996 (R)** Joey (Roth), who's mentally a little slow, returns to his tough Staten Island neighborhood after being paroled from prison. He goes to live with his low-level drug dealer older brother Tommy (Russo) and Tommy's wife, Lorrain (Unger), who's not too happy about the situation—at first. But Joey's basically a decent guy and Lorrain begins to respond to his consideration. Meanwhile, desperate Tommy's in debt to a loan shark and his behavior may once again find Joey taking the rap for his brother's misdeeds. The story's predictable but the cast definitely rises above the material. **101m/C; VHS, DVD.** Tim Roth; James Russo; Deborah Kara Unger; Catherine Kellner; Joe Ragno; *D:* Buddy Giovinazzo; *W:* Buddy Giovinazzo; *C:* Claudia Raschke; *M:* Ricky Giovinazzo.

No Way Out 🦴🦴 1/2 **1950** When bigoted bad guy Roy Biddle (Widmark) and his brother George (Bellaver) are shot, they're taken to a small hospital run by Dr. Wharton (McNally), who believes in giving all his doctors a fair chance. So black doctor Luther Brooks (Poitier) works on George, who dies. Naturally, Roy blames the doctor and gets his hoodlum pals to cause some bloody confrontations. **105m/B; VHS, DVD.** Sidney Poitier; Richard Widmark; Stephen McNally; Linda Darnell; Harry Bellaver; Stanley Ridges; Ruby Dee; Ossie Davis; *D:* Joseph L. Mankiewicz; *W:* Joseph L. Mankiewicz; Lesser Samuels; *C:* Milton Krasner; *M:* Alfred Newman.

No Way Out 🦴🦴🦴 **1987 (R)** Career Navy man Tom Farrel (Costner) is involved with a beautiful, sexy party girl, Susan (Young), who gets killed. Turns out she was also the mistress of Secretary of Defense Brice (Hackman), Tom's boss. Assigned to investigate her suspicious death, Tom suddenly finds himself set up as the chief suspect. A tight thriller based on 1948's "The Big Clock," with a new surprise ending. Costner looks fine in his Navy whites and there's a backseat limousine sex scene that's quite steamy. **114m/C; VHS, DVD, Blu-Ray; Open Captioned.** Kevin Costner; Sean Young; Gene Hackman; Will Patton; Howard Duff; George Dzundza; Iman; Chris D; Marshall Bell; Jason Bernard; Fred Dalton Thompson; David Paymer; Eugene Robert Glazer; *D:* Roger Donaldson; *W:* Robert Garland; *C:* John Alcott; *M:* Maurice Jarre.

No Way to Treat a Lady 🦴🦴🦴 **1968** Steiger is a psychotic master of disguise who stalks and kills various women in this suspenseful cat-and-mouse game. Segal, as the detective assigned to the case, uncovers clues, falls in love, and discovers that his new girl may be the killer's next victim. **108m/C; VHS, DVD.** Rod Steiger; Lee Remick; George Segal; Eileen Heckart; Murray Hamilton; *D:* Jack Smight; *W:* John Gay; *C:* Jack Priestley.

No Witness 🦴 1/2 **2004 (R)** Shady Senator Gene Haskell (Fahey) is having some problems staying on the right side of the law and makes his gopher Leiter (Feldman) his pawn in covering up the misdeeds. The thorough hit man Paul (Barnes) hired by gives even the senator the willies. All-too-familiar thriller-wannabe includes some familiar faces who don't further the cause. **95m/C; DVD.** Jeff Fahey; Corey Feldman; Michael Damian; Steve Barnes; Marisa Petroro; *D:* Michael Valverde; *W:* Michael Valverde; Steve Antczak. **VIDEO**

Noa at Seventeen 🦴🦴🦴 **1982** The political/social turmoil of Israel in 1951 is allegorically depicted by the school vs. kibbutz debate within a young girl's middle-class family. In Hebrew with English subtitles. **86m/C; VHS, DVD.** *IS* Dalia Shimko; Idit Zur; Shmuel Shilo; Moshe Havazelet; *D:* Isaac Yeshurun.

The Noah 🦴🦴 1/2 **1975** Bourla's only film, filmed in 1968 with a brief appearance on the festival circuit in 1975, is a murky B&W post-apocalyptic nightmare. Former soldier Noah (character actor Strauss) is the only survivor of a nuclear holocaust. He finds himself marooned on an island that once housed a Communist Chinese military facility, thus offering him shelter. Unable to cope with his solitude, Noah begins hearing voices that grow into an imaginary civilization complete with problems, including a war, which Noah must battle. A definite cinematic oddity. **107m/B; DVD.** Robert Strauss; *V:* Geoffrey Holder; Sally Kirkland; Jim Blackmore; *D:* Daniel Bourla; *W:* Daniel Bourla; *C:* Jerry Kalogeratos.

Noah 🦴🦴 1/2 **2014 (PG-13)** Visually striking, deeply emotional, and totally bizarre, director/writer Aronofsky's reinterpretation of the epic, classic tale of Noah and his Ark has been divisive since before its release. Church groups weren't happy because it's not religious enough, and fans of the auteur thought it too conservative. In fact, it's the work of a confident, daring, visionary filmmaker, one who spent decades on this passion project about the man (a powerful Crowe) who saved the natural world from God's wrath. Though religious themes abound, the story focuses more on the will of humans to survive what seems unsurvivable. And the amazing supporting cast, including Connelly, Watson, and Hopkins, do not disappoint. **138m/C; DVD, Blu-Ray.** Russell Crowe; Jennifer Connelly; Anthony Hopkins; Ray Winstone; Logan Lerman; Emma Watson; Douglas Booth; Nick Nolte; Mark Margolis; Kevin Durand; ***D:*** Darren Aronofsky; ***W:*** Darren Aronofsky; Ari Handel; ***C:*** Matthew Libatique; ***M:*** Clint Mansell.

Noah's Arc: Jumping the Broom ½ **2008 (R)** This feature film, based on the Logo network series, follows the preparations for the Martha's Vineyard nuptials of Noah and Wade. Of course the attendees indulge in the usual round of flirtations, secrets, jealousies, and sexual situations, with a satisfying happy ending for at least some. **101m/C; DVD.** Darryl Stephens; Jensen Atwood; Douglas Spearman; Christian Vincent; Rodney Chester; Gary LeRoi Gray; Jonathan Julian; Jason Steed; ***D:*** Patrik-Ian Polk; ***W:*** Patrik-Ian Polk; John R. Gordon; ***C:*** Christopher Porter; ***M:*** Adam S. Goldman; Julian Wass.

Noah's Ark **1928** Odd combo of a wartime romance and the parallel Bible story of Noah and the flood. Travelling in Europe, American buddies Travis and Al save German Marie and Travis falls in love. The lovebirds are separated because the boys enlist to fight in WWI and Marie is accused of being a spy after rejecting the advances of Russian Nickoloff. In the Bible story, a mysterious minister compares war atrocities to the Noah story, which gives the cast members dual roles. Filmed as a silent, Warner Bros. hastily added some awkward dialogue sequences when talkies became a hit. **100m/B; Silent; DVD.** George O'Brien; Guinn "Big Boy" Williams; Dolores Costello; Noah Beery, Sr.; Paul McAllister; Malcolm Waite; ***D:*** Michael Curtiz; ***W:*** Darryl F. Zanuck; Anthony Coldeway; ***C:*** Hal Mohr; Barney McGill.

Noah's Ark **1999** Made-for-TV biblical epic of the Old Testament story that doesn't exactly stay close to its biblical roots. It's eccentric, special effects-laden, and borders on the irreverent. Noah builds his ark, gathers the animals (and his family), watches as the world is destroyed, and survives the 40 days and nights of flooding. **178m/C; VHS, DVD.** Jon Voight; Mary Steenburgen; F. Murray Abraham; Carol Kane; James Coburn; Jonathan Cake; Alexis Denisof; Emily Mortimer; Sydney Tamiia Poitier; Sonya Walger; ***D:*** John Irvin; ***W:*** Peter Barnes; ***C:*** Mike Molloy; ***M:*** Paul Grabowsky. **TV**

Nob Hill ½ **1945** With dreams of moving up the social ladder, Barbary Coast saloon keeper Tony Angelo (Raft) dumps his chanteuse girlfriend Sally (Blaine) when San Francisco socialite Harriet Caruthers (Bennett) bats her eyelashes. He wises up but the songbird doesn't want to resume their romance until the orphan (Garner) they've been looking after butts in. **95m/C; DVD.** George Raft; Joan Bennett; Vivian Blaine; Peggy Ann Garner; Edgar Barrier; ***D:*** Henry Hathaway; ***W:*** Wanda Tuchock; Norman Reilly Raine; ***C:*** Edward Cronjager; ***M:*** David Buttolph.

Nobel Son ½ **2008 (R)** Professor Eli Michaelson (Rickson) was an egomaniacal jerk before being awarded the Nobel Prize in chemistry. Now, he's completely insufferable. So much so that he is uncaring when his only son Barkley (Greenberg), whom Eli regards as a complete disappointment, is kidnapped, and he won't pay the ransom. The abductor is no secret—Thaddeus James (Hatosy) is a mechanical genius claiming to be Eli's illegitimate son and he tries to force Barkley into aiding him in his revenge/extortion plot. However the characters are so tedious (as is the unfolding of the action) that it's hard to stay interested. **102m/C; DVD, Streaming.** Alan Rickman; Bryan Greenberg; Shawn Hatosy; Mary Steenburgen; Eliza Dushku; Bill Pullman; Danny DeVito; Ted Danson; ***D:*** Randall Miller; ***W:*** Randall Miller; Jody Slavin; ***C:*** Michael Ozier; ***M:*** Paul Oakenfold; Mark Adler.

Noble House ½ **1988** Continuation of James Clavell's Hong Kong series, following "Tai-Pan," and set in the present day. Ian Dunross (Brosnan) is the head of Struan and Company, Hong Kong's leading trading company, which is being undermined by the nefarious Quillan Gornt (Rhys-Davies) who plots to destroy his archrival. American businesswoman Casey Tcholok (the bland Raffin) serves as Dunross' love interest. Originally a four-part TV miniseries partially filmed on location. **350m/C; VHS, DVD.** Pierce Brosnan; John Rhys-Davies; Deborah Raffin; Ben Masters; Julia Nickson-Soul; Khigh Deigh; Tia Carrere; Gordon Jackson; ***D:*** Gary Nelson; ***W:*** Eric Bercovici; ***C:*** Cristiano Pogany; ***M:*** Paul Chihara.

Noble Things **2008 (R)** Family drama about love, loyalty, and regret. After four years away, troubled country singer Jimmy Wayne Collins returns to Blackwater, Texas to make peace with his dying father, imprisoned brother, and ex-girlfriend. **98m/C; DVD.** Brett Moses; Michael Parks; Ryan Hurst; Lee Ann Womack; Dominique Swain; James Parks; Ron Canada; ***D:*** Dan McMellen; ***W:*** Dan McMellen; ***C:*** Horacio Marquinez; ***M:*** Gaili Schoen.

Nobody **1999** Three businessmen get involved in a bar fight that isn't your average brawl. In fact, the situation begins to take over their lives and they're no longer certain even who they're fighting. Japanese with subtitles. **100m/C; VHS, DVD.** *JP* Masaya Kato; Jinpachi Nezu; Riki Takeuchi; Hideo Nakano; ***D:*** Shundo Ohkawa; Toshimichi Ohkawa; ***W:*** Shundo Ohkawa.

Nobody ½ **2007** Repetitious modern noir about an assassin who claims success on a kill to his mobster boss Toles. But Toles wants proof and it seems the dead man isn't so dead after all. Non-linear timeline and the lack of a coherent ending make this more of an indie experiment than cohesive storytelling. **88m/C; DVD.** *CA* Costas Mandylor; Ed O'Ross; Darren Wall; Dawn Johnson; ***D:*** Shawn Linden; ***W:*** Shawn Linden; ***M:*** James Robertson.

Nobody Else But You *Poupoupidou* **2011** Crime novelist David Rousseau shows up in a small town in the French Alps for the reading of a will and ends up investigating the alleged suicide of Candice Lecouer, whose body he finds in the snow. A locally famous model who did cheese ads, the appetizing blonde thought she was the reincarnation of Marilyn Monroe. David becomes obsessed and starts sleuthing while Candice's troubled history is revealed in flashbacks and beyond-the-grave narration. French with subtitles. **102m/C; DVD.** *FR* Jean-Paul Rouve; Sophie Quinton; Guillaume Gouix; Olivier Rabourdin; ***D:*** Gerald Hustache-Mathieu; ***W:*** Gerald Hustache-Mathieu; ***C:*** Pierre Cottereau; ***M:*** Stephane Lopez.

Nobody Knows ½ *Dare mo shiranai* **2004 (PG-13)** Inspired by a true story that happened in 1988, Koreeda's overly-long drama follows the lives of four abandoned children. Irresponsible Keiko (You) smuggles her brood into a Tokyo apartment, refusing to let them attend school and giving them bizarre rules to follow so they won't be discovered. 12-year-old Akira (Yuya) is the de facto head of the family, especially when mom leaves a little cash and takes off with her latest boyfriend. Akira soon realizes she isn't returning and struggles to keep the family together under increasingly dire circumstances. Japanese with subtitles. **141m/C; DVD.** Yuya Yagira; Ayu Kitaura; Momoko Shimizu; Hanae Kan; Hiei Kimura; ***D:*** Hirokazu Kore-eda; ***W:*** Hirokazu Kore-eda; ***C:*** Yutaka Yamazaki; ***M:*** Gontiti.

Nobody Lives Forever **1946** Garfield and Fitzgerald make a hot twosome in director Negulesco's film noir about postwar ennui and cynicism. Ex-GI Nick Blake (Garfield) is having trouble adjusting to civilian life and opts to not go back to his previous con man profession. Instead, he leaves New York for sunny California but, after reconnecting with former mentor Pop (Brennan), Nick is drawn into a scam involving wealthy widow Gladys (Fitzgerald). Except Nick really falls for the dame, which puts their lives in danger. **100m/B; DVD.** John Garfield; Geraldine Fitzgerald; Walter Brennan; George Coulouris; Faye Emerson; George Tobias; Robert Shayne; Richard Gaines; ***D:*** Jean Negulesco; ***W:*** W.R. Burnett; ***C:*** Arthur Edeson; ***M:*** Jerome Moross; Adolph Deutsch.

Nobody Walks ½ **2012 (R)** Great indie film actresses Thirlby and Dewitt work well with a script co-written by Lena Dunham, but the result is a film that's uneven in pace and tone more often than finds its stride. Martine (Thirlby) is a young artist who comes to live with Julie (Dewitt) and Peter (Krasinski) and amplifies cracks in the family foundation by her very presence. Director Russo-Young has a delicate touch that works well with her laid-back actors but the result is mostly forgettable soap opera wannabe. **83m/C; DVD, Blu-Ray.** Olivia Thirlby; John Krasinski; Rosemarie DeWitt; Dylan McDermott; Justin Kirk; India Ennenga; Rhys Wakefield; ***D:*** Ry Russo-Young; ***W:*** Ry Russo-Young; Lena Dunham; ***C:*** Christopher Blauvelt; ***M:*** Fall on Your Sword; Tiffany Anders.

Nobody's Baby **1937** Nursing students and roommates Kitty (Kelly) and Lena (Roberti) meet pregnant ballroom dancer Yvonne (Lawrence) during tryouts for an amateur competition. A furious Yvonne's left partner and husband Tony (Alvarado) because he thinks admitting they're married is bad for business. Then there's the baby's birth, a case of mistaken motherhood, and a couple of romantic overtures that neither gal is much interested in. **67m/B; DVD.** Patsy Kelly; Lyda Roberti; Rosina Lawrence; Lynne Overman; Robert Armstrong; Don Alvarado; ***D:*** Gus Meins; ***W:*** Hal Yates; Harold Law; Pat C. Flick; ***C:*** Norbert Brodine; ***M:*** Marvin Hartley.

Nobody's Baby **2001 (R)** Orphaned at a young age, hillbilly brothers Billy and Buford have turned to crime, facing hard prison time and a court-ordered separation from one another until they escape on the way to the big house. Splitting up, dim Billy triggers a car crash that kills everyone aboard except a baby. Absconding with the child, Billy gets aid caring for the tot from truck stop waitress Shauna (Mitchell). Buford joins the party and plans to ransom the kid off to still-living relatives, only to discover Billy has grown attached. Slapstick antics ensue as the two attempt to secure funds to raise the child as their own. Weak, patchy script and unmemorable performances. **113m/C; DVD.** Skeet Ulrich; Gary Oldman; Radha Mitchell; Mary Steenburgen; Gordon Tootoosis; Anna Gunn; Peter Greene; Ed O'Neill; Matthew Modine; ***D:*** David Seltzer; ***W:*** David Seltzer; ***C:*** Christopher Taylor; ***M:*** Brian Tyler; Joseph Vitarelli.

Nobody's Children *I Figli del Nessuno* **1952** Lies and tragedy. Count Guido Canali is the heir to his family's marble quarries while Luisa is the daughter of a humble watchman. Of course they fall in love, which causes outrage in Guido's family. An unmarried Luisa gives birth to a boy but Countess Canali schemes to separate Luisa from her son and grandson forever. Italian with subtitles; followed by "The White Angel" (1955). **96m/B; DVD.** *IT* Amedeo Nazzari; Yvonee Sanson; Francoise Rosay; Folco Lulli; Enrica Dyrell; Teresa Franchini; ***D:*** Raffaello Matarazzo; ***W:*** Aldo De Benedetti; ***C:*** Rodolfo Lombardi; ***M:*** Salvatoe Allegra.

Nobody's Fool **1986 (PG-13)** Another entry in the genre of quirky Americana, this romantic comedy concerns a hapless Midwestern waitress suffering from low-self esteem who falls in love with a traveling stage-hand. **107m/C; VHS, DVD.** Rosanna Arquette; Eric Roberts; Mare Winningham; Louise Fletcher; Jim Youngs; Gwen Welles; Stephen Tobolowsky; Charlie Barnett; Lewis Arquette; ***D:*** Evelyn Purcell; ***W:*** Beth Henley; ***C:*** Misha (Mikhail) Suslov; ***M:*** James Newton Howard.

Nobody's Fool ½ **1994 (R)** Newman shines as 60-year-old Donald "Sully" Sullivan, a construction worker who, in spite of himself, begins mending his many broken relationships over the course of the holiday season. Seemingly plotless scenario is sprinkled with enough humor, hope, and understated inspiration to become a delightfully modest celebration of a perfectly ordinary man. Character-driven story is blessed with commendable performances by supporting players—obviously inspired by Newman's brilliant portrayal. Based on the novel by Richard Russo. **110m/C; VHS, DVD.** Paul Newman; Jessica Tandy; Bruce Willis; Melanie Griffith; Dylan Walsh; Pruitt Taylor Vince; Gene Saks; Josef Sommer; Philip Seymour Hoffman; Philip Bosco; Margo Martindale; Jay Patterson; ***D:*** Robert Benton; ***W:*** Robert Benton; ***C:*** John Bailey; ***M:*** Howard Shore. Berlin Intl. Film Fest. '94: Actor (Newman); N.Y. Film Critics '94: Actor (Newman); Natl. Soc. Film Critics '94: Actor (Newman).

Nobody's Fool ½ **2018 (R)** Tiffany Haddish plays Tanya, a coarse, uncouth, LOUD ex-convict who moves in with her polar-opposite sister Danica (Sumpter), a buttoned-up, serious-minded executive. Tanya suspects that Danica is being catfished by her online boyfriend, leads the charge to unmask him, and hilarity ensues. Or not. Neither sister is likable nor, except for a couple of somewhat humorous spots, funny. Moreover, Perry's script is a mishmash without a clear direction. Don't be a fool: keep your expectations low. **110m/C; DVD, Blu-Ray.** Tiffany Haddish; Tika Sumpter; Omari Hardwick; Mehcad Brooks; Amber Riley; ***D:*** Tyler Perry; ***W:*** Tyler Perry; ***C:*** Richard J. Vialet; ***M:*** Philip White.

Nobody's Perfect **1990 (PG-13)** Where "Tootsie" and "Some Like It Hot" collide (or more likely crash and burn). A lovesick teenager masquerades as a girl and joins the tennis team to be near his dream girl. Takes its title from Joe E. Brown's famous last line in "Some Like It Hot." **90m/C; VHS, DVD.** Chad Lowe; Gail O'Grady; Patrick Breen; Kim Flowers; Robert Vaughn; ***D:*** Robert Kaylor; ***W:*** Joel Block.

Nobody's Perfekt **WOOF! 1979 (PG)** Supposed comedy about three psychiatric patients who decide to extort $650,000 from the city of Miami when their car is wrecked. Lacks laughs and generally considered a turkey. **95m/C; VHS, DVD.** Gabe Kaplan; Robert Klein; Alex Karras; Susan Clark; ***D:*** Peter Bonerz.

Nocturama ½ **2017** A dramatic thriller about terrorist teens in Paris that focuses on their thoughts and feelings over ideology and psychology. Using flashbacks, the film centers on a day in which they bomb and set fire to several targets. While highlighting the clock-like precision with which they execute their plot then hide overnight in a mall, filmmaker Bertrand Bonello shows the group loves consumer items and rap and pop music. Though each teen has different motivations, secrets, and feelings about their actions, they reveal much through the effective, but limited, dialogue. Meaningful, efficient symbolism and small gestures add to the film's depth. French with subtitles. **130m/C; DVD, Blu-Ray.** Finnegan Oldfield; Vincent Rottiers; Hazma Meziani; Manal Issa; Martin Petitguyot; ***D:*** Bertrand Bonello; ***W:*** Bertrand Bonello; ***C:*** Leo Hinstin; ***M:*** Bertrand Bonello.

Nocturnal Animals ½ **2016 (R)** Tom Ford's challenging drama is a star-studded examination of grief and revenge, with a beautifully constructed story within a story. Susan Morrow (Adams) is an art gallery owner who receives a manuscript from her ex-husband Edward (Gyllenhaal) called "Nocturnal Animals." We then see that story as she reads it, in which Gyllenhaal plays a man caught in a waking nightmare after his family is run off the road in the middle of the night by sociopaths. Shannon and Taylor-Johnson co-star in this riveting thriller, a movie about art and memory with fantastic performances from top to bottom. **116m/C; DVD, Blu-Ray.** Amy Adams; Jake Gyllenhaal; Michael Shannon; Aaron Taylor-Johnson; Isla Fisher; Jena Malone; ***D:*** Tom Ford; ***W:*** Tom Ford; ***C:*** Seamus McGarvey; ***M:*** Abel Korzeniowski. Golden Globes '17: Actor--Supporting (Taylor-Johnson).

Nocturne ½ **1946** A police lieutenant investigates the supposed suicide of a famous composer and uncovers dark secrets that suggest murder is afoot. An overlooked RKO production shines thanks to Raft's inimitable tough guy performance and some offbeat direction. For film noir completists. **88m/B; DVD.** George Raft; Lynn Bari; Virginia Huston; Joseph Pevney; Myrna Dell; Edward Ashley; Walter Sande; Mabel Paige; ***D:*** Edwin L. Marin; ***W:*** Rowland Brown; Frank Fenton; Jonathan Latimer; ***C:*** Harry Wild; ***M:*** Leigh Harline.

Noel ½ **2004 (PG)** Not designed for Christmas cheer, this coal-in-your-stocking drama (Palminteri's directorial debut) follows the intertwined stories of several lonely New Yorkers searching for happiness on Christmas Eve. Rose (Sarandon) is a divorced workaholic, desperately trying for a final reconciliation with her Alzheimer's-stricken mother; Mike's (Walker) jealousy is destroying his relationship with Nina (Cruz); Artie (Arkin) thinks Mike is the reincarnation of his dead wife (!) and constantly follows him; and homeless Jules's (Thomas) one happy holiday memory was a party in the hospital emergency room. When Robin Williams shows up (unbilled) to give advice, you know you're in trouble. **96m/C; Blu-Ray, On Demand.** Penelope Cruz; Susan Sarandon; Paul Walker; Alan Arkin; Marcus Thomas; Chazz Palminteri; Robin Williams; ***D:*** Chazz Palminteri; ***W:*** David Hubbard; ***C:*** Russell Carpenter; ***M:*** Alan Menken.

Noelle 🦴🦴 **2019 (G)** At the North Pole, Santa Claus is a role that passed down through the men in the Kringle family. Neurotic Nick (Hader) is to inherit the job, but does not want it and grows frustrated during the intensive training.Though his clever, talented sister Noelle (Kendrick) is better suited for the role, she accepts that women cannot become Santa. When Nick vanishes to Arizona, Noelle is sent to find him and convince him to return. Along the way, Noelle discovers her knack for Santa duties. The family Christmas film has a lovely message though the look is that of a TV movie, but Kendrick's energy rarely disappoints. **100m/C; DVD.** Anna Kendrick; Shirley MacLaine; Bill Hader; Kingsley Ben-Adir; Julie Hagerty; ***D:*** Marc Lawrence; ***W:*** Marc Lawrence; ***C:*** Russell Carpenter; ***M:*** Cody Fitzgerald; Clyde Lawrence. **VIDEO**

Noise 🦴 **1/2 2007** A recognizable situation turns one-note (and just what's the Russian chick all about?). Manhattanite David Owen (Robbins) is driven crazy by the city's noise pollution and starts taking a baseball bat to cars with constantly shrieking car alarms. He becomes a popular vigilante known as "The Rectifier" but blowhard Mayor Schneer (Hurt) is not one of his fans, and David's defiance becomes a real problem for City Hall. **88m/C; DVD.** Tim Robbins; William Hurt; Bridget Moynahan; Margarita Levieva; William Baldwin; ***D:*** Henry Bean; ***W:*** Henry Bean; ***C:*** Andrij Parekh; ***M:*** Philip Johnston.

Noises Off 🦴🦴 **1/2 1992 (PG-13)** An Americanization of a British farce about a group of second-rate actors touring in a sex comedy and their convoluted private lives. Wretched rehersals and equally disasterous preformances, backstage sniping, lovers' quarrels, and a beleaguered director all bumble along together. It worked better on stage, where it was a Broadway hit, but the actors at least have some fun with the material. Based on the play by Michael Frayn. **101m/C; VHS, DVD.** Michael Caine; Carol Burnett; Denholm Elliott; Julie Hagerty; Marilu Henner; Mark Linn-Baker; Christopher Reeve; John Ritter; Nicolette Sheridan; ***D:*** Peter Bogdanovich; ***W:*** Marty Kaplan; ***M:*** Phil Marshall.

Nomads 🦴🦴 **1/2 1986 (R)** A supernatural thriller set in Los Angeles about a French anthropologist who is mysteriously killed, and the woman doctor who investigates and becomes the next target of a band of strange street people with nomadic spirits. Nomad notables include pop stars Adam Ant and Josie Cotton. **91m/C; VHS, DVD, Blu-Ray.** Pierce Brosnan; Lesley-Anne Down; Adam Ant; Anna Maria Monticelli; Mary Woronov; Hector Mercado; ***D:*** John McTiernan; ***W:*** John McTiernan; ***C:*** Stephen Ramsey; ***M:*** Bill Conti.

Nomads of the North 🦴 **1/2 1920** Vintage silent melodrama set in the North Woods with the requisite young girl beset by evil villians, a climactic forest fire, and a dashing Mountie who allows a man wrongly sought by the law to be reunited with the woman he secretly loves. Also available at 75 minutes. **109m/B; Silent; VHS, DVD.** Lon Chaney, Sr.; Lewis Stone; Betty Blythe; ***D:*** David M. Hartford.

Non-Fiction 🦴 **1/2** ***Doubles vies*** **2018 (R)** A navel-gazer about infidelity and the publishing industry in the 21st century, incredibly billed as a comedy. The main characters are a mildly successful Parisian author (Spiegel) desperate for a bestseller, his pessimistic publisher (Danielson), who's cheating on his wife (Binoche), who herself is cheating with the above author; a young mistress and the author's put-upon wife round out the adulterous pentagon. If that setup doesn't have you guffawing, maybe the tedious conversations about eBooks and Kindles will. Non? C'est la vie. **108m/C; DVD.** *FR* Guillaume Canet; Juliette Binoche; Vincent Macaigne; Christa Theret; Nora Hamzawi; ***D:*** Olivier Assayas; ***W:*** Olivier Assayas; ***C:*** Yorick Le Saux.

Non-Stop 🦴🦴 **2014 (PG-13)** Collet-Serra reunites with Neeson, the most surprisingly robust action star in his sixties, in this thriller about a U.S. Air Marshal who could be the only man to stop a plane hijacking. Bill Marks receives a text that a passenger on their London-bound flight is going to be killed every 20 minutes until the terrorist is wired $150 million. Of course, no one will believe him. With a strong cast of suspects and top-notch claustrophobic cinematography, Collet-Serra keeps the engines humming for two acts until the nonsensical reveal of the villain and his motives puncture suspension of disbelief. **106m/C; DVD, Blu-Ray.** *US FR* Liam Neeson; Julianne Moore; Corey Stoll; Scoot McNairy; Omar Metwally; Michelle Dockery; Linus Roache; Jason Butler Harner; Lupita Nyong'o; Nate Parker; Anson Mount; ***D:*** Jaume Collet-Serra; ***W:*** John W. Richardson; Chris Roach; Ryan Engle; ***C:*** Flavio Martinez Labiano; ***M:*** John Ottman.

The Non-Stop Flight 🦴 **1/2 1926** The U.S. Navy's historic 1925 flight from San Francisco to Hawaii is a plot point in this silent adventure drama. Sea Captain Lars Larson becomes a bitter drunk after believing his pregnant wife has left him. He turns smuggler, which leads to an island, a hermit, a young girl, and the Navy going after white slavers. **71m/B; Silent; DVD.** Knute Erickson; Virginia Fry; Marcella Daly; David Dunbar; Harlan Hilton; Cecil Ogden; ***D:*** Emory Johnson; ***W:*** Emilie Johnson; ***C:*** Gilbert Warrenton.

Non-Stop New York 🦴🦴 **1/2 1937** Mystery tale with interesting twist. A wealthy woman can give an alibi for a murder suspect, but no one will listen, and she is subsequently framed. Pays homage to Hitchcock with its photography and humor. Quick and charming. **71m/B; VHS, DVD.** Anna Lee; John Loder; Francis L. Sullivan; Frank Cellier; Desmond Tester; Athene Seyler; William Dewhurst; Drusilla Wills; Jerry Verno; James Pirrie; Ellen Pollock; Arthur Goullet; James Carew; Alf Goddard; Danny Green; ***D:*** Robert Stevenson; ***W:*** Curt Siodmak; Roland Pertwee; Derek Twist; J.O.C. Orton; E.V.H. Emmett; ***C:*** Mutz Greenbaum.

NoNames 🦴 **1/2 2010** Depressing indie finds Kevin struggling with his decision to remain in his rural Wisconsin hometown. His girlfriend CJ is raped but refuses to press charges leaving Kevin to choose whether to escape from their going-nowhere lives or stay locked into the familar. **108m/C; DVD.** James Badge Dale; Gillian Jacobs; Barry Corbin; Darren E. Burrows; ***D:*** Kathy Lindboe; ***W:*** Kathy Lindboe; ***C:*** Kenneth Wilson, II.

None But the Brave 🦴🦴 **1965** During WWII, an American bomber plane crash-lands on an island already inhabited by stranded Japanese forces. After a skirmish, the two groups initiate a fragile truce, with the understanding that fighting will resume if one or the other sends for help. The Americans repair their radio unit and must decide on their next actions. Sinatra's directorial debut is a poor effort. **105m/C; VHS, DVD, Blu-Ray.** Frank Sinatra; Clint Walker; Tommy Sands; Brad Dexter; Tony Bill; Tatsuya Mihashi; Takeshi Kato; Sammy Jackson; ***D:*** Frank Sinatra; ***M:*** John Williams.

None But the Lonely Heart 🦴🦴🦴 **1944** In the days before WWII, a Cockney drifter (Grant) wanders the East End of London. When his get-rich-quick schemes fail, his dying shopkeeper-mother tries to help and lands in prison. Interesting characterization of life in the slums. Odets not only directed, but wrote the screenplay. **113m/B; VHS, DVD.** Cary Grant; Ethel Barrymore; Barry Fitzgerald; Jane Wyatt; Dan Duryea; George Coulouris; June Duprez; ***D:*** Clifford Odets; ***W:*** Clifford Odets; ***C:*** George Barnes. Oscars '44: Support. Actress (Barrymore).

Noon Sunday 🦴 **1975 (PG)** A cold war situation in the Pacific islands explodes into an orgy of death. **104m/C; VHS, DVD.** Mark Lenard; John Russell; Linda Avery; Keye Luke; ***D:*** Terry Bourke; ***W:*** Terry Bourke; ***C:*** Akira Mimura; ***M:*** Nick Demuth.

Noose for a Gunman 🦴🦴 **1/2 1960** In this solid B-western, gunslinger Case Britton (Davis) left town after being falsely accused of murder by cattle baron Carl Avery (MacLane). He returns after learning Avery's henchman Cantrell (de Corsia) is planning a robbery. Though the townsfolk don't believe him, Britton has Marshal Evans (Sande) on his side. **70m/B; DVD.** Jim Davis; Barton MacLane; Ted de Corsia; Walter Sande; Lyn Thomas; Leo Gordon; Harry Carey, Jr.; Lane Chandler; ***D:*** Edward L. Cahn; ***W:*** Robert E. Kent; ***C:*** Walter Strange; ***M:*** Paul Sawtell; Bert Shefter.

The Noose Hangs High 🦴🦴🦴 **1948** This broad comedy has our heroes as window washers mistaken for gamblers and getting involved with a bunch of gangsters. Much physical and verbal shenanigans as only these two can do it. The bits may be a bit old, but they're done with a fresh twist. Some good word play with the phrase "You can't be here" runs in the same vein as their classic "Who's on first?" routine. Genuinely funny. **77m/B; VHS, DVD, Blu-Ray.** Bud Abbott; Lou Costello; Cathy Downs; Joseph Calleia; Leon Errol; Mike Mazurki; Jack Overman; Fritz Feld; Vera Martin; Joe (Joseph) Kirk; Matt Willis; Benny Rubin; ***D:*** Charles T. Barton.

Nora 🦴🦴 **1/2 2000 (R)** In a film about the passionate relationship between two people, there's actually little heat to be found, although the leads are effective. Ambitious would-be writer James Joyce (McGregor) and hotel maid Nora Barnacle (Lynch) meet in Dublin in 1904. Nora soon becomes his muse, common-law wife, and the mother of his children but insecure Joyce is mistrustful of her faithfulness and the two are locked in a constant battle as they travel between Italy and Ireland and Joyce seeks to find a publisher for his work. Based on the book by Brenda Maddox. **106m/C; DVD.** *IR UK GE* Ewan McGregor; Susan Lynch; Peter McDonald; Roberto Citran; Andrew Scott; Vincent McCabe; Veronica Duffy; Aedin Moloney; Darragh Kelly; ***D:*** Pat Murphy; ***W:*** Gerard Stembridge; Pat Murphy; ***C:*** Jean-Francois Robin; ***M:*** Stanislas Syrewicz.

Nora Prentiss 🦴🦴 **1/2 1947** Staid San Francisco doctor Richard Talbot (Smith) is in a boring marriage and ripe to have an affair with nightclub singer Nora (Sheridan). When he dithers about a divorce, she moves to New York and the depressed Richard comes up with a radical idea when a patient unexpectedly dies in his office. Richard assumes another identity, fakes his own death, and goes to Nora. Unfortunately, the doctor's death is investigated as a murder and Richard later becomes paranoid, thinking the successful Nora is cheating on him. **111m/B; DVD.** Ken Smith; Ann Sheridan; Bruce Bennett; Robert Alda; Rosemary DeCamp; John Ridgely; ***D:*** Vincent Sherman; ***W:*** N. Richard Nash; ***C:*** James Wong Howe; ***M:*** Franz Waxman.

Nora's Hair Salon 🦴🦴 **2004 (R)** Girlfriends get together and dish the dirt at Nora's (Lewis) L.A. salon in this lively yet not quite as folksy female take on "Barbershop" where Nora plays mom to her staff and customers. Whitney Houston cameos. **84m/C; VHS, DVD.** Jenifer Lewis; Tatyana Ali; Bobby Brown; Christine Carlo; Tamala Jones; Pras; Kimberly (Lil' Kim) Jones; ***D:*** Jerry LaMothe; ***W:*** Jean-Claude La Marre; ***C:*** Robert Humphreys. **VIDEO**

Nora's Hair Salon 2: A Cut Above 🦴🦴 **2008 (PG-13)** Nora willed her beauty salon to her two nieces, but the estranged cousins have very different ideas for the business: Lilliana (Ali) wants to keep the shop open and Simone (Dash) wants to sell. There's some sassiness, some romance, and some thoughts on what it means to be family. **80m/C; DVD.** Stacey Dash; Tatyana Ali; Bobby Brown; Mekhi Phifer; Christine Carlo; Lucille Soong; Malik Barnhardt; ***D:*** Jill Maxcy; ***W:*** Jill Maxcy; Chanel Capra; ***C:*** Laura Beth Love; ***M:*** John "Flexx" Simeus. **VIDEO**

Nora's Will 🦴 **1/2** ***Five Days Without Nora; Cinco Dias Sin Nora*** **2009** Black comedy has chronically depressed Nora finally succeeding in her suicide, leading to a host of unexpected problems. Her ex-husband Jose finds the body as well as careful instructions for the Passover meal she's prepared, but there'll be a delay in burying her body because of the Sabbath. Religious clashes ensue between atheist Jose and the local orthodox rabbi as the family gathers. Spanish with subtitles. **92m/C; DVD.** *MX* Fernando Lujan; Silvia Mariscal; Max Kerlow; Enrique Arreola; ***D:*** Mariana Chenillo; ***W:*** Mariana Chenillo; ***C:*** Alberto Anaya Adalid; ***M:*** Dario Gonzalez Valderrama.

Norbit 🦴 **1/2 2007 (PG-13)** Eddie does triple duty as meek Norbit, raised in an orphanage by Mr. Wong (Murphy as the worst Asian stereotype since Mickey Rooney in "Breakfast at Tiffany's"), who is bullied into marriage with gargantuan Rasputia (yeah, it's Murphy inside the fat suit). But he's really in love with slender beauty Kate (Newton), whose fiance (Gooding Jr.) is in shady cahoots with Rasputia's intimidating brothers. Like you care, as long as Eddie delivers the predictable laughs. Rick Baker does the special effects makeup. **95m/C; DVD, Blu-Ray, HD-DVD.** Eddie Murphy; Thandie Newton; Terry Crews; Clifton Powell; Cuba Gooding, Jr.; Eddie Griffin; Katt Micah Williams; Marlon Wayans; Lester "Rasta" Speight; ***D:*** Brian Robbins; ***W:*** Charles Murphy; Jay Scherick; David Ronn; ***C:*** Clark Mathis; ***M:*** David Newman. Golden Raspberries '07: Worst Actor (Murphy), Worst Support. Actor (Murphy), Worst Support. Actress (Murphy).

The Norliss Tapes 🦴🦴 **1973** This failed NBC TV pilot is best viewed for its nostalgia value (especially those special effects). Troubled journalist David Norliss (Thinnes) disappears while investigating an attack by an alleged dead man. When his publisher (Porter) investigates, he finds only the recordings that Norliss left behind, which point to some supernatural forces at work. Curtis and Nolan were also responsible for "Kolchak: The Night Stalker." **72m/C; DVD.** Roy Thinnes; Don Porter; Angie Dickinson; Claude Akins; Vonetta McGee; Nick Dimitri; ***D:*** Dan Curtis; ***W:*** William F. Nolan; ***C:*** Ben Colman; ***M:*** Robert Cobert. **TV**

Norm of the North 🦴 **2016 (PG)** Norm (Schneider) is a polar bear who doesn't know how to hunt but can actually talk to humans. Norm travels to New York City to stop a wealthy villain from building luxury houses in the Arctic, and, oh, who cares? A cheap, aggressively annoying animated mess. The cut-rate animation wouldn't hold against most TV shows and the voice work meanders from lazy to irritating. Family animation, thanks to Pixar and DreamWorks, has come a long way in the last twenty years. This movie is a relic. **90m/C; DVD, Blu-Ray.** Maya Kay; Rob Schneider; Heather Graham; Ken Jeong; Bill Nighy; Colm Meaney; Gabriel "Fluffy" Iglesias; ***D:*** Trevor Wall; ***W:*** Daniel Altiere; Steven Altiere; Malcolm T. Goldman; Jamie Lissow; ***M:*** Stephen McKeon.

Norma Jean and Marilyn 🦴🦴 **1/2 1995 (R)** Blonde screen goddess Marilyn Monroe (Sorvino) is haunted by her past, literally, since she never escapes the legacy of ambitious Norma Jean Baker (Judd). As her relationships and career falter, Norma Jean is always there (thanks to drug-induced hallucinations) to remind Marilyn how worthless she is. Drama deals with Norma Jean's troubled past and how she was willing to do anything to be in the movies, although it (apparently) brought her little happiness. The dual stars work surprisingly well and director Fywell offers the proper camp flair. **133m/C; VHS, DVD.** Mira Sorvino; Ashley Judd; Josh Charles; Peter Dobson; Ron Rifkin; David Dukes; Taylor Nichols; Lindsay Crouse; John Rubinstein; Steven Culp; Perry Stephens; Earl Boen; ***D:*** Tim Fywell; ***W:*** Jill Isaacs; ***C:*** John Thomas; ***M:*** Christopher Young. **CABLE**

Norma Rae 🦴🦴🦴 **1979 (PG)** A poor, uneducated textile worker joins forces with a New York labor organizer to unionize the reluctant workers at a Southern mill. Field was a surprise with her fully developed character's strength, beauty, and humor; her Oscar was well-deserved. Ritt's direction is top-notch. Jennifer Warnes sings the theme song, "It Goes Like It Goes," which also won an Oscar. **114m/C; VHS, DVD, Blu-Ray.** Sally Field; Ron Leibman; Beau Bridges; Pat Hingle; ***D:*** Martin Ritt; ***W:*** Harriet Frank, Jr.; Irving Ravetch; ***C:*** John A. Alonzo; ***M:*** David Shire. Oscars '79: Actress (Field), Song ("It Goes Like It Goes"); Cannes '79: Actress (Field); Golden Globes '80: Actress--Drama (Field); L.A. Film Critics '79: Actress (Field); Natl. Bd. of Review '79: Actress (Field); Natl. Film Reg. '11; N.Y. Film Critics '79: Actress (Field); Natl. Soc. Film Critics '79: Actress (Field).

Normal 🦴🦴 **2003** No guts, no glory. And both Wilkinson and Lange had to have guts to make this story work. Roy and Irma Applewood have been married for 25 years and are respected members of their small Illinois farming community. Stress has Roy seeking counseling—and finally admitting that he has always felt like a woman trapped in a man's body. He's determined to undergo sex-change surgery, but tells Irma that he still loves her and wants them to continue living together. Irma's not unreasonably confused, resentful, angry, and, ultimately, loving and supportive as the community turns its back on them. Adapted from Anderson's play "Looking for Normal." **108m/C; DVD.** Tom Wilkinson; Jessica Lange; Hayden Panettiere; Joe Sikora; Clancy Brown; Richard Bull; Randall Arney; Mary Seibel; ***D:*** Jane Anderson; ***W:*** Jane Anderson; ***C:*** Alar Kivilo; ***M:*** Alex Wurman.

Normal **2007** University prof Walt (Rennie) drives drunk and gets involved in a car crash that kills a teenaged boy, but is acquitted of any wrongdoing. The dead boy's mother, Catherine (Moss), can't cope with her grief and ignores her remaining family. Troubled Jordie (Zegers), who was driving a stolen car and involved in the same accident, starts an affair with his stepmother to help him cope. There's a bunch of other people peripherally involved and a lot of overwrought guilt. **100m/C; DVD.** *CA* Carrie-Anne Moss; Kevin Zegers; Callum Keith Rennie; Lauren Lee Smith; Andrew Airlie; Tygh Runyan; Cameron Bright; Camille Sullivan; ***D:*** Carl Bessai; ***W:*** Travis McDonald; ***C:*** Carl Bessai; ***M:*** Clinton Shorter.

The Normal Heart **2014** Generally powerful HBO adaptation of Larry Kramer's play about the '80s AIDS crisis within and without the gay community. Kramer's surrogate is abrasive activist Ned Weeks (Ruffalo), continually frustrated by the lack of information about the mystery disease decimating those around him. Equally outraged is Dr. Emma Brookner (Roberts), wheelchair-bound by polio, and infuriated by the lack of concern among her peers for discovering the cause (and treatment) of the disease. Illness and death hits close to home for Ned when his lover Felix (Bomer) is diagnosed, but his fury makes him persona non grata among those looking for help. **130m/C; DVD, Blu-Ray.** Mark Ruffalo; Julia Roberts; Matt Bomer; Taylor Kitsch; Jim Parsons; Joe Mantello; Alfred Molina; Denis O'Hare; B.D. Wong; Jonathan Groff; ***D:*** Ryan Murphy; ***W:*** Larry Kramer; ***C:*** Daniel (Danny) Moder; ***M:*** Cliff Martinez. **CABLE**

Normal Life **1996 (R)** Straight-arrow, smalltown Illinois rookie cop Chris Anderson (Perry) comes to the aid of sexy, impetuous biker chick Pam (Judd) and they impulsively marry. Fast forward two years and the willfully irresponsible Pam has turned their lives into a disaster but for some reason Chris (now a security guard) sticks it out, even pulling bank jobs to afford Pam's luxuries. When she finds out what Chris has been doing, Pam insists on joining in, leading to a bitter end. Based on the true story of Jeffrey and Jill Erickson, who went on a bank robbing spree and were killed in 1991. Great lead performances though character motivation is lacking. **108m/C; DVD.** Luke Perry; Ashley Judd; Bruce A. Young; Jim True-Frost; Dawn Maxey; Penelope Milford; Tom Towler; Kate Walsh; ***D:*** John McNaughton; ***W:*** Bob Schneider; Peg Haller; ***C:*** Jean De Segonzac.

Norman **2010** Diffident high school loner Norman is having trouble accepting that his father is terminally ill and doesn't want to continue with his cancer treatment. When his best friend James accuses Norman of being self-absorbed, the teen blurbs out that he has cancer and is suddenly the center of attention, earning sympathy from dream girl Emily. Now Norman is finding it difficult to stop a lie that has gotten out of control. **98m/C; DVD.** Dan Byrd; Emily VanCamp; Richard Jenkins; Billy Lush; Adam Goldberg; ***D:*** Jonathan Segal; ***W:*** Talton Wingate; ***C:*** Darren Genet; ***M:*** Andrew Bird.

Norman **1/2** *Norman: The Moderate Rise and Tragic Fall of a New York Fixer* **2017 (R)** Defined by Gere's nuanced portrayal of Norman, the deft drama succeeds for those that buy into the spin. Norman is a fixer for business and politicians in the United States and Israel, and constantly works connections in hopes of achieving long-sought access and respect. Three years after helping Micha Eshel (Ashkenazi), an Israeli diplomat at a professional low point, he becomes Israel's prime minister and Norman gains the position and prestige he covets. However, the exaggerations and promises he cannot keep come back to affect him in unexpected ways that reflect the heart of this complicated, multi-layered film. **118m/C; DVD.** Richard Gere; Lior Ashkenazi; Michael Sheen; Steve Buscemi; Josh Charles; ***D:*** Joseph Cedar; ***W:*** Joseph Cedar; ***C:*** Yaron Scharf; ***M:*** Jun Miyake.

Norman Conquest *Park Plaza* **1953** Conway finds himself drugged and framed for murder in this bargain-basement thriller. Bartok is the leader of a diamond-smuggling operation who may be involved. **75m/B; VHS, DVD.** *GB* Tom Conway; Eva Bartok; Joy Shelton; Sidney James; Richard Wattis; Robert Adair; Ian Fleming; ***D:*** Bernard Knowles; ***W:*** Bernard Knowles.

The Norman Conquests, Part 1: Table Manners **1978** Part one of playwright Alan Ayckbourn's comic trilogy of love unfulfilled, as the charmingly unreliable Norman (Conti) works his amorous wiles on three women. **108m/C; VHS, DVD.** *GB* Tom Conti; Richard Briers; Penelope Keith; David Troughton; Fiona Walker; Penelope Wilton; ***D:*** Herbert Wise; ***W:*** Alan Ayckbourn; ***C:*** Peter Coombs.

The Norman Conquests, Part 2: Living Together **1978** Part two concerns the happenings in the living room during Norman's disastrous weekend of unsuccessful seduction. **93m/C; VHS, DVD.** *GB* Tom Conti; Penelope Keith; Richard Briers; Fiona Walker; David Troughton; Penelope Wilton; ***D:*** Herbert Wise; ***W:*** Alan Ayckbourn; ***C:*** Peter Coombs.

The Norman Conquests, Part 3: Round and Round the Garden **1978** Part three concerns Norman's furtive appearance in the garden, which suggests that the weekend is going to misfire. **106m/C; VHS, DVD.** *GB* Tom Conti; Penelope Keith; Richard Briers; David Troughton; Fiona Walker; Penelope Wilton; ***D:*** Herbert Wise; ***W:*** Alan Ayckbourn; ***C:*** Mike Hobbs.

Norman, Is That You? **1/2** **1976** Unsuccessful film adaptation based on the unsuccessful Broadway play about one family's sexual revolution. Revamped by a host of black stars, it's basically a one-joke affair when Foxx discovers his son is gay and living with his white lover. Shot on videotape and transferred to film. **91m/C; VHS, Streaming.** Redd Foxx; Pearl Bailey; Dennis Dugan; Michael Warren; Tamara Dobson; Vernee Watson-Johnson; Jayne Meadows; George Furth; ***D:*** George Schlatter; ***W:*** George Schlatter; Ron Clark; Sam Bobrick; ***M:*** William Goldstein.

Norman Rockwell's Shuffleton's Barbershop *Shuffleton's Barbershop* **2013** In this predictable Hallmark Channel drama, country singer Trey Cole returns to the Georgia hometown he abandoned long ago. Memories resurface as he enters Charlie Shuffleton's barbershop--only to learn his mentor recently died. Terry knows he must deal with his own family and past hurts in order to honor Charlie's memory. Based on a Norman Rockwell painting. **84m/C; DVD.** Austin Stowell; Danny Glover; Dash Pledger-Levine; Brett Rice; Kayla Ewell; ***D:*** Mark Jean; ***W:*** John Wilder; ***C:*** Tom Harting; ***M:*** Lawrence Shragge. **CABLE**

North and South Book 1 **1985** Lavish spectacle about a friendship tested by the turbulent times leading up to Civil War. Orry Main (Swayze) is a South Carolina plantation owner while his best friend George Hazard (Read) comes from a Pennsylvania industrial family. Orry is also involved in a doomed romance with the beautiful Madeline (Down), who's forced to marry the odious Justin LaMotte (Carradine). Lots of intrigue and excitement. Based on the novel by John Jakes. Filmed on location in Charleston, South Carolina. Originally broadcast as a six-part TV miniseries. **561m/C; VHS, DVD.** Patrick Swayze; James Read; Lesley-Anne Down; David Carradine; Kirstie Alley; Jean Simmons; Inga Swenson; Jonathan Frakes; Genie Francis; Terri Garber; Georg Stanford Brown; Olivia Cole; David Ogden Stiers; Robert Guillaume; Hal Holbrook; Gene Kelly; Robert Mitchum; Johnny Cash; Elizabeth Taylor; ***M:*** Bill Conti.

North and South Book 2 **1986** Equally dramatic sequel follows the southern Main clan and the northern Hazard family into the Civil War as friendship and romance struggle to survive the fighting. Casnoff is a notable presence as the aptly named Bent, who will go to any length to settle old scores with both families. Based on the John Jakes novel "Love and War." Originally broadcast as a six-part TV miniseries. The last of the Jakes trilogy, "Heaven and Hell," was finally filmed for TV in '94 but proved a major disappointment. **570m/C; VHS, DVD.** Patrick Swayze; James Read; Lesley-Anne Down; Terri Garber; Genie Francis; Jean Simmons; Kirstie Alley; Philip Casnoff; Hal Holbrook; Lloyd Bridges; James Stewart; Morgan Fairchild; Nancy Marchand; Parker Stevenson; Lewis Smith; ***M:*** Bill Conti.

The North Avenue Irregulars **1/2** **1979 (G)** Slapstick Disney comedy along the same lines as some of their earlier laugh-fests. A priest and three members of the local ladies' club try to bust a crime syndicate. Though the premise is silly, there are still lots of laughs in this family film. **99m/C; VHS, DVD.** Edward Herrmann; Barbara Harris; Susan Clark; Karen Valentine; Michael Constantine; Cloris Leachman; Melora Hardin; Alan Hale, Jr.; Ruth Buzzi; Patsy Kelly; Virginia Capers; ***D:*** Bruce Bilson; ***W:*** Don Tait; ***C:*** Leonard J. South; ***M:*** Robert F. Brunner.

North by Northwest **1959** Self-assured Madison Avenue ad exec Roger Thornhill (Grant) inadvertently gets involved with international spies when they mistake him for someone else. His problems are compounded when he's framed for murder and winds up on a cross-country train trip with pretty Eve Kendall (Saint) who offers her help. The movie where Grant and Saint dangle from the faces of Mount Rushmore and a plane chases Grant through farm fields. Exceptional performances, particularly Grant's. Plenty of plot twists are mixed with tongue-in-cheek humor. **136m/C; VHS, DVD, Blu-Ray.** Cary Grant; Eva Marie Saint; James Mason; Leo G. Carroll; Martin Landau; Jessie Royce Landis; Philip Ober; Adam Williams; Josephine Hutchinson; Edward Platt; ***D:*** Alfred Hitchcock; ***W:*** Ernest Lehman; ***C:*** Robert Burks; ***M:*** Bernard Herrmann. AFI '98: Top 100; Natl. Film Reg. '95.

North Country **1/2** **2005 (R)** Theron de-glamorizes to play Josey Aimes, a hard luck single mom who returns to her Minnesota home town to make a new start. Since the best-paying jobs are working in the mines, Josey decides to become a miner. Eventually fed up with the blatant sexual harassment of her male co-workers and the indifference of her employer, Josey files the first class action lawsuit for sexual harassment in the country (the actual plaintiff, Lois Jenson, sued her employer in 1984). An old-fashioned exercise in social responsibility and the search for justice. **123m/C; DVD.** Charlize Theron; Frances McDormand; Sean Bean; Richard Jenkins; Jeremy Renner; Michelle Monaghan; Woody Harrelson; Sissy Spacek; Rusty Schwimmer; Jillian Armenante; Thomas Curtis; Elizabeth Peterson; Linda Emond; Amber Heard; Cole Williams; ***D:*** Niki Caro; ***W:*** Michael Seitzman; ***C:*** Chris Menges; ***M:*** Gustavo Santaolalla.

North Dallas Forty **1/2** **1979 (R)** Based on the novel by former Dallas Cowboy Peter Gent, the film focuses on the labor abuses in pro-football. One of the best football movies ever made, it contains searing commentary and very good acting, although the plot is sometimes dropped behind the line of scrimmage. **119m/C; VHS, DVD.** Nick Nolte; Mac Davis; Charles Durning; Bo Svenson; John Matuszak; Dayle Haddon; Steve Forrest; Dabney Coleman; G.D. Spradlin; ***D:*** Ted Kotcheff; ***W:*** Ted Kotcheff; Frank Yablans; ***C:*** Paul Lohmann; ***M:*** John Scott.

North Face *Nordwand* **2008** Icy period piece loosely based on the 1936 attempt to climb the north face of Switzerland's Eiger Mountain. Hoping to gain publicity before the Olympic games, the Third Reich recruits mountaineers Toni (Furmann) and Andi (Lukas) to climb the last unconquered peak of the Alps. Their struggles and setbacks are contrasted with the luxury and ease of the propaganda brigade sent to cover the ascent. Director Stolzl plays rather fast-and-loose with the facts to heighten the tension and tie his story in with the Nazi ideology pervading Germany. The action and drama are riveting when focused on the men on the mountain, however. German with subtitles. **126m/C; DVD, Blu-Ray, On Demand.** *GE* Benno Furmann; Florian Lukas; Johanna Wokalek; Simon Schwarz; Georg Friedrich; Ulrich Tukur; ***D:*** Philipp Stolzl; ***W:*** Philipp Stolzl; Christoph Silber; Rupert Henning; Johannes Naber; ***C:*** Kolja Brandt; ***M:*** Christian Kolonovits.

North Shore **1/2** **1987 (PG)** A young surfer from Arizona hits the beaches of Hawaii and discovers love, sex, and adventure. Only redeeming quality is surfing footage. **96m/C; VHS, DVD.** Matt Adler; Nia Peeples; John Philbin; Gregory Harrison; Christina Raines; ***D:*** Will Phelps.

The North Star *Armored Attack* **1943** Gripping war tale of Nazis over-running an eastern Russian city, with courageous villagers fighting back. Colorized version available. **108m/B; VHS, DVD, Blu-Ray.** Dana Andrews; Walter Huston; Anne Baxter; Farley Granger; Walter Brennan; Erich von Stroheim; Jack Perrin; Dean Jagger; ***D:*** Lewis Milestone; ***W:*** Lillian Hellman; ***C:*** James Wong Howe; ***M:*** Aaron Copland.

North Star **1/2** **1996 (R)** Formulaic actioner where no one seems very enthusiastic. Half-breed trapper Hudson Ipsehawk (Lambert) refuses to mine the gold on his Alaskan property because the land is considered sacred. This doesn't concern greedy miner Sean McLennon (Caan) who wants the property for himself. Oh yeah, there's also a babe, Sarah (McCormack), that both men are interested in. Norway substitutes for Alaska. Based on the novel by Will Henry. **89m/C; VHS, DVD.** Christopher Lambert; James Caan; Catherine McCormack; Burt Young; ***D:*** Nils Gaup; ***W:*** Paul Ohl; Sergio Donati; Lorenzo Donati; ***C:*** Bruno de Keyzer; ***M:*** Bruce Rowland.

The North Star **1/2** **2016** Based on a true story, explores the journey of two runaway slaves seeking their freedom. In 1849, Benjamin "Big Ben" Jones (Trotter) and Moses Hopkins (Bartley) experience cruelty as slaves on a Virginia plantation. When Ben learns he will be sold to a new owner, he and Moses decide to run to freedom in the free state of Pennsylvania. Though they are pursued by slave hunters, the pair has benevolent assistance from the underground railroad. Welcomed by kind abolitionists at a church in Pennsylvania, Ben and Moses experience the life as free men yet the complexities of life as an African American in this time period. **88m/C; DVD, Streaming, Download.** Jeremiah Trotter; Thomas C. Bartley; Clifton Powell; John Diehl; Keith David; ***D:*** Thomas K. Philips; ***W:*** Thomas K. Philips; Tim O'Connell; ***C:*** Keiko Nakahara. **VIDEO**

North to Alaska **1960** A gold prospector encounters many problems when he agrees to pick up his partner's fiancee in Seattle to bring her home to Nome, Alaska, in the 1890s. Overly slapstick at times, but great fun nonetheless. Loosely based on Laszlo Fodor's play "The Birthday Gift." **120m/C; VHS, DVD, Blu-Ray.** John Wayne; Stewart Granger; Ernie Kovacs; Fabian; Capucine; ***D:*** Henry Hathaway; ***C:*** Leon Shamroy.

North West Frontier **1/2** *Flame Over India* **1959** Muslim rebels intend to kill a 6-year-old Hindu child to end the royal line, and a Captain of the British forces is asked to escort him to safety. But he's told the only way out is through rebel territory on an old rickety train. He still takes the job, unlike most people who would run away screaming. **129m/C; DVD.** *GB* Kenneth More; Lauren Bacall; Herbert Lom; Wilfrid Hyde-White; I.S. Johar; Ursula Jeans; Eugene Deckers; Ian Hunter; Jack (Gwyllam) Gwillim; Govind Raja Ross; ***D:*** J. Lee Thompson; ***W:*** Robin Estridge; Patrick Ford; Will Price; ***C:*** Geoffrey Unsworth; ***M:*** Mischa Spoliansky.

Northanger Abbey **1/2** **1987** Catherine is a young woman whose head is turned by her romance readings of dark secrets, sinister castles, dashing heroes, and helpless women. When the handsome Henry Tilney invites her to visit his ancestral home, Northanger Abbey, it seems all her fancies have come to life. A somewhat tepid adaptation of Jane Austen's parody of the popular Gothic romances of her day. **90m/C; VHS, DVD.** *GB* Peter Firth; Katherine Schlesinger; Googie Withers; Robert Hardy; *D:* Giles Foster; *W:* Maggie Wadey; *C:* Nat Crosby; *M:* Ilona Sekacz.

Northanger Abbey ♪♪ 1/2 **2007** Spirited teenager Catherine Morland (Jones) has an over-active imagination, fueled by the popular gothic romances she reads. Taken to fashionable Bath by family friends, Catherine falls in with two different families: the Thorpes and the Tilneys. Catherine becomes romantically interested in gentle Henry Tilney (Field) and is invited to their rather sinister family estate. Carried away by her surroundings, Catherine thoughtlessly upsets Henry and is then left to wonder about her future. Based on the novel by Jane Austen. **90m/C; DVD.** *GB* Felicity Jones; J.J. Feild; Carey Mulligan; Catherine Walker; Liam Cunningham; Hugh O'Connor; Sophie Vavasseur; Sylvestria Le Touzel; William Beck; Mark Dymond; Shauna Taylor; Desmond Barrit; Julia Dearden; *Nar:* Geraldine James; *D:* Jon Jones; *W:* Andrew Davies; *C:* Ciaran Tanham; *M:* Sue Wyatt. **TV**

Northern Extremes ♪ 1/2 *Buried on Sunday* **1993 (PG)** Silly comedy about an eccentric Canadian island village whose fishing livelihood is threatened. So the town mayor captures an errant nuclear submarine and uses it as a big bargaining chip. Filmed in Nova Scotia, Canada. **80m/C; VHS, DVD.** *CA* Paul Gross; Denise Virieux; Henry Czerny; Jeff Leder; Tommy Sexton; Louis Del Grande; Maury Chaykin; *D:* Paul Donovan; *W:* Bill Fleming.

Northern Lights ♪♪ **2009** Romantic suspense from Lifetime that's based on the book by Nora Roberts. After a tragedy, Baltimore detective Nate Burns (Cibrian) takes a job as the new sheriff of Lunacy, Alaska. When a long-dead body is found in a mountain cave, it's identified as the father of bush pilot Meg (Rimes)?a man everyone assumed ran out on his family. The murder stirs up long-buried secrets as well as feelings between Nate and Meg. **90m/C; DVD.** LeAnn Rimes; Eddie Cibrian; Rosanna Arquette; Greg Lawson; Jayne (Jane) Eastwood; Adrian Hough; Christianne Hirt; *D:* Mike Robe; *W:* Janet Brownell; *C:* Craig Wrobleski; *M:* Chris P. Bacon; Stuart M. Thomas. **CABLE**

Northern Pursuit ♪♪ 1/2 **1943** A Canadian Mountie disguises himself to infiltrate a Nazi spy ring in this exciting adventure film. Based on Leslie White's "Five Thousand Trojan Horses." **94m/B; VHS, DVD.** Errol Flynn; Helmut Dantine; Julie Bishop; Gene Lockhart; Tom Tully; *D:* Raoul Walsh.

Northfork ♪♪ **2003 (PG-13)** Surrealistic fairy tale, with pretensions of examining death and the afterlife, crossed with comical Americana circa 1955. The town of Northfolk is being evacuated to make way for an incoming hydroelectric plant, as a band of strange gypsy angels search for the "unknown angel," thought to be a sick orphan boy who has been left to the town preacher. Patchwork script is a jumble of pompous spiritual pronouncements, kitschy sitcom dialogue, and Lynchian confusion. At least the beautifully-filmed landscape gives you something nice to look at while wondering what the heck is going on. **103m/C; DVD.** James Woods; Nick Nolte; Claire Forlani; Duel Farnes; Mark Polish; Daryl Hannah; Ben Foster; Anthony Edwards; Robin Sachs; Graham Beckel; Peter Coyote; Jon(athan) Gries; Marshall Bell; Kyle MacLachlan; Michele Hicks; Josh Barker; *D:* Michael Polish; *W:* Mark Polish; Michael Polish; *C:* M. David Mullen; *M:* Stuart Matthewman.

Northman: A Viking Saga ♪♪ 1/2 **2015 (R)** An action-adventure drama about a ninth-century Viking experience in the British Isles. A group of Vikings travels to Britain with the goal of plundering the rich monasteries of the north. When their ship gets caught in a storm, it is broken to pieces on the rocks off the coast of Scotland. No Viking settlements yet exist in Scotland, but the Vikings seize the opportunity presented to them. They make the daughter of the Scottish king their hostage and demand a ransom for her return. In turn, the king sends mercenaries to attack them. As the Vikings take their hostage through the highlands to evade the mercenaries, they are in a race against time. **97m/C; DVD, Blu-Ray, Download.** Ed Skrein; James Norton; Ryan Kwanten; Tom Hopper; Ken Duken; *D:* Claudio Fah; *W:* Bastian Zach; Matthias Bauer; *C:* Lorenzo Senatore; *M:* Marcus Trumpp.

Northpole ♪♪ 1/2 **2014 (G)** Santa Claus' hometown is powered by holiday happiness that is in increasingly short supply given the frantic pace of everyday lives. Single mom Chelsea is stressed by her new reporter's job and 10-year-old son Kevin and his vivid imagination, which involves elves and sleigh rides. But Chelsea's the one who needs to believe. From the Hallmark Channel. **80m/C; DVD.** Tiffani(-Amber) Thiessen; Max Charles; Josh Charles; Bailee Madison; Candice Glover; Robert Wagner; Jill St. John; *D:* Douglas Barr; *W:* Gregg Rossen; Brian Sawyer; *C:* Pierre Jodoin; *M:* James Gelfand. **CABLE**

Northville Cemetery Massacre ♪ *The Northfield Cemetery Massacre* **1976 (R)** Gang of bikers comes to town and all hell breaks loose. The result is a horribly bloody war between the townsfolk and the gang. Yup, it was a massacre. **81m/C; VHS, DVD.** David Hyry; Craig Collicott; Jan Sisk; Carson Jackson; *D:* William Dear; Thomas L. Dyke; *C:* William Dear; Thomas L. Dyke; *M:* Michael Nesmith.

Northwest Passage ♪♪♪ **1940** The lavish first half of a projected two-film package based on Kenneth Roberts' popular novel, depicting the troop of Rogers' Rangers fighting the wilderness and hostile Indians. Beautifully produced; the second half was never made and the passage itself is never seen. **126m/C; VHS, DVD, Streaming.** Spencer Tracy; Robert Young; Ruth Hussey; Walter Brennan; Nat Pendleton; Robert Barrat; Lumsden Hare; *D:* King Vidor.

Northwest Trail ♪♪ **1946** Royal Canadian Mountie Steele's assignment is to escort Woodbury across the wilderness. She's carrying a large sum of money to save her uncle's business. Problem is, killers are on their trail. **75m/C; VHS, DVD.** Bob Steele; Joan Woodbury; John Litel; Raymond Hatton; Madge Bellamy; Charles Middleton; *D:* Derwin Abrahams.

Nosferatu the Vampyre ♪♪ *Nosferatu: Phantom der Nacht* **1979** Herzog's tribute to fellow countryman's F.W. Murnau's 1922 silent film interpretation of Bram Stoker's "Dracula" story. It features Kinski as the disgustingly rodent-like Count, with Ganz as Jonathan Harker, and Adjani as Harker's wife and the beautiful object of the Count's lust. Released in a German language version with subtitles and an English language version. **107m/C; VHS, DVD, Blu-Ray.** *FR GE* Klaus Kinski; Isabelle Adjani; Bruno Ganz; Roland Topor; Walter Ladengast; *D:* Werner Herzog; *W:* Werner Herzog; *C:* Jorge Schmidt-Reitwein; *M:* Popul Vuh; Florian Fricke.

Nostalghia ♪♪ **1983** Russian academic Jankovsky comes to Tuscany to research the life of an 18th-century composer and meets the mysterious Josephson, who's convinced the end of the world is near. And soon the homesick Russian is in a search for himself. Filled with Christian iconography and some extraordinary images. Tarkovsky's first film outside his native Russia. Russian and Italian with subtitles; the Russian sequences are filmed in B&W. **126m/C; VHS, DVD, Blu-Ray.** *IT* Oleg (Yankovsky) Jankowsky; Erland Josephson; Domiziana Giordano; Delia Boccardo; *D:* Andrei Tarkovsky; *W:* Andrei Tarkovsky; Tonino Guerra; *C:* Giuseppe Lanci.

Nostalgia ♪♪ **2018 (R)** A dramatic anthology exploring the power of the past. Widower Ronnie (Dern) stores a lifetime of objects in his Los Angeles home. His granddaughter (Tamblyn) asks insurance assessor Daniel (Ortiz) to see if anything has value. Daniel then visits widow Helen (Burstyn), who managed to save a Ted Williams signed baseball as her home burned down. Helen takes the ball to sports memorabilia dealer Will (Hamm) to get an estimate of its worth. Already grieving the end to his marriage, Will faces a new tragedy while cleaning out his childhood home. Though it has its moments, it falls short of being profound. **114m/C; DVD, Blu-Ray.** Jon Hamm; Catherine Keener; Ellen Burstyn; Bruce Dern; Nick Offerman; *D:* Mark Pellington; *W:* Alex Ross Perry; *C:* Matt Sakatani Roe; *M:* Laurent Eyquem.

The Nostradamus Kid ♪♪ **1992 (R)** Young man, convinced the world is about to end, decides his last goal will be to make love (for the first time) with his girlfriend. **120m/C; DVD.** Noah Taylor; Miranda Otto; Arthur Dignam; *D:* Bob Ellis; *W:* Bob Ellis; *C:* Geoff Burton; *M:* Chris Neal.

Not Another B Movie ♪ 1/2 **2010** In this Troma comedy, screenwriter Byron, director Larry, and producer James are meeting to discuss their latest low-budget exploitation flick. Byron wants to class things up but the other men just want to make money. As they talk about the script, various scenes come to life and get crazier the further away they get from the original idea. Angling for a part in whatever they decide to film is waitress/wannabe actress Holly. **85m/C; DVD.** Byron Thames; Larry Thomas; James Vallo; Lindsay Gareth; David Faustino; Joe Estevez; Erin Moran; Ed Asner; *D:* John Wesley Norton; *W:* John Wesley Norton; *C:* John Klein; *M:* Alan Jones. **VIDEO**

Not Another Happy Ending ♪ **2013** Poorly done rom com with irritating characters. Glasgow writer Jane had a big success with her first novel but has writer's block trying to finish her second book. This is causing major issues for her desperate publisher Tom, who decides the problem is Jane is too happy. He sets out to make her life miserable so she'll concentrate on her career and not her love life. **102m/C; DVD.** *UK* Karen Gillan; Stanley Weber; Henry Ian Cusick; Ian De Caestecker; Gary Lewis; *D:* John McKay; *W:* David Solomons; *C:* George Geddes; *M:* Lorne Balfe. **VIDEO**

Not Another Teen Movie ♪ 1/2 **2001 (R)** Unsuccessful parody of bad teen movies and the better John Hughes films of the '80s. Teen stereotypes are hammed up to the extreme, from the bitchy teenager to the dumb jock, nerdy beauty-in-waiting and fat guy for comic relief. Really obvious, unoriginal humor, including many bodily-function and base sexual jokes. Entertaining cameos by Molly Ringwald and John Vernon, though. **90m/C; DVD, Blu-Ray, UMD.** Chyler Leigh; Chris Evans; Eric Jungmann; Eric Christian Olsen; Cody McMains; Sam Huntington; Ron Lester; Samm Levine; Deon Richmond; Jaime Pressly; Lacey Chabert; Joanna Garcia; Mia Kirshner; *D:* Joel Gallen; *W:* Phil Beauman; Michael G. Bender; Adam Jay Epstein; Andrew Jacobson; Buddy Johnson; *C:* Reynaldo Villalobos; *M:* Theodore Shapiro.

Not as a Stranger ♪♪ 1/2 **1955** Glossy film about the medical profession and the varying degrees of dedication shown by doctors. Mitchum stars as an medical student who can't afford to pay his tuition, so he marries nurse de Havilland and continues going to school on her money, although their relationship is far from being a loving one. Producer Kramer's directorial debut. Based on the book by Morton Thompson. **135m/B; VHS, DVD, Blu-Ray.** Olivia de Havilland; Robert Mitchum; Frank Sinatra; Gloria Grahame; Broderick Crawford; Charles Bickford; Myron McCormick; Lon Chaney, Jr.; *D:* Stanley Kramer; *W:* Edward Anhalt.

Not Easily Broken ♪ 1/2 **2009 (PG-13)** Dave Johnson (Chestnut) is a remodeling contractor toiling in the shadow of his formidable wife Clarice (Henson), a successful real estate agent. Clarice and her live-in mom (Lewis) don't miss a beat in pointing out Dave's shortfalls, placing the marriage under constant strain. When Clarice is injured in an auto accident, Dave finds himself smitten by Clarice's single-mom physical therapist. Based on the book by T.D. Jakes, this marriage melodrama's attempt in spreading the bishop's theological message into the mainstream falls flat with zip for character development and a plodding, predictable plot. **100m/C; DVD, Blu-Ray, On Demand.** Morris Chestnut; Taraji P. Henson; Maeve Quinlan; Cannon Jay; Jenifer Lewis; Kevin Hart; Wood Harris; Eddie Cibrian; Niecy Nash; Albert Hall; *D:* Bill Duke; *W:* Brian Bird; *C:* Geary McLeod; *M:* Kurt Farquhar.

Not Fade Away ♪♪ 1/2 **2012 (R)** The Sopranos mastermind David Chase makes his big-screen debut with this heartfelt ode to a time when rock 'n' roll music was the chosen tool of youth expression. Magaro stars as the potential rock star in this tale of teen life in the 1960s in New Jersey as adolescence, responsibility, love, and friendship all came with a backbeat inspired by The Beatles, The Rolling Stones, and the other bands taking the world by storm. Chase has a nice, gentle touch with character but the film lacks focus, often feeling at arm's length when a warmer approach would have helped make the beat more memorable. **112m/C; DVD, Blu-Ray.** John Magaro; Jack Huston; Will Brill; James Gandolfini; Bella Heathcote; Christopher McDonald; Brad Garrett; *D:* David Chase; *W:* David Chase; *C:* Eigil Bryld.

Not for Publication ♪♪ **1984 (R)** A woman working as both a tabloid reporter and a mayoral campaign worker uncovers governmental corruption with the help of a shy photographer and a midget. Meant to be on par with older screwball comedies but lacking the wit and subtlety. **87m/C; VHS, DVD.** Nancy Allen; David Naughton; Richard Paul; Alice Ghostley; Laurence Luckinbill; *D:* Paul Bartel; *W:* Paul Bartel.

Not Forgotten ♪♪ **2009 (R)** Solid little thriller about the sins of the father. Businessman Jack Bishop (Baker) lives with his family in the border town of Del Rio, Texas. His 11-year-old daughter Toby (Moretz) goes missing and is presumed kidnapped and Jack crosses into Mexico in his search, but it seems his past isn't as squeaky-clean as everyone believes. **100m/C; DVD.** Simon Baker; Paz Vega; Chloë Grace Moretz; Michael Delorenzo; Ken Davitian; Mark Rolston; Gedde Watanabe; Claire Forlani; Benito Martinez; *D:* Dror Soref; *W:* Tomas Romero; *C:* Steven Bernstein; *M:* Mark Isham; Cynthia O'Connor.

Not Like Everyone Else ♪♪ **2006** Native American 15-year-old Brandi Blackbear (Shawkat) lashes out after being taunted at her Oklahoma high school and her injudicious remarks result in a modern-day witch hunt in this true story. A teacher's sudden illness and a notebook of Brandi's writings cause hysteria and her family must involve the ACLU in order to protect Brandi's civil rights after she is accused of witchcraft. **90m/C; DVD.** Alia Shawkat; Illeana Douglas; Eric Schweig; Ritchie Montgomery; Gary Grubbs; Lucas Till; *D:* Tom McLoughlin; *W:* Jamie Pachino; *C:* Lloyd Ahern, II; *M:* Sean Callery. **CABLE**

Not My Life ♪ 1/2 **2006** Alison's (Monroe) obsessed doctor kidnaps and drugs her so she forgets her past. Because of her amnesia, Alison believes Steve (Cohen) when he tells her about their married life but when her memories start returning, Alison turns to a PI to find the truth. **90m/C; DVD.** Meredith Monroe; Ari Cohen; Michael Woods; Ellie Harvie; Iris Paluly; *D:* John Terlesky; *W:* Paul A. Birkett; *C:* C. Kim Miles; *M:* Claude Foisy. **CABLE**

Not Now Darling ♪ 1/2 **1973** Silly British sex farce. Lecherous London furrier Gilbert Bodley (Phillips) wants to sell gangster Harry McMichael (Nesbitt) an expensive coat for his wife Janie (Ege) since Gilbert wants to make Janie his mistress. McMichael buys the fur, but for his own girlfriend Sue (Windsor). From there it's on to scantily-clad women hiding in closets, jealous spouses, and various other troubles. **97m/C; DVD.** *GB* Leslie Phillips; Julie Ege; Derren Nesbitt; Barbara Windsor; Moira Lister; *D:* Ray Cooney; *W:* Ray Cooney; *C:* John Rook; Alan Hume; *M:* Cyril Ornadel.

Not of This Earth ♪♪ 1/2 **1957** Sci-fi take on the vampire myth? Cold War paranoia? Did producer/director Corman and writers Griffith and Hanna really have an agenda or were they just making another B&W sci-fi quickie? However it's meant, this alien flick is effective. Paul Johnson (Birch) wears a dark suit and cool sunglasses and hires nurse Nadine (Garland) to give him constant blood transfusions. Seems Johnson is an alien from the planet Davana where his race is dying because they need fresh blood—and any way he can get the human kind will do just fine. Remade in 1988 and 1995. **67m/B; DVD.** Paul Birch; Beverly Garland; William Roerick; Morgan Jones; Jonathan Haze; Dick Miller; *D:* Roger Corman; *W:* Charles B. Griffith; Mark Hanna; *C:* John Mescall; *M:* Ronald Stein.

Not of This Earth 🦴 1/2 **1988 (R)** In a remake of the 1957 Roger Corman quickie, an alien wearing sunglasses makes an unfriendly trip to Earth. In order to save his dying planet he needs major blood donations from unsuspecting Earthlings. Not a match for the original version, some may nevertheless want to see ex-porn star Lords in her role as the nurse. **92m/C; VHS, DVD.** Traci Lords; Arthur Roberts; Lenny Juliano; Rebecca Perle; Ace Mask; Roger Lodge; Michael Delano; Monique Gabrielle; Becky LeBeau; ***D:*** Jim Wynorski; ***W:*** Jim Wynorski; R.J. Robertson; Charles B. Griffith; Mark Hanna; ***C:*** Zoran Hochstatter; ***M:*** Chuck Cirino.

Not of This Earth 🦴🦴 **1996 (R)** Corman remake of his own 1957 cheapie is both camp and sexy. Sunglass-wearing mystery millionaire Paul Johnson (York) apparently suffers from a rare condition and must have constant blood transfusions, so he hires a sexy live-in nurse (Barondes) to be at his beck-and-call. Yes, he does turn out to be a vampire but of the space alien-with-telepathic-powers variety who has a particular purpose for coming to earth. **92m/C; VHS, DVD.** Michael York; Elizabeth Barondes; Richard Belzer; Parker Stevenson; ***D:*** Terence H. Winkless; ***W:*** Charles Philip Moore. **CABLE**

Not of This World 🦴🦴 1/2 *Fuori dal Mondo* **1999** Sister Caterina (Buy) is about to take her final vows when she discovers an abandoned baby. She takes the baby to a hospital, learning the child will be put up for adoption. Caterina has a surge of maternal feelings and decides to search for the baby's parents, eventually finding Ernesto (Orlando), the middle-aged owner of a local laundry who suspects he may be the baby's father. The duo both take long looks at their lives and wonder if they should make some changes. Italian with subtitles. **100m/C; VHS, DVD.** *IT* Margherita Buy; Silvio Orlando; Carolina Freschi; Maria Cristina Minerva; ***D:*** Giuseppe Piccioni; ***W:*** Gualtiero Rosella; Giuseppe Piccioni; Lucia Maria Zei; ***C:*** Luca Bigazzi; ***M:*** Ludovico Einaudi.

Not One Less 🦴🦴 1/2 *Yi Ge Dou Bu Neng Shao* **1999 (G)** Gao is teaching in a rundown rural Chinese school when he is called away to visit his dying mother. The only substitute he can find is 13-year-old Wei Minzhi, who's scarcely older than her would-be students. Because so many children are forced to leave school because of their poverty-stricken families, Gao promises the girl extra money if she will keep all the pupils in class until he returns. When Zhang Huike must go to work in the city, Wei Minzhi is stubbornly determined to find and bring him back. Mandarin with subtitles. **106m/C; DVD.** *CH* Wei Minzhi; Zhang Huike; Gao Enman; ***D:*** Yimou Zhang; ***W:*** Shi Xiangsheng; ***C:*** Hou Yong; ***M:*** San Bao.

Not Quite Paradise 🦴 *Not Quite Jerusalem* **1986 (R)** A young American medical student falls in love with a young Israeli girl living on a kibbutz. **106m/C; VHS, DVD.** Sam Robards; Joanna Pacula; ***D:*** Lewis Gilbert.

Not Since You 🦴🦴 **2009 (PG-13)** A group of once-close college friends, who graduated from NYU in 2001, reunite for a weekend wedding in Athens, Georgia (though the wedding itself is unimportant to the plot). Sam hasn't been in contact since graduation but has never forgotten his feelings for onetime love Amy, who's not-so-contentedly married to Ryan. While she dithers, unresolved emotional conflicts surface among the others as well. **88m/C; DVD.** Desmond Harrington; Kathleen Robertson; Christian Kane; Jon Abrahams; Will Estes; Sunny Mabrey; Barry Corbin; Sara Rue; Elden (Ratliff) Henson; ***D:*** Jeff Stephenson; ***W:*** Jeff Stephenson; Jane Kelly Kosek; Brent Laffoon; ***C:*** Helge Gerull; ***M:*** Christopher Brody.

Not So Dusty 🦴 1/2 **1956** Director Rogers remade his own 1936 comedy but it's a tired affair the second time around. Cockney dustbin collectors Dusty (Owen) and Nobby (Dwyer) find a book in the trash that turns out to be quite valuable. Apparently thrown away by accident, its owners want it back before it can be sold but it's finders-keepers as far as the workers are concerned. **80m/B; DVD.** *GB* Bill Owen; Leslie Dwyer; Dandy Nichols; Roddy Hughes; Ellen Pollock; ***D:*** Maclean Rogers; ***W:*** Maclean Rogers; ***C:*** James Wilson; ***M:*** Wilfred Burns.

Not Suitable for Children 🦴 1/2 **2012** Lowbrow Aussie comedy. Jonah, Gus, and Stevie share a Sydney house and a party lifestyle until Jonah learns he has testicular cancer. After the operation, he'll be infertile, so in the intervening weeks, Jonah decides it's baby-making time if he can just find a woman to cooperate. **96m/C; DVD, Blu-Ray.** *AU* Ryan Kwanten; Ryan Corr; Sarah Snook; Bojana Novakovic; Kathryn Beck; Lewis Fitz-Gerald; ***D:*** Peter Templeman; ***W:*** Michael Lucas; ***C:*** Lachlan Milne; ***M:*** Matteo Zingales.

Not Tonight Darling 🦴 **1972 (R)** A bored suburban housewife becomes involved with a fast-talking businessman who leads her into a web of deceit and blackmail. **90m/C; VHS, DVD.** *GB* Luan Peters; Vincent Ball; Jason Twelvetrees; James Hayter; ***D:*** Anthony Sloman; ***W:*** Christopher Gregory; James Pillock; ***C:*** Harry Waxman.

Not Without My Daughter 🦴🦴 1/2 **1990 (PG-13)** Overwrought drama shot in Israel about American Field, who travels with her Arab husband and their daughter to his native Iran, where (he must have forgotten to tell her) she has no rights. He decides the family will stay, using beatings and confinement to persuade his uncooperative wife, but she risks all to escape with daughter. Based on the true story of Betty Mahmoody. **116m/C; VHS, DVD, Blu-Ray.** Sally Field; Alfred Molina; Sheila Rosenthal; Roshan Seth; Sarah Badel; Mony Rey; Georges Corraface; ***D:*** Brian Gilbert; ***W:*** David W. Rintels; ***C:*** Peter Hannan; ***M:*** Jerry Goldsmith.

The Note 🦴🦴 1/2 **2007** Widowed newspaper columnist Peyton Macgruder (Francis) may get the axe unless her readership picks up. When an airplane crashes nearby, Peyton goes to the site but is uncomfortable trying to get a story. Later she returns and finds a note in the debris that seems to have been written by a passenger to his child. Peyton wants to give the note to the intended recipient and makes her search the subject of her increasingly popular columns. Where the truth leads her, however, turns out to be very personal indeed. A Hallmark Channel original. **87m/C; DVD.** Genie Francis; Ted McGinley; Richard Leacock; Rick Roberts; Maria Ricossa; Katie Boland; Heather Hanson; Ginelle Williams; ***D:*** Douglas Barr; ***W:*** Paul W. Cooper; ***C:*** Derick Underschultz; ***M:*** Eric Allaman. **CABLE**

The Note 2: Taking a Chance on Love 🦴🦴 1/2 *Taking a Chance on Love* **2009** In this sequel to 2007's "The Note," sports writer King (McGinley) proposes to relationship-columnist Peyton (Francis) who tells him she needs to think about it. Peyton has commitment and family issues but swapping stories with a regretful reader who didn't follow her heart may help her make up her mind. **88m/C; DVD.** Genie Francis; Ted McGinley; Katie Boland; Genelle Williams; Maria Ricossa; ***D:*** Douglas Barr; ***W:*** Douglas Barr; ***C:*** Peter Benison; ***M:*** Eric Allaman. **CABLE**

The Note 3: Notes from the Heart Healer 🦴🦴 1/2 *Notes from the Heart Healer* **2012** From the Hallmark Channel. King Danville (McGinley) surprises his journalist wife Peyton MacGruder (Francis) by taking her on a cottage getaway for their first anniversary. They both get a surprise when Peyton finds a baby abandoned on their doorstep. Peyton tries to find the mother and is confronted by unexpected maternal feelings and her own painful memories. **87m/C; DVD; Closed Captioned.** Genie Francis; Ted McGinley; Laci Mailey; Brenda Crichlow; Rob Morton; ***D:*** Douglas Barr; ***W:*** Douglas Barr; ***C:*** Peter Benison; ***M:*** Hal Beckett. **CABLE**

The Notebook 🦴🦴 **2004 (PG-13)** An elderly man (Garner) tries patiently to reawaken his beloved wife's (Rowlands) failing memory of their life together by reading the story to her. Flashbacks detail their youthful romance. The story of the young lovers is romantic cliche in which noble blue collar boy (Gosling) overreaches his station, but pretty rich girl (McAdams) just can't help herself. They love, they lose one another, they're reunited again. When Garner and Rowlands share the screen there's true magic. Their chemistry is genuine and finally heartbreaking and too little time is spent exploring it. A frustrating schizophrenic letdown. **120m/C; DVD, Blu-Ray.** Rachel McAdams; Ryan Gosling; Gena Rowlands; James Garner; Joan Allen; James Marsden; Kevin Connolly; Sam Shepard; ***D:*** Nick Cassavetes; ***W:*** Jan Sardi; Jeremy Leven; ***C:*** Robert Fraisse; ***M:*** Aaron Zigman.

The Notebook 🦴🦴 1/2 *A Nagy Fuzet* **2013 (R)** An odd Hungarian WWII fairy tale following the misadventures of 13-year-old identical twin boys, simply credited as One (András Gyémánt) and Other (László Gyémánt). Sent off to live with their wicked grandmother (Molnár), the boys' behavior gets increasingly stranger and jaded as they adjust to the weirdoes around them. Their one task is to document everything that happens in a notebook. A surreal dark comedy that is a constant string of surprises; one minute light and playful, the next minute heavy and grave. Wartime criticism is rarely this fresh and off-kilter. **109m/C; DVD.** *HU GE* Andras Gyemant; Laszlo Gyemant; Piroska Molmar; Ulrich Thomsen; ***D:*** Janos Szasz; ***W:*** Janos Szasz; Andras Szeker; ***C:*** Christian Berger; ***M:*** Johan Johannson.

Notebook 🦴🦴 **2019** When military veteran Kabir (Iqbal) takes a position as a teacher in a secluded area of Kashmir, he struggles with his new life and new job. His life changes when he finds a notebook used by the school's previous teacher Firdous (Bahl) as a diary. As Kabir reads her emotional, passionate words, he is both inspired as a teacher and develops romantic feelings for her. An adaptation of the 2014 Thai film "The Teacher's Diary," the romantic drama has an uninspiring script despite the interesting concept. However, both Iqbal and Bahl give memorable performances and the Kashmir setting is beautifully depicted. Hindi with subtitles. **115m/C; DVD.** Zaheer Iqbal; Pranutan Bahl; Mir Mohammed Mehroos; Mir Mohammed Zayan; Soliha Maqbool; ***D:*** Nitin Kakkar; ***W:*** Darab Farooqui; ***C:*** Manoj Kumar Khatoi; ***M:*** Vishal Mishra.

Notes from Underground 🦴🦴 **1995** Modern adaptation of the Dostoevsky novella has Czerny starring as a nameless, alienated civil servant who can only find pleasure in the petty torments his job allows him to inflict on others. Everything he does to broaden his world backfires in humiliating ways. Most of the film consists of monologues that Czerny records on a homevideo camera as he recalls the worst moments in his life. Fortunately, Czerny is up to the nearly one-man task of carrying this odd film. **90m/C; VHS, DVD.** Henry Czerny; Sheryl Lee; Jon Favreau; Charles (Charlie) Stratton; ***D:*** Gary Walkow; ***W:*** Gary Walkow; ***C:*** Dan Gillham; ***M:*** Mark Governor.

Notes on a Scandal 🦴🦴🦴 **2006 (R)** Compelling look at obsession based on Zoe Heller's 2003 novel. Attractive Sheba Hart (Blanchett) is a novice art teacher given guidance by acerbic veteran Barbara Covett (Dench). Sheba has a vague dissatisfaction with her comfortable life, which leads her into a relationship with her very willing 15-year-old pupil Steven (Simpson). When the bitter, lonely Barbara discovers Sheba's indiscretion, she ruthlessly blackmails Sheba to tether the younger woman to her. Eventually, self-destructive Sheba has enough until the inevitable showdown. Disturbing and dazzling, thanks to the no-holds-barred performances of both Dench and Blanchett. **91m/C; DVD, Blu-Ray.** *GB US* Dame Judi Dench; Cate Blanchett; Bill Nighy; Andrew Simpson; Juno Temple; Max Lewis; ***D:*** Richard Eyre; ***W:*** Patrick Marber; ***C:*** Chris Menges; ***M:*** Philip Glass.

Nothin' 2 Lose 🦴 1/2 **2000** Kwame (Hooks) can't bring him himself to commit to marriage with his girlfriend, Yasmine (Bayete). He prefers to spend his time hanging with his friends, gambling on playground basketball games, and chattering illiterate gibberish about all things inane. Racist language serves for humor and women serve as objects in what proves to be a sad excuse for an urban comedy. **100m/C; DVD.** Brian Hooks; Shani Bayete; Cedric Pendleton; Crystal Sessoms; Michael A. LeMelle; Martin C. Jones; Rodney J. Hobbs; Sekenia Williams; Malik Jones; ***D:*** Barry Bowles; ***W:*** Barry Bowles.

Nothing but a Man 🦴🦴 1/2 **1964** Duff Anderson (Dixon) is a black laborer trying to make a life in a small Alabama town. He falls for the daughter of a minister, they marry, and he gets a job at a local sawmill. When he won't bend to his racist white employers, he's fired and labeled a troublemaker. Unsentimental depiction of the times. **95m/B; VHS, DVD.** Ivan Dixon; Abbey Lincoln; Gloria Foster; Julius W. Harris; Martin Priest; Yaphet Kotto; Leonard Parker; Stanley Greene; Helen Lounck; Helene Arrindell; ***D:*** Michael Roemer; ***W:*** Michael Roemer; Robert M. Young; ***C:*** Robert M. Young. Natl. Film Reg. '93.

Nothing But the Night 🦴 1/2 *The Devil's Undead; The Resurrection Syndicate* **1972 (PG)** Lee's company produced this convoluted story of orphans who are victims of a cult that uses them in their quest for immortality. **90m/C; VHS, DVD.** *GB* Christopher Lee; Peter Cushing; Diana Dors; Georgia Brown; Keith Barron; Fulton Mackay; Gwyneth Strong; John Robinson; ***D:*** Peter Sasdy.

Nothing But the Truth 🦴🦴 1/2 **1941** Stockbroker Steve Bennett (Hope) is the new guy at his Miami firm where he's approached by Gwen (Goddard), the niece of his boss T.T. Ralston (Arnold). She's raised $10,000 for charity and wants Steve to double the money since her uncle has promised to match the sum. Except Ralston is trying to welsh on his promise by betting Steve that he can't tell the truth for 24 hours, which gets Steve into all sorts of trouble. The third Hope/Goddard pairing. **90m/B; DVD.** Bob Hope; Paulette Goddard; Edward Arnold; Leif Erickson; Glenn Anders; Willie Best; Helen Vinson; ***D:*** Elliott Nugent; ***W:*** Don Hartman; Ken Englund; ***C:*** Charles B(ryant) Lang, Jr.

Nothing But the Truth 🦴🦴🦴 **2008 (R)** Very loosely based on the courtroom spectacle following the leak of CIA operative Valerie Plame's identity after her husband, a U.S. ambassador, publicly refuted President Bush's claim that Saddam Hussein was trying to buy uranium for nuclear weapons. Here, journalist Rachel (Beckinsale) leaks the classified CIA identity and is heavily prosecuted by the feds, represented in court by lawyer Patton Dubois (Dillon). Jailed for refusing to reveal her source, much like real-life New York Times reporter Judith Miller, her newspaper hires hotshot defense attorney Albert Burnside (Alda). Focused docudrama keeps to the cold, hard plotpoints and excels with its veteran cast. **108m/C; DVD, On Demand.** Kate Beckinsale; Matt Dillon; Alan Alda; Vera Farmiga; Angela Bassett; David Schwimmer; Courtney B. Vance; Noah Wyle; Floyd Abrams; ***D:*** Rod Lurie; ***W:*** Rod Lurie; ***C:*** Alik Sakharov; ***M:*** Lawrence Nash Groupe.

Nothing But Trouble 🦴🦴 1/2 **1944** Laurel & Hardy's last film for MGM is a complicated tale of two servants who wind up protecting an exiled boy king from the machinations of his power-mad uncle. **70m/B; VHS, DVD.** Stan Laurel; Oliver Hardy; Henry O'Neill; Mary Boland; David Leland; John Warburton; Connie Gilchrist; Philip Merivale; ***D:*** Sam Taylor.

Nothing But Trouble 🦴 **1991 (PG-13)** Yuppie couple out for weekend drive find themselves smoldering in small town hell thanks to a traffic ticket. Horror and humor mix like oil and water in Aykroyd's debut as director. **93m/C; VHS, DVD.** Dan Aykroyd; Demi Moore; Chevy Chase; John Candy; Taylor Negron; Bertila Damas; Valri Bromfield; ***D:*** Dan Aykroyd; ***W:*** Dan Aykroyd; Peter Aykroyd; ***C:*** Dean Cundey. Golden Raspberries '91: Worst Support. Actor (Aykroyd).

Nothing in Common 🦴🦴 1/2 **1986 (PG)** In his last film, Gleason plays the abrasive, diabetic father of immature advertising agency worker Hanks. After his parents separate, Hanks learns to be more responsible and loving in caring for his father. Comedy and drama are blended well here with the help of satirical pokes at the ad business and Hanks turns in a fine performance, but the unorganized, lengthy plot may lose some viewers. **119m/C; VHS, DVD.** Tom Hanks; Jackie Gleason; Eva Marie Saint; Bess Armstrong; Hector Elizondo; Barry Corbin; Sela Ward; John Kapelos; Jane Morris; Dan Castellaneta; Tracy Reiner; ***D:*** Garry Marshall; ***W:*** Rick Podell; ***C:*** John A. Alonzo; ***M:*** Patrick Leonard.

Nothing Like the Holidays 🦴🦴 1/2 **2008 (PG-13)** The holidays bring together the boisterous Puerto Rican Rodriguez clan at Mama Anna (Pena) and Papa Edy's (Molina) in Chicago's Humboldt Park. The kids are shocked when Anna asks Edy for a divorce over dinner, suspcting he's two-timing her, and she openly pines for a grandchild from her NY-based son Mauricio (Leguizamo) and his Jewish wife Sarah (Messing). Daughter Roxanna's (Ferlito) struggling with her L.A. acting career while younger son Jesse (Rodriguez) has PTSD from his Iraq service and doesn't want to take over the family bodega. Sure, it's a typical film family reunion but with an ethnic kick and a believable cast. **98m/C; DVD, Blu-Ray, On Demand.** Luis Guzman; John Leguizamo; Debra Messing; Freddy Rodriguez; Alfred Molina; Melonie Diaz; Vanessa Ferlito; Jay Hernandez; Elizabeth Pena; ***D:*** Alfredo de Villa; ***W:*** Rick Najera; Alison Swan; ***C:*** Scott Kevan; ***M:*** Paul Oakenfold.

Nothing Personal ½ **2009** Anne (Verbeek), an antisocial young Dutch woman hitchhiking through Ireland, is hired to do some gardening work for Martin (Rea), the owner of an isolated cottage. Both Anne and Martin rejoice in solitude and agree that there will be no personal contact between them, just work. A moving character study evolves by rookie director Antoniak—the struggle to overcome one's past and learning that unattached independence doesn't always equal freedom. Pacing isn't all that engaging, with chatter left to a minimum, a style that might not work for most audiences. English, Dutch, and Gaelic with subtitles. **84m/C; Blu-Ray.** *NL* Lotte Verbeek; Stephen Rea; ***D:*** Urszula Antoniak; ***W:*** Urszula Antoniak; ***C:*** Daniel Bouquet; ***M:*** Ethan Rose.

Nothing Sacred ½ **1937** Slick reporter Wally (March) takes advantage of small-town Hazel's (Lombard) situation, using a newspaper publicity stunt to bring her to the Big Apple to distract her from her supposedly imminent death in order to manipulate the public's sentiment and sell more copy. Not-so-innocent Hazel is far from death's door and deftly exploits her exploitation. Scathing indictment of the mass media and bovine mentality of the masses. Both hysterically funny and bitterly cynical; boasts Lombard's finest performance as the alleged rube who orchestrates the ruse. Remade in 1954 as "Living It Up." **75m/C; DVD, Blu-Ray.** Fredric March; Carole Lombard; Walter Connolly; Sig Rumann; Charles Winninger; Margaret Hamilton; ***D:*** William A. Wellman; ***W:*** Ben Hecht; ***C:*** William Howard Greene; ***M:*** Oscar Levant.

Nothing to Lose ½ **1996 (R)** Ad exec Nick Beam (Robbins) is having a very bad day. He loses his job, finds his wife is having an affair, then gets carjacked by street-wise but dim-witted thief T-Paul (Lawrence). T-Paul picked the wrong day to rob Nick, who ironically takes T-Paul hostage. The unlikely pair find they have more in common than realized. Screwball buddy comedy shows its originality in casting, and not much else. Robbins and Lawrence are an inspired pair with great comedic potential but are trapped in a mundane story. Filming was delayed due, in part, to Lawrence's constant run-ins with the law. **97m/C; VHS, DVD.** Tim Robbins; Martin Lawrence; John C. McGinley; Giancarlo Esposito; Kelly Preston; Michael McKean; Irma P. Hall; Susan Barnes; Rebecca Gayheart; Patrick Cranshaw; ***D:*** Steve Oedekerk; ***W:*** Steve Oedekerk; ***C:*** Donald E. Thorin; ***M:*** Robert Folk.

Nothing to Lose *TBS* **2008** Johan was convicted of murdering his father though he claimed self-defense. Escaping after years in a mental institution, Johan decides to find his mother whose testimony he believes will finally clear him. And to have some leverage with the police, he kidnaps 13-year-old Tessa to hold as a hostage. Dutch with subtitles. **87m/C; DVD.** *NL* Theo Maassen; Lisa Smit; Bob Schwarze; ***D:*** Peter Kuijpers; ***W:*** Peter Kuijpers; Paul Jan Nelissen; ***C:*** Bert Pot; ***M:*** Paleis Van Boem.

Nothing Too Good for a Cowboy ½ **1998** Family-oriented Canadian TV movie. In 1939, former stockbroker Richard Hobson partners with cowboy Panhandle Phillips to start a ranch in British Columbia. Richard soon marries debutante Gloria McIntosh but the start of WWII brings difficulties, including a lack of money and ranch hands. Followed by a 1999-2000 TV series. **90m/C; DVD.** *CA* Chad Willett; Ted Atherton; Sarah Chalke; Zachary Bennett; Ryan Gosling; ***D:*** Kari Skogland; ***W:*** David Barlow; ***C:*** Danny Nowak; ***M:*** Maribeth Solomon. **TV**

Notorious **1946** Post-WWII story of beautiful playgirl Alicia (Bergman), who's sent by the U.S. government to marry a suspected spy (Rains) living in Brazil. Cynical agent Devlin (Grant) is assigned to watch her. Duplicity and guilt are important factors in this brooding, romantic spy thriller. Suspenseful throughout, with a surprise ending. The acting is excellent all around and Hitchcock makes certain that suspense is maintained throughout this classy and complex thriller. **101m/B; VHS, DVD, Blu-Ray.** Cary Grant; Ingrid Bergman; Claude Rains; Louis Calhern; Leopoldine Konstantin; Reinhold Schunzel; Moroni Olsen; ***D:*** Alfred Hitchcock; ***W:*** Ben Hecht; ***C:*** Ted Tetzlaff; ***M:*** Roy Webb. Natl. Film Reg. '06.

Notorious **2009 (R)** That would be "Notorious" as in the rapper The Notorious B.I.G. (aka Christopher Wallace), his rise from the Brooklyn streets to fame in the 1990s, his rivalry with Tupac Shakur, and ultimately his murder. Biopic faithfully follows the all too familiar underdog-beats-odds, becomes-rich-star, dies-premature-death formula. Convincing, engaging performance by Woolard, who channels the bigger-than-life Biggie is the best part of an otherwise forgettable pic. Seen one rags-to-riches music biopic, seen this one. **122m/C; DVD, Blu-Ray, On Demand.** Derek Luke; Anthony Mackie; Angela Bassett; Marc John Jefferies; Jamal Woodard; Naturi Naughton; Antonique Smith; Sean Ringgold; ***D:*** George Tillman, Jr.; ***W:*** Reggie Rock Bythewood; Cheo Hodari Coker; ***C:*** Michael Grady; ***M:*** Danny Elfman.

The Notorious Bettie Page ½ **2006 (R)** The ultimate 50s fetish pinup, Bettie (Mol) is a sweet, religious Southern gal with a rocky past (bad childhood, bad men), who comes to the Big Apple to be an actress. She can't act, but Bettie looks great—dark hair, curvy body, come-hither smile, and an open sexuality that soon has her doing nude photo shoots. After Bettie meets the Klaws, Irving (Bauer) and his sister Paula (Taylor), she becomes a sensation in the specialty market of leather and bondage. This being the 50s, morality soon wags a disapproving finger when Senator Estes Kefauver (Strathairn) convenes his indecency hearings and Bettie gets caught in the crossfire. Mol is charming but Bettie remains a cipher. **91m/C; DVD.** Gretchen Mol; Chris Bauer; Jared Harris; Sarah Paulson; Cara Seymour; Lili Taylor; David Strathairn; John Cullum; Matt McGrath; Austin Pendleton; Norman Reedus; Dallas Roberts; Victor Slezak; Tara Subkoff; Kevin Carroll; Ann Dowd; Michael Gaston; Jefferson Mays; Peter McRobbie; Jonathan M. Woodward; ***D:*** Mary Harron; ***W:*** Mary Harron; Guinevere Turner; ***C:*** W. Mott Hupfel, III; ***M:*** Mark Suozzo.

Notorious But Nice **1933** Romantic crime melodrama. Richard and Jenny are in love but Richard's guardian John wants him to marry his daughter Constance. When Jenny realizes that Richard will lose his financial security, she does what's noble but worse troubles loom for her. **65m/B; DVD.** Marian Marsh; Donald Dillaway; Betty Compson; Rochelle Hudson; John St. Polis; J. Carrol Naish; ***D:*** Richard Thorpe; ***W:*** Carol Webster; ***C:*** M(ilton) A(rthur) Anderson.

The Notorious Lady ½ **1927** Englishman Stone kills the man he finds in Bedford's room, believing him to be his wife's lover. He's mistaken but she lies to save him and Stone takes off for the diamond mines in Africa. Bedford hears he's dead and sets out, seeking the truth. **79m/B; Silent; VHS, DVD.** Lewis Stone; Barbara Bedford; Earl Metcalfe; Francis McDonald; ***D:*** King Baggot; ***C:*** Gaetano Antonio "Tony" Gaudio.

The Notorious Landlady ½ **1962** State Department employee William Gridley (Lemmon) is transferred to London and rents a flat from Carlye Hardwicke (Novak). Her shady husband Miles (Reed) is missing and Gridley's boss Ambruster (Astaire) and Scotland Yard Inspector Oliphant (Jeffries) ask Gridley to snoop around. When Miles turns up, he threatens Carlye over some stolen jewels and she kills him and goes on trial. There's also a pawn ticket, a blackmail scheme, and an old lady (Winwood) who saw too much. Fast paced comic mystery. **123m/B; DVD.** Kim Novak; Jack Lemmon; Fred Astaire; Lionel Jeffries; Estelle Winwood; Maxwell Reed; Philippa Bevans; ***D:*** Richard Quine; ***W:*** Blake Edwards; Larry Gelbart; ***C:*** Arthur E. Arling; ***M:*** George Duning.

Notre Histoire ½ *Our Story; Separate Rooms* **1984** Confusing and frequently surreal drama. Middle-aged alcoholic Robert (Delon) is in despair about his life as he sits alone in a train compartment. Suddenly, beautiful Donatienne (Baye) enters and just as suddenly leaves (after they have sex, of course) with Robert soon obsessively chasing after her. French with subtitles. **110m/C; DVD.** *FR* Alain Delon; Nathalie Baye; ***D:*** Bernard Blier; ***W:*** Bernard Blier; ***C:*** Jean Penzer; ***M:*** Laurent Rossi.

Notting Hill **1999 (PG-13)** Romantic comedy that can coast by on charm alone. Roberts is not playing herself (okay, so there are, possibly, some similarities). She is playing a famous and neurotic movie star, Anna Scott, who's filming on location in London. She meets cute with shy travel bookstore owner William Thacker (Grant) and the unexpected twosome are soon spending a lot of time together. Trouble immediately begins when the paparazzi find out about their affair and William finds his face splashed all over the tabloids and reporters camped out in his garden. Ifans is a scene stealer as William's grubby and crazy housemate. **123m/C; DVD, Blu-Ray, HD-DVD.** Julia Roberts; Hugh Grant; Hugh Bonneville; Rhys Ifans; Tim (McInnerny) McInnery; Gina McKee; James Dreyfus; Richard McCabe; Emma Chambers; ***D:*** Roger Michell; ***W:*** Richard Curtis; ***C:*** Michael Coulter; ***M:*** Trevor Jones.

Novel Desires ½ **1992 (R)** Brian Freedman is a best-selling author who teams up with his writing rival, Vicky Chance. But it isn't just their imaginations they give free reign to, it's all their desires as well. **80m/C; VHS, DVD.** Tyler Gains; Caroline Monteith; Mitchell Clark; Lisa Hayland; ***D:*** Lawrence Unger.

Novel Romance **2006 (R)** Hearing her biological clock ticking very loudly, magazine editor Max (Lords) decides to have a baby and looks for a sperm donor. She picks a suitably charismatic unpublished writer (Johansson) and offers to make him a literary success if he will do his part (baby-making wise) and then get lost. He does, she does, and Max raises their daughter while he moves to France. But they just can't quite let go completely. **92m/C; DVD.** Traci Lords; Paul Johansson; Sherilyn Fenn; Mariette Hartley; Jacqueline Pinol; ***D:*** Emily Skopov; ***W:*** Emily Skopov; ***C:*** David Klein; ***M:*** Raney Shockne. **VIDEO**

A Novel Romance **2011** A humiliating romantic comedy that's generally embarrassing for all concerned. Middle-aged Nate (Guttenberg) is a would-be writer who meets cute with much-younger Jenny (Govich) while both are waiting for their inappropriate, current romantic interests to show. Adi (Elizabeth) and Buddy (Del Negro) are soon out of the picture, leaving Nate and Jenny to reconnect as more than platonic friends. **92m/C; DVD.** Steve Guttenberg; Milena Govich; Shannon Elizabeth; Matthew Del Negro; Kelly Bishop; Doug E. Doug; Jay O. Sanders; ***D:*** Allie Dvorin; ***W:*** Allie Dvorin; ***C:*** Jon Miguel Delgado; ***M:*** Michelangelo Sosnowitz.

November **2005 (R)** A young man (Le Gros) enters an L.A. convenience store to buy ice cream for his girlfriend Sophie (Cox) who is waiting in the car, but unwittingly walks into a holdup and is shot dead. The fateful date is replayed in three sections, "Denial," "Despair," and "Acceptance," each offering clues to what's behind the actual event, as Sophie begins to question her grip on her life and reality. Answers are beside the point in this psychological thriller—it's all about the quest. Fine acting by all and mindfully filmed. **73m/C; DVD.** Courteney Cox; James LeGros; Nora Dunn; Anne Archer; Michael Ealy; Nick Offerman; Matthew Carey; ***D:*** Greg Harrison; ***W:*** Benjamin Brand; ***C:*** Nancy Schreiber; ***M:*** Lew Baldwin.

November Christmas ½ **2010** Farmer Jess Sanford (Elliott) is confused by the odd requests of the Marks family until he realizes that their 8-year-old daughter Vanessa (Lind) has cancer. Tom (Corbett) and Beth (Paulson) want to give her all the holiday surprises they can so Jess leads the community in helping out. A tearjerker Hallmark Hall of Fame production but the first rate cast sells it all the way. **95m/C; DVD.** Emily Alyn Lind; John Corbett; Sarah Paulson; Sam Elliott; Max Charles; Richard Fitzpatrick; Elizabeth McLaughlin; Eric Keenleyside; Jeremy Akerman; Tegan Moss; Karen Allen; ***D:*** Robert Harmon; ***W:*** P'nenah Goldstein; ***C:*** Attila Szalay; ***M:*** Ernest Troost. **TV**

November Criminals **2017 (PG-13)** A combination teen angst and detective story, based on the novel by Sam Munson. Addison (Elgort) is a brainy high school senior whose mother has recently died. After his friend Kevin is killed in a coffee shop by a man on a motorcycle, Addison investigates with the help of his best friend Phoebe (Moretz), which worries his widower father (Straihairn) and annoying Phoebe's mother Fiona (Keener). Suspended by his high school principal (Kinney), Addison's investigation takes him to the drug underworld of Washington, D.C. Cliched, one-note characterizations strand the appealing cast in an underdeveloped film. **85m/C; DVD, Blu-Ray, Streaming.** Chloë Grace Moretz; Ansel Elgort; Catherine Keener; David Strathairn; Terry Kinney; ***D:*** Sacha Gervasi; ***W:*** Sacha Gervasi; Steven Knight; ***C:*** Mihai Malaimare, Jr.; ***M:*** David Norland.

The November Man ½ **2014 (R)** Brosnan tries to remind viewers that he was once James Bond. Sadly, he isn't any more. His latest action film from '80s director Donaldson feels archaic, the kind of action film that would have found an audience two decades before but doesn't really work in the '10s. Brosnan plays an ex-CIA operative brought back in on a very personal mission that puts him up against a former protégé with connections that link all the way up the power food chain. Moments of effective action are punctured by weak plots and weaker dialogue. **98m/C; DVD, Blu-Ray.** Pierce Brosnan; Olga Kurylenko; Luke Bracey; Lazar Ristovski; Bill Smitrovich; Eliza Taylor; Will Patton; ***D:*** Roger Donaldson; ***W:*** Michael Finch; Karl Gajdusek; ***C:*** Romain Lacourbas; ***M:*** Marco Beltrami.

Novitiate ½ **2017 (R)** A subtle look at aspiring nuns coming to terms with their futures as the changes in the era of Vatican II. Though the convent's Reverend Mother (Leo) rules the teen postulants with an iron fist, the young women try to please her while experiencing personal doubt. The film is filtered through the perspective of Cathleen (Qualley), a teenager who is initially sure of her devotion, but finds the strength of her faith severely tested. Like the other postulants, Cathleen's training deeply affects her body and soul. **123m/C; DVD, Blu-Ray.** Dianna Agron; Margaret Qualley; Liana Liberato; Julianne Nicholson; Eline Powell; Melissa Leo; ***D:*** Margaret Betts; ***W:*** Margaret Betts; ***C:*** Kat Westergaard; ***M:*** Christopher Stark.

Novocaine **2001 (R)** Ambitious, occasionally successful blend of black comedy and film noir framed in toothy imagery. Humdrum dentist Frank (Martin) has a thriving practice and perfect, if nutty, hygienist/fiancee (Dern). The normalcy is crushing and dread is palpable. Enter Susan (Bonham Carter), a grungy, seductive first-time patient with a need for painkillers. She appeals to Frank's latent desire for danger and soon he's playing the classic noir role of the stooge. Ultimately the plot stumbles and the dueling tones bump into each other. Laughing gas would've been preferable to the numbness of the film's ending, but points given for originality. **95m/C; DVD.** Steve Martin; Helena Bonham Carter; Laura Dern; Elias Koteas; Scott Caan; Keith David; Lynne Thigpen; Kevin Bacon; ***D:*** David Atkins; ***W:*** David Atkins; ***C:*** Vilko Filac; ***M:*** Steve Bartek.

Now and Forever ½ **1934** Penny (Temple) is the young daughter of charming widower and con man Jerry Day (Cooper). Penny's been in the care of her uncle but Jerry's decided to settle down in Paris with his lady love Toni (Lombard) and figures he can give the tyke a home. But the hard-up Jerry can't resist stealing a valuable necklace and there's much trouble ahead (and not your average happy ending). Temple steals the film from her elders. Adapted from the story "Honor Bright" by Jack Kirkland and Melville Baker. Colorized. **82m/C; DVD.** Gary

Cooper; Carole Lombard; Shirley Temple; Guy Standing; Charlotte Granville; Gilbert Emery; *D:* Henry Hathaway; *W:* Vincent Lawrence; Sylvia Thalberg; *C:* Harry Fischbeck.

Now and Forever 🦴 1/2 **1982 (R)** Young wife's life is shattered when her unfaithful husband is wrongly accused and convicted of rape. After he is sent to prison, she begins drinking and taking drugs. From the novel by Danielle Steel, it will appeal most to those who like their romances a la Harlequin. **93m/C; VHS, DVD.** *AU* Cheryl Ladd; Robert Coleby; Carmen Duncan; Christine Amor; Aileen Britton; *D:* Adrian Carr.

Now & Forever 🦴🦴 **2002** Childhood friends Angela Wilson and John Myron live in small-town Saskatchewan and come from different backgrounds (he's Cree, she's white). Angela's plagued by major family woes and longs to be an actress; John is mystical and grounded by his culture, and has loved Angela from the moment he met her. She takes up with a jerk who does the unthinkable and she leaves town. But the connection between Angela and John proves strong enough to bring them back together. Too many elements make the film convoluted, but it is earnest. **101m/C; DVD.** *CA* Mia Kirshner; Adam Beach; Theresa Russell; Gordon Tootoosis; Gabriel Olds; Callum Keith Rennie; Alexandra Purvis; Simon Baker; *D:* Bob (Benjamin) Clark; Billy Boyle; *C:* Jan Kiesser; *M:* Paul Zaza.

Now and Then 🦴🦴 **1995 (PG-13)** Four women hold a reunion 25 years after their most eventful childhood summer to relive the good ol' days of prepubescent triumphs and tragedies. Flashbacks, which thankfully comprise much of the movie, explore first kisses, budding breasts, death and divorce. Despite good intentions, this nostalgic coming-of-ager is a jumbled mass of borrowed formulas that just can't shake that feeling of forced sentimentality. The young actresses are talented and charming, but their adult counterparts are less convincing. **97m/C; DVD.** Rosie O'Donnell; Melanie Griffith; Demi Moore; Rita Wilson; Christina Ricci; Thora Birch; Gaby Hoffman; Ashleigh Aston Moore; Cloris Leachman; Lolita Davidovich; Bonnie Hunt; Brendan Fraser; *D:* Leslie Linka Glatter; *W:* I. Marlene King; *C:* Ueli Steiger; *M:* Cliff Eidelman.

NOW: In the Wings on a World Stage 🦴🦴 **2014** Spacey and Mendes mounted a daring, ambitious production of "Richard III" that travelled the globe, proving the international, cross-cultural appeal of Shakespeare's work and the overall power of theater. Watching Spacey perform the classic role in this documentary about the production has incredible power but not nearly enough is shown. Instead, NOW turns into a travelogue, a mildly interesting examination of how travelling theatre companies build community that misses the opportunity to point out the strengths of this specific production. Spacey is always fascinating but one wishes he treated viewers to more of the play itself and less of his co-stars anecdotes. **97m/C; On Demand.** *UK* Kevin Spacey; Sam Mendes; *D:* Jeremy Whelehan; *C:* Aadel Nodeh-Farahani; *M:* David M Saunders.

Now Is Good 🦴🦴 **2012 (PG-13)** Average teen weepie adapted from Jenny Downham's bestseller "Before I Die." Her terminal illness has Brit teen Tessa Scott's (Fanning) parents separated and unable to agree on her care and that's before she tries fulfilling her version of a bucket list. This includes partying with her friends and a romance with amiable new neighbor Adam (Irvine). **103m/C; DVD; Closed Captioned.** *UK* Dakota Fanning; Jeremy Irvine; Paddy Considine; Olivia Williams; Kaya Scodelario; *D:* Ol Parker; *W:* Ol Parker; *C:* Erik Alexander Wilson; *M:* Dustin O'Halloran.

Now, Voyager 🦴🦴🦴 1/2 **1942** Davis plays a lonely spinster who is transformed into a vibrant young woman by therapy. She comes out of her shell to have a romantic affair with a suave European (who turns out to be married) but still utters the famous phrase "Oh, Jerry, we have the stars. Let's not ask for the moon." Definitely melodramatic, but an involving story nonetheless. Based on a novel by Olive Higgins Prouty. **117m/B; VHS, DVD, Blu-Ray.** Bette Davis; Gladys Cooper; Claude Rains; Paul Henreid; Bonita Granville; Ilka Chase; *D:* Irving Rapper; *W:* Casey Robinson; *C:* Sol Polito; *M:* Max Steiner. Oscars '42: Orig. Dramatic Score; Natl. Film Reg. '07.

Now You Know 🦴 **2002 (R)** But you won't want to. Jeremy's (Sisto) fiancee Keri (Jones) suddenly calls off their wedding while he's at his bachelor party. He drowns his sorrows with buds Gil (Anderson) and Biscuit (Fehrman) while Keri talks it out with gal pal Marti (Kent). Finally, Jeremy just decides to ask Keri what went wrong. Lame comedy attempt from "Clerks" sidekick Anderson, making his directorial debut. **102m/C; DVD.** Jeremy Sisto; Rashida Jones; Trevor Fehrman; Paget Brewster; Heather Paige Kent; Anthony John (Tony) Denison; Jeff Anderson; *D:* Jeff Anderson; *W:* Jeff Anderson; *C:* Marco Cappetta; *M:* Lanny Cordola; Matt Sorum. **VIDEO**

Now You See Him, Now You Don't 🦴🦴 **1972 (G)** Light Disney comedy involving a gang of crooks who want to use a college student's invisibility formula to rob a local bank. Sequel to Disney's "The Computer Wore Tennis Shoes." **85m/C; VHS, DVD.** Kurt Russell; Joe Flynn; Cesar Romero; Jim Backus; Kelly Thordsen; *D:* Robert Butler; *M:* Robert F. Brunner.

Now You See Me 🦴🦴 **2013 (PG-13)** Director Leterrier's increasingly goofy caper film about a group of magicians (Eisenberg, Fisher, Franco, and Harrelson) who happen to pull off bank heists. With an ex-magician (Freeman), who now debunks tricks, and an FBI agent (Ruffalo) hot on their trail, the magicians continue to stay one step ahead of their pursuers and one step behind logic. Despite the undeniable charisma of the cast, Leterrier can't keep all of the plates spinning and the finale features more loose ends than a magic act can disguise. **115m/C; DVD, Blu-Ray.** Jesse Eisenberg; Isla Fisher; Woody Harrelson; Dave Franco; Morgan Freeman; Mark Ruffalo; Michael Caine; Melanie Laurent; *D:* Louis Leterrier; *W:* Edward Solomon; Boaz Yakin; *C:* Larry Fong; *M:* Tom Rowlands; Ed Simons.

Now You See Me 2 🦴 **2016 (PG-13)** An unfortunate and poorly made sequel. Set in a fictional world where the Four Horsemen of the first film have become worldwide celebrities for their actions, the magicians resurface for a performance designed to expose a tech magnate. Of course, they're framed and have to perform one final impossible heist to clear their names. See a star-studded cast given nothing to do! See magic tricks that are clearly CGI! See one of the most boring movies ever made! **115m/C; DVD, Blu-Ray.** Michael Caine; Jay Chou; Lizzy Caplan; Morgan Freeman; Jesse Eisenberg; Mark Ruffalo; Woody Harrelson; Dave Franco; Daniel Radcliffe; Ben Lamb; *D:* Jon M. Chu; *W:* Edward Solomon; *C:* Peter Deming; *M:* Brian Tyler.

Nowhere Boy 🦴🦴 **2009 (R)** Conventional bio of the unconventional family life of a teenaged John Lennon. In 1955, rebellious 15-year-old John (Taylor-Johnson), who's been raised by his Aunt Mimi (Scott-Thomas) and Uncle George (Threlfall), learns that his mother Julia (Duff) lives close by. She's a high-spirited, neurotic flirt, now married and with two young daughters, who introduces John to rock 'n' roll. However, the reserved Mimi becomes jealous of their closeness, especially after raising the immature Julia's son. A young Paul and George make appearances as John learns to play the guitar and decides to follow his musical impulses. **98m/C; DVD.** *GB* Aaron Taylor-Johnson; Kristin Scott Thomas; Anne-Marie Duff; Thomas Brodie-Sangster; David Threlfall; David Morrissey; Sam Bell; Josh Bolt; Ophelia Lovibond; *D:* Sam Taylor-Johnson; *W:* Matt Greenhalgh; Julia Baird; *C:* Seamus McGarvey; *M:* Alison Goldfrapp; Will Gregory.

Nowhere in Africa 🦴🦴 1/2 *Nirgendwo in Afrika* **2002 (R)** Walter Redlich (Ninidze), a German Jew, has fled Breslau for a job as a farm manager in British-colonized Kenya. In 1938, his wife Jettel (Koehler) and her 5-year-old daughter Regina (Kurka) join him. Jettel is unhappy with their harsh new life and isolation but Regina quickly adapts. When war is declared, Walter eventually joins the British Army, leaving Jettel behind to manage things. As Regina (Eckertz) grows up, she becomes ever-more adapted to life in Kenya and is dismayed when, in 1947, her father is offered a prestigious job and wants to return "home" to Germany. German with subtitles. From the novel by Stefanie Zweig. **141m/C; DVD, Blu-Ray.** *GE* Juliane Kohler; Merab Redlich; Karoline Eckertz; Lea Kurka; Matthias Habich; Sidede Onyulo; *D:* Caroline Link; *W:* Caroline Link; *C:* Gernot Roll; *M:* Niki Reiser. Oscars '02: Foreign Film.

Nowhere in Sight 🦴🦴 1/2 **2001** Rehash of "Wait until Dark" has little to add that masterpiece of suspense/horror. This time, Carly Bauer (Slater) is the blind woman who's tormented in her apartment by a couple of nasty thugs. The cast does credible work with familiar material. **94m/C; DVD.** Helen Slater; Mark Camacho; Richard Jutras; Max Perlus; Andrew McCarthy; *D:* Douglas Jackson; *W:* James (Momel) Lemmo; *C:* Bruno Philip; *M:* Helen Slater; David Findlay.

Nowhere Land 🦴🦴 **1998 (R)** If the feds want to make a case against the mob, they need to keep their witness alive and the dangerous beauty sent to provide protection is more than anyone bargained for. **88m/C; VHS, DVD.** Peter Dobson; Dina Meyer; Francesco Quinn; Jon Polito; Martin Kove; *D:* Rupert Hitzig; *W:* Dennis Manuel; *M:* Russ Landau.

Nowhere to Hide 🦴🦴 *On the Run* **1983 (R)** A widow whose Marine officer husband has been assassinated is chased by some bad guys who are after a helicopter part (say what?) and she must fight for survival for herself and her six-year-old son. **91m/C; VHS, DVD.** Amy Madigan; Daniel Hugh-Kelly; Michael Ironside; Beau Cox; Ray Meagher; *D:* Mario Azzopardi; Mende Brown; *W:* Michael Fisher; *C:* Paul Onorato; *M:* Brad Fiedel; Laurie Lewis.

Nowhere to Land 🦴🦴 1/2 **2000** Familiar plotline still manages to be suspenseful. A bomb filmed with nerve gas is stashed aboard a Boeing 747 flying from Australia to California. It's up to pilot John Prescott (Wagner) and the feds to get the situation under control. **90m/C; VHS, DVD.** Jack Wagner; Christine Elise; James B. Sikking; Ernie Hudson; Mark Lee; Helen Thomson; *D:* Armand Mastroianni. **CABLE**

Nowhere to Run 🦴 1/2 **1993 (R)** Kickboxer with heart seeks cross-over movie to establish real acting career. Unfortunately, even if such a movie existed, Van Damme wouldn't know what to do with it. Arquette plays the damsel in distress, facing eviction from the family farm with her two small children. Fortunately for Van Damme's escaped convict character, she is also a very lonely widow (nudge, nudge). He saves the day by abusing the daylights out of the big bad bankers, yet also finds time to play surrogate dad. Whatta guy. **95m/C; DVD, Blu-Ray.** Jean-Claude Van Damme; Rosanna Arquette; Kieran Culkin; Tiffany Taubman; Joss Ackland; Ted Levine; *D:* Robert Harmon; *W:* Joe Eszterhas; Leslie Bohem; Randy Feldman; *C:* David Gribble; Doug Milsome; Michael A. Benson; *M:* Mark Isham.

Nuclear Hurricane 🦴 **2007** Stupid sci-fi plot with limited CGI and acting abilities by the cast. A hurricane is on a collision course with an island that is the site of a nuclear power plant. The plant's cooling system goes haywire and the core is in danger of a meltdown. **85m/C; DVD.** Jamie Luner; Jack Scalia; David Millbern; Meredith McGeachie; Erin Gray; Gil Gerard; *D:* Fred Olen Ray; *W:* Anna Lorenzo; *C:* Theo Angell; *M:* Penka Kouneva. **VIDEO**

The Nude Bomb 🦴🦴 1/2 *The Return of Maxwell Smart* **1980 (PG)** Proof that old TV shows never die—they just get made into big screen movies. Maxwell Smart from "Get Smart" (would you believe?) tries to save the world from a bomb intended to destroy clothing and leave everyone in the buff. Old hat lines. Followed by the TV movie "Get Smart, Again!" **94m/C; VHS, DVD, Blu-Ray.** Don Adams; Dana Elcar; Pamela Hensley; Sylvia Kristel; Norman Lloyd; Rhonda Fleming; Joey Forman; *D:* Clive Donner; *W:* Bill Dana; *M:* Lalo Schifrin.

Nude on the Moon **WOOF!** **1961** Lunar expedition discovers moon inhabited by people who bare skin as hobby. Groovy theme song, "I'm Mooning Over You, My Little Moon Doll." Part of Joe Bob Brigg's "Sleaziest Movies in the History of the World" series. **83m/C; VHS, DVD.** Shelby Livingston; Pat Reilly; *D:* Doris Wishman; *W:* Doris Wishman; *C:* Raymond Phelan; *M:* Daniel Hart.

The Nude Set 🦴 1/2 *Mademoiselle Striptease* **1957** Silly and tame French sex comedy. Country girl Sophie (Laurent) chases after boyfriend Jacques (Nicaud) when he returns to Paris. She begins visiting nightclubs, including one that features striptease, and decides to liberate herself by getting up onstage. French with subtitles. **100m/B; DVD.** *FR* Agnes Laurent; Philippe Nicaud; Dora Doll; Simone Paris; Jack Ary; Michel Bardinet; *D:* Pierre Foucaud; *W:* Alice Colanis; *C:* Paul Cotteret; *M:* Rene Cloerec.

The Nugget 🦴 1/2 **2002 (R)** Aussie-made comedy's jokes may be better understood by the locals. Three working-class blokes spend their weekends out in the bush allegedly gold prospecting but mostly sitting around drinking beer. But on one trip, they finally find a huge nugget, and their greed leads to a disruption in their friendship, until their windfall gets stolen. **90m/C; DVD.** *AU* Eric Bana; Alan Brough; Max Cullen; Dave O'Neil; Stephen Currie; Peter Moon; Belinda Emmett; Sallyanne Ryan; Karen Pang; *D:* Bill Bennett; *W:* Bill Bennett; *C:* Danny Ruhlmann; *M:* Nigel Westlake.

The Nuisance 🦴🦴 1/2 **1933** Ambulance-chasing lawyer Joe Stevens (Tracy) works with alcoholic doc, Prescott (Morgan), who fixes x-rays as well as a 'flop man' who stages bogus accidents, and a team of paid-off 'witnesses' to bamboozle businesses with phony insurance claims. Beautiful PI Dorothy Mason (Evans) goes undercover to get the goods on the shyster but doesn't expect romance to follow. **83m/B; DVD.** Lee Tracy; Madge Evans; Frank Morgan; Charles Butterworth; John Miljan; *D:* Jack Conway; *W:* Bella Spewack; Samuel Spewack; *C:* Gregg Toland.

Numb 🦴🦴 1/2 **2007 (R)** Screenwriter Hudson Milbank (Perry) suffers from depersonalization disorder (DPD), a mental illness where the person cannot feel normal human emotion. Hudson feels neither love nor fear, just a depressed blank nothingness that permeates his life. He's tried many different drugs and therapies with no success until Sarah (Collins) enters his life. Hudson knows there's an attraction but cannot demonstrate it despite his desire to get better and Sarah's supportiveness. Funny rather than mawkish, and personal as director/writer Goldberg suffers from DPD himself. **94m/C; DVD.** Matthew Perry; Lynn Collins; Kevin Pollak; Mary Steenburgen; Bob Gunton; Helen Shaver; William B. Davis; *D:* Harris Goldberg; *W:* Harris Goldberg; *C:* Eric Steelberg; *M:* Ryan Shore.

#1 Cheerleader Camp **WOOF!** **2010** Strictly an excuse to showcase a lot of T and A to its intended audience of horny guys of all ages. College students Andy and Michael get summer jobs at a cheerleader camp and decide to recruit a group of strippers to help the cheerleaders take top prize in an upcoming competition. Ogle much? **95m/C; DVD.** Seth Cassell; Jay Gillespie; Erica Duke; Harmony Blossom; Diane Jay Blossom; Charlene Tilton; *D:* Mark Quod; *W:* Naomi L. Selfman; *C:* Alexander Yellen; *M:* Chris Ridenhour. **VIDEO**

Number One Fan 🦴 1/2 **1994 (R)** Hollywood action star Zane Barry (McQueen) is stalked by Blair (Ammann), a fan with whom he had a brief romance. Zane manages to patch things up when fiancee Holly (Stewart) finds out but Blair's determined to be the only woman in his life. **93m/C; VHS, Streaming.** Chad McQueen; Catherine Mary Stewart; Renee Griffin; Hoyt Axton; Paul Bartel; Eric (DaRe) Da Re; Charles Matthau; *D:* Jane Simpson; *W:* Anthony Laurence Greene.

Number One with a Bullet 🦴🦴 **1987 (R)** Two unorthodox "odd couple" detectives are demoted after losing a key witness, but still set out on their own to unearth a drug czar. Carradine and Williams are better than this standard action material. **103m/C; VHS, DVD, Streaming.** Robert Carradine; Billy Dee Williams; Peter Graves; Valerie Bertinelli; Bobby DiCicco; Doris Roberts; Mykelti Williamson; Jon(athan) Gries; Vanessa Bell Calloway; Shari Shattuck; *D:* Jack Smight; *W:* James Belushi; Andrew Kurtzman; Rob Riley; *C:* Alex Phillips, Jr.; *M:* Alf Clausen.

No. 3 🦴🦴 1/2 *Number Three* **1997** Gangster Tae-ju (suk-kyu Han) is a young triad member who resents being number three in the pecking order of his gang. His rival is a dumb guy who beats people with ashtrays, and his wife is cheating on him with a poet. This simply will not stand. **109m/C; DVD.** *NK* Min-Sik Choi; Suk-kyu Han; Mi-yeon Lee; Kang-ho Song; Kwang-jung Park; Sang-Myeon Park; ***D:*** Neung-han Song; ***W:*** Neung-han Song; ***C:*** Seung-bae Park; ***M:*** Dong-Ik Cho.

The Number 23 🦴 ½ **2007 (R)** Disappointing, gimmicky, and generally incoherent effort stars Carrey as dog catcher Walter Sparrow, who's given a mystery novel by wife Agatha (Madsen). It's about a noirish detective (also played by Carrey), and all the significant events in the book are oddly connected to the number 23. Walter also becomes obsessive about the number and begins to fear that he will follow the book's plot, which includes murder. Walter eventually gets a grip but the film never recovers. **95m/C; DVD.** Jim Carrey; Virginia Madsen; Logan Lerman; Danny Huston; Rhona Mitra; Lynn Collins; Mark Pellegrino; Ed Lauter; ***D:*** Joel Schumacher; ***W:*** Fernley Phillips; ***C:*** Matthew Libatique; ***M:*** Harry Gregson-Williams.

The Numbers Station 🦴 ½ **2013 (R)** Special Ops agent Emerson (Cusack) must leave field work after a mission goes awry and a witness becomes collateral damage. He gets stuck babysitting the operator (Akerman) of a numbers station, a remote locale that sends coded messages to agents in the field. Of course, the station is assaulted and Emerson has to fight for his life and that of the woman for whom he is a bodyguard. Director Barfoed can't figure out if he has made an action movie with no real action, a spy thriller with no thrills, and a character study with a half-asleep performance from Cusack. **89m/C; DVD, Blu-Ray.** John Cusack; Malin Akerman; Liam Cunningham; Hannah Murray; ***D:*** Kasper Barfoed; ***W:*** F. Scott Frazier; ***C:*** Ottar Gudnason; ***M:*** Paul Leonard-Morgan.

Numero Deux 🦴🦴 *Number Two* **1975** Godard explores politics, sex, and the trials of the modern family. A dissatisfied wife suffers from chronic constipation, her exhausted husband is impotent, they, their children, and grandparents all try to cope with daily life. For nine-tenths of the film Godard only used small portions of the screen (the upper left and lower right corners) to manipulate his message of frustration. It's only at the end that the full-screen is used to offer some sort of relief. In French with English subtitles. **90m/C; VHS, DVD.** *FR* Sandrine Battistella; Pierre Oudry; Alex(andre) Rignault; Rachel Stefanopol; ***D:*** Jean-Luc Godard; ***W:*** Anne-Marie Mieville; Jean-Luc Godard.

The Nun 🦴 ½ **2018 (R)** The origin story for "The Conjuring" franchise. At a cursed Roman Catholic abbey in 1952 Romania, a devout nun hangs herself. Her death compels the Vatican to send a demon hunter, Father Burke (Bichir), and a novitiate who has visions, Sister Irene (Farmiga), to investigate. They are guided by a local farmhand, Maurice (Bloquet). As they question the remaining nuns about the situation, it grows darker and more dire with frequent sightings of a menacing figure, The Nun (Aarons). Predictable and lacks the well-drawn characters and story of the first entries in the series. **96m/C; DVD, Blu-Ray.** Demian Bichir; Taissa Farmiga; Jonas Bloquet; Bonnie Aarons; Ingrid Bisu; ***D:*** Corin Hardy; ***W:*** Gary Dauberman; ***C:*** Maxime Alexandre; ***M:*** Abel Korzeniowski.

The Nun and the Sergeant 🦴 ½ **1962** Tough Sgt. McGrath chooses a group of convict soldiers who are considered expendable for a risky mission during the Korean War. When they reach their target, they are stymied by an injured American nun who's protecting a group of schoolgirls. **74m/B; DVD.** Robert Webber; Anna Sten; Hari Rhodes; Leo Gordon; Robert Easton; ***D:*** Frank (Franklyn) Adreon; ***W:*** Don Cerveris; ***C:*** Paul Ivano; ***M:*** Jerry Fielding.

Nun of That WOOF! **2009** Inspired by a short film, a murdered nun is taught to kill in Heaven by Jesus, Moses, and Gandhi before being resurrected to join a super-secret order of nuns who kill bad guys, and occasionally indulge in lesbianism. It also features Troma co-founder Lloyd Kaufman as The Pope. Low budget fare but it has its appeal. **90m/C; DVD.** Sarah Nicklin; Alexandra Cipolla; Shanette Wilson; Ruth Sullivan; Rich Treheway; Brandon Luis Aponte; Michael Reed; Debbie Rochon; Lloyd Kaufman; ***D:*** Richard Griffin; ***W:*** Richard Griffin; Ted Marr; ***C:*** Jacob Larimore; ***M:*** Daniel Hildreth; Tony Milano.

Nuns on the Run 🦴🦴 **1990 (PG-13)** Idle and Coltrane are two nonviolent members of a robbery gang who double-cross their boss during a hold-up and disguise themselves as nuns while on the run from both the Mob and the police. Catholic humor, slapstick, and much fun with habits dominate. Idle and Coltrane do their best to keep the so-so script moving with its one-joke premise. **95m/C; VHS, DVD; Open Captioned.** Eric Idle; Robbie Coltrane; Janet Suzman; Camille Coduri; Robert Patterson; Tom Hickey; Doris Hare; Lila Kaye; ***D:*** Jonathan Lynn; ***W:*** Jonathan Lynn; ***C:*** Mike Garfath.

The Nun's Story 🦴🦴🦴 ½ **1959** The melancholy tale of a young nun working in the Congo and Belgium during WWII, and struggling to reconcile her free spirit with the rigors of the order. Gabrielle (Hepburn) is the daughter of a Belgian doctor (Jagger), who leaves the convent as Sister Luke. Her assignment in the Congo is at a European hospital where's she influenced by dedicated surgeon, Dr. Fortunai (Finch). But Sister Luke comes to question her vocation as the Nazis rise to power and invade her homeland. Highly acclaimed; from the Kathryn Hulme novel. **152m/C; VHS, DVD.** Audrey Hepburn; Peter Finch; Edith Evans; Peggy Ashcroft; Mildred Dunnock; Dean Jagger; Beatrice Straight; Colleen Dewhurst; ***D:*** Fred Zinnemann; ***W:*** Robert Anderson; ***C:*** Franz Planer; ***M:*** Franz Waxman. British Acad. '59: Actress (Hepburn); Natl. Bd. of Review '59: Director (Zinnemann), Support. Actress (Evans); N.Y. Film Critics '59: Actress (Hepburn), Director (Zinnemann).

Nuremberg 🦴🦴 ½ **2000** A decent but not overly compelling intro to the allied prosecution of Nazi war criminals at Nuremberg, Germany in 1945/46. Supreme Court Justice Robert H. Jackson (Baldwin) is asked to take a leave from the bench to head up the prosecution and he decides to try a representative sample of Third Reich leaders, including Hitler's No. 2 man, Hermann Goering (the always chilling Cox). The trial scenes generally work but there's also the needless byplay of a romance between Jackson and his secretary Elsie (Hennessy). Based on the book "Nuremberg: Infamy on Trial" by Joseph E. Persico. **240m/C; DVD.** Alec Baldwin; Jill(ian) Hennessey; Brian Cox; Michael Ironside; Christopher Plummer; Matt Craven; Max von Sydow; Len Cariou; Len Doncheff; Herbert Knaup; ***D:*** Yves Simoneau; ***W:*** David W. Rintels; ***C:*** Alan Dostie; ***M:*** Richard Gregoire. **CABLE**

Nurse 🦴🦴 ½ **1980** A recently widowed woman resumes her career as a nurse in a large urban hospital, after her son leaves for college. Based on Peggy Anderson's book. Pilot for a TV series. **105m/C; VHS, DVD.** Michael Learned; Robert Reed; Antonio Fargas; ***D:*** David Lowell Rich. **TV**

The Nurse 🦴 ½ **1997 (R)** Nurse Laura Harriman (Zane) seeks revenge from the man she holds responsible for her father's suicide by destroying his family. **94m/C; VHS, DVD.** Lisa Zane; John Stockwell; Janet Gunn; William R. Moses; Nancy Dussault; Sherrie Rose; Jay Underwood; Michael Fairman; ***D:*** Rob Malenfant; ***W:*** Richard Brandes; ***C:*** Feliks Parnell; ***M:*** Richard Bowers.

Nurse 3D 🦴 ½ **2013 (R)** Twisted, perverse nurse Abby (de la Huerta) has a warped sense of justice--she lures married men into bed, then kills them as punishment for their infidelity. To cover up the mess, she drugs and romances rookie female nurse Danni (Bowden), blaming her for the murders. Danni's relationships and sense of reality spiral out of control, all under the guidance of nurse Abby. However, even with all the vindictive throat-slashing, Abby isn't having any fun. Her relentless voiceover talks about her depression and sadness. Making trash is fine as long as you sweeten it with a wink once in awhile. This trash just stinks. **84m/C; DVD, Blu-Ray.** Paz de la Huerta; Katrina Bowden; Corbin Bleu; Judd Nelson; Boris Kodjoe; Martin Donovan; Kathleen Turner; ***D:*** Douglas Aarniokoski; ***W:*** Douglas Aarniokoski; David Loughery; ***C:*** Boris Mojsovski; ***M:*** Anton Sanko.

Nurse Betty 🦴🦴🦴 **2000 (R)** Waitress Betty (Zellweger) fantasizes about her favorite soap opera doc David Ravell (Kinnear), but confuses fantasy and reality after witnessing the murder of her sleazoid husband (Eckhart). Thinking she's a character in the soap herself, Betty travels to Hollywood to be reunited with her true love, trailed by her husband's two killers (Rock, Freeman). LaBute's unpredictable black comedy represents a departure from his previous claustrophobic, misanthropic work, but retains a cynical edge. Zellweger and Freeman stand out in a stellar cast that includes Kinnear at his smarmy best. **110m/C; DVD.** Renée Zellweger; Morgan Freeman; Chris Rock; Greg Kinnear; Aaron Eckhart; Crispin Glover; Allison Janney; Pruitt Taylor Vince; Kathleen Wilhoite; Harriet Sansom Harris; Susan Barnes; Sheila Kelley; Tia Texada; ***D:*** Neil LaBute; ***W:*** John C. Richards; ***C:*** Jean-Yves Escoffier; ***M:*** Rolfe Kent. Golden Globes '01: Actress--Mus./Comedy (Zellweger).

Nurse Edith Cavell 🦴🦴🦴 **1939** Fine performances in this true story of Britain's famous nurse who aided the Belgian underground during WWI, transporting wounded soldiers out of the German-occupied country. Decidedly opposes war and, ironically, was released just as WWII began to heat up in 1939. **95m/B; VHS, DVD.** George Sanders; Edna May Oliver; Zasu Pitts; Robert Coote; May Robson; Anna Neagle; ***D:*** Herbert Wilcox.

The Nut Job 🦴 **2014 (PG)** Another lackluster slice of CGI kid's animation that furthers the case that the move from hand-drawn family films to computer-generated may have drained the genre of its soul. This awful, grating noise features a squirrel named Surly (Arnett), who gets caught up in a human caper when he tries to rob a nut store that is merely a front for bank robbers. The A-list voice cast can't help a script that doesn't go beyond bodily humor, physical hi-jinks, and silly voices. Bright colors and fast-talking characters won't keep even the littlest ones entertained for long. **86m/C; DVD, Blu-Ray.** *US CA SK V:* Will Arnett; Liam Neeson; Maya Rudolph; Brendan Fraser; Katherine Heigl; Stephen Lang; Jeff Dunham; ***D:*** Peter Lepeniotis; ***W:*** Peter Lepeniotis; Lorne Cameron; ***M:*** Paul Intson.

The Nut Job 2: Nutty by Nature 🦴🦴 **2017 (PG)** The sequel to the unexpected animated hit The Nut Job (2014) was guided to the screen by a new trio of writers but retains the appeal of its predecessor. While Surly Squirrel (Arnett) gains righteous praise for giving animals of Liberty Park unlimited access to an abandoned neighborhood nut shop, his friend Andie (Heigel) worries that they have forgotten how to forage for themselves. When Andie's words come to pass, Surly cannot find food for everyone and becomes entangled with the powerful city mouse Mr. Feng (Chan). The animals also must band together to face Oakton City's mayor (Moynihan), who wants to turn Liberty Park into an amusement park. **91m/C; DVD, Blu-Ray.** Will Arnett; Katherine Heigl; Maya Rudolph; Bobby Cannavale; Jackie Chan; ***D:*** Callan Brunker; ***W:*** Callan Brunker; Bob Barlen; Scott Bindley; ***M:*** Heitor Pereira.

The Nutcracker and the Four Realms 🦴🦴 **2018 (PG)** If Tchaikovsky scored the movies *The Chronicles of Narnia* and *Alice in Wonderland*, the result would be this ill-conceived confection. Mackenzie Foy plays Clara, a plucky, key-seeking girl who falls through a hollow tree into a magical, snowy world. There are nods to the famous Christmas-time ballet, but its directors aimed to incorporate more from the dark source material, a short story written by E.T.A. Hoffman in 1816. The costumes and set pieces are extravagant and inventive; plot and dialogue are mere afterthoughts. **99m/C; Blu-Ray, Streaming.** Mackenzie Foy; Keira Knightley; Morgan Freeman; Dame Helen Mirren; Matthew Macfadyen; ***D:*** Lasse Hallstrom; Joe Johnston; ***W:*** Ashleigh Powell; ***C:*** Linus Sandgren; ***M:*** James Newton Howard.

Nutcracker: Money, Madness & Murder 🦴🦴🦴 **1987** Remick is chillingly effective as sociopathic socialite Frances Bradshaw Schreuder in this true crime miniseries that's based on the book by Shana Alexander. Mentally unstable Frances comes from a wealthy family but impulsively marries outside her social strata. After divorcing two husbands, she takes her sons Marc and Larry and tries to establish herself in New York, using them to swindle money from her father. Frances eventually pressures a teenaged Marc (Donovan) into murder, leading to her own arrest and sensational trial. **286m/C; DVD.** Lee Remick; Tate Donovan; Frank Military; John Glover; Linda Kelsey; G.D. Spradlin; Elizabeth Wilson; Inga Swenson; ***D:*** Paul Bogart; ***W:*** William Hanley; ***C:*** Isidore Mankofsky; ***M:*** Billy Goldenberg. **TV**

The Nutcracker Prince 🦴🦴 **1991** The classic children's Christmas tale comes alive in this feature-length animated special. **75m/C; VHS, DVD.** *CA V:* Kiefer Sutherland; Megan Follows; Michael McDonald; Phyllis Diller; Peter O'Toole; ***D:*** Paul Schibli.

Nuts 🦴🦴🦴 **1987 (R)** A high-priced prostitute attempts to prove her sanity when she's accused of manslaughter. Ashamed of her lifestyle, and afraid of her reasons for it, her parents attempt to institutionalize her. A filmed version of Tom Topor's play that manages to retain its mesmerizing qualities. Fine performances, although the funnygirl goes over the top on several occasions. **116m/C; VHS, DVD.** Barbra Streisand; Richard Dreyfuss; Maureen Stapleton; Karl Malden; James Whitmore; Robert Webber; Eli Wallach; Leslie Nielsen; William Prince; Dakin Matthews; Hayley Taylor Block; ***D:*** Martin Ritt; ***W:*** Tom Topor; Darryl Ponicsan; Alvin Sargent; ***C:*** Andrzej Bartkowiak; ***M:*** Barbra Streisand.

Nuts! 🦴🦴🦴 **2016** The story of Dr. John Romulus Brinkley is so outlandish that only a mostly-animated, mostly-true documentary about him could do it justice. Brinkley was a con man in the 1920s who masqueraded as a doctor, building an empire out of promising to cure impotence with the use of goat testicles. While one might think this could be either a bore or an oddity, director Penny Lane delivers a film that is both playful and a warning against snake-oil salesman. It's funny and slightly disturbing, and a documentary that can be both is rare. **79m/C; DVD.** Gene Tognacci; ***D:*** Penny Lane; ***W:*** Thom Stylinski; ***C:*** Penny Lane; Hallie Kohler; Joseph Victorine; Angela Walley; Mark Walley.

Nuts in May 🦴🦴 **1976** Two smug, middle-aged, middle-class vegetarians go on a camping trip and totally alienate their cynical, working-class fellow campers. **84m/C; VHS, DVD.** *GB* Alison Steadman; Anthony O'Donnell; Roger Sloman; ***D:*** Mike Leigh; ***W:*** Mike Leigh; ***C:*** Michael Williams. **TV**

The Nutt House 🦴 ½ **1995 (PG-13)** Identical twins—separated at birth—grow up to be a slimy politician and a nutcase (living up to the family name) with multiple personalities. Naturally, when the two are reunited it makes for lots of outrageous complications. **90m/C; VHS, DVD.** Stephen Kearney; Traci Lords; Amy Yasbeck; ***Cameo(s):*** Stella Stevens; Robert Mandan; Catherine Bach; ***D:*** Adam Rifkin; ***W:*** Ron Zwang; Scott Spiegel; Sam Raimi; ***C:*** Bernd Heinl; ***M:*** Cameron Allan.

The Nutty Professor 🦴🦴🦴 **1963** A mild-mannered chemistry professor creates a potion that turns him into a suave, debonair, playboy type with an irresistible attraction to women. Lewis has repeatedly denied the slick character is a Dean Martin parody, but the evidence is quite strong. Easily Lewis's best film. **107m/C; VHS, DVD, Blu-Ray.** Jerry Lewis; Stella Stevens; Del Moore; Kathleen Freeman; Howard Morris; Les Brown; Med Flory; Norman Alden; Milton Frome; Buddy Lester; Henry Gibson; ***D:*** Jerry Lewis; ***W:*** Jerry Lewis; Bill Richmond; ***C:*** W. Wallace Kelley; ***M:*** Walter Scharf. Natl. Film Reg. '04.

The Nutty Professor 🦴🦴🦴 **1996 (PG-13)** Remake of the 1963 Jerry Lewis comedy stars Murphy as Professor Sherman Klump, a severely overweight but bright man whose heft gets in the way of his love life. He takes a swig of his own secret potion and is transformed into the slim and suave Buddy Love. Only the formula isn't perfect and seems to wear off at the worst possible times. Reminiscent of "Coming to America," Murphy plays eight different roles. The fat and fart jokes are plentiful and so are the laughs. **96m/C; DVD, Blu-Ray, HD-DVD.** Eddie Murphy; Jada Pinkett Smith; James Coburn; Dave Chappelle; ***D:*** Tom Shadyac; ***W:*** David Sheffield; Barry W. Blaustein; Steve Oedekerk; Tom Shadyac; ***C:*** Julio Macat; ***M:*** David Newman. Oscars '96: Makeup; Natl. Soc. Film Critics '96: Actor (Murphy).

Nutty Professor 2: The Klumps 🦴🦴 ½ **2000 (PG-13)** Sequel to the 1996 hit finds Murphy working overtime as Sherman Klump attempts to remove the DNA of his alter ego Buddy Love from his system. Once Buddy escapes, he steals Sherman's latest experiment, a youth serum. Buddy also complicates Sherman's relationship with a beautiful colleague (Jackson) and the entire Klump clan. Expanding a one-joke scene from the original is risky, but Murphy and the writers manage to pull it off rather impressively. Yes, the humor is crude, but the story is funny while the characters, if not always appealing, are sympathetic and genuine. **105m/C; DVD, Blu-Ray, HD-DVD.** Eddie Murphy; Janet Jackson; Anna Maria Horsford; Melinda McGraw; Richard Gant; John Ales; Larry Miller; Chris Elliott; Earl Boen; Kathleen Freeman; Charles Napier; Jamal Mixon; Nikki Cox; ***D:*** Peter Segal; ***W:*** Barry W. Blaustein; David Sheffield; Chris Weitz; Paul Weitz; Steve Oedekerk; ***C:*** Dean Semler; ***M:*** David Newman.

NYC: Tornado Terror 🦴 ½ **2008** Mediocre Sci Fi Channel disaster pic. NYC deputy mayor Jim Lawrence (Spence) and his meteorologist wife Cassie (de Boer) are picnicking in the park when Cassie notices that the dust devils kids are chasing are actually tiny tornadoes. They soon begin forming into one twister that threatens to become a super storm. And the Statue of Liberty gets it once again. **90m/C; DVD.** Sebastian Spence; Nicole de Boer; Jerry Wasserman; Tegan Moss; Colby Johannson; Winston Rekert; ***D:*** Tibor Takacs; ***W:*** T.S. Cook; ***C:*** Clinton Shorter. **CABLE**

NYC Underground 🦴 **2013 (R)** Typical drug-deal-gone bad flick. A bunch of rich teenage boys head out in NYC for the night led by Dylan (Mayes), who of course has ulterior motives for the group (cue the drug deal). They have to run for their lives from gangster Siman (Crawford) and naturally the best place to do that is via the subway. **87m/C; DVD.** Rob Mayes; Sean Faris; Clayne Crawford; Arielle Kebbel; Evan Ross; Dania Ramirez; ***D:*** Jessy Terrero; ***W:*** Andrew Klavan; ***C:*** Charles Minsky; ***M:*** Matthias Weber. **VIDEO**

A Nymphoid Barbarian in Dinosaur Hell **WOOF! 1994** Nuclear holocaust survivors, human and otherwise, vie for the affections of the last woman alive, a voluptuous nymphoid barbarian. **90m/C; VHS, DVD.** Linda Corwin; Paul Guzzi; ***D:*** Bret Piper; ***W:*** Bret Piper.

Nymphomaniac, Volume 1 🦴🦴 ½ **2013** The first half of director/writer Von Trier's four-hour epic about the numbing impact of sex addiction finds the director at his most playful in years. Joe (Gainsbourg) is found badly bruised in an alley by Seligman (Skarsgard). As she heals, Joe tells her story--that of a nymphomaniac--and the film flashes back to tales of sexual encounters. He brilliantly reduces her sex life to another obsessive hobby. It feels incomplete without the second half but also is a perfect set-up for it. **118m/C; DVD, Blu-Ray.** *DK* Charlotte Gainsbourg; Stellan Skarsgard; Stacy Martin; Shia LaBeouf; Christian Slater; Uma Thurman; ***D:*** Lars von Trier; ***W:*** Lars von Trier; ***C:*** Manuel Alberto Claro.

Nymphomaniac: Volume II 🦴🦴 **2014** Von Trier's second volume exploring a life in which sex becomes a numbing routine takes a darker turn. Joe (Gainsbourg) continues to convey her story to the kindly Seligman (Skarsgard), going through chapters of increasing intensity, such as when she engages in a masochistic affair with the mysterious K (Bell). Still top-notch filmmaking, but one misses the engaging Stacy Martin (Gainsbourg plays herself in flashbacks this time), and the switch from playful to dark isn't 100% successful. **123m/C; DVD, Blu-Ray.** *DK* Charlotte Gainsbourg; Stellan Skarsgard; Jamie Bell; ***D:*** Lars von Trier; ***W:*** Lars von Trier; ***C:*** Manuel Alberto Claro.

O 🦴🦴🦴 **2001 (R)** An exclusive South Carolina high school serves as background for this updated teen "Othello," which substitutes basketball for battle. Odin (Phifer) is the sole black student at Palmetto Grove Academy due to his hoops prowess. He has an intimate relationship with Desi (Stiles), the daughter of the school's dean. Hugo (Hartnett), the envious son of the basketball coach (Sheen), plots Odin's destruction by poisoning his mind against Desi. Although blasted by some critics as full of skimpy plot devices, there's not much that's not taken straight from the source material. Filmed in 1999, it was pulled following the Columbine shootings and not released until 2001. **94m/C; DVD.** Mekhi Phifer; Josh Hartnett; Julia Stiles; Elden (Ratliff) Henson; Andrew Keegan; Rain Phoenix; John Heard; A.J. (Anthony) Johnson; Martin Sheen; ***D:*** Tim Blake Nelson; ***W:*** Brad Kaaya; ***C:*** Russell Fine; ***M:*** Jeff Danna.

O Brother Where Art Thou? 🦴🦴 ½ **2000 (PG-13)** Chain gang escapee Ulysses Everett McGill (Clooney), who, along with fellow escapees Pete and Delmar (Turturro and Nelson), sets out on an "Odyssey"-like journey through Depression-era Mississippi bound for home and his wife, Penny (Hunter). What the trio encounter along the way are a number of Coenesque situations and characters that, when all is said and done, seem like just that—individual situations that never really add up to a cohesive whole. They fit well enough to comprise a pretty enjoyable film, though. Fine performances by Clooney, Nelson, and Coen regulars Goodman and Turturro. **103m/C; DVD, Blu-Ray.** George Clooney; Tim Blake Nelson; John Turturro; Holly Hunter; John Goodman; Charles Durning; Del Pentacost; Michael Badalucco; Brian Reddy; Wayne Duvall; Ed Gale; Ray McKinnon; Daniel von Bargen; Royce D. Applegate; Frank Collison; Lee Weaver; Stephen (Steve) Root; Musetta Vander; Chris Thomas King; Mia Tyler; Christy Taylor; ***D:*** Joel Coen; ***W:*** Ethan Coen; Joel Coen; ***C:*** Roger Deakins; ***M:*** T-Bone Burnett; Chris Thomas King; Carter Burwell. Golden Globes '01: Actor--Mus./Comedy (Clooney).

O Fantasma 🦴🦴 *Phantom* **2000** The darker side of sexuality is explored as lonely, twentysomething trash collector Sergio (Menses) drifts through his life in a dreamline haze, indulging in anonymous sexual encounters. He discovers a taste for the sexual extreme and becomes obsessed with the unobtainable Joao (Barbosa)?stalking him until Sergio can act on his desires. Explicit sex—fuzzy narrative. Portuguese with subtitles. **90m/C; VHS, DVD.** *PT* Ricardo Meneses; Andre Barbosa; Beatriz Torcato; Eurico Vieira; ***D:*** Joao Pedro Rodrigues; ***W:*** Joao Pedro Rodrigues; Jose Neves; Paulo Rebelo; Alexandre Melo; ***C:*** Rui Poças.

O Jerusalem 🦴 ½ **2007 (R)** Clunky retelling of the founding of Israel in 1948 that's based on the 1972 book by Dominique Lapierre and Larry Collins. When they lived in New York, Jewish Bobby (Feild) and Arab Said (Taghamaoui) were the best of friends. But in 1946 both travel to Palestine and find themselves in increasing opposition in a clash between the Brits, the Arabs, and the Jews for territory and legitimacy. **101m/C; DVD.** J.J. Feild; Said Taghmaoui; Ian Holm; Tovah Feldshuh; Tom Conti; Patrick Bruel; Maria Papas; Mel Raido; Jamie Harding; ***D:*** Elie Chouraqui; ***W:*** Elie Chouraqui; ***C:*** Giovanni Fiore Coltellacci; ***M:*** Stephen Endelman.

O Lucky Man! 🦴🦴🦴🦴 **1973 (R)** Surreal, black comedy following the rise and fall and eventual rebirth of a modern British coffee salesman. Several actors play multiple roles with outstanding performances throughout. Price's excellent score combines with the hilarity for an extraordinary experience. **178m/C; VHS, DVD.** *GB* Malcolm McDowell; Ralph Richardson; Rachel Roberts; Arthur Lowe; Alan Price; Dame Helen Mirren; Mona Washbourne; Warren Clarke; ***D:*** Lindsay Anderson; ***M:*** Alan Price. British Acad. '73: Support. Actor (Lowe).

O Pioneers! 🦴🦴 ½ **1991 (PG)** Lange plays Alexandra Bergson, an unmarried woman at the turn of the century, who inherits her family's Nebraska homestead because her father knows how much she loves the land. Although the family has prospered through Alexandra's smart investments, her brothers come to resent her influence. When her first love returns after 15 years and the romance is rekindled, family resentments surface once again. Based on the novel by Willa Cather. A Hallmark Hall of Fame presentation. **99m/C; VHS, DVD.** Jessica Lange; David Strathairn; Tom Aldredge; Reed Edward Diamond; Anne Heche; Heather Graham; Josh Hamilton; Leigh Lawson; Graham Beckel; ***D:*** Glenn Jordan; ***W:*** Glenn Jordan. **TV**

Oasis of the Zombies 🦴 *Bloodsucking Nazi Zombies; Treasure of the Living Dead* **1982** European students set out to find buried treasure in Saharan oasis but instead find bevy of hungry Nazis with eating disorders. Franco directed under the name "A.M. Frank." **75m/C; VHS, DVD, Blu-Ray.** *SP FR* Manuel Gelin; France Jordan; Jeff Montgomery; Miriam Landson; Eric Saint-Just; Caroline Audret; Henry Lambert; ***D:*** Jess (Jesus) Franco; ***W:*** Jess (Jesus) Franco.

Oasis: Supersonic 🦴🦴🦴 **2016 (R)** A feature-length, in-depth documentary about the British band Oasis. Focusing on the lives of the band members and the band's music, the documentary analyzes the struggles and conflicts for and within the band. The film also places the Manchester-based band in context, explaining how they defined an era. Concert footage and first-hand accounts of the tensions between the Gallagher brothers is in included as well. **122m/C; DVD, Blu-Ray, Streaming, Download.** ***D:*** Mat Whitecross; ***M:*** Rael Jones.

The Oath 🦴🦴🦴 ½ *El juramento* **2010** Poitra's highly-detailed documentary follows radical Islamic tactics through the eyes of Abu Jandal, a taxi driver in Yemen who was once Osama bin Laden's bodyguard. Intensely engaging, Jandal reveals much of what has been hidden from the American media following the World Trade Center attack. Unraveling his terrorist history, Jandal relates the chilling truths of the story of his brother-in-law and Al-Qaeda recruit Salim Hamdan, held at Guantanamo Bay on terrorism charges. The second in a planned trilogy on post-9/11 American policy, following Poitra's 2006 Iraq documentary "My Country, My Country." **97m/C; DVD.** ***D:*** Laura Poitras; ***C:*** Laura Poitras; Kirsten Boyd Johnson; ***M:*** Osvaldo Golijov.

The Oath 🦴🦴 ½ **2018 (R)** Family quarrels go to an extreme in this political satire, a pet project of Ike Barinholtz, its star, writer, director, and producer. U.S. citizens are given a deadline of Black Friday (the day after Thanksgiving) to sign a loyalty oath to the President, ensuring heated arguments at the family feast. The altercations become physical when federal agents arrive to interrogate non-signers. Part political commentary, part home invasion, this flick loses direction in the second half but remains mildly critical to both sides of the political spectrum. **93m/C; DVD, Blu-Ray.** Ike Barinholtz; Tiffany Haddish; John Cho; Carrie Brownstein; Billy Magnussen; ***D:*** Ike Barinholtz; ***W:*** Ike Barinholtz; ***C:*** Cary Lalonde; ***M:*** Bret Mazur.

Obituary 🦴 ½ **2006** Routine murder mystery with a somewhat silly lead. Newspaper obit writer Denise (Bisset) expects to be promoted to reporter, especially after stumbling onto a murder scene. Then Denise realizes she read an obit for the murder victim before the crime occurred. When the promotion goes to her ex-boyfriend Simon (Nickalls), Denise keeps investigating but can't get anyone to believe her theories about the crime until the killer targets her. **90m/C; DVD.** Josie Bissett; Grant Nickalls; Craig Olejnik; Alan C. Peterson; Joe Pingue; Amber Cull; ***D:*** John Bradshaw; ***W:*** Joanne Wannan; ***C:*** Russ Goozee; ***M:*** Stacey Hersh. **CABLE**

The Object of Beauty 🦴🦴🦴 **1991 (R)** Two Americans, trapped in Europe by their love of pleasure and their lack of money, bicker over whether to sell their one object of value—a tiny Henry Moore sculpture. When it disappears, their relationship is challenged. Excellent acting and telling direction. Forces an examination of one's own value placement. **105m/C; VHS, DVD.** Andie MacDowell; John Malkovich; Joss Ackland; Lolita Davidovich; Peter Riegert; Bill Paterson; Rudi Davies; Ricci Harnett; ***D:*** Michael Lindsay-Hogg; ***W:*** Michael Lindsay-Hogg; ***C:*** David Watkin; ***M:*** Tom Bahler.

The Object of My Affection 🦴🦴 ½ **1998 (R)** Brooklyn social worker Nina (Aniston) has an overbearing boyfriend, Vince (Pankow), she doesn't really love. Unfortunately, the man she does fall for is handsome gay teacher George (Rudd), who's broken up with his pretentious boyfriend, Joley (Daly), and is now renting Nina's spare room. When Nina discovers she's pregnant, she decides George would make a terrific father and asks him to raise the baby with her. But both turn out to have very unrealistic expectations about friendship and romance. Mix of humor and tears, with good performances, particularly by the appealing leads. Adapted from the novel by Stephen McCauley. **112m/C; DVD.** Jennifer Aniston; Paul Rudd; John Pankow; Timothy Daly; Alan Alda; Nigel Hawthorne; Allison Janney; Amo Gulinello; Steve Zahn; Daniel Cosgrove; ***D:*** Nicholas Hytner; ***W:*** Wendy Wasserstein; ***C:*** Oliver Stapleton; ***M:*** George Fenton.

Object of Obsession 🦴 ½ **1995 (R)** One wrong phone call propels divorcee Margaret into an affair with a stranger that leads to kinky psycho/sexual games and revenge. **91m/C; VHS, DVD.** Erika Anderson; Scott Valentine; ***D:*** Alexander Gregory (Gregory Dark) Hippolyte; ***W:*** Brad (Sean) Marlowe; ***C:*** Wally Pfister.

The Objective 🦴 ½ **2008** Stale and cliched supernatural thriller. CIA agent Benjamin Keynes (Ball) is sent on a secret mission to Afghanistan to figure out if a mysterious radioactive heat signal means Al Qaeda has nuclear weapons. Keynes heads into the mountains with a special forces team only to discover that their enemy isn't even human. **90m/C; DVD.** Jonas Ball; Jon Huertas; Michael C. Williams; Sam Hunter; Jeff Prewett; Chems-Eddine Zinoune; Matthew R. Anderson; ***D:*** Daniel Myrick; ***W:*** Daniel Myrick; Mark Patton; Wes Clark, Jr.; ***C:*** Stephanie Martin; ***M:*** Kays Al-Atrakchi.

Objective, Burma! 🦴🦴🦴🦴 **1945** Deemed by many to be the greatest and most moving WWII production released during the war. American paratroopers are dropped over Burma where their mission is to destroy a Japanese radar station. The Americans (led by Flynn) are successful in wiping out the station, but they are spotted and descended upon by Japanese forces. Impeded from returning to Allied lines, the American soldiers must try to survive enemy encounters, exhaustion, starvation, and the elements until they are rescued. Splendid performance by Flynn and exceptional direction from Walsh; excellent performances enhanced by energetic score. **142m/B; DVD.** Errol Flynn; James Brown; William Prince; George Tobias; Henry Hull; Warner Anderson; Richard Erdman; Mark Stevens; Anthony Caruso; Hugh Beaumont; John Alvin; William (Bill) Hudson; Lester Matthews; George Tyne; Erville Alderson; ***D:*** Raoul Walsh; ***W:*** Ranald MacDougall; Lester Cole; ***C:*** James Wong Howe; ***M:*** Franz Waxman.

Oblivion 🦴🦴 ½ **1994 (PG-13)** In this sci-fi western, set in the year 3031, its cowboys versus the aliens. A sheriff's son (Paul) returns to the town of Oblivion to avenge his father's murder and finds a reptilian extraterrestrial (Divoff) terrorizing the community. **94m/C; VHS, DVD.** Richard Joseph Paul; Andrew Divoff; Jackie Swanson; Meg Foster; Isaac Hayes; Julie Newmar; Carel Struycken; George Takei; ***D:*** Sam Irvin; ***W:*** Peter David; ***M:*** Pino Donaggio.

Oblivion 🦴🦴 ½ **2013 (PG-13)** In a post-apocalyptic future (is there any other kind?), a veteran named Jack (Cruise) has the unenviable task of going to Earth to repair the drones that mine the planet for resources to take back to outer space. A spacecraft crashes on the planet and Jack investigates, discovering an underground community led by the rebellious Malcolm (Freeman). Director/writer Kosinski's contribution to the sci-fi genre feels remarkably familiar but has enough style to spare. It's heavier on notable visuals than an actually memorable story but Cruise is at his engaging best. **124m/C; DVD, Blu-Ray.** Tom Cruise; Morgan Freeman; Olga Kurylenko; Nikolaj Coster-Waldau; Melissa Leo; Andrea Riseborough; ***D:*** Joseph Kosinski; ***W:*** Karl Gajdusek; Michael Arndt; ***C:*** Claudio Miranda; ***M:*** Anthony Gonzalez; Joseph Tranese.

Oblomov 🦴🦴🦴 ½ *A Few Days in the Life of I.I. Oblomov; Neskolko Dnel iz Zhizni I.I. Oblomov* **1981** A production of the classic Goncharov novel about a symbolically inert Russian aristocrat whose childhood friend helps him find a reason for action. Well made, with fine performances. In Russian with English subtitles. **145m/C; VHS, DVD.** *RU* Oleg Tabakov; Elena Solovei; ***D:*** Nikita Mikhalkov.

The Oblong Box 🦴🦴 *Edgar Allen Poe's The Oblong Box* **1969 (PG)** Coffins, blood, and live corpses fill drawn-out and lifeless adaptation of Edgar Allan Poe story. English aristocrat Price attempts to hide his disfigured brother in an old tower. Brother predictably escapes and rampages through town before being killed. **91m/C; VHS, DVD, Blu-Ray.** *GB* Vincent Price; Christopher Lee; Alister Williamson; Hilary Dwyer; Peter Arne; Harry Baird; Carl Rigg; Sally Geeson; Maxwell Shaw; ***D:*** Gordon Hessler; ***W:*** Lawrence Huntington; ***C:*** John Coquillon.

Obselidia **2010** Bell's debut feature is an eccentric indie drama about a man devoted to anything close to being extinct or obsolete. Brainy, rigid, and emotionally-stunted L.A. librarian George has a personal obsession with completing his book 'The Obselidia: An Encyclopedia of Obsolete Things.' When he interviews Sophie, the projectionist at the Silent Movie Theater, he discovers a like-minded soul, but one more conversant with the modern world. They begin an equally odd courtship that involves a road trip to Death Valley. **103m/C; DVD, Blu-Ray, Streaming.** Michael Piccirilli; Gaynor Howe; Frank Hoyt Taylor; Chris Byrne; Kim Beuche; ***D:*** Diane Bell; ***W:*** Diane Bell; ***C:*** Zak Mulligan; ***M:*** Liam Howe.

Observe and Report **½ 2009 (R)** Head of security Ronnie Barnhard (Rogen) patrols his shopping mall jurisdiction with an iron fist, combating skateboarders, shoplifters, and the occasional unruly customer while dreaming of the day when he can swap his flashlight for a badge and a gun. Ronnie's delusions of grandeur are tested when the mall is struck by a flasher. Plays way more dark than you'd expect and Rogen works against his everyman likability by relying on sexist, racist, homophobic, and sterotypical rent-a-cop mentality. Faris is genuinely funny as the ditzy blond object of Rogen's misguided affection. **86m/C; DVD, Blu-Ray.** Seth Rogen; Ray Liotta; Anna Faris; Patton Oswalt; Michael Peña; Jesse Plemons; ***D:*** Jody Hill; ***W:*** Jody Hill; ***C:*** Tim Orr; ***M:*** Joey Stephens.

Obsessed **2002** Based on a true crime story. Chicago medical writer Ellena Roberts (Elfman) is arrested for harassing married neurosurgeon David Stillman (Robards). Ellena claims to her lawyer Sara Miller (Burton) that they had an ongoing affair and David was leaving his wife for her but Stillman insists the affair never happened and Ellena is just nuts. Elfman's character spends a lot of the pic in her underwear, which might be one reason to watch. **90m/C; DVD.** Jenna Elfman; Sam Robards; Kate Burton; Jane Wheeler; Mark Camacho; Lisa Edelstein; Charles Powell; ***D:*** John Badham; ***W:*** Matthew Tabak; ***C:*** Ron Stannett; ***M:*** Joseph Conlan. **CABLE**

Obsessed **2009 (PG-13)** Cat fights between hot chicks! Successful L.A. businessman Derek (Elba) finds his idyllic married life with beautiful wife Sharon (Knowles) threatened when office temp Lisa (Larter) becomes obsessed and starts stalking him. Derek resists Lisa's vixenish charms but she makes certain that the jealous Sharon thinks something happened. But when Sharon comes to her senses she isn't about to let a delusional Lisa have her man. **101m/C; Blu-Ray, On Demand.** Idris Elba; Beyonce Knowles; Ali Larter; Christine Lahti; Bruce McGill; Scout Taylor-Compton; Jerry O'Connell; Matthew Humphreys; ***D:*** Steve Shill; ***W:*** David Loughery; ***C:*** Ken Seng; ***M:*** James Dooley.

Obsession **1949** A decent British noir creeper. Dr. Clive Riordan (Newton) goes crazy when he discovers his wife Storm (Gray) has taken yet another lover. He kidnaps Bill (Brown) and holds him captive, planning a protracted and grisly end (involving an acid bath) for the unfortunate fellow. However, Storm's curious poodle Monty and a Scotland Yard detective (Wayne) foil the plot. **96m/B; DVD.** *GB* Robert Newton; Phil Brown; Sally Gray; Naunton Wayne; James Harcourt; ***D:*** Edward Dmytryk; ***W:*** Alec Coppel; ***C:*** C.M. Pennington-Richards; ***M:*** Nino Rota.

Obsession **½ 1976 (PG)** A rich, lonely businessman meets a mysterious young girl in Italy, the mirror image of his late wife who was killed by kidnappers. Intriguing suspense film that's not quite up to comparisons with Hitchcock thrillers. Music by Hitchcock-collaborator Herrmann. **98m/C; VHS, DVD, Blu-Ray.** Cliff Robertson; Genevieve Bujold; John Lithgow; ***D:*** Brian De Palma; ***W:*** Paul Schrader; ***C:*** Vilmos Zsigmond; ***M:*** Bernard Herrmann.

Obsession **½ 1997** Pierre (Berling) is Miriam's (Makatsch) longtime lover. They seem happy until Miriam has a chance encounter at the Berlin train station with Jack McHale (Craig), who's investigating a family secret. The romantic triangle is inexplicable (Pierre's accepting, Jack's suddenly obsessed, and Miriam waffles) and John's family quest is confusing and ends in an unsatisfying manner. **105m/C; DVD.** *FR GE* Heike Makatsch; Charles Berling; Daniel Craig; Seymour Cassel; Allen Garfield; Marie-Christine Barrault; Daniel Gelin; ***D:*** Peter Sehr; ***W:*** Peter Sehr; Marie Noelle; ***C:*** David Watkin; ***M:*** Micki Meuser.

The Obsession **WOOF! 2006** Truly awful psycho-drama. Divorcee Deborah (Zuniga) discovers that her new boyfriend Reed (Spence) is actually obsessed with her teenage daughter Erika (Gatien), one of his ballet students. Since Gatien shows neither acting nor dancing skills (and there are way too many slow-motion dance montages), her character being the object of anyone's attention—let alone obsession—is unlikely. **90m/C; DVD.** Daphne Zuniga; Elise Gatien; Sebastian Spence; Nels Lennarson; ***D:*** David Winkler; ***W:*** Christopher Morro; ***C:*** Adam Sliwinski; ***M:*** Peter Allen. **CABLE**

Obvious Child **2014 (R)** Slate delivers a breakthrough performances as Donna Stern, a stand-up comedienne who gets dumped and rebounds into a one-night stand with the sweet Max (Lacy). Of course, Donna finds out a few weeks later that she's pregnant. She chooses to have an abortion but the decision and the general upheaval in her life forces her to rethink a few decisions and even draws her closer to Max. The brilliance of Slate and writer/director Robespierre's film is that it actually contains many of the tenets of the rom-com while still feeling more real than most Hollywood chick flicks. **84m/C; DVD, Blu-Ray.** Jenny Slate; Jake Lacy; Gaby Hoffman; Richard Kind; Polly Draper; ***D:*** Gillian Robespierre; ***W:*** Gillian Robespierre; ***C:*** Chris Teague; ***M:*** Chris Bordeaux.

O.C. and Stiggs **½ 1987 (R)** Two teens spend a summer harassing a neighbor and his family. Flimsy attempts at comedy fall flat. A failed adaptation of a National Lampoon short story, it was held for three years before release. **109m/C; VHS, DVD.** Daniel H. Jenkins; Neill Barry; Jane Curtin; Tina Louise; Jon Cryer; Dennis Hopper; Paul Dooley; Ray Walston; Louis Nye; Martin Mull; Melvin Van Peebles; ***D:*** Robert Altman; ***W:*** Donald Cantrell.

An Occasional Hell **½ 1996 (R)** Ernest DeWalt (Berenger) is an ex-cop turned writer and college professor. He investigates the death of a fellow professor (Lang) at the behest of the beautiful widow (Golino) and then learns the lady is the prime suspect. Filmed in South Carolina and based on the novel by Silvis, who wrote the screenplay. **93m/C; VHS, DVD.** Tom Berenger; Valeria Golino; Kari Wuhrer; Robert Davi; Stephen Lang; Richard Edson; Geoffrey Lewis; ***D:*** Salome Breziner; ***W:*** Randall Silvis; ***C:*** Mauro Fiore; ***M:*** Anton Sanko.

The Occultist **WOOF! 1989** Satan worshippers do the dance of death as they skin men alive for their evil purposes. **82m/C; VHS, DVD.** Rick Gianasi; ***D:*** Tim Kincaid; ***W:*** Tim Kincaid.

Occupation: Dreamland **2005** Documentary directors Scott and Olds spent six weeks in 2004 in the very dangerous city of Fallujah, following an eight-man squad of the Army's 82nd Airborne as they deal with hostile fire, isolation, bewildering customs, and whether their presence really will make any difference to the Iraqis. **78m/C; DVD.** ***D:*** Garrett Scott; Ian Olds.

Oceans *DisneyNature: Oceans* **2009 (G)** Another astonishing documentary from DisneyNature. Specially designed cameras follow a vast variety of sea creatures in this nature documentary that took four years of filming in some 54 locations. The directors offer a firm but understated reminder that three-quarters of the planet is water and the oceans should not be used as a garbage dump, a runoff for pollutants, and that endangered species are as important as commercial profits. **102m/C; Blu-Ray.** *FR SP SI* ***Nar:*** Jacques Perrin; ***D:*** Jacques Perrin; Jacques Cluzaud; ***W:*** Jacques Perrin; Jacques Cluzaud; ***M:*** Bruno Coulais.

Ocean's 8 **½ 2018 (PG-13)** This fourth installment of the Ocean's franchise capitalizes on a fresh infusion of characters. Debbie (Bullock), Danny Ocean's sister, leads a ring of crooks intent on swiping a necklace worth $150 million off the neck of flakey actress Daphne Kluger (Hathaway) at New York's annual Met Gala. A slick and fun romp that surpasses its predecessor (*Ocean's Thirteen*) in entertainment value, with chemistry among the all-female leads that's a joy to watch. **110m/C; DVD, Blu-Ray.** Sandra Bullock; Cate Blanchett; Anne Hathaway; Mindy Kaling; Sarah Paulson; Nora Lum; Rihanna; Helena Bonham Carter; ***D:*** Gary Ross; ***W:*** Gary Ross; Olivia Milch; ***C:*** Eigil Bryld; ***M:*** Daniel Pemberton.

Ocean's 11 **½ 1960** A Rat Pack romp. Spyros Acebos (Tamiroff) comes up with a plan to simultaneously rob five Las Vegas casinos on New Year's Eve. Danny Ocean (Sinatra) will lead his buddies—all of whom are veterans of the 82nd Airborne Division—in the action by shutting off all the electricity. The planning's elaborate but the plan itself goes wrong (so what else is new) and the gang can't get their stolen loot out of the city. **148m/C; VHS, DVD, Blu-Ray.** Frank Sinatra; Dean Martin; Sammy Davis, Jr.; Angie Dickinson; Peter Lawford; Richard Conte; Cesar Romero; Joey Bishop; Akim Tamiroff; Henry Silva; Buddy Lester; Norman Fell; Red Skelton; Shirley MacLaine; George Raft; ***D:*** Lewis Milestone; ***W:*** Harry Brown; Charles Lederer; ***C:*** William H. Daniels; ***M:*** Nelson Riddle.

Ocean's Eleven **2001 (PG-13)** Stylish, fun remake of the 1960 Rat Pack caper flick measures up to the original in Cool Factor and surpasses it in plot and action. In this version, Danny Ocean (Clooney) is an ex-con with a taste for the grift and a grudge against powerful casino owner Benedict (Garcia). Backed by an eclectic, amusingly quirky crew, he encounters complications when his ex (Roberts) turns out to be involved with Benedict. Great cast looks like they're having a blast (especially Gould and Reiner, who make the most of small but showy roles). **116m/C; DVD, Blu-Ray, UMD.** George Clooney; Brad Pitt; Andy Garcia; Matt Damon; Julia Roberts; Don Cheadle; Casey Affleck; Scott Caan; Elliott Gould; Bernie Mac; Carl Reiner; Edward Jemison; Shaobo Qin; ***Cameo(s):*** Henry Silva; Angie Dickinson; Holly Marie Combs; Joshua Jackson; Topher Grace; Steve Lawrence; Eydie Gorme; Wayne Newton; ***D:*** Steven Soderbergh; ***W:*** Ted Griffin; ***C:*** Steven Soderbergh; ***M:*** David Holmes.

Oceans of Fire **1986 (PG)** Average rehash of the tension-filled world of oil riggers. Lives of two ex-cons are threatened when they hire on as divers for world's deepest undersea oil rig. **100m/C; VHS, DVD; Open Captioned.** Gregory Harrison; Billy Dee Williams; Cynthia Sikes; Lyle Alzado; Tony Burton; Ray "Boom Boom" Mancini; David Carradine; Ken Norton; ***D:*** Steve Carver.

Ocean's Thirteen **2007 (PG-13)** The neo-Rat Pack returns to Vegas, baby, where they belong. Reuben (Gould) has been screwed out of his share of the strip's newest luxury hotel/casino by double-dealing egomaniac Willie Banks (Pacino). So Danny (Clooney) and Rusty (Pitt) assemble their usual team and concoct an elaborate plan (including simulating an earthquake) to sabotage the opening, bankrupt the casino, and ruin Banks. Old nemesis Garcia gets to join in on the fun this time out. Barkin comes in to cherchez la femme the boys club and everyone just has a cool, wink-wink good time. So should you. **122m/C; DVD, Blu-Ray, HD-DVD.** George Clooney; Brad Pitt; Matt Damon; Andy Garcia; Al Pacino; Bernie Mac; Ellen Barkin; Casey Affleck; Scott Caan; Elliott Gould; Shaobo Qin; Don Cheadle; Edward Jemison; Carl Reiner; Eddie Izzard; Michael Mantell; David Paymer; Vincent Cassel; Julian Sands; Bob Einstein; Noureen DeWulf; ***D:*** Steven Soderbergh; ***W:*** Brian Koppelman; David Levien; ***C:*** Steven Soderbergh; ***M:*** David Holmes.

Ocean's Twelve **½ 2004 (PG-13)** The gang's all back in this undemanding but fun sequel. It's taken three years but casino boss Terry Benedict (Garcia) has tracked down Danny Ocean (Clooney), now remarried to Tess (Roberts), and demands repayment of his $160 mil or else. Having spent his share of the dough, Danny gets the boys together and he and partner Rusty (Pitt) come up with a plan that takes them all a-thieving in various picturesque European cities. New to the adventure are Interpol agent Isabel Lahiri (Zeta-Jones), who has an amorous past with Rusty, and top Euro thief Francois Toulour (Cassel), out to prove just who's the best criminal. A frivolous, good-looking romp all the way. **125m/C; DVD, Blu-Ray.** George Clooney; Brad Pitt; Matt Damon; Catherine Zeta-Jones; Andy Garcia; Don Cheadle; Bernie Mac; Casey Affleck; Scott Caan; Vincent Cassel; Edward Jemison; Shaobo Qin; Carl Reiner; Elliott Gould; Robbie Coltrane; Eddie Izzard; Cherry Jones; Jeroen Krabbe; Julia Roberts; Jared Harris; ***D:*** Steven Soderbergh; ***W:*** George Nolfi; ***C:*** Steven Soderbergh; ***M:*** David Holmes.

Octagon **1980 (R)** Norris protects a woman from threatening Ninja warriors in average kung-fu adventure. Enough action and violence for fans of the genre. **103m/C; VHS, DVD, Blu-Ray, UMD.** Chuck Norris; Karen Carlson; Lee Van Cleef; Kim Lankford; Art Hindle; Jack Carter; ***D:*** Eric Karson; ***W:*** Paul Aaron; Leigh Chapman.

Octaman **½ 1971** Comical thriller featuring non-threatening octopus-man discovered by scientists in Mexico. Rip-off of director Essex's own "Creature from the Black Lagoon." Not without its curiosity factor: young Rick Baker designed the octopus man, while actress Angeli died of a drug overdose during filming. **79m/C; VHS, DVD, Blu-Ray.** Kerwin Mathews; Pier Angeli; Harry Guardino; David Essex; Jeff Morrow; Norman Fields; ***D:*** Harry Essex; ***W:*** Harry Essex; ***C:*** Robert Caramico.

Octane **½** *Dolphins* **2007 (R)** Brighton bad boy Brent Black discovers the adrenaline rush of illegal street racing but his success is challenged by the Bling London Boy Racers. Then Brent's car is mysteriously destroyed just a week before the big grudge match. **89m/C; DVD.** *GB* Frank Harper; Karl Davies; Lauren Steventon; Layke Anderson; Gemma Baker; Amy Blackburn; Roots Manuva; ***D:*** Mark Jay; ***W:*** Mark Jay; ***C:*** Simon Dennis; Brendan McGinty; ***M:*** Sacha Puttnam.

Octavia **1982 (R)** A contemporary fable about a blind girl who befriends a convict and learns about life and love. **93m/C; VHS, Streaming.** Susan Curtis; ***D:*** David Beaird; ***W:*** David Beaird.

October Baby **½ 2012 (PG-13)** Nineteen-year-old college student, Hannah (Hendrix), struggles from a host of physical and mental issues. She's adopted, and, it turns out, the product of a failed abortion. She road-trips with her pals to meet "real mom" on her way to spring break, and adoptive dad shows up to pick up the pieces. Nothing makes any sense here, but if you don't mind being walloped over the head with this propaganda piece, you probably won't care. **107m/C; DVD, Blu-Ray.** Rachel Hendrix; Jason Burke; John Schneider; Jennifer Price; Colleen Trussler; ***D:*** Andrew Erwin; Jon Erwin; ***W:*** Andrew Erwin; Jon Erwin; Cecil Stokes; Theresa Preston; ***C:*** Jon Erwin; ***M:*** Paul Mills.

October Sky **1999 (PG)** Relates the true story of young Homer Hickam Jr. (Gyllenhaal), who rose from a gloomy West Virginia mining town to become a NASA engineer. Spurred by the launch of Sputnik and a supportive teacher (Dern), Homer and three of his friends experiment with rockets with the hope of winning college scholarships. The boys battle the skepticism of their peers and families as well as the looming possibility of a future in the mines. Entertaining and uplifting without resorting to melodrama and sentimentality. Adapted from Hickam's memoir "Rocket Boys." **108m/C; VHS, DVD, Blu-Ray.** Jake Gyllenhaal; Chris Cooper; Laura Dern; Chris Owen; William Lee Scott; Chad Lindberg; Natalie Canerday; Scott Miles; Randy Stripling; Chris Ellis; ***D:*** Joe Johnston; ***W:*** Lewis Colick; ***C:*** Paul Murphy; ***M:*** Mark Isham.

Octopus **2000 (PG-13)** Giant mutant octopus lurking in the ocean depths is disturbed by a U.S. Navy submarine and decides to make it lunch. This, however, is not the only bad news. Seems the sub was transporting a terrorist who escapes in the confusion, and winds up on a cruise ship. He thinks he's safe but our eight-legged horror is just getting started. Special effects are pretty lame but the film doesn't take itself serously and the humor covers a lot of holes. **99m/C; VHS, DVD.** Carolyn Lowery; David Beecroft; Jay Harrington; Ravil Isyanov; ***D:*** John Eyres; ***W:*** Michael D. Weiss; ***C:*** Adolfo Bartoli; ***M:*** Marco Marinangelo. **VIDEO**

Octopus 2: River of Fear 🦴🦴 **2002 (R)** After two Russian tourists are killed on the waterfront off the Hudson River, scuba diver cop Nick (Burke) discovers a giant man-eating octopus. Not wanting to spoil the city's 4th of July celebrations, the mayor refuses to do anything. So Nick and his partner Walter (Lane) must stop the rampaging creature—who attacks the Statue of Liberty! That's just wrong. **95m/C; VHS, DVD.** Michael Reilly Burke; Frederic Lehne; Duncan Fraser; Meredith Morton; John Thaddeus; ***D:*** Yossi Wein; ***W:*** Michael D. Weiss; ***C:*** Peter Belcher; ***M:*** Bill Wandel. **VIDEO**

Octopussy 🦴🦴 **1983 (PG)** The Bond saga continues as Agent 007 is on a mission to prevent a crazed Russian general from launching a nuclear attack against the NATO forces in Europe. Lots of special effects and gadgets keep weak plot moving. **140m/C; VHS, DVD, Blu-Ray.** *GB* Roger Moore; Maud Adams; Louis Jourdan; Kristina Wayborn; Kabir Bedi; Steven Berkoff; Robert Brown; ***D:*** John Glen; ***W:*** Michael G. Wilson; ***C:*** Alan Hume; ***M:*** John Barry.

Oculus 🦴🦴 **2014 (R)** A few worthy ideas are wasted in this expansion of an acclaimed short film into a relatively generic feature length one. Gillan plays Kaylie Russell, the now-adult who watched her father (Cochrane) go crazy and kill her mother (Sackhoff) at the behest of a supernatural mirror. Years later, Kaylie and her brother Tim (Thwaites) track down the mirror and set out to prove its evil capabilities before destroying it. The current-day stuff works well enough but the flashbacks are depressingly routine and shallow. Some great scenes but they don't add up to a great movie. **104m/C; DVD, Blu-Ray.** Karen Gillan; Brenton Thwaites; Rory Cochrane; Katee Sackhoff; James Lafferty; Miguel (Michael) Sandoval; ***D:*** Mike Flanagan; ***W:*** Mike Flanagan; Jeff Howard; ***C:*** Michael Fimognari; ***M:*** The Newton Brothers.

The Odd Angry Shot 🦴🦴 1/2 **1979** Australian soldiers fighting in Vietnam discover the conflict is not what they expected. Ironic perspective of men struggling with their feelings about the war. More of an unremarkable drama with comic overtones than a combat film, it will appeal to those who prefer good direction to bloodshed. **90m/C; DVD, Blu-Ray.** *AU* Graham Kennedy; John Hargreaves; John Jarratt; Bryan Brown; Graeme Blundell; Richard Moir; Ian Gilmour; John Allen; Brandon Burke; Graham Rouse; Tony Barry; Max Cullen; John Fitzgerald; Ray Meagher; ***D:*** Tom Jeffrey; ***W:*** Tom Jeffrey; ***C:*** Donald McAlpine; ***M:*** Walter (Wendy) Carlos.

Odd Birds 🦴🦴 1/2 **1985** Coming of age drama set in 1965 California. Shy 15-year-old Joy Chan is a Chinese-American dreaming of becoming an actress. Her widowed immigrant mother wants Joy to have a practical profession—like nursing. Longing for someone to understand Joy meets Brother Murphy, a math teacher at the local boys school. Murphy's been trying to reconcile his religious commitment with his unorthodox views. It isn't long before these two individualists recognize a fellow kindred spirit. **87m/C; VHS, DVD, Streaming.** Michael Moriarty; Donna Lai Ming Lew; Nancy Lee; Bruce Gray; Karen Maruyama; Scott Crawford; ***D:*** Jeanne Collachia; ***W:*** Jeanne Collachia.

The Odd Couple 🦴🦴🦴 1/2 **1968 (G)** Two divorced men with completely opposite personalities move in together. Lemmon's obsession with neatness drives slob Matthau up the wall, and their inability to see eye-to-eye results in many hysterical escapades. A Hollywood rarity, it is actually better in some ways than Neil Simon's original Broadway version. Simon based the characters on brother Danny and his roommates. Basis for the hit TV series. **106m/C; VHS, DVD, Blu-Ray.** Jack Lemmon; Walter Matthau; Herb Edelman; John Fiedler; Monica Evans; Carol(e) Shelley; ***D:*** Gene Saks; ***W:*** Neil Simon; ***C:*** Robert B. Hauser.

The Odd Couple 2 🦴 1/2 *Neil Simon's The Odd Couple 2* **1998 (PG-13)** They waited too long and shouldn't have even bothered. Oscar (Matthau) and Felix (Lemmon) reunite when their respective kids (Silverman as Oscar's son, Waltz as Felix's daughter) marry. Meeting at LAX, the duo immediately falls into the old routine of annoying each other and, this time out, the audience. Simon fills his script with leftover road movie cliches and vaudeville jokes, leaving Lemmon and Matthau nothing to do but mug and yell. **96m/C; DVD.** Jack Lemmon; Walter Matthau; Jonathan Silverman; Lisa Waltz; Christine Baranski; Jean Smart; Barnard Hughes; Doris Belack; Ellen Geer; Jay O. Sanders; Rex Linn; Mary Beth Peil; Alice Ghostley; Rebecca Schull; Florence Stanley; Lou (Cutel) Cutell; ***D:*** Howard Deutch; ***W:*** Neil Simon; ***C:*** Jamie Anderson; ***M:*** Alan Silvestri.

Odd Jobs 🦴🦴 **1985 (PG-13)** When five college friends look for jobs during summer break, they wind up running their own moving business with the help of the mob. Good comic talent, but a silly slapstick script results in only a passable diversion. **89m/C; VHS, DVD.** Paul Reiser; Scott McGinnis; Rick Overton; Robert Townsend; ***D:*** Mark Story; ***W:*** Robert Conte; ***C:*** Arthur Albert; Peter Lyons Collister; ***M:*** Robert Folk.

The Odd Life of Timothy Green 🦴🦴 **2012 (PG)** Good intentions only go so far in family film. The creators of this fable about a couple (Edgerton, Garner) who scribble notes about the dream child they've been told they'll never have and bury the paper in the backyard only to see it sprout into an actual boy (Adams) try to create heartwarming drama for all ages. Sadly, they waste the opportunity with a cluttered script that has effective moments but too often dips into the melodrama handbook when it can't come up with its own ideas. **100m/C; DVD, Blu-Ray.** CJ Adams; Jennifer Garner; Joel Edgerton; Ron Livingston; Dianne Wiest; Rosemarie DeWitt; David Morse; M. Emmet Walsh; Lois Smith; ***D:*** Peter Hedges; ***W:*** Peter Hedges; ***C:*** John Toll; ***M:*** Geoff Zanelli.

Odd Man Out 🦴🦴🦴 1/2 *Gang War* **1947** An Irish revolutionary is injured during a robbery attempt. Suffering from gunshot wounds and closely pursued by the police, he must rely on the help of others who could betray him at any moment. A gripping tale of suspense and intrigue that will keep the proverbial seat's edge warm until the final credits. Adapted from F.L. Green's novel, previously filmed as "The Last Man." **111m/B; VHS, DVD, Blu-Ray.** *GB* James Mason; Robert Newton; Dan O'Herlihy; Kathleen Ryan; Cyril Cusack; ***D:*** Carol Reed; ***W:*** F.L. Green; R.C. Sherriff; ***C:*** Robert Krasker; ***M:*** William Alwyn. British Acad. '47: Film.

Odd Thomas 🦴 1/2 **2013** Dean Koontz's hit novel, which has inspired multiple sequels, gets a lackluster, long-delayed treatment from Sommers that relies far too much on cheesy special effects than the author's clever central character. The wisecracking fry cook (Yelchin) who can see dead people is little more than a cog in the machine in this cluttered mess about the supernatural warning signs that a massacre is soon to be befall the city of Pico Mundo, California. A love story that was the emotional core of the book has been rendered ineffective by poor casting but the film's biggest problems can be traced back to its CGI-heavy aesthetic. **100m/C; DVD, Blu-Ray.** Anton Yelchin; Addison Timlin; Willem Dafoe; Shuler Hensley; Gugu Mbatha-Raw; Leonor Varela; ***D:*** Stephen Sommers; ***W:*** Stephen Sommers; ***C:*** Mitchell Amundsen; ***M:*** John Swihart.

The Odd Way Home 🦴 **2013** Contrived, inconsistent drama. After fleeing her abusive L.A. boyfriend, pill-addicted Maya's truck breaks down in nowhere New Mexico. The nearest house is occupied by 20-something autistic savant Duncan, whose caretaker grandma has just died. Maya helps herself to cash and their old camper truck, only to discover Duncan has stowed away. After a series of misadventures, the odd couple head to a ghost town where Maya reunites with caring ex, Dave, and she and Duncan try to resolve some dysfunctional family issues. **87m/C; DVD.** Rumer Willis; Christopher Marquette; Brendan Sexton, III; Veronica Cartwright; Bruce Altman; ***D:*** Rajeev Nirmalakhandan; ***W:*** Rajeev Nirmalakhandan; Jason Ronstadt; ***C:*** Matt Wilson; ***M:*** Daniel James Chan.

Oddballs WOOF! **1984 (PG-13)** In another attempt to capitalize on the success of Bill Murray's "Meatballs," this summer camp story follows three campers and their pathetic attempts to lose their virginity. Brooks has his moments, but there is little else to recommend here. **92m/C; VHS, DVD.** Foster Brooks; Jason Sorokin; Wally Wodchis; Konnie Krome; ***D:*** Miklos Lente.

Odds Against Tomorrow 🦴🦴🦴 **1959** Compulsive gambler/nightclub singer Johnny Ingram (Belafonte) owes big money to gangster Bacco (Kuluva). He hooks up with racist ex-con Earl Slater (Ryan) and former policeman Dave Burke (Begley) to rob a bank but everything goes wrong. Ingram and Slater manage to escape to a nearby oil storage area but the racial tensions between the two are proving deadlier than the cops on their trail. Based on the novel by William P. McGivern; because of the blacklist screenwriter Polonsky was "fronted" by John O. Killens. Polonsky officially received credit for his work in 1996. **120m/B; DVD, Blu-Ray.** Harry Belafonte; Robert Ryan; Shelley Winters; Ed Begley, Sr.; Gloria Grahame; Will Kuluva; Richard Bright; ***D:*** Robert Wise; ***W:*** Abraham Polonsky; Nelson Gidding; ***C:*** Joseph Brun; ***M:*** John Lewis.

Ode to Billy Joe 🦴🦴 **1976 (PG)** The 1967 Bobby Gentry hit song of the same title is expanded to tell why a young man jumped to his death off the Tallahatchie Bridge. The problems of growing up in the rural South and teenage romance do not match the appeal of the theme song. Benson and O'Connor, however, work well together. **106m/C; VHS, DVD.** Robby Benson; Glynnis O'Connor; Joan Hotchkis; Sandy McPeak; James Best; ***D:*** Max Baer, Jr.

Ode to Joy 🦴🦴 1/2 **2019 (R)** Because he suffers from cataplexy, librarian Charlie (Freeman) faints the moment he experiences a large emotion and has avoided feeling of any deep love. Though he is likeable, Charlie's condition has made him neurotic, weary, and grumpy as he tries to avoid anything that will trigger his condition. Charlie's world is turned upside down when he meets the bold Francesca (Baccarin), who likes men for whom they are not. Though Charlie denies his feelings for her, his attempts to manipulate the situation only make it worse. The romantic comedy has an interesting premise that doesn't deliver. **98m/C; DVD.** Morena Baccarin; Melissa Rauch; Martin Freeman; Jake Lacy; Shannon Marie Woodward; ***D:*** Jason Winer; ***W:*** Max Werner; ***C:*** David Robert Jones; ***M:*** Jeremy Turner.

The Odessa File 🦴🦴 1/2 **1974 (PG)** During 1963, a German journalist attempts to track down some SS war criminals who have formed a secret organization called ODESSA. The story, from Frederick Forsyth's novel, drags in some places, but the scene where bad guy Schell and reporter Voight finally confront each other is a high point. **128m/C; VHS, DVD, Blu-Ray.** *GB GE* Jon Voight; Mary Tamm; Maximilian Schell; Maria Schell; Derek Jacobi; Peter Jeffrey; Klaus Lowitsch; Kurt Meisel; Hannes Messemer; Garfield Morgan; Shmuel Rodensku; Ernst Schroder; Noel Willman; Hans Caninenberg; Towje Kleiner; Gunnar Moller; ***D:*** Ronald Neame; ***W:*** Kenneth Ross; George Markstein; ***C:*** Oswald Morris; ***M:*** Andrew Lloyd Webber.

Odongo 🦴 **1956** Dated, sappy adventure drama that even the kids probably won't like because of the way the animals are treated. Steve Stratton captures African animals for zoos and circuses with hired native help, including young Odongo. After worker Walla is fired, he takes revenge by letting the caged animals loose. Odongo is wrongly accused and runs away, placing him in danger. **85m/C; DVD.** *UK* MacDonald Carey; Juma; Rhonda Fleming; Dan Jackson; ***D:*** John Gilling; ***W:*** John Gilling; ***C:*** Ted Moore; ***M:*** George Melachrino.

The Odyssey 🦴🦴 1/2 **1997 (PG-13)** Lavish TV miniseries based on Homer's epic poem, relating the adventures of King Odysseus of Ithaca. Odysseus (Assante) must leave faithful wife Penelope (Scacchi) when he's commanded by the goddess Athena (Rossellini) to battle the Trojans. Little does he realize that this is the beginning of a 20-year sojourn, where additional trials include sea monsters, the Cyclops, the Kingdom of the Dead, enchantress Circe (Peters), and getting shipwrecked on the isle of Calypso (Williams), who wants to keep the hunk around. But even Odysseus realizes there's no place like home. **203m/C; DVD.** Armand Assante; Greta Scacchi; Geraldine Chaplin; Eric Roberts; Bernadette Peters; Irene Papas; Vanessa L(ynne) Williams; Christopher Lee; Isabella Rossellini; Jeroen Krabbe; Nicholas Clay; Ron Cook; Michael J. Pollard; Paloma Baeza; Alan Cox; Heathcote Williams; ***D:*** Andrei Konchalovsky; ***W:*** Andrei Konchalovsky; Chris Solimine; ***C:*** Sergei Kozlov; ***M:*** Eduard Artemyev. **TV**

The Odyssey of the Pacific 🦴🦴 1/2 *The Emperor of Peru* **1982** Three young Cambodian refugees encounter retired train engineer Rooney living in the woods where a railway station once thrived. Together they work to restore an old locomotive. The ordinary, inoffensive script will not endanger quality family time. **82m/C; VHS, DVD, Blu-Ray.** *CA* Mickey Rooney; Monique Mercure; ***D:*** Fernando Arrabal.

Oedipus Rex 🦴🦴🦴 *Edipo Re* **1967** A new twist on the famous tragedy as Pasolini gives the story a modern prologue and epilogue. The classic plot has Oedipus spiraling downward into moral horror as he tries to avoid fulfulling the prophecy that he will murder his father and sleep with his mother. Cross-cultural curiosities include Japanese music and Lenin-inspired songs, some written by Pasolini, who also stars as the high priest. In Italian with English subtitles. **110m/C; VHS, DVD.** *IT* Franco Citti; Silvana Mangano; Alida Valli; Julian Beck; Pier Paolo Pasolini; ***D:*** Pier Paolo Pasolini.

Of Boys and Men 🦴🦴 **2008 (PG-13)** Holden Cole struggles to hold his family together after his wife is killed in a car accident. His sister Janey moves in to help but their grief is causing the family to pull apart rather than pull together. Youngest son Z gets tempted by a street thug's talk of easy money, which involves drugs. **86m/C; DVD.** Robert Townsend; Victoria Rowell; Angela Bassett; Dante Boens; Bobb'e J. Thompson; Vince Green; Scott Baity, Jr.; ***D:*** Carl Seaton; ***W:*** Michelle Amor; ***C:*** Joe Williams; ***M:*** Stephen James Taylor.

Of Fathers and Sons 🦴🦴🦴 *Kinder des Kalifats* **2018** Documentary sharing the story of Middle Eastern boys becoming militarized in Al-Nusra, Al-Qaeda's Syrian arm. Syrian-born filmmaker Derki posed as a war photographer with sympathies to the jihadist cause and spent over two years living with an Al-Nursa leader Abu Osama and his family. Derki captures how Abu's two oldest sons, 13-year-old Osama and 12-year-old Ayman, have experiences that militarize them yet are still children who play soccer and go to school. Though Abu Osama's involvement in the movement changes over time, Derki eloquently portrays how radicalization affects a family as well as the violence that is inherent to the process. **99m/C; DVD.** ***D:*** Talal Derki; ***C:*** Kahtan Hassoun; ***M:*** Karim Sebastian Elias.

Of Gods and Men 🦴🦴🦴 1/2 *Des Hommes et Des Dieux* **2010 (R)** Based on an actual 1996 event that took place in a Trappist monastery located near a Muslim village during the Algerian Civil War. After an outbreak of terrorist attacks on the city from Islamic extremists, the Christian monks decide to hold their ground, but are increasingly caught between the danger of the violence and the unsympathetic protection of the Algerian army. As little as the monks are defined, the nature of human spirit in the face of great wrath is enough to carry the weight of this adventure. Raises fundamental questions about religion and sacrifice without laying out too many answers. French and Arabic with subtitles. **122m/C; DVD, Blu-Ray.** *FR* Lambert Wilson; Michael (Michel) Lonsdale; Olivier Rabourdin; Philippe Laudenbach; Jacques Herlin; Loic Pichon; Xavier Maly; Jean-Marie Frin; Olivier Perrier; Sabrina Ouazani; Abdelhafid Metalsi; Abdallah Moundy; Adel Bencherif; Farid Larbi; ***D:*** Xavier Beauvois; ***W:*** Xavier Beauvois; Etienne Comar; ***C:*** Caroline Champetier.

Of Human Bondage **1934** The first movie version of W. Somerset Maugham's classic novel in which a young, handicapped medical student falls in love with a crude cockney waitress, in a mutually destructive affair. Established Davis's role as the tough, domineering woman. Remade in 1946 and 1964. **84m/B; VHS, DVD, Blu-Ray.** Bette Davis; Leslie Howard; Frances Dee; Reginald Owen; Reginald Denny; Alan Hale; *D:* John Cromwell; *W:* Lester Cohen; *C:* Henry W. Gerrard; *M:* Max Steiner.

Of Human Bondage **1964** An essentially decent man falls fatally in love with an alluring but heartless waitress, who subtly destroys him. Based on the W. Somerset Maugham novel. Miscast and least interesting of the three film versions, although Novak gives a good performance. **100m/B; DVD.** *UK* Kim Novak; Laurence Harvey; Robert Morley; Roger Livesey; Siobhan McKenna; *D:* Henry Hathaway; Ken Hughes; *W:* Bryan Forbes; *C:* Oswald Morris.

Of Human Hearts **1/2 1938** Rural life just before the Civil War sets up this cornpone tale of family strife. Huston is a stern preacher who has his family living in near poverty as an example of sacrifice to his flock. Son Stewart wants to study medicine and Bondi, defying her husband, manages to fund his dream. Only Stewart becomes so engrossed by his ambitions that he ignores the family, even after his father dies and his mother is left poor and alone. Then Stewart joins the Civil War as a doctor where he meets President Lincoln (Carradine), who tells him he should never neglect his mother. Oy. Well, the cast is good. Adapted from the story "Benefits Forgot" by Honore Morrow. **100m/B; DVD.** James Stewart; Beulah Bondi; Walter Huston; John Carradine; Guy Kibbee; Charles Coburn; Ann Rutherford; Charley Grapewin; Gene Lockhart; *D:* Clarence Brown; *W:* Bradbury Foote; *C:* Clyde De Vinna.

Of Love and Shadows **1994 (R)** Political photojournalist Francisco (Banderas) begins investigating the disappearance of a self-proclaimed saint after the bloody 1973 coup in Chile. He's aided by aristocratic Chilean Irene (Connelly), who's engaged to her Army captain cousin Gustavo (Gallardo) but can't resist Francisco's ever-smoldering charms. The intrepid duo naturally find lots of corruption. Based on the novel by Isabel Allende; shot on location in Argentina. **103m/C; VHS, DVD.** Antonio Banderas; Jennifer Connelly; Stefania Sandrelli; Camillo Gallardo; Patricio Contreras; *D:* Betty Kaplan; *W:* Donald Freed; *C:* Felix Monti; *M:* Jose Nieto.

Of Mice and Men **1939** A powerful adaptation of the classic Steinbeck tragedy about the friendship between two itinerant Southern ranch hands during the Great Depression. Chaney is wonderful as the gentle giant and mentally retarded Lenny, cared for by migrant worker Meredith. They both get into an irreversible situation when a woman is accidentally killed. **107m/C; VHS, DVD.** Lon Chaney, Jr.; Burgess Meredith; Betty Field; Bob Steele; Noah Beery, Jr.; Charles Bickford; *D:* Lewis Milestone; *W:* Eugene Solow; *C:* Norbert Brodine; *M:* Aaron Copland.

Of Mice and Men **1981** TV remake of the classic Steinbeck tale, casting TV's Baretta (Blake) as George and Quaid as Lenny. Worth watching. **150m/C; VHS, DVD.** Robert (Bobby) Blake; Randy Quaid; Lew Ayres; Mitchell Ryan; Ted Neeley; Cassie Yates; Pat Hingle; Whitman Mayo; Dennis Fimple; Pat Corley; *D:* Reza Badiyi. **TV**

Of Mice and Men **1/2 1992 (PG-13)** Set on the migratory farms of California, John Steinbeck's novel covers the friendship of the simple-minded Lenny, his protector George, and a flirtatious farm wife who doesn't know Lenny's strength. Director Sinise got permission from Steinbeck's widow to film the novel (actually the third adaptation). **110m/C; VHS, DVD, Blu-Ray.** John Malkovich; Sherilyn Fenn; Casey Siemaszko; Joe Morton; Ray Walston; Gary Sinise; John Terry; Richard Riehle; *D:* Gary Sinise; *W:* Horton Foote; *C:* Kenneth Macmillan; *M:* Mark Isham.

Of Time and the City **2008** Autobiographical filmmaker Terence Davies does a poetic visual memoir about his hometown of Liverpool. It's a free-association collage of archive material, original footage, and Davies' narration of his history and that of the city from the 1940s through approximately the 1960s, which often link up to his own feature films. **72m/C; On Demand.** *GB Nar:* Terence Davies; *D:* Terence Davies; *W:* Terence Davies; *C:* Tim Pollard; *M:* Ian Neil.

Of Two Minds **1/2 2012** Lifetime family drama with touching performances by both leads and no judgments. After their mother dies, Billie Clark (Davis) has her younger sister Elizabeth, better known as Baby (Blanchard), come to live with her and her family. Baby is schizophrenic and her fears and outbursts prove to be more disruptive than the Clarks can cope with as Billie tries to assuage her guilt and find Baby another place to live. **88m/C; DVD.** Kristin Davis; Tammy Blanchard; Joel Gretsch; Alexander Le Bas; Mackenzie Aladjem; Louise Fletcher; Bonnie Bartlett; *D:* Jim O'Hanlon; *W:* Richard Friedenberg; *C:* Ousama Rawi; *M:* Samuel Sim. **CABLE**

Of Unknown Origin **1/2 1983 (R)** Weller encounters a mutated rampaging rat in his New York townhouse while his family is away on vacation. His house becomes the battleground in a terror-tinged duel of survival. A well-done rat thriller not for those with a delicate stomach. Based on the novel "The Visitor." **88m/C; VHS, DVD, Blu-Ray.** *CA* Peter Weller; Jennifer Dale; Lawrence Dane; Kenneth Welsh; Louis Del Grande; Shannon Tweed; *D:* George P. Cosmatos; *W:* Brian Taggert; *C:* Rene Verzier.

The Off Hours **1/2 2011** Director Griffiths' debut is a bit of a snoozer, though some may be attracted by the melancholy atmosphere. Sex and alcohol are the two things that tie the denizens of a failing truck-stop diner together. Moody, longtime waitress Francine lives with her former foster brother Corey, who plays in a bar band, while being desultorily involved with his bandmate Ty. Diner owner Stu is an alcoholic while waitress Jelena is indiscriminate about her trucker sex partners. It's a low-budget, probably accurate, slice of some very stagnant lives. **93m/C; DVD.** Amy Seimetz; Scott NcNairy; Bret Roberts; Tony Doupe; Lynn Shelton; Madeline Elizabeth; Gergana Mellin; Ross Patridge; *D:* Megan Griffiths; *W:* Megan Griffiths; *C:* Benjamin Kasulke; *M:* Joshua Morrison; Jeramy Koepping.

Off Limits **1/2 1953** When a boxing manager is drafted into the Army, he freely breaks regulations in order to train a fighter as he sees fit. Hope and Rooney, while not in peak form, make a snappy duo in this amusing romp. **89m/B; VHS, DVD, Blu-Ray.** Bob Hope; Mickey Rooney; Marilyn Maxwell; Marvin Miller; *D:* George Marshall.

Off Limits **1/2 1987 (R)** A spree of murders involving Vietnamese hookers draws two cops from the Army's Criminal Investigation Department into the sleazy backstreets of 1968 Saigon. There is little mystery as to who the killer is in this tale that seems written more for the sake of foul language and gratuitous gunfights than actual plot. **102m/C; VHS, DVD.** Willem Dafoe; Gregory Hines; Fred Ward; Scott Glenn; Amanda Pays; Keith David; David Alan Grier; *D:* Christopher Crowe; *W:* Christopher Crowe; Jack Thibeau; *M:* James Newton Howard.

Off Season **1/2 2001** A Christmas movie set in July or, rather, a spirit of Christmas movie set in July. Recently orphaned Jackson (Culkin) is now living with his Aunt Patty in Florida. She tends bar in a tacky hotel where they also live and Jackson likes to make up stories about the guests. He decides that cranky Sam Clausner (Cronyn) is actually Santa Claus on vacation, although the elderly man is more Scrooge-like than jolly. Then hotel manager Mel Breskin (McBeath) gets the idea to use Jackson's tall tale in a tasteless promotion scheme and things just snowball from there. **95m/C; VHS, DVD.** Rory Culkin; Hume Cronyn; Sherilyn Fenn; Tom McBeath; Adam Arkin; Bruce Davison; *D:* Bruce Davison; *W:* Glen Gers; *C:* Tony Westman; *M:* Daniel Licht. **CABLE**

Off the Lip **1/2 2004 (R)** Rookie reporter Kat gets to rove the wilds of Hawaii when her first beat puts her in pursuit of slippery surfing legend The Monk. While the search might have stalled, what she learns about herself means so golly gosh more. **88m/C; VHS, DVD.** Marguerite Moreau; MacKenzie Astin; Adam Scott; Mark Fite; David Rasche; Jim Turner; Rick Overton; Matty Liu; *D:* Robert Mickelson; *W:* Shem Bitterman; *C:* Joey Forsyte; *M:* Andrew Gross. **VIDEO**

Off the Map **2003 (PG-13)** Folksy, quirky melodrama with strong performances. In 1974, eccentric IRS agent William Gibbs (True-Frost) is assigned to audit the Groden family, finally stumbling across their isolated New Mexico desert house. Living off the grid, the family's in crisis. Grizzled Charley (Elliott) is in a clinical depression and hasn't spoken in months while free-spirited wife Arlene (Allen) gardens in the nude and their preteen daughter Bo (de Angelis) longs for friends and normality. Gibbs becomes so involved that he throws his job aside and his presence alters the family's precarious balance. Film is narrated by the grown-up Bo (Brenneman); Ackermann adapted from her play. **111m/C; DVD, Streaming.** Joan Allen; Sam Elliott; J.K. Simmons; Amy Brenneman; Valentina de Angelis; Jim True-Frost; *D:* Campbell Scott; *W:* Joan Ackermann; *C:* Juan Ruiz-Anchia; *M:* Gary DeMichele.

The Offence *Something Like the Truth* **1973 (R)** Connery plays a London detective who beats a suspected child molester to death during a police interrogation. Turns out he's reacting to a long-buried molestation incident from his own childhood. A chilling psycho-drama highlighted by a strong lead performance by Connery. **108m/C; VHS, DVD, Blu-Ray.** *GB* Sean Connery; Trevor Howard; Vivien Merchant; Ian Bannen; Derek Newark; John Hallam; Peter Bowles; *D:* Sidney Lumet; *W:* John Hopkins.

Offensive Behaviour **1/2 2004** Odd little schlock comedy about the inhabitants of an apartment complex. One is a destitute filmmaker hoping to convince his friends to help him make some amateur, low-budget porn. The other is a gay hairdresser being bullied by his nun/assassin mother into helping her carry off one last murder before retirement. Give it props for trying to be different. **81m/C; DVD.** Richard Allom Coscrove; Janice Gray; Michael Maxwell; David Sheard; *D:* Patrick Gilles; *W:* Patrick Gilles; *C:* John Christoffels; *M:* Hamish Oliver.

Offerings **1989 (R)** After a boy is tormented by a gang of children who cause him to fall down a well, his resulting brain injuries turn him into a psychopathic killer. Seeking revenge ten years later, he systematically murders his oppressors, offering bits of their anatomy to the one girl who treated him kindly. A typical slasher movie, the plot is only slightly better than the worst examples of the genre. **96m/C; VHS, DVD, Blu-Ray.** G. Michael Smith; Loretta L. Bowman; *D:* Christopher Reynolds.

Office Christmas Party **1/2 2016 (R)** How could they screw this one up with this cast? An R-rated comedy about an office Christmas party gone out of control with some incredibly talented comedians in the cast should be a grand slam. At least a double. This one strikes out. The plot is right there in the title. Bateman, Munn, Aniston, McKinnon, Bayer, T.J. Miller and more people too talented for this nearly laughless script flounder around in directors Speck and Gordon's flick. **105m/C; DVD, Blu-Ray.** Jason Bateman; Olivia Munn; T.J. Miller; Jennifer Aniston; Kate McKinnon; Courtney B. Vance; *D:* Josh Gordon; Will Speck; *W:* Justin Malen; Laura Solon; Dan Mazer; *C:* Jeff Cutter; *M:* Theodore Shapiro.

Office Killer **1997 (R)** Meek copyeditor Dorine's (Kane) in danger of losing her job. After securing her position by accidentally electrocuting a fellow employee, Dorine begins some downsizing of her own. Pent up frustrations cause her sanity to take a personal leave of absence, and she begins to streamline her department by folding, spindling and mutilating her co-workers. Office tramp Kim (Ringwald) suspects the truth, but no one believes her. Stab at horror-black comedy isn't scary or funny. First directorial effort by still photographer Cindy Sherman, who didn't adapt very well to people moving around. **83m/C; DVD.** Carol Kane; Molly Ringwald; Jeanne Tripplehorn; Barbara Sukowa; Michael Imperioli; David Thornton; Alice Drummond; Mike Hodge; *Cameo(s):* Eric Bogosian; *D:* Cindy Sherman; *W:* Tom Kalin; Todd Haynes; Elise MacAdam; *C:* Russell Fine; *M:* Evan Lurie.

Office Space **1/2 1998 (R)** Satire of white collar corporate drudgery. Peter (Livingston) works for a software company and is on his way to a nervous breakdown when a hypnosis mishap opens his eyes. He becomes so apathetic that he can't even muster the energy to quit. His new no-work ethic is mistaken by a pair of corporate headhunters as "middle-management potential," and he is promoted as others are laid off. Frustrated in his attempts to be downsized, Peter hatches a plot to embezzle from the company. Adapted from animated shorts made by Judge, the film was a boxoffice bomb that's become a cult classic. **89m/C; DVD, Blu-Ray, UMD.** Ron Livingston; Jennifer Aniston; David Herman; Ajay Naidu; Gary Cole; Mike Judge; Diedrich Bader; Stephen (Steve) Root; Richard Riehle; John C. McGinley; Paul Willson; Orlando Jones; Alexandra Wentworth; Michael McShane; *D:* Mike Judge; *W:* Mike Judge; *C:* Tim Suhrstedt; *M:* John (Gianni) Frizzell.

An Officer and a Gentleman **1/2 1982 (R)** Young drifter Gere, who enters Navy Officer Candidate School because he doesn't know what else to do with his life, becomes a better person almost despite himself. Winger is the love interest who sets her sights on marrying Gere, and Gossett is the sergeant who whips him into shape. Strong performances by the whole cast made this a must-see in 1982 that is still appealing, despite the standard Hollywood premise. **126m/C; VHS, DVD, Blu-Ray.** Richard Gere; Louis Gossett, Jr.; David Keith; Lisa Eilbacher; Debra Winger; David Caruso; Robert Loggia; Lisa Blount; *D:* Taylor Hackford; *W:* Douglas Day Stewart; *C:* Donald E. Thorin; *M:* Jack Nitzsche. Oscars '82: Song ("Up Where We Belong"), Support. Actor (Gossett); Golden Globes '83: Song ("Up Where We Belong"), Support. Actor (Gossett).

Officer Down **1/2 2013 (R)** Detective Callahan (Stephen Dorff) is a former alcoholic trying to turn his life around when he arrests a rapist who turns out to be a fellow police officer. **97m/C; DVD, Blu-Ray, Streaming.** Stephen Dorff; AnnaLynne McCord; Dominic Purcell; Stephen Lang; David Boreanaz; *D:* Brian A. Miller; *W:* John Chase; *C:* Ryan Samul; *M:* Jerome Dillon.

Official Secrets **2019 (R)** Katherine Gun (Knightley) is working in a British government translating service in 2003 when she receives a memo related to the ramp up of war in Iraq. The memo calls for surveillance of United Nations member countries reluctant to support President Bush and Prime Minister Blair's efforts there. Already angry about the forthcoming war, she fails to get activist friends interested in the memo's explosive contents but has more success with newsman Peter Beaumont (Goode). Based on true events, it has the makings of a successful thriller but is instead mundane, though Knightley shines in telling Gun's powerful story. **112m/C; DVD.** Keira Knightley; Matt Smith; Matthew Goode; Rhys Ifans; Adam Bakri; *D:* Gavin Hood; *W:* Gavin Hood; Gregory Bernstein; Sara Bernstein; *C:* Florian Hoffmeister; *M:* Paul Hepker; Mark Kilian.

The Official Story **1/2** *La Historia Oficial; The Official History; The Official Version* **1985 (R)** A devastating drama about an Argentinian woman who realizes her young adopted daughter may be a child stolen from one of the thousands of citizens victimized by the country's repressive government. A powerful, important film. In Spanish with English subtitles or dubbed. **112m/C; VHS, DVD, Blu-Ray.** *AR* Norma Aleandro; Hector Alterio; Chunchuna Villafane; Patricio Contreras; *D:* Luis Puenzo; *W:* Luis Puenzo; Aida Bortnik. Oscars '85: Foreign Film; Cannes '85: Actress (Aleandro); Golden Globes '86: Foreign Film; L.A. Film Critics '85: Foreign Film; N.Y. Film Critics '85: Actress (Aleandro).

The Offspring *From a Whisper to a Scream* **1987 (R)** In four stories of past evils Price reveals his hometown can force folks to kill. Not the usual Price material: dismemberment, cannibalism, and necrophilia clash with his presence. Strong yuk factor. **99m/C; VHS, DVD, Blu-Ray, UMD.** Vincent Price; Cameron Mitchell; Clu Gulager; Terry Kiser; Susan Tyrrell; Harry Caesar; Rosalind Cash; Martine Beswick; Angelo Rossitto; Lawrence Tierney; *D:* Jeff Burr; *W:* Jeff Burr; C. Courtney Joyner; *M:* Jim Manzie.

The Ogre *Der Unhold* **1996** Misfit Abel (Malkovich) desperately believes in his own personal power to change the world around him. He winds up captured by the Germans in 1939 and is held in a POW camp until chance lands him in the service of a group of high-ranking Nazis, including Hermann Goring (Spengler). Goring sends Abel out to recruit young boys into becoming military conscripts and he gains the nickname of the Ogre, the mythic devourer of children. Adapted from Michael Tournier's novel "The Erl King." **117m/C; VHS, DVD.** *GE FR GB* John Malkovich; Volker Spengler; Armin Mueller-Stahl; Gottfried John; *D:* Volker Schlondorff; *W:* Volker Schlondorff; Jean-Claude Carriere; *C:* Bruno de Keyzer; *M:* Michael Nyman.

Oh, Alfie *Alfie Darling* **1975 (R)** In every man's life, there comes a time to settle down... but never when you're having as much fun as Alfie! Inadequate sequel to "Alfie." **99m/C; VHS, DVD.** *GB* Joan Collins; Alan Price; Jill Townsend; *D:* Ken Hughes; *W:* Ken Hughes.

Oh! Calcutta! ½ **1972** Film version of the first nude musical to play on Broadway, which caused a sensation in the late 1960s. It's really a collection of skits, some of which were written by such notables as John Lennon, Sam Shepard, and Jules Feiffer. And it's really not that funny or erotic. **105m/C; VHS, DVD.** Bill Macy; Mark Dempsey; Raina Barrett; Samantha Harper; Patricia Hawkins; Mitchell McGuire; *D:* Guillaume Martin Aucion; *W:* Robert Benton; Jules Feiffer; Dan Greenberg; John Lennon; Jacques Levy; Sam Shepard; Leonard Melfi; David Newman; Clovis Trouille; Sherman Yellen; *C:* Frank Biondo; Arnold Giordano; Jerry Sarcone; *M:* Prof. Peter Schickele; Robert Dennis.

Oh Christmas Tree! ½ *Fir Crazy* **2013** Driven career woman Elise MacReynolds loses her job and finds herself working in the family business again--selling Christmas trees from their tree farm in a Manhattan lot. Of course this leads to Elise figuring out the true meaning of the holiday, especially when scrooge-like exec Gary Dixon, who's bought the lot, demands the business be shut down immediately! From the Hallmark Channel. **87m/C; DVD.** Sarah Lancaster; Eric Johnson; Colin Mochrie; *D:* Craig Pryce; *W:* Elizabeth Hackett; Hilary Galanoy; *C:* John Berrie; *M:* Lawrence Shragge. **CABLE**

Oh, God! ½ **1977 (PG)** God, in the person of Burns, recruits Denver as his herald in his plan to save the world. Despite initial skepticism, Denver, in his film debut, keeps faith and is rewarded. Sincere performances and optimistic end make for satisfying story. Followed by "Oh God! Book 2" and "Oh God! You Devil." **104m/C; VHS, DVD.** George Burns; John Denver; Paul Sorvino; Ralph Bellamy; Teri Garr; William Daniels; Donald Pleasence; Barnard Hughes; Barry Sullivan; Dinah Shore; Jeff Corey; David Ogden Stiers; *D:* Carl Reiner; *W:* Larry Gelbart. Writers Guild '77: Adapt. Screenplay.

Oh, God! Book 2 **1980 (PG)** Burns returns as the "Almighty One" in strained sequel to "Oh God!" This time he enlists the help of a young girl to remind others of his existence. The slogan she concocts saves God's image, but not the movie. Followed by "Oh, God! You Devil." **94m/C; VHS, DVD.** George Burns; Suzanne Pleshette; David Birney; Louanne; Conrad Janis; Wilfrid Hyde-White; Hans Conried; Howard Duff; Anthony Holland; *D:* Gilbert Cates; *M:* Charles Fox.

Oh, God! You Devil **1984 (PG)** During his third trip to earth, Burns plays both the Devil and God as he first takes a struggling musician's soul, then gives it back. A few zingers and light atmosphere save unoriginal plot. The second sequel to "Oh, God!" **96m/C; VHS, DVD.** George Burns; Ted Wass; Roxanne Hart; Ron Silver; Eugene Roche; Robert Desiderio; *D:* Paul Bogart; *W:* Andrew Bergman; *M:* David Shire.

Oh, Heavenly Dog! **1980 (PG)** A private eye returns from the dead as a dog to solve his own murder. Man's best friend and intelligent to boot. The famous dog Benji's third film, and his acting improves with each one. Adults may find this movie slow, but kids will probably love it. **104m/C; VHS, DVD.** Chevy Chase; Jane Seymour; Omar Sharif; Robert Morley; Susan Kellerman; *D:* Joe Camp; *W:* Joe Camp; Rod Browning.

The Oh in Ohio **2006 (R)** Naughty trifle of an indie comedy with the 'oh' standing for orgasm. Frigid Priscilla (Posey) may say she's satisfied with the sex in her 10-year marriage to Jack (Rudd) but he isn't and she's lying. He's a high school teacher who succumbs to nubile student Kristen (Barton) while Priscilla finally decides to go to sex guru Alyssa (Minnelli) for advice. Once past the vibrator stage, Priscilla finds an unlikely sexual healer in lusty (and surprisingly sweet) swimming pool mogul Larry (DeVito). **88m/C; DVD.** Parker Posey; Paul Rudd; Danny DeVito; Mischa Barton; Liza Minnelli; Miranda Bailey; Keith David; Tim Russ; Linda Watkins; John McNamara; *D:* Danny DeVito; Billy Kent; Dan Milner; *W:* Billy Kent; Sarah Bird; Richard Bernstein; *C:* Ramsay Nickell; Brydon Baker; *M:* Darrell Calker.

Oh Lucy! *Ō Rûsh!* **2017 95m/C; Blu-Ray.** *JP US* Shinobu Terajima; Josh Hartnett; Shioli Kutsuna; Megan Mullally; Koji Yakusho; *D:* Atsuki Hirayanagi; *W:* Atsuki Hirayanagi; Boris Frumin; *C:* Paula Huidobro; *M:* Erik Friedlander.

Oh, Men! Oh, Women! ½ **1957** Frothy comedy based on Edward Chodorov's play. Shrink Alan Coles (Niven) discovers his would-be fiance Myra (Rush) gets around when neurotic patient Cobbler (Randall) complains about his former girlfriend and Mildred Turner (Rogers) is upset that her husband Arthur (Dailey) is apparently interested in a younger woman. Myra is a no-show for their wedding cruise, and Alan is certain their romance is over. **90m/C; DVD.** David Niven; Dan Dailey; Ginger Rogers; Barbara Rush; Tony Randall; Natalie Schafer; *D:* Nunnally Johnson; *W:* Nunnally Johnson; *C:* Charles G. Clarke; *M:* Cyril Mockridge.

Oh! What a Lovely War ½ **1969** Scathing musical re-creation of British soldiers in WWI using the era's popular songs and presenting the story as a music hall review as seen through the eyes of the working-class Smith family. All their sons are seduced into enlisting and get killed, while the generals and the politicians are safely behind the lines or complaining at home. Attenborough's directorial debut features an all-star cast but comes off as somewhat disjointed and obvious due to its adaptation from a stage production. Filmed on location in and around Brighton. **144m/C; DVD.** *GB* Colin Farrell; John Rae; Corin Redgrave; Maurice Roeves; Kim Smith; Angela Thorne; Mary Wimbush; Paul Daneman; Laurence Olivier; Michael Redgrave; Vanessa Redgrave; John Gielgud; Ralph Richardson; Maggie Smith; Susannah York; John Mills; Isabel Dean; Vincent Ball; Christian Doermer; Robert Flemyng; Ian Holm; David Lodge; Guy Middleton; Juliet Mills; Nanette Newman; *D:* Richard Attenborough; *W:* Len Deighton; *C:* Gerry Turpin; *M:* Alfred Ralston. British Acad. '69: Art Dir./Set Dec., Cinematog., Costume Des., Support. Actor (Olivier); Golden Globes '70: Foreign Film.

O'Hara's Wife ½ **1982** Loving wife Harley continues to care for her family even after her untimely death. Only husband Asner, however, can see her ghost. Lightweight drama traps good cast. **87m/C; VHS, DVD.** Ed Asner; Mariette Hartley; Jodie Foster; Tom Bosley; Perry Lang; Ray Walston; *D:* William S. Bartman; *W:* William S. Bartman; *M:* Artie Butler. **TV**

O'Horten **2009 (PG-13)** At 67, train engineer Odd Horten is forced into retirement and realizes that without his orderly existence he doesn't know what to do with his life. Norwegian with subtitles. **89m/C; On Demand.** *FR GE NO* Baard Owe; Espen Skjonberg; Ghita Norby; Henry Moan; *D:* Bent Hamer; *W:* Bent Hamer; *C:* John Christian Rosenlund; *M:* Kaada.

Oil **1978 (PG)** Seven men fight a raging oil fire that threatens to destroy an entire country. Unfortunately, the movie is unable to ignite any interest at all. **95m/C; VHS, DVD.** Ray Milland; Woody Strode; Stuart Whitman; Tony Kendall; William Berger; *D:* Mircea Dragan.

Oil for the Lamps of China ½ **1935** Stephen Chase (O'Brien) is fanatical about being a company man—in his case as an oil company rep in China who's constantly exploited by his firm. His fervor costs him his friends and nearly his marriage to his devoted wife Hester (Hutchinson). The communist Chinese figure into the plot as well and there's a foolish ending that negates much of what went on earlier. **98m/B; DVD.** Pat O'Brien; Josephine Hutchinson; Jean Muir; John Eldredge; Lyle Talbot; Donald Crisp; *D:* Mervyn LeRoy; *W:* Laird Doyle; *C:* Gaetano Antonio "Tony" Gaudio.

The Oil Raider **1934** Dave Warren (Crabbe) and his crew are trying to bring in a new oil well while trying to get rid of a troublemaker named Simmons (Wagner). To finance the digging Dave borrows five grand from banker J.T. Varley (Irving). Varley is in financial trouble and knows Dave is about to hit the jackpot, so he sends the aforementioned Simmons to sabotage the dig so Dave has to default on the loan and he can take over. **65m/B; DVD.** Buster Crabbe; Gloria Shea; George Irving; Max Wagner; Emmett Vogan; Harold Minjir; *D:* Spencer Gordon Bennett; *W:* Homer King Gordon; George Morgan; Rex Taylor; *C:* Edward Snyder.

Okinawa: The Afterburn *Okinawa: Urizun no ame* **2015** Based on the book by Koji Kobayashi, a feature-length documentary on the Battle of Okinawa and its long-term impact on Japan. The documentary details the battle from the perspectives of both Japanese and American soldiers, as well as the civilians who became part of the fighting. The post-war fate of Okinawa, including the long-term presence of the U.S. military, including bases and soldiers, is examined as well. The documentary looks at how the American military has led to increased crime, accidents, and pollution. Japanese and English with subtitles. **148m/C; DVD.** *D:* John Junkerman; *C:* Chuck France; Katanobu Kato; Takanobu Kato; Stephen McCarthy; Brett Wiley; *M:* Hitoshi Komuro. **VIDEO**

Okja **2017** A tale of a girl and her animal sidekick is given the typical treatment of writer/director Bong Joon Ho to become genre-bending, disturbing at times, yet ultimately entertaining. Young Mija has been the companion of Okja, a hippopotamus-like superpig developed by the evil Mirando Corp. as the meat source of the future. When CEO Mirando (Swinton) has Okja kidnapped, Mija pursues them to New York, where a not-so-merry band of animal activists assists in Okja's rescue. Slick and glossy cinematography are appealing, but parents be warned: extreme peril and critter cruelty may scare children into vegetarianism. **120m/C; DVD.** Tilda Swinton; Paul Dano; Seo-Hyun Ahn; Hee-Bong Byun; Steven Yeun; *D:* Joon-ho Bong; *W:* Joon-ho Bong; Jon Ronson; *C:* Darius Khondji.

Oklahoma! ½ **1955 (G)** Jones's film debut; a must-see for musical fans. A cowboy and country girl fall in love, but she is tormented by another unwelcomed suitor. At over two hours, cuteness wears thin for some. Actually filmed in Arizona. Adapted from Rodgers and Hammerstein's broadway hit with original score; choreography by Agnes de Mille. **145m/C; VHS, DVD, Blu-Ray.** Gordon MacRae; Shirley Jones; Rod Steiger; Gloria Grahame; Eddie Albert; Charlotte Greenwood; James Whitmore; Gene Nelson; Barbara Lawrence; Jay C. Flippen; *D:* Fred Zinnemann; *W:* Sonya Levien; William Ludwig; *C:* Robert L. Surtees; *M:* Richard Rodgers; Oscar Hammerstein. Oscars '55: Scoring/Musical, Sound; Natl. Film Reg. '07.

Oklahoma! *Rodger's and Hammerstein's Oklahoma!* **1999** 1999 London stage revival of the classic Rodgers and Hammerstein play filmed for television. Hugh Jackman stars as a singing cowboy. **180m/C; DVD, Blu-Ray.** *UK* Maureen Lipman; Hugh Jackman; Josefina Gabrielle; David Shelmerdine; Jimmy Johnston; *D:* Trevor Nunn; *W:* Lynn Riggs; *C:* Paul Wheeler. **TV**

Oklahoma Annie **1951** Storekeeper Canova joins the new sheriff in booting undesirables out of town, and tries to sing her way into his heart. Amazingly, it works—not for delicate ears. **90m/C; VHS, DVD.** Judy Canova; Fuzzy Knight; Grant Withers; John Russell; Denver Pyle; Allen Jenkins; Almira Sessions; *D:* R.G. Springsteen.

Oklahoma City **2017 90m/C; DVD, Streaming.** *D:* Barak Goodman; *W:* Barak Goodman; *C:* Stephen McCarthy; *M:* David Cieri.

The Oklahoma City Dolls ½ **1981** ABC TV movie. Factory worker Sally Jo (Blakeley) is after equal rights so she and her co-workers form a football team and hire broken-down coach Homer Sixx (Albert) to turn them into winners. **100m/C; DVD.** Susan Blakely; Eddie Albert; Ronee Blakley; Savannah Smith; David Huddleston; Waylon Jennings; *D:* E.W. Swackhamer; *W:* Ann Beckett; *C:* Edward R. Brown; *M:* Jerrold Immel. **TV**

Oklahoma Crude ½ **1973 (PG)** Sadistic oil trust rep Palence battles man-hating Dunaway for her well. Drifter Scott helps her resist on the promise of shared profits. In this 1913 setting, Dunaway tells Scott she wishes she could avoid men altogether, but later settles for him. **108m/C; VHS, Blu-Ray, Streaming.** George C. Scott; Faye Dunaway; John Mills; Jack Palance; Harvey Jason; Woodrow Parfrey; *D:* Stanley Kramer; *W:* Marc Norman; *C:* Robert L. Surtees; *M:* Henry Mancini.

Oklahoma Kid **1939** Offbeat, hilarious western with Bogie as the villain and gunfighter Cagney seeking revenge for his father's wrongful death. Highlight is Cagney's rendition of "I Don't Want To Play In Your Yard," complete with six-shooter accompaniment. **82m/B; DVD.** James Cagney; Humphrey Bogart; Rosemary Lane; Ward Bond; Donald Crisp; Charles Middleton; Harvey Stephens; *D:* Lloyd Bacon; *C:* James Wong Howe; *M:* Max Steiner.

The Oklahoman **1956** A routine western with some trivia value. Town doc McCrea helps Indian Pate keep his land. Talbott plays Indian maiden in same year as her title role in Daughter of Jekyll. Continuity buffs will note Hale wears the same outfit in most scenes. **80m/C; VHS, DVD.** Joel McCrea; Barbara Hale; Brad Dexter; Gloria Talbott; Verna Felton; Douglas Dick; Michael Pate; Scotty Beckett; *D:* Francis D. Lyon.

Okoge *Fag Hag* **1993** Rueful sexual comedy about a triangular friendship. Sayoko is a single young working woman living in a tiny Tokyo apartment. She meets the gay Noh and his older married lover Tochi and when they become friendly, Sayoko lets them use her apartment as their love nest—to the complications of all concerned. Title is a slang term used to refer to women who prefer the company of gay men. In Japanese with English subtitles. **120m/C; VHS, DVD.** *JP* Misa Shimizu; Takehiro Murata; Takeo Nakahara; Masayuki Shionoya; Noriko Sengoku; Kyozo Nagatsuka; Toshie Negishi; *D:* Takehiro Nakajima; *W:* Takehiro Nakajima; *C:* Yoshimasa Hakata; *M:* Hiroshi Ariyoshi.

Oktober **1998** A multinational pharmaceutical company is behind a sinister plot for global domination as a young teacher becomes both a walking experiment and a marked target in this medical thriller. **90m/C; DVD.** *GB* Stephen Tompkinson; Maria Lennon; James McCarthy; Lydzia Englert; *D:* Stephen Gallagher; *W:* Stephen Gallagher; *C:* Bruce McGowan; *M:* Alan Parker. **TV**

Old Acquaintance **1943** Onetime childhood friends Kit Marlowe (Davis) and Millie Drake (Hopkins) have a decades-long personal and professional rivalry. Serious writer Kit wins awards while Millie gets wealthy from her best-selling potboilers. Millie's neglected husband Preston (Loder) tells Kit he's in love with her although she doesn't feel the same. The boiling point is reached again years later thanks to Millie's teenage daughter Deirdre (Moran) and the two finally let it all out. Yep, Davis and Hopkins (who didn't like each other anyway) have an on-screen cat fight in this adaptation of the John Van Druten play. Remade in 1981 as "Rich and Famous." **110m/B; DVD.** Bette Davis; Miriam Hopkins; John Loder; Dolores Moran; Gig Young; Roscoe Karns; Phillip Reed; Anne Revere; *D:* Vincent Sherman; *W:* Lenore Coffee; John Van Druten; *C:* Sol Polito; *M:* Franz Waxman.

Old Boyfriends **1979 (R)** Shire is weak as a psychologist searching for old boyfriends in order to analyze her past. Strange combination of Carradine and Belushi may draw curious fans. **103m/C; VHS, DVD.** Talia Shire; Richard Jordan; John Belushi;

Keith Carradine; John Houseman; Buck Henry; ***D:*** Joan Tewkesbury; ***W:*** Leonard Schrader; Paul Schrader; ***M:*** David Shire.

The Old Curiosity Shop 1/2 **1994 (PG)** Another adaptation of Charles Dickens's 1840 tale about Grandfather Trent (Ustinov), an antiques dealer who has lost his fortune through gambling and makes matters worse by borrowing money from the miserable Mr. Quilp (Courtenay). Unable to repay the debt, Trent and young granddaughter Sally (Walsh) try to escape London, which turns Quilp's wrath upon them. Fine performances and a colorful production. **280m/C; VHS, DVD.** Peter Ustinov; Tom Courtenay; James Fox; Sally Walsh; William Mannering; Christopher Ettridge; Julia McKenzie; Anne White; Jean Marlow; Cornelia Hayes O'Herlihy; Michael Mears; ***D:*** Kevin Connor; ***W:*** John Goldsmith; ***C:*** Doug Milsome; ***M:*** Mason Daring. **CABLE**

The Old Curiosity Shop 1/2 **2007** Truncated BBC presentation of the Dickens novel. Ruthless moneylender Daniel Quilp (Jones) hounds the debt-ridden owner of the London antiques shop, causing the old man (Jacobi) and his teenaged granddaughter Little Nell (Vayasseur) to flee after their eviction. Since Quilp would rather see them in debtor's prison, they're relentlessly pursued as Grandfather's inveterate gambling makes their situation ever more dire. And then the ending gets changed! It's still tragic but not nearly so poignant. **100m/C; DVD.** *GB* Derek Jacobi; Toby Jones; Gina McKee; Bryan Dick; Martin Freeman; Adam Godley; Anna Madeley; Adrian Rawlins; Sophie Vayasseur; Geoff Breton; Zoe Wanamaker; George MacKay; ***D:*** Brian Percival; ***W:*** Martyn Hesford; ***C:*** Peter Greenhalgh; ***M:*** Stephen McKeon. **TV**

The Old Dark House **1932** An atmospheric horror film, with more than a touch of comedy, well-directed by Whale. In an old haunted house live the bizarre Femm family: the 102-year-old patriarch (Dudgeon), an atheist son (Thesinger), a religious fanatic daughter (Moore), and a crazed pyromanic son (Wills), all watched over by the mute, scarred, and psychotic butler (Karloff's first starring role). Into this strange group wander five stranded travelers who set all sorts of dastardly plots in motion. Based on the novel "Benighted" by J.B. Priestley. John Dudgeon is actually actress Elspeth Dudgeon who's playing in drag. Remade in 1963 by William Castle. **71m/B; DVD, Blu-Ray.** Boris Karloff; Melvyn Douglas; Charles Laughton; Gloria Stuart; Ernest Thesiger; Raymond Massey; Lillian Bond; Eva Moore; Brember Wills; Elspeth (John) Dudgeon; ***D:*** James Whale; ***W:*** Benn W. Levy; R.C. Sherriff; ***C:*** Arthur Edeson.

Old Dogs WOOF! **2009 (PG)** Divorcee Dan (Williams) and happy bachelor Charlie (Travolta) are best buds and business partners who have their lives upended when they suddenly become the guardians of mischievous 7-year-old twins. Hacked together, in a failed attempt to salvage any type of laughs, complete with four camera angles of Williams falling into a pond. Sad to say that none of them are funny. Regrettably, Travolta drags daughter Ella Bleu and wife Kelly Preston into this disastrous Disney flop. **88m/C; DVD, Blu-Ray.** Robin Williams; John Travolta; Conner Rayburn; Ella Bleu Travolta; Kelly Preston; Bernie Mac; Seth Green; Lori Loughlin; Matt Dillon; Rita Wilson; Laura Allen; Ann-Margret; Amy Sedaris; ***D:*** Walt Becker; ***W:*** David Diamond; David Weissman; ***C:*** Jeffrey L. Kimball; ***M:*** John Debney.

Old English **1930** Stagebound drama adapted from the John Galsworthy story and play. Octogenarian Sylvanus Heythorp is the managing director of a shipbuilding firm. He wants to provide for the widow and children of his deceased illegitimate son so he strikes a shady deal but is exposed. Unwilling to suffer a scandal Heythorp decides to commit gastronomic suicide (rich foods will kill him). **85m/B; DVD.** George Arliss; Ethel Griffies; Doris Lloyd; Leon Janney; Betty Lawford; Murray Kinnell; Reginald (Reggie, Reggy) Sheffield; ***D:*** Alfred E. Green; ***W:*** Maude Howell; Walter Anthony; ***C:*** James Van Trees.

Old Enough **1984 (PG)** Slow-moving coming-of-age comedy on the rich kid-poor kid friendship theme. Silver's directing debut. **91m/C; VHS, DVD.** Sarah Boyd; Rainbow Harvest; Neill Barry; Danny Aiello; Susan Kingsley; Roxanne Hart; Alyssa Milano; Fran Brill; Anne Pitoniak; ***D:*** Marisa Silver; ***W:*** Marisa Silver; ***C:*** Michael Ballhaus. Sundance '84: Grand Jury Prize.

An Old-Fashioned Thanksgiving 1/2 **2008** Hallmark Channel movie that's very loosely based on a short story by Louisa May Alcott and set after the Civil War. Wealthy Isabella (Bisset) has been estranged from her daughter Mary (Joy) ever since she ran away to marry a stablehand. With her husband dead, the widow and her children live in poverty so granddaughter Mathilda (Maslany) concocts a story to get Isabella to visit. **88m/C; DVD.** Jacqueline Bisset; Tatiana Maslany; Ted Atherton; Kristopher Turner; Helene Joy; Gage Munroe; Vivien Endicott Douglas; Paula Boudreau; ***D:*** Graeme Campbell; ***W:*** Shelley Evans; ***C:*** Mitchell Ness; ***M:*** James Gelfand. **CABLE**

The Old-Fashioned Way 1/2 **1934** McGonigle (Fields) is the hammy, debt-ridden manager of a third-rate traveling vaudeville troupe who needs to stay one step ahead of bill collectors and the local law. He cons wealthy small town widow Cleopatra Pepperday (Duggan) into paying the bills in return for a part in their latest production while her toddler son Albert (Baby LeRoy) harasses the curmudgeon. The best scenes include Fields' juggling act. **66m/B; DVD.** W.C. Fields; Jan Duggan; Baby LeRoy; Judith Allen; Joe Morrison; Tammany Young; ***D:*** William Beaudine; ***W:*** Garnett Weston; Jack Cunningham; ***C:*** Ben F. Reynolds.

Old Goats **2013** A bro-mantic comedy for the elder set. The semi-documentary follows three real-life well-past-retirement-age friends, Bob, Britton, and David, playing heightened versions of themselves as they navigate the world of dating and marriage in the new digital age. This unpolished indie relies on the charisma of its non-actor leads to carry the weight, as they bicker about sexuality and cell phones. A fun and quirky set-up but, as you might guess, it gets old after awhile. **94m/C; DVD.** Bob Burkholder; Britton Crosley; David Vander Wal; ***D:*** Taylor Guterson; ***W:*** Taylor Guterson; ***C:*** Taylor Guterson.

Old Gringo 1/2 **1989 (R)** Adapted from Carlos Fuentes' novelization of writer Ambrose Bierce's mysterious disappearance in Mexico during the revolution of 1913. Features Fonda in the unlikely role of a virgin schoolteacher, Smits as her revolutionary lover, and Peck as her hero. Soggy acting by all but Peck, whose presence is wasted in a sketchy character. Technical problems and cheesy sets and costumes—look for the dusk backdrop in the dance scene and Smits' silly moustache. Better to read the book. **119m/C; VHS, DVD, Blu-Ray.** Jane Fonda; Gregory Peck; Jimmy Smits; Patricio Contreras; Jenny Gago; Gabriela Roel; Sergio Calderon; Guillermo Rios; Anne Pitoniak; Pedro Armendariz, Jr.; Jim Metzler; ***D:*** Luis Puenzo; ***W:*** Aida Bortnik; Luis Puenzo; ***M:*** Lee Holdridge.

The Old Homestead **1935** Talent scout Wertheimer is impressed by the musical ability of country boy Bob and his fellow farmhands and offers them a new radio program. They head off to New York, along with Bob's gal Nancy and new manager Uncle Jed, but success swells Bob's head and he and Nancy break up, resulting in various other romantic and professional problems. **72m/B; DVD.** Mary Carlisle; Lawrence Gray; Willard Robertson; Dorothy Lee; Edward J. Nugent; Lillian Miles; Fuzzy Knight; Eddie Kane; ***D:*** William Nigh; ***W:*** Scott Darling; ***C:*** Harry Neumann.

Old Joy **2006** Two 30-something buddies who spent their younger days smoking pot and fighting the system embark on a reunion road trip to an Oregon natural hot springs. While their time together is pleasant enough, the pair doesn't quite reconnect—Kurt (Oldham) is still living in the past, while Mark (London) has a career, wife, and child on the way. Not much in the way of action but their talks—or, even, what isn't talked about—show how the glory days of friendship can't always be recaptured. Drawn from Jonathan Raymond's short story. **76m/C; DVD, Blu-Ray.** William Oldham; Daniel London; Tanya Smith; ***D:*** Kelly Reichardt; ***W:*** Kelly Reichardt; Jonathan Raymond; ***C:*** Peter Sillen.

The Old Maid **1939** After her beau is killed in the Civil War, a woman allows her cousin to raise her illegitimate daughter, and therein begins a years-long struggle over the girl's affections. High grade soaper based on Zoe Adkin's stage adaptation of Edith Wharton's novel. **96m/B; VHS, DVD.** Bette Davis; Miriam Hopkins; George Brent; Donald Crisp; Jane Bryan; Louise Fazenda; Henry Stephenson; ***D:*** Edmund Goulding; ***C:*** Gaetano Antonio "Tony" Gaudio; ***M:*** Max Steiner.

The Old Man & the Gun **2018 (PG-13)** Lifelong criminal Forrest Tucker (Redford) has been in and out of prison since his teens. Late in life, he robs banks with the manners of a gentleman. Forrest and his co-conspirators Teddy (Glover), and Waller (Waits) become known as the Over the Hill Gang. As this trio reaches the end of its days, Forrest becomes involved with Jewel (Spacek), a woman he meets after her car breaks down. The gang is pursued by officers led by John Hunt (Affleck), who admires Forrest's skill and attitude. Based on a true story, the final film of Redford is another well-crafted work by director/screenwriter Lowery. **93m/C; DVD, Blu-Ray.** Robert Redford; Sissy Spacek; Casey Affleck; Danny Glover; Tom Waits; ***D:*** David Lowery; ***W:*** David Lowery; ***C:*** Joe Anderson; ***M:*** Daniel Hart.

The Old Man and the Sea 1/2 **1958** Cuban fisherman Santiago hooks a giant marlin and battles sharks and the sea to bring his trophy home. Tracy's performance as the tough, aging fisherman garnered him his sixth Academy Award nomination and Tiomkin's beautiful score was an Oscar winner. **86m/C; DVD.** Spencer Tracy; Felipe Pazos; Harry Bellaver; Don Diamond; Don Blackman; Joey Ray; ***D:*** John Sturges; ***W:*** Peter Viertel; ***C:*** James Wong Howe; Floyd Crosby; ***M:*** Dimitri Tiomkin. Oscars '58: Orig. Dramatic Score.

The Old Man and the Sea 1/2 **1990** Quinn is wonderful as Hemingway's aging Cuban fisherman, Santiago, who battles a band of marauding sharks for a giant marlin in the Gulf Stream. Unfortunately, this made-for-TV adaptation is ordinary. **97m/C; VHS, DVD.** Anthony Quinn; Gary Cole; Alexis Cruz; Patricia Clarkson; Francesco Quinn; ***D:*** Jud Taylor; ***W:*** Roger O. Hirson; ***C:*** James Wong Howe; ***M:*** Bruce Broughton. **TV**

Old Man Rhythm **1935** Minor but diverting RKO musical. Overprotective dad worries about the effect girls are having on his son's grades, so pops enrolls as a college freshman to keep an eye on his progeny. A good thing since junior is being taken in by a gold-digger. Lyricist Johnny Mercer makes an appearance and Grable's coed tap dances en pointe. **75m/B; DVD.** Charles "Buddy" Rogers; George Barbier; Barbara Kent; Grace Bradley; Betty Grable; Eric Blore; Erik Rhodes; ***D:*** Edward Ludwig; ***W:*** Ernest Pagano; Sig Herzig; ***C:*** Nicholas Musuraca.

Old Mother Riley, Headmistress 1/2 **1950** Irish washerwoman Mrs. Riley (Lucan) winds up the headmistress of a girls' school that is threatened when a railroad line is planned to go through the property. **76m/B; VHS, DVD.** *GB* Arthur Lucan; Kitty McShane; Enid Hewitt; Jenny Mathot; Cyril Smith; ***D:*** John Harlow; ***W:*** Jack Marks; Con West; ***C:*** Ken Talbot.

Old Mother Riley in Paris 1/2 **1938** Brit comedy in drag. Irish washerwoman Mrs. Riley (Lucan) travels to Paris in search of daughter Kitty (McShane) and is mistaken for a spy before she stumbles upon a real spy ring. **73m/B; DVD.** *GB* Arthur Lucan; Kitty McShane; Jerry Verno; Magda Kun; C. Denier Warren; ***D:*** Oswald Mitchell; ***W:*** Con West; ***M:*** Percival Mackey.

Old Mother Riley, MP 1/2 **1939** Washerwoman Mrs. Riley (Lucan) gets fired from her job at the laundry and then learns that the same landlord is going to pull down houses on her street (including her own) as well as the local pub if he succeeds in winning election to Parliament. So Old Mother Riley decides to run against him. **73m/B; DVD.** *GB* Arthur Lucan; Kitty McShane; Torin Thatcher; Henry Longhurst; Patrick Ludlow; Dennis Wyndham; ***D:*** Oswald Mitchell; ***W:*** Oswald Mitchell; Con West; ***C:*** James Wilson.

Old Mother Riley's Ghosts **1941** A group of spies "haunt" Mother Riley's castle home in a futile attempt to scare her out; she turns the tables. Some good scares and laughs. Part of the Old Mother Riley series. Look for similarities to later Monty Python films. **82m/B; VHS, DVD.** *GB* Arthur Lucan; Kitty McShane; John Stuart; ***D:*** John Baxter.

Old Mother Riley's Jungle Treasure 1/2 **1951** Mother Riley (Lucan) and daughter Kitty (McShane) are working in an antiques shop where they discover a treasure map. So they head for the South Seas and find a pirate's ghost as well. **75m/B; VHS, DVD.** *GB* Arthur Lucan; Kitty McShane; Sebastian Cabot; Garry Marsh; Roddy Hughes; ***D:*** Maclean Rogers; ***W:*** Val Valentine; ***C:*** James Wilson.

Old Mother Riley's New Venture 1/2 **1949** Old Mother Riley (Lucan) is hired as the manager of a hotel that's been victimized by a series of robberies. But she's soon framed for a hotel jewel heist by the real thief. **80m/B; VHS, DVD.** *GB* Arthur Lucan; Kitty McShane; Chili Bouchier; Willer Neal; Sebastian Cabot; ***D:*** John Harlow; ***W:*** Jack Marks; Con West; ***C:*** James Wilson.

Old San Francisco 1/2 **1927** The Spanish Vasquez family was one of the original settlers of the San Francisco area, but now they are in financial difficulties. The evil and powerful Buckwell (Oland)?who is hiding a secret about his own origins—becomes interested in Dolores Vasquez (Costello) but she is in love with Irishman Terrence (Mack). When Dolores learns Buckwell's secret and threatens to expose him, he kidnaps her and Terrence. The 1906 San Francisco earthquake proves providential in their escape. The film's racial stereotyping of the Chinese community will appear offensively racist to modern eyes. **88m/B; Silent; DVD.** Dolores Costello; Warner Oland; Charles Emmet Mack; Josef Swickard; Anders Randolph; Anna May Wong; ***D:*** Alan Crosland; ***W:*** Anthony Coldeway; ***C:*** Hal Mohr.

Old School 1/2 **2003 (R)** Thirty-something pals Mitch (Wilson), Frank (Ferrell), and Beanie (Vaughn) start a frat at the nearby college so they can have a place to escape their everyday troubles. Mitch's girlfriend hosts orgies during his business trips, the recently married Frank longs for beery bachelor freedom, and Beanie has never grown up despite having a nice family and owning an electronics store chain. Despite the plot breakdowns and generally one-dimensional characters, everyone, including the audience, manages to have a pretty good time, thanks largely to the likeability of the cast. **90m/C; DVD, Blu-Ray, HD-DVD.** Luke Wilson; Will Ferrell; Vince Vaughn; Ellen Pompeo; Juliette Lewis; Leah Remini; Perrey Reeves; Elisha Cuthbert; Jeremy Piven; Rick Gonzalez; Terry O'Quinn; Artie Lange; Matthew Carey; Harve Presnell; Seann William Scott; Craig Kilborn; ***Cameo(s):*** Andy Dick; Snoop Dogg; ***D:*** Todd Phillips; ***W:*** Todd Phillips; Scot Armstrong; ***C:*** Mark Irwin; ***M:*** Theodore Shapiro.

The Old Settler 1/2 **2001** Elizabeth Barney (Rashad) is middleaged and has never been married, thus making her an old settler according to sister Quilly (Allen). Quilly has been abandoned by her husband and is living with Elizabeth in her Harlem apartment because times are hard. In fact to make a little extra cash, Elizabeth rents a room to handsome country boy Husband Witherspoon (Robinson), fresh off the bus from South Carolina. Eventually Husband, who's been disappointed in love, turns his attentions to Elizabeth, much to the bitter Quilly's astonishment. Based on the play by John Henry Redwood. **90m/C; VHS, DVD.** Phylicia Rashad; Debbie Allen; Bumper Robinson; Eartha D. Robinson; Crystal Fox; Randy J. Goodwin; ***D:*** Debbie Allen; ***W:*** Shauneille Perry. **TV**

Old Stone 1/2 *Lao Shi* **2016** The Chinese legal system when it comes to car accidents is literally one that encourages hit and runs, for the driver has to essentially become the keeper, financially and physically, of whomever he may accidentally hit in a crowded street. Such is the dilemma that cab driver Lao Shi (Gang Chen) finds himself in after a man jumps in front of his car. He does not flee the scene, but he arguably should have, given the legal problems, bureaucratic red tape, and medical bills that now pile up in front of him. This is a Kafkaesque examination of a broken system that envelopes a good man. **80m/C; DVD, Blu-Ray.** Gang Chen; Nai An; Hongwei Wang; Zebin Zhang; Xue'er Luo; ***D:*** Johnny Ma; ***W:*** Johnny Ma; ***C:*** Ming-Kai Leung; ***M:*** Lee Sanders.

Old Swimmin' Hole 🦴🦴 *When Youth Conspires* **1940** Small-town friends Moran and Jones try to bring their single parents together; his mother can't afford to finance his dream to be a doctor. Dull, melodramatic ode to heartland America, reminiscent of "Our Town." **78m/B; VHS, DVD.** Marcia Mae Jones; Jackie Moran; Leatrice Joy; Charles D. Brown; ***D:*** Robert McGowan.

The Old Testament 🦴 *Il Vecchio Testamento* **1962** Despite the title, this film only covers one small part of the Old Testament, specifically the Syrians driving the Jews out of Jerusalem. The transfer to DVD is not so good, which isn't as disappointing as the film itself which is cliche and poorly done. **88m/C; DVD.** *IT FR* Brad Harris; Franca Parisi; Mara Lane; Phillipe Hersent; Carlo Tamberlani; Jacques Berthier; Isarco Ravaioli; Enzo Doria; Vladimir Leib; ***D:*** Gianfranco Parolini; ***W:*** Gianfranco Parolini; Ghigo De Chiara; Luciano Martino; Giorgio Prosperi; Giovanni Simonelli; ***C:*** Francesco Izzarelli; ***M:*** Angelo Francesco Lavagnino.

Old Yeller 🦴🦴🦴½ **1957 (G)** Disney Studios' first and best boy-and-his-dog film, set in Texas in 1869. 15-year-old Travis Coates (Kirk) is left in charge of the family farm while dad Jim (Parker) is away on a cattle drive. When his younger brother Arliss (Corcoran) brings home a stray dog, Travis is displeased but lets him stay. Yeller saves Travis's life, but contracts rabies in the process. Keep tissue handy, especially for the kids. Strong acting, effective scenery—all good stuff. Based on the novel by Fred Gipson. Sequel "Savage Sam" released in 1963. **84m/C; VHS, DVD.** Dorothy McGuire; Fess Parker; Tommy Kirk; Kevin Corcoran; Jeff York; Beverly Washburn; Chuck Connors; ***D:*** Robert Stevenson; ***W:*** Fred Gipson; William Tunberg; ***C:*** Charles P. Boyle; ***M:*** Oliver Wallace. Natl. Film Reg. '19.

Oldboy 🦴🦴🦴🦴 **2003 (R)** After a drunken evening, Oh Dae-su (Choi, in a brilliant performance) awakens to find himself trapped inside a small room, barred from escape by a thick steel door. Oh spends the next 15 years in captivity, with no explanation ever offered from his jailers. With no warning, Oh—now half crazy from isolation and his thirst for vengeance—is suddenly freed and a mysterious figure gives him five days to figure out why he's been imprisoned. Park should be applauded for his vicious, unflinching insight into human sexuality and violence in this sad, surrealistic mystery. Korean with subtitles. **120m/C; DVD, Blu-Ray, UMD.** *NK* Min-Sik Choi; Yu Ji-tae; Hye-jeong Kang; ***D:*** Chan-wook Park; ***W:*** Chan-wook Park; Hwang Jo-yun; Lim Jun-hyeong; ***C:*** Jeong-hun Jeong; ***M:*** Yeong-wook Jo; Shim Hyeon-jeong; Lee Ji-su; Choi Sung-hyeon.

Oldboy 🦴½ **2013 (R)** Remaking a classic can be a tricky business though director Lee has the stature to do it. The story's the same and the horror is horrifically bloody. Brolin assumes the title role of Joe Doucett, who is inexplicably held captive for 20 years then just as bewilderingly let go. This sets him on a quest to find who did it and why. But the real "why" question remains--why redo what was so masterfully done? Neither Brolin nor Lee, as talented as they are, can capture what Chan Wook Park did in 2003's original. **104m/C; DVD, Blu-Ray.** Josh Brolin; Elizabeth Olsen; Sharlto Copley; Samuel L. Jackson; Michael Imperioli; James Ransone; ***D:*** Spike Lee; ***W:*** Mark Protosevich; ***C:*** Sean Bobbitt; ***M:*** Roque Baños.

Older Than America 🦴🦴 **2008** First-timer Lightning can't quite keep all the plots going in her feature but the premise is compelling. Rain lives on a Minnesota reservation with her tribal cop fiance Johnny. She begins having strange visions relating to an abandoned Catholic boarding school for Native American children and fears she's going crazy like her mother, but the truth is much more sinister. **102m/C; DVD.** Adam Beach; Bradley Cooper; Tantoo Cardinal; Stephen Yoakam; Wes Studi; Chris Mulkey; Georgia Lightning; ***D:*** Georgia Lightning; ***W:*** Georgia Lightning; Christine K. Walker; ***C:*** Shane Kelly; ***M:*** George S. Clinton.

Oldest Confederate Widow Tells All 🦴🦴🦴 **1995** TV drama starts with the recollections of 99-year-old Lucy Marsden (Bancroft), the widow of the title, as she revisits her marriage to troubled Civil War veteran Capt. William Marsden (Sutherland, sporting an impressive set of whiskers). In 1899, the teenaged Lucy (played by Lane) marries the eccentric 50-year-old, who constantly relives battlefield horrors and the loss of his boyhood friend, while she deals with family and various domestic crises. Somewhat meandering story with fine performances and subtle details. Based on Allan Gurganus' novel. **180m/C; VHS, DVD.** Diane Lane; Donald Sutherland; Anne Bancroft; Cicely Tyson; Blythe Danner; E.G. Marshall; Gwen Verdon; Maureen Mueller; Wil Horneff; ***D:*** Ken Cameron; ***W:*** Joyce Eliason; ***M:*** Mark Snow. **TV**

Oleanna 🦴½ **1994** Mamet directs the big-screen version of his controversial play about political correctness, sexual harrassment, and the gender gap. Pompous, burned-out college professor (Macy) is accused of sexual harassment by dense, shrill, academically weak student (Eisenstadt) after she misconstrues a self-important speech as a come-on. Unbalanced perspective, obvious stereotyping of unsympathetic characters, and weak performances remove any hint of the intended drama. **90m/C; VHS, DVD.** William H. Macy; Debra Eisenstadt; ***D:*** David Mamet; ***W:*** David Mamet; ***C:*** Andrzej Sekula; ***M:*** Rebecca Pidgeon.

Olga's Girls 🦴🦴 *Mme. Olga's Massage Parlor; Olga's Massage Parlor; Olga's Parlor* **1964** Sadistic Olga deals in narcotics and white slavery in New York's Chinatown. Her drug addicted girls turn to each other for comfort but Olga suspects there's a snitch in her outfit. She'll stop at nothing to get the informant but the girls think it's about time for revenge. Campy sexploitation. **72m/B; VHS, DVD.** Audrey Campbell; Alice Linville; ***D:*** Joseph P. Mawra; ***M:*** Claude Otis.

Olive Kitteridge 🦴🦴🦴 **2014** Adaptation of Elizabeth Sprout's Pulitzer Prize-winning novel, which is a series of interconnected stories set over a number of years. The HBO miniseries concentrates on depressed, disdainful Olive Kitteridge, who is contemplating suicide when we first see her. She's an unlikeable small town Maine math teacher who ignores her longtime marriage and is estranged from her son, but an unexpected development brings her in contact with equally lonely and grumpy widower Jack. Performances make this one work. **230m/C; DVD, Blu-Ray.** Frances McDormand; Richard Jenkins; Bill Murray; John Gallagher, Jr.; Zoe Kazan; Cory Michael Smith; Peter Mullan; ***D:*** Lisa Cholodenko; ***W:*** Jane Anderson; ***C:*** Frederick Elmes; ***M:*** Carter Burwell. **CABLE**

Oliver! 🦴🦴🦴½ **1968 (G)** Splendid big-budget musical adaptation of Dickens' "Oliver Twist." An innocent orphan is dragged into a life of crime when he is befriended by a gang of pickpockets. **145m/C; VHS, DVD, Blu-Ray.** *GB* Mark Lester; Jack Wild; Ron Moody; Shani Wallis; Oliver Reed; Hugh Griffith; ***D:*** Carol Reed; ***W:*** Vernon Harris; ***C:*** Oswald Morris; ***M:*** Lionel Bart. Oscars '68: Adapt. Score, Art Dir./Set Dec., Director (Reed), Film, Sound; Golden Globes '69: Actor--Mus./Comedy (Moody), Film--Mus./Comedy.

Oliver & Company 🦴🦴½ **1988 (G)** Animated animal retelling of Dicken's "Oliver Twist"--Disney style. Kitten Oliver (Lawrence) is left to fend for himself on the mean streets of New York until he's taken under the paw of Dodger (Joel) the dog. Dodger heads up a gang of doggy thieves, who help down-and-out human Fagin (DeLuise), who owes money to ruthless loan shark Sykes (Loggia). Out on his first job, Oliver's found by rich little Jenny (Gregory) and happily adopted. But his pals think he's been kidnapped and are off to rescue him. **72m/C; DVD, Blu-Ray.** ***V:*** Joseph Lawrence; Billy Joel; Richard "Cheech" Marin; Bette Midler; Dom DeLuise; Roscoe Lee Browne; Richard Mulligan; Sheryl Lee Ralph; Robert Loggia; Taurean Blacque; Carl Weintraub; Natalie Gregory; William Glover; ***D:*** George Scribner; ***W:*** Jim Cox; James Mangold.

Oliver Twist 🦴🦴🦴 **1922** Silent version of the Dickens classic is a vehicle for young Jackie Coogan. As orphan Oliver Twist, he is subjected to many frightening incidents before finding love and someone to care for him. Remade numerous times, most notably in 1933 and 1948 and as the musical "Oliver!" in 1968. **77m/B; Silent; VHS, DVD.** Jackie Coogan; Lon Chaney, Sr.; Gladys Brockwell; George Siegmann; Esther Ralston; James A. Marcus; Aggie Herring; Nelson McDowell; Lewis Sargent; Joan Standing; Carl Stockdale; Edouard Trebaol; Lionel Belmore; ***D:*** Frank Lloyd; ***W:*** Frank Lloyd; Henry Weil; ***C:*** Glen MacWilliams; Robert Martin.

Oliver Twist 🦴🦴 **1933** The first talking version of Dickens's classic about an ill-treated London orphan involved with youthful gang of pickpockets. Moore was too young—at seven—to be very credible in the lead role. The 1948 version is much more believable. **70m/B; VHS, DVD.** Dickie Moore; Irving Pichel; William "Stage" Boyd; Barbara Kent; ***D:*** William J. Cowen.

Oliver Twist 🦴🦴🦴🦴 **1948** Charles Dickens' immortal story of a workhouse orphan who is forced into a life of crime with a gang of pickpockets. The best of many film adaptations, with excellent portrayals by the cast. **116m/C; VHS, DVD.** *GB* Robert Newton; John Howard Davies; Alec Guinness; Francis L. Sullivan; Anthony Newley; Kay Walsh; Diana Dors; Henry Stephenson; ***D:*** David Lean; ***W:*** David Lean; ***C:*** Guy Green; ***M:*** Arnold Bax.

Oliver Twist 🦴🦴🦴 **1982** Good version of the classic Dicken's tale of a boy's rescue from a life of crime. Scott's Fagin is a treat, and period details are on the mark. **100m/C; DVD.** George C. Scott; Tim Curry; Michael Hordern; Timothy West; Lysette Anthony; Eileen Atkins; Cherie Lunghi; ***D:*** Clive Donner; ***W:*** James Goldman; ***C:*** Norman G. Langley; ***M:*** Nick Bicat. **TV**

Oliver Twist 🦴🦴🦴 **1985** Miniseries adaptation of the Charles Dickens classic about an orphan boy plunging into the underworld of 19th-century London. **333m/C; VHS, DVD.** *GB* Ben Rodska; Eric Porter; Frank Middlemass; Gillian Martell; ***D:*** Gareth Davies; ***W:*** Alexander Baron; ***C:*** Dudley Simpson. **TV**

Oliver Twist 🦴🦴½ **1997** Lavish TV version of the Dickens tale finds orphaned Oliver (Trench) escaping to 1837's London and being befriended by the wicked Fagin (Dreyfuss) and his gang of pickpocketing youngsters, including the Artful Dodger (Wood). **92m/C; VHS, DVD.** Alex Trench; Richard Dreyfuss; Elijah Wood; David O'Hara; Antoine Byrne; Olivia Caffrey; ***D:*** Tony Bill; ***W:*** Monte Merrick; ***C:*** Keith Wilson; ***M:*** Van Dyke Parks. **TV**

Oliver Twist 🦴🦴🦴 **2000** The umpteenth version of the Dickens saga is a well-done British miniseries that includes the backstory of Oliver's parents, an inheritance, scheming relatives, and finally young Oliver (Smith) himself and his adventures with Fagin (Lindsay) and the criminal elements of London. **360m/C; VHS, DVD.** Sam Smith; Robert Lindsay; Andy Serkis; Emily Woof; Julie Walters; Michael Kitchen; Annette Crosbie; Alex Crowley; David Ross; Tim Dutton; Lindsay Duncan; Sophia Myles; Keira Knightley; ***D:*** Renny Rye; ***W:*** Alan Bleasdale; ***C:*** Walter McGill; ***M:*** Elvis Costello; Paul Pritchard. **TV**

Oliver Twist 🦴🦴🦴 **2005 (PG-13)** Hey, what would happen if Roman Polanski took on a classic Charles Dickens' tale? Already a dark enough story, Polanski adds what he always adds: depth and details. What's new, or perhaps simply fitting, is Polanski's take, using his own experiences in a Jewish ghetto to inform his interpretation of 19th century London slums. Lavish sets and costumes are set to a lush orchestral score, Ben Kingsley portrays the suitably frightening Fagin. **130m/C; DVD.** *GB CZ FR IT* Ben Kingsley; Jamie Foreman; Harry Eden; Leanne Rowe; Edward Hardwicke; Ian McNeice; Mark Strong; Jeremy Swift; Frances Cuka; Alun Armstrong; Peter Copley; Liz Smith; Barney Clark; Michael Heath; Gillian Hanna; Andy De La Tour; ***D:*** Roman Polanski; ***W:*** Ronald Harwood; ***C:*** Pawel Edelman; ***M:*** Rachel Portman.

Oliver Twist 🦴🦴½ **2007** This grittier version of the Dickens saga is a typically well-done presentation from the BBC with the roles of criminal Fagin (Spall), violent Bill Sikes (Hardy), and tragic Nancy (Okonedo) particularly well-cast. Born in a workhouse, plucky orphan Oliver (Miller) has many misadventures in London, falls into bad company, is rescued, and has his true past and family revealed. **176m/C; DVD.** *GB* Timothy Spall; Tom (Thomas) Hardy; Sophie Okonedo; Edward Fox; Morven Christie; Julian Rhind-Tutt; Sarah Lancashire; Gregor Fisher; Anna Massey; John Sessions; Michelle Gomez; Adam Arnold; ***D:*** Coky Giedroyc; ***W:*** Sarah Phelps; ***C:*** Matt Gray; ***M:*** Martin Phipps. **TV**

Oliver's Story 🦴 **1978 (PG)** A "not so equal" sequel to "Love Story," where widower O'Neal wallows in grief until rich heiress Bergen comes along. He falls in love again, this time with money. **90m/C; VHS, DVD.** Ryan O'Neal; Candice Bergen; Ray Milland; Edward Binns; Nicola Pagett; Charles Haid; ***D:*** John Korty; ***W:*** Erich Segal.

Olivia 🦴½ **1983** Abused housewife moonlights as a prostitute and begins killing her customers. She falls in love with an American businessman and flees to America when her husband finds out about the affair. Revenge and murder are the result. **90m/C; VHS, DVD, Blu-Ray.** Suzanna Love; Robert Walker, Jr.; Jeff Winchester; ***D:*** Ulli Lommel.

Olly Olly Oxen Free 🦴🦴 *The Great Balloon Adventure* **1978** Junkyard owner Hepburn helps two boys fix up and fly a hot-air balloon, once piloted by McKenzie's grandfather, as a surprise for the man's birthday. Beautiful airborne scenes over California and a dramatic landing to the tune of the "1812 Overture," but not enough to make the whole film interesting. **89m/C; VHS, DVD.** Katharine Hepburn; Kevin McKenzie; Dennis Dimster-Denk; Peter Kilman; ***D:*** Richard A. Colla; ***M:*** Robert Alcivar.

Olympus Has Fallen 🦴🦴½ **2013 (R)** Butler returns to action mode as former Secret Service Agent Mike Banning who rushes into the chaos when a group of Korean terrorists assaults Washington, D.C., kills hundreds, and takes the President (Eckhart) hostage in the White House. As the bad guys threaten to plunge the planet into World War III, Banning is the only one who can save humanity from nuclear annihilation. Some of the action is well-staged and intense, particularly when the Koreans gain control. But the dialogue is stale, and some of the security breaches seem unlikely especially in light of 9/11. **120m/C; DVD, Blu-Ray.** Gerard Butler; Aaron Eckhart; Morgan Freeman; Rick Yune; Angela Bassett; Melissa Leo; Dylan McDermott; Radha Mitchell; Cole Hauser; Finley Jacobsen; Ashley Judd; Robert Forster; ***D:*** Antoine Fuqua; ***W:*** Creighton Rothenberger; Katrin Benedikt; ***C:*** Conrad W. Hall; ***M:*** Trevor Morris.

Omar 🦴🦴🦴 **2013** Evocative look from writer-director Abu-Assad at doomed love and violence. Palestinian Omar routinely climbs over the Israeli security wall that separates his West Bank home to secretly visit his young girlfriend, Nadja, the sister of his militant friend, Tarek. Along with buddy, Amjad, the young men impulsively go through with their plan to murder a border guard. Omar is imprisoned, but wily Israeli intelligence agent Rami offers him a way out. Omar thinks he can play Rami, but his life becomes more difficult as suspicion and betrayal follow him. Arabic and Hebrew with subtitles. **96m/C; DVD, Blu-Ray.** *PA* Adam Bakri; Leem Lubany; Eyad Hourani; Samer Bisharat; Waleed F. Zuaiter; ***D:*** Hany Abu-Assad; ***W:*** Hany Abu-Assad; ***C:*** Ehab Assal.

Omar Khayyam 🦴🦴 **1957** In medieval Persia, Omar (Wilde) becomes involved in a romance with the Shah of Persia's fiancee, while trying to fight off a faction of assassins trying to overthrow the Shah. Although this film has a great cast, the script is silly and juvenile, defeating the cast's fine efforts. **101m/C; VHS, Streaming.** Cornel Wilde; Michael Rennie; Debra Paget; Raymond Massey; John Derek; Yma Sumac; Margaret (Maggie) Hayes; Joan Taylor; Sebastian Cabot; ***D:*** William Dieterle.

The Omega Code 🦴½ **1999 (PG-13)** This entry in the God vs. Devil steel cage apocalypse smackdown genre was financed by the Christian cable network TBN. In this corner, representing good, is motivational speaker Gillen Lane (Van Dien), who believes that hidden truths may be discovered by applying mathematical equations to sections of the Bible or by overacting. In that corner, representing evil, is Stone Alexander (York), AKA The Antichrist, who uses the hidden codes for nefarious purposes such as taking over the world government and overacting. In the stunning climax, stolen from "Raiders of the Lost Ark," evil is overthrown. The whole thing was a fix from the beginning. **99m/C; DVD.** Casper Van Dien; Michael York; Catherine Oxenberg; Michael Ironside; Jan Triska; William Hootkins; Robert Ito; Janet Carroll; Gregory Wagrowski; Devon Odessa; George Coe; Robert F. Lyons; ***D:*** Robert Marcarelli; ***W:*** Stephan Bliss; Hollis Barton; ***C:*** Carlos Gonzalez; ***M:*** Harry Manfredini.

Omega Cop 🦴 *John Travis, Solar Survivor* **1990 (R)** In a post-apocalyptic future, there's only one cop left. He uses his martial arts skills and tons of guns attempting to rescue three women, but the violence doesn't cover the poor acting and shoddy production. Fans of TV's Batman might enjoy this for West's presence. **89m/C; VHS, DVD.** Ron Marchini; Adam West; Stuart Whitman; Troy Donahue; Meg Thayer; Jennifer Jostyn; Chrysti Jimenez; D.W. Landingham; Chuck Katzakian; ***D:*** Paul Kyriazi.

Omega Doom 🦴🦴 **1996 (PG-13)** Four hundred years after an apocalyptic war the most organic thing around are the cyborgs, who exist along with androids and robots in a world where humans no longer matter. Omega Doom (Hauer) is an android developed as a fighter who has no function except to kill. In a ruined amusement park, the Roms and Droids, two rival cyborg groups, maintain an uneasy truce and when Doom wanders in they unite to destroy the intruder. But they don't know what they're up against. **84m/C; VHS, DVD.** Rutger Hauer; Anna (Katerina) Katarina; Norbert Weisser; Jahi JJ Zuri; Shannon Whirry; Earl White; Tina Cote; Jill Pierce; ***D:*** Albert Pyun; ***W:*** Ed Naha; ***C:*** George Mooradian; ***M:*** Tony Riparetti.

Omega Man 🦴🦴 ½ **1971 (PG)** In post-holocaust Los Angeles, Heston is immune to the effects of a biologically engineered plague and battles those who aren't—an army of albino victims bent on destroying what's left of the world. Strong suspense with considerable violence, despite the PG rating. Based on the science fiction thriller "I Am Legend" by Richard Matheson, which is also the basis for the film "The Last Man on Earth." **98m/C; VHS, DVD, Blu-Ray.** Charlton Heston; Anthony Zerbe; Rosalind Cash; Paul Koslo; Eric Laneuville; Lincoln Kilpatrick; Anna Aries; John Dierkes; Monika Henreid; ***D:*** Boris Sagal; ***W:*** John W. Corrington; Joyce H. Corrington; ***C:*** Russell Metty; ***M:*** Ron Grainer.

The Omen 🦴🦴 ½ *Birthmark* **1976 (R)** American diplomat's family adopts a young boy who always seems to be around when bizarre and inexplicable deaths occur. Of course, what else would you expect of Satan's son? The shock and gore prevalent in "The Exorcist" is replaced with more suspense and believable effects. Well-done horror film doesn't insult the viewer's intelligence. Followed by three sequels: "Damien: Omen 2," "The Final Conflict," and "Omen 4." **111m/C; VHS, DVD, Blu-Ray.** Gregory Peck; Lee Remick; Harvey Stephens; Billie Whitelaw; David Warner; Holly Palance; Robert Rietty; Patrick Troughton; Martin Benson; Leo McKern; Richard Donner; ***D:*** Richard Donner; ***W:*** David Seltzer; ***C:*** Gilbert Taylor; ***M:*** Jerry Goldsmith. Oscars '76: Orig. Score.

The Omen 🦴🦴 ½ **2006 (R)** Robert Thorn (Schreiber), American ambassador to England, adopts an orphaned newborn after his own son dies, without telling his fragile wife Katherine (Stiles). Damien (newcomer Davey-Fitzpatrick) grows into a spooky little boy looked after by overprotective nanny Mrs. Baylock (Farrow). Sinister happenings lead Thorn to believe he's raising the antichrist. The remake uses the same screenwriter—David Seltzer—as the 1976 original with some modest updates so nothing's very surprising. But it's still pretty scary (and bloody). **110m/C; DVD, Blu-Ray.** Liev Schreiber; Julia Stiles; Mia Farrow; David Thewlis; Pete Postlethwaite; Michael Gambon; Seamus Davey-Fitzpatrick; ***D:*** John Moore; ***W:*** David Seltzer; ***C:*** Jonathan Sela; ***M:*** Marco Beltrami.

Omen 4: The Awakening 🦴🦴 **1991** It turns out Damien of Omens past had a daughter, Delia, who takes up where dear old devilish Dad left off. Delia is adopted by your basic clueless couple and proceeds to wreak havoc wherever she goes, including getting rid of several interfering adults. She also plans to make her adoptive father, a U.S. senator, President, so that his delightful child anti-Christ can have him carry out all her evil plans. **97m/C; VHS, DVD, Blu-Ray.** Faye Grant; Michael Woods; Michael Lerner; Asia Vieira; ***D:*** Jorge Montesi; Dominique Othenin-Girard. **TV**

On a Clear Day 🦴🦴 ½ **2005 (PG-13)** Frank (Mullan) is a 55-year-old Glasgow shipbuilder who has been laid off after 35 years. At odds with himself and his family, Frank regularly meets his mates at the local swimming pool, where an offhand remark sets him on his new goal—to swim the English Channel. He begins training in secret, thus causing his anxious wife Joan (Blethyn) to suspect he's having an affair. Frank also grapples with some past sorrows that have caused a rift between himself and son Rob (Sives). Mullan portrays Frank as such a gruff bloke that the mawkishness is kept at bay. **99m/C; DVD.** *GB* Peter Mullan; Brenda Blethyn; Sean McGinley; Jamie Sives; Billy Boyd; Ron Cook; Jodhi May; Benedict Wong; Shaun Dingwall; Anne-Marie Timoney; Tony Roper; Paul Ritter; ***D:*** Gaby Dellal; ***W:*** Alex Rose; ***C:*** David Johnson; ***M:*** Stephen Warbeck.

On a Clear Day You Can See Forever 🦴🦴 **1970 (G)** A psychiatric hypnotist helps a girl stop smoking and finds that in trances she remembers previous incarnations. He falls in love with one of the women she used to be. Alan Jay Lerner of "My Fair Lady" and "Camelot" wrote the lyrics and the book. Based on a musical by Lerner and Burton Lane. **129m/C; DVD, Blu-Ray.** Barbra Streisand; Yves Montand; Bob Newhart; Jack Nicholson; Simon Oakland; ***D:*** Vincente Minnelli; ***W:*** Alan Jay Lerner; ***C:*** Harry Stradling, Sr.

On Again-Off Again 🦴 ½ **1937** Late-career comedy finds Wheeler and Woolsey as feuding co-owners of a pill company who decide to settle their issues via a wrestling match. The winner operates the company without interference for a year while the loser becomes his valet. Remake of 1918's "A Pair of Sixes" and 1930's "Queen High." **68m/B; DVD.** Bert Wheeler; Robert Woolsey; Marjorie Lord; Patricia Wilder; Esther Muir; ***D:*** Edward F. (Eddie) Cline; ***W:*** Nat Perrin; Benny Rubin; ***C:*** Jack MacKenzie.

On an Island with You 🦴🦴 ½ **1948** Williams plays a movie star who finds romance on location in Hawaii in this musical extravaganza. Contains many of Williams' famous water ballet scenes and a bevy of bathing beauties. **107m/C; VHS, DVD.** Esther Williams; Peter Lawford; Ricardo Montalban; Jimmy Durante; Cyd Charisse; Leon Ames; ***D:*** Richard Thorpe.

On Any Sunday: The Next Chapter 🦴🦴 ½ **2014 (PG)** Taking its cue from the 1971 documentary "On Any Sunday," this film examines the breadth of motorcycle racing in 2014 and is created by the son of the documentarian behind the first film. This documentary looks at motorcycle racing and culture worldwide, such as motocross, Grand Prix, and many types of racers. The film also includes glimpses at custom bike shops, daredevils, and humanitarians using motorcycles to save lives. **90m/C; DVD, Blu-Ray, Streaming, Download.** ***D:*** Dana Brown; ***W:*** Dana Brown; Scott Rousseau; ***C:*** Alex Fostvedt; Brad McGregor; Nicholas Schrunk.

On Approval 🦴🦴🦴 **1944** Hilarious British farce in which two women trade boyfriends. Lillie's performace provides plenty of laughs. Brook runs the show as leading man, co-author, director, and co-producer. Based on the play by Frederick Lonsdale. **80m/B; VHS, DVD, Blu-Ray.** *GB* Clive Brook; Beatrice Lillie; Googie Withers; Roland Culver; O.B. Clarence; Lawrence Hanray; Elliot Mason; Hay Petrie; Marjorie Munks; Molly Munks; ***D:*** Clive Brook; ***W:*** Clive Brook; Terence Young; ***C:*** Claude Friese-Greene; ***M:*** William Alwyn.

On Body and Soul 🦴🦴🦴 *Teströl és Lélekröl* **2017** A dreamy, magical out-of-ordinary romantic drama. In a drab slaughterhouse located in a big city in Hungary, the facility's director, the introverted Endre (Morcsanyi), notices the government quality inspector, the timid Maria (Borbely). Though the two are attracted to each other, nothing comes of their interaction until an investigation after a theft at a slaughterhouse reveals that the pair have been having the exact same dream each night about a stag and a doe in a snowy forest. This revelation jumpstarts their unexpected, complicated pairing. The imaginative story gains depth with the dazzlingly performances of the lead actors. Hungarian with subtitles. **116m/C; DVD.** *HU* Alexandra Borbély; Géza Morcsányi; Réka Tenki; Zoltán Schneider; Ervin Nagy; ***D:*** Ildiko Enyedi; ***W:*** Ildiko Enyedi; ***C:*** Máté Herbai; ***M:*** Adam Balazs. **VIDEO**

On Borrowed Time 🦴🦴🦴 **1939** Engrossing tale of Death (Hardwicke) coming for an old man (Barrymore) who isn't ready to die so he traps him in his backyard apple tree. Performances are first rate in this good adaptation of the stage success (originally by Eugene O'Neill). Hardwicke is especially a standout; he gave up theatre for Hollywood after making this film. **99m/B; VHS, DVD.** Lionel Barrymore; Cedric Hardwicke; Beulah Bondi; Una Merkel; Bobs Watson; Henry Travers; ***D:*** Harold Bucquet; ***C:*** Joseph Ruttenberg.

On Chesil Beach 🦴🦴 **2017 (R)** A faithful, if lacking, adaptation of the 2007 Ian McEwan novella of the same name. In 1962 England, newlyweds Florence (Ronan) and Edward (Howle) spend their honeymoon at a hotel on the Dorset coast. Though the couple come from different backgrounds, they seem to enjoy each other's company. Both are sexually ignorant, and when it comes time to consummate their marriage, it is a disaster for both of them. Their lack of understanding of both sex and how to communicate about it creates further problems. **110m/C; DVD, Blu-Ray, Streaming.** *UK* Saoirse Ronan; Emily Watson; Anne-Marie Duff; Samuel West; Billy Howle; ***D:*** Dominic Cooke; ***W:*** Ian McEwan; ***C:*** Sean Bobbitt; ***M:*** Dan Jones.

On Dangerous Ground 🦴🦴🦴 **1951** A world-weary detective is sent to the countryside to investigate a murder. He encounters the victim's revenge-hungry father and the blind sister of the murderer. In the hateful father the detective sees a reflection of the person he has become, in the blind woman, he learns the redeeming qualities of humanity and compassion. A well-acted example of film noir that features the composer Herrman's favorite score. **82m/B; VHS, DVD.** Robert Ryan; Ida Lupino; Ward Bond; Ed Begley, Sr.; Cleo Moore; Charles Kemper; ***D:*** Nicholas Ray; ***M:*** Bernard Herrmann.

On Deadly Ground WOOF! **1994 (R)** Seagal nearly destroys Alaska in an effort to save it in this inane, preachy story of an oil-rig roughneck out to protect the landscape from an evil oil company's drilling habits. Directorial debut for Seagal lumbers from scene to scene. Violence is expected, as is silly dialogue—just try to keep from laughing when stoneyfaced Steven intones "What does it take to change the essence of man?" A better script, for one. **102m/C; VHS, DVD.** Steven Seagal; Michael Caine; Joan Chen; John C. McGinley; Billy Bob Thornton; R. Lee Ermey; ***D:*** Steven Seagal; ***W:*** Ed Horowitz; ***C:*** Ric Waite; ***M:*** Basil Poledouris. Golden Raspberries '94: Worst Director (Seagal).

On Each Side 🦴🦴 *A Cada Lado* **2007** An exploration of past and future through interconnected stories of characters affected by the building of the Rosario-Victoria Bridge across the Parana River in Argentina. Photographer Abel, hired to document the bridge's construction, meets a pair of thieves; two young boys grow into teenagers as the bridge building continues; an old man is constantly irritated by construction noise; and two elderly sisters take in a boarder—a German engineer secretly meeting a transvestite singer across the river. German and Spanish with subtitles. **95m/C; DVD.** *AR* Miguel Franchi; Miguel Bosco; Milagros Alacron; Julian Knab; Juan Pablo Garetto; Monica Alfonso; Monica Galan; Hector Bidonde; ***D:*** Hugo Grosso; ***W:*** Hugo Grosso; ***C:*** Sergio Garcia; ***M:*** Carlos Casazza.

On Edge 🦴🦴 **2003 (R)** Figure skaters Wendy (Winokur), Veda (Swatek), and J.C. (Langer) are three Olympic hopefuls vying for the Southern California regional figure skating championship amidst the usual jealousies and craziness. Alexander is the Zamboni driver who observes it all and a number of professional skaters play skating judges. **93m/C; VHS, DVD.** A.J. (Allison Joy) Langer; Jason Alexander; Barret Swatek; Marissa Jaret Winokur; John Glover; Kathy Griffin; Chris Hogan; Wallace (Wally) Langham; Sabrina Lloyd; Wendie Malick; ***D:*** Karl Slovin; ***W:*** Karl Slovin; Laura Wolf; ***C:*** Chris Squires; ***M:*** Jim Latham. **VIDEO**

On Golden Pond 🦴🦴🦴 ½ **1981 (PG)** Henry Fonda won his first—and long overdue—Oscar for his role as the curmudgeonly patriarch of the Thayer family. He and his wife have grudgingly agreed to look after a young boy while at their summer home in Maine. Through his gradually affectionate relationship with the boy, Fonda learns to allay his fears of mortality. He also gains an understanding of his semi-estranged daughter. Jane Fonda plays his daughter and Hepburn is his loving wife in this often funny adaptation of Ernest Thompson's 1978 play. Predictable but deeply moving. Henry Fonda's final screen appearance. **109m/C; VHS, DVD, Blu-Ray.** Henry Fonda; Jane Fonda; Katharine Hepburn; Dabney Coleman; Doug McKeon; William Lanteau; ***D:*** Mark Rydell; ***W:*** Ernest Thompson; ***C:*** Billy Williams; ***M:*** Dave Grusin. Oscars '81: Actor (Fonda), Actress (Hepburn), Adapt. Screenplay; British Acad. '82: Actress (Hepburn); Golden Globes '82: Actor--Drama (Fonda), Film--Drama, Screenplay; Natl. Bd. of Review '81: Actor (Fonda); Writers Guild '81: Adapt. Screenplay.

On Guard! 🦴🦴🦴 ½ *Le Bossu; En Garde* **2003** Thrilling story of revenge and swordplay set in 18th-century France. Lagardere (Auteuil) attempts to kill the Duke of Nevers (Perez) for money and ends up being taken in and trained by him. Nevers' cousin, the evil Gonzague (Luchini), murders him to grab the family fortune and Lagarderegoes into hiding to raise Nevers' daughter Aurore. Years later, Lagardere and grown Aurore (Gillain) are in the court of Gonzague, where they put their plot for vengeance into effect. Fantastic swordfighting scenes, complex intrigue, and excellent acting make this a world-class swashbuckler. Based on the frequently adapted 1857 French serial "Le Bossu" by Paul Feval. French with subtitles. **128m/C; VHS, DVD, Blu-Ray.** *FR IT GE* Daniel Auteuil; Fabrice Luchini; Vincent Perez; Marie Gillain; Jean-Francois Stevenin; Didier Pain; Claire Nebout; Philippe Noiret; Yann Collette; ***D:*** Philippe de Broca; ***W:*** Philippe de Broca; Jean Cosmos; Jerome Tonnerre; ***C:*** Jean-Francois Robin; ***M:*** Philippe Sarde.

On Her Majesty's Secret Service 🦴🦴🦴 **1969 (PG)** In the sixth 007 adventure, Bond again confronts the infamous Blofeld, who is planning a germ-warfare assault on the entire world. Australian Lazenby took a crack at playing the super spy, with mixed results. Many feel this is the best-written of the Bond films and might have been the most famous, had Sean Connery continued with the series. Includes the song "We Have All the Time In the World," sung by Louis Armstrong. **144m/C; VHS, DVD, Blu-Ray.** *GB* George Lazenby; Diana Rigg; Telly Savalas; Gabriele Ferzetti; Ilse Steppat; Bernard Lee; Lois Maxwell; Desmond Llewelyn; Catherine Schell; Julie Ege; Joanna Lumley; Mona Chong; Anouska (Anoushka) Hempel; Jenny Hanley; ***D:*** Peter Hunt; ***W:*** Richard Maibaum; ***M:*** John Barry.

On Moonlight Bay 🦴🦴 ½ **1951** Set in small-town Indiana in 1917 with Day as the tomboyish Marjorie who falls for college man MacRae. Her father (Ames) doesn't approve but the trouble really begins when Marjorie's younger brother gets into trouble at school. The incorrigible Wesley (Gray) blames everything on dear old dad and MacRae feels he must come to Marjorie's rescue! Gray steals the movie as the bratty brother—otherwise its business as usual. Based on Booth Tarkington's "Penrod" stories and followed by "By the Light of the Silvery Moon." **95m/C; DVD.** Doris Day; Gordon MacRae; Leon Ames; Billy Gray; Rosemary DeCamp; Mary Wickes; Ellen Corby; Esther Dale; ***D:*** Roy Del Ruth; ***W:*** Melville Shavelson; Jack Rose; ***M:*** Max Steiner.

On My Way 🦴🦴 *Elle S'en Va* **2014** Aging beauty queen Bettie (Deneuve) is thrown into a late-life crisis by a lover's betrayal and her restaurant's demise. When her estranged daughter asks Bettie to take her barely-known grandson to his paternal grandfather, it results in a road trip and even a reunion of her former pageant colleagues. Unfortunately the whole film feels like the scenes rarely connect to one another. Deneuve makes everything she does more interesting, but the film's tendency to waffle between improvised comedy and stark melodrama lets down the living legend. French with subtitles. **116m/C; DVD, Blu-Ray.** *FR* Catherine Deneuve; Nemo Schiffman; Gerard Garousle; Camille; *D:* Emmanuelle Bercot; *W:* Emmanuelle Bercot; Jerome Tonnerre; *C:* Guillaume Schiffman.

On Our Merry Way ♂♂ 1/2 *A Miracle Can Happen* **1948** Episodic comedy with Meredith starring as Oliver Pease, a would-be newspaper reporter (he actually works on the classifieds), asking the question "How has a child changed your life?" Among those queried are a couple of jazz musicians (Fonda, Stewart), Hollywood bit players (Lamour, Moore), and con men (Demerest, MacMurray). Goddard, who was married to Meredith at the time, plays his wife in the film. **107m/B; VHS, DVD.** Burgess Meredith; Paulette Goddard; Dorothy Lamour; Victor Moore; James Stewart; Henry Fonda; Fred MacMurray; William Demarest; Hugh Herbert; Eilene Janssen; Dorothy Ford; David Whorf; *D:* King Vidor; Leslie Fenton; *W:* Laurence Stallings; Lou Breslow; *C:* John Seitz; Ernest Laszlo; Gordon Avil; Joseph Biroc; Edward Cronjager; *M:* Heinz Roemheld.

On Strike for Christmas ♂♂ 1/2 **2010** Amusing holiday fare from Lifetime. Joy Robertson has always strived to do the best for her husband Stephen and their two sons, especially at Christmas. All her efforts are taken for granted and the unappreciated Joy decides to go out on strike. Her efforts inspire a holiday work stoppage by other moms throughout her town and chaos follows. Based on the 2007 book by Sheila Roberts. **86m/C; DVD.** Daphne Zuniga; David Sutcliffe; Victor Zinck, Jr.; Evan Williams; Chelah Horsdal; Julia Duffy; Ingrid Rogers; *D:* Robert Iscove; *W:* Jim Head; *C:* C. Kim Miles; *M:* Gary Koftinoff. **CABLE**

On the Avenue ♂♂♂ **1937** Broadway showman Powell opens up a new musical, starring Faye as the richest girl in the world, in this musical-comedy satirizing upper-crust society. Debutante Carroll is outraged because she realizes it's mocking her actual life. Carroll tries to get Powell to change the show, they fall in love, Faye gets her nose out of joint, and after lots of fuss everything ends happily. Fine Berlin score. **90m/B; DVD.** Dick Powell; Madeleine Carroll; Alice Faye; George Barbier; Al Ritz; Harry Ritz; Jimmy Ritz; Alan Mowbray; Cora Witherspoon; Walter Catlett; Stepin Fetchit; Sig Rumann; Douglas Fowley; Joan Davis; *D:* Roy Del Ruth; *W:* Gene Markey; *M:* Irving Berlin.

On the Basis of Sex ♂♂ 1/2 **2018 (PG-13)** An inspirational biopic of Ruth Bader Ginsburg as a young lawyer who strives to overturn federal laws allowing gender-based discrimination. It's a story that deserves to be told, especially to younger generations who take equal rights for granted, even if this film is a bit too formulaic to be groundbreaking or rousing. The motion picture premiered in the same year as Ginsburg's 25th anniversary as a Supreme Court Justice. **120m/C; DVD, Blu-Ray.** Felicity Jones; Armie Hammer; Justin Theroux; Kathy Bates; Sam Waterston; *D:* Mimi Leder; *W:* Daniel Stiepleman; *C:* Michael Grady; *M:* Mychael Danna.

On the Beach ♂♂♂ 1/2 **1959** A group of survivors attempt to live normal lives in post-apocalyptic Australia, waiting for the inevitable arrival of killer radiation. Astaire is strong in his first dramatic role. Though scientifically implausible, still a good anti-war vehicle. Based on the best-selling novel by Nevil Shute. **135m/B; VHS, DVD, Blu-Ray.** Gregory Peck; Anthony Perkins; Donna Anderson; Ava Gardner; Fred Astaire; *D:* Stanley Kramer; *W:* John Paxton; *C:* Daniel F. Fapp; *M:* Ernest Gold. Golden Globes '60: Score.

On the Beach ♂♂ 1/2 **2000** Remake of the 1959 anti-nuke film (based on the 1957 novel by Nevil Shute) is well-acted but so low-key that it never generates real tension. In 2006, the bomb has been dropped and Australia is the current refuge and the destination of sub commander Dwight Towers (Assante). A radio transmission from Alaska offers some hope but Towers needs the help of Melbourne scientist Julian Osborne (Brown), who happens to be the ex- of Towers' sultry love, Moira (Ward). **180m/C; VHS, DVD.** Armand Assante; Rachel Ward; Bryan Brown; Jacqueline McKenzie; Grant Bowler; *D:* Russell Mulcahy; *W:* David Williamson; Bill Kerby; *C:* Martin McGrath; *M:* Anna Borghesi. **CABLE**

On the Border ♂♂ 1/2 **1998 (R)** Familiar neo-noir revolves around a bank heist. Ex-bank robber Jake (Van Dien) is now a security guard. Kristin (Roos) entices him into a plot involving Brown, Baldwin, and Mitchum. The humor is intentional, and the Texas locations are well utilized. Overall, this is an overachieving video premiere. **103m/C; DVD.** Casper Van Dien; Bryan Brown; Bentley Mitchum; Camilla Overbye Roos; Rochelle Swanson; Daniel Baldwin; *D:* Bob Misiorowski; *W:* Josh Olson; *C:* Lawrence Sher; *M:* Serge Colbert. **VIDEO**

On the Borderline ♂♂ 1/2 **2001 (R)** On their way to California with their new baby, Luke (Mabius) and Nicole (Shelton) find themselves short of funds in a border town. She takes work as a waitress while he becomes involved with transporting Mexican aliens. Curious little road thriller actually works pretty well. The leads and a solid supporting cast handle the material well. Some scenes are curiously tinted to disguise the less-than-lavish production values. **93m/C; DVD.** Eric Mabius; Marley Shelton; Elizabeth Pena; R. Lee Ermey; *D:* Michael Oblowitz; *W:* Kevin R. Frech; *C:* Michael Barrow; *M:* Michael Wandmacher.

On the Doll ♂ 1/2 **2007** Jimmy (Ben-Victor) has a small-time sleaze business in L.A., including a strip club and a peep-show arcade. Tara (Sarafyan) owes Jimmy a lot of dough so she works the peep while boyfriend Jaron (Janowicz) tries to figure out a way to pay off her debt. To make some quick cash, he helps out hooker Balery (Snow) with an abusive client. Meanwhile, high schoolers Courtney (Domont) and Melody (Accola) get lured into Internet "modeling" for Jimmy, and streetwalker Chantal (Collins) works to provide for her unsuccessful musician boyfriend Wes (Crawford). **102m/C; DVD.** Brittany Snow; Josh Janowicz; Paul Ben-Victor; Marcus Giamatti; Edward Jemison; Clayne Crawford; Shanna Collins; Angela Sarafyan; Chloe Domont; Candice Accola; *D:* Thomas Mignone; *W:* Thomas Mignone; *C:* Nicole Hirsch; *M:* Paul D'Amour. **VIDEO**

On the Double ♂♂ 1/2 **1961** Suitably ridiculous WWII-set comedy from Kaye. GI Ernie Williams is caught impersonating an important English general and is then recruited to be his double to confuse the Nazis. Ernie must keep up the charade despite death, capture, an escape (using a number of disguises), and a return to England to expose a spy ring. **92m/C; DVD, Blu-Ray.** Danny Kaye; Dana Wynter; Wilfrid Hyde-White; Margaret Rutherford; Diana Dors; Rex Evans; Jesse White; Allan Cuthbertson; *D:* Melville Shavelson; *W:* Melville Shavelson; Jack Rose; *C:* Geoffrey Unsworth; Harry Stradling, Sr.; *M:* Leith Stevens.

On the Edge ♂♂ 1/2 **1986 (PG-13)** A drama about the inevitable Rocky-esque triumph of Dern as an aging marathon runner. Simultaneous to his running endeavor, Dern is trying to make up for lost time with his father. Available in two versions, one rated, the other unrated with a racy appearance by Pam Grier as the runner's interracial lover. **86m/C; VHS, DVD.** Bruce Dern; John Marley; Bill Bailey; Jim Haynie; Pam Grier; *D:* Rob Nilsson; *W:* Rob Nilsson.

On the Edge ♂♂ 1/2 **2000 (R)** Troubled 19-year-old Jonathan Breech (Murphy) deals with his depression over his father's death by stealing a car and driving it over a cliff. Surviving with very minor injuries, Jonathan is faced with prison or spending time in a mental institution. He chooses the latter, where he meets his caring therapist, Dr. Figure (Rea), and some fellow patients to bond with—Rachel (Vessey) and Toby (Jackson). Much teen angst is explored before the resolution and the material may not be fresh but it is heartfelt. **86m/C; VHS, DVD.** *IR* Cillian Murphy; Tricia Vessey; Jonathan Jackson; Stephen Rea; *D:* John Carney; *W:* Daniel James; John Carney; *C:* Eric Alan Edwards.

On the Edge ♂ 1/2 **2002 (R)** Community do-gooder Dakota Smith (Williamson) comes to the aid of basketball phenom Willie Jo Harris (Franklin) when he crosses drug dealer Slim Jim (Ice-T). Slim's goons mistakenly hit the family of Rex Stevens (Casey) so he teams up with Smith and Willie Jo's dad Frank (O'Neal) to start cleaning up the 'hood by first getting rid of hitman Felix (Busey). Fellow blaxploitation star Brown also makes an appearance. **90m/C; DVD.** Fred Williamson; Bernie Casey; Ron O'Neal; Gary Busey; Ice-T; Jim Brown; Derrick Franklin; *D:* Fred Williamson; *W:* Linda Williamson; *C:* John Dirlam. **VIDEO**

On the Inside ♂ **2011 (R)** In this unbelievable drama, revenge leads to murder and Allen (Stahl) ends up in a psychiatric hospital after a breakdown. He becomes part of a new program where patients are allowed to mingle and he meets schizophrenic Mia (Wilde). Another patient, psycho Carl (Mihok), is also planning a breakout. **90m/C; DVD, Blu-Ray.** Nick Stahl; Olivia Wilde; Dash Mihok; Pruitt Taylor Vince; Shohreh Aghdashloo; *D:* D.W. Brown; *W:* D.W. Brown; *C:* David A. Armstrong. **VIDEO**

On the Line ♂ 1/2 **1984** Laredo border patrolman Chuck (Delger) marries Mexican prostitute Engracia (Abril) and smuggles her into the U.S. where she gets turned in by Chuck's jealous boss (and Engracia's former client) Mitch (Wilson). Chuck follows his bride back to Mexico to work for his 'coyote' uncle Bryant (Carradine) and gets into more trouble, so his family seeks revenge. Unfortunately, Delger is an uncharismatic acting black hole; fortunately, the other leads are not. **95m/C; DVD.** David Carradine; Victoria Abril; Scott Wilson; Paul Richardson; Jesse Vint; Mitch Pileggi; Jeff Delger; *D:* Jose Luis Borau; *W:* Jose Luis Borau; *C:* Teodoro Escamilla; *M:* Armando Manzanero; George Michalski.

On the Line ♂ 1/2 **2001 (PG)** In this insipid romance, Kevin (Bass) meets Abbey (Chriqui), the girl of his dreams, on a Chicago train. How does he know she's the one for him? Well, they can both name all the presidents in order and they both like the Cubs. Gee! Ain't that sweet? But Kevin's too shy to ask for her number and he lets her slip away. He laments to his friends Rod (Fatone), Eric (GQ) and Randy (Bulliard) and they help him out by posting flyers all over town. A local reporter (Montgomery) picks up the story and a gaggle of girls claiming to be "The L Girl" respond. Tweens may tolerate the contrivances. **90m/C; DVD.** Lance Bass; Joey Fatone; Emmanuelle Chriqui; GQ; Al Green; Tamala Jones; Dave Foley; Dan Montgomery, Jr.; Jerry Stiller; *D:* Eric Bross; *W:* Paul Stanton; Eric Aronson; *C:* Michael Bernard; *M:* Stewart Copeland.

On the Other Hand, Death ♂♂ 1/2 **2008 (R)** Albany PI Donald Strachey (Allen) returns in this third mystery based on the Richard Stevenson series. Donald's husband Tim (Spence) is asked for help by ex-boyfriend Andrew (Runyan) when lesbian couple Dorothy (Kidder) and Edith (Rose) are apparently the targets of a hate crime. Strachey soon decides it's business rather than sexuality that's the issue since the women are the only ones who won't sell out to a rapacious developer, but it may not be that simple either. **85m/C; DVD.** Chad Allen; Sebastian Spence; Margot Kidder; Gabrielle Rose; Nelson Wong; Daryl Shuttleworth; Damon Runyan; *D:* Ron Oliver; *W:* Ron McGee; Gillian Horvath; *C:* C. Kim Miles; *M:* Peter Allen. **CABLE**

On the Outs ♂♂ **2005 (R)** Three teen girls find the mean streets more than they can handle. Suzette (Mariano) is pregnant by a crack dealer who leaves her literally holding the gun that killed a rival. Crack addict Marisol (Mendoza) is a single mom who loses her daughter to child welfare and learns that even if she stays clean it could take years to regain parental custody. Oz (Marte) is herself a crack dealer, trying to raise her mentally retarded younger brother. Based on case studies of young women who were held in a Jersey City juvenile detention center. **86m/C; DVD.** Judy Marte; Anny Mariano; Paola Mendoza; Dominic Colon; *D:* Lori Silverbush; Michael Skolnik; *W:* Lori Silverbush; *C:* Mariana Sanchez du Antunano; *M:* Richard Leigh; Brian Satz.

On the Road ♂♂ **2012 (R)** Walter Salles' adaptation of the beloved Jack Kerouac book mostly serves as proof that there were good reasons it took this long for a '60s classic to become a film. The young-man-lost aspect of Beat Generation writers is a tough, nearly impossible thing to translate to a medium that requires more dramatic urgency and so watching Sal Paradise (Riley), Dean Moriarty (Hedlund), and Marylou (Stewart) traverse the country trying to find themselves isn't as lyrical as it is printed form. The cast isn't bad and the technical elements are top-notch but the film is simply boring. **124m/C; DVD, Blu-Ray.** *US FR* Sam Riley; Garrett Hedlund; Kristen Stewart; Amy Adams; Tom Sturridge; Alice Braga; Elisabeth Moss; Danny Morgan; Kirsten Dunst; Viggo Mortensen; *D:* Walter Salles; *W:* Jose Rivera; *C:* Eric Gautier; *M:* Gustavo Santaolalla.

On the Run ♂ *Country Blue; One for the Money, Two for the Show* **1973 (R)** An ex-con and his gal cut a law-defying swath through the Bayou. **110m/C; VHS, DVD.** Jack Conrad; Rita George; Dub Taylor; David Huddleston; *D:* Jack Conrad; *W:* Jack Conrad; *C:* Emmett Alston.

On the Town ♂♂♂ 1/2 **1949** Kelly's directorial debut features three sailors on a one day leave search for romance in the Big Apple. Filmed on location in NYC, with uncompromisingly authentic flavor. Based on the successful Broadway musical. **98m/C; DVD, Blu-Ray.** Gene Kelly; Frank Sinatra; Vera-Ellen; Ann Miller; Betty Garrett; Jules Munshin; *D:* Gene Kelly; Stanley Donen; *W:* Betty Comden; Adolph Green; *M:* Leonard Bernstein. Oscars '49: Scoring/Musical; Natl. Film Reg. '18.

On the Waterfront ♂♂♂♂ **1954** A trend-setting, gritty portrait of New York dock workers embroiled in union violence. Cobb is the gangster union boss, Steiger his crooked lawyer, and Brando, Steiger's ex-fighter brother who "could've been a contender!" Intense performances and excellent direction stand up well today. The picture was a huge financial success. **108m/B; VHS, DVD, Blu-Ray.** Marlon Brando; Rod Steiger; Eva Marie Saint; Lee J. Cobb; Karl Malden; Pat Henning; Leif Erickson; Tony Galento; John Hamilton; Nehemiah Persoff; *D:* Elia Kazan; *W:* Budd Schulberg; *C:* Boris Kaufman; *M:* Leonard Bernstein. Oscars '54: Actor (Brando), Art Dir./Set Dec., B&W, B&W Cinematog., Director (Kazan), Film, Film Editing, Story & Screenplay, Support. Actress (Saint); AFI '98: Top 100; British Acad. '54: Actor (Brando); Directors Guild '54: Director (Kazan); Golden Globes '55: Actor--Drama (Brando), Director (Kazan), Film--Drama; Natl. Film Reg. '89; N.Y. Film Critics '54: Actor (Brando), Director (Kazan), Film.

On the Yard ♂♂ **1979 (R)** An attempt to realistically portray prison life. Focuses on a murderer who runs afoul of the leader of the prisoners and the system. A fairly typical prison drama with above average performances from Heard and Kellin. **102m/C; VHS, Streaming.** John Heard; Thomas G. Waites; Mike Kellin; Joe Grifasi; Dominic Chianese; *D:* Raphael D. Silver; *W:* Malcolm Braly.

On Thin Ice ♂♂ **2003** Based on a true crime story. When widowed mom Patsy McCartle (Keaton) loses her minimum wage waitress job, she struggles to support her two sons. A chance meeting with criminal Roger Hopkins (Rooker) leads Patsy to becoming one of his drug dealers but she gets hooked on crystal meth and only her sons can finally convince her to get clean. **90m/C; DVD.** Diane Keaton; Michael Seater; Colin Roberts; Michael Rooker; Lothaire Bluteau; *D:* David Attwood; *W:* Wesley Bishop; *C:* Jeffrey Jur; *M:* John Altman. **CABLE**

On Tour ♂♂ *Tournee* **2010** Amalric does triple duty as writer/director/star. Reckless would-be impresario Joachim decides to hit the French hinterlands with his group of American neo-Burlesque performers (prior to taking the show to Paris) but their tour results in a series of comic disasters. Oddly interesting, paints a rather unattractive picture of the rowdy life of Burlesque itself, but celebrates those who live it. Includes real-life performers of the craft. English and French with subtities. **111m/C; DVD.** *FR GE* Mathieu Amalric; Suzanne Ramsey; Miranda Colclasure; Linda Marraccini; Pierre Grimblat; Angela de Lorenzo; Alexander Craven; Damien Odoul; Julie Ann Muz; ***D:*** Mathieu Amalric; ***W:*** Mathieu Amalric; Philippe di Folco; Marcelo Novais Teles; Raphaelle Valbrune; ***C:*** Christophe Beaucarne.

On Valentine's Day 🦴🦴 ½ *Story of a Marriage* **1986 (PG)** Author Horton Foote based this story loosely on his parents' lives. A wealthy young Southern girl marries a poor but decent young man and finds herself ostracized from her family. A prequel to the same author's "1918." Produced with PBS for "American Playhouse." **106m/C; VHS, DVD.** Hallie Foote; Matthew Broderick; Michael Higgins; Steven Hill; William Converse-Roberts; Rochelle Oliver; Richard Jenkins; Horton Foote, Jr.; Carol Goodheart; ***D:*** Ken Harrison; ***W:*** Horton Foote; ***M:*** Jonathan Sheffer.

On with the Show 🦴🦴 ½ **1929** A frantic backstage—and onstage—musical that cuts between the behind the scenes efforts to manage the make-or-break production that is in rehearsals during an out-of-town tryout. Has a classic showbiz cliche of the diva leading lady refusing to perform so the chorus girl goes on instead. Ethel Waters debuts what would become her signature tune 'Am I Blue?' Filmed in two-strip Technicolor but those prints have been lost. **104m/B; DVD.** Betty Compson; Louise Fazenda; Sally O'Neil; Joe E. Brown; Arthur Lake; William "Billy" Bakewell; Purnell Pratt; Wheeler Oakman; Lee Moran; Sam Hardy; ***D:*** Alan Crosland; ***W:*** Robert Lord; ***C:*** Tony Gaudio.

On_Line 🦴🦴 **2001 (R)** Neurotic John Roth (Hamilton) and his partner Moe Curley (Perrineau) run an online sex site called InterconX. John is obsessive about documenting his life via a daily Webcam and becomes mesmerized by watching the beautiful Jordan (Ferlito), who does her own erotic fantasy thing on the website. He tries a real-live date with her but finds reality too much to handle. Other characters wander into the online world and Weintrob shows them (usually in split screen) interacting in various ways via computer and in person, but the characters aren't particularly appealing and it all seems dated. **87m/C; DVD.** Josh Hamilton; Harold Perrineau, Jr.; Isabel Gillies; Vanessa Ferlito; John Fleck; Eric Millegan; Liz Owens; ***D:*** Jed Weintrob; ***W:*** Andrew Osborne; Jed Weintrob; ***C:*** Toshiaki Ozawa; ***M:*** Roger Neill.

Onassis 🦴 ½ *The Richest Man in the World: The Story of Aristotle Onassis* **1988** Romanticized biography of Greek shipping magnate Aristotle Onassis, from the poverty of his youth to his later wealth and family and romantic liaisons and tragedies. Julia is adequate as the title character but English actress Annis is badly miscast as Jackie Kennedy Onassis. However, Seymour is terrific as Onassis's lover, opera star Maria Callas. Quinn, who played Onassis in "The Greek Tycoon," plays Onassis's father in this one. Miniseries based on the novel by Peter Evans. **120m/C; VHS, DVD.** Raul Julia; Jane Seymour; Francesca Annis; Anthony Quinn; Anthony Zerbe; Lorenzo Quinn; ***D:*** Waris Hussein. **TV**

Once 🦴🦴 **2006 (R)** Simple story, cool soundtrack. A nameless guy (singer-songwriter Hansard) works at his dad's vacuum repair shop and busks on the Dublin streets, still hoping to make his musical dreams come true. He meets a young Czech immigrant (Irglova), also a musician-songwriter, who wants them to team up. There's a hint of romance but it's the music that really draws them together. **86m/C; DVD, Blu-Ray.** *IR* Glen Hansard; Marketa Irglova; ***D:*** John Carney; ***W:*** John Carney; ***C:*** Tim Fleming; ***M:*** Glen Hansard; Marketa Irglova. Oscars '07: Song ("Falling Slowly"); Ind. Spirit '08: Foreign Film.

Once a Thief 🦴🦴 *Zong Heng Si Hai* **1990 (R)** Minor Woo. Three orphaned children are raised to be thieves by crime boss/surrogate father Chow (Tsang). As adults, Joe (Chow), Jim (Cheung), and Cherie (Chung) have just completed another successful art heist and Cherie thinks it's time they retire. Instead, they agree to one last job—stealing a painting from a heavily guarded French villa. But it turns out to be a set-up and Joe is apparently killed. He returns, in a wheelchair, two years later—seeking revenge against Chow, who betrayed them. Chinese with subtitles. Woo went on to use a variation of this premise for his TV movie/series of the same name. **108m/C; VHS, DVD.** *CH* Chow Yun-Fat; Leslie Cheung; Cherie Chung; Kenneth Tsang; ***D:*** John Woo; ***W:*** John Woo.

Once a Thief 🦴🦴🦴 **1996 (R)** A fun and action-packed TV movie finds adopted children Li Ann (Holt) and Mac (Sergei) being raised along with natural son Michael (Wong) by Hong Kong crime head Tang (Ito) and trained as daring professional thieves. A falling out finds Li Ann in Vancouver, involved with ex-cop Victor (Lea), and both of them working for a covert crime-fighting agency headed by a very tough director (Dale). Then Mac is forced to join the duo in an elaborate heist to bring down Michael and his family's criminal empire. Woo's director's cut contains additional footage. **101m/C; VHS, DVD.** Ivan Sergei; Sandrine Holt; Nicholas Lea; Michael Wong; Robert Ito; Jennifer Dale; Alan Scarfe; ***D:*** John Woo; ***W:*** Glenn Davis; William Laurin; ***C:*** Bill Wong; ***M:*** Amin Bhatia.

Once an Eagle 🦴🦴 ½ **1976** Originally shown as a seven-part NBC miniseries that follows more than 30 years in the lives of two career Army officers. Sam Damon (Elliot) is the straight arrow soldier who puts his duty before anything, including his marriage to Tommy (Carr). Conniving womanizer Courtney Massingale (Potts) drives his own wealthy wife Emily (Irving) into a breakdown and will stop at nothing to obtain the power he thinks he deserves. Based on the Anton Myrer novel. **510m/C; DVD.** Cliff (Potter) Potts; Darleen Carr; Amy Irving; Glenn Ford; Sam Elliot; Clu Gulager; Ralph Bellamy; Dane Clark; Lynda Day George; Juliet Mills; Kim Hunter; Robert Hogan; Andrew Duggan; John Saxon; Forrest Tucker; Melanie Griffith; ***D:*** E.W. Swackhamer; Richard Michaels; ***W:*** Dr. Peter Fischer; ***C:*** J.J. Jones; ***M:*** Dana Karpoff. **TV**

Once Around 🦴🦴 ½ **1991 (R)** 30ish, lonely Renata Bella (Hunter) meets boisterous, self-assured (read utterly obnoxious) Lithuanian salesman Sam Sharpe (Dreyfuss). He sweeps her off her feet, showers her with affection and gifts, and then tries hard—too hard—to please her close-knit Italian family. Casting doesn't get much better than the group assembled here and Hallstrom steers everyone to wonderful performances in his American directorial debut. The major flaw is the script, a light romantic comedy that then swerves into heavy drama. **115m/C; DVD.** Richard Dreyfuss; Holly Hunter; Danny Aiello; Gena Rowlands; Laura San Giacomo; Roxanne Hart; Danton Stone; Tim Guinee; Greg Germann; Griffin Dunne; ***D:*** Lasse Hallstrom; ***W:*** Malia Scotch Marmo; ***M:*** James Horner.

Once Before I Die 🦴🦴 ½ **1965** Army soldiers caught in the Philippines during WWII struggle to survive and elude the Japanese. A single woman traveling with them becomes the object of their spare time considerations. A brutal, odd, and gritty war drama. Director/actor Derek was Andress' husband at the time. **97m/C; VHS, DVD.** *PH* Ursula Andress; John Derek; Richard Jaeckel; Rod Lauren; Ron Ely; ***D:*** John Derek.

Once Bitten 🦴🦴 **1985 (PG-13)** Centuries-old though still remarkably youthful vampiress comes to LA to stalk male virgins. That may be the wrong city, but she needs their blood to retain her young countenance. Vampire comedy theme was more effectively explored in 1979s "Love at First Bite," notable, however for the screen debut of comic Carrey who would later gain fame for TV's "In Living Color" and "Ace Ventura, Pet Detective." **94m/C; VHS, DVD.** Lauren Hutton; Jim Carrey; Cleavon Little; Karen Kopins; Thomas Balltore; Skip Lackey; ***D:*** Howard Storm; ***W:*** Jonathan Roberts; David Hines; Jeffrey Hause; ***C:*** Adam Greenberg; ***M:*** John Du Prez.

Once in the Life 🦴🦴 ½ **2000 (R)** Fishburne transfers his 1995 Off Broadway play "Riff Raff" to the big screen but its stage antecedents are apparent. 20/20 Mike (Fishburne) has hooked up with his heroin-addicted white half-brother Torch (Welliver) and they have trouble over a drug score gone wrong that has enraged local boss Manny (Calderon). Manny sends henchman Tony the Tiger (Walker) to take care of things, even though Tony and Mike are old prison buddies. The film basically turns into a talky, one-set triangle leading to inevitable tragedy. **107m/C; DVD.** Laurence Fishburne; Titus Welliver; Eamonn Walker; Paul Calderon; Dominic Chianese; Gregory Hines; Annabella Sciorra; Michael Paul Chan; Nick (Nicholas) Chinlund; Jim Breuer; ***D:*** Laurence Fishburne; ***W:*** Laurence Fishburne; ***C:*** Richard Turner; ***M:*** Branford Marsalis.

Once Is Not Enough 🦴 ½ *Jacqueline Susann's Once is Not Enough* **1975 (R)** Limp trash-drama concerning the young daughter of a has-been movie producer who has a tempestuous affair with a writer who reminds her of her father. Based on the novel by Jacqueline Susann. **121m/C; VHS, DVD, Blu-Ray.** Kirk Douglas; Deborah Raffin; David Janssen; George Hamilton; Brenda Vaccaro; Alexis Smith; Melina Mercouri; ***D:*** Guy Green; ***W:*** Julius J. Epstein; ***C:*** John A. Alonzo; ***M:*** Henry Mancini. Golden Globes '76: Support. Actress (Vaccaro).

Once More, With Feeling 🦴🦴 ½ **1960** Amusing Brit rom com. Tempermental London conductor Victor Fabian (Brynner) needs his wife Dolly (Kendall) to help him control his bad behavior. When she leaves him because of an indiscretion, Victor can't work. He must win her back, but Dolly's now involved with another man (Toone). Kendall's last film, released posthumously. **92m/C; DVD.** *UK* Yul Brynner; Kay Kendall; Geoffrey Toone; Mervyn Johns; Shirley Anne Field; Gregory Ratoff; ***D:*** Stanley Donen; ***W:*** Harry Kurnitz; ***C:*** Georges Perinal.

Once More With Feeling 🦴🦴 **2008** A little too much (over-the-top) feeling in this family dramedy. Shrink Frank Gregorio (Palminteri) is having a midlife crisis and takes up karaoke because it reminds him of his youthful dreams of becoming a singer. He secretly starts entering karaoke contests and spending too much time with fan Lydia (Fiorentino). Meanwhile, Frank's insecure eldest daughter Lana (de Matteo) is obsessing over her appearance and decides to have an affair to boost her self-esteem. **105m/C; DVD.** Chazz Palminteri; Drea De Matteo; Linda Fiorentino; Maria Tucci; Chris Beetem; ***D:*** Jeff Lipsky; ***W:*** Gina O'Brien; ***C:*** Ruben O'Malley; ***M:*** Paul Hsu.

Once Upon a Brothers Grimm 🦴🦴 **1977** An original musical fantasy in which the Brothers Grimm meet a succession of their most famous storybook characters including Hansel and Gretel, the Gingerbread Lady, Little Red Riding Hood, and Rumpelstiltskin. **102m/C; VHS, DVD.** Dean Jones; Paul Sand; Cleavon Little; Ruth Buzzi; Chita Rivera; Teri Garr; ***D:*** Norman Campbell; ***M:*** Mitch Leigh. **TV**

Once Upon a Crime 🦴 ½ **1992 (PG)** Extremely disappointing comedy featuring a high profile cast set in Europe. The plot centers around Young and Lewis finding a dachshund and travelling from Rome to Monte Carlo to return the stray and collect a $5,000 reward. Upon arrival in Monte Carlo, they find the dog's owner dead and they end up getting implicated for the murder. Other prime suspects include Belushi, Candy, Hamilton, and Shepherd. Weak script is made bearable only by the comic genius of Candy. **94m/C; VHS, DVD, Blu-Ray.** John Candy; James Belushi; Cybill Shepherd; Sean Young; Richard Lewis; Ornella Muti; Giancarlo Giannini; George Hamilton; Joss Ackland; Elsa Martinelli; ***D:*** Eugene Levy; ***M:*** Richard Gibbs.

Once Upon a Forest 🦴🦴 **1993 (G)** Animated tale of three woodland creatures in a daring race against time when their young friend's life is at stake. Ecologically correct story is light on humor and heavy on gloom, as little animals encounter oppressive human society and their big, bad machines. Serviceable animation; Crawford, the voice of the wise old uncle, has a song, while Vereen breaks into a fervent gospel number as a marsh bird with a yen for preaching. **80m/C; DVD.** ***V:*** Michael Crawford; Ben Vereen; ***D:*** Charles Grosvenor; ***W:*** Mark Young; Kelly Ward.

Once Upon a Honeymoon 🦴🦴 ½ **1942** Set in 1938, Grant is an American radio broadcaster reporting on the oncoming war. Rogers is the ex-showgirl who unknowingly marries a Nazi. In this strange, uneven comedy, Grant tries to get the goods on him and also rescue Rogers. The plot is basic and uneven with Grant attempting to expose the Nazi and save Rogers. However, the slower moments are offset by some fairly surreal pieces of comedy. **116m/B; VHS, DVD.** Ginger Rogers; Cary Grant; Walter Slezak; Albert Dekker; ***D:*** Leo McCarey; ***C:*** George Barnes.

Once Upon a Scoundrel 🦴🦴 ½ **1973 (G)** A ruthless Mexican land baron arranges to have a young woman's fiancee thrown in jail so he can have her all to himself. **90m/C; VHS, Streaming.** Zero Mostel; Katy Jurado; Titos Vandis; Priscilla Garcia; A. Martinez; ***D:*** George Schaefer; ***M:*** Alex North.

Once Upon a Spy 🦴 **1980** Silly ABC TV movie plays like a James Bond spoof even though that's not its intention. Government computer genius Jack Chenault (Danson) is pushed into the field when a NASA supercomputer is stolen. The criminal mastermind is evil recluse Marcus Valorium (Lee), who's got a missile-equipped wheelchair AND a cosmic shrinking ray. All Jack's got is some blonde babe (Weller) in a tight jumpsuit. **91m/C; DVD.** Ted Danson; Christopher Lee; Mary Louise Weller; Eleanor Parker; Leonard Stone; ***D:*** Ivan Nagy; ***W:*** Jimmy Sangster; ***C:*** Dennis Dalzell; ***M:*** John Cacavas. **TV**

Once Upon a Time in America 🦴🦴🦴 ½ **1984 (R)** The uncut, original version of Leone's epic saga of five friends from a rough Jewish neighborhood in Brooklyn who grow up to be powerful Mob figures during Prohibition and try to keep their friendships and loyalties intact. Told, mostly in flashback, from the persepective of "Noodles" Aaronson (De Niro) as an old man looking back on a lifetime of crime, love, and death, with a sweeping and violent elegance. **229m/C; VHS, DVD, Blu-Ray.** Robert De Niro; James Woods; Elizabeth McGovern; Tuesday Weld; Treat Williams; James Hayden; Joe Pesci; Danny Aiello; William Forsythe; Burt Young; Darlanne Fluegel; Robert Harper; Richard Bright; Mario Brega; Frank Gio; Jennifer Connelly; Brian Bloom; James Russo; Tandy Cronyn; Marcia Jean Kurtz; Estelle Harris; ***D:*** Sergio Leone; ***W:*** Sergio Leone; Leonardo Benvenuti; Piero De Bernardi; Enrico Medioli; Franco Arcalli; Franco Ferrini; ***C:*** Tonino Delli Colli; ***M:*** Ennio Morricone. British Acad. '84: Costume Des., Orig. Score.

Once Upon a Time in Anatolia 🦴🦴🦴 *Bir zamanlar Anadolu'da* **2012** Three cars scour the gloomy Turkish countryside at night looking for a murder victim. A criminal has confessed but insists he's forgotten where he buried the body in his drunken haze and so police officers, a doctor, a prosecutor, and grave diggers search. Acclaimed director Ceylan focuses more on their conversations than their goal—illuminating the people and the philosophies of those who attempt to unearth crime instead of merely focusing on the crime itself. Beautifully shot and intellectually engaging. Turrkish with subtitles. **150m/C; DVD, Blu-Ray.** *TU* Firat Tanis; Burhan Yildiz; Yilmaz Erdogan; Taner Birsel; Muhammet Uzuner; ***D:*** Nuri Bilge Ceylan; ***W:*** Nuri Bilge Ceylan; Ercan Kesal; Ebru Ceylan; ***C:*** Gokhan Tiryaki.

Once Upon a Time in Brooklyn 🦴 *Goat* **2013 (R)** Derivative mob thriller about a convicted mobster trying to go straight on release from prison, but being told by the local crime family that it's a no go. **116m/C; DVD.** Armand Assante; William DeMeo; Cathy Moriarty; Ice-T; Vincent Pastore; ***D:*** Paul Borghese; ***W:*** Paul Borghese; ***C:*** Christopher Walters; ***M:*** Neil Berg. **VIDEO**

Once Upon a Time in China 🦴🦴🦴 *Wong Fei-hung* **1991** Martial arts expert Wong Fei-hung (Li) is dismayed as his country is overrun with western influences and the slave trade that provides labor to the California gold fields. When his aunt is kidnapped by slavers, Wong is determined to get revenge. The DVD edition clocks in at 134 minutes. **100m/C; VHS, DVD, Blu-Ray.** *CH* Jet Li; Yuen Biao; Jacky Cheung; Rosamund Kwan; Kent Cheng; ***D:*** Tsui Hark; ***W:*** Tsui Hark; ***C:*** Arthur Wong Ngok Tai; David Chung; ***M:*** James Wong.

Once Upon a Time in China II 🦴🦴🦴 *Wong Fei-hung Ji Yi: Naam Yi Dong Ji Keung* **1992 (R)** Wong (Li), his assistant Foon, and his aunt arrive in the city of Canton for a medical conference at which Wong is to demonstrate the Chinese art of acupuncture. But the city is on the brink of anarchy as a crumbling dynasty threatens its stability. So Wong joins the revolutionary Sun Yat Sen when a terrorist group initiates a campaign of violence. Dubbed into English. **112m/C; VHS, DVD.** *CH* Jet Li; Rosamund Kwan; Mok Siu Chung; Xin-Xin Xiong; John Chiang; Zhang Tie Lin; Yen Chi Tan; *D:* Tsui Hark; *W:* Tsui Hark; *C:* Wong Ngok Tai; *M:* Richard Yuen.

Once Upon a Time in China III 🦴🦴🦴 *Wong Fei-hung Tsi Sam: Si-wong Tsangba* **1993 (R)** Wong Fei-Hung, his young aunt-by-adoption Yee (to whom he is secretly engaged), and his friend Chung arrive in Peking just as the Empress announces an important martial arts contest. Wong faces rivals on two fronts: a brutal martial arts foe and a Russian diplomat who has a history with Yee. **105m/C; VHS, DVD.** *CH* Jet Li; Rosamund Kwan; Mok Siu Chung; Xin-Xin Xiong; Shun Lau; *D:* Tsui Hark; *W:* Tsui Hark; *C:* Wai Keung (Andrew) Lau; *M:* Wai Lap Wu.

Once Upon A Time... In Hollywood 🦴🦴🦴½ **2019 (R)** In 1969, television star Rick Dalton (DiCaprio) is struggling. He was the lead on a hit show, but is now facing uncertainty about his future. His laid back best friend/stunt double Cliff Booth (Pitt) helps him with the jobs he does get. Advised to go to Italy and appear in spaghetti westerns, anxious Rick is unsure. He also tries to connect with his new neighbors, film director Roman Polanski (Zawierucha) and his actress wife Sharon Tate (Robbie). The ninth film by Tarantino is a nostalgic look at 1960s Hollywood. Outstanding performances, especially by Pitt, and details from the period make the film worthwhile. **165m/C; DVD, Blu-Ray.** Leonardo DiCaprio; Brad Pitt; Margot Robbie; Emile Hirsch; Margaret Qualley; *D:* Quentin Tarantino; *W:* Quentin Tarantino; *C:* Robert Richardson. Oscars '19: Actor--Supporting (Pitt), Production Design; British Acad. '19: Actor--Supporting (Pitt); Golden Globes '20: Actor--Supporting (Pitt), Film--Mus./Comedy, Screenplay; Screen Actors Guild '19: Actor--Supporting (Pitt).

Once Upon a Time in Mexico 🦴🦴🦴 **2003 (R)** The last in Rodriguez's "El Mariachi" trilogy. Hitman El Mariachi (Banderas) is forced out of retirement by corrupt CIA agent Sands (Depp) when vicious cartel leader Barillo (Dafoe) plans a coup against the Preisdent of Mexico. Confusing twists and turns with flashbacks, doublecrosses, triplecrosses, and at least three different subplots keep you guessing about what's going on and who's on whose side. The top-notch cast keeps it all together (especially Depp, who walks away with all his scenes), under the playful guidance of Rodriguez, who doesn't disappoint with several spectacular action scenes. **101m/C; DVD, UMD.** Antonio Banderas; Johnny Depp; Willem Dafoe; Salma Hayek; Mickey Rourke; Eva Mendes; Danny Trejo; Enrique Iglesias; Marco Leonardi; Richard "Cheech" Marin; Ruben Blades; Pedro Armendariz, Jr.; Gerardo Vigil; *D:* Robert Rodriguez; *W:* Robert Rodriguez; *C:* Robert Rodriguez.

Once Upon a Time in the Midlands 🦴🦴 **2002 (R)** Small-time criminal Jimmy (Carlyle) takes a second chance on romance in this fitfully engaging comedy. Jimmy sees ex-girlfriend Shirley (Henderson) on a TV chat show where she's just turned down the marriage proposal of her current beau Dek (Ifans). He wants to win Shirley back—and he needs to get out of town after literally being left holding the bag after a bungled robbery. Jimmy tries to insinuate himself into Shirley's good graces and has several ineffectual showdowns with Dek before his pissed-off cohorts come to town looking for their share of the loot and more trouble ensues. **104m/C; DVD.** *UK* Robert Carlyle; Rhys Ifans; Shirley Henderson; Kathy Burke; Ricky Tomlinson; Finn Atkins; *D:* Shane Meadows; *W:* Shane Meadows; Paul Fraser; *C:* Brian Tufano; *M:* John Lunn.

Once Upon a Time in the West 🦴🦴🦴½ **1968 (PG)** The uncut version of Leone's sprawling epic about a band of ruthless gunmen who set out to murder a mysterious woman waiting for the railroad to come through. Filmed in John Ford's Monument Valley, it's a revisionist western with some of the longest opening credits in the history of the cinema. Fonda is cast against type as an extremely cold-blooded villain. Brilliant musical score. **165m/C; VHS, DVD, Blu-Ray.** *IT* Henry Fonda; Jason Robards, Jr.; Charles Bronson; Claudia Cardinale; Keenan Wynn; Lionel Stander; Woody Strode; Jack Elam; *D:* Sergio Leone; *W:* Sergio Leone; Bernardo Bertolucci; Dario Argento; *C:* Tonino Delli Colli; *M:* Ennio Morricone. Natl. Film Reg. '09.

Once Upon a Time . . . When We Were Colored 🦴🦴🦴 **1995 (PG)** Actor Reid makes a fine directorial debut with the story of a black youngster growing up parentless in '50s Mississippi. His family faces the usual troubles of the time, including poor wages and white bigotry, but manages to provide a positive and loving home life for him. Nostalgic, sensitive, and heartwarming adaptation of Clifton Taulbert's autobiographical book. **112m/C; VHS, DVD.** Al Freeman, Jr.; Paula Kelly; Phylicia Rashad; Polly Bergen; Richard Roundtree; Charles Taylor; Willie Norwood, Jr.; Damon Hines; Leon; *Nar:* Phill Lewis; *D:* Tim Reid; *W:* Paul Cooper; *C:* Johnny (John W.) Simmons; *M:* Steve Tyrell.

Once Upon a Wedding 🦴🦴 **2005 (PG)** Margarita (Ayanna), the daughter of an eccentric Caribbean dictator (Martinez), is just a week away from an arranged marriage to wealthy Manolo (de la Fuente). She accidentally runs over poor-but-handsome Rogelio (Becker) and takes him to the palace to recover. Of course when Margarita realizes she's fallen in love Dad isn't happy. **92m/C; DVD.** Charlotte Ayanna; A. Martinez; Kuno Becker; Christian de la Fuente; Esai Morales; *D:* Matia Karrell; *W:* Reuben Gonzalez; *C:* Steven Finestone; *M:* Ethan Holzman. **VIDEO**

Once Were Warriors 🦴🦴🦴 **1994 (R)** Violent story of the struggling Maori Heke family, who left their rural New Zealand roots to live in the city. Feisty mom Beth (Owen) struggles with five kids and volatile hubby Jake (Heke), who's continuously out of work, boozing, and fighting. Eldest son Nig (Arahanga) has left home and joined a street gang and the rest of the kids hate Jake for beating up on their mother. They also fall victim to his temper and his habit of bringing his brawling, drunk buddies home-leading to further tragedy. Intense drama showcases great performances. Based on the novel by Alan Duff. Feature-film directorial debut of Tamahori. **102m/C; DVD, Blu-Ray.** *NZ* Rena Owen; Temuera Morrison; Mamaengaroa Kerr-Bell; Julian (Sonny) Arahanga; Taungaroa Emile; Rachael Morris; Joseph Kairau; Pete Smith; *D:* Lee Tamahori; *W:* Riwia Brown; *C:* Stuart Dryburgh; *M:* Murray Grindlay; Murray McNabb. Australian Film Inst. '95: Foreign Film; Montreal World Film Fest. '94: Actress (Owen), Film.

Once You Kiss a Stranger 🦴½ **1969** This unacknowledged remake of Hitchcock's "Strangers on a Train," adapted from Patricia Highsmith's novel, is kitschy trash. Wealthy psycho Diana (Lynley) seduces SoCal golf pro Jerry (Burke) and then suggests she murder his rival (Carey) in return for Jerry killing her shrink Dr. Haggis (Bissell). She goes through with her part and then blackmails Jerry with sex and voice tapes but he's not quite the fool she assumes. **106m/C; DVD.** Carol Lynley; Paul Burke; Whit Bissell; Martha Hyer; Stephen McNally; Phil Carey; *D:* Robert Sparr; *W:* Norman Katkov; Frank Tarloff; *C:* Jacques "Jack" Marquette; *M:* Jimmie Fagas.

Ondine 🦴🦴½ **2009 (PG-13)** Unassuming, unhurried Irish folktale from Jordan, filmed in Castletownbere, Ireland. A reformed alcoholic with a hard-partying ex-wife and a 10-year-old daughter confined to a wheelchair because of kidney failure, troubled fisherman Syracuse (Farrell) is naturally surprised when he finds a young woman (Bachleda) caught in his fishing net. He takes her home and names the secretive lass Ondine after the selkie legend of a seal who can shed its skin and become human. It's easier than believing that she's just beautiful trouble. **110m/C; Blu-Ray, On Demand.** *US IR* Colin Farrell; Alicja Bachleda-Curus; Tony Curran; Emil Hostina; Dervla Kirwan; Stephen Rea; Alison Barry; *D:* Neil Jordan; *W:* Neil Jordan; *C:* Christopher Doyle; *M:* Kjartan Sveinsson.

The One 🦴🦴 **2001 (PG-13)** Action-intensive martial arts plot has 125 parallel universes with each person having a counterpart in all of them. Renegade agent Gabriel Yulaw (Li) is killing his fellow selves in order to absorb their energy. He has fellow agents Roedecker (Lindo) and Funsch (Statham) after him, but he only has one Gabe left to kill, this one a hardworking L.A. deputy sheriff, resulting in a showdown in a grungy factory. It's all just an excuse to have Jet Li kick Jet Li's butt on a catwalk to the sounds of grating techno/metal. Needed a touch of humor added to the ludicrous plot instead of special effects stolen from "The Matrix." **80m/C; DVD.** Jet Li; Delroy Lindo; Carla Gugino; Jason Statham; Dylan Bruno; Richard Steinmetz; James Morrison; *D:* James Wong; *W:* Glen Morgan; James Wong; *C:* Robert McLachlan; *M:* Trevor Rabin.

The One 🦴🦴½ **2011** Bittersweet gay romantic comedy with an ending that may upset the tender-hearted. Daniel has a successful career, a great family, and a loving fiancee in Jen. When he sees his former college classmate Tommy, who's gay, the two catch up at a bar and have drunken sex at Tommy's apartment. Daniel wants to be just friends, intending to go on with his 'straight' life and marry Jen, while Tommy's in love and convinced he can change Daniel's mind. **90m/C; DVD.** Jon Prescott; Ian Novick; Margaret Anne Florence; Christopher Cass; *D:* Caytha Jentis; *W:* Caytha Jentis; *C:* Ben Wolf; *M:* Kenneth Lampl. **VIDEO**

One After Another 🦴🦴🦴 *Day After Tomorrow; Uno dopo l'altro* **1968** Bounty hunter Stan (Richard Harrison) rides into town hoping to make money off a recent bank robbery by apprehending the bad guys. It quickly becomes apparent that there's more than one set of bad guys, and figuring out who is responsible will be a bigger task than anticipated. Currently only available as part of the 'Westerns Unchained' collection. **99m/C; Blu-Ray.** *IT SP* Richard Harrison; Pamela Tudor; Paolo Gozlino; Jose Bodalo; Jolanda Modio; *D:* Nick Nostro; *W:* Nick Nostro; Mariano de Lope; Carlos Emilio Rodriguez; Giovanni Simonelli; *C:* Mario Pacheco; *M:* Fred Bongusto; Berto Pisano. **VIDEO**

The One and Only 🦴🦴½ **1978 (PG)** An egotistical young man is determined to make it in show business. Instead, he finds himself in the world of professional wrestling. Most of the humor comes from the wrestling scenes, with Winkler and Darby's love story only serving to dilute the film. **98m/C; VHS, DVD, Blu-Ray.** Henry Winkler; Kim Darby; Gene Saks; William Daniels; Harold Gould; Herve Villechaize; *D:* Carl Reiner.

The One and Only, Genuine, Original Family Band 🦴🦴🦴 **1968 (G)** A harmonious musical family becomes divided when various members take sides in the presidential battle between Benjamin Harrison and Grover Cleveland, a political era that has been since overlooked. **110m/C; VHS, DVD.** Walter Brennan; Buddy Ebsen; Lesley Ann Warren; Kurt Russell; Goldie Hawn; Wally Cox; Richard Deacon; Janet Blair; *D:* Michael O'Herlihy; *W:* Lowell S. Hawley; *C:* Frank V. Phillips.

One Angry Juror 🦴🦴 **2010** In this average Lifetime drama, corporate lawyer Sarah Walsh is serving on a jury where young, black defendent Walter Byrd is accused of murder. Listening to the evidence and testimony has Sarah believing that the police invessigation wasn't handled properly. **89m/C; Streaming.** Jessica Capshaw; Shomari Downer; Jeremy Ratchford; Aaron Douglas; Michael Jai White; Jonathan Scarfe; *D:* Paul A. Kaufman; *W:* Rachel Abramowitz; *C:* Adam Sliwinski; *M:* Joseph Conlan. **CABLE**

One Arabian Night 🦴🦴🦴 *Sumurun* **1920** Hunchback Yeggar loves carnival dancer Yannaia who is willingly sold into an old sheik's harem to be near his handsome son. Rebellious harem favorite Sumurun loves a cloth merchant and various efforts are made to get the lovers together before the sheik takes his revenge on their betrayal. Melodrama secured a place in American filmmaking for director Lubitsch. **85m/B; Silent; DVD.** *GE* Pola Negri; Ernst Lubitsch; Paul Wegener; Jenny Hasselqvist; Harry Liedtke; *D:* Ernst Lubitsch; *W:* Ernst Lubitsch; *C:* Theodor Sparkuhl.

One Armed Executioner 🦴🦴 **1980 (R)** An Interpol agent seeks revenge on his wife's murderers. **90m/C; VHS, DVD.** Franco Guerrero; Jody Kay; *D:* Bobby A. Auarez.

The One-Armed Swordsman 🦴🦴🦴 *Dubei dao* **1967** Widely considered the first modern martial arts film produced in China (it's the first to show extended training sequences and use revenge as a central theme). An evil gang attacks the Golden Sword Kung Fu school and a student sacrifices himself to save it. His son is raise by the school in thanks, but the other students grow to resent him. So much so that the Master's daughter cuts off his arm. Nursed back to health, he learns a new style of Kung Fu. Will he use it to save his former school, which is now under attack? Chinese with subtitles. **109m/C; DVD.** *CH* Yu Wang; Chiao Chiao; Chung-Hsin Huang; Yin Tze Pan; Pei-Shan Chang; Lei Cheng; *D:* Cheh Chang; *W:* Cheh Chang; Kuang Ni; *C:* Chen San Yuan; *M:* Fu-ling Wang.

One Body Too Many 🦴🦴 **1944** A mystery spoof about a wacky insurance salesman who's mistaken for a detective. The usual comedy of errors ensues. A contrived mish-mash—but it does have Lugosi going for it. **75m/B; VHS, DVD, Blu-Ray.** Jack Haley; Jean Parker; Bela Lugosi; Lyle Talbot; Blanche Yurka; Douglas Fowley; Fay Helm; Lucien Littlefield; Dorothy Granger; *D:* Frank McDonald; *W:* Maxwell Shane; Winston Miller; *C:* Fred H. Jackman, Jr.; *M:* Alexander Laszlo.

One Chance 🦴🦴½ **2013 (PG-13)** Sweet, somewhat comedic, inspirational bio of Brit underdog Paul Potts (an appealing performance by Corden). A chubby everyman cell phone salesman in South Wales, tenor Paul has a love of singing and opera. His girlfriend, Julie-Ann (Roach), encourages him to attend an opera school in Venice where Paul's dreams are (momentarily) crushed. A lack of confidence plagues him until he becomes a contestant on the debuting 2007 reality TV show "Britain's Got Talent." Let's just say the judges are in for a surprise. **103m/C; DVD.** *UK* James Corden; Alexandra Roach; Julie Walters; Colm Meaney; Mackenzie Crook; Jemima Rooper; *D:* David Frankel; *W:* Justin Zachman; *C:* Florian Ballhaus; *M:* Theodore Shapiro.

One Child Nation 🦴🦴🦴 **2019 (R)** Documentary examining China's one child policy and the effects it had on life during the three decades it was enforced. Under the policy, a married couple could have one child though those in rural areas could have two. Having boys was strongly encouraged. Though filmmakers Wang and Zhang explain why the policy was needed--it was implemented at a time when the food supply could not keep up with population growth--the results of the policy were forced late term abortions and sterlizations, and child abandonment.The film's perspective is limited because no government officials were interviewed but this does not affect its potency. **89m/C; DVD.** Nanfu Wang; *D:* Nanfu Wang; Jialing Zhang; *C:* Nanfu Wang; Yuanchen Liu; *M:* Nathan Halpern; Chris Ruggiero.

One Christmas 🦴🦴½ *Truman Capote's One Christmas* **1995** Conman father uses his estranged son as a pawn to gain access to New Orleans high society. Based on the story "One Christmas" by Truman Capote. **91m/C; VHS, DVD.** Katharine Hepburn; Henry Winkler; Swoosie Kurtz; T.J. Lowther; Pat Hingle; Julie Harris; *D:* Tony Bill; *W:* Duane Poole; *M:* Van Dyke Parks. **TV**

One Crazy Summer 🦴🦴½ **1986 (PG)** A group of wacky teens spends a fun-filled summer on Nantucket Island in New England. Follow-up to "Better Off Dead" is offbeat and fairly charming, led by Cusack's perplexed cartoonist and with comic moments delivered by Goldthwait. **94m/C; VHS, DVD.** John Cusack; Demi Moore; William Hickey; Curtis Armstrong; Bobcat Goldthwait; Mark Metcalf; Joel Murray; Tom Villard; Joe Flaherty; *D:* Savage Steve Holland; *W:* Savage Steve Holland; *M:* Cory Lerios.

One Dark Night 🦴½ *Entity Force; Mausoleum* **1982 (R)** Two high school girls plan an initiation rite for one of their friends who is determined to shed her "goody-goody" image. West is the caped crusader of TV series "Batman" fame. **94m/C; VHS, DVD, Blu-Ray.** Meg Tilly; Adam West; David Mason Daniels; Robin Evans; Elizabeth Daily; ***D:*** Tom McLoughlin.

One Day 🦴 1/2 **2011 (PG-13)** The lives of idealistic Emma (Hathaway) and entitled Dexter (Sturgess) change forever after spending a romantic night together on their college graduation. Pic proceeds to track the pair over the next 20 years on that same date, showing their influences on one another as they develop into adults. They navigate a fine line between friendship and romance that ultimately defines them. Entertaining and charming on the surface, the story never ventures too far into legitimate emotional depth and often is excessively sentimental and predictable. Nicholls adapts from his novel. **107m/C; DVD, Blu-Ray, On Demand.** Anne Hathaway; Jim Sturgess; Romola Garai; Rafe Spall; Tom Mison; Jodie Whitaker; Patricia Clarkson; Josephine de la Baume; ***D:*** Lone Scherfig; ***W:*** David Nicholls; ***C:*** Benoit Delhomme; ***M:*** Rachel Portman.

One Day You'll Understand 🦴🦴 *Later; Plus Tard* **2008** Jewish WII survivor Rivka (Moreau) is quietly living in Paris in 1987 when her son Victor (Girardot) discovers an Aryan declaration among his late father's papers that was designed to protect the family from Nazi persecution. Since Rivka refuses to discuss the past, Victor and his family travel to the small French town where Rivka's parents sheltered before they were deported to Auschwitz. Increasingly agitated, Victor delves into his family's possibly anti-Semitic activities during the war. French with subtitles. **90m/C; DVD.** *FR* Jeanne Moreau; Hippolyte Giradot; Emmanuelle Devos; Dominique Blanc; ***D:*** Amos Gitai; ***W:*** Dan Franck; Jerome Clement; ***C:*** Caroline Champetier; ***M:*** Louis Sclavis.

One Deadly Summer 🦴🦴🦴 *L'Ete Meurtrier* **1983 (R)** Revenge drama about a young girl who returns to her mother's home village to ruin three men who had assaulted her mother years before. Very well acted. From the novel by Sebastien Japrisot. In French with English subtitles. **134m/C; VHS, DVD, Blu-Ray.** *FR* Isabelle Adjani; Alain Souchon; Suzanne Flon; ***D:*** Jean Becker; ***M:*** Georges Delerue. Cesar '84: Actress (Adjani), Support. Actress (Flon), Writing.

One Desire 🦴🦴 **1955** Steamy melodrama finds former madam Tacey Cromwell and her gambler lover Clint Saunders starting over in a new town and going legit. He gets a job at the local bank and they raise as couple of orphans, but banker's daughter Judith is determined to have Clint for herself. **94m/C; DVD.** Anne Baxter; Rock Hudson; Julie Adams; Carl Benton Reid; Natalie Wood; Barry Curtis; ***D:*** Jerry Hopper; ***W:*** Robert Blees; Lawrence Roman; ***C:*** Maury Gertsman; ***M:*** Frank Skinner.

One Direction: This Is Us 🦴🦴 **2013 (PG)** Cue the screaming teenage girls! Those boys from Britain--Niall, Zayn, Liam, Harry, and Louis--made it to the big screen, albeit in a documentary about their rise to fame. Discovered by Simon Cowell on Britain's "The X Factor" in 2010 and signed to his label, they hit the pop scene running. All the details are gushed out in between videos from their wildly successful concert tour. The promotional piece is mildly interesting for the non-1D fans, but heaven for those who are. **92m/C; DVD, Blu-Ray.** Niall Horan; Zayn Malik; Liam Payne; Harry Styles; Louis Tomlinson; ***D:*** Morgan Spurlock; ***C:*** Neil Harvey; ***M:*** Simon Franglen.

One Down, Two to Go! **WOOF!** **1982 (R)** When the mob is discovered to be rigging a championship karate bout, two dynamic expert fighters join in a climactic battle against the hoods. Example of really bad "blaxploitation" that wastes talent, film, and the audience's time. **84m/C; VHS, DVD.** Jim Brown; Fred Williamson; Jim Kelly; Richard Roundtree; Tom Signorelli; Joe Spinell; Paula Sills; Laura Loftus; ***D:*** Fred Williamson; ***W:*** Jeff Williamson; ***C:*** James (Momel) Lemmo; ***M:*** Herb Hetzer; Joe Trunzo.

187 🦴🦴 1/2 **1997 (R)** Jackson's a Brooklyn high school teacher who is brutally attacked by one of his students. His physical scars are healed, but his emotional state is marred as he takes some pretty unorthodox teaching methods to a troubled L.A. school. Very dark, psychological drama with a powerful performance by Jackson. Tough film whose title refers to the California penal code number for murder. First film from director Reynolds after his "Waterworld" fiasco. **119m/C; VHS, DVD.** Samuel L. Jackson; John Heard; Kelly Rowan; Clifton (Gonzalez) Collins, Jr.; Tony Plana; Lobo Sebastian; Jack Kehler; Demetrius Navarro; Karina Arroyave; ***D:*** Kevin Reynolds; ***W:*** Scott Yagemann; ***C:*** Ericson Core.

One-Eyed Jacks 🦴🦴🦴 1/2 **1961** An often engaging, but lengthy, psychological western about an outlaw who seeks to settle the score with a former partner who became a sheriff. Great acting by all, particularly Brando, who triumphed both as star and director. Stanley Kubrick was the original director, but Brando took over mid-way through the filming. The photography is wonderful and reflects the effort that went into it. **141m/C; VHS, DVD, Blu-Ray.** Marlon Brando; Karl Malden; Katy Jurado; Elisha Cook, Jr.; Slim Pickens; Ben Johnson; Pina Pellicer; Timothy Carey; ***D:*** Marlon Brando; ***W:*** Calder Willingham; ***C:*** Charles B(ryant) Lang, Jr. Natl. Film Reg. '18.

One-Eyed Soldiers 🦴 **1967** Young woman, criminal, and dwarf follow trail to mysterious key to unlock $15 million treasure. Much cheesy intrigue. **83m/C; VHS, DVD.** *GB YU* Dale Robertson; Luciana Paluzzi; ***D:*** Jean Christopher.

One False Move 🦴🦴🦴 **1991 (R)** Black psycho Pluto, his white-trash partner Ray, and Ray's biracial lover Fantasia are three low-level drug dealers on the L.A. streets who get involved in murder. Fleeing the city for Fantasia's small hometown in Arkansas, they come up against the local sheriff and two L.A. cops sent to bring them back. Not a typical crime thriller, first-time feature director Franklin is more interested in a psychological character study of racism and smalltown mores than in your average shoot 'em up action picture. Good performances, especially by Williams as the deceptive bad girl. **105m/C; DVD.** Bill Paxton; Cynda Williams; Michael Beach; Jim Metzler; Earl Billings; Billy Bob Thornton; Natalie Canerday; Robert Ginnaven; Robert Anthony Bell; Kevin Hunter; ***D:*** Carl Franklin; ***W:*** Billy Bob Thornton; Tom Epperson; ***C:*** James L. Carter; ***M:*** Peter Haycock; Derek Holt. Ind. Spirit '93: Director (Franklin); MTV Movie Awards '93: New Filmmaker (Franklin).

One Fine Day 🦴🦴 1/2 **1996 (PG)** A nod to classic screwball comedies throws harried single mom/architect Pfeiffer and political columnist/weekend dad Clooney together when their kids, who attend the same school, miss a class field trip. Naturally, they take an instant dislike to each other. An accidental cell phone mix-up provides the chance for repeated encounters, and growing mutual interest. Predictable, but pleasantly so. Pfeiffer always looks good and Clooney has that cocked head, devilish grin thing working overtime. Screenplay by Neil Simon's daughter Ellen supplies all the elements for a fine date movie. **108m/C; DVD, Blu-Ray.** Michelle Pfeiffer; George Clooney; Alex D. Linz; Mae Whitman; Charles Durning; Jon Robin Baitz; Ellen Greene; Joe Grifasi; Pete Hamill; Anna Maria Horsford; Sheila Kelley; Barry Kivel; Robert Klein; George Martin; Michael Massee; Amanda Peet; Bitty Schram; Holland Taylor; Rachel York; ***D:*** Michael Hoffman; ***W:*** Terrel Seltzer; Ellen Simon; ***C:*** Oliver Stapleton; ***M:*** James Newton Howard.

One Fine Day, When Django Met Sartana 🦴 1/2 *Quel maledetto giorno d'inverno... Django e Sartana all'ultimo sangue; One Damned Day at Dawn... Django Meets Sartana!; Django Meets Sartana* **1970** Inexperienced Sheriff Ronson (Fabio Testi) relies on the help of Bounty Hunter Django (Jack Betts) to put down a gang of outlaws invading his town. In some cases the character of Sheriff Ronson is changed to Sartana to take advantage of Sartana's popularity. Currently only available as part of the 'Westerns Unchained' collection. **90m/C; Blu-Ray.** *IT* Jack Betts; Fabio Testi; Dino Strano; Benito Pacifico; Luciano Conti; ***D:*** Demofilo Fidani; ***W:*** Demofilo Fidani; Mila Vitelli Valenza; ***C:*** Franco Villa. **VIDEO**

One Flew Over the Cuckoo's Nest 🦴🦴🦴🦴 **1975 (R)** Touching, hilarious, dramatic, and completely effective adaptation of Ken Kesey's novel. Nicholson is two-bit crook Randle Patrick McMurphy, who, facing a jail sentence, feigns insanity to be sentenced to a cushy mental hospital. The hospital is anything but cushy, with tyrannical head nurse Ratched (Fletcher) out to squash any vestige of the patients' independence. Nicholson proves to be a crazed messiah and catalyst for these mentally troubled patients and a worthy adversary for the head nurse. Classic performs superbly on numerous levels. **129m/C; VHS, DVD.** Jack Nicholson; Brad Dourif; Louise Fletcher; Will Sampson; William Redfield; Danny DeVito; Christopher Lloyd; Scatman Crothers; Vincent Schiavelli; Michael Berryman; Peter Brocco; Louisa Moritz; ***D:*** Milos Forman; ***W:*** Ken Kesey; Bo Goldman; ***C:*** Haskell Wexler; Bill Butler; William A. Fraker; ***M:*** Jack Nitzsche. Oscars '75: Actor (Nicholson), Actress (Fletcher), Adapt. Screenplay, Director (Forman), Film; AFI '98: Top 100; British Acad. '76: Actor (Nicholson), Actress (Fletcher), Director (Forman), Film, Support. Actor (Dourif); Directors Guild '75: Director (Forman); Golden Globes '76: Actor--Drama (Nicholson), Actress--Drama (Fletcher), Director (Forman), Film--Drama, Screenplay; Natl. Bd. of Review '75: Actor (Nicholson); Natl. Film Reg. '93; N.Y. Film Critics '75: Actor (Nicholson); Natl. Soc. Film Critics '75: Actor (Nicholson); Writers Guild '75: Adapt. Screenplay.

One Foot in Heaven 🦴🦴 1/2 **1941** Methodist minister William Spence strives to help struggling parishes, but this also means constantly moving his family from one new parish to another--something his children occasionally resent. While Spence and his wife maintain their faith in the face of constant struggle, he also isn't above recognizing when his own actions are at fault. Covers some 20 years in Spence's life, beginning at the turn of the 20th century. Based on a biography written by Spence's son. **107m/B; DVD.** Fredric March; Martha Scott; Beulah Bondi; Gene Lockhart; Harry Davenport; Grant Mitchell; ***D:*** Irving Rapper; ***W:*** Casey Robinson; ***C:*** Charles Rosher; ***M:*** Max Steiner.

One Foot in Hell 🦴🦴 **1960** Minor western that was one of Ladd's last films. Mitch Barrett (Ladd) holds an entire town responsible for the callous treatment and death of his wife when he can't afford the medicine to save her. The remorseful citizens offer him a deputy's badge and Barrett carefully plots his revenge by putting together a gang to rob the bank. **90m/B; DVD.** Alan Ladd; Don Murray; Dan O'Herlihy; Barry Coe; Dolores Michaels; Larry Gates; ***D:*** James B. Clark; ***W:*** Aaron Spelling; Sydney (Sidney) Boehm; ***C:*** William Mellor; ***M:*** Dominic Frontiere.

One for the Money 🦴 **2012 (PG-13)** A hit series of books (this time by Janet Evanovich) will not always translate to a hit series of films. A poorly cast and inept Heigl takes on the lead role of Stephanie Plum, a girl who goes from divorce to being a bail bondswoman (as if that's the easiest thing to do in the real world) tracking down dangerous scofflaws. Of course, her first case involves a former high school sweetheart. Grating, annoying, and aggressively unfunny, the film won't do any favors for Heigl's uneven movie career. **106m/C; DVD, Blu-Ray.** Katherine Heigl; Jason O'Mara; Daniel Sunjata; John Leguizamo; Sherri Shepherd; Debbie Reynolds; ***D:*** Julie Anne Robinson; ***W:*** Stacy Sherman; Karen Ray; Liz Brixius; ***C:*** Jim Whitaker; ***M:*** Deborah Lurie.

One for the Road 🦴 *Against All Hope* **1982** Michael Madsen's screen debut is unwatchable in this atrocious movie. He plays alcoholic Cecil Moe who's trying to straighten himself out. **90m/C; VHS, DVD.** Michael Madsen; Maureen McCarthy; Rex Flores; Tim Joosten; Herb Harms; Ron Schultz; ***D:*** Edward T. McDougal.

One Frightened Night 🦴🦴 1/2 **1935** An eccentric millionaire informs his family members that he is leaving each of them $1 million...as long as his long-lost granddaughter doesn't reappear. Guess who comes to dinner. **69m/B; VHS, DVD, Blu-Ray.** Mary Carlisle; Wallace Ford; Hedda Hopper; Charley Grapewin; ***D:*** Christy Cabanne.

One from the Heart 🦴🦴 **1982 (R)** The film more notable for sinking Coppola's Zoetrope Studios than for its cinematic context. Garr and Forrest are a jaded couple who seek romantic excitement with other people. An extravagant (thus Coppola's finance problems) fantasy Las Vegas set, pretty to look at but does little to enhance the weak plot. Score by Waits, a much-needed plus. **100m/C; VHS, DVD, Blu-Ray.** Teri Garr; Frederic Forrest; Nastassja Kinski; Raul Julia; Lainie Kazan; Rebecca De Mornay; Harry Dean Stanton; ***D:*** Francis Ford Coppola; ***W:*** Armyan Bernstein; Francis Ford Coppola; ***M:*** Tom Waits; Robert Alcivar.

One Girl's Confession 🦴 1/2 **1953** Waitress Mary (Moore) steals $25 thousand from her sleazy boss, buries the loot, confesses to the crime, and does her time knowing the money will be there upon her release. Out of the joint, Mary gets another waitressing job but her boss Damitrof (Haas) is a debt-ridden gambler and she decides to lend him some dough to save the diner. But when Damitrof starts spending a little too freely, Mary gets suspicious. **74m/B; DVD.** Cleo Moore; Hugo Haas; Glenn Langan; Ellen Stansbury; Anthony Jochim; ***D:*** Hugo Haas; ***W:*** Hugo Haas; ***C:*** Paul Ivano; ***M:*** Vaclav Divina.

One Good Cop 🦴🦴 1/2 **1991 (R)** A noble, inconsistent attempt to do a police thriller with a human face, as a young officer and his wife adopt the three little daughters of his slain partner from the force. But it reverts to a routine action wrapup, with 'Batman' Keaton even donning a masked-avenger getup to get revenge. **105m/C; DVD, Blu-Ray.** Michael Keaton; Rene Russo; Anthony LaPaglia; Kevin Conway; Rachel Ticotin; Grace Johnston; Blair Swanson; Rhea Silver-Smith; Tony Plana; Benjamin Bratt; Charlaine Woodard; Lisa Arrindell Anderson; ***D:*** Heywood Gould; ***W:*** Heywood Gould; ***C:*** Ralf Bode; ***M:*** William Ross.

One Good Turn 🦴🦴 **1995 (R)** Matt Forrest (Von Dohlen) and his wife Laura (Amis) seemingly have it all only to have their fortunes take a radical turn for the worse. Matt "accidentally" runs into Simon Jury (Remar), the man who saved his life 12 years before. But the seemingly friendly Jury is actually intent on destroying everything they have. **90m/C; VHS, DVD.** Lenny Von Dohlen; James Remar; Suzy Amis; John Savage; ***D:*** Tony Randel; ***W:*** Jim Piddock; ***C:*** Jacques Haitkin; ***M:*** Joel Goldsmith.

One Hour Photo 🦴🦴🦴 **2002 (R)** Creepy thriller with Williams treading new ground as Seymour Parrish, Sy the Photo Guy, a disturbed and disturbing one-hour photo clerk. While seemingly a milquetoast, Sy becomes a tad obsessed with the suburban Yorkin family, idealizing them in the process. After years of viewing their happiest moments frozen in time, he decides to get involved in their lives when he sees trouble brewing. Williams creates an off-kilter character that is surprisingly sympathetic. Romanek's direction is clever and extremely stylish, avoiding cliche, to craft a gripping psychodrama. **98m/C; DVD, Blu-Ray.** Robin Williams; Connie Nielsen; Michael Vartan; Gary Cole; Eriq La Salle; Dylan Smith; Erin Daniels; Andy Comeau; ***D:*** Mark Romanek; ***W:*** Mark Romanek; ***C:*** Jeff Cronenweth; ***M:*** Reinhold Heil; Johnny Klimek.

One Hour with You 🦴🦴 1/2 **1932** Lubitsch remade his 1924 silent, "The Marriage," into this musical comedy. Parisian doctor Andre Bertier (Chevalier) may be wed to Colette (MacDonald) but that doesn't stop his roving eye. Married Mitzi (Tobin) has designs on Andre and when her suspicious husband (Young) threatens to name him in a divorce suit, Andre is forced to reveal all to the miffed Colette, who decides to get even. Cukor started out as director but quit because of producer Lubitsch's interference and he finished the picture himself. **80m/B; DVD.** Maurice Chevalier; Charlie Ruggles; Jeanette MacDonald; Genevieve Tobin; Roland Young; Richard Carle; George Barbier; Joseph Dunn; ***D:*** Ernst Lubitsch; George Cukor; ***W:*** Samson Raphaelson; ***C:*** Victor Milner; ***M:*** Oscar Straus.

One Hundred and One Nights 🦴🦴 *Les Cent et Une Nuits; Les Cent et Une Nuits de Simon Cinema* **1995** Simon Cinema (Piccoli) is a 100-year-old producer/director whose memory is fading. So he hires young film student Camille (Gayet) to prompt his memory. Numerous celebrities make cameo appearances to talk about film and numerous film clips are shown. **101m/C; VHS, DVD.** *FR GB* Michel Piccoli; Marcello Mastroianni; Henri Garcin; Julie Gayet; Mathieu Demy; Emmanuel Salinger; ***D:*** Agnes Varda; ***W:*** Agnes Varda; ***C:*** Eric Gautier.

100 Bloody Acres **2012** Australian writer/directors Cameron and Colin Cairnes successfully manage that difficult balance between horror and comedy. The Morgan brothers (Herriman and Sampson) discover that their fertilizer company takes off when they use a few bodies stolen from a recent car accident nearby in the mix. What would happen if they use live bodies? A travelling love triangle (McGahan, Ackland, and Kristian) get sucked into this bizarre dynamic and could become their next business product but one of the brothers starts to have second thoughts. **91m/C; DVD, Blu-Ray.** *AU* Damon Herriman; Angus Sampson; Anna McGahan; Oliver Ackland; Jamie Kristian; ***D:*** Cameron Cairnes; Colin Cairnes; ***W:*** Cameron Cairnes; Colin Cairnes; ***C:*** John Brawley.

100 Feet **1/2 2008 (R)** Janssen makes a good woman-in-peril in this chiller. Marnie Watson was convicted of manslaughter for killing her abusive NYPD husband Mike (Pare) and must finish out her sentence under house arrest tethered to an ankle monitor. Her late husband's partner Shanks (Cannavale) still thinks the murder was deliberate and he's keeping a close eye on Marnie, hoping she screws up. Then Marnie starts getting abused again—from Mike's very vengeful ghost. She can't get away so Marnie has to get rid of Mike for good this time (which turns out to be the weakest part of the plot). **101m/C; DVD, Blu-Ray.** Famke Janssen; Bobby Cannavale; Michael Paré; Ed Westwick; John Fallon; Patricia Charbonneau; Kevin Geer; ***D:*** Eric Red; ***W:*** Eric Red; ***C:*** Ken Kelsch; ***M:*** John (Gianni) Frizzell. **VIDEO**

100 Girls **2000 (R)** College freshman Tucker (Tucker) scores an unexpected sexual encounter with a co-ed in the girls' dorm elevator during a blackout. He can't see her face and doesn't know her name, so he spends the semester investigating the 100 possibles in search of his mystery girl. Actually funny and not as sleazy as it may sound. **95m/C; VHS, DVD.** Jonathan Tucker; James DeBello; Emmanuelle Chriqui; Larisa Oleynik; Jaime Pressly; Katherine Heigl; ***D:*** Michael Davis; ***W:*** Michael Davis; ***C:*** James Lawrence Spencer; ***M:*** Kevin Bassinson.

100 Men and a Girl **1937** Charming musical features Durbin as the daughter of an unemployed musician, who decides she will try to persuade Leopold Stokowski to help her launch an orchestra that will employ her father and his musician friends. Beautiful mix of classical and pop music. Based on a story by Hans Kraly. **85m/B; VHS, DVD.** Deanna Durbin; Leopold Stokowski; Adolphe Menjou; Alice Brady; Eugene Pallette; Mischa Auer; Billy Gilbert; Alma Kruger; Christian Rub; Jed Prouty; Jack Mulhall; ***D:*** Henry Koster; ***W:*** Charles Kenyon; Bruce Manning; ***C:*** Joseph Valentine. Oscars '37: Score.

100 Mile Rule **1/2 2002 (R)** Dark comedy has a trio of salesman from Detroit discussing the "100 Mile Rule" en route to a business meeting in L.A. The rule states that a man is free to cheat on his girlfriend/spouse if he's over 100 miles away. Jerry is all for it, while family man Bobby wants no part of it. Bobby changes his tune when he meets Monica (Bello). After she seduces him, she blackmails him with a tape of the encounter, leading to murder and corporate backstabbing. Think "Very Bad Things" on business. Standard fare is helped along by McKean and Bello. **98m/C; VHS, DVD.** Jake Weber; Maria Bello; David Thornton; Michael McKean; Nick (Nicholas) Chinlund; David Dorfman; Shawn Huff; ***D:*** Brent Huff; ***W:*** Drew Pillsbury; ***C:*** Giovani Lampassi; ***M:*** Tor Hyams.

100 Million BC **2008 (R)** Scientist Frank Reno (Gross) still feels guilty for a 1940s time travel experiment that left a team stranded in the Cretaceous Period. In present-day L.A., some Navy SEALS are now being sent back on a rescue mission. Except when they return they just happen to be accompanied by a 100 million-year-old dino that's really hungry. **85m/C; DVD.** Michael Gross; Christopher Atkins; Greg Evigan; Mane Westbrook; Stephen Blackehart; Geoff Meed; Wendy Carter; ***D:*** Griff Furst; ***W:*** Paul Bates; ***C:*** Alexander Yellen; ***M:*** Ralph Rieckermann. **VIDEO**

100 Monsters *Yokai hyaku monogatari; The Hundred Monsters; Yokai Monsters 2: 100 Monsters* **1968** The second film in the Yokai Monsters trilogy is a little more serious than the first. An evil magistrate decides to demolish a shrine and some adjacent apartments to build a brothel. The peasants try fighting back, but their landlord is murdered. A lone samurai agrees to help them, and he summons the Yokai to teach the magistrate a lesson. Not as well done as the first, but still different enough to be worth attention. One of the few known horror films starring an umbrella monster. **90m/C; DVD.** *JP* Mikiko Tsubouchi; Keiko Kayanagi; Yoshio Yoshida; Ryutaro Gomi; Jun Fujimaki; Jun Hamamura; Tatsuo Hananuno; Masaru Hiraizumi; Takashi Kanda; ***D:*** Kimiyoshi Yasuda; ***W:*** Tetsuro Yoshida; ***C:*** Yasukazu Takemura; ***M:*** Michiaki Watanabe.

101 Ways (The Things a Girl Will Do to Keep Her Volvo) **1/2 2000** Actually, struggling writer Watson (Hoopes) doesn't seem to be trying too hard to keep that car, which her mother insisted she purchase because of its safety record. Watson has moved from the bright lights of the Big Apple to the suburbs of Connecticut in order to concentrate on her career but since she has to pay the bills, she works ineffectually at a couple of nothing jobs. The flick itself is ineffectual and Watson isn't terribly likeable so who cares what happens to her. **100m/C; DVD.** Wendy Hoopes; Glenn Fitzgerald; Jamie Harrold; Jack Gilpin; Patricia Elliott; Gabriel Macht; ***D:*** Jennifer B. Katz; ***W:*** Jennifer B. Katz; ***C:*** Jeffrey A. Splett; ***M:*** John Hodian.

100 Rifles **1969 (R)** Native American bank robber and Black American lawman join up with a female Mexican revolutionary to help save the Mexican Indians from annihilation by a despotic military governor. What it lacks in political correctness it makes up for in fits of action. Although quite racy in its day for its interracial sex sizzle of Brown and Rachel, it's tame and overblown by today's standards. **110m/C; VHS, DVD, Blu-Ray.** Jim Brown; Raquel Welch; Burt Reynolds; Fernando Lamas; Dan O'Herlihy; Eric Braeden; ***D:*** Tom Gries; ***W:*** Tom Gries; Clair Huffaker; ***C:*** Cecilio Paniagua; ***M:*** Jerry Goldsmith.

100 Streets **1/2 2017** An uneven ensemble drama that explores several intersecting stories set in a square mile of London. In one thread, Max (Elba) is a wealthy former rugby star who tries to find common ground and reconcile from his estranged wife (Arterton). In another, cab driver George (Creed-Miles) cannot escape bad luck and his wife Kathy (Wareing) attempts to improve his lot in life. In a third story, a petty criminal Kingsley (Drameh) has a chance encounter with middle-aged actor Terence (Stott) that changes his life. Though sometimes unoriginal, the film shows that strangers from different social classes can have parallel struggles. **93m/C; DVD.** Tom Cullen; Idris Elba; Gemma Arterton; Franz Drameh; Charlie Creed-Miles; ***D:*** Jim O'Hanlon; ***W:*** Leon Butler; ***C:*** Philipp Blaubach; ***M:*** Paul Saunderson.

The 100-Year-Old Man Who Climbed Out the Window and Disappeared **1/2 2015 (R)** A massive hit in its home country of Sweden, this slight, deadpan film may lose a little bit in translation for American audiences but its unique energy keeps it entertaining. The title really says it all. Allan Karlsson (Gustafsson) turns 100 and decides he needs an adventure. It's never too late to start over, as the saying goes. Where would a 100-year-old man go and what kind of trouble could he get into? Based on the Jonas Jonasson novel, this character-based comedy is so thin you can practically see through it. But it is a fun little film. And it's VERY Swedish. **114m/C; DVD, Blu-Ray.** Robert Gustafsson; Iwar Wiklander; David Wiberg; Mia Skaringer; Jens Hultén; ***D:*** Felix Herngren; ***W:*** Felix Herngren; Hans Ingemansson; ***C:*** Goran Hallberg; ***M:*** Matti Bye.

101 Dalmatians **1/2 1961 (G)** Disney classic has dogowners Roger and Anita, and their spotted pets Pongo and Perdita, shocked when their puppies are kidnapped by Cruella de Vil, villainess extraordinaire, to make a simply fabulous spotted coat. They enlist the aid of various animals to rescue the doomed pups, but find not only their own puppies, but 84 more as well. You can expect a happy ending and lots of spots—6,469,952 to be exact. Based on the children's book by Dodie Smith. Technically notable for the first time use of the Xerox process to transfer the animator's drawings onto celluloid, making the film's opening sequence of dots evolving into 101 barking dogs possible. **79m/C; DVD, Blu-Ray.** ***V:*** Rod Taylor; Betty Lou Gerson; Lisa Davis; Ben Wright; Frederick Worlock; J. Pat O'Malley; ***D:*** Clyde Geronimi; Wolfgang Reitherman; Hamilton Luske; ***W:*** Bill Peet; ***M:*** George Bruns.

101 Dalmatians **1/2 1996 (G)** Yes, it's the live-action Disney version of their own 1961 animated feature (based on the book by Dodie Smith) about dog-napping villainess Cruella De Vil (Close) and lots of spotted pups. They're absolutely adorable, of course, Cruella's costumes (and hair) are certainly eye-catching, and the bumbling crooks get their proper comeuppance. Daniels and Richardson have the thankless role of the dogs' human owners and get upstaged at every opportunity. Kids familiar with the cartoon pups may be surprised that the live pups don't talk—and keep in mind that Close, while terrific, may be too scary for the little ones. The Hound is always happy to see another dog movie but still feels some classics should be left alone. **103m/C; DVD, Blu-Ray.** Glenn Close; Jeff Daniels; Joely Richardson; Joan Plowright; Hugh Laurie; Mark Williams; ***D:*** Stephen Herek; ***W:*** John Hughes; ***C:*** Adrian Biddle; ***M:*** Michael Kamen.

102 Dalmatians **1/2 2000 (G)** Lackluster sequel to the 1996 live-action Disney film finds Cruella De Vil (Close) being released from prison and teaming up with fur designer Jean Pierre Le Pelt (Depardieu). She still wants that dalmatian fur coat (and this time a hood as well). The puppies are as cute as ever, with the addition of digitally de-spotted Oddball, but this one just seems like another excuse for Disney to print money and Close to chew scenery. Stick with the original (the 1961 cartoon version, that is). **100m/C; DVD.** Glenn Close; Gerard Depardieu; Ioan Gruffudd; Tim (McInnerny) McInnery; Ian Richardson; Ben Crompton; Jim Carter; Ron Cook; David Horovitch; Timothy West; Alice Evans; Carol MacReady; ***V:*** Eric Idle; ***D:*** Kevin Lima; ***W:*** Bob Tzudiker; Noni White; Kristen Buckley; Brian Regan; ***C:*** Adrian Biddle; ***M:*** David Newman.

127 Hours **1/2 2010 (R)** Based on adventurer Aron Ralston's book "Between a Rock and a Hard Place," in which Ralston recounts the five days he spent trapped in a Utah canyon with his right arm pinned against the canyon wall by a large rock. Franco's performance as Ralston is riveting, drawing viewers into his transformational journey of self-discovery as he struggles to find the strength to preserve his life by cutting off part of his trapped arm. Director Boyle crafts a compelling exploration of the universal will to live more than just one man's adventuring accident. **93m/C; DVD, Blu-Ray.** James Franco; Clemence Poesy; Amber Tamblyn; Kate Mara; Lizzy Caplan; Kate Burton; Sean Bott; Treat Williams; ***D:*** Danny Boyle; ***W:*** Danny Boyle; Simon Beaufoy; ***C:*** Enrique Chediak; Anthony Dod Mantle; ***M:*** A.R. Rahman. Ind. Spirit '11: Actor (Franco).

The One I Love **1/2 2014 (R)** Duplass and Moss do career-best work as a couple struggling to keep their marriage together who decide to spend a weekend to rekindle their flame and work on their union. One night they happen upon the coach house behind the cottage in which they're staying, and, well, they find something unique. Don't let anyone spoil the spectacular, "Twilight Zone"-esque twist of director McDowell's insightful commentary on how we long for perfect variations on our significant others but aren't really sure of what we're asking for. It falls a little short, but the set-up and performances make up for it. **91m/C; DVD, Blu-Ray.** Mark Duplass; Elisabeth Moss; Ted Danson; ***D:*** Charlie McDowell; ***W:*** Justin Lader; ***C:*** Doug Emmett; ***M:*** Danny Bensi; Saunder Jurriaans.

The One I Love **1/2 2014 (R)** A troubled couple tries to reconnect over a weekend trip but must face the unexpected when strange, if not paranormal, events occur which challenges them, their perceptions of the world, and their relationship. Ever since Ethan (Duplass) betrayed the trust of his wife Sophie (Moss), their marriage has become increasingly troubled. Following the advice of their marriage counselor (Danson), they go on a weekend retreat to a vacation home he recommended in the countryside. As the couple works on their marriage, odd things start to happen which affects how they view everything. **91m/C; DVD, Blu-Ray, Streaming, Download.** Mark Duplass; Elisabeth Moss; Ted Danson; Mary Steenburgen; Charlie McDowell; ***D:*** Charlie McDowell; ***W:*** Justin Lader; ***C:*** Doug Emmett; ***M:*** Danny Bensi; Saunder Jurriaans.

The One I Wrote For You **1/2 2014 (PG)** A family drama about a man who has a chance to fulfill his creative dreams but at a high cost. For much of his life, Ben (Jackson) wanted to be a singer/songwriter but life got in the way. Now he works in a coffee shop to support his family, which includes a ten-year-old daughter. Just after he is offered a manager position at the coffee shop, the reality television show "The Song" has auditions in town. Ben's daughter enters him in the competition. Though he makes to the show, he loses the first two rounds and must decide if he wants to risk himself to win. **110m/C; DVD, Download.** Cheyenne Jackson; Kevin Pollak; Christine Woods; Avi Lake; Christopher Lloyd; ***D:*** David Kauffman; ***W:*** David Kauffman; Andrew Lauer; Steven Sessions; ***C:*** Philip Roy; ***M:*** Keith Harter.

One in a Million **1936** Debut film of Norwegian skating star Henie centers around a Swiss girl whose father is training her for the Olympics. Features good comedy by the Ritz Brothers and Sparks, as well as the beautiful skating of Henie. **95m/B; DVD.** Sonja Henie; Adolphe Menjou; Jean Hersholt; Al Ritz; Harry Ritz; Jimmy Ritz; Arline Judge; Don Ameche; Ned Sparks; Montagu Love; Leah Ray; ***D:*** Sidney Lanfield; ***W:*** Leonard Praskins; Mark Kelly.

One In the Chamber **2012 (R)** Average Eurotrash action flick. Hitmen Carver (Gooding Jr.) and Andreev (Lundgren) are on opposite sides when Carver takes a job in Prague for the Russian mob and Andreev is hired to take him out. **91m/C; DVD, Blu-Ray.** Cuba Gooding, Jr.; Dolph Lundgren; Louis Mandylor; Claudia Bassols; Leo Gregory; ***D:*** William Kaufman; ***W:*** Derek Kolstad; ***C:*** Mark Rutledge; ***M:*** John Roome. **VIDEO**

One Kiss *Un bacio* **2016** Coming-of-age drama about three misfit teens. In a small town in northern Italy, teens Lorenzo (Grilo), Blu (Romani), and Antonio (Pazzagli) are outsiders in their high school. Though each one has a different reason for not belonging, they quickly bond and use their friendship to ward off bullying. The trio's tight-knit bond changes forever when Lorenzo reveals his attraction for Antonio, who feels that way about Blu. Antonio reacts poorly and the three become divided. When the bond is broken, unexpected outcomes occur. Italian with subtitles. **102m/C; DVD, Streaming, Download.** Rimau Ritzberger Grillo; Valentina Romani; Leonardo Pazzagli; Simonetta Solder; Giorgio Marchesi; ***D:*** Ivan Cotroneo; ***W:*** Ivan Cotroneo; Monica Rametta; ***C:*** Luca Bigazzi. **VIDEO**

One Last Ride **2003 (R)** Hard slice-of-life look at L.A. gambling addict Michael (Cupo), who's in deep to loan shark Tweat (Palminteri). Tweat tells the fabric salesman to do what he says or he and his unsuspecting pregnant wife Gina (Barone) will be harmed. Despite the threats, Michael is still sure he is just one win from everything going his way. Low-budget with a familiar story; Cupo adapted from his play. **90m/C; DVD.** Chazz Palminteri; Anita Barone; Mario Roccuzzo; Robert Davi; Charles Durning; Jack Carter; Pat Cupo; Joe Marinelli; ***D:*** Tony Vitale; ***W:*** Pat Cupo; ***C:*** Mark Doering-Powell; ***M:*** Josh G. Abrahams.

One Last Thing **1/2 2005 (R)** Dylan (Angarano) is 16 and dying from brain cancer. When a charity chooses to grant his final wish, he decides that rather than spending time with his football hero Jason O'Malley (Messner), he wants to meet supermodel Nikki Sinclair (Mabrey). Well, duh. Self-destructive Nikki needs the good publicity but bails as quickly as possible. Still, Jason offers

Dylan and his buddies Ricky (Bush) and Slap (Glick) a luxury weekend in New York during which Nikki is given a chance to redeem herself. Ping-pongs between sentiment and reality. Ethan Hawke appears uncredited in flashbacks as Dylan's dead father. **93m/C; DVD.** Cynthia Nixon; Michael Angarano; Sunny Mabrey; Michael Rispoli; Brian Stokes Mitchell; Gina Gershon; Nelust Wyclef Jean; Matthew Bush; Gideon Glick; ***D:*** Alex Steyermark; ***W:*** Barry Stringfellow; ***C:*** Christopher Norr; ***M:*** Anton Sanko.

One Little Indian ✂✂ **1973** AWOL cavalry man Garner and his Indian ward team up with a widow (Miles) and her daughter (Foster) in an attempt to cross the New Mexican desert. A tepid presentation from the usually high quality Disney studio. **90m/C; VHS, DVD.** James Garner; Vera Miles; Jodie Foster; Clay O'Brien; Andrew Prine; Bernard McEveety; ***D:*** Bernard McEveety; ***M:*** Jerry Goldsmith.

One Long Night ✂ ½ **2007** In 1994 (after the governor of California signs a controversial immigration bill), Mexican-American businessman Richard Macedo (Seda) is sent to Mexico City, witnesses a murder, goes on the run from a gang leader, gets attacked by drag queens, and tries to make it home all the while wondering about his Mexican heritage. **90m/C; DVD.** Jon Seda; Paul Rodriguez; Ed Begley, Jr.; Karen Black; Alison Eastwood; Mircea Monroe; Hector Suarez Gomez; Itati Cantoral; ***D:*** David Siqueiros; ***W:*** David Siqueiros; Chris Smernes; ***C:*** Reynaldo Villalobos; ***M:*** Gustavo Farias.

One Magic Christmas ✂✂ ½ **1985 (G)** Disney feel-good film about a disillusioned working woman whose faith in Christmas is restored when her guardian angel descends to Earth and performs various miracles. Somewhat cliched and tiresome, but partially redeemed by Stanton and Steenburgen's presence. **88m/C; VHS, DVD.** Mary Steenburgen; Harry Dean Stanton; Gary Basaraba; Michelle Meyrink; Arthur Hill; Elisabeth Harnois; Robbie Magwood; ***D:*** Phillip Borsos; ***W:*** Thomas Meehan; ***C:*** Frank Tidy; ***M:*** Michael Conway Baker.

One Man Army ✂ ½ **1993 (R)** Kickboxer goes to visit gramps in small town, only to discover the old guy has been murdered and corruption and cover-ups abound. So he decides to kick some butt and set things right. **95m/C; VHS, DVD.** Jerry Trimble; ***D:*** Cirio H. Santiago.

One Man Force ✂✂ **1989 (R)** L.A. narcotics cop Jake Swan goes on a vigilante spree. Huge in body and vengeful in spirit, he makes his partner's murderers pay! **92m/C; VHS, DVD.** John Matuszak; Ronny Cox; Charles Napier; Sharon Farrell; Sam Jones; Chance Boyer; Richard Lynch; Stacey Q; ***D:*** Dale Trevillion; ***W:*** Dale Trevillion; ***M:*** Charles Fox.

One Man's Hero ✂ ½ **1998 (R)** Heavy-handed retelling of the U.S.-Mexican war of the 1840s. Irish Catholic Army Sgt. John Riley (Berenger) is tired of the constant harassment he and his fellow Irishmen are subjected to. After disobeying an officer, Riley leads his men into Mexico where they eventually join the Mexican army as the St. Patrick's Battalion just in time to battle the U.S. troops of Gen. Zachary Taylor (Gammon). The history's confusing and isn't helped when the action stops for romantic interludes between Riley and rebel girl, Marta (Romo). **122m/C; DVD.** Tom Berenger; Joaquim de Almeida; Daniela Romo; James Gammon; Mark Moses; Stuart Graham; Stephen Tobolowsky; Carlos Carrasco; Patrick Bergin; ***D:*** Lance Hool; ***W:*** Milton S. Gelman; ***C:*** Joao Fernandes; ***M:*** Ernest Troost.

One Man's Journey ✂✂ ½ **1933** Barrymore plays it noble as widowed small town doctor Eli Watt. He's completely devoted to his practice though he doesn't make any money and sometimes feels unappreciated. But the doc comes to professional notice when he saves the town from a smallpox epidemic. Remade as "A Man to Remember" (1939). **72m/B; DVD.** Lionel Barrymore; May Robson; Dorothy Jordan; Joel McCrea; Frances Dee; David Landau; Hale Hamilton; James Rush; ***D:*** John S. Robertson; ***W:*** Lester Cohen; Samuel Ornitz.

One Man's Justice ✂✂ ½ **1995 (R)** Army drill sergeant John North (Bosworth) heads for the streets of Venice, California to get the drug-dealing, gun-running scum who killed his wife and daughter. And a streetwise 10-year-old may be his best chance for finding them. **100m/C; VHS, DVD.** Brian Bosworth; Bruce Payne; Jeff Kober; DeJuan Guy; Hammer; M.C. Gainey; ***D:*** Kurt Wimmer; ***W:*** Steven Selling; ***C:*** Jurgen Baum; John Huneck; ***M:*** Anthony Marinelli.

One Man's War ✂✂ ½ **1990 (PG-13)** A human-rights crusader in repressive Paraguay won't be silenced, even after government thugs torture and murder his son. He fights obsessively to bring the killers to justice. The true story of the Joel Filartiga family is heartfelt but ultimately a dramatic letdown; an epilogue proves that full story hasn't been told. **91m/C; VHS, DVD.** Anthony Hopkins; Norma Aleandro; Fernanda Torres; Ruben Blades; ***D:*** Sergio Toledo.

One Man's Way ✂✂ ½ **1963** Murray is appropriately devout as charasmatic religious leader Norman Vincent Peale. With the support of his wife (Hyland), he survives the adulations and accusations of blasphemy for his rather unorthodox theological ideas and his book, "The Power of Positive Thinking." Based on the book "Norman Vincent Peale: Minister to Millions" by Arthur Gordon. **105m/B; VHS, DVD.** Don Murray; Diana Hyland; William Windom; Virginia Christine; Carol Ohmart; Veronica Cartwright; Liam Sullivan; June Dayton; Ian Wolfe; ***D:*** Denis Sanders; ***W:*** Eleanore Griffin; John W. Bloch.

One Million B.C. ✂✂ ½ *The Cave Dwellers; Cave Man; Man and His Mate* **1940** The strange saga of the struggle of primitive cavemen and their battle against dinosaurs and other monsters. Curiously told in flashbacks, this film provided stock footage for countless dinosaur movies that followed. Portions of film rumored to be directed by cinematic pioneer D. W. Griffith. **80m/B; VHS, DVD, Blu-Ray.** Victor Mature; Carole Landis; Lon Chaney, Jr.; ***D:*** Hal Roach; Hal Roach, Jr.

One Million Years B.C. ✂✂ ½ **1966 (R)** It's Welch in a fur bikini and special FX expert Ray Harryhausen doing dinosaurs so who cares about a plot (which involves Welch and her boyfriend, who's from a rival clan). Remake of the 1940 film "One Million B.C." **100m/C; VHS, DVD, Blu-Ray.** *GB* Raquel Welch; John Richardson; Percy Herbert; Robert Brown; Martine Beswick; ***D:*** Don Chaffey.

One Minute to Zero ✂✂ **1952** Korean War action film divides its time between an army romance and war action. The lukwarm melodrama features Mitchum as a colonel in charge of evacuating American civilians but who ends up bombing refugees. **105m/B; VHS, DVD.** Robert Mitchum; Ann Blyth; William Talman; Charles McGraw; Margaret Sheridan; Richard Egan; Eduard Franz; Robert Osterloh; Robert Gist; ***D:*** Tay Garnett.

One Missed Call ✂✂✂ *Chakushin ari* **2003 (R)** Yoko receives a telephone message from 72 hours in the future, hearing herself in her last moments alive. The phone says the call comes from Yoko's own number, and sure enough 72 hours later she's dead. Investigating her friend's death, Yumi finds that Yoko isn't the only one to receive these calls. A vengeful spirit has been creeping onto people's cell phones, and killing those listed in their internal phone books. As Yumi struggles to find out why the killings are occurring, it begins to look like she herself is involved. A surprisingly straightforward Japanese horror film from director Miike. **111m/C; DVD, Blu-Ray.** *JP* Yutaka Matsushige; Goro Kishitani; Kou Shibasaki; Shin'ichi Tsutsumi; Kazue Fukiishi; Anna Nagata; Atsushi Ida; Mariko Tsutsui; Azusa; Karen Oshima; Yuna Mikuni; Renji Ishibashi; ***D:*** Takashi Miike; ***W:*** Yasushi Akimoto; Minako Daira; ***C:*** Hideo Yamamoto; ***M:*** Koji Endo.

One Missed Call WOOF! **2008 (PG-13)** Yet another technophobic Japanese horror remake, this one looking for scares from college students who receive cell phone calls from their future selves that capture the sounds of their own looming deaths. Burns and Cho are cringe-worthy as the good cop/bad cop tandem investigating at the behest of the dewy and earnest co-ed (Sossamon), who also brings a child-abuse subplot into play. Meanwhile, director Valette fails to conjure much oogidy-boogidy, and even the gore is boring. **87m/C; DVD, Blu-Ray.** *GE JP US UK* Shannyn Sossamon; Edward Burns; Ana Claudia Talancon; Ray Wise; Azura Skye; Jason Beghe; Margaret Cho; Meagan Good; ***D:*** Eric Valette; ***W:*** Andrew Klavan; ***C:*** Glen MacPherson; ***M:*** Reinhold Heil; Johnny Klimek.

One Missed Call 2 ✂✂ ½ *Chakushin ari 2* **2005 (R)** The survivors of the first film realize they haven't stopped the curse, which has now achieved urban legend status throughout Asia due to the live television death of a victim in the first film. Instead, it's begun to spread, and they begin to track its origins to the country of Taiwan in an effort to stop the ghost a second time before it manages to kill them. Unfortunately, the film suffers form the curse of being a horror movie sequel with a different director. **106m/C; DVD, Blu-Ray.** *JP* Haruko Wanibuchi; Kathryn Adams; Asako Seto; Karen Oshima; Renji Ishibashi; Peter Ho; ***D:*** Renpei Tsukamoto; ***W:*** Yasushi Akimoto; Minako Daira; ***C:*** Tokusho Kikumura.

One Missed Call 3: Final ✂ ½ *Final Call; One Missed Call Final; Chakushin ari Final* **2006** Asuka (Maki Horikita) is a young schoolgirl bullied by her classmates. On a trip to Korea all of them get a cell phone message from her saying to pass the message on and their life will be spared. No one takes much notice until people start dying then it's a mad rush to betray each other in order to live. **104m/C; DVD, Blu-Ray.** *JP* Maki Horikita; Meisa Kuroki; Yun-seok Jang; Erika Asakura; Yu Kamiwaki; Rie Tsuneyoshi; Arisa Naito; Rakuto Tochihara; Kazuma Yamane; Takashi Yamagata; Takanori Kawamoto; Yuta Ishida; Mami Hashimoto; Miho Amakawa; Sora Matsumoto; Ayumi Taahashi; Suna Ikeda; Ryu Morioka; Kenichi Okana; Haruki Itagashi; Chika Yada; Haruno Inoue; Mayu Sato; Yuki Takayasu; Mina Obata; Yuta Murakami; Ryoto Iwai; ***D:*** Manabu Asao.

One More Kiss ✂✂ **1999** Scottish immigrant Sarah (Edmond) leaves New York to return to her hometown when she learns she's dying from cancer. On her to-do list is getting closer to her father Frank (Cosmo) and spending time with old flame Sam (Butler), which doesn't please his wife Charlotte (Gogan). Tear-jerker, although Sarah comes across as selfish rather than your standard noble character. **98m/C; DVD.** *GB* Valerie Edmond; Gerard Butler; James Cosmo; Valerie Gogan; Carl Proctor; ***D:*** Vadim Jean; ***W:*** Suzie Halewood; ***C:*** Mike J. Fox; ***M:*** David A. Hughes; John Murphy.

One More Time ✂ ½ **1970 (PG)** Lewis' directorial effort is an uneven comedy follow-up to 1968's "Salt & Pepper." Salt (Davis Jr.) and Pepper's (Lawford) nightclub is having money trouble so Pepper goes to his wealthy twin brother Sydney (who lives in the family castle) for some dough. When Sydney is murdered, Pepper assumes his identity and learns that his brother was posing as a smuggler on behalf of Interpol. Then the duo gets chased through the countryside by Interpol agents and crooks after stolen diamonds. **95m/C; DVD.** Peter Lawford; Sammy Davis, Jr.; John Wood; Maggie Wright; Leslie Sands; Esther Anderson; Edward Evans; Sydney Arnold; ***Cameo(s):*** Peter Cushing; Christopher Lee; ***D:*** Jerry Lewis; ***W:*** Michael Pertwee; ***C:*** Ernest Steward; ***M:*** Les Reed.

One More Time ✂✂ **2015** This comedy-drama explores the humanity in a complicated father-daughter relationship. Paul Lombard (Walken) was once a somewhat successful singer in the mold of Frank Sinatra and a much better known ladies man. Now living alone in his mansion in the Hamptons, he must deal with havoc caused by his romantic life. Paul's life becomes more complicated when his daughter Jude (Heard), a punk rocker, comes in need of a place to live. Jude has her own issues, including a tense relationship with her sister, a difficult relationship with Paul, and her own difficult love life. **97m/C; DVD, Streaming, Download.** Christopher Walken; Amber Heard; Kelli Garner; Hamish Linklater; Ann Magnuson; ***D:*** Robert Edwards; ***W:*** Robert Edwards; ***C:*** Anne Etheridge; ***M:*** Joe McGinty. **VIDEO**

One Night at McCool's ✂✂ **2001 (R)** Quirky and inventive pic gets points for effort but the execution doesn't always live up to the ambition. Easygoing bartender Randy (Dillon) is involved in a murder by aggressively materialistic con artist Jewel (Tyler). Then his sleazy lawyer cousin (Reiser) and Det. Dehling (Goodman), who's investigating the murder of Jewel's former partner (Clay), get involved. All three fall in love and we see the preceding night's events through each set of love-struck eyes as they spill their guts to a hitman (Douglas), a shrink (McIntire), and a priest (Jenkins). Douglas's understated portrayal (and outlandish toupee), as well as some fine comic touches by Dillon, are highlights. **93m/C; DVD.** Liv Tyler; Matt Dillon; Paul Reiser; John Goodman; Michael Douglas; Reba McEntire; Richard Jenkins; Andrew Silverstein; Leo Rossi; Eric Schaeffer; ***D:*** Harald Zwart; ***W:*** Stan Seidel; ***C:*** Karl Walter Lindenlaub; ***M:*** Marc Shaiman.

One Night at Susie's ✂ ½ **1930** Sentimental drama finds Susie running a boardinghouse and offering advice to the local gangsters. They help her out with foster son Dick, who goes to prison for a murder committed by showgirl girlfriend Mary. Run times vary depending on the print. **85m/B; DVD.** Helen Ware; Billie Dove; Douglas Fairbanks, Jr.; James Crane; Tully Marshall; ***D:*** John Francis Dillon; ***W:*** Kathryn Scola; Forrest Halsey; ***C:*** Ernest Haller.

One Night in the Tropics ✂✂ ½ **1940** The film debut of radio stars Abbott & Costello who play secondary roles to a love triangle (set to music). Jones is an insurance salesman who falls in love with Kelly, the fiance of Cummings. Based on the novel "Love Insurance" by Earl Derr Biggers. **83m/B; VHS, DVD.** Allan Jones; Robert Cummings; Nancy Kelly; Bud Abbott; Lou Costello; Mary Boland; Peggy Moran; William Frawley; Leo Carrillo; ***D:*** Edward Sutherland; ***W:*** Kathryn Scola; Gertrude Purcell; Charles Grayson; Francis Martin.

One Night Stand ✂✂ ½ **1995 (R)** Lonely Michelle (Sheedy) visits a nightclub and allows herself to be picked up by your basic handsome stranger, Jack (Martinez) in this case. She wakes up alone and learns from building owner Josslyn (Forrest) that the apartment is up for lease. Obsessed with finding her mystery man, Michelle discovers Jack's wife was murdered—possibly by him or maybe by Josslyn, who turns out to be the dead woman's father. Debut feature for director Shire covers familiar territory, with Sheedy giving a strong performance. **92m/C; VHS, DVD.** Ally Sheedy; A. Martinez; Frederic Forrest; Don Novello; Diane Salinger; Millie Slavin; ***D:*** Talia Shire; ***W:*** Marty Casella; ***C:*** Arthur Albert; ***M:*** David Shire.

One Night Stand ✂✂✂ **1997 (R)** Max (Snipes) is in New York on business. While visiting his friend Charlie (Downey), a choreographer dying of AIDS, he meets willowy beauty Karen (Kinski). This leads to, you guessed it, a one night stand. When Max returns home to L.A., he realizes how empty his life is. One year later, he and wife Mimi (Wen) return to visit the quickly fading Charlie. They meet Charlie's brother Vernon (McLachlan) and his wife. . .Karen. Good performances and characterization make this more than a morality play about the ramifications of a sexual fling. Although paid for his original material, Joe Eszterhas didn't take any writing credit after Figgis totally rewrote the script. **103m/C; DVD.** Wesley Snipes; Nastassja Kinski; Ming Na; Robert Downey, Jr.; Kyle MacLachlan; Glenn Plummer; Amanda Donohoe; Thomas Haden Church; Julian Sands; John Ratzenberger; Annabelle Gurwitch; Donovan Leitch; ***D:*** Mike Figgis; ***W:*** Mike Figgis; ***C:*** Declan Quinn; ***M:*** Mike Figgis.

One Night with the King ✂ ½ **2006 (PG)** Re-telling of the Biblical story of Esther, a young Jewish girl who became the savior of her people by marrying the Persian king Xerxes. **123m/C; DVD, Blu-Ray.** Tiffany DuPont; Luke Goss; John Noble; Omar Sharif; John Rhys-Davies; ***D:*** Michael O. Sajbel; ***W:*** Stephen Blinn; ***C:*** Steven Bernstein; ***M:*** J.A.C. Redford.

One of My Wives Is Missing ✂✂ ½ **1976** An ex-New York cop tries to solve the mysterious disappearance of a newlywed socialite. Things become strange when she reappears but is discovered as an imposter. Above-average acting in a film adapted from the play "The Trap for a Lonely Man." **97m/C; DVD.** Jack Klugman; Elizabeth Ashley; James Franciscus; Joel Fabiani; ***D:*** Glenn Jordan; ***W:*** Peter Stone; ***C:*** Archie Dalzell; ***M:*** Billy Goldenberg. **TV**

One of Our Aircraft Is Missing 1/2 **1941** The crew of an R.A.F. bomber downed in the Netherlands, struggle to escape Nazi capture. A thoughtful study of wars and the men who fight them, with an entertaining melodramatic plot. Look for the British version, which runs 106 minutes. Some of the American prints only run 82 minutes. **103m/B; VHS, DVD, Blu-Ray.** *GB* Godfrey Tearle; Eric Portman; Hugh Williams; Pamela Brown; Googie Withers; Peter Ustinov; ***D:*** Emeric Pressburger; Michael Powell; ***W:*** Emeric Pressburger; Michael Powell; ***C:*** Ronald Neame.

One of Our Dinosaurs Is Missing **1975 (G)** An English nanny and her cohorts help British Intelligence retrieve a microfilm—concealing dinosaur fossil from the bad guys that have stolen it. Disney film was shot on location in England. **101m/C; VHS, Streaming.** Peter Ustinov; Helen Hayes; Derek Nimmo; Clive Revill; Joan Sims; ***D:*** Robert Stevenson; ***W:*** Bill Walsh; ***C:*** Paul Beeson; ***M:*** Ronald Goodwin.

One of Them WOOF! **2003 (R)** Really bad dead teen flick. Elizabeth (Carmichael) and her friends are trapped in a school of horrors (Satanism is involved). Uncle Don (Crenna) tries to come to the rescue. **93m/C; DVD.** Richard Anthony Crenna; Kelly Carmichael; Brian Sheridan; Erin Byron; Paul Geffre; ***D:*** Ralph Portillo; ***W:*** David Ciesielski; ***C:*** Keith Holland; ***M:*** Geoff Levin. **VIDEO**

One on One 1/2 **1977 (PG)** A Rocky-esque story about a high school basketball star from the country who accepts an athletic scholarship to a big city university. He encounters a demanding coach and intense competition. Light weight drama that is economically entertaining. **100m/C; VHS, DVD.** Robby Benson; Annette O'Toole; G.D. Spradlin; Gail Strickland; Melanie Griffith; ***D:*** Lamont Johnson; ***W:*** Robby Benson; ***M:*** Charles Fox.

One Perfect Day 1/2 **2004** Tommy (Dan Spielman) and Alysse (Leanna Walsman) split after the death of Tommy's younger sister. He goes on to achieve fame as a DJ, while she spirals into drug induced depression. Inevitably their paths cross again. **105m/C; DVD.** *AU* Dan Spielman; Leeanna Walsman; Nathan Phillips; Leigh Whannell; Abbie Cornish; ***D:*** Paul Currie; ***W:*** Paul Currie; Chip Richards; ***C:*** Gary Ravenscroft; ***M:*** Paul Van Dyk; David Hobson; Josh G. Abrahams. **VIDEO**

One Plus One *Exploring the Kinsey Report* **1961** A dramatization, believe it or not, of the Kinsey sex survey of the 1950s. Participants in a sex lecture talk about and demonstrate various "risque" practices, such as premarital sex and extramarital affairs. Despite this film, the sexual revolution went on as planned. **114m/B; VHS, DVD.** *CA* Leo G. Carroll; Hilda Brawner; William Traylor; Kate Reid; Ernest Graves; ***D:*** Arch Oboler; ***W:*** Arch Oboler.

One Rainy Afternoon **1936** A bit-player kisses the wrong girl in a Paris theatre causing a massive uproar that brands him as a notorious romantic "monster." Patterned after a German film, the story lacks depth and zest. **80m/B; VHS, DVD.** Francis Lederer; Ida Lupino; Hugh Herbert; Roland Young; Donald Meek; ***D:*** Rowland V. Lee.

One Romantic Night **1930** Princess Alexandra falls in love with her brother's plebian tutor Nicholas Haller, much to her mother's horror since she wants her daughter to marry Prince Albert. However, Alexandra knows her royal duty must trump her romantic feelings. Gish's first talkie is an adaptation of Ferenc Molnar's play "The Swan," which was remade in 1956 with Grace Kelly. **73m/B; DVD.** Lillian Gish; Conrad Nagel; Rod La Rocque; Marie Dressler; O.P. Heggie; Albert Conti; ***D:*** Paul Stein; ***W:*** Melville Baker; ***C:*** Karl Struss.

One Shoe Makes It Murder **1982** A shady casino owner hires ex-cop Mitchum to investigate the disappearance of his unfaithful wife. Adapted from Eric Bercovici's novel, the story does little to enhance Mitchum's TV debut. **100m/C; DVD.** Robert Mitchum; Angie Dickinson; Mel Ferrer; Howard Hesseman; Jose Perez; ***D:*** William (Billy) Hale; ***M:*** Bruce Broughton.

One Small Hero 1/2 **1999 (PG)** Dopey family entertainment might not be a complete waste of time for easygoing viewers. Joey Cooper (Kiley) can't pass the tests to become a member of the Wilderness Club and go on their camping trip. He fails once again (he's physically too small) but can't tell his mom after she surprises Joey with camping gear. So, he trails behind the campers and is the only one who can save them from kidnappers. **90m/C; VHS, DVD.** Nathan Kiley; Matthew Peters; Lindsay Lewis; Bonnie Burroughs; ***D:*** Jennifer Malchese; ***C:*** Denis Maloney; ***M:*** Herman Beeftink. **CABLE**

One Special Night 1/2 **1999 (PG)** Robert (Garner) is visiting his Alzheimer's-stricken wife in the hospital and is unable to get a taxi home because of a snowstorm. Doctor Catharine (Andrews) offers him a ride but her car gets stuck on a deserted road and they find shelter in a small cabin. The twosome are drawn to each other during their snowy refuge but will a romance be possible when they rejoin the real world? **90m/C; VHS, DVD.** Julie Andrews; James Garner; Patricia Charbonneau; Stacy Grant; Stewart Bick; ***D:*** Robert M. Young; ***W:*** Nancy Silvers; ***C:*** Guy Dufaux; ***M:*** Richard Bellis. **TV**

One Sunday Afternoon **1933** Told in flashbacks. Biff Grimes (Cooper) and Hugo Barnstead (Hamilton) are romantic rivals for selfish beauty Virginia Brush (Wray) while sweet Amy Lind (Fuller) pines for Biff to notice her. When Virginia and Hugo elope, Biff impulsively marries Amy. The rivalry takes a turn and one of the men goes to jail. Remade in 1941 as "The Strawberry Blonde" and again in 1948 under the original title. **90m/B; DVD.** Gary Cooper; Fay Wray; Frances Fuller; Neil Hamilton; Roscoe Karns; Jane Darwell; ***D:*** Stephen Roberts; ***W:*** Grover Jones; William Slavens McNutt; ***C:*** Victor Milner.

One Sunday Afternoon **1948** Technicolor musical remake of the Jean Hagan play that was previously filmed in 1933 and (by Walsh) as 1941's "The Strawberry Blonde." Turn-of-the-century dentist Biff Grimes (Morgan) loses strawberry blonde beauty Virginia (Paige) to smooth talking Hugo Barnstead (DeFore). They leave town, Biff marries sensible Amy (Malone) instead but pines for Virginia. The couple returns years later and Biff takes a second look at his life. **90m/C; DVD.** Dennis Morgan; Janis Paige; Don DeFore; Dorothy Malone; Alan Hale, Jr.; Ben Blue; ***D:*** Raoul Walsh; ***W:*** Robert L. Richards; ***C:*** Wilfred M. Cline; ***M:*** Ralph Blane.

One That Got Away **1957** A loyal German Luftwaffe pilot captured by the British becomes obsessed with escape. Fast paced and exciting. Based on a true story. **111m/B; DVD.** *UK* Hardy Kruger; Colin Gordon; Alec McCowen; Jack (Gwyllam) Gwillim; ***D:*** Roy Ward Baker; ***W:*** Howard Clewes; ***C:*** Eric Cross; ***M:*** Hubert Clifford.

The One That Got Away **1996** A badly prepared SAS patrol is dropped 300 miles behind enemy lines during the Gulf War to destroy Scud missile launchers that are aimed at Israel. Only when they are under fire, the soldiers discover that they cannot call for reinforcements and things get very bad indeed. Based on a true story. **104m/C; DVD.** *GB* Paul McGann; David Morrissey; Nick Brimble; Simon Burke; Steven Waddington; ***D:*** Paul Greengrass; ***W:*** Paul Greengrass; ***M:*** Barrington Pheloung. **TV**

One Third of a Nation 1/2 **1939** Depression era film contrasts the conditions of slum life with those in high society. A young entrepreneur inherits a city block in ruins, only to fall in love with a young woman who lives there and help her crippled brother. Timely social criticism. **79m/B; Streaming.** Sylvia Sidney; Leif Erickson; Myron McCormick; Sidney Lumet; ***D:*** Dudley Murphy; ***W:*** Oliver H.P. Garrett; ***C:*** William Miller; ***M:*** Nathaniel Shilkert.

1,000 Plane Raid 1/2 **1969** In 1943, U.S. Air Force Col. Greg Brandon (George) convinces the Allies to commit to a huge daylight bombing raid on Cologne, Germany. He also demands that the less-successful nightly bombing operations continue. His dangerous plan is approved but there are conflicts as Brandon's obsession is a problem for even his own men. **94m/C; DVD.** Christopher George; Gary Marshal; Ben Murphy; Bo Hopkins; Tim McIntire; J.D. Cannon; James Gammon; Gavin MacLeod; ***D:*** Boris Sagal; ***W:*** Donald S. Sanford; ***C:*** William W. Spencer; ***M:*** Jimmie Haskell.

1000 Rupee Note *Ek Hazarachi Note* **2016** A dramatic exploration of poverty, money, and conscience in India. In a small village in the Indian state of Maharashtra, the aged Budhi (Naik) is alone in the world. Her husband is dead and her son committed suicide over debt related to his farm. Despite these tragedies, she has happiness and finds comfort in her friendship with a neighbor, Sudma (Pathak). After a local politician (Yadav) presents Budhi with a 1000 rupee note at an election rally, her life is soon changed forever. She takes Sudma shopping at a nearby market but events there show that the politician's gift is a mixed blessing. Marathi with subtitles. **89m/C; DVD, Streaming, Download.** Usha Naik; Sandeep Pathak; Pooja Nayak; Ganesh Yadav; Devendra Gaikwad; ***D:*** Shrihari Sathe; ***W:*** Shrikant Bojewar; ***C:*** Ming-Kai Leung; ***M:*** Shailendra Barve.

1,000 Years From Now *Captive Women* **1952** Typical 50s sci fi set in a post-nuclear, rubble-strewn Manhattan in the year 3,000. Three tribes of humans are trying to survive: the brutal tunnel-living Upriver people, the cave-dwelling Norms, and the scarred-but-peaceful surface-living Mutes. With the Upriver tribe gone in a flood, it's up to the Norms and the Mutes to make sure mankind continues. **67m/B; DVD.** Margaret Field; Ron Randell; Robert Clarke; Gloria Saunders; Stuart Randall; Robert Bice; William Schallert; ***D:*** Stuart Gilmore; ***W:*** Aubrey Wisberg; Jack Pollexfen; ***C:*** Paul Ivano; ***M:*** Charles Koff.

1001 Arabian Nights 1/2 **1959** In this Arabian nightmare, the nearsighted Mr. Magoo is known as "Azziz" Magoo, lamp dealer and uncle of Aladdin. **76m/C; VHS, DVD.** ***V:*** Jim Backus; Kathryn Grant; Hans Conried; Herschel Bernardi; ***D:*** Jack Kinney; ***M:*** George Duning.

One to Another 1/2 *Chacun sa Nuit* **2006** Lucie investigates the beating death of her troubled bisexual brother Pierre, a member of a rock band made up of equally beautiful and bored teenagers. More of an excuse for bed-hopping and showing off good-looking bodies than a true murder mystery. French with subtitles. **95m/C; DVD.** *FR* Pierre Perrier; Valerie Mairesse; Lizzie Brochere; Arthur Dupont; Guillame Bache; Nicolas Nollet; ***D:*** Jean-Marc Barr; Pascal Arnold; ***W:*** Pascal Arnold; ***C:*** Jean-Marc Barr; ***M:*** Irina Decermic.

One Too Many *The Important Story of Alcoholism; Killer With a Label* **1951** Exploitation film depicting the evils of alcoholism. Campy, but slick. **110m/B; VHS, DVD.** Ruth Warrick; Richard Travis; Victor Kilian; Onslow Stevens; Lyle Talbot; ***D:*** Erle C. Kenton; ***W:*** Malcolm Stuart Boylan; ***C:*** Carl Berger; ***M:*** Bert Shefter.

One Touch of Venus 1/2 **1948** Love fills a department store when a window dresser kisses a statue of the goddess Venus—and she comes to life. Appealing adaptation of the Broadway musical. **82m/B; VHS, DVD, Blu-Ray.** Ava Gardner; Robert Walker; Eve Arden; Dick Haymes; Olga San Juan; Tom Conway; ***D:*** William A. Seiter; ***W:*** Harry Kurnitz; Frank Tashlin; ***C:*** Franz Planer; ***M:*** Kurt Weill.

One Tough Cop **1998 (R)** Headstrong NYPD detective Bo Dietl (Baldwin) and his partner Finnerty (Penn) investigate the brutal rape and mutilation of a nun in East Harlem. Despite Brazilian director Barreto's good eye for the mean streets of New York and Baldwin's stellar performance, this is just one more derivative police drama. Barreto's wife Irving makes an appearance as a mean-spirited federal agent. Based on the autobiography on real-life retired cop Dietl. **94m/C; DVD.** Stephen Baldwin; Gina Gershon; Christopher Penn; Mike McGlone; Paul Guilfoyle; Amy Irving; Victor Slezak; Luis Guzman; ***D:*** Bruno Barreto; ***W:*** Jeremy Iacone; ***C:*** Ron Fortunato; ***M:*** Bruce Broughton.

One Trick Pony 1/2 **1980 (R)** Once-popular rock singer/songwriter struggles to keep his head above water in a turbulent marriage and in the changing currents of popular taste. Simon wrote the autobiographical screenplay and score, but let's hope he is more sincere in real life. A good story. **100m/C; VHS, DVD.** Paul Simon; Blair Brown; Rip Torn; Joan Hackett; Mare Winningham; Lou Reed; Harry Shearer; Allen Garfield; Daniel Stern; ***D:*** Robert M. Young; ***C:*** Dick Bush.

One True Thing **1998 (PG-13)** Better check for the family-sized box of tissues before you take home this tearjerker about cancer-stricken mother Kate (Streep) and her relationship with arrogant, career-oriented daughter Ellen (Zellweger). After being guilted by her stuffy college professor dad (Hurt), Ellen agrees to care for Kate as the disease progresses and the two bridge their emotional distance. Lifted above the disease-of-the-week material by the presence of stars Streep and Hurt, and by the stellar performance of Zellweger. Based on the novel by Anna Quindlen. **128m/C; DVD, Blu-Ray.** Meryl Streep; Renée Zellweger; William Hurt; Tom Everett Scott; Nicky Katt; Lauren Graham; James Eckhouse; Patrick Breen; Gerrit Graham; ***D:*** Carl Franklin; ***W:*** Karen Croner; ***C:*** Declan Quinn; ***M:*** Cliff Eidelman.

One, Two, Three 1/2 **1961** Cagney, an American Coca-Cola exec in Germany, zealously pursues any opportunity to run Coke's European operations. He does this by promising to keep an eye on the boss's wild daughter, who promptly falls for an East German Communist. Fast-paced laughs, wonderful cinematography, and a fine score. **110m/B; VHS, DVD, Blu-Ray.** James Cagney; Horst Buchholz; Arlene Francis; Pamela Tiffin; ***D:*** Billy Wilder; ***W:*** Billy Wilder; I.A.L. Diamond; ***C:*** Daniel F. Fapp; ***M:*** Andre Previn.

One Way 1/2 **2006** Ad exec Eddie Schneider (Schweiger) is a womanizer despite his engagement to his boss' daughter Judy (von Pfetten). He's also always ready to put his career first even if it means lying so that his friend Angelina's (Smith) rapist Anthony (Roberts) is acquitted since Anthony is Judy's psycho brother. **117m/C; DVD.** Til Schweiger; Lauren Lee Smith; Stefanie von Pfetten; Sebastien Roberts; Art Hindle; Eric Roberts; Sonja Smits; Michael Clarke Duncan; ***D:*** Reto Salimbeni; ***W:*** Reto Salimbeni; ***C:*** Paul Sarossy; Mark Willis; ***M:*** Dirk Reichardt; Stefan Hansen.

One Way Out **1995** Frank (Gwaltney) gets out of jail, teams up with Bobby (Monahan) and his stripper girlfriend Eve (Golden), and the trio go to visit Frank's brother, Snooky (Turano). When Frank learns that Snooky's lowlife boss (Ironside) has been ripping him off, they plan to even the score. Naturally, the heist goes wrong and they wind up with a hostage (Gillies) and on the lam. **106m/C; VHS, DVD.** Jack Gwaltney; Jeff Monahan; Annie Golden; Robert Turano; Michael Ironside; Isabel Gillies; ***D:*** Kevin Lynn.

One Way Out **2002 (R)** Detective Harry Woltz (Belushi) is lax on the morality issues and has some gambling debts to the wrong people. They suggest Harry show unhappy hubby John Farrow (Bateman) how to murder his wife and get away with it. As an added incentive, they threaten Harry's girlfriend and partner, Gwen (Featherstone). But the subsequent murder investigation finds the evidence pointing Harry's way. **87m/C; VHS, DVD.** *CA* James Belushi; Jason Bateman; Angela Featherstone; Jack Langedijk; ***D:*** Allan Goldstein; ***W:*** John Salvati; ***C:*** Sylvain Brault. **VIDEO**

One Way Passage 1/2 **1932** Joan Ames (Francis) is dying and decides to spend her last days having fun aboard a cruise ship. She meets cute Dan Hardesty (Powell) but keeps her illness a secret from him. Dan's got a big secret of his own: he's an escaped killer being returned to San Francisco for execution by Steve (Hymer), who begins his own flirtation with con woman Betty (MacMahon). Betty and fellow con man Skippy (McHugh) hope to help Dan escape but when he learns of Joan's condition, he refuses to abandon her. **68m/B; VHS, DVD.** Kay Francis; William Powell; Aline MacMahon; Frank McHugh; Warren Hymer; Frederick Burton; ***D:*** Tay Garnett; ***W:*** Robert Lord; Wilson Mizner; Joe Jackson; ***C:*** Robert B. Kurrle.

One Way to Valhalla 1/2 **2009** Working-class Bo Durant (Macht) has his beloved 1970 Plymouth Barracuda impounded after he's arrested for drunk driving. He's forced to ride his stepdaughter Dale's (Pill) bike to work, is hit by a car, and suffers a serious head injury. This alters Bo's already volatile personality and alienates his wife and friends. The only one who's sympathetic is Dale, but when she tries to protect Bo, their lives take some unexpected turns. **94m/C; DVD.** Gabriel Macht; Alison Pill; Kim Dickens; Brad William Henke; Kate Walsh; *D:* Karen Goodman; *W:* Karen Goodman; *C:* John J. Campbell; *M:* Dave Nelson. **VIDEO**

One Week 🦴 ½ **2008** School teacher Ben Tyler (Jackson) learns he has stage four cancer. Deciding to delay debilitating treatment, he impulsively buys a motorcycle, leaves his fiancee (Balaban) behind in Toronto, and takes off on a trip across Canada as a distraction and perhaps a final chance at self-discovery. Hits all the Canadian signposts—Tim Horton's and the Stanley Cup among them—but the pic turns out to be as bland and amiable as its lead. **94m/C; DVD.** *CA* Joshua Jackson; Liane Balaban; Fiona Reid; Chuck Shamata; Emm Gryner; *Nar:* Campbell Scott; *D:* Michael McGowan; *W:* Michael McGowan; *C:* Arthur E. Cooper; *M:* Andrew Lockington.

One Wonderful Sunday 🦴🦴 *Subarashiki Nichiyobi* **1947** It's postwar Tokyo, so just how wonderful can things be? Well, perky Masako (Nakakita) is determined to make the day as bright as possible for her depressed fiance, Yuzo (Numasaki), despite the fact they have no money and can't afford to do much more than walk around together. More of a curiosity in Kurosawa's oeuvre than a substantial work. Japanese with subtitles. **108m/B; VHS, DVD.** *JP* Chieko Nakakita; Isao Numasaki; *D:* Akira Kurosawa; *W:* Akira Kurosawa; Keinosuke Uegusa; *C:* Asakazu Nakai; *M:* Tadashi Hattori.

Onegin 🦴🦴 **1999** Fiennes family affair, with Martha assuming directorial duties, brother Magnus providing the score, and Ralph starring as the titular 18th-century Russian aristocrat. The cynical sophisticate inherits a vast country estate in the 1820s, where Onegin befriends his young neighbor Lensky (Stephens) and his featherbrained fiancee, Olga (Headey). But Onegin is intrigued by Olga's older sister, lovely innocent Tatyana (Tyler), though he rejects her impulsive romantic gestures. This isn't the only mistake that Onegin makes—all of which cost him dearly. Film looks beautiful but doesn't have much soul. Based on the Aleksandr Pushkin novel "Eugene Onegin." **106m/C; DVD.** *UK* Ralph Fiennes; Liv Tyler; Toby Stephens; Lena Headey; Martin Donovan; Alun Armstrong; Harriet Walter; Irene Worth; Francesca Annis; *D:* Martha Fiennes; *W:* Peter Ettedgui; Michael Ignatieff; *C:* Remi Adefarasin; *M:* Magnus Fiennes.

101 Reykjavik 🦴🦴 **2000** Icelandic comedy about a slacker and his mom. The slacker is the pushing 30 Hlynur (Gudnason) who lives with indulgent mom Berglind (Karlsdottir). He's cynical, jobless and unambitious (though not unintelligent). Then Berglind invites her Spanish friend Lola (Abril), who's teaching flamenco at the local dance school, to stay. Hylnur falls for the hottie bigtime and they have a drunken New Year's Eve fling while Berglind is away—and before she manages to tell her son that Lola is her own lover. And then Lola finds out she's pregnant. Oh, the complications! Icelandic and English dialogue. **90m/C; VHS, DVD.** *IC DK FR NO* Hilmir Snaer Guonason; Victoria Abril; Baltasar Kormakur; Hanna Maria Karlsdottir; Olafur Darri Olafsson; Pruour Vilhjalmsdottir; *D:* Baltasar Kormakur; *W:* Baltasar Kormakur; *C:* Peter Stueger; *M:* Damon Albarn; Einar Orn Benediktsson.

The Ones Below 🦴 **2016 (R)** Pregnant women are crazy, right? Poesy plays Kate, a young Londoner about to have a child with Justin (Campbell Moore). Another couple with a pregnant spouse (Birn & Morrissey) moves in downstairs, but the female half of that partnership loses her baby. Then things get really weird, especially after they blame Kate and Justin for the baby's death. It's all well-made, but one can't shake the feeling that it's gross to riff on miscarriage and postpartum depression as thriller devices. **86m/C; DVD, Blu-Ray.** Clemence Poesy; David Morrissey; Stephen Campbell Moore; Laura Birn; Deborah Findlay; *D:* David Farr; *W:* David Farr; *C:* Ed Rutherford; *M:* Adem Ilhan.

Ong-Bak 🦴🦴🦴 **2003 (R)** Over-the-top action is the centerpiece of this breakthrough Thai martial arts film. Loose-cannon Thai kickboxer Ting (Jaa) travels to Bangkok in search of the stolen head to his tiny village's Buddha. Mayhem ensues. What little plot exists is just a vehicle for superb action sequences that are exceptionally violent yet highly inventive, especially when one considers that all the action was filmed without digital effects, wires, or other modern-day trickery. The result is a 70's-style martial-arts movie for the modern era, refreshingly real and a heck of a lot of fun. Thai with English subtitles. **107m/C; DVD, Blu-Ray.** *TH* Tony Jaa; Wannakit Siriput; Sukhaaw Phongwilai; Petchthai Wongkamlao; Pumwaree Yodkamol; Rungrawee Borrijindakul; *D:* Prachya Pinkaew; *W:* Suphachai Sithiamphian; *C:* Nattawut Kittikhun; *M:* Atomix Clubbing.

Ong Bak 2 🦴🦴 *Ong Bak: The Beginning* **2008 (R)** Set several hundred years in Thailand's past, when it was still known as Siam, Tien (Jaa) is a young orphan whose parents have been murdered. After beating up a crocodile, he is adopted by a band of thieves/martial arts masters and taught various fighting styles with the goal of merging them into one superior style. Eventually he learns of an opportunity for revenge and it's bone-crunching time. There's no real plot or character development, but no one is really looking for those in a martial arts revenge movie. Thai with subtitles. **115m/C; DVD, Blu-Ray.** *TH* Tony Jaa; Sorapong Chatree; Sarunyu Wongkrachang; Nirut Sirichanya; Dan Chupong; Santisuk Promsiri; Primorata Dejudom; *D:* Tony Jaa; Panna Rittikrai; *W:* Panna Rittikrai; *C:* Nattawhut Khittikhun; *M:* Terdsak Janpan.

Onibaba 🦴🦴🦴 *The Demon; The Devil Woman* **1964** A brutal parable about a mother and her daughter-in-law in war-ravaged medieval Japan who subsist by murdering stray soldiers and selling their armor. One soldier beds the daughter, setting the mother-in-law on a vengeful tirade. Review of the film varied widely, hailed by some as a masterpiece and by others as below average; in Japanese with subtitles. **103m/B; VHS, DVD.** *JP* Nobuko Otowa; Jitsuko Yoshimura; Kei Sato; *D:* Kaneto Shindo.

The Onion Field 🦴🦴🦴 ½ **1979 (R)** True story about the mental breakdown of an ex-cop who witnessed his partner's murder. Haunted by the slow process of justice and his own feelings of insecurity, he is unable to get his life together. Based on the novel by Joseph Wambaugh, who also wrote the screenplay. Compelling script and excellent acting. **126m/C; VHS, DVD, Blu-Ray.** John Savage; James Woods; Ronny Cox; Franklyn Seales; Ted Danson; David Huffman; Christopher Lloyd; Dianne Hull; Priscilla Pointer; Richard Venture; William Sanderson; Michael Pataki; *D:* Harold Becker; *W:* Eric Roth; *C:* Charles Rosher, Jr.; *M:* Eumir Deodato.

Onionhead 🦴 ½ **1958** Weak military comedy starring Griffith. Irresponsible Alvin Woods enlists in the Coast Guard after fighting with gal Josephine (O'Brien). He's assigned to be the junior cook aboard the U.S.S. Periwinkle under the tutelage of hostile Red (Matthau). Things get worse for Alvin because Red's would-be fiancée, Stella (Farr), makes eyes at Alvin. But all that is left behind after Pearl Harbor as the pic takes a serious turn when the Periwinkle must come to the aid of a battered ship and Alvin is forced to mature. **110m/B; DVD.** Andy Griffith; Walter Matthau; Felicia Farr; Ray Danton; Joey Bishop; Claude Akins; James Gregory; Erin O'Brien; *D:* Norman Taurog; *W:* Nelson Gidding; *C:* Harold Rosson; *M:* David Buttolph.

Only 🦴🦴 **2020** A mysterious ash falls upon the earth, delivering a virus that kills only females. Eva (Pinto) and Will (Odom) quarantine themselves in their apartment as a defense against both the bug and women-targeting bounty hunters, but when the isolation drives them crazy, they venture outdoors. It's well-acted yet hampered by a small budget, making it more a post-apocalyptic character study than a true thriller. **98m/C; DVD.** Freida Pinto; Leslie Odom, Jr.; Chandler Riggs; Jayson Warner Smith; Joshua Mikel; *D:* Takashi Doscher; *W:* Takashi Doscher; *C:* Sean Stiegemeier; *M:* John Kaefer; Michael Dean Parsons.

Only Angels Have Wings 🦴🦴🦴🦴 **1939** Melodramatic adventure about a broken-down Peruvian air mail service. Large cast adds to the love tension between Grant, a pilot, and Arthur, a showgirl at the saloon. Nominated for special effects, a category recognized by the Academy that year for the first time. William Rankin and Eleanor Griffin are uncredited writers. **121m/B; VHS, DVD, Blu-Ray.** Cary Grant; Thomas Mitchell; Richard Barthelmess; Jean Arthur; Noah Beery, Jr.; Rita Hayworth; Sig Rumann; John Carroll; Allyn Joslyn; *D:* Howard Hawks; *W:* Jules Furthman; *C:* Joseph Walker; *M:* Dimitri Tiomkin. Natl. Film Reg. '17.

Only God Forgives 🦴 ½ **2013 (R)** Stylized crime drama that is more style than substance. American fugitive Julian (Gosling) has spent a decade in Bangkok where he operates a boxing club and a drug smuggling business. Julian's life is turned upside down when his brother Billy (Burke) is murdered there by after he savagely killed an underage prostitute. Their mother, Crystal (Thomas), comes to claim Billy's body and seek vengeance for his death. Crystal is the head of a major international crime syndicate and demands the names of Billy's killers. At the same time, Julian must handle Chang (Pansringarm), a retired policeman who has taken it upon himself to clean up the city's brothels and other illegal underground enterprises as the Angel of Vengeance. **90m/C; DVD, Blu-Ray, Streaming.** *DK FR* Ryan Gosling; Kristin Scott Thomas; Vithaya Pansringarm; Tom Burke; Yayaying Rhatha Phongam; *D:* Nicolas Winding Refn; *W:* Nicolas Winding Refn; *C:* Larry Smith; *M:* Cliff Martinez.

The Only Living Boy in New York 🦴 ½ **2017 (R)** A polished coming-of-age drama of style but little substance as it observes the semi-interesting lives of its New York elite characters. Recent college grad Thomas Webb (Turner) uncovers an unexpected truth about his parents' marriage when he learns his father, Ethan (Brosnan) is involved with the much younger Johanna (Beckinsale). Furious Thomas' efforts to fix the situation have unintended consequences for everyone involved. Through the turmoil, Thomas finds solace in the guidance given by his opinionated neighbor, W.F. Gerald (Bridges). Despite a smart ensemble and tasteful attempts at depth, the film's exploration of family life and lonely relationships could have been so much more. **89m/C; DVD, Blu-Ray.** Callum Turner; Jeff Bridges; Kate Beckinsale; Pierce Brosnan; Cynthia Nixon; *D:* Marc Webb; *W:* Allan Loeb; *C:* Stuart Dryburgh; *M:* Ron Simonsen.

Only Love 🦴 ½ *Erich Segal's Only Love* **1998** Sappy made for TV romance adapted from the Segal novel. Neurosurgeon Matthew Heller (Morrow) is shocked by the reappearance of former fiancee Silvia Rinaldi (May) some 15 years after they broke up. She's dying of a brain tumor and needs his medical help. His longtime (platonic) female friend Evie (Tomei) can't understand his obsession and you won't either. (The scenery's nice though). **130m/C; VHS, DVD.** Rob Morrow; Marisa Tomei; Mathilda May; Jeroen Krabbe; Paul Freeman; Georges Corraface; *D:* John Erman; *W:* Gerald Christopher; *M:* John Morris. **TV**

Only Lovers Left Alive 🦴🦴 ½ **2013 (R)** Director/writer Jarmusch brings his unique vision to this unusual vampire tale of two people who have been alive for centuries and are getting a little bored by the passage of time. The amazing Hiddleston and Swinton play the perfectly named Adam and Eve, respectively, in a saga that spans from Detroit to Tangier. They have a relatively stable existence that falls apart when Eve's fiercely unruly sister Ava (Wasikowska) reappears on the scene. Can Adam and Eve find meaning in a life that never ends? Slow, for sure, but often mesmerizing. **123m/C; DVD.** *UK US GE* Tilda Swinton; Tom Hiddleston; Mia Wasikowska; Anton Yelchin; John Hurt; Jeffrey Wright; *D:* Jim Jarmusch; *W:* Jim Jarmusch; *C:* Yorick Le Saux; *M:* Jozef Van Wissem.

Only the Brave 🦴🦴 **2006 (R)** Patriotism triumphs over social prejudice in Nishikawa's feature directorial debut about a heroic all-volunteer WWII infantry unit, comprised of Hawaiian Nisei and Japanese-American internment camp residents, who were sent to North Africa, Italy, and France to fight. A tight budget and some too-modern dialogue as well as cliched war situations lessen the inspirational impact. **97m/C; DVD.** Jason Scott Lee; Mark Dacascos; Yuji Okumoto; Tamlyn Tomita; Greg Watanabe; Lane Nishikawa; Ken Narasaki; *D:* Lane Nishikawa; *W:* Lane Nishikawa; *C:* Michael G. Wojciechowski; *M:* Dan Kuramato; Kimo Cornwell. **VIDEO**

Only the Brave 🦴🦴🦴 **2017 (PG-13)** A disaster film centered on an Arizona firefighting crew known as the Granite Mountain Hotshots, based on a true story. Prescott, Arizona, fire chief Eric Marsh (Brolin) wants his municipal fire squad to be the first one certified as hotshots (elite forest firefighters). Despite a training error by Marsh, the group gains certification and becomes local heroes after fighting a series of fires, including the serious Yarnell Hill blaze. However, the cost of being part of the hotshots is high for all involved. An emotional and genuine portrayal of the men, their lives, and all that was lost. **133m/C; Blu-Ray, Streaming.** Josh Brolin; Miles Teller; Jeff Bridges; Jennifer Connelly; James Badge Dale; *D:* Joseph Kosinski; *W:* Ken Nolan; Eric Warren Singer; *C:* Claudio Miranda; *M:* Joseph Trapanese.

Only the Lonely 🦴🦴 ½ **1991 (PG)** Middle-aged cop, Candy, falls in love with a shy undertaker's assistant, Sheedy, and is torn between love and dear old Mom, O'Hara, in her first role in years. Candy is an unlikely leading man and even the jokes are forced. But the restaurant scene makes the whole thing well worth seeing. **104m/C; VHS, DVD.** John Candy; Ally Sheedy; Maureen O'Hara; Anthony Quinn; Kevin Dunn; James Belushi; Milo O'Shea; Bert Remsen; Macaulay Culkin; Joe V. Greco; *D:* Chris Columbus; *W:* Chris Columbus; *M:* Maurice Jarre.

Only the Strong 🦴 ½ **1993 (PG-13)** Louis (Dacascos) is a special forces officer who has mastered capoeira, a Brazilian form of kung fu. In Miami, he works with his old teacher (Lewis) to instill discipline in the 12 toughest punks in school by teaching them his martial arts skills. A neighborhood drug lord, related to two of the students, decides to cause trouble for Louis. Dascascos displays some charm along with his physical abilities but the story's ridiculous and the movie hastily put together. **96m/C; VHS, DVD.** Mark Dacascos; Stacey Travis; Todd Susman; Geoffrey Lewis; Paco Christian Prieto; *D:* Sheldon Lettich; *W:* Sheldon Lettich; Luis Esteban; *M:* Harvey W. Mason.

Only the Strong Survive 🦴🦴🦴 **2003 (PG-13)** Documentary filmmakers Hegedus and Pennebaker showcase R&B and soul legends of the late fifties to the early seventies in where-are-they-now features and in concert performances, including a number of performers from Memphis and Stax-Volt Records. Featured are Carla and Rufus Thomas, Issac Hayes, William Bell, the Chi-Lites, Jerry Butler, Sam Moore, Ann Peebles, Wilson Pickett, and Mary Wilson. **95m/C; DVD.** *D:* Chris Hegedus; D.A. Pennebaker; *C:* Chris Hegedus; D.A. Pennebaker; James Desmond; Nick Doob; Jehane Noujaim.

Only the Valiant 🦴🦴 **1950** Action-packed story of a cavalry officer who struggles to win his troops respect while warding off angry Apaches. Fast-paced Western fun requires little thought. **105m/B; DVD, Blu-Ray.** Gregory Peck; Ward Bond; Gig Young; Lon Chaney, Jr.; Barbara Payton; Neville Brand; *D:* Gordon Douglas; *W:* Edmund H. North; Harry Brown; *C:* Lionel Lindon; *M:* Franz Waxman.

The Only Thrill 🦴🦴 ½ *Tennessee Valley* **1997** Old-fashioned small town romance based on Ketron's play "The Trading Post." In 1966, Reece McHenry (Shepard) decides to open a used clothing store in his Tennessee hometown and hires widowed seamstress Carol Fitzsimmons (Keaton) to help him out. Reece is married but his wife is in an irreversible coma and soon the aw-shucks storekeeper is interested in romancing his new employee. Meanwhile, Reece's son Tom (Patrick) and Carol's daughter Katherine (Lane) have also discovered a reciprocated love. However, neither romance runs smoothly. **108m/C; DVD.** Sam Shepard; Diane Keaton; Robert Patrick; Diane Lane; Tate Donovan; Sharon Lawrence; Stacey Travis; *D:* Peter

Masterson; **W:** Larry Ketron; **C:** Don E. Fauntleroy; **M:** Peter Melnick.

The Only Way 1/2 **1970 (G)** A semi-documentary account of the plight of the Jews in Denmark during the Nazi occupation. Despite German insistence, the Danes succeeded in saving most of their Jewish population from the concentration camps. **86m/C; VHS, DVD.** Jane Seymour; Martin Potter; Benjamin Christiansen; **M:** Carl Davis.

Only When I Laugh *It Hurts Only When I Laugh* **1981 (R)** Neil Simon reworked his Broadway flop "The Gingerbread Lady" to produce this poignant comedy about the relationship between an aging alcoholic actress and her teenage daughters. **120m/C; VHS, Streaming.** Marsha Mason; Kristy McNichol; James Coco; Joan Hackett; David Dukes; Kevin Bacon; John Bennett Perry; **D:** Glenn Jordan; **W:** Neil Simon; **M:** David Shire. Golden Globes '82: Support. Actress (Hackett).

Only with Married Men **1974** Carne's hassle-free dating routine is disrupted when a sly bachelor pretends that he's married to get a date. A middle-aged persons answer to a teenage sex comedy. Pretty bad. **74m/C; DVD.** David Birney; Judy Carne; Gavin MacLeod; John Astin; Michele Lee; Dom DeLuise; **D:** Jerry Paris; **W:** Jerry Davis; **C:** Tim Southcott; **M:** Jack Elliott. **TV**

Only Yesterday *Omohide poro poro* **2016 (PG)** First produced in 1991, this animated film showcases 27-year-old Taeko, a Tokyo office worker who in 1982 visits the countryside, where she flashes back to her childhood in the 1960s and gains insight to the life she might have had. A beautiful and timeless story, thankfully (finally) shared with U.S. audiences in 2016. **118m/C; DVD.** Daisy Ridley; Dev Patel; Alison Fernandez; Hope Levy; Stephanie Sheh; **D:** Isao Takahata; **W:** Isao Takahata; **C:** Hisao Shirai; **M:** Katsu Hoshi.

Only You 1/2 **1992 (PG-13)** A shy guy has always searched for true romance. But his cup runneth over when he meets, and must choose between, two beautiful women—your basic beach babe and a sensible beauty. What's a guy to do? **85m/C; DVD.** Andrew McCarthy; Kelly Preston; Helen Hunt; **D:** Betty Thomas; **W:** Wayne Allan Rice; **C:** Bryan England; **M:** Peter Melnick.

Only You 1/2 *Him; Just in Time* **1994 (PG)** According to her ouija board, young Faith's (Tomei) soul mate is named Damon Bradley. But as the years pass, Faith is about to settle for a podiatrist—until an old school friend of her fiance's calls from Venice, Italy, with best wishes. Guess what his name is. So Faith and best friend Kate (Hunt) hop on a plane in search of Mr. Right. Then Faith meets charming shoe salesman Peter Wright (Downey) and wonders if ouija got things wrong. Slight romantic comedy with Jewison creating satisfactory chemistry with charming Downey and the somewhat miscast Tomei (and the Venetian scenery is gorgeous). **108m/C; VHS, DVD.** Marisa Tomei; Robert Downey, Jr.; Bonnie Hunt; Fisher Stevens; Billy Zane; Joaquim de Almeida; **D:** Norman Jewison; **W:** Diane Drake; **C:** Sven Nykvist; **M:** Rachel Portman.

Onmyoji *Onmyoji: The Yin Yang Master; The Yin Yang Masters* **2001 (R)** Onmyodo is a traditional Japanese form of occultism based on Chinese philosophy and influenced by Japanese culture and religion. Its professional practitioners were called the Onmyoji. Abe no Seimei is asked by a bumbling court noble to defend the emperor from an evil Onmyoji who is unleashing a horde of Yokai (spirit monsters) to bring about the government's downfall. Originally a novel, it became a comic and then a highly stylized film. With its strong cultural overtones most Western audiences will miss a lot of subtext if they aren't familiar with the Heian period of Japanese history. **116m/C; DVD, UMD.** *JP* Kenichi Yajima; Kenjiro Ishimaru; Houka Kinoshita; Akira (Tsukamoto) Emoto; Ittoku Kishibe; Hiroyuki (Henry) Sanada; Sachiko Kokubu; Mansai Nomura; Hideaki Ito; Eriko Imai; **D:** Yojiro Takita; **W:** Baku Yumemakura; **C:** Naoki Kayano; **M:** Shigeru Kumebayashi.

Onmyoji 2 **2003** The forces of the Daimyo brutally slaughter a small village, and a hidden priest invokes an ancient god to take revenge. Many years later, after a solar eclipse, mysterious events happen in the Heian capital. Demons are murdering members of the nobility by biting off parts of their body, and once again the famous Abe no Seimei is called upon to solve the problem. This sequel is more cinematic, and probably more accessible to viewers who aren't natives of Japan. **113m/C; DVD.** *JP* Mansai Nomura; Hideaki Ito; Eriko Imai; Kenji Yamaki; Kiichi Nakai; Kyoko Fukada; Hayato Ichihara; Yuko Kategawa; **D:** Yojiro Takita; **W:** Yojiro Takita; Baku Yumemakura; **C:** Harry Henderson; **M:** Shigeru Kumebayashi.

Onward **2020 (PG)** In suburbia, two teenage elf brothers have 24 hours to find a magical spell that will reunite them with their father, who died when they were young. In typical Pixar form, this animated family flick delivers heart and humor, even if this release isn't destined to be a classic. **102m/C; DVD, Blu-Ray.** **V:** Tom Holland; Chris Pratt; Julia Louis-Dreyfus; Octavia Spencer; Mel Rodriguez; **D:** Dan Scanlon; **W:** Dan Scanlon; Jason Headley; Keith Bunin; **C:** Sharon Calahan; Adam Habib; **M:** Jeff Danna.

The Oogieloves in the Big Balloon Adventure WOOF! 2012 (G) Tiny tots who like Barney may be persuaded to watch this interactive adventure that features three over-sized, primary-colored puppet kids while adults will likely cringe in disbelief. Gobie, Zoozie, and Toofie must recover the five magic balloons they got for their friend Schloofy's birthday. This leads them to some song-and-dance sequences that feature some really game actors. Actually filmed in 2009 with producer Kenn Viselman deciding to self-distribute his kid-friendly effort. **88m/C; DVD.** Christopher Lloyd; Jaime Pressly; Cary Elwes; Cloris Leachman; Chazz Palminteri; Toni Braxton; **D:** Matthew Diamond; **W:** Scott Stabile; **C:** Peter Klein; **M:** Joseph Alfuso; Robert Rettberg.

Opa! 1/2 **2005** Derivative romance with familiar characters. American archeologist Eric (Modine) wants to fulfill his deceased father's dream of finding the chalice of St. John the Divine. He's certain it's in a long-buried church that lies beneath a popular restaurant on the Greek isle of Patmos. Vivacious widowed mom Katerina (Scott) owns the place and takes a shine to the awkward Eric, who needs to makes a decision about what matters most. **93m/C; DVD.** *GB GR* Matthew Modine; Richard Griffiths; Alki David; Agni Scott; Hristos Valavanidis; **D:** Udayan Prasad; **W:** Raman Singh; Christina Concetta; **C:** Haris Zambarloukos; **M:** Stephen Warbeck.

Open Cam 1/2 *OpenCam* **2005** Lots of skin, but not too much mystery or plot logic in this gay crime thriller. A D.C. serial killer finds his victims through an adult webcam site, all of whom are somehow connected to aspiring artist Manny. Police detective Hamilton is investigating while behaving in a decidedly unprofessional manner with his protagonist. **100m/C; DVD.** Andreau Thomas; Amir Darvish; Ben Green; J. Matthew Miller; Christian Jones; **D:** Robert Gaston; **W:** Robert Gaston; **C:** Doug Gritzmacher; **M:** Jerry Walterick.

Open City *Roma, Citta Aperta; Rome, Open City* **1945** A leader in the Italian underground resists Nazi control of the city. A stunning film, making Rossellini's realistic style famous. In Italian with English subtitles. **103m/B; VHS, DVD.** *IT* Anna Magnani; Aldo Fabrizi; Marcel Pagliero; Maria Michi; Vito Annichiarico; Nando (Fernando) Bruno; Harry Feist; **D:** Roberto Rossellini; **W:** Federico Fellini; Sergio Amidei; **C:** Ubaldo Arata; **M:** Renzo Rossellini. N.Y. Film Critics '46: Foreign Film.

Open Graves **2009 (R)** Dumb horror from the Syfy Channel. Jason and his surfer buds are in Spain where Jason has a run-in with shopkeeper Malek. To supposedly make amends, Malek offers Jason an ancient board game called Mamba that turns out to be made of the skin and bones of an executed witch. The game is cursed and the losers die in horrible ways while the winner gets a wish granted. Naturally, Jason wants to win and use his wish to undo the curse that's costing his friends' lives. **88m/C; DVD.** Mike Vogel; Eliza Dushku; Lindsay Caroline Robba; Ethan Rains; Alex O'Dogherty; Boris Martinez; Gary Piquer; **D:** Alvaro de Arminan; **W:** Roderick Taylor; Bruce Taylor; **M:** Fernando Orti Salvador. **CABLE**

Open House **1986** Radio psychologist and beautiful real estate agent search for the killer of real estate agents and their clients. A mystery-thriller for the very patient. **95m/C; VHS, Streaming.** Joseph Bottoms; Adrienne Barbeau; Mary Stavin; Rudy Ramos; **D:** Jag Mundhra.

Open House **2010 (R)** Alice is trying to sell her L.A. house but winds up chained in the basement by sicko David. He and his dominating psycho/lover Lila play home invasion sex/murder games and Alice is supposed to be the latest victim. David has his own secrets though and Alice tries to use that to her advantage. Moyer and Paquin have very brief screen appearances; film is the directorial debut of Paquin's brother. **88m/C; DVD, Blu-Ray.** Rachel Blanchard; Brian Geraghty; Tricia Helfer; Gabriel Olds; Jessica Collins; Stephen Moyer; Anna Paquin; **D:** Andrew Paquin; **W:** Andrew Paquin; **C:** Joseph White; **M:** Nathan Barr. **VIDEO**

Open Range 1/2 **2003 (R)** Costner revives the glory of the classic Western with overwhelming success. Cowpokes Boss (a superb Duvall) and Charley (Costner) peacefully graze their cattle on the open range during the late 1800s. That is, until they run up against cranky, land-grabbing rancher Baxter (Gambon) who dislikes the free-spirited, free-grazers and Boss's posse in particular. Bening is excellent as Costner's love interest. Actor Costner handles his familiar role with aplomb, while director Costner displays an eye for detail and a reverence for the genre. Alberta, Canada subs for the Wild West. Based on the novel by Lauran Paine. **135m/C; VHS, DVD.** Robert Duvall; Kevin Costner; Annette Bening; Michael Gambon; Michael Jeter; Diego Luna; James Russo; Abraham Benrubi; Dean McDermott; Kim Coates; **D:** Kevin Costner; **W:** Craig Storper; **C:** J.(James) Michael Muro; **M:** Michael Kamen.

The Open Road 1/2 **2009 (PG-13)** Predictable reconciliation plot with some strong performances by leads Bridges and Timberlake. Kyle Garrett (Bridges) was a baseball superstar and a lousy family man. Retired, Kyle is thrown when his estranged son Carlton (Timberlake) shows up at an Ohio baseball convention to inform his dad that Carlton's mom Katherine (Steenburgen) insists on seeing Kyle before having a risky operation at a Houston hospital. It turns into a road trip—that gives them plenty of time to talk. Director Meredith (whose dad is football legend Don Meredith) doesn't resort to melodrama to get his story across. **90m/C; DVD.** Jeff Bridges; Justin Timberlake; Kate Mara; Mary Steenburgen; Harry Dean Stanton; **Cameo(s):** Lyle Lovett; Ted Danson; **D:** Michael Meredith; **W:** Michael Meredith; **C:** Yaron Orbach; **M:** Christopher Lennertz.

Open Road 1/2 *Angie* **2013** A young Brazilian artist abandons her old life to tour the United States in an old car searching for her long lost father and a purpose in life. Purpose comes in the form of a local sheriff and a drifter, both of them men. **86m/C; DVD, Blu-Ray.** *BR US* Juliette Lewis; Camilla Belle; Andy Garcia; Colin Egglesfield; John Savage; **D:** Marcio Garcia; **W:** Julia Camara; **C:** Jonathan Hall. **VIDEO**

Open Season **1995 (R)** Stuart Sain (Wuhl) is an ambitious executive at Fielding, a TV ratings company (think Nielsen) whose boxes turn out to be defective. The ratings error causes public television programming to be number one, forcing the networks to counter-program culturally in order to regain their market share. Meanwhile, the public TV executives get overconfident and everything's just up for grabs. Flawed satire. **97m/C; VHS, Streaming.** Robert Wuhl; Rod Taylor; Gailard Sartain; Maggie Han; Joe Piscopo; Helen Shaver; Dina Merrill; Saul Rubinek; Steven C. White; Timothy Arrington; Barry Flatman; Tom Selleck; Alan Thicke; Jimmie Walker; **D:** Robert Wuhl; **W:** Robert Wuhl; **C:** Stephen Lighthill; **M:** Marvin Hamlisch.

Open Season 1/2 **2006 (PG)** Harmless animated flick about the plight of animals vs. man. Boog (Lawrence) is a grizzly bear, raised in captivity, who's released into the woods a few days before the opening of hunting season. He relies on the help of his friend Elliot (Kutcher), a spastic mule deer, to find his way to safety, which means returning to human civilization since Boog really doesn't like this life-in-the-wild stuff. Abounds with standard bathroom humor, with sprinkles of wit for the grown-ups. **99m/C; DVD, Blu-Ray.** **V:** Martin Lawrence; Ashton Kutcher; Gary Sinise; Debra Messing; Billy Connolly; Jon Favreau; Georgia Engel; Jane Krakowski; Gordon Tootoosis; Patrick Warburton; **D:** Roger Allers; Jill Culton; **W:** Steve Bencich; Maurizio Merli; Nat Maudlin; **M:** Paul Westerberg; Ramin Djawadi.

Open Season 2 **2008 (PG)** In this animated sequel, nervous buck Elliot delays his marriage to doe Giselle when dachshund Mr. Weenie is enticed back to domesticity (thanks to a trail of dog biscuits). Toy poodle Fifi hates the wild and insists Mr. Weenie would be happier as a pampered pet. His forest friends set out to find him and the dog must make a decision about where he really does belong. **76m/C; DVD, Blu-Ray.** **V:** Joel McHale; Mike Epps; Jane Krakowski; Cody Cameron; Crispin Glover; Georgia Engel; Billy Connolly; Diedrich Bader; Steve Schirripa; Danny Mann; **D:** Matthew O'Callaghan; **W:** Daniel I. Stern; **M:** Ramin Djawadi. **VIDEO**

Open Season 3 1/2 **2010 (PG)** Third installment in the animated series. Boog the bear is feeling neglected by his buddies who have family commitments. So he takes off on a solo adventure and finds himself in a circus where he changes places with grizzly Doug. Boog finds fun under the big top as well as love with dancing bear Ursa, but Boog's friends realize that Doug is an imposter and they want Boog to come home. The circus is heading back to Russia so the race is on. **75m/C; DVD, Blu-Ray.** **V:** Matthew W. Taylor; Crispin Glover; Matthew J. Munn; Melissa Sturm; Karley Scott Collins; Dana Snyder; Georgia Engel; Steve Schirripa; Danny Mann; Andre Sogliuzzo; Cody Cameron; **D:** Cody Cameron; **W:** Daniel I. Stern; **M:** Jeff Cardoni. **VIDEO**

Open Secret **1948** Jewish residents are plagued by a gang of anti-semitic thugs. Violence and destruction escalate until a fed up police lieutenant, tenaciously played by Ireland, and a victimized shop owner (Tyne) join forces to just say no more. When the gang learns the shopkeeper has caught their dastardly deeds on camera, the battle begins in earnest. Fast-paced and intriguing suspense. **70m/B; VHS, DVD.** John Ireland; Jane Randolph; Roman Bohnen; Sheldon Leonard; George Tyne; Morgan Farley; Ellen Lowe; Anne O'Neal; Arthur O'Connell; **D:** John Reinhardt.

Open Water **2003 (R)** Daniel (Travis) and Susan (Ryan) are an overworked couple who badly need a vacation so they go on a group scuba diving excursion in the Caribbean. The boat crew screws up and the two resurface to find the boat has left without them. Fighting cold, hunger, dehydration, sharks, and worst of all, their own fear and insecurities, the couple stay afloat for more than 24 hours hoping the crew will discover they are missing. Kentis and his wife Laura Lua shot on location in the Bahamas using a digital camera. The resulting visceral images add to the realism and, subsequently, the fear and tension. Based on actual events. **79m/C; DVD, Blu-Ray, UMD.** Saul Stein; Blanchard Ryan; Daniel Travis; Estelle Lau; Michael E. Williamson; John Charles; Christina Zenaro; **D:** Chris Kentis; **W:** Chris Kentis; **C:** Chris Kentis; Laura Lau; **M:** Graeme Revell.

Open Window **2006 (R)** Peter (Edgerton) leaves the window open after fixing up a backyard studio for his photographer fiance Izzy (Tunney). She's working late one night and is raped by an intruder who enters through the open window. A guilt-ridden Peter feels helpless while trying to support a traumatized and deeply-depressed Izzy, and their relationship is soon at a breaking point. **98m/C; DVD.** Robin Tunney; Joel Edgerton; Cybill Shepherd; Elliott Gould; Scott Wilson; Shirley Knight; Matt Keeslar; **D:** Mia Goldman; **W:** Mia Goldman; **C:** Denis Maloney; **M:** Cliff Eidelman.

Open Windows **2014** Vigalondo tackles the lack of privacy in our information age in this clever thriller structured entirely around windows open on a laptop computer. The clever writer/director gives Hitchcock's privacy-breaking pane of glass from "Rear Window" a technological, 21st century spin. Wood stars as the #1 fan of a high-maintenance actress (Grey), with whom he believes he won a special dinner date. Before he knows it, he's ordered around by a man on the other end of the phone who seems to be giving this fanboy access to every part of another person's life. It's not perfect but it's smart, well-paced and definitely timely. **100m/C; Blu-Ray, Streaming.** *SP US* Elijah Wood; Sasha Grey; *V:* Neil Maskell; *D:* Nacho Vigalondo; *W:* Nacho Vigalondo; *C:* Jon D. Dominguez; *M:* Jorge Magaz.

Open Your Eyes *Abre Los Ojos* **1997 (R)** Reality gets taken for a mind-bending spin in this Spanish thriller. Gorgeous womanizer, Cesar (Noriega), meets equally gorgeous Sofia (Cruz) and thinks he's finally found the one. Only his crazy ex-girlfriend Nuria (Nimri) causes a car crash that kills her and disfigures Cesar. He awakens in a prison hospital wearing a mask, accused of murder, and with confused memories. But maybe he's had an operation to restore his looks and is actually back together with Sofia but then Cesar keeps seeing Nuria's ghost. So just what is going on? Spanish with subtitles. **117m/C; VHS, DVD, Blu-Ray.** *SP* Eduardo Noriega; Penelope Cruz; Najwa Nimri; Chete Lera; Fele Martinez; Gerard Barray; *D:* Alejandro Amenabar; *W:* Alejandro Amenabar; Mateo Gil; *C:* Hans Burman; *M:* Alejandro Amenabar; Mariano Marin.

Opening Night 1/2 **1977 (PG-13)** Very long study about an actress (Rowlands) and the play she's about to open in on Broadway. Backstage turmoil increases her own insecurities and the bad luck persists when an adoring fan is struck by a car while the play is in try-outs in New Haven. Performances carry this neurotic epic along, including Cassavettes as Rowland's co-star and Blondell as the playwright. **144m/C; VHS, DVD, Blu-Ray.** Gena Rowlands; John Cassavetes; Joan Blondell; Ben Gazzara; Paul Stewart; Zohra Lampert; Laura Johnson; *D:* John Cassavetes; *W:* John Cassavetes; *C:* Frederick Elmes; *M:* Bo Harwood.

Opening Night **2017** A musical comedy that explores the backstage happenings of a Broadway show's quirky cast and crew. Stressed out Nick (Grace) is a Broadway stage manager preparing for the first night of a new show, One Hit Wonderland. The musical includes chorus girl Chloe (Tal), Nick's ex-girlfriend for whom he still has feelings. After the show's star, aging actress Brooke (Heche), suffers a concussion right before curtain, Chloe must take her place. Nick must also manage situations such as prop master who loses track of concussed Brooke while the show goes on. The few effective funny moments do not make the film any less slight. **90m/C; DVD.** Topher Grace; Alona Tal; Paul Scheer; Anne Heche; Lauren Lapkus; *D:* Isaac Rentz; *W:* Gerry De Leon; Greg Lisi; *C:* Andre Lascaris; *M:* P.J. Hanke.

Opera 1/2 *Terror at the Opera* **1988 (R)** A bizarre staging of Verdi's "Macbeth" is plagued by depraved gore murders. But the show must go on, as one character chirps in badly dubbed English. Italian horrormeister Argento's ever-fluid camera achieves spectacular shots, but the lurid, ludicrous script make this one for connoisseurs only. The operatic scenes employ the voice of Maria Callas. Available in an edited "R" rated version. **107m/C; VHS, DVD, Blu-Ray.** *IT* Christina Marsillach; Ian Charleson; Urbano Barberini; William McNamara; Antonella Vitale; Barbara Cupisti; Coralina Cataldi-Tassoni; Daria Nicolodi; *D:* Dario Argento; *W:* Dario Argento; Franco Ferrini; *C:* Ronnie Taylor; *M:* Claudio Simonetti.

Operation Abduction *Rapt au Deuxieme Bureau* **1958** A government agency fakes a rocket scientist's kidnapping to protect him from foreign agents and then sends out one of their own to locate the bad guys. French with subtitles. **95m/B; DVD.** *FR* Frank Villard; Danielle Godet; George Lannes; Dalida; *D:* Jean Stelli; *W:* Jean Stelli; *C:* Marc Fossard; *M:* Marcel Landowski.

Operation Amsterdam **1960** Four agents have 14 hours to snare $10 million in diamonds from under the noses of local Nazis. Based on a true story. Full of 1940s wartime action and suspense. **103m/B; VHS, DVD.** *UK* Peter Finch; Eva Bartok; Tony Britton; Alexander Knox; *D:* Michael McCarthy; *W:* Michael McCarthy; John Eldridge; *C:* Reginald Wyer; *M:* Philip Green.

Operation Avalanche **2016 (R)** This should have been a slam dunk for Matt Johnson, the director of the underrated found footage horror flick "The Dirties." In this found footage follow-up, Johnson and his regular collaborators travel back to the golden era of the space race, imagining a behind-the-scenes expose about the faking of the moon landing. Johnson and Owen Williams star as a bumbling pair of A/V guys in the basement of a federal agency who basically get tapped to perform the cover-up of the century. What starts clever and fun quickly gets tiresome and repetitive. **94m/C; DVD.** Matt Johnson; Owen Williams; Josh Boles; Jared Raab; Andrew Appelle; *D:* Matt Johnson; *W:* Matt Johnson; Josh Boles; *C:* Jared Raab; Andrew Appelle; *M:* Jay McCarrol.

Operation Bikini 1/2 **1963** Although set in WWII, this AIP flick was aimed at the teen market with Avalon pop-singing his way through the unlikely action as part of a naval demolition team. Old salt Brady and his submarine crew must deliver Frankie and his pals to Bikini Island for a super-secret mission. **83m/C; VHS, DVD.** Frankie Avalon; Tab Hunter; Scott Brady; Jim Backus; Gary Crosby; Jody McCrea; Michael Dante; Eva Six; *D:* Anthony Carras; *W:* John Tomerlin; *C:* Gilbert Warrenton; *M:* Les Baxter.

Operation C.I.A. *Last Message From Saigon* **1965** A plot to assassinate the U.S. ambassador in Saigon inspires brave CIA agent Reynolds to wipe out the bad guys. Action-packed and somewhat exciting. **90m/C; VHS, DVD.** Burt Reynolds; John Hayt; Kieu Chinh; Danielle Aubry; *D:* Christian Nyby; *W:* Peter J. Oppenheimer; William Sanborn Ballinger; *C:* Richard Moore; *M:* Paul Dunlap.

Operation Condor **1991 (PG-13)** Secret agent Jackie (Chan) is sent by the United Nations to retrieve 240 tons of gold buried by the Nazis in a Moroccan desert during WWII. Naturally, he's not the only one after the treasure. Lots of typically exuberant stunts and laughable dialogue (dubbed into English from Cantonese). **92m/C; VHS, DVD, Blu-Ray.** *CH* Jackie Chan; Carol Cheng; Eva Cabo De Garcia; Ikeda Shoko; *D:* Jackie Chan; *W:* Jackie Chan; Edward Tang; *C:* Wong Ngok Tai; *M:* Stephen Endelman.

Operation Condor 2: The Armour of the Gods *Armour of God; Longxiong Hudi* **1986 (R)** Prequel to "Operation Condor" was re-released in 1997. Chan plays an adventurous treasure-hunter who is asked by his ex-girlfriend's new fiancee Alan (Tam), who used to be Jackie's best friend, to rescue her from an evil cult. The kidnappers want Jackie and Alan to deliver a priceless medieval set of armour, thought to contain mysterious powers, to them. Naturally, Chan must come up with some spectacular saves of both the armour and the girl. In Cantonese with English subtitles. **88m/C; VHS, DVD, Blu-Ray.** *CH* Jackie Chan; Alan Tam; Rosamund Kwan; Lola Forner; *D:* Jackie Chan; *W:* Jackie Chan; Edward Tang; John Sheppard; *C:* Peter Ngor; *M:* Michael Lai.

Operation Cross Eagles *Unakrsna Vatra* **1969** Routine WWII military thriller with Conte and Calhoun on a mission to rescue an American general in exchange for their German prisoner. Their mission is complicated by a traitor in the group. Conte's only directorship. **90m/C; VHS, DVD.** *YU* Richard Conte; Rory Calhoun; Aili King; Phil Brown; *D:* Richard Conte; *W:* Vincent Forte; *C:* Nenad Jovicic.

Operation Crossbow *The Great Spy Mission; Code Name: Operation Crossbow* **1965** Action-packed espionage tale in which a trio of agents are assigned to destroy a Nazi munitions installation. Exciting ending and sensational pyrotechnics. **116m/C; DVD, Blu-Ray.** *UK* Sophia Loren; George Peppard; Trevor Howard; John Mills; Richard Johnson; Tom Courtenay; Jeremy Kemp; Anthony Quayle; Helmut Dantine; *D:* Michael Anderson, Sr.; *W:* Ray Rigby; Emeric Pressburger; Derry Quinn; *C:* Erwin Hillier; *M:* Ronald Goodwin.

Operation Daybreak 1/2 *The Price of Freedom* **1975** Based on a true story and the Alan Burgess novel "Seven Men at Daybreak." In 1942, three British-trained Czech resistance fighters parachute into their homeland to assassinate SS General Reinhard Heydrich, the leader of the occupation forces. When they succeed, the Nazis brutally retaliate. There's a betrayal and resistance members are trapped in a cathedral fighting off a Nazi battalion. **118m/C; DVD.** Timothy Bottoms; Martin Shaw; Joss Ackland; Anton Diffring; Anthony Andrews; Nicola Pagett; Carl Duering; *D:* Lewis Gilbert; *W:* Ronald Harwood; *C:* Henri Decae; *M:* David Hentschel.

Operation Delta Force 2: Mayday 1/2 **1997 (R)** Russian terrorist Lukash (Campbell) is threatening atomic mayhem unless he's paid $25 billion and it's up to the elite combat unit, the Delta Force, to stop him. Standard actioner is less than memorable. **98m/C; VHS, DVD.** Michael McGrady; J. Kenneth Campbell; Dale Dye; Simon Jones; *D:* Yossi Wein; *W:* David Sparling; *C:* Peter Belcher; *M:* Russell Stirling; Wessel Van Rensburg. **VIDEO**

Operation Delta Force 3: Clear Target 1/2 **1998 (R)** When the Delta Force destroys a billion-dollar cocaine operation, the drug cartel is out for revenge. Drug lord Umberto Salvatore steals a submarine and programs its warheads to fire on New York City. Of course, Delta Force has to get to the sub first. **96m/C; VHS, DVD.** Bryan Genesse; Danny Keogh; Jim (James) Fitzpatrick; Greg Collins; Darcy La Pier; *D:* Mark Roper; *W:* David Sparling; *C:* John Scheepers; *M:* Serge Colbert. **VIDEO**

Operation Delta Force 5: Random Fire **2000 (R)** With this film director Wein is well on his way to becoming the new Uwe Boll. Delta Force is sent to stop Osama Bin Laden from brainwashing prisoners into becoming human bombs. Everything about this film is bad, from the plot to the acting to the messed up insignias on the uniforms. **97m/C; DVD.** Todd Jensen; Anthony Bishop; David Lee; Nick Boraine; Cliff Simon; Ron Smerczak; Pepper Sweeney; Trae Thomas; *D:* Yossi Wein; *W:* Danny Lerner; Bernard Stone; *C:* Peter Belcher; *M:* Serge Colbert.

Operation Dumbo Drop 1/2 *Dumbo Drop* **1995 (PG)** It's 1968 and tough Green Beret captain (Glover), rescued by Vietnamese villagers, promises to replace their prized elephant, which was killed during his mission. He and a group of commandos use land, sea, and air to transport the reluctant beast, learning way more about elephant hygiene and eating habits than they ever wanted to know in the process. Wincer, who also directed "Free Willy," seems to be going for the title of "greatest large mammal director of all time." Anything with good-guy U.S. troops, a paratrooper elephant, and a family-friendly plot should be a Bob Dole favorite. **107m/C; VHS, DVD, Blu-Ray.** Danny Glover; Ray Liotta; Doug E. Doug; Denis Leary; Corin "Corky" Nemec; Thein Le Dihn; *D:* Simon Wincer; *W:* Jim Kouf; Gene Quintano; *C:* Russell Boyd; *M:* David Newman.

Operation Eichmann 1/2 **1961** First half of the pic focuses on Eichmann's WWII exploits while the second half deals with the real-life hunt for the infamous Nazi war criminal as Israeli agents go on a 15-year manhunt. Quickie production released just weeks before Eichmann's actual trial began in Jerusalem. **92m/B; DVD.** Werner Klemperer; Ruta Lee; Donald Buka; Steve Gravers; John Banner; *D:* R.G. Springsteen; *W:* Lester Cole; *C:* Joseph Biroc.

Operation: Endgame **2010 (R)** Overly-ambitious spy spoof finds two rival teams of government assassins (with Tarot code names) accidentally put into lockdown in their office cubicle underground bunker. A seriously disturbed bunch, they start knocking each other off (creatively using office supplies) while looking for an escape route. **82m/C; DVD.** Zach Galifianakis; Emilie de Ravin; Rob Corddry; Ellen Barkin; Brandon T. Jackson; Maggie Q; Adam Scott; Odette Annable; Joe Anderson; Ving Rhames; Bob Odenkirk; Jeffrey Tambor; Michael Hitchcock; Tim Bagley; *D:* Fouad Mikati; *W:* Sam Levinson; Brian Watanabe; *C:* Arnaud Stefani; *M:* Ian Honeyman. **VIDEO**

Operation Finale 1/2 **2018 (PG-13)** In the mid-twentieth century, Israeli intelligence agent Peter Malkin (Isaac) locates former Nazis so they can be brought to justice. Though he kills the wrong Nazi on a 1954 raid, he is tapped to investigate when the Israelis are given information that Holocaust architect Adolf Eichmann (Kingsley) is living under an assumed name with his family. As Malkin pursues Eichmann and takes action to bring him before an international court, he is assisted by associate Rossi (Kroll) and an anesthesiologist/Malkin's former girlfriend (Laurent). Engrossing and tense, it explores the outfall from World War II and features a strong performance by Isaac. **122m/C; DVD, Blu-Ray.** Oscar Isaac; Ben Kingsley; Melanie Laurent; Lior Raz; Nick Kroll; *D:* Chris Weitz; *W:* Matthew Orton; *C:* Javier Aguirresarobe; *M:* Alexandre Desplat.

Operation Haylift **1950** The true story of the U.S. Air Force's efforts to rescue starving cattle and sheep herds during Nevada's blizzards of 1949. The Air Force provided realism for the film with planes, equipment, and servicemen. **73m/B; VHS, DVD.** Bill Williams; Tom Brown; Ann Rutherford; Jane Nigh; Joseph (Joe) Sawyer; Dean Riesner; Richard Travis; Raymond Hatton; Jimmy Conlin; Tommy "T.V." Ivo; *D:* William Berke; *W:* Joseph (Joe) Sawyer; Dean Riesner; *C:* Benjamin (Ben H.) Kline.

Operation Heartbeat *U.M.C.* **1969** The alternate title—U.M.C.?stands for University Medical Center, the setting for this TV pilot movie for the "Medical Center" series. Widow Joanna Hanson (Stanley) files a lawsuit against the hospital and surgeon Joe Gannon (Bradford) because she believes Gannon let her husband die so his heart could be transplanted into his ailing mentor Lee Forestman (Robinson). **97m/C; DVD.** Edward G. Robinson; Richard Bradford; Kim Stanley; Maurice Evans; Kevin McCarthy; Shelley Fabares; James Daly; William Windom; J.D. Cannon; *D:* Boris Sagal; *W:* Al C. Ward; *C:* Joseph LaShelle; *M:* George Romanis; Lalo Schifrin. **TV**

Operation Mad Ball 1/2 **1957** Lemmon plays a conniving enlisted man in this military comedy. Bored WWII GIs, stationed at an Army medical unit in France, decide to liven things up by throwing a party for the nurses at a local hotel. Fast-talking Pvt. Hogan (Lemmon) must sneak around by-the-book Capt. Locke (Kovacs) since the nurses are officers and the enlisted men can't fraternize with them. Kovacs's screen debut. **105m/B; DVD.** Jack Lemmon; Ernie Kovacs; Kathryn Grant; Mickey Rooney; Arthur O'Connell; Dick York; James Darren; Roger Smith; L.Q. Jones; Jeanne Manet; *D:* Richard Quine; *W:* Blake Edwards; Arthur Carter; Jed Harris; *C:* Charles Lawton, Jr.; *M:* George Duning.

Operation Petticoat 1/2 **1959** Submarine captain Grant teams with wheeler-dealer Curtis to make his sub seaworthy. They're joined by a group of Navy women, and the gags begin. Great teamwork from Grant and Curtis keeps things rolling. Jokes may be considered sexist these days. Later remake and TV series couldn't hold a candle to the original. **120m/C; VHS, DVD, Blu-Ray.** Cary Grant; Tony Curtis; Joan O'Brien; Dina Merrill; Gene Evans; Arthur O'Connell; Virginia Gregg; *D:* Blake Edwards; *W:* Stanley Shapiro; Maurice Richlin; *C:* Russell Harlan; *M:* David Rose.

Operation Secret **1952** A former French Legionnaire and Marine, Peter Forrester (Wilde) assisted the French Resistance during WWII but, after his presumed death in Germany, he is accused of murdering leader Armand (Picerni). A tribunal is set up to investigate the crime and reports of a traitor and flashbacks reveal each witness' part in Forrester's life, but are they telling the truth? **108m/B; DVD.** Cornel Wilde; Steve Cochran; Phyllis Thaxter; Karl Malden; Paul Picerni; Dan O'Herlihy; Jay Novello; Lester Matthews; *D:* Lewis Seiler; *W:* Harold Medford; James R. Webb; *C:* Ted D. McCord.

Operation Thunderbolt 1/2 *Entebbe: Operation Thunderbolt; Mivtsa Yonatan* **1977** Israeli-produced depiction of Israel's July 14, 1976 commando raid on Entebbe, Uganda to rescue the passengers of a hijacked plane. Better than the American versions "Raid on Entebbe" and "Victory at Entebbe" in its performances as well as the information provided, much of it unavailable to the American filmmakers. **120m/C; DVD.** *IS* Yehoram Gaon; Assi Dayan; Ori Levy; Klaus

Kinski; ***D:*** Menahem Golan; ***W:*** Menahem Golan; ***C:*** Adam Greenberg; ***M:*** Dov Seltzer.

Operation Valkyrie 1/2 *Stauffenberg* **2004** German television movie based on the true story of a 1944 plot to assassinate Hitler by placing a bomb in his war office. The plot is hatched by decorated Army Colonel Claus von Stauffenberg but we all know how it ends. German with subtitles. The same incident was filmed with Tom Cruise as 2008's "Valkyrie." **92m/C; DVD.** *GE* Sebastian Koch; Christopher Buchholz; Hardy Kruger; Stefania Rocca; Ulrich Tukur; Nina Kunzendorf; Olli Dittrich; Axel Milberg; ***D:*** Jo Baier; ***W:*** Jo Baier; ***C:*** Gunnar Fuss; ***M:*** Enjott Schneider. **TV**

The Operative **2019** After a year of silence, Mossad agent Thomas (Freeman) hears from guarded Rachel (Kruger), a fellow agent for whom he acted as handler. On assignment, Rachel had gone undercover to Tehran. Though Rachel posed as an English teacher, she was there to infiltrate an electronics company with the ultimate goal of selling tracked technology to Iran's intelligence forces. During the course of her mission, Rachel's humanity and mistakes put her life in danger. Based on the novel by Atir, the standard espionage thriller finds some suspense thanks to Kruger. **117m/C; DVD.** Diane Kruger; Martin Freeman; Cas Anvar; Rotem Keinan; Lana Ettinger; ***D:*** Yuval Adler; ***W:*** Yuval Adler; ***C:*** Kolja Brandt; ***M:*** Haim Frank Ilfman.

The Operator **2001** Scumdog lawyer Gary Whelan (Laurence) gets his comeuppance when he insults the wrong telephone operator (Kim). Calling herself Shiva (the Hindu goddess of destruction), she decides to even the karmic balance by stripping Gary of all his worldly possessions, breaking up his marriage, and framing him for murder. Set in Dallas, Texas. **102m/C; VHS, DVD.** Jacqueline Kim; Michael Laurence; Christa Miller; Stephen Tobolowsky; Brion James; Frances Bay; ***D:*** Jon Dichter; ***W:*** Jon Dichter.

Operator 13 **1934** Implausible plot, and the title role is not a good fit for natural comedienne Davies as she plays an actress turned Union spy during the Civil War. Gail assumes a couple of identities (including that of a mulatto washerwoman) to get information and later discovers a mutual attraction with Confederate captain, Jack Gailliard (Cooper). The Oscar-nominated cinematography by George Folsey is the best thing about the film. **86m/B; DVD.** Marion Davies; Gary Cooper; Douglass Dumbrille; Katherine Alexander; Jean Parker; Sidney Toler; William Robertson; ***D:*** Richard Boleslawski; ***W:*** Eve Greene; Zelda Sears; Harvey Thew; ***C:*** George J. Folsey; ***M:*** William Axt.

Ophelia 1/2 **2019 (PG-13)** Raised by her widowed father Polonius (Mafham) in their native Denmark, the neglected yet fearless Ophelia (Ridley) becomes a lady in waiting to the queen, Gertrude (Watts), after speaking her mind. Ophelia learns the rules of courtly behavior, but she retains her independent spirit and becomes a favorite of the lonely Gertrude. Though Ophelia and the prince, Hamlet (McKay), fall in love, the treachery in the court threatens their relationship and their lives. Based on the Lisa Klein novel, the film provides insight into a tragic figure from Shakespeare's Hamlet as well as into the events in the play from her point of view. **114m/C; DVD, Blu-Ray.** Daisy Ridley; Naomi Watts; Clive Owen; Tom Felton; George MacKay; ***D:*** Claire McCarthy; ***W:*** Semi Chellas; ***C:*** Denson Baker; ***M:*** Steven Price.

Opium and Kung-Fu Master *Hung Kuen Dai See; Lightning Fists of Shaolin; Hong quan da shi* **1984** Martial arts hero Ti Lung (Chao-San) and his students have long protected the local village they dwell in. But the arrival of a rival Kung Fu school does not bode well, as its master pushes Opium on the local populace who initially don't realize just how bad it truly is. Even Ti Lung himself becomes an addict, and must go cold turkey if he is to fight off the growing menace. **86m/C; DVD, Blu-Ray.** *CH* Master Teih Chao-san; Kuan Tai Chen; Philip Ko; Shen Chan; Ying Huang; ***D:*** Chia Tang; ***C:*** Hui-chi Tsao; ***M:*** Chin Yung Shing; Chen-hou Su.

Opium: Diary of a Madwoman 1/2 **2007** A perverse look at addiction, madness, and obsession that's set in 1913 in a remote and nightmarish mental institution for women. Morphine-addicted Dr. Joszef Brenner comes to the clinic under the guise of psychoanalyzing the patients. The beautiful Gizella attracts his attention as she is convinced that the devil has possessed her and she compulsively fills diaries with her ramblings. Suffering from writer's block himself, Brenner is both jealous and sexually obsessed with Gizella. Based on the diaries of Hungary's first neurologist, writing under the pen name Geza Csath. **109m/C; DVD.** *HU GE* Ulrich Thomsen; Kirsti Stubo; Zsolt Laszlo; ***D:*** Janos Szasz; ***W:*** Andras Szeker; ***C:*** Tibor Mathe.

The Opponent *Qualcuno Paghera* **1989 (R)** A young boxer saves a young woman's life, not realizing that she has mob connections, thus embroiling him in a world of crime. **102m/C; DVD.** *IT* Daniel Greene; Ernest Borgnine; Julian Gemma; Mary Stavin; Kelly Shaye Smith; ***D:*** Sergio Martino; ***W:*** Sergio Martino; ***C:*** Giancarlo Ferrando; ***M:*** Luciano Michelini.

The Opponent 1/2 **2001 (R)** After years of domestic violence, Patty (Eleniak) finds an outlet for her anger in the boxing ring of the community center. With the encouragment of her trainer (Colby), she decides to take it to the next level and go for a pro career. But when Patty embarks on a romance with the guy, she also gets distracted from her goals. **90m/C; VHS, DVD.** Erika Eleniak; Aunjanue Ellis; James Colby; John Doman; ***D:*** Eugene Jarecki; ***W:*** Eugene Jarecki; ***C:*** Joe Di Gennaro. **VIDEO**

Opportunity Knocks 1/2 **1990 (PG-13)** Carvey's first feature film has him impersonating a friend of a rich suburbanite's family while hiding from a vengeful gangster. They buy it, and give him a job and the daughter. Not hilarious, but not a dud either. **105m/C; VHS, DVD, Blu-Ray.** Dana Carvey; Robert Loggia; Todd Graff; Milo O'Shea; Julia Campbell; James Tolkan; Doris Belack; Sally Gracie; Del Close; ***D:*** Donald Petrie; ***W:*** Mitchel Katlin; Nat Bernstein; ***M:*** Miles Goodman.

Opposing Force 1/2 *Hellcamp* **1987 (R)** The commander of an Air Force camp simulates prisoner-of-war conditions for realistic training, but he goes too far, creating all too real torture situations. He preys on the only female in the experiment, raping her as part of the training. A decent thriller. **97m/C; VHS, DVD, Blu-Ray.** Tom Skerritt; Lisa Eichhorn; Anthony Zerbe; Richard Roundtree; Robert Wightman; John Considine; George Kee Cheung; Paul Joynt; Jay Louden; Ken Wright; Dan Hamilton; ***D:*** Eric Karson; ***W:*** Gil Cowan; ***M:*** Marc Donahue.

Opposite Day 1/2 **2009 (G)** Innocuous family comedy of no particular distinction. Sammy's frazzled parents decide that he and younger sister Carla should spend a weekend away with their grandparents and Sammy wishes that kids could be in charge. His wish comes true but Sammy soon realizes being a grown-up isn't so great and he wants to change things back. **81m/C; DVD.** Billy Unger; Ariel Winter; Pauly Shore; Colleen Crabtree; Dylan Cash; Dick Van Patten; Renee Taylor; French Stewart; ***D:*** R. Michael Givens; ***W:*** Max Botkin; ***C:*** R. Michael Givens; ***M:*** Misha Segal. **VIDEO**

The Opposite of Sex 1/2 **1998 (R)** Teenaged terror Dedee (Ricci) wreaks havoc with the life of gay half-brother Bill (Donovan). She seduces his boyfriend Matt (Sergei), gets pregnant, steals his savings, and nearly costs Bill his high school teacher's job. Then she takes off for L.A., with Bill, his best friend Lucia (Kudrow), and sheriff Carl (Lovett) in pursuit. Quirky black comedy isn't shy, especially when Ricci's vamping across the screen, and features fine work by Ricci and Kudrow (in a welcome departure from the dumb blonde roles). Dedee's acerbic narration is another highlight. **105m/C; DVD.** Christina Ricci; Martin Donovan; Lisa Kudrow; Ivan Sergei; Lyle Lovett; Johnny Galecki; William Lee Scott; Colin Ferguson; ***D:*** Don Roos; ***W:*** Don Roos; ***C:*** Hubert Taczanowski; ***M:*** Mason Daring. Ind. Spirit '99: First Feature, Screenplay; Natl. Bd. of Review '98: Support. Actress (Ricci); N.Y. Film Critics '98: Support. Actress (Kudrow).

The Opposite Sex **1956** Bevy of women battle mediocre script in adaptation of 1939's "The Women." **115m/C; VHS, DVD.** June Allyson; Joan Collins; Dolores Gray; Ann Sheridan; Ann Miller; Leslie Nielsen; Agnes Moorehead; Joan Blondell; ***D:*** David Miller; ***W:*** Fay Kanin; Michael Kanin.

The Opposite Sex and How to Live With Them **1993 (R)** Yuppies (Gross and Cox) from different backgrounds (he's Jewish, she's a WASP) meet, fall in love, fight, break up, and reunite, inspiring yawning disinterest. All this while their two best buddies (Pollak and Brown) offer what are meant to be "candid insights" delivered directly to the camera. Flat and formulaic romantic comedy wants to sparkle, but script lacks both purpose and point, and worse, takes way too much time not getting there. Winner of the annual Grammar Police award for the worst example of a semantically incorrect title in recent years. **86m/C; VHS, Streaming.** Arye Gross; Courteney Cox; Kevin Pollak; Julie Brown; Mitchell Ryan; Philip Bruns; Mitzi McCall; B.J. Ward; ***D:*** Matthew Meshekoff; ***W:*** Noah Stern; ***M:*** Ira Newborn.

The Optimists 1/2 **1973** Sentimental story finds Sam (Sellers), an old vaudeville performer, reduced to performing with his dog on London street corners. He befriends young Liz (Mullane) and her brother Mark (Chaffey), offering friendship and an optimistic view to their poverty-stricken lives on the wrong side of the tracks. Simmons directed from his novel "The Optimists of Nine Elms." **110m/C; DVD, Blu-Ray.** Peter Sellers; David Daker; Marjorie Yates; Donna Mullane; John Chaffey; ***D:*** Anthony Simmons; ***W:*** Anthony Simmons; Tudor Gates; ***C:*** Larry Pizer; ***M:*** Lionel Bart.

The Oracle **1985** A woman takes a new apartment only to find that the previous occupant's spirit is still a resident. The spirit tries to force her to take revenge on his murderers. Not bad for a low-budget thriller, but bad editing is a distraction. **94m/C; VHS, DVD.** Caroline Capers Powers; Roger Neil; ***D:*** Roberta Findlay; ***W:*** R. Allen Leider; ***C:*** Roberta Findlay; ***M:*** Walter Sear.

Orange County 1/2 **2002 (PG-13)** Typical Orange County, California teen Shaun Brumder (Hanks) trades his surf board for a pen when he accidentally discovers the joys of literature via a Marcus Skinner (an uncredited Kline) novel on the beach. Determined to study under Skinner at Stanford, Brumder is bummed when the wrong test scores are submitted to the college who summarily rejects him. Enter stoner brother Lance (Black), to help him straighten everything out. Dynamic comedy with character development of a surprisingly sophisticated nature for this type of film. **81m/C; DVD.** Colin Hanks; Jack Black; Schuyler Fisk; Catherine O'Hara; John Lithgow; Harold Ramis; Jane Adams; Garry Marshall; Dana Ivey; Chevy Chase; Lily Tomlin; George Murdock; Leslie Mann; Kyle Howard; Kevin Kline; ***D:*** Jake Kasdan; ***W:*** Mike White; ***C:*** Greg Gardiner; ***M:*** Michael Andrews.

The Oranges 1/2 **2012 (R)** Too polite dysfunctional comedy-drama. David (Laurie) and Paige (Keener) Welling and Terry (Platt) and Cathy (Janney) Ostroff are longtime Jersey neighbors and friends. When the Ostroff's prodigal daughter Nina (Meester) returns home, David makes an impulsive move and she responds. So now what happens to the families and friendships? There's little energy to the pic and less chemistry between Laurie and Meester to make their affair believable except the obvious midlife crisis of a middle-aged man. **91m/C; DVD, Blu-Ray.** Hugh Laurie; Catherine Keener; Oliver Platt; Allison Janney; Leighton Meester; Alia Shawkat; Adam Brody; ***D:*** Julian Farino; ***W:*** Ian Helfer; Jay Reiss; ***C:*** Steven Fierberg; ***M:*** Klaus Badelt; Andrew Raiher.

Oranges and Sunshine **2010 (R)** Heartbreaking true story set in the 1980s. British social worker Margaret Humphreys (Watson) is confronted by Australian Charlotte (Holmes) who's trying to find out about her past. Margaret's probing uncovers a shameful bureaucratic decision where thousands of British children were illegally removed from allegedly unfit mothers and sent to Australian children's homes in the 1940s and '50s. As the scandal grows, Margaret gets hundred of inquiries and seeks to reunite as many families as she can. Based on the book "Empty Cradles" by Humphreys. **105m/C; DVD, Blu-Ray.** *UK AU* Emily Watson; Hugo Weaving; David Wenham; Federay Holmes; Lorraine Ashbourne; Richard Dillane; Tara Morice; ***D:*** Jim Loach; ***W:*** Rona Munro; ***C:*** Denson Baker; ***M:*** Lisa Gerrard.

Oranges Are Not the Only Fruit 1/2 **1989** Lesbian coming of age story about young Jess (Coleman), who must escape her evangelical religious upbringing and mother (McEwan) in order to be true to herself. When the teenaged Jess gets a schoolgirl crush on her friend Melanie, the congregation finds out and condemns the girls until Jess finds the strength to break away. Based on the novel by Winsterson, who also wrote the screenplay. Made for TV. **165m/C; VHS, DVD.** *GB* Charlotte Coleman; Geraldine McEwan; Cathryn Bradshaw; Kenneth Cranham; Freda Dowie; Richard Henders; Elizabeth Spriggs; Sophie Thursfield; ***D:*** Beeban Kidron; ***W:*** Jeanette Winterson; ***M:*** Rachel Portman. **TV**

Orca **WOOF!** *Orca—Killer Whale; The Killer Whale* **1977 (PG)** Ridiculous premise has a killer whale chasing bounty hunter Harris to avenge the murder of its pregnant mate. Great for gore lovers, especially when the whale chomps Derek's leg off. **92m/C; VHS, DVD.** Richard Harris; Charlotte Rampling; Bo Derek; Keenan Wynn; Will Sampson; Robert Carradine; ***D:*** Michael Anderson, Sr.; ***W:*** Sergio Donati; Luciano Vincenzoni; ***C:*** Ted Moore; ***M:*** Ennio Morricone.

Orchestra Rehearsal *Prova d'Orchestra* **1978** Italian orchestra musicians gather in a 13th-century chapel to film a TV documentary, protest the increasing authoritarianism of their German conductor, but are eventually persuaded to play amidst the chaos. Rota's last score. Italian with subtitles. **72m/C; VHS, DVD, Blu-Ray.** *IT* Balduin Baas; Clara Colosimo; Elisabeth Labi; Ronaldo Bonacchi; Ferdinando Villella; Giovanni Javarone; David Mauhsell; Francesco Aluigi; ***D:*** Federico Fellini; ***W:*** Federico Fellini; Brunello Rondi; ***C:*** Giuseppe Rotunno; ***M:*** Nino Rota.

Orchestra Wives **1942** A drama bursting with wonderful Glenn Miller music. A woman marries a musician and goes on the road with the band and the other wives. Trouble springs up with the sultry singer who desperately wants the woman's new husband. The commotion spreads throughout the group. **98m/B; DVD.** George Montgomery; Glenn Miller; Lynn Bari; Carole Landis; Jackie Gleason; Cesar Romero; Ann Rutherford; Virginia Gilmore; Mary Beth Hughes; Harry (Henry) Morgan; ***D:*** Archie Mayo; ***W:*** Karl Tunberg; Darrell Ware; ***C:*** Lucien Ballard.

Orchids to You 1/2 **1935** Very minor Fox romantic drama. Flower shop owner Camelia Rand is furious when she's informed that a developer plans to tear down the building. Despite her anger, Camelia takes an interest in the developer's lawyer, Thomas Bentley, but backs off because he's married. When another man sends orchids to Mrs. Bentley, Camelia is unwillingly drawn into their divorce case. **74m/B; DVD.** Jean Muir; John Boles; Ruthelma Stevens; Charles Butterworth; Sidney Toler; Harvey Stephens; Spring Byington; ***D:*** William A. Seiter; ***W:*** Bartlett Cormack; Glenn Tryon; Howard Estabrook; William Hurlbut; ***C:*** Merritt B. Gerstad.

Orde Wingate **1976** Capable biography of Orde Wingate (Foster), who was one of Britain's most celebrated and unorthodox commanders during WWII. While serving in Palestine, Wingate becomes a passionate Zionist and develops guerrilla tactics he teaches to the future leaders of the Israeli Defense Force. **174m/C; DVD.** *GB* Barry Foster; James Cosmo; Denholm Elliott; Bernard Hepton; Sheila Ruskin; Arnold Diamond; ***D:*** Bill Hays; ***W:*** Don Shaw. **TV**

Ordeal in the Arctic 1/2 **1993 (PG)** Military transport plane, piloted by Capt. John Couch (Chamberlain), crashes into the remote glaciers of the Arctic. The survivors face a blizzard and freezing to death unless a rescue team can get to them quickly. Based on the book "Death and Deliverance" by Robert Mason Lee. **93m/C; VHS, DVD.** *CA* Richard Chamberlain; Melanie Mayron; Catherine Mary Stewart; Scott Hylands; Page Fletcher; Christopher Bolton; Richard McMillan; ***D:*** Mark Sobel; ***W:*** Paul F. Edwards; ***C:*** Miklos Lente; ***M:*** Amin Bhatia. **CABLE**

The Ordeal of Dr. Mudd 🦴🦴🦴 **1980** His name was Mudd—a fitting moniker after he unwittingly aided President Lincoln's assassin. Dr. Mudd set John Wilkes Boothe's leg, broken during the assassination, and was jailed for conspiracy. He became a hero in prison for his aid during yellow fever epidemics and was eventually released. A strong and intricate performance by Weaver keeps this TV drama interesting. Mudd's descendants are still trying to completely clear his name of any wrongdoing in the Lincoln assassination. **143m/C; VHS, DVD.** Dennis Weaver; Susan Sullivan; Richard Dysart; Michael McGuire; Nigel Davenport; Arthur Hill; ***D:*** Paul Wendkos. **TV**

The Order 🦴 *Sin Eater* **2003 (R)** Religious wannabe thriller stars a dour and underwhelming Ledger as Alex, a Catholic priest investigating the death of his mentor (Carnelutti). His sleuthing leads to a character known as a "Sin Eater" (Furmann), who literally ingests a wide range of normally unforgivable sins. These sins are represented by creatures similar to those in "Alien," as they also come bursting out of the chests of the unfortunate, but soon to be forgiven, souls. A poor man's "Exorcist" lacking in action, pacing, and a believable story line with heavy-handed dialogue and humorless characters. **102m/C; DVD, Blu-Ray.** Heath Ledger; Shannyn Sossamon; Benno Furmann; Mark Addy; Peter Weller; Francesco Carnelutti; ***D:*** Brian Helgeland; ***W:*** Brian Helgeland; ***C:*** Nicola Pecorini; ***M:*** David Torn.

Order of Chaos 🦴 **1/2 2010 (R)** Vincent Vieluf's writer/director debut psycho-thriller is overly-ambitious but shows promise. Workaholic tax attorney John (Coiro) is a pushover for the women in both his professional and private lives. Then devious, party-loving new hire Rick (Ventimiglia) talks John into not letting anyone push him around anymore with some violent consequences. **88m/C; DVD.** Milo Ventimiglia; Samantha Mathis; Rhys Coiro; Mimi Rogers; Susan Ward; Maggie Kiley; Chip Joslin; Anna Campbell; ***D:*** Vince Vieluf; ***C:*** Thomas M. (Tom) Harting. **VIDEO**

Order to Kill 🦴🦴 **1/2 1973** A gambling boss puts out a contract on a hit man. **110m/C; VHS, DVD.** Jose Ferrer; Helmut Berger; Sydne Rome; Kevin McCarthy; ***D:*** Jose Maesso.

Ordet 🦴🦴🦴 **1/2** *The Word* **1955** A man who believes he is Jesus Christ is ridiculed until he begins performing miracles, which result in the rebuilding of a broken family. A statement on the nature of religious faith vs. fanaticism by the profoundly religious Dreyer, and based on the play by Kaj Munk. In Danish with English subtitles. **126m/B; VHS, DVD.** *DK* Henrik Malberg; Birgitte Federspiel; Cay Kristiansen; Emil Hass Christiansen; ***D:*** Carl Theodor Dreyer; ***W:*** Carl Theodor Dreyer; Kaj Munk; ***C:*** Henning Bendtsen. Golden Globes '56: Foreign Film; Venice Film Fest. '55: Film.

Ordinary Decent Criminal 🦴🦴 **1999 (R)** Lightweight caper flick loosely based on the life of Irish thief Martin Cahill was shot in 1998 but only recently received limited runs abroad. Spacey is Michael Lynch, a self-styled blue collar criminal who enjoys high-profile heists and making the local cops look bad. When he steals a Caravaggio painting worth $45 million, he gets caught up with the IRA and an obsessive cop (Dillane) bent on catching him. Passes the time pleasantly enough, with a jovial performance by Spacey, but John Boorman's "The General" tells this story better. **90m/C; VHS, DVD, Blu-Ray.** *IR GB* Kevin Spacey; Linda Fiorentino; Helen Baxendale; Stephen (Dillon) Dillane; Peter Mullan; Patrick Malahide; Gerard McSorley; Colin Farrell; ***D:*** Thaddeus O'Sullivan; ***W:*** Gerard Stembridge; ***C:*** Andrew Dunn; ***M:*** Damon Albarn.

Ordinary Love 🦴🦴 **1/2 2020 (R)** Married for decades, Tom (Neeson) and Joan (Manville) are devoted to each other and have a loving, affectionate relationship. Their world is turned upside down when Joan is unexpectedly diagnosed with breast cancer. As she goes through brutal treatments, including surgery, radiation, and chemotherapy, Tom remains supportive and steadfast, even shaving Joan's head as her hair begins to fall out due to the chemo. At the same time, Joan also finds comfort in communications with others, including fellow cancer patients such as Peter (Wilmot). The first script by Irish playwright McCafferty, the detail-rich drama is highlighted by a courageous, realistic performance by Manville. **92m/C; DVD.** Liam Neeson; Lesley Manville; David Wilmot; Amit Shah; Stella McCusker; ***D:*** Lisa Barros D'Sa; Glenn Leyburn; ***W:*** Owen McCafferty; ***C:*** Piers McGrail; ***M:*** David Holmes; Brian Irvine.

An Ordinary Man 🦴 **1/2 2018 (R)** Kingsley chews up the scenery as the General, a war criminal evading capture for his crimes in the former Yugoslavia, and whose young new maid reveals herself to be his undercover bodyguard. With little action, it's meant to be a psychological and/or character study, but there's little meaningful contemplation of either. The nature of the General's atrocities is never explained, and his monologue-esque delivery of lines rings as phony as his puzzling British/Scottish accent. **90m/C; DVD.** Ben Kingsley; Hera Hilmar; Peter Serafinowicz; Robert Blythe; Bojan Bajcetic; ***D:*** Brad Silberling; ***W:*** Brad Silberling; ***C:*** Magdalena Gorka; ***M:*** Christophe Beck.

Ordinary People 🦴🦴🦴 **1/2 1980 (R)** Powerful, well-acted story of a family's struggle to deal with one son's accidental death and the other's subsequent guilt-ridden suicide attempt. Features strong performances by all, but Moore is especially believable as the cold and rigid mother. McGovern's film debut as well as Redford's directorial debut. Based on the novel by Judith Guest. **124m/C; VHS, DVD.** Mary Tyler Moore; Donald Sutherland; Timothy Hutton; Judd Hirsch; M. Emmet Walsh; Elizabeth McGovern; Adam Baldwin; Dinah Manoff; James B. Sikking; Frederic Lehne; ***D:*** Robert Redford; ***W:*** Alvin Sargent; ***C:*** John Bailey; ***M:*** Marvin Hamlisch. Oscars '80: Adapt. Screenplay, Director (Redford), Film, Support. Actor (Hutton); Directors Guild '80: Director (Redford); Golden Globes '81: Actress--Drama (Moore), Director (Redford), Film--Drama, Support. Actor (Hutton); L.A. Film Critics '80: Support. Actor (Hutton); Natl. Bd. of Review '80: Director (Redford); N.Y. Film Critics '80: Film; Writers Guild '80: Adapt. Screenplay.

Ordinary Sinner 🦴🦴 **1/2 2002** Peter (Hines) drops out of an Episcopal seminary after his faith's shaken while working as a teen counselor. He comes to a small Vermont college town where his shy childhood friend Alex (Park) has a crush on sexy student Rachel (Banks), who's more interested in the depressed Peter. Meanwhile, Peter's one-time mentor Father Ed (Martinez) publicly reveals he's gay when a series of gay-bashing incidents strike the campus. A death causes more emotional upheaval and adds some unnecessary whodunit elements to an already overstuffed plot. Well-meaning plea for tolerance borders on the preachy. **92m/C; VHS, DVD.** Brendan P. Hines; Kris Park; Elizabeth Banks; A. Martinez; Peter Onorati; Nathaniel Marston; ***D:*** John Henry Davis; ***W:*** William Mahone; ***C:*** Mathieu Roberts; ***M:*** Brian Adler.

Ordinary World 🦴🦴 *Geezer* **2016** Perry Miller (Billie Joe Armstrong of Green Day) is an aging musician who left his punk rock band for an ordinary life. In the midst of a midlife crisis he decides to hold a party at a fancy NY hotel to cheer himself, only to find out his old friends have moved on to bigger and better things. Fans of Green Day will love the music, but others will find a pretty ordinary story. **87m/C; DVD, Blu-Ray, Streaming.**

Orfeu 🦴🦴 **1999** Diegues's musical drama is adapted from the Vinicius de Moraes play that also inspired Marcel Camus's 1959 film "Black Orpheus." The retelling of the Greek Orpheus and Eurydice tragedy is set during carnivale in Rio and features pop singer Garrido as egotistical songwriter Orfeu who becomes smitten with country girl Eurydice (Franca). Portuguese with subtitles. **112m/C; VHS, DVD.** *BR* Toni Garrido; Patricia Franca; Murilo Benicio; Zeze Motta; Milton Goncalves; Isabel Fillardis; ***D:*** Carlos Diegues; ***W:*** Carlos Diegues; ***C:*** Affonso Beato; ***M:*** Caetano Veloso.

Organ 🦴 **1/2 1996** Two detectives bust into what they believe is the lair of a street gang, but end up in the middle of a group of organ thieves. One is dissected before help arrives, but the surviving partner loses his mind and decides to take down the gang's ringleader, Yoko What follows is an incoherent bloody mess of organ thieves, deviant sex murders, and a biology experiment kept alive on the blood of young virgins. Be warned: if you vomit easily this film ain't for you. It's uncut on DVD, but it was censored heavily before theatrical release, even in Japan (where they're more tolerant of gore). **104m/C; DVD.** *JP* Kei Fujiwara; Shun Sugata; ***D:*** Kei Fujiwara; ***W:*** Kei Fujiwara; ***C:*** Kei Fujiwara; ***M:*** Video Rodeo.

The Organization 🦴🦴🦴 **1971 (PG)** Poitier's third and final portrayal of Detective Virgil Tibbs, first seen in "In the Heat of the Night." This time around he battles a drug smuggling ring with a vigilante group. Good action scenes and a realistic ending. **108m/C; VHS, DVD, Blu-Ray.** Sidney Poitier; Barbara McNair; Sheree North; Raul Julia; ***D:*** Don Medford; ***W:*** James R. Webb; ***C:*** Joseph Biroc; ***M:*** Gil Melle.

Organized Crime & Triad Bureau 🦴🦴 *Chungon Satluk Linggei* **1993** Determined Lee and his cop team seal off crowded Hong Kong island Cheung Chai to trap mob boss Tung and his tootsie. And the bystanders better just get out of the way. Lots of action; Chinese with subtitles. **91m/C; VHS, DVD.** *CH* Danny Lee; Anthony Wong; Cecilia Yip; Roy Cheung; Elizabeth Lee; ***D:*** Kirk Wong; ***W:*** Winky Wong; ***C:*** Wing-Hung Wong; Kwong-Hung Chan; ***M:*** Danny Chung; Ding-Yat Tsung.

The Organizer 🦴🦴 *I Compagni; Comrades* **1964** In 19th-century Turin, impoverished aristocratic professor Mastroianni unites a group of textile workers striking against unsafe working conditions. Italian with subtitles. **127m/B; VHS, DVD, Blu-Ray.** *IT* Marcello Mastroianni; Annie Girardot; Renato Salvatori; Bernard Blier; Francois Perier; Folco Lulli; ***D:*** Mario Monicelli; ***W:*** Mario Monicelli; ***C:*** Giuseppe Rotunno.

Organizm 🦴 **1/2** *Living Hell* **2008 (R)** Typically underwhelming Sci-Fi Channel original. When Frank Sears was a kid, his dad worked at a New Mexico army base doing weird experiments that his crazy mom ranted about. She knew they kept something dangerous locked in an underground lab and carved the section's numbers into the palms of Frank's hands. When the adult Frank (Schaech) learns the base is to be demolished, he finally gets someone to look in the lab and they accidentally unleash a deadly organism that feeds on light and energy. Naturally, Frank is the only one that can stop the creature. **92m/C; DVD.** Johnathon Schaech; Erica Leerhsen; James McDaniel; Jason Wiles; Frederick Lopez; ***D:*** Richard Jefferies; ***W:*** Richard Jefferies; ***C:*** Eric Leach; ***M:*** Terence Jay. **CABLE**

The Orgasm Diaries 🦴 *Brilliantlove* **2010** Boring borderline porn with a sorta plot. Wannabe photographer Manchester is living in a dirty squat with his lover Noon. He takes a series of explicit shots detailing their sex lives (and they have a lot of sex) only to leave some behind after a drunken night in a pub. After shady Franny sees them, he makes Manchester an offer to display them at a swank gallery but Manchester neglects to tell Noon about his nudie art show. **101m/C; DVD.** *GB* Liam Browne; Nancy Trotter Landry; Michael Hodgson; Arabella Arnott; Stephen Bent; ***D:*** Ashley Horner; ***W:*** Sean Conway; ***C:*** Simon Tindall; ***M:*** Sol Seppy.

Orgazmo 🦴 **1/2 1998 (NC-17)** "South Park" co-creator Trey Parker plays Morman porn star Joe Young in this tale of sinners and Latter Day Saints in the dirty movie biz. When his sidekick (Bachar) invents an orgasm ray gun, they become superheroes and ride the one-joke premise like a rented Ferrari. Although hung with an NC-17 rating, it's guilty of bad humor more than bad taste. Parker is likeable, however, and provides intermittent laughs. **95m/C; VHS, DVD, Blu-Ray.** Trey Parker; Dian Bachar; Ron Jeremy; Matt Stone; Robyn Lynne; Michael Dean Jacobs; Andrew W. Kemler; David Dunn; ***D:*** Trey Parker; ***W:*** Trey Parker; ***C:*** Kenny Gioseffi; ***M:*** Paul Robb.

Orgy of the Dead **WOOF!** **1965** Classic anti-canon film scripted by Ed Wood Jr., from his own novel. Two innocent travelers are forced to watch an even dozen nude spirits dance in a cardboard graveyard. Hilariously bad. **90m/C; VHS, DVD, Blu-Ray.** Criswell; Fawn Silver; William Bates; Pat Barrington; John Andrews; Colleen O'Brien; ***D:*** A.C. (Stephen Apostoloff) Stephen; ***W:*** Edward D. Wood, Jr.; ***C:*** Robert Caramico.

Orgy of the Vampires 🦴 *Vampire's Night Orgy* **1973 (R)** Tourists wander into village during cocktail hour. **86m/C; VHS, DVD, Blu-Ray.** *SP IT* Jack Taylor; Charo Soriano; Dianik Zurakowska; John Richard; ***D:*** Leon Klimovsky; ***W:*** Antonio Fos; ***C:*** Antonio Ballesteros.

Oriana 🦴🦴 **1985** Marie (Silverio) learns that her Aunt Oriana (Wells) has willed her the family estate, a remote Venezuelan hacienda she visited as a girl. While preparing the house for sale and going through her aunt's things, Marie remembers her long-ago stay and tries to discover why Oriana never left the property, what happened to her first love, and what other secrets she kept. Spanish and French with subtitles. **88m/C; DVD.** *FR VZ* Daniela Silverio; Doris Wells; Rafael Briceno; Luis Armando Castillo; Maya Oloe; Mirtha Borges; ***D:*** Fina Torres; ***W:*** Fina Torres; Antoine Lacomblez; ***C:*** Jean-Claude Larrieu; ***M:*** Eduardo Marturet.

Original Gangstas 🦴🦴 **1996 (R)** John Bookman (Williamson) returns to his old Gary, Indiana 'hood after his father is brutally shot by a gang leader. Things have changed from Bookman's days of gang banging, with the streets swarming with young machine gun-toting lowlifes. Bent on revenge, Bookman's aided by childhood friends Jake (Brown), Slick (Roundtree), and Bubba (O'Neal) in taking back their streets with a little help from greiving mother, Laurie (Grier). The nostalgia quotient is high watching these '70s blaxploitation stars together--older, grayer, and a little wider, but still able to kick butt in a conventional vigilante vehicle. **98m/C; VHS, DVD, Blu-Ray.** Jim Brown; Fred Williamson; Pam Grier; Ron O'Neal; Richard Roundtree; Paul Winfield; ***D:*** Larry Cohen; ***W:*** Aubrey Rattan; ***C:*** Carlos Gonzalez; ***M:*** Vladimir Horunzhy.

Original Intent 🦴🦴 **1991 (PG)** A successful lawyer, facing a mid-life crisis, jeopardizes both his family and career when he decides to defend a homeless shelter from eviction proceedings. What might have been a powerful drama about one man's crusade to help the homeless instead merely melodramtic. Actor/activist Sheen appears briefly as a homeless man. **97m/C; VHS, DVD.** Jay Richardson; Candy Clark; Kris Kristofferson; Vince Edwards; Cindy Pickett; Robert DoQui; Joseph Campanella; ***Cameo(s):*** Martin Sheen; ***D:*** Robert Marcarelli; ***W:*** Robert Marcarelli.

Original Sin 🦴🦴 **2001 (R)** 1880s Cuban coffee-plantation owner Luis (Banderas) sends for a mail-order bride and beautiful Julia (Jolie) shows up. What follows is betrayal, murder, and theft for starters. Soon he's cleaned out, shamed, and on the trail of his former "wife." Banderas and Jolie torch the screen as the couple in lust, but the ham-handed dialogue and direction derail this period potboiler. Loosely based on the Cornell Woolrich novel "Waltz Into Darkness," which was also the source for Truffaut's "Mississippi Mermaid." **112m/C; VHS, DVD.** Antonio Banderas; Angelina Jolie; Thomas Jane; Jack Thompson; Gregory Itzin; Joan Pringle; Allison Mackie; Cordelia Richards; Pedro Armendariz, Jr.; ***D:*** Michael Cristofer; ***W:*** Michael Cristofer; ***C:*** Rodrigo Prieto; ***M:*** Terence Blanchard.

Orlando 🦴🦴🦴 **1992 (PG-13)** Potter's sumptuous film adaptation of Virginia Woolf's 1928 novel, which covers 400 years in the life of an English nobleman, who not only defies death but evolves from a man to a woman in the intervening years. Orlando (Swinton) is first seen as a young man in the court of Queen Elizabeth I (Crisp) but after a deep sleep it's suddenly 40 years later. Things like this just keep happening and by 1750 he is now a she (and remains so), finding and losing love, and eventually gaining fulfillment in the 20th century. Elaborate productions never overwhelm Swinton's serene, self-assured performance. **93m/C; VHS, DVD.** *UK* Tilda Swinton; Charlotte Valandrey; Billy Zane; Lothaire Bluteau; John Wood; Quentin Crisp; Heathcote Williams; Dudley Sutton; Thom Hoffman; Peter Eyre; Jimmy Somerville; ***D:*** Sally Potter; ***W:*** Sally Potter; ***C:*** Alexei Rodionov; ***M:*** Bob Last.

Orloff and the Invisible Man *Orloff Against the Invisible Man; The Invisible Dead; Dr. Orloff's Invisible Monster* **1970** So many invisible man movies, so little time. A scientist creates an invisible man, imprisons and tortures him. A bit miffed with his host, he who can't be seen escapes, and vents his invisible spleen. **76m/C; VHS, DVD.** *IT FR* Howard Vernon; Brigitte Carva; Fernando (Fernand) Sancho; Isabel Del Rio; Paco Valladares; ***D:*** Pierre Chevalier; ***W:*** France Villon; ***M:*** Camile Sauvage.

The Orphan ½ *Friday the 13th: The Orphan* **1979** A young orphaned boy seeks revenge against his cruel aunt who is harassing him with sadistic discipline. Based on the Saki story and sold as "Friday the 13th: The Orphan" though it has nothng to do with that franchise. **80m/C; VHS, Streaming.** Mark Evans; Joanna Miles; Peggy (Margaret) Feury; ***D:*** John Ballard; ***W:*** John Ballard; ***C:*** Bedrich Batka; ***M:*** Teo Macero.

Orphan ½ **2009 (R)** Gory and somewhat repulsive killer kiddie flick. When their third child is stillborn it takes a toll on John (Sarsgaard) and Kate's (Farmiga) marriage and Kate's sanity as well, tipping her farther over the edge into alcoholism. So of course it makes sense (only in movie plot land) to decide it would be a great time to adopt. They choose extremely polite but obviously odd nine-year-old orphan Esther (Fuhrman) but Kate becomes increasingly alarmed that something evil lurks beneath the girl's prim facade. Passive-aggressive John (and everyone else) seems to think Kate is the one needing a timeout. **101m/C; Blu-Ray, On Demand.** Vera Farmiga; Peter Sarsgaard; Jimmy Bennett; Isabelle Fuhrman; Aryana Engineer; CCH Pounder; Margo Martindale; Karel Roden; Rosemary Dunsmore; ***D:*** Jaume Collet-Serra; ***W:*** David Leslie Johnson; ***C:*** Jeff Cutter; ***M:*** John Ottman.

The Orphanage *El Orfanato* **2007 (R)** Laura (Rueda) returns to the orphanage of her youth with husband Carlos (Cayo) and adopted son Simon (Princep). They've purchased the abandoned building with plans to establish a home for sick and disabled children, but their plans are preempted by Simon's new imaginary playmate, forcing long-repressed memories to surface for Laura and leading to Simon's disappearance. Laura attempts to sort reality from haunting fantasy as she desperately tries to find her son and cling to sanity. Well-acted and well-crafted, this terrifying ghost story is gripping, anxious, and truly scary. **100m/C; DVD, Blu-Ray.** *SP* Belen Rueda; Geraldine Chaplin; Mabel Rivera; Fernando Cayo; Roger Princep; Montserrat Carulla; ***D:*** Juan Antonio Bayona; ***W:*** Sergio G. Sanchez; ***C:*** Oscar Fauna; ***M:*** Fernando Velazquez.

Orphans **1987 (R)** A gangster on the run is kidnapped by a tough New York orphan but soon takes control by befriending his abductor's maladjusted brother. Eventually each brother realizes his need for the older man, who has become a father figure to them. This very quirky film is salvaged by good performances. Based on the play by Lyle Kessler. **116m/C; VHS, DVD.** Albert Finney; Matthew Modine; Kevin Anderson; ***D:*** Alan J. Pakula; ***W:*** Lyle Kessler; ***M:*** Michael Small.

Orphans **1997** Three brothers and their handicapped sister come unraveled in the 24-hour period following their mother's death. The four Flynn siblings head for the pub the night before the funeral where eldest brother Thomas (Lewis) takes to singing, drawing amusement from the onlookers. This upsets Michael (Henshall), who then gets stabbed in the subsequent bar fight, leading youngest brother John (McCole) to vow to get revenge. Meanwhile, angry, wheelchair-bound Sheila (Stevenson) is bored and decides to take a little roll around Glasgow on her own. Feature directorial debut of actor Mullan. **102m/C; VHS, DVD.** *GB* Douglas Henshall; Gary Lewis; Stephen McCole; Rosemarie Stevenson; Alex Norton; Frank Gallagher; Malcolm Shields; ***D:*** Peter Mullan; ***W:*** Peter Mullan; ***C:*** Grant Scott Cameron; ***M:*** Craig Armstrong.

Orphans of the Storm ½ **1921** Two sisters are separated and raised in opposite worlds—one by thieves, the other by aristocrats. Gish's poignant search for her sister is hampered by the turbulent maelstrom preceding the French Revolution. Silent. Based on the French play "The Two Orphans." **190m/B; Silent; VHS, DVD.** Lillian Gish; Dorothy Gish; Monte Blue; Joseph Schildkraut; ***D:*** D.W. Griffith; ***W:*** D.W. Griffith; ***C:*** Billy (G.W.) Bitzer; Hendrik Sartov; ***M:*** Louis F. Gottschalk; William F. Peters.

Orpheus ½ *Orphee* **1949** Cocteau's fascinating, innovative retelling of the Orpheus legend in a modern, though slightly askew, Parisian setting. Classic visual effects and poetic imagery. In French with English subtitles. **95m/B; VHS, DVD, Blu-Ray.** Jean Marais; Francois Perier; Maria Casares; Marie Dea; Edouard Dermithe; Juliette Greco; ***D:*** Jean Cocteau; ***W:*** Jean Cocteau; ***C:*** Nicolas Hayer; ***M:*** Georges Auric.

Orwell Rolls in His Grave **2003** Wordy talking-head dominated movie parallels George Orwell's Big Brother totalitarianism in "1984" with the current relationship of U.S. media and government. Interviews conducted in dull settings and comically ominous soundtrack music detract from the main objective. Basically a poor rehashing of other Republication-bashing docs like "Fahrenheit 9/11," "The Corporation," and "Outfoxed." **95m/C; DVD.** ***D:*** Robert Kane Pappas; ***W:*** Robert Kane Pappas; Tom Blackburn; ***C:*** Robert Kane Pappas; Alan Hostetter; ***M:*** Eric Wood.

Osaka Elegy ½ *Woman of Osaka* **1936** A study of Japanese cultural rules when society condemns a woman for behavior that is acceptable for a man. Japanese with subtitles. **71m/B; VHS, DVD.** *JP* Isuzu Yamada; Benkei Shiganoya; Eitaro Shindo; ***D:*** Kenji Mizoguchi; ***W:*** Yoshikata Yoda; ***C:*** Minoru Miki; ***M:*** Koichi Takagi.

Osama **2003** First post-Taliban movie produced in Afghanistan shows the oppression suffered by women under that regime in the story of Osama (Golbahari) who breaks the law, disguising herself as a boy to support her family after her father and brother are killed. She's rounded up with all the boys of her village and forced into the local religious/military training camp where she does everything she can to keep her disguise from being discovered. Director Barmak has an exceptional eye for detail and uses hand-held cameras and nonprofessional actors on the streets of Kabul to create a brutally realistic portrait of Afghanistan under the Taliban. A brilliant, intense portrait of one girl's quest to survive hopelessness, horrible cruelty, and overbearing oppression. Dari with subtitles. **82m/C; DVD.** *JP IR* Marina Golbahari; Arif Herati; Zubaida Sahar; ***D:*** Siddiq Barmak; ***W:*** Siddiq Barmak; ***C:*** Ebraheem Ghafouri; ***M:*** Mohammad Reza Darvishi.

Oscar **1991 (PG)** The improbable casting of Stallone in a 1930s style crime farce (an attempt to change his image) is hard to imagine, and harder to believe. Stallone has little to do as he plays the straight man in this often ridiculous story of a crime boss who swears he'll go straight. Cameos aplenty, with Curry's the most notable. Based on a French play by Claude Magnier. **109m/C; VHS, DVD, Blu-Ray.** Sylvester Stallone; Ornella Muti; Peter Riegert; Vincent Spano; Marisa Tomei; Kirk Douglas; Art LaFleur; Ken Howard; Chazz Palminteri; Tim Curry; Don Ameche; Richard Romanus; ***D:*** John Landis; ***W:*** Michael Barrie; Jim Mulholland; ***C:*** Mac Ahlberg; ***M:*** Elmer Bernstein.

Oscar and Lucinda ½ **1997 (R)** A priest and a glassworks heiress are united by a shared passion for gambling; together they attempt to transport a glass church through 1860s Australian wilderness. Fiennes' performance as the vulnerable and flailing Oscar is particularly good. Narrated by Geoffrey Rush. Based on the Booker Prize-winning novel by Peter Carey. **131m/C; VHS, DVD.** Ralph Fiennes; Cate Blanchett; Ciaran Hinds; Tom Wilkinson; Richard Roxburgh; Clive Russell; Bille Brown; Josephine Byrnes; Barnaby Kay; Barry Otto; Linda Bassett; ***Nar:*** Geoffrey Rush; ***D:*** Gillian Armstrong; ***W:*** Laura Jones; ***C:*** Geoffrey Simpson; ***M:*** Thomas Newman. Australian Film Inst. '98: Cinematog., Score.

Oslo, August 31st **2011** A once-promising writer, 30-something Anders screwed up his life with his addictions to alcohol and drugs. Having cleaned up in a country rehab center, he takes a day trip to Oslo, ostensibly for a job interview but really to review his past and his prospects. He meets his former best friend Thomas, who has gone from wild partying to a respectable life, and wonders if it's possible for him to do the same. Or if his continuing shame and depression will make this literally his last day alive. Norwegian with subtitles. **96m/C; DVD.** *NO* Anders Danielsen Lie; Hans Olav Brenner; ***D:*** Joachim Trier; ***W:*** Joachim Trier; Eskil Vogt; ***C:*** Jakob Ihre; ***M:*** Ola Flottum; Torgny Amadam.

Osmosis Jones ½ **2001 (PG-13)** Combo of animation and live-action concerns a slob named Frank (Murray) who's suffering from an evil virus (Fishburne) that's taking over his body. To the rescue are white blood cell Osmosis Jones (Rock) and cold tablet Drix (Pierce). The Farrellys push the gross-out humor, but the live-action sequences suffer when compared to the clever, high-energy animated sequences. Kids will enjoy the lively animation and gross stuff while adults should have a good enough time with the puns and references to other movies. Murray goes to heroic lengths to portray Frank's devotion to self-degradation. **95m/C; VHS, DVD.** Bill Murray; Molly Shannon; Chris Elliott; Elena Franklin; ***V:*** Chris Rock; Laurence Fishburne; David Hyde Pierce; Brandy Norwood; William Shatner; Ron Howard; ***D:*** Bobby Farrelly; Peter Farrelly; Piet Kroon; Tom Sito; ***W:*** Marc Hyman; ***C:*** Mark Irwin; ***M:*** Randy Edelman.

Osombie *Ozombie; Osombie: Axis of the Evil Dead* **2012** A yoga instructor heads for Afghanistan to rescue her conspiracy theorist brother who believes Osama bin Laden is alive. Unbelievably, he's half right, and Osama is a zombie swiftly infecting everything in his path. **94m/C; DVD, Blu-Ray, Streaming.** Corey Sevier; Eve Mauro; Jasen Wade; Danielle Chuchran; William Rubio; ***D:*** John Lyde; ***W:*** Kurt Hale; ***C:*** Airk Thaughbaer; ***M:*** Jimmy Schafer. **VIDEO**

OSS 117: Cairo, Nest of Spies *OSS 117: Le Caire Nid d'Espions* **2006** This spy spoof has a long history in France, beginning with Jean Bruce's first novel in 1949 (pre-James Bond), with the character previously appearing in seven films. A suavely deadpan OSS 117 (Dujardin) is sent to Cairo in 1955 to protect French interests in the Suez crisis and investigate the murder of a fellow agent. He's condescending to the locals, thinks he's irresistible to women, and his dumb luck is surpassed only by his ignorance. French with subtitles. **99m/C; DVD.** *FR* Berenice Bejo; Philippe Lefebvre; Aure Atika; Jean Dujardin; Constantin Alexandrev; ***D:*** Michel Hazanavicius; ***W:*** Jean-Francois Halin; ***C:*** Guillaume Schiffman; ***M:*** Ludovic Bource.

OSS 117: Lost in Rio *OSS 117: Rio Ne Repond Plus* **2009** Equally silly spy comedy sequel to 2006's "OSS 117: Cairo, Nest of Spies" based on a series of novels by Jean Bruce. Bumbling, preening spy OSS 117's (Dujardin) mission is defending his country against foreigners and sticking up for Charles de Gaulle. In 1967, he's sent to Brazil to get some microfilm that names Frenchmen who collaborated with the Nazis. OSS 117 is teamed with Mossad agent Dolores (Morot), who's after escaped Nazis, but his anti-Semitism and sexism keeps surfacing and screwing things up. French with subtitles. **101m/C; DVD, Streaming.** *FR* Jean Dujardin; Louise Monot; Alex Lutz; Rudiger Volger; Ken Samuels; Reem Kherici; Pierre Bellemare; Serge Hazanavicius; ***D:*** Serge Hazanavicius; ***W:*** Serge Hazanavicius; Jean-Francois Halin; ***C:*** Guillaume Schiffman; ***M:*** Ludovic Bource.

Ossessione ½ **1942** An adaptation of "The Postman Always Rings Twice," transferred to Fascist Italy, where a drifter and an innkeeper's wife murder her husband. Visconti's first feature, which initiated Italian neo-realism, was not released in the U.S. until 1975 due to a copyright dispute. In Italian with English subtitles. **135m/B; VHS, DVD.** *IT* Massimo Girotti; Clara Calamai; Juan deLanda; Elio Marcuzzo; ***D:*** Luchino Visconti; ***W:*** Guiseppe de Santis; Mario Alicata; ***C:*** Aldo Tonti; Domenico Scala.

Osso Bucco ½ **2008** A comedy with romance and mobsters. Misfit mobster Jelly and his trigger-happy cousin Nick go to Jelly's favorite Chicago restaurant so Jelly can have his favorite meal and moon over waitress Megan. They're soon snowbound by a blizzard with a couple of police detectives with arrest warrants when the power in the restaurant goes out as well. **86m/C; DVD.** Mike Starr; Illeana Douglas; Christian Stolte; Antoine McKay; Mike Nussbaum; Aaron Roman Weiner; ***D:*** Gary Taylor; Fred Blurton; ***W:*** Gary Taylor; ***C:*** David Kessler; ***M:*** Karen Martin.

The Osterman Weekend **1983 (R)** Peckinpah was said to have disliked the story and the script in this, his last film, which could account for the convoluted and confusing end result. Adding to the problem is the traditional difficulty of adapting Ludlum's complex psychological thrillers for the screen. The result: cast members seem to not quite "get it" as they portray a group of friends, one of whom has been convinced by the CIA that the others are all Soviet spies. **102m/C; VHS, DVD, Blu-Ray.** Burt Lancaster; Rutger Hauer; Craig T. Nelson; Dennis Hopper; John Hurt; Chris Sarandon; Meg Foster; Helen Shaver; ***D:*** Sam Peckinpah; ***M:*** Lalo Schifrin.

Otaku No Video *Fan's Video* **1991** Satirized bio of Gainax animation studio and its founders containing two installments, one made in 1982 and one in 1985. In 1982, college freshman Kubo is reunited with his old friend Tanaka and gets sucked into the world of hopelessly obsessed anime and science fiction fans (or "otaku") that examines the social costs of his new hobby. The second installment finds Kubo and Tanaka starting two different businesses directly related to their beloved hobby. As if the animated stories weren't hilarious enough, tthere are live-action, fake documentary segments focusing on different aspects of "otakudom." **100m/C; VHS, DVD.** *JP* ***V:*** Kohi Tsujitani; Toshiharu Sakurai; ***D:*** Takeshi Mori; ***W:*** Toshio Okada; ***C:*** Tadashi Sano; ***M:*** Kohei Tanaka.

Otello ½ **1986 (PG)** An uncommon film treat for opera fans, with a stellar performance by Domingo as the troubled Moor who murders his wife in a fit of jealous rage and later finds she was never unfaithful. Be prepared, however, for changes from the Shakespeare and Verdi stories, necessitated by the film adaptation. Highly acclaimed and awarded; in Italian with English subtitles. **123m/C; VHS, DVD.** *IT* Placido Domingo; Katia Ricciarelli; Justino Diaz; ***D:*** Franco Zeffirelli.

Othello ½ **1922** A silent version of Shakespeare's tragedy, featuring Jannings as the tragic Moor. Titles are in English; with musical score. **81m/B; Silent; VHS, DVD.** *GE* Emil Jannings; Lya de Putti; Werner Krauss; ***D:*** Dimitri Buchowetzki.

Othello *Orson Welles's Othello; The Tragedy of Othello: The Moor of Venice* **1952** Welles's striking adaptation of the Shakespeare tragedy casts him as the self-deluding Moor, with MacLiammoir as the despicable Iago and Cloutier as innocent victim, Desdemona. Welles filmed his epic over a four-year period due to budget difficulties, which also resulted in his filming in a number of different countries and settings. The film underwent a $1 million restoration, supervised by Welles's daughter, prior to its limited theatrical re-release in 1992. **90m/B; VHS, DVD.** Orson Welles; Micheal MacLiammoir; Suzanne Cloutier; Robert Coote; Hilton Edwards; Michael Lawrence; Nicholas Bruce; Fay Compton; Doris Dowling; Jean Davis; Joseph Cotten; Joan Fontaine; ***D:*** Orson Welles; ***W:*** Orson Welles; ***C:*** Anchise Brizzi; George Fanto; Alberto Fusi; Aldo (G.R. Aldo) Graziatti; Oberdan Troiani; ***M:*** Alberto Barberis; Angelo Francesco Lavagnino. Cannes '52: Film.

Othello ½ **1965** Olivier (in blackface) gives another towering performance as Shakespeare's tragic Moor, led to disaster by his own jealousy. He's ably supported by Finlay's insinuating performance as Iago, Smith as a sweetly vulnerable Desdemona, and Jacobi as unwitting rival Cassio. The production, however, doesn't stray far from its stage-bound roots. **150m/C; VHS, DVD.** Laurence Olivier; Frank Finlay; Maggie Smith; Derek Jacobi; Joyce Redman; Anthony Nicholls; Sheila Reid; Roy Holder; ***D:*** Stuart Burge; ***W:*** Margaret Unsworth; ***C:*** Geoffrey Unsworth; ***M:*** Richard Hampton.

Othello **1995 (R)** Fishburne stars as Shakespeare's tragic Moor, with Branagh as silken agitator Iago, and Jacob as the tragic Desdemona. First time director Oliver Parker (brother Nathaniel is also in the film) drastically cut the play, rearranging scenes (and even adding material)--purists will no doubt scream, but performances carry the production. Through the clever use of asides directed at the camera, Iago makes the viewer feel like an accomplice in the plot. French-speaking Jacob, however, seems to have a hard time pronouncing the Shakespearean dialogue. **125m/C; DVD.** Laurence Fishburne; Irene Jacob; Kenneth Branagh; Nathaniel Parker; Michael Maloney; Anna Patrick; Nicholas Farrell; Indra Ove; Michael Sheen; Andre Oumansky; Philip Locke; John Savident; Gabriele Ferzetti; Pierre Vaneck; ***D:*** Oliver Parker; ***W:*** Oliver Parker; ***C:*** David C(lark) Johnson; ***M:*** Charlie Mole.

Othello **2001** Updated version (with modern dialogue) of Shakespeare's "Othello" set in contemporary London. John Othello (Walker) is a respected police officer who has just been installed as the first black commissioner of the Metropolitan force. His promotion comes at the expense of his mentor/friend Ben Jago (Eccleston) who does not handle the slight well as he is now second-in-command. So Ben plays the race card and works on John's jealousy of his heiress white wife, Dessie (Hawley), by suggesting that she is unfaithful. Walker is convincingly impassioned but Eccleston's slimy manipulation is rather too obvious. **96m/C; VHS, DVD.** *GB* Eamonn Walker; Christopher Eccleston; Keeley Hawes; Richard Coyle; Del Synnott; Christopher Fox; Allan Cutts; Patrick Myers; ***D:*** Geoffrey Sax; ***W:*** Andrew Davies; ***C:*** Daf Hobson; ***M:*** Debbie Wiseman. **TV**

The Other **1972 (PG)** Eerie, effective thriller adapted by Tyron from his supernatural novel. Twin brothers represent good and evil in a 1930s Connecticut farm town beset with gruesome murders and accidents. A good scare. **100m/C; VHS, DVD, Blu-Ray; Open Captioned.** Martin Udvarnoky; Chris Udvarnoky; Uta Hagen; Diana Muldaur; Norma Connolly; Victor French; John Ritter; Loretta Leversee; Lou Frizzell; Portia Nelson; Jenny Sullivan; ***D:*** Robert Mulligan; ***W:*** Tom Tryon; ***C:*** Robert L. Surtees; ***M:*** Jerry Goldsmith.

The Other Boleyn Girl **2003** Truncated, low-budget TV version of Philippa Gregory's novel about Mary Boleyn (McElhone), who first won the favor of King Henry VIII (Harris) while a young married woman at court. When Mary becomes pregnant, the restless Henry turns his attentions to Mary's older and much-more ambitious sister Anne (May), who refuses to give in until Henry is free to marry her. **90m/C; DVD.** *GB* Natascha (Natasha) McElhone; Jodhi May; Jared Harris; Jack Shepherd; Philip Glenister; John Woodvine; Ron Cook; Anthony Howell; Yolanda Vazquez; Steven Mackintosh; Jane Gurnett; ***C:*** Graham Smith; ***M:*** Peter Salem. **TV**

The Other Boleyn Girl 1/2 **2008 (PG-13)** Big-budget Elizabethan period piece that comes off more like a Hollywood soap opera, starring three non-British leads who seem too hip and contemporary for this kind of melodramatic material. Sisters Anne (Portman) and Mary (Johansson) Boleyn compete for the love of King Henry VIII (Bana) with a fast-forward through history showing Anne's ascent to the throne. The costumes and scenery are expectedly great and script is surprisingly tight (if occasionally anachronistic), but the direction is often confusing and awkward. Based on the novel by Phillipa Gregory. **115m/C; DVD, Blu-Ray.** *GB US* Eric Bana; Natalie Portman; Scarlett Johansson; David Morrissey; Mark Rylance; Jim Sturgess; Eddie Redmayne; Benedict Cumberbatch; Ana Torrent; Juno Temple; Oliver Coleman; Kristin Scott Thomas; ***D:*** Justin Chadwick; ***W:*** Peter Morgan; ***C:*** Kieran McGuigan; ***M:*** Paul Cantelon.

The Other Brother 1/2 **2002 (R)** Nice guy Martin (Phifer) is shocked to discover his girlfriend in bed with another woman. Uncertain about his judgement of the fair sex, he reluctantly agrees to listen to his player brother Junnie's (Blake) advice, which results in some awkward pickup moments. Of course, Martin has already meet the perfect new girlfriend, his new upstairs neighbor Paula (Miller), if only he would listen to what his own heart says. **94m/C; VHS, DVD.** Mekhi Phifer; Andre B. Blake; Michele Morgan; Tangi Miller; Ebony Jo-Ann; Regina Hall; Collette Wilson; ***D:*** Mandel Holland; ***W:*** Mandel Holland; ***C:*** Matthew Clark.

The Other End of the Line 1/2 **2008 (PG-13)** Charming cross-cultural romantic comedy. Priya (Saran) has the best American accent of all the Indian employees at the Bangalore call center. Good enough to fool regular client Granger Woodruff (Metcalfe) who thinks Priya also lives in San Francisco. A series of contrivances takes Priya to the city by the bay and a chance for true love. **106m/C; DVD.** Jesse Metcalfe; Austin Basis; Larry Miller; Anupam Kher; Shriya Saran; ***D:*** James Dodson; ***W:*** Tracey Jackson; ***C:*** Harlan Bosmajian; ***M:*** B.C. Smith.

The Other Guys 1/2 **2010 (PG-13)** Intentionally dumb buddy-cop leaves no cliche untouched, scoring plenty of laughs in the process. Generally mild-mannered New York detective and forensic accountant Allen Gamble (Ferrell) prefers to work a desk rather than the streets while his new partner, testy and trigger-happy Terry Hoitz (Wahlberg), can't get enough action. They try to emulate supercops Danson (Johnson) and Highsmith (Jackson) but things don't work out as planned as they go after white collar Wall Street criminal Ershon (Coogan). **107m/C; DVD, Blu-Ray, On Demand.** Will Ferrell; Mark Wahlberg; Dwayne "The Rock" Johnson; Samuel L. Jackson; Steve Coogan; Eva Mendes; Lindsay Sloane; Michael Keaton; Damon Wayans, Jr.; Paris Hilton; Rob Riggle; Bobby Cannavale; Anne Heche; ***Nar:*** Ice-T; ***D:*** Adam McKay; ***W:*** Adam McKay; Chris Henchy; ***C:*** Oliver Wood; ***M:*** Jon Brion.

The Other Half **2006** Englishman Mark surprises his American bride Holly with her dream honeymoon in Portugal. Then Holly discovers that the country is hosting an international soccer tournament and the English national team just happens to be playing. Mark protests his innocence but Holly is convinced her soccer-mad hubby is lying, which isn't a great way to start a marriage. **101m/C; DVD.** *GB* Danny Dyer; Gillian Kearney; Vinnie Jones; Mark Lynch; Jonathan Broke; Katie Cromer; ***D:*** Marlowe Fawcett; Richard Nockles; ***W:*** Marlowe Fawcett; Richard Nockles; ***C:*** John Behrens.

The Other Half 1/2 **2017** Few films have addressed mental illness and emotional devastation in as raw as fashion as Joey Klein's romantic drama, which takes the realism a step further by casting real-life couple Maslany and Cullen in the leading roles. Maslany plays Emily, a woman struggling with bipolar disorder; Cullen plays Nickie, a man overcome with grief. The film is really just about how the two of them battle their issues to live normal lives. Both performers are very good here, but Klein's script too often uses real issues for heartstring-tugging effect. See it for Maslany and Cullen though. **103m/C; DVD.** Tatiana Maslany; Tom Cullen; Henry Czerny; Suzanne Clément; Diana Bentley; ***D:*** Joey Klein; ***W:*** Joey Klein; ***C:*** Bobby Shore.

The Other Love 1/2 **1947** Maudlin melodrama based on a story by Erich Marie Remarque. A surprisingly healthy-looking concert pianist, Karen Duncan (Stanwyck), is actually dying of TB and goes to a Swiss sanitarium for treatment. She falls for her dashing doctor, Anthony Stanton (Niven), who tries to get her to rest and stay calm. Instead, Karen decides to leave and have a fling with race car driver, Paul (Conte), before coming back to her true love. **93m/B; DVD, Blu-Ray.** Barbara Stanwyck; David Niven; Richard Conte; Joan Lorring; Natalie Schafer; ***D:*** Andre de Toth; ***W:*** Ladislas Fodor; Harry Brown; ***C:*** Victor Milner; ***M:*** Miklos Rozsa.

The Other Man **2008 (R)** Fussy, minor romantic melodrama/thriller with silly plot twists. Successful software exec Peter (Neeson) and his longtime wife, upscale shoe designer Lisa (Linney), live with their daughter Abigail (Garai) in Cambridge, England. Lisa apparently disappears after dropping hints about marital infidelity and Peter learns by snooping on her computer that she's having an affair with Ralph (Banderas), who lives in Milan. Jealous, Peter heads to Italy, befriends Ralph over chess games in a local cafe, and tries to press him for details on the affair without divulging who he is. **89m/C; DVD, Blu-Ray, On Demand.** *UK* Liam Neeson; Antonio Banderas; Laura Linney; Romola Garai; ***D:*** Richard Eyre; ***W:*** Richard Eyre; Charles Wood; ***C:*** Haris Zambarloukos; ***M:*** Stephen Warbeck.

Other Men's Women **1931** Railroad engineer Jack (Toomey) and his wife Lily (Astor) agree to let his pal Bill (Withers) stay with them. The flirtatious Bill starts up with Lily, which leads to a quarrel with Jack and a train accident that leaves Jack blind. Unwilling to be a burden to Lily, Jack comes up with a radical solution when a railroad bridge is threatened with collapse during a flood. **70m/B; DVD.** Regis Toomey; Mary Astor; Grant Withers; Joan Blondell; James Cagney; Fred Kohler, Sr.; J. Farrell MacDonald; ***D:*** William A. Wellman; ***W:*** Maude Fulton; William K. Wells; ***C:*** Barney McGill.

Other People 1/2 **2016** David (Plemons) is a young man returning home when his mother Joanne (career-best work from Shannon) is diagnosed with terminal cancer. Ultimately, it's yet another one of those dramedies in which a selfish man learns how to be a better person by facing the death of his beloved parent. But yet writer/director Kelly finds a way to make you empathize with David as he faces personal struggles in the wake of his extreme grief. **97m/C; DVD.** Jesse Plemons; Molly Shannon; Bradley Whitford; Maude Apatow; Madisen Beaty; ***D:*** Chris Kelly; ***W:*** Chris Kelly; ***C:*** Brian Burgoyne; ***M:*** Julian Wass. Ind. Spirit '17: Actress--Supporting (Shannon).

Other People's Money 1/2 **1991 (R)** DeVito is "Larry the Liquidator," a corporate raider with a heart of stone and a penchant for doughnuts. When he sets his sights on a post-smokestack era, family-owned cable company, he gets a taste of love for the first time in his life. He and Miller, the daughter of the company president and also its legal advisor, court one another while sparring over the fate of the company. Unbelievably clipped ending mars otherwise enterprising comedy about the triumph of greed in corporate America. Based on the off-Broadway play by Jerry Sterner. **101m/C; DVD.** Danny DeVito; Penelope Ann Miller; Dean Jones; Gregory Peck; Piper Laurie; Tom Aldredge; R.D. Call; ***D:*** Norman Jewison; ***W:*** Alvin Sargent; ***C:*** Haskell Wexler; ***M:*** David Newman.

The Other Side of Heaven **2002 (PG)** Well-meaning if heavy-handed biodrama based on Groberg's memoir "In the Eye of the Storm." John Groberg (Gorham) is a Mormon college student at Brigham Young University in 1953, who's pining for Jean (Hathaway), the girl of his dreams. Then he receives his missionary assignment—to Tonga in the South Seas. He struggles with native culture, the language barrier, and various hardships and natural disasters before he can accomplish his goals. Film's sincere but you never get much of an idea of how Groberg feels about what befalls him except for his enduring faith. Filmed in the Cook Islands. **113m/C; VHS, DVD.** Christopher Gorham; Anne Hathaway; Joe Folau; Miriama Smith; Nathaniel Lees; Whetu Fala; ***D:*** Mitch Davis; ***W:*** Mitch Davis; ***C:*** Brian J. Breheny; ***M:*** Kevin Kiner.

The Other Side of Heaven 2: Fire of Faith 1/2 **2019 (PG-13)** In the mid-1960s, Mormon missionary Elder John Groberg (Gorham) returns to Tonga, where he had been a missionary a decade earlier, to become the mission's president. This time, he brings his wife (Medlock) and children. John faces conflict with Methodist minister Sione (Baker), who is concerned he will lose followers to the Mormons. When John's son is born with a serious illness and Sione faces a dilemma with his adult son, the pair tries to find common ground. This sequel has better production quality than most faith-based films but features clunky dialogue and stiff performances. **110m/C; DVD.** Christopher Gorham; Natalie Medlock; Russell Dixon; Joe Folau; Ian Mune; ***D:*** Mitch Davis; ***W:*** Mitch Davis; ***C:*** T.C. Christensen; ***M:*** Christian Davis.

The Other Side of Hope 1/2 *Toivon Tuolla Puolen* **2017** A warmly humorous comedy-drama about an aspiring restrainer and the tribulations of a Syrian refugee in Finland. After ending his marriage and winning money in poker, Wikstrom (Kuosmanen) invests in a small bar/restaurant. He transforms his business into a sushi bar with the help of Syrian refugee Khaled (Haji), who has his own troubles. Rejected by the Finnish immigration system, he stays in the country illegally to help get his sister out of Syria. Khaled also must manage the racist skinheads who attack him, though they get his ethnicity wrong. Reveals much about immigration through an interesting story. Finnish with subtitles. **100m/C; DVD, Blu-Ray.** Ville Virtanen; Dome Karukoski; Kati Outinen; Tommi Korpela; Sakari Kuosmanen; ***D:*** Aki Kaurismaki; ***W:*** Aki Kaurismaki; ***C:*** Timo Salminen.

The Other Side of Midnight **WOOF!** **1977 (R)** The dreary, depressingly shallow life story of a poor French girl, dumped by an American GI, who sleeps her way to acting stardom and a profitable marriage, then seeks revenge for the jilt. Based on Sidney Sheldon's novel, it's not even titillating—just a real downer. **160m/C; VHS, DVD, Blu-Ray.** Susan Sarandon; Marie-France Pisier; John Beck; Raf Vallone; Clu Gulager; Sorrell Booke; ***D:*** Charles Jarrott; ***W:*** Daniel Taradash; ***C:*** Fred W. Koenekamp.

The Other Side of Sunday *Sondagsengler* **1996** A small town in 1959 Norway is the setting for this coming of age comedy. Maria (Thiesen) is the eldest daughter of conservative priest Johannes (Sundquist). Fun doesn't seem to be part of their religion but puberty is hitting Maria hard and she longs to join in with the livelier crowd of her school friend Brigit (Salvesen), who listens to rock 'n' roll, wears makeup, and makes out with boys. Maria does find a compassionate listener in Mrs. Tunheim (Riise), who urges the teenager to learn how to think for herself. Based on the novel "Sunday" by Reidun Nortvedt. Norwegian with subtitles. **103m/C; VHS, DVD.** *NO* Marie Theisen; Bjorn Sundquist; Hildegunn Riise; Sylvia Salvesen; ***D:*** Berit Nesheim; ***W:*** Berit Nesheim; Lasse Glomm; ***C:*** Arne Borsheim; ***M:*** Geir Bohren; Bent Aserud.

The Other Side of the Door 1/2 **2016 (R)** After her son dies in a car accident, grieving mother Maria (Callies) opens the door to the afterlife, inadvertently bringing forth more than just her son. Nothing new in terms of horror material, and director/co-writer Roberts opts too often for the typical scary movie tricks. Which saps the life out of Callies' strong performance. **96m/C; DVD, Blu-Ray.** Sarah Wayne Callies; Jeremy Sisto; Sofia Rosinsky; Logan Creran; Suchitra Pillai; ***D:*** Johannes Roberts; ***W:*** Johannes Roberts; Ernest Riera; ***C:*** Maxime Alexandre; ***M:*** Joseph Bishara.

The Other Side of the Law **1995 (R)** Man makes a wilderness hideout with his son after killing his wife's murderer. But when the boy grows up, dad decides to send him back into civilization for education, leading to nothing but trouble. **96m/C; DVD.** *CA* Jurgen Prochnow; Johnny Morina; Maggie Castle; Yves Renier; Xavier DeLuc; ***D:*** Gilles Carle; ***W:*** Gilles Carle; ***M:*** Jean Delorme.

The Other Side of the Mountain *A Window to the Sky* **1975 (PG)** Tear-jerking true story of Olympic hopeful skier Jill Kinmont, paralyzed in a fall. Bridges helps her pull her life together. A sequel followed two years later. Based on the book "A Long Way Up" by E. G. Valens. **102m/C; VHS, DVD.** Marilyn Hassett; Beau Bridges; Dabney Coleman; John David Garfield; Griffin Dunne; ***D:*** Larry Peerce; ***W:*** David Seltzer; ***M:*** Charles Fox.

The Other Side of the Mountain, Part 2 **1978 (PG)** Quadriplegic Jill Kinmont, paralyzed in a skiing accident that killed her hopes for the Olympics, overcomes depression and the death of the man who helped her to recover. In this chapter, she falls in love again and finds happiness. More tears are jerked. **99m/C; VHS, DVD.** Marilyn Hassett; Timothy Bottoms; ***D:*** Larry Peerce.

The Other Side of the Wind 1/2 **2018 (R)** Finally released from a Paris vault, the footage of Orson Welles's last, unfinished film was assembled and released, decades after his death. It's both Hollywood satire and mockumentary, focusing on an aging movie director (Huston) trying to stay relevant in a changing world. Shot between 1970 and 1976, the original footage is otherworldly at times, giving Welles's fans a new glimpse into the mind of a master director. **122m/C; Streaming.** John Huston; Oja Kodar; Peter Bogdanovich; Susan Strasberg; Norman Foster; ***D:*** Orson Welles; ***W:*** Oja Kodar; Orson Welles; ***C:*** Gary Graver; ***M:*** Michel Legrand. **TV**

The Other Sister 🦴🦴 **1998 (PG-13)** Carla (Lewis) is the mentally challenged but exuberant member of the repressed Tate family. After leaving a "special school," she convinces her uptight parents Elizabeth (Keaton) and Radley (Skerritt) to let her enroll in a vocational program. She meets and falls for fellow retarded student Danny (Ribisi), much to her parents' dismay. Love wins out, but the script is so sappy that a maple syrup factory could be built on it. Lewis and Ribisi do an admirable job of rising above the material, which was co-written by schmaltz-meister director Garry Marshall. **129m/C; VHS, DVD.** Juliette Lewis; Giovanni Ribisi; Diane Keaton; Tom Skerritt; Poppy Montgomery; Linda Thorson; Juliet Mills; Hector Elizondo; Sarah Paulson; Joe Flanigan; Dina Merrill; ***D:*** Garry Marshall; ***W:*** Garry Marshall; Bob Brunner; ***C:*** Dante Spinotti; ***M:*** Rachel Portman.

The Other Son 🦴🦴🦴 *Le fils de l'autre* **2012 (PG-13)** Two young men, one Palestinian, one Israeli, discover they were switched at birth and must now deal with the fact that the culture they live in violently opposes the culture that gave birth to them. **105m/C; DVD, Blu-Ray, Streaming.** *FR* Emmanuelle Devos; Pascal Elbe; Jules Sitruk; Mehdi Dehbi; Areen Omari; ***D:*** Lorraine Levy; ***W:*** Lorraine Levy; Noam Fitoussi; Nathalie Saugeon; ***C:*** Emmanuel Soyer; ***M:*** Dhafer Youssef.

The Other Story 🦴🦴 **1/2 2019** Though Shachar (Goshen) was a singer with a rock star lifestyle and Anat (Rieger) was a free-spirited Jewish woman, the couple have joined an ultra-Orthodox community and decide to marry. Anat's secular parents try to stop the nuptials despite years of post-divorce acrimony. Simultaneously, Anat's father Yonaton (Segal) and grandfather Shlomo (Gabai), both psychologists, work on a case of Shlomo's involving a custody battle between a Jewish-turned-pagan mother and a Jewish father worried about losing his young son. Though the filmmaker successfully weaves stories that make a broad comment on Israeli life, his exploration of busyness and human connection is equally effective. Hebrew with subtitles. **112m/C; DVD.** Joy Rieger; Yuval Segal; Maya Dagan; Sasson Gabai; Nathan Goshen; ***D:*** Avi Nesher; ***W:*** Avi Nesher; Noam Shpancer; ***C:*** Michel Abramowicz; ***M:*** Cyrille Aufort.

Other Voices, Other Rooms 🦴🦴 **1/2 1995** Adaptation of Truman Capote's 1948 first novel, a semi-autobiographical story of a young boy's search for his father set against the backdrop of a decaying Bayou mansion. Narrated by Capote sound-alike Kingdom, it starts when 12-year-old Joel's (Speck) mother dies and he's sent to live with his father. He's greeted by cousins Amy (Thomson), a fragile and pretty Southern belle, and Randolph (Bluteau), an effete and charming alcoholic. Pic deals with the secrets of the father's illness and what lies behind the unhappiness of the cousins. Lacks the danger and suspense of Capote's novel, but sets a proper mood and shows off the actors' talents. **98m/C; VHS, DVD.** Lothaire Bluteau; Anna Thomson; David Speck; April Turner; Aubrey Dollar; ***Nar:*** Bob Kingdom; ***D:*** David Rocksavage; ***W:*** David Rocksavage; Sara Flanigan; ***C:*** Dr. Paul Ryan; ***M:*** Chris Hajian.

The Other Woman 🦴 **1/2** *Joy Fielding's The Other Woman* **2008** There's two other women—one acts stupidly and one's a blatant vamp tramp. After having an affair, Jill (Bissett) marries now-divorced David Plumley (Whittall), an ambitious lawyer. At a party, his hottie intern Nicole (Caruk) announces to Jill that she plans on being the third Mrs. Plumley. Sounds intriguing but is actually a dull marital mess. **90m/C; DVD.** Josie Bissett; Ted Whittall; Lisa Marie Caruk; Alan C. Peterson; Judith Buchan; Mackenzie Porter; Jason Priestley; ***D:*** Jason Priestley; ***W:*** Dave Schultz; ***C:*** Craig Wrobleski; ***M:*** Zack Ryan. **CABLE**

The Other Woman 🦴 **1/2 2014 (PG-13)** Why do they make so many comedies, especially those starring women, that waste the talents of their cast? When you have two comedians with such perfect timing as Mann and Diaz, one expects a few more laughs than this Cassavetes comedy has to offer. Diaz plays Carly, the boyfriend to Mark (Coster-Waldau), who happens to be married to Mann's Kate. When the two discover that the man between them has yet ANOTHER girlfriend in Amber (Upton), the wheels of comedic revenge begin a-spinning. Mann can do no wrong, even in bad movies, which this definitely is. **109m/C; DVD, Blu-Ray.** Cameron Diaz; Leslie Mann; Kate Upton; Nikolaj Coster-Waldau; Nicki Minaj; Taylor Kinney; Don Johnson; ***D:*** Nick Cassavetes; ***W:*** Melissa Stack; ***C:*** Robert Fraisse; ***M:*** Aaron Zigman. Golden Raspberries '14: Worst Actress (Diaz).

Otherhood 🦴🦴 **2019 (R)** When three suburban mothers who feel neglected by their adult sons gather for a boozy Mother's Day brunch, they decide to visit their boys in New York City to confront them. Each mother has an issue. Piano teacher Gillian (Arquette) has alienated writer son Daniel (Hoffman) by criticizing his girlfriend. Appearance-oriented Helen (Huffman) is hurt that her son Paul (Lacy) told his father he was gay and not her. Artistic Carol struggles with widowhood. The trip becomes about the women's identities and friendship as much as their sons. Strong performances by Huffman and Hoffman can't overcome the superficial flick. **100m/C; DVD.** Angela Bassett; Patricia Arquette; Felicity Huffman; Jake Hoffman; Jake Lacy; ***D:*** Cindy Chupack; ***W:*** Cindy Chupack; Mark Andrus; ***C:*** Declan Quinn; ***M:*** Marcelo Zarvos.

The Others 🦴🦴🦴 **2001 (PG-13)** Twisting Gothic haunt-fest centers on Grace (Kidman) and her two children Anne (Mann) and Nicholas (Bentley), living in a mansion on Britain's remote Isle of Jersey. After her servants suddenly leave, Grace's surprised when a trio of domestics show up, claiming to have worked in the house before. They soon discover why their predecessors left as Grace is demanding and high-strung and, because of rare allergies, the kids must be kept out of the sunlight. Maybe the solitude is preying on Grace's mind, maybe she's crazy, or maybe their house is haunted. Kidman is at her chilly best as the audience is kept guessing. **101m/C; VHS, DVD, Blu-Ray.** Nicole Kidman; Fionnula Flanagan; Alakina Mann; James Bentley; Christopher Eccleston; Elaine Cassidy; Eric Sykes; Renee Asherson; ***D:*** Alejandro Amenabar; ***W:*** Alejandro Amenabar; ***C:*** Javier Aguirresarobe; ***M:*** Alejandro Amenabar.

Otis 🦴🦴 **2008** A pizza delivery guy kidnaps women and forces them to act out the prom night he always wished had happened to him. Unfortunately for him the family of his latest kidnap victim goes unhinged and decides to hunt him down. **100m/C; DVD, Blu-Ray, Streaming.** Bostin Christopher; Ashley Johnson; Daniel Stern; Illeana Douglas; Kevin Pollack; ***D:*** Tony Krantz; ***W:*** Erik Jendresen; Thomas Schnauz; ***C:*** Tom Yatsko; ***M:*** James S. Levine. **VIDEO**

Otley 🦴🦴 **1968** Spy spoof finds bumbling antiques picker Otley (Courtenay) getting repeatedly captured by various groups who believe he has info on stolen state secrets. They also mistakenly believe that he's some spy/counterspy/defector and Otley's not the only one who's confused. Based on the first in the book series by Martin Waddell. **91m/C; DVD.** *GB* Tom Courtenay; Romy Schneider; Alan Badel; James Villiers; Leonard Rossiter; Freddie Jones; ***D:*** Dick Clement; ***W:*** Dick Clement; Ian La Frenais; ***C:*** Austin Dempster; ***M:*** Stanley Myers.

Otto: Or, Up with Dead People 🦴🦴 **2008** A sexually explicit gay zombie film from provocateur LaBruce that's not for the squeamish. Young zombie Otto lives in Berlin and subsists on roadkill. He gets a role in a queer zombie movie, directed by pretentiously avant-garde Medea Yarn, and his fellow cast members think Otto's taking his 'method acting' quite seriously. English and German with subtitles. **95m/C; DVD.** *CA GE* Jay Crisfar; Katharina Klewinghaus; Marcel Schlutt; Christophe Chemin; ***D:*** Bruce LaBruce; ***W:*** Bruce LaBruce; ***C:*** James Carman.

Ouija 🦴 **2014 (PG-13)** Just another poorly made piece of horror nonsense trying to make a few bucks in the Halloween season, this one playing off the classic children's toy that most of us outgrew decades ago. Yes, it's about a deadly Ouija board, believe it or not. A girl is killed after playing with an ancient Ouija board, leading her friends to investigate what really happened to her. In this PG-13 vision of horror, it's not much. The only real mystery is why anyone spent any money making it or why anyone would spend any time watching it. **89m/C; DVD, Blu-Ray.** Olivia Cooke; Ana Coto; Bianca Santos; Daren Kagasoff; Douglas Smith; Shelley Hennig; Lin Shaye; ***D:*** Stiles White; ***W:*** Stiles White; Juliet Snowden; ***C:*** David Emmerichs; ***M:*** Anton Sanko.

Ouija: Origin of Evil 🦴🦴 **1/2 2016 (PG-13)** Horror sequels are almost never better than the original, especially when they're based on board games, but this is a true exception. The main reason was the hiring of the talented Flanagan as director. This is more of a prequel, focusing on a widow who works as a medium in 1967 who employs a Ouija board in her scam. Of course, it's not long before the Ouija board is accessing something otherworldly but Flanagan knows how to play for honest creepiness instead of cheap jump scares. A solid horror flick that actually makes one excited for another entry in the series. **99m/C; DVD, Blu-Ray.** Annalise Basso; Elizabeth Reaser; Lulu Wilson; Henry Thomas; ***D:*** Mike Flanagan; ***W:*** Mike Flanagan; Jeff Howard; ***C:*** Michael Fimognari; ***M:*** The Newton Brothers.

Our America 🦴🦴 **1/2 2002 (R)** In 1993, Chicago teens LeAlan Jones (Pannell) and Lloyd Newman (Hammond) are living in a notorious southside housing project. They are approached by white NPR producer David Isay (Charles) to record an audio diary of their daily lives, which becomes the radio series "Ghetto Life 101." Stung by the controversy the program receives, the boys pull back until the suspicious death of a five-year-old boy has them looking into neighborhood problems once again. **95m/C; DVD.** Brandon Hammond; Josh Charles; Vanessa Williams; Mykelti Williamson; Peter Paige; Irma P. Hall; Roderick Pannell; Serena Lee; ***D:*** Ernest R. Dickerson; ***W:*** Gordon Rayfield; ***C:*** Ernest R. Dickerson; ***M:*** Patrice Rushen. **CABLE**

Our Blushing Brides 🦴🦴 **1/2 1930** Risqué talkie follows 1928's "Our Dancing Daughters" and 1929's "Our Modern Maidens." Crawford stars as Jerry in this go-round, who works in a department store with her two girlfriends, Connie and Franky, and each have different ideas about romance. Jerry wants a wedding ring from wealthy boyfriend Tony before she'll permit any liberties while Franky falls for a crook with cash and Connie agrees to be a rich young man's mistress with unhappy consequences. **79m/B; DVD.** Joan Crawford; Robert Montgomery; Anita Page; Dorothy Sebastian; Raymond Hackett; John Miljan; Hedda Hopper; ***D:*** Harry Beaumont; ***W:*** Bess Meredyth; John Howard Lawson; Edwin Justus Mayer; ***C:*** Merritt B. Gerstad.

Our Brand Is Crisis 🦴🦴🦴 **2005** Unsettling documentary follows the American political consultancy firm of Greenberg Carville and Shrum as they work on the 2002 Bolivian presidential campaign. Their candidate is unpopular former president Gonzalo Sanchez de Lozada, and the consultants work to spin him as the new and improved version, with the focus ("brand") being that Bolivia is in crisis and needs an experienced politico at the helm. English and Spanish with subtitles. **87m/C; DVD.** ***D:*** Rachel Boynton; ***C:*** Michael Anderson; Tom Hurwitz; Christine Burrill; Jerr Risius; ***M:*** Marcelo Zarvos.

Our Brand is Crisis 🦴🦴 **2015 (R)** David Gordon Green directs this adaptation of Rachel Boynton's documentary about American political campaign strategists playing the games they play during the 2002 Bolivian presidential election. Pedro Castillo is the fictional politician who hires Jane Bodine (Sandra Bullock) to manage his campaign, drawing her nemesis Pat Candy (Billy Bob Thornton) into the fray on the other side. Playing a version of Primary Colors south of the border, Green's film doesn't have the satirical teeth it needed to work, coming off as a limp version of political satire that we've seen so many times before. Politicians will do anything to get elected. Tell me something new. **107m/C; DVD, Blu-Ray, Streaming.** Sandra Bullock; Billy Bob Thornton; Anthony Mackie; Ann Dowd; Scoot McNairy; Zoe Kazan; ***D:*** David Gordon Green; ***W:*** Peter Straughan; ***C:*** Tim Orr; ***M:*** David Wingo.

Our Children 🦴🦴 **1/2** *A perdre la raison* **2012** Based on true events, this French drama with psychological overtones explores the sometimes tragic impact of interdependent human relationships. From childhood, Mounir (Rahim) has resided with his adoptive father, Dr. Pinget (Arestrup). The doctor has given Mounir an enviable life of comfort. As an adult, Mounir continues to live with the doctor and brings his love Murielle (Dequenne) into the situation. She is full of life with a promising future ahead of her. After the couple marries and has children, they become overly dependent on the Pinget and frictions emerge. As Murielle becomes intertwined in the emotional climate in the home and understands that her family must leave, the situation takes a darker turn. French and Arabic with subtitles. **111m/C; DVD, Blu-Ray.** Emilie Dequenne; Niels Arestrup; Tahar Rahim; Stephane Bissot; Jean-Charles Hautera; ***D:*** Joachim Lafosse; ***W:*** Joachim Lafosse; Mathieu Reynaert; Thomas Bidegain; ***C:*** Jean-Francois Hensgens.

Our Daily Bread 🦴🦴🦴 *Miracle of Life* **1934** Vidor's sequel to the 1928 "The Crowd." A young couple inherit a farm during the Depression and succeed in managing the land. A near-classic, with several sequences highly influenced by directors Alexander Dovshenko and Sergei Eisenstein. Director Vidor also co-scripted this film, risking bankruptcy to finance it. **80m/B; DVD, Blu-Ray.** Karen Morley; Tom Keene; John Qualen; Barbara Pepper; Addison Richards; ***D:*** King Vidor; ***W:*** King Vidor; Elizabeth Hill; ***C:*** Robert Planck. Natl. Film Reg. '15.

Our Dancing Daughters 🦴🦴 **1/2 1928** Flapper (Crawford on the brink of stardom) falls hard for millionaire who's forced into arranged marriage, but obliging little missus kicks bucket so Crawford can step in. **98m/B; Silent; VHS, DVD.** Joan Crawford; Johnny Mack Brown; Nils Asther; Dorothy Sebastian; Anita Page; ***D:*** Harry Beaumont; ***C:*** George Barnes.

Our Family Wedding 🦴 **1/2** *Family Wedding* **2010 (PG-13)** Playing like an overlong sitcom episode, this ham-fisted tale of interracial marriage is a wedding album best left unseen. Lucia (Ferrara) and Marcus (Gross) are two college grads who are itching to tie the knot. The problem is that she's Mexican-American and he's African-American. At least that's a problem for her father Miguel (Mencia) and his father Brad (Whitaker). The two dads engage in a battle of stereotypes and slapstick until the inevitable "kiss-and-make-up" ending. **101m/C; DVD, Blu-Ray.** Forest Whitaker; Carlos Mencia; America Ferrera; Lance Gross; Regina King; Lupe Ontiveros; Anna Maria Horsford; Warren Sapp; ***D:*** Rick Famuyiwa; ***W:*** Rick Famuyiwa; Wayne Conley; Malcolm Spellman; ***C:*** Julio Macat; ***M:*** Transcenders.

Our Hospitality 🦴🦴🦴🦴 **1923** One of Keaton's finest silent films. William McKay travels to the American South on a quaint train (a near-exact replica of the Stephenson Rocket), to claim an inheritance as the last survivor of his family. En route, a young woman (Talmadge) informs him that her family has had a long, deadly feud with his, and that they intend to kill him. McKay resolves to get the inheritance, depending on the Southern rule of hospitality to guests to save his life until he can make his escape. Watch for the river scene where, during filming, Keaton's own life was really in danger. **74m/B; Silent; VHS, DVD, Blu-Ray.** Buster Keaton; Natalie Talmadge; Joe Keaton; Buster Keaton, Jr.; Kitty Bradbury; Joe Roberts; Monte (Monty) Collins; ***D:*** Buster Keaton; John Blystone; ***W:*** Jean C. Havez; Joseph A. Mitchell; Clyde Bruckman; ***C:*** Elgin Lessley; Gordon Jennings.

Our Idiot Brother 🦴🦴 *My Idiot Brother* **2011 (R)** Ned (Rudd) is a mellow and happy idiot—unlike his three unhappy and unfulfilled sisters. After being released on parole following a pot bust, the amiable screw-up seeks temporary shelter from his self-absorbed siblings: uptight, married-with-kids Liz (Mortimer), ruthless careerist writer Miranda (Banks), and would-be standup comedian and promiscuous lesbian Natalie (Deschanel). Ned innocently learns secrets about their respective lives, blurts them out at inopportune moments, and proceeds to drive them crazy while remaining unaware of the havoc he's causing. **96m/C; DVD, Blu-Ray.** Paul Rudd; Emily Mortimer; Elizabeth Banks; Zooey Deschanel; Shirley Knight; Steve Coogan; Hugh Dancy; Rashida Jones; T.J. Miller; Kathryn Hahn; Adam Scott; ***D:*** Jesse Peretz; ***W:*** Evgenia Peretz; David Schisgall; ***C:*** Yaron Orbach; ***M:*** Nathan Larson; Eric Johnson.

Our Italian Husband 2004 Lame comedy. Vincenzo is a struggling artist living with his pregnant American wife Charlene in New York. Except Vincenzo is a bigamist, as everyone discovers when his Italian wife Maria arrives with their two kids. **?m/CDVD.** *IT* Brooke Shields; Maria Grazia Cucinotta; Chevy Chase; Pierfrancesco Favino; ***D:*** Ilaria Berrelli; ***W:*** Ilaria Berrelli; ***C:*** Benjamin Morgan; ***M:*** Brian Burnam.

Our Kind of Traitor 🦴🦴 **2016 (R)** Peter (McGregor) meets a Russian on a Moroccan vacation. The Russian tells Peter that the mob wants him dead and that only Peter can get him to the safety of the British intelligence service. However, that group may be corrupt as well. Susanna White directs this variation on the classic tale of an everyman caught up in the spy game. An A-list cast still can't quite bring together all the complex elements in yet another John le Carre thriller that doesn't really thrill. **108m/C; DVD, Blu-Ray.** Ewan McGregor; Stellan Skarsgard; Damian Lewis; Naomie Harris; Jeremy Northam; ***D:*** Susanna White; ***W:*** Hossein Amini; ***C:*** Anthony Dod Mantle; ***M:*** Marcelo Zarvos.

Our Lady of the Assassins 🦴🦴 *La Virgen de los Sicarios* **2001 (R)** Based on Vallejo's 1994 autobiographical novel. Fernando's (Jaramillo) an older gay man and a writer who has returned to his hometown of Medellin, Colombia to die. After 30 years away, Fernando discovers a crime-ridden city with drug trafficking, gangs, and violence to be the norm. At a party, he's introduced to 16-year-old street tough Alexis (Ballesteros), who soon moves in with him. But when Alexis's past catches up with him, Fernando seeks the truth in a city of lies. Not for the faint-hearted; Spanish with subtitles. **98m/C; VHS, DVD.** *CO FR* German Jaramillo; Anderson Ballesteros; Juan David Restrepo; Manuel Busquets; ***D:*** Barbet Schroeder; ***W:*** Fernando Vallejo; ***C:*** Rodrigo Lalinde; ***M:*** Jorge Arriagada.

Our Life 🦴🦴 *La Nostra Vita* **2010** Awkward, working-class melodrama. Construction worker Claudio is suddenly left a widower with three kids when his wife dies in childbirth. He becomes obsessed with making money to support his family, including blackmailing his boss for a building contract when Claudio discovers the body of an undocumented Romanian worker on a work site, borrowing money from a decidedly shady friend, and his hiring of more illegal workers he can take advantage of. Italian with subtitles. **100m/C; DVD.** *IT FR* Elio Germano; Raoul Bova; Luca Zingaretti; Isabella Ragonese; Stefania Montorsi; Giorgio Colangeli; Marius Ignat; ***D:*** Daniele Luchetti; ***W:*** Daniele Luchetti; Sandro Petraglia; Stefano Rulli; ***C:*** Claudio Collepiccolo; ***M:*** Franco Piersanti.

Our Little Sister 🦴🦴 1/2 *Umimachi Diary* **2016 (PG)** Three close sisters in Kamakura have their routine shattered when they learn their estranged father has passed away, leaving a half-sister they never knew existed. They allow the young teenage girl to move in with them and she gently and quietly changes their lives. Koreeda is a master of delicate observation, never allowing this family drama to turn melodramatic, allowing the characters to feel completely real at every turn. **128m/C; DVD.** Haruka Ayase; Masami Nagasawa; Kaho; Suzu Hirose; Ryo Kase; ***D:*** Hirokazu Kore-eda; ***W:*** Hirokazu Kore-eda; Akimi Yoshida; ***C:*** Mikiya Takimoto; ***M:*** Yoko Kanno.

Our Man Flint 🦴🦴 **1966** James Bond clone Derek Flint uses gadgets and his ingenuity to save the world from an evil organization, GALAXY, that seeks world domination through control of the weather. The plot moves quickly around many bikini-clad women, but still strains for effect. Spawned one sequel: "In Like Flint." **107m/C; DVD, Blu-Ray.** James Coburn; Lee J. Cobb; Gila Golan; Edward Mulhare; Benson Fong; Shelby Grant; Sigrid Valdis; Gianna Serra; James Brolin; Helen Funai; Michael St. Clair; ***D:*** Daniel Mann; ***W:*** Hal Fimberg; Ben Starr; ***C:*** Daniel F. Fapp; ***M:*** Jerry Goldsmith.

Our Man in Havana 🦴🦴🦴 **1959** Excellent noir—with plenty of veddy British black comedy—has ordinary, but not very successful, Havana-based vacuum salesman Guinness joining the British spy service to make some extra money. He begins spinning elaborate tails of intrigue to justify himself, and his lies eventually spiral out of control and into some very real, very dangerous situations. Kovacs, Richardson, and Coward stand out among a great cast. See "The Tailor of Panama" for a post-Cold War re-telling of the tale, but see this one first. **111m/B; VHS, DVD, Blu-Ray.** *GB* Alec Guinness; Burl Ives; Maureen O'Hara; Noel Coward; Ernie Kovacs; Ralph Richardson; Jo Morrow; Paul Rogers; Gregoire Aslan; Joseph Prieto; Timothy Bateson; Duncan MacRae; Maurice Denham; Raymond Huntley; Ferdinand "Ferdy" Mayne; Rachel Roberts; ***D:*** Carol Reed; ***W:*** Graham Greene; ***C:*** Oswald Morris.

Our Miss Brooks 🦴🦴 1/2 **1956** Quietly pleasing version of the TV series. Miss Brooks pursues the "mother's boy" biology professor. The father of the child she begins tutoring appears taken with her. The professor takes notice. **85m/B; VHS, DVD.** Eve Arden; Gale Gordon; Nick Adams; Richard Crenna; Don Porter; ***D:*** Al Lewis; ***W:*** Al Lewis; ***C:*** Joseph LaShelle; ***M:*** Roy Webb.

Our Modern Maidens 🦴🦴 1/2 **1929** Scandalous jazz-age drama in which Crawford and Fairbanks both fall in love with other people before their wedding is to take place. This sequel to "Our Dancing Daughters" features beautiful gowns and lush, opulent Art Deco interiors. Based on a story by Josephine Lovett. **75m/B; VHS, DVD.** Joan Crawford; Rod La Rocque; Douglas Fairbanks, Jr.; Anita Page; Josephine Dunn; ***D:*** Jack Conway; ***W:*** Josephine Lovett.

Our Mother's House 🦴🦴 **1967** Creepy chiller. When their invalid, Bible-obsessed mother dies, the seven Hook children fear being separated and sent to an orphanage. They bury mom in the backyard and carry on as if nothing has changed. But when their n'er-do-well, long-lost father Charlie turns up, plans change, especially when the kids discover Charles trying to defraud them and sell the house. **105m/C; DVD.** Dirk Bogarde; Margaret Leclere; Louis Sheldon Williams; Pamela Franklin; Mark Lester; Phoebe Nicholls; ***D:*** Jack Clayton; ***W:*** Haya Harareet; Jeremy Brooks; ***C:*** Larry Pizer; ***M:*** Georges Delerue.

Our Music 🦴🦴 *Our Music* **2004** Godard divides his film into three kingdoms, using Dante's "The Divine Comedy" as his structure. First there's Hell, with a montage showing war and genocide throughout history. Next is the longest section, Purgatory, set in Sarajevo and featuring Godard at a literary conference where we meet Israeli journalist Judith (Adler), and Olga (Dieu), a Russian Jew now living in Israel, and the theme is reconciliation and sacrifice. Then we get to Heaven, which again features Olga under very different circumstances. If you're a Godard fan, you'll know what strangeness you're getting into: others beware. French with subtitles. **80m/C; DVD.** *FR SI* Nade Dieu; Sarah Adler; ***D:*** Jean-Luc Godard; ***W:*** Jean-Luc Godard; ***C:*** Julien Hirsch; Jean-Christophe Beauvallet.

Our Mutual Friend 🦴🦴 1/2 **1998** Charles Dickens' last completed novel follows the complicated saga of John Harmon (Mackintosh), who must consent to a prearranged marriage if he's to inherit a fortune. But when fate allows Harmon to assume a new identity, he decides to see what anonymity will bring him. Meanwhile, Harmon's life and death also brings together low-born Lizzie Hexum and wastrel lawyer Eugene Wrayburn, who develops an unexpected affection for the lovely young woman. On 3 cassettes. **339m/C; VHS, DVD.** *GB* Steven Mackintosh; Anna Friel; Paul McGann; Keeley Hawes; David Morrissey; Dominic Mafham; Peter Vaughan; Pam Ferris; Kenneth Cranham; Timothy Spall; David Bradley; Margaret Tyzack; ***D:*** Julian Farino; ***W:*** Sandy Welch; ***C:*** David Odd; ***M:*** Adrian Johnston. **TV**

Our Paradise 🦴 1/2 *Notre Paradis* **2011** In this violent sex and crime drama, aging Paris hustler Vassili finds young Angelo in the park, beaten, and takes him home. Before long they're teaming up--in bed and out--to get clients. Robbery and, possibly, murder follows as the two flee Paris and try to leave their old lives behind. French with subtitles. **100m/C; DVD.** *FR* Stephane Rideau; Dimitri Durdaine; Beatrice Dalle; Didier Flamand; ***D:*** Gael Morel; ***W:*** Gael Morel; ***C:*** Nicolas Dixmier.

Our Relations 🦴🦴🦴 1/2 **1936** Confusion reigns when Stan and Ollie meet the twin brothers they never knew they had, a pair of happy-go-lucky sailors. Laurel directs the pair through madcap encounters with their twins' wives and the local underworld. One of the pair's best efforts, though not well-remembered. Based on a story by W.W. Jacobs. **94m/B; DVD.** Stan Laurel; Oliver Hardy; Alan Hale; Sidney Toler; James Finlayson; Daphne Pollard; ***D:*** Harry Lachman; ***W:*** Jack Jevne; ***C:*** Rudolph Mate; ***M:*** Leroy Shield.

Our Song 🦴🦴🦴 **2001 (R)** Quietly affecting, poetic and solid teen drama. First-time actors Washington, Simpson and Martinez bring poignancy and realism to their roles as high school friends living in the Brooklyn projects and rehearsing for a marching band competition. The expected issues are present, but pic forgos major plot drama in favor of finding powerful moments in small places. Real-life marching band the Jackie Robinson Steppers, who were the inspiration for the film, provide a focal point for the story and punch to the sometimes languid pacing. **96m/C; VHS, DVD.** Kerry Washington; Anna Simpson; Melissa Martinez; Marlene Forte; Rosalyn Coleman; Ray Anthony Thomas; D'Monroe; Kim Howard; Carmen Lopez; ***D:*** Jim McKay; ***W:*** Jim McKay; ***C:*** Jim Denault.

Our Sons 🦴🦴 1/2 **1991** Two middle-aged moms strike up an unlikely friendship over their gay sons in this TV weeper. Arkansas waitress Luanna (Ann Margret) hasn't talked to son Donald (Ivanek) in years—now he's dying of AIDS. Successfull career woman Audrey (Andrews in her TV-movie debut) has seemingly accepted son James' (Grant) life with Donald and it's James who urges his mother to make contact with Luanna and persuade her to see Donald one last time. **100m/C; VHS, DVD.** Julie Andrews; Ann-Margret; Hugh Grant; Zeljko Ivanek; Tony Roberts; ***D:*** John Erman; ***W:*** John Erman; William Hanley.

Our Time 🦴🦴 1/2 *Death of Her Innocence* **1974** An exclusive girls finishing school in the '50s is the setting for the friendship of Abby (Martin) and Muffy (Slade) and their first stirrings of romance. But when Muffy gets pregnant, tragedy awaits. Sappy. **91m/C; VHS, DVD.** Pamela Sue Martin; Betsey Slade; Parker Stevenson; George O'Hanlon, Jr.; Roderick Cook; Edith Atwater; Meg Wyllie; Debralee Scott; Nora Heflin; Kathryn Holcomb; Robert Walden; Helene Winston; Karen Balkin; Helen Baron; Michael Gray; ***D:*** Peter Hyams; ***W:*** Peter Hyams; Jane C. Stanton; ***C:*** Jules Brenner; ***M:*** Michel Legrand.

Our Town 🦴🦴🦴 **1940** Small-town New England life in Grover's Corners in the early 1900s is celebrated in this well-performed and directed adaptation of the Pulitzer Prize-winning play by Thornton Wilder. Film debut of Scott. **90m/B; VHS, DVD.** Martha Scott; William Holden; Thomas Mitchell; Fay Bainter; Guy Kibbee; Beulah Bondi; Frank Craven; ***D:*** Sam Wood; ***W:*** Frank Craven; Harry Chandlee; ***C:*** Bert Glennon; ***M:*** Aaron Copland.

Our Town 🦴🦴🦴 **1977** TV version of Thornton Wilder's classic play about everyday life in Grovers Corners, a small New England town at the turn of the century. It hews more closely to the style of the stage version than the earlier film version. **120m/C; VHS, DVD.** Ned Beatty; Sada Thompson; Ronny Cox; Glynnis O'Connor; Robby Benson; Hal Holbrook; John Houseman; ***D:*** Franklin J. Schaffner. **TV**

Our Town 🦴🦴 1/2 **1989** Filmed TV version of the Tony Award-winning Lincoln Center production of the Thornton Wilder play focusing on small-town life in Grover's Corners, New Hampshire. Gray is the omniscient Stage Manager, with Stolz and Miller as the young couple brought together by the everyday cycle of happiness and hardship. **104m/C; VHS, DVD.** Eric Stoltz; Penelope Ann Miller; Spalding Gray; ***D:*** Gregory Mosher. **TV**

Our Town 🦴🦴 1/2 **2003** Filmed version of the 1938 Thornton Wilder play as staged by the Westport County Playhouse. Newman makes his first stage appearance in nearly 40 years as the Stage Manager, who narrates the story of the townspeople of Grover's Corners, New Hampshire at the turn of the 20th century. At the play's heart are Emily Webb and George Gibbs, who will grow up, marry, and start a family with tragic results as the ghosts of the town watch the lives of those they've left behind. **120m/C; DVD.** Paul Newman; Margaret Lacey; Frank Converse; Jayne Atkinson; Jeffrey DeMunn; Jane Curtin; Stephen Spinella; Mia Dillon; ***D:*** James Naughton; ***W:*** Thornton Wilder; ***C:*** Phil Abraham. **CABLE**

Our Vines Have Tender Grapes 🦴🦴🦴 1/2 **1945** A change of pace role for the volatile Robinson who plays a kind Norwegian farmer, living in Wisconsin with his daughter, the spunky O'Brien. The film is made-up of small-town moments as O'Brien learns a few of life's lessons, eased by the thoughtful compassion of Robinson. Based on the novel "For Our Vines Have Tender Grapes" by George Victor Martin. **105m/B; VHS, DVD.** Edward G. Robinson; Margaret O'Brien; James Craig; Agnes Moorehead; Jackie "Butch" Jenkins; Morris Carnovsky; Frances Gifford; Sara Haden; Louis Jean Heydt; ***D:*** Roy Rowland; ***W:*** Dalton Trumbo; ***C:*** Robert L. Surtees.

Our Wild Hearts 🦴🦴 1/2 **2013** It's a family affair for the Scroeder clan in this predictable 'girl-and-her-horse' Hallmark Channel movie. Willow Johnson leaves Malibu to live with her father Jack Thomas in the Sierra Nevada mountains. But her first adventure after settling in is with a wild mustang she names Bravo. **86m/C; DVD, Blu-Ray.** Cambrie Schroder; Rick Schroder; Cliff (Potter) Potts; Martin Kove; ***D:*** Rick Schroder; ***W:*** Rick Schroder; Andrea Schroder; ***C:*** Steve Gainer; ***M:*** Michael Lord. **CABLE**

Out 🦴🦴 1/2 *Deadly Drifter* **1982** A drifter's travels throughout the U.S. from the '60s to the '80s. Successfully manages to satirize just about every conceivable situation but keeps from posturing by not taking itself too seriously. Adapted from an experimental novel by Ronald Sukenick. **88m/C; VHS, DVD.** Peter Coyote; Danny Glover; O-Lan Shepard; Jim Haynie; Scott Beach; Semu Haute; ***D:*** Eli Hollander; ***W:*** Eli Hollander; ***M:*** David Cope.

Out at the Wedding 🦴🦴 **2007** Alex Houston tells her Jewish, African-American fiance Dana that her family is dead because she believes they'll disapprove. Then she quietly heads home to South Carolina to be a bridesmaid in her sister Jeannie's wedding, taking along her gay best friend Jonathan. Jonathan mentions Dana to her family and they think Dana is a woman. Alex is so surprised by their supportive attitude that she lets the lie stand. But things spin out of control when Jeannie decides to come to New York to meet her sister's 'girlfriend.' **96m/C; DVD.** Charlie Schlatter; Mystro Clark; Mike Farrell; Mink Stole; Andrea Marcellus; Desi Lydic; Cathy DeBuono; Jill Bennett; ***D:*** Lee Friedlander; ***W:*** Paula Goldberg; ***C:*** Alex Vendler; ***M:*** Laura Karpman.

Out Cold 🦴 1/2 **1989 (R)** Black comedy follows the misadventures of a butcher who believes he has accidentally frozen his business partner; the iced man's girlfriend, who really killed him; and the detective who tries to solve the crime. Too many poor frozen body jokes may leave the viewer cold. **91m/C; VHS, DVD; Open Captioned.** John Lithgow; Teri Garr; Randy Quaid; Bruce McGill; ***D:*** Malcolm Mowbray; ***W:*** Leonard Glasser; ***C:*** Tony Pierce-Roberts; ***M:*** Michel Colombier.

Out Cold 🦴 1/2 **2001 (PG-13)** Dumb snowboarding comedy (the snowboarding scenes are the only cool things about the movie) focuses on a ragged ski resort in Bull Mountain, Alaska that developer Jack Majors (Majors) wants to turn into a family-oriented resort. That means getting rid of the resort's raucous loser employees, including Rick (London) and his buddies. **90m/C; VHS, DVD.** Jason London; Willie Garson; Lee Majors; A.J. Cook; Derek Hamilton; Zach Galifianakis; Flex Anderson; Caroline Dhavernas; Victoria Silvstedt; ***D:*** Brendan Malloy; Emmett Malloy; ***W:***

Jon Zack; **C:** Richard Crudo; **M:** Michael Andrews.

Out For a Kill ½ **2003 (R)** Seagal plays an archaeologist who is framed for a murder after he digs up priceless artifacts in China. He's turned loose by the cops to lure out the real killers who promptly off his wife, and he goes after them hell-bent on revenge. One can only wonder why Mr. Seagal continues to torture his well-meaning fans. **90m/C; DVD.** Steven Seagal; Corey Johnson; Elaine Tan; Michael J. Reynolds; Kata Dobo; Ray Charleson; Michelle Goh; Tom Wu; Ozzie Yue; Bruce Wang; Chike Chan; Hon Ping Tang; Dave Wong; Chooi Kheng-Beh; Vincent Wong; **D:** Michael Oblowitz; **W:** Dennis Dimster; Danny Lerner; Sam Hayes; **C:** Mark Vargo; **M:** Roy Hay.

Out for Blood **1993 (R)** Attorney John Decker is living a happy life until his family is murdered by drug dealers. He turns vigilante, dubbed "Karateman" by the press, and finds himself hunted by the cops and the criminals. **90m/C; VHS, DVD, On Demand.** Don "The Dragon" Wilson; Shari Shattuck; Michael Delano; Kenneth McLeod; Todd Curtis; Timothy Baker; Howard Jackson; Bob Schott; Eric Lee; **D:** Richard W. Munchkin; **W:** David S. Green.

Out for Justice ½ **1991 (R)** A psycho Brooklyn hood goes on a murder spree, and homeboy turned lone-wolf cop Seagal races other police and the mob to get at him. Bloodthirsty and profane, it does try to depict N.Y.C.'s Italian-American community—but 90 percent of them are dead by the end so what's the point? Better yet, why does it open with a quote from Arthur Miller? Better still, what's Daffy Duck doing on this tape peddling Warner Bros. T-shirts to kid viewers?! **91m/C; VHS, DVD, Blu-Ray, HD-DVD.** Steven Seagal; William Forsythe; Jerry Orbach; Julianna Margulies; Gina Gershon; John Leguizamo; Julie Strain; Dominic Chianese; **D:** John Flynn; **W:** David Lee Henry; **C:** Ric Waite; **M:** David Michael Frank.

Out in Fifty ½ **1999 (R)** Con is released from prison only to be pursued by a psycho detective who wants him back in the slammer and a mystery babe who has her own plans for the guy. **95m/C; VHS, DVD.** Mickey Rourke; Bojesse Christopher; Christina Applegate; Scott Leet; Balthazar Getty; Peter Greene; **D:** Bojesse Christopher; Scott Leet; **W:** Bojesse Christopher; Scott Leet; **C:** Sharone Meir; **M:** Stephen (Steve) Edwards. **VIDEO**

Out in the Dark **2012** Debut feature for Israeli director Mayer is a subtle romantic drama dealing with harsh political realities. Palestinian grad student Nimr meets Jewish lawyer Roy in a Tel Aviv bar and a relationship soon begins. Nimr has a student visa but his life is complicated by the fact that his conservative family would never accept his sexuality and his radical brother, Nabil, has come under the scrutiny of Israeli security forces. Roy offers a lifeline but Nimr sees his situation dangerously narrow. Hebrew and Arabic with subtitles. **96m/C; DVD.** *IS* Nicholas Jacob; Michael Aloni; Jamil Khouri; Alon Pudt; Loai Noufi; **D:** Michael Mayer; **W:** Michael Mayer; Yael Shafrir; **C:** Ran Aviad; **M:** Mark Holden; Michael Lopez.

Out of Africa **1985 (PG)** An epic film of the years spent by Danish authoress Isak Dinesen (her true name is Karen Blixen) on a Kenya coffee plantation. She moved to Africa to marry, and later fell in love with Denys Finch-Hatten, a British adventurer. Based on several books, including biographies of the two lovers. Some critics loved the scenery and music; others despised the acting and the script. A definite "no" for those who love action. **161m/C; VHS, DVD, Blu-Ray.** Meryl Streep; Robert Redford; Klaus Maria Brandauer; Michael Kitchen; Malick Bowens; Michael Gough; Suzanna Hamilton; Rachel Kempson; Graham Crowden; Shane Rimmer; Donal McCann; Iman; Joseph Thiaka; Stephen Kinyanjui; **D:** Sydney Pollack; **W:** Kurt Luedtke; **C:** David Watkin; **M:** John Barry. Oscars '85: Adapt. Screenplay, Art Dir./Set Dec., Cinematog., Director (Pollack), Film, Orig. Score, Sound; British Acad. '86: Adapt. Screenplay; Golden Globes '86: Film--Drama, Score, Support. Actor (Brandauer); L.A. Film Critics '85: Actress (Streep), Cinematog.; Natl. Bd. of Review '85: Support. Actor (Brandauer); N.Y. Film Critics '85: Cinematog., Support. Actor (Brandauer).

Out of Line ½ **2000 (R)** A convict is sprung early from prison to pull off a murder, but he decides to start a relationship with his parole officer instead. Granted his PO is played by Beals, so his decision is understandable. **96m/C; DVD.** Jennifer Beals; Holt McCallany; Michael Moriarty; Christopher Judge; Rick Ravanello; William B. Davis; Pablo Bryant; Alonso Oyarzun; Darcy Laurie; Keegan Connor Tracy; **D:** Johana Demetrakas; **W:** Johana Demetrakas; **C:** David Pelletier; **M:** John Philip Shenale; Bob Thiele, Jr.

Out of Order **2003 (R)** The pilot episode of the Showtime series finds Stoltz and Huffman starring as a long-married, successful Hollywood screenwriting couple Mark and Lorna Colm. Lorna is going through a deep depression, which leaves Mark caring for their son and vulnerable to the unhappily married Danni (Dickens). Meanwhile, Lorna finds some solace with bitter best pal Steven (Macy), a not very successful producer. **97m/C; VHS, DVD.** Eric Stoltz; Felicity Huffman; Kim Dickens; William H. Macy; Justine Bateman; Peter Bogdanovich; **D:** Wayne Powers; **W:** Wayne Powers; Donna Powers. **CABLE**

Out of Reach ½ *The Rescue; Poza zasiegiem* **2004 (R)** Seagal teams with veteran Asian director Leung to make an action film about a retired government agent (which he's played in almost all of his films) who comes out of retirement to find a kidnapped girl. If this sounds a lot like "Belly of the Beast", that's because the plot is pretty similar except the girl is his pen pal as opposed to his daughter. How many ex government agents in their fifties are pen pals with young girls? And why do they need to have other actors dubbing their voice over their own lines? **100m/C; DVD.** *PL* Steven Seagal; Ida Nowakowska; Agnieszka Wagner; Matt Schulze; Krzysztof Pieczynski; Robbie Gee; Murat Yilmaz; Nick Brimble; Jan Plazalski; Hanna Dunowska; **D:** Po-Chih Leung; **W:** Trevor Miller; James Townsend; **C:** Richard Crudo; **M:** Alex Heffes.

Out of Season *Winter Rates* **1975 (R)** Mother and teenage daughter compete for the attentions of the mother's mysterious ex-lover. We never know who wins the man in this enigmatic drama set in an English village, and hints of incest make the story even murkier. Had only a short run in the U.S. **90m/C; VHS, DVD.** *GB* Cliff Robertson; Vanessa Redgrave; Susan George; **D:** Alan Bridges.

Out of Sight **1998 (R)** Soderbergh turns up the heat in this fine adaptation (with fine performances) of the Elmore Leonard crime caper. Jack Foley (Clooney) is a charming bank robber with bad luck and three prison terms—his current one being served in a Florida pen from which he escapes with the aid of partner Buddy (Rhames). Even the escape doesn't go as planned when federal marshal Karen Sisco (Lopez) becomes a temporary hostage. Sparks fly, but Karen's still determined to bring Jack to justice, even as he plans his next heist involving shady financier Richard Ripley (Brooks) that takes Jack and Buddy to Detroit and more complications. **122m/C; VHS, DVD, HD-DVD.** George Clooney; Jennifer Lopez; Ving Rhames; Don Cheadle; Albert Brooks; Steve Zahn; Dennis Farina; Catherine Keener; Luis Guzman; Isaiah Washington, IV; Keith Loneker; Nancy Allen; **Cameo(s):** Michael Keaton; Samuel L. Jackson; **D:** Steven Soderbergh; **W:** Scott Frank; **C:** Elliot Davis; **M:** Cliff Martinez. Natl. Soc. Film Critics '98: Director (Soderbergh), Film, Screenplay; Writers Guild '98: Adapt. Screenplay.

Out of Sync ½ **1995 (R)** Deejay Jason St. Julian gets in trouble with his bookies and L.A. detectives, one of whom forces him into an undercover job with a drug-dealing club owner. Then Jason falls for the dealer's girlfriend. Hip-hop soundtrack may provide the only interest. **105m/C; VHS, DVD.** LL Cool J; Victoria Dillard; Howard Hesseman; Ramy Zada; Don Yesso; Yaphet Kotto; **D:** Debbie Allen; **W:** Robert E. Dorn; **C:** Isidore Mankofsky; **M:** Steve Tyrell.

Out of the Ashes ½ **2003 (R)** Based on actual events. Dr. Gisella Perl (Lahti) is a Hungarian Jew who is sent to Auschwitz, along with her family, in 1944. Perl survives by working as a doctor in the camp, but when she tries to immigrate to the U.S. in 1947 she is accused of being a Nazi collaborator by immigration officials. **113m/C; DVD.** Christine Lahti; Beau Bridges; Richard Crenna; Bruce Davison; Jonathan Cake; Jolyon Baker; Jessica Beitchman; **D:** Joseph Sargent; **W:** Anne Meredith; **C:** Donald M. Morgan; **M:** Charles Bernstein. **CABLE**

Out of the Black ½ **2001** In 1976, 10-year-old Cole Malby is told to forget everything he thinks he saw regarding the death of his Pennsylvania coal miner father and the shooting that paralyzed his mother (Kirkland). Thirteen years later, Cole (Christopher) and his younger brother Patrick (Widener) struggle on the family farm and decide it's past time to find out the truth. Naturally, there are a lot of people determined to make the brothers sorry for their interference. **105m/C; VHS, DVD.** Tyler Christopher; Sally Kirkland; Dee Wallace; Jason Widener; Jacqueline Aries; Jack Conley; Michael J. Pollard; Miles O'Keeffe; Sally Struthers; Allison Lange; John Capodice; Tom Atkins; **D:** Karl Kozak; **W:** Karl Kozak; Joel Eisenberg; **C:** Maximo Munzi; **M:** Lawrence Nash Groupe.

Out of the Blue ½ **1947** There's trouble in paradise for a married man when a shady lady passes out in his apartment. Thinking she's dead, he tries to get rid of the body. The antics with his neighbor and wife provide plenty of laughs. **86m/B; VHS, DVD, Blu-Ray, Streaming.** George Brent; Virginia Mayo; Carole Landis; Turhan Bey; Ann Dvorak; **D:** Leigh Jason; **W:** Vera Caspary; Walter Bullock; **C:** Jackson Rose; **M:** Carmen Dragon.

Out of the Blue **1980 (R)** A harsh, violent portrait of a shattered family. When an imprisoned father's return fails to reunite this Woodstock-generation family, the troubled teenage daughter takes matters into her own hands. "Easy Rider" star Hopper seems to have reconsidered the effects of the 1960s. **94m/C; VHS, DVD.** Dennis Hopper; Linda Manz; Raymond Burr; **D:** Dennis Hopper; **W:** Gary Jules Jouvenat; Brenda Nielson; Leonard Yakir; **C:** Marc Champion; **M:** Tom Lavin.

Out of Blue **2019** Prominent astrophysicist Jennifer Rockwell (Gummer) is found dead at an observatory. Her research focused on the secrets of black holes and how they related to humanity. As female detective Mike Hoolihan (Clarson) investigates Jennifer's murder, she wants know not only who shot the scientist but why. During the course of Mike's work, she is also investigating what happened to her because she has no memory of her life before she joined the force. Based on the 1997 Martin Amis novel "Night Train," the film is a murder mystery folded into a musing about the nature of the universe but does not adequately address either. **109m/C; DVD.** Jacki Weaver; Patricia Clarkson; Mamie Gummer; James Caan; Aaron Tveit; **D:** Carol Morley; **W:** Carol Morley; **C:** Conrad W. Hall; **M:** Clint Mansell.

Out of the Cold ½ **1999 (R)** Jewish tap dancer Dan Scott (Carradine) decides to take his fading cabaret act to his family's homeland of Estonia on the eve of WWII. Bad idea. Trapped between the Nazis and the Soviets, Dan still finds time to romance local beauty Deborah (Kirshner), although their love affair is cut short by tragedy. Blah film whose plot goes nowhere quickly. **111m/C; VHS, DVD.** Keith Carradine; Mia Kirshner; Judd Hirsch; Brian Dennehy; Mercedes Ruehl; Bronson Pinchot; Kim Hunter; Mark Sheppard; **D:** Aleksandr (Sasha) Buravsky; **W:** Aleksandr (Sasha) Buravsky; Alex Kustanovich; **C:** Vladimir Klimov; **M:** Maksim Dunayevsky.

Out of the Dark ½ **1988 (R)** The female employees of a telephone-sex service are stalked by a killer wearing a clown mask in this tongue-in-cheek thriller. A few laughs amid the slaughter. Look for Divine. **98m/C; VHS, DVD, Streaming.** Cameron Dye; Divine; Karen Black; Bud Cort; Lynn Danielson-Rosenthal; Geoffrey Lewis; Paul Bartel; Tracey Walter; Silvania Gallardo; Starr Andreeff; Lainie Kazan; Tab Hunter; John DeBello; **D:** Michael Schroeder; **W:** James DeFelice; Zane W. Levitt; **C:** Julio Macat; **M:** Paul Antonelli; David Wheatley.

Out of the Fog **1941** Garfield stars as an irredeemable racketeering louse who shakes down the fishermen of Sheepshead Bay. Elderly friends Jonah (Mitchell) and Olaf (Qualen) have big dreams and small means but pay protection money to Harold Goff for safety's sake. Harold woos Jonah's bored daughter Stella (Lupino) and continues to threaten the two men so they plot Harold's death. Fate intervenes so the good guys don't become bad guys. Based on the Irwin Shaw play "The Gentle People." **93m/B; DVD.** John Garfield; Thomas Mitchell; John Qualen; Ida Lupino; Eddie Albert; George Tobias; Aline MacMahon; Leo Gorcey; Paul Harvey; **D:** Anatole Litvak; **W:** Jerry Wald; Robert Rossen; Richard Macaulay; **C:** James Wong Howe.

Out of the Furnace ½ **2013 (R)** Rodney Baze Jr. (Affleck) is a PTSD-addled vet who can't find happiness in the traditional workforce and so gets involved with an underground fight scene that includes the loathsome Harlan DeGroat (Harrelson). When Baze crosses too many bad guys, his brother Russell (Bale) must avenge his brother and maybe win back the love of his life (Saldana). Scott Cooper has assembled a fantastic cast but given them nothing believable to do. The small, character-driven moments are effective but the dialogue is melodramatic. Overall, it's a massive disappointment given the talent of the people involved. **116m/C; DVD, Blu-Ray.** Christian Bale; Casey Affleck; Woody Harrelson; Zoe Saldana; Willem Dafoe; Forest Whitaker; **D:** Scott Cooper; **W:** Scott Cooper; Brad Ingelsby; **C:** Masanobu Takayanagi; **M:** Dickon Hinchliffe.

Out of the Inferno *Out of Inferno* **2013 (PG-13)** A high-rise disaster film centered on a fire out of control. Brothers Taikwan (Lau) and Keung (Koo) have spent their whole careers as dedicated firefighters albeit in different ways. While Tai-kwan follows the rules and works for the fire department, Keung is a rebel who works for their uncle's up-and-coming fire protection business. When Keung meets with some people interested in investing in the enterprise meet in the company's offices, the skyscraper catches on fire. As Keung tries to take care of survivors on the inside, Tai-kwan and the fire department work to control the blaze from the outside. Chinese with subtitles. **107m/C; DVD, Streaming, Download.** Sean Lau; Louis Koo; Angelica Lee; Sicheng Chen; Natalie Tong; **D:** Danny Pang; Oxide Pang; **W:** Danny Pang; Oxide Pang; Tang Nicholl; Kam-yuen Szeto; MengZhang Wu; **C:** Anthony Pun; **M:** Peter Kam; Kin-wai Wong.

Out of the Past ½ *Build My Gallows High* **1947** A private detective gets caught in a complex web of love, murder, and money in this film noir classic. The plot is torturous but clear thanks to fine directing. Mitchum became an overnight star after this film, which was overlooked but now considered one of the best in its genre. Based on Geoffrey Homes's novel "Build My Gallows High." Remade in 1984 as "Against All Odds." **97m/B; VHS, DVD, Blu-Ray.** Robert Mitchum; Kirk Douglas; Jane Greer; Rhonda Fleming; Steve Brodie; Dickie Moore; Richard Webb; Virginia Huston; Ken Niles; Paul Valentine; **D:** Jacques Tourneur; **W:** Daniel Mainwaring; **C:** Nicholas Musuraca; **M:** Roy Webb. Natl. Film Reg. '91.

Out of the Woods ½ **2005** Hallmark Channel family drama. Hotshot young attorney Matt (London) travels to his curmudgeonly grandfather's (Asner) remote cabin when he believes the old man is squandering his estate. Jack wants to buy the surrounding land and deed it outside the family and Matt thinks he's become incompetent. Of course, it's Matt who needs to learn some life lessons. **87m/C; DVD.** Ed Asner; Jason London; Missy (Melissa) Crider; Mel Harris; Meredith Salenger; **D:** Stephen Bridgewater; **W:** Jeff Schechter; **C:** Maximo Munzi; **M:** Roger Bellon. **CABLE**

Out of Time ½ **2000** Dull update of the Rip Van Winkle legend. While walking in the woods outside his small Oregon town, Jack Epson (McDaniels) takes a drink from a spring and falls asleep for 20 years. He wakes up to find his natural surroundings are under siege from developers and his now-grown daughter has a child of her own. **94m/C; VHS, DVD.** James McDaniel; Mel Harris; August Schellenberg; Ken Pogue; **D:** Ernest Thompson; **W:** Ernest Thompson; Rob Gilmer; **C:** Stephen McNutt; **M:** Terry Frewer. **CABLE**

Out of Time ½ **2003 (PG-13)** Far-fetched thriller gets by on the charms of its lead. Matt Lee Whitlock (Washington) is an easy-going police chief in a sleepy Florida town who's having an affair with Ann (Lathan), who's married to jealous Chris (Cain). Ann reveals she has cancer and Matt "borrows" money from a drug bust and gives it to her to help with her treatment. There's a mysterious fire, a couple of charred bodies, and soon Matt is trying to stay one step ahead of a criminal investigation being lead by his estranged wife Alex (Mendes). He may not be an innocent but Matt's not a murderer either, and he has to figure out who's setting him up. **114m/C; VHS, DVD, Blu-Ray.** Denzel Washington; Eva Mendes; Sanaa Lathan; Dean Cain; Robert Baker; Alex Carter; John Billingsley; ***D:*** Carl Franklin; ***W:*** Dave Collard; ***C:*** Theo van de Sande; ***M:*** Graeme Revell.

The Out-of-Towners **1970 (G)** A pair of Ohio rubes travels to New York City and along the way everything that could go wrong does. Lemmon's performance is excellent and Simon's script is, as usual, both wholesome and funny. **98m/C; VHS, DVD.** Jack Lemmon; Sandy Dennis; Anne Meara; Sandy Baron; Billy Dee Williams; ***D:*** Arthur Hiller; ***W:*** Neil Simon. Writers Guild '70: Orig. Screenplay.

The Out-of-Towners **1999 (PG-13)** Hawn and Martin are Nancy and Henry Clark, middle-aged Ohio empty-nesters headed for Henry's job interview in New York. Along the way, they're thwarted by every tourist nightmare obstacle imaginable: rerouting to Boston, missed trains, rental car mishaps, muggings, maxed credit cards, snooty hotel personnel, etc, etc. Martin's seen all this before (in "Planes, Trains, and Automobiles") and so have we, in any number of movies, including the original 1970 Neil Simon script. Mostly uninspired and inconsistent, with flashes of fine physical comedy from Hawn and Martin. Cleese plays a familiar role as a needlessly pompous hotel manager. **92m/C; VHS, DVD.** Goldie Hawn; Steve Martin; John Cleese; Mark McKinney; Oliver Hudson; ***D:*** Sam Weisman; ***W:*** Marc Lawrence; ***C:*** John Bailey; ***M:*** Marc Shaiman.

Out to Sea **1/2** **1997 (PG-13)** Charlie (Matthau) persuades brother-in-law Herb (Lemmon) to become a dance instructor aboard a cruise ship so they can meet women and con them out of money. Charlie sets his sights on feisty socialite Liz (Cannon), while Herb romances Vivian (DeHaven), who's tagging along on her daughter's honeymoon. Both of these "salty old dogs" have to avoid the wrath of militaristic cruise director Gil (Spiner). The duo still has great comic timing; great supporting cast, including O'Connor in a couple of nifty dance scenes, seems to be having a great time. **109m/C; VHS, DVD.** Walter Matthau; Jack Lemmon; Dyan Cannon; Gloria De Haven; Brent Spiner; Elaine Stritch; Hal Linden; Donald O'Connor; Edward Mulhare; Rue McClanahan; Joe (Johnny) Viterelli; ***D:*** Martha Coolidge; ***W:*** Robert Nelson Jacobs; Danny Jacobson; ***C:*** Lajos Koltai; ***M:*** David Newman.

Out West With the Hardys **1/2** **1938** The fifth in the series finds Judge Hardy and his family heading west so the judge can help an old school friend save the family's Arizona ranch. Andy tries to be a cowboy and sister Marian falls for the ranch foreman. **84m/B; DVD.** Mickey Rooney; Lewis Stone; Fay Holden; Cecilia Parker; Sara Haden; Ann Rutherford; Ralph Morgan; Nana Bryant; Don Castle; Virginia Weidler; Gordon Jones; ***D:*** George B. Seitz; ***W:*** Kay Van Riper; Agnes Christine Johnston; William Ludwig; ***C:*** Lester White.

Outback *Wake in Fright* **1971** A horror movie about beer in a film that manages to be unnerving while containing a lot of sunlight. An Australian schoolteacher (Bond) on summer vacation, gets off his train at a stop just to stretch, promptly gambles away his money, and finds himself stranded among beer-swilling, kangaroo-hunting dimwits. One is a vaguely depraved, alcoholic ex-doctor (Pleasance), who meets the teacher in a bar. At first the teacher tries to drink and hunt with "the boys" because he's afraid they'll pummel himt, but soon his civilized veneer begins to crack and his newly macho brutality starts to suit him. **109m/C; DVD, Blu-Ray.** *AU* Gary Bond; Donald Pleasence; John Armstrong; Charles Hughes; John Meillon; Chips Rafferty; Al Thomas; Jack Thompson; John Dalleen; Slim De Gray; Maggie Dence; Norman Erskine; Buster Fiddess; Tex Foote; Mark "Jacko" Jackson; Sylvia Kay; ***D:*** Ted Kotcheff; ***W:*** Evan Jones; ***C:*** Brian West; ***M:*** John Scott.

Outbreak **1994 (R)** Smuggled African monkey spits on someone who kisses someone else who sneezes on a bunch of people, thus initiating the spread of a highly infectious mystery disease in a northern California 'burb. Hoffman leads a team of scientists in a search for the antidote, but it's a secret government plot to exterminate the victims, sending Hoffman and crew into action movie cliche overdrive. Not that that's so bad—if the beat-the-clock tempo doesn't grab you, paranoia certainly will. Based on two books: Richard Preston's "The Hot Zone" and Laurie Garrett's "The Coming Plague." **128m/C; VHS, DVD.** Dustin Hoffman; Rene Russo; Morgan Freeman; Donald Sutherland; Cuba Gooding, Jr.; Kevin Spacey; J.T. Walsh; Dale Dye; ***D:*** Wolfgang Petersen; ***W:*** Laurence Dworet; Robert Roy Pool; ***C:*** Michael Ballhaus; ***M:*** James Newton Howard. N.Y. Film Critics '95: Support. Actor (Spacey).

Outerworld **1/2** *Beyond the Rising Moon; Star Quest: Beyond the Rising Moon* **1987 (R)** A female cyborg and a trader team up to prevent bad guys from getting their hands on an alien ship that crashes on Earth. **84m/C; DVD, Streaming.** Tracy Davis; Hans Bachmann; Michael Mack; Rick Foucheux; Ron Ikejiri; ***D:*** Philip J. Cook; ***W:*** Philip J. Cook; ***C:*** Philip J. Cook; ***M:*** David Bartley. **VIDEO**

The Outfit **1973** Ex-con Earl comes home to discover his brother has been killed by mobsters in retaliation for the bank heist that sent Earl to prison. Earl learns that the bank was mob-controlled and boss Mailer wants Earl and his other partner Cody eliminated as well. Earl and Cody have another plan in mind. Based on a novel by Donald E. Westlake (writing as Richard Stark). **102m/C; DVD.** Robert Duvall; Joe Don Baker; Karen Black; Robert Ryan; Timothy Carey; Richard Jaeckel; Marie Windsor; Elisha Cook, Jr.; Joanna Cassidy; Jane Greer; ***D:*** John Flynn; ***W:*** John Flynn; ***C:*** Bruce Surtees; ***M:*** Jerry Fielding.

Outfoxed: Rupert Murdoch's War on Journalism **2004** Greenwald's doc rails against what he views as manipulation, political bias, and smear-campaign tactics used to further the conservative agenda of Fox News Channel. Uses internal Fox News Department memos to illustrate and ask hard questions about the line between news coverage and commentary. **77m/C; DVD.** ***D:*** Robert Greenwald; ***C:*** Bob Sullivan; James Curry; Will Miller; Glen Pearcy; Richard Perez; Luke Riffle; Eugene Thompson; ***M:*** Nicholas O'Toole.

Outing Riley **2004** Chicago architect Bobby Riley (Jones) is a regular guy in his thirties from an Irish-Catholic family. At the urging of his sister (Pearl) and his boyfriend (McDonald), Bobby finally decides to come out to his three brothers. Only they don't believe him. **86m/C; DVD.** Pete Jones; Nathan Fillion; Michael McDonald; Stoney Westmoreland; Dev Kennedy; Julie R. Pearl; Dana Gilhooley; ***D:*** Pete Jones; ***W:*** Pete Jones; ***C:*** Pete Biagi.

Outland **1981 (R)** On a volcanic moon of Jupiter, miners begin suffering from spells of insanity. A single federal marshal begins an investigation that threatens the colony's survival. No more or less than a western in space, and the science is rather poor. Might make an interesting double feature with "High Noon," though. **109m/C; VHS, DVD, Blu-Ray.** Sean Connery; Peter Boyle; Frances Sternhagen; James B. Sikking; Kika Markham; Clarke Peters; Steven Berkoff; John Ratzenberger; Manning Redwood; Angus MacInnes; ***D:*** Peter Hyams; ***W:*** Peter Hyams; ***C:*** Stephen Goldblatt; ***M:*** Jerry Goldsmith.

Outlander **1/2** **2008 (R)** We're in aliens vs. Vikings territory. In 709 AD, human-looking alien Kainan (Caviezel) crashes his spacecraft in a Norwegian fjord. Unbeknownst to him, a vicious alien called a Moorwen was hiding aboard and promptly decides to destroy the local Norse settlements. Kainan convinces the Viking king Rothgar (Hurt) that he can kill the monster. Some flashbacks explain the Kainan/Moorwen connection and there's finally some action in the last half of the pic but it's a slow slog to get there. **115m/C; Blu-Ray, On Demand.** *US GE* James (Jim) Caviezel; John Hurt; Sophia Myles; Jack Huston; Ron Perlman; Cliff Saunders; Patrick Stevenson; ***D:*** Howard McCain; ***W:*** Howard McCain; Dirk Blackman; ***C:*** Pierre Gill; ***M:*** Geoff Zanelli.

The Outlaw **1943** Hughes's variation on the saga of Billy the Kid, which spends more time on Billy's relationship with girlfriend Rio than the climactic showdown with Pat Garrett. The famous Russell vehicle isn't as steamy as it must have seemed to viewers of the day, but the brouhaha around it served to keep it on the shelf for six years. Also available colorized. **123m/B; VHS, DVD, Blu-Ray.** Jane Russell; Jack Buetel; Walter Huston; Thomas Mitchell; Mimi Aguglia; Gene Rizzi; Joseph (Joe) Sawyer; ***D:*** Howard Hughes; ***W:*** Jules Furthman; ***C:*** Gregg Toland; ***M:*** Victor Young.

Outlaw **1/2** **2007 (R)** Good Brit cast in a revenge flick with lots and lots (and lots) of violence. Embittered ex-soldier Danny Bryant (Bean) forms a vigilante group after becoming disgusted by the brazenness of the city's criminals and the weakness of the PC judicial system. His recruits have all been victimized by violence and Danny has an inside man with longtime copper Lewis (Hoskins), who passes along information on the whereabouts of various scum that need dealing with. **105m/C; DVD.** *GB* Sean Bean; Bob Hoskins; Danny Dyer; Rupert Friend; Sean Harris; Lennie James; ***D:*** Nick Love; ***W:*** Nick Love; ***C:*** Sam McCurdy; ***M:*** David Julyan.

The Outlaw and His Wife **1/2** *You and I* **1917** An early silent film about a farmer, accused of a petty crime, who flees with his wife into the mountains to escape the police. This powerful drama was a breakthrough film for the early Swedish movie industry. **73m/B; Silent; VHS, DVD.** *SW* Victor Sjostrom; Edith Erastoff; ***D:*** Victor Sjostrom; ***W:*** Victor Sjostrom; ***C:*** Julius Jaenzon.

Outlaw Blues **1977 (PG)** An ex-convict becomes a national folk hero when he sets out to reclaim his stolen hit song about prison life. St. James is charming in her first major movie role. A grab bag of action, drama, and tongue-in-cheek humor. **101m/C; VHS, DVD.** Peter Fonda; Susan St. James; Johnny Crawford; Michael Lerner; James Callahan; ***D:*** Richard T. Heffron; ***W:*** Bill L. Norton; ***C:*** Jules Brenner; ***M:*** Charles Bernstein.

The Outlaw Josey Wales **1976 (PG)** Eastwood plays a farmer with a motive for revenge—his family was killed by Union guerillas, and he was betrayed and hunted. His desire to play the lone killer is, however, tempered by his need for family and friends. He kills plenty, but in the end finds peace. Considered one of the last great Westerns, with many superb performances. Eastwood took over directorial chores during filming from Kaufman, who co-scripted. Adapted from "Gone To Texas" by Forest Carter. **135m/C; VHS, DVD, Blu-Ray.** Clint Eastwood; Chief Dan George; Sondra Locke; Matt Clark; John Vernon; Bill McKinney; Sam Bottoms; Will Sampson; Woodrow Parfrey; Royal Dano; John Quade; John Russell; John Mitchum; Kyle Eastwood; ***D:*** Clint Eastwood; ***W:*** Philip Kaufman; ***C:*** Bruce Surtees; ***M:*** Jerry Fielding. Natl. Film Reg. '96.

Outlaw Justice **1/2** **1998 (R)** Aging gunslingers Nelson and Kristofferson meet up with buddy Tritt in order to avenge the death of their old partner. Nothing new storywise but the cast is certainly comfortable with the material. **94m/C; VHS, DVD.** Kris Kristofferson; Willie Nelson; Sancho Garcia; Travis Tritt; Chad Willet; Waylon Jennings; ***D:*** Bill Corcoran; ***W:*** Gene Quintano; ***C:*** Federico Ribes; ***M:*** Jay Gruska. **TV**

Outlaw King **1/2** **2018 (R)** The true story of Robert the Bruce, a 14th-century nobleman who is crowned king of Scotland and leads the charge against the occupying, massive British army. Pine, aptly cast as the titular leader of legends, delivers a performance that's both impassioned and compassioned. The sets are magnificent and the battle scenes are realistic, i.e., bloody. It essentially picks up where the 1995 epic *Braveheart* leaves off, but is more historically accurate than that predecessor. **121m/C; DVD.** Chris Pine; Aaron Taylor-Johnson; Florence Pugh; Billy Howle; Sam Spruell; ***D:*** David Mackenzie; ***W:*** David Mackenzie; Bathsheba Doran; James MacInnes; ***C:*** Barry Ackroyd; ***M:*** Grey Dogs.

Outlaw Prophet **2001** An intergalactic reality TV star is sent to Earth, befriends a little girl, and discovers Christianity. Obviously this doesn't set well with his producers. **90m/C; DVD.** David Heavener; Rebecca Holden; Ric White; Davita Sharone; Aimee Tenaglia; DJ Perry; ***D:*** David Heavener; ***W:*** David Heavener; ***C:*** R. Mark Ramey; ***M:*** Russ Long; Steve Yeaman. **VIDEO**

Outlaw Prophet: Warren Jeffs **2014** Sleazy Lifetime pic based on a true crime story. Warren Jeffs was a fundamentalist, polygamous Mormon leader who was convicted for his sexual abuse of underage girls within his sect. Goldwyn does what he can but pic reeks of exploitation. Based on Stephen Singular's nonfiction book. **88m/C; DVD.** Tony Goldwyn; Molly Parker; Joey King; Martin Landau; ***D:*** Gabriel Range; ***W:*** Steve Kornacki; Alyson Evans; Bryce Kass; ***C:*** Graham Smith; ***M:*** Tony Morales. **CABLE**

Outlaw Women **1952** A western town is run by a woman who won't let male outlaws in—until one wins her heart. **76m/C; VHS, DVD.** Marie Windsor; Jackie Coogan; Carla Balenda; Richard Rober; ***D:*** Sam Newfield; ***W:*** Orville H. Hampton; ***C:*** Harry Neumann; ***M:*** Walter Greene.

Outlaws and Angels **1/2** **2016 (R)** As in so many Westerns, the set-up is simple: bank robbers hold in an isolated farmhouse, basically terrorizing the pastor and his family who live there while bounty hunters try and track them down. There's not a single character to care about and the long running time isn't justified by the filmmaking. The period details don't feel genuine and the performances are boring. This is one for diehard genre fans only. **120m/C; DVD.** Chad Michael Murray; Francesca Ruth Eastwood; Madisen Beaty; Ben Browder; Luke Wilson; Teri Polo; ***D:*** JT Mollner; ***W:*** JT Mollner; ***C:*** Matthew Irving; ***M:*** Colin Stetson.

The Outlaws Is Coming! **1/2** **1965** Three magazine staffers (Larry, Moe, and Curly Joe) and their editor (West) encounter Wyatt Earp, Wild Bill Hickock, Jesse James, and Annie Oakley when they journey out West to save the buffalo. Last, and one of the best, of the Three Stooges feature films. **90m/B; VHS, DVD.** Moe Howard; Larry Fine; Joe DeRita; Adam West; Nancy Kovack; Emil Sitka; Henry Gibson; ***D:*** Norman Maurer; ***W:*** Elwood Ullman; ***C:*** Irving Lippman; ***M:*** Paul Dunlap.

Outlaw's Son **1957** Outlaw Nate Burke (Clark) comes to town to reunite with his son Jeff, who's been raised by his sister-in-law Ruth (Drew). Fearful the boy will become a criminal too, she frames Nate for a robbery and murder and he's sent away. Nate eventually escapes but a now-grown Jeff (Cooper) has learned the truth and decides to live up to his father's bad reputation by planning a stagecoach heist. **88m/B; DVD.** Dane Clark; Ben Cooper; Ellen Drew; Lori Nelson; Charles Watts; Robert Knapp; ***D:*** Lesley Selander; ***W:*** Richard Alan Simmons; ***C:*** William Margulies; ***M:*** Les Baxter.

Outpost **2007 (R)** In a small East European town devastated by war, a man hires a group of mercenaries to protect him while he does a mineralogical survey of an old WWII Nazi bunker on land he's come into possession of. Their thoughts that he might just be lying are confirmed when they arrive to find a pile of corpses. **90m/C; DVD.** *UK* Ray Stevenson; Julian Wadham; Richard Brake; Paul Blair; Brett Fancy; Enoch Frost; Julian Rivett; Michael Smiley; ***D:*** Steve Barker; ***W:*** Steve Barker; Rae Brunton; Kieran Parker; ***C:*** Gavin Struthers; ***M:*** James Seymour Brett.

Outpost: Black Sun **2012** Dull, dreary sequel to Barker's 2007 "Outpost" features more Nazi stormtroopers who were turned into a zombie army. A present-day NATO special forces unit in Eastern Europe must deal with an old bunker full of the creatures. **101m/C; DVD, Blu-Ray.** *UK* Catherine Steadman; Richard Coyle; Julian Wadham; Daniel Caltagirone; Clive Russell; Michael Byrne; ***D:*** Steve Barker; ***W:*** Steve Barker; Rae Brunton; ***C:*** Darran Tiernan; ***M:*** Theo Green. **VIDEO**

Outpost in Morocco **1/2** **1949** A desert soldier is sent to quiet the restless natives and falls for the rebel leader's daughter. The good guys win, but the love interest is sacrificed. Glory before love boys, and damn the story. **92m/B; VHS, DVD.** George Raft; Marie Windsor; Akim Tamiroff; John Litel; Eduard Franz; ***D:*** Robert Florey; ***W:*** Charles Grayson; Paul de Sainte-Colombe; ***C:*** Lucien N. Andriot; ***M:*** Michel Michelet.

Outpost: Rise of the Spetsnaz 🦴 1/2 *Outpost 3: Rise of the Spetsnaz* **2013** Prequel to the first two "Outpost" films, in which Russian special forces scuffle with dead Nazis in the aftermath of WWII. First directorial effort by Parker, who successfully caters to gore fans but otherwise it's the same old zombie stuff. **84m/C; DVD, Blu-Ray.** *UK* Michael McKell; Bryan Larkin; Ivan Kamaras; Velibor Topic; Laurence Possa; Patrick Jonsson; ***D:*** Kieran Parker; ***W:*** Rae Brunton; ***C:*** Carlos De Carvalho; ***M:*** Al Hardiman. **VIDEO**

The Outrage 🦴 1/2 **1964** Paul Newman plays a Mexican bandit with a bad accent in this dreary western remake of "Rashomon." A con man (Robinson), preacher (Shatner), and prospector (Da Silva) wait at a railway station. They were all witnesses at the trial of bandit Juan (Newman), who was convicted of rape and murder. But the three men give divergent accounts as to what happened (shown in flashbacks). **95m/B; DVD.** Paul Newman; Laurence Harvey; Claire Bloom; Edward G. Robinson; William Shatner; Howard da Silva; Albert Salmi; Paul Fix; Thomas Chalmers; ***D:*** Martin Ritt; ***W:*** Michael Kanin; ***C:*** James Wong Howe; ***M:*** Alex North.

Outrage 🦴🦴 *Dispara* **1993 (R)** Journalist Marco Vallez's (Banderas) latest assignment is a story about a traveling circus. Bored with the usual acts, he's intrigued by equestrian/sharpshooter Anna (Neri) and asks her for an interview, which leads to passion. While Marco is on assignment in Barcelona, Anna is attacked and raped in her trailer. Rather than calling the police, Anna decides to take her own revenge. Spanish with subtitles or dubbed. **108m/C; VHS, DVD.** *SP* Antonio Banderas; Francesca Neri; Eulalia Ramon; Walter Vidarte; Coque Malla; ***D:*** Carlos Saura; ***W:*** Carlos Saura; ***C:*** Javier Aguirresarobe; ***M:*** Alberto Iglesias.

Outrage 🦴🦴 1/2 **1998** Average guy Tom Casey (Lowe) thinks he's being a good citizen when he reports some teens stealing from cars to the cops. Instead, he and wife Sally (Grey) are terrorized by the punks and Tom decides the best solution is to take care of the miscreants himself. **90m/C; VHS, DVD.** Rob Lowe; Jennifer Grey; Eric Michael Cole; Shane Meier; Nathaniel DeVeaux; Kathryn Harrold; Robert Wisden; ***D:*** Robert Allan Ackerman; ***W:*** Ellen Weston; ***C:*** Tobias Schliessler; ***M:*** David Mansfield. **TV**

Outrage 🦴🦴 **2009 (R)** Controversial documentarian Kirby Dick focuses on politicians (mainly Republicans) who campaign and vote against gay rights legislation while living closeted lives. Dick offers interviews (such as with gay blogger Michael Rogers who specializes in outing politicos), television clips, and commercials although it can come across as manipulative, including Dick's presumptions of a media conspiracy. **98m/C; DVD.** ***D:*** Kirby Dick; ***C:*** Thaddeus Wadleigh; ***M:*** Peter Golub.

Outrage 🦴🦴 *Autoreiji* **2010 (R)** Takeshi Kitano, a one-man Japanese movie machine, stars in his Beat Takeshi acting persona as super-cool Otomo, a yakuza clean-up man, in this stylishly ultraviolent drama. Three Tokyo crime families are fighting for power and Otomo is told by his boss to make sure they come out on top. Japanese with subtitles. **109m/C; DVD, Blu-Ray.** *JP* Takeshi "Beat" Kitano; Renji Ishibashi; Jun Kunimura; Soichiro Kitamura; Tetta Sugimoto; Ryo Kase; ***D:*** Takeshi "Beat" Kitano; ***W:*** Takeshi "Beat" Kitano; ***C:*** Katsumi Yanagijima; ***M:*** Keiichi Suzuki.

Outrage Born in Terror 🦴 **2009 (R)** Low-budget action banality finds Christine and boyfriend Trey heading to an isolated mansion she's inherited. However, it's already occupied by nutjob ex-military sniper Farragute and his crew who are planning a robbery. **89m/C; DVD, Blu-Ray.** Ace Cruz; Michael Madsen; Katie Fountain; Natasha Lyonne; Derek Lee Nixon; Michael Berryman; ***W:*** Chris Soth; ***C:*** Michael Mansouri; ***M:*** Taylor Uhler. **VIDEO**

Outrageous! 🦴🦴🦴 **1977 (R)** An offbeat, low-budget comedy about the strange relationship between a gay female impersonator and his pregnant schizophrenic friend. The pair end up in New York, where they feel right at home. Russell's impersonations of female film stars earned him the best actor prize at the Berlin Film Festival. **100m/C; VHS, DVD.** *CA* Craig Russell; Hollis McLaren; Richard Easley; Allan Moyle; Helen Shaver; Martha Gibson; Helen Hughes; David McIlwraith; Andree Pelletier; ***D:*** Richard Benner; ***W:*** Richard Benner; ***C:*** James Kelly; ***M:*** Paul Hoffert.

Outrageous Fortune 🦴🦴 **1987 (R)** Two would-be actresses—one prim and innocent and one wildly trampy—chase after the same two-timing boyfriend and get involved in a dangerous CIA plot surrounding a deadly bacteria. Tired plot. Mediocre acting and formula jokes, but somehow still funny. Disney's first foray into comedy for grownups. **112m/C; VHS, DVD.** Shelley Long; Bette Midler; George Carlin; Peter Coyote; ***D:*** Arthur Hiller; ***W:*** Leslie Dixon; ***C:*** David M. Walsh; ***M:*** Alan Silvestri.

The Outriders 🦴🦴 1/2 **1950** Well-played, fast-paced Technicolor western filmed at Kanab, Utah. Confederate soldiers Will, Jesse, and Clint escape from a Union POW camp and soon join a rebel gang led by Keeley. The ruthless raiders target a wagon train secretly carrying gold bullion and the trio gets hired on as escorts. Will becomes interested in widow Jen Gort and when he realizes that Keeley doesn't care about killing innocents, he has second thoughts about going through with the ambush. **93m/C; DVD.** Joel McCrea; Barry Sullivan; James Whitmore; Jeff Corey; Arlene Dahl; Claude Jarman, Jr.; Ramon Novarro; Ted de Corsia; ***D:*** Roy Rowland; ***W:*** Irving Ravetch; ***C:*** Charles E. Schoenbaum; ***M:*** Andre Previn.

Outside Bet 🦴 1/2 **2012** Strained, low-budget Brit comedy. During the financial meltdown of the 1980s, a typesetter, union rep, barmaid, and others worried about their economic survival decide to make a risky investment in a racehorse. **101m/C; DVD.** *UK* Calum MacNab; Bob Hoskins; Emily Atack; Jenny Agutter; Philip Davis; Jason Maza; Adam Deacon; ***D:*** Sacha Bennett; ***W:*** Nigel Smith; ***C:*** Nic Lawson; ***M:*** Greg Hatwell.

Outside In 🦴🦴 1/2 **2017** A subtle, empathetic drama about the outfall from a man released after a long unjust prison sentence. Carol (Falco) has spent two decades working to free her former student Chris (Duplass) from prison. In this period, she not only neglected her teaching but also her husband Tom (Leggett) and daughter Hildy (Dever). After Chris's release, he lacks the understanding he needs from family and friends, while Carol's attempt to reconnect with her family is strained. Chris's romantic feelings for Carol add to the tension. **109m/C; DVD.** Edie Falco; Jay Duplass; Kaitlyn Dever; Ben Schwartz; Aaron Blakely; ***D:*** Lynn Shelton; ***W:*** Jay Duplass; Lynn Shelton; ***C:*** Nathan M. Miller; ***M:*** Andrew Bird.

Outside of Paradise 🦴 1/2 **1938** New York bandleader Danny O'Toole inherits a half-interest in an Irish castle. He and his pals show up and want to turn the place into a restaurant/nightclub but co-owner Mavourneen isn't pleased with their idea and then gets downright stubborn when Danny starts flirting with wealthy Dorothy. **68m/B; DVD.** Phil Regan; Penny Singleton; Ruth Coleman; Leonid Kinskey; Mary Forbes; Lionel Pape; Bert Gordon; ***D:*** John H. Auer; ***W:*** Harry Sauber; ***C:*** Jack Marta.

Outside Providence 🦴🦴 1/2 **1999 (R)** Based on Peter Farrelly's semi-autobiographical novel, it tells the story of Dunph (Hatosy), a stoner teen from Pawtucket who's sent to a snooty prep school by his father (Baldwin) after he and his druggie friends crash into a police car. Dunph has immediate trouble fitting in, although he manages to hook up with coed Jane (Smart) whose book smarts help his anemic GPA. Unfortunately, his pranks put her Ivy League hopes in danger. Baldwin gives a good performance as the gruff-but-loving dad, but too many of the characters are merely skimmed over before they have a chance to develop. **103m/C; VHS, DVD.** Shawn Hatosy; Alec Baldwin; George Wendt; Jonathan Brandis; Amy Smart; Gabriel Mann; Jon Abrahams; Adam LaVorgna; Mike Cerrone; Richard Jenkins; ***D:*** Michael Corrente; ***W:*** Peter Farrelly; Michael Corrente; Bobby Farrelly; ***C:*** Richard Crudo; ***M:*** Sheldon Mirowitz.

Outside the Law 🦴🦴 **1921** Lon Chaney plays dual roles of the underworld hood in "Black Mike Sylva," and a Chinese servant in "Ah Wing." Silent. **77m/B; Silent; VHS, DVD.** Lon Chaney, Sr.; Priscilla Dean; Ralph Lewis; Wheeler Oakman; ***D:*** Tod Browning; ***W:*** Lucien Hubbard; ***C:*** William Fildew.

Outside the Law 🦴 1/2 **1995 (R)** Maverick cop Brad Kingsbury (Bradley) crosses the line when he falls for luscious Tanya Borgman (Thomson), who's the prime suspect in a murder investigation. Also available unrated. **94m/C; VHS, DVD.** David Bradley; Anna Thomson; Ashley Laurence; ***D:*** Boaz Davidson; ***W:*** Dennis Dimster-Denk; ***C:*** Avi (Avraham) Karpik; ***M:*** Blake Leyh.

Outside the Law 🦴🦴 *Hors-la-Loi* **2010** Controversial Algerian drama takes on the struggle for independence against the French (from the 1920s to the early 1960s) through well-worn plot devices. A poor family, who have been dispossessed of their home in Algeria, immigrate to France. The three brothers grow up resentful of the French colonists and become radicalized to various degrees through the guerilla National Liberation Front. The Front's violence is matched by a French secret counterterrorist organization that employs the same brutal tactics. French and Arabic with subtitles. **138m/C; Blu-Ray.** *AL* Roschdy Zem; Sami Bouajila; Bernard Blancan; Jean-Pierre Lorit; Samir Guesmi; Jamel Debouze; Assâad Bouabl; Chafia Boudraa; Ahmed Benaissa; ***D:*** Rachid Bouchareb; ***W:*** Rachid Bouchareb; Olivier Lorelle; ***C:*** Christophe Beaucarne; ***M:*** Armand Amar.

The Outsider 🦴🦴 1/2 **2002 (R)** Rebecca Yoder (Watts) is part of a relgious community that has settled in Montana in 1886, hoping to escape the prejudice that plagued them in Ohio. But the local cattle ranchers are angry over a land dispute and kill Rebecca's husband, hoping to force her to sell her farm. Then, a wounded stanger staggers onto her property, whom Rebecca nurses back to health. Of course, Johnny Gault (Daly) is not only worldly but dangerous and Rebecca may be forced to choose between her new man and the religious community that disapproves. Adapted from the book by Penelope Williamson. **119m/C; VHS, DVD.** Timothy Daly; Naomi Watts; Keith Carradine; David Carradine; Jason Clarke; Grant Piro; ***D:*** Randa Haines; ***W:*** Jenny Wingfield; ***C:*** Ben Nott; ***M:*** Todd Boekelheide. **CABLE**

The Outsider 🦴 **2014** Lex Walker (Fairbrass) is the title character, a British mercenary who travels to Los Angeles to find his daughter. He hires a local detective (Patric) and crosses paths with an Internet tycoon (Caan) on his way into the dark side of the city of angels. Echoes of the brilliant "The Limey" do the film no favors in comparison. Miller's thriller is a snooze, wasting a talented supporting cast in service of a plot that's increasingly impossible to care. By the time the film reaches its climax, you'll have given up entirely. **94m/C; DVD, Blu-Ray.** Craig Fairbrass; James Caan; Jason Patric; Shannon Elizabeth; Johnny Messner; Melissa Ordway; ***D:*** Brian A. Miller; ***W:*** Brian A. Miller; ***C:*** Eduardo Enrique Mayen; ***M:*** Patrick Savage.

The Outsider 🦴🦴 **2019** After serving in the American military in World War II, veteran Nick Lowell (Leto) is in a Japanese prison in 1954 when he saves the life of yazuka (organized crime gang) member Kiyoshi (Asano). Because of his actions, Nick is invited to join the Shiramatsu gang and is taught specialized fighting skills by the gang boss (Manaka). As he is accepted by the Shiramatsu, he is drawn into their deadly turf war with the Seizu gang. The action crime drama wants to be an epic but its story and action scenes don't hold up. **86m/C; DVD.** Jon Foo; Trace Adkins; Sean Patrick Flanery; Kaiwi Lyman; Danny Trejo; ***D:*** Timothy Woodward, Jr.; ***W:*** Sean Ryan; ***C:*** Pablo Diez; ***M:*** Samuel Joseph Smythe.

The Outsiders 🦴🦴 1/2 **1983 (PG)** Based on the popular S.E. Hinton book, the story of a teen gang from the wrong side of the tracks and their conflicts with society and each other. Melodramatic and over-done, but teenagers still love the story. Good soundtrack and cast ripples with up and coming stars. Followed by a TV series. Coppola adapted another Hinton novel the same year, "Rumble Fish." **91m/C; VHS, DVD, Blu-Ray.** C. Thomas Howell; Matt Dillon; Ralph Macchio; Patrick Swayze; Diane Lane; Tom Cruise; Emilio Estevez; Rob Lowe; Tom Waits; Leif Garrett; ***D:*** Francis Ford Coppola; ***W:*** Kathleen Rowell; ***C:*** Stephen Burum; ***M:*** Carmine Coppola.

The Outskirts 🦴🦴🦴 *Okraina* **1998** An epic political thriller with darkly humorous edge. In Russia at a time of violent transformation, a group of farmers in the Ural Mountains find their land has been sold to oil companies. Taking up arms, they try to discover who stole their land and fight injustice in the process. As they seek information, they travel from their countryside to the heights of political power in the form of the Soviet oil ministry. Along they way, they experience corruption and sadness but also have romantic and religious experiences. Russian with subtitles. **95m/C; DVD.** Yuriy Dubrovin; Nikolay Olyalin; Aleksei Pushkin; Aleksey Vanin; Rimma Markova; ***D:*** Pyotr Lutsik; ***W:*** Pyotr Lutsik; ***C:*** Nikolay Ivasiv; ***M:*** Gavriil Popov; Georgi Sviridov.

Outsourced 🦴🦴 1/2 **2006 (PG-13)** Romantic comedy makes it cultural points with a light touch. Todd Anderson (Hamilton) manages a Seattle call center filling orders for cheap novelties. Told his department is being shut down because the jobs have been outsourced to India, Todd is then informed he's expected to travel to the country and train his replacements. He reluctantly labors to instruct his confused new employees until he finds a bittersweet romance with co-worker Asha (Dharker), who introduces him to her culture. **103m/C; DVD.** Josh Hamilton; Ayesha Dharker; Larry Pine; Matt Smith; Asif Basra; ***D:*** John Jeffcoat; ***W:*** John Jeffcoat; George Irving; ***C:*** Teodoro Maniaci; ***M:*** B.C. Smith.

Outta Time 🦴🦴 *The Courier* **2001 (R)** Tijuana native David Morales (Lopez) has gottan an athletic scholarship to the University of San Diego but loses it because of a knee injury. Needing cash to pay his tuition, David doesn't ask a lot of questions when ex-professor Darabont (Saxon) asks David to transport some sealed packages of serum for testing across the border. Naturally, this job isn't as easy as David has been told. **90m/C; VHS, DVD.** Mario Lopez; John Saxon; Ali Landry; Nancy O'Dell; Tava Smiley; Tim Sitarz; ***D:*** Lorena David; ***W:*** Scott Duncan; Ned Kerwin; ***C:*** Lisa Wiegand; ***M:*** Scott Gilman.

Over-Exposed 🦴🦴 **1956** Alcoholic shutterbug Max (Greenleaf) teaches ambitious Lila (cleavage-baring Moore) the tricks of his trade and she finds success in the big city and romance with newshound Russell (Crenna). But Lila also gets involved with blackmail and mobsters thanks to working for a sleazy tabloid and that's not good for a dame's health. **80m/B; DVD.** Cleo Moore; Richard Crenna; Raymond Greenleaf; James O'Rear; Donald Randolph; Isobel Elsom; Jeanne Cooper; ***D:*** Lewis Seiler; ***W:*** Gil Orlovitz; James Gunn; ***C:*** Henry Freulich; ***M:*** Mischa Bakaleinikoff.

Over Her Dead Body 🦴 1/2 **2008 (PG-13)** Henry (Rudd) and Kate (Longoria Parker) are about to tie the knot at their perfectly orchestrated wedding when a freak ice sculpture accident leads to the bee-otchy bridezilla's untimely demise. A year later, the still-mourning Henry is encouraged by his sister Chloe (Sloane) to see her psychic friend Ashley (Bell) to help him get over his grief. Of course sparks fly, but ghostly Kate shows up to put the kibosh on Henry's new romance. Bell's charming and Rudd's likable in a premise that's been done to death, but the inexplicably top-billed Longoria Parker grates in every scene she stomps through. **95m/C; Blu-Ray, On Demand.** Eva Longoria; Paul Rudd; Lake Bell; Jason Biggs; Lindsay Sloane; Stephen (Steve) Root; William Morgan Sheppard; ***D:*** Jeff Lowell; ***W:*** Jeff Lowell; ***C:*** John Bailey; ***M:*** David Kitay.

Over the Edge 🦴🦴🦴 1/2 **1979 (PG)** The music of Cheap Trick, The Cars, and The Ramones highlights this realistic tale of alienated suburban youth on the rampage. Dillon makes his screen debut in this updated, well-done "Rebel Without a Cause." Shelved for several years, the movie was finally released after Dillon made it big. Sleeper with excellent direction and dialogue. **91m/C; VHS, DVD.** Michael Kramer; Matt Dillon; Pamela Ludwig; Vincent Spano; Tom Fergus; Harry Northrup; Andy Romano; Ellen Geer; Richard Jamison; Julia Pomeroy; Tiger Thompson; ***D:*** Jonathan Kaplan; ***W:*** Charles F. Haas; Tim Hunter; ***C:*** Andrew Davis; ***M:*** Sol Kaplan.

Over the Hedge 🦴🦴🦴 **2006 (PG)** Hilarious though shallow comedy has a group of woodland creatures awakening from their winter hibernation, surprised to see a subdivision has sprouted up just beyond a hedge. Opportunistic raccoon RJ (Willis) tells his pals, including cautious turtle Verne (Shandling), that humans equal the good life and that they should venture into this strange new world. Of course, the humans, in the form of harpie Gladys (Janney) and "Verminator" Dwayne (Church) view these new neighbors as pests. Plenty of laughs and excellent voice performances, but trades some of the satire of Michael Fry and T. Lewis's source comic strip for fuzzy sentimentality. **84m/C; DVD, Blu-Ray.** ***V:*** Bruce Willis; Garry Shandling; Steve Carell; William Shatner; Catherine O'Hara; Eugene Levy; Wanda Sykes; Nick Nolte; Thomas Haden Church; Allison Janney; ***D:*** Tim Johnson; Karey Kirkpatrick; ***W:*** Karey Kirkpatrick; Len Blum; Lorne Cameron; David Hoselton; ***M:*** Rupert Gregson-Williams.

Over the Hill 🦴🦴 **1/2 1993 (PG)** Dukakis stars as Alma, an eccentric widow who decides to leave her well-meaning son's restrictive home in Maine to visit her estranged daughter Elizabeth in Sydney, Australia. Embarassed by her peculiarities Elizabeth arranges a holiday away but Mom has her own plans. She wants to "loop the loop," and make a complete circuit around the Australian continent. Soon Alma is on the road, meeting fellow eccentrics and experiencing a variety of adventures. **102m/C; VHS, Streaming.** Olympia Dukakis; Sigrid Thornton; Derek Fowlds; Pippa Grandison; ***D:*** George Miller; ***W:*** Robert Caswell; ***C:*** David Connell.

The Over-the-Hill Gang 🦴🦴 **1/2 1969** In this TV movie western, originally shown on ABC, retired Texas Ranger Oren Hayes calls on three equally time-worn buddies for help. Seems his son-in-law Jeff Rose got roughed up by corrupt officials during a mayoral race and Hayes thinks the law should prevail. **75m/C; DVD.** Pat O'Brien; Walter Brennan; Chill Wills; Edgar Buchanan; Ricky Nelson; Edward Andrews; Jack Elam; Andy Devine; Kristin Harmon; Gypsy Rose Lee; ***D:*** Jean Yarbrough; ***W:*** Jameson Brewer; ***C:*** Henry Cronjager, Jr.; ***M:*** Hugo Friedhofer. **TV**

The Over-the-Hill Gang Rides Again 🦴🦴 **1/2 1970** In this sequel to the 1969 ABC TV comic western, retired Texas Ranger Nash Crawford (Brennan) gathers the gang together to rescue The Baltimore Kid (Astaire) from murder charges in Waco. It involves mistaken identity and a stagecoach robbery. **75m/C; DVD.** Walter Brennan; Fred Astaire; Edgar Buchanan; Andy Devine; Chill Wills; Lana Wood; ***D:*** George McCowan; ***W:*** Richard Carr; ***C:*** Fleet Southcott; ***M:*** David Raskin. **TV**

Over the Top 🦴 **1/2 1986 (PG)** The film that started a nationwide arm-wrestling craze. A slow-witted trucker decides the only way he can retain custody of his estranged son, as well as win the boy's respect, is by winning a big arm-wrestling competition. Stallone is an expert at grinding these movies out by now, and the kid (General Hospital's Mikey) is all right, but the end result is boredom, as it should be with an arm-wrestling epic. **94m/C; VHS, DVD, Blu-Ray.** Sylvester Stallone; Susan Blakely; Robert Loggia; David Mendenhall; ***D:*** Menahem Golan; ***W:*** Sylvester Stallone; Gary Conway; Stirling Silliphant. Golden Raspberries '87: Worst New Star (Mendenhall), Worst Support. Actor (Mendenhall).

Over the Waves 🦴🦴 **1/2** *Sobre las Olas* **1949** Biography of sorts based loosely on the life of violinist and composer Juventino Rosas (Infante) and named after his most famous waltz. Sadly Juventino died poor as he sold much of his work for a paltry sum, and his most famous work was mistakenly believed to be Viennese in origin. While the film is not entirely accurate, it does stay true to the tragedy of the life of the man it depicts. **128m/B; DVD.** *MX* Pedro Infante; Alicia Neira; Beatriz Aguirre; Bertha Lomeli; Beatriz Jimeno; Prudencia Grifell; Andres Soler; Jose Luis Jimenez; Antonio F. Frausto; Miguel Manzano; Pedro Elviro; ***D:*** Ismael Rodriguez; ***W:*** Ismael Rodriguez; Rogelio A. Gonzalez; Pedro De Urdimalas; ***C:*** Jack Draper; ***M:*** Raul Lavista.

Over the Wire 🦴 **1/2 1995** Telephone lineman Bruce (Christensen) accidentally overhears a conversation where a woman hires a hitman to kill her sister. He finds out that the sisters live together and tries to figure out just who the target is before it's too late (of course, he has to seduce both of them to accomplish this). Ray used the pseudonym Nicholas Medina. **90m/C; VHS, DVD.** David Christensen; Shauna O'Brien; Landon Hall; Tim Abell; John Lazar; Bob Dole; ***D:*** Fred Olen Ray; ***W:*** Pete Slate; ***C:*** Howard Wexler.

Over 21 🦴🦴 **1/2 1945** Satirical wartime comedy that's an adaptation of the Ruth Gordon play and based on her experiences with husband Garson Kanin. Middle-aged newspaper editor Max Wharton (Knox) decides to do his WWII bit by signing up for Office Candidate School. His screenwriter wife Paula (Dunne) follows him to a Florida Army base, trying to adjust to being a military wife, while Max worries he'll embarrass himself before the much-younger recruits and flunk out. **102m/B; DVD.** Irene Dunne; Alexander Knox; Charles Coburn; Jeff Donnell; Loren Tindall; Phil Brown; Pierre Watkin; ***D:*** Charles Vidor; ***W:*** Sidney Buchman; ***C:*** Rudolph Mate; ***M:*** Marlin Skiles.

Overboard 🦴🦴 **1987 (PG)** A wealthy, spoiled woman falls off of her yacht and into the arms of a low-class carpenter who picks her up and convinces her she is in fact his wife, and mother to his four brats. Just when she learns to like her life, the tables are turned again. Even though it's all been done before, you can't help but laugh at the screwy gags. **112m/C; VHS, DVD, Blu-Ray.** Goldie Hawn; Kurt Russell; Katherine Helmond; Roddy McDowall; Edward Herrmann; ***D:*** Garry Marshall; ***W:*** Leslie Dixon; ***C:*** John A. Alonzo; ***M:*** Alan Silvestri.

Overboard 🦴 **1/2 2018 (PG-13)** A gender-switching remake of the 1987 farce. When financially struggling single mom Kate (Faris) takes a job on the yacht of lazy playboy Leonardo (Derbez), he insults her and pushes her overboard. After he falls in himself and wakes up with amnesia, Kate convinces him that they are married and he is a blue-collar construction worker. Leonardo believes her lies and works hard, though his memory eventually starts to return. The remake does not match the laughs of the original film and Derbez seems too old to play Leonardo, but his work in the role is the highlight of the film. **112m/C; DVD, Blu-Ray.** Eugenio Derbez; Anna Faris; Eva Longoria; Mel Rodriguez; John Hannah; ***D:*** Rob Greenberg; ***W:*** Rob Greenberg; Bob Fisher; Leslie Dixon; ***C:*** Michael Barrett; ***M:*** Lyle Workman.

The Overbrook Brothers 🦴🦴 **2009** Deadpan dark comedy. Immature Jason and aggressive Todd have had a nasty sibling rivalry since they were kids with Todd doing most of the troublemaking. A holiday gathering has Jason reluctantly introducing fiancee Shelly into the mix but Todd won't be outdone in news: his bombshell is that Jason is adopted. So the battling bros (along with the third wheel girlfriend) go on a road trip from Colorado to Texas so Jason can introduce himself to his biological parents. **92m/C; DVD.** Steve Zissis; Nathan Harlan; Mark Reeb; Laurel Whitsett; John Jones; Kerbey Smith; ***D:*** John E. Bryant; ***W:*** John E. Bryant; Jason Foxworth; ***C:*** Mike Washlesky; ***M:*** Adam Blau. **VIDEO**

Overcomer 🦴🦴 **2019 (PG)** When the local manufacturing plant lays off most of its employees, a small town faces economic disaster and many families leave. The local Christian high school is particularly hard hit, including the basketball team coached by John Harrison (Kendrick). When the school's principal asks him to coach the cross country team, John balks because he does not believe running is a sport and only Hannah (Wright-Thompson) is interested. As he takes the job and Hannah trains for the state championship, John changes her life in unexpected ways. The faith-based film is disorganized but still uplifting. **?m/C; DVD, Blu-Ray.** Alex Kendrick; Priscilla C. Shirer; Shari Rigby; Ben Davies; Elizabeth Becka; ***D:*** Alex Kendrick; ***W:*** Alex Kendrick; Stephen Kendrick; ***C:*** Bob Scott; ***M:*** Paul Mills.

Overdrive 🦴🦴 **2017 (PG-13)** An escapist action thriller in the mold of the Fast and the Furious franchise. Based in Marseille, half-brothers Andrew (Eastwood) and Garrett (Thorp) finance their high-end lifestyle by stealing expensive classic sport cars for shifty customers. When the brothers hijack a $41 million 1937 Bugatti from local crime boss Morier (Abkarian), they face his wrath. To save their lives, they agree to steal a priceless 1962 Ferrari from Morier's German rival (Schick). The duo must evade cops and mobsters to secure the vehicle and survive. Though the plot is unbelievable and the dialogue trite, the car chases are relatively effective. **93m/C; DVD.** Scott Eastwood; Freddie Thorp; Ana de Armas; Gaia Weiss; Simon Abkarian; ***D:*** Antonio Negret; ***W:*** Michael Brandt; Derek Haas; ***C:*** Laurent Bares; ***M:*** Pascal Lengagne.

Overkill 🦴🦴 **1996 (R)** Burnt-out cop Jack Hazard (Norris) heads for vacation in Costa Rica and winds up being the prey for demented hunter Lloyd Wheeler (Nouri). **92m/C; VHS, Streaming.** Aaron Norris; Michael Nouri; ***D:*** Dean Ferrandini; ***W:*** Dean Ferrandini.

Overland Mail 🦴🦴 **1942** Fifteen episodes of the vintage serial filled with western action. **225m/B; VHS, DVD.** Lon Chaney, Jr.; Helen Parrish; Don Terry; Bob Baker; Noah Beery, Sr.; Noah Beery, Jr.; Tom Chatterton; Charles Stevens; ***D:*** Ford Beebe; John Rawlins; ***W:*** Paul Huston; ***C:*** George Robinson; William Sickner.

Overlanders 🦴🦴🦴 **1946** The Japanese may invade, but rather than kill 1,000 head of cattle, these Aussies drive the huge herd across the continent, facing danger along the way. Beautifully photographed, featuring the "Australian Gary Cooper" and a stampede scene to challenge "Dances with Wolves." **91m/B; VHS, DVD.** *AU* Chips Rafferty; Daphne Campbell; Jean Blue; John Nugent Hayward; ***D:*** Harry Watt; ***W:*** Harry Watt; ***C:*** Osmond H. Borradaile.

Overlord 🦴🦴 **1/2 2018 (R)** The story of two American soldiers behind enemy lines on D Day. **109m/C; DVD, Blu-Ray, Streaming.** *CA US* Jovan Adepo; Wyatt Russell; Mathilde Ollivier; Pilou Asbaek; John Magaro; ***D:*** Julius Avery; ***W:*** Billy Ray; Mark L . Smith; ***C:*** Laurie Rose; Fabian Wagner; ***M:*** Jed Kurzel.

Overnight 🦴🦴🦴 **2003 (R)** Troy Duffy's "The Boondock Saints" has garnered a cult following on video, but this documentary about the story behind the film will make viewers recoil in disbelief at how one man's hubris and self-delusion can sink a promising career. During the indie film boom of the 1990s, Miramax offered Duffy $1 million for his "Boondock" script and signed his band to a record deal. Convinced of his own greatness, Duffy alienates and bullies everyone around him until he loses every opportunity he's been handed. It's hard to sympathize with Duffy, particularly because he originally hired Montana and Smith to direct the doc as a chronicle of his rise to the top. Weak in spots, but it's still schadenfreude at its best. **81m/C; DVD.** ***D:*** Mark Smith; ***C:*** Mark Smith; ***M:*** Troy Duffy.

The Overnight 🦴🦴 **1/2 2015 (R)** Why is it so hard for adults to make friends? And why do they fail to understand that they can have fun and change their relationship even after they have kids? These are the questions at the core of Patrick Brice's hilarious "one crazy night" comedy about a transplanted couple (Schilling & Scott) who have a dinner play date with new friends (Schwartzman & Godreche) that gets unpredictably out of control. A lot of drinking, some frank discussion, and even some skinny dipping lead to insightful conversations about how we all need to be willing to change, even after someone starts calling us mommy or daddy. **78m/C; DVD, Streaming.** Adam Scott; Taylor Schilling; Jason Schwartzman; Judith Godreche; ***D:*** Patrick Brice; ***W:*** Patrick Brice; ***C:*** John Guleserian; ***M:*** Julian Wass.

Overnight Delivery 🦴🦴 **1996 (PG-13)** Convinced his girlfriend (Taylor) has been cheating on him, Wyatt (Rudd) sends her a nasty breakup letter via overnight mail. But when he realizes he's been wrong, Wyatt enlists the aid of friendly stripper Ivy (Witherspoon) to help him retrieve the letter. **87m/C; VHS, DVD.** Reese Witherspoon; Paul Rudd; Christine Taylor; Larry Drake; Tobin Bell; ***D:*** Jason Bloom; ***W:*** Steven L. Bloom; ***C:*** Edward Pei; ***M:*** Andrew Gross.

The Overnighters 🦴🦴🦴 **2014** Director Moss stumbled on to a documentarian's dream in Pastor Jay Reinke and this tale of a modern Deadwood taking place in North Dakota. Due to fracking, this part of the country has become an oil-rich community, bringing men from around the United States looking for work and a place to sleep. Reinke allows them room on his church floor but then local crime rates rise. Where do charity and community concerns intersect? Reinke is a fascinating character, seemingly charitable but also hiding a major secret of his own and seemingly enjoying the power. **100m/C; DVD, Blu-Ray.** ***D:*** Jesse Moss; ***W:*** Jesse Moss; ***C:*** Jesse Moss; ***M:*** T. Griffin.

An Oversimplification of Her Beauty 🦴🦴 **1/2 2013** A comedy-drama about a couple on the verge of a romantic relationship told through both live action and animation.Terence (Nance) is an artist who is trying to understand his relationship with a young woman (Minter) whom he met on a mystery date. Their relationship is on the balance between being platonic and romantic, and the film explores the vulnerability, humor, and complex emotions in the situation. **84m/C; DVD.** Terence Nance; Namik Minter; Chanelle Pearson; Alisa Becher; Dexter Jones; ***D:*** Terence Nance; ***W:*** Terence Nance; ***C:*** Matthew Bray; Shawn Peters; ***M:*** Flying Lotus.

Overtime 🦴 **1/2 2011** Raph (Al Snow) and Max (John Wells) are hit men working for a defense attorney. Once she gets her clients off in court she assigns the guys to go kill them, and it seems to work until one of her clients has some alien zombie infestation problems. **81m/C; DVD, Blu-Ray, Streaming.** Al Snow; John Wells; Sebrina Siegel; Erica Goldsmith; James Tackett; ***D:*** Brian Cunningham; Matt Niehoff; ***W:*** Brian Cunningham; Matt Niehoff; ***C:*** Brian Cunningham; ***M:*** Jason Paige. **VIDEO**

Owd Bob 🦴🦴 **1/2 1997** Fine family drama is a loose remake of the 1938 film and adaptation of the book by Alfred Ollivant. Newly-orphaned David (Provencher) goes to live with his bitter grandfather Adam (Cromwell) on his Isle of Man sheep farm. David begins working with Adam's sheepdogs but there's a long-standing grudge with neighbor Keith Moore (Meaney) until the champion dogs of both men are accused of being sheep killers. Title refers to one of the dogs. **105m/C; DVD.** *GB* James Cromwell; Colm Meaney; Jemima Rooper; John Benfield; Anthony Booth; Dylan Provencher; Paul Moulton; ***D:*** Rodney Gibbons; ***W:*** Sharon Buckingham; ***C:*** Keith Young; ***M:*** Alan Reeves.

The Owl and the Pussycat 🦴🦴🦴 **1970 (PG)** Nerdy author gets the neighborhood hooker evicted from her apartment. She returns the favor, and the pair hit the street—and the sack—in Buck Henry's hilarious adaptation of the Broadway play. Streisand's first non-singing role. **96m/C; VHS, DVD.** Barbra Streisand; George Segal; Robert Klein; Allen Garfield; ***D:*** Herbert Ross; ***W:*** Buck Henry; ***C:*** Harry Stradling, Sr.; Andrew Laszlo; ***M:*** Dick Halligan.

The Owl and the Sparrow 🦴🦴 *Cu Va Chim Se Se* **2007 (PG)** Ten-year-old orphan Thuy, who works in a bamboo factory, runs away to Saigon where she learns how to survive on the streets. She becomes a flower seller and is befriended by Hai, a young zookeeper (and his baby elephant charge), as well as lonely air hostess Lan and the girl decides to play matchmaker. Vietnamese with subtitles. **97m/C; DVD.** *VT* Thi Han Pham; The Lu Le; Cat Ly; ***D:*** Stephane Gauger; ***W:*** Stephane Gauger; ***C:*** Stephane Gauger; ***M:*** Pete Nguyen.

The Owls 🦴 **1/2 2009** Short niche romantic/crime drama whose title is an acronym for Older, Wiser Lesbians. The four middle-aged women here may be older but they're certainly no wiser when a drug-fueled party results in a death, which is covered up. A year later, the guilt is still causing problems when a young woman appears looking for her missing friend. **65m/C; DVD.** V.S. Brodie; Guinevere Turner; Lisa Gornick; Skyler Cooper; Deak Evgenikos; Cheryl Dunye; ***D:*** Cheryl Dunye; ***W:*** Cheryl Dunye; Sarah Schulman; ***C:*** Alison Kelly; ***M:*** Ysanna Spevack.

Owning Mahowny 1/2 **2003 (R)** Dan Mahowny (Hoffman) is a vice president at a Toronto bank. He's also a compulsive gambler and in order to clear his debts, he embezzles millions of dollars. Even Dan's fiancee Belinda (Driver) can't pull him away from the casino tables when they are supposed to be on a romantic getaway. Hoffman excels as an everyday schlub who's completely absorbed in his addiction and Hurt is fascinatingly reptilian as the Atlantic City casino boss who's happy to enable Mahowny's addiction. Based on a true story; adapted from the book "Stung: The Incredible Obsession of Brian Molony" by Gary Ross. **107m/C; VHS, DVD.** *CA UK* Philip Seymour Hoffman; Minnie Driver; Maury Chaykin; John Hurt; Sonja Smits; Ian Tracey; Roger Dunn; Jason Blicker; Chris Collins; ***D:*** Richard Kwietniowski; ***W:*** Richard Kwietniowski; Maurice Chauvet; ***C:*** Oliver Curtis; ***M:*** Richard Grassby-Lewis.

The Ox 1/2 **1991** Slow-moving, simple tale, set in rural Sweden in the 1860s during a famine. Desperate to feed his family a tenant farmer kills his employer's ox. Consumed by guilt, the man is quickly found out and sentenced to life imprisonment. Pardoned after six years, the farmer returns to his family, to find out his wife has survived by doing things he finds difficult to forgive. Based on a true story. Directorial debut of Nykvist, the longtime cinematographer for Ingmar Bergman, well displays his familiarity with composition and lighting to heighten mood. In Swedish with English subtitles. **93m/C; VHS, DVD.** *SW* Stellan Skarsgard; Ewa Froling; Lennart Hjulstrom; Max von Sydow; Liv Ullmann; Bjorn Granath; Erland Josephson; ***D:*** Sven Nykvist; ***W:*** Lasse Summanen; Sven Nykvist.

The Ox-Bow Incident *Strange Incident* **1943** A popular rancher is murdered, and a mob of angry townspeople can't wait for the sheriff to find the killers. They hang the young man, despite the protests of Fonda, a cowboy with a conscience. Excellent study of mob mentality with strong individual characterizations. A brilliant western based on a true story by Walter Van Tilburg Clark. Also see "Twelve Angry Men"?less tragic but just as moving. **75m/B; VHS, DVD, Blu-Ray.** Henry Fonda; Harry (Henry) Morgan; Dana Andrews; Anthony Quinn; Frank Conroy; Harry Davenport; Jane Darwell; William Eythe; Mary Beth Hughes; ***D:*** William A. Wellman; ***W:*** Lamar Trotti; ***C:*** Arthur C. Miller; ***M:*** Cyril Mockridge. Natl. Bd. of Review '43: Director (Wellman); Natl. Film Reg. '98.

Oxford Blues **1984 (PG-13)** An American finagles his way into England's Oxford University and onto the rowing team in pursuit of the girl of his dreams. Beautiful scenery, but the plot is wafer-thin. Remake of "Yank at Oxford." **98m/C; VHS, DVD.** Rob Lowe; Ally Sheedy; Amanda Pays; Julian Sands; Michael Gough; Gail Strickland; Cary Elwes; Jeffrey S. (Jeff) Perry; ***D:*** Robert Boris; ***W:*** Robert Boris; ***C:*** John Stanier; ***M:*** John Du Prez.

The Oxford Murders 1/2 **2008 (R)** American grad student Martin (Wood) arrives at Oxford hoping that philosopher Arthur Seldom (Hurt) will be his thesis advisor. After Seldom discovers his murdered landlady, he and Martin team up, attempting to use logic to find the killer. The philosophy discussions get tedious and Wood struggles with a dull character while Hurt gets to be arrogant and hammy. **109m/C; DVD.** *GB SP* Elijah Wood; John Hurt; Leonor Watling; Julie Cox; Jim Carter; Alex Cox; Dominique Pinon; Burn Gorman; Anna Massey; ***D:*** Alex de la Iglesia; ***W:*** Alex de la Iglesia; Jorge Guerricaechevarria; ***C:*** Kiko de la Rica; ***M:*** Roque Baños.

Oxygen **1999 (R)** Madeline (Tierney) is a troubled police detective who's married to another cop (Kinney) and involved in a kinky extramarital affair. Harry (Brody) is an escape artist who fancies himself the new Houdini—he kidnaps the wife (Robbins) of wealthy Clarke Hannon (Naughton) and buries her alive. Madeline's assigned to the case and Harry takes to taunting her and their dangerous game could have more than one victim. **92m/C; VHS, DVD.** Adrien Brody; Maura Tierney; Terry Kinney; James Naughton; Laila Robins; Dylan Baker; ***D:*** Richard Shepard; ***W:*** Richard Shepard; ***C:*** Sarah Cawley; ***M:*** Rolfe Kent.

Oy Vey! My Son is Gay! 1/2 **2009 (PG-13)** Exuberantly clichéd family comedy. The Long Island Hirsch family are shocked when only son Nelson reveals he's gay and that his partner, Angelo, isn't even Jewish. Nelson's parents, Shirley and Martin, decide to get to know Angelo's Italian family and his parents, Carmine and Teresa, so they can all bond. But what really brings the families together is when the two men come under attack for adopting a baby and you know where family loyalty lies. **90m/C; DVD.** Lainie Kazan; Saul Rubinek; John Lloyd Young; Jai Rodriguez; Vincent Pastore; Shelly Birch; Bruce Vilanch; Carmen Electra; ***D:*** Evgeny Afineevsky; ***W:*** Evgeny Afineevsky; ***C:*** Peter N. Green; ***M:*** Eddie Grimberg; Lilo Fedida. **VIDEO**

Oz the Great and Powerful 1/2 **2013 (PG)** Director Raimi's prequel to "The Wizard of Oz" is visually striking but is deflated by a pretty boring, uninspired script. Oscar Diggs (Franco) is just an average circus magician when he's whisked from Kansas to the Land of Oz. He meets three witches (Kunis, Weisz, and Williams) and his path to the inevitable Wizard of Emerald City becomes pretty clear. Franco is dull and most of the supporting cast is uninspired. The visual magic may be there but none of the storytelling power that has made Frank L. Baum's fantasies so timeless. **130m/C; DVD, Blu-Ray.** James Franco; Michelle Williams; Mila Kunis; Rachel Weisz; Zach Braff; Bill Cobbs; Tony Cox; ***Cameo(s):*** Bruce Campbell; ***V:*** Zach Braff; Joey King; ***D:*** Sam Raimi; ***W:*** David Lindsay-Abaire; Mitchell Kapner; ***C:*** Peter Deming; ***M:*** Danny Elfman.

P2 **2007 (R)** Late on Christmas Eve, Angela (Nichols) decends to level PS of her office's parking garage, only to find that her car won't start and the parking lot attendant Thomas (Bentley) is a homicidal maniac obsessed with her. After she initially escapes, she again finds herself trapped, with Thomas menacingly creeping her out. Standard gory "woman in danger" thriller fare with the occasional imaginative twist. **98m/C; DVD.** Wes Bentley; Rachel Nichols; ***D:*** Franck Khalfoun; ***W:*** Franck Khalfoun; Alexandre Aja; Gregory Levasseur; ***C:*** Maxime Alexandre; ***M:*** tomandandy.

Pace That Kills **1928** An anti-drug cautionary drama from the Roaring '20s, one of many now marketed on cassette as campy fun. Beware, though, a little bit of this stuff goes a long way. A young man goes to the big city to find his missing sister and winds up hooked on heroin. **87m/B; Silent; VHS, DVD.** Owen Gorin; Virginia Roye; Florence Turner; ***D:*** William A. O'Connor; Norton S. Parker; ***W:*** Ruth Todd; ***C:*** Ernest Laszlo.

The Pacific 1/2 **2010** An equally meticulous follow-up to 2001's "Band of Brothers" that shifts the WWII action to the Pacific islands shortly after Pearl Harbor. The narrative focuses on the combat experiences of three Marines: Robert Leckie (Dale) at Guadalcanal, Eugene Sledge (Mazzello) at Peleliu and Okinawa, and John Basilone (Seda), whose heroism at Guadalcanal earns him the Medal of Honor; he later voluntarily returns to fight at Iwo Jima. The miniseries gets stronger once the exposition of the early episodes is out of the way though the narrative jumps somewhat confusingly between the characters. However, the action is every bit as bewildering, brutal, and relentless as you might expect. **400m/C; DVD, Blu-Ray.** James Badge Dale; Joseph Mazzello; Jon Seda; Ashton Holmes; Rami Malek; William Sadler; Jacob Pitts; Martin McCann; Keith Nobbs; Annie Parisse; Josh Helman; ***D:*** Timothy Van Patten; David Nutter; Jeremy Podeswa; Carl Franklin; Tony To; Graham Yost; ***W:*** Graham Yost; Bruce McKenna; Robert Schenkkan; George Pelecanos; Michelle Ashford; Laurence Andries; ***C:*** Remi Adefarasin; Stephen F. Windon; ***M:*** Hans Zimmer; Blake Neely; Geoff Zanieli. **CABLE**

The Pacific and Eddy 1/2 **2007** Eddy (Donowho) skips out of his seaside hometown after the death of a friend for which he feels responsible. After living life as a struggling musician, he decides to return and tries to reconnect with the people he left behind, but they aren't that interested in making nice. **87m/C; DVD.** Ryan Donowho; Dominique Swain; James Duval; Baelyn Neff; Mark Gregg; Nikki Sudden; ***D:*** Matthew Nourse; ***W:*** Matthew Nourse; ***C:*** Aaron Platt; ***M:*** Kelli Scarr.

Pacific Heights **1990 (R)** Young San Francisco couple takes on mammoth mortgage assuming tenants will write their ticket to the American dream, but psychopathic tenant Keaton moves in downstairs and redecorates. He won't pay the rent and he won't leave. Creepy psycho-thriller has lapses but builds to effective climax. It's a treat to watch mother/daughter actresses Hedren and Griffith work together. Watch for D'Angelo as Keaton's lover. **103m/C; VHS, DVD, Blu-Ray.** Melanie Griffith; Matthew Modine; Michael Keaton; Mako; Nobu McCarthy; Laurie Metcalf; Carl Lumbly; Dorian Harewood; Luca Bercovici; Tippi Hedren; Beverly D'Angelo; Dan Hedaya; ***D:*** John Schlesinger; ***W:*** Daniel Pyne; ***C:*** Amir M. Mokri; ***M:*** Hans Zimmer.

Pacific Inferno **1985** During WWII, American POWs endeavor to break out of a Japanese prison camp in the Philippines. Their goal is to prevent their captors from retrieving millions of dollars worth of sunken U.S. gold. **90m/C; VHS, DVD.** Jim Brown; Richard Jaeckel; Timothy Brown; ***D:*** Rolf Bayer. **CABLE**

Pacific Rim 1/2 **2013 (PG-13)** Giant monsters called the Kaiju are coming up through a dimensional rift in the Pacific Ocean and deliberately homing in on human cities. Incredibly toxic, they're unstoppable by conventional military so humankind builds giant robots known as Jaegers to stop them. These work for a while, but a desperate world sees the end in sight. A visual treat and great fun for fans of giant robots and monsters fighting one another, but it doesn't offer much else and the human pilots inside the robots are characterless. An unapologetic homage to the Japanese Kaiju genre, featuring shout-outs to Godzilla, Gamera, Go Nagai, and others. **131m/C; DVD, Blu-Ray.** Charlie Hunnam; Idris Elba; Rinko Kikuchi; Charlie Day; Ron Perlman; Clifton (Gonzalez) Collins, Jr.; ***D:*** Guillermo del Toro; ***W:*** Guillermo del Toro; Travis Beacham; ***C:*** Guillermo Navarro; ***M:*** Ramin Djawadi.

Pacific Rim: Uprising 1/2 **2018 (PG-13)** Jake Pentecost (Boyega) follows in the footsteps of his father, Stacker, in "piloting" the Jaeger robots to fight the monstrous Kaiju, who've paid a return visit to Earth to cause more mayhem and destruction. The action is predictably large and loud, but with none of the emotional stakes of the original flick, it's easily forgettable. **111m/C; DVD, Blu-Ray.** John Boyega; Scott Eastwood; Cailee Spaeny; Burn Gorman; Charlie Day; ***D:*** Steven S. DeKnight; ***W:*** Steven S. DeKnight; Emily Carmichael; Kira Snyder; T.S. Nowlin; ***C:*** Dan(iel) Mindel; ***M:*** Lorne Balfe.

The Pacifier 1/2 **2005 (PG)** Shane Wolfe (Diesel) is a Navy SEAL who fails to prevent the death of a scientist at the hands of terrorists and is then assigned to protect the scientist's five kids and find some top-secret disk hidden in their home. Mom (Ford) is conveniently absent for much of the time. He retrofits his gadgets to hold baby formula and other child-friendly necessities and tries to promote military discipline on the bratty, unwilling clan. There's also a pet duck who doesn't like the new babysitter. It's all obvious and silly. **95m/C; VHS, DVD.** Vin Diesel; Lauren Graham; Faith Ford; Brittany Snow; Max Thieriot; Chris Potter; Morgan York; Scott Thompson; Carol Kane; Brad Garrett; Tate Donovan; Denis Akiyama; Mung-Ling Tsui; ***D:*** Adam Shankman; ***W:*** Robert Ben Garant; ***C:*** Peter James; ***M:*** John Debney.

The Pack 1/2 *The Long, Dark Night* **1977 (R)** A group of dogs become wild when left on a resort island. A marine biologist leads the humans who fight to keep the dogs from using vacationers as chew toys. Fine production valves keep it from going to the dogs. Made with the approval of the American Humane Society who helped with the treatment of stage hands. **99m/C; VHS, DVD.** Joe Don Baker; Hope Alexander-Willis; R.G. Armstrong; Richard B. Shull; ***D:*** Robert Clouse; ***W:*** Robert Clouse.

Pack of Lies 1/2 **1987** In the early 1960s, MI5 agents manipulate a British family, quietly living in the suburbs, into allowing them to use their home for a surveillance mission. Only it turns out they're watching the Jackson's neighbors and best friends, who are actually Soviet spies. Based on a true story. **100m/C; DVD.** Ellen Burstyn; Teri Garr; Alan Bates; Ronald Hines; Daniel Benzali; Sammi Davis; Clive Swift; ***D:*** Anthony Page; ***W:*** Hugh Whitemore; ***C:*** Kenneth Macmillan; ***M:*** Stanley Myers. **TV**

Pack Up Your Troubles 1/2 *We're in the Army Now* **1932** Laurel and Hardy make good on a promise to help find the grandfather of a girl whose father was killed in WWI. All they know is the grandfather's last name though—Smith. Wholesome R and R. **68m/B; VHS, DVD.** Stan Laurel; Oliver Hardy; James Finlayson; Jacquie Lyn; ***D:*** George Marshall; ***W:*** H.M. Walker; ***C:*** Art Lloyd.

The Package 1/2 **1989 (R)** An espionage thriller about an army sergeant who loses the prisoner he escorts into the U.S. When he tries to track him down, he uncovers a military plot to start WWIII. Hackman is believable in his role as the sergeant. **108m/C; VHS, DVD, Blu-Ray.** Gene Hackman; Tommy Lee Jones; Joanna Cassidy; Dennis Franz; Pam Grier; John Heard; Reni Santoni; Thalmus Rasulala; Ike Pappas; Kevin Crowley; Wilhelm von Homburg; ***D:*** Andrew Davis; ***W:*** John Bishop; ***M:*** James Newton Howard.

The Package **2012 (R)** Predictable but fun B-actioner filled with mayhem. Tommy Wick is the enforcer for Seattle mobster/loan shark Big Doug. Doug tells Tommy to deliver a package to a crime boss, called The German, in British Columbia, but Tommy's soon dogged by heavily-armed killers who want the package for themselves. **95m/C; DVD, Blu-Ray.** Steve Austin; Dolph Lundgren; Eric Keenleyside; Mike Dopud; Lochlyn Munro; ***D:*** Jesse Johnson; ***W:*** Derek Kolstad; ***C:*** C. Kim Miles; ***M:*** Sean Murray. **VIDEO**

A Packing Suburbia 1/2 **1999 (R)** An ultra-low budget film of teen angst (it was filmed for 60 grand), this one nevertheless managed to win awards at a few Indie movie festivals. James (Brandise) has to move to a rougher high school than he's used to when his family falls on hard times. He tries to fit in, but when the girl he likes is gang-raped and murdered as a gang initiation he learns how to use a gun on the Internet and goes off for bloody vengeance. Not exactly a subtle film. **90m/C; DVD.** Thomas Brandise; Mariana Carreno; ***D:*** Stephen Szklarski; ***W:*** Stephen Szklarski; ***C:*** Robbie Anderson.

Paco 1/2 **1975 (G)** A young, South American boy heads for the city, where he meets his uncle. He discovers his uncle is the leader of a gang of youthful thieves. Predictable and sluggish. **89m/C; VHS, DVD.** Jose Ferrer; Panchito Gomez; Allen Garfield; Pernell Roberts; Andre Marquis; ***D:*** Robert Vincent O'Neil; ***W:*** Robert Vincent O'Neil; ***C:*** Andrew Davis; ***M:*** Mariano Moreno.

The Pact *The Secret Pact* **1999 (R)** When teenager Greg (Frost) witnesses his parents' murder by the mob, he's sent to a private school in Montreal as part of the witness protection program. He makes a new best friend with a fellow student (Strong) but discovers his fellow teen is actually a hit man sent to kill him. Only they come to a strange sort of deal instead. **94m/C; VHS, DVD.** *CA* Rider Strong; Adam Frost; John Heard; Nick Mancuso; Jack Langedijk; Lisa Zane; ***D:*** Rodney Gibbons; ***W:*** William Lee; Brian Cameron Fuld; ***C:*** Bert Tougas; ***M:*** Antonio Battista. **VIDEO**

The Pact 1/2 **2012 (R)** Two sisters return to their family home to attend their mother's funeral but people begin disappearing and accusations of a ghost haunting begin. **89m/C; DVD, Blu-Ray, Streaming.** Caity Lotz; Kathleen Rose Perkins; Haley Hudson; Sam Ball; Mark Steger; ***D:*** Nicholas Mccarthy; ***W:*** Nicholas Mccarthy; ***C:*** Bridger Nielson; ***M:*** Ronen Landa. **VIDEO**

Paddington **2014 (PG)** This surprisingly delightful adaptation of Michael Bond's hit family books features most of the best traits of British family films—dry wit, whimsical humor, and a genuine sense of heart. Ben Whishaw voices the titular Marmalade-loving bear (filmed in CGI), who is actually found deep in the jungles of Peru before joining the Brown family in London, where he gets into a series of slapsticky but sweet adventures. A lot of warm fuzzies that don't feel forced like so many family films with just enough physical humor for the kids and clever wordplay for their parents. The Hound dares you NOT to like it! **95m/C; DVD, Blu-Ray.** *UK* Hugh Bonneville; Sally Hawkins; Madeleine Harris; Samuel Joslin; Nicole Kidman; Peter Capaldi; Julie Walters; ***V:*** Ben Whishaw; ***D:*** Paul King; ***W:*** Paul King; ***C:*** Erik Wilson; ***M:*** Nick Urata.

Paddington 2 🦴🦴🦴 **2017 (PG)** In a sequel just as delightful as the original, the marmalade-loving Paddington, now a happy member of the Brown family, takes odd jobs to earn enough money to buy his Aunt Lucy an expensive birthday present. But when that rare book gets stolen before he can get his paws on it, Paddington himself gets branded the thief. A main character who exhibits manners and kindness may sound like an unbear-able drip, but Paddington's cheer, charm, and humor make him a furry friend for all ages. **104m/C; DVD, Blu-Ray.** Hugh Grant; Brendan Gleeson; Hugh Bonneville; Sally Hawkins; ***V:*** Ben Whishaw; ***D:*** Paul King; ***W:*** Paul King; Simon Farnaby; ***C:*** Erik Alexander Wilson; ***M:*** Dario Marianelli.

Paddleton 🦴🦴 **1/2 2019** When Mike (Duplass) learns that he has cancer and his health starts to fail, he spends much time with his best friend Andy (Romano). The pair remembers old times and argues about favorite movies. Though laid back Mike often has to soothe the more anxious, often annoying Andy, Andy believes that Mike should fight his illness instead choosing to end his life before his cancer does. However, when Mike is ready to die, they take one last roadtrip to pick up his right-to-die drugs. This buddy comedy-drama is a moving exploration of close male friendships and features stellar performances by the leads. **89m/C; DVD.** Mark Duplass; Ray Romano; Christine Woods; Jen Sung; Stephen Oyoung; ***D:*** Alexandre Lehmann; ***W:*** Mark Duplass; Alexandre Lehmann; ***C:*** Nathan M. Miller; ***M:*** Julian Wass. **VIDEO**

Paddy O'Day 🦴🦴 **1/2 1935** Spunky young Irish immigrant Paddy O'Day (Withers) travels to New York to reunite with her mother only to learn that she's died. Paddy makes her way to the mansion of the Ford family (where her mother worked), the servants hide the kid to foil the immigration officials. Young Roy Ford (Tomlin) is charmed by Paddy and falls in love with Paddy's shipboard friend, dancer Tamara (Hayworth, then still Rita Casino). Things eventually work out for everyone in true '30s fashion. **73m/B; DVD.** Jane Withers; Rita Hayworth; Pinky Tomlin; Jane Darwell; Vera Lewis; Louise Carter; ***D:*** Lewis Seiler; ***W:*** Lou Breslow; Edward Eliscu; ***C:*** Arthur C. Miller.

Padmaavat 🦴🦴🦴 **2018** A disturbing, though visually impressive, drama based on an epic poem from thirteenth century India. After accidentally hitting king Ratan Singh (Kapoor) with her arrow while hunting, the extraordinarily beautiful Rajput (Padukone) marries him and returns to his kingdom. Though Rajput faces jealousy when she displaces Singh's first wife, she faces a far greater danger when sultan Allaudin (Singh) hears of her beauty and decides to conquer her kingdom to possess her. The film sparked controversy in India, and its extreme violence overwhelms its appealing qualities. Hindi with subtitles. **164m/C; DVD.** Deepika Padukone; Ranveer Singh; Shahid Kapoor; Aditi Rao Hydari; Jim Sarbh; ***D:*** Sanjay Leela Bhansali; ***W:*** Sanjay Leela Bhansali; Prakash Kapadia; ***C:*** Sudeep Chatterjee; ***M:*** Sanjay Leela Bhansali; Sanchit Balhara.

The Padre 🦴🦴 **2018 (R)** The Padre (Roth) is a British con man wearing priest garb and on the run in Mexico. He is trying to elude Nemes (Nolte), an American determined to get vengeance on the Padre. The situation is further complicated by Lena (Henriquez), a Mexican in her late teens who is determined to get to the United States any way that she can. Lena becomes entangled in the situation when she joins the Padre as he steals a car to escape the angry American. While Henriquez has appeal, Roth and Nolte play character types they have played before. **98m/C; DVD.** Tim Roth; Valeria Henriquez; Nick Nolte; Luis Guzman; Benjamin Petersen; ***D:*** Jonathan Sobol; ***W:*** Stephen Kunc; ***C:*** Paul Sarossy.

Padre Padrone 🦴🦴🦴 **1/2** *Father Master; My Father, My Master* **1977** The much acclaimed adaptation of the Gavino Ledda autobiography about his youth in agrarian Sardinia with a brutal, tyrannical father. Eventually he overcomes his handicaps, breaks the destructive emotional ties to his father and successfully attends college. Highly regarded although low budget; in an Italian dialect (Sardinian) with English subtitles. **113m/C; VHS, DVD.** *IT* Omero Antonutti; Saverio Marconi; Marcella Michelangeli; Fabrizio Forte; ***D:*** Paolo Taviani; Vittorio Taviani; ***W:*** Paolo Taviani; Vittorio Taviani; ***C:*** Mario Masini; ***M:*** Egisto Macchi. Cannes '77: Film.

The Pagan 🦴🦴 **1929** In his South Seas paradise, wealthy half-caste Henry (Novarro) has no cares until the lecherous white guardian (Crisp) of Tilo (Janis), the native girl Henry loves, decides it's his Christian duty to marry her. Director Van Dyke filmed on location in Tahiti and the silent was released with synchronized musical sequences. Novarro can be heard crooning snippets of 'Pagan Love Song.' **78m/B; Silent; DVD.** Ramon Novarro; Dorothy Janis; Donald Crisp; Renee Adoree; ***D:*** W.S. Van Dyke; ***W:*** Dorothy Farnum; ***C:*** Clyde De Vinna.

Pagan Island 🦴 **1960** A man is stranded on a desert island with 30 beautiful girls who tie him up and abandon him. Maki, to be sacrificed by the rest, saves Dew and they fall in love. They go off in search of a reputed treasure, which they find, but at a deadly cost. **67m/B; VHS, DVD.** Eddie Dew; Nani Maka; Yanka (Doris Keating) Mann; ***D:*** Barry Mahon; ***W:*** Clelle Mahon; ***C:*** Mark Dennis.

Pagan Love Song 🦴🦴 **1950** A dull musical which finds Keel in Tahiti taking over his uncle's coconut plantation and falling in love with Williams. Surprise! Williams performs one of her famous water ballets, which is the only saving grace in this lifeless movie. **76m/C; DVD.** Esther Williams; Howard Keel; Minna Gombell; Rita Moreno; ***D:*** Robert Alton; ***W:*** Jerry Davis; Robert Nathan; ***C:*** Charles Rosher.

The Pagan Queen 🦴 **2009** Based vaguely on the Slavic myths about the founding of Prague, a witch is forced into marriage by her people after they decide to turn from peaceful Pagans into brutal modernistic sociopaths obsessed with land and money. **99m/C; DVD.** *CZ US* Winter Ave Zoli; Csaba Lucas; Lea Mornar; Vera Filatova; Veronika Bellova; ***D:*** Constantin Werner; ***W:*** Constantin Werner; Lance Daly; ***C:*** Bobby Bukowski; ***M:*** Benedikt Brydem.

Page Eight 🦴🦴 **1/2** *Worricker: Page Eight* **2011** British political thriller with long-time, world-weary MI5 spooks Johnny Worricker (Nighy) and Benedict Baron (Gambon) knowing they're dealing with info obtained illegally from the Americans that the Prime Minister (Fiennes) wants kept quiet. Benedict dies and Johnny thinks the circumstances are suspicious. So he decides that a controversial report should be published and, as it happens, Johnny's lovely neighbor Nancy (Weisz) is an activist/publisher willing to help him out. A little too contrived but the performances make up for that. **105m/C; DVD, Blu-Ray.** *GB* Bill Nighy; Michael Gambon; Rachel Weisz; Ralph Fiennes; Judy Davis; Saskia Reeves; Alice Krige; Felicity Jones; Ewen Bremner; Holly Aird; ***D:*** David Hare; ***W:*** David Hare; ***C:*** Martin Ruhe; ***M:*** Paul Englishby. **TV**

The Page Turner 🦴🦴 *La Tourneuse de Pages* **2006** As a child, aspiring pianist Melanie has her dreams carelessly ruined by concert pianist Ariane (Frot). She nurses a grudge and when Melanie (Francois) grows up, she puts her plan for revenge into action by insinuating herself into Ariane's family life. Okay thriller, but nothing that hasn't been seen before. French with subtitles. **85m/C; DVD.** *FR* Deborah Francois; Catherine Frot; Pascal Greggory; Clothilde Mollet; ***D:*** Denis Dercourt; ***W:*** Denis Dercourt; Jacques Sotty; ***C:*** Jerome Peyrebrune; ***M:*** Jacques Lemonnier.

The Pagemaster 🦴 **1/2 1994 (G)** Timid Richard (Macauley) is basically scared of his own shadow but, during a storm, he's forced to take refuge in a mysterious library with an even odder librarian, Mr. Dewey (Lloyd). Richard's intrigued by the library's mural, which turns out to be the doorway to an animated universe where the wizardlike Pagemaster (voiced by Lloyd) and other literary characters help Richard discover his strengths and overcome his fears. Mildly amusing but kids may not know who the characters refer to unless they're readers (a good intro, perhaps?) **76m/C; VHS, DVD, Blu-Ray.** Macaulay Culkin; Christopher Lloyd; Ed Begley, Jr.; Mel Harris; ***V:*** Christopher Lloyd; Whoopi Goldberg; Patrick Stewart; Frank Welker; Leonard Nimoy; ***D:*** Joe Johnston; Maurice Hunt; ***W:*** David Casci; David Kirschner; Ernie Contreras; ***M:*** James Horner.

Paid 🦴🦴 **1/2 1930** Remake of the 1923 silent "Within the Law." Mary Turner (Crawford) vows revenge on the men who sent her to the slammer after a false conviction for theft. Thanks to friend Agnes' (Prevost) connections, she meets racketeer Joe Garson (Armstrong) but Mary sticks to her own plans, which include marrying Bob (Montgomery), the son of department store owner Edward Gilder (Pratt), one of the men who sent her to prison. **83m/B; DVD.** Joan Crawford; Robert Armstrong; Marie Prevost; Douglass Montgomery; Purnell Pratt; John Miljan; Hale Hamilton; Polly Moran; ***D:*** Sam Wood; ***W:*** Charles MacArthur; Lucien Hubbard; ***C:*** Charles Rosher.

Paid 🦴🦴 **2006** French hooker Paula Gireaux is working in Amsterdam where she gets involved with young hitman Michel. Both of them would like to start new lives together but Paula made a deal with drug lord Rudi Dancer. Now Rudi's rivalry with fellow drug baron William Montague threatens Paula and Michel's futures. **91m/C; DVD.** Annie Charrier; Murilo Benicio; Tom Conti; Corbin Bernsen; Guy Marchand; Marie-France Pisier; Beppe Chierici; ***D:*** Laurence Lamers; ***W:*** Laurence Lamers; ***C:*** Tom Erisman; ***M:*** Jaques Morelembaum. **VIDEO**

Paid in Full 🦴🦴 **1/2 2002 (R)** Based on the true story of the rise and fall of three Harlem drug dealers in the mid '80s during the height of the crack cocaine trade and the beginnings of "Gangsta" culture. Ace (Harris), Mitch (Phifer), and Rico (Cam'ron) deal with the issues of staying friends while also becoming rivals. Highlights the unsavory side of a business that makes former good kid Ace a fortune, but steals his soul. Acting all around is admirable and story is well told but revisits too-familiar territory about the price of greed and the politics of poverty. **93m/C; VHS, DVD, Blu-Ray.** Wood Harris; Mekhi Phifer; Kevin Carroll; Esai Morales; Chi McBride; Cynthia Martells; Elise Neal; Cam'ron; Regina Hall; Remo Greene; Anthony Clark; ***D:*** Charles Stone, III; ***W:*** Azie Faison, Jr.; Austin Phillips; Matthew Cirulnick; Thulani Davis; ***C:*** Paul Sarossy; ***M:*** Vernon Reid; Frank Fitzpatrick.

Paid to Kill 🦴🦴 *Five Days* **1954** A failing businessman hires a thug to kill him in order to leave his family insurance money, but when the business picks up, he can't contact the thug to cancel the contract. The actors' lack of talent is matched only by the characters' lack of motivation. **71m/B; VHS, DVD.** *GB* Dane Clark; Paul Carpenter; Thea Gregory; Howard Marion-Crawford; Peter Gawthorne; ***D:*** Montgomery Tully; ***W:*** Paul Tabori; ***C:*** Walter J. (Jimmy W.) Harvey.

Pain & Gain 🦴 **1/2 2013 (R)** Director Bay proves that he doesn't know how to handle satire in this broad comedy version of a story so ridiculous it has to be true. Daniel Lugo (Wahlberg) works hard to get his body into perfect shape as a personal trainer but the true American dream of fancy cars, beautiful women, and McMansions eludes him. With the help of fellow bodybuilders Paul Doyle (Johnson) and Adrian Doorbal (Mackie), Lugo decides to take it any way he can. An emphasis on juvenile, homophobic, gross-out humor along with a bloated running time damages what the truly charismatic cast brings to the project. **129m/C; DVD, Blu-Ray.** Mark Wahlberg; Dwayne "The Rock" Johnson; Anthony Mackie; Tony Shalhoub; Ed Harris; Rob Corddry; Rebel Wilson; Ken Jeong; ***D:*** Michael Bay; ***W:*** Christopher Markus; Stephen McFeely; ***C:*** Ben Seresin; ***M:*** Steve Jablonsky.

Pain and Glory 🦴🦴🦴 *Dolor y gloria* **2019 (R)** Famous Spanish director Salvador Mallo (Banderas) reunites with Alberto Crespo (Etxeandia) an actor he worked with decades earlier but lost touch with because of bad blood related to Alberto's performance in a film and heroin use. When they reunite for a panel discussion, Salvador uses heroin to address his chronic pain. As Salvador deals with his pain, drug use, and worsening health, he has flashbacks to his childhood, especially his mother (Cruz), people he has met during his life, his mortality, and the creation of his art. Almodovar's highly personal, semi-autobiographical drama is a moving and impressive story, as well as a career-defining performance by Banderas. **112m/C; DVD, Blu-Ray.** Antonio Banderas; Asier Etxeandia; Penelope Cruz; Leonardo Sbaraglia; Julieta Serrano; ***D:*** Pedro Almodóvar; ***W:*** Pedro Almodóvar; ***C:*** José Luis Alcaine; ***M:*** Alberto Iglesias.

Painkillers 🦴🦴 **2015** A science fiction exploration of memory and truth. When a squad of marines is sent to war-torn Afghanistan on a mission to find an object, they discover it is not what thought it was going to be. Before they can react, the surviving squad members find themselves waking up in a military medical facility. All have lost their memories, not only of what happened but even of who they are. When the doctors try to use an experimental drug to help them recover their memories, the soldiers experience hallucinations and fits of rage. When squad member Major Cafferty (Penikett) starts to remember, he has doubts about the medical staff and what they really found. **102m/C; DVD, Streaming, Download.** Tahmoh Penikett; Lesley-Ann Brandt; Colm Feore; Erica Durance; Julia Voth; ***D:*** Peter Winther; ***W:*** Peter Winther; Jason Groce; Kirk Roos; ***C:*** Kamal Derkaoui; ***M:*** Alec Harrison.

Paint and Powder 🦴🦴 **1925** Risque silent. Jimmy winds up with the stolen wallet of Broadway producer Mark Kelsey and uses the money to help his struggling dancer/singer girlfriend Mary get her shot in a show. She becomes an overnight star while Jimmy's in jail for theft. Jimmy gets out and he wants to start over with Mary but there's more heartbreak ahead. **70m/B; Silent; DVD.** Elaine Hammerstein; Theodore von Eltz; John St. Polis; Stuart Holmes; ***D:*** Hunt Stromberg; ***W:*** Harvey Gates; ***C:*** Sol Polito.

Paint Your Wagon 🦴🦴 **1/2 1969 (PG)** Big-budget western musical-comedy about a gold mining boom town, and two prospectors sharing the same Mormon wife complete with a classic Lerner and Lowe score. Marvin chews up the sagebrush and Eastwood attempts to sing, although Seberg was mercifully dubbed. Overlong, with patches of interest, pretty songs, and plenty of panoramic scenery. Adapted from the L & L play. **164m/C; VHS, DVD.** Lee Marvin; Clint Eastwood; Jean Seberg; Harve Presnell; ***D:*** Joshua Logan; ***W:*** Paddy Chayefsky; ***M:*** Frederick Loewe; Andre Previn; ***M:*** Alan Jay Lerner.

The Painted Desert 🦴🦴 **1931** Gable's first film role of any consequence came in this early sound western. Gable plays a villain opposite "good guy" William Boyd. **80m/B; VHS, DVD.** William Boyd; Helen Twelvetrees; George O'Brien; Clark Gable; William Farnum; ***D:*** Howard Higgin; ***W:*** Howard Higgin; ***C:*** Edward Snyder.

Painted Faces 🦴 **1/2 1929** Circus clown Hermann (Brown in an early talkie and a non-comedic role) is the lone jury holdout for a guilty verdict after a performer is murdered and another is put on trial for the crime. **74m/B; DVD.** Joe E. Brown; Helen Foster; Barton Hepburn; Dorothy Gulliver; Lester Cole; William B. Davidson; Richard Tucker; Purnell Pratt; ***D:*** Albert Rogell; ***W:*** Frederic Hatton; Fanny Hatton; ***C:*** Jackson Rose.

Painted Hero 🦴🦴 **1/2 1995 (R)** Rodeo clown Virgil Kidder (Yoakum) has to watch out for more than rampaging bulls when he returns to Waco, where he's accused of murder and reunites with the mother of his now-dead son. **105m/C; VHS, DVD.** Dwight Yoakam; Bo Hopkins; Cindy Pickett; Michelle Joyner; ***D:*** Terry Benedict; ***W:*** Terry Benedict; ***C:*** David Bridges; ***M:*** Rick Marotta.

The Painted Hills 🦴🦴 **1/2 1951 (G)** Lassie outsmarts crooked miners and rescues her friends. Surprise, Surprise! Overly sentimental, but action packed and beautifully shot. Lassie's last outing with MGM. **70m/C; VHS, DVD.** Paul Kelly; Bruce Cowling;

Gary Gray; Art Smith; Ann Doran; *D:* Harold F. Kress; *W:* True Boardman; *C:* Alfred Gilks; *M:* Daniele Amfitheatrof.

A Painted House 2003 Loose adaptation of the John Grisham novel finds 10-year-old Luke Chandler (Lerman) living on a struggling Arkansas farm in 1952 with his parents and grandparents. The family needs to hire local "hill" people and Mexican migrant workers to pick their cotton crop and there's trouble between the groups as well as with Luke and his family. Title refers to the fact that the Chandler's bare clapboard farmhouse gets mysteriously painted (they can't afford to do it themselves). **110m/C; DVD.** Scott Glenn; Melinda Dillon; Robert Sean Leonard; Logan Lerman; Geoffrey Lewis; Arija Bareikis; Pablo Schreiber; Luis Esteban Garcia; Luke Eberl; Diane Delano; Audrey Marie Anderson; *D:* Alfonso Arau; *W:* Patrick Sheane Duncan; *C:* Xavier Perez Grobet; *M:* Ruy Folguera. **TV**

The Painted Lady 1997 Maggie Sheridan (Mirren) is a hard-living ex-blues singer with some destructive habits. After bottoming out some years before, she was taken in by Sir Charles Stafford (Cuthbertson), the father of childhood friend Sebastian (Glen). Sir Charles is murdered during a botched robbery, a 16th-century painting stolen, and Sebastian becomes the victim of a brutal attack, so Maggie decides to get involved. And finds herself deeply enmeshed in the illegal art trade, posing as a collector, and romancing a very dangerous man (Nero). **204m/C; VHS, DVD.** *GB* Dame Helen Mirren; Franco Nero; Iain Glen; Michael Maloney; Lesley Manville; Roland Gift; Iain Cuthbertson; Michael Liebman; Indro Montanelli; *D:* Julian Jarrold. **TV**

Painted Skin *Hua Pi Zhi Yinyang Fawang* **1993** Historical supernatural tale concerns a ghost (Joey Wang) who's trapped on Earth and must paint her skin to pass among humans. The evil Demon King is responsible. Sammo Hung co-stars as a monk. **93m/C; DVD.** *CH* Adam Cheng; Joey Wang; Sammo Hung; *D:* King Hu; *W:* King Hu; Chang A. Cheng; *C:* Stephen Yip; *M:* Ng Tai Kong.

Painted Skin: The Resurrection ½ *Hua pi 2; Painted Skin 2* **2012** An ancient fox spirit becomes bound to a disfigured princess on her quest to become human in this lavish supernatural epic of modern Chinese fantasy. **132m/C; DVD, Blu-Ray, Streaming.** *CH* Xun Zhou; Kun Chen; Wei Zhao; Mi Yang; Shaofeng Feng; Fei Xiang; Tingjia Chen; *D:* Wuershan; *W:* Ping Ran; Jia'nan Ran; *C:* Yue-Tai Huang; *M:* Shi-Tian Shin-Fang. **VIDEO**

The Painted Veil ½ **1934** Adaptation of a W. Somerset Maugham novel. Garbo, once again the disillusioned wife turning to the affections of another man, is magnificent, almost eclipsing the weak script. Lost money at the box office, but for Garbo fans, an absolute must. **83m/B; DVD.** Greta Garbo; Herbert Marshall; George Brent; Warner Oland; Jean Hersholt; *D:* Richard Boleslawski; *W:* John Meehan; Salka Viertel; Edith Fitzgerald; *C:* William H. Daniels; *M:* Herbert Stothart.

The Painted Veil **2006 (PG-13)** The third version of Maugham's 1925 novel takes some liberties and the leads can't engender much sympathy for their self-absorbed characters, although the locations are eye-catching. Flirty Kitty (Watts) impulsively marries serious bacteriologist Walter Fane (Norton) and travels with him to Shanghai. When Walter discovers bored Kitty's affair with British consul Charlie Townsend (Schreiber), he forces her to join him in a remote area beset by a cholera outbreak. Kitty helps out a group of nuns at their orphanage amidst the rise of Chinese nationalism (as if an epidemic and problematic marriage aren't trouble enough). **125m/C; DVD.** *CH US* Naomi Watts; Edward Norton; Liev Schreiber; Toby Jones; Diana Rigg; Anthony Wong; *D:* John Curran; *W:* Ron Nyswaner; *C:* Stuart Dryburgh; *M:* Alexandre Desplat. Golden Globes '07: Orig. Score.

The Painting *Le Tableau* **2011** Animated feature focusing on three groups inhabiting a painting. Its expressionistic style gives it freedom to explore social issues in a loose and surprisingly coherent manner. The Allduns are fully detailed, vibrant, and at the top of this bizarre social ladder; the Halfies are incomplete and not allowed in the Allduns castle; while the Sketchies exist only as outlines, often hunted down by the Allduns. Yearning for answers one member of each group join up to seek out their creator to ask why they have been painted in this way. A fascinating experiment in morals that often gets too bogged down in over-simplified metaphors. French with subtitles. **76m/C; DVD, Blu-Ray.** *FR V:* Adrien Larmande; Chloe Berthier; Thierry Jahn; Jessica Monceau; *D:* Jean-Francois Laguionie; *W:* Jean-Francois Laguionie; Anik Le Ray; *M:* Pascal Le Pennec.

Painting the Clouds With Sunshine **1951** Average MGM musical comedy has Abby (Norman) dumping her gambler boyfriend Vince (Morgan) to join friends Carol (Mayo) and June (Gibson) in Vegas in a search for rich husbands. The girls get a job as a singing trio and Abby is pursued by dancer Ted Lansing (Nelson)?only he's really a millionaire in disguise. Then Ted's banker cousin Bennington (Conway) shows up and Ted tries to keep him quiet until he can get Abby to the altar but Vince isn't ready to give up his claim to her heart. **86m/C; DVD.** Dennis Morgan; Lucille Norman; Virginia Mayo; Virginia Gibson; Gene Nelson; S.Z. Sakall; Tom Conway; Wallace Ford; *D:* David Butler; *W:* Roland Kibbee; Peter Milne; Harry Clork; *C:* Wilfred M. Cline.

Paisan **1946** Six episodic tales of life in Italy, several featuring Allied soldiers and nurses during WWII. One of the stories tells of a man who tries to develop a relationship without being able to speak Italian. Another focuses on a young street robber who is confronted by one of his victims. Strong stories that covers a wide range of emotions. In Italian with English subtitles. **115m/B; VHS, DVD.** *IT* Maria Michi; Carmela Sazio; Gar Moore; William Tubbs; Harriet White; Robert Van Loon; Dale Edmonds; Carlo Pisacane; Dots Johnson; *D:* Roberto Rossellini; *W:* Federico Fellini; Roberto Rossellini. Natl. Bd. of Review '48: Director (Fellini); N.Y. Film Critics '48: Foreign Film.

The Pajama Game ½ **1957** A spritely musical about the striking workers of the Sleeptite Pajama Ffactory and their plucky negotiator, Katie (Day), who falls in love with the new foreman, Sid (Raitt). Based on the hit Broadway musical, which was based on Richard Bissell's book "Seven and a Half Cents" and adapted for the screen by Bisell and Abbott. Bob Fosse choreographed the dance numbers. **101m/C; VHS, DVD.** Doris Day; John Raitt; Eddie Foy, Jr.; Reta Shaw; Carol Haney; *D:* Stanley Donen; George Abbott; *W:* George Abbott; Richard Bissell; *C:* Harry Stradling, Sr.

Pajama Party **1964** Followup to "Bikini Beach" takes the party inside in this fourth entry in the popular "Beach Party" series. Plot is up to beach party realism. Funicello is Avalon-less (although he does have a cameo) so she falls for Martian Kirk instead. He's scouting for an alien invasion, but after he falls into Annette's lap decides to save the planet instead. Typical fluff with the usual beach movie faces present; look for a young Garr as a dancer. Followed by the classic "Beach Blanket Bingo." **82m/C; VHS, DVD.** Tommy Kirk; Annette Funicello; Elsa Lanchester; Harvey Lembeck; Jesse White; Jody McCrea; Donna Loren; Susan Hart; Bobbi Shaw; Cheryl Sweeten; Luree Holmes; Candy Johnson; Dorothy Lamour; Toni Basil; Frankie Avalon; Don Rickles; Teri Garr; Ben Lessy; *Cameo(s):* Buster Keaton; *D:* Don Weis; *W:* Louis M. Heyward; *C:* Floyd Crosby; *M:* Les Baxter.

Pal Joey **1957** Musical comedy about an opportunistic singer who courts a wealthy socialite in hopes that she will finance his nightclub. His play results in comedic complications. Stellar choreography, fine direction, and beautiful costumes complement performances headed by Hayworth and Sinatra. Oscar overlooked his pal Joey when awards were handed out. Songs include some of Rodgers and Hart's best. Based on John O'Hara's book and play. **109m/C; VHS, DVD.** Frank Sinatra; Rita Hayworth; Kim Novak; Barbara Nichols; Hank Henry; Elizabeth Patterson; *D:* George Sidney; *W:* Dorothy Kingsley; *C:* Harold Lipstein; *M:* Richard Rodgers. Golden Globes '58: Actor--Mus./Comedy (Sinatra).

Pale Flower *Kawaita Hana* **1964** Nihilistic Yakuza enforcer Muraki, just released from prison, returns to his old Tokyo gambling spots. He attempts to acclimate himself to the shift in power amongst the gangsters while becoming intrigued with beautiful, upper-class Saeko, a self-destructive thrill-seeker who likes hanging around bad guys. Japanese with subtitles. **96m/B; DVD, Blu-Ray.** *JP* Ryo Ikebe; Mariko Kaga; Takashi Fujiki; Seiji Miyaguchi; Eijiro Tono; *D:* Masahiro Shinoda; *W:* Masahiro Shinoda; Masuru Baba; *C:* Masao Kosugi; *M:* Toru Takemitsu.

Pale Rider **1985 (R)** A mysterious nameless stranger rides into a small California gold rush town to find himself in the middle of a feud between a mining syndicate and a group of independent prospectors. Christ-like Eastwood evokes comparisons to "Shane." A classical western theme treated well complemented by excellent photography and a rock-solid cast. **116m/C; VHS, DVD, Blu-Ray.** Clint Eastwood; Michael Moriarty; Carrie Snodgress; Sydney Penny; Richard Dysart; Richard Kiel; Christopher Penn; John Russell; Charles Hallahan; Douglas McGrath; Fran Ryan; *D:* Clint Eastwood; *W:* Michael Butler; Dennis Shryack; *C:* Bruce Surtees; *M:* Lennie Niehaus.

Pale Saints ½ **1997 (R)** Small-time hoods Louis (Flanery) and Dody (Riley) decide that they will do one last job for crime broker Quick Vic and use their share of the money to head off to California. They travel to Montreal and wind up with a botched heist, a case of mistaken identity, and a lot of double-dealing. The plot gets too convoluted, although it's so fast-paced you may not notice the holes. **98m/C; VHS, DVD.** *CA* Sean Patrick Flanery; Michael Riley; Saul Rubinek; Maury Chaykin; Rachael Crawford; Gordon Pinsent; *D:* Joel Wyner; *W:* Joel Wyner; *C:* Barry Stone; *M:* Michel Theriault.

The Paleface **1948** A cowardly dentist becomes a gunslinging hero when Calamity Jane starts aiming for him. A rip-roarin' good time as the conventions of the Old West are turned upside down. Includes the Oscar-winning song "Buttons and Bows." The 1952 sequel is "Son of Paleface." Remade in 1968 as "The Shakiest Gun in the West." **91m/C; VHS, DVD.** Jane Russell; Bob Hope; Robert Armstrong; Iris Adrian; Robert Watson; *D:* Norman Z. McLeod; *C:* Ray Rennahan. Oscars '48: Song ("Buttons and Bows").

Palindromes **2004** As if having abortion as his central topic wasn't challenging enough, Solondz raises the ante by having his teenaged protagonist, Aviva, played by eight different actors, including Jennifer Jason Leigh, an African-American woman, and a boy. Aviva dreams of motherhood, but after she's impregnated, her overbearing parents insist she get an abortion. To keep the baby, Aviva runs away, meeting an eccentric cast of characters on the road. Solondz masterfully conducts this postmodern morality play, showing the pitfalls of both sides of the abortion issue until the audience's moral compass is helplessly askew. **100m/C; DVD.** Jennifer Jason Leigh; Ellen Barkin; Richard Masur; Debra Monk; Emani Sledge; Valerie Shusterov; Hannah Freiman; Rachel Corr; Will Denton; Shayna Levine; Sharon Wilkins; Stephen Adly Guirgis; Matthew Faber; Steve Singer; Richard Riehle; Robert Agri; John Gemberling; Alexander Brickel; Walter Bobbie; *D:* Todd Solondz; *W:* Todd Solondz; *C:* Tom Richmond; *M:* Nathan Larson.

Palio **2015** A documentary chronicling the oldest horse race in the world, the Palio. Held twice a year in Siena, Italy, the documentary follows the twice yearly race from four days before the race when the horses are allocated to the race itself. The culture behind the race—and Italy—is examined as well, including the strategy, bribery, and corruption. Gigi Bruschelli, the legendary rider who won 13 Palios in a 16-year period, and his former protege and current rival, Giovanni Atzeni, are profiled as well. Italian with subtitles. **91m/C; DVD, Blu-Ray, Streaming, Download.** *D:* Cosima Spender; *W:* Cosima Spender; John Hunt; *C:* Stuart Bentley; *M:* Alex Heffes.

The Pallbearer ½ **1995 (PG-13)** You probably liked this one better when it was called "The Graduate," as it shares some key plot points with, but lacks the edge and cultural impact of the 1967 classic. Tom's (Schwimmer) asked to be a pallbearer for an old high school classmate he can't quite remember. He's seduced by the mother (Hershey) of the deceased, while trying to kindle a romance with the fabulous Julie DeMarco (Paltrow), an old classmate who can't quite remember him. The spurned older woman then begins to exact her revenge, while Tom tries to figure out how to court Julie while living at home with his mom. Good performances make it watchable. **98m/C; VHS, DVD.** David Schwimmer; Gwyneth Paltrow; Barbara Hershey; Michael Rapaport; Carol Kane; Toni Collette; Michael Vartan; Joseph (Joe) D'Onofrio; *D:* Matt Reeves; *W:* Matt Reeves; Jason Katims; *C:* Robert Elswit; *M:* Stewart Copeland.

The Palm Beach Story **1942** Young architect Tom Jeffers (McCrea) dreams of building an airport and his adoring wife Gerry (Colbert) decides to help him out—by divorcing him. That way she can head to Palm Beach, marry rich, and finance Tom's ambitions. So Gerry sets her considerable charms on catching eccentric J.D. Hackensacker (Vallee). When Tom follows, he becomes prey for J.D.'s tart-tongued sister (Astor). Takes amusing aim at the idle rich with Sturges's trademark witty, sophisticated dialogue. **88m/B; VHS, DVD, Blu-Ray.** Claudette Colbert; Joel McCrea; Mary Astor; Rudy Vallee; William Demarest; Franklin Pangborn; *D:* Preston Sturges; *W:* Preston Sturges; *C:* Victor Milner; *M:* Victor Young.

Palm Springs Weekend ½ **1963** A busload of love-hungry kids head south and get involved in routine hijinks. Actually shot in Palm Springs with above average performances by a handful of stars. **100m/C; VHS, DVD.** Troy Donahue; Ty Hardin; Connie Stevens; Stefanie Powers; Robert Conrad; Jack Weston; Andrew Duggan; *D:* Norman Taurog; *W:* Earl Hamner; *C:* Harold Lipstein; *M:* Frank Perkins.

Palmetto ½ **1998 (R)** Contempo-noir that misses the mark has bitter ex-con Harry (Harrelson) partnered with seductress Rhea (Shue) in a phony kidnapping of her stepdaughter Odette (Sevigny). Newly released from the joint after a frame-up, Harry's ex, Nina (Gershon), lures him to the backwater town that sent him up, where he's again the patsy as all three women go to work on him. Originality and character development go AWOL, as the normally adept Harrelson flounders for an identity. From Rene Raymond's (a.k.a. James Hadley Chase) novel, "Just Another Sucker." **114m/C; DVD.** Woody Harrelson; Elisabeth Shue; Michael Rapaport; Angela Featherstone; Gina Gershon; Chloë Sevigny; Rolf Hoppe; Tom Wright; *D:* Volker Schlondorff; *W:* E. Max Frye; *C:* Thomas Kloss; *M:* Klaus Doldinger.

Palo Alto **2007 (R)** Not the trashy teens-gone-wild flick you might expect from the rating. Four longtime buds, who have gone off to separate colleges, reunite at their first Thanksgiving break to catch up. They not only discover how much they're changing but how much their hometown actually does mean to them. **95m/C; DVD.** Ben Savage; Aaron Ashmore; Johnny Lewis; Autumn Reeser; Justin Mentell; Tom Arnold; *D:* Brad Leong; *W:* Tony Vallone; *C:* Rachel Morrison.

Palo Alto **2014 (R)** Gia Coppola, granddaughter of Francis Ford Coppola, makes her directorial debut with this mediocre adaptation of James Franco's series of short stories about teenage apathy and ennui in the city of angels. April (Roberts) is the class virgin, harboring a not-so-secret crush on classmate Teddy (Kilmer), even as she flirts openly with her soccer coach (played by Franco himself). Friend Emily (Levin) is the more outgoing one while Fred (Wolff) is the reckless one in this dazed and confused quartet. It's just another tale of youthful indiscretion and adults who turn predator if they're paying attention at all. **100m/C; DVD.** Emma Roberts; Jack Kilmer; Nat Wolff; Zoe Levin; James Franco; Val Kilmer; *D:* Gia Coppola; *W:* Gia Coppola; *C:* Autumn Cheyenne Durald; *M:* Devonte Hynes; Robert Schwartzman.

Palooka ½ *Joe Palooka; The Great Schnozzle* **1934 (G)** Based on the comic strip, this film portrays a fast-talking boxing manager and his goofy, lovable protege. The young scrapper fights James Cagney's little brother. Durante sings his classic tune, "Inka-Dinka-Doo," and packs a punch in the lead. A two-fisted comedy with a witty dialogue and fine direction. Not a part of the Palooka series of the 1940s. **86m/B; VHS, DVD.** Jimmy Durante; Stuart Erwin; Lupe Velez; Robert Armstrong; Thelma Todd; William Cagney; ***D:*** Ben Stoloff.

Palookaville 🦴🦴🦴 **1995 (R)** Nostalgic comedy of three under-employed friends who take up crime, temporarily, just until they can secure legit work. Using a little-known 1950s crime movie as their tutor, criminal cretins Jerry (Trese), Russ (Gallo), and Sid (Forsythe) encounter a variety of setbacks on their way to financial security as they plan an elaborate scheme to rob an armored car. Adapted from short stories written in the 1940s by the Italian Italo Calvino, modern adaptation manages to retain an old-fashioned feel and charm. **92m/C; VHS, DVD.** William Forsythe; Vincent Gallo; Adam Trese; Lisa Gay Hamilton; Frances McDormand; Davis Boulton; James David Hilton; Gareth Williams; Bridget Ryan; Kim Dickens; Suzanne Shepherd; Robert LuPone; ***D:*** Alan Taylor; ***W:*** David Epstein; ***C:*** John Thomas; ***M:*** Rachel Portman.

Pals 🦴🦴 **1987** Old friends stumble across $3 million in cash and learn the predictable lesson that money can't buy happiness. A terribly trite CBS TV-movie with an exceptional cast. **90m/C; VHS, DVD.** Don Ameche; George C. Scott; Sylvia Sidney; Susan Rinell; James Greene; ***D:*** Lou Antonio; ***W:*** Michael Norell; ***C:*** Steve Yaconelli; ***M:*** Mark Snow. **TV**

Pampered Youth 🦴🦴 **1925** Adaptation of Booth Tarkington's "The Magnificent Ambersons." Major Amberson is the wealthiest man in his Midwestern town. Daughter Isabel settles for marrying Wilbur Minafer after true love Eugene Morgan departs in disgrace. She thoroughly spoils only son George, who nearly bankrupts the family with his profligate ways. Wilbur returns to a widowed Isabel but the familial troubles don't stop. **70m/B; Silent; DVD.** Alice Calhoun; Cullen Landis; Allan Forrest; Emmett King; Wallace MacDonald; Charlotte Merriam; ***D:*** David Smith; ***W:*** Jay Pilcher; ***C:*** W. Steve Smith, Jr.

Pan 🦴 **2015 (PG)** At least this hunk of garbage will make people think more fondly of Steven Spielberg's Hook. While that notorious box office bomb has its issues, it's not as soulless as Joe Wright's stunning 3D misfire, a movie that tries to fly without a heart. It's a Peter Pan origin story as a young Petey (Levi Miller) encounters magical pirates and is transported to the land of Neverland. He is forced to mine fairy dust for a ruthless pirate named Blackbeard (Hugh Jackman) and gets close to a fellow miner named James Hook (Garrett Hedlund), who, well, you know. Rooney Mara plays Tiger Lily. **135m/C; DVD, Blu-Ray.** Levi Miller; Rooney Mara; Amanda Seyfried; Hugh Jackman; Garrett Hedlund; Cara Delevingne; ***D:*** Joe Wright; ***W:*** Jason Fuchs; ***C:*** John Mathieson; Seamus McGarvey; ***M:*** John Powell.

Panama Hattie 🦴🦴 **1942** Screen adaptation of Cole Porter's delightful Broadway musical. Unfortunately, something (like a plot) was lost in transition. Southern runs a saloon for our boys down in Panama. Among the musical numbers and vaudevillian acts some spies show up. Several screenwriters and directors, including Vincente Minnelli, worked uncredited on this picture, to no avail. Horne's second screen appearance. **79m/B; VHS, DVD.** Ann Sothern; Dan Dailey; Red Skelton; Virginia O'Brien; Rags Ragland; Alan Mowbray; Ben Blue; Carl Esmond; Lena Horne; ***D:*** Norman Z. McLeod; ***C:*** George J. Folsey; ***M:*** George Bassman; Cole Porter.

Pancho Villa 🦴 ½ **1972 (PG)** Savalas has the lead in this fictional account of the famous Mexican, He leads his men in a raid on an American fort after being hoodwinked in an arms deal. Connors tries to hold the fort against him. The finale, in which two trains crash head on, is the most exciting event in the whole darn movie. **92m/C; VHS, DVD.** *SP* Telly Savalas; Clint Walker; Anne Francis; Chuck Connors; Angel Del Pozo; Luis Davila; ***D:*** Eugenio (Gene) Martin; ***W:*** Julian Zimet; ***C:*** Alejandro Ulloa; ***M:*** Anton Abril.

Pandaemonium 🦴🦴 ½ **2000 (PG-13)** Friendship, rivalry, and jealousy between 19th-century English romanticists William Wordsworth (Hannah) and Samuel Taylor Coleridge (Roache). In 1813, debilitated by opium abuse, Coleridge remembers his first meeting with the now-distant Wordsworth some 20 years before. Coleridge and wife Sara (Morton) move to a country cottage with Wordworth and his sister Dorothy (Woof) living nearby as the two men collaborate. Coleridge becomes (mutually) attracted to Dorothy and a rift between the two men deepens when Wordsworth marries and Coleridge dependency on drugs worsens—even as his poetry soars. **125m/C; VHS, DVD.** *UK* Linus Roache; John Hannah; Samantha Morton; Emily Woof; Emma Fielding; Andy Serkis; Samuel West; Guy Lankester; ***D:*** Julien Temple; ***W:*** Frank Cottrell-Boyce; ***C:*** John Lynch; ***M:*** Dario Marianelli.

Pandas 🦴🦴🦴 **2018 (G)** Narrated by Kristen Bell, this documentary short follows the call of the wild for one young panda. Born in captivity, Qian Qian is guided by a team of Chinese and American experts to venture outside the limits of the only environment she's ever known, the first step in the larger vision of reintroducing giant pandas in China. In true IMAX form, the cinematography is gorgeous and perfectly scored, but all eyes remain glued on the ridiculously cute star. **40m/C; DVD.** Kristen Bell; Wen Lei Bi; Rong Hou; Ben Kilham; Jacob Owens; ***D:*** David Douglas; Drew Fellman; ***W:*** Drew Fellman; ***C:*** David Douglas; ***M:*** Mark Mothersbaugh.

Pandemic 🦴 ½ **2007** Dr. Kayla Martin (Thiessen) and her partner Carl (Stewart) fear the frightening effects of a biological attack when a young man dies on a plane following a fever and violent convulsions. Other passengers on board are now filtering into the city and infecting areas of Los Angeles. The virus and panic continue to spread. Fairly entertaining but overly saturated with unsupported improbability (starting with Thiessen as a doctor). **170m/C; DVD.** Tiffani(-Amber) Thiessen; Vincent Spano; Eric Roberts; Faye Dunaway; French Stewart; Bruce Boxleitner; Bob Gunton; Renee Taylor; Tamlyn Tomita; Clyde Kusatsu; ***D:*** Armand Mastroianni; ***W:*** Bruce Zabel; Jackie Zabel; ***C:*** Amit Bhattacharya. **CABLE**

Pandemic 🦴 ½ **2009 (R)** Action-thriller about a New Mexico community where humans and animals are both stricken with a gory contagious virus. The area is quarantined by the military and all outside communication is cut off so veterinarian Sydney Stevens teams up with conspiracy theorist Spenser to figure out what's going on and reveal the truth. **90m/C; DVD.** Alesha Rucci; Peter Holden; Ray Wise; Graham McTavish; Kristi Culbert; ***D:*** Jason Connery; ***W:*** Aaron Pope; ***C:*** Miguel Bunster; ***M:*** Christian Henson. **VIDEO**

Pandora and the Flying Dutchman 🦴🦴 ½ **1951** Feverish romantic fantasy has playgirl/nightclub singer Pandora Reynolds (Gardner) living in '30s Spain and being romanced by every man in sight. Naturally, she cares for none of them until she meets enigmatic Dutch captain Hendrick van der Zee (Mason) who is, in fact, the legendary Flying Dutchman—condemned to wander the seas forever unless a woman is willing to give up her life for him. Gardner is, as usual, exotically lovely. **123m/C; VHS, DVD, Blu-Ray.** Ava Gardner; James Mason; Nigel Patrick; Sheila Sim; Harold Warrender; Mario Cabre; ***D:*** Albert Lewin; ***W:*** Albert Lewin; ***C:*** Jack Cardiff; ***M:*** Alan Rawsthorne.

Pandora Machine 🦴 **2004 (R)** In a corrupt dystopian future, surveillance is universal and the police are a for-profit corporation. Somehow, despite the insane levels of security, a serial killer is on the loose and there is no track record of who it is. **84m/C; DVD.** Daryl Boling; Doris Hick; Margaret Dodge; Jason Howard; Monica Russell; ***D:*** Andrew Bellware; ***W:*** Andrew Bellware; Laura Schlachtmeyer; ***C:*** Andrew Bellware; ***M:*** Andrew Bellware. **VIDEO**

Pandora's Box 🦴🦴🦴🦴 *Die Buechse der Pandora; Lulu* **1928** This silent classic marked the end of the German Expressionist era and established Brooks as a major screen presence. She plays the tempestuous Lulu, who destroys everyone she comes in contact with, eventually sinking to prostitution and a fateful meeting with Jack the Ripper. Silent with orchestral score. **110m/B; Silent; VHS, DVD.** *GE* Louise Brooks; Fritz Kortner; Francis Lederer; Carl Goetz; Alice Roberts; Gustav Diesl; ***D:*** G.W. Pabst; ***W:*** G.W. Pabst; ***C:*** Gunther Krampf.

Pandora's Clock 🦴🦴 **1996** Over-extended but often suspenseful disaster flick. Quantum Airlines flight 66 is traveling from Frankfurt to New York when a passenger dies. Capt. Holland (Anderson) radios to make an emergency landing in London but is informed that the passenger was infected with a doomsday virus and the plane must be quarantined. No country will let them land and then the CIA and various shady government types get involved, proposing much more drastic solutions. Based on the novel by John J. Nance. **178m/C; DVD.** Richard Dean Anderson; Daphne Zuniga; Jane Leeves; Richard Lawson; Edward Herrmann; Robert Guillaume; Robert Loggia; Stephen (Steve) Root; ***D:*** Eric Laneuville; ***W:*** David Israel; ***C:*** Paul Pollard; ***M:*** Don Davis. **TV**

Pandora's Promise 🦴🦴 **2013** Well-intentioned but incredibly dry and one-sided, Stone's documentary is an interesting start to a conversation but an incomplete one on its own. The director offers a number of scientists and environmentalists who once opposed nuclear power but have now come around to defending it as the only answer to a future that contains decreasing fossil fuels. Arguing that the risk of nuclear power is overstated, Stone makes some convincing arguments but presents no one on the other side of the debate to counterbalance, leading to a film that feels more like a pitch or propaganda. **90m/C; DVD.** ***D:*** Robert Stone; ***W:*** Robert Stone; ***C:*** Robert Stone; Howard Shack; ***M:*** Gary Lionelli.

Pandorum 🦴 ½ **2009 (R)** Two space shuttle crew members, Payton (Quaid) and Bower (Foster), awake from a cryogenic snooze to find that they have no memory of why they're in outer space and little recollection of their own identity. While trying to piece together their mystery they realize they're sharing quarters with flesh-eating alien rodents. Any shot at being a genuine sci-fi thriller is undone by these unimaginative creatures that push it into nothing more than "Alien" knock-off territory. **108m/C; Blu-Ray, On Demand.** Dennis Quaid; Ben Foster; Norman Reedus; Cam Gigandet; Cung Le; Eddie Rouse; Antje Traue; ***D:*** Christian Alvart; ***W:*** Christian Alvart; Travis Milloy; ***C:*** Wendigo von Schultzendorff; ***M:*** Michi Britsch.

Panhandle 🦴🦴 **1948** Trading post owner John Sands (Cameron) wound up in Mexico after he went from lawman to gunslinger. Learning his brother was murdered, Sands heads north to hunt down the killers but old adversary Matt Garson (Hadley) has no intention of making it a fair fight. Co-star (and co-writer) Edwards, playing a gunfighter, became better-known as a writer-director. **85m/B; DVD.** Rod Cameron; Reed Hadley; Anne Gwynne; Cathy Downs; Blake Edwards; J. Farrell MacDonald; Dick Crockett; ***D:*** Lesley Selander; ***W:*** Blake Edwards; John C. Champion; ***C:*** Harry Neumann; ***M:*** Rex Dunn.

Panic 🦴🦴 ½ **2000 (R)** Hangdog Macy is perfect as middle-aged Alex, who is not having your usual midlife crisis since he's a hit man. As a matter of fact, he learned his trade from his ruthless dad Michael (Sutherland), who still calls the shots. But Alex has been keeping the truth from his wife Martha (Ullman) and his beloved son Sammy (Dorfman) and he needs to talk. So he goes to shrink Josh Parks (Ritter) and, in the waiting room, Alex meets neurotic Sarah (Campbell), with whom he contemplates an affair. Alex wants to make some changes but when you're a professional killer, it's not that easy. **93m/C; VHS, DVD.** William H. Macy; John Ritter; Neve Campbell; Donald Sutherland; Tracey Ullman; Barbara Bain; David Dorfman; ***D:*** Henry Bromell; ***W:*** Henry Bromell; ***C:*** Jeffrey Jur; ***M:*** Brian Tyler.

Panic Button 🦴 ½ **1962** Mel Brooks took the plot from this film and made "The Producers," which was much better. Italian gangsters produce a TV show and stack the deck so that it will fail. Unbeknownst to them, the star has figured out what they are doing and works to make it a success. Shot in Italy, mainly in Venice and Rome. **90m/B; DVD.** *IT* Maurice Chevalier; Eleanor Parker; Jayne Mansfield; Mike Connors; Akim Tamiroff; ***D:*** George Sherman; ***W:*** Hal Biller; ***C:*** Enzo Serafin; ***M:*** Georges Garvarentz.

Panic in Echo Park 🦴🦴 **1977** A doctor races against time to find the cause of an epidemic that is threatening the health of a city. Good performances compensate for a predictable plot. **78m/C; VHS, DVD.** Dorian Harewood; Robin Gammell; Catlin Adams; Ramon Bieri; Movita; ***D:*** John Llewellyn Moxey; ***W:*** Dalene Young; ***C:*** Robert B. Hauser. **TV**

Panic in Needle Park 🦴🦴🦴 **1971 (R)** Drugs become an obsession for a young girl who goes to New York for an abortion. Her new boyfriend is imprisoned for robbery in order to support both their habits. She resorts to prostitution to continue her drug habit, and trouble occurs when her boyfriend realizes she was instrumental in his being sent to jail. Strikes a vein in presenting an uncompromising look at drug use. May be too much of a depressant for some. Pacino's first starring role. **90m/C; VHS, DVD, Blu-Ray.** Al Pacino; Kitty Winn; Alan Vint; Richard Bright; Kiel Martin; Warren Finnerty; Raul Julia; Paul Sorvino; ***D:*** Jerry Schatzberg; ***W:*** Joan Didion; John Gregory Dunne; ***C:*** Adam Holender. Cannes '71: Actress (Winn).

Panic in the City 🦴 ½ **1968** A man collapses on the street and is pronounced to be radioactive at a hospital. Claiming to be a scientist, he is murdered before he can speak to authorities. Buyers should be aware that Dennis Hopper has only a bit part in this film, despite being used as an advertisement on the cover. **97m/C; DVD.** Howard Duff; Linda Cristal; Stephen McNally; Nehemiah Persoff; Anne Jeffreys; ***D:*** Eddie Davis; ***W:*** Eddie Davis; ***C:*** Alan Stensvold; ***M:*** Paul Dunlap.

Panic in the Skies 🦴🦴 **1996** The cockpit of a Boeing 747 is struck by lightning in mid-flight, killing the pilot and co-pilot. Flight attendant Jackson and passenger Marinaro try to figure out a way to safely land the passenger-filled jet. **90m/C; VHS, DVD.** Kate Jackson; Ed Marinaro; Erik Estrada; Maureen McCormick; Billy Warlock; Robert Guillaume; ***D:*** Paul Ziller; ***W:*** Robert Hamilton; ***C:*** Rod Parkhurst; ***M:*** Todd Hayen. **TV**

Panic in the Streets 🦴🦴🦴 **1950** The Black Death threatens New Orleans in this intense tale. When a body is found on the waterfront, a doctor (Widmark) is called upon for a diagnosis. The carrier proves to be deadly in more ways than one. Fine performances, taut direction (this was one of Kazan's favorite movies). Filmed on location in New Orleans. **96m/B; VHS, DVD, Blu-Ray.** Richard Widmark; Jack Palance; Barbara Bel Geddes; Paul Douglas; Zero Mostel; ***D:*** Elia Kazan; ***W:*** Edward Anhalt. Oscars '50: Story.

Panic in Year Zero! 🦴🦴 ½ *End of the World* **1962** Milland and family leave Los Angeles for a fishing trip just as the city is hit by a nuclear bomb. Continuing out into the wilderness for safety, the family now must try to survive as their world crumbles around them. Generally considered the best of Milland's five directorial efforts. **92m/B; VHS, DVD, Blu-Ray.** Ray Milland; Jean Hagen; Frankie Avalon; Mary Mitchell; Joan Freeman; Richard Garland; Rex Holman; Richard Bakalyan; Willis Bouchey; Neil Nephew; ***D:*** Ray Milland; ***W:*** Jay Simms; John Morton; ***C:*** Gilbert Warrenton; ***M:*** Les Baxter.

Panic Room 🦴🦴 ½ **2002 (R)** Meg (Foster) moves with daughter Sarah (Stewart) into an ominous four-story brownstone in New York, complete with a fortress-like panic room the paranoid billionaire previous occupant had built. Three intruders come looking for something that happens to be in the room, where the women have holed up. And thus the cat-and-mouse game begins. Fincher's talents for visual style, creative camera work, and squirmy set pieces are well-used here as the tension mounts. The plot isn't especially original, but the twists are well-done and the performers acquit themselves nicely. **112m/C; VHS, DVD.** Jodie Foster; Forest Whitaker; Dwight Yoakam; Jared Leto; Kristen Stewart; Ann Magnuson; Patrick Bauchau; Ian Buchanan; Paul Schulze; ***D:*** David Fincher; ***W:*** David Koepp; ***C:*** Conrad W. Hall; Darius Khondji; ***M:*** Howard Shore.

Pan's Labyrinth 🦴🦴🦴🦴 *El Laberinto del Fauno* **2006 (R)** Young Ofelia (Baquero) is stuck with a brutal stepfather (Lopez) when her mother (Gil) remarries. Ofelia sees an escape from her miserable situation when she stumbles upon a garden labyrinth leading to a freakish-yet-bewitching underground fantasy world inhabited by strange creatures led by Pan (Jones), who is part goat, part man. He tells Ofelia that she might be their lost princess but must perform three tasks in order to prove herself worthy of the crown. Eventually the line between the two worlds blurs, causing dire consequences. Complex and entertaining adult fairytale mixes vivid scenery with computer-generated effects. Spanish with subtitles. **112m/C; DVD, Blu-Ray, HD-DVD.** *MX SP* Sergi Lopez; Maribel Verdu; Doug Jones; Alex Angulo; Ivana Baquero; Ariadna Gil; Roger Casamajor; ***D:*** Guillermo del Toro; ***W:*** Guillermo del Toro; ***C:*** Guillermo Navarro; ***M:*** Javier Navarrete. Oscars '06: Art Dir./Set Dec., Cinematog., Makeup; British Acad. '06: Costume Des., Foreign Film, Makeup; Ind. Spirit '07: Cinematog.

Panther **1995 (R)** A fictionalized account of the Black Panthers' emergence as a voice for African Americans and as a fixture on the FBI's most wanted list in the late '60s. Vietnam vet Judge's (Hardison) forced by the FBI to become an informant, chronicles the activities of leaders Bobby Seale (Vance) and Huey P. Newton (Chong) and serves as witness to the Panthers' rise and subsequent fall into corruption and disintegration. Scatter-shot editing is meant to signify the chaos of the times; instead it adds to the action-flick feel and further detracts from the professed intent of being a message movie. **124m/C; VHS, DVD.** Kadeem Hardison; Marcus Chong; Courtney B. Vance; Bokeem Woodbine; Joe Don Baker; Anthony Griffith; Nefertiti; James Russo; Richard Dysart; M. Emmet Walsh; Mario Van Peebles; ***D:*** Mario Van Peebles; ***W:*** Melvin Van Peebles; ***C:*** Edward Pei; ***M:*** Stanley Clarke.

The Panther's Claw **1942** Murder befalls an opera troupe, but a sleuth with the memorable name of Thatcher Colt is on the case. A quick-moving mystery quickie that delivers on its own modest terms. **72m/B; VHS, DVD.** Sidney Blackmer; Byron Foulger; Rick Vallin; Herbert Rawlinson; ***D:*** William Beaudine; ***W:*** Martin Mooney; ***C:*** Marcel Le Picard.

Panzer *Panzer Chocolate* **2013** A horror drama centered on items stolen by the Nazis. When a student archaeologist and her friends go looking for art stolen by the Nazis, they find the Nazi bunker called Valhalla and so much more. The bunker has a beast as a guard and the seekers soon learn that their lives are in danger. The film also has interactive elements involving cellphone technology to bring the horror into the real world. **84m/C; DVD, Streaming, Download.** Melina Matthews; Geraldine Chaplin; Ariadna Cabrol; Tony Corvillo; Mark Schardan; ***D:*** Robert Figueras; ***W:*** Robert Figueras; Gemma Dunjo; Pep Garrido; ***C:*** Inigo Zubicaray; ***M:*** Pep Sala. **VIDEO**

Papa: Hemingway in Cuba **2016 (R)** The true story of how Ed Myers (Ribisi), a young journalist, travels to Cuba in the 1950s to seek the guidance of his hero, Ernest Hemingway (Sparks), in the midst of the Cuban Revolution. Director Yari's film is a vision to watch, particularly since Cuba itself serves as the backdrop (the first U.S. movie filmed there since Castro took over in 1959). If only the script lived up to the story and the scenery. A murky recounting combined with flat performances makes this a disappointing venture. **110m/C; DVD.** Giovanni Ribisi; Joely Richardson; Adrian Sparks; Minka Kelly; Shaun Toub; ***D:*** Bob Yari; ***W:*** Denne Bart Petitclerc; ***C:*** Ernesto Melara; ***M:*** Mark Isham.

Paparazzi **1/2 2004 (PG-13)** An actor's revenge? Produced by Mel Gibson (who has a cameo) and his Icon production company, this overheated melodrama follows newly-crowned action star Bo Laramie (Hauser), whose celebrity has led to his being stalked by those degenerate paparazzi. When Bo's family is critically injured in a car crash caused by the relentless shutterbug pursuit, Bo turns vigilante to get revenge. Sizemore is at his slimy nastiest as the lead sleazy photog. **85m/C; VHS, DVD.** Cole Hauser; Robin Tunney; Dennis Farina; Daniel Baldwin; Tom Hollander; Kevin Gage; Tom Sizemore; Duane Davis; Blake Bryan; Andrea Baker; Jordan Baker; ***Cameo(s):*** Mel Gibson; Chris Rock; Matthew McConaughey; Vince Vaughn; ***D:*** Paul Abascal; ***W:*** Forrest Smith; ***C:*** Daryn Okada; ***M:*** Brian Tyler.

Papa's Delicate Condition **1963** Based on the autobiographical writings of silent screen star Corinne Griffith. Gleason is Papa whose "delicate condition" is a result of his drinking. His antics provide a constant headache to his family. A paean to turn-of-the-century family life. No I.D.s required as the performances are enjoyable for the whole family. Features the Academy Award-winning song "Call Me Irresponsible." **98m/C; VHS, DVD, Blu-Ray.** Jackie Gleason; Glynis Johns; Charlie Ruggles; Laurel Goodwin; Elisha Cook, Jr.; Murray Hamilton; Ned Glass; Charles Lane; Don Beddoe; Juanita Moore; Trevor Bardette; Ken Renard; ***D:*** George Marshall; ***W:*** Jack Rose; ***C:*** Loyal Griggs; ***M:*** Joseph J. Lilley. Oscars '63: Song ("Call Me Irresponsible").

The Paper **1994 (R)** Follows a red letter day in the life of an editor at the tabloid New York Sun. Fresh, fast-moving script by the Koepp brothers offers a fairly accurate portrayal of the business of journalism with a few Hollywood exceptions. Pace suffers from cutaways to life outside, while script and direction sometimes coast past targets. Propelled by a fine cast, with cola-swigging editor Keaton the focus as he juggles his personal and professional lives. As a managing editor married to her work and ready to run over anyone in her way, Close is both funny and scary. Duvall contributes salt as the old newsroom warhorse. **112m/C; VHS, DVD, Blu-Ray.** Michael Keaton; Robert Duvall; Marisa Tomei; Glenn Close; Randy Quaid; Jason Robards, Jr.; Jason Alexander; Spalding Gray; Catherine O'Hara; Lynne Thigpen; ***D:*** Ron Howard; ***W:*** David Koepp; Steven Koepp; ***C:*** John Seale; ***M:*** Randy Newman.

Paper Bullets **1/2** *Gangs, Inc.* **1941** Too many plots make for confusion. Rita takes a hit-and-run rap for her playboy boyfriend and then shakes down his wealthy father when she gets out of the joint, using his influence to get her in with the mobsters who control the city. Then there are a couple of Rita's old pals from the orphanage, an undercover agent after gangsters, and Rita deciding to go straight for love. **72m/B; DVD.** Joan Woodbury; Jack La Rue; John Archer; Philip Trent; George Pembroke; Alan Ladd; Linda Ware; Gavin Gordon; ***D:*** Phil Rosen; ***W:*** Martin Mooney; ***C:*** Arthur Martinelli.

Paper Bullets **1999 (R)** Cop John Rourke's son is kidnapped by a Chinese drug lord and, naturally, he'll do anything to get his boy back. Including aligning himself with a beautiful woman who has an equal obsession for revenge. **95m/C; VHS, DVD.** James Russo; William McNamara; Ernie Hudson; Nicole Bilderback; Jeff Wincott; Francois Chan; ***D:*** Serge Rodnunsky; ***W:*** Serge Rodnunsky; ***C:*** Greg Patterson; ***M:*** Jeff Walton. **VIDEO**

The Paper Chase **1973 (PG)** Students at Harvard Law School suffer and struggle through their first year. A realistic, sometimes acidly humorous look at Ivy League ambitions, with Houseman stealing the show as the tough professor. Wonderful adaptation of the John Jay Osborn novel which later became the basis for the acclaimed TV series. **111m/C; VHS, DVD.** Timothy Bottoms; Lindsay Wagner; John Houseman; Graham Beckel; Edward Herrmann; James Naughton; Craig Richard Nelson; Bob Lydiard; ***D:*** James Bridges; ***W:*** James Bridges; ***C:*** Gordon Willis; ***M:*** John Williams. Oscars '73: Support. Actor (Houseman); Golden Globes '74: Support. Actor (Houseman); Natl. Bd. of Review '73: Support. Actor (Houseman).

Paper Heart **2009 (PG-13)** What's fake and what's real and do you care? What started out as an alleged documentary turned into something else as skeptical, chipmunk-cheeked performance artist Yi takes a road trip to ask the question 'Does true love really exist?' Her director/crew is played by an actor (Johnson) who is portraying the actual co-writer/director (Jasenovec). Then Yi meets actor Michael Cera and just might have the answer to her own question, although they act like a couple of grade-school kids playing at romance without any actual understanding of adult relationships. And then there are the puppets. We don't get it either. **88m/C; Blu-Ray, On Demand.** Michael Cera; Charlyne Yi; Jake M. Johnson; ***D:*** Nicholas Jasenovec; ***W:*** Charlyne Yi; Nicholas Jasenovec; ***C:*** Jay Hunter; ***M:*** Michael Cera; Charlyne Yi.

Paper Lion **1/2 1968** A comedy "documentary" about bestselling writer George Plimpton's tryout game as quarterback with the Detroit Lions. Film debut of Alan Alda. Helped Karras make the transition from the gridiron to the silver screen. Moves into field goal range but doesn't quite score. **107m/C; VHS, Streaming.** Alan Alda; Lauren Hutton; Alex Karras; Ann Turkel; John Gordy; Roger Brown; "Sugar Ray" Robinson; Roy Scheider; David Doyle; ***D:*** Alex March; ***W:*** Lawrence Roman; ***M:*** Roger Kellaway.

Paper Man **1971** A group of college students create a fictitious person in a computer for a credit card scam. The scheme snowballs, resulting in murder and hints of possible artificial intelligence. But it's just standard fare, with a creepy performance by Stockwell as a computer whiz. CBS TV movie. **90m/C; VHS, DVD.** Dean Stockwell; Stefanie Powers; James Stacy; Elliot Street; Tina Chen; James Olson; Ross Elliott; ***D:*** Walter Grauman; ***W:*** Ronald Austin; ***C:*** Jack Woolf; ***M:*** Duane Tatro. **TV**

Paper Man **1/2 2009 (R)** Ungainly, gimmicky drama. Self-absorbed, middle-aged writer Richard (Daniels) is sequestered in a Long Island cabin by wife Claire (Kudrow) in an effort to get him over his writer's block. Richard prefers communing with his imaginary friend since childhood, a bleached-blond superhero knockoff he calls Captain Excellent (a nearly-unrecognizable Reynolds). Then he impulsively hires lonely teenager Abby (Stone) as a babysitter and she sticks around even after realizing it's Richard that needs the company. They bond over soup and conversation—it's that kind of flick. **110m/C; Blu-Ray, On Demand.** Jeff Daniels; Emma Stone; Ryan Reynolds; Lisa Kudrow; Kieran Culkin; Hunter Parrish; Arabella Field; Chris Parnell; ***D:*** Kieran Mulroney; Michele Mulroney; ***W:*** Kieran Mulroney; Michele Mulroney; ***C:*** Eigil Bryld; ***M:*** Mark McAdam.

Paper Mask **1/2 1991 (R)** When a promising young doctor is killed in an auto accident, an unscrupulous, psychotic porter assumes his identity. He uses said identity to, among other things, initiate an affair with a sultry co-worker. How long will this madman play his unholy game, and at what cost? **105m/C; DVD.** *UK* Paul McGann; Amanda Donohoe; Frederick Treves; Barbara Leigh-Hunt; Jimmy Yuill; Tom Wilkinson; ***D:*** Christopher Morahan; ***W:*** John Collee; ***C:*** Nat Crosby; ***M:*** Richard Harvey.

Paper Moon **1/2 1973 (PG)** Award-winning story set in depression-era Kansas with Ryan O'Neal as a Bible-wielding con who meets up with a nine-year-old orphan. During their travels together, he discovers that the orphan (his daughter, Tatum) is better at "his" game than he is. Irresistible chemistry between the O'Neals, leading to Tatum's Oscar win (she is the youngest actor ever to take home a statue). Cinematically picturesque and cynical enough to keep overt sentimentalism at bay. Based on Joe David Brown's novel, "Addie Pray." The director's version contains a prologue by director Bogdanovich. **102m/B; VHS, DVD.** Ryan O'Neal; Tatum O'Neal; Madeline Kahn; John Hillerman; Randy Quaid; ***D:*** Peter Bogdanovich; ***W:*** Alvin Sargent. Oscars '73: Support. Actress (O'Neal); Writers Guild '73: Adapt. Screenplay.

Paper Soldiers **1/2 2002 (R)** An action comedy about a burglar whose trying to improve his game. Though Shawn (Hart) is on parole, he wants to become a better burglar to help support his struggling family. Shawn convinces a more experienced thief Will (Lee) to train him. When Shawn's girlfriend Monique (Withers) learns what he is doing, he feels her wrath while managing some wannabe criminal friends and the neighborhood sociopath Stu (Sigel). **88m/C; DVD, Streaming, Download.** Kevin Hart; Beanie Sigel; Capone Lee; Tiffany Withers; Stacey Dash; ***D:*** David Daniel; Damon Dash; ***W:*** Terrence Mosley; ***C:*** Phil Oetiker.

Paper Towns **2015 (PG-13)** Hollywood goes back to the John Green well, hoping for a bit of the magic gleaned from the adaptation of his bestselling "The Fault in Our Stars" a year earlier. Wolff plays Quentin, shy and long-obsessed with his beautiful neighbor Margo (Delevingne). After spending an unusual night of adventure with her, Margo up and disappears, leaving behind a trail of clues for Quentin to follow. He gets a group of friends together to do just that. There's nothing particularly wrong with this Young Adult adaptation, but it's just not as memorable or emotional. **109m/C; DVD, Blu-Ray, Streaming.** Nat Wolff; Cara Delevingne; Austin Abrams; Justice Smith; Halston Sage; ***D:*** Jake Schreier; ***W:*** Scott Neustadter; Michael H. Weber; ***C:*** David Lanzenberg; ***M:*** Son Lux.

A Paper Wedding *Les Noces de Papier* **1989** A middle-aged literature professor with a dead-end career and equally dead-end romance with a married man is persuaded by her lawyer sister to marry a Chilean political refugee to avoid his deportation. Of course, they must fool an immigration official and their fake marriage does turn into romance, but this is no light-hearted "Green Card." Bujold shines. In French and Spanish with English subtitles. **90m/C; VHS, DVD.** *CA* Genevieve Bujold; Manuel Aranguiz; Dorothee Berryman; ***D:*** Michel Brault; ***C:*** Sylvain Brault.

Paperback Romance **1/2** *Lucky Break* **1996 (R)** Sophie (Carides) is a writer of erotica who doesn't act on her own impulses because she's embarassed by her polio-crippled leg. But when she breaks her leg, the cast allows her to pass the injury off as a skiing accident and Sophie decides to go after the man of her dreams, a charmingly shady jewelry dealer named Eddie (LaPaglia)?who just happens to be engaged. **99m/C; VHS, DVD.** *AU* Gia Carides; Anthony LaPaglia; Rebecca Gibney; ***D:*** Ben Lewin; ***W:*** Ben Lewin; ***C:*** Vincent Monton; ***M:*** Paul Grabowsky.

The Paperboy **1994 (R)** Melissa Thorpe (Paul) returns to her small hometown to settle her mother's estate, only to become the obsession of Johnny (Marut), the 12-year-old paperboy she mistakenly befriends. Seems he becomes psychotically jealous when Melissa takes up with an old flame (Katt) and dead bodies become as common as old newspapers. **93m/C; VHS, Streaming.** Alexandra Paul; Marc Marut; William Katt; Brigid Tierney; ***D:*** Douglas Jackson; ***W:*** David Peckinpah; ***M:*** Milan Kymlicka.

The Paperboy **1/2 2012 (R)** Set in 1969, Miami reporter Ward Jansen (McConaughey) travels to his small Florida hometown to write a piece about a venomous convict (Cusack) on Death Row, who he believes is innocent. Ward recruits his younger brother Jack (Efron) to help out, who is soon seduced by the inmate's trashy blonde lover Charlotte (Kidman). The investigation takes them waist-deep through swamps and the steamy underbelly of criminal Florida. A murky and lurid passion project from director Daniels that works without being taken too seriously. Adapted from Pete Dexter's 1995 novel. **107m/C; DVD, Blu-Ray.** Nicole Kidman; Zac Efron; Matthew McConaughey; John Cusack; Macy Gray; David Oyelowo; ***D:*** Lee Daniels; ***W:*** Lee Daniels; ***C:*** Roberto Schaefer; ***M:*** Mario Grigorov.

Papillon **1973 (PG)** McQueen is a criminal sent to Devil's Island in the 1930s determined to escape from the Lemote prison. Hoffman is the swindler he befriends. A series of escapes and recaptures follow. Boxoffice winner based on the autobiographical writings of French thief Henri Charriere. Excellent portrayal of prison life and fine performances from the prisoners. Certain segments would have been better left on the cutting room floor. The film's title refers to the lead's butterfly tattoo. **150m/C; VHS, DVD, Blu-Ray.** Steve McQueen; Dustin Hoffman; Victor Jory; George Coulouris; Anthony Zerbe; ***D:*** Franklin J. Schaffner; ***W:*** Dalton Trumbo; Lorenzo Semple, Jr.; ***C:*** Fred W. Koenekamp; ***M:*** Jerry Goldsmith.

Papillon **2017 (R)** After being framed for the murder of a pimp, charismatic criminal Henri "Papillon" Charriere (Hunnam) is sent to a brutal, violent penal colony in French Guinea. On the way there, he meets counterfeiter Dega (Malek). When Papillon learns that Dega has hidden money, he conceives a plan for them both to stay alive and escape. Though life in the colony is torturous, the pair maintain hope. This remake of the 1973 hit does not have the star power of the original, Malek's character is underdeveloped, and the film lacks an original take on the familiar story. But Hunnam gives an impressive performance. **133m/C; DVD, Blu-Ray.** Rami Malek; Charlie Hunnam; Tommy Flanagan; Eve Hewson; Roland Moller; ***D:*** Michael Noer; ***W:*** Aaron Guzikowski; ***C:*** Hagen Bogdanski; ***M:*** David Buckley.

Paprika 1/2 **2006 (R)** "Tokyo Godfathers" creator Satoshi Kon is back with the warped tale of a company that has created a machine that allows therapists to enter their patient's dreams. Head researcher Dr. Chiba—known to her patients as Paprika—enlists the help of a police detective because a madman has stolen a prototype and is mucking about with the minds of her colleagues. The animation is mind-blowing, but the surreal and disturbing nature of the dream sequences will make it too spicy for some. **90m/C; DVD.** *JP V:* Akio Ohtsuka; Toru Furuya; Satoshi Kon; ***D:*** Seishi Minakimi; ***W:*** Seishi Minakimi; ***C:*** Michiya Kato; ***M:*** Susumu Hirasawa.

Parachute Jumper **1932** Jobless stenographer Patricia 'Alabama' Brent (Davis) meets equally jobless pilot Bill Keller (Fairbanks, Jr.) and his buddy Toodles Cooper (McHugh) in Central Park as they exchange woes about the Depression. Bill gets work with bootlegger Kurt Weber (Carrillo) flying booze from Canada to the U.S. and Alabama works as the gangster's secretary. Then Bill finds out he's also flying in drug shipments and wants to teach the criminal a lesson. Some good aerial footage. Davis disliked the film and gave a lackluster performance but her role is little more than the generic 'girl.' **72m/B; DVD.** Douglas Fairbanks, Jr.; Bette Davis; Frank McHugh; Leo Carrillo; Claire Dodd; ***D:*** Alfred E. Green; ***W:*** John Larkin; ***C:*** James Van Trees.

The Paradine Case 1/2 **1947** A passable Hitchcock romancer about a young lawyer who falls in love with the woman he's defending for murder, not knowing whether she is innocent or guilty. Script could be tighter and more cohesive. $70,000 of the $3 million budget were spent recreating the original Bailey courtroom. Based on the novel by Robert Hichens. **125m/B; VHS, DVD, Blu-Ray.** Gregory Peck; Alida Valli; Ann Todd; Louis Jourdan; Charles Laughton; Charles Coburn; Ethel Barrymore; Leo G. Carroll; ***D:*** Alfred Hitchcock; ***W:*** David O. Selznick; ***C:*** Lee Garmes; ***M:*** Franz Waxman.

Paradise **1982 (R)** Young American boy and beautiful English girl on a 19th-century jaunt through the Middle East are the sole survivors when their caravan is massacred. Left to their own devices, they discover a magnificent oasis and the joys of frolicking naked and experience (surprise) their sexual awakening. Do a double-take: it's the "Blue Lagoon" all over, with a bit more nudity and a lot more sand. **96m/C; VHS, DVD.** Phoebe Cates; Willie Aames; Richard Curnock; Tuvio Tavi; ***D:*** Stuart Gillard; ***W:*** Stuart Gillard; ***C:*** Adam Greenberg; ***M:*** Paul Hoffert.

Paradise **1991 (PG-13)** Young boy is sent to the country to live with his pregnant mother's married friends (Johnson and Griffith). From the outset it is clear that the couple are experiencing marital troubles, making the boy's assimilation all the more difficult. Help arrives in the form of a sprightly 10-year-old girl, with whom he forms a charming relationship. Largely predictable, this remake of the French film "Le Grand Chemin" works thanks to the surprisingly good work of its ensemble cast, and the gorgeous scenery of South Carolina, where the movie was filmed. **112m/C; VHS, DVD, Blu-Ray.** Melanie Griffith; Don Johnson; Elijah Wood; Thora Birch; Sheila McCarthy; Eve Gordon; Louise Latham; Greg Travis; Sarah Trigger; ***D:*** Mary Agnes Donoghue; ***W:*** Mary Agnes Donoghue; ***M:*** David Newman.

Paradise Alley **1978 (PG)** Rocky tires of boxing, decides to join the WWF. Three brothers brave the world of professional wrestling in an effort to strike it rich and move out of the seedy Hell's Kitchen neighborhood of New York, circa 1946. Stallone wrote, stars in, and makes his directorial debut in addition to singing the title song. He makes a few good moves as director, but is ultimately pinned to the canvas. **109m/C; VHS, DVD, Blu-Ray.** Sylvester Stallone; Anne Archer; Armand Assante; Lee Canalito; Kevin Conway; ***D:*** Sylvester Stallone; ***W:*** Sylvester Stallone; ***M:*** Bill Conti.

Paradise: Faith 1/2 *Paradies: Glaube* **2012** Bludgeoning drama without nuance is the second part of Siedl's trilogy following "Paradise: Love." Middle-aged Austrian Anna Maria is part of an ultra-religious Catholic community. When not working at her hospital job, she does missionary work in the mostly-immigrant neighborhoods in Vienna. Anna Maria's own life is upended when her Egyptian-born, Muslim husband Nabil returns after a two-year absence, confined to a wheelchair after a work accident. He doesn't like the changes in his wife and she doesn't seem to want him around at all. German and Arabic with subtitles. **115m/C; DVD.** *AT GE FR* Maria Hofsatter; Nabil Saleh; ***D:*** Ulrich Seidl; ***W:*** Ulrich Seidl; Veronika Franz; ***C:*** Edward Lachman; Wolfgang Thaler.

Paradise for Three **1938** Convoluted story of mistaken identity and romance. Wealthy Rudolph Tobler (Morgan) uses an assumed name when he goes on vacation to an Alpine resort and he is thought to be a poor nobody while poor Fritz Hagedorn (Young) is mistaken for the wealthy Tobler. Predatory Mrs. Mallebre (Astor) is looking for a wealthy meal ticket and goes after both men (just in case) while Fritz romances Rudolph's daughter Hilde (Rice), who's also hiding her identity. **75m/B; DVD.** Frank Morgan; Robert Young; Mary Astor; Florence Rice; Edna May Oliver; Reginald Owen; Sig Rumann; Herman Bing; ***D:*** Edward Buzzell; ***W:*** George Oppenheimer; Harry Ruskin; ***C:*** Leonard Smith; ***M:*** Edward Ward.

Paradise, Hawaiian Style 1/2 **1966 (G)** Out-of-work pilot returns to Hawaii, where he and a buddy start a charter service with two helicopters. Plenty of gals are wooed by "the Pelvis." Filmed four years after Elvis's first Pacific piece, "Blue Hawaii." Presley, showing the first signs of slow-down, displays no surprises here. **91m/C; VHS, DVD.** Elvis Presley; Suzanna Leigh; James Shigeta; Donna Butterworth; Irene Tsu; Julie Parrish; Philip Ahn; Mary Treen; Marianna Hill; John Doucette; Grady Sutton; ***D:*** Michael D. Moore; ***W:*** Anthony Lawrence; Allan Weiss; ***C:*** W. Wallace Kelley; ***M:*** Joseph J. Lilley.

Paradise: Hope *Paradies: Hoffnung* **2013** Unlike the two earlier films, the last pic in Seidl's trilogy is a surprisingly wistful, affectionate (occasionally queasy) drama. Since her mother is traveling in Kenya and her aunt is busy with her missionary work, overweight, 13-year-old Melanie is packed off to a fat camp for the summer. Indifferent to the program, Melanie bonds with her dorm mates, especially 16-year-old Verena, who boasts about her sexual experience. Melanie's own sexual curiosity manifests in her single-minded, inappropriate would-be seduction of the decades-older camp doctor. German with subtitles. **91m/C; DVD.** *AT GE* Melanie Lenz; Verena Lehbauer; Joseph Lorenz; ***D:*** Ulrich Seidl; ***W:*** Ulrich Seidl; Veronika Franz; ***C:*** Edward Lachman; Wolfgang Thaler.

Paradise in Harlem 1/2 **1940** All-black musical in which a cabaret performer witnesses a gangland murder, sees his sick wife die, and is pressured into leaving town by the mob. Have a nice day. **83m/B; VHS, DVD.** Frank Wilson; Mamie Smith; Edna Mae Harris; Juanita Hall; ***D:*** Joseph Seiden; ***W:*** Vincent Valentini; ***C:*** Don Malkames; ***M:*** Lucky Millinder.

Paradise Island **1930** Down-scale musical romance about an ingenue on her way to join her fiance in the South Seas, only to find that he has gambled away his money. The opportunistic saloon owner tries to put the moves on her. Will the two lovers be reunited? **68m/B; VHS, DVD.** Kenneth Harlan; Marceline Day; Thomas Santschi; Paul Hurst; Victor Potel; Gladden James; Will Stanton; ***D:*** Bert Glennon.

Paradise Lost: The Child Murders at Robin Hood Hills **1995** True crime documentary follows the arrest and trial of three misfit teenagers, supposed involved in satanism, for the brutal 1993 murders of three eight-year-old boys in the Arkansas community of West Memphis. They were convicted although no physical evidence placed them at the scene. The filmmakers provide interviews with the teens, their families, and investigators. **150m/C; VHS, DVD.** ***D:*** Joe Berlinger; Bruce Sinofsky; ***C:*** Robert Richman.

Paradise Lost 2: Revelations **1999** Documentary sequel continues to investigate the case of the West Memphis Three, accused of killing three second graders in 1993. This film looks at their appeal, and offers another suspect, the clearly unstable father of one of the victims. **133m/C; DVD.** ***D:*** Joe Berlinger; Bruce Sinofsky; ***M:*** Metallica.

Paradise Lost 3: Purgatory **2011** This third HBO documentary follows 1996's "Paradise Lost: The Child Murders at Robin Hood Hills" and 2000's "Paradise Lost 2: Revelations." Echols, Baldwin, and Miskelly—known as the West Memphis 3—are released in August 2011 after 18 years in prison (Echols was also on Death Row) and agreeing to a plea deal with the Arkansas prosecutor's office. Directors Berliner and Sinofsy summarize the case and offer more evidence pointing to a severe miscarriage of justice in the arrest and murder trial as well as forensic and DNA evidence presented in 2007 pointing to a new suspect. **110m/C; DVD.** ***D:*** Joe Berlinger; Bruce Sinofsky; ***C:*** Robert Richman; ***M:*** Wendy Blackstone. **CABLE**

Paradise Now *Al-Jenna-An* **2005 (PG-13)** Recounts how two young Palestinians go from garage mechanics to suicide bombers preparing for a mission to Tel Aviv. Best friends Said (Nashef) and Khaled (Suliman) live in Nablus on the West Bank and apparently have guerrilla ties. They are informed that they have been chosen and have 24 hours to prepare; the men seem more resigned than fanatical. Director Abu-Assad pays close attention to the details. **90m/C; DVD.** Lubna Azabal; Hiam Abbass; Kais Nashef; Ali Suliman; Amer Hlehel; Ashraf Barhoum; ***D:*** Hany Abu-Assad; ***W:*** Hany Abu-Assad; Bero Beyer; ***C:*** Antoine Heberle. Golden Globes '06: Foreign Film; Ind. Spirit '06: Foreign Film; Natl. Bd. of Review '05: Foreign Film.

Paradise Road **1997 (R)** Fleeing Singapore during WWII, a group of British, American, and Australian women straggle to the shore of Sumatra after their ship is bombed, where they're taken prisoner by the Japanese. The prisoners form a vocal ensemble that crosses their collective national differences and attempts to lift the spirits of the brutalized women. Familiar ground is trod in this prisoner-of-war saga, but the music is genuinely moving, and excellent performances from the cast help sustain interest. The symphonic choral pieces were taken from actual sheet music used by a similar group of real-life WWII prisoners. **115m/C; VHS, DVD.** Glenn Close; Frances McDormand; Julianna Margulies; Pauline Collins; Jennifer Ehle; Elizabeth Spriggs; Tessa Humphries; Sab Shimono; Cate Blanchett; Wendy Hughes; Johanna Ter Steege; Pamela Rabe; Clyde Kusatsu; Stan(ford) Egi; ***D:*** Bruce Beresford; ***W:*** Bruce Beresford; David Giles; ***C:*** Peter James; ***M:*** Margareth Dryburgh; Ross Edwards.

Paradise, Texas **2005 (PG)** Mack Cameron (Bottoms) is an action actor whose career has faded, which is why he agrees to star in an indie drama being made in his Texas hometown. Mack also hopes that bringing his family along will help him reestablish the bonds with his wife (Baxter) and sons. He even mentors his star-struck young co-star (Estus), until a professional setback turns Mack into a morose drunk who needs some tough love (personal and professional). **90m/C; DVD.** Timothy Bottoms; Meredith Baxter; Sheryl Lee; Polly Bergen; Ben Estus; Rider Strong; Brandon Smith; ***D:*** Lorraine Senna; ***W:*** Joe Conway; ***C:*** Shane F. Kelley; ***M:*** Jay Ferguson.

The Paradise Virus **2003** A virologist goes on vacation in the Bahamas just in time for a virus outbreak that threatens to destroy the United States if it escapes the island. Been there, done that—and sadly some version of it will be done again. **95m/C; DVD.** Lorenzo Lamas; Melody Thomas Scott; Ralph (Ralf) Moeller; David Millbern; Gregory Wooddell; Kristen Honey; Jessica Steen; Kimberley Huie; Cling Jung; Arthur Smith; Dennis Banes; ***D:*** Brian Trenchard-Smith; ***W:*** Peter Layton; ***C:*** Albert J. Dunk; ***M:*** David Reynolds. **TV**

The Parallax View 1/2 **1974 (R)** Lee (Prentiss) was a witness to the assassination of a senator and is worried for her own safety, so she goes to newspaper reporter Joe Frady (Beatty) with her fears. He becomes suspicious after her alleged suicide and starts to investigate, discovering a mysterious corporation that hires assassins. As Joe digs deeper, he uncovers more than he bargained for and becomes a pawn in the conspirators' further plans. Beatty is excellent and the conspiracy is never less than believable. A compelling political thriller based on the novel by Loren Singer. **102m/C; VHS, DVD.** Warren Beatty; Hume Cronyn; William Daniels; Paula Prentiss; Kenneth Mars; Bill McKinney; Anthony Zerbe; Walter McGinn; Kelly Thordsen; ***D:*** Alan J. Pakula; ***W:*** David Giler; Lorenzo Semple, Jr.; ***C:*** Gordon Willis; ***M:*** Michael Small. Natl. Soc. Film Critics '74: Cinematog.

Parallel Sons **1995** No-budget first feature from Young has an awkward construction but a couple of fine performances. Teen Seth (Mick) lives in a conservative upstate New York farming community—exactly the wrong place for a young gay white man with a penchant for black culture. He's working at the local diner, which is held up by Knowledge (Mason), a black con shot during an escape from the local prison. Seth shelters Knowledge, whose hostility is gradually overcome by both Seth's concern and a mutual sexual attraction. However, more plot complications lead to melodrama. **93m/C; VHS, DVD.** Gabriel Mick; Laurence Mason; Murphy Guyer; Graham Alex Johnson; Heather Gottlieb; ***D:*** John G. Young; ***W:*** John G. Young; ***C:*** Matt Howe; ***M:*** E.D. Menasche.

Paranoia *Orgasmo; A Beautiful Place to Kill; A Quiet Place to Kill* **1969** Beautiful jet-set widow is trapped in her own Italian villa by a young couple who drug her to get her to perform in various sex orgies, which are probably the most interesting part of this muddled affair. **94m/C; VHS, DVD.** *IT* Carroll Baker; Lou Castel; Colette Descombes; ***D:*** Umberto Lenzi.

Paranoia **1998 (R)** An imprisoned killer uses a computer to harass the surviving member of the family he murdered. **86m/C; VHS, DVD.** Larry Drake; Sally Kirkland; Scott Valentine; Brigitte Bako; ***D:*** Larry Brand; ***W:*** Larry Brand; ***M:*** Martin Trum. **VIDEO**

Paranoia **2013 (PG-13)** Adam Cassidy (Hemsworth) becomes a pawn in a high-stakes game of corporate espionage when the Steve Jobs-esque Nicholas Wyatt (Oldman) forces him to work for him by getting a job at his closest competitor, a tech firm run by Jock Goddard (Ford), and stealing company secrets. This kind of lifeless thriller only makes viewers feel sorry for the talented cast members involved as it fails miserably at producing a single moment of actual suspense. Unrealistic and unentertaining, it only succeeds at making no one care about Adam's fate--a stunningly ineffective protagonist in every way. **106m/C; DVD, Blu-Ray.** Liam Hemsworth; Amber Heard; Gary Oldman; Harrison Ford; Richard Dreyfuss; Lucas Till; Angela Sarafyan; Embeth Davidtz; Julian McMahon; Josh Holloway; ***D:*** Robert Luketic; ***W:*** Jason Hall; Barry L. Levy; ***C:*** David Tattersall; ***M:*** Junkie XL.

Paranoia 1.0 *One Point O* **2004 (R)** Computer programmer Simon J (Sisto) keeps finding mysterious empty packages left in his rundown apartment. Are the boxes really empty? (Maybe they contain an airborne contaminant.) Is one of his freaky neighbors leaving them? Is Simon J just nuts? Well, he's paranoid and having hallucinations, so he's got a reason. Note the tagline: "Are you infected?" **92m/C; DVD.** *RO IC US* Jeremy Sisto; Deborah Kara Unger; Lance Henriksen; Udo Kier; Eugene Byrd; Bruce Payne; Richard Rees; ***D:*** Jeff Renfroe; Marteinn Thorsson; ***W:*** Jeff Renfroe; Marteinn Thorsson; ***C:*** Christopher Soos; ***M:*** Terry Huud.

Paranoiac 1/2 **1962** Greed and terror set in a country mansion. Simon (Reed) wants the family inheritance all to himself even if it means driving sister Eleanor (Scott) insane. This may not be so hard—she's claiming to see their dead brother Tony. Surprise! Tony (Davion) shows up (really throwing Simon for a loop). Reed's evil is tinged with humor although the numerous plot twists can get confusing. First directorial effort for cinematographer Francis. **80m/B; VHS, DVD, Blu-Ray.** *GB* Oliver Reed; Janette Scott; Alex Davion; Liliane Brousse; Sheila Burrell; Maurice Denham; *D:* Freddie Francis; *W:* Jimmy Sangster; *C:* Arthur Grant; *M:* Elisabeth Lutyens.

Paranoid Park 🦴🦴 ½ **2007 (R)** A security guard is murdered at Portland, Oregon's famous skater hangout, Paranoid Park, and police hone in on high school student Alex (Nevins) as a suspect. As the investigation continues, the pieces fall into place both for viewers and for Alex, who finds his own outlets to cope with the consequences of his actions. Clean 35-millimeter is interspersed with grainy Super-8 footage of Alex and friends at the skate park, and a mostly newcomer cast is a plus, giving the teen characters a natural, easy credibility, but with a dark, ambivalent tone. **90m/C; DVD.** Taylor Momsen; Scott Green; Gabe Nevins; Lauren McKinney; Jake Miller; Richard Lu; *D:* Gus Van Sant; *W:* Gus Van Sant; *C:* Christopher Doyle; Rain Kathy Li.

The Paranoids 🦴 ½ **2008** Off-putting, offbeat debut from Medina. Loser hypochondriac Luciano is also an aspiring screenwriter living in Buenos Aires. His childhood buddy Manuel visits with his glum girlfriend Sofia and needles Luciano about his successful Madrid TV series, which Manuel wants to turn into a movie. He offers Luciano the chance to adapt the series but Luciano discovers he's the model for the unsuccessful lead character. Spanish with subtitles. **98m/C; DVD.** *AR* Daniel Hendler; Walter Jakob; Jazmin Stuart; Martin Feldman; Miguel Dedovich; *D:* Gabriel Medina; *W:* Gabriel Medina; Nicolas Gueilburt; *C:* Lucio Bonelli; *M:* Guillermo Guareschi.

Paranormal Activity 🦴🦴🦴 **2009 (R)** Katie (Featherston) and Micah (Sloat) are an otherwise boring, argumentative young couple—except when night comes around and bizarre otherworldly things start happening. A skeptical and ornery Micah sets up a camera to basically shut Katie up, and Katie's admission that this isn't the first supernatural episode in her lifetime doesn't help matters. Director Peli used his low budget (only $15, 000), low special effects, and low gore to go higher on the scare factor. At times slow-moving, the "found" footage and the unknown leads more than make up for the pace. **99m/C; DVD, Blu-Ray, On Demand.** Katie Featherston; Micah Sloat; Michael Bayouth; Amber Armstrong; Mark Fredrichs; Ashley Palmer; Randy McDowell; Tim Piper; Crystal Cartwright; *D:* Oren Peli; *W:* Oren Peli.

Paranormal Activity 2 🦴🦴 ½ **2010 (R)** It's the sequel law of diminishing returns in the more-of-the-same, only-on-a-bigger-budget, popcorn pic. The tie-in is that it's (first flick) Katie's sister Kristi's family who's now in spooky peril. She's the second wife of Daniel, mother to cute toddler Hunter, and stepmom to teenager Ali. This time there's a Latina maid and the family's loyal german shepherd as well. Daniel installs a video security system after their home is broken into but it reveals...well that would be telling, wouldn't it. **91m/C; DVD, Blu-Ray.** Brian Boland; Molly Ephraim; Sprague Grayden; Katie Featherston; Micah Sloat; Vivis; Seth Ginsberg; *D:* Tod Harrison Williams; *W:* Christopher Landon; Michael R. Perry; Tom Pabst; *C:* Michael Simmonds.

Paranormal Activity 3 🦴🦴 ½ **2011 (R)** A paranormal prequel set in 1988 that shows how young sisters Katie and Kristi had their first encounter with demon Toby. The girls' videographer dad Dennis becomes obsessed with figuring out the source of the bump-in-the-night sounds in their house and sets up surveillance cameras while their mother Julie refuses to believe anything supernatural is happening. It's still a creepy horror show that likes to escalate the dread in a low-key manner. **84m/C; DVD, Blu-Ray.** Christopher Nicholas Smith; Katie Featherston; Jessica Tyler Brown; Sprague Grayden; *D:* Lauren Bittner; Chloe Csengery; Oren Peli; *W:* Oren Peli; *C:* Magdalena Gorka.

Paranormal Activity 4 🦴 **2012 (R)** The low-budget horror series that seemed to defy the general law of diminishing returns dives headfirst into the disappointment pool with easily its most ineffective installment. The plot is secondary to the gimmick--another found footage film about ghostly occurrences caught in such a way as to tease the audience for most of the running time and then throw loud scares at them in the last five minutes. Even the least jaded, most loyal fans of this hit franchise must admit that this has grown old (and not so scary). **88m/C; DVD, Blu-Ray.** Kathryn Newton; Matt Shively; Aiden Lovekamp; Brady Allen; Stephen Dunham; Alexondra Lee; Katie Featherston; *D:* Henry Joost; Ariel Schulman; *W:* Christopher Landon; *C:* Doug Emmett.

Paranormal Activity 5: The Ghost Dimension 🦴 **2015 (R)** This franchise has reached its end both creatively and narratively with what has been advertised as the mercifully final installment (although an international gross seven times its budget could change that). The plot that promise to answer all your burning questions centers on a ghost figure named Toby, who has been behind all these paranormal shenanigans. Ryan (Chris J. Murray) finds some video tapes in his house that cross time and space, and, oh, who cares? It's all about jump scares and shoddy editing, as this franchise which wore out its welcome at least three movies ago comes to an end. **88m/C; DVD, Blu-Ray.** Chris Murray; Brit Shaw; Ivy George; Dan Gill; Chloe Csengery; *D:* Gregory Plotkin; *W:* Jason Pagan; Andrew Deutschman; Adam Robitel; Gavin Heffernan; *C:* John Rutland.

Paranormal Activity: The Marked Ones 🦴 ½ **2014 (R)** Breaking from the haunted family tree at the root of the series, this unoriginal spin-off of the found-footage horror hits falsely advertises itself as a standalone film. While security cameras were catching the chaos of the first four films, Jesse (Jacobs) was experiencing a haunting of his own as the target of a coven seeking to possess young men with demons. It's more standard shaky-cam horror with a bit more personality than your standard sequel--and yet also nowhere near enough to make it memorable. **84m/C; DVD, Blu-Ray.** Andrew Jacobs; Jorge Diaz; Gabrielle Walsh; Molly Ephraim; Gloria Sandoval; Richard Cabral; *D:* Christopher Landon; *W:* Christopher Landon; *C:* Gonzalo Amat.

The Paranormal Diaries: Clophill 🦴 ½ **2013** Faux documentary of filmmakers conducting an investigation into the most haunted places in the world experiencing the unexpected in England. Six supernatural investigators travel to the most haunted places in the world to examine such phenomena in person. The group meets their match in the ruins of St. Mary's Church in Clophill, which has attracted darker forces, grave robbers, and body snatchers for centuries. Seeking the truth, the researchers bring their cameras into the darkness around the site for three nights and become ensnared with an ancient evil seeking a passage into our world. **88m/C; DVD, Streaming, Download.** Michael Bartlett; Kevin Gates; Bill King; Mark Knight; Gerry McGovern; *D:* Michael Bartlett; *W:* Kevin Gates; *C:* George Carpenter; *M:* Pete Renton. **VIDEO**

Paranormal Movie 🦴 **2013** A a couple moves into a new house and finds some weird stuff happening and decide to film their swiftly approaching doom for posterity. **86m/C; DVD, Streaming.** Kevin Farley; Carly Craig; Nicky Whelan; Eric Roberts; William Katt; *D:* Kevin Farley; *W:* Lisa Baget; *C:* Alexander Yellen; *M:* Richard Figone. **VIDEO**

ParaNorman 🦴🦴🦴 ½ **2012 (PG)** Stop-motion 3D animated kiddy fright-fest that all ages will enjoy. Norman (Smit-McPhee) sees ghosts and may be the key to saving his small New England town from complete zombie destruction. Using school life in a way that blends John Hughes with John Carpenter was a stroke of genius. And so was everything after that, including the marvelous voice work, perfect design, fantastic score, and clever storytelling. **92m/C; DVD, Blu-Ray.** *V:* Kodi Smit-McPhee; Casey Affleck; John Goodman; Jeff Garlin; Leslie Mann; Elaine Stritch; Anna Kendrick; Tempestt Bledsoe; *D:* Sam Fell; Chris Butler; *W:* Chris Butler; *C:* Tristan Oliver; *M:* Jon Brion.

Parasite WOOF! **1982 (R)** A small town is beset by giant parasites. An "Alien" ripoff originally filmed in 3-D, during that technique's brief return in the early '80s. Bad films like this killed it both the first and second times. An unpardonable mess that comes off as a stinky sixth-grade film project. **90m/C; VHS, DVD, Blu-Ray.** Bob Glaudini; Demi Moore; Luca Bercovici; Cherie Currie; Gale Robbins; James Davidson; Al Fann; Cheryl "Rainbeaux" Smith; Vivian Blaine; *D:* Charles Band; *W:* Alan J. Adler; Frank Levering; Michael Shoob; *C:* Mac Ahlberg; *M:* Richard Band.

Parasite 🦴 ½ **2003 (R)** Ah, the far reaches of the North Sea...what a perfect spot to gather a team of engineers on an old oil rig to test out some cleaning fluid. But those pesky environmental do-gooders have to come and ruin the fun by hijacking the rig and holding them captive. Then to really top things off there's the parasite that's absolutely famished and happy to see so many items on the menu. **93m/C; VHS, DVD.** *GB* Saskia Gould; Conrad Whitaker; G.W. Stevens; Gary Condes; Margaret Thompson; Oliver Price; Michelle Acuna; *D:* Andrew Prendergast; *W:* Andrew Prendergast; Alan Coulson; Paul Mackman; *C:* Tom Wright; *M:* Tom Bible. **VIDEO**

Parasite 🦴🦴🦴 ½ *Gisaengchung* **2019 (R)** A genre-bending masterpiece that demands to be watched with minimal advance knowledge of plot. Living in a basement hovel in Seoul, the unambitious yet creatively scheming Kim family stays afloat through odd jobs and leeching off their neighbors' amenities. After the son wrangles a job as private tutor to the wealthy Parks family, the two families become intertwined in a symbiotic relationship. That is, until an unexpected element is introduced. The result is a gorgeously filmed, socially satirical, darkly comedic thriller. **132m/C; Blu-Ray, Download.** *SK* Kang-ho Song; Sun-kyun Lee; Yeo-jeong Jo; Woo-sik Choi; Hye-jin Jang; *D:* Joon-ho Bong; *W:* Joon-ho Bong; Jin Won Han; *C:* Kyung-Pyo Hong; *M:* Jaeil Jung. Oscars '19: Director (Bong), Film, Foreign Film, Screenplay; British Acad. '19: Foreign Film, Orig. Screenplay; Golden Globes '20: Foreign Film; Ind. Spirit '20: Foreign Film; Screen Actors Guild '19: Cast; Writers Guild '19: Orig. Screenplay.

Parasite Eve 🦴🦴🦴 **1997** Scientist Dr. Nagashima (Mikami) has discovered that mitochondria, the organisms which provide energy for cells, appear to have their own DNA and life-cycle. Nagashima puts this theory to work in his research, as he attempts to cure diseases in lab animals, using the mitochondrian energy. When Nagashima's young wife Kiyomi (Hakuzi) is killed in an auto accident, Nagashima takes her liver in order to try and clone her, using the energy of the mitochondria. He doesn't realize is that her death may be the first step in an evolutionary leap, in which the mitochondria will rise up and dominate the world. **120m/C; DVD.** *JP* Hiroshi Mikami; Riona Hazuki; Tomoko Nakajima; *D:* Masayuki Ochiai.

Parasomnia 🦴🦴 **2008 (R)** Effective, twisted horror fairytale with a literal Sleeping Beauty. Laura suffers from parasomnia—a rare sleep disorder in which she rarely regains consciousness. This plays into the sicko needs of imprisoned serial killer/mesmerist Volpe, who's in the same mental hospital and can enter her unconsciousness. Laura has a protector in Danny but Volpe isn't so easily thwarted. **98m/C; DVD, Blu-Ray.** Cherilyn Wilson; Patrick Kilpatrick; Dylan Purcell; Jeffrey Combs; Timothy Bottoms; Kathryn Leigh Scott; *D:* William Malone; *W:* William Malone; *C:* Christian Sebaldt; *M:* Nicholas Pike. **VIDEO**

Pardners 🦴🦴 ½ **1956** Spoiled New York millionaire (Lewis) becomes the sheriff of small western town, with Martin as a ranch foreman. The two team up to rid the town of bad guys and romance two local cuties. Western spoof (with music) is a remake of 1936's "Rhythm on the Range." **88m/C; DVD.** Jerry Lewis; Dean Martin; Lori Nelson; Jackie Loughery; Jeff Morrow; John Baragrey; Agnes Moorehead; Lon Chaney, Jr.; Milton Frome; Lee Van Cleef; Jack Elam; Bob Steele; Emory Parnell; *D:* Norman Taurog; *W:* Sidney Sheldon; Jerry Davis.

Pardon My Sarong 🦴🦴 ½ **1942** Bud and Lou star as Chicago bus drivers who end up shipwrecked on a South Pacific island when they get involved with notorious jewel thieves. The island natives think Lou is a god! Standard Abbott & Costello fare. **83m/B; VHS, DVD.** Bud Abbott; Lou Costello; Virginia Bruce; Robert Paige; Lionel Atwill; Leif Erickson; William Demarest; Samuel S. Hinds; *D:* Erle C. Kenton; *C:* Milton Krasner.

Pardon Us 🦴🦴 ½ *Jail Birds* **1931** Laurel and Hardy are thrown into prison for bootlegging. Plot meanders along aimlessly, but the duo have some inspired moments. The first Laurel and Hardy feature. **78m/B; VHS, DVD.** Stan Laurel; Oliver Hardy; June Marlowe; James Finlayson; *D:* James Parrott; *W:* H.M. Walker; *C:* Jack Stevens.

The Parent Trap 🦴🦴 ½ **1961** Mills plays a dual role in this heartwarming comedy as twin sisters Susan and Sharon, who were separated at birth by their divorcing parents Mitch (Keith) and Maggie (O'Hara), discover each other during a stay a summer camp. They decide to switch lives and when they realize that dear old dad is about to get married to just the wrong woman (Barnes), the twins conspire to bring their divorced parents back together. Well-known Disney fluff. Followed by several made-for-TV sequels featuring the now grown-up twins (Mills reprised her role). **127m/C; VHS, DVD.** Hayley Mills; Maureen O'Hara; Brian Keith; Charlie Ruggles; Una Merkel; Leo G. Carroll; Joanna Barnes; Cathleen Nesbitt; Ruth McDevitt; *D:* David Swift; *W:* David Swift; *C:* Lucien Ballard; *M:* Paul J. Smith.

The Parent Trap 🦴🦴 ½ **1998 (PG)** Updated remake of Disney's 1961 family film about long-separated identical twins, Hallie and Annie (Lohan), who meet accidentally at camp and decide to reunite their divorced parents. Quaid is Napa vineyard-owning dad while Richardson is London fashion designer mom. The twins switch places and foil gold-digger publicist Meredith (Hendrix) in order to get their parents back together. Since it's both Disney and a remake, you can assume that it works. "Let's Get Together," the song that the guitar strummin' Hayley Mills made popular with the original, makes a cameo in an elevator. **128m/C; VHS, DVD, Blu-Ray.** Dennis Quaid; Natasha Richardson; Lindsay Lohan; Polly Holliday; Elaine Hendrix; Joanna Barnes; Ronnie Stevens; Lisa Ann Walter; Simon Kunz; Maggie Wheeler; *D:* Nancy Meyers; *W:* Nancy Meyers; Charles Shyer; David Swift; *C:* Dean Cundey; *M:* Alan Silvestri.

The Parent Trap II 🦴🦴 ½ **1986 (G)** Mills returns to her dual roles from the 1961 Disney movie with a charm that the ABC sequel doesn't possess (although it's still a cute flick). Tween Nikki doesn't want to move from Florida to New York with divorced mom Sharon. So she and best friend Mary scheme to get Sharon romantically involved with Mary's widowed dad, Bill. When they don't strike sparks, Nikki calls in married Aunt Susan, mom's identical twin, to rescue their plan. **81m/C; DVD.** Hayley Mills; Tom Skerritt; Carrie Kei Helm; Bridgette Andersen; Alex Harvey; *D:* Ronald F. Maxwell; *W:* Stu Krieger; *C:* Peter Stein; *M:* Charles Fox. **TV**

Parental Guidance 🦴🦴 *Kinfolks* **1998 (R)** Sean (Lee) is part of a crazy extended family in South Central L.A. who is reluctant to bring his upscale girlfriend Lisa (Johnson) home for the family's Christmas dinner. **87m/C; VHS, DVD.** Maia Campbell; Stacii Jae Johnson; Casey Lee; *D:* A.M. Cali; *W:* A.M. Cali; *C:* Scott Edelstein; *M:* Horace Washington.

Parental Guidance 🦴 **2012 (PG)** Bette Midler and Billy Crystal return to the big screen for the first time in years and seem to have brought a script from the '80s peak of their comedy popularity. The pair play grandparents tasked with taking care of their daughter's rugrats as their old-fashioned child-rearing techniques clash with 21st-century kids. To call the film stale would be a compliment as Crystal and Midler mug their way through a truly horrendous script that only reminds one that they used to make broad family comedies more often, like back when Billy Crystal was a star. **104m/C; DVD, Blu-Ray.** Billy Crystal; Bette Midler; Marisa Tomei; Tom Everett Scott; Bailee Madison; Joshua Rush; Kyle Harrison Breitkopf; *D:* Andy Flickman; *W:* Lisa Addario; Joe Syracuse; *C:* Dean Semler; *M:* Marc Shaiman.

Parenthood 🦴🦴🦴 **1989 (PG-13)** Four grown siblings and their parents struggle with various levels of parenthood. From the college drop-out, to the nervous single mother, to the yuppie couple raising an overachiever, every possibility is explored, including the perspective from the older generation, portrayed by Robards. Genuinely funny with dramatic moments that work most of the time, with an affecting performance from Martin and Wiest. Director Howard has four kids and was inspired to make this film when on a European jaunt with them. **124m/C; VHS, DVD, Blu-Ray.** Steve Martin; Mary Steenburgen; Dianne Wiest; Martha Plimpton; Keanu Reeves; Tom Hulce; Jason Robards, Jr.; Rick Moranis; Harley Jane Kozak; Joaquin Rafael (Leaf) Phoenix; Paul (Link) Linke; Dennis Dugan; ***D:*** Ron Howard; ***W:*** Ron Howard; Lowell Ganz; Babaloo Mandel; ***C:*** Donald McAlpine; ***M:*** Randy Newman.

Parents **1989 (R)** Dark satire of middle class suburban life in the '50s, centering on a young boy who discovers that his parents aren't getting their meat from the local butcher. Gives new meaning to leftovers and boasts a very disturbing barbecue scene. Balaban's debut is a strikingly visual and creative gorefest with definite cult potential. The eerie score is by Badalamenti, who also composed the music for "Blue Velvet," "Wild at Heart," and "Twin Peaks." **81m/C; VHS, DVD, Blu-Ray.** Randy Quaid; Mary Beth Hurt; Bryan Madorsky; Sandy Dennis; Kathryn Grody; Deborah Rush; Graham Jarvis; Juno Mills-Cockell; ***D:*** Bob Balaban; ***W:*** Christopher Hawthorne; ***C:*** Robin Vidgeon; Ernest Day; ***M:*** Angelo Badalamenti; Jonathan Elias; Sherman Foote.

Pariah **1998 (R)** A drama based on real events. An interracial couple, Steve (Jones) and Sam (Williams), is attacked by a gang of neo-Nazi skinheads one evening, forever changing their lives. Sam is also gang raped and later commits suicide. To enact his own revenge, Steve decides to join the gang and undermine them from within their ranks. After becoming part of the group, Steve better understands their motivations, including poverty and being rejected by society, and starts to feel a kinship with them. When Steve is asked to kill someone, his loyalty to the gang wavers. **105m/C; DVD, Streaming.** Damon Jones; David Oren Ward; David Lee Wilson; Aimee Chaffin; Angela Jones; Anna Padgett; Dan Weene; Anne Zupa; Brandon Slater; Jason Posey; Elexa Williams; ***D:*** Randolph Kret; ***W:*** Randolph Kret; ***C:*** Nils Erickson; ***M:*** Scott Grusin. **VIDEO**

Pariah **2011 (R)** Driven by honest performances from Oduye and Wayans, this sensitive and heartfelt low-budget debut feature from writer/director Rees tackles a subject that film has not really dealt with before, being an African-American teenage lesbian in the inner city. Set in Brooklyn, Alike (Oduye) is a 17-year-old coming to terms with her own homosexuality while knowing that she needs to hide it from her family and classmates. Walks a tightrope that could have easily descended into cliche and stereotype but instead Rees and her talented cast find the truth. **86m/C; DVD, Blu-Ray.** Adepero Oduye; Pernell Walker; Aasha Davis; Kim Wayans; Charles Parnell; Sahra Mellesse; Raymond Anthony Thomas; Shamika Cotton; ***D:*** Dee Rees; ***W:*** Dee Rees; ***C:*** Bradford Young.

Paris **2008 (R)** French family dramedy. Professional chorus dancer Pierre (Duris) is forced to quit his cabaret job because of serious heart problems. His frumpy, divorced social worker sister Elise (Binoche) and her three kids move into his small Paris apartment so she can care for him while Pierre awaits a heart transplant. Meanwhile, he mostly stares out his window or interacts with various characters while wandering the streets. English and French with subtitles. **128m/C; DVD, Blu-Ray, On Demand.** *FR* Romain Duris; Juliette Binoche; Fabrice Luchini; Melanie Laurent; Albert Dupontel; Francois Cluzet; Olivia Bonamy; Gilles Lellouche; Julie Ferrier; ***D:*** Cedric Klapisch; ***W:*** Cedric Klapisch; ***C:*** Christophe Beaucarne; ***M:*** Loik Dury.

Paris After Dark **1943** After being released from a POW camp, Jean Blanchard (Dorn) returns home and thinks his nurse wife, Yvonne (Marshall), is having an affair with her doctor boss, Andre Marbel (Sanders). Instead, he learns they are both working for the resistance and he finally decides to fight the Nazis by joining himself. **84m/B; DVD.** George Sanders; Brenda Marshall; Philip Dorn; Marcel Dalio; Madeleine LeBeau; ***D:*** Leonide Moguy; ***W:*** Harold Buchman; ***C:*** Lucien N. Andriot; ***M:*** Hugo Friedhofer.

Paris Blues **1/2 1961** Two jazz musicians, one white, one black, strive for success in Paris and become involved with American tourists who want to take them back to the States. Score by Duke Ellington and an appearance by Armstrong make it a must-see for jazz fans. **100m/B; DVD, Blu-Ray.** Paul Newman; Sidney Poitier; Joanne Woodward; Diahann Carroll; Louis Armstrong; Barbara Lange; ***D:*** Martin Ritt; ***W:*** Jack Sher; Walter Bernstein; ***M:*** Duke Ellington.

Paris Can Wait *Bonjour Anne* **2017 (PG)** Eleanor Coppola's solo writing/directing debut seems semi-autobiographical in the set-up of a plot. Anne (Lane), wife of a Hollywood producer, ventures to Paris from Cannes with hubby's stereotypically French partner (Viard), learning to appreciate France and herself along the way. Lane is radiant and charming, and the film is beautifully and seductively filmed, but the trite circumstances and overly cheesy dialogue (especially Viard's), takes away from the enjoyment of what could have been a nice summer counter-programming date flick. **92m/C; DVD, Blu-Ray.** Diane Lane; Alec Baldwin; Arnaud Viard; Cedric Monnet; Elodie Navarre; ***D:*** Eleanor Coppola; ***W:*** Eleanor Coppola; ***C:*** Crystel Fournier; ***M:*** Laura Karpman.

Paris, France **1994 (NC-17)** Lucy (Hope) is a frustrated writer, living in Toronto, who decides the pursuit of sexual passion will unleash her blocked creative urges. Her main partner is poet Sloan (Outerbridge), the young man Lucy is trying to fashion in the image of a deceased Parisian lover, and also the man whose poetry her husband (and publisher) Michael (Ertmanis) is promoting. Lots of self-delusion and literary pretensions as well as erotic grappling. Adapted from the novel by Tom Walmsley. **111m/C; VHS, DVD.** *CA* Leslie Hope; Peter Outerbridge; Victor Ertmanis; Raoul Trujillo; Dan Lett; ***D:*** Gerard Ciccoritti; ***W:*** Tom Walmsley; ***M:*** John McCarthy.

Paris Holiday **1/2 1957** An actor heading for Paris to buy a noted author's latest screenplay finds mystery and romance. Entertaining chase scenes as the characters try to find the elusive script. **100m/C; VHS, DVD, Blu-Ray.** Bob Hope; Fernandel; Anita Ekberg; Martha Hyer; Preston Sturges; ***D:*** Gerd Oswald; ***W:*** Edmund Beloin; Dean Reisner; ***C:*** Roger Hubert.

Paris Is Burning **1991 (R)** Livingston's documentary portrayal of New York City's transvestite balls where men dress up, dance, and compete in various categories. Filmed between 1985 and 1989, this is a compelling look at a subculture of primarily black and Hispanic men and the one place they can truly be themselves. Madonna noted this look and attitude (much watered down) in her song "Vogue." **71m/C; VHS, DVD, Blu-Ray.** Dorian Corey; Pepper Labeija; Venus Xtravaganza; Octavia St. Laurant; Willi Ninja; Anji Xtravaganza; Freddie Pendavis; Junior Labeija; ***D:*** Jennie Livingston; ***C:*** Paul Gibson. Natl. Film Reg. '16; Natl. Soc. Film Critics '91: Feature Doc.; Sundance '91: Grand Jury Prize.

Paris, je t'aime *Paris, I Love You* **2006 (R)** Eighteen—count 'em—eighteen uneven vignettes by 20 international directors all set in various Parisian neighborhoods. Some are little slice of life tales while others are fantasies (vampires?). Some are about love and some about friendship and some are serious while some are lighthearted. All are so brief that if one doesn't strike your fancy, the next one may, especially given the variety of the cast. English and French with subtitles. **120m/C; DVD.** *FR SI* Leila Bekhti; Marianne Faithfull; Elias McConnell; Gaspard Ulliel; Steve Buscemi; Catalina Sandino Moreno; Barbet Schroeder; Sergio Castellitto; Miranda Richardson; Leonor Watling; Juliette Binoche; Willem Dafoe; Hippolyte Girardot; Yolande Moreau; Nick Nolte; Ludivine Sagnier; Bob Hoskins; Fanny Ardant; Maggie Gyllenhaal; Aïssa Maïga; Elijah Wood; Emily Mortimer; Rufus Sewell; Natalie Portman; Melchior Beslon; Gerard Depardieu; Ben Gazzara; Gena Rowlands; Margo Martindale; Bruno Podalydes; Florence Muller; Cyril Descours; Julie Bataille; Axel Kiener; Li Xin; Paul Putner; Lionel Dray; Seydou Boro; Olga Kurylenko; ***D:*** Gerard Depardieu; Gurinder Chadha; Gus Van Sant; Joel Coen; Ethan Coen; Walter Salles; Daniela Thomas; Christopher Doyle; Isabel Coixet; Sylvain Chomet; Alfonso Cuarón; Richard LaGravenese; Olivier Assayas; Oliver Schmitz; Vincenzo Natali; Wes Craven; Alexander Payne; Tom Tykwer; Noburhiro Suwa; ***W:*** Gurinder Chadha; Gus Van Sant; Joel Coen; Ethan Coen; Walter Salles; Daniela Thomas; Christopher Doyle; Isabel Coixet; Sylvain Chomet; Alfonso Cuarón; Richard LaGravenese; Olivier Assayas; Oliver Schmitz; Vincenzo Natali; Wes Craven; Alexander Payne; Tom Tykwer; Noburhiro Suwa; ***C:*** Christopher Doyle; Mathieu Poirot-Delpech; Pascal Rabaud; Bruno Delbonnel; Eric Gautier; Jean-Claude Larrieu; Pascal Marti; Eric Guichard; Gerard Sterin; Michel Amathieu; Michael Seresin; Pierre Aim; J. Eddie Peck; Tetsuo Nagata; David Quesemand; Frank Greibe; ***M:*** Tom Tykwer; Michael Andrews; Reinhold Heil; Johnny Klimek.

Paris, Texas **1/2 1983 (PG)** After four years a drifter returns to find his son is being raised by his brother because the boy's mother has also disappeared. He tries to reconnect with the boy. Introspective script acclaimed by many film critics, but others found it to be too slow. **145m/C; VHS, DVD, Blu-Ray.** *FR GE* Harry Dean Stanton; Nastassja Kinski; Dean Stockwell; Hunter Carson; Aurore Clement; ***D:*** Wim Wenders; ***W:*** Sam Shepard; L.M. Kit Carson; ***M:*** Ry Cooder. British Acad. '84: Director (Wenders); Cannes '84: Film.

Paris 36 **1/2** *Faubourg 36* **2008 (PG-13)** Old-fashioned musical drama about workers' rights and politics in 1930s Paris. Labor/management tensions escalate after the Popular Front left-wing party is elected. Working-class stage manager Germain Pigoli (Jugnot) is distraught when scheming bigwig Galapiat (Donnadieu) closes down the theater but he manages to reopen it with the help of a couple of performers and a political activist. French with subtitles. **120m/C; DVD.** *FR* Gerard Jugnot; Barnard Pierre Donnadieu; Kad Merad; Clovis Cornillac; Elisabeth Vitali; Maxence Perrin; Nora Arnezeder; ***D:*** Christophe Barratier; ***W:*** Christophe Barratier; ***C:*** Tom Stern.

Paris When It Sizzles **1964** A screenwriter and his secretary fall in love while working on a film in Paris, confusing themselves with the script's characters. Star-studded cast deserves better than this lame script. Shot on location in Paris. Holden's drinking—he ran into a brick wall while under the influence—and some unresolved romantic tension between him and Hepburn affected shooting. Dietrich, Sinatra, Astaire, Ferrer, and Curtis show up for a party on the set. **110m/C; VHS, DVD.** William Holden; Audrey Hepburn; Gregoire Aslan; Raymond Bussieres; Tony Curtis; Fred Astaire; Frank Sinatra; Noel Coward; Marlene Dietrich; Mel Ferrer; ***D:*** Richard Quine; ***W:*** George Axelrod; ***C:*** Charles B(ryant) Lang, Jr.; ***M:*** Nelson Riddle.

A Parisian Romance **1/2 1932** A playboy Baron finds himself actually falling in love with Claudette but thinks she would have a more secure life with his rival Victor. **76m/B; DVD.** Lew Cody; Marion Shilling; Gilbert Roland; Joyce Compton; Yola D'Avril; Nicholas Soussanin; ***D:*** Chester M. Franklin; ***W:*** Frederick Hugh Herbert; ***C:*** Tom Galligan; Harry Neumann.

The Park Is Mine **1985** A deranged and desperate Vietnam vet takes hostages in Central Park. Semi-infamous film, notable for being the first movie made for HBO, and for being filmed in Toronto, before the inexpensive practice of filming in Canada became widespread. **102m/C; VHS, Blu-Ray, Streaming.** Tommy Lee Jones; Yaphet Kotto; Helen Shaver; ***D:*** Steven Hilliard Stern; ***W:*** Stephen Peters; ***C:*** Laszlo George; ***M:*** Tangerine Dream. **CABLE**

Park Row **1/2 1952** Writer/director Samuel Fuller also financed his unsuccessful, old-fashioned independent film, which is set in 1880s New York City. Dedicated reporter Phineas Mitchell (Evans) starts his own small muckraking newspaper, which angers his former employer, Charity Hackett (Welch). She uses multiple dirty tricks to try to put the upstart out of business. **83m/B; DVD.** Gene Evans; Mary Welch; Bela Kovacs; Herbert (Hayes) Heyes; J.M. Kerrigan; Forrest Taylor; ***D:*** Samuel Fuller; ***W:*** Samuel Fuller; ***C:*** John L. Russell; ***M:*** Paul Dunlap.

Parked **1/2** *Jumissa* **2010** Fred (Colm Meaney) is a native Irishman temporarily homeless while awaiting public housing. He befriends another homeless man, a drug addicted youth who may be the low down criminal everyone believes Fred to be. **94m/C; DVD, Blu-Ray.** *FI IR* Colm Meaney; Colin Morgan; Milka Ahlroth; Stuart Graham; Michael McElhatton; ***D:*** Darragh Byrne; ***W:*** Ciaran Creagh; ***C:*** John Conroy; ***M:*** Niall Byrne. **VIDEO**

Parker **1/2 2013 (R)** Master of disguise and expert thief Parker (Statham) is left for dead when his brothers-in-crime double-cross him. Going undercover, he tracks his former associates to Florida where they're about to pull off a big score. He recruits real estate agent Leslie (Lopez) to help him hide out as a wealthy Texan as he plots his revenge. Some flat action scenes and bloody awkward brutality add up to a barely competent clunker of a crime thriller. Luckily, Statham and Lopez's chemistry and natural charisma save it from complete collapse. Adapted from a Donald E. Westlake novel. **118m/C; DVD, Blu-Ray.** Jason Statham; Jennifer Lopez; Michael Chiklis; Clifton (Gonzalez) Collins, Jr.; Wendell Pierce; Nick Nolte; ***D:*** Taylor Hackford; ***W:*** John J. McLaughlin; ***C:*** J. Michael Muro; ***M:*** David Buckley.

Parkland **2013 (PG-13)** Busy drama looks at the ordinary people caught up in the 11/22/63 JFK assassination in Dallas, Texas. Secret Service agent Roy Kellerman is riding in the presidential limo; businessman Abraham Zapruder brings his home movie camera to film the motorcade; Parkland Hospital doctors Jim Carrico and Malcom Perry, along with head nurse Doris Nelson, are working the ER; FBI agent James Hosty is told to destroy his Oswald file; while Robert Oswald and his wacko mom, Marguerite, each deal with the aftermath of Lee Harvey's crime in very different ways. And that's only some of what Landesman tries to put into his overstuffed pic. **93m/C; DVD, Blu-Ray.** Zac Efron; James Badge Dale; Marcia Gay Harden; Colin Hanks; Jacki Weaver; Ron Livingston; Paul Giamatti; Tom Welling; Billy Bob Thornton; Jeremy Strong; ***D:*** Peter Landesman; ***W:*** Peter Landesman; ***C:*** Barry Ackroyd; ***M:*** James Newton Howard.

Parlor, Bedroom and Bath *Romeo in Pyjamas* **1931** A family tries to keep a young woman from seeing that her love interest is flirting with other prospects. Doesn't live up to the standard Keaton set in his silent films. Keaton spoke French and German for foreign versions. **75m/B; VHS, DVD.** Buster Keaton; Charlotte Greenwood; Cliff Edwards; Reginald Denny; ***D:*** Edward Sedgwick; ***W:*** Richard Schayer; ***C:*** Leonard Smith.

Parnell **1937** Overstuffed, expensive boxoffice failure starring a miscast Gable as Irish nationalist Charles Stuart Parnell. Amidst his tireless battles with Great Britain for home rule, he falls in love with married Katie O'Shea (Loy). Her estranged husband Willie (Marshal) tries blackmailing Parnell and then names him in the divorce suit, causing a scandal and ruining his political career. **118m/B; DVD.** Clark Gable; Myrna Loy; Alan Marshal; Edna May Oliver; Edmund Gwenn; Billie Burke; Donald Crisp; ***D:*** John M. Stahl; ***W:*** John Van Druten; S.N. Behrman; ***C:*** Karl Freund; ***M:*** William Axt.

Parole, Inc. **1949** FBI takes on the underground in this early crime film. Criminals on parole have not served their sentences, and the mob is responsible. A meagerly financed yawner. **71m/B; VHS, DVD.** Michael O'Shea; Evelyn Ankers; Turhan Bey; Lyle Talbot; ***D:*** Alfred Zeisler; ***W:*** Sherman Lowe; ***C:*** Gilbert Warrenton; ***M:*** Alexander Laszlo.

Parrish **1/2 1961** Parrish McLean (Donohue) is a very ambitious young man, determined to make it in the rich world of the tobacco growers of the Connecticut River Valley. But his ruthless tobacco king stepfather (Malden) would like to thwart his plans. As befits Donohue's teen idol status, he also gets to romance three beautiful girls. Very silly and much too long. Based on the novel by Mildred Savage. **138m/C; VHS, DVD.** Troy Donahue; Claudette Colbert; Karl Malden; Dean Jagger; Diane McBain; Connie Stevens; Sharon Hugueny; Dub Taylor; Hampton Fancher; Bibi Osterwald; Madeline Sherwood; Sylvia Miles; Carroll O'Connor; Vincent Gardenia; ***D:*** Delmer Daves; ***W:*** Delmer Daves; ***C:*** Harry Stradling, Sr.; ***M:*** Max Steiner.

Parting Glances 🦴🦴🦴 **1986 (R)** Low-budget but acclaimed film shows the relationship between two gay men and how they deal with a close friend's discovery of his exposure to the AIDS virus. Touching and realistic portrayals make this a must see. In 1990 Sherwood died of AIDS without completing any other films. **90m/C; VHS, DVD.** John Bolger; Richard Ganoung; Steve Buscemi; Adam Nathan; Patrick Tull; Kathy Kinney; ***D:*** Bill Sherwood; ***W:*** Bill Sherwood; ***C:*** Jacek Laskus.

Parting Shots 🦴 1/2 **1998** Harry's feeling like a bunch of folks have done him wrong—from his ex-wife to his thieving best buddy to the local chef—so once he learns he's only got six weeks to live, he aims to settle the score...with a gun. "Death Wish" director Winner shoots for edgy humor but misses. **98m/C; VHS, DVD.** Chris Rea; Felicity Kendal; Bob Hoskins; Ben Kingsley; Joanna Lumley; Oliver Reed; Diana Rigg; John Cleese; Gareth Hunt; Peter Davison; Patrick Ryecart; Edward Hardwicke; Nicholas Gecks; Ruby Snape; Nicola Bryant; Brian Poyser; Nicky Henson; Caroline Langrishe; Taryn Kay; Alison Reynolds; Roland Curram; Craig Jelley; Jenny Logan; Sarah Reeves; Anthony Smee; Donald Standen; Nathan Weaver; ***D:*** Michael Winner; ***W:*** Michael Winner; Nick Mead; ***C:*** Ousama Rawi; ***M:*** Chris Rea; Les Reed. **VIDEO**

Partition 🦴🦴 **2007** Predictable historical romance/drama. Gian Singh (Mistry) is an ex-soldier from a Sikh regiment who fought for the Brits in WWII. In 1947, when India and Pakistan have become separate countries, Gian watches the violent upheavals from his Punjab village and then rescues Muslim refugee Naseem (Kruek) from an angry mob. The two fall in love and marry despite the religious complications but Naseem eventually hears word of her family in Pakistan and goes to see them. Her brothers are horrified that she's married an enemy and hold her prisoner, which causes more trouble when Gian travels to bring his wife home. **115m/C; DVD.** *CA* Jimi Mistry; Kristin Kreuk; Neve Campbell; John Light; Madhur Jaffrey; Irfan Khan; Jesse Moss; ***D:*** Vic Sarin; ***W:*** Vic Sarin; Patricia Finn; ***C:*** Vic Sarin; ***M:*** Brian Tyler.

Partner 🦴🦴🦴 **1968** An extremely shy young man invents a strong alter ego to cope with the world but this second personality comes to dominate—with tragic results. In Italian with English subtitles. **110m/C; VHS, DVD.** *IT* Pierre Clementi; Stefania Sandrelli; Tina Aumont; ***D:*** Bernardo Bertolucci; ***W:*** Bernardo Bertolucci; ***C:*** Ugo Piccone; ***M:*** Ennio Morricone.

Partners 🦴🦴 **1982 (R)** A straight, macho cop must pose as the lover of a gay cop to investigate the murder of a gay man in Los Angeles' homosexual community. Sets out to parody "Cruising"; unfortunately, the only source of humor the makers could find was in ridiculous homosexual stereotypes that are somewhat offensive and often unfunny. **93m/C; VHS, DVD, Blu-Ray.** Ryan O'Neal; John Hurt; Kenneth McMillan; Robyn Douglass; Jay Robinson; Rick Jason; ***D:*** James Burrows; ***W:*** Francis Veber; ***M:*** Georges Delerue.

Partners 🦴🦴 **1999 (R)** All of the usual suspects are rounded up for this action comedy. Mild-mannered Bob (Paymer) steals a super-secret computer program from his company. Then it's stolen from him by hunky thief Axel (Van Dien). A series of double-crosses and chases—involving the obligatory Caddy convertible—ensue. Toss in the sexy girlfriend (Angel) and a cheap L.A. motel with a heart-shaped bed. **90m/C; VHS, DVD.** Casper Van Dien; Vanessa Angel; David Paymer; Jenifer Lewis; Yuji Okumoto; Donna Pescow; ***D:*** Joey Travolta; ***W:*** Jeff Ferrell; ***C:*** Kristian Bernier; ***M:*** Jeff Lass.

Partners 🦴 **2009** Brooklyn police detectives Perez (Iengo) and Clarkson (Piacente) naively believe they can stem the rising tide of crime after a new criminal decides he can take on the Mafia and drug gangs for control of crime in the city. Predictable buddy crime drama. **100m/C; DVD.** Christopher Iengo; Adam Piacente; ***D:*** Peter James Iengo; ***W:*** Peter James Iengo; ***C:*** Peter James Iengo; Joe Janasiewicz; ***M:*** Guy Michelmore.

Partners in Crime 🦴🦴 **1999 (R)** Local detective Gene Reardon (Hauer) is assigned to investigate the kidnapping of a wealthy man from a small town. But soon the FBI is called in, including Reardon's ex-wife Wallis Longworth (Porizkova). Then the victim turns up dead on Reardon's property and he's suddenly suspect numero uno. Since Wallis doesn't think Gene's guilty, she decides to secretly help him prove who really done it. **90m/C; VHS, DVD.** Rutger Hauer; Paulina Porizkova; Michael Flynn; Andrew Dolan; ***D:*** Jennifer Warren; ***W:*** Brett Lewis; ***C:*** Stevan Larner. **VIDEO**

Parts Per Billion 🦴 **2014 (R)** A biohazard used in a terrorist war is spreading and may wipe out humanity. The threat is intertwined with that of three couples (played by actors such as Hartnett, Rowlands, Bledel, Langella, and Dawson, who all probably regret the decision) coming to terms with the end of the world. It's a very dull doomsday. **102m/C; DVD, Blu-Ray.** Josh Hartnett; Teresa Palmer; Penn Badgley; Rosario Dawson; Frank Langella; Alexis Bledel; ***Cameo(s):*** Gena Rowlands; ***D:*** Brian Horiuchi; ***W:*** Brian Horiuchi; ***C:*** John Guleserian; ***M:*** Mark Kilian. **VIDEO**

The Parts You Lose 🦴🦴 **2019** Wesley (Murphy) is an observant deaf boy living in rural North Dakota. Though his mother Gail (Winstead) has learned sign language to communicate with her son, Wesley's father Ronnie (McNairy) will not and sees his son's disability as something that is unfair to him personally. One winter day, Wesley finds an injured criminal (Paul) in the snow. As the man hides out, Wesley helps him even though Wesley knows the authorities are searching for him. Told from Wesley's perspective, it's an engrossing thriller highlighted by Murphy and Paul. **93m/C; DVD, Blu-Ray.** Danny Murphy; Mary Elizabeth Winstead; Aaron Paul; Scoot McNairy; Kristen Harris; ***D:*** Christopher Cantwell; ***W:*** Darren Lemke; ***C:*** Evans Brown; ***M:*** Austin Fray; Bleeding Fingers Music.

The Party 🦴🦴🦴 **1968** Disaster-prone Indian actor wreaks considerable havoc at a posh Hollywood gathering. Laughs come quickly in this quirky Sellers vehicle. **99m/C; VHS, DVD, Blu-Ray.** Peter Sellers; Claudine Longet; Marge Champion; Sharron Kimberly; Denny Miller; Gavin MacLeod; Carol Wayne; ***D:*** Blake Edwards; ***W:*** Blake Edwards; ***C:*** Lucien Ballard; ***M:*** Henry Mancini.

Party 🦴🦴 **1996** Leonor (Silveira) and Rogerio (Samora) are having a 10th anniversary party at their seaside villa. As the celebration continues, Leonor is pursued by aging playboy Michel (Piccoli) while her husband stands idly by. Maybe that has something to do with the secret Rogerio's about to reveal. French and Portuguese with subtitles. **91m/C; VHS, DVD.** *FR PT* Leonor Silveira; Michel Piccoli; Rogerio Samora; Irene Papas; ***D:*** Manoel de Oliveira; ***W:*** Manoel de Oliveira; Augustina Bessa-Luis; ***C:*** Renato Berta.

The Party 🦴🦴 1/2 **2017 (R)** An effective chamber comedy-drama with a touch of tragedy about a set of dysfunctional yet socially and politically committed characters. When progressive politician Janet (Scott Thomas) receives a promotion in the British government, she throws a small party. The guests include her romantic partner, the struggling Bill (Spall), a couple, April (Clarkson) and Gottfried (Ganz), who are separating, and Tom (Murphy), a gun-carrying drug user. Tensions escalate as politics are discussed, the food in the oven burns, and the group's complicated relationships reveal serious dysfunction. In addition to featuring a talented cast, Potter's compact film balances social purpose with revealing humor. **71m/B; DVD, Streaming.** *UK* Patricia Clarkson; Bruno Ganz; Cherry Jones; Emily Mortimer; Cillian Murphy; Kristin Scott Thomas; Timothy Spall; ***D:*** Sally Potter; ***W:*** Sally Potter; Walter Donohue; ***C:*** Aleksei Rodionov; ***M:*** Matt Biffa.

Party Animal 🦴 **1983 (R)** A college stud teaches a shy farm boy a thing or two about the carnal aspects of campus life. **78m/C; VHS, DVD.** Timothy Carhart; Matthew Causey; Robin Harlan; ***D:*** David Beaird; ***W:*** David Beaird; ***C:*** Bryan England.

Party Girl 🦴 1/2 **1930** A wealthy young man gets caught up in an escort service and is targeted for marriage by a young party girl and her conniving mother in this melodrama. **67m/B; VHS, DVD.** Douglas Fairbanks, Jr.; Jeanette Loff; Judith Barrie; Marie Prevost; John St. Polis; Lucien Prival; ***D:*** Victor Halperin; ***W:*** Victor Halperin; ***C:*** Henry Cronjager.

Party Girl 🦴🦴🦴 1/2 **1958** A crime drama involving an attorney representing a 1920s crime boss and his henchmen when they run afoul of the law. The lawyer falls in love with a nightclub dancer who successfully encourages him to leave the mob, but not before he is wounded in a gang war attack, arrested, and forced to testify against the mob as a material witness. The mob then takes his girlfriend hostage to prevent his testifying, leading to an exciting climax. Must-see viewing for Charisse's steamy dance numbers. **99m/C; VHS, DVD.** Robert Taylor; Cyd Charisse; Lee J. Cobb; John Ireland; Kent Smith; Claire Kelly; Corey Allen; ***D:*** Nicholas Ray.

Party Girl 🦴🦴 1/2 **1994 (R)** In the "girls just wanna have fun" category comes this spritely saga of 20-something Manhattan club gal Mary (Posey), who needs some steady income after the cops bust her for throwing an illegal rent party. So, since Mary's godmother is a librarian, she gets a job as a library clerk and discovers the wonders of the Dewey Decimal system (no, I'm not joking but presumably director Mayer is). Parker's Mary is a properly flaunting poseur but a little nightlife tends to go a long way. **94m/C; VHS, DVD.** Parker Posey; Omar Townsend; Anthony De Sando; Guillermo Diaz; Sasha von Scherler; Liev Schreiber; ***D:*** Daisy von Scherler Mayer; ***W:*** Harry Birckmayer; Daisy von Scherler Mayer; ***C:*** Michael Slovis; ***M:*** Anton Sanko.

Party Girls for Sale 🦴🦴 *Violated; Mannequins for Rio* **1954** Mystery thriller in which a young girl's body is found on the beach in Rio de Janeiro. Part of the 'Forgotten Noir, Vol. 1' collection. **80m/B; VHS, DVD.** *US GE* Raymond Burr; Scott Brady; Johanna (Hannerl) Matz; Kurt Meisel; Gert Frobe; ***D:*** Kurt Neumann; ***W:*** Kurt Neumann; ***C:*** Ekkehard Kyrath; ***M:*** Michael Jary.

Party Husband 🦴 1/2 **1931** Ex-Ziegfeld Follies beauty Laura (Mackaill) and her husband Jay (Rennie) find having an 'open' modern marriage isn't all it's cracked up to be. Jay succumbs to another woman's charms and Laura is pursued by another man. It's up to Laura's mother to set things right. **73m/B; DVD.** Dorothy Mackaill; James Alan Rennie; Mary Doran; Donald Cook; Dorothy Peterson; ***D:*** Clarence Badger; ***W:*** Charles Kenyon; ***C:*** Sidney Hickox.

Party Line 🦴 **1988 (R)** A veteran police captain and a district attorney team up to track down a pair of killers who find their victims through party lines. **90m/C; VHS, DVD, Blu-Ray.** Richard Hatch; Shawn Weatherly; Richard Roundtree; Leif Garrett; Greta Blackburn; ***D:*** William Webb; ***W:*** Richard Brandes.

Party Monster 🦴🦴 1/2 **2003 (R)** Michael Alig's (Culkin) a club kid turned murderer in this gaudy true crime drama. The misunderstood midwestern kid travels to the Big Apple where he quickly finds his niche in the decadent and flamboyant club scene of the 1990s. He hooks up with mentor James St. James (Green), who teaches him the ropes, but Alig surpasses him, becoming a celebrated party promoter at the famed disco Limelight. As Michael spirals out of control both in his addictions and emotionally, St. James attempts to intervene to little avail. Green provides superb support to Culkin's lead. Based on the book "Disco Bloodbath" by St. James. **98m/C; VHS, DVD.** Macaulay Culkin; Seth Green; Chloë Sevigny; Natasha Lyonne; Wilson Cruz; Wilmer Valderrama; Dylan McDermott; Justin Hagan; Diana Scarwid; Marilyn Manson; ***D:*** Fenton Bailey; Randy Barbato; ***W:*** Fenton Bailey; Randy Barbato; ***C:*** Teodoro Maniaci; ***M:*** Jimmy Harry.

The Party Never Stops 🦴 1/2 **2007** Clunky teen drama from Lifetime. Shy college freshman Jessie Brenner (Paxton) intends to study hard, make the track team, and have an active social life. She doesn't intend to indulge in non-stop partying and binge drinking, which causes numerous consequences. **90m/C; DVD.** Sara Paxton; Chelsea Hobbs; James Kirk; Jared Keeso; Nancy Travis; Alexia Fast; ***D:*** David Wu; ***W:*** Matt Dorff; ***C:*** Tony Westman; ***M:*** Lawrence Shragge. **CABLE**

The Passage 🦴 1/2 **1979** Simplistic and cliched WWII adventure-drama. A Basque shepherd is approached by the French Resistance to lead an escaped scientist and his family across the Pyrenees to safety in Spain. They're pursued by an SS officer. **101m/C; DVD.** *GB* Anthony Quinn; James Mason; Malcolm McDowell; Patricia Neal; Kay Lenz; Paul Clemens; Michael (Michel) Lonsdale; Christopher Lee; ***D:*** J. Lee Thompson; ***W:*** Bruce Nicolaysen; ***C:*** Michael Reed; ***M:*** Michael Lewis.

A Passage to India 🦴🦴🦴 **1984 (PG)** An ambitious adaptation of E.M. Forster's complex novel about relations between Brits and Indians in the 1920s. Drama centers on a young British woman's accusations that an Indian doctor raped her while serving as a guide in some rather ominous caves. Film occasionally flags, but is usually compelling. Features particularly strong performances from Bannerjee, Fox, and Davis. **163m/C; VHS, DVD, Blu-Ray.** *GB* Peggy Ashcroft; Alec Guinness; James Fox; Judy Davis; Victor Banerjee; Nigel Havers; ***D:*** David Lean; ***W:*** David Lean; ***C:*** Ernest Day; ***M:*** Maurice Jarre. Oscars '84: Orig. Score, Support. Actress (Ashcroft); British Acad. '85: Actress (Ashcroft); Golden Globes '85: Foreign Film, Score, Support. Actress (Ashcroft); L.A. Film Critics '84: Support. Actress (Ashcroft); Natl. Bd. of Review '84: Actor (Banerjee), Actress (Ashcroft), Director (Lean); N.Y. Film Critics '84: Actress (Ashcroft), Director (Lean), Film.

Passage to Marseilles 🦴🦴🦴 **1944** Hollywood propaganda in which convicts escape from Devil's Island and help French freedom fighters combat Nazis. Routine but entertaining. What else could it be with Bogart, Raines, Greenstreet, and Lorre, who earlier had made a pretty good film set in Casablanca? **110m/B; VHS, DVD, Blu-Ray.** Humphrey Bogart; Claude Rains; Sydney Greenstreet; Peter Lorre; Helmut Dantine; George Tobias; John Loder; Eduardo Ciannelli; Michele Morgan; Hans Conried; Philip Dorn; Victor Francen; ***D:*** Michael Curtiz; ***W:*** Casey Robinson; Jack Moffitt; ***C:*** James Wong Howe; ***M:*** Max Steiner.

Passchendaele 🦴 1/2 **2010** Unfortunately melodramatic, though well-intentioned, Canadian retelling of the 1917 Allied debacle in the Belgian town, which was part of the larger Third Battle of Ypres. Shell-shocked Sgt. Michael Dunne (Gross) falls for his hospital nurse Sarah (Dhavernas), whose asthmatic brother is conscripted and taken under Dunne's wing. The film then moves unsuccessfully between the personal and the wartime action. **114m/C; DVD.** *CA* Paul Gross; Caroline Dhavernas; Joe Dinicol; Jim Mezon; Meredith Bailey; Michael Greyeyes; Adam Harrington; Gil Bellows; James Kot; ***D:*** Paul Gross; ***W:*** Paul Gross; ***C:*** Gregory Middleton; ***M:*** Jan A.P. Kaczmarek.

Passed Away 🦴 1/2 **1992 (PG-13)** Family patriarch Jack Scanlan dies and his family gets together for the funeral and a big Irish wake. The family, of course, is made up of a weird group of characters, good steadfast son Hoskins, dim-witted but good-looking son Petersen, rebellious daughter Reed, and a left-wing nun (McDormand) who works in Central America and is accompanied by an illegal immigrant. Throw in a mysterious female mourner and a pregnant granddaughter who goes into labor at the graveside and you come up with a movie that manages to use every comic death cliche ever imagined and wastes a talented cast **96m/C; VHS, Streaming.** Bob Hoskins; Jack Warden; William L. Petersen; Helen Lloyd Breed; Maureen Stapleton; Pamela Reed; Tim Curry; Peter Riegert; Blair Brown; Patrick Breen; Nancy Travis; Teri Polo; Frances McDormand; ***D:*** Charlie Peters; ***W:*** Charlie Peters; ***C:*** Arthur Albert; ***M:*** Richard Gibbs.

The Passenger 🦴🦴🦴 1/2 *Profession: Reporter* **1975 (PG)** A dissatisfied TV reporter changes identities with a dead man while on assignment in Africa, then learns that he is posing as a gunrunner. Mysterious, elliptical production from Italian master Antonioni, who co-wrote. Nicholson is fine in the low-key role, and Schneider is surprisingly winning as the woman drawn to him. The object of much debate, hailed by some as quintessential cinema and by others as slow and unrewarding. **119m/C; VHS, DVD.** *IT* Jack Nicholson; Maria Schneider; Ian Hendry; Jenny Runacre; Steven Berkoff; ***D:*** Michelangelo Antonioni; ***W:*** Mark Peploe; Michelangelo Antonioni; ***M:*** Claude Bolling.

Passenger 57 🦴 **1992 (R)** Classic movie-of-the-week fare. Anti-terrorist specialist John Cutter (Snipes) leaves his profession because of his wife's murder, and coincidentally boards the same plane as Charles Rane (Payne), an apprehended evil terrorist headed to trial in L.A. Somehow, Rane's thugs have also sneaked aboard with plans to hijack the plane, and it's up to Cutter to use his skills and save the day. Athletic Snipes is convincing in his role but can't make up for the plot's lack of premise. **84m/C; VHS, DVD, Blu-Ray.** Wesley Snipes; Bruce Payne; Tom Sizemore; Alex Datcher; Bruce Greenwood; Robert Hooks; Elizabeth Hurley; Michael Horse; ***D:*** Kevin Hooks; ***W:*** Dan Gordon; David Loughery; ***C:*** Mark Irwin; ***M:*** Stanley Clarke.

Passenger Side **2009** Absurdist road movie set in L.A. (title is taken from the Wilco song). It's Michael Brown's birthday and he gets a call from his irresponsible, ex-druggie younger brother Tobey who needs a ride (apparently to nowhere). It turns into an all-day journey and run-ins with an assortment of oddball characters as the semi-estranged brothers carry on semi-awkward conversations. **95m/C; DVD.** Adam Scott; Joel Bissonnette; Robin Tunney; Gale Harold; Rachel Santhon; Kimberley Huie; ***D:*** Matthew Bissonnette; ***W:*** Matthew Bissonnette; ***C:*** Jonathan Cliff.

Passengers 1/2 **2008 (PG-13)** Grief counselor Claire Summers (Hathaway) is assigned to treat a group of plane crash survivors, who she suspects are involved in a cover-up. The life-long lonely workaholic soon finds romance with her patient Eric (Wilson), who begins to reveal the mystery behind the crash. Marketed as a horror/thriller, but the obvious absence of both horrors and thrills plainly put it in drama territory. Be warned, the twist ending isn't very twisted. **92m/C; Blu-Ray, On Demand.** Anne Hathaway; Patrick Wilson; David Morse; Andre Braugher; Clea DuVall; Dianne Wiest; Chelah Horsdal; Ryan Robbins; ***D:*** Rodrigo Garcia; ***W:*** Ronnie Christensen; ***C:*** Igor Jadue-Lillo; ***M:*** Ed Shearmur.

Passengers **2016 (PG-13)** Jim Preston (Pratt) and Aurora Lane (Lawrence) are passengers on a starship on which colonists are supposed to stay in hibernation for 120 years. Unfortunately the attractive pair wakes up 90 years too early. As they search for answers, naturally love blooms. But the differing circumstances which disrupted their slumber cause the lovebirds much strife. More significant issues spell possible doom for not just themselves but the thousands of others aboard still in dreamland. This big-budget sci-fi by director Spaihts that should have been more than it was. Technically well-made but a bit halfhearted. **116m/C; DVD, Blu-Ray.** Jennifer Lawrence; Chris Pratt; Michael Sheen; Laurence Fishburne; Andy Garcia; ***D:*** Morten Tyldum; ***W:*** Jon Spaihts; ***C:*** Rodrigo Prieto; ***M:*** Thomas Newman.

The Passing 1/2 **1988** Two men find themselves trapped in the darker vicissitudes of life. The two lead almost parallel lives until an extraordinary event unites them. **96m/C; VHS, DVD, Blu-Ray.** James Plaster; Welton Benjamin Johnson; Lynn Dunn; Albert B. Smith; ***D:*** John Huckert.

Passing Glory **1999** The script may not be a three-pointer but the acting is a slam-dunk in this fact-based drama. Joseph Verrett (Braugher) is a black priest in segregationist New Orleans in the early '60s, teaching at St. Augustine High and coaching the school's unbeaten varsity basketball squad. Verrett is a go-getter who wants to integrate the league now, while his boss, Father Robert Grant (Torn) preaches patience. Despite numerous obstacles, Verrett manages to challenge white Jesuit High to an unofficial city championship game. **94m/C; VHS, DVD.** Andre Braugher; Rip Torn; Bill Nunn; Sean Squire; Ruby Dee; Daniel Hugh-Kelly; Anderson Bourell; Khalil Kain; ***D:*** Steve James; ***W:*** Harold Sylvester; ***C:*** Bill Butler; ***M:*** Stephen James Taylor. **CABLE**

The Passing of Evil 1/2 *The Grasshopper; Passions* **1970 (R)** Bisset is a starstruck Canadian undone by the bright lights and big cities of America. By age 22, she's a burnt-out prostitute in Las Vegas. Cheerless but compelling. **96m/C; VHS, DVD.** Jacqueline Bisset; Jim Brown; Joseph Cotten; Corbett Monica; Ramon Bieri; Christopher Stone; Roger Garrett; Stanley Adams; Dick Richards; Tim O'Kelly; Ed Flanders; ***D:*** Jerry Paris; ***C:*** Sam Leavitt; ***M:*** Billy Goldenberg.

The Passing of the Third Floor Back **1935** Boarding house tenants improve their lives after being inspired by a mysterious stranger. They revert, though, when he leaves. Now you know. Based on a Victorian morality play. **80m/B; DVD.** *UK* Conrad Veidt; Rene Ray; Frank Cellier; Anna Lee; John Turnbull; Cathleen Nesbitt; ***D:*** Berthold Viertel; ***W:*** Michael Hogan; Alma Reville; ***C:*** Curt Courant.

Passion 1/2 **1919** Paris, and the decadent Louis XV falls for the lovely Jeanne, making her his mistress, much to the scandal of the nation. Respectable silent version of "Madame DuBarry" is a relatively realistic costume drama, but it doesn't rate with the best German films of this period. **135m/B; Silent; VHS, DVD.** *GE* Pola Negri; Emil Jannings; Harry Liedtke; ***D:*** Ernst Lubitsch.

Passion **1954** When a rancher's young family falls victim to rampaging desperadoes, he enlists an outlaw's aid to avenge the murders of his loved ones. **84m/C; VHS, DVD.** Raymond Burr; Cornel Wilde; Yvonne De Carlo; Lon Chaney, Jr.; John Qualen; ***D:*** Allan Dwan.

Passion **1982 (R)** A Polish film director (Radziwilowicz) is making a movie called "Passion" and practicing what he's filming by having an affair with the motel owner (Schygulla) where the film crew are staying. Then the money for the film begins to run out. Meanwhile, Schygulla's husband, Piccoli, is having problems at his factory because of a labor dispute called by worker Huppert. French with subtitles. **88m/C; VHS, DVD.** *FR* Jerzy Radziwilowicz; Hanna Schygulla; Michel Piccoli; Isabelle Huppert; Laszlo Szabo; ***D:*** Jean-Luc Godard; ***W:*** Jean-Luc Godard; ***C:*** Raoul Coutard.

Passion **1999** Over-the-top bio of Aussie-born composer Percy Grainger (1882-1961). Although born in Melbourne and starting his career as a concert pianist, Grainger (Roxburgh) spent most of his life in Europe and the U.S. and was involved in recovering English and Celtic folk songs. But his home life is a twisted psychosexual drama as his devoted mother, Rose (Hershey), suffers from syphilitic fits amid rumors of their incestuous relationship and Grainger's own masochistic impulses, which are catered to by his piano student, Karen (Woof). **98m/C; VHS, DVD.** *AU* Richard Roxburgh; Barbara Hershey; Emily Woof; Claudia Karvan; Simon Burke; Linda Cropper; Julia Blake; ***D:*** Peter Duncan; ***W:*** Don Watson; ***C:*** Martin McGrath. Australian Film Inst. '99: Art Dir./Set Dec., Cinematog., Costume Des.

Passion **2013 (R)** High-powered advertising exec Christine (McAdams) takes credit for an idea brought to her by co-worker Isabelle (Rapace). The corporate crime leads to an escalating series of sabotages by each of the ladies, spinning out of control in ways that only director/writer De Palma's heroines could possibly do. Both stars seem out of place here but De Palma replaces character with style in entertaining ways. Not quite a return to form, this remake of 2010's "Love Crime" (France) shows glimpses of the life that its auteur burst through every frame in the '70s and '80s. **102m/C; DVD, Blu-Ray.** *FR GE* Rachel McAdams; Noomi Rapace; Karoline Herfurth; Paul Anderson; Rainer Bock; ***D:*** Brian De Palma; ***W:*** Brian De Palma; ***C:*** Jose Luis Alcaine; ***M:*** Pino Donaggio.

Passion Fish **1992 (R)** McDonnell plays May-Alice, a soap opera actress who is paralyzed after a taxi accident in New York. Confined to a wheelchair, the bitter woman moves back to her Louisiana home and alienates a number of live-in nurses until Chantelle (Woodard), who has her own problems, comes along. Blunt writing and directing by Sayles overcome the story's inherent sentimentality as do the spirited performances of the leads, including Curtis-Hall as the rogue romancing Chantelle and Strathairn as the Cajun bad boy McDonnell once loved. **136m/C; VHS, DVD.** Mary McDonnell; Alfre Woodard; David Strathairn; Vondie Curtis-Hall; Nora Dunn; Sheila Kelley; Angela Bassett; Mary Portser; Maggie Renzi; Leo Burmester; Shauntisa Willis; John Henry; Michael Laskin; ***D:*** John Sayles; ***W:*** John Sayles; ***C:*** Roger Deakins; ***M:*** Mason Daring. Ind. Spirit '93: Support. Actress (Woodard).

Passion in the Desert *Simoom: A Passion in the Desert* **1997 (PG-13)** Definitely one of the stranger plots going. Augustin Roberts (Daniels) is a French officer in Napoleon's Egyptian campaign. He's escorting artist Venture de Paradis (Piccoli), who's been commissioned to record the country's monuments. The duo are lost and separated in a desert sandstorm, with Roberts eventually finding shelter in the ruins of an ancient city. But he's not alone—his dangerous companion is a female leopard, who decides to help out the two-legged interloper. Based on a novella by Honore de Balzac. **93m/C; VHS, DVD.** Ben Daniels; Michel Piccoli; ***D:*** Lavinia Currier; ***W:*** Lavinia Currier; Martin Edmunds; ***C:*** Alexei Rodionov; ***M:*** Jose Nieto.

The Passion of Anna **1970 (R)** A complicated psychological drama about four people on an isolated island. Von Sydow is an ex-con living a hermit's existence when he becomes involved with a crippled widow (Ullmann) and her two friends—all of whom have secrets in their pasts. Brutal and disturbing. Wonderful cinematography by Sven Nykvist. Filmed on the island of Faro. In Swedish with English subtitles. **101m/C; VHS, DVD, Blu-Ray.** *SW* Max von Sydow; Liv Ullmann; Bibi Andersson; Erland Josephson; Erik Hell; ***D:*** Ingmar Bergman; ***W:*** Ingmar Bergman; ***C:*** Sven Nykvist. Natl. Soc. Film Critics '70: Director (Bergman).

The Passion of Ayn Rand 1/2 **1999** Warts-and-all bio of the Russian-born novelist/philosopher that focuses on the 20-year friendship between Rand (Mirren) and psychoanalyst Nathaniel Branden (Stoltz). When the pic opens in 1951, self-important Rand is already famous for "The Fountainhead" and has a longtime marriage to the overshadowed Frank (Fonda). Nathaniel and Barbara (Delpy) are college students pushed to marry by mentor Rand, who soon becomes Nathaniel's lover and encourages his ambitions—to the dismay of both spouses. Based on the 1986 memoir by Barbara Branden, so there's an axe to grind. **104m/C; VHS, DVD.** Dame Helen Mirren; Eric Stoltz; Julie Delpy; Peter Fonda; Tom McCamus; Sybil Temchen; Don McKellar; David Ferry; ***D:*** Christopher Menaul; ***W:*** Howard Korder; Mary Gallagher; ***C:*** Ronald Orieux; ***M:*** Jeff Beal. **CABLE**

The Passion of Darkly Noon 1/2 **1995** Strange religious/sexual allegory. Running through the woods, Darkly Noon (Fraser) stumbles across the rural home of Callie (Judd) and Clay (Mortensen). Callie sees that the young man is ill and allows him to stay, discovering his parents have recently died and he's escaped from the ultra-religious community where he was raised. The sexy Callie is an uncomfortable attraction for the naive lad and when he meets a crazy old woman (Zabriskie) in the woods, he's inclined to listen to her ravings against Callie, leading Darkly to believe he's been sent to punish the transgressors. **106m/C; VHS, DVD, Blu-Ray, Streaming.** *GB GE BE* Brendan Fraser; Ashley Judd; Viggo Mortensen; Grace Zabriskie; Loren Dean; ***D:*** Philip Ridley; ***W:*** Philip Ridley; ***C:*** John de Borman; ***M:*** Nick Bicat.

Passion of Joan of Arc **1928** Dreyer's version of the life of France's Joan of Arc ignores all the battlefield dramatics and confines itself to showing Joan in her cell and at her trial, with only one exterior shot—that of Joan (stage actress Falconetti in her only film role) on her way to the stake. The script is drawn from the Latin text of the heresy trial itself and Dreyer uses numerous close-ups (the actors wore no makeup) to show the bewilderment, fear, and anger of the participants. Dreyer refused to have his film shown with musical accompaniment but the tape includes Richard Einhron's oratoria, "Voices of Light." **114m/B; Silent; VHS, DVD, Blu-Ray.** *FR* Renee (Marie) Falconetti; Eugena Sylvaw; Maurice Schutz; Antonin Artaud; Michel Simon; ***D:*** Carl Theodor Dreyer; ***W:*** Carl Theodor Dreyer; Joseph Delteil; ***C:*** Rudolph Mate.

Passion of Mind 1/2 **2000 (PG-13)** Moore plays two roles: Marie is an American widow and mother living in France while Marty is a hard-charging single New York literary agent. Marie falls asleep and wakes up as Marty and vice versa. Marie/Marty can't tell anymore which of her two worlds is real and things get even more complicated when each persona falls for an appealing man (Skarsgard in France, Fichtner in New York). It's not really confusing since the script is so simplistic and both her lives turn out to be remarkably dull (as is Moore's performance). English-language debut for Berliner and Moore's first film since 1997's "G.I. Jane." **105m/C; VHS, DVD.** Demi Moore; Stellan Skarsgard; William Fichtner; Peter Riegert; Joss Ackland; Sinead Cusack; ***D:*** Alain Berliner; ***W:*** Ronald Bass; David Field; ***C:*** Eduardo Serra; ***M:*** Randy Edelman.

The Passion of the Christ **2004 (R)** Gibson's controversial version of the last 12 hours in the life of Jesus Christ. Film begins as Jesus (Caveizel) is arrested and taken before Hebrew and Roman authorities for crimes of heresy. Although some backstory is told in flashback, the movie focuses on giving as graphic a portrayal of his torture and crucifixion as possible. Very bold and well-crafted, but the obsessive focus on gore and violence will leave many asking where the spirituality is and pic drew complaints for its negative depiction of the Hebrew leaders, as well as some violent scenes that Gibson invented. Gibson funded the film with $30 million of his own money. Aramaic, Latin, and Hebrew with subtitles. **126m/C; DVD, Blu-Ray.** James (Jim) Caviezel; Monica Bellucci; Maia Morgenstern; Claudia Gerini; Sergio Rubini; Toni Bertorelli; Mattia Sbragia; Hristo Naumov Shopov; Rosalinda Celentano; Luca De Dominicis; Francesco De Vito; Giancinto Ferro; Luca Lionello; ***D:*** Mel Gibson; ***W:*** Mel Gibson; Benedict Fitzgerald; ***C:*** Caleb Deschanel; ***M:*** John Debney.

Passion Play 1/2 **2010 (R)** Oddball, at-odds pairing of Rourke and Murray while Fox's display of her physical assets may attract some attention to Glazer's eccentric directorial debut. Jazz trumpeter Nate Poole (Rourke) is in trouble for fooling with gangster Happy Shannon's (Murray) wife. After escaping a hitman, he stumbles across a crazy carnival and its main attraction, Lily the Bird Girl (Fox), a young beauty who literally has wings. Nate decides he can profit from their association in more ways than one. **92m/C; DVD, Blu-Ray.** Mickey Rourke; Megan Fox; Bill Murray; Kelly Lynch; Rhys Ifans; ***D:*** Mitch Glazer; ***W:*** Mitch Glazer; ***C:*** Christopher Doyle; ***M:*** Dickon Hinchliffe.

Passionada **2002 (PG-13)** An offbeat yet sensual romantic comedy with a sense of adventure. Set in New Bedford, Massachusetts, in its Portugeuese fishing community, widow Sally Amonte (Milos) is a long-time widow raising a teenage daughter, Vicky (Rossum) and refusing to date. Sally does let go in the evenings, singing entrancing fado songs. Her vocals impress Charlie Beck (Isaacs), a British gambler who is new in town. Vicky aspires to be a professional gambler herself, and makes a deal with him to find new love for her mother while learning how to count cards. **108m/C; DVD, Streaming.** Sofia Milos; Emmy Rossum; Lupe Ontiveros; Jason Isaacs; Theresa Russell; Seymour Cassel; ***D:*** Dan Ireland; ***W:*** Stephen Jermanok; Jim Jermanok; ***C:*** Claudio Rocha; ***M:*** Harry Gregson-Williams. **VIDEO**

The Passionate Plumber 1/2 **1932** Silent screen star Keaton didn't make a particularly successful transition to sound films and this blustery, inconsistent comedy did him no favors. Plumber Elmer Tuttle is called to fix the shower of Paris socialite Patricia Alden (Purcell) and before long she's using him to try to make her Spanish boyfriend Tony (Roland) jealous. Only Tony is already two-timing Patricia with Nina. Based on the Frederick Lonsdale play "Her Cardboard Lover." **73m/B; DVD.** Buster Keaton; Irene Purcell; Gilbert Roland; Mona Maris; Jimmy Durante; Polly Moran; Maude Eburne; ***D:*** Edward Sedgwick; ***W:*** Laurence E. Johnson; Ralph Spence; ***C:*** Norbert Brodine.

Passport to Pimlico 1/2 **1949** Farce about a London neighborhood's residents who discover an ancient charter proclaiming their right to form their own country within city limits. Passable comedy. **81m/B; VHS, DVD, Blu-Ray.** *UK* Stanley Holloway; Margaret Rutherford; Hermione Baddeley; Naunton Wayne; Basil Radford; ***D:*** Henry Cornelius; *W:* T.E.B. Clarke; *C:* Lionel Banes; *M:* Georges Auric.

Passport to Suez 1/2 **1943** The ninth and last film for Williams as The Lone Wolf. Michael Lanyard is in Alexandria, Egypt working undercover to foil a Nazi scheme to steal Allied plans for fortifying the Suez Canal. **72m/B; DVD.** Warren William; Ann Savage; Eric Blore; Robert Stanford; Sheldon Leonard; Lloyd Bridges; Gavin Muir; *D:* Andre de Toth; *C:* L. William O'Connell.

The Password Is Courage **1962** Based on a true story. British Sgt. Maj. Charles Coward is a POW at Stalag 8-B. He plans a break out with fellow prisoner Billy Pope by digging a tunnel, which means first gathering information by any means necessary. **115m/B; DVD.** *UK* Dirk Bogarde; Alfred Lynch; Maria Perschy; Nigel Stock; *D:* Andrew L. Stone; *W:* Andrew L. Stone; *C:* Davis Boulton.

The Past *Le Passe* **2013 (PG-13)** Ahmad (Mosaffa) is returning home to his family after an extended separation to grant his wife Marie (Bejo) a divorce. He learns that Marie has taken up with another married man named Samir (Rahim), whose wife is in a coma. Children from both relationships complicate matters even further. Writer/director Farhadi works in the space between what people say and what they mean as relationships fall apart. The conclusion is a bit unsatisfying but there's still a lot to discuss when it's over. **130m/C; DVD, Blu-Ray.** *FR IA* Berenice Bejo; Tahar Rahim; Ali Mosaffa; Pauline Burlet; Elyes Aguis; *D:* Asghar Farhadi; *W:* Asghar Farhadi; *C:* Mahmoud Kalari; *M:* Evgueni Galperine.

Past Midnight **1992 (R)** Richardson plays a social worker who believes recently paroled killer Hauer was wrongly convicted. She attempts to prove his innocence while also falling in love—a dangerous combination. Richardson's beautiful and Hauer's making a successful career out of playing handsome psychos. **100m/C; VHS, DVD.** Natasha Richardson; Rutger Hauer; Clancy Brown; Guy Boyd; *D:* Jan Eliasberg; *W:* Frank Norwood; *M:* Steve Bartek.

Past Sins 1/2 **2006** Ambitious criminal attorney Donna Erickson (Bell) gets a headline case when soccer mom Janice Bradford (Jenkins) is charged with a notorious 30-year-old crime. As part of a protest group, Janice was involved in a deadly bombing but insists they were framed, so Donna has to find the truth in a very cold case. **90m/C; DVD.** Lauralee Bell; Rebecca Jenkins; Woody Jeffreys; Peter Hall; Michael Kopsa; Kevin McNulty; Timothy Webber; Philip Granger; *D:* David Winning; *W:* Don Nelson; *C:* Eric Goldstein; *M:* Brent Belke. **CABLE**

Past Tense 1/2 **2006** Widowed mom Kim Shay (Trickey) tries to comfort her 10-year-old daughter Sara (Fast) who has nightmares about a murder. Only the murder turns out to be real and the killer may also be responsible for the death of Kim's cop husband. **90m/C; DVD.** Paula Trickey; Alexia Fast; Michael Rogers; Adrian Hough; Donnelly Rhodes; Zara Taylor; *D:* Penelope Buitenhuis; *W:* Alex Campbell; *C:* Adam Sliwinski; *M:* John Sereda; Paul Michael Thomas. **CABLE**

Pastime *One Cup of Coffee* **1991 (PG)** A bittersweet baseball elegy set in the minor leagues in 1957. A boyish 41-year-old pitcher can't face his impending retirement and pals around with the team pariah, a 17-year-old black rookie. Splendidly written and acted, it's a melancholy treat whether you're a fan of the game or not, and safe for family attendance. The only drawback is a grungy, low-budget look. **94m/C; VHS, DVD.** William Russ; Scott Plank; Glenn Plummer; Noble Willingham; Jeffrey Tambor; Deirdre O'Connell; Ricky Paull Goldin; ***Cameo(s):*** Ernie Banks; Harmon Killebrew; Duke Snider; Bob Feller; Bill Mazeroski; Don Newcombe; *D:* Robin B. Armstrong; *W:* David Eyre; *C:* Tom Richmond. Sundance '91: Aud. Award.

The Pastor's Wife **2011** Lifetime true crime with a strong lead performance by McGowan. In 2006, Mary Winkler took a shotgun to her husband Matthew in their Tennessee home. He was a popular pastor, but she claims self-defense because (as we're shown in flashbacks) she was an abused wife. With little evidence to support her, Mary and her lawyer have a hard time convincing the court. **90m/C; Streaming.** Rose McGowan; Michael Shanks; Martin Cummins; *D:* Norma Bailey; *W:* Robert L. Freedman; *C:* C. Kim Miles; *M:* Schaun Tozer. **CABLE**

Pat and Mike **1952** War of the sexes rages in this comedy about a leathery sports promoter who futilely attempts to train a woman for athletic competition. Tracy and Hepburn have fine chemistry, but supporting players contribute too. Watch for the first on-screen appearance of Bronson (then Charles Buchinski) as a crook. **95m/B; VHS, DVD.** Spencer Tracy; Katharine Hepburn; Aldo Ray; Jim Backus; William Ching; Sammy White; Phyllis Povah; Charles Bronson; Chuck Connors; Mae Clarke; Carl "Alfalfa" Switzer; *D:* George Cukor; *W:* Ruth Gordon; Garson Kanin; *C:* William H. Daniels; *M:* David Raksin.

Pat Garrett & Billy the Kid **1973** Coburn is Garrett, one-time partner of Billy the Kid (Kristofferson), turned sheriff. He tracks down and eventually kills the outlaw. The uncut director's version released on video is a vast improvement over the theatrical and TV versions. Dylan's soundtrack includes the now famous "Knockin' on Heaven's Door." **106m/C; VHS, DVD.** Kris Kristofferson; James Coburn; Bob Dylan; Richard Jaeckel; Katy Jurado; Chill Wills; Charles Martin Smith; Slim Pickens; Harry Dean Stanton; *D:* Sam Peckinpah; *W:* Rudy Wurlitzer; *M:* George Duning.

Patch Adams **1998 (PG-13)** Maverick medical student Hunter "Patch" Adams (Williams) takes the expression "laughter is the best medicine" literally and treats terminally ill patients with slapstick routines. Naturally, the medical establishment frowns on his antics, but Patch thumbs his fake nose and defends his unorthodox ways to fellow students, including the requisite love interest (Potter). Director Shadyac and screenwriter Oedekerk let Williams unleash his rapid-fire wackiness without much direction and the flick is brought down by sappy melodrama and emotional manipulation under the guise of sincere emotion. **115m/C; VHS, DVD, Blu-Ray, HD-DVD.** Robin Williams; Philip Seymour Hoffman; Monica Potter; Bob Gunton; Josef Sommer; Irma P. Hall; Daniel London; Frances Lee McCain; Harve Presnell; Peter Coyote; Michael Jeter; Harold Gould; Richard Kiley; Alan Tudyk; Barry (Shabaka) Henley; *D:* Tom Shadyac; *W:* Steve Oedekerk; *C:* Phedon Papamichael; *M:* Marc Shaiman.

A Patch of Blue 1/2 **1965** A kind-hearted blind girl falls in love with a black man without acknowledging racial differences. Good performances from Hartman and Poitier are film's strongest assets. **108m/C; DVD, Blu-Ray.** Sidney Poitier; Elizabeth Hartman; Shelley Winters; Wallace Ford; Ivan Dixon; John Qualen; Elisabeth Fraser; Kelly Flynn; *D:* Guy Green; *W:* Guy Green; *C:* Robert Burks; *M:* Jerry Goldsmith. Oscars '65: Support. Actress (Winters).

Patchwork Girl of Oz **1914** You wonder what Baum might have been imbibing when he wrote some of his Oz books. In this story a mysterious Emerald City doctor is working on a powder of life that his wife accidentally tests on a patchwork servant doll that suddenly comes alive. **80m/B; Silent; VHS, DVD.** Frank Moore; Violet MacMillan; Raymond Russell; Leontine Dranet; Pierre Couderc; Richard Rosson; Bobbie Gould; Marie Wayne; *D:* J. Farrell MacDonald; *W:* L. Frank Baum; *C:* James A. Crosby.

Paterson **2016 (R)** Paterson (Driver) is a bus driver who happens to live in Paterson, New Jersey. Paterson writes poetry as breaks from his routine, which writer/director Jarmusch captures beautifully, highlighting how much poetry there is in everyday, mundane life. An exceptional Driver anchors a story that's so incredibly simple and yet astoundingly moving. Jarmusch has created an ode to dreamers and poets everywhere, whether they're household names or driving a bus in New Jersey. **118m/C; DVD, Blu-Ray.** Adam Driver; Golshifteh Farahani; Barry (Shabaka) Henley; Method Man; William Jackson Harper; *D:* Jim Jarmusch; *W:* Jim Jarmusch; *C:* Frederick Elmes; *M:* Jim Jarmusch; Carter Logan; Sqürl.

Path to Paradise **1997 (R)** Based on the true story of the 1993 World Trade Center bombing, which focuses on both the terrorists and the FBI investigators. FBI agent John Anticev (Gallagher) is investigating a rabbi's murder, which leads him to Islamic extremists. An informant warns Anticev that the group are planning terroristt activities in Manhattan but the conspirators are closer to their target than the FBI imagine. **95m/C; VHS, DVD.** Peter Gallagher; Art Malik; Ned Eisenberg; Marcia Gay Harden; Paul Guilfoyle; Andreas Katsulas; Shiek Mahmud-Bey; Mike Starr; *D:* Larry Williams; Leslie Libman; *W:* Ned Curren; *C:* Jean De Segonzac. **CABLE**

Path to War 1/2 **2002** Covers the period from the night of President Lyndon B. Johnson's (Gambon) inauguration in 1965 to his 1968 decision not to seek re-election because of the escalating war in Vietnam. While the British Gambon has Johnson's mannerisms down, he can't manage the Texas drawl, which is a real handicap. Baldwin plays Defense Secretary Robert McNamara and Sutherland is Johnson adviser Clark Clifford. **160m/C; VHS, DVD.** Michael Gambon; Alec Baldwin; Donald Sutherland; John Aylward; Cliff DeYoung; Christopher Eigeman; Frederic Forrest; James Frain; Philip Baker Hall; Felicity Huffman; Patricia Kalember; Bruce McGill; Tom Skerritt; Diana Scarwid; Gary Sinise; *D:* John Frankenheimer; *W:* Daniel Giat; *C:* Stephen Goldblatt; Nancy Schreiber; *M:* Gary Chang. **CABLE**

Pather Panchali *The Song of the Road; The Saga of the Road; The Lament of the Path* **1954** Somber, moving story of a young Bengali boy growing up in impoverished India. Stunning debut from India's master filmmaker Ray, who continued the story in "Aparajito" and "World of Apu." A truly great work. In Bengali with English subtitles. **112m/B; VHS, DVD, Blu-Ray.** *IN* Kanu Bannerjee; Karuna Bannerjee; Uma Das Gupta; Subir Banerji; Runki Banerji; Chunibala Devi; *D:* Satyajit Ray; *W:* Satyajit Ray; *M:* Ravi Shankar.

The Pathfinder 1/2 **1996 (PG-13)** TV adaptation of the 1840 James Fenimore Cooper novel that finds legendary woodsman Natty Bumppo, his adoptive Indian father Chingachgook, and lovely Mabel Dunham trying to aid a beseiged British fort during the French and Indian wars. If this sounds familiar, it's because Cooper's "Leatherstocking Tales" were also the basis for "The Last of the Mohicans." **104m/C; VHS, DVD.** Kevin Dillon; Graham Greene; Jaimz Woolvett; Laurie Holden; Russell Means; Stacy Keach; *D:* Donald Shebib; *W:* James Mitchell Miller; Thomas W. Lynch; *M:* Reg Powell.

Pathfinder **2007 (R)** Shelved for a year and then released after blockbuster "300." Coincidence? We think not. Violent and gory (although with fewer ripped abs), this epic wannabe doesn't even have the camp factor to save it. Abandoned by his father during a North American raid, a Viking lad is raised by a peaceful Native American tribe. When the Vikings return for more pillaging and slaughter, now-grown Ghost (Urban) takes on the intruders. Soon all the action cliches commence. Loosely inspired by the 1988 Norwegian pic "Ofelas." **99m/C; DVD, Blu-Ray.** Karl Urban; Russell Means; Moon Bloodgood; Clancy Brown; Ralph (Ralf) Moeller; Jay Tavare; *D:* Marcus Nispel; *W:* Laeta Kalogridis; *C:* Daniel Pearl; *M:* Jonathan Elias.

Pathology **2008 (R)** Grisly, perverse horror thriller finds amoral young doctor Ted Grey (Ventimiglia) beginning his residency in pathology. His fellow docs are a sex-and-drugs crazed bunch led by loony Jack (Weston). Jack has devised a game in which one of the team commits a murder and then the others perform an autopsy to decide how it was done (so much for the Hippocratic Oath). Ted's soon involved up to his scalpel but discovers getting out of Jack's band of merry killers isn't so easy. **93m/C; DVD.** Milo Ventimiglia; Michael Weston; Alyssa Milano; Lauren Lee Smith; Johnny Whitworth; John de Lancie; Mei Melancon; Keir O'Donnell; *D:* Marc Schoelermann; *C:* Ekkehart Pollack; *M:* Johannes Kobilke; Robert Williamson.

Paths of Glory **1957** Classic anti-war drama set in WWI France. A vain, ambitious officer imposes unlikely battle strategy on his hapless troops, and when it fails, he demands that three soldiers be selected for execution as cowards. Menjou is excellent as the bloodless French officer, with Douglas properly heroic as the French officer who knows about the whole disgraceful enterprise. Fabulous, wrenching fare from film-making great Kubrick, who co-wrote. Based on a true story from Humphrey Cobb's novel of the same name. **86m/B; VHS, DVD, Blu-Ray.** Kirk Douglas; Adolphe Menjou; George Macready; Ralph Meeker; Richard Anderson; Wayne Morris; Timothy Carey; Susanne Christian; Bert Freed; Joe Turkel; Peter Capell; *D:* Stanley Kubrick; *W:* Stanley Kubrick; Calder Willingham; Jim Thompson; *C:* Georg Krause; *M:* Gerald Fried. Natl. Film Reg. '92.

Paths to Paradise **1925** Compson and Griffith share criminal past, reunite at gala event to snatch priceless necklace, and head south of the border. World-class chase scene. **78m/B; Silent; VHS, DVD.** Raymond Griffith; Betty Compson; Thomas Santschi; Bert Woodruff; Fred Kelsey; *D:* Clarence Badger; *W:* Keene Thompson; *C:* H. Kinley Martin.

The Patience Stone **2013 (R)** Farahani gives a star-making turn in this slow but rewarding drama adapted from director Rahimi's bestselling novel. A Muslim woman faithfully sits by the side of her comatose husband, transforming him into a magical force that protects her from the increasing dangers of war. As she weathers the world around her, she tells her husband all of the issues she has remained silent about and what is happening to her now. In a part of the world where women are not allowed to express themselves in any way, it captures the passion and pain behind the veil. Persian with subtitles. **102m/C; DVD.** *FR GE UK AF* Golshifteh Farshani; Hamid Djavadan; *D:* Atiq Rahimi; *W:* Jean-Claude Carriere; *C:* Thierry Arbogast.

Patient Zero 1/2 **2018 (R)** When a super strain of rabies turns much of humanity into zombies, a small group of soldiers and scientists survive in an underground bunker. Among them is Dr. Gina Rose (Dormer), who is trying to engineer an antivirus from the blood of the infected and locate the disease's initial victim. Soldier Morgan (Smith) was bitten but did not turn rabid, so Gina uses his blood as part of her tests on the captive infected, including Morgan's wife Janet (Deyn). Similar to "28 Days Later," it's an interesting concept but lackluster in character development with a disorganized story. **93m/C; DVD, Blu-Ray.** Natalie Dormer; Matt Smith; Stanley Tucci; Clive Standen; Agyness Deyn; *D:* Stefan Ruzowitzky; *W:* Mike Le; *C:* Benedict Neuenfels; *M:* Michael Wandmacher.

Patricia Cornwell's At Risk 1/2 *At Risk* **2010** Originally written as a 15-part magazine serial, Patricia Cornwell's wannabe mystery is convoluted and anticlimactic. Ambitious Boston D.A. Monique 'Money' Lamont (MacDowell) has her eyes on the Massachusetts governor's office by pushing an anti-crime initiative. Her reluctant go-to guy is state investigator Win Garano (Sunjata) and she shoves a 20-year-old cold case at him involving the murder of a Tennessee grandmother that supposedly has ties to a current-day political conspiracy. Followed by "Patricia Cornwell's The Front." **100m/C; DVD.** Andie MacDowell; Daniel Sunjata; Annabeth Gish; Barclay Hope; Zak Santiago; Ashley Williams; Diahann Carroll; *D:* Tom McLoughlin; *W:* John Pielmeier; *C:* Alwyn Kumst; *M:* Christopher Ward. **CABLE**

Patricia Cornwell's The Front 1/2 *The Front* **2010** In this equally nonsensical Lifetime sequel to "Patricia Cornwell's At Risk," Boston D.A. Monique Lamont (MacDowell) is having an affair with the current Massachusetts governor while hoping to revive her own political ambitions. Once again she has state investigator Win Garano (Sunjata) looking into a cold case; this time it's the 40-year-old unsolved murder of blind Janie Brolin. The prime suspect at the time was Janie's boyfriend but Monique would prefer to believe that Janie was a victim of the Boston Strangler. **100m/C; DVD.** Andie MacDowell; Daniel Sunjata; Ashley Williams; Joe Grifasi; Dane DeHaan; Diahann Carroll; Zak Santiago; *D:* Tom McLoughlin; *W:* John Pielmeier; *C:* Alwyn Kumst; *M:* Christopher Ward. **CABLE**

Patrick 1/2 **1978 (PG)** Coma patient suddenly develops strange powers and has a weird effect on the people he comes in contact with. **115m/C; VHS, DVD, Blu-Ray.** *AU* Robert Helpmann; Susan Penhaligon; Rod Mullinar; *D:* Richard Franklin; *M:* Brian May.

Patrick 1/2 **2013** Remake of the cult 1978 Australian film. A a mad scientist (Dance) experiments on an insane patient with psychic powers who lies comatose in his hospital. Using modern gore techniques definitely ups the ante, but the talented cast wakes this one up the most. **93m/C; DVD, Blu-Ray, Streaming.** *AU* Charles Dance; Rachel Griffiths; Sharni Vinson; Peta Sergeant; Martin Crewes; ***D:*** Mark Hartley; ***W:*** Justin King; ***C:*** Garry Richards; ***M:*** Pino Donaggio.

The Patriot 1/2 **1986 (R)** An action film about an ex-Navy commando who battles a band of nuclear-arms smuggling terrorists. Edited via George Lucas' electronic editor, Edit Droid. **88m/C; VHS, DVD.** Jeff Conaway; Michael J. Pollard; Leslie Nielsen; Gregg Henry; Simone Griffeth; ***D:*** Frank Harris; ***W:*** Andy Ruben; Katt Shea; ***M:*** Jay Ferguson.

The Patriot **1999 (R)** Wesley McClaren (Seagal) is a former government immunologist who's now the local doctor for a small ranching community. The peaceful community becomes a plague town when an extremist militia group take over and turn out to be carriers of a mysterious disease. McClaren might be a healer but he also can kick some extremist butt when necessary. **90m/C; VHS, DVD.** Steven Seagal; Gailard Sartain; L.Q. Jones; ***D:*** Dean Semler; ***C:*** Stephen F. Windon; ***M:*** Stephen (Steve) Edwards.

The Patriot 1/2 **2000 (R)** Bloody, long, and melodramatic Revolutionary War revenge pic with a strong lead by Gibson and a notably hissable villain in Isaacs. Benjamin Martin (Gibson) is a former guerilla soldier in the French and Indian wars who just wants to raise his family in peace. Unfortunately, local redcoat leader, Col. Tavington (Isaacs), has other ideas and when Martin's idealistic soldier son Gabriel (Ledger) is captured, dad gets caught up in the action. Film gave the British critics apoplexy with its inaccuracies. but who won, anyway? **164m/C; VHS, DVD, Blu-Ray.** Mel Gibson; Heath Ledger; Jason Isaacs; Chris Cooper; Tcheky Karyo; Joely Richardson; Tom Wilkinson; Donal Logue; Rene Auberjonois; Adam Baldwin; Logan Lerman; Gregory Edward Smith; ***D:*** Roland Emmerich; ***W:*** Robert Rodat; ***C:*** Caleb Deschanel; ***M:*** John Williams.

Patriot Games **1992 (R)** Jack Ryan, retired CIA analyst, takes his wife and daughter to England on a holiday and ends up saving a member of the Royal Family from assassination by IRA extremists. Ryan, who has killed one of the terrorists, then becomes the target of revenge by the dead man's brother. Good action sequences but otherwise predictable adaptation of the novel by Tom Clancy. Companion to "The Hunt for Red October," with Ford taking over the role of Ryan from Alec Baldwin. Followed by "Clear and Present Danger." **117m/C; VHS, DVD, Blu-Ray.** Harrison Ford; Anne Archer; Patrick Bergin; Thora Birch; Sean Bean; Richard Harris; James Earl Jones; James Fox; Samuel L. Jackson; Polly Walker; Theodore (Ted) Raimi; ***D:*** Phillip Noyce; ***W:*** Donald Stewart; W. Peter Iliff; ***C:*** Donald McAlpine; ***M:*** James Horner.

The Patriots **1933** A German prisoner works as a shoemaker in a small village during WWI. A lyrical drama in German and Russian with English titles. **82m/B; VHS, DVD.** *RU* Sergei Komarov; Nikolai Kryuchkov; Aleksandr Chistyakov; Yelena Kuzmina; ***D:*** Boris Barnet; ***W:*** Boris Barnet; ***C:*** Mikhail Kirillov; ***M:*** Sergei Vasilenko.

Patriots Day 1/2 **2017 (R)** Director Berg makes rock-solid dramas based on true stories, even though the liberties with the truth here border on unforgivable. Berg's partner in drama, Wahlberg, plays Police Sergeant Tommy Saunders, who survives and investigates the bombing of the Boston Marathon in 2013. The problem is that Berg's film makes him a fictional hero, adding to the true story with Hollywood exaggerations, and some questionable racism regarding the wife of one of the bombers. Adapting history is difficult, but it's downright dangerous when filmmakers make this much up. **133m/C; DVD, Blu-Ray.** Mark Wahlberg; John Goodman; Kevin Bacon; J.K. Simmons; Michelle Monaghan; ***D:*** Peter Berg; ***W:*** Peter Berg; Matt Cook; Joshua Zetumer; ***C:*** Tobias A. Schliessler; ***M:*** Trent Reznor; Atticus Ross.

The Patsy 1/2 **1928** Patricia (Davies) has fallen for glamorous older sister Grace's (Winton) boyfriend Tony (Caldwell). Grace seems more interested in rich playboy Bill (Gray), but she's stringing Tony along and she and their domineering mother (Dressler) want baby sis to butt out. Tony unwittingly gives Patricia romantic advice that she uses on him although not quite as intended. Davies was a charming comedienne and her character's attempts to act sophisticated are amusing. **78m/B; Silent; DVD.** Marion Davies; Jane Winton; Marie Dressler; Orville Caldwell; Lawrence Gray; Dell Henderson; ***D:*** King Vidor; ***W:*** Ralph Spence; ***C:*** John Seitz.

The Patsy **1964** Shady producers attempt to transform a lowly bellboy into a comedy superstar. Not one of Lewis's better efforts; Lorre's last film. **101m/C; VHS, DVD.** Jerry Lewis; Ina Balin; Everett Sloane; Phil Harris; Keenan Wynn; Peter Lorre; John Carradine; Hans Conried; Richard Deacon; Scatman Crothers; Del Moore; Neil Hamilton; Buddy Lester; Nancy Kulp; Norman Alden; Jack Albertson; ***D:*** Jerry Lewis; ***W:*** Jerry Lewis.

Pattern for Plunder 1/2 *The Bay of Saint Michel* **1962** Ex-commando leader rounds up his former comrades to head back to Normandy in search of buried Nazi plunder. **73m/B; VHS, DVD.** *GB* Keenan Wynn; Mai Zetterling; Ronald Howard; Edward Underdown; ***D:*** John Ainsworth; ***W:*** Christopher Davis.

Patterns *Patterns of Power* **1956** Realistic depiction of big business. Heflin starts work at a huge New York office that is under the ruthless supervision of Sloane. Serling's astute screenplay (adapted from his TV play) is adept at portraying ruthless, power-struggling executives and the sundry workings of a large corporation. Film has aged slightly, but it still has some edge to it. Originally intended for television. **83m/B; VHS, DVD, Blu-Ray.** Van Heflin; Everett Sloane; Ed Begley, Sr.; Beatrice Straight; Elizabeth Wilson; ***D:*** Fielder Cook; ***W:*** Rod Serling; ***C:*** Boris Kaufman.

Patti Cake$ 1/2 **2017 (R)** Dynamic indie drama that explores the power of music and belief in yourself and your goals, driven by the gritty performance of Macdonald in the titular role. Living in Jersey with her singer mother (Everett) and her grandmother (Moriarty), Patricia "Patti" Dombroski (Macdonald) is an aspiring rapper who writes her rhymes while working in the service industry. With best friend Jheri (Dhananjay) and new collaborator Basterd (Athie), Patti fights for her dream of rap stardom and a way out of her working class life. An authentic story of an underdog searching for her way to success. **109m/C; DVD.** Danielle MacDonald; Bridget Everett; Siddharth Dhananjay; Mamoudou Athie; Cathy Moriarty; ***D:*** Geremy Jasper; ***W:*** Geremy Jasper; ***C:*** Federico Cesca; ***M:*** Geremy Jasper; Jason Binnick.

Patton 1/2 *Patton: Lust for Glory; Patton: A Salute to a Rebel* **1970 (PG)** Lengthy but stellar bio of the vain, temperamental American general who masterminded significant combat triumphs during WWII. "Old Blood and Guts," who considered himself an 18th-century commander living in the wrong era, produced victory after victory in North Africa and Europe, but not without a decided impact upon his troops. Scott is truly magnificent in the title role, and Malden shines in the supporting role of General Omar Bradley. Not a subtle film, but neither is its subject. Interesting match-up with the 1986 TV movie "The Last Days of Patton," also starring Scott. **171m/C; VHS, DVD, Blu-Ray.** George C. Scott; Karl Malden; Stephen Young; Michael Strong; Frank Latimore; James Edwards; Lawrence (Larry) Dobkin; Michael Bates; Tim Considine; Edward Binns; John Doucette; Morgan Paull; Siegfried Rauch; ***D:*** Franklin J. Schaffner; ***W:*** Edmund H. North; Francis Ford Coppola; ***C:*** Fred W. Koenekamp; ***M:*** Jerry Goldsmith. Oscars '70: Actor (Scott), Art Dir./Set Dec., Director (Schaffner), Film, Film Editing, Sound, Story & Screenplay; AFI '98: Top 100; Directors Guild '70: Director (Schaffner); Golden Globes '71: Actor--Drama (Scott); Natl. Bd. of Review '70: Actor (Scott); Natl. Film Reg. '03; N.Y. Film Critics '70: Actor (Scott); Natl. Soc. Film Critics '70: Actor (Scott); Writers Guild '70: Orig. Screenplay.

Patty Hearst 1/2 **1988 (R)** Less than fascinating, expressionistic portrait of Hearst from her kidnapping through her brainwashing and eventual criminal participation with the SLA. An enigmatic film that seems to only make Hearst's transformation into a Marxist terrorist all the more mysterious. Based on Hearst's book, "Every Secret Thing." **108m/C; VHS, DVD, Blu-Ray; Open Captioned.** Natasha Richardson; William Forsythe; Ving Rhames; Frances Fisher; Jodi Long; Dana Delany; ***D:*** Paul Schrader; ***W:*** Nicholas Kazan; ***C:*** Bojan Bazelli.

Paul **2011 (R)** British sci-fi geeks Graeme (Pegg) and Clive (Frost) travel to America to attend Comic-Con and then go on an RV road trip to check out UFO sites. They don't expect to rescue wisecracking alien Paul (voiced by Rogen), a big-headed, big-eyed, skinny 'grey' (but wearing board shorts and flip-flops), who's escaped from Area 51 where he's been kept for 60 years. He wants to go home and asks the Brits to drive him to his long-hidden spaceship. Naturally, the trio is pursued by the men in black in this good-natured, surprisingly gentle comic sci fi adventure. **104m/C; Blu-Ray, On Demand.** *US GB* Simon Pegg; Nick Frost; Jason Bateman; Kristen Wiig; Bill Hader; Jane Lynch; Jeffrey Tambor; John Lynch; Sigourney Weaver; Blythe Danner; David Koechner; Jesse Plemons; Mia Stallard; Joe Lo Truglio; ***V:*** Seth Rogen; ***D:*** Greg Mottola; ***W:*** Simon Pegg; Nick Frost; ***C:*** Lawrence Sher; ***M:*** David Arnold.

Paul, Apostle of Christ 1/2 **2018 (PG-13)** A moving telling of the story of the Apostle Paul's imprisonment and martyrdom. Set in ancient Rome, at a time when Christ's first followers were often brutally persecuted and killed, Paul (Faulkner), the newly arrived Luke the Evangelist (Caviezel), and fellow Christians deliberate on the best way to ensure they--and the gospel--survive. Much of the story centers on the jailed Paul sharing his teachings and his personal story, including his conversion on the road to Damascus, with Luke. Focusing on the cost and value of sacrificial love, compassion, and the power of faith, the film thoughtfully explores the message of Christ. **108m/C; DVD, Blu-Ray.** Jim Caviezel; James Faulkner; Olivier Martinez; Joanne Whalley; John Lynch; ***D:*** Andrew Hyatt; ***W:*** Andrew Hyatt; Terence Berden; ***C:*** Gerardo Madrazo; ***M:*** Jan A.P. Kaczmarek.

Paul Blart: Mall Cop 1/2 **2009 (PG)** Mild-mannered single dad and security guard Paul Blart must save the day when a gang of crooks (dressed as Santa's helpers) takes over his New Jersey shopping mall with a plan to rob all the stores. Like the comedy of the 3 Stooges, flick relies upon slapstick and pratfalls to pry loose a few mindless laughs, which get old after the first 20 minutes, not coincidently the approximate running time of a TV sitcom, a venue more suited to James' limited range. **91m/C; Blu-Ray, On Demand.** Kevin James; Keir O'Donnell; Jayma Mays; Erik Avari; Shirley Knight; Peter Gerety; Bobby Cannavale; Adam Ferrara; Raini Rodriguez; Stephen Rannazzisi; ***D:*** Steve Carr; ***W:*** Kevin James; Nicky Bakay; ***C:*** Russ T. Alsobrook; ***M:*** Waddy Wachtel.

Paul Blart: Mall Cop 2 **WOOF!** **2015 (PG)** The lovable mall cop from the first film has been replaced by a misogynist, smarmy jerk in this completely laughless sequel that nobody asked for. Paul Blart gets invited to Las Vegas for a security officers convention and stumbles upon another crime. The plot is a thin excuse for more pratfalls and boring physical humor, and even that stuff is poorly handled. Star James has proven that he has solid comic timing in the past but he falls victim to the horrendous script, one of the worst in years, and leaden direction that most sitcom producers would call inadequate. **94m/C; DVD, Blu-Ray.** Kevin James; Raini Rodriguez; Eduardo Verastegui; Daniella Alonso; Neal McDonough; DB Woodside; Nicholas Turturro; ***D:*** Andy Fickman; ***W:*** Kevin James; Nick Bakay; ***C:*** Dean Semler; ***M:*** Rupert Gregson-Williams.

Paul Robeson **1977** Major events in the life of the popular actor are recounted in this one-man performance. Originally staged by Charles Nelson Reilly. **118m/C; VHS, DVD.** James Earl Jones; ***D:*** Lloyd Richards.

Paula 1/2 **1952** A weepy played with sincerity. A hit-and-run accident leaves young David (Rettig) mute. Driver Paula (Young) wants to hide her involvement but is still guilt-ridden so she works to help David learn to speak again. As he improves, David figures out Paula was responsible and the police investigation takes a new turn. **80m/B; DVD.** Loretta Young; Tommy Rettig; Ken Smith; Alexander Knox; Otto Hulett; ***D:*** Rudolph Mate; ***W:*** William Sackheim; James Poe; ***C:*** Charles Lawton, Jr.; ***M:*** George Duning.

Paulie 1/2 **1998 (PG)** Dreamworks tale of a conversant parrot (voiced by Mohr) whose mouth keeps getting him in trouble. Trapped in a dingy basement, Paulie tells a lonely Russian janitor (Shalhoub) the story of his cross-country quest to return to his original owner, the little girl (Eisenberg) who raised him from a fledgling. After the girl's parents send him away, Paulie goes through a succession of owners. Not a whole lot of action for a kiddie movie and some of the jokes may go over their heads, but fine performances and a charming story keep pic aloft. **91m/C; VHS, DVD.** Jay Mohr; Gena Rowlands; Tony Shalhoub; Richard "Cheech" Marin; Hallie Kate Eisenberg; Bruce Davison; Trini Alvarado; Buddy Hackett; Matt Craven; Bill Cobbs; Laura Harrington; Tia Texada; ***V:*** Jay Mohr; ***D:*** John Roberts; ***W:*** Laurie Craig; ***C:*** Tony Pierce-Roberts; ***M:*** John Debney.

Pauline and Paulette **2001 (PG)** Pauline (van der Groen) is a 66-year-old mentally retarded woman living happily with her sister Martha (De Bruyn) is a Flemish town near Brussels. When Martha dies, her will states that her estate will be divided in thirds on condition that one of the two remaining sisters, Paulette (Petersen) or Cecile (Bergmans) take in Pauline. Otherwise the money will go to set Pauline up in a special care facility. Paulette agrees to care for Pauline, at least temporarily, and finds there are some obligations that aren't easy to get rid of. French and Flemish with subtitles. **78m/C; VHS, DVD.** *BE FR NL* Dora van der Groen; Ann Petersen; Rosemarie Bergmans; Julienne De Bruyn; Idwig Stephane; ***D:*** Lieven Debrauwer; ***W:*** Lieven Debrauwer; Jacques Boon; ***C:*** Michael Van Laer; ***M:*** Frederic Devreese.

Pauline at the Beach 1/2 *Pauline a la Plage* **1983 (R)** Fifteen-year-old Pauline (Langlet) accompanies her more experienced divorced cousin Marion (Dombasle) to the French coast for a summer of sexual hijinks. Contemplative, not coarse, though the leads look great in—and out—of their swimsuits. Breezy, typically talky fare from small-film master Rohmer. Third film in the director's Comedies & Proverbs series. French with subtitles. **95m/C; VHS, DVD, Blu-Ray.** *FR* Amanda Langlet; Arielle Dombasle; Pascal Greggory; Rosette; Feodor Atkine; Simon de la Brosse; ***D:*** Eric Rohmer; ***W:*** Eric Rohmer; ***C:*** Nestor Almendros.

Pavarotti 1/2 **2019 (PG-13)** An inviting look at popular Italian opera singer Luciano Pavarotti—his life, marriage, and family, and the beginnings of his successful career in the 1960s. Though the growth of his career affects his family, Pavaraotti's personal warmth and personality bring more people to opera. Features the operas he performs in, his time with The Three Tenors, and his charity work. As directed by Howard, the appealing documentary includes the expected talking heads and archive footage of Pavarotti but offers a comprehensive, honest look at him and his place in music history. **114m/C; DVD, Blu-Ray.** Luciano Pavarotti; Spike Lee; Stevie Wonder; ***D:*** Ron Howard; ***W:*** Mark Monroe; ***C:*** Michael Dwyer; ***M:*** Ric Markmann; Matter Music; Dan Pinnella; Chris Wagner.

Pavilion of Women 1/2 **2001 (R)** Dull adaptation of the 1946 Pearl S. Buck novel. As the Japanese prepare to invade Manchuria in 1938, Madame Wu (Luo), tired of her husband's brutality, decides to give him a peasant girl concubine, Chiuming (Ding), whom he promptly rejects. However, the pretty girl attracts the interest of the Wu's youngest son, Fengmo (Cho), just as Madame becomes interested in American missionary doctor, Father Andre (Dafoe), who runs the local orphanage. The film is in English and the Chinese actors do struggle with their dialogue which doesn't help the emotional balance of the production. **120m/C; VHS, DVD.** Luo Yan; Willem Dafoe; John Cho; Yi Ding; Shek Sau; Amy Hill; Anita Loo; Kate McGregor-Stewart; ***W:*** Luo Yan; Paul R. Collins; ***C:*** Hang-Seng Poon; ***M:*** Conrad Pope.

Pawn 1/2 **2013 (R)** By-the-numbers hostage crime thriller mostly notable for Chiklis' odd English accent as bad guy Derrick. A nondescript diner is a mob front and Derrick and his two thugs are hired to steal a backroom hard drive. Derrick decides on an old-fashioned stick-up of the customers as well, resulting in a hostage situation, good and bad cops, ex-cons, gangsters, and violence. **88m/C; DVD, Blu-Ray.** Michael Chiklis; Forest Whitaker; Sean Faris; Stephen Lang; Nikki Reed; Common; Jessica Szohr; Marton Csokas; Ray Liotta; ***D:*** David A. Armstrong; ***W:*** Jay Anthony White; ***C:*** Keith Dunkerley; ***M:*** Jacob Yoffee.

Pawn Sacrifice **2015 (PG-13)** The true story of the battle between Cold War superpowers embodied in the competition between Bobby Fischer (Maguire) and Boris Spassky (Schreiber) is a fascinating one, but the film by Zwick is a surprisingly flat one, coming off more like a TV movie take on the subject than a cinematic one. In 1972, Fischer was at the top of the chess game but also dealing with serious mental illness. Zwick's film captures some of Fischer's rise and how it was his mental demons that he hid from the world as everyone watched him take on Spassky in the most famous chess match of all time. **114m/C; DVD.**

Pawn Sacrifice 1/2 **2015 (PG-13)** Though the story has been told before, Maguire shines as the lead in this recounting of the famous chess match in 1972 between Bobby Fischer and Boris Spassky (Schreiber). The event was powerful for what it represented during the Cold War -- an intellectual faceoff between the two opposing superpowers. But director Zwick falls short of capturing the essence of this true-life story. Though Maguire is worth watching as the tormented Fischer struggles with his emotional state. **114m/C; DVD.** Liev Schreiber; Lily Rabe; Tobey Maguire; Peter Sarsgaard; Michael Stuhlbarg; ***D:*** Edward Zwick; ***W:*** Steven Knight; ***C:*** Bradford Young; ***M:*** James Newton Howard.

The Pawnbroker 1/2 **1965** A Jewish pawnbroker in Harlem is haunted by his grueling experiences in a Nazi camp during the Holocaust. Powerful and well done. Probably Steiger's best performance. Adapted from a novel by Edward Lewis Wallant. **120m/B; DVD, Blu-Ray.** Rod Steiger; Brock Peters; Geraldine Fitzgerald; Jaime Sanchez; Thelma Oliver; ***D:*** Sidney Lumet; ***C:*** Boris Kaufman; ***M:*** Quincy Jones. Berlin Intl. Film Fest. '65: Actor (Steiger); British Acad. '66: Actor (Steiger); Natl. Film Reg. '08.

Pay It Forward **2000 (PG-13)** Seventh-grade student Trevor (Osment) takes his social studies assignment very seriously. His teacher Eugene (Spacey) has his students think of an idea to change the world and tells them to put it into action. Trevor comes up with the idea of doing a good deed for someone who is then supposed to do a favor for someone else as a way to "pay the favor forward." Trevor's cocktail waitress/recovering alcoholic mom Arlene (Hunt) finds herself wary of both the project and the teacher. Cloyingly emotional and more than a little manipulative. Based on the novel by Catherine Ryan Hyde. **122m/C; VHS, DVD.** Haley Joel Osment; Kevin Spacey; Helen Hunt; David Ramsey; Jay Mohr; James (Jim) Caviezel; Jon Bon Jovi; Angie Dickinson; Gary Werntz; ***D:*** Mimi Leder; ***W:*** Leslie Dixon; ***C:*** Oliver Stapleton; ***M:*** Thomas Newman.

Pay the Ghost **2015** Based on a work of fiction by Tim Lebbon thriller about the terror surrounding a missing child for one determined father. During a Halloween carnival, a young boy is abducted and has not been found a year later. One year later, the boy's father, workaholic professor Mike Lawford (Cage), struggles with visions of his son and odd messages sent his way. Still looking for his son, Mike partners with his estranged wife Kristen (Callies) to find him. Along the way, they encounter a legend from the past that is still haunting people in present day. **94m/C; DVD, Blu-Ray, Streaming, Download.** Nicolas Cage; Sarah Wayne Callies; Veronica Ferres; Lyriq Bent; Lauren Beatty; ***D:*** Uli Edel; ***W:*** Dan Kay; ***C:*** Sharone Meir; ***M:*** Joseph LoDuca. **VIDEO**

Payback **1998 (R)** Mel's very, very mean. Of course, his character has every reason to be in this loose remake of 1967's "Point Blank" and the novel "The Hunter" by Richard Stark. Porter (Gibson) is double-crossed by partner Val (Henry), who steals the loot from their latest heist as well as Porter's junkie wife, Lynn (Unger), and then leaves Porter for dead. Porter becomes obsessed with getting his money back, and he'll take on anyone who gets in his way. Very cold, violent neo-noir with a pro lead and interesting supporting cast. **110m/C; VHS, DVD, Blu-Ray, HD-DVD.** Mel Gibson; Gregg Henry; Maria Bello; David Paymer; Deborah Kara Unger; William Devane; Kris Kristofferson; Bill Duke; Jack Conley; John Glover; Lucy Liu; James Coburn; ***D:*** Brian Helgeland; ***W:*** Brian Helgeland; Terry Hayes; ***C:*** Ericson Core; ***M:*** Chris Boardman.

Paycheck **2003 (PG-13)** Michael Jennings (Affleck) is a brilliant engineer hired by his old friend Jimmy Rethrick (Echkart) to work on a top-secret project. The one condition is that he gets his mind erased after his job is completed. Three years later, Jennings, sans memories, finds that he had forfeited his fee of $90 million in exchange for a manila envelope full of seemingly random objects that become clues to figuring out why his employers now want him dead. Surprisingly lackluster adaption of a Phillip K. Dick short story, considering that John Woo is the director. **110m/C; DVD, Blu-Ray.** Ben Affleck; Aaron Eckhart; Uma Thurman; Paul Giamatti; Colm Feore; Joe Morton; Michael C. Hall; ***D:*** John Woo; ***W:*** Dean Georgaris; ***C:*** Jeffrey L. Kimball; ***M:*** John Powell. Golden Raspberries '03: Worst Actor (Affleck).

Payday 1/2 **1973** Torn stars as a declining country music star on tour in this portrayal of the seamy side of show business, from groupies to grimy motels. Well-written script and fine performances make this an engaging, if rather draining, drama not easily found on the big screen. **98m/C; VHS, DVD.** Rip Torn; Ahna Capri; Michael C. Gwynne; Jeff Morris; Sonny Shroyer; ***D:*** Daryl Duke; ***W:*** Don Carpenter; ***C:*** Richard C. Glouner; ***M:*** Ed Bogas; Shel Silverstein; Ian Tyson.

Payment on Demand 1/2 **1951** Bette plays social climbing bitch Joyce Ramsey who, nonetheless, is stunned when David (Sullivan), her husband of 20 years, calmly asks her for a divorce. She's livid when she learns that he has been seeing another woman (Dee) and threatens a scandal unless David coughs up a large settlement. While taking a cruise, Joyce gets a glimpse into the lonely life of a divorcee so before the final decree can be granted, she asks David for another chance. Definitely a movie suited to the conservative Hollywood times. **90m/B; DVD.** Bette Davis; Frances Dee; Kent Taylor; John Sutton; Jane Cowl; Barry Sullivan; Betty Lynn; Peggy Castle; Otto Kruger; Richard Anderson; ***D:*** Curtis Bernhardt; ***W:*** Curtis Bernhardt; ***C:*** Bruce Manning; Leo Tover; ***M:*** Victor Young.

The Payoff 1/2 **1943** The old-fashioned newspaper-reporter-as-crime-fighter routine. When the city's special prosecutor is murdered a daring newshawk investigates and tracks the bad guys. But will he spell their names right? **74m/B; VHS, DVD.** Lee Tracy; Tom Brown; Tina Thayer; Evelyn Brent; Jack La Rue; Ian Keith; John Maxwell; ***D:*** Arthur Dreifuss.

P.C.U. **1994 (PG-13)** Satire on campus political correctness follows freshman Tom Lawrence's (Young) adventures as he navigates the treacherous waters of Port Chester University (PCU). He falls in with the gang from the Pit, the militantly non-PC dorm, who encourage bizarre and offensive behavior. Essentially a modern update of "National Lampoon's Animal House," but without the brilliance; add half a bone for tackling the thorny sensitivity issue in a humorous way that parodies, but shouldn't offend. Actor Bochner's directorial debut. **81m/C; VHS, DVD.** Jeremy Piven; Chris Young; David Spade; Sarah Trigger; Jessica Walter; Jon Favreau; Megan Ward; Jake Busey; Alex Desert; ***Cameo(s):*** George Clinton; ***D:*** Hart Bochner; ***W:*** Adam Leff; Zak Penn; ***M:*** Steve Vai.

P.D. James: Death in Holy Orders 1/2 *Death in Holy Orders* **2003** When murder and suicide overtake St. Anselm's, a remote theological college, one victim's wealthy father pressures Scotland Yard to investigate. Adam Dalgleish (Shaw), who spent childhood summers at the school, is sent and discovers that the Church of England wishes to close the school, and Archdeacon Matthew Crampton (Wood) is particularly interested in seeing that its valuable art works have more suitable settings. What the widowed Dalgleish doesn't expect to encounter is potential romance with visiting professor Emma Lavenham (Dee). **180m/C; DVD.** *GB* Martin Shaw; Jesse Spencer; Alan Howard; Clive Wood; Hugh Fraser; Robert Hardy; Janie Dee; ***D:*** John J. Campbell; ***W:*** Robert C. Jones; ***C:*** Martin Fuhrer; ***M:*** Julian Nott. **TV**

P.D. James: The Murder Room 1/2 *The Murder Room* **2004** A macabre family legacy leads to murder and other crimes. London's Dupayne Museum houses exhibits from some of Britain's most gruesome real-life homicides. When Neville (Maloney), one of the Dupayne heirs, dies in a terrible fire, Adam Dalgleish (Shaw) investigates and discovers that the killing is similar to a notorious case on display. But there are also family secrets the remaining Dupaynes don't want exposed. **180m/C; DVD.** *GB* Martin Shaw; Samantha Bond; Michael Maloney; Nicholas Le Prevost; Sian Phillips; Kerry Fox; Janie Dee; ***D:*** Diarmuid Lawrence; ***W:*** Robert C. Jones; ***C:*** Simon Richards; ***M:*** John Lunn. **TV**

Peace, Love & Misunderstanding **2011 (R)** Undemanding, predictable family comedy finds aged hippie Grace (Fonda) playing mother figure to the folks of Woodstock, who apparently got trapped in the '60s. Her own long-estranged daughter, straitlaced Diane (Keener), makes a sudden appearance with her two teenagers to cope with her almost-finalized divorce issues. They seem to settle right in and before long find romance to go along with Grandma's pot. **92m/C; DVD, Blu-Ray, Streaming.** Catherine Keener; Nat Wolff; Kyle MacLachlan; Elizabeth Olsen; Jane Fonda; Jeffrey Dean Morgan; Marissa O'Donnell; Chace Crawford; ***D:*** Bruce Beresford; ***W:*** Christina Mengert; Joseph Muszynski, PhD; ***C:*** Andre Fleuren; ***M:*** Spencer David Hutchings.

Peace, Propaganda & the Promised Land **2004** Expose lashing out at the American media's coverage of the Israeli-Palestinian conflict. Another long-winded attempt at a Michael Moore-style "documentary." Cites twists on terms, such as "retaliate" when Israel makes a move, but using the word "attack" when describing Palestinian operations. On-camera interviews come from unabashedly biased academics and advocates. Makes some stirring observations, but its lack of humor and tunnel-visioned hoopla will turn off most audiences. Ironically, it falls into the category it sets out to derail: juicy propaganda. **80m/C; DVD.** ***D:*** Sut Jhally; Bathsheba Ratzkoff; ***C:*** Kelli Garner; ***M:*** Thom Monahan.

Peaceful Warrior **2006 (PG-13)** It's not quite the new "Karate Kid" despite that whole Zen mentor aspect that Nolte brings to the role of Socrates. Dan (Mechlowicz) is a hotshot college gymnast who is told his dreams are over after a bad motorcycle crash. Socrates offers his own spiritual take on Dan's dilemma and Dan goes on to'well, the actual Dan Millman goes on to write a 1980 New Age memoir called "Way of the Peaceful Warrior," which this film is based on. **121m/C; DVD.** Nick Nolte; Scott Mechlowicz; Amy Smart; Tim DeKay; Paul Wesley; Ashton Holmes; Agnes Bruckner; Ray Wise; B. J. Britt; ***D:*** Victor Salva; ***W:*** Victor Salva; Kevin Bernhardt; ***C:*** Sharone Meir; ***M:*** Bennett Salvay.

The Peacekeeper **1998 (R)** Frank Cross (Lundgren) is one unlucky man. While guarding the president (Scheider), he manages to lose the briefcase containing nuclear launch codes to a terrorist group. Now, they're blackmailing the government and Cross needs to breach the terrorist's stronghold to save the day. **98m/C; VHS, DVD.** *CA* Dolph Lundgren; Roy Scheider; Michael Sarrazin; Montel Williams; Monica Schnarre; ***D:*** Frederic Forestier; ***W:*** James H. Stewart; Robert Geoffrion; ***C:*** John Berrie; ***M:*** Francois Forestier.

Peacekillers 1/2 **1971** A mean bunch of bikers visit a commune to kidnap a young woman. The gang has a big surprise in store for them when the girl escapes. **86m/C; VHS, Streaming.** Michael Ontkean; Clint Ritchie; Paul Krokop; ***D:*** Douglas Schwartz.

Peacemaker **1990 (R)** Two aliens masquerading as human cops stalk each other through a major city. **90m/C; VHS, DVD; Open Captioned.** Robert Forster; Lance Edwards; Hilary Shepard; Bert Remsen; Robert Davi; ***D:*** Kevin S. Tenney; ***W:*** Kevin S. Tenney.

The Peacemaker 1/2 **1997 (R)** First-time feature director Leder teams up with fellow "ER" vet Clooney on the first theatrical release for Dreamworks SKG. Army Intel officer Lt. Col. Thomas Devoe (Clooney) works with White House nuke expert Dr. Julia Kelly (Kidman) when a renegade Russian colonel diverts some nuclear warheads, scheduled for dismantling, into the hands of a Bosnian diplomat (Iures) with a grudge against the West. Plenty of well-constructed action set pieces and a reasonably plausible plot overcome a lack of snappy dialogue. Extra credit for making the terrorist human instead of the usual evil caricature, and for letting the two leads work together without having to sleep together. **123m/C; VHS, DVD.** George Clooney; Nicole Kidman; Armin Mueller-Stahl; Marcel Iures; Alexander Baluyev; Randall Batinkoff; Jim Haynie; Michael Boatman; Gary Werntz; Holt McCallany; Joan Copeland; Carlos Gomez; Rene Medvesek; Alexander Strobele; ***D:*** Mimi Leder; ***W:*** Michael Schiffer; ***C:*** Dietrich Lohmann; ***M:*** Hans Zimmer.

Peacock **2009 (PG-13)** Oddball drama set in the 1950s in the small town of Peacock, Nebraska. Meek bank clerk John Skillpa (Murphy) is living quietly until the caboose of a derailed train lands in his backyard. When the locals survey the accident, they notice a young woman running into the house and assume it's John's previously unseen wife. Actually, it's the disturbed John's alter ego Emma and the accident leads the personalities to start clashing. **90m/C; DVD.** Cillian Murphy; Ellen Page; Josh(ua) Lucas; Susan Sarandon; Keith Carradine; Graham Beckel; Bill Pullman; ***D:*** Michael Lander; ***W:*** Michael Lander; Ryan Roy; ***C:*** Philippe Rousselot; ***M:*** Brian Reitzell. **VIDEO**

The Peanut Butter Falcon 1/2 **2019 (PG-13)** Placed in a nursing home by the state because he lacks family and resources, young Zac (Gottsagen) has Down Syndrome and dreams of becoming a professional wrestler. Though he is friends with the elderly residents and worker Eleanor (Johnson), he wants to attend a wrestling school run by Salt Walter Redneck (Haden Church). One night, Zac flees and stows away on a crabbing ship owned by Tyler (LaBeouf). Though Tyler has problems of his own, he bonds with Zac and helps him work towards his goal. The adventure buddy film looks and feels like a fable and allows cast members, including Gottsagen, to shine. **93m/C; DVD, Blu-Ray.** Shia LaBeouf; Dakota Johnson; Zack Gottsagen; John Hawkes; Thomas Haden Church; ***D:*** Tyler Nilson; Michael Schwartz; ***W:*** Tyler Nilson; Michael Schwartz; ***C:*** Nigel Bluck; ***M:*** Zachary Dawes; Noam Pikelny; Jonathan Sadoff; Gabe Witcher.

The Peanuts Movie **2015 (G)** It's nice to spend some time with the gang created by Charles M. Schulz, but rarely has a film existed on more of a foundation of pure nostalgia. The team behind Charlie Brown's CGI-animated debut literally crib from some of the most famous Peanuts cartoons of the past, lifting bits wholesale, resulting in a film that's bizarrely episodic. If you don't mind films that lack originality or play on your sentimental heartstrings, there are parts of Martino's film that are pretty cute. But that's not quite enough in an era of fantastic, original animation. **92m/C; DVD, Blu-Ray.** Noah Schnapp; Bill Melendez; Rebecca Bloom; Anastasia Bredikhina; Francesca Capaldi; ***D:*** Steve Martino; ***W:*** Bryan Schulz; Craig A. Schulz; Cornelius Uliano; ***C:*** Renato Falcao; ***M:*** Christophe Beck.

Pearl 1/2 **1978** Sweeping miniseries covers the careers and private lives of those who live and work at the naval base at Pearl Harbor, Hawaii, from right before the Japanese attack to its aftermath. **233m/C; VHS, DVD.** Robert Wagner; Dennis Weaver; Lesley Ann Warren; Brian Dennehy; Max Gail; Mary Crosby; Gregg Henry; Katherine Helmond; Angie Dickinson; Tiana Alexandra; Richard Anderson; Adam Arkin; Marion Ross; Allan Miller; David Elliott; ***Nar:*** Joseph Campanella; ***D:*** Hy Averback; Alexander Singer; ***W:*** Stirling Silliphant; ***C:*** Gayne Rescher; ***M:*** John Addison. **TV**

Pearl Diver ♪♪ **2004** Sisters Hannah and Marian were raised on the family's farm in a Mennonite community in rural Indiana. Their mother's murder has caused them to drift apart as Hannah has moved to the city and become a writer and Marian has married and stayed at home. When Marian's daughter is severely injured in a farm accident, Hannah returns to help out and the two sisters also attempt to confront what really happened the night their mother died. **90m/C; DVD.** Eugene (Yevgeny) Lazarev; Joey Honja; Amy Jean Johnson; Kim Stauffer; Brian Boland; Maddie Abshire; Christopher Collard; ***D:*** Sidney King; ***W:*** Sidney King; ***C:*** John Rotan; ***M:*** Jay Lapp; Frances Miller.

Pearl Harbor ♪♪ **2001 (PG-13)** Director Bay knows his way around big-budget, action-packed event movies. The problem, besides his usual difficulties with characterization and subtlety, is that we have to wade through the trite romantic triangle between U.S. Army Air aviator Hartnett, flyboy Affleck, and Navy nurse Beckinsale before we get to the well-done spectacle of the bombing on December 7, 1941, as well as the subsequent U.S. raid on Tokyo led by James Doolittle (Baldwin). It's probably quicker, and more enjoyable, just to skip to the attack sequence. **183m/C; VHS, DVD.** Ben Affleck; Josh Hartnett; Kate Beckinsale; Alec Baldwin; Dan Aykroyd; Colm Feore; Mako; Scott Wilson; Cuba Gooding, Jr.; Jon Voight; Tom Sizemore; Glenn Morshower; Peter Firth; Michael Shannon; William Lee Scott; Jennifer Garner; Catherine Kellner; Jaime King; ***D:*** Michael Bay; ***W:*** Randall Wallace; ***C:*** John Schwartzman; ***M:*** Hans Zimmer.

Pearl Jam Twenty ♪♪ 1/2 **2011** Director Crowe moved to Seattle at just the moment that the music scene there was about to explode in the 1990s. Essentially, he's been tracking Pearl Jam for the two decades since (over 12,000 hours of footage) and he's perfectly cut together never-before-seen archival footage with recently-shot interviews. Crowe has made a rock and roll documentary for more than pure fans of the band, as even those who long ago gave up on the grunge icons could find inspiration in the story of their creative integrity and impressive drive. **109m/C; DVD, Blu-Ray.** Cameron Crowe; Edward Vedder; Stone Gossart; Jeff Ament; Matt Cameron; Mike McCready; Chris Cornell; ***D:*** Cameron Crowe; ***W:*** Cameron Crowe; ***C:*** Nicola Marsh; ***M:*** Pearl Jam.

The Pearl of Death ♪♪ 1/2 **1944** Holmes and Watson investigate the theft of a precious pearl. **69m/B; VHS, DVD.** Basil Rathbone; Nigel Bruce; Dennis Hoey; Miles Mander; Rondo Hatton; Evelyn Ankers; ***D:*** Roy William Neill; ***W:*** Bertram Millhauser; ***C:*** Virgil Miller.

Pearl of the South Pacific ♪♪ *South Sea Woman* **1955** A trio of adventurers destroy a quiet and peaceful island when they ransack it for pearl treasures. **85m/C; VHS, DVD.** Dennis Morgan; Virginia Mayo; David Farrar; ***D:*** Allan Dwan; ***W:*** Edwin Blum; ***C:*** John Alton; ***M:*** Louis Forbes.

Peau D'Ane ♪♪♪ **1971** Charming fairy tale about a widowed king in search of a beautiful wife. Gorgeous color production. In French with English subtitles. **90m/C; VHS, DVD.** *FR* Catherine Deneuve; Jacques Perrin; Jean Marais; Delphine Seyrig; ***D:*** Jacques Demy.

The Pebble and the Penguin ♪♪ 1/2 **1994 (G)** Animated musical about a shy, romantic penguin named Hubie (Short), who must present his lady love Marina (Golden) with a beautiful pebble to win her hand before the villainous Drake (Curry) can claim her. Hubie is helped along by a cantankerous new friend (Belushi) he meets when stranded on a boat to Tahiti. Together, the two race back to Antarctica fighting enemies and the elements along the way. Based on the mating customs of the Adeli penguins, the story is satisfying for younger viewers, but won't keep adults interested. Beware of the sugary Manilow tunes. **74m/C; VHS, DVD, Blu-Ray.** ***V:*** Martin Short; Annie Golden; Tim Curry; James Belushi; ***Nar:*** Shani Wallis; ***D:*** Don Bluth; ***W:*** Rachel Koretsky; Steve Whitestone; ***M:*** Barry Manilow; Bruce Sussman; Mark Watters.

Pecker ♪♪ 1/2 **1998 (R)** A kinder, gentler Waters? To be sure, he doesn't laugh at, but with, his working-class Baltimoreans. Still, you've got strippers (of both sexes), a "talking" statue of the Virgin Mary, and rats having sex. Pecker (Furlong), who gets his name from pecking at his food, is a sweet teenager and amateur photog, who takes pictures of what's around him. His work catches the eye of New York art dealer Rorey Wheeler (Taylor), who wants to showcase the next hot trend, and Pecker becomes an overnight superstar in the fickle art world. But his celeb status has unexpected repercussions on his hometown friends and family. **87m/C; VHS, DVD.** Edward Furlong; Lili Taylor; Christina Ricci; Jean Schertler; Martha Plimpton; Mary Kay Place; Brendan Sexton, III; Patty (Patricia Campbell) Hearst; Mark Joy; Mink Stole; Bess Armstrong; ***V:*** John Waters; ***D:*** John Waters; ***W:*** John Waters; ***C:*** Robert M. Stevens; ***M:*** Stewart Copeland. Natl. Bd. of Review '98: Support. Actress (Ricci).

Peck's Bad Boy ♪♪ 1/2 **1934** A wedge is driven between a young boy and his adoptive father when the man's sister and her son move in. The aunt wants her son to be number one, causing much discord. Cooper is excellent in his role as the adopted son. **70m/B; VHS, DVD.** Thomas Meighan; Jackie Cooper; Dorothy Peterson; Jackie Searl; O.P. Heggie; Harvey Clark; Lloyd Ingraham; ***D:*** Edward F. (Eddie) Cline.

Peck's Bad Boy with the Circus ♪♪ **1938** The circus will never be the same after the mischievous youngster and his buddies get done with it. Gilbert and Kennedy provide the high points. **67m/B; VHS, DVD.** Tommy Kelly; Ann Gillis; George "Spanky" McFarland; Edgar Kennedy; Billy Gilbert; ***D:*** Edward F. (Eddie) Cline.

Pee-wee's Big Adventure ♪♪♪ 1/2 **1985 (PG)** Zany, endearing comedy about an adult nerd's many adventures while attempting to recover his stolen bicycle. Chock full of classic sequences, including a barroom encounter between Pee-wee and several ornery bikers, and a tour through the Alamo. A colorful, exhilarating experience. **92m/C; VHS, DVD, Blu-Ray.** Paul (Pee-wee Herman) Reubens; Elizabeth Daily; Mark Holton; Diane Salinger; Judd Omen; Cassandra Peterson; James Brolin; Morgan Fairchild; Tony Bill; Jan Hooks; Phil Hartman; Jason Hervey; John Paragon; ***D:*** Tim Burton; ***W:*** Paul (Pee-wee Herman) Reubens; Michael Varhol; Phil Hartman; ***C:*** Victor Kemper; ***M:*** Danny Elfman.

Peep World ♪ 1/2 **2010** The dysfunctional Meyerowitz siblings attempt to celebrate the 70th birthday of their despicable father Henry (Rifkin) while dealing with personal crises in Blausteins's hackneyed black comedy. The characters are strained caricatures: eldest brother Jack (Hall), the supposedly responsible married one, is addicted to peep-show porn; Joel (Wilson) is a constantly in-and-out of rehab mooch; wannabe showbiz-hyphenate Cheryl (Silverman) is an obnoxious diva; and youngest Nathan (Schwartz) is a smug writer who has just published a roman a clef about the family that isn't going over well on the homefront. An unpleasant group unworthy of your time. **89m/C; DVD, Blu-Ray.** Michael C. Hall; Sarah Silverman; Rainn Wilson; Ben Schwartz; Judy Greer; Kate Mara; Ron Rifkin; Alicia Witt; Taraji P. Henson; Nicholas Hormann; ***Nar:*** Lewis Black; ***D:*** Barry W. Blaustein; ***W:*** Peter Himmelstein; ***C:*** Tobias Datum; ***M:*** Jeff Cardoni.

Peeping Tom ♪♪♪ 1/2 *Face of Fear; The Fotographer of Panic* **1960** Controversial, unsettling thriller in which psychopath Mark Lewis (Boehm) lures women before his film camera, then records their deaths at his hand. Unnerving subject matter is rendered impressively by British master Powell, who plays the part of Mark's abusie father who's shown in home movies tormenting the boy. A classic of its kind, but definitely not for everyone. Critical brickbats effectively derailed Powell's career and the original uncut version was not released until 1979. **88m/C; VHS, DVD.** *GB* Karl-Heinz Boehm; Moira Shearer; Anna Massey; Maxine Audley; Esmond Knight; Shirley Anne Field; Brenda Bruce; Pamela Green; Jack Watson; Nigel Davenport; Susan Travers; Veronica Hurst; Martin Miller; Miles Malleson; Michael Powell; ***D:*** Michael Powell; ***W:*** Leo Marks; ***C:*** Otto Heller; ***M:*** Brian Easdale.

Peeples ♪ 1/2 **2013 (PG-13)** The polarizing writer/actor/director Perry produces this inert, dopey comedy that plays like an African-American version of "Meet the Parents" but can't even live up to that film's modest standards. The talented Robinson is left afloat as Wade Walker, the fiancé of Grace (way-too-good-for-this Washington), who happens to be vacationing with her family in the Hamptons, an annual tradition, when the poor protagonist stumbles into the sitcomish set-up. The cast is so likeable that they allow viewers to get over some of the rough patches of bizarre melodrama and broad comedy, but not enough to recommend. **95m/C; DVD, Blu-Ray.** Craig Robinson; Kerry Washington; David Alan Grier; S. Epatha Merkerson; Melvin Van Peebles; Diahann Carroll; ***D:*** Tina Gordon Chism; ***W:*** Tina Gordon Chism; ***C:*** Alexander Gruszynski; ***M:*** Aaron Zigman.

Peggy Sue Got Married ♪♪ 1/2 **1986 (PG-13)** Uneven but entertaining comedy about an unhappily married woman seemingly unable to relive her life when she falls unconscious at a high school reunion and awakens to find herself back in school. Turner shines, but the film flags often, and Cage isn't around enough to elevate entire work. O'Connor scores, though, as a sensitive biker. Look for musician Marshall Crenshaw as part of the reunion band. **103m/C; VHS, DVD, Blu-Ray.** Kathleen Turner; Nicolas Cage; Catherine Hicks; Maureen O'Sullivan; John Carradine; Helen Hunt; Lisa Jane Persky; Barbara Harris; Joan Allen; Kevin J. O'Connor; Barry Miller; Don Murray; Leon Ames; Sofia Coppola; Sachi (MacLaine) Parker; Jim Carrey; ***D:*** Francis Ford Coppola; ***W:*** Jerry Leichtling; Arlene Sarner; ***C:*** Jordan Cronenweth; ***M:*** John Barry. Natl. Bd. of Review '86: Actress (Turner).

The Peking Blond ♪ 1/2 *The Blonde From Peking; Le Blonde de Pekin* **1968** French-fried spyfilm boasts lousy acting unencumbered by plot. Amnesiac may or may not hold secrets coveted by Americans, Russians and Chinese. **80m/C; VHS, DVD.** *FR* Mireille Darc; Claudio Brook; Edward G. Robinson; Pascale Roberts; ***D:*** Nicolas Gessner; ***W:*** Nicolas Gessner; Marc Behm.

The Pelican Brief ♪♪ 1/2 **1993 (PG-13)** Tulane law student Darby Shaw (Roberts) writes a speculative brief on the murders of two Supreme Court justices that results in more murder and sends her running for her life. Fairly faithful to the Grisham bestseller, but the multitude of characters is confusing. Pakula adds style and star-power, but much will depend on your tolerance for paranoid political thrillers. Washington is sharp as reporter Gray Grantham, the guy Roberts looks like she falls hard for (but the book's romance is nowhere to be seen). **141m/C; VHS, DVD, Blu-Ray.** Julia Roberts; Denzel Washington; John Heard; Tony Goldwyn; Stanley Tucci; James B. Sikking; William Atherton; Robert Culp; John Lithgow; Sam Shepard; Hume Cronyn; ***D:*** Alan J. Pakula; ***W:*** Alan J. Pakula; ***C:*** Stephen Goldblatt; ***M:*** James Horner.

Pelle the Conqueror ♪♪♪♪ **1988** Overpowering tale of a Swedish boy and his widower father who serve landowners in late 19th-century Denmark. Compassionate saga of human spirit contains numerous memorable sequences. Hvenegaard is wonderful as young Pelle, but von Sydow delivers what is probably his finest performance as a sympathetic weakling. American distributors foolishly trimmed the film by some 20 minutes (140 minute version). From the novel by Martin Anderson Nexo. In Swedish with English subtitles. **160m/C; VHS, DVD, Blu-Ray.** *SW DK* Max von Sydow; Pelle Hvenegaard; Erik Paaske; Bjorn Granath; Axel Strobye; Astrid Villaume; Troels Asmussen; John Wittig; Anne Lise Hirsch Bjerrum; Kristina Tornqvist; Morten Jorgensen; ***D:*** Bille August; ***W:*** Bille August. Oscars '88: Foreign Film; Cannes '88: Film; Golden Globes '89: Foreign Film.

The Penalty ♪♪ 1/2 **1920** Chaney's properly creepy as madman Blizzard who had his legs needlessly amputated as a child and who has grown up seeking revenge on the doctor and society. A brain operation leads to a radical change in personality and the flick's ridiculous ending. **93m/B; Silent; DVD, Blu-Ray.** Lon Chaney, Sr.; Claire Adams; Kenneth Harlan; Charles Clary; ***D:*** Wallace Worsley, II; ***W:*** Charles Kenyon; Philip Lonergan; ***C:*** Don Short.

Penelope ♪♪ 1/2 **2006 (PG)** Modern-day retelling of a fairytale casts Ricci as Penelope, the lonely girl cursed with a pig's snout. Raised by overbearing and bizarre upper-crust parents (O'Hara, Grant), Penelope is presented with a long line of suitors, all of whom hope to marry into the family's wealth but immediately bail at the sight of their daughter's schnoz. Penelope flees to the Big Apple in search of a companion equally cursed, but instead meets Max (McAvoy), a sweet and charming rocker who sees her inner beauty. First-time director Palansky successfully blends fantasy with the modern world, even throwing in a few political jabs along the way. **101m/C; DVD.** *GB* Christina Ricci; James McAvoy; Catherine O'Hara; Peter Dinklage; Richard E. Grant; Reese Witherspoon; Simon Woods; Michael Feast; Nigel Havers; Lenny Henry; Ronni Ancona; ***D:*** Mark Palansky; ***W:*** Leslie Caveny; ***C:*** Michel Amanthieu; ***M:*** Joby Talbot.

Penguin Pool Murder ♪♪ 1/2 **1932** The first of six Hildegarde Withers comic mysteries from RKO Pictures, based on the Stuart Palmer novel. Schoolteacher Hildegarde (Oliver) turns amateur sleuth when she spots a dead man in the penguin tank at NYC's Battery Park Aquarium. She then butts into gruff Inspector Oscar Piper's (Gleason) investigation. "Followed by "Murder On the Blackboard." **70m/B; DVD.** Edna May Oliver; James Gleason; Mae Clarke; Robert Armstrong; Donald Cook; Edgar Kennedy; ***D:*** George Archainbaud; ***W:*** Willis Goldbeck; ***C:*** Henry W. Gerrard.

Penguins ♪♪♪ *Disneynature: Penguins* **2019 (G)** In the Antarctic tundra, Steve, an Adelie penguin, makes the annual 100-mile trek with thousands of other male penguins to a colony. There, they will find female partners, build nests, mate, and start families. Along the way, Steve faces challenges such as when he gets lost and finds himself in danger from predators. At the colony, he and his mate Adeline have two babies but the danger continues for all the penguins. When a powerful storm hits, the penguins must survive the elements. The nature documentary tells a tidy story, and features spectacular images, engrossing storytelling, and appealing animals. **76m/C; DVD.** Ed Helms; ***D:*** Alastair Fothergill; Jeff Wilson; ***W:*** David Fowler; ***C:*** Rolf Steinmann; ***M:*** Harry Gregson-Williams.

Penguins of Madagascar ♪♪ **2014 (PG)** The scene-stealing penguins of the Madagascar franchise were popular enough to get their own TV show leading up to their return to the big screen in this sometimes-funny, mostly-unnecessary spin-off. Skipper, Kowalski, Rico, and Private are forced to battle an undercover organization known as The North Wind and the villainous Dr. Octavius Brine. The animated film flies by on a non-stop rollercoaster of physical jokes and clever puns for the adults, but it's not that distinctly different from watching a few episodes of the TV show. For some that may be enough. **92m/C; DVD, Blu-Ray.** ***V:*** Tom McGrath; Christopher Knights; Chris Miller; Conrad Vernon; John Malkovich; Benedict Cumberbatch; Peter Stormare; Ken Jeong; Annet Mahendru; ***D:*** Eric Darnell; Simon J. Smith; ***W:*** Michael Colton; John Aboud; Brandon Sawyer; ***M:*** Lorne Balfe.

The Penitent Man ♪ 1/2 **2010** In Gyeney's talky speculative fiction drama, psychologist Jason Pratt (Walker) is confronted by Mr. Darnell (Henriksen), a patient who insists he comes from the future. He tells Pratt he has invented a time-viewing machine that looks into the past and has resulted in a lot of trouble. Henriksen's presence keeps things somewhat interesting. **92m/C; DVD.** Lance Henriksen; Lathrop Walker; Andrew Keegan; Melissa Roberts; ***D:*** Nichlas Gyeney; ***W:*** Nichlas Gyeney; Trevor Tillman; ***C:*** Michael Boydstun; ***M:*** Daniel Bernstein.
VIDEO

Penitentiary ♪♪ 1/2 **1979 (R)** A realistic story of a black fighter who survives his prison incarceration by winning bouts against the other prisoners. Well-made and executed, followed by two progressively worse sequels. **99m/C; VHS, DVD, Blu-Ray.** Leon Isaac Kennedy; Jamaa Fanaka; Badja (Medu) Djola; Chuck "Porky" Mitchell; ***D:*** Jamaa Fanaka; ***W:*** Jamaa Fanaka; ***C:*** Marty Ollstein.

Penitentiary 2 ♪ **1982 (R)** A welterweight fighter is after the man who murdered his girlfriend, who, luckily, is incarcerated in the same prison as Our Hero. Sometimes things just work out right. **108m/C; VHS, DVD, Blu-Ray.** Leon Isaac Kennedy; Mr. T; Leif Erickson; Ernie Hudson; Glynn Turman; *D:* Jamaa Fanaka; *W:* Jamaa Fanaka; *C:* Stephen Posey; *M:* Jack Wheaton.

Penn and Teller Get Killed
1990 (R) The comedy team with a cult following are pursued by an assassin through dozens of pratfalls in this dark comedy. **91m/C; VHS, DVD.** Penn Jillette; Teller; Caitlin Clarke; Leonardo Cimino; David Patrick Kelly; *D:* Arthur Penn.

Pennies from Heaven ½ **1936** Bing plays Larry, a singer wrongly imprisoned, who promises to help the family of a man killed by a death row inmate Larry has befriended. Once on the outside, Larry finds the family, sassy little girl Patsy (Fellows) and her grandfather (Meek), enduring hard times. A social worker (Evans) is trying to keep Patsy out of the orphanage, and the gift of a home that Larry brings may help accomplish that. Complications arrive, however, when they try to turn the place into a cafe and find it may even be haunted. Typical of Crosby's 1930s work, it's pleasant enough and relies on Bing's charm and singing. He sings the Oscar-nominated title song no less than three times. Louis Armstrong appears to great effect, for the film and his subsequent career. **80m/C; DVD.** Bing Crosby; Madge Evans; Edith Fellows; Donald Meek; Louis Armstrong; John Gallaudet; Tom Dugan; Nana Bryant; Charles C. Wilson; Harry Tyler; William Stack; *D:* Norman Z. McLeod; *W:* Jo Swerling; *C:* Robert Pittack; *M:* Johnny Burke; Arthur Johnston; John Scott Trotter. Oscars '36: Song ("Pennies from Heaven").

Pennies from Heaven ½ **1981 (R)** Underrated, one-of-a-kind musical about a horny sheet-music salesman in Chicago and his escapades during the Depression. Extraordinary musical sequences have stars lip-synching to great effect. Martin is only somewhat acceptable as the hapless salesman, but Peters and Harper deliver powerful performances as the women whose lives he ruins. Walken brings down the house in a stunning song-and-dance sequence. Adapted by Dennis Potter from his British TV series. **107m/C; VHS, DVD.** Steve Martin; Bernadette Peters; Christopher Walken; Jessica Harper; Vernel Bagneris; *D:* Herbert Ross; *W:* Dennis Potter; *C:* Gordon Willis; *M:* Ralph Burns; Marvin Hamlisch. Golden Globes '82: Actress--Mus./Comedy (Peters); Natl. Soc. Film Critics '81: Cinematog.

Penny Princess **1952** Romantic comedy was not Bogarde's forte but he tries in this silly venture from writer/director Guest. American Lindy Smith (Donlan) is shocked to inherit the tiny, bankrupt European country of Lompidorra, which barely survives on smuggling and producing a cheese with a heavy alcohol content. British cheese salesman Tony Craig (Bogarde) happens along on his way to Switzerland and works with Lindy to market the cheese to solve the country's money woes. **91m/C; DVD.** *GB* Yolande Donlan; Dirk Bogarde; A.E. Matthews; Mary Clare; Reginald Beckwith; Kynaston Reeves; Edwin Styles; *D:* Val Guest; *W:* Val Guest; *C:* Geoffrey Unsworth; *M:* Ronald Hanmer.

Penny Serenade **1941** Newlyweds adopt a child, but tragedy awaits. Simplistic story nonetheless proves to be a moving experience. They don't make 'em like this anymore, and no one plays Grant better than Grant. Dunne is adequate. Also available colorized. **120m/B; VHS, DVD, Blu-Ray.** Cary Grant; Irene Dunne; Beulah Bondi; Edgar Buchanan; Ann Doran; Wallis (Clarke) Clark; *D:* George Stevens; *W:* Morrie Ryskind; *C:* Joseph Walker; *M:* W. Franke Harling.

Penrod and Sam **1931** The first talkie version of the Booth Tarkington novel (following a 1923 silent). Best friends Penrod and Sam are growing up in a small Indiana town as the leaders of the neighborhood's boys-only secret society. They play various pranks and have trouble when they lose their clubhouse because the property is sold. Some aspects will probably be offensive to modern viewers, including George being called a 'pansy' and refused membership in the boys' club. **71m/B; DVD.** Leon Janney; Frank "Junior" Coghlan; Billy (Billie) Lord; Margaret Marquis; Matt Moore; Dorothy Peterson; Zasu Pitts; *D:* William Beaudine; *W:* Waldemar Young; *C:* Roy F. Overbaugh.

The Pentagon Wars ½ **1998 (R)** Based on the true story of Air Force Col. James G. Burton (Elwes) whose mandate in the 1980s was to monitor weapons testing. What he discovers is the ultimate in white elephants—the Bradley Fighting Vehicle, an armored troop transport project that cost the taxpayers $14 billion over 17 years. Grammer is the scheming and pompous Army General Patridge (a composite character) who'll brook no interference. Adapted from the book "The Pentagon Wars" by James Burton. **104m/C; VHS, DVD.** Cary Elwes; Kelsey Grammer; Olympia Dukakis; Richard Benjamin; John C. McGinley; Tom Wright; Clifton Powell; Richard Schiff; *D:* Richard Benjamin; *W:* Martyn Burke; Jamie Malanowski; *C:* Robert Yeoman; *M:* Joseph Vitarelli. **CABLE**

Pentathlon ½ **1994 (R)** East German Olympic athlete Eric Brogar (Lundgren) defects to the U.S. a year before the crash of the Berlin Wall, causing embarassed German authorities to seek revenge on him and his family. **101m/C; VHS, Streaming.** Dolph Lundgren; David Soul; Roger E. Mosley; Renee Coleman; *D:* Bruce Malmuth.

Penthouse *Crooks in Clover* **1933** Baxter is a corporation lawyer who, for a change of pace, defends a gangland boss (Pendleton). His success loses him his high-society clientele but wins him Pendleton's respect and protection. But Baxter then gets involved in a further series of gang-related crimes, which nearly cost him his life. Also aiding Baxter is Loy, playing a smart-cookie gun moll, who would take her wisecracks to "The Thin Man" the following year. Good combo of melodrama, suspense, and humor. **90m/B; DVD.** Warner Baxter; Myrna Loy; Nat Pendleton; C. Henry Gordon; Mae Clarke; Charles Butterworth; Phillips Holmes; *D:* W.S. Van Dyke.

The Penthouse **1989** Givens stars as a wealthy young woman stalked by an old boyfriend who just happens to have escaped from a mental institution. When he traps her in her home, she has two choices—love him or die. Based on the novel by Elleston Trevor. **93m/C; VHS, DVD.** Robin Givens; David Hewlett; Cedric Smith; Donnelly Rhodes; Robert Guillaume; *D:* David Greene. **TV**

The Penthouse **2010 (R)** Party-loving Tyler wins an L.A. penthouse on a reality TV show and persuades his best buds, dopey Heath and slightly-more mature Kieran, to move in with him. Kieran actually has a girlfriend, but Erica wants a grown-up commitment that Kieran is reluctant to make. To up the ante, Tyler's hot younger sister Trista comes to visit and decides to move in as well. **85m/C; DVD.** Corey Large; James DeBello; Rider Strong; Kaley Cuoco; Mya; Lochlyn Munro; April Scott; *D:* Chris Levitus; *W:* Chris Levitus; *C:* Roger Chingirian; *M:* Ralph Rieckermann. **VIDEO**

The People ½ **1971** A young teacher takes a job in a small town and finds out that her students have telepathic powers and other strange qualities. Adapted from a novel by Zenna Henderson. Good atmosphere, especially for a TV movie. **74m/C; VHS, DVD.** Kim Darby; Dan O'Herlihy; Diane Varsi; William Shatner; *D:* John Korty; *M:* Carmine Coppola.

People **2004** Charles (Everett) is party planner for the jet set in Paris until a jealous rival brings him down. Desperate, Charles heads off to hedonistic Ibiza in order to persuade flamboyant club owner John John (Garcia) to join forces so Charles can restore his reputation. French with subtitles. **88m/C; DVD.** *FR SP* Rupert Everett; Jose Garcia; Ornella Muti; Lambert Wilson; Rossy de Palma; Marisa Berenson; Jean-Claude Brialy; Patrice Cols; *D:* Fabien Onteniente; *W:* Fabien Onteniente; *C:* Josep Civit; *M:* Joachim Garraud; Bernard Grimaldi; David Guetta; Pascal Lemaire.

The People Against O'Hara
1951 Downbeat legal drama. Widower James Curtayne (Tracy) was a brilliant defense attorney until alcohol ruined his life. So he left his practice and is being cared for by his daughter Virginia (Lynn). Neighborhood kid John O'Hara (Arness) is accused of murder and his poor parents ask James to take his case. A mistake since his booze-addled efforts get John convicted. How will Curtayne make amends? **102m/B; DVD.** Spencer Tracy; James Arness; Diana Lynn; John Hodiak; Richard Anderson; Jay C. Flippen; *D:* John Sturges; *W:* John Monks, Jr.; *C:* John Alton; *M:* Carmen Dragon.

People Are Funny **1946** Battling radio producers vie to land the big sponsor with an original radio idea. Comedy ensues when one of them comes up with a great idea—stolen from a local station. **94m/B; VHS, DVD.** Jack Haley; Rudy Vallee; Ozzie Nelson; Art Linkletter; Helen Walker; *D:* Sam White.

People I Know ½ **2002 (R)** Pacino forgoes the over-the-top style that's been his forte lately for a more restrained, meticulous portrayal of burned-out publicist Eli Wurman, and his performance saves the intriguing but muddled character study/political caper. Wurman's down to his last bigtime client, movie star Cary Launer (O'Neal), a shallow, womanizing, preening actor trying to break into politics. His bid for office is endangered when an actress with whom Launer had a drug-fueled fling is arrested. Eli is sent to bail her out, but becomes entangled in her murder and mysterious political hijinks, all while trying to stage a benefit for African refugees. Fine supporting cast delivers but plot gets a little busy for its own good when not focused on Eli's inner struggle. **95m/C; VHS, DVD, Blu-Ray.** Al Pacino; Kim Basinger; Ryan O'Neal; Tea Leoni; Richard Schiff; Bill Nunn; Robert Klein; Mark Webber; Polly Adams; *D:* Daniel Algrant; *W:* Jon Robin Baitz; *C:* Peter Deming; *M:* Terence Blanchard.

The People I've Slept With ½
2009 Unabashedly promiscuous Angela Young finds herself preggers and has five possible baby daddies. Since she always photographs her bed partners, she goes on a DNA who's-the-daddy hunt even though she's still not convinced she should change her ways despite her family's pleas. **89m/C; DVD.** Karin Anna Cheung; Archie Kao; Wilson Cruz; Chris Zylka; Lynn Chen; Randall Park; Rane Jameson; *D:* Quentin Lee; *W:* Koji Steven Sakai; *C:* Quyen Tran; *M:* Steven Pranoto.

People Like Us **2012 (PG-13)** Sam (Pine) and his girlfriend Hannah (Wilde) go to his estranged father's funeral and he immediately tangles with his unhappy mother, Lillian (Pfeiffer). The next shock comes when he learns his dad has left his previously unknown half-sister Frankie (Banks) money that Sam is to deliver. He tracks her down, a recovering alcoholic single mom, and strikes up a friendship with her and her preteen son Josh (D'Addario) without revealing their connection. The characters are frustrating, and so is the film, but the actors' sincerity for the material goes a long way to make it palatable. **113m/C; DVD, Blu-Ray, Streaming.** Chris Pine; Elizabeth Banks; Michael Hall D'Addario; Michelle Pfeiffer; Olivia Wilde; Mark Duplass; Philip Baker Hall; *D:* Alex Kurtzman; *W:* Alex Kurtzman; Roberto Orci; Jody Lambert; *C:* Salvatore Totino; *M:* A.R. Rahman.

People Places Things ½ **2015 (R)** Will Henry (Clement) is struggling to put his life back together after catching his wife cheating on him. He tries to be a good male role model to his two kids (Aundrea & Gia Gadsby) while encouraging his students to find their own way in the world. One of his students, Kat (Williams), likes Will enough to introduce him to her mother Diane (Hall)—potential love blossoms. This is a remarkably simple, delicate slice-of-life story without much in the way of drama but likable characters and confident direction. It's forgettable but never a waste of time. **85m/C; DVD.** Jemaine Clement; Regina Hall; Jessica Williams; Stephanie Allynne; Michael Chernus; *D:* James C. Strouse; *W:* James C. Strouse; *C:* Chris Teague; *M:* Mark Orton.

The People That Time Forgot ½ **1977 (PG)** Sequel to "The Land That Time Forgot," based on the Edgar Rice Burroughs novel. A rescue team returns to a world of prehistoric monsters to rescue a man left there after the first film. **90m/C; VHS, DVD, Blu-Ray.** *GB* Doug McClure; Patrick Wayne; Sarah Douglas; Dana Gillespie; Thorley Walters; Shane Rimmer; *D:* Kevin Connor; *W:* Patrick Tilley; *C:* Alan Hume; *M:* John Scott.

The People under the Stairs ½ **1991 (R)** Adams is part of a scheme to rob a house in the slums owned by a mysterious couple (Robie and McGill, both of "Twin Peaks" fame). After his friends are killed off in a gruesome fashion, he discovers that the couple aren't the house's only strange inhabitants—homicidal creatures also lurk within. **102m/C; VHS, DVD, Blu-Ray.** Everett McGill; Wendy Robie; Brandon Adams; Ving Rhames; A.J. (Allison Joy) Langer; Sean M. Whalen; Kelly Jo Minter; *D:* Wes Craven; *W:* Wes Craven; *C:* Sandi Sissel; *M:* Don Peake.

The People vs. Dr. Kildare ½
1941 In this seventh and lesser entry in the series, Kildare spends more time in the courtroom than the hospital defending himself from a malpractice charge. He saved the life of pro ice skater Frances Marlow after an auto accident, but one of her legs is paralyzed. She blames Kildare but Dr. Gillespie thinks there's another reason for her medical condition. **78m/B; DVD.** Lew Ayres; Lionel Barrymore; Laraine Day; Bonita Granville; Red Skelton; Paul Stanton; Tom Conway; *D:* Harold Bucquet; *W:* Harry Ruskin; Willis Goldbeck; *C:* Clyde De Vinna; *M:* David Snell.

The People vs. George Lucas ½
2010 Just who does "Star Wars" belong to? Apparently not creator George Lucas, who is vilified by the zealous fan community every time he makes changes to (or comments on) the franchise. Director Philippe amassed fan-created footage, interviews, and emails after an open call for submissions, but his fractured documentary results in too many participants and too many clips (and a lot of carping). **97m/C; DVD.** *D:* Alexandre O. Philippe; *C:* Robert Muratore; *M:* Jon Hegel.

The People vs. Jean Harris
1981 Follows the trial of Jean Harris. Shortly before this film was released, she had been convicted of murder in the death of Dr. Herman Tarnower, the author of "The Scarsdale Diet." Harris was headmistress in a private school all the while. Burstyn was nominated for an Emmy Award for best actress. **147m/C; VHS, DVD.** Ellen Burstyn; Martin Balsam; Richard Dysart; Peter Coyote; Priscilla Morrill; Sarah Marshall; Millie Slavin; *D:* George Schaefer; *M:* Brad Fiedel. **TV**

The People vs. Larry Flynt
1996 (R) Controversy surrounded director Forman's look at unrepentant pornographer and Hustler Magazine publisher, Larry Flynt (Harrelson). While feminists decried what they saw as a whitewash of Flynt's career, Forman insisted his movie was about Flynt's legal battles concerning the First Amendment and freedom of speech. If you can set aside your prejudices, you'll find a master storyteller at work and some great performances from Harrelson as Flynt, Love as his drug-addicted and ultimately tragic wife Althea, and Norton as Flynt's sometimes impatient attorney, Alan Isaacman, who does get his big moment before the U.S. Supreme Court (his speeches are taken from actual court transcripts). **130m/C; VHS, DVD, Blu-Ray.** Woody Harrelson; Courtney Love; Edward Norton; James Cromwell; Crispin Glover; Brett Harrelson; James Carville; Vincent Schiavelli; Richard Paul; Donna Hanover; Norm MacDonald; Miles Chapin; Jan Triska; *Cameo(s):* Larry Flynt; *D:* Milos Forman; *W:* Larry Karaszewski; Scott M. Alexander; *C:* Philippe Rousselot; *M:* Thomas Newman. Golden Globes '97: Director (Forman), Screenplay; L.A. Film Critics '96: Support. Actor (Norton); Natl. Bd. of Review '96: Support. Actor (Norton); N.Y. Film Critics '96: Support. Actress (Love).

People Will Talk ½ **1951** Grant plays Dr. Noah Praetorius, a doctor and educator who believes that the mind is a better healer than medicine. Archenemy Cronyn is the fellow instructor with a vengeance. Sickened by Grant's goodwill and the undying attention he receives, Cronyn reports Grant's unconventional medical practices to the higher-ups in hopes of ruining his reputation as doctor/educator. Witty and satirical, this well-crafted comedy-drama is chock-full of interesting characters and finely tuned dialogue. Adapted from the play "Dr. Praetorius" by Curt Goetz. **110m/B; VHS, DVD.**

Cary Grant; Jeanne Crain; Finlay Currie; Hume Cronyn; Walter Slezak; Sidney Blackmer; Basil Ruysdael; Katherine Locke; Margaret Hamilton; Carleton Young; Billy House; Stuart Holmes; ***D:*** Joseph L. Mankiewicz; ***W:*** Joseph L. Mankiewicz; ***C:*** Milton Krasner.

Pep Squad 1/2 **1998 (R)** Director Steve Balderson does a John Waters riff with the story of evil Cherry (Brooke Balderson) who reacts inappropriately when she's not chosen for the high school pep squad. The Kansas production is driven by broad, nasty slapstick humor. **97m/C; DVD.** Brooke Balderson; Jennifer Dreiling; Adrian Pujoi; Summer Makovkin; ***D:*** Steve Balderson; ***W:*** Steve Balderson; ***C:*** Rhet W. Bear; ***M:*** Johnette Napolitano.

Pepe El Toro **1953** In the sequel to "Ustedes los Ricos," Pepe (Infante) is now a widower (Blanca Estela Pavon, who played his wife, died before this film could be made). Taking up boxing to settle a debt, Pepe must comfort the wife of his best friend after accidentally killing him in the ring. A fourth film was planned, but Infante passed away before it could be filmed. **108m/B; DVD.** *MX* Pedro Infante; Evita Munoz; Amanda Del Llano; Irma Dorantes; Freddy Fernandez; Fernando Soto Mantequilla; Joaquin Cordero; Juan Orraca; Wolf Ruvinskis; ***D:*** Ismael Rodriguez; ***W:*** Ismael Rodriguez; Carlos Orellana; Pedro De Urdimalas; ***C:*** Ignacio Torres; ***M:*** Manuel Esperon.

Pepe Le Moko **1937** An influential French film about a notorious gangster holed up in the Casbah, emerging at his own peril out of love for a beautiful woman. Stirring film established Gabin as a matinee idol. Cinematography is particularly fine too. Based upon the D'Ashelbe novel. The basis for both "Algiers," the popular Boyer-Lamarr melodrama, and the musical "The Casbah." In French with English subtitles. **87m/B; VHS, DVD.** *FR* Jean Gabin; Mireille Balin; Gabriel Gabrio; Lucas Gridoux; ***D:*** Julien Duvivier; ***W:*** Julien Duvivier; Henri Jeanson; ***C:*** Jules Kruger; ***M:*** Vincent Scotto.

Pepper and His Wacky Taxi 1/2 **1972 (G)** Father of four buys a '59 Cadillac and starts a cab company. Time-capsule fun. **79m/C; VHS, DVD.** John Astin; Frank Sinatra, Jr.; Jackie Gayle; Alan Sherman; ***D:*** Alex Grasshof.

Peppermint **2018 (R)** After the husband (Hephner) and young daughter of bank employee Riley North (Garner) are murdered by a group of Latino drug-dealers, she is traumatized and psychologically unstable. Though Riley remembers the faces of the three men who destroyed her family, no one in the justice system believes her. Going underground to take matters into her own hands, Riley exacts her own form of vengeance against drug lord Diego Garcia (Raba), his lawyer (Mosley), a corrupt judge (Harlan), and anyone else who has contributed to the situation. This revenge thriller fails to live up to its promise and Garner's stellar abilities as an action actress. **101m/C; DVD, Blu-Ray.** Jennifer Garner; John Gallagher, Jr.; John Ortiz; Juan Pablo Raba; Annie Ilonzeh; ***D:*** Pierre Morel; ***W:*** Chad St. John; ***C:*** David Lanzenberg; ***M:*** Simon Franglen.

Percentage **WOOF!** **2013** Inept gangsta pic filled with clichés and posturing rather than actual acting. Thugs Ant and Carter doublecross the Russian mob and have to get out of New York. They head to Miami and are soon involved in a credit card scam with Carter's cousin Flaco that has them living large and upsetting the city's leading crime diva, who expects her share of the action if they want to keep living at all. Rhames takes the throwaway role of an enforcer. **86m/C; DVD.** Cam'ron; Omar Gooding; Antwon Tanner; Macy Gray; Malinda Williams; Ving Rhames; ***D:*** Alex Merkin; ***W:*** Cam'ron; Elya Ottenberg; ***C:*** Thomas Callaway. **VIDEO**

Perception **2006** The perception is that this comedy pretty much stinks. Weirdo Jen (Perabo) lives with her equally weird parents (Hurt, Rasche) in Brooklyn. She also has a weird possessive girlfriend, Ramona (Burns); during an argument, Jen runs into the street and gets hit by a car, which leaves her in a wheelchair. There's also something about Jen's ex-boyfriend who's back from Iraq and her befriending an ex-heroin addict but the story is so incoherent, you probably won't care. **101m/C; DVD.** Piper Perabo; Heather Burns; Aunjanue Ellis; Mary Beth Hurt; Seth Meyers; Kate Mulgrew; Ajay Naidu; David Rasche; Nick Scotti; Mark Dobies; Carolina Hoyos; ***D:*** Irving Schwartz; ***W:*** Irving Schwartz; ***C:*** John Darbonne; ***M:*** Joel Someillan.

Perceval *Perceval Le Gallois* **1978** Rohmer's extremely stylized version of Chretien de Troyes unfinished 12th century poem. Young Welsh knight Perceval (Luchini) comes to a mysterious castle where he sees a vision of the Holy Grail, although he doesn't recognize it. In the morning, the castle is deserted and Perceval resumes his wanderings. When he finally realizes what he has seen, the castle has disappeared and Perceval continues with his search for the Grail. French with subtitles. **140m/C; VHS, DVD.** *FR* Fabrice Luchini; Andre Dussollier; Arielle Dombasle; Marie-Christine Barrault; ***D:*** Eric Rohmer; ***W:*** Eric Rohmer; ***C:*** Nestor Almendros.

Percy Jackson & The Olympians: The Lightning Thief 1/2 **2010 (PG)** Based on a popular series of children's books, this tale of Greek gods and awkward teens can't escape comparison to the Harry Potter movies. Percy (Lerman) is a student struggling with learning disabilities when he discovers that he is the son of the sea god Poseidon and a mortal woman. He is sent to a special school for demi-gods along with his pal Grover (Jackson). When his mother (Keener) disappears and he is accused of stealing the lightning bolt of Zeus (Bean), Percy must go on a quest to return Zeus' property and prevent civil war between the gods. Director Columbus, who also directed the first two Potter films, makes some significant changes to the story and tone of Rick Riordan's novel, which may bother fans of the book. **118m/C; Blu-Ray.** Logan Lerman; Pierce Brosnan; Uma Thurman; Sean Bean; Kevin McKidd; Melina Kanakaredes; Catherine Keener; Steve Coogan; ***D:*** Chris Columbus; ***W:*** Craig Titley; ***C:*** Stephen Goldblatt; ***M:*** Christophe Beck.

Percy Jackson: Sea of Monsters **2013 (PG)** Where the first Percy Jackson film had some clever fun in its mix of mythology and adolescent angst, the follow-up, also based on Rick Riordan's book, feels more like a bland obligation. Percy (Lerman) must travel to the Sea of Monsters with Annabeth (Daddario), Clarisse (Rambin), and newfound half-brother-and-a-Cyclops Tyson (Smith) to retrieve the Golden Fleece and save Camp Half-Blood. A harmless but lackluster action-adventure flick that might entertain the tweeners even if it falls short of Riordan's work. Pleasantly humorous cameos by veterans Fillion and Tucci. **106m/C; DVD, Blu-Ray.** Logan Lerman; Leven Rambin; Jake Abel; Douglas Smith; Alexandra Daddario; Brandon T. Jackson; Anthony Head; Stanley Tucci; Paloma Kwiatkowski; Nathan Fillion; ***D:*** Thor Freudenthal; ***W:*** Marc Guggenheim; ***C:*** Shelly Johnson; ***M:*** Andrew Lockington.

Perestroika **2009** In 1992, middle-aged astrophysicist Sasha Greenberg (Robards) returns to Moscow after the fall of communism and after spending 17 years in New York working for the U.S. military. He's scheduled to give the keynote address at a physics conference but his time is taken up by old friends and ex-lovers who are both happy and suspicious to see him. His mentor was/is Professor Gross (Abraham), an American defector who helped the Soviets develop nuclear weapons much as Greenberg did for the Americans. Sasha's life is depicted with numerous flashbacks while director Tsukerman overstuffs the plot as Sasha is beset by his past and present. **116m/C; DVD.** Sam Robards; F. Murray Abraham; Oksana Stashenko; Ally Sheedy; Maria Andreyeva; Jicky Schnee; ***D:*** Slava Tsukerman; ***W:*** Ally Sheedy; Slava Tsukerman; ***C:*** Mikhail Iskandarov; ***M:*** Alexander Zhurbin. **VIDEO**

The Perez Family 1/2 **1994 (R)** Juan Paul Perez (Molina) has spent 20 years in Cuban jails, dreaming of being reunited with wife Carmela (Huston) and daughter Teresa (Alvarado) who successfully escaped to Miami. Part of the 1980 Mariel exodus, Juan meets exuberant Dottie (Tomei), who learns families get sponsored first at the refugee camps. She convinces Juan to pose as her husband, while Carmela, who's being wooed by cop Pirelli (Palminteri), mistakenly believes Juan has literally missed the boat. Tomei's spunky (but with a garish accent), Huston's regal, Palminteri courtly, and Molina morose. The film's inconsistently whimsical, wistful, and clunky. From the novel by Christine Bell. **135m/C; VHS, DVD.** Marisa Tomei; Alfred Molina; Anjelica Huston; Chazz Palminteri; Trini Alvarado; Celia Cruz; ***D:*** Mira Nair; ***W:*** Robin Swicord; ***C:*** Stuart Dryburgh; ***M:*** Alan Silvestri.

Perfect 1/2 **1985 (R)** A "Rolling Stone" reporter goes after the shallowness of the Los Angeles health club scene, and falls in love with the aerobics instructor he is going to write about. "Rolling Stone" publisher Wenner plays himself. As bad as it sounds. **120m/C; VHS, DVD, Blu-Ray.** John Travolta; Jamie Lee Curtis; Carly Simon; Marilu Henner; Laraine Newman; Jann Wenner; Anne DeSalvo; ***D:*** James Bridges; ***W:*** James Bridges; Aaron Latham; ***C:*** Gordon Willis; ***M:*** Ralph Burns.

The Perfect Age of Rock 'n' Roll **2010 (R)** The soundtrack is of some interest but the plot's too cliched to be more than occasionally trashy fun. A framing device finds reporter Clifton Hanger (Haas) interviewing aging rocker Spyder (Zegers). In the 1980s, self-destructive Spyder's debut album was a huge hit but his second was just as big a flop. He goes back to his hometown for a reunion with former friend and songwriter Eric (Ritter), hoping for another chance. This soon involves a road trip along Route 66 to rekindle some musical mojo. **92m/C; DVD.** Kevin Zegers; Jason Ritter; Taryn Manning; Peter Fonda; Lukas Haas; Ruby Dee; Lauren Holly; Billy Dee Williams; Michael K(enneth) Williams; ***D:*** Scott Rosenbaum; ***W:*** Scott Rosenbaum; ***C:*** Tom Richmond; ***M:*** Andrew Hollander.

The Perfect Date **2019** Handsome, ambitious high schooler Brooks Rattigan (Centineo) gets along with everyone. Such qualities become important when he agrees to go on a pity date with Celia (Marano) paid for by her parents who want her to go out. After this experience, Brooks and his best friend Murph (Gerogiadis) create an app so that people can book Brooks to be a stand-in boyfriend and he can save money for college. Based on "The Stand-In" by Steve Bloom, the feel-good romantic comedy is predictable but pleasant. **89m/C; DVD.** Noah Centineo; Laura Marano; Odiseas Georgiadis; Camilla Mendes; Matt Walsh; ***D:*** Chris Nelson; ***W:*** Steve Bloom; Randall Green; ***C:*** Bartosz Nalazek. **VIDEO**

A Perfect Day **2006** Rather maudlin story based on the novel by Richard Paul Evans. Author Rob Harlan (Lowe) writes an unexpected bestseller and his fame has him ignoring his wife and daughter. Then his supposed guardian angel (Lloyd) appears to show Mr. Selfish the error of his ways, especially when he tells Rob that if he doesn't change his attitude, he dies on Christmas. Fear—what an incentive to become a better person. **91m/C; DVD.** Rob Lowe; Christopher Lloyd; Paget Brewster; Frances Conroy; Jude Ciccolella; Rowena King; Kevin Dunn; ***D:*** Peter Levin; ***W:*** Joyce Eliason; ***C:*** Kees Van Oostrum; ***M:*** Jeff Beal. **CABLE**

A Perfect Day 1/2 **2016 (R)** Two award-winning actors elevate a relatively routine Spanish dramedy in this film from Fernando Leon de Aranoa from the book by Paula Farias. There's a body in the well in this "MASH"-esque examination of aid workers dealing with bureaucracy, the military, local criminals and general stupidity. Robbins and Del Toro co-star in the story of a group trying to save the local water supply and the struggle they face just trying to get a body out of the well. It doesn't help that one of their ex-lovers has flown in to shut the whole aid organization down. **106m/C; DVD, Blu-Ray.** Benicio Del Toro; Tim Robbins; Olga Kurylenko; Mélanie Thierry; Sergi Lopez; ***D:*** Fernando Leon de Aranoa; ***W:*** Fernando Leon de Aranoa; ***C:*** Alex Catalan; ***M:*** Arnau Bataller.

A Perfect Ending **2012** Unhappy, middle-aged Rebecca Westridge (Niven) admits to her girlfriends that her longtime marriage has always left her sexually unsatisfied. They arrange an informational tryst with a high-end female escort (who better to understand the anatomy) but Rebecca is uncomfortable with much-younger Paris (Clark). She runs away--and keeps coming back. More emotional than sexual with its share of stale moments. **106m/C; DVD.** Barbara Niven; Jessica Clark; John Heard; Morgan Fairchild; Rebecca Staab; ***D:*** Nicole Conn; ***W:*** Nicole Conn; ***C:*** Tal Lazar; ***M:*** Stephen Ridley. **VIDEO**

The Perfect Family 1/2 **2011 (PG-13)** Family dramedy whose sincerity occasionally falls into the predictable. Devoutly Catholic Eileen Cleary (Turner) learns she has been nominated for the 'Catholic Woman of the Year' award as has her arch-rival Agnes Dunn (Lawrence). Qualifications include a family life of traditional beliefs and Eileen's has a number of flaws she can either try to hide or finally accept. Turner gives a dynamic performance but the rest of the cast has some stirring moments of their own. **84m/C; DVD.** Kathleen Turner; Michael McGrady; Emily Deschanel; Jason Ritter; Richard Chamberlain; Angelique Cabral; Kristen Dalton; Elizabeth Pena; Sharon Lawrence; ***D:*** Anne Renton; ***W:*** Paula Goldberg; Claire V. Riley; ***C:*** Andre Lascaris; ***M:*** Andrew Kaiser.

The Perfect Furlough 1/2 *Strictly for Pleasure* **1959** Paul Hodges (Curtis) is an Army corporal who wins three weeks in Paris with a movie star (Cristal) as a publicity gimmick. It's the idea of a female Army psychologist (Leigh), who thinks the guys need a morale booster, and she accompanies Hodges on his trip. Pretty bizarre, but it works. **93m/C; DVD.** Tony Curtis; Janet Leigh; Keenan Wynn; Linda Cristal; Elaine Stritch; Marcel Dalio; King Donovan; ***D:*** Blake Edwards; ***W:*** Stanley Shapiro.

Perfect Game 1/2 **2000** Kanin Crosby (Finley) and his equally uncoordinated friends are determined to make it into the winning park league baseball team, the Bulldogs, but they're all surprised when they're chosen by the team's arrogant coach, Bobby Geiser (Duffy). Eventually the kids learn that Geiser is only playing and coaching his best players, leaving the others to warm the bench. A confrontation leads to Kanin's mom Diane (Nelson) taking over along with grumbling retired coach Billy Hicks (Asner) and the kids are on their way once again. **99m/C; VHS, DVD.** Cameron Finley; Tracy Nelson; Patrick Duffy; Ed Asner; ***D:*** Dan Guntzelman; ***W:*** Dan Guntzelman; ***M:*** David Benoit. **VIDEO**

The Perfect Game 1/2 **2009 (PG)** Earnest junior sports drama based on a true story. In 1957, Cesar Faz has returned to his Monterrey, Mexico hometown after having held a minor baseball job in the States. This encourages the local kids to have Cesar coach them and they're surprisingly successful—so much so that they earn a spot playing at the Little League World Championship in Williamsport, Pennsylvania. They encounter prejudice on their road trip but the title will give you a big clue as to the inspirational outcome. **118m/C; DVD.** Clifton (Gonzalez) Collins, Jr.; Moises Arias; Ryan Ochoa; Jake T. Austin; Jansen Panettiere; Cheech Marin; Louis Gossett, Jr.; Emilie de Ravin; David Koechner; Bruce McGill; Frances Fisher; ***D:*** William Dear; ***W:*** W. William Winokur; ***C:*** Bryan Greenberg; ***M:*** Bill Conti.

A Perfect Getaway **2009 (R)** . A Hawaiian honeymoon hike to a remote beach turns into a nightmare for newlyweds Cliff (Zahn) and Cydney (Jovovich) when they're joined by fellow hikers Nick (Olyphant) and Gina (Sanchez) and confronted by belligerent hitchhikers Cleo (Shelton) and Kale (Hemsworth). Screenwriter Cliff and survivalist Nick discuss movie red herrings (or 'red snappers' as Nick calls them) and viewers will probably want a second look at Twohy's flick to check them out. Offers cheap and mindless B-movie thrills with gratuitous nudity and violence. Really, what more could you want? **98m/C; DVD, Blu-Ray.** Milla Jovovich; Steve Zahn; Timothy Olyphant; Kiele Sanchez; Marley Shelton; Chris Hemsworth; ***D:*** David N. Twohy; ***W:*** David N. Twohy; ***C:*** Mark Plummer; ***M:*** Boris Elkis.

The Perfect Guy **2015 (PG-13)** Another cheesy thriller targeting minority audiences that falls completely flat, and didn't screen for critics for good reason. The way-too-talented-for-this Lathan stars as Leah Vaughn, a successful lobbyist who careens into an affair with a hunky new guy (Ealy) after breaking up with the stable one (Chestnut) in her life. When the new guy starts to act funny, she goes back to the old one to protect her, because, of course, women in these films always need male protectors. This is insultingly nonsense. **100m/C; DVD, Blu-Ray.** Sanaa Lathan; Michael Ealy; Morris Chestnut; Kathryn Morris; Shannon Lucio; Charles S. Dutton; Alan B. McElroy; *D:* David Rosenthal; *W:* Tyger Williams; *C:* Peter Simonite; *M:* Dave Fleming; Atli Orvarsson.

Perfect Harmony 🦴🦴 1/2 **1991** Racial conflict at an exclusive Southern boys school in 1950s South Carolina is overcome through friendship and the love of music in this sentimental tale. **93m/C; VHS, DVD.** Peter Scolari; Darren McGavin; Catherine Mary Stewart; Moses Gunn; Cleavon Little; Justin Whalin; David Faustino; Richie Havens; Eugene Boyd; *D:* Will MacKenzie. **CABLE**

Perfect Hideout 🦴 1/2 **2008** Nick and Celia are lovers on the lam who take a hostage after they invade a remote villa. He says he's Victor, the homeowner, but then the twosome notice the dead bodies and realize that they're trapped with a killer while the police surround the property. **93m/C; DVD.** Billy Zane; Cristian Solimeno; Ken Bones; Melinda Y. Cohen; Scarlett Sabet; *D:* Stephen Manuel; *W:* Andreas Brune; Sven Frauenhoff; *C:* Oliver Staack; *M:* Eckart Gadow. **VIDEO**

The Perfect Holiday 🦴 1/2 **2007 (PG)** Nancy (Union), a struggling single mother of three who is desperately searching for a good man, finds love in Benjamin (Chestnut), a mall Santa and aspiring songwriter. The only problem is that Nancy's ex-husband and famous rapper, J-Jizzy (Murphy), is recording one of Benjamin's songs and doesn't know Nancy and Benjamin have fallen in love. Benjamin doesn't know J-Jizzy is Nancy's ex and Nancy is just plain clueless. A predictable and lukewarm romantic comedy saved in part by Queen Latifah's cameo appearance. Despite the marketing ploy, this is not a sequel to "The Last Holiday." **96m/C; On Demand.** Gabrielle Union; Morris Chestnut; Queen Latifah; Terrence Howard; Charlie (Charles Q.) Murphy; Faizon Love; Katt Micah Williams; Jill Jones; Malik Hammond; Khail Bryant; Jeremy Gumbs; Rachel True; *D:* Lance Rivera; *W:* Lance Rivera; Nat Mauldin; Jeff Stein; Marc Calixte; *C:* Teodoro Maniaci; *M:* Christopher Lennertz.

The Perfect Host 🦴🦴 **2010 (R)** Contradictory psycho-thriller that doesn't let reality get in the way of its plot. Prim L.A. bachelor Warwick Wilson (Pierce) is preparing for a dinner party when John Taylor (Crawford) shows up at his door, conning his way inside. Charming John has just robbed a bank and needs a place to lay low but his meticulous host changes dramatically (and not quite convincingly) over the course of the evening. Even after John's true identity is revealed and he turns threatening, you're not quite sure just who the hostage is. **93m/C; DVD, Blu-Ray, On Demand.** David Hyde Pierce; Clayne Crawford; Nathaniel Parker; Helen Reddy; Megahn Perry; *D:* Nick Tomnay; *W:* Nick Tomnay; Krishna Jones; *C:* John Brawley; *M:* John Swihart.

The Perfect Husband 🦴🦴 *El Marido Perfecto* **1992** Womanizing 19th-century opera singer Milan (Roth) finally falls in love—only it's to a woman he can't have. **90m/C; VHS, DVD.** *SP GB* Tim Roth; Peter Firth; Aitana Sanchez-Gijon; Ana Belen; *D:* Beda Docampo Feijoo; *W:* Beda Docampo Feijoo; Juan Bautista Stagnaro; *C:* Frantisek Uldrich; *M:* Jose Nieto.

Perfect Killer 🦴 1/2 *Satanic Mechanic* **1977 (R)** Van Cleef stars as a world weary Mafia hit-man who is double-crossed by his girl, set up by his best friend, and hunted by another hired assassin. **85m/C; VHS, DVD.** Lee Van Cleef; Tita Barker; John Ireland; Robert Widmark; *D:* Marlon Sirko.

Perfect Love 🦴🦴 *Parfait Amour* **1996** Divorced Frederique (Renauld) has an affair with volatile younger man, Christophe (Renaud). When she realizes he's also seeing other women, she's angry and the tension builds as each seeks to psychologically wound the other. The only thing they still agree upon is sex but then Christophe loses control. French with subtitles. **110m/C; VHS, DVD.** *FR* Isabelle Renauld; Francis Renaud; Laura Saglio; *D:* Catherine Breillat; *W:* Catherine Breillat; *C:* Laurent Dailland.

The Perfect Man 🦴 **2005 (PG)** Whenever 16-year-old Holly's (Duff) single mom, the gloomy Jean (Locklear), loses at love she packs up Holly and younger sister Zoe to a brand new city in a desperate search for a fresh start. Fed up with the chaos, Holly concocts a secret admirer—based on her best friend Amy's suave Uncle Ben (Noth)?when she sees another potentially lame suitor on the horizon in the form of Styx-loving Lenny (O'Malley). Naturally the ruse gets dicey and Holly must scurry to cover her you-know-what. Feeble humor, plus it's hard to believe the knockout Locklear would have trouble finding a decent man. **100m/C; DVD, Blu-Ray.** Hilary Duff; Heather Locklear; Chris Noth; Vanessa Lengies; Aria Wallace; Ben Feldman; Michael O'Malley; Caroline Rhea; Kym E. Whitley; *D:* Mark Rosman; *W:* Gina Wendkos; *C:* John R. Leonetti; *M:* Christophe Beck.

The Perfect Man 🦴🦴 **2011 (PG-13)** Romantic drama centered on the complicated feelings surrounding marriage and post-marriage relationships. Russell (Keys) and Bailey (Lewis) Thomas were married for years and had a son. Though their marriage essentially fell apart when their son was young, the couple decided to remain married until he went to college. Russell leaves after his son begins his young adulthood, but he finds himself re-considering the decision when his wife begins dating a good-lucking younger man. Russell soon learns Bailey's new beau is not all that he seems, and works win back his wife and his marriage. **90m/C; DVD, Streaming, Download.** Christian Keys; Jazsmin Lewis; Malika Blessing; Maya Gilbert; Elise Neal; *D:* Paul D. Hannah; *W:* Paul D. Hannah; *M:* Theodore Gearring. **VIDEO**

A Perfect Man 🦴 **2013 (R)** Sour, off-putting marital drama. When Nina (Tripplehorn) catches husband James (Schreiber) cheating again, she finally leaves him. The compulsive, apparently sex addicted, James laments his marital failings over phone conversations with an allegedly friend of Nina's, except it's merely Nina pretending so she can figure out if James deserves another chance. He doesn't and neither does the pic. **94m/C; DVD, Blu-Ray.** Liev Schreiber; Jeanne Tripplehorn; Joelle Carter; Louise Fletcher; Renee Soutendijk; Katie Carr; *D:* Kees Van Oostrum; *W:* Larry Brand; Peter Elkoff; *C:* Joost van Gelder; *M:* Jeff Cardoni.

A Perfect Murder 🦴🦴 **1998 (R)** Steven Taylor (Douglas), a rich commodities trader about to lose his fortune, is married to young, rich, Emily (Paltrow), who's having a torrid affair with hippie artist David (Mortensen). The love triangle gets shaken when Steven devises a solution to both his wife's infidelities and his financial woes by paying David to kill Emily. Things go a little bit astray, and the psychological cat and mouse game begins. Glossy production is only eye candy while the unsympathetic characters (led by a weak protagonist in Paltrow) march to the beat of many plot points that all come together in a rushed and dull climax. Douglas, the aged yet sturdy centerpiece of the film, shines as the pompous rich dude devoid of morals, and overpowers his youthful supporting players. Inspired by Hitchcock's 1954 film, "Dial M for Murder." **105m/C; VHS, DVD, Blu-Ray.** Michael Douglas; Gwyneth Paltrow; Viggo Mortensen; David Suchet; Sarita Choudhury; Constance Towers; Novella Nelson; *D:* Andrew Davis; *W:* Patrick Smith Kelly; *C:* Dariusz Wolski; *M:* James Newton Howard.

Perfect Murder, Perfect Town 🦴🦴 **2000** Re-telling of the (still unsolved) murder of six-year-old JonBenet Ramsey in Boulder, Colorado, the subsequent investigation and the media frenzy that descended on the community. Miniseries is based on the book by director Schiller. **178m/C; VHS, DVD.** Marg Helgenberger; Ronny Cox; Kris Kristofferson; Ken Howard; John Heard; Ann-Margret; Scott Cohen; John Rubinstein; Dennis Boutsikaris; Sean M. Whalen; *D:* Lawrence Schiller; *W:* Tom Topor; *C:* Peter Sova; *M:* John Cacavas. **TV**

The Perfect Nanny 🦴🦴 **2000** Andrea McBride (Nelson) gets released from a mental institution and manages to get a job as a nanny to the children of a wealthy widower (Boxleitner). But Andrea expects a fairy-tale life and will do anything to make her romantic happy ending come true. **90m/C; VHS, DVD.** Tracy Nelson; Bruce Boxleitner; Dana Barron; Susan Blakely; Katherine Helmond; *D:* Rob Malenfant; *W:* Victor Schiller; Christine Conradt; Richard Gilbert Hill; *C:* Don E. Fauntleroy; *M:* Richard Bowers. **VIDEO**

Perfect Parents 🦴🦴 1/2 **2006** After learning about the violence their 10-year-old daughter Lucy (Garrood) has witnessed at her public school, Stuart (Eccleston) and Allison (Harker) are anxious to get her into a respected private Catholic school despite being atheists. Willing to lie, they enlist the aid of a dodgy priest (Warner) and others to vouch for them, but that first fib spirals into fraud, blackmail, and murder. **92m/C; DVD.** *GB* Christopher Eccleston; Susannah Harker; Lesley Manville; David Warner; Brendan Coyle; Maddy Garrood; Michelle Joseph; Isha Joseph; *D:* Joe Ahearne; *W:* Joe Ahearne; *C:* Peter Greenhalgh; *M:* Murray Gold. **TV**

The Perfect Score 🦴🦴 1/2 **2004 (PG-13)** Anxious high school seniors stressing about the SATs decide to steal the answers in this average teen movie. Kyle (Evans), worried that his lousy test scores will derail his future, assembles a crew of stereotypes to do the crime, including slacker buddy Matty (Greenberg), angry rich girl Francesca (Johansson), overachiever Anna (Christiansen), star athlete Desmond (Miles) and stoner Roy (Nam), who's the smartest of the bunch. The plot takes a backseat to the interaction between the misfits, but none of it adds up to much, with the exception of scene-stealers Johansson and Nam. **93m/C; DVD.** Erika Christensen; Chris Evans; Scarlett Johansson; Tyra Ferrell; Bryan Greenburg; Darius Miles; Leonardo Nam; Matthew Lillard; Vanessa Angel; Fulvio Cecere; *D:* Brian Robbins; *W:* Mark Schwahn; Marc Hyman; Jon Zack; *C:* Clark Mathis; *M:* John Murphy.

Perfect Sense 🦴🦴 1/2 **2011** Another case in the plague of disease-oriented apocalypse movies. Glasgow epidemiologist Susan (Green) can't explain why people across Europe are losing their senses one at a time. This is also bad news for her boyfriend Michael (McGregor), who happens to be a chef. Complicating matters is that the loss of each sense seems to be tied to intense feelings of a particular emotion. As the world unravels like faulty DNA around them, the two become more obsessed with each other and their sensory deprivation gets more acute. **88m/C; DVD, Blu-Ray.** *GB DK IR* Ewan McGregor; Eva Green; Ewen Bremner; Stephen (Dillon) Dillane; Denis Lawson; Connie Nielsen; *D:* David Mackenzie; *W:* Kim Fupz Aakeson; *C:* Giles Nuttgens; *M:* Max Richter.

Perfect Sisters 🦴 1/2 **2014** A truly disturbing 2003 crime in Toronto—in which two sisters planned and executed the murder of their mother—gets a rather lackluster treatment that's only curious in that it continues the surprising decline of the career of the once-promising Abigail Breslin. The child star appears as Sandra, sister to Beth (Henley), who reports the death of her alcoholic mother as an accidental drowning. The police believe the girls until rumors continue to persist that this death may have been planned. The story is interesting but the filmmaking is flat, boring and nondescript in every way. **100m/C; DVD.** *CA* Abigail Breslin; Georgie Henley; Mira Sorvino; James Russo; Jeffrey Ballard; Zoe Belkin; *D:* Stan Brooks; *W:* Fabrizio Filippo; Adam Till; *C:* Stephanie Weber-Biron; *M:* Carmen Rizzo.

The Perfect Sleep 🦴 **2008 (R)** Pretentious film noir homage. An unnamed man (Pardue) returns to being an assassin to save the woman (Sanchez) he loves but can never have. There's revenge, a Russian crime boss, a sinister doctor, and way too much narration in a plot that ultimately makes no sense. **90m/C; DVD.** Roselyn Sanchez; Patrick Bauchau; Peter J. Lucas; Tony Amendola; Cameron Daddo; Michael Paré; Sam Thakur; Anton Pardue; *D:* Jeremy Alter; *W:* Anton Pardue; *C:* Charles Papert; *M:* David Vanian.

The Perfect Son 🦴🦴 1/2 **2000** When their father dies, estranged brothers Theo (Cubitt) and Ryan (Feore) are reluctantly reunited. Theo is out of rehab and hoping to make a fresh start with ex-lover Sarah (West) but it's his "perfect brother" Ryan who has some revelations. The overly responsible, successful lawyer reveals to his younger bro that he is gay and dying of AIDS. They try to set aside old rivalries as one struggles to start over and the other struggles with facing his mortality. Strong drama with two exceptional lead performances, although the story is simple and somewhat old-fashioned. **93m/C; VHS, DVD.** *CA* David Cubitt; Colm Feore; Chandra West; *D:* Leonard Farlinger; *W:* Leonard Farlinger; *C:* Barry Stone; *M:* Ron Sures.

A Perfect Spy 🦴🦴 1/2 *John Le Carre's A Perfect Spy* **1988** In this BBC miniseries, John Le Carre takes a break from the world of George Smiley to take a look at spying from a personal view. Magnus Pym (Evan) would seem to be the perfect English gentleman; having gone to the right schools he proceeds to join the covert world of espionage. But Magnus hides the secret that his estranged father is a con man par excellence and it leads him to his own betrayals. Adapted from the novel, which Le Carre is said to have drawn from his own past. On three cassettes. **360m/C; VHS, DVD.** *GB* Peter Egan; Ray McAnally; Frances Tomelty; Benedict Taylor; Tim Healy; *W:* Arthur Hopcraft.

The Perfect Storm 🦴🦴 1/2 **2000 (PG-13)** Based on the true story of the Andrea Gail, a swordfishing boat lost at sea in 1991 during a freak storm—one of the biggest of the century—off the coast of Newfoundland. Film briefly sets up the backgrounds of the six men who will be the captain and crew on the tragic voyage, but not even Clooney and Wahlberg can compete with the watery special effects and it turns into a stereotypical disaster flick. Adapted from Sebastian Junger's bestselling nonfiction account of the tragedy. **129m/C; VHS, DVD, Blu-Ray, HD-DVD.** George Clooney; Mark Wahlberg; Mary Elizabeth Mastrantonio; John C. Reilly; Diane Lane; William Fichtner; Allen Payne; John Hawkes; Karen Allen; Bob Gunton; Cherry Jones; Christopher McDonald; Dash Mihok; Josh Hopkins; Michael Ironside; Janet Wright; Rusty Schwimmer; *D:* Wolfgang Petersen; *W:* William D. Wittliff; *C:* John Seale; *M:* James Horner.

Perfect Stranger 🦴🦴 1/2 **2007 (R)** Efficient, if routine, thriller. Rowena (Berry) is an investigative reporter whose childhood friend Grace (Aycox) is murdered shortly after admitting to an affair with married corporate hotshot Harrison Hill (Willis). She goes undercover at Hill's ad firm, with the help of sorta creepy/geeky tech whiz Miles (Ribisi), to get to the truth and double-plays Hill by also posing as an online tart (which is how Grace met him). Rowena is unethical, Hill is smug, but at least director Foley won't leave viewers frustrated. **109m/C; DVD, Blu-Ray.** Halle Berry; Bruce Willis; Giovanni Ribisi; Richard Portnow; Nicki Aycox; Gary Dourdan; Kathleen Chalfant; Florencia Lozano; *D:* James Foley; *W:* Todd Komarnicki; *C:* Anastas Michos; *M:* Antonio Pinto.

Perfect Strangers 🦴🦴 **1950** Divorcee Terry (Rogers) and unhappily married David (Morgan) fall for each other when they're sequestered jurors on an L.A. murder trial. But will the romance last once the verdict is reached? **88m/B; DVD.** Ginger Rogers; Dennis Morgan; Thelma Ritter; Margalo Gillmore; Anthony Ross; Howard Freeman; Paul Ford; *D:* Bretaigne Windust; *W:* Edith Sommer; *C:* J. Peverell Marley; *M:* Leigh Harline.

Perfect Strangers 🦴🦴 *Blind Alley* **1984 (R)** Thriller develops around a murder and the child who witnesses it. The killer attempts to kidnap the young boy, but problems arise when he falls in love with the lad's mother. **90m/C; VHS, DVD.** Anne Carlisle; Brad Rijn; John Woehrle; Matthew Stockley; Ann Magnuson; Stephen Lack; *D:* Larry Cohen; *W:* Larry Cohen.

Perfect Strangers 🦴🦴 1/2 **2003** It's too bad when a girl (Blake) can't go out on the town, get plastered, and pick up an honorable, upstanding guy. No, he (Neill) has to turn out to be a charming kidnapper (aren't those the worst kind?) who holds her hostage at his shack on a desolate island (off of New Zealand's west coast). But, this captivating yet contorted tale might just reveal that there's just no escaping the true bliss that demented love brings. **96m/C; VHS, DVD.** Sam Neill; Rachael Blake; Joel Tobeck; Robyn Malcolm; Madeleine Sami; *D:* Gaylene Preston; *W:* Gaylene Preston; *C:* Alun Bollinger; *M:* Neil Finn. **VIDEO**

The Perfect Student 🦴 **2011 (R)** Sub-par crime thriller. Criminology professor Nicole Johnson defends student Jordan against a charge of murdering her college roommate. Jordan's found not guilty, but new evidence emerges and it seems the professor was dead wrong. **88m/C; DVD.** Natasha Henstridge; Brea Grant; Robert Neary; Josie Davis; Jay Pickett; Michael Bowen; ***D:*** Michael Feifer; ***W:*** Peter Sullivan; ***C:*** Denis Maloney; ***M:*** Marc Jovani. **VIDEO**

Perfect Target ½ **1998 (R)** An ex-CIA agent is forced to work as a mercenary, protecting the president of Santa Brava. Naturally, this assignment doesn't go well and he becomes the fall guy for the politico's murder. Only he doesn't intend to stay that way. **97m/C; VHS, DVD.** Daniel Bernhardt; Robert Englund; Brian Thompson; Dara Tomanovich; ***D:*** Sheldon Lettich. **VIDEO**

The Perfect Teacher **2010** Psycho student goes nuts for teacher in this overly-familiar thriller from the Lifetime channel. High schooler Devon wants her divorced teacher Jim Wilkes and doesn't care that he has a new girlfriend. As usual, the guy is too dumb to realize what's going on until things turn deadly. **94m/C; DVD.** Megan Park; David Charvet; Boti Ann Bliss; Keeva Lynk; Amanda Tilson; Kimberly-Sue Murray; ***D:*** Jim Donovan; ***W:*** Christine Conradt. **CABLE**

Perfect Tenant ½ **1999 (R)** Overly familiar thriller. Because of financial problems Jessica (Purl) is forced to rent out her guesthouse. She thinks she's found the perfect tenant in Bryan (Caulfield) since he's not only handsome but polite and tidy. But it's all a facade since Bryan actually wants revenge on the woman he blames for his father's suicide. **93m/C; VHS, DVD.** Linda Purl; Maxwell Caulfield; Tracy Nelson; Earl Holliman; Melissa Behr; Stacy Hogue; ***D:*** Doug Campbell; ***W:*** Jim Vines; M. Todd Bonin; ***C:*** M. David Mullen. **VIDEO**

Perfect Understanding **1933** Rom com was a financial and critical mishap for Swanson and her British production company. While on holiday in London, Judy (Swanson) meets and quicky marries aristocrat Nicholas Randall (Olivier) although both insist on maintaining their freedom and friends. This 'perfect understanding' falls apart when Nicholas dallies with an old flame (Swinburne) and, in retaliation, Judy sees admirer Ivan (Halliday). Olivier--who was still a novice screen actor--is too callow compared to scene-stealing veteran Swanson. **80m/B; DVD, Blu-Ray.** *UK* Gloria Swanson; Laurence Olivier; John Halliday; Nora Swinburne; Genevieve Tobin; ***D:*** Cyril Gardner; ***W:*** Miles Malleson; Michael Powell; ***C:*** Curt Courant.

Perfect Victims *Perfect Life* **2008 (R)** Drug and alcohol-addicted college student Jack is longtime pals with wealthy Brit Freddy and they are both in love with Anne, though Jack keeps his interest quiet. Jack starts having blackouts and things get more confusing when he and Anne are guests of Freddy's at his family's country home. The plot gets confusing too. **98m/C; DVD.** Jesse Bradford; Sienna Guillory; Scot Williams; Emily Hamilton; Justin Urich; ***D:*** Josef Rusnak; ***W:*** Hilde Eynikel; ***C:*** Tony Imi; ***M:*** Tom Batoy; Franco Tortora. **VIDEO**

The Perfect Weapon **1991 (R)** Kenpo karate master Speakman severs family ties and wears funny belt in order to avenge underworld murder of his teacher. **85m/C; VHS, DVD, Blu-Ray.** Jeff Sanders; Jeff Speakman; ***D:*** Mark DiSalle; ***W:*** David Wilson; ***C:*** Russell Carpenter; ***M:*** Gary Chang.

The Perfect Wedding **2012** Likeable--if bland--indie rom com. Recovering alcoholic Paul is living with his parents in Florida, waiting for his adopted sister, Alana, to come home for the holidays. Recently engaged, Alana wants to plan out her wedding, which means inviting her best friends, Vicki and Roy to stay. Only Roy is Paul's ex, whom he hasn't seen since their messy break-up, so he asks Gavin to come along and pretend to be his new boyfriend. One problem is Gavin and Paul's instant attraction to one another. **82m/C; DVD.** Eric Aragon; Jason T. Gaffney; Roger Stewart; James Rebhorn; Kristine Sutherland; Apolonia Davalos; Brendan Griffin; Annie Kerins; ***D:*** Scott Gabriel; ***W:*** Jason T. Gaffney; Suzanne Brockmann; Ed Gaffney; ***C:*** Lauretta Prevost; ***M:*** Jack Gavina.

The Perfect Wife **2000** Liza (Sturges) is another of those vengeful blondes who, in the wake of "Hand that Rocks the Cradle," thrive on video premieres. She goes after everyone she blames for her beloved brother's death, including the doctor (King) who did not save his life after an auto accident. How does she get close to the good doctor? She marries him, of course, and sets about to ruin everyone he cares for. The pace moves along briskly while production values are strictly of the made-for-TV level. **92m/C; DVD.** Shannon Sturges; Perry King; Lesley-Anne Down; William R. Moses; ***D:*** Don E. Fauntleroy; ***W:*** Frank Rehwaldt; George Saunders.

Perfect Witness ½ **1989** A restaurant owner witnesses a mob slaying and resists testifying against the culprit to save his family and himself. Filmed in New York City. **104m/C; VHS, DVD; Open Captioned.** Brian Dennehy; Aidan Quinn; Stockard Channing; Laura Harrington; Joe Grifasi; ***D:*** Robert Mandel; ***M:*** Brad Fiedel. **CABLE**

The Perfect Witness *The Ungodly* **2007 (R)** Wannabe documentary filmmaker Mickey thinks he's gotten his big break when he accidentally tapes serial killer James in the act. Mickey doesn't go the cops but to James; he'll interview him and film his crimes until James is either caught or killed. (Way to be a good citizen, Mickey!) But it's the serial killer who turns out to have the upper hand. **100m/C; DVD.** Kenny Johnson; Mark Borkowski; Wes Bentley; Joanne Baron; Beth Grant; ***D:*** Thomas Dunn; ***W:*** Mark Borkowski; Thomas Dunn; ***C:*** Paco Fremenia.

A Perfect World ½ **1993 (PG-13)** Butch Haynes (Costner) is an escaped con who takes eight-year-old fatherless Phillip (Lowther) as a hostage in 1963 Texas and is pursued by Texas Ranger Red Garnett (Eastwood). Butch is a bad guy and the film never tries to make him heroic but it also allows him to grow attached to Phillip and acknowledge him as a surrogate son. Costner gives a quiet and strong performance and the remarkable Lowther never goes wrong in his role as the needy little boy. Eastwood's role is strictly secondary as the well tested lawman who understands justice without seeking vengeance. Somewhat draggy—especially the protracted final scene. **138m/C; VHS, DVD, Blu-Ray.** Kevin Costner; T.J. Lowther; Clint Eastwood; Laura Dern; Keith Szarabajka; Leo Burmester; Paul Hewitt; Bradley Whitford; Ray McKinnon; Wayne Dehart; Jennifer Griffin; Linda Hart; ***D:*** Clint Eastwood; ***W:*** John Lee Hancock; ***C:*** Jack N. Green; ***M:*** Lennie Niehaus.

The Perfection **2019** Charlotte (Williams) was once a star pupil at an elite music school until she had to drop out to care for her dying mother. Joining her former mentor, Anton Bachoff (Weber), and his wife Paloma (Huffman), at a competition for new students in China, Charlotte meets one of his new proteges, Lizzie (Browning). Lizzie is professionally successful in a way that Charlotte was not. Charlotte convinces Lizzie to go on a trip through western China that puts Lizzie's life in jeopardy. The horror film effectively combines aspect of grindhouse with upper crust themes while telling a twisted story where nothing is what it seems. **90m/C; DVD.** Allison Williams; Logan Browning; Alaina Huffman; Steven Weber; Graeme Duffy; ***D:*** Richard Shepard; ***W:*** Richard Shepard; Eric C. Charmelo; Nicole Snyder; ***C:*** Vanja Cernjul; ***M:*** Paul Haslinger. **VIDEO**

Performance ½ **1970 (R)** Grim and unsettling psychological account of a criminal who hides out in a bizarre house occupied by a peculiar rock star and his two female companions. Entire cast scores high marks, with Pallenberg especially compelling as a somewhat mysterious and attractive housemate to mincing Jagger. A cult favorite, with music by Nitzsche under the direction of Randy Newman. **104m/C; DVD, Blu-Ray.** *UK* James Fox; Mick Jagger; Anita Pallenberg; Michele Breton; Ann Sidney; John Bindon; Stanley Meadows; Allan Cuthbertson; Antony Morton; ***D:*** Donald Cammell; Nicolas Roeg; ***W:*** Donald Cammell; ***C:*** Nicolas Roeg; ***M:*** Jack Nitzsche.

Perfume **2001 (R)** Rymer worked from an outline rather than a complete script and had his actors improvise this satire on the fashion world but the film fumbles on fuzzy plots and characters. English photog Anthony (Harris) deals with professional and personal crises; gay fashion mogul Lorenzo (Sorvino) learns he has terminal cancer and draws closer to his family and lover; magazine editor Janice (Baron) is suddenly confronted by the daughter (Williams) she hasn't seen in years; and various designers (Epps, Wilson, Mann) have various problems. **106m/C; VHS, DVD.** Rita Wilson; Leslie Mann; Jared Harris; Michelle Forbes; Paul Sorvino; Peter Gallagher; Sonia Braga; Omar Epps; Jeff Goldblum; Harris Yulin; Michelle Williams; Carmen Electra; Mariel Hemingway; Robert Joy; ***D:*** Michael Rymer; ***W:*** Michael Rymer; L.M. Kit Carson; ***C:*** Rex Nicholson; ***M:*** Adam Plack.

The Perfume of Yvonne ½ *Le Parfum d'Yvonne; The Scent of Yvonne* **1994** Pretty but languid story told in flashbacks. Victor (Giradot) is staying at a Swiss hotel in 1958 and begins a flirtation with aspiring actress Yvonne (Majani), who's there with her gay companion, Dr. Meinthe (Mareille). To Victor it turns into an unforgettable romance, but the only person Yvonne loves is herself. French with subtitles. **90m/C; DVD.** *FR* Richard Bohringer; Hippolyte Giradot; Sandra Majani; Jean-Pierre Mareille; ***D:*** Patrice Leconte; ***W:*** Patrice Leconte; ***C:*** Eduardo Serra; ***M:*** Pascal Esteve.

Perfume: The Story of a Murderer **2006 (R)** Patrick Susskind's "unfilmable" 1985 novel offered a unique challenge to director Tykwer: how do you visualize the sense of smell? Jean-Baptiste Grenouille (Whishaw), orphaned in filthy, smelly 18th-century Paris, has two unique characteristics: he has no natural body odor and he possesses an unparalleled sense of smell that leads to an apprenticeship with perfumer Baldini (Hoffman). Grenouille's obsessed with the natural scent of young women and becomes a serial killer to preserve that smell and turn it into the perfect perfume. Ironically, the flick may be too faithful to the book and could have used some judicious editing. **145m/C; DVD.** *SP FR GE* Ben Whishaw; Dustin Hoffman; Alan Rickman; Rachel Hurd-Wood; Corinna Harfouch; ***Nar:*** John Hurt; ***D:*** Tom Tykwer; ***W:*** Tom Tykwer; Andrew Birkin; Bernd Eichinger; ***C:*** Frank Griebe; ***M:*** Tom Tykwer; Johnny Klimek; Reinhold Heil.

Perhaps Love *Ruguo Ai* **2005** Marketed as the first Chinese musical in 40 years, the premise is that everyone's life is a film, and they are the star only in that film. In the "life movies" of others they are at best a bit part. Famous director Nie Wen (Jacky Cheung) is directing a musical about a romantic triangle starring his lover Sun (Zhou) and her former lover Lin (Kaneshiro). **108m/C; DVD, Blu-Ray.** *CH CH* Takeshi Kaneshiro; Jacky Cheung; Xun Zhou; Jin-hee Ji; ***D:*** Peter Chan; ***W:*** Oi Wah Lam; Raymond To; ***C:*** Christopher Doyle; Peter Pau; ***M:*** Peter Kam; Leon Ko.

Peril **2000 (R)** Out-of-control plot dooms this women-in-peril saga. Terry (Fairchild) and her semi-disabled hubby Scott (James) are facing financial ruin but have one chance to save themselves. Unfortunately, Scott falls and gets trapped in a storm drain and when Terry goes for help, she gets captured by an escaped mental patient (Pare) who uses her as a hostage against the cops. Oh, and the water is rising in the storm drain, so Scott's gonna drown unless Terry can get free. Very dumb. **90m/C; VHS, DVD.** Morgan Fairchild; Michael Paré; John James; Steve Eastin; Thom Christopher; ***D:*** David Giancola. **VIDEO**

The Perils of Gwendoline ½ *Gwendoline; The Perils of Gwendoline in the Land of the Yik-Yak* **1984 (R)** A young woman leaves a convent to search for her long-lost father, in this adaptation of a much funnier French comic strip of the same name. What ends up on the screen is merely a very silly rip-off of the successful "Raiders of the Lost Ark," and of primary interest for its numerous scenes of amply endowed Kitaen in the buff. **88m/C; VHS, DVD, Blu-Ray.** *FR* Tawny Kitaen; Brent Huff; Zabou; Bernadette LaFont; Jean Rougerie; ***D:*** Just Jaeckin; ***M:*** Pierre Bachelet.

The Perils of Pauline ½ **1934** All 12 episodes of this classic melodrama/adventure serial in one package, featuring dastardly villains, cliff-hanging predicaments, and worldwide chases. **238m/B; VHS, DVD.** Evalyn Knapp; Robert "Tex" Allen; James Durkin; Sonny Ray; Pat O'Malley; ***D:*** Ray Taylor.

The Perils of Pauline **1947** A musical biography of Pearl White, the reigning belle of silent movie serials. Look for lots of silent film stars. **96m/C; VHS, DVD.** Betty Hutton; John Lund; Constance Collier; William Demarest; Billy DeWolfe; ***D:*** George Marshall; ***C:*** Ray Rennahan; ***M:*** Frank Loesser.

Period of Adjustment **1962** Heartwarming comedy about young newlyweds adjusting to the pressures of domestic life and trying to help the troubled marriage of an older couple. Based on the play by Tennessee Williams. **112m/B; VHS, DVD.** Anthony (Tony) Franciosa; Jane Fonda; Jim Hutton; Lois Nettleton; John McGiver; Jack Albertson; ***D:*** George Roy Hill; ***W:*** Isobel Lennart.

The Perks of Being a Wallflower ½ **2012 (PG-13)** Stephen Chbosky brilliantly adapts his hit, semi-autobiographical, young adult novel about the tumultuous high school years in a way that brings back memories of Cameron Crowe and John Hughes' best work with its stunning blend of wit and sentiment. Charlie (Lerman) is a troubled young man who is plucked from the wall by a group of theatrical kids including an unrequited crush (Watson) and flamboyant protector (Miller). Charlie has a dark past that Chbosky reveals delicately, never once conveying that sense of manipulation that mars so many similar films. He likes these characters and it becomes impossible not to do the same. **103m/C; DVD, Blu-Ray.** Logan Lerman; Emma Watson; Ezra Miller; Mae Whitman; Nina Dobrev; Johnny Simmons; Melanie Lynskey; Dylan McDermott; Kate Walsh; ***D:*** Stephen Chbosky; ***W:*** Stephen Chbosky; ***C:*** Andrew Dunn; ***M:*** Michael Brook. Ind. Spirit '13: First Feature.

Permanent **2017 (PG-13)** A teen angst comedy set in 1982 that uses a bad hair experience to explore issues of adolescence, class, and family. After moving to a Virginia suburb, young Aurelie (McLean) wants to create a new identity at her new school by getting a permanent. After a salon trainee gives her a disastrous perm, Aurelie becomes even more bullied than she was before. Because her parents cannot afford to pay for her hair to be straightened, she schemes to get the funds with the help of determined friend Lydia (Daniels). Though the film's humor comes from nostalgia, it lacks solid storytelling. **93m/C; DVD, Blu-Ray.** Patricia Arquette; Rainn Wilson; Kira McLean; Nena Daniels; Brian Bremer; ***D:*** Colette Burson; ***W:*** Colette Burson; ***C:*** Paula Huidobro; ***M:*** Craig Wedren.

Permanent Midnight ½ **1998 (R)** Film version of TV writer Jerry Stahl's 1995 autobiography, which follows his plunge from a guy who has it all to a loser junkie who's as unlikable as this movie. There are some great flashes of dark humor—Jerry's (Stiller) obsessed with exercising and eating right even while pumping himself full of drugs—and some truly horrific sequences, but the problem is that we don't care. Stiller's comic timing makes most of the bleak jokes work; however, his brooding performance lacks any charisma. Watch for Stahl himself as a pessimistic doctor at a methadone clinic. **85m/C; VHS, DVD.** Ben Stiller; Elizabeth Hurley; Maria Bello; Owen Wilson; Lourdes Benedicto; Peter Greene; Cheryl Ladd; Fred Willard; Charles Fleischer; Janeane Garofalo; Jerry Stahl; ***D:*** David Veloz; ***W:*** David Veloz; ***C:*** Robert Yeoman; ***M:*** Daniel Licht.

Permanent Record ½ **1988 (PG-13)** Hyper-sincere drama about a popular high schooler's suicide and the emotional reactions of those he left behind. Great performance from Reeves. **92m/C; DVD.** Alan Boyce; Keanu Reeves; Michelle Meyrink; Jennifer Rubin; Pamela Gidley; Michael Elgart; Richard Bradford; Barry Corbin; Kathy Baker; ***D:*** Marisa Silver; ***W:*** Jarre Fees; Alice Liddle; Larry Ketron; ***C:*** Frederick Elmes; ***M:*** Joe Strummer.

Permission **2018** Childhood sweethearts Anna (Hall) and Will (Stevens) are on an inevitable path to marriage when a friend drunkenly plants a seed about sowing their heretofore unsown oats before hitting the altar. Anna takes the comment to heart, and suggests that she and Will pursue farming...er, sex with other partners as a way of confirming their devotion to each other. Hall and Stevens give outstanding, heartbreaking performances in this exploration of modern, adult relationships. **96m/C; DVD.** Rebecca Hall; Dan Stevens; Jason Sudeikis; Gina Gershon; François Arnaud; ***D:*** Brian Crano; ***W:*** Brian Crano; ***C:*** Adam Bricker; ***M:*** Jason Kramer.

Perpetrators of the Crime 🦴🦴 **1998 (R)** Dumb criminals—dumb crime. Jones (Burgess) comes up with a kidnapping scheme but his sidekicks, Phil (Strong) and Ed (Devine), kidnap the wrong girl (Spelling) and take her to the wrong hideout. That makes things difficult when Jones tries to shake down their mark (Davis) for the ransom. **85m/C; VHS, DVD.** *CA* Danny Strong; Tori Spelling; Mark Burgess; Sean Devine; William B. Davis; ***D:*** John Hamilton; ***W:*** Max Sartor.

Perrier's Bounty 🦴 1/2 **2009** Violent and familiar Irish crime comedy. Petty criminal Michael McCrea (Murphy) borrows money from Dublin gangster Perrier (Gleeson) and gets beaten up by Perrier's goons when he can't repay the debt. This leads to an accidental shooting by his suicidal neighbor Brenda (Whittaker), Michael's estranged and crazy father Jim (Broadbent) as an unexpected witness, and a bounty being placed on all their heads. **88m/C; DVD, Blu-Ray.** *GB IR* Cillian Murphy; Jim Broadbent; Brendan Gleeson; Jodie Whitaker; Liam Cunningham; Michael McElhatton; ***V:*** Gabriel Byrne; ***D:*** Ian Fitzgibbon; ***W:*** Mark O'Rowe; ***C:*** Seamus Deasy; ***M:*** David Holmes.

Perry Mason Returns 🦴🦴🦴 **1985** Perry Mason returns to solve another baffling mystery. This time he must help his longtime assistant, Della Street, when she is accused of killing her new employer. **95m/C; VHS, DVD.** Raymond Burr; Barbara Hale; William Katt; Patrick O'Neal; Richard Anderson; Cassie Yates; Al Freeman, Jr.; ***D:*** Ron Satlof.

Persepolis 🦴🦴🦴 **2007 (PG-13)** Animated tale about a young Iranian girl's life from the end of the Shah's rule through the abrupt transition to the fundamentalist Muslim regime that followed. The profound impact of the many changes Marjane (Mastroianni) endures is heartrending. Although part of a progressive family, she's forced to don a face-covering veil. After fleeing to Austria, she's stereotyped as a fanatical Muslim. When she returns to Iran, she's now an outsider and she flees yet again. Adapted from Satrapi's semi-autobiographical graphic novel, the characters are expressed as rather low-tech line drawings, but the resulting images and storyline are relatable. **95m/B; DVD, Blu-Ray.** *FR* ***V:*** Chiara Mastroianni; Danielle Darrieux; Simon Abkarian; Gabrielle Lopes; Catherine Deneuve; Francois Jerosme; ***D:*** Marjane Satrapi; Vincent Paronnauel; ***W:*** Marjane Satrapi; Vincent Paronnauel; ***M:*** Olivier Bernet.

Persona 🦴🦴🦴🦴 **1966** A famous actress turns mute and is treated by a talkative nurse at a secluded cottage. As their relationship turns increasingly tense, the women's personalities begin to merge. Memorable, unnerving—and atypically avant garde—fare from cinema giant Bergman. First of several collaborations between the director and leading lady Ullman. In Swedish with English subtitles. **100m/C; VHS, DVD, Blu-Ray.** *SW* Bibi Andersson; Liv Ullmann; Gunnar Bjornstrand; Margareta Krook; Jorgen Lindstrom; ***D:*** Ingmar Bergman; ***W:*** Ingmar Bergman; ***C:*** Sven Nykvist; ***M:*** Lars Johan Werle. Natl. Soc. Film Critics '67: Actress (Andersson), Director (Bergman), Film.

Personal Best 🦴🦴🦴 **1982 (R)** Lesbian lovers compete while training for the 1980 Olympics. Provocative fare often goes where few films have gone before, but overly stylized direction occasionally overwhelms characterizations. It gleefully exploits locker-room nudity, with Hemingway in her pre-implant days. Still, an ambitious, often accomplished production. Towne's directorial debut. **126m/C; DVD.** Mariel Hemingway; Scott Glenn; Patrice Donnelly; ***D:*** Robert Towne; ***W:*** Robert Towne; ***C:*** Michael Chapman; ***M:*** Jack Nitzsche.

Personal Effects 🦴 1/2 **2005** Crime drama that takes an obvious path. Attorney Bonnie Locke (Miller) is looking into her brother's (Van Dien) disappearance and the stalker who is frightening her friend Nicole (Mennell). Bonnie soon realizes that the two situations are related. **90m/C; DVD.** Penelope Ann Miller; Casper Van Dien; Laura Mennell; Christopher Judge; William Macdonald; ***D:*** Michael Scott; ***W:*** David Golden; ***C:*** Adam Sliwinski; ***M:*** Tim Jones. **CABLE**

Personal Effects 🦴 1/2 **2009 (R)** A clumsily-told combo of tragedy and romance. Kutcher goes from comedy to drama (with middling success) as a college wrestler whose life is upended when his twin sister is murdered. Walter meets equally grief-stricken Linda (Pfeiffer) at a support group and the two are bonded by circumstance as well as Linda's deaf teen son Clay (Hudson) who is heading down a dangerous path of his own. **110m/C; DVD.** Ashton Kutcher; Michelle Pfeiffer; Kathy Bates; John Mann; David Lewis; Spencer Hudson; ***D:*** David Hollander; ***W:*** David Hollander; ***C:*** Elliot Davis; ***M:*** Johann Johannsson. **VIDEO**

Personal Property 🦴🦴 1/2 *The Man in Possession* **1937** Taylor tries every trick in the book to win Harlow over in this MGM romantic fluff. Not that big on laughs, but plenty of good shots of Harlow and a beefcake scene of Taylor in a bathtub, who was the darling of the MGM lot and worked with every leading lady. This was the only film Harlow and Taylor made together. Remake of the 1931 film "The Man in Possession." **84m/B; VHS, DVD.** Robert Taylor; Jean Harlow; Reginald Owen; Una O'Connor; E.E. Clive; Henrietta Crosman; Cora Witherspoon; ***D:*** W.S. Van Dyke; ***W:*** Hugh Mills.

Personal Services 🦴🦴 1/2 **1987 (R)** A bawdy satire loosely based on the life and times of Britain's modern-day madam, Cynthia Payne, and her rise to fame in the world of prostitution. Payne's earlier years were featured in the film "Wish You Were Here." **104m/C; VHS, DVD.** *GB* Julie Walters; Alec McCowen; Shirley Stelfox; Tim Woodward; Dave Atkins; Danny Schiller; Victoria Hardcastle; ***D:*** Terry Jones; ***W:*** David Leland; ***C:*** Roger Deakins; ***M:*** John Du Prez.

Personal Shopper 🦴🦴🦴 **2017 (R)** Stewart continues to be one of the most interesting actresses in indie cinema in this reunion with her "Clouds of Sils Maria" director, Olivier Assayas. She plays Maureen, the personal shopper for a celebrity in Paris. Against the backdrop of beautiful people in beautiful places, Assayas unfolds a unique ghost story when Maureen starts to believe she's communicating with her dead twin brother, sometime via text message and e-mail. The idea that we are haunted by our lost loved ones, especially in places as hollow as the world of high fashion, is a fascinating one, and Stewart gives a career-best performance. **105m/C; DVD, Blu-Ray.** Kristen Stewart; Lars Eidinger; Sigrid Bouaziz; Anders Danielsen Lie; Ty Olwin; ***D:*** Olivier Assayas; ***W:*** Olivier Assayas; ***C:*** Yorick Le Saux.

Personal Velocity: Three Portraits 🦴🦴🦴 **2002 (R)** Story of three New York women undergoing life-changing moments. Delia (Sedgwick) takes her children and leaves her abusive spouse and Catskill trailer life. Greta (Posey), a Manhattan cookbook editor, realizes that in order to move forward she needs to leave her slouch of a husband. Paula (Balk), a pregnant, misdirected young woman driving nowhere in particular, connects with her maternal instincts through an encounter with a hitchhiker. Ellen Kuras's cinematography is notable and Miller (playwright Arthur's daughter) mixes great storytelling with flashbacks, montages, and narrator commentary to provide a well-rounded understanding of each situation. **86m/C; VHS, DVD.** Kyra Sedgwick; David Warshofsky; Leo Fitzpatrick; Brian Tarantina; Mara Hobel; Parker Posey; Tim Guinee; Joel de la Fuente; Wallace Shawn; Ron Leibman; Josh Weinstein; Ben Shankman; Fairuza Balk; Seth Gilliam; David Patrick Kelly; Lou Taylor Pucci; Patti D'Arbanville; ***Nar:*** John Ventimiglia; ***D:*** Rebecca Miller; ***W:*** Rebecca Miller; ***C:*** Ellen Kuras; ***M:*** Michael Rohatyn.

Personal Vendetta 🦴 **1996** A housewife decides to end years of abuse by finally pressing charges against her husband with the help of a kindly police officer who inspires her to join the force. The abuse angle would be a little more believable if the battered wife wasn't being player by former wrestler "Magnificent Mimi" Lesseos. **89m/C; DVD.** Mimi Lesseos; Timothy Bottoms; Mark Wilson; Bill Douglas; Lisa Marie Hayes; Kennon Raines; Frank Trejo; ***D:*** Stephen Lieb; ***W:*** Mimi Lesseos; Thomas Quinn; ***C:*** Bodo Holst; ***M:*** Howard Shear. **TV**

The Personals 🦴🦴 1/2 **1983 (PG)** A recently divorced young man takes out a personal ad in a newspaper to find the woman of his dreams. But it isn't quite that simple in this independent comedy shot entirely in Minneapolis. **90m/C; VHS, DVD.** Bill Schoppert; Karen Landry; Paul Eiding; Michael Laskin; Vickie Dakil; ***D:*** Peter Markle.

The Personals 🦴🦴 1/2 **1998** Fed up with her boring love life, Dr. Du Jia-zhen (Liu) takes out a personal ad and gets 100 responses. The body of the film is made up of the interviews she conducts with these men—well, most of them are men. Other filmmakers have made more of the same premise, but director Kuo-fu Chen keeps his camera squarely on his characters. The Taiwan setting is a bit exotic. Liu's performance is a model of restraint. Mandarin with subtitles. **104m/C; VHS, DVD.** *TW* Rene Liu; Wu Bai; ***D:*** Kuo-fu Chen; Shih-chich Chen; ***W:*** Kuo-fu Chen; Shih-chich Chen; ***C:*** Nan-hong Ho.

Personals 🦴🦴 1/2 *Hook'd Up* **2000** New Yorker Keith (Yoba) is juggling two girlfriends and a writing job and sucking at all three endeavors. So it's no big surprise when he loses it all. Keith then decides to write an expose of personal ads but finds out more about himself then the women who answer his ad. Entertaining debut for filmmaker Sargent. **91m/C; VHS, DVD.** Malik Yoba; Stacey Dash; Sheryl Lee Ralph; Rhonda Ross Kendrick; Monteria Ivey; ***D:*** Mike Sargent; ***W:*** Mike Sargent. **VIDEO**

Persons Unknown 🦴🦴 **1996** Melodramatic noir with a decent cast. Disgraced ex-cop Jim Holland (Mantegna) now runs a security firm in Long Beach, CA. He has a one-nighter with foxy Amanda (Lynch) and wakes up to discover she's stolen confidential files. So, with colleague Cake (Walsh), he tracks Amanda down and discovers that she and her wheelchair-bound sister, Molly (Watts), are planning a robbery that involves ripping off Columbian drug lords. But, as usual, nothing works out as intended. **99m/C; VHS, DVD.** Joe Mantegna; Kelly Lynch; J.T. Walsh; Naomi Watts; Xander Berkeley; Jon Favreau; Channon Roe; Michael Nicolosi; ***D:*** George Hickenlooper; ***W:*** Craig Smith; ***C:*** Richard Crudo; ***M:*** Ed Tomney.

Persuasion 🦴🦴 1/2 **1971** Practical Anne Elliott is always at the beck-and-call of her snobbish and helpless family. She even turned down a marriage proposal for their sake. Now Captain Wentworth has come back into Anne's life and she has a second chance. But will she be strong enough to take it? Made for BBC TV. **225m/C; VHS, DVD.** *GB* Ann(e) Firbank; Basil Dignam; Valerie Gearon; Marian Spence; Charlotte Mitchell; ***D:*** Howard E. Baker; ***W:*** Julian Mitchell. **TV**

Persuasion 🦴🦴🦴 1/2 **1995 (PG)** Charming British costume romance, based on Jane Austen's final novel, deals with the constricted life of practical, plain, put-upon Anne Elliot (Root). Thanks to well-meaning interference, Anne refused the marriage proposal of the manly Frederick Wentworth (Hinds) and instead stuck by her snobbish and demanding family. Eight years later, Anne is given a second chance at love when the now-wealthy Wentworth happens back into her life—but she still has her obnoxious relations to contend with. It's wonderful to see Anne blossom although the swirl of supporting players (and settings) provide some confusion. **104m/C; VHS, DVD.** *UK* Amanda Root; Ciaran Hinds; Susan Fleetwood; Corin Redgrave; Fiona Shaw; John Woodvine; Phoebe Nicholls; Samuel West; Sophie Thompson; Judy Cornwell; Felicity Dean; Simon Russell Beale; Victoria Hamilton; ***D:*** Roger Mitchell; ***W:*** Nick Dear; Jeremy Sams; ***C:*** John Daly; ***M:*** Jeremy Sams.

Persuasion 🦴🦴 1/2 **2007** Poor, put-upon spinster Anne Elliot (Hawkins)! Some years before, having respected the wishes of family and friends, she turned down the marriage proposal of Captain Wentworth (Penry-Jones) to care for her selfish and self-centered family. But Wentworth unexpectedly re-enters the scene—now a wealthy, rather dashing, and very eligible bachelor. Can Anne still catch his eye? And will she allow her own feelings to rule what's still expected of her? Based on the novel by Jane Austen. **90m/C; DVD.** *GB* Sally Hawkins; Rupert Penry-Jones; Anthony Head; Julia Davis; Amanda Halle; Sam Hazeldine; Alice Krige; Michael Fenton-Stevens; Mary Stockley; Maisie Dimbelby; ***D:*** Adrian Shergold; ***W:*** Simon Burke; ***C:*** David Odd; ***M:*** Martin Phipps. **TV**

The Perverse Countess 🦴 *La Comtesse Perverse; Countess Perverse* **1973** Romay is a bored tourist who spends a free weekend on a fling with Woods, who procures human flesh for the cannibalistic Count and Countess Zaroff (Vernon and Arno). Romay accompanies her lover to the haunted castle on a delivery, not realizing she is the package. When the Countess sees what a succulent bon-bon Romay is, she faces difficult choices. Subtitled in English. **86m/C; VHS, DVD, Blu-Ray.** *FR* Lina Romay; Robert Woods; Howard Vernon; Alice Arno; Caroline Riviere; ***D:*** Jess (Jesus) Franco.

The Pest 🦴 **1996 (PG-13)** Movie certainly lives up to its title. A hyperkinetic Leguizamo stars as Pestario (Pest) Vargas, a small-time Miami con man, who owes 50 large to the mob. Eccentric German businessman Gustav Shank (Jones) offers the money to Pest—the catch being that Pest will become the human prey for Gustav's private island hunting party. You'll be rooting for the hunter. **85m/C; VHS, DVD.** John Leguizamo; Jeffrey Jones; Edoardo Ballerini; Freddy Rodriguez; Joe Morton; Charles Hallahan; Tammy Townsend; Aries Spears; ***D:*** Paul Miller; ***W:*** David Bar Katz; ***C:*** Roy Wagner; ***M:*** Kevin Kiner.

Pet Sematary 🦴 1/2 **2019 (R)** After the Creed family moves to their new home in rural Maine, the family cat Church is killed by a truck and neighbor Jude (Lithgow) offers to help Louis Creed (Clarke) bury him. Assured that Louis's young daughter Ellie (Laurence) loved him, Jud has Louis bury Church in a certain part of the woods. The next day, Church returns from the dead, though is not quite the same. Louis soon learns the secret of the burial ground. Based on the Stephen King novel, the film is forgettable in its easy scares and meaningless plot twists but Lithgow and Laurence do their best. **101m/C; DVD, Blu-Ray.** Jason Clarke; Amy Seimetz; John Lithgow; Jeté Laurence; Obssa Ahmed; ***D:*** Kevin Kölsch; Dennis Widmyer; ***W:*** Jeff Buhler; ***C:*** Laurie Rose; ***M:*** Christopher Young.

Pet Sematary 🦴🦴 **1989 (R)** A quirky adaptation of Stephen King's bestseller about a certain patch of woods in the Maine wilderness that rejuvenates the dead, and how a newly located college MD eventually uses it to restore his dead son. Mildly creepy. **103m/C; VHS, DVD, Blu-Ray.** Dale Midkiff; Fred Gwynne; Denise Crosby; Blaze Berdahl; Brad Greenquist; Miko Hughes; Stephen King; ***D:*** Mary Lambert; ***W:*** Stephen King; ***C:*** Peter Stein; ***M:*** Elliot Goldenthal.

Pet Sematary 2 🦴 1/2 **1992 (R)** Lame sequel to original Stephen King flick. After seeing his mother electrocuted, a teen and his veterinarian father move to the Maine town where the legendary Pet Sematary is located. Horror begins when the boy's friend's dog is shot by his stepfather, and the boys bury the dog in the "sematary." King wasn't involved with this film, so the story isn't very coherent, but shock value and special effects are great. Not recommended for those with a weak stomach. **102m/C; VHS, DVD, Blu-Ray.** Anthony Edwards; Edward Furlong; Clancy Brown; Jared Rushton; Darlanne Fluegel; Lisa Waltz; Jason McGuire; Sarah Trigger; ***D:*** Mary Lambert; ***W:*** Richard Outten; ***C:*** Russell Carpenter.

Petals on the Wind 🦴 1/2 **2014** Lifetime sequel to "Flowers in the Attic" still doesn't live up to its lurid origins, especially since crazy granny is now bedridden and dying so Burstyn doesn't have much to do. It's all about revenge as 10 years have past and the surviving Dollanganger kids have scattered to try and get on with their lives. Cathy is studying ballet in New York but is determined to make mommy dearest pay by seducing her trophy husband. Which doesn't mean that she and brother Christopher have let go of all those incestuous feelings. **90m/C; DVD.** Rose McIver; Wyatt Nash; Bailey Buntain; Heather Graham; Ellen Burstyn; Dylan Bruce; Will(iam) Kemp; Whitney Hoy; Ross Phillips; ***D:*** Karen Moncrieff; ***W:*** Kayla Alpert; ***C:*** Anastas Michos; ***M:*** Mario Grigorov. **CABLE**

Pete Kelly's Blues 1955 A jazz musician in a Kansas City speakeasy is forced to stand up against a brutal racketeer. The melodramatic plot is brightened by a nonstop flow of jazz tunes sung by Lee and Fitzgerald and played by an all-star lineup that includes Dick Cathcart, Matty Matlock, Eddie Miller and George Van Eps. **96m/C; VHS, DVD, Blu-Ray.** Jack Webb; Janet Leigh; Edmond O'Brien; Lee Marvin; Martin Milner; Peggy Lee; Ella Fitzgerald; Jayne Mansfield; ***D:*** Jack Webb.

Pete 'n' Tillie 1/2 **1972 (PG)** Amiable comedy turns to less appealing melodrama as couple meets, marries, and endures tragedy. Film contributes little to director Ritt's hitt-and-miss reputation, but Matthau and Burnett shine in leads. Adapted by Julius J. Epstein from a Peter de Vries' story. **100m/C; VHS, DVD.** Walter Matthau; Carol Burnett; Geraldine Page; Barry Nelson; Rene Auberjonois; Lee Montgomery; Henry Jones; Kent Smith; ***D:*** Martin Ritt; ***W:*** Julius J. Epstein; ***C:*** John A. Alonzo; ***M:*** John Williams. British Acad. '73: Actor (Matthau).

Pete Smalls Is Dead 1/2 **2010** Crass would-be comedy with obnoxious characters. Former screenwriter KC Munk is now running a laundromat in New York and is in such trouble with his bookie that his dog is kidnapped and held as collateral. KC heads back to Hollywood with old pal Jack to attend the funeral of their one-time friend Pete Smalls, a successful director who screwed them out of a business deal. The pals hope to parley Pete's unfinished movie into a windfall but it's gone missing. **95m/C; DVD.** Peter Dinklage; Mark Boone, Jr.; Theresa Wayman; Seymour Cassel; Ritchie Coster; Rosie Perez; Michael Lerner; Steve Buscemi; Tim Roth; ***D:*** Alexandre Rockwell; ***W:*** Alexandre Rockwell; Brandon Cole; ***C:*** Kai Orion; ***M:*** Mader.

Peter and Paul 1/2 **1981** TV miniseries follows the lives of the two apostles, Peter (Foxworth) and Paul (Hopkins), from the Crucifixion through the next three decades as they travel spreading the word of Christ, until both are executed in Rome. Tries valiantly, but falls a bit short. **194m/C; VHS, DVD.** Anthony Hopkins; Robert Foxworth; Eddie Albert; Raymond Burr; Jose Ferrer; Jon Finch; David Gwillim; Herbert Lom; Jean Peters; ***D:*** Robert Day; ***W:*** Christopher Knopf.

Peter and Vandy 1/2 **2009** New Yorker Peter (Ritter) is constantly apologizing for all his actions, which annoys his girlfriend Vandy (Weixler). Of course he needs to since his insecurities cause Peter to behave like a jerk although Vandy's a passive-aggressive pill so maybe they deserve each other. They bicker—a lot—in a non-linear timeframe that gets old really, really quickly. Some romance. DiPetro already did his own two-character play. **78m/C; On Demand.** Jason Ritter; Jess Weixler; Jesse L. Martin; Noah Bean; Zak Orth; Dana Ekelson; Bruce Altman; Maryann Plunkett; ***D:*** Jay DiPietro; ***W:*** Jay DiPietro; ***C:*** Frank DeMarco.

Peter Gunn **1989** Detective Peter Gunn returns, only to find himself being hunted by both the mob and the Feds. A TV movie reprise of the vintage series that has none of the original cast members. **97m/C; VHS, DVD.** Peter Strauss; Barbara Williams; Jennifer Edwards; Charles Cioffi; Pearl Bailey; Peter Jurasik; David Rappaport; ***D:*** Blake Edwards; ***M:*** Henry Mancini. **TV**

Peter Ibbetson **1935** Convoluted fantasy romance—much of which takes place in prison, where the wrongly convicted Peter (Cooper) is serving a life sentence. He's accidentally killed the Duke of Towers (Halliday), the jealous husband of Peter's childhood friend, Mary (Harding). She stands by him and claims they can always be young and together in his dreams. Somewhat stilted, but if the viewer can accept Peter's dream world there is some emotional impact. **88m/B; DVD.** Gary Cooper; Ann Harding; John Halliday; Ida Lupino; Douglass Dumbrille; Dickie Moore; Virginia Weidler; Donald Meek; ***D:*** Henry Hathaway; ***W:*** Vincent Lawrence; Waldemar Young; ***C:*** Charles B(ryant) Lang, Jr.; ***M:*** Ernst Toch.

Peter Lundy and the Medicine Hat Stallion 1/2 *The Medicine Hat Stallion; Pony Express* **1977** A teenaged Pony Express rider must outrun the Indians and battle the elements in order to carry mail from the Nebraska Territory to the West Coast. Good family entertainment. **85m/C; VHS, DVD.** Leif Garrett; Mitchell Ryan; Bibi Besch; John Quade; Milo O'Shea; ***D:*** Michael O'Herlihy. **TV**

Peter Pan 1/2 **1924** The first film adaptation of James M. Barrie's children's classic stars Bronson as the title character (in a performance endorsed by Barrie himself) that of an adventurous boy who refuses to grow up. Torrence is a scene-stealer as Captain Hook. A little on the stagy side but it still shines. **102m/B; Silent; VHS, DVD, Blu-Ray.** Betty Bronson; Ernest Torrence; Mary Brian; Virginia Brown Faire; Anna May Wong; Esther Ralston; Cyril Chadwick; Philippe De Lacey; Jack Murphy; ***D:*** Herbert Brenon; ***W:*** Willis Goldbeck; ***C:*** James Wong Howe; ***M:*** Philip Carli. Natl. Film Reg. '00.

Peter Pan **1953 (G)** Disney classic about a boy who never wants to grow up. Based on J.M. Barrie's book and play. Still stands head and shoulders above any recent competition in providing fun family entertainment. Terrific animation and lovely hummable music. **76m/C; VHS, DVD, Blu-Ray.** ***V:*** Bobby Driscoll; Kathryn Beaumont; Hans Conried; Heather Angel; Candy Candido; Bill Thompson; ***Nar:*** Tom Conway; ***D:*** Hamilton Luske; ***W:*** Milt Banta; William Cottrell; Winston Hibler; Bill Peet; Erdman Penner; Joe Rinaldi; Ted Sears; Ralph Wright; ***M:*** Edward Plumb; Oliver Wallace.

Peter Pan 1/2 **1960** A TV classic, this videotape of a performance of the 1954 Broadway musical adapted from the J.M. Barrie classic features Mary Martin in one of her most famous incarnations, as the adolescent Peter Pan. Songs include "I'm Flying," "Neverland," and "I Won't Grow Up." **100m/C; VHS, DVD.** Mary Martin; Cyril Ritchard; Sondra Lee; Heather Halliday; Luke Halpin; ***D:*** Vincent J. Donehue. **TV**

Peter Pan 1/2 **2003 (PG)** Much more literal adaptation of the J.M. Barrie novel is surprisingly serious in its tone. Peter Pan (Sumpter), played by an actual boy this time around, teaches the Darling children how to fly and leads them to Neverland. Newcomer Rachel Hurd-Wood shines as Wendy Darling. Goes deeper into the relationships and emotions between the characters, including Peter and Hook, than in previous versons. **113m/C; VHS, DVD, Blu-Ray.** Jason Isaacs; Jeremy Sumpter; Rachel Hurd-Wood; Olivia Williams; Ludivine Sagnier; Richard Briers; Lynn Redgrave; Geoffrey Palmer; Harry Newell; Freddie Popplewell; ***Nar:*** Saffron Burrows; ***D:*** P.J. Hogan; ***W:*** P.J. Hogan; Michael Goldenberg; ***C:*** Donald McAlpine; ***M:*** James Newton Howard.

Peter Pan Live! 1/2 **2014** NBC offers a solid version of the musical with Williams appropriately spunky in the title role. Walken does less well as the foppish Captain Hook, forgetting more than a few lines, but clearly enjoying himself. All the flying wire work and lighting (we believe, Tinkerbell) add to the general energy. **132m/C; DVD.** Allison Williams; Christopher Walken; Taylor Louderman; Christian Borle; Kelli O'Hara; Minnie Driver; ***D:*** Rob Ashford; Glenn Weiss; ***W:*** Irene Mecchi. **TV**

Peter Rabbit 1/2 **2018 (PG)** A combination live-action/animation feature that brings to life Beatrix Potter's classic characters, though you may not recognize them. Peter Rabbit is living the good life, basking in the friendship of his fellow animals, the affection of his neighbor Bea (Byrne), and the bounty of the vegetable garden. But when boundary-loving Mr. McGregor (Gleeson) moves in, he not only bars the bunnies from his garden, he puts the moves on Bea, so the CGI critters launch a counterattack. In this inter-species feud, which is a hare too violent, the quiet charm of Potter's illustrations and characters was collateral damage. **93m/C; DVD, Blu-Ray.** Rose Byrne; Domhnall Gleeson; Sam Neill; ***V:*** James Corden; Daisy Ridley; ***D:*** Will Gluck; ***W:*** Will Gluck; Rob Lieber; ***C:*** Peter Menzies, Jr.; ***M:*** Dominic Lewis.

Peterloo 1/2 **2018 (PG-13)** In Britain in 1819, members of the working class demand more workers' rights and parliamentary reform. As their calls grow stronger, the prime minister (Wilfort), Prince Regent (McInnerny), and home secretary Lord Sidmouth (Johnson) become concerned. Events reach a climax when 80,000 protestors gather in St. Peter's Field in Manchester to call for these changes and hear speakers like Henry Hunt (Kinnear). In response, the British government sends in the calvary to restore order but the result is chaos. Based on historical events, writer/director Leigh has created a visually striking passion project though the dialogue is often clichéd. **154m/C; DVD.** *UK* Rory Kinnear; Maxine Peake; Pearce Quigley; David Moorst; Rachel Finnegan; ***D:*** Mike Leigh; ***W:*** Mike Leigh; ***C:*** Dick Pope; ***M:*** Gary Yershon.

Peter's Friends 1/2 **1992 (R)** Peter has recently inherited a grand manor house located outside London and invites some chums to celebrate a New Year's Eve weekend, ten years after they've been at university together. So begins another nostalgic trip down memory lane ala "The Big Chill," but this one can stand on its own, with a lightweight and sly script by talented comedienne Rudner (in her film debut) and her husband Bergman. If the script sometimes falls a little flat, the fine cast makes up for it. Thompson's mother, actress Law, plays the housekeeper. **102m/C; VHS, DVD.** *GB* Kenneth Branagh; Rita Rudner; Emma Thompson; Stephen Fry; Hugh Laurie; Imelda Staunton; Alphonsia Emmanuel; Tony Slattery; Alex Lowe; Alex Scott; Phyllida Law; Richard Briers; ***D:*** Kenneth Branagh; ***W:*** Rita Rudner; Martin Bregman.

Pete's Dragon 1/2 **1977 (G)** Elliot, an enormous, bumbling dragon with a penchant for clumsy heroics, becomes friends with poor orphan Pete. Combines brilliant animation with the talents of live actors for an interesting effect. **128m/C; VHS, DVD, Blu-Ray.** Helen Reddy; Shelley Winters; Mickey Rooney; Jim Dale; Red Buttons; Sean Marshall; Jim Backus; Jeff Conaway; ***V:*** Charlie Callas; ***D:*** Don Chaffey; ***W:*** Malcolm Marmorstein; ***C:*** Frank V. Phillips; ***M:*** Irwin Kostal.

Pete's Dragon 1/2 **2016 (PG)** In 1977, a young boy named Pete is on a road trip with his parents when an accident happens and they're both killed. Pete flees into a nearby forest, where he meets a dragon, who essentially becomes his new guardian in this riff on The Jungle Book with a magical twist. This is one of those rare remakes that feels artistically designed. Director Lowery brings a graceful, natural touch to the story, allowing it to work for both adults and little ones, although there may be a few deep conversations about death following a viewing. **103m/C; DVD, Blu-Ray.** Bryce Dallas Howard; Robert Redford; Oakes Fegley; Oona Laurence; Wes Bentley; ***D:*** David Lowery; ***W:*** David Lowery; Toby Halbrooks; ***C:*** Bojan Bazelli; ***M:*** Daniel Hart.

Pete's Meteor 1/2 **1998 (R)** A meteor lands in the Dublin backyard where Mickey and his two siblings are living with their grandmother (Fricker) after the death of their parents. They think the rock is a gift from mom and dad (who now live up in the stars). But when the government takes the meteor and sends it to a university scientist (Molina) for study, the kids decide to get it back. And if this wasn't plot enough, the trio's junkie Uncle Pete (Myers) is in trouble with the mob. Don't be fooled—this is a gritty and thoughtful drama, not a kid flick or a comedy despite Myers presence. **103m/C; VHS, DVD.** Mike Myers; Brenda Fricker; Alfred Molina; Ian Costello; ***D:*** Joe O'Byrne; ***W:*** Joe O'Byrne; ***C:*** Paul Sarossy.

Petits Freres 1/2 *Little Fellas* **2000** Troubled 13-year-old Talia (Touly) takes her pitbull Kim and runs away from her brutal stepfather. She hangs out in the projects with a group of boys her own age whom she warily befriends, only to be victimized when they steal and sell Kim to a dogfighting ring. Despite their denials, Talia knows what they did, even when they promise to help her rescue the dog. Kids, who are non-professionals, do fine but the story meanders it's way to a predictable ending. French with subtitles. **92m/C; VHS, DVD.** *FR* Stephanie Touly; Ilies Sefraoui; Mustapha Goumane; Nassim Izem; Rachid Mansouri; Gerald Dantsoff; ***D:*** Jacques Doillon; ***W:*** Jacques Doillon; ***C:*** Manuel Teran.

Petrified Forest **1936** Writer Alan Squier (Howard) is hitchhiking through the Arizona desert when he stops at a rundown gas station/diner run by Maple (Hall) and his daughter Gabrielle (Davis). Once an idealist, Alan now feels he has little to live for, which may explain his attitude when the diner patrons and employees are held hostage by on the lam gangster Duke Mantee (Bogart) and his boys. Often gripping, with memorable performances from Davis, Howard, and Bogart. Based on the play by Robert Sherwood with Howard and Bogart re-creating their stage roles. **83m/B; VHS, DVD, Blu-Ray.** Bette Davis; Leslie Howard; Humphrey Bogart; Dick Foran; Charley Grapewin; Porter Hall; Genevieve Tobin; Joseph (Joe) Sawyer; ***D:*** Archie Mayo; ***W:*** Delmer Daves; ***C:*** Sol Polito; ***M:*** Bernhard Kaun.

Petticoat Planet **1996 (R)** A man crashlands on a wild-west themed planet ruled by women who immediately proceed to fight over who owns him. **78m/C; DVD.** Elizabeth Kaitan; Troy Vincent; Lesli Kay; Betsey Lynn George; ***D:*** David DeCoteau; ***W:*** Matthew Jason Walsh; ***C:*** Viorel Sergovici, Jr.; ***M:*** Reg Powell. **VIDEO**

Petty Crimes *Aller-Simple Pour Manhattan* **2002** Evading jail time in France, two-bit thief Michel immigrates to the Big Apple and falls for the zesty Zoe who works on his deportation battle when his visa expires. But he needs to scrounge up some major coinage pronto. Enter the persistent old partner tempting him back into his rotten ways of yore. All goes pleasantly enough until the Frenchman faces a puzzling, perturbing twist at the end—mais non! **78m/C; VHS, DVD.** *FR* Andrew Pang; Ann Hu; Jeremie Covillault; Sarah Zoe Canner; ***D:*** Michel Ferry; ***W:*** Sarah Zoe Canner; Michel Ferry; ***C:*** Jean Coudsi; ***M:*** Jean-Claude Ghrenessia. **VIDEO**

Petulia **1968 (R)** Overlooked, offbeat drama about a flighty woman who spites her husband by dallying with a sensitive, recently divorced surgeon. Classic '60s document and cult favorite offers great performance from the appealing Christie, with Scott fine as the vulnerable surgeon. Onscreen performances by the Grateful Dead and Big Brother. Among idiosyncratic director Lester's best. From the novel "Me and the Arch Kook Petulia" by John Haase. **105m/C; VHS, DVD.** George C. Scott; Richard Chamberlain; Julie Christie; Shirley Knight; Arthur Hill; Joseph Cotten; Pippa Scott; Richard Dysart; Kathleen Widdoes; Austin Pendleton; Rene Auberjonois; Roger Bowen; Ellen Geer; ***D:*** Richard Lester; ***W:*** Lawrence B. Marcus; ***C:*** Nicolas Roeg; ***M:*** John Barry.

Petunia **2013** Nervous New Yorker Charlie Petunia is part of a dysfunctional family--his psychotherapist parents can't stand each other, his brother Adrian is a sex addict, and his other brother Michael has just married party girl Vivian, who's as unsure about the marriage as she is about her pregnancy (the dad could be Adrian). Charlie lets himself be pulled into dating Vivian's cousin George, who turns out to be a married man whose unhappy wife Robin is passive-agressive about his gay affairs. It's a somewhat contrived, decidely crazy, and biting ensemble comedy. **92m/C; DVD.** Tobias Segal; Michael Urie; Brittany Snow; Christine Lahti; David Rasche; Eddie Kaye Thomas; Jimmy Heck; Thora Birch; ***D:*** Ash Christian; ***W:*** Ash Christian; Theresa Bennett; ***C:*** Austin F. Schmidt; ***M:*** Douglas J. Cuomo.

Peyton Place **1957** Passion, scandal, and deception in a small New England town set the standard for passion, scandal, and deception in soap operadom. Shot on location in Camden, Maine. Performances and themes now seem dated, but produced a blockbuster in its time. Adapted from Grace Metalious' popular novel and followed by "Return to Peyton Place." **157m/C; VHS, DVD, Blu-Ray.** Lana Turner; Hope Lange; Lee Philips; Lloyd Nolan; Diane Varsi; Lorne Greene; Russ Tamblyn; Arthur Kennedy; Terry Moore; Barry Coe; David Nelson; Betty Field; Mildred Dunnock; Leon Ames; Alan Reed, Jr.; ***D:*** Mark Robson; ***W:*** John Michael Hayes; ***C:*** William Mellor; ***M:*** Franz Waxman.

Phaedra **1961** Loose and updated adaptation of Euripides' "Hipploytus." Mercouri, the second wife of a rich Greek shipping magnate, is dispatched to London to convince her husband's adult son (Perkins) to come home to Greece. Mercouri and Perkins immediately begin a steamy affair but their return home brings problems for all.

Dubbed. **116m/B; VHS, DVD, Blu-Ray.** *GR FR* Melina Mercouri; Anthony Perkins; Raf Vallone; Elizabeth Ercy; ***Cameo(s):*** Jules Dassin; ***D:*** Jules Dassin; ***W:*** Jules Dassin; Margarita Liberaki; ***M:*** Mikis Theodorakis.

Phantasm 🦴🦴 1/2 *The Never Dead* **1979 (R)** A small-budgeted, hallucinatory horror fantasy about two parentless brothers who discover weird goings-on at the local funeral parlor, including the infamous airborne, brain-chewing chrome ball. Creepy, unpredictable nightmare fashioned on a shoestring by young independent producer Coscarelli. Scenes were cut out of the original film to avoid "X" rating. Followed by "Phantasm II." **90m/C; VHS, DVD, Blu-Ray.** A. Michael Baldwin; Bill Thornbury; Reggie Bannister; Kathy Lester; Terrie Kalbus; Kenneth V. Jones; Susan Harper; Lynn Eastman; David Arntzen; Angus Scrimm; Bill Cone; ***D:*** Don A. Coscarelli; ***W:*** Don A. Coscarelli; ***C:*** Don A. Coscarelli; ***M:*** Fredric Myrow; Malcolm Seagrave.

Phantasm 2 🦴🦴 **1988 (R)** Teen psychic keeps flashing on villainous Tall Man. A rehash sequel to the original, cultishly idiosyncratic fantasy, wherein more victims are fed into the inter-dimensional abyss and Mike discovers that the horror is not all in his head. Occasional inspired gore; bloodier than its predecessor. More yuck for the buck. **97m/C; DVD, Blu-Ray.** James LeGros; Reggie Bannister; Angus Scrimm; Paula Irvine; Samantha (Sam) Phillips; Ken Tigar; ***D:*** Don A. Coscarelli; ***W:*** Don A. Coscarelli; ***C:*** Daryn Okada; ***M:*** Christopher L. Stone.

Phantasm 3: Lord of the Dead 🦴 1/2 **1994 (R)** Murderous mortician The Tall Man and his killer silver spheres return once again in this continuing gore fest. Mike, whose brother Jody was one of The Tall Man's victims, teams up with the cynical Reggie and martial arts expert Rocky to try to defeat the creep. That's if they can get past his zombie cohorts and flesh-eating ghouls. **91m/C; VHS, DVD, Blu-Ray.** Reggie Bannister; A. Michael Baldwin; Bill Thornbury; Gloria Lynne Henry; Kevin Connor; Angus Scrimm; ***D:*** Don A. Coscarelli; ***W:*** Don A. Coscarelli; ***M:*** Christopher L. Stone.

Phantasm 4: Oblivion 🦴 1/2 **1998 (R)** At least this sequel can boast the original's lead actors, which allows for footage from the first movie to be used in telling a familiar story. The Tall Man (Scrimm) is still transporting corpses and Mike (Baldwin) is now becoming one of the evil guy's minions. But some time travel takes Mike back to the Tall Man's origins and he tries to take care of the problem at the source. **90m/C; VHS, DVD, Blu-Ray.** Angus Scrimm; A. Michael Baldwin; Reggie Bannister; Bill Thornbury; Bob Ivy; ***D:*** Don A. Coscarelli; ***W:*** Don A. Coscarelli; ***C:*** Chris Chomyn; ***M:*** Christopher L. Stone. **VIDEO**

Phantasm: Ravager 🦴🦴 **2016** The fifth and final film in a series that started decades ago, Ravager is a fun flick for hardcore fans of the franchise only. They will likely be satisfied in a way that allows them to overlook the film's many flaws. Angus Scrimm, in his last film role, returns as The Tall Man, the mythical figure with supernatural powers. Explaining the plot of a fifth film in a series based on so much mythology and general insanity would be worthless. Don't start here if you're unfamiliar with the series, but fifth chapters in horror franchises have been worse. **85m/C; DVD, Blu-Ray.** Reggie Bannister; A. Michael Baldwin; Dawn Cody; Gloria Lynne Henry; Angus Scrimm; ***D:*** David Hartman; ***W:*** David Hartman; Don A. Coscarelli; ***C:*** David Hartman; ***M:*** Christopher L. Stone.

Phantom 🦴🦴 **1922** A mild-mannered clerk, dreaming of bettering himself by becoming a famous poet, becomes obsessed with a wealthy beauty. Restored and hand-tinted silent from legendary German director Murnau with a 2003 orchestral score by Israel. **120m/B; Silent; DVD.** *GE* Alfred Abel; Lya de Putti; Lil Dagover; ***D:*** F.W. Murnau; ***W:*** Thea von Harbou; ***C:*** Axel Graatkjaer; Theophan Ouchakoff; ***M:*** Robert Israel.

The Phantom 🦴🦴 1/2 **1996 (PG)** Based on the Lee Falk comic created in 1936. Deep in the Bengalla jungle, a mysterious costumed figure honors a 400-year-old legacy by fighting piracy, greed, and cruelty. With the help of a beautiful newspaper heiress (Swanson), the latest guardian (Zane) must keep an American industrialist (Williams) and a secret brotherhood of pirates from finding three sacred skulls that contain the power to dominate the world. Old-fashioned swashbuckling story is helped along by Zane's enthusiastic portrayal of the stalwart hero. Action set pieces are fun and exciting even though the story's a bit hokey. **100m/C; VHS, DVD.** Billy Zane; Kristy Swanson; Treat Williams; Catherine Zeta-Jones; James Remar; Jon Tenney; Patrick McGoohan; Samantha Eggar; Cary-Hiroyuki Tagawa; Robert Coleby; David Proval; ***D:*** Simon Wincer; ***W:*** Jeffrey Boam; ***C:*** David Burr; ***M:*** David Newman.

The Phantom 🦴 1/2 **2009** Originally shown on the Syfy Channel as a two-part movie that updates the costumed hero from the comics to the 21st century and gives him an origin story. New York law student Chris Moore learns his life has been a lie: his real name is Kit Walker and he's the latest in a long line of crime fighters who have opposed the evil machinations of the Singh Brotherhood. **175m/C; DVD.** Ryan Carnes; Jean Marchand; Sandrine Holt; Cas Anvar; Isabella Rossellini; Cameron Goodman; Ron Lea; Anthony Lemke; ***D:*** Paolo Barzman; ***W:*** Daniel Knauf; Charles Knauf; ***C:*** Pierre Jodoin; ***M:*** Michel Corriveau. **CABLE**

Phantom 🦴 **2013 (R)** Laughable military thriller. Cold War Soviet missile submarine captain Demi (Harris) is charged with one last mission before retirement. The captain is confronted by Bruni (Duchovny) and his rogue KBG group intent on taking control of the sub and kicking off WWIII. Cheap and cliched, full of corny pseudo-spiritual pleas from Demi to a god who just doesn't give a damn. Writer-director Robinson claims it's inspired by true events. Yes, a Russian sub mysteriously sank in 1968 and was recovered years later on the ocean floor. And that's about it. All of these Russians speaking with American accents don't help. **97m/C; DVD, Blu-Ray.** Ed Harris; David Duchovny; William Fichtner; Lance Henriksen; Johnathon Schaech; Jason Beghe; Sean Patrick Flanery; Dagmara Dominczyk; ***D:*** Todd Robinson; ***W:*** Todd Robinson; ***C:*** Byron Werner; ***M:*** Jeff Rona.

Phantom Boy 🦴🦴 1/2 **2016 (PG)** The writer and directors of the Oscar-nominated "A Cat in Paris" return for this sweet and fun tale of triumph over tragedy, designed as a thrilling take on the superhero genre. This is the story of Leo (Gaspard Gagnol), a very ill young man who has prolonged out-of-body experiences, and how he uses that superpower to help Alex (Baer), a cop confined to a wheelchair, bring down a mob kingpin. The film uniquely references classic French cinema and modern superhero movies. Though it might have worked better as a short, it's original and clever more often than not. **84m/C; DVD.** Gaspard Gagnol; Audrey Tautou; Edouard Baer; Jean-Pierre Marielle; Fred Armisen; ***D:*** Jean-Loup Felicioli; Alain Gagnol; ***W:*** Alain Gagnol; ***M:*** Serge Besset.

The Phantom Carriage 🦴🦴🦴 *The Phantom Chariot; Korkarlen* **1921** A supernatural silent morality tale, based on the 1912 novel by Selma Lagerlof, that was heavily influential on director Ingmar Bergman, among others. Mean drunk David Holm (writer/director Sjostrom) tells his equally drunken buddies about a Scandinavian legend that has the last sinner to die on New Year's Eve condemned to drive Death's carriage and collect the souls of the dead for the next year. When David suddenly dies, it's his old friend Georges driving the carriage, and he shows David (ala "A Christmas Carol") how his miserable life has affected others, with the possibility that David may still be able to redeem himself. **107m/B; Silent; DVD, Blu-Ray.** *SW* Victor Sjostrom; Tore Svennberg; Astrid Holm; Lisa Lundholm; Hilda Borgstrom; Einar Axelsson; Concordia Selander; Tor Weijden; ***D:*** Victor Sjostrom; ***W:*** Victor Sjostrom; ***C:*** Julius Jaenzon.

The Phantom Chariot 🦴🦴 1/2 **1920** A fantasy depicting the Swedish myth about how Death's coach must be driven by the last man to die each year. Silent. **89m/B; Silent; VHS, DVD, Blu-Ray.** *SW* Hilda Borgstrom; Tore Svennberg; Astrid Holm; ***D:*** Victor Sjostrom; ***W:*** Victor Sjostrom; ***C:*** Julius Jaenzon.

The Phantom Creeps 🦴🦴 **1939** Evil Dr. Zorka, armed with a meteorite chunk which can bring an army to a standstill, provides the impetus for this enjoyable serial in 12 episodes. **235m/B; VHS, DVD, Blu-Ray.** Bela Lugosi; Dorothy Arnold; Robert Kent; Regis Toomey; ***D:*** Ford Beebe; Saul Goodkind.

The Phantom Empire 🦴🦴 *Radio Ranch* **1935** Autry faces the futuristic "Thunder Riders" from the subterranean city of Murania, located 20,000 feet beneath his ranch. A complete serial in 12 episodes. If you only see one science-fiction western in your life, this is the one. Also available in an edited theatrical version at 80 minutes. **245m/B; VHS, DVD.** Gene Autry; Frankie Darro; Betsy King Ross; Smiley Burnette; ***D:*** B. Reeves Eason; Otto Brower.

Phantom Empire 🦴🦴 **1987 (R)** A woman who rules over a lost city takes a bunch of scientists prisoner and forces them to be slaves. **85m/C; VHS, DVD, Blu-Ray.** Ross Hagen; Jeffrey Combs; Dawn Wildsmith; Robert Quarry; Susan Stokey; Michelle (McClellan) Bauer; Russ Tamblyn; Sybil Danning; ***D:*** Fred Olen Ray; ***W:*** Fred Olen Ray; T.L. Lankford.

Phantom Fiend 🦴 1/2 **1935** A gentle musician becomes a suspect when a series of Jack-the-Ripper type murders terrorize London. Is he the nice guy known by his girlfriend and the people in his lodging house, or is the musician really JTR? Based on the novel "The Lodger" by Marie Belloc-Lowndes. **70m/B; VHS, DVD.** *GB* Ivor Novello; Elizabeth Allan; A.W. Baskcomb; Jack Hawkins; Barbara Everest; Peter Gawthorne; Kynaston Reeves; ***D:*** Maurice Elvey.

Phantom from Space 🦴 1/2 **1953** An invisible alien lands on Earth, begins killing people, and is pursued by a pair of scientists. **72m/B; VHS, DVD.** Ted Cooper; Rudolph Anders; Noreen Nash; James Seay; Harry Landers; ***D:*** W. Lee Wilder; ***C:*** William Clothier.

The Phantom from 10,000 Leagues 🦴 **1956** Slimy sea monster attacks swimmers and fishermen; investigating oceanographer pretends not to notice monster is hand puppet. Early AIP release, when still named American Releasing Company. **80m/B; VHS, DVD, Blu-Ray.** Kent Taylor; Cathy Downs; Michael Whalen; Helene Stanton; Phillip Pine; ***D:*** Dan Milner; ***W:*** Lou Rusoff; ***C:*** Brydon Baker; ***M:*** Ronald Stein.

Phantom Lady 🦴🦴🦴 **1944** After an argument with his wife Scott Henderson (Curtis) walks into a bar and chats up a mystery woman (Helm). When he returns home, the police are there and his wife has been strangled with his necktie. Since he doesn't know his bar mate's name and no one professes to remember her, Scott is quickly convicted of the crime. Only his loyal secretary Carol (Raines) believes him and she sets out to solve the crime. Based on the novel by Cornell Woolrich. **87m/B; DVD, Blu-Ray.** Ella Raines; Alan Curtis; Franchot Tone; Thomas Gomez; Elisha Cook, Jr.; Fay Helm; Aurora Miranda; Andrew Tombes; Regis Toomey; Joseph Crehan; Virginia Brissac; Milburn Stone; ***D:*** Robert Siodmak; ***W:*** Bernard C. Schoenfeld; ***C:*** Elwood "Woody" Bredell.

The Phantom Light 🦴🦴 1/2 **1935** A lighthouse keeper is murdered under strange circumstances and a mysterious light keeps appearing at the scene. Detective Hale joins up with a navy man and another lighthouse keeper to solve the crime. A low-budget mystery with good atmosphere and some humor. **75m/B; VHS, DVD.** *GB* Binnie Hale; Gordon Harker; Ian Hunter; Donald Calthrop; ***D:*** Michael Powell.

The Phantom Lover 🦴🦴 1/2 *Ye Bang Ge Sheng* **1995** It's "The Phantom of the Opera" Hong Kong style, although it's a adult fairytale rather than a horror story. In 1936 a theatrical troupe hopes to restore a burned-out opera house for their performances. Legendary singer Sung Dan-Ping (Cheung) was thought to have died in the fire, instead, horribly disfigured, he hides out in the ruins and dreams of his lost love (Chein-Lien). Chinese with subtitles or dubbed. **102m/C; VHS, DVD.** *CH* Leslie Cheung; Chien-Lien Wu; Philip Kwok; Roy Szeto; ***D:*** Ronny Yu; ***W:*** Roy Szeto; Raymond Wong; ***C:*** Peter Pau; ***M:*** Chris Babida.

The Phantom of Crestwood 🦴 1/2 **1932** Beginning as a six-week radio serial, the solution to the murder mystery was only available by seeing the motion picture. Jenny Wren's (Morley) shady past is revealed in flashbacks as she asks a number of her male 'friends' to a dinner party where she intends to blackmail them. Jenny is one dead dame and criminal Gary Curtis (Cortez) is set up to take the fall. **76m/B; DVD.** Ricardo Cortez; Karen Morley; H.B. Warner; Pauline Frederick; Robert McWade; Richard "Skeets" Gallagher; Anita Louise; ***D:*** J. Walter Ruben; ***W:*** Bartlett Cormack; ***C:*** Henry W. Gerrard.

The Phantom of Hollywood 🦴 1/2 **1974** MGM studios took advantage of its abandoned backlots, which were being sold off, and its movie heritage in this showbiz horror pic. Venerable Worldwide Films is being decimated piece-by-piece by its quick buck owner, much to the disgust of the mysterious Phantom. The movie-loving vigilante secretly calls the studio home and is willing to kill to prevent its destruction. **73m/C; DVD.** Peter Lawford; Skye Aubrey; Jack Cassidy; Jackie Coogan; Broderick Crawford; Peter Haskell; John Ireland; ***D:*** Gene Levitt; ***W:*** George Schenck; ***C:*** Gene Polito; ***M:*** Leonard Rosenman.

Phantom of Liberty 🦴🦴🦴 1/2 *Le Fantome de la Liberte; The Specter of Freedom* **1974** Master surrealist Bunuel's episodic film wanders from character to character and from event to event. Animals wander through a man's bedroom, soldiers conduct military exercises in an inhabited area, a missing girl stands before her parents even as they futilely attempt to determine her whereabouts, and an assassin is found guilty, then applauded and led to freedom. They don't get much more surreal than this. Bunuel is among the firing squad vicitms in the film's opening enactment of Goya's May 3, 1808. French with subtitles. **104m/C; VHS, DVD.** *FR* Adriana Asti; Jean-Claude Brialy; Michel Piccoli; Adolfo Celi; Monica Vitti; Milena Vukotic; Michael (Michel) Lonsdale; Claude Pieplu; Julien Bertheau; Paul Frankeur; Paul Le Person; Bernard Verley; ***D:*** Luis Bunuel; ***W:*** Luis Bunuel; Jean-Claude Carriere; ***C:*** Edmond Richard.

The Phantom of Paris 🦴 1/2 **1931** Bibi (Gilbert), a world-class French escape artist, attempts to escape a false murder charge trumped up by an evil marquis (Keith) who has murdered the wealthy father of Bibi's fiancee (Hyams) in a plot to lay claim to her and her father's wealth. Bibi uses his talent for escape to elude the law while he attempts to clear his name. Featuring one of John Gilbert's first talking roles after a successful career in silent film. **73m/B; DVD.** John Gilbert; Leila Hyams; Lewis Stone; Jean Hersholt; Sir C. Aubrey Smith; Ian Keith; ***D:*** John S. Robertson; ***W:*** Gaston Leroux; ***C:*** Oliver Marsh.

The Phantom of Santa Fe 🦴 *The Hawk* **1936** Rare poverty-row western shot in color in 1931 and released as "The Hawk"; it didn't improve with age. An outlaw is troubling a prairie community and is apparently behind the theft of some priceless mission treasures. **75m/C; DVD.** Norman Kerry; Nina Quartero; Frank Mayo; Carmelita Geraghty; Jack Mower; ***D:*** Jacques Jaccard; ***W:*** Charles Francis Royal; ***C:*** Otto Himm.

The Phantom of Soho 🦴🦴 *Das Phantom von Soho* **1964** A Scotland Yard detective investigates the murders of several prominent businessmen and is assisted by a beautiful mystery writer. **92m/B; VHS, DVD.** *GE* Dieter Borsche; Barbara Rutting; Hans Sohnker; Peter Vogel; Helga Sommerfeld; Werner Peters; ***D:*** Franz Gottlieb.

Phantom of the Mall: Eric's Revenge 🦴 **1989** A murderous spirit haunts the local mall. Gore flows like water. **91m/C; VHS, DVD.** Morgan Fairchild; Kari Whitman; Jonathan Goldsmith; Derek Rydall; Pauly Shore; Rob(ert) Estes; Brinke Stevens; ***D:*** Richard Friedman; ***W:*** Robert King; ***C:*** Harry Mathias; ***M:*** Stacy Widelitz.

The Phantom of the Opera 🦴🦴🦴 **1925** Deranged, disfigured music lover haunts the sewers of a Parisian opera house and kills to further the career of an unsuspecting young soprano. First of many film versions still packs a wallop, with fine playing from Chaney Sr. Silent with two-color Technicolor "Bal Masque" sequence. Versions with different running times are also available, including 79 and 88 minutes. **101m/B;**

Silent; VHS, DVD, Blu-Ray. Lon Chaney, Sr.; Norman Kerry; Mary Philbin; Gibson Gowland; Arthur Edmund Carewe; John St. Polis; Snitz Edwards; Virginia Pearson; ***D:*** Lon Chaney, Sr.; Rupert Julian; Edward Sedgwick; ***W:*** Elliot J. Clawson; Raymond L. Schrock; Frank M. McCormack; ***C:*** Virgil Miller; Charles Van Enger; Milton Bridenbecker. Natl. Film Reg. '98.

The Phantom of the Opera 🦴🦴🦴
1943 Second Hollywood version (following the 1925 silent) of Gaston Leroux's novel, remade by the same studio (Universal), suffers by dispersing the chills with too many opera scenes (no doubt to give Eddy something to do) and weak comedy. Enrique (a sympathetic Rains) is a disfigured musician in the Paris Opera who sacrifices himself for the love of young singer Christine (DuBois), who doesn't even know he exists. Rains is only briefly seen in his horror visage. **92m/C; VHS, DVD, Blu-Ray.** Nelson Eddy; Susanna Foster; Claude Rains; Edgar Barrier; Leo Carrillo; Hume Cronyn; J. Edward Bromberg; ***D:*** Arthur Lubin; ***W:*** Samuel Hoffenstein; Eric Taylor; ***C:*** Hal Mohr; William Howard Greene; ***M:*** Edward Ward. Oscars '43: Color Cinematog.

The Phantom of the Opera 🦴🦴 1/2
1962 Hammer version of the Gaston Leroux novel transfers the action from Paris to London but keeps the basic story of a young singer (Sears) and her masked benefactor (Lom), who lives in the sewers beneath the opera house. There's also the wimpy fiance (De Souza) to come between them. Good gothic melodrama. Sears' singing was dubbed by opera performer Pat Clark; producer Hinds used the pseudonym John Elder for his screenplay. **85m/C; VHS, DVD, Blu-Ray.** Herbert Lom; Heather Sears; Edward De Souza; Thorley Walters; Michael Gough; Martin Miller; Ian Wilson; ***D:*** Terence Fisher; ***W:*** John (Anthony Hinds) Elder; ***C:*** Arthur Grant; ***M:*** Edwin Astley.

The Phantom of the Opera 🦴 1/2
1989 (R) A gory, "Elm Street"-ish version of the Gaston Leroux classic, attempting to cash in on the success of the Broadway musical. **93m/C; VHS, DVD, Blu-Ray.** Robert Englund; Jill Schoelen; Alex Hyde-White; Bill Nighy; Terence Harvey; Stephanie Lawrence; Nathan Lewis; Peter Clapham; Molly Shannon; ***D:*** Dwight Little; ***W:*** Duke Sandefur; ***C:*** Elemer Ragalyi; ***M:*** Misha Segal.

The Phantom of the Opera 🦴🦴 1/2
1990 Yet another version of the tragic tale of a disfigured mask-wearing opera lover, who lurks in the depths of the Paris Opera House, and his desire for lovely young singer, Christine. Dance plays the Phantom as doomed romantic, with Lancaster his protective father. Kopit adapted from his 1983 play. Made for TV drama, originally shown in two parts. **200m/C; VHS, DVD.** *GB* Charles Dance; Burt Lancaster; Teri Polo; Ian Richardson; Andrea Ferreol; Adam Storke; Jean-Pierre Cassel; ***D:*** Tony Richardson; ***W:*** Arthur Kopit; ***C:*** Steve Yaconelli; ***M:*** John Addison. **TV**

The Phantom of the Opera 🦴 1/2
Dario Argento's Phantom of the Opera; Il Fantasma dell'Opera **1998 (R)** Campy excess (and lots of gore) overwhelms Gaston Leroux's often-filmed chiller. This Phantom (Sands) doesn't have a facial disfigurement and goes unmasked but he's weird nonetheless. Abandoned as a baby, he's raised by rats (ewwww) beneath the Paris Opera where he becomes smitten by young singer, Christine (Argento), and does his best to make her his alone. **100m/C; VHS, DVD, Blu-Ray.** *IT* Julian Sands; Asia Argento; Andrea Di Stefano; Nadia Rinaldi; Coralina Cataldi-Tassoni; Istvan Bubik; Zoltan Barabas; ***D:*** Dario Argento; ***W:*** Dario Argento; Gerard Brach; ***C:*** Ronnie Taylor; ***M:*** Ennio Morricone.

The Phantom of the Opera 🦴🦴
2004 (PG-13) Andrew Lloyd Webber's London musical hits the big screen in this extravagant version from director Schumacher that ramps up the romance. The title character, as played here by brawny Scottish actor Butler, is positively swoon-worthy. Story is simple: Paris Opera ingenue Christine (Rossum) gets her big break and is then torn between two would-be loves; well-mannered opera patron Raoul de Chagny (Wilson) and that mystery man. Some changes are made from stage to screen but fans won't be unduly alarmed although the film's cheesy romanticism is unlikely to find new converts. Sets and costumes are eye-catching. **143m/C; VHS, DVD, Blu-Ray, HD-DVD.** Gerard Butler; Emmy Rossum; Patrick Wilson; Miranda Richardson; Minnie Driver; Simon Callow; Ciaran Hinds; James Fleet; Kevin McNally; Murray Melvin; Victor McGuire; Jennifer Ellison; ***D:*** Joel Schumacher; ***W:*** Joel Schumacher; Andrew Lloyd Webber; ***C:*** John Mathieson; ***M:*** Andrew Lloyd Webber.

Phantom of the Paradise 🦴🦴 **1974 (PG)** A rock 'n' roll parody of "Phantom of the Opera." Splashy, only occasionally horrific spoof in which cruel music executive Williams, much to his everlasting regret, swindles a songwriter. Violence ensues. Not for most, or even many, tastes. Graham steals the film as rocker Beef. A failure at the boxoffice, and now a small cult item for its oddball humor and outrageous rock star parodies. Williams also wrote the turgid score. **92m/C; VHS, DVD, Blu-Ray.** Paul Williams; William Finley; Jessica Harper; Gerrit Graham; George Memmoli; Archie Hahn; ***D:*** Brian De Palma; ***W:*** Brian De Palma; ***C:*** Larry Pizer; ***M:*** Paul Williams; George Aliceson Tipton.

Phantom of the West 🦴🦴 **1931** Ten-episode serial about a rancher who becomes "The Phantom of the West" in order to smoke out his father's killer. **166m/B; VHS, DVD.** William Desmond; Thomas Santschi; Tom Tyler; ***D:*** David Ross Lederman.

Phantom Pain 🦴 1/2 *Phantomschmerz* **2009** Conventional inspirational drama—complete with montages—that's based on a true story. Marc Sumner is a 30-something slacker with some dad issues whose only passion is for cycling. He gets into a traffic accident and his left leg is amputated, which means he has to reevaluate his life. **97m/C; DVD.** *GE* Til Schweiger; Jana Pallaske; Stipe Erceg; Luna Schweiger; Julia Brendler; ***D:*** Matthias Emcke; ***W:*** Matthias Emcke; ***C:*** The Chau Ngo; ***M:*** Martin Todsharow.

The Phantom Planet 🦴 1/2 **1961** An astronaut crash-lands on an asteroid and discovers a race of tiny people living there. Having breathed the atmosphere, he shrinks to their diminutive size and aids them in their war against brutal invaders. Infamously peculiar. **82m/B; VHS, DVD.** Dean Fredericks; Coleen Gray; Tony Dexter; Dolores Faith; Francis X. Bushman; Richard Kiel; ***D:*** William Marshall; ***W:*** Fred De Gorter; Fred Gebhardt; William Telaak; ***C:*** Elwood J. Nicholson; ***M:*** Hayes Pagel.

Phantom Punch 🦴 1/2 **2009 (R)** Disappointingly shallow biopic of heavyweight boxing champ Sonny Liston that does have a compelling lead performance from Rhames. The ex-con is allegedly a mob-backed, cheating husband with a controversial career thanks to a possible dive (the so-called 'phantom punch') when he loses his title to Cassius Clay in 1965. However, director Townsend never really gives you a sense of the man or where Liston stands in boxing history. **104m/C; DVD.** Ving Rhames; Nicholas Turturro; Stacey Dash; David Proval; Bridgette Wilson; Rick Roberts; Alan Van Sprang; ***D:*** Robert Townsend; ***W:*** Ryan Combs; ***C:*** John Dyer; ***M:*** Stephen James Taylor. **VIDEO**

Phantom Racer 🦴 1/2 **2009** Gory and somewhat silly possessed killer car flick from the Syfy Channel. Ex-stock car racer J.J. Sawyer (Evigan) still blames himself for the fiery death of rival Cutter (Battrick) and, after 15 years, returns to his hometown to confront the past. He sees that Cutter's red 66 car has been restored but Cutter's vengeful spirit is restored as well. **87m/C; DVD.** Greg Evigan; Nicole Eggert; Chad Willett; Winston Rekert; Luciana Carro; Brenna O'Brien; Adam Battrick; ***D:*** Terry Ingram; ***W:*** Jason Bourque; ***C:*** Michael Balfry; ***M:*** John Sereda. **CABLE**

Phantom Raiders 🦴🦴 **1940** Detective Nick Carter (Walter Pidgeon) is on vacation when he is called to Panama to investigate cargo ships being sunk off the coast. **70m/C; DVD.** Walter Pidgeon; Donald Meek; Joseph Schildkraut; Florence Rice; Nat Pendleton; ***D:*** Jacques Tourneur; ***W:*** William R. Lipman; ***C:*** Clyde De Vinna; ***M:*** David Snell; Daniele Amfitheatrof. **VIDEO**

Phantom Thread 🦴🦴🦴 1/2 **2017 (R)** A dense, visually stunning romantic drama by writer/director Paul Thomas Anderson. Highly respected couturier Reynolds Woodcock (Day-Lewis) is at the height of his career as a dressmaker and lives an ordered, meticulous life. While breakfasting at a local hotel, he meets waitress Alma (Krieps) with whom he becomes unconventionally involved. Their relationship becomes a battle of wills and confrontations, and includes the additional perspective of Reynolds' sister Cyril (Manville). Though Reynolds becomes the man that Alma wants, the difficult alliance comes at a cost. **130m/C; DVD, Blu-Ray.** Vicky Krieps; Daniel Day-Lewis; Lesley Manville; Sue Clark; Joan Brown; ***D:*** Paul Thomas Anderson; ***W:*** Paul Thomas Anderson; ***C:*** Paul Thomas Anderson; ***M:*** Jonny Greenwood. Oscars '17: Costume Des.; British Acad. '17: Costume Des.

Phantom Tollbooth 🦴🦴🦴 **1969 (G)** A young boy drives his car into an animated world, where the numbers are at war with the letters and he has been chosen to save Rhyme and Reason, to bring stability back to the Land of Wisdom. Completely unique and typically Jonesian in its intellectual level and interests. Bright children will be interested, but this is really for adults who will understand the allegory. Based on Norman Justers' metaphorical novel. **89m/C; VHS, DVD.** ***V:*** Mel Blanc; Hans Conried; ***D:*** Chuck Jones.

Phantom 2040 Movie: The Ghost Who Walks 🦴🦴 1/2 **1995** Teenager Kit Walker discovers his destiny when a mysterious stranger tells him about his late father and how Kit must carry on his father's legacy as a superhero called the Phantom. A purple suit renders Kit invisible and he finds himself battling his dad's old nemesis, Rebecca Madison, who's out to destroy the Earth's resources. Based on the TV and comic book series. **97m/C; VHS, DVD.** ***V:*** Scott Valentine; Margot Kidder; Ron Perlman; Carrie Snodgress; Mark Hamill.

Phantoms 🦴 **1997 (R)** Dr. Jennifer Pailey (Going) and her sister Lisa (McGowan) arrive in a Colorado resort town and discover that the entire population has been wiped out by a mysterious force. They team up with local sheriff Hammond (Affleck) and his odd deputy (Schrieber) to battle the evil force thingie, which also seems to have an adverse affect on acting ability, except for O'Toole as an expert on ancient plagues. Will they stop the amorphous monster who is taking over the corpses of its victims? You'll hope not. Based on the novel by Dean Koontz, who also adapted it for the screen and produced. **91m/C; VHS, DVD, Blu-Ray.** Peter O'Toole; Joanna Going; Rose McGowan; Ben Affleck; Liev Schreiber; Nicky Katt; Clifton Powell; Adam Nelson; John Hammil; John Scott Clough; ***D:*** Joe Chappelle; ***W:*** Dean Koontz; ***C:*** Richard Clabaugh; ***M:*** David Williams.

The Pharaoh's Curse 🦴 1/2 **1957** Not your typical mummy tale but a low budget and a dull execution dilutes the horror. A young Egyptian, a member of a British archeological expedition, is turned into a deadly mummy-creature after being possessed by the pharaoh's spirit. The pharaoh isn't pleased after the royal tomb is desecrated and starts a killing spree. **66m/B; DVD.** Mark Dana; Ziva Rodann; Diane Brewster; George Neise; Alvaro Guillot; Ben Wright; Guy Prescott; ***D:*** Lee Sholem; ***W:*** Richard H. Landau; ***C:*** William Margulies; ***M:*** Les Baxter.

Pharoah's Army 🦴🦴 1/2 **1995 (PG-13)** Five Union soldiers are foraging for food at a small Kentucky farm when one young soldier (Fox) is badly injured and his captain, John Abston (Cooper), is forced to stay put while he treats the wounds. The farm is home to Sarah Anders (Clarkson) and her young son (Lucas), while her husband is off fighting for the Confederates. Sarah isn't happy about the arrangement but the decent Alston, a farmer himself in peacetime, begins slowly to win her over. Their friendship, however, doesn't sit well with either his men nor Sarah's son. Fine performances in a restrained drama. **90m/C; VHS, DVD.** Chris Cooper; Patricia Clarkson; Kris Kristofferson; Richard Tyson; Huckleberry Fox; Will Lucas; ***D:*** Robby Henson; ***W:*** Robby Henson; ***C:*** Doron Schlair.

Phase 4 🦴🦴 **1974 (PG)** A tale of killer ants retaliating against the humans attempting to exterminate them. **84m/C; VHS, DVD, Blu-Ray.** Nigel Davenport; Michael Murphy; Lynne Frederick; ***D:*** Saul Bass; ***C:*** Dick Bush.

Phat Beach 🦴🦴 1/2 **1996 (R)** Generic but harmless buddies-at-the-beach comedy with a hip-hop beat. Fast-talking, slickster Durrell (Hooks) manipulates sensitive, overweight pal Benny (Hopkins) into emptying his savings, "borrowing" his dad's Mercedes convertible, and taking off for some Southern California fun. Scores of scantily clad beach bunnies aren't the only ones threadbare—so's the whole premise of this flick—but the likable Hopkins/Hooks comedy team is a hit with precise, lowbrow humor. Coolio, prominent in the ads, is barely window dressing with minimal screen time. Kickin' soundtrack. **99m/C; VHS, DVD.** Jermaine "Huggy" Hopkins; Brian Hooks; Jennifer Lucienne; Claudia Kaleem; Gregg D. Vance; Tommy (Tiny) Lister; Erick Fleeks; Alma Collins; Candice Merideth; Sabrina De Pina; Coolio; ***D:*** Doug Ellin; ***W:*** Doug Ellin; Brian E. O'Neal; Ben Morris; ***C:*** Jurgen Baum; ***M:*** Paul Stewart.

Phat Girlz 🦴🦴 **2006 (PG-13)** Sassy, plus-sized comedienne Mo'Nique stars as Jazmin, a salesclerk at a store catering to the snooty skinny, who has designs on creating her own plus-sized fashion line. Her self-esteem a little battered, Jazmin and her equally-fleshy best friend Stacey (Johnson) are happy to indulge themselves at a Palm Springs resort, especially when they meet a couple of buff Nigerian doctors (Jean-Louis, Godfrey) who happen to like their ladies with some extra curves. Thus inspired, Jazmin decides to pursue her fashion dream. **99m/C; DVD.** Mo'Nique; Jimmy Jean-Louis; Godfrey; Jack Noseworthy; Kendra C. Johnson; Joyful Drake; Eric Roberts; ***D:*** Nnegest Likke; ***W:*** Nnegest Likke; ***C:*** Dean Lent; John L. (Ndiaga) Demps, Jr.; ***M:*** Stephen Endelman.

Phedre 🦴 1/2 **1968** Jean Racine's adaptation of the Greek legend involving Phedre, Theseus, and Hippolyte. Bell is the only one worth watching in this weak and stagy picture. In French with English subtitles. **93m/C; VHS, DVD.** Marie Bell; Claude Giraud; Jacques Dacqmine; Jean Chevrier; ***D:*** Pierre Jourdan; ***C:*** Michel Kelber.

The Phenix City Story 🦴🦴 1/2 **1955** This Alabama sin city has drugs, prostitution, and a number of other vices all run by crime boss Rhett Tanner (Andrews), who has the cops on his payroll and the local politicians in his pocket. This doesn't stop some reform-minded citizens from pushing honest Albert Patterson (McIntire) to take on the DA's job. And when Albert is murdered, his lawyer son John (Kiley) steps right in. Gritty docudrama based on a true story that happened in 1954. **100m/B; DVD.** John McIntire; Richard Kiley; Edward Andrews; Kathryn Grant; James Edwards; John Larch; Lenka Peterson; Biff McGuire; Truman Smith; ***D:*** Phil Karlson; ***W:*** Crane Wilbur; Daniel Mainwaring; ***C:*** Harry Neumann; ***M:*** Harry Sukman. Natl. Film Reg. '19.

The Phenom 🦴🦴 1/2 **2016** The excellent Simmons plays Hopper Gibson, a Major League rookie pitcher who has lost his control and is sent down to the minors to find it again. No mere sports procedural, Hooper is forced to confront his relationship with his overbearing father (a great Hawke) by dealing with a team shrink played by Giamatti. It's more "Good Will Hunting" than "Major League." All three of the leading men avoid the clichés that could have sunk the drama. This is one of those character-driven dramas that deserved a much bigger audience through word of mouth. **90m/C; DVD, Blu-Ray.** Ethan Hawke; Paul Giamatti; Johnny Simmons; Paul Adelstein; Elizabeth Marvel; ***D:*** Noah Buschel; ***W:*** Noah Buschel; ***C:*** Ryan Samul; ***M:*** Aleks de Carvalho.

Phenomenon 🦴🦴 1/2 **1996 (PG)** Average small town schmoe George Malley (Travolta) is turned into a genius when he's struck by a bright light on his 37th birthday. This development brings him to the attention of the scientific community and, of course, the military. The locals scorn him, thus fulfilling the Hollywood stereotype of rural folks fearing anything they don't understand. Good-natured weeper plays the Gump card (but turns too paranoid) and wins as Travolta gets to be the nice guy, while attractive Sedgwick is fine as romantic interest Lace. **123m/C; VHS, DVD, Blu-Ray.** John Travolta; Robert Duvall; Kyra Sedgwick; Forest Whitaker; Richard Kiley; Brent Spiner; David Gallagher; Jeffrey DeMunn; ***D:*** Jon Turteltaub; ***W:*** Gerald Di Pego; ***C:*** Phedon Papamichael; ***M:*** Thomas Newman.

Phffft! 🦴🦴 1/2 **1954** Holliday and Lemmon are a bored couple who decide to divorce, date others, and take mambo lessons.

By no stretch of plausibility, they constantly run into each other and compete in the same mambo contest. **91m/B; VHS, DVD.** Judy Holliday; Jack Lemmon; Jack Carson; Kim Novak; Luella Gear; Merry Anders; ***D:*** Mark Robson; ***W:*** George Axelrod; ***C:*** Charles B(ryant) Lang, Jr.

Phil Spector 🦴🦴 **2013** Pacino was criticized for his cartoonish portrayal in this HBO drama, but who better to convey the wackiness that was Spector at his 2003 murder trial. Writer-director Mamet actually focuses on the relationship between Spector and his (at-first) skectical new lawyer, Linda Kenney Braden (Mirren), who comes to believe that Spector was innocent but doesn't want to put the eccentric on the witness stand. The pic had a disclaimer that it was a work of fiction to get past any of those pesky defamation lawsuits. **92m/C; DVD.** Al Pacino; Dame Helen Mirren; Jeffrey Tambor; Rebecca Pidgeon; ***D:*** David Mamet; ***W:*** David Mamet; ***C:*** Juan Ruiz Anchia; ***M:*** Marcelo Zarvos. **CABLE**

Philadelphia 🦴🦴🦴 1/2 **1993 (PG-13)** AIDS goes Hollywood as hot-shot corporate attorney Andrew Beckett (Hanks), fired because he has the disease, hires brilliant but homophobic personal injury attorney Washington as his counsel when he sues for discrimination. Boxoffice winner was criticized by some gay activists as too mainstream, which is the point. It doesn't probe deeply into the gay lifestyle, focusing instead on justice and compassion. Boasts a good script, make-up that transforms Hanks, sure direction, great soundtrack, and a strong supporting cast, but all would mean little without Hanks' superb performance. **125m/C; DVD, Blu-Ray.** Tom Hanks; Denzel Washington; Antonio Banderas; Jason Robards, Jr.; Joanne Woodward; Mary Steenburgen; Ron Vawter; Robert Ridgely; Obba Babatunde; Robert Castle; Daniel Chapman; Roger Corman; John Bedford Lloyd; Roberta Maxwell; Warren Miller; ***D:*** Jonathan Demme; ***W:*** Ron Nyswaner; ***C:*** Tak Fujimoto; ***M:*** Howard Shore. Oscars '93: Actor (Hanks), Song ("Streets of Philadelphia"); Berlin Intl. Film Fest. '94: Actor (Hanks); Golden Globes '94: Actor--Drama (Hanks), Song ("Streets of Philadelphia"); MTV Movie Awards '94: Male Perf. (Hanks); Blockbuster '95: Drama Actor, V. (Hanks).

The Philadelphia Experiment 🦴🦴 1/2 **1984 (PG)** A WWII sailor falls through a hole in time and lands in the mid-1980s, whereupon he woos a gorgeous woman. Sufficient chemistry between Pare and Allen, but PG rating is an indication of the film's less-than-graphic love scenes. **101m/C; VHS, DVD.** Michael Paré; Nancy Allen; Eric Christmas; Bobby DiCicco; ***D:*** Stewart Raffill; ***W:*** Don Jakoby; ***C:*** Dick Bush; ***M:*** Kenneth Wannberg.

Philadelphia Experiment 2 🦴🦴 1/2 **1993 (PG-13)** Melodramatic sci-fi what-ifer has Germany winning WWII by dropping a bomb on Washington. So southern California is now one big labor camp with an evil mad scientist (Graham) and a beleagured hero (Johnson) who must time-travel back to 1943 to prevent the Germans from dropping that bomb. **98m/C; VHS, DVD.** Brad Johnson; Gerrit Graham; Marjean Holden; James Greene; Geoffrey Blake; John Christian Grass; Cyril O'Reilly; ***D:*** Stephen Cornwell; ***W:*** Kevin Rock; Nick Paine; ***M:*** Gerald Gouriet.

The Philadelphia Story 🦴🦴🦴🦴 **1940** A woman's plans to marry again go awry when her dashing ex-husband arrives on the scene. Matters are further complicated when a loopy reporter—assigned to spy on the nuptials—falls in love with the blushing bride. Classic comedy, with trio of Hepburn, Grant, and Stewart all serving aces. Based on the hit Broadway play by Philip Barry, and remade as the musical "High Society" in 1956 (stick to the original). Also available colorized. **112m/B; VHS, DVD, Blu-Ray.** Katharine Hepburn; Cary Grant; James Stewart; Ruth Hussey; Roland Young; John Howard; John Halliday; Virginia Weidler; Henry Daniell; Hillary Brooke; Mary Nash; ***D:*** George Cukor; ***W:*** Donald Ogden Stewart; ***C:*** Joseph Ruttenberg; ***M:*** Franz Waxman. Oscars '40: Actor (Stewart), Screenplay; AFI '98: Top 100; Natl. Film Reg. '95; N.Y. Film Critics '40: Actress (Hepburn).

Philby, Burgess and MacLean: Spy Scandal of the Century 🦴🦴 1/2 **1984** The true story of the three infamous British officials who defected to the Soviet Union in 1951, after stealing some vital British secrets for the KGB. **83m/C; VHS, DVD.** *GB* Derek Jacobi; Anthony Bate; Michael Culver; ***D:*** Gordon Flemyng; ***W:*** Ian Curteis.

The Philly Kid 🦴🦴 **2012 (R)** Conventional sports drama provides modest entertainment. Dillon (Chatham) gets out of prison and gets a job with the help of his old pal, Jake (Sawa). Jake has a big gambling debt and persuades Dillon to help him out by fighting in underground cage matches. His winning ways cause Dillon to draw attention from the wrong sort of guys. **90m/C; DVD, Blu-Ray.** Wes Chatham; Devon Sawa; Neal McDonough; Chris Browning; Sarah Butler; Michael Jai White; ***D:*** Jason Connery; ***W:*** Adam Mervis; ***C:*** Marco Fargnoli; ***M:*** Ian Honeyman. **VIDEO**

Philomena 🦴🦴 1/2 **2013 (PG-13)** Costar Coogan co-adapts this true story of disgraced journalist Martin Sixsmith, who's just looking for a rebound story after a scandal. Instead, he finds the most important article he'll ever write when he meets Philomena (Dench). The quiet, reserved, older woman tells Martin a shocking tale of teen pregnancy that resulted in her child being sold into adoption from the Catholic institution at which she lived. As Martin and Philomena search for her long-lost son, betrayals and the complex way in which men and women deal with past regrets boil to the surface. Well-performed and well-intentioned, but a bit duller than it should be. **98m/C; DVD, Blu-Ray.** *UK* Dame Judi Dench; Steve Coogan; Mare Winningham; Michelle Fairley; Sophie Kennedy Clark; Barbara Jefford; Ruth McCabe; Peter Hermann; Sean Mahon; ***D:*** Stephen Frears; ***W:*** Steve Coogan; Jeff Pope; ***C:*** Robbie Ryan; ***M:*** Alexandre Desplat. British Acad. '13: Adapt. Screenplay.

Phobia WOOF! **1980 (R)** Patients at a hospital are mysteriously being murdered. Stupid and unpleasant story that lasts too long and probably should never have started. **91m/C; VHS, Blu-Ray, Streaming.** *CA* Paul Michael Glaser; Susan Hogan; ***D:*** John Huston; ***W:*** Peter Bellwood; Lew Lehman; Gary Sherman; Ronald Shusett; Jimmy Sangster.

Phobia 🦴🦴 *Alone* **2013** A horror-thriller with a mystery twist about a troubled man with a troubled mind. The life of Jonathan MacKinley (Jefferson) changed forever after a car accident led to the death of his beloved wife. Suffering from extreme agoraphobia, he is trapped at home with days which repeat over and over again. The boredom of his barely sane existence takes a sinister turn after a home invasion. Jonathan then starts experiencing dark visions and twisted waking nightmares that include his dead wife. He wonders if personal demons or true evil now haunts his home, if not his mind. **91m/C; DVD, Streaming, Download.** Michael Jefferson; Emma Dubery; Sarah Schoofs; Peter Gregus; Debbie Rochon; Rory Douglas Abel; ***D:*** Rory Douglas Abel; ***W:*** Rory Douglas Abel; Matthew Barnes; ***C:*** Mike Aransky; ***M:*** John Avarese.

Phobic 🦴 **2002 (R)** A kid who sees his sister murdered by a serial killer develops a phobia of leaving his house. Probably because he keeps seeing her killer outside everywhere. **88m/C; DVD, Streaming.** Billy Parish; Anthony Azizi; ***D:*** Alexandra Lief; ***W:*** Tim Munson; ***C:*** Lisa Stoll; ***M:*** Brandon Roberts. **VIDEO**

Phoebe in Wonderland 🦴🦴 **2008 (PG-13)** Nine-year-old Phoebe (Fanning) is bright but troubled, though her protective mother (Huffman) prefers to believe her child is merely high-spirited and imaginative. Phoebe's imagination works to her advantage when she's cast in the lead role in her school's production of "Alice in Wonderland" and taken under the wing of charismatic, nonconformist drama teacher Miss Dodger (Clarkson). But as Phoebe's fantasies get more self-destructive, it becomes clear she needs serious help and not adults mouthing platitudes. Fanning and Clarkson are compelling but the story suffers from shrillness and a tendency towards artistic preaching. **96m/C; DVD, On Demand.** Elle Fanning; Felicity Huffman; Bill Pullman; Patricia Clarkson; Campbell Scott; Peter Gerety; Caitlin Sanchez; Tessa Albertson; ***D:*** Daniel Barnz; ***W:*** Daniel Barnz; ***C:*** Bobby Bukowski; ***M:*** Christophe Beck.

Phoenix 🦴 1/2 *Hi No Tori; The Firebird* **1978** Aging queen summons her marksman to find the Phoenix, a mythical bird that she believes will bring her eternal life. With English subtitles. **137m/C; VHS, DVD.** *JP* Tomisaburo Wakayama; Ken Tanaka; Reiko Ohara; Micko Takamine; Tatsuya Nakadai; ***D:*** Kon Ichikawa; ***W:*** Shuntaro Tanikawa; ***C:*** Kiyoshi Hasegawa; ***M:*** Jun Fukamachi.

Phoenix 🦴🦴 **1995** The Titus 4 deep-space outpost has problems when the creators of a killing machine are targeted for death by their creation, which has begun to think for itself. **94m/C; VHS, DVD.** Stephen Nichols; Billy Drago; William Sanderson; Brad Dourif; ***D:*** Troy Cook; ***W:*** Troy Cook; Jimmy Lifton.

Phoenix 🦴🦴 **1998 (R)** With a cast like this, you hope for a bit more than the usual cliched crime drama. Gambling addict/Phoenix cop Harry Collins (Liotta) is in big debt to loansharks. He decides the best way to get the money is to rob the nightclub of a local sleaze where fellow corruptible officer Mike Henshaw (LaPaglia) moonlights. But beyond the inherent stupidity of such a plan is the lurking presence of internal affairs officer Clyde Webber (Berkely). **104m/C; VHS, DVD.** Ray Liotta; Anthony LaPaglia; Daniel Baldwin; Jeremy Piven; Xander Berkeley; Giancarlo Esposito; Anjelica Huston; Tom Noonan; Kari Wuhrer; Brittany Murphy; ***D:*** Danny Cannon; ***W:*** Eddie Richey; ***C:*** James L. Carter; ***M:*** Graeme Revell.

Phoenix 🦴 1/2 **2006** Low-budget indie with a couple of attractive, if amateurish, leads and some plausibility issues. Kenneth shows up in L.A. at his young boyfriend Dylan's birthday party, but leaves after an argument. Wanting to make things right, Dylan flies to Phoenix and discovers Kenneth isn't to be found. But his longtime boyfriend Demetrius is. **90m/C; DVD.** Chad Bartley; Jeff Castle; Gaetano Jones; ***D:*** Michael D. Akers; ***W:*** Michael D. Akers; Sandon Berg; ***C:*** Chris Brown; ***M:*** Aram Mandossian. **VIDEO**

Phoenix 🦴🦴🦴 **2014 (PG-13)** Nelly (Hoss) is an unexpected survivor of a concentration camp, but her face has been destroyed. She has it reconstructed not to become a new person and disappear but to look exactly as she had. She wants to reconcile with her husband Johnny, even though she knows in her heart that he sold her out to the Nazis. When he sees her, he doesn't believe it's his dead wife, but thinks she looks enough like her to get her inheritance. The result is a noir that also serves as a brilliant commentary on denial of atrocity and how we deal with life-changing events. **98m/C; DVD, Blu-Ray.** *GE PL* Nina Hoss; Ronald Zehrfeld; Nina Kunzendorf; Michael Maertens; Imogene Kogge; ***D:*** Christian Petzold; ***W:*** Christian Petzold; Harun Farocki; ***C:*** Hans Fromm; ***M:*** Stefan Will.

The Phenix City Story 🦴🦴🦴 **1955** In the notorious community of Phenix City, Alabama, lawyer Albert Patterson (McIntire) runs for public office to counteract local organized crime after his Korean War veteran son John (Kiley) is attacked on the street. As Albert announces his candidacy for state attorney general, mobsters, including Rhett Tanner (Andrews), threaten and commit acts of violence to intimidate him. When Albert wins the Democratic party nomination, the situation grows more dire. Based on true events and shot in the real Phenix City, the intense film noir does not shy away from examining racial violence and features performances by locals. **100m/B; DVD.** John McIntire; Richard (Paul) Kiley; Kathryn Grant; Edward Andrews; Lenka Peterson; ***D:*** Phil Karlson; ***W:*** Crane Wilbur; Daniel Mainwaring; ***C:*** Harry Neumann; ***M:*** Harry Sukman. Natl. Film Reg. '55.

Phoenix Forgotten 🦴🦴 **2017 (PG-13)** Based partially on a real event, this science fiction thriller does not live up to the found-footage success of The Blair Witch. In March 1997, lights believed to be from a UFO were seen over Phoenix and three teens who were shooting a home movie went missing in the nearby desert. Two decades later, Sophie (Hartigan), a sister of one of the teens, begins to shoot her own project investigating the Phoenix Lights and the disappearance. Through interviews and a lucky finding, Sophie learns the truth about what happened. Despite a few memorable moments, the film lacks an original punch. **87m/C; DVD.** Florence Hartigan; Luke Spencer Roberts; Chelsea Lopez; Justin Matthews; Clint Jordan; ***D:*** Justin Barber; ***W:*** Justin Barber; T.S. Nowlin; ***C:*** Jay Keitel; ***M:*** Mondo Boys.

Phoenix the Warrior 🦴 *She Wolves of the Wasteland* **1988** Sometime in the future, female savages battle each other for control of the now ravaged earth. A newcomer seeks the tribe most worthy of receiving the last man on the planet, thereby continuing the human race. **90m/C; VHS, DVD.** Persis Khambatta; James H. Emery; Peggy Sands; Kathleen Kinmont; ***D:*** Robert Hayes; ***W:*** Robert Hayes.

Phone Booth 🦴🦴 **2002 (R)** After slimy publicist Stu (Farrell) hangs up the phone in the booth he's been using, the phone rings and he answers, only to be told that if he hangs up or runs, he'll be shot. To prove his point, the unseen sniper (voiced by Sutherland), kills a pimp who's been wanting the booth for himself. After the interesting premise and set-up, what follows is a disappointing mix of suspense thriller cliches and Schumacher's trademark visual stunts filmed in real time. It all adds up to nothing more than a showcase for Farrell, who does a great job. Whitaker, Holmes and Mitchell are wasted in one-dimensional roles. **81m/C; VHS, DVD, Blu-Ray.** Colin Farrell; Forest Whitaker; Katie Holmes; Radha Mitchell; Kiefer Sutherland; Richard T. Jones; Keith Nobbs; John Enos; James MacDonald; Josh Pais; Paula Jai Parker; Tia Texada; ***D:*** Joel Schumacher; ***W:*** Larry Cohen; ***C:*** Matthew Libatique; ***M:*** Harry Gregson-Williams.

Phone Call from a Stranger 🦴🦴 1/2 **1952** After a plane crash, a survivor visits the families of three of the victims whom he met during the flight. **96m/B; VHS, DVD.** Bette Davis; Gary Merrill; Michael Rennie; Shelley Winters; Hugh Beaumont; Keenan Wynn; Eve Arden; Craig Stevens; ***D:*** Jean Negulesco; ***W:*** Nunnally Johnson; ***C:*** Milton Krasner.

Photograph 🦴🦴 1/2 **2019 (PG-13)** Photographer Rafi (Siddiqui) makes his living at Mumbai's Gateway monument, taking pictures of tourists and selling them the photos. Accounting student Miloni (Malhotra) visits the Gateway and allows Rafi to take her picture, but her family calls her away before she can get the photo from him. When Rafi learns that his grandmother (Jaffar) won't take her medicine until he makes progress on getting married, he sends Miloni's photo as proof he is dating someone. The situation becomes complicated when his grandmother decides to visit to meet her. The charming film has a gentle tone, interesting storytelling, and lovely visuals, especially of Mumbai. Hindi with subtitles. **110m/C; DVD.** Nawazuddin Siddiqui; Sanya Malhotra; Sachin Khedekar; Denzil Smith; Brinda Trivedi; ***D:*** Ritesh Batra; ***W:*** Ritesh Batra; ***C:*** Tim Gillis; Ben Kutchins; ***M:*** Peter Raeburn.

The Photograph 🦴🦴 1/2 **2020 (PG-13)** In the process of doing a story on now-deceased famous photographer Christina Eames (Adams), Michael (Stanfield) interviews her one-time paramour, Isaac (Morgan), in rural Louisiana. Though Isaac does not reveal the depth of their relationship, Michael tries to learn more from her surviving daughter, curator Mae (Rae). As the pair work together to discover more about Christina, including her time with Isaac and the true identity of Mae's father, Michael and Mae feel their own passions. Occasionally intriguing, the romantic drama is mostly a straightforward story with uneven chemistry between Stanfield and Rae. **106m/C; DVD, Blu-Ray.** Chelsea Peretti; Lakeith Stanfield; Issa Rae; Courtney B. Vance; Teyonah Parris; ***D:*** Stella Meghie; ***W:*** Stella Meghie; ***C:*** Mark Schwartzbard; ***M:*** Robert Glasper.

Photographing Fairies 🦴🦴 **1997 (R)** Haunting story that's not quite compelling enough. After the wife of photographer Charles Castle (Stephens) is killed, he shuts down emotionally. He eventually sets up a London studio, becoming an expert in unmasking doctored photos. When Beatrice (Barber) shows him photos of fairies taken by her young daughters, Charles travels to her country home to expose them as fakes. Instead, he comes to believe that they are real and the fairies represent the "Other Side." Based on the novel by Steve Szilagyi. The premise involving the young girls and the faked fairy photos is also the basis of the film "Fairytale: A True Story." **107m/C; VHS, Streaming.** *UK* Toby Stephens; Frances Barber; Ben Kingsley; Emily Woof; Philip Davis; Rachel Shelley; Edward Hardwicke; Hannah Bould; Miriam Grant; Clive Merrison; ***D:*** Nick Willing; ***W:*** Nick Willing; Chris Harrald; ***C:*** John de Borman; ***M:*** Simon Boswell.

The Phynx WOOF! 1970 Incoherent, out-of-touch, crass mess of a spy spoof/musical has the US government's Super Secret Agency fabricating a rock band to go to communist Albania. They'll play a gig at a castle where a number of celebrities are being held hostage and rescue them. Even the music by Stoller and Leiber is atrocious. **81m/C; DVD.** Michael A. Miller; Ray Chippeway; Dennis Larden; Lonny Stevens; Michael Ansara; Lou Antonio; Mike Kellin; ***D:*** Lee H. Katzin; ***W:*** Stan Cornyn; ***C:*** Michael Hugo; ***M:*** Mike Stoller; Jerry Leiber.

Physical Evidence **1989 (R)** A lawyer finds herself falling for an ex-cop turned murder suspect while she tries to defend him for a crime he doesn't remember committing. **99m/C; VHS, DVD, Blu-Ray.** Burt Reynolds; Theresa Russell; Ned Beatty; Kay Lenz; Ted McGinley; ***D:*** Michael Crichton; ***W:*** Bill (William) Phillips; ***C:*** John A. Alonzo; ***M:*** Henry Mancini.

Pi **1998 (R)** Definitely a first—a religious/mathematical thriller about a man obsessed with decoding the real name of God. Max (Gullette) is a genius mathematician who believes everything can be understood in terms of numbers, so he works on his homebuilt supercomputer to unravel the stock market. Max begins to suffer hallucinations and blackouts just as his work draws the interest of both a high-powered Wall Street firm and a Hasidic cabalistic sect. **85m/B; VHS, DVD.** Sean Gullette; Mark Margolis; Ben Shenkman; Pamela Hart; Stephen Perlman; Samia Shoaib; Ajay Naidu; ***D:*** Darren Aronofsky; ***W:*** Sean Gullette; Darren Aronofsky; Eric Watson; ***C:*** Matthew Libatique; ***M:*** Clint Mansell. Ind. Spirit '99: First Screenplay; Sundance '98: Director (Aronofsky).

The Pianist **1991** As teenagers in Toronto, sisters Jean (Travers) and Colette (Grenon) become infatuated with Yoshi Takahashi (Okuda), a Japanese concert pianist who lived across the street. Ten years later, they have a family reunion in Vancouver and learn Yoshi is giving a concert in the city. Jean is excited to renew their ties but Colette is reluctant—and Jean reveals that she knows her sister and the pianist had a sexual relationship. Is Jean jealous? Or does she plan on establishing her own claims? Based on Ann Ireland's novel "A Certain Mr. Takahashi." **90m/C; VHS, DVD.** *CA* Gail Travers; Macha Grenon; Eiji Okuda; Maury Chaykin; Dorothee Berryman; Carl Alacchi; ***D:*** Claude Gagnon; ***W:*** Claude Gagnon.

The Pianist **1/2 2002 (R)** Polanski effectively turns his personal knowledge of the Holocaust into a spellbinding portrait of fellow Holocaust survivor Wladyslaw Szpilman (based on his autobiography), the renowned Polish-Jewish pianist of the title. Brody's dead-on portrayal of Szpilman, who as a gifted artist scarcely believes he will be affected by the war, effectively registers the horrifying transition from life of luxury to ending up in the Warsaw ghetto. An interesting feeling of hopefulness lying beneath the barbarism shows Polanski's attention to the humanity and kindness that still may be found in the most savage conditions. **148m/C; VHS, DVD, HD-DVD, On Demand.** *FR PL GE UK* Adrien Brody; Thomas Kretschmann; Frank Finlay; Maureen Lipman; Emilia Fox; Ed Stoppard; Julia Rayner; Jessica Kate Meyer; Ruth Platt; ***D:*** Roman Polanski; ***W:*** Ronald Harwood; ***C:*** Pawel Edelman; ***M:*** Wojciech Kilar. Oscars '02: Actor (Brody), Adapt. Screenplay, Director (Polanski); British Acad. '02: Director (Polanski), Film; Cannes '02: Film; Natl. Soc. Film Critics '02: Actor (Brody), Director (Polanski), Film, Screenplay.

The Piano **1/2 1993 (R)** In the 1850s, Ada (Hunter), a mute Scottish widow with a young daughter, agrees to an arranged marriage with Stewart (Neill), a colonial landowner in New Zealand. The way she expresses her feelings is by playing her cherished piano, left behind on the beach by her new husband. Another settler, George (Keitel), buys it, arranges for lessons with Ada, and soon the duo begin a grand passion leading to a cruelly calculated revenge. Fiercely poetic and well acted (with Keitel in a notably romantic role), though the film may be too dark and intense for some. Fine original score with Hunter doing her own piano playing. **120m/C; VHS, DVD, Blu-Ray.** *AU* Holly Hunter; Harvey Keitel; Sam Neill; Anna Paquin; Kerry Walker; Genevieve Lemon; ***D:*** Jane Campion; ***W:*** Jane Campion; ***C:*** Stuart Dryburgh; ***M:*** Michael Nyman. Oscars '93: Actress (Hunter), Orig. Screenplay, Support. Actress (Paquin); Australian Film Inst. '93: Actor (Keitel), Actress (Hunter), Cinematog., Costume Des., Director (Campion), Film, Film Editing, Score, Screenplay, Sound; British Acad. '93: Actress (Hunter); Cannes '93: Actress (Hunter), Film; Golden Globes '94: Actress--Drama (Hunter); Ind. Spirit '94: Foreign Film; L.A. Film Critics '93: Actress (Hunter), Cinematog., Director (Campion), Screenplay, Support. Actress (Paquin); Natl. Bd. of Review '93: Actress (Hunter); N.Y. Film Critics '93: Actress (Hunter), Director (Campion), Screenplay; Natl. Soc. Film Critics '93: Actress (Hunter), Screenplay; Writers Guild '93: Orig. Screenplay.

The Piano Lesson **1994 (PG)** The prized heirloom of the Charles family is an 80-year-old, ornately carved upright piano, jealously guarded by widowed Berniece (Woodard), and housed in the Pittsburgh home of Uncle Doaker (Gordon). When Berniece's brother Willie Boy (Dutton) visits from Mississippi, it's to persuade her to sell the piano in order to buy some land that their grandfather had worked as a slave. But the past, carved into the piano's panels, has a strong hold—one that Berniece refuses to give up. Set in 1936. Adaptation by Wilson of his 1990 Pulitzer Prize-winning play. **99m/C; VHS, DVD.** Alfre Woodard; Charles S. Dutton; Courtney B. Vance; Carl Gordon; Tommy Hollis; Zelda Harris; Lou Myers; Rosalyn Coleman; Tommy La Fitte; ***D:*** Lloyd Richards; ***W:*** August Wilson; ***M:*** Stephen James Taylor; Dwight Andrews. **TV**

Piano Man **1/2 1996** The police have begun to discover bodies so horribly mutilated that they've become unidentifiable—along with small toy pianos stuffed in them. Eventually the killer gets tired of waiting for the police to quit fumbling and figure things out and begins sending them clues. Unfortunately what follows is all too predictable despite a promising start. **120m/C; DVD.** *NK* Seung-yeon Lee; Kyoung-In Hong; Cheol Park; Min-su Choi; ***D:*** Sang-wook Yu; ***W:*** Sang-wook Yu; Jae-ho Heo; ***C:*** Jeong-min Seo; ***M:*** Baek-sang Nam.

The Piano Teacher *La Pianiste* **2001** Middle-aged Erika (Huppert) teaches piano at the Vienna Conservatory where she is demanding—if not cruel—to her students. Erika lives with her controlling mother (Girardot) and spends her off hours mutiliating herself, watching porn, and engaging in other bizarre behavior. Which doesn't improve when she agrees to a questionable sexual relationship (on her masochistic terms) with hot new student Walter (Magimel). Not for the faint-hearted; adapted from the 1983 novel by Effriede Jelinek. French with subtitles. **130m/C; VHS, DVD, Blu-Ray.** *FR AT* Isabelle Huppert; Benoît Magimel; Annie Girardot; Udo Samel; Susanne Lothar; Anna Sigalenteh; ***D:*** Michael Haneke; ***W:*** Michael Haneke; ***C:*** Christian Berger. Cannes '01: Actor (Magimel), Actress (Huppert), Grand Jury Prize.

Piano Tuner of Earthquakes *L'Accordeur de tremblements de terre* **2005** Appropriately bizarre but unfortunately stale experimental film from the Quay brothers has beautiful opera star Malvina (Casar) killed before her weding by the evil Dr. Droz (John), who then steals her corpse to revive it. He then hires piano tuner Felsiberto (Sasachu) to write and choreograph an opera depicting the events. Since he resembles her former love, Malvina falls in love with him and he plots their escape. Interesting staging and visuals can't make up for the many weaknesses. **99m/C; DVD.** *FR GB GE* Amira Casar; Gottfried John; Assumpta Serna; Cesar Sarachu; ***D:*** Stephen Quay; Timothy Quay; ***W:*** Stephen Quay; Timothy Quay; ***C:*** Nicholas D. Knowland; ***M:*** Christopher Slaski.

The Picasso Summer **1/2 1969** A pretty travelogue but a dull and rather frustrating flick. Disenchanted architect George Smith (Finney) is disgusted by the smug San Francisco art scene so he and loyal wife Alice (Mimieux) take off for France so George can meet the one artist he does admire—Pablo Picasso, who proves elusive. Includes animated sequences of Picasso's work. Based on a story by Ray Bradbury, who co-wrote the screenplay under the pseudonym Douglas Spaulding. **90m/C; DVD.** Albert Finney; Yvette Mimieux; Luis Miguel Dominguin; ***D:*** Robert Sallin; Serge Bourguignon; ***W:*** Edwin Boyd; Ray Bradbury; ***C:*** Vilmos Zsigmond; ***M:*** Michel Legrand.

Picasso Trigger **1989 (R)** An American spy tries to catch an elusive murderer. The sequel to "Hard Ticket to Hawaii" and "Malibu Express." **99m/C; VHS, DVD, Blu-Ray.** Steve Bond; Dona Speir; John Aprea; Hope Marie Carlton; Guich Koock; Roberta Vasquez; Bruce Penhall; Harold Diamond; Rodrigo Obregon; ***D:*** Andy Sidaris; ***W:*** Andy Sidaris; ***C:*** Howard Wexler; ***M:*** Gary Stockdale.

Piccadilly **1929** Diva nightclub performer Mabel (Gray) is riding high since her lover is London club owner Valentine Wilmot (Thomas) and her dance act with partner Victor (Ritchard) is a hit. At least until Val fires Victor for trying to get Mabel to quit and work in America. Mabel isn't a success on her own so Val takes a chance on Asian kitchen drudge Shosho (Wong) whom Victor sees entertaining her fellow workers which fuels Mabel's insecurities. Originally shot as a silent but director Dupont did reshoots for a sound version. **108m/B; DVD.** *GB* Anna May Wong; Gilda Gray; Jameson Thomas; King Hou Chang; Cyril Ritchard; Charles Laughton; Hannah Janes; ***D:*** Ewald Andre Dupont; ***W:*** Arnold Bennett; ***C:*** Werner Brandes.

Pick a Star *Movie Struck* **1937** Lawrence is a small-town girl who wins a contest and is off to Hollywood. Only no one pays any attention to her except for publicity man Haley, who arranges her screen test. Naturally, she knocks the studio bosses for a loop and becomes a star. Laurel & Hardy are featured in a couple of comedy segments showing the newcomer some backstage silliness and movie business on the set of a Western they're filming (with Finlayson, better known as a director, cast as the duo's director). **70m/B; VHS, DVD.** Rosina Lawrence; Jack Haley; Patsy Kelly; Mischa Auer; Stan Laurel; Oliver Hardy; Charles Halton; Tom Dugan; Russell Hicks; James Finlayson; ***D:*** Edward Sedgwick.

The Pick-Up Artist **1/2 1987 (PG-13)** The adventures of a compulsive Don Juan who finds he genuinely loves the daughter of an alcoholic who's in debt to the mob. Standard story with no surprises. **81m/C; VHS, DVD, Blu-Ray.** Robert Downey, Jr.; Molly Ringwald; Dennis Hopper; Harvey Keitel; Danny Aiello; Vanessa L(ynne) Williams; Robert Towne; Mildred Dunnock; Lorraine Bracco; Joe Spinell; Victoria Jackson; Polly Draper; Brian Hamill; Christine Baranski; Bob Gunton; G. Anthony "Tony" Sirico; Victor Argo; Reni Santoni; ***D:*** James Toback; ***W:*** James Toback; ***C:*** Gordon Willis; ***M:*** Georges Delerue.

Pick-Up Summer *Pinball Summer; Pinball Pick-Up* **1979 (R)** Two suburban boys cruise their town after school lets out, chasing a pair of voluptuous sisters. **99m/C; VHS, DVD.** *CA* Michael Zelniker; Carl Marotte; ***D:*** George Mihalka.

Picking Up the Pieces **1999 (R)** Tex (Allen) is a kosher cowboy in a New Mexico town, who's also a butcher. This trade comes in handy when he dismembers unfaithful wife, Candy (Stone), and scatters her remains in the desert. When a blind woman stumbles on Candy's severed hand and miraculously has her sight restored, she delivers the hand to the local church where it becomes a shrine for pilgrims seeking miracle cures. Meanwhile, Tex just wants to rebury the evidence. If you can buy Allen as any kind of cowboy, you can buy the rest of this would-be comedy. **95m/C; VHS, DVD.** Woody Allen; David Schwimmer; Maria Grazia Cucinotta; Kiefer Sutherland; Sharon Stone; Alfonso Arau; Richard "Cheech" Marin; Lou Diamond Phillips; Danny De La Paz; Andy Dick; Fran Drescher; Joseph Gordon-Levitt; Elliott Gould; Eddie Griffin; Lupe Ontiveros; ***D:*** Alfonso Arau; ***W:*** Bill Wilson; ***C:*** Vittorio Storaro; ***M:*** Ruy Folguera.

The Pickle **1993 (R)** Self-indulgent comedy about a midlife crisis. Aiello stars as a middle-aged manic-depressive director certain that his new film is going to be an abysmal flop (as have all his recent pictures). He seeks comfort and reassurance from various ex-wives, children, lovers, and others, though he abuses them all. This dispirited tale also shows clips of the director's dreadful film about children who launch a giant pickle into space. It couldn't possibly be worse that what Mazursky actually put up on the screen. **103m/C; VHS, DVD.** Danny Aiello; Dyan Cannon; Clotilde Courau; Shelley Winters; Barry Miller; Jerry Stiller; Christopher Penn; Rebecca Miller; ***Cameo(s):*** Ally Sheedy; Little Richard; Spalding Gray; Griffin Dunne; Isabella Rossellini; Dudley Moore; ***D:*** Paul Mazursky; ***W:*** Paul Mazursky; ***M:*** Michel Legrand.

Pickpocket **1/2 1959** Slow moving, documentary-like account of a petty thief's existence is a moral tragedy inspired by "Crime and Punishment." Ending is particularly moving. Classic filmmaking from Bresson, France's master of austerity. In French with English subtitles. **75m/B; VHS, DVD, Blu-Ray.** *FR* Martin LaSalle; Marika Green; Pierre Leymarie; Pierre Etaix; Jean Pelegri; Dolly Scal; ***D:*** Robert Bresson; ***W:*** Robert Bresson; ***C:*** Leonce-Henri Burel.

Pickup Alley **1957** Dull crime drama that does take advantage of its many European settings, including Rome's catacombs. FBI agent Sturgis wants revenge on international drug smuggler McNally who killed Sturgis' sister. He gets sent to London to assist Interpol and starts tracking McNally's courier Gina. **91m/B; DVD, Blu-Ray.** *GB* Victor Mature; Trevor Howard; Anita Ekberg; Lionel Murton; ***D:*** John Gilling; ***W:*** John Paxton; ***C:*** Ted Moore; ***M:*** Richard Rodney Bennett.

Pickup on South Street **1953** Petty thief Widmark lifts woman's wallet only to find it contains top secret Communist micro-film for which pinko agents will stop at nothing to get back. Intriguing look at the politics of the day. The creme of "B" movies. **80m/B; VHS, DVD.** Richard Widmark; Jean Peters; Thelma Ritter; Murvyn Vye; Richard Kiley; Milburn Stone; ***D:*** Samuel Fuller; ***W:*** Samuel Fuller; ***C:*** Joe MacDonald; ***M:*** Leigh Harline. Natl. Film Reg. '18.

The Pickwick Papers **1/2 1954** Comedy based on the Dickens classic wherein Mrs. Bardell sues the Pickwick Club for breach of promise. **109m/B; VHS, DVD.** *GB* James Hayter; James Donald; Nigel Patrick; Hermione Gingold; Hermione Baddeley; Kathleen Harrison; ***D:*** Noel Langley.

Picnic **1/2 1955** Drifter Hal Carter (Holden) arrives in a small town and immediately wins the love of his friend's girl, Madge (Novak). The other women in town seem interested too. Strong, romantic work, with Holden excelling in the lead. Novak provides a couple pointers too. Lavish Hollywood adaptation of the William Inge play, including the popular tune "Moonglow/Theme from Picnic." Remade for TV in 2000 with Josh Brolin in the Holden role. **113m/C; VHS, DVD; Open Captioned.** William Holden; Kim Novak; Rosalind Russell; Susan Strasberg; Arthur O'Connell; Cliff Robertson; Betty Field; Verna Felton; Reta Shaw; Nick Adams; Phyllis Newman; Raymond Bailey; ***D:*** Joshua Logan; ***W:*** Daniel Taradash; ***C:*** James Wong Howe; ***M:*** George Duning. Oscars '55: Art Dir./Set Dec., Color, Film Editing; Golden Globes '56: Director (Logan).

Picnic at Hanging Rock **1975 (PG)** School outing in 1900 into a mountainous region ends tragically when three girls disappear. Eerie film is strong on atmosphere, as befits mood master Weir. Lambert is extremely photogenic—and suitable subdued—as one of the girls to disappear. Otherwise beautifully photographed on location. From the novel by Joan Lindsey. **110m/C; VHS, DVD, Blu-Ray.** *AU* Margaret Nelson; Rachel Roberts; Dominic Guard; Helen Morse; Jacki Weaver; Vivean Gray; Anne Louise Lambert; ***D:*** Peter Weir; ***W:*** Clifford Green; ***C:*** Russell Boyd; ***M:*** Bruce Smeaton.

Picture Bride ☌☌ 1/2 **1994 (PG-13)** Familiar immigrant saga finds 17-year-old Japanese Riyo (Kudoh) setting off for Hawaii in 1918 as a "picture bride" to a husband she's never met but with whom she's exchanged photos (hence the title). Riyo's shocked to discover her intended, sugar-cane worker Matsuji (Takayama), has deceived her with an out-of-date picture and is at least 25 years older than she. She refuses to consummate the marriage and goes to work in the fields, intending to earn money for her passage home but of course things don't work out quite as Riyo intends. Japanese with subtitles. **95m/C; VHS, DVD.** *JP* Youki Kudoh; Akira Takayama; Tamlyn Tomita; Cary-Hiroyuki Tagawa; Yoko Sugi; ***Cameo(s):*** Toshiro Mifune; ***D:*** Kayo Hatta; ***W:*** Kayo Hatta; Mari Hatta; Diane Mark; ***C:*** Claudio Rocha; ***M:*** Cliff Eidelman. Sundance '95: Aud. Award.

Picture Claire ☌ **2001 (R)** Lewis is miscast as the independent French-speaking Claire, who leaves Montreal for Toronto to find a one-time boyfriend. Instead, Claire gets in the middle of a diamond heist between shady lady Lily (Gershon), sleazy Eddie (Rourke), and sadistic thug Laramie (Rennie)?all because she can't speak English. Bleech. English and French with subtitles. **90m/C; VHS, DVD.** *CA* Juliette Lewis; Callum Keith Rennie; Gina Gershon; Mickey Rourke; ***D:*** Bruce McDonald; ***W:*** Semi Chellas; ***C:*** Miroslaw Baszak; ***M:*** Paul Haslinger.

Picture Day ☌☌ **2013 (R)** A comedy-drama about a rebellious teen who must repeat her senior year of high school and the unexpected impact it has on several lives. Though she had a reputation as a bad ass, Claire (Maslany) finds it has taken a hit because she was held back and not allowed to graduate on time. Despite her still-present snarky wit and headphones to keep the world at bay, Claire faces social difficulties and takes freshman Henry (Van Wyck) under her wing. Claire once babysat the nerdy Henry and helps him re-invent himself as a mysterious rebel. At night, Claire finds release in live music and becomes involved with a 33-year-old musician, Jim (McCarthy), who takes her into the partying world of musicians. Through these relationships, Claire learns difficult truths about real friends and true intimacy. **93m/C; DVD, Streaming, Download.** Tatiana Maslany; Spencer Van Wyck; Steven McCarthy; Susan Coyne; Fiona Highet; ***D:*** Kate Melville; ***W:*** Kate Melville; ***C:*** Celiana Cardenas. **VIDEO**

Picture Mommy Dead ☌☌ **1966** Well acted melodrama involving a scheming shrew who struggles to drive her mentally disturbed stepdaughter insane for the sake of cold, hard cash. **85m/C; VHS, DVD.** Don Ameche; Zsa Zsa Gabor; Martha Hyer; Susan Gordon; ***D:*** Bert I. Gordon; ***C:*** Ellsworth Fredericks.

Picture of Dorian Gray ☌☌☌ **1945** Hatfield plays the rake who stays young while his portrait ages in this adaptation of Oscar Wilde's classic novel. Lansbury steals this one. **110m/B; VHS, DVD, Blu-Ray.** Hurd Hatfield; George Sanders; Donna Reed; Angela Lansbury; Peter Lawford; Lowell Gilmore; Miles Mander; ***D:*** Albert Lewin; ***W:*** Albert Lewin; ***C:*** Harry Stradling, Sr. Oscars '45: B&W Cinematog.; Golden Globes '46: Support. Actress (Lansbury).

Picture of Dorian Gray ☌☌☌ **1974** Another version of Wilde's renowned novel about a man who retains his youthful visage while his portrait shows the physical ravages of aging. Davenport is particularly appealing in the lead. **130m/C; VHS, DVD.** Shane Briant; Nigel Davenport; Charles Aidman; Fionnula Flanagan; Linda Kelsey; Vanessa Howard; ***D:*** Glenn Jordan. **TV**

Picture Perfect ☌☌ 1/2 **1996 (PG-13)** While trying to impress her new boss, ad exec Kate (Aniston) claims Nick (Mohr), the man standing with her in a photo, is her fiance. Unfortunately, the boss now wants to meet the guy (a stranger who was at the same party) and she must find him and get him to play along. The story's cliched, but Aniston's appealing screen presence perks things up a bit. **100m/C; VHS, DVD.** Jennifer Aniston; Jay Mohr; Kevin Bacon; Illeana Douglas; Olympia Dukakis; Kevin Dunn; Faith Prince; Anne Twomey; ***D:*** Glenn Gordon Caron; ***W:*** Glenn Gordon Caron; ***C:*** Paul Sarossy; ***M:*** Carter Burwell.

Picture Snatcher ☌☌ **1933** Former gangster Danny Kean (Cagney) tries to make himself over as a photographer for a tabloid, using his criminal know-how to get scoops. But his sometimes underhanded ways cause problems when Danny romances Patricia (Ellis), who happens to be the daughter of the cop (O'Connor) who once put Danny behind bars. **76m/B; DVD.** James Cagney; Patricia Ellis; Ralph Bellamy; Alice White; Robert Emmett O'Connor; Ralf Harolde; ***D:*** Lloyd Bacon; ***W:*** P.J. Wolfson; Allen Rivkin; ***C:*** Sol Polito.

Picture This! **2008** High school senior Mandy (chipper blonde Tisdale) isn't one of the popular girls but she does know what she wants. And it's within reach when very popular guy Drew (Amell) asks her to the biggest party of the year. Too bad Mandy's overprotective dad (Pollak) has grounded her. But with some help from her friends and her new video phone, Mandy is determined to go to the ball—uh, party. **?m/CDVD.** Ashley Tisdale; Maxim Roy; Lauren Collins; Robbie Amell; Kevin Pollak; Shenae Grimes; Cindy Busby; ***D:*** Stephen Herek; ***W:*** Temple Mathews; ***C:*** Bernard Couture; ***M:*** Richard (Rick) Marvin. **VIDEO**

Picture Windows ☌☌ **1995 (R)** Three short cable movies inspired by works of art. "Lightning," based on Frederic Remington sketches and a Zane Grey short story, finds western codger Keith striking gold with the help of his trusty mule. A David Hockney painting suggested "Armed Response," which features a confrontation between a wealthy lawyer (Loggia) and a burglar (Zahn). And an anonymous 16th-century canvas "Two Nudes Bathing" is given an imaginative history. **95m/C; VHS, DVD.** Brian Keith; Robert Loggia; Steve Zahn; Charley Boorman; ***D:*** Joe Dante; Bob Rafelson; John Boorman. **CABLE**

Pictures of Hollis Woods ☌☌ 1/2 **2007** Twelve-year-old Hollis Woods (Ferland) was found abandoned as a baby and has spent her life in various foster homes. Her dedicated social worker Edna (Woodard) had hoped that Hollis' last family, the Reagans, would be permanent but an incident put Hollis on the move again and into the care of retired schoolteacher Josie (Spacek). Only Josie's forgetfulness turns out to be the early stages of Alzheimer's—a fact Hollis tries to cover up so she won't be moved again. Adapted from Patricia Reilly Giff's novel. **110m/C; DVD.** Jodelle Ferland; Sissy Spacek; Alfre Woodard; Judith Ivey; James Tupper; Julie Ann Emery; Ridge Canipe; ***D:*** Tony Bill; ***W:*** Ann Peacock; Daniel Petrie, Jr.; ***C:*** Camille Thomasson; ***M:*** Paul Sarossy; Van Dyke Parks. **TV**

Pie in the Sky ☌☌ 1/2 **1995 (R)** Charles Dunlap (Charles) is a traffic geek, fascinated by the flow of cars on the nearby freeway, whose hero is local traffic reporter Alan Davenport (Goodman), with whom he eventually gets a job in L.A. Charles' other interest is dancer/waitress Amy (Heche)?their first attempt at romance goes awry but persistence pays off. Optimistic and corny. **94m/C; VHS, DVD.** Josh Charles; Anne Heche; John Goodman; Christine Lahti; Peter Riegert; Christine Ebersole; Wil Wheaton; Bob Balaban; Dey Young; ***D:*** Bryan Gordon; ***W:*** Bryan Gordon; ***C:*** Bernd Heinl; ***M:*** Michael Covertino.

Piece of Cake ☌☌ 1/2 **1988** Adaptation of the Derek Robinson novel follows the flyboys of the RAF Hornet Squadron during the early years of WWII. They have trouble taking the war seriously but tangles with the Luftwaffe and increasing casualties put a strain on everyone. Great aerial photography and the British planes are vintage Spitfires not repros. Made for British TV miniseries on six cassettes. **312m/C; VHS, DVD.** *GB* Tom Burlinson; Tim Woodward; Boyd Gaines; Nathaniel Parker; Neil Dudgeon; David Horovitch; Richard Hope; Jeremy Wortham; Michael Elwyn; Corinne Dacla; Helena Michell; ***D:*** Ian Toynton; ***W:*** Leon Griffiths; ***C:*** Peter Jessop; ***M:*** Peter Martin. **TV**

A Piece of Pleasure ☌☌☌ *Un Partie de Plaisir* **1974** Marriage declines due to a domineering husband in this familiar domestic study from French master Chabrol. Good, but not among the director's best efforts. In French with English subtitles. **100m/C; VHS, DVD.** *FR* Paul Gegauff; Danielle Gegauff; Clemence Gegauff; Paula Moore; Michel Valette; Cecile Vassort; ***D:*** Claude Chabrol; ***W:*** Paul Gegauff; ***C:*** Jean Ralsier; ***M:*** Pierre Jansen.

Piece of the Action ☌☌ 1/2 **1977 (PG)** An ex-cop beats two con men at their own game when he convinces them to work for a Chicago community center. **135m/C; VHS, DVD.** Sidney Poitier; Bill Cosby; James Earl Jones; Denise Nicholas; Hope Clarke; Tracy Reed; Titos Vandis; Ja'net DuBois; ***D:*** Sidney Poitier; ***M:*** Curtis Mayfield.

Pieces **WOOF!** **1983 (R)** Chain-saw wielding madman roams a college campus in search of human parts for a ghastly jigsaw puzzle. Gory and loathsome. **90m/C; VHS, DVD, Blu-Ray.** *IT SP* Christopher George; Lynda Day George; Paul Smith; ***D:*** J(uan) Piquer Simon.

Pieces of April ☌☌ 1/2 **2003 (PG-13)** Delightfully dysfunctional family meets for a chaotic Thanksgiving when tattooed New Yorker April (Holmes) has her suburban family join her for holiday dinner. The family trip to NYC is rife with humorous dramas and sidetracks while domestically-challenged April's oven breaks down and seemingly nice new boyfriend Bobby's (Luke) behavior hints that something dark is afoot. Despite the misleading and slightly disturbing subplot, and a somewhat hasty ending, film is entertaining and original. Completed in three weeks on a limited budget ($200,000) with surprisingly slick digital camerawork. **81m/C; VHS, DVD.** Katie Holmes; Patricia Clarkson; Oliver Platt; Derek Luke; Alison Pill; Alice Drummond; Sean P. Hayes; John Gallagher, Jr.; Sisqo; Isiah Whitlock, Jr.; Lillias White; ***D:*** Peter Hedges; ***W:*** Peter Hedges; ***C:*** Tami Reiker; ***M:*** Stephin Merritt. Natl. Bd. of Review '03: Support. Actress (Clarkson); Natl. Soc. Film Critics '03: Support. Actress (Clarkson).

Pieces of Dreams ☌☌ **1970** Predictable and maudlin romantic drama. Father Gregory Lind (Forster) questions his priestly commitment after working with divorced social worker Pamela Gibson (Hutton). They eventually have an affair and Lind contemplates whether he and Pamela have a future, which would mean his leaving the church. **100m/C; DVD.** Robert Forster; Lauren Hutton; Will Geer; Ivor Francis; Richard O'Brien; Edith Atwater; Mitzi Hoag; ***D:*** Daniel Haller; ***W:*** Roger O. Hirson; ***C:*** Charles F. Wheeler; ***M:*** Michel Legrand.

Pied Piper ☌ 1/2 **1972** Weird and violent not-for-the-kiddies retelling of the legend of the Pied Piper of Hamelin. Donovan minimally stars as the mysteriously musical rat catcher who offers to rid the grubby 14th-century town of Hamelin of its plague-carrying rodents for a price. When the town reneges, the piper plays his tunes for the town's children instead. **90m/C; DVD, Blu-Ray.** *GB* Jack Wild; Donald Pleasence; John Hurt; Michael Hordern; Roy Kinnear; Peter Vaughan; Diana Dors; Cathryn Harrison; Donovan; ***D:*** Jacques Demy; ***W:*** Jacques Demy; Andrew Birkin; Mark Peploe; ***C:*** Peter Suschitzky; ***M:*** Donovan.

The Pied Piper of Hamelin ☌☌ **1957** The evergreen classic of the magical piper who rids a village of rats and then disappears with the village children into a mountain when the townspeople fail to keep a promise. **90m/C; VHS, DVD.** Van Johnson; Claude Rains; Jim Backus; Kay Starr; Lori Nelson; ***D:*** Bretaigne Windust.

Piercing ☌☌ 1/2 **2018 (R)** On a business trip away from his family, Reed makes plans to murder a prostitute in his hotel room. When the would-be victim arrives, though, the two engage in an erotic power struggle that will make you question who's in charge and what's real. The physical and psychological terrors are brutal and disturbing, but they'd be more so if the characters elicited greater investment from the viewer. Based on the novel by Ryû Murakami. **81m/C; DVD, Blu-Ray.** Christopher Abbott; Mia Wasikowska; Laia Costa; Marin Ireland; Wendell Pierce; ***D:*** Nicolas Pesce; ***W:*** Nicolas Pesce; ***C:*** Zack Galler.

Pierrot le Fou ☌☌☌ 1/2 **1965** A woman fleeing a gangster joins a man leaving his wife in this stunning, occasionally confusing classic from iconoclast Godard. A hallmark in 1960s improvisational filmmaking, with rugged Belmondo and always-photogenic Karina effortlessly excelling in leads. In French with English subtitles. **110m/C; VHS, DVD.** *FR IT* Samuel Fuller; Jean-Pierre Leaud; Jean-Paul Belmondo; Anna Karina; Dirk Sanders; ***D:*** Jean-Luc Godard; ***W:*** Jean-Luc Godard; ***C:*** Raoul Coutard; ***M:*** Antoine Duhamel.

Pieta ☌☌☌ **2013** Director Kim Ki-Duk became the first Korean to win the Golden Lion at the Venice Film Festival for this incredibly dark tale of revenge and redemption. Gang-Do, an enforcer for the Korean mob, enjoys collecting on his employer's debts a bit too much. When a mysterious woman, claiming to be his mother, arrives, Gang-Do falls into a trap related to his past. The first half of Kim's film has a mesmerizingly dirty tone and pitch-black dark sense of humanity but the second half gets a bit standard. Still incredibly well-done. Korean with subtitles. **104m/C; DVD, Blu-Ray.** *SK* Jeong-jin Lee; Min-soo Jo; ***D:*** Ki-Duk Kim; ***W:*** Ki-Duk Kim; ***C:*** Jo Young-Jik; ***M:*** In-young Park.

Pigalle ☌☌ **1995** Dridi's feature debut focuses on the red light district of Paris and the company of various lowlifes, including pickpocket Fifi (Renaud), who's involved with both stripper Vera (Brile) and transvestite hooker Divine (Li). There's also an increasingly violent turf war between a couple of drug dealers that takes in everyone around. Violent and sordid melodrama. French with subtitles. **93m/C; VHS, DVD.** *FR* Francis Renaud; Vera Briole; Bianca Li; Raymond Gil; Younesse Boudache; Philippe Ambrosini; Jean-Claude Grenier; ***D:*** Karim Dridi; ***W:*** Karim Dridi; ***C:*** John Mathieson.

A Pigeon Sat on a Branch Reflecting on Existence ☌☌☌ *En duva satt på en gren och funerade på tillvaron* **2014 (PG-13)** The final part of Roy Andersson's "Living Trilogy"—after 2002's "Songs From the Second Floor" and 2007's "You, the Living"—ends this series about "what it means to be a human" on a deadpan, deeply philosophical note. Again, Andersson eschews plot for a series of vignettes, most of them dryly humorous, but laced with social and class commentary more than ever before. The filmmaking here is impressive but there is a bit of law of diminishing returns in how much it feels like the other two films. Having said that, Andersson's style is something to behold. One wishes he made films more often. **100m/C; Streaming.** *DK FR GE NO SW* Holger Andersson; Nils Westblom; Charlotta Larsson; Viktor Gyllenberg; ***D:*** Roy Andersson; ***W:*** Roy Andersson; ***C:*** István Borbás; Gergely Pálos; ***M:*** Gorm Sunderberg.

Piglet's Big Movie ☌☌ 1/2 **2003 (G)** An adaptation of three stories by A.A. Milne. Piglet (voiced by Fielder) is a very small animal and something of a fraidy pig. He's feeling too small to be of help to his friends and decides to take a little hike into the Hundred Acre Woods when he's ignored once again. However, when best bud Pooh (Cummings) thinks Piglet is missing, he organizes a search party and everyone realizes how important Piglet is to them. Best for the wee ones with its gentle lessons on friendship, even if it can't live up to the original shorts of the '60s and early '70s. **75m/C; VHS, DVD.** ***V:*** John Fiedler; Jim (Jonah) Cummings; Kath Soucie; Nikita Hopkins; Andre Stoja; Thomas Wheatley; Peter Cullen; Ken Sansom; ***D:*** Francis Glebas; ***W:*** Brian Hohlfeld; ***M:*** Carly Simon; Carl Johnson; ***M:*** Carly Simon.

Pigs ☌ 1/2 *Daddy's Deadly Darling; The Killers* **1973** Young woman who has escaped from a mental hospital teams up with an evil old man to go on a murdering spree. They complement each other beautifully. She kills them and he disposes of the bodies by making pig slop out of them. **90m/C; VHS, DVD, Blu-Ray.** Toni Lawrence; Marc Lawrence; Jesse Vint; Katharine Ross; ***D:*** Marc Lawrence; ***M:*** Charles Bernstein.

Pigs ☌ **2007** In this lame oink-fest about young men behaving, well, like pigs, Miles (Brown) takes a bet from his best buddy Cleaver (Lucio) that he can have sex with 26 girls, alphabetically A-Z. Only he doesn't intend to fall for Miss X—Gaby Xeropolus (Marden). Tries to go from wacky sex romp to heartfelt romance but can't really pull it off.

85m/C; DVD. Chris Elliott; Jefferson Brown; Melanie Marden; Darryn Lucio; **D:** Karl DiPelino; **W:** Karl DiPelino; Chris Ragonetti; **C:** Gurjeet Mann; **M:** John Jamieson. **VIDEO**

Pigskin Parade 1/2 **1936** Fifteen-year-old Garland's first feature is a light-hearted musical combining college and football. Winston Winters (Haley) coaches the Texas State U team, which has been mistakenly invited to play Yale, and goes to great lengths to give his team a chance by recruiting a farmboy (Erwin) who's a natural phenom. (Garland's the boy's singing sister.) **95m/B; VHS, DVD.** Jack Haley; Patsy Kelly; Stuart Erwin; Judy Garland; Johnny Downs; Betty Grable; Arline Judge; Tony Martin; Fred Kohler, Jr.; Elisha Cook, Jr.; **D:** David Butler; **W:** Harry Tugend; Jack Yellen; **C:** Arthur C. Miller.

Pilgrimage **1933** Overbearing Hannah Jessop (Crosman) is horrified when her son Jim (Foster) takes up with the unsuitable Mary (Nixon), so she sends him off to fight in WWI. Jim doesn't know Mary is pregnant and after he is killed, Hannah refuses to have anything to do with her grandson. It's not until she takes a trip to France to visit her son's grave that she realizes her heartlessness and makes amends. Crosman was a grand dame of the theater and well-suited to her part. **96m/B; DVD.** Henrietta Crosman; Marion (Marian) Nixon; Norman Foster; Heather Angel; Charley Grapewin; Lucille LaVerne; Maurice Murphy; Hedda Hopper; **D:** John Ford; **W:** Philip Klein; Barry Connors; Dudley Nichols; **C:** George Schneiderman; **M:** R. H. Bassett.

Pillars of the Earth 1/2 **2010** Lavish miniseries based on the novel by Ken Follett. In 12th-century England, King Henry's heirs start a civil war fighting over the throne while pious Philip, the prior of Kingsbridge, wants to build a new cathedral that will take decades to complete. The large cast takes time to sort out amidst much scheming by the clergy, the nobles, and the royals while the commoners just get on with the work (and some romance). **428m/C; DVD, Blu-Ray.** Ian McShane; Rufus Sewell; Eddie Redmayne; Donald Sutherland; Matthew Macfadyen; Hayley Atwell; Sam Claflin; Alison Pill; Tony Curran; Natalia Woerner; Sarah Paris; Gordon Pinsent; **D:** Sergio Mimica-Gezzan; **W:** John Pielmeier; **C:** Attila Szalay; **M:** Trevor Morris. **CABLE**

Pillars of the Sky 1/2 **1956** Army Sgt. Emmett Bell (Chandler) is in charge of maintaining order on an Oregon Indian reservation where missionary Joseph Holden (Bond) converted several tribes. An uprising occurs when Col. Stedlow (Bouchey) and his cavalry troop arrive to build a road through tribal land. Malone is Chandler's token love interest. **95m/C; DVD.** Jeff Chandler; Dorothy Malone; Ward Bond; Willis Bouchey; Lee Marvin; Keith Andes; Michael Ansara; **D:** George Marshall; **W:** Sam Rolfe; **C:** Harold Lipstein.

The Pillow Book **1995 (NC-17)** Greenaway's usual chilliness gives way to some true erotic heat that still keeps to arcane subjects, violence, and dazzling visuals. Japanese model Nagiko (Wu) longs for the childhood rituals enacted by her calligrapher father (Ogata) and, as an adult, she searches out lovers willing to use her body as their paper. She's unsatisfied until she meets bisexual Englishman Jerome (McGregor), who insists Nagiko write on him. But a chance connection to the past triggers Nagiko's jealousy, with tragic consequences. Title refers to the 10th-century diary "The Pillow Book of Sei Shonagon." Some subtitled Japanese dialogue. **126m/C; VHS, DVD, Blu-Ray.** *NL FR UK* Vivian Wu; Ewan McGregor; Yoshi Oida; Ken Ogata; Hideko Yoshida; Judy Ongg; Ken Mitsuishi; Yutaka Honda; Ronald Guttman; **D:** Peter Greenaway; **W:** Peter Greenaway; **C:** Sacha Vierny.

Pillow Talk 1/2 **1959** Sex comedy in which a man woos a woman who loathes him. By the way, they share the same telephone party line. Narrative provides minimal indication of the film's strengths, which are many. Classic '50s comedy with masters Day and Hudson exhibiting considerable rapport, even when fighting. Lighthearted, constantly funny. **102m/C; VHS, DVD, Blu-Ray.** Rock Hudson; Doris Day; Tony Randall; Thelma Ritter; Nick Adams; Lee Patrick; **D:** Michael Gordon; **W:** Maurice Richlin; Stanley Shapiro; **C:** Arthur E. Arling; **M:** Frank DeVol. Oscars '59: Story & Screenplay; Natl. Film Reg. '09.

Pilot No. 5 1/2 **1943** Wartime propaganda. In Java, pilot Geoge Collins (Tone) takes on a suicide mission when he flies his squadron's only airworthy plane to drop a bomb on a Japanese aircraft carrier. The pilots left behind share their stories about the airman, including how Collins' hatred of fascism led to his joining the Air Corps. **71m/B; DVD.** Franchot Tone; Gene Kelly; Van Johnson; Alan Baxter; Dick Simmons; Marsha Hunt; Steven Geray; **D:** George Sidney; **W:** David Hertz; **C:** Paul Vogel; **M:** Lennie Hayton.

Pilot X 1/2 *Death in the Air* **1937** World War I ace Carl has been driven crazy by combat-related stress and thinks every former wartime pilot is out to kill him. So he decides to get them first. The airmen suspects all gather in the mansion owned by shrink Dr. Norris but the body count keeps growing. **69m/B; DVD.** Leon Ames; John Carroll; Lona Andre; Henry Hall; Wheeler Oakman; Pat Somerset; Reed Howes; Gaston Glass; Hans Joby; John Elliott; **D:** Elmer Clifton; **W:** Charles Condon; **C:** James Diamond; Arthur Reed.

The Pilot's Wife **2001 (PG-13)** Kathryn Lyons (Lahti) learns that her husband Jack (Heard), a commercial airline pilot, has died in a crash over Ireland. She's angry when she discovers investigators think he caused the crash and bewildered when she finds out Jack led a double life. Accompanied by union rep Robert Hart (Scott), Kathryn heads to England and Ireland to get some answers. Shreve co-scripted the teleplay from her own novel. **89m/C; VHS, DVD.** Christine Lahti; Campbell Scott; John Heard; Alison Pill; Nigel Bennett; **D:** Robert Markowitz; **W:** Anita Shreve; Christine Berardo; **C:** Rudolf Blahacek; **M:** Lee Holdridge. **TV**

Pimp **2018 (R)** The daughter of pimp Midnight John (DMX), Wen (Palmer) was prepared from an early age to take over his business. After his murder when she was ten, she began pimping herself. By adulthood, Wen is successful and supporting both her alcoholic mother (Ellis) and her girlfriend Nikki (Ramm). When Wen's mother needs bail money, Nikki offers to prostitute herself to help pay the bills. Wen's world becomes even more complicated when the beautiful Destiny (Morgan) defects from rival pimp Kenny (Gathegi), setting off a conflict between them. The riveting feature directorial debut by Crokos recalls '70s blaxploitation films. **86m/C; DVD.** Keke Palmer; Lyrica Okano; Vanessa Morgan; Aunjanue Ellis; Edi Gathegi; **D:** Christine Crokos; **W:** Christine Crokos; **C:** Rik Zang; **M:** Alec Puro.

Pin. . . 1/2 **1988 (R)** A boy's imaginary friend assists in the slaying of various enemies. Horror effort could be worse. **103m/C; VHS, DVD.** Cynthia (Cyndy, Cindy) Preston; David Hewlett; Terry O'Quinn; Bronwen Mantel; Helene Udy; Patricia Collins; Steven Bednarski; Katie Shingler; Jacob Tierney; Michelle Anderson; **D:** Sandor Stern; **W:** Sandor Stern; **C:** Guy Defaux.

Pin Down Girls *Racket Girls; Pin Down Girl* **1951** Great schlock about girl wrestlers. **81m/B; VHS, DVD.** Clara Mortensen; Rita Martinez; Peaches Page; Timothy Farrell; **D:** Robert Derteno; **W:** Robert Derteno; **C:** William C. Thompson.

Pin-Up Girl **1944** Grable plays a secretary who becomes an overnight sensation during WWII. Loosely based on her famous pinup poster that was so popular at the time, the movie didn't even come close to being as successful. The songs aren't particularly memorable, although Charlie Spivak and his Orchestra perform. **83m/C; VHS, DVD, Blu-Ray.** Betty Grable; Martha Raye; Jon Harvey; Joe E. Brown; Eugene Pallette; Mantan Moreland; **D:** H. Bruce Humberstone; **C:** Ernest Palmer.

Pina **2011 (PG)** In this tribute, Wenders uses 3D technology to highlight German modern dance choreographer Pina Bausch and her company, the Tanztheater Wuppertal. Although Wenders and Bausch discussed their collaboration, Bausch died in 2009 before the film went into production and the film emphasizes her work rather than a biography about her. German with subtitles. **106m/C; DVD, Blu-Ray.** *FR GE* **D:** Wim Wenders; **W:** Wim Wenders; **C:** Helene Louvart; Joerg Widmer; **M:** Thomas Hanreich.

Pineapple Express **2008 (R)** After scoring some super-robust dope—the "Pineapple Express" of the title—from his buddy/dealer Saul (a high-spirited Franco), process server/burnout Dale (Rogen, also a co-writer) heads to subpoena Ted (Cole), who coincidentally is Saul's supplier. Panicked by the sight of a cop car outside the house, Dale catches sight of Ted and corrupt policewoman Carol (Perez) in the middle of a murder. When Ted makes the reefer connection, the constantly stoned buddies end up on the run. Think Cheech and Chong, but with more consistent laughs and lots of action-movie violence. And explosions. **111m/C; DVD, Blu-Ray, UMD, On Demand.** Seth Rogen; James Franco; Gary Cole; Rosie Perez; Amber Heard; James Remar; Bill Hader; Danny McBride; Nora Dunn; Kevin Corrigan; Ed Begley, Jr.; Bobby Lee; Craig Robinson; Jack Kehler; Ken Jeong; **D:** David Gordon Green; **W:** Seth Rogen; Evan Goldberg; **C:** Tim Orr; **M:** Graeme Revell.

Pinero **2001 (R)** Change of pace role for Bratt. Although he physically did not resemble the Puerto Rican poet/playwright/actor Miguel Pinero, Bratt gives a dynamic performance as the street smart hustler/heroin addict who died at age 40 in 1988. An ex-con who did time at Sing-Sing, Pinero put his experience to use with the Tony Award-nominated play, "Short Eyes," and was one of the founders of the Nuyorican Cafe. Film is non-chronological, which can get confusing, and few of the secondary characters have enough screen time to make strong impressions. **103m/C; VHS, DVD.** Benjamin Bratt; Talisa Soto; Giancarlo Esposito; Rita Moreno; Mandy Patinkin; Michael Irby; Michael Wright; Nelson Vasquez; Jaime Sanchez; Rome Neal; **D:** Leon Ichaso; **W:** Leon Ichaso; **C:** Claudio Chea.

Ping! **1999 (PG)** Silly family comedy that gets an extra half-bone from the Hound for being about a dog—in this case, smart little chihuahua Ping who's been rescued from the pound by Ethel. And the little guard dog is not about to let a couple of inept burglars (Reinhold, Howard) cause problems on his new turf. **93m/C; VHS, DVD.** Judge Reinhold; Clint Howard; Shirley Jones; Lou Ferrigno; **D:** Chris Baugh; **W:** Albert Ruis. **VIDEO**

Ping Pong **2002** Based on the comic by Taiyo Matsumoto, this is the story of two friends (and polar opposites) who are competitive ping pong players. Peco (Yosuke Kubozuka) is arrogant and always trash talks his opponents. Smile (Arata) is a quiet player who let's his opponents win so they don't feel bad. After both are beaten soundly in a tournament they must pick themselves back up and train for their inevitable rematch with their opponents. **114m/C; DVD.** *JP* Arata; Sam Lee; Shido Nakamura; Naoto Takenaka; Mari Natsuki; Yosuke Kobuzuka; Koji Ookura; **D:** Fumihiko Sori; **W:** Kankuro Kudo; Taiyo Matsumoto; **C:** Akira Sakoh.

Ping Pong Summer **2014** The summer of 1985 was all about parachute pants, hip hop, and good times, but for shy 13-year-old Rad (Conte), it's also about ping pong. During a typically dull family vacation, Rad scuffles with the town bullies (and reigning ping pong champs), who challenge him and his new best friend (Massey) to a tabletop tournament. The shy challenger seeks out the wisdom of oddball neighbor Randi Jammer (Sarandon), who turns out to be a ping pong master. In a diluted attempt to capture "Karate Kid" magic, director Tully plays it too safe, serving up little more than an affectionate love-letter to his days on the pier. **92m/C; DVD, Blu-Ray.** Marcello Conte; Myles Massey; Susan Sarandon; Lea Thompson; John Hannah; Emmi Shockley; Joseph McCaughtry; **D:** Michael Tully; **W:** Michael Tully; **C:** Wyatt Garfield; **M:** Michael Montes.

Pink Cadillac 1/2 **1989 (PG-13)** A grizzled, middle-aged bondsman is on the road, tracking down bail-jumping crooks. He helps the wife and baby of his latest target escape from her husband's more evil associates. Eastwood's performance is good and fun to watch, in this otherwise lightweight film. **121m/C; VHS, DVD.** Clint Eastwood; Bernadette Peters; Timothy Carhart; Michael Des Barres; William Hickey; John Dennis Johnston; Geoffrey Lewis; Jim Carrey; Tiffany Gail Robinson; Angela Louise Robinson; **D:** Buddy Van Horn; **W:** John Eskow; **M:** Steve Dorff.

The Pink Chiquitas **1986 (PG-13)** Sci-fi spoof about a detective battling a mob of meteorite-traveling Amazons. **86m/C; VHS, DVD.** Frank Stallone; Eartha Kitt; Bruce Pirrie; McKinlay Robinson; Elizabeth Edwards; Claudia Udy; **D:** Anthony Currie.

The Pink Conspiracy **2007** David thinks his girlfriend Jamie is cheating on him so he follows her and discovers the truth is worse. She has teamed up with his ex-girlfriends to make David's life miserable. Since David doesn't seem like that bad a guy and since Jamie targeted her previous boyfriend Frank before, the chicks just come across as crazy. **98m/C; DVD.** Mercedes McNab; Sarah Thompson; MacKenzie Firgens; James Russo; Chad Everett; Bradley Snedeker; Frank Krueger; **D:** Brian Scott Miller; Marc Clebanoff; **W:** Brian Scott Miller; Marc Clebanoff; **C:** Tim Otholt; **M:** Vashi Nedomansky.

Pink Flamingos **1972 (NC-17)** Divine, the dainty 300-pound transvestite, faces the biggest challenge of his/her career when he/she competes for the title of World's Filthiest Person. Tasteless, crude, and hysterical film; this one earned Waters his title as "Prince of Puke." If there are any doubts about this honor—or Divine's rep—watch through to the end to catch Divine chewing real dog excrement, all the time wearing a you-know-what-eating grin. **95m/C; VHS, DVD.** Divine; David Lochary; Mary Vivian Pearce; Danny Mills; Mink Stole; Edith Massey; Cookie Mueller; Channing Wilroy; Paul Swift; Susan Walsh; Linda Olgierson; Elizabeth Coffey; Steve Yeager; Pat Moran; George Figgs; **Nar:** John Waters; **D:** John Waters; **W:** John Waters; **C:** John Waters.

Pink Floyd: The Wall 1/2 **1982 (R)** Film version of Pink Floyd's 1979 LP, "The Wall." A surreal, impressionistic tour-de-force about a boy who grows up numb from society's pressures. The concept is bombastic and overwrought, but Geldof manages to remain somewhat likeable as the cynical rock star and the Gerald Scarfe animation perfectly complements the film. **95m/C; VHS, DVD.** *GB* Bob Geldof; Christine Hargreaves; Bob Hoskins; James Laurenson; Eleanor David; Kevin McKeon; David Bingham; Jenny Wright; Alex McAvoy; Nell Campbell; Joanne Whalley; **D:** Alan Parker; **W:** Roger Waters; **C:** Peter Biziou; **M:** Michael Kamen; David Gilmour; Roger Waters.

The Pink Panther **1964** Bumbling, disaster-prone inspector invades a Swiss ski resort and becomes obsessed with capturing a jewel thief hoping to lift the legendary "Pink Panther" diamond. Said thief is also the inspector's wife's lover, though the inspector doesn't know it. Slick slapstick succeeds on strength of Sellers' classic portrayal of Clouseau, who accidentally destroys everything in his path while speaking in a funny French accent. Followed by "A Shot in the Dark," "Inspector Clouseau" (without Sellers), "The Return of the Pink Panther," "The Pink Panther Strikes Again," "Revenge of the Pink Panther," "Trail of the Pink Panther," and "Curse of the Pink Panther." Memorable theme supplied by Mancini. **113m/C; VHS, DVD, Blu-Ray.** *GB* Peter Sellers; David Niven; Robert Wagner; Claudia Cardinale; Capucine; Brenda de Banzie; **D:** Blake Edwards; **W:** Blake Edwards; **C:** Philip H. Lathrop; **M:** Henry Mancini. Natl. Film Reg. '10.

The Pink Panther **2006 (PG)** Martin returns to his slapstick roots as he takes over the character of bumbling Inspector Jacques Clouseau. When soccer coach Gluant (Statham) is murdered, the Pink Panther diamond he was about to give his girlfriend, hottie pop diva Xania (Knowles), disappears. Ambitious Inspector Dreyfus (Kline) assigns the case to Clouseau and his partner Ponton (Reno), knowing they will botch it and he can take over and save the day. Martin maintains a ridiculous accent and leaves destruction in his wake, but the effort is wasted in a tired retread. Clive Owen has a cameo as Agent 006, spoofing superspy James Bond. **92m/C; DVD, Blu-Ray, UMD.** Steve Martin; Kevin Kline; Jean Reno; Emily Mortimer; Henry Czerny; Kristin Chenoweth; Roger Rees; Beyonce Knowles; Clive Owen; **D:** Shawn Levy; **W:** Steve Martin; Len Blum; **C:** Jonathan Brown;

George Folsey, Jr.; ***M:*** Christophe Beck; Randall Poster.

The Pink Panther 2 🦴 1/2 **2009 (PG)** Martin returns as the bumbling French inspector Clouseau to stop an international artifacts thief who's out for France's prized Pink Panther diamond. Along for the wacky ride is his new assistant Nicole (Mortimer), who's head-over-heels (literally) for the inspector. John Cleese replaces Kevin Kline as Dreyfus, Clouseau's boss, with too many other stars vying for screen time with not enough material for any of them. The sight gags and language barrier jokes are still there, and much like the first, Martin never lives up to his potential. **92m/C; Blu-Ray, On Demand.** Steve Martin; Jean Reno; Emily Mortimer; John Cleese; Andy Garcia; Alfred Molina; Aishwarya Rai; Yuki Matsuzaki; Lily Tomlin; Geoffrey Palmer; Jeremy Irons; Johnny Hallyday; ***D:*** Harald Zwart; ***W:*** Steve Martin; Scott Neustadter; Michael H. Weber; ***C:*** Denis Crossan; Rick Butler; ***M:*** Christophe Beck.

The Pink Panther Strikes Again 🦴🦴🦴 **1976 (PG)** Fifth in the series has the incompetent inspector tracking his former boss, who has gone insane and has become preoccupied with destroying the entire world. A must for Sellers buffs and anyone who appreciates slapstick. **103m/C; VHS, DVD, Blu-Ray.** *GB* Peter Sellers; Herbert Lom; Lesley-Anne Down; Colin Blakely; Leonard Rossiter; Burt Kwouk; ***D:*** Blake Edwards; ***W:*** Edwards Waldman; Frank Waldman; ***C:*** Harry Waxman; ***M:*** Henry Mancini. Writers Guild '76: Adapt. Screenplay.

Pinky 🦴🦴🦴 **1949** Early Hollywood treatment of the tragic choice made by some black Americans to pass as white in order to attain a better life for themselves and their families. The story is still relevant today. Waters and Barrymore also star, but the lead black character is portrayed by a white actress. Based on the novel "Quality" by Cyd Ricketts Sumner. **102m/B; VHS, DVD.** Jeanne Crain; Ethel Barrymore; Ethel Waters; Nina Mae McKinney; William Lundigan; ***D:*** Elia Kazan; ***W:*** Philip Dunne; Dudley Nichols; ***M:*** Alfred Newman.

Pinocchio 🦴🦴🦴🦴 **1940 (G)** Second Disney animated film featuring Pinocchio, a little wooden puppet, made with love by the old woodcarver Geppetto, and brought to life by a good fairy. Except Pinocchio isn't content to be just a puppet—he wants to become a real boy. Lured off by a sly fox, Pinocchio undergoes a number of adventures as he tries to return safely home. Has some scary scenes, including Geppetto, Pinocchio, and their friend Jiminy Cricket getting swallowed by a whale, and Pleasure Island, where naughty boys are turned into donkeys. An example of animation at its best and a Disney classic that has held up over time. **87m/C; VHS, DVD, Blu-Ray.** ***V:*** Dick(ie) Jones; Cliff Edwards; Evelyn Venable; Walter Catlett; Frankie Darro; Charles (Judel, Judells) Judels; Don Brodie; Christian Rub; ***D:*** Ben Sharpsteen; Hamilton Luske; ***W:*** Aurelius Battaglia; William Cottrell; Otto Englander; Erdman Penner; Joseph Sabo; Ted Sears; Webb Smith. Oscars '40: Orig. Score, Song ("When You Wish Upon a Star"); Natl. Film Reg. '94.

Pinocchio 🦴 1/2 **2002 (G)** Benigni's faithful version of Carlo Collodi's Italian fairy tale suffers from his self-consciously manic and forced portrayal of the little wooden boy. Set against this wall-to-wall performance, the rest of the proceedings seem lifeless and dull, with the exception of the opening sequence (before Benigni shows up). One thing that is not a problem is Spinotti's wonderful cinematography. There's the original version in Italian and a disastrous English-dubbed version. **108m/C; VHS, DVD.** *IT* Roberto Benigni; Nicoletta Braschi; Mino Bellei; Carlo Guiffre; Peppe Barra; ***D:*** Roberto Benigni; ***W:*** Roberto Benigni; Vincenzo Cerami; ***C:*** Dante Spinotti; ***M:*** Nicola Piovani. Golden Raspberries '02: Worst Actor (Benigni).

Pinocchio's Revenge 🦴 **1996 (R)** Man murders his child and buries the body with a wooden Pinocchio puppet. Somehow before his execution, his lawyer, Jennifer Garrick (Allen), and her cute daughter Zoe (Smith) wind up with the grisly toy and Jennifer allows her daughter to keep it. Naturally, this is not a good thing. **96m/C; VHS, DVD.** Rosalind Allen; Brittany Alyse Smith; Todd Allen; Lewis Van Bergen; Aaron Lustig; Ron Canada; ***D:*** Kevin S. Tenney; ***W:*** Kevin S. Tenney; ***M:*** Dennis Michael Tenney.

Pinochet's Last Stand 🦴🦴 *Pinochet in Suburbia* **2006** In 1973, General Augusto Pinochet took control of Chile in a violent coup and ruled as a dictator for 17 years. But in 1998, in a surprise move, the elderly ex-leader (Jacobi) was arrested in Britain (where he was seeking medical treatment) and charged with crimes against humanity. Confined to a house in a London suburb, Pinochet waited in exile while government ministers vacillated and the judicial system took over. **77m/C; DVD.** *GB* Derek Jacobi; Peter Capaldi; Phyllida Law; Michael Maloney; Jessica Stevenson; Pip Torrens; Yolanda Vasquez; Anna Massey; Susan Woolridge; ***D:*** Richard Curson Smith; ***W:*** Richard Curson Smith; ***C:*** Jeff Baynes; ***M:*** Jeff Beal.

Pioneer 🦴 1/2 **2013 (R)** Obvious wannabe conspiracy thriller set in the early 1980s when enormous oil and gas deposits are discovered in the North Sea. Professional diver Petter is hired to work on a pipeline to bring the oil from below the ocean to the Norwegian coast. An accident has him questioning the perilous work because maybe it wasn't an accident after all. English and Norwegian with subtitles. **110m/C; DVD, Blu-Ray.** *NO* Aksel Hennie; Wes Bentley; Stephen Lang; Jonathan LaPaglia; Andre Eriksen; ***D:*** Erik Skjoldbjaerg; ***W:*** Erik Skjoldbjaerg; Hans Gunnarsson; ***C:*** Jallo Faber.

Pioneer Woman 🦴🦴 *Pioneers* **1973** A family encounters hostility when they set up a frontier homestead in Nebraska in 1867. Told from the feminine perspective, the tale is strewn with hurdles, both personal and natural. **74m/C; VHS, DVD.** Joanna Pettet; William Shatner; David Janssen; Helen Hunt; ***D:*** Buzz Kulik. **TV**

Pipe Dream 🦴🦴 1/2 **2002 (R)** David (Donovan) is a New York City plumber who is tired of being taken for granted by snobs. So he steals the unproduced screenplay of writer/neighbor Toni (Parker) and pretends to be a casting director with the help of industry pal R.J. (Carroll). He holds auditions for his nonexistent movie and suddenly the buzz is that the film is hot and everyone wants a piece of the action, including Toni, who feeds the clueless David appropriate showbiz lines. The cast is good but the film turns out to be mildly amusing rather than satiric. **94m/C; VHS, DVD.** Martin Donovan; Mary-Louise Parker; Kevin Carroll; Rebecca Gayheart; Peter Jacobson; Cynthia Kaplan; Tim Hopper; Guinevere Turner; Marla Sucharetza; ***D:*** John C. Walsh; ***W:*** Cynthia Kaplan; John C. Walsh; ***C:*** Peter Nelson; ***M:*** Alexander Lasarenko.

Pippi Goes on Board 🦴🦴 1/2 **1969 (G)** The fourth and last film in the Swedish series finds Pippi's father arriving one day to take her sailing to Taka-Kuka, his island kingdom. She can't bear to leave her friends and jumps off the ship to return home. The series is poorly dubbed and technically flawed, which the kids probably won't notice. Based on the books by Astrid Lindgren. Preceded by "Pippi Longstocking," "Pippi in the South Seas," and "Pippi on the Run." **83m/C; VHS, DVD, Blu-Ray.** *SW* Inger Nilsson; Maria Persson; Par Sundberg; Margot Trooger; Hans Clarin; ***D:*** Olle Hellbom; ***W:*** Astrid Lindgren; ***C:*** Kalle Bergholm; ***M:*** Christian Bruhn.

Pippi in the South Seas 🦴🦴 1/2 *Pippi Langstrump Pa de Sju Haven* **1970 (G)** Pippi, a fun-loving, independent, red haired little girl, and her two friends decide to rescue her father, who is being held captive by a band of pirates on a South Sea island. Naturally, clever Pippi saves the day. Poorly dubbed and edited. Based on the children's book by Astrid Lindgren. Follows "Pippi Longstocking" and precedes "Pippi on the Run" and "Pippi Goes on Board." **99m/C; VHS, DVD, Blu-Ray.** *SW* Inger Nilsson; Maria Persson; Par Sundberg; Beppe Wolgens; ***D:*** Olle Hellbom; ***W:*** Olle Hellbom; ***C:*** Kalle Bergholm; ***M:*** Jan Johansson.

Pippi Longstocking 🦴🦴 1/2 **1969 (G)** This little red-headed, pigtailed terror is left alone by her sailor father as he heads out to sea. Not that Pippi minds, since it gives her the chance to create havoc in her town through the antics of her pets, a monkey and a horse. Pippi's antics may amuse the kiddies but adults will find her obnoxious. Poorly dubbed and technically somewhat shaky. Based on the children's book by Astrid Lindgren. Followed by "Pippi in the South Seas," "Pippi on the Run," and "Pippi Goes on Board." **99m/C; VHS, DVD, Blu-Ray.** *SW* Inger Nilsson; Maria Persson; Par Sundberg; Margot Trooger; Hans Clarin; ***D:*** Olle Hellbom; ***W:*** Astrid Lindgren; ***C:*** Kalle Bergholm; ***M:*** Konrad Elfers.

Pippi on the Run 🦴🦴 1/2 **1970 (G)** The third film in the series finds Pippi on the trail of two friends who have run away from home. The three have many adventures before deciding home is best. Preceded by "Pippi Longstocking" and "Pippi in the South Seas," followed by "Pippi Goes on Board." Films lacks technical and dubbing skills. Based on the children's book by Astrid Lindgren. **99m/C; VHS, DVD, Blu-Ray.** *SW* Inger Nilsson; Hans Alfredson; Maria Persson; Par Sundberg; ***D:*** Olle Hellbom; ***W:*** Astrid Lindgren; ***C:*** Kalle Bergholm; ***M:*** Christian Bruhn.

Pippin 🦴🦴🦴 **1981** Video version of the stage musical about the adolescent son of Charlemagne finding true love. Adequate record of Bob Fosse's Broadway smash. Features Vereen re-creating his original Tony Award-winning role. **120m/C; VHS, DVD.** Ben Vereen; William Katt; Martha Raye; Chita Rivera; Leslie Denniston; Benjamin Rayson; ***D:*** David Sheehan; ***W:*** Roger O. Hirson; ***M:*** Stephen Schwartz. **TV**

Piranha 🦴🦴 1/2 **1995 (R)** Genetically enhanced piranha terrorize the resort community of Lost River. Scientists Paul (Katt) and Maggie (Paul) have accidentally released the vicious fishies but everyone ignores their warnings until some swimmers become dindin. Remake of Roger Corman's 1978 cult item and based on John Sayles' original screenplay. **81m/C; VHS, DVD.** Alexandra Paul; William Katt; Soleil Moon Frye; Monte Markham; Darleen Carr; James Karen; Lincoln Kilpatrick; ***D:*** Scott Levy; ***W:*** Alex Simon; ***C:*** Christopher Baffa; ***M:*** Christopher Lennertz.

Piranha 🦴🦴 1/2 **1978 (R)** A rural Texas resort area is plagued by attacks from ferocious man-eating fish which a scientist created to be used as a secret weapon in the Vietnam War. Spoofy horror film features the now-obligatory Dante film in-jokes in the background. **90m/C; VHS, DVD, Blu-Ray.** Bradford Dillman; Heather Menzies; Kevin McCarthy; Keenan Wynn; Barbara Steele; Dick Miller; Paul Bartel; John Sayles; Richard Deacon; ***D:*** Joe Dante; ***W:*** John Sayles; ***C:*** Jamie Anderson; ***M:*** Pino Donaggio.

Piranha 2: The Spawning 🦴 1/2 *Piranha 2: Flying Killers; The Spawning* **1982 (R)** Diving instructor and a biochemist seek to destroy piranha mutations that are murdering tourists at a club. Early Cameron exercise in gore tech that's a step down from original "Piranha." **88m/C; VHS, DVD, Blu-Ray.** Steve Marachuk; Lance Henriksen; Ricky Paul; Tricia O'Neil; ***D:*** James Cameron; ***W:*** H.A. Milton; ***C:*** Roberto D'Ettorre Piazzoli.

Piranha 3D 🦴🦴 **2010 (R)** What more do you need to know than babes in bikinis get chomped on in bloody, graphic 3D, by the title killer fish. This shameless exploitation flick finds the prehistoric piranha swimming through a fault line into Lake Victoria over a wild July 4th weekend that sees the town also invaded by tourists. Since becoming fish food would be bad for business, the townspeople must band together to stop the hungry critters. **88m/C; Blu-Ray, On Demand.** Elisabeth Shue; Adam Scott; Jerry O'Connell; Jessica Szohr; Dina Meyer; Cody Longo; Christopher Lloyd; ***Cameo(s):*** Ving Rhames; Richard Dreyfuss; ***D:*** Alexandre Aja; ***W:*** Alexandre Aja; Josh Stolberg; ***C:*** John R. Leonetti; ***M:*** Michael Wandmacher.

Piranha 3DD WOOF! **2011 (R)** The follow-up to Aja's 3D gore orgy make its predecessor look like a horror masterpiece. Completely worthless from its lack of a single interesting character to the fact that David Hasselhoff has difficulty playing himself believably, this is an absolute mess, a movie that gives a bad name to horror, 3D, sequels, swimming, and killer fish. The "plot" involves the titular man-eating fish being sucked into a pool complex and devouring all the women and children. Barely runs 70 minutes before ten minutes of the most painful outtakes/bloopers in film history. **83m/C; DVD, Blu-Ray, Streaming.** Danielle Panabaker; Matthew Bush; Gary Busey; Katrina Bowden; Jean-Luc Bilodeau; David Koechner; Chris Zylka; Meagan Tandy; Christopher Lloyd; Ving Rhames; ***Cameo(s):*** David Hasselhoff; ***D:*** John Gulager; ***W:*** Marcus Dunstan; Patrick Melton; Joel Soisson; ***C:*** Alexandre Lehmann; ***M:*** Elia Cmiral.

Piranhas 🦴🦴 *La paranza dei bambini* **2019** In working class Naples, Italy, a group of teenage boys form a gang with criminal aspirations. Though they are typical teens who are proficient with technology and want to impress their idols, they gradually become more deeply criminal and involved with drugs, weapons, money, and women. Led by underdog leader/mobster in the making Nicola (Di Napoli), their energy is infectious until serious life or death choices must be made. Based on Roberto Saviano's novel, the organized crime drama has similarities to gangster films like Scarface, but nowhere near the quality. Italian with subtitles. **112m/C; DVD, Blu-Ray.** Francesco Di Napoli; Viviana Aprea; Mattia Piano Del Balzo; Ciro Vecchione; Ciro Pellechia; ***D:*** Claudio Giovannesi; ***W:*** Claudio Giovannesi; Roberto Saviano; Maurizio Braucci; ***C:*** Daniele Cipri; ***M:*** Andrea Moscianese.

The Pirate 🦴🦴🦴 **1948** A traveling actor poses as a legendary pilot to woo a lonely woman on a remote Caribbean island. Minnelli always scores with this type of fare, and both Garland and Kelly make the most of the Cole Porter score. **102m/C; VHS, DVD.** Judy Garland; Gene Kelly; Walter Slezak; Gladys Cooper; George Zucco; Reginald Owen; ***D:*** Vincente Minnelli; ***C:*** Harry Stradling, Sr.

Pirate Movie 🦴🦴 1/2 **1982 (PG)** Gilbert and Sullivan's "The Pirates of Penzance" is combined with new pop songs in this tale of fantasy and romance. Feeble attempt to update a musical that was fine the way it was. **98m/C; VHS, DVD.** Kristy McNichol; Christopher Atkins; Ted Hamilton; Bill Kerr; Garry McDonald; ***D:*** Ken Annakin; ***M:*** Tony Britten. Golden Raspberries '82: Worst Director (Annakin), Worst Song ("Pumpin' and Blowin'").

Pirate Radio 🦴🦴 1/2 *The Boat That Rocked* **2009 (R)** In '60s England, Quentin (Nighy) and his crew of raucous deejays (Hoffman, Ifans, Frost) set up a ship in the North Sea to beam rock songs back to Blighty in defiance of uptight government minister Dormandy (Branagh). Most of the action revolves around the hijinks of the outlaw band and the story drags at times, but the excellent cast and soundtrack keeps the good times rolling. Released in Great Britain as "The Boat That Rocked," this love letter to rock and roll was trimmed substantially for American release. **134m/C; DVD, Blu-Ray.** *US UK* Philip Seymour Hoffman; Bill Nighy; Rhys Ifans; Nick Frost; Kenneth Branagh; Rhys Darby; Katherine Parkinson; Tom Wisdom; Thomas Sturridge; Jack Davenport; Emma Thompson; Tom Brooke; Chris O'Dowd; ***D:*** Richard Curtis; ***W:*** Richard Curtis; ***C:*** Danny Cohen.

The Pirates! Band of Misfits 🦴🦴 1/2 *The Pirates! In an Adventure with Scientists!* **2012 (PG)** Aardman Animation tackles the high seas with this stop-motion 3-D adaptation of one of Gideon Defoe's books. The Pirate Captain (Grant) leads a ragtag crew on an adventure to win The Pirate of the Year Award that involves Queen Victoria (Staunton), Charles Darwin (Tennant), a clever chimp, and the last dodo bird on Earth. Smart, funny, and never talking down to its target audience, this is great family entertainment. **88m/C; DVD, Blu-Ray.** *UK US* ***V:*** Hugh Grant; Martin Freeman; Imelda Staunton; David Tennant; Jeremy Piven; Salma Hayek; Brian Blessed; Anton Yelchin; Brendan Gleeson; Lenny Henry; ***D:*** Peter Lord; Jeff Newitt; ***W:*** Gideon Defoe; ***C:*** Frank Passingham; ***M:*** Theodore Shapiro.

Pirates of Blood River 🦴🦴 **1962** Pirate story is mostly land-locked since it's a low-budget Hammer production but Lee gets a lot of mileage out of his role as the evil, eye-patch wearing LaRoche. The pirate leader forces exiled Jonathan Standing (Mathews) to take him to his island home to find reputed buried treasure. LaRoche kills many in his search and Standing finally escapes to gather support. **87m/C; DVD, Blu-Ray.** *UK* Christopher Lee; Kerwin Mathews; Glenn Corbett; Marla Landi; Oliver Reed; Andrew

Keir; Michael Ripper; Peter Arne; *D:* John Gentil; *W:* John Gentil; John Hunter; *C:* Arthur Grant; *M:* Gary Hughes.

The Pirates of Capri 🦴 1/2 *The Masked Pirate* **1949** Swashbuckler has Count Amalfi (Hayward) using his secret identity as Captain Sirocco to protect the peasants in Naples from the excesses of the oppressive aristocracy. Naturally, the pirate is hunted--in this case by evil Baron Von Holstein (Serato). **94m/B; DVD.** *IT US* Louis Hayward; Binnie Barnes; Mariella Lotti; Massimo Serato; Alan Curtis; Mikhail Rasumny; *D:* Edgar G. Ulmer; *W:* Giorgio Moser; *C:* Anchise Brizzi; *M:* Nino Rota.

The Pirates of Penzance 🦴🦴 **1983 (G)** Gilbert and Sullivan's comic operetta is the story of a band of fun-loving pirates, their reluctant young apprentice, the "very model of a modern major general," and his lovely daughters. An adaptation of Joseph Papp's award-winning Broadway play. **112m/C; VHS, DVD, Blu-Ray.** Kevin Kline; Angela Lansbury; Linda Ronstadt; Rex Smith; George Rose; *D:* Wilford Leach.

The Pirates of Silicon Valley 🦴🦴 1/2 **1999** Fact-based docudrama covering the early days of Apple and Microsoft. The partners in both companies tend to get the short end of the story as the telepic focuses on charismatic manipulator Steve Jobs (Wyle) and shrewd geek kingpin Bill Gates (Hall), who not only kept an eye on each other but outmaneuvered industry giants such as IBM and Xerox to virtually begin the personal computer market. **95m/C; VHS, DVD.** Noah Wyle; Anthony Michael Hall; Joey Slotnick; John DiMaggio; Josh Hopkins; Gema Zamprogna; Allan Royal; Bodhi (Pine) Elfman; Gailard Sartain; *D:* Martyn Burke; *W:* Martyn Burke; *C:* Ousama Rawi; *M:* Frank Fitzpatrick. **CABLE**

The Pirates of Somalia 🦴🦴 1/2 **2017 (R)** A dramatic look at a Canadian man's quest to become a respected journalist by courting danger in Somalia, based on the memoir by Jay Bahadur. Though Jay (Peters) longs to become a journalist like his heroes Bob Woodward and Carl Bernstein, he lives in his parents' basement. After a chance meeting with respected journalist Seymour Toubin (Pacino), Jay travels to Somalia in 2008 to make a name for himself by writing a first-hand account of the pirates coming from that country. By doing so, he provides previously unknown information on them. Strong performances by Somali actors add to the realism of the film. **116m/C; DVD, Blu-Ray.** Evan Peters; Al Pacino; Melanie Griffith; Barkhad Abdi; Coral Pena; *D:* Bryan Buckley; *W:* Bryan Buckley; *C:* Scott Henriksen; *M:* Andrew Feltenstein; John Nau.

Pirates of the Caribbean: At World's End 🦴🦴 1/2 **2007 (PG-13)** Familiar heroes and villains band together to fight even worse villains, perform rescues, and serve up 168 minutes of non-stop spectacle. Lord Cutler Beckett (Hollander) and tentacle-faced Davy Jones (Nighy) are trying to wipe out pirates and only Captain Jack Sparrow (Depp), Will (Bloom), and Elizabeth (Knightley) can stop him. Captain Barbossa (Rush, who steals every scene) is back, Captain Jack's swallowed by a sea monster, and Keith Richards is his dad. The plot is largely nonsensical and much is lost to the hectic pace and CGI effects. Still, the swashbuckling and action are excellent, and it all adds up to a fun, if overstuffed, mess of a movie. **168m/C; DVD, Blu-Ray.** Johnny Depp; Keira Knightley; Orlando Bloom; Geoffrey Rush; Bill Nighy; Chow Yun-Fat; Jack Davenport; Stellan Skarsgard; Jonathan Pryce; Naomie Harris; Tom Hollander; Kevin McNally; Mackenzie Crook; Martin Klebba; Lee Arenberg; Marshall Manesh; *D:* Gore Verbinski; *W:* Terry Rossio; Ted Elliott; *C:* Dariusz Wolski; *M:* Hans Zimmer.

Pirates of the Caribbean: Dead Man's Chest 🦴🦴 1/2 **2006 (PG-13)** The second installment of Disney's amusement-park-ride-turned-flick finds Capt. Jack Sparrow (Depp) swishing and swashbuckling in and out of one perilous predicament after another. This time he must contend with a ghost ship full of half-men/half-sea creatures in an attempt to repay a debt. Depp hams one scene more than the next and the pic seems to aspire merely to showing off the tens of millions likely spent on CGI and special effects. Somewhat effective follow-up doesn't have the charm of the first. This and the third installment were shot back-to-back. **150m/C; DVD, Blu-Ray.** Johnny Depp; Orlando Bloom; Keira Knightley; Stellan Skarsgard; Bill Nighy; Naomie Harris; Jack Davenport; Jonathan Pryce; Kevin McNally; Tom Hollander; Mackenzie Crook; Lee Arenberg; Alex Norton; David Bailie; Martin Klebba; David Schofield; *D:* Gore Verbinski; *W:* Ted Elliott; Terry Rossio; *C:* Dariusz Wolski; *M:* Hans Zimmer. Oscars '06: Visual FX; British Acad. '06: Visual FX.

Pirates of the Caribbean: Dead Men Tell No Tales 🦴 **2017 (PG-13)** The fifth installment has Captain Jack (Depp, duh) and this flick's designated nemesis, Captain Armando Salazar (Bardem), vying for the Trident of Poseidon so Salazar can undo his undead crew's curse and kill all the other pirates, or something. A feisty female astronomer (Scodelario) and Will Turner's kid (Thwaites) play straight men for Depp's mugging. At this point, no one should really care, because it's clear that the writers and directors don't. Bardem brings the only spark of life to the proceedings. **129m/C; DVD, Blu-Ray.** Johnny Depp; Orlando Bloom; Kaya Scodelario; Javier Bardem; Geoffrey Rush; *D:* Joachim Ronning; Espen Sandberg; *W:* Jeff Nathanson; *C:* Paul Cameron; *M:* Geoff Zanelli.

Pirates of the Caribbean: On Stranger Tides 🦴 1/2 **2011 (PG-13)** Having tied up the romantic plots in 2007's "At World's End," the fourth flick focuses firmly on flamboyant, drunken Captain Jack Sparrow (Depp). Angelica (Cruz), the daughter of the feared pirate Blackbeard (McShane), shares a past with Captain Jack and may be using him to find the legendary Fountain of Youth. A litany of overdone, exaggerated special effects action tries to mask a predictable and drawn out storyline. It seems it might be time for the Captain to sail out to sea, though it might not be the end of the series. **136m/C; DVD, Blu-Ray.** Johnny Depp; Penelope Cruz; Ian McShane; Geoffrey Rush; Kevin McNally; Sam Claflin; Richard Griffiths; Gemma Ward; Dame Judi Dench; *D:* Rob Marshall; *W:* Ted Elliott; Terry Rossio; *C:* Dariusz Wolski; *M:* Hans Zimmer.

Pirates of the Caribbean: The Curse of the Black Pearl 🦴🦴🦴 **2003 (PG-13)** Yes, the film was inspired by the Disney theme park ride. Star Depp swashes his buckle with addled glee as pirate captain Jack Sparrow—a cross, Depp said, between Keith Richards and Pepe Le Pew—whose ship has been commandeered by Capt. Barbossa (Rush, having an equally good teeth-gnashing time). He and his crew are cursed and need a gold medallion, unwittingly held by feisty Governor's daughter Elizabeth (Knightley), to break the spell. This involves kidnapping the girl and a rescue mission led by her true love, blacksmith Will (Bloom), and Sparrow. A few too many plot twists and extended sword fights but the action and humor keep things moving. **134m/C; DVD, Blu-Ray, UMD.** Johnny Depp; Geoffrey Rush; Orlando Bloom; Keira Knightley; Jonathan Pryce; Jack Davenport; Kevin McNally; Zoe Saldana; Treva Etienne; Lee Arenberg; Trevor Goddard; David Bailie; Mackenzie Crook; Isaac C. Singleton, Jr.; Brye Cooper; *D:* Gore Verbinski; *W:* Ted Elliott; Terry Rossio; *C:* Dariusz Wolski; *M:* Klaus Badelt. British Acad. '03: Actor (Depp), Makeup; Screen Actors Guild '03: Actor (Depp).

Pirates of the Coast 🦴 1/2 **1961** A Spanish naval commander teams up with a group of pirates to even the score with an evil governor during the 1500s. **102m/C; VHS, DVD.** Lex Barker; Estella Blain; Livio Lorenzon; Liana Orfei; *D:* Domenico Paolella.

Pirates of the Seven Seas 🦴 1/2 *Sandokan, Pirate of Malaysia* **1962** In the further tales of "Sandokan the Great," the pirate hero helps save the heroine's father from an evil English Imperialist. **90m/C; VHS, DVD, Streaming.** Steve Reeves; Jacqueline Sassard; Andrea Bosic; *D:* Umberto Lenzi.

Pirates of Tortuga 🦴 1/2 **1961** Bland action flick. The British government recruits Captain Bart Paxton (Scott) to find and take out notorious pirate captain Henry Morgan (Stephens). Things are slightly complicated by a female stowaway. **97m/C; DVD.** Ken Scott; Robert Stephens; Leticia Roman; Rafer Johnson; John Richardson; *D:* Robert D. Webb; *W:* Jesse Lasky, Jr.; Melvin Levy; *C:* Ellis W. Carter; *M:* Paul Sawtell; Bert Shefter.

Pirates of Treasure Island 🦴 **2006 (PG-13)** Technically inspired by the Robert Louis Stevenson story of the same name, it veers wildly off course as usual with Asylum's movies. After all, the novel didn't include a giant alien-looking bug. The story is mostly the same as any other version of 'Treasure Island' but falls short of its intended attempt at spoofing it, as well as featuring less-than-competent acting performances. **82m/C; DVD.** Lance Henriksen; Tom Nagel; Rebekah Kochan; Rhett Giles; Justin L. Jones; *D:* Leigh Scott; *W:* Leigh Scott; Carlos De Los Rios; *C:* Steven Parker; *M:* Mel Lewis.

The Pirates Who Don't Do Anything: A VeggieTales Movie 🦴🦴 **2008 (G)** Three produce-aisle pals—a cucumber, a gourd, and a giant grape—find themselves transformed from dinner theater waiters into 17th-century pirates charged with the task of saving a princess and thwarting the bad guy. The faith-based, kid-friendly franchise backs off on its usual religiosity in favor of a more Oz-like tone to convey the virtues of moral fortitude, but the young'uns will be too into the bright colors, silly voices, and funny faces to care about the message, let alone the fact that the characters are fresh from the middle strata of the food pyramid. **85m/C; On Demand.** *V:* Cam(eron) Clarke; Mike Nawrocki; Phil Vischer; Laura Gerow; Yuri Lowenthal; *M:* Kurt Heinecke.

Pistol: The Birth of a Legend 🦴🦴 1/2 **1990 (G)** Biography of "Pistol" Pete Maravich, the basketball star who defied age limitations in the 1960s to play on his varsity team. **104m/C; VHS, DVD, Blu-Ray.** Adam Guier; Nick Benedict; Boots Garland; Millie Perkins; *D:* Frank C. Schroeder; *W:* Darrel A. Campbell.

Pistol Whipped 🦴 **2008 (R)** Seagal lumbers through with his usual inexpressiveness. Alcoholic ex-cop Matt has a gambling problem and big debts. So when a stranger (Henriksen) offers to take care of Matt's money issues in exchange for his assassinating some mobsters, he's not as unwilling as you might imagine. Of course, it's just not that simple. The real problem is that there's not enough Henriksen onscreen. **96m/C; DVD.** Steven Seagal; Lance Henriksen; Paul Calderon; Blanchard Ryan; Renee Goldsberry; Lydia Grace Jordan; *D:* Roel Reine; *W:* J.D. Zeik; *C:* Richard Crudo; *M:* Jerry Brunskill.

The Pit 🦴 1/2 **1981 (R)** Autistic boy gets his chance for revenge. The townspeople who humiliate him are in for a surprise after he stumbles across a huge hole in the forest, at the bottom of which are strange and deadly creatures. **96m/C; VHS, DVD, Blu-Ray.** Sammy Snyders; Sonja Smits; Jeannie Elias; Laura Hollingsworth; *D:* Lew Lehman.

The Pit and the Pendulum 🦴🦴🦴 **1961** A woman and her lover plan to drive her brother mad, and he responds by locking them in his torture chamber, which was built by his loony dad, whom he now thinks he is. Standard Corman production only remotely derived from the classic Poe tale, with the cast chewing on a loopy script. A landmark in Gothic horror. **80m/C; VHS, DVD, Blu-Ray.** Vincent Price; John Kerr; Barbara Steele; Luana Anders; Antony Carbone; Charles Victor; Lynn Bernay; Patrick Westwood; *D:* Roger Corman; *W:* Richard Matheson; *C:* Floyd Crosby; *M:* Les Baxter.

The Pit & the Pendulum 🦴🦴 1/2 **1991 (R)** Retelling of the classic Poe short story, mixed with his "A Cask of Amantillado" and set during the Spanish Inquisition. Great special effects and professional scary guy, Lance Henriksen. **97m/C; VHS, DVD.** Lance Henriksen; Rona De Ricci; Jonathan Fuller; Jeffrey Combs; Tom Towler; Stephen Lee; Frances Bay; Oliver Reed; *D:* Stuart Gordon; *W:* Dennis Paoli; *M:* Richard Band.

The Pit and the Pendulum 🦴 *Edgar Allan Poe's the Pit and the Pendulum* **2009** Yeah, there's a pendulum because crazy scientist/dominatrix Divay is obsessed with clocks but that's as close to Poe as it gets. Another of director DeCoteau's 'underwear acting' flicks has his scantily-clad group of college students volunteering for a hypnosis experiment at a creepy house that used to be an insane asylum. The experiments are all about surviving pain but Divay isn't too concerned if her subjects actually do survive. **86m/C; DVD.** Lorielle New; Stephen Hansen; Jason-Shane Scott; Danielle Demski; Tom Sandoval; Amy Paffrath; Bart Voitila; *D:* David DeCoteau; *W:* Simon Savory; *C:* Howard Wexler; *M:* Jerry Lambert. **VIDEO**

Pit Fighter 🦴🦴 **2005 (R)** A pit fighter suffering from amnesia, now living in Mexico, comes under the gun once old enemies find out he's not dead. Over-the-top low budget fight flick manages to pack a decent punch/dropkick combo. Its exaggerated style whoops its doofus plot. **84m/C; DVD.** Steven Bauer; Stephen Graham; Stana Katic; Dominiquie Vandenberg; *D:* Jesse Johnson; *W:* Jesse Johnson; *C:* Robert Hayes; *M:* Marcello De Francisci. **VIDEO**

Pit of Darkness 🦴 1/2 **1961** Safe designer Richard Logan is found unconscious and has no memory of the previous three weeks. A safe his firm installed in a country house has been opened and its contents are missing. Accused of helping the thieves, Richard and his worried wife Julie try to discover the truth. **76m/B; DVD.** *GB* William Franklyn; Moira Redmond; Bruno Barnabe; Leonard Sachs; Nigel Green; Bruce Beeby; *D:* Lance Comfort; *W:* Lance Comfort; *C:* Basil Emmott; *M:* Martin Slavin.

Pit Stop 🦴🦴🦴 **1967** On the DVD commentary track, director Jack Hill admits that he made this movie quickly to capitalize on the short-lived phenomenon of figure-8 racing, where the shape of the track guarantees many crashes. Brian Donlevy is the promoter who involves young racers Sid Haig and Dick Davalos in his plans. **91m/B; DVD, Blu-Ray.** Brian Donlevy; Richard (Dick) Davalos; Ellen Burstyn; Sid Haig; Beverly Washburn; *D:* Jack Hill; *W:* Jack Hill; *C:* Austin McKinney.

Pitch Black 🦴🦴🦴 **2000 (R)** Scary scifier with some familiar elements. Freak meteor storm causes a spaceship to make a crash landing on an unknown planet with three suns and apparently no life. Hah! In this version of "they only come out at night," the survivors discover that very nasty hunting creatures attack after dark—and the planet is in for a total eclipse. Diesel gives a hard-ass performance as a convicted murderer who has nothing to lose. Shot in Queensland, Australia. **108m/C; VHS, DVD, Blu-Ray, UMD, HD-DVD.** Vin Diesel; Radha Mitchell; Cole Hauser; Keith David; Lewis Fitz-Gerald; John Moore; Simon Burke; Claudia Black; Rhiana Griffith; *D:* David N. Twohy; Jim Wheat; Ken Wheat; *W:* David N. Twohy; *C:* David Eggby; *M:* Graeme Revell.

Pitch Perfect 🦴🦴 1/2 **2012 (PG-13)** It's easier to swallow a formulaic movie when the performances are this charismatic and the musical numbers are charming and engaging. The remarkably camera-friendly Kendrick plays Beca, a girl who unites the many cliques at her new college through an a cappella singing group. Like the best films of this type, director Moore's comedy never takes itself overly seriously, recognizing that movies about singing competitions work best with their musical tongue firmly in their cheek. Could have been a little smarter and more genre-busting, but it's too catchy to notice while it's playing. **112m/C; DVD, Blu-Ray.** Anna Kendrick; Rebel Wilson; Brittany Snow; Adam Devine; Anna Camp; Alexis Knapp; Freddie Stroma; Elizabeth Banks; Christopher Mintz-Plasse; *D:* Jason Moore; *W:* Kay Cannon; *C:* Julio Macat; *M:* Christophe Beck.

Pitch Perfect 2 🦴 1/2 **2015 (PG-13)** The first pic became a massive hit on DVD and cable, largely through the likable performance from Kendrick as the little acapella singer who could. The sequel, which made a fortune and marked the directorial debut of actress Banks, makes a miscalculation by going more "Mean Girls," unnecessarily mocking its characters in a way that sounds fake. The plot? It's unessential but it has something to do with the Bellas, led by Kendrick, losing their right to perform status after a horrible show and competing to get it back. **115m/C; DVD, Blu-Ray.** Anna Kendrick; Rebel Wilson; Hailee Steinfeld; Brittany Snow;

Skylar Astin; *D:* Elizabeth Banks; *W:* Kay Cannon; *C:* Jim Denault; *M:* Mark Mothersbaugh.

Pitch Perfect 3 🦴🦴 1/2 **2017 (PG-13)** The ambitious final film in the trilogy features the Barden Bellas experiencing misadventures during an international tour. Though all the Bellas, except Emily (Steinfeld), are out of school, each woman is struggling in their post-college life. Beca (Kendrick) has quit her job, Fat Amy (Wilson) has never had a job, and Chloe (Snow) is making plans to attend vet school. To delay adulthood, they agree to a three-country USO tour where the Bellas find themselves competing with the other acts involved. A stretch into action is challenging, but the strong cast still has the singing chops and comic timing to make it work. **93m/C; DVD, Blu-Ray.** Anna Kendrick; Rebel Wilson; Brittany Snow; Anna Camp; Hailee Steinfeld; *D:* Trish Sie; *W:* Kay Cannon; Mike White; *C:* Matthew Clark; *M:* Christopher Lennertz.

Pittsburgh 🦴🦴 **1942** Slow-moving drama about a love triangle combined with class differences. Dietrich loves Wayne, but he's more interested in the coal and steel business, so rival Scott steps in. Although limited by standard plot, picture works because of excellent performances by leads. Based on a screen story by George Owen and Tom Reed. **98m/B; DVD, Blu-Ray.** Marlene Dietrich; Randolph Scott; John Wayne; Frank Craven; Louise Allbritton; Shemp Howard; Thomas Gomez; Ludwig Stossel; *D:* Lewis Seiler; *W:* Kenneth Gamet; Tom Reed; John Twist.

Pittsburgh 🦴 1/2 **2006** Actor Goldblum (playing himself) agrees to do a two-week regional theater production of "The Music Man" in his Pennsylvania hometown, because he's in love with the young actress (Wreford) who's cast as Marion the Librarian. He drags a bunch of friends into the production as well and, since Goldblum is hardly a natural for the singing/dancing title role, he undergoes quite a bit of humiliation before opening night. **84m/C; DVD.** Jeff Goldblum; Illeana Douglas; Ed Begley, Jr.; Moby; Catherine Wreford; Richard Sabellico; *D:* Christopher Bradley; Kyle LaBrache; *C:* Christopher Bradley; Kyle LaBrache; *M:* David Byrne.

Pixels 🦴 1/2 **2015 (PG-13)** Sandler stars as Brenner, a former video game champion called in to save the planet when an alien race misinterprets footage of '80s video games as threats of war and attacks in kind, sending down giant Pac-Man characters, Donkey Kong, and other iconic gaming nightmares. Brenner recruits a team of unlikely adults, who were hardcore video arcade players in the 1980s (including Gad, James, and Monaghan) to save the day. This short film idea's upgrade to action comedy feature might be painful and insulting to some, but others might enjoy the throwback gamer humor. **106m/C; DVD, Blu-Ray, Streaming.** Adam Sandler; Peter Dinklage; Kevin James; Michelle Monaghan; Josh Gad; *D:* Chris Columbus; *W:* Timothy Dowling; Tim Herlihy; *C:* Amir M. Mokri; *M:* Henry Jackman.

Pixote 🦴🦴🦴🦴 *Pixote: A Lei do Mais Fraco* **1981** Wrenching, documentary-like account of an orphan-boy's life on the streets in a Brazil metropolis. Graphic and depressing, it's not for all tastes but nonetheless masterfully done. In Portuguese with English subtitles. **127m/C; VHS, DVD.** *BR* Fernando Ramos Da Silva; Marilia Pera; Jorge Juliao; Gilberto Moura; Jose Nilson dos Santos; Edilson Lino; *D:* Hector Babenco; *W:* Hector Babenco; *C:* Rodolfo Sanchez; *M:* John Neschling. L.A. Film Critics '81: Foreign Film; N.Y. Film Critics '81: Foreign Film; Natl. Soc. Film Critics '81: Actress (Pera).

Pizza 🦴 1/2 **2005** This pizza has a lot of extra cheese. An overweight misfit, Cara-Ethyl (Sparks) throws herself an 18th birthday party, but none of the guests show up. Finally, pizza delivery guy Matt (Embry) arrives. Maybe he feels sorry for her, 'cause Matt invites C-E to come along on his pizza runs. Misadventure and strangeness ensue while the two bond. **82m/C; DVD.** Kylie Sparks; Ethan (Randall) Embry; Julie Hagerty; Joey Kern; Alexis Dziena; Mary Birdsong; Marylouise Burke; Richard Easton; Miriam Shor; Judah Friedlander; *D:* Mark Christopher; *W:* Mark Christopher; *C:* Ken Ferris; *M:* John Kimbrough.

Pizza Man 🦴 1/2 **1991 (PG-13)** Pizza deliveryman Elmo Bunn is minding his own business, delivering an extra large with anchovies and sausage, when he finds himself mixed up in a political scandal. Lawton directed under alias "J.D. Athens." **90m/C; VHS, DVD, Streaming.** Bill Maher; Annabelle Gurwitch; *D:* J.F. Lawton; *W:* J.F. Lawton.

A Place at the Table 🦴🦴🦴 **2013 (PG)** Hunger is a more prominent problem in America than most people believe, and directors Jacobson and Silverbush do an admirable job of shining a light on what should be a national concern as it affects 49 million people--one fourth of those are children. Focuses on three subjects in different parts of the country to highlight the growing hunger epidemic, while also using interview footage from experts that range from nutrition policy leaders to famous chefs to Jeff Bridges. **84m/C; DVD, Blu-Ray.** Jeff Bridges; Tom Colicchio; *D:* Kristie Jacobson; Lori Silverbush; *C:* Daniel B. Gold; Kirsten Johnson; *M:* T-Bone Burnett.

The Place Beyond the Pines 🦴🦴🦴 **2013 (R)** In a misguided effort to take care of his kid with former girlfriend Romina (a striking Mendes), edgy drifter Luke (Gosling) robs banks and winds up being pursued by flawed-but-ambitious policeman Avery (Cooper). Not a standard thriller, this epic film is played out in three parts with themes as much as action, which it doesn't lack. An ambitious piece about family, fatherhood, and the mistakes we make to protect those we love. It's fascinating, perfectly acted, and riveting, making clear that the creative partnership of Gosling and director Cianfrance (2010's "Blue Valentine") is one that should continue. **141m/C; DVD, Blu-Ray.** Ryan Gosling; Bradley Cooper; Eva Mendes; Rose Byrne; Ray Liotta; Bruce Greenwood; Mahershala Ali; Ben Mendelsohn; Harris Yulin; Dane DeHaan; Emory Cohen; *D:* Derek Cianfrance; *W:* Derek Cianfrance; Ben Coccio; Darius Marder; *C:* Sean Bobbitt; *M:* Mike Patton.

A Place Called Glory 🦴🦴 *Die Holle von Manitoba* **1966** Barker comes to the aid of the local townsfolk in Glory city who have their hands full with a gang of bloodthirsty outlaws. **92m/C; VHS, DVD.** *GE SP* Lex Barker; Pierre Brice; Marianne Koch; *D:* Sheldon Reynolds; *W:* Edward Di Lorenzo; *C:* Federico G. Larraya; *M:* Angel Arteaga.

A Place Called Home 🦴🦴 1/2 **2004** Aging, widowed Tula (Ann-Margret) is going blind but is reluctant to see an eye specialist even though a social work is determining whether Tula can still live on her own. Her late husband's greedy relatives would like to put Tula in a nursing home so they can sell her valuable property. To help her out at home, Tula hires drifter Hank (Settle), who is looking for a place to settle with his young daughter. Made for the Hallmark Channel. **88m/C; DVD.** Ann-Margret; Matthew Settle; Shailene Woodley; Gary Sandy; Hunter Tylo; Sean O'Bryan; *D:* Michael Tuchner; *W:* J.P. Martin; *C:* James W. Wrenn; *M:* Joe Kraemer. **CABLE**

A Place in the Sun 🦴🦴🦴 **1951** Melodramatic adaptation of "An American Tragedy," Theodore Dreiser's realist classic about an ambitious laborer whose aspirations to the high life with a gorgeous debutante are threatened by his lower-class lover's pregnancy. Clift is magnificent in the lead, and Taylor and Winters also shine in support. Burr, however, grossly overdoes his role of the vehement prosecutor. Still, not a bad effort from somewhat undisciplined director Stevens. **120m/B; VHS, DVD.** Montgomery Clift; Elizabeth Taylor; Shelley Winters; Raymond Burr; Anne Revere; Keefe Brasselle; Shepperd Strudwick; Herbert (Hayes) Heyes; Frieda Inescort; *D:* George Stevens; *W:* Harry Brown; Michael Wilson; *C:* William Mellor; *M:* Franz Waxman. Oscars '51: B&W Cinematog., Costume Des. (B&W), Director (Stevens), Film Editing, Orig. Dramatic Score, Screenplay; AFI '98: Top 100; Directors Guild '51: Director (Stevens); Golden Globes '52: Film--Drama; Natl. Film Reg. '91.

A Place in the World 🦴🦴🦴 **1992** Returning from exile to their native Argentina during a military dictatorship, Mario and Ana (Luppi and Roth) work to help the less advantaged in their society, determined to make a difference. Story is seen as a flashback from point-of-view of the couples' son Ernesto (Batyi). Well-crafted, finely acted piece exploring political, social, and interpersonal themes. 1993 Oscar bid retracted due to controversy over country of film's origin. **120m/C; VHS, DVD.** *AR* Jose Sacristan; Federico Luppi; Cecilia (Celia) Roth; Leonor Benedetto; Gaston Batyi; Lorena Del Rio; *D:* Adolfo Aristarain; *W:* Alberto Lecchi; Adolfo Aristarain; *C:* Ricardo De Angelis; *M:* Emilio Kauderer.

Place of Execution 🦴🦴 1/2 **2009** In 1963, 13-year-old Alison goes missing and young inspector George Bennett (Ingleby) becomes obsessed with the case. Alison's bloody clothing is eventually found (but no body) and her wealthy, pervy stepfather Philip Hawkin (Wise) is convicted of her murder. Forty years later, filmmaker Catherine Heathcote (Stevenson) is making a documentary about the case with extensive interviews with the retired Bennett (Jackson) who suddenly withdraws his cooperation. Obsessive herself, Catherine starts digging deeper and discovers a miscarriage of justice may have occurred. Based on the novel by Val McDermid. **140m/C; DVD.** *GB* Juliet Stevenson; Lee Ingleby; Philip Jackson; Greg Wise; Emma Cunniffe; Tony Maudsley; David Hill; Elizabeth Day; Zoe Telford; Danny Sapani; *D:* Daniel Percival; *W:* Patrick Harbinson; *C:* Steve Lawes; *M:* The Insects. **TV**

Place Vendome 🦴🦴🦴 **1998** Deneuve stars as elegant alcoholic Marianne Malivert, who finds a new interest after her husband's (Fresson) suicide. A prominent jeweler with a shop on the fashionable Place Vendome, he was unable to confess that the business is bankrupt and his connections shady. Instead, he leaves Marianne with seven priceless diamonds that turn out to be stolen, which rekindles her business instincts (she's a former gem broker) and places her in danger. French with subtitles; originally released at 117 minutes. **105m/C; VHS, DVD.** *FR* Catherine Deneuve; Jean-Pierre Bacri; Emmanuelle Seigner; Jacques Dutronc; Bernard Fresson; Francois Berleand; Philippe Clevenot; *D:* Nicole Garcia; *W:* Nicole Garcia; Jacques Fieschi; *C:* Laurent Dailland; *M:* Richard Robbins.

Places in the Heart 🦴🦴🦴 **1984 (PG)** A young widow determines to make the best of a bad situation on a small farm in Depression-era Texas, fighting poverty, racism, and sexism while enduring back-breaking labor. Support group includes a blind veteran and a black drifter. Hokey but nonetheless moving film is improved significantly by strong performances by virtually everyone in the cast. In his debut, Malkovich shines through this stellar group. Effective dust-bowl photography by Nestor Almendros. **113m/C; VHS, DVD, Blu-Ray.** Sally Field; John Malkovich; Danny Glover; Ed Harris; Lindsay Crouse; Amy Madigan; Terry O'Quinn; Ned Dowd; Ray Baker; *D:* Robert Benton; *W:* Robert Benton; *C:* Nestor Almendros; *M:* Howard Shore. Oscars '84: Actress (Field), Orig. Screenplay; Golden Globes '85: Actress--Drama (Field); Natl. Bd. of Review '84: Support. Actor (Malkovich); N.Y. Film Critics '84: Screenplay; Natl. Soc. Film Critics '84: Support. Actor (Malkovich).

The Plague Dogs 🦴🦴 1/2 **1982** Two dogs carrying a plague escape from a research center and are tracked down in this unlikely animated film. A bit ponderous. And yes, that is Hurt's voice. From the novel by Richard Adams, author of "Watership Down." **99m/C; VHS, DVD, Blu-Ray.** *V:* John Hurt; Christopher Benjamin; Judy Geeson; Barbara Leigh-Hunt; Patrick Stewart; *D:* Martin Rosen; *W:* Martin Rosen; *M:* Patrick Gleeson.

Plague of the Zombies 🦴🦴 1/2 **1966** The local doctor in a Cornish village gets suspicious when its inhabitants begin suddenly dying off and the local squire refuses to allow any autopsies. That's because he's learned voodoo rites while staying in Haiti and is turning the dead locals into zombies. **90m/C; VHS, DVD, Blu-Ray.** *GB* Andre Morell; John Carson; Diane Clare; Alex Davion; Jacqueline Pearce; Brook Williams; Michael Ripper; Marcus Hammond; Roy Royston; *D:* John Gilling; *W:* Peter Bryan; John (Anthony Hinds) Elder; *C:* Arthur Grant; *M:* James Bernard.

Plain Dirty 🦴🦴 *Briar Patch; Killing Edgar* **2004 (R)** Abused wife Inez (Swain) has smitten local hermit Flowers (Verveen) help kill her husband (Thomas) then runs of with a rich lawyer (Urbaniak). Well, Flowers is none too pleased with that development, and sets out to vent his displeasure. Allusions to Shakespeare's MacBeth somehow work for this literate Southern Gothic tale, and the cinematography makes great use of the Virginia setting. **103m/C; VHS, DVD.** Dominique Swain; Henry Thomas; Arie Verveen; James Urbaniak; Karen Allen; Debra Monk; Blake Lindsley; *D:* Zev Berman; *W:* Christian Carion; *C:* Scott Kevan; *M:* Nathan Barr. **VIDEO**

Plain Jane 🦴🦴 1/2 **2002** In 1911, David Bruce (Whately) has just moved to London with his wife (Manville) and baby daughter. Newly prosperous, the family can afford to hire live-in maid, Jane (Cunniffe). But David begins to take too much of an interest in Jane (and doesn't realize that his grown son is also involved with her) and sexual obsession leads to murder. **75m/C; VHS, DVD.** *GB* Kevin Whately; Emma Cunniffe; Lesley Manville; Jason Hughes; Keith Barron; Celia Imrie; Corin Redgrave; *D:* John Woods; *W:* Lucy Gannon; *C:* John McGlashan; *M:* Ray Russell. **TV**

Plain Truth 🦴🦴 1/2 **2004** Lifetime movie based on the book by Jodi Picoult. Amish teenager Katie Finch is accused of killing her baby and Philadelphia defense attorney Ellie Harrison is called in to represent her. In order to get Katie out of jail, Ellie becomes her legal guardian and moves into the Fitch family home. Ellie also needs Katie to open up about her pregnancy, which Katie has been denying. **90m/C; DVD.** Mariska Hargitay; Alison Pill; Jan Niklas; Kate Trotter; Robert Bockstael; Jonathan LaPaglia; Alex McClure; *D:* Paul Shapiro; *W:* Matthew Tabak; *C:* David (Robert) A. Greene; *M:* Yves Laferriere. **CABLE**

The Plainsman 🦴🦴 1/2 **1937** Western legends Wild Bill Hickock, Buffalo Bill, and Calamity Jane team up for adventure in this big, empty venture. Just about what you'd expect from splashy director DeMille. **113m/B; VHS, DVD.** Gary Cooper; Jean Arthur; Charles Bickford; Anthony Quinn; George "Gabby" Hayes; Porter Hall; James Mason; *D:* Cecil B. DeMille; *C:* Victor Milner.

Plan B 🦴🦴 **2009** Touchingly awkward and amusing comedy set in Buenos Aires. When Bruno's girlfriend Laura dumps him for handsome Pablo, who Bruno hears is bisexual, he comes up with the strange notion of seducing Pablo so he can get Laura back. Of course Bruno thinks of himself as straight, but his plan causes an unexpected realization. Spanish with subtitles. **103m/C; DVD.** *FR* Manuel Vignau; Lucas Ferraro; Mercedes Quinteros; Ana Lucia Anthony; Carolina Stegmayer; *D:* Marco Berger; *W:* Marco Berger; *C:* Tomas Perez Silver; *M:* Pedro Irusta.

Plan 9 from Outer Space **WOOF!** *Grave Robbers from Outer Space* **1956** Two or three aliens in silk pajamas conspire to resurrect several slow-moving zombies from a cardboard graveyard in order to conquer the Earth. Spaceships that look suspiciously like paper plates blaze across the sky. Pitiful, inadvertently hilarious fright is in the running for the "dumbest movie ever made" award. Lugosi's actual screen time is under two minutes, since he had died before the film was complete. Enjoy the taller and younger replacement (the chiropractor of Wood's wife) they found for Lugosi, who remains hooded to protect his identity. **78m/B; VHS, DVD, Blu-Ray.** Bela Lugosi; Tor Johnson; Lyle Talbot; Vampira; Gregory Walcott; Tom Keene; Dudley Manlove; Mona McKinnon; Duke Moore; Joanna Lee; Bunny Breckinridge; Criswell; Carl Anthony; Paul Marco; Norma McCarty; David DeMering; Bill Ash; Conrad Brooks; Karl Johnson; Edward D. Wood, Jr.; *D:* Edward D. Wood, Jr.; *W:* Edward D. Wood, Jr.; *C:* William C. Thompson; *M:* Trevor Duncan; Van Phillips; James Stevens; Bruce Campbell.

Planes 🦴 *Disney's Planes* **2013 (PG)** A blatant, crass, commercial attempt to cash in on the still-loyal fans of Pixar's "Cars," this non-Pixar product displays all the creativity of a karaoke version by someone who can't carry a tune. Cook, whose voice grates even more in animated form, takes on the part of Dusty Crophopper, a plane with a fear of heights. Dusty must tackle his phobia, of course, when he gets to live his dream of competing in an around-the-world race. The globetrotting settings allow for the film to play better in international markets and the characters feel designed merely to sell more toys. **91m/C; DVD, Blu-Ray.** *V:* Dane Cook; Brad

Garrett; Teri Hatcher; Priyanka Chopra; Stacy Keach; John Cleese; Julia Louis-Dreyfus; Cedric the Entertainer; Roger Craig Smith; Carlos Alazraqui; *D:* Klay Hall; *W:* Jeffrey M. Howard; *M:* Mark Mancina.

Planes: Fire & Rescue 🦴 1/2 **2014 (PG)** A sequel to a film that even kids thought was pretty awful actually improves on the original, although that's the most backhanded compliment possible. In a move designed to pull heartstrings, Dusty (Cook) goes from racer to life-saver when he trains to join the squad of firefighting planes who drop water on Mother Nature when it burns. Lessons about heroism naturally follow. A strong voice cast and more of a visual personality helps, but this is still bland, by-the-number, kids' film storytelling. Your kids deserve better. **83m/C; DVD, Blu-Ray.** *V:* Dane Cook; Julie Bowen; Ed Harris; Wes Studi; Curtis Armstrong; John Michael Higgins; Hal Holbrook; Teri Hatcher; Stacy Keach; Brad Garrett; Cedric the Entertainer; *D:* Bobs Gannaway; *W:* Bobs Gannaway; Jeffrey M. Howard; *M:* Mark Mancina.

Planes, Trains & Automobiles 🦴🦴 1/2 **1987 (R)** One-joke Hughes comedy saved by Martin and Candy. Strait-laced businessman Neal Page (played straight by Martin) on the way home for Thanksgiving meets up with a oafish, bad-luck-ridden boor Del Griffith (Candy) who turns his efforts to get home upside down. Martin and Candy both turn in fine performances, and effectively straddle a thin line between true pathos and hilarious buffoonery. Bacon and McClurg, both Hughes alumni, have small but funny roles. **93m/C; VHS, DVD, Blu-Ray.** Steve Martin; John Candy; Edie McClurg; Kevin Bacon; Michael McKean; William Windom; Laila Robins; Martin Ferrero; Charles Tyner; Dylan Baker; Ben Stein; Lyman Ward; *D:* John Hughes; *W:* John Hughes; *C:* Don Peterman; *M:* Ira Newborn.

The Planet 🦴 **2006 (R)** A group of mercenaries are ambushed by aliens and crash-land on a strange planet. They quickly discover it's hostile, and somehow manifesting the ghosts of their dead comrades. You'll wish you could escape this sci-fi mess too. **80m/C; DVD.** *UK* Mike Mitchell; Patrick Wight; Scott Ironside; Shawn Paul Hastings; Steve Campbell; *D:* Mark Stirton; *W:* Mark Stirton; *C:* Mark Stirton; *M:* Nicky Fraser. **VIDEO**

Planet Burg 🦴🦴 1/2 **1962** A classic Soviet sci-fi flick about a space exploration team landing on Venus. Their job becomes a rescue mission when one of the crew is stranded. Although there are some silly moments, some good plot twists and acting make up for them. In Russian with English subtitles. **90m/C; VHS, DVD.** *RU* Vladimir Temelianov; Gennadi Vernov; Kyunna Ignatova; *D:* Pavel Klushantsev.

Planet Earth 🦴🦴 1/2 **1974** In the year 2133, a man who has been in suspended animation for 154 years is revived to lead the troops against a violent group of women (and mutants, too!). **78m/C; VHS, DVD.** John Saxon; Janet Margolin; Ted Cassidy; Diana Muldaur; Johana DeWinter; Christopher Gary; *D:* Marc Daniels.

Planet 51 🦴 1/2 **2009 (PG)** American astronaut Chuck Baker (Johnson) thinks he's the first to walk on Planet 51, but quickly discovers he's not alone. The green inhabitants are nice, suburban families who live with only one fear—being invaded by aliens. Now all Chuck wants to do is avoid capture and get his spaceship back to Earth. Luckily, friendly teen Lem (Long) helps him out when General Grawl (Oldman) and wacky scientist Kipple (Cleese) tell the locals that Chuck is out to get them and the pursuit begins. A 1950s Hollywood sci-fi idea turned into a cute vice-versa animated family cartoon loaded with '50s pop references that kids won't get. **91m/C; DVD, Blu-Ray, On Demand.** *V:* Dwayne "The Rock" Johnson; Jessica Biel; Justin Long; Seann William Scott; Gary Oldman; John Cleese; *D:* Jorge Blanco; Javier Abad; Marcos Martinez; *W:* Joe Stillman; *M:* James Seymour Brett.

Planet of Blood 🦴🦴 *Queen of Blood* **1966** Space opera about an alien vampire discovered on Mars by a rescue team. If you've ever seen the Soviet film "Niebo Zowiet," don't be surprised if some scenes look familiar; the script was written around segments cut from that film. **81m/C; VHS, DVD.** John Saxon; Basil Rathbone; Judi Meredith; Dennis Hopper; Florence Marly; Forrest J Ackerman; *D:* Curtis Harrington; *W:* Curtis Harrington; *C:* Vilis Lapenieks; *M:* Leonard Morand.

Planet of the Apes 🦴🦴🦴 1/2 **1968 (G)** Astronauts crash land on a planet where apes are masters and humans are merely brute animals. Superior science fiction with sociological implications marred only by unnecessary humor. Heston delivers one of his more plausible performances. Superb ape makeup creates realistic pseudo-simians of McDowall, Hunter, Evans, Whitmore, and Daly. Adapted from Pierre Boulle's novel "Monkey Planet." Followed by four sequels and two TV series. **112m/C; VHS, DVD, Blu-Ray.** Charlton Heston; Roddy McDowall; Kim Hunter; Maurice Evans; Linda Harrison; James Whitmore; James Daly; *D:* Franklin J. Schaffner; *W:* Rod Serling; Michael Wilson; *C:* Leon Shamroy; *M:* Jerry Goldsmith. Natl. Film Reg. '01.

Planet of the Apes 🦴🦴🦴 **2001 (PG-13)** Burton's "re-imagining" looks more to the original novel by Pierre Boulle than to the 1968 classic. Wahlberg takes over the Heston role, but without the bravado or screen presence. Roth excels as Gen. Thade, an angry militarist with a loathing for all humans and a contempt for polite ape society. All of the actors in the ape makeup do a fine job and the makeup effects, courtesy of Rick Baker, are astounding. The action moves along at a satisfyingly brisk pace and the screenplay provides plenty of clever references to the original, but without its sense of social commentary. What it does have is a twist ending that seems tacked on. **125m/C; VHS, DVD, Blu-Ray, UMD.** Mark Wahlberg; Tim Roth; Helena Bonham Carter; Michael Clarke Duncan; Paul Giamatti; Estella Warren; Cary-Hiroyuki Tagawa; David Warner; Kris Kristofferson; Erik Avari; Luke Eberl; Charlton Heston; Evan Dexter Parke; Michael Jace; *D:* Tim Burton; *W:* William Broyles, Jr.; Larry Konner; Mark Rosenthal; *C:* Philippe Rousselot; *M:* Danny Elfman. Golden Raspberries '01: Worst Remake/Sequel, Worst Support. Actor (Heston), Worst Support. Actress (Warren).

Planet of the Dinosaurs 🦴 1/2 **1980 (PG)** Survivors from a ruined spaceship combat huge savage dinosaurs on a swampy uncharted planet. **85m/C; VHS, DVD.** James Whitworth; Max (Michael) Thayer; Louie Lawless; Pamela Bottaro; Charlotte Speer; *D:* James K. Shea; *W:* Ralph Lucas.

Planet of the Vampires 🦴🦴 1/2 *The Demon Planet; The Haunted Planet; The Outlawed Planet; Planet of Blood; Planet of Terror; Planet of the Damned; Space Mutants; Terror in Space; Terrore nello Spazio; Terreur dans l'Espace* **1965** Astronauts search for missing comrades on a planet dominated by mind-bending forces. Acceptable atmospheric filmmaking from genre master Bava, but it's not among his more compelling ventures. **86m/C; VHS, DVD, Blu-Ray.** *IT SP* Barry Sullivan; Norma Bengell; Angel Aranda; Evi Marandi; Stelio Candelli; Ivan Rassimov; Fernando Villena; *D:* Mario Bava; *W:* Mario Bava; Alberto Bevilacqua; Callisto Cosulich; Louis M. Heyward; Ib Melchior; Antonio Roman; Rafael J. Salvia; *C:* Antonio Rinaldi; *M:* Gino Marinuzzi, Jr.

Planet on the Prowl 🦴 *War Between the Planets* **1965** A fiery planet causes earthly disasters, so a troop of wily astronauts try to destroy it with the latest technology. They fail, leading one sacrificial soul to do it himself. **80m/C; VHS, DVD.** *IT* Giacomo "Jack" Rossi-Stuart; Amber Collins; Peter Martellanza; John Bartha; Halina Zalewska; James Weaver; *D:* Anthony M. Dawson.

Planet Terror 🦴🦴 1/2 *Robert Rodriguez's Planet Terror; Grindhouse: Planet Terror* **2007** The better half of the Weinstein Bros. B-movie double-feature "Grindhouse." Almost every schlock-film cliche makes an appearance, which is the point, really. After a rogue military team sets loose a nerve gas that turns people into surprisingly gross zombies, it's up to El Wray (Rodriguez), his gal Cherry Darling (McGowan), and a gaggle of terrified Texans to try to stop the gas from spreading. McGowan steals the show with her M16-prosthetic leg, but the flurry of cheap thrills starts to feel... well... "cheap" after an hour or so. **105m/C; DVD, Blu-Ray.** Rose McGowan; Freddy Rodriguez; Josh Brolin; Marley Shelton; Jeff Fahey; Michael Biehn; Bruce Willis; Naveen Andrews; Julio Oscar Mechoso; Stacy "Fergie" Ferguson; Nicky Katt; Tom Savini; Carlos Gallardo; Michael Parks; Quentin Tarantino; Rebel Rodriguez; *D:* Robert Rodriguez; *W:* Robert Rodriguez; *C:* Robert Rodriguez; *M:* Graeme Revell.

Plastic 🦴🦴 1/2 **2014 (R)** Based on a true story, this caper comedy centers two hustlers who pay a steep price when they steal from the wrong man. For a long time, Sam (Spleeers) and Fordy (Poulter) have been quite successful at running a blackmail and credit card fraud scheme with other young white collar criminals. The result is a life of luxury. However, when they steal from a gangster with a sadistic streak who tracks them down, they must raise millions in two weeks to pay him back. To do so, they must complete a challenging, if not impossible, diamond heist. **102m/C; DVD, Blu-Ray, Streaming, Download.** Ed Speleers; Will Poulter; Alfie Allen; Sebastian De Souza; Ms. Emma Rigby; *D:* Julian Gilbey; *W:* Julian Gilbey; Sacha Bennett; Will Gilbey; Chris Howard; *C:* Peter Wignall; *M:* Chad Hobson.

The Plastic Age 🦴🦴 1/2 **1925** Cynthia (Bow) is a flapper college babe who likes boys and parties. She easily manages to charm naive newcomer Hugh (Keith), who pays more attention to her than his athletic career. But Cynthia's not heartless—when she sees that Hugh is ruining his chances, she decides to give him up. **73m/B; Silent; VHS, DVD.** Clara Bow; Donald Keith; Gilbert Roland; Henry B. Walthall; Mary Alden; *D:* Wesley Ruggles; *W:* Eve Unsell; Frederica Sagor; *C:* Gilbert Warrenton; Allen Siegler.

Platinum Blonde 🦴🦴🦴 **1931** Screwball comedy in which a newspaper journalist (Williams) marries a wealthy girl (Harlow) but finds that he doesn't like the restrictions and confinement of high society. Yearning for a creative outlet, he decides to write a play and hires a reporter (Young) to collaborate with him. The results are funny and surprising when Young shows up at the mansion flanked by a group of hard-drinking, fun-loving reporters. **86m/B; VHS, DVD.** Loretta Young; Robert Williams; Jean Harlow; Louise Closser Hale; *D:* Frank Capra; *W:* Jo Swerling; Dorothy Howell.

Platoon 🦴🦴🦴 1/2 **1986 (R)** A grunt's view of the Vietnam War is provided in all its horrific, inexplicable detail. Sheen is wooden in the lead, but both Dafoe and Berenger are resplendent as, respectively, good and bad soldiers. Strong, visceral filmmaking from fearless director Stone, who based the film on his own GI experiences. Highly acclaimed; considered by many to be the most realistic portrayal of the war on film. **113m/C; VHS, DVD, Blu-Ray.** Charlie Sheen; Willem Dafoe; Tom Berenger; Francesco Quinn; Forest Whitaker; John C. McGinley; Kevin Dillon; Richard Edson; Reggie Johnson; Keith David; Johnny Depp; Dale Dye; Mark Moses; Chris Pederson; David Neidorf; Tony Todd; Ivan Kane; Paul Sanchez; Corey Glover; Oliver Stone; *D:* Oliver Stone; *W:* Oliver Stone; *C:* Robert Richardson; *M:* Georges Delerue. Oscars '86: Director (Stone), Film, Film Editing, Sound; AFI '98: Top 100; British Acad. '87: Director (Stone); Directors Guild '86: Director (Stone); Golden Globes '87: Director (Stone), Film--Drama, Support. Actor (Berenger); Ind. Spirit '87: Cinematog., Director (Stone), Film, Screenplay; Natl. Film Reg. '19.

Plato's Run 🦴🦴 **1996 (R)** Ex-CIA agent agrees to free a Cuban who's been falsely imprisoned. But once the job is done, the agent learns he's been doublecrossed and the prisoner turns out to be a professional assassin. **96m/C; VHS, DVD.** Gary Busey; Roy Scheider; Steven Bauer; Jeff Speakman; *D:* James Becket; *W:* James Becket; *C:* Richard Clabaugh; *M:* Robert O. Ragland.

Play Dead 🦴 *Satan's Dog* **1981** Poor Yvonne De Carlo plays a psychotic woman who trains a dog to rip people to shreds. **89m/C; VHS, DVD, Blu-Ray.** Yvonne De Carlo; Stephanie Dunham; David Cullinane; Glenn Kezer; Ron Jackson; Carolyn Greenwood; *D:* Peter Wittman.

Play Dead 🦴 1/2 **2009** Ronnie Reno (Klein) is a washed-up action star who gets stranded in the middle of nowhere. He finds a dead FBI agent, and quickly runs afoul of the meth dealers running the town and their goober henchman. To save his own behind he calls up some acting buddies and convinces them to play DEA agents instead of, you know, calling the real DEA. **85m/C; DVD.** Chris Klein; Fred Durst; Jake Busey; Michael Beach; Paul Francis; *D:* Jason Wiles; *W:* Jason Wiles; Shem Bitterman; *C:* Mike O'Shea; *M:* Jeremy C. Grody.

Play for Me 🦴🦴 *Toca Para Mi* **2001** Punk rock drummer Carlos goes on a search for identity after his adoptive father dies. He travels to the town of his birth in the Argentine pampas and meets hooker Fabiana who helps him on his journey. Spanish with subtitles. **101m/C; VHS, DVD.** *AR* Hermes Gaido; Maria Laura Frigerio; Alejandro Fiore; Emilio Urdapilleta; *D:* Rodrigo Furth; *W:* Rodrigo Furth; Eduardo Ruderman; *C:* Paula Grandio; *M:* Fernando Manuel Dieguez.

Play Girl 🦴 1/2 **1941** Minor RKO rom com with an abrupt ending. Longtime gold-digger Grace (Francis) realizes age is catching up with her scamming abilities. She takes on young protege Ellen (Coles), who makes the mistake of falling in love with her mark, wealthy young Texas rancher Tom Dice (Ellison). Fits of conscience figure in before there's allegedly a happy ending for everyone. **76m/B; DVD.** Kay Francis; Mildred Coles; James Ellison; Nigel Bruce; Margaret Hamilton; Kane Richmond; *D:* Frank Woodruff; *W:* Jerome Cady; *C:* Nicholas Musuraca; *M:* Paul Sawtell.

Play It Again, Sam 🦴🦴🦴 1/2 **1972 (PG)** Allen is—no surprise—a nerd, and this time he's in love with his best friend's wife. Modest story line provides a framework of endless gags, with Allen borrowing heavily from "Casablanca." Bogey even appears periodically to counsel Allen on the ways of wooing women. Superior comedy isn't hurt by Ross directing instead of Allen, who adapted the script from his own play. **86m/C; VHS, DVD.** Woody Allen; Diane Keaton; Tony Roberts; Susan Anspach; Jerry Lacy; Jennifer Salt; Joy Bang; Viva; Herbert Ross; *D:* Herbert Ross; *W:* Woody Allen; *C:* Owen Roizman; *M:* Billy Goldenberg.

Play It to the Bone 🦴🦴 **1999 (R)** Vince (Harrelson) and Cesar (Banderas) are fading boxers and best friends, who unexpectedly wind up in an undercard bout against each other. Since they need to get to Vegas, and didn't think to get travel money from the promoter, Cesar's girlfriend (and Vince's ex) Grace (Davidovich) agrees to drive them. Along the way, she uses her wiles to whip up their competitive juices to use in the fight. It works, as the excessively brutal fight sequence shows. Shelton's film doesn't quite connect as it's mostly an uninteresting road movie with boxing cliches tacked onto both ends. **124m/C; VHS, DVD, Blu-Ray.** Woody Harrelson; Antonio Banderas; Lolita Davidovich; Lucy Liu; Tom Sizemore; Robert Wagner; Richard Masur; Willie Garson; Cylk Cozart; Jack Carter; *D:* Ron Shelton; *W:* Ron Shelton; *C:* Mark Vargo; *M:* Alex Wurman.

Play Misty for Me 🦴🦴🦴 **1971 (R)** A radio deejay obliges a psychotic woman's song request and suddenly finds himself the target of her obsessive behavior, which rapidly turns from seductive to murderous. Auspicious directorial debut for Eastwood, borrowing from the Siegel playbook (look for the director's cameo as a barkeep). Based on a story by Heims. **102m/C; VHS, DVD, Blu-Ray.** Jessica Walter; Donna Mills; John Larch; Irene Hervey; Jack Ging; Clint Eastwood; *Cameo(s):* Donald Siegel; *D:* Clint Eastwood; *W:* Jo Heims; Dean Riesner; *C:* Bruce Surtees; *M:* Dee Barton.

Play Nice 🦴 1/2 **1992 (R)** A detective hunts down a murderous psychopath but is shocked when he discovers his suspect is a woman—and someone he knows. Also available in an unrated version. **90m/C; VHS, DVD.** Ed O'Ross; Michael Zand; Bruce McGill; Ron Canada; Louise Robey; *D:* Terri Treas; *W:* Michael Zand; Chuck McCollum; *M:* Gary Stevan Scott.

Play the Game 🦴 1/2 **2009 (PG-13)** Multigenerational comedy with some unfortunate cringe-inducing moments. Octogenarian widower Joe (Griffith) is looking for some companionship in his retirement community but mistakenly takes the advice of his callow womanizing grandson David (Campbell). This leads to some Viagra moments better left undiscovered until Joe goes with his own instincts and woos neighbor Rose (Roberts) who happens to have a granddaughter (Sokoloff) who'll teach David a few lessons as well. **105m/C; DVD.** Andy Griffiths; Paul Campbell; Doris Roberts; Marla Sokoloff; Liz Sheridan; Clint Howard; Rance Howard; ***D:*** Marc Fienberg; ***W:*** Marc Fienberg; ***C:*** Gavin Kelly; ***M:*** Jim Latham.

Play Time **1994** Jeannie, Lindsay, and their husbands are on vacation in Palm Springs where they get up to some naughty sexual games that test the limits of friendship. Available in an unedited version at 95 minutes. **90m/C; VHS, DVD.** Monique Parent; Craig Stepp; Jennifer Burton; Elliot David; Julie Strain; Tammy Parks; Ashlie Rhey; ***D:*** Dale Trevillion; ***W:*** Mary Ellen Hanover; ***C:*** Sven Kirsten; ***M:*** Joel Derouin.

The Playaz Court **1/2 2007 (R)** An aspiring lawyer returns home and ends up playing a pickup game of basketball with his younger brother who has some hoodlum friends. One of the players is shot dead in the bathroom, the lone white man is accused of killing him, and a makeshift trial begins in the gym. **91m/C; DVD.** Arlen Escarpeta; Charles Malik Whitfield; Kirk "Sticky Fingaz" Jones; Charles Robinson; Robert David Cochrane; ***D:*** Greg Morgan; ***W:*** Robert David Cochrane; ***C:*** Jessica Gallant; ***M:*** Gregory Darryl Smith.

Playback **1/2 2012 (R)** Over-stuffed, dull teen horror. Aspiring filmmaker Julian decides to make a movie about the 1994 Diehl murders for his journalism assignment. Julian borrows the film equipment from Quinn (Hemingway), who works at a TV station, and asks him to look for news footage. Quinn watches the material himself, becomes possessed (which happened to Diehl), and goes on a killing spree starting with Julian's friends. Slater briefly plays a perv cop. **98m/C; DVD, Blu-Ray.** Johnny Pacar; Toby Hemingway; Jonathan Keltz; Jennifer Missoni; Ambyr Childers; Christian Slater; ***D:*** Michael A. (M.A.) Nickles; ***W:*** Michael A. (M.A.) Nickles; ***C:*** Mark Petersen; ***M:*** Woody Pak. **VIDEO**

The Playboys **1992 (PG-13)** In 1957 in a tiny Irish village, unmarried Tara Maguire (Wright) has a baby. Her beauty attracts lots of men, including obsessive, middle-aged Sgt. Hegarty (Finney) and Tom Castle (Quinn), an actor with a rag-tag theatrical troupe called the Playboys. Slow-moving and simple story with particularly good performances by Wright as the strong-willed Tara and Finney as Hegarty, clinging to a last chance at love and family. The Playboys' hysterically hammy version of "Gone With the Wind" is a gem. Directorial debut of Mackinnon. Filmed in the village of Redhills, Ireland, the hometown of co-writer Connaughton. **114m/C; VHS, DVD.** Albert Finney; Aidan Quinn; Robin Wright; Milo O'Shea; Alan Devlin; Niamh Cusack; Ian McElhinney; Niall Buggy; Adrian Dunbar; ***D:*** Gilles Mackinnon; ***W:*** Shane Connaughton; Kerry Crabbe; ***C:*** Jack Conroy; ***M:*** Jean-Claude Petit.

Played **2006 (R)** Dull, low-budget crime drama that the name actors seem to have done as a favor to Rossi. Ray (Rossi), the fall guy for a botched heist, gets out of prison and is hired by London crime boss Rawlings (Dotrice) to take out rival gangster Riley (Bergin) who was behind the bungled job. **87m/C; DVD.** *GB* Patrick Bergin; Roy Dotrice; Val Kilmer; Gabriel Byrne; Mick Rossi; Vinnie Jones; Anthony LaPaglia; Bruno Kirby; Joanne Whalley; Patsy Kensit; ***D:*** Sean Stanek; ***W:*** Mick Rossi; Sean Stanek; ***C:*** Michael Pavlisan; ***M:*** Danny Saber.

The Player **1/2 1992 (R)** Clever, entertaining, and biting satire of the movie industry and the greed that controls it. Robbins is dead-on as Griffin Mill, a young studio exec who becomes the chief suspect in a murder investigation. He personifies Hollywood's ethics (or lack thereof) in a performance both cold and vulnerable, as he looks for the right buttons to push and the proper back to stab. Strong leading performances are supplemented by 65 star cameos. Some viewers may be put off by the inside-Hollywood jokes, but Altman fans will love it. **123m/C; VHS, DVD, Blu-Ray.** Tim Robbins; Greta Scacchi; Fred Ward; Whoopi Goldberg; Peter Gallagher; Brion James; Cynthia Stevenson; Vincent D'Onofrio; Dean Stockwell; Richard E. Grant; Dina Merrill; Sydney Pollack; Lyle Lovett; Michael Tolkin; Randall Batinkoff; Gina Gershon; Nick Nolte; Jack Lemmon; Lily Tomlin; Marlee Matlin; Julia Roberts; Bruce Willis; Anjelica Huston; Elliott Gould; Sally Kellerman; Steve Allen; Richard Anderson; Harry Belafonte; Shari Belafonte; Karen Black; Gary Busey; Robert Carradine; James Coburn; Cathy Lee Crosby; John Cusack; Brad Davis; Peter Falk; Teri Garr; Leeza Gibbons; Scott Glenn; Jeff Goldblum; Joel Grey; Buck Henry; Kathy Ireland; Sally Kirkland; Andie MacDowell; Martin Mull; Mimi Rogers; Jill St. John; Susan Sarandon; Rod Steiger; Joan Tewkesbury; Robert Wagner; Louise Fletcher; Dennis Franz; Malcolm McDowell; Ray Walston; Rene Auberjonois; David Alan Grier; Jayne Meadows; Michael Bowen; Steve James; Brian Tochi; Natalie Strong; ***Cameo(s):*** Burt Reynolds; Cher; ***D:*** Robert Altman; ***W:*** Michael Tolkin; ***C:*** Jean Lepine; ***M:*** Thomas Newman. British Acad. '92: Adapt. Screenplay; Cannes '92: Actor (Robbins), Director (Altman); Golden Globes '93: Actor--Mus./Comedy (Robbins), Film--Mus./Comedy; Ind. Spirit '93: Film; N.Y. Film Critics '92: Cinematog., Director (Altman), Film; Writers Guild '92: Adapt. Screenplay.

Player 5150 **1/2 2008 (R)** Bookie Tony (McDonald) gives all his bettors a number and that's the one given to gambling addict Joey (Embry). He's a day-trader who likes risky investment strategies and he owes Tony a lot of money. Vegas denizen Nick (Gunton) leaves a duffle bag of cash for Joey to discreetly invest but of course he's going to put the money to another use. **91m/C; DVD.** Ethan (Randall) Embry; Bob Gunton; Christopher McDonald; Kelly Carlson; Bob Sapp; Kathleen Roberson; ***D:*** David Michael O'Neill; ***W:*** David Michael O'Neill; ***C:*** Patrice Lucien Cochet; ***M:*** Michael Muhlfriedel. **VIDEO**

Players **1/2** *Pledge of Allegiance* **2003 (R)** Star high school football player Sean (Rodriguez) dates Sophia (Marsala), the daughter of local Nevada wiseguy Salvi (Dobson). Then Sean discovers that having dad's friendship means throwing some championship games to help the sports betting line. Trouble follows. **90m/C; DVD.** Freddy Rodriguez; Peter Dobson; Rena Owen; Carmine D. Giovinazzo; Melissa Marsala; Joseph Bologna; John Doe; Theodore (Ted) Raimi; James DeBello; James Duval; ***D:*** Lee Madsen; ***W:*** Lee Madsen; ***C:*** Ben Kufrin; ***M:*** Adam Sanborne.

The Players Club **1998 (R)** Rapper-turned-auteur Ice Cube directs (from his own screenplay) this look at the seamy and steamy world of strip clubs. Diana (LisaRaye) is a single mom and college student by day and a dancer at a strip club owned by the bombastic Dollar Bill (Mac) by night. When her naive cousin Ebony (Calhoun) is lured into turning tricks by fellow stripper Ronnie (Wilson), trouble starts. Blue (Foxx) is the deejay who falls for Diana and is persuaded to act honorably by Diana's disapproving father (Williams). Ice Cube appears as a customer who inadvertently lights the fuse for the movie's climax. **103m/C; VHS, DVD.** LisaRaye; Bernie Mac; Monica Calhoun; A.J. (Anthony) Johnson; Jamie Foxx; Ice Cube; Dick Anthony Williams; Tommy (Tiny) Lister; John Amos; Faizon Love; Alex Thomas; Chrystale Wilson; Adele Givens; Larry McCoy; ***D:*** Ice Cube; ***W:*** Ice Cube; ***C:*** Malik Hassan Sayeed; ***M:*** Hidden Faces.

Playgirl Killer *Decoy for Terror* **1966** After impulsively murdering a restless model, an artist continues to kill indiscriminately, keeping his spoils on ice. Sedaka croons between kills and luxuriates poolside—seemingly oblivious to the plot of the film—while a female decoy is sent to bait the killer for the police. For adult viewers. **86m/C; VHS, DVD.** *CA* William Kerwin; Jean Christopher; Andree Champagne; Neil Sedaka; Allan Nicholls; ***D:*** Erick Santamaria.

Playin' For Love **2015** A high school basketball/romantic comedy centering on a coach who meets his match in a player's mother. For much of his career, Coach Banks (Townsend) has lead his Jackson High teams to championships following his own path. His world is turned upside down when a star player transfers to Jackson. The player's strong-willed, single mother Talisa McCoy (Richardson-Whitfield) has very specific ideas on how to make a winning team. Talisa also challenges Coach Banks' ideas on romance and how to be an ideal man. **84m/C; DVD, Streaming, Download.** Robert Townsend; Salli Richardson-Whitfield; Esai Morales; Jenifer Lewis; Lawrence-Hilton Jacobs; ***D:*** Robert Townsend; ***W:*** Robert Townsend; Michelle Amor; Cheryl L. West; ***C:*** John L. (Ndiaga) Demps, Jr. **VIDEO**

Playing by Heart *Dancing about Architecture* **1998 (R)** Excellent ensemble cast doesn't save this episodic film about several L.A. couples falling in and out of love. Theatre director Anderson tries to avoid becoming involved with architect Stewart; loud-mouthed night-clubber Jolie won't give up on Phillippe; Quaid uses bad lines and lies on Kinski and Clarkson, while his wife, Stowe, fools around with Edwards; Connery and Rowlands (in the best-acted segments) find their 40-year marriage threatened by emotional and health problems; and Burstyn tries to comfort her son Mohr, in the last stages of AIDS. **121m/C; DVD.** Sean Connery; Gena Rowlands; Ryan Phillippe; Angelina Jolie; Ellen Burstyn; Gillian Anderson; Dennis Quaid; Jay Mohr; Anthony Edwards; Madeleine Stowe; Jon Stewart; Patricia Clarkson; Nastassja Kinski; Jeremy Sisto; ***D:*** Willard Carroll; ***W:*** Willard Carroll; ***C:*** Vilmos Zsigmond; ***M:*** John Barry.

Playing for Keeps **1986 (PG-13)** Three high school grads turn a dilapidated hotel into a rock 'n' roll resort. Music by Pete Townshend, Peter Frampton, Phil Collins, and others. **103m/C; VHS, DVD.** Daniel Jordano; Matthew Penn; Leon Grant; Harold Gould; Jimmy Baio; ***D:*** Bob Weinstein.

Playing for Keeps *Playing the Field* **2012 (PG-13)** So many talented people, so little talent on display. Butler gives a half-asleep leading man performance as George, a soccer player who becomes the romantic target of all the soccer moms in his new neighborhood. Biel, Quaid, Thurman, Zeta-Jones, and Greer deserve better than this misogynistic tripe masquerading as a romantic comedy. Like far too many films in this wanting genre, it's neither romantic nor a comedy, unless you find pathetic excuses for what Hollywood thinks of suburban love lives hilarious. **105m/C; DVD, Blu-Ray.** Gerard Butler; Jessica Biel; Noah Lomax; Dennis Quaid; Uma Thurman; Catherine Zeta-Jones; James Tupper; Judy Greer; ***D:*** Gabriele Muccino; ***W:*** Robbie Fox; ***C:*** Peter Menzies, Jr.; ***M:*** Andrea Guerra.

Playing for Time **1980** Compelling, award-winning TV drama based on actual experiences of a Holocaust prisoner who survives by leading an inmate orchestra. Strong playing from Redgrave and Mayron. Pro-Palestinian Redgrave's political beliefs made her a controversial candidate for the role of Jewish Fania Fenelon, but her stunning performance is on the mark. **148m/C; VHS, DVD, Blu-Ray.** Vanessa Redgrave; Jane Alexander; Maud Adams; Verna Bloom; Melanie Mayron; ***D:*** Daniel Mann; ***M:*** Brad Fiedel. **TV**

Playing God **1/2 1996 (R)** Eugene (Duchovny), a disgraced junkie doctor who has lost his license, saves the life of a hood in a bar. This brings him to the attention of Raymond (Hutton), the head of a counterfeiting and smuggling ring, who hires Eugene as his own personal emergency room. While patching up crooks, Eugene develops more than a doctor-patient relationship with Raymond's pillow-lipped girlfriend Claire (Jolie). Things begin to get a little slicey and dicey for Eugene, until he saves the life of an undercover cop. While sufficiently bloody and nasty, flick tries too hard to be offbeat and hip. **94m/C; VHS, DVD, Blu-Ray.** David Duchovny; Timothy Hutton; Angelina Jolie; Michael Massee; Peter Stormare; Andrew Tiernan; John Hawkes; Gary Dourdan; Stacey Travis; ***D:*** Andy Wilson; ***W:*** Mark Haskell Smith; ***C:*** Anthony B. Richmond; ***M:*** Richard Hartley.

Playing House **1/2 2006** Lifetime movie with an especially appealing lead in Kelly. Canadian Frannie has a job as a book editor in New York. She also has a romance with jazz musician Calvin, who's off on a European tour when Frannie learns she's pregnant. She goes to visit her parents and then can't re-cross the border because of an expired visa so Frannie must juggle her new/old life in Canada, including working with writer Michael, who's taking a personal interest in his new editor. **90m/C; DVD.** Joanne Kelly; Lucas Bryant; Colin Ferguson; Michael Murphy; Rosemary Dunsmore; Kristin Lehman; ***D:*** Kelly Makin; ***W:*** Michelle A. Lovretta; ***C:*** Thom Best; ***M:*** Robert Carli. **CABLE**

Playing House **2010** Predictable would-be erotic thriller. Newlyweds Jen and Mitch invite Mitch's best friend Danny to move in with them to help meet the expenses of their new house. Single Danny hooks up with Blair and soon she is hanging around a lot. Jen doesn't like the scantily-clad trouble-maker flirting with Mitch but no one knows how crazy Blair really is. **84m/C; DVD.** Craig Welzbacher; Sarah Prikyl; Matt Lusk; Mayra Leal; ***D:*** Tom Vaughan; ***W:*** Tom Vaughan; Kristy Dobkin; ***C:*** Sean Maxwell; ***M:*** Austin Wintory. **VIDEO**

Playing It Cool **2014 (R)** Yet another wannabe rom com where the leads remain nameless and clichés abound (despite the appealing cast). A cynical screenwriter is prodded by his manager to write a rom com to further his career, but the guy knows zip about love until he meets 'the one.' Her being engaged doesn't stop his pursuit nor the generally useless advice given by his friends. **94m/C; DVD.** Chris Evans; Michelle Monaghan; Aubrey Plaza; Ioan Gruffudd; Anthony Mackie; Patrick Warburton; Topher Grace; Luke Wilson; ***D:*** Justin Reardon; ***W:*** Chris Shafer; Paul Vicknair; ***C:*** Jeff Cutter; ***M:*** Jake Monaco. **VIDEO**

Playing Mona Lisa **1/2 2000 (R)** Piano prodigy Claire (Witt) gets dumped by her boyfriend on the night of her college graduation and then is humiliated at a piano competition. So, while trying to cope with her problems, Claire decides to adopt a Mona Lisa smile and see what life has to offer. **97m/C; VHS, DVD.** Alicia Witt; Ivan Sergei; Brooke Langton; Johnny Galecki; Elliott Gould; Marlo Thomas; Harvey Fierstein; Molly Hagan; Estelle Harris; Sandra Bernhard; Shannon Finn; ***D:*** Matthew Huffman; ***W:*** Marni Freedman; Carlos De Los Rios; ***C:*** James Glennon.

Playing with Fire **2019 (PG)** A crew of rugged fighters meet their match when attempting to rescue three rambunctious kids. **95m/C; DVD, Blu-Ray.** John Cena; Keegan Michael Key; John Leguizamo; Brianna Hildebrand; Judy Greer; ***D:*** Andy Fickman; ***W:*** Dan Ewen; Matt Lieberman; ***C:*** Dean Semler; ***M:*** Nathan Wang.

Playmates **1941** Barrymore is practically wasted in his last film as a down-on-his-luck actor who agrees to turn bandleader Kyser into a Shakespearean actor. Bizarre comedy is funny at times, but leaves the audience wondering what Barrymore thought he was doing. Currently only available as part of a collection. **96m/B; VHS, DVD.** Kay Kyser; John Barrymore; Ginny Simms; Lupe Velez; May Robson; Patsy Kelly; Peter Lind Hayes; George Cleveland; ***D:*** David Butler.

Playmobil: The Movie **1/2 2019 (PG)** Four years after the unexpected death of their parents, 22-year-old Marla (Taylor-Joy) is exhausted by the responsibilities of life as she raises her 10-year-old brother Charlie (Bateman). When Charlie runs away, she tracks him to a soon-to-open toy fair with a large Playmobil toy display. A lighthouse with a magical light ray transports Marla and Charlie into the world of toys, where the Playmobil version of Marla must rescue Charlie, now a Playmobil viking, from an evil emperor (Lambert). Based on a line of toys, it's boring and inconsistent, making even the Playmobils seem not particularly fun to play with. **110m/C; DVD.** Anya Taylor-Joy; Gabriel Bateman; Jim Gaffigan; Daniel Radcliffe; Meghan Trainor; ***D:*** Lino DiSalvo; ***W:*** Blaise Hemingway; Greg Erb; Jason Oremland; ***M:*** Heitor Pereira.

Playtime **1967** Occasionally enterprising comedy in which the bemused Frenchman Hulot tries in vain to maintain an appointment in an urban landscape of glass and steel. The theme of cold, unfeeling civilization is hardly unique, but the film is nonetheless enjoyable. The third in the Hulot trilogy, preceded by "Mr. Hulot's Holiday" and "Mon Oncle." In French with English subtitles. **108m/C; VHS, DVD, Blu-Ray.** *FR* Jacques Tati; Barbara Dennek; Jacqueline Lecomte; Jack Gautier; ***D:*** Jacques Tati.

Plaza Suite **1971 (PG)** Three alternating skits from Neil Simon's play about different couples staying at the New York hotel. Matthau shines in all three vignettes. Some of Simon's funnier stuff, with the first sketch being the best: Matthau and Stapleton are a couple celebrating their 24th anniversary. She's sentimental, while he's yearning for his mistress. Number two has producer Matthau putting the make on old flame Harris, while the finale has father Matthau coaxing his anxious daughter out of the bathroom on her wedding day. **114m/C; VHS, DVD.** Walter Matthau; Maureen Stapleton; Barbara Harris; Lee Grant; Louise Sorel; ***D:*** Arthur Hiller; ***W:*** Neil Simon; ***M:*** Maurice Jarre.

Pleasantville 1/2 **1998 (PG-13)** David (Maguire) and his sister Jennifer (Witherspoon) are sucked into the sterile world of Pleasantville, a 1950s B/W TV show in constant reruns. They find themselves in the roles of Bud and Mary Sue, the blandly adorable children of George and Betty Parker (Macy, Allen). After Jennifer shows a classmate what lovers' lane is really for, the townspeople begin to lose their innocence and their world becomes more colorful as each new human passion is realized. The performances are dead-on and the transition from straight comedy to social commentary is adeptly handled. The great character actor J.T. Walsh gives his usual excellent (and sadly, last) performance as the stubborn head of the chamber of commerce. **124m/C; VHS, DVD.** Tobey Maguire; Reese Witherspoon; William H. Macy; Joan Allen; Jeff Daniels; J.T. Walsh; Don Knotts; Paul Walker; Jane Kaczmarek; Marley Shelton; ***D:*** Gary Ross; ***W:*** Gary Ross; ***C:*** John Lindley; ***M:*** Randy Newman. L.A. Film Critics '98: Support. Actress (Allen); Broadcast Film Critics '98: Support. Actress (Allen).

Please Don't Eat My Mother
WOOF! *Hungry Pets; Glump* **1972** A softcore remake of "Little Shop of Horrors" in which a lonely voyeur plays host to a human-eating plant. **95m/C; VHS, DVD.** Buck Kartalian; Lynn Lundgren; Art Hedberg; Alice Fredlund; Adam Blair; Flora Wiesel; Ric Lutze; Renee Bond; Dash Fremont; ***D:*** Carl Monson; ***W:*** Eric Norden; ***C:*** Jack Beckett; ***M:*** Dan Foly.

Please Don't Eat the Daisies 1/2 **1960** City couple and kids leave the Big Apple for the country and are traumatized by flora and fauna. Goofy '60s fluff taken from Jean Kerr's book and the basis for the eventual TV series. **111m/C; VHS, DVD.** Doris Day; David Niven; Janis Paige; Spring Byington; Richard Haydn; Patsy Kelly; Jack Weston; Margaret Lindsay; ***D:*** Charles Walters; ***W:*** Isobel Lennart; ***C:*** Robert J. Bronner; ***M:*** David Rose.

Please Give **2010 (R)** Awkwardly shy Rebecca (Hall) is devoted to her ornery, bitter 91-year-old grandmother Andra (Guilbert) whose coveted New York apartment is owned by her next-door neighbors, successful vintage furniture dealers Kate (Keener) and Alex (Platt). They are not-so-subtly waiting for Andra to die so they can expand and renovate their own living quarters. A wannabe do-gooder suffering from liberal guilt, Kate invites Andra, Rebecca and her tactless, beauty-obsessed sister Mary (Peet) over for a birthday dinner and an embarrassing clash of personalities ensues, to acerbic, if somewhat wearying, effect. **91m/C; Blu-Ray, On Demand.** Catherine Keener; Amanda Peet; Oliver Platt; Rebecca Hall; Ann Guilbert; Sarah Steele; Lois Smith; Thomas Ian Nicholas; ***D:*** Nicole Holofcener; ***W:*** Nicole Holofcener; ***C:*** Yaron Orbach; ***M:*** Marcelo Zarvos.

Please Not Now! *Only for Love; La Bride sur le Cou* **1961** Parisian model Bardot discovers her boyfriend Riberolles is cheating on her and she decides to shoot him. He's warned by Subor, who wants Bardot for himself, and takes off with new gal pal James, but Bardot and Subor are in pursuit. Then Bardot and James commiserate over the fact that men are scum and decide to team up against their lovers. French with subtitles. **74m/B; VHS, DVD.** *FR IT* Brigitte Bardot; Josephine James; Michel Subor; Jacques Riberolles; Mireille Darc; Serge Marquand; Claude Brasseur; Jean Tissier; Bernard Fresson; Claude Berri; ***D:*** Roger Vadim; J(ack) D(unn) Trop; ***W:*** Roger Vadim; Claude Brule; J(ack) D(unn) Trop; ***C:*** Robert Lefebvre; ***M:*** James Campbell.

Please Stand By **2017 (PG-13)** A comedy-drama about a Star Trek-obsessed autistic woman. Though Wendy has a menial job and a supportive therapist/caregiver in Scottie (Collette), she struggles in day-to-day life. Because of her sudden rages, Wendy (Fanning) must live apart from her sister Audrey (Eve) and Audrey's infant child. However, Wendy uses her extensive knowledge of Star Trek to write a 500-page-long script that she wants to enter in a contest. When she realizes that she has missed the mailing deadline, she breaks the rules she has been given to deliver it herself. Though Fanning's performance is memorable, the story itself is quite predictable. **93m/C; DVD, Blu-Ray, Streaming.** Dakota Fanning; Toni Collette; Alice Eve; River Alexander; Marla Gibbs; ***D:*** Ben Lewin; ***W:*** Michael Golamco; ***C:*** Geoffrey Simpson; ***M:*** Heitor Pereira.

The Pleasure Drivers 1/2 **2005** Disjointed plot follows the efforts of caregiver Daphne (Holly) to get what's due from cult leader Marvin (Zane), who refuses to pay for his son's care. Daphne decides to kidnap her patient's mentally unstable sister to get dad's attention. Meanwhile, psychology professor Bill (Macfadyen) takes a road trip with sex-obsessed student Faruza (Chabert) after his wife leaves him for another woman. Somehow a lesbian hitwoman (Bennett) becomes involved. All ultimately meet in the desert where justice is meted out. **99m/C; DVD.** Lauren Holly; Lacey Chabert; Billy Zane; Jill Bennett; Angus MacFadyen; Steffany Huckaby; Angelo Spizzirri; Meat Loaf Aday; Jason Mewes; Rachel Dratch; Harrison Young; ***D:*** Andrzej Sekula; ***W:*** Adam Haynes; ***C:*** Andrzej Sekula; ***M:*** Steve Gutheinz. **VIDEO**

The Pleasure Garden **1925** In this early Hitchcock flick, the Pleasure Garden is a London music hall where sweet Patsy gets gold-digging Jill a job. Jill quickly dumps her fiance Hugh for a richer man and Hugh returns to working on a plantation in the Far East. Patsy has married Hugh's friend Levett though he soon leaves her behind in London. Eventually, a worried Patsy follows and finds a shocking situation that leads to much silent romantic melodrama. **75m/B; Silent; DVD.** *GB* Virginia Valli; Carmelita Geraghty; Miles Mander; John Stuart; Nita Naldi; ***D:*** Alfred Hitchcock; ***W:*** Eliot Stannard; ***C:*** Gaetano di Ventimiglia.

The Pledge **2000 (R)** Retired Reno homicide detective Nicholson is obsessed with the unsolved murder of a little girl, which bares a resemblance to past unsolved child murders. Unconventional thriller's dark subject matter will no doubt dissuade some potential viewers, but Penn's third (and best) directorial outing is impressive, thanks in large part to Nicholson's subtle, intense work. **124m/C; VHS, DVD.** Jack Nicholson; Robin Wright; Aaron Eckhart; Vanessa Redgrave; Benicio Del Toro; Patricia Clarkson; Harry Dean Stanton; Tom Noonan; Dame Helen Mirren; Lois Smith; Sam Shepard; Mickey Rourke; ***D:*** Sean Penn; ***W:*** Mary Olson-Kromolowski; Jerzy Kromolowski; ***C:*** Chris Menges; ***M:*** Hans Zimmer.

The Pledge 1/2 **2008** Sheriff Matt Austin (Perry) goes after the escaped criminal who murdered his wife and son and finds he's been hired by greedy land developer Horn (Howell) to harass widowed Gail (Brenner) until she sells. Pretty standard stuff, done better elsewhere. **85m/C; DVD.** Luke Perry; C. Thomas Howell; Lisa Brenner; Kim Coates; Francesco Quinn; ***D:*** Armand Mastroianni; ***W:*** Jim Byrnes; ***C:*** James W. Wrenn. **CABLE**

Plenty 1/2 **1985 (R)** Difficult but worthwhile film with Streep in top form as a former member of the French Resistance, who upon returning to England finds life at home increasingly tedious and banal and begins to fear her finest hours may be behind her. Gielgud is flawless as the aging career diplomat. Adapted by David Hare from his play, an allegory to British decline. **119m/C; VHS, DVD.** Meryl Streep; Tracey Ullman; Sting; John Gielgud; Charles Dance; Ian McKellen; Sam Neill; Burt Kwouk; ***D:*** Fred Schepisi; ***W:*** David Hare; ***C:*** Ian Baker; ***M:*** Bruce Smeaton. L.A. Film Critics '85: Support. Actor (Gielgud); Natl. Soc. Film Critics '85: Support. Actor (Gielgud).

The Plot Against Harry **1969** Jewish racketeer Harry Plotnik checks out of prison, and finds the outside world ain't what it used to be. Attempting to lead an honest life only makes matters worse. Completely overlooked when first released in 1969 (and quickly shelved) because it was considered to have no commercial potential, Roemer's crime comedy found an enthusiastic audience when it was rediscovered 20 years later. **81m/B; VHS, DVD.** Martin Priest; Ben Lang; Maxine Woods; Henry Nemo; Jacques Taylor; Ellen Herbert; Sandra Kazan; ***D:*** Michael Roemer; ***W:*** Michael Roemer; ***C:*** Robert M. Young; ***M:*** Frank Lewin.

The Plot Thickens 1/2 **1936** Pitts takes over the role of Hildegarde Withers for the final two entries in the rapidly deteriorating RKO series. In the 5th entry, the now-dithery Hildegarde and gruff Inspector Piper (Gleason) investigate two murders that tie together over a stolen emerald and a museum art theft. Followed by "Forty Naughty Girls." **67m/B; DVD.** Zasu Pitts; James Gleason; Owen Davis, Jr.; Louise Latimer; Arthur Aylesworth; Paul Fix; Richard Tucker; ***D:*** Ben Holmes; ***W:*** Clarence Upson Young; Jack Townley; ***C:*** Nicholas Musuraca.

The Plot to Kill Hitler **1990** In 1944 the war began to turn against Germany and several members of the government decided to assassinate Hitler before he destroyed the country. It failed, and 5,000 Germans lost their lives merely for being friends or family of the conspirators. The film has some slight historical inaccuracies but remains true overall. **97m/C; DVD.** *YU* Brad Davis; Madolyn Smith; Ian Richardson; Rupert Graves; Kenneth Colley; Mike Byrne; Mike Gwilym; ***D:*** Lawrence Schiller; ***W:*** Steven Elkins; ***C:*** Freddie Francis; ***M:*** Laurence Rosenthal. **TV**

The Ploughman's Lunch **1983** A BBC news reporter claws and lies his way to the top. He then discovers that he is the victim of a far more devious plan. Engrossing and well made, although some of the political views are simplistic. **107m/C; VHS, DVD.** Jonathan Pryce; Charlie Dore; Tim Curry; Rosemary Harris; Frank Finlay; Bill Paterson; ***D:*** Richard Eyre.

Plucking the Daisy 1/2 *Please! Mr. Balzac; While Plucking the Daisy; En Effeuillant la Marguerite; Mademoiselle Striptease* **1956** Agnes Dumont (Bardot) anonymously writes a scandalous romantic novel that becomes a best-seller and causes her straitlaced father to send Agnes to a convent school. Only she escapes to her brother's in Paris instead, where she decides to earn some money by entering a striptease contest (which serves to put enticing Bardot's ample charms on display). French with subtitles. **100m/B; VHS, DVD.** *FR* Brigitte Bardot; Robert Hirsch; Daniel Gelin; Jacques Dumesnil; ***D:*** Marc Allegret; ***W:*** Marc Allegret; Roger Vadim; ***C:*** Louis Page; ***M:*** Paul Misraki.

Plughead Rewired: Circuitry Man 2 *Circuitry Man 2* **1994 (R)** Earth's atmosphere has been destroyed and survivors are forced underground, where they're terrorized by the humanoid Plughead, who likes to literally plug into the minds of his victims. Plughead wants to rule what's left of life on Earth and all that stands in his way is the android Circuitry Man and FBI agent Kyle. Special effects are strictly bargain basement level. **97m/C; VHS, DVD.** Vernon Wells; Deborah Shelton; Jim Metzler; Dennis Christopher; Nicholas Worth; Traci Lords; ***D:*** Steven Lovy; Robert Lovy; ***W:*** Steven Lovy; Robert Lovy; ***C:*** Stephen Timberlake; ***M:*** Tim Kelly.

Plum Role 1/2 **2007** Struggling actor Jacob (Hardie) lives in Perth in western Australia, where gigs aren't so plentiful. He's just gotten his big break by getting cast in a cop show filming in Sydney. The week before he leaves, Jacob meets vulnerable Cheryl (Henderson) and a series of unexpected complications threaten not only his potential career but his life. **80m/C; DVD.** *AU* Matt Hardie; Laura Henderson; Luke Jago; Adam McGurk; Tom Stokes; ***D:*** Zak Hilditch; ***W:*** Zak Hilditch; ***C:*** Antony Webb; ***M:*** Ash Gibson Greig.

Plumber 1/2 **1979** A plumber who makes a house call extends his stay to psychologically torture the woman of the house. Originally made for Australian TV. **76m/C; VHS, DVD.** *AU* Judy Morris; Ivar Kants; Robert Coleby; ***D:*** Peter Weir; ***W:*** Peter Weir. **TV**

A Plumm Summer 1/2 **2008 (PG)** You try saying no to a cute five-year-old when he needs your help. Young Elliott (Massaglia) is heartbroken when his favorite local children's TV show is forced off the air when Happy Herb's (Winkler) sidekick puppet Froggy Doo is kidnapped. Elliott insists his teen brother Rocky (Pearce) help him investigate but Rocky doesn't agree until pretty neighbor Haley (Flynn) wants to help with their sleuthing. The story takes a strange turn because the Plumm's dad (Baldwin) is a bitter alcoholic constantly fighting with their mother (Guerrero) but gets back on track by the third act. **101m/C; DVD.** William Baldwin; Brenda Strong; Henry Winkler; Peter Scolari; Rick Overton; Tim Quill; Chris Massoglia; Owen Pearce; Morgan Flynn; Lisa Guerrero; ***D:*** Caroline Zelder; ***W:*** Caroline Zelder; T.J. Lynch; Frank Antonelli; ***C:*** Mark Vargo; ***M:*** Tom Hiel.

Plump Fiction **1997 (R)** Lame spoof attacks Quentin Tarantino's already over-the-top characters from "Pulp Fiction" and "Natural Born Killers." Julius (Davidson) and Jimmy (Dinello) are the loser hit men and Mimi (Brown) is the gangster's wife. Mimi's substance abuse problem is food--she's fat, get it? Ha ha ha? Intersecting storylines feature Nicky (Glave) and Vallory (Segall) as "Natural Blonde Killers." The only redeeming scene is that of Kane Picoy as "Christopher Walken character," doing an uncanny impersonation of the king of the psychos. **82m/C; VHS, DVD.** Tommy Davidson; Julie Brown; Sandra Bernhard; Paul Dinello; Dan Castellaneta; Colleen Camp; Pamela Segall; Kevin Meaney; Matthew Glave; Jennifer Rubin; Robert Costanzo; Phillipe Bergerone; ***D:*** Bob Koherr; ***W:*** Bob Koherr; ***C:*** Rex Nicholson; ***M:*** Michael Muhlfriedel.

Plunder Road 1/2 **1957** Eddie (Raymond)masterminds a plan to rob a train bound for the San Francisco Mint that's carrying a fortune in gold bullion. The heist's a success but actually getting away with the loot becomes a problem. Top notch B-film noir. **76m/B; DVD, Blu-Ray.** Gene Raymond; Jeanne Cooper; Wayne Morris; Elisha Cook, Jr.; Stafford Repp; Steven Ritch; ***D:*** Hubert Cornfield; ***W:*** Steven Ritch; ***C:*** Ernest Haller; ***M:*** Irving Gertz.

The Plunderers 1/2 **1960** Four young toughs try to terrorize a small western town but bitter one-armed Civil War hero-turned-rancher Sam (Chandler) finds the courage to oppose them. **94m/B; DVD.** Jeff Chandler; John Saxon; Ray Stricklyn; Dee Pollock; Marsha Hunt; Dolores Hart; Jay C. Flippen; Joseph Pevney; Roger Torrey; ***D:*** Joseph Pevney; ***W:*** Bob Barbash; ***C:*** Gene Polito; ***M:*** Leonard Rosenman.

Plunkett & Macleane **1998 (R)** Will Plunkett (Carlyle) is a lower-class thief who teams up with wastrel aristocrat Macleane (Miller) for careers as highwaymen in 18th-century London. The rogues are aided by hedonistic Lord Rochester (Cumming) and opposed by Lord Chief Justice Gibson (Gambon), whose vixenish niece, Lady Rebecca (Tyler), becomes Macleane's inamorata. Carlyle and Miller make a fine criminal duo but the film has lots of flaws to distract the viewer. (Son of Ridley) Scott's directorial debut. **102m/C; VHS, DVD.** *GB* Robert Carlyle; Jonny Lee Miller; Liv Tyler; Michael Gambon; Alan Cumming; Ken Stott; Terence Rigby; Claire Rushbrook; Iain Robertson; Dave Atkins; ***D:*** Jake Scott; ***W:*** Robert Wade; Neal Purvis; Charles McKeown; ***C:*** John Mathieson; ***M:*** Craig Armstrong.

Plus One 1/2 **2019** When Ben (Quaid) has to give a best man toast at his close friend's wedding, he tries it out on his college friend Alice (Erskine) and takes her advice to make it humorous so he can impress a girl from his past. Though his toast goes over well, the girl is engaged. Because Alice is also single after going through a terrible breakup, Ben and Alice agree to be each other's plus one at the series of 10 weddings they must attend in the near future. Though the plot is somewhat predictable, the romantic comedy is endearing and Quaid displays skill as a romantic comedy actor. **99m/C; DVD, Blu-Ray.** Maya Erskine; Jack Quaid; Ed Begley, Jr.; Beck Bennett; Rosalind Chao; ***D:*** Jeff Chan; Andrew Rhymer; ***W:*** Jeff Chan; Andrew Rhymer; ***C:*** Guy Godfree; ***M:*** Leo Birenberg.

Plush **2013 (R)** Trashy, clunky thriller. When her brother and bandmate Jack dies from a drug overdose and their commercial prospects fail, lead singer Hayley goes into a depression. It only lifts when she hires replacement guitarist Enzo and the two get busy off stage during a tour. After getting home, married mom Hayley's spooked when Enzo shows up at her house, seemingly obsessed and making demands. **99m/C; DVD, Blu-Ray.** Emily Browning; Xavier Samuel; Cam Gigandet; Thomas Dekker; Frances Fisher; ***D:*** Catherine Hardwicke; ***W:*** Catherine Hardwicke; Arty Nelson; ***C:*** Daniel (Danny) Moder; ***M:*** Nick Launay. **VIDEO**

Plutonium Baby **1987** A mutated kid, whose mother was killed by the same radiation exposure that infected him, tracks down the guilty party in New York in this comic-book style film. **85m/C; VHS, DVD.** Patrick Molloy; Danny Guerra; ***D:*** Ray Hirschman.

Pocahontas **1995 (G)** In 1607, spirited Powhatan maiden Pocahontas (Bedard) and British settler Capt. John Smith have an unlikely romance in Disney's 33rd animated feature, its first based on the life of an historical figure. Lovely Poca, a virtual post-adolescent Native American superbabe, introduces the roguish captain (spoken and sung by Gibson) to the wonders of unspoiled nature and serves as peacemaker in the clash of European and Native American cultures. Disney puts its spin on history but maintains cultural sensitivity. Stunningly animated, but its mediocre soundtrack and decidedly somber tone leave it lacking in typical Disney majesty and charm. **90m/C; VHS, DVD, Blu-Ray.** ***V:*** Irene Bedard; Judy Kuhn; Mel Gibson; Joe Baker; Christian Bale; Billy Connolly; James Apaumut Fall; Linda Hunt; John Kassir; Danny Mann; Bill Cobbs; David Ogden Stiers; Michelle St. John; Gordon Tootoosis; Frank Welker; ***D:*** Mike Gabriel; Eric Goldberg; ***W:*** Carl Binder; Susannah Grant; Philip LaZebnik; ***M:*** Alan Menken; ***M:*** Stephen Schwartz. Oscars '95: Orig. Score, Song ("Colors of the Wind"); Golden Globes '96: Song ("Colors of the Wind").

Pocahontas: The Legend **1/2** **1995** Live-action version of the increasingly familiar story of the Native American girl who aids Virginia settler, John Smith. **101m/C; VHS, DVD.** *CA* Sandrine Holt; Miles O'Keeffe; Tony Goldwyn; Gordon Tootoosis; ***D:*** Daniele Suissa; ***W:*** Daniele Suissa.

Pocket Money **1972 (PG)** Down-on-their-luck cowpokes foolishly do business with crooked rancher in attempt to make comeback in faltering acting careers. Star-powered, moderately entertaining modern western-comedy based on the novel "Jim Kane" by J.K.S. Brown. **100m/C; VHS, DVD.** Paul Newman; Lee Marvin; Strother Martin; Christine Belford; Wayne Rogers; Hector Elizondo; Gregory Sierra; ***D:*** Stuart Rosenberg; ***W:*** Terrence Malick; ***M:*** Alex North.

Pocketful of Miracles **1961** Capra's final film, a remake of his 1933 "Lady for a Day," is just as corny and sentimental but doesn't work quite as well. Davis is delightful as Apple Annie, a down-on-her-luck street vendor who will go to any extreme to hide her poverty from the well-married daughter she adores. Ford is terrific as the man who transforms Annie into a lady in time for her daughter's visit. Touching. Maybe too touching. Also marks Ann-Margret's film debut. **136m/C; VHS, DVD, Blu-Ray.** Bette Davis; Glenn Ford; Peter Falk; Hope Lange; Arthur O'Connell; Ann-Margret; Thomas Mitchell; Jack Elam; Edward Everett Horton; David Brian; Mickey Shaughnessy; ***D:*** Frank Capra; ***W:*** Hal Kanter; Harry Tugend; ***C:*** Robert J. Bronner; ***M:*** Walter Scharf. Golden Globes '62: Actor--Mus./Comedy (Ford).

Poetic Justice **1/2** **1993 (R)** Justice (Jackson in her movie debut) gives up college plans to follow a career in cosmetology after her boyfriend's brutal murder. She copes with her loss by dedicating herself to poetry writing (provided by no less than poet Maya Angelou) and meets postal worker Shakur. Singleton's second directorial effort is about the girlz n the hood and boasts a lighter script, focusing less on the Boyz-style morality and more on the trials and tribulations of Justice. Production stopped on the South Central L.A. set during the '92 riots, but the aftermath produced poignant pictures for later scenes. **109m/C; VHS, DVD.** Janet Jackson; Tupac Shakur; Tyra Ferrell; Regina King; Joe Torry; Norma Donaldson; ***D:*** John Singleton; ***W:*** John Singleton; ***C:*** Peter Lyons Collister; ***M:*** Stanley Clarke. MTV Movie Awards '94: Female Perf. (Jackson), Most Desirable Female (Jackson); Golden Raspberries '93: Worst New Star (Jackson).

Poetry *Shi* **2010** Sixty-something Mija lives in a suburb of Seoul and looks after her sullen teenage grandson Jongwook for her divorced daughter. Mija's just learned she's in the early stages of Alzheimer's and decides to take a poetry class at the local community center where she pesters the teacher about finding poetic inspiration. It comes unexpectedly when Jongwook and his equally-apathetic friends are accused of driving a female classmate to suicide after raping her. Korean with subtitles. **139m/C; DVD, Blu-Ray.** *NK* Jeong-hie Yun; Da-wit (David) Lee; Hira Kim; Yong-taek Kim; Nae-sang Ahn; ***D:*** Chang-dong Lee; ***W:*** Chang-dong Lee; ***C:*** Hyun-seok Kim.

Poil de Carotte **1/2** *The Red Head* **1931** A semi-famous French melodrama about a young boy harassed by his overbearing mother to the point of disaster, redeemed finally by the love of his father. In French with English subtitles. **90m/B; VHS, DVD.** *FR* Harry Baur; Robert Lynen; Catherine Fontenoy; ***D:*** Julien Duvivier.

The Point **1/2** **1971** Charming and sincere animated feature about the rejection and isolation of a round-headed child in a world of pointy-headed people. Excellent score. **74m/C; VHS, DVD.** ***V:*** Paul Frees; ***Nar:*** Ringo Starr; ***D:*** Fred Wolf; ***M:*** Harry Nilsson. **TV**

Point Blank **1/2** **1967** Adapted from Stark's "The Hunter." The film's techniques are sometimes compared to those of Resnais and Godard. Double-crossed and believed dead, gangster Marvin returns to claim his share of the loot from the Organization. Hard-nosed examination of the depersonalization of a mechanized urban world. Plus, Lee Marvin is a complete badass. **92m/C; VHS, DVD, Blu-Ray.** Lee Marvin; Angie Dickinson; Keenan Wynn; Carroll O'Connor; Lloyd Bochner; Michael Strong; James B. Sikking; John Vernon; Sid Haig; Kathleen Freeman; ***D:*** John Boorman. Natl. Film Reg. '16.

Point Blank **1/2** **1998 (R)** A bus carrying death-row convicts is ambushed but the cons don't go their separate ways. Instead, they take over a shopping mall and begin fighting among themselves. **90m/C; VHS, DVD.** Mickey Rourke; Danny Trejo; Kevin Gage; Michael Wright; Frederic Forrest; James Gammon; ***D:*** Matt Earl Beesley. **VIDEO**

Point Blank *A Bout Pourtant* **2010 (R)** Fast-paced, if unlikely, French thriller. Career thief Hugo Sartet's life is saved by nurse Samuel Pierret, which gets Samuel in a whole lot of trouble since Sartet's been double-crossed by his employers. The bad guys kidnap Samuel's very pregnant wife in order to force him to do their bidding while he and Sartet try to stay alive. French with subtitles. **84m/C; DVD, Blu-Ray.** *FR* Gilles Lellouche; Roschdy Zem; Gerard Lanvin; Elena Anaya; Mireille Perrier; ***D:*** Fred Cavaye; ***W:*** Fred Cavaye; Guillaume Lemans; ***C:*** Alain Duplantier; ***M:*** Klaus Badelt.

Point Break **1/2** **1991 (R)** If you can suspend your disbelief—and you'd need a crane—then this crime adventure is just dandy. Reeves is a young undercover FBI kid sent to infiltrate a gang of bank-robbing surfer dudes. Swayze is the leader of the beach subculture, a thrillseeker who plays cat-and-mouse with the feds in a series of excellent action scenes. Silly brain candy. **117m/C; VHS, DVD, Blu-Ray.** Patrick Swayze; Keanu Reeves; Gary Busey; Lori Petty; John C. McGinley; Chris Pederson; Bojesse Christopher; Julian Reyes; Daniel Beer; Sydney Walsh; Vincent Klyn; James LeGros; John Philbin; Jack Kehler; Lee Tergesen; Christopher Pettiet; Elizabeth Berkley; Tom Sizemore; Anthony Mangano; ***D:*** Kathryn Bigelow; ***W:*** W. Peter Iliff; ***C:*** Don Peterman; ***M:*** Mark Isham. MTV Movie Awards '92: Most Desirable Male (Reeves).

Point Break **2015 (PG-13)** What's the point of remaking a movie that was kind of mediocre in the first place? Kathryn Bigelow's original tapped into something about the era in which it was made, especially with the pretty-boy-turned-action-star performances at its center to carry it. No one involved in the 2015 version ever seemed to ask why make the movie again if they can't tap the same cultural vein? So, we get a by the numbers remake of an action movie with lackluster actors replacing the charismatic ones, and such numbingly flat set pieces that it's not even a guilty pleasure. It never justifies its existence. **114m/C; DVD, Blu-Ray.** Edgar Ramirez; Luke Bracey; Ray Winstone; Teresa Palmer; Matias Varela; Delroy Lindo; ***D:*** Ericson Core; ***W:*** Kurt Wimmer; ***C:*** Ericson Core; ***M:*** Junkie XL.

Point of Impact *Spanish Rose* **1993 (R)** A Miami customs officer is killed in an explosion and his partner is blamed. He knows a Cuban crime boss was actually behind it and goes undercover to bring the criminal organization down. But there's also the temptation of the the criminal's sexy ladyfriend. Also available in an unrated version. **96m/C; VHS, DVD.** Michael Paré; Barbara Carrera; Michael Ironside; ***D:*** Bob Misiorowski; ***W:*** George Fernandez; ***C:*** Yossi Wein; ***M:*** Vladimir Horunzhy.

Point of No Return **1/2** **1993 (R)** Fonda is Maggie, a drugged-out loser condemned to death for her part in a murder spree, but if she agrees to work as a government assassin, she'll be given a reprieve. Fonda displays a certain perkiness as the assassin and is better in her early surly scenes; Keitel is creepy as another assassin. Flashy, exacting, but ultimately innocuous remake of the 1990 French thriller "La Femme Nikita." **108m/C; VHS, DVD, Blu-Ray.** Bridget Fonda; Gabriel Byrne; Dermot Mulroney; Miguel Ferrer; Anne Bancroft; Olivia D'Abo; Harvey Keitel; Richard Romanus; Lorraine Toussaint; Geoffrey Lewis; Calvin Levels; ***D:*** John Badham; ***W:*** Robert Getchell; Alexandra Seros; ***C:*** Michael Watkins; ***M:*** Hans Zimmer.

Point of Origin **1/2** **2002** Captain John Orr (Liotta) is an arson investigator with the Glendale fire department. He's investigating a six-year string of fires in southern California (in the 1980s) along with protege/inspector Keith Lang (Leguizamo). Everyone's a suspect, including the firefighters themselves. Based on a true story. **86m/C; VHS, DVD.** Ray Liotta; John Leguizamo; Colm Feore; Clifford Curtis; Bai Ling; Illeana Douglas; Ronny Cox; ***D:*** Newton Thomas (Tom) Sigel; ***W:*** Matthew Tabak; ***C:*** Anthony G. Nakonechnyi; ***M:*** John Ottman. **CABLE**

Point of Terror **1971 (R)** A handsome rock singer seduces a record company executive's wife in order to further his career. **88m/C; VHS, DVD.** Peter Carpenter; Dyanne Thorne; Lory Hansen; Leslie Simms; ***D:*** Alex Nicol.

Poison **1991 (R)** A controversial, compelling drama weaving the story of a seven year-old boy's murder of his father with two other tales of obsessive, fringe behavior. From the director of the underground hit "Superstar: The Karen Carpenter Story," which was shot using only a cast of "Barbie" dolls. **85m/C; VHS, DVD.** Edith Meeks; Larry Maxwell; Susan Norman; Scott Renderer; James Lyons; Millie White; Buck Smith; Anne Giotta; Al Quagliata; Michelle Sullivan; John R. Lombardi; Tony Pemberton; Andrew Harpending; ***D:*** Todd Haynes; ***W:*** Todd Haynes; ***C:*** Maryse Alberti; ***M:*** James Bennett. Sundance '91: Grand Jury Prize.

Poison **1/2** *Thy Neighbor's Wife* **2001 (R)** Ann believes that an ordinary housewife is responsible for the death of her husband. So Ann disguises herself, gets a job with the family, and decides to extract the proper revenge. Of course, Ann's crazy. **92m/C; VHS, DVD.** Kari Wuhrer; Jeff Trachta; Barbara Crampton; Michael Cavanaugh; Larry Poindexter; ***D:*** Jim Wynorski; ***W:*** Sean O'Bannon; ***C:*** Andrea V. Rossotto. **VIDEO**

Poison Ivy **1992 (R)** Barrymore is right on target as a junior femme fatale in this trashy tale of a wayward teenager and her takeover of her best friend's family. Ivy has no discernable family life and quickly attaches herself to the lonely, neglected Cooper (Gilbert) who ends up watching as she systematically seduces both her mother (emotionally) and her father (physically). But when Ivy's homewrecking turns lethal, Cooper must fight her "friend" to save herself. Glossy, over-done pulp. An unrated version is also available. **91m/C; VHS, DVD, Blu-Ray.** Drew Barrymore; Sara Gilbert; Tom Skerritt; Cheryl Ladd; ***D:*** Katt Shea; ***W:*** Katt Shea; Andy Ruben; ***C:*** Phedon Papamichael; ***M:*** David Michael Frank.

Poison Ivy 2: Lily **1/2** **1995 (R)** Art student Lily (Milano) finds the provocative Ivy's diary and becomes intrigued enough to decide to take a walk on the wild side herself, which gets her into all sorts of trouble. Also available unrated. **110m/C; VHS, DVD, Blu-Ray.** Alyssa Milano; Xander Berkeley; Johnathon Schaech; Belinda Bauer; ***D:*** Anne Goursaud; ***W:*** Chloe King; ***C:*** Suki Medencevic; ***M:*** Joseph Williams.

Poison Ivy 3: The New Seduction **1/2** **1997 (R)** Now Ivy has a long-lost sister, appropriately named Violet (Pressly), who heads to their childhood home to get revenge on those she believes betrayed them. Naturally, it's all sex and men being led around by their...zippers. Also available unrated. **93m/C; VHS, DVD, Blu-Ray.** Jaime Pressly; Megan Edwards; Michael Des Barres; Greg Vaughan; ***D:*** Kurt Voss; ***W:*** Karen Kelly; ***C:*** Feliks Parnell; ***M:*** Reg Powell.

Poison Ivy 4: The Secret Society **2008** Has no connection to the previous trashy flicks except for that whole flower name thing. Freshman Daisy Brooks is really enjoying her time at Beckshire College, especially when she is invited to join the exclusive Ivy Society. But Daisy soon learns the members have no scruples when it comes to getting what they want, including blackmail and murder. **96m/C; DVD, Blu-Ray.** Miriam McDonald; Shawna Waldron; Ryan Kennedy; Greg Evigan; Catherine Hicks; ***D:*** Jason Hreno; ***W:*** Peter Sullivan; Liz Maverick; ***C:*** Kamal Derkaoui. **VIDEO**

The Poison Rose **1/2** **2019 (R)** In 1978 Los Angeles, private investigator Carson Phillips (Travolta) is hired by a woman to check on her aunt because no one has heard from her in a while. The aunt lives at a sanitarium in Galveston, Texas. At the facility, Carson is prevented from seeing her by Dr. Miles Mitchell (Fraser). As Carson digs deeper into the case, he must deal with his own past, including vengeful nightclub owner Doc (Freeman), and help his former girlfriend Jayne (Janssen) protect her daughter from an abusive husband. In this predictable neo-noir even the actors look bored. **98m/C; DVD, Blu-Ray.** Brendan Fraser; Famke Janssen; John Travolta; Ella Bleu Travolta; Morgan Freeman; ***D:*** Francesco Cinquemani; George Gallo; ***W:*** Francesco Cinquemani; George Gallo; Richard Salvatore; ***C:*** Terry Stacey; ***M:*** Aldo Shllaku; Marcus Sjowall.

Pokemon 3: The Movie **2001 (G)** As opposed to what, "Pokemon 3: The Dinner Theater?" This installment of the interminable franchise has a young girl, who's father has disappeared, turning her surroundings into a land of icy crystal. Ash, Pikachu and the other Pokemon (Pokemen?) show up to save the day with various pocket monster battles. Lessons are learned, battles are fought and won or lost, and days are saved, except for the days wasted by parents who have to sit throught it all. **88m/C; VHS, DVD, Blu-Ray.** ***V:*** Veronica Taylor; Eric Stuart; Rachael Lillis; Maddie (Maddeleine) Blaustein; Ikue Otani; ***D:*** Kunihiko Yuyama; Michael Haigney; ***W:*** Michael Haigney; Norman Grossfeld; Takeshi Shudo; Hideki Sonoda.

Pokémon Detective Pikachu *Detective Pikachu* **2019 (PG)** In a world where people collect Pokemon to do battle, a former Pokemon trainer-turned-insurance salesman must investigate the death of his estranged father, a famous detective. Fortunately his father's partner is Deadpo...er, we mean Pikachu (voiced by Reynolds). Unfortunately the litttle fluffball has amnesia. Monster fighting hijinks ensue. This first live action-animated outing for the franchise may not be for everyone, but fans will rejoice. And Reynolds, who lives for these roles, doesn't disappoint. **104m/C; DVD, Blu-Ray, Streaming.** *JP US CA* Justice Smith; Kathryn Newton; Bill Nighy; Ken(saku) Watanabe; ***V:*** Ryan Reynolds; ***D:*** Rob Letterman; ***W:*** Rob Letterman; Derek Connolly; Dan Hernandez; Benji Samit; ***C:*** John Mathieson; ***M:*** Henry Jackman.

Pokemon: The First Movie 🦴🦴 **1999 (G)** If your kid is saying things like "Pikachu," "Squirtle," and "Charizard," then you've already been introduced to the multimedia world of Pokemon. In this full-length version of the popular cartoon series (video game, trading card game, toy line, etc...), hero Ash and his pals Misty and Brock go to New Island to do battle with a twisted genetically engineered Pokemon called Mewtwo. Mewtwo defeats all the Pokemon trainers in battle, and is ready to clone hideous monsters from the defeated critters when he is challenged by the mysterious and rare Mew. Several new characters are introduced. **75m/C; VHS, DVD, Blu-Ray.** *V:* Veronica Taylor; Rachael Lillis; Eric Stuart; Philip Bartlett; *D:* Kunihiko Yuyama; Michael Haigney; *W:* Michael Haigney; Takeshi Shudo; *C:* Hisao Shirai.

Pokemon the Movie: The Power of Us 🦴🦴 *Gekijouban Poketto monsuta: Minna no Monogatari* **2018** Ash Ketchum (Natochenny) and his Pokemon Pikachu travel to Fula City to attend the Wind Festival. This event honors the history of the city, specifically when it saved from a destructive fire by Pokemon Lugia and given the power source of wind by him. At the festival, Ash and Pikachu meet new friends, including teenage Risa (Paschall) who wants to catch a Pokemon for her sick brother. The fun ends when Team Rocket steals a vial of Effect Spore that explodes in nearby forests and puts everyone at risk. The enjoyable animated feature features a positive story about friendship, responsibility, and environmental consciousness. **97m/C; DVD.** Sarah Natochenny; Haven Paschall; Eddy Lee; Kathryn Cahill; Erica Schroeder; *D:* Tetsuo Yajima; *W:* Aya Takaha; Eiji Umehara; *M:* Shinji Miyazaki.

Pokemon the Movie 2000: The Power of One 🦴🦴 *Poketto Monsutaa: Maboroshi No Pokemon X: Lugia Bakudan* **2000 (G)** As with the first Pokemon movie, considerations such as quality, plot, characterization, or dialogue do not matter. If you have kids under ten years old, you will be forced to rent (or more likely buy) this movie and watch it repeatedly. If you don't have any kids under ten, you most likely don't know or care what a Pokemon is anyway. If you do, for some strange reason, need to know the plot, here it is: Ash must stop the Collector from capturing Pokemon. If the kiddies like the Pokemon, they'll enjoy this little exercise in media overkill. **103m/C; VHS, DVD, Blu-Ray.** *JP V:* Ikue Ootani; Rica Matsumoto; Mayumi Iizuka; Tomokazu Seki; *D:* Kunihiko Yuyama; Michael Haigney; *W:* Michael Haigney; Takeshi Shudo; *M:* Ralph Schuckett; John Loeffler.

Poker Alice 🦴🦴 **1987** A lively Western starring Elizabeth Taylor as a sometime gambler who wins a brothel in a poker game. **100m/C; VHS, DVD.** Elizabeth Taylor; George Hamilton; Tom Skerritt; Richard Mulligan; David Wayne; Susan Tyrrell; Pat Corley; *D:* Arthur Allan Seidelman; *W:* James Lee Barrett.

The Poker Club 🦴 **2008 (R)** For years, Aaron and his three buds have been getting together for a Monday night poker game that's an excuse to get drunk and high. On this night, a burglar tries to break into the house and is accidentally bashed to death. The guys panic and dump the body in the river but someone witnessed their crime and the cops eventually come into the picture as well. Clumsy twists in a story you've seen before. Adapted from the Ed Gorman novel. **82m/C; DVD.** Johnathon Schaech; Johnny Messner; Loren Dean; Michael Risley; Lori Heuring; Judy Reyes; Lenny Levi; *D:* Tim McCann; *W:* Johnathon Schaech; *C:* Frank Barrera; *M:* Evan Evans. **VIDEO**

The Poker House 🦴 ½ **2009 (R)** In 1976, 14-year-old Agnes is living in a rundown house with her two young sisters, her druggie, drunk hooker mom Sarah, and Sarah's pimp Duval, who runs poker games in the living room. Agnes tries to protect her sisters while struggling to find a way to get them a better life. Petty's directorial debut is allegedly based on incidents from her own childhood. **93m/C; DVD.** Jennifer Lawrence; Selma Blair; Bokeem Woodbine; David Alan Grier; *D:* Lori Petty; *W:* David Alan Grier; Lori Petty; *C:* Ken Seng; *M:* Mike Post. **VIDEO**

Pola X 🦴🦴 **1999** French film continues to push the sexual envelope even when it's inspired by Herman Melville's 1852 novel, "Pierre, or, the Ambiguities." Rich boy Pierre (Depardieu) lives with his beautiful widowed mother, Marie (Deneuve), in a country chateau. He's about to marry his faithful girlfriend, Lucie (Chuillot), when a strange woman named Isabelle (Golubeva) shows up, claiming to be Pierre's half-sister. Soon Pierre is living the grunge life with Isabelle in Paris and the two are involved in an incestuous relationship (some of which is explicitly displayed). Another bizarre film from auteur Carax. French with subtitles. **134m/C; VHS, DVD.** *FR* Guillaume Depardieu; Yekaterina (Katia) Golubeva; Catherine Deneuve; Delphine Chuillot; Laurent Lucas; *D:* Leos Carax; *W:* Leos Carax; Jean-Pol Fargeau; Lauren Sedofsky; *C:* Eric Gautier; *M:* Scott Walker.

Polar 🦴🦴 **2019** Deadly assassin Duncan Vizla (Mikkelsen) is being forced to retire on his 50th birthday. Though he will receive a generous pension package like those before him, the organization that employs him struggles to pay everyone reaching retirement age. Organization head Mr. Blut (Lucas) sends out his own killers to murder those employees. Blut tries to eliminate Duncan through his final job, but Duncan sees through the plot, kills his attackers, and gets his money. Though Ducan retires to his comfortable Montana cabin, he is not free of his past. Based on a graphic novel, it's full of cheesy gore. **118m/C; DVD.** Mads Mikkelsen; Vanessa Anne Hudgens; Katheryn Winnick; Fei Ren; Ruby O. Fee; *D:* Jonas Akerlund; Doobie White; *W:* Jayson Rothwell; *C:* Par M. Ekberg; *M:* Deadmau5. **VIDEO**

The Polar Bear King 🦴🦴 ½ **1994 (PG)** When a handsome prince refuses to marry the evil witch of Summerland, the wicked woman uses her power to turn him into a polar bear. The polar bear prince embarks on a journey to Winterland where he meets and falls in love with a beautiful princess. Together they return to Summerland and try to break the witch's spell. Filmed on location in Norway and Sweden. **87m/C; VHS, DVD.** Maria Bonnevie; Jack Fjeldstad; Tobias Hoesl; Anna-Lotta Larsson; *D:* Ola Solum.

The Polar Express 🦴🦴 ½ **2004 (G)** Your capacity to enjoy this Christmas story will depend on whether or not you find motion capture animation enthralling or creepy. An extended version of Chris Van Allsburg's popular children's book, the story opens on Christmas Eve when nameless skeptic Hero Boy is suddenly awakened by a steam train appearing outside his window. The train is leaving for the North Pole and Hero Boy, encouraged by a kindly conductor (one of Hanks' many roles), joins the passengers on their journey to meet Santa. There are various adventures intended to offer life-affirming lessons but this is a rather melancholy tale with which to entertain the tykes. **100m/C; DVD, Blu-Ray, HD-DVD.** Tom Hanks; Michael Jeter; Nona Gaye; Peter Scolari; Eddie Deezen; Charles Fleischer; Steven Tyler; Daryl Sabara; Leslie Zemeckis; Andre Sogliuzzo; Jimmy Bennett; Isabella Peregrina; *V:* Daryl Sabara; *D:* Robert Zemeckis; *C:* Don Burgess; Robert Presley; *M:* Alan Silvestri.

Polar Storm 🦴 **2009 (PG-13)** SciFi Channel disaster flick. Pieces of a comet strike the Earth, playing havoc with our planet's electromagnetic fields. Astrophysicist James Mayfield (Colman) realizes the danger is spreading while the government tries to cover up the seriousness of the situation. **93m/C; DVD.** Jack Coleman; Holly Dignard; Tyler Johnston; Terry David Mulligan; Roger R. Cross; David Lewis; Jay Brazeau; *D:* Paul Ziller; *W:* Paul Ziller; Jason Bourque; *C:* Mahlon Todd Williams; *M:* Michael Richard Plowman. **CABLE**

Poldark 🦴🦴🦴 **1975** Tempestuous love, political intrigue, and family struggles all set in 18th-century Cornwall, then the copper-producing center of England. Heroic Ross Poldark has just returned from fighting upstart Americans in the Revolutionary War only to discover that his father has died and the family mines are about to be sold to the scheming Warleggan family. Ross struggles to pay off family debts, reclaim his heritage, resolve his feelings for an old love, and fight his attraction to the beguiling, but completely unsuitable, Demelza. Adapted from the novels by Winston Graham. **720m/C; DVD.** *UK* Robin Ellis; Angharad Rees; Jill Townsend; Judy Geeson; Ralph Bates; Richard Morant; Clive Francis; John Baskcomb; Paul Curran; Tilly Tremayne; Mary Wimbush; *D:* Paul Annett; Christopher Barry; Kenneth Ives; *W:* Paul Wheeler; Peter Draper; Jack Pulman. **TV**

Poldark 🦴🦴 **1996** Picks up the story of Ross and Demelza Poldark and their family from where the 1970s BBC series ended. It's 1810 and Ross is spending most of his time in London as a Member of Parliament while at their Cornwall home, Demelza deals with the continuing Warleggan feud. Poldark son, Jeremy, struggles to keep the mine going and daughter Clowance is in the throes of her first romance. Based on the novel "The Stranger from the Sea" by Winston Graham. **105m/C; VHS, DVD.** *GB* John Bowe; Mel Martin; Ioan Gruffudd; Michael Attwell; Kelly Reilly; Hans Matheson; Amanda Ryan; Nicholas Gleaves; Gabrielle Lloyd; Sarah Carpenter; *D:* Richard Laxton; *W:* Robin Mukherjee; *M:* Ian Hughes. **TV**

Poldark 2 🦴🦴🦴 **1975** The further adventures of Ross Poldark, wife Demelza, and assorted family, friends, and enemies, all set in 18th-century Cornwall. Demelza's two meddlesome younger brothers come to live at Nampara, enemy George Warleggan and Ross' old love Elizabeth move too close for comfort, and the uncertainties of the copper mining economy all bring their share of trouble. Adapted from the novels by Winston Graham. Made for British TV; six cassettes. **720m/C; VHS, DVD.** *GB* Robin Ellis; Angharad Rees; Jill Townsend; Judy Geeson; Ralph Bates; Kevin McNally; Brian Stirner; Michael Cadman; Jane Wymark; David Delve; Christopher Biggins; Trudie Styler; *D:* Philip Dudley; Roger Jenkins; *W:* Alexander Baron; John Wiles; Martin Worth. **TV**

Police 🦴🦴 ½ **1985** French police drama with the intense Depardieu as a cop hunting an Algerian drug boss. Matters grow complicated when he falls for the elusive crook's girlfriend. Sometimes gripping, but unveven; the actors were encouraged to improvise. Inspired by the novel "Bodies Are Dust" by P.J. Wolfson. In French with English subtitles. **113m/C; DVD, Blu-Ray.** *FR* Gerard Depardieu; Sophie Marceau; Sandrine Bonnaire; Richard Anconina; Pascale Rocard; *D:* Maurice Pialat; *W:* Catherine Breillat. Venice Film Fest. '85: Actor (Depardieu).

Police Academy 🦴 ½ **1984 (R)** In an attempt to recruit more cops, a big-city police department does away with all its job standards. The producers probably didn't know that they were introducing bad comedy's answer to the "Friday the 13th" series, but it's hard to avoid heaping the sins of its successors on this film. Besides, it's just plain dumb. **96m/C; VHS, DVD, Blu-Ray.** Steve Guttenberg; Kim Cattrall; Bubba Smith; George Gaynes; Michael Winslow; Leslie Easterbrook; Georgina Spelvin; Debralee Scott; *D:* Hugh Wilson; *W:* Hugh Wilson; Pat Proft; Neal Israel; *C:* Michael D. Margulies; *M:* Robert Folk.

Police Academy 2: Their First Assignment 🦴 **1985 (PG-13)** More predictable idiocy from the cop shop. This time they're determined to rid the precinct of some troublesome punks. No real story to speak of, just more high jinks in this mindless sequel. **87m/C; VHS, DVD, Blu-Ray.** Steve Guttenberg; Bubba Smith; Michael Winslow; Art Metrano; Colleen Camp; Howard Hesseman; David Graf; George Gaynes; *D:* Jerry Paris; *W:* Barry W. Blaustein.

Police Academy 3: Back in Training 🦴 **1986 (PG)** In yet another sequel, the bumbling cops find their alma mater is threatened by a budget crunch and they must compete with a rival academy to see which school survives. The "return to school" plot allowed the filmmakers to add new characters to replace those who had some scruples about picking up yet another "Police Lobotomy" check. Followed by three more sequels. **84m/C; VHS, DVD, Blu-Ray.** Steve Guttenberg; Bubba Smith; David Graf; Michael Winslow; Marion Ramsey; Art Metrano; Bobcat Goldthwait; Leslie Easterbrook; Tim Kazurinsky; George Gaynes; Shawn Weatherly; *D:* Jerry Paris; *W:* Gene Quintano; *M:* Robert Folk.

Police Academy 4: Citizens on Patrol 🦴 **1987 (PG)** The comic cop cutups from the first three films aid a citizen's patrol group in their unnamed, but still wacky, hometown. Moronic high jinks ensue. Fourth in the series of five (or is it six?) that began with "Police Academy." **88m/C; VHS, DVD, Blu-Ray.** Steve Guttenberg; Bubba Smith; Michael Winslow; David Graf; Tim Kazurinsky; George Gaynes; Colleen Camp; Bobcat Goldthwait; Sharon Stone; James Carroll; *D:* Jim Drake; *W:* Gene Quintano; *M:* Robert Folk.

Police Academy 5: Assignment Miami Beach WOOF! **1988 (PG)** The fourth sequel, wherein the misfits-with-badges go to Miami and bumble about in the usual manner. It's about time these cops were retired from the force. **89m/C; VHS, DVD, Blu-Ray.** Bubba Smith; David Graf; Michael Winslow; Leslie Easterbrook; Rene Auberjonois; Marion Ramsey; Janet Jones; George Gaynes; Matt McCoy; *D:* Alan Myerson; *W:* Stephen J. Curwick; *M:* Robert Folk.

Police Academy 6: City under Siege 🦴 **1989 (PG)** In what is hoped to be the last in a series of bad comedies, the distinguished graduates pursue three goofballs responsible for a crime wave. **85m/C; VHS, DVD, Blu-Ray.** Bubba Smith; David Graf; Michael Winslow; Leslie Easterbrook; Marion Ramsey; Matt McCoy; Bruce Mahler; G.W. Bailey; George Gaynes; *D:* Peter Bonerz; *W:* Stephen J. Curwick; *M:* Robert Folk.

Police Academy 7: Mission to Moscow 🦴 **1994 (PG)** The seventh in the series is another inept comedy, which finds the chaotic crew tackling a Russian mobster on his Moscow turf—all because of a popular computer game with some sinister software. Like you'll care about the plot anyway. **83m/C; VHS, DVD, Blu-Ray.** George Gaynes; Michael Winslow; David Graf; Leslie Easterbrook; G.W. Bailey; Charlie Schlatter; Ron Perlman; Christopher Lee; *D:* Alan Metter; *W:* Michele S. Chodos; Randolph Davis; *M:* Robert Folk.

Police, Adjective 🦴🦴 *Politist, Adj.* **2009** Undercover cop Cristi (Bacur) is on a dull surveillance assignment, following alleged pot-selling teen Victor (Costin) through the streets of the stagnating, post-communist city of Vasliu. Cristi's officious boss Nelu (Stoica) wants to know who's supplying the teen's drugs but Victor turns out to be just indulging his own tastes. However, Nelu is unwilling to let the situation drop. Cristi and Nelu actually have a linguistic discussion (hence the title) about conscience and justice and the job of the police. Romanian with subtitles. **113m/C; DVD, Streaming.** *RO* Vlad Ivanov; Dragos Bucur; Ion Stoica; Irina Saulescu; Cosmin Selesi; George Remes; Dan Cogalniceanu; Radu Costin; *D:* Corneliu Porumboiu; *W:* Corneliu Porumboiu; *C:* Marius Panduru; *M:* Mirabela Dauer; Yan Raiburg.

Police Story 🦴🦴 ½ *Jackie Chan's Police Force; Police Force; Jackie Chan's Police Story; Ging Chaat Goo Si* **1985 (PG-13)** Chopsocker Chan's assigned to protect a witness in a drug case. Faced by unsavory thugs, he flies through the air with the greatest of ease. Very cool stunts. **92m/C; VHS, DVD, Blu-Ray.** *CH* Jackie Chan; Brigitte Lin; Maggie Cheung; Cho Yuen; Bill Tung; Kenneth Tong; *D:* Jackie Chan; *C:* Yiu-tsou Cheung.

Policewomen 🦴 ½ **1973 (R)** Female undercover agent must stop a ring of gold smugglers. **99m/C; VHS, DVD.** Sondra Currie; Tony Young; Phil Hoover; Elizabeth Stuart; Jeannie Bell; *D:* Lee Frost.

A Polish Vampire in Burbank 🦴🦴 **1980** A shy vampire in Burbank tries again and again to find blood and love. Wacky. **84m/C; VHS, DVD.** Mark Pirro; Lori Sutton; Eddie Deezen; *D:* Mark Pirro.

Polish Wedding 🦴🦴 ½ **1997 (PG-13)** Strong-willed teenager Hala (Danes) throws her working-class Polish/American family into a tizzy when she becomes pregnant and the family decides she must get married. But Hala's not the only one whose life is romntically complicated—her mom Jadzia's (Olin) had a longtime affair with Roman (Serbedzja), which husband Bolek (Byrne) tolerates because he's afraid of losing her. Too slapsticky but the cast is game and it does have heart. **107m/C; VHS, DVD.** Claire Danes; Lena Olin; Gabriel Byrne; Adam Trese; Rade Serbedzija; Mili Avital; Daniel Lapaine; Kristen Bell; *D:* Theresa Connelly; *W:* Theresa Connelly; *C:* Guy Dufaux; *M:* Luis Bacalov.

Polisse ♪♪♪ **2011** Based on the real-life cases and daily lives of the men and women who work the Child Protection Unit in Paris, France. This results in this complex drama falling victim to the common flaw of a screenplay trying to tell interlocking stories--some are more interesting than others. But for every arc or subplot that falls flat, there's one that rings true. A promising drama about people whose real lives are more intense than the average police flick. French with subtitles. **128m/C; DVD.** *FR* Maiwenn; Joey Starr; Karin Viard; Marina Fois; Nicolas Duvauchelle; Karole Rocher; Emmanuelle Bercot; ***D:*** Maiwenn; ***W:*** Maiwenn; Emmanuelle Bercot; ***C:*** Pierre Aim; ***M:*** Stephen Warbeck.

Politics ♪♪ **1931** Widowed Hattie (Dressler) decides to run for mayor because the incumbent is doing nothing about the town's crime problem with bootleggers and other gangsters. Unbeknownst to Hattie, her daughter Myrtle (Morley) is involved with Benny (Bakewell), who wants to get out of the mob. Hattie persuades the town's married women to withhold domestic services so they can influence their husbands (shades of Lysistrata). Her campaign is going fine until the Benny problem comes to light. **73m/B; DVD.** Marie Dressler; Karen Morley; William "Billy" Bakewell; Polly Moran; Roscoe Ates; John Miljan; Tom McGuire; Joan Marsh; Kane Richmond; ***D:*** Charles Reisner; ***W:*** Wells Root; ***C:*** Clyde De Vinna.

The Polka King ♪♪ **2018** A biopic of the Polish immigrant Jan Lewan (Black), who was a successful amateur criminal and upbeat polka bandleader. The owner of a strip mall trinket shop, he dreams of building his own business empire. He starts taking investments from fans, offering to pay interest, and truly believing that he will pay them back. He learns that he did not file the correct paperwork after a visit from the feds. Lying to the government, Jan continues to take more investments and to expand his ventures. A generally strong cast and worthwhile performances do not fully compensate for the script's shortcomings. **95m/C; DVD.** Jack Black; Jenny Slate; Jason Schwartzman; Jacki Weaver; J.B. Smoove; ***D:*** Maya Forbes; ***W:*** Maya Forbes; M. Wallace Wolodarsky; ***C:*** Andrei Bowden Schwartz; ***M:*** Theodore Shapiro. **VIDEO**

Pollock ♪♪♪ **2000 (R)** First-time director Harris (who also stars) scores a personal triumph with his bio of abstract expressionist artist Jackson Pollock (whom the actor resembles quite astonishingly). Pollock is a troubled soul, beset by alcoholism and insecurity, who leads himself down a self-destructive path. The film covers 1941-1956 as Pollock struggles to find his artistic breakthrough and marries fellow artist Lee Krasner (Harden), a tough New Yorker who takes his career in hand, but his success only exacerbates Pollock's problems. Solid production with a couple of great leading performances. **122m/C; VHS, DVD.** Ed Harris; Marcia Gay Harden; Amy Madigan; Jennifer Connelly; Jeffrey Tambor; Bud Cort; John Heard; Val Kilmer; ***D:*** Ed Harris; ***W:*** Barbara Turner; Susan J. Emshwiller; ***C:*** Lisa Rinzler; ***M:*** Jeff Beal. Oscars '00: Support. Actress (Harden); N.Y. Film Critics '00: Support. Actress (Harden).

Polly of the Circus ♪♪ ½ **1932** Circus aerialist Polly Fisher (Davies) suffers a fall and is taken to the nearby home of Rev. John Hartley (Gable). The two are immediately smitten and soon marry, shocking his prudish parishoners. The preacher even loses his job, which upsets his bride so much that she leaves him, thinking he will be reinstated. Davies is charming but Gable is somewhat miscast as the earnest clergyman. Remake of the 1917 silent. **72m/B; DVD.** Marion Davies; Clark Gable; Sir C. Aubrey Smith; Raymond Hatton; David Landau; ***D:*** Alfred Santell; ***W:*** Laurence E. Johnson; Carey Wilson; ***C:*** George Barnes.

Pollyanna ♪♪♪ ½ **1960** Based on the Eleanor Porter story about an enchanting young girl whose contagious enthusiasm and zest for life touches the hearts of all she meets. Mills is perfect in the title role and was awarded a special Oscar for outstanding juvenile performance. A distinguished supporting cast is the icing on the cake in this delightful Disney confection. Original version was filmed in 1920 with Mary Pickford. **134m/C; VHS, DVD, Blu-Ray.** Hayley Mills; Jane Wyman; Richard Egan; Karl Malden; Nancy Olson; Adolphe Menjou; Donald Crisp; Agnes Moorehead; Kevin Corcoran; ***D:*** David Swift; ***W:*** David Swift; ***C:*** Russell Harlan; ***M:*** Paul J. Smith.

Poltergeist ♪ ½ **2015 (PG-13)** The latest remake that nobody asked for basically serves as a sped-up cover version of the original, lacking the heart and depth. The Bowen family (headed by Rockwell and DeWitt) stumble first on tough times economically and then an all-out haunting in their new home. Hands reach up from the ground, trees grab kids, and their youngest daughter gets sucked into her closet into a space in between reality and the afterlife. Only real ghost hunters and a family's love can save her. Tobe Hooper's original was a commentary on technology and the power of family. Gil Kenan's remake is hollow. **93m/C; DVD, Blu-Ray.** Sam Rockwell; Rosemarie DeWitt; Saxon Sharbino; Kyle Catlett; Kennedi Clements; ***D:*** Gil Kenan; ***W:*** David Lindsay-Abaire; ***C:*** Javier Aguirresarobe; ***M:*** Marc Streitenfeld.

Poltergeist ♪♪♪♪ **1982 (PG)** This production has Stephen Spielberg written all over it. A young family's home becomes a house of horrors when they are terrorized by menancing spirits who abduct their five-year-old daughter...through the TV screen! Roller-coaster thrills and chills, dazzling special effects, and perfectly timed humor highlight this stupendously scary ghost story. **114m/C; VHS, DVD, Blu-Ray.** JoBeth Williams; Craig T. Nelson; Beatrice Straight; Heather O'Rourke; Zelda Rubinstein; Dominique Dunne; Oliver Robins; Richard Lawson; James Karen; Michael McManus; ***D:*** Tobe Hooper; ***W:*** Steven Spielberg; Michael Grais; Mark Victor; ***C:*** Matthew F. Leonetti; ***M:*** Jerry Goldsmith.

Poltergeist 2: The Other Side ♪♪ ½ **1986 (PG-13)** Adequate sequel to the Spielburg-produced venture into the supernatural, where demons follow the Freeling family in their efforts to recapture the clairvoyant young daughter Carol Anne. The film includes sojourns into Indian lore and a four-foot high agave worm designed by H.R. Giger. The movie was followed by "Poltergeist 3" in 1988. **92m/C; VHS, DVD, Blu-Ray.** Craig T. Nelson; JoBeth Williams; Heather O'Rourke; Will Sampson; Julian Beck; Geraldine Fitzgerald; Oliver Robins; Zelda Rubinstein; ***D:*** Brian Gibson; ***W:*** Mark Victor; Michael Grais; ***C:*** Andrew Laszlo; ***M:*** Jerry Goldsmith.

Poltergeist 3 ♪ ½ **1988 (PG-13)** Wrestling with the supernatural has finally unnerved Carol Ann and she's sent to stay with her aunt and uncle in Chicago where she attends a school for gifted children with emotional disorders. Guess who follows her? Uninspired acting, threadbare premise, and one ghastly encounter too many. Oddly, O'Rourke died suddenly four months before the film's release. **97m/C; VHS, DVD, Blu-Ray.** Tom Skerritt; Nancy Allen; Heather O'Rourke; Lara Flynn Boyle; Zelda Rubinstein; ***D:*** Gary Sherman; ***W:*** Gary Sherman; Brian Taggert; ***C:*** Alex Nepomniaschy.

The Poltergeist of Borley Forest ♪ ½ *You Will Love Me* **2013** A horror-thriller centered on a poltergeist with boundary issues. After Paige Pritchard (Petrano) spends an evening of teenage partying in the woods, she finds her overwhelmed by visitations from the supernatural that grow ever more violent. As she tries to understand what is happening, she learns a dark secret related to this evil poltergeist who has chosen to haunt her. Paige tries to stop it before she and her friends suffer any more at its hands. **102m/C; DVD, Streaming, Download.** Marina Petrano; Christopher Ingle; Rhea Rossiter; Weston Adwell; Nicholas Barrera; ***D:*** Stephen McKendree; ***W:*** R. Presley Stephens; ***C:*** Stephen McKendree; ***M:*** Chris Harper; Geoff Langhans.

Poltergeist: The Legacy ♪♪ ½ **1996** Pilot for the cable series about a secret international society, the Legacy, which is devoted to the paranormal and to protecting mankind from supernatural evil. Derek Rayne (De Lint), the head of the San Francisco Legacy house, must find the last of five sepulchers containing the evil spirits of five fallen angels. This takes him and his cohorts to Ireland where Rachel Corrigan (Shaver) and her young psychic daughter Kat (Purvis) come into unwitting possession of the fifth box and untold danger. **86m/C; VHS, DVD.** Derek de Lint; Helen Shaver; Alexandra Purvis; Martin Cummins; Robbi Chong; Patrick Fitzgerald; Jordan Bayne; William Sadler; Daniel Pilon; Chad Krowchuk; ***D:*** Stuart Gillard; ***W:*** Brad Wright; ***C:*** Manfred Guthe. **CABLE**

Polyester ♪♪ ½ **1981 (R)** Amusing satire on middle-class life, described by producer, director and writer Waters as "'Father Knows Best' gone berserk." Forlorn housewife Divine pines for the man of her dreams while the rest of her life is falling apart at the seams. Filmed in "Odorama," a hilarious gimmick in which theatre goers were provided with scratch-n-sniff cards, containing specific scents corresponding to key scenes. Video watchers will have to use their imagination in experiencing a wide range of smells. The first of Waters' more mainstream films. Features songs by Murray and Harry. **86m/C; VHS, DVD, Blu-Ray.** Divine; Tab Hunter; Edith Massey; Mink Stole; Stiv Bators; David Samson; Mary Garlington; Kenneth King; Joni-Ruth White; Jean Hill; Hans Kramm; Mary Vivian Pearce; Cookie Mueller; Susan Lowe; George Stover; George Figgs; Steve Yeager; ***D:*** John Waters; ***W:*** John Waters; ***C:*** David Insley; ***M:*** Deborah Harry; Michael Kamen.

Pom Poko ♪♪ ½ *Heisei tanuki gassen pompoko; The Raccoon War* **1994 (PG)** Despite being referred to as the Raccoon War, this film actually stars Tanuki—a sort of wild dog native to Japan that resembles a raccoon. The humans are encroaching upon the Tanuki's forest realm with new urban development, and they've decided to fight for their forest homes any way they can. Not necessarily a children's film despite being animated. A working knowledge of Japanese myth will aid greatly in understanding. **112m/C; DVD, Blu-Ray.** *JP V:* Maurice LaMarche; Jonathan Taylor Thomas; J.K. Simmons; Tress MacNeille; Clancy Brown; Jess Harnell; Kevin M. Richardson; Olivia D'Abo; Marc Donato; Brian George; Brian Posehn; Jillian Bowen; David Oliver Cohen; John Di Maggio; Wally Kurth; ***D:*** Isao Takahata; ***W:*** Isao Takahata.

Pom Pom Girls ♪ ½ **1976 (R)** High school seniors, intent on having one last fling before graduating, get involved in crazy antics, clumsy romances, and football rivalries. **90m/C; VHS, DVD, Blu-Ray.** Robert Carradine; Jennifer Ashley; Michael Mullins; Cheryl "Rainbeaux" Smith; Dianne Lee Hart; Lisa Reeves; Bill Adler; ***D:*** Joseph Ruben; ***W:*** Joseph Ruben; ***C:*** Stephen M. Katz; ***M:*** Michael Lloyd.

POM Wonderful Presents: The Greatest Movie Ever Sold ♪♪ ½ *The Greatest Movie Ever Sold* **2011 (PG-13)** Writer/director Spurlock's often humorous documentary on advertising and product placement. It's brought to you by a pomegranate juice company because he financed the film through such endeavors to convey the ubiquity of advertising in current culture. Spurlock, who includes himself as a brand, then demonstrates successful pitching and marketing techniques and deconstructs audience manipulations, including for such companies as JetBlue and Hyatt, and for shampoo Mane 'N Tail and Merrell Shoes among other products. **86m/C; DVD, Blu-Ray, On Demand.** Morgan Spurlock; ***D:*** Morgan Spurlock; ***W:*** Morgan Spurlock; Jeremy Chilnick; ***C:*** Daniel Marracino; ***M:*** Jon Spurney.

The Pompatus of Love ♪♪ ½ **1995 (R)** Remember Steve Miller's song "The Joker"??well, that's where the title comes from—and we still don't know what it means. But the film's about four New York guys and the mystery of women. They may be (reasonably) bright and literate but they still don't have a clue about love or how to grow-up. Naturally, the women they know—or meet—are all too smart for them. **99m/C; VHS, DVD.** Jon Cryer; Tim Guinee; Adrian Pasdar; Adam Oliensis; Kristen Wilson; Dana Wheeler-Nicholson; Paige Turco; Mia Sara; Kristin Scott Thomas; Arabella Field; Jennifer Tilly; Roscoe Lee Browne; ***D:*** Richard Schenkman; ***W:*** Jon Cryer; Adam Oliensis; Richard Schenkman; ***C:*** Russell Fine; ***M:*** John Hill. **VIDEO**

Pompeii ♪ **2014 (PG-13)** Perhaps enjoyable as a so-bad-it's-good guilty pleasure, Anderson delivers another cinematic turd by revisiting the swords-and-sandals genre that has produced so many wastes of time. It is 79 A.D. and Milo (Harington) is a slave-turned-gladiator who wants to save his love Cassia (Browning) before the city of Pompeii is frozen in time by a volcano's eruption. Milo has to fight his way out of the gladiator's arena to get to Cassia before it's too late and you'll have to fight eye-rolling and yawns to care whether or not he makes it. **105m/C; DVD, Blu-Ray.** *CA GE* Kit Harington; Kiefer Sutherland; Emily Browning; Adewale Akinnuoye-Agbaje; Jared Harris; Carrie-Anne Moss; Jessica Lucas; ***D:*** Paul W.S. Anderson; ***W:*** Janet Scott Batchler; Lee Batchler; Michael Robert Johnson; ***C:*** Glen MacPherson; ***M:*** Clinton Shorter.

Poms ♪♪ **2019 (PG-13)** After a long career as a teacher, Martha (Keaton) moves to a cheery retirement community in Georgia. Suffering from cancer, she is not interested in joining any of the clubs as required or being friendly with other community members. When neighbor Sheryl (Weaver) learns that Martha was selected to be a cheerleader in high school but never got to perform because of her mother's illness, she encourages Martha to organize her own squad and the idea gives Martha new life. Though predictable, director Hayes debut is well-paced and performances by Keaton and her co-stars are enjoyable. **91m/C; DVD, Blu-Ray.** *UK US* Diane Keaton; Jacki Weaver; Celia Weston; Alisha Boe; Charlie Tahan; ***D:*** Zara Hayes; ***W:*** Shane Atkinson; ***C:*** Tim Orr; ***M:*** Deborah Lurie.

Ponette ♪♪ **1995** Four-year-old Ponette (Thivisol) is hard-pressed to understand what's happening to her family after her mother is killed in a car accident. Her father can't seem to explain it properly, so Ponette comes to her own acceptance with the help of some school friends. Film drew some controversy when the very young Thivisol was awarded the best actress award at the Venice Film Festival—since Thivisol was thought by some critics to be too young to "act," director Doillon was accused of manipulating the youngster in order to get a performance. French with subtitles. **92m/C; VHS, DVD.** *FR* Victorie Thivisol; Marie Trintignant; Claire Nebout; Xavier Beauvois; ***D:*** Jacques Doillon; ***W:*** Jacques Doillon; ***C:*** Caroline Champetier; ***M:*** Philippe Sarde. N.Y. Film Critics '97: Foreign Film; Venice Film Fest. '96: Actress (Thivisol).

Pontiac Moon ♪ ½ **1994 (PG-13)** Danson plays a high school teacher who takes his son on a road trip to Spires of the Moon National Park hoping to arrive simultaneously with the astronauts' first lunar landing. His wife (Steenburgen) decides to follow them, although she's phobic about leaving the house and hasn't set foot outside in seven years. Sincere yet tedious film about father-son bonding has a few heartfelt moments, but not enough to sustain interest for entire viewing period. Best (and only) reason for watching: Monument Valley scenery. **108m/C; VHS, DVD.** Ted Danson; Mary Steenburgen; Ryan Todd; Eric Schweig; Cathy Moriarty; Max Gail; Lisa Jane Persky; ***D:*** Peter Medak; ***W:*** Finn Taylor; Jeffrey Brown; ***M:*** Randy Edelman.

Pontypool ♪ ½ **2009** The staff of radio station CLSY broadcasts from a church basement in the rural Ontario town of the title. On Valentine's Day, the station is besieged by callers reporting cases of extreme violence in the town and it turns out tainted English language (especially endearments) is making zombies out of the listeners. So to prevent the spread of the infection, hard-drinking DJ Grant (McHattie) and his cohorts resort to broken French to get by (only in bilingual Canada). Burgess adapted from his novel "Pontypool Changes Everything." English and French with subtitles. **95m/C; Blu-Ray.** *CA* Stephen McHattie; Rick Roberts; Grant Alianak; Lisa Houle; Georgina Reilly; ***D:*** Bruce McDonald; ***W:*** Tony Burgess; ***C:*** Miroslaw Baszak; ***M:*** Claude Foisy.

Pony Express ♪♪♪ **1953** Buffalo Bill Cody and Wild Bill Hickok join forces to extend the Pony Express mail route west to California through rain and sleet, snow and hail. Far from a factual account but good for extending the myth of the Old West. **101m/C; VHS, DVD.** Charlton Heston; Rhonda Fleming; Jan Sterling; Forrest Tucker; ***D:*** Jerry Hopper; ***C:*** Ray Rennahan.

Pony Express Rider ♪♪♪ **1976 (G)** Young man with a mission joins up with the Pony Express hoping to bag the male responsible for killing his pa. The well-produced script boasts a bevy of veteran western character actors, all lending, solid, rugged performances. **100m/C; VHS, DVD.** Stewart Petersen; Henry Wilcoxon; Buck Taylor; Maureen McCormick; Joan Caulfield; Ken Curtis; Slim Pickens; Dub Taylor; Jack Elam; ***D:*** Robert Totten.

Ponyo 🦴🦴🦴 *Gake no Ue no Ponyo; Ponyo on the Cliff by the Sea* **2008 (G)** Miyazaki's wonderfully joyous animated story (a variation of "The Little Mermaid") finds young fish princess Ponyo so curious about the surface world that she goes exploring and needs to be rescued by Sosuke, a five-year-old boy who promises to protect her. So Ponyo decides to become human and stay awhile, but Ponyo's sorcerer father eventually takes her home, only to have his willful daughter escape again. The Japanese film was redone with an English-language cast. **100m/C; DVD, Blu-Ray.** *JP V:* Cate Blanchett; Tina Fey; Liam Neeson; Betty White; Lily Tomlin; Cloris Leachman; Noah Lindsey Cyrus; Matt Damon; Frankie Jonas; ***D:*** Hayao Miyazaki; ***W:*** Hayao Miyazaki; ***M:*** Joe Hisaishi.

Poodle Springs 🦴🦴 **1998** In 1963, Philip Marlowe (Caan) has a wealthy young wife (Meyer) and is living in Palm Springs. Bored, he decides to get back into the PI biz and is soon dealing with land swindlers and dead bodies (and a confusing plot) that lead to a political conspiracy. Raymond Chandler died before finishing his novel and his estate eventually hired Robert B. Parker to complete it from Chandler's outline. **96m/C; DVD.** James Caan; Dina Meyer; David Keith; Brian Cox; Julia Campbell; Nia Peeples; Joe Don Baker; ***D:*** Bob Rafelson; ***W:*** Tom Stoppard; ***C:*** Stuart Dryburgh; ***M:*** Michael Small. **CABLE**

The Pool Boys 🦴 **2010 (R)** Pointless, derivative sex comedy. Needing a summer job to make his college tuition, Alex goes to Beverly Hills to work with his supposedly successful cousin Roger. Roger turns out to be a lazy, dope-smoking pool cleaner but, thanks to a client needing a mansion sitter and Alex falling for heart-of-gold call girl Laura, they figure out a way to make some dough. **88m/C; DVD, Blu-Ray.** Matthew Lillard; Brett Davern; Rachelle Lefevre; Jay Thomas; Efrem Ramirez; Tom Arnold; ***D:*** James B. Rogers; ***W:*** Justin Ware; ***C:*** Tom Priestly, Jr. **VIDEO**

Poolhall Junkies 🦴🦴 **1/2 2002 (R)** Johnny Doyle (writer-director Callahan) is a pool hustler who aspired to greatness until his mentor/backer Joe (Palminteri) sabotaged his chance at the pro tour and found himself a new boy, Brad (Schroder). Johnny impresses his girlfriend's Uncle Mike (Walken), who agrees to bankroll his road to the final showdown with Brad and Joe. Gritty but enthusiastic debut for Callahan doesn't wallow in cliches, it revels in 'em. Fortunately, it all works because of the talents of the elder actors (including Steiger in his last role) and the good sense of the younger ones to stay out of their way. Excellent pool hall action. **94m/C; VHS, DVD.** Mars Callahan; Michael Rosenbaum; Chazz Palminteri; Rod Steiger; Christopher Walken; Rick Schroder; Alison Eastwood; Glenn Plummer; Ernie Reyes, Jr.; Peter Mark Richman; Anson Mount; ***D:*** Mars Callahan; ***W:*** Mars Callahan; Chris Corso; ***C:*** Robert Morris; ***M:*** Richard Glasser.

Poor Little Rich Girl: The Barbara Hutton Story 🦴🦴 **1/2 1987** Biodrama of the one-time richest woman in America, Woolworth heiress Hutton (Fawcett), and her extravagant lifestyle. She married seven times (including actor Cary Grant) until falling into self-destructive alcohol and drug addictions. Lavishly presented but superficial. Based on the book by C. David Heymann. **98m/C; VHS, DVD.** Farrah Fawcett; Bruce Davison; Kevin McCarthy; Burl Ives; James Read; Stephane Audran; Anne Francis; David Ackroyd; Tony Peck; Zoe Wanamaker; Amadeus August; ***D:*** Charles Jarrott; ***W:*** Dennis Turner; ***M:*** Richard Rodney Bennett. **TV**

Poor Man's Game 🦴🦴🦴 *Poor Boy's Game* **2006 (R)** Provocative look at racism and redemption. White working-class Donnie Rose (Sutherland) is released from prison after serving 10 years for the brutal beating of a black man named Keith Carvery, who was left brain damaged. The racially-motivated incident has continued to divide the Halifax communities. Having boxed in the joint, Donnie agrees to a grudge match with local fisticuffs star Ossie (Alexander), but, after much soul-searching, George Carvery (a strong Glover) decides that an eye-for-an-eye has to stop and he offers to become Donnie's trainer so he'll have a chance to survive. **104m/C; DVD.** *CA* Danny Glover; Rossif Sutherland; Flex Alexander; Stephen McHattie; Tonya Lee Williams; Greg Bryk; K.C. Collins; Laura Reagan; ***D:*** Clement Virgo; ***W:*** Chaz Thorne; Clement Virgo; ***C:*** Luc Montpellier; ***M:*** Bryon Kent Wong.

Poor Pretty Eddie 🦴 **1/2** *Black Vengeance; Heartbreak Motel; Redneck County* **1973 (R)** A young black singer gets waylaid and taken in by a twisted white Southern clan. An incredibly sleazy movie which boasts Shelly Winters performing a strip act. **90m/C; DVD, Blu-Ray.** Leslie Uggams; Shelley Winters; Michael Christian; Ted Cassidy; Slim Pickens; Dub Taylor; ***D:*** Richard Robinson.

Poor White Trash 🦴 **1/2 2000 (R)** One-note comedy. Buddies Mike (Denman) and Lennie's (Tierney) prank on a local store owner backfires and the boys are in bigtime trouble that could be eased if they had money for defense attorney Ron (Devane). So Mike's trailer-trash mom, Linda (Young), and her boy toy Brian (London) agree to help the dummies raise the money through some burglaries that, of course, get botched. The gags are repeated so often that they lose what humor they minimally possessed. **85m/C; VHS, DVD.** Jacob Tierney; Sean Young; Jason London; Tony Denman; William Devane; Jaime Pressly; M. Emmet Walsh; Tim Kazurinsky; Charles Solomon, Jr.; ***D:*** Michael Addis; ***W:*** Michael Addis; ***C:*** Peter Kowalski; ***M:*** Tree Adams.

Pootie Tang 🦴 **1/2 2001 (PG-13)** The gibberish-babbling Pootie Tang (Crouther) was mildly amusing as a one-joke sketch on "The Chris Rock Show." The premise here is that Pootie talks so cool, no one wants to admit they don't have a clue what he's saying. He's also a role model to all the kids and fights crime with his whip-crackin' belt, which he wields like a kung-fu master. Evil Lecter (Vaughn) tricks Pootie into endorsing his empire of cigarettes, booze and junk food by using the feminine wiles of slinky Ireenie (Coolidge). Pootie retires in disgrace before coming back to make everything wambly again. **81m/C; VHS, DVD.** Lance Crouther; Jennifer Coolidge; Robert Vaughn; Chris Rock; Reg E. Cathey; Wanda Sykes; Dave Attell; Mario Joyner; J.B. Smoove; Cathy Trien; Andy Richter; Kristen Bell; ***Cameo(s):*** Bob Costas; ***D:*** Louis CK; ***W:*** Louis CK; ***C:*** Willy Kurant.

Popcorn 🦴🦴 **1989 (R)** A killer stalks a movie audience who is unaware that his crimes are paralleling those in the very film they are watching. **93m/C; VHS, DVD, Blu-Ray.** Jill Schoelen; Tom Villard; Dee Wallace; Derek Rydall; Elliott Hurst; Kelly Jo Minter; Malcolm Danare; Ray Walston; Tony Roberts; Karen Witter; ***D:*** Mark Herrier; Alan Ormsby; ***W:*** Alan Ormsby; ***C:*** Ronnie Taylor.

Pope Dreams 🦴🦴 **1/2 2006** Quiet, aimless teenager Andy works for his dad and drums in a garage band. His devoutly Catholic mother Kristina is dying and Andy (who's closest to her) is trying to come up with a way to fulfill her dream of seeing the Vatican. Meanwhile, might-be girlfriend Brady discovers the guy she chose to date because she thought it would upset her dad is really a keeper. **105m/C; DVD.** Marne(tte) Patterson; Stephen Tobolowsky; Noel Fisher; Rex Smith; Phillip Vaden; Julie Hagerty; David Shatraw; Larisa Oleynik; ***D:*** Patrick Hogan; ***W:*** Patrick Hogan; ***C:*** John Ealer; ***M:*** Joel J. Richard. **VIDEO**

The Pope of Greenwich Village 🦴🦴 **1/2 1984 (R)** Two Italian-American cousins (Rourke and Roberts) struggle to escape the trap of poverty in New York's Greenwich Village. When a small crime goes wrong in a big way, the two must learn about deception and loyalty. Mostly character study; Page is exceptional. Inferior re-run of the "Mean Streets" idea does have its moments. **122m/C; VHS, DVD, Blu-Ray.** Eric Roberts; Mickey Rourke; Daryl Hannah; Geraldine Page; Tony Musante; M. Emmet Walsh; Kenneth McMillan; Burt Young; Jack Kehoe; Philip Bosco; Val Avery; Joe Grifasi; Tony DiBenedetto; ***D:*** Stuart Rosenberg; ***W:*** Vincent Patrick; ***C:*** John Bailey; ***M:*** Dave Grusin.

Popeye 🦴🦴 **1980 (PG)** The cartoon sailor brought to life is on a search to find his long-lost father. Along the way, he meets Olive Oyl and adopts little Sweet Pea. Williams accomplishes the near-impossible feat of physically resembling the title character, and the whole movie does accomplish the maker's stated goal of "looking like a comic strip," but it isn't anywhere near as funny as it should be. **114m/C; VHS, DVD.** Robin Williams; Shelley Duvall; Ray Walston; Paul Dooley; Bill Irwin; Paul Smith; Linda Hunt; Richard Libertini; Ned Dowd; Allan Nicholls; ***D:*** Robert Altman; ***W:*** Jules Feiffer; ***M:*** Harry Nilsson.

Popi 🦴🦴🦴 **1969 (G)** Arkin is the heart and soul of this poignant charmer in his role as a Puerto Rican immigrant hell-bent on securing a better life outside the ghetto for his two sons. His zany efforts culminate in one outrageous scheme to set them adrift off the Florida coast in hopes they will be rescued and raised by a wealthy family. Far fetched, but ultimately heartwarming. **115m/C; VHS, DVD.** Alan Arkin; Rita Moreno; Miguel Alejandro; Reuben Figueroa; ***D:*** Arthur Hiller.

The Poppy Is Also a Flower 🦴 **1/2** *Poppies Are Also Flowers; Opium Connection* **1966 (PG)** A star-laden, anti-drug drama produced by the United Nations. Filmed on location in Iran, Monaco, and Italy. Based on a drug trade thriller by Ian Fleming that explains how poppies, converted into heroin, are brought into the United States. **100m/C; VHS, DVD.** E.G. Marshall; Trevor Howard; Gilbert Roland; Eli Wallach; Marcello Mastroianni; Angie Dickinson; Rita Hayworth; Yul Brynner; Trini Lopez; Bessie Love; ***D:*** Terence Young. **TV**

Popstar: Never Stop Never Stopping 🦴🦴🦴 **2016 (R)** Acting as a modern-day "This is Spinal Tap" for the Justin Bieber crowd, Andy Samberg's musical comedy, working with the other members of the SNL-based comedy troupe known as The Lonely Island, is funny and clever. Samberg plays a pop prince known as conner4real, whose new album fails to catch on with his loyal fan base, forcing a reunion with the boy band group that made him famous in the first place, The Style Boyz. The loose plot is just the structure on which to hang jabs at the self-obsession of the music industry and fill this laugh-out-loud comedy with a stunning number of cameos. **86m/C; DVD, Blu-Ray.** Andy Samberg; Jorma Taccone; Akiva Schaffer; Sarah Silverman; Tim Meadows; ***D:*** Jorma Taccone; Akiva Schaffer; ***W:*** Andy Samberg; Jorma Taccone; Akiva Schaffer; ***C:*** Brandon Trost; ***M:*** Matthew Compton.

Population 436 🦴🦴 **2006 (R)** Census investigator Steve Kady (Sisto) is sent to the reclusive town of Rockwell Falls, where the population has remained unchanged at 436 people for more than 100 years. The town seems idyllic although excess residents have a tendency to succumb to a strange fever. Can Steve stay alive long enough to figure out what's really going on? Sisto plays the horror straight and Limp Bizkit frontman Durst is amiable as the town law. **92m/C; DVD.** *CA* Jeremy Sisto; Fred Durst; R.H. Thomson; Peter Outerbridge; Charlotte Sullivan; David Ames; David Fox; ***D:*** Michelle Maxwell MacLaren; ***W:*** Michael Kingston; ***C:*** Thomas Burstyn. **VIDEO**

Porcile 🦴🦴 *Pigsty; Porcherie* **1969** Pasolini intertwines the story of a soldier cannibal living in a medieval age with the son of an ex-Nazi industrialist in present day Germany. Both the soldier and the young German (who prefers pigs to his fiance) become sacrificial victims of their differing societies. A grotesque fable on Pasolini's hatred of middle class mores and the 20th century. In Italian with English subtitles. **90m/C; VHS, DVD.** *IT FR* Pierre Clementi; Franco Citti; Jean-Pierre Leaud; Anna Wiazemsky; Ugo Tognazzi; Alberto Lionello; ***D:*** Pier Paolo Pasolini; ***W:*** Pier Paolo Pasolini; ***C:*** Tonino Delli Colli; Armando Nannuzzi; Giuseppe Ruzzolini.

Pork Chop Hill 🦴🦴🦴 **1959** A powerful, hard-hitting account of the last hours of the Korean War. Peck is totally believable as the man ordered to hold his ground against the hopeless onslaught of Chinese Communist hordes. A chilling, stark look in the face of a no-win situation. Top notch cast and masterful directing. **97m/B; VHS, DVD, Blu-Ray.** Gregory Peck; Harry Guardino; Rip Torn; George Peppard; James Edwards; Bob Steele; Woody Strode; Robert (Bobby) Blake; Martin Landau; Norman Fell; Bert Remsen; George Shibata; Biff (Elliott) Elliot; Barry Atwater; Martin Garth; Lew Gallo; Charles Aidman; Leonard Graves; Ken Lynch; Paul Comi; Cliff Ketchum; Abel Fernandez; Gavin MacLeod; ***D:*** Lewis Milestone; ***W:*** James R. Webb; ***C:*** Sam Leavitt; ***M:*** Leonard Rosenman.

Porky's 🦴🦴 **1/2 1982 (R)** Investigation of teen horniness set in South Florida during the fab '50s. Irreverent comedy follows the misadventures of six youths imprisoned in Angel Beach High School who share a common interest: girls. Their main barrier to sexual success: the no-touch babes they lust after and the incredibly stupid adults who run the world. Fairly dumb and tasteless with occasional big laughs that earned mega bucks at the drive-in. **94m/C; VHS, DVD, Blu-Ray.** *CA* Dan Monahan; Wyatt Knight; Scott Colomby; Tony Ganios; Mark Herrier; Cyril O'Reilly; Roger Wilson; Alex Karras; Kim Cattrall; Kaki Hunter; Nancy Parsons; Boyd Gaines; Douglas McGrath; Susan Clark; Art Hindle; Wayne Maunder; Chuck "Porky" Mitchell; Eric Christmas; Bob (Benjamin) Clark; ***D:*** Bob (Benjamin) Clark; ***W:*** Bob (Benjamin) Clark; ***C:*** Reginald Morris; ***M:*** Paul Zaza; Carl Zittrer.

Porky's 2: The Next Day 🦴🦴 **1983 (R)** More tame tomfoolery about teenage sex drives, Shakespeare, fat high school teachers, the Ku Klux Klan, and streaking in the Florida high school where it all began. Outright caricature shares the stage with juvenile humor, some of which may induce laughter. **100m/C; VHS, DVD, Blu-Ray.** *CA* Bill Wiley; Dan Monahan; Wyatt Knight; Cyril O'Reilly; Roger Wilson; Tony Ganios; Mark Herrier; Scott Colomby; Kaki Hunter; Nancy Parsons; Eric Christmas; Art Hindle; ***D:*** Bob (Benjamin) Clark; ***W:*** Alan Ormsby; Bob (Benjamin) Clark; Roger E. Swaybill; ***C:*** Reginald Morris; ***M:*** Carl Zittrer.

Porky's Revenge 🦴 **1985 (R)** The Angel Beach High School students are out to get revenge against Porky who orders the school basketball coach to throw the championship game. The second of the "Porky's" sequels. **95m/C; VHS, DVD, Blu-Ray.** *CA* Dan Monahan; Wyatt Knight; Tony Ganios; Nancy Parsons; Chuck "Porky" Mitchell; Kaki Hunter; Kimberly Evenson; Scott Colomby; Mark Herrier; Eric Christmas; Rose McVeigh; ***D:*** James Komack; ***W:*** Ziggy Steinberg; ***C:*** Robert C. Jessup; ***M:*** Dave Edmunds.

The Pornographer 🦴🦴 **2000 (R)** In his introduction, director Atchison says that the inspiration for this story of lonely guy Paul Ryan (Degood) who becomes a porno filmmaker almost by accident came from his own situation. While trying to raise money for his own legitimate movies, Atchison briefly considered trying to make skin flicks to raise money. Instead, he came up with an intriguing little video premiere. **88m/C; VHS, DVD.** Michael Degood; Craig Wasson; Monique Parent; Katheryn Cain; ***D:*** Doug Atchison; ***W:*** Doug Atchison; ***C:*** Christopher Mosio; ***M:*** Warner David Jansen.

The Pornographers 🦴🦴🦴 **1966** Bizzare, black comedy focuses on a part-time porno filmmaker lusting after the daughter of the widow he lives with and trying to cope with his family, the world, and himself. A perversely fascinating exploration of contemporary Japanese society and the many facets of sexual emotion. In Japanese with English subtitles. **128m/B; VHS, DVD.** *JP* Shoichi Ozawa; Massaomi Konda; Sumiko Sakamoto; Haruo Tanaka; Keiko Sagowa; ***D:*** Shohei Imamura.

Pornography: A Thriller 🦴 **1/2 2010** Confusing tri-part storytelling. Gay porn star Mark Anton (Grey) disappeared in 1995 after giving an interview. Fourteen years later, writer Michael Castigan (Montgomery), who's working on a history of porn, discovers a tape in the wall of his Brooklyn apartment (where Mark lived) that may be the key to his fate. Then porn star-turned-director Matt Stevens (Scherer) decides to make a movie about Mark but starts having terrible nightmares and is seemingly haunted by Mark's ghost. **113m/C; DVD.** Matthew Montgomery; Pete Scherer; Jared Grey; Walter Delmar; Dylan Vox; Nick Salamone; ***D:*** David Kittredge; ***W:***

David Kittredge; *C:* Ivan Corona; *M:* Robb Williamson.

Porridge ✌✌ *Doing Time* **1991** A British comedy inspired by the popular BBC situation comedy of the title, about a habitual criminal and convict who makes the most of his time in prison. **105m/C; VHS, DVD.** *GB* Ronnie Barker; Fulton Mackay; Peter Vaughan; Julian Holloway; Geoffrey Bayldon; *D:* Dick Clement.

Port of Call ✌✌✌ **1948** Early Bergman drama about a seaman on the docks who falls for a troubled woman whose wild, unhappy past has earned her an unsavory reputation. The hopeful, upbeat tone seems incongruous with the grim harbor/slum setting. It's minor Bergman but the seeds of his trademark themes can be seen taking shape, making it a must-see for avid fans. In Swedish with English subtitles. **100m/B; VHS, DVD, Blu-Ray.** *SW* Ivine-Christine Jonsson; Bengt Eklund; Erik Hell; Berta Hall; Mimi Nelson; *D:* Ingmar Bergman.

Port of New York ✌✌ **1949** A narcotics gang is smuggling large quantities of drugs into New York. A government agent poses as a gang member in order to infiltrate the mob and get the goods on them. Brynner's film debut. **82m/B; VHS, DVD.** Scott Brady; Yul Brynner; K.T. Stevens; *D:* Laszlo Benedek.

Portland Expose ✌ 1/2 **1957** Stilted noir supposedly based on an actual expose of mob/union corruption. George Madison owns a Portland, Oregon tavern and is being pressured by mobsters and corrupt union members to add some sleazy action to his joint. When his daughter is attacked by a goon, George decides to get evidence to put them all in jail. **72m/B; DVD.** Edward Binns; Carolyn Craig; Virginia Gregg; Frank Gorshin; Lawrence (Larry) Dobkin; Joseph Marr; *D:* Harold Schuster; *W:* Jack DeWitt; *C:* Carl Berger; *M:* Paul Dunlap.

Porto ✌✌ 1/2 **2017** A moody exploration of the emotional outfall of a one-night stand. Heartsick American Jake (Yelchin) has drifted to the Portuguese city of Porto where he meets French archaeology student Mati (Lucas), who has her own sorrows. The pair share a one-night stand. The film shows these events from Jake's perspective, Mati's perspective, and combination of two--all several years after the fact. In doing so, conversations, gestures, and errors are highlighted, explaining why Jake is still mournful years later. Lovingly shot on film stock and featuring one of Yelchin's last performances, the film nonetheless struggles with a thin plot and somewhat problematic editing. **76m/C; DVD, Blu-Ray.** Anton Yelchin; Lucie Lucas; Paulo Calatre; Francoise Lebrun; Florie Auclerc; *D:* Gabe Klinger; *W:* Gabe Klinger; Larry Gross; *C:* Wyatt Garfield.

The Portrait ✌ 1/2 **1999 (R)** A distaff version of "The Picture of Dorian Gray." Beautiful woman meets strange photographer whose work is weird. Nevertheless, she poses for him and, after seeing the results, unwittingly vows to remain as eternally youthful as her portrait. But the photo shows the real story as time passes by. **85m/C; VHS, DVD.** Gabriella Hall; Jenna Bodnar; Avalon Anders; Christopher Johnston; *D:* David Goldner; *W:* David Goldner; *C:* Rocky Dijon. **VIDEO**

Portrait in Black ✌✌ 1/2 **1960** Invalid shipping magnate Matthew Cabot (Nolan) is contemptuous of second wife Sheila (Turner), who can't leave the marriage because of young son Peter (Kohler). She finds comfort in the arms of her husband's doctor, David Rivera (Quinn), and the duo decide the only way to find happiness is to kill off Cabot, which they do. Then Sheila begins to get anonymous letters accusing her of murder. Turner's glamor can't hide the gaping holes in the contrived plot. Adapted from the Goff/Roberts play. **113m/C; VHS, DVD, Blu-Ray.** Lana Turner; Lloyd Nolan; Anthony Quinn; Richard Basehart; Sandra Dee; John Saxon; Ray Walston; Anna May Wong; Virginia Grey; Dennis Kohler; *D:* Michael Gordon; *W:* Ivan Goff; Ben Roberts; *C:* Russell Metty; *M:* Frank Skinner.

Portrait in Terror ✌ 1/2 **1966** A master thief and a deranged artist plan a heist of a Titian painting in an oddball suspense piece. Not a great success, but atmospheric and weird. **81m/B; VHS, DVD.** Patrick Magee; William Campbell; Anna Pavane; *D:* Jack Hill.

Portrait of a Hitman ✌ *Jim Buck* **1977** Aspiring painter leads a double life as a professional hitman. Ragged feature feels more abandoned than finished, as if most of the movie had been shot and then the money ran out. All leads turn in paycheck performances, no more. **85m/C; VHS, DVD.** Jack Palance; Rod Steiger; Richard Roundtree; Bo Svenson; Ann Turkel; *D:* Allan A. Buckhantz.

Portrait of a Lady ✌✌ 1/2 **1967** A spirited young American woman is taken to England and insists on complete freedom to choose her own future and make her own choices. Based on the 1881 novel by Henry James. On two cassettes. **240m/C; VHS, DVD.** *GB* Richard Chamberlain; Suzanne Neve; Edward Fox; *D:* James Cellan Jones; *W:* Jack Pulman.

Portrait of a Lady ✌✌✌ **1996 (PG-13)** Adapted from the Henry James novel. Independent and newly wealthy American, Isabel Archer (Kidman), is abroad in Europe where she falls under the influence of the bitter, opportunistic Madame Merle (Hershey, in a strong performance), who steers the innocent Isabel into a disastrous marriage with Gilbert Osmond (Malkovich). The film then deals with Isabel's efforts to flee the domineering Osmond and find herself again. Kidman plays her role with efficiency; Malkovich is suitably evil; and director Campion's modern voice carries the film, but is sometimes out of place. Filmed in England and Italy. **142m/C; VHS, DVD, Blu-Ray.** *GB* Nicole Kidman; John Malkovich; Barbara Hershey; Martin Donovan; Christian Bale; Shelley Winters; Shelley Duvall; Mary-Louise Parker; Richard E. Grant; John Gielgud; Viggo Mortensen; *D:* Jane Campion; *W:* Laura Jones; *C:* Stuart Dryburgh; *M:* Wojciech Kilar. L.A. Film Critics '96: Support. Actress (Hershey); Natl. Soc. Film Critics '96: Support. Actor (Donovan), Support. Actress (Hershey).

Portrait of a Lady on Fire ✌✌✌ *Portrait de la jeune fille en feu* **2019 (R)** In 1770s Brittany, Heloise (Haenel) does not know she is to be a bride in an arranged marriage to a nobleman. Her mother (Golino) brings for-hire portrait painter Marianne (Merlant) to their remote home to paint a portrait of Heloise to be sent to her future husband. Because of Heloise's stubbornness, she is told that Marianne's job is to keep her company during daily walks while Marianne paints her from memory in secret. When the truth is revealed, the portrait and their relationship are transformed. The romantic drama is magnetic in its intimacy and depiction of a woman-focused world. French and Italian with subtitles. **119m/C; DVD.** Noémie Merlant; Adèle Haenel; Luana Bajrami; Valeria Golino; Armande Boulanger; *D:* Céline Sciamma; *W:* Céline Sciamma; *C:* Claire Mathon; *M:* Jean-Baptiste de Laubier; Arthur Simonini.

Portrait of a Showgirl ✌✌ **1982** Inexperienced showgirl learns the ropes of Las Vegas life from a veteran of the Vegas stages. **100m/C; VHS, DVD.** Lesley Ann Warren; Rita Moreno; Tony Curtis; Dianne Kay; Howard Morris; *D:* Steven Hilliard Stern. **TV**

Portrait of an Assassin ✌✌ **1949** Unhappy with his marriage to a nagging wife (Arletty), carnival daredevil Fabius (Brasseur) goes so far as to tell her that he killed a woman by mistake, thinking it was her. Can this marriage be saved? Before it's over, more infidelity and the paralyzed Eric (the inimitable Von Stroheim) have come into play. French with subtitles. **86m/B; VHS, DVD.** *FR* Pierre Brasseur; Arletty; Maria Montez; Erich von Stroheim; *D:* Bernard Roland; *W:* Marcel Rivet; *C:* Roger Hubert; *M:* Maurice Thiriet.

Portrait of an Escort ✌✌ **1980** In this luridly plotted CBS TV movie, divorced mom Jordan West (Anspach) attempts to solve her financial problems by joining her friend Sandy (Frann) as an escort at a professional dating service. Jordan insists on a 'no sex' proviso but becomes concerned when one of her dates seems to have turned stalker. **96m/C; DVD.** Susan Anspach; Tony Bill; Edie Adams; Mary Frann; Cyd Charisse; Debbie Lytton; Kevin McCarthy; Todd Susman; *D:* Steven Hilliard Stern; *W:* Ann Beckett; *C:* Howard Schwartz; *M:* Hagood Hardy. **TV**

A Portrait of James Dean: Joshua Tree, 1951 ✌✌ *Joshua Tree, 1951: A Portrait of James Dean* **2012** Non-linear B&W mythologizing of the actor (well-played by handsome Preston), shown in vignettes as he's just about to break big into films. Writer/director Mishory doesn't shy away from Dean's complicated sexuality or the predatory nature of '50s Hollywood and what Dean was willing to do to bcome a star. Those familiar with Dean's life can play 'name that person' with the characters, including the roommate he travels with to Joshua Tree. **93m/B; DVD.** James Preston; Dan Glenn; Edward Singletary, Jr.; Dalilah Rain; Robert Gant; Erin Daniels; *D:* Matthew Mishory; *W:* Matthew Mishory; *C:* Michael Marius Pessah; *M:* Arban Ornelas; Steven Severin.

Portrait of Jennie ✌✌✌ 1/2 *Jennie; Tidal Wave* **1948** In this haunting, romantic fable, a struggling artist is inspired by and smitten with a strange and beautiful girl who he also suspects may be the spirit of a dead woman. A fine cast works wonders with what could have been a forgettable story. The last reel was tinted green in the original release with the last scene shot in technicolor. Oscar-winning special effects. Based on a novella by Robert Nathan. **86m/B; DVD, Blu-Ray.** Joseph Cotten; Jennifer Jones; Cecil Kellaway; Ethel Barrymore; David Wayne; Lillian Gish; Henry Hull; Florence Bates; Felix Bressart; Anne Francis; *D:* William Dieterle; *W:* Leonardo Bercovici; Peter Berneis; Paul Osborn; *C:* Joseph August; *M:* Dimitri Tiomkin. Venice Film Fest. '49: Actor (Cotten).

Portraits Chinois ✌✌ 1/2 *Shadow Play* **1996** Uneven romantic drama finds English fashion designer Ada (Bonham Carter) living in Paris with her screenwriter boyfriend Paul (Ecoffey). They have just moved into an apartment together though dissatisfaction looms. Paul's writing parter, Guido (Castellito), has broken up with his girlfriend thus complicating their latest assignment, and Ada's fellow designer Lise (Bohringer) has not only impressed their boss Rene (Brialy) but has fallen for Paul. Various other friends interact and everything breaks apart and re-forms over the course of several months. French with subtitles. **105m/C; VHS, DVD.** *FR* Helena Bonham Carter; Jean-Philippe Ecoffey; Romane Bohringer; Sergio Castellitto; Marie Trintignant; Elsa Zylberstein; Yvan Attal; Miki (Predrag) Manojlovic; Jean-Claude Brialy; *D:* Martine Dugowson; *W:* Martine Dugowson; Peter Chase; *C:* Vincenzo Marano; *M:* Peter Chase.

Portraits of a Killer ✌✌ *Portraits of Innocence* **1995** Attorney Elaine Taylor (Grey) is getting all hot and bothered by her client—photographer George Kendell (Mandylor), who's suspected in the murders of five hookers. But the detective (Ironside) on the case thinks she's just asking for trouble. **93m/C; VHS, Streaming.** Jennifer Grey; Costas Mandylor; Michael Ironside; Patricia Charbonneau; Kenneth Welsh; M. Emmet Walsh; *D:* Bill Corcoran.

Posed for Murder ✌✌ **1989 (R)** A young centerfold is stalked by a psycho who wants her all for himself. **90m/C; VHS, DVD.** Charlotte J. Helmkamp; Carl Fury; Rick Gianasi; Michael Merrins; *D:* Brian Thomas Jones.

Poseidon ✌ 1/2 **2006 (PG-13)** Uninspired remake of 1972's "The Poseidon Adventure" sunk faster at the box office than the flick's luxury cruise ship. A rogue wave capsizes the liner on New Year's Eve but a few of the passengers defy the captain's orders to remain in the ballroom and await rescue and decide to make their own way to the surface through the treacherous wreckage. The cast is stuck with recognizable genre types (hero, coward, protective parent) but no one stands out amidst the watery rubble. **99m/C; DVD, HD-DVD.** Josh(ua) Lucas; Kurt Russell; Emmy Rossum; Jacinda Barrett; Jimmy Bennett; Mia Maestro; Andre Braugher; Richard Dreyfuss; Mike Vogel; Kevin Dillon; Freddy Rodriguez; Gabe Jarret; Stacy "Fergie" Ferguson; *D:* Wolfgang Petersen; *W:* Mark Protosevich; *C:* John Seale; *M:* Klaus Badelt.

The Poseidon Adventure ✌✌ 1/2 **1972 (PG)** The cruise ship Poseidon is on its last voyage from New York to Athens on New Year's Eve when it is capsized by a tidal wave. The ten survivors struggle to escape the water-logged tomb. Oscar-winning special effects, such as Shelley Winters floating in a boiler room. Created an entirely new genre of film making—the big cast disaster flick. **117m/C; VHS, DVD, Blu-Ray.** Gene Hackman; Ernest Borgnine; Shelley Winters; Red Buttons; Jack Albertson; Carol Lynley; Roddy McDowall; *D:* Ronald Neame; *W:* Wendell Mayes; Stirling Silliphant; *C:* Harold E. Stine; *M:* John Williams. Oscars '72: Song ("The Morning After"), Visual FX; Golden Globes '73: Support. Actress (Winters).

The Poseidon Adventure ✌ **2005** The 1972 original was a commentary on the effects of corporate greed, as cruise ship passengers found themselves stranded at sea on a boat that should have long since been retired. This sadly inadequate TV miniseries remake shifts the focus from sociopathic corporations to evil terrorists who are now responsible for sinking the ship. It's just another disaster flick. **174m/C; DVD, Blu-Ray.** Adam Baldwin; Rutger Hauer; Steve Guttenberg; Bryan Brown; C. Thomas Howell; *D:* John Putch; *W:* Bryce Zabel; *C:* Ross Berryman; *M:* Joe Kraemer. **CABLE**

Posers ✌ 1/2 *Viperes* **2002 (R)** An unwary woman is fatally pummeled in a nightclub bathroom by four jealous party chicks. When the leader of the pack is suspiciously AWOL the terrible trio just totally freaks out thinking that—gasp!?someone is after them to avenge the killing. Cue the customary finger-pointing as the girls disintegrate along with this tale of woe. **85m/C; VHS, DVD.** *CA* Jessica Pare; Stefanie von Pfetten; Emily Hampshire; Adam Beach; Sarain Boylan; Chad Connell; Danielle Kind; Adrian Langley; Alexandra Sinclair; *D:* Katie Tallo; *W:* Katie Tallo; *C:* Claudine Sauve; *M:* Serge Cote. **VIDEO**

Positive I.D. ✌✌ **1987 (R)** A troubled housewife learns that the man who raped her years before is getting released on parole. She devises a second persona for herself with which to entrap him and get her revenge. **96m/C; VHS, DVD.** Stephanie Rascoe; John Davies; Steve Fromholz; *D:* Andy Anderson; *W:* Andy Anderson; *C:* Paul Barton.

The Positively True Adventures of the Alleged Texas Cheerleader-Murdering Mom ✌✌✌ 1/2 **1993 (R)** Satirical melodrama about Texas housewife Wanda Holloway (Hunter), accused of hiring a hitman to murder the mother of her daughter's chief cheerleading rival. She figures the girl will be so distraught that her own daughter can easily replace her. Ruthless and hilarious, this fact-based cable movie goes way over the top in satirizing suburban lifestyle excess and media overkill. Hunter, complete with whiney Texas twang, is perfect in her role as self-absorbed Wanda and Bridges is great as her loopy ex-brother-in-law and partner in planned homicide. A riot compared to the usual dramatic movies served up by the networks. **99m/C; VHS, DVD.** Holly Hunter; Beau Bridges; Swoosie Kurtz; Gregg Henry; Matt Frewer; Frankie Ingrassia; Elizabeth Ruscio; Megan Berwick; Andy Richter; Jack Kehler; *D:* Michael Ritchie; *W:* Jane Anderson; *M:* Lucy Simon. **CABLE**

Posse ✌✌✌ **1975 (PG)** There's a hidden agenda, fueled by political ambition, in a lawman's (Douglas) dauntless pursuit of an escaped bandit (Dern). An interesting contrast between the evil of corrupt politics and the honesty of traditional lawlessness. Well performed, well photographed, and almost insightful. **94m/C; DVD.** Kirk Douglas; Bruce Dern; James Stacy; Bo Hopkins; Luke Askew; David Canary; Alfonso Arau; Kate Woodville; Mark Roberts; *D:* Kirk Douglas; *W:* William Roberts; *C:* Fred W. Koenekamp; *M:* Maurice Jarre.

Posse ✌✌✌ **1993 (R)** Big, brawny western telling the tale of how more than 8,000 black cowboys helped tame the American frontier. Or, spaghetti western meets blaxploitation meets the magnificent seven meets the L.A. riots. However categorized, the intent is to show a side of Americana seldom seen. Strode appears at both the beginning and ending, while several other veteran black performers appear in cameos. Hunky Van Peebles is the leader of the usual misfits--infantry deserters holding a load of gold. Between them and freedom is a gang of goons led by Zane. Lots of flash and dash, but lacking soul. **113m/C; VHS, DVD.** Mario

Van Peebles; Stephen Baldwin; Charles Lane; Tommy (Tiny) Lister; Big Daddy Kane; Billy Zane; Blair Underwood; Tone Loc; Salli Richardson-Whitfield; Reginald (Reggie) Hudlin; Richard Edson; Reginald VelJohnson; Warrington Hudlin; ***Cameo(s):*** Melvin Van Peebles; Pam Grier; Isaac Hayes; Robert Hooks; Richard Jordan; Paul Bartel; Nipsey Russell; Woody Strode; Aaron Neville; Stephen J. Cannell; ***D:*** Mario Van Peebles; ***W:*** Sy Richardson; Dario Scardapane; ***C:*** Peter Menzies, Jr.; ***M:*** Michel Colombier.

Possessed ½ **1931** A poor factory girl becomes a wealthy Park Avenue sophisticate when she falls in love with a rich lawyer who wants to be governor. Not to be confused with Crawford's 1947 movie of the same name, but worth a look. Gable and Crawford make a great couple! **77m/B; VHS, DVD.** Joan Crawford; Clark Gable; Wallace Ford; Richard "Skeets" Gallagher; John Miljan; ***D:*** Clarence Brown.

The Possessed **1947** Crawford is at her melodramatic best as a crazed gal who can't find happiness with either hunk Heflin or bland Massey. First film for Brooks. From the story "One Man's Secret" by Rita Weiman. **109m/B; DVD, Blu-Ray.** Joan Crawford; Van Heflin; Raymond Massey; Geraldine Brooks; Stanley Ridges; John Ridgely; Nana Bryant; Moroni Olsen; ***D:*** Curtis Bernhardt; ***C:*** Joseph Valentine.

The Possessed ½ **1977 (PG-13)** Farentino is a priest who loses his faith, but regains it after an apparently fatal auto accident. Hackett is the headmistress of a private girls' school which is in need of an exorcist, since one of her student's appears to be possessed, and Farentino seems just the man for the job. Fairly tame, though originally made for TV. **75m/C; VHS, DVD.** James Farentino; Joan Hackett; Diana Scarwid; Claudette Nevins; Eugene Roche; Ann Dusenberry; Dinah Manoff; P.J. Soles; ***D:*** Jerry Thorpe. **TV**

Possessed **2000** William Bowdern (Dalton) is a troubled priest in 1949 St. Louis, who has taken to drink because of his WWII nightmares. He's called on to help 11-year-old Robbie (Malen) who is apparently possessed by a demon. Will reluctant Archbishop Hume (Plummer) allow Bowdern to performan an arcane exorcism and does Robbie's strange Aunt Hanna (Laurie) have anything to do with his condition? Based on the true story of the only documented exorcism performed by the Catholic Church in the U.S. **111m/C; VHS, DVD.** Timothy Dalton; Christopher Plummer; Henry Czerny; Jonathan Malen; Shannon Lawson; Piper Laurie; Michael Rhoades; ***D:*** Steven E. de Souza; ***W:*** Steven E. de Souza; Michael Lazarou; ***C:*** Edward Pei; ***M:*** John (Gianni) Frizzell. **CABLE**

Possessed *Deadly Visions* **2005** After being blinded in a car accident, Anne Culver (Sheridan) is given a new pair of eyes from a donor. The only problem is that now she's seeing visions of her donor's murder. Ho-hum thriller with few surprises. Should please fans of the genre. **95m/C; VHS, DVD.** Nicolette Sheridan; Gordon Currie; Sarah Deakins; Philip Granger; ***D:*** Michael Scott; ***W:*** John Murlowski; ***C:*** Adam Sliwinski; ***M:*** Sophia Morizet. **VIDEO**

Possessing Piper Rose **2011** Lifetime horror (in more ways than one since it's dull and dumb) has Joanne and Ben Maxwell adopting young Piper Rose, one of those unexpectedly creepy TV kids. The girl acts weird because she sees her dead birth mom, who possesses Joanne's own mother and--as shocking as it might seem--bad things happen. **89m/C; Streaming.** Rebecca Romijn; David Cubitt; Isabelle Cramp; Christine Willes; Sarah Jane Redmond; ***D:*** Kevin Fair; ***W:*** Scott Nimerfro; ***M:*** Michael Richard Plowman. **CABLE**

Possession **1981 (R)** Returned from a long mission, a secret agent notices that his wife is acting very strangely. She's about to give birth to a manifestation of the evil within her! Gory, hysterical, over-intellectual and often unintelligible. **123m/C; VHS, DVD, Blu-Ray.** *FR GE* Isabelle Adjani; Sam Neill; Heinz Bennent; Margit Carstensen; Shaun Lawtor; Johanna Hofer; ***D:*** Andrzej Zulawski; ***W:*** Andrzej Zulawski; Frederic Tuten; ***C:*** Bruno Nuytten; ***M:*** Andrzej Korzynski; Art Phillips. Cesar '82: Actress (Adjani).

Possession **2002 (PG-13)** English lit lite in this uninvolving romance based on the 1990 novel by A.S. Byatt. Brash and scruffy American scholar Roland Michell (Eckhart) finds letters from 19th-century poet Randolph Henry Ash (Northam)--possibly to feminist poet Christabel LaMotte (Ehle). Michell hooks up with repressed Brit scholar Maud Bailey (bun-wearing Paltrow), an expert on Christabel, to investigate the connection. They discover the married Ash and LaMotte had a brief, passionate affair that changed their lives. The modern-day duo are too wary to get involved the same way—at least at first. Looks beautiful but is utterly predictable. **102m/C; VHS, DVD.** *US UK* Gwyneth Paltrow; Aaron Eckhart; Jeremy Northam; Jennifer Ehle; Lena Headey; Toby Stephens; Tom Hickey; Trevor Eve; Tom Hollander; Graham Crowden; Anna Massey; Holly Aird; Georgia Mackenzie; ***D:*** Neil LaBute; ***W:*** Neil LaBute; David Henry Hwang; Laura Jones; ***C:*** Jean-Yves Escoffier; ***M:*** Gabriel Yared.

Possession **2008 (PG-13)** Lame and boring American remake of the Korean horror pic "Addicted." Jessica (Gellar) is married to perfect romantic guy Ryan (Landes) although she has to put up with his creepy, violent brother Roman (Pace) who is living with them after being released from prison. Roman and Ryan both wind up in comas after a car crash but when Roman regains consciousness he seems to have Ryan's personality and memories. This upsets Jessica until she comes to believe that Ryan is now trapped in Roman's body. **85m/C; DVD, Blu-Ray.** Sarah Michelle Gellar; Lee Pace; Michael Landes; Chelah Horsdal; William B. Davis; Veena Sood; ***D:*** Joel Bergvall; Simon Sandquist; ***W:*** Michael Petroni; ***C:*** Gregory Middleton; ***M:*** Christian Sandquist.

The Possession **2012 (PG-13)** Yet another ghost story allegedly based on a true story, Bornedal's film has some high caliber set pieces but too often falls back on genre trappings. Clyde (Morgan) and Stephanie (Sedgwick) panic when their daughter Em (Calis) starts acting, well, odd, after a Dibbuk (a Jewish demon) escapes from an antique box and possesses the poor girl. To call the film a "Jewish Exorcist" isn't far from the truth. A talented cast and visually strong director save it from disaster but there's not enough personality here to make it memorable. **91m/C; DVD, Blu-Ray.** Jeffrey Dean Morgan; Kyra Sedgwick; Natasha Calis; Grant Show; Jay Brazeau; Madison Davenport; Matisyahu; ***D:*** Ole Bornedal; ***W:*** Juliet Snowden; Stiles White; ***C:*** Dan Laustsen; ***M:*** Anton Sanko.

The Possession of Joel Delaney ½ **1972 (R)** Blend of occult horror and commentary on social mores works for the most part, but some viewers may be put off by the low production values and spottiness of the script. MacLaine is a wealthy divorcee who must deal with the mysterious transformations affecting her brother. Skeptical at first, she begins to suspect he is the victim of Caribbean voodoo. **105m/C; VHS, DVD.** Shirley MacLaine; Perry King; Michael Hordern; David Elliott; Robert Burr; ***D:*** Waris Hussein; ***W:*** Matt Robinson; ***C:*** Arthur Ornitz; ***M:*** Joe Raposo.

The Possession of Michael King **2014 (R)** A promising set-up for yet another found-footage film (darn you, Blair Witch!) falls apart when the creators of this nearly straight-to-video bomb go for cheap camera tricks instead of actual characters or genuine scares. Michael King (Johnson) has a religious crisis after the death of his wife. He chooses to make a documentary that disproves the afterlife, which, of course, takes him across to the dark side of the occult and possession. Poor Michael gets possessed. The skeptic in need of an exorcist makes for a great concept but the execution fails it. **83m/C; DVD, Blu-Ray.** Shane Johnson; Ella Anderson; ***D:*** David Jung; ***W:*** David Jung; Tedi Sarafian; ***C:*** Phil Parmet; ***M:*** Mark Binder.

Possible Loves *Amores Possiveis* **2000** Rom com with a Brazilian beat and three possible outcomes. College student Carlos (Benicio) is waiting for his girlfriend Julia (Ferraz) outside a Rio cinema. Fifteen years later, the viewer learns what happens if she does—or doesn't—show up. In the first, Julia doesn't, so Carlos has a dull marriage to Maria (Goulart) until he and Julia have a chance meeting. Scenario two has Julia and Carlos married but he leaves his family Pedro (de Mello) as he tries to decide whom he loves. In the third plot, Julia doesn't show again and Carlos is a swinging bachelor looking for the perfect woman. Portuguese with subtitles. **98m/C; VHS, DVD.** *BR* Murilo Benicio; Carolina Ferraz; Beth Goulart; Emilio de Mello; Irene Ravache; ***D:*** Sandra Werneck; ***W:*** Paulo Halm; ***C:*** Walter Carvalho; ***M:*** Chico Buarque; Joao Nabuco.

Possums ½ **1999 (PG)** Beat-up small town can't endure the local high school football team's quarter-century of losing seasons and pulls the plug on the pathetic Possums. But their announcer, Will (Davis), breathes new life into the downtrodden fans by calling fictional wins. It's all high-fives until the real champs want to square off and Will has to assemble a first-rate squad. **97m/C; VHS, DVD.** Mac Davis; Cynthia Sikes; Greg Coolidge; Andrew Prine; Dennis Burkley; Monica Creel; Jay Underwood; Clive Revill; ***D:*** J. Max Burnett; ***W:*** J. Max Burnett; ***C:*** Christopher Duskin; ***M:*** Justin Caine Burnett. **VIDEO**

The Post **2017 (PG-13)** A timely drama by director Steven Spielberg about the Pentagon Papers and the Washington Post in the early 1970s. After Daniel Ellsberg (Rhys) takes sensitive papers from the Pentagon that reveal the U.S. government had been lying about the Vietnam war, the New York Times prints some of the documents before being stopped in court. When Washington Post reporter Ben Bagdikian (Odenkirk) gains the same sources, his paper's publisher Kay Graham (Streep) and editor Ben Bradlee (Hanks) must decide if they should risk being charged with treason by printing the papers themselves. A well-constructed script and inspired performances give depth to this message-focused film. **115m/C; DVD, Blu-Ray.** Meryl Streep; Tom Hanks; Sarah Paulson; Bob Odenkirk; Tracy Letts; ***D:*** Steven Spielberg; ***W:*** Liz Hannah; Josh Singer; ***C:*** Janusz Kaminski; ***M:*** John Williams.

Post Concussion **1999 (PG-13)** Matthew (Yoon) is a ruthless corporate "consultant" who specializes in downsizing and layoffs until he's hit by a car and suffers a severe head injury. Unable to work because of lingering symptoms, he re-evaluates his life, starts a romance with a neighbor, and explores New Age remedies. Writer-director Yoon based his refreshing, inventive, and gently humorous debut on his own experience with a brain-injuring accident and its subsequent effect on his own life and career. **82m/C; VHS, DVD.** Daniel Yoon; Michael Hohmeyer; Destry Miller; Niloufar Talebi; Jennifer Welch; ***D:*** Daniel Yoon; ***W:*** Daniel Yoon; ***C:*** Daniel Yoon.

Post Grad ½ *Ticket to Ride; The Post Grad Survival Guide* **2009 (PG-13)** Mediocre comedy finds overachieving Ryden Malby (Bledel) getting a rude awakening to the real world when she graduates from college, misses out on the perfect job (which goes to a rival), and so must move back in with her eccentric family. One thing that does seem to make sense is maybe Ryden and her platonic buddy Adam (Gilford) shouldn't be so platonic anymore only Ryden is more interested in ogling flirty, hunky Brazilian neighbor David (Santoro). Flick features the protracted burial arrangements for a squished cat (it's funny in a sick sorta way). **88m/C; DVD.** Alexis Bledel; Michael Keaton; Jane Lynch; Rodrigo Santoro; Zach Gilford; Craig Robinson; Carol Burnett; Fred Armisen; Andrew Daly; Catherine Reitman; Bobby Coleman; ***D:*** Victoria Jenson; ***W:*** Kelly Fremon Craig; ***C:*** Charles Minsky; ***M:*** Christophe Beck.

Post Impact **2004 (R)** After a meteor impact brings Earth into a new ice age, most of civilization is destroyed. The survivors journey into the frozen wastes in search of a rumored military satellite designed to control the weather that may save the human race. **90m/C; DVD.** *GE US* Dean Cain; Bettina Zimmermann; Joanna Taylor; Nigel Bennett; John Keough; Torsten Dewi; ***D:*** Cristoph Schrewe; ***W:*** Cristoph Schrewe; ***C:*** Lorenzo Senatore; ***M:*** Guy Farley. **VIDEO**

Post Tenebras Lux ½ **2012** Although the title translates literally from Latin as "after darkness, light" there won't be much for viewers of this metaphysical head-scratcher that disdains a cohesive narrative. Juan and his wife Natalia live with their two children in an isolated house in rural Mexico. There's an alcoholic handyman, an extended scene of the couple as regulars in a French-speaking sex club, and something about a devil, dogs and other animals, and well, Reygadas obviously is going his own filmic way. English, Spanish and French with subtitles. **115m/C; DVD, Blu-Ray, On Demand.** *MX FR GE NL* Adolfo Jimenez Castro; Nathalia Acevedo; Willebaldo Torres; ***D:*** Carlos Reygadas; ***W:*** Carlos Reygadas; ***C:*** Alexis Zabe.

Postal **WOOF!** **2007 (R)** Energetically tasteless, fitfully amusing farce, adapted from the videogame, satirizes our post-9/11 world and skewers its targets equally. Unemployed Dude (Ward) turns to his Uncle Dave (Foley), the leader of an apocalyptic cult, for money, and the two plot to steal a truckload of dirty dolls—a must-have toy in short supply. The same idea has occurred to Osama bin Laden follower Mohammed (Benyaer), and the two factions collide at the Third Reich-themed amusement park Little Germany (with director Boll appearing as the park's manager). **109m/C; DVD.** *US CA GE* Zack (Zach) Ward; Dave Foley; Christopher Coppola; J.K. Simmons; Larry Thomas; Verne Troyer; Michael Benyaer; Brent Mendenhall; ***Cameo(s):*** Uwe Boll; ***D:*** Uwe Boll; ***W:*** Uwe Boll; Bryan C. Knight; ***C:*** Mathias Neumann; ***M:*** Jessica de Rooij. Golden Raspberries '08: Worst Director (Boll).

Postcards from America **1995 (R)** Traces the non-artistic aspects of the life of writer/artist David Wojnarowicz, who died of AIDS. Neophyte McLean concentrates on troubled childhood with an abusive father and teen years spent as a street hustler years. Choppy narrative uses little of Wojnarowicz's dialogue, save the voice-over narration by the lead character. Based on two semi-autobiographical novels by the artist. **93m/C; VHS, DVD.** James Lyons; Michael Tighe; Olmo Tighe; Michael Imperioli; Michael Ringer; Maggie Low; ***D:*** Steve McLean; ***W:*** Steve McLean; ***C:*** Ellen Kuras; ***M:*** Stephen Endelman.

Postcards from the Edge ½ **1990 (R)** Fisher adapted her best-selling novel, tamed and tempered, for the big screen with a tour-de-force of talent. Streep very fine as a delightfully harried actress struggling with her career, her drug dependence, and her competitive, overwhelming show-biz mother. Autobiographical script is bitingly clever and filled with refreshingly witty dialogue. Lots of cameos by Hollywood's hippest. **101m/C; VHS, DVD, Blu-Ray.** Meryl Streep; Shirley MacLaine; Dennis Quaid; Gene Hackman; Richard Dreyfuss; Rob Reiner; Mary Wickes; Conrad Bain; Annette Bening; Michael Ontkean; Dana Ivey; Robin Bartlett; Anthony Heald; Oliver Platt; CCH Pounder; ***D:*** Mike Nichols; ***W:*** Carrie Fisher; ***C:*** Michael Ballhaus; ***M:*** Shel Silverstein; Carly Simon; Stephen Sondheim; Howard Shore; Paul Shaffer; Gilda Radner.

Poster Boy **2004 (R)** Right-wing senator Jack Kray (Lerner) decides to use his college- student son Henry (Newton) in his reelection campaign in order to attract the youth vote. Except Henry's gay, and while he's living it up within his college confines, he's not out to the rest of the world, including his parents. Over-the-top soapiness and preachiness ensue as secrets and truth affect the dynamics of family, friendship, and public image. Allen is excellent as the smile-and-wave political wife who likes a cocktail, but the good performances are crushed by a heavy-handed script. **98m/C; DVD.** Matt Newton; Karen Allen; Michael Lerner; Jack Noseworthy; Valerie Geffner; Ian Reed Kesler; Sheff Stevens; ***D:*** Zak Tucker; ***W:*** Ryan Shiraki; Lecia Rosenthal; ***C:*** Wolfgang Held; ***M:*** Mark Garcia.

The Postman ½ *Il Postino* **1994 (PG)** Bittersweet, charming film about Mario (Troisi), a shy villager who winds up the personal postman of poet Pablo Neruda (Noiret), who is exiled from his beloved Chile in 1952. Granted asylum by the Italian government, he's living in the tiny Italian community of Isla Negra. The tongue-tied Mario has fallen in love with barmaid Beatrice (Cucinotta) and asks the poet's help in wooing the dark-eyed beauty, striking up an unlikely friendship with the worldly Neruda. Based on the novel "Burning Patience" by Antonio Skarmeta. Italian with subtitles. Troisi, a beloved comic actor in his native Italy, was gravely ill, needing a heart transplant, during the making of the film (all-too apparent from his gaunt appearance) and died the day after filming was completed. **115m/C; VHS, DVD.** *IT* Massimo Troisi; Philippe Noiret; Maria Grazia Cucinotta; Linda Moretti; Renato Scarpa; Anna Buonaiuto; Mariano Rigillo; ***D:*** Michael Radford; ***W:*** Massimo Troisi; Michael Radford; Furio Scarpelli; Anna Pavignano; Giacomo Scarpelli; ***C:*** Franco Di Giacomo; ***M:*** Luis Bacalov. Oscars '95: Orig. Dramatic Score; British Acad. '95: Director (Radford), Foreign Film, Score; Broadcast Film Critics '95: Foreign Film.

The Postman **1997 (R)** It's postapocalypse time (the year's 2013), with a nameless drifter (Costner, also directing) assuming the role of a postal carrier in order to bring hope to a devasted town terrorized by maruading hooligans, led by General Bethlehem (Patton). If you fancy deadpan dialogue and can swallow the image of a mail carrier as the symbol for patriotism, then this one's for you. Overall, Costner offers nothing new to the genre of the stranger offering hope, and soon the flick becomes a cornball exercise and extravagant waste of time for all involved. **170m/C; VHS, DVD.** Kevin Costner; Larenz Tate; Will Patton; Olivia Williams; James Russo; Tom Petty; Daniel von Bargen; Scott Bairstow; Giovanni Ribisi; Roberta Maxwell; Joe Santos; Peggy Lipton; Ron McLarty; Rex Linn; Todd Allen; Shawn Hatosy; ***D:*** Kevin Costner; ***W:*** Brian Helgeland; Eric Roth; ***C:*** Stephen F. Windon; ***M:*** James Newton Howard. Golden Raspberries '97: Worst Actor (Costner), Worst Director (Costner), Worst Picture, Worst Screenplay, Worst Song (Entire Song Score).

The Postman Always Rings Twice **1/2 1946** Even without the brutal sexuality of the James M. Cain novel, Garfield and Turner sizzle as the lust-laden lovers in this lurid tale of fatal attraction. Garfield steals the show as the streetwise drifter who blows into town and lights a fire in Turner. As their affair steams up the two conspire to do away with her husband and circumstances begin to spin out of control. Tense and compelling. A classic. **113m/B; VHS, DVD, Blu-Ray.** Lana Turner; John Garfield; Cecil Kellaway; Hume Cronyn; Leon Ames; Audrey Totter; Alan Reed; ***D:*** Tay Garnett; ***W:*** Harry Ruskin; Niven Busch; ***C:*** Sidney Wagner; ***M:*** George Bassman.

The Postman Always Rings Twice **1981 (R)** It must be true because he's ringing again in Mamet's version of James M. Cain's depression-era novel. This time Nicholson plays the drifter and Lange the amoral wife with an aged husband. Truer to the original story than the 1946 movie in its use of brutal sex scenes, it nevertheless lacks the power of the original. Nicholson works well in this time era and Lange adds depth and realism to the character of Cora. But in the end it remains dreary and easily forgettable. **123m/C; VHS, DVD, Blu-Ray.** Jack Nicholson; Jessica Lange; John Colicos; Anjelica Huston; Michael Lerner; John P. Ryan; Christopher Lloyd; ***D:*** Bob Rafelson; ***W:*** David Mamet; ***C:*** Sven Nykvist; ***M:*** Michael Small.

Postman Pat: The Movie **1/2 2014** Mild-mannered Postman Pat (voiced by Mangan), enters a TV singing contest with the hopes of taking his wife on a belated honeymoon to Italy. Turns out, Pat has serious pipes and becomes an overnight celebrity. Now here's where the big-screen adaptation of the beloved British animated kids' series plunges into strange waters. While away, the evil entrepreneur Carbuncle (Woodward) replaces the postman with a ultra-efficient robot in a scheme for world domination. What starts as a charming adaptation turns unncessarily convoluted and overly-eager to please the kids, while still winking at the parents. **88m/C; DVD.** *UK* ***V:*** Stephen Mangan; Peter Woodward; Rupert Grint; David Tennant; Robin Atkin Downes; ***D:*** Mike Disa; ***W:*** Nicole Dubuc; ***M:*** Rupert Gregson-Williams.

Postman's Knock **1962** Chaotic comic Milligan is stuck in a conventional slapstick comedy. Village postman Harold Petts (Milligan) is so efficient he gets transferred to London. He meets pretty art student Jean (Shelley) and thwarts an attempted mail train robbery but becomes a suspect despite his alibi. And while Harold is being trailed by the coppers, the inept gang decides to try again. **87m/B; DVD.** *GB* Spike Milligan; Barbara Shelley; John Wood; Warren Mitchell; Archie Duncan; Lance Percival; Arthur Mullard; John Bennett; ***D:*** Robert Lynn; ***W:*** John Briley; Jack Trevor Story; Robert Kinnoch; ***C:*** Gerald Moss; ***M:*** Ronald Goodwin.

Postmark for Danger **1/2** *Portrait of Alison* **1956** Detectives do their best to smash a diamond smuggling ring that operates between Britain and the U.S. Along the way a number of people are killed. **84m/B; VHS, DVD.** *GB* Terry Moore; Robert Beatty; William Sylvester; Josephine Griffin; Geoffrey Keen; Henry Oscar; ***D:*** Guy Green.

Postmortem **1998 (R)** Sheen is an FBI serial killer profiler who leaves the job to become a novelist and find peace in a small town. But his quiet life is shattered by a murderer who writes the obituaries of his victims before he kills. **105m/C; VHS, DVD.** Charlie Sheen; Michael Halsey; Stephen McCole; Gary Lewis; Hazel Ann Crawford; ***D:*** Albert Pyun; ***W:*** John Lamb; ***C:*** George Mooradian; ***M:*** Tony Riparetti.

Pot o' Gold *The Golden Hour* **1941** Stewart plays a wealthy young man who signs on with a struggling band. He convinces his uncle, who has a radio program, to let the band perform during a radio giveaway show he has concocted. Slight comedy, Stewart notwithstanding. **87m/B; VHS, DVD.** Paulette Goddard; James Stewart; Charles Winninger; Horace Heidt; Art Carney; ***D:*** George Marshall; ***W:*** Walter DeLeon; ***C:*** Hal Mohr.

Potiche **2010 (R)** Sparkling, warm-hearted feminist comedy from Ozon, set in pastel and polyester 1977, with eye-catching performances from Deneuve and Depardieu. The French title translates to "trophy wife," which is what Suzanne Pujol (Deneuve) has always been in her marriage to her unfaithful, arrogant schmuck husband Robert (Luchini). But when the workers at the family umbrella factory go on strike, it's up to Suzanne to become management's negotiator. She calls on her communist union leader ex-beau Maurice Babin (Depardieu) for help and it's clear he still harbors romantic feelings. French with subtitles. **103m/C; DVD, Blu-Ray.** *BE FR* Catherine Deneuve; Gerard Depardieu; Fabrice Luchini; Karin Viard; Judith Godreche; Jeremie Renier; Evelyne Dandry; Bruno Lochet; ***D:*** Francois Ozon; ***W:*** Francois Ozon; ***C:*** Yorick Le Saux; ***M:*** Philippe Rombi.

Pound of Flesh **2010** Professor Noah Melville teaches at an exclusive and expensive private college. He helps attractive young women in his classes pay for their tuition by moonlighting for his escort service. A student turns up dead and troubled detective Patrick Kelly threatens the entire enterprise. Cliched crime drama with a poor script and mediocre acting (at best). **97m/C; DVD.** Malcolm McDowell; Angus MacFadyen; Elizabeth Rodriguez; Dee Wallace; Timothy Bottoms; Whitney Able; ***D:*** Tamar Simon Hoffs; ***W:*** Tamar Simon Hoffs; ***C:*** Peter N. Green; ***M:*** Seth Podowitz. **VIDEO**

Poverty, Inc. **1/2 2014** This insightful, revealing documentary explores the "poverty industry," that is, charity or the business of doing good. In arguing that the West has made itself the protagonist of development, it has also given rise to a multi-billion dollar industry of doing good. Yet, the results of these efforts are mixed at best. Some actions of the poverty industry are catastrophic in the developing world. Through 200 interviews in 20 countries, the documentary explores the challenges created by this industry and the calls of the leaders of the developing world in seeking a change in how charities and charitable companies do business. **94m/C; DVD, Streaming, Download.** ***D:*** Michael Matheson Miller; ***W:*** Michael Matheson Miller; Simon Scionka; Jonathan Witt; ***C:*** Simon Scionka.

Powaqqatsi: Life in Transformation **1/2 1988 (G)** Director Reggio's follow-up to "Koyaanisqatsi" doesn't pack the wallop of its predecessor. Still, the cinematography is magnificent and the music of Philip Glass is exquisitely hypnotic as we are taken on a spellbinding video collage of various third world countries and see the price they've paid in the name of progress. Part 2 of a planned trilogy. **95m/C; VHS, DVD, Blu-Ray.** ***D:*** Godfrey Reggio; ***M:*** Philip Glass.

Powder **1995 (PG-13)** An electromagnetic albino with an I.Q. off the charts is discovered living in his grandparents' cellar and brought to live in a school for troubled teens. Despite harrassment, Powder (Flanery) manages to exude compassion and electricity all over the place with the help of sensitive school director Steenbergen and wacky science teacher Goldblum. Hypersentimentality, convoluted and contradictory writing, absurd messianic overtones, and a cop-out climax barely scratch the surface of film's problems. Revelations of Salva's criminal conviction for child molestation cast some scenes in a disturbing light. **111m/C; VHS, DVD.** Sean Patrick Flanery; Mary Steenburgen; Lance Henriksen; Jeff Goldblum; Brandon Smith; Bradford Tatum; Susan Tyrrell; Missy (Melissa) Crider; Ray Wise; Esteban Louis Powell; ***D:*** Victor Salva; ***W:*** Victor Salva; ***C:*** Jerzy Zielinski; ***M:*** Jerry Goldsmith.

Powder Blue **2009 (R)** Manages to make Jessica Biel as a stripper boring. Intersecting drama, set during Christmas, about said stripper, an ex-priest, an ex-con, and a mortician who are all in crisis. It sounds like a bad bar joke and it is. It not only snows in L.A. but the snow is blue-colored. **106m/C; DVD.** Jessica Biel; Eddie Redmayne; Forest Whitaker; Ray Liotta; Lisa Kudrow; Patrick Swayze; Kris Kristofferson; Sanaa Lathan; ***D:*** Timothy Linh Bui; ***W:*** Stephane Gauger; Timothy Linh Bui; ***C:*** Jonathan Sela; ***M:*** Didier Rachou.

Powder River **1953** Former Marshall Chino Bullock (Calhoun) has taken up gold prospecting. But when his partner is killed, he becomes the new law in town to get his revenge although it takes an unexpected turn. **77m/C; DVD.** Rory Calhoun; Cameron Mitchell; Corinne Calvet; Carl Betz; John Dehner; Penny Edwards; ***D:*** Louis King; ***W:*** Daniel Mainwaring; ***C:*** Edward Cronjager; ***M:*** Lionel Newman.

Power **1/2** *Jew Suss* **1934** A Jewish ghetto inhabitant in 18th-century Wurtemburg works his way out of the gutter and into some authority by pleasing the whims of an evil duke. Based on the novel by Leon Fuechtwangler. **105m/B; VHS, DVD.** *GB* Conrad Veidt; Benita Hume; Frank Vosper; Cedric Hardwicke; Gerald du Maurier; Pamela Ostrer; Joan Maude; Paul Graetz; Mary Clare; Percy Parsons; Dennis Hoey; Gibb McLaughlin; Francis L. Sullivan; ***D:*** Lothar Mendes.

The Power **1/2 1968** Solid B-movie sci fi with echoes of Hitchcock. Members of a scientific research team are murdered and biochemist Tanner (Hamilton) becomes the prime suspect. Turns out the team members have developed super-psychic powers and one of them decides to test them out before taking over the world. **108m/C; DVD.** George Hamilton; Suzanne Pleshette; Richard Carlson; Yvonne De Carlo; Arthur O'Connell; Earl Holliman; Gary Merrill; Nehemiah Persoff; Michael Rennie; Aldo Ray; ***D:*** Byron Haskin; ***W:*** John Gay; ***C:*** Ellsworth Fredricks; ***M:*** Miklos Rozsa.

Power **1/2 1986 (R)** A study of corporate manipulations. Gere plays a ruthless media consultant working for politicians. Fine cast can't find the energy needed to make this great, but it's still interesting. Lumet did better with same material in "Network." **111m/C; VHS, DVD.** Richard Gere; Julie Christie; E.G. Marshall; Gene Hackman; Beatrice Straight; Kate Capshaw; Denzel Washington; Fritz Weaver; Michael Learned; E. Katherine Kerr; Polly Rowles; Matt Salinger; J.T. Walsh; ***D:*** Sidney Lumet; ***W:*** David Himmelstein; ***C:*** Andrzej Bartkowiak; ***M:*** Cy Coleman.

Power and Beauty **1/2 2002** A titillating topic turns into a dull telepic. Judith Campbell Exner (Henstridge) is a beauty who, afer a fling with Frank Sinatra (Ralston), becomes the mistress of JFK (Anderson). Sinatra is also the one who introduced Judith to wiseguy Sam Giancana (Friedman) and FBI honcho Herbert Hoover is convinced that the babe is some kind of messenger service between the White House and the Chicago crime boss. (In 1975, the real Exner is subpoenaed by a Senate committee who wants details and is briefly in the public eye.) **94m/C; VHS, DVD.** Natasha Henstridge; Kevin Anderson; Peter Friedman; Grant Nickalls; John Ralston; ***D:*** Susan Seidelman; ***W:*** William Bast; Dave Erickson; Paul Huson; ***C:*** Derick Underschultz; ***M:*** Patrick Williams. **CABLE**

The Power and the Glory **1933** Preston Sturges' first screenplay is a glum drama told in the (then) new style of narrated flashbacks. Railroad magnate Tom Garner (Tracy) rises from humble beginnings but he neglects his wife (Moore) and son (Trent) for success, which only brings unhappiness and betrayal. After his funeral, Tom's lifelong friend, Henry (Morgan), debates his merits as a man (showcasing the flashbacks). **76m/B; DVD.** Spencer Tracy; Colleen Moore; Ralph Morgan; Helen Vinson; Philip Trent; Henry Kolker; Sarah Padden; ***D:*** William K. Howard; ***W:*** Preston Sturges; ***C:*** James Wong Howe. Natl. Film Reg. '14.

The Power and the Prize **1956** Power turns out not to be a prize worth having for businessman Cliff Barton (Taylor) who's sent to London by his boss/mentor George Salt (Ives) to broker a suspicious deal. Cliff has also been asked to check on a charity that Mrs. Salt (Astor) supports, which is how Cliff meets refugee Miriam (Muller), who may have communist leanings. Still, Cliff falls hard and is suddenly thwarting Salt's plans, getting him into trouble back home. The plot shifts are unbelievable as is the romance since Muller seems to be suffering from hysterics. **98m/B; DVD.** Robert Taylor; Elisabeth Mueller; Burl Ives; Mary Astor; Charles Coburn; Cedric Hardwicke; Niki Dantine; ***D:*** Henry Koster; ***W:*** Robert Ardrey; ***C:*** George J. Folsey; ***M:*** Bronislau Kaper.

Power Dive **1941** Test pilot Brad (Arlen) must show that a new plane commissioned by the army that was designed and constructed of plastic by Professor Blake (Ross) is safe to fly. Brad's gal is Blake's daughter Carol (Parker) and Brad has a romantic rival in his own brother, engineer Doug (Castle), which makes things sticky on and off the ground. **71m/B; DVD.** Richard Arlen; Jean Parker; Don Castle; Thomas Ross W.; Roger Pryor; Cliff Edwards; Helen Mack; Louis Jean Heydt; ***D:*** James Hogan; ***W:*** Edward Churchill; Maxwell Shane; ***C:*** John Alton; ***M:*** C. Bakaleinikoff.

Power of Attorney **1994 (R)** Ambitious up-from-the-streets lawyer Paul Diehl (Koteas) decides to defend Mafia don Joseph Scassi (Aiello) against federal charges of murder and extortion, convincing himself that the mobster is telling the truth. But Scassi decides to make certain his lawyer will do his best by threatening Diehl's drug-dealing brother Frankie (Wilson). **97m/C; VHS, DVD.** Danny Aiello; Elias Koteas; Nina Siemaszko; Rae Dawn Chong; Roger Wilson; ***D:*** Howard Himelstein; ***W:*** George Erschbamer; Jeff Barmash; ***M:*** Hal Beckett.

The Power of Few **2013 (R)** Problematic, jumbled narrative that's supposedly taking place over a mere 20 minutes as diverse characters' lives converge on the streets of the Big Easy after a violent act. It was a movie literally made by committee--online users could vote on casting, narrative, and editing--and too many cooks made this gumbo inedible. **96m/C; DVD, Blu-Ray.** Tione Johnson; Q'orianka Kilcher; Jesse Bradford; Christopher Walken; Devon Gearhart; Moon Bloodgood; Christian Slater; Nicky Whelan; Anthony Anderson; ***D:*** Leone Marucci; ***W:*** Leone Marucci; ***C:*** Reinhart Peschke; ***M:*** Michael Simpson. **VIDEO**

The Power of One **1992 (PG-13)** Good cast is generally wasted in liberal white look at apartheid. Set in South Africa during the 1940s, P.K. is a white orphan of British descent who is sent to a boarding school run by Afrikaaners (South Africans of German descent). Humiliated and bullied, particularly when England and Germany go to war, P.K. is befriended by a German pianist and a black boxing coach who teach him to box and stand up for his rights. Preachy and filled with stereotypes. Based on the novel by Bryce Courtenay. **126m/C; VHS, DVD.** Stephen Dorff; Armin Mueller-Stahl; Morgan Freeman; John Gielgud; Fay Masterson; Marius Weyers; Tracy Brooks Swope; John Osborne; Daniel Craig; Dominic Walker; Alois Mayo; Ian Roberts; Maria Marais; ***D:*** John G. Avildsen; ***W:*** Robert Mark Kamen; ***C:*** Dean Semler; ***M:*** Hans Zimmer.

Power, Passion & Murder **1/2 1983** A young, glamorous movie star has an affair with a married man which begins the end of her career in 1930s Hollywood. **104m/C; VHS, DVD.** Michelle Pfeiffer; Darren McGavin; Stella Stevens; ***D:*** Paul Bogart; Leon Ichaso.

Power Play 1/2 *Operation Overthrow; A State of Shock* **1978** Young army colonel from a small European country joins forces with rebels to overthrow the government. After the coup, the group discovers that in their midst is a traitor. So who is it? Suspense never builds adequately. **95m/C; VHS, DVD.** *CA GB* Peter O'Toole; David Hemmings; Donald Pleasence; Barry Morse; ***D:*** Martyn Burke; ***W:*** Martyn Burke.

Power Play 1/2 **2002 (R)** Connecting an energy company's greed to massive earthquakes in southern California is no small feat but reporter Matt Nash puts his life on the line to do just that. B-movie disaster flick is decidedly low-energy. **100m/C; VHS, DVD.** Dylan Walsh; Alison Eastwood; Tobin Bell; Julia Davis; Jaimz Woolvett; ***D:*** Joseph Zito; ***W:*** B.J. Davis; Brent Huff; Adrian Fulle; ***C:*** Gideon Porath. **VIDEO**

Power Rangers 1/2 *Saban's Power Rangers* **2017 (PG-13)** The hit TV and action-figure series is rebooted as a grittier, teen-pitched flick with mixed results. A group of five troubled teens finds the Power Coins, the source of power for the legendary Rangers, and become superheroes. The problem with this take is that it's too self-serious, never recognizing the campy aspect of the source material that connected with so many viewers. Most of all, it's pretty dull, which is the last thing a film about superpowered teenagers can possibly be. **124m/C; DVD, Blu-Ray.** Dacre Montgomery; Naomi Scott; R.J. Cyler; Ludi Lin; Becky G; Elizabeth Banks; ***D:*** Dean Israelite; ***W:*** John Gatins; ***C:*** Matthew Lloyd; ***M:*** Brian Tyler.

The Power Within 1/2 **1995 (PG-13)** Evil Raymond Vonn has stolen an ancient ring of power but to acquire its complete strength he needs to find a second, matching ring. This is in the possession of teenaged Stan Dryer (Roberts), who must discover the ring's power if he expects to defeat Vonn. **97m/C; VHS, DVD.** Ted Jan Roberts; Karen Valentine; Keith Coogan; John O'Hurley; Gary Morgan; Sean Fitzgerald; William Zabka; ***D:*** Art Camacho; ***W:*** Jacobsen Hart; Susan Bowen; ***M:*** Jim Halfpenny.

The Powerpuff Girls Movie **2002 (G)** Blossom, Buttercup, and Bubbles, the big-eyed trio of superpowered kindergartners, came into existence after a botched experiment by Professor Utonium, who mixed his sugar, spice, and everything nice recipe with a little Chemical X (thanks to Jojo the lab chimp), leaving the tots with super powers. After a mishap puts their father/creator in jail, the girls join up with Jojo, genetically altered by Chemical X himself and acquiring a taste for world domination, unbeknownst to the Power Pack. Runs a bit long, but creator/director McCracken's cool retro animation, fast-paced editing, and satiric fun makes the spunky girls' action-packed film debut a winner. **74m/C; VHS, DVD.** ***V:*** Catherine Cavadini; Tara Strong; Elizabeth Daily; Roger L. Jackson; Tom Kane; Tom Kenny; Jennifer Hale; Jennifer Martin; ***Nar:*** Tom Kenny; ***D:*** Craig McCracken; ***W:*** Craig McCracken; Charlie Bean; Lauren Faust; Paul Rudish; John Roarke.

Powwow Highway 1/2 **1989 (R)** Remarkably fine performances in this unusual, thought-provoking, poorly titled foray into the plight of Native Americans. Farmer shines as the unassuming, amiable Cheyenne traveling to New Mexico in a beat-up Chevy with his Indian activist buddy, passionately portrayed by Martinez. On the journey they are constantly confronted with the tragedy of life on a reservation. A sobering look at government injustice and the lingering spirit of a people lost inside their homeland. **105m/C; VHS, DVD.** Gary Farmer; A. Martinez; Amanda Wyss; Sam Vlahos; Joanelle Romero; Graham Greene; ***D:*** Jonathan Wacks; ***W:*** Janet Heaney; Jean Stawarz; ***C:*** Toyomichi Kurita; ***M:*** Barry Goldberg. Sundance '89: Filmmakers Trophy.

Practical Magic 1/2 **1998 (PG-13)** Gillian (Kidman) and Sally (Bullock) are modern-day witch sisters whose family suffers from an unfortunate 100-year-old curse. Any man they fall in love with is doomed to an early death. One more dead body, Gillian's abusive boyfriend Jimmy (Visnjic), brings out detective Gary Hallet (Quinn) and his charms prove mighty attractive to the frantic Sally. Good cast, weak story. Based on the 1995 novel by Alice Hoffman. **105m/C; VHS, DVD.** Sandra Bullock; Nicole Kidman; Aidan Quinn; Stockard Channing; Dianne Wiest; Goran Visnjic; ***D:*** Griffin Dunne; ***W:*** Robin Swicord; Akiva Goldsman; Adam Brooks; ***C:*** Andrew Dunn; ***M:*** Alan Silvestri.

Prairie Fever **2008** Grieving the death of his wife, former sheriff Preston Biggs (Sorbo) has become a drunk. Needing money, Biggs takes a job transporting several rejected mail-order brides said to be suffering from "prairie fever" (or mental illness) to the train depot in Carson City. Meanwhile, card cheat Olivia (Allman) has dumped partner Monte (Henriksen) and stolen their money. Needing a way out of town, she takes a place with Biggs. They're trailed by some outlaws with a grudge against Biggs and Olivia hasn't seen the last of Monte either. **80m/C; DVD.** Kevin Sorbo; Jillian Armenante; Dominique Swain; Lance Henriksen; Silas Weir Mitchell; Don Swayze; Chris(topher) McKenna; Felecia Day; Jamie Anne Allman; ***D:*** Stephen Bridgewater; David S. Cass, Sr.; ***W:*** Steven H. Berman; ***C:*** Al Lopez. **TV**

A Prairie Home Companion 1/2 **2006 (PG-13)** Leisurely-paced adaptation of Keillor's radio show begins at the Fitzgerald Theater in St. Paul on a Saturday night. Only this night is the program's last broadcast because the radio station has been sold. Emcee Keillor (more or less playing himself) doesn't want to spoil things by making a fuss so the show goes on with the singing Johnson sisters—ditsy Yolanda (Streep) and caustic Rhonda (Tomlin)?and risque cowboy duo Lefty (Reilly) and Dusty (Harrelson), while backstage P.I. Guy Noir (Kline) wonders about the mysterious blonde in white (Madsen). Ensemble master Altman just lets his 39th feature meander gently along. **105m/C; DVD.** Meryl Streep; Lily Tomlin; Lindsay Lohan; Woody Harrelson; John C. Reilly; Kevin Kline; Tommy Lee Jones; L.Q. Jones; Virginia Madsen; Maya Rudolph; Garrison Keillor; Marylouise Burke; ***D:*** Robert Altman; ***W:*** Garrison Keillor; ***C:*** Edward Lachman.

Praise **1998** First-time director Curran scores big with this downbeat sex-and-drugs saga. Gordan (Fenton) has quit his convenience store job to spend his time drinking with his mates in his grubby Brisbane apartment. Former co-worker Cynthia (Holder) invites Gordon to her parents' empty house where the duo spend their time with various chemical substances, alcohol, and sex. They wind up sticking together out of mutual need and never rise above their marginal existence. Still, both director and actors deliver a powerful production. Adapted from the novel by McGahan, who wrote the screenplay. **97m/C; VHS, DVD.** *AU* Peter Fenton; Sacha Horler; ***D:*** John Curran; ***W:*** Andrew McGahan; ***C:*** Dion Beebe. Australian Film Inst. '99: Actress (Horler), Adapt. Screenplay.

Prancer **1989 (G)** An eight-year-old girl whose mother has recently died thinks an injured reindeer she has found belongs to Santa. She lovingly nurses him back to health. Harmless family entertainment. **102m/C; VHS, DVD, Blu-Ray.** Sam Elliott; Rebecca Harrell; Cloris Leachman; Rutanya Alda; John Joseph Duda; Abe Vigoda; Michael Constantine; Ariana Richards; Mark Rolston; ***D:*** John Hancock; ***W:*** Greg Taylor; ***C:*** Misha (Mikhail) Suslov; ***M:*** Maurice Jarre.

Prancer Returns 1/2 **2001 (G)** When dad cuts out, 8-year-old Charlie, his mom and his brother move to a small Michigan town where Charlie hears about a local legend. Seems a young girl nursed a wounded deer back to health and set it free on Christmas Eve. The deer turned out to be Prancer and he rejoined Santa just in time to help pull the sleigh. So when Charlie finds a baby reindeer in the woods, he decides it must be a new Prancer and he has to make sure that the deer gets to Santa in time for Christmas. **90m/C; VHS, DVD.** Jack Palance; John Corbett; Stacy Edwards; Gavin Fink; Michael O'Keefe; ***D:*** Joshua Butler; ***W:*** Greg Taylor. **CABLE**

The Prankster 1/2 **2010** High school misfits calling themselves The Pranksters battle cliques through social anarchy. This starts backfiring for leader Chris who has fallen for Hispanic cheerleader Mariah and then discovers he needs some legitimate extracurricular activities if he expects to get a needed college scholarship. **117m/C; DVD.** Ken Davitian; Georges Corraface; Devon Werkheiser; Madison Riley; Robert Adamson; Jareb Dauplaise; Kurt Fuller; Matt Angel; Veronica Sixtos; ***D:*** Tony Vidal; ***W:*** Tony Vidal; ***C:*** Martin Rosenberg; ***M:*** Charles David Denler. **VIDEO**

Pray for Death **1985 (R)** When a mild-mannered Japanese family is victimized by a crime syndicate in L.A., a master ninja comes to the rescue. Higher quality production than most ninja adventures. **93m/C; VHS, DVD, Blu-Ray.** James Booth; Robert Ito; Sho Kosugi; Shane Kosugi; Kane (Takeshi) Kosugi; Donna Kei Benz; ***D:*** Gordon Hessler; ***W:*** James Booth.

Pray TV *KGOD* **1980 (PG)** A sly con man turns a failing TV station into a profitable one when the station starts to broadcast around-the-clock religious programming. **92m/C; VHS, DVD.** Dabney Coleman; Archie Hahn; Joyce Jameson; Nancy Morgan; Roger E. Mosley; Marcia Wallace; ***D:*** Rick Friedberg; ***W:*** Nick Castle. **TV**

A Prayer Before Dawn **2018 (R)** Boxer Billy (Cole) is jailed in a brutal Thai prison after police raid his drug-filled apartment. Once inside, he is isolated because he does not speak the language and has no family or visitors other than a young boxer he was training. The self-destructive Billy continues to buy and use drugs, but comes into conflict with other prisoners because he cannot pay. He soon realizes that boxing may be his only hope for salvation. Based on a true story, the depiction of violence is relentless yet the story is unabashedly powerful and realistic. **116m/C; DVD, Blu-Ray.** Joe Cole; Vithaya Pansringarm; Panya Yimmumphai; Sura Sirmalai; Pornchanok Mabklang; ***D:*** Jean-Stephane Sauvaire; ***W:*** Jonathan Hirschbein; Nick Saltrese; ***C:*** David Ungaro; ***M:*** Nicolas Becker.

Prayer for the Dying 1/2 **1987 (R)** An IRA hitman longs to quit, but he has to complete one last assignment. The hit is witnessed by a priest who becomes an unwitting associate when the hitman hides out at the church. Fine performances from Bates and Rourke, though Hodges and Rourke were not satisfied with finished film. **104m/C; VHS, DVD, Blu-Ray.** Mickey Rourke; Alan Bates; Bob Hoskins; Sammi Davis; Liam Neeson; Alison Doody; Christopher Fulford; ***D:*** Mike Hodges; ***W:*** Edmund Ward; Martin Lynch; ***M:*** Bill Conti.

Prayer of the Rollerboys 1/2 **1991 (R)** Violent, futuristic, funky action as Haim infiltrates a criminal gang of syncopated roller-blading neo-nazi youth with plans for nationwide domination. Though routinely plotted and predictable, it's got great skating stunts and a wry vision of tomorrow's shattered USA—broke, drug-soaked, homeless, foreign-owned; even sharper when you realize this is a Japanese-American co-production. **94m/C; DVD.** Corey Haim; Patricia Arquette; Christopher Collet; Julius W. Harris; J.C. Quinn; Jake Dengel; Devin Clark; Mark Pellegrino; Morgan Weisser; ***D:*** Rick King; ***W:*** W. Peter Iliff; ***C:*** Phedon Papamichael; ***M:*** Stacy Widelitz.

Prayers for Bobby **2009** Haunting Lifetime drama based on a true story. In 1979, conservative, religious mom Mary Griffith (Weaver) is appalled to learn that her teenage son Bobby (Kelley) is gay. She forces him into therapy but all that does is eventually drive him away from home and into a suicidal despair. What follows is Mary's tearjerking quest to understand what happened and reconcile it with her spiritual beliefs. **86m/C; DVD.** Sigourney Weaver; Ryan Kelley; Henry Czerny; Austin Nicols; Carly Schroeder; Shannon Eagan; Scott Bailey; Susan Ruttan; Dan E. Butler; ***D:*** Russell Mulcahy; ***W:*** Katie Ford; ***C:*** Thom Best; ***M:*** Christopher Ward. **CABLE**

Preacherman 1/2 **1983 (R)** Phony preacher travels through the South, fleecing gullible congregations (and providing for their sexual desires) wherever he goes. **90m/C; VHS, DVD.** Amos Huxley; Marian Brown; Adam Hesse; Ilene Kristen; W. Henry Smith; ***D:*** Albert T. Viola; ***W:*** Albert T. Viola; Harvey Flaxman; ***M:*** W. Henry Smith; Roland Pope.

Preacher's Kid 1/2 **2010 (PG-13)** Inexperienced Angie King (Luckett) is not so content being the dutiful daughter of stern Bishop King (Williams). With some singing ambitions, Angie is ripe for the attention of Devlin (Babbs), the star of a travelling gospel show, who gets her an audition. Director Ike (Powell) hires Angie as an understudy even though her father strongly disapproves of Angie leaving. Not perfect, but not preachy, with an appealing lead and a hardworking cast. **110m/C; DVD.** Clifton Powell; Gregory Alan Williams; Tammy Townsend; Rae'ven (Alyia Larrymore) Kelly; LeToya Luckett; Durrel Babbs; Sharif Atkins; Essence Atkins; Ella Joyce; ***D:*** Stan Foster; ***W:*** Stan Foster; ***C:*** Dave Perkal; ***M:*** Tim Miner. **VIDEO**

The Preacher's Wife **1996 (PG)** Remake of 1947's "The Bishop's Wife" finds troubled Newark minister Henry Biggs (Vance) praying for heavenly intervention. His prayers are answered with angel Dudley (Washington)--who isn't so holy that he can't appreciate the minister's choir-leading wife Julia (Houston). While trying to save his cash-strapped church from a greedy developer (Hines), Rev. Biggs is so mired in material problems that he doesn't believe Dudley is actually an angel. Washington is the dictionary definition of debonair, but the real stars of this Christmas tale are Houston's vocal cords. Fans of her singing will love this movie; others may prefer the original. **124m/C; VHS, DVD, Blu-Ray.** Denzel Washington; Whitney Houston; Courtney B. Vance; Gregory Hines; Jenifer Lewis; Loretta Devine; Lionel Richie; Paul Bates; Justin Pierre Edmund; Darvel Davis, Jr.; William James Stiggers, Jr.; Shari Headley; ***D:*** Penny Marshall; ***W:*** Nat Mauldin; Allan Scott; ***C:*** Miroslav Ondricek; ***M:*** Hans Zimmer.

Preaching to the Choir **2005 (PG-13)** Twin brothers Teshawn (Greene) and Wesley (Sills-Evans) Tucker have been estranged since the death of their parents. Te is the gangsta hip hop star Zulu while Wes is a minister at a Harlem church. When Te gets into big trouble with his LA record producer Bull Sharkey (Akinnoyye-Agbaje), he flees to Harlem to hide out and he and Wes try to reconcile their differences, especially when Te offers to whip the church's raggedy gospel choir into shape in time for a competition. **100m/C; DVD.** Darien Sills-Evans; Billoah Greene; Tichina Arnold; Adewale Akinnuoye-Agbaje; Eartha Kitt; Patti LaBelle; Novella Nelson; Janine Green; ***D:*** Olga San Juan; ***W:*** Kevin Heffernan; Peter E. Lengyel; ***C:*** Robert Barocci; ***M:*** Nona Hendryx.

Preaching to the Perverted **1997 (R)** Silly sex comedy finds politician Henry Harding (Bell) crusading against smut with his intention to close down London's S&M clubs. First up is the House of Thwax, run by New York fetish queen, Tanya (Turner). To get evidence of naughtiness, Henry sends in virginal volunteer Peter (Anholt), who becomes obsessed with Tanya. Tanya's intrigued by his innocence and teaches Peter a few sexual tricks, which soon means he has to choose between his job and his newly acquired interest in kink. **99m/C; DVD.** *GB* Guinevere Turner; Christien Anholt; Tom Bell; Julie Graham; Julian Wadham; Georgina Hale; Ricky Tomlinson; Don Henderson; ***D:*** Stuart Urban; ***W:*** Stuart Urban; ***C:*** Sam McCurdy; ***M:*** Magnus Fiennes.

Precious: Based on the Novel 'Push' by Sapphire 1/2 **2009 (R)** Multi-award winner's a graphic and uncompromising urban nightmare that offers a sliver of hope. In 1987 Harlem, obese, 16-year-old African-American Claireece "Precious" Jones (Sidibe) is precious to no one—certainly not to her monster mom Mary (Mo'Nique) or the unseen father who raped her and got Precious pregnant again. Withdrawn Precious has her fantasies, which the audience sees and hears, while being nearly illiterate. She enrolls at an alternative school with the prerequisite caring teacher (Patton) and also comes to the attention of a welfare counselor (Carey) who tries to show her something more. As the title states, based on the 1996 novel by Sapphire. **109m/C; DVD.** Gabourney "Gabby" Sidibe; Mo'Nique; Paula Patton; Mariah Carey; Lenny Kravitz; Sherri Shepherd; ***D:*** Lee Daniels; ***W:*** Geoffrey "Damien

Paul" Fletcher; *C:* Andrew Dunn; *M:* Mario Grigorov. Oscars '09: Adapt. Screenplay, Support. Actress (Mo'Nique); British Acad. '09: Support. Actress (Mo'Nique); Golden Globes '10: Support. Actress (Mo'Nique); Ind. Spirit '10: Actress (Sidibe), Director (Daniels), Film, First Screenplay, Support. Actress (Mo'Nique); Screen Actors Guild '09: Support. Actress (Mo'Nique).

Precious Cargo **2016 (R)** A crime drama about a heist gone bad and tense aftermath. Karen (Forlani) is a thief whose robbery for Eddie (Willis), a crime boss, did not go as planned. A vengeful sort, Eddie begins to search for Karen to gain his revenge. Hoping to mollify Eddie, Karen convinces her ex-lover Jack (Goesselaar), also a talented thief, to steal rare gems. During and after the job, however, the alliances shift between Karen, Eddie, and Jack, leading to an unexpected showdown between the three master criminals. **90m/C; DVD, Blu-Ray, Streaming, Download.** Mark-Paul Gosselaar; Bruce Willis; Claire Forlani; John Brotherton; Daniel Bernhardt; *D:* Max Adams; Paul V. Seetachitt; *W:* Max Adams; Paul V. Seetachitt; *C:* Brandon Cox; *M:* James Edward Barker; Tim Despic.

The Predator **2018 (R)** As an alien predator ship approaches Earth, sniper Quinn McKenna (Holbrook) is nearly hit by its escape pod. Before the government captures the predator and Quinn, he steals some of the alien gear, which ends up in the hands of his autistic son Rory (Tremblay). At the same time, biologist Casey Bracket (Munn) examines the alien, while captured Quinn connects with a group of military prisoners dubbed "The Loonies." With help of them and Casey, Quinn tries to find the predator and protect Rory. A loose sequel to the 1987 classic, the well-paced film is a fun throwback to 1980s action films. **107m/C; DVD, Blu-Ray.** Boyd Holbrook; Trevante Rhodes; Jacob Tremblay; Keegan Michael Key; Olivia Munn; *D:* Shane Black; *W:* Shane Black; Fred Dekker; *C:* Larry Fong; *M:* Henry Jackman.

Predator 1/2 **1987 (R)** Schwarzenegger leads a team of CIA-hired mercenaries into the Central American jungles to rescue hostages. They encounter an alien force that begins to attack them one by one. Soon it's just Arnold and the Beast in this attention-grabbing, but sometimes silly, suspense film. **107m/C; VHS, DVD, Blu-Ray, UMD.** Arnold Schwarzenegger; Jesse Ventura; Sonny Landham; Bill Duke; Elpidia Carrillo; Carl Weathers; R.G. Armstrong; Richard Chaves; Shane Black; Kevin Peter Hall; *D:* John McTiernan; *W:* Jim Thomas; John Thomas; *C:* Donald McAlpine; *M:* Alan Silvestri.

Predator 2 **1990 (R)** Tough cop takes time away from battling drug dealers to deal with malicious extraterrestrial who exterminated Arnold's band of commandos in "Predator." Miss-billed as sequel, its only resemblance to the original is that the predator has inexplicably returned (this time to the thick of L.A.). Gory action aplenty, little logic. Fine cast dominated by minority performers can't save this one. **105m/C; VHS, DVD, Blu-Ray.** Danny Glover; Gary Busey; Ruben Blades; Maria Conchita Alonso; Bill Paxton; Robert Davi; Adam Baldwin; Kent McCord; Morton Downey, Jr.; Calvin Lockhart; Teri Weigel; Kevin Peter Hall; Steve Kahan; Michael (Mike) Papajohn; Jsu Garcia; *D:* Stephen Hopkins; *W:* John Thomas; Jim Thomas; *C:* Peter Levy; *M:* Alan Silvestri.

Predator Island *Hell's Beacon* **2005 (R)** Teens and aliens-what could be more fun? A group of teens head off for a lovely weekend boat trip off the New England Coast. A meteor crash spurs bad weather and throws the crew off-course, stranding them on an island inhabited only by a creepy lighthouse keeper and his wife. The aliens, presumably having hitched a ride on the meteor, terrorize all. **75m/C; DVD.** Daniel Gordon; Hank Torrance; Libby Krall; Thomas Dahl; Ilana Becker; Michael Wrann; *D:* Steven Charles Castle; *W:* Steven Charles Castle; *C:* Andrew Gernhard; *M:* Tony Bitten. **VIDEO**

Predators 1/2 **2010 (R)** A group of elite soldiers and professional killers are hunted by alien trackers in this gory, fast-paced, but needless franchise reboot from producer Robert Rodriguez and his Troublemaker studio. Mercenary Royce (Brody) unexpectedly finds himself in a jungle game preserve with some other terrestrial toughs who soon realize it isn't easy to survive when you're the prey. **107m/C; DVD, Blu-Ray.** Adrien Brody; Laurence Fishburne; Topher Grace; Alice Braga; Danny Trejo; Walton Goggins; Mahershala Ali; Oleg Nikolai; Louis Ozawa Changchien; *D:* Nimrod Antal; *W:* Michael Finch; Alex Litvak; *C:* Gyula Pados; *M:* John Debney.

Predestination **2015 (R)** Based on Robert A. Heinlein's short story "All You Zombies," this wraps around itself so many times some viewers might get a headache but it's certainly not standard sci-fi thriller. It's hard to even recap. The main crux of the story centers on a conversation between a bartender (Hawke) and a customer (Snook), who explains his story, which includes time travel, gender reassignment, and the kind of Twilight Zone-esque twists that sci-fi fans adore. Smart, fun, and just a little bit crazy. The final act gets a bit too ridiculous, but definitely worth a look for genre fans. **97m/C; DVD, Blu-Ray.** *AU* Ethan Hawke; Sarah Snook; Noah Taylor; *D:* Michael Spierig; Peter Spierig; *W:* Michael Spierig; Peter Spierig; *C:* Ben Nott; *M:* Peter Spierig.

Prefontaine 1/2 **1996 (PG-13)** Sports bio has appeal, thanks to lead actor Leto, in covering the brief career of early '70s runner Steve Prefontaine. Cocky and outspoken, the charismatic University of Oregon star soon owns every American record for distances between 2,000 and 10,000 meters. He's expected to gold at the 1972 Munich Olympics but falters, thanks in part to the tragedy surrounding the games. Returning home, the flamboyant Pre becomes a sports activist for athletes' rights before dying in a car crash in 1975 at the age of 24. Relatively straight narrative and little psychological insight make for few lasting impressions. **107m/C; VHS, DVD, Blu-Ray.** Jared Leto; R. Lee Ermey; Ed O'Neill; Amy Locane; Lindsay Crouse; Laurel Holloman; Breckin Meyer; Kurtwood Smith; Brian McGovern; Peter Anthony Jacobs; *D:* Steve James; *W:* Steve James; Eugene Corr; *C:* Peter Gilbert; *M:* Mason Daring.

The Pregnancy Pact **2010** Lifetime teen drama 'inspired by' a true story. After one girl in their clique becomes pregnant, her naive teen friends, who all have fantasy ideas of mommyhood, also decide to get preggers and raise their babies together. Internet blogger Sydney (Birch) comes back to her hometown to get the story, which becomes a media sensation causing scandal in the conservative community. Production raises some valid points but then turns wishy-washy. **83m/C; DVD.** Thora Birch; Madisen Beaty; Nancy Travis; James McCaffrey; Kelly Heyer; Michelle DeFraites; Jenna Leigh Hall; Camryn Manheim; David Clayton Rogers; Max Ehrich; Tim Powell; *D:* Rosemary Rodriguez; *W:* Teena Booth; Pamela Davis; *C:* John Aronson; *M:* Richard (Rick) Marvin. **CABLE**

The Pregnancy Project **2012** This Lifetime movie, based on the memoir by Gaby Rodriguez, sits in the unbelievable-but-true category. Smart high school senior Gaby (Vega) chooses stereotyping for her senior project. She tells her family, friends, and teachers that she is pregnant and records how she is treated. And it's not pretty. **96m/C; DVD; Closed Captioned.** Alexa Vega; Judy Reyes; Walter Perez; Michael Mando; Peter Benson; Sarah Strange; *D:* Norman Buckley; *W:* Teena Booth; *C:* Adam Sliwinski; *M:* James Jandrisch. **CABLE**

Prehistoric Bimbos in Armageddon City **WOOF! 1993** Trianna and her tribe of Prehistoric Bimbos must prevent post-nuclear domination in Old Chicago City, the last remaining civilization after WWIII, by defeating the evil ruler Nemesis and his cyborgs. "Enough bimbos to fill two post-nuclear action comedies." So bad its gotta be good. **70m/C; VHS, DVD.** Robert Vollrath; Tonia Monahan; Deric Bernier; *D:* Todd Sheets; *W:* Roger Williams.

Prehistoric Women **WOOF! 1950** A tribe of prehistoric women look for husbands the old-fashioned way—they drag them back to their caves from the jungle. So bad it's almost good. **74m/C; VHS, DVD.** Laurette Luez; Allan Nixon; Mara Lynn; Joan Shawlee; Judy Landon; *D:* Gregg Tallas.

Prehistoric Women *Slave Girls* **1967** Essentially, an equally tacky remake of the 1950 woofer. Great white hunter David Marchant (Latimer) gets lost in a jungle where the local tribe worship the white rhino. He escapes from one group, only to recapture by some Amazons, who take the hunter to their queen, Kari (Beswick—the only reason to waste your time), who gives him two options—satisfy her or die. **90m/C; VHS, DVD.** *GB* Michael Latimer; Martine Beswick; Edina Ronay; Carol White; *D:* Michael Carreras; *W:* Michael Carreras; *C:* Michael Reed; *M:* Carlo Martelli.

Prelude to a Kiss **1992 (PG-13)** Disappointing screen adaptation of Craig Lucas' hit play features Baldwin and Ryan as young lovers in this romantic fantasy. Rita, a free-spirited bartender and Peter, a conservative writer, decide to marry after a whirlwind courtship. At their wedding reception, Rita obligingly kisses one of their guests, an old man (Walker). Then, on their honeymoon, Peter begins to notice a number of changes to Rita's character and comes to realize this is truly not the girl he married. The delicate fantasy which worked on stage struggles to survive the "opening up" of the screen adaptation though Baldwin (who reprises his stage role) and Ryan are appealing. **106m/C; VHS, DVD.** Alec Baldwin; Meg Ryan; Sydney Walker; Ned Beatty; Patty Duke; Kathy Bates; Stanley Tucci; *D:* Norman Rene; *W:* Craig Lucas; *C:* Stefan Czapsky; *M:* Howard Shore.

Premature 1/2 **2020** In Harlem, young adults Ayanna (Howard) and Isaiah (Boone) meet and have their first conversation at a laundromat. After sharing their first kiss in a park and becoming romantically involved, their relationship grows stronger as they experience personal growth. Throughout it all, Ayanna also deals with family difficulties and writes poetry, while Isaiah works on his music with powerful singer Dymond (Herrold). Refreshing, direct, and honest, the low budget film is an engaging exploration of the ups and downs of a relationship with strong cinematography and editing. The film is also a love letter to Harlem and New York City. **90m/C; DVD.** Zora Howard; Joshua Boone; Michelle Wilson; Alexis Marie Wint; Imani Lewis; *D:* Rashaad Ernesto Green; *W:* Zora Howard; Rashaad Ernesto Green; *C:* Laura Valladao; *M:* Patrick Cannell; Stefan Swanson.

Premature Burial **1962** A cataleptic Englishman's worst fears come true when he is buried alive. He escapes and seeks revenge on his doctor and his greedy wife. Based upon the story by Edgar Allan Poe. **81m/C; VHS, DVD, Blu-Ray.** Ray Milland; Richard Ney; Hazel Court; Heather Angel; Alan Napier; John Dierkes; Dick Miller; Brendan Dillon, Jr.; Clive Halliday; *D:* Roger Corman; *W:* Charles Beaumont; Ray Russell; *C:* Floyd Crosby; *M:* Ronald Stein.

Premium Rush **2012 (PG-13)** Bike messenger Wilee (the always-spectacular Gordon-Levitt) is at the top of his game, weaving through New York traffic and getting his packages to their location before the recipient even knows they've been shipped. When his final shipment of the day turns out to be more than he bargained for, he has to race for his life. A great cast and incredible sense of pace make the formulaic aspects of the film easier to overlook. Writer/director Koepp and his talented cast pump up the adrenalin in this surprisingly effective thrill ride. **90m/C; DVD, Blu-Ray.** Joseph Gordon-Levitt; Michael Shannon; Jamie Chung; Aasif Mandvi; *D:* David Koepp; *W:* David Koepp; John Kamps; *C:* Mitchell Amundsen; *M:* David Sardy.

The Premonition 1/2 **1975 (PG)** Parapsychologist searching for a missing child is drawn into a frightening maze of dream therapy and communication with the dead. Well-done paranorm tale filmed in Mississippi. **94m/C; VHS, DVD, Blu-Ray.** Richard Lynch; Sharon Farrell; Jeff Corey; Ellen Barber; Edward Bell; Danielle Brisebois; *D:* Robert Allen Schnitzer; *W:* Anthony Mahon.

Premonition **1998 (R)** Lloyd and Preston are tabloid reporters who investigate supernatural phenomena. Their latest find is a mental patient who predicts events that wind up leading back to a past they both share. Unfortunately, the film is more a series of horror cliches and makes little sense. **93m/C; VHS, DVD.** Christopher Lloyd; Adrian Paul; Cynthia (Cyndy, Cindy) Preston; Blu Mankuma; *D:* Gavin Wilding; *W:* Gavin Wilding; Raul Inglis; John Fairley; *C:* Glen Winter. **VIDEO**

Premonition 1/2 **2007 (PG-13)** He's dead! No, he's not! He's in the shower! He's being buried! Whew—no wonder Linda (Bullock) thinks she's going nuts. Seems every time she wakes up the fate of her husband Jim (McMahon) has changed. Linda finally realizes her days are mysteriously out of order and if she can figure out the pattern (or have a little faith), maybe she can save her man. It's confusing however you look at it, though Bullock tries her best. **97m/C; DVD, Blu-Ray.** Sandra Bullock; Julian McMahon; Nia Long; Kate Nelligan; Amber Valletta; Peter Stormare; Courtney Taylor Burness; Shyann McClure; *D:* Mennan Yapo; *W:* Bill Kelly; *C:* Torsten Lippstock; *M:* Klaus Badelt.

Preppies 1/2 **1982 (R)** Yet another teen sex comedy, but this time Ivy Leaguer Drake must pass his exams to receive his $50 million inheritance. Lots of skirt chasing as his conniving cousin leads him astray. **83m/C; VHS, DVD.** Dennis Drake; Peter Brady Reardon; Steven Holt; Nitchie Barrett; Cindy Manion; Katt Shea; Lynda Wiesmeier; *D:* Chuck Vincent.

Prescription Thugs 1/2 **2016** This feature-length documentary explores and exposes the prescription drug industry in North America. In this no-holds-barred and thought-provoking film, filmmaker Chris Bell looks at the pharmaceutical companies themselves and their marketing efforts. More deeply, he examines how this industry has created a culture of addiction to and abuse of prescription drugs, and considers the nature of addiction in North American culture. **86m/C; DVD, Blu-Ray, Streaming, Download.** *D:* Chris Bell; Josh Alexander; Greg Young; *W:* Josh Alexander; *C:* Greg Young; *M:* Joel Goodman.

Presenting Lily Mars **1943** A small-town girl comes to New York to make it on Broadway. Based on the Booth Tarkington novel. **105m/B; VHS, DVD.** Judy Garland; Van Heflin; Fay Bainter; Richard Carlson; Tommy Dorsey; *D:* Norman Taurog; *C:* Joseph Ruttenberg.

Presenting Princess Shaw 1/2 **2016** This strong documentary captures the connective power of the Internet through the story of Samantha Montgomery, a woman who cares for the elderly in New Orleans during the day and writes and sings her own songs as a YouTube sensation known as Princess Shaw at night. Halfway around the world, a composer named Kutiman stumbles on Princess Shaw online and becomes entranced with her, working with Shaw to elevate her persona and profile even higher. Not only is this an interesting study of the newly connected world but a commentary on how artistic genius may be around every corner. **83m/C; DVD.** *D:* Ido Haar; *W:* Ido Haar; *C:* Ido Haar.

Preservation 1/2 **2014** Wit (movie-stealing Schmidt) and her husband Mike (Staton) are on a camping trip with Mike's brother Sean (Schreiber) when they awaken to find their clothes stolen. They're being stalked and hunted through the woods. What would you do to survive? Would you kill? Of course the pacifistic Mike and the vet Sean have different answers. What starts as an engaging drama about three very different people becomes a predictable, generic mess that tries to comment on the violent culture of today's youth with all the subtlety of a claw hammer to the head. **90m/C; Streaming.** Aaron Staton; Wrenn Schmidt; Pablo Schreiber; *D:* Christopher Denham; *W:* Christopher Denham; *C:* Nicola Marsh; *M:* Samuel Jones; Alexis Marsh.

The President's Analyst 1/2 **1967** A superbly written, brilliantly executed satire from the mind of Theodore J. Flicker, who wrote as well as directed. Coburn steals the show as a psychiatrist who has the dubious honor of being appointed "secret shrink" to the President of the U.S. Pressures of the job steadily increase his paranoia until he suspects he is being pursued by agents and counter agents alike. Is he losing his sanity or...? Vastly entertaining. **104m/C; VHS, DVD.** James Coburn; Godfrey Cambridge; Severn Darden; Joan Delaney; Pat Harrington, Jr.; Will Geer; William Daniels; Barry McGuire; Jill

Banner; Arte Johnson; *D:* Theodore J. Flicker; *W:* Theodore J. Flicker; *C:* William A. Fraker; *M:* Lalo Schifrin.

The President's Man 1/2 **2000 (PG-13)** Joshua McCord (Norris) is an aging Secret Service agent who decides to train his replacement while he still can. During training the first lady gets snatched by terrorists and the pair must rescue her in time. Chuck was 60 when he did this so it's quite interesting that he's able to pull it off. **95m/C; DVD.** Chuck Norris; Dylan Neal; Marla Adams; Jennifer Tung; *D:* Eric Norris; *W:* Bob Gookin; *C:* Rick Anderson; *M:* Christopher L. Stone. **TV**

The President's Man 2: A Line in the Sand 1/2 **2002 (PG-13)** Terrorists smuggle plutonium to Texas in teensy statues and make a toaster-sized nuclear weapon. The President calls in an aging McCord (Norris) and his protege to go find them and put a stop to the operation before they detonate in Dallas. **93m/C; DVD.** Chuck Norris; Judson Mills; Jennifer Tung; Robert Urich; Roxanne Hart; Philip Casnoff; *D:* Eric Norris; *W:* John Lansing; *C:* Rick Anderson; *M:* Kevin Kiner. **TV**

The President's Mystery 1/2 *One For All* **1936** A lawyer decides to turn his back on society by giving up his practice and his marriage. Eventually he meets and falls in love with another woman. The most interesting aspect of the film is that it is based on a story by Franklin D. Roosevelt, which was published in "Liberty" magazine. The story was supposedly better than its screen adaptation. **80m/B; VHS, DVD.** Henry Wilcoxon; Betty Furness; Sidney Blackmer; Evelyn Brent; *D:* Phil Rosen.

The Presidio **1988 (R)** An easy going police detective must investigate a murder on a military base where he and the base commander have sparred before. The commander becomes downright nasty when his daughter shows an interest in the detective. Good action scenes in San Francisco almost covers up script weaknesses, but not quite. **97m/C; VHS, DVD, Blu-Ray.** Sean Connery; Mark Harmon; Meg Ryan; Jack Warden; Mark Blum; Jenette Goldstein; *D:* Peter Hyams; *W:* Larry Ferguson; *M:* Bruce Broughton.

Pressed 1/2 **2011** Passable crime drama. Investment banker Brian sets up a drug deal when he needs some quick cash. It goes wrong when his car, containing the payoff money, is stolen by a couple of joyriding teens. Brian owes the drug thug and the teens realize they've make a big mistake. **88m/C; DVD.** Luke Goss; Tyler Johnston; Jef-f(rey) Ballard; Michael Eklund; *D:* Justin Donnelly; *W:* Justin Donnelly; *C:* Norm Li; *M:* Peter Allen. **VIDEO**

Pressure 1/2 **2002 (R)** Med students Steve (Smith) and Patrick (Munro) find themselves on a road trip to hell when they make a stop in a smalltown bar. Patrick spends his time dancing with the cheerleaders inhabiting the premises while Steve is lured outside by vampy Amber (Featherstone). He's then knocked unconscious and set-up by her beau, Bo (Dorval), who accidentally shoots himself. This puts our boys in big trouble since Bo is the local corrupt sheriff's (Rhodes) kid. Then the chase is on! **90m/C; VHS, DVD.** Kerr Smith; Lochlyn Munro; Angela Featherstone; Adrien Dorval; Donnelly Rhodes; Michelle Harrison; *D:* Richard Gale; *W:* Richard Gale; Craig Brewer; *M:* Christopher Brady. **VIDEO**

Pressure Point **1962** Poitier stars as a prison psychiatrist treating an inmate who is a racist and a member of the Nazi party. Darin gives an excellent performance as the Nazi patient in this intelligent drama based on a true case. **87m/B; VHS, DVD, Blu-Ray.** Sidney Poitier; Bobby Darin; Peter Falk; Carl Benton Reid; Barry J. Gordon; Howard Caine; Mary Munday; *D:* Hubert Cornfield; *M:* Ernest Gold.

The Prestige **2006 (PG-13)** Perplexing, complicated, and lavish period mystery focuses on the increasingly violent rivalry between two London magicians. Posh Robert Angier (Jackman) is the more natural showman while Cockney Alfred Borden (Bale) is the risk taker; both are mentored by the conciliatory Cutter (Caine). One of Borden's risks causes the death of Robert's wife Julia (Perabo) and their feud is on. Eventually, it will involve Alfred's unhappy missus, Sarah (Hall), lush magician's assistant Olivia (Johansson), reclusive inventor Nikola Tesla (Bowie), and murder. Situations turn fantastical but clues are apparent if you pay attention. Definitely worth a second look. **128m/C; DVD, Blu-Ray.** *GB US* Christian Bale; Hugh Jackman; Michael Caine; Scarlett Johansson; Piper Perabo; Rebecca Hall; David Bowie; Andy Serkis; Roger Rees; Ricky Jay; Samantha Mahurin; William Morgan Sheppard; *D:* Christopher Nolan; *W:* Christopher Nolan; Jonathan Nolan; *C:* Wally Pfister; *M:* David Julyan.

Presumed Dead **2006** Overly-complicated crime drama. When crime novelist Seth Harmon's (Regehr) protege Paige (Dent) disappears, the evidence points to murder and he is arrested by detective Mary Anne Cooper (Fenn). The courtroom drama makes Harmon's latest book a bestseller and Mary Anne soon realizes she's been the victim of a publicity stunt. Except that Paige is really missing and Mary Anne is certain that Harmon is guilty. **90m/C; DVD.** Sherilyn Fenn; Duncan Regehr; Rhonda Dent; Jay Brazeau; Pascale Hutton; Blu Mankuma; *D:* George Mendeluk; *W:* Keith Shaw; *C:* Mahlon Todd Williams; *M:* Clinton Shorter. **CABLE**

Presumed Guilty **1991** An innocent man is released from prison only to find he is once again a wanted man! So he gets his gal, who happens to be the sheriff's daughter, is beaten up and in the end winds up living happily ever after. **91m/C; VHS, DVD.** Jack Vogel; Holly Floria; Sean Holton; Wayne Zanelotti; Bradley Rockwell; Sharon Young; Al Schuerman; *D:* Lawrence L. Simeone; *W:* Lawrence L. Simeone.

Presumed Innocent **1990 (R)** Assistant district attorney is the prime suspect when a former lover turns up brutally murdered. Cover-ups surround him, the political climate changes, and friends and enemies switch sides. Slow-paced courtroom drama with excellent performances from Ford, Julia, and Bedelia. Skillfully adapted from the best-seller by Chicago attorney Scott Turow. **127m/C; VHS, DVD.** Harrison Ford; Brian Dennehy; Bonnie Bedelia; Greta Scacchi; Raul Julia; Paul Winfield; John Spencer; Joe Grifasi; Anna Maria Horsford; Sab Shimono; Christine Estabrook; Michael (Lawrence) Tolan; Tom Mardirosian; Bradley Whitford; Jesse Bradford; Joseph Mazzello; Jeffrey Wright; Ron Frazier; *D:* Alan J. Pakula; *W:* Alan J. Pakula; Frank Pierson; *C:* Gordon Willis; *M:* John Williams.

The Pretender 1/2 **1947** Embezzling investment broker Kenneth Holden thinks he can get square by marrying wealthy young Claire Worthington. He has a romantic rival so Kenneth arranges a hit through a third party and there's a not-so-unexpected twist to this stilted, paranoid minor noir. **70m/B; DVD.** Albert Dekker; Catherine Craig; Charles Drake; Alan Carney; Tom Kennedy; *D:* W. Lee Wilder; *W:* Don Martin; Doris Miller; *C:* John Alton; *M:* Paul Dessau.

Pretenders **2019** In 1970s America, film student and aspiring auteur Terry (Kilmer) meets beautiful wannabe actress Catherine (Levy) and photographer Phil (Moore) at a French New Wave film screening. The three become friends and collaborate and share secrets. Though Terry is obsessively in love with Catherine and makes her the stars of his student film, a love triangle with Phil develops. By the 1980s, the realities of the movie business have changed their lives, and nothing in Terry's life has turned out as expected. Though the superficial dramedy intends to honor New Wave filmmakers like Truffaut and Godard, Franco's production is generally clumsy. **95m/C; DVD.** Jane Levy; Brian Cox; Juno Temple; James Franco; Dennis Quaid; *D:* James Franco; *W:* Josh Boone; *C:* Peter Zeitlinger; *M:* Mark Kozelek.

Pretty Baby **1950** Silly workplace comedy. All Patsy (Drake) wants is a seat on the subway and a chance to advance at the ad agency where she works. When a baby food campaign fails, Patsy takes the life-sized baby doll from the ad and uses it to pass herself off as a young mother so she can finally sit down. Baby food manufacturer Baxter (Gwenn) just happens to sit next to Patsy and her subterfuge leads to his insisting that she take over his ad campaign much to the dismay of her bosses. **92m/B; DVD.** Betsy Drake; Edmund Gwenn; Dennis Morgan; Zachary Scott; William Frawley; *D:* Bretaigne Windust; *W:* Everett Freeman; Harry Kurnitz; *C:* J. Peverell Marley; *M:* David Buttolph.

Pretty Baby **1978 (R)** Shield's launching pad and Malle's first American film is a masterpiece of cinematography and style, nearly upstaged by the plodding story line. Carradine manages to be effective but never succeeds at looking comfortable as the New Orleans photographer besotted with, and subsequently married to, an 11-year-old prostitute (Shields). Low key, disturbingly intriguing story, beautifully photographed by Sven Nykvist. **109m/C; VHS, DVD.** Brooke Shields; Keith Carradine; Susan Sarandon; Barbara Steele; Diana Scarwid; Antonio Fargas; Frances Faye; Gerrit Graham; Mae Mercer; *D:* Louis Malle; *W:* Polly Platt; *C:* Sven Nykvist; *M:* Jerry Wexler.

Pretty Bird 1/2 **2008 (R)** Crazy entrepreneur Curtiss (Crudup) returns to his hometown and manages to convince old buddy Kenny (Hornsby) to invest in his plan to manufacture and market a rocket belt. Curtiss gets some practical assistance from gruff, unemployed rocket scientist Rick (Giamatti) but Schneider's pic never gets off the ground. **120m/C; DVD.** Billy Crudup; Paul Giamatti; Elizabeth Marvel; David Hornsby; Denis O'Hare; Garret Dillahunt; *D:* Paul Schneider; *W:* Paul Schneider; *C:* Igor Martinovic; *M:* Wim Mertens.

Pretty Dead Things **2006** Four adult film actors-turned-vampires return to the town that made them famous so one of them can find the director who was her one true love. **120m/C; DVD.** Patrick Pitu; William DeCoff; Ross Kelly; Jason Witter; Caleb Emerson; Donald C. Foley; Robin L. Watkins; Daniel Lozeau; *D:* Richard Griffin; *W:* Richard Griffin; Sandeep Padmakant Parikh; *C:* Caleb Emerson; *M:* Daniel Hildreth. **VIDEO**

Pretty in Pink 1/2 **1986 (PG-13)** More teen angst from the pen of Hughes. Poor girl falls for a rich guy. Their families fret, their friends are distressed, and fate conspires against them. If you can suspend your disbelief that a teenager with her own car and answering machine is financially inferior, then you may very well be able to accept the entire premise. Slickly done and adequately, if not enthusiastically, acted. In 1987, Hughes essentially rewrote this film with "Some Kind of Wonderful," the same story with the rich/pauper characters reversed by gender. **96m/C; VHS, DVD.** Molly Ringwald; Andrew McCarthy; Jon Cryer; Harry Dean Stanton; James Spader; Annie Potts; Andrew Silverstein; Margaret Colin; Alexa Kenin; Gina Gershon; Dweezil Zappa; Kristy Swanson; *D:* Howard Deutch; *W:* John Hughes; *C:* Tak Fujimoto; *M:* Michael Gore.

Pretty Maids All In a Row 1/2 **1971 (R)** Hudson attempts to go the sex and psycho-killer route with poor results in this sleazy black comedy from director Vadim. When married high school football coach and guidance counselor Tiger McDrew has sex with a cheerleader and she threatens to expose him, he strangles her. Then he keeps going with the rendezvous and the murders if any of the girls seem likely to endanger his marriage or job. **91m/C; DVD.** Rock Hudson; Angie Dickinson; John David Carson; Telly Savalas; Keenan Wynn; Roddy McDowall; James Doohan; Barbara Leigh; *D:* Roger Vadim; *W:* Gene Roddenberry; *C:* Charles Rosher, Jr.; *M:* Lalo Schifrin.

The Pretty One 1/2 **2014 (R)** A modest and somewhat ludicrous comedy that's salvaged by the always-delightful Kazan, this time getting two roles with which her to show her remarkable screen charisma. She plays twins Laurel and Audrey. The pair get into a horrible car accident and Audrey dies. After a mix-up at the hospital, Laurel takes Audrey's identity, and learns something about herself by becoming her sister. It's a dark premise that's still handled in a bizarrely light tone, befitting the charms of its lead. Kazan is great but the script gets clunky and the direction can be leaden. **90m/C; DVD.** Zoe Kazan; Jake Johnson; Ron Livingston; John Carroll Lynch; Frances Shaw; *D:* Jenee LaMarque; *W:* Jenee LaMarque; *C:* Polly Morgan; *M:* Julian Wass.

Pretty Persuasion **2005** Toxic Kimberly (Wood) rules her private high school roost, dragging along airhead best pal Brittany (Harnois) and new student Randa (Schnall) in her wake. The vicious teen targets her English teacher, Mr. Anderson (Livingston), who harbors fantasies about his female students, accusing him of sexual abuse and persuading her friends to back her up. The ensuing scandal and trial are played up by preening tabloid reporter Emily Klein (Krakowski). Woods is around as Kimberly's wealthy, aggressively nasty dad. Smug and offensive. **104m/C; DVD.** Evan Rachel Wood; Ron Livingston; James Woods; Jane Krakowski; Elisabeth Harnois; Selma Blair; Danny Comden; Stark Sands; Michael Hitchcock; Robert Joy; Jaime King; Adi Schnall; Alex Desert; *D:* Marcos Siega; *W:* Skander Halim; *C:* Ramsay Nickell; *M:* Gilad Benamram.

Pretty Poison 1/2 **1968** You won't need an antidote for this one. Original, absorbing screenplay, top-notch acting, and on target direction combine to raise this low-budget, black comedy above the crowd. Perkins at his eerie best as a burned-out arsonist who cooks up a crazy scheme and enlists the aid of a hot-to-trot high schooler, only to discover too late she has some burning desires of her own. Weld is riveting as the turbulent teen. **89m/C; VHS, DVD, Blu-Ray.** Anthony Perkins; Tuesday Weld; Beverly Garland; John Randolph; Dick O'Neill; Joe (Joseph) Bova; Ken Kercheval; *D:* Noel Black; *W:* Lorenzo Semple, Jr.; *C:* David Quaid; *M:* Johnny Mandel. N.Y. Film Critics '68: Screenplay.

Pretty Ugly People **2008 (R)** Perky Lucy (Pyle) uses deception to get her one-time college friends together for a reunion in the Montana wilderness. Morbidly obese back then, Lucy plays the health card but actually wants them to help her celebrate her dramatic weight loss with a four-day wilderness hike. The old friendships were already strained by time and distance and the cracks become craters as everyone unwillingly examines where they now are in their lives. **98m/C; DVD.** Missi Pyle; Melissa McCarthy; Josh Hopkins; Octavia Spencer; Jack Noseworthy; Larry Sullivan; Phill Lewis; Philip Littell; Allison Janney; William Sanderson; *D:* Tate Taylor; *W:* Tate Taylor; *C:* J.P. Lipa; *M:* Lucian Piane. **VIDEO**

Pretty Village, Pretty Flame *Lepa Sela, Lepo Gore* **1996** Powerful story of the Bosnian conflict that is loosely based on a true incident. Story flashes from the days of Yugoslavian unity under Marshal Tito to 1992 when members of a Serbian patrol are trapped (along with an American journalist) by Muslim militiamen in a tunnel connecting Zagreb and Belgrade with no hope for escape. Serbo-Croatian with subtitles. **125m/C; VHS, DVD.** Dragan Bjelogric; Nikola Kojo; Bata Zivojinovic; Dragan Maksimovic; Zoran Cvijanovic; Nikola Pejakovic; Lisa Moncure; *D:* Srdjan Dragojevic; *W:* Nikola Pejakovic; Srdjan Dragojevic; Vanja Bulic; *C:* Dusan Joksimovic; *M:* Lazar Ristovski.

Pretty Woman **1990 (R)** An old story takes a fresh approach as a successful but stuffy business man hires a fun-loving, energetic young hooker to be his companion for a week. The film caused some controversy over its upbeat portrayal of prostitution, but its popularity at the boxoffice catapulted Roberts to stardom. **117m/C; VHS, DVD, Blu-Ray.** Richard Gere; Julia Roberts; Ralph Bellamy; Jason Alexander; Laura San Giacomo; Hector Elizondo; Alex Hyde-White; Elinor Donahue; Larry Miller; Jane Morris; *D:* Garry Marshall; *W:* J.F. Lawton; *C:* Charles Minsky; *M:* James Newton Howard. Golden Globes '91: Actress--Mus./Comedy (Roberts).

Prey *Proie* **2010** Chemist Claire's family owns a massive fertilizer company and her father demands she come and work on a secret project. It may have to do with the fact that the animals on the family's country property have been acting strangely, including a supersized wild boar. Claire's boyfriend Nathan is forced into joining the men on a hunt but soon they're not the ones being stalked. French with subtitles. **79m/C; DVD.** *FR* Gregoire Colin; Berenice Bejo; Isabelle Renauld; Francois Levantal; Fred Ulysse; Joseph Malerba; *D:* Antoine Blossier; *W:* Antoine Blossier; Erich Vogel; *C:* Pierre Aim; *M:* Romaric Laurence.

The Prey 1/2 *La Proie* **2011 (R)** Low-level grifter Franck (Dupontel) is stuck in prison for a bank heist, patiently waiting until he can return to his family and reclaim the loot he'd stashed from the job. After foolishly revealing the whereabouts of the money to his cellmate (Debac), who he later discovers is a child molester and serial killer, he must suddenly escape his brickwall confines in order to beat the killer to the punch and to protect his family. Silly and formulaic, but in a good way. It comes off like the best trashy romance novel of the summer, relying on Dupontel's sheer charisma and ability to hot-foot through oncoming freeway traffic. In French with subtitles. **105m/C; DVD, Blu-Ray.** *FR* Albert Dupontel; Stephane Debac; Alice Taglioni; Sergi Lopez; Natacha Regnier; Caterina Murino; ***D:*** Eric Valette; ***W:*** Laurent Turner; Luc Bossi; ***C:*** Vincent Mathias; ***M:*** Noko.

Prey 1/2 **2019 (PG-13)** After his father is murdered, teen Toby (Miller) becomes disaffected and is sent to an outdoor program for troubled youth. As part of the program, Toby is left alone on a remote jungle island near Malaysia by guide Kay (Lai). Lacking survival skills, he immediately loses his provisions to a monkey but is rescued by the more equipped Madeleine (Froseth). Though Toby learns much from Madeleine, he also must deal with her murderous mother (Anderson) after finding himself stranded. An unbelievable and unoriginal horror thriller , though Froseth's performance is better than the material. **85m/C; DVD.** Logan Miller; Kristine Froseth; Jolene Anderson; Anthony Jensen; Jody Mortara; ***D:*** Franck Khalfoun; ***W:*** Franck Khalfoun; David Coggeshall; ***C:*** Eric Robbins; ***M:*** Richard Breakspear.

Prey for Rock and Roll **2003 (R)** Jacki (Gershon) is a punk rocker who heads the all-girl band Clam Dandy in the L.A. club scene. She's been trying to make it big for the past twenty years, and, fast approaching 40, wonders if it's time to call it quits. While the movie has heart and an authentic rock and roll attitude, it falls on some conventional tactics. That doesn't undermine the raw performance of Gershon, who co-produced the film, and sang her own songs, but it does have a buzz-killing effect on the rest of the proceedings. Adapted from the autobiographical play by Cheri Lovedog. **104m/C; VHS, DVD.** Gina Gershon; Drea De Matteo; Lori Petty; Shelly Cole; Marc Blucas; Ivan Martin; ***D:*** Alex Steyermark; ***W:*** Cheri Lovedog; Robin Whitehouse; ***C:*** Antonio Calvache.

Prey of the Chameleon **1991 (R)** A female serial killer escapes from her asylum, ready to rip more men to shreds. However a tough lady cop has other ideas and goes all out to put an end to the madwoman's doings. Can she stop this fiend before the man she loves becomes the next victim? **91m/C; VHS, DVD.** Daphne Zuniga; James Wilder; Alexandra Paul; Don Harvey; ***D:*** Fleming Fuller.

Prey of the Jaguar 1/2 **1996 (R)** Derek Leigh (Caulfield) is an ex-Special Ops agent who's the target of revenge-minded drug lord Damien Bandera (Goddard). When Bandera slaughters his family, Leigh transforms himself into costumed avenger, the Jaguar (after his son's drawing), and first goes after Bandera's drug network before hunting the man himself. Dopey costume but this vigilante prefers putting people to sleep (via a dart) rather than killing them so there's reduced gore and the violence is more martial-arts than slice-and-dice. **96m/C; VHS, DVD.** Maxwell Caulfield; Trevor Goddard; Linda Blair; Stacy Keach; Paul Regina; ***D:*** David DeCoteau; ***W:*** Rory Johnston; Bud Robertson; Nick Spagnoli; ***C:*** Howard Wexler; ***M:*** Jeff Walton.

A Price Above Rubies 1/2 **1997 (R)** An Orthodox Jewish wife seeks fulfillment outside the lonely and oppressive world in which she lives. Sonia (Zellweger) defies her frigid Hasidic husband Mendel (Fitzgerald) to take a job as a jeweler, then falls in love with a Puerto Rican artist (Payne). Eccleston is Mendel's brother, who has a strange relationship with Sonia, and Margulies is his more traditional wife who tries to help Sonia fit in. Interesting, though characterization beyond film's female lead is scanty, including the one-dimensional males. **117m/C; VHS, DVD.** Renée Zellweger; Christopher Eccleston; Glenn Fitzgerald; Allen Payne; Julianna Margulies; Kim Hunter; John Randolph; Kathleen Chalfant; Edie Falco; Tim Jerome; Phyllis Newman; ***D:*** Boaz Yakin; ***W:*** Boaz Yakin; ***C:*** Adam Holender; ***M:*** Lesley Barber.

The Price of Fear 1/2 **1956** Dog-track owner Dave Barrett (Barker) learns his partner sold out to (and has been bumped off by) the mob and he must go on the lam when they frame him for the murder. He hops into the unattended car of Jessica Warren (Oberon) and lands in even more trouble. A drunken Jessica committed a fatal hit-and-run and now has a patsy in Dave. Oberon's glamorous but she does more posing than acting and Barker is a standard '50s hunk. **79m/B; DVD, Blu-Ray.** Lex Barker; Merle Oberon; Charles Drake; Gia Scala; Warren Stevens; ***D:*** Abner Biberman; ***W:*** Robert Tallman; ***C:*** Irving Glassberg.

Price of Glory **2000 (PG-13)** After seeing hs promising boxing career destroyed by an unscrupulous manager, Arturo Ortega (Smits) tries to live his dreams through his three sons. Sonny (Seda) is the best boxer but can't please his father, Jimmy (Collins) is the rebel, and Johnny (Hernandez) shares his dad's passion and has talent. Complicating matters are a powerful promoter (Perlman) and Arturo's self-destructive tendencies. You've seen this story before, even if the setting is changed to the Southwest, and except for excellent performances by Smits and Seda, there's nothing here to cover for the lack of originality and less-than-stellar execution. **118m/C; VHS, DVD.** Jimmy Smits; Jon Seda; Clifton (Gonzalez) Collins, Jr.; Maria Del Mar; Sal Lopez; Louis Mandylor; Paul Rodriguez; Ron Perlman; Danielle Camastra; Ernesto Hernandez; ***D:*** Carlos Avila; ***W:*** Phil Berger; ***C:*** Affonso Beato; ***M:*** Joseph Julian Gonzalez.

The Price of Milk **2000 (PG-13)** Quirky modern fairy tale has Rob and Lucinda living a happy idyllic life on a New Zealand dairy farm when Lucinda becomes worried that they've become too happy. She decides to test Rob's love, first by jumping into an expensive vat of fresh cow's milk. Rob forgives her, but things are about to get strange. Lucinda accidently runs over a local Maori woman. The woman is unharmed but upset and later has her nephews steal Lucinda's prized patchwork quilt, demanding the entire dairy herd in exchange for its return. Sinclair worked from a 30-page outline instead of a script, and it shows. Robust performances and the beautiful scenery help make up for it, though. **87m/C; VHS, DVD.** *NZ* Danielle Cormack; Karl Urban; Willa O'Neill; Michael Lawrence; Rangi Motu; ***D:*** Harry Sinclair; ***W:*** Harry Sinclair; ***C:*** Leon Narbey.

The Price of the Bride 1/2 **1990** The CIA and MI-6 team up to get information from a KGB defector. Only they start to suspect that the defector is only a decoy for an assassination plot. Based on a Frederick Forsyth story. **98m/C; DVD.** *UK* Mike Farrell; Peter Egan; Diana Quick; Robert Foxworth; Alan Howard; ***D:*** Tom Clegg; ***W:*** Murray Smith; ***C:*** Cristiano Pogany; ***M:*** Paul Chihara. **TV**

Priceless 1/2 *Hors de Prix* **2006 (PG-13)** French fluff. Slinky/sweet gold digger Irene (Tautou) mistakes soulful hotel employee Jean (Elmaleh) for a wealthy mark and they spend a night together before she realizes her mistake. But Jean is smitten and circumstances eventually lead to another meeting in Monte Carlo where a rich widow (Adam) wants to make Jean her boy toy. So Jean asks for gigolo lessons from Irene, who's surprised to find herself miffed that someone else wants him. French with subtitles. **106m/C; DVD, Blu-Ray, On Demand.** *FR* Audrey Tautou; Gad Elmaleh; Vernon Dobtcheff; Annelise Hesme; Marie-Christine Adam; Jacques Spiesser; ***D:*** Pierre Salvadori; ***W:*** Pierre Salvadori; Benoit Graffin; ***C:*** Gilles Henry; ***M:*** Camille Bazbaz.

Priceless **2016 (PG-13)** An underwhelming faith-based thriller about human trafficking, based on true events. After his wife's death, James Stevens (Smallbone) focuses on drinking and fighting to the point that he loses his job and custody of his young daughter. Eager to make money, he takes a job driving a box truck with unknown contents cross country. James eventually learns that his cargo is two Mexican sisters. After delivering the sisters to a seedy motel, James tries to save them with the help of a local named Dale (Koechner). **97m/C; DVD.** Joel Smallbone; Bianca Santos; David Koechner; Jim Parrack; Amber Midthunder; ***D:*** Ben Smallbone; ***W:*** Chris Dowling; Tyler Poelle; ***C:*** Daniel Stilling.

Prick Up Your Ears **1987 (R)** Film biography of popular subversive playwright Joe Orton depicts his rise to fame and his eventual murder at the hands of his homosexual lover in 1967. Acclaimed for its realistic and sometimes humorous portrayal of the relationship between two men in a society that regarded homosexuality as a crime, the film unfortunately pays scant attention to Orton's theatrical success. The occasional sluggishness of the script detracts a bit from the three leads' outstanding performances. **110m/C; VHS, DVD.** *GB* Gary Oldman; Alfred Molina; Vanessa Redgrave; Julie Walters; Lindsay Duncan; Wallace Shawn; James Grant; Frances Barber; Janet Dale; Dave Atkins; ***D:*** Stephen Frears; ***W:*** Alan Bennett; ***C:*** Oliver Stapleton; ***M:*** Stanley Myers. N.Y. Film Critics '87: Support. Actress (Redgrave).

Pride 1/2 **2007 (PG)** Yet another inspirational true sports flick. Jim Ellis (Howard) experiences racism as a black collegiate swimmer in the 1960s and the same problem when he tries to get a job coaching in the early '70s. He finally accepts work at a dismal Philly rec center that does have an unused pool (the kids prefer basketball). Jim decides to pull a team together, instilling discipline and a winning attitude in his kids. It's predictable and is more Hollywood than factual, but you can't fault the performances. **108m/C; DVD.** Terrence Howard; Bernie Mac; Kimberly Elise; Tom Arnold; Alphonso McAuley; Nathaniel Parker; Kevin Phillips; Scott Reeves; Brandon Fobbs; Regine Nehy; Evan Ross; Gary Sturgis; ***D:*** Sunu Gonera; ***W:*** J. Mills Goodloe; Norman Vance, Jr.; Kevin Michael Smith; Michael Gozzard; ***C:*** Matthew F. Leonetti; ***M:*** Aaron Zigman.

Pride **2014 (R)** Based on a true story, director Warchus' dramedy tells the tale of a British miners' strike in 1984 and how it intersected with the fight for gay and lesbian rights in the country. A group of gay activists decided to help raise money for the families of the out-of-work mine workers on strike in opposition to Margaret Thatcher's reign. As a result, the very unique "Lesbians and Gays Support the Miners" campaign was born. The film about this remarkable chapter in UK history is remarkably crowd-pleasing, and even moving. And the heartstring-tugging, albeit intentional, works. **120m/C; DVD, Blu-Ray.** *UK* Dominic West; Bill Nighy; Paddy Considine; Imelda Staunton; George MacKay; Ben Schnetzer; Lisa Palfrey; Andrew Scott; Joseph Gilgun; Faye Marsay; ***D:*** Matthew Warchus; ***W:*** Stephen Beresford; ***C:*** Tat Radcliffe; ***M:*** Christopher Nightingale.

Pride and Extreme Prejudice **1990** West German agent Bruno Morenz is also working for Sam McCready at MI-6. Sam needs Bruno to get into East Germany and meet a Soviet military attache selling secrets. Sam doesn't know Bruno is in the midst of a breakdown after murdering his cheating girlfriend and her lover. The situation gets even more complicated and Sam decides to go to Bruno's aid. Based on a Frederick Forsyth story. **98m/C; DVD.** *UK* Brian Dennehy; Alan Howard; Malcolm Storry; Simon Cadell; Lisa Eichhorn; Michael J. Shannon; ***D:*** Ian Sharp; ***W:*** Murray Smith; ***C:*** Cristiano Pogany; ***M:*** Paul Chihara. **TV**

Pride and Glory **2008 (R)** Ray Tierney (Norton) is from an Irish-American family of NYC cops. Reluctantly, the detective is assigned to a task force investigating a drug bust gone awry that cost the lives of four cops, which also involves his bad-guy brother-in-law Jimmy (Farrell). Lots of drinking and swearing ensues amid the angst and double-crossing that threatens both family ties and the Thin Blue Line. Norton's talent is wasted in this paint-by-numbers rehash, but his presence makes the pic watchable. **129m/C; Blu-Ray.** John Ortiz; Edward Norton; Colin Farrell; Jon Voight; Noah Emmerich; Jennifer Ehle; Shea Whigham; Frank Grillo; Lake Bell; Rick Gonzalez; Wayne Duvall; Carmen Ejogo; ***D:*** Gavin O'Connor; ***W:*** Gavin O'Connor; Joe Carnahan; ***C:*** Declan Quinn; ***M:*** Mark Isham.

Pride and Prejudice 1/2 **1940** Classic adaptation of Austen's classic novel of manners as a young marriageable woman spurns the suitor her parents choose for her. Excellent cast vividly re-creates 19th-century England, aided by the inspired set design that won the film an Oscar. **114m/B; VHS, DVD.** Greer Garson; Laurence Olivier; Edmund Gwenn; Edna May Oliver; Mary Boland; Maureen O'Sullivan; Ann Rutherford; Frieda Inescort; Marsha Hunt; ***D:*** Robert Z. Leonard; ***C:*** Karl Freund.

Pride and Prejudice 1/2 **1985** BBC miniseries adaptation of Jane Austen's novel about 19th-century British mores and the attempts of five sisters to get married. **226m/C; VHS, DVD.** *GB* Elizabeth Garvie; David Rintoul; ***D:*** Cyril Coke. **TV**

Pride and Prejudice **1995** Lavish TV adaptation of the Jane Austen novel finds bright Elizabeth Bennet (Ehle) unwillingly smitten by the wealthy, mysterious, and arrogant Mr. Darcy (Firth). Her family, filled with unmarried daughters, is rather silly and, of course, Elizabeth should be looking to get married (or at least not hinder her sisters' chances). Filmed on location in Derbyshire. On six cassettes. **300m/C; VHS, DVD, Blu-Ray.** *GB* Jennifer Ehle; Colin Firth; Susannah Harker; Alison Steadman; Julia Sawalha; Benjamin Whitrow; Crispin Bonham Carter; Anna Chancellor; David Bamber; David Bark-Jones; Polly Maberly; Lucy Briers; Barbara Leigh-Hunt; Adrian Lukis; ***D:*** Simon Langton; ***W:*** Andrew Davies; ***C:*** John Kenway; ***M:*** Carl Davis.

Pride and Prejudice **2005 (PG)** In 19th century England, Mrs. Bennet (Blethyn) must marry her daughters off to the right men, but headstrong daughter Elizabeth (Knightley) proves difficult. More manageable in scope than the BBC miniseries, this version is gorgeous and classic nonetheless, losing none of the essence of the story. Knightley brings a welcomed force and passion to her portrayal of Lizzie that, for some reason, brought mixed reviews. Sutherland is excellent as the brood's bemused patriarch. **127m/C; DVD, Blu-Ray, HD-DVD.** Keira Knightley; Matthew Macfadyen; Brenda Blethyn; Donald Sutherland; Tom Hollander; Dame Judi Dench; Rosamund Pike; Jena Malone; Kelly Reilly; Claudie Blakley; Peter Wight; Penelope Wilton; Simon Woods; Rupert Friend; Carey Mulligan; Talulah Riley; Tamzin Merchant; ***D:*** Joe Wright; ***W:*** Deborah Moggach; ***C:*** Roman Osin; ***M:*** Dario Marianelli.

Pride and Prejudice and Zombies **2016 (PG-13)** Didn't we learn anything from "Abraham Lincoln: Vampire Hunter"? The kind of parody that works on the page doesn't always work on the screen, and again a hit novel (this one by Grahame-Smith) comes to the movies completely flat. Burr Steers' film is surprisingly loyal to the Jane Austen source material on to which the undead have been grafted, but that's part of the problem. Imagine watching one of the many adaptations of "Pride and Prejudice" and flipping to a George Romero movie every fifteen minutes for an action scene. The effect would be jarring. Now you have an idea what this movie is like. **107m/C; DVD, Blu-Ray.** Lily James; Sam Riley; Bella Heathcote; Ellie Bamber; Millie Brady; ***D:*** Burr Steers; ***W:*** Burr Steers; ***C:*** Remi Adefarasin; ***M:*** Fernando Velazquez.

The Pride and the Passion **1957** A small group of resistance fighters battling for Spanish independence in 1810 must smuggle a 6-ton cannon across the rugged terrain of Spain. Miscasting, especially of Sinatra as a Spanish peasant, hurts this film. **132m/C; VHS, DVD, Blu-Ray.** Cary Grant; Frank Sinatra; Sophia Loren; Theodore Bikel; John Wengraf; Jay Novello; Philip Van Zandt; ***D:*** Stanley Kramer; ***W:*** Edward Anhalt; ***C:*** Franz Planer; ***M:*** George Antheil.

Pride of Africa **1997** When the luxury train, Pride of Africa, is targeted by a thief who steals passengers' valuables, the owner is afraid its reputation will be ruined. Local tour guide David Webb is hired to quietly catch the criminal but with shady travelers, a kidnapping, and possibly a murder, David's job gets very dangerous indeed. Set in the 1930s; made for British TV. **103m/C; DVD.** *GB* Robert Powell; Ashley Hayden; Jeremy Crutchley; Clive Scott; Nthati Moshesh; Anthony Fridjhon; ***D:*** Herman Binge; ***W:*** Paul Wheler; ***C:*** Andrzej Slazak; ***M:*** Pip Burley. **TV**

Pride of Jesse Hallum 1/2 **1981** An illiterate man (played by country singer Cash) learns, after much trial and tribulation, to read. **105m/C; VHS, DVD.** Johnny Cash; Brenda Vaccaro; Eli Wallach; ***D:*** Gary Nelson. **TV**

Pride of St. Louis ☙☙ **1952** A romanticized and humorous portrait of famed baseball player-turned-commentator Dizzy Dean. **93m/B; VHS, Streaming.** Dan Dailey; Joanne Dru; Richard Crenna; Richard Haydn; Hugh Sanders; ***D:*** Harmon Jones; ***W:*** Herman J. Mankiewicz; ***C:*** Leo Tover; ***M:*** Arthur Lange.

Pride of the Clan ☙☙ ½ **1918** Silent drama with Pickford and Moore as Scottish sweethearts battling a bit of adversity. When Pickford's father is lost at sea, she moves onto his fishing boat. She meets Moore, a fishing boy, and falls in love. But, he inherits a fortune and his parents forbid him to see Pickford. He goes off to live the good life but comes back to dramatically rescue Pickford. **80m/B; Silent; VHS, DVD.** Mary Pickford; Matt Moore; ***D:*** Maurice Tourneur.

Pride of the Legion ☙ ½ **1932** Rin Tin Tin shows why dogs are man's best friend when he aids troubled cop Jerry (Jory) who's suffering from job-related trauma. **70m/B; DVD.** Victor Jory; Barbara Kent; Lucien Littlefield; J. Farrell MacDonald; Sally Blane; ***D:*** Ford Beebe; ***W:*** Ford Beebe; ***C:*** Ernest Miller.

Pride of the Marines ☙☙☙ **1945** True story notable for its war scenes and its depiction of returning wounded vets (as well as Garfield's outstanding performance). Al Schmid meets Ruth (Parker) on a blind date and becomes engaged to her just before enlisting in the Marines and getting shipped off to Guadalcanal. His machine gun crew defeats a Japanese assault but Al is blinded by a grenade. Hospitalized, depressed, and bitter, Al tells Ruth the engagement is off and can't be persuaded to try rehab until he gets told some hard truths by buddy Lee (Clark) and Ruth reassures him of her love. Director Daves uses a number of visual techniques to showcase Al's blindness and recovery. **119m/B; DVD.** John Garfield; Eleanor Parker; Dane Clark; John Ridgely; Ann Doran; Anthony Caruso; Rosemary DeCamp; Ann E. Todd; ***D:*** Delmer Daves; ***W:*** Albert (John B. Sherry) Maltz; ***C:*** J. Peverell Marley; ***M:*** Franz Waxman.

The Pride of the Yankees ☙☙☙ ½ **1942** Excellent portrait of baseball great Lou Gehrig. Beginning as he joined the Yankees in 1923, the film follows this great American through to his moving farewell speech as his career was tragically cut short by the disease that bears his name. Cooper is inspiring in the title role. **128m/B; VHS, DVD.** Gary Cooper; Teresa Wright; Babe Ruth; Walter Brennan; Dan Duryea; Vinton (Hayworth) Haworth; ***D:*** Sam Wood; ***W:*** Herman J. Mankiewicz; Jo Swerling; ***C:*** Rudolph Mate; ***M:*** Leigh Harline. Oscars '42: Film Editing.

Priest ☙☙ **1994 (R)** Brit TV movie. Father Greg (an intense performance by Roache) is a young, idealistic priest who gets a rude awakening when he's assigned to a tough inner-city Liverpool parish. His superior, Father Matthew (Wilkinson), is a middle-aged rabble rouser who's openly having an affair with their black housekeeper Maria (Tyson). But Father Greg has a secret of his own—despite struggles with his sexuality, he gets involved with Graham (Carlyle), a man he meets in the local gay bar. Director Bird walks a fine line between criticism and condemnation of Catholic doctrine. **98m/C; VHS, DVD.** *UK* Linus Roache; Tom Wilkinson; Cathy Tyson; Robert Carlyle; James Ellis; John Bennett; Rio Fanning; Jimmy Coleman; Lesley Sharp; Robert Pugh; Christine Tremarco; ***D:*** Antonia Bird; ***W:*** Jimmy McGovern; ***C:*** Fred Tammes; ***M:*** Andy Roberts.

Priest ☙ **2011 (PG-13)** A group of priests imprisoned the vampires who threatened human existence years before but an uprising is on the horizon. Enter legendary warrior Priest (Bettany) who must save his niece from becoming a bloodsucker after the ghouls kidnap her. Director Stewart's adaptation of the graphic novels by Min-Woo Hyung is good to look at, but the story itself is messy, inconsistent, and unoriginal—definitely disappointing for an intriguing concept. An unfortunate mishmash of western, sci-fi, horror, action, and thriller that, at only 87 minutes, seems to give up on itself. **87m/C; DVD, Blu-Ray, On Demand.** Paul Bettany; Maggie Q; Cam Gigandet; Lily Collins; Karl Urban; Stephen Moyer; Brad Dourif; Christopher Plummer; Madchen Amick; ***D:*** Scott Stewart; ***W:*** Scott Stewart; Cory Goodman; ***C:*** Don Burgess; ***M:*** Christopher Young.

Priest of Love ☙☙ ½ **1981 (R)** Arty account of the final years of the life of then-controversial author D.H. Lawrence, during which time he published "Lady Chatterly's Lover." A slow-moving but interesting portrayal of this complex man and his wife as they grapple with his imminent death from tuberculosis. **125m/C; VHS, DVD, Blu-Ray, Streaming.** *GB* Ian McKellen; Janet Suzman; John Gielgud; Dame Helen Mirren; Jorge (George) Rivero; ***D:*** Christopher Miles; ***W:*** Alan Plater; ***C:*** Ted Moore.

The Priest's Wife ☙☙ *La Moglie del Prete* **1971** Moderately amusing comic collaboration between Loren and Mastroianni. Don Mario finds his priestly vows sorely tested when pulchritudinous singer Valeria gets romantic designs on him after he rescues her from a suicide attempt. Marco succumbs, has doubts, asks for advice, and is finally summoned to the Vatican. So will the beauty or God win out? Italian with subtitles. **106m/C; DVD.** *IT FR* Marcello Mastroianni; Sophia Loren; Gianni Cavalieri; Giuseppe Maffioli; Venantino Venantini; Augusto Mastrantoni; Jacques Stany; ***D:*** Dino Risi; ***W:*** Ruggero Maccari; Bernardino Zapponi; ***C:*** Alfio Contini; ***M:*** Armando Trovajoli.

Primal ☙☙ **2019 (R)** Frank Walsh (Cage) is a former zookeeper who has turned to animal smuggling after falling on hard times. After he captures a ghost jaguar and other animals in South America, he transports them to the United States via freighter. Also aboard is a psychopathic escaped prisoner, Richard Loffler (Durrand), who is accompanied by a team that includes U.S. Marshals, an attorney, and a neurologist. At sea, Richard acts out, terrorizing the animals and humans on the ship, compelling Frank to take action. Harmless-yet-silly action-thriller with somewhat interesting characters. **97m/C; DVD, Blu-Ray.** Nicolas Cage; Famke Janssen; Kevin Durand; Michael Imperioli; LaMonica Garrett; ***D:*** Nick Powell; ***W:*** Richard Leder; ***C:*** Vern Nobles; ***M:*** Guillaume Roussel.

Primal Fear ☙☙ **1996 (R)** Chicago defense attorney Martin Vail (Gere) is torn between justice and fame. He finds the spotlight when a gentle altar boy (newcomer Norton is a standout) is accused of savagely murdering an archbishop. This leads to some courtroom fireworks due, in part, to the fact that the prosecutor (Linney) is Vail's former lover. Gere turns in a satisfying performance but can't keep the script afloat. Lame plot revelations and an obvious "shocker" ending don't help matters. Feature film debut of TV director Hoblit. Adapted from the book by William Diehl. **130m/C; VHS, DVD, Blu-Ray.** Richard Gere; Laura Linney; Edward Norton; John Mahoney; Alfre Woodard; Frances McDormand; Terry O'Quinn; Andre Braugher; Steven Bauer; Joe Spano; Tony Plana; Stanley Anderson; Maura Tierney; Jon Seda; ***D:*** Gregory Hoblit; ***W:*** Steve Shagan; Ann Biderman; ***C:*** Michael Chapman; ***M:*** James Newton Howard. Golden Globes '97: Support. Actor (Norton); L.A. Film Critics '96: Support. Actor (Norton); Natl. Bd. of Review '96: Support. Actor (Norton).

Primal Impulse ☙ ½ *Footprints* **1974** An astronaut, stranded on the moon because of a sinister experimental double-cross, unleashes a mental scream which possesses a young woman's mind back on earth. **90m/C; VHS, DVD.** *IT* Klaus Kinski; Florinda Bolkan; Peter McEnery; Lila Kedrova; Nicoletta Elmi; ***D:*** Luigi Bazzoni; ***W:*** Mario Fanelli; ***C:*** Vittorio Storaro; ***M:*** Nicola Piovani.

Primal Scream ☙ ½ *Hellfire* **1987 (R)** The Year is 1993. Earth's fuel sources are rapidly decaying and the top secret project to mine a revolutionary new energy source is underway—independently managed by a corrupt corporation. **95m/C; VHS, DVD, Blu-Ray.** Kenneth John McGregor; Sharon Mason; Julie Miller; Jon Maurice; Mickey Shaughnessy; ***D:*** William Murray.

Primal Secrets ☙☙ ½ *Trick of the Eye* **1994** Artist Tilly, who specializes in illusionary trompe l'oeil paintings, is commissioned to paint a mural for reclusive socialite/widow Burstyn but there's a lot of mystery surrounding the job, especially when Burstyn begins to take an overly avid interest in Tilly's life. Based on the novel by Jane Stanton Hitchcock. Made for TV. **93m/C; VHS, DVD.** Meg Tilly; Ellen Burstyn; Barnard Hughes; ***D:*** Ed Kaplan. **TV**

Primary Colors ☙☙ ½ **1998 (R)** Adaptation of Joe Klein's anonymously published political satire that starts off humorously and shifts into somber. Southern good ole boy, Gov. Jack Stanton (Travolta), and his savvy wife (Thompson) are after the presidential nomination and surrounded by crazy associates, including skeptical first-time campaign manager Henry Burton (Lester). More about Henry's political baptism by fire than anything else, as he tries to accommodate his conscience to the continuous scandals and double-dealing. The change in tone is jarring, characters and situations disappear without warning. Still the goings-on will hold your attention until they're over—and you realize it's all smoke-and-mirrors. **138m/C; VHS, DVD, Blu-Ray.** John Travolta; Emma Thompson; Adrian Lester; Kathy Bates; Billy Bob Thornton; Larry Hagman; Maura Tierney; Stacy Edwards; Diane Ladd; Gia Carides; Paul Guilfoyle; Tommy Hollis; Robert Klein; J.C. Quinn; Rob Reiner; Caroline Aaron; Allison Janney; Mykelti Williamson; Tony Shalhoub; John Vargas; Ben Jones; Bonnie Bartlett; ***D:*** Mike Nichols; ***W:*** Elaine May; ***C:*** Michael Ballhaus; ***M:*** Ry Cooder. British Acad. '98: Adapt. Screenplay; Screen Actors Guild '98: Support. Actress (Bates); Broadcast Film Critics '98: Support. Actress (Bates).

Prime ☙☙ ½ **2005 (PG-13)** Streep plays Lisa, an interfering Jewish mama, fretting over her handsome 23-year-old son, David (Greenberg). Lisa's a shrink; one of her needier patients is newly divorced Rafi (Thurman) who's beautiful but insecure. Rafi is happy but fretful over a new romance with a much-younger guy, who, of course, turns out to be Lisa's son David. Lisa is the first to realize this and suffers agonies of embarrassment as Rafi enthusiastically describes her rejuvenated sex life. Lots more embarrassment is to come for all concerned. Harmless comedic fluff. **105m/C; DVD.** Meryl Streep; Uma Thurman; Bryan Greenberg; Jon Abrahams; Zak Orth; Annie Parisse; ***D:*** Ben Younger; ***W:*** Ben Younger; ***C:*** William Rexer; ***M:*** Ryan Shore.

Prime Cut ☙☙ ½ **1972 (R)** Veritable orgy of drug trafficking, prostitution, extortion, loan sharking, fisticuffs and gangsters getting ground into mincemeat. Sleazy but well-made crime melodrama has its followers, but is best known as Spacek's film debut. **86m/C; VHS, DVD, Blu-Ray.** Lee Marvin; Gene Hackman; Sissy Spacek; Angel Tompkins; Gregory Walcott; ***D:*** Michael Ritchie; ***W:*** Robert Dillon; ***M:*** Lalo Schifrin.

Prime Evil ☙☙ **1988 (R)** A brave and determined nun infiltrates a sect of devil worshipping monks in an attempt to end their demonic sacrifices. The question is, will this sister slide beneath Satan's cleaver? **87m/C; VHS, DVD, Blu-Ray.** William Beckwith; Christine Moore; ***D:*** Roberta Findlay.

The Prime Gig ☙☙ **2000** Wise (Vaughn) works a telephone scam for a rundown company manafed by Mick (Tobolowsky) that soon goes under. He's then recruited by Caitlin (Ormond) for a telemarketing scheme involving selling stocks in a gold mine for guru Kelly Grant (Harris), whose previous schemes cost him jail time. Wise is a success but despite the money (and the girl) you know there's trouble ahead. Predictable plot with Harris giving the strong performance. **96m/C; VHS, DVD.** Vince Vaughn; Julia Ormond; Ed Harris; Rory Cochrane; Wallace Shawn; George Wendt; Stephen Tobolowsky; ***D:*** Gregory Mosher; ***W:*** William Wheeler; ***C:*** John A. Alonzo; ***M:*** David Robbins.

The Prime of Miss Jean Brodie ☙☙☙ **1969 (PG)** Oscar-winning performance by Smith as a forward-thinking teacher in an Edinburgh girls' school in 1932. She captivates her impressionable young students with her fascist ideals and free-thinking attitudes in this adaptation of the play taken from Muriel Spark's novel. **116m/C; VHS, DVD, Blu-Ray.** *GB* Maggie Smith; Pamela Franklin; Robert Stephens; Celia Johnson; Gordon Jackson; Jane Carr; ***D:*** Ronald Neame; ***W:*** Jay Presson Allen; ***C:*** Ted Moore; ***M:*** Rod McKuen. Oscars '69: Actress (Smith); British Acad. '69: Actress (Smith), Support. Actress (Johnson); Golden Globes '70: Song ("Jean"); Natl. Bd. of Review '69: Support. Actress (Franklin).

The Prime of Miss Jean Brodie ☙☙ **1978** Cheap-looking miniseries for Scottish TV, adapted from the Muriel Sparks novel, benefits from McEwan's performance. Imperious, eccentric Jean Brodie teaches at the Marcia Blaine School for Girls in Edinburgh in the 1930s. She seeks to inspire her students although her defense of fascism and her outsized personality ruffle more than a few. **366m/C; DVD.** *UK* Geraldine McEwan; John Castle; Lynsey Baxter; ***D:*** Christopher Hodson; ***M:*** Marvin Hamlisch. **TV**

Prime of Your Life ☙ ½ **2010** Low-budget indie, with a fairly unlikeable female lead, that doesn't quite go down the usual romantic path. Jobless slacker Sandy uses her looks—and sponging off her older sister—to get by. She meets charming con man Keith at a funeral and decides to get into the grifter game when Keith offers her a job. **92m/C; DVD.** Ryan Donowho; Brett Rice; Nicole Abisinio; Georgia Chris; Jennifer Rapp; Melinda Lee; ***D:*** Kelly L. King; ***W:*** Brandon Cotter; ***C:*** Curtis Graham; ***M:*** Eric Baines. **VIDEO**

Prime Suspect ☙☙ **1982** An honest citizen becomes the prime suspect after the coverage of a murder by an over-ambitious television reporter. **100m/C; VHS, DVD.** Mike Farrell; Teri Garr; Veronica Cartwright; Lane Smith; Barry Corbin; James Sloyan; Charles Aidman; ***D:*** Noel Black; ***C:*** Reynaldo Villalobos; ***M:*** Charles Gross. **TV**

Prime Suspect ☙☙ **1988** A young man escapes from a mental institution to clear his name after being wrongfully accused of murdering his girlfriend. **89m/C; VHS, DVD.** Susan Strasberg; Frank Stallone; Billy Drago; Doug McClure; ***D:*** Mark Rutland.

Prime Suspect ☙☙☙ **1992** Mirren stars as Detective Chief Inspector Jane Tennison in this British TV police procedural. When a male inspector dies of a heart attack while investigating a rape-murder, Tennison, the only women of senior police status, wants the case. But she runs into multiple obstructions, not the least being the smug male police system. Then the case really takes a turn when it appears Tennison is searching for a serial killer. But Jane is no quitter and she has both the brains and the guts to back up her orders. Adapted from the book by Lynda La Plante, who also wrote the teleplay. A number of other TV seasons followed. **240m/C; VHS, DVD.** *GB* Dame Helen Mirren; Tom Bell; Zoe Wanamaker; John Bowe; Tom Wilkinson; Ralph Fiennes; ***D:*** Christopher Menaul; ***W:*** Lynda La Plante. **TV**

Prime Target ☙☙ **1991 (R)** Small-town cop John Bloodstone (Heavener) is recruited by the FBI to transfer a mafia boss (Curtis) from a safehouse to the courthouse. He has to keep the former mobster alive long enough to testify against the "family." Their cross-country adventure is heightened by a murderous confrontation with evil forces that want them both dead. **87m/C; VHS, DVD, Streaming.** David Heavener; Tony Curtis; Isaac Hayes; Jenilee Harrison; Robert Reed; Andrew (Andy) Robinson; Don Stroud; ***D:*** David Heavener; ***W:*** David Heavener; ***M:*** Chris Boardman.

The Prime Time **WOOF!** **1960** Horrid film about a teen girl who leaves home and gets involved with a teen gang and a slimy detective. She's also kidnapped by a weird beatnik artist who forces her to pose nude. Black's film debut. Also known as "Hellkitten." **76m/B; VHS, DVD.** JoAnn LeCompte; Frank Roche; James Brooks; Ray Gronwold; Maria Pavelle; Robert Major; Karen Black; ***D:*** Herschell Gordon Lewis.

Prime Time ☙ ½ *American Raspberry* **1977 (R)** Forgotten satirical comedy about what would happen if the censors took a day off from American TV. **73m/C; VHS, DVD.** Warren Oates; David Spielberg; Robert Ridgely; Joanna Cassidy; Harry Shearer; Harris Yulin; Dick O'Neill; George Furth; Stephen Furst; Larry Gelman; Fred (John F.) Dryer; ***D:*** Bradley R. Swirnoff; ***W:*** Steve Feinberg; Bradley R. Swirnoff; ***C:*** Matthew F. Leonetti; ***M:*** Ken Lauber.

Prime Time Murder ☙ ½ **1992 (R)** Freelance TV journalist hooks up with eccentric ex-cop to trail a psycho stalking street people. **95m/C; VHS, DVD.** Tim Thomerson; Sally Kirkland; Anthony Finetti; Laura Reed; ***D:*** Gary Skeen Hall.

Primer ☙☙☙ ½ **2004 (PG-13)** Writer/director Carruth's debut film is a thinking-man's time travel movie, beautifully shot for an absurdly low $7,500. The plot revolves around two engineers, Aaron (Carruth) and Abe (Sullivan), who accidentally construct a box that allows them to move backwards through time. Carruth piles on the technical jargon, which will either hopelessly confuse viewers or make them love the director for respecting their intelligence. At its core, Carruth's film is a meditation on trust, obsession, power, and the chaos surrounding innovation, combined with a nonlinear storyline that should inspire repeated viewings. **80m/C; DVD.** Shane Carruth; David Sullivan; Casey Gooden; Anand Upadhyaya; Carrie Crawford; Samantha Thomson; Brandon Blagg; ***D:*** Shane Carruth; ***W:*** Shane Carruth; ***C:*** Shane Carruth; Anand Upadhyaya.

Primeval ½ **2007 (R)** What a croc—literally. Weird fact-based combo of horror and politics set in pre-2005, war-torn Burundi. Cynical reporter Tim (Purcell) is pressured into a tabloid story—capture a 25-foot croc, nicknamed Gustave, that has been eating the locals for years. The area is also the province of a vicious warlord who has nicknamed himself after the beastie. Brooding guide Jacob (Prochnow) takes Tim and his crew to the croc's favorite dining spot, but things don't go as planned. Neither as campy nor as gruesome as most of its ilk. **94m/C; DVD, Blu-Ray.** Dominic Purcell; Orlando Jones; Brooke Langton; Jurgen Prochnow; Gideon Emery; Dumisani Mbebe; Gabriel Malema; ***D:*** Michael Katleman; ***W:*** John Brancato; Michael Ferris; ***C:*** Edward Pei; ***M:*** John (Gianni) Frizzell.

The Primitive Lover **1922** Early silent comedy finds romantic Phyllis Tomley (Talmadge) thinking her husband Hector (Ford) is just too dull to live with anymore. She wants a divorce so she can marry author Donald Wales (Harlan), whom she thinks is the perfect adventurous hero. Hector decides to prove her wrong. **70m/B; Silent; DVD.** Constance Talmadge; Kenneth Harlan; Harrison Ford; Joe Roberts; Chief John Big Tree; ***D:*** Sidney Franklin; ***W:*** Frances Marion; ***C:*** David Abel.

Primrose Path ½ **1940** Melodramatic soaper with comedic touches about a wrong-side-of-the-tracks girl falling for and then losing an ambitious young go-getter running a hamburger stand. **93m/B; VHS, DVD.** Ginger Rogers; Joel McCrea; Marjorie Rambeau; Henry Travers; Miles Mander; Queenie Vasser; Joan Carroll; Vivienne Osborne; ***D:*** Gregory La Cava.

The Prince **2014 (R)** Willis and Cusask continue to prove that they'll do literally anything for a paycheck with another straight-to-DVD action dud. Stop me if you heard this before! A retired assassin is forced back into action when his daughter is kidnapped by a former rival. And the lackluster filmmaking and half-asleep performances do nothing beyond that cookie-cutter plot description. You can practically see the actors signing their paychecks and calling it a day. **93m/C; DVD, Blu-Ray.** Jason Patric; Bruce Willis; John Cusack; Gia Mantegna; Jessica Lowndes; ***D:*** Brian A. Miller; ***W:*** Andre Fabrizio; Jeremy Passmore; ***C:*** Yaron Levy; ***M:*** The Newton Brothers.

The Prince & Me ½ **2004 (PG)** Dairy farmer's daughter Paige (Stiles) is a driven pre-med student who dreams of a future with Doctors Without Borders until Prince Charming shows up disguised as an average Joe. In this case his name is Eddie—actually Prince Edvard of Denmark (Mably)--and they fall in love, but as these young romance stories go the truth inevitably surfaces and the conflicts begin. Should she give up on her life's passion? Or live the supposed fairy tale life of a princess? Of does she really have to choose? Only Stiles' engaging performance makes this sweet-yet-typical story at all worth watching. **110m/C; VHS, DVD.** Julia Stiles; Luke Mably; Ben Miller; James Fox; Miranda Richardson; Eliza Bennett; Alberta Watson; John Bourgeois; Joanne Baron; ***D:*** Martha Coolidge; ***W:*** Mark Amin; Jack Amiel; Katherine Fugate; Michael Begler; ***C:*** Alex Nepomniaschy; ***M:*** Jennie Muskett.

The Prince & Me 2: Royal Wedding **2006 (PG)** In this dull fluff sequel, Danish Prince Edvard (Mably) runs into a problem with his wedding plans to American commoner Paige (Heskin). Conniving cousin Albert (Holt) uses an ancient obscure law to proclaim that Edvard must marry someone of royal blood or he can't become king—and Albert offers his daughter, the equally sly Princess Kirsten (Burton-Hill), as a substitute. Apparently, Edvard is just too stupid to ask the Danish parliament to change the law, so Paige must find a loophole. **97m/C; DVD, Blu-Ray.** Luke Mably; Kam Heskin; Jim Holt; Maryam D'Abo; Clemency Burton-Hill; Jonathan Firth; ***D:*** Catherine Cyran; ***W:*** Allison Robinson; ***C:*** Blake T. Evans; ***M:*** Andrew Gross. **VIDEO**

The Prince & Me 3: A Royal Honeymoon ½ **2008 (PG)** They met, they married, and finally newly crowned Danish king Edvard (Geere) and his American bride Paige (Heskin) can take their honeymoon. To avoid the paparazzi, Edvard takes them to a resort at Belaria, a remote Danish protectorate. Too bad that evil Prime Minister Polonius' (Jensen) flunky Oliver (Rubin) is already there and they suspiciously run into Paige's ex-fiance Scott (Croasdell). Edvard learns that Polonius is planning to bulldoze the local forest to drill for oil and he and Paige intend to stop the nefarious plot. **92m/C; DVD, Blu-Ray.** Kam Heskin; Todd Jensen; Jonathan Firth; Chris Geere; Joshua Rubin; Adam Croasdell; ***D:*** Catherine Cyran; ***W:*** Blayne Weaver; ***C:*** Emil Topuzov; ***M:*** Andrew Gross. **VIDEO**

The Prince & Me 4: The Elephant Adventure **2010 (PG)** About to celebrate their first wedding anniversary, King Edward and Queen Paige of Denmark receive an invitation to attend the royal wedding of Princess Myra of Sangyoon. Except Myra isn't happy about the arranged marriage since she's in love with elephant handler Alu. Then the sacred wedding elephant goes missing and Paige and Edward must find the pachyderm and show that true love matters. **92m/C; DVD.** Kam Heskin; Chris Geere; Jonathan Firth; Ase Wang; Amarin Cholvibul; Vithaya Pansringarm; Prinya Intachai; Selina Lo; ***D:*** Catherine Cyran; ***W:*** Blayne Weaver; ***C:*** Picha Srisansanee; ***M:*** Andrew Gross. **VIDEO**

The Prince and the Pauper **1937** Satisfying adaptation of the classic Mark Twain story of a young street urchin who trades places with the young king of England. Wonderful musical score by noted composer Korngold who provided the music for many of Flynn's adventure films. Also available in a computer-colorized version. **118m/B; VHS, DVD.** Errol Flynn; Claude Rains; Alan Hale; Billy Mauch; Montagu Love; Henry Stephenson; Barton MacLane; Anne Howard; ***D:*** William Keighley; ***M:*** Erich Wolfgang Korngold.

The Prince and the Pauper **1962** A prince and a poor young boy swap their clothes and identities, thus causing a lot of confusion for their families. Based on the story by Mark Twain. **93m/C; VHS, Streaming.** Guy Williams; Laurence Naismith; Donald Houston; Jane Asher; Sean Scully; ***D:*** Don Chaffey; ***W:*** Jack Whittingham; ***C:*** Paul Beeson; ***M:*** Tristram Cary. **TV**

The Prince and the Pauper ½ *Crossed Swords* **1978 (PG)** Remake of the 1937 Errol Flynn film employing lavish sets and a tongue-in-cheek attitude among the all-star cast, who occasionally wander adrift when the director stops for tea. When an English prince and a pauper discover that they have identical appearances, they decide to trade places with each other. From Mark Twain's classic. **113m/C; VHS, DVD.** *GB* Oliver Reed; Raquel Welch; Mark Lester; Ernest Borgnine; George C. Scott; Rex Harrison; Charlton Heston; Sybil Danning; ***D:*** Richard Fleischer; ***W:*** Berta Dominguez; George MacDonald Fraser; Pierre Spengler; ***C:*** Jack Cardiff; ***M:*** Maurice Jarre.

The Prince and the Pauper ½ **2001** Yet another version of the Mark Twain classic covers all the familiar bases but is briskly paced and has a good cast. Prince Edward (Jonathan Timmins) exchanges identities with peasant Tom Canty (Robert Timmins) and both learn that whether you're rich or poor life will always be a challenge. **90m/C; VHS, DVD.** Jonathan Timmins; Robert Timmins; Aidan Quinn; Alan Bates; Jonathan Hyde; ***D:*** Giles Foster; ***W:*** Duke Fenady; Dominic Minghella. **CABLE**

The Prince and the Pauper ½ **2007 (PG)** A modern-day retelling of the Mark Twain classic, starring the Sprouse twins. Tom Canty wants to be an actor so he sneaks onto the set of his favorite show to meet its lead, Eddie Tutor. A spoiled child star, Eddie is about to get fired for his antics until the look-alikes decide to trade places and see how the other half lives. But neither of the boys expects the TV production to suddenly go on location to Miami, leaving the duo in their assumed identities. **92m/C; DVD.** Dylan Sprouse; Cole Sprouse; Vincent Spano; Kay Panabaker; Dedee Pfeiffer; Ed Lauter; Sally Kellerman; Nick Vallelonga; ***D:*** James Quattrochi; ***W:*** Amanda Moresco; ***C:*** Jeff Baustert; ***M:*** Dennis McCarthy. **VIDEO**

The Prince and the Showgirl ½ **1957** An American showgirl in 1910 London is wooed by the Prince of Carpathia. Part of the "A Night at the Movies" series, this tape simulates a 1957 movie evening, with a Sylvester the Cat cartoon, "Greedy for Tweety," a newsreel and coming attractions for "Spirit of St. Louis." **127m/C; VHS, DVD.** Laurence Olivier; Marilyn Monroe; Sybil Thorndike; Jeremy Spenser; Richard Wattis; ***D:*** Laurence Olivier; ***W:*** Terence Rattigan; ***C:*** Jack Cardiff.

The Prince and the Surfer ½ **1999 (PG)** A modern young prince, Edward, wants a chance to be a regular guy and changes places with his surfer teen double, Cash. Updated version of the Mark Twain story. **90m/C; VHS, DVD, On Demand.** Vincent Schiavelli; Arye Gross; Robert Englund; Timothy Bottoms; C. Thomas Howell; Linda Cardellini; ***D:*** Gregory Gieras. **VIDEO**

Prince Avalanche ½ **2013 (R)** A simple, conversational--though slow at times--tale of two men spending a summer together tasked with the unique job of repainting lines on the highway after forest fires destroy miles of land. Alvin (Rudd) and Lance (Hirsch) have little in common, even if the latter is the brother of the former's girlfriend. Lance is younger, more restless and eager to go to town on breaks and let off steam. Alvin is more relaxed although it masks an uptight anxiety. After a few studio-produced creative misfires, Sundance darling director/writer Gordon Green returns to his roots here bolstered by two first-class leads. **94m/C; DVD, Blu-Ray.** Paul Rudd; Emile Hirsch; ***D:*** David Gordon Green; ***W:*** David Gordon Green; ***C:*** Tim Orr; ***M:*** David Wingo; Explosions in the Sky.

Prince Brat and the Whipping Boy *The Whipping Boy* **1995 (G)** Orphaned Jemmy (Munro) is living on the streets of the 18th-century German town of Brattenburg with his younger sister Annyrose (Salt). Neglected, spoiled Prince Horace (Knight) has been causing mischief in the castle but instead of being punished himself, the king's men catch Jemmy and use him as a punishment stand-in. Jemmy escapes the castle to get back to his sister and the Prince decides to go along for the adventure. Filmed on location in North Rhine-Westphalia and Burgundy, Germany. Adventurous TV movie with spunky leads; adapted from Sid Fleischman's novella. **96m/C; VHS, DVD, Streaming.** Truan Munro; Nic Knight; Karen Salt; George C. Scott; Kevin Conway; Vincent Schiavelli; Andrew Bicknell; Jean Anderson; Mathilda May; ***D:*** Syd Macartney; ***W:*** Max Brindle; ***M:*** Lee Holdridge.

Prince of Bel Air ½ **1987 (R)** A pool-cleaning playboy who makes a habit of one night stands meets a woman and starts falling in love with her. **95m/C; VHS, DVD.** Mark Harmon; Kirstie Alley; Robert Vaughn; Patrick Laborteaux; Deborah Harmon; ***D:*** Charles Braverman; ***M:*** Robert Folk. **TV**

The Prince of Central Park **1977** Two young orphans are forced by circumstance to live in a tree in New York's Central Park until they are befriended by a lonely old woman. An above-average adaptation of the novel by Evan H. Rhodes, the story was later used for a Broadway play. **76m/C; VHS, DVD, Streaming.** Ruth Gordon; T(imothy) J(ohn) Hargrave; Lisa Richards; Brooke Shields; Marc Vahanian; Dan Hedaya; ***D:*** Harvey Hart. **TV**

Prince of Central Park ½ **2000 (PG-13)** JJ Somerled (Nasso) is a 12-year-old stuck in the abusive foster home of Mrs. Ardis (Moriarty). Fed up, he takes off for the carousel at Central Park, where he had his last happy memory of his long-gone mother. In the park, JJ is befriended by all sorts of do-gooders and eccentrics. Bland non-musical reworking of a musical play. **105m/C; VHS, DVD.** Frank Nasso; Kathleen Turner; Danny Aiello; Harvey Keitel; Cathy Moriarty; Lauren Velez; Jerry Orbach; Tina Holmes; ***D:*** John Leekley; ***W:*** John Leekley; ***C:*** Jonathan Herron; ***M:*** Theodore Shapiro.

Prince of Darkness ½ **1987 (R)** University students release Satan, in the form of a mysterious chemical, unwittingly on the world. Written by Martin Quatermass (a pseudonym of Carpenter). Strong personnel does not save this dreary and slow-moving cliche plot. **102m/C; VHS, DVD, Blu-Ray.** Donald Pleasence; Lisa Blount; Victor Wong; Jameson Parker; Dennis Dun; Susan Blanchard; Alice Cooper; Anne Marie Howard; Ken Wright; Dirk Blocker; ***D:*** John Carpenter; ***W:*** John Carpenter; ***C:*** Gary B. Kibbe; ***M:*** John Carpenter.

Prince of Egypt **1998 (PG)** First animated musical from Dreamworks manages to tell the story of the Exodus without turning it into Mickey Moses. Young Moses (Kilmer) is adopted by the royal family: imperious pharaoh Seti (Stewart), his stately Queen (Mirren) and jockish son Rameses (Fiennes). Happily wed to Tzipporah (Pfeiffer), he's living it up until a chance meeting with his real sister Miriam (Bullock) twists his conscience and destiny. Steve Martin and Martin Short provide a short comic break, but overall the joking is kept to a minimum. Successful in combining epic feeling with stylized animation. **93m/C; VHS, DVD, Blu-Ray.** ***V:*** Val Kilmer; Michelle Pfeiffer; Dame Helen Mirren; Steve Martin; Martin Short; Ralph Fiennes; Sandra Bullock; Jeff Goldblum; Danny Glover; Patrick Stewart; Ofra Haza; James Avery; Eden Riegel; ***D:*** Simon Wells; Brenda Chapman; Steve Hickner; ***M:*** Hans Zimmer. Oscars '98: Song ("When You Believe"); Broadcast Film Critics '98: Song ("When You Believe").

Prince of Foxes ½ **1949** In 16th-century Italy, rascally Orsini (Power) is sent by his boss, the power-hungry Cesare Borgia (Welles), to seduce Camilla (Hendrix), the insipid young wife of an old duke (Aylmer), and turn the town over to the Borgias. But Orsini likes Count Varano and decide to switch sides, which doesn't please his now ex-boss. The story is plodding, the dialogue is deadly, and although it's lavishly picturesque (and filmed on location), it's a shame that Fox didn't shoot the film in Technicolor. Based on the novel by Samuel Shellabarger. **107m/B; DVD, Blu-Ray.** Tyrone Power; Orson Welles; Wanda Hendrix; Felix Aylmer; Everett Sloane; Marina Berti; Katina Paxinou; ***D:*** Henry King; ***W:*** Milton Krims; ***C:*** Leon Shamroy; ***M:*** Alfred Newman.

Prince of Pennsylvania ½ **1988 (R)** A mild comedy about a spaced-out youth who kidnaps his own father in hopes of nabbing a family inheritance. **113m/C; VHS, DVD.** Keanu Reeves; Fred Ward; Amy Madigan; Bonnie Bedelia; Jeff Hayenga; ***D:*** Ron Nyswaner; ***W:*** Ron Nyswaner; ***M:*** Thomas Newman.

Prince of Persia: The Sands of Time **2010 (PG-13)** A rogue prince (a considerably bulked-up Gyllenhaal) joins forces with a feisty princess (Tamina) to safeguard an ancient dagger from evil forces. The dagger can release a 'gift' from the gods that can reverse time and allow the possessor unimagined power as well as turn the locals into demons. Jerry Bruckheimer-produced adaptation of the videogame (for Disney). Family-friendly, somewhat bland swashbuckler-lite. **116m/C; Blu-Ray.** Jake Gyllenhaal; Gemma Arterton; Ben Kingsley; Alfred Molina; ***D:*** Mike Newell; ***W:*** Doug Miro; Carlo Bernard; ***C:*** John Seale; ***M:*** Harry Gregson-Williams.

Prince of Poisoners: The Life and Crimes of William Palmer ½ **1998** A true crime story set in mid-19th century England. Dr. William Palmer (Allen) appears to be a successful surgeon with a devoted wife, Annie (Ashbourne), and happy family. But the doctor has a secret passion for racehorses and gambling and his good life is about to crumble because of his debts. So what's his solution? Why, murder of course, so Palmer can collect on various insurance policies and dispose of his gambling rivals. **180m/C; VHS, DVD.** *GB* Keith Allen; Jayne Ashbourne; Judy Cornwell; Richard Coyle; Freddie Jones; Stephen Moore; *D:* Alan Dossor; *W:* Glenn Chandler; *C:* Allan Pyrah; *M:* Christopher Gunning. **TV**

Prince of the City 1981 **(R)** Docu-drama of a police officer who becomes an informant in an effort to end corruption within his narcotics unit, but finds he must pay a heavy price. Based on the true story told in Robert Daly's book, the powerful script carries the tension through what would otherwise be an overly long film. Excellent performances make this a riveting character study. **167m/C; VHS, DVD.** Treat Williams; Jerry Orbach; Richard Foronjy; Don Billett; Ken Marino; Lindsay Crouse; Lance Henriksen; *D:* Sidney Lumet; *W:* Jay Presson Allen; Sidney Lumet; *C:* Andrzej Bartkowiak. N.Y. Film Critics '81: Director (Lumet).

The Prince of Thieves 1948 Robin Hood helps Lady Marian extricate herself from a forced marriage in this adventure made with younger audiences in mind. **72m/C; VHS, DVD.** Jon Hall; Patricia Morison; Adele Jergens; Alan Mowbray; Michael Duane; *D:* Howard Bretherton; *W:* Charles Schnee; Maurice Tombragel; *C:* Fred H. Jackman, Jr.

The Prince of Tides 1/2 1991 **(R)** Pat Conroy's sprawling southern-fried saga is neatly pared down to essentials in this tale of the dysfunctional Wingo family, whose dark tragedies are gradually revealed as twins Tom and Savannah come to grips with personal demons under the ministering aid of psychiatrist Susan. Bravura performance by Nolte and Streisand's generally restrained in both her performance and direction although a subplot dealing with her character's bad marriage and rebellious son is a needless distraction. The South Carolina low country, and even New York City, never looked better. Conroy co-wrote the screenplay. **132m/C; VHS, DVD, Blu-Ray.** Nick Nolte; Barbra Streisand; Blythe Danner; Kate Nelligan; Jeroen Krabbe; Melinda Dillon; George Carlin; Jason Gould; Brad Sullivan; *D:* Barbra Streisand; *W:* Pat Conroy; Becky Johnston; *C:* Stephen Goldblatt; *M:* James Newton Howard. Golden Globes '92: Actor--Drama (Nolte); L.A. Film Critics '91: Actor (Nolte).

Prince Valiant 1/2 1954 **(PG-13)** When his royal dad is exiled by an evil tyrant, brave young Wagner brushes aside bangs and journeys to Camelot to seek the help of King Arthur. Based on Harold Foster's classic comic strip. **100m/C; VHS, DVD.** James Mason; Janet Leigh; Robert Wagner; Debra Paget; Sterling Hayden; Victor McLaglen; Donald Crisp; Brian Aherne; Barry Jones; Mary (Phillips) Philips; *D:* Henry Hathaway; *W:* Dudley Nichols.

Princess: A Modern Fairytale 1/2 2008 Cute ABC Family movie. Mysterious Princess Ithaca makes her annual appearance at a fund-raising ball where William Humphrey hopes to get a date with her. But Ithaca must pass on the power of speech to a bunch of CGI animals as well as find a new princess to take over her duties when Ithaca turns 25 so she doesn't think she has time to fall in love as well. **88m/C; DVD.** Nora Zehetner; Kip Pardue; *D:* Mark Rosman; *W:* Heidi Ferrer; *C:* David Makin; *M:* Richard (Rick) Marvin. **CABLE**

The Princess & the Call Girl 1984 Call girl Lucy Darling asks her look-alike college girlfriend Audrey Swallow (Levy in a dual role) to take her place in Monaco for a lavishly erotic weekend. Then when Audrey gets delayed, Lucy winds up taking her place in New York—at Audrey's engagement party. Weaker than Metzger's usual sexual romps. **90m/C; VHS, DVD.** Carol Levy; Shannah Hall; Victor Bevine; *D:* Radley Metzger.

The Princess and the Frog 2009 **(G)** Hand-drawn animated musical comedy featuring Disney's first African-American heroine. Living in New Orleans during the Jazz Age, orphan and aspiring chef Tiana (Rose) finds a talking frog in the bayou who claims to be Prince Naveen (Campos), under a curse until a kiss can break the spell and turn him human again. Of course, there's a twist, and with the help of some bayou animals, the two must find a way to stop sinister voodoo priest Dr. Facilier (David) and break the curse before it's too late. Kids and adults will like this charming story supported by animation in the old Disney style and inspiring musical numbers. **97m/C; DVD, Blu-Ray, On Demand.** *V:* Anika Noni Rose; Bruno Campos; Terrence Howard; John Goodman; Keith David; Jim (Jonah) Cummings; Jenifer Lewis; Oprah Winfrey; Jennifer Cody; Michael-Leon Wooley; Peter Bartlett; *D:* Ron Clements; John Musker; *W:* Ron Clements; John Musker; *M:* Randy Newman.

The Princess and the Goblin 1/2 1994 **(G)** Little kiddies may enjoy this animated adventure but it's a bland story with mediocre animation. Groups of ugly, underground-dwelling goblins like nothing better than to scare humans, especially castle-dwelling Princess Irene. Brave working-class Curdie helps to save the day. Based on a book by George MacDonald. **82m/C; VHS, DVD.** *GB HU V:* Sally Ann Marsh; Peter Murray; Claire Bloom; *D:* Jozsef Gemes; *W:* Robin Lyons; *M:* Istvan Lerch.

The Princess and the Pirate 1944 Hope at his craziest as a vaudvillian who falls for a beautiful princess while on the run from buccaneers on the Spanish Main. Look for Crosby in a closing cameo performance. Available in digitally remastered stereo with original movie trailer. **94m/C; VHS, DVD.** Bob Hope; Walter Slezak; Walter Brennan; Virginia Mayo; Victor McLaglen; Bing Crosby; *D:* David Butler; *W:* Everett Freeman; Don Hartman; Melville Shavelson; *C:* Victor Milner; *M:* David Rose.

The Princess and the Warrior *Der Krieger und die Kaiserin* **2000 (R)** Nurse Sissi's (Potente) life is saved by small-time crook Bodo (Furmann) after she's run over by a truck in an accident that he helped cause. He crawls under the truck to avoid the police (he was about to rob the bank), but ends up saving her as she's about to choke to death. After Sissi recovers, she sets out to find Bodo, feeling that he's her one true love. Bodo, still grieving the loss of his wife, resists. Impossible to pigeonhole as Twyker is clearly more concerned with his characters than with shoving them into a conveniently labeled plot. German with subtitles. **130m/C; VHS, DVD.** *GE* Franka Potente; Benno Furmann; Joachim Krol; Marita Breuer; Lars Rudolph; Jurgen Tarrach; Melchior Beslon; Ludger Pistor; *D:* Tom Tykwer; *W:* Tom Tykwer; *C:* Frank Griebe; *M:* Tom Tykwer; Johnny Klimek; Reinhold Heil.

The Princess Blade 1/2 *Shura Yukihime* **2002 (R)** It is the future in Japan, and the reigning monarchy employs a group of sword fighting samurai assassins to hunt down the rebels opposing them. Yuki (Shaku) is the last of a noble line, and an assassin herself. She quits the clan after finding out they killed her mother, and ends up hiding with the rebels in a gas station awaiting the inevitable bloody showdown. **95m/C; DVD.** *JP* Hideaki Ito; Shiro Sano; Yoichi Numata; Yoko Chosokabe; Yoko Maki; Naomasa Musaka; Yutaka Matsushige; Yumiko Shaku; Kyusaku Shimada; *D:* Shinsuke Sato; *W:* Kazuo Kamimura; Kazuo Koike; Shinsuke Sato; Kei Kunii; *C:* Taro Kawazu; *M:* Kenji Kawai.

The Princess Bride 1/2 1987 **(PG)** A modern update of the basic fairy tale crammed with all the cliches, this adventurously irreverent love story centers around beautiful maiden Buttercup (Wright Penn) and her young swain Westley (Elwes) as they battle the evils of the mythical kingdom of Florin to be reunited with one another. Great dueling scenes and offbeat satire of the genre make this fun for adults as well as children. Based on William Goldman's cult novel. **98m/C; VHS, DVD, Blu-Ray, UMD.** Cary Elwes; Mandy Patinkin; Robin Wright; Wallace Shawn; Peter Falk; Andre the Giant; Chris Sarandon; Christopher Guest; Billy Crystal; Carol Kane; Fred Savage; Peter Cook; Mel Smith; *D:* Rob Reiner; *W:* William Goldman; *C:* Adrian Biddle; *M:* Mark Knopfler. Natl. Film Reg. '16.

Princess Caraboo 1/2 1994 **(PG)** Fluffy quasi-fairy tale (but based on a true story) finds an exotic beauty (Cates) appearing in an English village in 1817. She speaks a language no one understands and is taken under the wing of the local gentry, the Worralls, who believe she is an Asian princess washed ashore during a shipwreck. Meanwhile, the local jouralist (Rea) is suspicious but protective, an Oxford linguist (Lithgow) is determined to prove her a fraud, and she must put up with the Worrall family's pompous Greek butler (Cate's husband Kline at his showy best). **97m/C; VHS, DVD.** Phoebe Cates; Stephen Rea; John Lithgow; Kevin Kline; Jim Broadbent; Wendy Hughes; Peter Eyre; Jacqueline Pearce; John Lynch; John Sessions; Arkie Whiteley; John Wells; *D:* Michael Austin; *W:* John Wells; Michael Austin; *C:* Freddie Francis; *M:* Richard Hartley.

The Princess Comes Across 1936 Deft comedy-mystery finds Brooklyn actress Lombard deciding to take an ocean voyage and pass herself off as a Swedish princess in the hopes of furthering her career. Bandleader MacMurray is smitten but an old beau recognizes the ruse and demands hush money. Then he turns up dead and the duo fall under the suspicious eye of a German passenger (Rumann) who happens to be a detective. From the novel by Louis Lucien Rogger. **77m/B; DVD.** Carole Lombard; Fred MacMurray; Alison Skipworth; Sig Rumann; Douglass Dumbrille; William Frawley; Porter Hall; George Barbier; Lumsden Hare; Mischa Auer; Tetsu Komai; *D:* William K. Howard; *W:* Walter DeLeon; Francis Martin; Frank Butler; Don Hartman; *C:* Ted Tetzlaff.

Princess Daisy 1983 A beautiful model claws her way to the top of her profession while trying to find true love and avoid the clutches of her rotten half-brother. Adapted from Judith Krantz's glitzy bestselling novel. **200m/C; VHS, DVD.** Merete Van Kamp; Lindsay Wagner; Claudia Cardinale; Stacy Keach; Ringo Starr; Barbara Bach; *D:* Waris Hussein. **TV**

The Princess Diaries 1/2 2001 **(G)** Gently amusing comedy perfect for tweenies who worry about being misfits. Modern-day Cinderella story finds brainy-but-clumsy San Francisco teen Mia (newcomer Hathaway, who's a real find) learning that she's the heir to the European kingdom of Genovia after the death of her long-absent dad. And to teach her the ways of royalty is her very regal grandmama (Andrews). Think Henry Higgins and Eliza Doolittle. Of course, Mia has her doubts about being a princess, especially when the kids at school learn her secret. There's even a little first romance thrown in for good measure. Based on the novel by Meg Cabot. **114m/C; DVD, Blu-Ray.** Anne Hathaway; Julie Andrews; Hector Elizondo; Heather Matarazzo; Erik von Detten; Mandy Moore; Robert Schwartzman; Caroline Goodall; Larry Miller; Sandra Oh; Sean O'Bryan; *D:* Garry Marshall; *W:* Gina Wendkos; *C:* Karl Walter Lindenlaub; *M:* John Debney.

The Princess Diaries 2: Royal Engagement 2004 **(G)** College grad Princess Mia (Hathaway), still sweet and klutzy, is on her way to Genovia to live with grandma, Queen Clarisse (Andrews), and assume her royal duties. But Clarisse is being forced to abdicate and ancient law dictates that Mia must first marry before she can become queen. If not, sneaky Viscount Mabrey's (Rhys-Davies) plastic-handsome nephew, Nicholas (Pine), is the next rightful heir. Nicholas tries to charm Mia while she dutifully agrees to marry affable British nobleman Andrew (Blue). There's a little too much slapstick but it's all very nice and innocent and little princesses should be enchanted once again. **120m/C; DVD, Blu-Ray.** Anne Hathaway; Julie Andrews; Hector Elizondo; John Rhys-Davies; Heather Matarazzo; Chris Pine; Callum Blue; Kathleen Marshall; Tom Poston; Joel McCrary; Kim Thomson; Larry Miller; Raven; Caroline Goodall; Sean O'Bryan; Matthew (Matt) Walker; Elinor Donahue; Paul Williams; Lorraine Nicholson; *D:* Garry Marshall; *W:* Shonda Rhimes; *C:* Charles Minsky; *M:* John Debney.

A Princess for Christmas 2011 Jules (McGrath) is overwhelmed when she becomes the guardian for niece Maddie (de Meza) and nephew Milo Huntington (Turner) when their parents are killed in an accident. An invitation to spend Christmas with the kids' estranged grandfather (Moore), an English duke, turns into an adventure, especially when Jules meets a handsome young prince (Heughan). **87m/C; DVD.** Katie McGrath; Roger Moore; Sam Heughan; Miles Richardson; Travis Turner; Leilah de Meza; *D:* Michael Damian; *W:* Michael Damian; Janeen Damian; *C:* Viorel Sergovici, Jr.; *M:* Mark Thomas. **CABLE**

Princess Kaiulani 1/2 *Barbarian Princess* **2009 (PG)** Drama about the slow overthrow of Hawaii's monarchy, beginning in 1888, when foreign businessmen force King David Kalakaua to restrict royal powers. His young niece Princess Kaiulani (Kilcher), who expects one day to rule herself, is then taken to Scotland and raised as an English gentlewoman. However, Kaiulani never forgets her heritage and becomes a political activist when she learns that the U.S. military has placed her uncle's successor under house arrest. Hints at some interesting conflict but really provides little character depth or insight. Plays instead like a bland, melodramatic story with all the weight of a cable TV biopic. **102m/C; On Demand.** Barry Pepper; Shaun Evans; Jimmy Yuill; Julian Glover; Tamzin Merchant; Will Patton; Q'orianka Kilcher; Ocean Kaowili; Leo Anderson Akana; *D:* Marc Forby; *W:* Marc Forby; *C:* Gabriel Beristain; *M:* Stephen Warbeck.

Princess Mononoke 1998 **(PG-13)** Stunning animated feature by Japanese master Hayao Miyazaki is a bit too long and graphic for children, but a must-see for fans of anime. Dubbed into English by an all-star cast, the tale follows the plight of Ashitaka (Crudup), who's cursed after he accidentally kills a rampaging forest spirit. He discovers the cause is the encroaching civilization of Iron Town, led by the cold Lady Eboshi (Driver), and its conflict with the forest spirits and their champion San (Danes)--the princess of the title. Became the first feature of any kind to gross over $150 million at the boxoffice in its native Japan. **133m/C; VHS, DVD, Blu-Ray.** *V:* Claire Danes; Billy Crudup; Minnie Driver; Gillian Anderson; Jada Pinkett Smith; Billy Bob Thornton; *D:* Hayao Miyazaki; *W:* Neil Gaiman; *M:* Joe Hisaishi.

Princess of Mars 2009 Low-budget, rip-off sci fi (with bad acting and a nonsensical plot) is a loosely updated version of the 1912 novel by Edgar Rice Burroughs. Left for dead after a mission, Special Forces Op John Carter (Sabato Jr.) is used in an experimental program that allows his mind to be uploaded to a flash drive while his body recovers. Carter is then sent to explore the newly-discovered Mars 216 planet and its reptilian inhabitants, the Tharks, who are in conflict with Princess Dejah (Lords) and her people. **90m/C; DVD, Blu-Ray.** Antonio Sabato, Jr.; Traci Lords; Matt Lasky; Chacko Vadaketh; Mitchell Gordon; Matt Lagan; Noelle Perris; *D:* Mark Atkins; *W:* Mark Atkins; *C:* Mark Atkins; *M:* Chris Ridenhour. **VIDEO**

The Princess of Montpensier *Le Princesse de Montpensier* **2010** The savage religious war between France's Catholics and Huguenots provides a fitting backdrop to this 16th-century love story. Marie (Thierry) is bartered off by her father to marry the privileged prince Philippe (Leprince-Ringuet), even though the new princess is secretly in love with her dashing cousin Henri (Ulliel). Philippe is called to duty and Marie struggles to stay true to a husband she doesn't love. Adapted from Madame de La Fayette's 1662 novella. Visually stunning, with flawless costume design and period settings. The military warfare is just as captivating as the romantic warfare. French with subtitles. **139m/C; DVD, Streaming.** *FR GE* Mélanie Thierry; Gregoire Leprince-Ringuet; Gaspard Ulliel; Lambert Wilson; Raphael Personnaz; Antatole de Bodinat; Eric Bulliat; *D:* Bertrand Tavernier; *W:* Bertrand Tavernier; Jean Cosmos; Francois Olivier Rousseau; *C:* Bruno de Keyzer; *M:* Philippe Sarde.

The Princess of Nebraska 2007 Meandering indie sketch from Wang with an ambiguous ending. Sasha, a sullen Chinese exchange student studying in Omaha, travels to San Francisco to look up her Beijing one-night stand's American lover. Sasha's pregnant and thinks she wants an abortion but she seems to spend most of her time wandering aimlessly around the city doing stuff she shouldn't. **77m/C; DVD.** Li Ling; Brian Danforth; Pamelyn Chee; *D:* Wayne Wang; *W:* Michael Ray; *C:* Richard Wong; *M:* Kent Sparling.

Princess of the Nile 1954 Technicolor costume adventure. In 13th-century Egypt, Prince Haidi (Hunter) stops in Halwan, which has been conquered by evil Bedouin leader Rama Khan (Rennie). Princess Shalimar (Paget) , daughter of the rightful ruler, disguises herself as a dancing girl to plot revenge, aided by the smitten Haidi. Lovely Paget shakes and shimmies in see-thru finery, courtesy of costume designer Travilla. **71m/C; DVD.** Debra Paget; Jeffrey Hunter; Michael Rennie; Michael Ansara; Jack Elam; Dona Drake; ***D:*** Harmon Jones; ***W:*** Gerald Drayson Adams; ***C:*** Lloyd Ahern; ***M:*** Lionel Newman.

Princess of Thieves 🦴🦴 ½ **2001** An aging Robin Hood and Will Scarlett return to England with a mortally wounded King Richard. Robin knows that Prince John will stop at nothing to assume the throne, including killing Richard's son Phillip. Unfortunately, the duo are captured by the Sheriff of Nottingham and it's up to Robin's feisty daughter Gwyn, who disguises herself as a boy, to rescue her father and Will and stop the bad guys from taking over the kingdom. **88m/C; VHS, DVD.** Malcolm McDowell; Keira Knightley; Roger Ashton-Griffiths; Jonathan Hyde; Del Synnott; Stephen Moyer; Stuart Wilson; ***D:*** Peter Hewitt; ***W:*** Sally Robinson; Robin Lerner. **TV**

Princess O'Rourke 🦴🦴 ½ **1943** European diplomat Holman (Coburn) is living in wartime exile in New York with his royal niece Maria (de Havilland). He's determined to marry her off because their country needs a male heir, but an incident with sleeping pills has Maria chastely spending the night in the apartment of flyboy Eddie O'Rourke (Cummings). Eddie thinks Maria is some kind of war refugee and they fall in love. Uncle Holman is happy to see them together and arranges a White House wedding but things get a little complicated. FDR makes a cameo appearance and his Scottie dog Fala actually has a part as a romantic go-between. **95m/B; DVD.** Olivia de Havilland; Robert Cummings; Charles Coburn; Jack Carson; Jane Wyman; Gladys Cooper; Minor Watson; Curt Bois; Harry Davenport; ***D:*** Norman Krasna; ***W:*** Norman Krasna; ***C:*** Ernest Haller; ***M:*** Frederick "Friedrich" Hollander.

Princess Protection Program 🦴🦴 ½ **2009 (G)** Charming Disney cable flick about an imperiled young princess and the tomboyish teen who befriends her. Princess Rosalinda Marie Montoya Fiore (Lovato) must go into hiding when her island home of Costa Luna is threatened by a neighboring dictator's political coup. Unbeknownst to his daughter Carter (Gomez), Joe Mason (Verica) is an agent for the Princess Protection Program and spirits the newly-named Rosie to his home in Lake Monroe, Louisiana for safekeeping. She doesn't exactly fit in so Carter, despite some hesitation, helps Rosie navigate high school and typical teen life. **89m/C; DVD.** Selena Gomez; Demi Lovato; Tom Verica; Nicholas Braun; Jamie Chung; Samantha Droke; Robert Adamson; ***D:*** Allison Liddi-Brown; ***W:*** Annie DeYoung; ***C:*** David Makin; ***M:*** John Van Tongeren. **CABLE**

Princess Raccoon 🦴🦴 ½ *Operetta tanuki goten* **2005** The Tanuki (the film's protagonist) is a species of wild dog in Japan that resembles raccoons, and is thought to be an evil shape-shifter in Japanese folklore. Partly inspired by the Tanukigoten musicals popular in Japan in the 40s and 50s, it is a strange cross between a modern musical, traditional Japanese opera, and folklore/myth. The Princess of the Tanuki falls in love with a human prince who has been exiled from his father's kingdom, and their respective parents are, to say the least, disapproving. Especially his, since he's been prophesied to be the end of his own father's reign. **110m/C; DVD.** *JP* Ziyi Zhang; Joe Odagiri; ***D:*** Seijun Suzuki; ***W:*** Yoshiro Urasawa.

Princess Tam Tam 🦴🦴🦴 **1935** Pleasing French adaptation of Shaw's "Pygmalion," as a beautiful native African woman is "westernized" by a handsome writer and then introduced to high society as an exotic princess. A musical notable for its spectacular choreography and on-location Tunisian scenery. Story by Pepito Abatino, who was then Baker's husband. In French with English subtitles. **77m/B; VHS, DVD.** *FR* Josephine Baker; Albert Prejean; Germaine Aussey; Viviane Romance; ***D:*** Edmond T. Greville.

The Principal 🦴🦴 ½ **1987 (R)** A tough, down-on-his-luck high school teacher is hired as the principal of a relentlessly violent, uncontrollable high school. Naturally he whips it into shape. **109m/C; VHS, DVD, Blu-Ray.** James Belushi; Louis Gossett, Jr.; Rae Dawn Chong; Michael Wright; Esai Morales; J.J. (Jeffrey Jay) Cohen; Troy Winbush; Jacob Vargas; ***D:*** Christopher Cain; ***W:*** Frank Deese; ***C:*** Arthur Albert; ***M:*** Jay Gruska.

Prison Break 🦴🦴 **1938** A convict plans a daring prison escape in order to clear his name for a murder he did not commit. **72m/B; VHS, DVD.** Barton MacLane; Glenda Farrell; Paul Hurst; Constance Moore; Edmund MacDonald; Ward Bond; Guy Usher; Victor Kilian; ***D:*** Arthur Lubin; ***W:*** Dorothy Davenport Reid; ***C:*** Harry Neumann; ***M:*** Frank Sanucci; Hayes Pagel.

Prison Break: The Final Break 🦴🦴 **2009** Takes place in the time frame of the TV series' fourth season finale after the company is defeated and before the four year flash-forward coda. Pregnant Sara is now in prison (for the murder of Christina Scofield) and Michael reunites with his cohorts to break her out. Explains some of the questions left hanging in the last TV episode but some of the silly plot points won't please fans. **88m/C; DVD, Blu-Ray.** Wentworth Miller; Sarah Wayne Callies; Dominic Purcell; Amaury Nolasco; William Fichtner; Robert Knepper; Jodi Lyn O'Keefe; Leon Russom; Kim Coates; Chris Bruno; ***D:*** Brad Turner; ***W:*** Nick Santora; Christian Trokey; ***C:*** Jeffrey Mygatt; ***M:*** Ramin Djawadi. **VIDEO**

Prison of Secrets 🦴🦴 ½ **1997** Mom Zimbalist gets convicted of racketeering and sent to the big house where she learns that some of the prison guards are pimping the inmates. After suffering degradation herself, Zimbalist finally decides to expose the abuse but she needs the other women to testify as well. **91m/C; VHS, DVD.** Stephanie Zimbalist; Dan Lauria; Finola Hughes; Rusty Schwimmer; Gary Frank; Kimberly Russell; ***D:*** Fred Gerber; ***W:*** Layce Gardner; ***C:*** John Fleckenstein; ***M:*** Nan Miskin. **CABLE**

Prison on Fire 🦴🦴 **1987** A mobster sent to prison for murdering his wife becomes friends with an innocent prisoner who has been framed. Violent portrayal of prison life. In Cantonese with English subtitles. **98m/C; VHS, DVD.** *CH* Chow Yun-Fat; Tony Leung Ka-Fai; ***D:*** Ringo Lam; ***W:*** Yin Nam; ***M:*** Lowell Lo.

Prison on Fire 2 🦴🦴 *Tao Fan; Jian Yu Feng Yun Xu Ji* **1991** Ching is a hard-timer in a Hong Kong prison troubled by an ongoing battle between local inmates and those from Mainland China. He manages to escape to see his young son but is soon returned to prison where evil security chief Zau sets him up against the Mainland gang, led by Dragon. There are more escapes, a riot, revenge, and lots of action. Subtitled. **107m/C; DVD.** *CH* Chow Yun-Fat; Elvis Tsui; Kam-Kong Tsui; Yu Li; ***D:*** Ringo Lam; ***M:*** Lowell Lo.

Prison Shadows 🦴 **1936** Contrived programmer about a fighter (Nugent) who attempts to make a comeback after having served three years of a five-year sentence for killing an opponent in the boxing ring. He makes his comeback, but deals yet another mortal blow. Turns out that a gambling ring is behind the bizarre murders of the fighters and Nugent is their next victim. **67m/B; VHS, DVD.** Eddie Nugent; Lucille Lund; Joan Barclay; Forrest Taylor; Syd Saylor; Monte Blue; ***D:*** Robert F. "Bob" Hill; ***W:*** Al Martin.

Prison Train 🦴🦴 ½ *People's Enemy* **1938** Travelogue of a convicted murderer's cross-country journey to begin his prison sentence at Alcatraz. **84m/B; VHS, DVD.** Fred Keating; Dorothy Comingore; Clarence Muse; Faith Bacon; Alexander Leftwich; Nestor Paiva; Franklyn Farnum; ***D:*** Gordon Wiles.

The Prisoner 🦴🦴🦴 **1955** Gritty drama about a Cardinal imprisoned in a Soviet bloc country as his captors attempt to break his determination not to be used as a propaganda tool. Interactions between the prisoner and his interogator are riveting. Based on the real-life experiences of Cardinal Mindszenty, a Hungarian activist during and after WWII. **91m/B; VHS, DVD, Blu-Ray.** *GB* Alec Guinness; Jack Hawkins; Raymond Huntley; Wilfred Lawson; ***D:*** Peter Glenville.

The Prisoner 🦴🦴 *Jackie Chan Is the Prisoner; Huo Shao Dao* **1990 (R)** Even though the cover of this bizarre import says "Jackie Chan Is The Prisoner," he doesn't even show up for the first 20 minutes or so. Actually, the film is something of an ensemble piece that cheerfully borrows from American prison movies (most blatantly "Cool Hand Luke") between action scenes. The free-wheeling plot has Jackie, Sammo Hung, and Tony Leung battling fellow prisoners and corrupt officials. **94m/C; DVD.** *CH* Jackie Chan; Sammo Hung; Tony Leung Ka-Fai; ***D:*** Yen Ping Chu; ***W:*** Fu Lai; Yeh Yuen Chiao; ***C:*** Chan Wing Su; ***M:*** Eckart Seeber.

Prisoner 🦴 ½ **2007** Controversial director Derek Plato (McMahon) checks out the location for his next violent film—an abandoned prison that's not so empty when a deranged man locks Derek up in a cell on death row. His jailer (Koteas) then starts filming Derek and asking him questions about his sordid past and career. Every unanswered question moves Derek closer to a presumably-working electric chair. **94m/C; DVD.** Julian McMahon; Elias Koteas; Dagmara Dominczyk; Tom Guiry; ***D:*** David Alford; Robert Lynn; ***W:*** David Alford; Robert Lynn; ***C:*** Armanda Costanza. **VIDEO**

The Prisoner 🦴🦴 **2009** If you are unfamiliar with the surreal 1967 British cult series, co-created by and starring a powerful Patrick McGoohan, you may be moderately interested in Gallagher's reinterpretation of the material. Otherwise, this miniseries is self-conscious, somewhat incoherent, and frustrating. After abruptly resigning from some giant corporation, Michael (Caviezel) awakens in someplace called the Village where everyone has numbers instead of names. He's now Six and Two (McKellan) runs the show. Naturally a baffled, angry Six doesn't want to be there, wants to know what's going on, and wants to escape. You'll probably feel the same way yourself. **276m/C; DVD.** *GB* James (Jim) Caviezel; Ian McKellen; Jamie Campbell; Hayley Atwell; Lennie James; Ruth Wilson; Rachael Blake; ***D:*** Nick Hurran; ***W:*** Bill Gallagher; ***C:*** Florian Hoffmeister. **CABLE**

Prisoner in the Middle 🦴🦴 **1974 (PG)** Janssen is the only man who can stop a nuclear warhead from falling into the hands of rival Middle East factions. Originally released as "Warhead." **87m/C; VHS, DVD.** David Janssen; Karin Dor; Christopher Stone; Turia Tan; David Semadar; Art Metrano; ***D:*** John O'Conner.

Prisoner of Honor 🦴🦴🦴 **1991 (PG)** A cable retelling of notorious Dreyfus Affair, in which a Jewish officer in the 19th-century French military was accused of treason based on little evidence and lots of bigotry. George Piquart (Dreyfuss), the anti-semitic counterintelligence head, grows to realize Dreyfuss's innocence and fights zealously for the truth. Russell's flamboyant direction takes the heroic tale into the realm of the surreal; this may not be a thoroughly accurate account, but it's one of the more eye-filling. **90m/C; VHS, DVD.** Richard Dreyfuss; Oliver Reed; Peter Firth; Jeremy Kemp; Brian Blessed; Peter Vaughan; Kenneth Colley; Lindsay Anderson; ***D:*** Ken Russell. **CABLE**

Prisoner of Love 🦴 ½ **1999 (R)** After bartender Tracy (Campbell) witnesses a shakedown gone wrong, low-level stooge Jonny (Thal) is told to get rid of her. But since he's fallen in lust with Tracy after flirting with her in a nightclub, Jonny kidnaps her and holds her prisoner in a warehouse until he can figure out how to keep them both alive. Not nearly as kinky as it sounds—in fact the sheer blandness makes this a miss. **100m/C; VHS, DVD.** Eric Thal; Naomi Campbell; Beau Starr; Carl Marotte; ***D:*** Steve DiMarco; ***M:*** Norman Orenstein.

Prisoner of Paradise 🦴🦴🦴 **2002** Stark PBS documentary profiling German singer/actor/director Kurt Gerron who gained fame during the 1920s and 1930s in "The Blue Angel," but, as a Jew, was not allowed to work with the Nazis in power and oddly declined a chance to escape. After being captured while touring with gypsies and sent to a camp, the Nazis forced him to create a pro-Nazi film, "The Fuhrer Gives a City to the Jews." His 23-minute work is curiously omitted. **96m/C; DVD.** ***D:*** Malcolm Clarke; Stuart Sender; ***W:*** Malcolm Clarke; Ian Holm. **TV**

Prisoner of Second Avenue 🦴🦴 ½ **1974 (PG)** A New Yorker in his late 40s faces the future, without a job or any confidence in his ability, with the help of his understanding wife. Based on the Broadway play by Neil Simon. **98m/C; VHS, DVD, Blu-Ray.** Jack Lemmon; Anne Bancroft; Gene Saks; Elizabeth Wilson; Sylvester Stallone; F. Murray Abraham; ***D:*** Melvin Frank; ***W:*** Neil Simon; ***M:*** Marvin Hamlisch.

The Prisoner of Shark Island 🦴🦴 ½ **1936** Dr. Samuel Mudd (Baxter) is wrongly convicted of conspiring to assassinate President Lincoln after he unwittingly sets the broken leg of assassin John Wilkes Booth (McDonald). He's sent to the titular island where Mudd cares for the inmates and guards, saving many during a yellow fever epidemic. Thanks to his heroism, Mudd's case is then re-opened. Baxter elicits audience sympathy without over-playing his role. **86m/B; DVD.** Warner Baxter; Gloria Stuart; Claude Gillingwater; Frank McGlynn; Francis McDonald; Harry Carey, Sr.; John Carradine; Fred Kohler, Jr.; Douglas Wood; Paul Fix; ***D:*** John Ford; ***W:*** Nunnally Johnson; ***C:*** Bert Glennon.

Prisoner of the Mountains 🦴🦴🦴 *Kavkazsky Plennik; Prisoner of the Caucasus* **1996 (R)** A modern-day, freely adapted version of Leo Tolstoy's novella "Prisoner of the Caucasus." Two Russian soldiers find themselves taken hostage in a remote Muslim village high in the Caucasus Mountains. Their captor, Abdul-Mourant (Sikharulidze), wishes to exchange them for his own captive son. Seasoned veteran Sacha (Menshikov) and young recruit Vanya (Bodrov Jr.) slowly form a bond, not only with each other but gradually with their captors. But there's a tragic inevitability to the entire untenable situation. Russian with subtitles. **98m/C; VHS, DVD.** *RU* Sergei Bodrov, Jr.; Oleg Menshikov; Jemal Sikharulidze; Susanna Mekhraliyeva; Alexander Burejev; Alexei Zharkov; Valentina Fedotova; ***D:*** Sergei Bodrov; ***W:*** Sergei Bodrov; Arif Aliev; Boris Giller; ***C:*** Pavel Lebeshev; ***M:*** Leonid Desyatnikov.

The Prisoner of Zenda 🦴🦴 ½ **1922** The third silent film adaptation of Anthony Hope's popular adventure novel. Stone stars in the dual role of King Rudolf of Ruritania and his lookalike English cousin, Rudolf Rassendyll. The King is drugged and thrown into the dungeon of Zenda by his evil half-brother Michael (Holmes) who wants the throne. Imagine Michael's surprise when the imposter shows up for the coronation. Novarro steals the flick as monocle-wearing baddie Rupert. **115m/B; Silent; DVD.** Lewis Stone; Stuart Holmes; Ramon Novarro; Alice Terry; Barbara La Marr; Robert Edeson; ***D:*** Rex Ingram; ***W:*** Mary O'Hara; ***C:*** John Seitz.

Prisoner of Zenda 🦴🦴🦴 ½ **1937** An excellent cast and splendid photography make this the definitive film adaptation of Anthony Hope's swashbuckling novel. A British commoner is forced to pose as his cousin, the kidnapped king of a small European country, to save the throne. Complications of the romantic sort ensue when he falls in love with the queen. Excellent acting, robust sword play, and beautifully designed costumes make this an enjoyable spectacle. **101m/B; VHS, DVD.** Ronald Colman; Douglas Fairbanks, Jr.; Madeleine Carroll; David Niven; Raymond Massey; Mary Astor; Sir C. Aubrey Smith; Montagu Love; Byron Foulger; Alexander D'Arcy; Charles Halton; ***D:*** John Cromwell; ***W:*** Donald Ogden Stewart; John Lloyd Balderston; Wells Root; ***C:*** James Wong Howe. Natl. Film Reg. '91.

Prisoner of Zenda 🦴🦴 ½ **1952** Less-inspired remake of the 1937 version of Anthony Hope's novel, of a man resembling the monarch of a small country who is forced to pose as King during the coronation ceremony, becomes enamored with the queen, and finds himself embroiled in a murder plot. Worth watching for the luxurious costumes and lavish sets. Cast as a Cardinal here, Stone starred in the 1922 version. **101m/C; VHS, DVD.** Stewart Granger; Deborah Kerr; Louis Calhern; James Mason; Jane Greer; Lewis

Stone; *D:* Richard Thorpe; *C:* Joseph Ruttenberg.

Prisoner of Zenda **1979 (PG)** Flat comedic interpretation of Anthony Hope's swashbuckling tale of two identical men who switch places, only to find things complicated by a murder. Sellers stars in the double role of Prince Rudolph of Ruritania and Syd, the cockney cab driver who doubles for Rudolph when the Prince is imprisoned by his jealous brother Michael. **108m/C; DVD.** Peter Sellers; Jeremy Kemp; Lynne Frederick; Lionel Jeffries; Elke Sommer; *D:* Richard Quine; *W:* Dick Clement; Ian La Frenais; *M:* Henry Mancini.

Prisoners **2013 (R)** Dark, dense, and remarkably well-made, director Villeneuve's drama offers a harrowing look at the lengths one man will go to when his family's safety is at risk. Two little girls are kidnapped on Thanksgiving. The father of one, Keller Dover (Jackman), is frustrated when the police, led by Detective Loki (Gyllenhaal), lets the main suspect (Dano) free. Stellar performances are framed by award-worthy cinematography from Deakins. The final act is a bit traditional but the film is still unforgettable. **153m/C; DVD, Blu-Ray.** Hugh Jackman; Jake Gyllenhaal; Viola Davis; Maria Bello; Terrence Howard; Melissa Leo; Paul Dano; *D:* Denis Villeneuve; *W:* Aaron Guzikowski; *C:* Roger Deakins; *M:* Johan Johannsson.

Prisoners of the Lost Universe 1/2 **1984** Talk-show hostess and her buddy are transported to a hostile universe by a renegade scientist. The two terrified humans search desperately for the dimensional door that is their only hope of escape. **94m/C; VHS, DVD.** Richard Hatch; Kay Lenz; John Saxon; *D:* Terry Marcel. **TV**

Prisoners of the Sun *Blood Oath* **1991 (R)** Right after WWII an Australian captain fights to convict Japanese officers for atrocities against Allied POWs, but he's stonewalled by both the U.S. military and still-defiant enemy prisoners. This fiery drama from Down Under packs a punch as it questions whether wartime justice even exists; similar in that way to Brown's earlier "Breaker Morant." Takei (Sulu of the original "Star Trek") makes an imposing Japanese admiral. **109m/C; VHS, DVD.** *AU* Bryan Brown; George Takei; Terry O'Quinn; John Back; Toshi Shioya; Deborah Kara Unger; *D:* Stephen Wallace.

The Private Affairs of Bel Ami **1947** "This is the story of a scoundrel," proclaims the opening. Sanders is ideally cast as a suave cad who rises in 1880s Parisian society, largely through the strategic seduction of prominent women. Moralistically minded Old Hollywood toned down the talky adaptation of the Guy de Maupassant novel, but it's still drama of a high order. **112m/B; VHS, Blu-Ray, Streaming.** George Sanders; Angela Lansbury; Ann Dvorak; Frances Dee; John Carradine; Susan Douglas; Hugo Haas; Marie Wilson; Albert Bassermann; Warren William; Katherine Emery; Richard Fraser; *D:* Albert Lewin; *W:* Albert Lewin.

Private Benjamin 1/2 **1980 (R)** Lighthearted fare about a pampered New York Jewish princess who impulsively enlists in the U.S. Army after her husband dies on their wedding night. Hawn, who also produced, creates a character loveable even at her worst moments and brings a surprising amount of depth to this otherwise frivolous look at high society attitudes. Basis for a TV series. **110m/C; VHS, DVD.** Goldie Hawn; Eileen Brennan; Albert Brooks; Robert Webber; Armand Assante; Barbara Barrie; Mary Kay Place; Sally Kirkland; Craig T. Nelson; Harry Dean Stanton; Sam Wanamaker; *D:* Howard Zieff; *W:* Nancy Meyers; Charles Shyer; Harvey Miller; *C:* David M. Walsh; *M:* Bill Conti. Writers Guild '80: Orig. Screenplay.

Private Buckaroo **1942** War time entertainment in which Harry James and his orchestra get drafted. They decide to put on a show for the soldiers and get help from the Andrews Sisters. **70m/B; VHS, DVD.** Andrews Sisters; Harry James; Joe E. Lewis; Dick Foran; Shemp Howard; Mary Wickes; Donald O'Connor; *D:* Edward F. (Eddie) Cline.

Private Duty Nurses 1/2 *Young L.A. Nurses 1* **1971 (R)** Three nurses take on racism, war wounds, and a menage-a-trois (between one nurse, a doctor, and a drug addict). Second in Roger Corman's "nurse" quintet takes itself too seriously to be entertaining, but the gals make good use of those exciting new inventions, waterbeds. Preceded by "The Student Nurses" and followed by "Night Call Nurses," "The Young Nurses," and "Candy Stripe Nurses." **80m/C; VHS, DVD.** Katherine (Kathy) Cannon; Joyce Williams; Pegi Boucher; Joseph Kaufmann; Dennis Redfield; Herbert Jefferson, Jr.; Paul Hampton; Paul Gleason; *D:* George Armitage; *W:* George Armitage; *C:* John McNichol; *M:* Sky.

The Private Eyes 1/2 **1980 (PG)** Light and uneven comedic romp with Knotts and Conway as bungling sleuths engaged to investigate two deaths. They're led on a merry chase through secret passages to a meeting with a ghostly adversary. **91m/C; VHS, DVD.** Don Knotts; Tim Conway; Trisha Noble; Bernard Fox; *D:* Lang Elliott; *W:* Tim Conway; John Myhers; *C:* Jacques Haitkin; *M:* Peter Matz.

Private Fears in Public Places 1/2 *Coeurs* **2006** Short scenes make for a fitful stop-and-start story about six essentially lonely people in Paris. Nicole (Morante) is looking for a new apartment for herself and fiance Dan (Wilson) with the help of broker Thierry (Dussollier). Thierry works with Charlotte (Azema), who knows bartender Lionel (Arditi) at the hotel where Dan likes to drink. Dan's drinking causes him to split with Nicole and he meets Gaelle (Carre), who happens to be Thierry's unhappy younger sister. The actors are pros but the production feels flat and constricted. French with subtitles. **120m/C; DVD.** *FR IT* Laura Morante; Lambert Wilson; Pierre Arditti; Isabelle Carre; Andre Dussollier; Azema; *D:* Alain Resnais; *W:* Alain Resnais; Alan Ayckbourn; Jean-Michel Ribes; *C:* Eric Gautier; *M:* Mark Snow.

The Private Files of J. Edgar Hoover 1/2 **1977 (PG)** Scandalmongering "biography" of J. Edgar Hoover's private, sex-filled life. **112m/C; VHS, DVD.** Broderick Crawford; Dan Dailey; Jose Ferrer; Rip Torn; Michael Parks; Raymond St. Jacques; Ronee Blakley; *D:* Larry Cohen; *W:* Larry Cohen.

A Private Function 1/2 **1984 (PG)** A ribald gag-fest dealing with Palin as a Yorkshireman who steals and fattens a wily contraband pig against the backdrop of post-WWII rationing. The satire ranges from biting to downright nasty, but Palin is always likeable in the center of it all. **96m/C; VHS, DVD.** *GB* Michael Palin; Maggie Smith; Denholm Elliott; Bill Paterson; Liz Smith; Richard Griffiths; Tony Haygarth; John Normington; Alison Steadman; Pete Postlethwaite; *D:* Malcolm Mowbray; *W:* Alan Bennett; *C:* Tony Pierce-Roberts; *M:* John Du Prez. British Acad. '84: Actress (Smith), Support. Actor (Elliott), Support. Actress (Smith).

Private Hell 36 **1954** Two detectives become guilt-ridden after keeping part of some stolen money recovered after a robbery. Co-produced by Lupino. **81m/B; DVD, Blu-Ray, Streaming.** Ida Lupino; Howard Duff; Steve Cochran; Dean Jagger; Dorothy Malone; Bridget Duff; Jerry Hausner; Dabbs Greer; Chris O'Brien; Kenneth Patterson; George Dockstader; Jimmy Hawkins; King Donovan; *D:* Donald Siegel; *W:* Ida Lupino; *C:* Burnett Guffey; *M:* Leith Stevens.

Private Lessons **1975 (R)** Teenage boy is left alone for the summer in the care of an alluring maid and a scheming chauffeur. **83m/C; VHS, DVD, Blu-Ray.** *IT* Eric Brown; Sylvia Kristel; Howard Hesseman; Ed Begley, Jr.; *D:* Alan Myerson; Vittorio De Sisti; *W:* Vittorio De Sisti; *C:* Jan De Bont; Mario Masini; *M:* Franco Micalizzi.

Private Life of Don Juan *Don Juan* **1934** Appropriately slow-moving British costume drama set in 17th-century Spain finds an aging Don Juan struggling to maintain his usual antics in the pursuit of beautiful women. Furthermore, his reputation is being upstaged by a young imposter. Notable only as the last film appearance by Douglas Fairbanks Sr., and based on the play by Henri Bataille. **87m/B; VHS, DVD.** *GB* Douglas Fairbanks, Sr.; Merle Oberon; Binnie Barnes; Melville Cooper; Joan Gardner; Benita Hume; Athene Seyler; *D:* Alexander Korda; *C:* Georges Perinal.

The Private Life of Henry VIII **1933** Lavish historical spectacle lustily portraying the life and lovers of notorious British Monarch, King Henry VIII. A tour de force for Laughton as the robust 16th-century king, with outstanding performances by the entire cast. **97m/B; VHS, DVD.** *GB* Charles Laughton; Binnie Barnes; Elsa Lanchester; Robert Donat; Merle Oberon; Miles Mander; Wendy Barrie; John Loder; Lady Tree; Franklin Dyall; Claud Allister; William Austin; Gibb McLaughlin; Sam Livesey; Lawrence Hanray; Everley Gregg; Judy Kelly; John Turnbull; Frederick Culley; Hay Petrie; Wally Patch; *D:* Alexander Korda; *W:* Arthur Wimperis; Lajos Biro; *C:* Georges Perinal. Oscars '33: Actor (Laughton).

The Private Life of Sherlock Holmes 1/2 **1970 (PG-13)** A unique perspective on the life of the famous detective reveals a complex character. Beautifully photographed, with fine performances by the supporting cast, the film boasts a haunting musical score but received suprisingly little recognition despite Wilder's high caliber direction. **125m/C; VHS, DVD, Blu-Ray.** *GB* Robert Stephens; Colin Blakely; Genevieve Page; Irene Handl; Stanley Holloway; Christopher Lee; Clive Revill; Catherine Lacey; Tamara Toumanova; Mollie Maureen; Michael Balfour; *D:* Billy Wilder; *W:* Billy Wilder; I.A.L. Diamond; *C:* Christopher Challis; *M:* Miklos Rozsa.

Private Lives 1/2 **1931** Stylish adaptation of Noel Coward play starring Shearer and Montgomery as a couple with a tempestuous relationship. Although once married, they have since divorced and married other mates. While honeymooning at the same french hotel (Quelle coincidence!), they have trouble showing affection to their new spouses and realize they still feel passionately about one another. Excellent acting combined with Coward's witty dialogue makes this film a treat. **92m/B; VHS, DVD.** Norma Shearer; Robert Montgomery; Reginald Denny; Una Merkel; Jean Hersholt; *D:* Sidney Franklin; *W:* Hans Kraly; Richard Schayer; *C:* Ray Binger.

The Private Lives of Elizabeth & Essex **1939** Cast reads like a Who's Who in Hollywood in this lavishly costumed dramatization of the love affair between Queen Elizabeth I (Davis) and Robert Devereaux (Flynn), the second Earl of Essex. Forced to choose between her Kingdom and her lover, Davis' monarch is the epitome of a regal women. Fabray made her first film appearance as an adult in this adaptation of Maxwell Anderson's 1930 play "Elizabeth the Queen." **106m/C; VHS, DVD.** Bette Davis; Errol Flynn; Vincent Price; Nanette Fabray; Olivia de Havilland; Alan Hale; Donald Crisp; Leo G. Carroll; *D:* Michael Curtiz.

The Private Lives of Pippa Lee **2009 (R)** Miller adapted her own novel for this mild dysfunctional family drama. At 50, placid Pippa Lee (Wright) thought she has the perfect life. Then her dominating, 30-years-older husband Herb (Arkin) moves them from their Manhattan apartment into a Connecticut retirement community because of his failing health. Pippa thinks about her troubled past with her drug addict mom (Bello), which lead to her own druggie-runaway youth in New York and starts confiding in neighbor's son Chris (Reeves) that she's lost her own identity while devoting her life to placating everyone else. Now she wonders just where it got her. **93m/C; DVD, Blu-Ray, On Demand.** Robin Wright; Alan Arkin; Keanu Reeves; Shirley Knight; Robin Weigert; Julianne Moore; Blake Lively; Maria Bello; Tim Guinee; Winona Ryder; Monica Bellucci; Zoe Kazan; Ryan McDonald; *D:* Rebecca Miller; *W:* Rebecca Miller; *C:* Declan Quinn; *M:* Michael Rohatyn.

A Private Matter **1992 (PG-13)** Based on the true story of Sherri Finkbine (hostess of TV's "Romper Room") and the controversy surrounding her decision to terminate her pregnancy in 1962. Pregnant with her fifth child, she discovered her sleeping medication contained thalidomide, known to cause severe birth defects. Although technically illegal, her doctor agreed to quietly perform an abortion. Sherri warned a local newspaper reporter about the drug's dangers and her identity was mistakenly revealed. A storm of adverse publicity forced her to Sweden for the abortion. Great performances highlight this complex and traumatic issue. **89m/C; VHS, DVD.** Sissy Spacek; Aidan Quinn; Estelle Parsons; Sheila McCarthy; Leon Russom; William H. Macy; *D:* Joan Micklin Silver; *W:* William Nicholson. **CABLE**

Private Navy of Sgt. O'Farrell **1968** Serviceable World War II service comedy casts Hope as the titular NCO who must salvage a cargo ship full of beer that was sunk by the Japanese. He also tries to get some nurses assigned to the remote Pacific island where he's stationed. But Phyllis Diller proves to be a poor morale booster. The film doesn't come close to the "Road" comedies, but it's still worth a mild recommendation to the star's fans. **92m/C; DVD.** Bob Hope; Phyllis Diller; Jeffrey Hunter; Dick Sargent; Mako; Gina Lollobrigida; *D:* Frank Tashlin; *W:* Frank Tashlin; *C:* Alan Stensvold.

Private Number 1/2 **1936** Creaky romantic drama that eliminated what was interesting about the 1915 play "Common Clay" and earlier film adaptations. Poor-but-lovely teenager Ellen (Young) is hired as a maid for the wealthy Winfield family. Handsome heir Richard (Taylor) falls for the nobody and they secretly marry before Richad heads back to college. Ellen's pregnant, loses her job, and is kept apart from Richard through various machinations, including evil butler, Wroxton (Rathbone). **80m/B; DVD.** Loretta Young; Robert Taylor; Basil Rathbone; Marjorie Gateson; Patsy Kelly; Paul Harvey; Jane Darwell; *D:* Roy Del Ruth; *W:* William Conselman; Gene Markey; *C:* J. Peverell Marley.

Private Obsession 1/2 **1994 (R)** Model Emanuelle Griffith (Whirry) is missing—kidnapped by obsessed admirer Richard (Christian) who wants the beauty for himself alone. Emanuelle may be blonde but she's not dumb and she decides to turn the tables on her captor. **93m/C; VHS, DVD.** Shannon Whirry; Michael Christian; Bo Svenson; Rip Taylor; *D:* Lee Frost; *W:* Lee Frost; *C:* William Boatman; *M:* Dean Andre.

Private Parts **1972 (R)** A bizarre first attempt at feature length for Bartel. Black comedy featuring a runaway, a voyeuristic photographer and a hotel full of strange people who participate in murder and a variety of freakish sexual acts. **87m/C; VHS, DVD.** Ayn Ruymen; Lucille Benson; John Ventantonio; Laurie Main; Stanley Livingston; Charles Woolf; John Lupton; Dorothy Neumann; Gene Simms; *D:* Paul Bartel; *W:* Philip Kearney; Les Rendelstein; *C:* Andrew Davis; *M:* Hugo Friedhofer.

Private Parts 1/2 *Howard Stern's Private Parts* **1996 (R)** Stern makes his movie debut as...himself! Self-effacing yet self-aggrandizing bio traces Stern's rise from gawky kid to gawky college student to awkward small-market DJ to New York madman to inauguration as self-proclaimed King of All Media. Funny, and at times, touching flick features good performances by the rookie actors in Stern's inner circle, as well as by the pros. Giamatti is exceptional as the WNBC exec assigned to tame Howard. Script manages to show Stern's outrageousness and still make him likeable. **109m/C; VHS, DVD.** Howard Stern; Robin Quivers; Mary McCormack; Paul Giamatti; Fred Norris; Gary Dell'Abate; Bobby Boriello; Michael Maccarone; Matthew Friedman; Jackie Martling; Henry Goodman; Jonathan Hadary; Kelly Bishop; Allison Janney; *D:* Betty Thomas; *W:* Len Blum; Michael Kalesniko; *C:* Walt Lloyd; *M:* Van Dyke Parks.

Private Passions **1985** A sultry woman gives her teenaged cousin a lesson in love during his European vacation. **86m/C; VHS, DVD.** Sybil Danning; David J. Siegel; Susanne Ashley; Gavin Brennan; *D:* Kikuo Kawasaki; *W:* Kikuo Kawasaki; *C:* Ramon Suarez.

Private Peaceful **2012** Ernest Brit war drama plays like TV fare. Impoverished brothers Charlie and teenaged Tommo Peaceful are rivals for beautiful Molly, who marries more-mature Charlie. This sends Tommo to enlist as a WWI soldier with Charlie soon following to protect his brother. They quickly find themselves on the battlefields of Flanders. Flashbacks show one of the brothers facing a court martial and firing squad. **102m/C; DVD.** *UK* Jack O'Connell; George MacKay; Alexandra Roach; Richard Griffiths;

Frances de la Tour; John Lynch; Maxine Peake; *D:* Pat O'Connor; *W:* Simon Reade; *C:* Jerzy Zielinski; *M:* Rachel Portman.

Private Property 1/2 *Nue Propriete* **2006** Unpleasant dysfunctional family drama. Pascale lives with her lay-about twin sons Francois and Thierry in a rundown farmhouse that was part of her acrimonious divorce settlement. She and her sons have never cut those apron strings and the boys are appalled when Pascale hints at selling the dump, in part because she's found a boyfriend. Lots of bickering (and more) follows. French with subtitles. **95m/C; DVD.** *BE FR LU* Isabelle Huppert; Jeremie Renier; Patrick Descamps; Yannick Renier; Kris Cuppens; *D:* Joachim Lafosse; *W:* Joachim Lafosse; Francois Pirot; *C:* Hichame Alaouie.

Private Resort **1984 (R)** Curious house detective and a bumbling thief interrupt the highjinks of two girl-crazy teens on a quest for fun at an expensive Miami hotel. Occasionally funny plodder. **82m/C; VHS, DVD, Blu-Ray.** Johnny Depp; Rob Morrow; Karyn O'Bryan; Emily Longstreth; Tony Azito; Hector Elizondo; Dody Goodman; Leslie Easterbrook; Andrew Silverstein; *D:* George Bowers.

Private Romeo **2011** Modern update of Shakespeare's "Romeo and Juliet" set in a military academy. A four-day weekend finds eight cadets, basically left unsupervised, taking their rehearsals outside the classroom. The emotions bleed over into real life with the play's family rivalry turned into institutional homophobia as cadet Sam/Romeo is confused when he realizes he's in love with Glenn/Juliet. **98m/C; DVD; Closed Captioned.** Seth Numrich; Matt Doyle; Hale Appleman; Charlie Barnett; Adam Barrie; Bobby Moreno; Sean Hudock; Chris Bresky; *D:* Alan Brown; *W:* Alan Brown; *C:* Derek McKane; *M:* Nicholas Wright.

Private School 1/2 **1983 (R)** Two high school girls from the exclusive Cherryvale Academy for Women compete for the affections of a young man from nearby Freemount Academy for Men, while Cherryvale's headmistress is trying to raise funds to build a new wing. Banal teen sexploitation comedy with better-than-average cast. **89m/C; VHS, DVD, Blu-Ray.** Phoebe Cates; Betsy Russell; Kathleen Wilhoite; Sylvia Kristel; Ray Walston; Matthew Modine; Michael Zorek; Fran Ryan; Jonathan Prince; Kari Lizer; Richard Stahl; *D:* Noel Black; *C:* Walter Lassally.

Private Valentine: Blonde & Dangerous *Major Movie Star* **2008 (PG-13)** Simpson pulls a Goldie Hawn/"Private Benjamin" moment with a lot less talent involved but an amiable presence. Megan Valentine is a fluff bunny movie star whose latest effort is a flop. Adding to her woes is a bad breakup and a crooked accountant who's left her broke. So what's a busty blonde to do? Hey, Megan is a nice girl—so she decides to join the Army. **98m/C; DVD.** Jessica Simpson; Vivica A. Fox; Steve Guttenberg; Cheri Oteri; Bryce Johnson; *D:* Steve Miner; *W:* April Blair; Kelly Bowe; *C:* Patrick Cady; *M:* Dennis Smith.

Private Violence **2014** Domestic violence is still too often seen as "someone else's problem." Director Hill tackles the subject by presenting two women forever impacted by it--victim's rights advocate Kit Gruelle, herself a survivor of abuse, and a young mother named Deanna, who underwent unimaginable real-life horrors. Hill lets her subjects tell their stories without title cards of statistics or narration, resulting in a documentary that feels important instead of like it's teaching a lesson. She also allows for hope and change if people are willing to listen to women like Kit and Deanna. **81m/C; DVD.** *D:* Cynthia Hill; *C:* Rex Miller; *M:* Chuck Johnson.

A Private War 1/2 **2018 (R)** An American from Long Island, journalist Marie Colvin travels the world covering wars and interviewing rebels and despots. Working for the London Sunday Times, she describes the brutality to make her readers understand what is at stake. Though Marie loses an eye in Sri Lanka and is later hospitalized for PTSD, she draws on her personal courage and puts her life at risk as she challenges the status quo in war torn regions like Syria, Iraq, and Libya. The first feature film from documentarian Heineman tells the real life story of the remarkable, fearless journalist, driven by Pike's dynamic performance. **106m/C; DVD.** Rosamund Pike; Jamie Dornan; Greg Wise; Alexandra Moen; Tom Hollander; *D:* Matthew Heineman; *W:* Arash (A.E.) Amel; *C:* Robert Richardson; *M:* H. Scott Salinas.

Private Wars **1993 (R)** A law-abiding community falls victim to gangland violence until the inhabitants hire a down-and-out private eye (Railsback) to show them how to fight back. He finds out that a greedy land developer (Whitman) has bribed the Chief of Police (Champion) to let his goons do anything to get the people out so he can redevelop the land. **94m/C; VHS, DVD.** Steve Railsback; Michael Champion; Stuart Whitman; Holly Floria; Dan Tullis, Jr.; Michael Delano; James Lew; Brian Patrick Clarke; *D:* John Weidner; *W:* Ken Lamplugh; John Weidner.

Privates on Parade 1/2 **1984 (R)** Film centering around the comic antics of an Army song-and-dance unit entertaining the troops in the Malayan jungle during the late '40s. Occasionally inspired horseplay based on Peter Nichols play. **107m/C; VHS, DVD.** *GB* John Cleese; Denis Quilley; Simon Jones; Joe Melia; Nicola Pagett; Julian Sands; *D:* Michael Blakemore.

Privilege **1967** The acting's poor but the situations are still relevant. British pop star Steve Shorter (debut of singer Jones) is immensely popular but also easily manipulated and exploited. In this nightmare future oddity, the government decides to use Steve as a symbol of national unity and conformity. Artist Vanessa (model Shrimpton in her only film role) becomes Steve's lover and makes him see how he's been used so he'll stage a social revolt. **103m/C; DVD.** *GB* Paul Jones; Mark London; Jeremy Child; William Job; Jean Shrimpton; Max Bacon; *D:* Peter Watkins; *W:* Peter Watkins; Norman Bogner; *C:* Peter Suschitzky; *M:* Mike Leander.

Prix de Beaute 1/2 *Miss Europe* **1930** A woman's boyfriend does not know that she has won a beauty contest. Brooks' last starring role and the only film she did in France. In French with English subtitles. **93m/B; VHS, DVD.** *FR* Louise Brooks; Jean Bradin; George Charlia; Gaston Jacquet; *D:* Augusto Genina.

The Prize **1963** Gripping spy story laced with laughs based on a novel by Irving Wallace (adapted by Lehman). In Stockholm, writer accepts the Nobel prize for dubious reasons and then finds himself in the midst of political intrigue. Newman and Sommer turn in great performances in this action drama. **136m/C; VHS, DVD, Blu-Ray.** Paul Newman; Edward G. Robinson; Elke Sommer; Leo G. Carroll; Diane Baker; Micheline Presle; Gerard Oury; Sergio Fantoni; *D:* Mark Robson; *W:* Ernest Lehman; *C:* William H. Daniels; *M:* Jerry Goldsmith.

Prize Fighter **1979 (PG)** Comedy team of Knotts and Conway take on Depression-era boxing. Fight manager Knotts and his pugilistic protege Conway unknowingly get involved with a powerful gangster, who convinces them to fight in a fixed championship match. Most enjoyable if intelligence is suspended at onset. **99m/C; VHS, DVD.** Tim Conway; Don Knotts; *D:* Michael Preece; *W:* Tim Conway.

The Prize Pulitzer *Roxanne: The Prize Pulitzer* **1989** Watered-down account of the scandalous divorce between publishing heir Herbert "Pete" Pulitzer and his young wife Roxanne. Based on the book "The Prize Pulitzer" by Roxanne Pulitzer. **95m/C; VHS, DVD.** Perry King; Chynna Phillips; Courteney Cox; Betsy Russell; Sondra Blake; Caitlin Brown; *D:* Richard A. Colla. **TV**

The Prize Winner of Defiance, Ohio **2005 (PG-13)** Based on a memoir by Terry Adams. The "prize winner" is Terry's mother Evelyn (Moore, who filmmakers seem to love casting as a 1950s housewife). The mother of ten children and the wife of a drunk (Harrelson), ever-cheerful Evelyn figures out how to (barely) hold it all together by becoming a successful jingle writer, winning money and prizes for her catchy advertising tunes. Maybe a little heavy and nostalgic at moments, but charming nonetheless. **99m/C; DVD.** Julianne Moore; Woody Harrelson; Laura Dern; Trevor Morgan; Simon Reynolds; *D:* Jane Anderson; *W:* Jane Anderson; *C:* Jonathan Freeman; *M:* John (Gianni) Frizzell.

The Prizefighter and the Lady *Every Woman's Man* **1933** In his first film role boxer Baer (who won the heavyweight boxing crown in 1934) is a natural as a fighter who falls for a beautiful nightclub singer (Loy). Baer and Loy get, but don't stay, together but she does turn out to be his lucky charm in the big fight finale. Fellow professional boxer Carnera, Baer's opponent in the climactic fight scene, refused to lose as the script indicated and the film ending was eventually rewritten. The likeable Baer later earned his living as an actor. **102m/B; DVD.** Max Baer, Sr.; Myrna Loy; Otto Kruger; Primo Carnera; Walter Huston; Vince Barnett; Muriel Evans; *D:* W.S. Van Dyke.

Prizzi's Honor **1985 (R)** Highly stylized, sometimes leaden black comedy about Vharley Partana (Nicholson), an aging and none-to-bright hit man from a New York mob family who breaks with family loyalties when he falls for Irene Walker (Turner), an upwardly mobile tax consultant who's also a hired killer. Skirting caricature in every frame, Nicholson is excellent in his portrayal of the thick-skulled mobster, as are Angelica Huston as the hot-to-trot Mafia daughter Maerose and Hickey as Don Prizzi. Adapted by Condon and Roach from Condon's novel. **130m/C; VHS, DVD, Blu-Ray.** Jack Nicholson; Kathleen Turner; Robert Loggia; John Randolph; Anjelica Huston; Lawrence Tierney; William Hickey; Lee Richardson; Michael Lombard; Joseph Ruskin; CCH Pounder; *D:* John Huston; *W:* Richard Condon; Janet Roach; *C:* Andrzej Bartkowiak; *M:* Alex North. Oscars '85: Support. Actress (Huston); British Acad. '85: Adapt. Screenplay; Golden Globes '86: Actor--Mus./Comedy (Nicholson), Actress--Mus./Comedy (Turner), Director (Huston), Film--Mus./Comedy; L.A. Film Critics '85: Support. Actress (Huston); N.Y. Film Critics '85: Actor (Nicholson), Director (Huston), Film, Support. Actress (Huston); Natl. Soc. Film Critics '85: Actor (Nicholson), Director (Huston), Support. Actress (Huston); Writers Guild '85: Adapt. Screenplay.

Probable Cause **1995 (R)** A knife-wielding serial killer specializes in murdering cops and the clues seem to point to a troubled veteran cop (Ironside), newly paired with a beautiful detective (Vernon). Some unexpected twists and a surprise ending. **90m/C; VHS, Streaming.** Michael Ironside; Kate Vernon; Kirk Baltz; Craig T. Nelson; M. Emmet Walsh; *D:* Paul Ziller; *W:* Hal Salwen; *C:* Danny Nowak.

Probe 1/2 **1972** A detective uses computer-age technology to apprehend criminals. Pilot for the TV series "Search." **95m/C; VHS, DVD.** Hugh O'Brian; Elke Sommer; John Gielgud; Burgess Meredith; Angel Tompkins; Lilia Skala; Kent Smith; Alfred Ryder; Jaclyn Smith; *D:* Russ Mayberry; *W:* Leslie Stevens. **TV**

Problem Child 1/2 **1990 (PG)** Ritter decides to adopt Oliver out of the goodness of his heart, but it seems young Oliver's already got a father figure named Beelzebub. Potential for laughs is unmet. **81m/C; VHS, DVD.** John Ritter; Michael Oliver; Jack Warden; Amy Yasbeck; Gilbert Gottfried; Michael Richards; Peter Jurasik; *D:* Dennis Dugan; *W:* Scott M. Alexander; Larry Karaszewski; *C:* Peter Lyons Collister; *M:* Miles Goodman.

Problem Child 2 **1991 (PG-13)** Ritter and his nasty adopted son are back, but this time there's an equally malevolent little girl. They team up to prevent Ritter's upcoming marriage to a socialite. Low slapstick junk. **91m/C; VHS, DVD, Blu-Ray.** John Ritter; Michael Oliver; Laraine Newman; Amy Yasbeck; Jack Warden; Ivyann Schwan; Gilbert Gottfried; James Tolkan; Charlene Tilton; Alan Blumenfeld; Paul Sutera; *D:* Brian Levant; *W:* Scott M. Alexander; Larry Karaszewski.

The Prodigal 1/2 **1955** Luke's New Testament Bible story of the son seduced by greed slickly transfered to the silver screen by MGM. A colorful cast is the main attraction. **113m/C; DVD.** Lana Turner; Edmund Purdom; Louis Calhern; Audrey Dalton; Neville Brand; Walter Hampden; Taina Elg; Francis L. Sullivan; Joseph Wiseman; Sandy Descher; John Dehner; Cecil Kellaway; Henry Daniell; Paul Cavanagh; Tracey Roberts; Jay Novello; Dorothy Adams; Richard Devon; *D:* Richard Thorpe; *C:* Joseph Ruttenberg.

The Prodigal Planet **1988** Small group of believers continue their struggle against the world government UNTIE by disrupting their communication network. Sequel to "Thief in the Night," "A Distant Thunder," and "Image of the Beast." **67m/C; VHS, DVD.** William Wellman, Jr.; Linda Beatie; Cathy Wellman; Thom Rachford; *D:* Donald W. Thompson.

The Prodigal Son 1/2 **1982** Small-town martial arts champ Biao learns all his fights were fixed by his wealthy father. Determined to prove himself fairly, Biao learns the true wisdom and skills of kung fu from traveling entertainer Ying. Typically over-the-top fight scenes. Chinese with subtitles or dubbed. **100m/C; VHS, DVD.** *CH* Yuen Biao; Ching-Ying Lam; Sammo Hung; *D:* Sammo Hung; *W:* Jing Wong.

The Prodigy **1998** Well-intentioned but far-fetched drama posits that Nathan Jones (Earl), an illiterate 12-year-old black boy, is "adopted" by a fraternity and enrolled as a student as a child prodigy. Sounds like an after-school special gone tragically awry. **104m/C; DVD.** Robert Foreman; Jeremy Isiah Earl; Jennifer Rochester; *D:* Edward T. McDougal; *W:* Edward T. McDougal; Dale Chapman; Christopher Panneck; *C:* Ben Kufrin.

The Prodigy **2019 (R)** Though 8-year-old Miles (Scott) is very intelligent, his mother Sarah (Schilling) has been concerned about him since his birth because of his violent, sometimes unexplainable actions. Though doctors have assured her about Miles, his increasingly odd behavior leads to her to consult spiritualist Arthur (Feore). Arthur is sure that Miles is possessed by evil, which Sarah does not believe until Miles' actions force her to accept what her son has become. The predictable, formulaic story, uninspired directing, and Miles' poorly defined character combine to make a film that is too much like many other, better horror films. **92m/C; DVD, Blu-Ray.** *CA US* Jackson Robert Scott; Taylor Schilling; Peter Mooney; Colm Feore; Paul Fauteux; *D:* Nicholas McCarthy; *W:* Jeff Buhler; *C:* Bridger Nielson; *M:* Joseph Bishara.

The Producers 1/2 **1968** A hilarious farce follows an attempted swindle by theater producer/con artist Max Bialystock (Mostel), who convinces his meek accountant Leo Bloom (Wilder) to go along with a scheme to deliberately stage a Broadway flop and abscond with the investors' money. They pick what they believe will be a surefire disaster, a musical entitled "Springtime for Hitler," only to see their plan backfire. Film achieved cult status and is considered one of Brooks' best. The phony play was later actually produced by Alan Johnson. **90m/C; VHS, DVD, Blu-Ray.** Zero Mostel; Gene Wilder; Dick Shawn; Kenneth Mars; Estelle Winwood; Lee Meredith; Frank Campanella; Mel Brooks; *D:* Mel Brooks; *W:* Mel Brooks; *C:* Joseph Coffey; *M:* John Morris. Oscars '68: Story & Screenplay; Natl. Film Reg. '96; Writers Guild '68: Orig. Screenplay.

The Producers 1/2 **2005 (PG-13)** The wildly funny Mel Brooks 1968 film showed up in 2001 as a hit Broadway musical—this is the film version of that, cast with most of the originals from Broadway. Shifty producer Max (Lane) and his accountant Leo (Broderick) hatch a scheme to get rich by producing a flop and pocketing the leftover investor money after the show surely closes. Hideous Nazi musical "Springtime for Hitler" not only doesn't flop, it's a major success, which means trouble. Yes, it's all rehashed, and old-schoolers will go back to the original film with a renewed fondness. Fun cast and hilarious musical numbers help to somewhat mask the weaknesses. **129m/C; DVD, Blu-Ray.** Nathan Lane; Matthew Broderick; Uma Thurman; Will Ferrell; Roger Bart; Eileen Essell; David Huddleston; Michael McKean; Debra Monk; Andrea Martin; Jon Lovitz; Mel Brooks; Gary Beach; *D:* Susan Stroman; *W:* Mel Brooks; Thomas Meehan; *C:* John Bailey; Charles Minsky; *M:* Mel Brooks.

The Professional *Leon; The Cleaner* **1994 (R)** Leon (Reno) is an eccentric French hit man, working New York's mean streets, when his 12-year-old neighbor Mathilda (Portman) comes knocking. Seems her family has been murdered by minions of crooked drug enforcement agent Stansfield (Oldman) and she'd like Leon to teach her how to be a "cleaner" so she can get revenge. And Leon obliges. The lovely young Portman (in her film debut) is a little too Lolita-ish for comfort as she manipulates the stolid Reno, with Oldman suitably extravagant in the role of sadistic psycho. **109m/C; VHS, DVD, Blu-Ray.** *FR* Jean Reno; Natalie Portman; Gary Oldman; Danny Aiello; Michael Badalucco; Ellen Greene; ***D:*** Luc Besson; ***W:*** Luc Besson; ***C:*** Thierry Arbogast; ***M:*** Éric Serra.

Professional Soldier **1935** Tough guy McLaglen stars as ex-Marine Michael Donovan who's hired to kidnap the boy king of one of those movie European countries in a political coup.Discovering that Peter (Bartholomew) is going to be killed by his opponents, Donovan tries to save the kid instead. Based on a Damon Runyon story. **75m/B; DVD.** Victor McLaglen; Freddie Bartholomew; Michael Whalen; Gloria Stuart; Constance Collier; ***D:*** Tay Garnett; ***W:*** Gene Fowler, Sr.; ***C:*** Rudolph Mate; ***M:*** Louis Silvers.

The Professionals 1/2 **1966 (PG-13)** Action and adventure count for more than a story line in this exciting western about four mercenaries hired by a wealthy cattle baron to rescue his young wife from Mexican kidnappers. Breathtaking photography recreates turn-of-the-century Mexico in this adaptation of the Frank O'Rourke novel. **117m/C; VHS, DVD.** Burt Lancaster; Lee Marvin; Claudia Cardinale; Jack Palance; Robert Ryan; Woody Strode; Ralph Bellamy; ***D:*** Richard Brooks; ***W:*** Richard Brooks; ***C:*** Conrad L. Hall; ***M:*** Maurice Jarre.

The Professor 1/2 **2019 (R)** When professor Richard (Depp) learns he is dying of lung cancer, he rejects the diagnosis and tells only one colleague. Living defiantly, he ignores his own syllabus when he teaches his English class, kicks students out of class who don't read books in their spare time, and smokes marijuana with his students on campus. As Richard comes to terms with his mortality, those around him believe he is having a meltdown. Depp is well-suited to the role and brings some charisma, but overall nothing quite works well. **91m/C; DVD, Blu-Ray.** Johnny Depp; Rosemarie DeWitt; Odessa Young; Danny Huston; Zoey Deutch; ***D:*** Wayne Roberts; ***W:*** Wayne Roberts; ***C:*** Tim Orr; ***M:*** Aaron Dessner; Bryce Dessner.

The Professor and the Madman 1/2 **2019** When language expert Professor James Murray (Gibson) becomes the unlikely editor of the Oxford English Dictionary project, he becomes obsessed with the work despite the lack of support of his peers. The workload proves to be too much, so he devises the idea of having others submit words with definitions. One of his most talented helpers is Dr. William Minor (Penn), an American and Civil War veteran seeking redemption while imprisoned in a mental hospital. Based on a true story, it's ambitious but struggles to be engaging. **124m/C; DVD.** Natalie Dormer; Mel Gibson; Sean Penn; Jennifer Ehle; Ioan Gruffudd; ***D:*** Farhad Safinia; ***W:*** Farhad Safinia; John Boorman; Todd Komarnicki; ***C:*** Kasper Tuxen; ***M:*** Bear McCreary.

Professor Marston and the Wonder Women 1/2 **2017 (R)** The true story of the origins of the Wonder Woman character. In the late 1920s, Harvard psychology professor William Marston (Evans) conducts research with his brilliant wife Elizabeth (Hall). Their relationship is changed forever when they become professionally and sexually involved with their lab assistant, Radcliffe student Olive Byrne (Heathcote). Inspired by their costumed sexual play and Byrne's personal style, Marston creates Wonder Woman, though all involved pay a price. Effectively gives full reign to the complex sexual relationships among the main characters and affirms the potency of feminine power. **108m/C; Blu-Ray.** Luke Evans; Rebecca Hall; Bella Heathcote; Connie Britton; J.J. Feild; ***D:*** Angela Robinson; ***W:*** Angela Robinson; ***C:*** Bryce Fortner; ***M:*** Tom Howe.

Progeny **1998** Familiar horror ground with some scary creatures. Craig (Vosloo) and Sherry (McWhirter) are zapped by a bright light while in bed and don't remember what happened until a shrink (Crouse) and UFO investigator Clavell (Dourif) hypnotize them. Then Sherry remembers she was abducted and apparently impregnated by some slimy, tentacled aliens and it's all just kind of predictably gross from there on out. **100m/C; VHS, DVD.** Arnold Vosloo; Jillian McWhirter; Brad Dourif; Lindsay Crouse; Wilford Brimley; ***D:*** Brian Yuzna; ***W:*** Aubrey Solomon; ***C:*** James Hawkinson; ***M:*** Steven Morrell. **VIDEO**

The Program 1/2 **1993 (R)** Sensitive tearjerker about college football players getting caught up in the drive for a championship. As the season takes its toll on both mind and body, players prepare for the Big Game. Caan is the team's gruff coach, who's willing to look the other way as long as his boys are winning. Film sparked controversy when the Disney studio pulled and recut it after release because one scene, where Sheffer's character lies down in traffic, sparked copy-cat actions and several deaths. The scene was not restored for the video version. **110m/C; VHS, DVD.** James Caan; Craig Sheffer; Kristy Swanson; Halle Berry; Omar Epps; Duane Davis; Abraham Benrubi; Jon Maynard Pennell; Andrew Bryniarski; Joey Lauren Adams; ***D:*** David S. Ward; ***W:*** David S. Ward; Aaron Latham; ***M:*** Michel Colombier.

The Program **2015 (R)** There may be a great movie in the deception by world-renowned cyclist Lance Armstrong, who was proven to have used performance-enhancing drugs during his notorious streak of Tour de France wins. Sadly, this ain't it. Stephen Frears can't quite find the drama in the true story, hinging his film on an Irish journalist named David Walsh (O'Dowd), who grows increasingly suspicious of Armstrong (Foster) and seeks to prove his drug use. We all know how this story ends, and so there's no suspense, and too little artistry in the telling. Foster's committed performance is the only thing worth seeing here. **103m/C; DVD, Blu-Ray, Streaming.** *FR UK* Ben Foster; Chris O'Dowd; Guillaume Canet; Jesse Plemons; Lee Pace; ***D:*** Stephen Frears; ***W:*** John Hodge; ***C:*** Danny Cohen; ***M:*** Alex Heffes.

Project A 1/2 *Jackie Chan's Project A; A Gai Waak* **1983 (PG-13)** This period piece has several excellent physical routines. As Dragon Ma, a coast guard officer in 19th-century Hong Kong, Jackie Chan (who also directed) performs some of his most ingenious stunts, and pays overt homage to one of his greatest influences, Harold Lloyd. **105m/C; VHS, DVD, Blu-Ray.** *CH* Jackie Chan; Sammo Hung; Yuen Biao; ***D:*** Jackie Chan; ***W:*** Jackie Chan; Edward Tang; ***M:*** Nicholas Rivera.

Project A: Part 2 *Jackie Chan's Project A2* **1987** Dragon Ma, the only honest cop in Hong Kong on the high seas at the turn of the century is back with a new set of adventures. In Cantonese with English subtitles. **101m/C; VHS, DVD.** *CH* Jackie Chan; Maggie Cheung; Carina Lau; David Lam; ***D:*** Jackie Chan; ***W:*** Jackie Chan; Edward Tang.

Project Almanac 1/2 **2015 (PG-13)** Another found-footage, low-budget affair trying to mimic the critical and commercial success of others with decidedly less satisfying results. This one centers on time travel as 17-year-old David (Weston) is watching a video from his birthday party ten years earlier and sees the current version of himself in a mirror. Maybe his father's experiments with time travel actually worked? He investigates his dad's research with a few buddies, and before you know it they're hopping through time like they never saw The Butterfly Effect. Reasonably well-made and somewhat entertaining but ultimately forgettable. **106m/C; DVD, Blu-Ray.** Jonny Weston; Allen Evangelista; Sam Lerner; Virginia Gardner; Sofia Black-D'Elia; Amy Landecker; Gary Weeks; ***D:*** Dean Israelite; ***W:*** Jason Harry Pagan; Andrew Deutschman; ***C:*** Matthew Lloyd.

Project: Eliminator 1/2 **1991 (R)** A group of terrorists kidnap a designer of "smart" weapons, and it's up to a hard-hitting special forces unit to get him back. Filmed in New Mexico. **89m/C; VHS, DVD.** David Carradine; Frank Zagarino; Drew Snyder; Hilary English; Vivian Schilling; ***D:*** H. Kaye Dyal; ***W:*** H. Kaye Dyal; Morris Asgar; ***C:*** Gerry Lively; ***M:*** Jon McCallum.

Project: Kill! **1977** Head of a murder-for-hire squad suddenly disappears and his former assistant is hired to track him down dead or alive. **94m/C; VHS, DVD, Blu-Ray.** Leslie Nielsen; Gary Lockwood; Nancy Kwan; Vic Silayan; Vic Diaz; Donald G. Thompson; ***D:*** William Girdler; ***W:*** Donald G. Thompson; ***C:*** Frank Johnson; ***M:*** Robert O. Ragland.

Project Nim 1/2 **2011 (PG-13)** An attempt to further illuminate the link between man and simian results in deep tragedy in this devastating documentary. Using home movies and archival footage intercut with present-day interviews, Oscar-winning director Marsh chronicles what was essentially animal abuse under the guise of science as a project to raise a chimp named Nim as a human companion leads to inevitable disaster. Playing up the similarities between chimps and humans led Columbia University professor Herb Terrace to both international fame and obvious regret at how the 1970s experiment turned out. **93m/C; DVD, Blu-Ray.** *UK* Bob Angelini; Bern Cohen; Reagan Leonard; ***D:*** James Marsh; ***C:*** Michael Simmonds; ***M:*** Dickon Hinchliffe. Directors Guild '11: Documentary Director (Marsh).

Project Shadowchaser 3000 1/2 **1995 (R)** Deep space satellite station collides with a mining vessel carrying a killer android. The seven surviving crew are then hunted by the android as the ship's nuclear core is also threatening to explode. **99m/C; VHS, DVD.** Frank Zagarino; Sam Bottoms; Christopher Atkins; Musetta Vander; Christopher Neame; ***D:*** John Eyres; ***W:*** Nick Davis; ***M:*** Stephen (Steve) Edwards.

Project Solitude: Buried Alive **2009** Volunteers on a woodsy wilderness survival course find themselves stranded with no transportation out, no cell phone service, and a missing participant. Familiar happenings that have been done better in other flicks. **96m/C; DVD.** Eric Roberts; Michelle Belegrin; Vanessa Lee Evigan; David Frye; Stacy Stas; Jenna Zablocki; Danny Vasquez; ***D:*** Rustam Branaman; ***W:*** Rustam Branaman; ***C:*** John Disalvo; ***M:*** Randy Mitchell. **VIDEO**

Project Vampire 1/2 **1993** Vampire concocts a serum that will change humans into vampires within three days. His first guinea pig fights to stop the evil from succeeding. **90m/C; VHS, DVD.** Brian Knudson; Mary-Louise Gemmill; Christopher Cho; Myron Natwick; ***D:*** Peter Flynn.

Project Viper **2002 (R)** A genetic organism designed to terraform Mars goes berserk en route and the order goes out to destroy the second prototype still in a lab on Earth. Predictably it is stolen before this can happen and the race is on to get it back before it escapes, or the government nukes the area to put it down. **85m/C; DVD, Streaming.** Patrick Muldoon; Theresa Russell; Curtis Armstrong; John Beck; Tamara Davies; ***D:*** Jim Wynorski; ***W:*** Curtis Joseph; David Mason; ***C:*** Mario D'Ayala; ***M:*** Neal Acree. **CABLE**

Project X **1968** A spy frozen in cryogenic suspension is revived when it's learned he may contain information about an Asian superweapon that will be used to destroy the West. Unfortunately he's lost his memory, and his revivers must resort to virtual reality in an attempt to bring him back to normal. **97m/C; DVD, Blu-Ray, Streaming.** Christopher George; Greta Baldwin; Henry Jones; Monte Markham; Harold Gould; ***D:*** William Castle; ***W:*** Edmund Morris; ***C:*** Harold E. Stine; ***M:*** Van Cleave. **VIDEO**

Project X 1/2 **1987 (PG)** A bemused Air Force pilot is assigned to a special project involving chimpanzees. He must decide where his duty lies when he realizes the semi-intelligent chimps are slated to die. **107m/C; VHS, DVD.** Matthew Broderick; Helen Hunt; William Sadler; Johnny Rae McGhee; Jonathan Stark; Robin Gammell; Stephen Lang; Jean Smart; Dick Miller; ***D:*** Jonathan Kaplan; ***W:*** Stanley Weiser; Lawrence Lasker; ***C:*** Dean Cundey; ***M:*** James Horner.

Project X 1/2 **2011 (R)** Updating the low-brow beer-and-babes teen movie for the smartphone set, this raucous comedy follows the adventures of Tom (Mann), JD (Brown) and Costa (Cooper) as they throw a hormone and drug-fueled birthday party in order to climb the high school social ladder. Documenting the festivities is their friend Dax (Flame), who captures the debauchery on a shaky handheld camera. Costa advertises the party online and things quickly get out of the boys' control. They are forced to deal with the ramifications of a groin-targeting dwarf, a flamethrower and a trashed prized Mercedes. **87m/C; DVD, Blu-Ray.** Brendan Miller; Jonathan Daniel Brown; Alexis Knapp; Kirby Bliss Blanton; Thomas Mann; Martin Klebba; Oliver Cooper; Dax Flame; Miles Teller; ***D:*** Nima Nourizadeh; ***W:*** Matt Drake; Michael Bacall; ***C:*** Ken Seng.

The Projectionist **1971 (PG)** A must-see for movie buffs, Dangerfield made his screen debut in this story about a projectionist in a seedy movie house whose real-life existence begins to blur into the films he continuously watches. Made on a limited budget, this creative effort by Hurwitz was the first film to utilize the technique of superimposition. **84m/C; VHS, DVD.** Rodney Dangerfield; Chuck McCann; Ina Balin; Jara Kohout; Harry Hurwitz; Stephen Phillips; Clara Rosenthal; Jacquelyn Glenn; Robert Staats; ***D:*** Harry Hurwitz; ***W:*** Harry Hurwitz; ***C:*** Victor Petrashevich; ***M:*** Igo Kantor; Erma E. Levin.

Prom 1/2 **2011 (PG)** Bland Disney teen comedy tells the different stories of high school seniors as they prepare for that momentous rite of passage: Prom. Drama and cliches ensue as the teens re-evaluate their relationships and personal identities, the party is threatened by a fire, and various break-ups and crushes play out along the way. The characters are superficial, leading up to the underwhelming "night of all nights." Too goody-two-shoes for its own good, this is more suited for the tweener crowd. **109m/C; DVD, Blu-Ray, On Demand.** Aimee Teegarden; Thomas McDonell; Yin Chang; DeVaughn Nixon; Danielle Campbell; Christine Elise; Nicholas Braun; Faith Ford; Jere Burns; ***D:*** Joe Nussbaum; ***W:*** Katie Wech; ***C:*** Byron Shah; ***M:*** Deborah Lurie.

Prom Night **1980 (R)** A masked killer stalks four high school girls during their senior prom as revenge for a murder which occurred six years prior. Sequelled by "Hello Mary Lou: Prom Night 2," "Prom Night 3: The Last Kiss," and "Prom Night 4: Deliver Us from Evil." **91m/C; VHS, DVD, Blu-Ray.** *CA* Jamie Lee Curtis; Leslie Nielsen; Casey Stevens; Eddie Benton; Antoinette Bower; Michael Tough; Pita Oliver; David Mucci; Joy Thompson; Mary Beth Rubens; ***D:*** Paul Lynch; ***W:*** William Gray; ***C:*** Robert New; ***M:*** Paul Zaza.

Prom Night **2008 (PG-13)** Scream, run, die. Director McCormick's feature debut is a watered-down but slick sorta remake of the R-rated 1980 slasher with Snow a merely adequate substitute in the Jamie Lee Curtis scream queen role. Donna's (Snow) family was slain by obsessed teacher Richard Fenton (Schaech) and, three years later, he's escaped from prison to finish his work while Donna and her friends party in their hotel suite on prom night. **88m/C; DVD, Blu-Ray.** Brittany Snow; Johnathon Schaech; Idris Elba; Dana Davis; Jessica Stroup; ***D:*** Nelson McCormick; ***W:*** J.S. Cardone; ***C:*** Checco Varese; ***M:*** Paul Haslinger.

Prom Night 3: The Last Kiss **1989 (R)** The second sequel, in which the reappearing high school ghoul beguiles a lucky teenager. **97m/C; VHS, DVD.** Tim Conlon; Cynthia (Cyndy, Cindy) Preston; Courtney Taylor; David Stratton; Dylan Neal; Jeremy Ratchford; ***D:*** Ron Oliver; Peter Simpson; ***W:*** Ron Oliver; ***C:*** Rhett Morita.

Prom Night 4: Deliver Us from Evil **1991 (R)** Yet another gory entry in the Prom series (one would hope it will be the last). Another group of naive teens decide that they can have more fun at a private party than at the prom. They host the party in a summer home that was once a monastery, but the festive affair soon turns into a night of terror when an uninvited guest crashes the party. For true fans of slasher flicks. **95m/C; VHS, DVD.** *CA* Nicole de Boer; Alden Kane; Joy Tanner; Alle Ghadban; James Carver; ***D:*** Clay Borris; ***W:*** Richard Beattie.

Prom Queen **2004** Based on the actual 2002 Canadian Supreme Court case of Ontario gay teen Marc Hall (Ashmore). An out blue-haired rebel in a small town who attends Catholic school, Marc is a popular student who only wants to take his boyfriend Jason (Fyfe) to the senior prom. When he's denied by the homophobic school board, Marc and his lawyer (Thompson) decide to sue the Catholic Church for discrimination. **92m/C; DVD.** *CA* Dave Foley; Tamara Hope; Fiona Reid; Aaron Ashmore; Scott Thompson; Mak Fyfe; Marie Tifo; Peter Zabriskie; Victoria Adilman; ***D:*** John L'Ecuyer; ***W:*** Kent Staines; ***C:*** Glenn Warner; ***M:*** Gary Koftinoff. **TV**

Prom Wars 1/2 **2008 (R)** Teen comedy about dopey boys and smarter girls. Two all-boys' private schools (one for nerds, the other for jocks) are in a competition to get prom dates with the beauties at an exclusive all-girls' school. Since the girls know they have the upper-hand, they design a series of challenges and to the winning school go the dates. **89m/C; DVD.** *CA* Rachelle Lefevre; Alia Shawkat; Raviv (Ricky) Ullman; Kevin Coughlin; Chad Connell; Nicholas Wright; Minal Rath; David Eberts; ***D:*** Kenneth Price; ***W:*** William Haines; ***C:*** Michael Martin; ***M:*** Jamel Sassi.

Promare 1/2 *Promare: Puromea* **2019 (PG-13)** On a futuristic chaotic Earth, people suffering from a mutation get extremely angry then spontaneously combust, shoot a flame, and burn what is nearby. Three decades later, the mutants, dubbed Burnishers, have been tamed. The Burning Rescue—groups of firefighting children led by charismatic Galo Thymos (Matsuyama)—plays a significant role in this with the blessing of the governor. When the Burning Rescue captures a Burnisher leader Lio Fotia (Saotome), he makes them question if they are fighting for the right side. The animated feature has memorable design and animation, but is marred by constant battle scenes and cheesy omnipresent music. Japanese with subtitles. **111m/C; DVD.** John Bentley; Steve Blum; Johnny Yong Bosch; Melissa Fahn; Crispin Freeman; ***D:*** Hiroyuki Imaishi; ***W:*** Kazuki Nakashima; Michael Schneider; ***C:*** Shinsuke Ikeda; ***M:*** Hiroyuki Sawano.

Prometheus 1/2 **2012 (R)** Visually elaborate but narratively weak sci-fi from director Scott about the search for the origins of our species. In 2093, skeptic Charlie Holway (Marshall-Green) and believer Elizabeth Shaw (Rapace) are aboard the Prometheus on a deep-space mission. Also aboard is ship's commander Janek (Elba), corporate pain Vickers (Theron), and the film's best character, android David (Fassbender), who takes the lead in the film "Lawrence of Arabia" as his ideal for human behavior. Landing on an alien planet then provides stock dangers when they meet the inhabitants, who aren't happy with mankind. **124m/C; DVD, Blu-Ray.** Noomi Rapace; Michael Fassbender; Guy Pearce; Idris Elba; Logan Marshall-Green; Charlize Theron; Rafe Spall; ***D:*** Ridley Scott; ***W:*** Damon Lindelof; Jon Spaihts; ***C:*** Dariusz Wolski; ***M:*** Marc Streitenfeld.

The Promise 1/2 *Face of a Stranger* **1979 (PG)** Weepie outdated story about star-crossed lovers Michael (Collins) and Nancy (Quinlan). A car accident leaves Michael comatose and Nancy badly disfigured. Michael's mother (Straight), who loathes Nancy, sees her chance to finally break them up. She offers to pay for Nancy's plastic surgery if she'll leave Michael forever, then Mom tells her son his girlfriend's dead. A year later Nancy, with her new face and new identity, and Michael meet. From the novel by Danielle Steele. **97m/C; VHS, DVD.** Stephen Collins; Kathleen Quinlan; Beatrice Straight; Laurence Luckinbill; William Prince; Michael O'Hare; ***D:*** Gilbert Cates; ***W:*** Garry Michael White; ***M:*** David Shire.

Promise **1986** Keep the tissues handy for this Hallmark Hall of Fame presentation that has particularly strong performances from Garner and Woods. When his mother dies, middle-aged Bob Buehler (Garner) must make good on his promise to take custody of his schizophrenic younger brother DJ (Woods). The two are long-estranged since Bob couldn't cope with his sibling but they now must find a way to reunite. **97m/C; DVD.** James Garner; James Woods; Piper Laurie; Alan Rosenberg; Peter Michael Goetz; ***D:*** Glenn Jordan; ***W:*** Richard Friedenberg; ***C:*** Gayne Rescher; ***M:*** David Shire. **TV**

The Promise 1/2 *Wu Ji; Master of the Crimson Armor* **2005 (PG-13)** Complicated and stylized martial arts fantasy in which a young orphan is offered a life of riches by a goddess (Hong) with the caveat that she will lose every man she loves. Qingcheng (Cheung) lives with her bargain until she falls for General Guangming (Sanada), he of the crimson armor. Except it was his slave, Kunlun (Dong-Gun), who was wearing the armor and actually rescued the princess. Never really makes any sense (at least to Westerners). Mandarin with subtitles; also released at 121 minutes. **103m/C; DVD.** *CH US* Hiroyuki (Henry) Sanada; Dong-gun Jang; Cecilia Cheung; Nicholas Tse; Liu Yeh; Chen Hong; Qian Bo; Yu Xiaowei; Cheng Qian; ***D:*** Chen Kaige; Zhang Tan; ***W:*** Chen Kaige; ***C:*** Peter Pau; ***M:*** Klaus Badelt.

A Promise **2013** Bland period piece set in pre-WWI Germany, with wealthy factory owner Herr Hoffmeister (Rickman) hiring a young male secretary, Friedrich (Madden) as his right-hand man. Without fail, the new employee catches the eye of Hoffmeister's young wife, Lotte (Hall) and the two try to resist their mutual attraction. Friedrich's job requires him to move around, and Lotte is married. From here, the melodrama oozes off the screen. The actors look right, sound right, but don't feel right. For all the romantic trappings and swooning and pretty scenery, there's very little passion, in front of, or behind the camera. **94m/C; On Demand.** *BE FR* Alan Rickman; Rebecca Hall; Richard Madden; ***D:*** Patrice Leconte; ***W:*** Patrice Leconte; Jerome Tonnere; ***C:*** Eduardo Serra; ***M:*** Gabriel Yared.

The Promise 1/2 **2017 (PG-13)** In 1914, Michael (Isaac) is an Armenian medical student in Constantinople. He meets Ana (LeBon), an Armenian artist who has lived in Paris, and her boyfriend Chris (Bale), an American photojournalist covering the war. Ana and Michael's shared heritage sparks romance, and the three must deal with that and try to survive together as the situation of the Armenian people in Turkey deteriorates into chaos. Terry George's flawed epic can't quite deliver on the long untold story of the Armenian genocide in Turkey during WWI. While it features excellent performances by the leads, beautiful, sweeping cinematography, and an epic story with a heartbreaking love triangle at its center, it doesn't quite add up to the sum of its parts. **133m/C; DVD.** Oscar Isaac; Charlotte Le Bon; Christian Bale; Daniel Gimenez Cacho; Shohreh Aghdashloo; ***D:*** Terry George; ***W:*** Terry George; Robin Swicord; ***C:*** Javier Aguirresarobe; ***M:*** Gabriel Yared.

Promised Land *Young Hearts* **1988 (R)** Two high school friends from the rural northwestern U.S. come together several years after graduation under tragic circumstances. Writer Hoffman's semi-autobiographical, disillusioned look at the American Dream was re-discovered by movie goers due to its excellent dramatic performances, notable also as the first film produced by Robert Redford's Sundance Institute. **110m/C; VHS, DVD.** Kiefer Sutherland; Meg Ryan; Tracy Pollan; Jason Gedrick; Googy Gress; Deborah Richter; Sandra Seacat; Jay Underwood; Oscar Rowland; ***D:*** Michael Hoffman; ***W:*** Michael Hoffman; ***M:*** James Newton Howard.

Promised Land **2012 (R)** Van Sant delivers an old-fashioned pic with an attractive, interesting cast that misses its chance to be something more memorable than its bare-bones plot and relative caricatures allows. Steve Butler (Damon) comes to a small town to try and convince its residents that the natural gas company he works for isn't going to ruin their way of life with fracking and, of course, he gets drawn in by the locals, including the lovely Alice (DeWitt). Damon's a solid lead and most films would be improved with McDormand and Holbrook in their supporting casts but Van Sant's drama is surprisingly predictable and inert. **106m/C; DVD, Blu-Ray.** Matt Damon; Terry Kinney; Joe Coyle; Hal Holbrook; Frances McDormand; John Krasinski; ***D:*** Gus Van Sant; ***W:*** Matt Damon; John Krasinski; Dave Eggers; ***C:*** Linus Sandgren; ***M:*** Danny Elfman.

Promises in the Dark 1/2 **1979 (PG)** Drama focusing on the complex relationship between a woman doctor and her 17-year-old female patient who is terminally ill with cancer. Hellman's directorial debut. **118m/C; VHS, DVD.** Marsha Mason; Ned Beatty; Kathleen Beller; Susan Clark; Paul Clemens; Donald Moffat; Michael Brandon; ***D:*** Jerome Hellman.

Promises! Promises! 1/2 *Promise Her Anything* **1963** Having difficulty getting pregnant, a woman goes on a cruise with her husband. While on board, they meet another couple, all get drunk, and change partners. Of course, both women find themselves pregnant, leaving the paternity in doubt. Famous primarily as the movie Mansfield told "Playboy" magazine she appeared "completely nude" in. **90m/B; VHS, DVD.** Jayne Mansfield; Marie McDonald; Tommy Noonan; Fritz Feld; Claude Stroud; Mickey Hargitay; Marjorie Bennett; Vic Lundin; ***D:*** King Donovan; ***W:*** Tommy Noonan; William Welch; ***C:*** Joseph Biroc.

Promises to Keep 1/2 **1985** Three generations of the Mitchum clan star in this CBS TV drama. Wyoming ranch foreman Jack Palmer learns he has a life-threatening illness. Before he begins treatment, he visits the family he deserted 30 years before. While his ex-wife Sally is willing to forgive and his grandson Johnny is happy to meet the old man, Jack's son Tom remains bitter. **93m/C; DVD.** Robert Mitchum; Chris Mitchum; Bentley Mitchum; Claire Bloom; Tess Harper; Merritt Butrick; ***D:*** Noel Black; ***W:*** Phil Penningroth; ***C:*** Dennis Dalzell; ***M:*** Michel Legrand. **TV**

The Promoter *The Card* **1952** Horatio Alger comedy stars Guinness as an impoverished student who gives himself a surreptitious leg up in life by altering his school entrance exam scores. Outstanding performances enliven this subtle British comedy of morals. Sold as part of a collection only. **87m/B; VHS, DVD.** *GB* Alec Guinness; Glynis Johns; Petula Clark; Valerie Hobson; Michael Hordern; ***D:*** Ronald Neame; ***W:*** Eric Ambler.

The Promotion **2008 (R)** Murky comedy focusing on two down-and-out supermarket employees desperate to win the managerial spot at a new store. Doug (Scott) is convinced he'll get the promotion and invests all his money in a non-refundable deposit on a new house, while Richard (Reilly), a recovering addict, fights for the position to prove to his wife he's a trustworthy husband and father. A human story at its core, but only mildly amusing as a comedy. Reilly and Scott are good, but never seem to find their groove. Directorial debut for writer Conrad, who penned "The Pursuit of Happyness." **85m/C; DVD, Streaming.** Seann William Scott; John C. Reilly; Jenna Fischer; Lili Taylor; Fred Armisen; Gil Bellows; Bobby Cannavale; Rick Gonzalez; Chris Conrad; ***D:*** Steve Conrad; ***W:*** Steve Conrad; ***C:*** Lawrence Sher; ***M:*** Alex Wurman.

Proof **1991 (R)** Directorial debut of Moorhouse tells a tale of manipulation, friendship, and obsessive love between a blind photographer, his housekeeper, and the young man he befriends. Martin, mistrustful of the world around him, takes photographs as "proof" of the reality of his life. A chance meeting with Andy provides Martin with his "eyes" and the opportunity to expand his world and emotions—something his housekeeper, Celia, would be only too happy to help him with. Unhealthy triangle leads all three to a re-evaluation of their lives. Propelled by terrific performances and enough humor to balance its emotional content. **90m/C; VHS, DVD.** *AU* Hugo Weaving; Genevieve Picot; Russell Crowe; Heather Mitchell; Jeffrey Walker; Frank Gallacher; ***D:*** Jocelyn Moorhouse; ***W:*** Jocelyn Moorhouse. Australian Film Inst. '91: Actor (Weaving), Director (Moorhouse), Film, Film Editing, Screenplay, Support. Actor (Crowe).

Proof 1/2 **2005 (PG-13)** Film adaptation of David Auburn's award-winning Broadway play makes the most of its four-character construct. Catherine (Paltrow), the gifted daughter of a once-brilliant mathematician (Hopkins), who in the final years of his life suffered with dementia, sits at the center of the film. A brainy introvert by nature, Catherine is forced in the wake of her father's death to seek redeeming personal value as both an academic and a daughter, while contemplating her own fragile grip on sanity. **99m/C; DVD, Blu-Ray.** Gwyneth Paltrow; Anthony Hopkins; Jake Gyllenhaal; Hope Davis; Roshan Seth; Gary Houston; ***D:*** John Madden; ***W:*** David Auburn; ***C:*** Alwin Kuchler; ***M:*** Stephen Warbeck.

Proof of Lies 1/2 **2006** Research scientist Christine Hartley's (Detmer) latest breakthrough points to a genetic cause for addictive behavior. It could make her rich and famous but her greedy husband Chuck (Lemke) may have other plans and he isn't the only one involved. **90m/C; DVD.** Amanda Detmer; Anthony Lemke; Jonathan Scarfe; Serge Houde; Cindy Sampson; ***D:*** Peter Svatek; ***W:*** Rene Baker; ***C:*** Stephen Reizes; ***M:*** James Gelford. **CABLE**

Proof of Life 1/2 **2000 (R)** When Alicia's (Ryan) engineer husband (Morse) is kidnapped by anti-government guerrillas in South America, she hires professional negotiator Terry Thorne (Crowe) to get him back. Complications arise when Terry falls for the wife. Complications also arose when Ryan fell for Crowe and her marriage to Dennis Quaid fell apart and then Crowe and Ryan subsequently broke up just before the pic's release and wouldn't do publicity. Didn't matter, the movie's a lot better when dealing with the husband's predicament and the rescue operations than when exploring Ryan's angst and the budding romance. **135m/C; VHS, DVD.** Russell Crowe; Meg Ryan; David Morse; David Caruso; Margo Martindale; Pamela Reed; Anthony Heald; Stanley Anderson; Gottfried John; Alun Armstrong; Michael Kitchen; ***D:*** Taylor Hackford; ***W:*** Tony Gilroy; ***C:*** Slawomir Idziak; ***M:*** Danny Elfman.

Prophecy 1/2 **1979 (PG)** A doctor and his wife travel to Maine to research the effects of pollution caused by the lumber industry. They encounter several terrifying freaks of nature and a series of bizarre human deaths. Laughable horror film. **102m/C; VHS, DVD, Blu-Ray.** Talia Shire; Robert Foxworth; Armand Assante; Victoria Racimo; Richard Dysart; George Clutesi; ***D:*** John Frankenheimer; ***W:*** David Seltzer; ***C:*** Harry Stradling, Jr.

The Prophecy 1/2 **1995 (R)** Modern variation of "Paradise Lost" carries a heavy load including possession, Native American mythology, and Walken as the archangel Gabriel. Not surprisingly, it stumbles under the weight. Gabriel is at odds with good angel Simon (Stolz) over the souls of humans, a battle that has its final showdown in a small Arizona community and crosses the paths of homicide detective Thomas Dagget (Koteas) and school teacher Katherine (Madsen). Successfully mixes humor and horror, but biblical jargon can lose horror fans just looking for a cheap thrill. Directorial debut of screenwriter Widen. **97m/C; VHS, DVD, Blu-Ray.** Christopher Walken; Eric Stoltz; Elias Koteas; Virginia Madsen; Amanda Plummer; Viggo Mortensen; ***D:*** Gregory Widen; ***W:*** Gregory Widen; ***C:*** Bruce Douglas Johnson; Richard Clabaugh; ***M:*** David Williams.

The Prophecy 2: Ashtown 1/2 *The Prophecy II: God's War* **1997 (R)** It's post-apocalyptic L.A. and power-hungry fallen angel Gabriel (Walken) returns from hell to stop the creation of a half-human/half-angelic child who's prophesized as the new savior of mankind. Angel Danyael (Wong) is intended as the dad while nurse Valerie (Beals) is the woman chosen as the mother. The good guys get some help from angel Michael (Roberts). Lots of action and good special effects, though viewers who haven't seen the first film may be confused. **83m/C; VHS, DVD, Blu-Ray.** Christopher Walken; Russell Wong; Eric Roberts; Jennifer Beals; Bruce Abbott; Brittany Murphy; Steve Hytner; Glenn Danzig; ***D:*** Greg Spence; ***W:*** Greg Spence; Matt Greenberg; ***C:*** Richard Clabaugh; ***M:*** David Williams. **VIDEO**

The Prophecy 3: The Ascent **1999 (R)** Half-human/half-angel Danyael (Buzzotta) has grown up to be an anti-religious street preacher and is out to destroy new angel, Piriel (Cleverdon). This doesn't sit well with angel Zophael (Spano) who decides to stop him. Walken seems to be having the most fun as he once again appears as Gabriel, who's become content in his mortal guise and with human pleasure. **83m/C; VHS, DVD, Blu-Ray.** Christopher Walken; Vincent Spano; Brad Dourif; Dave Buzzotta; Steve Hytner; Scott Cleverdon; Kayren Ann Butler; ***D:*** Patrick Lussier; ***W:*** Joel Soisson; Carl DuPre; ***C:*** Nathan Hope. **VIDEO**

A Prophet *Un Prophete* **2009 (R)** Audiard's powerful coming-of-age prison drama finds illiterate, 19-year-old French-

Arab Malik (Rahim) sentenced to six years in prison, which is where he truly gets his education in life in a continual effort to survive. Malik is forced by Cesar Luciani (Arestrup), the Corsican crime boss who runs one of the two prison gangs, to kill a fellow Arab. He does so but is still regarded as an outsider by both the Corsicans and the prison's Muslim bloc. However, Malik is nothing if not a quick study and gradually gains some power of his own as the time passes. French, Arabic, and Corsican with subtitles. **155m/C; DVD, Blu-Ray, On Demand.** *FR IT* Niels Arestrup; Tahar Rahim; Adel Bencherif; Gilles Cohen; Antoine Basler; Reda Kateb; Hichem Yacoubi; Jean-Philippe Ricci; Pierre Leccia; ***D:*** Jacques Audiard; ***W:*** Jacques Audiard; Thomas Bidegain; ***C:*** Stephane Fontaine; ***M:*** Alexandre Desplot. British Acad. '09: Foreign Film.

The Prophet's Game **1999 (R)** Retired Seattle detective Vincent Swan (Hopper) gets a message from the Prophet, a serial killer that Swan supposedly killed years before. Then new victims turn up in L.A., killed in the Prophet's distinctive manner. So Swan heads south to help with the investigation and figure out is he dealing with a copycat—or did he just kill the wrong man? **107m/C; VHS, DVD.** Dennis Hopper; Geoffrey Lewis; Stephanie Zimbalist; Joe Penny; Greg Lauren; Shannon Whirry; Michael Dorn; Don Swayze; Robert Ginty; Sondra Locke; ***D:*** David Worth; ***W:*** Carol Chrest; ***C:*** David Worth. **VIDEO**

The Proposal 1/2 **2000 (R)** Moran is an undercover cop who's forced to take on partner Esposito, who has no such experience, because he needs someone to pose as his wife in order to trap crime boss Lang. Only Esposito and Lang are starting to get a little too friendly, so Moran wonders how much she can be trusted. **90m/C; VHS, DVD.** Nick Moran; Jennifer Esposito; Stephen Lang; William B. Davis; ***D:*** Richard Gale; ***W:*** Maurice Hurley; ***C:*** Curtis Petersen; ***M:*** Joseph Conlan.

The Proposal 1/2 **2009 (PG-13)** Tyrannical New York book editor Margaret Tate (Bullock) has overstayed her visa and is going to be deported. She proposes a green card marriage to her put-upon younger assistant Andrew Paxton (Reynolds) and he agrees, although immigration official Gilbertson (O'Hare) is suspicious. To make things look good, Andrew takes Margaret to meet his wealthy family in Sitka, Alaska so they can celebrate his wacky grandma Annie's (White) 90th birthday. Familiar rom-com situations are given a light touch by director Fletcher through likeable leads and pro supporting players. **107m/C; DVD, Blu-Ray.** Sandra Bullock; Ryan Reynolds; Craig T. Nelson; Mary Steenburgen; Betty White; Denis O'Hare; Malin Akerman; Osmar Nunez; Michael Nouri; Aasif Mandvi; ***D:*** Anne Fletcher; ***W:*** Peter Chiarelli; ***C:*** Oliver Stapleton; ***M:*** Aaron Zigman.

The Proposition 1/2 **1996 (R)** Unless widow Catherine Morgan (Russell) can find the money to pay her late husband's gambling debts, she and her two daughters will be evicted from their Welsh farm. She refuses to take the easy way and marry local sheriff Huw (Lynch), instead making a bargain with his rakish, drunken bastard brother Rhys (Bergin) to drive her cattle to Gloucester market. Huw takes exception to this plan and tries every dirty trick he can to thwart them and naturally, Catherine and Rhys become more than antagonistic allies along the rough journey. **99m/C; VHS, DVD.** Theresa Russell; Patrick Bergin; Richard Lynch; Richard Harrington; Jennifer Vaughan; Ifan Huw Dafydd; Nick McGaughey; Owen Garmon; ***D:*** Strathford Hamilton; ***W:*** Paul Matthews; ***C:*** David Lewis; ***M:*** Ben Heneghan; Ian Lawson.

The Proposition *Tempting Fate; Shakespeare's Sister* **1997 (R)** Convoluted and clunky story centering on wealthy-but-sterile Boston industrialist Hurt and his feminist writer wife Stowe, who hire a surrogate (Harris) to get Stowe pregnant. But faltering priest Branagh, whom the couple consult, has some concerns. After the surrogate is murdered, the melodrama starts to fly, complete with dirty little secrets and earth-shaking revelations dropped with the sublety usually reserved for an anvil on Wile E. Coyote. Hurt and Stowe give their characters a little fire, but everybody else seems to be wandering around on their own little acting planet. **115m/C; VHS, DVD.** Kenneth Branagh; William Hurt; Madeleine Stowe; Blythe Danner; Neil Patrick Harris; Robert Loggia; Josef Sommer; David Byrd; Pamela Hart; ***D:*** Leslie Linka Glatter; ***W:*** Rick Ramage; ***C:*** Peter Sova; ***M:*** Stephen Endelman.

The Proposition **2005 (R)** Brutal Aussie western set in the outback in the 1880s. Capt. Stanley (Winstone) is obsessed with bringing law to his patch of dirt, which means getting rid of the Burns brothers and their gang. He gets a break when he captures Charlie Burns (Pearce) and his younger brother, Mikey (Wilson). Stanley offers Charlie a devil's bargain—he will spare both brothers if Charlie will track and kill vicious older brother Arthur (a poetically psychotic Huston). Charlie has no choice but to agree but all that can be expected is more violence, blood, and death. **104m/C; DVD, Blu-Ray.** *AU GB* Guy Pearce; Ray Winstone; Emily Watson; Danny Huston; John Hurt; David Wenham; Noah Taylor; David Gulpilil; Leah Purcell; Tommy (Tom E.) Lewis; ***D:*** John Hillcoat; ***W:*** Nick Cave; ***C:*** Benoit Delhomme; ***M:*** Warren Ellis.

Pros & Cons **1999 (R)** Opposites help each other out as new cellmates Davidson and Miller (both doing time for crimes they didn't commit) bumble their way into the good graces of convict kingpin Lindo. **103m/C; VHS, DVD.** Larry Miller; Tommy Davidson; Delroy Lindo; ***D:*** Boris Damast; ***W:*** Larry Miller; ***C:*** Jonathan Brown; ***M:*** Michel Colombier.

Pros and Ex-cons 1/2 *Fink!* **2005 (R)** Willing (Bastoni) and Able (Worthigton) are two ex-cons who don't exactly lives up to their names. They become hitmen for crime boss Fink (Wheeler) but are told they killed the wrong person and must correct their mistake. There's also a bunch of confusing subplots in this Aussie crime comedy that only add to its mediocrity. **92m/C; DVD.** *AU* Steve Bastoni; David Wheeler; Sam Worthington; John Boxer; ***D:*** Tim Boyle; ***W:*** Tim Boyle; ***C:*** Casimir Dickson; ***M:*** Michael Lira.

Prosecuting Casey Anthony **2013** Lifetime true crime pic is a competent recreation of the lurid trial of Florida mom Casey Anthony who was accused of murdering her young daughter Caylee. Prosecuting attorneys Jeff Ashton and Linda Burdick feel the evidence and Anthony's less-experienced lawyer will work to their advantage but changing defense strategy confuses the situation. The pic also relies on the constant media coverage of the case to frame the story, which is based on Ashton's book. **90m/C; DVD.** Rob Lowe; Elizabeth Mitchell; Virginia Welch; Oscar Nunez; Marisa Ramirez; Kevin Dunn; ***D:*** Peter Werner; ***W:*** Alison Cross; ***C:*** James Chressanthis; ***M:*** Richard Marvin. **CABLE**

Prospero's Books **1991 (R)** Greenaway's free-ranging adaptation of Shakespeare's "The Tempest" has all his usual hallmarks of the bizarre. Gielgud is the aged Propsero, exiled to a magical island with his innocent daughter, Miranda, and 24 beloved books containing the magician's recipe for life, each of which becomes a separate chapter in the film. Greenaway mixes film and high-definition video to create, with cinematographer Sacha Vierny, dazzling visuals that threaten to overwhelm but don't quite, thanks to both Greenaway's skill and the astonishing performance of the then 87-year-old Gielgud. **129m/C; VHS, DVD.** John Gielgud; Michel Blanc; Erland Josephson; Isabelle Pasco; Tom Bell; Kenneth Cranham; Michael Clark; Mark Rylance; ***D:*** Peter Greenaway; ***W:*** Peter Greenaway; ***C:*** Sacha Vierny; ***M:*** Michael Nyman.

Protecting the King **2007** When he was four, David Stanley's mother married widower Vernon Presley and the boy became Elvis's (Dobson) stepbrother. In 1972, David (Barr) began working as the singer's bodyguard until Presley's death five years later. In this biographical take, David witnesses the King's ever-increasing drug use and watches hopelessly as the singer's life spirals downward. **90m/C; DVD.** Peter Dobson; John Bennett Perry; Tom Sizemore; Brian Krause; Matt Barr; Max Perlich; Mark Rolston; Dey Young; ***D:*** David Edward Stanley; ***W:*** David Edward Stanley; ***C:*** Philip Lee; ***M:*** Joe Cruz.

Protection 1/2 **2001 (R)** Mobster Sal (Baldwin) and his family are relocated into the witness protection program and Sal gets a job with real estate broker Ted (Gallagher), who's putting together a low-income housing project. But Sal can't resist using his past and brings in local crime boss Lujack (Tager) to finance the deal. **97m/C; VHS, DVD.** Stephen Baldwin; Peter Gallagher; Katie Griffin; Deborah Odell; Vlasta Vrana; Aron Tager; ***D:*** John Flynn; ***W:*** Jack Kelly; ***C:*** Marc Charlebois; ***M:*** Richard (Rick) Marvin. **VIDEO**

Protector **1985 (R)** A semi-martial arts cops 'n' robbers epic about the cracking of a Hong Kong-New York heroin route. **94m/C; VHS, DVD, Blu-Ray.** Jackie Chan; Danny Aiello; ***D:*** James Glickenhaus.

Protector *Valentine's Day* **1997 (R)** Undercover cop Jack Valentine (Van Peebles) is supposed to be protecting a witness, who winds up being murdered. The cop is given 10 days to solve the crime or lose his badge. **97m/C; VHS, DVD.** Mario Van Peebles; Randy Quaid; Rae Dawn Chong; Ben Gazzara; ***D:*** Duane Clark. **VIDEO**

Proteus **1995 (R)** Survivors of a boat wreck wash up on an off-shore oil rig that's actually a secret lab financed by loony millionaire Brinkstone (Bradley), who's seeking immortality. His DNA experiments have led to the creation of a disgusting parasite that travels from body to body. Naturally, the boat survivors also seek to survive this latest health threat. Based on the novel "Slimer" by Harry Adam Knight. **97m/C; VHS, Streaming.** *GB* Doug Bradley; Craig Fairbrass; Toni Barry; ***D:*** Bob Keen.

Protocol **1984 (PG)** A series of comic accidents lead a Washington cocktail waitress into the U.S. State Department's employ as a protocol official. Once there she is used as a pawn to make an arms deal with a Middle Eastern country. Typical Hawn comedy with an enjoyable ending. **100m/C; VHS, DVD.** Goldie Hawn; Chris Sarandon; Andre Gregory; Cliff DeYoung; Ed Begley, Jr.; Gail Strickland; Richard Romanus; Keith Szarabajka; James Staley; Kenneth Mars; Kenneth McMillan; Archie Hahn; Amanda Bearse; ***D:*** Herbert Ross; ***W:*** Charles Shyer; Buck Henry; Nancy Meyers; Harvey Miller; ***C:*** William A. Fraker; ***M:*** Basil Poledouris.

Prototype **1983** TV revision of the Frankenstein legend has award-winning scientist Plummer as the creator of the first android. Fearful of the use the military branch of government has in mind for his creation, he attempts to steal back his discovery, in this suspenseful adventure. **100m/C; VHS, DVD.** Christopher Plummer; David Morse; Frances Sternhagen; James Sutorius; ***D:*** David Greene; ***M:*** Billy Goldenberg. **TV**

The Proud and Profane *The Proud and the Profane* **1956** Genteel widow Lee Ashley (Kerr) comes to the South Pacific as part of a Red Cross group to get information on her husband's death. She meets, and is seduced by, tough Marine Colin Black (Holden). Lee gets pregnant and discovers the louse is married. More trauma follows before things work out in this wartime weepie. **111m/B; Streaming.** Deborah Kerr; William Holden; Thelma Ritter; Dewey Martin; William Redfield; Marion Ross; ***D:*** George Seaton; ***W:*** George Seaton; ***C:*** John F. Warren; ***M:*** Victor Young.

The Proud and the Damned *Proud, Damned, and Dead* **1972 (PG)** Five Civil-War-veteran mercenaries wander into a Latin American war and get manipulated by both sides. **95m/C; VHS, DVD.** Chuck Connors; Aron Kincaid; Cesar Romero; ***D:*** Ferde Grofe, Jr.

The Proud Family Movie **2005 (G)** The Disney Channel's original television series featuring an animated African American family gets a feature-length storyline. Teenager Penny Proud's parents treat her like a kid, banning her from dancing in a hip-hop half time show and dragging her off to a tropical island for a family vacation. The family finds themselves in trouble when their "vacation" turns out to be an excuse for the evil Dr. Carver to get his hands on dad's hot sauce recipe. Hijinks abound as Penny saves the recipe--and the day. Short enough to sit through for most pre-teens. **91m/C; VHS, DVD.** ***V:*** Kyla Pratt; Tommy Davidson; Paula Jai Parker; Soleil Moon Frye; Omari (Omarion) Grandberry; Arsenio Hall; Orlando Brown; Jo Maria Payton; ***D:*** Bruce Smith; ***W:*** Calvin Brown, Jr.; ***M:*** Elik Alvarez. **CABLE**

Proud Mary 1/2 **2018 (R)** An action-drama about the Boston underworld centered on a hitwoman, Mary (Henson). When Mary was a lost teenager, she was rescued by crime boss Benny (Glover) and trained as an assassin. Decades later, she has grown weary of the life, and her perspective is further changed when she takes 13-year-old Danny (Winston) into her protection. Danny works for a local criminal but has crossed the wrong people. Despite the routine action sequences and B-movie script, Henson's soulful, swaggering performance gives the film depth and passion. **89m/C; DVD, Blu-Ray.** Taraji P. Henson; Billy Brown; Jahi Di'Allo Winston; Neal McDonough; Margaret Avery; ***D:*** Babak Najafi; Steve Antin; ***W:*** John Stuart Newman; Christian Swegal; ***C:*** Dan Laustsen; ***M:*** Fil Eisler.

Proud Men **1987** A cattle rancher and his expatriate son are separated by bitterness toward each other. Good acting from Heston and Strauss, and good action sequences, but ordinary script. **95m/C; VHS, DVD.** Charlton Heston; Peter Strauss; Nan Martin; Alan Autry; Belinda Balaski; Red West; ***D:*** William A. Graham.

Proud Rebel **1958** A character study of a stubborn widower who searches for a doctor to aid him in dealing with the problems of his mute son, and of the woman who helps to tame the boy. Ladd's real-life son makes his acting debut. **99m/C; VHS, DVD.** Alan Ladd; Olivia de Havilland; Dean Jagger; Harry Dean Stanton; ***D:*** Michael Curtiz; ***W:*** Lillie Hayward; Joseph Petracca; ***C:*** Ted D. McCord; ***M:*** Jerome Moross.

Provocateur *Agent Provocateur* **1996 (R)** Story revolves around the 1994 power struggle in North Korea. Spy Sook Hee (March), with close ties to dictator Kim Il Sung, takes a job as a nanny in South Korea in order to get access to sensitive info from her boss, a U.S. colonel. But her loyalties are torn when she befriends her young charge and then falls in love with the colonel's teenaged son Chris (Brancato). When her true identity is revealed, there's trouble for all. **104m/C; VHS, Streaming.** Jane March; Nick Mancuso; Lillo Brancato; Cary-Hiroyuki Tagawa; ***D:*** Jim Donovan.

Prowl **2010 (R)** Amber persuades her friends to join her on a road trip to Chicago, but when their car breaks down they accept a ride from trucker Bernard. He locks them in the back and delivers them to an abandoned slaughterhouse populated by vampires. There Amber discovers her inner viciousness in a throwdown with vamp leader Veronica. **85m/C; DVD.** Courtney Hope; Saxon Trainor; Bruce Payne; Joshua Bowman; Ruta Gedmintas; Perdita Weeks; Jamie Blackley; ***D:*** Patrick Syversen; ***W:*** Tim Tori; ***C:*** Havard Andre Byrkjeland; ***M:*** Theo Green.

The Prowler **1951** Taut film noir. Cynical, ambitious cop Webb Garwood (Heflin) is always looking for that lucky break. He responds to a prowler complaint at the L.A. home of wealthy, lonely, married Susan (Keyes) and soon they are hot-and-heavy. Not about to let his chance slip away when Susan gets the guilts, an obsessed Webb goes to deadly lengths to get what he wants. **92m/B; DVD, Blu-Ray.** Van Heflin; Evelyn Keyes; Emerson Treacy; John Maxwell; Katherine Warren; Sherry Hall; Madge Blake; Wheaton Chambers; ***D:*** Joseph Losey; ***W:*** Dalton Trumbo; Hugo Butler; ***C:*** Arthur C. Miller; ***M:*** Lyn Murray.

The Prowler *Rosemary's Killer* **1981 (R)** A soldier returns from duty during WWII, only to find his girl in bed with another guy. He kills them, and for unclear reasons, returns to the same town 35 years later to kill more people. An effects-fest for Tom Savini. **87m/C; VHS, DVD, Blu-Ray.** Vicky Dawson; Christopher Goutman; Cindy Weintraub; Farley Granger; John Seitz; Lawrence Tierney; ***D:*** Joseph Zito; ***W:*** Neal Barbera; ***M:*** Richard Einhorn.

Proximity 1/2 **2000 (R)** William Conroy (Lowe) gets prison time for vehicular manslaughter and learns that the big house is hazardous to his health. Seems the inmates have a bad habit of getting killed and Conroy is next when he learns too much about what's going on. Conroy manages to escape and seeks help to expose the whole sleazy situation. Unfortunately, the movie is really dopey and dull. **86m/C; VHS, DVD.** Rob Lowe; James Coburn; Kelly Rowan; Sonya A. Avakian; ***D:*** Scott Ziehl; ***W:*** Ben Queen; Seamus Ruane; ***M:*** Stephen Cullo.

Proxy 🦴🦴 **2013** Esther Woodhouse (Rasmussen) is nearly nine months pregnant when she is savagely attacked. Seeking comfort in a support group, she meets a kind woman there named Melanie (Havins), who has some remarkable secrets of her own. Director/writer Parker's film very intentionally takes a sharp right turn every twenty minutes or so, almost resetting itself with a scene of such shocking intensity that the viewer loses their bearings. This take on the dark heart of human need is not for the faint of heart but rewards those willing to go on its unusual, well-crafted journey. **120m/C; DVD, Blu-Ray.** Alexia Rasmussen; Alexa Havins; Joe Swanberg; Kristina Klebe; ***D:*** Zack Parker; ***W:*** Zack Parker; Kevin Donner; ***C:*** Jim Timperman; ***M:*** The Newton Brothers.

Prozac Nation 🦴🦴 **1/2 2001 (R)** Drama based on Elizabeth Wurtzel's (Ricci) memoir of her depression, drug, and booze fueled college breakdown, which led her to seek the help of therapist Dr. Sterling (Heche). Unfocused script detracts from fine performance by Ricci, Williams and Biggs. **99m/C; DVD.** Christina Ricci; Michelle Williams; Jason Biggs; Anne Heche; Jonathan Rhys Meyers; Jessica Lange; Nicholas (Nick) Campbell; Emily Perkins; ***D:*** Erik Skjoldbjaerg; ***W:*** Frank Deasy; ***C:*** Erling Thurmann-Andersen; ***M:*** Nathan Larson.

P.S. 🦴🦴 **2004 (R)** Linney is a treasure but the same can't be said for the film, based on co-screenwriter Schulman's novel, "P.S. I Love You." Louise (Linney) is a quiet divorcee who works as a Columbia University admissions officer. She's intrigued by a young grad school applicant who bears the same name, F. Scott Feinstadt, as her lost first love. The young man (a game Grace) is bewildered but flattered by this attractive, lonely woman's attentions, but he's negligible since it's Louise's emotional baggage we're supposed to be interested in, and she's got a lot of it. Unfortunately, neither the movie nor the viewer can really handle all that weight without buckling. **97m/C; DVD.** Laura Linney; Topher Grace; Paul Rudd; Lois Smith; Gabriel Byrne; Marcia Gay Harden; ***D:*** Dylan Kidd; ***W:*** Helen Schulman; ***C:*** Joaquin Baca-Asay; ***M:*** Craig Wedren.

P.S. I Love You 🦴 **2007 (PG-13)** In this painfully sappy romantic drama, happily marrieds Holly (Swank) and Gerry (Butler) soon aren't so happy when Gerry dies of a brain tumor. Ah, but good ol' Gerry had enough time to plot out his widow's life for the next year—sending her a series of letters with various instructions to, you know, get out there and live! Kudrow and Gershon are gal pals while Connick and Morgan are potential new romances. Swank is game but Butler looked a lot more comfortable in leather and muscles in "300." **126m/C; DVD, Blu-Ray, On Demand.** Hilary Swank; Gerard Butler; Lisa Kudrow; Gina Gershon; Harry Connick, Jr.; Jeffrey Dean Morgan; Kathy Bates; James Marsters; ***D:*** Richard LaGravenese; ***W:*** Richard LaGravenese; Steven Rogers; ***C:*** Terry Stacey; ***M:*** John Powell.

P.S. Your Cat is Dead! 🦴 **1/2 2002 (R)** A moldy oldie. James Kirkwood's 1975 off-Broadway play was based on his 1972 novel and its attitudes towards gays appear quaint at best if not outright insulting. Jimmy Zoole (Guttenberg) is a failed actor/writer with a dead cat and a girlfriend, Kate (Watros), who's just dumped him. This leaves Jimmy alone in his L.A. apartment on New Year's Eve. Except for gay burglar Eddie (Boyar), who has the misfortune to be caught by a distraught Jimmy, who takes his gun and ties the man face down on a kitchen counter. Eddie proceeds to taunt Jimmy about his manhood, various humiliating things happen, and somehow male bonding occurs. **92m/C; DVD.** Steve Guttenberg; Lombardo Boyar; Cynthia Watros; Shirley Knight; Tom Wright; A.J. Benza; ***D:*** Steve Guttenberg; ***W:*** Steve Guttenberg; Jeff Korn; ***C:*** David A. Armstrong; ***M:*** Dean Grinsfelder.

Psych: 9 🦴 **1/2 2010 (R)** Troubled Roslyn works a night shift clerical job at a closed hospital in an area haunted by a serial killer who bludgeons women. Creepy things happen and Roslyn voices her concerns to Dr. Clement but maybe she's just experiencing delusions and paranoia. **98m/C; DVD.** Sara Foster; Cary Elwes; Gabriel Mann; Michael Biehn; Colleen Camp; ***D:*** Andrew Shortell; ***W:*** Lawrence Robinson; ***C:*** Shane Daly; ***M:*** James Edward Barker.

Psych-Out 🦴🦴 **1/2 1968** A deaf girl searches Haight-Ashbury for her runaway brother. She meets hippies and flower children during the Summer of Love. Psychedelic score with Strawberry Alarm Clock and The Seeds. Somewhere in the picture, Nicholson whangs on lead guitar. **95m/C; VHS, DVD, Blu-Ray.** Jack Nicholson; Bruce Dern; Susan Strasberg; Dean Stockwell; Henry Jaglom; ***D:*** Richard Rush; ***W:*** Richard Rush.

Psyche 59 🦴🦴 **1964** Allison (Neal) supposedly went blind because of a fall but it was actually a hysterical reaction to discovering that her husband Eric (Jurgens) and sexy younger sister Robin (Eggar) were fooling around. As Allison finally begins to regain her eyesight, she has to deal with their betrayal and Robin's return to their London lives after a five-year absence. **94m/B; DVD.** *GB* Patricia Neal; Curt Jurgens; Samantha Eggar; Ian Bannen; Beatrix Lehmann; Elspeth March; ***D:*** Alexander Singer; ***W:*** Julian Zimet; ***C:*** Walter Lassally; ***M:*** Kenneth V. Jones.

The Psychic WOOF! *Copenhagen's Psychic Loves* **1968** An ad executive gains psychic powers after he falls off a ladder and tries to conquer the world. A later effort by gore-king Lewis, notable only for sex scenes inserted by Lewis to make the movie salable. **90m/C; VHS, DVD.** Dick Genola; Robin Guest; Bobbi Spencer; Carol Saenz; Sandra Wolsfeld; ***D:*** Herschell Gordon Lewis; James F. Hurley; ***C:*** Herschell Gordon Lewis; ***M:*** Vincent Oddo.

Psychic 🦴 **1/2 1991 (R)** A college student with psychic powers believes he knows who the next victim of a demented serial killer will be. The problem is: no one will believe him. And the victim is the woman he loves. **92m/C; VHS, Streaming.** Michael Nouri; Catherine Mary Stewart; Zach Galligan; ***D:*** George Mihalka; ***W:*** Paul Koval; ***C:*** Ludek Bogner; ***M:*** Milan Kymlicka.

Psychic Experiment WOOF! 2010 (R) A woofer for its sheer incompetence and ultimately confusing plot. Evil doctors take control of a small community and implant chips to record all the inhabitants' sinister thoughts. They use that knowledge to terrorize the residents. **93m/C; DVD.** Adrienne King; Debbie Rochon; Denton Blane Everett; Reggie Bannister; Glenn Morshower; Katie Featherston; ***D:*** Meli House; ***W:*** Meli House; ***C:*** Philip Roy; ***M:*** Dwayne Cathey. **VIDEO**

Psychic Killer 🦴 **1/2 1975 (PG)** A wrongfully committed asylum inmate acquires psychic powers and decides to use them in a deadly revenge. Good cast in cheapie horror flick. **89m/C; VHS, DVD, Blu-Ray.** Jim Hutton; Paul Burke; Julie Adams; Neville Brand; Aldo Ray; Rod Cameron; Della Reese; ***D:*** Ray Danton; ***W:*** Ray Danton; Mikel Angel; Greydon Clark; ***C:*** Herb Pearl; ***M:*** William Craft.

Psycho 🦴 **1/2 1998 (R)** Redundant is a fitting description of Gus Van Sant's shot-for-shot recreation and ya pretty much have to ask, "what's the point?" Significant to the success of the original was that it pushed the envelope in 1960, but by today's standards, "Psycho" is utterly tame. As talented as Vaughn is, the inevitable comparison between him and Anthony Perkins reveals that Vaughn is just too cool for this role. Perkins' Norman Bates was geeky and frail, Vaughn just isn't. As the saying goes, "if it ain't broke, don't fix it." **106m/C; VHS, DVD, Blu-Ray.** Vince Vaughn; Anne Heche; Julianne Moore; William H. Macy; Viggo Mortensen; Robert Forster; Philip Baker Hall; Anne Haney; Chad Everett; Rance Howard; Rita Wilson; James Remar; James LeGros; ***D:*** Gus Van Sant; ***W:*** Joseph Stefano; ***C:*** Christopher Doyle. Golden Raspberries '98: Worst Director (Van Sant), Worst Remake/Sequel.

Psycho 🦴🦴🦴🦴 **1960** Hitchcock counted on his directorial stature and broke all the rules in this story of violent murder, transvestism, and insanity. Based on Robert Bloch's novelization of an actual murder, Leigh plays a fleeing thief who stops at the secluded Bates Motel where she meets her death in Hitchcock's classic "shower scene." Shot on a limited budget in little more than a month, "Psycho" changed the Hollywood horror film forever. Followed by "Psycho 2" (1983), "Psycho 3" (1986), "Psycho 4: The Beginning" (1990), and a TV movie. **109m/B; VHS, DVD, Blu-Ray.** Anthony Perkins; Janet Leigh; Vera Miles; John Gavin; John McIntire; Martin Balsam; Simon Oakland; Ted (Edward) Knight; John Anderson; Frank Albertson; Patricia Hitchcock; Alfred Hitchcock; ***V:*** Virginia Gregg; Jeannette Nolan; ***D:*** Alfred Hitchcock; ***W:*** Joseph Stefano; ***C:*** John L. "Jack" Russell; ***M:*** Bernard Herrmann. AFI '98: Top 100; Golden Globes '61: Support. Actress (Leigh); Natl. Film Reg. '92.

Psycho 2 🦴🦴 **1983 (R)** This sequel to the Hitchcock classic finds Norman Bates returning home after 22 years in an asylum to find himself haunted by "mother" and caught up in a series of murders. In a surprisingly good horror film, Perkins and Miles reprise their roles from the original "Psycho." Perkins went on to direct yet another sequel, "Psycho 3." **113m/C; VHS, DVD, Blu-Ray.** Anthony Perkins; Vera Miles; Meg Tilly; Robert Loggia; Dennis Franz; Claudia Bryar; Oz (Osgood) Perkins, II; ***D:*** Richard Franklin; ***W:*** Tom Holland; ***C:*** Dean Cundey; ***M:*** Jerry Goldsmith.

Psycho 3 🦴🦴 **1986 (R)** The second sequel to Hitchcock's "Psycho" finds Norman Bates drawn into his past by "mother" and the appearance of a woman who reminds him of this original victim. Perkins made his directorial debut in this film that stretches the plausibility of the storyline to its limits, but the element of parody throughout makes this an entertaining film for "Psycho" fans. **93m/C; VHS, DVD, Blu-Ray.** Anthony Perkins; Diana Scarwid; Jeff Fahey; Roberta Maxwell; Robert Alan Browne; Hugh Gillin; Lee Garlington; ***D:*** Anthony Perkins; ***W:*** Charles Edward Pogue; ***C:*** Bruce Surtees; ***M:*** Carter Burwell.

Psycho 4: The Beginning 🦴🦴 **1990 (R)** Prequels "Psycho" when, at the behest of a radio talk show host, Norman Bates recounts his childhood and reveals the circumstances that aided in the development of his peculiar neuroses. Stefano wrote the original screenplay and the original score is used, but this doesn't even come close to the original. **96m/C; VHS, DVD, Blu-Ray.** Anthony Perkins; Henry Thomas; Olivia Hussey; CCH Pounder; Warren Frost; Donna Mitchell; ***D:*** Mick Garris; ***W:*** Joseph Stefano; ***C:*** Rodney Charters; ***M:*** Graeme Revell.

Psycho Beach Party 🦴🦴 **1/2 2000** Busch adapted his own play—a spoof of 60s teen beach movies and psycho/thrillers. Perky teen tomboy Florence (Ambrose) desperately wants to fit into her SoCal ocean lifestyle by becoming the first female accepted into the local surfers who are led by hipster Kanaka (Gibson). The newly christened "Chicklet" has a dark side, however, a separate sultry personality named Anne that she fears is responsible for a series of murders that are thinning out the teen population. Busch plays the investigating officer, and former Kanaka girlfriend, Capt. Monica Stark. **95m/C; VHS, DVD, Blu-Ray.** Lauren Ambrose; Thomas Gibson; Nicholas Brendon; Charles Busch; Kimberly Davies; Matt Keeslar; Nathan Bexton; Buddy Quaid; Beth Broderick; Amy Adams; Danni Wheeler; Kathleen Robertson; ***D:*** Robert Lee King; ***W:*** Charles Busch; ***C:*** Arturo Smith; ***M:*** Ben Vaughn.

Psycho Cop 2 🦴 **1/2 1994 (R)** Four buddies plan a raunchy bachelor party, commandeering the company conference room for an after-hours orgy. Only Psycho Cop is on their case. Gore. Rifkin used the pseudonym Rif Coogan. **80m/C; VHS, DVD.** Robert (Bobby Ray) Shafer; Barbara Niven; Julie Strain; ***D:*** Adam Rifkin.

Psycho Sisters 🦴🦴 **1/2 1998** As children, Jackie (North) and Jane (Lynn) witness shocking events that traumatize them into the titular killers. Actually, after seeing so many young women pursued by homicidal maniacs, it's nice that a couple of them get to turn the tables. This low-budget horror has developed a strong cult following. **90m/C; DVD.** J.J. North; Theresa Lynn; ***D:*** Pete Jacelone; ***W:*** Pete Jacelone; James L. Edwards; ***C:*** Timothy Healy.

Psychomania 🦴 **1/2** *Violent Midnight* **1963** Semi-limpid mystery thriller about a former war hero and painter who is suspected of being the demented killer stalking girls on campus. To prove his innocence, he tracks the killer himself. **95m/C; VHS, DVD.** Lee Philips; Shepperd Strudwick; Jean Hale; Dick Van Patten; Sylvia Miles; James Farentino; ***D:*** Richard Hilliard.

Psychomania 🦴🦴 *The Death Wheelers* **1973 (R)** A drama of the supernatural, the occult, and the violence which lies just beyond the conventions of society for a group of dead motorcyclists, the Living Dead, who all came back to life after committing suicide with the help of the devil. **89m/C; VHS, DVD, Blu-Ray.** *GB* George Sanders; Beryl Reid; Nicky Henson; Mary Laroche; Patrick Holt; ***D:*** Don Sharp; ***W:*** Arnaud d'Usseau; ***C:*** Ted Moore.

The Psychopath 🦴🦴 **1966** Four men are found murdered--each with a lookalike doll left at the crime scene. Inspector Holloway (Wymark) learns that the men were part of a commission that convicted a German industrialist of war crimes. The man's family has moved to England so Holloway pays a call on the wheelchair-bound, doll-collecting widow (Johnston) and her violent son (Standing). But which one is the likely killer? Entertaining Brit shocker (and dolls are creepy). **82m/C; DVD, Blu-Ray.** *UK* Patrick Wymark; Margaret Johnston; John Standing; Alexander Knox; Judy Huxtable; ***D:*** Freddie Francis; ***W:*** Robert Bloch; ***C:*** John Wilcox; ***M:*** Philip Martell; Elisabeth Lutyens.

Psychopath 🦴🦴 **1/2** *Twist of Fate* **1997 (R)** D.A. Rachel Dwyer (Amick) needs the help of serial killer Lennox (Mulkey), who targets female law students, in solving another crime. Low on the histrionics and high on the courtroom drama as well as being well-acted. **95m/C; VHS, DVD.** Madchen Amick; Chris Mulkey; Bruce Dinsmore; Don Jordan; Lynne Adams; Cas Anvar; Tara Slone; James Bradford; ***D:*** Max Fischer; ***W:*** Cameron Kent; William Lee; ***C:*** Guy Kinkead; ***M:*** Normand Corbeil. **CABLE**

Psychos in Love WOOF! 1987 A psychotic murderer who hates grapes of any kind finds the woman of his dreams—she's a psychotic murderer who hates grapes! Together they find bliss—until the plumber discovers their secret! **90m/C; VHS, DVD, Blu-Ray.** Carmine Capobianco; Debi Thibeault; Frank Stewart; ***D:*** Gorman Bechard.

Psychosis 🦴 **1/2 2010 (R)** Old-fashioned, sometimes ludicrous horror with a conventional plot (and an out-of-place and unnecessary prologue). Successful-but-troubled horror novelist Susan Gordon moves from California to a remote country estate in England with her cheating husband David. Before you can say 'boo,' Susan is having terrifying visions, but is she seeing actual episodes of past violence or is she having a mental breakdown? **93m/C; DVD.** *GB* Charisma Carpenter; Paul Sculfor; Ricci Harnett; Justin Hawkins; Katrena Rochell; Ty Glaser; ***D:*** Reg Traviss; ***W:*** Reg Traviss; ***C:*** Bryan Loftus; ***M:*** Scott Shields. **VIDEO**

Psychotica 🦴 *Nostrum* **2010** A group of addicts decides to shoot up one last time before going straight, only to find their stash has been laced with an experimental new drug designed to make addicts suicidal. Unfortunately for the mad scientist who hopes to cleanse the world of junkies it instead has a nasty habit of turning users into psychopathic killers. **?m/CDVD, Blu-Ray.** *CA* Megan Hutchings; Mike Webster; Aimee Feler; Shamier Anderson; Kevin Jake Walker; ***D:*** Jonathan Wright; ***W:*** Jonathan Wright; Robert Allaire; ***C:*** Michael Jari Davidson; ***M:*** Wes Hambright. **VIDEO**

PT 109 🦴🦴 **1963** The WWII exploits of Lieutenant (j.g.) John F. Kennedy in the South Pacific. Part of the "A Night at the Movies" series, this tape simulates a 1963 movie evening, with a Foghorn Leghorn cartoon ("Banty Raids"), a newsreel on the JFK assassination, and coming attractions for "Critic's Choice" and "Four for Texas." **159m/C; VHS, DVD.** Cliff Robertson; Ty Hardin; Robert (Bobby) Blake; Robert Culp; James Gregory; ***D:*** Leslie Martinson.

P.T. Barnum 🦴🦴 **1/2 1999** Bio of Phineas Taylor Barnum (Beau Bridges) and his development of "The Greatest Show on Earth." A shopkeeper from Connecticut, P.T. was determined to make his fortune in New York, eventually purchasing Scudder's American Museum and its exhibits, which he turned into a traveling big top event, thanks to his promotional skills. Barnum's zest for work, however, made for a less than happy home life. Beau's son Jordan plays the young Barnum. Filmed in Montreal and Vancouver, Canada. **138m/C; VHS, DVD.** Beau Bridges; Cynthia Dale; Natalie Radford; Jordan Bridges; George Hamilton; Henry Czerny; Charles Martin Smith; Josh Ryan Evans; R.H. Thomson; Stephanie Morgenstern; Isabelle Cyr; Michelle-Barbara Pelletier; Victoria Sanchez; ***D:*** Simon Wincer; ***W:*** Lionel Chetwynd; ***C:*** Pierre Mignot. **CABLE**

Pterodactyl **2005** A dormant Turkish volcano warms up and hatches a bunch of millions-years-old giant Pterodactyl eggs. Quickly growing hungry, they sample the local buffet in the form of a U.S. Special Forces team. **89m/C; DVD.** Cameron Daddo; Coolio; Amy Sloan; George Calil; Ivo Cutzarida; ***D:*** Mark L. Lester; ***W:*** Mark Sevi; ***C:*** George Mooradian; ***M:*** John Dickson. **VIDEO**

Pterodactyl Woman from Beverly Hills **1997 (R)** California housewife Pixie Chandler (D'Angelo) is the victim of an eccentric witch doctor (James) when her paleontologist husband Dick (Wilson) disturbs an ancient burial site and the doc curses Pixie by turning her into a dinosaur. This is the first so-called family release from those madcap Troma people who brought you the Toxic Avenger. **97m/C; VHS, DVD.** Beverly D'Angelo; Brion James; Brad Wilson; Moon Zappa; Aron Eisenberg; ***D:*** Philippe Mora; ***W:*** Philippe Mora; ***C:*** Walter Bal; ***M:*** Roy Hay.

PU-239 1/2 *The Half Life of Timofey Berezin* **2006** Nuclear plant worker Timofey Berezin (Considine) is dosed with a lethal amount of radiation and becomes the victim of an administrative cover-up. To provide for his family, Timofey steals a tube of plutonium and turns to smalltime Moscow gangster Shiv (Isaac) to help him sell it on the black market. But Shiv's general ineptitude just gets them into trouble with mob boss Starkov (Berkoff). Set in 1995. **107m/C; DVD.** *GB* Paddy Considine; Radha Mitchell; Oscar Isaac; Jason Flemyng; Steven Berkhoff; Nikolaj Lie Kaas; Michael Fisher; ***D:*** Scott Burns; ***W:*** Scott Burns; ***C:*** Eigil Bryld; ***M:*** Abel Koreniowski.

The Public **2018 (PG-13)** Librarian Gordon (Estevez) works in Cincinnati at a large public library where many local homeless spend their days. When the city experiences extremely cold weather, local shelters get filled up and many of the homeless who regularly spend time at the library decide to stay after close. Gordon sides with them, leading to a standoff that involves the police, including sympathetic police negotiator/detective Bill Ramstead (Baldwin), politicians, including mayoral candidate Josh Davis (Slater), and the media. Though the film has some compelling moments, it's a little too preachy for it's own good. **119m/C; DVD.** Alec Baldwin; Taylor Schilling; Emilio Estevez; Jena Malone; Christian Slater; ***D:*** Emilio Estevez; ***W:*** Emilio Estevez; ***C:*** Juanmi (Juan Miguel) Azpiroz; ***M:*** Tyler Bates; Joanne Higginbottom.

Public Access **1993 (R)** Newcomer Whiley Pritcher (Marquette) manages to cause trouble in the small town of Brewster when he begins broadcasting a call-in program over a public-access cable station that encourages complaining about the town's problems. Skeletons start falling out of closets, leading to unexpected tragedy. Feature-film directorial debut of Singer. **90m/C; VHS, DVD.** Ron Marquette; Dina Brooks; Burt Williams; Charles Kavanaugh; Larry Maxwell; Brandon Boyce; ***D:*** Bryan Singer; ***W:*** Bryan Singer; Christopher McQuarrie; Michael Feit Dougan; ***C:*** Bruce Douglas Johnson; ***M:*** John Ottman. Sundance '93: Grand Jury Prize.

The Public Defender **1931** Tidy RKO thriller is about a playboy with a secret identity. Pike Winslow (Dix), an ex-military intelligence officer, is the Reckoner who leaves behind a calling card printed with the scales of justice. Along with his two associates, Pike goes after crooked bank officials who framed Barbara Gerry's (Grey) father for causing the bank's collapse--a hot topic for this Depression-era pic. **70m/B; DVD.** Richard Dix; Boris Karloff; Paul Hurst; Shirley Grey; Purnell Pratt; Frank Sheridan; Carl Gerard; ***D:*** J. Walter Ruben; ***W:*** Bernard Schubert; ***C:*** Edward Cronjager.

Public Enemies **2009 (R)** Stylish but cold crime drama from Mann centers on Depression-era gangster John Dillinger (Depp), here an enigmatic guy who likes to rob banks. The director dispenses with background and psychological insights so it's all meticulous surface as the pic hops from his prison break in 1933 to his 1934 death outside a Chicago movie theater. In an effort to bring attention to his fledging FBI operation, ambitious J. Edgar Hoover (Crudup) assigns his top agent, tightly-wound Melvin Purvis (Bale), to get Dillinger, the Bureau's first 'Public Enemy.' **140m/C; DVD, Blu-Ray, On Demand.** Christian Bale; Johnny Depp; Stephen Graham; Channing Tatum; Billy Crudup; Leelee Sobieski; Stephen Dorff; Giovanni Ribisi; David Wenham; Marion Cotillard; Emilie de Ravin; Rory Cochrane; Shawn Hatosy; ***D:*** Michael Mann; ***W:*** Ronan Bennett; Ann Biderman; ***C:*** Dante Spinotti; ***M:*** Elliot Goldenthal.

Public Enemy 1/2 *Enemies of the Public* **1931** Cagney's acting career was launched by this story of two Irish boys growing up in a Chicago shantytown to become hoodlums during the prohibition era. Tom (Cagney) and Matt (Woods) work their way up the criminal ladder, hooking up with molls Kitty (Clarke) and Mamie (Blondell) on their rise to the top. Harlow's a tough blonde who knows how to handle Cagney when he gets tired of Clarke. Considered the most realistic "gangster" film, Wellman's movie is also the most grimly brutal due to its release prior to Hollywood censorship. The scene where Cagney smashes a grapefruit in Clarke's face was credited with starting a trend in abusing film heroines. **85m/B; VHS, DVD, Blu-Ray.** James Cagney; Edward (Eddie) Woods; Leslie Fenton; Joan Blondell; Mae Clarke; Jean Harlow; Donald Cook; Beryl Mercer; ***D:*** William A. Wellman; ***W:*** Harvey Thew; John Bright; Kubec Glasmon; ***C:*** Devereaux Jennings. Natl. Film Reg. '98.

Public Enemy 1/2 *Gonggongui jeog* **2002** Detective Kang (Sol Kyung-gu) is a corrupt officer whose partner has committed suicide in shame after Internal Affairs announces they are being investigated for criminal activities. While on a stakeout a young man he bumps into slashes Kang's face with a knife. Later on he realizes the man may be responsible for a horrible double murder nearby. He becomes obsessed with bringing the man to justice, and puts aside his own illegal activities to hunt him down. **138m/C; DVD.** *NK* Kyung-gu Sol; Shin-il Kang; Sung-jae Lee; Jeong-hak Kim; Yong-gu Do; ***D:*** Woo-suk Kang; ***W:*** Hyeong-jeon Kim; ***C:*** Sung-bok Kim; ***M:*** Yeong-wook Jo.

The Public Eye 1/2 **1992 (R)** Underappreciated film noir homage casts Pesci as a crime photographer with an unsuspected romantic streak. It's 1942 in NYC and cynical freelancer Leon "Bernzy" Bernstein's always looking for the perfect shot. Hershey's the recent widow whose nightclub-owner husband had mob ties and decides Pesci would be a likely patsy for helping her out. Hershey seems decorative and the romantic angle never quite develops, but Pesci delivers a rich, low-key performance as the visionary, hard-boiled artist. Climatic mob shootout is cinematic bullet ballet. Based loosely on the career of '40s photog Weegee, who defined New York and its times in his work. **98m/C; VHS, DVD.** Joe Pesci; Barbara Hershey; Stanley Tucci; Richard Foronjy; Richard Riehle; Jared Harris; Jerry Adler; Dominic Chianese; Gerry Becker; ***D:*** Howard Franklin; ***W:*** Howard Franklin; ***M:*** John Barry.

Public Menace 1/2 **1935** Cocky reporter Red Foster (Murphy) is trailing gangster Tonelli (Dumbrille) aboard an ocean liner but neglects work to romance manicurist Cassie (Arthur). He loses his job but marries the girl, although he starts divorce proceedings after Red believes he's a dolt because Cassie's tips about the mobster's whereabouts are wrong. They're not. **72m/B; DVD.** Jean Arthur; George Murphy; Douglass Dumbrille; George McKay; Robert Middlemass; Victor Kilian; ***D:*** Erle C. Kenton; ***W:*** Ethel Hill; Lionel Houser; ***C:*** Henry Freulich.

Puccini for Beginners **2006** Snappy, droll, if occasionally labored comedy. Opera-loving Allegra (Reaser) breaks up with girlfriend Samantha (Nicholson) and drunkenly decides to have an affair after meeting appealing Philip (Kirk), who's dumped girlfriend Grace (Mol), who soon has her own rebound romance—with Allegra. Obviously, New York is a very small town. **82m/C; DVD.** Elizabeth Reaser; Justin Kirk; Gretchen Mol; Jennifer (Jennie) Dundas Lowe; Julianne Nicholson; Tina Benko; Brian Letscher; ***D:*** Maria Maggenti; ***W:*** Maria Maggenti; ***C:*** Mauricio Rubinstein; ***M:*** Terry Dame.

Puerto Ricans in Paris 1/2 **2016 (R)** A fish-out-of-water comedy about two Puerto Rican police detectives from New York City working a case in Paris. Luis (Guzman) and Eddie (Garcia) are recruited by a fashion agency to locate the blackmarket thief who has pilfered its latest handbag designs. To claim the large bounty that has been offered, the pair must travel to Paris to find the thief. In the process, the pair they must move through unfamiliar territory, including fashion shows, night clubs, and hip cafes, to find their thief. **82m/C; DVD, Blu-Ray, Download.** Luis Guzman; Edgar Garcia; Miriam Shor; Rosario Dawson; Brian Tyree Henry; ***D:*** Ian Edelman; ***W:*** Ian Edelman; Neel Shah; ***C:*** Damian Acevedo; ***M:*** Jonathan Sadoff.

Puerto Vallarta Squeeze 1/2 **2004 (R)** Failed American writer Danny Paster (Wasson) is living in Mexico with his girlfriend Maria (Zacarias). Needing money, Danny agrees to drive Clayton Price (Glenn) to the border though he knows something is off and that officials are on high alert following two assassinations. Seems Price is a government hitman gone rogue and CIA operative Walter McGrane (Keitel) has been sent in to clean up the mess, which includes getting rid of Price. Based on the novel by Robert James Waller. **120m/C; DVD.** Scott Glenn; Harvey Keitel; Craig Wasson; Jonathan Brandis; Giovanna Zacarias; ***D:*** Arthur Allan Seidelman; ***W:*** Richard Alfieri; ***C:*** Chuy Chavez; ***M:*** Lee Holdridge.

Puff, Puff, Pass **WOOF!** **2006 (R)** Excretal comedy about a couple of tokers who get locked out of their apartment for nonpayment of rent and then get into various unpleasant situations as they seek a place to hang out. Not even worth watching stoned. **95m/C; DVD.** Danny Masterson; Mekhi Phifer; Ronnie Warner; ***D:*** Mekhi Phifer; ***W:*** Ronnie Warner; Kent George; ***C:*** Arthur Albert.

Pufnstuf 1/2 **1970 (G)** Surreal theatrical feature based on the "H.R. Pufnstuff" children's series by Sid and Marty Kroft. Jimmy (Wild) takes his talking flute to Living Island, where objects, plants, and animals can speak and where he meets mayor Pufnstuf, a dragon. But Jack's magic flute is stolen by Witchiepoo (Hayes) who wants to be named "Witch of the Year" at the annual witches convention. **95m/C; VHS, DVD.** Jack Wild; Billie Hayes; Martha Raye; "Mama" Cass Elliott; Billy Barty; ***D:*** Hollingsworth Morse; ***W:*** John Fenton Murray; ***C:*** Kenneth Peach, Sr.; ***M:*** Charles Fox.

Pulling Strings 1/2 **2013 (R)** Still strung out after his wife's death, Mariachi singer Alejandro (an appealing Camil) thinks it best to scoot his daughter out of Mexico City and into the United States to stay with the grandparents for a while. After being turned away by uptight immigration officer Rachel (Ramsey), the singer finds himself gigging an embassy party later that night and helping the intoxicated nitpicker onto the couch at his place. A hunt for her missing laptop becomes the couple's mission, and, sure enough, romance is in the air. A predictable, but harmless bilingual rom com. **111m/C; DVD.** *MX* Jaime Camil; Laura Ramsey; Omar Chaparro; Tom Arnold; Stockard Channing; Roberto Sosa; ***D:*** Pedro Pablo Ibarra; ***W:*** Issa Lopez; Georgina Garcia Riedel; Gabriel Ripstein; Oscar Orlando; ***C:*** Alejandro Perez Gavilan; ***M:*** Áureo Baqueiro.

Pulp 1/2 **1972 (PG)** Caine, playing a mystery writer, becomes a target for murder when he ghostwrites the memoirs of a movie gangster from the 1930s, played deftly by Rooney. **95m/C; VHS, DVD, Blu-Ray.** *GB* Michael Caine; Mickey Rooney; Lionel Stander; Lizabeth Scott; Nadia Cassini; Dennis Price; Al Lettieri; ***D:*** Mike Hodges; ***W:*** Mike Hodges.

Pulp Fiction **1994 (R)** Tarantino moves into the cinematic mainstream with his trademark violence and '70s pop culture mindset intact in this stylish crime trilogy. A day in the life of a criminal community unexpectedly shifts from outrageous, esoteric dialogue to violent mayhem with solid scripting that takes familiar stories to unexplored territory. Offbeat cast offers superb performances, led by Travolta in his best role to date as a hit man whose adventures with partner Jackson tie the seemingly unrelated stories together. Clever, almost gleeful look at everyday life on the fringes of mainstream society. Inspired by "Black Mask" magazine. **154m/C; VHS, DVD, Blu-Ray, UMD.** John Travolta; Samuel L. Jackson; Uma Thurman; Harvey Keitel; Tim Roth; Amanda Plummer; Maria De Medeiros; Ving Rhames; Eric Stoltz; Rosanna Arquette; Christopher Walken; Bruce Willis; Frank Whaley; Steve Buscemi; Peter Greene; Alexis Arquette; Julia Sweeney; Quentin Tarantino; Angela Jones; ***D:*** Quentin Tarantino; ***W:*** Roger Avary; Quentin Tarantino; ***C:*** Andrzej Sekula; ***M:*** Karyn Rachtman. Oscars '94: Orig. Screenplay; AFI '98: Top 100; British Acad. '94: Orig. Screenplay, Support. Actor (Jackson); Cannes '94: Film; Golden Globes '95: Screenplay; Ind. Spirit '95: Actor (Jackson), Director (Tarantino), Film, Screenplay; L.A. Film Critics '94: Actor (Travolta), Director (Tarantino), Film, Screenplay; MTV Movie Awards '95: Dance Seq. (John Travolta/Uma Thurman), Film; Natl. Bd. of Review '94: Director (Tarantino), Film; Natl. Film Reg. '13; N.Y. Film Critics '94: Director (Tarantino), Screenplay; Natl. Soc. Film Critics '94: Director (Tarantino), Film, Screenplay.

Pulse **1988 (PG-13)** Electricity goes awry in this science-fiction thriller about appliances and other household devices that become super-charged and destroy property and their owners. **90m/C; VHS, DVD, Blu-Ray.** Cliff DeYoung; Roxanne Hart; Joseph Lawrence; Charles Tyner; Dennis Redfield; Robert Romanus; Myron Healey; ***D:*** Paul Golding; ***C:*** Peter Lyons Collister; ***M:*** Jay Ferguson.

Pulse 1/2 *Kairo* **2001** Set in dirty and industrial Tokyo, a great example of Japanese horror. Don't look for logic because its not here. Instead there's tension and dread surrounding disquieting images hosted by a malevolent website. A group of friends are shocked by the suicide of another friend and are then haunted by ghostly computer images. Other people continue to die or disappear in strange ways, as Tokyo becomes an increasingly desolate place. **118m/C; DVD, Blu-Ray.** *JP* Kumiko Aso; Koyuki; Shun Sugata; Masayuki Shionoya; Shinji Takeda; Koji Yakusho; Haruhiko Kato; Kurume Arisaka; Masatoshi Matsuo; Kenji Mizuhashi; Jun Fubuki; ***D:*** Kiyoshi Kurosawa; ***W:*** Kiyoshi Kurosawa; ***C:*** Junichiro Hayashi; ***M:*** Takefumi Haketa.

Pulse *Octane* **2003 (R)** Weirdo traveling vampire cult kidnaps teenage girl causing her anguished mom to descend into their world to attempt her rescue. **90m/C; VHS, DVD.** Madeleine Stowe; Norman Reedus; Bijou Phillips; Mischa Barton; Jonathan Rhys Meyers; Samuel Froler; Tom Hunsinger; Leo Gregory; Amber Batty; Jenny Jules; Patrick O'Kane; Martin McDougall; Shauna Shim; David Menkin; Nigel Whitmey; Stephen Lord; Dean Gregory; Sarah Drews; Raffaello Degruttola; Glenn Wrage; Monika Hudgins; Emma Drews; Marcus Adams; ***D:*** Marcus Volk; ***W:*** Stephen Volk; ***C:*** Robin Vidgeon; ***M:*** Paul Hartnoll; Phil Hartnoll; Orbital. **VIDEO**

Pulse 1/2 **2006 (R)** Remake of the 2001 Japanese horror flick "Kairo" that features an evil website. When the unsuspecting click on the creepy images of the dead, the supernatural force behind the site invades the lives of those who log on and makes them commit suicide. Technology is bad, but not as bad as this watered-down version, which forgoes creepy atmospherics and conceptualized plot for the occasional scare. **90m/C; DVD, Blu-Ray, HD-DVD.** Kristen Bell; Ian Somerhalder; Christina Milian; Rick Gonzalez; Zach Grenier; Ron Rifkin; Jonathan Tucker; Brad Dourif; Samm Levine; ***D:*** Jim Sonzero; ***W:*** Wes Craven; Ray Wright; ***C:*** Mark Plummer; ***M:*** Elia Cmiral.

Pulse 2: Afterlife 1/2 *Pulse: Afterlife and Invasion* **2008 (R)** After the events of the first film, what little is left of the world's population is hiding out in the woods or mountains to escape the soul-eating phantoms that have been using technology to access our world. One of the survivors must protect his daughter from his ex-wife's spirit and fend off his jealous, possessive girlfriend. What seems like a sound premise is ruined by the cinematography, which makes it look like a student film with a decent budget. **89m/C; DVD.** Jamie Bamber; Boti Ann Bliss; Laura Cayouette; Noureen DeWulf; Jackie Arnold; Karley Scott Collins; Georgina Rylance; ***D:*** Joel Soisson; ***W:*** Joel Soisson; ***C:*** Brandon Trost; ***M:*** Elia Cmiral. **VIDEO**

Pump Up the Volume ½ **1990 (R)** High school newcomer leads double life as Hard Harry, sarcastic host of an illegal radio broadcast and Jack Nicholson soundalike. Anonymously popular with his peers, he invites the wrath of the school principal due to his less than flattering comments about the school administration. Slater seems to enjoy himself as defiant deejay while youthful cast effectively supports. **105m/C; VHS, DVD.** Christian Slater; Scott Paulin; Ellen Greene; Samantha Mathis; Cheryl Pollak; Annie Ross; Andy Romano; Mimi Kennedy; ***D:*** Allan Moyle; ***W:*** Allan Moyle; ***C:*** Walt Lloyd; ***M:*** Cliff Martinez.

Pumpkin **2002 (R)** Ambitious but over-reaching satire. California blonde sorority sister Carolyn McDuffy (Ricci) is a reluctant participant in the group's charity activity—helping to coach "special" athletes. Then Carolyn gets to know Pumpkin (Harris), who's confined to a wheelchair and seems to be mentally retarded as well (this isn't very clear). Soon, Pumpkin is smitten and Carolyn falls for his inner beauty—thus alienating her boyfriend, sorority sisters, and Pumpkins's mother. Too bad all the characters are little more than stereotypes. **118m/C; VHS, DVD.** Christina Ricci; Brenda Blethyn; Dominique Swain; Hank Harris; Marisa Coughlan; Samuel Ball; Harry J. Lennix; Nina Foch; Caroline Aaron; Lisa Banes; Julio Oscar Mechoso; Amy Adams; ***D:*** Adam Larson Broder; Tony R. Abrams; ***W:*** Adam Larson Broder; ***C:*** Tim Suhrstedt; ***M:*** John Ottman.

The Pumpkin Eater **1964** British housewife Jo (Bancroft) has seemingly found contentment with her third husband, famous and wealthy writer Jake (Finch), and her eight children. But as Jo struggles to face middle age she discovers Jake is chronically unfaithful and goes into an emotional tailspin. Last film for Hardwicke. Slow-paced film with fine performances; based on the novel by Penelope Mortimer. **110m/C; VHS, DVD, Blu-Ray.** *GB* Anne Bancroft; Peter Finch; James Mason; Richard Johnson; Cedric Hardwicke; Maggie Smith; Alan Webb; Eric Porter; ***D:*** Jack Clayton; ***W:*** Harold Pinter; ***C:*** Oswald Morris; ***M:*** Georges Delerue. British Acad. '64: Screenplay.

Pumpkinhead ½ *Vengeance: The Demon* **1988 (R)** A farmer evokes a demon from the earth to avenge his son's death. When it continues on its murdering rampage, the farmer finds he no longer has any control over the vicious killer. **89m/C; VHS, DVD, Blu-Ray.** Lance Henriksen; John DiAquino; Kerry Remsen; Matthew Hurley; Jeff East; Kimberly Ross; Cynthia Bain; Joel Hoffman; Florence Schauffler; George "Buck" Flower; Tom Woodruff, Jr.; ***D:*** Stan Winston; ***W:*** Mark Patrick Carducci; Gary Gerani; ***C:*** Bojan Bazelli; ***M:*** Richard Stone.

Pumpkinhead 2: Blood Wings ½ **1994 (R)** Five typically stupid teenagers resurrect a demon and the creature goes on a bloodthirsty rampage. His leaves his signature, a calling card in the shape of wings, at each murder scene. **88m/C; VHS, DVD, Blu-Ray.** Ami Dolenz; Andrew (Andy) Robinson; Kane Hodder; R.A. Mihailoff; Linnea Quigley; Steve Kanaly; Caren Kaye; Gloria Hendry; Soleil Moon Frye; Mark McCracken; Roger Clinton; ***D:*** Jeff Burr; ***W:*** Ivan Chachornia; Constantin Chachornia.

Pumpkinhead 3: Ashes to Ashes **2006 (R)** Cheapie forgettable franchise entry starts 20 years after the original although dead Ed Harley (Henriksen) still manages to return. Local mortician Doc Frasier (Bradley) has been stealing body parts from the dead and throwing the remains in the swamp rather than giving them a proper burial. After his desecration is discovered, outraged townsfolk turn to Haggis the witch to summon the demonic Pumpkinhead to give them revenge. **95m/C; DVD.** Doug Bradley; Lance Henriksen; Douglas Roberts; Lisa McAllister; Tess Panzer; ***D:*** Jake West; ***W:*** Jake West; ***C:*** Erik Wilson; ***M:*** Robert Lord. **VIDEO**

Pumpkinhead 4: Blood Feud ½ **2007 (R)** Jody Hatfield and Ricky McCoy fall in love despite their families' ongoing feud. But when Ricky's younger sister dies, he decides to get the local witch to call up Pumpkinhead to kill all the Hatfields except for lover Jody. A ghostly Ed Harley tries to convince 'em that this is a bad idea since Pumpkinhead isn't going to check IDs before he starts his slaughter. Better than the previous entry but still standard monster fare. **95m/C; DVD.** Rob Freeman; Richard Durden; Lance Henriksen; Bradley Taylor; Amy Manson; Claire Lams; ***D:*** Michael Hurst; ***W:*** Michael Hurst; ***C:*** Eric Wilson; ***M:*** Robert Lord. **VIDEO**

Punch-Drunk Love **2002 (R)** Barry Egan (Sandler), owner of a novelty toilet-plunger company, is prone to sudden outbreaks of physical violence (mostly to glass doors and public bathrooms), but still finds a woman (Watson) attracted to him. Amid the budding love stuff, Egan battles with a phone sex company's extortion attempts and his discovery of a marketing mistake allowing him to obtain millions of frequent flyers miles for the price of some pudding cups (based on a true incident). Anderson arranges scenes like musical numbers, escalating sound and spectacle to a dizzying point, to good effect. **97m/C; VHS, DVD, Blu-Ray.** Adam Sandler; Emily Watson; Philip Seymour Hoffman; Luis Guzman; Mary Lynn Rajskub; Ashley Clark; ***D:*** Paul Thomas Anderson; ***W:*** Paul Thomas Anderson; ***C:*** Robert Elswit; ***M:*** Jon Brion.

Punchline **1988 (R)** A look at the lives of stand-up comics, following the career ups-and-downs of an embittered professional funny-man and a frustrated housewife hitting the stage for the first time. Some very funny and touching moments and some not-so-funny and touching as the movie descends into melodrama without a cause. **100m/C; VHS, DVD, Blu-Ray.** Tom Hanks; Sally Field; John Goodman; Mark Rydell; Kim Greist; Barry Sobel; Paul Mazursky; Pam Matteson; George Michael McGrath; Taylor Negron; Damon Wayans; ***D:*** David Seltzer; ***W:*** David Seltzer; ***C:*** Reynaldo Villalobos. L.A. Film Critics '88: Actor (Hanks).

Puncture **2011 (R)** Mike Weiss (a convincing Evans) is a functioning drug addict and personal injury lawyer in Houston, who falls into a case that makes him question his own demons and his ability to overcome them to do what's right. Weiss represents a nurse (Shaw) who becomes the face for all health care workers pricked by infected needles in the work place, exposing a massive cover-up by the medical industry to keep safe needles out of the market. A true story with noble goals and sentiments but falls short emotionally given its strong subject matter. **100m/C; DVD, Blu-Ray.** Chris Evans; Mark Kassen; Vinessa Shaw; Brett Cullen; Michael Biehn; Jesse L. Martin; Kate Burton; Marshall Bell; Tess Parker; Roxanna Hope; ***D:*** Mark Kassen; Adam Kassen; ***W:*** Chris Lopata; ***C:*** Helge Gerull; ***M:*** Ryan Ross Smith.

The Punisher **1990 (R)** Lundgren portrays Frank Castle, the Marvel Comics anti-hero known as the Punisher. When his family is killed by the mob Castle set his eyes on revenge. Filmed in Australia. **92m/C; VHS, DVD.** Dolph Lundgren; Louis Gossett, Jr.; Jeroen Krabbe; Kim Miyori; ***D:*** Mark Goldblatt; ***W:*** Boaz Yakin; ***C:*** Ian Baker; ***M:*** Dennis Dreith.

The Punisher **2004 (R)** Revenge pic filled with gloomy, dour punishment, drunken brooding, and grisly deaths. The Punisher AKA Frank Castle (Jane) is an FBI agent turned vigilante after a sting kills a wealthy mobster's son and triggers the murder of Castle's entire family while he survives the slaughter. Rest of pic is his plot against Mr. Saint (an uninspired Travolta), his right hand man (Patton) and assorted evil cohorts. Based on the Marvel comic books. **124m/C; VHS, DVD, Blu-Ray, UMD.** Thomas Jane; John Travolta; Edward Jemison; Samantha Mathis; Will Patton; Laura Elena Harring; Roy Scheider; Rebecca Romijn; Geoff Wallace; Mark Collie; Ben Foster; Russell Andrews; ***D:*** Jonathan Hensleigh; ***W:*** Jonathan Hensleigh; Michael France; ***C:*** Conrad W. Hall; ***M:*** Carlo Siliotto.

Punisher: War Zone ½ **2008 (R)** In this Marvel Comics sequel, director Alexander gleefully surpasses her predecessors in the how-many-different-gory-ways-can-they-die category. When Castle (Stevenson) unwittingly knocks off an undercover FBI agent, his guilty conscience forces him to protect the family from escaped mobsters Billy Russoti (West) and his brother Loony Bin Jim (Hutchison). It seems that Billy is upset that the Punisher caused him to have a horribly disfiguring encounter with a glass-crushing machine and he reemerges as the aptly named Jigsaw, recruiting a criminal army. **107m/C; DVD, Blu-Ray, On Demand.** *US GE* Ray Stevenson; Dominic West; Julie Benz; Wayne Knight; Doug Hutchison; Dash Mihok; Colin Salmon; ***D:*** Lexi Alexander; ***W:*** Nick Santora; Art Marcum; Mat Holloway; ***C:*** Steve Gainer; ***M:*** Michael Wandmacher.

Punk Love ½ **2006** Sarah is an aimless 15-year-old, living in a bad home situation in a dreary factory town. She hooks up with drug addicted musician Spike and they turn to petty crime to support themselves. Things start looking up when Spike's band audition actually pays off but they head downwards soon enough. **96m/C; DVD.** Chad Lindberg; Max Perlich; Emma Bing; ***D:*** Nick Lyon; ***W:*** Nick Lyon; ***C:*** Rene Richter; ***M:*** Miles Mosley. **VIDEO**

P.U.N.K.S. ½ **1998 (PG)** Preteen Drew (Redwine) and his friends are regularly beaten up by school bullies. Then they realize that evil industrialist Edward Crow (Winkler) has stolen an invention that turns weaklings into hulks and they decide to steal it back. **99m/C; VHS, DVD.** Randy Quaid; Cathy Moriarty; Henry Winkler; Ted Redwine; Patrick Renna; ***D:*** Sean McNamara. **VIDEO**

Puppet Master ½ **1989 (R)** Four psychics are sent to investigate a puppet maker who they think may have discovered the secret of life. Before they know it, they are stalked by evil puppets. Great special effects, not-so-great script. **90m/C; VHS, DVD, Blu-Ray.** Paul LeMat; Jimmie F. Skaggs; Irene Miracle; Robyn Frates; Barbara Crampton; William Hickey; Matt Roe; Kathryn O'Reilly; ***D:*** David Schmoeller; ***W:*** Joseph G. Collodi; ***C:*** Sergio Salvati; ***M:*** Richard Band.

Puppet Master 2 **1990 (R)** Puppets on a rampage turn hotel into den of special effects. Less effective string pulling than in original. Long live Pinocchio. **90m/C; VHS, DVD, Blu-Ray.** Elizabeth MacLellan; Collin Bernsen; Greg Webb; Charlie Spradling; Nita Talbot; Steve Welles; Jeff Weston; ***D:*** Dave Allen; ***W:*** David Pabian; ***C:*** Thomas Denove; ***M:*** Richard Band.

Puppet Master 3: Toulon's Revenge **1990 (R)** Prequel about the origin of the whole gory Puppet Master shebang, set in Nazi Germany. The weapon-hungry Third Reich tries to wrest secrets of artificial life from sorceror Andre Toulon, who sics his deadly puppets on them. Toulon's a good guy here, one of many contradictions in the series. Fine cast, but strictly for the followers. **86m/C; VHS, DVD, Blu-Ray.** Guy Rolfe; Ian Abercrombie; Sarah Douglas; Richard Lynch; Walter Gotell; ***D:*** David DeCoteau; ***W:*** C. Courtney Joyner; ***C:*** Adolfo Bartoli; ***M:*** Richard Band.

Puppet Master 4 **1993 (R)** It's the puppets versus the totems, equally loathsome midget creatures who derive their power from the same eternal force as the puppets. No one wants to share and there's lots of gore while they battle for supremacy. **80m/C; VHS, DVD, Blu-Ray.** Gordon Currie; Chandra West; Jason Adams; Teresa Hill; Guy Rolfe; ***D:*** Jeff Burr; ***W:*** Todd Henschell; Steven E. Carr; Jo Duffy; Douglas Aarniokoski; Keith Payson; ***M:*** Richard Band.

Puppet Master 5: The Final Chapter ½ **1994** Greedy Dr. Jennings has come to Bodega Bay Inn to capture the puppets and discover the secret formula for their animation so he can sell it to the highest bidder. But he's not the only threat, it seems the demonic Eyad, a being from another dimension, also wants the secret and has sent his own evil puppet to kill the puppet master and steal their magic. **81m/C; VHS, DVD, Blu-Ray.** Gordon Currie; Chandra West; Ian Ogilvy; Teresa Hill; Nicholas Guest; Willard Pugh; Diane McBain; Kaz Garas; Guy Rolfe; ***D:*** Jeff Burr; ***W:*** Douglas Aarniokoski; Jo Duffy; Todd Henschell; Keith Payson; Steven E. Karr; ***C:*** Adolfo Bartoli; ***M:*** Richard Band.

Puppet Master: The Littlest Reich ½ **2018** Reboots the '90s franchise with gruesome glee. When Edgar and pals find a discarded puppet, they decide to sell it at a convention where other puppets are also brought to auction and, mysteriously, to life. The effects and acting are improved, and the bloodbath scores a 9 on the gore-ometer, but purists will notice a significant change in its legacy: Toulon, who originally crafted his puppets to kill Nazis, is recast as a homicidal Nazi, undoubtedly to support the puppets' butchery of certain types of victims. A slasher that delights in grisly political incorrectness. **84m/C; DVD, Blu-Ray.** Thomas Lennon; Udo Kier; Michael Paré; Nelson Franklin; Jenny Pellicer; ***D:*** Sonny Laguna; Tommy Wiklund; ***W:*** S. Craig Zahler; ***M:*** Richard Band; Fabio Frizzi.

The Puppet Masters *Robert A. Heinlein's The Puppet Masters* **1994 (R)** Government official (Sutherland) discovers aliens are taking over the bodies of humans and if he doesn't find a way to stop the parasites they'll soon rule the Earth. Yes, it does sound like "Invasion of the Body Snatchers" but the film is based on Robert A. Heinlein's 1951 novel, written five years before. The parasites are sufficiently yucky but, unfortunately, this adaptation is mediocre and generally wastes a talented cast. **109m/C; VHS, DVD, Blu-Ray.** Donald Sutherland; Eric Thal; Julie Warner; Keith David; Will Patton; Richard Belzer; Yaphet Kotto; Dale Dye; ***D:*** Stuart Orme; ***W:*** Terry Rossio; David S. Goyer; Ted Elliott; ***M:*** Colin Towns.

Puppet on a Chain **1972 (PG)** American narcotics officer busts an Amsterdam drug ring and the leader's identity surprises him. Slow-moving thriller based on the Alistair MacLean novel. **97m/C; VHS, DVD, Blu-Ray.** *GB* Sven-Bertil Taube; Barbara Parkins; Alexander Knox; Patrick Allen; Geoffrey Reeve; ***D:*** Geoffrey Reeve; ***C:*** Jack Hildyard.

Pups **1999** Surburban 13-year-old Stevie (Van Hoy) finds his mom's gun, which he shows to equally young girlfriend, Rocky (Barton). Instead of going to school, Stevie impulsively decides to rob a nearby bank, and nearly gets away with it until the cops and the FBI show up. Now the kids have hostages and no clue as to what they're doing, while hostage negotiator Daniel Bender (Reynolds) tries to get a volatile Stevie to listen to reason. **103m/C; VHS, DVD.** Cameron Van Hoy; Mischa Barton; Burt Reynolds; Darling Narita; ***D:*** Ash; ***W:*** Ash; ***C:*** Carolos Arguello.

Purana Mandir *The Old Temple* **1984** The Ramsay brothers are considered the fathers of Bollywood horror, and this is one of their better efforts. A demon is ordered beheaded, but before dying he curses the Raja and his family for all time. Flash forward to modern-day India, where the Raja's great-great-grandson has a daughter who wishes to marry and he doesn't know how to explain why she can't. Bollywood films tend to follow a very different formula than Hollywood and their style may not make sense to a western audience as they shift from one genre to another. **145m/C; DVD.** *IN* Mohnish Bahl; Arti Gupta; Sadashiv Amrapurkar; Puneet Issar; Rajendra Nath; Satish Shah; Ajay Agarwal; ***D:*** Shyam Ramsay; Tulsi Ramsay; ***W:*** J. K. Ahuja; Dr. Gurdeep; Kumar Ramsay; ***C:*** Gangu Ramsay; ***M:*** Ajit Singh.

The Purchase Price **1932** After a less than amorous beginning, farmer Brent and mail order bride Stanwyck fall into love and financial despair in this drama bordering on comedy. Good neighbor Landau is willing to help the poor agriculturalist out in exchange for Stanwyck. Tragedy strikes again when Stanwyck's bootlegger ex-boyfriend shows up and further disasters continue to test the couple's commitment. Based on the story "The Mud Lark" by Arthur Stringer. **70m/B; VHS, DVD.** Barbara Stanwyck; George Brent; Lyle Talbot; Hardie Albright; David Landau; ***D:*** William A. Wellman; ***W:*** Robert Lord.

Pure **2002 (R)** Sentimental and brutal tale about Paul (Eden), a 10-year-old boy trying to stay in control of his life and save his mother from her addiction to heroin. Everyone around him is either an addict, a prostitute, or a pusher, yet he remains in confident denial of his true situation. The bad choices and ludicrous behavior of the adults in his life are perpetual and heartbreaking. Fine acting, especially by Eden; well shot but story on the whole is emotionally unsatisfying. **94m/C; DVD.** *GB* Molly Parker; David Wenham; Geraldine McEwan; Keira Knightley; Kate Ashfield; Gary Lewis; Marsha Thomason; Karl Johnson; Harry Eden; Nitin Ganatra; Levi Hayes; Vinni Hunter; ***D:*** Gilles Mackinnon; ***W:*** Alison Hume; ***C:*** John de Borman; ***M:*** Nitin Sawhney.

Pure Country 🦴🦴 ½ **1992 (PG)** An easygoing movie about a familiar subject is held together by the charm of Strait (in his movie debut) and the rest of the cast. Strait plays a country music superstar, tired of the career glitz, who decides to get out and go back to his home in Texas. He falls in love with the spunky Glasser and decides to run his career his own way. Warren is effective as his tough manager and old-time cowboy Calhoun is finely weathered as Glasser's gruff dad. **113m/C; VHS, DVD, Blu-Ray.** George Strait; Isabel Glasser; Lesley Ann Warren; Rory Calhoun; Kyle Chandler; John Doe; Molly McClure; ***D:*** Christopher Cain; ***W:*** Rex McGee; ***C:*** Rick Bota; ***M:*** Steve Dorff.

Pure Country 2: The Gift 🦴 ½ **2010 (PG)** In-name-only, faith-based sequel starts off with three angels bestowing a beautiful singing voice on newborn Bobbie Thomas. There are three rules: never lie, always be fair, and never break a promise. Unfortunately, the adult Bobbie (Elam) has trouble with these as she tries to find her way to country music success in Nashville. George Strait is briefly seen as himself and not the character he played in the 1992 original. **111m/C; DVD, Blu-Ray.** Katrina Elam; Travis Fimmel; Jackie Welch; Michael McKean; Cheech Marin; Bronson Pinchot; Todd Truly; J.D. Parker; William Katt; George Strait; ***D:*** Christopher Cain; ***W:*** Christopher Cain; Dean Cain; ***C:*** Juan Ruiz-Anchia; ***M:*** Steve Dorff. **VIDEO**

Pure Danger 🦴🦴 ½ **1996 (R)** Short order cook Johnny (Howell) and his waitress girlfriend Becky (Linn) stumble upon a bag of diamonds and think all their troubles are over. Wrong—they're just beginning, since some very nasty men want the jewels and don't care who they kill to get them. Howell keeps his directorial debut fast-paced and surprisingly entertaining. **99m/C; VHS, DVD.** C. Thomas Howell; Teri Ann Linn; Leon; Michael Russo; ***D:*** C. Thomas Howell; ***W:*** William Applegate, Jr.; Joseph John Barmettler, Jr.; ***C:*** Ken Blakey; ***M:*** K. Alexander (Alex) Wilkinson.

A Pure Formality 🦴🦴 *Una Pura Formalita; Une Pure Formalite* **1994 (PG-13)** Murky psycho-drama finds a disheveled man (Depardieu) winding up at an isolated police station in a nameless country (in the middle of a rainstorm, no less). The Inspector (Polanski) suspects him of a local murder, especially after he claims to be a famous writer named Onoff, yet, can remember nothing. The Inspector wants a confession and spends the night trying to exact one from his guileful suspect. French with subtitles. Film is rated at a much younger level than will possibly understand or enjoy it. **111m/C; VHS, Blu-Ray, Streaming.** *FR IT* Gerard Depardieu; Roman Polanski; Sergio Rubini; ***D:*** Giuseppe Tornatore; ***W:*** Giuseppe Tornatore; Pascal Quignard; ***C:*** Blasco Giurato; ***M:*** Ennio Morricone.

The Pure Hell of St. Trinian's 🦴🦴 ½ **1961** In this sequel to "Blue Murder at St. Trinian's," a sheik who desires to fill out his harem tries recruiting at a rowdy girls' school. Although it isn't as funny as the first, due to the lack of Alistair Sim, it is still humorous. Followed by "The Great St. Trinian's Train Robbery." Based on the cartoon by Ronald Searle. **94m/B; VHS, DVD, Streaming.** *GB* Cecil Parker; Joyce Grenfell; George Cole; Thorley Walters; ***D:*** Frank Launder; ***M:*** Malcolm Arnold.

Pure Luck 🦴 ½ **1991 (PG)** A who-asked-for-it remake of a 1981 Franco-Italian film called "La Chevre." The premise is the same: an accident-prone heiress disappears in Mexico, and her father tries to locate her using an equally clumsy accountant. The nebbish and an attendant tough private eye stumble and bumble south of the border until the plot arbitrarily ends. Pure awful. **96m/C; VHS, DVD.** Martin Short; Danny Glover; Sheila Kelley; Scott Wilson; Sam Wanamaker; Harry Shearer; ***D:*** Nadia Tass; ***W:*** Herschel Weingrod; Timothy Harris.

Purgatory 🦴🦴 ½ **1999** A group of desperadoes head for what they think is the defenseless town of Refuge, where the sheriff (Shepard) doesn't carry a gun or allow cussing. But the town and its inhabitants are not what they seem and these cowpoke bad guys are in for quite a surprise. **94m/C; VHS, DVD.** Sam Shepard; Eric Roberts; Randy Quaid; Peter Stormare; Donnie Wahlberg; ***D:*** Uli Edel; ***W:*** Gordon Dawson. **CABLE**

Purgatory House 🦴🦴 ½ **2004 (R)** Unable to bear her miserable drug-addled and Goth-wannabe existence, 14-year-old Silver Strand (Davis) offs herself, only to become stranded with other similarly-troubled teens between heaven and hell, where she is made to attend daily group sessions while watching the televised earthly sufferings of the loved ones she left behind. With the help of Saint James (Hanks) she must either cope with the fallout or be stuck there. Frank discussion of teen angst by first-time director Baer and written by lead Davis, who was 14 years old at the time. **95m/C; DVD.** Celeste Davis; Jim Hanks; Johnny Pacar; Devin Witt; Cindy Baer; ***D:*** Cindy Baer; ***W:*** Celeste Davis. **VIDEO**

The Purge 🦴🦴 **2013 (R)** In an attempt to curb crime, our future America commissions one night a year for full-on anarchy, letting the criminals run amok and citizens regulate their own punishment. Family man James Sandin (Hawke) has made a killing by selling military-like home security and must decide how far he'll go to protect his home against a vicious gang led by a man (Wakefield) who wields a smile as well as a weapon. What seems like an intelligent take on claustrophobia and paranoia turns into a fairly straightforward home invasion genre clunker. A fascinating concept that doesn't push its ideas far enough. **85m/C; DVD, Blu-Ray.** Ethan Hawke; Lena Headey; Adelaide Kane; Max Burkholder; Rhys Wakefield; Edwin Hodge; ***D:*** James DeMonaco; ***W:*** James DeMonaco; ***C:*** Jacques Jouffret; ***M:*** Nathan Whitehead.

The Purge: Anarchy 🦴🦴 **2014 (R)** The sequel to the surprising 2013 hit action "what if" film about a world in which all crime is legal for 12 hours a year works reasonably well as a B-movie grindhouse flick, not so much when it tries to get serious. The idea to expand the concept of The Purge from one house under siege to how the lawlessness impacts the general population was a smart one. This time, a poor couple's (Gilford & Ejogo) car breaks down just as The Purge is commencing, leading them on a perilous journey back to safety. **103m/C; DVD, Blu-Ray.** Frank Grillo; Carmen Ejogo; Zoe Soul; Zach Gilford; Kiele Sanchez; Michael K(enneth) Williams; ***D:*** James DeMonaco; ***W:*** James DeMonaco; ***C:*** Jacques Jouffret; ***M:*** Nathan Whitehead.

The Purge: Election Year 🦴 ½ **2016 (R)** The series that started with a clever idea—all crime is legal for 12 hours—has devolved into pure ultra-violent nonsense, the kind of junk that pretends to hold a message about human nature but really just plays to gore lover's desires to see people killed. Barnes (Grillo), the protagonist and best thing about the last film, returns as the head of security for Senator Charlie Roan (Mitchell), who has been targeted for assassination on the night of the Purge because she's vowed to end it. After this, the Hound hopes any plans for a fourth film are purged. **109m/C; DVD, Blu-Ray.** Frank Grillo; Elizabeth Mitchell; Mykelti Williamson; Edwin Hodge; Joseph Julian Soria; ***D:*** James DeMonaco; ***W:*** James DeMonaco; ***C:*** Jacques Jouffret; ***M:*** Nathan Whitehead.

The Purifiers 🦴 **2004 (R)** In a near-future Glasgow, rival gangs like to show off by holding martial arts battles. Crime boss Moses (McKidd) wants to organize the gangs but the Purifiers, led by John (Alexander), are eager to keep crime out of their 'hood and don't want to go along. Chop-socky with a Scottish brogue. **85m/C; DVD.** Kevin McKidd; Dominic Monaghan; Gordon Alexander; Rachel Grant; ***D:*** Richard Jobson; ***W:*** Richard Jobson; ***C:*** John Rhodes; ***M:*** Steven Severin.

Purlie Victorious 🦴🦴 ½ *Gone are the Days!; The Man from C.O.T.T.O.N.* **1963** Preacher Purlie (Davis) returns to Georgia and tries to get an inheritance from the plantation owner, "Ol' Cap'n" Cotchipee (Booke), he used to serve. Cotchipee's progressive son (Alda) unexpectedly helps him in his cause. Presentation of Davis's award-winning Broadway hit. **93m/C; VHS, DVD.** Ossie Davis; Ruby Dee; Godfrey Cambridge; Alan Alda; Sorrell Booke; Beah Richards; ***D:*** Nicholas Webster; ***W:*** Ossie Davis; ***C:*** Boris Kaufman.

Purple Butterfly 🦴🦴🦴 ½ *Zi Hudie* **2003 (R)** Stunning political thriller/noir set in 1930s Shanghai. Cynthia/Ding Hui (Zhang) is an operative in the anti-Japanese underground Purple Butterfly. A fearless and dedicated patriot, her past comes to haunt her in the form of former lover Itami (Nakamura), now a Japanese agent assigned to bring down Purple Butterfly. Soon enough, the two are caught in a delicate balancing act, struggling between their duty and the love that may still exist between them. Director Lou mixes Western noir style with a distinct, dreamlike moodiness that ensnares while shocking with interesting twists in the complex plot. Chinese with subtitles. **127m/C; DVD.** Ziyi Zhang; Toru Nakamura; Yuanzheng Feng; Ye Liu; ***D:*** Ye Lou; ***W:*** Ye Lou; ***C:*** Yu Wang; ***M:*** Jorg Lemberg.

The Purple Gang 🦴🦴 **1959** Teenage hoodlum Honeyboy Willard (Blake) and his gang take on Police Lt. William Harley (Sullivan) and Prohibition rum runners in Detroit. Honeyboy is soon running the action so merchants turn to Al Capone in Chicago to set the situation right. When the vicious hothead is responsible for the deaths of two women, it's Harley who'll stop at nothing to put him down. **85m/B; DVD.** Robert (Bobby) Blake; Barry Sullivan; Elaine Edwards; Jody Lawrance; Marc Cavell; Suzanne Ridgeway; Joseph Turkel; Victor Creatore; Paul Dubov; ***D:*** Frank McDonald; ***W:*** Jack DeWitt; ***C:*** Ellis W. Carter; ***M:*** Paul Dunlap.

The Purple Heart 🦴🦴 ½ **1944** An American Air Force crew is shot down over Tokyo and taken into brutal POW camps. Intense wartime melodramatics. **99m/B; VHS, DVD.** Dana Andrews; Richard Conte; Farley Granger; Donald (Don "Red") Barry; Sam Levene; Kevin O'Shea; Tala Birell; Nestor Paiva; Benson Fong; Marshall Thompson; Richard Loo; ***D:*** Lewis Milestone; ***C:*** Arthur C. Miller.

Purple Heart 🦴 **2005 (R)** What obligation does the military have to care for its damaged soldiers while simultaneously hiding the truth about its operations? Colonel Allen (Sadler) leads a covert unit into Iraq with orders to kill Saddam Hussein prior to the 2003 invasion. Marine sniper Oscar Padilla (Navarro) is chosen for the job, but he's captured and tortured. After his rescue, the troubled Padilla is locked in a military psych ward from which he escapes. Allen is sent after him since if word of their illegal mission gets out it would cause a political firestorm. **91m/C; DVD.** William Sadler; Demetrius Navarro; Mel Harris; ***D:*** Bill Birrell; ***W:*** Russell Gannon; Bill Birrell; ***C:*** Guy Livneh; ***M:*** Ralph Rieckermann. **VIDEO**

Purple Hearts 🦴 ½ **1984 (R)** Wahl stars as a Navy doctor who falls in love with nurse Ladd against the backdrop of the Vietnam war. Overlong and redundant. **115m/C; VHS, DVD.** Cheryl Ladd; Ken Wahl; Stephen Lee; Annie McEnroe; Paul McCrane; Cyril O'Reilly; ***D:*** Sidney J. Furie; ***W:*** Sidney J. Furie; Ron Nyswaner; ***M:*** Robert Folk.

The Purple Monster Strikes 🦴🦴 *D-Day on Mars; The Purple Shadow Strikes* **1945** A martian plots to conquer Earth to save his dying planet. Serial in 15 episodes. **188m/B; VHS, DVD.** Dennis Moore; Linda Stirling; Roy Barcroft; ***D:*** Spencer Gordon Bennet; Fred Brannon; ***W:*** Barney A. Sarecky; Basil Dickey; Lynn Perkins; Joseph Poland; Albert DeMond; ***C:*** Bud Thackery.

Purple Noon 🦴🦴🦴 *Plein Soleil; Lust for Evil* **1960 (PG-13)** Don't let the rating fool you, this isn't teen fodder. The gorgeous Delon stars as opportunistic Tom Ripley, who's hired by the father of his rich, arrogant playboy friend Philippe (Ronet) to persuade him to return home to San Francisco. Instead, Ripley covets the man's yacht, beautiful girlfriend Marge (Laforet), and money, so when Philippe pushes Tom too far he disposes of him and tries to divert police suspicions. Film noir set in the hedonistic Mediterranean sun. Based on the novel "The Talented Mr. Ripley" by Patricia Highsmith, although the ending of novel and film differ greatly. French with subtitles. **118m/C; VHS, DVD, Blu-Ray.** *FR* Alain Delon; Maurice Ronet; Marie Laforet; Erno Crisa; Billy Kearns; ***D:*** Rene Clement; ***W:*** Rene Clement; Paul Gegauff; ***C:*** Henri Decae; ***M:*** Nino Rota.

The Purple Plain 🦴🦴 **1954** Psychologically troubled pilot Bill Forrester is stationed in Burma in 1945. A plane crash in Japanese-occupied territory leaves Forrester, his injured navigator Carrington, and medical officer Blore to make a dangerous trek through the jungle to safety. Based on the H.E. Bates novel. **100m/C; DVD, Blu-Ray.** *UK* Gregory Peck; Lyndon Brook; Maurice Denham; Bernard Lee; ***D:*** Robert Parrish; ***W:*** Eric Ambler; ***C:*** Geoffrey Unsworth; ***M:*** John Veale.

Purple Rain 🦴🦴 ½ **1984 (R)** A quasi-autobiographical video showcase for the pop-star Prince. Film tells the tale of his struggle for love, attention, acceptance, and popular artistic recognition in Minneapolis. Not a bad film, for such a monumentally egotistical movie. **113m/C; VHS, DVD, Blu-Ray, HD-DVD.** Prince; Apollonia; Morris Day; Olga Karlatos; Clarence Williams, III; ***D:*** Albert Magnoli; ***W:*** William Blinn; ***C:*** Donald E. Thorin; ***M:*** Michel Colombier. Oscars '84: Orig. Song Score and/or Adapt.; Natl. Film Reg. '19.

The Purple Rose of Cairo 🦴🦴🦴 **1985 (PG)** A diner waitress, disillusioned by the Depression and a lackluster life, escapes into a film playing at the local movie house where a blond film hero, tiring of the monotony of his role, makes a break from the celluloid to join her in the real world. The ensuing love story allows director-writer Allen to show his knowledge of old movies and provide his fans with a change of pace. Farrow's film sister is also her real-life sister Stephanie, who went on to appear in Allen's "Zelig." **82m/C; VHS, DVD, Blu-Ray.** Mia Farrow; Jeff Daniels; Danny Aiello; Dianne Wiest; Van Johnson; Zoe Caldwell; John Wood; Michael Tucker; Edward Herrmann; Milo O'Shea; Glenne Headly; Karen Akers; Deborah Rush; ***D:*** Woody Allen; ***W:*** Woody Allen; ***C:*** Gordon Willis; ***M:*** Dick Hyman. British Acad. '85: Film, Orig. Screenplay; Cesar '86: Foreign Film; Golden Globes '86: Screenplay; N.Y. Film Critics '85: Screenplay.

Purple Violets 🦴 ½ **2007** Yet another of Burns' New York-set comedy-dramas, but this time he takes a supporting role to the somewhat more appealing story of Blair and Wilson. Patti (Blair) is a failed novelist in a bad marriage, unhappily working as a real estate agent. Out for a drink with girlfriend Kate (Messing), she runs into her college beau Brian (Wilson), a successful writer who's had a professional setback. With Brian is his best friend, Murph (Burns), who used to be Kate's college love until an incident she refuses to forgive. Meanwhile, Patti and Brian decide to explore the possibilities of renewing their romance. **93m/C; DVD.** Selma Blair; Patrick Wilson; Debra Messing; Edward Burns; Donal Logue; Elizabeth Reaser; Dennis Farina; ***D:*** Edward Burns; ***W:*** Edward Burns; ***C:*** William Rexer; ***M:*** P.T. Walkley. **VIDEO**

Purpose 🦴🦴 ½ **2002 (R)** College dropout turned Internet entrepreneur John Elias (Light) finds fame and fortune during the dot.com boom but things turn rough when his girlfriend (Dodds) and dad (Coyote) question his business ethics and John must prevent a hostil takeover of his company. **96m/C; VHS, DVD.** John Light; Megan Dodds; Peter Coyote; Jeffrey Donovan; Hal Holbrook; Mia Farrow; Paul Reiser; ***D:*** Alan Ari Lazar; ***W:*** Alan Ari Lazar; ***M:*** Alan Ari Lazar.

Pursued 🦴🦴🦴 **1947** Excellent performances by Mitchum and Wright mark this suspenseful Western drama of a Spanish-American war veteran in search of his father's killer. **105m/B; DVD, Blu-Ray.** Teresa Wright; Robert Mitchum; Judith Anderson; Dean Jagger; Alan Hale; Harry Carey, Jr.; John Rodney; ***D:*** Raoul Walsh; ***C:*** James Wong Howe; ***M:*** Max Steiner.

Pursuit 🦴🦴🦴 **1972** A terrorist threatens to release a toxic nerve gas throughout a city hosting a political convention. Tension mounts as federal agents must beat the extremists' countdown to zero. Based on the novel by Crichton. **73m/C; VHS, DVD, Blu-**

Ray. Ben Gazzara; E.G. Marshall; Martin Sheen; Joseph Wiseman; William Windom; ***D:*** Michael Crichton; ***M:*** Jerry Goldsmith.

The Pursuit of Happiness 1/2 **1970 (PG)** An idealistic man is convicted of manslaughter after accidentally running down a woman. Once in prison, he's faced with the decision to try to escape. **85m/C; VHS, DVD.** Michael Sarrazin; Arthur Hill; E.G. Marshall; Barbara Hershey; Robert Klein; ***D:*** Robert Mulligan.

Pursuit of Happiness 1/2 **2001** L.A. ad exec Alan Oliver (Whaley) always has his longtime best platonic friend Marissa (Gish) to turn to when his life spins out of control. And it's about to'his boss (Stapleton) takes him off his biggest account, his girlfriend moves out, and he's suddenly in a rebound romance with Tracy (Johnson). What Alan fails to realize is that Marissa is also having trouble since her marriage is falling apart. Oh, and as Alan pursues happiness, he should also realize that it's closer than he thinks. **93m/C; VHS, DVD.** Frank Whaley; Annabeth Gish; Amy Jo Johnson; Patrick Van Horn; Jean Stapleton; Alex Hyde-White; Cress Williams; Liz Vassey; Kieran Mulroney; Anne-Marie Johnson; ***D:*** John Putch; ***W:*** John Robert Zaring; ***C:*** Ross Berryman.

The Pursuit of Happyness 1/2 **2006 (PG-13)** Smith and too-cute son Jaden (in his film debut) easily fill the shoes of real-life father and son as Chris Gardner and 5-year-old Christopher. When Chris' bad decisions leave the family broke and mom (Newton) bails, father and son are soon homeless, until Chris pins his hopes on a six-month unpaid competitive internship at a brokerage firm that could lead to a full-time job and a stable life. The usual feel-good, never-give-up path ensues, and the Smiths make it a worthwhile journey. A misspelling on a mural at Christopher's daycare center supplied the film's title. **120m/C; DVD, Blu-Ray.** Will Smith; Thandie Newton; Brian Howe; James Karen; Jaden Smith; Dan Castellaneta; Kurt Fuller; ***D:*** Gabriele Muccino; ***W:*** Steve Conrad; ***C:*** Phedon Papamichael; ***M:*** Andrea Guerra.

Pursuit of the Graf Spee 1/2 *The Battle of the River Plate* **1957** Three small British ships destroy the mighty Graf Spee, a WWII German battleship. **106m/C; VHS, DVD.** *GB* Anthony Quayle; Peter Finch; Ian Hunter; ***D:*** Michael Powell.

Pursuit to Algiers 1/2 **1945** The modernized Holmes and Watson guard over the King of fictional Rovenia during a sea voyage, during which assassins close in. **65m/B; VHS, DVD.** Basil Rathbone; Nigel Bruce; Martin Kosleck; Marjorie (Reardon) Riordan; Rosalind Ivan; John Abbott; ***D:*** Roy William Neill.

Push **2006 (R)** Unoriginal drug story set in Miami. Bartender Joe (Lindberg) gets his greedy pals Micky (DePaolo) and Kevin (Forsythe) involved in a scheme to push Ecstasy for drug lord Paul (Sanchez). Naturally, they get in too deep and bad things happen. **105m/C; DVD.** Chad Lindberg; Otto Sanchez; Chazz Palminteri; Charlotte Ayanna; William DePaolo; Pierce Forsythe; Michael Rappaport; ***D:*** Dave Rodriguez; ***W:*** Dave Rodriguez; Ben Carlin; ***C:*** Steve Goodman; ***M:*** Tommy Finno.

Push 1/2 **2009 (PG-13)** Operating in a shadowy spy world of paranormals are the subsequent generations of the subjects of a Nazi experiment gone awry, battling over world supremacy. A government agency known as "the Division" seeks to exploit these gifted individuals to carry out their dastardly plans, but young Cassie (Fanning), a "watcher," teams up with Nick (Evans), a "telekinetic," who is underground in Hong Kong to rescue Kira (Belle). Kira is a "pusher" (one who can push thoughts and beliefs into others' minds) who the Division wants dead. Slick and sophisticated cinematography but the performances and plot fall flat. **111m/C; DVD, Blu-Ray, On Demand.** Chris Evans; Dakota Fanning; Camilla Belle; Djimon Hounsou; Clifford Curtis; Neil Jackson; Maggie Siff; Ming Na; Nate Mooney; ***D:*** Paul McGuigan; ***W:*** David Bourla; ***C:*** Peter Sova; ***M:*** Neil Davidge.

Pushed to the Limit 1/2 **1992 (R)** Harry Lee, the most feared gangster in Chinatown, is about to meet his match in martial-arts queen Lesseos. She's out for revenge when she learns that Lee is responsible for her brother's murder but first she must get by Lee's lethal bodyguard, the equally skilled Inga. **88m/C; VHS, DVD.** Mimi Lesseos; Henry Hayashi; Verrel Reed; Barbara Braverman; Greg Ostrin; ***D:*** Michael Mileham; ***W:*** Mimi Lesseos; ***C:*** Bodo Holst; ***M:*** Miriam Cutler.

Pusher **1996** Violent thriller was the directorial debut of 24-year-old Refn. Frank (Bodnia) and his buddy Tonny (Mikkelsen) sell heroin in Copenhagen. Their drug supplier is a Serbian gangster named Milo (Buric), to whom Frank owes money. Things get worse when Frank dumps his latest supply before being arrested—Milo warns him if he doesn't pay his debts in the next couple of days, he's a dead man. The more Frank tries to get the money, the worse things get for him. Danish with subtitles. **105m/C; VHS, DVD.** *DK* Kim Bodnia; Zlatko Buric; Mads Mikkelsen; Laura Drasbaek; Slavko Labovic; Lisbeth Rasmussen; ***D:*** Nicolas Winding Refn; ***W:*** Nicolas Winding Refn; Jens Dahl; ***C:*** Morten Soborg; ***M:*** Povl Kristian Mortensen.

Pushing Hands 1/2 **1992** Aging tai chi master Mr. Chu (Lung) leaves Beijing to live with his son Alex (Wang) and daughter-in-law Martha (Snyder) in suburban New York. High-strung Martha doesn't understand her tranquilly stubborn father-in-law, nor does Chu find disposable American society much to his liking. Naturally, and slowly, some accomodations are made. The title is a tai chi reference to keeping your opponent off-balance while maintaining your own equilibrium. Director Lee's debut feature is also the first in his trilogy of family films—followed by the more accomplished "The Wedding Banquet" and "Eat Drink Man Woman." English and Mandarin Chinese with subtitles. **100m/C; VHS, DVD.** Sihung Lung; Deb Snyder; Bo Z. Wang; Lai Wang; ***D:*** Ang Lee; ***W:*** Ang Lee; ***C:*** Jong Lin; ***M:*** Xiao-Song Qu.

Pushing Tin **1999 (R)** Nick (Cusack) and Russell (Thornton) are rival air traffic controllers at the Long Island tower that oversees New York's three main airports. Nick's a cool professional and a family man with a stay-at-home wife, Connie (Blanchett), and kids. Russell's a cowboy whose wife Mary (Jolie) is young, wild, and usually drunk. The guys' rivalry is intensified when Nick sleeps with Mary and his paranoia gets to him. The technical and journalistic aspects (it's based on a New York Times article) of the tower scenes get things started in surprisingly exciting fashion, and the four leads keep the intensity going despite some script lapses and questionable plot devices. **124m/C; VHS, DVD.** John Cusack; Billy Bob Thornton; Cate Blanchett; Angelina Jolie; Vicki Lewis; Jake Weber; Kurt Fuller; Matt Ross; Jerry Grayson; Michael Willis; ***D:*** Mike Newell; ***W:*** Glen Charles; Les Charles; ***C:*** Gale Tattersall; ***M:*** Anne Dudley.

Pushover **1954** It's all because of a dame. Detective Paul Sheridan (MacMurray) is assigned to befriend moll Lona (Novak) in the hopes she'll lead him to her gangster boyfriend Wheeler (Richards), who was involved in a bank robbery. However, Sheridan and Lona get a little too friendly. After Sheridan and two cohorts stake out Lona's apartment, he agrees to the femme's plan to kill Wheeler and keep the dough instead. The plan goes wrong. **88m/B; DVD.** Fred MacMurray; Kim Novak; Phil Carey; Paul Richards; Allen Nourse; Dorothy Malone; E.G. Marshall; ***D:*** Richard Quine; ***W:*** Roy Huggins; ***C:*** Lester White; ***M:*** Arthur Morton.

Puss in Boots **2011 (PG)** An animated fairy tale adventure taking place before the Shrek series, with the crafty Puss in Boots (voiced by Banderas) trying to rectify his unwarranted fugitive status. In route to retrieve magic beans from criminal tag team Jack and Jill, Puss meets his female nemesis Kitty Softpaws (Hayek) who convinces him to join her quest in helping Humpty Dumpty (Galifianakis) steal the Goose that lays the golden eggs. The animation is as slick as it gets, and the jokes are great for old and young alike. Not too shabby for a spin-off prequel based on a character from a sequel. **90m/C; DVD, Blu-Ray.** ***V:*** Antonio Banderas; Salma Hayek; Zach Galifianakis; Billy Bob Thornton; Amy Sedaris; Constance Marie; ***D:*** Christopher Miller; ***W:*** Tom Wheeler; ***M:*** Henry Jackman.

Pussycat, Pussycat, I Love You **1970** Title is taken from Woody Allen's 1965 pic "What's New Pussycat?" and this British sex comedy is allegedly a remake but it's very poorly done. Egotistical, womanizing American playwright Fred C. Dobbs (McShane) is living in Rome and suffering from fears of going bald and being attacked by a sex-starved gorilla. He finds quack shrink Dr. Fahrquardt (Darden) to help him with both problems. **100m/C; DVD.** *UK* Ian McShane; Severn Darden; Anna Calder-Marshall; John Gavin; Joyce Van Patten; Beba Loncar; ***D:*** Rod Amateau; ***W:*** Rod Amateau; ***C:*** Tonino Delli Colli; ***M:*** Lalo Schifrin.

Putney Swope **1969 (R)** Comedy about a token black ad man mistakenly elected Chairman of the board of a Madison Avenue ad agency who turns the company upside-down. A series of riotous spoofs on commercials is the highpoint in this funny, though somewhat dated look at big business. **84m/B; VHS, DVD, Blu-Ray.** Arnold Johnson; Laura Greene; Stanley Gottlieb; Mel Brooks; ***D:*** Robert Downey; ***W:*** Robert Downey; ***C:*** Gerald Cotts; ***M:*** Charles Cura. Natl. Film Reg. '16.

Puzzle 1/2 **2018 (R)** Agnes (Macdonald) is a timid housewife and mother of two who discovers a hidden talent for completing jigsaw puzzles. To the consternation of her husband (Denman), she partners with another avid puzzler (Khan) to compete in jigsaw tournaments. The pair form an unlikely duo that simultaneously fuels her spirit as a competitor and as a person. A low-key character study, delivered with quiet vulnerability by Macdonald. Adapted from the 2009 Argentinian film, *Rompecabezas.* **103m/C; DVD.** Kelly Macdonald; Irfan Khan; David Denman; Bubba Weiler; Austin Abrams; ***D:*** Marc Turtletaub; ***W:*** Oren Moverman; Natalia Smirnoff; ***C:*** Chris Norr; ***M:*** Dustin O'Halloran.

Puzzlehead 1/2 **2005** Hitchcock and Frankenstein collide in this ill-fated fable. Walter creates an android that not only looks like him but also has his psyche downloaded into its hard drive. As Puzzlehead starts to experience more of Walter's emotions, things get complicated and the two find themselves in love with the same Russian woman from the shop down the street. Conceptually and visually stunning with a regrettably flat-lined plot. **81m/C; DVD.** Stephen Galaida; Robbie Shapiro; ***D:*** James Bai; ***W:*** James Bai; ***C:*** Jeffrey Scott Lando; ***M:*** Max Lichtenstein.

Pygmalion 1/2 **1938** Oscar-winning film adaptation of Shaw's play about a cockney flower-girl who is transformed into a "lady" under the guidance of a stuffy phonetics professor. Shaw himself aided in writing the script in this superbly acted comedy that would be adapted into the musical, "My Fair Lady," first on Broadway in 1956 and for the screen in 1964. **96m/B; VHS, DVD.** *UK* Leslie Howard; Wendy Hiller; Wilfred Lawson; Marie Lohr; Scott Sunderland; David Tree; Everley Gregg; Leueen McGrath; Jean Cadell; Eileen Beldon; Frank Atkinson; O.B. Clarence; ***D:*** Leslie Howard; Anthony Asquith; ***W:*** Cecil Lewis; W.P. Lipscomb; George Bernard Shaw; ***C:*** Harry Stradling, Sr. Oscars '38: Screenplay; Venice Film Fest. '38: Actor (Howard).

Pygmy Island **1950** In this 5th Jungle Jim adventure, Jim (Weissmuller) rescues missing WAC Capt. Ann Kingsley (Savage). Then they work together to defend the local tribe of white pygmies who are being threatened by evil enemy agents after a special type of plant that can be used in the war effort. **69m/B; DVD.** Johnny Weissmuller; Ann Savage; David Bruce; Billy Barty; Steven Geray; William Tannen; Billy Curtis; ***D:*** William Berke; ***W:*** Carroll Young; ***C:*** Ira Morgan.

The Pyramid **2014 (R)** This nonsense was barely released in theaters at the end of 2014 for a reason. Buried by the studio, it's the story of a group of archaeologists who discover a vast, unusually shaped pyramid buried the desert in Giza, and, well, you can imagine where it goes from there. Egyptian history/relics as fodder for a horror film might have worked if the creators of this one had any style whatsoever. Instead, it's just a series of jump scares, poorly shot scenes in the dark, and a plot that becomes increasingly less possible to care about. The studio pretty much ignored it. You should too. **89m/C; DVD, Blu-Ray.** Denis O'Hare; Ashley Hinshaw; Christa Nicola; James Buckley; Amir K; ***D:*** Gregory Levasseur; ***W:*** Nick Simon; Daniel Meersand; ***C:*** Laurent Tangy; ***M:*** Nima Fakhrara.

A Pyromaniac's Love Story **1995 (PG)** Offbeat tale of romance has a neigborhood bakery burning down and every major character confessing to the crime. Earnest working stiffs, snotty rich kids, and kindly old shop owners all have really confusing reasons for wanting to take the heat, most of which have to do with unrequited love. At times charming, but ultimately too whimsical for its own good. The quirky characters and goofy plot twists sabotage any attempt to ignite much interest. **99m/C; VHS, DVD, Blu-Ray.** John Leguizamo; Sadie Frost; William Baldwin; Erika Eleniak; Michael Lerner; Joan Plowright; Armin Mueller-Stahl; Richard Crenna; ***D:*** Joshua Brand; ***W:*** Morgan Ward; ***C:*** John Schwartzman; ***M:*** Rachel Portman.

Python 1/2 **2000 (R)** Intelligence organization develops a perfect weapon in a gigantic python. Of course, the government screws up, the snake gets loose, and there's hell to pay. **90m/C; VHS, DVD.** Robert Englund; Casper Van Dien; Jenny McCarthy; Wil Wheaton; Frayne Rosenoff; ***D:*** Richard Clabaugh; ***W:*** Chris Neal; Gary Hershberger; Paul J.M. Bogh; ***C:*** Patrick Rousseau; ***M:*** David J. Nelsen. **VIDEO**

Python 2 **WOOF!** **2002 (R)** HISSSSSSSSS!!! No, not the titular snake, the unfortunate viewer who picks up this woofer. American cargo plane carrying a secret weapon is shot down over war-torn Chechnya and Russian scientists go to investigate. The "weapon" turns out to be a biogenetically enhanced python that has a taste for human flesh. **85m/C; VHS, DVD.** William Zabka; Dana Ashbrook; Simmone MacKinnon; Alex Jolig; ***D:*** Jeff Rank; ***W:*** Lee McConnell. **CABLE**

The Pyx *The Hooker Cult Murders* **1973 (R)** Canadian suspense thriller about the murder of a prostitute with satanic overtones. Poice sergeant investigates the crime and enters a world of devil worship and decadence. Based on the novel by John Buell. **111m/C; VHS, DVD.** *CA* Karen Black; Christopher Plummer; Donald Pilon; ***D:*** Harvey Hart.

Q & A **1990 (R)** Semi-taut thriller with Nolte playing a totally corrupt, hair-trigger cop trying to make his murder of a drug dealer look like self-defense. Assigned to the case is an ex-cop turned assistant DA (Hutton) who's supposed to sweep the case under the rug. Then he finds out another dealer (Assante) is a witness and he happens to be romancing Hutton's former girlfriend (film debut of director Lumet's daughter). Lots of violence and raw language. **132m/C; VHS, DVD.** Nick Nolte; Timothy Hutton; Armand Assante; Patrick O'Neal; Lee Richardson; Luis Guzman; Charles S. Dutton; Jenny Lumet; Paul Calderon; Fyvush Finkel; Dominic Chianese; ***D:*** Sidney Lumet; ***W:*** Sidney Lumet; ***C:*** Andrzej Bartkowiak; ***M:*** Ruben Blades.

Q (The Winged Serpent) *Q; The Winged Serpent* **1982 (R)** A cult of admirers surrounds this goony monster flick about dragonlike Aztec god Quetzlcoatl, summoned to modern Manhattan by gory human sacrifices, and hungry for rooftop sunbathers and construction teams. Direction and special effects are pretty ragged, but witty script helps the cast shine, especially Moriarty as a lowlife crook who's found the beast's hidden nest. **92m/C; VHS, DVD, Blu-Ray.** Michael Moriarty; Candy Clark; David Carradine; Richard Roundtree; Malachy McCourt; James Dixon; Eddie Jones; Bruce Carradine; Tony Page; Fred J. Scollay; Mary Louise Weller; ***D:*** Larry Cohen; ***W:*** Larry Cohen; ***C:*** Fred Murphy; ***M:*** Robert O. Ragland.

QB VII 1/2 **1974** A knighted physician brings a suit for libel against a novelist for implicating him in war crimes. Hopkins as the purportedly wronged doctor and Gazzara as the writer are both superb. Ending is stunning. Adapted from the novel by Leon Uris. **313m/C; VHS, DVD.** Anthony Hopkins; Ben Gazzara; Lee Remick; Leslie Caron; Juliet Mills; John Gielgud; Anthony Quayle; ***D:*** Tom Gries; ***W:*** Edward Anhalt; ***M:*** Jerry Goldsmith. **TV**

Quackser Fortune Has a Cousin in the Bronx *Fun Loving* **1970 (R)** An Irish fertilizer salesman meets an exchange student from the U.S., who finds herself attracted to this unlearned, but not unknowing, man. An original love story with drama and appeal. **88m/C; VHS, DVD.** *IR* Gene Wilder; Margot Kidder; Eileen Colgan; May Ollis; Seamus Ford; Danny Cummins; Liz Davis; ***D:*** Waris Hussein; ***W:*** Gabriel Walsh; ***C:*** Gilbert Taylor; ***M:*** Michael Dress.

Quadrophenia 🦴🦴🦴 **1979 (R)** Pete Townshend's excellent rock opera about an alienated youth looking for life's meaning in Britain's music scene circa 1963. Jimmy (Daniels) and his pals are Mods who brawl with their rivals, the Rockers. Music by The Who is powerful and apt. Fine performance by Sting in his acting debut as The Ace Face. **115m/C; VHS, DVD, Blu-Ray.** *GB* Phil Daniels; Mark Wingett; Philip Davis; Leslie Ash; Sting; Garry Cooper; Gary Shail; Toyah Willcox; Trevor Laird; Ray Winstone; ***D:*** Franc Roddam; ***W:*** Franc Roddam; Martin Stellman; Dave Humphries; Pete Townshend; ***C:*** Brian Tufano; ***M:*** John Entwhistle; Pete Townshend.

Quality Street 🦴🦴 **1937** English lovers Tone and Hepburn are separated when he leaves to fight in the Napoleonic Wars. When Tone returns years later, he's forgotten his erstwhile heartthrob. He also fails to recognize that the 16-year old coquette who's caught his eye is his old beloved in disguise. Cast works hard to overcome the absurd premise, based on the play by Sir James Barrie. **84m/B; VHS, DVD.** Katharine Hepburn; Franchot Tone; Fay Bainter; Eric Blore; Cora Witherspoon; Estelle Winwood; Florence Lake; Bonita Granville; ***D:*** George Stevens; ***W:*** J.M. Barrie.

Quantez 🦴 ½ **1957** Dull western has a group of bank robbers (plus the leader's girlfriend) heading to the town of Quantez only to discover it's now deserted. Forced to rest their horses, the thieves hope to get away before Apaches, a posse, or their mistrust of each other gets to them. **80m/C; DVD.** Fred MacMurray; Dorothy Malone; John Larch; Syd Chaplin; John Gavin; Michael Ansara; ***D:*** Harry Keller; ***W:*** R. Wright Campbell; ***C:*** Carl Guthrie; ***M:*** Herman Stein.

Quantum of Solace 🦴🦴 ½ **2008 (PG-13)** Bond 24 picks up where "Casino Royale" left off as 007 seeks answers to the late Vesper Lynd's betrayal. An MI6 traitor leads Bond to Dominic Greene, a ruthless businessman who's part of the mysterious Quantum organization, although this time the quest for world domination isn't the issue; it's the water supply that's in jeopardy. Craig gives another excellent performance, lending greater depth and emotion to the character with his steely, angst-ridden depiction. The usual Bond requisites (the gadgets, the car, the explosions, and of course, the femme fatale) are also top-shelf and worth watching. **105m/C; DVD, Blu-Ray, On Demand.** Daniel Craig; Dame Judi Dench; Mathieu Amalric; Olga Kurylenko; Jeffrey Wright; Giancarlo Giannini; Jesper Christensen; Stana Katic; Gemma Arterton; Joaquin Cosio; David Harbour; ***D:*** Marc Foster; ***W:*** Paul Haggis; Neal Purvis; Robert Wade; ***C:*** Roberto Schaefer; ***M:*** David Arnold.

Quarantine 🦴 **2008 (R)** TV reporter Angela Vidal (Carpenter) and her faithful cameraman Scott (Harris) have been assigned to follow two veteran L.A. firefighters, Jake (Hernandez) and Fletcher (Schaech). After responding to a 911 call at a rundown apartment building, the four are suddenly locked inside, trapped with the residents, all of whom are now bloodthirsty zombies, thanks to a mutant virus. And, you guessed it, cameraman Scott films the entire thing, complete with nauseating handheld camera and panicked confessionals. Supposedly a remake of the terrifying Spanish horror flick "Rec," but it plays like a cheap knock-off. **89m/C; Blu-Ray, On Demand, Download.** Jennifer Carpenter; Dania Ramirez; Johnathon Schaech; Jay Hernandez; Columbus Short; Marin Hinkle; Rade Serbedzija; Denis O'Hare; Greg Germann; Steve Harris; ***D:*** John Erick Dowdle; ***W:*** John Erick Dowdle; Drew Dowdle; ***C:*** Ken Seng.

The Quare Fellow 🦴🦴 **1962** Thomas Crimmin (McGoohan), the new warden in a Dublin prison, believes in capital punishment. Two condemned men ("quares" in prison slang) are on death row and one kills himself. Crimmin visits Kathleen (Syms), the other prisoner's wife, and learns the real circumstances behind her husband's crime. He then tries to get the man a reprieve after finding his own views changing. Based on a play by Brendan Behan. **85m/B; DVD.** *GB* Patrick McGoohan; Sylvia Syms; Hilton Edwards; Dermot Kelly; Philip O'Flynn; Walter Macken; Jack Cunningham; ***D:*** Arthur Dreifuss; ***W:*** Jacqueline Sundstrom; ***C:*** Peter Hennessy; ***M:*** Alexander Faris.

The Quarrel 🦴🦴 ½ **1993** Chaim Kovler is a New York poet visiting Montreal in 1948. In a park he notices a group of Orthodox Jews and discovers one is his childhood friend Hersh. Fifteen years earlier their friendship broke over Chaim's decision to give up the religious life for his writing. Having lost their families to the Holocaust in Poland, both men have immigrated to new lives in North America. They immediately pick up their quarrel over religious faith and its value. The two characters serve too much as careful ideologues to be compelling and the story turns cloyingly sentimental. Based on a short story by Yiddish writer Chaim Grade. **88m/C; VHS, DVD.** *CA* Saul Rubinek; R.H. Thomson; Arthur Grosser; ***D:*** Eli Cohen; ***W:*** David Brandes; ***M:*** William Goldstein.

The Quarry 🦴🦴 **1998** A nameless fugitive (Lynch) accepts a ride from a minister, whom he accidentally kills. He takes over the man's identity and possessions and journeys to the minister's new posting in an isolated South African town. When his goods are in turn stolen by a poor young black man, Valentine, the town's racist white police chief not only arrests Valentine for the theft but links him to the murder when the minister's body is discovered. The original fugitive is consumed by guilt but will justice prevail? Based on the novel by Damon Galgut. English and Afrikaans with subtitles. **112m/C; VHS, DVD.** *SA* John Lynch; Serge-Henri Valcke; Jonny Phillips; Oscar Petersen; Jody Abrahams; Sylvia Esau; ***D:*** Marion Hansel; ***W:*** Marion Hansel; ***C:*** Bernard Lutic; ***M:*** Takashi Kako.

Quartet 🦴🦴🦴 **1981 (R)** A young French woman is taken in by an English couple after her husband goes to prison. The husband seduces her, and she becomes trapped emotionally and socially. Superbly acted, claustrophobic drama based on a Jean Rhys novel. **101m/C; VHS, DVD, Blu-Ray.** *GB FR* Isabelle Adjani; Alan Bates; Maggie Smith; Anthony (Corlan) Higgins; ***D:*** James Ivory; ***W:*** Ruth Prawer Jhabvala. Cannes '81: Actress (Adjani).

Quartet 🦴🦴 **2012 (PG-13)** The legendary Hoffman makes a solid directorial debut with this dramedy about an old folks' home for opera singers. Reg (Courtenay), Wilf (Connolly), and Cissy (Collins) live at Beecham House, where they put on a concert for Verdi's birthday every year. Reg's ex-wife Jean (Smith) arrives at the home, causing old rivalries to be raised and relationships tested. Smith and Michael Gambon go a long way in making the clichés of a relatively unsatisfactory script easier to take. **98m/C; DVD, Blu-Ray.** *UK* Maggie Smith; Tom Courtenay; Billy Connolly; Pauline Collins; Michael Gambon; Sheridan Smith; Trevor Peacock; ***D:*** Dustin Hoffman; ***W:*** Ronald Harwood; ***C:*** John de Borman; ***M:*** Dario Marianelli.

Quatermass 2 🦴🦴🦴 *Enemy from Space* **1957** In the well made sequel to "Quatermass Experiment," (also known as "The Creeping Unknown") Professor Quatermass battles blobs and brainwashed zombies to rescue government officials whose bodies have been invaded by aliens. "Five Million Years to Earth" concluded the trilogy. **84m/B; VHS, DVD, Blu-Ray.** *GB* Brian Donlevy; John Longden; Sidney James; Bryan Forbes; William Franklyn; Vera Day; John Van Eyssen; Michael Ripper; Michael Balfour; ***D:*** Val Guest; ***W:*** Val Guest; Nigel Kneale; ***C:*** Gerald Gibbs; ***M:*** James Bernard.

Quatermass Conclusion 🦴🦴 **1979** An elderly British scientist comes out of retirement to stop an immobilizing death ray from outer space from destroying Earth. Edited version of a TV miniseries continues earlier adventures of Quatermass on film and television. **105m/C; VHS, DVD.** *GB* John Mills; Simon MacCorkindale; Barbara Kellerman; Margaret Tyzack; ***D:*** Piers Haggard. **TV**

The Quatermass Experiment 🦴🦴🦴 *The Creeping Unknown* **1956** Excellent British production about an astronaut who returns to Earth carrying an alien infestation that causes him to turn into a horrible monster. Competent acting and tense direction. Followed by "Enemy From Space." **78m/B; VHS, DVD, Blu-Ray.** *GB* Brian Donlevy; Margia Dean; Jack Warner; Richard Wordsworth; ***D:*** Val Guest; ***M:*** James Bernard.

Que Viva Mexico 🦴🦴🦴 *Da Zdravstvuyet Meksika* **1932** Eisenstein's grand unfinished folly on the history of Mexico, reconstructed and released in 1979 by his protege, Grigori Alexandrov. Divided into four sections: "Sandunga" covers the Tehuantepec jungles and its inhabitants; "Manguei" is about a peasant and his bride; "Fiesta" devotes itself to bullfighting and romance; and "Soldadera" depicts the 1910 Mexican revolution through frescoes. Along with "Greed" and "Napoleon," it remains as one of cinema's greatest irrecoverable casualties. Russian narration with English subtitles. **85m/B; VHS, DVD.** *RU* ***D:*** Sergei Eisenstein; ***W:*** Sergei Eisenstein; Grigori Alexandrov; ***C:*** Eduard Tisse.

Queen 🦴🦴🦴 **1993** Epic miniseries from Alex Haley chronicles the life of his paternal great-grandmother, who bore a baby girl, Queen, to her white slave master. At the heart is Queen's quest for identity as she experiences problems due to her mixed race. She finally finds love with a ferry operator (Glover) and it's this union that produces Alex's father, Simon. Although Haley died during production, he had spent considerable time sharing his vision with the staff, who also worked with him on the original "Roots." Good casting and a nice interpretation of Haley's tale. **360m/C; VHS, DVD.** Halle Berry; Ann-Margret; Jasmine Guy; Timothy Daly; Danny Glover; Madge Sinclair; Martin Sheen; Paul Winfield; Ossie Davis; Raven; Victor Garber; Lonette McKee; Sada Thompson; Elizabeth Wilson; ***D:*** John Erman; ***W:*** David Stevens. **TV**

The Queen 🦴🦴🦴 **2006 (PG-13)** Mirren is royalty personified as Britain's Queen Elizabeth II, who maintains her regal authority while dealing with her gossip-prone family and those annoying politicians. The timeline begins in 1997 with the election of Tony Blair (Sheen) as Labor prime minister and moves onto what happens when Princess Diana is killed in that car crash a few months later. Frankly, the Queen can't understand the fuss but, thanks to her professionalism, when she realizes the effect the tragedy has on the country, its politics, and, ultimately, her family, she rallies to put the best royal face on the public grief. **101m/C; DVD, Blu-Ray.** *GB FR IT* Dame Helen Mirren; Michael Sheen; James Cromwell; Helen McCrory; Alex Jennings; Sylvia Sims; ***D:*** Stephen Frears; ***W:*** Peter Morgan; ***C:*** Affonso Beato; ***M:*** Alexandre Desplat. Oscars '06: Actress (Mirren); British Acad. '06: Actress (Mirren), Film; Golden Globes '07: Actress--Drama (Mirren), Screenplay; Screen Actors Guild '06: Actress (Mirren).

Queen and Country 🦴🦴 ½ **2014** Reportedly the final film of the legendary John Boorman's career, this drama is a direct sequel to the director's Best Picture-nominated 1987 film "Hope and Glory." It picks up the story of that film as Bill Rohan (Turner), John Boorman's alter ego for these biographical tales, is ten years older and enlisting. It is the early '50s and England is going through a major time of change as Boorman captures the development of a country through the eyes of a young man forced to train for the Korean War. In basic training, Bill and his best buddy Percy (Jones) match wits with superiors played eloquently by Richard E. Grant and David Thewlis. **115m/C; DVD.** *UK* Callum Turner; Caleb Landry Jones; Tamsin Egerton; David Thewlis; Richard E. Grant; Sinead Cusack; David Hayman; John Standing; Vanessa Kirby; ***D:*** John Boorman; ***W:*** John Boorman; ***C:*** Seamus Deasy; ***M:*** Stephen McKeon.

Queen & Slim 🦴🦴🦴 **2019 (R)** After an awkward Tinder date, the man (Kaluuya) is driving his companion (Turner-Smith) home when they are pulled over by an aggressive cop on a minor traffic violation. The situation escalates because of the trigger happy, racist officer, who ends up dead. The terrified couple leaves the scene and goes on the run together. As they travel south to flee the country, they grow closer. At the same time, dash cam footage of the incident goes viral turning them into folk heroes. Matsoukas's feature debut is stylish and visually interesting, with characters and situations who are given time and space to develop. **133m/C; DVD, Blu-Ray.** Daniel Kaluuya; Jodie Turner-Smith; Bokeem Woodbine; Chloë Sevigny; Flea; ***D:*** Melina Matsoukas; ***W:*** Lena Waithe; ***C:*** Tat Radcliffe.

Queen Bee 🦴🦴 ½ **1955** Crawford is at her manipulative best as Southern belle Eva Phillips, married to wealthy Georgia mill owner Avery (Sullivan). The ruthless Eva is despised by her bitter, tippling husband who finds a chance at romance when cousin Jennifer (Marlow) comes to visit. Naturally, Eva can't stand any competition, though she doesn't care about Avery, and tries to break up the duo even as she seeks to renew her own affair with a former lover (Ireland). Based on the novel by Edna Lee. **94m/B; VHS, DVD.** Joan Crawford; Barry Sullivan; John Ireland; Lucy Marlow; Betsy Palmer; Fay Wray; ***D:*** Ranald MacDougall; ***W:*** Ranald MacDougall; ***C:*** Charles B(ryant) Lang, Jr.; ***M:*** George Duning.

Queen Christina 🦴🦴🦴 ½ **1933** A stylish, resonant star vehicle for Garbo, portraying the 17th-century Swedish queen from ascension to the throne to her romance with a Spanish ambassador. Alternately hilarious and moving, it holds some of Garbo's greatest and most memorable moments. Gilbert's second to last film and his only successful outing after the coming of sound. **101m/B; VHS, DVD.** Greta Garbo; John Gilbert; Lewis Stone; Sir C. Aubrey Smith; Ian Keith; Reginald Owen; Elizabeth Young; ***D:*** Rouben Mamoulian; ***C:*** William H. Daniels.

Queen for a Day 🦴🦴 ½ *Horsie* **1951** Three differing vignettes, based on a rather notorious radio and TV game show of the time, in which "deserving" (or sufficiently pathetic) working-class women were rewarded for their selflessness. Part one concerns a perfect suburban family whose son contracts polio. Part two has a teen spooking his immigrant parents by working as a carnival high diver to earn college cash. The finale is a Dorothy Parker farce about a homely but kindhearted nurse caring for the child of an unappreciative couple. So popular was this segment that the film was retitled after the main character. Overall, not bad considering the source. **107m/B; DVD.** Phyllis Avery; Darren McGavin; Tristram Coffin; Adam Williams; Tracey Roberts; Jack Bailey; Jim Morgan; Fort Pearson; ***D:*** Arthur Lubin; ***W:*** Seton I. Miller; ***C:*** Guy Roe; ***M:*** Hugo Friedhofer.

Queen Kelly 🦴🦴🦴 **1929** The popularly known, slapdash version of von Stroheim's famous final film, in which an orphan goes from royal marriage to white slavery to astounding wealth. Never really finished, the film is the edited first half of the intended project, prepared for European release after von Stroheim had been fired. Even so, a campy, extravagant and lusty melodrama. Silent. **113m/B; Silent; VHS, DVD.** Gloria Swanson; Walter Byron; Seena Owen; Tully Marshall; Madam Sul Te Wan; ***D:*** Erich von Stroheim; ***W:*** Erich von Stroheim; ***C:*** Paul Ivano; Gordon Pollock.

Queen Margot 🦴🦴🦴 ½ *La Reine Margot* **1994 (R)** Beautiful Catholic Princess Marguerite de Valois (Adjani) is the pawn of her devious mother, the widowed queen Catherine de Medici (Lisi). Mom manipulates unstable son Charles IX (Anglade), the nominal ruler of 1570s France, while she marries Margot off to Protestant Henri de Navarre (Auteuil). Margot is contemptuous of Henri and takes a lover, de la Mole (Perez). But both Margot and Henri are united against Catherine's orders to murder the rival Huguenots—a violent affair known as the St. Bartholomew's Day Massacre. The history's confusing, the violence graphic, the acting flamboyant, and the visuals top-notch. Based on the Alexandre Dumas novel. French with subtitles. **135m/C; VHS, DVD, Blu-Ray.** *FR* Isabelle Adjani; Daniel Auteuil; Virna Lisi; Jean-Hugues Anglade; Vincent Perez; Pascal Greggory; Miguel Bose; Dominique Blanc; Claudio Amendola; Asia Argento; Julien Rassam; Jean-Claude Brialy; Carlos Lopez; ***D:*** Patrice Chereau; ***W:*** Patrice Chereau; Daniele Thompson; ***C:*** Philippe Rousselot; ***M:*** Goran Bregovic. Cannes '94: Actress (Lisi), Special Jury Prize; Cesar '95: Actress (Adjani), Cinematog., Costume Des., Support. Actor (Anglade), Support. Actress (Lisi).

Queen of Blood 1966 Cheap AIP sci fi. In 1990, a rescue ship is sent to Mars to look for survivors of the crash of an alien spaceship. The astronauts find a green-skinned alien queen who starts draining them of blood, which she needs to survive. Oh yeah, her planet is dying and her people want to make Earth their new home (sound familiar?) Executive producer Roger Corman bought footage from one (or maybe two) Russian sci fi flicks and just incorporated it with enough new scenes to make a plot. **81m/C; DVD.** Florence Marly; Judi Meredith; John Saxon; Basil Rathbone; Dennis Hopper; ***D:*** Curtis Harrington; ***W:*** Curtis Harrington; ***C:*** Vilis Lapenieks; ***M:*** Leonard Morand.

Queen of Diamonds 1991 The "Queen of Diamonds" is an alienated blackjack dealer in Vegas who, in between dealing cards, casually searches for her missing husband and looks after an old man in a motel. **77m/C; VHS, DVD, Streaming.** Tinka Menkes; ***D:*** Nina Menkes; ***W:*** Nina Menkes.

Queen of Earth 2015 Writer/director Alex Ross Perry draws two amazing performances from his leads: Moss and Waterston. Catherine (Moss) is a woman dealing with the emotional turmoil after the one-two punch of her father's suicide and her boyfriend breaking up with her. She goes to spend time with friend Virginia (Waterston) at a lake house, and Perry flashes back to a year earlier when "Ginny" was the troubled one and Catherine the happy one. As the current Catherine gets more and more unstable, Perry's film becomes something closer to a thriller than the relationship drama one might expect. It's fantastic. **90m/C; DVD.** Elisabeth Moss; Katherine Waterston; Patrick Fugit; Kentucker Audley; Keith Poulson; ***D:*** Alex Ross Perry; ***W:*** Alex Ross Perry; ***C:*** Sean Price Williams; ***M:*** Keegan DeWitt.

Queen of Hearts 1/2 **1989 (PG)** Excellent, original romantic comedy is a directorial triumph for Amiel in his first feature. An Italian couple defy both their families and marry for love. Four children later, we find them running a diner in England. Humorous, dramatic, sad—everything a movie can and should be. Fine performances. **112m/C; VHS, DVD; Open Captioned.** *GB* Anita Zagaria; Joseph Long; Eileen Way; Vittorio Duse; Vittorio Amandola; Ian Hawkes; ***D:*** Jon Amiel; ***M:*** Michael Convertino.

Queen of Hearts 1/2 *Dronningen* **2019** A successful, married attorney and mother of two seduces her teenage stepson, wreaking havoc in both her personal and professional life. Writer/director May el-Toukhy delivers a disturbing character study of a narcissist who transforms from merely unethical to downright evil. Denmark's submission to the International Feature Film category of the 92nd Academy Awards. **127m/C; DVD.** Trine Dyrholm; Gustav Lindh; Magnus Krepper; Liv Esmår Dannemann; Silja Esmår Dannemann; ***D:*** May el-Toukhy; ***W:*** May el-Toukhy; Maren Louise Käehne; ***C:*** Jasper Spanning; ***M:*** Jon Ekstrand.

Queen of Katwe **2016 (PG)** Director Nair, who lives in Uganda, tells one of her country's most crowd-pleasing stories, that of the grandmaster in chess who came from one of its slums. Phiona Mutesi (Nalwanga) helps her mother (a perfect Nyong'o) sell food on the streets just to make ends meet. At a sports club, she learns about chess, and is trained by one of its leaders, Robert Katende (Oyelowo). Quickly, Katende realizes that Phiona is no ordinary chess player, and she becomes the first African grandmaster in the sport. This is smart, heartfelt and moving filmmaking, a film that feels real instead of manipulative. **124m/C; DVD, Blu-Ray.** Madina Nalwanga; David Oyelowo; Lupita Nyong'o; Martin Kabanza; Taryn Kyaze; ***D:*** Mira Nair; ***W:*** William Wheeler; ***C:*** Sean Bobbitt; ***M:*** Alex Heffes.

The Queen of Mean 1/2 *Leona Helmsley: The Queen of Mean* **1990** Tabloid TV-movie based on Ransdell Pierson's scandal-sheet bio of the hotel magnate and convicted tax cheat. See Leona connive. See Leona bitch. See Leona gets hers. What's the point? If you ask that you're too bright to watch. Currently available as 'Leona Helmsely: The Queen of Mean'. **94m/C; VHS, Streaming.** Suzanne Pleshette; Lloyd Bridges; Bruce Weitz; Joe Regalbuto; ***D:*** Richard Michaels; ***C:*** Hanania Baer. **TV**

Queen of Outer Space WOOF! **1958** Notorious male-chauvinist sci-fi cheapie starts out slow, but then the laughs keep coming as the cast plays the hyperdumb material straight. Space cadets crash on Venus, find it ruled by women—and the dolls have wicked plans in store for mankind. Don't be surprised if you've seen the sets before since they were borrowed from "Forbidden Planet," "World Without End," and "Flight to Mars." **80m/C; VHS, DVD, Blu-Ray.** Zsa Zsa Gabor; Eric Fleming; Laurie Mitchell; Paul Birch; Barbara Darrow; Dave Willcock; Lisa Davis; Patrick Waltz; Marilyn Buferd; Marjorie Durant; Lynn Cartwright; Gerry Gaylor; ***D:*** Edward L. Bernds; ***W:*** Charles Beaumont; ***C:*** William F. Whitley; ***M:*** Marlin Skiles.

The Queen of Spades 1949 Mystical drama about a Russian soldier who ruins his life searching for winning methods of card playing. Well-made version of the Pushkin story. **95m/B; VHS, DVD, Blu-Ray.** *GB* Anton Walbrook; Edith Evans; Ronald Howard; Mary Jerrold; Yvonne Mitchell; Anthony Dawson; ***D:*** Thorold Dickinson.

Queen of the Damned **2002 (R)** Adaptation of the third book in Anne Rice's "Vampire Chronicles" resurrects vampire Lestat (Townsend) to rock the new millennium after a 200-year nap. He becomes the lead singer of a goth band and soon meets up with Jesse (Moreau) a reckless vampire researcher and fellow vampires Marius (Perez), and Maharet (Olin). Lestat's new lady love is Akasha (late pop star Aaliyah), the mother of all the vampires, who has big plans to (what else?) rule the world. Her followers feel differently, however. Camp, but not camp enough. One dimensional characters and lackluster plot leave this drag of a "Queen" to Rice and vampire fans only. **101m/C; VHS, DVD, Blu-Ray.** *US AU* Aaliyah; Stuart Townsend; Marguerite Moreau; Vincent Perez; Lena Olin; Paul McGann; Claudia Black; Bruce Spence; Christian Manon; ***D:*** Michael Rymer; ***W:*** Scott Abbott; ***C:*** Ian Baker; ***M:*** Richard Gibbs; Jonathan Davis.

Queen of the Jungle 1935 Re-edited adventure serial featuring a white woman cast off in a hot-air balloon and landing in Africa, where she is hailed as a Queen. High camp, starring ex-Our Ganger Kornman. **85m/B; VHS, DVD.** Mary Kornman; Reed Howes; ***D:*** Robert F. "Bob" Hill.

Queen of the Stardust Ballroom 1975 Well-made drama about a lonely widow who goes to a local dance hall, where she meets a man and begins an unconventional late love. **98m/C; DVD, Blu-Ray.** Maureen Stapleton; Charles Durning; Michael Strong; Charlotte Rae; Sam O'Steen; ***D:*** Michael Brandon; ***M:*** Billy Goldenberg. **TV**

The Queen of Versailles **2012 (PG)** Documentary filmmaker Greenfield turns the bizarre story of Jackie and David Siegel into more than just a commentary on the pitfalls of excess but a character-driven piece about how the economic downfall impacted both the little and very, very big people. The Siegels were big enough that they could realistically plan to build the largest private home in America, their own modern Versailles. As the housing crisis deflates David Siegel's fortune like a punctured balloon, Greenfield captures their world falling apart in all its comic tragedy. **100m/C; DVD, Blu-Ray.** ***D:*** Lauren Greenfield; ***C:*** Tom Hurwitz; ***M:*** Jeff Beal.

Queen Sized 2008 Maggie (Blonsky) is a fat (which she prefers to plus-sized) high school senior constantly humiliated by the popular clique. She's also nagged about her weight by her worried mom (Potts) since her overweight dad died of diabetes. As a cruel prank, Maggie is nominated for homecoming queen but her friend Casey (Holleman) encourages her to let the other social outcasts organize a real campaign. Blonsky shines in a predictable but fact-based story, letting her insecurities and triumphs all show on her expressive face. **120m/C; DVD.** Nicole Blonsky; Annie Potts; Lilly Holleman; Jackson Pace; Fabian Morena; Kimberly Matula; Liz McGeever; Kelsey Schultz; ***D:*** Peter Levin; ***W:*** Richard Kletter; Rodney Johnson; Nora Kletter; ***C:*** Neil Roach. **CABLE**

Queen to Play *Joueuse* **2009** Assured debut about reinvention from writer/director Bottaro. Middle-aged Corsican hotel maid and house cleaner Helene (Bonnaire) becomes intrigued by an American couple's flirtatious chess game. Sexual sparks are sadly lacking in her own marriage and neither her husband or daughter understand her sudden obsession. When she realizes that reclusive expatriate Dr. Kroger (Kline) is a chess player, Helene persuades him to be her mentor. English and French with subtitles. **101m/C; DVD.** *FR GE* Sandrine Bonnaire; Kevin Kline; Francis Reanud; Valerie Lagrange; Jennifer Beals; Dominic Gould; ***D:*** Caroline Bottaro; ***W:*** Caroline Bottaro; ***C:*** Jean-Claude Larrieu.

Queenie 1/2 **1987** Miniseries loosely based on the life of actress Merle Oberon, exploring her rise to stardom. Based on the best-selling novel by Michael Korda, Oberon's nephew by marriage. Many long, dry passages fit for leaving the room for snacks. **233m/C; VHS, DVD.** Mia Sara; Kirk Douglas; Martin Balsam; Claire Bloom; Topol; Joel Grey; Sarah Miles; Joss Ackland; ***D:*** Larry Peerce; ***M:*** Georges Delerue. **TV**

The Queens 1/2 *Sex Quartet* **1966** Italian sex comedy consisting of four short stories with four different female leads filmed by four different directors. After some trouble, a young woman hitchhiker has a perverse reaction to the third man who offers her a ride; a gypsy, who uses a neighbors' children to get money, seduces a doctor; a man is happy to indulge a housewife whose husband is away until he discovers his own wife is unfaithful; and a drunken woman seduces her butler and then forgets their night together. Italian with subtitles. **110m/C; DVD.** *IT* Monica Vitti; Claudia Cardinale; Raquel Welch; Capucine; Jean Sorel; Alberto Sordi; Gastone Moschin; Enrico Maria Salerno; ***D:*** Mario Monicelli; Mauro Bolognini; Luciano Salce; Antonio Pietrangeli; ***W:*** Suso Cecchi D'Amico; Roberto Sonego; Ruggero Maccari; Luigi Magni; ***C:*** Dario Di Palma; Carlo Di Palma; Armando Nannuzzi; Leonida Barboni.

Queens Logic 1/2 **1991 (R)** Ensemble comedy in the tradition of "The Big Chill" featuring the trials and tribulations of the "old-neighborhood" gang, who gather again on hometurf and reminisce. Most of the film centers around Olin and girlfriend Webb and whether or not he will chicken out of their wedding. Not bad comedy, with Mantegna delivering most of the good lines. **116m/C; VHS, DVD.** John Malkovich; Kevin Bacon; Jamie Lee Curtis; Linda Fiorentino; Joe Mantegna; Ken Olin; Tom Waits; Chloe Webb; Ed Marinaro; Kelly Bishop; Tony Spiridakis; ***D:*** Steve Rash; ***W:*** Tony Spiridakis; ***C:*** Amir M. Mokri; ***M:*** Joe Jackson.

Queen's Messenger II *Witness to a Kill* **2001 (R)** Super-suave-James-Bond-wannabe Captain Strong's mission is to free two gorgeous women from their captors while cracking an international smuggling ring and preventing an African country's government from being overthrown. **90m/C; VHS, DVD.** Gary Daniels; Norman Anstey; Vusi Kunene; Ron Smerczak; Nick Boraine; Lindelani Buthelezi; Isaac Chokwe; Gideon Emery; Moagi Modise; Robert Whitehead; John Whiteley; ***D:*** Darrell Roodt; Mark Roper; ***W:*** Peter Jobin; Harry Alan Towers; Michael Swan; ***C:*** Adolfo Bartoli; Giulio Biccari; ***M:*** Rene Veldsman. **VIDEO**

Queens of Comedy 1/2 **2001 (R)** This "sort of" companion piece to Spike Lee's "Original Kings of Comedy" is a concert recorded at the Orpheum Theatre in Memphis starring four black stand-up comediennes—Miss Laura Hayes, Adel Givens, Sommore, and Mo'Nique. **79m/C; DVD.** Adele Givens; Mo'Nique; Miss Laura Hayes; Sommore; ***D:*** Steve Purcell.

Queens of the Ring 1/2 *Wrestling Queens; Les reines du ring* **2013** A French wrestling comedy about a mother's extreme efforts to connect with her son. A cashier by trade, Rose (Berry) has become estranged from her son, whose primary interest is WWE wrestling. Looking for any way to reach him, she signs up for an intense training program to learn how to wrestle just like the professionals in the WWE. Along the way, she gets her co-workers to join the program as well, they become engrossed in the training, and develop their own popular ring personas. French with subtitles. **97m/C; DVD, Streaming, Download.** Marilou Berry; Nathalie Baye; Andre Dussollier; Audrey Fleurot; Corinne Masiero; ***D:*** Jean-Marc Rudnicki; ***W:*** Manon Dillys; Helene Le Gall; Marie Pavlenko; ***C:*** Antoine Monod.

The Queen's Sister 2005 The queen would be the never-seen Elizabeth and the sister would be perennial tabloid fodder, Princess Margaret (Cohu), a fun-loving sort who never let royal restrictions impinge on her having a good time. Unable to marry her true love (a divorced man), Margaret settles for photographer Anthony Armstrong-Jones (Stephens), eventually leading to her own divorce (the first in the royal family) and a series of controversial liaisons. Cohu is properly flamboyant but, ultimately, Margaret's life is a sad decline. **155m/C; DVD.** Toby Stephens; David Threlfall; Simon Woods; Meredith MacNeill; Lucy Cohu; Aden Gillet; ***D:*** Simon Cellan Jones; ***W:*** Craig Warner; ***C:*** David Katznelson; ***M:*** John Altman. **TV**

Queer Duck: The Movie 2006 An extension of the Showtime cartoons featuring a gay duck. Queer Duck breaks up with his partner Openly Gator for an unlikely love interest—aging diva Lola Buzzard. But this turn towards heterosexuality proves to be a mistake. Raucous humor and musical numbers further liven the rude proceedings. **72m/C; DVD.** ***V:*** Kevin M. Richardson; Maurice LaMarche; Billy West; Jackie Hoffman; Tim Curry; Conan O'Brien; David Duchovny; Jim J. Bullock; ***D:*** Xeth Feinberg; ***W:*** Mike Reiss; ***M:*** Sam Elwitt. **VIDEO**

Quentin Durward 1/2 **1955** In 1465, dashing Quentin (Taylor) is sent from Scotland by his elderly uncle (Thesinger) to pick up his French bride-to-be Isabelle (Kendall). She is a pawn at Louis XI's (Morley) court because of her previous association with the power-hungry Duke of Burgundy (Clunes) and gets kidnapped. Quentin, who has nobly refrained from expressing his own love for the lovely, comes to her rescue and much swashbuckling follows. Based on a novel by Sir Walter Scott. **100m/C; DVD.** Robert Taylor; Kay Kendall; Robert Morley; Alec Clunes; George Cole; Duncan Lamont; Marius Goring; Wilfrid Hyde-White; Ernest Thesiger; ***D:*** Richard Thorpe; ***W:*** Robert Ardrey; George Froeschel; ***C:*** Christopher Challis; ***M:*** Bronislau Kaper.

Querelle 1/2 **1983 (R)** Querelle, a handsome sailor, finds himself involved in a bewildering environment of murder, drug smuggling, and homosexuality in the port of Brest. Highly stylized and erotic sets, along with a dark look, give the film an interesting feel. Nice performances by Davis, Nero, and Moreau. Fassbinder's controversial last film, based on the story by Jean Genet. Strange, difficult narrative (such as it is), alternately boring and engrossing. **106m/C; VHS, DVD.** *GE* Brad Davis; Jeanne Moreau; Franco Nero; Laurent Malet; ***D:*** Rainer Werner Fassbinder; ***W:*** Rainer Werner Fassbinder; Burkhard Driest; ***C:*** Xaver Schwarzenberger; Josef Vavra; ***M:*** Peer Raben.

The Quest **1996 (PG-13)** In his directorial debut, Van Damme plays pick-pocket Christopher Dubois, who hops a freighter heading for the Far East in order to escape police trouble. He learns about a prestigious martial arts competition, where the prize could set him up for life, if he can manage to get into the invitation-only event. Van Dammesets this in the 1920s, with fairly good results, piling on the beautiful location shots until the inevitable martial arts melee toward the end. Pacing is sketchy but Van Damme does display directorial talent. **95m/C; VHS, DVD, Blu-Ray.** Jean-Claude Van Damme; Roger Moore; Aki Aleong; James Remar; Jack McGee; Janet Gunn; Abdel Qissi; Louis Mandylor; ***D:*** Jean-Claude Van Damme; ***W:*** Stuart Klein; Paul Mones; ***C:*** David Gribble; ***M:*** Randy Edelman.

Quest 1/2 **2017** An insightful documentary look at Christopher "Quest" Rainey, who uses the small music studio in the basement of his North Philadelphia home to support and encourage young men in his African-American community. Shot over a decade, the film explores Quest's family life, including his marriage to Christine'a, their adult children from previous relationships, and their young daughter, P.J. Through many family moments--good and bad--the film shows the couple's deep and thoughtful perspective on life. Quest's interactions with the young aspiring hip-hop artists are also meaningful and revealing. A moving film that effectively shows the complexities of life, both tragic and joyful. **104m/C; DVD.** ***D:*** Jonathan Olshefski; ***M:*** T. Griffin.

Quest for Camelot 1/2 **1998 (G)** Camelot's future lies in the hands of heroine Kayley, who sees an opportunity to win a spot at King Arthur's roundtable when Excalibur is stolen by evil knight Ruber. On her quest to recover the sword, she meets blind hermit Garrett and two-headed dragon Devon and Cornwall. Ffirst full-length animated feature from Warner Bros. can't quite overcome its familar story, one-dimensional villain, and forgettable songs. However, Kayley and Garrett are strong, non-stereotypical characters. Based on the children's novel "The King's Damosel" by Vera Chapman. **85m/C; VHS, DVD.** ***V:*** Jessalyn Gilsig; Cary Elwes; Gary Oldman; Eric Idle; Don Rickles; Jane Seymour; Pierce Brosnan; Gabriel Byrne; Bronson Pinchot; Jaleel White; John Gielgud; ***D:*** Frederick Du Chau; ***W:*** Kirk De Micco; William Schifrin; David Seidler; ***M:*** Patrick Doyle. Golden Globes '99: Song ("The Prayer").

Quest for Fire **1982 (R)** An interesting story sans the usual dialogue thing. A group of men (McGill, Perlman, El-Kadi) during the Ice Age must wander the land searching for fire after they lose theirs fending off an attack. During their quest, they encounter and battle various animals and tribesmen in order to survive. The special language they speak was developed by Anthony Burgess, while the primitive movements were Desmond "The Naked Ape" Morris. Perlman went on to become the Beast in TV's "Beauty and the Beast"; Chong, as a primitive babe, is the daughter of Tommy Chong of the comic duo Cheech and Chong. **75m/C; VHS, DVD.** *FR* Everett McGill; Ron Perlman; Nameer El-Kadi; Rae Dawn Chong; ***D:*** Jean-Jacques Annaud; ***W:*** Gerard Brach. Oscars '82: Makeup; Genie '83: Actress (Chong).

Quest for Love 1/2 **1971** Quirky sci-fi story of a man who passes through a time warp and finds himself able to maintain two parallel lives. Based on John Wyndham's short story. **90m/C; VHS, DVD.** *GB* Joan Collins; Tom Bell; Denholm Elliott; Laurence Naismith; ***D:*** Ralph Thomas.

A Question of Attribution 1/2 **1991** Sir Anthony Blunt (Fox) is an internationally respected art expert who also serves as an art adviser to Queen Elizabeth II. His life unravels when an on-going British Intelligence investigation reveals him to be the fourth man in the Burgess-Maclean-Philby scandal involving Englishmen who spied for the USSR. The investigation of Blunt's covert past is paralleled with his own art investigation of a painting attributed to Titian. Three men are depicted in the art work—with a fourth male figure discovered to have been painted over. Bennett adapted his play for this TV drama. Part of the 'The Alan Bennett Collection'. **90m/C; VHS, DVD.** *UK* James Fox; David Calder; Geoffrey Palmer; Prunella Scales; Mark Payton; Jason Flemyng; Edward De Souza; Ann Beach; ***D:*** John Schlesinger; ***W:*** Alan Bennett. **TV**

A Question of Faith 1/2 **2017 (PG)** Three sets of parents turn to their faith for comfort when tragedy strikes their children in simultaneous yet distinct ways. Delivers heaps of pro-God sentiment that only believers will find moving; for others, it's as uninspired as its title. **104m/C; DVD, Blu-Ray.** Richard T. Jones; Kim Fields; C. Thomas Howell; Renee O'Connor; Gregory Alan Williams; ***D:*** Kevan Otto; ***W:*** Ty Manns; ***C:*** Chase Bowman.

The Questor Tapes 1/2 **1974** Reclusive genius Dr. Vaslovik (Ayres) disappears, leaving the programming for his lifelike android Questor (Foxworth) incomplete. Questor then leaves the lab in search of his maker in this failed TV pilot from Gene Roddenberry. **100m/C; DVD.** Robert Foxworth; Mike Farrell; John Vernon; Lew Ayres; James Shigeta; Dana Wynter; Majel Barrett; ***D:*** Richard A. Colla; ***W:*** Gene Roddenberry; Gene L. Coon; ***C:*** Michael D. Margulies; ***M:*** Gil Melle. **TV**

Quick 1/2 **1993 (R)** Polo stars as Quick, a professional assassin whose latest job is Herschel (Donovan), a mob accountant turned federal witness. When Quick is double-crossed, she takes off with Herschel as her insurance and a couple of bad guys (Fahey and Davi) on her trail. Not too much sex and lots of violence to go along with the fast pacing. **99m/C; VHS, DVD.** Teri Polo; Martin Donovan; Jeff Fahey; Robert Davi; Tia Carrere; ***D:*** Rick King; ***W:*** Frederick Bailey; ***M:*** Robert Sprayberry.

The Quick and the Dead **1987** Based on a Louis L'Amour story, this cable western features a lone gunslinger who protects a defenseless settler's family from the lawless West, only to become a source of sexual tension for the wife. **91m/C; VHS, DVD.** Sam Elliott; Tom Conti; Kate Capshaw; Kenny Morrison; Matt Clark; ***D:*** Robert Day; ***C:*** Dick Bush; ***M:*** Steve Dorff. **CABLE**

The Quick and the Dead 1/2 **1995 (R)** Stone is a tough gal gunslinger out to avenge the murder of her father. Ellen arrives in the frontier town of Redemption where arch-villain Herod (Hackman) rules by means of violence and intimidation. Director Raimi packs in so many cliches that you're amazed that it's not a parody of the spaghetti westerns it tries to emulate. Maybe if Stone and Raimi didn't take this film so seriously, it would have been a better movie, but it's still entertaining. Sit back and enjoy the wildly staged gunfights, interesting camera angles, and excellent work by Hackman and Crowe. **105m/C; VHS, DVD, Blu-Ray.** Sharon Stone; Gene Hackman; Leonardo DiCaprio; Russell Crowe; Kevin Conway; Lance Henriksen; Roberts Blossom; Pat Hingle; Keith David; Michael Stone; Stacey Linn Ramsower; Gary Sinise; ***D:*** Sam Raimi; ***W:*** Simon Moore; ***C:*** Dante Spinotti; ***M:*** Alan Silvestri.

Quick Change 1/2 **1990 (R)** Murray, Davis, and Quaid form bumbling trio of New York bank robbers who can't seem to exit the Big Apple with loot. Based on Jay Cronley's book, it's Murray's directing debut (with help from screenwriter Franklin). Engaging minor caper comedy displaying plenty of NYC dirty boulevards. **89m/C; VHS, DVD.** Bill Murray; Geena Davis; Randy Quaid; Jason Robards, Jr.; Bob Elliott; Victor Argo; Kathryn Grody; Philip Bosco; Phil Hartman; Kurtwood Smith; Jamey Sheridan; Tony Shalhoub; Stanley Tucci; Jack Gilpin; Reg E. Cathey; ***D:*** Bill Murray; Howard Franklin; ***W:*** Howard Franklin; ***C:*** Michael Chapman; ***M:*** Randy Edelman; Howard Shore.

The Quick Gun 1/2 **1964** Routine western finds gunslinger Clint Cooper (Murphy) returning to his father's ranch, which he's just inherited. First he stumbles across the Spangler gang planning to rob the local bank. Most of the men are off on a cattle drive, so Cooper must defend the remaining inhabitants with a few volunteers. **88m/C; DVD.** Audie Murphy; Ted de Corsia; Merry Anders; James Best; Walter Sande; ***D:*** Sidney Salkow; ***W:*** Robert E. Kent; ***C:*** Lester Shorr; ***M:*** Richard LaSalle.

Quick, Let's Get Married WOOF! *Seven Different Ways; The Confession* **1971** Quick, let's not watch this movie. Even the people who made it must have hated it: they waited seven years to release it. Rogers runs a whorehouse; Eden is a gullible, pregnant prostitute; Gould in his big-screen debut(!) is a deaf-mute. A must-not see. **96m/C; VHS, DVD.** Ginger Rogers; Ray Milland; Barbara Eden; Carl Schell; Michael Ansara; Walter Abel; Scott Meyer; Cecil Kellaway; Elliott Gould; ***D:*** William Dieterle.

The Quickie 1/2 **2001 (R)** Get your minds out of the gutter! Actually, this mob soap opera would have been a lot more fun if it had wallowed in the gutter itself. Conflicted Russian mobster Oleg (Mashkov) is celebrating his retirement with his family on New Year's Eve at their Malibu beach house. But Oleg has been targeted for extermination and maybe exterminator Lisa (Leigh), who is supposedly at the house to get rid of the vermin, is there to do the job. Bodrov's first English-language venture. **95m/C; VHS, DVD.** Vladimir Mashkov; Jennifer Jason Leigh; Dean Stockwell; Lesley Ann Warren; Henry Thomas; Sergei Bodrov, Jr.; Brenda Bakke; Jsu Garcia; ***D:*** Sergei Bodrov; ***W:*** Sergei Bodrov; Carolyn Cavallero; ***C:*** Sergei Kozlov; ***M:*** Gia Kancheli.

Quicksand 1/2 **1950** Mechanic Rooney borrows $20 from his boss's cash register, intending to return it. One thing leads to another, the plot thickens, and it's downhill (for Rooney) from there. Good, tense suspense drama. **79m/B; VHS, DVD.** Mickey Rooney; Peter Lorre; Jeanne Cagney; ***D:*** Irving Pichel; ***W:*** Robert Smith; ***C:*** Lionel Lindon; ***M:*** Louis Gruenberg.

Quicksand **2001 (R)** Bill Turner (Dudikoff) is the new shrink on a marine base and one of his patients is Randi Stewart (Theiss), who's not only a sergeant but the commanding officer's (Hedaya) daughter. When General Stewart is murdered, Randi becomes the prime suspect. Turner, who has taken more than a professional interest in his patient, begins investigating and learns that the base has had an unusually high number of suicides as well. **92m/C; VHS, DVD.** Michael Dudikoff; Brooke Theiss; Dan Hedaya; Michael O'Hagan; Douglas Weston; Richard Kind; Pamela Salem; ***D:*** Sam Firstenberg; ***W:*** Steve Schoenberg; Ruben Gordon; ***C:*** Sameer Reddy; ***M:*** Curt Harpel. **VIDEO**

Quicksand **2001 (R)** Bank exec Martin (Keaton) is sent to Monaco to investigate some questionable offshore accounts. Apparently the money is being laundered through financing various film productions—one of which is the currently filming "Quicksand" that stars washed-up actor Jake (Caine). Soon both are in over their heads in some real-life drama. **93m/C; VHS, DVD.** *GB FR* Michael Caine; Michael Keaton; Rade Serbedzija; Judith Godreche; Xander Berkeley; Elina Lowensohn; Kathleen Wilhoite; ***D:*** John MacKenzie; ***W:*** Tim Prager; ***C:*** Walter McGill; ***M:*** Hal Lindes; Anthony Marinelli. **VIDEO**

Quicksand: No Escape **1991 (PG-13)** Scott Reinhardt (Matheson) is a successful architect whose partner decides to secure a building contract by bribing a city official. When his partner is murdered Reinhardt is approached by a former cop (Sutherland) asking a lot of money for some incriminating evidence. Reinhardt is then drawn ever deeper into the illicit dealings, endangering his life. **93m/C; VHS, DVD.** Tim Matheson; Donald Sutherland; Jay Acovone; Timothy Carhart; John Finn; Marc Alaimo; Felicity Huffman; Al Pugliese; ***D:*** Michael Pressman; ***W:*** Peter Baloff; Dave Wollert.

Quicksilver 1/2 **1986 (PG)** A young stockbroker loses all, then quits his job to become a city bicycle messenger. Pointless, self-indulgent yuppie fantasy. **106m/C; VHS, DVD, Blu-Ray.** Kevin Bacon; Jami Gertz; Paul Rodriguez; Rudy Ramos; Andrew Smith; Gerald S. O'Loughlin; Laurence Fishburne; Louie Anderson; ***D:*** Thomas Michael Donnelly; ***W:*** Thomas Michael Donnelly; ***M:*** Tony Banks.

Quicksilver Highway 1/2 **1998 (R)** Storyteller Aaron Quicksilver (Lloyd) entertains with two horror tales, based on the stories "The Body Politic" by Clive Barker and "Chattery Teeth" by Stephen King. The Barker story has been re-set in America and now features a plastic surgeon whose hands decide to become independent from the rest of his body, while the King story is about a traveling salesman who purchases a pair of steel teeth at a Arizona gas station, which turn out to be lifesavers when he makes the mistake of picking up a nightmarish hitchhiker. **90m/C; VHS, DVD.** Christopher Lloyd; Matt Frewer; Raphael Sbarge; Missy (Melissa) Crider; Veronica Cartwright; Bill Nunn; Amelia Heinle; ***Cameo(s):*** Clive Barker; ***D:*** Mick Garris; ***W:*** Mick Garris; ***C:*** Shelly Johnson; ***M:*** Mark Mothersbaugh. **TV**

Quid Pro Quo **2008 (R)** Kinky drama with a stunning performance by Farmiga. Isaac Knott (Stahl) has been in a wheelchair since a childhood car accident. Now a reporter for a New York public radio station, Isaac gets a tip about a fetish group whose members suffer from paralysis envy and will pay to become disabled. His informer is slinky femme Fiona (Farmiga), who finds his wheelchair a turn-on. As they begin a edgy romance, things really turn weird when Isaac starts regaining feeling in his legs while he encourages Fiona to live out her fantasies. **82m/C; DVD.** Nick Stahl; Vera Farmiga; Kate Burton; Dylan Bruno; Aimee Mullins; ***D:*** Carlos Brooks; ***W:*** Carlos Brooks; ***C:*** Michael McDonough; ***M:*** Mark Mothersbaugh.

The Quiet **2005 (R)** Dot (Belle), an orphaned deaf-mute teen, goes to live with her godparents (Donovan and Falco), much to the disdain of their catty cheerleader daughter Nina (Cuthbert). Dad twitches and mom self-medicates, Nina snarks, and Dot sulks, but then the otherwise socially rejected Dot becomes a convenient confessor for Nina and others, and the secrets they reveal are doozies. Too heavy to be a teen sex farce, too outlandish and gross to be poignant, the movie melts into cheesy ick despite good turns by the main players. **96m/C; DVD.** Camilla Belle; Elisha Cuthbert; Martin Donovan; Edie Falco; Shawn Ashmore; Katy Mixon; ***D:*** Jamie Babbit; ***W:*** Abdi Nazemian; Micah Schraft; ***C:*** M. David Mullen; ***M:*** Jeff Rona.

The Quiet American **2002 (R)** Caine well-deserves accolades for his role as the aging and cynical English journalist Thomas Fowler, a long-time correspondent based in 1950s Saigon. He's obsessed with his beautiful young Vietnamese mistress Phuong (Yen) who also becomes a romantic object for brash American Alden Pyle (Fraser). There's something about this dogooder, who's supposedly on a medical mission, that makes Fowler both suspicious and jealous. Set amidst the communist insurgence of Ho Chi Minh into French-held Indo-China, which will then lead to American involvement. Based on the novel by Graham Greene. **118m/C; VHS, DVD.** Michael Caine; Brendan Fraser; Do Thi Hai Yen; Rade Serbedzija; Tzi Ma; Robert Stanton; Holmes Osborne; Pham Thai Mai Hoa; Quang Hai; Ferdinand Hoang; ***D:*** Phillip Noyce; ***W:*** Christopher Hampton; Robert Schenkkan; ***C:*** Christopher Doyle; ***M:*** Craig Armstrong. Natl. Bd. of Review '02: Director (Noyce).

Quiet Chaos 1/2 *Caos Calmo* **2008** While on vacation, Pietro (Moretti) rescues a woman from drowning only to learn on his return home that his wife has died in an accident. Grief-stricken, Pietro must adjust to being a single dad to 10-year-old Claudia (Yoshimi) and can scarcely bear to let his daughter out of his sight. So he begins spending his days in a park by her school while quietly attempting to come to terms with his loss. Italian with subtitles. **105m/C; DVD.** *IT* Nanni Moretti; Valeria Golino; Isabella Ferrari; Blu Yoshimi; Alessandro Gassman; Hippolyte Girardot; Kasia Smutniak; ***D:*** Antonello Grimaldi; ***W:*** Nanni Moretti; Francesco Piccolo; Laura Paolucci; ***C:*** Alessandro Pesci; ***M:*** Paolo Buonvino.

Quiet Cool **1986 (R)** When his former girlfriend's family is killed, a New York cop travels to a sleepy California town run by a pot-growing tycoon. He subsequently kills the bad guys in a Rambo-like fit of vengeance. Dopey exercise in sleepy-eyed bloodshed. **80m/C; VHS, DVD.** James Remar; Daphne Ashbrook; Adam Coleman Howard; Jared Martin; Fran Ryan; ***D:*** Clay Borris; ***W:*** Clay Borris; ***M:*** Jay Ferguson.

Quiet Days in Clichy *Jours Tranquilles a Clichy* **1990** Chabrol's ludicrous adaptation (previously filmed in 1970) of Henry Miller's autobiographical novel, which followed the sexually obsessed writer (young and poor at the time) and his friend through various exploits in the French town of Clichy in the 1930s. Chabrol's version features the horrendously miscast McCarthy as Miller, who now has money to throw around, as he and his pal Alfred (Havers) spend most of their time in a fancy brothel with various girls. French with subtitles. **100m/C; VHS, DVD, Blu-Ray.** *FR* Andrew McCarthy; Nigel Havers; Stephane Audran; Isolde Barth; Eva Grimaldi; Stephanie Cotta; Barbara De Rossi; ***D:*** Claude Chabrol; ***W:*** Claude Chabrol; Ugo Leonzio; ***C:*** Jean Rabier; ***M:*** Matthieu Chabrol.

Quiet Days in Hollywood *The Way We Are* **1997 (R)** Sexual roundelay in Hollywood involves a prostitute, an actor, a crook, a waitress, a rape, a gay triangle, various affairs, and related sexual experimentation. Less titillating than it sounds; German director Rusnak was making his U.S. feature debut. Maybe something got lost in the translation. **95m/C; VHS, DVD.** Peter Dobson; Chad Lowe; Steven Mailer; Daryl (Chill) Mitchell; Bill Cusack; Meta Golding; Hilary Swank; Natasha Gregson Wagner; ***D:*** Josef Rusnak; *W:* Josef Rusnak; *C:* Dietrich Lohmann; *M:* Harald Kloser.

A Quiet Duel *Akira Kurosawa's The Quiet Duel; Shizuka Naru Ketto* **1949** Kyoji (Mifune), a young, idealistic doctor working as an army surgeon, contracts syphillis from the blood of a patient during an operation. Because the disease was virtually incurable at the time, the tormented Kyoji abandons his fiance and decides to dedicate himself to his work. Based on a play by Kazuo Kikuta. Japanese with subtitles. **95m/B; VHS, DVD.** *JP* Toshiro Mifune; Takashi Shimura; Kenjiro Uemura; *D:* Akira Kurosawa; *W:* Senkichi Taniguchi; Akira Kurosawa; *M:* Akira Ifukube.

The Quiet Earth **1985 (R)** Serious science fiction film about a scientist who awakens to find himself seemingly the only human left on earth as the result of a misfired time/space government experiment. He later finds two other people, a girl and a Maori tribesman, and must try to repair the damage in order to save what's left of mankind. **91m/C; VHS, DVD, Blu-Ray.** *NZ* Bruno Lawrence; Alison Routledge; Peter Smith; Norman Fletcher; Tom Hyde; *D:* Geoff Murphy; *W:* Bruno Lawrence; Sam Pillsbury; Bill Baer; *C:* James Bartle; *M:* John Charles.

The Quiet Family *Choyonghan kajok* **1998** The Kang family buy a mountain lodge after hearing a major road will be getting built there. But there's a problem: no customers. And they've spent all the money they have on the lodge. One night a guest finally arrives, but commits suicide and the family buries him in the woods to avoid bad publicity. Unfortunately their soon-to-be arriving waves of guests all inexplicably snuff it in the night (willingly or not). The Kangs continue to bury them all, wondering how long they can keep it up. Eventually remade as "The Happiness of the Katakuris" by Takashi Miike. **105m/C; DVD.** *NK* Kang-ho Song; Min-Sik Choi; In-hwan Park; Mun-hee Na; Ho-kyung Go; Yun-seong Lee; *D:* Ji-woon Kim; *W:* Ji-woon Kim; *C:* Kwang-Seok Jeong.

Quiet Fire ½ **1991 (R)** A health-club owner tries to get the goods on the arms-dealing congressman who killed his best friend. Hilton-Jacobs looks properly pumped up since his sweathog days on TV's "Welcome Back Kotter." **100m/C; VHS, DVD.** Lawrence-Hilton Jacobs; Robert Z'Dar; Nadia Marie; Karen Black; Lance Lindsay; *D:* Lawrence-Hilton Jacobs.

The Quiet Man **1952** The classic incarnation of Hollywood Irishness, and one of Ford's best and funniest films. Sean Thornton's (Wayne) a weary American ex-boxer who returns to the Irish hamlet of his childhood and tries to take spirited lass Mary Kate (O'Hara) as his wife, despite the strenuous objections of her brawling brother Red Will (McLaglen). Thornton's aided by the leprechaun-like Michaleen Flynn (Fitzgerald) and the local parish priest (Bond). A high-spirited and memorable film filled with Irish stew, wonderful banter, and shots of the lush countryside. **129m/C; DVD, Blu-Ray.** John Wayne; Maureen O'Hara; Barry Fitzgerald; Victor McLaglen; Arthur Shields; Jack MacGowran; Ward Bond; Mildred Natwick; Ken Curtis; Mae Marsh; Sean McClory; Francis Ford; D.R.O. Hatswell; *D:* John Ford; *W:* Frank Nugent; *C:* Archie Stout; *M:* Victor Young. Oscars '52: Color Cinematog., Director (Ford); Directors Guild '52: Director (Ford); Natl. Film Reg. '13; Venice Film Fest. '52: Director (Ford).

The Quiet Ones ½ **2014 (PG-13)** The resurgence of Hammer Films hits a speed bump here with a dull, forgettable scare flick about a professor who, of course, finds a way to contact the other side. Joseph Coupland (Harris) works at an estate outside London to conduct an experiment designed to reach the great beyond. Working on a special, very disturbed, girl named Jane (Cooke), they open a door that allows dark forces into our world and, well, you can imagine what happens next. PG-13 ghost stories have to offer copious atmosphere to really work and director Pogue forgot that. **98m/C; DVD, Blu-Ray.** *UK* Jared Harris; Olivia Cooke; Sam Claflin; Erin Richards; Rory Fleck-Byrne; *D:* John Pogue; *W:* John Pogue; Craig Rosenberg; Oren Moverman; *C:* Mátyás Erdély; *M:* Lucas Vidal.

A Quiet Passion ½ **2017 (PG-13)** An effective biopic of the lauded American poet Emily Dickinson (Nixon). Beginning with a questioning young Emily (Bell) at school, the film explores her family life, outspoken nature, and mostly secret poem writing. Emily's usually happy relationships with her sister Vinnie (Ehle) and friend Vryling Buffman (Bailey) are contrasted with her defined sense of self, strong personal values, and dedication to her carefully crafted work. Though Emily suffers from illness, seems mentally ill at times, and does not live to see the impact and legacy of her work, Nixon's measured, revealing performance brings the American literary icon to full life. **125m/C; DVD.** Cynthia Nixon; Jennifer Ehle; Duncan Duff; Keith Carradine; Joanna Bacon; *D:* Terence Davies; *W:* Terence Davies; *C:* Florian Hoffmeister.

A Quiet Place **2018 (PG-13)** Fans of horror movies brace themselves when things suddenly go quiet, because that's when the true scares come. This film extends that tension for its entire length, as a family's survival depends on utter silence. Krasinski and real-life wife Blunt play parents whose family of four lives in an isolated forest, desperate to remain aurally invisible to terrifying creatures that hunt by sound. An original, white-knuckler that showcases Blunt's acting abilities and establishes Krasinski as an up-and-coming director. **90m/C; DVD, Blu-Ray.** Emily Blunt; John Krasinski; Millicent Simmonds; Noah Jupe; Cade Woodward; *D:* John Krasinski; *W:* John Krasinski; Bryan Woods; Scott Beck; *C:* Charlotte Bruus Christensen; *M:* Marco Beltrami. Screen Actors Guild '18: Actress--Supporting (Blunt).

A Quiet Place in the Country ½ *Un Tranquillo Posto di Campagna* **1969** Successful abstract artist Leonardo (Nero) decides to get away from his hectic life in Milan and rents an old mansion in the country. He's joined by his married lover/agent Flavia (Redgrave) but Leonardo becomes obsessed with a caretaker's story about a young woman's ghost haunting the property and decides to hold a seance. Italian with subtitles. **106m/C; DVD, Blu-Ray.** *IT* Franco Nero; Vanessa Redgrave; Georges Geret; Gabriella Grimaldi; *D:* Elio Petri; *W:* Elio Petri; Luciano Vincenzoni; *C:* Luigi Kuveiller; *M:* Ennio Morricone.

The Quiet Room **1996 (PG)** A nameless seven-year-old girl (Chloe Ferguson) refuses to speak when she learns her constantly quarreling parents are separating. Film is shown from only the child's perspective and her fantasies of a different life as she goes about her daily routine. Although the girl remains silent, she answers her parents in her thoughts (the voiceover lets the viewer into the girl's world) and she has flashbacks to her younger self (played by Ferguson's sister Phoebe) and when her parents loved each other. **91m/C; VHS, DVD.** *AU* Chloe Ferguson; Celine O'Leary; Paul Blackwell; Phoebe Ferguson; *D:* Rolf de Heer; *W:* Rolf de Heer; *C:* Tony Clark; *M:* Graham Tardif.

Quigley ½ **2003 (G)** When a ruthless, stinking-rich businessman suddenly dies, the powers-that-be won't let him into heaven unless he goes back and fixes his wrongdoings—as a cutesy pup named Quigley. **89m/C; VHS, DVD.** Gary Busey; Oz (Osgood) Perkins, II; Curtis Armstrong; Christopher Atkins; P.J. Ochlan; Kieran Mulroney; Bill Fagerbakke; Jessica Ferrarone; Caryn Greenhut; *D:* William B. Hillman; *W:* William B. Hillman; *C:* Gary Graver; *M:* Eric Lundmark. **VIDEO**

Quigley Down Under ½ **1990 (PG-13)** A Western sharpshooter moves to Australia in search of employment. To his horror, he discovers that he has been hired to kill aborigines. Predictable action is somewhat redeemed by the terrific chemistry between Selleck and San Giacomo and the usual enjoyable theatrics from Rickman as the landowner heavy. **121m/C; VHS, DVD, Blu-Ray.** *AU* Tom Selleck; Laura San Giacomo; Alan Rickman; Chris Haywood; Ron Haddrick; Tony Bonner; Roger Ward; Ben Mendelsohn; Jerome Ehlers; Conor McDermottroe; *D:* Simon Wincer; *W:* John Hill; *C:* David Eggby; *M:* Basil Poledouris.

The Quiller Memorandum **1966** An American secret agent travels to Berlin to uncover a deadly neo-Nazi gang. Refreshingly different from other spy tales of its era. Good screenplay adapted from Adam Hall's novel, "The Berlin Memorandum." **103m/C; VHS, DVD, Blu-Ray.** George Segal; Senta Berger; Alec Guinness; Max von Sydow; George Sanders; *D:* Michael Anderson, Sr.; *W:* Harold Pinter; *M:* John Barry.

Quills ½ **2000 (R)** Follows the last years of the life of the Marquis de Sade (Rush), which he spent in an insane asylum as punishment for his erotic writings. Sade continues to write while imprisoned and, with the help of his secret courier, Madeleine (Winslet), is able to distribute his stories to the public. The movie uses Sade's imprisonment as a lesson about freedom of expression and the perils of censorship, sacrificing a more interesting story about the man's boiling imagination. Worth viewing for the performances. Based on the off-Broadway play by David Wright. **123m/C; VHS, DVD.** Geoffrey Rush; Kate Winslet; Joaquin Rafael (Leaf) Phoenix; Michael Caine; *D:* Philip Kaufman; *W:* Doug Wright; *C:* Rogier Stoffers; *M:* Stephen Warbeck. Natl. Bd. of Review '00: Film, Support. Actor (Phoenix).

Quilombo ½ **1984** The title refers to a legendary settlement of runaway slaves in 17th-century Brazil; an epic chronicles its fortunes as leadership passes from a wise ruler to a more militant one who goes to war against the government. Stunning scenery, tribal images, and folk songs, but the numerous characters seldom come to life as personalities. One of Brazil's most expensive films, in Portuguese with English subtitles. **114m/C; VHS, DVD.** *BR* Vera Fischer; Antonio Pompeo; Zeze Motta; Toni Tornado; *D:* Carlos Diegues; *W:* Carlos Diegues.

Quincannon, Frontier Scout **1956** Standard western, filmed in Utah, with singer Martin unbelievable and badly miscast in the title role. Frontier scout Quincannon (Martin) is sent to a remote fort to find a missing shipment of rifles that may be in the hands of the local Cheyenne tribe. Also along is Maylene Mason (Castle), who wants to know if her younger brother died in an Indian attack. **85m/C; DVD.** Tony Martin; Peggie Castle; John Bromfield; John Smith; John Doucette; Morris Ankrum; Ron Randell; *D:* Lesley Selander; *W:* Don Martin; John C. Higgins; *C:* Joseph Biroc; *M:* Les Baxter.

Quinceanera **2006 (R)** Quinceanera is a traditional celebration that marks a coming-of-age at 15 for Mexican-American girls. Magdalena (newcomer Rios) reaches this milestone with the revelation that she's pregnant. Banished from home by her devout father, she takes refuge with her Uncle Tomas (Gonzalez), a wise octogenarian who is also sheltering his gay nephew Carols (Garcia). Meanwhile, Tomas's modest home is threatened by his new landlords, adding to a complex story of tradition versus change, the definition of family, and gentrification. Effective docu-stylings illuminate life in L.A.'s Echo Park community and make the flick's ending utterly satisfying. **90m/C; DVD.** David W. Ross; Emily Rios; Jesse Garcia; Chalo Gonzalez; J.R. Cruz; Jason L. Wood; Araceli Guzman-Rico; Jesus Castanos-Chima; *D:* Richard Glatzer; Wash Westmoreland; *W:* Richard Glatzer; Wash Westmoreland; *C:* Eric Steelberg; *M:* Victor Block.

Quintet **1979** Atypical Altman sci-fi effort. The stakes in "Quintet," a form of backgammon, are high—you bet your life. Set during the planet's final ice age. Newman and wife Fossey wander into a dying city and are invited to play the game, with Fossey losing quickly. Bizarre and pretentious, with heavy symbolic going. **118m/C; VHS, DVD.** Paul Newman; Bibi Andersson; Fernando Rey; Vittorio Gassman; David Langton; Nina Van Pallandt; Brigitte Fossey; *D:* Robert Altman; *W:* Lionel Chetwynd; Patricia Resnick; Frank Barhydt; Robert Altman.

The Quitter ½ **1934** Small town newspaper publisher Ed Tilford goes to France in 1918 to report on WWI and doesn't return home. His widow Cordelia keeps the paper running until her two sons are old enough to take over. However, eldest son Russell turns the paper into a financial disaster and it must be sold. **68m/B; DVD.** Charley Grapewin; Emma Dunn; William "Billy" Bakewell; Glen Boles; Lafe (Lafayette) McKee; Mary Kornman; Barbara Weeks; Hale Hamilton; *D:* Richard Thorpe; *W:* Robert Ellis; *C:* M(ilton) A(rthur) Anderson.

Quitters ½ **2016 (R)** Teenager Clark Rayman (Konigsberg) is witnessing his family fall apart. His father (Germann) is distant and apathetic; his mother (Sorvino) is addicted to pills. Rather than try to keep his family together, he decides to just try to join another. If only happiness were that easy to find. Noah Pritzker's debut is well-intentioned and promising but shows the amateur signs of its production. **95m/C; DVD.** Ben Konigsberg; Greg Germann; Mira Sorvino; Kara Hayward; Morgan Turner; *D:* Noah Pritzker; *W:* Noah Pritzker; Ben Tarnoff; *C:* Jakob Ihre; *M:* David Shire.

Quiz Show **1994 (PG-13)** Redford's intelligent, entertaining, and morally complex film about the TV game show scandals of the late '50s. Charles Van Doren (Fiennes), an intellectual golden boy, dethrones Herbert Stempel (Turturro), the reigning champion of the rigged "Twenty-One." The program's sponsor felt the Jewish Stempel's appeal was waning and wanted a more polished image, which they found in handsome, sophisticated Van Doren. Federal investigator Goodwin (Morrow) suspects Van Doren's reign is a sham and sets out to expose him as a fraud. Acting is of the highest caliber, with a strong script and gorgeous lensing. Based on the book "Remembering America: A Voice From the Sixties" by Richard N. Goodwin. **133m/C; VHS, DVD.** John Turturro; Rob Morrow; Ralph Fiennes; Paul Scofield; David Paymer; Hank Azaria; Christopher McDonald; Johann Carlo; Elizabeth Wilson; Mira Sorvino; Griffin Dunne; Martin Scorsese; Barry Levinson; *D:* Robert Redford; *W:* Paul Attanasio; *C:* Michael Ballhaus; *M:* Mark Isham. British Acad. '94: Adapt. Screenplay; N.Y. Film Critics '94: Film.

Quo Vadis **1951** Larger-than-life production about Nero and the Christian persecution. Done on a giant scale: features exciting fighting scenes, romance, and fabulous costumes. Definitive version of the classic novel by Henryk Siekiewicz. Remade for Italian TV in 1985. **171m/C; VHS, DVD.** Robert Taylor; Deborah Kerr; Leo Genn; Peter Ustinov; Patricia Laffan; Finlay Currie; Abraham Sofaer; Marina Berti; Buddy Baer; Felix Aylmer; Nora Swinburne; Sophia Loren; Elizabeth Taylor; Elspeth March; *Nar:* Walter Pidgeon; *D:* Mervyn LeRoy; *C:* Robert L. Surtees; *M:* Miklos Rozsa. Golden Globes '52: Support. Actor (Ustinov).

R100 **2015** An absurd, if not bizarre, Japanese dark sex comedy by acclaimed director Hitoshi Matsumoto. Though Takafumi Katayama (Ohmori) is a mild-mannered family man employed as a store clerk, he has a secret fetish for S&M. Signing a year-long contract with an agency that specializes in humiliation, he is ambushed by a series of dominatrices known as the queens of control. Each dominatrix has an interesting gift, and uses it on Takefumi at random times in public and private. As the situation grows out of control, he tries, and fails, to get out of his iron-clad contract. Japanese with subtitles. **99m/C; DVD, Blu-Ray, Streaming, Download.** Nao Ohmori; Mao Daichi; Lindsay Hayward; Mao Asou; Hairi Katagiri; *D:* Hitoshi Matsumoto; *W:* Hitoshi Matsumoto; Mitsuyoshi Takasu; Tomoji Hasegawa; Koji Ema; Mitsuru Kuramoto; *C:* Kazunari Tanaka; *M:* Shuichi Sakamoto; Shuichiro Toki.

'R Xmas **2001** Brancato and de Matteo star as the unnamed husband and wife whose idyllic Manhattan days disguise their shady heroin dealings by night in the Bronx. It's Christmas and everything is just swell for the twosome until they attempt to illegally obtain a hard-to-find toy for their daughter (Valens). Dad gets kidnapped by a thug (Ice-T) who wants a huge ransom and that they stop dealing. Some racial issues are explored as well as the obvious moral and financial issues. De Matteo makes her character complex and eminently watchable through somewhat predictable and tired material. **83m/C; VHS, DVD.** *US FR* Lillo Brancato; Drea De Matteo; Ice-T; Victor Argo; Lisa Valens; *D:* Abel Ferrara; *W:* Abel Ferrara; Scott Pardo; *C:* Ken Kelsch.

The Rabbi's Cat ½ *Le chat du rabbin* **2011** Set in 1920s Algeria, a cat eats the family parrot and develops the ability to speak much to the consternation of his owner's father, a local Rabbi. When a painter convinces the Rabbi of a lost Israelite city in Africa, they all travel in search of it, being subjected to the cat's wit at every turn. Based on the famous graphic novel of the same name. **89m/C; DVD, Blu-Ray.** *AT FR* ***V:*** Francois Morel; Maurice Benichou; Hafsia Herzi; Francois Damiens; Mathieu Amalric; ***D:*** Antoine Delesveaux; Joann Sfar; ***W:*** Joann Sfar; Sandrina Jardel; ***C:*** Jerome Brezillon; ***M:*** Olivier Daviaud.

Rabbit Hole 🦴🦴🦴 **2010 (PG-13)** Grief combines with melancholy humor and exceptional performances by the leads in Mitchell's family drama, an expanded version of Lindsay-Abaire's prize-winning play that the writer adapted for the screen. Since the accidental death of their four-year-old son Danny, Howie (Eckhart) and Becca (Kidman) find themselves coping in very different ways. Becca wants to sell the house and move on but Howie can't bear changing anything relating to their son. They try group grief therapy but angry Becca can't abide the sharing while Howie finds it cathartic. Since both turn away from each other, the marriage may also not survive. **91m/C; DVD, Blu-Ray, On Demand.** Nicole Kidman; Aaron Eckhart; Dianne Wiest; Miles Teller; Tammy Blanchard; Sandra Oh; Giancarlo Esposito; Jon Tenney; ***D:*** John Cameron Mitchell; ***W:*** David Lindsay-Abaire; ***C:*** Frank DeMarco; ***M:*** Anton Sanko.

The Rabbit Is Me 🦴🦴 *Das Kaninchen Bin Ich; I Am the Rabbit* **1965** Maria's life in East Germany is tainted when her brother is jailed for subversive political activity. She has an affair with an older man, only to discover he's the judge who sent her brother to prison. This doesn't help her self-esteem. German with subtitles. **109m/B; DVD.** *GE* Angelika Waller; Alfred Muller; Irma Munch; Ilse Voight; Wolfgang Winkler; Willi Narloch; ***D:*** Kurt Maetzig; ***W:*** Manfred Bieler; ***C:*** Erich Gusko; ***M:*** Reiner Bredemeyer; Gerhard Rosenfeld.

Rabbit-Proof Fence 🦴🦴🦴 ½ **2002 (PG)** Fascinating, true story of three mixed-race Aboriginal girls in 1930s Australia, who escape their forced incarceration at an institution designed to train such children, snatched from their parents by the government, as domestic workers. Embarking on an incredible 1,500 mile journey to return home, Molly, Daisy, and Gracie follow the line of a fence—the longest unbroken piece of fence ever created—built by the government to keep out the rabbits that had overrun the farmlands. Branagh plays Neville, a bigot who oversaw the racist policies that the Australian government enforced until 1970. Based on a book by Doris Pilkington, daughter of one of the girls. **95m/C; VHS, DVD.** *AU GB* Everlyn Sampi; Tianna Sansbury; Laura Monaghan; Kenneth Branagh; David Gulpilil; Deborah Mailman; Jason Clarke; Garry McDonald; Ningali Lawford; Myarn Lawford; ***D:*** Phillip Noyce; ***W:*** Christine Olsen; ***C:*** Christopher Doyle; ***M:*** Peter Gabriel. Natl. Bd. of Review '02: Director (Noyce).

Rabbit, Run 🦴 ½ **1970** Adaptation of the 1960 John Updike novel that's the first of four books featuring Harry 'Rabbit' Angstrom. Rabbit (Caan) can't get past his glory days as a high school basketball star despite his suburban life, dead-end job, marriage to Janice (Snodgress), and impending (unwanted) fatherhood. No wonder the equally unhappy Janice has turned into an alcoholic. After another marital spat, Rabbit moves in with his retired coach Marty (Albertson) who introduces him to hooker Ruth (Comer). But she just brings more adult problems into his life. **94m/C; DVD.** James Caan; Carrie Snodgress; Jack Albertson; Anjanette Comer; Arthur Hill; Melodie Johnson; Henry Jones; Josephine Hutchinson; Ken Kercheval; ***D:*** Jack Smight; ***W:*** Howard B. Kreitsek; ***C:*** Philip H. Lathrop.

Rabid 🦴🦴 ½ *Rage* **1977 (R)** A young girl undergoes a radical plastic surgery technique and develops a strange and unexplained lesion in her armpit. She also finds she has an unusual craving for human blood. **90m/C; VHS, DVD, Blu-Ray.** *CA* Marilyn Chambers; Frank Moore; Joe Silver; Howard Ryshpan; Patricia Gage; Susan (Suzan) Roman; Roger Periard; Victor Desy; ***D:*** David Cronenberg; ***W:*** David Cronenberg; ***C:*** Rene Verzier.

Rabid Grannies **WOOF!** **1989 (R)** Wicked satire about two aging sisters who receive a surprise birthday gift from their devilworshipping nephew. The gift turns their party into a gorefest as they rip into various family members—literally. Any humor will be lost on any but the most diehard Troma fans. Dubbed. **89m/C; VHS, DVD, Blu-Ray.** *BE* Catherine Aymerie; Caroline Brackman; Danielle Daven; Raymond Lescot; Anne Marie Fox; Richard Cotica; Patricia Davie; ***D:*** Emmanuel Kervyn; ***W:*** Emmanuel Kervyn; ***C:*** Hugh Labye; ***M:*** Jean-Bruno Castelain; Pierre-Damien Castelain.

Rabies 🦴🦴 *Kalevet* **2010** Twisted Israeli slasher pic (with some nasty violence) with several character stories coming together because of a psycho killer. Four teens take a wrong turn and get lost in a nature preserve; two cops aren't so helpful; a brother tries to rescue his sister who's trapped in a mine shaft; and the park ranger doesn't know what's going on. Title refers to rabid behavior not the disease. Hebrew with subtitles. **90m/C; DVD.** *IS* Lior Ashkenazi; Danny Geva; Ran Danker; David Henry; Menashe Noy; Yaron Motola; ***D:*** Aharon Keshales; Navot Papushado; ***W:*** Aharon Keshales; Navot Papushado; ***C:*** Guy Raz; ***M:*** Frank Ilfman.

Race 🦴🦴 ½ **1999 (R)** Serious low-budget film attempts to take a serious look at practical politics on the local level. L.A. councilman Durman (Robertson) comes in third in the primary after redistricting. Tied for first are Lucinda Davis (Pounder), a black woman, and Gustavo Alvarez (Rodriguez), a Latino house painter. Their race touches all of the Southern California racial and ethnic hot buttons, and quickly turns nasty. **103m/C; VHS, DVD.** Paul Rodriguez; CCH Pounder; Cliff Robertson; Annette Murphy; ***D:*** Tom Musca; ***W:*** Tom Musca; Mark Kemble; ***C:*** Arturo Smith; ***M:*** Stan Ridgway.

The Race 🦴🦴 ½ **2009** Eleven-year-old Mary lives on a County Antrim farm with her bickering parents, who are too worried over money troubles to take much notice of their daughter. Mary's dream is to become a race-car driver and she has built her own go-cart just in time for a local race. However, her resolve wavers when she's teased at school about her choices (because girls can't be race drivers). **84m/C; DVD.** *IR* Colm Meaney; Susan Lynch; Niamh McGirr; ***D:*** Andre F. Nebe; ***W:*** Rowan O'Neill; ***C:*** Dirk Morgenstern; ***M:*** Mortiz Denis.

Race 🦴🦴 **2016 (PG-13)** A strong performance from future star Stephan James is wasted on a standard, safe Hollywood interpretation of the story of Jesse Owens. James stars as Owens, and Stephen Hopkins film chronicles the runner's record-breaking four medals won at the 1936 Olympic Games in Berlin, on the cusp of World War II. The movie hits most of the expected biopic beats focusing on the conflict when Owens struggled with even going to the Olympics in Germany, but turned his victories there into a statement for diversity. There's nothing overtly wrong with this telling of this story, but the whole thing has that TV movie feel that often sinks traditional biopics. **134m/C; DVD, Blu-Ray.** Stephan James; Jason Sudeikis; Eli Goree; Shanice Banton; Carice van Houten; ***D:*** Stephen Hopkins; ***W:*** Joe Shrapnel; Anna Waterhouse; ***C:*** Peter Levy; ***M:*** Rachel Portman.

Race Against Time 🦴🦴 **2000** Another bleak futuristic thriller but with fast-paced and suspenseful action. When Gabriel's (Roberts) son is diagnosed with a deadly virus, Gabirel learns that the vaccine will cost him mucho dinero'and he has only 12 hours to come up with the cash. So he agrees to sell his organs to Lifecorps for harvesting in a year's time, then it's bye-bye for Gabe. But when his son dies anyway, Gabriel tries to get out of the agreement, especially when it seems his son's death wasn't so straightforward. **90m/C; VHS, DVD.** Eric Roberts; Cary Elwes; Sarah Wynter; Chris Sarandon; ***D:*** Geoff Murphy. **CABLE**

Race for Life 🦴 ½ *Mask of Dust* **1955** A race car driver attempts to make a comeback despite objections from his wife. He races around Europe (great scenery); she leaves him; he tries to win her back and salvage his career. Standard, un-gripping story. Car scenes are great. **69m/B; VHS, DVD.** *GB* Richard Conte; Mari Aldon; George Coulouris; Alec Mango; Meredith Edwards; Richard Marner; Jeremy Hawk; ***D:*** Terence Fisher; ***W:*** Richard H. Landau; ***C:*** Walter J. (Jimmy W.) Harvey; ***M:*** Leonard Salzedo.

Race Street 🦴🦴 **1948** Serviceable RKO crime drama. In postwar San Francisco, honorable bookie Dan Gannin (Raft) maintains an independent operation, resisting the mob's attempts to muscle in. He intends to go straight since he's fallen for Robbie (Maxwell), but gets bamboozled instead and Dan's life is further shaken when his friend, Hal (Morgan), is murdered. So Dan finally agrees to work with boyhood pal Barney Runson (Bendix), who's now a police detective. **79m/C; DVD.** George Raft; William Bendix; Marilyn Maxwell; Harry (Henry) Morgan; Frank Faylen; Gale Robbins; ***D:*** Edwin L. Marin; ***W:*** Martin Rackin; ***C:*** J. Roy Hunt; ***M:*** Roy Webb.

Race the Sun 🦴🦴 **1996 (PG)** There's nothin' new under this sun. Tired story of a group of young losers who band together to beat the odds and compete in an unusual contest is trotted out once again for populist amusement. This time it's a Hawaiian high school solar car team traveling to Australia to go for the prize against the big shots and snobs. Based on true events, it features some nice scenery from Berry and the main locations, but not much else. Uninspired but basically harmless, this one's fine for the kids. **100m/C; VHS, DVD.** Halle Berry; James Belushi; Casey Affleck; Eliza Dushku; Kevin Tighe; Anthony Michael Ruivivar; J. Moki Cho; Dion Basco; Sara Tanaka; Nadja Pionilla; Steve Zahn; Bill Hunter; ***D:*** Charles Kanganis; ***W:*** Barry Morrow; ***C:*** David Burr; ***M:*** Graeme Revell.

Race to Freedom: The Story of the Underground Railroad 🦴🦴 ½ **1994** Story of four fugitive slaves, in 1850, who struggle to get from North Carolina to the safety of Canada through a network of safe-houses and people willing to risk smuggling them to asylum. **90m/C; DVD.** *CA* Courtney B. Vance; Janet Bailey; Glynn Turman; Tim Reid; Michael Riley; Dawnn Lewis; Ron White; Alfre Woodard; ***D:*** Don McBrearty; ***W:*** Nancy Trite Botkin; Diana Braithwaite; ***M:*** Christopher Dedrick. **CABLE**

Race to Space 🦴🦴 ½ **2001 (PG)** German rocket scientist Wilhelm Von Huber (Woods) and his young son Billy (Linz) move to Cocoa Beach, Florida, in 1960 so dad can work for NASA on the Mercury program. Billy, who's been lonely since his mother's death, is taken under the wing of vet Donni McGuinness (Gish), and bonds with Mac, one of the chimps being trained to go into space, which in turn helps him get closer to his father. The chimp steals the movie, which is heavy on the sentimentality. **104m/C; VHS, DVD.** Alex D. Linz; James Woods; William Devane; William Atherton; John O'Hurley; Barry Corbin; Annabeth Gish; Jake Lloyd; ***D:*** Sean McNamara; ***W:*** Eric Gardner; Steven H. Wilson; ***C:*** Christian Sebaldt; ***M:*** John Coda. **VIDEO**

Race to Witch Mountain 🦴🦴 **2009 (PG)** Reworking of the 1975 Disney classic "Escape from Witch Mountain" adds muscle, firearms, and non-stop action while sacrificing plot and character development. Jack Bruno (Johnson), an ex-con Vegas cabbie, finds sweet-looking teenaged siblings Sara (Robb) and Seth (Ludwig) in his cab, needing his help after their spaceship crashes. Cash persuades the skeptical Bruno to drive into the desert with bad guys following, including Bruno's former underworld associates, a nasty extraterrestrial terminator, and well-armed agents in black SUVs, while they pick up a kooky UFO-seeking astrophysicist (Gugino). **98m/C; DVD, Blu-Ray.** AnnaSophia Robb; Alexander Ludwig; Carla Gugino; Ciaran Hinds; Dwayne "The Rock" Johnson; Tom Everett Scott; Richard "Cheech" Marin; Garry Marshall; ***D:*** Andy Fickman; ***W:*** Matt Lopez; Mark Bomback; ***C:*** Greg Gardiner; ***M:*** Trevor Rabin.

Race with the Devil 🦴 ½ **1975 (PG)** Vacationers are terrorized by devil worshippers after they witness a sacrificial killing. Heavy on car chases; light on plot and redeeming qualities. Don't waste your time. **88m/C; VHS, DVD, Blu-Ray.** Peter Fonda; Warren Oates; Loretta Swit; Lara Parker; R.G. Armstrong; ***D:*** Jack Starrett; ***W:*** Wes Bishop; Lee Frost; ***C:*** Robert C. Jessup.

Rachel Getting Married 🦴🦴🦴 ½ **2008 (R)** Rachel (DeWitt) is indeed getting married, but here comes the bride's junkie sister Kym (Hathaway), attending the wedding after her umpteenth rehab stint. The impending nuptials force a reluctant reunion of a family fragmented by the weight of accumulated self-inflicted wounds but held together by a desire to belong. Kym's habit of hogging a spotlight that should finally be on Rachel anchors the sibs' caustic relationship, which is further eroded by father Paul (Irwin) and his second wife (Winger). An ensemble cast delivers their best work, while director Demme's documentary-like approach provides an at times uncomfortable intimacy. **111m/C; DVD, Blu-Ray, On Demand.** Anne Hathaway; Rosemarie DeWitt; Bill Irwin; Debra Winger; Tunde Adebimpe; Mather Zickel; Anisa George; Anna Deavere Smith; ***D:*** Jonathan Demme; ***W:*** Jenny Lumet; ***C:*** Declan Quinn; ***M:*** Zafer Tawil; Donald Harrison, Jr.

The Rachel Papers 🦴🦴🦴 **1989 (R)** Based on the Martin Amis novel, this is the funny/sad tale of an Oxford youth who plots via his computer the seduction of a beautiful American girl. For anyone who has ever loved someone just out of their reach. **92m/C; VHS, DVD.** Dexter Fletcher; Ione Skye; James Spader; Jonathan Pryce; Bill Paterson; Michael Gambon; Lesley Sharp; ***D:*** Damian Harris; ***W:*** Damian Harris; ***M:*** Chaz Jankel.

Rachel, Rachel 🦴🦴🦴 ½ **1968 (R)** Rachel teaches by day, wearing simple, practical dresses and her hair up. By night she caters to her domineering mother by preparing refreshments for her parties. This sexually repressed, spinster schoolteacher, however, gets one last chance at romance in her small Connecticut town. Woodward mixes just the right amounts of loneliness and sweetness in the leading role. A surprising award-winner that was an independent production of Newman. Based on Margaret Laurence's "A Jest of God." **102m/C; VHS, DVD.** Joanne Woodward; James Olson; Estelle Parsons; Geraldine Fitzgerald; Donald Moffat; ***D:*** Paul Newman; ***W:*** Stewart Stern. Golden Globes '69: Actress--Drama (Woodward), Director (Newman); N.Y. Film Critics '68: Actress (Woodward), Director (Newman).

Rachel's Man 🦴 **1975** A big-screen version of the Biblical love story of Jacob and Rachel. **115m/C; VHS, DVD.** Mickey Rooney; Rita Tushingham; Leonard Whiting; Michal Bat-Adam; ***D:*** Moshe Mizrahi.

Rachida 🦴🦴🦴 **2005** Rachida is a young school teacher in terror-stricken 1990s Algeria. When stopped by street kids who demand she place a bomb in her classroom, she refuses. Shot point-blank and left for dead, Rachida miraculously survives. Under the care of her mother, far from the dangers of the city life, she begins to recover. Still, the struggle to find hope in such a violent world proves difficult for everyone. An unflinching portrait of fear with a brave performance from Djouadi; promising debut from writer/director Bachir. Arabic and French with English subtitles. **100m/C; DVD.** *FR AL* Ibtissem Djouadi; Bahia Rachedi; Rachida Messaoui En; Zaki Boulenafed; Hamid Remas; ***D:*** Yamina Bachir; ***W:*** Yamina Bachir.

Racing Daylight 🦴🦴 **2007** Sadie Stokes (Leo) is caring for her ill grandma in the family's longtime Hudson River Valley home when a ghostly presence makes itself known. As Sadie starts researching her family's past, she believes that she and handyman Henry (Strathairn) are reincarnations of Stokes ancestors who have unfinished business and are determined to be reunited. **83m/C; DVD.** Melissa Leo; David Strathairn; Sabrina Lloyd; Giancarlo Esposito; Jason Downs; Sigrid Heath; ***D:*** Nicole Quinn; ***W:*** Nicole Quinn; ***C:*** Stephen Harris; ***M:*** Sarah Plant. **VIDEO**

Racing for Time 🦴🦴 **2008** Lifetime drama based on a true story. Texas Correctional Youth Authority guard Cleveland Stackhouse (Dutton) is tired of seeing the destructive choices and racial tensions perpetuated by the teen girl offenders. So he chooses a racially-mixed group to become part of a track team to promote discipline and responsibility. **86m/C; DVD.** Charles S. Dutton; Aunjanue Ellis; Elizabeth Pena; Yaya DaCosta; Saige Thompson; Tiffany Haddish; Zulay Henao; Dequina Moore; ***W:*** Glenn German; Adam Rodgers; ***C:*** William Wages. **CABLE**

Racing Stripes 🦴🦴 **2005 (PG)** Farmer Nolan Walsh (Greenwood), finds a baby zebra (voiced by Muniz) left by a traveling circus in rural Kentucky and raises him on his farm. Stripes grows up yearning to be a racing horse, just as Channing (Panettiere), the farmer's daughter, yearns to be a jockey. The plot thickens as Walsh is a former horse trainer whose wife died in a riding accident and has since forbidden Channing from racing. Strange combination uses live animals with creepy computer-enhanced mouths for the speaking parts. Kids will enjoy it, but it's routine fare. **102m/C; DVD.** Bruce Greenwood; Hayden Panettiere; M. Emmet Walsh; Wendie Malick; ***V:*** Frankie Muniz; Mandy Moore; Michael Clarke Duncan; Joshua Jackson; Jeff Foxworthy; Joe Pantoliano; Michael Rosenbaum; Steve Harvey; David Spade; Snoop Dogg; Fred Dalton Thompson; Dustin Hoffman; Whoopi Goldberg; ***D:*** Frederick Du Chau; ***W:*** Frederick Du Chau; David F. Schmidt; ***C:*** David Eggby; ***M:*** Mark Isham.

Racing with the Moon **1984 (PG)** Sweet, nostalgic film about two buddies awaiting induction into the Marines in 1942. They have their last chance at summer romance. Benjamin makes the most of skillful young actors and conventional story. Great period detail. Keep your eyes peeled for glimpses of many rising young stars including Hannah and Carvey. **108m/C; VHS, DVD.** Sean Penn; Elizabeth McGovern; Nicolas Cage; John Karlen; Rutanya Alda; Max (Casey Adams) Showalter; Crispin Glover; Page Hannah; Michael Madsen; Carol Kane; Dana Carvey; Michael Talbott; Suzanne Adkinson; Michael Schoeffling; Victor Rendina; ***D:*** Richard Benjamin; ***W:*** Steve Kloves; ***C:*** John Bailey; ***M:*** Dave Grusin.

The Rack **1956** Former Korean War POW, Army Capt. Edward W. Hall Jr. (Newman) is placed on trial for collaborating with the enemy after being tortured and brainwashed by his Chinese captors. Some of his accusers faced the same conditions and didn't break, so how culpable is Hall? Adapted from a Rod Serling teleplay. **100m/B; DVD.** Paul Newman; Walter Pidgeon; Wendell Corey; Lee Marvin; Edmond O'Brien; Anne Francis; Cloris Leachman; ***D:*** Arnold Laven; ***W:*** Stewart Stern; ***C:*** Paul Vogel; ***M:*** Adolph Deutsch.

The Racket **1951** Police captain Mitchum tries to break up mob racket of gangster Ryan. Internecine strife on both sides adds complexity. Mitchum and especially Ryan are super; fine, tense melodrama. **88m/B; VHS, DVD.** Robert Ryan; Robert Mitchum; Lizabeth Scott; Ray Collins; William Conrad; Don Porter; ***D:*** John Cromwell.

The Racketeer **½ 1929** A racketeer falls in love with a pretty girl and attempts to win her over. As part of his plan, the gangster arranges to help the girl's boyfriend begin his musical career in exchange for the girl's promise to marry him. **68m/B; VHS, DVD.** Carole Lombard; Robert Armstrong; Hedda Hopper; ***D:*** Howard Higgin.

Radar Men from the Moon *Retik, the Moon Menace* **1952** Commando Cody, with his jet-pack, fights to defend the earth from invaders from the moon. Twelve-episode serial on two tapes. Silly sci-fi. **152m/B; VHS, DVD.** George D. Wallace; Aline Towne; Roy Barcroft; William "Billy" Bakewell; Clayton Moore; ***D:*** Fred Brannon.

Radio **½ 2003 (PG)** Feelgooder inspired by the true story of the mentally disabled James "Radio" Kennedy (Gooding Jr.), who befriends the kindly local football coach (Harris) and becomes a beloved mascot of sorts in Anderson, South Carolina circa 1976. Coach Jones finds Radio (so named for his ample, much-loved collection of discarded radios) locked in a storage shed after being taunted by a few players and is determined to help him. Radio, in turn, ends up teaching the town a lesson or two about the Golden Rule. Top notch cast and script can't completely save the somewhat saccharine but nonetheless inspirational story. Based on a "Sports Illustrated" story by Gary Smith. **109m/C; VHS, DVD.** Cuba Gooding, Jr.; Ed Harris; Alfre Woodard; S. Epatha Merkerson; Chris Mulkey; Sarah Drew; Riley Smith; Patrick Breen; Brent Sexton; Debra Winger; ***D:*** Mike Tollin; ***W:*** Mike Rich; ***C:*** Don Burgess; ***M:*** James Horner.

Radio Cab Murder **½ 1954** Fred (Hanley) was a safecracker who's trying to go straight by getting a job as a London cabbie. When an anonymous note informs his boss of Fred's past, the police deduce a gang wants Fred fired so they can recruit him. Fred plays along to infiltrate the gang and learn their plans for a bank heist but then his ruse is discovered. **70m/B; DVD.** *GB* Lana Morris; Jimmy Hanley; Sam Kydd; Elizabeth Seal; Jack Allen; Rupert Holliday; Bruce Beeby; ***D:*** Vernon Sewell; ***W:*** Vernon Sewell; ***C:*** Geoffrey Faithfull.

Radio Days **1987 (PG)** A lovely, unpretentious remembrance of the pre-TV radio culture. Allen tells his story in a series of vignettes centering around his youth in Brooklyn, his eccentric extended family, and the legends of radio they all followed. The ubiquitous Farrow is a young singer hoping to make it big. **89m/C; VHS, DVD, Blu-Ray; Open Captioned.** Mia Farrow; Dianne Wiest; Julie Kavner; Michael Tucker; Wallace Shawn; Josh Mostel; Tony Roberts; Jeff Daniels; Kenneth Mars; Seth Green; William Magerman; Diane Keaton; Renee Lippin; Danny Aiello; Gina DeAngelis; Kitty Carlisle Hart; Mercedes Ruehl; Tito Puente; ***Nar:*** Woody Allen; ***D:*** Woody Allen; ***W:*** Woody Allen; ***C:*** Carlo Di Palma.

Radio Flyer **1992 (PG-13)** It's 1969 and Mike and Bobby have just moved to northern California with their divorced mom. Everything would be idyllic if only their mother hadn't decided to marry a drunken child abuser who beats Bobby whenever the mood strikes him. Mike decides to help Bobby escape by turning their Radio Flyer wagon into a magic rocketship that will carry Bobby to safety, but ultimately proves tragic. Appealing version of childhood dreams sans the child abuse angle (toned down though it was), which is abruptly and unsatisfactorily handled. **114m/C; VHS, DVD, Blu-Ray.** Elijah Wood; Joseph Mazzello; Lorraine Bracco; Adam Baldwin; John Heard; Ben Johnson; ***Nar:*** Tom Hanks; ***D:*** Richard Donner.

Radio Inside **½ 1994** Aimless Matthew (McNamara) comes to live with older brother Michael (Walsh) after their dad's death. Matthew needs someone to listen to him but, unfortunately, his picks his brother's neglected girlfriend Natalie (Shue). Aimless story, as well. **91m/C; VHS, DVD.** William McNamara; Dylan Walsh; Elisabeth Shue; Gil Goldstein; ***D:*** Jeffrey Bell; ***W:*** Jeffrey Bell. **CABLE**

Radio Patrol **1937** Plenty of action and thrills abound in this 12-chapter serial. Pinky Adams, radio cop, is assisted by his trusty canine partner, Irish (Silverwolf). A cop's best friend is his dog. **235m/B; VHS, DVD.** Mickey Rentschler; Adrian Morris; Monte Montague; Jack Mulhall; Grant Withers; Catherine Hughes; ***D:*** Ford Beebe; Cliff(ord) Smith.

Radio Rebel **½ 2012** In this Disney Channel teen comedy painfully shy high schooler Tara (Ryan) has a secret identity as the confident host of a daily podcast she does from her bedroom. Her stepfather, the owner of SLAM radio, finds out and offers Tara a chance to broadcast from the studio. As her influence grows among her peers, it sparks a rebellion that school principal Moreno (Robertson) is determined to squelch. **89m/C; DVD.** Debby Ryan; Adam DiMarco; Sarena Parmar; Merritt Patterson; Nancy Robertson; Martin Cummins; ***D:*** Peter Hewitt; ***W:*** Erik Patterson; Jessica Scott; ***C:*** Kamal Derkaoui; ***M:*** James Jandrisch. **CABLE**

Radio Stars on Parade **1945** Tired and trite pic finds RKO comedy duo Brown and Carney playing a couple of jobless comedians who take over an L.A. talent agency. They get songbird Sally Baker (Langford) some radio work, but Chicago mobster Lucky Maddox (Leonard) wants Sally back working at his nightclub and shows up in town to make that happen. **70m/B; DVD.** Wally Brown; Alan Carney; Frances Langford; Sheldon Leonard; Ralph Edwards; ***D:*** Leslie Goodwins; ***W:*** Monte Brice; Robert E. Kent; ***C:*** Harry Wild; ***M:*** Roy Webb.

Radioland Murders **½ 1994 (PG)** Looks overwhelm weak plot in this mystery-comedy about 1939 Chicago radio station WBN. Lots of stock types (befuddled director, preening announcer, lusty vamp) with Masterson as Penny, the secretary holding everything together except for her marriage to head writer Roger (Benben). Then bodies start piling up during the live broadcast and everyone runs around frantically trying to solve the crimes and keep the broadcast going. Tiring and cliched. **112m/C; VHS, DVD, Blu-Ray.** Brian Benben; Mary Stuart Masterson; Ned Beatty; George Burns; Brion James; Michael Lerner; Michael McKean; Jeffrey Tambor; Scott Michael Campbell; Anita Morris; Stephen Tobolowsky; Christopher Lloyd; Larry Miller; Corbin Bernsen; ***Cameo(s):*** Robert Klein; Harvey Korman; Peter MacNichol; Joseph Lawrence; Bobcat Goldthwait; ***D:*** Mel Smith; ***W:*** Willard Huyck; Gloria Katz; Jeff Reno; Ron Osborn; ***C:*** David Tattersall; ***M:*** Joel McNeely.

Raffles **1930** Debonair and dashing gentleman thief A.J. Raffles (Coleman) is a famed cricket player by day and a cat burglar by night, who's always been successful at eluding Scotland Yard. Then he falls for beautiful socialite Lady Gwen Manders (Francis) and gets invited to a weekend house party where Lady Kitty Melrose (Skipworth) just happens to own a very valuable necklace and one of the other guests is suspicious Scotland Yard inspector McKenzie (Torrance). Naturally Raffles goes after the jewels. Based on the novel "The Amateur Cracksman" by Ernest William Hornung. Director D'Arrast was fired by producer Goldwyn and Fitzmaurice finished the film. **72m/B; DVD.** Ronald Colman; Kay Francis; Alison Skipworth; David Torrence; Bramwell Fletcher; Frances Dade; ***D:*** Harry D'Abbadie D'Arrast; George Fitzmaurice; ***W:*** Sidney Howard; ***C:*** George Barnes; Gregg Toland.

Raffles **1939** Dashing cricketer Raffles (Niven) is also an infamous burglar who gives Scotland Yard's Inspector MacKenzie (Digges) fits. When Raffles falls in love with Gwen (de Havilland), he decides to go straight after first helping out Gwen's broke brother, Bunny (Walton). He plans to steal Lady Melrose's (Whitty) emerald necklace, but this time MacKenzie is on to him. Niven is properly roguish but it's a too-close remake of the 1930 pic. **72m/B; DVD.** David Niven; Olivia de Havilland; Dudley Digges; May Whitty; Douglas Walton; E.E. Clive; Lionel Pape; ***D:*** Sam Wood; ***W:*** John Van Druten; Sidney Howard; ***M:*** Gregg Toland; Victor Young.

Rafter Romance **½ 1933** When neither Mary (Rogers) nor Jack (Foster) can afford their separate Greenwich Village apartments any longer, landlord Max (Sidney) moves them both into the same attic room. He figures the arrangement will be manageable because Mary works days and Jack nights and they will never see each other. But this doesn't mean they can't snipe with caustic notes and play practical jokes (oh, and fall in love). Remade as "Living on Love" (1937). **72m/B; DVD.** Ginger Rogers; Norman Foster; George Sidney; Robert Benchley; Laura Hope Crews; Guinn "Big Boy" Williams; Sidney Miller; ***D:*** William A. Seiter; ***W:*** Sam Mintz; H. W. Hanemann; ***C:*** David Abel.

Rage **½ 1972** Never the subtlest of actors, Scott goes over-the-top in this self-directed melodrama. Dan (Logan) and his son Chris (Beauvy) are camping when an Army helicopter accidentally sprays the area with a nerve gas. Dan rushes Chris to the hospital (he's in a coma) where he's separated from his son by Army medico Holliford (Sheen). Chris dies but Holliford keeps the news from Dan because he's not only trying to cover-up the incident but he wants to figure out why Dan survived a supposedly fatal gas. It's just a delayed reaction, and when the terminal Dan discovers the truth, he decides to get some serious revenge. **99m/C; DVD.** George C. Scott; Martin Sheen; Richard Basehart; Barnard Hughes; Nicolas Beauvy; Paul Stevens; Stephen Young; ***D:*** George C. Scott; ***W:*** Dan Kleinman; Philip Friedman; ***C:*** Fred W. Koenekamp; ***M:*** Lalo Schifrin.

Rage **½ 1995 (R)** When Alex Gainer (Daniels) is kidnapped he becomes the target of a high-tech lab experiment. Injected with chemicals that induce blind and killing rages, Alex escapes and unwillingly goes on a murderous rampage. Now he must find the antidote and clear his name before it happens again. **94m/C; VHS, DVD.** Gary Daniels; Ken Tigar; Jillian McWhirter; Fiona Hutchinson; Peter Jason; Mark Metcalf; ***D:*** Joseph Merhi; ***W:*** Jacobsen Hart; Joseph John Barmettler, Jr.; ***C:*** Ken Blakey; ***M:*** Louis Febre.

The Rage **1996 (R)** Nick Travis (Lamas) is a burned-out FBI agent with a brand new partner Kelly McCord (Cloke), who has no field experience, and a tough assignment. He's after a gang of anti-government killers led by psycho Dacy (Busey). Good action sequences substitute for the lack of plot sense. **95m/C; VHS, DVD.** Lorenzo Lamas; Gary Busey; Kristen Cloke; Roy Scheider; David Carradine; Jenny (Jennifer) McShane; ***D:*** Sidney J. Furie; ***W:*** Greg Mellott; ***C:*** Donald M. Morgan; ***M:*** Paul Zaza.

The Rage **2007** Old-fashioned gorefest about a mad scientist and a deadly mutating virus. Russian scientist Viktor (Divoff) get the pharmaceutical shaft after discovering a cancer cure. To get even he develops the rage virus, which turns the infected into flesh-eating mutants. One of his test subjects escapes, dies in the woods, and becomes dinner for vultures. The infected birds then attack any unfortunates they find, some of whom eventually turn up at Viktor's cabin. There's lots of limb-ripping, blood-gushing, and flesh-noshing with some decent special effects. **89m/C; DVD.** Andrew Divoff; Misty Mundae; Reggie Bannister; Robert Kurtzman; Ryan Hooks; ***W:*** John Bisson; ***M:*** Edward Douglas. **VIDEO**

Rage **½** *Tokarev* **2014** Action-drama-thriller about the lengths a father will go to protect his daughter, even if it means facing issues long-buried. Though he was once a violent criminal, Paul Maguire (Cage) is now a widowed father and legitimate businessman. When his teenaged daughter Caitlin (Peeples) is kidnapped from their home, Paul goes to extraordinary lengths to find and rescue her. He even puts his old crew back together, though this choice results in bloody revenge and coming to terms with past secrets. **98m/C; DVD, Blu-Ray, Streaming, Download.** Nicolas Cage; Rachel Nichols; Max Ryan; Michael McGrady; Aubrey Peeples; ***D:*** Paco Cabezas; ***W:*** Jim Agnew; Sean Keller; ***C:*** Andrzej Sekula; ***M:*** Laurent Eyquem.

Rage **2014** Cage plays a reformed criminal whose daughter is kidnapped, forcing him into violent action Chuck Bronson style. It's something that nearly everyone on Earth has seen before, done better. Poor Stormare and Glover are dragged along for the remarkably boring ride. Some of the later bits in which Cage gets to launch over-the-top feel designed for no reason other than YouTube supercuts of the scenery-chewing actor. **92m/C; DVD, Blu-Ray.** Nicolas Cage; Danny Glover; Max Ryan; Michael McGrady; Peter Stormare; Pasha D. Lychnikoff; Rachel Nichols; Aubrey Peeples; ***D:*** Paco Cabezas; ***W:*** Jim Agnew; Sean Keller; ***C:*** Andrzej Sekula; ***M:*** Laurent Eyquem.

Rage and Honor **1992 (R)** Rothrock stars as Kris Fairfield, a high-school teacher who spends her spare time tutoring students in the martial-arts. Her present students are a group of cops, including Aussie visitor Preston Michaels. When Michaels witnesses a drug deal, he gets set-up by the dealers for a murder he didn't commit and only Kris can help him prove his innocence. **93m/C; VHS, DVD.** Cynthia Rothrock; Richard Norton; Brian Thompson; Terri Treas; Catherine Bach; Alex Datcher; ***D:*** Terence H. Winkless; ***W:*** Terence H. Winkless.

Rage and Honor 2: Hostile Takeover **½ 1993 (R)** Rothrock returns as black-belt CIA operative Kris Fairfield, whose latest assignment takes her to Jakarta where a banker is involved in a large-scale drug money laundering operation. She teams up with Preston Michaels (Norton), a renegade Australian cop, and winds up following a trail that leads to a fortune in diamonds and lots of trouble. **98m/C; VHS, DVD.** Cynthia Rothrock; Richard Norton; Patrick Muldoon; Frans Tumbuan; Ron Vreeken; Alex Tumundo; ***D:*** Guy Norris; ***W:*** Louis Sun; Steven Reich.

Rage at Dawn **½** *Seven Bad Men* **1955** An outlaw gang is tracked by a special agent who must "bend" the rules a little in order to get the bad guys. Not surprisingly, he gets his girl as well. A solid standard of the genre, with some clever plot twists. **87m/C; VHS, DVD.** Randolph Scott; Forrest Tucker; Mala Powers; J. Carrol Naish; Edgar Buchanan; ***D:*** Tim Whelan; ***W:*** Horace McCoy; ***C:*** Ray Rennahan; ***M:*** Paul Sawtell.

The Rage: Carrie 2 *Carrie 2* **1999 (R)** You don't need psychic powers to know that things probably aren't going to end well for the tormenting teens in this slightly altered sequel. Rachel's (Bergl), a semi-Goth outcast who has a crush on good guy jock Jesse (London). She also has the ability to rattle and explode things when she's upset. Sue (Irving), the sole survivor from Carrie White's little tantrum years earlier, discovers that Rachel is related to the late telekinetic prom queen and tries to warn her. Too late. Jesse's bitchy girlfriend sets out to humiliate Rachel at a big party held at an all too flammable mansion. Lacks the character development and shock value of the original. **97m/C; VHS, DVD, Blu-Ray.** Emily Bergl; Amy Irving; Jason London; J. Smith-Cameron; Zachery Ty Bryan; John Doe; Gordon Clapp; Rachel Blanchard; Mena Suvari; Eddie Kaye Thomas; ***D:*** Katt Shea; ***W:*** Rafael Moreu; ***C:*** Donald M. Morgan; ***M:*** Danny P. Harvey.

A Rage in Harlem **1991 (R)** The crime novels of Chester A. Himes were translated into the best movies of the early '70s blaxploitation era. Now, a Himes story gets the big budget Hollywood treatment with juice and aplomb. A voluptuous lady crook enters Harlem circa 1950 with a trunkful of stolen gold sought by competing crooks, and the chase is on, with one virtuous soul (Whitaker) who only wants the girl. Great cast and characters, much humor, but unsparing in its violence. **108m/C; VHS, DVD, Blu-Ray.** Forest Whitaker; Gregory Hines; Robin Givens; Zakes Mokae; Danny Glover; Tyler Collins; Ron Taylor; T.K. Carter; Willard Pugh; Samm-Art Williams; Screamin' Jay Hawkins; Badja (Medu) Djola; John Toles-Bey; Stack Pierce; George D. Wallace; ***D:*** Bill Duke; ***W:*** John Toles-Bey; Bobby Crawford; ***M:*** Elmer Bernstein.

Rage in Heaven **1/2 1941** Stilted melodrama based on a James Hilton novel. Wealthy Philip Monrell (Montgomery) hides the fact he escaped from a Paris mental hospital when he returns home to London. After quickly marrying his mother's secretary, Stella (Bergman), Philip becomes obsessively jealous, convinced that his friend Ward Andrews (Sanders) and Stella are having an affair. As his madness grows, Philip actually plots his own death so Ward will be accused of murder! **85m/B; DVD.** Robert Montgomery; George Sanders; Ingrid Bergman; Oscar Homolka; Lucile Watson; Philip Merivale; ***D:*** W.S. Van Dyke; ***W:*** Christopher Isherwood; Robert Thoeren; ***C:*** Oliver Marsh; ***M:*** Bronislau Kaper.

The Rage In Placid Lake **2003** After being humiliated by his hippy parents all his life, Placid Lake (Ben Lee) decides to go in the opposite direction of them by becoming a corporate stooge after his graduation. **89m/C; DVD, Streaming.** *AU* Ben Lee; Rose Byrne; Miranda Richardson; Garry McDonald; Stephen James King; ***D:*** Tony McNamara; ***W:*** Tony McNamara; ***C:*** Ellery Ryan; ***M:*** Cezary Skubiszewski. **VIDEO**

Rage of Honor **1987 (R)** A high-kicking undercover cop seeks vengeance on bad guys for his partner's murder. Standard of its type; why bother? **92m/C; VHS, DVD, Blu-Ray.** Sho Kosugi; Lewis Van Bergen; Robin Evans; Gerry Gibson; ***D:*** Gordon Hessler; ***W:*** Wallace C. Bennett.

The Rage of Paris **1938** Scheming ex-actress and head waiter hope to gain by helping a beautiful French girl (Darrieux) snag a rich hubby. She comes to her senses, realizing that love, true love, matters more than wealth. Well-acted, quaint comedy. **78m/B; VHS, DVD.** Danielle Darrieux; Douglas Fairbanks, Jr.; Mischa Auer; Helen Broderick; ***D:*** Henry Koster; ***C:*** Joseph Valentine.

A Rage to Live **1/2 1965** Trashy, moralistic adaptation of the John O'Hara novel. Wealthy nympho Grace (Pleshette) marries dull, nice Sidney (Dillman) after he convinces her she can be faithful. This works for awhile until she fools around with the unstable Roger (Gazzara) and gets caught. Sidney gives her a last-chance ultimatum but there's more crying to come. **101m/B; DVD.** Suzanne Pleshette; Bradford Dillman; Ben Gazzara; Peter Graves; Bethel Leslie; Carmen Mathews; Linden Chiles; Mark Goddard; ***D:*** Walter Grauman; ***W:*** John T. Kelley; ***C:*** Charles Lawton, Jr.; ***M:*** Nelson Riddle.

Raggedy Man **1981 (PG)** Spacek in her signature role as a lonely small-town woman. Here she's raising two sons alone in a small Texas town during WWII. Spacek's strong acting carries a well-scripted story, unfortunately marred by an overwrought ending. **94m/C; VHS, DVD.** Sissy Spacek; Eric Roberts; Sam Shepard; Tracey Walter; William Sanderson; Henry Thomas; ***D:*** Jack Fisk; ***W:*** William D. Wittliff; ***C:*** Ralf Bode; ***M:*** Jerry Goldsmith.

The Raggedy Rawney **1/2 1990 (R)** A young Army deserter dresses in women's clothing and hides out as a mad woman with a band of gypsies. Good first directing effort by English actor Bob Hoskins. Unpretentious and engaging. **102m/C; VHS, DVD.** Bob Hoskins; Dexter Fletcher; Zoe Nathenson; David Hill; Ian Dury; Zoe Wanamaker; J.G. Devlin; Perry Fenwick; ***D:*** Bob Hoskins; ***W:*** Bob Hoskins; Nicole De Wilde; ***M:*** Michael Kamen.

Ragin' Cajun **1990** Retired kickboxer is forced into a death match to save his girlfriend. **91m/C; VHS, DVD.** David Heavener; Charlene Tilton; Sam Bottoms; Samantha Eggar; ***D:*** William B. Hillman.

Raging Bull **1980 (R)** Scorsese's depressing but magnificent vision of the dying American Dream and suicidal macho codes in the form of the rise and fall of middleweight boxing champ Jake LaMotta, a brutish, dull-witted animal who can express himself only in the ring and through violence. A photographically expressive, brilliant drama, with easily the most intense and brutal boxing scenes ever filmed. De Niro provides a vintage performance, going from the young LaMotta to the aging has-been, and is ably accompanied by Moriarty as his girl and Pesci as his loyal, much beat-upon bro. **128m/B; VHS, DVD, Blu-Ray.** Robert De Niro; Cathy Moriarty; Joe Pesci; Frank Vincent; Nicholas Colasanto; Theresa Saldana; ***D:*** Martin Scorsese; ***W:*** Paul Schrader; Mardik Martin; ***C:*** Michael Chapman; ***M:*** Robbie Robertson. Oscars '80: Actor (De Niro), Film Editing; AFI '98: Top 100; Golden Globes '81: Actor--Drama (De Niro); L.A. Film Critics '80: Actor (De Niro), Film; Natl. Bd. of Review '80: Actor (De Niro), Support. Actor (Pesci); Natl. Film Reg. '90; N.Y. Film Critics '80: Actor (De Niro), Actor (De Niro), Support. Actor (Pesci), Support. Actor (Pesci); Natl. Soc. Film Critics '80: Cinematog., Director (Scorsese), Support. Actor (Pesci).

Raging Hormones **1999** Florida teen Peter Broadhurst thinks he's died and gone to hormone heaven when his beautiful neighbor Sally decides to make him her personal sex toy. At least until his mother finds out. Strictly low-budget, amateur night. **93m/C; DVD.** Antoni Corone; Topher Hopkins; Della Hobby; Darlene Demko; Rene Orobello; ***D:*** Michael Dugan; ***W:*** Michael Dugan; ***C:*** Anthony Foy. **VIDEO**

Raging Phoenix *Deu Suay Doo* **2009 (R)** Deu (JeeJa Yanin) is coping with the loss of being abandoned by both her family and her rock band, when a group of kidnappers who want women for the sex trade or organ harvesting try kidnapping her. She is saved by a ragtag band of martial artists who teach her 'Meyraiyuth', and odd blend of Muay Thai, break dancing, and Drunken Style kung Fu. The story is preposterous of course, but most people will be watching to see the vengeance as opposed to the plot. **112m/C; DVD, Blu-Ray.** *TH* Jeeja Yanin; Kazu Patrick Tang; ***D:*** Rashane Limtrakul; ***W:*** Sompope Vejchapipat; ***C:*** Thanachart Boonla; Tiwa Moeithaisong; Teerawat Rujintham; Chalerm Wongpim; ***M:*** Kanisorn Phuangjin.

Rags **1/2 2012** A sweet, gender-reversal Cinderella teen musical from Nickelodeon. Charlie is left to toil in the nightclub owned by his deceased mother that's being mismanaged by his greedy stepfather, Arthur. Arthur's latest plan is to promote his two sons as the next hot boy band even though Charlie is the one with the talent. Charlie meets cute with teen pop star Kadee and, thanks to Charlie's fairy god-dude Shawn and a talent contest, things work out as expected. **90m/C; DVD.** Max Schneider; Keke Palmer; Drake Bell; Robert Moloney; Isaiah Mustafa; ***D:*** Bille Woodruff; ***W:*** Jason Fuchs; ***C:*** Glen Winter; ***M:*** Rodney Jenkins. **CABLE**

Rags to Riches **1987** A wealthy Beverly Hills entrepreneur decides to improve his public image by adopting six orphan girls. TV pilot. **96m/C; VHS, DVD.** Joseph Bologna; Tisha Campbell; ***D:*** Bruce Seth Green; ***W:*** David Garber. **TV**

Ragtime **1981 (PG)** The lives and passions of a middle class family weave into the scandals and events of 1906 America. A small, unthinking act represents all the racist attacks on one man, who refuses to back down this time. Wonderful period detail. From the E.L. Doctorow novel, but not nearly as complex. Features Cagney's last film performance. **156m/C; VHS, DVD.** Howard E. Rollins, Jr.; Kenneth McMillan; Brad Dourif; Mary Steenburgen; James Olson; Elizabeth McGovern; Pat O'Brien; James Cagney; Debbie Allen; Jeff Daniels; Moses Gunn; Donald O'Connor; Mandy Patinkin; Norman Mailer; Jeffrey DeMunn; Robert Joy; Fran Drescher; Frankie Faison; Samuel L. Jackson; Michael Jeter; John Ratzenberger; ***D:*** Milos Forman; ***W:*** Michael Weller; ***C:*** Miroslav Ondricek; ***M:*** Randy Newman.

Raid on Entebbe **1977 (R)** Dramatization of the Israeli rescue of passengers held hostage by terrorists at Uganda's Entebbe Airport in 1976. A gripping actioner all the more compelling because true. Finch received an Emmy nomination in this, his last film. **113m/C; VHS, DVD.** Charles Bronson; Peter Finch; Horst Buchholz; John Saxon; Martin Balsam; Jack Warden; Yaphet Kotto; Sylvia Sidney; ***D:*** Irvin Kershner; ***C:*** Bill Butler; ***M:*** David Shire. **TV**

Raid on Rommel **1/2 1971 (PG)** A British soldier (Burton) poses as a Nazi and tries to infiltrate Rommel's team with his rag-tag brigade of misfits. Predictable drivel. Contains action footage from the 1967 film "Tobruk." **98m/C; DVD.** Richard Burton; John Colicos; Clinton Greyn; Wolfgang Preiss; ***D:*** Henry Hathaway; ***W:*** Richard M. Bluel; ***C:*** Earl Rath; ***M:*** Hal Mooney.

The Raid: Redemption *Serbuan maut* **2011 (R)** Indonesian director/writer Evans shows Hollywood how to make a memorable—and incredibly savage—action film with his remarkable martial arts choreography. Tells the tale of a SWAT team trying to take down Jakarta drug lord Tama (the amazingly evil Sahetapy) who happens to have an entire building worth of reprobates on his side. As the team faces wave after wave of enemies, creative set pieces include an exploding fridge and a pitch-black stairwell shoot-out. Indonesian with subtitles. **101m/C; DVD, Blu-Ray.** Iko Uwais; Joe Taslim; Doni Alamsyah; Yayan Ruhian; Pierre Gruno; Tegar Satrya; Ray Sahetapy; ***D:*** Gareth Evans; ***W:*** Gareth Evans; ***C:*** Matt Flannery; Dimas Imam Subhono; ***M:*** Fajar Yuskemal; Aria Prayogi.

Raiders from Beneath the Sea **1964** The title sounds like a sci-fi monster flick but it's actually a crime drama about thieves planning to rob a Catalina Island bank using scuba gear. A minor, cheap B programmer that's barely watchable. **74m/B; DVD.** Ken Scott; Merry Anders; Garth Benton; Russ Bender; Booth Colman; ***D:*** Maury Dexter; ***W:*** Harry Spalding; ***C:*** Floyd Crosby; ***M:*** Harry Levine.

Raiders of Ghost City **1/2 1944** Serial in 13 chapters involves a Union Secret Service Agent after a ring of gold robbers who are posing as Confederate soldiers during the end of the Civil War. **225m/B; VHS, DVD.** Dennis Moore; Lionel Atwill; Regis Toomey; Wanda McKay; Joseph (Joe) Sawyer; Virginia Christine; ***D:*** Lewis D. Collins; Ray Taylor; ***W:*** Morgan Cox; ***C:*** Harry Neumann; William Sickner.

Raiders of Leyte Gulf **1963** Long-unavailable Philippine film from the early 1960s is a throwback to the propaganda that Hollywood produced during WWII. This one features sadistic bucktoothed Japanese soldiers. The protagonists are American POWs and Philippine guerrillas who are setting the stage for MacArthur's return. Director Romero would go on to a busy career in horror and other genres. **80m/B; VHS, DVD.** *PH* Leopold Salcedo; Michael Parsons; Jennings Sturgeon; Liza Moreno; ***D:*** Eddie Romero; ***W:*** Carl Kuntze; E.F. Romero; ***C:*** Felipe Sacdalan; ***M:*** Tito Arevalo.

Raiders of the Lost Ark *Indiana Jones and the Raiders of the Lost Ark* **1981 (PG)** Classic '30s-style adventure reminiscent of early serials spawned sequels and numerous rip-offs and made Ford a household name as dashing hero and intrepid archeologist Indiana Jones. Set in 1936, Indy battles mean Nazis, decodes hieroglyphics, fights his fear of snakes, and even has time for a little romance in his quest for the biblical Ark of the Covenant. Allen is perfectly cast as his feisty ex-flame Marion, more than a little irritated with the smooth talker who dumped her years earlier. Asks viewers to suspend belief as every chase and stunt tops the last. Unrelated opening sequence does a great job of introducing the character. **115m/C; VHS, DVD, Blu-Ray.** Harrison Ford; Karen Allen; Wolf Kahler; Paul Freeman; John Rhys-Davies; Denholm Elliott; Ronald Lacey; Anthony (Corlan) Higgins; Alfred Molina; ***D:*** Steven Spielberg; ***W:*** George Lucas; Philip Kaufman; ***C:*** Douglas Slocombe; ***M:*** John Williams. Oscars '81: Art Dir./Set Dec., Film Editing, Sound, Visual FX; AFI '98: Top 100; Natl. Film Reg. '99.

Raiders of the Seven Seas **1953** Payne makes a dashing rogue of a pirate but Reed is miscast (though lovely) as a Spanish countess in this routine swashbuckler. Pirate Barbarossa takes Countess Alida hostage, intending to ransom her to her fiance Salcedo (Mohr). Only he falls in love and decides to expose her intended for the scheming coward he is. **88m/C; DVD.** John Payne; Donna Reed; Gerald Mohr; Lon Chaney, Jr.; Anthony Caruso; Henry (Kleinbach) Brandon; ***D:*** Sidney Salkow; ***W:*** Sidney Salkow; John O'Dea; ***C:*** William Howard Greene; ***M:*** Paul Sawtell.

Raiders of the Sun **1992 (R)** After the Earth has been ruined in a biological disaster, a futuristic warrior arrives to help restore world peace and order. Cheap "Mad Max" ripoff. **80m/C; VHS, DVD.** Richard Norton; Rick Dean; William (Bill) Steis; Blake Boyd; Brigitta Stenberg; Ned Hourani; Nick Nicholson; Nigel Hogge; Paul Holmes; Ernie Satana; ***D:*** Cirio H. Santiago; ***W:*** Frederick Bailey; Thomas McKelvey Cleaver; ***C:*** Joe Batac; ***M:*** Gary Earl; Odette Springer.

Raiders!: The Story of the Greatest Fan Film Ever Made **2016** In 1989, three Mississippi teenagers nearly finished a project they had been working on most of their lives, a shot-for-shot recreation of their favorite film, Steven Spielberg's "Raiders of the Lost Ark." They came so close to finishing the movie, but real life got in the way. Decades later, they reunited to finish the film, and the documentary about their fan project captures both the glory of fandom and how much their lives changed since those innocent days of childhood. It's a surprisingly moving documentary about the glory of youthful joy and how tightly we have to hold on to that feeling as adults. **106m/C; DVD.** ***D:*** Jeremy Coon; Tim Skousen; ***W:*** Jeremy Coon; Tim Skousen; ***C:*** Tim Irwin; Ed Stephenson; ***M:*** Anton Sanko.

Railroad Tigers **2017** In 1941, Chinese railroad workers ambush a Japanese military train to steal food for the starving. It might work as a war/action movie, but doesn't gel for slapstick humor and overly choreographed fight scenes. Jackie Chan is still kicking butt, though at age 62 his kicks aren't as high as they were during his heyday. Chan's son Jaycee gives ol' dad a hand, but it's not enough to pull this mediocre fare from the tracks. **124m/C; DVD.** Jackie Chan; Zitao Huang; Jaycee Chan; Kai Wang; Ping Sang; ***D:*** Ding Sheng; ***W:*** Ding Sheng; He Keke; ***C:*** Yu Ding; ***M:*** Zai Lao.

Railroaded **1947** The police suspect an innocent man in the botched robbery of a bookie joint. Complications arise when the detective investigating the case falls for the man's sister. Tense, excellent noir Anthony Mann crime drama. **72m/B; VHS, DVD.** John Ireland; Sheila Ryan; Hugh Beaumont; Ed Kelly; Jane Randolph; ***D:*** Anthony Mann; ***W:*** John C. Higgins; ***C:*** Guy Roe; ***M:*** Alvin Levin.

Rails & Ties **1/2 2007 (PG-13)** Despite good performances, this drama goes off track with some unbelievable plot machinations in (daughter of Clint) Eastwood's directorial debut. Emotionally distant train engineer Tom Stark (Bacon) can't cope with his wife Megan's (Harden) terminal cancer diagnosis and escapes through work. At a rail crossing, a disturbed young woman (Root) parks her car on the tracks; the crash kills her but her son Danny (Heizer) survives. A suspended Tom is brooding at home when Danny shows up, having run away from foster care. They take the boy in and Tom and Danny are soon bonding over their mutual love of trains. **101m/C; DVD.** Kevin Bacon; Marcia Gay Harden; Marin Hinkle; Eugene Byrd; Miles Heizer; Margo Martindale; Bonnie Root; Micky Levy; ***D:*** Alison Eastwood; ***W:*** Micky Levy; ***C:*** Tom Stern; ***M:*** Kyle Eastwood; Michael Stevens.

The Railway Children ½ **1970** At the turn of the century in England, the father of three children is framed and sent to prison during Christmas. The trio and their mother must survive on a poverty stricken farm near the railroad tracks. They eventually meet a new friend who helps them prove their father's innocence. Wonderfully directed by Jeffries. From the classic Edith Nesbitt children's novel. **104m/C; VHS, DVD.** *GB* Jenny Agutter; William Mervyn; Bernard Cribbins; Dinah Sheridan; Iain Cuthbertson; Sally Thomsett; Peter Bromilow; Ann Lancaster; Gary Warren; Gordon Whiting; David Lodge; ***D:*** Lionel Jeffries; ***W:*** Lionel Jeffries; ***C:*** Arthur Ibbetson.

The Railway Children **2000** Heart-tugger about the three Waterbury children, who must move to a small village and live in reduced circumstances with their mother (Agutter) when their father (Kitchen) is wrongfully imprisoned. The threesome spend much of their time by the railroad with its stationmaster (Russell) and a kindly railroad tycoon (Attenborough), who takes an interest in their situation. Based on the novel by Edith Nesbitt. Agutter played the role of the eldest daughter in the 1970 film version. **90m/C; VHS, DVD.** *GB* Jenny Agutter; Michael Kitchen; Jemima Rooper; Jack Blumenau; Clare Thomas; Richard Attenborough; Clive Russell; David Bamber; Gregor Fisher; ***D:*** Catherine Morshead; ***W:*** Simon Nye; ***C:*** John Daly; ***M:*** Simon Lacey. **TV**

The Railway Man **2013 (R)** Well-intentioned melodrama that tells an interesting story but nonetheless feels flat. Firth plays Eric Lomax, a British Army officer who was tormented as a prisoner of war at a Japanese labor camp during World War II. Decades later, he revisits that camp with his love interest Patti (Kidman), only to learn that the Japanese interpreter who dealt much of the torture is still alive. It's a period piece about horrible memories, vengeance, and forgiveness. Admirable and well-made but there's a line between understated and dull that this flick crosses more than once. **116m/C; DVD, Blu-Ray.** *UK* Colin Firth; Nicole Kidman; Stellan Skarsgard; Hiroyuki (Henry) Sanada; Jeremy Irvine; Tanroh Ishida; Sam Reid; ***D:*** Jonathan Teplitzky; ***W:*** Frank Cottrell Boyce; Andy Paterson; ***C:*** Garry Phillips; ***M:*** David Hirschfelder.

Rain ½ **1932** W. Somerset Maugham's tale of a puritanical minister's attempt to reclaim a "lost woman" on the island of Pago Pago. Crawford and Huston work up some static. Remake of the 1928 silent film "Sadie Thompson." Remade again in 1953 as "Miss Sadie Thompson." **92m/B; VHS, DVD.** Joan Crawford; Walter Huston; William Gargan; Guy Kibbee; Beulah Bondi; Walter Catlett; ***D:*** Lewis Milestone; ***W:*** Maxwell Anderson; ***C:*** Oliver Marsh; ***M:*** Alfred Newman.

Rain **2001** Coming-of-age drama based on the 1994 novel by Kirsty Gunn. In 1972, 13-year-old Janey (Fulford-Wierzbicki) is spending the summer at a New Zealand beach cottage with her depressed mom Kate (Peirse), ineffectual father Ed (Browning), and her younger brother, Jim (Murphy). Trouble comes in the form of too much booze and the attentions of photographer Cady (Csokas), who not only catches Kate's eye but blossoming Janey's as well. Tensions build as the betrayals multiply. **90m/C; VHS, DVD.** *AU* Alicia Fulford-Wierzbicki; Sarah Peirse; Marton Csokas; Alistair Browning; Aaron Murphy; ***D:*** Christine Jeffs; ***W:*** Christine Jeffs; ***C:*** John Toon; ***M:*** Neil Finn; Edmund McWilliams.

Rain *V.C. Andrews' Rain* **2006** Rain is a musical prodigy living with her family in the projects. She inadvertently witnesses the gangland slaying of her sister. In order to protect Rain, her mother reveals that the teenager is adopted and her biological mother is white and rich. Rain is taken into the home of her wealthy grandparents and offered a privileged new life but it's not easy. Very loosely based on the V.C. Andrews novel. **99m/C; DVD.** Brooklyn Sudano; Faye Dunaway; Robert Loggia; Khandi Alexander; Giancarlo Esposito; ***D:*** Craig De Bona; ***W:*** Andrew Neiderman; ***C:*** Craig De Bona. **VIDEO**

Rain Fall ½ **2009 (R)** Freelance assassin John Rain (Shiina) is being hunted by the yakuza and by Holtzer (Oldman), the head of the CIA's Tokyo office, since both believe that Rain has a flash drive containing information on corrupt bureaucrats. Rain is a subdued guy for being so lethal and feared while Holtzer makes up for it by yelling all the time. There are some subplots that don't really go anywhere and the flick doesn't have as much action or thrills as an action-thriller should. Based on the first of Barry Eisler's 'John Rain' novels. **111m/C; DVD.** Kippei Shiina; Gary Oldman; Kyoko Hasegawa; Misa Shimizu; Akira (Tsukamoto) Emoto; ***D:*** Max Mannix; ***W:*** Max Mannix; ***C:*** John Wareham, MD; ***M:*** Kenji Kawai. **VIDEO**

Rain Man ½ **1988 (R)** When his father dies, ambitious and self-centered Charlie Babbit finds he has an older autistic brother who's been institutionalized for years. Needing him to claim an inheritance, he liberates him from the institution and takes to the road, where both brothers undergo subtle changes. The Vegas montage is wonderful. Critically acclaimed drama and a labor of love for the entire cast. Cruise's best performance to date as he goes from cad to recognizing something wonderfully human in his brother and himself. Hoffman is exceptional. **128m/C; VHS, DVD, Blu-Ray.** Dustin Hoffman; Tom Cruise; Valeria Golino; Jerry Molen; Jack Murdock; Michael D. Roberts; Ralph Seymour; Lucinda Jenney; Bonnie Hunt; Kim Robillard; Beth Grant; ***D:*** Barry Levinson; ***W:*** Ronald Bass; Barry Morrow; ***C:*** John Seale; ***M:*** Hans Zimmer. Oscars '88: Actor (Hoffman), Director (Levinson), Film, Orig. Screenplay; Berlin Intl. Film Fest. '88: Golden Berlin Bear; Directors Guild '88: Director (Levinson); Golden Globes '89: Actor--Drama (Hoffman), Film--Drama.

Rain or Shine ½ **1930** Mary Rainey (Peers) inherits the family circus and works to save it from bankruptcy with the aid of manager Smiley (Cook). Adapted from Cook's Broadway musical comedy--minus the music and with more slapstick courtesy of Cook and his colleagues Howard and Chasen. Capra ends the entertainment by burning down the big top! **86m/B; DVD.** Joan Peers; Joe Cook; William "Buster" Collier, Jr.; Louise Fazenda; Tom Howard; Dave Chasen; Alan Roscoe; ***D:*** Frank Capra; ***W:*** Jo Swerling; Dorothy Howell; ***C:*** Joseph Walker.

The Rain People **1969 (R)** Pregnant housewife Knight takes to the road in desperation and boredom; along the way she meets retarded ex-football player Caan. Well directed by Coppola from his original script. Pensive drama. **102m/C; VHS, DVD.** Shirley Knight; James Caan; Robert Duvall; Tom Aldredge; Marya Zimmet; Andrew Duncan; Sally Gracie; Alan Manson; Laura Hope Crews; ***D:*** Francis Ford Coppola; ***W:*** Francis Ford Coppola; ***C:*** Bill Butler; ***M:*** Ronald Stein.

Rain Without Thunder ½ **1993 (PG-13)** Imagine the year 2042, a time when abortion is illegal and a fertilized egg has full Constitutional rights. Now imagine sitting through an 87 minute fake documentary that follows the story of a mother and daughter team who have been jailed for trying to go to Sweden so that the daughter can get an abortion. A one-sided, militant pro-choice effort that is neither entertaining nor informational. **87m/C; VHS, Streaming.** Betty Buckley; Jeff Daniels; Ali Thomas; Frederic Forrest; Carolyn McCormick; Linda Hunt; Robert Earl Jones; Graham Greene; Iona Morris; Austin Pendleton; ***D:*** Gary T. Bennett; ***W:*** Gary T. Bennett; ***M:*** Randall Lynch; Allen Lynch.

The Rainbow **1989 (R)** Mature, literate rendering of the classic D.H. Lawrence novel about a young woman's sexual awakening. Beautiful cinematography. Companion/prequel to director Russell's earlier Lawrence adaptation, "Women in Love" (1969). **104m/C; VHS, DVD.** *GB* Sammi Davis; Amanda Donohoe; Paul McGann; Christopher Gable; David Hemmings; Glenda Jackson; Kenneth Colley; ***D:*** Ken Russell; ***W:*** Vivian Russell; Ken Russell; ***C:*** Billy Williams; ***M:*** Carl Davis.

Rainbow Bridge **1971 (R)** The adventures of a group of hippies searching for their consciousness in Hawaii. Features concert footage from Jimi Hendrix's final performance. **74m/C; VHS, DVD.** Chuck Wein; Herbie Fletcher; Pat Hartley; ***D:*** Chuck Wein; ***C:*** Vilis Lapenieks.

The Rainbow Tribe ½ **2011** Feel good family comedy. Morgan is in the midst of a health crisis when he reconnects with childhood buddy Sunny, who's now the director of the summer camp they attended as kids. Morgan becomes a counselor and is determined to make the summer a memorable one for the not-so-happy 10-year-olds under his care. **90m/C; DVD.** David James Elliott; Ed Quinn; Max Burkholder; Grayson Russell; Julie Ann Emery; Rebecca Mader; Gabriel Mann; Renee Taylor; ***D:*** Christopher R. Watson; ***W:*** Daniel Frisch; ***C:*** Shane Daly; ***M:*** Ken Stange. **VIDEO**

Raining Stones **1993** A hard-up plumber becomes obsessed with buying an expensive first communion dress for his daughter and gets involved in numerous misadventures trying to get the money. Another of Loach's comedy-dramas about the British working class and their struggle to survive with dignity. **90m/C; VHS, DVD, Blu-Ray.** *GB* Bruce Jones; Julie Brown; Ricky Tomlinson; Tom Hickey; Gemma Phoenix; Jonathan James; ***D:*** Ken Loach; ***W:*** Jim Allen; ***C:*** Barry Ackroyd; ***M:*** Stewart Copeland. Cannes '93: Special Jury Prize.

The Rainmaker **1956** Reminiscent of "Elmer Gantry" in his masterful performance, Lancaster makes it all believable as a con man who comes to a small midwestern town and works miracles not only on the weather but on spinster Hepburn, although both were a little long in the tooth for their roles. Written by Nash from his own play. **121m/C; VHS, DVD.** Burt Lancaster; Katharine Hepburn; Wendell Corey; Lloyd Bridges; Earl Holliman; Cameron Prudhomme; Wallace Ford; ***D:*** Joseph Anthony; ***W:*** N. Richard Nash; ***C:*** Charles B(ryant) Lang, Jr.; ***M:*** Alex North. Golden Globes '57: Support. Actor (Holliman).

The Rainmakers ½ **1935** Roscoe the Rainmaker (Woolsey) and his partner Billy (Wheeler) come to drought-stricken Lima Junction, CA with their patented Magno-Magnetizer. Land speculator Simon Parker (Churchill) and his son Orville (Meeker) don't want a cloudburst ruining their plans, and they sabotage the equipment. A runaway train features into the climax. **78m/B; DVD.** Bert Wheeler; Robert Woolsey; Berton Churchill; George Meeker; Dorothy Lee; ***D:*** Fred Guiol; ***W:*** Leslie Goodwins; ***C:*** Ted D. McCord.

The Rains Came ½ **1939** Living within a loveless marriage in the mythical Indian city of Ranchipur, English socialite Loy pursues extramarital love interests, including the compassionate doctor Power, potential heir to the maharajah's throne. When an earthquake hits and brings major destruction to the city, Loy aids the doctor in helping the injured. Hankies should be kept handy. Adapted from the Louis Bromfield novel. **104m/B; VHS, DVD.** Myrna Loy; Tyrone Power; George Brent; Brenda Joyce; Nigel Bruce; Maria Ouspenskaya; Joseph Schildkraut; Laura Hope Crews; Marilyn Nash; Jane Darwell; Marjorie Rambeau; Henry Travers; H.B. Warner; William Royle; C. Montague Shaw; Harry Hayden; Abner Biberman; George Regas; ***D:*** Clarence Brown; ***W:*** Philip Dunne; Julien Josephson; ***C:*** Arthur C. Miller; ***M:*** Alfred Newman.

The Rains of Ranchipur ½ **1955** A wealthy American socialite flies to India with her husband, only to fall in love with the local doctor. Which is fortunate as disease spreads quickly after a natural disaster lays waste to the area. **104m/C; Blu-Ray, Streaming.** Lana Turner; Richard Burton; Fred MacMurray; Joan Caulfield; Michael Rennie; ***D:*** Jean Negulesco; ***W:*** Merle Miller; ***C:*** Milton Krasner; ***M:*** Hugo Friedhofer. **VIDEO**

Raintree County ½ **1957** A lavish, somewhat overdone epic about two lovers caught up in the national turmoil of the Civil War. An Indiana teacher (Clift) marries a southern belle (Taylor) just after the outbreak of war. The new wife battles mental illness. Producers had hoped this would be another "Gone with the Wind." Adapted from the novel by Ross Lockridge Jr. Film was delayed in mid-production by Clift's near-fatal and disfiguring car crash. **175m/C; VHS, DVD.** Elizabeth Taylor; Montgomery Clift; Eva Marie Saint; Lee Marvin; Nigel Patrick; Rod Taylor; Agnes Moorehead; Walter Abel; ***D:*** Edward Dmytryk; ***C:*** Robert L. Surtees.

Raise the Red Lantern ½ **1991 (PG)** Set in 1920s China, Zhang explores its claustrophobic world of privilege and humiliation. Songlian, an educated 19-year-old beauty, is forced into marriage as the fourth wife of a wealthy and powerful old man. She discovers that the wives have their own separate quarters and servants, and spend most of their time battling to attract their husband's attention. Over the course of a year, Songlian's fury and resentment grow until self-defeating rebellion is all she has. Gong Li is exquisite as the young woman struggling for dignity in a portrayal which is both haunting and tragic. **125m/C; VHS, DVD.** *CH* Gong Li; Ma Jingwu; He Caifei; Cao Cuifeng; Jin Shuyuan; Kong Lin; Ding Weimin; ***D:*** Yimou Zhang. British Acad. '92: Foreign Film; L.A. Film Critics '92: Cinematog.; N.Y. Film Critics '92: Foreign Film; Natl. Soc. Film Critics '92: Cinematog., Foreign Film.

Raise the Titanic WOOF! **1980 (PG)** A disaster about a disaster. Horrible script cannot be redeemed by purported thrill of the ship's emergence from the deep after 70 years. It's a shame, because the free world's security hangs in the balance. Based on Clive Cussler's best seller. **112m/C; VHS, DVD, Blu-Ray.** Jason Robards, Jr.; Richard Jordan; Anne Archer; Alec Guinness; J.D. Cannon; ***D:*** Jerry Jameson; ***M:*** John Barry.

Raise Your Voice ½ **2004 (PG)** Contrived tweenie fluff has eager 16-year-old Terri (Duff, blonde and bubbly as usual) longing to expand her singing talents by attending a performing arts summer school in L.A. Terri is encouraged by everyone but her overprotective dad (Keith) but finds the highly competitive atmosphere an eye-opener. Can sweet Terri realize her dreams and find mild romance with nice guy Jay (James)? Since this flick hits every teen cliche the answer should be obvious but it will still appeal to Duff's fans. **103m/C; VHS, DVD.** Hilary Duff; Oliver James; David Keith; Rita Wilson; Rebecca De Mornay; John Corbett; Jason Ritter; Robert Trebor; Dana Davis; Johnny Lewis; Kat Dennings; Lauren C. Mayhew; ***D:*** Sean McNamara; ***W:*** Sam Schreiber; ***C:*** John R. Leonetti; ***M:*** Machine Head; Aaron Zigman.

A Raisin in the Sun **1961** Outstanding story of a black family trying to make a better life for themselves in an all-white neighborhood in Chicago. The characters are played realistically and make for a moving story. Each person struggles with doing what he must while still maintaining his dignity and sense of self. Based on the 1959 Broadway play by Hansberry, who also wrote the screenplay. Remade for TV in 1989 with Danny Glover. **128m/B; VHS, DVD, Blu-Ray.** Diana Sands; John Fiedler; Ivan Dixon; Louis Gossett, Jr.; Sidney Poitier; Claudia McNeil; Ruby Dee; ***D:*** Daniel Petrie; ***W:*** Lorraine Hansberry; ***C:*** Charles Lawton, Jr.; ***M:*** Laurence Rosenthal. Natl. Bd. of Review '61: Support. Actress (Dee); Natl. Film Reg. '05.

A Raisin in the Sun **1989** An "American Playhouse" presentation of the Lorraine Hansberry play about a black family threatened with dissolution by the outside forces of racism and greed when they move into an all-white neighborhood in the 1950s. **171m/C; VHS, DVD.** Danny Glover; Esther Rolle; Starletta DuPois; ***D:*** Bill Duke. **TV**

A Raisin in the Sun ½ **2008** The leads reprise their roles from the 2004 Broadway revival of Lorraine Hansberry's 1959 play. The Youngers live in a crowded Chicago tenement: mother Lena (Rashad) is a maid, daughter Beneatha (Lathan) is attending college, and son Walter (Combs) is a chauffeur with a long-suffering wife, Ruth (McDonald), and young son, Travis (Martin). When Lena receives a substantial insurance check, she decides to use the money to buy a house in a nice middle-class—and white—neighborhood. Walter wants to spend the money to open a family business, a liquor store, but Lena disapproves. **87m/C; DVD.** Phylicia Rashad; Sean (Puffy, Puff Daddy, P. Diddy) Combs; Audra McDonald; Sanaa Lathan; Justin Martin; Sean Patrick Thomas; David Oyelowo; John Stamos; Bill Nunn; ***Nar:*** Morgan Freeman; ***D:*** Kenny Leon; ***W:*** Paris Qualles; ***C:*** Ivan Strasburg; ***M:*** Mervyn Warren. **TV**

Raising Arizona ✓✓✓ 1/2 **1987 (PG-13)** Hi's an ex-con and the world's worst hold-up man. Ed's a policewoman. They meet, fall in love, marry, and kidnap a baby (one of a family of quints). Why not? Ed's infertile and the family they took the baby from has "more than enough," so who will notice? But unfinished furniture tycoon Nathan Arizona wants his baby back, even if he has to hire an axe murderer on a motorcycle to do it. A brilliant, original comedy narrated in notorious loopy deadpan style by Cage. Innovative camera work by Barry Sonnenfeld. Wild, surreal, and hilarious. **94m/C; VHS, DVD, Blu-Ray.** Nicolas Cage; Holly Hunter; John Goodman; William Forsythe; Randall "Tex" Cobb; Trey Wilson; M. Emmet Walsh; Frances McDormand; Sam McMurray; T.J. Kuhn; Peter Benedek; ***D:*** Joel Coen; ***W:*** Ethan Coen; Joel Coen; ***C:*** Barry Sonnenfeld; ***M:*** Carter Burwell.

Raising Cain ✓✓ **1992 (R)** Thriller evoking poor man's Hitchcock about a child psychiatrist who just happens to be nuts features Lithgow in five roles. Seems his supposedly dead Norwegian father has come to the United States and needs his son's help to steal babies for a child development experiment, so the son's alter ego, Cain, shows up to commit the nasty deed. Unfortunately Lithgow also catches his wife with another man, and that's when the bodies start piling up. **95m/C; VHS, DVD, Blu-Ray.** John Lithgow; Lolita Davidovich; Steven Bauer; Frances Sternhagen; Tom Bower; Mel Harris; Gabrielle Carteris; Barton Heyman; ***D:*** Brian De Palma; ***W:*** Brian De Palma; ***C:*** Stephen Burum; ***M:*** Pino Donaggio.

Raising Flagg ✓✓ **2006 (PG-13)** Flagg Purdy (Arkin) is a small-town handyman with a stubborn streak and a continuing feud with his neighbor Gus (Pendleton). Their latest fracas causes a public humiliation and a crisis for Flagg and he takes to his bed, sure he's about to meet his maker. So his family reluctantly gathers to figure out what to do about dad now. **102m/C; DVD.** Alan Arkin; Austin Pendleton; Barbara Dana; Lauren Holly; Glenne Headly; Matthew Arkin; Daniel Quinn; Stephanie Lemelin; Dawn Maxey; Richard Kind; Clifton James; Vana O'Brien; ***D:*** Neal Miller; ***W:*** Nancy Miller; Dorothy Velasco; ***C:*** Erich Roland; ***M:*** Alan Barcus; Les Hooper.

Raising Genius ✓ 1/2 **2004 (R)** Weird teenaged math genius Hal (Long) locks himself in the bathroom to work on an equation that involves watching his cheerleader neighbor Lacy (McKellar) bounce on a trampoline. And it also upsets his overbearing mother Nancy (Malick). But things get out of hand when a burglary brings out the cops who think Hal is being kept prisoner. **83m/C; DVD.** Justin Long; Wendie Malick; Stephen (Steve) Root; Danica McKellar; Tippi Hedren; Shirley Jones; ***D:*** Linda Voorhees; Bess Wiley; ***W:*** Linda Voorhees; ***C:*** Chris W. Johnson. **VIDEO**

Raising Helen ✓✓ 1/2 **2004 (PG-13)** Helen (Hudson) has a successful, carefree life as a modeling agency exec, and is the favorite "cool" aunt of her sis Lindsay's (Huffman) three kids. However, Helen's shocked when Lindsay and her husband are killed in a car accident and she is given custody of the kids over perfect homemaker sis Jenny (Cusack). Helen soon gets fired, moves from Manhattan to Queens, finds a new job (working for Elizondo), and enrolls the kids at a nearby school run by the single and hunky Pastor Dan (Corbett). Hudson is as winsome as ever, but this is just another notch in her romantic comedy belt and it's all-too-familiar attire. **119m/C; DVD.** Kate Hudson; Joan Cusack; John Corbett; Dame Helen Mirren; Hayden Panettiere; Spencer Breslin; Felicity Huffman; Sean O'Bryan; Hector Elizondo; Sakina Jaffrey; Abigail Breslin; Kevin Kilner; ***D:*** Garry Marshall; ***W:*** Jack Amiel; Michael Begler; ***C:*** Charles Minsky; ***M:*** John Debney.

Raising Heroes ✓✓ **1997** Josh (Sistillio) and Paul (White) are about to finalize their adoption of a child when Josh witnesses a mob hit. Now he's a target, trying to stay alive and protect his family as well. **85m/C; VHS, DVD.** Troy Sistillio; Henry White; ***D:*** Douglas Langway; ***W:*** Douglas Langway.

Raising the Heights ✓ 1/2 **1997 (R)** Tensions escalate in the Brooklyn neighbor of Crown Heights when a drug deal, involving a high school teacher, results in the death of a young girl. So the victim's brother, Michael, decides to take revenge by taking a teacher hostage, with reporter Judy Burke leading a media barrage about the tense situation. Good intentions can't quite make up for the amateur filmmaking. **86m/C; VHS, DVD.** Gilbert Brown, Jr.; John Knox; Fia Perera; ***D:*** Max Gottlieb; ***W:*** Max Gottlieb.

Raising Victor Vargas ✓✓ 1/2 *Long Way Home* **2003 (R)** Fifteen-year-old Latino Victor (Rasuk) thinks he's pretty hot stuff in his Lower East Side New York neighborhood as he spends his summer vacation chasing the local hotties. His feisty old-world Grandma (Guzman), who's raising Victor and his two younger siblings, begs to differ but the kids try to keep Grandma in the dark. Then Victor meets Judy (Marte), who's too smart to fall for his lines, and Victor really gets some lessons in love. **87m/C; VHS, DVD.** Victor Rasuk; Judy Marte; Melonie Diaz; Altagracia Guzman; Silvestre Rasuk; Krystal Rodriguez; Kevin Rivera; ***D:*** Peter Sollett; ***W:*** Peter Sollett; ***C:*** Tim Orr; ***M:*** Roy Nathanson.

Rally 'Round the Flag, Boys! ✓ 1/2 **1958** Badly dated satire (from the novel by Max Shulman) turned slapstick comedy. Harry (Newman) and Grace (Woodward) Bannerman live in the quiet commuter community of Putnam's Landing, CT. When the Air Force chooses the town as the site of a new missile base, civic-minded Grace joins a committee to halt the project, much to the initial embarrassment of reservist Harry, who's chosen as the government's liaison. Local vamp Angela (Collins) regards their marital misunderstandings as her chance to console handsome Harry. Unfortunately, Newman was never good at flat-out comedy and the strain shows. **106m/C; DVD.** Paul Newman; Joanne Woodward; Joan Collins; Jack Carson; Tuesday Weld; Dwayne Hickman; Gale Gordon; O.Z. Whitehead; ***D:*** Leo McCarey; ***W:*** Leo McCarey; Claude Binyon; George Axelrod; ***C:*** Leon Shamroy; ***M:*** Cyril Mockridge.

Ralph Breaks the Internet ✓✓ 1/2 *Ralph Breaks the Internet: Wreck-It Ralph 2* **2018 (PG)** In this family-friendly sequel, Ralph and his BFF Vanellope travel into the Internet to find a replacement for her broken video game part, but their friendship is tested when Vanellope considers staying in that exciting, new world. Amid the colorful imagery, tomfoolery around online-isms, and meta-Disney gags exist powerful lessons in relationships and growing up. **112m/C; Blu-Ray, Streaming.** ***V:*** John C. Reilly; Sarah Silverman; Gal Gadot; Jack McBrayer; Jane Lynch; ***D:*** Phil Johnston; ***W:*** Phil Johnston; Rich Moore; Pamela Ribon; Josie Trinidad; Jim Reardon; ***C:*** Nathan Warner; ***M:*** Henry Jackman.

Rampage ✓✓ 1/2 **2018 (PG-13)** A CGI-heavy action-adventure drama centered on giant animals destroying Chicago, based on a video game. Samples from a genetically altered rat survive a spaceship crash, and land on Earth in three places. One hits near an animal sanctuary run by Davis Okoye (Johnson), who has bonded with an albino gorilla named George. George finds the sample, becomes infected, and grows to an enormous size with aggression and hunger to match. After escaping, he and the two other infected animals create havoc as scientists and Okoye work to contain them. Johnson's charisma cannot overcome the ludicrous plot, though the film has some appealing over-the-top humor. **107m/C; DVD, Blu-Ray.** Dwayne "The Rock" Johnson; Naomie Harris; Malin Akerman; Jeffrey Dean Morgan; Jake Lacy; ***D:*** Brad Peyton; ***W:*** Ryan Engle; Carlton Cuse; Ryan Condal; Adam Sztykiel; ***C:*** Jaron Presant; ***M:*** Andrew Lockington.

The Rambler ✓ **2013 (R)** Surreal and silly road movie features a bunch of nameless characters, starting with the title ex-con who gets out of prison, finds out you can't go home again, and hits the road. Among those who offer him a ride are a scientist who records dreams on VHS tapes and the participants' heads explode. The viewer should be so lucky. **99m/C; DVD, Blu-Ray.** Dermot Mulroney; James Cady; Lindsay Pulsipher; Natasha Lyonne; ***D:*** Calvin Lee Reeder; ***W:*** Calvin Lee Reeder; ***C:*** Dave McFarland; ***M:*** Heather McIntosh. **VIDEO**

Rambling Rose ✓✓✓ **1991 (R)** Rose (Dern) is a free-spirited, sexually adventurous young woman taken in by a Southern family in 1935. Rose immediately has an impact on the males of the clan, thanks to her insuppressible sexuality. This causes consternation with the strait-laced patriarch (Duvall), who attempts to control his desire for the girl. Eventually Rose decides she must try to stick to one man, but this only causes further problems. Excellent period piece withl solid performances, including Dern's real-life mother Ladd. **115m/C; VHS, DVD.** Laura Dern; Diane Ladd; Robert Duvall; Lukas Haas; John Heard; Kevin Conway; Robert John Burke; Lisa Jakub; Evan Lockwood; ***D:*** Martha Coolidge; ***W:*** Calder Willingham; ***C:*** Johnny E. Jensen; ***M:*** Elmer Bernstein. Ind. Spirit '92: Director (Coolidge), Film, Support. Actress (Ladd).

Rambo ✓✓ **2008 (R)** World-weary killing machine John Rambo (Stallone) is back, and the body count is higher than ever. Seemingly forgotten by the American military that used him in Vietnam and Afghanistan, Rambo's retired to isolation in the swamps of Thailand, but he's soon sucked back into the life of a mercenary when a group of missionaries recruit him to take them to Myanmar. Before the group has much time to help the innocents affected by the ongoing civil war, they're kidnapped by soldiers and Rambo swings into action, wiping out anyone in his way. Passable, if over-the-top, action sequences highlight Stallone's freakishly buff 60-year-old bod. **93m/C; DVD, Blu-Ray.** Sylvester Stallone; Julie Benz; Paul Schulze; Ken Howard; Tim Kang; Graham McTavish; Rey Gallegos; Jake La Botz; Maung Maung Khin; ***D:*** Sylvester Stallone; ***W:*** Sylvester Stallone; Art Monterastelli; ***C:*** Glen MacPherson; ***M:*** Brian Tyler; Ashley Miller.

Rambo: First Blood, Part 2 ✓✓ **1985 (R)** If anyone can save Our Boys still held prisoner in Asia it's John Rambo. Along the way he's tortured, flexes biceps, grunts, and then disposes of the bad guys by the dozen in one of filmdom's bigger dead body parades. Mindless action best enjoyed by testosterone-driven fans of the genre. Sequel to "First Blood" (1982); followed by "Rambo 3" (1988). **93m/C; VHS, DVD, Blu-Ray.** Sylvester Stallone; Richard Crenna; Charles Napier; Steven Berkoff; Julia Nickson-Soul; Martin Kove; ***D:*** George P. Cosmatos; ***W:*** Sylvester Stallone; James Cameron; ***C:*** Jack Cardiff; ***M:*** Jerry Goldsmith. Golden Raspberries '85: Worst Actor (Stallone), Worst Picture, Worst Screenplay, Worst Song ("Peace In Our Life").

Rambo: Last Blood ✓✓ **2019 (R)** The quiet life that PTSD-suffering Vietnam vet John Rambo (Stallone) has built on his Arizona ranch includes a close relationship with his adopted family, Maria (Barraza) and her college-bound daughter Gabrielle (Monreal). After learning that her long lost father is in Mexico, Gabrielle plans a trip to see him despite Rambo's warnings about the dangers involved. Shortly after crossing the border, she is kidnapped by a sex trafficking ring run by the Martinez gang, and Rambo must take action to save her. Not the strongest entry in the Rambo series but will satisfy fans. **89m/C; DVD, Blu-Ray.** Sylvester Stallone; Paz Vega; Sergio Peris-Mencheta; Adriana Barraza; Yvette Monreal; Fenessa Pineda; ***D:*** Adrian Grunberg; ***W:*** Sylvester Stallone; Matthew Cirulnick; ***C:*** Brendan Galvin; ***M:*** Brian Tyler. Golden Raspberries '19: Worst Remake/ Sequel.

Rambo 3 ✓ 1/2 **1988 (R)** John Rambo, the famous Vietnam vet turned Buddhist monk, this time invades Afghanistan to rescue his mentor. Meets up with orphan and fights his way around the country. Typically exploitative, kill now, ask questions later Rambo attack, lacking the sheer volume of no-brainer action of the first two Rambos. At the time, the most expensive film ever made, costing $58 million. Filmed in Israel. **102m/C; VHS, DVD, Blu-Ray.** Sylvester Stallone; Richard Crenna; Marc De Jonge; Kurtwood Smith; Spiros Focas; ***D:*** Peter McDonald; ***W:*** Sylvester Stallone; ***C:*** John Stanier; ***M:*** Jerry Goldsmith. Golden Raspberries '88: Worst Actor (Stallone).

The Ramen Girl ✓✓ **2008 (PG-13)** Abby (Murphy) gets dumped and stranded just after she's moved to Tokyo. Depressed, she wanders into a noodle shop and decides it's her destiny, pestering Maezumi (Nishida), the demanding chef, until he agrees to teach her his ramen secrets. Abby regains her self-confidence but after meeting Toshi (Park), Abby needs to decide her priorities, especially since he's moving to Shanghai. **102m/C; DVD.** Brittany Murphy; Toshiyuki Nishida; Tammy Blanchard; Kimiko Yo; Sohee Park; ***D:*** Robert Allan Ackerman; ***W:*** Becca Topol; ***C:*** Yoshitaka Sakamoto; ***M:*** Carlo Siliotto.

Ramona ✓ 1/2 **1936** In old Spanish-held California, beautiful Ramona (Young) is the illegitimate daughter of a Spanish rancher and a Native American woman. She's raised in the hacienda and eventually falls in love with Alessandro (Ameche). They run off and marry but it all turns tragic because of rampant racism (which is downplayed sympathetically). Both leads are badly miscast even given the times. 20th Century Fox's first feature shot completely in Technicolor. **84m/C; DVD.** Loretta Young; Don Ameche; Kent Taylor; Jane Darwell; John Carradine; Katherine DeMille; ***D:*** Henry King; ***W:*** Lamar Trotti; ***C:*** William V. Skall; ***M:*** Alfred Newman.

Ramona and Beezus ✓✓ 1/2 **2010 (G)** Inviting family comedy is an adaptation of the first book in Beverly Cleary's Newberry Award-winning series. Nine-year-old third-grader Ramona Quimby's (King) overactive imagination is always getting her in trouble and embarrassing her teenaged sister Beezus (Gomez). In the nominal plot, Mr. Quimby (Corbett) becomes a stay-at-home dad after losing his job, Mrs. Quimby (Moynahan) goes back to work, and Ramona tries (unsuccessfully) to not irritate anyone. **103m/C; Blu-Ray.** Joey King; Selena Gomez; John Corbett; Bridget Moynahan; Ginnifer Goodwin; Josh Duhamel; Sandra Oh; Hutch Dano; Jason Spevack; Janet Wright; Sierra McCormick; ***D:*** Elizabeth Allen; ***W:*** Laurie Craig; Nick Pustav; ***C:*** John Bailey; ***M:*** Mark Mothersbaugh.

Rampage ✓ 1/2 **1963** Predictable plot has Mitchum going through the motions as big game trapper Harry Stanton. He's hired by a German zoo to bring back a legendary Malaysian cat that's half-tiger/half-leopard. Stanton is teamed with aging hunter Otto Abbott (Hawkins) who brings along his beautiful and much-younger mistress, Anna (Martinelli). The paranoid Otto believes the duo are betraying him and they may not survive their jungle trek. **98m/C; DVD.** Robert Mitchum; Jack Hawkins; Elsa Martinelli; Sabu; ***D:*** Phil Karlson; ***W:*** Marguerite Roberts; Robert I. Holt; ***C:*** Harold Lipstein; ***M:*** Elmer Bernstein.

Rampage ✓✓ **1987 (R)** Seemingly all-American guy Charles Reece (McArthur) goes on a murder spree, killing and then mutilating his victims. Fraser (Biehn) is a liberal district attorney who questions his own views as he argues that Reece was sane when he committed the murders and deserves the death penalty. Director Friedkin makes no bones about his concerns that the criminal insanity defense often spares the perpetrator while denying justice to the victims. Adapted from the book by William P. Wood and loosely based on killer Richard Chase. Filmed in 1987, the movie wasn't released until 1992 due to the production company's financial difficulties. **92m/C; VHS, Streaming.** Michael Biehn; Alex McArthur; Nicholas (Nick) Campbell; Deborah Van Valkenburgh; John Harkins; Art LaFleur; ***D:*** William Friedkin; ***W:*** William Friedkin; ***M:*** Ennio Morricone.

Rampage ✓ **2009** Overly-familiar story about a small town misfit who snaps and goes on a killing spree. Frustrated 20-something Bill (Fletcher) loses it when his parents nag him to stop freeloading and move out and his boss won't give him a raise. So he puts on Kevlar body armor and begins shooting random strangers. **85m/C; DVD.** *CA* Brendan Fletcher; Shaun Sipos; Lynda Boyd; Matt Frewer; Michael Paré; ***D:*** Uwe Boll; ***W:*** Uwe Boll; ***C:*** Mathias Neumann; ***M:*** Jessica de Rooij. **VIDEO**

Rampage: Capital Punishment ✓ **2014** Psycho Bill Williamson (Fletcher) finally comes out of hiding in Boll's sequel to his 2009 flick. This time the disturbed Bill takes hostages at a DC TV station where he uses the media to decry mankind's moral failings. Talky and violent. **93m/C; DVD, Blu-Ray.** *CA GE* Brendan Fletcher; Lochlyn Munro; *D:* Uwe Boll; *W:* Uwe Boll; *C:* Mathias Neumann; *M:* Jessica de Rooij. **VIDEO**

Rampage: President Down **2016** In the third installment of the Rampage trilogy, the president of the United States is threatened. Still alive, Bill Williamson (Fletcher) wants to live up to his promise to tear up Washington. To that end, he does recon work in the city to bring down the U.S. president and his Secret Service detail. If all goes according to his plan, he will negatively impact the population of the United States and the world. **99m/C; DVD, Blu-Ray, Streaming, Download.** Brendan Fletcher; Steve Baran; Ryan McDonell; Crystal Lowe; Bruce Blain; *D:* Uwe Boll; *W:* Brendan Fletcher; Uwe Boll; *C:* Mathias Neumann; *M:* Jessica de Rooij; Pale Christian Thomas. **VIDEO**

Rampage: The Hillside Strangler Murders **2004 (R)** Has only the most tenuous connection with the true serial killer story involving the rape and strangulation deaths of young women in L.A. in the late 1970s. Detective Jillian Dunne (Bell) calls in troubled shrink Samantha Stone (Daniel) to examine prime suspect Kenneth Bianchi (Collins). Samantha is led to believe that Bianchi is suffering from multiple personalities but the killer is only playing head games. **85m/C; DVD.** Clifton (Gonzalez) Collins, Jr.; Brittany Daniel; Lake Bell; Bret Roberts; Michael G. (Mike) Hagerty; Tomas Arana; Channon Roe; *D:* Chris Fisher; *W:* Chris Fisher; Aaron Pope; *C:* Eliot Rockett; *M:* Ryan Beveridge. **VIDEO**

Rampart **1/2 2011 (R)** Following up his critical smash "The Messenger," director/writer Moverman teams again with Harrelson but dips into a bit of a sophomore slump with this "bad cop" drama based on a real-life event (co-written by James Ellroy). Nearly saving it with his stellar performance is Harrelson as Dave Brown, an abusive cop caught up in the LAPD Rampart division scandal of 1999. Attempting to present a realistic portrait of a relic of a police officer basically being forced into retirement, it gets off-track and jumbled by meandering to numerous supporting characters and subplots. **108m/C; DVD, Blu-Ray.** Woody Harrelson; Robin Wright; Sigourney Weaver; Ice Cube; Ned Beatty; Steve Buscemi; Cynthia Nixon; Anne Heche; Brie Larson; Ben Foster; Sammy Boyarsky; *D:* Oren Moverman; *W:* Oren Moverman; James Ellroy; *C:* Bobby Bukowski; *M:* Dickon Hinchliffe.

Ramrod **1947** Lake is a tough ranch owner at odds with her father, who is being manipulated by a big-time cattleman into trying to put them out of business. She fights back, and McCrea is caught in the middle as the only good guy. Nothing special. **94m/B; DVD, Blu-Ray.** Veronica Lake; Joel McCrea; Arleen Whelan; Don DeFore; Preston Foster; Charlie Ruggles; Donald Crisp; Lloyd Bridges; *D:* Andre de Toth; *W:* Jack Moffitt; Cecile Kramer; *C:* Russell Harlan; *M:* Adolph Deutsch.

Ran **1985 (R)** The culmination of Kurosawa's career stands as his masterpiece. Loosely adapting Shakespeare's "King Lear," with plot elements from "Macbeth," he's fashioned an epic, heartbreaking statement about honor, ambition, and the futility of war. Aging medieval warlord Hidetora gives control of his empire to his oldest son, creating conflict with two other sons. Soon he's an outcast, as ambition and greed seize the two sons. Stunning battle scenes illuminate the full-blown tragedy of Kurosawa's vision. Superb acting with a scene-stealing Harada as the revenge-minded Lady Kaede; period costumes took three years to create. Japanese with English subtitles. **160m/C; VHS, DVD, Blu-Ray.** *JP FR* Tatsuya Nakadai; Akira Terao; Jinpachi Nezu; Daisuke Ryu; Meiko Harada; Hisashi Igawa; Peter; Kazuo Kato; Takeshi Kato; Jun Tazaki; Toshiya Ito; Yoshiko Miyazaki; Masayuki Yui; Norio Matsui; Takashi Nomura; *D:* Akira Kurosawa; *W:* Akira Kurosawa; Hideo Oguni; Masato Ide; *C:* Asakazu Nakai; Takao Saito; Masaharu Ueda; *M:* Toru Takemitsu. Oscars '85: Costume Des.; British Acad. '86: Foreign Film; L.A. Film Critics '85: Foreign Film; Natl. Bd. of Review '85: Director (Kurosawa); N.Y. Film Critics '85: Foreign Film; Natl. Soc. Film Critics '85: Cinematog., Film.

Rana: The Legend of Shadow Lake **1975** Gold at the bottom of a lake is guarded by a frog-monster, but treasure hunters try to retrieve it anyway. **96m/C; VHS, DVD.** Alan Ross; Karen McDiarmid; Jerry Gregoris; *D:* Bill Rebane; *W:* Lyoma Denetz; *C:* Bill Rebane; *M:* Bruce Malm.

Rancho Deluxe **1975** Off-beat western spoof starring Bridges and Waterston as two carefree cowpokes. Cult favorite featuring music by Buffett, who also appears in the film. **93m/C; VHS, DVD.** Jeff Bridges; Sam Waterston; Elizabeth Ashley; Charlene Dallas; Clifton James; Slim Pickens; Harry Dean Stanton; Richard Bright; Jimmy Buffett; *D:* Frank Perry; *W:* Thomas McGuane; *C:* William A. Fraker; *M:* Jimmy Buffett.

Rancho Notorious **1952** Kennedy, on the trail of his girlfriend's murderer, falls for dance hall girl Dietrich. Fine acting. A "period" sample oF '50s westerns, but different. A must for Dietrich fans. **89m/C; VHS, DVD.** Marlene Dietrich; Arthur Kennedy; Mel Ferrer; William Frawley; Jack Elam; George Reeves; *D:* Fritz Lang; *W:* Daniel Taradash; *C:* Hal Mohr.

Rancid **1/2 2004 (R)** Not terribly thrilling crime thriller. Failed writer (but successful drunk) James Hayson (Settle) hooks up with former flame Monica (Masterson) at a class reunion. This upsets her wealthy, controlling husband Crispin (Graham) and James winds up in a room with Monica's corpse. He learns he's been set-up but maybe not by who you think. **102m/C; DVD.** Matthew Settle; Fay Masterson; Jay Acovone; Patrick Ersgard; Graham Currie; Siena Goines; Jarmo Makinen; *D:* Joakim (Jack) Ersgard; *W:* Patrick Ersgard; Joakim (Jack) Ersgard; Jesper Ersgard; *C:* Kjell Lagerros; *M:* Lars Anderson.

Rancid Aluminium **1/2 2000** Druggie Pete Thompson (Ifans) inherits his family's failing publishing business, ticking off his friend (and the company's accountant) Sean Deeny (Fiennes). So Sean decides to take over the busines and borrows money from Russian mobster, Mr. Kant (Berkoff). Pete thinks Sean is just getting an additonal source of capital, but eventually learns what Sean is really up to. The Russian wants a return on his investment. And the viewer will wonder why he's wasting his time since this movie is dumb. Based on the novel by Hawes, who did the screenplay. **91m/C; VHS, DVD.** *GB* Rhys Ifans; Joseph Fiennes; Steven Berkoff; Tara Fitzgerald; Sadie Frost; Dani Behr; Keith Allen; Nick Moran; *D:* Edward Thomas; *W:* James Hawes; *C:* Tony Imi; *M:* John E.R. Hardy.

Random Encounter **1/2 1998** Executive Berkley becomes invovled in extortion and a murder cover-up all because she takes a shine to a mystery man. **100m/C; VHS, DVD.** *CA* Elizabeth Berkley; Joel Wyner; Frank Schorpion; Barry Flatman; Mark Walker; Ellen David; Susan Glover; Frank Fontaine; *D:* Douglas Jackson; *W:* Matt Dorff; *C:* Georges Archambault; *M:* Daniel Scott. **VIDEO**

Random Harvest **1942** A masterful, tearjerking film based on the James Hilton novel. A shell-shocked WWI amnesiac meets and is made happy by a beautiful music hall dancer. He regains his memory and forgets about the dancer and their child. This is Garson's finest hour, and a shamelessly potent sobfest. **126m/B; VHS, DVD.** Greer Garson; Ronald Colman; Reginald Owen; Philip Dorn; Susan Peters; Henry Travers; Margaret Wycherly; Bramwell Fletcher; *D:* Mervyn LeRoy; *W:* Claudine West; George Froeschel; Arthur Wimperis; *C:* Joseph Ruttenberg; *M:* Herbert Stothart.

Random Hearts **1999 (R)** If this film had stuck to overcoming tragedy and finding new love, it could have been a good romantic weepie. But the addition of some police corruption malarkey and a slow pace undermine the emotional payoff. Congresswoman Kay Chandler (Scott Thomas) and internal affairs cop Dutch Van Den Broeck (Ford) discover that their respective spouses, who were killed in the same airliner crash, had been having an affair. Dutch needs to know all the sordid details when Kay, who's up for re-election, wants the potentially scandalous situation to remain quiet. Based on the novel by Warren Adler. **133m/C; VHS, DVD.** Harrison Ford; Kristin Scott Thomas; Sydney Pollack; Charles S. Dutton; Bonnie Hunt; Dennis Haysbert; Richard Jenkins; Paul Guilfoyle; Susanna Thompson; Peter Coyote; Dylan Baker; Lynne Thigpen; Bill Cobbs; Susan Floyd; Edie Falco; Kate Mara; *D:* Sydney Pollack; *W:* Kurt Luedtke; *C:* Philippe Rousselot; *M:* Dave Grusin.

Range of Motion **1/2 2000** After an accident, Lainie Berman's (De Mornay) husband slips into a coma but she's positive he can recover if she has enough faith. Based on the book by Elizabeth Berg. **120m/C; VHS, DVD.** Rebecca De Mornay; Henry Czerny; Melanie Mayron; Barclay Hope; Kimberly Roberts; *D:* Donald Wrye; *W:* Grace McKeaney; *C:* Malcolm Cross; *M:* Gary Chang. **CABLE**

Rangers **2000 (R)** McCoy leads an Army Rangers team in capturing a terrorist bomber and while they accomplish their mission, the unit is forced to leave behind Plummer, which turns out to be part of a government setup. Not happy about this, Plummer joins the terrorists to get revenge and goes after his ex-buddies while McCoy realizes there's a conspiracy going on. **100m/C; VHS, DVD.** Matt McCoy; Glenn Plummer; Corbin Bernsen; Dartanyan Edmonds; Rene Rivera; *D:* Jim Wynorski; *W:* Steve Latshaw; *C:* Ken Blakey; *M:* David Wurst; Eric Wurst. **VIDEO**

Rango **1/2 2011 (PG)** Note-perfect animated Western follows the misadventures of Rango (voiced by Depp), an ordinary lizard and imaginary thespian, caught up in saving the village of Dirt, which is desperately short on water and overrun by reptilian bandits. Rango sees the village as a giant stage where he can finally play the hero and make a name for himself. Director Verbinski and writer Logan brilliantly pay homage to the Western genre, and to countless other classics along the way. Inspired and genuinely odd, and works for all age groups. **107m/C; Blu-Ray, On Demand.** *V:* Johnny Depp; Bill Nighy; Timothy Olyphant; Ned Beatty; Isla Fisher; Abigail Breslin; Ray Winstone; Alfred Molina; Stephen (Steve) Root; Harry Dean Stanton; *D:* Gore Verbinski; *W:* John Logan; *M:* Hans Zimmer. Oscars '11: Animated Film; British Acad. '11: Animated Film.

Ransom! **1956** Self-made millionaire David Stannard's (Ford) son is kidnapped, but David doesn't think paying the ransom will keep the boy safe. Instead, he goes on TV to offer the money to anyone who'll help him get his son back unharmed and capture the kidnappers. Neither his wife Edith (Reed) nor the cops think David's announcement is a great idea. Based on the 1954 TV play "Fearful Decision" and remade in 1996. **102m/B; DVD.** Glenn Ford; Donna Reed; Leslie Nielsen; Robert Keith; Juano Hernandez; Ainslie Pryor; *D:* Alex Segal; *W:* Cyril Hume; Richard Maibaum; *C:* Arthur E. Arling; *M:* Jeff Alexander.

Ransom **1996 (R)** Tight and crafty thriller proves airline magnate Tom Mullen (Gibson) is a force to be reckoned with when son Sean (Nolte) is kidnapped. Mullen treats this like a high-stakes business deal and decides to get his kid back by announcing on TV that the $2 million ransom demand will instead become a bounty on the kidnappers. Wife Kate (Russo) flips out but Mullen, after a few encounters with the heinous abductors, has sized them up and is convinced he's done the right thing. Lindo is a by-the-book fed and Sinise is a bad cop. Based on the 1956 flick starring Glenn Ford. **121m/C; VHS, DVD, Blu-Ray.** Mel Gibson; Rene Russo; Gary Sinise; Delroy Lindo; Brawley Nolte; Lili Taylor; Liev Schreiber; Evan Handler; Dan Hedaya; Paul Guilfoyle; Jose Zuniga; Donnie Wahlberg; Michael Gaston; Nancy Ticotin; ***Cameo(s):*** Richard Price; *D:* Ron Howard; *W:* Richard Price; Alexander Ignon; *C:* Piotr Sobocinski; *M:* James Horner.

Ranson's Folly **1/2 1926** Barthelmess makes a wager that he can impersonate a famous outlaw well enough to rob a stage with only a pair of scissors. When the army paymaster is killed, guess who gets caught with his swash unbuckled? **80m/B; Silent; VHS, DVD.** Richard Barthelmess; Dorothy Mackaill; Anders Randolph; Pat Hartigan; Brooks Benedict; *D:* Sidney Olcott.

Rapa Nui **1/2 1993 (R)** The title refers to the Polynesian name for Easter Island, with the film set in the 17th century (before Dutch explorers discovered the island). It depicts the annual rituals of the mysterious people who built the Island's moai—the famous giant stone statues. Lee plays the heroic Noroinia, with Morales as his rival Make, and Holt as Ramana, the object of their desires. Faux primitive but with some great on-location filming. **107m/C; VHS, Streaming.** Jason Scott Lee; Esai Morales; Sandrine Holt; *D:* Kevin Reynolds; *W:* Kevin Reynolds; Tim Rose Price; *M:* Stewart Copeland.

The Rape of the Sabines WOOF! *El Rapto de las Sabinas; The Mating of the Sabine Women; Shame of the Sabine Women* **1961** The story of Romulus, king of Rome, and how he led the Romans to capture the women of Sabina. The battles rage, the women plot, and Romulus fights and lusts. Dubbed in English. **101m/C; VHS, DVD.** *IT FR* Roger Moore; Mylene Demongeot; Jean Marais; *D:* Richard Pottier.

Rapid Assault **1999 (R)** Terrorist Lars Rynark (Scribner) is set to detonate a biochemical agent in the Atlantic Ocean that will decimate the population—unless he gets paid a lot of cash. Three government ops are sent to get to the terrorist first. Typical action fodder—the plot making any sense is besides the point. **90m/C; VHS, DVD.** Tim Abell; Don Scribner; Jeff Rector; Lisa Mazzetti; *D:* Fred Olen Ray. **VIDEO**

Rapid Fire **1989** Cheap, made-for-video quickie about a good guy U.S. agent who battles terrorists. Easy to skip. **90m/C; VHS, DVD.** Joe Spinell; Michael Wayne; Ron Waldron; *D:* David A. Prior.

Rapid Fire **1/2 1992 (R)** Lee (son of martial arts cult film star Bruce Lee) is a Chinese-American art student who also happens to be a martial arts expert. He's tapped by the police to help stem the violence between the Asian and Italian gangs fighting for control over Chicago's drug trade. Typical martial arts movie is made better by uniquely choreographed action sequences and Lee's attractive presence. **96m/C; VHS, DVD, Blu-Ray.** Brandon Lee; Powers Boothe; Nick Mancuso; Raymond J. Barry; Kate Hodge; Tzi Ma; Tony Longo; Michael Paul Chan; Dustin Nguyen; John Vickery; *D:* Dwight Little; *W:* Alan B. McElroy; Cindy Cirile; Paul Attanasio; *M:* Christopher Young.

Rappin' **1985 (PG)** Ex-con Van Peebles gets into it with the landlord and a street gang leader. Forgettable action/music drivel. **92m/C; VHS, DVD, Blu-Ray.** Mario Van Peebles; Tasia Valenza; Harry Goz; Charles Flohe; *D:* Joel Silberg.

Rapt **2009** Based on a true crime from 1978 but set in present-day Paris. Jetsetting businessman Stanislas Graff is kidnapped and to make certain they're taken seriously, the kidnappers send one of Graff's fingers along with their hefty ransom demand. Revelations leaked to the press about Graff's lurid private life and large gambling debts make him a less-than-sympathetic victim. As the kidnapping drags on, Graff's physical and psychological state worsens. French with subtitles. **126m/C; DVD, Blu-Ray.** *FR BE* Yvan Attal; Anne Consigny; Gerard Meylan; Andre Marcon; Alex Descas; *D:* Lucas Belvaux; *W:* Lucas Belvaux; *C:* Pierre Milon; *M:* Ricardo Del Fra.

Raptor Island **2004** Navy SEALS chase terrorists onto an island in the South China Sea looking to rescue a comrade. Unfortunately for both sides the island is inhabited by vicious mutant dinosaurs who have no sense of hospitality. **89m/C; DVD.** Lorenzo Lamas; Steven Bauer; Hayley DuMond; Michael Cory Davis; Peter Jason; *D:* Stanley Isaacs; *W:* Stanley Isaacs; Dean Widenmann; *C:* David Worth; *M:* Peter Bernstein. **CABLE**

Rapture **1965** Unsettling drama. Embittered, widowed, retired judge Frederick Larbaud (Douglas) lives in seclusion with his unstable 15-year-old daughter Agnes (Gazzi) and their housekeeper Karen (Lindblom) on an isolated Brittany farm. Escaped convict Joseph (Stockwell) shows up seeking shelter and Agnes is fascinated but it's Karen he seduces until Agnes threatens her. Joseph and Agnes soon flee to Paris but the city is too overwhelming and Agnes heads home. Things don't end well for Joseph when he follows her. **104m/B; DVD, Blu-Ray.** *FR* Melvyn Douglas; Dean Stockwell; Patricia Gozzi; Gunnel Linbdlom; Sylvia Kay; ***D:*** John Guillermin; ***W:*** Stanley Mann; ***C:*** Marcel Grignon; ***M:*** Georges Delerue.

The Rapture **1991 (R)** A beautiful telephone operator engages in indiscriminate sexual adventures to relieve the boredom of her job and life. She becomes curious by, and eventually converted to, evangelical Christianity, which leads her to a contented marriage and the birth of a daughter. When her husband is tragically killed she becomes convinced that she and her child will be taken by God into heaven if she only waits for the proper sign. **100m/C; VHS, DVD.** Mimi Rogers; David Duchovny; Patrick Bauchau; Will Patton; ***D:*** Michael Tolkin; ***W:*** Michael Tolkin; ***C:*** Bojan Bazelli.

Rapturious **2007** Surprisingly entertaining supernatural thriller. White rapper Rapturious (Oppel) takes a new street drug that causes murderous hallucinations, only to discover that the murders are real. As it turns out, the rapper is the reincarnation of a 19th-century western serial killer hanged for his crimes and sent to Hell. And Hell wants him back. **95m/C; DVD.** Robert Oppel; Debbie Rochon; Cinque Lee; Joe Bob Briggs; Amin Joseph; Hoya Guerra; ***D:*** Kamal Ahmed; ***W:*** Kamal Ahmed; ***C:*** Tom Agnello; ***M:*** Kamal Ahmed; Timo Elliston. **VIDEO**

Rare Birds **1/2 2001** Quirky Canadian comedy finds Dave Purcell (Hurt) depressed. His restaurant, located in the small town of Cape Spear, Newfoundland, is failing as is his long-distance marriage. But his eccentric neighbor Alphonse (Jones) comes up with a plan—he spreads the word among birders that a rare duck has been sighted and soon the area is flooded with amateur ornithologists, which isgood for Dave's business and his love life as he gets together with waitress Alice (Parker). Oh yeah, there's also Alphonse's plans for a cocaine shipment he's salvaged from a sunken boat, if he can keep away from the product himself. Based on the novel by Riche. **101m/C; VHS, DVD.** *CA* William Hurt; Molly Parker; Andy Jones; Cathy Jones; Sheila McCarthy; Vicky Hynes; Greg Malone; ***D:*** Sturla Gunnarsson; ***W:*** Edward Riche; ***C:*** Jan Kiesser; ***M:*** Jonathan Goldsmith.

The Rare Breed **1/2 1966** Plodding but pleasant Western. A no-strings ranch hand (Stewart) agrees to escort a Hereford Bull to Texas, where the widow of an English breeder plans to crossbreed the bull with longhorn cattle. The widow (O'Hara) insists that she and her daughter accompany Stewart on the trip, which features every kind of western calamity imaginable. When all others believe the attempt to crossbreed has failed, Stewart sets out to prove them wrong. **97m/C; VHS, DVD, Blu-Ray.** James Stewart; Maureen O'Hara; Brian Keith; Juliet Mills; Jack Elam; Ben Johnson; ***D:*** Andrew V. McLaglen; ***C:*** William Clothier; ***M:*** John Williams.

Rare Exports: A Christmas Tale **2010 (R)** Genre spoof of Christmas horror set in the Finnish Arctic and based on pagan mythology. A scientific expedition uncovers the remains of the very malevolent Santa of local lore in a block of ice. He unthaws and soon has his naked demon elves snatching up the town's kiddies. Young Pietari (Tommila) finds a field of slaughtered reindeer, realizes the kids are missing, and needs a way to fight back. English and Finnish with subtitles. **84m/C; Blu-Ray.** *FI NO SW FR* Onni Tommila; Jorma Tommila; Ilmari Jarvenpaa; Peeter Jakobi; ***D:*** Jalmari Helander; ***W:*** Jalmari Helander; ***C:*** Mika Orasmaa; ***M:*** Juri Seppa; Miska Seppa.

Rascals **1938** Mediocre miscast comedy. Margaret (Hudson) has amnesia when she wanders into a gypsy camp and becomes their fortune teller. She's successful enough to earn the money to have an operation that restores her memory, revealing she's a society dame engaged to a cad only after her fortune. Naturally, Gypsy the gypsy (Withers) knows Margaret can do better. **78m/B; DVD.** Jane Withers; Rochelle Hudson; Robert Wilcox; Jose Crespo; ***D:*** H. Bruce Humberstone; ***W:*** Helen Logan; Robert Ellis; ***C:*** Edward Cronjager.

Rasen **1/2 1998** The original sequel to "Ringu," directed and released at the same time, is closer to the actual book and attempts to explain the first film with pseudo science, which is probably why it bombed at the Japanese boxoffice and is largely forgotten. Taking place directly after the first film, the body of Reiko's ex husband is being examined by his longtime friend Dr. Ando, a pathologist. Ando finds a cryptic note in his friend's stomach, which leads him to discover the dreaded video tape. Depressed over the death of his own child, Ando watches the tape, only to discover that Sadako has very different plans for him. **90m/C; DVD, Blu-Ray.** *JP* Koichi Sato; Hiroyuki (Henry) Sanada; Yutaka Matsushige; Hitomi Sato; Hinako Saeki; Shingo Tsurumi; Nanako Matsushima; Tomohiro Okada; Koji Suzuki; ***D:*** Joji Iida; ***W:*** Koji Suzuki; Joji Iida; ***C:*** Makoto Watanabe.

Rashomon *In the Woods* **1951** In 12th century Japan, two travelers attempt to discover the truth about an ambush/rape/murder. They get four completely different versions of the incident from the three people involved in the crime and the single witness. An insightful masterpiece that established Kurosawa and Japanese cinema as major artistic forces. Fine performances, particularly Mifune as the bandit. Visually beautiful and rhythmic. Remade as a western, "The Outrage," in 1964. In Japanese with English subtitles. **83m/B; VHS, DVD, Blu-Ray.** *JP* Machiko Kyo; Toshiro Mifune; Masayuki Mori; Takashi Shimura; Minoru Chiaki; Kichijiro Ueda; Daisuke Kato; ***D:*** Akira Kurosawa; ***W:*** Akira Kurosawa; Shinobu Hashimoto; ***C:*** Kazuo Miyagawa; ***M:*** Fumio Hayasaka. Oscars '51: Foreign Film; Natl. Bd. of Review '51: Director (Kurosawa); Venice Film Fest. '51: Film.

Rasputin *Agoniya* **1985** The long-censored and banned film of the story of the mad monk and his domination of the royal family before the Russian Revolution. Petrenko is superb. First released in the United States in 1988. In Russian with English subtitles. **104m/C; VHS, DVD.** *RU* Alexei Petrenko; Anatoly Romashin; Velta Linne; Alice Freindlikh; ***D:*** Elem Klimov; ***W:*** Semyon Lunghin; Ilya Nusinov; ***M:*** Alfred Shnitke.

Rasputin and the Empress *Rasputin: The Mad Monk* **1933** Lavish historical epic teamed the three Barrymore sibs for the first and only time, as they vied for scene-stealing honors. Ethel is Empress Alexandra of Russia, tied to the weak-willed Nicholas II (Morgan) and under the spell of Rasputin, played by Lionel. John is a nobleman who seeks to warn the Russian rulers of their perilous perch on the throne, made only worse by Rasputin's spreading power and corruption. Ethel's first talkie and Wynyard's first film role. Uncredited director Charles Brabin was replaced by Boleslawski due to his incompatability with the imperious Ethel. **123m/B; VHS, DVD.** Ethel Barrymore; John Barrymore; Lionel Barrymore; Ralph Morgan; Diana Wynyard; Tad Alexander; C. Henry Gordon; Edward Arnold; Gustav von Seyffertitz; Anne Shirley; Jean Parker; Henry Kolker; ***D:*** Richard Boleslawski; ***W:*** Charles MacArthur; ***C:*** William H. Daniels.

Rasputin the Mad Monk **1966** Hammer's version of Russian history of course emphasizes the evil powers of the mad Russian monk (Lee) who gains entry into the court of the czar. Poor script but Lee's good. **90m/B; VHS, DVD, Blu-Ray.** *GB* Christopher Lee; Barbara Shelley; Richard Pasco; Francis Matthews; Suzan Farmer; Nicholas Pennell; Renee Asherson; Derek Francis; ***D:*** Don Sharp; ***W:*** John (Anthony Hinds) Elder; ***C:*** Michael Reed; ***M:*** Don Banks.

The Rat Pack **1/2 1998 (R)** Warts-and-all bio of ole blue eyes, Frank Sinatra (Liotta) and his pals, including Dean Martin (Mantegna), Sammy Davis Jr. (Don Cheadle), Joey Bishop (Slayton), and Peter Lawford (McFayden). Story focuses on the time when Sinatra decides to support John F. Kennedy's (Petersen) bid for the presidency but his mobster ties eventually end their would-be association. TV effort is unauthorized and scorned by the late Sinatra's family. **120m/C; VHS, DVD.** Ray Liotta; Don Cheadle; Angus MacFadyen; Joe Mantegna; Bobby Slayton; William L. Petersen; Zeljko Ivanek; Robert Miranda; Dan O'Herlihy; Deborah Kara Unger; Phyllis Lyons; Megan Dodds; ***D:*** Rob Cohen; ***W:*** Kario Salem; ***C:*** Shane Hurlbut; ***M:*** Mark Adler. **CABLE**

Rat Pfink a Boo-Boo WOOF! *Rat Pfink and Boo Boo* **1966** Parody on "Batman" in which a bumbling superhero and his sidekick race around saving people. Notoriously inept. Title story is legendary—it was misspelled accidentally and Steckler didn't have the cash to fix it. **72m/B; VHS, DVD.** Ron Haydock; Carolyn Brandt; Titus Moede; Mike Kannon; James Bowie; George Caldwell; Keith Wester; ***D:*** Ray Dennis Steckler; ***W:*** Ron Haydock; ***C:*** Ray Dennis Steckler; ***M:*** Andre Brummer.

The Rat Race **1960** A dancer and a musician venture to Manhattan to make it big, and end up sharing an apartment. Their relationship starts pleasantly and becomes romantic. Enjoyable farce. Well photographed and scripted, with the supporting characters stealing the show. **105m/C; VHS, DVD, Streaming.** Tony Curtis; Debbie Reynolds; Jack Oakie; Kay Medford; Don Rickles; Joe Bushkin; ***D:*** Robert Mulligan; ***C:*** Robert Burks; ***M:*** Elmer Bernstein.

Rat Race **1/2 2001 (PG-13)** Eccentric Las Vegas casino tycoon Sinclair (Cleese) sends six ordinary gamblers on a treasure hunt for two million bucks while rich gamblers wager on the outcome. It's old-fashioned, but in a good, solidly funny, anything-for-a-laugh way. The mostly B-list cast has a lot of fun with the material, which is well-paced and expertly carried out by writer Breckman and director Zucker, who returns to the zany wall-to-wall comedy that put him on the map. **92m/C; VHS, DVD.** John Cleese; Whoopi Goldberg; Cuba Gooding, Jr.; Jon Lovitz; Breckin Meyer; Amy Smart; Seth Green; Kathy Najimy; Rowan Atkinson; Wayne Knight; Dean Cain; Vince Vieluf; Lanei Chapman; Paul Rodriguez; ***D:*** Jerry Zucker; ***W:*** Andy Breckman; ***C:*** Thomas Ackerman; ***M:*** John Powell.

Ratatouille **2007 (G)** Remy the rat (Oswalt) has a very refined palate, too refined for the garbage his colony hoards to survive. So he sneaks into the best restaurant in Paris to forage while he dreams of becoming a chef himself. This makes him odd-rat-out with his dad and the sewer-dwelling rodent community, not to mention the rodent-averse employees of the restaurant. He gets an in when he helps the klutzy new guy, a kitchen helper named Linguini (Romano), to become a renowned chef. Provides plenty to entertain all ages, with beautiful animation, excellent voice work, well-developed characters, and some surprising plot twists. **110m/C; DVD, Blu-Ray.** ***V:*** Patton Oswalt; Brian Dennehy; Brad Garrett; Janeane Garofalo; Ian Holm; Peter O'Toole; Will Arnett; James Remar; Lou Romano; John Ratzenberger; Brad Bird; Peter Sohn; ***Nar:*** Stephane Roux; ***D:*** Brad Bird; ***W:*** Brad Bird; Jan Pinkava; Jim Capobianco; ***C:*** Sharon Calahan; Robert Anderson; ***M:*** Michael Giacchino. Oscars '07: Animated Film; British Acad. '07: Animated Film; Golden Globes '08: Animated Film.

Ratboy **1/2 1986 (PG-13)** An unscrupulous woman attempts to transform a boy with a rat's face into a celebrity, with tragic results. First directorial effort by Locke that gradually loses steam. **105m/C; DVD.** Sondra Locke; Sharon Baird; Robert Townsend; ***D:*** Sondra Locke; ***W:*** Rob Thompson; ***C:*** Bruce Surtees; ***M:*** Lennie Niehaus.

Ratcatcher **1/2 1999** Twelve-year-old James (Eadie) gets into a fight with another boy on the banks of the canal that runs through their 1970s working-class Glasgow neighborhood. Ryan falls in and drowns and James keeps quiet while being endlessly drawn back to the scene. Meanwhile there's trouble at home and the family's hopes for a better life (by moving to new council housing) is also in jeopardy. **93m/C; VHS, DVD.** *GB* William Eadie; Tommy Flanagan; Mandy Matthews; Leanne Mullen; John Miller; ***D:*** Lynne Ramsay; ***W:*** Lynne Ramsay; ***C:*** Alwin Kuchler; ***M:*** Rachel Portman.

Ratchet & Clank **1/2 2016 (PG)** The 2002 Sony video game that spawned several hit sequels finally gets a movie and it follows in a long line of films based on video games. In other words, don't waste your time. Just play it instead. Ratchet (voiced by James Arnold Taylor) wants desperately to join the Galactic Rangers, but he's first turned away by the egotistical Captain Qwark (Jim Ward). Meanwhile, Clank knows the secret plans of the nefarious Drek, so when he basically falls into Ratchet's lap, the young Lombax becomes an important figure in this galactic war. **94m/C; DVD, Blu-Ray.** James Arnold Taylor; David Kaye; Jim Ward; Rosario Dawson; Paul Giamatti; ***D:*** Kevin Munroe; Jericca Cleland; ***W:*** Kevin Munroe; T.J. Fixman; Gerry Swallow; ***C:*** Anthony Di Ninno; ***M:*** Evan Wise.

Rated X **2000 (R)** True story of smut kings, the Mitchell Brothers, as portrayed by brothers Sheen and Estevez. Porno pioneer Jim (Estevez) sees dollar signs and joins with younger brother Artie (Sheen) to film skin flicks in San Francisco, including their hard-core classic "Behind the Green Door." They get busted a lot on obscenity charges and fall victim to booze and drugs but while Jim finally cleans up his act, Artie just sinks deeper, leading to a deadly confrontation between the two. The brothers do a surprisingly impressive job but it's grim going. Based on the book by David McCumber. **114m/C; VHS, DVD.** Emilio Estevez; Charlie Sheen; Megan Ward; Danielle Brett; Rafer Weigel; Terry O'Quinn; Nicole de Boer; Peter Bogdanovich; Tracy Hutson; ***D:*** Emilio Estevez; ***W:*** Norman Snider; Anne Meredith; David Hollander; ***C:*** Paul Sarossy; ***M:*** Tyler Bates. **CABLE**

A Rather English Marriage **1/2 1998** Aging Reggie (Finney) and Roy (Courtenay) meet in a hospital waiting room after their wives have just died. The odd couple (Reggie is blustery ex-military while Roy was a milkman) are further thrown together when a social worker suggests that both should share Reggie's house to help with chores and expenses (and neither man is used to living alone). The rest of the subdued drama is their adjustment to each other and their new situations with flashbacks to their younger selves. Based on the novel by Angela Carter. Finney and Courtenay starred together in 1983's "The Dresser." **104m/C; VHS, DVD.** *UK* Albert Finney; Tom Courtenay; Joanna Lumley; ***D:*** Paul Seed; ***W:*** Andrew Davies; ***C:*** Gavin Finney; ***M:*** Jim Parker. **TV**

Ratings Game *The Mogul* **1984** A bitter, out-of-work actor and a woman who works at the ratings service manage to mess up the TV industry. Early directorial effort by DeVito is uneven but funny. **102m/C; VHS, DVD, Blu-Ray.** Danny DeVito; Rhea Perlman; Gerrit Graham; Kevin McCarthy; Jayne Meadows; Steve Allen; Ronny Graham; George Wendt; Barry Corbin; Huntz Hall; Louis Giambalvo; Basil Hoffman; Michael Richards; Ron Rifkin; Joe Santos; Vincent Schiavelli; Frank Sivero; Daniel Stern; Randi Brooks; Robert Costanzo; Allyce Beasley; Selma Diamond; Jason Hervey; James LeGros; Jerry Seinfeld; Damon Hines; ***D:*** Danny DeVito; ***W:*** Michael Barrie; Jim Mulholland; ***C:*** Tim Suhrstedt; ***M:*** Bruce Kimmel; David Spear. **CABLE**

Raton Pass **1951** Workmanlike western with a surprisingly devious performance by Neal. Ambitious Ann Challon, who received a half-share of a large ranch upon her marriage, now wants to take complete control from husband Marc. She seduces railroad man Prentice into buying out her husband, who changes his mind about selling, so Ann hires a gunslinger while Marc rallies the other homesteaders. **84m/B; DVD.** Patricia Neal; Dennis Morgan; Scott Forbes; Steve Cochran; Dorothy Hart; ***D:*** Edwin L. Marin; ***W:*** James R. Webb; Thomas W. Blackburn; ***C:*** Wilfred M. Cline; ***M:*** Max Steiner.

The Rats **2001 (R)** Manhattan department store manager Susan Costello (Amick) calls in exterminator Jack Carver (Spano) to get rid of some rats but they discover these aren't the usual critters. Turns out these pesky rodents are genetically altered lab rats who have gotten loose and they're very aggressive—and very hungry. **94m/C; VHS, DVD.** Vincent Spano; Madchen Amick; Daveigh Chase; Shawn Michael Howard; Sheila McCarthy; ***D:*** John Lafia; ***W:*** Frank Deasy; ***M:*** Elia Cmiral. **TV**

Ratter **2016 (R)** A dramatic psychological thriller about being observed in modern life. Having moved from the Midwest to New York City for graduate school, Emma (Benson) is enjoying her new life on her own in the city. But Emma's sense of security is eroded by a stalker who starts to hack into all her devices, including her cell phone, computer, and other web-enabled devices. The hacker not only erases her data but records her intimately. The situation only grows more dangerous when the hacker takes more drastic action. **80m/C; DVD, Blu-Ray,**

Streaming, Download. Ashley Benson; Matt McGorry; Kaili Vernoff; Rebecca Naomi Jones; Alex Cranmer; ***D:*** Branden Kramer; ***W:*** Branden Kramer; ***C:*** Stefan Haverkamp.

Rattlers 1976 **(PG)** TV movie featuring poisonous rattlesnakes who attack at random. **82m/C; VHS, DVD.** Sam Chew; Elizabeth Chauvet; Dan Priest; ***D:*** John McCauley. **TV**

Rattlesnake 2019 During a road trip, Katrina (Ejogo) blows a tire in a remote area without cell phone service. As she changes it, her young daughter Clara (Pratt) gets bitten by a rattlesnake. Desperate, Katrina runs to a nearby trailer where a mysterious woman saves Clara's life. When Katrina takes her daughter to the nearest hospital, there is no evidence of Clara being bitten but a bizarre man tells Katrina that she must kill someone by sundown or Clara will die. Starting off strong, this horror flick dies a slow death, despite an interesting premise and a strong performance by Ejoggo. **85m/C; DVD.** Carmen Ejogo; Theo Rossi; Emma Greenwell; Apollonia Pratt; Debrianna Mansini; ***D:*** Zak Hilditch; ***W:*** Zak Hilditch; ***M:*** Ian Hultquist. **VIDEO**

Ratz 1/2 **1999** Dumb teen film about best friends Marci and Summer who get involved with a magic ring, an eccentric shopkeeper, and two rats (yes, the rodent kind) who are transformed into a couple of datable young hunks so the girls will have escorts to the big spring dance. **95m/C; VHS, DVD.** Caroline Elliott; Vanessa Lengies; Jake Seeley; Levi James; Kathy Baker; Ron Silver; Barbara Tyson; ***D:*** Thom Eberhardt; ***W:*** Thom Eberhardt; ***C:*** Ric Waite. **CABLE**

The Ravagers 1965 Capt. Kermit Dowling (Saxon) and ex-con Gaudiel (Poe) led Filipino guerrillas against remnants of the Japanese forces on the Philippines. The Japanese have taken over a convent in their search for a ship of gold bullion and Gaudiel manages to sneak inside where he encounters American Shelia (Fitzsimmons), who's been sheltered by the nuns. In between the action, they take a liking to each other. **80m/B; VHS, DVD.** John Saxon; Fernando Poe, Jr.; Bronwyn Fitzsimons; Robert Arevalo; Mike Parsons; ***D:*** Eddie Romero; ***W:*** Eddie Romero; Cesar Amigo; ***M:*** Tito Arevalo.

The Raven 1915 An early, eccentric pseudo-biography of author Edgar Allan Poe. The film opens with a look at Poe's ancestors and follows the author to maturity when he turns to alcohol for solace. His drunken stupor produces hallucinations that lead to his tale of "The Raven." Silent with added music track. **80m/B; Silent; VHS, DVD.** Henry B. Walthall; Wanda Howard; ***D:*** Charles Brabin.

The Raven 1963 This could-have-been monumental teaming of horror greats Karloff, Lorre, and Price is more of a satire than a true horror film. One of the more enjoyable of the Corman/Poe adaptations, the movie takes only the title of the poem. As for the story line: Price and Karloff play two rival sorcerers who battle for supremacy, with Lorre as the unfortunate associate turned into the bird of the title. **86m/C; VHS, DVD, Blu-Ray.** Vincent Price; Boris Karloff; Peter Lorre; Jack Nicholson; Hazel Court; Olive Sturgess; ***D:*** Roger Corman; ***W:*** Richard Matheson; ***C:*** Floyd Crosby; ***M:*** Les Baxter.

Raven 1/2 **1997 (R)** Covert mercenary team codenamed Raven is after a Soviet satellite decoder. They're double-crossed by renegade CIA agents and their leader Reynolds decides to get his own brand of justice. **93m/C; VHS, DVD, Blu-Ray.** Burt Reynolds; Krista Allen; Matt Battaglia; David Ackroyd; Richard Gant; ***D:*** Russell Solberg; ***W:*** Jacobsen Hart; ***C:*** John Dirlam; ***M:*** Harry Manfredini.

The Raven 2007 Somewhere in this happily cheesy gay horror film there's an acknowledgement of the Edgar Allan story. Roderick is hosting a masquerade ball in the same house that was the scene of the Ravenswood massacre 50 years before. Soon his guests are being slaughtered by a man wearing a raven costume. **96m/C; DVD.** Rick Armando; Ivan Botha; Litha Booi; Traverse Le Goff; ***Nar:*** Richard Johnson; ***D:*** David DeCoteau; ***W:*** Matthew Jason Walsh; ***C:*** Vincent Cox; ***M:*** Richard Band; Joe Silva.

The Raven 2012 **(R)** Turning Edgar Allen Poe into just another crime-solver, director McTeigue's thriller commits crimes against history, literature, and celluloid all at once. Cusack plays Poe in the last weeks of his life as the writers imagine a macabre tale to explain how the Baltimore-based author was found dead on a park bench. In their version, Poe was chasing a serial killer working from his own works as the inspiration for his elaborate crimes. Horribly paced and tediously dull, it fails on every level. **110m/C; DVD, Blu-Ray, Streaming.** John Cusack; Luke Evans; Alice Eve; Brendan Gleeson; Oliver Jackson-Cohen; Pam Ferris; ***D:*** James McTeigue; ***W:*** Ben Livingston; Hannah Shakespeare; ***C:*** Danny Ruhlmann; ***M:*** Lucas Vidal.

Ravenous 1/2 **1999 (R)** Off-kilter tale of cannibalism in the American West in 1847 (loosely based on the Donner Party) loses its way when it begins to use man-eating as a metaphor for settlers carving up the land. When stringy, twitching Colqhoun (Carlyle) shows up starving and nearly frozen at an army fort in the Sierra Nevadas, he tells Captain John Boyd (Pearce) that he was with a party that resorted to eating their dead when stranded. When a team is sent to investigate, more than the facts are digested. The unusual subject and offbeat attempts at humor make this a recipe not for all tastes. **100m/C; VHS, DVD, Blu-Ray.** Guy Pearce; Robert Carlyle; Jeremy Davies; Jeffrey Jones; John Spencer; Stephen Spinella; Neal McDonough; David Arquette; ***D:*** Antonia Bird; ***W:*** Ted Griffin; ***C:*** Anthony B. Richmond; ***M:*** Michael Nyman; Damon Albarn.

Raven's Ridge 1/2 **1997 (R)** Imagine an exceptionally low-budget combination of Stanley Kubrick's heist movie "The Killing" and "Deliverance." That's essentially what this story boils down to. A group of friends knock over an armored car at a racetrack then stash the loot out in the woods. When they go to retrieve it, they're attacked by a grizzled local. **77m/C; DVD.** William Kendall; Dawn Howard; John Rizzi; ***D:*** Mike Upton.

Ravishing Idiot *Agent 38-24-36; Adorable Idiot; The Warm-Blooded Spy; Bewitching Scatterbrain* **1964** An unemployed bank clerk becomes mixed up with Soviet spies. **99m/B; VHS, DVD.** ***FR*** Brigitte Bardot; Anthony Perkins; ***D:*** Edouard Molinaro.

Raw 1/2 *Grave* **2017 (R)** Justine (Marillier) has been a lifelong vegetarian but everything changes when she enters a veterinary school and must eat a raw rabbit kidney during a hazing ritual. It's the beginning of a slide into meat-eating that progresses to grave extremes in Julia Ducournau's shocking indie hit that was so disturbing that people reportedly became physically ill during its Toronto Film Festival premiere. The extent of its shock value may have been exaggerated but this is a confident, memorable debut nonetheless that offers an original take on the cannibal-horror genre, filtered through a feminist perspective. **99m/C; DVD.** Garance Marillier; Ella Rumpf; Rabah Nait Oufella; Laurent Lucas; Joana Preiss; ***D:*** Julia Ducournau; ***W:*** Julia Ducournau; ***C:*** Ruben Impens; ***M:*** Jim Williams.

Raw Deal 1948 Sadistic Rick Coyle (Burr) framed one-time associate Joe Sullivan (O'Keefe), who wound up in prison. Joe's moll Pat (Trevor) helps him to escape and they take prison social worker Ann (Hunt), who's befriended Joe, as a hostage. They go after Coyle and Joe begins to fall for the demure dame, who finds the underworld life exciting and even saves Joe from one of Coyle's henchmen. No good guys here but it is fine film noir. **79m/B; VHS, DVD, Blu-Ray.** Dennis O'Keefe; Claire Trevor; Raymond Burr; Marsha Hunt; John Ireland; Curt Conway; Whit Bissell; ***D:*** Anthony Mann; ***W:*** John C. Higgins; Leopold Atlas; ***C:*** John Alton; ***M:*** Paul Sawtell.

Raw Deal 1/2 **1986 (R)** Don't ever give Schwarzenegger a raw deal! FBI agent Schwarzie infiltrates the mob and shoots lots of people. **106m/C; VHS, DVD.** Arnold Schwarzenegger; Kathryn Harrold; Darren McGavin; Sam Wanamaker; Paul Shenar; Steven Hill; ***D:*** John Irvin; ***W:*** Gary De Vore; Patrick Edgeworth; ***C:*** Alex Thomson.

Raw Force *Shogun Island* **1981 (R)** Three karate buffs visit an island inhabited by a sect of cannibalistic monks who have the power to raise the dead (it could happen). They fix the villains by kicking them all in the head. **90m/C; VHS, DVD, Blu-Ray.** ***PH*** Cameron Mitchell; Geoffrey Binney; John Dresden; John Locke; Ralph Lombardi; ***D:*** Edward Murphy.

Raw Justice **1993 (R)** When the daughter of a powerful Southern mayor is murdered, tough ex-cop Mace (Keith) is hired to get the killer. Mace enlists the reluctant help of call girl Sarah (Anderson) to help him trap Mitch (Hayes), his prime suspect. Only things don't work out as Mace planned and the wary threesome must work together to save themselves from certain death. **92m/C; VHS, DVD.** David Keith; Pamela Anderson; Robert Hays; Leo Rossi; Charles Napier; Stacy Keach; ***D:*** David A. Prior; ***W:*** David A. Prior.

Raw Meat *Death Line* **1972** British creepfest. Two college students (Ladd, Gurney) find a body on the steps of London's Russell Square subway platform but it has disappeared by the time Scotland Yard shows up. Inspector Calhoun (Pleasence) investigates since it's not the first time something strange has happened there. He learns he's chasing the remaining survivor of a long-ago cave-in who has mutated into a cannibal-zombie creature. **88m/C; DVD, Blu-Ray.** ***GB*** Donald Pleasence; David Ladd; Sharon Gurney; Norman Rossington; Clive Swift; Christopher Lee; Hugh Armstrong; ***D:*** Gary Sherman; ***W:*** Ceri Jones; ***C:*** Alex Thomson; ***M:*** Wil Mallone; Jeremy Rose.

Raw Nerve **1991 (R)** A cast with possibilities can't overcome this poorly reasoned suspenser. A young man has visions of the local serial killer, but when he reports them to police he becomes the suspect. There are a few twists beyond that, none too thrilling. **91m/C; VHS, DVD.** Glenn Ford; Traci Lords; Sandahl Bergman; Randall "Tex" Cobb; Ted Prior; Jan-Michael Vincent; ***W:*** David A. Prior.

Raw Nerve 1/2 **1999 (R)** Rogue cop Blair (Van Peebles) has crossed the line one too many times and is being investigated for money laundering. He's in trouble with IAD and the mob, which also puts girlfriend Izabel (Sheridan) in danger. Blair turns for help to ex-cop buddy Ethan (Galligan) but won't change his violent ways and keeps sinking down. **102m/C; VHS, DVD.** Mario Van Peebles; Nicolette Sheridan; Zach Galligan; ***D:*** Avi Nesher. **VIDEO**

Raw Target 1/2 **1995 (R)** Ex-kickboxer Johnny Rider (Cook) finds himself a police decoy in a drug bust and then learns that the drug gang's leader Sparks (Hill) was also involved in his brother's death. **92m/C; VHS, DVD.** Dale "Apollo" Cook; Ron Hall; Nick (Nicholas, Niko) Hill; Mychelle Charters; ***D:*** Tim Spring; ***W:*** Larry Maddox; ***C:*** Bruce Dorfman; ***M:*** Jun Lupito.

Rawhead Rex 1/2 **1987 (R)** An ancient demon is released from his underground prison in Ireland by a plowing farmer, and begins to decapitate and maim at will. Adapted by Clive Barker from his own short story. But Barker later disowned the film, so make your own judgment. **89m/C; VHS, DVD, Blu-Ray.** David Dukes; Kelly Piper; Niall Toibin; Niall O'Brien; Donal McCann; Gladys Sheehan; Cora Lunny; Heinrich von Schellendorf; ***D:*** George Pavlou; ***W:*** Clive Barker; ***C:*** John Metcalfe; ***M:*** Colin Towns.

Rawhide *Desperate Siege* **1950** Four escaped convicts hijack a stagecoach way station and hold hostages while waiting for a shipment of gold. A suspenseful B-grade western with a bang-up ending. Well paced and cast with an abundance of good talent. A remake of "Show Them No Mercy" (1938). **86m/B; VHS, DVD, Blu-Ray.** Tyrone Power; Susan Hayward; Hugh Marlowe; Jack Elam; Dean Jagger; George Tobias; Edgar Buchanan; Jeff Corey; ***D:*** Henry Hathaway; ***C:*** Milton Krasner.

Ray **2004 (PG-13)** Foxx won an Oscar for his depiction of the legendary Ray Charles in an extended biography that covers 1930 to 1966. After an education at a school for the blind, Ray finds musical success in the Seattle jazz scene but also gets firsthand knowledge of the dark side of the biz. While touring, he picks up a 20-year heroin habit and an equally destructive addiction to women, although it's supportive wife Della Bea (Washington) who encourages Ray to develop his own style, a heady fusion of gospel and R&B. Hackford doesn't skimp on Ray's charms or faults and finds a workable balance between showcasing the musician's professional and personal lives. **152m/C; VHS, DVD, HD-DVD.** Jamie Foxx; Kerry Washington; Regina King; Clifton Powell; Aunjanue Ellis; Harry J. Lennix; Terrence Howard; Larenz Tate; Bokeem Woodbine; Curtis Armstrong; Richard Schiff; Wendell Pierce; Chris Thomas King; David Krumholtz; Warwick Davis; Robert Wisdom; Denise Dowse; Thomas Jefferson Byrd; Rick Gomez; Kurt Fuller; Sharon Warren; C.J. Sanders; Patrick Bauchau; ***D:*** Taylor Hackford; ***W:*** James L. White; ***C:*** Pawel Edelman; ***M:*** Craig Armstrong. Oscars '04: Actor (Foxx), Sound; British Acad. '04: Actor (Foxx), Sound; Golden Globes '05: Actor--Mus./Comedy (Foxx); Screen Actors Guild '04: Actor (Foxx).

Ray & Liz 1/2 **2019** Though they have two young sons, Ray (Salinger) and Liz (Smith) are mostly concerned with meeting their own needs. One day, they go out and leave the boys in the care of Ray's intellectually impaired brother Lol (Way). Neighbor Will (Gittens) gets Lol drunk, leading to an act of abuse. Seven years later, the younger son is again put in a seriously risky situation. Years later, the effects of these actions impact the lives of all involved. Inspired by filmmaker Billingham's life and family and shot in his childhood apartment, his debut feature explores emotionally complex ideas but the arty cinematography limits its appeal. **108m/C; DVD.** Justin Salinger; Ella Smith; Tony Way; Richard Ashton; James Eeles; ***D:*** Richard Billingham; ***W:*** Richard Billingham; ***C:*** Daniel Landin.

Razor Blade Smile **1998 (R)** Kinky vampire tale with a really killer babe fond of leather fetish wear. She's Lilith Silver (Daley), a vampire hitwoman working in London. Lilith has been hired to murder members of the Illuminati—a secret society that has made inroads into the highest levels of business and government. Turns out the head of the Illuminati is Sethane Blake (Adamson), the vampire who originally made Lilith one of the undead. Low-budget, bloody camp with some watchable twists and turns. Also available in an unrated version. **101m/C; VHS, DVD.** ***GB*** Eileen Daly; Chris(topher) Adamson; Kevin Howarth; Jonathan Coote; Heidi James; David Warbeck; ***D:*** Jake West; ***W:*** Jake West; ***C:*** James Solan; ***M:*** Richard Wells.

Razorback **1984 (R)** Young American travels to the Australian outback in search of his missing journalist wife. During his quest, he encounters a giant killer pig that has been terrorizing the area. Firmly establishes that pigs, with little sense of natural timing, make lousy movie villains. **95m/C; VHS, DVD.** ***AU*** Gregory Harrison; Bill Kerr; Arkie Whiteley; Judy Morris; Chris Haywood; David Argue; ***D:*** Russell Mulcahy; ***W:*** Everett De Roche; ***C:*** Dean Semler.

The Razor's Edge **1946** Adaptation of the W. Somerset Maugham novel. A rich young man spends his time between WWI & WWII searching for essential truth, eventually landing in India. A satisfying cinematic version of a difficult novel, supported by an excellent cast. Remade in 1984 with Bill Murray in the lead role. **146m/B; VHS, DVD, Blu-Ray.** Tyrone Power; Gene Tierney; Anne Baxter; Clifton Webb; Herbert Marshall; John Payne; Elsa Lanchester; Lucile Watson; Frank Latimore; Cecil Humphreys; Harry Pilcer; Cobina Wright, Sr.; Noel Cravat; John Wengraf; ***D:*** Edmund Goulding; ***W:*** Lamar Trotti; ***C:*** Arthur C. Miller; ***M:*** Alfred Newman. Oscars '46: Support. Actress (Baxter); Golden Globes '47: Support. Actor (Webb), Support. Actress (Baxter).

The Razor's Edge 1/2 **1984 (PG-13)** A beautifully filmed but idiosyncratic version of the W. Somerset Maugham novel. WWI-ravaged Larry Darrell combs the world in search of the meaning of life. Murray is a little too old and sardonic to seem really tortured. Russell is great as the loser he rescues. Subtly unique, with real shortcomings. **129m/C; VHS, DVD.** Bill Murray; Catherine Hicks; Theresa Russell; Denholm Elliott; James Keach; Peter Vaughan; Saeed Jaffrey; Brian Doyle-Murray; ***D:*** John Byrum; ***W:*** John Byrum; ***M:*** Jack Nitzsche.

Razorteeth WOOF! 2005 No budget digital film rip-off of the 1978 cult classic "Piranha." **75m/C; DVD, On Demand.** Todd Carpent; Stevan Anselmi; Brian Berry; Brice Kennedy; *D:* John Polonia; *W:* John Polonia; *C:* Paul Alan Steele; *M:* Jon McBride. **VIDEO**

RBG **2018 (PG)** A documentary about Ruth Bader Ginsburg, Associate Justice of the U.S. Supreme Court since 1993. The woman is diminutive in size only -- her impact on law, politics, and gender equality is immeasurable. Features footage of her personal and professional life, as well as comments by friends (and foes). An inspirational tale for everyone, regardless of political leanings. **98m/C; DVD, Blu-Ray.** Ruth Bader Ginsburg; William J. Clinton; Gloria Steinem; Rush Limbaugh; Antonin Scalia; *D:* Julie Cohen; Betsy West; *C:* Claudia Raschke; *M:* Miriam Cutler.

Re-Animator **1984** Black humor cult classic, based on the H.P. Lovecraft story "Herbert West, The Re-Animator." Med student Herbert West (Combs) is determined to make a medical breakthrough by bringing the dead back to life. His experimental green goo is finally successful on a corpse from the med school morgue but, as usual, any resurrected cadaver becomes difficult to control. Grisly if somewhat self-conscious but there's an unforgettable sex scene invovling a lustful severed head and heroine Megan (Crampton). Followed by "Bride of Re-Animator." **86m/C; VHS, DVD, Blu-Ray.** Jeffrey Combs; Bruce Abbott; Barbara Crampton; David Gale; Robert Sampson; Gerry Black; Carolyn Purdy-Gordon; *D:* Stuart Gordon; *W:* Stuart Gordon; Dennis Paoli; William J. Norris; *C:* Mac Ahlberg; *M:* Richard Band.

Re-Cycle **1/2** *Gwai wik; Gui yu* **2006 (R)** A successful romance writer is working on a horror novel as a change of pace, and the creepy things she describes keep happening. Soon she is sucked into another universe in a scene that is sort of like "Alice in Wonderland" meets "Silent Hill." Gore hounds will be disappointed, but Terry Gilliam fans might want to give it a chance. **97m/C; DVD, Blu-Ray.** Lawrence Chou; Angelica Lee; Yaqi Zeng; *D:* Oxide Pang Chun; Danny Pang; *W:* Oxide Pang Chun; Danny Pang; Cub Chin; SirLaosson Dara; Sam Lung; Thomas Pang; *C:* Decha Srimantra; *M:* Payont Permsith. **VIDEO**

Re-Generation **1/2** *The Limb Salesman* **2004** Unconvincing, low-budget Canadian sci-fi. After a series of eco disasters, water has become a prized and expensive commodity. Abe Fielder (Johnson) and his family run a remote northern underground mining operation that extracts water from ice. So he's wealthy enough to afford to hire roving genetic specialist Dr. Gabriel Goode (Stebbings) to manufacture legs for Abe's daughter Clara (Veninger) who was born without them. **79m/C; DVD.** *CA* Clark Johnson; Peter Stebbings; Ingrid Veninger; Charles Officer; Jackie Burroughs; *D:* Anais Granofsky; *W:* Ingrid Veninger; Anais Granofsky; *C:* D. Gregor Hagey; *M:* John Weisman.

Reach for Me **2008** Conventional, though well-cast, tearjerker. Irascible senior Alvin has terminal cancer and his behavior makes him the bane of the hospice staff and the other patients. The codger is disconcerted when his new roomie is young Kevin, whose love for his girlfriend Sarah inspires Alvin to warm to flirty fellow patient Valerie. **90m/C; DVD.** Seymour Cassel; Adrienne Barbeau; Johnny Whitworth; Lacey Chabert; Alfre Woodard; LeVar Burton; *D:* LeVar Burton; *W:* Michael Bruce Adams; *C:* Kris Krosskove; *M:* Julio Reyes Copello.

Reach for the Sky **1/2 1956** WW II flying ace loses both legs in an accident and learns to fly again. He becomes a hero during the Battle of Britain, then is shot down over France and held prisoner by the Germans. At war's end he returns to England to lead 3,000 planes over London in a victory flight. Inspirationaly told true story. **123m/B; VHS, DVD.** *GB* Kenneth More; Alexander Knox; Nigel Green; *D:* Lewis Gilbert; *M:* John Addison. British Acad. '56: Film.

Reach Me **2014 (PG-13)** Kickstarter-funded indie about a reclusive author whose self-help book has taken the world by storm. A group of seemingly unrelated people have their lives changed while searching for him and somehow link up. It has tons of cameos, but their subplots merely make it feel disjointed and incoherent. **92m/C; DVD, Blu-Ray.** Kyra Sedgwick; Danny Aiello; Cary Elwes; Kevin Connolly; Sylvester Stallone; *D:* John Herzfeld; *W:* John Herzfeld; *C:* Vern Nobles; *M:* Tree Adams. **VIDEO**

Reaching for the Moon *Flores Rares; Rare Flowers* **2013** Beset by writer's block, 40-year-old prize-winning American poet Elizabeth Bishop (Otto) takes up a 1951 invitation from Vassar friend Mary Morse (Middendorf) to visit Rio de Janiero. Mary is living with her lover, architect Lota de Macedo Soares (Pires), on Lota's lavish estate where Elizabeth's priggishness clashes with Lota's bohemian life. But their mutual attraction soon leads to a long-but-uneasy triangle, punctuated by Mary's unhappiness, Elizabeth's increasing alcoholism, and Lota's depression and right-wing politics. English and Portuguese with subtitles. **118m/C; DVD.** *BR* Miranda Otto; Gloria Pires; Tracy Middendorf; Marcello Airoldi; Treat Williams; *D:* Bruno Barreto; *W:* Carolina Kotscho; Matthew Chapman; *C:* Mauro Pinheiro, Jr.; *M:* Marcelo Zarvos.

Reactor *War of the Robots; La Guerra dei Robot* **1978** A low-budget sci-fi film about kidnapped scientists, alien ships and an activated nuclear reactor. **90m/C; VHS, DVD.** *IT* Yanti Somer; Melissa Long; Giacomo "Jack" Rossi-Stuart; Robert Barnes; Aldo Canti; Antonio (Tony) Sabato; *D:* Alfonso Brescia; *W:* Alfonso Brescia; *C:* Silvio Fraschetti; *M:* Marcello Giombini.

Read My Lips **1/2** *Sur Mes Levres* **2001** Hearing-impaired Carla (Devos) is an office worker for a real-estate firm who is tired of being either ignored or used. When her boss has her hire an assistant, Carla chooses ex-con Paul (Cassel), who has no discernable office skills but does retain his shady criminal associations. He wants to heist some loot from an old associate, she wants revenge on a weaselly co-worker and it seems Carla's lip-reading skills are the key to both plans. French with subtitles. **115m/C; VHS, DVD.** *FR* Emmanuelle Devos; Vincent Cassel; Olivier Gourmet; Olivier Perrier; Olivia Bonamy; Pierre Diot; *D:* Jacques Audiard; *W:* Jacques Audiard; Tonino Beranacquista; *C:* Mathieu Vadepied; *M:* Alexandre Desplat. Cesar '01: Actress (Devos), Screenplay.

The Reader **1/2 2008 (R)** In postwar Germany, middle-aged Hanna (Winslet) and 15-year-old Michael (Kross) become sexually involved, with her insisting he read to her before their encounters (hence the title). She breaks off the forbidden relationship abruptly and the story leaps ahead to an older Michael (Fiennes), now a law student, witnessing Hanna on trial for war crimes. Her involvement in atrocities, her concealed illiteracy, and her past relationship with Michael serve as an attempt to understand how awful things can be done by seemingly decent people. Film adaptation of Bernard Schlink's best-selling novel has high aspirations, with Winslet's performance somber and convincing. **123m/C; DVD, Blu-Ray, On Demand.** *US GE* Ralph Fiennes; Kate Winslet; Bruno Ganz; Alexandra Maria Lara; Lena Olin; Karoline Herforth; David Kross; Matthias Habich; Susanne Lothar; *D:* Stephen Daldry; *W:* David Hare; *C:* Chris Menges; Roger Deakins; *M:* Nico Muhly. Oscars '08: Actress (Winslet); British Acad. '08: Actress (Winslet); Golden Globes '09: Support. Actress (Winslet); Screen Actors Guild '08: Support. Actress (Winslet).

The Reading Room **1/2 2005 (PG)** Businessman William Campbell (Jones) fulfills his deceased wife's last wish by opening a free reading room in the gang-ridden inner-city neighborhood where he grew up. But his generosity is resented, and his dream threatened, by some in the neighborhood. **87m/C; DVD.** James Earl Jones; Douglas Spain; Joanna Cassidy; Lynne Moody; Spencir Bridges; Tim Reid; Georg Stanford Brown; *D:* Georg Stanford Brown; *W:* Randy Feldman; *C:* James W. Wrenn; *M:* Elia Cmiral. **CABLE**

Ready or Not **2019 (R)** To marry her love Alex Le Domas (O'Brien), Grace (Weaving) puts up with his eccentric family and their antisocial efforts to drive her away. The ceremony does take place at the Le Domas family mansion, but after the nuptials, Grace is forced to be part of one more ceremony with the family that is a tradition--playing a game. When Grace draws a card that indicates the group will play hide and seek, she finds not only her new marriage -- but her very life -- is at risk. Quite fun, the comedy-horror-thriller satire has subtle anti-wealthy theme brought home by Weaving's full-bodied performance. **95m/C; DVD, Blu-Ray.** Samara Weaving; Adam Brody; Mark O'Brien; Henry Czerny; *Cameo(s):* Andie MacDowell; *D:* Matt Bettinelli-Olpin; Tyler Gillett; *W:* Guy Busick; Ryan Murphy; *C:* Brett Jutkiewicz; *M:* Brian Tyler.

Ready Player One **2018 (PG-13)** Reality in the year 2045 is so grim that people escape into the Oasis, a virtual universe brimming with 80s pop culture. Before his death, its creator devised a contest that would grant control of the Oasis to the first player to complete three challenges, so Wade Watts and his pals immerse themselves in the game to locate the prized Easter Egg. Who better than Spielberg to whisk us back to the 1980s? This movie, based on the novel by Ernest Cline, recaptures the look, sound, and feel of that generation of filmmaking. There's not much beneath the surface, but it's a pulsing, entertaining ride up top. **140m/C; DVD, Blu-Ray.** Tye Sheridan; Olivia Cooke; Ben Mendelsohn; Lena Waithe; T.J. Miller; *D:* Steven Spielberg; *W:* Zak Penn; Ernest Cline; *C:* Janusz Kaminski; *M:* Alan Silvestri.

Ready to Rumble **2000 (PG-13)** Sanitation workers and best buds Gordie (Arquette) and Sean (Caan) decide to mastermind the comeback of their favorite wrestler, Jimmy "the King" King (Platt). The reason he needs a comeback is that promoter Titus Sinclair (Pantaliano) has decided that he's outlasted his usefulness. Sort of like this movie. Arquette and wrestling are annoying enough individually, but put 'em together and it's almost painful to watch. The two buddies make Bill and Ted look like Rhodes scholars, and it's not like there's any point to further parodying the "sport" of wrestling. Hopefully, this was a worth a few mortgage payments to supporting players Platt, Landau, and Pantaliano. **100m/C; VHS, DVD.** David Arquette; Scott Caan; Oliver Platt; Rose McGowan; Joe Pantoliano; Martin Landau; Richard Lineback; Chris Owen; Kathleen Freeman; Lewis Arquette; Dallas Page; *D:* Brian Robbins; *W:* Steven Brill; *C:* Clark Mathis; *M:* George S. Clinton.

Ready to Wear *Pret-a-Porter* **1994 (R)** Altman travels to Paris to take on the fashion industry with his trademark satire, ensemble cast, and cameo players in tow. The untimely death of a major industry player begins a swirl of random subplots involving a head-spinning array of fashion industry stereotypes. Loren and Mastroianni recreate their "Yesterday, Today and Tomorrow" boudoir striptease scene. Coterie of one-dimensional characters is set adrift with no discernable plot, which might make for interesting people watching, but results in a tedious movie. Altman did it better with "The Player" and "Short Cuts." **132m/C; VHS, DVD.** Sophia Loren; Marcello Mastroianni; Julia Roberts; Tim Robbins; Kim Basinger; Stephen Rea; Anouk Aimee; Lauren Bacall; Lili Taylor; Sally Kellerman; Tracey Ullman; Linda Hunt; Rupert Everett; Forest Whitaker; Richard E. Grant; Danny Aiello; Teri Garr; Lyle Lovett; Jean Rochefort; Michel Blanc; Anne Canovos; Jean-Pierre Cassel; Francois Cluzet; Rossy de Palma; Kasia (Katarzyna) Figura; Sam Robards; Cher; Harry Belafonte; Issey Miyake; Sonia Rykiel; Jean-Paul Gaultier; Thierry Mugler; *D:* Robert Altman; *W:* Barbara Shulgasser; Robert Altman; *C:* Jean Lepine; Pierre Mignot; *M:* Michel Legrand.

Ready? OK! **2008** Sweet-natured comedy about a young boy who's very sure of what he likes even if the grown-up implications escape him. San Diego single mom Andy is struggling to raise her strong-willed 10-year-old son Joshua with the help of her deadbeat brother Alex and gay neighbor Charlie. Joshua, who likes dolls and dresses, is determined to join the all-girl cheerleading squad at his Catholic school, which results in a number of parent-teacher conferences as Sister Vivian tries to steer Joshua into more manly pursuits with some unexpected results. **91m/C; DVD.** Carrie Preston; John Preston; Michael Emerson; Kali Rocha; Lurie Poston; Tara Karsian; *D:* James Vasquez; *W:* James Vasquez; *C:* Elizabeth Santoro; *M:* Lance Horne.

The Reagans **2004** Despite it being pulled from network broadcast due to allegations of character assassination, the production presents a compassionate and charitable portrayal of Ronald and Nancy Reagan's assent from Hollywood couple to First Family. Starting with their first date in 1949 and follows them through two White House terms. **180m/C; DVD.** James Brolin; Judy David; Zeljko Ivanek; Mary Beth Peil; Bill Smitrovich; Shad Hart; Tom Barnett; Stewart Bick; Sean McCann; John Stamos; Lisa Bronwyn Moore; Zoie Palmer; Claudia Besso; *D:* Robert Allan Ackerman; *W:* Thomas (Tom) Rickman; *C:* James Chressanthis; *M:* John Altman. **TV**

A Real American Hero **1/2** *Hard Stick* **1978** Story of Tennessee sheriff Buford Pusser, the subject of three "Walking Tall" films. Here, he battles moonshiners, with the usual violence. **94m/C; VHS, DVD.** Brian Dennehy; Brian Kerwin; Forrest Tucker; *D:* Lou Antonio. **TV**

The Real Blonde **1/2 1997 (R)** DiCillo's entertaining ensemble pic exposes the business behind the show. There's disillusioned actor Joe (Modine), his beleaguered girlfriend Mary (Keener), and successful soap star Bob (Caulfield), who's searching for a peroxide-free blonde in New York. Intelligent writing and caustic wit provide a few memorable scenes, including Bob's resolution to his blonde quest and Joe's emotional improv. Thomas stands out from the crowd as a pretentious fashion photog who's Mary's boss. **105m/C; DVD.** Matthew Modine; Catherine Keener; Daryl Hannah; Maxwell Caulfield; Elizabeth Berkley; Marlo Thomas; Buck Henry; Bridgette Wilson-Sampras; Christopher Lloyd; Kathleen Turner; Denis Leary; Steve Buscemi; *D:* Tom DiCillo; *W:* Tom DiCillo; *C:* Frank Prinzi; *M:* Jim Farmer.

The Real Charlotte **1/2 1991** When young, lovely, and flirtatious Francie Fitzpatrick (Roth) is romantically betrayed by a young English officer, she then sets her mind on the one man (Bergin) whom her plain and middle-aged cousin Charlotte (Crowley) has long loved. Set in Victorian-era Ireland; made for British TV. **240m/C; VHS, DVD.** *GB* Joanna Roth; Jeananne Crowley; Patrick Bergin; *D:* Tony Barry; *W:* Bernard MacLaverty; *M:* Paul Corbett. **TV**

The Real Dirt on Farmer John **2006** Eccentric John Peterson is the titular Illinois farmer whose life has been documented since the 1950s when his mother, Anna, began shooting Super 8 home movies. John, who embraced the counterculture of the 1960s, later took over filming—and the farm—after his father died. Director Siegel befriended and started filming John in the 1980s after a number of financial crises led him to sell most of the acreage, though the farm eventually rebounded as an organic co-op. **83m/C; On Demand.** *D:* Taggart Siegel; *W:* John Peterson; *C:* Taggart Siegel; *M:* Mark Orton.

Real Genius **1985 (PG)** Brainy kids in California work with lasers on a class project that is actually intended for use as an offensive military weapon. When they learn of the scheme, they use their brilliant minds to mount an amusingly elaborate strategic defense initiative of their own. Eccentric characters and an intelligent script provide a bevy of laughs for the family. **108m/C; VHS, DVD, Blu-Ray.** Val Kilmer; Gabe Jarret; Jon(athan) Gries; Michelle Meyrink; William Atherton; Patti D'Arbanville; Severn Darden; Robert Prescott; Deborah Foreman; Ed Lauter; Tommy Swerdlow; Dean Devlin; *D:* Martha Coolidge; *W:* Peter Torokvei; Neal Israel; Pat Proft; *M:* Thomas Newman.

The Real Glory **1939** After the U.S. capture of the Philippine islands during the Spanish-American war, an uprising of Moro tribesmen spreads terror. After most of the islands are evacuated only a small group of Army officers is left to lead the Filipino soldiers against the rebels. Cooper plays the heroic doctor, who is not afraid to fight, especially when he comes to the rescue of the beseiged Army fort. Great action sequences and particularly good performances by Cooper and Niven. **95m/B; VHS, DVD.** Gary Cooper; David Niven; Andrea Leeds; Reginald Owen; Broderick Crawford; Kay Johnson; Russell Hicks; Vladimir Sokoloff; Rudy Robles; Tetsu Komai; Roy Gordon; Henry Kolker; Soledad Jiminez; *D:* Henry Hathaway; *W:* Robert Presnell, Sr.; Jo Swerling; *C:* Rudolph Mate; *M:* Alfred Newman.

The Real Howard Spitz 1/2 **1998 (PG)** Cranky has-been detective turned writer Spitz (Grammer) finds unlikely success with a children's book about a crime-solving cow, despite the fact that Howard hates kids. But even he can't resist 8-year-old Samantha's (Tessier) pleas to help her find her missing father. Amusing and Grammer even dresses in a cow costume. **93m/C; VHS, Streaming.** Kelsey Grammer; Amanda Donohoe; Genevieve Tessier; Cathy Lee Crosby; ***D:*** Vadim Jean; ***W:*** Jurgen Wolff; ***C:*** Glen MacPherson; ***M:*** John Murphy. **VIDEO**

The Real Joan of Arc 1/2 *Vraie Jeanne, fausse Jeanne* **2008** An insightful, feature-length documentary look at a persistent story involving the death, and perhaps life, of Joan of Arc. Though it is generally believed that the teenage shepherd girl was burned at the stake at Rouen, 15th century documents tell another story. These papers show that many people at the time that another girl was burned instead of Joan. Five years after the incident, there were rumors that Joan was back and alive. The documentary offers a full portrait of all that is known about Joan, her life, and her death.French with subtitles. **94m/C; DVD.** ***D:*** Martin Meissonnier; ***C:*** Christophe Petit; ***M:*** Martin Meissonnier. **VIDEO**

Real Life **1979 (R)** Writer/comedian Brooks's first feature sags in places, but holds its own as a vehicle for his peculiar talent. Brooks plays a pompous director whose ambition is to make a documentary of a "typical" American family. Good, intelligent comedy. **99m/C; VHS, DVD.** Charles Grodin; Frances Lee McCain; Albert Brooks; ***D:*** Albert Brooks; ***W:*** Albert Brooks; Monica Johnson; Harry Shearer; ***C:*** Eric Saarinen; ***M:*** Mort Lindsey.

The Real McCoy 1/2 **1993 (PG-13)** Generally awful crime-caper film about female bank robber Karen McCoy (Basinger). Just out of prison, all Karen wants to do is go straight and raise her young son but her plans are thwarted by former associates who kidnap the child to force her into one last heist. Kilmer is the small-time thief, with a crush on Karen, who tries to help her out. Dumb, slow-moving story with a vapid performance by Basinger. **104m/C; VHS, DVD, Blu-Ray.** Kim Basinger; Val Kilmer; Terence Stamp; Zach English; Gailard Sartain; ***D:*** Russell Mulcahy; ***W:*** William Davies; William Osborne; ***C:*** Denis Crossan; ***M:*** Brad Fiedel.

Real Men 1/2 **1987 (PG-13)** The junior Belushi brother is a spy forced to recruit ordinary guy Ritter to help him negotiate with aliens to save the world. Bizarre premise shows promise, but spy spoof doesn't fire on all comedic pistons. Nice try. **86m/C; VHS, DVD, Blu-Ray.** James Belushi; John Ritter; Barbara Barrie; ***D:*** Dennis Feldman; ***C:*** John A. Alonzo; ***M:*** Miles Goodman.

Real Steel 1/2 **2011 (PG-13)** Audience-pleasing, underdog-cheering Disney popcorn flick. Set in the not-so-distant future, the sport of boxing loses the human element replaced with hi-tech robots. In a one last chance effort, ex-fighter, smalltime promoter, and selfish deadbeat dad Charlie Kenton (Jackson) teams up with his 11-year-old estranged son Max (Goyo) to re-build and train an obsolete robot as a contender for the Bot Boxing Championship. Sugar Ray Leonard served as a boxing consultant for the fight sequences, which were filmed using motion-capture techniques. **127m/C; DVD.** Hugh Jackman; Dakota Goyo; Kevin Durand; Evangeline Lilly; Anthony Mackie; Hope Davis; James Rebhorn; Karl Yune; ***D:*** Shawn Levy; ***W:*** John Gatins; ***C:*** Mauro Fiore; ***M:*** Danny Elfman.

Real Time **2008 (R)** Andy (Baruchel) is a whiny, chronic screw-up and compulsive gambler who's upset his creditors for the last time. They send thoughtful Aussie hit man Reuben (Quaid) to take care of him but Reuben allows Andy one last hour to settle his affairs. **78m/C; DVD.** *CA* Jay Baruchel; Randy Quaid; Jayne (Jane) Eastwood; Jeff Pustil; Ella Chan; ***D:*** Randel Cole; ***W:*** Randel Cole; ***C:*** Rudolf Blahacek; ***M:*** Jim Guthrie.

Real Time: Siege at Lucas Street Market **2000** Deals with an armed robbery at a convenience store, which escalates into a hostage situation. What makes "Real Time" unique is that the story is played out through in-store security video, police-car cameras, and TV news footage. While this approach is interesting, it also depersonalizes the action, deflating the drama. At times, it feels like an extended episode of "Cops." On DVD, every scene can be viewed from a second angle, giving the movie the extra kick that it needs. Unfortunately, the inventiveness behind the camera never matches the on-screen action. **72m/C; DVD.** Michael Cornelison; Chadrick Hoch; Tom Keane; Carol German; Sandy Grillet; ***D:*** Max Allan Collins; ***W:*** Max Allan Collins; ***C:*** Phillip W. Dingeldein.

Real Women Have Curves **2002 (PG-13)** Coming-of-age comedy marks the debut of Ferrara as the young, headstrong and slightly plump Mexican-American Ana, who has decided to attend college despite her overbearing mother Carmen (Ontiveros), who's decided that Ana would be better off married with children. Ana's plans are put on hold when she has to help her sister Estela (Oliu) meet deadlines in a dress factory. While featuring such themes as the body image of larger women, work in a sweatshop and the rigid roles assigned to ethnic youngsters by their elders, the film manages to avoid cliches and preachiness. **93m/C; VHS, DVD.** America Ferrera; Lupe Ontiveros; Ingrid Oliu; George Lopez; Soledad St. Hilaire; Brian Sites; Jorge Cerera, Jr.; ***D:*** Patricia Cardoso; ***W:*** George LaVoo; Josefina Lopez; ***C:*** Jim Denault; ***M:*** Hector Pereira. Natl. Film Reg. '19.

A Real Young Girl **1975** Breillat's explicit film was never commercially released—being too weird even for French cinema (at least at the time). It deals with the budding sexuality of the teenaged Alice (Alexandra) during her summer vacation as she becomes infatuated with Jim (Keller), a hunky laborer at her father's saw mill. Based on the director's novel "Le Soupirail" ("The Air Duct"). In French with subtitles. **93m/C; VHS, DVD.** *FR* Charlotta Alexandra; Hiram Keller; Rita Meiden; Bruno Balp; Shirley Stoler; ***D:*** Catherine Breillat; ***W:*** Catherine Breillat; ***C:*** Pierre Fattori; ***M:*** Mort Shuman.

Reality Bites 1/2 **1994 (PG-13)** Humorous look at four recent college grads living, working, and slacking in Houston. Script by newcomer Childress is at its best when highlighting the trends: 7-Eleven Big Gulps, tacky '70s memorabilia, and games revolving around episodes of old TV shows like "Good Times," to name a few. Definite appeal for those in their early 20s, but anyone over 25 may encounter a "Generation X-er" gap, a noticeable problem since "Reality" claims to speak for the entire twenty-something generation. Decent directorial debut for Stiller; good cast, particularly Garofalo, in her film debut. **99m/C; DVD, Blu-Ray.** Winona Ryder; Ethan Hawke; Ben Stiller; Janeane Garofalo; Steve Zahn; Swoosie Kurtz; Joe Don Baker; John Mahoney; ***Cameo(s):*** David Pirner; Anne Meara; Jeanne Tripplehorn; Karen Duffy; ***D:*** Ben Stiller; ***W:*** Helen Childress; ***C:*** Emmanuel Lubezki; ***M:*** Karl Wallinger.

Reap the Wild Wind 1/2 **1942** DeMille epic about salvagers off the Georgia coast in the 1840s featuring Wayne as the captain and Massey and a giant squid as the villains. Good cast, lesser story, fine underwater photography. **123m/C; VHS, DVD, Blu-Ray.** Ray Milland; John Wayne; Paulette Goddard; Raymond Massey; Robert Preston; Lynne Overman; Susan Hayward; Charles Bickford; Walter Hampden; Louise Beavers; Martha O'Driscoll; Elisabeth Risdon; Hedda Hopper; Raymond Hatton; Barbara Britton; ***D:*** Cecil B. DeMille; ***W:*** Charles Bennett; Jesse Lasky, Jr.; Alan LeMay; ***C:*** Victor Milner; ***M:*** Victor Young.

The Reaper **1997 (R)** A crime writer's most famous novel seems to be the basis for a copycat serial killer. Since the author is nearby the scene of every crime as well, he becomes the prime suspect. The investigating detective asks for his help but if the killer stays true to the plot, she's likely to become the next victim. **97m/C; VHS, DVD.** *CA* Chris Sarandon; Catherine Mary Stewart; Vlasta Vrana; Joanna Noyes; ***D:*** John Bradshaw; ***W:*** Matt Dorff; ***C:*** Bruce Chun. **TV**

Reaper **2015** A supernatural science fiction/horror/crime drama hybrid set in a small town hotel. When a serial killer meets his demise as a death row inmate, he does not die during his execution. Instead, he returns as the supernatural Reaper, a creature from hell. Settling in a rundown hotel full of drifters and criminals, the Reaper begins enact his sinister agenda. The residents must band together to survive the onslaught and come out of the experience alive. **90m/C; DVD, Streaming, Download.** Danny Trejo; Vinnie Jones; Jake Busey; Shayla Beesley; James Jurdi; ***D:*** Philip Shih; ***W:*** James Jurdi; Mark James; ***C:*** Hiroyuki Haga; ***M:*** Sean Murray.

The Reaping 1/2 **2007 (R)** Southern gothic revisits the 10 plagues from the book of Exodus that are being felt in the Louisiana bayou town of Haven. Having lost her own faith, professor Katherine Winter (Swank), now a professional debunker of alleged miracles and religious phenomena, is called in to offer scientific explanations. Of course, she can't. CGI's decent, Swank's stoic, but the story is so much familiar hooey (and not very scary). **98m/C; DVD, Blu-Ray, HD-DVD.** Hilary Swank; David Morrissey; Idris Elba; AnnaSophia Robb; William Ragsdale; Stephen Rea; ***D:*** Stephen Hopkins; ***W:*** Carey Hayes; Chad Hayes; ***C:*** Peter Levy; ***M:*** John (Gianni) Frizzell; John Frizzell.

Rear Window **1954** A newspaper photographer with a broken leg (Stewart) passes the time recuperating by observing his neighbors through the window. When he sees what he believes to be a murder, he decides to solve the crime himself. With help from his beautiful girlfriend and his nurse, he tries to catch the murderer without getting killed himself. Top-drawer Hitchcock blends exquisite suspense with occasional on-target laughs. Based on the story by Cornell Woolrich. **112m/C; VHS, DVD, Blu-Ray.** James Stewart; Grace Kelly; Thelma Ritter; Wendell Corey; Raymond Burr; Judith Evelyn; ***D:*** Alfred Hitchcock; ***W:*** John Michael Hayes; ***C:*** Robert Burks; ***M:*** Franz Waxman. AFI '98: Top 100; Natl. Film Reg. '97.

A Reason to Believe **1995 (R)** Campus date rape drama filmed at writer/director Tirola's alma mater, Miami University. Charlotte (Smith) goes to her boyfriend Wesley's (Quinn) big frat party, even though he's away. She drinks and flirts (a lot) with his best friend Jim (Underwood) and eventually leaves to collapse in a stupor on Wesley's bed. Jim follows and rapes her, though he'll tell his buddies Charlotte was a willing participant, which Wesley angrily believes. Meanwhile, the traumatized Charlotte is taken up by Linda (Emelin), the leader of the student feminist organization who wants the fraternities disbanded. Somewhat preachy and predicatable. **109m/C; VHS, DVD.** Allison Smith; Jay Underwood; Daniel Quinn; Georgia Emelin; Obba Babatunde; ***D:*** Douglas Tirola; ***W:*** Douglas Tirola; ***C:*** Sarah Cawley.

A Reason to Live, a Reason to Die *Massacre at Fort Holman; Una Ragione Per Vivere e Una Per Morire* **1973** A bland Italian-French-German-Spanish western in which a group of condemned men attempt to take a Confederate fort. **90m/C; VHS, DVD, Blu-Ray.** James Coburn; Telly Savalas; Bud Spencer; Guy Mairesse; ***D:*** Tonino Valerii.

Reasonable Doubt 1/2 **2014 (R)** Hotshot district attorney Mitch (Cooper) has it all, but one tequila-fueled night leads to a booze cruise that comes to a sobering head after hitting a man with his car. Mitch carefully sets aside the body and continues on. Honest, hard-working mechanic Clinton (Jackson) discovers it, and the police assume he's the killer. The juicy irony to this moral noir? Mitch must prosecute Clinton. There's a reason the director took his name off this project, as the proceeding becomes an awkward jumble of "Law & Order" snippets, switching motives every twenty minutes. The reasonable doubt should've started in the studio. **91m/C; DVD, Blu-Ray.** *GE CA* Dominic Cooper; Samuel L. Jackson; Erin Karpluk; Gloria Reuben; Ryan Robbins; ***D:*** Peter Howitt; ***W:*** Peter A. Dowling; ***C:*** Brian Pearson; ***M:*** James Jandrisch.

Rebecca **1940** Based on Daphne Du Maurier's best-selling novel about a young unsophisticated girl who marries a moody and prominent country gentleman haunted by the memory of his first wife. Fontaine and Olivier turn in fine performances as the unlikely couple. Suspenseful and surprising. Hitchcock's first American film and only Best Picture Oscar. **130m/B; VHS, DVD, Blu-Ray.** Joan Fontaine; Laurence Olivier; Judith Anderson; George Sanders; Nigel Bruce; Florence Bates; Gladys Cooper; Reginald Denny; Leo G. Carroll; Sir C. Aubrey Smith; Melville Cooper; ***D:*** Alfred Hitchcock; ***W:*** Joan Harrison; Robert Sherwood; ***C:*** George Barnes; ***M:*** Franz Waxman. Oscars '40: B&W Cinematog., Film; Natl. Film Reg. '18.

Rebecca **1997** Daphne du Maurier's tale of marriage and jealousy makes its second TV incarnation. Worldly widower Maxim de Winter (Dance) takes his nameless, shy young bride (Fox) back to Manderley, the family estate. There she must compete with the ghost of the first Mrs. de Winter—the glamorous Rebecca—family secrets, and obsessive housekeeper, Mrs. Danvers (Rigg). The 1980 TV version (with Jeremy Brett as Maxim) starred Joanna David in the title role, coincidentally newcomer Fox's mother. **240m/C; VHS, DVD.** *GB* Emilia Fox; Charles Dance; Diana Rigg; Faye Dunaway; Geraldine James; Jonathan Cake; ***D:*** Jim O'Brien; ***W:*** Arthur Hopcraft; ***C:*** Rex Maidment. **TV**

Rebecca of Sunnybrook Farm **1917** The original film version of the tale about an orphan who spreads sunshine and good cheer to all those around her. Silent with organ score. Based on the popular novel by Kate Douglas Wiggin; remade with Shirley Temple in 1938. Part of the 'The Actors: Rare Films of Mary Pickford, Vol. 2' collection. **77m/B; Silent; DVD.** Mary Pickford; Eugene O'Brien; Marjorie Daw; Helen Jerome Eddy; ***D:*** Marshall Neilan; ***W:*** Frances Marion; ***C:*** Walter Stradling.

Rebecca of Sunnybrook Farm 1/2 **1938** Temple becomes a radio star over her aunt's objections in this bouncy musical that has nothing to do with the famous Kate Douglas Wiggin novel. Temple sings a medley of her hits, and dances the finale with Bill "Bojangles" Robinson. **80m/B; VHS, DVD.** Shirley Temple; Randolph Scott; Jack Haley; Phyllis Brooks; Gloria Stuart; Slim Summerville; Bill Robinson; Helen Westley; William Demarest; ***D:*** Allan Dwan; ***C:*** Arthur C. Miller.

Rebel 1/2 **1985 (R)** A U.S. Marine falls in love with a Sydney nightclub singer and goes AWOL during WWII. Stylish but empty and badly cast. **93m/C; VHS, DVD.** *AU* Matt Dillon; Debbie Byrne; Bryan Brown; Bill Hunter; Ray Barrett; ***D:*** Michael Jenkins.

The Rebel *Dong Mau Anh Hung* **2008** In 1920's French Colonial Vietnam, a government agent is trying to stop a rebellion caused by the injustices of his masters. Feeling sympathy for the rebel leader's daughter, he sets her free, becoming a wanted man himself. Low budget actioner looks spectacular, and as one of the few Vietnamese martial arts films, it's a treat for fans looking for something beyond kung fu. **103m/C; DVD.** *VT* Dustin Nguyen; Stephane Gauger; Johnny Nguyen; Thanh Van Ngo; David Minetti; Thang Nguyen; ***D:*** Truc 'Charlie' Nguyen; ***W:*** Johnny Nguyen; Truc 'Charlie' Nguyen; Dominic Pereira; ***C:*** Dominic Pereira; ***M:*** Christopher Wong. **VIDEO**

Rebel in the Rye 1/2 **2017 (PG-13)** A problematic biography of J.D. Salinger (Hoult) that assumes the audience has read his 1951 masterpiece, "The Catcher in the Rye." Focusing on Salinger as author, it explores his time at Columbia, as a World War II soldier, and as a short story writer. The success of his novel and his later years of seclusion are also depicted. These moments of biography serve as launching points to offer theories about Salinger's genius, creative process, and inspirations, using Catcher as the lens. Though Salinger's romantic life is considered as well, it is formulaic and limited in scope like the rest of the film. **106m/C; DVD, Blu-Ray.** Nicholas Hoult; Kevin Spacey; Zoey Deutch; Lucy Boynton; Sarah Paulson; ***D:*** Danny Strong; ***W:*** Danny Strong; ***C:*** Kramer Morgenthau; ***M:*** Bear McCreary.

Rebel in Town **1956** Ex-Confederate soldier Bedloe Mason and his four sons are starting over after the Civil War by turning to robbery. They have to hightail it out of town when Wesley Mason accidentally kills a young boy playing with a cap pistol. Only youngest son Gray feels remorse and returns to see how the devastated Willoughby family is doing without revealing his part in the tragedy. **79m/B; DVD.** J. Carrol Naish; John Payne; Ruth Roman; Ben Cooper; John Smith; Ben Johnson; James J. Griffith; ***D:*** Alfred Werker; ***W:*** Danny Arnold; ***C:*** Gordon Avil; ***M:*** Les Baxter.

Rebel Rousers ✓✓ **1969** A motorcycle gang wreaks havoc in a small town where a drag-race is being held to see who will get the pregnant girlfriend of Dern's high-school buddy as the prize. Young Nicholson in striped pants steals the show. **81m/C; VHS, DVD.** Jack Nicholson; Cameron Mitchell; Diane Ladd; Bruce Dern; Harry Dean Stanton; ***D:*** Martin B. Cohen; ***W:*** Martin B. Cohen; Abe Polsky; Michael Kars; ***C:*** Laszlo Kovacs; Glen R. Smith; ***M:*** William Loose.

Rebel Run ✓ *Bolt* **1994 (R)** Biker Grieco moves west in order to escape his violent past but is then drawn into a rumble with arch-rival Ironside. **93m/C; VHS, DVD.** Richard Grieco; Sean Young; Michael Ironside; ***D:*** Henri Colline; ***W:*** Henri Colline; ***C:*** Gerald Wolfe; ***M:*** Chris Squire. **VIDEO**

The Rebel Set ✓✓ 1/2 *Beatsville* **1959** The owner of a beat generation coffeehouse plans an armed robbery with the help of some buddies. Genuinely suspenseful, competently directed. **72m/B; VHS, DVD.** Gregg (Hunter) Palmer; Kathleen Crowley; Edward Platt; John Lupton; Ned Glass; Don Sullivan; Vicki Dougan; I. Stanford Jolley; ***D:*** Gene Fowler, Jr.; ***W:*** Bernard Girard; Louis Vittes; ***C:*** Karl Struss; ***M:*** Paul Dunlap.

Rebel Vixens WOOF! *The Scavengers* **1969** Even though the war is over, ex-confederate soldiers continue looting and raping, until a brothel-full of prostitutes concoct a plan that has a lot to do with softcore sex. **94m/C; VHS, DVD.** Maria Lease; Roda Spain; Jonathan Bliss; Michael Divoka; Wes Bishop; Bruce (Kemp) Kimball; ***D:*** Lee Frost; ***W:*** Robert W. Cresse; ***C:*** Robert Maxwell; ***M:*** Lee Frost; Robert W. Cresse.

Rebel without a Cause ✓✓✓✓ **1955** James Dean's most memorable screen appearance. In the second of his three films (following "East of Eden"), he plays troubled teen Jim Stark, who's alienated from both his parents and peers. He befriends outcasts Judy (Wood) and Plato (Mineo) in a police station and together they find a common ground. Many memorable scenes, including the "chickie run" between Jim and black leather-jacketed Buzz (Allen). Superb young stars carry this in-the-gut story of adolescence. All three leads met with real-life tragic ends. **111m/C; VHS, DVD, Blu-Ray.** James Dean; Natalie Wood; Sal Mineo; Jim Backus; Nick Adams; Dennis Hopper; Ann Doran; William Hopper; Rochelle Hudson; Corey Allen; Edward Platt; ***D:*** Nicholas Ray; ***W:*** Stewart Stern; Irving Shulman; ***C:*** Ernest Haller; ***M:*** Leonard Rosenman. AFI '98: Top 100; Natl. Film Reg. '90.

Rebirth of Mothra ✓✓ *Mosura; Mothra* **1996** A lumber company working in the Hokkaido rain forest accidently unearths the secret lair of Desghidorah, a three-headed monster, who teams up with the evil Belvera. It's up to twins More and Mona to call on Mothra to rescue the earth from their demonic powers. **106m/C; VHS, DVD, Blu-Ray.** *JP* Megumi Kobayashi; Sayaka Yamaguchi; Hano Aki; ***D:*** Okihiro Yoneda.

Rebirth of Mothra 2 ✓ 1/2 *Mosura 2; Mothra 2* **1997** Garbage-eating monster Degehra and mutant marine lifeforms threaten Earth's oceans and it's up to Mothra and a magical treasure hidden in the underwater city of Nelikani to save the day. **103m/C; VHS, DVD, Blu-Ray.** *JP* Megumi Kobayashi; Sayaka Yamaguchi; Hano Aki; ***D:*** Kunio Miyoshi; ***W:*** Masumi Suetani.

Reborn ✓✓ *Renacer* **1981** A faith healer and a talent scout hire actors to be cured of fake ailments. **105m/C; VHS, Streaming.** *SP* Dennis Hopper; Michael Moriarty; Francisco Rabal; Antonella Murgia; ***D:*** Bigas Luna; ***W:*** Bigas Luna; ***C:*** Juan Ruiz-Anchia; ***M:*** Scott Harper.

Rebound ✓✓ **2005 (PG)** Dumped as a college basketball coach after his usual sideline histrionics lead to the demise of an opposing team's avian mascot, Roy McCormick (Lawrence) decides to accept his old middle school's offer to take over their woeful team. From there, the tired, warm and fuzzy sports tale plays out as hard-nosed Roy becomes a softy while fashioning the losing squad into winners and finding love, too. Lawrence curbs his customary foul language for this family flick. **103m/C; DVD.** Martin Lawrence; Steven Anthony Lawrence; Horatio Sanz; Megan Mullally; Patrick Warburton; Wendy Raquel Robinson; Breckin Meyer; Fred Stoller; ***D:*** Steve Carr; ***W:*** Jon Lucas; Scott Moore; ***C:*** Glen MacPherson; ***M:*** Teddy Castellucci.

The Rebound ✓ 1/2 **2009 (R)** Predictable, somewhat crude, romantic comedy that has some charm because of its leads. 40-year-old suburban housewife Sandy (Zeta-Jones) discovers her husband's infidelity and moves into Manhattan with their two kids. She gets an apartment above a coffee shop where 25-year-old Aram (Bartha) is working. Aram's also disillusioned after divorcing his French wife when he learned she only married him for a green card. Sandy gets a job and Aram becomes her babysitter and the two start a romance everyone around them assumes is just a rebound affair. **95m/C; DVD, Blu-Ray.** Catherine Zeta-Jones; Justin Bartha; Kelly Gould; Andrew Cherry; Lynn Whitfield; Art Garfunkel; Joanna Gleason; Sam Robards; ***D:*** Bart Freundlich; ***W:*** Bart Freundlich; ***C:*** Jonathan Freeman; ***M:*** Clint Mansell.

Rebound: The Legend of Earl "The Goat" Manigault ✓✓ 1/2 **1996 (R)** Earl "The Goat" Manigault (Cheadle) was a '60s Harlem playground basketball phenom who was taken under the wing of parks director Holcomb Rucker (Whitaker), who tries to steer the young man towards college and a career in the NBA. Unfortunately, the easily influenced Manigault also attracts the attention of local drug dealer Legrand (Beach) and when Manigault's life starts to fall apart, he drops out of college and turns to heroin, eventually winding up in prison. Since this is an inspirational true story, Manigault does turn his life around to found his own basketball tournament in Harlem. **111m/C; VHS, DVD.** Don Cheadle; Michael Beach; James Earl Jones; Loretta Devine; Glynn Turman; Clarence Williams, III; Ronny Cox; Forest Whitaker; Tamara Tunie; Eriq La Salle; ***Cameo(s):*** Kareem Abdul-Jabbar; ***D:*** Eriq La Salle; ***W:*** Larry Golin; Alan Swyer; ***C:*** Alar Kivilo; ***M:*** Kevin Eubanks. **CABLE**

Rec ✓✓ **2007 (R)** Spanish horror with TV reporter Angela and her cameraman doing a segment on firemen for a reality show. Angela goes with them on a rescue call at an apartment house and it's zombie time as a flesh-eating disease infects the inhabitants, the building is sealed off, and Angela continues reporting as the camera keeps recording. Spanish with subtitles. Remade as 2008's "Quarantine." **80m/C; DVD.** Manuela Velasco; Ferran Terraza; David Vert; Carlos Vicente; Carlos Lesarte; ***D:*** Jaume Balaguero; Paco Plaza; ***W:*** Jaume Balaguero; Paco Plaza; Luis Berdejo; ***C:*** Pablo Rosso; ***M:*** Carlos Ann.

Rec 2 ✓ 1/2 **2009 (R)** Spanish shaky-cam sequel immediately picks up where 2007's "REC" left off as a SWAT team is brought into the quarantined Barcelona apartment building to get rid of its inhabitants, who have been turned into vicious zombie-like creatures because of an unknown virus. Again every move is recorded by cameras and the sequel is repetitive in both story and violence. Spanish with subtitles. **84m/C; DVD, Blu-Ray, Streaming.** *SP* Pablo Rosso; Manuela Velasco; Jonathan Mellor; Oscar Sanchez Zafra; Ariel Casas; Alejandro Casaseca; Andrea Ros; Alex Batllori; Pau Poch; ***D:*** Jaume Balaguero; Paco Plaza; ***W:*** Jaume Balaguero; Paco Plaza; Manu Diez; ***C:*** Pablo Rosso.

REC 3: Genesis ✓✓ 1/2 **2012 (R)** After two claustrophobic international hits, director and co-writer Plaza takes his concept out of the apartment building and transfers the brain-eating frenzy to what should be the happiest of locations, a lavish wedding. After a found footage set-up of wedding videos, the third film abandons the over-used concept for what is a straight-up gore fest. Some of it is generic, but star Dolera sells the scream-queen-with-a-chainsaw angle with enough charisma that genre fans should enjoy the short, bloody ride. Spanish with subtitles. **80m/C; DVD, Blu-Ray.** *SP* Leticia Dolera; Diego Martin; Ismael Martinez; Alex Monner; Borja Glez. Santaolalla; ***D:*** Paco Plaza; ***W:*** Paco Plaza; Luiso Berdejo; David Gallart; ***C:*** Pablo Rosso; ***M:*** Mikel Salas.

REC 4: Apocalyse ✓ **2014 (R)** The enjoyable third outing in this surprising franchise is completely discarded by this stupid sequel, which moves the zombie action of the series to the open seas. Taking place immediately after the second film, Manuela Velasco returns as the embattled reporter with the worst assignment of her life—investigating ground zero of the undead apocalypse. She ends up on a ship under military quarantine where further experiments are being done—the kind that end up with zombie monkeys. The Hound wishes it was as fun as that sounds; instead, it's loud, annoying, and just dumb. Spanish with subtitles. **96m/C; Blu-Ray, Streaming.** *SP* Manuela Velasco; Hector Colome; Paco Manzanedo; Ismael Fritschi; ***D:*** Jaume Balaguero; ***W:*** Jaume Balaguero; Manu Diez; ***C:*** Pablo Rossu; ***M:*** Arnau Bataller.

The Recall ✓ **2017 (R)** Five bland friends spend a weekend at a remote cabin, where they encounter a weird hunter (Snipes), who prepares them for an alien invasion. Excited to see Snipes on the big screen again? Too bad--he's on it for roughly 15 minutes and mostly just gives gravely exposition. Happy to waste your time with bad acting, predictable plot, laughable writing, and mediocre effects? You're in luck! Hey aliens, leave the people; abduct this flick instead. **90m/C; DVD, Blu-Ray.** Wesley Snipes; R.J. Mitte; Jedidiah Goodacre; Laura Bilgeri; Niko Pepaj; ***D:*** Mauro Borrelli; ***W:*** Reggie Keyohara, III; ***C:*** Mark Dobrescu; ***M:*** Todd Bryanton.

The Reception ✓✓ 1/2 **2005** Jeannette, a wealthy, alcoholic Frenchwoman, lives with African American gay painter, Martin, under sadly codependent circumstances. Sierra, her estranged daughter, shows up one winter day with her new husband, coincidently also African American, to collect on a promised inheritance. What unfolds is a scenario of shifting alliances that shadow the entanglement of racial prejudice, sexual orientation and addiction. Shooting in eight days on a $5,000 budget, Young presents an admirable effort. **75m/C; DVD.** Pamela Stewart; Darien Sills-Evans; Wayne Lamont Sims; Margaret Burkwit; ***D:*** John G. Young; ***W:*** John G. Young; ***C:*** Derek Wiesehahn.

Recipe for a Perfect Christmas ✓✓ 1/2 **2005** Easy to digest Christmas fare with Baranski the best reason to watch. On a tight deadline, strait-laced J.J. Jenner (Pope) has a chance at a dream promotion to magazine food critic when her exuberant mother Lee (Baranski) suddenly shows up for the holidays. So she can find some time to work, J.J. pawns Lee off on ambitious chef Alex (Cannavale) in exchange for a review but things don't go exactly as planned. **90m/C; DVD.** Carly Pope; Christine Baranski; Bobby Cannavale; Monica Parker; Kristen Hager; Tracy Dawson; ***D:*** Sheldon Larry; ***W:*** Rachel Feldman; Susan Nanus; ***C:*** Albert J. Dunk; ***M:*** Amin Bhatia; Ari Psoner. **CABLE**

Recipe for Disaster ✓✓ 1/2 **2003 (G)** The kids have to save the day when Mom (Warren) and Dad (Larroquette) get lost on their way home on the eve of their new restaurant's grand opening. Snooty owners of a neigboring restaurant complicate matters by trying to sabotage the kids' efforts at keeping the opening night crowd happy. Fun, well-paced family flick should go over well although younger children may be scared by the villains, who are a little more mean than they have to be for this type of movie. **92m/C; VHS, DVD.** Lesley Ann Warren; John Larroquette; Michelle Brookhurst; Margo Harshman; Devon Werkheiser; Bill Dawes; Andrew James Allen; Melissa Peterman; ***D:*** Harvey Frost; ***W:*** William Propp; ***C:*** Christopher Pearson; ***M:*** William Goodrum. **TV**

Recipe for Revenge ✓ 1/2 **1998** Caterer Carly (Huffman) is cooking dinner for her friend Sophie (Hallier) so Sophie can impress her new beau. She shockingly witnesses Sophie's murder by Dr. Winnifield (Bernsen) but he gives the cops a solid alibi and convinces them that Carly is unstable. However, Detective Jack Brannigan (Carter) gives Carly the benefit of the doubt, especially when her own life is threatened. From the Harlequin Romance Series; adapted from the Kristin Gabriel novel. **95m/C; DVD.** *CA* Alex Carter; Corbin Bernsen; Lori Hallier; Hugh Thompson; Kim Huffman; ***D:*** Stacey Stewart Curtis; ***W:*** Peter Lauterman; Jennifer Black; ***C:*** Michael Storey; ***M:*** John McCarthy. **TV**

Reckless ✓✓ **1935** Harlow, in a role originally intended for Joan Crawford, plays a showgirl coveted by a millionaire and secretly loved by her manager. Unfortunately, Harlow couldn't pull off the acting (much less the singing and dancing), although the plot strangely paralleled her own life. Songs include "Reckless," "Ev'rything's Been Done Before," "Trocadero," "Hear What My Heart Is Saying" and "Cyclone." **96m/B; VHS, DVD, Streaming.** Jean Harlow; William Powell; Franchot Tone; May Robson; Ted Healy; Nat Pendleton; Rosalind Russell; ***D:*** Victor Fleming; ***C:*** George J. Folsey.

Reckless ✓✓ 1/2 **1984 (R)** A sincere movie about a "good" girl who finds herself obsessed with a rebel from the wrong side of her small town. Differs from 1950s' wrong-side-of-the-track flicks only in updated sex and music. **93m/C; VHS, DVD.** Aidan Quinn; Daryl Hannah; Kenneth McMillan; Cliff DeYoung; Lois Smith; Adam Baldwin; Dan Hedaya; Jennifer Grey; Pamela Springsteen; ***D:*** James Foley; ***W:*** Chris Columbus; ***C:*** Michael Ballhaus; ***M:*** Thomas Newman.

Reckless ✓✓✓ **1997** Brit TV production's a combo of farce, romance, and drama that finds young doctor Owen Springer (Green) returning to Manchester to look after his feisty-but-ailing father (Bradley). He has a chance meeting with a beautiful middle-aged woman, Anna Fairley (Annis), who turns out to be his job interviewer. Reckless Owen falls impulsively in love—before learning Anna is also the wife of his new boss, Dr. Richard Crane (Kitchen). When he learns Crane is having an affair, Owen arranges for Anna to discover her husband's infidelity, leading to Owen and Anna hitting the sheets and things getting very complicated. **312m/C; DVD.** *UK* Robson Green; Francesca Annis; Michael Kitchen; David Bradley; Julian Rhind-Tutt; Daniela Nardini; Margery Mason; Conor Mullen; ***D:*** David Richards; Sarah Harding; ***W:*** Paul Abbott. **TV**

The Reckless Hour ✓✓ **1931** Jersey girl Margaret (Mackaill) is working as a Fifth Avenue fashion shop model. She wants to bag a rich husband but wealthy playboy Allen (Byron) promises marriage and leaves her alone and pregnant instead. Margaret's hard-working family get into financial trouble trying to help her out, making her willing to negotiate a monetary deal with divorced artist Edward (Nagel). Only he turns out to be an honorable guy. **70m/B; DVD.** Dorothy Mackaill; Walter Byron; Conrad Nagel; Joan Blondell; H.B. Warner; Helen Ware; ***D:*** John Francis Dillon; ***W:*** Robert Lloyd; Florence Ryerson; ***C:*** James Van Trees.

Reckless Kelly ✓✓ 1/2 **1993 (PG)** Australian bank robber, pop culture hero, and local video store owner Kelly is upset when his gang's island retreat is about to be sold to a Japanese conglomerate, unless he can come up with a higher offer. So he prepares for a last-ditch defense of his home. Slapstick homage to legendary Australian outlaw Ned Kelly. **81m/C; VHS, Streaming.** *AU* Yahoo Serious; Hugo Weaving; Melora Hardin; Alexei Sayle; Bob Maza; Kathleen Freeman; ***D:*** Yahoo Serious; ***W:*** Yahoo Serious.

Reckless Moment ✓✓✓ **1949** A mother commits murder to save her daughter from an unsavory older man, and finds herself blackmailed. Gripping, intense thriller. **82m/B; VHS, DVD.** James Mason; Joan Bennett; Geraldine Brooks; ***D:*** Max Ophuls; ***C:*** Burnett Guffey.

Reckless: The Sequel ✓✓✓ **1998** Brit TV follow-up to the 1997 miniseries. A year later, Anna (Annis) has divorced philandering Richard (Kitchen) and is living with Owen (Green). The duo decide, somewhat impulsively, to marry, which drives the chronically jealous Richard into a frenzy and he vows to use any dirty trick necessary to break them up. But family interference and Anna and Owen's own doubts may do the job for him. **120m/C; DVD.** *UK* Robson Green; Francesca Annis; Michael Kitchen; David Bradley; ***D:*** David Richards; ***W:*** Paul Abbott; ***C:*** Lawrence Jones; ***M:*** Hal Lindes. **TV**

The Reckless Way ½ **1936** A young woman struggles for her big break into the movies. **72m/B; VHS, DVD.** Marion (Marian) Nixon; Kane Richmond; Inez Courtney; Malcolm McGregor; Harry Harvey; Arthur Howard; ***D:*** Bernard B. Ray.

The Reckoning **1969** Dark Brit drama about class, prejudice, and family ties. Ruthless Michael Marler (Williamson) grew up working-class Irish in Liverpool and bulldozed his way to success in London. When his father dies, Marler returns home for the first time in many years and learns his dad was insulted and then beaten in a pub brawl by some teenage Teddy Boys. Becoming increasingly furious, Marler decides to get revenge. **111m/C; DVD.** *GB* Nicol Williamson; Ann Bell; Lilita De Barros; Tom Kempinski; Kenneth Hendel; Douglas Wilmer; Rachel Roberts; Paul Rogers; ***D:*** Jack Gold; ***W:*** John McGrath; ***C:*** Geoffrey Unsworth; ***M:*** Malcolm Arnold.

The Reckoning **2003 (R)** Nicholas (Bettany) is a 14th-century priest on the run from charges of adultery who joins a band of actors led by the bored Martin (Dafoe). They come upon a town where a deaf-mute woman is on trial for a boy's murder and the actors decide to perform a play based on the crime. Nicholas discovers other boys have been killed in a similar manner and he becomes obsessed with uncovering the secrets of the village's "protector" Lord De Guise (Cassel). McGuigan makes excellent use of a deft story and exciting but not intrusive visuals to build suspense. Bettany and Dafoe shine. **110m/C; DVD.** Paul Bettany; Sarah Henderson; Tom (Thomas) Hardy; Willem Dafoe; Gina McKee; Stuart Wells; Vincent Cassel; Elvira Minguez; Ewen Bremner; ***D:*** Paul McGuigan; ***W:*** Mark Mills; ***C:*** Peter Sova; ***M:*** Adrian Lee; Mark Mancina.

The Reckoning **2014 (R)** A crime/mystery thriller centered on a police detective investigating a case involving himself. Troubled police detective Robbie Green (LaPaglia) is investigating the mysterious roadside execution-style murder of his partner Jason (Hemsworth). The most importance piece of evidence in the case is video camera footage shot by two teenagers. After looking at the footage, Green finds that it shows murky details about the drug-related death of a sibling in an unsolved hit-and-run case. When the teens go missing, Green must find them by retracing their journey, discovers a bloody trail of murder, and is startled to find that it leads back to police headquarters and Green himself. **86m/C; DVD, Blu-Ray.** Jonathan LaPaglia; Luke Hemsworth; Viva Bianca; Hanna Mangan Lawrence; Alex Williams; ***D:*** John V. Soto; ***W:*** John V. Soto; ***C:*** Jason Thomas; ***M:*** Thomas Rouch. **VIDEO**

Reclaim **2014 (R)** Formulaic thriller that comes across as 'doing it for the paycheck.' Steven and Shannon travel to Puerto Rico to pick up the Haitian orphan they've adopted, but discover it's a scam. The local cops shrug off the crime until the wealthy Americans are threatened by the crooks, who are involved in human trafficking. **96m/C; DVD, Blu-Ray.** Ryan Phillipe; Rachelle Lefevre; John Cusack; Jacki Weaver; Luis Guzman; ***D:*** Alan White; ***W:*** Luke Davies; ***C:*** Scott Kevan; ***M:*** Inon Zur.

Recoil **1953** Tense Brit crime drama. Jean Talbot (Sellars) witnesses her father's murder by Nicholas Conway (Moore) during a jewel heist. Nicholas works for gangster Farnborough (Benson), but decides to keep some of the gems for himself although Farnborough soon learns of his thievery. Nicholas also uses his unwitting brother Michael (Underdown) as his alibi. So Jean decides to secretly help the police to get evidence to arrest Nicholas, never expecting that both brothers will fall for her. **79m/B; DVD.** *GB* Elizabeth Sellars; Kieron Moore; Edward Underdown; Martin Benson; John Horsley; Robert Reglan; Ian Fleming; ***D:*** John Gilling; ***W:*** John Gilling; ***C:*** Monty Berman; ***M:*** Stanley Black.

Recoil **1997 (R)** L.A. detective Ray Morgan (Daniels) gets in trouble with a crime family and they target his wife and family. So, for Ray it's a kill or be killed situation. **96m/C; VHS, DVD.** Gary Daniels; Gregory McKinney; ***D:*** Art Camacho; ***W:*** Richard Preston, Jr.; ***C:*** Ken Blakey; ***M:*** Tim Wynn. **VIDEO**

Recoil ½ **2011 (R)** Ex-cop Ryan Varrett (Austin) tracks the men who murdered his family to the small town of Hope. It's run by a drug- and gun-dealing biker gang led by Drayke (Trejo), whose brother is the man Ryan wants dead. And if the body count rises, he doesn't care. **93m/C; DVD, Blu-Ray.** Steve Austin; Danny Trejo; Noel Guglielmi; Serinda Swan; Lochlyn Munro; ***D:*** Terry Miles; ***W:*** John Sullivan; ***C:*** Bruce Chun; ***M:*** Eiko Ishiwata. **VIDEO**

Recon 2023: The Gauda Prime Conspiracy **WOOF!** **2008** Bizarre sci fi sequel in which a military squad teams up with a group of robots to destroy an alien super weapon guarded by sand people and mutant chickens. **101m/C; DVD.** Andy (Anderson) Bradshaw; Deke Richards; Heidi Hawkins; John Fallon; ***D:*** Christian Viel; ***W:*** John Fallon; Christian Viel; ***C:*** Tommy Douglas.

Reconstruction **2003** One evening, photographer Alex (Kaas) dumps girlfriend Simone (Bonnevie) to follow blonde Swedish beauty Aimee (also Bonnevie) through the streets of Copenhagen. She's married to an older author, August (Henriksson), who also serves as narrator. Or is August actually narrating the plot of the book he's currently writing? After a one-night stand, Alex's world is completely changed-no one recognizes him and all he can think to do is find Aimee again. Danish and Swedish with subtitles. **91m/C; DVD.** Nikolaj Lie Kaas; Maria Bonnevie; Krister Henriksson; ***D:*** Christoffer Boe; ***W:*** Mogens Rukov; Christoffer Boe; ***C:*** Manuel Alberto Claro; ***M:*** Thomas Knak.

Recount ½ **2008** Just in time for the 2008 presidential election is a retelling of the 2000 election battle and the infamous hanging chads in Florida. Dern is scary as Florida's secretary of state Katherine Harris and Spacey is effective as Al Gore's chief of staff Ron Klain. Actual broadcast news clips are interspersed to show that the entire farcical situation (which was ultimately decided in Florida's Supreme Court) was really that insane. **116m/C; DVD.** Kevin Spacey; Laura Dern; Tom Wilkinson; Bob Balaban; Ed Begley, Jr.; John Hurt; Denis Leary; Bruce McGill; Bruce Altman; Mitch Pileggi; ***D:*** Jay Roach; ***W:*** Danny Strong; ***C:*** Jim Denault; ***M:*** Dave Grusin. **CABLE**

The Recruit ½ **2003 (PG-13)** James Clayton's (Farrell) an MIT graduate who's approached by CIA "talent scout" Walter Burke (Pacino). Walter tells James he has the goods to be a top agent and entices him with the promise of info on his dad, who died in a plane crash. Once on the Farm, the CIA training center, James lmeets beautiful spook-wannabe Layla (Moynahan), who may not be what she appears. Pacino is in full-on scenery-chewing mode, which helps when the plot heads into spy cliche territory. Farrell and Moynihan provide good chemistry, which helps pick up the slack when Pacino's not around. **105m/C; DVD, Blu-Ray.** Al Pacino; Colin Farrell; Bridget Moynahan; Gabriel Macht; Karl Pruner; Eugene Lipinski; ***D:*** Roger Donaldson; ***W:*** Roger Towne; Mitch Glazer; Kurt Wimmer; ***C:*** Stuart Dryburgh; ***M:*** Klaus Badelt.

The Rector's Wife **1994** Anna Bouverie (Duncan) has spent 20 years as a clergyman's wife, scrimping and slaving to raise a family, serve God, and work for the parish on limited means. Tired of the financial strain she takes a job at a local supermarket causing additional disturbances in her already shaky marriage, disapproval of the parish, and the sudden interest of three different men. Based on the novel by Joanna Trollope; on four cassettes. **208m/C; VHS, DVD.** *GB* Lindsay Duncan; Jonathan Coy; Simon Fenton; Lucy Dawson; Joyce Redman; Stephen (Dillon) Dillane; Ronald Pickup; Miles Anderson; Prunella Scales; Jonathan Cecil; ***D:*** Giles Foster; ***W:*** Hugh Whitemore; ***M:*** Richard Hartley.

Red **2008 (R)** Small-town widowed veteran Avery Ludow's best friend is his dog Red. When three teens kill the dog for kicks, Avery first turns to the law and when that fails, he decides to mete out his own justice. Based on the Jack Ketchum novel. **98m/C; DVD.** Tom Sizemore; Noel Fisher; Kyle Gallner; Shiloh Fernandez; Robert Englund; Amanda Plummer; Kim Dickens; Richard Riehle; ***D:*** Lucky McKee; Trygve Allister Diesen; ***W:*** Stephen Susco; ***C:*** Harald Gunnar Paalgard; ***M:*** Soren Hyldgaard.

RED ½ **2010 (PG-13)** Gleeful action/spy comedy with the cast apparently having a fine old time wielding machine guns and kicking bad guy butt. The title stands for 'retired and extremely dangerous,' the status of CIA vet Frank (Willis) who is suddenly fending off a team of hitmen. Frank then reunites with his former colleagues to figure out who wants them dead. Based on the DC Comics graphic novel by Warren Ellis and Cully Hamner. **111m/C; DVD, Blu-Ray.** Bruce Willis; Morgan Freeman; John Malkovich; Dame Helen Mirren; Karl Urban; Mary-Louise Parker; Brian Cox; Julian McMahon; Richard Dreyfuss; James Remar; Ernest Borgnine; Rebecca Pidgeon; ***D:*** Robert Schwentke; ***W:*** Erich Hoeber; Jon Hoeber; ***C:*** Florian Ballhaus; ***M:*** Christophe Beck.

RED 2 ½ **2013 (PG-13)** This sequel that no one really asked for continues the development of the premise that old people acting like action stars is inherently funny. Frank Moses (Willis) returns, aided again by Marvin (Malkovich), Sarah (Parker), and Victoria (Mirren). Director Parisot has no idea how to pace an action-comedy, presenting a choppy, ineffective affair that doesn't work as either genre. It's not exciting enough to be called an action movie and certainly isn't terribly funny. Only the charisma of its stars makes it watchable at all but they're buried under a boring sequel that only makes the first film look like a classic. **116m/C; DVD, Blu-Ray.** Bruce Willis; John Malkovich; Mary-Louise Parker; Dame Helen Mirren; Catherine Zeta-Jones; Anthony Hopkins; Neal McDonough; Brian Cox; Byung-hun Lee; David Thewlis; Tim Pigott-Smith; ***D:*** Dean Parisot; ***W:*** Jon Hoeber; Erich Hoeber; ***C:*** Enrique Chediak; ***M:*** Alan Silvestri.

The Red and the White *Csillagosok, Katonak* **1968** Epic war drama about the civil war between the Red Army and the non-communist Whites in Russia in 1918. Told from the perspective of Hungarians who fought alongside the Reds. Little dialogue. In Hungarian with English subtitles. **92m/B; VHS, DVD.** *HU* Tibor Molnar; Andras Kozak; Josef Madaras; ***D:*** Miklos Jancso; ***W:*** Miklos Jancso; Gyula Hernadi; Giorgi Mdivani; ***C:*** Tamas Somlo.

The Red Badge of Courage ½ **1951** John Huston's adaptation of the Stephen Crane Civil War novel is inspired, despite cutting room hatchet job by the studio. A classic study of courage and cowardice. Sweeping battle scenes and intense personal drama. **69m/B; VHS, DVD.** Audie Murphy; Bill Mauldin; Douglas Dick; Royal Dano; Andy Devine; Arthur Hunnicutt; John Dierkes; Richard Easton; Tim Durant; ***D:*** John Huston; ***W:*** Albert Band; ***C:*** Harold Rosson; ***M:*** Bronislau Kaper.

The Red Baron *Der Rote Baron* **2008 (PG-13)** Biopic of WWI German flying ace Baron Manfred von Richthofen (Schweighoefer) looks good but is flat on storytelling. In 1916, Manfred is the leader of a group of flyers and follows a personal code of honor. This includes rescuing Canadian pilot Capt. Roy Brown (Fiennes) when he gets shot down, which leads to Manfred meeting nurse Kaete (Headey) although the romance is equally dull going. The aerial combat sequences are the only thing of interest. **129m/C; DVD.** *GE* Volker Bruch; Maxim Mehmet; Steffen Schroeder; Matthias Schweighofer; Lena Headey; Til Schweiger; Joseph Fiennes; Brano Holicek; Ralph Misske; ***D:*** Nikolai Muellerschoen; ***W:*** Nikolai Muellerschoen; ***C:*** Klaus Merkel; ***M:*** Dirk Reichardt; Stefan Hansen.

Red Beard *Akahige* **1965** An uncharacteristic drama by Kurosawa, about a young doctor in Japan awakening to life and love under the tutelage of a compassionate old physician. Highly acclaimed; in Japanese with English subtitles. **185m/B; VHS, DVD.** *JP* Toshiro Mifune; Yuzo Kayama; Yoshio Tsuchiya; Reiko Dan; ***D:*** Akira Kurosawa.

Red Blooded American Girl **1990 (R)** A scientist develops a virus that turns people into vampires. Those infected hit the streets in search of blood. **89m/C; VHS, DVD.** *CA* Christopher Plummer; Andrew Stevens; Heather Thomas; Kim Coates; ***D:*** David Blyth.

Red Cliff *Chi Bi* **2008 (R)** Woo's epic historical action-drama is based on a 208 A.D. battle foretelling the end of the 400-year-old Han dynasty. General Coa Coa (Zhang) gets the emperor's permission to crush the rebel warlords Bei Liu (You) and Quan Sun (Chang). Bei's military strategist Zhuge (Kaneshiro) knows they must ally with their rival to survive and parlays with Quan's advisor Zhao (Leung Chiu-wai) to mount a campaign against Coa Coa's numerically-superior forces. In Chinese-speaking territories, Woo released a two-part, four-and-a-half-hour version. Mandarin with subtitles. **131m/C; DVD.** *CH JP NK TW US* Tony Leung Chiu-Wai; Takeshi Kaneshiro; Fengyi Zhang; Chen "Chang Chen" Chang; You Yong; Vicki Zhao; Jun Hu; Shido Nakamura; Ning Wang; Chiling Lin; ***D:*** John Woo; ***W:*** John Woo; Khan Chan; Cheng Kuo; Heyu Sheng; ***C:*** Lu Yue; Li Zhang; ***M:*** Taro Iwashiro.

Red Clover *Leprechaun's Revenge* **2012 (R)** Teenager Karen is hunting in the creepy woods with her crazy grandpa when she finds a red four-leaf clover and picks it up--only to be attacked by some icky leprechaun. The mark of the clover is burned into her skin and Karen starts having nightmares while the creature she's let loose is out killing townsfolk for their gold. Glowing horseshoes are involved so you know you're watching a lame Syfy Channel pic. **89m/C; DVD.** Courtney Halverson; Billy Zane; William Devane; Dave Davis; ***D:*** Drew Daywalt; ***W:*** Anthony C. Ferrante; ***C:*** Robert Morris; ***M:*** Gregory Burkart. **CABLE**

Red Corner ½ **1997 (R)** Wrongman scenario finds Jack (Gere), an American entertainment lawyer on business in China, being framed for murdering the model he spent the night with. Jack's beautiful, court-appointed attorney (Ling) explains the formidable Chinese legal process while gruesome jail scenes and a hell-on-wheels female judge don't help his case much. Pic suffers from some of the usual cliches but is aided by an acclaimed performance by Ling and one of the better recent Gere turns. Beijing was recreated on the DreamWorks studio lot in California. **118m/C; VHS, DVD.** Richard Gere; Bai Ling; Byron Mann; Bradley Whitford; Peter Donat; Robert Stanton; Tsai Chin; James Hong; Tzi Ma; Richard Venture; ***D:*** Jon Avnet; ***W:*** Robert King; ***C:*** Karl Walter Lindenlaub; ***M:*** Thomas Newman.

The Red Danube ½ **1950** Cold War/Red Scare flick with some romance and religion thrown in. British Major John McPhimister (Lawford) works in internationally partitioned post-WWII Vienna on repatriation, which can mean reuniting families or sending unwilling refugees back to the countries they fled. He falls in love with a ballet dancer calling her Maria Buhlen (Leigh), who appears to be wanted by the Soviets. **119m/B; DVD.** Peter Lawford; Janet Leigh; Walter Pidgeon; Angela Lansbury; Ethel Barrymore; Louis Calhern; ***D:*** George Sidney; ***W:*** Gina Kaus; ***C:*** Charles Rosher; ***M:*** Miklos Rozsa.

Red Dawn ½ **1984 (PG-13)** During WWIII, Russian invaders overrun America's heartland and take over the country. Eight small-town teenagers, calling themselves the Wolverines, hide out in the rugged countryside and fight the Russians. Swayze and Grey met again in "Dirty Dancing." **114m/C; VHS, DVD, Blu-Ray.** Patrick Swayze; C. Thomas Howell; Harry Dean Stanton; Powers Boothe; Lea Thompson; Charlie Sheen; Ben Johnson; Jennifer Grey; Ron O'Neal; William (Bill) Smith; ***D:*** John Milius; ***W:*** John Milius; Kevin Reynolds; ***C:*** Ric Waite; ***M:*** Basil Poledouris.

The Red Desert *Il Deserto Rosso* **1964** Antonioni's first color film, depicting an alienated Italian wife who searches for meaning in the industrial lunar landscape of northern Italy, to no avail. Highly acclaimed, and a masterpiece of visual form. In Italian with English subtitles. **120m/C; VHS, DVD, Blu-Ray.** *IT* Monica Vitti; Richard Harris; Carlos Chionetti; ***D:*** Michelangelo Antonioni; ***W:*** Michelangelo Antonioni; Tonino Guerra; ***C:*** Carlo Di Palma; ***M:*** Giovanni Fusco. Venice Film Fest. '64: Film.

Red Dirt ½ **1999** Teenaged cousins Griffith (Montgomery) and Emily (Palladino) spent their days lazying around their Mississippi town, sometimes in the company of their crazy Aunt Summer (Black). That is until the older Lee (Goggins) rents a cottage from the family and Griffith has some confused reactions to the newcomer, much to Emily's dismay. Unfortunately, this coming of age story is tritely told with laborious performances. **111m/C; VHS, DVD.** Dan Montgomery, Jr.; Walton Goggins; Aleksa Palladino; Karen Black; Glenn Shadix; John Mese; Peg O'Keef; *D:* Tag Purvis; *W:* Tag Purvis; *C:* Ted Cohen; *M:* Nathan Barr.

Red Dog 1/2 **2011** Based on the true story of a small red dog who wanders the Australian outback looking for his master and inspiring those he meets. **92m/C; DVD, Blu-Ray.** *AU US* Josh(ua) Lucas; Rachael Taylor; Rohan Nichol; Luke Ford; Arthur Angel; *D:* Kriv Stenders; *W:* Daniel Taplitz; *C:* Geoffrey Hall; *M:* Cezary Skubiszewski. **VIDEO**

Red Doors 1/2 **2005 (R)** A cultural-clash family comedy. A red door is supposed to mean good luck in Chinese culture but it doesn't seem to be working for the Chinese-American Wong family. Dad Ed (Ma) is in a suicidal funk since his retirement, wondering what happened to the three little girls he and his wife (Shen) raised, since they are so absorbed in their own lives and seem oblivious to his pain. Ed suddenly decides to immure himself in a monastery and then the family really gets crazy. **90m/C; DVD.** Tzi Ma; Jacqueline Kim; Freda Foh Shen; Sebastian Stan; Kathy Shao-Lin Lee; Elaine Kao; Jayce Bartok; Rossif Sutherland; Mia Riverton; *D:* Georgia Lee; *W:* Georgia Lee; *C:* Zeus Morand; *M:* Robert Miller.

Red Dragon 1/2 **2002 (R)** Prequel to "Silence of the Lambs" with filmdom's favorite man-eater pitted against former FBI agent Will Graham (Norton). Graham needs the charismatic cannibal to crack the case of a serial killer (Fiennes) dubbed the Tooth Fairy. Graham and Lecter have a history, as Graham helped to put Hannibal away after coming this close to becoming a plate-mate of some fava beans. As usual, Hopkins steals the show and the pic has good character development and a rare look at Lecter before incarceration. Second movie telling of Harris's first Lecter novel, following 1986's "Manhunter." **124m/C; DVD, Blu-Ray, HD-DVD.** Anthony Hopkins; Edward Norton; Ralph Fiennes; Harvey Keitel; Emily Watson; Mary-Louise Parker; Philip Seymour Hoffman; Frankie Faison; Anthony Heald; Bill Duke; Stanley Anderson; Ken Leung; *V:* Ellen Burstyn; *D:* Brett Ratner; *W:* Ted Tally; *C:* Dante Spinotti; *M:* Danny Elfman.

Red Dust **1932** Dennis Carson (Gable) is the overseer of a rubber plantation in Indochina who causes all kinds of trouble when he falls in love with an engineer's (Raymond) new wife, Barbara (Astor). Harlow's the tart also interested in the big lug. Filled with free-spirited humor and skillfully directed; remarkably original. Remade in 1940 as "Congo Maisie" and Gable did his own remake with 1954's "Mogambo," co-starring Ava Gardner and Grace Kelly. **83m/B; DVD.** Clark Gable; Jean Harlow; Mary Astor; Gene Raymond; Donald Crisp; Tully Marshall; *D:* Victor Fleming; *W:* John Lee Mahin. Natl. Film Reg. '06.

The Red Dwarf **1999 (R)** Somewhat mawkish melodramatic fantasy about love-starved dwarf Lucien Lhotte (Thual) who works as a law clerk. He's summoned by aging opera singer Countess Paola Bendoni (Ekberg), who wants a divorce. The duo become improbable lovers, although he's humiliated (and vengeful) when the Countess returns to her husband. Lucien is also innocently loved by young circus acrobat, Isis (Gauzy), and her profession leads Lucien to an unexpected escape from his restricted world. French with subtitles. **101m/B; VHS, DVD.** *FR* Anita Ekberg; Jean-Yves Thual; Dyna Gauzy; Arno Chevrier; *D:* Yvan Le Moine; *W:* Yvan Le Moine; *C:* Danny Elsen; *M:* Alexei Shelegin; Daniel Brandt.

Red 11 **2019** After filmmaker Rob (Attal) borrows money for a project, he learns that the money came from a Mexican drug cartel. To quickly come up with the $7,000 he needs to pay them back, Rob decides to spend a week in a medical lab as a human guinea pig for drug testing. Like the other patients, Rob wears color-coded attire to distinguish what drug he is testing. He soon learns something sinister is occurring at the facility. Made by Rodriguez for $6,800 while shooting Alita: Battle Angel, the thriller suffers from an uninspiring script and boring dialogue despite some interesting ideas. **77m/C; DVD.** Roby Attal; Alejandro Rose-Garcia; Lauren Hatfield; Carlos Gallardo; Jasmine Balais; *D:* Robert Rodriguez; *W:* Robert Rodriguez; Racer Rodriguez; *C:* Robert Rodriguez; *M:* Rebel Rodriguez. **VIDEO**

Red Ensign 1/2 **1934** A low-budget British quota quickie that served as a good apprenticeship for director Powell. Obsessed ship builder David Barr (Banks) is determined to launch a new kind of vessel and save the industry despite the company's board of directors refusing financing. When Barr runs out of his own money, he's caught forging a check and goes to jail while fiancee June (Goodner) stands loyally by, waiting for his release and eventual triumph. **69m/B; DVD.** *GB* Leslie Banks; Carol Goodner; Frank Vosper; Alfred Drayton; Donald Calthrop; Allan Jeayes; *D:* Michael Powell; *W:* Michael Powell; Jerome Jackson; *C:* Leslie Rowson.

Red Eye **2005 (PG-13)** Lisa (McAdams) deftly handles calls, questions, and customers at the front desk of the high-end Miami hotel where she works. Jackson Rippner (Murphy) appears to be like any other guest—until he shows up next to her on her red-eye flight. Turns out she's his target, and Lisa's dad Joe (Cox) and an official of the Department of Homeland Security are at stake if Lisa doesn't figure out how to deal with the high-flying madman. Psychological thrills and chills at high-altitude don't disappoint, with McAdams scoring as a feisty and crafty heroine. **85m/C; DVD, UMD.** Rachel McAdams; Cillian Murphy; Brian Cox; Kyle Gallner; Brittany Oaks; Jack Scalia; ***Cameo(s):*** Wes Craven; Carl Ellsworth; *D:* Wes Craven; *W:* Carl Ellsworth; Dan Foos; *C:* Robert Yeoman; *M:* Marco Beltrami.

Red Faction: Origins **2011** Syfy Channel adaptation of the video game. It's 25 years since Alec Mason (Patrick) led the Mars colonies to freedom, although that also led to the eventual death of his wife and the kidnapping of his daughter. Alec's son Jake (Smith) discovers that his long-lost sister Lyra (Merchant) is still alive but has been trained to be an enemy solider. The two opposing factions could start a fight that undermines the political stability of the planet. **93m/C; DVD.** Brian J. Smith; Tamzin Merchant; Robert Patrick; Gareth David-Lloyd; Kate Vernon; Devon Graye; Danielle Nicolet; *D:* Michael Nankin; *W:* Andrew Kreisberg; *M:* Jonathan Ortega. **CABLE**

Red Firecracker, Green Firecracker 1/2 *Paoda Shuang Deng* **1993 (R)** Set in northern China before the 1911 revolution, this gorgeous saga focuses on the fortunes of the Cai family. The family, whose wealth depends on their fireworks business, has no male heirs and is headed by daughter Chun Zhi (Jing). To assume this lofty position, Chun Zhi must dress like a man and is forbidden to marry but that doesn't stop her from falling in love with bold young travelling artist Nie Bao (Gang). The household is thrown into a frenzy by their affair and it's decided that all Chun Zhi's potential suitors must undergo a firecracker ritual in order to win her hand. Mandarin Chinese with subtitles. **111m/C; VHS, DVD.** *CH CH* Ning Jing; Wu Gang; Zhao Xiaorui; Gai Yang; *D:* He Ping; *W:* Da Ying; *C:* Yang Lun.

The Red Fury **1984** Young Indian boy struggles to overcome prejudice and caring for his horse shows him the way. Good family viewing. **105m/C; VHS, DVD.** William Jordan; Katherine (Kathy) Cannon; *D:* Lyman Dayton; *W:* Joe Elliott; *C:* Arch Bryant; *M:* Merrill Jenson.

Red Garters 1/2 **1954** A musical parody of old-time westerns which doesn't quite come off. Mitchell palys the cowpoke who comes to town to avenge the death of his brother with Clooney as the saloon singer who uses him to make boyfriend Carson jealous. The adequate songs include "Red Garters," "Man and Woman," "A Dime and a Dollar," and "Vaquero." **91m/C; DVD.** Guy Mitchell; Rosemary Clooney; Jack Carson; Gene Barry; Pat(ricia) Crowley; Joanne Gilbert; Frank Faylen; Reginald Owen; Buddy Ebsen; *D:* George Marshall; *W:* Michael Fessier; *C:* Arthur E. Arling; *M:* Joseph J. Lilley.

The Red-Haired Alibi 1/2 **1932** A naive newcomer to the big city, red-haired Lynn keeps gangster Trent Travers company and he uses her as a very visible alibi while his hoods carry out his criminal orders. **72m/B; DVD.** Merna Kennedy; Theodore von Eltz; Grant Withers; Purnell Pratt; Huntley Gordon; Fred Kelsey; Shirley Temple; *D:* Christy Cabanne; *W:* Edward T. Lowe; *C:* Harry Forbes.

Red Headed Woman **1932** Unscrupulous Lil (sultry Harlow in a red wig) vamps her boss Bill Legendre (Morris) into divorcing his wife (Hyams) and marrying her. But then she gets bored and takes up with the wealthier Gaerste (Stephenson), while keeping his chauffeur Albert (Boyer) on the side. Bill finally divorces her and Lil heads for Europe (with Albert) to play among the nobility. Audiences loved the scandalous material, but the Hays Office objected to the fact that the immoral woman goes unpunished. Boyer took the small but notable role in his third American film because of studio MGM's prestige and it made his career. **79m/B; DVD.** Jean Harlow; Chester Morris; Lewis Stone; Leila Hyams; Una Merkel; Henry Stephenson; May Robson; Charles Boyer; Harvey Clark; *D:* Jack Conway; *W:* Anita Loos; *C:* Harold Rosson.

Red Heat 1/2 **1985** Blair is a tourist in East Germany mistakenly arrested and sent to a rough women's prison. Her fiance tries to free her. Meanwhile, she has to deal with tough-lady fellow jail bird Kristel. Familiar and marginal. **104m/C; VHS, DVD.** Linda Blair; Sylvia Kristel; Sue Kiel; William Ostrander; *D:* Robert Collector.

Red Heat **1988 (R)** Two cops—one from the Soviet Union, one from Chicago team up to catch the Eastern Bloc's biggest drug czar. Lots of action, but at times it seems too similar to Hill's earlier hit "48 Hours." Film claims to be the first major U.S. production shot in Red Square, Moscow. **106m/C; VHS, DVD, Blu-Ray.** Arnold Schwarzenegger; James Belushi; Peter Boyle; Ed O'Ross; Laurence Fishburne; Gina Gershon; Richard Bright; *D:* Walter Hill; *W:* Walter Hill; *C:* Matthew F. Leonetti; *M:* James Horner.

Red Hill 1/2 **2010 (R)** Strong contemporary Aussie western. New constable Shane Cooper thinks working for the police department in the small town of Red Hill will mean a quiet life for him and his pregnant wife. However, on Shane's first day convicted murderer, Aborigine Jimmy Conway, escapes from prison and heads to town on a revenge kill with one of his targets being Shane's boss Old Bill Jones. **97m/C; DVD.** *AU* Ryan Kwanten; Tommy (Tom E.) Lewis; Steve Bisley; Christopher Davis; Kevin Harrington; Claire Van Der Boom; *D:* Patrick Hughes; *W:* Patrick Hughes; *C:* Tim Hudson; *M:* Dimitri Golovko.

Red Hook Summer **2012 (R)** Spike Lee returns to Brooklyn for his sixth film, set in the New York borough he knows and loves in this divisive quasi-sequel to "Do the Right Thing" that centers on a young man (Brown) who is forced to spend a summer with his preacher grandfather (Peters). When Lee is vibrantly painting a portrait of a community he clearly feels passionate about or commenting on how religion can be used as a crutch against personal responsibility, his film works. But a controversial final act twist is misguided, as are multiple subplots and unconnected scenes that give a feeling of improvisation. **121m/C; DVD, Blu-Ray.** Jules Brown; De'Adre Aziza; Clarke Peters; Nate Parker; Thomas Jefferson Byrd; Heather Alicia Simms; Toni Lysaith; James E. Ransome; Spike Lee; *D:* Spike Lee; *W:* Spike Lee; James McBride; *C:* Kerwin Devonish; *M:* Bruce Hornsby.

The Red House **1947** Robinson plays a crippled farmer who, after his daughter brings home a suitor, attempts to keep everyone from a mysterious red house located on his property. Madness and murder prevail. Strange film noir about tangled relationships and unsuccessful attempts to bury the horrid past. Based on the novel by George Agnew Chamberlain. **100m/B; VHS, DVD, Blu-Ray.** Edward G. Robinson; Lon (Bud) McCallister; Judith Anderson; Allene Roberts; Rory Calhoun; Ona Munson; Julie London; Harry Shannon; Arthur Space; Walter Sande; Pat Flaherty; *D:* Delmer Daves; *W:* Delmer Daves; *C:* Bert Glennon; *M:* Miklos Rozsa.

The Red Inn *L'Auberge Rouge* **1951** Yes, it is a comedy. An innkeeper and his wife have a second career involving the robbery and murder of stagecoach travellers staying at their isolated inn. And it's up to a monk (Fernandel) to stop the mayhem. French with subtitles. Yves Montand sings on the soundtrack. **95m/B; VHS, DVD, Streaming.** *FR* Fernandel; Francoise Rosay; Julien Carette; Gregoire Aslan; Marie-Claire Olivia; Lud Germain; *D:* Claude Autant-Lara; *W:* Jean Aurenche; Pierre Bost; *C:* Andre Bac; *M:* Rene Cloerec.

Red Joan **2019 (R)** A biopic of Joan Stanley, a British physics student who funneled nuclear bomb secrets to the Russians in the 1940s. Forty years later, she was arrested by the MI5 as a spy. It's a fascinating true story, full of international intrigue, undercover ops, and life-or-death consequences, but the screenplay reduces her to a lovesick patsy. The real onscreen crime is the sparsity and brevity of Dench's scenes as the elderly Stanley. Read Jennie Rooney's novel of the same name instead. **101m/C; DVD, Blu-Ray.** Dame Judi Dench; Sophie Cookson; Stephen Campbell Moore; Tom Hughes; Ben Miles; *D:* Trevor Nunn; *W:* Lindsay Shapero; *C:* Zac Nicholson; *M:* George Fenton.

Red Kimono **1925** Exploitative silent melodrama about a young woman ditched by her husband. She becomes a prostitute, but is redeemed by true love. Interesting slice of its period. **95m/B; Silent; VHS, DVD.** Tyrone Power, Sr.; Priscilla Boner; Nellie Bly Baker; Mary Carr; *D:* Walter Lang.

Red Letters **2000 (R)** The plot veers wildly but the performances are worth a watch. Widowed college prof Dennis Burke (Coyote) has an eye for the ladies. He flirts with the dean's sexy young daughter, Gretchen (Balk), and is so taken with the imprisoned Lydia (Kinski) that he helps her escape so she can prove her innocence in a murder conviction. Not a good idea. **102m/C; VHS, DVD.** Peter Coyote; Nastassja Kinski; Fairuza Balk; Jeremy Piven; Ernie Hudson; Udo Kier; *D:* Bradley Battersby; *W:* Bradley Battersby; Tom Hughes; *C:* Steven Fierberg. **VIDEO**

Red Light 1/2 **1949** Trucking company owner John Torno is targeted by Nick Cherney, an ex-employee who went to prison for embezzlement. Nick starts his revenge plan by having John's priest brother, Jess, murdered. A missing Gideon bible figures into the plot, which never amounts to much. **83m/B; DVD.** George Raft; Raymond Burr; Virginia Mayo; Gene Lockhart; Harry (Henry) Morgan; Arthur Franz; *D:* Roy Del Ruth; *W:* George Callahan; *C:* Bert Glennon; *M:* Dimitri Tiomkin.

Red Lights *Feux rouges* **2004** Troubled couple embarks on a trip to pick up their children from camp. They argue viciously as hubby repeatedly stops to drink along the way. When the missus finally ditches him and takes the train, the volatile and smashed husband continues by car but picks up an ominous stranger. Story of a man who regains his dignity through surprisingly violent twist of fate. Terrific French thriller in the vein of Hitchcock, with solid acting and direction. **106m/C; VHS, DVD.** *FR* Jean-Pierre Darroussin; Carole Bouquet; Jean-Pierre Gos; *D:* Cedric Kahn; *W:* Cedric Kahn; *C:* Patrick Blossier; *M:* Arvo Part.

Red Lights 1/2 **2012 (R)** De Niro gets to bring out the ham with his performance as blind psychic Simon Silver, who also has telekinetic abilities, in director Cortes' creepy, slick horror flick. Tom Buckley (Murphy) and Margaret Matheson (Weaver) are a couple of scientists devoted to debunking the odd with rational explanations. They meet Silver and things turn, well, unbelievable as the ending undermines what's gone before. **113m/C; DVD, Blu-Ray, Streaming.** *US SP* Cillian Murphy; Sigourney Weaver; Robert De Niro; Toby Jones; Joely Richardson; Elizabeth Olsen; *D:* Rodrigo Cortés; *W:* Rodrigo Cortés; *C:* Xavi Gimenez; *M:* Victor Reyes.

The Red Lily **1924** Marise La Noue (Bennett) is a poor cobbler's daughter while her beau, Jean Leonnec (Navarro), is the son of the mayor. To be together they must run away to Paris and Jean promises to meet Marise at the train station so they can be married. But fate intervenes and they are destined to spend years apart with Marise forced into prostitution while Jean falls in with thief Bo-Bo (Beery). When they finally reunite, both are bitterly disappointed although Marise still comes to Jean's aid when the police come after him. **80m/B; Silent; DVD.** Enid Bennett; Ramon Novarro; Wallace Beery; Frank Currier; Mitchell Lewis; ***D:*** Fred Niblo, Jr.; ***W:*** Bess Meredyth; ***C:*** Victor Milner.

Red Line 1/2 **1996 (R)** Stock-car racer Jim (McQueen) loses his sponsorship, turns to petty crime to settle his debts, and winds up in trouble with the mob when he hooks up with a couple of hoods to steal some diamonds. **102m/C; VHS, DVD.** Chad McQueen; Michael Madsen; Corey Feldman; Jan-Michael Vincent; Roxana Zal; Dom DeLuise; Julie Strain; Robert Z'Dar; ***D:*** John Sjogren; ***W:*** John Sjogren; Scott Ziehl; Rolfe Kanefsky; ***C:*** Kevin McKay; ***M:*** Craig Carothers; Junior Walker.

Red Line 1/2 **2013 (R)** Generic thriller. Passengers aboard an L.A. subway train are trapped in a tunnel by an explosion. As some look for anything to help the injured as they wait for rescue, they find an IED with an hour left on the timer. Passenger Al is picked as the terrorist and is beaten to get him to confess and disarm the device, but he swears he's innocent, so what do they do next? **87m/C; DVD.** Nicole Gale Anderson; Kunal Sharma; John Billingsley; Keena Ferguson; ***D:*** Robert Kirbyson; ***W:*** Robert Kirbyson; ***C:*** Robert Kirbyson; ***M:*** Alan Derian. **VIDEO**

Red Line 7000 **1965** High stakes auto racers drive fast cars and date women. Excellent racing footage in otherwise routine four-wheel fest. **110m/C; VHS, DVD, Blu-Ray.** James Caan; Laura Devon; Gail Hire; Charlene Holt; Marianna Hill; George Takei; ***D:*** Howard Hawks; ***C:*** Milton Krasner.

Red Lion 1/2 *Akage* **1969** A bumbling horse-tender in feudal Japan impersonates a military officer to impress his family, only to be swept into leading a liberating revolution. In Japanese with English subtitles. **115m/C; VHS, DVD.** *JP* Toshiro Mifune; Shima Iwashita; ***D:*** Kihachi Okamoto.

Red Meat 1/2 **1998** Stefan (Slattery) and Chris (Mailer) are the last remaining members of the Red Meat Club, buddies who get together for macho posturing over steak dinners. This time, they run into Victor (Frain) who's been out of touch. Stefan and Chris boast of their dating games (which are shown in flashback) and then it's Victor's turn to regale them with a lurid sexual saga. Only Victor's story involves his tender relationship with a dying woman, Ruth (Boyle). **94m/C; VHS, DVD.** James Frain; John Slattery; Steven Mailer; Lara Flynn Boyle; Jennifer Grey; Traci Lind; ***D:*** Allison Burnett; ***W:*** Allison Burnett; ***C:*** Charlie Lieberman.

The Red Menace **WOOF!** **1949** Anti-Communist propaganda, made with unknown actors in documentary style has little to offer today's viewers other than unintentional laughs. Picture the Commies offering naive Americans money and sex to join the party, and you'll have an idea of the intellectual talent that went into this one. **87m/B; DVD, Blu-Ray.** Robert Rockwell; Hannelore Axman; Shepard Menken; Betty Lou Gerson; Barbara Fuller; ***D:*** R.G. Springsteen; ***W:*** Albert DeMond; Gerald Geraghty; ***C:*** John MacBurnie; ***M:*** Nathan Scott.

Red Mercury 1/2 **2005 (R)** Three Islamic terrorists, planning a London bombing, have their cover blown and flee into a Greek restaurant, taking hostages. They're still carrying materials for their dirty bomb but the tension heightens as time passes and the bombers are forced to interact with their hostages as the police and government officials await the outcome. Rather too talky and obvious. **113m/C; DVD.** *GB* Stockard Channing; Ron Silver; Pete Postlethwaite; Juliet Stevenson; David Bradley; Nigel Terry; Navin Chowdhry; Honeysuckle Weeks; Alex Caan; San Shella; ***D:*** Roy Battersby; ***W:*** Farrukh Dhondy; ***C:*** Colin Towns; Uday Tiwari. **VIDEO**

The Red Mill **1927** Makes good use of Davies' comedic talents as she portrays Cinderella-like Dutch barmaid Tina, who hopes that handsome newcomer Dennis (Moore) will be her Prince Charming. Instead, he falls for her friend Gretchen (Faenda), the burgomaster's daughter, who is being forced into an arranged marriage. When Tina and Dennis interfere, the burgomaster locks all three into the haunted mill of the title. Loosely based on the Victor Herbert operetta. Davies championed the hiring of a post-scandal Arbuckle as director, through he used the pseudonym "William Goodrich" for the film's release. **73m/B; Silent; DVD.** Marion Davies; Owen Moore; George Siegmann; Karl (Daen) Dane; Snitz Edwards; Louise Faenda; ***D:*** Fatty Arbuckle; ***W:*** Frances Marion; ***C:*** Hendrik Sartov.

Red Planet 1/2 **2000 (PG-13)** It's 2050, Earth is dying, and the crew of the Mars-1 has been sent to the red planet to find out what went wrong with a previous colonization mission. Something goes wrong again (those pesky gamma rays), and the crew are forced to shuttle to the surface of Mars, where yet another mishap leaves them stranded. Then, the crew's AMEE (Autonomous Mapping Evaluation and Evasion) robot turns nasty and intends to further endanger them and their mission. Heavy with visual effects, but the film tries to keep the focus on the human elements. **110m/C; VHS, DVD, Blu-Ray.** Val Kilmer; Tom Sizemore; Carrie-Anne Moss; Benjamin Bratt; Simon Baker; Terence Stamp; ***D:*** Antony Hoffman; ***W:*** Jonathan Lemkin; Chuck Pfarrer.

Red Planet Mars **1952** Anti-communist, pro-Christianity story about scientists discovering that the Voice of Radio Free Mars belongs to God. Incoherent film overburdened with messages about politics, religion, and science was ahead of its time. Based on the play "Red Planet" by John L. Balderson and John Hoare. **87m/B; VHS, DVD.** Peter Graves; Andrea King; Marvin Miller; Herbert Berghof; House Peters, Jr.; Vince Barnett; ***D:*** Harry Horner; ***W:*** Anthony Veiller; John Lloyd Balderston.

The Red Pony **1949** A young boy escapes from his family's fighting through his love for a pet pony. Based on the novel by John Steinbeck. Timeless classic that the whole family can enjoy. **89m/C; DVD, Blu-Ray.** Myrna Loy; Robert Mitchum; Peter Miles; Louis Calhern; Shepperd Strudwick; Margaret Hamilton; Beau Bridges; ***D:*** Lewis Milestone; ***W:*** John Steinbeck; ***C:*** Gaetano Antonio "Tony" Gaudio; ***M:*** Aaron Copland.

Red Riding Hood 1/2 **1988** Musical version of story of wolf who has little girl fetish. **81m/C; VHS, DVD.** Isabella Rossellini; Craig T. Nelson; Rocco Sisto; ***D:*** Adam Brooks; ***W:*** Carole Lucia Satrina; ***C:*** Yuri Neyman; ***M:*** Stephen Lawrence.

Red Riding Hood **2003 (R)** Freakshow fairytale. Jenny (Satta) is a 12-year-old American who has been abandoned in a Rome apartment by her mother. She watched her politician father get assassinated, which obviously twisted her little psyche since Jenny roams the streets handing out her own brand of vigilante justice. She's accompanied by a big bad wolf named George (Dipascasio), who could be a figment of her crazy imagination. Then Granny (Archebald) shows up to take the little darling home, but Jenny's got other plans. English and Italian with subtitles. **90m/C; DVD.** *IT* Susan Satta; Kathleen Archebald; Simone K. Dipascasio; Iaon Gunn; Roberto Purvis; Marco Firini; Justine Powell; ***D:*** Giacomo Cimini; ***W:*** Ovidio G. Assonitis; Andrew Benker; ***C:*** Sergio Salvati; Roberto Benvenuti; ***M:*** Alessandro Molinari.

Red Riding Hood 1/2 **2011 (PG-13)** Beautiful Seyfried bats those big baby blues and we're as lost as any wolf in this tame, swoony version of the Little Red Riding Hood fairytale. Teenaged Valerie plans to run away with orphaned woodcutter Peter (Fernandez) rather than marry blacksmith Henry (Irons) until her sister is killed by the werewolf who lives in the woods surrounding their medieval village. Hunter Father Solomon (Oldman) informs the villagers that the werewolf can assume human form and could be anyone, which rouses Valerie's suspicions. That big red cape sure is pretty as is the movie itself. **100m/C; DVD, Blu-Ray, On Demand.** Amanda Seyfried; Shiloh Fernandez; Max Irons; Gary Oldman; Julie Christie; Michael Shanks; Billy Burke; Virginia Madsen; Lukas Haas; ***D:*** Catherine Hardwicke; ***W:*** David Leslie Johnson; ***C:*** Mandy Walker; ***M:*** Brian Reitzell; Alex Heffes.

Red Riding, Part 1: 1974 **2009** Deeply disturbing contemporary noir, the first in a trilogy (from three different directors), that was originally filmed for British TV's Channel 4 and based on four crime novels from David Pearce. Events are inspired by the sadistic murders of young girls and women in Yorkshire with Riding referring to the trio of administrative areas in the county. In this first film, cocky Leeds crime reporter Eddie Dunford links a series of torture deaths of little girls together, leading him to surly police detective Bill Molloy, one of the coppers bought off by powerful local developer John Dawson, who commit and cover-up various crimes. Also involved are vicar Martin Laws, young rent boy BJ, and grieving mother Paula Garland. **102m/C; DVD, Blu-Ray, On Demand.** *UK* Sean Bean; Warren Clarke; Andrew Garfield; David Morrissey; Sean Harris; Rebecca Hall; Robert Sheehan; Tony Mooney; Eddie Marsan; Peter Mullan; ***D:*** Julian Jarrold; Peter Mullan; ***W:*** Tony Grisoni; ***C:*** Rob Hardy; ***M:*** Adrian Johnston.

Red Riding, Part 2: 1980 **2009** After a second series of murders occur, this time on women, the Home Office is dismayed by the pace of the Yorkshire investigation and sends in Manchester outsider Peter Hunter to conduct an internal review that includes resentful detective Bob Craven. Local on-the-take detective Maurice Jobson also takes a more active role as does vicar Martin Laws. **93m/C; DVD, Blu-Ray, On Demand.** *UK* Paddy Considine; Maxine Peake; Andrew Garfield; David Morrissey; Tony Pitts; Peter Mullan; Robert Sheehan; Sean Harris; Tony Mooney; Warren Clarke; James Fox; Sean Bean; Eddie Marsan; Joseph Mawle; ***D:*** James Marsh; ***W:*** Tony Grisoni; ***C:*** Igor Martinovic; ***M:*** Dickon Hinchliffe.

Red Riding, Part 3: 1983 **2009** In the final film, another young girl goes missing, involving remorseful Leeds detective Maurice Jobson and lawyer John Piggott as well as scared rent boy BJ, who turns out to be a witness to some of the crimes. They all get closer to the overwhelming police corruption and cover-ups as well as to exposing another killer. **100m/C; DVD, Blu-Ray, On Demand.** *UK* Mark Addy; David Morrissey; Peter Mullan; Robert Sheehan; Sean Harris; Tony Mooney; Lisa Howard; Warren Clarke; Andrew Garfield; Sean Bean; Daniel Mays; ***D:*** Anand Tucker; ***W:*** Tony Grisoni; ***C:*** David Higgs; ***M:*** Barrington Pheloung.

Red River **1948** The classic Hawks epic about a gruelling cattle drive and the battle of wills between father and son. Tom Dunston (Wayne), who owns a sprawling cattle empire, decides to make a difficult trek north, refusing to listen to any advice from his adopted son, Matthew Garth (Clift, in his first film). Matt is eventually forced to take over the drive from the obsessed Dunston, who swears revenge. Generally regarded as one of the best westerns ever made, with a great supporting cast headed by Brennan and Ireland, although Dru is a very nominal love interest. Restored version has eight minutes of previously edited material. Remade for TV in 1988 with James Arness and Bruce Boxleitner. **133m/B; DVD, Blu-Ray.** John Wayne; Montgomery Clift; Walter Brennan; Joanne Dru; John Ireland; Noah Beery, Jr.; Paul Fix; Coleen Gray; Harry Carey, Jr.; Harry Carey, Sr.; Chief Yowlachie; Hank Worden; ***D:*** Howard Hawks; ***W:*** Borden Chase; Charles Schnee; ***C:*** Russell Harlan; ***M:*** Dimitri Tiomkin. Natl. Film Reg. '90.

Red Road **2006** Debut feature for Brit helmer Arnold heightens suspense but fumbles the ending. Widowed Jackie (Dickie) works for a private security firm monitoring cameras that maintain surveillance on a rough North Glasgow neighborhood. She becomes obsessed watching ex-con Clyde (Curran) and his friends, who live in the decrepit Red Road housing estate. She contrives to meet him but it turns out Jackie has specific reasons for her interest in Clyde and they aren't going to make him happy. **113m/C; DVD.** *GB CZ* Tony Curran; Martin Compston; Nathalie Press; Kate Dickie; Andrew Armour; ***D:*** Andrea Arnold; ***W:*** Andrea Arnold; ***C:*** Robbie Ryan.

Red Rock West 1/2 **1993 (R)** Nothing is what it seems in this stylish and entertaining film noir set in a desolate Wyoming town. Perennial loser and nice guy Michael (Cage) is headed to a job at an oil rig, but blows his chance by admitting he has a bad leg. Landing in the tiny burg of Red Rock, he's mistaken for the hit man hired by local barkeep Walsh to kill his pretty wife (Boyle). Then Boyle doubles Walsh's offer—what's a film noir boy to do? And Hopper, the real killer, strides into town. Full of twists and turns, this enjoyable, well-acted thriller is a real gem that escaped directly to cable before being rescued by a San Francisco exhibitor. **98m/C; DVD.** Nicolas Cage; Dennis Hopper; Lara Flynn Boyle; J.T. Walsh; Timothy Carhart; Dan Shor; Dwight Yoakam; Bobby Joe McFadden; Craig Reay; Vance Johnson; Robert Apel; Dale Gibson; Ted Parks; Babs Bram; Robert Guajardo; Sarah Sullivan; ***D:*** John Dahl; ***W:*** John Dahl; Rick Dahl; ***C:*** Marc Reshovsky; ***M:*** William Olvis.

Red Roses and Petrol 1/2 **2003 (R)** Flashbacks and home videos are used to fill in details of the life of patriarch Enda Doyle (McDowell) as his widow and estranged children reunite at his Dublin wake. Dysfunctional family revelations are all too commonplace. Based on a play by Joseph O'Connor. **97m/C; DVD.** Malcolm McDowell; Olivia Tracey; Heather Jurgenson; Max Beesley; Greg Ellis; Susan Lynch; Arie Verveen; Sean Lawlor; Catherine Farrell; ***D:*** Tamar Simon Hoffs; ***W:*** Tamar Simon Hoffs; Gail Wager Stayden; ***C:*** Nancy Schreiber; ***M:*** Seth Pedowitz.

Red Sands *The Stone House* **2009 (R)** In Afghanistan, a group of soldiers is dispatched to take control of a road that runs past an abandoned house. They find an ancient stone statue and destroy the relic by using it for target practice but they've released a supernatural force that proves to be deadly. **89m/C; DVD.** Callum Blue; Noel Guglielmi; Shane West; Brendan Miller; Leonard Roberts; Aldis Hodge; Theo Rossi; ***D:*** Alex Turner; ***W:*** Simon Barrett; ***C:*** Sean O'Dea; ***M:*** Luke Rothschild. **VIDEO**

Red Scorpion **1989 (R)** A Soviet soldier journeys to Africa where he is to assassinate the leader of a rebel group. Will he succeed or switch allegiances? Poor acting and directing abound. **102m/C; VHS, DVD, Blu-Ray, UMD.** Dolph Lundgren; M. Emmet Walsh; Al White; T.P. McKenna; Carmen Argenziano; Brion James; Regopstann; ***D:*** Joseph Zito; ***W:*** Arne Olsen; Jack Abramoff; Robert Abramoff; ***C:*** Joao Fernandes; ***M:*** Jay Chattaway.

Red Serpent *Blood Money* **2002 (R)** A group of criminals tries hijacking drugs from a train guarded by a KGB squad and predictably things go bad. The KGB commander ends up with a dead family, a job shoveling elephant poop in the circus, and a certain need for revenge. He gets his chance when the bad guys kidnap the daughter of an American businessman. **90m/C; DVD.** Michael Paré; Roy Scheider; Oleg Taktarov; Alexander Nevsky; ***D:*** Gino Tanasescu; ***W:*** Alex Kustanovich; ***C:*** Andrei Zhegalov; ***M:*** Kenneth Burgomaster.

Red Shadow *Akakage* **2001** Director Hiroyuki Nakano parodies ninja films with this remake of a 60's TV series (which was itself based on a manga). Red Shadow, Blue Shadow, and Asuka are beginner ninjas under the tutelage of their master White Shadow. When one of them is killed, the other two decide to go their own way to get revenge. Ninja fans looking for gore and non-stop violence will be disappointed as this is more of a slapstick satire (though the second half is darker in tone once the revenge plot takes hold). **108m/C; DVD.** *JP* Mansanobu Ando; Megumi Okina; Kumiko Aso; Jun Murakami; Naoto Takenaka; Fumiya Fujii; Shuhei Mainoumi; Kei Tani; Ryoko Shinohara; Kitaro; Denden; Shigeru Koyama; Seizo Fukomoto; ***D:*** Takashi Miike; ***W:*** Hiroyuki Nakano; ***C:*** Mitsuteru Yokoyama; ***M:*** Tomoyasu Hotei.

Red Shoe Diaries **1992 (R)** After a woman's suicide her grieving lover discovers her diaries and finds out she led a secret erotic life, revolving around her shoe-salesman lover and a pair of sexy red shoes. Also available in an unrated version. **105m/C; VHS, DVD.** David Duchovny; Billy Wirth; Brigitte Bako; ***D:*** Zalman King. **CABLE**

Red Shoe Diaries 2: Double Dare **1992 (R)** The erotic sequel to "Red Shoe Diaries" follows the libidinous fancies of three women. Severance begins a sexual affair with a stranger only to be torn between love and lust. Johnson gets naked to tease an office worker in the building next door. Crosby is a cop who is rejected by the man she desires—so she arrests and handcuffs him in order to play some kinky games. Also available in an unrated version. **92m/C; VHS, DVD, Streaming.** Joan Severance; Laura Johnson; Denise Crosby; Steven Bauer; Arnold Vosloo; David Duchovny; ***D:*** Zalman King; Tibor Takacs. **CABLE**

Red Shoe Diaries 3: Another Woman's Lipstick ♂♂ **1993 (R)** Another sexual anthology focusing on three stories of desire. In "Another Woman's Lipstick" Zoey finds out her husband is having an affair and follows him to his liaison—only to become intrigued with his lover herself. "Just Like That" finds the up-tight Trudie falling for two very opposite men. "Talk to Me Baby" finds Ida and her lover Bud caught up in a very obsessional relationship. Also available in an unrated version. **90m/C; VHS, Streaming.** Nina Siemaszko; Matt LeBlanc; Tcheky Karyo; Maryam D'Abo; Richard Tyson; Lydie Denier; Christina (Kristina) Fulton; Kevin Haley; David Duchovny; ***D:*** Ted Kotcheff; Rafael Eisenman; Zalman King; ***W:*** Zalman King; Chloe King. **CABLE**

Red Shoe Diaries 4: Auto Erotica ♂♂ **1993 (R)** Yet another compilation of erotic tales courtesy of the Zalman King series. The first story finds a maid finding her employer's secret chamber and uncovering a very private fantasy. The second has an architect lured by a mystery woman into a game of seduction and the third finds a couple engaged in competitive obsessions. Also available in an unrated version. **83m/C; VHS, DVD, Streaming.** Ally Sheedy; Scott Plank; David Duchovny; Sheryl Lee; Nick (Nicholas) Chinlund; ***D:*** Zalman King. **CABLE**

Red Shoe Diaries 5: Weekend Pass ♂♂ **1995 (R)** Yet another erotic saga from the cable series that features a model (Barbieri) hustling a pool hustler, a bounty hunter (Stansfield) becoming captivated by her prey, and an army recruit (Pouget) whose furlough involves a sexy drifter. **85m/C; VHS, DVD, Streaming.** Paula Barbieri; Claire Stansfield; Ely Pouget; Francesco Quinn; Ron Marquette; Anthony Addabbo; ***D:*** Ted Kotcheff. **CABLE**

Red Shoe Diaries 6: How I Met My Husband ♂♂ **1995 (R)** Three more erotic vignettes from the cable series. "How I Met My Husband" finds Alice enrolling in a course on becoming a domanitrix and falling for Giuseppe, who's one of the training objects. Camille has inherited her father's vast fortune in "Naked in the Moonlight" on the condition that she take special care of his '57 Cadillac convertible—and the one mechanic allowed to work on the car. In "Midnight Bells," Claire reminisces about the mystery lover she meets on only one night of the year—New Year's Eve. **85m/C; VHS, DVD, Streaming.** Luigi Amodeo; Neith Hunter; Raven Snow; Carsten Norgaard; John Enos; Charlotte Lewis; David Duchovny; ***D:*** Anne Goursaud; Philippe Angers; Bernard Auroux. **CABLE**

Red Shoe Diaries 7: Burning Up ♂♂ **1996 (R)** Yet another trilogy of TV eroticism. "Burning Up" finds Lynn becoming obsessed with a handsome fireman, "Kidnap" features the workaholic Sara taken hostage during a bank robbery and finding out that her captor has decided to marry her, Alia is a top model in "Runway," who falls in lust with a cabby. **90m/C; VHS, DVD, Streaming.** Udo Kier; Ron Marquette; Jennifer Ciesar; Amber Smith; Anthony Guidera; Daniel Blasco; Alexandra Tydings; David Duchovny; ***D:*** Rafael Eisenman. **CABLE**

Red Shoe Diaries 8: Night of Abandon ♂♂ **1997 (R)** Three more erotic adventures from the cable series. "Night of Abandon" finds Isabelle visiting her grandma in Rio de Janeiro and indulging in Carnival. "Liar's Table" has photojournalist Corey assigned to record L.A.'s sex scene and becoming intrigued by a very expensive call girl. Married Kathryn's life changes "In the Blink of an Eye" when she meets a young boxer who's in training with her husband. **86m/C; VHS, DVD.** Erika Anderson; Audie England; Daniel Leza; Ann Cockburn; Terrence Sheahan; Laurie Simpson; Julien Maurel; Brian Edwards; David Duchovny; ***D:*** Rafael Eisenman; Rene Manzor; James Gavin Bedford. **CABLE**

Red Shoe Diaries: Four on the Floor ♂♂ **1996** The late-night cable series continues with three more stories concerning a psychiatrist and her patient, two couples stranded on a rainy night, and the meeting of a rap star and a dancer. Contents:" The Psychiatrist," "Four on the Floor," "Emily's Dance." **85m/C; DVD.** Denise Crosby; Georges Corraface; Christopher Atkins; Jsu Garcia; David Duchovny; Demetra Hampton; Rachel Palieri; Freedom Williams; Marry Morrow; Kent Masters-King; ***D:*** Rafael Eisenman; Zalman King; David Womark; ***W:*** Richard Baskin; Nellie Allard; Joelle Bentolila; ***C:*** Etienne Fauduet; Manuel Teran; Marco Mazzei; ***M:*** George S. Clinton. **CABLE**

Red Shoe Diaries: Luscious Lola ♂♂ ½ **2000** In these three stories, shy Mimi (Phillips) fantasizes about winning her dream guy; a sailor on shore leave winds up with more women than he can handle; and a young woman toys with men. **87m/C; DVD.** Bobbie Phillips; Michael C. Bendetti; Christina (Kristina) Fulton; Perrey Reeves; Ernie Banks; John Enos; Joseph Whipp; David Duchovny; Andrew Bilgore; Heidi Mark; Michael Reilly Burke; ***D:*** Zalman King; Stephen Halbert; ***W:*** John Enos; Chloe King; Pascal Franchot; Elize D'Haene; ***C:*** Eagle Egilsson; David Stockton; ***M:*** George S. Clinton. **CABLE**

Red Shoe Diaries: Strip Poker ♂♂ **1996** Contains the episodes "Strip Poker," "Slow Train," "Hard Labor". **87m/C; DVD.** Athena Massey; Jennifer Ciesar; Carolyn Seymour; David Duchovny; Anfisa Nezinskaya; Larisa Tipikina; Andrew Calder; Mark Suelke; Maximo Morrone; ***D:*** Zalman King; Rafael Eisenman; ***W:*** Zalman King; Patricia Louisianna Knop; Julie Marie Myatt; Elize D'Haene; ***C:*** Eagle Egilsson; Alexei Rodionov; ***M:*** George S. Clinton. **CABLE**

Red Shoe Diaries: Swimming Naked ♂♂ ½ **2000** The mother of all late-night cable series is still the artsiest. As such, these stories about a lifeguard, a skydiver, and a dancer are told with lots of smoke and gauzy focus. Contents: "Swimming Naked," "Jump," "Tears." **83m/C; DVD.** Michael Woods; Cyia Batten; Carolyn Seymour; Arabella Holzbog; David Duchovny; Kristi Frank; Omry Reznik; Sonya Ryzy-Ryski; Todd Gordon; Daniel Ezralow; ***D:*** Zalman King; Rafael Eisenman; ***W:*** Zalman King; Melanie Finn; Chloe King; Katarina Wittich; Kathryn MacQuarrie; ***C:*** Eagle Egilsson; David Knaus; ***M:*** George S. Clinton. **CABLE**

The Red Shoes ♂♂♂♂ **1948** British classic about a young ballerina torn between love and success. Boris Lermontov (Walbrook) is the impresario of a ballet company who hires dancer Victoria Page (Shearer) and composer Julian Craster (Goring), giving them the chance at a new ballet inspired by the Hans Christian Andersen fairy tale. But when the endeavor becomes a major success, Boris become jealous over the closeness that develops between his proteges. Noted for the 20-minute ballet at the heart of the film and for the lavish use of Technicolor. **136m/C; DVD.** *UK* Anton Walbrook; Moira Shearer; Marius Goring; Leonide Massine; Robert Helpmann; Albert Bassermann; Ludmilla Tcherina; Esmond Knight; ***D:*** Emeric Pressburger; Michael Powell; ***W:*** Emeric Pressburger; Michael Powell; ***C:*** Jack Cardiff; ***M:*** Brian Easdale. Oscars '48: Art Dir./Set Dec., Color, Orig. Dramatic Score; Golden Globes '49: Score.

The Red Shoes ♂♂ *Bunhongsin* **2005** Korean horror film based on a fairy tale by Hans Christian Andersen, though you wouldn't know that by watching it. Sun Jae leaves her cheating husband and moves with her daughter into an old apartment building. She finds a pair of red high heels on the subway and takes them home, not knowing they are cursed to destroy anyone they come in contact with. The race is on to discover the origin of the shoes and somehow end the curse before everyone dies. **103m/C; DVD.** *NK* Hye-su Kim; Seong-su Kim; Yeon-ah Park; ***D:*** Yong-gyun Kim; ***W:*** Yong-gyun Kim; Ma Sang-Ryeol; ***M:*** Byung-woo Lee.

Red Siren ♂ ½ *La Sirene Rouge* **2002 (R)** A 12-year-old girl tells the French police her mother is a murderer and asks for them to take her to her father in Portugal. She has no evidence so the police can't touch her mother, who sends a paramilitary force to fetch her daughter who has since given up on the police and is now relying on a hitman for protection. **119m/C; DVD.** *FR* Jean-Marc Barr; Asia Argento; Frances Barber; Andrew Tiernan; Vernon Dobtcheff; ***D:*** Olivier Megaton; ***W:*** Olivier Megaton; ***C:*** Denis Rouden.

Red Skies of Montana ♂♂ **1952** Tragedy occurs when smoke jumpers die in a forest fire in the Montana mountains. The only survivor, Cliff Mason (Widmark), can't remember what happened, but young Ed Miller (Hunter) accuses Cliff of cowardice. The Forestry Serivce has Cliff training new recruits, including Ed, and Cliff must then take his rookies to battle another blaze. The plot's standard but the fire action is exciting. **98m/C; DVD.** Richard Widmark; Jeffrey Hunter; Constance Smith; Richard Boone; Warren Stevens; ***D:*** Joseph M. Newman; ***W:*** Harry Kleiner; ***C:*** Charles G. Clarke; ***M:*** Sol Kaplan.

Red Sky ♂ **2014 (PG-13)** Top gun pilots are dishonorably discharged after following some questionable orders. They're later given the chance to clear their names by recovering a WMD. A couple of decent action sequences don't make up for the plot clichés. **108m/C; DVD, Blu-Ray.** Cam Gigandet; Shane West; Rachael Leigh Cook; Brian Krause; Troy Garity; ***D:*** Mario Van Peebles; ***W:*** Mario Van Peebles; Adam Prince; ***C:*** Ronald Hersey; ***M:*** Tim Williams. **VIDEO**

The Red Sneakers ♂♂ ½ **2001** Reggie Reynolds (Pappion) is a high-school math whiz who figures he'll get more respect as a basketball star. He meets junkman Zeke (Hines), who gives Reggie a pair of worn red high-tops that he insists were worn by a legendary Harlem hoopster. When Reggie puts the shoes on, he suddenly seems to have inherited all the skill of their former owner and is suddenly drawing lots of attention as a star player. But there's a price to be paid. **109m/C; VHS, DVD.** Gregory Hines; Vincent D'Onofrio; Vanessa Bell Calloway; Dempsey Pappion; Ruben Santiago-Hudson; Philip Akin; ***D:*** Gregory Hines; ***W:*** Mark Saltzman; ***C:*** John Berrie; ***M:*** Stanley Clarke. **CABLE**

Red Snow ♂ **1991** High in the Cascade Mountains, Kyle Lewis is the new snowboard instructor for the Hurricane Ridge Ski Resort. The job is fine in the beginning, until Kyle learns of the tragic fate of the last instructor. Before he knows it, Kyle is the next target and is framed for two murders. He secures the help of his fellow snowboard buddies in hopes of solving the mystery and getting the girl, too. High speed ski scenes and dangerous stunts are the film's only redeeming qualities. **86m/C; VHS, Streaming.** Carlo Scandiuzzi; Scott Galloway; Darla Haun; Mitchell Cox; Tamar Tibbs; Brian Mahoney; ***D:*** Phillip J. Roth.

Red Sonja ♂ ½ **1985 (PG-13)** Two warriors join forces against an evil queen in this sword and sorcery saga. Big, beautiful bodies everywhere, with Bergman returning from her Conan adventures. Little humor, few special effects, and weak acting make this a poor outing. **89m/C; VHS, DVD.** Arnold Schwarzenegger; Brigitte Nielsen; Sandahl Bergman; Paul Smith; ***D:*** Richard Fleischer; ***M:*** Ennio Morricone. Golden Raspberries '85: Worst New Star (Nielsen).

Red Sparrow ♂♂ ½ **2018 (R)** With her ballerina dreams crushed, Dominika Egorova (Lawrence) is recruited by the Russian government to join the Sparrows, an elite intelligence agency that uses sex and manipulation (and horrifyingly, a potato peeler) as weapons. Lawrence gives it her all physically and emotionally, even if her accent sometimes drifts into Natasha's moose-and-squirrel territory. It's Haythe's script that fails to rise to the movie's potential -- twists and turns are mandatory for spy stories, but the plot is too convoluted to capitalize on them. Based on the book by Jason Matthews. **140m/C; DVD, Blu-Ray.** Jennifer Lawrence; Joel Edgerton; Matthias Schoenaerts; Charlotte Rampling; Mary-Louise Parker; ***D:*** Francis Lawrence; ***W:*** Justin Haythe; ***C:*** Jo Willems; ***M:*** James Newton Howard.

Red State ♂♂ **2011 (R)** Director Kevin Smith takes a step in a new direction with this entry in the horror genre. After being lured by internet siren Sara (Leo), three horny teenagers are kidnapped by extreme right-wing preacher Abin Cooper (Parks) and his lunatic congregation. The flock has gotten the attention of an ATF agent (Goodman) and a sketchy sheriff (Root), however. The inevitable bloody showdown features a high body count and some surprising twists. Smith chose to release the film independently in protest to the studio distribution system. **88m/C; DVD, Blu-Ray, On Demand.** Michael Parks; John Goodman; Stephen (Steve) Root; Michael Angarano; Kyle Gallner; Nicholas Braun; Melissa Leo; ***D:*** Kevin Smith; ***W:*** Kevin Smith; ***C:*** David Klein.

Red Sun ♂♂ **1971** A gunfighter, a samurai, and a French bandit fight each other in various combinations in the 1860s. Ludicrous and boring. **115m/C; VHS, DVD.** *FR IT SP* Charles Bronson; Toshiro Mifune; Alain Delon; Ursula Andress; ***D:*** Terence Young; ***W:*** William Roberts; ***M:*** Maurice Jarre.

Red Surf ♂♂ **1990 (R)** Action abounds in this surfer film. A couple of hard-nosed wave-riders get involved with big money drug gangs and face danger far greater than the tide. **104m/C; VHS, DVD.** George Clooney; Doug Savant; Dedee Pfeiffer; Gene Simmons; Rick Najera; Philip McKeon; ***D:*** H. Gordon Boos; ***W:*** Vincent Robert; ***C:*** John Schwartzman; ***M:*** Sasha Matson.

Red Tails ♂♂ ½ **2012 (PG-13)** Executive producer George Lucas brings this tale of African-American fighter squadron, the Tuskegee Airmen, to the big screen after 23 years in development limbo, but these heroes are brought down by the script. The film alternates between the efforts of the pilots' commanders (Howard, Gooding) to get the unit a meaningful combat mission and the exploits of the flyers, led by hothead "Lightning" (Oyelowo) and squadron leader "Easy" (Parker). The aerial dogfight scenes are spectacular, but the overall shine is dulled with characters that are one-dimensional and dialogue that would seem trite in a WWII-era B-movie. **125m/C; DVD, Blu-Ray.** Terrence Howard; Cuba Gooding, Jr.; Nate Parker; David Oyelowo; Ne-Yo; Tristan Wilds; Bryan Cranston; Lee Terjesen; ***D:*** Anthony Hemingway; ***W:*** John Ridley; Aaron McGruder; ***C:*** John Aronson; ***M:*** Terence Blanchard.

Red Tent ♂♂♂ *Krasnaya Palatka* **1969 (G)** A robust, sweeping man-versus-nature epic based on the true story of the Arctic stranding of Italian explorer Umberto Nobile's expedition in 1928. A Russian-Italian co-production. **121m/C; DVD.** Sean Connery; Claudia Cardinale; Peter Finch; Hardy Kruger; Massimo Girotti; Luigi Vannucchi; ***D:*** Mikhail Kalatozov; ***M:*** Ennio Morricone.

The Red Tent ♂♂ **2014** Biblical melodrama from Lifetime, based on Anita Diamant's bestseller. The emphasis is on Jacob's wives and his one daughter, Dinah, who share their rituals under a red tent. When Jacob wants to return to his home in Canaan, family strife follows as Dinah catches the eye of a prince and her brothers increasingly resent youngest son Joseph. The changes from the Old Testament version may upset the faithful. **176m/C; DVD.** Rebecca Ferguson; Minnie Driver; Morena Baccarin; Debra Winger; Iain Glen; Will Tudor; ***D:*** Roger Young; ***W:*** Elizabeth Chandler; Anne Meredith; ***C:*** Michael Snyman; ***M:*** Laurent Eyquem. **CABLE**

The Red Turtle ♂♂♂ *La tortue rouge* **2017 (PG)** The first non-Japanese film produced by Studio Ghibli continues their emphasis on man's relationship to the natural world. Michael Dudok de Wit's dialogue-less animated fairy tale is the story of a man who wakes up on a deserted island. He tries to build a raft to escape, but a red turtle keeps stopping him from doing so, destroying that which he builds. The turtle dies, turning into a woman, with whom the man forms a relationship. This is a simple, daring film, which tells a story through pictures without a single word spoken. **80m/C; DVD, Blu-Ray.** *BE FR FR* ***D:*** Michael Dudok de Wit; ***W:*** Michael Dudok de Wit; Pascale Ferran; ***M:*** Laurent Perez Del Mar.

The Red Violin ♂♂ ½ *Le Violon Rouge* **1998 (R)** Spans 300 years in the life of one famed musical instrument that winds up in present-day Montreal on the auction block. Crafted by the Italian master Bussotti (Cecchi) in 1681, the red violin derives its unusual color from the human blood mixed into the finish. With this legacy, the violin travels to Austria, England, China, and Canada, leaving both beauty and tragedy in its wake. Most of the vignettes are dull, with the Montreal-set framing story holding the most interest. **131m/C; VHS, DVD.** *CA* Samuel L. Jackson; Don McKellar; Carlo Cecchi; Irene Grazioli; Jean-Luc Bideau; Jason Flemyng; Greta Scacchi; Christoph Koncz; Sylvia Chang; Colm Feore; Monique Mercure; Liu Zi Feng; ***D:*** Francois Girard; ***W:*** Don McKellar; Francois Girard; ***C:*** Alan Dostie; ***M:*** John Corigliano. Oscars '99: Orig. Score; Genie '98: Art Dir./Set Dec., Cinematog., Costume Des., Director (Girard), Film, Score, Screenplay.

Red Water 🦴 **2001 (R)** Sanders is a Louisiana fisherman and ex-oil company worker who hooks up with his scientist wife to find natural gas in a Louisiana river. At the same time, gangsters and an ex-con are heading to the same place looking for buried loot, and a freshwater shark picks the spot as well, looking for a human buffet. The too-complicated plot only serves as a reason for everyone to show up and become shark bait for the ridiculously fake-looking maneater. If you're gonna spend time watching a shark movie, make it "Jaws" instead of this made-for-TV waste. **92m/C; VHS, DVD.** Lou Diamond Phillips; Kristy Swanson; Coolio; Jaimz Woolvett; ***D:*** Charles Robert Carner; ***W:*** J.D. Feigelson; Chris Mack; ***C:*** Michael Goi. **TV**

Red: Werewolf Hunter 🦴 **1/2 2010** Syfy Channel original has FBI agent Virginia bringing home fellow agent/fiance Nathan to meet her family and learn their secret. They're descendents of Little Red Riding Hood and werewolf hunters. Rogue werewolf Gabriel breaks a peace pact between humans and werewolves so Virginia has to go hunting, especially after Nathan is bitten and becomes a potential threat. There's more melodrama than bloody horror, so it's not nearly as frightening as it should be. **88m/C; DVD.** Felicia Day; Kavan Smith; Stephen McHattie; Rosemary Dunsmore; Greg Bryk; David Reale; ***D:*** Sheldon Wilson; ***W:*** Brook Durham; ***C:*** Russ Goozee; ***M:*** Stacey Hersh. **CABLE**

Red White & Blue 🦴 **1/2 2010** Every night, nympho Erica (Fuller) picks up a different guy in a bar and has a one-night stand. Nate (Taylor), who lives in the same boarding house and admits to a violent past, takes an interest but Erica won't have sex with him. Instead, she beds would-be rocker Franki (Senter) and eventually goes missing, prompting Nate to investigate. Cult Brit director Rumley filmed his derivative slasher pic in Austin, Texas. **104m/C; DVD.** *GB* Noah Taylor; Amanda Fuller; Marc Senter; Sally Jane Jackson; Nick Ashy Holden; Patrick Crovo; Jon Michael Davis; ***D:*** Simon Rumley; ***W:*** Simon Rumley; ***C:*** Milton Kam; ***M:*** Richard Chester.

Redacted 🦴🦴 **2007 (R)** A group of soldiers find themselves in increasingly brutal and amoral situations, culminating in the group rape and murder of a 15-year-old girl. Izzy Diaz (Salazar), who's filming his experiences in Iraq in hopes of getting into film school, is disgusted but fears retribution if he reports them. DePalma uses true stories from the Iraq War as inspiration and a "fictional documentary" technique, in which the entire film appears to be composed of various assembled footage. Story is powerful but ultimately heavy-handed, and the performances are inconsistent. Intense, depressing, and divisive, pic received accusations of anti-American bias and bombed at the box office. **90m/C; DVD, On Demand.** *US CA* Kel O'Neill; Pat Carroll; Izzy Diaz; Rob Devaney; Daniel Stewart Sherman; Ty Jones; ***D:*** Brian De Palma; ***W:*** Brian De Palma; ***C:*** Jonathan Cliff.

Redbelt 🦴🦴🦴 **1/2 2008 (R)** Gulf War vet Mike Terry's (Ejiofor) a small-time L.A. jujitsu instructor who follows the strict code of honor of a samurai. Money worries cause ethical dilemmas when a Hollywood action star (Allen, in a surprisingly venomous role) and his producer (Mantegna) offer to pay Mike for ideas they plan on stealing. Terrific performances all around, especially from Ejiofor. Writer/director Mamet wisely takes a philosophical approach, rather than making a formulaic fight flick, and shelves his usual twists and trickery for a story that's human and honest. (Still, the fight scenes are pretty cool.) **99m/C; DVD, Blu-Ray, On Demand.** Chiwetel Ejiofor; Alice Braga; Tim Allen; Emily Mortimer; Rodrigo Santoro; Joe Mantegna; Rebecca Pidgeon; David Paymer; Ricky Jay; Jose Pablo Cantillo; Ray "Boom Boom" Mancini; Maximillian Martini; John Machado; ***D:*** David Mamet; ***W:*** David Mamet; ***C:*** Robert Elswit; ***M:*** Stephen Endelman.

Redeemer 🦴🦴 **1/2 2002** Paul Freeman is a writing teacher in a prison program who decides to help inmate Charles Henderson (Babatunde), an articulate ex-Black Panther serving life for murder. After 20 years, Charles wants to write a letter to his victim's sister, Sharon Davidson (Greene), asking her forgiveness. The reaction to the letter turns out to be a catalyst for a second chance for each of them. **90m/C; VHS, DVD.** Matthew Modine; Obba Babatunde; Michele Greene; ***D:*** Graeme Clifford; ***W:*** James Ricci; ***C:*** Norayr Kasper; ***M:*** Frankie Blue. **CABLE**

Redemption 🦴🦴 **1/2 2013 (R)** Statham makes a solid return to drama, proving again that he has more range than the action vehicles he stars in usually allow him to display. Writer Knight's directorial debut is the tale of a soldier dealing with serious PTSD and hiding on the London streets from a potential court martial. When Joey literally crashes into an apartment that he learns will be abandoned for the season, he steals an identity and tries to right his past wrongs with the help of a beautiful nun named Cristina (Buzek). **100m/C; DVD, Blu-Ray.** *UK* Jason Statham; Agata Buzek; Vicky McClure; Benedict Wong; Ger Ryan; ***D:*** Steven Knight; ***W:*** Steven Knight; ***C:*** Chris Menges; ***M:*** Dario Marianelli.

Redemption: Kickboxer 5 🦴 *Kickboxer 5* **1995 (R)** Retired kickboxer Matt Reeves (Dacascos) goes after the scum who murdered a friend. No surprises here. **87m/C; VHS, DVD.** Mark Dacascos; James Ryan; ***D:*** Kristine Peterson; ***M:*** John Massari.

The Redemption of General Butt Naked 🦴 **1/2 2011** Documentary covers the unlikely conversion of Liberian warlord Joshua Milton Blahyl, who was responsible for unbelievable atrocities and the slaughter of some 20,000 people during the country's civil war as his army forcibly recruited child soldiers. The flamboyant Blahyl underwent a self-proclaimed conversion to become an evangelical preacher offering public amends and rehabilitation. He was forced to flee the country after being granted amnesty for testifying before the Truth and Reconciliation Commission. **85m/C; DVD.** ***D:*** Eric Strauss; Daniele Anastasion; ***C:*** Eric Strauss; Peter Hutchens; Ryan Hill; ***M:*** Justin Melland.

Redemption Road 🦴🦴 *Black, White and Blues* **2010 (PG-13)** Down-and-out blues musician Jefferson Bailey (Simpson) takes off on a road trip from Texas to Alabama after a relative leaves him an inheritance. He's accompanied by the mysterious Augie (Duncan) and both men have some issues to work through as you might gather from the title. **95m/C; DVD.** Morgan Simpson; Michael Clarke Duncan; Kiele Sanchez; Tom Skerritt; Luke Perry; Taryn Manning; Melvin Van Peebles; ***D:*** Mario Van Peebles; ***W:*** Morgan Simpson; George Richards; ***C:*** Matthew Irving; ***M:*** Tree Adams.

Redemption Trail 🦴🦴 **2013** Tess, the daughter of a murdered Black Panther revolutionary, lives off the grid as a Sonoma vineyard manager. Reluctant to have emotional ties, Tess still gives refuge to desperate Anna, who has attempted suicide. The two find themselves forming an unlikely bond as they redefine themselves in this simple drama. **91m/C; DVD.** Lisa Gay Hamilton; Lily Rabe; Hamish Linklater; Jake Weber; ***D:*** Britta Sjogren; ***W:*** Britta Sjogren; ***C:*** Bradley Sellers; ***M:*** Mark Orton. **VIDEO**

The Redhead from Wyoming 🦴🦴 **1/2 1953** Spirited sagebrush adventure with fiery-tempered O'Hara as a saloon proprietress with feelings for both a local cattle rustler and the town's sheriff. Based on a story by James. **81m/C; VHS, DVD.** Maureen O'Hara; Alex Nicol; William Bishop; Robert Strauss; Alexander Scourby; Jack Kelly; Jeanne Cooper; Dennis Weaver; Stacy Harris; ***D:*** Lee Sholem; ***W:*** Polly James; Herb Meadow.

Redline 🦴🦴 *Deathline* **1997 (R)** John Wade (Hauer) is double-crossed and murdered by his partner Merrick (Dacascos), who's involved with a Russian crime syndicate. But Wade is resurrected as a bionically enhanced creation and hunts for revenge in a seedily futuristic Moscow. **96m/C; VHS, DVD.** Rutger Hauer; Mark Dacascos; Yvonne Scio; ***D:*** Tibor Takacs; Brian Irving; ***W:*** Tibor Takacs; Brian Irving; ***C:*** Zoltan David; ***M:*** Guy Zerafa. **VIDEO**

Redline 🦴 **2007 (PG-13)** Self-financed and distributed by real estate tycoon Sadek, this action pic is most notable for its conspicuous consumption. Dissolute Michael (Macfadyen) instigates an illegal $100 million winner-take-all race with high-rollers Infamous (Griffin), a rapper, and movie producer Jerry (Matheson), and such drivers as the vengeful Natasha (Bjorlin) and daredevil Jason (Johnson). Plot—such as it is—is an excuse to watch some of the world's most expensive cars become scrap metal. **95m/C; DVD.** Nathan Phillips; Angus MacFadyen; Tim Matheson; Eddie Griffin; Nadia Bjorlin; Jesse Johnson; Barbara Niven; Louis Mandylor; Denyce Lawton; Neill Skylar; ***D:*** Andy Cheng; ***W:*** Richard Foreman; ***C:*** Bill Butler; ***M:*** Ian Honeyman; Andrew Raiher.

Redneck Zombies 🦴 **1988 (R)** A bunch of backwoods rednecks become zombies after chug-a-lugging some radioactive beer. Eating local tourists becomes a hard habit to break. Betcha can't have just one! **83m/C; VHS, DVD.** Lisa DeHaven; W.E. Benson; Floyd Piranha; William-Livingston Dekkar; Zoofeet; James Housely; Anthony Burlington-Smith; Martin J. Wolfman; Boo Teasdale; Darla Deans; Tyrone Taylor; Frank Lantz; Pericles Lewnes; ***D:*** Pericles Lewnes; ***W:*** Fester Smellman; ***C:*** Ken Davis; ***M:*** Adrian Bond.

Reds 🦴🦴🦴 **1981 (PG)** The re-creation of the life of author John Reed ("Ten Days that Shook the World"), his romance with Louise Bryant, his efforts to start an American Communist party, and his reporting of the Russian Revolution. A sweeping, melancholy epic using dozens of "witnesses" who reminisce about what they saw. See director Sergei Eisenstein's silent masterpiece "Ten Days that Shook the World," based on Reed's book, for the Russian view of some of the events depicted in Beatty's film. **195m/C; VHS, DVD, Blu-Ray, HD-DVD.** Warren Beatty; Diane Keaton; Jack Nicholson; Edward Herrmann; Maureen Stapleton; Gene Hackman; Jerzy Kosinski; George Plimpton; Paul Sorvino; William Daniels; M. Emmet Walsh; Dolph Sweet; Josef Sommer; ***D:*** Warren Beatty; ***W:*** Warren Beatty; ***C:*** Vittorio Storaro; ***M:*** Dave Grusin; Stephen Sondheim. Oscars '81: Cinematog., Director (Beatty), Support. Actress (Stapleton); British Acad. '82: Support. Actor (Nicholson), Support. Actress (Stapleton); Directors Guild '81: Director (Beatty); Golden Globes '82: Director (Beatty); L.A. Film Critics '81: Cinematog., Director (Beatty), Support. Actress (Stapleton); Natl. Bd. of Review '81: Director (Beatty), Support. Actor (Nicholson); N.Y. Film Critics '81: Film; Natl. Soc. Film Critics '81: Support. Actress (Stapleton); Writers Guild '81: Orig. Screenplay.

Reducing 🦴🦴 **1931** Polly owns a ritzy New York beauty and reducing salon and when her Midwestern sister Marie's family falls on hard times, she offers her a job and the chance to live with Polly and her daughter Joyce. Joyce is dating wealthy Johnnie but Marie's daughter Vivian makes a play for him. **77m/B; DVD.** Marie Dressler; Polly Moran; Anita Page; Sally Eilers; William "Buster" Collier, Jr.; Lucien Littlefield; William "Billy" Bakewell; ***D:*** Charles Reisner; ***W:*** Beatrice Banyard; William Mack; ***C:*** Leonard Smith.

Redwoods 🦴🦴 **2009** Everett (Bradley) and Miles (Coughenour) are long-term partners, raising their son Billy. Everett thinks the relationship has stagnated and when Miles and Billy are away, he stays home and starts a flirtation with writer Chase (Montgomery) who is driving through Northern California. Their attraction is instantaneous but neither man may be able to deal with more than a vacation fling. **90m/C; DVD.** Matthew Montgomery; Brendan Bradley; Tad Coughenour; Laurie Burke; ***D:*** David Lewis; ***W:*** David Lewis; ***C:*** Joe Rivera; ***M:*** Jack Curtis Dubowsky. **VIDEO**

The Reeds 🦴 **1/2 2009 (R)** Murky and muddled Brit horror. Three London couples go on a weekend boating trip through the Norfolk Broads tidewater but run their boat aground. While one goes for help, the others discover skeletons caged and chained to the river floor and then they are hunted by something terrifying coming out of the reeds. **90m/C; DVD.** *GB* Geoff Bell; Daniel Caltagirone; Emma Catherwood; Karl Ashman; Anna Brewster; ***D:*** Nick Cohen; ***W:*** Chris Baker; Simon Sprackling; ***C:*** Dennis Madden; ***M:*** Vincent Watts.

The Reef 🦴🦴 **2010 (R)** Suspenseful people vs. sharks plot. Luke meets his friends to take them sailing around the Great Barrier Reef. The boat gets damaged and overturns and soon everyone has to make a decision: hope they get rescued before it sinks or swim to a not-so-nearby island. Either way they face attack by the sharks that are starting to circle. **94m/C; DVD.** *AU* Damian Walshe-Howling; Gyton Grantley; Adrienne Pickering; Zoe Naylor; Mark Simpson; Kieran Darcy-Smith; ***D:*** Andrew Traucki; ***W:*** Andrew Traucki; ***C:*** Daniel Ardilley; ***M:*** Rafael May.

Reef 2: High Tide 🦴 **1/2 2012 (PG)** Sequel to the animated feature The Reef. Fish Pi (Bell) and Cordelia (Philipps) have become parents to a new son Junior (Jonas), but Pi's shark enemy Troy (Logue) is free and on the hunt with his shark gang. Because Troy's attack will come with high tide, Pi begins to train his family and others on the reef in water fu so they are prepared for the attack. Pi's plan is disrupted by a spy sent by Troy in the form of a new reef fish, Ronny (Kennedy). Soon after, Troy kidnaps Cornelia, setting off a search for the missing fish and a wider plan to save everyone on the reef. **80m/C; DVD, Blu-Ray.** Drake Bell; Busy Philipps; Frankie Jonas; Donal Logue; Jamie Kennedy; ***D:*** Mark Dippe; Taedong Park; ***W:*** Chris Denk; Johnny Hartmann; ***M:*** Todd Haberman. **VIDEO**

Reefer Madness WOOF! *Tell Your Children; Dope Addict; Doped Youth; Love Madness; The Burning Question* **1938 (PG)** Considered serious at the time of its release, this low-budget depiction of the horrors of marijuana has become an underground comedy favorite. Overwrought acting and lurid script contribute to the fun. **67m/B; VHS, DVD, Blu-Ray.** Dave O'Brien; Dorothy Short; Warren McCollum; Lillian Miles; Thelma White; Carleton Young; Josef Forte; Harry Harvey, Jr.; Pat Royale; ***D:*** Louis Gasnier; ***W:*** Paul Franklin; Arthur Hoerl; ***C:*** Jack Greenhalgh; ***M:*** Abe Meyer.

Reel Love 🦴 **1/2 2011** CMT cable rom com with a familiar story and a lot of fishing gags (as you can tell from the title). Southern gal Holly (Rimes) heads home from the big city after her fishing-obsessed dad Wade (Reynolds) has a heart attack. She has to hang around town where she starts a 'catch and release' romance with hunky Jay (Roberts) although maybe neither of them really wants to go free. **90m/C; DVD.** LeAnn Rimes; Burt Reynolds; Shawn Roberts; Christian Potenza; Jeff Roop; ***D:*** Brian K. Roberts; ***W:*** Sharon Weil; ***C:*** Gerald Packer; ***M:*** Carlos Lopes. **CABLE**

Reel Paradise 🦴🦴🦴 **2005 (R)** Follows film industry insider, John Pierson, and his family during the final month of a one-year sabbatical in Taveuni, Fiji, from their suburban New York home. In Taveuni, the Piersons established the self-proclaimed "most remote theatre in the world" in the 180 Meridian Cinema, Taveuni's 52-year-old 288-seat theatre. Taps into the unbridled enthusiasm as the local Fijians pack the seats to view such films as "Jackass: The Movie" (later banned in Fiji), "Apocalypse Now Redux," "Bend it Like Beckham" and the Hindi film "Kaante." With free admission, the Piersons received little support from the Local Catholic mission—apparently the films were in competition with attendance at religious services. **110m/C; DVD.** ***D:*** Steve James; ***C:*** P.H. O'Brien; ***M:*** Norman Arnold.

Reet, Petite and Gone 🦴🦴🦴 **1947** All-Black musical featuring the music of neglected jive singer Louis Jordan, and his band, The Tympany Five. A girl's mother dies; sneaky lawyer tries to cheat her. Slick and enjoyable. **75m/B; VHS, DVD.** Louis Jordan; June Richmond; ***D:*** William Forest Crouch.

The Ref 1993 (R) The couple from hell turn the tables on Gus (Leary), a hard-nosed fugitive who takes Caroline (Davis) and her husband Lloyd (Spacey) hostage. Gus then finds himself trapped in the traditional Christmas ordeal of a family suffering from industrial-strength dysfunction. He plots his getaway while masquerading as the couple's marriage counselor, hence the film's title. This sometimes brutal, frequently hysterical satire of male-female relationships, family ties, and compulsory holiday rituals uses consistently sharp dialogue and superb acting to tell an absurd but convincing tale. **97m/C; VHS, DVD.** Denis Leary; Judy Davis; Kevin Spacey; Glynis Johns; Robert J. Steinmiller, Jr.; Christine Baranski; Raymond J. Barry; Richard Bright; J.K. Simmons; ***D:*** Ted (Edward) Demme; ***W:*** Richard LaGravenese; Marie Weiss; ***C:*** Adam Kimmel; ***M:*** David A. Stewart.

The Reflecting Skin 1991 In a 1950s prairie town a small boy sees insanity, child-murder, and radiation sickness, leading him to fantasize that the tormented young widow next door is a vampire. The pretentious drama/freak show rationalizes its ghastly events as symbolizing the hero's loss of youthful innocence. But the Hound knows the score; this is "Faces of Death" for the arts crowd, a grotesque menagerie that dares you to watch. The exploding-frog opener is already notorious. Beautiful photography, with vistas inspired by the painting of Andrew Wyeth. **116m/C; VHS, DVD, Blu-Ray.** *GB* Viggo Mortensen; Lindsay Duncan; Jeremy Cooper; Duncan Fraser; Shiela Moore; David Longworth; Robert Koons; David Bloom; Evan Hall; ***D:*** Philip Ridley; ***W:*** Philip Ridley; ***C:*** Dick Pope; ***M:*** Nick Bicat.

A Reflection of Fear *Labyrinth* 1973 Young Marguerite has been secluded in the grim family mansion with her mother and grandmother. Her only companion is a doll Marguerite believes can kill. The girl loses all semblance of sanity when her estranged dad Michael suddenly shows up with his girlfriend Anne. The doll has a weird sexual vibe as well. **89m/C; VHS, DVD.** Sondra Locke; Robert Shaw; Sally Kellerman; Mary Ure; Signe Hasso; Mitchell Ryan; ***D:*** William A. Fraker; ***W:*** Lewis John Carlino; Edward Hume; ***C:*** Laszlo Kovacs; ***M:*** Fred Myrow.

Reflections 1/2 2008 Generally predictable Euro-thriller. Interpol agent Tom Brindle heads to Barcelona when a body turns up and is apparently the work of serial killer Pygmalion. DNA evidence brings in soldier Marco Soler for questioning but Marco insists the killer is his estranged twin brother. Brindle then asks shrink Elena to figure out if the troubled Marco is telling the truth. **94m/C; DVD.** *SP* Timothy Hutton; Dominik Garcia-Lorido; Miguel Angel Silvestre; Tania Sarrias; Fernando Guillen-Cuervo; Ivana Mino; ***D:*** Bryan Goeres; ***W:*** Jay Beattie; ***C:*** Jacques Haitkin; ***M:*** Sean Murray. **VIDEO**

Reflections in a Golden Eye 1/2 1967 Huston's film adaptation of Carson McCullers novel about repressed homosexuality, madness, and murder at a Southern Army base in 1948. Star-studded cast cannot consistently pull off convoluted lives of warped characters; not for everyone, though it holds some interest. **109m/C; VHS, DVD, Blu-Ray.** Elizabeth Taylor; Marlon Brando; Brian Keith; Julie Harris; ***D:*** John Huston; ***C:*** Oswald Morris.

Reform Girl 1/2 1933 Lydia isn't reformed when she gets out of prison since she joins a gang of crooks trying to frame honest politico Putnam. It's only when Lydia falls for Putnam's campaign manager Joe that she decides to go straight and then discovers a secret about her own past. **70m/B; DVD.** Noel Francis; Richard "Skeets" Gallagher; Hale Hamilton; Dorothy Peterson; Robert Ellis; DeWitt Jennings; ***D:*** Sam Newfield; ***W:*** George Wallace Sayre; ***C:*** Harry Forbes.

Reform School Girls 1986 (R) Satiric raucous women's prison film, complete with tough lesbian wardens, brutal lesbian guards, sadistic lesbian inmates, and a single, newly convicted heterosexual heroine. Wendy O. Williams as a teenager? Come on. Overdone, over-campy, exploitative. **94m/C; VHS, DVD.** Linda Carol; Wendy O. Williams; Pat Ast; Sybil Danning; Charlotte McGinnis; Sherri Stoner; ***D:*** Tom De Simone; ***W:*** Tom De Simone; ***C:*** Howard Wexler.

The Reformer and the Redhead 1950 Lawyer Andrew (Powell) is running for mayor on a political reform platform. Kathleen Maguire (Allyson) is upset that her zoo keeper father (Kellaway) lost his job because of political cronyism and works with Andrew until she discovers he's more ambitious than noble. Two full-grown lions--one a pet named Herman and one a zoo escapee--figure into the light-hearted comedy. **90m/B; DVD.** Dick Powell; June Allyson; David Wayne; Cecil Kellaway; Ray Collins; Robert Keith; ***D:*** Melvin Frank; Norman Panama; ***W:*** Melvin Frank; Norman Panama; ***C:*** Ray June; ***M:*** David Raksin.

Regarding Henry 1991 (PG-13) A cold-hearted lawyer gets shot in the head during a holdup and survives with memory and personality erased. During recovery the new Henry displays compassion and conscience the old one never had. Though too calculated in its yuppie-bashing ironies, the picture works thanks to splendid acting and low-key, on-target direction. **107m/C; VHS, DVD.** Harrison Ford; Annette Bening; Bill Nunn; Mikki Allen; Elizabeth Wilson; Robin Bartlett; John Leguizamo; Donald Moffat; Nancy Marchand; ***D:*** Mike Nichols; ***W:*** J.J. (Jeffrey) Abrams; ***C:*** Giuseppe Rotunno; ***M:*** Hans Zimmer.

Regeneration 1915 Irish hoodlum Owen (Fellowes) is saved from his life of crime by social worker Mamie Rose (Nilsson). Walsh filmed on location in New York's Bowery district and used actual gangsters in roles. Also features the 10-minute 1910 short "The Police Force of New York City," produced by Thomas Edison. **72m/B; Silent; VHS, DVD.** Rockliffe Fellowes; Anna Q. Nilsson; ***D:*** Raoul Walsh; ***W:*** Raoul Walsh; Carl Harbaugh; ***C:*** Georges Benoit. Natl. Film Reg. '00.

Regina 1/2 *Regina Roma* 1983 A woman controls all the activities of her husband and son. At age 36, her son is ready to leave home and she refuses to let him. Fine performances in this strange and disturbing film. **86m/C; VHS, DVD.** *IT* Anthony Quinn; Ava Gardner; Ray Sharkey; Anna Karina; ***D:*** Jean-Yves Prate.

Regression 2016 (R) John Gray (Dencik) cannot recall having done the crime his daughter Angela (Watson) implicates him in, nonetheless he admits to being guilty. Hawke plays Det. Bruce Kenner who teams up with psychologist Dr. Raines (Thewlis) to probe the mystery, which involves delving into Angela's memories. All of which eventually leads to more questions and the exposure of a wider conspiracy possibly involving Satanic rituals. While Watson and Hawke work well together, this thriller is less than thrilling. **106m/C; DVD, Blu-Ray.** Emma Watson; Ethan Hawke; David Thewlis; Aaron Ashmore; Devon Bostick; ***D:*** Alejandro Amenabar; ***W:*** Alejandro Amenabar; ***C:*** Daniel Aranyo; ***M:*** Rocque Banos.

Regular Guys 1/2 *Echte Kerle; Real Men* 1996 Macho Frankfurt cop Christoph (Ohrt) gets blindingly drunk after discovering his girlfriend with another guy. She kicks him out—sans belongings—and after a very long night, Christoph wakes up in the bed of stud car mechanic, Edgar (Bergmann). Christoph can't remember anything and Edgar won't say if something happened between them, although he agrees to let Christoph stay awhile while he sorts things out. Meanwhile, the cop's new colleague Helen (Tietze) is making eyes at him and rumors are flying at the police station about his living arrangements and sexual orientation. German with subtitles. **102m/C; VHS, DVD.** *GE* Christoph M. Ohrt; Tim Bergmann; Carin C. Tietze; Oliver Stokowski; ***D:*** Rolf Silber; ***W:*** Rolf Silber; Rudolf Bergmann; ***C:*** Jurgen Herrmann; ***M:*** Peter W. Schmitt.

Rehearsal for Murder 1/2 1982 Movie star Redgrave is murdered on the night of her Broadway debut. Seems it might have been someone in the cast. Brought to you by the creative team behind "Columbo." Challenging whodunit a twist. Good cast. **96m/C; VHS, DVD.** Robert Preston; Lynn Redgrave; Patrick Macnee; Lawrence Pressman; Madolyn Smith; Jeff Goldblum; William Daniels; ***D:*** David Greene; ***W:*** Richard Levinson; William Link; ***C:*** Stevan Larner; ***M:*** Billy Goldenberg. **TV**

Reign of Assassins 1/2 *Jian Yu* 2010 (R) A martial arts action thriller that combines Face/Off and Mr. and Mrs. Smith. In ancient China, Drizzle (Yeoh) is an elusive assassin who takes on the identity of modest shop owner Zeng Jing as part of her mission. She is to help transport the remains of a mystical Buddhist monk to its resting place. She is needed to guard the remains, which are believed to have powers, from the Dark Stone gang. The situation grows more complicated when she falls in love with Jiang (Jung), a warrior and trained martial artist posing as a messenger. As a romantic triangle forms between, her story unravels and assassins come after the remains. Chinese with subtitles. **117m/C; DVD, Blu-Ray, Streaming, Download.** Michelle Yeoh; Woo-sung Jung; Xueqi Wang; Barbie Hsu; Shawn Yue; ***D:*** Chao-Bin Su; ***W:*** Chao-Bin Su; ***C:*** Wing-Hang Wong; ***M:*** Anthony Chue; Peter Kam.

Reign of Fire 1/2 2002 (PG-13) In a post-apocalyptic world, fire-breathing dragons rule. These long dormant, London tunnel-dwelling beasties are out to incinerate what's left of humankind, which ain't much. Enter a multi-tattooed, macho American (McConaughey), a British fireman (Bale), and a foxy blond helicopter pilot (Scorupco) who hook up to give the nasty critters a taste of their own medicine. Character development and a semi-believable plot are as lacking as the reptile posse's personal hygiene, but the humor scores points for the humans although the cool FX dragons definitely come out on top. **101m/C; DVD, Blu-Ray, UMD.** Matthew McConaughey; Christian Bale; Izabela Scorupco; Gerard Butler; Scott James Moutter; Alexander Siddig; David Kennedy; Alice Krige; Ned Dennehy; Rory Kennan; Terence Maynard; Ben Thornton; ***D:*** Rob Bowman; ***W:*** Matt Greenberg; Gregg Chabot; Kevin Peterka; ***C:*** Adrian Biddle; ***M:*** Ed Shearmur.

Reign of Terror *The Black Book* 1949 British-made adventure set during the French Revolution, with everyone after the black book that holds the names of those arch-fiend Robespierre plans to guillotine in his ruthless bid for power. Well-mounted, but historical personages and events are reduced to cartoon form. **89m/B; DVD.** Robert Cummings; Arlene Dahl; Richard Hart; Arnold Moss; Richard Basehart; ***D:*** Anthony Mann; ***W:*** Philip Yordan; ***C:*** John Alton.

Reign Over Me 1/2 2007 (R) Why is Adam Sandler wearing Bob Dylan's hair? NYC dentist Alan (Cheadle) is mildly bored with his successful life and perfect family. Then he runs into his old college roommate, Charlie (Sandler), whose family was killed in 9/11. Charlie won't even acknowledge he had a family and flies into a rage whenever the past is brought up. However, Alan's a compassionate guy and tries to do some male bonding, resulting in bringing Charlie back to reality. Sandler restrains from doing shtick, although he's done the angry boy-man thing before, and Binder rushes his predictable ending. **128m/C; DVD, Blu-Ray.** Adam Sandler; Don Cheadle; Jada Pinkett Smith; Liv Tyler; Saffron Burrows; Donald Sutherland; Robert Klein; Melinda Dillon; Jonathan Banks; Mike Binder; ***D:*** Mike Binder; ***W:*** Mike Binder; ***C:*** Russ T. Alsobrook; ***M:*** Rolfe Kent.

Reilly: Ace of Spies 1987 Covers the exploits of the real-life superspy and womanizer Sydney Reilly who uncovers Russian secrets in 1901, allowing the Japanese to sink the Russian fleet and invade China. After a lively spying career for the British, Reilly eventually plots against the Bolsheviks and comes close to overthrowing Lenin and installing himself as the new leader of the Russian government. Eleven episodes on four cassettes. **572m/C; VHS, DVD.** *GB* Sam Neill; Sebastian Shaw; Jeananne Crowley; ***D:*** Jim (James) Goddard.

The Reincarnate 1971 (PG) Cult guarantees lawyer will live forever if he can find a new body. Enter gullible sculptor; lawyer uses skill at persuasion. **89m/C; VHS, DVD.** *CA* Jack Creley; Jay Reynolds; Trudy Young; Terry Tweed; ***D:*** Don Haldane.

Reindeer Games 2000 (R) Too much talking and not nearly enough gun-toting action bog down this already inane crime thriller. A miscast Affleck is Rudy Duncan, a just released convict who assumes the identity of his recently deceased cellmate in order to get cozy with the guy's prison pen pal, Ashley (Theron). The couple has aerobic sex until Ashley's sadistic "brother" Gabriel (Sinise) forces Rudy to help him and his skanky gang rob an Indian casino on Christmas Eve. Pic is surprisingly flat, deadening the impact of the surprise endings that come in rapid succession, which unintentionally transform the film into a parody of itself. **98m/C; VHS, DVD, Blu-Ray.** Ben Affleck; Charlize Theron; Gary Sinise; Clarence Williams, III; Dennis Farina; Donal Logue; James Frain; Isaac Hayes; Danny Trejo; ***D:*** John Frankenheimer; ***W:*** Ehren Kruger; ***C:*** Alan Caso; ***M:*** Alan Silvestri.

The Reivers 1/2 1969 (PG) Young boy and two adult pals journey from small town Mississippi (circa 1905) to the big city of Memphis in a stolen car. Picaresque tale is delightful onscreen, as in William Faulkner's enjoyable last novel. **107m/C; VHS, DVD, Blu-Ray.** Steve McQueen; Sharon Farrell; Will Geer; Michael Constantine; Rupert Crosse; ***D:*** Mark Rydell; ***W:*** Harriet Frank, Jr.; Irving Ravetch; ***M:*** John Williams.

Relative Fear 1/2 1995 (R) Little Adam has bad luck with his friends and relatives—they keep getting murdered all around him. His mother begins to suspect something unnatural is going on, and discovers Adam is not her natural child, but the son of a homicidal madwoman. Has Adam inherited some deadly traits? **94m/C; VHS, DVD.** Darlanne Fluegel; M. Emmet Walsh; James Brolin; Denise Crosby; Martin Neufeld; Linda Sorensen; Matthew Dupuis; ***D:*** George Mihalka; ***W:*** Kurt Wimmer.

Relative Stranger 2009 One-time football star Walter (La Salle) walked out on wife Charlotte (Michele) and their two kids after an injury ended his career and he couldn't cope. He returns to his hometown for his dad's funeral and learns that Charlotte is now involved with his brother James (Beach), who wants Walter to leave again as soon as possible. Their mother Pearl (Tyson) would like to see a reconciliation and since this is a Hallmark Channel movie, you know mama knows best. **88m/C; DVD.** Eriq La Salle; Michael Beach; Cicely Tyson; Michael Michele; Dana Davis; Dan Castellaneta; Carlos McCullers, II; ***D:*** Charles Burnett; ***W:*** Eric Haywood; ***C:*** Todd Barron; ***M:*** Nathan Furst. **CABLE**

Relative Strangers 1999 Newly widowed Maureen Lessing is devastated to learn her husband was a bigamist, maintaining a second household with a wife and young son. Maureen goes to confront the other woman and learns her child is seriously ill. So she tries to set aside her anger when the boy's only chance to live may hinge on Maureen's own children. **178m/C; DVD.** *GB IR* Brenda Fricker; Lena Stolze; Harriet Owen; Robin Laing; Adrian Dunbar; Benjamin Butler; Paul Copley; ***D:*** Giles Foster; ***W:*** Eric Deacon; ***C:*** Rex Maidment; ***M:*** Nick Bicat. **TV**

Relative Strangers 1/2 2006 (PG-13) Ticky-tacky and too familiar. Uptight self-help author Richard Clayton (Livingston) learns from his oh-so-proper parents (Baranski, Herrmann) that he was adopted. But when Richard finds his birth parents, the Menures (Bates, DeVito) turn out to be less-than-couth trailer park denizens. His fiancee Ellen (Campbell) thinks Richard should just roll with it but he's horrified. **86m/C; DVD.** Ron Livingston; Neve Campbell; Kathy Bates; Danny DeVito; Christine Baranski; Edward Herrmann; Ed Begley, Jr.; Beverly D'Angelo; ***D:*** Greg Glienna; ***W:*** Greg Glienna; Jeff Baynes; ***C:*** Jeffrey Greeley; Tim Suhrstedt; ***M:*** David Kitay; Arnold Diamond.

Relative Values 1/2 1999 (PG-13) The upper crusty Countess of Marshwood (Andrews) is appalled when her son Nigel (Atterton) wants to marry American starlet Miranda (Tripplehorn). And she isn't the only one—Miranda has jilted her Hollywood star boyfriend Don (Baldwin), who shows up at the Marshwood's country house to change her mind, and she also has a long-lost sister, Moxie (Thompson), who happens to be the Countess' maid. Slight but witty confection, based on a 1951 Noel Coward play. **92m/C; VHS, DVD.** *GB* Julie Andrews; Edward Atterton; Jeanne Tripplehorn; William Baldwin; Sophie Thompson; Colin Firth; Stephen Fry; ***D:*** Eric

Styles; ***W:*** Paul Rattigan; Michael Walker; ***C:*** Jimmy Dibling; ***M:*** John Debney.

Relax. . . It's Just Sex! 1/2 **1998 (R)** Love and sex in the '90s surround gay looking-for-love writer Vincey (Anderson). His self-made extended family include best gal pal Tara (Tilly) and her boyfriend Gus (Perez), whose HIV-positive brother Javi (Garcia) has just attracted the attention of Buzz (Carson), the man Vincey had his eye on. Then there's troubled lesbian couple Megan (Scott Thomas) and her girlfriend Sarina (Williams). But romantic complications take a back seat when Javi and Vincey are subjected to a fag bashing in which Vincey violently turns the tables on one of his attackers. **110m/C; VHS, DVD.** Mitchell Anderson; Jennifer Tilly; Cynda Williams; Serena Scott Thomas; Lori Petty; Eddie Garcia; Terrence "T.C." Carson; Timothy Paul Perez; Billy Wirth; Susan Tyrrell; Chris Cleveland; Gibbs Toldsdorf; Seymour Cassel; Paul Winfield; ***D:*** P.J. Castellaneta; ***W:*** P.J. Castellaneta; ***C:*** Lon Magdich; ***M:*** Lori Eschler Frystak.

Relentless **1989 (R)** Twisted psycho Nelson, once rejected by the LAPD Academy on psychological grounds, takes his revenge by murdering people and using his police training to cover his tracks. Good acting keeps sporadically powerful but cliched thriller afloat. **92m/C; VHS, DVD.** Judd Nelson; Robert Loggia; Meg Foster; Leo Rossi; Pat O'Bryan; Mindy Seeger; Angel Tompkins; Ken Lerner; George "Buck" Flower; Edward (Eddie) Bunker; ***D:*** William Lustig.

Relentless 2: Dead On **1991 (R)** Rossi, the detective from the first film, tracks yet another murderer whose occult-style mutilations mask an international political conspiracy. So-so slaughter with artsy camera work. Honestly, how many "Relentless" fans can you name who've been waiting with anticipation? **93m/C; VHS, DVD.** Leo Rossi; Ray Sharkey; Meg Foster; Miles O'Keeffe; Dale Dye; ***D:*** Michael Schroeder.

Relentless 3 **1993 (R)** A serial killer (Forsythe) likes to carve up his women victims and send various body parts to taunt the police. Then this sicko decides to really drive the cops crazy by stalking the beautiful girlfriend of the detective (Rossi) investigating the crimes. **84m/C; VHS, DVD.** William Forsythe; Leo Rossi; Tom Bower; Robert Costanzo; Signy Coleman; ***D:*** James (Momel) Lemmo; ***W:*** James (Momel) Lemmo.

Relentless 4 1/2 **1994 (R)** A psychiatrist with a secret (Janssen) is the only clue Detective Sam Dietz (Rossi) has to a serial killer. Seems all the victims knew the shrink but what does she know? **91m/C; VHS, DVD.** Leo Rossi; Famke Janssen; Ken Lerner; Colleen T. Coffey; ***D:*** Oley Sassone; ***W:*** Mark Sevi; Terry Plumeri.

The Relic **1996 (R)** A ship from Brazil arrives in Chicago with a headless crew and crates intended for a local museum. Superstitious police detective Vincent D'Agosto (Sizemore) wants to close the place down, but museum director Ann Cuthbert (Hunt) won't agree. The decapitating South American monster proceeds to suck brains until the sassy scientist (Miller) helping out decides she's had enough and takes off her high heels, which everyone knows means the end is near for the creature. **110m/C; VHS, DVD.** Penelope Ann Miller; Tom Sizemore; Linda Hunt; James Whitmore; Clayton Rohner; Thomas Ryan; Lewis Van Bergen; Chi Muoi Lo; Robert Lesser; ***D:*** Peter Hyams; ***W:*** Amy Holden Jones; John Raffo; Rick Jaffa; Amanda Silver; ***C:*** Peter Hyams; ***M:*** John Debney.

Religulous **2008 (R)** Comedian/talk show host Maher and director Charles' pic revolves around Maher's disdain of organized religion. Maher attempts to apply thoughtful reason to issues of faith, but it's really just a launch pad for his typical sharp-witted skewering of willing ignorance and delusional acceptance of what appear to be, to him at least, ridiculous fairy tales. One-sided and at times both hilarious and offensive, Maher's larger conclusion is that these absurd belief systems are responsible for the world's conflicts and suffering and will eventually push us into mutually-assured annihilation. A must for Maher fans, although certain to upset the devout. **101m/C; DVD.** Bill Maher; ***D:*** Larry Charles; ***C:*** Anthony Hardwick.

The Reluctant Agent *Double Your Pleasure* **1989** Waitress Linda (Jackee) is persuaded to take the place of injured twin sister Charlene, an FBI agent hot on the trail of shady-but-attractive businessman C. Gabriel Dash (Lawson). So, she goes undercover with the questionable assistance of agent John Fraser (Hedaya) to bring their criminal to justice. **94m/C; VHS, DVD.** Jackee; Richard Lawson; Dan Hedaya; Bill Fagerbakke; Harold Sylvester; Cynthia Stevenson; Sharon Barr; Eda Reiss Merin; ***D:*** Paul Lynch; ***W:*** Jeff Cohn; Kristi Kane; ***M:*** Tim Truman. **TV**

The Reluctant Astronaut 1/2 **1967** Roy Fleming (Knotts) is a carnvial worker who operates the spaceship ride. Dad's upset the kid has no ambition and sends an application for Roy to NASA. Everyone's surprised when Roy gets accepted and he heads off to Florida but it turns out the job is janitorial. Still Roy does make friends with astronaut Red (Nielsen), who persuades NASA that Roy would be the perfect civilian to send up in an experimental capsule. Too bad Roy's terrified to fly in anything. **103m/C; VHS, DVD, Blu-Ray.** Don Knotts; Leslie Nielsen; Joan Freeman; Arthur O'Connell; Jesse White; Jeannette Nolan; Joan Shawlee; ***D:*** Edward Montagne; ***W:*** James Fritzell; Everett Greenbaum; ***C:*** Rexford Wimpy; ***M:*** Vic Mizzy.

The Reluctant Debutante **1958** Harrison and Kendall are the urbane parents of Dee who are trying to find a suitable British husband for their girl. It seems their choices just won't do however, and Dee falls for American bad boy musician Saxon. A very lightweight yet extremely enjoyable romantic comedy thanks to Harrison and in particular his real-life wife Kendall, who unfortunately died the following year. **96m/C; VHS, DVD, Blu-Ray.** Rex Harrison; Kay Kendall; John Saxon; Sandra Dee; Angela Lansbury; Diane Clare; ***D:*** Vincente Minnelli; ***C:*** Joseph Ruttenberg.

The Remains of the Day **1993 (PG)** If repression is your cup of tea then this is the film for you. Others may want to shake British butler par excellence Stevens (Hopkins). In the 1930s, Stevens is the rigidly traditional butler to Lord Darlington (Fox). When new housekeeper, Miss Kenton (Thompson) , expresses a quietly personal interest in Stevens, his loyalty to an unworthy master prevents him from a chance at happiness. A quiet movie, told in flashback. Hopkins' impressive performance gets by strictly on nuance with Thompson at least allowed a small amount of natural charm. Based on the novel by Kazuo Ishiguro. **135m/C; VHS, DVD, Blu-Ray.** *UK* Anthony Hopkins; Emma Thompson; James Fox; Christopher Reeve; Peter Vaughan; Hugh Grant; Michael (Michel) Lonsdale; Tim Pigott-Smith; ***D:*** James Ivory; ***W:*** Ruth Prawer Jhabvala; ***C:*** Tony Pierce-Roberts; ***M:*** Richard Robbins. British Acad. '93: Actor (Hopkins); L.A. Film Critics '93: Actor (Hopkins); Natl. Bd. of Review '93: Actor (Hopkins).

The Remarkable Mr. Pennypacker **1959** It's the 1890s and Horace Pennypacker (Webb) is a bigamist. Working for his family's company means he travels between Harrisburg and his wife Emily (Maguire) and their children and Philadelphia where a widowed Horace deals with more kids (there's 17 little Pennypackers in all.) Then an unexpected family emergency exposes his double life. Adapted from Liam O'Brien's Broadwy play. **87m/C; DVD.** Clifton Webb; Dorothy McGuire; Charles Coburn; Jill St. John; Ray Stricklyn; Ron Ely; Larry Gates; ***D:*** Henry Levin; ***W:*** Walter Reisch; ***C:*** Milton Krasner; ***M:*** Leigh Harline.

Remarkable Power **2008 (R)** Two parallel storylines converge in the final act of writer/director Beckner's plot-filled black comedy. First there's a news report about the death of L.A. late-night talk show host Jack West (Nealon). Flashbacks reveal that Jack's show was cancelled and he hired PI Van Hagen (Arnold) after learning that his wife was cheating on him. Meanwhile, loner Ross (Peters) accidentally kills an infomercial actor and then takes over his life. Oh, and Van Hagen teams up with blogger Athena (Zehetner) to find the connection between Ross, Jack, and Russian mobsters. **91m/C; DVD.** Kevin Nealon; Tom Arnold; Evan Peters; Nora Zehetner; Kip Pardue; Dulé Hill; Whitney Able; Jack Plotnick; Johnny Messner; Christopher Titus; ***D:*** Brandon Beckner; ***W:*** Brandon Beckner; Scott Sampila; ***C:*** Damian Acevedo; ***M:*** Tony Tisdale. **VIDEO**

Rembrandt **1936** Necessarily very visual biography of the great Dutch painter, Rembrandt. Superb acting by Laughton. **86m/B; VHS, DVD.** *GB* Charles Laughton; Elsa Lanchester; Gertrude Lawrence; Walter Hudd; ***D:*** Alexander Korda; ***C:*** Georges Perinal.

Remedy 1/2 **2005** Will's life is perfect until his friend is fatally shot while the two are out partying. Too doped up to remember anything, he appears guilty thus forcing him to find the real killers amid New York City's sleaziest players. **82m/C; VHS, DVD.** Christian Maelen; Arthur J. Nascarella; Vincent Pastore; Nicholas Reiner; ***D:*** Christian Maelen; ***W:*** Jonathan Hanser; ***C:*** Brendan Flynt; ***M:*** Jon Doscher. **VIDEO**

Remedy for Riches **1940** The fourth "Dr. Christian" comedy, has the small-town doctor trying to uncover a real estate fraud before it bankrupts his community. Mildly funny. **66m/B; VHS, DVD.** Jean Hersholt; Dorothy Lovett; Edgar Kennedy; Jed Prouty; Walter Catlett; ***D:*** Erle C. Kenton.

Remember 1/2 **2015 (R)** Zev Guttman (Plummer) is a man sent on a mission by fellow old folks' home resident Max Rosenbaum (Landau). The two Holocaust survivors think they have learned the location of one of the SS Guards who caused their families so much pain and death. Zev seeks vengeance not just for himself but for his people. Director Egoyan's story twists and turns and even gets a little implausible along the way to a final twist that makes the whole thing feel like an exercise in exploitation. The true treasure is the superbly talented leads. **94m/C; DVD, Blu-Ray.** *CA GE* Christopher Plummer; Dean Norris; Martin Landau; Bruno Ganz; Henry Czerny; ***D:*** Atom Egoyan; ***W:*** Benjamin August; ***C:*** Paul Sarossy; ***M:*** Mychael Danna.

Remember Me **2010 (PG-13)** Pattinson takes a break from playing a mopey vampire to play a mopey hipster in this story of star-crossed love. Tyler (Pattinson) is a chain-smoking, beer-drinking rebel who's arrested by police Sgt. Craig (Cooper) after a drunken brawl. He plans to date Craig's daughter Ally (de Ravin) and dump her as revenge, but true love starts to bloom. A veritable avalanche of misfortune then befalls nearly every character, including Tyler's cold father Charles (Brosnan) and sensitive little sis Caroline (Jerins). Sighs are heaved, but at least no one gets all glittery. **113m/C; DVD, Blu-Ray, On Demand.** Robert Pattinson; Emilie de Ravin; Chris Cooper; Martha Plimpton; Lena Olin; Pierce Brosnan; Caitlyn Rund; ***D:*** Allen Coulter; ***W:*** Will Fetters; Jenny Lumet; ***C:*** Jonathan Freeman; ***M:*** Marcelo Zarvos.

Remember Sunday 1/2 **2013** Hallmark Hall of Fame romantic drama. Lonely waitress Molly (Bledel) meets quirky jewelry store clerk Gus (Levi), but he has an unusual problem. Three years before, a brain aneurysm destroyed astrophysicist Gus's short-term memory, though he can remember everything before that just fine. In order to function day-to-day, he relies on sticky notes and other aids. Meeting Molly and falling in love with her is always new, but can she live like that? **95m/C; DVD.** Zachary Levi; Alexis Bledel; Merritt Wever; Barry (Shabaka) Henley; David Hoffman; Jerry Adler; ***D:*** Jeff Bleckner; ***W:*** Barry Morrow; ***C:*** Michael Lohmann; ***M:*** Christopher Lennertz. **TV**

Remember the Day 1/2 **1941** In this bittersweet drama (told in flashback), elderly schoolteacher Nora Trinell (Colbert) is waiting for a glimpse of Presidential candidate Dewey Roberts (Strudwick). In 1916, Nora was young Dewey's (Croft) dedicated teacher and he has a boyish crush that turns to jealousy when he discovers that Nora is secretly maried to fellow teacher, Dan Hopkins (Payne). To prevent a scandal, Dan enlists with Canadian troops to fight in WWI. **86m/B; DVD.** Claudette Colbert; John Payne; Shepperd Strudwick; Ann Todd; Douglas Croft; Anne Revere; ***D:*** Henry King; ***W:*** Tess Slesinger; Frank Davis; Allan Scott; ***C:*** George Barnes.

Remember the Daze 1/2 *The Beautiful Ordinary* **2007 (R)** Starts with four teenaged girls on the last day at their suburban high school in 1999 and expands to include various groups of geeks, jocks, divas, and stoners as they get ready for the first we're-out-of-school summer party. Manafort's debut basically looks back at her own school years (she graduated in 2000) as aimlessly as the kids themselves. **101m/C; DVD.** Amber Heard; Melonie Diaz; Alexa Vega; Leighton Meester; Douglas Smith; Wesley Jonathan; Marne(tte) Patterson; Christopher Marquette; Sean Marquette; John Robinson; Moira Kelly; Lyndsy Fonseca; Charles Chen; ***D:*** Jess Manafort; ***W:*** Jess Manafort; ***C:*** Steve Gainer; ***M:*** Dustin O'Halloran.

Remember the Night **1940** Another Sturges-scripted winner in which assistant D.A. MacMurray falls for sophisticated shoplifter Stanwyck, who has stolen a diamond bracelet amidst the Christmas holiday bustle. On a promise that she will return for the trial MacMurray postpones the trial and offers her a ride home for the holidays. Stanwyck is turned away by her mother and MacMurray brings her home for a real family Christmas, where love blooms. A sentimental, funny romance that boisters holiday cheer any time of year. **94m/B; DVD, Blu-Ray.** Barbara Stanwyck; Fred MacMurray; Beulah Bondi; Elizabeth Patterson; Willard Robertson; Sterling Holloway; ***D:*** Mitchell Leisen; ***W:*** Preston Sturges; ***C:*** Ted Tetzlaff; ***M:*** Frederick "Friedrich" Hollander.

Remember the Titans **2000 (PG)** Black coach Herman Boone (Washington) is hired to lead the football team at a racially tense Alexandria, Virginia high school that has been forced to integrate in 1971. White coach Bill Yoast (Patton) is now the assistant coach and he and his former players warily show up for the first practices. The team works through initial stages of mistrust and ignorance, but finally learn to work together. As the school year begins, racial tensions are eased by the success of the team, who go on to the state championship. A bit predictable and cliche-ridden, but heartfelt. Based on a true story. **114m/C; DVD, Blu-Ray, UMD.** Denzel Washington; Will Patton; Donald Adeosun Faison; Wood Harris; Ethan Suplee; Nicole Ari Parker; Hayden Panettiere; Kate (Catherine) Bosworth; Ryan Hurst; Kip Pardue; Craig Kirkwood; Burgess Jenkins; Earl C. Poitier; Ryan Gosling; ***D:*** Boaz Yakin; ***W:*** Gregory Allen Howard; ***C:*** Philippe Rousselot; ***M:*** Trevor Rabin.

Rememory **2017 (PG-13)** Professor Gordon Dunn (Donovan) has invented a machine that can extract people's memories and show their life events objectively. After Gordon is found dead, a mysterious friend of his, Sam Bloom (Dinklage) begins investigating Gordon's death as a homicide to protect his business interests. First, Sam meets with Gordon's widow Carolyn (Ormond), then steals a prototype of the memory machine and talks to Gordon's patients--most of whom regret becoming involved with him. While Sam seeks a suspect among them, he lies about how he is. This sci-fi mystery's muddled high-concept plotting undermine the actors' performances. **111m/C; DVD.** Peter Dinklage; Matt Ellis; Jordana Largy; Martin Donovan; Julia Ormond; ***D:*** Mark Palansky; ***W:*** Mark Palansky; Mike Vukadinovich; ***C:*** Gregory Middleton; ***M:*** Gregory Tripi.

Remo Williams: The Adventure Begins *Remo: Unarmed and Dangerous* **1985 (PG-13)** Adaptation of "The Destroyer" adventure novel series with a Bond-like hero who can walk on water and dodge bullets after being instructed by a Korean martial arts master. Funny and diverting, and Grey is excellent (if a bit over the top) as the wizened oriental. The title's assumption is that the adventure will continue. **121m/C; VHS, DVD, Blu-Ray.** Fred Ward; Joel Grey; Wilford Brimley; Kate Mulgrew; J.A. Preston; George Coe; Charles Cioffi; Patrick Kilpatrick; Michael Pataki; Marv Albert; Reginald VelJohnson; William Hickey; ***D:*** Guy Hamilton; ***W:*** Warren B. Murphy; Christopher Wood; ***C:*** Andrew Laszlo; ***M:*** Craig Safan.

Renaissance 1/2 **2006 (R)** Stark noir/sci-fi animation set in 2054 Paris, a city that has become a gigantic labyrinth run by Avalon, a company and entity more like Big Brother, Inc. A female scientist who works for the company goes missing, setting off a classic noir adventure with the brooding cop hero, femme fatale, and enemies around every corner. The B&W design is striking but the story drags after awhile. The film was originally voiced by French actors and redone for the English-language market. **103m/B; DVD, Blu-Ray.** *GB FR LU* Romola Garai; Ian Holm; Jonathan Pryce; ***V:*** Daniel Craig; Catherine McCormack; ***D:*** Christian Volckman; ***W:*** Alexandre de la Patelliere; Matthieu Delaporte; ***M:*** Nicholas Dodd.

Renaissance Man 1/2 **1994 (PG-13)** Skeptical new teacher inspires a classroom of underachievers and finds his true calling that's based loosely on the experiences of screenwriter Burnstein. Civilian Bill Rago (DeVito) is an unemployed ad exec assigned to teach Shakespeare to a group of borderline Army recruits. Add half a bone for the recruits and their Hamlet rap, a breath of fresh air in an otherwise stale plot. Some funny moments, reminiscent of "Stripes," but not quite as wacky. Shot with the cooperation of the Army. **128m/C; VHS, DVD.** Danny DeVito; Gregory Hines; James Remar; Stacey Dash; Ed Begley, Jr.; Mark Wahlberg; Lillo Brancato; Kadeem Hardison; Richard T. Jones; Khalil Kain; Peter Simmons; Jenifer Lewis; ***Cameo(s):*** Cliff Robertson; ***D:*** Penny Marshall; ***W:*** Jim Burnstein; Ned Mauldin; ***M:*** Hans Zimmer.

The Rendering **2002** Art student Sarah (Doherty) is attacked by a man who's obsessed with her. Recovering in the hospital, she renders a sketch that has Theodore Grey (Outerbridge) arrested and sent to prison. Ten years later, Sarah is married to Boston businessman Michael (Brennan) but has never told him what happened to her and her continued paranoia has caused a rift. Sarah has also continued to help the police as a sketch artist and her latest drawing of a suspect looks suspiciously like Michael. Has he committed a crime or is this a set-up by Grey, who happens to be out on parole. **93m/C; VHS, DVD.** *CA* Shannen Doherty; Peter Outerbridge; John Brennan; Tammy Isabell; Conrad Pla; Sean Devine; ***D:*** Peter Svatek; ***W:*** David Amann; ***C:*** Francois Dagenais; ***M:*** James Gelfand. **CABLE**

Rendez-vous **1985 (R)** A racy, dark film about the sensitive balance between sex and exploitation, the real world and the stage world. Some may be disturbed by chillingly explicit scenes. Impressive tour de force of imagination, direction, and cinematography. In French with English subtitles. **82m/C; VHS, DVD.** *FR* Juliette Binoche; Lambert Wilson; Wadeck Stanczak; Jean-Louis Trintignant; ***D:*** Andre Techine; ***W:*** Olivier Assayas; ***C:*** Philippe Angers. Cannes '85: Director (Techine).

Rendezvous **1935** In this comic thriller, Bill Gordon (Powell) is a deskbound WWI Army cryptographer working to break the codes the German agents. His girlfriend Joel Carter (Russell), whose uncle is a government bigwig, keeps interfering to make sure Bill is safe in DC when he wants to get on the front lines. As it turns out, there are spies in the capitol meaning Bill will see some action after all. Based on "American Black Chamber" by Herbert O. Yardley, who was the head of the U.S. Secret Service. **94m/B; DVD.** William Powell; Rosalind Russell; Binnie Barnes; Cesar Romero; Lionel Atwill; Samuel S. Hinds; Henry Stephenson; Charley Grapewin; ***D:*** William K. Howard; ***W:*** Bella Spewack; Samuel Spewack; George Oppenheimer; P.J. Wolfson; ***C:*** William H. Daniels; ***M:*** William Axt.

Rendition 1/2 **2007 (R)** Egyptian-born American citizen Anwar El-Ibrahimi (Metwally) is ripped from his suburban Chicago existence to the confusion of his pregnant wife Isabella (Witherspoon), who worries when he doesn't return from a business trip. Turns out Anwar's in North Africa being tortured by the local authorities for what they believe is his involvement in a terrorist bombing. Meanwhile, newly-promoted CIA analyst Douglas Freeman (Gyllenhaal) is privy to Anwar's situation and begins to have second thoughts about the rendition program (an actual government policy allowing suspected terrorists to be extradited for interrogation). Unfortunately even the brilliant cast can't make the story convincing. **120m/C; DVD, Blu-Ray.** Meryl Streep; Reese Witherspoon; Jake Gyllenhaal; Peter Sarsgaard; Alan Arkin; Omar Metwally; Igal Naor; Moa Khouas; Zineb Oukach; ***D:*** Gavin Hood; ***W:*** Kelley Sane; ***C:*** Dion Beebe; ***M:*** Paul Hepker; Mark Killian.

Renegade Girl **1946** A special agent is sent west to capture the female head of a band of outlaws. **65m/B; VHS, DVD.** Alan Curtis; Ann Savage; Edward Brophy; Ray Corrigan; Jack Holt; Russell Wade; Claudia Drake; John "Dusty" King; Chief Thundercloud; Edmund Cobb; ***D:*** William Berke; ***W:*** Edwin Westrate; ***C:*** James S. Brown, Jr.; ***M:*** Darrell Calker.

Renegades **1989 (R)** A young cop from Philadelphia and a Lakota Indian begrudgingly unite to track down a gang of ruthless crooks. Good action, and lots of it; not much story. **105m/C; VHS, DVD.** Kiefer Sutherland; Lou Diamond Phillips; Robert Knepper; Jami Gertz; Bill Smitrovich; ***D:*** Jack Sholder; ***C:*** Phil Meheux; ***M:*** Michael Kamen.

Renegades **2017 (PG-13)** In wartime Sarajevo, Navy Seals go off mission when they find millions of dollars in Nazi gold at the bottom of a lake and decide to retrieve it and return it to its owners. To complete their operation in the few hours they have before being sent home, they rely on local help to avoid enemy and other peacekeeping forces and get the job done. This action thriller features an interesting premise in its military heist but lacks effective dialogue, characterizations, and understanding of military norms. A technically dazzling underwater sequence does not compensate for the film's other failings. **105m/C; DVD.** Ewen Bremner; J.K. Simmons; Sullivan Stapleton; Charlie Bewley; Sylvia Hoeks; ***D:*** Steven Quale; ***W:*** Richard Wenk; Luc Besson; ***C:*** Brian Pearson; ***M:*** Éric Serra.

Reno 1/2 **1939** Sappy family drama. When the silver-mining town of Reno goes bust, gambling and lenient divorce laws turn it around. Lawyer Bill Shayne (Dix) has a good divorce practice until his neglected wife Jessie (Patrick) uses the law to dump Bill and take their daughter back east. Then Bill gets disbarred, changes his name, and becomes a casino owner. When his grown daughter Joanna (Louise) shows up in town for her own divorce, Bill tries to teach her a couple of life lessons before they reconcile. **73m/B; DVD.** Richard Dix; Gail Patrick; Anita Louise; Paul Cavanagh; Laura Hope Crews; ***D:*** John Farrow; ***W:*** John Twist; ***C:*** J. Roy Hunt.

Reno 911! Miami **2007 (R)** If you're a fan of the Comedy Central TV show, you'll enjoy this expanded version in all its raunchy, silly glory. The Reno sheriffs go to a police convention in Miami and are left to patrol the city's streets (with their usual complete incompetence) when all the other cops are quarantined at the hotel. Improv is hit-or-miss and involves alligators, topless beaches, crazy mobsters, sexual frustration—and Lt. Dangle (Lennon) in his short-shorts. **84m/C; DVD.** Thomas Lennon; Robert Ben Garant; Niecy Nash; Nick Swardson; Kerri Kenney-Silver; Carlos Alazraqui; Mary Birdsong; Wendi McLendon-Covey; Cedric Yarbrough; Paul Rudd; ***Cameo(s):*** Danny DeVito; Dwayne "The Rock" Johnson; ***D:*** Robert Ben Garant; ***W:*** Thomas Lennon; Robert Ben Garant; Kerri Kenney-Silver; ***C:*** Joe Kessler; ***M:*** Craig Wedren.

Renoir **2012 (R)** Old-fashioned, elegant drama. In 1915, Pierre-Auguste Renoir (Bouquet), 74, a recent widower, and crippled with arthritis, is living on his estate and still painting. His current (and final) muse is beautiful-but-rude, red-headed teenager Andree (Theret) who also catches the eye of 21-year-old Jean Renoir (Rottiers), home convalescing from serious war wounds. Not much happens, but it certainly is lovely. French and Italian with subtitles. **111m/C; DVD.** *FR* Michel Bouquet; Vincent Rottiers; Christa Theret; Thomas Doret; Romane Bohringer; ***D:*** Gilles Bourdos; ***W:*** Gilles Bourdos; Jerome Tonnerre; ***C:*** Mark Ping Bin Lee; ***M:*** Alexandre Desplat.

Rent **2005 (PG-13)** Hit Broadway show makes its screen debut, though it all feels just a bit too late. For the uninitiated, the story follows a group of New York squatters and struggling artists in an update of La Boheme. The passion isn't an act—the film cast is the same group that developed the characters on stage. If you dug the musical or have ever been a little lost, young, and broke in a big city, the timing and uber-sentimentality won't matter. Themes of AIDS, homosexuality and drugs may be too much for stuffier viewers. **128m/C; DVD, Blu-Ray, UMD.** Anthony Rapp; Adam Pascal; Rosario Dawson; Taye Diggs; Jesse L. Martin; Wilson Jermaine Heredia; Idina Menzel; Tracie Thoms; ***D:*** Chris Columbus; ***C:*** Stephen Goldblatt; ***M:*** Rob Cavallo.

Rent-A-Cop **1988 (R)** A cop (Reynolds) is bounced from the force after he survives a drug-bust massacre under suspicious circumstances. He becomes a security guard and continues to track down the still-at-large killer with help from call girl Minnelli. **95m/C; VHS, DVD.** Burt Reynolds; Liza Minnelli; James Remar; Richard Masur; Bernie Casey; John Stanton; John P. Ryan; Dionne Warwick; Robby Benson; ***D:*** Jerry London; ***W:*** Michael Blodgett; ***C:*** Giuseppe Rotunno; ***M:*** Jerry Goldsmith. Golden Raspberries '88: Worst Actress (Minnelli).

Rentadick **1972** A precursor to the Monty Python masterpieces, written by future members Chapman and Cleese. Private eye spoof isn't as funny as later Python efforts; but it is an indication of what was yet to come and fans should enjoy it. **94m/C; DVD.** *UK* James Booth; Julie Ege; Ronald Fraser; Donald Sinden; Michael Bentine; Richard Briers; Spike Milligan; Tsai Chin; Kenneth Cope; John Wells; ***D:*** Jim Clark; ***W:*** Graham Chapman; John Cleese; ***C:*** John Coquillon; ***M:*** Carl Davis.

Repentance *Pokayaniye; Confession* **1987 (PG)** A popular, surreal satire of Soviet and Communist societies. A woman is arrested for repeatedly digging up a dead local despot, and put on trial. Wickedly funny and controversial; released under the auspices of glasnost. In Russian with English subtitles. **151m/C; VHS, DVD.** *RU* Avtandil Makharadze; Zeinab Botsvadze; Ia Ninidze; Edisher Giorgobiani; Ketevan Abuladze; Kakhi Kavsadze; ***D:*** Tengiz Abuladze. Cannes '87: Grand Jury Prize.

Repentance **2014 (R)** Tommy (Mackie) has reinvented himself as a spiritual advisor and life coach years after a drunken car crash that almost took his life. He becomes the focus of a truly troubled man named Angel (Whitaker), a guy who the life coach takes on as a client but learns that he may not have the tools to deal with his severe issues. A great cast can't save this tedious drama that's weighed down by a mediocre, morally heavy-handed script. **90m/C; DVD.** Forest Whitaker; Anthony Mackie; Mike Epps; Sanaa Lathan; Nicole Ari Parker; ***D:*** Philippe Caland; ***W:*** Shintaro Shimosawa; ***C:*** Denis Maloney; ***M:*** Mark Kilian.

The Replacement Killers 1/2 **1998 (R)** Hong Kong action star Chow makes his American debut in this derivative first feature from director Fuqua. John Lee, an assassin working for crime boss Mr. Wei (Tsang), decides not to carry out a hit on a cop's (Rooker) son and becomes the target of the men sent to replace him. There are many high body count gun battles and Fuqua, who was heavily influenced by John Woo, does a passable job of conveying the style of Chow and Woo's Hong Kong work. Chow's sublety and charisma are crammed into a mechanical action plot and only his talent saves the whole thing from imploding. **86m/C; DVD, Blu-Ray, UMD.** Chow Yun-Fat; Mira Sorvino; Michael Rooker; Kenneth Tsang; Jurgen Prochnow; Danny Trejo; Til Schweiger; Clifton (Gonzalez) Collins, Jr.; Carlos Gomez; Frank Medrano; ***D:*** Antoine Fuqua; ***W:*** Ken Sanzel; ***C:*** Peter Lyons Collister; ***M:*** Harry Gregson-Williams.

The Replacements 1/2 **2000 (PG-13)** An NFL players' strike finds coach Hackman stuck with a bunch of replacement players, including washed-up quarterback Shane Falco (Reeves) and never-was receiver Clifford Franklin (Jones). If you can get past the fact that the heroes are scabs, this silly cliche-fest still isn't very good. It's better than it oughta be, but only because of Hackman's presence and Jones's comic talents. The odd assortment of misfits and goofballs is occasionally amusing, but nothing you haven't seen in all the other "rag-tag-team-fights-the-odds" sports comedies. Based on the 1987 strike when players filling in for the Washington Redskins won three straight games. **105m/C; VHS, DVD, Blu-Ray.** Keanu Reeves; Gene Hackman; Jon Favreau; Orlando Jones; Jack Warden; Brooke Langton; Rhys Ifans; Brett Cullen; Gailard Sartain; Art LaFleur; Troy Winbush; David Denman; Keith David; Faizon Love; ***D:*** Howard Deutch; ***W:*** Vince McKewin; ***C:*** Tak Fujimoto; ***M:*** Alan Silvestri.

Repli-Kate 1/2 *National Lampoon Presents Repli-Kate* **2001 (R)** Reporter Kate (Landry) is accidentally cloned by grad student Max (Roday) while she's doing a story on his professor's (Levy) genetic experiments. Since Kate is a hot babe, Max's pal Henry (Askew) thinks this is a wonderful thing and promptly teaches Repli-Kate about the important things in every guy's life—sports, beer, and sex. **90m/C; VHS, DVD.** Ali Landry; James Roday; Desmond Askew; Eugene Levy; ***D:*** Frank Longo; ***W:*** Stuart Gibbs; ***C:*** Alan Caso; ***M:*** Teddy Castellucci. **VIDEO**

Replicant 1/2 **2001 (R)** It takes a killer to catch a killer. In this case Van Damme is cloned by the government so he can go after himself (the original is a vicious serial killer). Cop Rooker, who's been unsuccessfully hunting the psycho for several years, teams up with the duplicate to get results. Lots of chases, fights, and high-tech thrills. **100m/C; VHS, DVD, Blu-Ray.** Jean-Claude Van Damme; Michael Rooker; Ian Robinson; Catherine Dent; ***D:*** Ringo Lam; ***W:*** Lawrence Riggins; Les Weldon; ***C:*** Mike Southon; ***M:*** Guy Zerafa. **VIDEO**

Replicas **2018 (PG-13)** Will Foster (Reeves) is a scientist who is working on technology to transplant the human consciousness with lab partner Ed (Middleditch), an expert in cloning. While on vacation with his wife Mona (Eve) and their three young children, Will's family is killed in a car accident on a rainy night. After their deaths, Will calls on Ed to use their collective expertise to make clones of Will's family and implant their consciousness in the clones. Their experiment does not turn out as they expect. Explores somewhat interesting ideas, but doesn't deliver. **107m/C; DVD.** Keanu Reeves; Alice Eve; Thomas Middleditch; John Ortiz; Emjay Anthony; ***D:*** Jeffrey Nachmanoff; ***W:*** Chad St. John; ***C:*** Checco Varese; ***M:*** Mark Kilian; Jose Ojeda.

Replikator: Cloned to Kill 1/2 **1994 (R)** In the 21st century, a ruthless criminal gets hold of replication techology that can duplicate anything, including people. So it's up to a cop and two cyberpunks to stop the destruction. **96m/C; VHS, DVD.** Michael St. Gerard; Brigitte Bako; Ned Beatty; ***D:*** G. Philip Jackson; ***W:*** Tony Johnston; Michelle Bellerose; John Dawson.

Repo Chick 1/2 **2009** Disappointingly futile in-name-only sequel from Cox. Rich girl Pixxi gets cut off from the family funds after one too many screw-ups. She needs money and when her car is repossessed, she finds her calling and becomes a success. Until she tries to claim a bounty on some antique railroad cars that are being occupied by vegan terrorists who threaten to blow-up L.A. unless golf is outlawed (among other demands). **85m/C; DVD.** Jacklyn Jonet; Rosanna Arquette; Karen Black; Xander Berkeley; Miguel (Michael) Sandoval; Chloe Webb; Robert Beltran; ***D:*** Alex Cox; ***W:*** Alex Cox; ***C:*** Steven Fierberg; ***M:*** Dan Wool.

Repo Jake 1/2 **1990** Jake Baxter learns the myth of the carefree life of a repossession man in this action thriller. His illusion is destroyed by angry clients, pornography, a deadly underworld racetrack, and a sinister crime boss. **90m/C; VHS, Streaming.** Dan Haggerty; Robert Axelrod; ***D:*** Joseph Merhi; ***W:*** Joe Hart; ***C:*** Richard Pepin; ***M:*** John Gonzalez.

Repo Man 1/2 **1983 (R)** An inventive, perversely witty portrait of sick modern urbanity, following the adventures of punk stock boy Otto (Estevez), who takes a job as a car repossessor under the jaundiced eye of veteran Bud (Stanton). Then there's the lobotomized physicist Parnell (Harris), who carries around a strang glowing object in the trunk of his car that's wanted by the government. The L.A. landscape is filled with pointless violence, no-frills packaging, media hypnosis, and aliens. Executive producer: none other than ex-Monkee Michael Nesmith. **93m/C; VHS, DVD.** Emilio Estevez; Harry Dean Stanton; Sy Richardson; Tracey Walter; Olivia Barash; Fox Harris; Jennifer Balgobin;

Vonetta McGee; Angelique Pettyjohn; Biff Yeager; **D:** Alex Cox; **W:** Alex Cox; **C:** Robby Muller; **M:** Tito Larriva; Iggy Pop.

Repo Men 🦴🦴 **2010 (R)** In the near future, a giant corporation supplies the world with artificial organs but they're pricey, and not covered by medical insurance. And just like buying a house or a car, if payments aren't made, then the merchandise gets repossessed. After a fall out with his employer, ex-repo man Remy (Law) joins forces with drugged-out singer Beth (Braga), going up against his former partner Jake (Whitaker) to protect his own artificial parts. While lifting a generic hyper-active style from Guy Ritchie, first-time director Sapochnik isn't as confident with the film's mood or purpose, wobbling along as part sci-fi, part satire, part action, but never committing to much of anything. **111m/C; DVD, Blu-Ray.** Jude Law; Forest Whitaker; Alice Braga; Carice van Houten; Liev Schreiber; **D:** Miguel Sapochnik; **W:** Eric Garcia; Garrett Lerner; **C:** Enrique Chediak; **M:** Marco Beltrami.

Repo! The Genetic Opera 🦴 **2008 (R)** Truly awful although it may pass muster for inclusion in the midnight movie madness genre. Sometime in the future, organs may be bought for transplantation purposes—and repossessed if you're late with your payments. Villainous Rotti Largo (Sorvino) has manipulated guilt-ridden scientist Nathan (Head) into becoming a repo man so Nathan can care for his sickly daughter, the angelic Shilo (Vega). **98m/C; Blu-Ray, On Demand.** Anthony Head; Alexa Vega; Paul Sorvino; Bill Moseley; Paris Hilton; Sarah Brightman; Terrance Zdunich; Nivek Ogre; **D:** Darren Lynn Bousman; **W:** Darren Smith; **C:** Joseph White; **M:** Darren Smith. Golden Raspberries '08: Worst Support. Actress (Hilton).

The Report 🦴🦴 ½ **2019 (R)** Working for the U.S. Senate Intelligence Committee, lead investigator Daniel J. Jones (Driver) has been charged with looking into the CIA's suspect detention and interrogation program after the 9/11 terrorist attacks. For the next five years, he devotes the whole of his life to this work, finding and examining an endless stack of documents that detail many examples of torturing detainees as he writes his 6,700 page report for the committee. Though the real-life story being told is important and features an impressive cast, it does not easily lend itself to film and is overloaded with information. **118m/C; DVD.** Adam Driver; Corey Stoll; Jon Hamm; Linda Powell; Annette Bening; **D:** Scott Z. Burns; **W:** Scott Z. Burns; **C:** Eigil Bryld; **M:** David Wingo.

Report to the Commissioner 🦴🦴🦴 *Operation Undercover* **1975 (R)** A rough, energetic crime-in-the-streets cop thriller. A young detective accidentally kills an attractive woman who turns out to have been an undercover cop, then is dragged into the bureaucratic cover-up. **112m/C; VHS, DVD, Blu-Ray.** Michael Moriarty; Yaphet Kotto; Susan Blakely; Hector Elizondo; Richard Gere; Tony King; Michael McGuire; Stephen Elliott; William Devane; Bob Balaban; **D:** Milton Katselas; **W:** Abby Mann; **M:** Elmer Bernstein.

The Reports on Sarah and Saleem 🦴🦴🦴 **2019** In Jerusalem, Sarah (Kretchner) is a cafe owner who is married to an Israeli army officer, David (Golan). Sarah receives deliveries for her cafe from a Palestinian named Saleem (Safadi) who lives in East Jerusalem with his pregnant wife. The pair are having a sexual affair. Their lives and freedoms are threatened when Saleem invites her to join him on his night job running goods to Bethlehem and her identity as an Israeli is unintentionally revealed. The well-constructed psychological drama/thriller offers deep insights into tensions between Israelis and Palestinians though the characters are sometimes unbelievable. **127m/C; DVD.** Sivane Kretchner; Adeeb Safadi; Maisa Abd Elhadi; Kamel El Basha; Hanan Hillo; **D:** Muayad Alayan; **W:** Rami Musa Alayan; **C:** Sebastian Bock; **M:** Frank Gelat; Charlie Rishmawi; Tarek Abu Salameh.

Repossessed 🦴🦴 **1990 (PG-13)** A corny, occasionally funny takeoff on the human-possessed-by-the-devil films with Blair, as usual, as the afflicted victim. Nielsen, in another typecast role, plays the goofy man of the cloth who must save the day. Numerous actors appear in brief comedy sequences which lampoon current celebrities and constitute the film's highlights. For fans of "Airplane" and "The Naked Gun"; not necessarily for others. **89m/C; VHS, DVD.** Linda Blair; Ned Beatty; Leslie Nielsen; Anthony Starke; Jesse Ventura; **D:** Bob Logan; **W:** Bob Logan; **M:** Charles Fox. Golden Raspberries '90: Worst Song ("He's Comin' Back (The Devil!)").

Reprisal 🦴 ½ **2018 (R)** During a robbery spree in Cincinnati, the bank managed by Jacob (Grillo) is hit and a security guard is shot to death. Haunted by the event, Jacob pulls away from his wife (Culpo) and young daughter. He reaches out to his ex-cop neighbor James (Willis) to find the robber, take him down, and prevent him from pulling off another heist. The robber, Gabriel (Schaech), has his own issues. He is robbing banks to give his ill father, a veteran, better nursing home care. Full of endless chases and shoot-outs, the film is an unoriginal and endless game of cat and mouse. **89m/C; DVD.** Bruce Willis; Frank Grillo; Johnathon Schaech; Olivia Culpo; Natali Yura; **D:** Brian A. Miller; **W:** Bryce Hammons; **C:** Peter Holland; **M:** Sonya Belousova; Giona Ostinelli.

Reprise 🦴🦴 **2006 (R)** Feature film debut of Trier follows the fortunes of two 20-something childhood buds, Erik (Klouman-Hoiner) and Phillip (Lie). They share the same literary ambitions but only Phillip's first novel gets published and becomes a success. However, he can't deal with the attention, develops an obsession with girlfriend Kari (Winge), and has a breakdown that lands him in a mental hospital. Meanwhile, Erik neglects his girlfriend Lillian (Hagen) for his literary pursuits and tries to remain loyal to Phillip. Norwegian with subtitles. **105m/C; DVD.** *NO SW* Anders Danielsen Lie; Espen Klouman-Hoiner; Viktoria Winge; Silje Hagen; Sigmund Saeverud; **D:** Joachim Trier; **W:** Joachim Trier; Eskil Vogt; **C:** Jakob Ihre; **M:** Ola Flottum; Knut Schreiner.

The Reptile 🦴🦴 **1966** The inhabitants of yet another Cornish village are turning up dead—mysteriously from snakebite. When Harry (Barrett) investigates his brother's death, he finds out Anna (Pearce) is the victim of a curse, which causes her to turn into a snake. Rather sympathetic characters for the horror genre. **90m/C; VHS, DVD, Blu-Ray.** *GB* Jacqueline Pearce; Ray Barrett; Noel Willman; Jennifer Daniel; Michael Ripper; John Laurie; Marne Maitland; Charles Lloyd-Pack; George Woodbridge; **D:** John Gilling; **W:** John (Anthony Hinds) Elder; **C:** Arthur Grant; **M:** Don Banks.

Reptilian 🦴 **1999 (PG-13)** Archeologists Campbell (Livingston) and Hughes (Young) are searching for remains of a gigantic dinosaur. But guess who gets to them first? Evil aliens! Who want to take over the earth! So they ray-zap the dino remains back to life and the creature goes on a rampage until the military puts him down. But it doesn't end there—although you'll certainly wish it had. **99m/C; VHS, DVD.** *NK* Harrison Young; Donna Philipson; Richard B. Livingston; **D:** Hyung Rae Shim; **W:** Marty Poole; **C:** Hong Kim An; **M:** Chris Desmong; Seung Woo Cho.

Reptilicus 🦴🦴 **1962** Oil drillers in Lapland bring up a sample of prehistoric flesh from a frozen bog and it's transported to Copenhagen. It proves to be alive and a lightning storm frees it from its holding tank as a completely regenerated monster, crawling across the landscape, crushing buildings and eating farmers. The authorities have no luck ridding themselves of the scaly, snake-like dragon until they corner it in the main square in downtown Copenhagen. The several hundred extras running politely through the streets look bored or amused and most of the scenes are artlessly shot in broad daylight, making its general artificiality even more obvious. **90m/C; DVD, Blu-Ray.** *DK* Carl Ottosen; Ann Smyrner; Mimi Heinrich; Asbjorn Andersen; Bodil Miller; Bent Mejding; Dirch Passer; Ole Wisborg; **D:** Sidney W. Pink; **W:** Sidney W. Pink; Ib Melchior; **C:** Aage Wiltrup; **M:** Sven Gyldmark.

The Republic of Love 🦴🦴 ½ **2003** Set in Toronto and based on the novel by Carol Shields. Late-night radio talk show host Tom had an unconventional upbringing that has led to his being impulsive about love and marriage (including three ex-wives). Academician Fay views her parents' 40-year marriage as perfect so she has impossibly high standards for her own relationships. When their lives finally intersect, there is instant attraction and a lot of unrealistic expectations. **96m/C; DVD.** *CA* Bruce Greenwood; Emilia Fox; Edward Fox; Martha Henry; Lloyd Owen; Jackie Burroughs; Gary Farmer; Jan Rubes; **D:** Deepa Mehta; **W:** Deepa Mehta; Esta Spalding; **C:** Douglas Koch; **M:** Talvin Singh.

Repulsion 🦴🦴🦴 ½ **1965** Character study of a young French girl who is repulsed and attracted by sex. Left alone when her sister goes on vacation, her facade of stability begins to crack, with violent and bizarre results. Polanski's first film in English and his first publicly accepted full-length feature. Suspenseful, disturbing and potent. **105m/B; VHS, DVD, Blu-Ray.** *GB* Catherine Deneuve; Yvonne Furneaux; Ian Hendry; John Fraser; Patrick Wymark; James Villiers; Renee Houston; Helen Fraser; Mike Pratt; Valerie Taylor; **D:** Roman Polanski; **W:** Roman Polanski; Gerard Brach; David Stone; **C:** Gilbert Taylor.

Requiem for a Dream 🦴🦴🦴 ½ **2000** Amazing performances from the entire cast propel this harrowing story of drug addiction and crumbled dreams. Harry (Leto) and his friend Tyrone (Wayans) become small-time drug dealers so Harry can get the cash to help his girlfriend Marion (Connelly) open a clothing store. Unfortunately, they begin to sample the merchandise until all they can plan is how to get their next fix. In a parallel storyline, Harry's mother Sara (Burstyn) learns she may be a contestant on her favorite game show. So she begins gobbling diet pills to improve her appearance and soon can't live without them. Based on the novel by Hubert Selby, Jr. **102m/C; VHS, DVD.** Jared Leto; Ellen Burstyn; Jennifer Connelly; Marlon Wayans; Christopher McDonald; Louise Lasser; Keith David; Sean Gullette; **D:** Darren Aronofsky; **W:** Darren Aronofsky; Hubert Selby, Jr.; **C:** Matthew Libatique; **M:** Clint Mansell. Ind. Spirit '01: Actress (Burstyn), Cinematog.

Requiem for a Heavyweight 🦴🦴🦴 **1956** Original TV version of the story about an American Indian heavyweight boxer played by Palance who risks blindness in order to help his manager pay off bookies. Highly acclaimed teleplay written for "Playhouse 90." **90m/B; VHS, DVD.** Jack Palance; Keenan Wynn; Ed Wynn; Kim Hunter; Ned Glass; **D:** Ralph Nelson; **W:** Rod Serling. **TV**

Requiem for a Heavyweight 🦴🦴🦴 *Blood Money* **1962** After 17 years, Mountain Rivera (Quinn) is a washed-up heavyweight risking his life if he continues boxing. He tries to find another job but his manager, Maish Rennick (Gleason), owes the mob big, and persuades the fighter to help him pay off his debts by joining the wrestling circuit, so Mountain humiliates himself to help out his old friend. The 1956 TV version is still more compelling but the film's performances are all first-rate. **100m/B; VHS, DVD.** Anthony Quinn; Jackie Gleason; Mickey Rooney; Julie Harris; Stanley Adams; Spivy Levoe; Muhammad Ali; Jack Dempsey; **D:** Ralph Nelson; **W:** Rod Serling; **C:** Arthur Ornitz; **M:** Laurence Rosenthal.

Requiem for Murder 🦴 ½ **1999 (PG-13)** Psychotic fan of a classical radio DJ decides to murder her competition. **95m/C; VHS, DVD.** Molly Ringwald; Christopher Heyerdahl; Lynne Adams; Chris Mulkey; Jayne Heitmeyer; **D:** Douglas Jackson; **W:** Matt Dorff; **C:** Barry Gravelle; **M:** Milan Kymlicka. **VIDEO**

The Rescue 🦴 ½ **1988 (PG)** An elite team of U.S. Navy Seals is captured after destroying a disabled submarine. When the U.S. government writes off the men, their children decide to mount a rescue. Puerile, empty-headed trash for teens. **97m/C; VHS, Streaming.** Marc Price; Charles Haid; Kevin Dillon; Christina Harnos; Edward Albert; **D:** Ferdinand Fairfax; **W:** Jim Thomas; John Thomas; **C:** Russell Boyd; **M:** Bruce Broughton.

Rescue Dawn 🦴🦴🦴 **2006 (PG-13)** Brutal true survival story of Dieter Dengler, the only American POW to ever escape from a prison camp in the Laotian jungle and return alive to his own side. Director Herzog—who also helmed a documentary version of Dengler's epic experience a decade earlier with "Little Dieter Needs to Fly"?forgoes the flashy effects and plot complications of most modern war films in favor of raw storytelling. Funny guy Zahn is notable in a rare non-comic screen role. **125m/C; DVD, Blu-Ray.** Christian Bale; Steve Zahn; Jeremy Davies; Evan Jones; Marshall Bell; Zach Grenier; Toby Huss; Abhijati Jusakul; Pat Healy; Galen Yuen; Chaiyan Chunsuttiwat; **D:** Werner Herzog; **W:** Werner Herzog; **C:** Peter Zietlinger; **M:** Klaus Bartle.

Rescue from Gilligan's Island 🦴 ½ **1978** Fifteen years after the cancellation of "Gilligan's Island" came this TV movie that reunited the principal cast (minus Tina Louise's original Ginger). After a tsunami sweeps the group's huts into the sea, they're discovered by the Coast Guard and return to civilization. The former castaways face difficulties assimilating with modern life, while at the same time Gilligan is pursued by Russian spies sent to retrieve an information disc that landed on the island. A dated, awkward return to the lame jokes and slapstick of the TV series, although the cast's chemistry is still evident. **92m/C; VHS, DVD.** Bob Denver; Alan Hale, Jr.; Russell Johnson; Jim Backus; Natalie Schafer; Dawn Wells; Judith Baldwin; **D:** Leslie Martinson; **W:** David Harmon; Sherwood Schwartz; Elroy Schwartz; Al Schwartz; **C:** Robert Primes; **M:** Gerald Fried. **TV**

The Rescuers 🦴🦴🦴 **1977 (G)** Bernard and Miss Bianca, two mice who are members of the Rescue Aid Society, attempt to rescue an orphan named Penny from the evil Madame Medusa, who's after the world's biggest diamond. They are aided by comic sidekick, Orville the albatross, and a group of lovable swamp creatures. Very charming in the best Disney tradition. Based on the stories of Margery Sharp. Followed by "The Rescuers Down Under." **76m/C; VHS, DVD, Blu-Ray.** **V:** Bob Newhart; Eva Gabor; Geraldine Page; Jim Jordan; Joe Flynn; Jeannette Nolan; Pat Buttram; **D:** Wolfgang Reitherman; John Lounsbery; **M:** Artie Butler.

The Rescuers Down Under 🦴🦴 ½ **1990 (G)** "Crocodile" Dundee goes Disney; the followup to "The Rescuers" places its characters in Australia with only mild results for a Magic Kingdom product. Heroic mice Bernard and Bianca protect a young boy and a rare golden eagle from a poacher. The great bird closely resembles the logo of Republic Pictures. **77m/C; VHS, DVD, Blu-Ray.** **V:** Bob Newhart; Eva Gabor; John Candy; Tristan Rogers; George C. Scott; Frank Welker; Adam Ryen; **D:** Hendel Butoy; Mike Gabriel; **W:** Jim Cox; Karey Kirkpatrick; Joe Ranft; Byron Simpson; **M:** Bruce Broughton.

Reservation Road 🦴🦴 **2007 (R)** Dwight Arno (Ruffalo) is a small town Connecticut lawyer. Already running late returning his son to his ex-wife's home at the end of a visitation day, he accidentally strikes and kills a young boy with his car, then flees the scene in panic. The dead boy's grief-stricken father, Ethan Learner (Phoenix), is filled with anger and dissatisfied with local law enforcement's inability to find his son's killer. So he seeks the assistance of an attorney—the conficted Dwight. An unfortunate series of coincidences stretch believability and derail this overly melodramatic story. **102m/C; DVD, Blu-Ray.** Joaquin Rafael (Leaf) Phoenix; Mark Ruffalo; Jennifer Connelly; Christopher Sorvino; Elle Fanning; John Slattery; Antoni Corone; Sean Curley; Eddie Alderson; **D:** Terry George; **W:** John Burnham Schwartz; **C:** John Lindley; **M:** Mark Isham.

Reservoir Dogs 🦴🦴🦴 ½ **1992 (R)** Ultraviolent tale of honor among thieves. Six professional criminals known by code names to protect their identities (Misters Pink, White, Orange, Blonde, Blue, and Brown) are assembled by Joe Cabot (Tierney) to pull off a diamond heist. But two of the gang are killed in a police ambush. The survivors regroup in an empty warehouse and try to discover the informer in their midst. In probably the most stomach-churning scene, a policeman is tortured (by Madsen) just for the heck of it to the tune of the Stealers Wheel "Stuck in the Middle with You." Unrelenting; auspicious debut for Tarantino with strong ensemble cast anchored by Keitel as the very professional Mr. White. **100m/C; DVD, Blu-Ray.** Harvey Keitel; Tim Roth; Michael Madsen; Steve Buscemi; Christopher Penn; Lawrence Tierney; Kirk Baltz; Quentin Tarantino; Edward (Eddie) Bunker; Randy Brooks; **V:** Steven Wright; **D:**

Quentin Tarantino; ***W:*** Quentin Tarantino; ***C:*** Andrzej Sekula; ***M:*** Karyn Rachtman. Ind. Spirit '93: Support. Actor (Buscemi).

The Resident 1/2 **2010 (R)** Mediocre woman-in-peril thriller with only a few scares. Juliet (Swank) moves into a suspiciously perfect apartment after breaking up with boyfriend Jack (Pace). Landlord Max (Morgan) is oh-so-helpful but Juliet soon gets the feeling she's being watched. Unfortunately, she's not paranoid since it's all too clear Max is an obsessed stalker. **91m/C; DVD, Blu-Ray.** Hilary Swank; Jeffrey Dean Morgan; Lee Pace; Christopher Lee; Aunjanue Ellis; ***D:*** Antti Jokinen; ***W:*** Antti Jokinen; Robert Orr; ***C:*** Guillermo Navarro; ***M:*** John Ottman. **VIDEO**

Resident Evil **2002 (R)** Yet another noisy movie adapted from a videogame, which never gets as creepy as a zombie movie should. Umbrella Corp. (AKA the Hive) is the front for a secret military tech and genetics operations. Its security operations are controlled by a A.I. computer known as the Red Queen, which instigates a series of defensive measures to contain a virus (that can reanimate the dead) that has been released. A group of containment specialists (including heroine babe Jovanovich) are sent in and have to battle workers who have been contaminated and turned into flesh-munching creatures. **100m/C; VHS, DVD, Blu-Ray, UMD.** *GE GB* Milla Jovovich; Michelle Rodriguez; Colin Salmon; Eric Mabius; James Purefoy; Stephen Billington; ***D:*** Paul W.S. Anderson; ***W:*** Paul W.S. Anderson; ***C:*** David C(lark) Johnson; ***M:*** Marco Beltrami.

Resident Evil: Afterlife 1/2 *Resident Evil: Afterlife: An IMAX 3D Experience* **2010 (R)** Hoping to breathe new life into a floundering franchise (unsuccessfully), this fourth (but not last) installment also hops onto the 3D bandwagon with mixed results. Alice (Jovovich) and sidekick Claire (Larter) fly to L.A. to meet up with other survivors in search of sanctuary from the zombie plague but instead they (gasp!) walk straight into a city swarming with undead creatures! Plot continues its backseat ride with femme fatale buttkicking aggressively in the driver's seat. Fans should note the return of Anderson as director. **97m/C; Blu-Ray, On Demand.** Milla Jovovich; Ali Larter; Wentworth Miller; Kim Coates; Boris Kodjoe; Shawn Roberts; Sienna Guillory; Fulvio Cecere; ***D:*** Paul W.S. Anderson; ***W:*** Paul W.S. Anderson; ***C:*** Glen MacPherson; ***M:*** tomandandy.

Resident Evil: Apocalypse **2004 (R)** While its predecessor was a moderately successful return to pulp science-fiction films, this outing is nothing of the kind. It's less of a sequel than a regurgitating of the earlier installment but with fewer thrills, less action, and an inconsequential story. Alice and a new batch of survivors are trying to escape the city above The Hive, which has been re-infected with the T-virus. By simply rehashing the first film, any fresh conflict is forgone. Lack of suspense and characterization make for an uninspired, unoriginal, and thoroughly unenjoyable genre pic. **93m/C; VHS, DVD, Blu-Ray, UMD.** *GB CA* Milla Jovovich; Sienna Guillory; Oded Fehr; Thomas Kretschmann; Sophie Vavasseur; Jared Harris; Mike Epps; Sandrine Holt; Raz Adoti; Zack (Zach) Ward; Iain Glen; ***D:*** Alexander Witt; ***W:*** Paul W.S. Anderson; ***C:*** Christian Sebaldt; Derek Rogers; ***M:*** Jeff Danna.

Resident Evil: Extinction 1/2 **2007 (R)** Video game franchise trades claustrophobic underground sets for "Road Warrior" style wasteland, but star Jovovich is stuck battling the same old zombies. This time super-powered Alice meets up with a convoy of refugees trying to stay one step ahead of the zombie virus. Between the zombies and the evil corporation that created them, there's not much hope that they'll make it to safety unscathed. Instead, they must make a stand in a mostly sand-buried Las Vegas (created by Oscar-winning production designer Caballero). Short on originality, the movie depends on its mostly dull action scenes and its franchise status to keep viewers interested. **94m/C; DVD, Blu-Ray.** *CA GB* Milla Jovovich; Oded Fehr; Ali Larter; Iain Glen; Ashanti; Christopher Egan; Spencer Locke; Matthew Marsden; Linden Ashby; Mike Epps; Jason O'Mara; ***D:*** Russell Mulcahy; ***W:*** Paul W.S. Anderson; ***C:*** David Johnson; ***M:*** Charlie Clouser.

Resident Evil: Retribution 1/2 **2012 (R)** In this fifth franchise installment, Alice (Jovovich) once again provides familar, butt-kicking action as she's still after the Umbrella Corporation, hunting those responsible for the T-virus, which is turning the world's population into zombies. Characters who died in previous films are alive in a plot where Alice has to explain to the viewer what happened previously and it still makes no sense. But there are lots of explosions, chases, automatic weapons fire, and the inevitability of another sequel. **96m/C; DVD, Blu-Ray.** *CA GE* Milla Jovovich; Sienna Guillory; Michelle Rodriquez; Li Bingbing; Boris Kodjoe; Johann Urb; Kevin Durand; Oded Fehr; Colin Salmon; Shawn Roberts; ***D:*** Paul W.S. Anderson; ***W:*** Paul W.S. Anderson; ***C:*** Glen MacPherson; ***M:*** tomandandy.

Resident Evil: The Final Chapter **2016 (R)** Purportedly the final chapter in the series of films loosely based on the Capcom video game series. Director Anderson's decent CGI action orgy returns to the scene of the first film to tie up loose ends. Alice (Jovovich) is one of the last survivors of the worldwide plague unleashed by the Umbrella Corporation. She now must go back to where it all began, Raccoon City, and face the creators of the disease head on to stop them from eliminating the last vestige of human life on Earth. **106m/C; DVD, Blu-Ray, Streaming.** *AU US GE FR UK JP CA SA* Milla Jovovich; Ali Larter; Iain Glen; Shawn Roberts; William Levy; ***D:*** Paul W.S. Anderson; ***W:*** Paul W.S. Anderson; ***C:*** Glen MacPherson; ***M:*** Paul Haslinger.

Resident Evil: Vendetta **2017 (R)** An animated take on the action-horror Resident Evil series. Evil scientist Glenn Arias (DeMita) makes plans to get revenge by spreading a deadly virus in New York City. After BSAA co-founder Chris Redfield (Dorman) fails to contain Arias in his rundown mansion, Chris teams up with shell-shocked government agent Leon S. Kennedy (Mercer) and brainy professor Rebecca Chambers (Cahill), an expert in viral outbreaks. As Rebecca finishes a vaccine and cure for the manufactured disease, Chris and Leon must keep those who want to stop them at bay. More action than horror, the film features beautiful animation but a heavy-handed script. **97m/C; DVD.** Kevin Dorman; Matthew Mercer; Erin Cahill; John De Mita; Fred Tatasciore; ***D:*** Takanori Tsujimoto; ***W:*** Makoto Fukami; ***M:*** Kenji Kawai.

Resilience 1/2 **2006** Corporate manager Jimmy finds doing a good deed brings lots of trouble. He fakes the work record of his destitute Uncle Hodge to get him a job and then gets blackmailed by his shifty cousin Andrew. Jimmy learns a drug dealer has put a contract out on the troublesome Andrew and he can't decide whether to warn him or let the hit take place, which would solve Jimmy's own problems with the sleazebag. **96m/C; DVD.** Henry LeBlanc; Steve Wilcox; Al Rossi; Julie Alexander; Amy Arce; ***D:*** Paul Bojack; ***W:*** Paul Bojack; ***C:*** Michael Parry; ***M:*** Markian Federowycz.

Resistance **1992** Apocalyptic tale of rebels and soldiers. The poor have been driven from abandoned cities into working as farm hands for a large corporation. When the workers rebel, anti-terrorist squads manage to make the situation worse and a full-scale rebellion begins. **112m/C; VHS, DVD.** Jack Thompson; Stephen Leeder; Robyn Nevin; Harold Hopkins; Helen Jones; Kris McQuade; Hugh Keays-Byrne; ***D:*** Paul Elliot.

Resistance **2003 (R)** Wartime romance based on the novel by Anita Shreve. American fighter pilot Ted Brice (Paxton) is shot down over Belgium in 1944. He's badly injured but brought to safety by members of the resistance. Hidden and cared for by Claire (Ormond), whose husband Henri (Volter) is away on a mission, they soon find love. When their affair is discovered by Henri, it sets up more than one betrayal. **92m/C; DVD.** Bill Paxton; Julia Ormond; Philippe Volter; Sandrine Bonnaire; Jean-Michel Vovk; Antoine Van Lierde; ***D:*** Todd Komarnicki; ***W:*** Todd Komarnicki; ***C:*** Marc Felperlaan; ***M:*** Angelo Badalamenti.

Resistance **2020 (R)** In late 1930s France, Marcel (Eisenberg) works as a mime in a cabaret despite his father's disapproval. At the same time, he is already involved with the French Resistance as the threat of Nazi Germany looms. As the war tears his country apart, Marcel fights Nazi oppression by saving war orphans, including Elsbeth (Ramsey), while working with the Boy Scouts and Girl Scouts. By the end of the war, Marcel serves as a liaison officer for U.S. General George Patton (Harris). A biopic about mime Marcel Marceau, the film expertly weaves many story threads while showing Marcel's toughness and humanity. **120m/C; DVD.** Jesse Eisenberg; Clemence Poesy; Felix Moati; Vica Kerekes; Matthias Schweighofer; ***D:*** Jonathan Jakubowicz; ***W:*** Jonathan Jakubowicz; ***C:*** Miguel Ioann Littin Menz; ***M:*** Angelo Milli.

A Respectable Trade 1/2 **1998** Frances Scott (Fielding) has lost her position as a governess in 1788 Bristol, England. A job-search letter gathers Frances a marriage proposal from Josiah Cole (Clarke), an older, earnest, social climbing businessman whose trade happens to be slaves. Josiah wishes Frances to teach English to some of his property so they may be sold as house servants and Frances begins to feel something special for one of the group—Moses (Bakare)--who turns out to be much more of an educated gentleman than her own husband. Based on Gregory's 1995 novel. **240m/C; DVD.** *UK* Emma Fielding; Warren Clarke; Ariyon Bakare; Anna Massey; ***D:*** Suri Krishnamma; ***W:*** Philippa Gregory. **TV**

Respire 1/2 **2009 (R)** Cross' flick starts off as a thriller and turns into horror. A doctor researches a Roman legend about bottling a person's dying breath. He discovers it can prevent sickness and aging for the next person who breathes it in, although not without serious consequences. Terminally ill antiques dealer Sue has a couple of very interested customers for a wooden box containing the vial but she uses it herself and bloody havoc follows. **90m/C; DVD.** Tracy Teague; Matthew J. Wright; Vince Eustace; Ellie Torrez; Timothy Dykes; ***D:*** David A. Cross; ***W:*** David A. Cross; ***C:*** Nick Gardner; ***M:*** Dimitris Plagiannis.

Respiro *I Breathe; Respiro: Grazia's Island* **2002 (PG-13)** Grazia (Golino'the only professional in the cast) doesn't fit into the usual life of the Sicilian fishing village of Lempedusa. Although devoted to her husband Pietro (Amato) and their children, Grazia's emotions are volatile (even by Italian standards). When Pietro tries to send his wife to Milan for treatment, she runs away to hide out in a local cave, depending on her 13-year-old son Pasquale (Casisa) to protect her. The film replaces reality (the fact that Grazia has a mental illness) with poetics (she's really just a free-spirit) but you'll be lulled by its charms. Italian with subtitles. **95m/C; VHS, DVD.** *IT FR* Valeria Golino; Vincenzo Amato; Francesco Casisa; Veronica D'Agostino; Filippo Pucillo; Muzzi Loffredo; Elio Germano; ***D:*** Emanuele Crialese; ***W:*** Emanuele Crialese; ***C:*** Fabio Zamarion; ***M:*** John Surman.

Rest Stop *Rest Stop: Dead Ahead* **2006** The dumbest woman of all time and her boyfriend pause at a rest stop while en route to California. When she returns from the loo he's gone, and then she finds a torture victim in the restroom who apparently couldn't speak up before. Eventually she gets chased by a psycho, tries to escape by hitching a ride with a family of psychos, and makes other unfortunate choices, including getting drunk and passing out instead of going for help. **85m/C; DVD, Blu-Ray.** Joey Mendicino; Deanna Russo; Joseph Lawrence; Mikey Post; Diane Salinger; Jaimie Alexander; Michael Childers; Nick Orefice; ***D:*** John Shiban; ***W:*** John Shiban; ***C:*** Mark Vargo; ***M:*** Bear McCreary.

Rest Stop: Don't Look Back 1/2 *Rest Stop 2* **2008** One year after the events of the first film, the brother of one of the victims returns from Iraq and goes looking for her. He and his companions immediately find an eyewitness who proceeds to give the stereotypical "y'all wanna leave this place" explanation germane to all bad horror films. The killers from the original return, and once again you have an average torture flick, spiced up only by the appearance of ghosts from the victims killed in the first go-round. **89m/C; DVD, Blu-Ray.** Richard Tillman; Jessie Ward; Mikey Post; Julie Mond; Joey Mendicino; Graham Norris; ***D:*** Shawn Papazian; ***C:*** Jas Shelton; ***M:*** Bear McCreary. **VIDEO**

Restaurant 1/2 **1998 (R)** Would-be showbiz types all work at the same swanky New Jersey restaurant while exploring their relationships and ambitions. Recovering alcoholic and aspiring playwright Chris (Brody) is still carrying a torch for ex-girlfriend, Leslie (Hill) who slept with actor/co-worker Kenny (Baker), who's been cast in Chris' new play, much to his dismay. Meanwhile, Chris is trying a new romance with singer/waitress Jeanine (Neal). Although race doesn't seem to be a problem in personal relations (Chris is white, both his girlfriends are black), it starts to raise ugly problems at work (and change the tenor of the movie). **107m/C; DVD.** Adrien Brody; Elise Neal; David Moscow; Simon Baker; Catherine Kellner; Malcolm Jamal Warner; Lauryn Hill; John Carroll Lynch; Sybil Temchen; Vonte Sweet; Michael Stoyanov; ***D:*** Eric Bross; ***W:*** Tom Cudworth; ***C:*** Horacio Marquinez; ***M:*** Theodore Shapiro.

Resting Place **1986** Filmed as part of Hallmark's Hall of Fame series, the story follows Maj. Kendall Laird as he accompanies home the body of a black soldier who fell in Vietnam. He is to arrange for a burial but the soldier's racist hometown refuses to let an African-American soldier be buried there. An investigation into the town's secrets turns up some pretty ugly truths before all is over. **100m/C; DVD.** John Lithgow; Richard Bradford; Morgan Freeman; G.D. Spradlin; CCH Pounder; Frances Sternhagen; M. Emmet Walsh; ***D:*** John Korty; ***W:*** Walter Halsey Davis; ***C:*** William Wages; ***M:*** Paul Chihara. **TV**

Restless **2011 (PG-13)** Two young people who are overly familiar with death fall for each other—Enoch (Hopper) recently lost both of his parents in a car accident and briefly died himself, a situation leading to a funeral obsession and talking to ghosts, while alluring Annabel (Wasikowska) is herself terminally ill. Following their doomed romance, director Van Sant is meditative and poetic yet at times too twee and hipster. **91m/C; DVD, Blu-Ray.** Mia Wasikowska; Henry Hopper; Ryo Kase; Schuyler Fisk; Jane Adams; Lusia Strus; ***D:*** Gus Van Sant; ***W:*** Jason Lew; ***C:*** Harris Savides; ***M:*** Danny Elfman.

Restless Spirits 1/2 *Dead Aviators* **1999** Sullen Katie (Wimbles) and her young brother Simon (Swan) are staying with their grandmother Lydia (Mason) in Porter's Point, Newfoundland. Both children are still grieving the death of their aviator father in a crash four years before. While exploring a remote pond, Katie encounters the ghosts of French airmen Nungesser (Bluteau) and Coli (Monty). In 1927, they left Paris in a biplane on a nonstop trans-Atlantic flight to New York and disappeared. It seems their plane crashed into Porter's Pond and until it can be recovered they are doomed to wander the area. Katie's determined to help, though no one believes her story. **95m/C; VHS, DVD.** *CA* Juliana Wimbles; Lothaire Bluteau; Michel Monty; Marsha Mason; Leslie Hope; Ben Cook; Eugene Lipinski; Nickolas Swan; ***D:*** David Wellington; ***W:*** Semi Chellas; ***C:*** Andre Pienaar; ***M:*** Ron Sures. **CABLE**

The Restless Years **1958** Typical '50s teenage melodrama with a couple of angsty leads. Her neurotic mom is going crazy and she's illegitimate, so Melinda (Dee) is an outcast in her disapproving hometown. This means she and wrong-side-of-the-tracks Will Henderson (Saxon) are made for each other--if their young love can survive high school bullies and the town gossips. **87m/B; DVD.** Sandra Dee; John Saxon; Teresa Wright; James Whitmore; Margaret Lindsay; ***D:*** Helmut Kautner; ***W:*** Edward Anhalt; ***C:*** Ernest Laszlo; ***M:*** Frank Skinner.

Restoration **1994 (R)** After curing one of King Charles II's (Neill) dogs, physician Robert Merivel (Downey) is elevated to courtier and falls into drunken debauchery. He's forced to marry (but not touch) the king's favorite mistress, but disobeys and is banished from the court. Cast among the common rabble, he encounters the plague and the Great Fire of London while trying to redeem himself. Strong cast and sumptuous set design help to propel Downey's performance. Adapted from Rose Tremain's 1989 novel. **118m/C; VHS, DVD.** Robert Downey, Jr.; Meg Ryan; Sam Neill; Hugh Grant; David Thewlis; Polly Walker; Ian McKellen; ***D:*** Michael Hoffman; ***W:*** Rupert Walters; ***C:***

Oliver Stapleton; ***M:*** James Newton Howard. Oscars '95: Art Dir./Set Dec., Costume Des.

Restraining Order **1999 (R)** Lawyer Robert Woodfield (Roberts) witnesses a murder that's committed by a former client. He contacts a friend in the D.A.'s office but when that friend is also murdered and Woodfield's efforts to bring the killer to justice are futile, he decides to personally avenge the crimes. **95m/C; VHS, DVD.** Eric Roberts; Hannes Jaenicke; Tatjana Patitz; Dean Stockwell; ***D:*** Lee H. Katzin; ***W:*** John Jarrell; ***M:*** David Wurst; Eric Wurst. **VIDEO**

Restraint **2008 (R)** Ron and Dale are a couple of not-so-bright criminals who get into a mess and need a place to hide out. They come across what they think is an abandoned mansion, only wealthy agoraphobic Andrew actually lives there and the duo take him hostage. Except Andrew is really willing and starts telling Dale how much she looks like his ex-fiancee, who just happened to leave all her things behind when she supposedly left him. So who's really got the upper hand? **92m/C; DVD.** *AU* Stephen Moyer; Teresa Palmer; Travis Fimmel; ***D:*** David Denneen; ***W:*** David T. Wagner; ***C:*** Simon Duggan; ***M:*** Elliott Wheeler.

Restrepo **2010 (R)** Beginning in June 2007, reporter/author Sebastian Junger and war photographer Tim Hetherington began shadowing the Second Platoon, Battle Company, 173rd Airborne Brigade through their 15-month deployment in Afghanistan's isolated and dangerous Korengal Valley. The two made 10 trips (until July 2008) to film and interview the soldiers, and their documentary is told from the soldiers' POV. The title refers to the name of the platoon's first casualty, Pfc. Juan S. Restrepo, and the mountain outpost that the platoon dedicates to him. **92m/C; Blu-Ray, On Demand.** ***D:*** Tim Hetherington; Sebastian Junger; ***C:*** Tim Hetherington; Sebastian Junger.

Results **1/2 2015 (R)** Danny (Corrigan) is newly rich and with no idea what to do with his money. He hires a trainer named Kat (Smulders) really just out of boredom, but Kat's boss Trevor (Pearce) doesn't take to Danny's flirtations with his employee, realizing he himself has feelings for her. Andrew Bujalski makes an unexpected stab at mainstream success with this romantic comedy but the loose, jangly style he brought to his mumblecore films remains, resulting in a bizarre but entertaining piece similar to James L. Brooks' timeless "Broadcast News." Smulders is fantastic here, and the film has a clever, winking energy to it. **105m/C; DVD.** Guy Pearce; Cobie Smulders; Kevin Corrigan; Giovanni Ribisi; Brooklyn Decker; ***D:*** Andrew Bujalski; ***W:*** Andrew Bujalski; ***C:*** Matthias Grunsky; ***M:*** Justin Rice.

The Resurrected **1/2 1991 (R)** One of the best recent H.P. Lovecraft horror adaptations, a fairly faithful try at "The Case of Charles Dexter Ward." Ward learns he has a satanic ancestor who possessed the secret of resurrection and eternal life—but, as the warlock says, it is very messy. Surprisingly tasteful even with occasional gore and truly ghastly monsters; in fact this pic could have used a bit more intensity. **108m/C; VHS, DVD, Blu-Ray.** John Terry; Jane Sibbett; Chris Sarandon; Robert Romanus; ***D:*** Dan O'Bannon; ***M:*** Richard Band.

Resurrecting the Champ **2007 (PG-13)** Denver sports reporter Erik Kernan (Hartnett) is looking for a big story and thinks he's found it in homeless Bob "Champ" Satterfield (Jackson), a former contender. Erik pursues his big chance to make a name for himself without much concern for Champ, but after his feature story is published, Erik realizes that everything might not be what it seems. Of course there's a valuable lesson to be learned, but Hartnett ultimately can't give his flawed character depth. Any energy Jackson gives disappears the second he's not on the screen. Loosely based on a true story about writer J.R. Moehringer and real-life boxer Satterfield. **111m/C; DVD, Blu-Ray.** Samuel L. Jackson; Josh Hartnett; Teri Hatcher; Kathryn Morris; Alan Alda; David Paymer; Rachel Nichols; Dakota Goyo; Harry J. Lennix; Peter Coyote; Ryan McDonald; ***D:*** Rod Lurie; ***W:*** Michael Bortman; Allison Burnett; ***C:*** Adam Kane; ***M:*** Lawrence Nash Groupe.

Resurrection **1/2 1980 (PG)** After a near-fatal car accident, a woman finds she has the power to heal others by touch. She denies that God is responsible, much to her Bible Belt community's dismay. Acclaimed and well-acted. **103m/C; VHS, DVD, Blu-Ray.** Ellen Burstyn; Sam Shepard; Roberts Blossom; Eva LeGallienne; Clifford David; Richard Farnsworth; Pamela Payton-Wright; ***D:*** Daniel Petrie; ***W:*** Lewis John Carlino; ***M:*** Maurice Jarre. Natl. Bd. of Review '80: Support. Actress (LeGallienne).

Resurrection **1999 (R)** Chicago detectives John Prudhomme (Lambert) and Andrew Hollinsworth (Orser) are tracking a serial killer (Joy) who is killing men named after Christ's 12 apostles. He intends to use parts of his victims to reassemble the body of Christ in time for Easter Sunday resurrection. **108m/C; VHS, DVD.** Christopher Lambert; Leland Orser; Robert Joy; Rick Fox; Barbara Tyson; James Kidnie; David Cronenberg; ***D:*** Russell Mulcahy; ***W:*** Brad Mirman; ***C:*** Jonathan Freeman; ***M:*** Jim McGrath.

The Resurrection of Gavin Stone **1/2 2017 (PG)** A faith-based comedy-drama centered on a prodigal son given a chance for redemption. Once a child star, Gavin Stone (Dalton) is now a self-destructive actor landing few roles. After being sentenced to community service for an incident the last time he visited his hometown, he returns to complete his sentence. Assigned to do janitorial work at a local church, Gavin wins the role of Jesus Christ in a church production directed by the pastor's daughter, Kelly Richardson (Johnson-Reyes). Preparing for the play seems to change Gavin, but the offer of a comeback role in Hollywood makes him question his commitment. Predictable yet pleasant. **91m/C; DVD.** Brett Dalton; Anjelah Johnson-Reyes; Neil Flynn; D.B. Sweeney; Shawn Michaels; ***D:*** Dallas Jenkins; ***W:*** Andrea Gyertson Nasfell; ***C:*** Lyn Moncrief; ***M:*** Jeehun Hwang.

Resurrection of Zachary Wheeler **1/2 1971 (G)** A presidential candidate, who narrowly escaped death in an auto crash, is brought to a mysterious clinic in New Mexico. A reporter sneaks into the clinic and discovers the horrors of cloning. **100m/C; VHS, DVD.** Angie Dickinson; Bradford Dillman; Leslie Nielsen; Jack Carter; James Daly; ***D:*** Bob Wynn.

Retour Chez Ma Mere *Back to Mom's* **2016** A French comedy-drama. Once a successful architect, Stephanie (Lamy) has lost her job and her money. To get back on her feet, she moves home with her mother, Jacqueline (Balasko). Stephanie struggles at first, as her mother treats her as a child, finding a job proves difficult, and her siblings are jealous. The situation becomes more difficult for Stephanie when she has to ask her siblings for money. The family situation grows more complicated when it becomes clear that Stephanie's mother is keeping an unexpected secret from her children. French, with subtitles. **97m/C; DVD.** Alexandra Lamy; Josiane Balasko; Mathilde Seigner; Philippe Lefebvre; Didier Flamand; ***D:*** Eric Lavaine; ***W:*** Eric Lavaine; Hector Cabello Reyes; ***C:*** Francois Hernandez; ***M:*** Fabien Cahen. **VIDEO**

Retreat **1/2 2011 (R)** In a last ditch effort to save their failing marriage, Martin (Murphy) and Kate (Newton) return to the isolated island where their romance began. Instead, they get an unwelcome visitor when alleged soldier Jack (Bell) washes ashore with a fantastic tale that a pandemic has suddenly been wiping out humanity and they must continue to stay on the island if they want to survive. His story is never quite believable, although they can't contact anyone on the mainland, and Kate and Martin generally behave like fools. This thriller doesn't hold up but the actors try their best. **90m/C; DVD.** *GB* Cillian Murphy; Thandie Newton; Jamie Bell; ***D:*** Carl Tibbetts; ***W:*** Carl Tibbetts; Janice Hallett; ***C:*** Chris Seager; ***M:*** Ilan Eshkeri.

Retribution **1/2 1988 (R)** Struggling artist survives suicide attempt only to find himself possessed by the spirit of a criminal who was tortured to death. Seeing the hood's gruesome demise in his dreams, the survivor sets out to bring his murderers face-to-face with their maker. **106m/C; VHS, DVD, Blu-Ray.** Dennis Lipscomb; Hoyt Axton; Leslie Wing; Suzanne Snyder; ***D:*** Guy Magar.

Retribution *Complicity* **1998 (R)** Cameron Colley (Miller) is an investigative journalist who constantly runs into trouble with his editors. He's also addicted to cigarettes, cocaine, computer games, and sex with the married Yvonne (Hawes). Now he's looking into a series of grisly murders that possibly lead back to the youthful protests of a group of activists. Tends to be confusing more than compelling. Based on the novel by Iain Banks. **99m/C; VHS, DVD.** *GB* Jonny Lee Miller; Brian Cox; Keeley Hawes; Paul Higgins; Bill Paterson; Samuel West; Rachael Stirling; Jason Hetherington; ***D:*** Gavin Millar; ***W:*** Bryan Elsley; ***C:*** David Odd; ***M:*** Colin Towns.

Retribution Road **1/2** *Blue Eyes* **2007 (PG-13)** A bank robbery gone wrong lands Wardlaw, Texas sheriff Gimbol with notorious outlaw Johnny Rios as a prisoner in his jail. However, Rios' family will stop at nothing to break him out, even if it means they destroy the town trying. **75m/C; DVD.** Michael Gregory; Leslie Easterbrook; Peter Sherayko; John Castellanos; Eduardo Enriquez, Jr.; Mark Enriquez; ***D:*** Chuck Walker; ***W:*** Chuck Walker. **VIDEO**

Retrievers **1982** Young man and a former CIA agent team up to expose the unsavory practices of the organization. **90m/C; VHS, DVD.** Max (Michael) Thayer; Roselyn Royce; Richard Anderson; Shawn Hoskins; Mary McCormick; Lenard Miller; ***D:*** Elliot Hong; ***W:*** Elliot Hong; ***C:*** Stephen Kim; ***M:*** Ted Ashford.

Retro Puppet Master **1999 (PG-13)** Most recent entry in the "Puppet Master" series is officially the first, finding a young Toulon in pre-World War I Paris where he falls in love with the daughter of the Swiss ambassador. Of course, the puppets and other mini-critters are involved too. **90m/C; DVD, Blu-Ray.** Guy Rolfe; Greg Sestero; Brigitta Dau; Jack Donner; Stephen Blackehart; ***D:*** Joseph Tennent; ***W:*** Benjamin Carr; ***C:*** Viorel Sergovici, Jr.; ***M:*** John Massari.

Retroactive **1997 (R)** Scientist Brian (Whaley) has been experimenting with reversing time and finally manages to make his project work. Meanwhile, police psychologist Karen (Travis) has has car trouble and been given a ride by Frank (Belushi) and his wife Rayanne (Whirry). Karen soon realizes Frank is a psycho and escapes, stumbling into Brian's lab. But Brian's just reversed time and Karen winds up back in Frank's car, trying to change the sequence of events. **91m/C; VHS, DVD, Blu-Ray.** James Belushi; Kylie Travis; Shannon Whirry; Frank Whaley; Jesse Borrego; M. Emmet Walsh; Guy Boyd; ***D:*** Louis Morneau; ***W:*** Robert Strauss; Phillip Badger; ***C:*** George Mooradian; ***M:*** Tim Truman.

Retrograde **1/2 2003 (R)** A meteor carrying an alien virus is discovered in Antarctica and quickly begins wiping out humanity. Time travelers immune to the virus travel back to prevent it being found and have to deal with the fact that each of them has ulterior motives, which will quickly put a halt to their mission. **94m/C; DVD.** Dolph Lundgren; Silvia De Santis; Gary Daniels; Joe Sagal; ***D:*** Christopher Kulikowski; ***W:*** Tom Reeve; ***C:*** Carlo Thiel; ***M:*** Stephen Melillo.

The Return **1/2 2006 (PG-13)** Supernatural thriller that substitutes atmospheric moodiness for actual plot and dialogue. Joanna (Gellar) is a sales rep who uses the constant movement of her job to escape the visions and blackouts that have plagued her since her childhood. When business brings her back to her hometown, her hallucinations intensify. She begins seeing visions of a woman and the mysterious dirtbag who may have murdered her. Soon Joanna is being stalked by the killer, as well as by a jilted ex and a sexy stranger who also seems wrapped up in the mystery. **85m/C; DVD, Blu-Ray.** Sarah Michelle Gellar; Peter O'Brien; Adam Scott; Kate Beahan; Sam Shepard; J.C. MacKenzie; Erinn Allison; ***D:*** Asif Kapadia; ***W:*** Adam Sussman; ***C:*** Roman Osin; ***M:*** Dario Marianelli.

Return **2011** Familiar, though not unworthy, back-from-war family drama. Kelli (Cardellini), an Ohio National Guard reservist, has returned home after a non-combatant tour of duty. She thinks she can easily readjust to life with her husband and daughters, as well as her family, friends, and old job. She can't. Increasinlgy depressed, Kelli begins to drink and her struggles increase. **97m/C; DVD, Blu-Ray.** Linda Cardellini; Michael Shannon; John Slattery; Talia Balsam; Paul Sparks; ***D:*** Liza Johnson; ***W:*** Liza Johnson; ***C:*** Anne Etheridge.

Return from Witch Mountain **1/2 1978 (G)** A pair of evil masterminds use a boy's supernatural powers to place Los Angeles in nuclear jeopardy. Sequel to Disney's ever-popular "Escape to Witch Mountain." **93m/C; VHS, DVD, Blu-Ray.** Christopher Lee; Bette Davis; Ike Eisenmann; Kim Richards; Jack Soo; Helene Winston; ***D:*** John Hough; ***W:*** Malcolm Marmorstein.

The Return of a Man Called Horse **1976 (PG)** Sequel to "A Man Called Horse" tells the story of an English aristocrat who was captured and raised by Sioux Indians, and then returned to his native homeland. Contains more of the torture scenes for which this series is famous, but not much of Harris. **125m/C; VHS, DVD, Blu-Ray.** Richard Harris; Gale Sondergaard; Geoffrey Lewis; ***D:*** Irvin Kershner; ***W:*** Jack DeWitt; ***C:*** Owen Roizman.

The Return of Boston Blackie **1/2 1927** The oft-filmed crook/detective tries to retrieve an heiress's stolen jewels. Silent. **77m/B; Silent; VHS, DVD.** Raymond Glenn; Corliss Palmer; Strongheart; Rosemary Cooper; Coit Albertson; ***D:*** Harry Hoyt.

Return of Captain Invincible **1/2** *Legend in Leotards* **1983 (PG)** Arkin is a derelict superhero persuaded to fight crime again in this unique spoof. One liners fly faster than a speeding bullet. Lee gives one of his best performances as the mad scientist. Musical numbers by Rocky Horror's O'Brien and Hartley sporadically interrupt. Made on a shoe-string budget, offbeat film is entertaining but uneven. **102m/C; VHS, DVD.** *AU* Alan Arkin; Christopher Lee; Kate Fitzpatrick; Bill Hunter; Graham Kennedy; Michael Pate; Hayes Gordon; Max Phipps; Noel Ferrier; ***D:*** Philippe Mora; ***W:*** Steven E. de Souza; Andrew Gaty; ***C:*** Louis Irving; Mike Molloy; ***M:*** William Motzing; Richard O'Brien.

Return of Chandu **1934** This serial in 12 chapters features Bela Lugosi as Chandu, who exercises his magical powers to conquer a religious sect of cat worshippers inhabiting the island of Lemuria. In the process, he fights to save the Princess Nadji from being sacrificed by them. **156m/B; VHS, DVD.** Bela Lugosi; Maria Alba; Clara Kimball Young; ***D:*** Ray Taylor.

The Return of Count Yorga **1971 (R)** The vampire Count returns, taking up residence in a decrepit mansion nearby an orphanage. There he spies the toothsome Cynthia and Yorga decides to make her a vampiric bride. But the Count reckons without Cynthia's noble boyfriend who wants to keep his honey on this side of the grave. Preceded by "Count Yorga, Vampire." **97m/C; VHS, DVD, Blu-Ray.** Robert Quarry; Mariette Hartley; Roger Perry; Yvonne Wilder; Rudy DeLuca; George Macready; Walter Brooke; Tom Toner; Karen Huston; Paul Hansen; Craig T. Nelson; ***D:*** Bob Kelljan; ***W:*** Yvonne Wilder; Bob Kelljan; ***C:*** Bill Butler.

The Return of Dr. Mabuse **1/2** *Im Stahlnetz Des Dr. Mabuse; Phantom Fiend* **1961** The evil doctor is back, this time sending his entranced slaves to attack a nuclear power plant. Frobe, the inspector, and Barker, the FBI man, team up to thwart him. Fun for fans of serial detective stories. **88m/B; VHS, DVD.** *GE FR IT* Gert Frobe; Lex Barker; Daliah Lavi; Wolfgang Preiss; Fausto Tozzi; Rudolph Forster; ***D:*** Harald Reinl.

Return of Dracula *The Curse of Dracula; The Fantastic Disappearing Man* **1958** Low-budget film about the Count killing a Czech artist and assuming his identity as he makes his way to the States. Once there, he moves in with the dead man's family and begins acting rather strangely. Retitled "The

Curse of Dracula" for TV. **77m/C; VHS, DVD, Blu-Ray.** Francis Lederer; Norma Eberhardt; Ray Stricklyn; Jimmy Baird; John Wengraf; Virginia Vincent; Greta Granstedt; *D:* Paul Landres; *W:* Pat Fielder; *C:* Jack MacKenzie.

The Return of Eliot Ness 1/2 **1991 (R)** Ness comes out of retirement in 1947 Chicago to track down a friend's killer. And with Al Capone dead, Chicago mob bosses are fighting for their piece of illegal turf. Stack reprises his "The Untouchables" TV role from the early '60s in this made for TV movie. **94m/C; VHS, DVD.** Robert Stack; Charles Durning; Philip Bosco; Jack Coleman; Lisa Hartman Black; Anthony De Sando; *D:* James A. Contner. **TV**

Return of Frank James **1940** One of Lang's lesser Hollywood works, this is nonetheless an entertaining sequel to 1939's "Jesse James." Brother Frank tries to go straight, but eventually has to hunt down the culprits who murdered his infamous outlaw sibling. Tierney's first film. **92m/C; VHS, DVD, Blu-Ray.** Henry Fonda; Gene Tierney; Jackie Cooper; Henry Hull; John Carradine; Donald Meek; J. Edward Bromberg; *D:* Fritz Lang.

The Return of Jafar 1/2 **1994 (G)** Clumsy thief Abis Mal inadvertently releases evil sorcerer Jafar from his lamp prison and now the powerful "genie Jafar" plots his revenge. So it's up to Aladdin and friends to save the Sultan's kingdom once again. Contains five new songs. **66m/C; VHS, DVD, Blu-Ray.** *V:* Scott Weinger; Linda Larkin; Gilbert Gottfried; Val Bettin; Dan Castellaneta; Jason Alexander; *W:* Kevin Campbell; Mirith J.S. Colao.

Return of Jesse James **1950** Look-alike of dead outlaw Jesse James joins in with some former members of the James Gang, leading townsfolk to believe the notorious bank robber never died. It's up to brother Frank James, now an upstanding citizen, to set the record straight. A little slow moving at times, but still worth viewing. **77m/B; VHS, DVD.** John Ireland; Ann Dvorak; Reed Hadley; Henry Hull; Hugh O'Brian; Tommy Noonan; Peter Marshall; *D:* Arthur Hilton.

The Return of Joe Rich 1/2 **2011** Joe (Witwer) loses his job and his wife leaves him, so he returns to his Chicago hometown and asks his mob-connected Uncle Dominic (Assante) for help. Joe isn't a natural gangster (he's squeamish), but he watches and learns. Assante's an asset but the most original part of Auster's pic is having 10 elderly, former wiseguys serve as a Greek chorus. **90m/C; DVD.** Sam Witwer; Armand Assante; Talia Shire; Vanessa Vander Pluym; Joe Minoso; Tim Kazurinsky; *D:* Sam Auster; *W:* Sam Auster; *C:* Lance Catania; *M:* Danny Tuss; David Tuss. **VIDEO**

The Return of Martin Guerre 1/2 *Le Retour de Martin Guerre* **1983** In this medieval tale, a dissolute village husband disappears soon after his marriage. Years later, someone who appears to be Martin Guerre returns, allegedly from war, and appears much kinder and more educated. Starring in a love story of second chances, Depardieu does not disappoint, nor does the rest of the cast. In French with English subtitles. Based on an actual court case. Remade in 1993 as "Sommersby." **111m/C; VHS, DVD, Blu-Ray.** *FR* Gerard Depardieu; Roger Planchon; Maurice Jacquemont; Barnard Pierre Donnadieu; Nathalie Baye; *D:* Daniel Vigne; *W:* Daniel Vigne; Jean-Claude Carriere; *C:* Andre Neau; *M:* Michel Portal. Cesar '83: Score, Writing; Natl. Soc. Film Critics '83: Actor (Depardieu).

Return of Sabata 1/2 **1971 (PG)** Van Cleef is back in this thoroughly confusing mishmash. Sabata is working as a trick-shot performer in a circus that arrives in the town of Hobsonville. Robber baron Joe McIntock heavily taxes the community, secretly turning his ill-gotten gains into gold so he can skip town with a fortune. Sabata discovers his plan. **100m/C; DVD, Blu-Ray.** *IT* Lee Van Cleef; Giampiero Albertini; Reiner Schone; Pedro Sanchez; Annabella Incontrera; *D:* Gianfranco Parolini; *W:* Gianfranco Parolini; Renato Izzo; *C:* Sandro Moncori; *M:* Marcello Gombini.

The Return of Spinal Tap 1/2 **1992** Cult-fave mock rock group Spinal Tap is back with a feature-length video of performance and backstage footage from its recent reunion concert tour promoting their album "Break Like the Wind." Sequel to "This Is Spinal Tap" features lots of heavy metal songs including the title track, "Majesty of Rock," "Bitch School," "Diva Fever," "Clam Caravan," and "Stinkin' Up the Great Outdoors." Not as great as the original satire, but will appeal to Spinal Tap fans. **110m/C; VHS, DVD.** Christopher Guest; Michael McKean; Harry Shearer; Rick Parnell; C.J. Vanston; June Chadwick; *Cameo(s):* Paul Anka; Jeff Beck; Jamie Lee Curtis; Richard Lewis; Martha Quinn; Kenny Rogers; Martin Short; Mel Torme; Rob Reiner; Paul Shaffer; Fred Willard; Bob Geldof; *W:* Christopher Guest; Michael McKean; Harry Shearer.

The Return of Swamp Thing 1/2 **1989 (PG-13)** The DC Comics creature rises again out of the muck to fight mutants and evil scientists. Tongue-in-cheek, and nothing at all like the literate, ecologically oriented comic from which it was derived. **95m/C; VHS, DVD.** Louis Jourdan; Heather Locklear; Sarah Douglas; Dick Durock; *D:* Jim Wynorski.

Return of the Aliens: The Deadly Spawn *The Deadly Spawn* **1983 (R)** Aliens infect the earth and violently destroy humans. Extremely violent and gory. Watch out for those officious offspring. **90m/C; VHS, DVD.** Charles George Hildebrandt; *D:* Douglas McKeown.

Return of the Bad Men **1948** Scott is a retired marshall who must fight against a gang of outlaws lead by the Sundance Kid. Sequel to "Badman's Territory." **90m/C; VHS, DVD.** Randolph Scott; Robert Ryan; Anne Jeffreys; George "Gabby" Hayes; Jason Robards, Sr.; Jacqueline White; *D:* Ray Enright; *W:* Charles "Blackie" O'Neal.

The Return of the Beverly Hillbillies **1981** The Clampett clan, along with now-government official Miss Jane help to solve the energy crisis using Granny's 'white lightening.' Adding to the whoops and hollers is Miss Jane's downhome Ozark wedding to her boss Mr. Medford. Entertaining enough but not quite the same with the loss of key players in the parts of Granny, Mr. Drysdale and Jethro. **100m/C; VHS, DVD.** Buddy Ebsen; Donna Douglas; Nancy Kulp; Ray Young; Imogene Coca; *D:* Robert M. Leeds; *W:* Paul Henning. **VIDEO**

The Return of the Cisco Kid 1/2 **1939** The Cisco Kid (Baxter) helps lovely Ann (Bari) whose property has been swindled from her by the land-grabbing sheriff (Barrat). Baxter's third and last time in the role following "In Old Arizona" (1928) and "The Cisco Kid" (1931). **71m/B; DVD.** Warner Baxter; Lynn Bari; Robert Barrat; Henry Hull; Kane Richmond; Cesar Romero; *D:* Herbert I. Leeds; *W:* Milton Sperling; *C:* Charles G. Clarke.

Return of the Dragon 1/2 **1973 (R)** In Lee's last picture, a Chinese restaurant in Rome is menaced by gangsters who want to buy the property. On behalf of the owners, Lee duels an American karate champ in the Roman forum. The battle scenes between Lee and Norris are great and make this a must-see for martial arts fans. **91m/C; VHS, DVD, Blu-Ray.** *CH* Bruce Lee; Nora Miao; Chuck Norris; *D:* Bruce Lee; *W:* Bruce Lee; *C:* Ho Lang Shang; *M:* Joseph Koo.

Return of the Evil Dead *Return of the Blind Dead; El Ataque de los Muertos Sin Ojos* **1975** The sightless dead priests return to attack still more 1970s' Europeans in this second installment of the "blind dead" trilogy. Preceded by "Tombs of the Blind Dead" and followed by "Horror of the Zombies." Not to be confused with Raimi's "Evil Dead" slasher flicks. **85m/C; VHS, DVD.** *SP PT* Tony Kendall; Esther Roy; Frank Blake; Fernando (Fernand) Sancho; Lone Fleming; Loreta Tovar; Jose Canalejas; *D:* Armando de Ossorio; *W:* Armando de Ossorio; *C:* Miguel Mila; *M:* Anton Abril.

Return of the Fly **1959** The son of the scientist who discovered how to move matter through space decides to continue his father's work, but does so against his uncle's wishes. He soon duplicates his dad's experiments with similar results. This sequel to "The Fly" doesn't buzz like the original. Followed by "Curse of the Fly." **80m/B; VHS, DVD, Blu-Ray.** Vincent Price; Brett Halsey; John Sutton; Dan Seymour; David Frankham; Danielle De Metz; Ed Wolff; *D:* Edward L. Bernds; *W:* Edward L. Bernds; Brydon Baker.

Return of the Frontiersman 1/2 **1950** Sheriff's son Logan Barrett (MacRae) is falsely accused and convicted of numerous crimes and sent to jail. He escapes to find the man who framed him with the help of girlfriend Janie (London). MacRae croons a couple of western ditties to pass the time. **74m/C; DVD.** Edwin Rand; *W:* Edna Anhalt.

Return of the Gunfighter 1/2 **1967** Released from prison after a wrongful murder conviction, aging gunslinger Ben Wyatt (Taylor) wants a quiet life. After an old friend and his wife are murdered, Ben and the couple's daughter, Anisa (Martin), want to find the killers. They should ask Lee Sutton (Everett), the young gun that Ben is mentoring, since he knows more than he's saying. Taylor's final Western was originally shown as an ABC TV movie. **96m/C; DVD.** Robert Taylor; Ana Martin; Chad Everett; Lyle Bettger; Mort Mills; *D:* James Neilson; *W:* Robert Buckner; *C:* Ellsworth Fredericks; *M:* Hans J. Salter. **TV**

Return of the Jedi 1/2 *Star Wars: Episode 6—Return of the Jedi* **1983 (PG)** Third film in George Lucas' popular space saga. Against seemingly fearsome odds, Luke Skywalker battles such worthies as Jabba the Hut and heavy-breathing Darth Vader to save his comrades and triumph over the evil Galactic Empire. Han and Leia reaffirm their love and team with C3PO, R2-D2, Chewbacca, Calrissian, and a bunch of furry Ewoks to aid in the annihilation of the Dark Side. The special effects are still spectacular, even the third time around. Sequel to "Star Wars" (1977) and "The Empire Strikes Back" (1980). **132m/C; VHS, DVD, Blu-Ray.** Mark Hamill; Carrie Fisher; Harrison Ford; Billy Dee Williams; David Prowse; James Earl Jones; Kenny Baker; Denis Lawson; Anthony Daniels; Peter Mayhew; Sebastian Shaw; Jeremy Bulloch; Toby Philpot; *V:* Alec Guinness; Frank Oz; *D:* Richard Marquand; *W:* George Lucas; Lawrence Kasdan; *C:* Alan Hume; *M:* John Williams. Oscars '83: Visual FX.

Return of the Killer Tomatoes! **1988 (PG)** The man-eating plant-life from 1977's "Attack of the Killer Tomatoes" is back, able to turn into people due to the slightly larger budget. Astin is mad as the scientist. Not as bad as "Attack," representing a small hurdle in the history of filmdom. Followed by "Killer Tomatoes Strike Back." **98m/C; VHS, DVD, Blu-Ray.** Anthony Starke; George Clooney; Karen Mistal; Steve Lundquist; John Astin; Charlie Jones; Rock Peace; Frank Davis; C.J. Dillon; Teri Weigel; *D:* John DeBello; *W:* John DeBello; Constantine Dillon; Steve Peace; *C:* Stephen Kent Welch; *M:* Neal Fox; Rick Patterson.

The Return of the King 1/2 **1980** The third and final animated episode of J.R.R Tolkien's Middle Earth Trilogy. This saga features Frodo, relative to Hobbit Bilbo Baggins, and his faithful servant, making middle Earth safe from Orcs, Gollums and other ooky creatures. **120m/C; VHS, DVD.** *V:* Orson Bean; Roddy McDowall; John Huston; Theodore Bikel; William Conrad; Glen Yarborough; Paul Frees; Casey Kasem; Sonny Melendrez; *D:* Arthur Rankin, Jr.; Jules Bass; *M:* Maury Laws.

Return of the Living Dead 1/2 **1985 (R)** Poisonous gas revives a cemetery and a morgue rendering an outrageous spoof on the living-dead sub-genre with fast-moving zombies, punk humor, and exaggerated gore. Its humor does not diminish the fear factor, however. Sequel follows. Directed by "Alien" writer O'Bannon. **90m/C; VHS, DVD, Blu-Ray.** Clu Gulager; James Karen; Linnea Quigley; Don Calfa; Jewel Shepard; Beverly Randolph; Miguel A. Nunez, Jr.; Brian Peck; *D:* Dan O'Bannon; *W:* Dan O'Bannon; John A. Russo; Russell Streiner; *C:* Jules Brenner.

Return of the Living Dead 2 1/2 **1988 (R)** An inevitable sequel to the original Dan O'Bannon satire about George Romero-esque brain-eating zombies attacking suburbia with zest and vigor. **89m/C; VHS, DVD, Blu-Ray.** Dana Ashbrook; Marsha Dietlein; Philip Bruns; James Karen; Thom Mathews; Suzanne Snyder; Michael Kenworthy; Thor Van Lingen; *D:* Ken Wiederhorn; *W:* Ken Wiederhorn; *C:* Robert Elswit.

Return of the Living Dead 3 1/2 **1993 (R)** When Curt's girlfriend Julie dies in a motorcycle accident you'd think that would be the end of romance. But not when your dad heads a secret project that involves reviving corpses. Only problem is now Julie's a zombie with long metal claws and glass spikes sticking out of various body parts. Hey, if it's true love Curt will get over it. Macabre special effects. Also available unrated. **97m/C; VHS, DVD, Blu-Ray.** Melinda (Mindy) Clarke; J. Trevor Edmond; Kent McCord; Basil Wallace; Fabio Urena; *D:* Brian Yuzna; *W:* John Penney; *C:* Gerry Lively; *M:* Barry Goldberg.

Return of the Living Dead: Rave to the Grave **2005 (R)** Don't expect much from the franchise and you won't be disappointed. In this fifth installment, university chemist Garrison (Coyote) creates a toxin that is discovered by a group of buds who make their own designer drug. One pill gets you high but use too many and you become a brain-eating zombie. Just in time to party at the campus Halloween rave. **86m/C; DVD.** Peter Coyote; Aimee-Lynn Chadwick; John Keefe; Cory Hardrict; Jenny Mollen; *D:* Ellory Elkayem; *W:* William Butler; Aaron Strongoni; *C:* Gabriel Kosuth. **VIDEO**

Return of the Magnificent Seven *Return of the Seven* **1966** The first sequel to "The Magnificent Seven" features the group liberating a compatriot who is held hostage. Yawn. **97m/C; VHS, DVD, Blu-Ray.** Yul Brynner; Warren Oates; Robert Fuller; Claude Akins; Julian Mateos; Elisa Montes; Emilio Fernandez; *D:* Burt Kennedy; *W:* Larry Cohen; *C:* Paul Vogel; *M:* Elmer Bernstein.

Return of the Man from U.N.C.L.E. **1983** Those dashing super agents Napoleon Solo and Illya Kuryakin come out of retirement to settle an old score with their nemesis THRUSH. **96m/C; VHS, DVD.** Robert Vaughn; David McCallum; Patrick Macnee; Gayle Hunnicutt; Geoffrey Lewis; *D:* Ray Austin. **TV**

The Return of the Native 1/2 **1994 (PG)** Wind-swept moors, a tempestuous heroine, two loves, and requisite tragedy all courtesy of Thomas Hardy's 1878 novel. Beautiful Eustacia Vye (Jones) longs to leave the boredom of Egdon Heath—even though she's involved with the roguish Damon Wildeve (Owen). Then businessman Clym Yeobright (Stevenson) returns from Paris and captures Eustacia's fancy. She marries him in the hope they'll return to the continent but she's bitterly disappointed when they remain in Egdon. Meanwhile, Damon has married Clym's gentle cousin Thomasin (Skinner) but he and Eustacia can't stay away from each other. **99m/C; VHS, DVD.** Catherine Zeta-Jones; Clive Owen; Ray Stevenson; Claire Skinner; Joan Plowright; Steven Mackintosh; Celia Imrie; Paul Rogers; *D:* Jack Gold; *W:* Robert W. Lenski; *M:* Carl Davis. **TV**

Return of the Pink Panther 1/2 **1974 (G)** Bumbling Inspector Clouseau is called upon to rescue the Pink Panther diamond stolen from a museum. Sellers manages to produce mayhem with a vacuum cleaner and other devices that, in his hands, become instruments of terror. Clever opening credits. Fourth installment in the Pink Panther series but the first with Sellers since 1964's "A Shot in the Dark." **113m/C; VHS, DVD, Blu-Ray.** Peter Sellers; Christopher Plummer; Catherine Schell; Herbert Lom; Victor Spinetti; *D:* Blake Edwards; *W:* Frank Waldman; Blake Edwards; *C:* Geoffrey Unsworth; *M:* Henry Mancini.

Return of the Rebels **1981** TV fluff with Eden as a motorcycle matron whose campground is rid of riff-raff by the crow-lined participants in a 25-year reunion of a biker gang. **100m/C; VHS, DVD.** Barbara Eden; Robert Mandan; Jamie Farr; Patrick Swayze; Don Murray; Christopher Connelly; *D:* Noel Nosseck. **TV**

The Return of the Scarlet Pimpernel 1/2 **1937** Barnes is a lackluster replacement for Leslie Howard (of the 1934 original "The Scarlet Pimpernel") in this tepid historical adventure. Sir Percy returns to France and disguises himself once again in order to rescue his kidnapped wife Marguerite from evil Robespierre and the Reign of Terror. **80m/B; DVD.** Barry K. Barnes; Sophie Stewart; Henry Oscar; Anthony Bushnell; Francis Lister; James Mason; Margaretta Scott; ***D:*** Hanns Schwarz; ***W:*** Lajos Biro; Adrian Brunel; Arthur Wimperis; ***C:*** Mutz Greenbaum.

Return of the Secaucus 7 1/2 **1980** Centers around a weekend reunion of seven friends who were activists during the Vietnam War in the turbulent '60s. Now turning 30, they evaluate their present lives and progress. Writer and director Sayles plays Howie in this excellent example of what a low-budget film can and should be. A less trendy predecessor of "The Big Chill" (1983) which, perhaps, was a few years ahead of its time. **110m/C; VHS, DVD.** Mark Arnott; Gordon Clapp; Maggie Cousineau-Arndt; David Strathairn; Adam LeFevre; Bruce MacDonald; Maggie Renzi; Jean Passanante; Karen Trott; John Sayles; ***D:*** John Sayles; ***W:*** John Sayles; ***C:*** Austin De Besche; ***M:*** Mason Daring. L.A. Film Critics '80: Screenplay; Natl. Film Reg. '97.

Return of the Soldier **1982** A shell-shocked WWI veteran has no memory of his marriage, leaving his wife, his childhood flame, and an unrequited love to vie for his affections. Adapted from the novel by Rebecca West. **101m/C; VHS, DVD.** *GB* Glenda Jackson; Julie Christie; Ann-Margret; Alan Bates; Ian Holm; Frank Finlay; ***D:*** Alan Bridges; ***M:*** Richard Rodney Bennett.

Return of the Street Fighter 1/2 *Satsujin-ken 2* **1974** Sequel to "The Street Fighter," finds Terry Tsuguri (Chiba) hired by a gang to silence a jailed informer. So, Terry gets arrested, practices his karate and does the guy in, and finds out the gang now wants to silence him. Big mistake! Notice a pattern yet? Followed by "The Street Fighter's Last Revenge" and "Sister Street Fighter." **88m/C; VHS, DVD, Blu-Ray.** *JP* Sonny Chiba; Claude Gannyon; ***D:*** Shigehiro (Sakae) Ozawa; ***W:*** Hajjime Koiwa; Koji Takada; ***C:*** Teiji Yoshida.

The Return of the Swamp Thing 1/2 **1989 (PG-13)** Swampy (Durock) is back to once again battle the evil Dr. Arcane (Jourdan), who's doing a Dr. Moreau impression with a bigger lab and a hot, blonde stepdaughter (Locklear). The intentional campiness doesn't make up for the bad writing, inept effects, and unintentional chuckles. **84m/C; DVD, Blu-Ray.** Dick Durock; Louis Jourdan; Heather Locklear; Santiago Douglas; Joe Sagal; Monique Gabrielle; RonReaco Lee; Ace Mask; ***D:*** Jim Wynorski; ***W:*** Neil Cuthbert; Grant Morris; ***C:*** Zoran Hochstatter; ***M:*** Chuck Cirino. Golden Raspberries '89: Worst Actress (Locklear).

Return of the Vampire **1943** A Hungarian vampire and his werewolf servant seek revenge on the family who drove a spike through his heart two decades earlier. **69m/B; VHS, DVD, Blu-Ray.** Bela Lugosi; Nina Foch; Miles Mander; Matt Willis; Frieda Inescort; Roland Varno; Gilbert Emery; Ottola Nesmith; ***D:*** Lew Landers; ***W:*** Griffin Jay; ***C:*** L. William O'Connell; John Stumar.

Return to Africa **1989** Rebels threaten the familial paradise of the tightknit Mallory clan. **95m/C; VHS, DVD.** Stan Brock; Anne Collings; David Tors; Ivan Tors; Peter Tors; Steven Tors; ***D:*** Leslie Martinson.

Return to Boggy Creek **1977 (PG)** Townspeople in a small fishing village learn from a photographer that a "killer" beast, whom they thought had disappeared, has returned and is living in Boggy Creek. Some curious children follow the shutterbug into the marsh, despite hurricane warnings, and the swamp monster reacts with unusual compassion. OK for the kiddies. Fictitious story unlike other "Boggy Creek" films, which are billed as semi-documentaries. Sequel to "Legend of Boggy Creek" and features Mary Ann from "Gilligan's Island." **87m/C; VHS, DVD.** Dawn Wells; Dana Plato; Louise Belaire; John Hofeus; ***D:*** Tom (Thomas R.) Moore.

Return to Cabin by the Lake 1/2 **2001** Psychos never die—they always return to do the sequel. Presumed dead writer/ serial killer Stanley Caldwell (Nelson) isn't dead at all. In fact, he infiltrates a movie crew making a film adaptation of the circumstances of his killing spree. But Stanley doesn't like the way events are being portrayed, so he bumps off the director (Krause) and takes control. Campy rather than scary. **89m/C; VHS, DVD.** Judd Nelson; Brian Krause; Dahlia Salem; Michael P. Northey; Emmanuelle Vaugier; ***D:*** Po-Chih Leung; ***W:*** Jeffrey Reddick; ***C:*** Stephen M. Katz; ***M:*** Frankie Blue. **CABLE**

Return to Cranford 1/2 **2009** Picks up where "Cranford" left off as Miss Matty (Dench) and her gossiping cronies enjoy the social life of their close-knit mid-Victorian-era village. However, inevitable progress is chugging along just outside of town as the railroad comes ever closer to linking Cranford to the wider world despite some community opposition. The usual mixture of reunions, romance, and tragedy also plays a part. Based on the stories by Elizabeth Gaskell. **175m/C; DVD.** *GB* Dame Judi Dench; Julia McKenzie; Barbara Flynn; Imelda Staunton; Jim Carter; Jonathan Pryce; Tom Hiddleston; Michelle Dockery; Lesley Sharp; Jodie Wittaker; Matthew McNulty; Emma Fielding; Alex Etel; Celia Emrie; Francesca Annis; Greg Wise; Nicholas Le Prevost; Tim Curry; Alex Jennings; Claudie Blakley; ***D:*** Simon Curtis; ***W:*** Heidi Thomas; ***C:*** Ben Smithard; ***M:*** Carl Davis. **TV**

Return to Fantasy Island 1/2 **1977** Boss, boss, it's da plane! The second full-length TV treatment of the once-popular series wherein three couples get their most cherished fantasy fulfilled by Mr. Roarke and company. **100m/C; VHS, DVD.** Ricardo Montalban; Herve Villechaize; Adrienne Barbeau; Pat(ricia) Crowley; Joseph Campanella; Karen Valentine; Laraine Day; George Maharis; Horst Buchholz; France Nuyen; Joseph Cotten; Cameron Mitchell; George Chakiris; ***D:*** George McCowan. **TV**

Return to Frogtown WOOF! 1992 (PG-13) Sequel to "Hell Comes to Frogtown" finds Texas Rocket Ranger Ferrigno captured by mutant frogs. As unbelievably bad as it sounds. **90m/C; VHS, DVD.** Lou Ferrigno; Charles Napier; Robert Z'Dar; Denice Duff; Don Stroud; ***D:*** Donald G. Jackson.

Return to Halloweentown *Halloweentown 4* **2006** Marnie (now played by Paxton) has enrolled at Halloweentown's Witch University along with nerdy brother Dylan and her boyfriend Ethan. But she runs into trouble with the three Sinister sisters and their evil father, who want to take Marnie's powers. **88m/C; DVD.** Sara Paxton; Lucas Grabeel; Joey Zimmerman; Keone Young; Kristy Wu; Summer Bishil; Millicent Martin; Judith Hoag; Katie Cockrell; Kellie Cockrell; Debbie Reynolds; ***D:*** David S. Jackson; ***W:*** Max Enscoe; Annie DeYoung; ***C:*** Denis Maloney; ***M:*** Kenneth Burgomaster. **CABLE**

Return to Horror High **1987 (R)** A horror movie producer makes a film in an abandoned and haunted high school, where a series of murders occurred years earlier. As in most "return" flicks, history repeats itself. **95m/C; VHS, DVD.** Alex Rocco; Vince Edwards; Philip McKeon; Brendan Hughes; Lori Lethin; Scott Jacoby; George Clooney; Maureen McCormick; ***D:*** Bill Froelich; ***W:*** Bill Froelich; Mark Lisson; Dana Escalante; Greg H. Sims; Nancy Forner; ***C:*** Roy Wagner; ***M:*** Stacy Widelitz.

Return to House on Haunted Hill 1/2 **2007 (R)** Typical haunted house flick. Sarah survived the massacre at Vanacutt Mansion only to later commit suicide. Now her sister Ariel is investigating, aided by the diary of Dr. Vanacutt, which speaks of a diabolical evil inhabiting the house. But the mansion also contains a relic worth millions, and several treasure-seekers come to claim it, although the house has other ideas. **81m/C; DVD, Blu-Ray, HD-DVD.** Erik Palladino; Cerina Vincent; Tom Riley; Jeffrey Combs; Amanda Righetti; Andrew Lee Potts; Steven Pacey; ***D:*** Victor Garcia; ***W:*** William Massa; ***C:*** Lorenzo Senatore; ***M:*** Frederik Wiedmann. **VIDEO**

Return to Lonesome Dove 1/2 **1993** Routine sequel to successful western saga "Lonesome Dove" picks up after the burial of Gus McCrae in Texas by his friend, ex-Texas Ranger Woodrow F. Call (now played by Voight). The original dealt with a cattle drive, this one with horses. Along the way you'll run into the usual sidewinders as well as McCrae's lost love Clara (now Hershey) and Schroder, returning as Call's unacknowledged son Newt. Filmed on loction in Montana. TV production was already underway when author Larry McMurtry gave the producers his then unpublished sequel "Streets of Laredo" which differed from the script. Some changes were made but the book and miniseries don't match. **330m/C; DVD.** Jon Voight; William L. Petersen; Rick Schroder; Barbara Hershey; Louis Gossett, Jr.; Oliver Reed; Reese Witherspoon; Nia Peeples; Dennis Haysbert; Timothy Scott; Barry Tubb; Chris Cooper; CCH Pounder; William Sanderson; ***D:*** Mike Robe; ***W:*** John Wilder. **TV**

Return to Mayberry **1985** Andy Taylor returns to Mayberry after 20 years to obtain his old job as sheriff. Sixteen of the original actors reappeared for this nostalgia-fest. **95m/C; VHS, DVD.** Andy Griffith; Ron Howard; Don Knotts; Jim Nabors; Aneta Corsaut; Jack Dodson; George Lindsey; Betty Lynn; ***D:*** Bob Sweeney. **TV**

Return to Me 1/2 **2000 (PG)** Widowed building contractor Bob (Duchovny) is uneasy about getting involved in a new romance (particularly after some pathetic blind dates) but meets waitress Grace (Driver) and suddenly love is in the air. However, Grace is reluctant to reveal that she's had a heart transplant. What's she going to do when she discovers that the donor heart came from Bob's beloved late wife? The best romance, however, might be between the testily loving marrieds, the Daytons (Hunt, Belushi), who are Grace's best friends. Directorial debut of Hunt is soapy without being sappy. **113m/C; VHS, DVD, Blu-Ray.** David Duchovny; Minnie Driver; James Belushi; Bonnie Hunt; Carroll O'Connor; Robert Loggia; David Alan Grier; Joely Richardson; Eddie Jones; Marianne Muellerleile; William Bronder; ***D:*** Bonnie Hunt; ***W:*** Bonnie Hunt; Don Lake; ***C:*** Laszlo Kovacs; ***M:*** Nicholas Pike.

Return to Never Land 1/2 **2002 (G)** Losing much of the charm and magic of the 1953 Disney animated classic "Peter Pan," this sequel picks up years later. Wendy (Soucie) is now grown and married with a daughter of her own, the spunky Jane (Owen), whose skepticism about her mother's wild tales fades after she is kidnaped by Captain Hook (Burton), still on a quest for the treasure he believes Pan stole. She soon finds her way to Peter (Weaver) and more adventures. Innocuous and generic but this Disney entry works for the youngest viewers, although older children and parents won't find anything deeper for them. Nice blend of digital and traditional animation. **72m/C; VHS, DVD.** ***V:*** Blayne Weaver; Harriet Owen; Corey Burton; Jeff Glenn Bennett; Kath Soucie; Roger Rees; Spencer Breslin; Andrew McDonough; ***D:*** Robin Budd; ***W:*** Temple Mathews; ***M:*** Joel McNeely.

Return to Nim's Island **2013 (PG)** In this Hallmark Channel picture, teenager Nim (Irwin) faces off with animal poachers and land developers hoping to buy her family's island. Based on the stories by author Wendy Orr. **90m/C; DVD, Blu-Ray.** *AU* Matthew Lillard; Bindi Irwin; Toby Wallace; John Waters; Sebastian Gregory; ***D:*** Brendan Maher; ***W:*** Ray Boseley; Cathy Randall; ***C:*** Judd Overton; ***M:*** Nerida Tyson-Chew. **CABLE**

Return to Oz 1/2 **1985 (PG)** Picking up where "The Wizard of Oz" left off, Auntie Em and Uncle Ed place Dorothy in the care of a therapist to cure her "delusions" of Oz. A natural disaster again lands her in the land of the yellow brick road, where the evil Nome King and Princess Mombi are spreading terror and squalor. Based on a later L. Frank Baum book. Enjoyable for the whole family although some scenes may frighten very small children. **109m/C; VHS, DVD, Blu-Ray.** Fairuza Balk; Piper Laurie; Matt Clark; Nicol Williamson; Jean Marsh; ***D:*** Walter Murch; ***W:*** Walter Murch; Gill Dennis; ***C:*** David Watkin; ***M:*** David Shire.

Return to Paradise **1953** Cooper is a soldier of fortune wandering through the Polynesian islands in the late 1920s. On a remote atoll he comes across a crazy missionary intent upon subduing the native population. Cooper falls in love with a native beauty (Haynes in her screen debut) and leads the natives in a revolt against authority. Cliched but with nice scenery from the location shoot in Samoa. Loose adaptation of the short story "Mr. Morgan" by James Michener. **100m/C; VHS, DVD.** Gary Cooper; Roberta Haynes; Barry Jones; John Hudson; Moira MacDonald; ***D:*** Mark Robson; ***W:*** Charles A. Kaufman.

Return to Paradise *All for One* **1998 (R)** Sheriff (Vaughn) and Tony (Conrad), along with their new friend Lewis (Phoenix), take a vice-filled vacation in Malaysia. Two years later, lawyer Beth (Heche) tracks Sheriff down to say Lewis has been in a Malaysian prison, now facing execution for the hashish found by the police after he and Tony left. In order to save Lewis, Sheriff and Tony must return and take their share of the responsibility and prison time. As an ambitious reporter, Pinkett Smith contirbutes an important twist to the extremely powerful climax, but it feels too contrived. Loose retelling of the 1989 French film "Force Majeure." **112m/C; VHS, DVD, Blu-Ray.** Vince Vaughn; Joaquin Rafael (Leaf) Phoenix; Anne Heche; David Conrad; Jada Pinkett Smith; Vera Farmiga; Nick Sandow; ***D:*** Joseph Ruben; ***W:*** Wesley Strick; Bruce Robinson; ***C:*** Reynaldo Villalobos; ***M:*** Mark Mancina.

Return to Peyton Place 1/2 **1961** A young writer publishes novel exposing town as virtual Peyton Place, and the townsfolk turn against her and her family. Sequel to the scandalously popular '50s original and inspiration for the just-as-popular soap opera. Astor is excellent as the evil matriarch. **122m/C; VHS, DVD.** Carol Lynley; Jeff Chandler; Eleanor Parker; Mary Astor; Robert Sterling; Luciana Paluzzi; Tuesday Weld; Brett Halsey; Bob Crane; ***D:*** Jose Ferrer.

Return to Salem's Lot **1987 (R)** Enjoyable camp sequel to the Stephen King tale, this time involving a cynical scientist and his son returning to the town only to find it completely run by vampires. **101m/C; VHS, DVD.** Michael Moriarty; Ricky Addison Reed; Samuel Fuller; Andrew Duggan; Evelyn Keyes; Jill Gatsby; June Havoc; Ronee Blakley; James Dixon; David Holbrook; ***D:*** Larry Cohen; ***W:*** James Dixon; Larry Cohen; ***C:*** Daniel Pearl.

Return to Savage Beach 1/2 **1997 (R)** Top secret government agency LE.T.H.A.L. is sent to retrieve a computer disk containing the location of a hidden treasure. Lots of action, babes, and hard-bodies (you're not expecting acting talent, are you?). **98m/C; VHS, DVD.** Julie Strain; Julie K. Smith; Shae Marks; Cristian Letelier; ***D:*** Andy Sidaris; ***W:*** Andy Sidaris; ***C:*** Howard Wexler. **VIDEO**

Return to Sender 1/2 **2015** A dramatic thriller exploring the impact of assault on a woman's life and the lengths she goes through for closure. Though Miranda Wells (Pike) has a fulfilling career as a nurse, she wants more in her life, including love. Mistaking a stranger who shows up on her porch for her blind date, she is sexually assaulted and traumatized. Though her attacker, William Finn (Fernandez), is caught, convicted, and imprisoned, Miranda becomes depressed and her life becomes disordered. Her mood improves when she learns that William is in a nearby prison, and she begins to contact him, visit him, and build a relationship with him. After William is paroled and seeks her out, Miranda exacts her revenge. **95m/C; DVD, Blu-Ray, Streaming, Download.** Rosamund Pike; Shiloh Fernandez; Nick Nolte; Camryn Manheim; Alexi Wasser; ***D:*** Fouad Mikati; ***W:*** Patricia Beauchamp; Joe Gossett; ***C:*** Russell Carpenter; ***M:*** Daniel Hart.

Return to Sleepaway Camp *Nightmare Vacation 5; Sleepaway Camp 5: The Return* **2008 (R)** The original's director returns for a sequel that's finally as mean-spirited and seedy as the first film. One of the survivors of Angela's massacre has become a camp counselor, and he runs herd over some of the meanest kids ever. Eventually they start dying and it's feared that the original killer has returned, but it's verified she's locked away in an asylum. So the hunt is on for who's doing away with the campers. Definitely a must-see for fans of the original, but everyone else will feel kinda icky watching this, as the actors playing kids actually are kids for a change. **90m/C; DVD.** Vincent Pastore; Jonathan Tiersten; Isaac Hayes; Adam Wylie; Christopher Violette; Felissa Rose; Paul DeAngelo; Mary Elizabeth King; Paul

Iacono; Jenny Coyle; *D:* Robert Hiltzik; *W:* Robert Hiltzik; *C:* Ken Kelsch; Bryan Pryzpek; *M:* Rodney Whittenberg. **VIDEO**

Return to Snowy River **1988 (PG)** Continues the love story of the former ranch hand and the rancher's daughter in Australia's Victoria Alps that began in "The Man From Snowy River." Dennehy takes over from Kirk Douglas as the father who aims to keep the lovers apart. The photography of horses and the scenery is spectacular, making the whole film worthwhile. **99m/C; VHS, DVD; Open Captioned.** *AU* Tom Burlinson; Sigrid Thornton; Brian Dennehy; Nicholas Eadie; Mark Hembrow; Bryan Marshall; *D:* Geoff Burrowes; *W:* Geoff Burrowes.

Return to the Blue Lagoon **1991 (PG-13)** Neither the acting nor the premise has improved with age. Another photogenic adolescent couple experiences puberty on that island; for continuity, the young man is the son of the lovers in the first "Blue Lagoon." Breathtaking scenery—just turn down the sound. **102m/C; VHS, DVD.** Milla Jovovich; Brian Krause; Lisa Pelikan; *D:* William A. Graham; *C:* Robert Steadman.

Return to the Lost World 1/2 **1993 (PG)** Rival scientists Challenger and Summerlee set out for the Lost World and find it threatened by oil prospectors. With a volcano about to explode the scientists set out to save their prehistoric paradise and its dinosaur inhabitants. Based on a story by Sir Arthur Conan Doyle. Sequel to "The Lost World." **99m/C; VHS, DVD.** John Rhys-Davies; David Warner; Darren Peter Mercer; Geza Kovacs; *D:* Timothy Bond.

Return to Treasure Island 1/2 **1954** Jamie Hawkins (Addams), a descendant of Jim Hawkins, inherits a treasure map. Aided by archeology student Clive Stone (Hunter), they travel to Treasure Island to see if any of Long John Silver's booty got left behind. However, they're not the only ones looking. Mild adventure flick is frequently confused with 1954's "Long John Silver's Return to Treasure Island" starring Robert Newton. **75m/C; DVD.** Dawn Addams; Tab Hunter; Porter Hall; James Seay; William Cottrell; *D:* Ewald Andre Dupont; *W:* Jack Pollexfen; Aubrey Wisberg; *C:* William Bradford; *M:* Paul Sawtell.

Return to Waterloo **1985 (PG-13)** Experimental musical concept from the Kinks' Ray Davies about an everyman commuter (Colley) who is either having a nervous breakdown or living in a fantasy world or both. As he rides the train between the Guildford and Waterloo stations, his fellow passengers burst into song and things get increasingly violent. Also includes "Come Dancing with the Kinks," with videos of eight songs, including "Lola" and "Come Dancing." **95m/C; VHS, DVD.** *GB* Ray Davies; Gretchen Franklin; Tim Roth; *D:* Ray Davies; *W:* Ray Davies; *C:* Roger Deakins; *M:* Ray Davies.

Return to Zero 1/2 **2014** Lifetime drama based on a true story has some strong performances. Maggie (Driver) and Aaron (Adelstein) Royal are eagerly anticipating the birth of their first child when they learn that the baby boy has died in the womb. Grief drives them apart and they don't know if their marriage can survive when Maggie unexpectedly becomes pregnant again. Can they make it through the pregnancy together? **107m/C; DVD.** Paul Adelstein; Minnie Driver; Alfred Molina; Connie Nielsen; Kathy Baker; *D:* Sean Hanish; *W:* Sean Hanish; *C:* Harris Charalambous; *M:* James T. Sale. **CABLE**

The Returned 1/2 *Retornados* **2014** Long after the zombie apocalypse has died down and the outbreak controlled, things still aren't business as usual. If it's not enough that those who have been bitten in the past must administer a daily antidote to ward off the zombie virus, but they must also endure the social stigmas of being one of The Returned. Things get ugly when the antidote supply runs low, forcing Alex (Holden-Ried) and Kate (Hampshire) to fight for their meds while still hiding their secret from violent bigots. A fairly obvious Reagan-era allegory, but as silly as the events unfold, it's refreshing to see more brains behind the camera than smeared across the mouths of zombies. **98m/C; DVD, Streaming, On Demand.** *US CA SP* Emily Hampshire; Kris Holden-Ried; Shawn Doyle; Claudia Bassols; Melina Matthews; *D:* Manuel Carballo; *W:* Hatem Khraiche; *C:* Javier Salomes; Javier Salmones; *M:* Jonathan Goldsmith.

Returned 1/2 **2015** An indie scifi drama about one man's unexpected return. While flying to New York, the flight that Benjamin Lathan (Kimble) is on disappears. Twelve years later, he is found floating on the ocean alone. Guided by a mysterious woman, he goes on a journey to understand his past and the future. **90m/C; DVD, Streaming, Download.** Blue Kimble; Aaron Harris; Edgar Zanabria; Michael Casey; Theresa Sullivan; *D:* Lamont Gant; *W:* Lamont Gant; Victoria Marie; Marlon McCaulsky; *C:* Lamont Gant. **VIDEO**

The Reunion **2011 (PG-13)** Sam, Leo, and Douglas are estranged half-brothers who will each get a substantial inheritance if they can work together for two years. When one of bail bondsman Leo's clients skips out and heads to Mexico, the trio find themselves involved in a billionaire's kidnapping plot. A lot less action than one would expect and the family aspects are just boring. **96m/C; DVD, Blu-Ray.** John Cena; Ethan (Randall) Embry; Boyd Holbrook; Amy Smart; Gregg Henry; Michael Rispoli; *D:* Michael Pavone; *W:* Michael Pavone; *C:* Kenneth Zunder; *M:* Jim Johnston. **VIDEO**

Reunion at Fairborough 1/2 **1985** HBO romantic drama. After 40 years, U.S. Air Force buddies return to the English village where they were stationed during WWII. Carl Hostrup (Mitchum) goes on a whim with crewmate Jiggs Quealy (Buttons), hoping to find out what happened to his then-love Sally and they meet again. **113m/C; DVD.** Robert Mitchum; Deborah Kerr; Red Buttons; Barry Morse; Judi Trott; Shane Rimmer; *D:* Herbert Wise; *W:* Albert Ruben; *C:* Tony Imi; *M:* Nigel Hess. **CABLE**

Reunion in France *Mademoiselle France; Reunion* **1942** Parisian dress designer sacrifices her lifestyle to help an American flier flee France after the Nazis invade. Dated patriotic flag-waver. **104m/B; VHS, DVD.** Joan Crawford; John Wayne; Philip Dorn; Reginald Owen; Albert Bassermann; John Carradine; Ann Ayars; J. Edward Bromberg; Henry Daniell; Moroni Olsen; Howard da Silva; Ava Gardner; John Considine; *D:* Jules Dassin.

Revak the Rebel *The Barbarians* **1960** Giggle-inducing sword and sandal pic filled with stiffs and scenery-chewing. Penda, an island kingdom, is conquered by the Carthaginians during their war against Rome. Prince Revak (Palance) is captured and put on board a slave ship, but he escapes and vows revenge. **84m/C; DVD.** Jack Palance; Milly Vitale; Deirdre Sullivan; *D:* Rudolph Mate; *W:* Martin Rackin; John Lee Martin; *C:* Carl Guthrie; *M:* Franco Ferrara.

Revelation **2000** In the continuing adventures based on the "Left Behind" novels (a conservative Christian interpretation of the Book of Revelation), a counter-terrorism expert (Fahey) goes up against a Messiah (Mancuso) out to rule the world, etc., etc. **97m/C; DVD.** Jeff Fahey; Nick Mancuso; Carol Alt; Leigh Lewis; *D:* Andre Van Heerden; *W:* Peter LaLonde; Paul LaLonde; *C:* Jiri (George) Tirl.

Revelation Road: The Beginning of the End **2013** A business man saves a shop owner from bikers and finds religion just in time for the end of the world. **88m/C; DVD, Blu-Ray.** David A.R. White; Brian Bosworth; Eric Roberts; Noell Coet; Bruce Marchiano; Sean Paul Murphy; *D:* Gabriel Sabloff; *W:* Gabriel Sabloff; *C:* Darren Rydstrom; *M:* William Musser. **VIDEO**

The Revenant **2015 (R)** Taken from a true story, Inarritu and his team spent nine months in the wilderness shooting this epic tale of fur trapper Hugh Glass, a man who refuses to die until he gets the vengeance this world demands. Set in the bleak terrain of the 19th-century Great Plains, Glass (DiCaprio) endures a horrific attack by a bear (a special effects masterpiece in itself). While his group eventually leaves him for dead, he suffers a more horrifying tragedy at the hands of conniving cohort John Fitzgerald (a truly possessed Hardy). Glass literally crawls from the ground and confronts unimaginable conditions on a quest for justice. The result is a harrowing journey, captured beautifully by Inarritu. It's unforgettable. **156m/C; DVD, Blu-Ray.** Leonardo DiCaprio; Tom (Thomas) Hardy; Domhnall Gleeson; Will Poulter; Forrest Goodluck; Paul Anderson; Lukas Haas; *D:* Alejandro Gonzalez Inarritu; *W:* Alejandro Gonzalez Inarritu; Mark L. Smith; *C:* Emmanuel Lubezki; *M:* Carsten Nicolaisen; Ryuichi Sakamoto. Oscars '15: Actor (DiCaprio), Cinematog., Director (Inarritu); British Acad. '15: Actor (DiCaprio), Cinematog., Director (Inarritu), Film, Sound; Directors Guild '15: Director (Inarritu); Golden Globes '16: Actor--Drama (DiCaprio), Director (Inarritu), Film--Drama; Screen Actors Guild '15: Actor (DiCaprio).

Revenge *Adauchi* **1964** Gritty samurai movie focuses on tradition, honor, and betrayal. Poor samurai Ezaki Shinpachi is insulted by the eldest brother of the wealthy Okumo clan. He kills him in a private duel and the magistrates are more worried about appearances than tradition, so they declare Shinpachi insane and send him to a monastery. Shume Okumo takes over his clan and wants revenge, which eventually leads to a formal public duel, but the Okumos have no intention of behaving honorably to win the fight. Japanese with subtitles. **104m/B; DVD.** *JP* Kinnosuke Nakamura; Tetsuro Tanba; Yoshiko Mita; Eitaro Shindo; Takahiro Tamura; *D:* Tadashi Imai; *W:* Shinobu Hashimoto; *C:* Shunichiro Nakao; *M:* Mayuzumi Toshiro.

Revenge 1/2 *Terror under the House; After Jenny Died; Inn of the Frightened People* **1971** The parents of a girl who was brutally killed take the law into their own hands in this bloody, vengeful thriller. **89m/C; VHS, DVD, Streaming.** *GB* Joan Collins; James Booth; Ray Barrett; Sinead Cusack; Kenneth Griffith; *D:* Sidney Hayers.

Revenge WOOF! **1986 (R)** Sequel to "Blood Cult" about a cult led by horror king Carradine. Seems these dog worshippers want McGowan's land and Senator Carradine will stop at nothing to get it. Woofer filled with gratuitous violence. **104m/C; VHS, DVD.** Patrick Wayne; John Carradine; Bennie Lee McGowan; Josef Hanet; Stephanie Kropke; *D:* Christopher Lewis; *W:* Christopher Lewis; *C:* Steve McWilliams; *M:* Rod Slane.

Revenge **1990 (R)** Retired pilot Costner makes the mistake of falling in love with another man's wife. Quinn gives a first-rate performance as the Mexican crime lord who punishes his spouse and her lover, beginning a cycle of vengeance. Sometimes contrived, but artfully photographed with tantalizing love scenes. Based on the Jim Harrison novel. **123m/C; VHS, DVD, Blu-Ray; Open Captioned.** Kevin Costner; Anthony Quinn; Madeleine Stowe; Sally Kirkland; Joe Santos; Miguel Ferrer; James Gammon; Tomas Milian; *D:* Tony Scott; *W:* Jim Harrison; *M:* Jack Nitzsche.

Revenge 1/2 **2017 (R)** An action thriller in the form of a rape-revenge fantasy. When Jen (Lutz) goes on a remote desert getaway with her wealthy boyfriend Richard (Janssens), two of his shady friends, Stan (Colombe) and Dimitri (Bouchede), show up a day early for a hunting weekend with him. The next morning, when Richard is gone, Stan rapes her, Dimitri ignores her screams, and Richard does not try to save her when he returns. Though her situation is dire, Jen fights back. Director/screenwriter Fargeat's debut stuns in its intensity, with strong pacing, stylish visuals, a timely, emotionally complex story, and Lutz's brilliant performance. **108m/C; Blu-Ray, Streaming.** *FR* Matilda Anna Ingrid Lutz; Kevin Janssens; Vincent Colombe; Guillaume Bouchède; *D:* Coralie Fargeat; *W:* Coralie Fargeat; *C:* Robrecht Hayvaert; *M:* Robin Coudert.

Revenge for Jolly! 1/2 **2012 (R)** Harry (Brian Petsos) hires his cousin to help track down the murderer of his tiny dog Jolly. **84m/C; DVD, Streaming.** Brian Petsos; Oscar Isaac; Elijah Wood; Ryan Phillippe; Kristen Wiig; *D:* Chadd Harbold; *W:* Brian Petsos; *C:* Daniel Katz; *M:* Dave Fleming; Justin Hori. **VIDEO**

Revenge in the House of Usher *Neurosis; Zombie 5* **1982** Mad Eric Usher, the last of his equally insane family, lives in a creepy cliffside house with vampire-ghost Helen. Then he invites Alan Harker for a visit, and Alan's accepting is a big mistake on his part. **90m/C; VHS, DVD.** *FR* Howard Vernon; Anthony (Jose, J. Antonio, J.A.) Mayans; Dan Villers; Lina Romay; *D:* Jess (Jesus) Franco; *C:* Alain Hardy; *M:* Daniel White.

Revenge Is My Destiny 1/2 **1971 (PG)** Vietnam veteran Ross Archer (Robinson) returns from duty missing an eye and then his wife is found dead the next day. The authorities list her as a suicide and a defiant Ross investigates what happened to his wife while he was gone. **95m/C; DVD.** Chris Robinson; Sidney Blackmer; Elisa Ingram; Joe E. Ross; *D:* Joseph Adler; *W:* Mardik Martin; *C:* Ares Demertzis; *M:* Stu Phillips.

The Revenge of Frankenstein 1/2 **1958** Frankenstein (Cushing) is rescued from the guillotine by his dwarf servant and decides to relocate to Carlsbruck where he becomes the popular society physician, Dr. Stein. But the misunderstood doc just can't stop his ghoulish experiments and plans to transfer his servant's brain into another sewn together creature. Nicely macabre sequel to "The Curse of Frankenstein"; followed by "The Evil of Frankenstein." **89m/C; VHS, DVD, Blu-Ray.** *GB* Peter Cushing; Michael Gwynn; Francis Matthews; Oscar Quitak; Lionel Jeffries; Eunice Gayson; John Welsh; *D:* Terence Fisher; *W:* Jimmy Sangster.

Revenge of Sartana 1/2 *Joaquin Murrieta; Murieta* **1965** Murrieta (Jeffrey Hunter) and his wife move to California to prospect for gold. When his wife is murdered by bandits, Murieta forms a band of outlaws and leaves a path of destruction in revenge. Currently only available as part of the 'Westerns Unchained' collection. **107m/C; Blu-Ray.** *SP* Jeffrey Hunter; Arthur Kennedy; Diana Lorys; Sara Lezana; Roberto Camardiel; *D:* George Sherman; *W:* James O'Hanlon; *C:* Miguel Fernandez Mila; *M:* Antonio Perez Olea. **VIDEO**

Revenge of the Barbarians *La Vendetta dei Barbari* **1960** As the barbarians descend on Rome, Olympus must decide whether to save the empire or the beautiful Gallo, the woman he loves. Decisions, decisions. **104m/C; VHS, DVD.** *IT* Robert Alda; Anthony Steel; Tom Felleghi; Daniela Rocca; *D:* Giuseppe Vari; *W:* Gastone Ramazzotti; *C:* Sergio Pesce; *M:* Roberto Nicolosi.

Revenge of the Bridesmaids 1/2 **2010** ABC Family Channel comedy. When Abigail and Parker visit their hometown, they learn wealthy ex-friend Caitlin has stolen Tony, the longtime beau of their gal pal Rachel, and is about to marry him. The two connive their way into being bridesmaids, intending to sabotage the wedding so that Rachel has another shot with foolish Tony. **90m/C; DVD.** Raven; Joanna Garcia; Virginia Williams; Chryssie Whitehead; Beth Broderick; David Clayton Rogers; Lyle Brocato; *D:* James Hayman; *W:* David Kendall; Bob Young; *C:* Neil Roach; *M:* Danny Lux. **CABLE**

Revenge of the Cheerleaders **1976 (R)** The cheerleaders pull out all the stops to save their school from a ruthless land developer. What spirit. **86m/C; VHS, DVD, Blu-Ray.** Jerii Woods; Cheryl "Rainbeaux" Smith; Helen Lang; Patrice Rohmer; Susie Elene; Eddra Gale; William Bramley; Carl Ballantine; David Hasselhoff; *D:* Richard Lerner.

Revenge of the Creature **1955** In this follow up to "The Creature from the Black Lagoon," the Gill-man is captured in the Amazon and taken to a Florida marine park. There he is put on display for visitors and subjected to heartless experiments. Growing restless in his captive surroundings, the creature breaks free and makes for the ocean. Includes screen debut of Clint Eastwood as a lab technician. Originally shot in 3-D. Based on a story by William Alland. **82m/B; VHS, DVD, Blu-Ray.** John Agar; Lori Nelson; John Bromfield; Nestor Paiva; Clint Eastwood; Robert B. Williams; Grandon Rhodes; Charles Cane; *D:* Jack Arnold; *W:* Martin Berkeley; *C:* Charles S. Welbourne; *M:* Joseph Gershenson.

Revenge of the Dead **1984 (R)** European archeological team discovers the existence of a powerful force that allows the dead to return to life. **100m/C; VHS, DVD, Blu-Ray.** *IT* Gabriele Lavia; Anne Canoras; ***D:*** Pupi Avati.

Revenge of the Green Dragons 1/2 **2014 (R)** Crime drama centering on the escapades of two Chinese immigrant brothers--Sonny and Steven--rising through the underworld ranks in 1980's New York. Trouble follows and Sonny finally turns on the gang. Martin Scorsese was one of the executive producers. **94m/C; DVD, Blu-Ray, Streaming.** *CH US* Justin Chon; Kevin Wu; Harry Shum, Jr.; Ray Liotta; Shuya Chang; ***D:*** Wai Keung (Andrew) Lau; Andrew Loo; ***W:*** Andrew Loo; Michael Di Jiacomo; ***C:*** Martin Ahlgren; ***M:*** Mark Kilian.

Revenge of the Living Zombies **1988 (R)** Teens on a Halloween hayride run headlong into flesh-craving zombies. Available in a slightly edited version. **85m/C; VHS, DVD.** Bill (William Heinzman) Hinzman; John Mowod; Leslie Ann Wick; Kevin Kindlin; ***D:*** Bill (William Heinzman) Hinzman.

Revenge of the Musketeers *D'Artagnan Contro I Tre Moschettieri* **1963** A lighthearted (dubbed) swashbuckler. D'Artagnan (Lamas) is reunited with his musketeer comrades to help out Charles II (Antonini), the English king who's been exiled to France during Cromwell's rule. Naturally there are evil plots to thwart. **90m/C; DVD.** *IT* Fernando Lamas; Gloria Milland; Roberto Risso; Walter Barnes; Franco Fantasia; Gabriel Antonio; Folco Lulli; Andreina Paul; ***D:*** Fulvio Tului; ***W:*** Roberto Gianviti; Tito Carpi; Robert Gianviti.

Revenge of the Musketeers 1/2 *D'Artagnan's Daughter; La Fille de D'Artagnan* **1994 (R)** Exciting swashbuckler that finds the beautiful Eloise (Marceau) uncovering a dastardly plot by the Duc of Crassac (Rich) to kill King Louis XIV (Legros). She goes to her father, aging Musketeer D'Artagnan (Noiret), and he seeks the aid of old compatriots Athos (Bideau), Porthos (Billerey), and Aramis (Frey). Since Eloise can handle a sword as well as any of the Musketeers, she gets her own share of dering-do. French with subtitles. **130m/C; VHS, DVD.** *FR* Sophie Marceau; Philippe Noiret; Jean-Luc Bideau; Raoul Billerey; Sami Frey; Claude Rich; Nils (Niels) Tavernier; Charlotte Kady; Stephane Legros; Luigi Proietti; ***D:*** Bertrand Tavernier; ***W:*** Michel Leviant; ***C:*** Patrick Blossier; ***M:*** Philippe Sarde.

Revenge of the Nerds 1/2 **1984 (R)** When nerdy college freshmen are victimized by jocks, frat boys and the school's beauties, they start their own fraternity and seek revenge. Carradine and Edwards team well as the geeks in this better than average teenage sex comedy. Guess who gets the girls? Sequel was much worse. **89m/C; VHS, DVD, Blu-Ray.** Robert Carradine; Anthony Edwards; Timothy Busfield; Andrew Cassese; Curtis Armstrong; Larry B. Scott; Brian Tochi; Julia Montgomery; Michelle Meyrink; Ted McGinley; John Goodman; Bernie Casey; ***D:*** Jeff Kanew; ***W:*** Tim Metcalfe; Jeff Buhai; ***C:*** King Baggot; ***M:*** Thomas Newman.

Revenge of the Nerds 2: Nerds in Paradise **1987 (PG-13)** The nerd clan from the first film (minus Edwards who only makes a brief appearance) travels to Fort Lauderdale for a fraternity conference. They fend off loads of bullies and jocks with raunchy humor. Boy can Booger belch. Not as good as the first Nerds movie; a few laughs nonetheless. **89m/C; VHS, DVD.** Robert Carradine; Curtis Armstrong; Timothy Busfield; Andrew Cassese; Ed Lauter; Larry B. Scott; Courtney Thorne-Smith; Anthony Edwards; James Hong; ***D:*** Joe Roth; ***W:*** Dan Guntzelman; Steve Marshall; ***C:*** Charles Correll; ***M:*** Mark Mothersbaugh.

Revenge of the Nerds 3: The Next Generation 1/2 **1992** Adams College has nerd-loathing trustee Downey Jr. mobilizing those frat boys against the bespectacled geeks, who turn to founding nerd Carradine to save them. Cookie-cutter characters and the gags won't hold your attention. Let's hope this is the last in the series. **100m/C; VHS, DVD.** Robert Carradine; Curtis Armstrong; Ted McGinley; Morton Downey, Jr.; Julia Montgomery; ***D:*** Roland Mesa; ***W:*** Steve Zacharias; Jeff Buhai; ***C:*** Zoran Hochstatter; ***M:*** Garry Schyman.

Revenge of the Nerds 4: Nerds in Love 1/2 **1994** Yes, even nerds deserve a little love. This time the gang get together for Booger's (Armstrong) wedding—complete with nerd bachelor party and wedding shower. Too bad Booger's future father-in-law is so reluctant to have a nerd in the family that he hires a sleazy detective to dig up some dirt. Made for TV. **90m/C; VHS, DVD.** Curtis Armstrong; Robert Carradine; Ted McGinley; Larry B. Scott; Donald Gibb; Joseph Bologna; Julia Montgomery; Corinne Bohrer; Christina Pickles; Jessica Tuck; Robert Picardo; ***D:*** Steve Zacharias; ***W:*** Steve Zacharias; Steve Buhai. **TV**

Revenge of the Ninja 1/2 **1983 (R)** Ninja Kosugi hopes to escape his past in Los Angeles. A drug trafficker, also ninja-trained, prevents him. The two polish off a slew of mobsters before their own inevitable showdown. Better-than the standard chopsocky fest from Cannon with amusing surreal touches like a battling grandma ninja. Sequel to "Enter the Ninja," followed by "Ninja III." **90m/C; VHS, DVD, Blu-Ray.** Sho Kosugi; Arthur Roberts; Keith Vitali; Virgil Frye; Ashley Ferrare; Kane (Takeshi) Kosugi; John Lamotta; Grace Oshita; Melvin C. Hampton; Mario Gallo; ***D:*** Sam Firstenberg; ***W:*** James R. Silke; ***M:*** Rob Walsh; W. Michael Lewis.

Revenge of the Pink Panther 1/2 **1978 (PG)** Inspector Clouseau survives his own assassination attempt, but allows the world to think he is dead in order to pursue an investigation of the culprits in his own unique, bumbling way. The last "Pink Panther" film before Sellers died, and perhaps the least funny. **99m/C; VHS, DVD, Blu-Ray.** Peter Sellers; Herbert Lom; Dyan Cannon; Robert Webber; Burt Kwouk; Robert Loggia; ***D:*** Blake Edwards; ***W:*** Blake Edwards; Ron Clark; Frank Waldman; ***C:*** Ernest Day; ***M:*** Henry Mancini.

Revenge of the Red Baron 1/2 **1993 (PG-13)** Jim Spencer (Rooney) is the WWI pilot who shot down Germany's fearsome Red Baron. Now aged and infirm he's tormented by what he thinks is his enemy's ghost. A vengeful ghost who takes after Spencer's family. **90m/C; VHS, DVD.** Mickey Rooney; Tobey Maguire; Laraine Newman; Cliff DeYoung; ***D:*** Robert Gordon; ***W:*** Michael James McDonald; ***C:*** Christian Sebaldt.

Revenge of the Teenage Vixens from Outer Space **1986** A low-budget film about three sex starved females from another planet who come to earth to find men. When the ones they meet do not live up to their expectations, the frustrated females turn the disappointing dudes into vegetables. **84m/C; VHS, DVD.** Lisa Schwedop; Howard Scott; ***D:*** Jeff Ferrell.

Revenge Quest **1996** In the year 2031, Trent McCormic, L.A.'s most violent serial killer, escapes from a maximum security prison on Mars. He's determined to kill Julie Myers, the woman who testified against him. LAPD detective Rick Castle is equally determined to protect her. **90m/C; VHS, DVD.** Brian Gluhak; Christopher Michael Egger; Jennifer Agular; ***D:*** Alan De Herrera; ***W:*** Alan De Herrera; ***C:*** Alan De Herrera; ***M:*** Joseph Andalino. **VIDEO**

The Revenger **1990** A framed man returns from prison and finds that a mobster has kidnapped his wife and wants $50,000 to give her back. **91m/C; VHS, DVD.** Oliver Reed; Frank Zagarino; ***D:*** Cedric Sundstrom.

The Revengers **1972** Predictable and dull western. John Benedict (Holden) returns home to his ranch to find his family slaughtered by Comanches led by renegade white man, Tarp (Vanders). Holden hires some convicts to come with him to the Mexican town where Tarp is hiding out, so he can get his revenge. Things don't go as planned (this is where Hayward's nominal character briefly comes in), but Benedict gets another chance when the Army captures Vanders and has him confined at an outpost. **110m/C; DVD, Blu-Ray.** William Holden; Susan Hayward; Ernest Borgnine; Woody Strode; Warren Vanders; Jorge Luke; ***D:*** Daniel Mann; ***W:*** Wendell Mayes; ***C:*** Gabriel Torres; ***M:*** Pino Calvi.

Reversal of Fortune 1/2 **1990 (R)** True tale of wealthy socialite Claus von Bulow (Irons) accused of deliberately giving his wife Sunny (Close) a near-lethal overdose of insulin. Comatose Sunny narrates history of the couple's courtship and married life, a saga of unhappiness and substance abuse, while lawyer Dershowitz (Silver) et al prepare von Bulow's defense. An unflattering picture of the idle rich that never spells out what really happened. Irons is excellent as the eccentric and creepy defendant and richly deserved his Best Actor Oscar. From the book by Dershowitz. **112m/C; DVD.** Jeremy Irons; Glenn Close; Ron Silver; Annabella Sciorra; Uta Hagen; Fisher Stevens; Julie Hagerty; Jack Gilpin; Christine Baranski; John David (J.D.) Cullum; Felicity Huffman; Lisa Gay Hamilton; Christine Dunford; Steven Mailer; ***D:*** Barbet Schroeder; ***W:*** Nicholas Kazan; ***C:*** Luciano Tovoli; ***M:*** Mark Isham. Oscars '90: Actor (Irons); Golden Globes '91: Actor--Drama (Irons); L.A. Film Critics '90: Actor (Irons), Screenplay; Natl. Soc. Film Critics '90: Actor (Irons).

Reviving Ophelia 1/2 **2010** Lifetime teen drama based on psychologist Mary Pipher's book "Reviving Ophelia: Saving the Selves of Adolescent Girls." Middle-class 15-year-old Elizabeth is seemingly the perfect girl with the perfect boyfriend while her rebellious cousin Kelli lives with her single mom and indulges in risky behavior. Kelli suspects Elizabeth's boyfriend Mark is abusive, but until Elizabeth lands in the hospital no one takes her seriously. **100m/C; DVD.** Rebecca Williams; Carleigh Beverly; Nick Thurston; Kim Dickens; Jane Kaczmarek; ***D:*** Bobby Roth; ***W:*** Teena Booth; ***C:*** Michael Storey; ***M:*** Christopher Franke; Edgar Rothermich. **CABLE**

Revolt **2017 (R)** An African-set futuristic alien invasion thriller. American soldier Bo (Pace) wakes up in a jail cell in Nairobi with selective amnesia. Because he cannot remember his name, Bo was given to him by fellow prisoner Nadia (Marlohe), a French army medic. Bo and Nadia escape and finds themselves in the middle of an invasion by alien killing machines that have already destroyed a large part of Africa. As they pair try to reach the border, they must battle both poachers and aliens, and learn Bo's identity in the process. An entertaining, fast-moving genre film. English, Swahili, and Kikuyu with subtitles. **87m/C; DVD.** Lee Pace; Berenice Marlohe; Jason Flemyng; Sibulele Gcilitshana; Wandile Molebatsi; ***D:*** Joe Miale; ***W:*** Joe Miale; Rowan Athale; ***C:*** Karl Walter Lindenlaub; ***M:*** Bear McCreary.

Revolt in the Big House 1/2 **1958** Cheapie prison pic. Rudy is trying to stay out of trouble in the joint so he can get early parole. His mob boss cellmate Lou Gannon has other ideas, planning to use Rudy as a patsy in a prison break, but Rudy learns about the doublecross. **79m/B; DVD.** Robert (Bobby) Blake; Gene Evans; Timothy Carey; John Qualen; ***D:*** R.G. Springsteen; ***W:*** Daniel James; Eugene Lourie; ***C:*** William Margulies.

Revolt of the Zombies **1936** A mad scientist learns the secret of bringing the dead to life and musters the zombies into an unique, gruesome military unit during WWI. Strange early zombie flick looks silly by today's standards. **65m/B; VHS, DVD.** Dorothy Stone; Dean Jagger; Roy D'Arcy; Robert Noland; George Cleveland; ***D:*** Victor Halperin; ***W:*** Howard Higgin; ***C:*** Jockey A. Feindel; Arthur Martinelli.

Revolution **1985 (R)** The American Revolution is the setting for this failed epic centering on an illiterate trapper and his son who find themselves caught up in the fighting. Long and dull, which is unfortunate, because the story had some potential. The cast is barely believable in their individual roles. Where did you get that accent, Al? **125m/C; VHS, DVD.** *GB* Al Pacino; Donald Sutherland; Nastassja Kinski; Annie Lennox; Joan Plowright; Steven Berkoff; Dave King; ***D:*** Hugh Hudson; ***W:*** Robert Dillon.

Revolution #9 1/2 **2001** James Jackson (Risley) is a NYC worker drone who's just become engaged to Kim (Shelly) when his behavior undergoes a radical transformation. He believes he's receiving subliminal messages via commercials for a perfume called Revolution #9 and his mental breakdown is diagnosed as schizophrenia. Kim bears the brunt of James's paranoia and self-destructive behavior while also trying to deal with the bureaucracy and inadequacies of the mental health system. Risley forgoes histrionics in playing a mentally ill character while Shelly displays the toughness of an ordinary woman confronted by a difficult situation. **91m/C; VHS, DVD.** Michael Risley; Adrienne Shelly; Spalding Gray; Callie (Calliope) Thorne; Sakina Jaffrey; Michael Rodrick; ***D:*** Tim McCann; ***W:*** Tim McCann; ***C:*** Tim McCann; ***M:*** Douglas J. Cuomo.

Revolutionary Road 1/2 **2008 (R)** Frank (DiCaprio) and April Wheeler (Winslet) are certain they'll lead lives filled with excitement. Seven years and two kids later, they're entrenched in Connecticut leading a typical 1950's suburban life. The oppression eventually leads them to infidelity and a combative relationship. Pressed to the breaking point, Frank agrees to April's plan to flee to Paris to find themselves and their abandoned dreams, but their self-loathing is exposed by John (Shannon), the mentally ill son of their neighbor (Bates). Based on Richard Yates' novel, the film captures the buttoned-up look and feel of mid-1950s America though by-passing the nostalgia. **119m/C; DVD, Blu-Ray, On Demand.** Leonardo DiCaprio; Kate Winslet; Kathy Bates; Kathryn Hahn; Michael Shannon; David Harbour; Dylan Baker; Richard Easton; Zoe Kazan; Jay O. Sanders; Max Casella; ***D:*** Sam Mendes; ***W:*** Justin Haythe; ***C:*** Roger Deakins; ***M:*** Thomas Newman. Golden Globes '09: Actress--Drama (Winslet).

Revolver *Blood in the Streets; In the Name of Love; La Poursuite Implacable* **1975** Vito Cipriani (Reed) is a prison warden called from home to quell a riot. When he finally gets back, his wife is missing, and he gets a message telling him to release small time crook Milo Ruiz (Testi) if he ever wishes to see his wife alive. He does so, then turns the tables on Milo in order to ensure he gets his wife back. **111m/C; DVD.** *FR GE IT* Oliver Reed; Fabio Testi; Agostina Belli; Peter Berling; Calisto Calisti; Steffen Zacharias; Paola Pitagora; Frederic De Pasquale; Daniel Beretta; ***D:*** Sergio Sollima; ***W:*** Sergio Sollima; Massimo De Rita; Arduino (Dino) Maiuri; ***C:*** Aldo Scavarda; ***M:*** Ennio Morricone.

Revolver **2005** Director Ritchie sticks to lowlife criminals with little return. Ex-con Jake Green (Statham) decides to get even with casino-owning baddie Macha (Liotta), who set him up for a prison stint. Jake wins big at the casino and Macha orders a hit to soothe his humiliation. Then Jake is picked up by loan shark Zack (Pastore) and his partner Avi (Benjamin), who dispense a lot of silly psychobabble to no known purpose, which is par for the flick's general incoherence. **115m/C; DVD.** *GB FR* Jason Statham; Ray Liotta; Vincent Pastore; Andre Benjamin; Francesca Annis; Terence Maynard; Mark Strong; Andrew Howard; ***D:*** Guy Ritchie; ***W:*** Guy Ritchie; ***C:*** Tim Maurice-Jones; ***M:*** Nathaniel Mechaly.

The Rewrite 1/2 *The Reluctant Professor* **2015** A romantic comedy about a screenwriter finding an unexpected life. Though Keith Michaels (Grant) is an award-winning screenwriter, his career and personal life have both fallen apart. In debt and unable to write, he takes a job as screenwriting professor in upstate New York. His original plan of writing his own script and doing only the minimum as a professor goes awry and he becomes deeply involved in the lives of his students. One in particular, a single mother named Holly (Tomei), leads to a deeper connection and romance, making him question his whole life. **97m/C; DVD, Blu-Ray, Streaming, Download.** Hugh Grant; Marisa Tomei; Chris Elliott; J.K. Simmons; Allison Janney; ***D:*** Marc Lawrence; ***W:*** Marc Lawrence; ***C:*** Jonathan Brown; ***M:*** Clyde Lawrence. **VIDEO**

Reykjavik-Rotterdam **2008** Straightforward crime thriller. Ex-con Kristofer (Komakur) is trying to go straight until his dumb brother-in-law Amor (Ragnarsson) screws up a job for thug Eirikur (Johannesson). Needing some extra cash, Kristofer reluctantly agrees to go in on a smuggling run from Reykavik to Rotterdam. It goes wrong, in part because of a betrayal. If this sounds familiar it's because star Kormakur directed the remake, 2012's U.S. release "Contraband." English, Icelandic, and Dutch with subtitles. **86m/C; DVD.** *IC* Baltasar Kormakur; Jorundur Ragnarsson; Jóhannes Haukur Jóhannesson; Ingvar Sigurdsson; ***D:*** Oskar Jonasson; ***W:*** Oskar Jonasson; Amaldur Indridason; ***C:*** Bergsteinn Bjorgulfsson; ***M:*** Bardi Johannsson.

RFK 🦴🦴 1/2 **2002** Focuses on the years following the assassination of President John F. Kennedy (Donovan) as his brother Robert (Roache) pursued his own political career until his own assassination. **90m/C; VHS, DVD.** Linus Roache; James Cromwell; David Paymer; Martin Donovan; Ving Rhames; Marnie McPhail; Jacob Vargas; Sean Gregory Sullivan; Kevin Hare; ***D:*** Robert Dornhelm; ***W:*** Hank Steinberg; ***C:*** Derick Underschultz; ***M:*** Harald Kloser; Thomas Wanker. **CABLE**

Rhapsody 🦴🦴 1/2 **1954** Taylor plays a wealthy woman torn between a famous young violinist and an equally talented pianist in this long and overdrawn soap opera. Although Taylor gives a superb performance, it's not enough to save this sugarcoated musical romance. Includes lush European scenery and sequences of classical music dubbed in by Claudio Arrau and Michael Rabin. Based on the adaptation of the Henry Handel Richardson novel "Maurice Guest." **115m/C; VHS, DVD.** Elizabeth Taylor; Vittorio Gassman; John Ericson; Louis Calhern; Michael Chekhov; Barbara Bates; Celia Lovsky; ***D:*** Charles Vidor; ***W:*** Michael Kanin; Fay Kanin.

Rhapsody 🦴🦴 **2001 (R)** In 1986, young hoods Jelly and Roughneck are caught out by an undercover cop in a drug deal. Jelly escapes arrests while Roughneck does time. Released from prison, Roughneck (Plummer) thinks his ex-partner (Phillips), who's now a successful music producer, owes him. **95m/C; VHS, DVD.** Glenn Plummer; Fred Williamson; Ice-T; Tee Phillips; Tone Loc; Freda Payne; ***D:*** Don Abernathy; ***W:*** Don Abernathy. **VIDEO**

Rhapsody in August 🦴🦴 1/2 *Hachigatsu no Kyoshikyoku* **1991 (PG)** Talky family drama has four children spending the summer with their grandmother Kane in Nagasaki. They become obsessed with the memorials and bomb sites commemorating the dropping of the atomic bomb in 1945 and their grandmother's experiences. Then Kane's Eurasian nephew (Gere) comes for a visit, inciting more family discussions. Adapted from the novel "Nabe-no-Naka" by Kiyoko Murata. Minor Kurosawa; in Japanese with English subtitles. **98m/C; VHS, DVD.** *JP* Sachiko Murase; Narumi Kayashima; Hisashi Igawa; Richard Gere; ***D:*** Akira Kurosawa; ***W:*** Akira Kurosawa; ***C:*** Takao Saito; Masaharu Ueda; ***M:*** Shinichiro Ikebe.

Rhapsody in Blue 🦴🦴🦴 **1945** Standard Hollywood biography of the great composer features whitewashed and non-existent characters to deal with the spottier aspects of George Gershwin's life. Still, the music is the main attraction and it doesn't disappoint. **139m/B; DVD.** Robert Alda; Joan Leslie; Alexis Smith; Charles Coburn; Julie Bishop; Albert Bassermann; Morris Carnovsky; Rosemary DeCamp; Herbert Rudley; Charles Halton; Robert Shayne; Johnny Downs; Al Jolson; ***D:*** Irving Rapper; ***W:*** Howard Koch; ***M:*** Max Steiner; ***M:*** Ira Gershwin.

Rhapsody of Spring 🦴🦴 **1998** Inspired by the life of one of China's most-respected composers. Zhao (Shao) comes of age during the Cultural Revolution and is torn between preserving the past and living in the present. He studies China's indigenous musical forms and becomes determined to compose a new type of opera that will combine traditional songs within a westernized orchestral arrangement, despite any disapproval. Mandarin with subtitles. **120m/C; DVD.** *CH* Bing Shao; Ying Qu; Quan Yuan; ***D:*** Wenji Teng; ***W:*** Wenji Teng; Ping He; Wu Hanqing; ***C:*** Lei Zhi; ***M:*** Yuhong Chang.

Rhinestone 🦴 **1984 (PG)** A country singer claims she can turn anyone, even a cabbie, into a singing sensation. Stuck with Stallone, Parton prepares her protege to sing at New York City's roughest country-western club, The Rhinestone. Only die-hard Dolly and Rocky fans need bother with this bunk. Some may enjoy watching the thick, New York accented Stallone learn how to properly pronounce dog ("dawg") in country lingo. Yee-haw. **111m/C; VHS, DVD.** Sylvester Stallone; Dolly Parton; Ron Leibman; Richard Farnsworth; Tim Thomerson; ***D:*** Bob (Benjamin) Clark; ***W:*** Sylvester Stallone; Phil Alden Robinson. Golden Raspberries '84: Worst Actor (Stallone), Worst Song ("Drinkenstein").

Rhubarb 🦴🦴 1/2 **1951** Eccentric millionaire T.J. Banner (Lockhart) adopts tough alley cat Rhubarb, making him the mascot of his losing baseball team, the Brooklyn Loons. When Banner dies, he leaves his fortune to the cat, with his lawyer Eric Yeager (Milland) as the feline's guardian. Yeager's also the press agent for the ball club and after he convinces the superstitious players that Rhubarb is good luck, the team starts winning. But then disgruntled gamblers kidnap the fur ball just before the championship game. Leonard Nimoy can be spotted as one of the ball players. **95m/B; DVD.** Ray Milland; Jan Sterling; Gene Lockhart; William Frawley; Strother Martin; Taylor Holmes; Elsie Holmes; Leonard Nimoy; Billie Bird; Willard Waterman; ***D:*** Ray Milland; Arthur Lubin; ***W:*** Dorothy Davenport Reid; Francis Cockrell; ***C:*** Lionel Lindon; ***M:*** Nathan Van Cleave.

Rhythm on the Range 🦴🦴 1/2 **1936** Crosby stars as a singing cowboy who befriends freight car stowaway Farmer while transporting his prize steer back to his ranch in California. He invites her to his domicile and she falls in love with life on the range and with the rancher himself. Filled with lots of musical numbers, including an appearance from the Sons of the Pioneers featuring Roy Rogers. Comedy from Burns and Raye, who makes her feature film debut here, is as entertaining as always. Remade by Dean Martin and Jerry Lewis in 1956 as "Pardners." **88m/B; VHS, DVD.** Bing Crosby; Frances Farmer; Bob Burns; Martha Raye; Samuel S. Hinds; Warren Hymer; Lucile Watson; ***D:*** Norman Taurog; ***W:*** John Moffitt; Sidney Salkow; Walter DeLeon; Francis Martin; ***C:*** Karl Struss.

Rhythm on the River 🦴🦴 1/2 **1940** Famous Broadway songwriter Rathbone has lost his magic touch so he hires melody maker Crosby to ghost for him while also hiring Martin to be the wordsmith. When the two fall in love they decide to strike off on their own but can't get their music heard since everyone assumes they've been copying Rathbone. Lots of backstage jokes with Rathbone terrific as an insecure egomaniac. **94m/B; VHS, DVD.** Bing Crosby; Mary Martin; Basil Rathbone; Oscar Levant; Oscar Shaw; Charley Grapewin; William Frawley; Charles Lane; ***D:*** Victor Schertzinger; ***W:*** Dwight Taylor; ***M:*** Victor Young.

Rhythm Parade 🦴🦴 **1943** A woman takes off for Hawaii, leaving her infant in the care of an L.A. nightclub singer. A jealous rival of the singer takes the opportunity to cause problems. The thin plot serves as a vehicle for lots of singing. **68m/B; VHS, DVD.** Nils T. Granlund; Gale Storm; Robert Lowery; Margaret Dumont; Chick Chandler; Cliff Nazarro; Jan Wiley; Candy Candido; Yvonne De Carlo; ***D:*** Howard Bretherton.

The Rhythm Section 🦴 1/2 **2019 (R)** The tragic death of her family in a plane crash causes an ordinary young woman, Stephanie Patrick (Lively), to fall apart. She goes into a downward spiral of depression, substance abuse, and prostitution in a London brothel. A visit from an investigative journalist (Jeffrey) changes her life as he believes the crash was a terrorist incident. Stephanie transforms herself to seek justice. While Lively gives her performance her all, it's a bland adaptation of the 1999 Burnell novel. **109m/C; DVD.** Blake Lively; Jude Law; Sterling K. Brown; Max Casella; Daniel Mays; ***D:*** Reed Morano; ***W:*** Mark Burnell; ***C:*** Sean Bobbitt; ***M:*** Steve Mazzaro.

Rhythm Thief 🦴🦴 **1994** No-budget independent film finds alienated New York hustler Simon (Andrews) eking out a living selling tapes of local underground bands he has illegally recorded. He wants to be left alone but circumstances won't allow it. He's got one of the enraged bands after him, he's pestered by local "admirers," and his eccentric former girlfriend Marty (Daniels) suddenly turns up—severely shaking Simon's emotionally barren existence. Quirky character study gets lots of impact from tiny bucks. **88m/B; VHS, DVD.** Jason Andrews; Eddie Daniels; Kimberly Flynn; Kevin Corrigan; Sean Haggerty; Mark Alfred; Christopher Cooke; ***D:*** Matthew Harrison; ***W:*** Matthew Harrison; Christopher Grimm; ***C:*** Howard Krupa; ***M:*** Danny Brenner. Sundance '95: Special Jury Prize.

Rica 🦴🦴 *Konketsuji Rika; Rika the Mixed Blood Girl* **1972** A good example of Japan's Pinky violence films in the 1970s. Rica is a half-Japanese girl, whose mother was raped by American G.I.s, who is sent to reform school after murdering a yakuza who left her friend after getting her pregnant (the poor girl soon commits suicide). While in school most of her gang is kidnapped and sold by rivals, so she decides to bust out and raise hell. **90m/C; DVD.** *JP* Masami Souda; Ryohei Uchida; Masane Tsukayama; Rika Aoki; Mich Nono; Yasuo Harakayama; Satoshi Moritsuka; Yoshihiro Nakdai; Jun Otomo; ***D:*** Ko Nakahira; ***W:*** Taro Bonten; Kaneto Shindo; ***C:*** Aguri Sugita; ***M:*** Jiro Takemura.

Rica 2: Lonely Wanderer 🦴🦴 1/2 *Konketsuji Rika: Hitoriyuku sasuraitabi* **1973** Rica (Rika Aoki) has left her old life behind until a friend dies in a mysterious boat explosion. When she tries to investigate what happened by talking to the survivors they all end up dying. Her only clue is that a drug cartel is behind the killings Pairing with a private detective, the two take the cartel on. **83m/C; DVD.** *JP* Taiji Tonoyama; Hitoshi Takagi; Rika Aoki; Ryunosuke Minagishi; Eiji Karasawa; Wolf Otsuki; Haruhiko Tazaki; Kentaro Kaji; Yushi Nishi; Koichi Kubo; ***D:*** Ko Nakahira; ***W:*** Kaneto Shindo; Taro Bonten; ***C:*** Yasushi Sasakibara; Shigenari Hanamura; Tadashi Saijo; Aguri Sugita; ***M:*** Jiro Takemura.

Rica 3: Juvenile's Lullaby 🦴🦴 **1973** In trouble again, Rica is sent to a reform school, and then to a mental institution where the people running things are selling the worst girl delinquents into slavery—where they are forced to produce pornographic films. Yet again, young Rica must use all her Karate skills to defeat an army of intimidating but physically useless goobers. Third film in the series, with a bit more comedy than the rest. **85m/C; DVD.** *JP* Taiji Tonoyama; Rika Aoki; Masami Souda; Boss Alstrom; Mammoth Suzuki; ***D:*** Oxide Pang Chun; Kozabura Yoshimura; ***W:*** Kaneto Shindo; Taro Bonten; ***C:*** Aguri Sugita; ***M:*** Jiro Takemura.

Ricco 🦴🦴 *Summertime Killer* **1974 (PG)** A young man swears vengeance against the mobsters who killed his father. He kidnaps the daughter of a mafia kingpin and the battle begins. **90m/C; VHS, DVD.** *FR IT SP* Chris Mitchum; Karl Malden; Olivia Hussey; Raf Vallone; Claudine Auger; Gerard Tichy; ***D:*** Antonio (Isasi-Isasmendi) Isasi.

R.I.C.C.O. 🦴 1/2 **2002 (R)** When a defense attorney saves a beautiful young woman from the clutches of sinister hitmen, they both become pawns in a deadly game of hide and seek, running from R.I.C.C.O., Detroit's mysterious ganglord. No budget action piece acts more like a decent tour video of Detrot. Other than that, there's not much to look at. Dismal acting and a silly score. **108m/C; VHS, DVD.** Walter Harris; Sophia Taylor; ***D:*** Shawn Woodard; ***W:*** Shawn Woodard. **VIDEO**

Rich and Famous 🦴🦴 **1981 (R)** The story of the 25-year friendship of two women, through college, marriage, and success. George Cukor's last film. **117m/C; VHS, DVD.** Jacqueline Bisset; Candice Bergen; David Selby; Hart Bochner; Meg Ryan; Steven Hill; Michael Brandon; Matt Lattanzi; ***D:*** George Cukor; ***W:*** Gerald Ayres; ***M:*** Georges Delerue. Writers Guild '81: Adapt. Screenplay.

Rich and Strange 🦴🦴 1/2 *East of Shanghai* **1932** Early Hitchcock movie is not in the same class as his later thrillers. A couple inherits a fortune and journeys around the world. Eventually the pair gets shipwrecked. **92m/B; VHS, DVD.** *GB* Henry Kendall; Joan Barry; Betty Amann; Percy Marmont; Elsie Randolph; ***D:*** Alfred Hitchcock; ***W:*** Alfred Hitchcock; Alma Reville; ***C:*** Jack Cox; Charles Martin.

The Rich Are Always With Us 🦴🦴 **1932** Wealthy Caroline (Chatterton) can't buy herself happiness in her marriage to Greg Grannard (Miljan). He's unfaithful and Caroline gets a divorce and goes to Paris to be comforted by longtime admirer Julian (Brent). When Greg falls on hard times, Caroline can't quite let go and it looks like their finally requited love won't last. Davis has a minor role as a woman Julian briefly romances. **71m/B; DVD.** Ruth Chatterton; George Brent; John Miljan; Adrienne Dore; Bette Davis; John Wray; ***D:*** Alfred E. Green; ***W:*** Austin Parker; ***C:*** Ernest Haller.

Rich Hill 🦴🦴🦴 **2014** The Grand Jury Prize winner for Documentary at the 2014 Sundance Film Festival chronicles three young residents of a rural American town and becomes a statement on poverty, youth, and social class in the '10s. While technology has redefined the youth generation, there are still parts of the country in which people struggle to make ends meet in a more rural, old-fashioned way. Directors Tracy Droz Tragos and Andrew Droz Palermo tap into the youthful indiscretion and endless dreams of childhood in this moving, compassionate glimpse at American poverty. **91m/C; Streaming.** ***D:*** Tracy Droz Tragos; Andrew Droz Palermo; ***C:*** Andrew Droz Palermo; ***M:*** Nathan Halpern.

Rich in Love 🦴🦴 1/2 **1993 (PG-13)** Light-hearted look at the changes in a Southern family after matriarch Helen Odom leaves to pursue her own life, shattering the peaceful existence of those around her. Seen through the eyes of 17-year-old daughter Lucille who assumes the role of "mother" for her sister and father while trying to come to terms with her own confused feelings. Nice performances by newcomer Erbe and Finney can't overcome a mediocre script. Based on the novel by Josephine Humphreys. **105m/C; VHS, DVD.** Albert Finney; Jill Clayburgh; Kathryn Erbe; Kyle MacLachlan; Piper Laurie; Ethan Hawke; Suzy Amis; Alfre Woodard; ***D:*** Bruce Beresford; ***W:*** Alfred Uhry; ***M:*** Georges Delerue.

Rich Man, Poor Man 🦴🦴🦴 **1976** Classic TV miniseries covers 20 (sometimes bitter) years in the lives of the two Jordache brothers. It's 1945 in quiet Port Phillip, New York with embittered German baker Axel (Asner), his unfulfilled wife Mary (McGuire), and sons Tom (Nolte) and Rudy (Strauss). Tom is wild and irresponsible, Rudy is ambitious and college-bound, and Julie Prescott (Blakely), Rudy's girl, overshadows both their lives. Based on the novel by Irwin Shaw. The first series contained 12 episodes. A second series of 21 episodes primarily followed the tribulations of the next generation, although Strauss returned as Rudy. **720m/C; VHS, DVD.** Peter Strauss; Nick Nolte; Susan Blakely; Ed Asner; Dorothy McGuire; Bill Bixby; Robert Reed; Ray Milland; Kim Darby; Talia Shire; Lawrence Pressman; Kay Lenz; ***M:*** Alex North. **TV**

The Rich Man's Wife 🦴 1/2 **1996 (R)** Modern noir strands unhappy wife Josie (Berry) on Martha's Vineyard without her loathsome spouse (McDonald), where she makes the mistake of confiding her marital woes to sympathetic, yet obviously deranged stranger Cole (Greene). She tells Cole sometimes she wishes her husband was dead. Poof! Before you can say "foreshadowing," hubby's murdered and she's the prime suspect. Increasingly nutso Cole stalks our heroine, seemingly innocent, but possibly not as blameless as it appears. Failed mystery/thriller delivers little of either and the attempt at a "Strangers on a Train" premise and a "Usual Suspects" type ending fail miserably. **95m/C; VHS, DVD, Blu-Ray.** Halle Berry; Christopher McDonald; Clive Owen; Peter Greene; Charles Hallahan; Frankie Faison; Clea Lewis; ***D:*** Amy Holden Jones; ***W:*** Amy Holden Jones; ***C:*** Haskell Wexler; ***M:*** John (Gianni) Frizzell.

Rich, Young and Pretty 🦴🦴 1/2 **1951** Light-hearted, innocuous musical starring Powell as a Texas gal visiting Paris with her rancher father (Corey). Powell finds romance with Damone (in his screen debut) and a secret—the mother she has never known (Darrieux). Lamas (in his American screen debut) plays Darrieux's new heartthrob. **95m/C; VHS, DVD.** Jane Powell; Danielle Darrieux; Wendell Corey; Vic Damone; Fernando Lamas; Marcel Dalio; Una Merkel; Richard Anderson; Jean Murat; Hans Conried; ***D:*** Norman Taurog; ***W:*** Sidney Sheldon; Dorothy Cooper; ***M:*** Sammy Cahn; Nicholas Brodszky.

Richard Jewell 🦴🦴🦴 **2019 (R)** After being fired as a college security guard, Richard Jewell (Hauser) is hired to provide security for music events held at Centennial Park during the 1996 Summer Olympics. The overzealous Richard saves lives when a pipe bomb is set off during an event. Initially lauded, he is soon investigated by the FBI and falsely accused of setting off the bomb. He is vilified in the press and finds his life spinning out of control. Inspired by true events, director Eastwood and Hauser have aptly reflected the frenzy around Jewell and what that says about society as a whole. **129m/C; DVD, Blu-Ray.** Paul Walter Hauser; Sam Rockwell; Kathy Bates; Charles Green; Olivia Wilde; *D:* Clint Eastwood; *W:* Billy Ray; *C:* Yves Bélanger; *M:* Arturo Sandoval.

Richard Petty Story 🦴 **1972 (G)** The biography of race car driver Petty, played by himself, and his various achievements on the track. **83m/C; VHS, DVD.** Richard Petty; Darren McGavin; Kathie Browne; Lynn(e) Marta; Noah Beery, Jr.; L.Q. Jones; *D:* Ed Lasko.

Richard III 🦴🦴🦴 ½ **1955** This landmark film version of the Shakespearean play features an acclaimed performance by Laurence Olivier, who also directs. The plot follows the life of the mentally and physically twisted Richard of Gloucester and his schemes for the throne of England. **138m/C; VHS, DVD, Blu-Ray.** *GB* Laurence Olivier; Cedric Hardwicke; Ralph Richardson; John Gielgud; Stanley Baker; Michael Gough; Claire Bloom; *D:* Laurence Olivier. British Acad. '55: Actor (Olivier), Director (Olivier), Film; Golden Globes '57: Foreign Film.

Richard III 🦴🦴🦴 ½ **1995 (R)** The Brits once again bring the Bard's most notorious monarch to the screen, this time in a new setting. McKellen stars in the title role of the deformed and ruthless English king, now in an imagined 1930s London of swanky Art Deco, Black Shirt thugs and modern media. Purists may resent major dialogue cuts, but famous speeches (such as the "winter of our discontent" opener) are amusingly staged in this modern take. Gorgeously polished visuals are perfect foil for the slimy, evil goings-on. Based on both Shakespeare's play and Richard Eyre's stage adaptation (in which McKellen also starred). **105m/C; VHS, DVD, Blu-Ray.** *GB* Ian McKellen; Annette Bening; Jim Broadbent; Robert Downey, Jr.; Nigel Hawthorne; Kristin Scott Thomas; Maggie Smith; John Wood; *D:* Richard Loncraine; *W:* Ian McKellen; Richard Loncraine; *C:* Peter Biziou; *M:* Trevor Jones.

Richie Rich 🦴🦴 ½ **1994 (PG)** Yet another adaptation from the comics. Richie (Culkin), the world's richest boy, takes over the family business when his madcap parents Richard (Herrmann) and Regina (Ebersole) disappear thanks to the devious Laurence Van Dough (Larroquette). But there's kindly valet Cadbury (Hyde) and eccentric live-in inventor Keenbean (McShane) to help Richie save the day. Some silliness but Culkin has clearly outgrown this type of kid role. Biltmore, the 8,000 acre Vanderbilt estate in Asheville, North Carolina, serves as the Rich family home. **94m/C; VHS, DVD.** Macaulay Culkin; John Larroquette; Edward Herrmann; Christine Ebersole; Jonathan Hyde; Michael McShane; Stephi Lineburg; *Cameo(s):* Reggie Jackson; Claudia Schiffer; *D:* Donald Petrie; *W:* Tom S. Parker; Jim Jennewein; *C:* Don Burgess; *M:* Alan Silvestri.

Rick 🦴🦴 ½ **2003 (R)** Drawing from Verdi's "Rigoletto," the widower Rick is a detestable corporate exec who despises his annoying and much younger boss Duke yet degrades himself to score points. He's pushed past the breaking point when he learns that the punk has been sex-chatting online with his teenage daughter and figures putting a hit out on him is the only answer. **93m/C; VHS, DVD.** Bill Pullman; Aaron Stanford; Agnes Bruckner; Sandra Oh; Dylan Baker; Emmanuelle Chriqui; Marianne Hagan; Jamie Harris; Paz de la Huerta; P.J. Brown; Haviland (Haylie) Morris; Dan Moran; Jerome Preston Bates; Marin Rathje; William Ryall; Daniel Handler; Dennis Parlato; Todd A. Kovner; Kimberly Anne Thompson; Vita Haas; Ben Hauck; *W:* Daniel Handler; *C:* Lisa Rinzler; *M:* Ted Reichman. **VIDEO**

Ricki and the Flash 🦴🦴 **2015 (PG-13)** Director Demme and screenwriter Cody prove to be an awkward fit in this tale of parental drama headlined by another strong performance from Streep as Ricki, and an even better one by her daughter. Ricki is the singer of a bar band who has been estranged from her family for years. She's forced back into their lives when her daughter (Gummer) tries to commit suicide. Ricki must take some responsibility for her past mistakes and help her child get her head above water. Demme loves the healing power of music and both Streep and Gummer are great, but the tale is too predictable. **101m/C; DVD, Blu-Ray.** Meryl Streep; Rick Springfield; Kevin Kline; Mamie Gummer; Benjamin Platt; *D:* Jonathan Demme; *W:* Diablo Cody; *C:* Declan Quinn.

Ricky 🦴 ½ **2009** Weird combo of fantasy and family drama about factory worker Katie (Lamy) who's a single mom to officious 7-year-old Lisa (Mayance). Katie falls for her Spanish co-worker Paco (Lopez) but Lisa gets a bad case of sibling rivalry when they have a baby they name Ricky (Peyret). After Paco babysits, Katie notices odd marks on Ricky and accuses Paco of abuse, but it turns out Ricky is literally about to sprout wings and begins to fly around. No one finds this particularly odd—although there's something of a media frenzy—but the story is underwritten at best. Based on the short story "Moth" by Rose Tremain. French with subtitles. **89m/C; DVD.** *FR* Alexandra Lamy; Sergi Lopez; Melusine Mayance; Arthure Peyret; Andre Wilms; Jean-Claude Bolle-Reddat; *D:* Francois Ozon; *W:* Francois Ozon; Emmanuele Bernheim; *C:* Jeanne Lapoirie; *M:* Philippe Rombi.

Ricky Nelson: Original Teen Idol 🦴 ½ **1999** Made-for-TV showbiz bio with the adult Rick talking to a fan shortly before his plane crash death in 1985. Flashbacks depict his life working on the family TV show in the 1950s, which launched Ricky Nelson as a teen singing idol. There are the usual family struggles as he tries to break away from his parents' control and expectations and the hard-partying, drug-fueled interludes as Ricky grows up and his career stalls. **93m/C; DVD.** Gregory Calpakis; Jamey Sheridan; Sara Botsford; Anthony Lemke; Anne Openshaw; *D:* Sturla Gunnarsson; *W:* Arlene Sarner; *C:* Tony Westman; *M:* Jonathan Goldsmith. **TV**

Ricky 1 🦴 ½ **1988** Mumbling pugilist spoof. Da Mob wants to make Ricky da fall guy, but uh, he's not as dumb as he looks. **90m/C; VHS, DVD.** Michael Michaud; Maggie Hughes; James Herbert; Lane Montano; *D:* Bill Naud; *M:* Joel Goldsmith.

Ricochet 🦴🦴🦴 **1991 (R)** Rookie cop Washington causes a sensation when he singlehandedly captures notorious psychopath Lithgow. But this particular criminal is a twisted genius, and from his prison cell he comes up with a plan to destroy the young cop. Teaming up with old friend Ice-T, the rookie tries to outwit his evil arch-nemesis. Genuinely scary, tense and violent thriller. **104m/C; VHS, DVD.** Denzel Washington; John Lithgow; Ice-T; Jesse Ventura; Kevin Pollak; Lindsay Wagner; Mary Ellen Trainor; Josh Evans; Victoria Dillard; John Amos; John Cothran, Jr.; *D:* Russell Mulcahy; *W:* Steven E. de Souza; *C:* Peter Levy; *M:* Alan Silvestri.

Ricochet River 🦴🦴 **1998 (R)** High school senior Lorna (Hudson) has big dreams that don't include staying around her tiny Oregon community, even if she is dating hotshot school quarterback Wade. The duo are also the only two to accept newcomer Jesse, a Native American who falls victim to the town's prejudice. **111m/C; VHS, DVD.** Kate Hudson; Douglas Spain; Jason James Richter; Matthew Glave; Dan Lauria; John Cullum; *D:* Deborah Del Prete. **VIDEO**

Riddick 🦴🦴 ½ **2013 (R)** Diesel returns in the third film to feature the exploits of the killing machine who can see in the dark. After the failed effort to expand the mythology around the title character into something more epic in "The Chronicles of Riddick," writer/director Twohy returns to basics with a film that plays like a remake of "Pitch Black." It's simple, but mostly effective stuff as Riddick battles mercenaries who want the head of the most infamous criminal in the universe and waves of monsters that are deadly enough to take them all out. It's undeniably silly and way too long but the action centerpieces work well enough to entertain. **119m/C; DVD, Blu-Ray.** *US UK* Vin Diesel; Jordi Molla; Matt Noble; Katee Sackhoff; Bokeem Woodbine; Dave Bautista; Karl Urban; Raoul Trujillo; Conrad Pla; Nolan Gerard Funk; *D:* David N. Twohy; *W:* David N. Twohy; *C:* David Eggby; *M:* Graeme Revell.

The Riddle 🦴🦴 **2007 (PG-13)** Thames-side pub landlady Sadie (Day) is murdered after discovering an unpublished Charles Dickens manuscript in her cellar. But she's already turned it over to her friend, sports reporter Mike (Jones), who's trying to reinvent himself as an investigative journalist. He's willing to hook up with police press officer Kate (Cox) and even a dockside tramp (Jacobi) if they can help him. But a century-old crime described by Dickens (played in flashbacks by Jacobi) might lead Mike to solving Sadie's murder and figuring out who's trying to grab the manuscript from him. **116m/C; DVD.** *GB* Vinnie Jones; Julie Cox; Derek Jacobi; Vanessa Redgrave; Jason Flemyng; P. H. Moriarty; Mel Smith; Vera Day; *D:* Brendan Foley; *W:* Brendan Foley; *C:* Mark Moriarty; *M:* Graham Sack.

Riddle 🦴 **2013** Sluggish, underdeveloped slasher horror. College student Holly Teller (Hanois) goes to the small, nearly-abandoned town of Riddle, PA in search of her missing brother. Sheriff Richards (Kilmer) and others try to discourage her snooping. Kilmer's barely in the pic in an "I show up and you pay me" performance. **116m/C; DVD.** Elisabeth Harnois; Diora Baird; Val Kilmer; William Sadler; *D:* John O. Hartman; Nicholas Mross; *W:* John O. Hartman; Nicholas Mross; *C:* Jeff Garton; *M:* Scott Glasgow. **VIDEO**

The Riddle of the Sands 🦴🦴 ½ **1979** Two English yachtsmen in 1903 inadvertently stumble upon a German plot to invade England by sea. British film based on the Erskine Childers spy novel. **99m/C; VHS, DVD.** *GB* Michael York; Jenny Agutter; Simon MacCorkindale; Alan Badel; *D:* Tony Maylam; *M:* Howard Blake.

Riddler's Moon 🦴 ½ *Nightworld: Riddler's Moon* **1998** Widow Victoria Riddler and her teenaged, wheelchair-bound son Elias are barely surviving on the family's unproductive Indiana farm. But after Elias has a vision—the crops suddenly start growing—and the neighbors start talking. **90m/C; DVD.** Kate Mulgrew; Daniel Newman; Corbin Bernsen; William Armstrong; *D:* Don McBrearty; *W:* Karl Schiffman; *C:* Jon Joffin; *M:* John Welsman. **TV**

Ride 🦴🦴 **1998 (R)** This sometimes-amusing but mostly rude road comedy seems to be merely an excuse for getting MTV veejays and rap stars together without actually showing any videos. Freddy B (Campbell) is a superstar looking for street cred, so his director Bleau (Brown) sends Leta (DeSousa) to Harlem to bring a group of young street talents to Miami for a video shoot. There are too many storylines in the busload of passengers to develop fully, so they are skimmed over and defused with a mixture of generic road movie brawls and narrow escapes combined with sexual and scatalogical humor. Yoba does a good job as Poppa, who's trying to watch over reckless little brother Geronimo (Starr) while keeping the rest of the crew in line. **83m/C; VHS, DVD.** Malik Yoba; Melissa De Sousa; Fredro Starr; John Witherspoon; Cedric the Entertainer; Kirk "Sticky Fingaz" Jones; Kellie Williams; Idalis de Leon; Julia Garrison; Guy Torry; Reuben Asher; Lady of Rage; Dartanyan Edmonds; Julie Brown; *Cameo(s):* Snoop Dogg; *D:* Millicent Shelton; *W:* Millicent Shelton; *C:* Frank Byers; *M:* Dunn Pearson, Jr.

Ride a Crooked Trail 🦴 ½ **1958** Bank robber Joe Maybe (Murphy) rides into town and drunken Judge Kyle (Matthau) mistakes him for the U.S. Marshal he's been expecting. Joe pins on a badge and then is nearly exposed by Tessa (Scala), the girlfriend of fellow robber Sam Teeler (Silva). She's arrived to case the local bank for Teeler. She poses as Joe's wife to allay suspicions and both like the respectability of their new identities until Sam and his gang show up. **87m/C; DVD.** Audie Murphy; Walter Matthau; Gia Scala; Henry Silva; Joanna Moore; Leo Gordon; Eddie Little; Mort Mills; *D:* Jesse Hibbs; *W:* Borden Chase; *C:* Harold Lipstein; *M:* Joseph Gershenson.

Ride a Wild Pony 🦴🦴🦴 **1975 (G)** A poor Australian farmer's son is allowed to pick a horse of his own from a neighboring rancher's herd. After he trains and grows to love the pony, the rancher's daughter, a handicapped rich girl, decides to claim it for herself. Enjoyable Disney story is based on the tale "Sporting Proposition," by James Aldridge. **86m/C; VHS, DVD.** *AU* John Meillon; Michael Craig; Robert Bettles; Eva Griffith; Graham Rouse; *D:* Don Chaffey; *C:* Jack Cardiff; *M:* John Addison.

Ride Along 🦴🦴 **2014 (PG-13)** Ben (Hart) wants to marry James' (Cube) sister Angela (Sumpter). James is a cop. Ben rides along with James. Hilarity is intended to ensue. Proving that comedic charisma can go a very long way to make a film bearable, almost all of any perceived success of this buddy flick comes down to the fun repartee between the two leads. Sadly, too much of the film is directed like a TBS sitcom to really rise above its boring script. **99m/C; DVD, Blu-Ray.** Kevin Hart; Ice Cube; Tika Sumpter; John Leguizamo; Bryan Callen; Bruce McGill; Laurence Fishburne; *D:* Tim Story; *W:* Greg Coolidge; Phil Hay; Jason Mantzoukas; Matt Manfredi; *C:* Larry Blanford; *M:* Christopher Lennertz.

Ride Along 2 🦴 ½ **2016 (PG-13)** The law of diminishing returns that most comedy sequels are guilty of (jokes are never funny twice because you know the punchline) seems amplified in this limp sequel for Atlanta cop James (Ice Cube) and his brother-in-law Ben (Hart). To say that the writers basically just reprinted their last screenplay would be an understatement—it steals scenes and bits wholesale. The only thing that averts complete disaster is that Hart still throws himself into all of the ridiculousness and Ice Cube maintains his easygoing charm. **102m/C; DVD, Blu-Ray.** Ice Cube; Kevin Hart; Tika Sumpter; Benjamin Bratt; Olivia Munn; *D:* Tim Story; *W:* Phil Hay; Matt Manfredi; *C:* Mitchell Amundsen; *M:* Christopher Lennertz.

The Ride Back 🦴🦴 ½ **1957** Well-done western about lawman Hamish (Conrad) who decides to take outlaw Kallen (Quinn) across the Mexican border back to Texas—a four days' journey through hostile territory. At the site of a massacre they discover a lone survivor, a little girl whom they take with them. Then they are attacked by Apaches and when Hamish is wounded, Kallen sees his chance for escape. Good performances by the leads; feature debut for director Miner. **80m/B; VHS, DVD.** William Conrad; Anthony Quinn; Lita Milan; Ellen Hope Monroe; *D:* Allen Miner; *W:* Antony Ellis; *C:* Joseph Biroc; *M:* Frank DeVol.

Ride Clear of Diablo 🦴🦴 ½ **1954** Crooked Sheriff Kenyon (Birch) and equally crooked lawyer Meredith (Pullen) murder Clay O'Mara's (Murphy) father and brother. He vows to get revenge, aided by gunslinger Whitey Kincade (Duryea). Then Laurie (Cabot), Kenyon's niece and Meredith's fiance, comes to Clay's attention. Macho Technicolor western with a likeable cast. **80m/C; VHS, DVD.** Audie Murphy; Dan Duryea; Susan Cabot; Paul Birch; William Pullen; Abbe Lane; Russell Johnson; Jack Elam; Lane Bradford; Holly Bane; Denver Pyle; *D:* Jesse Hibbs; *W:* George Zuckerman; D.D. Beauchamp; *C:* Irving Glassberg.

Ride 'Em Cowboy 🦴🦴 ½ **1942** Two peanut and hotdog vendors travel west to try their hand as cowpokes. Usual Abbott and Costello fare with a twist—there are lots of great musical numbers. **86m/B; VHS, DVD.** Bud Abbott; Lou Costello; Anne Gwynne; Samuel S. Hinds; Dick Foran; Richard Lane; Johnny Mack Brown; Ella Fitzgerald; Douglass Dumbrille; *D:* Arthur Lubin.

Ride for Lance 🦴🦴 **2014** A documentary look at the cross-country experiences of the Lance Vaccaro Ride. A Navy SEAL, Vaccaro died while serving his country in 2008. To pay tribute to his sacrifice, several friends of Vaccaro organized a month-long motorcycle ride from Virginia to Alaska. The documentary chronicles the experiences of the riders themselves and the many people they meet along the way. **85m/C; DVD, Download.** *D:* Scott Mactavish; *W:* Scott Mactavish. **VIDEO**

Ride in the Whirlwind 🦴🦴 **1966** Three cowboys are mistaken for members of a gang by a posse. Screenplay for the offbeat western by Nicholson. **83m/C; DVD, Blu-Ray.** Jack Nicholson; Cameron Mitchell; Millie Perkins; Katherine Squire; Harry Dean Stanton;

Rupert Crosse; *D:* Monte Hellman; *W:* Jack Nicholson; *C:* Gregory Sandor; *M:* Robert Drasnin.

Ride Lonesome 🦴🦴 ½ **1959** The heroic Scott is a bounty hunter looking for a killer (Best). It's not just the money, Scott hopes Best will lead him to the man who murdered Scott's wife. Along the trail he meets a pretty widow and two outlaws who hope if they capture Best, they'll get a pardon. A well-done example of a "B" western with good performances; Coburn's film debut. **73m/C; VHS, DVD.** Randolph Scott; James Best; Karen Steele; Pernell Roberts; Lee Van Cleef; James Coburn; *D:* Budd Boetticher; *W:* Burt Kennedy.

Ride the High Country 🦴🦴🦴🦴 *Guns in the Afternoon* **1962** The cult classic western about two old friends who have had careers on both sides of the law. One, Joel McCrea, is entrusted with a shipment of gold, and the other, Randolph Scott, rides along with him to steal the precious cargo. Although barely promoted by MGM, the film became a critics' favorite. Grimacing and long in the tooth, McCrea and Scott enact a fitting tribute and farewell to the myth of the grand ol' West. **93m/C; VHS, DVD, Blu-Ray.** Randolph Scott; Joel McCrea; Mariette Hartley; Edgar Buchanan; R.G. Armstrong; Ronald Starr; John Anderson; James Drury; L.Q. Jones; Warren Oates; Jenie Jackson; John Davis Chandler; *D:* Sam Peckinpah; *W:* N.B. Stone, Jr.; *C:* Lucien Ballard; *M:* George Bassman. Natl. Film Reg. '92.

Ride the Pink Horse 🦴🦴🦴 **1947** Unsettling film noir moodiness, adapted from the Dorothy B. Hughes novel. Embittered WWII vet Lucky Gagin (Montgomery, who also directed) comes to a small New Mexico town during its busy annual fiesta. He's looking to blackmail gangster Frank Hugo, who killed Lucky's friend, only to find interfering FBI agent Retz wants Lucky's incriminating evidence to put Hugo away. Lucky doesn't have much luck despite help from a couple of locals--genial carousel owner Pancho and lovestruck young Pila. **101m/B; DVD, Blu-Ray.** Robert Montgomery; Thomas Gomez; Wanda Hendrix; Art Smith; Fred Clark; *D:* Robert Montgomery; *W:* Ben Hecht; Charles Lederer; *C:* Russell Metty; *M:* Frank Skinner.

Ride the Wild Fields 🦴🦴 ½ **2000** Tender adaptation of Vacarro's play "And the Home of the Brave" finds 11-year-old Opal Miller (Vega) and her mother Ruby (Whalley) struggling to manage their small North Carolina farm while Opal's dad serves overseas during WWII. Ruby is grateful for the help of drifter Tom (Flanery), though others are suspicious of the young man, but complications arise when the adults develop stronger feelings for one another. **101m/C; VHS, DVD.** Joanne Whalley; Sean Patrick Flanery; Alexa Vega; Cotter Smith; *D:* Paul A. Kaufman; *W:* Rodney Vaccaro; *C:* Thom Best; *M:* Laura Kaufman. **CABLE**

Ride the Wild Surf 🦴🦴 ½ **1964** It's fun in the sun when surfers Fabian, Hunter, and Brown head to Hawaii in search of the ultimate waves. Throw in a little romance and a cool title song by Jan and Dean and you've got your better than average beach movie. The surfing footage is excellent. Cowabunga! **101m/C; VHS, DVD.** Fabian; Tab Hunter; Barbara Eden; Peter Brown; Susan Hart; Shelley Fabares; Jim Mitchum; *D:* Don Taylor.

Ride to Glory 🦴🦴 *The Deserter; La Spina Dorsale del Diavolo* **1971** In 1886, a cavalry officer deserts his troops to seek revenge on the Apaches that brutally killed his family. Hearing this, a general offers to pardon him if he will lead a dangerous group of men on a mission against the Apaches. Fast-paced and very bloody. **90m/C; VHS, DVD.** Bekim Fehmiu; Richard Crenna; Chuck Connors; Ricardo Montalban; Ian Bannen; Slim Pickens; Woody Strode; Patrick Wayne; John Huston; *D:* Burt Kennedy.

Ride, Vaquero! 🦴🦴 **1953** Violent bandito leader Esqueda vows to burn any new ranch going up along the Rio Grande border after the Civil War ends. His quiet-but-menacing foster brother Rio is indifferent until he gets involved with rancher King Cameron and his beautiful, suspicious wife Cordelia. As Rio's alliance with Esqueda becomes increasingly uneasy, Cordelia wants to know which side Rio will choose. **90m/C; DVD.** Robert Taylor; Anthony Quinn; Ava Gardner; Howard Keel; Kurt Kasznar; Ted de Corsia; Jack Elam; *D:* John Farrow; *W:* Frank Fenton; *C:* Robert L. Surtees; *M:* Bronislau Kaper.

Ride with the Devil 🦴🦴 ½ **1999 (R)** Clunky Civil War saga adapted from Daniel Woodrell's novel "Woe to Live On." Lee concentrates on the 1862 Border Wars between the Southern-sympathizers known as the Bushwhackers and the pro-Union Jayhawkers. Best pals Jack Bull Chiles (Ulrich) and Jake Roedel (Maguire) join a group of Bushwhackers and both become involved with a young farm widow, Sue Lee (singer Jewel in her acting debut). After some losses, Jake and the remaining band join in Quantrill's (Ales) infamous raid on the abolitionist stronghold of Lawrence, Kansas. Film serves as a coming-of-age story for the teenaged Jake and Maguire is up to the challenge. **139m/C; VHS, DVD, Blu-Ray.** Tobey Maguire; Skeet Ulrich; Jeffrey Wright; Jewel Kilcher; Tom Wilkinson; Simon Baker; Jonathan Rhys Meyers; James (Jim) Caviezel; Tom Guiry; John Ales; Jonathan Brandis; Mark Ruffalo; Matthew Faber; Margo Martindale; Zach Grenier; *D:* Ang Lee; *W:* James Schamus; *C:* Frederick Elmes; *M:* Mychael Danna.

The Rider 🦴🦴 ½ **2017 (R)** A moving drama about rodeo riders living on a South Dakota reservation. Though at the top of his field as a bronco rider and horse trainer, Brady Blackburn (Jandreau) had a bad fall, suffered a head injury, and is unsure if he will ride again. As he considers his future, he continues to break horses. A visit to his paralyzed best friend Lane (Scott), clarifies the idea that Brady should not give up on his dreams. This non-traditional, beautiful film that mesmerizes through its look, mood, and performances from the non-actors, many who live on the reservation where the film was shot. **104m/C; DVD.** Brady Jandreau; Tim Jandreau; Lilly Jandreau; Cat Clifford; Lane Scott; *D:* Chloé Zhao; *W:* Chloé Zhao; *C:* Joshua James Richards; *M:* Nathan Halpern.

The Rider of Death Valley 🦴 ½ **1932** Larribe and Grant plot to steal Bill Joyce's desert gold mine after he dies and leaves the property to his sister Helen and young daughter Betty. Knowing something shady is going on rancher Tom Rigby tries to protect the claim but Helen gets the wrong idea. **78m/B; DVD.** Tom Mix; Lois Wilson; Fred Kohler, Jr.; Forrest Stanley; Edith Fellows; Willard Robertson; Mae Busch; *D:* Albert Rogell; *W:* Jack Cunningham; *C:* Daniel B. Clark.

Rider on a Dead Horse 🦴 ½ **1962** Three prospectors strike it rich, then bury their gold in the Arizona desert to hide it from hostile Apaches. However, one of the men decides to kill his partners to claim it all. **72m/B; DVD.** John Vivyan; Bruce Gordon; Charles Lampkin; Kevin Hagen; Lisa Lu; *D:* Herbert L. Strock; *W:* Stephen Longstreet; *C:* Frank V. Phillips.

Rider on the Rain 🦴🦴🦴 *Lepassager de la Pluie* **1970** A young housewife is viciously raped by an escaped sex maniac. She kills him and disposes of his body, not knowing that he is being relentlessly pursued by mysterious American Bronson. Suspenseful, French-made thriller featuring one of Bronson's best performances. **115m/C; VHS, DVD.** *FR* Marlene Jobert; Charles Bronson; Jill Ireland; *D:* Rene Clement. Golden Globes '71: Foreign Film.

Riders 🦴 *Jilly Cooper's Riders* **1988** Enemies since childhood, aristocratic Rupert Campbell-Black (Gilbert) and half-gypsy Jake Lovell (Praed) have carried their rivalry into the competitive equestrian field. Of course, there's the added complication of Rupert's wife, whom Jake is also interested in. Based on Jilly Cooper's steamy novel. **210m/C; VHS, DVD.** *GB* Marcus Gilbert; Michael Praed; Stephanie Beacham; Gabrielle Beaumont; Serena Gordon; John Standing; Anthony Valentine; Cecile Paoli; *D:* Gabrielle Beaumont; *W:* Charlotte Bingham; *C:* Michael J. Davis; *M:* Roger Webb.

Riders of Death Valley 🦴🦴 ½ **1941** Splendid western action serial in 15 episodes. Foran, Jones, and Carillo head a passel o'men watching for thieves and claim jumpers in a mining area. **320m/B; VHS, DVD.** Dick Foran; Buck Jones; Leo Carrillo; Lon Chaney, Jr.; *D:* Ford Beebe; Ray Taylor.

Riders of the Purple Sage 🦴🦴 ½ **1996** Legendary gunman (are there any other kind?) Lassiter (Harris) helps save Bern (Thomas) from a beating in a town run by a conservative religious sect, led by Deacon Tull (Weisser). Seems Bern's befriended ranch owner (and nonmember) Jane (Madigan) and the Deacon is not only after Jane but her considerable land and cattle holdings. Lassiter rides to the rescue. Properly brooding TV adaptation of the 1912 Zane Grey novel (the Grey novel specifies that the sect are Mormons but this caused considerable fuss). Filmed in Utah. **90m/C; DVD.** Ed Harris; Amy Madigan; Henry Thomas; Norbert Weisser; Robin Tunney; G.D. Spradlin; *D:* Charles Haid; *W:* Gill Dennis; *C:* William Wages; *M:* Arthur Kempel. **TV**

Riders of the Storm 🦴 ½ *The American Way* **1988 (R)** A motley crew of Vietnam vets runs a covert TV broadcasting station from an in-flight B-29, jamming America's legitimate airwaves. Interesting premise with boring result. **92m/C; VHS, DVD.** Dennis Hopper; Michael J. Pollard; Eugene Lipinski; James Aubrey; Nigel Pegram; *D:* Maurice Phillips; *W:* Scott Roberts.

Ridicule 🦴🦴🦴 ½ **1996 (R)** Minor country aristocrat Malavoy (Berling) enters the depraved world of the 18th-century court at Versailles, discovering the weapons of success are wit, deadly ridicule, and impeccable lineage. After initial missteps, he quickly adapts and finds some influential allies: the beautiful Madame de Blayac (Ardant) and sympathetic Marquis de Bellegarde (Rochefort). When the Marquis's spirited, attractive daughter, Mathilde (Godreche), arrives, the smitten Malavoy must stop her loveless marriage of convenience. Perfectly cast, director Leconte's period piece has all the emotional and technical elements needed for an engaging film. French with subtitles. **102m/C; VHS, DVD.** *FR* Charles Berling; Jean Rochefort; Fanny Ardant; Bernard Giraudeau; Judith Godreche; Bernard Dheran; Carlo Brandt; Jacques Mathou; *D:* Patrice Leconte; *W:* Remi Waterhouse; Michel Fessler; Eric Vicaut; *C:* Thierry Arbogast; *M:* Antoine Duhamel. Cesar '97: Director (Leconte), Film; Broadcast Film Critics '96: Foreign Film.

Ridin' on a Rainbow 🦴 ½ **1941** Has-been performer on a steamboat decides to rob a bank in the hopes of starting a new life for himself and his daughter. The money he robs had just been deposited by some cattlemen, one of whom joins the steamboat's crew, wins the daughter's heart, and gets to the father. Slow and dull, with too much singing, and too little plot and scenery. **79m/B; VHS, DVD.** Gene Autry; Smiley Burnette; Mary Lee; *D:* Lew Landers.

Riding Alone for Thousands of Miles 🦴🦴 *Qian Li Zou Dan Ji* **2005 (PG)** Small-scale, compelling human drama from Zhang. Japanese fisherman Gou-ichi Takata (Takakura) is called to Tokyo by his daughter-in-law, where his estranged son Ken-ichi (Nakai) is hospitalized with terminal cancer. Grief-stricken, Gou-ichi vows to fulfill his son's dying dream—to film celebrated Chinese opera star Li Jiamin (appearing as himself) in performance. This involves the elderly man traveling to a remote Chinese province and ultimately reuniting Li with his own illegitimate son. Hope triumphs amidst the hardships. Japanese and Chinese with subtitles. **108m/C; DVD.** *CH CH JP* Ken Takakura; Kiichi Nakai; Shinobu Terajima; Li Jiamon; *D:* Yimou Zhang; *W:* Zou Jingzhi; *C:* Xiaoding Zhao; *M:* Guo Wenjing.

Riding Giants 🦴🦴 **2004 (PG-13)** Director Stacy Peralta does for surfing what she did for skateboarding in "Dogtown and Z-Boys" by capturing the consummate skill and infectious enthusiasm of those who dominate the sport. Includes an animated mini-history that sardonically traces surfing from its Polynesian roots through the 20th century. **105m/C; DVD.** Jeff Clark; Darrick Doerner; Mickey Munoz; Brian L. Keaulana; Dick Brewer; Buzzy Kerbox; Ricky Grigg; Pat Curren; Laird Hamilton; Lyon Hamilton; Dave Kalama; Randy Rarick; Buffalo Keaulana; Evan Slater; Kelly Slater; ***Cameo(s):*** Sam George; Gabrielle Reece; Dr. Mark Renneker; Mike Stange; *D:* Stacy Peralta; *W:* Sam George; Stacy Peralta; *C:* Peter Pilafian; *M:* Alan Barker.

Riding High 🦴🦴 ½ **1950** Capra remade his 1934 film "Broadway Bill" as this light-hearted musical. Horse trainer Crosby falls for the wealthy Gray who demands he choose between her and his horse. Bing chooses the horse who proves his loyalty by winning the big race and making Crosby a rich man. **112m/B; DVD.** Bing Crosby; Coleen Gray; Charles Bickford; William Demarest; Frances Gifford; Raymond Walburn; James Gleason; Ward Bond; Percy Kilbride; Harry Davenport; Margaret Hamilton; Douglass Dumbrille; *D:* Frank Capra; *W:* Robert Riskin; Jack Rose; Melville Shavelson; *C:* George Barnes.

Riding in Cars with Boys 🦴🦴 **2001 (PG-13)** Based on the memoir of Beverly Donofrio, the plot follows Beverly (Barrymore) from 1965, when she becomes pregnant at age 15, to 1986, when her son has grown up and she has completed her book. The pic is more concerned with the way parents treat their children, and, unfortunately, Beverly comes off as a whiner who blames her loser husband Ray (Zahn) for getting her pregnant, her own parents (Woods, Bracco) for not talking to her, and even her son Jason (Garcia) for merely being around. Barrymore still gives a good performance and Zahn adds texture to the woeful Ray. **132m/C; VHS, DVD.** Drew Barrymore; Steve Zahn; Brittany Murphy; Adam Garcia; Lorraine Bracco; James Woods; Sara Gilbert; Desmond Harrington; David Moscow; Maggie Gyllenhaal; Peter Facinelli; Marisa Ryan; Mika Boorem; Skye McCole Bartusiak; Logan Lerman; *D:* Penny Marshall; *W:* Morgan Ward; *C:* Miroslav Ondricek; *M:* Hans Zimmer.

Riding the Bullet 🦴 ½ **2004 (R)** A death-obsessed young man (Jackson) keeps running from and into the Grim Reaper and his agents. Lame Garris/King collaboration relying on obvious shocks instead of suspense for its thrills. Tired horror movie cliches abound, so it never gets under your skin the way it should. **98m/C; DVD.** Jonathan Jackson; David Arquette; Cliff Robertson; Barbara Hershey; Erika Christensen; *D:* Mick Garris; *W:* Mick Garris; *C:* Robert New; *M:* Nicholas Pike.

Riff Raff 🦴🦴 *Riffraff* **1935** Melodramatic story about the relationship of two waterfront workers in the tuna fishing business. Confusing script saddled with too many characters, but there is some good sharp dialogue between the leads. Also features the scenic California waterfront. **80m/B; VHS, DVD.** Jean Harlow; Spencer Tracy; Joseph Calleia; Una Merkel; Mickey Rooney; Victor Kilian; J. Farrell MacDonald; Roger Imhof; *D:* J. Walter Ruben.

Riff Raff 🦴🦴🦴 **1992** Unsparing black comedy about the British working class by director Loach. Ex-con Stevie comes to London from Scotland to look for work and escape his thieving past. He finds a nonunion job on a construction site, takes up squatter's rights in an abandoned apartment, and finds a girlfriend in equally struggling singer Susie, who turns out to be a junkie. Loach's characters deal with their unenviable lot in life through rough humor and honest sentiment. Regional accents are so thick that the film is subtitled. **96m/C; VHS, DVD.** *GB* Robert Carlyle; Emer McCourt; Jimmy Coleman; George Moss; Ricky Tomlinson; David Finch; Bill Jesse; *D:* Ken Loach; *W:* Bill Jesse; *M:* Stewart Copeland.

Rififi 🦴🦴🦴 ½ *Du Rififi Chez les Hommes* **1954** Perhaps the greatest of all "heist" movies. Four jewel thieves pull off a daring caper, only to fall prey to mutual distrust. The long scene of the actual theft, completely in silence, will have your heart in your throat. In French with English subtitles. **115m/B; VHS, DVD, Blu-Ray.** *FR* Jean Servais; Carl Mohner; Robert Manuel; Jules Dassin; *D:* Jules Dassin; *W:* Jules Dassin; *C:* Philippe Agostini; *M:* Georges Auric. Cannes '55: Director (Dassin).

The Rig 🦴 ½ **2010 (R)** A skeleton crew on an offshore oil rig is riding out a hurricane when crew members start to go missing. Seems the rig has disturbed some alien creature on the ocean floor and the monster is now aboard and on a killing spree. **94m/C; DVD, Blu-Ray.** William Forsythe; Art LaFleur; Serah D'Laine; Marcus T. Paulk; Stacey Hinnen; Carmen Perez; Scott Martin; Dan Benson; *D:*

Peter Atencio; **W:** Marilee Benson; Lori Chavez; **C:** Douglas E. Davis; **M:** Bruce Fowler. **VIDEO**

The Right Approach 1961 Cliched showbiz drama with Brit singer Vaughan playing a completely unlikeable character. Wannabe actor Leo Mark (Vaughan) comes to California to sponge off his brother and his pals who are sharing a pad. The amoral hustler fools around with equally hard-boiled Ursula (Prowse), who's looking to marry money, and then tries to take advantage of journalist Anne (Hyer), who's too smart for him. Adapted from the Garson Kanin play, "The Live Wire." **91m/B; DVD.** Frankie Vaughan; Juliet Prowse; Martha Hyer; Gary Crosby; Jane Withers; David McLean; **D:** David Butler; **W:** Fay Kanin; Michael Kanin; **C:** Sam Leavitt; **M:** Dominic Frontiere.

Right at Your Door 2006 (R) Brad (Cochrane) is forced to seal up his house and lock his wife Lexi (McCormack) outside after she is exposed to deadly toxins caused by dirty bombs hitting Los Angeles. Basically a disaster flick with only two major characters, and that gets dull real fast (especially since Brad is obnoxious). **96m/C; DVD.** Rory Cochrane; Mary McCormack; Tony Perez; **D:** Chris Gorak; **W:** Chris Gorak; **C:** Tom Richmond; **M:** tomandandy.

Right Cross 1/2 1950 Prejudice is part of the plot as Mexican boxer Johnny Monterez (Montalban) is sure he's not getting his due despite being a champ. A hand injury threatens his career, so Johnny panics and dumps his longime manager Sean O'Malley (Barrymore), despite his romance with Sean's daughter Pat (Allyson), and signs with a promoter who promises him big bucks for a last bout. Powel's the cynical sports reporter buddy. **90m/B; DVD.** Ricardo Montalban; Dick Powell; June Allyson; Lionel Barrymore; Teresa Celli; Barry Kelley; **D:** John Sturges; **W:** Charles Schnee; **C:** Norbert Brodine; **M:** David Raksin.

The Right Hand Man 1/2 1987 (R) A brother and sister must deal with their crusty patriarch's demise in the Victorian-era Australian outback. Disappointing and overwrought. **101m/C; VHS, DVD.** *AU* Rupert Everett; Hugo Weaving; Arthur Dignam; **D:** Di Drew.

The Right Kind Of Wrong 1/2 2013 (R) Leo (Kwanten) is a sweet, ridiculously stubborn romantic idealist and dreamer. So much so that his somewhat nasty ex-wife Julie (Hager) has made a successful career of blogging about his faults. So it's no surprise that when he sees Collette (Canning), he immediately believes she's his soul mate. Of course, it happens to be her wedding day, but that doesn't stop Leo from pursuing her. It helps that Colette's new hubby (McPartlin) turns out to be a complete jerk so Leo doesn't look like a deranged stalker. Based on Tim Sandlin's novel "Sex and Sunsets." **97m/C; DVD, Blu-Ray.** *CA* Ryan Kwanten; Sara Canning; Ryan McPartlin; Kristen Hager; Will Sasso; Catherine O'Hara; **D:** Jeremiah S. Chechik; **W:** Megan Martin; **C:** Luc Montpellier; **M:** Rachel Portman. **VIDEO**

The Right of the People 1986 Heavy-handed ABC TV movie. District Attorney Christopher Wells' (Ontkean) wife and daughter are among the 10 victims of an attempted armed robbery in a restaurant. Distraught, Wells pushes through legislation allowing everyone in town to carry a gun. Only the violence increases because every argument seems to escalate into an armed confrontation. **95m/C; DVD.** Michael Ontkean; Jane Kaczmarek; Billy Dee Williams; John Randolph; M. Emmet Walsh; **D:** Jeffrey Bloom; **C:** Gil Hubbs; **M:** Billy Goldenberg. **TV**

The Right of Way 1931 Creaky, melodramatic early talkie. Charles Steele (Nagel) is a successful Quebec lawyer and a louse. After a severe beating, he's rescued by grateful ex-client Joe (Kohler), who takes Steele to his remote cabin where Charles is nursed back to health by lovely Rosalie (Young). Charles has amnesia and Joe keeps his past a secret since the louse has turned over a new leaf, but the past won't stay in the past. **68m/B; DVD.** Conrad Nagel; Loretta Young; Fred Kohler, Sr.; Olive Tell; William Janney; Snitz Edwards; **D:** Frank Lloyd; **W:** Francis Edwards Faragoh; **C:** John Seitz.

The Right Stuff 1983 (PG) A rambunctious adaptation of Tom Wolfe's nonfiction book about the beginnings of the U.S. space program, from Chuck Yeager's breaking of the sound barrier to the last of the Mercury missions. Featuring an all-star cast and an ambitious script. Rowdy, imaginative, and thrilling, though broadly painted and oddly uninvolving. Former astronaut John Glenn was running for president when this was out. **193m/C; VHS, DVD, Blu-Ray.** Ed Harris; Dennis Quaid; Sam Shepard; Scott Glenn; Fred Ward; Charles Frank; William Russ; Kathy Baker; Barbara Hershey; Levon Helm; David Clennon; Kim Stanley; Mary Jo Deschanel; Veronica Cartwright; Pamela Reed; Jeff Goldblum; Harry Shearer; Donald Moffat; Scott Paulin; Lance Henriksen; Scott Wilson; John P. Ryan; Royal Dano; **D:** Philip Kaufman; **W:** Philip Kaufman; **C:** Caleb Deschanel; **M:** Bill Conti. Oscars '83: Film Editing, Orig. Score, Sound; Natl. Film Reg. '13.

The Right Temptation 1/2 2000 (R) Female PI Derian (De Mornay) is hired by a jealous wife (Delaney) to get the dirt on her adulterous rich husband (Sutherland). Too bad the PI then falls for her target, who may also be in bed with the mob. **93m/C; VHS, DVD.** Kiefer Sutherland; Rebecca De Mornay; Dana Delany; Adam Baldwin; **D:** Lyndon Chubbuck.

The Right to Live 1935 Controversial drama based on W. Somerset Maugham's 1928 play "The Sacred Flame." Wealthy Maurice Trent (Clive) becomes an invalid shortly after his marriage to Stella (Hutchinson). He invites his brother Colin (Brent) to visit and escort Stella around town while he recovers. His sudden death leads to trouble for Stella when Maurice's nurse (Wood) makes accusations. **70m/B; DVD.** Josephine Hutchinson; George Brent; Colin Clive; Peggy Wood; Sir C. Aubrey Smith; Leo G. Carroll; Henrietta Crosman; **D:** William Keighley; **W:** Ralph Block; **C:** Sidney Hickox.

Righteous Kill 2008 (R) Turk (De Niro) and Rooster (Pacino), long-time friends and partners, have been assigned to investigate the recent murders of violent criminals who've gotten off on legal technicalities. Neither is too motivated to solve the case, almost grateful for the vigilante's sense of justice. Keeping them in check are detectives Perez (Leguizamo) and Riley (Wahlberg), who begin to suspect one of the two. Unfortunately, it's a routine police drama. De Niro and Pacino's third film together, but only the second time they've actually shared screen time. **100m/C; DVD, Blu-Ray, On Demand.** Robert De Niro; Al Pacino; Brian Dennehy; Carla Gugino; Donnie Wahlberg; John Leguizamo; 50 Cent; Melissa Leo; Trilby Glover; Alan Rosenberg; Barry Primus; Alan Blumenfeld; Oleg Taktarov; Shirly Brener; Ajay Naidu; Saidah Arrika Ekulona; **D:** Jon Avnet; **W:** Russell Gewirtz; **C:** Denis Lenoir; **M:** Ed Shearmur.

Rikisha-Man 1/2 *Rickshaw Man; Muhomatsu no Issho* 1958 A tragic melodrama about a rickshaw puller who helps raise a young boy after his father has died, and loves the boy's mother from afar. Inagaki's remake of his original 1943 version. In Japanese with English subtitles. **105m/B; VHS, DVD.** *JP* Toshiro Mifune; **D:** Hiroshi Inagaki.

Rikky and Pete 1/2 1988 (R) An engaging Australian comedy about a bizarre, precociously eccentric brother and sister. He's a Rube Goldberg-style mentor; she's a scientist-cum-country singer. They move together to the outback and meet a score of weird characters. A worthy follow-up to director Tass's "Malcolm." **103m/C; VHS, DVD.** *AU* Nina Landis; Stephen Kearney; Tetchie Agbayani; Bruce Spence; Bruno Lawrence; Bill Hunter; Dorothy Allison; Don Reid; Lewis FitzGerald; **D:** Nadia Tass; **W:** David Parker; **M:** Phil Judd.

Rikyu 1990 Set in 16th century Japan, Rikyu is a Buddhist priest who elevated the tea ceremony to an art form. To him it is a spiritual experience, to his master, Lord Hideyoshi Toilyotomi, the ruler of Japan, mastery of the ceremony is a matter of prestige. Conflict arises between Rikyu's ideal of profound simplicity, symbolized by the ceremony, and Toilyotomi's planned conquest of China, which Rikyu opposes. In Japanese with English subtitles. **116m/C; VHS, DVD.** *JP* Rentaro Mikuni; Tsutomu Yamazaki; **D:** Hiroshi Teshigahara; **W:** Hiroshi Teshigahara; Genpei Akasegawa; **C:** Fujio Morita; **M:** Toru Takemitsu.

Rimfire 1/2 1949 An undercover agent tracks down some stolen U.S. Army gold, aided by the ghost of a wrongly hanged gambler. Fun B western. **65m/B; VHS, DVD.** Mary Beth Hughes; Henry Hull; Fuzzy Knight; James Millican; Victor Kilian; Margia Dean; Jason Robards, Sr.; Reed Hadley; Chris-Pin (Ethier Crispin Martini) Martin; John Cason; George Cleveland; I. Stanford Jolley; Stanley Price; **D:** B. Reeves Eason; **W:** Ron Ormond; Arthur St. Claire; Frank Wisbar; **C:** Ernest Miller; **M:** Walter Greene.

The Ring 1/2 1927 Very early Hitchcock about boxer who marries carnival girl, loses carnival girl, and wins carnival girl back again. Standard romantic punch and roses yarn interesting as measure of young director's developing authority. **82m/B; Silent; VHS, DVD, Blu-Ray.** *GB* Carl Brisson; Lillian Hall-Davis; Ian Hunter; Gordon Harker; **D:** Alfred Hitchcock; **W:** Alfred Hitchcock; **C:** Jack Cox.

The Ring 1/2 1952 Poignant early fight movie that gives a lesson in prejudice against Chicanos. The main character feels that the only way to get respect from the world is to fight for it. Well-directed and perceptive. **79m/B; DVD.** Gerald Mohr; Rita Moreno; Lalo Rios; Robert Arthur; Robert Osterloh; Jack Elam; **D:** Kurt Neumann; **W:** Irving Shulman; **C:** Russell Harlan; **M:** Herschel Burke Gilbert.

The Ring 1/2 2002 (R) American adaptation of the film that took Japan by storm in 1998. Upon hearing of an allegedly lethal videotape in urban legend fashion, teen Katie (Tamblyn) and her friends get a copy and watch it. A week later all four teens are dead. Katie's reporter aunt Rachel (Watts) investigates, but has only one week to do so after also viewing the tape. She is also racing to save her son (Dorfman) and ex-husband (Henderson), who she has stupidly exposed to the tape as well. While the look is suitably atmospheric and creepy, the plot stretches plausibility to the breaking point. **115m/C; VHS, DVD, Blu-Ray.** Naomi Watts; Martin Henderson; David Dorfman; Brian Cox; Jane Alexander; Lindsay Frost; Amber Tamblyn; Rachael Bella; Daveigh Chase; Pauley Perrette; Sara Rue; Shannon Cochran; **D:** Gore Verbinski; **W:** Ehren Kruger; **C:** Bojan Bazelli; **M:** Hans Zimmer.

The Ring 2 1/2 2005 (PG-13) Creepy demon-child Samara (Chase) continues to pursue reporter Rachel (Watts) and her son (Dorfman). This time around the killer videotape is dispensed with early on in favor of a more traditional possession theme. Samara wants all the comforts of Mommy and home, and seems to find them in the son's body. Excruciatingly slow, confused, and almost totally unfrightening wreck, this time helmed by the director of the original Japanese film, who should have known better. **111m/C; DVD.** Naomi Watts; Simon Baker; David Dorfman; Elizabeth Perkins; Gary Cole; Sissy Spacek; Ryan Merriman; Emily Van Camp; Daveigh Chase; Kelly Overton; Kelly Stables; James Lesure; **D:** Hideo Nakata; **W:** Ehren Kruger; Hideo Nakata; **C:** Gabriel Beristain; **M:** Henning Lohner; Martin Tillman.

Ring-a-Ding Rhythm 1/2 *It's Trad, Dad* 1962 There's a generation gap in a small English town when the Mayor forces a coffeeshop used as a teen hangout to shut off its jukebox. Helen and Craig fight back by putting together a music fest that will showcase Dixieland jazz and rock 'n' roll. Richard Lester's first feature is best seen for the musical talent, including Del Shannon, Chubby Checkers, Gene Vincent, and others. **78m/C; DVD.** *UK* Helen Shapiro; Craig Douglas; Felix Felton; Timothy Bateson; Arthur Mullard; **D:** Richard Lester; **W:** Milton Subotsky; **C:** Gilbert Taylor; **M:** Ken Thorne.

Ring of Bright Water 1969 (G) Well done story of a pet otter from Gavin Maxwell's autobiography. The film stars the couple that made the delightful "Born Free." Beautiful Scottish Highlands photography adds to this captivating and endearing tale of a civil servant who purchases an otter from a pet store and moves to the country. **107m/C; VHS, DVD, Blu-Ray.** *GB* Bill Travers; Virginia McKenna; Peter Jeffrey; Archie Duncan; **D:** Jack Couffer; **W:** Bill Travers; Jack Couffer; **C:** Wolfgang Suschitzky; **M:** Frank Cordell.

Ring of Darkness WOOF! 2004 (R) Boy band zombies. Pop singer Shawn (Martines) reluctantly agrees to girlfriend Stacy's (Starr) demands that he try out to be the replacement lead singer of boy band Take Ten. Shawn and two other finalists are whisked away to a secluded island and discover that the band members are zombies who use black magic to stay young and on the charts. An unfortunate Barbeau plays their evil manager. Grating music and no frights—except for that plotline. **85m/C; DVD.** Jeremy Jackson; Adrienne Barbeau; Mink Stole; Stephen Martines; Ryan Starr; Eric Dearborn; Greg Cipes; **D:** David DeCoteau; **W:** Mathew Jason Walsh; Ryan Carrasi; Michael Gingold; **C:** Mateo Londono. **CABLE**

Ring of Death 1/2 *The Detective* 1969 (R) A tough cop investigating a routine case becomes a hunted man after someone kills the man he is following. **103m/C; VHS, DVD.** *IT* Franco Nero; Florinda Bolkan; Adolfo Celi; Delia Boccardo; Susanna Martinkova; **D:** Romolo Guerrieri; **W:** Massimo D'Avak; **C:** Roberto Gerardi; **M:** Fred Bongusto.

Ring of Death 1/2 2008 Disgraced ex-cop Burke Wyatt (Messner) is trying to rebuild his life and get back together with estranged wife Mary (Ross). He agrees to go undercover for the feds, getting himself tossed in prison to bust up a crime ring. Then Wyatt finds himself caught up in a deadly underground fight league. **86m/C; DVD.** Johnny Messner; Stacy Keach; Charlotte Ross; **D:** Bradford May; **W:** Matthew Chernov; David Rosiak; **C:** Maximo Munzi. **CABLE**

Ring of Fire 1/2 1991 (R) Wilson is one of very few modern American kung-fu heroes of Asian descent, and he works messages against prejudice into this interracial Romeo-and-Juliet chopsocky tale. What foot through yonder window breaks? **100m/C; VHS, DVD.** Don "The Dragon" Wilson; Maria Ford; Vince Murdocco; Dale Jacoby; Michael Delano; Eric Lee; **D:** Richard W. Munchkin.

Ring of Fire 1/2 2013 Jewel is indeed a jewel as June Carter Cash in this Lifetime biopic of the country duo's romance that's based on the book by their son John Carter Cash. It's a version of 'stand-by-your-man' even as June recognizes her anger over her tumultous relationship with 'dope fiend' Johnny (well-played by Ross). The two actors are convincing as a couple and there's the music to enjoy as well. **90m/C; DVD.** Jewel Kilcher; Matt Ross; John Doe; Frances Conroy; **D:** Allison Anders; **W:** Richard Friedenberg; **C:** Joseph E. Gallagher; **M:** Anton Sanko. **CABLE**

Ring of Fire 2: Blood and Steel 1/2 1992 (R) Wilson returns as Dr. Johnny Wu in this martial-arts actioner which finds the good doctor the witness to a robbery. When one of the robbers is killed, the gang's leader kidnaps Johnny's fiance and holds her for ransom. He decides to bypass the police and use his own expertise to rescue her. **94m/C; VHS, DVD, On Demand.** Don "The Dragon" Wilson; Maria Ford; Sy Richardson; Michael Delano; Dale Jacoby; Vince Murdocco; Evan Lurie; Charlie Ganis; Ron Yuan; **D:** Richard W. Munchkin.

Ring of Fire 3: Lion Strike 1/2 1994 (R) Johnny Wu is supposed to be on vacation with his son and a beautiful forest ranger when they find themselves in the way of a violent group known as the Global Mafia. Seems Johnny has a computer disk that the gangsters want. **90m/C; VHS, DVD, On Demand.** Don "The Dragon" Wilson; Bobbie Phillips; Robert Costanzo; **D:** Rick Jacobson.

Ring of Terror 1962 College boy who wants to join a fraternity must survive the initiation rights, which include stealing a ring from a corpse. Unfortunately, this seemingly invincible guy has a deadly terror of the dead. Cheaply made flop alledgedly based on a composite of actual hazing incidents. **72m/B; VHS, DVD.** George Mather; Esther Furst; Austin Green; Joseph Conway; **D:** Clark Paylow.

Ring of the Musketeers 1/2 1993 (PG-13) Contemporary spoof of the Musketeers saga finds three descendants of the swashbuckling heroes carrying on the family tradition of protecting the weak and innocent. They even get stuck with a Musketeer-wanna-be when they come to the resuce of a young boy who is kidnapped to prevent his dad from testifying against mobsters. **86m/C; VHS, Streaming.** David Hasselhoff; Alison Doody; Thomas Gottschalk; Richard "Cheech" Marin; Corbin Bernsen; John Rhys-Davies; *D:* John Paragon; *W:* Joel Surnow.

Ring the Bell 🦴🦴 **2013 (PG)** A sports-tinged drama about the power of the unexpected. Sports agent Rob Decker (Scharoun) is used to a fast life in a big city and seems to have it all. Sent to a small town to sign a high school baseball superstar in the making, Rob becomes stranded in the community for a time to complete the transaction. There, Rob is exposed to a more simple life and more people of faith living their lives by their beliefs. Rob feels torn between the two ways of life and considers which would really make him happier and truly fulfilled. **97m/C; DVD, Streaming, Download.** Ryan Scharoun; Ashley Nicole Anderson; Casey Bond; Madison Miller; Robert Caso; *D:* Thomas Weber; *W:* Thomas Weber; Mark Miller; *C:* Mr. Samson Chan; *M:* Evan Frankfort. **VIDEO**

The Ring Virus 🦴🦴 **1999** South Korea's remake of "Ringu" is ironically closer to the novel than the Japanese film. On the same day, four people die under similar circumstances. Reporter Sun-Joo discovers they all knew each other. Believing this can't be a coincidence, she investigates., and ends up watching a supposedly cursed videotape that tells her she has one week to live. She teams with a neurologist who has also seen the tape, eventually being led to a remote island and the demonic girl Eun-Suh. Not quite as good as the Japanese version, it still has its moments. Korean with subtitles. **95m/C; DVD.** *NK* Du-na Bae; Eun-Kyung Shin; Jin-yeong Jong; Seung-Hyeon Lee; Chang-wan Kim; Ggoch-ji Kim; Yeon-Su Yu; *D:* Dong-bin Kim; *W:* Koji Suzuki; Dong-bin Kim; *C:* Mauricio Dortona; Chul-hyun Hwang; *M:* Il Won.

The Ringer 🦴 ½ **2005 (PG-13)** Throughout their film careers, the Farrelly Brothers have consistently showcased their un-ironic affection for both toilet humor and the mentally handicapped. However, their attempt (as the producers) to bring the two together fails miserably. Steve (Knoxville) is a nice guy who, thanks to money woes, gets talked into posing as a retarded athlete, so his uncle Gary (Cox) can fix the Special Olympics. The script is completely toothless, vacillating between mocking the handicapped and telling us how awesome they are. Hypocrisy is rarely funny, and this dud is no exception. **94m/C; DVD, Blu-Ray.** Johnny Knoxville; Brian Cox; Katherine Heigl; Geoffrey Arend; Leonard Earl Howze; Jed Rees; John Taylor; Edward Barbanell; Bill Chott; Leonard Flowers; *D:* Barry W. Blaustein; *W:* Ricky Blitt; *C:* Mark Irwin; *M:* Mark Mothersbaugh.

Ringmaster WOOF! *Jerry Springer's Ringmaster* **1998 (R)** Okay, this is it. It's the apocalypse. Jerry Springer's made a movie. And the first question would be: Why? To cash in, of course. The second question is: Why should you bother? The answer is a resounding "You shouldn't." In case you couldn't guess the plot, Jerry welcomes a stepdad (Dudikoff) who's doing it with his 15-year-old stepdaughter (Pressly), and a woman (Robinson) who caught her man (White) with her best friend. Sexual escapades and the thrill of being on "the TEE-vee" ensue. **89m/C; VHS, DVD.** Jerry Springer; John Capodice; Jaime Pressly; Molly Hagan; Michael Dudikoff; Michael Jai White; William McNamara; Dawn Maxey; Wendy Raquel Robinson; Tangie Ambrose; Nicki Micheaux; Ashley Holbrook; *D:* Neil Abramson; *W:* Jon Bernstein; *C:* Russell Lyster; *M:* Kennard Ramsey. Golden Raspberries '98: Worst New Star (Springer).

Ringo, the Lone Rider 🦴🦴 *Two Brothers, One Death; Dos hombres van a morir; Ringo, il cavaliere solitario* **1968** Spaghetti western. Eight soldiers feel the Civil War has ended too early and begin robbing banks to continue harassing their enemies (or as an excuse to get rich). Unfortunately for them infamous outlaw Ringo and a friend have just escaped from jail and are looking for something to do and taking on the bank robbers seems like fun. **87m/C; DVD.** *IT SP* Pietro Martellanza; Piero Lulli; Armando Calvo; Jose Jaspe; *D:* Rafael Romero Marchent; *W:* Mario Caiano; *C:* Emanuele Di Cola; *M:* Manuel Parada.

Ringo's Big Night 🦴 ½ *La grande notte di Ringo* **1966** Jack (aka Ringo) is jailed for a stagecoach robbery he didn't commit, so he opts to break out of jail, steal the money from the bad guys, and subsequently kill them all off. Currently only available as part of the 'Westerns Unchained' collection. **93m/C; Blu-Ray.** *IT SP* William Berger; Adriana Ambesi; Eduardo Fajardo; Walter Maestosi; George Rigaud; *D:* Mario Maffei; *W:* Mario Maffei; David Moreno; Eduardo Brochero; *C:* Carlo Bellero; Emilio Foriscot; *M:* Carlo Rustichelli. **VIDEO**

Ringo's Mark of Vengeance 🦴🦴 *Los cuatro salvajes; Ringo: Face of Revenge* **1967** Two drifters save the life of an ex-con with half a treasure map tattoed on his back and set off to find the owner of the other half. Currently only available as part of the 'Westerns Unchained' collection. **102m/C; Blu-Ray.** *IT SP* Anthony Steffen; Frank Wolff; Eduardo Fajardo; Armando Calvo; Alejandro Nilo; *D:* Mario Caiano; *W:* Mario Caiano; Eduardo Brochero; *C:* Julio Ortas; *M:* Francesco De Masi. **VIDEO**

Rings WOOF! **2017 (PG-13)** Twelve years after the last English-language Ring film, Hollywood returns to this horror franchise for no apparent reason. The basic premise of the films based on the Japanese Ringu series remains intact—a video tape is viewed, the viewer dies seven days later—but any sense of character, atmosphere, or even logic is cast off for a film that feels more like a cheap attempt to cash-in on a brand of nostalgia than anything remotely creative. There are bad, nearly straight-to-video horror movies all the time but this could be the new low bar. **102m/C; DVD, Blu-Ray.** Matilda Anna Ingrid Lutz; Alex Roe; Johnny Galecki; Vincent D'Onofrio; Aimee Teegarden; *D:* F. Javier Gutierrez; *W:* David Loucka; Jacob Aaron Estes; Akiva Goldsman; *C:* Sharone Meir; *M:* Matthew Margeson.

Rings on Her Fingers 🦴🦴 ½ **1942** Con artists Maybelle (Byington) and Warren (Cregar) head to Palm Springs and enlist pretty shopgirl Susan (Tierney) in their schemes. They think accountant John Wheeler (Fonda) is rich since he wants to buy a boat. Susan and John fall in love, but Susan's would-be partners aren't ready to give up on her landing a better prospect, which results in a lot of confusion (and marriage proposals). **85m/B; DVD.** Henry Fonda; Gene Tierney; Laird Cregar; Spring Byington; Henry Stephenson; Shepperd Strudwick; *D:* Rouben Mamoulian; *W:* Ken Englund; *C:* George Barnes; *M:* Cyril Mockridge.

Ringside Maisie 🦴🦴 ½ **1941** As usual, Brooklyn showgirl Maisie (Sothern) is broke and stranded--this time in upstate New York near a boxing training camp. She becomes the confidante of up-and-coming fighter Terry Dolan (Sterling), who tells Maisie he wants to get out of the game. Instead, Terry's sleazy manager Skeets (Murphy) is pushing him into the big time with unexpected results. Fifth in the MGM series. **96m/B; DVD.** Ann Sothern; Robert Sterling; George Murphy; Natalie Thompson; Margaret Moffatt; Maxie "Slapsie" Rosenbloom; Rags Ragland; Jack LaRue; *D:* Edwin L. Marin; *W:* Mary C. McCall; *C:* Charles Lawton, Jr.; *M:* David Snell.

Ringu 🦴🦴🦴 **1998** Based on Koji Suzuki's novel, although the film relies far less on its pseudo-science and more heavily on the supernatural, making it more effective. Western audiences unfamiliar with Japanese culture may miss several of the mythology references, though. One week after renting a cabin and watching a strange tape, a group of students die. The cousin of one, Reiko Asakawa, is a reporter, and she asks her estranged husband for help investigating the deaths due to his psychic abilities. Together they search for the meaning behind the mysterious tape and the deadly spirit known as Sadako. Japanese with subtitles. **96m/C; DVD, Blu-Ray.** *JP* Hiroyuki (Henry) Sanada; Yutaka Matsushige; Hiroyuki Watanabe; Masako; Katsumi Muramatsu; Rikiya Otaka; Nanako Matsushima; Miki Nakatani; Kiriko Shimizu; Hitomi Sato; Yoichi Numata; Yuko Takeuchi; *D:* Hideo Nakata; *W:* Koji Suzuki; Hiroshi Takahashi; *C:* Junichiro Hayashi; *M:* Kenji Kawai.

Ringu 0 🦴🦴 ½ *Ringu 0: Basudei* **2001** In this prequel to "Ringu," a young Sadako has gone off to college. Despite being shy and withdrawn, she joins the drama club, but the members hate her, especially when a lead actress dies and the director nominates Sadako to replace her. They plot to get rid of her some way, except for Hiroshi who has fallen in love with her. To make matters worse, a reporter who believes Sadako is a murderer begins nosing around. Eventually the cast members assault Sadako before traveling to her home for the apocalyptic finale. Creepy and effective, the only sequel that is on par with the original. Japanese with subtitles. **99m/C; DVD, Blu-Ray.** *JP* Seichi Tanabe; Kumiko Aso; Yoshiko Tanaka; Takeshi Wakamatsu; Kazue Tsunogae; Ryuji Mizukami; Kaoru Okunuki; Daisuke Ban; Tsukasa Kimura; Junko Takahata; Masako; Yasuji Kimura; Masami Hashimoto; *D:* Norio Tsuruta; *W:* Koji Suzuki; Hiroshi Takahashi; *C:* Takahide Shinbanushi; *M:* Shinichiro Ogata.

Ringu 2 🦴🦴 **1999** Taking off right after the end of the first film, Reiko and her son have gone into hiding after surviving their encounter with Sadako while the authorities try to explain the deaths. Unfortunately, it seems Sadako's spirit has not been laid to rest and Reiko's son appears to be developing psychic powers like his father. Reiko fears the ghost now has some connection to her son. Like the first film, the sequel relies on growing suspense as opposed to gore or shocks, but it doesn't do it nearly as well. Japanese with subtitles. **92m/C; DVD, Blu-Ray.** *JP* Miki Nakatani; Hitomi Sato; Kyoko Fukada; Fumiyo Kohinata; Kenjiro Ishimaru; Yurei Yanagi; Rikiya Otaka; Yoichi Numata; Nanako Matsushima; Hiroyuki (Henry) Sanada; Masako; Rie Inou; Katsumi Muramatsu; *D:* Hideo Nakata; *W:* Hideo Nakata; Koji Suzuki; Hiroshi Takahashi; *C:* Hideo Yamamoto; *M:* Kenji Kawai.

Rio 🦴🦴 ½ **2011 (G)** In this lively, upbeat animated 3D comedy, lonely yet happily domesticated Macaw Blu (Eisenberg) never learned to fly. When owner/best friend Linda (Mann) reluctantly takes him to Brazil to mate in order to save the species, he meets independent and adventurous Jewel (Hathaway). But kidnappers intercede and the pair is on the run—literally, since they are bound together and Blu can't fly. Lots of adventures abound in the visually lovely Rio de Janeiro, paired with lots of foot-tapping tunes, making it an enjoyable romp for all ages. **96m/C; DVD, Blu-Ray, On Demand.** *V:* Jesse Eisenberg; Anne Hathaway; Leslie Mann; George Lopez; Jake T. Austin; Will I Am; Jamie Foxx; *D:* Carlos Saldanha; *W:* Carlos Saldanha; Don Rhymer; Todd R. Jones; *C:* Renato Falcao; *M:* John Powell.

Rio 2 🦴 ½ **2014 (G)** Why bother? Sure, the first Rio was a serviceable animated adventure but it's not a film that demanded a sequel to flesh out the story. Knowing that, the producers of Rio 2 weigh their adventure down with lots of noise and color. Bright birds! Drum playing! Bruno Mars! It's a crowded movie as Blu (Eisenberg) and Jewel (Hathaway) deal with family drama when more of their species are discovered deep in the rainforest. The cast is bigger, the musical numbers louder, and the jokes flatter in a movie that bores even the youngest viewers. **101m/C; DVD, Blu-Ray.** *V:* Jesse Eisenberg; Anne Hathaway; Andy Garcia; Jemaine Clement; Rodrigo Santoro; Jamie Foxx; Leslie Mann; Kristin Chenoweth; Bruno Mars; George Lopez; *D:* Carlos Saldanha; *W:* Jenny Bicks; Yoni Brenner; Carlos Kotkin; *C:* Renato Falcao; *M:* John Powell.

Rio Bravo 🦴🦴🦴 ½ **1959** John T. Chance (Wayne) is the sheriff of a Texas border town who takes murderer Joe (Akins) into custody. Since Joe is the brother of powerful local cattle baron Nathan Burdette (Russell), the sheriff faces a blockade of gunmen hired to keep his prisoner from being brought to justice. Chance has to make do with the help of a cripple (Brennan), a drunk (Martin), and a hot-headed kid (Nelson). Long, but continually entertaining film that didn't impress critics at the time but its reputation has improved over the years. Hawks and Wayne basically remade this one with "El Dorado." **140m/C; VHS, DVD, Blu-Ray, HD-DVD.** John Wayne; Dean Martin; Angie Dickinson; Ricky Nelson; Walter Brennan; Ward Bond; Claude Akins; Bob Steele; John Russell; Harry Carey, Jr.; Pedro Gonzalez-Gonzalez; *D:* Howard Hawks; *W:* Leigh Brackett; Jules Furthman; *C:* Russell Harlan; *M:* Dimitri Tiomkin. Natl. Film Reg. '14.

Rio Conchos 🦴🦴🦴 **1964** Nifty nonstop action in this western set in Texas after the Civil War. Three Army buddies search for 2,000 stolen rifles. Boone is understated, O'Brien is good, and Brown memorable in his debut. **107m/C; VHS, DVD, Blu-Ray.** Richard Boone; Stuart Whitman; Edmond O'Brien; Anthony (Tony) Franciosa; Jim Brown; *D:* Gordon Douglas; *M:* Jerry Goldsmith.

Rio Diablo 🦴🦴 ½ **1993** Country Western singers abound in—what else—a made-for-TV Western movie. A bounty hunter (Rogers) and newlywed groom (Tritt) set off after a gang of thieving kidnappers who have snatched the young bride (Harring). Judd shows up as the owner of a desert hostelry, who happens to cross paths with the hunters. Watch out—this could be more fun than a Partridge Family reunion. **120m/C; VHS, DVD.** Kenny Rogers; Travis Tritt; Naomi Judd; Stacy Keach; Brion James; Bruce Greenwood; Laura Elena Harring; *M:* Larry Brown.

Rio Grande 🦴🦴🦴 **1950** The last entry in Ford's cavalry trilogy following "Fort Apache" and "She Wore a Yellow Ribbon." A U.S. cavalry unit on the Mexican border conducts an unsuccessful campaign against marauding Indians. The commander of the lonely outpost, Lt. Col. Kirby Yorke (Wayne), plays no favorites when his only son, Jeff (Jarman Jr.), arrives as a new recruit and is soon followed by Yorke's estranged wife, Kathleen (O'Hara). Featuring an excellent Victor Young score and several songs by the Sons of the Pioneers. **105m/B; VHS, DVD, Blu-Ray.** John Wayne; Maureen O'Hara; Ben Johnson; Claude Jarman, Jr.; Harry Carey, Jr.; Victor McLaglen; Chill Wills; J. Carrol Naish; *D:* John Ford; *W:* James Kevin McGuinness; *C:* Bert Glennon; *M:* Victor Young.

Rio, I Love You 🦴 ½ *Rio, Eu Te Amo* **2014 (R)** In this anthology set in Rio de Janeiro, the 10 short films each feature an expression of love in a different neighborhood in the Brazilian city. Following on the heels of the acclaimed 2006 film "Paris, je t'aime" and its less-acclaimed 2009 follow-up, "New York, I Love You," comes the third film in the so-called "Cities of Love" franchise, films that assemble short films by notable directors. This one includes works by Fernando Meirelles ("City of God"), Paolo Sorrentino ("The Great Beauty"), and Guillermo Arriaga ("Babel"), among others, but it's the least inspired and least dramatically engaging of the three films by some stretch. **110m/C; DVD.** Basil Hoffman; Emily Mortimer; Rodrigo Santoro; Nadine Labaki; Harvey Keitel; *D:* Nadine Labaki; Vicente Amorim; Guillermo Arriaga; Stephan Elliott; Sang-soo Im; Fernando Meirelles; Jose Padilha; Carlos Saldanha; Paolo Sorrentino; John Turturro; Andrucha Waddington; Cesar Charlone; *W:* Nadine Labaki; Guillermo Arriaga; Stephan Elliott; Sang-soo Im; Paolo Sorrentino; John Turturro; Andrucha Waddington; Mauricio Zacharias; Antonio Prata; Chico Mattoso; Elena Soarez; Otavio Leonidio; Rodney El Haddad; Khaled Mouzannar; Fellipe Barbosa; *C:* Daria D'Antonio; Ricardo Della Rosa; Yves Sehnaoui; Adrian Teijido; *M:* Khaled Mouzannar; Pedro Bromfman.

Rio Lobo 🦴🦴 ½ **1970 (G)** Hawks's final film takes place after the Civil War, when Union Colonel Wayne goes to Rio Lobo to take revenge on two traitors. Disappointing. The Duke has to carry weak supporting performances on his brawny shoulders—and nearly does. **114m/C; VHS, DVD, Blu-Ray.** John Wayne; Jorge (George) Rivero; Jennifer O'Neill; Jack Elam; Chris Mitchum; David Huddleston; George Plimpton; *D:* Howard Hawks; *C:* William Clothier; *M:* Jerry Goldsmith.

Rio Rita 🦴🦴 ½ **1929** RKO's film version of producer Florenz Ziegfeld's 1928 Broadway musical with sequences filmed in two-strip Technicolor. Irish-Mexican ranch owner Rita (Daniels) is being wooed by disguised, singing Texas Ranger Jim (Boles) who thinks her brother (Alvarado) is a notorious bandit. There's also a subplot with comic duo Wheeler & Woolsey with Wheeler hiring shyster lawyer Woolsey to get him a quickie Mexican divorce. Loosely remade in 1942. **102m/C; DVD.** Bebe Daniels; John Boles; Bert Wheeler; Robert Woolsey; Don Alvarado; Dorothy Lee; Georges Renavent; Helen Kaiser; *D:*

Luther Reed; *W:* Luther Reed; *C:* Robert B. Kurrle.

Rio Rita ½ **1942** Abbott & Costello are working on a ranch and somehow become involved with Nazi spies. Provides a few original comic bits for the duo but is otherwise mediocre. An updated remake of the 1929 Wheeler & Woolsey comedy. **91m/B; VHS, DVD.** Bud Abbott; Lou Costello; Kathryn Grayson; John Carroll; Patricia Dane; Tom Conway; Peter Whitney; *D:* S. Sylvan Simon; *C:* George J. Folsey.

Rio Sex Comedy ½ **2010** This mostly improvised comedy is neither very sexy nor very funny as it follows various expats around the city. Married filmmaker Irene has an affair with her brother-in-law but her husband can't confront them. New American ambassador William finds a sleazy tour guide so he can explore the more dangerous side of Rio, but the authorities think he's been kidnapped. Fearing the cosmetic surgery craze, plastic surgeon Charlotte opens an office to counsel would-be patients. English, French, and Portuguese with subtitles. **126m/C; DVD.** *BR FR* Charlotte Rampling; Bill Pullman; Fisher Stevens; Irene Jacob; Jerome Kircher; *D:* Jonathan Nossiter; *W:* Jonathan Nossiter; *C:* Lubomir Bakchev.

Riot ½ **1969 (R)** Men in cages throw tantrums until warden returns from vacation. Filmed in Arizona State Prison with real convicts as extras. Strong performances by fullback Brown and durable Hackman. Based on story by ex-con Frank Elli. Too oft-played theme song sung by Bill Medley of the Righteous Brothers. **97m/C; VHS, DVD, Blu-Ray, Streaming.** Gene Hackman; Jim Brown; Mike Kellin; Ben Carruthers; Frank Eyman; *D:* Buzz Kulik; *W:* James Poe.

Riot **1996 (R)** Dumb actioner set on Christmas Eve, 1999, amidst some L.A. riots. British Special Air Service officer Shane Alcott (Daniels) must rescue his kidnapped ex-girlfriend Anna-Lisa (Rowland), who just happens to be the British ambassador's daughter. She's being held by ghetto gangster Leon (Sanders), whose gang turn out to be pawns for IRA leader O'Flaherty (Kilpatrick), who has a score to settle. Predictable fights, lots of explosions. **95m/C; VHS, DVD.** Gary Daniels; Ray "Sugar Ray" Leonard; Patrick Kilpatrick; Paige Rowland; Dex Elliot Sanders; Charles Napier; *D:* Joseph Merhi; *W:* Joseph John Barmettler, Jr.; William Applegate, Jr.; *C:* Ken Blakey; *M:* Jim Halfpenny.

Riot **2015** An action crime centered on one cop's quest for revenge. To get put into prison, police officer Jack Stone (Reese) deliberately orchestrates a bank robbery. Stone's only goal is to be put in the same prison with Russian criminal kingpin Balam (Liddell). Balam not only controls the police force but the whole city from his lavish private cell. Though Balam is surrounded by security and henchmen, Stone wants to get his revenge on Balam for murdering Stone's family in cold blood and will stop at nothing to see Balam dead. **87m/C; DVD, Blu-Ray, Streaming, Download.** Matthew Reese; Dolph Lundgren; Danielle Chuchran; Chuck Liddell; Michael Flynn; *D:* John Lyde; *W:* Spanky Dustin Ward; *C:* Airk Thaughbaer; *M:* James Schafer. **VIDEO**

The Riot Club ½ **2015 (R)** Milo (Irons) is a privileged first-year Oxford student who is invited to join The Riot Club by former schoolmate Hugo (Reid). Club members must come from certain elite schools, including Milo and Hugo's alma mater Winchester. When Milo and fellow new member Alistair (Clafin) are inducted, the club holds a raucous party at a country pub, where issues of class and conscience emerge as activities become more heinous. Adapted from a play, it's a familiar story of spoiled rich people behaving badly, but it's too muddled for anyone to care. **107m/C; DVD.** Thomas Arnold; Harry Lloyd; Amber Anderson; Max Irons; Sam Clarfin; *D:* Lone Scherfig; *W:* Laura Wade; *C:* Sebastian Blenkov; *M:* Kasper Winding.

Riot in Cell Block 11 **1954** A convict leads four thousand prisoners in an uprising to improve prison conditions. Based on producer/ex-con Walter Wanger's own experience. Powerful and still timely. Filmed at Folsom Prison. **80m/B; DVD, Blu-Ray.** Neville Brand; Leo Gordon; Emile Meyer; Frank Faylen; *D:* Donald Siegel; *W:* Richard Collins; *C:* Russell Harlan; *M:* Herschel Burke Gilbert.

Riot in Juvenile Prison ½ **1959** Title says it all. After two teenage inmates at a male juvenile detention center are shot, psychologist Dr. Paul Furman (Thor) is brought in, to the dismay of Warden Walton (Hoyt). Furman decides to make the center co-ed, but this triggers more trouble initially and the juvies start a riot. **72m/B; DVD.** Jerome Thor; Scott Marlowe; John Hoyt; Marcia Henderson; Richard Tyler; Dorothy Provine; Virginia Aldridge; *D:* Edward L. Chan; *W:* Orville H. Hampton; *C:* Maury Gertsman; *M:* Emil Newman.

Riot in the Streets *Riot* **1996 (R)** Four intertwined stories revolving around the 1992 Los Angeles riots, on the day the Rodney King verdict was announced. Concerned are an African-American family, a white police officer, a Latino family, and Asian-American shopowners. Documentary footage of the actual riots is also included. **95m/C; VHS, DVD.** John Ortiz; Mario Van Peebles; Melvin Van Peebles; Cicely Tyson; Luke Perry; Peter Dobson; Dante Basco; Mako; Kieu Chinh; Alexis Cruz; Douglas Spain; Yelba Osorio; *D:* C. David Johnson; Richard Dilello; Galen Yuen; Alex Munoz; *W:* C. David Johnson; Richard Dilello; Galen Yuen; Joe Vasquez; *C:* Paul Elliott. **CABLE**

Riot on 42nd Street **1987** The owner of a grindhouse theater returns from a stint in prison and plans on re-opening his nightclub, only to have his employees massacred on opening night by an old rival. Reverting to his old ways, he goes out for revenge. **89m/C; DVD.** John Hayden; Jeff Fahey; Michael Speero; Carl Fury; Kate Collins; Frances Raines; *D:* Tim Kincaid; *W:* Tim Kincaid; *C:* Arthur D. Marks.

Riot on Sunset Strip **1967** AIP teen-exploitation that takes its cue from the actual 1966 riots. Rebellious teens and hippies cause problems for business owners along the Strip and they complain to the cops. Lt. Walt Lorimer (Ray) brokers a truce between them until his estranged daughter Andy (Farmer) gets into trouble with the wrong hard-partying crowd that hang out in one of the local clubs. A bad acid trip leads to Andy being raped and Lorimer putting a beat-down on the perps. **86m/C; DVD.** Aldo Ray; Mimsy Farmer; Michael Evans; Laurie Mock; Schuyler Haydn; Tim Rooney; Anna Strasberg; Gene Kirkwood; Hortense Petra; *D:* Arthur Dreifuss; *W:* Orville H. Hampton; *C:* Paul Vogel; *M:* Fred Karger.

Rip It Off *Beyond the City Limits* **2002 (R)** Lexi (Hannigan) and Misha (Kinski) have a couple of loser thug boyfriends (Denisof, McCardie) who are planning a casino heist with a couple of dirty cops. When the gals get fed up by the way they're treated, they hook up with pal Helena (Esposito) and decide to pull off the heist first and leave the guys out in the cold. Told from the POV of Helena's own dirty cop, Toretti (Field). **91m/C; VHS, DVD.** Nastassja Kinski; Alyson Hannigan; Jennifer Esposito; Brian McCardie; Alexis Denisof; Todd Field; Steve Harris; Freddy Rodriguez; Sophie B. Hawkins; *D:* Gigi Gaston; *W:* John McMahon; *C:* David Bridges.

The Rip Off *The Squeeze* **1978 (R)** A colorful gang of hoodlums goes for the biggest heist of their lives—six million bucks in diamonds! **99m/C; VHS, DVD.** Lee Van Cleef; Karen Black; Robert Alda; Edward Albert; *D:* Anthony M. Dawson.

R.I.P.D. **2013 (PG-13)** A mega-budget train wreck, Schwentke's box office bomb comes across as a lazy attempt all around--all CGI, no actual writing. Reynolds plays Nick, a recently slain police officer who joins the R.I.P.D., a group of supernatural/undead cops who fight crime in much the same way the Men in Black fought aliens right under our nose. Nick is partnered with the irascible Roy (Bridges). The two stars are engaging but offer nothing fresh here, and they're buried under a film that bombards its audience with noisy special effects. **96m/C; DVD, Blu-Ray.** Ryan Reynolds; Jeff Bridges; Mary-Louise Parker; Robert Knepper; James Hong; Mike O'Malley; Kevin Bacon; Stephanie Szostak; *D:* Robert Schwentke; *W:* Matt Manfredi; Phil Hay; *C:* Alwin Kuchler; *M:* Christophe Beck.

Ripe **1997 (R)** Fourteen-year-old fraternal twins Violet (Keena) and Rosie (Eagan) decide to make it on their own after their abusive parents are killed in a car crash. They wind up on a derelict southern army base where they're befriended by caretaker Pete (Currie) and M.P. Ken (Brice), who may not have the most innocent of intentions. **93m/C; VHS, DVD.** Monica Keena; Daisy Eagan; Gordon Currie; Ron Brice; Karen (Lynn) Gorney; Vincent Laresca; *D:* Mo Ogrodnik; *W:* Mo Ogrodnik; *C:* Wolfgang Held; *M:* Anton Sanko.

Ripley's Game **2002 (R)** Tom Ripley (Malkovich) is still a sociopath, but now he's older, more refined, icier, married, and successful. When he overhears his dinner party host, Trevanny (Scott), insult him, Ripley decides to make him pay. His opportunity comes when British gangster Reeves (Winstone) needs an anonymous assassin to take out a Russian mobster. Ripley, knowing Trevanny is terminally ill and broke, suggests him, but Trevanny is betrayed by Reeves. This conflicts with Ripley's sense of honor and he intervenes. There's an enjoyably intricate plot and Malkovich is perfectly cast. Based on the Patricia Highsmith novel. **100m/C; VHS, DVD.** John Malkovich; Dougray Scott; Ray Winstone; Lena Headey; Chiara Caselli; *D:* Liliana Cavani; *W:* Liliana Cavani; Charles McKeown; *C:* Alfio Contini; *M:* Ennio Morricone. **VIDEO**

The Ripper **WOOF!** **1986** The spirit of Jack the Ripper possesses a university professor's body. Ultra-violent. Shot on videotape for the video market. **90m/C; VHS, DVD.** Wade Tower; Tom Schreir; Mona Van Pernis; Andrea Adams; *D:* Christopher Lewis.

Ripper: Letter from Hell **2001 (R)** Thankfully, there's more terror than gore in this slasher, which could be a bummer if you prefer the bloodier the better. Molly Keller (Cook) enrolls in a forensic science program taught by criminologist Marshall Kane (Payne). There's a spate of recent campus murders that Molly and her study group are investigating and the modus operandi resembles that of Jack the Ripper. Then they start becoming the killer's next victims. **113m/C; VHS, DVD.** A.J. Cook; Bruce Payne; Ryan Northcott; Jurgen Prochnow; Claire Keim; Derek Hamilton; Emmanuelle Vaugier; *D:* John Eyres; *W:* Patrick Bermel; *C:* Thomas M. (Tom) Harting; *M:* Peter Allen. **VIDEO**

Ripple Effect **2007 (R)** Lebanese-born American fashion mogul Amer Atrash (writer/director Caland) is having money troubles and a bailout by a friend falls through. Convinced that it's karmic payback for covering up a 15-year-old hit-and-run, Amer is determined to make amends to the wheelchair-bound Philip (Whitaker). Except to Philip, his accident was a blessing in disguise. **87m/C; DVD.** Forest Whitaker; Virginia Madsen; Minnie Driver; John Billingsley; Philippe Caland; Kip Pardue; Kali Rocha; *D:* Philippe Caland; *W:* Philippe Caland; *C:* Daron Keet; *M:* Anthony Marinelli.

Riptide **1934** Shearer is a carefree American married to stuffy English lord Marshall. He goes off to America on a business trip, she's bored and goes to a costume party (everyone dresses as insects!) where she meets old flame Montgomery. He gets drunk, follows her home in an effort to rekindle their passion, and winds up in the hospital after a drunken fall. The returning Marshall is appalled by the scandalous press and instigates divorce proceedings. Eventually, they come to their senses and decide they do love each other. Quality production with an entertaining cast. **90m/B; VHS, DVD.** Norma Shearer; Herbert Marshall; Robert Montgomery; Richard "Skeets" Gallagher; Ralph Forbes; Lilyan Tashman; *D:* Edmund Goulding; *W:* Edmund Goulding.

The Rise and Fall of Legs Diamond ½ **1960** Not quite historically accurate but fast-paced and entertaining gangster bio of legendary booze trafficker Legs Diamond. Danton's debut. **101m/B; VHS, DVD.** Ray Danton; Karen Steele; Jesse White; Simon Oakland; Robert Lowery; Elaine Stewart; Warren Oates; Judson Pratt; Dyan Cannon; *D:* Budd Boetticher.

The Rise and Rise of Michael Rimmer **1970** Deadpan social satire follows the ever-rising career of ambitious Michael Rimmer (Cook). He turns around a failing ad agency by his constant use of opinion polls and parleys the polls into a political career with a seat in Parliament and then a cabinet position. Through his constant manipulation of the public, Rimmer continues his upward climb to an ultimate prize. **94m/C; DVD.** *GB* Peter Cook; Denholm Elliott; Ronald Fraser; Arthur Lowe; Vanessa Howard; Harold Pinter; John Cleese; Roland Culver; *D:* Kevin Billington; *W:* Peter Cook; John Cleese; Kevin Billington; Graham Chapman; *C:* Alex Thompson; *M:* John Cameron.

Rise: Blood Hunter **2007** Reporter Sadie (Liu) becomes a victim of the underground vampire cult she was investigating. She's not happy and, armed with a crossbow, she decides to get revenge on the vamp leader (D'Arcy) and anyone else who brutalized her. Lots of violence, gore, and nakedness. **94m/C; DVD.** Lucy Liu; Michael Chiklis; Carla Gugino; James D'Arcy; Nick Lachey; Robert Forster; Mako; *D:* Sebastian Gutierrez; *W:* Sebastian Gutierrez; *C:* John Toll; *M:* Nathan Barr.

The Rise of Louis XIV *La Prise de Pouvoir Par Louis XIV* **1966** A masterful docudrama detailing the life and court intrigues of Louis XIV of France. Successfully captures the attitudes and mores of the royalty at the time. One of a series of historical films directed by Rossellini. Made for French TV; subtitled. **100m/C; VHS, DVD.** *FR* Jean-Marie Patte; Raymond Jourdan; Dominique Vincent; Giorgio Silvagni; Pierre Barrat; *D:* Roberto Rossellini. **TV**

Rise of the Dinosaurs *Jurassic Attack* **2013 (R)** A beautiful bio-geneticist is kidnapped by a South American terrorist so she can make him a bioweapon. An elite group of soldiers are sent to rescue her, but their helicopter crashes in a remote valley that's filled with carnivorous dinosaurs. Syfy Channel nonsense with lousy CGI, a ho-hum plot, and characters that deserve to be dino chow. **83m/C; DVD.** Natascha Berg; Israel Saez de Miguel; Corin "Corky" Nemec; Gary Stretch; Michael Worth; Vernon Wells; *D:* Anthony Fankhauser; *W:* Rafael Jordan; *C:* Stuart Brereton; *M:* Mario Salvucci. **CABLE**

Rise of the Footsoldier **2007 (R)** Brit crime flick, based on a true story, that has nothing going for it but violence. Carlton Leach goes from football hooligan in the 1980s to criminal muscle and gangster in the 1990s and is ultimately involved in the discovery of three murdered drug dealers who were found in rural Essex. **119m/C; DVD.** *GB* Ricci Harnett; Craig Fairbrass; Terry Stone; Roland Manookian; *D:* Julian Gilbey; *W:* Julian Gilbey; Will Gilbey; *C:* Ali Asad.

Rise of the Gargoyles **2009** Part of the Syfy Channel's "Maneater" series. Workers in an ancient Paris church discover an underground passage and fall prey to a gargoyle guarding its treasures. American prof Jack Randall (Balfour) soon figures out what is suddenly swooping over the Paris streets, killing random citizens, but no one believes him. You don't see much of the gargoyle, probably because there's no budget for decent CGI. **94m/C; DVD.** Eric Balfour; Caroline Neron; Ifan Huw Dafydd; Tanya Clarke; Justin Salinger; Nick Mancuso; *D:* Bill Corcoran; *W:* Andy Briggs; *C:* Pierre Jodoin; *M:* Ned Bouhalassa. **CABLE**

Rise of the Guardians ½ **2012 (PG)** William Joyce adapts his book series in which Santa Claus (Baldwin), the Easter Bunny (Jackman), and the Tooth Fairy (Fisher)--as well as the silent Sandman and Jack Frost (Pine)--are re-imagined as protectors for the children of the world, now at risk with the return of the bogeyman Pitch (Law). Pleasantly inoffensive, visually interesting, with an incredibly talented voice cast and a clever, though simplistic, concept. An unusual children's film that will entertain the young ones and can be appreciated by adults. **97m/C; DVD, Blu-Ray.** *V:* Chris Pine; Alec Baldwin; Jude Law; Isla Fisher; Hugh Jackman; *D:* Peter Ramsey; *W:* David Lindsay-Abaire; *M:* Alexandre Desplat.

The Rise of the Krays **2016 (R)** A biographical crime drama about the notorious British criminals, the twin brothers Reggie (Leslie) and Ronnie (Cotton) Kray. Told from the perspective of one of the brothers' closest friends, the story of the Krays is offered from their years as amateur boxers to their involvement with crime to their years as violent criminal masterminds and enthusiastic participants in gang wars in 1960s London. The film also explores their fall and the aftermath of their years of terror. **110m/C; DVD, Blu-Ray, Streaming, Download.** Simon Cotton; Kevin Leslie; Dan Parr; Phil Dunster; Danny Midwinter; ***D:*** Zackary Adler; ***W:*** Ken Brown; Sebastian Brown; ***C:*** Luke Palmer. **VIDEO**

Rise of the Planet of the Apes *Rise of the Apes* **2011 (PG-13)** Superb prequel to the classic Charlton Heston sci-fi flick that weaves modern visual effects (not one actual ape appears) around the mythological story. In an attempt to stave off his father's (Lithgow) Alzheimer's, medical researcher Will Rodman's (Franco) drug has a surprising intellectual effect on the test apes. Things go haywire and Will ends up raising baby chimp Caesar (Serkis via motion-capture) though an incident causes a string of events leading to the iconic uprising of the species. Humans aren't the headliners here—director Wyatt perfectly captures Caesar's arc from family member to caged animal to future leader. **105m/C; DVD, Blu-Ray.** James Franco; Freida Pinto; Andy Serkis; Tyler Labine; John Lithgow; David Hewlett; Brian Cox; Tom Felton; ***D:*** Rupert Wyatt; ***W:*** Amanda Silver; Rick Jaffa; ***C:*** Andrew Lesnie; ***M:*** Patrick Doyle.

Rise of the Zombies **2012** The zombie apocalypse finally lands in San Francisco and a group of people make the decision to wait it out in nearby Alcatraz prison. **90m/C; DVD, Blu-Ray.** Mariel Hemingway; Ethan Suplee; LeVar Burton; Danny Trejo; Heather Hemmens; ***D:*** Nick Lyon; ***W:*** Keith Allan; Delondra Williams; ***C:*** Alexander Yellen; ***M:*** Chris Ridenhour. **CABLE**

Risen **2016 (PG-13)** Reynolds delivers a faith-based action film with a bit more bite than most in recent years but one that still ultimately succumbs to the tropes of the genre. His film tracks the Resurrection from the perspective a non-believer named Clavius (Fiennes), a Roman Military Tribune assigned the case of the missing body when Jesus Christ goes missing after death. At first, the gladiator sets out to disprove the rumors of a risen savior, but, of course, he eventually becomes a believer himself. This wannabe blockbuster is decently well-made but devolves into something so self-serious that it approaches parody. **107m/C; DVD, Blu-Ray.** Joseph Fiennes; Tom Felton; Peter Firth; Clifford Curtis; Maria Botto; ***D:*** Kevin Reynolds; ***W:*** Kevin Reynolds; Paul Aiello; ***C:*** Lorenzo Senatore; ***M:*** Rocque Banos.

The Rising of the Moon **1957** John Ford's three-story anthology on Irish culture introduced by Tyrone Power. In "The Majesty of the Law," a policeman is sent to arrest an elderly man who refuses to pay a fine. "A Minute's Wait" has a passenger train stopping at a station to pick up some fresh lobsters and the waiting time getting extended for a variety of reasons. "1921" has players from the Abbey Theatre disguising themselves to smuggle an Irish patriot out of prison before his execution. **81m/B; DVD.** Cyril Cusack; Noel Purcell; Jimmy O'Dea; Donal Donnelly; ***D:*** John Ford; ***W:*** Frank Nugent; ***C:*** Robert Krasker; ***M:*** Eamonn O'Gallagher.

The Rising Place **2002 (PG-13)** Nostalgia and tears. Dying Emily Hodge (Drummond) recalls her sometimes unconventional life to her niece Virginia (Fisher) in a series of flashbacks. The young Emily (Holloman) is a smalltown Southern belle who gets pregnant by her boyfriend who goes off to WWII, never to return. Having scandalized her conventional parents (Harper, Cole), Emily agrees to give her baby up for adoption but refuses to go into hiding. Instead, she becomes a schoolteacher along with her black best friend, Wilma (Neal), who encourages Emily to get involved in the civil rights movement. Based on the novel by David Armstrong. **93m/C; VHS, DVD.** Laurel Holloman; Elise Neal; Mark Webber; Billy Campbell; Gary Cole; Tess Harper; Alice Drummond; Frances Fisher; ***D:*** Tom Rice; ***W:*** Tom Rice; ***C:*** Jim Dollarhide; ***M:*** Conrad Pope.

Rising Sun **1993 (R)** When a prostitute is found murdered in the boardroom of a powerful Japanese-owned corporation, seasoned cop (and Japanese expert) Connery and new partner Snipes are sent to investigate. Complicated yarn about business, prejudice, cops, and the differences between east and west. Filmed with stylized camera techniques, quick action, and good rapport between the two leads. Based on the book by Crichton, which offered ominous theories about international politics and business. These aspects had the film labeled as Japan-bashing, one of the reasons the script was rewritten to focus more on the murder mystery. **129m/C; VHS, DVD.** Sean Connery; Wesley Snipes; Tia Carrere; Harvey Keitel; Kevin Anderson; Stan(ford) Egi; Mako; Cary-Hiroyuki Tagawa; Ray Wise; Steve Buscemi; Dan E. Butler; Tatjana Patitz; ***D:*** Philip Kaufman; ***W:*** Philip Kaufman; Michael Backes; Michael Crichton; ***C:*** Michael Chapman; ***M:*** Toru Takemitsu.

Risk 1/2 **2000 (R)** Shady insurance guy John Kriesky (Brown) is tutoring young Ben (Long) in money, sex, and shifty deals, including involving him in insurance fraud. Then Kriesky's lawyer/girlfriend Louise (Karvan) decides to give Ben a few personal lessons as well. Fast-paced thriller with a cast that's well worth watching. **89m/C; VHS, DVD.** *AU* Bryan Brown; Tom Long; Claudia Karvan; Jason Clarke; ***D:*** Alan White; ***W:*** John Armstrong; ***C:*** Simon Duggan; ***M:*** Don Miller-Robinson. **CABLE**

Risky Business **1983 (R)** With his parents out of town and awaiting word from the college boards, a teenager becomes involved in unexpected ways with a quick-thinking prostitute, her pimp, and assorted others. Cruise is likeable, especially when dancing in his underwear. Funny, well-paced, stylish prototypical '80s teen flick reintroduced Ray-Bans as the sunglasses for the wanna-be hip. What a party! **99m/C; VHS, DVD, Blu-Ray.** Tom Cruise; Rebecca De Mornay; Curtis Armstrong; Bronson Pinchot; Joe Pantoliano; Kevin Anderson; Richard Masur; Raphael Sbarge; Nicholas Pryor; Janet Carroll; ***D:*** Paul Brickman; ***W:*** Paul Brickman; ***C:*** Reynaldo Villalobos; Bruce Surtees; ***M:*** Tangerine Dream.

Rita, Sue & Bob Too **1987 (R)** A middle-aged Englishman gets involved in a menage a trois with two promiscuous teenagers, until the whole town gets wind of it. A raunchy, amoral British comedy. **94m/C; VHS, DVD, Blu-Ray.** *GB* Michelle Holmes; George Costigan; Siobhan Finneran; Lesley Sharp; Willie Ross; Patti Nicholls; Kulvinder Ghir; ***D:*** Alan Clarke; ***W:*** Andrea Dunbar; ***C:*** Ivan Strasburg; ***M:*** Michael Kamen.

The Rite *The Ritual; Riten* **1969** Members of a famous theatrical troupe are called before a judge to answer charges that a production is obscene. The judge's interrogation exposes their private and painful neuroses until the performers decide to turn on their accuser. Pessimistic even by Bergman standards and the first film the director made specifically for TV. Swedish with subtitles. **75m/B; VHS, DVD, Blu-Ray.** *SW* Ingrid Thulin; Gunnar Bjornstrand; Erik Hell; Anders Ek; ***D:*** Ingmar Bergman; ***W:*** Ingmar Bergman; ***C:*** Sven Nykvist.

The Rite 1/2 **2011 (PG-13)** American seminary student Michael (O'Donoghue) reluctantly attends an exorcism school at the Vatican and meets an unorthodox priest, Father Lucas (Hopkins). Michael contends that the possessed need to be treated through psychiatric means and is unconvinced of any merits of exorcism. But when Father Lucas shows him the darker elements of his faith, Michael learns that science can't explain everything. Poorly directed supernatural thriller falls flat and lacks suspense or surprises. Loosely taken from Matt Baglio's book, "The Rite: The Making of a Modern Exorcist." **112m/C; DVD, Blu-Ray, On Demand.** Colin O'Donoghue; Anthony Hopkins; Alice Braga; Ciaran Hinds; Toby Jones; Rutger Hauer; ***D:*** Mikael Hafstrom; ***W:*** Michael Petroni; ***C:*** Benjamin Davis; ***M:*** Alex Heffes.

Rites of Frankenstein *Erotic Rites of Frankenstein* **1972 (R)** Ultra-low budget remake with plenty of blood, sex and perversions required of surreal horrors. Frankenstein (Price) is murdered and his monster creation is stolen by his archenemy Dr. Cagliostro, a mad genius taken to kidnapping girls for their body parts, which he uses in dastardly experiments. Frankenstein's daughter (Savon) seeks to avenge her father's death through unconventional methods, of course. Just wacky enough to become a euro-trash classic. In Spanish with English subtitles. **94m/C; DVD, Blu-Ray.** Jess (Jesus) Franco; Dennis Price; Howard Vernon; Anne Libert; Britt Nichols; Alberto Dalbes; Luis Barboo; Lina Romay; Daniel White; Beatriz Savon; ***D:*** Jess (Jesus) Franco; ***W:*** Jess (Jesus) Franco; ***C:*** Raul Artigot; ***M:*** Daniel White. **VIDEO**

Rites of Passage **1999 (R)** Suspenser about fathers, sons, and masculinity has both awkwardness and intensity. Del Farraday (Stockwell) and his son D.J. (Keith) travel to their secluded mountain cabin for a heart-to-heart chat, only to discover the place is being used by Farley's estranged gay son, Campbell (Behr). As if there weren't enough family angst, the trio are joined by violent escaped cons Frank (Remar) and Red (Woolvett). Tempers flare between Del and Frank and the entire situation is worsened by a secret that Campbell is keeping. Good performances. **94m/C; VHS, DVD.** Dean Stockwell; James Remar; Jaimz Woolvett; Jason Behr; Robert Keith; ***D:*** Victor Salva; ***W:*** Victor Salva; ***C:*** Don E. Fauntleroy; ***M:*** Bennett Salvay.

Rites of Passage 1/2 **2012 (R)** Psycho-thriller with a too-busy plot and a lot of weak elements that don't add up. Anthropology student Nathan invites his prof and classmates to his family's abandoned ranch for the weekend. Since the property was once a Chumash burial ground, his excuse is that they can re-create an ancient Native American ceremony. Really, they plan to drink, do drugs, and party, but Nathan's psycho older brother Benny and his drug dealer Delgado have other ideas. **103m/C; DVD, Blu-Ray.** Wes Bentley; Christian Slater; Stephen Dorff; Ryan Donowho; Kate Maberly; Briana Evigan; ***D:*** W. Peter Iliff; ***W:*** W. Peter Iliff; ***C:*** Alex Nepomniaschy; ***M:*** Elia Cmiral. **VIDEO**

Rituals 1/2 *The Creeper* **1979** Group of five calm, rational men suddenly turn desperate after a chain of nightmarish events on a camping trip. Yet another low-budget "Deliverance" rip off. **100m/C; VHS, DVD, Blu-Ray.** *CA* Hal Holbrook; Lawrence Dane; ***D:*** Peter Carter.

The Ritz **1976 (R)** Weston tries to get away from his gangster brother-in-law by hiding out in a gay bathhouse in New York. Moreno plays a talentless singer Googie Gomez, who performs in the bathhouse while waiting for her big break. Moreno is great reprising her Tony-winning stage role, and Lester's direction is spiffy. Written by Terence McNally from his play. **91m/C; DVD.** Rita Moreno; Jack Weston; Jerry Stiller; Kaye Ballard; Treat Williams; F. Murray Abraham; ***D:*** Richard Lester; ***W:*** Terrence McNally; ***C:*** Paul Wilson; ***M:*** Ken Thorne.

Rivals 1/2 *Deadly Rivals* **1972 (R)** Shallow, unconvincing drama about a stepfather challenged by his stepson, who wants to kill this new contender for his mother's love. Nice handling of cast credits, but other details—like acting, directing and photography—leave much to be desired. **103m/C; VHS, DVD.** Robert Klein; Joan Hackett; Scott Jacoby; ***D:*** Krishna Shah.

The River **1951** A massively lauded late film by Renoir about three British girls growing up in Bengal, India, all developing crushes on a one-legged American vet. Lyrical and heartwarming, with hailed cinematography by Claude Renoir. Rumer Godden wrote the novel, and co-scripted the screenplay with director Renoir. Satyajit Ray, one of India's greatest filmmakers, assisted Renoir. **99m/C; VHS, DVD, Blu-Ray.** *FR* Patricia Walters; Adrienne Corri; Nora Swinburne; Radha; Arthur Shields; Thomas E. Breen; Esmond Knight; ***Nar:*** June Hillman; ***D:*** Jean Renoir; ***W:*** Jean Renoir; ***C:*** Claude Renoir.

The River **1984 (PG)** Farmers battle a river whose flood threatens their farm. Spacek, as always, is strong and believable as the wife and mother, but Gibson falters. Beautiful photography. The third in an onslaught of films in the early '80s that dramatized the plight of the small American farmer. "The River" isn't as strong as "Country" and "Places in the Heart" which managed to convey important messages less cloyingly. **124m/C; VHS, DVD, HD-DVD.** Mel Gibson; Sissy Spacek; Scott Glenn; Billy Green Bush; ***D:*** Mark Rydell; ***W:*** Julian Barry; Robert Dillon; ***C:*** Vilmos Zsigmond; ***M:*** John Williams.

A River Called Titas *Titas Ekti Nodir Naam* **1973** An insightful, revealing documentary look at the harsh life of fisherman who make their living on the Titas River in Brahmanbaria, Bangladesh. In this time period, Bangladesh was a newly formed country, and the tensions between traditional culture and wider changes are explored. Some of the documentary is focused on a fisherman named Kishore who marries Basanti, but she is kidnapped on their wedding night. She has amnesia and only remembers the name of his village, and it is a decade before she tries to find him with their son. Her return is complicated as some members of Kishore's village will not share food with her and her son, in part because of the threat of starvation. Bengali with subtitles. **159m/C; DVD.** ***D:*** Ritwik Ghatak; ***W:*** Ritwik Ghatak; ***C:*** Baby Islam; ***M:*** Ustad Bahadur Khan.

The River King **2005 (R)** Muddled and dull crime drama based on the novel by Alice Hoffman. Small town police detective Abel Grey (Burns) doesn't believe that the drowning death of a private school student was suicide. His investigation leads him to the boy's photography teacher, Betsy Chase (Ehle), who aids in Abel's sleuthing. **99m/C; DVD.** *GB CA* Edward Burns; Jennifer Ehle; Julian Rhind-Tutt; Jaime King; Rachelle Lefevre; Sean McCann; ***D:*** Nick Willing; ***W:*** David Kane; ***C:*** Paul Sarossy; ***M:*** Simon Boswell.

A River Made to Drown In **1997** When wealthy lawyer Thaddeus MacKenzie (Chamberlain) learns he is dying from AIDS, he decides to get in touch with the two people he once loved, Allen and Jaime. Allen (Imperioli) is a struggling artist who once worked the streets and is now involved with gallery owner Eva (Lemper), who knows nothing about his former life. But he agrees to look for the still-hustling Jaime (Duval), even if this means confronting a past he'd rather forget. **98m/C; VHS, DVD.** Michael Imperioli; Richard Chamberlain; James Duval; Ute Lemper; Austin Pendleton; Talia Shire; Mike Starr; Michael Saucedo; James Karen; Lewis Arquette; ***D:*** James Merendino; ***W:*** Paul Marius; ***C:*** Thomas Callaway.

The River Murders 1/2 **2011 (R)** Generic thriller but Slater's oddball FBI agent is worth watching. Horndog homicide detective Jack Verdon (Liotta) becomes the prime suspect in a series of murders since the female victims were all sexually involved with him. **92m/C; DVD.** Ray Liotta; Christian Slater; Ving Rhames; Gisele Fraga; Melora Walters; Raymond J. Barry; ***D:*** Rich Cowan; ***W:*** Steve Anderson; ***C:*** Dan Heigh; ***M:*** Pinar Toprak. **VIDEO**

The River Niger 1/2 **1976 (R)** Jones is riveting, and Tyson is good in an otherwise muddling adaptation of the Tony-award winning play about black ghetto life. Realistic emotions and believable characters. **105m/C; VHS, DVD.** James Earl Jones; Cicely Tyson; Glynn Turman; Louis Gossett, Jr.; Roger E. Mosley; Jonelle Allen; ***D:*** Krishna Shah.

River of Death 1/2 **1990 (R)** Absurd adventure, based on an Alistair McLean novel, about a white man entering the Amazon jungle world of a forgotten tribe in search of wealth, tripping over Neo-Nazi scientists and war criminals. Too complex to be harmlessly enjoyable; too mindless for the complexity to be worth unraveling. **103m/C; VHS, DVD, Blu-Ray.** Michael Dudikoff; Robert Vaughn; Donald Pleasence; Herbert Lom; L.Q. Jones; Cynthia Erland; Sarah Maur-Thorp; ***D:*** Steve Carver.

River of Evil 1/2 **1964** Action/adventure in which a young girl travels through the Amazon jungle searching for clues to her father's death. **83m/C; VHS, DVD.** *GE* Barbara Rutting; Harald Leipnitz; Oswaldo Loureiro; Cyl Farney; Tereza Raquel; ***D:*** Franz Eichhorn; ***W:*** Franz Eichhorn; ***C:*** Edgar Eichhorn; ***M:*** Catulo Cearense.

River of Grass 1/2 **1994** No-budget noirish crime/romance set in the swampy, low-rent Florida area between Miami and the Everglades. Uncaring and frankly dumb housewife/mom Cozy (Bowman) hooks up with the boozing Lee Ray (Fessenden) and the dim duo take an illegal dip in a private pool. Cozy manages to fire off Lee's gun and thinks she hit a man who suddenly appeared. Not bothering to find out if this is true, they decide to hold up in a motel until they can figure out what to do. You won't really care but director Reichardt does have a way with visuals so things aren't a total loss. **80m/C; VHS, DVD, Blu-Ray.** Lisa Bowman; Larry Fessenden; Dick Russell; **D:** Kelly Reichardt; **W:** Kelly Reichardt; Jesse Hartman; **C:** Jim Denault.

River of No Return 🦴🦴 1/2 **1954** During the gold rush, an itinerant farmer and his young son help a heart-of-gold saloon singer search for her estranged husband. Rather crummy script is helped by the mere presence of Mitchum and Monroe. Marilyn sings the title song, as well as "Down in the Meadow," and "I'm Going to File My Claim." **91m/C; DVD, Blu-Ray.** Robert Mitchum; Marilyn Monroe; Tommy Rettig; Rory Calhoun; Murvyn Vye; Douglas Spencer; **D:** Otto Preminger; **W:** Frank Fenton; **C:** Joseph LaShelle; **M:** Cyril Mockridge.

River Queen 🦴 1/2 **2005 (R)** A wannabe epic that turns out to be a snoozer. In 1854, the native Maori population is clashing with European settlers in New Zealand. At a garrison post, Sarah (Morton) has an affair with the son of a Maori tribal leader and bears his son. Her lover dies and eventually the boy is kidnapped by his grandfather so he can be raised according to Maori tradition. Sarah isn't reunited with her son until he's a teenager torn between the two cultures. **114m/C; DVD.** *GB NZ* Samantha Morton; Clifford Curtis; Temuera Morrison; Kiefer Sutherland; Anton Lesser; Stephen Rea; David Rawiri Pene; **D:** Vincent Ward; **W:** Vincent Ward; Toa Fraser; **C:** Alun Bollinger; **M:** Karl Jenkins.

River Red 🦴🦴 **1998 (R)** Dave Holden (Scott) kills their abusive dad to save his younger brother Tom (Moscow) from being beaten. Tom takes the rap since he's a minor and gets a lighter sentence, being sent to a juvenile home. However, Dave's guilt and his being deeply in debt lead him into a life of crime. When the brothers reunite, emotions come to a head. Based on Drilling's one-act stage play, film boasts fine performances but fails to take advantage of its controversial plot and deep psychological themes. **104m/C; DVD.** Tom Everett Scott; David Moscow; Cara Buono; Denis O'Hare; Leo Burmester; Tibor Feldman; James Murtaugh; David Lowery; Michael Kelly; **D:** Eric Drilling; **W:** Eric Drilling; **C:** Steven Schlueter; **M:** Johnny Hickman.

A River Runs Through It 🦴🦴🦴 1/2 **1992 (PG)** Contemplative exploration of family ties and coming of age with impact falling just short of the novel's is another well-crafted American tale directed by Redford. Set in Montana during the early part of the century, a Presbyterian minister teaches his two sons, one troubled and one on his way to success, about life and religion via fly-fishing. Based on the novel by Norman Maclean. **123m/C; VHS, DVD.** Craig Sheffer; Brad Pitt; Tom Skerritt; Brenda Blethyn; Emily Lloyd; Edie McClurg; Stephen Shellen; Susan Taylor; **D:** Robert Redford; **W:** Richard Friedenberg; **C:** Philippe Rousselot; **M:** Mark Isham. Oscars '92: Cinematog.

River Street 🦴🦴 **1995** Ambitious real estate agent Ben Egan (Young) is engaged to marry Sharon (MacIntosh), his shady boss Vincent Pierce's (Hunter) daughter. But when he blows a big deal and winds up striking a cop, Ben's sentenced to community service at a dilapidated center for street kids. He takes an interest in good-hearted center director Wendy (Davis) but can't change his ways so easily. The center stands on valuable river front property and if Ben can get the land, he'll get back both his job and Sharon. The relationships don't convince and Ben's change of heart seems forced. **88m/C; VHS, DVD.** *AU* Aden Young; Bill Hunter; Essie Davis; Tammy MacIntosh; Sullivan Stapleton; Lois Ramsey; **D:** Tony Mahood; **W:** Philip Ryall; **C:** Martin McGrath; **M:** David Bridie; John Phillips.

River: The Legend of La Llorona WOOF! **2006** Spanish legend of the Weeping Woman who drowned her children after being deserted by their father becomes a no-budget ghost story. Miguel is hired to bring back runaway Luciana but she escapes when he gets into a car accident. He goes to the nearby town to find her and there's some foolishness about a curse involving Luciana and La Llorona. But it makes no sense and the flick is bad in every possible way. **73m/C; DVD.** Will Morales; Reshma Freeman; Maria Sanchez; Ed Diaz; Denise Gossett; **D:** Terence Williams; **W:** Terence Williams; **C:** Terence Williams; **M:** Lukasz Brzostek. **VIDEO**

The River Why 🦴 1/2 **2010 (PG-13)** A slow-moving and bland family drama best seen by those who admire northwestern Oregon and fishing. Gloomy young Gus leaves his bickering parents behind in the city to commune with nature in rural Oregon and take up fly fishing. There's a perfunctory romantic interest with pretty Eddy. **101m/C; DVD.** Zach Gilford; Amber Heard; William Hurt; Dallas Roberts; Kathleen Quinlan; William Devane; **D:** Matthew Leutwyler; **W:** Thomas A. Cohen; **C:** Karsten Gopinath; **M:** Austin Wintory.

The River Wild 🦴🦴 1/2 **1994 (PG-13)** Dissatisfied wife Gail (Streep) plans a family white-water rafting vacation with 10-year-old son Roarke (Mazzello) and workaholic husband Tom (Strathairn). A former guide (and white-water expert) Gail comes to the aid of river novices Wade (boyishly menacing Bacon) and Terry (Reilly), who quickly turn out to be violent criminals needing Gail's help with their escape. Slow start leads to nonstop thrills with Streep an adept action heroine, though undercut by the flic's need to do something with Strathairn's thankless role. Beautiful Montana and Oregon settings. **111m/C; VHS, DVD.** Meryl Streep; David Strathairn; Joseph Mazzello; Kevin Bacon; John C. Reilly; Benjamin Bratt; **D:** Curtis Hanson; **W:** Raynold Gideon; **C:** Robert Elswit; **M:** Jerry Goldsmith.

The River Within 🦴🦴 **2009** Christian-oriented first feature from writer/director Heath. Law school grad Jason returns to his hometown for the summer to study for the bar exam and reconnects with old friends Layla and Paul. Though engaged, Layla has some unresolved romantic feelings for Jason and Paul is trying to make some tough personal decisions. Meanwhile, Jason is asked by Pastor David to lead the local youth group and he befriends Marcus. After learning something disturbing about the young man, Jason starts questioning his own purpose in life. **92m/C; DVD.** Josh Odor; Jacklyn Friedlander; Craig Luttrell; Maurice Mejia; Craig Morris; Geoffrey Falk; **D:** Zac Heath; **W:** Zac Heath; **C:** Derrick Smith; **M:** Craig Morris; Megan McCauley. **VIDEO**

The Riverman 🦴🦴 1/2 **2004 (R)** In 1982, Washington state detective Dave Reichert (Jaeger) is investigating the unsolved murders of 13 women in the Green River area. Needing help, Reichert turns to obsessive homicide detective/profiler Robert Keppel (Greenwood) who worked on the Ted Bundy case. Awaiting execution in Florida, Bundy (Elwes) contacts Keppel, offering his own ideas on the Green River killer but he wants something in exchange. Focuses more on the Keppel/Bundy connection that the Green River case itself but Greenwood and Elwes are excellent and the A&E cable pic is inevitably disturbing. Based on Keppel's book. **91m/C; DVD.** Bruce Greenwood; Cary Elwes; Sam Jaeger; Kathleen Quinlan; David Brown; **D:** Bill Eagles; **W:** Tom Towler; **C:** Steve Cossens; **M:** Jeff Rona. **CABLE**

River's Edge 🦴🦴🦴 **1987 (R)** Drug-addled high school student strangles his girlfriend and casually displays the corpse to his apathetic group of friends, who leave the murder unreported for days. Harrowing and gripping; based on a true story. Aging biker Hopper is splendid. **99m/C; VHS, DVD, Blu-Ray.** Keanu Reeves; Crispin Glover; Daniel Roebuck; Joshua John Miller; Dennis Hopper; Ione Skye; Roxana Zal; Tom Bower; Constance Forslund; Leo Rossi; Jim Metzler; **D:** Tim Hunter; **W:** Neal Jimenez; **C:** Frederick Elmes; **M:** Jurgen Knieper. Ind. Spirit '88: Film, Screenplay; Sundance '87: Special Jury Prize.

River's End 🦴🦴 1/2 *Molding Clay* **2005 (PG)** Texas teen Clay Watkins has gotten into scrapes ever since his father died. When things get too bad, his sheriff grandfather Buster gives Clay a choice: go to jail or make a 60-mile wilderness trip along the Pecos River and do some serious thinking. Clay decides on the latter but his path eventually crosses a couple of fugitive drug dealers who are trying to get to Mexico with Buster tracking them. **94m/C; DVD.** Sam Huntington; Barry Corbin; Caroline Goodall; Rudolf Martin; Joe Stephens; Amanda Brooks; Greg Evigan; Charles Durning; Clint Howard; William Katt; **D:** William Katt; **W:** Samuel Benedict; Glen Stephens; **C:** John-Paul Beeghly; **M:** Jay Michael Ferguson; Paul Cristo. **VIDEO**

Riverworld 🦴 1/2 **2010** Two-part miniseries from the SyFy channel that's a loose adaptation of the sci fi novels by Philip Jose Farmer. American journalist Matt Elman and his fiancee Jessie are killed in a suicide bombing. Matt awakens on a riverbank on an alien planet in some kind of afterlife. There are two rival bands of blue-skinned aliens, resurrected Earthlings in a good vs. evil battle, and a long river that bisects the planet that Matt must travel while he tries to reunite with Jessie. **178m/C; DVD.** Tahmoh Penikett; Mark Deklin; Peter Wingfield; Laura Vandervoort; Jeananne Goossen; Bruce Ramsay; Alan Cumming; **D:** Stuart Gillard; **W:** Randall Badat; Robert Hewitt Wolfe; Hans Beimler; **C:** Thomas Burstyn; **M:** Jim Gutteridge. **CABLE**

Rize 🦴🦴🦴 **2005 (PG-13)** Intensely uptempo, hyped-up L.A. dancing form called "clowning" or "krumping" is vividly chronicled in this David LaChappelle documentary. Born from the 1992 riots as a peaceful means of expression by poverty-stricken inner-city dwellers, krumping was the invention of Tom Johnson, or Tommy the Clown, a reformed drug dealer who started the movement by dressing as a clown and, later, reenacting the Rodney King footage. Payoff comes in the form of a grand krumping contest held annually at the Great Western Forum. **85m/C; DVD.** **D:** David LaChapelle; **C:** Morgan Susser; **M:** Red Ronin Prods; Amy Marie Beauchamp; Jose Cancella.

RKO 281 🦴🦴🦴 **1999 (R)** This retelling of Orson Welles' (Schrieber) battles to make 1941's "Citizen Kane" is all about egos. Welles had the arrogance of youth and Hearst the arrogance of power. The film, written with Herman J. Mankiewicz (Malkovich), was a thinly disguised look at newspaper magnate William Randolph Hearst (Cromwell) and his life with longtime mistress, blond actress Marion Davies (Griffith). Hearst was so outraged by Welles' movie that he tried to use his considerable influence with the Hollywood studios to have the film destroyed. Naturally, the story is both streamlined and altered but the leading roles are dramatically well served. **87m/C; VHS, DVD.** Liev Schreiber; John Malkovich; James Cromwell; Melanie Griffith; Brenda Blethyn; Roy Scheider; David Suchet; Fiona Shaw; Liam Cunningham; Tim Woodward; **D:** Ridley Scott; **W:** John Logan; **C:** Mike Southon; **M:** John Altman. **CABLE**

R.L. Stine's The Haunting Hour: Don't Even Think About It 🦴 1/2 *The Haunting Hour: Don't Even Think About It* **2007 (PG)** Cassie (Osment) is a young Goth girl whose family has moved to a new town, and she has no friends in school. Spending her time playing pranks on the popular kids, she eventually gains possession of a book called "The Evil Thing." What happens next is pretty much just for the kiddies. **87m/C; DVD.** Emily Osment; Brittany Curran; Cody Linley; Tobin Bell; **D:** Alex Zamm; **W:** Dan Angel; **C:** Jacques Haitkin; **M:** Chris Hajian.

The Road 🦴🦴 *El Camino* **2000** Manuel is on his way to a family funeral (by motorcycle) when he meets photographer Caroline on the road. Their romance is tested when Manuel is suddenly arrested and thrown in jail—only to escape after seeing a cop beat an inmate to death. The lovers are on the run but the end of the road is not the end of the journey. Spanish with subtitles. **107m/C; VHS, DVD.** *AR* Ezequiel Rodriquez; Antonella Costa; Daniel Valenzuela; Hector Anglada; Alejandro Awada; Ruben Patagonia; **D:** Javier Olivera; **W:** Hector Olivera; Javier Olivera; **C:** Cristian Cottet; **M:** Axel Krygier.

The Road 🦴🦴 **2009 (R)** A post-apocalyptic nightmare road trip taken by a father and son that's based on Cormac McCarthy's Pulitzer Prize-winning novel. An unnamed man (Mortenson) and young boy (Smit-McPhee) trudge along towards the sea in a daily quest for food, shelter, and survival while trying to avoid violent, and probably cannibalistic, roving gangs. Mortensen is haunted and determined and Smit-McPhee convincingly acts fearful and stunned. It's relentlessly grim (although how could it not be?), with limited dialogue, and the appropriately scorched and desolate look but it's also emotionally distancing and as much of a slog as the duo's walk itself. **119m/C; Blu-Ray, On Demand.** Viggo Mortensen; Kodi Smit-McPhee; Charlize Theron; Guy Pearce; Robert Duvall; Garret Dillahunt; Michael K(enneth) Williams; **D:** John Hillcoat; **W:** Joe Penhall; **C:** Javier Aguirresarobe; **M:** Nick Cave.

Road Ends 🦴🦴 1/2 **1998 (R)** Small town sheriff Hopper and local innkeeper Hemingway unwittingly offer refuge to runaway FBI informant, Maceda (Sarandon), who's supposed to testify against his drug trafficking boss. FBI agent Gere (Coyote) is after Maceda as well as his ex-employers—and it's just a matter of who catches up to him first. **98m/C; VHS, DVD.** Chris Sarandon; Peter Coyote; Dennis Hopper; Mariel Hemingway; Joanna Gleason; **D:** Rick King; **W:** Bill Mesce, Jr.; **C:** Bruce Douglas Johnson; **M:** David Mansfield.

The Road from Coorain 🦴🦴 1/2 **2002** Based on the 1989 memoir by historian Jill Ker Conway who was born and raised on a vast and isolated Australian sheep ranch called Coorain. The story, which opens in the early 1940s, deals with Jill's difficult relationship with her stoical mother Eve (Stevenson), who keeps Coorain even after being widowed and moving her family to Sydney. Jill proves to be an exceptional student and excels at university but family tragedies continue to haunt the Kers. **120m/C; VHS, DVD.** *AU* Juliet Stevenson; Richard Roxburgh; Katherine Slattery; Alex Tomasetti; Tim Guinee; John Howard; Bernard Curry; Sean Hall; **D:** Brendan Maher; **W:** Sue Smith; **C:** Tristan Milani; **M:** Stephen Rae. **TV**

Road Games 🦴🦴 **1981 (PG)** Trucker Keach is drawn into a web of intrigue surrounding a series of highway "Jack the Ripper"-style murders. Curtis is a hitchhiker. Nothing special. Director Franklin later helmed "Psycho II." **100m/C; VHS, DVD, Blu-Ray.** *AU* Stacy Keach; Jamie Lee Curtis; Marion Edwards; Grant Page; Bill Stacey; Thaddeus Smith; Alan Hopgood; **D:** Richard Franklin; **W:** Everett De Roche; **C:** Vincent Monton; **M:** Brian May.

Road Hard 🦴🦴 **2015** A comedy about the difficulties about being a not-so-successful stand-up comedian. Though Bruce Madsen (Carolla) moved from stand-up comedy to acting in film and television, his career has hit a downward cycle. To try to bring his career back to life, he goes back on the road playing comedy clubs, flying coach, and spending nights in budget hotel rooms. Also trying to have a love life and put his daughter through college, Bruce finds the comedy grind unbearable and does all he can to get off the road. **98m/C; DVD, Blu-Ray, Streaming, Download.** Adam Carolla; Larry Clarke; Jonathan Klein; Jim O'Heir; Jay Mohr; **D:** Adam Carolla; Kevin Hench; **W:** Adam Carolla; Kevin Hench; **C:** Marten Tedin; **M:** Andrew Johnson.

The Road Home 🦴🦴🦴 *Wo De Fu Qin Mu Qin* **2001 (G)** Sweet story about enduring love. Luo Yuseng (Honglei) returns to his Chinese village to bury his father. He learns his mother wants to have a funeral ritual performed as a mark of respect, which involves carrying the coffin to the cemetery. Flashbacks show how young illiterate beauty Zhao Di (Ziyi) caught the eye of Luo Changyu (Hao), the new schoolteacher, who comes from the city and is of a higher class. But Changyu falls victim to the political climate of the '50s and must leave her behind, promising to return. And she promises to wait. The flashbacks are filmed in color while the present is filmed in B&W. Chinese with subtitles. **89m/C; DVD.** *CH* Ziyi Zhang; Honglei Sun; Zheng Hao; Zhao Yuelin; Bin Li; **D:** Yimou Zhang; **W:** Bao Shi; **C:** Hou Yong; **M:** San Bao.

Road House 🦴🦴 1/2 **1948** Nightclub singer Lupino inspires noir feelings between jealous road house owner Widmark and his partner Wilde. Widmark sets up Wilde to take the fall for a faked robbery, convinces the law to release him into his custody, then dares him to escape. **95m/B; VHS, DVD, Blu-Ray.** Richard Widmark; Ida Lupino; Cornel Wilde; Celeste Holm; O.Z. Whitehead; **D:** Jean Negulesco; **W:** Edward Chodorov; Oscar Saul; **C:** Joseph LaShelle; **M:** Cyril Mockridge.

Road House 🦴 1/2 **1989 (R)** Bouncer Swayze is hired to do the impossible: clean up the toughest bar in Kansas City. When he lays down his rules he makes a lot of enemies, including ex-bar employees and local organized crime. Ample violence; an example of formula filmmaking at its most brain-numbing, with a rock soundtrack. **115m/C; VHS, DVD, Blu-Ray, UMD; Open Captioned.** Patrick Swayze; Sam Elliott; Kelly Lynch; Ben Gazzara; Kevin Tighe; Marshall Teague; Julie Michaels; Jeff Healey; ***D:*** Rowdy Herrington; ***C:*** Dean Cundey; ***M:*** Michael Kamen.

Road House 2: Last Call 🦴 1/2 **2006 (R)** Dopey sequel to the 1989 cheese-fest. Nate Tanner (Patton) is the owner of a rowdy Louisiana road house called the Black Pelican. When local drug runner Wild Bill (wildly overacted by Busey) and his minions want to take over the place, Nate's DEA nephew Shane (Schaech) decides to forcibly discourage them. Many brawls follow. **86m/C; DVD, Blu-Ray.** Johnathon Schaech; Jake Busey; Will Patton; William Ragsdale; Ellen Hollman; ***D:*** Scott Ziehl; ***W:*** Johnathon Schaech; Richard Chizmar; ***M:*** Amotz Plessner. **VIDEO**

The Road Killers 🦴🦴 **1995 (R)** Sickening psycho Cliff (well-played by Sheffer) is head of a brutal quartet that terrorizes a family driving along a remote desert highway. Cliff kidnaps the family daughter and her mild-mannered dad (Lambert) must rescue her. **89m/C; VHS, DVD.** Christopher Lambert; Craig Sheffer; Adrienne Shelly; ***D:*** Deran Sarafian; ***W:*** Tedi Sarafian.

Road Movie 🦴🦴 1/2 **1972** Cult favorite about a pair of brutish truck drivers (Bostwick and Drivas) who pick up a prostitute (Baff) on a trip across America. Baff delivers an emotional performance as the beaten and furious hooker who, after being abused and rejected, seeks her revenge. **82m/C; DVD.** Barry Bostwick; Robert Drivas; Regina Baff; ***D:*** Joseph Strick; ***W:*** Judith Rascoe; ***C:*** Don Lenzer.

Road of No Return 🦴 **2009** They might be prominently featured in the promo material, but Carradine and Madsen only have small supporting roles. Four hit men are hired by a shady government agency to eliminate drug traffickers the agency can't get to legally. Then the government guys decide to cover their own backsides by eliminating the hit men. **94m/C; DVD.** Shane Woodson; Ernest Anthony; Jose Andrews; Michael Blain-Rozgay; David Carradine; Michael Madsen; ***D:*** Parviz Saghizadeh; ***W:*** Parviz Saghizadeh; ***M:*** Gerard Barbut. **VIDEO**

Road Racers 🦴🦴 **1959** The roar of the engine, fast cars, and family ties combine in this movie about the thrill of speed. **73m/B; VHS, DVD.** Joel Lawrence; Marian Collier; Skip Ward; ***D:*** Arthur Swerdloff; ***W:*** Stanley Kallis; Ed Lasko.

Road Rage WOOF! *A Friday Night Date* **2001** The familiar plot wouldn't be so bad if there was some suspense or twists to this flick but there's not. Jim offers Sonia a ride home after breaking up a fight between Sonia and her possessive ex-boyfriend Bo. While driving, Jim cuts off a big rig, whose driver decides to get even. It won't be any surprise to discover the truck's driver is Bo. Blah. **96m/C; VHS, DVD.** Casper Van Dien; Danielle Brett; Catherine Oxenberg; Joseph Griffin; ***D:*** Sidney J. Furie; ***W:*** Greg Mellott; ***C:*** Curtis Petersen; ***M:*** Robert Carli. **VIDEO**

Road Show 🦴🦴 1/2 **1941** Hubbard stars as a young man wrongfully committed to an insane asylum. He escapes and joins a bankrupt carnival owned by Landis. Some really zany stuff keeps this from being just standard fare. Co-written by silent film comic Langdon. **87m/B; VHS, DVD.** Adolphe Menjou; Carole Landis; John Hubbard; Charles Butterworth; Patsy Kelly; George E. Stone; Polly Ann Young; Edward Norris; Marjorie Woodworth; Florence Bates; ***D:*** Hal Roach; ***W:*** Harry Langdon.

The Road to Bali 🦴🦴🦴 **1953** Sixth Bob-n-Bing road show, the only one in color, is a keeper. The boys are competing for the love of—that's right—Lamour. She must be some gal, cuz they chase her all the way to Bali, where they meet cannibals and other perils, including the actual Humphrey Bogart. Jones's debut, in a bit role. **90m/C; VHS, DVD, Blu-Ray.** Bob Hope; Bing Crosby; Dorothy Lamour; Murvyn Vye; Ralph Moody; Jane Russell; Jerry Lewis; Dean Martin; Carolyn Jones; ***D:*** Hal Walker; ***W:*** Frank Butler; Hal Kanter; William Morrow; ***C:*** George Barnes.

The Road to Coronation Street 🦴🦴 1/2 **2010** The TV movie celebrates the 50th anniversary of the popular Brit series. In 1960, former child actor turned scriptwriter Tony Warren is pitching a new soap opera series that's set in working-class Manchester. The network execs are reluctant to take the gamble and only order 13 episodes, so Tony has to make sure his cast and story catch the viewers' attention quickly. **101m/C; DVD.** *GB* David Dawson; Steven Berkoff; Jane Horrocks; Lynda Baron; Shaun Dooley; Henry Goodman; Christian McKay; John Thompson; ***D:*** Charles Sturridge; ***W:*** Daran Little; ***C:*** Tim Palmer; ***M:*** Adrian Johnston. **TV**

The Road to El Dorado 🦴🦴 1/2 **2000 (PG)** Spanish con men Tulio (Kline) and Miguel (Branagh) search for the legendary Lost City of Gold in this animated adventure. The duo hitch a ride with Cortes' expedition to South America, land among the natives, and are mistaken for gods. They also run into a beautiful local (Perez) who's onto their game, and run afoul of a priest (Assante), who's fond of human sacrifice and wants to overthrow the kindly chief (Olmos). As usual, the DreamWorks animation is superb and there are enjoyable moments, but a weak plot and nondescript characters add up to a somewhat disappointing outing. **90m/C; VHS, DVD, Blu-Ray.** ***V:*** Kevin Kline; Kenneth Branagh; Rosie Perez; Armand Assante; Edward James Olmos; ***Nar:*** Sir Elton John; ***D:*** Eric Bergeron; Don Paul; ***W:*** Ted Elliott; Terry Rossio; ***M:*** Sir Elton John; Hans Zimmer; John Powell; ***M:*** Tim Rice.

The Road to Glory 🦴🦴 **1936** A WWI French regiment deals with life in the trenches. Capt. LaRoche (Baxter) turns to drink as he continually sends his recruits out to be slaughtered. His only solace is young nurse Monique (Lang), but even this is taken away when she prefers carefree newcomer Lt. Denet (March), who quickly becomes disillusioned. Remake of the 1932 French film "Les Croix des Bois." **101m/B; DVD.** Fredric March; Warner Baxter; Lionel Barrymore; June Lang; Gregory Ratoff; Victor Kilian; ***D:*** Howard Hawks; ***W:*** William Faulkner; Joel Sayre; ***C:*** Gregg Toland.

The Road to Guantanamo 🦴🦴 **2006 (R)** Political docudrama from Winterbottom and Whitecross focuses on the misfortunes of the "Tipton Three." These young British Muslims are in Pakistan for a wedding immediately after 9/11 and then travel to Afghanistan (apparently for humanitarian reasons). Big mistake—they get rounded up by Northern Alliance troops and are guilty until proven innocent, which takes years of military imprisonment and interrogation at Gitmo (film covers 2001-2004). **95m/C; DVD.** *GB* Rizwan Ahmed; Farhad Harun; Waqar Siddiqui; Afran Usman; ***D:*** Michael Winterbottom; Mat Whitecross; ***C:*** Marcel Zyskind; ***M:*** Molly Nyman; Harry Escott. Ind. Spirit '07: Feature Doc.

The Road to Hong Kong 🦴🦴 1/2 **1962** Last of the Crosby/Hope team-ups shows some wear, but still manages charm and humor. Lamour appears only briefly in this twisted comedy of hustlers caught in international espionage and cosmic goingson. **91m/B; VHS, DVD, Blu-Ray.** Bob Hope; Bing Crosby; Joan Collins; Dorothy Lamour; Peter Sellers; ***D:*** Norman Panama; ***W:*** Norman Panama; ***C:*** Jack Hildyard.

The Road to Morocco 🦴🦴🦴 1/2 **1942** The third in the road movie series finds Hope and Crosby in Morocco, stranded and broke. To get some money, Crosby sells Hope into slavery to be the princess's (Lamour) personal plaything. Feeling guilty, Crosby returns to the palace to rescue Hope, only to find that he and the princess are getting married because the royal astrologer said it was in the stars. Crosby then tries to woo Lamour and, when the astrologer discovers the stars were mistaken, those two decide to marry. Quinn, however, also wants her and hilarious scenes ensue when the boys rescue Lamour from him. One of the funniest in the series. Watch for the camel at the end. **83m/B; VHS, DVD, Blu-Ray.** Bing Crosby; Bob Hope; Dorothy Lamour; Anthony Quinn; Dona Drake; Vladimir Sokoloff; Yvonne De Carlo; ***D:*** David Butler; ***W:*** Frank Butler; Don Hartman; ***C:*** William Mellor. Natl. Film Reg. '96.

Road to Nashville 🦴🦴 **1967 (G)** An agent travels to Nashville to enlist talent for a new musical. Why do so many of these semi-musicals insist on having a plot? Good music. **110m/C; VHS, DVD.** Marty Robbins; Johnny Cash; Doodles Weaver; Connie Smith; Richard Arlen; ***D:*** Robert Patrick.

Road to Paloma 🦴🦴 1/2 **2014 (R)** The directorial debut of Jason Momoa, this dramatic thriller road movie of one man being chased after serving up justice. After avenging the murder of his mother, Wolf (Momoa) goes on the run across the American West on a motorcycle. Traveling across desolate regions, his quest for redemption leads him to discover unexpected secrets, experience roads with unforeseen turns, and pay a price he could not have anticipated. **91m/C; DVD, Blu-Ray.** Jason Momoa; Lisa Bonet; Lance Henriksen; Timothy V. Murphy; Kelly Noonan; ***D:*** Jason Momoa; ***W:*** Jason Momoa; Robert Homer Mollohan; Jonathan Hirschbein; ***C:*** Brian Mendoza; ***M:*** Ohad Benchetrit; Justin Small.

Road to Paradise 🦴 1/2 **1930** This early talkie has a completely nonsensical story but a charming turn by Young in a dual role. Orphaned Mary Brennan was raised by a couple of good-natured crooks who plan to rob the mansion of the wealthy Waring family. As it turns out, Margaret Waring is Mary's long-lost twin, the scheme goes awry, and Mary tries impersonating Margaret to keep them out of trouble. **76m/B; DVD.** Loretta Young; Jack Mulhall; Raymond Hatton; George Barraud; Kathlyn Williams; Purnell Pratt; ***D:*** William Beaudine; ***W:*** F. Hugh Herbert; ***C:*** John Seitz.

Road to Perdition 🦴🦴🦴🦴 **2002 (R)** Michael Sullivan (Hanks) is a Depression-era hitman who must take his teenage son Michael Jr. (Hoechlin) on the run as he seeks revenge on the people who betrayed him and killed his wife and youngest son. Dark, atmospheric tale excels on the strength of the brilliantly understated screenplay and outstanding performances, highlighted by Hanks's tormented hitman/father and Newman's conflicted mob boss. Based on the 1998 graphic novel by Max Allan Collins and Richard Piers Rayner. **116m/C; VHS, DVD, Blu-Ray.** Tom Hanks; Paul Newman; Jude Law; Tyler Hoechlin; Jennifer Jason Leigh; Stanley Tucci; Daniel Craig; Liam Aiken; Ciaran Hinds; Dylan Baker; David Darlow; Mina Badie; ***D:*** Sam Mendes; ***W:*** David Self; ***C:*** Conrad L. Hall; ***M:*** Thomas Newman. Oscars '02: Cinematog.; British Acad. '02: Cinematog.

Road to Riches 🦴🦴🦴 *Strange Hearts* **2001 (R)** This independent feature by first-timer Gallagher is a happy surprise, thanks especially to McGowan and Forster. Middle-aged Jack (Forster) is very protective of the emotionally disturbed Moira (McGowan). Then cocky, handsome, and exceptionally lucky young Henry (Pardue) comes along and takes Moira away without realizing the extent of her problems. Jack is not about to let her go so easily, but he needs some good luck of his own to get her back. **90m/C; VHS, DVD.** Robert Forster; Rose McGowan; Kip Pardue; Harry Hamlin; ***D:*** Michelle Gallagher; ***W:*** Michelle Gallagher; ***C:*** Adam Holender; ***M:*** Fletcher Beasley.

The Road to Rio 🦴🦴🦴 1/2 **1947** The wisecracking duo travel to Rio De Janeiro to prevent Spanish beauty Lamour (there she is again) from going through with an arranged marriage. Top-notch entry; fifth in the "Road" series. **100m/B; VHS, DVD, Blu-Ray.** Bing Crosby; Bob Hope; Dorothy Lamour; Gale Sondergaard; Frank Faylen; Andrews Sisters; ***D:*** Norman Z. McLeod; ***W:*** Jack Rose; ***C:*** Ernest Laszlo.

The Road to Singapore 🦴🦴 1/2 **1940** This is the movie that started it all. Crosby and Hope decide to swear off women and escape to Singapore to enjoy the free life. There they meet Lamour, a showgirl who is abused by Quinn. The boys rescue Lamour, but soon find they are both falling for her. She's in love with one of them, but won't reveal her feelings. Who will get the girl? Not as funny as some of the other road movies, but it's great for a first try. **84m/C; VHS, DVD, Blu-Ray.** Bing Crosby; Bob Hope; Dorothy Lamour; Charles Coburn; Judith Barrett; Anthony Quinn; Jerry Colonna; Johnny Arthur; Pierre Watkin; ***D:*** Victor Schertzinger; ***W:*** Frank Butler; Don Hartman; ***C:*** William Mellor.

The Road to Utopia 🦴🦴🦴 **1946** Fourth of the "Road" films, wherein the boys wind up in Alaska posing as two famous escaped killers in order to locate a secret gold mine. One of the series' funniest and most spontaneous entries, abetted by Benchley's dry, upper-crust comments. **90m/B; VHS, DVD, Blu-Ray.** Bing Crosby; Bob Hope; Dorothy Lamour; Jack La Rue; Robert Benchley; Douglass Dumbrille; Hillary Brooke; Robert Barrat; Nestor Paiva; ***D:*** Hal Walker; ***W:*** Norman Panama; Melvin Frank; ***C:*** Lionel Lindon; ***M:*** Johnny Burke; Leigh Harline; James Van Heusen.

The Road to Wellville 🦴🦴 **1994 (R)** Corn flake magnate John Harvey Kellogg takes good health to an intestine-invading extreme in this spa satire featuring Hopkins as the buck-toothed Kellogg. Broderick and Fonda portray a wealthy couple who visit the turn-of-the-century sanitarium in search of Kellogg's cure, but receive only sexual frustration and anal humiliations. Bowel jokes and an essentially plotless scenario overshadow a gifted, but helpless cast. Adapted from T. Coraghessan Boyle's not-so-easily-adaptable novel. **120m/C; VHS, DVD.** Anthony Hopkins; Bridget Fonda; Matthew Broderick; John Cusack; Dana Carvey; Michael Lerner; Colm Meaney; John Neville; Lara Flynn Boyle; Traci Lind; Roy Brocksmith; Norbert Weisser; ***D:*** Alan Parker; ***W:*** Alan Parker; ***C:*** Peter Biziou; ***M:*** Rachel Portman.

The Road to Yesterday 🦴🦴 1/2 **1925** Two couples together on a crashing train are somehow thrown into the 18th century in roles parallel to their own lives. DeMille's first independent film; intriguing action/melodrama. Silent with musical soundtrack. **136m/B; Silent; VHS, DVD.** Joseph Schildkraut; William Boyd; Jetta Goudal; Vera Reynolds; Iron Eyes Cody; ***D:*** Cecil B. DeMille.

The Road to Zanzibar 🦴🦴🦴 **1941** After selling a fake diamond mine to a criminal, Crosby and Hope flee to Zanzibar, where they meet up with Lamour and Merkel. The guys put up the money for a safari, supposedly to look for Lamour's brother, but they soon discover that they too have been tricked. Deciding to head back to Zanzibar, Crosby and Hope find themselves surrounded by hungry cannibals. Will they survive, or will they be someone's dinner? Not as funny as the other road movies, but amusing nonetheless. **92m/C; VHS, DVD, Blu-Ray.** Bing Crosby; Bob Hope; Dorothy Lamour; Una Merkel; Eric Blore; Iris Adrian; Lionel Royce; ***D:*** Victor Schertzinger; ***W:*** Frank Butler; Don Hartman; ***C:*** Ted Tetzlaff.

Road Trip 🦴🦴 1/2 **2000 (R)** Extremely low-brow comedy about four college buddies who set out on an 1,800-mile road trip (from New York to Texas) in order to intercept an incriminating videotape Josh (Meyer) has mistakenly mailed to his long-distance girlfriend. Green does disgusting things to a defenseless white mouse, and there's the usual frat-house sexual humor, but like most teen comedies these days, it's quotable, laugh-even-though-you-know-better funny, and basically harmless. **91m/C; DVD, Blu-Ray.** Breckin Meyer; Seann William Scott; Rachel Blanchard; DJ Qualls; Fred Ward; Andy Dick; Paulo Costanzo; Tom Green; Amy Smart; Anthony Rapp; Ethan Suplee; ***D:*** Todd Phillips; ***W:*** Todd Phillips; Scot Armstrong; ***C:*** Mark Irwin; ***M:*** Mike Simpson.

Road Trip: Beer Pong 🦴 **2009 (R)** Usual dumb raunchy comedy with Qualls taking over as the framing device narrator from the first flick. Graduate student Kyle is giving a campus tour to prospective students when he relates a story about a legendary road trip (shown in flashbacks). Andy and some buds are headed out to a national beer pong championship with Andy's secondary mission to hook up with hottie ex-girlfriend Jenna. **96m/C; DVD.** Preston Jones; Danny Pudi; Michael Trotter; Daniel Newman; Nestor Aaron Absera; DJ Qualls; Julianna Guill; Julia Levy-Boeken; ***D:*** Steve Rash; ***W:*** Brad Riddell; ***C:*** Levie Isaacks. **VIDEO**

The Road Warrior 🦴🦴🦴 1/2 *Mad Max 2* **1982 (R)** The first sequel to "Mad Max" takes place after nuclear war has destroyed

Australia. Max helps a colony of oil-drilling survivors defend themselves from the roving murderous outback gangs and escape to the coast. The climactic chase scene is among the most exciting ever filmed; this film virtually created the "action-adventure" picture of the 1980s. **95m/C; VHS, DVD, Blu-Ray, HD-DVD.** *AU* Mel Gibson; Bruce Spence; Emil Minty; Vernon Wells; Virginia Hey; Max Phipps; Mike (Michael) Preston; William Zappa; *D:* George Miller; *W:* George Miller; Terry Hayes; *C:* Dean Semler; *M:* Brian May. L.A. Film Critics '82: Foreign Film.

Roadblock ✌✌ **1951** Low-budget pulp noir plot about a schnook who's done in by a dame. L.A. insurance investigator Joe falls for Diane, who has a taste for the good life that he can't afford. He gets involved in a mail train robbery to get some dough and his partner Harry figures out Joe was the inside man so Joe tries to make a run for it. **73m/B; DVD.** Charles McGraw; Joan Dixon; Louis Jean Heydt; Milburn Stone; Lowell Gilmore; *D:* Harold Daniels; *W:* George Bricker; Steve Fisher; *C:* Nicholas Musuraca; *M:* Paul Sawtell.

Roadhouse 66 ✌ 1/2 **1984 (R)** Utterly unoriginal broke-down-in-a-hick-town nonsense. Snooty Reinhold and scruffy Dafoe go through the motions, and of course find a pair of female companions. Soundtrack features Los Lobos, the Pretenders, and Dave Edmunds. **90m/C; VHS, DVD.** Willem Dafoe; Judge Reinhold; Karen Lee; Kate Vernon; Stephen Elliott; *D:* John Mark Robinson; *C:* Thomas Ackerman.

Roadie ✌ 1/2 **1980 (PG)** Supposedly a look at the back-stage world of rock 'n' roll, but the performance and direction leave a lot to be desired. Meatloaf is a roadie who desperately wants to meet Alice Cooper, and spends the movie trying to do so. Features Art Carney, and musical names like Blondie, Roy Orbison, Hank Williams Jr., and Don Cornelius (of "Soul Train" fame). **105m/C; VHS, DVD, Blu-Ray.** Meat Loaf Aday; Kaki Hunter; Art Carney; Gailard Sartain; Alice Cooper; Roy Orbison; Hank Williams, Jr.; Ramblin' Jack Elliot; *D:* Alan Rudolph; *W:* Alan Rudolph; Michael Ventura.

Roadie ✌✌ **2011 (R)** Awkward, uneven drama. After 20 years as a roadie for Blue Oyster Cult, 40-year-old burnout Jimmy is fired before the band's latest tour. With nowhere else to go, he returns to his ailing Mom's home in Queens to help care for her. Jimmy's been lying about his success in the music business, which comes back to bite him when he tries to rekindle a romance with ex-flame Nikki, whose overbearing husband Randy, who bullied Jimmy in high school, is still a jerk. **96m/C; DVD, Blu-Ray.** Ron Eldard; Jill Hennessy; Bobby Cannavale; Lois Smith; David Margulies; Catherine Wolf; *D:* Michael Cuesta; *W:* Michael Cuesta; Gerald Cuesta; *C:* Andrew Lilian; *M:* Chris Seefried.

Roadkill ✌ **1989** Cheap thriller about Ramona (Buhagiar), a concert promoter who tries to find a lost band, "The Children of Paradise," in the Canadian north woods. Along the way, she meets a would-be serial killer and other assorted weirdos. **85m/B; VHS, DVD.** *CA* Valerie Buhagiar; Don McKellar; Bruce McDonald; *D:* Bruce McDonald; *W:* Don McKellar. Toronto-City '89: Canadian Feature Film.

Roadkill ✌ **2011** Nonsense from the Syfy Channel involving an RV road trip in Ireland taken by a bunch of clueless Americans. They manage to run over an old gypsy woman on a back road and she curses them before dying by declaring the Simuroc will get her revenge. They flee the scene and soon find out that the Simuroc is an ancient bird of prey who's eager to hunt, kill, and devour. **88m/C; DVD.** Kacey Barnfield; Colin Maher; Oliver James; Eliza Bennett; Ned Dennehy; Stephen Rea; *D:* Johannes Roberts; *W:* Rick Suvalle; *C:* Peter Robinson; *M:* Ray Harman. **CABLE**

Roadracers ✌✌ **1994 (R)** Made as part of Showtime's "Rebel Highway" series, Rodriguez basically takes the title from the 1959 AIP low-budgeter and goes his own way. Leather-clad rebel Dude Delaney (Arquette) has a voluptuous Latino dreamgirl named Donna (Hayek) and a gang which faces off against the clique led by rival Teddy Leather (Wiles) in drag races and roller rinks all around town. Great rockabilly soundtrack. **95m/C; VHS, DVD, Blu-Ray.** David Arquette; Jason Wiles; Salma Hayek; John Hawkes; William Sadler; O'Neal Compton; Lance LeGault; Karen Landry; Tommy Nix; *D:* Robert Rodriguez; *W:* Robert Rodriguez; Tommy Nix; *C:* Roberto Schaefer; *M:* Paul Boll; Johnny Reno. **CABLE**

Roadside ✌✌ **2015** A suspenseful thriller centered on a couple stuck in a dangerous game with a gunmen. Traveling along an isolated mountain road, Dan Summers (Marrero) and his pregnant wife Mindy (Stegeman) must stop because of a tree in the road. When Dan leaves their vehicle to remove the object, he and his wife find themselves trapped by a mysterious gunman before he can get back inside. Stuck in unforgiving darkness and terrified by their unknown attacker, the hostage couple struggles to survive the game they do not fully understand. **100m/C; DVD, Streaming, Download.** Ace Marrero; Katie Stegeman; Lionel D. Carson; Marshall Yates; Jack Curenton; *D:* Eric England; *W:* Eric England; *C:* Dan Hertzog; *M:* Igor Nemirovsky. **VIDEO**

Roadside Prophets ✌✌ **1992 (R)** Counter-culture road trip, striving to be the '90s version of "Easy Rider," follows factory worker/biker Joe (Doe) on his mission to transport the ashes of a fellow biker to Nevada. He is accompanied by the pesky younger Sam (Horovitz), and together they meet up with lots of eccentrics and stay at lots of cheap motels. Interesting cast meanders through sentimental and slow-moving buddy flick from debut director Wool, who wrote "Sid and Nancy." Cusack completes the cameo hat trick, with appearances here and in 1992's "The Player" and "Shadows and Fog." **96m/C; VHS, DVD.** John Doe; Adam Horovitz; David Carradine; Timothy Leary; Arlo Guthrie; Barton Heyman; Jennifer Balgobin; John David (J.D.) Cullum; *Cameo(s):* John Cusack; *D:* Abbe Wool; *W:* Abbe Wool.

The Roaring Twenties ✌✌✌ 1/2 **1939** Eddie (Cagney), George (Bogart), and Lloyd (Lynn) are three WWI buddies who find their lives intersecting unexpectedly in Prohibition-era New York. Eddie becomes a bootlegger and vies with George for status as crime boss. Lloyd is the attorney working to prosecute them. Great gangster flick was the last time Bogart and Cagney worked together after "Angels with Dirty Faces" (1938) and "The Oklahoma Kid" (1939). Cheesy script delivered with zest by top pros. **106m/B; VHS, DVD.** James Cagney; Humphrey Bogart; Jeffrey Lynn; Priscilla Lane; Gladys George; Frank McHugh; Paul Kelly; Joseph (Joe) Sawyer; *D:* Raoul Walsh; *W:* Robert Rossen; Richard Macaulay; *C:* Ernest Haller; *M:* Heinz Roemheld; Ray Heindorf.

Rob Roy ✌✌✌ **1995 (R)** Overlong tale of legendary Scot Robert Roy MacGregor mixes love and honor with bloodlust and revenge. Neeson's rugged clan leader fends off a band of dastardly nobles led by Cunningham (Roth), a foppish twit with an evil bent. Misty highland scenery and intense romantic interplay between Neeson and Lange as the spirited Mary MacGregor lend a passionate twist to an otherwise earthy, robust adventure of lore capped by one of the best sword fights ever. Visually stunning, with location shooting in the Scottish Highlands. More ambience is provided by Buswell's evocative score. **144m/C; VHS, DVD, Blu-Ray.** Liam Neeson; Jessica Lange; Tim Roth; John Hurt; Eric Stoltz; Andrew Keir; Brian Cox; Brian McCardie; Gilbert Martin; Vicki Masson; David Hayman; Jason Flemyng; Shirley Henderson; Gilly Gilchrist; John Murtagh; Ewan Stewart; *D:* Michael Caton-Jones; *W:* Alan Sharp; *C:* Karl Walter Lindenlaub; Roger Deakins; *M:* Carter Burwell. British Acad. '95: Support. Actor (Roth).

Rob Roy—The Highland Rogue ✌ 1/2 *Rob Roy* **1953** In the early 18th century, Scottish Highlander Rob Roy must battle against the King of England's secretary, who would undermine the MacGregor clan to enact his evil deeds. Dull Disney drama. **84m/C; VHS, DVD.** Richard Todd; Glynis Johns; James Robertson Justice; Michael Gough; *D:* Harold French.

Rob the Mob ✌✌ 1/2 **2014 (R)** Tommy (Pitt) and Rosie (Arianda) are a pair of simple criminals who make the arguably unwise decision to start robbing Mafia-owned clubs and stumble upon a closely guarded mob secret. Big Al (Garcia) wants to return the secret to its rightful place while the Feds want to use the crooks to their legal advantage. Hijinks ensue. Another tale of small-time crooks gets a bit of energy from a talented cast and a director who never allows the story to turn into the stereotypical Big Apple caper that it could have become. **104m/C; DVD, Blu-Ray.** Michael Pitt; Nina Arianda; Andy Garcia; Ray Romano; Griffin Dunne; Burt Young; Frank Whaley; Michael Rispoli; Aida Turturro; *D:* Raymond De Felitta; *W:* Jonathan Fernandez; *C:* Christopher Norr; *M:* Stephen Endelman.

Robbers' Roost ✌✌ **1955** Cattle rustler Hank Hays (Boone) and his rival Heesman (Graves) have been hired by crippled cattle baron Herrick (Bennett) to get his cows to market. Herrick thinks the thieves will be too busy watching each other to rustle his cows although his sister Helen (Findley) doesn't agree. Jim Wall (Montgomery) is after the last of three men who murdered his wife, and it leads him to the cattle drive. Based on a Zane Grey story; remake of the 1933 film. **82m/C; DVD, Blu-Ray.** George Montgomery; Richard Boone; Peter Graves; Bruce Bennett; Sylvia Findley; Leo Gordon; *D:* Sidney Salkow; *W:* Sidney Salkow; John O'Dea; Maurice Geraghty; *C:* Jack Draper; *M:* Paul Dunlap.

Robbery under Arms ✌✌ 1/2 **1957** From Australia in the 1800s, similar to the American wild west, comes a tale of love and robbery. Finch is the leader of a band of outlaws. Rather dull story redeemed by excellent photography of beautiful landscape. **83m/C; VHS, DVD.** *GB* Peter Finch; Ronald Lewis; Laurence Naismith; Maureen Swanson; David McCallum; Jill Ireland; *D:* Jack Lee.

The Robe ✌✌ 1/2 **1953** This moving, religious portrait follows the career and religious awakening of drunken and dissolute Roman tribune Marcellus (Burton), after he wins the robe of the just-crucified Christ in a dice game. Mature plays Burton's slave surprisingly well, and reprised the role in the sequel, "Demetrius and the Gladiators"; Burton is wooden. "The Robe" was the first movie to be filmed in CinemaScope. Based on the novel by Lloyd C. Douglas. **133m/C; VHS, DVD, Blu-Ray.** Richard Burton; Jean Simmons; Victor Mature; Michael Rennie; Richard Boone; Dean Jagger; Jeff Morrow; Jay Robinson; Dawn Addams; Ernest Thesiger; Torin Thatcher; *D:* Henry Koster; *W:* Albert (John B. Sherry) Maltz; Philip Dunne; *C:* Leon Shamroy. Oscars '53: Art Dir./Set Dec., Color, Costume Des. (C); Golden Globes '54: Film--Drama; Natl. Bd. of Review '53: Actress (Simmons).

The Robert Benchley Miniatures Collection ✌✌ 1/2 **1935** Writer and humorist Robert Benchley made 30 theatrical shorts for MGM between 1935 and 1944 as he commented on such everyday subjects as training a dog, figuring out income taxes, and enjoying a movie. Also included is Benchley's debut short, "How to Sleep," which won an Academy Award. **267m/B; DVD.** Robert Benchley; *D:* Jules White; *W:* Robert Benchley.

Robert Kennedy and His Times ✌✌ 1/2 **1990** Another look at the Kennedy clan, this time from the Bobby angle. Good acting. Based on the book by Arthur Schlesinger. **309m/C; VHS, DVD.** Brad Davis; Veronica Cartwright; Cliff DeYoung; Ned Beatty; Beatrice Straight; Jack Warden; *D:* Marvin J. Chomsky.

Robert Louis Stevenson's The Game of Death ✌✌ 1/2 *The Suicide Club; The Game of Death; Robert Louis Stevenson's The Suicide Club* **1999 (R)** This version sticks to the spirit of Stevenson's story (which was filmed in 1936 as "Trouble for Two") but adds plotlines and characters. It's 1899 and Henry Joyce (Morrissey) has decided to kill himself because of his lover's betrayal. He and pal, Captain May (Shuke), meet the equally suicidal Shaw (Bettany), who takes them along to the Suicide Club. Run by the mysterious Bourne (Pryce), its members willingly want to die—and both the next victim and their murderer are selected by a drawing of the cards. And you aren't allowed to change your mind. **89m/C; VHS, DVD.** David Morrissey; Jonathan Pryce; Paul Bettany; Neil Stuke; Catherine Siggins; *D:* Rachel Samuels; *W:* Lev L. Spiro; *C:* Chris Manley; *M:* Adrian Johnston.

Roberta ✌✌✌ **1935** A football player inherits his aunt's Parisian dress shop and finds himself at odds with an incognito Russian princess. Dumb plot aside, this is one of the best Astaire-Rogers efforts. A later remake was titled "Lovely to Look At." **85m/B; VHS, DVD.** Fred Astaire; Ginger Rogers; Irene Dunne; Lucille Ball; Randolph Scott; *D:* William A. Seiter; *M:* Max Steiner.

Robin and Marian ✌✌ **1976 (PG)** After a separation of 20 years, Robin Hood is reunited with Maid Marian, who is now a nun. Their dormant feelings for each other are reawakened as Robin spirits her to Sherwood Forest. In case you wanted to see Robin Hood robbed of all magic, spontaneity, and fun. Connery is dull, dull, dull, working with an uninspired script. **106m/C; VHS, DVD, Blu-Ray.** *GB* Sean Connery; Audrey Hepburn; Robert Shaw; Richard Harris; Denholm Elliott; Ian Holm; Nicol Williamson; Ronnie Barker; *D:* Richard Lester; *C:* David Watkin; *M:* John Barry.

Robin and the 7 Hoods ✌✌ 1/2 **1964** Runyon-esque Rat Pack version of 1920s Chicago, with Frank and the boys as do-good gangsters in their last go-round. Fun if not unforgettable. **124m/C; VHS, DVD, Blu-Ray.** Frank Sinatra; Bing Crosby; Dean Martin; Sammy Davis, Jr.; Peter Falk; Barbara Rush; Victor Buono; Hank Henry; Robert Foulk; Allen Jenkins; Jack La Rue; Edward G. Robinson; Hans Conried; Tony Randall; *D:* Gordon Douglas; *W:* John Fenton Murray; David R. Schwartz; *C:* William H. Daniels; *M:* Nelson Riddle; James Van Heusen.

Robin-B-Hood ✌✌ *Rob-B-Hood* **2006** Goofy two-men-and-a-baby crime comedy. Compulsive gamblers Thongs (Chan) and Octopus (Koo) steal to support their addiction. Their boss wants them to kidnap an infant for big bucks but they have to babysit the tyke until arrangements for transfer can be made. Despite many mishaps, the duo bond with baby and are reluctant to turn him over to a Triad leader, who thinks the boy is his grandson. Cantonese with subtitles. **134m/C; DVD.** *CH CH* Jackie Chan; Michael Hui; Yuen Biao; Chen Baoguo; Louis Koo; Yuanyuan Gao; *D:* Benny Chan; *W:* Jackie Chan; Benny Chan; *C:* Anthony Pun; *M:* Fai-young Chan.

Robin Cook's Invasion ✌✌ 1/2 *Invasion* **1997** College student Beau Stark (Perry) is one of many sickened by some kind of strange viral infection after being exposed to rocks of interstellar origin. The virus induces mutations and Beau works with scientists to find an antidote to the alien threat. A familiar story slickly done. **180m/C; VHS, DVD.** Luke Perry; Kim Cattrall; Rebecca Gayheart; Christopher Orr; Jon Polito; Neal McDonough; Jason Schombing; *D:* Armand Mastroianni; *W:* Rockne S. O'Bannon; *C:* Bryan England; *M:* Don Davis. **TV**

Robin Cook's Terminal ✌✌ *Terminal* **1996** Mediocre medical thriller. Cancer researcher Sean O'Grady (Savant) has just gotten an internship at a medical clinic that has a phenomenal cure rate for a particular type of brain cancer. Sean gets suspicious about the treatment and works with ex-girlfriend (and nurse) Janet (Peeples) to find out the truth. Which is always a bad idea in these sorts of movies because then lots of unsavory, suspicious types come after you. **90m/C; VHS, DVD.** Doug Savant; Nia Peeples; Michael Ironside; James Eckhouse; Roy Thinnes; Jenny O'Hara; Khandi Alexander; Gregg Henry; *D:* Larry Elikann; *W:* Nancy Isaak; *C:* Eric Van Haren Noman; *M:* Garry Schyman. **TV**

Robin Hood ✌✌✌ 1/2 **1922** Extravagant production casts Fairbanks as eponymous gymnastic swashbuckler who departs for Crusades as Earl of Huntington and returns as the hooded one to save King Richard's throne from the sinister Sheriff of Nottingham. Best ever silent swashbuckling. **110m/B; Silent; VHS, DVD.** Douglas Fairbanks, Sr.; Wallace Beery; Sam De Grasse; Enid Bennett; Paul Dickey; William E. (W.E., William A., W.A.) Lowery; Roy Coulson; Bill Bennett; Merrill McCormick; Wilson Benge; Willard Louis; Alan Hale; Maine Geary; Lloyd Talman; *D:* Allan

Dwan; *W:* Douglas Fairbanks, Sr.; *C:* Arthur Edeson.

Robin Hood 🦴🦴🦴 **1973** This time the Sherwood Forest crew are portrayed by appropriate cartoon animals, hence, Robin is a fox, Little John a bear, etc. Good family fare, but not as memorable as other Disney features. **83m/C; VHS, DVD, Blu-Ray.** *V:* Roger Miller; Brian Bedford; Monica Evans; Phil Harris; Andy Devine; Carol(e) Shelley; Peter Ustinov; Terry-Thomas; Pat Buttram; George Lindsey; Ken Curtis; *D:* Wolfgang Reitherman; *M:* George Bruns.

Robin Hood 🦴🦴🦴 **1991** Dark version of the medieval tale. Bergin's Prince of Thieves is well developed and Thurman is a graceful Marion. Three studios announced plans to remake "Robin Hood" in 1990 and two were completed, including this one which was scaled down for cable TV. **116m/C; VHS, DVD.** Patrick Bergin; Uma Thurman; Jurgen Prochnow; Edward Fox; Jeroen Krabbe; Jeff Nuttal; David Morrissey; Owen Teale; *D:* John Irvin; *M:* Geoffrey Burgon. **CABLE**

Robin Hood 🦴🦴 **2010 (PG-13)** This 5th collaboration between star Crowe and director Scott takes on the legendary English folk hero in a less-than-swashbuckling manner. Robin (Crowe) is an ex-crusader who has returned home to England after the death of King Richard. The newly-crowned King John (Isaac) is weak and the country is suffering so Robin gathers together a band of mercenaries to confront corruption, beginning with the despotic Sheriff of Nottingham (Macfadyen) though the widowed Marian (Blanchett) is suspicious of Robin's motives. Film loses much of the traditional "rob-from-the-rich" mythology for a more generic actioner full of battle scenes and speeches. **140m/C; DVD, Blu-Ray.** Russell Crowe; Cate Blanchett; Matthew Macfadyen; William Hurt; Mark Strong; Mark Addy; Scott Grimes; Kevin Durand; Eileen Atkins; Oscar Isaac; Danny Huston; Alan Doyle; *D:* Ridley Scott; *W:* Brian Helgeland; *C:* John Mathiesen; *M:* Marc Streitenfeld.

Robin Hood 🦴🦴 **2018 (PG-13)** This latest iteration of the public domain legend brings little new to the table aside from costuming (look Ma, no tights!) and racial diversity among the leads. Egerton has his charms as the title character, and he enjoys a bromance with his Foxx's Little John, but the love triangle with Maid Marian (Hewson) is a non-starter and the overuse of CGI effects is tiresome. **116m/C; DVD, Blu-Ray.** Taron Egerton; Jamie Foxx; Ben Mendelsohn; Eve Hewson; Jamie Dornan; *D:* Otto Bathurst; *W:* Ben Chandler; Daavid James Kelly; *C:* George Steel; *M:* Joseph Trapanese.

The Robin Hood Gang 🦴🦴 **1/2** *Angels in the Attic* **1998 (PG)** Brad (Taylor) and Frankie (Losack) are enterprising youngsters who collect empty soda cans to raise money to buy new bikes. But when they discover a suitcase full of cash in the attic of their apartment, they decide to share the wealth with their equally hard-up neighbors. When they learn that it's stolen bank loot, they must figure out how to catch the criminal and return the money. Nobody's going to mistake this modest kidvid for "Home Alone" but it's an acceptable time-waster for the short set. **86m/C; DVD.** Clayton Taylor; Steven Losak; Dalin Christiansen; Brenda Price; Scott Christopher; *D:* Eric Hendershot; *W:* Eric Hendershot; *C:* T.C. Christensen; *M:* Allen Williams. **VIDEO**

Robin Hood: Men in Tights 🦴🦴 **1/2** *Men in Tights* **1993 (PG-13)** Brooksian rendition of the classic legend inspires guffaws, but doesn't hit the bullseye on all it promises. Hood afficionados will appreciate the painstaking effort taken to spoof the 1938 Errol Flynn classic while leaving plenty of room to poke fun at the more recent Costner non-classic "Robin Hood: Prince of Thieves." Elwes, last seen swinging swords in "The Princess Bride," is well cast as the Flynn look-alike. Expect the usual off-color humor that's so prevalent in all Brooks outings. **105m/C; VHS, DVD, Blu-Ray.** Cary Elwes; Richard Lewis; Roger Rees; Tracey Ullman; Isaac Hayes; Amy Yasbeck; Mark Blankfield; Megan Cavanagh; Eric Allen Kramer; Tony Griffin; Dick Van Patten; Dave Chappelle; Mel Brooks; Patrick Stewart; Dom DeLuise; Robert Ridgely; Avery Schreiber; *D:* Mel Brooks; *W:* Mel Brooks; J. David Shapiro; Evan Chandler; *M:* Hummie Mann.

Robin Hood of Texas 🦴🦴 **1/2 1947** Autry finds his calm life disturbed when he is falsely accused of robbing a bank. Pretty good plot for once, in Autry's last Republic western, and plenty of action. **71m/B; VHS, DVD.** Gene Autry; Lynne Roberts; Sterling Holloway; Adele Mara; *D:* Lesley Selander.

Robin Hood: Prince of Thieves 🦴🦴 **1/2 1991 (PG-13)** Costner is a politically correct rebel, but a thinker, not a doer—and that's a problem. His quiet thoughtfulness doesn't add up to leadership and Rickman easily overpowers him as the wicked, crazed Sheriff of Nottingham. Freeman is excellent as a civilized Moor who finds England, and its people, inhospitable, dangerous, and not a little stupid, while Mastrantonio excels as the lovely Lady Marian. Great action sequences, a gritty and morbid picture of the Middle Ages, and some fun scenes with the Merry Men. Revisionist in its ideas about the times and people, critics generally disapproved of the changes in the story. **144m/C; VHS, DVD.** Kevin Costner; Morgan Freeman; Mary Elizabeth Mastrantonio; Christian Slater; Alan Rickman; Geraldine McEwan; Michael McShane; Brian Blessed; Michael Wincott; Nick Brimble; Harold Innocent; Jack Wild; *Cameo(s):* Sean Connery; *D:* Kevin Reynolds; *W:* Pen Densham; John Watson; *C:* Billy Milton; *M:* Michael Kamen. British Acad. '91: Support. Actor (Rickman); MTV Movie Awards '92: Song ("(Everything I Do) I Do for You"); Golden Raspberries '91: Worst Actor (Costner).

Robin Hood. . . The Legend: Robin Hood and the Sorcerer 🦴🦴 **1/2 1983** Robin Hood is chosen by the mystical Herne the Hunter to thwart the evil Sheriff of Nottingham and protect the English peasantry. He must defeat the supernatural powers of a sorcerer and gather together his men in this pilot for British TV. **115m/C; VHS, DVD.** *GB* Michael Praed; Anthony Valentine; Nickolas Grace; Clive Mantle; Peter Williams; *D:* Ian Sharp. **TV**

Robin of Locksley 🦴🦴 **1/2 1995 (PG)** A modern-day, teenaged Robin Hood (Sawa) battles the bullies at his private boys school (thanks to his archery prowess), meets a girl named Marian, and takes on sinister FBI agent Nottingham. **97m/C; VHS, DVD.** Devon Sawa; Sarah Chalke; Joshua Jackson; *D:* Michael Kennedy.

Robin's Hood 🦴🦴 **2003** Robin (Turner) is a black social worker in Oakland who is about to lose her job for caring too much about her clients. She meets thief Brooklyn (Cates) and together they start robbing banks and distributing the money to the neighborhood needy. But their crime spree can't last for long. **81m/C; DVD.** Khahtee V. Turner; Clody Cates; *D:* Sara Millman; *W:* Khahtee V. Turner; Sara Millman; *C:* Howard Shack.

Robinson Crusoe 🦴🦴 *The Adventures of Robinson Crusoe* **1954** Spanish surrealist Bunuel's only English-language film (and his first in color) is an unsentimental adaptation of the Daniel Defoe adventure classic. Slave trader Crusoe (O'Herlihy) is washed ashore on a deserted island after a shipwreck in 1659. He must learn to survive years of being alone until a cannibal band comes to the island and decides to make one of the group their next meal. Crusoe rescues the man, who becomes his servant/companion Friday (Fernandez). **90m/C; DVD.** *MX* Dan O'Herlihy; Jaime Fernandez; Felipe de Alba; Chel Lopez; *D:* Luis Bunuel; *W:* Luis Bunuel; Hugo Butler; *C:* Alex Phillips; *M:* Anthony Collins.

Robinson Crusoe 🦴🦴 **1/2** *Daniel Defoe's Robinson Crusoe* **1996 (PG-13)** Originally intended as a TV production, film got pushed to the big screen thanks to Brosnan's success as James Bond. He's the shipwrecked seaman and Takaku is Friday. First film to be shot in Papua, New Guinea. **105m/C; DVD.** Pierce Brosnan; William Takaku; Polly Walker; Ian Hart; Damian Lewis; Lysette Anthony; *D:* George Miller; *W:* Tracy Keenan Wynn; Christopher Canaan; *C:* David Connell.

Robinson Crusoe & the Tiger 🦴 **1/2 1972 (G)** A tiger tells the famous story of how Robinson Crusoe became stranded on a desert island. **109m/C; VHS, DVD.** Hugo Stiglitz; Ahui; *D:* Rene Cardona, Jr.

Robinson Crusoe of Clipper Island 🦴🦴 *Robinson Crusoe of Mystery Island* **1936** Fourteen-episode serial featuring the investigative expertise of Mala, a Polynesian in the employ of the U.S. Intelligence Service. Each episode runs 16 minutes. Shortened version titled "Robinson Crusoe of Mystery Island." **256m/B; VHS, DVD.** Mala; Rex; Buck; Kate Greenfield; John Ward; Ray Taylor; Tracy Lane; Robert F. (Bob) Kortman; Herbert Rawlinson; *D:* Mack V. Wright.

Robinson Crusoe on Mars 🦴 **1964** Sci-fi interpretation of Defoe classic. West is one of two daring scientists who take a monkey with them on a mission to outer space. When a meteor strikes their ship, it hurtles out of control towards the red planet and only Mantee and Mona survive the wreckage. They meet Lundin, an escaped slave and teach him English until evil slave traders spoil the fun. **109m/C; DVD, Blu-Ray.** Adam West; Vic Lundin; Paul Mantee; *D:* Byron Haskin; *W:* Ib Melchior; John C. Higgins; *C:* Winton C. Hoch; *M:* Nathan Van Cleave.

Robinson Crusoe: The Great Blitzkrieg 🦴 **2008** Bizarre re-interpretation of Daniel Defoe's novel which has Robinson Crusoe as humanity's savior in a far-flung future in which Earth is being invaded by time traveling alien Nazis who have resurrected Hitler. **102m/C; DVD.** Kaiwi Lyman; *D:* George Anton; *W:* George Anton; *C:* George Anton.

Robo-Dog 🦴🦴 **1/2 2015** A family-friendly, dog-centered robot film. When the family dog dies in a tragic incident, Tyler Austin (Campion) feels like he has lost his best friend. Fortunately, his father Tom (Muldoon) is an inventor. Using spare parts and his new invention called the super battery, Tom builds a new robot dog for his son. However, Mr. Willis (Shawn), Tom's former employer, wants this super battery and goes to extremes to obtain it. After getting his hands on an unstable version of the super battery, Willis uses it and puts the town in jeopardy, until the robot dog uses his special abilities to help save everyone. **90m/C; DVD, Blu-Ray, Streaming, Download.** Wallace Shawn; Olivia D'Abo; Michael Campion; James Arnold Taylor; Patrick Muldoon; *D:* Jason Murphy; *W:* Anthony Steven Giordano; *C:* Kraig Swisher; *M:* Danny Fontana. **VIDEO**

RoboCop 🦴🦴 **2014 (PG-13)** A reimagining of the 1987 sci-fi classic, done up with a bigger budget and a new, boring suit. The set-up is the same--set in 2028, madman Pat Novak (Jackson) spins controversy into ratings, hyping drone destruction and mass terrorism. Seeking a solution to the global threats, scientist Dennett Norton (Oldman) teams with OmniCorp CEO Raymond Sellars (Keaton) to combat Detroit's escalating violence by fusing half-dead police officer Alex Murphy (Kinnaman) with the body of an indestructable machine of justice. Not as bad as it seems, but riddled with overly-serious techo babble and paper-thin characters. Any laughs are unintentional. **117m/C; DVD, Blu-Ray.** Joel Kinnaman; Samuel L. Jackson; Gary Oldman; Michael Keaton; Abbie Cornish; Marianne Jean-Baptiste; Jennifer Ehle; Jackie Earle Haley; Jay Baruchel; Michael K(enneth) Williams; *D:* Jose Padilha; *W:* Joshua Zetumer; *C:* Lula Carvalho; *M:* Pedro Bromfman.

RoboCop 🦴🦴🦴 **1987 (R)** A nearly dead Detroit cop, Alex Murphy (Weller), is used as the brain for a crime-fighting robot in this bleak vision of the future. Humor, satire, action, and violence keep this moving in spite of its underlying sadness. Slick animation techniques from Phil Tippet. Verhoeven's first American film. **103m/C; VHS, DVD, Blu-Ray, UMD.** Peter Weller; Nancy Allen; Ronny Cox; Kurtwood Smith; Ray Wise; Miguel Ferrer; Dan O'Herlihy; Robert DoQui; Felton Perry; Paul McCrane; Del Zamora; *D:* Paul Verhoeven; *W:* Michael Miner; Edward Neumeier; *C:* Jan De Bont; *M:* Basil Poledouris.

RoboCop 2 🦴🦴 **1990 (R)** Grimer, more violent sequel to the initial fascinating look at the future, where police departments are run by corporations hungry for profit at any cost. A new and highly addictive drug has made Detroit more dangerous than ever. Robocop is replaced by a stronger cyborg with the brain of a brutal criminal. When the cyborg goes berserk, Robocop battles it and the drug lords for control of the city. Dark humor and graphic savagery, with little of the tenderness and emotion of the original. **117m/C; VHS, DVD, Blu-Ray.** Peter Weller; Nancy Allen; Belinda Bauer; Dan O'Herlihy; Tom Noonan; Gabriel Damon; Galyn Gorg; Felton Perry; Patricia Charbonneau; *D:* Irvin Kershner; *W:* Walon Green; *C:* Mark Irwin; *M:* Leonard Rosenman.

RoboCop 3 🦴 **1/2 1991 (PG-13)** Robocop's new Japanese owners plan to build a huge, new, ultra-modern city (in place of the decrepit 21st-century Detroit) but first must evict thousands of people in this third installment of the "Robocop" films (which sat on the studio shelf before finally being released in 1993). There's an android Ninja warrior to do battle with Robo, who's gone over to the rebel underground. Plot and action sequences are rehashed from better films. Watch the original. **104m/C; VHS, DVD, Blu-Ray.** Robert John Burke; Nancy Allen; John Castle; CCH Pounder; Bruce Locke; Rip Torn; Remi Ryan; Felton Perry; Stephen (Steve) Root; *D:* Fred Dekker; *W:* Fred Dekker; Frank Miller; *C:* Gary B. Kibbe; *M:* Basil Poledouris.

RoboGeisha 🦴 **1/2 2006** Noboru Iguchi was asked to tone down the splatterfest for this latest effort, but it's still bloodier than most American films would be. Two geishas are kidnapped, re-engineered as cyborgs, and trained as assassins with robotic weapons hidden in their various bodily orifices. The story and acting are pretty so-so, but no one will notice once the machine gun bosoms, giant robots, and half clothed geisha women with chainsaw tongues pop up. **120m/C; DVD, Blu-Ray.** *JP* Naoto Takenaka; Takuma Saito; Suzuki Matsuo; Aya Kiguchi; Hitomi Hasebe; Demo Tanaka; Yuya Ishikawa; Kentaro Shimazu; Asami Kumakiri; Taro Shigaki; Shoko Nakahara; Kentaro Kishi; Etsuko Ikuta; Mariko Takayama; Shigeki Terao; *D:* Noboru Iguchi; *W:* Noboru Iguchi; *C:* Yasatako Nagano; *M:* Yasuhiko Fukuda.

Robot & Frank 🦴🦴🦴 **2012 (PG-13)** Perhaps the oddest buddy comedy in years is raised up by yet-another terrific performance from Langella. The versatile actor stars as a retired cat burglar who is in the twilight of his years in the near future. His son Hunter (Marsden) wants to place him in assisted living but they compromise after Frank gets a robot assistant to help out around the house and keep an eye out for his safety. The thought of seeing a retiree argue with a mechanical man might sound like a recipe for bad comedy disaster, but director Schreier makes the characters relatable. **90m/C; DVD.** Frank Langella; James Marsden; Liv Tyler; Susan Sarandon; Jeremy Strong; Jeremy Sisto; *V:* Peter Sarsgaard; *D:* Jake Schreier; *W:* Christopher Ford; *C:* Matthew Lloyd; *M:* Francis and the Lights.

Robot Jox 🦴 **1/2 1990 (PG)** Two futuristic warriors battle to the finish in giant mechanical robots. Preteen fare. **84m/C; VHS, DVD, Blu-Ray.** Gary (Rand) Graham; Anne-Marie Johnson; Paul Koslo; Robert Sampson; Danny Kamekona; Hilary Mason; Michael Alldredge; *D:* Stuart Gordon; *W:* Joe Haldeman; *C:* Mac Ahlberg.

Robot Monster 🦴🦴 **1/2** *Monster from Mars; Monsters from the Moon* **1953** Ludicrous cheapie is widely considered one of the worst films of all time, as a single alien dressed in a moth-eaten gorilla suit and diving helmet conspires to take over the Earth from his station in a small, bubble-filled California cave. Available in original 3-D format. **84m/B; VHS, DVD.** George Nader; Claudia Barrett; Gregory Moffett; Selena Royle; John (Jack) Mylong; George Barrows; *V:* John Brown; *D:* Phil Tucker; *W:* Wyott Ordung; *C:* Jack Greenhalgh; *M:* Elmer Bernsteih.

Robot Pilot 🦴 *Emergency Landing* **1941** Tucker stars as a WWII test pilot trying to promote a friend's invention. Along the way, he's involved in a subplot with enemy agents who steal a bomber. He also finds time to become romantically entangled with the boss' spoiled daughter. **68m/B; VHS, DVD.** Forrest Tucker; Carol Hughes; Evelyn Brent; Emmett Vogan; William (Bill) Halligan; *D:* William Beaudine.

Robot Stories 🦴🦴 **1/2 2003** Writer-director Pak's first theatrical venture gazes into the future and imagines the impact that robots and artificial intelligence will have on society via four short stories. Though the central theme is sci-fi, at its core each piece is really an intriguing exploration of timeless human emotions such as grief, death, family, and love. **85m/C; DVD.** Tamlyn Tomita; James Saito; Joshua Spafford; Rea Tajiri; Vin Knight; Gina Quintos; Karen Tse Lee; Glen Kubota; Tim Kang; Tanisha Eanes; Catherine Carota; Norma Fire; Cindy Cheung; Louis Ozawa Changchien; Angel Desai; Greg Pak; ***D:*** Greg Pak; ***W:*** Greg Pak; ***C:*** Peter Olsen; ***M:*** Rick Knutsen.

Robot Wars **1993 (PG)** When what seems to be the last mega-robot on earth falls into enemy hands, a renegade pilot unearths another with the help of an engineer and archeologist to fight for the future of mankind. **106m/C; VHS, DVD.** Don Michael Paul; Barbara Crampton; James Staley; Lisa Rinna; Danny Kamekona; Yuji Okumoto; J. Downing; Peter Haskell; ***D:*** Albert Band.

Robot World 1/2 **2015** A scifi thriller centered on a pilot marooned on an alien planet. When a pilot (Rowe) is sent through the galaxy, his mission is simple. He is supposed to orbit an alien planet and gain information about it, then return home. The only thing the pilot knows about this planet is that it has intelligent life. Once there, the pilot became trapped on the planet. He soon learns that only predatory machines live there and that other truths about the planet change his perspective on Earth itself. **82m/C; DVD, Download.** Ian Rowe; Claire Soper; Paul Soper; Lisa Mitchell; Tony Mitchell; ***D:*** Neil Rowe; ***W:*** Neil Rowe; ***M:*** Amanda Rowe. **VIDEO**

Robots 1/2 **2005 (PG)** Animated tale of a small-town robot in the big city. Idealistic Rodney Copperbottom (McGregor) travels to Robot City to present his inventions to Bigweld (Brooks), the beloved president of Bigweld Industries. However, Ratchet (Kinnear) and Madame Gasket (Broadbent) have taken over and are forcing old robots to upgrade or perish. Rodney organizes a motley band of rejects, including Williams' predictably schticky Fender, to topple the heartless duo. The outcome is predictable, but the CGI work is dazzling (the kitschy character design is the highlight), although the generic story and characters fail to inspire. **91m/C; VHS, DVD, Blu-Ray, UMD.** ***V:*** Ewan McGregor; Halle Berry; Robin Williams; Greg Kinnear; Mel Brooks; Drew Carey; Jim Broadbent; Amanda Bynes; Jennifer Coolidge; Stanley Tucci; Dianne Wiest; Paul Giamatti; Natasha Lyonne; Lowell Ganz; Dan Hedaya; Jackie Hoffman; ***D:*** Chris Wedge; ***W:*** Lowell Ganz; Babaloo Mandel; David Lindsay-Abaire; ***M:*** John Powell.

Rocco and His Brothers 1/2 *Rocco et Ses Freres; Rocco E I Suoi Fratelli* **1960** A modern classic from top director Visconti, about four brothers who move with their mother from the Italian countryside to Milan. Very long, sometimes ponderous, but engrossing, complex drama. Available shortened to 90 minutes, but the unedited version is much more rewarding. In Italian with English subtitles. **168m/B; VHS, DVD, Blu-Ray.** *IT* Alain Delon; Renato Salvatori; Annie Girardot; Katina Paxinou; Claudia Cardinale; Roger Hanin; Alessandra Panaro; Spiros Focas; Max Cartier; ***D:*** Luchino Visconti; ***W:*** Luchino Visconti; Suso Cecchi D'Amico; Pasquale Festa Campanile; Enrico Medioli; Massimo Franciosa; ***C:*** Giuseppe Rotunno; ***M:*** Nino Rota.

The Rock **1996 (R)** In an attempt to get benefits for the families of soldiers killed in various covert operations, a decorated general (Harris) and his commando squad occupy Alcatraz, taking hostages and threatening to unleash a deadly gas bomb on San Francisco. Biochemical weapons expert Stanley Goodspeed (Cage) is called in to disarm the rockets, aided by John Patrick Mason (Connery), the only man to successfully escape from the island prison. Credibility is stretched to the limit, but the action scenes and crisp pacing don't leave much time for pondering details, anyway. Connery is as cool as ever and Cage effectively plays up his character's inexperience at being the hero. **136m/C; DVD, Blu-Ray.** Nicolas Cage; Sean Connery; Ed Harris; Michael Biehn; William Forsythe; David Morse; John Spencer; John C. McGinley; Tony Todd; Bokeem Woodbine; Danny Nucci; Claire Forlani; Vanessa Marcil; Gregory Sporleder; Steve Harris; Jim Maniaci; Brendan Kelly; Todd Louiso; Willie Garson; Stuart Wilson; Anthony Clark; James (Jim) Caviezel; Xander Berkeley; Sam Whipple; Raymond Cruz; David Marshall Grant; Philip Baker Hall; ***D:*** Michael Bay; ***W:*** Jonathan Hensleigh; ***C:*** John Schwartzman; ***M:*** Nick Glennie-Smith. MTV Movie Awards '97: On-Screen Duo (Sean Connery/ Nicolas Cage).

Rock-A-Bye Baby 1/2 **1957** Clayton Poole (Lewis) is a big fan of glamorous movie star Carla Naples (Maxwell), a recent widow who gives birth to triplets—a fact she wants kept hush-hush since she's starring as a virgin in a religious epic. So Clayton comes to the rescue by agreeing to be the little bundles' babysitter. And as a job bonus he gets to fall in love with Carla's sweet sister, Sandy (Stevens). A very loose adaptation of the Preston Sturges comedy "The Miracle of Morgan's Creek." **103m/C; VHS, DVD, Blu-Ray.** Jerry Lewis; Marilyn Maxwell; Connie Stevens; Salvatore Baccaloni; Reginald Gardiner; Hans Conried; Ida Moore; George Sanders; James Gleason; ***D:*** Frank Tashlin; ***W:*** Frank Tashlin; ***C:*** Haskell Boggs; ***M:*** Walter Scharf.

Rock-a-Doodle 1/2 **1992 (G)** Little Edmond is knocked out during a storm and has an Elvis-influenced vision. He sees Chanticleer, the sun-raising rooster, tricked into neglecting his duties by an evil barnyard owl. Humiliated and scorned, the earnest young fowl leaves the farm and winds up in a Las Vegas-like city as an Elvis-impersonating singer (complete with pompadour) where he meets with success and all its trappings. Mildly amusing, but bland by today's standards of animation, with music which is certainly nothing to crow about. **77m/C; VHS, DVD, Blu-Ray.** ***V:*** Glen Campbell; Christopher Plummer; Phil Harris; Sandy Duncan; Ellen Greene; Charles Nelson Reilly; Eddie Deezen; Toby Scott Granger; Sorrell Booke; ***D:*** Don Bluth; ***W:*** David N. Weiss; ***M:*** Robert Folk.

Rock & Rule **1983** Animated sword & sorcery epic with a rock soundtrack. Voices are provided by Deborah Harry, Cheap Trick, Lou Reed, and Iggy Pop. **85m/C; VHS, DVD.** ***V:*** Paul LeMat; Susan (Suzan) Roman; Don Francks; Dan Hennessey; Chris Wiggins; Catherine Gallant; Catherine O'Hara; ***D:*** Clive A. Smith; ***M:*** Deborah Harry; Lou Reed; Iggy Pop.

Rock, Baby, Rock It **1957** Weak and silly rock-and-roll crime drama about teens trying to fight the Mafia in Dallas in 1957. Features performances by many regional bands including Kay Wheeler, the Cell Block Seven, Johnny Carroll, Preacher Smith and the Deacons, and the Five Stars. If you grew up in Dallas in the '50s, the musical groups may bring back some fond memories; otherwise, this obscure film probably isn't worth your time. **84m/B; VHS, DVD.** Kay Wheeler; John Carroll; ***D:*** Murray Douglas Sporup.

Rock Dog 1/2 **2017 (PG)** Wilson voices the title character, a dog Tibetan Mastiff sheepdog who, well, rocks after he finds a radio literally falls on him from the sky, teaching him about the power of music and sending him on a journey to become a rock star himself. It's somewhat difficult to come down too hard on an animated film that includes a character voiced by Sam Elliott named Fleetwood Yak, but this is a pretty dull. The voice cast is surprisingly excellent (also including Izzard, Simmons, and Black), but the animation and script are the kind of thing more likely seen on a Saturday morning cartoon. **90m/C; DVD, Blu-Ray.** J.K. Simmons; Luke Wilson; Eddie Izzard; Lewis Black; Kenan Thompson; ***D:*** Ash Brannon; ***W:*** Ash Brannon; ***M:*** Rolfe Kent.

Rock Haven **2007** A devout Christian, 18-year-old Bradley has just moved with his overprotective mother to the titular coastal town in northern California. Settling in, he's surprised to find himself attracted to athletic neighbor Clifford. But will Bradley's beliefs cause him to turn away from his first romance? Sentimental story that doesn't negate the importance of Bradley's spirituality. **78m/C; DVD.** Sean Hoagland; Owen Alabado; Laura Jane Coles; Katheryn Hecht; Erin Daly; ***D:*** David Lewis; ***W:*** David Lewis; ***C:*** Christian Bruno; ***M:*** Jack Curtis Dubowsky.

Rock Jocks **2012** The Asteroid Management Initiative, part of the DoD, is tasked with spotting and then shooting down asteroids heading towards Earth. Except the profane 'rock jocks' are competitive, bored, and under threat from a government bureaucrat who wants to shut them down. Oh, yeah, there's also an alien, nicknamed 'smoking jesus,' who lives in the facility's basement. **91m/C; DVD.** Justin Chon; Kevin Wu; Felicia Day; Andrew Bowen; Gerry Bednob; Mark Woolley; ***D:*** Paul V. Seetachitt; ***W:*** Paul V. Seetachitt; ***C:*** Polly Morgan; ***M:*** S. Peace Nistades. **VIDEO**

Rock My World *Global Heresy* **2002 (R)** Amazingly bad would-be comedy finds one-hit American band Global Heresy forced to hire new bassist Nat (Silverstone) when their original player suddenly disappears. The group is headed to a English country mansion to relax and rehearse and it turns out the cash-poor aristocratic owners (O'Toole, Plowright) are secretly posing as the butler and cook. Every culture clash cliche is trotted out. **106m/C; VHS, DVD, On Demand.** *GB CA* Peter O'Toole; Joan Plowright; Alicia Silverstone; Jaimz Woolvett; Lochlyn Munro; Martin Clunes; ***D:*** Sidney J. Furie; ***W:*** Mark Mills; ***C:*** Curtis Petersen.

Rock 'n' Roll High School **1979 (PG)** The music of the Ramones highlights this non-stop high-energy cult classic about a high school out to thwart the principal at every turn. If it had been made in 1957, it would have been the ultimate rock 'n' roll teen movie. As it is, its 1970s' milieu works against it, but the performances are perfect for the material and the Ramones are great. Songs include "Teenage Lobotomy," "Blitzkrieg Bop," "I Wanna Be Sedated," and the title track, among others. Followed less successfully by "Rock 'n' Roll High School Forever." **94m/C; VHS, DVD, Blu-Ray.** P.J. Soles; Vincent Van Patten; Clint Howard; Dey Young; Mary Woronov; Alix Elias; Dick Miller; Paul Bartel; Don Steele; Dee Dee Ramone; Joey Ramone; Johnny Ramone; Marky Ramone; ***D:*** Allan Arkush; ***W:*** Joe Dante; Russ Dvonch; Joseph McBride; Richard Whitley; ***C:*** Dean Cundey; ***M:*** Ramones.

Rock 'n' Roll High School Forever **1991 (PG-13)** Jesse Davis and his band just want to rock 'n' roll, but the new principal doesn't share their enthusiasm. Way late, way lame sequel to "Rock 'n' Roll High School" doesn't come close to the originality that made it a cult classic. Soundtrack includes music from The Divinyls, Dee Dee Ramone, Mojo Nixon, Will and the Bushmen, The Pursuit of Happiness, and more. **94m/C; VHS, DVD.** Corey Feldman; Mary Woronov; Mojo Nixon; Evan Richards; Michael Ceveris; Patrick Malone; Larry Linville; Sarah Buxton; Liane (Alexandra) Curtis; Lewis Arquette; Jason Lively; ***D:*** Deborah Brock; ***W:*** Deborah Brock; ***C:*** James Mathers.

Rock 'n' Roll Nightmare 1/2 *The Edge of Hell* **1985 (R)** A rock band is pursued by demons from another dimension. The usual lame garbage. **89m/C; VHS, DVD.** *CA* Jon Mikl Thor; Paula Francescatto; Rusty Hamilton; Jillian Peri; Frank Dietz; David Lane; Teresa Simpson; Liane Abel; Nancy Bush; ***D:*** John Fasano; ***W:*** Jon Mikl Thor; ***C:*** Mark MacKay.

Rock of Ages **2012 (PG-13)** Director Shankman can't get a grip on the cheese factor of hair metal and mistakenly plays his adaptation of the Broadway hit completely straight, leading to embarrassment more than entertainment. Naïve newcomer Sherrie (Hough) moves to L.A. in 1987 with stars in her eyes and soon finds love with city boy Drew (newcomer Boneta). It's all an excuse for musical numbers built around '80s rock hits with an A-list supporting cast, including the rock/sex god played by Cruise. But the film is unbearable for those not into its music while also kind of insulting for those who are. **123m/C; DVD, Blu-Ray, Streaming.** Julianne Hough; Diego Boneta; Russell Brand; Alec Baldwin; Bryan Cranston; Catherine Zeta-Jones; Paul Giamatti; Tom Cruise; ***D:*** Adam Shankman; ***W:*** Chris D'Arienzo; Allan Loeb; Justin Theroux; ***C:*** Bojan Bazelli; ***M:*** Adam Anders; Peer Astrom.

Rock, Pretty Baby **1956** Early rock-'n'-roll movie about a teenage band and high school riots. **89m/B; VHS, DVD.** Sal Mineo; John Saxon; Rod McKuen; Luana Patten; Fay Wray; Edward Platt; Alan Reed, Jr.; ***D:*** Richard Bartlett; ***M:*** Henry Mancini.

Rock, Rock, Rock 1/2 **1956** A young girl tries to earn enough money for a prom gown after her father closes her charge account. Screen debut of Tuesday Weld. Ultra-low-budget, but a classic after a fashion. Includes classic musical numbers performed by Chuck Berry and other rock 'n' roll pioneers. **78m/B; VHS, DVD.** Alan Freed; Chuck Berry; Fats Domino; Tuesday Weld; ***D:*** Will Price.

Rock School **2005 (R)** Director Argott's dynamic documentary lays bare the life of offbeat and intense music teacher Paul Green and his School of Rock Music, an after-school program in Philadelphia for highly-skilled nine to 17-year-olds. Flipping between cursing and berating his pupils to chumming around with them, Green prepares his most gifted group for an inspired appearance at the annual Zappanale festival in Germany (a tribute to the late rocker Frank Zappa). Green is often thought to be the basis for Jack Black's comedy "School of Rock," though its creators have refuted the claim. **93m/C; DVD.** ***D:*** Don Argott; ***C:*** Don Argott.

Rock Slyde: Private Eye **2009 (PG-13)** Contemporary film noir spoof. Clueless hard-boiled PI Slyde (Warburton) has his office in the same building as the ever-expanding House of Bartology run by quasi-cult leader Bart (Dick). Bart wants Slyde's office space and starts by brainwashing Slyde's secretary Judy (Hendrix). Then femme fatale Sara Lee (Sofer) comes slinking in, asking Slyde to help her with a stalker. There's also a gay pirate porn musical and an overly-attentive postal worker among other silliness. **96m/C; DVD.** Patrick Warburton; Andy Dick; Elaine Hendrix; Rena Sofer; Jamie Alexander; Jason Alexander; Eric Roberts; Brian Bosworth; Tom Bergeron; ***D:*** Chris Dowling; ***W:*** Chris Dowling; ***C:*** Alexandre Lehmann. **VIDEO**

Rock Star **2001 (R)** Working class Chris (Wahlberg) spends his off hours as the lead singer in Blood Pollution, a "tribute band" to heavy metal demigods Steel Dragon. He gets a little too obsessive, alienates the rest of the band, and is finally replaced. In a fantastical twist (and a none-too-subtle reference to real-life rockers Judas Priest), the musicians in Steel Dragon fire their secretly gay lead singer Bobby Beers (Flemyng) and recruit the amazed Chris to replace him. Real rock musicians and former rock star wives are scattered throughout the cast, but they don't add any glam to a bland depiction of a raunchy time period. **106m/C; VHS, DVD, Blu-Ray.** Mark Wahlberg; Jennifer Aniston; Timothy Olyphant; Timothy Spall; Jason Flemyng; Dominic West; Matthew Glave; Beth Grant; Stephan Jenkins; Jason Bonham; Heidi Mark; Michael Shamus Wiles; Dagmara Dominczyk; Rachel Hunter; Colleen (Ann) Fitzpatrick; ***D:*** Stephen Herek; ***W:*** John Stockwell; ***C:*** Ueli Steiger; ***M:*** Trevor Rabin.

Rock the Kasbah **2015 (R)** The once-talented Barry Levinson delivers one of the most offensively inept films of the last decade from a major filmmaker. Bill Murray lazily brings out his schtick as music producer Richie Lanz, a borderline con artist who discovers a true talent named Salima (Leem Lubany) in a cave in Afghanistan, and works against cultural issues related to gender to get her on Afghani Idol. The hijinks involve a local escort (Kate Hudson) and a mercenary (Bruce Willis) in the area. Culturally insensitive, and stunningly flat in terms of humor, rarely has suh a talented cast been given so little interesting material to worth with. **100m/C; DVD, Blu-Ray.** Bill Murray; Bruce Willis; Kate Hudson; Zooey Deschanel; Scott Caan; ***D:*** Barry Levinson; ***W:*** Mitch Glazer; ***C:*** Sean Bobbitt; ***M:*** Marcelo Zarvos.

Rock the Paint 1/2 **2005 (R)** High school sports pic would work better if co-star Smith wasn't such a blank onscreen. Josh Sendler (Smith) is a white star basketball player from rural Indiana who must move to Newark, New Jersey, with his loud-mouthed younger brother Tim (Stone) when their widowed dad (Innvar) gets a new job. Josh gets some hard lessons learning to deal with his black teammates, despite the help of Antwon (Phillips), amidst the city's overall racial tensions. The team has a shot at the state championship but things go south during the big game when Josh loses his cool and blurts out exactly the wrong thing. **90m/C; DVD.** Douglas Smith; Kevin Phillips; John Doman; Christopher Innvar; Sam Oz Stone; Jas Anderson; Tom Brennan; *D:* Phil Bertelsen; *W:* Dallas Brennan; *C:* John Foster; *M:* Wyclef Jean. **VIDEO**

The Rocker 2008 **(PG-13)** Aging, bitter, unemployed former rocker Robert "Fish" Fishman (Wilson) gets roped into a drumming gig with his teenage nephew's rock band (aptly named A.D.D.). Fish schools the adolescents in all things rock and A.D.D. gains notoriety, eventually landing an opening gig for Fish's former band, Vesuvius. Fish needs to grow up in order to impress A.D.D. bandmate Curtis' (Geiger) hot single mom (Applegate) and outdo Vesuvius. Unapologetically retro with the requisite immature gags you'd expect, but plenty fun nonetheless. Hader steals the movie as a slimy manager. **102m/C; DVD, Blu-Ray, On Demand.** Rainn Wilson; Christina Applegate; Josh Gad; Emma Stone; Teddy Geiger; Jane Lynch; Jeff Garlin; Jason Sudeikis; Howard Hesseman; Will Arnett; Bradley Cooper; Fred Armisen; Lonny Ross; Jane Krakowski; *D:* Peter Cattaneo; *W:* Maya Forbes; M. Wallace Wolodarsky; *C:* Anthony B. Richmond; *M:* Chad Fischer.

The Rocket *Maurice Richard* **2005 (PG)** Inspiring biopic of hockey legend Maurice "The Rocket" Richard (perfectly portrayed by Dupuis), who, in the 1940s and 50s, rises from the Quebec working-class to stardom with the Montreal Canadiens and winner of multiple Stanley Cups. Although his speed and skill make him popular with the fans, Richard has to battle prejudice against French-speaking players from the controlling, Anglo hockey establishment. Injuries lead to constant trade talk and Richard also isn't afraid to push for much-needed NHL reforms, which doesn't endear him to the suits. English and French with subtitles. **124m/C; DVD.** *CA* Roy Dupuis; Stephen McHattie; Charles Biname; Serge Roude; Patrice Robitaille; Julie Le Breton; Francois Langlois Vallieres; Ian Laperriere; Vincent Lecavalier; Ted Dillon; *C:* Pierre Gill; *M:* Michel Cusson.

Rocket Attack U.S.A. WOOF! 1958 Antiquated and ridiculous tale of nuclear warfare about the time of Sputnik, with Russia's first strike blowing up New York City and environs. Mercifully short, with time for a little romance. Everything about this movie is so bad it's good for a laugh. **70m/B; VHS, DVD.** Monica Davis; John MacKay; Dan Kern; Edward Czerniuk; Art Metrano; *D:* Barry Mahon.

Rocket Gibraltar 1988 **(PG)** On the occasion of a crusty patriarch's birthday, a large family unites on his remote estate to carry out his special birthday wish. Fine performance by Lancaster. Supported by a solid cast, overcomes a slim story. Culkin, later of "Home Alone," is loveable as the precocious five-year-old. Picturesque Long Island scenery. **92m/C; VHS, DVD.** Burt Lancaster; Bill Pullman; John Glover; Suzy Amis; Macaulay Culkin; Patricia Clarkson; Frances Conroy; Sinead Cusack; Bill Martin; Kevin Spacey; *D:* Daniel Petrie; *W:* Amos Poe; *M:* Andrew Powell.

The Rocket Man 1/2 **1954** An orphan comes into possession of a powerful ray gun that makes people shot by it tell the truth. **79m/B; DVD.** Charles Coburn; Spring Byington; Anne Francis; John Agar; George Winslow; Stanley Clements; Emory Parnell; *D:* Oscar Rudolph; *W:* Lenny Bruce; George W. George; Jack Henley; George F. Slavin; *C:* John F. Seitz; *M:* Lionel Newman.

Rocket Science 2007 **(R)** Hal (Thompson) is having a tough time: his dad (O'Hare) has just walked out on his family, his brother Earl (Piazza) is a domineering bully, and his stutter is so intense that it gets him mocked at school. Along comes ambitious Ginny (Kendrick), who recruits him for the debate club. Hal slowly falls for Ginny, all the time unsure if she likes him or if she's just using him. Sweet and quirky meditation on first love and teenage awkwardness provides plenty of laughs, but director Blitz has a genuine sense of feeling for the characters as well in his first feature film; he previously directed the spelling bee documentary "Spellbound." **98m/C; DVD.** Reece Thompson; Anna Kendrick; Margo Martindale; Nicholas D'Agosto; Vincent Piazza; *D:* Jeffrey Blitz; *W:* Jeffrey Blitz; *C:* Jo Willems; *M:* Eef Barzelay.

The Rocketeer 1991 **(PG)** Light-headed fun. A stunt flyer in the 1930s finds a prototype jet backpack sought by Nazi spies. Donning a mask, he becomes a flying superhero. Breezy family entertainment with stupendous effects; even better if you know movie trivia, as it brims with Hollywood references, like a great villain (Dalton) clearly based on Errol Flynn. **109m/C; VHS, DVD.** Billy Campbell; Jennifer Connelly; Alan Arkin; Timothy Dalton; Paul Sorvino; Melora Hardin; Tiny Ron; Terry O'Quinn; Ed Lauter; James Handy; *D:* Joe Johnston; *W:* Danny Bilson; Paul DeMeo; *C:* Hiro Narita; *M:* James Horner.

RocketMan 1/2 *Rocket Man* **1997 (PG)** Houston, we have a gastrointestinal problem. Well, dumb astronaut Fred Z. Randall (Williams) does, anyway. The bumbling computer geek is picked to go on the first manned mission to Mars, much to the dismay of crew commander "Wild Bill" Overbeck (Sadler) and specialist Julie Ford (Lundy). Bud Nesbitt (Bridges), the veteran astronaut back at NASA headquarters, is Randall's only supporter. While too much of the humor revolves around flatulence, Williams shows some talent while raiding the Disney archive for impressions. **93m/C; VHS, DVD, Blu-Ray.** Harland Williams; Jessica Lundy; Beau Bridges; William Sadler; Jeffrey DeMunn; James Pickens, Jr.; Peter Onorati; *D:* Stuart Gillard; *W:* Craig Mazin; Greg Erb; *C:* Steven Poster; *M:* Michael Tavera.

Rocketman 2019 **(R)** Egerton is astounding as Elton John in this unbelievably satisfying biography chronicling the surprisingly turbulent life of Elton John. Told as a sort of musical fantasy, utilizing many of John's most beloved songs, the story follows the metamorphosis of a shy, self-taught piano prodigy named Reginald Dwight into a world-renown superstar. Egerton performed all of John's music featured in the film, giving the film an air of authenticity and credibility missing in many musical biopics. Bell stars as John's writing partner Bernie Taupin, whose friendship and collaboration helps mold John and his music. **121m/C; DVD, Blu-Ray.** *UK US* Taron Egerton; Jamie Bell; Richard Madden; Bryce Dallas Howard; Gemma Jones; *D:* Dexter Fletcher; *W:* Lee Hall; *C:* George Richmond; *M:* Matthew Margeson. Oscars '19: Song ("I'm Gonna Love Me Again"); Golden Globes '20: Actor--Mus./Comedy (Egerton), Song ("I'm Gonna Love Me Again").

Rocketship *Flash Gordon: Rocketship* **1936** Flash Gordon battles sea monsters, ray guns, and robots in this sci-fi adventure, which is an edited version of a Flash serial. **97m/B; VHS, DVD.** Buster Crabbe; Jean Rogers; Charles Middleton; *D:* Frederick Stephani; *W:* Frederick Stephani; *C:* Jerome Ash; *M:* Clifford Vaughan.

Rocketship X-M 1/2 *Expedition Moon* **1950** A lunar mission goes awry and the crew lands on Mars, where they discover ancient ruins. Well acted and nicely photographed. Contains footage, a tinted sequence and previews of coming attractions from classis science fiction files. **77m/B; VHS, DVD, Blu-Ray.** Lloyd Bridges; Osa Massen; John Emery; Hugh O'Brian; Noah Beery, Jr.; *D:* Kurt Neumann; *W:* Kurt Neumann; Dalton Trumbo; *C:* Karl Struss; *M:* Ferde Grofe, Jr.

Rockin' Road Trip 1985 **(PG-13)** A guy meets a girl in a Boston bar, and finds himself on a drunken, slapstick road trip down the Eastern seaboard with a rock band. **101m/C; VHS, DVD.** Garth McLean; Katherine Harrison; Margeret Currie; Steve Boles; *D:* William Olsen; *W:* William Olsen; *C:* Austin McKinney; *M:* Ricky Keller.

The Rocking Horse Winner 1/2 **1949** Poignant tale of a young boy who discovers he can predict racehorse winners by riding his rocking horse. His spendthrift mother's greed leads to tragedy. Based on the short story by D.H. Lawrence. **91m/B; VHS, DVD.** *GB* John Howard Davies; Valerie Hobson; Hugh Sinclair; *D:* Anthony Pelissier.

RocknRolla 1/2 **2008 (R)** Ritchie's usual fast-talking, overly complicated methods are again at work when the London and Russian criminal underworlds go to war with each other over $350 million in real estate that has slipped through the fingers of a major corporation. Motley crews of eclectic gangsters are all out to cheat one another, along with sexy accountant Stella (Newton), who swoops in to turn the con around. And just when things begin to click, a drugged-out rock 'n' roller, known simply as Rocker (Bower), enters to mess with everyone. **114m/C; DVD, Blu-Ray, On Demand.** Gerard Butler; Tom Wilkinson; Thandie Newton; Mark Strong; Idris Elba; Tom (Thomas) Hardy; Karel Roden; Toby Kebbell; Jeremy Piven; Chris Bridges; Jimi Mistry; *D:* Guy Ritchie; *W:* Guy Ritchie; *C:* David Higgs; *M:* Steve Isles.

Rockula 1/2 **1990 (PG-13)** Teen rock comedy about a young-yet-300-year-old vampire looking to lose his virginity. Recommended only for hard-core Diddley fans. **90m/C; VHS, DVD, Blu-Ray.** Dean Cameron; Bo Diddley; Tawny (Ellis) Fere; Susan Tyrrell; Thomas Dolby; Toni Basil; *D:* Luca Bercovici; *W:* Luca Bercovici.

Rockwell: A Legend of the Wild West 1/2 **1993** Black heroics in the wild west. U.S. Marshall Porter Rockwell and his posse of sharp shooters are after a vicious gang murdering supposed claim jumpers who just happen to be Rockwell's friends. **105m/C; VHS, DVD.** Randy Gleave; Karl Malone; Michael Rudd; George Sullivan; *D:* Richard Lloyd Dewey; *W:* Richard Lloyd Dewey.

Rocky 1/2 **1976 (PG)** Boxoffice smash about a young man from the slums of Philadelphia who dreams of becoming a boxing champion. Stallone plays Rocky, the underdog hoping to win fame and self-respect. Rags-to-riches story seems to parallel Stallone's life; he had been previously virtually unknown before this movie. Intense portrayal of the American Dream; loses strength in the subsequent (and numerous) sequels. **125m/C; VHS, DVD, Blu-Ray.** Sylvester Stallone; Talia Shire; Burgess Meredith; Burt Young; Carl Weathers; Pedro Lovell; Joe Spinell; Thayer David; Tony Burton; Michael Dorn; *D:* John G. Avildsen; *W:* Sylvester Stallone; *C:* James A. Crabe; *M:* Bill Conti. Oscars '76: Director (Avildsen), Film, Film Editing; AFI '98: Top 100; Directors Guild '76: Director (Avildsen); Golden Globes '77: Film--Drama; L.A. Film Critics '76: Film; Natl. Bd. of Review '76: Support. Actress (Shire); Natl. Film Reg. '06; N.Y. Film Critics '76: Support. Actress (Shire).

Rocky 2 1979 **(PG)** Time-marking sequel to the boxoffice smash finds Rocky frustrated by the commercialism that followed his match to Apollo, but considering a return bout. Meanwhile, his wife fights for her life. The overall effect is to prepare you for the next sequel. **119m/C; VHS, DVD, Blu-Ray.** Sylvester Stallone; Talia Shire; Burt Young; Burgess Meredith; Carl Weathers; *D:* Sylvester Stallone; *W:* Sylvester Stallone; *C:* Bill Butler; *M:* Bill Conti.

Rocky 3 1/2 **1982 (PG)** Rocky is beaten by big, mean Clubber Lang (played to a tee by Mr. T). He realizes success has made him soft, and has to dig deep to find the motivation to stay on top. Amazingly, Stallone regains his underdog persona here, looking puny next to Mr. T, who is the best thing about the second-best "Rocky" flick. **103m/C; VHS, DVD, Blu-Ray.** Sylvester Stallone; Talia Shire; Burgess Meredith; Carl Weathers; Mr. T; Leif Erickson; Burt Young; Hulk Hogan; *D:* Sylvester Stallone; *W:* Sylvester Stallone; *C:* Bill Butler; *M:* Bill Conti.

Rocky 4 1/2 **1985 (PG)** Rocky travels to Russia to fight the Soviet champ who killed his friend during a bout. Will Rocky knock the Russkie out? Will Rocky get hammered on the head a great many times and sag around the ring? Will Rocky ever learn? Lundgren isn't nearly as much fun as some of Rocky's former opponents and Stallone overdoes the hyper-patriotism and relies too heavily on uplifting footage from earlier "Rocky" movies. **91m/C; VHS, DVD, Blu-Ray.** Sylvester Stallone; Talia Shire; Dolph Lundgren; Brigitte Nielsen; Michael Pataki; Burt Young; Carl Weathers; *D:* Sylvester Stallone; *W:* Sylvester Stallone; *C:* Bill Butler; *M:* Bill Conti; Vince DiCola. Golden Raspberries '85: Worst Actor (Stallone), Worst Director (Stallone), Worst New Star (Nielsen), Worst Screenplay, Worst Support. Actress (Nielsen).

Rocky 5 1990 **(PG)** Brain damaged and broke, Rocky finds himself back where he started on the streets of Philadelphia. Boxing still very much in his blood, Rocky takes in a protege, training him in the style that made him a champ (take a lickin' and keep on tickin'). However an unscrupulous promoter has designs on the young fighter and seeks to wrest the lad from under the former champ's wing. This eventually leads to a showdown between Rocky and the young boxer in a brutal streetfight. Supposedly the last "Rocky" film, it's clear the formula has run dry. **105m/C; VHS, DVD, Blu-Ray.** Sylvester Stallone; Talia Shire; Burt Young; Sage Stallone; Tom Morrison; Burgess Meredith; *D:* John G. Avildsen; *W:* Sylvester Stallone; *C:* Steven Poster; *M:* Bill Conti.

Rocky Balboa 1/2 **2006 (PG)** A retired Rocky is running the restaurant he's named after his late wife when a computer simulation predicts that the 50-something former champ would beat the current heavyweight title holder, Mason "The Line" Dixon (Tarver). The new bout stirs up all that was good about the olden days—the music, the punching bag, and those infamous museum steps. But what about Rocky's previous brain damage? Why is Rocky Jr. (Ventimiglia) so whiny? Are those muscles or implants? None of it seems to matter in this somewhat cheerworthy effort that at least doesn't embarrass the franchise. **101m/C; DVD, Blu-Ray.** Sylvester Stallone; Burt Young; Milo Ventimiglia; Tony Burton; Antonio Tarver; Geraldine Hughes; A.J. Benza; James Francis Kelly, III; Henry Sanders; Lahmard Tate; Pedro Lovell; Ana Gerena; *D:* Sylvester Stallone; *W:* Sylvester Stallone; *C:* Clark Mathis; *M:* Bill Conti.

The Rocky Horror Picture Show 1975 **(R)** When a young couple take refuge in a haunted castle, they find themselves the unwilling pawns in a warped scientist's experiment. Cult camp classic has been a midnight movie favorite for years and has developed an entire subculture built around audience participation. Includes a seven-minute short detailing the story behind the movie's popularity. May not be as much fun watching it on the little screen unless you bring the rice and squirt guns. **105m/C; VHS, DVD, Blu-Ray.** *GB* Tim Curry; Susan Sarandon; Barry Bostwick; Nell Campbell; Richard O'Brien; Patricia Quinn; Jonathan Adams; Peter Hinwood; Meat Loaf Aday; Charles Gray; Koo Stark; *D:* Jim Sharman; *W:* Richard O'Brien; Jim Sharman; *C:* Peter Suschitzky; *M:* Richard O'Brien; Richard Hartley. Natl. Film Reg. '05.

Rocky Marciano 1/2 **1999 (R)** Boxing biopic about the up-from-poverty Rocky (Favreau) who, as heavyweight champ, had 43 knockouts and who retired in 1956 undefeated. (He was killed in a 1969 plane crash.) Marciano has the usual tribulations—greedy managers and overly interested mobsters—and a climatic bout with his childhood hero, an aging Joe Louis (Davis). LoBianco, who plays a mobster, starred as Marciano in the 1979 TV movie, "Marciano." **90m/C; VHS, DVD.** Jon Favreau; Judd Hirsch; Penelope Ann Miller; George C. Scott; Tony LoBianco; Duane Davis; Rhoda Gemignani; Rino Romano; *D:* Charles Winkler; *W:* Charles Winkler; Larry Golin; *C:* Paul Sarossy; *M:* Stanley Clarke. **CABLE**

Rocky Mountain 1950 The hard-living Flynn was looking mighty weather-beaten by the time he filmed his last western. Confederate officer Lafe Barstow and his men are sent to California to contact southern sympathizers in hopes that the territory can still be claimed for the south. The soldiers come to the aid of a stagecoach besieged by Indians and Barstow is taken with pretty passenger Johanna (Wymore). But his interest doesn't stop him from using her when he learns her fiance is a Union Army commander. Flynn also fell for the much-younger Wymore offscreen and she became Mrs. Flynn (no. 3) the same year. **83m/B; DVD.** Errol Flynn; Patrice Wymore; Scott Forbes; Guinn "Big Boy" Williams; Slim Pickens; Dick(ie) Jones; Chubby Johnson; Howard Petrie; *D:* William Keighley; *W:* Winston Miller; Alan LeMay; *C:* Ted D. McCord; *M:* Max Steiner.

Rodan *Radon; Radon the Flying Monster* **1956** A gigantic prehistoric bird is disturbed from his slumber by H-bomb tests. He awakens to wreak havoc on civilization. Big bugs also run amok. From the director of "Godzilla" and a host of other nuclear monster movies. **74m/C; VHS, DVD.** *JP* Kenji Sahara; Yumi Shirakawa; *D:* Inoshiro Honda.

Rodeo Girl 1/2 **1980** Ross is a restless housewife who joins the rodeo in this drama based on the life of cowgirl Sue Pirtle.

Particularly strong supporting cast of Hopkins, Clark, and Brimley. **100m/C; VHS, DVD.** Katharine Ross; Bo Hopkins; Candy Clark; Jacqueline Brookes; Wilford Brimley; Parley Baer; ***D:*** Jackie Cooper. **TV**

Rodeo Rhythm **1942** Scott's last starring role as a singing cowboy is a cheap and terrible grade-Z western slightly redeemed by the riding talents of Roy Knapp's Juvenile Rough Riders. Buck (Scott) tries to prevent mortgage-holding Twitchell (Frank) from foreclosing on his sister Tillie's (Bridge) orphanage, while the kids put on a rodeo to raise money. **72m/B; DVD.** Fred Scott; Loie Bridge; Patricia Redpath; John Frank; Pat Dunn; ***D:*** Fred Newmeyer; ***W:*** Eugene Allen; Gene Tuttle; ***C:*** Edward Kull.

Rodgers & Hammerstein's South Pacific 1/2 *South Pacific* **2001** Close may be a little mature to be cockeyed optimist and smalltown nurse Nellie Forbush but she gives it her all (and served as one of the exective producers) in this TV remake of the Rodgers and Hammerstein musical. Filmed in Australia and Tahiti, the scenery, music, and capable cast (who can sing just fine), all contribute. Of course, Connick Jr. (as romantic Lt. Cable) has an advantage in the vocal area but Serbedzija's plantation owner Emile de Becque has charisma to spare. **135m/C; VHS, DVD.** Glenn Close; Rade Serbedzija; Harry Connick, Jr.; Robert Pastorelli; Jack Thompson; Ilene Graff; Lori Tan Chinn; Natalie Mendoza; Simon Burke; Steve Le Marquand; Steve Bastoni; Damon Herriman; ***D:*** Richard Pearce; ***W:*** Lawrence D. Cohen; ***C:*** Stephen F. Windon; ***M:*** Richard Rodgers. **TV**

Roger & Me 1/2 **1989 (R)** Hilarious, controversial and atypical semi-documentary details Moore's protracted efforts to meet General Motors president Roger Smith and confront him with the poverty and despair afflicting Flint, Michigan, after GM closed its plants there. Includes some emotionally grabbing scenes: a Flint family is evicted just before Christmas; a woman makes a living by selling rabbits for food or pets; and a then soon-to-be Miss America addresses the socioeconomic impact of GM's decision. One of the highest-grossing non-fiction films ever released, and Moore's first. **91m/C; VHS, DVD, Blu-Ray.** Michael Moore; Anita Bryant; Bob Eubanks; Pat Boone; ***D:*** Michael Moore; ***W:*** Michael Moore; ***C:*** Kevin Rafferty; Chris Beaver; John Prusak; Bruce Schermer. Natl. Film Reg. '13.

Roger Corman's Death Race 2050 1/2 *Death Race 2050* **2017 (R)** Another entry in the Death Race series that includes up-to-date social and political commentary amidst gory, over-the-top silliness. In the future, the United Corporations of America holds an annual Death Race to curb overpopulation. Racers gain points doing such things as killing people or blowing things up. Every move and every kill is recorded by the camera-carrying journalists who ride with every driver. Because everyone wears VR helmets, the races are universally watched and many people put themselves in harm's way for their moment of fame. Though the film is inexpensive looking, high octane pacing and a sense of fun add to its appeal. **90m/C; DVD.** Manu Bennett; Malcolm McDowell; Marci Miller; Burt Grinstead; Folake Olowofoyeku; ***D:*** G.J. Echternkamp; ***W:*** G.J. Echternkamp; Matt Yamashita; ***M:*** John Alexander Rushie. **VIDEO**

Roger Dodger **2002 (R)** Roger's (Scott) a slightly sleazy ad copywriter who believes he can talk his way into or out of anything, especially when it comes to women. But after he's dumped by boss/girlfriend Joyce (Rossellini), he realizes that he's been cheating himself. When his eager nephew Nick (Eisenberg) arrives unannounced, Roger tutors him in his cynical pickup methods, but the hotties respond more to Nick's innocence and honesty than to Roger's bag of tricks. Scott's performance adds a touch of warmth and compassion to a character who could have been totally odious. **104m/C; VHS, DVD.** Campbell Scott; Jesse Eisenberg; Isabella Rossellini; Elizabeth Berkley; Jennifer Beals; Ben Shenkman; Mina Badie; Chris Stack; Colin Fickes; ***D:*** Dylan Kidd; ***W:*** Dylan Kidd; ***C:*** Joaquin Baca-Asay; ***M:*** Craig Wedren. Natl. Bd. of Review '02: Actor (Scott), Actor (Scott); N.Y. Film Critics '02: First Feature.

Rogue 1/2 **2007 (R)** Competent Aussie horror about a killer croc. American travel writer Pete McKell (Vartan) heads to the Northern Territory and joins a river cruise run by Kate Ryan (Mitchell) along with various disposable passengers. The unseen croc rams the vessel, leaving everyone stranded on a tiny river island that's disappearing under a rising tide with the beast just waiting to pick them off. **92m/C; DVD, Blu-Ray.** *AU US* Michael Vartan; Radha Mitchell; Sam Worthington; Stephen Curry; John Jarratt; Heather Mitchell; Geoff Morrell; Mia Wasikowska; ***D:*** Greg Mclean; ***W:*** Greg Mclean; ***C:*** William Gibson; ***M:*** Francois (Frank) Tetaz.

Rogue Force 1/2 **1999 (R)** A renegade SWAT commander (Patrick) leads a vigilante group of ex-police officers in assassinating a number of mobsters. The murders are being investigating by federal agent Rooker and homicide detective DiLascio, who have no idea where their assignment is leading them. Predictable but delivers the action required of the genre. **90m/C; VHS, DVD.** Robert Patrick; Michael Rooker; Louis Mandylor; Diane DiLascio; ***D:*** Martin Klinert. **VIDEO**

Rogue Male 1/2 **1976** TV movie finds '30s British aristocrat O'Toole plotting to assassinate Hitler. When his plan fails, he's on the run from both the Gestapo and the British police. Based on the novel by Geoffrey Household. **100m/C; VHS, DVD.** *GB* Peter O'Toole; Alastair Sim; John Standing; Cyd Hayman; ***D:*** Clive Donner; ***W:*** Frederic Raphael.

Rogue One: A Star Wars Story 1/2 **2016 (PG-13)** The surprising resurgence of the Star Wars franchise after the generally disliked prequels continues with this semi-prequel, a film that takes place between the third and fourth episodes in the legendary series. Did you ever wonder how the Alliance got the plans to eventually destroy the Death Star? Wonder no more. This intense action film about the stealing of those plans is a smart, character-driven blockbuster that feels like it has actual stakes and tension, something often missing from the Star Wars universe. And the talented cast definitely is one with the Force and the Force is with them. **133m/C; DVD, Blu-Ray.** Felicity Jones; Diego Luna; Alan Tudyk; Donnie Yen; Ben Mendelsohn; ***D:*** Gareth Edwards; ***W:*** Chris Weitz; Tony Gilroy; ***C:*** Greig Fraser; ***M:*** Michael Giacchino.

Rogue Trader **1998 (R)** Unremarkable recreation of the true story of futures trader Nick Leeson (McGregor), who singlehandedly brought down the Barings Merchant Bank in 1995. Working the floor of the Singapore International Money Exchange, Leeson quickly realizes he's completely out of his depth but can't admit it, so he hides his losses and continues to gamble until the deficit adds up to a $1 billion. Based on the book by Nicholas Leeson and Edward Whitley. The real Leeson was paroled from a Singapore jail in 1999. **101m/C; VHS, DVD.** *GB* Ewan McGregor; John Standing; Anna Friel; Yves Beneyton; Tim (McInnerny) McInnery; Betsy Brantley; Caroline Langrishe; ***D:*** James Dearden; ***W:*** James Dearden; ***C:*** Jean-Francois Robin; ***M:*** Richard Hartley.

Rogues of Sherwood Forest **1950** Despite the fact that pretty-boy Derek doesn't appear to know which end of the sword to use, this Technicolor swashbuckler is still fun. Greedy King John (Macready) is taxing the poor so Robin (Derek) gathers his father's merry men to go back to stealing from the rich. Naturally, King John is either plotting to kill Robin or frame him for other crimes so he can be executed. **80m/C; DVD.** John Derek; Diana Lynn; George Macready; Alan Hale; Paul Cavanagh; Lowell Gilmore; Billy House; Lester Matthews; Billy Bevan; ***D:*** Gordon Douglas; ***W:*** George Bruce; ***C:*** Charles Lawton, Jr.; ***M:*** Arthur Morton; Heinz Roemheld.

Rogue's Tavern **1936** In this grade B curio, a blood-thirsty killer stalks the occupants of a country inn, bodies are found with their throats crushed, and a psycho psychic is on the loose. Surprise ending. **70m/B; VHS, DVD.** Wallace Ford; Joan Woodbury; Clara Kimball Young; Barbara Pepper; Jack Mulhall; John Elliott; ***D:*** Robert F. "Bob" Hill.

Role Models **2008 (R)** After some trouble, Danny (Rudd) and Wheeler (Scott) choose community service over jail time and wind up in the "Sturdy Wings" program as reluctant role models to at-risk kids. They're matched with Augie (Mitz-Plasse), an awkward geek whose life revolves around a medieval role-playing game, and Ronnie (Thompson), a pint-sized troublemaker with the attitude and vocabulary of a hardened convict. The two mentors stumble from one gaffe to another but, ultimately, they're all the better for the experience as is required by the formula, although this one is funnier than most on the way there. **99m/C; DVD, Blu-Ray, On Demand.** Paul Rudd; Seann William Scott; Elizabeth Banks; Jane Lynch; Ken Marino; Christopher Mintz-Plasse; Bobb'e J. Thompson; ***D:*** David Wain; ***W:*** Paul Rudd; Ken Marino; David Wain; Timothy Dowling; ***C:*** Russ T. Alsobrook; ***M:*** Craig Wedren.

Role/Play **2010** Static and talky gay drama. Soap opera actor Graham Windsor (Callaghan) is outed and fired after his sex tape gets on the Internet. To escape the tabloids, he retreats to a Palm Springs resort. Also hiding out there is outspoken Trey Reed (Montgomery), a gay marriage activist who was caught cheating on his spouse. Though there's more to their respective scandals than the media knows. **85m/C; Streaming.** Steve Callahan; Matthew Montgomery; David Pevsner; ***D:*** Rob Williams; ***W:*** Rob Williams; ***C:*** Ruben Russ; ***M:*** Jay Monaco. **VIDEO**

Roll Bounce **2005 (PG-13)** Even if you don't remember the roller-disco craze of the 70s, you'll relive it here. South-side Chicago kid Xavier (Bow Wow) and his buddies find their turf rink closes, so they're forced to go North to the swankier Sweetwater rink where the super-cool Sweetness (Jonathan) holds court. The summer rolls by with skating, flirting, and a growing rivalry until the kids square off in an end-of-summer skate-off. Based on fact, this third film directed by Malcolm Lee (Spike's cousin) is more than worthwhile, rooted in true heart and offering a sweetness that sets it apart. **107m/C; DVD.** Bow Wow; Chi McBride; Mike Epps; Wesley Jonathan; Kellita Smith; Meagan Good; Khleo Thomas; Nick Cannon; Rick Gonzalez; Jurnee Smollett; Charlie (Charles Q.) Murphy; Wayne Brady; ***D:*** Malcolm Lee; ***W:*** Norman Vance, Jr.; ***C:*** J.(James) Michael Muro; ***M:*** Stanley Clarke.

Roller Boogie **WOOF! 1979 (PG)** A truly awful film made at the time of the mercifully brief roller-disco craze. Blair runs away from home and winds up helping some friends thwart a businessman looking to close the local roller rink. Everything about this one reeks amateur. **103m/C; DVD, Blu-Ray.** Linda Blair; Jim Bray; Beverly Garland; Roger Perry; James Van Patten; Kimberly Beck; Mark Goddard; Stoney Jackson; Sean McClory; ***D:*** Mark L. Lester; ***W:*** Barry Schneider; ***C:*** Dean Cundey.

Rollerball 1/2 **1975 (R)** Caan is utterly convincing in this futuristic tale in which a brutal sport assumes alarming importance to a sterile society. Flashy, violent, sometimes exhilirating. **123m/C; DVD, Blu-Ray.** James Caan; John Houseman; Maud Adams; Moses Gunn; John Beck; ***D:*** Norman Jewison; ***W:*** William Harrison; ***C:*** Douglas Slocombe; ***M:*** Andre Previn.

Rollerball **2002 (PG-13)** This combosport of the near-future attracts extreme sports enthusiast Jonathan Cross (Klein). He's fleeing U.S. law enforcement and ends up in a former Soviet republic where the league is run by ex-KGB agent Petrovich (Reno), who wants to increase the sport's blood and gore factor to gain a stateside cable TV deal. Laughable scenarios, seriously ailing editing, corny script, lackluster performances, and grave miscasting (the sensitive Klein as a macho macho man) make this re-imagining of the 1975 cult classic laughable. **98m/C; DVD.** Chris Klein; LL Cool J; Rebecca Romijn; Jean Reno; Naveen Andrews; Oleg Taktarov; David Hemblen; ***D:*** John McTiernan; ***W:*** Larry Ferguson; John Pogue; ***C:*** Steve Mason; ***M:*** Éric Serra.

Rollercoaster **1977 (PG)** A deranged extortionist threatens to sabotage an amusement park ride. Plucky Segal must stop him. Video renters will be spared the nauseating effects of film's original "Sensurround." **119m/C; VHS, DVD, Blu-Ray.** George Segal; Richard Widmark; Timothy Bottoms; Henry Fonda; Susan Strasberg; Harry Guardino; Helen Hunt; Craig Wasson; Steve Guttenberg; ***D:*** James Goldstone; ***W:*** William Link; ***C:*** David M. Walsh; ***M:*** Lalo Schifrin.

Rolling Family *Familia Rodante* **2004** Aged matriarch Emilia is invited to be the guest of honor at her grandniece's wedding. So she gathers four squabbling generations of her family and packs them into a worn-out motor home so they can travel cross-country from Buenos Aires to the ceremony. It's hot, there's no air-conditioning, they have repeated motor trouble, and all those smelly people packed into tight quarters leads to some temperamental behavior. Spanish with subtitles. **103m/C; DVD.** *AR* Graciana Chironi; Liliana Capuro; Ruth Dobel; Bernardo Forteza; Carlos Resta; Raul Vinoles; Leila Gomez; Laura Glave; Federico Esqurro; ***D:*** Pablo Trapero; ***W:*** Pablo Trapero; ***C:*** Guillermo Nieto; ***M:*** Leon Giecco.

Rolling Home **1948** Tame tale about aging cowpoke, his grandson, and a really swell horse. Saddle up and snooze. **71m/B; VHS, DVD.** Jean Parker; Russell Hayden; Pamela Blake; Buss Henry; Raymond Hatton; ***D:*** William Berke; ***W:*** Edwin Westrate; ***C:*** Benjamin (Ben H.) Kline; ***M:*** Kierstin Koppell.

Rolling Thunder 1/2 **1977 (R)** Vietnam vet turns vigilante when he arrives home from POW camp and sees his family slaughtered. Graphically violent, potentially cathartic. Typical of screenwriter Paul Schrader. **99m/C; VHS, DVD, Blu-Ray.** William Devane; Tommy Lee Jones; Linda Haynes; ***D:*** John Flynn; ***W:*** Paul Schrader; Heywood Gould; ***C:*** Jordan Cronenweth.

Rolling Thunder Revue: A Bob Dylan Story by Martin Scorsese **2019** Nine years after being seriously injured in a motorcycle accident, musical icon Bob Dylan organized a 1975 tour of the United States with a cavalcade that included musicians, poets, and photographers. Though Dylan believed that the tour had little positive cultural or financial impact, Scorsese's rollicking documentary uses tour footage, reproductions, and interviews to explore its importance on Dylan's career and wider culture. Scorsese adds fictional characters talking about the footage, the tour, and Dylan to enhance the discussion. **142m/C; DVD.** Bob Dylan; Allen Ginsberg; Joan Baez; ***D:*** Martin Scorsese; ***C:*** Howard Alk; Paul Goldsmith; Ellen Kuras; David Myers. **VIDEO**

Rollover 1/2 **1981 (R)** Turgid big-budget drama about Arab undermining of American economy. Kristofferson is lifeless, Fonda is humorless. Supporting players Sommer and Cronyn fare better. **117m/C; VHS, DVD.** Jane Fonda; Kris Kristofferson; Hume Cronyn; Bob Gunton; Josef Sommer; Martha Plimpton; ***D:*** Alan J. Pakula.

Roma **2018 (R)** In 1970s Mexico City, dedicated Cleo (Aparicio) works as a domestic servant for a wealthy family. Though the young woman is almost part of the family and even travels with them, she is constantly reminded in small ways that she is only an employee. Cleo's situation becomes more complicated when she becomes pregnant after having an affair as the family she works for begins to fall apart. A personal story inspired by the filmmaker's early life, the film successfully brings a time, place, and characters to life while also fully blending a sense of the humane with the artistic in each frame. **135m/B; DVD, Blu-Ray.** *US MX* Yalitza Aparicio; Marina de Tavira; Diego Cortina Autrey; Carlos Peralta; Marco Graf; ***D:*** Alfonso Cuarón; ***W:*** Alfonso Cuarón; ***C:*** Alfonso Cuarón; ***M:*** Lynn Fainchtein. Oscars '18: Cinematog., Director (Cuarón), Foreign Film; British Acad. '18: Cinematog., Director (Cuarón), Film, Foreign Film; Directors Guild '18: Director (Cuarón); Golden Globes '18: Director (Cuarón); Golden Globes '19: Foreign Film; Ind. Spirit '19: Foreign Film.

Roman **2006** Alienated Roman (McKee) exists in his own lonely world until he becomes interested in his blonde neighbor (Bell). Too bad he accidentally kills her. Not knowing what to do, Roman starts dismembering the corpse and disposing of it piece by piece. Then death-obsessed Eva (Rose) becomes his new neighbor but maybe Roman should be careful about inviting her to visit. **92m/C; DVD, Blu-Ray.** Lucky McKee; Nectar Rose; Kristen Bell; James Duval; Jesse Hlubik; Ben Boyer; ***D:*** Angela Bettis; ***W:*** Lucky McKee; ***C:*** Kevin Ford; ***M:*** Jaye Barnes Luckett.

Roman de Gare 🦴🦴 *Crossed Tracks* **2007 (R)** The French title is slang for the type of pulp literature sold in railway stations for waiting travelers to pass the time. In this just-as-pulpy thriller, successful crime novelist Judith (Ardant) is being interrogated about her connection to a serial killer called the Magician, who has escaped from prison. Only it turns out that Judith's books are ghostwritten—possibly by the mysterious Louie (Pinon). And what does Louie want from unhappy hairdresser Huguette (Dana), who's just been abandoned by her boyfriend at a highway service station? Is he looking for a ride, romance, or a new victim? Ah, fate makes fools of us all. French with subtitles. **103m/C; DVD.** *FR* Dominique Pinon; Fanny Ardant; Zinedine Soualem; Audrey Dana; Michele Bernier; ***D:*** Claude Lelouch; ***W:*** Claude Lelouch; Pierre Uytterhoeven; ***C:*** Gerard de Battista; ***M:*** Gilbert Becaud; Alex Jaffray.

Roman Holiday 🦴🦴🦴 1/2 **1953** Hepburn's first starring role is a charmer as a princess bored with her official visit to Rome who slips away and plays at being an "average Jane." A reporter discovers her little charade and decides to cash in with an exclusive story. Before they know it, love calls. Blacklisted screenwriter Trumbo was "fronted" by Ian McLellan Hunter, who accepted screen credit and the Best Story Oscar in Trumbo's stead. The Academy voted to posthumously award Trumbo his own Oscar in 1993. **118m/B; VHS, DVD.** Audrey Hepburn; Gregory Peck; Eddie Albert; Tullio Carminati; ***D:*** William Wyler; ***W:*** Dalton Trumbo. Oscars '53: Actress (Hepburn), Costume Des. (B&W), Story; British Acad. '53: Actress (Hepburn); Golden Globes '54: Actress--Drama (Hepburn); Natl. Film Reg. '99; N.Y. Film Critics '53: Actress (Hepburn).

Roman J. Israel, Esq. 🦴🦴 **2017 (PG-13)** An unfocused lawyer drama that attempts to explore issues like civil rights, the court system, and racial injustice, but fails to form a cohesive whole. Lawyer Roman J. Israel (Washington) spends his days writing briefs for the civil rights cases of his law firm partner until his unexpected death. After the firm is closed by his partner's relative, Roman eventually ends up working for a defense lawyer, George Pierce (Farrell), with a corporate law firm and serving as inspirational figure for Pierce and civil rights activist Maya (Ejogo). Washington's performance does not add enough to save the film. **122m/C; DVD, Blu-Ray.** Denzel Washington; Colin Farrell; Carmen Ejogo; Lynda Gravatt; Amanda Warren; ***D:*** Dan Gilroy; ***W:*** Dan Gilroy; ***C:*** Robert Elswit; ***M:*** James Newton Howard.

Roman Polanski: Wanted and Desired 🦴🦴 1/2 **2008** Roman Polanski's life is already close to a Hollywood drama, with his parents' death in the Holocaust, his childhood on the streets of Poland, his directorial fame in America, and the murder of his pregnant wife, Sharon Tate, at the hands of the Manson family. Then in 1977, he was arrested and tried for unlawful sex with a 13-year-old girl. After numerous court mishaps and misunderstandings, Polanski fled to Europe to avoid prison time. Perhaps his tragic background is the motive behind HBO's slightly biased spin. **99m/C; DVD, On Demand.** ***D:*** Marina Zenovich; ***W:*** Marina Zenovich; Joe Bini; P.G. Morgan; ***C:*** Tanya Koop; ***M:*** Mark De Gli Antoni.

Roman Spring of Mrs. Stone 🦴🦴🦴 *The Widow and the Gigolo* **1961** An aging actress determines to revive her career in Rome but finds romance with a gigolo instead in this adaptation of Tennessee Williams's novella. Leigh and Beatty are compelling, but Lenya nearly steals the show as Leigh's distinctly unappealing confidant. **104m/C; VHS, DVD.** Warren Beatty; Vivien Leigh; Lotte Lenya; Bessie Love; Jill St. John; Elspeth March; ***D:*** Jose Quintero; ***W:*** Gavin Lambert.

The Roman Spring of Mrs. Stone 🦴🦴 1/2 *Tennessee Williams: The Roman Spring of Mrs. Stone* **2003 (R)** In this slightly revised remake of the 1961 original, older actress Karen Stone (Mirren) becomes infatuated with conniving gigolo Paolo (Martinez) as she tries to rebound from the death of her rich husband while in Italy. **108m/C; VHS, DVD.** Dame Helen Mirren; Olivier Martinez; Anne Bancroft; Rodrigo Santoro; Brian Dennehy; Suzanne Bertish; Jane Bertish; Roger Allam; Victor Alfieri; Dona Granata; Aldo Signoretti; ***D:*** Robert Allan Ackerman; ***W:*** Martin Sherman; Tennessee Williams; ***C:*** Ashley Rowe; ***M:*** John Altman. **TV**

Romance 🦴🦴 **1930** In only her second talkie, Garbo stars as an Italian opera star who seduces a young priest. Poor story and weak acting from everyone with the exception of Garbo. Even she can't save this one. Adapted from the play "Signora Cacllini." **77m/B; VHS, DVD.** Greta Garbo; Lewis Stone; Gavin Gordon; Elliott Nugent; Florence Lake; Clara Blandick; ***D:*** Clarence Brown; ***C:*** William H. Daniels.

Romance 🦴🦴 **1999** This journey of erotic self-discovery caused raised eyebrows even among the blase French. Schoolteacher Marie (Ducey) is sexually rejected by her bored male model boyfriend Paul (Stevenin). This so distresses her that Marie flings herself into sexual escapades, including bar-pickup Paolo (Italian porn star Siffredi) and bondage sessions with school principal Robert (Berleand). Very talky, very self-serious, and very explicit. French with subtitles. **93m/C; VHS, DVD.** *FR* Caroline Ducey; Sagamore Stevenin; Francois Berleand; Rocco Siffredi; ***D:*** Catherine Breillat; ***W:*** Catherine Breillat; ***C:*** Yorgos Arvanitis; ***M:*** D.J. Valentin; Raphael Tidas.

Romance & Cigarettes 🦴🦴 **2005 (R)** Although made in 2005, Turturro's musical comedy didn't get much of a release until 2007 although it's not really bad—just, well, odd. Queens ironworker Nick (Gandolfini) is cheating on wife Kitty (Sarandon) with a slinky redhead—lingerie shop owner Tula (a foul-mouthed Winslet). When Kitty finds out, she decides to get even, aided by Cousin Bo (Walken) and the couple's three daughters (Aida Turturro, Parker, Moore). The score is mainly recognizable pop tunes, which the actors either sing or lip-synch to. **106m/C; DVD, Blu-Ray.** James Gandolfini; Susan Sarandon; Kate Winslet; Christopher Walken; Mary-Louise Parker; Aida Turturro; Mandy Moore; Bobby Cannavale; Steve Buscemi; Eddie Izzard; Elaine Stritch; ***D:*** John Turturro; ***W:*** John Turturro; ***C:*** Tom Stern; ***M:*** Paul Chihara.

Romance and Rejection 🦴🦴 *So This Is Romance?* **1996** Sad-sack Mike (Dinsdale) is looking for love in London. His father tells him to settle for good sex but Mike wants more. Then he meets a woman (Bellar) who may fulfill both parts of the equation. **98m/C; VHS, DVD.** *GB* Reece Dinsdale; Clara Bellar; John Hannah; Victoria Smurfit; Frank Finlay; Susannah York; Maryam D'Abo; Rowena King; ***D:*** Kevin W. Smith; ***W:*** Kevin W. Smith; ***C:*** Ian Savage; ***M:*** Howard J. Davidson.

Romance in Manhattan 🦴🦴 **1934** Recent immigrant to New York struggles to build new life, in spite of unemployment, language barriers, and loneliness. He meets Broadway chorine Rogers and song and dance ensues. America, ain't it a great place? **78m/B; VHS, DVD.** Ginger Rogers; Francis Lederer; J. Farrell MacDonald; ***D:*** Stephen Roberts; ***M:*** Max Steiner.

Romance of a Horsethief 🦴🦴 1/2 **1971 (PG)** Brynner leads this entertaining but slow-paced "Fiddler on the Roof" comedic romp without the music. In 1904 Poland, a Cossack captain takes horses for the Russo-Japanese war. The residents of the town rise up, goaded on by Birkin. **100m/C; VHS, DVD.** *YU* Yul Brynner; Eli Wallach; Jane Birkin; Oliver Tobias; Lainie Kazan; David Opatoshu; ***D:*** Abraham Polonsky.

The Romance of Astrea and Celadon 🦴🦴 *Les Amours d'Astree et de Celadon* **2007** A pastoral romance, set in a mythic 5th-century Gaul, based on the 17th-century novel by Honore d'Urfe. Shepherd Celadon (Gillet) is in love with shepherdess Astrea (Crayencour). She thinks he's unfaithful and banishes him, so Celadon tries to drown himself. He is saved by nymph Galathee (Reymoud), who wants him for herself. Celadon sulks until a druid (Renko) persuades him to dress in drag so he can befriend Astrea. Although the courtly discourse is frequently amusing, the artificial setting and subject will probably be of interest to only director Rohmer's fans. French with subtitles. **106m/C; DVD.** *FR IT SP* Serge Renko; Rodolphe Pauly; Andy Gillet; Stephanie Crayencour; Veronique Reymond; Cecile Cassel; Jocelyn Quivrin; ***D:*** Eric Rohmer; ***W:*** Eric Rohmer; ***C:*** Diane Baratier; ***M:*** Jean-Louis Valero.

The Romance of Rosy Ridge 🦴🦴 **1947** Post-Civil War romantic drama. Henry Carson (Johnson) rides into a Missouri community and gets a job working on the farm of fervent Confederate Gill MacBean (Mitchell). Henry falls in love with MacBean's daughter Lissy Anne (Leigh in her film debut) but Gill becomes suspicious that his new hand fought for the Union. Barns are being burned by night riders and the Rebs are convinced their Yankee neighbors are to blame, but someone may be stirring up trouble for other reasons. **109m/B; DVD.** Van Johnson; Janet Leigh; Thomas Mitchell; Selena Royle; Dean Stockwell; Charles Dingle; Jim Davis; Guy Kibbee; Elisabeth Risdon; Marshall Thompson; ***D:*** Roy Rowland; ***W:*** Lester Cole; ***C:*** Sidney Wagner; ***M:*** George Bassman.

Romance of the Limberlost 🦴 1/2 **1938** Orphaned wrong-side-of-the-bayou beauty Laurie (Parker) is pushed into an engagement with wealthy bully Corson (Pawley) by her greedy Aunt Nora (Main). She loves lawyer Wayne (Linden), whose very first trial case is the defense of young Chris (Jewell), who's accused of murdering Corson. **75m/B; DVD.** Jean Parker; Eric Linden; Marjorie Main; Edward Pawley; Hollis Jewell; Betty Blythe; ***D:*** William Nigh; ***W:*** Marion Orth; ***C:*** Gilbert Warrenton.

Romance on the High Seas 🦴🦴🦴 **1948** A woman is scheduled to take a cruise vacation but skips the boat when she believes her husband is cheating on her. Her husband believes she is taking the cruise to cheat on him and hires a private detective to follow her. Pleasant comedy features the film debut of Doris Day. **99m/C; VHS, DVD.** Jack Carson; Janis Paige; Don DeFore; Doris Day; Oscar Levant; S.Z. Sakall; Eric Blore; Franklin Pangborn; Leslie Brooks; William "Billy" Bakewell; ***D:*** Michael Curtiz; ***W:*** Julius J. Epstein.

Romancing the Stone 🦴🦴🦴 **1984 (PG)** Uptight romance novelist Joan (Turner) lives out her fantasies after she receives a mysterious map from her murdered brother-in-law and her sister is kidnapped in South America—the ransom being the map. Out to rescue her sister, she's helped and hindered by American soldier of fortune Jack (Douglas) whose main concern is himself and the hidden treasure described in the map. Great chemistry between the stars and loads of clever dialogue in this appealing adventure comedy. First outing with Turner, Douglas, and DeVito. Followed by "The Jewel of the Nile." **106m/C; VHS, DVD, Blu-Ray.** Michael Douglas; Kathleen Turner; Danny DeVito; Zack Norman; Alfonso Arau; Ron Silver; Mary Ellen Trainor; ***D:*** Robert Zemeckis; ***W:*** Diane Thomas; ***C:*** Dean Cundey; ***M:*** Alan Silvestri. Golden Globes '85: Actress--Mus./Comedy (Turner), Film--Mus./Comedy; L.A. Film Critics '84: Actress (Turner).

Romantic Comedy 🦴🦴 **1983 (PG)** Writing duo never seem to synchronize their desires for each other in this dull comedy. Engaging stars don't inspire each other much, and supporting cast can't make up the difference. Adapted from the Bernard Slade play. **102m/C; VHS, DVD.** Dudley Moore; Mary Steenburgen; Frances Sternhagen; Ron Leibman; ***D:*** Arthur Hiller; ***W:*** Bernard Slade; ***C:*** David M. Walsh; ***M:*** Marvin Hamlisch.

Romantic Englishwoman 🦴🦴🦴 **1975 (R)** Literate comedy-drama about the intertwined lives of several sophisticated and restrained Brits. Caine is a successful novelist with writer's block whose wife falls for another man while on a trip alone. He then invites his wife's lover to stay with them in order to generate ideas for his writing until his jealousy begins to surface. **117m/C; VHS, Blu-Ray.** *GB* Glenda Jackson; Michael Caine; Helmut Berger; Kate Nelligan; ***D:*** Joseph Losey; ***W:*** Tom Stoppard; Thomas Wiseman.

The Romantics 🦴 1/2 **2010 (PG-13)** Members of a Yale clique reunite for Lila (Paquin) and Tom's (Duhamel) wedding and, absurdly, Lila asks Laura (Holmes) to be Maid of Honor despite her passionate past and unsurprising current hang-up with the groom. A yuppie love triangle that could have been funny or dramatic instead sinks to self-indulgence and gooey melodrama. Even Bergen is dismal as the stereotypically controlling mother of the bride. Directorial debut of the book's author, Niederhoffer, with cheap, handheld camerawork that makes the sometimes grand landscapes look as dull as these preppy schmucks. **95m/C; DVD.** Katie Holmes; Josh Duhamel; Anna Paquin; Adam Brody; Malin Akerman; Elijah Wood; Jeremy Strong; Rebecca Lawrence; Dianna Agron; Candice Bergen; ***D:*** Galt Niederhoffer; ***W:*** Galt Niederhoffer; ***C:*** Sam Levy; ***M:*** Jonathan Sadoff.

Romantics Anonymous 🦴🦴 1/2 *Les Emotifs Anonymes* **2010** Chocolate brings together two awkward souls in this too-sweet French rom com. Work-at-home chocolatier Angelique is so shy she becomes jobless after failing to assert her abilities to a new boss. Easily panicked Jean-Rene is about to lose his chocolate factory unless he can hire a go-getter salesperson. He mistakenly hires Angelique but their mutual love of chocolate is a starting point for romance if only they can get past their pathological anxiety. French with subtitles. **80m/C; DVD.** *FR* Benoit Poelvoorde; Isabelle Carre; Lorella Cravotta; Pierre Niney; ***D:*** Jean-Pierre Ameis; ***W:*** Jean-Pierre Ameis; Philippe Blasband; ***C:*** Gerard Simon; ***M:*** Pierre Adenot.

Rome Adventure 🦴🦴 *Lovers Must Learn* **1962** Spinster librarian Pleshette takes Roman vacation hoping to meet handsome prince. Donahue takes shine to her while girlfriend Dickinson is away, as does suave Roman Brazzi. Soapy, ill-paced romance. **119m/C; VHS, DVD.** Troy Donahue; Angie Dickinson; Suzanne Pleshette; Rossano Brazzi; Constance Ford; Al Hirt; Chad Everett; Pam(ela) Austin; ***D:*** Delmer Daves; ***W:*** Delmer Daves; ***M:*** Max Steiner.

Rome Express 🦴 1/2 **1932** Thriller on a train as French detective Jolif (Vosper) investigates murder and the theft of a valuable painting aboard the Paris-Rome Express. Naturally everyone's a suspect. **94m/B; DVD.** *UK* Frank Vosper; Conrad Veidt; Esther Ralston; Joan Barry; Gordon Harker; Cedric Hardwicke; ***D:*** Walter Forde; ***W:*** Sidney Gilliat; ***C:*** Gunther Krampf.

Romeo and Juliet 🦴🦴🦴 1/2 **1936** One of MGM producer Irving Thalberg's pet projects (and starring Thalberg's wife, Norma Shearer), this Shakespeare classic was given the spare-no-expense MGM treatment. Physically too old to portray teenage lovers, both Howard and Shearer let their acting ability supply all necessary illusions. Also notable is Barrymore's over-the-top portrayal of Mercutio. **126m/B; VHS, DVD.** Leslie Howard; Norma Shearer; John Barrymore; Basil Rathbone; Edna May Oliver; ***D:*** George Cukor; ***C:*** William H. Daniels.

Romeo and Juliet 🦴🦴 **1954** Unfulfilling adaptation of Shakespeare's timeless drama of young love cast against family antagonisms. Peculiar supporting cast features both Cabot and ubiquitous master Gielgud. **138m/C; VHS, DVD.** *IT* Laurence Harvey; Susan Shantall; Aldo Zollo; Sebastian Cabot; Flora Robson; Mervyn Johns; Bill Travers; John Gielgud; ***D:*** Renato Castellani; ***C:*** Robert Krasker. Natl. Bd. of Review '54: Director (Castellani).

Romeo and Juliet 🦴🦴🦴 1/2 **1968 (PG)** Young couple share love despite prohibitive conflict between their families in this adaptation of Shakespeare's classic play. Director Zeffirelli succeeds in casting relative novices Whiting and Hussey in the leads, but is somewhat less proficient in lending air of free-wheeling '60s appeal to entire enterprise. Kudos, however, to cinematographer Pasquale De Santis and composer Nina Rota. Also available in a 45-minute edited version. **138m/C; VHS, DVD.** *GB IT* Olivia Hussey; Leonard Whiting; Michael York; Milo O'Shea; ***Nar:*** Laurence Olivier; ***D:*** Franco Zeffirelli; ***W:*** Franco Zeffirelli; Franco Brusati; Maestro D'Amico; ***C:*** Pasqualino De Santis; ***M:*** Nino Rota. Oscars '68: Cinematog., Costume Des.; Golden Globes '69: Foreign Film; Natl. Bd. of Review '68: Director (Zeffirelli).

Romeo & Juliet 🦴🦴 **2013 (PG-13)** This umpteenth adaptation keeps the setting but loses the dialogue, choosing to rewrite the Bard's brilliant language and keep the plot. The choice was a daring and misguided one even if Booth and Steinfeld do a decent job as arguably the two most legendary doomed teenaged lovers in history. The film isn't annoyingly bad but does leave one to wonder where it stands in the long legacy of Shakespeare adaptations. It's just too forgettable when there are already so many versions of this tale. **118m/C; DVD, Blu-Ray.** *UK* Douglas Booth; Hailee Steinfeld; Damian Lewis; Natascha (Natasha) McElhone; Stellan Skarsgard; Laura Morante; Tomas Arana; Christian Cooke; Ed Westwick; Tom Wisdom; Kodi Smit-McPhee; Lesley Manville; Paul Giamatti; ***D:*** Carlo Carlei; ***W:*** Julian Fellowes; ***C:*** David Tattersall; ***M:*** Abel Koreniowski.

Romeo Is Bleeding 🦴🦴 1/2 **1993 (R)** Jack (Oldman) is a police detective accepting mobster payoffs from boss Falcone (Scheider) for fingering federally protected witnesses. But the next target proves Jack's undoing—hitwoman Mona (Olin), who's more than a match for any man. Oldman's character is played for a patsy by everyone while Olin's is a kinky psycho-villainess with an enjoyment of violence, red lipstick, and a constant, maniacal laugh. Sciorra is generally wasted as Jack's unhappy wife while Lewis is annoying as his young and vacuous mistress. Part homage, part satire of film noir is overly stylized with intrusive narration but some effective shocks. **110m/C; VHS, DVD, Blu-Ray.** Gary Oldman; Lena Olin; Annabella Sciorra; Juliette Lewis; Roy Scheider; Michael Wincott; David Proval; Paul Butler; Will Patton; Larry Joshua; James Cromwell; Ron Perlman; ***D:*** Peter Medak; ***W:*** Hilary Henkin; ***C:*** Dariusz Wolski; ***M:*** Mark Isham.

Romeo Must Die 🦴🦴 1/2 **2000 (R)** Romance is decidedly secondary to action in this kung fu/hip hop hybrid. Black crime lord Isaak O'Day (a magnetic Lindo) and Asian crime boss Ch'u Sing (O) are maintaining an uneasy truce in order to do a mega-business deal. Into the mix springs good guy/ex-cop Han Sing (Li), who's out to avenge his brother's death, and lovely Trish O'Day (Aaliyah), who wants the same for her brother. (This is the chastest romantic pairing in modern movies.) The action sequences are frequent and frequently amazing and Li has minimal English dialogue to worry about. There's also humor, including Han's introduction to touch football. **115m/C; DVD, Blu-Ray, UMD.** Jet Li; Aaliyah; Delroy Lindo; Henry O; Isaiah Washington, IV; Russell Wong; DMX; DB Woodside; Edoardo Ballerini; Anthony Anderson; Jon Kit Lee; Francoise Yip; ***D:*** Andrzej Bartkowiak; ***W:*** Eric Bernt; John Jarrell; ***C:*** Glen MacPherson; ***M:*** Stanley Clarke; Timbaland.

Romero 🦴🦴 1/2 **1989** Julia is riveting as the Salvadoran archbishop who championed his destitute congregation despite considerable political opposition. A stirring biography financed by the United States Roman Catholic Church. **102m/C; VHS, DVD.** Raul Julia; Richard Jordan; Ana Alicia; Eddie Velez; Alejandro Bracho; Tony Plana; Lucy Reina; Harold Gould; Al Ruscio; Robert Viharo; ***D:*** John Duigan; ***W:*** John Sacret Young; ***C:*** Geoff Burton; ***M:*** Gabriel Yared.

Romola 🦴🦴 1/2 **1925** Silent adventure. After Powell and his father are attacked by pirates, Powell escapes. But instead of rescuing his father, he opts for a life of corruption. Dad eventually escapes and returns to exact vengeance. A rather expensive film in its day, troubled by modern-day sights in what was supposed to be old Florence. Gish's drowning scene had to be re-shot because she wouldn't sink. Colman arranged for his then-wife Raye to have a bit part, but they were divorced soon after the film was finished. **120m/B; Silent; VHS, DVD.** Lillian Gish; Dorothy Gish; William Powell; Ronald Colman; Charles Lane; Herbert Grimwood; Bonaventure Ibanez; Frank Puglia; Thelma Raye; ***D:*** Henry King.

Romper Stomper 🦴🦴 **1992 (R)** Violent confrontations between Australian skinheads and the Vietnamese community mixed in with a disturbing love story. Suburban rich girl Gabe (McKenzie) is drawn to the charasmatic Hando (Crowe), the certifiably loony leader of a group of Melbourne's skinheads. Any romance is secondary to the carnage brought by the skinheads' attacks on the local Asian community, who fight back with equal force. Disquieting look at a brutal world that can't be ignored. Film caused a furor upon its Australian release with debates about whether the extreme violence was intended to titilate or explicate the plot. **85m/C; VHS, DVD.** *AU* Russell Crowe; Jacqueline McKenzie; Daniel Pollock; Alex Scott; Leigh Russell; Daniel Wyllie; James McKenna; Samantha Bladon; ***D:*** Geoffrey Wright; ***W:*** Geoffrey Wright; ***C:*** Ron Hagen; ***M:*** John Clifford White. Australian Film Inst. '92: Actor (Crowe), Score, Sound.

Romulus, My Father 🦴🦴🦴 **2007 (R)** Opening in Australia's 1961 economic struggles, 10-year old Raimond (Smit-McPhee) and his eccentric Yugolasvian father Romulus (Bana) are comfortable as the town oddballs. Things begin to spiral out of control once Raimond's emotional German mother, Christina (Potente), briefly returns and leaves again, leading Romulus into a mental institution. Told in vignettes, the story spans years in the course of Raimond's life, as he discovers his strengths and fights to keep his father at his side. Melodramatic and often predictable, but it's got guts and an emotional punch. Based on the memoir by philosopher Raimond Gaita. **109m/C; DVD, On Demand.** *AU* Eric Bana; Franka Potente; Russell Dykstra; Marton Csokas; Kodi Smit-McPhee; Jacek Koman; ***D:*** Richard Roxburgh; ***W:*** Nick Drake; ***C:*** Geoffrey Simpson; ***M:*** Basil Hogios.

Romy and Michele's High School Reunion 🦴 1/2 **1997 (R)** Two vacuous ditz queens, Romy (Sorvino) and Michele (Kudrow), best friends and roommates since high school, decide they must impress at their 10-year Tucson high school reunion by passing themselves off as wealthy and successful. This proves to be a challenge, especially when cynical Heather (Garofalo), who knows the truth, threatens their deception. Music's good, and there are a (very) few funny moments, but you don't laugh with these would-be babes, you laugh at them. And even then, not all that much. Based on Schiff's play "The Ladies' Room." **91m/C; DVD, Blu-Ray.** Mira Sorvino; Lisa Kudrow; Janeane Garofalo; Alan Cumming; Julia Campbell; Elaine Hendrix; Jacob Vargas; Camryn Manheim; ***D:*** David Mirkin; ***W:*** Robin Schiff; ***C:*** Reynaldo Villalobos; ***M:*** Steve Bartek.

Ronin 🦴🦴 1/2 **1998 (R)** Disappointing despite the cast, writers, and director, although the scenery's spectacular (the action takes place between Paris and Nice) and there are some amazing car chases. But, they go on much too long and the story's less than involving. Sam (De Niro) is a world-weary, possibly ex-spy who gets involved with several international players (including Reno, Skarsgard, and Bean) to do a job for tough Irish lass Deirdre (McElhone) whose's fronting (for the violent Pryce) a project to retrieve a mysterious suitcase from some Russian bad guys. Title refers to a Japanese legend concerning 47 masterless samurai. **118m/C; DVD, Blu-Ray, UMD.** Robert De Niro; Jean Reno; Stellan Skarsgard; Natascha (Natasha) McElhone; Jonathan Pryce; Skipp (Robert L.) Sudduth; Michael (Michel) Lonsdale; Sean Bean; Jan Triska; Feodor Atkine; Bernard Bloch; Katarina Witt; ***D:*** John Frankenheimer; ***W:*** David Mamet; J.D. Zeik; ***C:*** Robert Fraisse; ***M:*** Elia Cmiral.

Ronin Gai 🦴🦴 1/2 *Ronin-Gai* **1990** Filmed as a tribute to Shozo Makino (regarded as the father of the Japanese Period Drama), this is the fourth version of the original film. It is 1836, and the Samurai are being tossed aside and forgotten. Outside of Edo four former Samurai are drowning their sorrows in sake and prostitutes, until the local whores begin to get cut up by the retainers of the local Shogun. When asked for help, the disgraced Samurai must shrug off their drunkenness for a chance at redemption. **121m/C; DVD.** *JP* Yoshio Harada; Kanako Higuchi; Shintaro Katsu; ***D:*** Kazuo Kiroki; ***W:*** Kazuo Kasahara; Itaro Yamagami; ***C:*** Hitoshi Takaiwa; ***M:*** Teizo Matsumura.

Ronnie and Julie 🦴🦴 1/2 **1997 (PG)** Yet another contemporary variation of "Romeo & Juliet" with high-school sweethearts Ronnie (Jackson) and Julie's (Finley) relationship threatened by their respective parents political rivalry in a mayoral campaign. At least this one has a happy ending. **99m/C; VHS, DVD.** Teri Garr; Joshua Jackson; Margot Finley; Alexandra Purvis; Tom Butler; Garwin Sanford; ***D:*** Philip Spink; ***C:*** Bruce Worrall.

Rooftops 🦴 1/2 **1989 (R)** Peculiar but predictable, centering on love between Hispanic girl and white youth who has mastered martial arts dancing. Director Wise is a long way from his earlier "West Side Story." See this one and be the only person you know who has. **108m/C; VHS, DVD.** Jason Gedrick; Troy Beyer; Eddie Velez; Tisha Campbell; ***D:*** Robert Wise; ***W:*** Allan Goldstein; Terrence (Terry) Brennan; ***M:*** Michael Kamen.

The Rook 🦴 1/2 **1999 (R)** Freaky yet flat crime thriller with drab Donovan as religious detective out to solve a young woman's murder in a rural community whose residents are as kooky (and not in that "fun to be around" way) as the evidence he uncovers. **85m/C; VHS, DVD.** Martin Donovan; John MacKay; Michael Finesilver; Fritz Fox; Karen Abrahams; ***D:*** Eran Palatnik; ***W:*** Richard Lee Purvis; ***C:*** Zack Winestine; ***M:*** Robert Een. **VIDEO**

The Rookie WOOF! **1959** This miserably unfunny military comedy is a misfire all the way. New recruit Noonan is eager to impress his boot camp sarge. He gets the chance when they are stranded on a Pacific isle with an actress and two Japanese soldiers who don't realize World War II is over. **86m/B; DVD.** Tommy Noonan; Peter Marshall; Julie Newmar; Jerry Lester; ***D:*** George O'Hanlon; ***W:*** Tommy Noonan; George O'Hanlon; ***C:*** Floyd Crosby; ***M:*** Paul Dunlap.

The Rookie 🦴🦴 **1990 (R)** Routine cop drama has worldly veteran and wide-eyed newcomer team to crack stolen-car ring managed by Germans. Eastwood and Sheen are reliable, but Hispanics Julia and Braga, though miscast, nonetheless steal this one as the German villains. **121m/C; VHS, DVD.** Clint Eastwood; Charlie Sheen; Raul Julia; Sonia Braga; Lara Flynn Boyle; Pepe Serna; Marco Rodriguez; Tom Skerritt; Roberta Vasquez; ***D:*** Clint Eastwood.

The Rookie 🦴🦴🦴 1/2 **2002 (G)** Texas high school teacher and baseball coach Jim Morris (Quaid) challenges his also-ran team by promising to go on a major league tryout if they win the regional championship. The team wins, and the former minor-leaguer attends a Devil Rays tryout and finds his now-rejuvenated arm can throw a baseball 98 mph. During his journey to the majors, he deals with his relationship with his old man, and life on the other side of 30. If this were't a true story, it'd be one of the hokiest movies ever, but because you know it's real, it's, well...inspiring. It helps that Quaid nails the role, and Jones, as son Hunter, walks off with every scene he's in. Based on Morris's book "The Oldest Rookie." **127m/C; VHS, DVD.** Dennis Quaid; Rachel Griffiths; Angus T. Jones; Brian Cox; Beth Grant; Chad Lindberg; Royce D. Applegate; Jay Hernandez; Russell Richardson; Raynor Scheine; David Blackwell; Edward "Blue" Deckert; Dan Kamin; Trevor Morgan; Rick Gonzalez; Angelo Spizzirri; ***D:*** John Lee Hancock; ***W:*** Mike Rich; ***C:*** John Schwartzman; ***M:*** Carter Burwell.

Rookie of the Year 🦴🦴 1/2 **1993 (PG)** Kid's fluff fantasy come true. Twelve-year-old baseball fanatic Henry has dreams of making it to the big league. He falls, breaks his arm, and when it heals strangely is blessed with a pitching arm so spectacular he finds himself not only playing for the Chicago Cubs, but leading them to the World Series. Enjoyable family outing for first-time director Stern (who also plays a seasoned and very incredulous ballplayer). Keep your eyes peeled for appearances by real-live sluggers Pedro Guerrero, Barry Bonds, and others. **103m/C; VHS, DVD.** Thomas Ian Nicholas; Daniel Stern; Gary Busey; Dan Hedaya; ***D:*** Daniel Stern; ***W:*** Sam Harper; ***C:*** Jack N. Green; ***M:*** Bill Conti. Blockbuster '95: Family Movie, V.

The Room WOOF! **2003 (R)** This unintentional laugher/vanity project has become a strange Hollywood cult item among the midnight movie crowd because of its sheer chutzpah and ineptitude. There's a plot in there somewhere (something about love and betrayal) but the Hound is certain that you won't care (and it doesn't make sense anyway). **99m/C; DVD, Blu-Ray.** Greg Sestero; Tommy Wiseau; Juliette Danielle; Philip Haldiman; Carolyn Minnott; ***D:*** Tommy Wiseau; ***W:*** Tommy Wiseau; ***C:*** Todd Barron; ***M:*** Mladen Milicevic.

Room 🦴🦴 1/2 **2015 (R)** Brie Larson and Jacob Tremblay are both revelations as Ma and her five-year-old son Jack, who has lived his whole life in the shed in which his mother has been kept prisoner at the hands of the sadistic Old Nick (Sean Bridgers). When she finally sees an opportunity to escape her imprisonment, Ma sends Jack out for help, and both of them are rescued. Readjusting to life proves understandably difficult for Ma, even with the support of the parents (Joan Allen & William H. Macy) with whom she is now reunited. The first half is harrowing and intense, but director Lenny Abrahamson loses the second half a bit. **113m/C; Streaming.** *CA IR* Brie Larson; Jacob Tremblay; Sean Bridges; Amanda Brugel; Joan Allen; William H. Macy; ***D:*** Lenny Abrahamson; ***W:*** Emma Donoghue; ***C:*** Danny Cohen; ***M:*** Stephen Rennicks. Oscars '15: Actress (Larson); Golden Globes '16: Actress--Drama (Larson); Ind. Spirit '16: Actress (Larson), First Screenplay; Screen Actors Guild '15: Actress (Larson).

Room at the Top 🦴🦴🦴 1/2 **1959** Ambitious factory man forsakes true love and marries boss's daughter instead in this grim drama set in industrial northern England. Cast excels, with Harvey and Sears as the worker and his wife. Signoret is also quite compelling as the abandoned woman. Adapted from John Braine's novel and followed by "Life at the Top" and "Man at the Top." **118m/B; VHS, DVD, Blu-Ray.** *GB* Laurence Harvey; Simone Signoret; Heather Sears; Hermione Baddeley; Avril Ungar; Donald Wolfit; Wendy Craig; Allan Cuthbertson; Ian Hendry; Donald Houston; Raymond Huntley; Miriam Karlin; Wilfred Lawson; Richard Pasco; Mary Peach; Prunella Scales; Beatrice Varley; John Westbrook; Delena Kidd; ***D:*** Jack Clayton; ***W:*** Neil Paterson; ***C:*** Freddie Francis; ***M:*** Mario Nascimbene. Oscars '59: Actress (Signoret), Adapt. Screenplay; British Acad. '58: Actress (Signoret), Film; Cannes '59: Actress (Signoret).

Room for One More 🦴🦴 **1951** Anna Rose (Drake) can't resist taking in strays, which her husband George (Grant) and their three children are used to. Then Anna comes to the rescue of orphaned Jane (Mann), a problem child in need of a foster family, and later to handicapped Jimmy-John (Tatum, Jr.) despite her husband's initial objections. Shameless heart-tugger based on a true story; Grant and Drake were married at the time of filming. **95m/B; DVD.** Cary Grant; Betsy Drake; Iris Mann; Clifford Tatum, Jr.; Lurene Tuttle; Randy Stuart; John Ridgely; ***D:*** Norman Taurog; ***W:*** Jack Rose; Melville Shavelson; ***C:*** Robert Burks; ***M:*** Max Steiner.

Room Service 🦴🦴 1/2 **1938** The Marx Brothers provide less than the usual mayhem here with Groucho as a penniless theatrical producer determined to remain in his hotel room until he can secure funds for his next play. Ball doesn't help matters much either. Not bad, but certainly not up to the zany Marx clan's usual stuff. **78m/B; VHS, DVD.** Groucho Marx; Harpo Marx; Chico Marx; Lucille Ball; Ann Miller; Frank Albertson; Donald MacBride; Charles Halton; ***D:*** William A. Seiter; ***W:*** Morrie Ryskind; ***C:*** J. Roy Hunt; ***M:*** Roy Webb.

Room 314 🦴🦴 **2007** Micro-budget drama, which Knowles adapted from his play, where a hotel room is the scene of five couples' stories. Stacey can't remember her drunken one-nighter with Nick; alcoholic Harry is contemplating suicide, not adultery, when his suspicious wife Gretchen shows up; salesman Jack tries to sell co-worker Kathy on an affair; luckless Matt's pickup Tracey seems to be a psycho; and needy David tries to define his relationship with his moody girlfriend Caly. **100m/C; DVD.** Joelle Carter; Michael Laurence; Michael Mosley; Sarah Bennett; Robyn Myhr; Monique Vukovic; Jennifer Marlowe; Matthew Del Negro; Todd Swenson; Michael Knowles; ***D:*** Michael Knowles; ***W:*** Michael Knowles; ***C:*** Michael Knowles; Shawn Regruto.

A Room with a View 🦴🦴🦴🦴 **1986** Engaging adaptation of E.M. Forster's novel of requited love. Lucy Honeychurch (Bonham Carter) is the feisty British idealist who rejects dashing George (Sands) for supercilious Cecil (Day-Lewis), then repents and finds (presumably) eternal passion. A multi-Oscar nominee, with great music (courtesy of Puccini), great scenery (courtesy of Florence), and great performances (courtesy of practically everybody, but supporters Smith,

Dench, Callow, and Elliott must be particularly distinguished). Truly romantic, and there's much humor too. **117m/C; DVD, Blu-Ray, HD-DVD.** *UK* Helena Bonham Carter; Julian Sands; Denholm Elliott; Maggie Smith; Dame Judi Dench; Simon Callow; Daniel Day-Lewis; Rupert Graves; Rosemary Leach; ***D:*** James Ivory; ***W:*** Ruth Prawer Jhabvala; ***C:*** Tony Pierce-Roberts; ***M:*** Richard Robbins. Oscars '86: Adapt. Screenplay, Art Dir./Set Dec., Costume Des.; British Acad. '86: Actress (Smith), Film, Support. Actress (Dench); Golden Globes '87: Support. Actress (Smith); Ind. Spirit '87: Foreign Film; Natl. Bd. of Review '86: Support. Actor (Day-Lewis); N.Y. Film Critics '86: Cinematog., Support. Actor (Day-Lewis); Writers Guild '86: Adapt. Screenplay.

A Room With a View 🦴🦴 **2008** BBC version of E.M. Forster's 1908 novel leaves a bad taste thanks to an unfortunate coda added by writer Davies, allegedly from later material by Forster. Prim (but secretly passionate) Lucy Honeychurch (Cassidy) is touring Italy with her fluttery chaperone Charlotte (Thompson). In Florence they meet garrulous working-class Mr. Emerson and his son George (played by the father/son Spalls) and Lucy is tempted into unexpected romance with the totally unsuitable young man. Lucy's terribly conflicted, weighed down by others' expectations, but will she follow her heart? **86m/C; DVD.** *GB* Elaine Cassidy; Rafe Spall; Timothy Spall; Sophie Thompson; Laurence Fox; Mark Williams; Timothy West; Elizabeth McGovern; Sinead Cusack; ***D:*** Nicholas Renton; ***W:*** Andrew Davies; ***C:*** Alan Almond; ***M:*** Gabriel Yared. **TV**

Roommate 🦴🦴 **1984** A valedictorian church-goer and a rebellious iconoclast room together at Northwestern University in 1952, with the expected humorous results. Public TV presentation based on a John Updike story. **96m/C; VHS, DVD.** Lance Guest; Barry Miller; Elaine Wilkes; Melissa Ford; David Bachman; ***D:*** Nell Cox. **TV**

The Roommate WOOF! 2011 (PG-13) Psychopathic college freshman Rebecca (Meester) becomes violently obsessed with her new roommate, Sara (Kelly). The two lead actresses are likeable but nothing can save this trite, inconsistent film that is utterly lacking in suspense. It's a stretch to even call it a guilty pleasure, due to the bland predictability of the plot. An extremely dreadful attempt at remaking the classic roommate suspense film, "Single White Female." **91m/C; Blu-Ray.** Leighton Meester; Minka Kelly; Cam Gigandet; Alyson Michalka; Danneel Harris; Matt Lanter; Frances Fisher; Tomas Arana; Billy Zane; ***D:*** Christian E. Christiansen; ***W:*** Sonny Malihi; ***C:*** Phil Parmet; ***M:*** John (Gianni) Frizzell.

Roommates 🦴🦴 **1/2 1995 (PG)** Rocky Holeczek (Falk) is a cantankerous coot who, at age 75, decides to care for orphaned seven-year-old grandson Michael. Over the 30 years they are together, they fight over Rocky's old school ways and a grown-up Michael's (Sweeney) attempt to have a family of his own. But despite their bickering, Michael soon realizes that his 107-year-old grandfather's words are truly pearls of wisdom when faced with tragedy. Film hits the right sentimental buttons without going overboard with the tissues and Falk's performance, underneath the layers of latex makeup, is charmingly irascible. Based on cowriter Apple's own grandfather. **108m/C; VHS, DVD, Blu-Ray.** Peter Falk; D.B. Sweeney; Julianne Moore; Ellen Burstyn; ***D:*** Peter Yates; ***W:*** Max Apple; Stephen Metcalfe; ***C:*** Mike Southon; ***M:*** Elmer Bernstein.

Rooms for Tourists 🦴🦴 *Habitaciones para Turistas* **2004** Creepy, gory feature (made more so by being filmed in B&W) set in a backwater section of Buenos Aires. Five girls miss their train and find room in a hostel owned by two brothers. Soon they're hunted by a masked killer throughout the dark, decrepit house. Spanish with subtitles. **90m/B; DVD.** *AR* Jimena Krouco; Elena Siritto; Mariela Mujica; Brenda Vera; Victoria Witemburg; Rolf Garcia; Alejandro Lise; ***D:*** Adrian Garcia-Bogliano; ***W:*** Adrian Garcia-Bogliano; Ramiro Garcia-Bogliano; ***C:*** Dario Bermeo; Veronica Padron; ***M:*** Rodrigo Franco.

Rooster Cogburn 🦴🦴 **1/2 1975 (PG)** A Bible-thumping schoolmarm joins up with a hard-drinking, hard-fighting marshal in order to capture a gang of outlaws who killed her father. Tired sequel to "True Grit" but the chemistry between Wayne and Hepburn is right on target. **107m/C; VHS, DVD, Blu-Ray.** John Wayne; Katharine Hepburn; Richard Jordan; Anthony Zerbe; John McIntire; Strother Martin; Paul Koslo; Tommy Lee; ***D:*** Stuart Millar; ***W:*** Martin Julien; ***C:*** Harry Stradling, Jr.; ***M:*** Laurence Rosenthal.

Roosters 🦴🦴 **1/2 1995 (R)** Gallo Morales (Olmos) is returning home, after serving seven years in prison for manslaughter, anxiously awaited by wife Juana (Braga), 20-year-old rebellious son Hector (Nucci), neglected adolescent daughter Angela (Lassez), and sexy sister Chata (Alonso). Gallo is a noted breeder of fighting cocks, which for him represent machismo and power but, to his resentment, it's Hector who owns a potential prize-winning bird, precipitating some explosive family conflicts. Adapted by Sanchez-Scott from her 1987 play. **93m/C; VHS, DVD.** Edward James Olmos; Sonia Braga; Maria Conchita Alonso; Danny Nucci; Sarah Lassez; ***D:*** Robert M. Young; ***W:*** Milcha Sanchez-Scott; ***C:*** Reynaldo Villalobos; ***M:*** David Kitay.

Roots 🦴🦴🦴🦴 **1977** The complete version of Alex Haley's saga following a black man's search for his heritage, revealing an epic panorama of America's past. Dramatizing the shared heritage of millions of African Americans in an ennobling fashion, this milestone miniseries brought together dozens of black actors to create an accurate, if simplified, picture of several generations in one black family. The story begins with Kunta Kinte (Burton) going through his manhood trials in his Gambian village in Africa, only to be captured by slavers and shipped away to America. **573m/C; VHS, DVD, Blu-Ray.** John Amos; Maya Angelou; Ed Asner; Lloyd Bridges; LeVar Burton; Chuck Connors; Cicely Tyson; Ben Vereen; Sandy Duncan; Tanya Boyd; Lynda Day George; Lorne Greene; Burl Ives; O.J. Simpson; Todd Bridges; Georg Stanford Brown; MacDonald Carey; Olivia Cole; Leslie Uggams; Ossie Davis; ***D:*** David Greene; Marvin J. Chomsky; John Erman; Gilbert Moses; ***W:*** William Blinn; Ernest Kinoy; M. Charles Cohen; James H. Lee; ***C:*** Stevan Larner; Joseph M. Wilcots; ***M:*** Quincy Jones; Gerald Fried. **TV**

Roots: The Gift 🦴🦴 **1988** It's Christmas 1770, and Kunte Kinte (Burton) and Fiddler (Gossett) try to escape slavery via the Underground Railroad. In their attempt, they wind up giving the gift of freedom to several of their fellow slaves. **94m/C; VHS, Streaming.** Louis Gossett, Jr.; LeVar Burton; Michael Learned; Avery Brooks; Kate Mulgrew; Shaun Cassidy; John McMartin; ***D:*** Kevin Hooks; ***C:*** John A. Alonzo. **TV**

Roots: The Next Generation 🦴🦴🦴 **1979** Sequel to the landmark TV miniseries continuing the story of author Alex Haley's ancestors from the Reconstruction era of the 1880s to 1967, culminating with Haley's visit to West Africa where he is told the story of Kunta Kinte. **685m/C; VHS, DVD.** Georg Stanford Brown; Lynne Moody; Henry Fonda; Richard Thomas; Marc Singer; Olivia de Havilland; Paul Koslo; Beah Richards; Stan Shaw; Harry (Henry) Morgan; Irene Cara; Dorian Harewood; Ruby Dee; Paul Winfield; James Earl Jones; Debbie Allen; ***Cameo(s):*** Al Freeman, Jr.; Marlon Brando; ***D:*** John Erman; ***W:*** Sydney Glass; ***C:*** Joseph M. Wilcots; ***M:*** Gerald Fried. **TV**

Rope 🦴🦴🦴 **1/2 1948 (PG)** In New York City, two gay college students murder a friend for kicks and store the body in a living room trunk. They further insult the dead by using the trunk as the buffet table and inviting his parents to the dinner party in his honor. Very dark humor is the theme in Hitchcock's first color film, which he innovatively shot in uncut ten-minute takes, with the illusion of a continuous scene maintained with tricky camera work. Based on the Patrick Hamilton play and on the Leopold-Loeb murder case. **81m/C; VHS, DVD, Blu-Ray.** James Stewart; John Dall; Farley Granger; Cedric Hardwicke; Constance Collier; ***D:*** Alfred Hitchcock; ***W:*** Arthur Laurents; ***C:*** William V. Skall; Joseph Valentine; ***M:*** David Buttolph.

Rope of Sand 🦴🦴 **1949** In a South African mining town, hunting guide Mike Davis' (Lancaster) client trespasses on mining property, finds a cache of diamonds, and then dies. Sadistic company cop Paul Vogel (Henried) tries to whip the gems location out of Mike, but he doesn't talk. Two years later, he returns to collect the diamonds and mine owner Arthur Martingale (Rains) sends whore Suzanne (Calvert) to seduce the info from Mike instead, but Vogel still has his own ideas. **104m/B; DVD, Blu-Ray.** Burt Lancaster; Paul Henreid; Claude Rains; Corinne Calvet; Peter Lorre; Sam Jaffe; John Bromfield; Mike Mazurki; ***D:*** William Dieterle; ***W:*** Walter Doniger; John Paxton; ***C:*** Charles B(ryant) Lang, Jr.; ***M:*** Franz Waxman.

Rory O'Shea Was Here 🦴🦴 **1/2** *Inside I'm Dancing* **2004 (R)** Rory is the independence-seeking, fun-loving, skirt-chasing new arrival at Carrigmore nursing home. A muscular dystrophy patient, he befriends cerebral palsy sufferer Michael because he seems to be the only one who can understand him. When Rory is denied an independent-living grant because of his recklessness, he persuades Michael to apply, tagging along as his interpreter. They hire Siobhan, a cute supermarket clerk as their helper. Inevitably, they both fall for her. Excellent performances and some genuinely funning and touching scenes help elevate this Irish import above the usual disease-of-the-week fare. **104m/C; DVD.** *IR GB FR* Steven Robertson; James McAvoy; Romola Garai; Brenda Fricker; Gerard McSorley; Tom Hickey; Ruth McCabe; ***D:*** Damien O'Donnell; ***W:*** Jeffrey Caine; ***M:*** David Julyan.

The Rosa Parks Story 🦴🦴 **1/2 2002** Rather prosaic bio on Rosa Parks (Bassett) goes into detail on her life (beginning when she was the new girl at a Montgomery school) to her involvement in the N.A.A.C.P. and the Montgomery, Alabama bus boycott sparked by her arrest. **90m/C; VHS, DVD.** Angela Bassett; Peter Francis James; Tonea Stewart; Cicely Tyson; Sonny Shroyer; ***D:*** Julie Dash; ***W:*** Paris Qualles. **TV**

Rosalie 🦴🦴 **1/2 1938** A gridiron great from West Point falls for a mysterious beauty from Vassar. He soon learns that her father reigns over a tiny Balkan nation. Expensive, massive, imperfect musical; exotic romantic pairing fails to conceal plot's blah-ness. Oh well, at least Porter's music is good. **118m/B; VHS, DVD.** Nelson Eddy; Eleanor Powell; Frank Morgan; Ray Bolger; Ilona Massey; Reginald Owen; Edna May Oliver; Jerry Colonna; ***D:*** W.S. Van Dyke; ***M:*** Cole Porter.

Rosalie Goes Shopping 🦴🦴🦴 **1989 (PG-13)** Satire about American consumerism hiding behind slapstick comedy, and it works, most of the time. Misplaced Bavarian (Sagebrecht) moves to Arkansas and begins spending wildly and acquiring "things." Twisty plot carried confidently by confident wackiness from Sagebrecht and supporters. **94m/C; VHS, Streaming.** *GE* Marianne Sagebrecht; Brad Davis; Judge Reinhold; Willie Harlander; Alex Winter; Erika Blumberger; Patricia Zehentmayr; ***D:*** Percy Adlon; ***W:*** Eleonore Adlon; Percy Adlon; ***M:*** Bob Telson.

Roseanne for President! 🦴🦴 **2016** A feature-length documentary about controversial comedian Roseanne Barr. The film ostensibly follows Barr as she runs an unexpected and unusual presidential campaign as the candidate of the Peace and Freedom Party. Her platform focuses on her ability to fix everything. it reveals more about her persona as a comedian and a portrait of her as complex person. The film also includes interviews with such comedy luminaries as Rosie O'Donnell, Michael Moore, and Tommy Smothers. **96m/C; DVD, Streaming, Download.** Roseanne Barr; ***D:*** Eric Weinrib; ***C:*** Vernon Hunnings, Jr; Nick Junkersfeld; Jayme Roy; Shane Sigler.

The Rose 🦴🦴🦴 **1979 (R)** Modeled after the life of Janis Joplin, Midler plays a young, talented and self-destructive blues/rock singer. Professional triumphs don't stop her lonely restlessness and confused love affairs. The best exhibition of the rock and roll world outside of documentaries. Electrifying film debut for Midler features an incredible collection of songs. **134m/C; VHS, DVD, Blu-Ray.** Bette Midler; Alan Bates; Frederic Forrest; Harry Dean Stanton; David Keith; ***D:*** Mark Rydell; ***C:*** Vilmos Zsigmond. Golden Globes '80: Actress--Mus./Comedy (Midler), Song ("The Rose"); Natl. Soc. Film Critics '79: Support. Actor (Forrest).

The Rose and the Jackal 🦴🦴 **1990** Well-done TNT historical drama that's an intriguing fictionalization about the founder of the Pinkerton detective agency. In 1861, President Lincoln forms the secret service agency headed by Allen Pinkerton. He goes after Southern society belle Rose Greenhow, who is suspected of giving Union military secrets to the Confederacy. The two find a doomed romance when Pinkerton imprisons Rose as a spy. **94m/C; DVD.** Christopher Reeve; Madolyn Smith; Granville Van Dusen; Carrie Snodgress; Kevin McCarthy; ***D:*** Jack Gold; ***W:*** Eric Edson; ***C:*** Dietrich Lohmann; ***M:*** Michael J. Lewis. **CABLE**

The Rose Garden 🦴🦴 **1/2 1989 (PG-13)** In modern Germany, a Holocaust survivor is put on trial for assaulting an elderly man. The victim, it turns out, was a Nazi guilty of heinous war crimes. Ullmann and Schell lend substance, though treatment of a powerful theme is inadequate. **112m/C; VHS, DVD.** Liv Ullmann; Maximilian Schell; Peter Fonda; Jan Niklas; Kurt Hubner; ***D:*** Fons Rademakers; ***W:*** Paul Hengge; ***M:*** Egisto Macchi.

Rose Hill 🦴🦴 **1/2 1997 (PG)** Adam, Travis, Douglas, and Cole are (unrelated) orphans, living on the streets of 1860s New York City, when they find an abandoned baby girl. They adopt the baby, whom they name Mary Rose, and decide to head west to start a new life as a family. As the years pass the boys build a cattle ranch in Montana they name Rose Hill and over-protect their headstrong teenaged sister, who would like the chance to flirt with some beaus without her brothers hovering around. TV movie based on the Julie Garwood novel "For the Roses." **90m/C; VHS, DVD.** Jennifer Garner; Jeffrey D. Sams; Tristan Tait; Zak Orth; Justin Chambers; Casey Siemaszko; David Newcom; ***D:*** Christopher Cain; ***W:*** Earl W. Wallace. **TV**

Rose Marie 🦴🦴🦴 *Indian Love Call* **1936** An opera star falls in love with the mountie who captured her escaped convict brother. Hollywood legend has it that when a British singer was presented with the first line in "Indian Love Song," which is "When I'm calling you-oo-oo-oo-oo-oo-oo," the confused performer sang, "When I'm calling you, double oh, double oh, double oh..." Maybe true, maybe not, but funny anyway. Classic MacDonald-Eddy operetta. Remade in 1954. **112m/B; VHS, DVD.** Jeanette MacDonald; Nelson Eddy; James Stewart; Allan Jones; David Niven; Reginald Owen; ***D:*** W.S. Van Dyke; ***C:*** William H. Daniels; ***M:*** Rudolf Friml.

Rose Marie 🦴🦴🦴 **1954 (G)** Blyth is a lonely Canadian woman wooed by a mean spirited fur trapper and a gallant mountie. Unremarkable remake of the Eddy/MacDonald musical is saved by specatular technicolor and CinemaScope photography. Choreography by Busby Berkeley. **115m/C; VHS, DVD.** Ann Blyth; Howard Keel; Fernando Lamas; Bert Lahr; Marjorie Main; Joan Taylor; Chief Yowlachie; Abel Fernandez; Al Ferguson; Dabbs Greer; Lumsden Hare; ***D:*** Mervyn LeRoy; ***C:*** Paul Vogel.

Rose of Washington Square 🦴🦴 **1/2 1939** Singer Faye gets involved with the no-account Power, much to the dismay of her friend Jolson. They marry, and she becomes a singing sensation in the Ziegfeld Follies while he becomes an embarassment, eventually winding up on the wrong side of the law. Jolson stole the movie, singing some of his best numbers. This thinly disguised portrait of Fanny Brice caused the performer to sue for defamation of character; she eventually settled out of court. **86m/B; VHS, DVD.** Alice Faye; Tyrone Power; Al Jolson; William Frawley; Joyce Compton; Hobart Cavanaugh; Moroni Olsen; ***D:*** Gregory Ratoff; ***W:*** Nunnally Johnson; ***C:*** Karl Freund.

The Rose Tattoo 🦴🦴🦴 **1/2 1955** Magnani, in her U.S. screen debut, is just right as a Southern widow who cherishes her husband's memory, but falls for virile trucker Lancaster. Williams wrote this play and screenplay specifically for Magnani, who was never as successful again. Interesting character studies, although Lancaster doesn't seem right as an Italian longshoreman. **117m/B; DVD.** Anna Magnani; Burt Lancaster; Marisa Pavan; Ben Cooper; Virginia Grey; Jo Van Fleet; ***D:*** Daniel Mann; ***W:*** Tennessee Williams;

Hal Kanter; ***C:*** James Wong Howe; ***M:*** Alex North. Oscars '55: Actress (Magnani), Art Dir./Set Dec., B&W, B&W Cinematog.; British Acad. '56: Actress (Magnani); Golden Globes '56: Actress--Drama (Magnani), Support. Actress (Pavan); N.Y. Film Critics '55: Actress (Magnani).

Rosebud Beach Hotel 🦴 *The Big Lobby; The No-Tell Hotel* **1985 (R)** Wimpy loser tries his hand at managing a run-down hotel in order to please his demanding girlfriend. Camp is okay, but this soft-porn excuse is horrible in every other way. **82m/C; VHS, DVD.** Colleen Camp; Peter Scolari; Christopher Lee; Fran Drescher; Eddie Deezen; Chuck McCann; Hank Garrett; Hamilton Camp; Cherie Currie; ***D:*** Harry Hurwitz; ***C:*** Joao Fernandes.

Roseland 🦴🦴🦴 **1977 (PG)** Three interlocking stories, set at New York's famous old Roseland Ballroom, about lonely people who live to dance. Not fully successful, but strong characters, especially in the second and third stories, make it worth watching, although it lacks energy. **103m/C; VHS, DVD.** Christopher Walken; Geraldine Chaplin; Joan Copeland; Teresa Wright; Lou Jacobi; ***D:*** James Ivory; ***W:*** Ruth Prawer Jhabvala.

Rosemary's Baby 🦴🦴🦴🦴 **1968 (R)** A young woman, innocent and religious, and her husband, ambitious and agnostic, move into a new apartment. Soon the woman is pregnant, but she begins to realize that she has fallen into a coven of witches and warlocks, and that they claim the child as the antichrist. Gripping and powerful, subtle yet utterly horrifying, with luminous performances by all. Polanski's first American film; from Levin's best-seller. **134m/C; VHS, DVD, Blu-Ray.** Mia Farrow; John Cassavetes; Ruth Gordon; Sidney Blackmer; Maurice Evans; Patsy Kelly; Elisha Cook, Jr.; Ralph Bellamy; Charles Grodin; Hanna Landy; Emmaline Henry; William Castle; ***V:*** Tony Curtis; ***D:*** Roman Polanski; ***W:*** Roman Polanski; ***C:*** William A. Fraker; ***M:*** Krzysztof Komeda. Oscars '68: Support. Actress (Gordon); Golden Globes '69: Support. Actress (Gordon); Natl. Film Reg. '14.

Rosemary's Baby 🦴🦴 **2014** NBC TV miniseries remake of the 1968 film relocates the story from New York to Paris as a lonely Rosemary (Saldana) adjusts to the changes in her life with husband Guy (Adams), who's teaching at the Sorbonne for a year. The couple is soon taken up by sophisticated Roman (Isaacs) and Margaux (Bouquet) who are overly-attentive to the young couple. Weak-willed Guy lets his ambitions get the best of him and soon a pregnant Rosemary is very worried that their new friends are part of a Satanic cult. Gorier than the original movie and a little too long, but Saldana makes for a fierce mommy-to-be. **176m/C; DVD, Blu-Ray.** Zoe Saldana; Patrick J. Adams; Jason Isaacs; Carole Bouquet; Christina Cole; ***D:*** Agnieszka Holland; ***W:*** Scott Abbott; James Wong; ***C:*** Michel Amathieu; ***M:*** Antoni Lazarkiewicz. **TV**

Rosencrantz & Guildenstern Are Dead 🦴🦴🦴 **1990 (PG)** Playwright Stoppard adapted his own absurdist 1967 play to film—which at first look makes as much sense as a "Swan Lake" ballet on radio. Patience is rewarded for those who stick with it. Two tragicomic minor characters in "Hamlet" squabble rhetorically and misperceive Shakespeare's plot tightening fatally around them. Uprooted from the stage environment, it's arcane but hilarious if you're paying attention. Roth and Oldman are superb as the doomed duo. **118m/C; VHS, DVD, Blu-Ray.** *GB* Gary Oldman; Tim Roth; Richard Dreyfuss; Iain Glen; Joanna Roth; Donald (Don) Sumpter; Sven Medvesck; Joanna Miles; Ian Richardson; John Burgess; Vili Matula; Ljubo Zecevic; ***D:*** Tom Stoppard; ***W:*** Tom Stoppard; ***C:*** Peter Biziou; ***M:*** Stanley Myers. Venice Film Fest. '91: Picture.

Rosencrantz & Guildenstern Are Undead 🦴 ½ **2010** Low-budget indie with a minor slacker charm. Mopey and broke New Yorker Julian (Hoffman, son of actor Dustin) answers an ad to work on an off-Broadway production of "Hamlet" and soon discovers that the others involved in the production are vampires. Writer Theo (Ventigmiglia) is hoping to lure the real Hamlet (another vampire) out of hiding so they can finally settle a longstanding grudge over Ophelia. Title is a nod to the (much better) Tom Stoppard play (and film). **83m/C; Blu-Ray.** Jake Hoffman; Devon Aoki; John Ventimiglia; Kris Lemche; Graeme Malcolm; Chip Zien; Joey Kern; Ralph Macchio; Jeremy Sisto; Geneva Carr; Mike Landry; Carlos Velazquez; Azie Tesfai; Carmen Goodine; ***D:*** Jordan Galland; ***W:*** Jordan Galland; ***C:*** Christopher LaVasseur; ***M:*** Sean Lennon.

Rosenstrasse 🦴🦴🦴 **2003 (PG-13)** Fact-based account of a forgotten incident of heroism in WWII Germany. When Berlin's remaining Jews are rounded up for deportation to death camps in 1943, those married to non-Jewish women, or children of such couples are diverted to temporary prison on Rosenstrasse ("Street of Roses"). Many of the detainees' wives gather outside the prison to show support to families inside and demand their release. Film tells this story through families directly involved in event. Moving and well-acted retelling of lost piece of history. **136m/C; DVD.** *GE NL* Katja Riemann; Maria Schrader; Martin Feifel; Jutta Lampe; Doris Schade; Fedja Van Huet; Carola Regnier; Jan Decleir; Thekla Reuten; Lena Stolze; Isolde Barth; Martin Wuttke; Jurgen Vogel; Svea Lohde; Jutta Wachowiak; Nina Kunzendorf; ***D:*** Margarethe von Trotta; ***W:*** Margarethe von Trotta; Pamela Katz; ***C:*** Jan Betke; ***M:*** Loek Dikker.

Roses Are for the Rich 🦴🦴 **1987** CBS TV miniseries adapted from the Jonell Lawson novel. Autumn McAvin's (Hartman) husband dies in a suspicious mine explosion and she vows revenge on coal baron Douglas Osborne (Dern). Eventually, she blackmails Osborne into marrying her but when he suddenly dies, Autumn goes on trial for murder. **182m/C; Download.** Lisa Hartman Black; Bruce Dern; Joe Penny; Richard Masur; Howard Duff; Morgan Stevens; Sharon Wyatt; Betty Buckley; ***D:*** Michael Miller; ***W:*** Judith Paige Mitchell; ***C:*** Kees Van Oostrum; ***M:*** Arthur B. Rubinstein. **TV**

Rosetta 🦴🦴 **1999 (R)** Rosetta (Dequenne) is a desperate 17-year-old Belgian who lives in a trailer with her alcoholic mother. Her joyless routine includes caring for her passed-out mom and frantically searching for some kind of employment, even if it means betraying her one friend, Riquet (Rongione), who works at a waffle stand and whose job Rosetta comes to covet. Claustrophobic and depressing. French with subtitles. **95m/C; VHS, DVD, Blu-Ray.** *FR BE* Emilie Dequenne; Fabrizio Rongione; Anne Yernaux; Olivier Gourmet; ***D:*** Jean-Pierre Dardenne; Luc Dardenne; ***W:*** Jean-Pierre Dardenne; Luc Dardenne; ***C:*** Alain Marcoen. Cannes '99: Actress (Dequenne), Film.

Rosewater 🦴 ½ **2014 (R)** Comedian/tv host Stewart adapts and directs the fascinating story of Maziar Bahari, an Iranian-Canadian journalist imprisoned by his dictatorial government after he went on Stewart's "The Daily Show" and his captors mistook satire for fact. This interesting act of a theatrical apology falls apart due to a few key errors by Stewart (in his directorial debut), including casting too many non-Iranians in an Iranian story, and, more damagingly, never presenting the true stakes of Bahari's plight. It's a movie rendition without any actual sense of danger. Based on Bahari's best-selling memoir, "Then They Came for Me: A Family's Story of Love, Captivity, and Survival." **103m/C; DVD, Blu-Ray.** Gael Garcia Bernal; Kim Bodnia; Shohreh Aghdashloo; Claire Foy; ***D:*** Jon Stewart; ***W:*** Jon Stewart; ***C:*** Bobby Bukowski; ***M:*** Howard Shore.

Rosewood 🦴🦴🦴 **1996 (R)** Based on the true story of the African American community of Rosewood, Florida, which was destroyed by a white mob in 1923. War vet Mr. Mann (Rhames) and white shopkeeper Wright (Voight) try to save innocent people from the tragedy that begins when a white woman falsely accuses a black man of rape. Accurately shows the tensions of the time; both leads are strong, and film succeeds as a detailed visual reminder of country's tragic history. Real-life survivors of the bloodshed finally won reparation from the Florida legislature in 1993. Singleton shot on location in the Florida swamps. **142m/C; VHS, DVD.** Ving Rhames; Jon Voight; Don Cheadle; Michael Rooker; Bruce McGill; Loren Dean; Esther Rolle; Elise Neal; Catherine Kellner; Akosua Busia; Paul Benjamin; Mark Boone, Jr.; Muse Watson; Badja (Medu) Djola; Kathryn Meisle; Jaimz Woolvett; ***D:*** John Singleton; ***W:*** Gregory Poirier; ***C:*** Johnny E. Jensen; ***M:*** John Williams.

Roswell: The Aliens Attack 🦴 **1999 (PG)** Two aliens escape from Roswell intent on detonating a nuclear device that will clear humanity off the planet. One of the two falls in love with a local woman despite the biological unlikelihood of this possibility. **88m/C; DVD.** *CA* Steven Flynn; Kate Greenhouse; Heather Hanson; Brent Strait; ***D:*** Brad Turner; ***W:*** Jim Makichuk; ***C:*** Robert Steadman; ***M:*** Fred Mollin. **TV**

Roswell: The U.F.O. Cover-Up 🦴🦴 ½ **1994 (PG-13)** Fact-based TV drama finds intelligence officer Maj. Jesse Marcel (McLachlan) investigating the wreckage of a craft near his Roswell air base in the summer of 1947. Marcel believes the craft is extraterrestrial—as are the strange bodies recovered from the wreckage. An Air Force press release announces a UFO but is quickly retracted and Marcel's suspicions ridiculed. A 30-year reunion still finds him obsessed and seeking to clear his name but this time Marcel's investigations may finally lead to the truth. Based on the book "UFO Crash at Roswell" by Kevin D. Randle and Donald R. Schmitt. **91m/C; VHS, DVD.** Kyle MacLachlan; Dwight Yoakam; Kim Greist; Martin Sheen; Xander Berkeley; J.D. Daniels; Doug Wert; John M. Jackson; Peter MacNichol; Bob Gunton; Charles Martin Smith; ***D:*** Jeremy Paul Kagan; ***W:*** Jeremy Paul Kagan; Arthur Kopit; Paul Davids; ***C:*** Steven Poster; ***M:*** Elliot Goldenthal. **TV**

The Rough and the Smooth 🦴 ½ *Portrait of a Sinner* **1959** Mike is engaged to heiress Margaret but falls for nympho Ila who proceeds to nearly ruin his life when they have an affair, taunting him about the other men she's also seeing. Based on a novel by Robin Maugham. **96m/B; DVD.** *GB* Tony Britton; Nadja Tiller; William Bendix; Natasha Parry; Tony Wright; Norman Wooland; Donald Wolfit; Adrienne Corri; ***D:*** Robert Siodmak; ***W:*** Dudley Leslie; Audrey Erskine-Lindop; ***C:*** Otto Heller; ***M:*** Douglas Gamley.

Rough Magic 🦴🦴 *Miss Shumway; Jette un Sort* **1995 (PG-13)** Fantasy-noir-romance-comedy-on-the-road-movie-nostalgia-fest can't decide what it wants to be when it grows up. A magician's assistant (Fonda), with latent powers of her own, flees to Mexico after witnessing a murder. Her fiance (Moffett) turns out to be the culprit and he hires drifter Crowe to track her down. Along the way, they meet a quack doctor (Broadbent) trying to find a magic Mayan potion, a garage owner who becomes a sausage, and a shaman. Sure, it's confusing, but the performances are good. Adapted from the novel "Miss Shumway Waves a Wand" by James Hadley Chase. **104m/C; VHS, DVD.** *UK FR* Bridget Fonda; Russell Crowe; Jim Broadbent; D.W. Moffett; Paul Rodriguez; Euva Anderson; ***D:*** Clare Peploe; ***W:*** Clare Peploe; Robert Mundy; William Brookfield; ***C:*** John J. Campbell; ***M:*** Richard Hartley.

Rough Night 🦴🦴 **2017 (R)** Five college besties reunite in Miami for a killer bachelorette party, but when that turns literal, they have to scramble to dispose of a stripper's corpse. Inevitable comparisons to "The Hangover" aside, this female ode to drunken raucousness has a few laughs but ultimately misses opportunities and underuses the comedic talents of the cast. **101m/C; DVD, Blu-Ray.** Scarlett Johansson; Jillian Bell; Zoë Kravitz; Ilana Glazer; Kate McKinnon; ***D:*** Lucia Aniello; ***W:*** Lucia Aniello; Paul W. Downs; ***C:*** Sean Porter; ***M:*** Dominic Lewis.

Rough Night in Jericho 🦴 ½ **1967** Martin plays unredeemable scum in this cliched western. He's an ex-lawman trying to take over the town of Jericho and all that's left to own is the stagecoach line run by Simmons and McIntire. Coming to Simmons aid is Peppard, a former deputy marshall turned gambler. Predicatably violent. **104m/C; VHS, DVD.** Dean Martin; Jean Simmons; George Peppard; John McIntire; Slim Pickens; Don Galloway; ***D:*** Arnold Laven; ***W:*** Sydney (Sidney) Boehm; Marvin H. Albert; ***C:*** Russell Metty; ***M:*** Don Costa.

Rough Riders 🦴🦴 ½ **1997** Miniseries covering the adventures of the Volunteer Cavalry, led by a pre-presidential Teddy Roosevelt (Berneger), and their travails during the Spanish-American War in 1898. Fighting in Cuba, the Calvary were a mixture of western outlaws and cowboys and eastern bluebloods—all of whom would have to learn to fight together. Filmed on locations in Texas. **240m/C; VHS, DVD.** Tom Berenger; Sam Elliott; Gary Busey; Brad Johnson; Chris Noth; Brian Keith; George Hamilton; R. Lee Ermey; Nick (Nicholas) Chinlund; Dale Dye; Holt McCallany; Illeana Douglas; Geoffrey Lewis; William Katt; Adam Storke; Dakin Matthews; Francesco Quinn; Titus Welliver; Mark Moses; ***D:*** John Milius; ***W:*** John Milius; Hugh Wilson; ***C:*** Anthony B. Richmond; ***M:*** Peter Bernstein. **CABLE**

Roughly Speaking 🦴🦴 **1945** Sentimental domestic drama based on Randall Pierson's autobiography. Independent-minded Louise (Russell) is taking business classes when she marries conventional Rodney Crane (Woods). They have four kids, but Rodney's a cheat and they get divorced so Louise must support her family any way she can. Then she meets amiable Harold Pierson (Carson) and they marry but their happy family life is frequently plagued by financial difficulties as the story continues through the Depression into World War II. **117m/B; DVD.** Rosalind Russell; Jack Carson; Donald Woods; Ann Doran; Alan Hale; ***D:*** Michael Curtiz; ***W:*** Louise R. Pierson; ***C:*** Joseph Walker; ***M:*** Max Steiner.

Round Midnight 🦴🦴🦴 **1986 (R)** An aging, alcoholic black American jazz saxophonist comes to Paris in the late 1950s seeking an escape from his self-destructive existence. A devoted young French fan spurs him to one last burst of creative brilliance. A moody, heartfelt homage to such expatriate bebop musicians as Bud Powell and Lester Young. In English and French with English subtitles. Available in a Spanish-subtitled version. **132m/C; VHS, DVD.** *FR* Dexter Gordon; Lonette McKee; Francois Cluzet; Martin Scorsese; Herbie Hancock; Sandra Reaves-Phillips; ***D:*** Bertrand Tavernier; ***W:*** Bertrand Tavernier; David Rayfiel; ***C:*** Bruno de Keyzer. Oscars '86: Orig. Score.

The Rounders 🦴🦴 ½ **1965** Two aging, no-account cowboys (Ford and Fonda) dream of giving up their bronco-busting ways to open a bar in Tahiti where they can watch the world go by. But they have a habit of blowing all their money on women, whiskey, and bad bets. An ornery unbreakable horse may be the key to changing their luck. Mild-mannered comedy with beautiful Arizona scenery. **85m/C; VHS, DVD, Blu-Ray, UMD.** Glenn Ford; Henry Fonda; Sue Ane Langdon; Hope Holiday; Chill Wills; Edgar Buchanan; Kathleen Freeman; Joan Freeman; Denver Pyle; ***D:*** Burt Kennedy; ***W:*** Burt Kennedy; ***C:*** Paul Vogel.

Rounders 🦴🦴 ½ **1998 (R)** Law student Mike (Damon) used to be a poker hustler, but he's now ready to leave the game and settle down with girlfriend Jo (Mol). His good intentions are undermined by his "friend" Worm (Norton), whose gambling debts are mounting. Mike's return to the table doesn't reduce the debt; instead, he loses money and his reputation. So Mike sets up a final showdown with Teddy KGB (Malkovich). Damon holds his own, while Norton and Malkovich add a lot of spark. It's all style over substance, but that's what makes it (mostly) work. **120m/C; VHS, DVD, Blu-Ray.** Matt Damon; Edward Norton; John Turturro; Gretchen Mol; Famke Janssen; John Malkovich; Martin Landau; Michael Rispoli; Melina Kanakaredes; Josh Mostel; Lenny Clarke; Tom Aldredge; Lenny Venito; Goran Visnjic; ***D:*** John Dahl; ***W:*** David Levien; Brian Koppelman; ***C:*** Jean-Yves Escoffier; ***M:*** Christopher Young.

Rounds 🦴🦴 **2008** Three friends living in Hollywood find their individual concepts of friendship tested by a series of events. **110m/C; Blu-Ray.** Mark Atienza; Drew Allyn; Josh Chacona; Jill Curran; Billy Drago; ***D:*** Mark Atienza; ***W:*** Mark Atienza; ***C:*** Yasu Tanida; ***M:*** Mark Brandon Hill. **VIDEO**

Roustabout 🦴🦴 ½ **1964 (PG)** A roving, reckless drifter joins a carnival and romances the owner's daughter. Elvis rides on good support from Stanwyck et al. Welch has a bit part in her film debut; look for Terri Garr as a dancer. **101m/C; VHS, DVD.** Elvis Presley; Barbara Stanwyck; Joan Freeman; Leif Erickson; Sue Ane Langdon; Pat Buttram; Joan Staley; Dabbs Greer; Steve Brodie; Jack Albertson; Marianna Hill; Beverly Adams; Billy Barty; Richard Kiel; Raquel Welch; *D:* John Rich.

The Rousters 🦴🦴 1/2 **1990 (PG)** Descendants of Wyatt Earp run a carnival in a small Western town. Comic misadventures arise when a modern varmint named Clayton comes looking for action. Cannell (of "The A-Team" and "Riptide" fame) co-wrote and produced—with his usual extraordinary mix of the absurd and the dangerous. Unusual vehicle for Rogers, but she keeps her style and humor. Made for TV. **72m/C; VHS, DVD.** Jim Varney; Mimi Rogers; Chad Everett; Maxine Stuart; Hoyt Axton; *D:* E.W. Swackhamer; *W:* E.W. Swackhamer; Stephen J. Cannell. **TV**

Route 9 🦴🦴 **1998 (R)** Cliched story has some decent performances. Two smalltown sheriff's deputies (MacLachlan and Williams) discover a couple of dead bodies, drugs, and a stash of cash, which they decide to keep. But their boss (Coyote) gets suspicious and then the feds come investigating. **102m/C; VHS, DVD.** Kyle MacLachlan; Wade Andrew Williams; Peter Coyote; Roma Maffia; Amy Locane; Miguel (Michael) Sandoval; Scott Coffey; *D:* David Mackay; *W:* Brendan Broderick; Rob Kerchner; *C:* Brian Sullivan; *M:* Don Davis. **CABLE**

Route 666 🦴🦴 1/2 **2001 (R)** Some very slick stylistic touches are brought to this action/horror that aspires to be another "From Dusk Til Dawn." Marshals Jack (Phillips) and Stephanie (Petty) are escorting a witness to a grand jury in Los Angeles when they become lost on a remote highway. Years ago, a chain gang was murdered there, and they return as inmates of the living dead for revenge. The ultra-violence is silly but some of the visual tricks are pretty cool. **90m/C; DVD.** Lou Diamond Phillips; Lori Petty; Steven Williams; Dale Midkiff; Alex McArthur; Mercedes Colon; L.Q. Jones; *D:* William Wesley; *W:* William Wesley; Thomas N. Weber; Scott Fivelson; *C:* Philip Lee; *M:* Terry Plumeri.

Route 30 🦴🦴 **2008** Putch's loosely interconnected stories are set along the Lincoln highway in south-central Pennsylvania. In "Deer Hunters Wives," Civil War tour guide Mandy (Boltt) is obsessed with the story of a female civilian killed at the battle of Gettysburg. "What I Believe" has a man explaining to a Christian Scientist that he injured his back after being chased through the mountains by Bigfoot. And in "Original Bill," writer Bill (DeLuise) buys a farmhouse hoping for quiet and inspiration but discovers his Amish neighbor Martha (Delany) isn't what he expected. **83m/C; DVD.** David DeLuise; Dana Delany; Nathalie Boltt; Christine Elise; Curtis Armstrong; Robert Romanus; Kevin Rahm; *D:* John Putch; *W:* John Putch; *C:* Keith J. Duggan; *M:* Alexander Baker.

The Rover 🦴🦴 1/2 **2014 (R)** Michod's follow-up to the hit "Animal Kingdom" is yet another story of a post-apocalyptic future without much of a human population but the writer/director's commitment to his vision and two great central performances make it work. Eric (Pearce) is having a drink when his car is stolen by a group of criminals led by Henry (McNairy). He sets out to get it back at any cost, crossing paths with the car thief's dim-witted brother, Rey (Pattinson). A road movie through a desolate future without much hope may sound too familiar but Pearce and Pattinson carry it. **103m/C; DVD, Blu-Ray.** *AU US* Guy Pearce; Robert Pattinson; Scoot McNairy; *D:* David Michod; *W:* David Michod; *C:* Natasha Brajer; *M:* Antony Partos.

Rover Dangerfield 🦴🦴 **1991 (G)** Lovable Las Vegas hound Rover Dangerfield searches for respect but finds none. The results are hilarious. Quality animation from a project developed by Rodney Dangerfield and Harold Ramis. **78m/C; VHS, DVD.** *V:* Rodney Dangerfield; *D:* Jim George; *W:* Harold Ramis; *M:* David Newman.

Row Your Boat 🦴🦴 **1998** Ex-con Jamey (Bon Jovi), who took a burglary rap for his brother (Forsythe), is determined to go straight after his release from prison. He gets a job as a census taker, which is how he meets Asian immigrant single mom Chun Hua (Ling) who will become a part of a scheme by Jamey's no-good brother. **106m/C; VHS, DVD.** Jon Bon Jovi; William Forsythe; Bai Ling; Jill(ian) Hennessey; John Ventimiglia; *D:* Sollace Mitchell; *W:* Sollace Mitchell; *C:* Michael Barrow; Zoltan David; *M:* Phil Ramone.

The Rowdy Girls 🦴🦴 **2000** Sharpshooting Tweed disguises herself as a nun and meets up with bullwhip-wielding wild woman Strain and runaway bride Brooks in order to cross the western frontier. And no amount of scurvy outlaws are going to stop them. Ogle to your heart's content. **88m/C; VHS, DVD.** Shannon Tweed; Julie Strain; Deanna Brooks; Laszlo Vargo; *D:* Steve Nevius; *W:* India Allen. **VIDEO**

Rowing Through 🦴🦴 **1996** Tiff Wood (Ferguson) is a top sculler at Harvard who is sacrificing everything in his obession to win gold at the 1980 Moscow Olympics. And he has the best chance—until the U.S. decides to boycott the games. But Tiff refuses to give up his dream and struggles four more years towards the '84 Olympics—even though it means proving himself against a younger group of competitors. **115m/C; VHS, DVD.** *CA JP* Colin Ferguson; Leslie Hope; Peter Murnik; Kenneth Welsh; Michiko Hada; Helen Shaver; James Hyndman; Christopher Jacobs; *D:* Masato Harada; *W:* Masato Harada; Will Aitken; *C:* Sylvain Brault; *M:* Masahiro Kawasaki.

Rowing with the Wind 🦴🦴 *Remando al Viento* **1988 (R)** The story behind Mary Shelley's (McInnerny) writing of "Frankenstein," amidst the decadence of Mary and Percy B.'s (Pelka) 1816 Swiss sojourn with Lord Byron (Grant). Hurley has the relatively small role of Claire, Mary's half-sister and Byron's former lover. **95m/C; VHS, DVD.** *SP* Lizzy McInnerny; Hugh Grant; Valentine Pelka; Elizabeth Hurley; Jose Luis Gomez; Aitana Sanchez-Gijon; *D:* Gonzalo Suarez; *W:* Gonzalo Suarez; *C:* Carlos Suarez.

Roxanne 🦴🦴🦴 **1987 (PG)** A modern comic retelling of "Cyrano de Bergerac." The romantic triangle between a big nosed, small town fire chief, a shy fireman and the lovely astronomer they both love. Martin gives his most sensitive and believable performance. Don't miss the bar scene where he gets back at a heckler. A wonderful adaptation for the modern age. **107m/C; VHS, DVD, Blu-Ray.** Steve Martin; Daryl Hannah; Rick Rossovich; Shelley Duvall; Michael J. Pollard; Fred Willard; John Kapelos; Max Alexander; Damon Wayans; Matt Lattanzi; Kevin Nealon; *D:* Fred Schepisi; *W:* Steve Martin; *C:* Ian Baker; *M:* Bruce Smeaton. L.A. Film Critics '87: Actor (Martin); Natl. Soc. Film Critics '87: Actor (Martin); Writers Guild '87: Adapt. Screenplay.

Roxie Hart 🦴🦴 1/2 **1942** Sassy '20s Chicago dance hall girl Roxie (Rogers) decides to take the fall when hubby (Chandler) murders a man. (She sees it as a publicity boost to her career). Slick lawyer Billy Flynn (Menjou) knows he can get the tootsie off if she justs flashes the jury her considerable sex appeal. Montgomery's a smitten reporter who catches Roxie's eye. Based on the play "Chicago" by Maurine Watkins and previously filmed in 1927. Bob Fosse later adapted the play for a Broadway musical. **75m/B; VHS, DVD.** Ginger Rogers; Adolphe Menjou; George Montgomery; Lynne Overman; Nigel Bruce; Phil Silvers; Sara Allgood; William Frawley; Spring Byington; George Chandler; *D:* William A. Wellman; *W:* Nunnally Johnson; *C:* Leon Shamroy; *M:* Alfred Newman.

Roy Colt and Winchester Jack 🦴 **1970** Bava's flat and padded attempt at a spaghetti western comedy. Gunslinging former partners become rivals when one discovers a map that leads to gold hidden in an Indian burial ground. Of course they aren't the only ones who want the treasure. Italian with subtitles. **85m/C; DVD, Blu-Ray.** *IT* Brett Halsey; Charles Southwood; Marilu Tolo; Giorgio Gargiullo; Teodoro Corra; Isa Miranda; *D:* Mario Bava; *W:* Mario di Nardo; *C:* Antonio Rinaldi; *M:* Pierro Umiliani.

A Royal Affair 🦴🦴🦴 1/2 *En kongelig affaere* **2012 (R)** Possibly insane, or at least seriously disturbed, Danish King Christian VII (Folsgaard) marries young English princess Caroline (Vikander). He's lousy company, and Caroline ends up falling for his personal physician Johann Struensee (Mikkelsen) who is far more interesting and, well, not insane. Caroline finds fun again, and the doc ends up as de facto ruler for at least a little while. Lively version of this true story with superb visuals, showy clothing, and a fine choice of cast. **137m/C; DVD, Blu-Ray.** *DK SW CZ* Alicia Vikander; Mads Mikkelsen; Mikkel Boe Folsgaard; Trine Dyrholm; David Dencik; *D:* Nikolaj Arcel; *W:* Nikolaj Arcel; Rasmus Heisterberg; *C:* Rasmus Videbaek; *M:* Cyrille Aufort; Gabriel Yared; Mikkel E.G. Nielsen.

The Royal Bed 🦴🦴 1/2 *The Queen's Husband* **1931** King Eric's queen really wears the pants in the family, and when she leaves on a trip, he's left helpless and hapless. A revolution erupts, and his daughter announces she plans to marry a commoner. What's a king to do? **74m/B; VHS, DVD.** Lowell Sherman; Nance O'Neil; Mary Astor; Anthony Bushell; Gilbert Emery; Robert Warwick; J. Carrol Naish; *D:* Lowell Sherman; *W:* J. Walter Ruben; *C:* Leo Tover.

A Royal Christmas 🦴 1/2 **2014** Hallmark Channel schmaltz with a heroine who's something of a drip. Philadelphia seamstress Emily (Chabert) is in love with Leo, who finally reveals he's actually Prince Leopold of Cordinia. He takes her home to meet his formidable mama (Seymour), who's completely appalled Leo wants to marry a commoner. Emily feels out of place and hangs out with the servants while Queen Isadora schemes to have Leo marry his royal ex-girlfriend (Flynn) instead. **85m/C; DVD.** Lacey Chabert; Stephen Hagan; Jane Seymour; Katie Flynn; *D:* Alex Zamm; *W:* Janeen Damian; Michael Damian; *C:* Viorel Sergovici, Jr.; *M:* Chris Hajian. **CABLE**

Royal Deceit 🦴 1/2 *Prince of Jutland* **1994 (R)** Young Amled (Bale) is heir to the 6th century kingdom of Jutland. But when his father is murdered by Amled's jealous uncle Fenge (Byrne), the youth feigns insanity to save himself and then begins to plot his revenge. Very familiar story doesn't arouse more than mild interest despite the cast. **85m/C; VHS, DVD.** Gabriel Byrne; Dame Helen Mirren; Christian Bale; Brian Cox; Kate Beckinsale; Steven Waddington; Tom Wilkinson; Tony Haygarth; Saskia Wickham; Brian Glover; *D:* Gabriel Axel; *C:* Henning Kristiansen; *M:* Per Norgard.

Royal Flash 🦴🦴🦴 **1975 (PG)** Satirical adventure picture, witty and fast paced, with a few real life period characters thrown in for good measure. Cowardly swashbuckler Flashman, wanting to enter high society, is used to advance a political cause when he is forced to impersonate a Prussian nobleman and marry a duchess. Script by Fraser and based on his series of novels featuring the Flashman character. **98m/C; VHS, DVD, Blu-Ray.** *GB* Malcolm McDowell; Alan Bates; Florinda Bolkan; Oliver Reed; Britt Ekland; Lionel Jeffries; Tom Bell; Alastair Sim; Michael Hordern; Joss Ackland; Christopher Cazenove; Bob Hoskins; *D:* Richard Lester; *W:* George MacDonald Fraser; *C:* Geoffrey Unsworth.

A Royal Night Out 🦴🦴🦴 **2015 (PG-13)** A romantic comedy based on real events in the life of the British royal family. On V-E day, Great Britain is celebrating the end of World War II in Europe. Young royals Princess Elizabeth (Gadon) and Princess Margaret (Powley) are allowed to leave Buckingham Palace and join in the festivities. Soon freeing themselves from their chaperones, the sisters experience a few normal hours of excitement, danger, and romance. **97m/C; DVD, Blu-Ray, Streaming, Download.** Sarah Gadon; Bel Powley; Emily Watson; Rupert Everett; Mark Hadfield; *D:* Julian Jarrold; *W:* Trevor De Silva; Kevin Hood; *C:* Christophe Beaucarne; *M:* Paul Englishby.

A Royal Scandal 🦴🦴 1/2 **1945** Enthusisastic young officer Chertov (William Eythe) is promoted to Chief of Russia's Imperial Guard. At first this sems like a great thing, but he quickly finds himself navigating the various plots and schemes of the court official, the miltary, and most frustratingly the Queen (Tallulah Bankhead) herself who may have certain intentions towards him. **93m/B; DVD.** Tallulah Bankhead; Charles Coburn; Anne Baxter; William Eythe; Vincent Price; *D:* Otto Preminger; Ernst Lubitsch; *W:* Edward Mayer; Bruno Frank; *C:* Arthur C. Miller; *M:* Alfred Newman. **VIDEO**

The Royal Tenenbaums 🦴🦴🦴 1/2 **2001 (R)** Anderson and Wilson's third and most ambitious film concerns a wildly eccentric family of kid geniuses who converge upon their childhood home as unhappy adults, just as their long-estranged father shows up looking for handouts and understanding, and mother is considering remarriage to the family accountant. Inventive script and quirky dialogue carry a story that sometimes becomes cartoonish, as most of the characters are one-dimensional. Some may find the film's overt weirdness a bit much, but there's a heart underneath it all. Hackman's performance as the dastardly, tactless, and yet wholly lovable Royal is a supreme comic feat. Depression has never been so fun. **108m/C; VHS, DVD, Blu-Ray.** Gene Hackman; Anjelica Huston; Gwyneth Paltrow; Ben Stiller; Luke Wilson; Owen Wilson; Bill Murray; Danny Glover; Seymour Cassel; Kumar Pallana; Grant Rosenmeyer; Jonah Meyerson; Stephen Lea Sheppard; *Nar:* Alec Baldwin; *D:* Wes Anderson; *W:* Owen Wilson; Wes Anderson; *C:* Robert Yeoman; *M:* Mark Mothersbaugh. Golden Globes '02: Actor--Mus./Comedy (Hackman); Natl. Soc. Film Critics '01: Actor (Hackman).

Royal Warriors 🦴🦴 *In the Line of Duty; Police Assassins; Ultra Force; Huang Jia Zhan Shi* **1986** Watch Michelle kick major butt! Policewoman Yeoh teams up with a retired Japanese cop and an airport security officer to prevent a terrorist highjacking. When the terrorist's associates decide to get even, the three must continue to fight together to save themselves. Chinese with subtitles or dubbed. **85m/C; VHS, DVD.** *CH* Michelle Yeoh; Hiroyuki (Henry) Sanada; Michael Wong; *D:* David Chung.

Royal Wedding 🦴🦴🦴 *Wedding Bells* **1951** Astaire and Powell play a brother-and-sister dance team who go to London during the royal wedding of Princess Elizabeth, and find their own romances. Notable for the inspired songs and Astaire's incredible dancing on the ceiling and walls; Lerner's first screenplay. The idea came from Adele Astaire's recent marriage to a British Lord. **93m/C; VHS, DVD.** Fred Astaire; Jane Powell; Peter Lawford; Keenan Wynn; Sarah Churchill; *D:* Stanley Donen; *W:* Alan Jay Lerner; *C:* Robert Planck; *M:* Johnny Green; Burton Lane; Albert Sendrey.

R.P.M. 🦴🦴 **1997 (R)** Professional car thief Luke (Arquette) takes up an offer to steal a prototype fuel-less supercar for a very large sum of money. However, he's not the only one after the goods. **91m/C; VHS, DVD.** David Arquette; Famke Janssen; Emmanuelle Seigner; Jerry Hall; *D:* Ian Sharp; *C:* Harvey Harrison; *M:* Alan Lisk. **VIDEO**

R.P.M.* (*Revolutions Per Minute) 🦴 1/2 **1970 (R)** Another chance to relive the '60s. Student activists force the university hierarchy to appoint their favorite radical professor president. Hip profturned-prez Quinn is between a rock and a hard place, and allows police to crack down. Could have been intriguing, but loses steam; in any case, the script and direction both stink. **90m/C; VHS, DVD.** Anthony Quinn; Paul Winfield; Gary Lockwood; Ann-Margret; Rigg Kennedy; *D:* Stanley Kramer; *W:* Erich Segal; *M:* Perry Botkin.

R.S.V.P. 🦴 1/2 **2002 (R)** Slacker college student Nick (Otto), who has an unhealthy interest in criminology and the Leopold and Loeb case, decides to invite ten friends to a Vegas penthouse for a going away party. His guests start disappearing (as in permanently 'cause they're dead) and the viewers know the killer's identity while the potential victims struggle to figure things out. Steals from master suspenser Hitchcock (see "Rope"), which is good, but is generally obvious and unpleasant, which is bad. **98m/C; VHS, DVD.** Rick Otto; Jason Mewes; Majandra Delfino; Glenn Quinn; Grace Zabriskie; Jonathan Banks; Reno Wilson; *D:* Mark Anthony Galluzzo; *W:* Mark Anthony Galluzzo; *C:* Mark Anthony Galluzzo; *M:* Michael Muhlfriedel.

Rubber 🦴 1/2 **2010 (R)** Intentionally silly French horror flick about a murderous telekinetic tire. People are gathered in the desert when an old tubeless car tire (which the credits list as Robbie) suddenly starts rolling along in an increasingly deadly frenzy, including blowing up rabbits and people's heads. Eventually, there's a murder at a motel, meaning Lt. Chad (Spinella) has to come and investigate. Some phone voice instructs an accountant (Plotnick) to poison the witnesses who are left—among other irrationalities.

English and French with subtitles. **85m/C; DVD, Blu-Ray, On Demand.** *FR* Stephen Spinella; Roxane Mesquida; Jack Plotnick; Wings Hauser; Tara Jean O'Brien; Ethan Cohn; Charley Koontz; David Bowe; Remy Thorne; ***D:*** Quentin Dupieux; ***W:*** Quentin Dupieux; ***C:*** Quentin Dupieux; ***M:*** Gaspard Auge.

Rubber's Lover 1/2 **1997** Two scientists are attempting to create psychic powers by hopping up their victims on psychotropic drugs and torturing them with sound waves to create altered mental states. Unfortunately all they do is make people explode or go crazy or commit horrible acts. When the company funding the scientists sends an investigator to find out what they're up to, the loonies decide to rape her and make her a test subject (maybe they've been taking a few drugs themselves). Then everything suddenly goes bad. Highly disturbing and there's lots of screaming, so turn the volume down. **90m/B; DVD.** *JP* Nao; Norimizu Ameya; Youta Kawase; Mika Kunihiro; Sosuke Saito; ***D:*** Shozin Fukui; ***W:*** Hiroshi Saito; Shozin Fukui; ***M:*** Tanizaki Tetora.

Ruben Brandt, Collector 1/2 **2018 (R)** The operator of an art therapy institute, Ruben Brandt (Kamaras) is well known for treating people with artistic leanings. However, he suffers from intense dreams in which he is attacked by figures in famous paintings that he loves. Because of his pain, Ruben's patients take action to help him heal. Among them is Mimi (Hamori), a burglar, who helps Ruben steal these paintings so that they can be hung on his wall and their threat to him will be neutralized. This innovative animated film features memorable animation, a zippy plot that takes place in locations around the world, and a cheeky sense of humor. **96m/C; DVD.** Ivan Kamaras; Gabriella Hamori; Zalan Makranczi; Csaba Marton; Matt Devere; ***D:*** Milorad Krstic; ***W:*** Milorad Krstic; Radmila Roczkov; ***M:*** Tibor Cari.

Ruby **1977 (R)** A young woman, christened in blood and raised in sin, has a love affair with the supernatural and murders up a storm at a drive-in. Confused, uneven horror a step up from most similar flicks. **85m/C; VHS, DVD, Blu-Ray.** Roger Davis; Janit Baldwin; Piper Laurie; Stuart Whitman; ***D:*** Curtis Harrington; ***W:*** Barry Schneider; ***C:*** William Mendenhall; ***M:*** Don Ellis.

Ruby 1/2 **1992 (R)** Another in the increasing number of Kennedy assassination and conspiracy dramas—this one told from the viewpoint of Jack Ruby, Lee Harvey Oswald's killer. Confusing plot, somewhat redeemed by the performances of Aiello and Fenn. Combines actual footage of Ruby shooting Oswald with black-and-white filmed scenes. Based on the play "Love Field" by Stephen Davis. **111m/C; VHS, DVD.** Danny Aiello; Sherilyn Fenn; Arliss Howard; Tobin Bell; David Duchovny; Richard Sarafian; Joe Cortese; Marc Lawrence; Joe (Johnny) Viterelli; ***D:*** John MacKenzie; ***W:*** Stephen Davis; ***C:*** Phil Meheux; ***M:*** John Scott.

Ruby Blue 1/2 **2007** Grumpy widower Jack has no interest in life until eight-year-old Florrie and her mom move in next door. Soon Jack is looking after Florrie and then, at the instigation of neighbor Stephanie, he offers to help troubled teen Ian train his racing pigeon Ruby Blue. But someone always has to be a busybody and Jack's relationship with the youngsters is subjected to whispers. **112m/C; DVD.** *GB* Bob Hoskins; Josiane Balasko; Jody Latham; Jessica Stewart; ***D:*** Jan Dunn; ***W:*** Jan Dunn; ***C:*** Ole Bratt Birkeland; ***M:*** Janette Mason.

Ruby Bridges 1/2 **1998** On November 14, 1960, six-year-old Ruby Bridges (Monet) became the first black student to integrate the New Orleans public school system. She started her first day of first grade classes at William Frantz Elementary School escorted by four federal marshals, enduring hostile crowds and death threats because of her mother Lucielle's (Rochon) desire for her daughter to get an equal education despite what the Bridges family would endure. **90m/C; VHS, DVD.** Michael Beach; Penelope Ann Miller; Lela Rochon; Chaz Monet; Kevin Pollak; Diana Scarwid; ***D:*** Euzhan Palcy; ***W:*** Toni Johnson. **TV**

Ruby Gentry 1/2 **1952** White-trash girl Jones, cast aside by man-she-loves Heston, marries wealthy Malden to spite him, then seeks revenge. Classic Southern theme of comeuppance, good direction and acting lift it a notch. **82m/B; VHS, DVD, Blu-Ray.** Charlton Heston; Jennifer Jones; Karl Malden; ***D:*** King Vidor.

Ruby in the Smoke 1/2 *Sally Lockhart Mysteries: Ruby in the Smoke* **2006** It's 1872 in London and Sally Lockhart has just learned that her father has died while investigating suspicious activity in his shipping business. Spunky Sally is told about the Ruby of Agrapur and her father's part in the gem's disappearance decades before. It seems the cursed stone is leading Sally straight into danger with the city's most ruthless criminals. Based on the mystery by Philip Pullman. **90m/C; DVD.** *GB* Julie Walters; J.J. Feild; David Harewood; Hayley Atwell; Billie Piper; Matt Smith; Ramon Tikaram; ***V:*** Martin Jarvis; ***D:*** Brian Percival; ***W:*** Adrian Hodges; ***C:*** Peter Greenhalgh; ***M:*** Martin Phipps. **TV**

Ruby Sparks 1/2 **2012 (R)** A compelling examination of the controlling nature of the writer, Kazan proves to be as promising a screenwriter as she is a stunning young actress. She stars as the title character, someone who literally sprouts from the imagination of a once-promising young author (Dano), a man who can use his typewriter to control his girlfriend/creation's actions and personality. While he thinks he can be mature enough to let her develop naturally, his ability to warp his own romantic future ultimately sinks him. Directors Dayton and Faris offer a funny, romantic, fascinating, and insightful dramedy. **105m/C; DVD, Blu-Ray.** Zoe Kazan; Paul Dano; Elliott Gould; Chris Messina; Annette Bening; Antonio Banderas; Steve Coogan; Alia Shawkat; Aasif Mandvi; ***D:*** Jonathan Dayton; Valerie Faris; ***W:*** Zoe Kazan; ***C:*** Matthew Libatique; ***M:*** Nick Urata.

Ruby's Bucket of Blood 1/2 **2001 (PG-13)** Life's not easy for Ruby Delacroix (Bassett), the sultry owner of a bayou roadhouse, colorfully called the "Bucket of Blood," especially since she's a black woman in the segregated south of 1960. Neglected by her husband Earl (Mitchell) and constantly battling with her teenaged daughter, Emerald (Smollett), Ruby is feeling vulnerable. Which may be why she allows Johnny (Plummer), the leader of the house band, to hire Billy Dupre (Anderson) as a replacement singer. Billy's white—and married. But Ruby and Billy have an undeniable attraction—and when Earl leaves Ruby, it becomes harder and harder to resist. **96m/C; VHS, DVD.** Angela Bassett; Kevin Anderson; Brian Stokes Mitchell; Glenn Plummer; Jurnee Smollett; Angelica Torn; ***D:*** Peter Werner; ***W:*** Julie Hebert. **CABLE**

Ruby's Dream *Dear Mr. Wonderful* **1982** A bowling alley and nightclub owner dreams of making it big in Las Vegas. After his dreams crash to the ground, however, he realizes what is truly important in life. **100m/C; VHS, DVD.** Joe Pesci; Ed O'Ross; Evan Handler; Ivy Ray Browning; ***D:*** Peter Lilienthal; ***W:*** Sam Koperwas; ***C:*** Michael Ballhaus; ***M:*** Claus Bantzer.

Ruckus *The Loner* **1981 (PG)** A Vietnam vet uses his training to defend himself when he runs into trouble in a small Alabama town. Less obnoxious than "First Blood," (which came later), but basically the same movie. **91m/C; VHS, DVD.** Dirk Benedict; Linda Blair; Ben Johnson; Richard Farnsworth; Matt Clark; ***D:*** Max Kleven; ***W:*** Max Kleven; ***C:*** Don Burgess; ***M:*** Willie Nelson.

Rudderless **2014 (R)** Macy's directorial debut is a bland drama about grief and dreams. After the murder of his son Josh, Sam's life has fallen apart and he's taken to living on a boat and drowning in alcohol. Then his ex-wife gives him a box of Josh's original music recordings and Sam is inspired to perform one at a bar's open mike night. He then gains the unwanted attention of aspiring musician Quentin, who bullies Sam into forming the titular band to play 'Sam's' songs. Pic meanders along until Macy gives in to a misguided third-act surprise that nearly derails the film. **105m/C; Streaming.** Billy Crudup; Anton Yelchin; Laurence Fishburne; Felicity Huffman; Selena Gomez; William H. Macy; ***D:*** William H. Macy; ***W:*** William H. Macy; Casey Twenter; Jeff Robison; ***C:*** Eric Lin; ***M:*** Eef Barzelay.

Ruddigore **1982** The Lords of Ruddigore have been bound for centuries by a terribly inconvenient curse; they must commit a crime every day or die a horribly painful death. When the Lord of Ruddigore passes his mantle on to the new heir, the young heir loses both his good reputation and his very proper fiancee. A new version of Gilbert and Sullivan's opera. **112m/C; VHS, DVD.** *GB* Vincent Price; Keith Michell; Paul Hudson; John Trevelyan; Sandra Dugdale; ***D:*** Barrie Gavin. **TV**

Rude **1996 (R)** Rude (Lewis) is a Jamaican-Canadian pirate-radio DJ in Toronto, who narrates three stories about urban life: window dresser Maxine (Crawford) struggles to recover from an abortion after her lover leaves her; frightened boxer Jordan (Chevolleau) tries to deal with his own homosexuality after participating with friends in a gay bashing; and ex-con Luke (Wint) returns to his wife (now a police officer) and young son. He tries to resist returning to his drug dealing past and cope with a jealous younger brother (Johnson). Debut for director Virgo. **90m/C; VHS, DVD.** *CA* Sharon M. Lewis; Richard Chevolleau; Rachael Crawford; Maurice Dean Wint; Stephen Ellen; Clark Johnson; Melanie Nicholls-King; Stephen Shellen; ***D:*** Clement Virgo; ***W:*** Clement Virgo; ***C:*** Barry Stone; ***M:*** Aaron David.

Rude Boy: The Jamaican Don **2003 (R)** Wanting to escape his life of crime in Jamaica, DJ Julius instead becomes ensnared with a big-time L.A. drug lord/music producer who promises to make all his rap-reggae dreams come true if Julius serves as his personal hitman. Not much hop when the bullets aren't flying. **92m/C; VHS, DVD.** Jimmy Cliff; Mark Danvers; Michael "Bear" Taliferro; John Cornelius; Marcia Griffith; Beenie Man; Ninja Man; ***D:*** Desmond Gumbs. **VIDEO**

Rudo y Cursi 1/2 **2009 (R)** A genially ragged rags-to-riches comedy. Half-brothers Tato (Garcia Bernal) and Beto (Luna) are working on a banana plantation in rural Mexico, dreaming of a better life. Spotted during a pickup soccer game, sly sports agent Batuta (Francella) offers to take them to Mexico City, getting big league positions for Tato as a forward and Beto as a goalie—on rival teams. Of course this leads to sibling rivalry and a showdown at the big game. Title refers to the boys' nicknames: 'Rudo' means tough and 'Cursi' means corny. Spanish with subtitles. **103m/C; Blu-Ray, On Demand.** *MX* Gael Garcia Bernal; Diego Luna; Dolores Heredia; Guillermo Francella; Adriana Paz; Jessica Mas; ***D:*** Carlos Cuaron; ***W:*** Carlos Cuaron; ***C:*** Adam Kimmel; ***M:*** Felipe Perez Santiago.

Rudy 1/2 **1993 (PG)** Likeable, true story about a little guy who triumphs over big odds. Daniel "Rudy" Ruettiger (Astin) dreams of playing football for Notre Dame, no matter how farfetched the dream. He's a mediocre student, physically unsuitable for big time college ball, but sheer determination helps him attain his dream. Astin delivers an engaging performance and is backed up by a good supporting cast. Sentimental story stretches the truth with typical shameless Hollywood manipulation, but is still entertaining. From the director and writer of another David beats Goliath sports film, "Hoosiers." **112m/C; VHS, DVD, Blu-Ray.** Sean Astin; Ned Beatty; Charles S. Dutton; Lili Taylor; Robert Prosky; Jason Miller; Ron Dean; Chelcie Ross; Jon Favreau; Greta Lind; Scott Benjaminson; Christopher Reed; Robert J. Steinmiller, Jr.; Vince Vaughn; ***D:*** David Anspaugh; ***W:*** Angelo Pizzo; ***C:*** Oliver Wood; ***M:*** Jerry Goldsmith.

Rudy: The Rudy Giulani Story 1/2 **2003** Warts and all bio of former New York mayor Rudy Giuliani (Woods, in an Emmy-nominated performance). The bio begins on September 10, 2001 as the mayor is on his second and last term and what happens during the World Trade Center disaster. Flashbacks highlight Giuliani's political rise as well as his abrasive personality and his controversial private life. **120m/C; VHS, DVD.** James Woods; Penelope Ann Miller; Michelle Nolden; John Bourgeois; Kirsten Bishop; Maxim Roy; Michael Woods; ***D:*** Robert Dornhelm; ***W:*** Stanley Weiser; ***C:*** Serge Ladouceur; ***M:*** Harald Kloser. **CABLE**

Rudyard Kipling's The Jungle Book 1/2 *The Jungle Book* **1994 (PG)** Respectable live-action version from Disney of the Rudyard Kipling tale of Mowgli (Lee), the boy who's raised by a wolf pack after getting lost in an Indian jungle. This time around Mowgli gets to grow up—enough to have a romantic interest in the lovely Kitty (Headey), the daughter of British officer, Major Brydon (Neill). His rival is the supercilious Captain Boone (Elwes), who learns Mowgli knows the location of a hidden jungle treasure. Now Mowgli must count on his friends, Grey Brother the wolf, Baloo the bear, and Bagheera the black panther, to defeat the greedy Boone and win Kitty. Filmed in India. **111m/C; VHS, DVD.** Jason Scott Lee; Cary Elwes; Sam Neill; Lena Headey; John Cleese; ***D:*** Stephen Sommers; ***W:*** Stephen Sommers.

Rudyard Kipling's the Second Jungle Book: Mowgli and Baloo *Mowgli and Baloo: Jungle Book 2; The Second Jungle Book: Mowgli and Baloo* **1997 (PG)** Actually a prequel to "Rudyard Kipling's The Jungle Book," the story centers on 10-year-old Mowgli (Williams) and his efforts to stay among his animal friends. After he's spotted by a scout for P.T. Barnum's circus, he must elude the hastily organized group that's out to capture and exploit him. Mowgli must also dodge the Bandars, a group of funky monkeys who want to make Mowgli their unwilling leader. The special effects are nowhere near as good as its predecessor, with matte shots that make some of the animals look like they were added with magic markers. The story is a classic, however, and the performances are good. **88m/C; VHS, DVD.** Jamie Williams; Billy Campbell; Roddy McDowall; Cornelia Hayes O'Herlihy; David Paul Francis; Gulshan Grover; Dyrk Ashton; B.J. Hogg; Amy Robbins; Hal Fowler; ***D:*** Duncan McLachlan; ***W:*** Bayard Johnson; Matthew Horton; ***C:*** Adolfo Bartoli; ***M:*** John Scott.

The Rue Morgue Massacres 1/2 **1973 (R)** A modern reprise of the Poe story with touches of Frankensteinia thrown in; plenty of gore. **90m/C; VHS, DVD.** *SP* Paul Naschy; Rossana Yanni; Maria Perschy; Vic Winner; Mary Ellen Arpon; ***D:*** Javier Aguirre.

Ruggles of Red Gap **1935** Classic comedy about an uptight British butler who is "won" by a barbarous American rancher in a poker game. Laughton as the nonplussed manservant is hilarious; supporting cast excellent. Third and far superior filming of Harry Leon Wilson story. One of the all-time great comedies, the film was remade musically with Bob Hope and Lucille Ball as "Fancy Pants" (1950). **90m/B; VHS, DVD, Streaming.** Charles Laughton; Mary Boland; Charlie Ruggles; Zasu Pitts; Roland Young; Leila Hyams; James Burke; Maude Eburne; ***D:*** Leo McCarey; ***W:*** Walter DeLeon; ***M:*** Ralph Rainger. Natl. Film Reg. '14; N.Y. Film Critics '35: Actor (Laughton).

Rugrats Go Wild! **2003 (PG)** Two Nickelodeon animated series combine in this adventure when the Rugrats, who are vacationing with their parents, get stranded on an island and the Wild Thornberries, on the island to find a rare leopard for their TV show, come to the rescue. Less charming than previous outings for both series, there's just too many characters competing for too little screen time, and the wandering plotlines don't help the situation. Less-discriminating kids may enjoy it, but there's nothing for adults or older kids. **81m/C; VHS, DVD.** ***V:*** Elizabeth Daily; Michael Bell; Jodi Carlisle; Nancy Cartwright; Lacey Chabert; Melanie Chartoff; Tim Curry; Cheryl Chase; Flea; Danielle Harris; Tom Kane; Bruce Willis; Chrissie Hynde; Tara Strong; Jack Riley; Kath Soucie; Tress MacNeille; Cree Summer; Dionne Quan; LL Cool J; ***D:*** Norton Virgien; John Eng; ***W:*** Kate Boutilier; ***M:*** Mark Mothersbaugh.

Rugrats in Paris: The Movie **2000 (G)** Enough pop culture references and sly humor for the parents and enough diaper, booger and barf jokes for the kids make this sequel entertaining viewing. Tommy, Chuckie and the rest of the gang from the animated Nickelodeon series are off to France as Tommy's inventor dad tries to fix a mechanical dinosaur at a very EuroDisney-style theme park. Also, Chuckie's dad is wooed by the kid-hating park operator Coco La Bouche, who only wants to marry him because she thinks that there's a promotion in it for her. This all leads to a bizarre chase through Paris involving the giant dinosaur and a huge escargot. **80m/C; VHS, DVD.** ***V:*** Elizabeth Daily; Christine Cavanaugh; Susan Sarandon; Jack Riley; Michael Bell; Melanie Chartoff; Tara Strong; Kath Soucie; John Lithgow; Debbie Reynolds; Mako; James D. Stern; Cheryl Chase; Julia Kato; Lisa McClowry; ***D:*** Stig Bergqvist; Paul Demeyer; ***W:*** David N. Weiss; Jill Gorey; Barbara Herndon; Kate Boutilier; ***M:*** Mark Mothersbaugh.

The Rugrats Movie **1998 (G)** Precocious one-year-old Tommy is afraid he'll be forgotten by his parents with the arrival of baby brother Dil, so he and his pals decide to return the infant to the hospital. Boarding a talking wagon named Reptar (invented by Tommy's father), they embark on an adventure that takes them to a scary forest where they run into wolves, a "wizard," and a band of escaped circus monkeys that kidnap Dil in the film's most frightening sequence. While dishing out lessons about responsibility, bravery, friendship, and jealousy, film also contains parodies of and homages to several films. The humor works on many levels, so this one is enjoyable for all ages. **79m/C; VHS, DVD.** ***V:*** Elizabeth Daily; Christine Cavanaugh; Tara Strong; Melanie Chartoff; Jack Riley; Joe Alaskey; Phil(ip) Proctor; Whoopi Goldberg; David Spade; Kath Soucie; Cheryl Case; Cree Summer; Michael Bell; Tress MacNeille; Busta Rhymes; ***D:*** Norton Virgien; Igor Kovalyov; ***W:*** David N. Weiss; J. David Stem; ***M:*** Mark Mothersbaugh.

The Ruins **½ 2008 (R)** Rather than being content hanging by the pool at their Mexican seaside resort, Jeff (Tucker), Amy (Malone), Eric (Ashmore), and Stacy (Ramsay) accept the questionable invite of Mathias (Anderson) to visit an archeological dig at a Mayan ruin. The armed locals are very unhappy by these turistas and chase them up the vine-covered pyramid, but it's definitely not to safety. There's a gruesomely creepy twist to what attacks them but otherwise it's horror business as usual. Scott B. Smith adapted his novel. **90m/C; DVD, Blu-Ray.** Jonathan Tucker; Jena Malone; Shawn Ashmore; Laura Ramsey; Joe Anderson; ***D:*** Carter Smith; ***W:*** Scott B. Smith; ***C:*** Darius Khondji; ***M:*** Graeme Revell.

Rulers of the City *I Padroni della Citta; The Big Boss; Blood and Bullets; Mister Scarface* **1976** Young gangster avenges his father's death. **91m/C; VHS, DVD.** *IT* Jack Palance; Edmund Purdom; Al Cliver; Harry Baer; Gisela Hahn; Vittorio Caprioli; ***D:*** Fernando Di Leo; ***W:*** Fernando Di Leo; Peter Berling; ***C:*** Erico Menczer; ***M:*** Luis Bacalov.

Rulers of the City **½** *Mr. Scarface; I padroni della città; Big Boss* **1977 (R)** A hoodlum climbs to the top of a crime syndicate as he searches for the man who murdered his father years earlier in a dark alley. An Italian film previously titled "Mr. Scarface." **90m/C; VHS, DVD.** *IT* Jack Palance; Edmund Purdom; Al Cliver; Harry Baer; Gisela Hahn; ***D:*** Fernando Di Leo.

Rules Don't Apply **2016 (PG-13)** The legendary Beatty's first directorial effort in over a decade is a well-meaning but oddly-ineffective look at the golden era of Hollywood in which its creator became a star. Beatty stars as Howard Hughes, a lynchpin to the story here, but this is really a love story between Frank Forbes (Ehrenreich) and Marla Mabrey (Collins), two people caught in Hughes' circle of influence and dealing with the Puritan sexual restrictions of the day. There's a good period drama here but it's edited in a clunky fashion and feels unfocused and inconsistent. Maybe a Director's Cut will improve it. **127m/C; DVD, Blu-Ray.** Warren Beatty; Lily Collins; Alden Ehrenreich; Matthew Broderick; Alec Baldwin; Annette Bening; ***D:*** Warren Beatty; ***W:*** Warren Beatty; ***C:*** Caleb Deschanel.

The Rules of Attraction **2002 (R)** Follows a group of shallow, overprivileged, drug-addled college students apparently attending Hedonism University. Drug dealer Sean (Van Der Beek) is in lust with campus goddess Lauren (Sossamon) whose bisexual ex-boyfriend Paul (Somerhalder) has a crush on the straight Sean. Lauren yearns for coked-up Victor (Pardue), who once slept with Paul. Everyone does drugs and sleeps with everyone else. Avary uses production tricks and a fluctuating timeline in order to convey the feeling of the Bret Easton Ellis novel, but the characters are completely unlikable and uninteresting. **104m/C; VHS, DVD.** James Van Der Beek; Ian Somerhalder; Shannyn Sossamon; Jessica Biel; Kip Pardue; Thomas Ian Nicholas; Kate (Catherine) Bosworth; Fred Savage; Eric Stoltz; Clifton (Gonzalez) Collins, Jr.; Faye Dunaway; Swoosie Kurtz; Russell Sams; Matthew Lang; ***D:*** Roger Avary; ***W:*** Roger Avary; ***C:*** Robert Brinkmann; ***M:*** tomandandy.

Rules of Engagement **½ 2000 (R)** Marine Childers (Jackson) is assigned the task of rescuing an ambassador and his family from a hostile area in Yemen. The mission goes terribly wrong and results in the deaths of 83 women and children. To keep the U.S. from suffering any terrorist backlash, Childers is charged with mass murder. Effective courtroom drama, although it merely grazes the complex issues of military decision-making due to its skeletal script. Intensity and momentum is sustained by the towering performances of leads Jackson and Jones as Childers's buddy and lawyer. Based on a story by ex-Secretary of the Navy James Webb. **128m/C; VHS, DVD.** Samuel L. Jackson; Tommy Lee Jones; Guy Pearce; Bruce Greenwood; Blair Underwood; Philip Baker Hall; Anne Archer; Ben Kingsley; Mark Feuerstein; Dale Dye; Elayne J. Taylor; ***D:*** William Friedkin; ***W:*** Stephen Gaghan; ***C:*** Nicola Pecorini; William A. Fraker; ***M:*** Mark Isham.

The Rules of the Game *Le Regle du Jeu* **1939** Renoir's masterpiece, in which a group of French aristocrats, gathering for a weekend of decadence and self-indulgence just before WWII, becomes a metaphor for human folly under siege. The film was banned by the French government, pulled from distribution by the Nazis, and not restored to its original form until 1959, when it premiered at the Venice Film Festival. A great, subtle, ominous film landmark. In French with English subtitles. Heavily copied and poorly remade in 1989 as "Scenes from the Class Struggle in Beverly Hills." **110m/B; VHS, DVD, Blu-Ray.** Marcel Dalio; Nora Gregor; Jean Renoir; Mila Parely; Julien Carette; Gaston Modot; Roland Toutain; Paulette Dubost; Odette Talazac; ***D:*** Jean Renoir; ***W:*** Jean Renoir.

The Ruling Class **½ 1972 (PG)** The classic cult satire features O'Toole as the unbalanced 14th Earl of Gurney, who believes that he is either Jesus Christ or Jack the Ripper. Tongue-in-cheek look, complete with dance and music, at eccentric upper-class Brits and their institutions. Uneven, chaotic, surreal and noteworthy. **154m/C; VHS, DVD.** *GB* Peter O'Toole; Alastair Sim; Arthur Lowe; Harry Andrews; Coral Browne; Nigel Green; Michael Bryant; William Mervyn; Carolyn Seymour; James Villiers; ***D:*** Peter Medak; ***W:*** Peter Barnes; ***C:*** Ken Hodges; ***M:*** John Cameron. Natl. Bd. of Review '72: Actor (O'Toole).

The Rum Diary **2011 (R)** Johnny Depp covers familiar ground, returning to the world of Hunter S. Thompson in this disjointed adaptation of a disjointed book. Depp plays Paul Kemp, a journalist who leaves the hustle of New York life behind to find himself (like most Thompson heroes) in Puerto Rico in 1959. An episodic comedy of booze, babes, and bad behavior finds Depp having his typical amount of fun in roles like this one. Just as unsteady as the author's debut novel. **110m/C; DVD, Blu-Ray.** Johnny Depp; Amber Heard; Aaron Eckhart; Richard Jenkins; Michael Rispoli; Giovanni Ribisi; Marshall Bell; Amaury Nolasco; ***D:*** Bruce Robinson; ***W:*** Bruce Robinson; ***C:*** Dariusz Wolski; ***M:*** Christopher Young.

Rumble Fish **1983 (R)** A young street punk worships his gang-leading older brother, the only role model he's known. Crafted by Coppola into an important story of growing up on the wrong side of town, from the novel by S.E. Hinton. Ambitious and experimental, with an atmospheric music score; in black and white. **94m/B; VHS, DVD, Blu-Ray.** Matt Dillon; Mickey Rourke; Dennis Hopper; Diane Lane; Vincent Spano; Nicolas Cage; Diana Scarwid; Christopher Penn; Tom Waits; ***D:*** Francis Ford Coppola; ***W:*** Francis Ford Coppola; ***C:*** Stephen Burum; ***M:*** Stewart Copeland.

Rumble in the Bronx **½ 1996 (R)** Singapore action star Chan plays a Hong Kong cop who comes to the South Bronx to attend his uncle's wedding and winds up caught in a crime war between the mob and a vicious motorcycle gang. Chan choreographed and performed all of his own stunts, and they are remarkable (pay special attention to the hovercraft scene). Over-the-top cheesy dubbing and streets that are obviously not New York (filmed in Vancouver) add to the cartoonish fun. After several attempts to break into the American market, this is Chan's first release in the United States. **91m/C; VHS, DVD, Blu-Ray.** *CH* Jackie Chan; Anita (Yim-Fong) Mui; Francoise Yip; Bill Tung; Morgan Lam; Marc Akerstream; ***D:*** Stanley Tong; ***W:*** Edward Tang; Fibe Ma; ***C:*** Jingle Ma; ***M:*** J. Peter Robinson.

Rumble on the Docks **½ 1956** Darren, in his first film, stars as New York juvenile delinquent Jimmy, who moves up the criminal ladder by working for corrupt longshoremen union leader Brindo. Jimmy's dad Pete was crippled in a union riot with Brindo's thugs and he throws his son out of the house. The kid comes to his senses when Brindo's attacks on a rival union lead to death. **82m/B; DVD, Blu-Ray.** James Darren; Michael Granger; Edgar Barrier; Laurie Carroll; Celia Lovsky; Jerry Janger; Robert (Bobby) Blake; David Bond; Timothy Carey; ***D:*** Fred F. Sears; ***W:*** Jack DeWitt; Louis Morheim; ***C:*** Benjamin (Ben H.) Kline; ***M:*** Mischa Bakaleinikoff.

Rumor Has It. . . **2005 (PG-13)** Rumor has it... this movie blows. And, unfortunately, that ain't gossip. Rob Reiner continues to explore the latter, significantly crappier stage of his directorial career in this monumental waste of time and talent. It's a nifty concept—at her sister's wedding, the engaged Sarah (Aniston) discovers that her family was the basis for "The Graduate" and finds herself falling for the man (Costner) who seduced both her mother and grandmother (MacLaine)?but everyone involved in the production looks uncomfortable and there are no laughs to be found. Nice job, Meathead. **96m/C; DVD, Blu-Ray, HD-DVD.** Jennifer Aniston; Kevin Costner; Shirley MacLaine; Mark Ruffalo; Richard Jenkins; Christopher McDonald; Mena Suvari; Steve Sandvoss; ***D:*** Rob Reiner; ***W:*** T.M. Griffin; ***C:*** Peter Deming; ***M:*** Marc Shaiman.

The Rumor Mill **½** *Malice in Wonderland* **1986** The careers and titanic rivalry of influential Hollywood gossip writer Hedda Hopper and Louella Parsons, played with verve by Taylor and Alexander. Fictionalized script based on the book "Hedda and Louella" by George Eels. **94m/C; VHS, DVD.** Elizabeth Taylor; Jane Alexander; Richard Dysart; Joyce Van Patten; ***D:*** Gus Trikonis; ***W:*** Jacqueline Feather; David Seidler; ***M:*** Charles Bernstein. **TV**

A Rumor of Angels **2000 (PG-13)** Cloying coming-of-age tale somewhat redeemed by Redgrave's performance as eccentric recluse Maddy Bennett. 12-year-old James (Morgan) is spending the summer on the Maine coast. His mother died in a car accident, he resents his new stepmom Mary (McCormack), doesn't get along with his neglectful father Nathan (Liotta), and also has his misfit Uncle Charlie (Livingston) to deal with. After James vandalizes Maddy's property, the two become unlikely confidantes and Maddy helps him to deal with his problems. **94m/C; VHS, DVD.** Vanessa Redgrave; Trevor Morgan; Ray Liotta; Catherine McCormack; Ron Livingston; ***D:*** Peter O'Fallon; ***W:*** Peter O'Fallon; James Eric; Jamie Horton; ***C:*** Roy Wagner; ***M:*** Tim Simonec.

Rumpelstiltskin **1986 (G)** Musical retelling of the classic Brother Grimm fairy tale. Irving plays a young girl who says she can spin straw into gold. Barty is a dwarf who helps her. The catch: she must give up her first born to pay him. Lackluster direction and uninspired acting make this version a yawner. Irving's real-life mother (Pointer) and brother have roles too. **84m/C; VHS, DVD.** Amy Irving; Billy Barty; Robert Symonds; Priscilla Pointer; Clive Revill; John Moulder-Brown; ***D:*** David Irving.

Rumpelstiltskin **WOOF! 1996 (R)** First director Jones inflicts "Leprechaun" upon us and now there's another warped dwarf on the loose. Single L.A. mom Shelly (Johnston-Ulrich) finds a wishing stone in a thrift shop and unwittingly summons up the little demon, who immediately tries to steal her young son. **91m/C; VHS, DVD.** Kim Johnston-Ulrich; Tommy Blaze; Max Grodenchik; Allyce Beasley; ***D:*** Mark Jones; ***W:*** Mark Jones; ***C:*** Doug Milsome; ***M:*** Charles Bernstein.

Run All Night **½ 2015 (R)** The best of the three collaborations between director Jaume Collet-Serra and star Liam Neeson (after Unknown and Non-Stop) is an entertaining and well-made action thriller with few gimmicks and tight editing. Hit man Jimmy Conlon (Neeson) has become something of a worthless drunk but he's forced back into action when his son (Kinnaman) witnesses a murder by the offspring (Holbrook) of Conlon's mob boss (Harris). Jimmy and his kid have to keep moving to stay ahead of the cops and criminals trying to bring them down, while they try to figure out what to do next. **110m/C; DVD, Blu-Ray.** Liam Neeson; Ed Harris; Joel Kinnaman; Boyd Holbrook; Bruce McGill; ***D:*** Jaume Collet-Serra; ***W:*** Brad Ingelsby; ***C:*** Martin Ruhe; ***M:*** Junkie XL.

Run & Jump **½ 2013** Carefully underplaying potential melodrama, this confident indie follows stiff American neuropsychologist, Ted (Forte), to Ireland where he cares for Conor (MacLiam)--a man who's suffered a rare type of stroke. After a month in a coma and four months of rehab, Conor returns to his family and wife (Peake). Ted goes through his own rehab as he helps the family adjust to Conor's new frame of mind. Tender and optimistic, with an incredible performance from Peake as Conor's vivacious wife. **105m/C; DVD.** *IR GE* Maxine Peake; Will Forte; Edward MacLiam; Sharon Horgan; ***D:*** Steph Green; ***W:*** Steph Green; Ailbhe Keogan; ***C:*** Kevin Richey; ***M:*** Sebastian Pille.

Run, Angel, Run! **½ 1969 (R)** Ex-biker Angel is on the run from his former gang after he helps expose them in a magazine article. He settles on a sheep ranch with his girl and then the gang shows up with revenge in mind. Prime drive-in fare with title song sung by none other than Ms. Tammy Wynette. **90m/C; VHS, DVD.** William (Bill) Smith; Margaret Markov; Valerie Starrett; ***D:*** Jack Starrett; ***W:*** V.A. Furlong; Jerome Wish; ***C:*** John Stephens; ***M:*** Stu Phillips.

Run, Fatboy, Run **½ 2007 (PG-13)** Schwimmer makes his directorial debut, oddly enough, in British territory, but very much in the vein of a "Friends" episode. Like the bonehead he is, Dennis (Pegg) leaves pregnant Libby (Newton) at the altar for no good reason. Five years later, somehow still friends with Libby and working as a security guard in a lingerie shop, out-of-shape, lazy Dennis desperately tries to win her back as she's about to marry Whit (Azaria), a rich American marathon runner. Of course, the way to win her heart is to challenge the fiance to a race. Cute and charming, but never laugh-out-loud funny. **100m/C; DVD, Blu-Ray, On Demand.** *UK* Simon Pegg; Thandie Newton; Hank Azaria; Dylan Moran; Harish Patel; India de Beaufort; Matthew Festoon; ***D:*** David Schwimmer; ***W:*** Michael Ian Black; Michael Parker; ***C:*** Richard Greatrex; ***M:*** Alex Wurman.

Run for Cover **1955** Generally standard western with a couple of surprises thrown in by director Ray. Drifters Matt (Cagney) and Davey (Derek) are mistaken for train robbers by the local sheriff and Davey is shot. After clearing their names, Matt stays in town and takes over as the new sheriff with the now-crippled Davey as his deputy. The bitter Davey eventually betrays his surrogate father by throwing in with the real criminals. **93m/C; DVD, Blu-Ray.** James Cagney; John Derek; Viveca Lindfors; Jean Hersholt; Grant Withers; Jack Lambert; Ernest Borgnine; John Miljan; ***D:*** Nicholas Ray; ***W:*** Winston Miller; ***C:*** Daniel F. Fapp; ***M:*** Howard Jackson.

Run for the Sun **1956** Journalist Katie Connors (Greer) is tracking down adventure writer Mike Latimer (Widmark) who's gone into exile in Mexico. They wind up surviving a plane crash in a jungle area and are rescued by Mr. Browne (Howard) and his brother-in-law Van Anders (Van Eyck). Mike has his suspicions about the two men and he and Katie end up running for their lives. **99m/C; DVD.** Richard Widmark; Jane Greer; Trevor Howard; Peter Van Eyck; ***D:*** Roy Boulting; ***W:*** Roy Boulting; Dudley Nichols; ***C:*** Joseph La Shelle; ***M:*** Fred Steiner.

Run Hide Die *The Anniversary* **2015** A horror-thriller centered on a girls' weekend trip gone very, very wrong. On the anniversary of her husband's brutal murder, Addison Davenport (Monda) takes her former in-laws up on their offer to use their summer cabin and take time to reflectively heal. Accompanied by four close friends, Addison initially finds peace and relaxation at the picturesque cabin located far in the forest. The fun is cut short as the women realize they are not alone, and each one of them is captured and tormented. It soon becomes clear that one of the friends has a dark secret, their captor wants revenge, and they will all pay a bloody price. **104m/C; DVD, Streaming, Download.** Alison Monda; Alicia Mendez; Ivey Bronwen; Tabitha Bastien; Keiko Green; ***D:*** Collin Joseph Neal; ***W:*** Alison Monda; ***C:*** Alan Certeza; ***M:*** Matt Menovcik. **VIDEO**

Run If You Can **1987 (R)** A woman sees a brutal murderer killing his victims on her TV. Will she be next? **92m/C; VHS, DVD.** Martin Landau; Yvette Nipar; Jerry Van Dyke; ***D:*** Virginia Lively Stone; ***M:*** Christopher L. Stone.

Run Lola Run 1/2 *Lola Rennt* **1998 (R)** Berlin punkette Lola (Potente) receives a frantic phone call from her smalltime criminal boyfriend Manni (Bleibtreu). He's lost a bag of money he was delivering to his boss and has only 20 minutes to make good or he's history. Lola then sprints off in a manic attempt to find the money needed to save her man. The plot comes roaring to a halt, and is then repeated with different outcomes based on small changes in Lola's path, with different styles to match. Writer/director Tom Tykwer's energetic style helps push this creative and technically brilliant thriller across the winner's line. German with subtitles. **81m/C; VHS, DVD, Blu-Ray.** *GE* Franka Potente; Moritz Bleibtreu; Joachim Krol; Herbert Knaup; Armin Rohde; ***D:*** Tom Tykwer; ***W:*** Tom Tykwer; ***C:*** Frank Griebe; ***M:*** Tom Tykwer. Ind. Spirit '00: Foreign Film.

The Run of the Country **1995 (R)** Amid the scenic splendor of a small Irish town in County Cavan, Danny (Keeslar) comes of age, sometimes the hard way. After his relationship with his bullying dad (Finney) crumbles, he runs away to live with town malcontent Prunty (Brophy) and falls in love with the beautiful Annagh (Smurfit). Life gets more complicated when Annagh learns she's pregnant. The usual themes of family dysfunction, religious rebellion and moral dilemma are augmented by the occasional appearance of the IRA. As the frustrated, violent father, Finney shines. In their debut, Keeslar and Smurfit are fine, but Brophy's Prunty is the one you'll remember. Adapted by Connaughton from his novel. **109m/C; Streaming.** Albert Finney; Matt Keeslar; Victoria Smurfit; Anthony Brophy; David Kelly; ***D:*** Peter Yates; ***W:*** Shane Connaughton; ***C:*** Mike Southon; ***M:*** Cynthia Millar.

Run Silent, Run Deep **1958** Submarine commander Gable battles his officers, especially the bitter Lancaster who vied for the same command, while stalking the Japanese destroyer that sunk his former command. Top-notch WWII sub action, scripted from Commander Edward L. Beach's novel. **93m/B; VHS, DVD, Blu-Ray.** Burt Lancaster; Clark Gable; Jack Warden; Don Rickles; Brad Dexter; Nick Cravat; Joe Maross; Mary Laroche; Eddie Foy, III; Rudy Bond; H.M. Wynant; Joel Fluellen; Ken Lynch; John Bryant; ***D:*** Robert Wise; ***W:*** John Gay; ***C:*** Russell Harlan; ***M:*** Franz Waxman.

Run the Race **2019 (PG)** Star high school football player Zach Truett (Shine) seems to have it all, but he questions God's plan for his life. He and his younger brother Davd (Hofer) have lived by themselves in a rundown house for several years because their mother died of cancer and their absent father (Polaha) is an alcoholic. Though Zach hopes football will provide a way for him and his brother to escape their situation and improve their lives. However, circumstances, including Dave's illness, may prevent Zach from achieving his goal. Standard faith-based fare that will appeal to its target audience despite an uneven script. **101m/C; DVD, Blu-Ray.** Tanner Stine; Kristoffer Polaha; Evan Hofer; Kelsey Reinhardt; Mario Van Peebles; ***D:*** Chris Dowling; ***W:*** Chris Dowling; Jake McEntire; Jason Baumgardner; ***C:*** Kristopher S. Kimlin; ***M:*** Paul Mills.

Run This Town 1/2 **2020 (R)** The true story of Toronto mayor Rob Ford, a 2013 video that his aides want to suppress, and a young, ambitious journalist (Platt) hellbent on exposing the scandal. What was intended as a political thriller ends up as an overly verbose, confusing, and weirdly edited snore. **99m/C; DVD.** Benjamin Platt; Mena Massoud; Damian Lewis; Nina Dobrev; Scott Speedman; ***D:*** Ricky Tollman; ***W:*** Ricky Tollman; ***C:*** Nick Haight; ***M:*** Ali Shaheed Muhammad; Adrian Younge.

Runaway 1/2 **1984 (PG-13)** A cop and his sidekick track down a group of killer robots wreaking havoc. Self-serious, sorry sci-fi. Features Simmons of the rock group KISS. **100m/C; VHS, DVD.** Tom Selleck; Cynthia Rhodes; Gene Simmons; Stan Shaw; Kirstie Alley; ***D:*** Michael Crichton; ***W:*** Michael Crichton; ***C:*** John A. Alonzo; ***M:*** Jerry Goldsmith.

The Runaway 1/2 **2000** Luke Winter (Newton) and Joshua Monroe (McLaughlin) are best friends growing up in 1940s rural Georgia despite the fact that one is black and one white. While on an adventure, they make a discovery that leads new sheriff Frank Richards (Cain) into reopening the investigation into the unsolved murders of three local black men. The town wants to hush up the whole incident but the sheriff wants justice to prevail. **98m/C; VHS, DVD.** Dean Cain; Maya Angelou; Debbi (Deborah) Morgan; Pat Hingle; Kathryn Erbe; Cliff DeYoung; Cody Newton; Duane McLaughlin; Roxanne Hart; Sonny Shroyer; ***D:*** Arthur Allan Seidelman; ***W:*** Ron Raley; ***C:*** Ron Garcia; ***M:*** Ernest Troost. **TV**

Runaway **2005** Michael is hiding out in a rural community, secretly caring for his younger brother Dylan after having run away from their abusive dad. He's working at a gas station where co-worker Carly is romantically interested in him and eventually Michael begins confiding in her. Flashbacks show how bad things were for Michael and it all ends with a dramatic flourish. **80m/C; DVD.** Aaron Stanford; Robin Tunney; Zack Savage; Peter Gerety; Melissa Leo; Michael Gaston; Terry Kinney; ***D:*** Tim McCann; ***W:*** Bill True; ***C:*** Frank Barerra; ***M:*** Robert Miller.

Runaway Bride **1999 (PG)** If you don't mind being manipulated, the predictability of this romantic comedy won't bother you. New York columnist Ike Graham (Gere) is fired when it's discovered that his story on bolting bride Maggie Carpenter (Roberts) is filled with errors. So Ike goes to Maggie's hometown, where she's on her fourth engagement, to get the real scoop. Of course, he falls for the would-be bride and she for him but things aren't all hearts and flowers. Appealing performances and boy, does Roberts know how to wear a wedding dress. **116m/C; VHS, DVD, Blu-Ray.** Julia Roberts; Richard Gere; Joan Cusack; Hector Elizondo; Christopher Meloni; Rita Wilson; Paul Dooley; Laurie Metcalf; Jean Schertler; Donal Logue; Reg Rogers; Yul Vazquez; Lisa Roberts Gillan; Sela Ward; Tom Mason; ***D:*** Garry Marshall; ***W:*** Josann McGibbon; Sara Parriott; ***C:*** Stuart Dryburgh; ***M:*** James Newton Howard.

The Runaway Bus **1954** Filled with the requisite motley crew of passengers, including a gold-carrying thief and the ever-befuddled Margaret Rutherford, a bus gets lost between airports and ends up in a deserted village. Would-be wacky comedy. **78m/B; VHS, DVD.** *GB* Frankie Howerd; Margaret Rutherford; Petula Clark; George Coulouris; Belinda Lee; Reginald Beckwith; Terence Alexander; Toke Townley; John Horsley; Anthony Oliver; Stringer Davis; Lisa Gastoni; ***D:*** Val Guest; ***W:*** Val Guest; ***C:*** Stanley Pavey; ***M:*** Ronald Binge.

Runaway Daughters **1994 (PG-13)** Part of Showtime's "Rebel Highway" remakes of '50s flicks, in this case the 1956 AIP juvie drama (although the similarities are minimal). Three small town teen babes (Bowen, Lewis, Fields) fake their own kidnappings so they can steal a car and head out on the highway to catch the runaway beau (Young) of one babe who's knocked up. **82m/C; DVD.** Julie Bowen; Holly Fields; Jenny Lewis; Paul Rudd; Chris Young; Dick Miller; Fabian; Joe Flaherty; Belinda Balaski; Robert Picardo; Dee Wallace; ***Cameo(s):*** Cathy Moriarty; ***D:*** Joe Dante; ***W:*** Charles S. Haas; ***C:*** Richard Bowen; ***M:*** Hummie Mann. **CABLE**

Runaway Father 1/2 **1991** Pat Bennett's husband fakes his own death in an attempt to abandon his family. When Bennett discovers he's alive she works to set a legal precedent—17 years worth of back child support. Based on a true story. **94m/C; VHS, DVD.** Donna Mills; Jack Scalia; Chris Mulkey; Jenny Lewis; ***D:*** John Nicolella. **TV**

Runaway Jury **2003 (PG-13)** Grisham-penned legal thriller has the goods. Hot-shot jury consultant Rankin Fitch (Hackman) is hired by a gun manufacturer on trial after an office massacre. The unscrupulous Fitch spies on potential jurors and isn't above using blackmail in his quest to find a totally sympathetic jury. His goal of a totally biased jury is endangered when he's forced to include Nicholas (Cusack), a man with a secret. A-list cast, interesting supports, well-rounded characters, and top-notch direction more than make up for the lacking plot development and a less than satisfying ending. **127m/C; VHS, DVD.** John Cusack; Gene Hackman; Dustin Hoffman; Rachel Weisz; Bruce Davison; Bruce McGill; Jeremy Piven; Nick Searcy; Stanley Anderson; Clifford Curtis; Nestor Serrano; Leland Orser; Jennifer Beals; Gerry Bamman; Joanna Going; Bill Nunn; Juanita Jennings; Marguerite Moreau; Nora Dunn; Guy Torry; Rusty Schwimmer; ***D:*** Gary Fleder; ***W:*** Brian Koppelman; David Levien; Rick Cleveland; Matthew Chapman; ***C:*** Robert Elswit; ***M:*** Christopher Young.

Runaway Train **1985 (R)** A tough jailbird and his sidekick break out of the hoosegow and find themselves trapped aboard a brakeless freight train heading for certain derailment in northwestern Canada. Harrowing existential action drama based on a screenplay by Akira Kurosawa. Voight is superb. **112m/C; VHS, DVD, Blu-Ray.** Jon Voight; Eric Roberts; Rebecca De Mornay; John P. Ryan; T.K. Carter; Kenneth McMillan; John Bloom; Edward (Eddie) Bunker; ***D:*** Andrei Konchalovsky; ***W:*** Andrei Konchalovsky; Djordje Milicevic; Edward (Eddie) Bunker; Paul Zindel; ***C:*** Alan Hume; ***M:*** Trevor Jones. Golden Globes '86: Actor--Drama (Voight).

Runaways *Fugitive Lovers* **1975** A corrupt politician's wife falls in love with the man who saved her when she attempted suicide. The two try to escape her husband's wrathful vengeance. **95m/C; VHS, DVD.** Steve Oliver; Sondra Currie; John Russell; Virginia Mayo; Doodles Weaver; Juanita Moore; Frankie Darro; Vincent Barbi; ***D:*** John Carr; ***W:*** John Carr; ***C:*** Michael Mileham; ***M:*** Alex Barnhardt.

The Runaways **2010 (R)** This coming-of-age music bio about the '70s all-girl hard rock band "The Runaways" focuses on guitarist Joan Jett (Stewart) and lead singer Cherie Currie (Fanning) while letting the other band members fade into the background. Overall, it's a pretty rockin' tale of the excessive music business of the day. Driven by egomaniacal Svengali Kim Fowley (Shannon), the girls rise from obscurity to success before the inevitable downward spiral caused by the temptations of rock 'n roll life. Good performances from Fanning and Stewart, who nails Jett's swagger. The script was largely drawn from Currie's memoir "Neon Angel." **109m/C; DVD, Blu-Ray, On Demand.** Kristen Stewart; Dakota Fanning; Scout Taylor-Compton; Stella Maeve; Alia Shawkat; Hannah Marks; Michael Shannon; Brett Cullen; Tatum O'Neal; ***D:*** Floria Sigismondi; ***W:*** Floria Sigismondi; ***C:*** Benoît Debie.

The Rundown 1/2 **2003 (PG-13)** Amusing buddy/action comedy works because of Johnson's self-deprecating charm (and physical abilities) and Scott's insolent exuberance. Bounty hunter Beck takes one last job: retrieve his boss' wastrel son. Archeology student Travis is in the Amazon seeking a priceless golden artifact, which is also sought by his ex-girlfriend Marianna (Dawson), who wants to use it against manic mine owner Hatcher (Walken). The action (and there's lots of it) is briskly paced, and Hawaii's rain forests and the San Gabriel Mountains provide appropriate substitutes for the Amazon. Watch for the scene with the Rock and some amorous monkeys. **104m/C; VHS, DVD, Blu-Ray, UMD, HD-DVD.** Dwayne "The Rock" Johnson; Seann William Scott; Rosario Dawson; Christopher Walken; Ewen Bremner; Jon(athan) Gries; William Lucking; Ernie Reyes, Jr.; Stuart Wilson; ***Cameo(s):*** Arnold Schwarzenegger; ***D:*** Peter Berg; ***W:*** R.J. Stewart; James Vanderbilt; ***C:*** Tobias Schliessler; ***M:*** Harry Gregson-Williams.

The Runner **1999 (R)** Eldard stars as a compulsive Vegas gambler who's so deeply in debt he agrees to his shady uncle's (Mantegna) offer to get him a job with gangster Goodman. Eldard places bets with sports bookies (with mob money) and falls for cocktail waitress Cox, using some of Goodman's money to buy her a diamond ring. The vengeful Goodman doesn't take kindly to this. **95m/C; VHS, DVD.** Ron Eldard; John Goodman; Courteney Cox; Joe Mantegna; Bokeem Woodbine; ***D:*** Ron Moler; ***W:*** Anthony E. Zuiker; Dustin Lee Abraham; ***C:*** James Glennon; ***M:*** Anthony Marinelli.

The Runner **2015 (R)** A political and personal drama set after the 2010 BP oil spill. Louisiana Congressman Colin Pryce (Cage) is prepared to make a run for the U.S. Senate after delivering a passionate speech about the effects of the spill on the Louisiana coastline. His campaign, however, is over before it can get started as a sex scandal involving Pryce comes to light and becomes media fodder. Faced with the choice of making a real difference in the restoration of the region or playing politics as usual, Pryce handles issues of corruption and deceit both in his professional and his personal life as he decides what kind of person he wants to be. **94m/C; DVD, Blu-Ray, Streaming, Download.** Nicolas Cage; Sarah Paulson; Connie Nielsen; Peter Fonda; Wendell Pierce; ***D:*** Austin Stark; ***W:*** Austin Stark; ***C:*** Elliot Davis; ***M:*** The Newton Brothers.

Runner Runner 1/2 **2013 (R)** Richie (Timberlake) is a Princeton grad student with a gift for online gambling. When he believes he's been swindled in an online game by a gambling tycoon named Ivan Block (Affleck), he tracks him down and gets sucked into his world of beautiful women and immense privilege. Before he knows it, Block is turning the tables on him. Can Richie turn the tables back with the help of the FBI and take down his new nemesis? The cast is beautiful, the settings are gorgeous, and the story is impossible to care about for even a second. Just boring. **91m/C; DVD, Blu-Ray.** Justin Timberlake; Ben Affleck; Gemma Arterton; Anthony Mackie; John Heard; ***D:*** Brad Furman; ***W:*** Brian Koppelman; David Levien; ***C:*** Mauro Fiore; ***M:*** Christophe Beck.

Running Brave **1983 (PG)** The true story of Billy Mills, a South Dakota Sioux Indian who won the Gold Medal in the 10,000 meter run at the 1964 Tokyo Olympics. Not bad, but hokey in the way of many of these plodding true-story flicks. **90m/C; VHS, DVD.** Robby Benson; Claudia Cron; Pat Hingle; Denis Lacroix; ***D:*** D.S. Everett; ***W:*** Henry Bean.

Running for Grace 1/2 *Jo, the Medicine Runner* **2018** Jo, an orphaned Asian boy, finds a vocation in running medicines from a doctor to coffee pickers throughout the mountainous fields of Hawaii. As he grows, he falls for the Caucasian daughter of the plantation owner, and the two must transcend the overt racism of the 1920s to realize their love. A pleasant enough tale of romance and overcoming prejudice in a highly scenic setting. **110m/C; DVD.** Matt Dillon; Jim Caviezel; Ryan Potter; Olivia Ritchie; Juliet Mills; ***D:*** David L. Cunningham; ***W:*** David L. Cunningham; Christian Parkes; ***C:*** Akis Konstantakopoulos; ***M:*** Elia Cmiral.

Running Free 1/2 **1994 (PG)** Sullen Garrett joins his naturalist mother in the Alaskan wilderness and establishes a friendship with a wolverine cub (who's smarter than the kid). **90m/C; VHS, DVD.** Jesse Montgomery Sythe; Jayme Lee Misfeldt; Michael Peña; ***D:*** Steve Kroschel.

Running Free 1/2 **2000 (G)** Inspiring story of the friendship between an orphaned servant boy and an abandoned colt named Lucky who is destined for a life of hard labor. Their quest for freedom from their proscribed lives creates a visually stunning tale about the triumph of the human spirit. **85m/C; DVD.** Chase Moore; Jan Decleir; Arie Verveen; Maria Geelbooi; Lukas Haas; ***D:*** Sergei Bodrov; ***W:*** Jeanne Rosenberg; ***C:*** Dan Laustsen; ***M:*** Nicola Piovani.

Running From Crazy **2013** Intimate documentary of family and mental illness as actress Mariel Hemingway allows viewers a window into her desire to know more about her family history, including grandfather Ernest Hemingway. The Hemingway clan is a deeply troubled one, as they have battled addictions, mental illness, and suicide for generations. Watching Hemingway come to terms with these tragedies while also hoping for a better future for herself and subsequent generations has an easygoing charm even if the pic isn't terribly relatable. **100m/C; DVD.** Mariel Hemingway; ***D:*** Barbara Kopple; ***C:*** Phil Parmet; Andrew Young; ***M:*** Joel Goodman.

Running Hot 1/2 *Highway to Hell; Lucky 13* **1983 (R)** Seventeen-year-old convicted murderer Stoltz gets love letter in prison from older woman Carrico. When he escapes, they flee the law together. Quick-paced and entertaining. **88m/C; VHS, DVD.** Monica Carrico; Eric Stoltz; Stuart Margolin; Virgil Frye; Richard Bradford; Sorrels Pickard; Juliette Cummins; ***D:*** Mark Griffiths; ***W:*** Mark Griffiths.

The Running Man 1/2 **1987 (R)** Special-effects-laden adaptation of the Stephen King novel (under his Richard Bachman pseud) about a futuristic TV game show. Convicts are given a chance for pardon—all they have to do is survive a battle with specially trained assassins in the bombed-out sections of Los Angeles. Sci-fi with an attitude. **101m/C; VHS, DVD, Blu-Ray.** Arnold Schwarzenegger; Richard Dawson; Maria Conchita Alonso; Yaphet Kotto; Mick Fleetwood; Dweezil Zappa; Jesse Ventura; Jim Brown; Edward (Eddie) Bunker; Kurt Fuller; Lin Shaye; Toru Tanaka; Erland van Lidth; Gus Rethwisch; ***D:*** Paul Michael Glaser; ***W:*** Steven E. de Souza; ***C:*** Thomas Del Ruth; ***M:*** Harold Faltermeyer.

Running Mates **1992 (PG-13)** Cynically amusing political satire about a bachelor politician and his too intelligent lady love. Harris is Hugh, a U.S. senator looking forward to the presidential primaries when he meets widowed children's novelist Aggie (Keaton). She hates politics and he's Mr. Slick, although decent enough behind the political expediency. Aggie, however, has a potentially damaging secret in her past which causes the scandal-scenting pack of press hounds to bay in salivating anticipation. Will Hugh stick by Aggie and will Aggie overcome her natural political distaste for everything to end happily? A well-played romp. **88m/C; VHS, DVD.** Ed Harris; Diane Keaton; Ed Begley, Jr.; Ben Masters; Robert Harper; Brandon Maggart; Russ Tamblyn; ***D:*** Michael Lindsay-Hogg; ***W:*** A.L. Appling. **CABLE**

Running Mates 1/2 **2000** Liberal governor James Pryce (Selleck) is a shoo-in for the presidential nomination at the L.A. Democratic convention. But he still has to choose his veep running mate. And he's got four powerful women giving him opinions, including his wife Jenny (Travis), his campaign manager Lauren (Linney), Hollywood fundraiser Shawna (Hatcher), and boozy socialite Meg (Dunaway), who's the wife of Pryce's mentor (Culp). So will he go with the idealistic senator (Gunton) or the power broker (McGill)? **90m/C; VHS, DVD.** Tom Selleck; Laura Linney; Nancy Travis; Teri Hatcher; Bruce McGill; Bob Gunton; Faye Dunaway; Robert Culp; Caroline Aaron; Matt Malloy; ***D:*** Ron Lagomarsino; ***W:*** Claudia Salter; ***C:*** Alan Caso; ***M:*** John Debney. **CABLE**

Running on Empty **1988 (PG-13)** Two 1960s radicals are still on the run in 1988 for a politically motivated Vietnam Warera crime. Though they have managed to stay one step ahead of the law, their son wants a "normal" life, even if it means never seeing his family again. Well-performed, quiet, plausible drama. **116m/C; DVD, Blu-Ray.** Christine Lahti; River Phoenix; Judd Hirsch; Martha Plimpton; Jonas Arby; Ed Crowley; L.M. Kit Carson; Steven Hill; Augusta Dabney; David Margulies; Sidney Lumet; ***D:*** Sidney Lumet; ***W:*** Naomi Foner; ***C:*** Gerry Fisher; ***M:*** Tony Mottola. Golden Globes '89: Screenplay; L.A. Film Critics '88: Actress (Lahti); Natl. Bd. of Review '88: Support. Actor (Phoenix).

Running on Karma 1/2 *Da zhi lao; Daai chek liu; An Intelligent Muscle Man* **2003** Big is a former Buddhist monk who has taken up competitive weightlifting and stripping despite having gained psychic powers from his former religious vocation after killing a sparrow in a fit of rage. He can see the sins committed in past lives (karma) by those who are about to die. And the perky young female cop who has just arrested him for indecent exposure is one such individual. Knowing that karma can't be opposed, Big decides to help her do so anyway, along with helping her track down a murderer. Buddhist theology, muscle suits, and neat fights abound. **93m/C; DVD.** *CH* Andy Lau; Cecilia Cheung; Siu-fai Cheung; Wen Zhong Yu; Lian Sheng Hou; Meng Zhang; ***D:*** Johnny To; Kai-Fai Wai; ***W:*** Kai-Fai Wai; Nai-Hoi Yau; Tin-Shing Yip; Kin-Yee Au; ***C:*** Siu-keung Cheng; ***M:*** Cacine Wong.

Running Out of Time *Dias Contados; Numbered Days* **1994** Antonio (Gomez) is a Basque who belongs to a terrorist organization. He's sent to Madrid to carry out an assignment, winds up getting involved with drug-addicted prostitute Charo (Gabriel), and finds that his mission overlaps with his relationship. Spanish with subtitles. **93m/C; VHS, DVD.** *SP* Carmelo Gomez; Ruth Gabriel; Javier Bardem; Karra Elejalde; Candela Pena; ***D:*** Imanol Uribe; ***W:*** Imanol Uribe; ***C:*** Javier Aguirresarobe; ***M:*** Jose Nieto.

Running out of Time **1999** Jewel thief Andy (Lau) knows that he has only two weeks to live. He goes ahead and pulls a job that sets him against Sean (Wan), a canny police negotiator. Director Johnny To employs some flashy visuals in this overachieving crime movie and he got first-rate performances from his leads, particularly Lau Ching Wan, a tremendous character actor. **89m/C; DVD.** *CH* Andy Lau; Lau Ching Wan; Waise Lee; Hui Siu Hung; Yoyo Mung; ***D:*** Johnny To; ***W:*** Yau Nai Hoi; ***C:*** Cheng Siu Keung; ***M:*** Wong Ying Wah.

Running Out of Time 2 *Am zin 2; Am zhan 2; Hidden War 2* **2006** Inspector Ho (Lau Ching-Wan) from the original film has been promoted to a desk job, but he inevitably winds up on the streets again when a magician-turned-art thief tries a series of heists. Not as well done as the original, it's often thought of as more of an overly complicated parody of the first film than a sequel to it (proving that even in China, sequels usually suck). **91m/C; DVD.** *CH* Ching-Wan Lau; Ekin Cheng; Kelly Lin; Suet Lam; Ruby Wong; Shiu Hung Hui; Yun Shang Ding; ***D:*** Johnny To; Wing-cheong Law; ***W:*** Nai-Hoi Yau; Kin-Yee Au; Laurent Cortiaud; Julien Carbon; ***C:*** Siu-keung Cheng; ***M:*** Raymond Wong.

Running Red **1999 (R)** Gregori was once a member of an elite Soviet commando team. Sickened by the corruption, he quits and eventually sets up a new life for himself in the U.S. But his past comes back when his ex-boss contacts him and threatens to kill his family unless Greg does an assassination job for him. **92m/C; VHS, DVD.** Jeff Speakman; Angie Everhart; Stanley Kamel; Elya Baskin; Geoffrey Rivas; DeLane Matthews; Bart Braverman; ***D:*** Jerry P. Jacobs; ***W:*** David Stauffer; ***C:*** Ken Blakey; ***M:*** Jim Halfpenny. **VIDEO**

Running Scared 1/2 **1986 (R)** Hip, unorthodox Chicago cops Hines and Crystal have to handle an important drug arrest before taking an extended vacation in Key West. Not as relentless as "48 Hrs," but more enjoyable in some ways. Ever wonder what it's like to ride in a car at high speed on the tracks? Find out here. **107m/C; VHS, DVD, Blu-Ray.** Gregory Hines; Billy Crystal; Dan Hedaya; Jimmy Smits; Darlanne Fluegel; Joe Pantoliano; Steven Bauer; ***D:*** Peter Hyams; ***W:*** Gary De Vore; ***C:*** Peter Hyams.

Running Scared 1/2 **2006 (R)** Frenetic actioner has small-time hood Joe (Walker) charged with disposing of a gun for his Mob cronies after a drug deal gone bad that involves dead crooked cops. When a neighbor kid takes the gun and uses it to shoot his Russian mob-affiliated, abusive stepdad, things go sideways for everyone. Joe must race the clock, the cops, his associates, and the Russians to find the kid and the gun, both of which change hands with astonishing regularity over the course of the night. What this one lacks in cohesion and plausibility, it makes up for in pacing (which rarely slackens) and urgency. **122m/C; DVD, Blu-Ray.** Paul Walker; Cameron Bright; Vera Farmiga; Karel Roden; Johnny Messner; Ivana Milicevic; Chazz Palminteri; Alex Neuberger; Michael Cudlitz; Bruce Altman; Elizabeth Mitchell; Arthur J. Nascarella; John Noble; David Warshofsky; Idalis DeLeon; ***D:*** Wayne Kramer; ***W:*** Wayne Kramer; ***C:*** Jim Whitaker; ***M:*** Mark Isham.

Running Target **1956** Sheriff Scott (Franz) is leading a posse into the Colorado Rockies after some escaped convicts. Included are trigger-happy bar owner Jaynes (Reeves) and Smitty (Dowling), whose gas station was allegedly robbed. The sheriff thinks Smitty has another reason for coming along. **82m/C; DVD.** Arthur Franz; Doris Dowling; Richard Reeves; Myron Healey; Charles Delaney; James Anderson; ***D:*** Marvin R. Weinstein; ***W:*** Marvin R. Weinstein; Jack Couffer; Conrad L. Hall; ***C:*** Lester Shorr; ***M:*** Ernest Gold.

Running Wild 1/2 **1973 (G)** A freelance photographer becomes involved in a dispute to save a corral of wild mustang horses. The usual great Colorado scenery enhances a good, family-view story. **102m/C; VHS, DVD.** Lloyd Bridges; Dina Merrill; Pat Hingle; Gilbert Roland; Morgan Woodward; ***D:*** Robert McCahon; ***W:*** Robert McCahon.

Running Wild 1/2 **1999** Retired Air Force pilot Matt Robinson (Harrison) takes a job with the U.N. tracking elephant migrations in Africa. He takes his children, Angela (Nevin) and Nicholas (Jones), and they soon meet pretty veternarian Rachel (Hallier) and guide,Isaac (Kanaventi). They enjoy a great adventure until Matt realizes that there are poachers in the area. When the kids are threatened, the adults spring into action. Fun film for the entire family, although a bit too preachy at times. Contains fine performances as well as breathtaking nature photography. **92m/C; VHS, DVD.** Gregory Harrison; Lori Hallier; Cody Jones; Brooke Nevin; Munyaradzi Kanaventi; ***D:*** Timothy Bond. **CABLE**

Running with Scissors **2006 (R)** Sex, drugs, and insanity are manifest in the debuting Murphy's adaptation of Burrough's memoirs of his screwed-up adolescence. Narcissist monster mom Deirdre (Bening) has divorced Augusten's (Cross) alcoholic dad and is in therapy with bizarre shrink Dr. Finch (Cox). Augusten moves into the Finch's ramshackle Victorian house, where everyone is odd, including depressed Mrs. Finch (Clayburgh) and adoptive son Neil (Fiennes), who seduces the willing teen. Also ensconced are Bible-reading Hope (Paltrow) and her rebellious younger sister Natalie (Wood), who befriends Augusten. Flick is more scenic than coherent. **121m/C; DVD, Blu-Ray.** Joseph Cross; Annette Bening; Brian Cox; Joseph Fiennes; Evan Rachel Wood; Alec Baldwin; Jill Clayburgh; Gwyneth Paltrow; Gabrielle Union; Kristin Chenoweth; Patrick Wilson; Jack Kaeding; Gabriel Guedj; ***D:*** Ryan Murphy; ***W:*** Ryan Murphy; ***C:*** Christopher Baffa; ***M:*** James Levine.

Running with the Devil **2019 (R)** After family members die from a cocaine overdose, a federal agent (Bibb) takes the war on drugs very seriously. Because of quality control issues, which also impact the life of a cocaine-loving dealer (Fishburne), another drug smuggler (Cage) is sent to Columbia to find the source of the problem. Going down the supply chain, the whole cocaine operation is considered from the harvesting of the coca leaves and initial processing by a farmer (Collins) and his wife (Reyes) to the street. An impressive cast falls prey to a poorly written and trite story. **100m/C; DVD.** Nicolas Cage; Leslie Bibb; Cole Hauser; Peter Facinelli; Laurence Fishburne; ***D:*** Jason Cabell; ***W:*** Jason Cabell; ***C:*** Cory Geryak; ***M:*** Reinhold Heil.

Running Woman **1998 (R)** Emily Russo (Russell) is accused of the mysterious death of her young son and goes on the lam to prove her inncence. With the police on her trail, Emily's quest leads her to a gang that's terrorizing some seedier parts of L.A. **84m/C; VHS, DVD.** Theresa Russell; Andrew (Andy) Robinson; Gary (Rand) Graham; Eddie Velez; Anthony Crivello; Robert LaSardo; Chris Pennock; ***D:*** Rachel Samuels; ***W:*** Rachel Samuels; ***C:*** Chris Manley; ***M:*** Christopher Lennertz. **VIDEO**

Rush **1991 (R)** Texas drug culture, circa 1975, is portrayed in this bleak cop drama. Rookie narcotics officer Kristen Cates (Leigh) goes undercover with the experienced Raynor (Patric) to catch a big-time dealer, menancingly played by Allman, and their bosses don't much care how they do it. Cates falls in love with Raynor and is drawn ever deeper into the drug-addicted world they are supposed to destroy. Fine performances and a great blues score by Clapton. The directorial debut of Zanuck. Based on ex-narcotics cop Kim Wozencraft's autobiographical novel. **120m/C; VHS, DVD, Blu-Ray.** Jason Patric; Jennifer Jason Leigh; Gregg Allman; Max Perlich; Sam Elliott; Tony Frank; William Sadler; Special K. McCray; ***D:*** Lili Fini Zanuck; ***W:*** Pete Dexter; ***C:*** Kenneth Macmillan; ***M:*** Eric Clapton.

Rush **2013 (R)** A true story of the peak of Formula 1 racing when two potential stars drove for fame and glory. English playboy James Hunt (Hemsworth) and Austrian driver Niki Lauda (Bruhl) had distinctly different styles both behind the wheel and outside of the driver's seats. They were bitter rivals during the 1976 racing season when it looked like either could become world champion, even after Lauda is seriously burned in a horrendous crash. Howard delivers a surprisingly sleek film with a streamlined style that fits the story of two men who pushed themselves to the limit to become the best. **123m/C; DVD, Blu-Ray.** *US UK* Chris Hemsworth; Daniel Brühl; Olivia Wilde; Alexandra Maria Lara; Natalie Dormer; ***D:*** Ron Howard; ***W:*** Peter Morgan; ***C:*** Anthony Dod Mantle; ***M:*** Hans Zimmer. British Acad. '13: Film Editing.

Rush Hour 1/2 **1998 (PG-13)** Cliched buddy film that's sauced up a bit with the unlikely pairing of loud-mouthed Tucker and swift-footed Chan. Motormouth L.A. detective James Carter is temporarily assigned to the FBI to babysit Hong Kong detective Lee and keep him away from a kidnapping case that Lee is anxious to solve for personal reasons. Chan is more subdued stuntwise than in his own pictures but nonetheless a charmer against the abrasive Tucker. The culture clash scenes and some high gloss action moments make for a rousing action-comedy. **98m/C; VHS, DVD, Blu-Ray, UMD.** Jackie Chan; Chris Tucker; Tzi Ma; Julia Hsu; Philip Baker Hall; Rex Linn; Elizabeth Pena; Mark Rolston; Tom Wilkinson; ***D:*** Brett Ratner; ***W:*** Jim Kouf; Ross LaManna; ***C:*** Adam Greenberg; ***M:*** Lalo Schifrin. MTV Movie Awards '99: On-Screen Duo (Chris Tucker/Jackie Chan).

Rush Hour 2 **2001 (PG-13)** Director Ratner and stars Tucker and Chan all reteam for the sequel to their $250 million comedy. Det. Carter travels to Hong Kong with his new buddy, Det. Lee and they get involved in a criminal conspiracy. The jokes aren't as funny or fresh, and that situation isn't helped by the fact that before the movie's half over you just want Tucker to shut up. Chan does a fine job, which are to continue to amusingly mangle the English language and do some more of those great martial-arts stunts. He gets some help in the acrobatic martial-arts department from Ziyi, Lone, and a nice cameo by Cheadle. **91m/C; DVD, Blu-Ray, UMD.** Chris Tucker; Jackie Chan; Harris Yulin; Ziyi Zhang; John Lone; Alan King; Roselyn Sanchez; Kenneth Tsang; Ernie Reyes, Jr.; Jeremy Piven; Saul Rubinek; Don Cheadle; ***D:*** Brett Ratner; ***W:*** Jeff Nathanson; ***C:*** Matthew F. Leonetti; ***M:*** Lalo Schifrin; Kathy Nelson.

Rush Hour 3 1/2 **2007 (PG-13)** Third pic brings nothing fresh to the table except a new location, Paris, for Chan and Tucker's wacky culture clash schtick. After the attempted murder of the Chinese ambassador (Ma), the two travel to Paris to track the assassin, protect his daughter, and make a bunch of jokes that constantly refer back to the previous, better entries in the series. Chan and Tucker still have chemistry but director Ratner doesn't give them much to work with. The fight scenes seem slowed-down, shorter, and less fun, and even the standard end-of-movie blooper reel is a yawn. Roman Polanski cameos as a particularly nasty French commissioner. **91m/C; DVD, Blu-Ray.** Jackie Chan; Chris Tucker; Max von Sydow; Hiroyuki (Henry) Sanada; Yvan Attal; Roselyn Sanchez; Roman Polanski; Noemie Lenoir; Vinnie Jones; Tzi Ma; Julie Depardieu; Youki Kudoh; Dana Ivey; Zhang Jingchu; ***D:*** Brett Ratner; ***W:*** Jeff Nathanson; ***C:*** J.(James) Michael Muro; ***M:*** Lalo Schifrin.

Rush Week **1988 (R)** Dead coeds populate campus during frat week. Greg Allman has bit part and the Dickies perform two songs. **93m/C; VHS, DVD.** Dean Hamilton; Gregg Allman; Kathleen Kinmont; Roy Thinnes; Pamela Ludwig; ***D:*** Bob Bravler; ***W:*** Michael W. Leighton; Russell V. Manzatt; ***C:*** Jeff Mart.

Rushlights **2013 (R)** Neo-noir indie with too many would-be plot twists and a couple of greedy and stupid lead characters.

They would be Billy (Henderson) and Sarah (Webb) who find out when Sarah's lookalike roommate dies of a heroin overdose that she was about to inherit a fortune from a barely-known uncle. So the two head to smalltown Texas to run a scam and claim the money by having Sarah impersonate the dead roomie, but their plan doesn't work out so well. **95m/C; DVD, Blu-Ray, On Demand.** Josh Henderson; Haley Webb; Beau Bridges; Aidan Quinn; Jordan Bridges; Crispian Belfrage; ***D:*** Antoni Stutz; ***W:*** Antoni Stutz; Ashley Scott Meyers; ***C:*** Gregg Easterbrook; ***M:*** Jeffrey Coulter.

Rushmore 1/2 **1998 (R)** Fresh and original comedy from Anderson follows 15-year-old Max (Schwartzman), an under-achieving yet overconfident student at Rushmore Academy. He has romantic designs on teacher Miss Cross (Williams), and enlists the help of wealthy alum Herman Blume (Murray) in his quest to impress her. Blume also falls for the woman, instigating a war of nasty tricks between the two quirky rivals. Murray drops his trademark smirk and he and newcomer Schwartzman shine. **93m/C; VHS, DVD.** Bill Murray; Jason Schwartzman; Olivia Williams; Seymour Cassel; Brian Cox; Mason Gamble; Sara Tanaka; Connie Nielsen; Kim Terry; Stephen McCole; Ronnie McCawley; Keith McCawley; ***D:*** Wes Anderson; ***W:*** Wes Anderson; Owen Wilson; ***C:*** Robert Yeoman; ***M:*** Mark Mothersbaugh. Ind. Spirit '99: Director (Anderson), Support. Actor (Murray); L.A. Film Critics '98: Support. Actor (Murray); Natl. Film Reg. '16; N.Y. Film Critics '98: Support. Actor (Murray); Natl. Soc. Film Critics '98: Support. Actor (Murray).

Ruslan *Driven to Kill* **2009 (R)** Ruslan Drachev (Seagal) is an ex-mobster turned crime writer whose past comes back to bite him when his daughter decides to marry his bitterest rival and his family is threatened. But Ruslan hasn't forgotten how to be a bad guy. **98m/C; DVD, Blu-Ray, Streaming.** *CA RU US* Steven Seagal; Laura Mennell; Igor Jijikine; Mike Dopud; Robert Wisden; Dan Payne; Holly Eglington; Zak Santiago; Inna Korobkina; ***D:*** Jeff King; ***W:*** Mark James; ***C:*** Thomas M. (Tom) Harting; Tom Harting; ***M:*** Peter Allen. **VIDEO**

Russell Mulcahy's Tale of the Mummy *Tale of the Mummy; Talos the Mummy* **1999 (R)** Archeologists break open the sealed tomb of an Egyptian prince and are destroyed by the curse of Talos. Fifty years later, Samantha Turkel (Lombard) discovers her grandfather's logbook and decides to retrace the course of his deadly expedition. She recovers a sacred amulet and suddenly the power of Talos threatens again. The film was originally released at 119 minutes under the title "Talos the Mummy." **87m/C; VHS, DVD, Blu-Ray.** Jason Scott Lee; Louise Lombard; Sean Pertwee; Lysette Anthony; Michael Lerner; Jack Davenport; Honor Blackman; Christopher Lee; Shelley Duvall; Jon Polito; ***D:*** Russell Mulcahy; ***W:*** Russell Mulcahy; John Esposito; ***C:*** Gabriel Beristain. **VIDEO**

The Russia House 1/2 **1990 (R)** Russian scientist Brandauer attempts to publish book debunking Soviet Union's claims of military superiority by passing it through ex-lover Pfeiffer to British editor Connery. Star-studded spy thriller aspires to heights it never quitereaches. Adapted from John Le Carre's novel, Stoppard's screenplay is very fine, actually making some aspects of the novel work better. **122m/C; VHS, DVD, Blu-Ray.** Sean Connery; Michelle Pfeiffer; Roy Scheider; James Fox; John Mahoney; Klaus Maria Brandauer; Ken Russell; J.T. Walsh; Michael Kitchen; David Threlfall; Ian McNeice; Christopher Lawford; ***D:*** Fred Schepisi; ***W:*** Tom Stoppard; ***C:*** Ian Baker; ***M:*** Jerry Goldsmith.

Russian Dolls 1/2 *Les Poupees Russes* **2005** Set five years after Klapisch's 2002 comedy "L'Auberge Espagnole," the roommates of the Barcelona apartment are older but only a little wiser. Narrator Xavier (Duris) is now 30 and writing for a TV soap in Paris while maintaining a friendship with his exasperating ex Martine (Tautou). His co-writer is Brit Wendy (Reilly), whose brother William (Bishop) is engaged to Russian ballerina Natacha (Obraztsova). The friends are reuniting in St. Petersburg for the wedding. Generally picturesque froth. English, French, Spanish, and Russian with subtitles. **125m/C; DVD.** *FR GB* Romain Duris; Audrey Tautou; Cecile de France; Kelly Reilly; Kevin Bishop; Lucy Gordon; Aïssa Maïga; Eugenya Obraztsova; ***D:*** Cedric Klapisch; ***W:*** Cedric Klapisch; ***C:*** Dominique Colin; ***M:*** Loik Dury; Laurent Levesque.

Russian Roulette **1975** The Russian premier is visiting Vancouver in 1970, and the Mounties must prevent a dissident KGB terrorist from assassinating him. Unthrilling spy yarn fails to deliver on intriguing premise. **100m/C; VHS, DVD.** George Segal; Christina Raines; Bo Brundin; Denholm Elliott; Louise Fletcher; ***D:*** Lou Lombardo.

Russian Roulette 1/2 **1993** Routine story about an American woman on vacation in Russia who finds herself in the middle of a plot to locate a hidden Czarist artifact and smuggle it out of the country. Everyone on her tour group is suspect, an American businessman becomes involved, and a killer starts eliminating the number of players. Great location scenery. **89m/C; VHS, DVD.** Susan Blakely; Barry Bostwick; E.G. Marshall; Jeff Altman; ***D:*** Greydon Clark.

The Russian Specialist *The Mechanik* **2005 (R)** Nikolai (Lundgren) is a Russian Special Ops veteran, who moves to America after his family is murdered by a drug dealer. A fellow expatriate threatens to expose him as an illegal immigrant if he doesn't bring back her kidnapped daughter. Once he finds out the men responsible for his family's death are responsible for the kidnapping he agrees and begins plotting his revenge. **94m/C; DVD.** Dolph Lundgren; Ben Cross; Ivan Petrushinov; Olivia Lee; ***D:*** Dolph Lundgren; ***W:*** Bryan Edward Hill; ***C:*** Ross W. Clarkson; ***M:*** Elia Cmiral.

The Russian Woodpecker **2015** During the Ukrainian revolution and war with Russia, Fedor Alexandrovich, a Ukrainian survivor of the Chernobyl nuclear disaster, learns a dark secret that could impact himself and his war-torn nation if revealed. **80m/C; DVD.** ***D:*** Chad Garcia; ***W:*** Chad Garcia; ***C:*** Artem Ryzhykov; ***M:*** Katya Mihailova.

The Russians Are Coming, the Russians Are Coming **1966** Based on the comic novel "The Off-Islanders" by Nathaniel Benchley, this is the story of a Russian sub which accidentally runs aground off the New England coast. The residents falsely believe that the nine-man crew is the beginning of a Soviet invasion, though the men are only looking for help. A memorable set of silly events follows the landing, engineered by a gung-ho police chief and a town filled with overactive imaginations. **126m/C; VHS, DVD, Blu-Ray.** Alan Arkin; Carl Reiner; Theodore Bikel; Eva Marie Saint; Brian Keith; Paul Ford; Jonathan Winters; Ben Blue; Tessie O'Shea; Doro Merande; John Phillip Law; ***D:*** Norman Jewison; ***C:*** Joseph Biroc. Golden Globes '67: Actor--Mus./Comedy (Arkin), Film--Mus./Comedy.

Russkies 1/2 **1987 (PG)** A jolly comedy about three adorable American kids who capture, and eventually grow to like, a stranded Russian sailor. Friendly and peace-loving, but dull. **98m/C; VHS, DVD.** Joaquin Rafael (Leaf) Phoenix; Whip Hubley; Peter Billingsley; Stefan DeSalle; Susan Walters; ***D:*** Rick Rosenthal; ***M:*** James Newton Howard.

Rust 1/2 **2009 (PG)** Suffering a crisis of faith, former pastor James Moore returns to his hometown but his family isn't so happy to see him. He learns a newcomer family has been killed in a suspicious fire and Moore's childhood friend Travis is in a psychiatric prison ward as the culprit. James believes Travis is innocent but can he help anyone else when he can't seem to help himself? Filmed on location in Kipling, Saskatchewan. **94m/C; DVD.** Corbin Bernsen; Lloyd Allen Warner; Lorne Cardinal; Frank Gall; Audrey Lynn Tennant; Kirsten Collins; Rev. John G. Hutchinson; Judith Davies; Nolan Hubbard; Ryder Debreceni; ***D:*** Corbin Bernsen; ***W:*** Corbin Bernsen; ***M:*** Brandon McCormick; Mike Post. **VIDEO**

Rust and Bone *De rouille et d'os* **2012 (R)** After being given sole custody of his estranged son, down and out loner Ali (Schoenaerts) leaves the south of France for his sister's house in Antibes to begin anew. The indifferent former fighter takes a job as a bouncer where meets a cocky, gorgeous, and out-of-his-league orca trainer in Stephanie (a convincing Cotillard). A tragic accident upends her and a chance phone call leads the damaged pair to one another. Stark and occasionally rough, the leads were up to the task of director Audiard's shamelessly worthy love story. **120m/C; DVD, Blu-Ray.** *FR BE* Marion Cotillard; Matthias Schoenaerts; Armand Verdure; Celine Sallette; Corinne Masiero; Bouli Lanners; Jean-Michel Correia; Mourad Frarema; Yanick Choirat; ***D:*** Jacques Audiard; ***W:*** Jacques Audiard; Thomas Bidegain; Craig Davison; ***C:*** Stephanie Fontaine; ***M:*** Alexandre Desplat.

Rust Creek **2019 (R)** When college student Sawyer (Corfield) drives to Washington, DC, for a job interview, her GPS takes her to a closed road. Trying to find her way back through the woods, she stops to check her directions when two untrustworthy looking men offer to help. Though they attack her, Sawyer fights them off, gets a knife, and becomes stranded into the woods. As she tries to find her way out, Sawyer encounters police officers with a hidden agenda and gains an ally in Lowell (Paulson). A thriller-wannabe. **108m/C; DVD, Blu-Ray.** Hermione Corfield; Denise Dal Vera; Jeremy Glazer; Laura Guzman; Micah Hauptman; ***D:*** Jen McGowan; ***W:*** Julie Lipson; ***C:*** Michelle Lawler; ***M:*** H. Scott Salinas.

Rustin 1/2 **2001 (PG-13)** Every cliche possible appears in this cross between an afterschool special and a movie-of-the-week. Billy Stagen (Johnson) is a former pro football player who's becomes the sheriff of his Alabama hometown, Rustin. He slides by on charm and local celebrity until troubled teen Lee (Johnson) shows up, claiming to be his daughter. Now it's time to see if Billy can handle adult responsibilities. Meat Loaf is the current high school coach and Bryan is the latest football player-hero (in case you're wondering why they're featured on the box cover). **100m/C; VHS, DVD.** Rick Johnson; Meat Loaf Aday; Ashley Johnson; Zachery Ty Bryan; Michael (Mike) Papajohn; Shawn Weatherly; ***D:*** Rick Johnson; ***W:*** Jon Lucas; ***C:*** Wally Pfister; ***M:*** Jonathan Price.

Rustlers of Red Dog 1/2 **1935** A 12-chapter western serial about Indian wars and cattle rustlers. **235m/B; VHS, DVD.** Johnny Mack Brown; Raymond Hatton; Joyce Compton; Walter Miller; Harry Woods; William Desmond; Wally Wales; Chief Thundercloud; Art Mix; Bill(y) (William Patten) Patton; Bud Osborne; Lafe (Lafayette) McKee; ***D:*** Lew Landers.

Rustler's Rhapsody **1985 (PG)** A singing cowboy rides into a small western town and encounters all kinds of desperados in this earnest would-be satire of '40s B-movie westerns. **89m/C; VHS, DVD.** Tom Berenger; Patrick Wayne; G.W. Bailey; Andy Griffith; Marilu Henner; ***D:*** Hugh Wilson; ***W:*** Hugh Wilson; ***C:*** Jose Luis Alcaine; ***M:*** Steve Dorff.

Ruthless **1948** Mostly done in flashbacks, Ulmer's flick is a rise-and-fall melodrama. Horace Vendig (Scott) starts off as a poor boy determined to obtain money, power, and social status by any means necessary, including using several women. Former pal Vic (Hayward) relates the beginning of Horace's machinations to his fiance Mallory (Lynn), the lookalike of Martha, the first supposed love of Horace's life. From there it's on to socialite Susan (Vickers) and married Christa (Bremer), but Horace's ruthlessness finally catches up with him. **104m/B; DVD, Blu-Ray.** Zachary Scott; Louis Hayward; Diana Lynn; Sydney Greenstreet; Lucille Bremer; Martha Vickers; Raymond Burr; ***D:*** Edgar G. Ulmer; ***W:*** S.K. Lauren; Gordon Kahn; ***C:*** Bert Glennon; ***M:*** Werner Janssen.

Ruthless People **1986 (R)** DeVito and his mistress spend a romantic evening plotting his obnoxious wife's untimely demise. Before he can put his plan into action, he's delighted to discover she's been kidnapped by some very desperate people—who don't stand a chance with Bette. High farcical entertainment is a variation on the story "The Ransom of Red Chief," by O. Henry. **93m/C; VHS, DVD.** Bette Midler; Danny DeVito; Judge Reinhold; Helen Slater; Anita Morris; Bill Pullman; ***D:*** David Zucker; Jim Abrahams; Jerry Zucker; ***W:*** Dale Lanner; ***C:*** Jan De Bont; ***M:*** Michel Colombier.

RV **2006 (PG)** When Bob Munro (Williams) is forced to cancel a vacation for a business trip to Colorado, he decides it's the perfect opportunity to reconnect with his over-scheduled family. Bob rents a hideously gaudy RV and tricks wife Jamie (Hines), grumpy teen daughter Cassie (Levesque), and macho young son Carl (Hutcherson) into a road trip. Bob is basically clueless, and they run into various calamities (generally involving raw sewage) as well as the goofy, constantly upbeat Gornicke family, who live in their RV and really want to bond with the Munros. Williams does shtick but at least the schmaltz is minimal. **98m/C; DVD, Blu-Ray, UMD.** Robin Williams; Jeff Daniels; Cheryl Hines; Kristin Chenoweth; Joanna "JoJo" Levesque; Josh Hutcherson; Will Arnett; Brendan Fletcher; Brian Markinson; Barry Sonnenfeld; Hunter Parrish; Rob LaBelle; Chloe Sonnenfeld; Alex Ferris; Tony Hale; Brian Howe; ***D:*** Barry Sonnenfeld; ***W:*** Geoff Rodkey; ***C:*** Fred Murphy; ***M:*** James Newton Howard.

Rx 1/2 *Simple Lies* **2006** When his parents face financial ruin, Andrew (Balfour) decides to head south of the border with two friends, Jonny (Hanks) and Melissa (German), to pull off a big-money drug deal. Things take a bad turn for the twentysomethings, however, and their only hope of returning home from Mexico is in the form of a perilous pact with gay German drug dealers—who enjoy partying dressed as Nazis—that also endangers their lives. Predictable but definitely not dull. **86m/C; DVD.** Eric Balfour; Colin Hanks; Lauren German; Danny Pino; Lulu Molina; ***D:*** Ariel Vromen; ***W:*** Ariel Vromen; Morgan Land. **VIDEO**

Ryan's Daughter 1/2 **1970 (PG)** Irish woman (Miles) marries a man she does not love and then falls for a shell-shocked British major who arrives during the 1916 Irish uprising to keep the peace. Not surprisingly, she is accused of betraying the local IRA gunrunners to her British lover. Tasteful melodrama with lots of pretty scenery that goes on a bit too long. **194m/C; VHS, DVD.** *GB* Sarah Miles; Robert Mitchum; John Mills; Trevor Howard; Christopher Jones; Leo McKern; ***D:*** David Lean; ***W:*** Robert Bolt; ***C:*** Frederick A. (Freddie) Young; ***M:*** Maurice Jarre. Oscars '70: Cinematog., Support. Actor (Mills); Golden Globes '71: Support. Actor (Mills).

Ryder P.I. **1986 (PG-13)** P.I Ryder and his sidekick fight crime and solve weird cases in the big city. **92m/C; VHS, DVD.** Bob Nelson; Dave Hawthorne; John Mulrooney; Howard Stern; ***D:*** Karl Hosch; Chuck Walker; ***W:*** Bob Nelson; Dave Hawthorne; Karl Hosch; Chuck Walker; ***C:*** Phil Arfman; ***M:*** Kevin Kelly.

Ryna **2005** In rural Romania, beautiful teenager Ryna (Petre) is forced to dress as a boy and work as a mechanic by her abusive father (Popescu). But she asserts her independence after a tragedy. Romanian and French with subtitles. **94m/C; DVD.** *RO SI* Doroteea Petre; Valentin Popescu; Nicolae Praida; Matthieu Roze; ***D:*** Ruxandra Zenide; ***W:*** Ruxandra Zenide; Marek Epstein; ***C:*** Marius Panduru; ***M:*** Antoine Auberson.

S. Darko: A Donnie Darko Tale **2009 (R)** Tedious repetition and dull characters doom this bad sequel to the cult original. Donnie's younger sister Samantha (Chase) has yet to recover from her brother's death. She and her best pal Corey (Evigan) decide to drive to L.A. but their car breaks down in a small Utah town that's soon hit by a meteor. While Corey is partying with the locals, Samantha starts having end-of-the-world visions. **103m/C; DVD, Blu-Ray.** Daveigh Chase; Briana Evigan; Ed Westwick; James Lafferty; John Hawkes; Elizabeth Berkley; Matthew Davis; Jackson Rathbone; Bret Roberts; ***D:*** Chris Fisher; ***W:*** Nathan Atkins; ***C:*** Marvin V. Rush; ***M:*** Ed Harcourt. **VIDEO**

S21: The Khmer Rouge Killing Machine *S21: La Machine De Mort Khmere Rouge; S21: The Khmer Rouge Death Machine* **2003** From 1975-1979, the Khmer Rouge, led by Pol Pot, instituted a series of murderous purges that took place at S21, a high school turned interrogation and torture center in Phnom Penh where 17,000 prisoners were "processed." Only three lived to tell about it. Vahn Nath, an artist, relates his story of survival by painting flattering portraits of the guards. Journals kept by guards and re-creations describe the painful techniques used on prisoners. Director Rithy Panh (himself an inmate at S21) takes an unvarnished look at the horrors perpetrated in the name of the state. **105m/C; DVD.** *FR* ***D:*** Rithy Panh; ***W:*** Rithy Panh; ***C:*** Rithy Panh; Prum Mesar; ***M:*** Mark Marder.

Saadia 🦴 ½ **1953** French doctor Henrik (Ferrer) is working in Morocco when he saves the life of young and beautiful Saadia (Gam) who's been poisoned by jealous local witch Fatima (Rotha). Henrik falls in love but Saadia is already enamored of Henrik's friend, the provincial ruler Lahssen (Wilde). **82m/C; DVD.** Rita Gam; Mel Ferrer; Cornel Wilde; Wanda Rotha; Cyril Cusack; Michel Simon; ***D:*** Albert Lewin; ***W:*** Albert Lewin; ***C:*** Christopher Challis; ***M:*** Bronislau Kaper.

Sabaka 🦴🦴 *The Hindu* **1955** Adventure set in India about a scary religious cult. Karloff and the cast of stalwart "B" movie performers have fun with this one, and you should, too. **81m/C; VHS, DVD.** Boris Karloff; Reginald Denny; Victor Jory; Lisa Howard; Jeanne Bates; Jay Novello; June Foray; ***D:*** Frank Ferrin.

Sabata 🦴 ½ **1969 (PG-13)** Van Cleef is the man in black as gunslinger Sabata in this exuberant, if confusing, spaghetti western. Sabata enters the town of Daugherty just after a robbery of Union Army funds. Sabata wants the reward but quickly discovers that three of the town's leaders funded the theft so he decides to blackmail them. They send numerous assassins after Sabata with no luck. **111m/C; DVD, Blu-Ray.** *IT* Lee Van Cleef; William Berger; Pedro Sanchez; Frank Ressel; Aldo Canti; Gianni Rizzo; Antonio Gradoli; ***D:*** Gianfranco Parolini; ***W:*** Gianfranco Parolini; Renato Izzo; ***C:*** Sandro Moncori; ***M:*** Marcello Giombini.

Sabotage 🦴🦴🦴 *A Woman Alone; Hidden Power* **1936** Early Hitchcock thriller based on Conrad's "The Secret Agent." A woman who works at a movie theatre (Sidney) suspects her quiet husband (Homolka) might be the terrorist planting bombs around London. Numerous sly touches of the Master's signature humor. **81m/B; VHS, DVD, Blu-Ray.** Oscar Homolka; Sylvia Sidney; John Loder; Desmond Tester; Joyce Barbour; Matthew Boulton; S.J. Warmington; William Dewhurst; Austin Trevor; Torin Thatcher; Aubrey Mather; Peter Bull; Charles Hawtrey; Martita Hunt; Hal Walters; Frederick Piper; ***D:*** Alfred Hitchcock; ***W:*** Charles Bennett; Ian Hay; Alma Reville; E.V.H. Emmett; Helen Simpson; ***C:*** Bernard Knowles.

Sabotage 🦴🦴 **1996 (R)** A disgraced ex-Navy counterterrorism operative and bodyguard is on the trail of the man who murdered his boss, along with the FBI agent assigned to the case. Standard-issue shoot-em-up with decent action. **99m/C; VHS, DVD.** *CA* Mark Dacascos; Carrie-Anne Moss; Tony Todd; Graham Greene; John Neville; James Purcell; ***D:*** Tibor Takacs; ***W:*** Michael Stokes; ***C:*** Curtis Petersen; ***M:*** Guy Zerafa.

Sabotage 🦴 ½ **2014 (R)** Excessively violent and excessively stupid, this action-cop drama is the latest piece of evidence that Ah-nuld never should have returned to Hollywood after his political stint ended. Schwarzenegger stars as John "Breacher" Wharton, a tough-as-nails DEA agent with his own group of "edgy cops" who fight drugs but skirt the law themselves. They're using a cartel safe house as a cover to steal $10 million in drug money. That doesn't end well (gasp!). And then members of the group start ending up in body bags. It's a messy, silly film with gigantic plot holes and little entertainment. **109m/C; DVD, Blu-Ray.** Arnold Schwarzenegger; Mireille Enos; Sam Worthington; Joe Manganiello; Terrence Howard; Olivia Williams; Josh Holloway; Maximillian Martini; ***D:*** David Ayer; ***W:*** David Ayer; Skip Woods; ***C:*** Bruce McCleery; ***M:*** David Sardy.

Saboteur 🦴🦴🦴 **1942** A man wrongly accused of sabotaging an American munitions plant during WWII sets out to find the traitor who framed him. Hitchcock uses his locations, including Boulder Dam, Radio City Music Hall, and the Statue of Liberty, to greatly intensify the action. Stunning resolution. **108m/B; VHS, DVD, Blu-Ray.** Priscilla Lane; Robert Cummings; Otto Kruger; Alan Baxter; Norman Lloyd; Charles Halton; ***D:*** Alfred Hitchcock; ***W:*** Alfred Hitchcock; Peter Viertel; ***C:*** Joseph Valentine; ***M:*** Frank Skinner.

Sabretooth **WOOF! 2001 (R)** Stupid scientist uses fossil DNA to genetically re-create the sabretooth tiger, loses control of the new beastie, which goes on a killing spree (of campers no less). Supremely dumb, unintentionally humorous, with bad acting (by actors who certainly have done better work), bad special effects...well, if you like cheap horror flicks, this woof is for you. **90m/C; VHS, DVD.** David Keith; Vanessa Angel; John Rhys-Davies; Lahmard Tate; ***D:*** James D.R. Hickox; ***W:*** Tom Woolsley; ***C:*** Christopher Pearson. **VIDEO**

Sabrina 🦴🦴🦴🦴 *Sabrina Fair* **1954** Two wealthy brothers, one an aging businessman (Bogart) and the other a dissolute playboy (Holden), vie for the attention of their chauffeur's daughter (Hepburn), who has just returned from a French cooking school. Typically acerbic, in the Wilder manner, with Bogart and Holden cast interestingly against type (but it's Hepburn's picture anyway). Based on the play "Sabrina Fair" by Samuel Taylor. **113m/B; VHS, DVD, Blu-Ray.** Audrey Hepburn; Humphrey Bogart; William Holden; Walter Hampden; Francis X. Bushman; John Williams; Martha Hyer; Marcel Dalio; ***D:*** Billy Wilder; ***W:*** Billy Wilder; Ernest Lehman; ***C:*** Charles B(ryant) Lang, Jr. Oscars '54: Costume Des. (B&W); Directors Guild '54: Director (Wilder); Golden Globes '55: Screenplay; Natl. Bd. of Review '54: Support. Actor (Williams); Natl. Film Reg. '02.

Sabrina 🦴🦴 ½ **1995 (PG)** Updated version of Billy Wilder's 1954 fairytale that starred a luminous Audrey Hepburn. This time around the pretty Ormond is the chauffeur's daughter who gets closely involved with the wealthy Larrabees. And this time the emphasis is more on workaholic business mogul Linus (Ford), who plays a dangerous game when he decides to transfer Sabrina's affections from his feckless engaged brother David (Kinnear) to himself in order to protect a business merger. Ford's a little too stodgy (you'll wonder why Sabrina bothers except she's probably just too nice to say no) but Kinnear's suitably charming (in his film debut) and Marchand properly matriarchal. **127m/C; VHS, DVD.** Harrison Ford; Julia Ormond; Greg Kinnear; Nancy Marchand; John Wood; Richard Crenna; Angie Dickinson; Lauren Holly; Fanny Ardant; Dana Ivey; Patrick Bruel; Miriam Colon; Elizabeth Franz; ***D:*** Sydney Pollack; ***W:*** David Rayfiel; Barbara Benedek; ***C:*** Giuseppe Rotunno; ***M:*** John Williams.

Sabrina the Teenage Witch 🦴🦴 ½ **1996 (PG)** Based on the Archie Comics, this lighthearted movie finds 16-year-old Sabrina (Hart) being told by her two eccentric aunts, Hilda (Miller) and Zelda (Fernetz), that she is a witch, descended from a long line of good witches and warlocks. Sabrina's having enough trouble fitting in at Riverdale High without this kind of news but she does find that her magical powers have their advantages. Pilot for the TV series. **90m/C; VHS, DVD.** Melissa Joan Hart; Charlene Fernetz; Sherry Miller; Michelle Beaudoin; Ryan Reynolds; Tobias Mehler; Lalainia Lindbjerg; ***D:*** Tibor Takacs; ***W:*** Barney Cohen; Kathryn Wallack; Nicholas Factor. **CABLE**

Sabu 🦴🦴 **2004** Eiji (Tatsuya Fujiwara) is framed for a crime he didn't commit, and his friend Sabu (Satoshi Tsumabuki) must somehow find a way to prove his innocence. Adapted from a classic Japanese novel by Shugoro Yamamoto, it is surprisingly conventional considering the director (Takashi Miike) is well known for films including lurid violence, sexuality, or just plain weirdness. A period drama about two friends that's made for television is about as far from his usual work as you can get. **122m/C; DVD.** *JP* Tatsuya Fujiwara; Satoshi Tsumabuki; Tomoko Tabata; Kazue Fukiishi; Kenji Sawada; Naomasa Rokudaira; Tatsuo Yamada; Yoshiki Arizono; ***D:*** Takashi Miike; ***W:*** Hiroshi Takeyama; Shugoro Yamamoto; ***C:*** Hideo Yamamoto; ***M:*** Koji Endo.

Sacco & Vanzetti 🦴🦴 *Sacco e Vanzetti* **1971 (PG)** Two Italian immigrants and acknowledged anarchists are caught amidst communist witch-hunts and judicial negligence when they are tried and executed for murder in 1920s America. Based on the true-life case, considered by some a flagrant miscarriage of justice and political martyrdom, by others, honest American judicial-system proceedings. Well-made and acted. Joan Baez sings the title song "The Ballad of Sacco and Vanzetti." **120m/C; VHS, DVD.** Gian Marie Volonte; Riccardo Cucciolla; Milo O'Shea; Cyril Cusack; Geoffrey Keen; ***D:*** Guiliano Montaldo; ***M:*** Ennio Morricone. Cannes '71: Actor (Cucciolla).

The Sacketts 🦴🦴 ½ **1979** Follows the adventures of three Tennessee brothers who migrate to the West after the Civil War. Based on two Louis L'Amour novels. **198m/C; VHS, DVD.** Jeffery Osterhage; Tom Selleck; Sam Elliott; Glenn Ford; Ben Johnson; Mercedes McCambridge; Ruth Roman; Jack Elam; Gilbert Roland; ***D:*** Robert Totten. **TV**

The Sacrament 🦴🦴 **2013 (R)** Sam (Bowen), Jake (Swanberg), and Patrick (Audley) travel to a distant religious settlement to find Patrick's sister, who has been inducted into a cult. At first, it seems that life in this close-knit community is utopia. They all support each other. Patrick's sister is happy. They're self-sufficient and live off the land. What could possibly go wrong here? Of course, anyone knows what will go awry and it's a shame to see director West--a horror festival star--work so predictably. **100m/C; DVD, Blu-Ray.** Joe Swanberg; AJ Bowen; Kentucker Audley; Amy Seimetz; Gene Jones; Kate Lyn Sheil; ***D:*** Ti West; ***W:*** Ti West; ***C:*** Eric Robbins; ***M:*** Tyler Bates.

Sacred Ground 🦴🦴 **1983 (PG)** A trapper and his pregnant Apache wife unknowingly build shelter on the Paiute Indians' sacred burial ground. When the wife dies in childbirth, the pioneer is forced to kidnap a Paiute woman who has just buried her own deceased infant. Average western drama. **100m/C; VHS, DVD.** Tim McIntire; Jack Elam; L.Q. Jones; Mindi Miller; ***D:*** Charles B. Pierce; ***W:*** Charles B. Pierce.

The Sacrifice 🦴🦴🦴 **1986 (PG)** Tarkovsky's enigmatic final film, released after his death. Deals with a retired intellectual's spiritually symbolic efforts at self-sacrifice in order to save his family on the eve of a nuclear holocaust. Stunning cinematography by Nykvist. Acclaimed, but sometimes slow going; not everyone will appreciate Tarkovsky's visionary spiritualism. In Swedish and Russian with English subtitles. **145m/C; VHS, DVD, Blu-Ray.** *FR SW* Erland Josephson; Susan Fleetwood; Valerie Mairesse; Allan Edwall; Gudrun Gisladottir; Sven Wollter; Filippa Franzen; ***D:*** Andrei Tarkovsky; ***W:*** Andrei Tarkovsky; ***C:*** Sven Nykvist. British Acad. '87: Foreign Film.

Sacrifice 🦴🦴 **2000 (R)** Serial killer has murdered the daughter of felon Tyler Pearce, who escapes from prison to get revenge. He hooks up with an ex-prostitute (Luner) but he'll have to avoid an FBI agent who wants to put Tyler back behind bars. **91m/C; VHS, DVD.** Michael Madsen; Bokeem Woodbine; Jamie Luner; Joshua Leonard; ***D:*** Mark L. Lester. **VIDEO**

The Sacrifice 🦴 ½ **2005** Low-budget indie horror from first-timer Fessenden. Teenager Jonathan Kelly and his widowed mom Laura move to the small New Hampshire town of Dunkirk. Jonathan quickly becomes friends with David, who shares his interest in the occult. As they investigate a local ghost story, they find someone has been digging up graves in the old cemetery and plans to use the bones for a ritual, but bones may not be enough. **95m/C; DVD.** Robert Kersey; David L. Snyder; Kymra McCarthy; Jamie Fessenden; ***D:*** Jamie Fessenden; ***W:*** Jamie Fessenden; ***C:*** Jamie Fessenden.

Sacrifice 🦴 ½ **2011 (R)** Undercover cop John Hebron (Gooding Jr.) has become an unreliable drunk after the murders of his wife and daughter. He's given a chance at redemption when he's asked to protect Angel, the baby sister of mule Mike (Bostick), who's trying to get out of the heroin trade. Also involved is Father Porter (Slater)--he's been counseling John and his church is missing a statue of the Virgin Mary. How everything ties together is obvious but there's enough action to keep up a mild interest. **99m/C; DVD, Blu-Ray.** *CA US* Cuba Gooding, Jr.; Christian Slater; Kim Coates; Devon Bostick; Lara Daans; Arcadia Kendal; Zion Lee; Athena Karkanis; ***D:*** Damian Lee; ***W:*** Damian Lee; ***C:*** David Pelletier. **VIDEO**

The Sad Sack 🦴🦴 **1957** A bumbling hero with a photographic memory winds up in Morocco as a member of the French Foreign Legion. Although a success at the box office, Lewis's second movie (without partner Dean Martin) seems jerky and out of sorts today. Based on the comic strip character by George Baker, but not effectively. **98m/B; VHS, Streaming.** Jerry Lewis; Phyllis Kirk; David Wayne; Peter Lorre; Gene Evans; Mary Treen; ***D:*** George Marshall; ***C:*** Loyal Griggs; ***M:*** Burt Bacharach; Hal David.

The Saddest Music in the World 🦴🦴 ½ **2003** Arty but amusing take on the classic musicals and screwball comedies of the 1930s set in Depression-era Winnipeg, Canada. Eccentric plot has legless beer baroness Lady Helen Port-Huntly (Rossellini) proclaiming she will offer a prize of $25,000 and a crown of frozen tears to any nation that comes up with the world's saddest music. Americans Chester Kent (McKinney), a failed Broadway producer and Canadian ex-pat, and Narcissa (de Medeiros), his amnesiac, nymphomanic muse, decide to take a crack at it. Truly stylish, madcap and clever, zaniness nonetheless wears thin by the conclusion. Appropriately eclectic soundtrack. Based on an original screenplay by Kazuo Ishigura. **99m/B; DVD.** *CA* Isabella Rossellini; Mark McKinney; Maria De Medeiros; Ross McMillan; David Fox; Claude Dorge; Darcy Fehr; ***D:*** Guy Maddin; ***W:*** Guy Maddin; George Toles; Kazuo Ishiguro; ***C:*** Luc Montpellier; ***M:*** Christopher Dedrick.

Saddle the Wind 🦴🦴 ½ **1958** Taylor's exceptionally good as ex-gunfighter Steve Sinclair who's given up his guns for ranching. His quiet life is upset when his quick-tempered, trigger-happy younger brother Tony (Cassavetes) suddenly returns home with dancehall gal Joan (London), whom he says is his fiance. Soon Tony is getting into scrapes showing off his gun skills, which causes trouble for Steve with big landowner Deneen (Crisp), who likes things peaceful in his town. **84m/C; DVD.** Robert Taylor; John Cassavetes; Julie London; Donald Crisp; Royal Dano; Richard Erdman; Douglas Spencer; Ray Teal; Charles McGraw; Robert Parrish; ***D:*** John Cassavetes; Donald Crisp; Robert Parrish; ***W:*** John Cassavetes; Rod Serling; ***C:*** George J. Folsey; ***M:*** Elmer Bernstein.

Saddle Tramp 🦴 ½ **1947** Carefee cowpoke Chuck Conner (McCrea) is suddenly saddled with four kids after his best friend (a widower and the boys' father) is killed riding Chuck's horse. He takes a job at a ranch but has to keep the kids on the down-low, which is made more difficult by the addition of Della—a runaway girl from a neighboring ranch. To make matters worse, Chuck finds evidence of cattle rustling and the rustlers don't much like Chuck snooping around. **90m/C; DVD.** Joel McCrea; Wanda Hendrix; John Russell; John McIntire; Jeannette Nolan; Russell Simpson; Ed Begley, Sr.; ***D:*** Hugo Fregonese; ***W:*** Harold Shumate; ***C:*** Charles P. Boyle; ***M:*** Joseph Gershenson.

Sade 🦴🦴 **2000** Director Jacquot takes a low-key approach to a short period in the life of the notorious Marquis de Sade. In 1794, Sade (Auteuil), depicted as a manipulative bon vivant rather than a sexual libertine, is one of many aristocrats imprisoned at a former convent during the Reign of Terror. His relatively luxurious abode is thanks to the machinations of a former mistress (Denicourt), who's now under the protection of Fournier (Colin), one of Robespierre's men. Sade enjoys his situation by staging sexual tableaus and plotting the seduction of virginal teen Emilie (Le Besco) by handsome gardener Augustin (Lespert). Based on the novel "La Terreur du Boudoir" by Serge Bramly. French with subtitles. **100m/C; DVD.** *FR* Daniel Auteuil; Marianne (Cuau) Denicourt; Gregoire Colin; Islid Le Besco; Jeanne Balibar; Jean-Pierre Cassel; Jalil Lespert; ***D:*** Benoit Jacquot; ***W:*** Jacques Fieschi; Bernard Minoret; ***C:*** Benoit Delhomme.

Sadie McKee 🦴🦴🦴 **1934** A melodrama with Crawford as a maid searching for love in the big city. She falls for a self-destructive ne'er-do-well, marries an alcoholic millionaire, and eventually finds true love with the wealthy Tone (who would become Crawford's third husband). Professional acting and directing elevate the story. **90m/B; VHS, DVD.** Joan Crawford; Franchot Tone; Gene Raymond; Edward Arnold; ***D:*** Clarence Brown.

Sadie Thompson 🦴🦴🦴 **1928** Swanson plays a harlot with a heart of gold, bawdy and good-natured, in the South Seas. A zealot missionary (Barrymore) arrives and falls in love with her. The last eight minutes of footage have been recreated by using stills and the original title cards, to replace the last reel which had decomposed. Remade as "Rain," "Dirty Gertie From Harlem," and "Miss Sadie Thompson." Based on W. Somerset Maugham's "Rain." **97m/B; Silent; VHS, DVD.** Gloria Swanson; Lionel Barrymore; Raoul Walsh; Blanche Frederici; Charles Lane; James A. Marcus; ***D:*** Raoul Walsh; ***W:*** Raoul Walsh; ***C:*** George Barnes; Robert B. Kurrle; Oliver Marsh.

The Sadist 1/2 *The Profile of Terror* **1963** Three teachers on their way to Dodger Stadium find themselves stranded at a roadside garage and terrorized by a snivelling lunatic. Tense and plausible. **95m/B; VHS, DVD.** Arch Hall, Jr.; Helen Hovey; Richard Alden; Marilyn Manning; ***D:*** James Landis; ***W:*** James Landis; ***C:*** Vilmos Zsigmond.

Safari Drums **1953** A movie company on safari comes to the jungle to make a wildlife film but Larry Conrad secretly is arranging to film a fight between two big cats, which Bomba won't allow. But the jungle boy is busy looking for a murderer in Conrad's crew at Commissioner Barnes' request. 9th in the series. **71m/B; DVD.** John(ny) Sheffield; Emory Parnell; Barbara Bestar; Douglas Kennedy; Leonard Mudie; ***D:*** Ford Beebe; ***W:*** Ford Beebe; ***C:*** Harry Neumann; ***M:*** Marlin Skiles.

Safe **1995 (R)** Surburban California housewife Carol (Moore) literally becomes allergic to her environment and winds up seeking relief in a holistic center in Albuquerque, where director Haynes takes a shot at the New Age and finds a link to the AIDS crisis. Serious, stylistically detached look at a near future riddled with environmental toxins is led by Moore's performance as the sunny suburbanite undone by the unseen. **119m/C; VHS, DVD, Blu-Ray.** Julianne Moore; Peter Friedman; Xander Berkeley; Susan Norman; James LeGros; Mary Carver; Kate McGregor-Stewart; Jessica Harper; Brandon Cruz; ***D:*** Todd Haynes; ***W:*** Todd Haynes; ***C:*** Alex Nepomniaschy; ***M:*** Ed Tomney.

Safe Conduct 1/2 *Laissez-Passer* **2001** Tavernier beautifully tells the true story of French filmmakers during the Nazi occupation of WWII. Follows the stories of Jean Devaivre, an assistant director who rises to become a feature director while trying to inject some personal view into his films, and writer Jean Aurenche, who refuses to work for the German-controlled studio. Important, but generally overlooked, part of French film history is beautifully told, directed, and acted. **170m/C; VHS, DVD.** *FR GE SP* Jacques Gamblin; Denis Podalydes; Marie Gillain; Christian Berkel; Charlotte Kady; Marie Desgranges; Maria Pitarresi; Thierry Gibault; Philippe Morier-Genoud; Christophe Odent; Ged Marlon; Laurent Schilling; ***D:*** Bertrand Tavernier; ***W:*** Bertrand Tavernier; Jean Cosmos; ***C:*** Alain Choquart; ***M:*** Antoine Duhamel.

Safe Harbor 1/2 **2006** Detective Carly Segan (Gold) is after a possible serial killer who targets women who were once residents of Safe Harbor, a home for abused children. Evidence points to blackmailing pedophile and former handyman Ray (Heindl) but Carly has kept quiet about growing up in the home herself and her past may be affecting her judgment. **90m/C; DVD.** Tracey Gold; Mitchell Kosterman; Steve Bacic; Daryl Shuttleworth; Pamela Perry; Stacy Grant; Scott Heindl; ***D:*** Mark Griffiths; ***W:*** David Golden; ***C:*** Richard Walden. **CABLE**

Safe Harbor 1/2 **2009** Hallmark Channel original. Doug (Williams) and Robbie (Travis) Smith are about to fulfill their retirement houseboat trip dream when the stock market bottoms out and keeps them at home. A family friend, Judge Roberts (Bean), asks the couple to take in three juvies to save them from adult lockup. They reluctantly agree and Doug puts the boys to work but the other members of the marina community aren't happy and when problems arise, Doug and Robbie have to show that their safe harbor for the boys is a good arrangement. Based on the Safe Harbor program in Jacksonville, Florida. **90m/C; DVD.** Treat Williams; Nancy Travis; Charlie McDermott; Sam Jones, III; Orson Bean; Reiley McClendon; ***D:*** Jerry Jameson; ***W:*** Josef Anderson; ***C:*** Dane Peterson; ***M:*** Bruce Broughton. **CABLE**

Safe Harbour 1/2 *Danielle Steel's Safe Harbour* **2007 (PG-13)** Ophelie's (Gilbert) husband and son are killed in a plane crash and she retreats with 14-year-old daughter Pip (Liberato) to a rented beach house to grieve. While walking the beach, Pip meets artist Matt (Johnson) but Ophelie is horrified that her daughter is talking to strangers until Matt introduces himself. (Naturally, he has family problems of his own to work through.) Her best friend Andrea (Staab) urges Ophelie to have a little fun with Matt but she thinks it's too soon and then she finds out a secret. It's all really nice and stilted and passion-free and Gilbert tries to use a French accent (since the character in Danielle Steel's book was French) but doesn't pull it off. **101m/C; DVD.** Melissa Gilbert; Brad Johnson; Rebecca Staab; Edithe Swensen; Liana Liberato; Katie Walder; ***D:*** William Corcoran; ***C:*** Curtis Petersen; ***M:*** Joey Newman. **VIDEO**

Safe Haven **2013 (PG-13)** The Nicholas Sparks book-to-film machine keeps turning, spitting out another horrendous romantic drama aimed at audiences who just want to see pretty people behave sentimentally and won't care that none of it makes any sense. Katie (Hough) is a newcomer to a North Carolina town who is trying to escape a dark past. Hunky Alex (Duhamel) plays her savior, a man who will protect her and give her "safe haven" from the abuse she has suffered. Of course, Alex has emotional wounds of his own. So will viewers after watching this dreck. **115m/C; DVD, Blu-Ray.** Julianne Hough; Josh Duhamel; Cobie Smulders; David Lyons; ***D:*** Lasse Hallstrom; ***W:*** Dana Stevens; Leslie Bohem; ***C:*** Terry Stacey; ***M:*** Deborah Lurie.

Safe House 1/2 **1999** Comedy-thriller with a terrific lead performance by Stewart. A retiree succumbing to Alzheimer's, Mace Sowell becomes increasingly paranoid and taken to carrying a gun and maintaining an elaborate security system around his L.A. home. Mace claims to be an ex-government agent, marked for death by his former boss who's now a presidential candidate. His fears are dismissed by his shrink (Elizondo) and his daughter forces him to get an in-home caregiver, Andi Travers (Williams). But soon Andi begins to think her charge may not be crazy after all. **125m/C; VHS, DVD.** Patrick Stewart; Kimberly Williams; Hector Elizondo; Craig Shoemaker; ***D:*** Eric Steven Stahl; ***W:*** Eric Steven Stahl; Sean McLain; ***C:*** Vincent Donohue; ***M:*** Kevin Kiner. **CABLE**

Safe House **2012 (R)** Infamous CIA-agent-turned-rogue-criminal Tobin Frost (Washington) ends up at a South African safe house run by relative rookie Matt Weston (Reynolds) when his enemies come to track him down and the pair is forced to escape. As Weston tries to figure out the mystery behind his controversial guest, the film goes through predictable motions. Washington brings the piece some energy but falters from a clear refusal to turn him into a real villain. Nothing particularly wrong with this "Bourne" wannabe, except the generic, cliched script with a nonsensical plot, which makes it a little too safe for its own good. **115m/C; DVD, Blu-Ray.** Denzel Washington; Ryan Reynolds; Brendan Gleeson; Sam Shepard; Robert Patrick; Liam Cunningham; Vera Farmiga; Ruben Blades; Nora Arnezeder; ***D:*** Daniel Espinosa; ***W:*** Davis Guggenheim; ***C:*** Oliver Wood; ***M:*** Ramin Djawadi.

Safe in Hell 1/2 **1931** Melodramatic morality tale. New Orleans prostitute Gilda (Mackaill) thinks she's killed a client and goes on the lam. She winds up with sweet sailor Carl (Cook) and they take refuge on an island with no extradition but a lot of shady characters. The two pledge to be faithful while Carl is away at sea but Gilda is besieged by every sleaze in town and gets into big trouble. **74m/B; DVD.** Dorothy Mackaill; Donald Cook; Ralf Harolde; John Wray; Morgan Wallace; Victor Varconi; Ivan Simpson; ***D:*** William A. Wellman; ***W:*** Maude Fulton; Joseph Jackson; ***C:*** Sidney Hickox.

Safe Men **1998 (R)** Goofy, low-budget indie comedy whose pieces don't quite fit together. Set in Providence, R.I., talentless would-be singers Sam (Rockwell) and Eddie (Zahn) are mistaken by the local Jewish mafia for a couple of expert safecrackers. The inept duo are pressured by Big Fat Bernie Gayle (Lerner) and his henchman Veal Chop (Giamatti) to break into the home of Bernie's rival, Good Stuff Leo (Fierstein). Some dumb luck and a lot of coincidence work in the guys favor. But then the real safecracking team turns up. **89m/C; VHS, DVD.** Sam Rockwell; Steve Zahn; Paul Giamatti; Michael Lerner; Harvey Fierstein; Mark Ruffalo; ***D:*** John Hamburg; ***W:*** John Hamburg; ***C:*** Michael Barrett; ***M:*** Theodore Shapiro.

Safe Passage **1994 (PG-13)** Grueling family drama with Sarandon and Shepherd portraying an unhappily married couple who are the parents of seven sons, one of whom is missing and presumed dead in the Sinai Desert war. One by one the grown boys arrive home to await any further news. They rehash memories, watch old videos, open old wounds, and generally affirm life. None of the performances, with the exception of Sarandon, are truly believable. She is the only one that brings any depth to her character as the tough matriarch that holds the family together. Feels like a TV movie, albeit one with classier names. Based on the novel by Ellyn Bache. **98m/C; DVD.** Susan Sarandon; Sam Shepard; Robert Sean Leonard; Sean Astin; Marcia Gay Harden; Nick Stahl; Jason London; Philip Bosco; Matt Keeslar; ***D:*** Robert Allan Ackerman; ***W:*** Deena Goldstone; ***C:*** Ralf Bode; ***M:*** Mark Isham.

A Safe Place **1971** Jaglom made his directorial debut in this muddled story of Weld regressing to her childhood—the only time she felt safe. Welles' role as the magician refers to a character the child Susan met in Central Park. Most of the pic was filmed in the apartment of Jaglom's parents. **94m/C; DVD.** Tuesday Weld; Orson Welles; Jack Nicholson; Phil(ip) Proctor; Gwen Welles; ***D:*** Henry Jaglom; ***W:*** Henry Jaglom.

Safehouse **WOOF!** **2008 (R)** FBI agent Cooper O'Neil watches his partner get killed when an operation goes wrong and decides to retire. When another agent associate of Cooper's turns up dead, he gets suspicious. You'll be suspicious as to how a movie this stupid and amateurish actually got made. **80m/C; DVD.** Robert Miano; Sheila Cutchlow; Carolina Hoyos; Clayton Mears; Thomas Calabro; Johnny Alonso; ***D:*** John Poague; ***W:*** David Stever; ***C:*** Joe O' Ferrel; ***M:*** Geoff Knorr. **VIDEO**

Safelight **2015 (R)** This drama explores the development of an unexpected teen romance and its consequences. Living in a small desert community, teenager Charlie (Peters) lives with his father, has physical challenges, and has little hope after being beaten down in life. His life changes forever when he meets Vickie (Temple), a runaway with issues and who works as a prostitute. Charlie is smitten by her and what he sees beneath her tough exterior. Their mutual interest is tempered by Vickie's crazy, abusive pimp Skid (Alejandro), who does all he can to end their relationship. To escape Skid, Charlie and Vickie travel down the California coast to take pictures of lighthouses. Though their feelings for each other grow stronger, Skid goes over the edge and threatens their very lives. **84m/C; DVD, Streaming, Download.** Evan Peters; Juno Temple; Kevin Alejandro; Jason Beghe; Christine Lahti; ***D:*** Tony Aloupis; ***W:*** Tony Aloupis; ***C:*** Gavin Kelly; ***M:*** Joel P. West.

Safety Last **1923** Lloyd silent comedy about an average guy who goes to the big city to become a success, and his misadventures. Hilarious and still awe-inspiring building climbing scene set new standards for movies in sight gags and comedy-thrill stunts, which became Lloyd's trademark. **78m/B; Silent; VHS, DVD, Blu-Ray.** Harold Lloyd; Mildred Davis; Bill Strothers; Noah Young; ***D:*** Fred Newmeyer; Sam Taylor; ***W:*** Sam Taylor; Jean C. Havez; Tim Whelan. Natl. Film Reg. '94.

Safety Not Guaranteed **2012 (R)** Quirky indie comedy. Cynical Seattle magazine intern Darius, shy fellow intern Arnau, and their horny, self-centered boss Jeff head out of town after seeing a classified ad for a time-travelling companion. The seeker is somewhat paranoid Kenneth, a grocery store clerk who has a time machine he claims to have already used successfully. Darius manages to win him over to get her story (and ultimately more) as everyone gets some soul-searching lessons on what's important in life. Newcomer director Trevorrow blends sci-fi, drama, and romance to deliver a fascinating and engaging film. **86m/C; DVD, Blu-Ray, Streaming.** Aubrey Plaza; Jake M. Johnson; Karan Soni; Mark Duplass; Jenica Bergere; ***D:*** Colin Trevorrow; ***W:*** Derek Connolly; ***C:*** Benjamin Kasulke; ***M:*** Ryan Miller. Ind. Spirit '13: First Screenplay.

The Safety of Objects 1/2 **2001 (R)** The lives of four suburban families intersect in Troche's third feature, based on stories by A.M. Homes. Esther Gold (Close) is committed to caring for her comatose son Paul (Jackson), who was the secret lover of divorcee Annette (Clarkson), who makes a pass at lawn & pool guy Randy (Olyphant). Then there's Jim (Mulroney) who doesn't tell wife Susan (Kelly) he's left his job and whose young son is obsessed with his sister's Barbie-like doll. And Esther and Susan get involved in a contest to win an SUV and still the neighborhood's tentacles continue to spread among the inhabitants. **121m/C; DVD.** Glenn Close; Dermot Mulroney; Jessica Campbell; Patricia Clarkson; Joshua Jackson; Moira Kelly; Robert Klein; Timothy Olyphant; Mary Kay Place; Kristen Stewart; Alex House; ***D:*** Rose Troche; ***W:*** Rose Troche; ***C:*** Enrique Chediak.

Sahara **1943** A British-American unit must fight the Germans for their survival in the Libyan desert during WWII. Plenty of action and suspense combined with good performances makes this one a step above the usual war movie. **97m/B; VHS, DVD.** Humphrey Bogart; Dan Duryea; Bruce Bennett; Lloyd Bridges; Rex Ingram; J. Carrol Naish; Richard Nugent; Pat O'Moore; Kurt Kreuger; John Wengraf; Carl Harbord; Louis Mercier; Guy Kingsford; Peter Lawford; ***D:*** Zoltan Korda; ***W:*** Zoltan Korda; John Howard Lawson; James O'Hanlon; ***C:*** Rudolph Mate; ***M:*** Miklos Rozsa.

Sahara **1995** Remake of the 1943 pic. In 1942, tank commander Sgt. Joe Gunn (Belushi) and some fellow soldiers are forced into the desert after a German attack. They pick up other survivors but soon run out of water. When the group discovers a fabled well, they must fend off the Germans who are also searching for a water source. **106m/C; DVD.** James Belushi; Paul Empson; Mark Lee; Alan David Lee; Simon Westaway; Jerome Ehlers; Michael Massee; Robert Wisdom; ***D:*** Brian Trenchard-Smith; ***W:*** David Phillips; ***C:*** John Stokes; ***M:*** Garry McDonald.

Sahara 1/2 **2005 (PG-13)** Second attempt to construct a franchise around Clive Cussler's popular Dirk Pitt character (the first was 1980's "Raise the Titanic"). Pitt (McConaughey) and his buddy, Al Giordino (Zahn), are ex-Navy treasure-hunters searching for a lost Civil War battleship off the coast of West Africa. Cruz is a UN doctor who enlists Pitt in helping her find the source of a virulent African plague. The plot reeks of modern-day Indiana Jones and, thankfully, doesn't try to hide it, helped along by McConaughey and Zahn's boisterous chemistry. Eisner wisely chooses to keep things light throughout, which makes the film both charmingly self-aware and easily dismissible. **127m/C; DVD, Blu-Ray, UMD, HD-DVD.** Matthew McConaughey; Steve Zahn; Penelope Cruz; Lambert Wilson; Glynn Turman; William H. Macy; Delroy Lindo; Lennie James; Rainn Wilson; Patrick Malahide; ***D:*** Breck Eisner; ***W:*** John C. Richards; Thomas Dean Donnelly; Joshua Oppenheimer; James V. Hart; ***C:*** Seamus McGarvey; ***M:*** Clint Mansell.

Saigon 1/2 **1947** In Shanghai after WWII, pilots Larry (Ladd) and Pete (Cassell) are informed that their pal Mike (Dick) doesn't have much time left. Instead of giving Mike the bad news, they intend to spend the rest of Mike's time living it up. To finance the fun, they accept a shady deal and end up crash-landing in the Asian jungle with the financier's secretary and her briefcase full of cash. **93m/B; DVD.** Alan Ladd; Veronica Lake; Douglas Dick; Wally Cassell; Luther Adler; Morris Carnovsky; ***D:*** Leslie Fenton; ***W:*** Julian Zimet; Arthur Sheekman; ***M:*** Robert Emmett Dolan.

Saigon: Year of the Cat **1987** Drama about an American ambassador, a CIA operative, and a British bank clerk who try to leave Saigon in 1974 before the Vietcong enter the city. **106m/C; VHS, DVD.** *GB* Frederic Forrest; E.G. Marshall; Dame Judi Dench; ***D:*** Stephen Frears; ***W:*** David Hare; ***M:*** George Fenton. **TV**

Sail a Crooked Ship **1961** gag-filled comedy, adapted from the Nathaniel Benchley novel, that doesn't quite work despite the cast. Ex-Naval officer Gilbert Barrows has a job piloting mothballed ships to the scrap heap. A group of inept criminals shanghai a ship in order to have Burrows sail them into Boston harbor so they can pull off a bank heist and use the vessel as their getaway craft. Naturally, things don't go as planned. **88m/B; DVD.** Robert Wagner; Dolores Hart; Ernie Kovacs; Frank Gorshin; Carolyn Jones; Frankie Avalon; Jesse White; Harvey Lembeck; **D:** Irving Brecher; **W:** Bruce Geller; Ruth Brooks Flippen; **C:** Joseph Biroc; **M:** George Duning.

Sailing Along **1938** British musical finds Kay Martin dreaming of becoming a music hall star. She gets her chance when she's spotted by a producer but her London success causes problems in her romance with barge skipper's son, Steve. **80m/B; DVD.** *UK* Jessie Matthews; Barry Mackay; Jack Whiting; Roland Young; Noel Madison; Athene Seyler; Frank Pettingell; Alastair Sim; **D:** Sonnie Hale; **W:** Sonnie Hale; Lesser Samuels; **C:** Glen MacWilliams.

Sailor Beware **1952** Naive Melvin Jones (Lewis) is inducted into the Navy along with lothario singer Al Crowthers (Martin). In this typical slapstick mishmash of comedy and music, Lewis causes havoc aboard a submarine and becomes the judge of the most kissable girl contest in Hawaii while Martin romances singer Calvert (playing herself). Betty Hutton has a cameo as one of Dean's gals during the recruitment scene. **108m/B; DVD.** Jerry Lewis; Dean Martin; Marion Marshall; Robert Strauss; Corrine Calvert; Leif Erickson; Don Wilson; Vince Edwards; **Cameo(s):** Betty Hutton; **D:** Hal Walker; **W:** Martin Rackin; James Allardice; **C:** Daniel F. Fapp; **M:** Joseph J. Lilley.

Sailor of the King **1953** A British naval ship is torpedoed in the Pacific during WWII and survivor Andrew Brown (Hunter) is rescued by the German cruiser Essen. The damaged ship pulls into a cove at a Galapagos island to make emergency repairs and Brown escapes (with a rifle), determined to delay their departure until a force of British ships get closer. There's a framing story that involves Rennie and Hiller but it's so much filler. Adapted from the C.S. Forester novel "Brown on Resolution." **85m/B; DVD.** *GB* Jeffrey Hunter; Peter Van Eyck; Michael Rennie; Wendy Hiller; Bernard Lee; Victor Maddern; **D:** Roy Boulting; **W:** Valentine Davies; **C:** Gilbert Taylor; **M:** Clifton Parker.

The Sailor Who Fell from Grace with the Sea **1976 (R)** Perverse tale of a disillusioned sailor who rejects the sea for the love of a lonely young widow and her troubled son. Graphic sexual scenes. Based on the novel by Yukio Mishima, the film suffers from the transition of Japanese culture to an English setting. **105m/C; VHS, DVD, Blu-Ray.** *GB* Sarah Miles; Kris Kristofferson; Jonathan Kahn; Margo Cunningham; **D:** Lewis John Carlino; **W:** Lewis John Carlino.

The Saint 1/2 **1997 (PG-13)** The plot makes little sense, the villains are average ego-driven bad guys, and Shue's naive scientist/babe is totally unbelieveable. The only reason the movie works is due to the debonair, if angst-ridden, charms of Kilmer as super-thief and master of disguise Simon Templar. He's hired by Russian strongman Ivan Tretiak (Serbedzija) to steal the formula for cold fusion from scientist Emma Russell so that Tretiak can deliver cheap energy and make Russia a formidable power once again. Only problem is Templar, who names all his alter egos after saints, falls for Emma and tries to get them out of harm's way by double-crossing Tretiak. Templar's exploits are featured in a series of novels by Leslie Charteris, and previously appeared in earlier movies and on TV. **118m/C; DVD.** Val Kilmer; Elisabeth Shue; Rade Serbedzija; Valery (Valeri Nikolayev) Nikolaev; Henry Goodman; Alun Armstrong; Michael Byrne; Eugene (Yevgeny) Lazarev; **D:** Phillip Noyce; **W:** Jonathan Hensleigh; Wesley Strick; **C:** Phil Meheux; **M:** Graeme Revell.

St. Benny the Dip 1/2 *Escape If You Can* **1951** Three con-men evade police by posing as clergymen, and end up going straight after a series of adventures in a skid row mission. Funny in parts but extremely predictable. Still, good for a few laughs. **80m/B; VHS, DVD.** Dick Haymes; Nina Foch; Roland Young; Lionel Stander; Freddie Bartholomew; **D:** Edgar G. Ulmer.

St. Elmo's Fire 1/2 **1985 (R)** Seven Georgetown graduates confront adult problems during their first post-graduate year. Reminiscent of "The Big Chill," but a weak story wastes lots of talent and time. **110m/C; VHS, DVD, Blu-Ray.** Rob Lowe; Demi Moore; Andrew McCarthy; Judd Nelson; Ally Sheedy; Emilio Estevez; Mare Winningham; Martin Balsam; Jenny Wright; Joyce Van Patten; Andie MacDowell; Anna Maria Horsford; **D:** Joel Schumacher; **W:** Carl Kurlander; Joel Schumacher; **C:** Stephen Burum; **M:** David Foster. Golden Raspberries '85: Worst Support. Actor (Lowe).

The St. Francisville Experiment **2000 (PG-13)** Psychic, amateur ghost hunter, history student, and filmmaker fly to Louisiana to investigate a haunted house plagued by the spirit of slaves. **79m/C; VHS, DVD.** Tim Baldini; Madison Charap; Ryan Larson; Paul Palmer; Paul James; Paul Salamoff; Troy Taylor; **D:** Tim Thompson.

St. Helen's, Killer Volcano 1/2 **1982** A young man and an old man develop a deep friendship amid the devastation, fear, greed, and panic surrounding the eruption of the Mt. St. Helen's volcano. Based on the true story of Harry Truman (!), who refused to leave his home. Pretty good. **95m/C; VHS, DVD.** Art Carney; David Huffman; Cassie Yates; Bill McKinney; Ron O'Neal; Albert Salmi; Cesare Danova; **D:** Ernest Pintoff.

The Saint in London **1939** The Saint investigates a gang trying to pass counterfeit banknotes. The third in "The Saint" series. Sol as part of the 'The George Sanders Saint Movie Collection'. **72m/B; VHS, DVD.** George Sanders; Sally Gray; **D:** Jack Paddy Carstairs.

The Saint in Palm Springs **1941** Inspector Fernack (Hale) asks Simon Templar (Sanders) to help a friend who smuggled three priceless stamps out of occupied Europe. The friend is killed first but Simon takes the stamps from New York to Palm Springs to give to Elna Johnson (Barrie) as her inheritance. Naturally others are also after the goods. Loosely based on a Leslie Charteris story, this was the fifth and last for Sanders in the RKO series. **65m/B; DVD.** George Sanders; Paul Guilfoyle; Wendy Barrie; Jonathan Hale; Linda Hayes; Harry Shannon; Ferris Taylor; **D:** Jack B. Hively; **W:** Jerome Cady; **C:** Harry Wild; **M:** Roy Webb.

St. Ives **1976 (PG)** Former police reporter Bronson agrees to recover some stolen ledgers and finds himself dealing with betrayal and murder. Bisset is sultry and the tale is slickly told, but dumb. Co-stars Travanti, later of TV's "Hill Street Blues." **94m/C; VHS, DVD.** Charles Bronson; Jacqueline Bisset; John Houseman; Harry Guardino; Maximilian Schell; Harris Yulin; Elisha Cook, Jr.; Daniel J. Travanti; **D:** J. Lee Thompson; **W:** Barry Beckerman; **M:** Lalo Schifrin.

St. Ives 1/2 *Robert Louis Stevenson's St. Ives; All for Love* **1998 (R)** During the Napoleonic Wars, dashing French officer, Captain Jacques St. Ives (Barr), is captured during battle and sent to a POW camp in the Scottish Highlands that is run by Major Chevening (Grant). St. Ives and the Major become friends but that doesn't mean that he won't try to escape, especially since Jacques has the aid of plucky lassie Flora (Friel). A leisurely paced costume romp. **90m/C; VHS, DVD.** *GB* Jean-Marc Barr; Anna Friel; Richard E. Grant; Miranda Richardson; Michael Gough; Jason Isaacs; Tim Dutton; Cecile Pallas; **D:** Harry Hook; **W:** Allan Cubitt; **C:** Robert Alazraki.

Saint Jack **1979 (R)** The story of a small-time pimp with big dreams working the pleasure palaces of late-night Singapore. Engrossing and pleasant. Based on Paul Theroux's novel. **112m/C; VHS, DVD, Blu-Ray.** Ben Gazzara; Denholm Elliott; Joss Ackland; George Lazenby; Peter Bogdanovich; **D:** Peter Bogdanovich; **W:** Peter Bogdanovich; **C:** Robby Muller.

Saint Joan **1957** Film of the George Bernard Shaw play, adapted by Graham Greene, about the French Maid of Orleans at her trial. Otto Preminger went on a nationwide talent hunt for his leading actress and chose the inexperienced Seberg (her screen debut). A good thing for her career, but not for this ill-begotten, overambitious opus. Seberg doesn't fit. Also available colorized. **131m/B; VHS, DVD.** Jean Seberg; Anton Walbrook; Richard Widmark; John Gielgud; Harry Andrews; Felix Aylmer; Richard Todd; **D:** Otto Preminger; **W:** Graham Greene; **C:** Georges Perinal.

Saint John of Las Vegas **2009 (R)** Did someone lose a bet? How else would a completely unfunny, whimsical roadtrip comedy loosely based on Dante's Inferno get made? Ex-gambler John (Buscemi) falls under the influence of insurance fraud investigator Virgil (Malco) and is lured back to Vegas under the guise of investigating a stripper's injury claim. Along the way they meet a series of wacky characters who don't seem to fit anywhere unless you have a working knowledge of Dante. Appallingly bad and made worse by the disappointing use of its usually dependable cast and involvement of high-profile producers Spike Lee and Stanley Tucci. **85m/C; On Demand.** Steve Buscemi; Romany Malco; Tim Blake Nelson; Sarah Silverman; Peter Dinklage; John Cho; Emmanuelle Chriqui; **D:** Hue Rhodes; **W:** Hue Rhodes; **C:** Giles Nuttgens; **M:** David Torn.

Saint Judy 1/2 **2019 (PG-13)** When successful defense lawyer Judy Wood (Monaghan) moves to Los Angeles so her son Alex (Bateman) can be closer to his father (Krause), she unexpectedly finds success in immigration law. Though her new boss Ray (Molina) wants her to focus on easy cases, she takes the case of an imprisoned Afghani woman, former teacher and activist Asefa (Lubany), who is about to be deported from the United States. Judy faces unexpected challenges, both inside and outside of court as she seeks justice for Asefa. Based on real events, the film's preachy and storytelling is uninspired. **106m/C; DVD.** Michelle Monaghan; Leem Lubany; Common; Alfred Molina; Alfre Woodard; **D:** Sean Hanish; **W:** Dmitry Portnoy; **C:** Richard Wong; **M:** James T. Sale.

St. Louis Woman 1/2 **1934** Medical student and college football star Jim Warren and his teammates head to a nightclub to hear singer Lou. The boys get into a brawl that becomes a newspaper scandal and Jim gets kicked out of school. He lands on skid row, where Lou finds him and she decides to call in some favors to help Jim out. **70m/B; DVD.** Jeanette Loff; Johnny Mack Brown; Earle Foxe; Roberta Gale; **D:** Albert Ray; **W:** Jack Natteford; **C:** George Meehan, Jr.

The Saint Meets the Tiger **1943** A dying man collapses on Simon Templar's (Sinclair) doorstep, and it leads The Saint to a seaside village to find a gold smuggling criminal mastermind called The Tiger. The eighth film in the series and Sinclair's second (and last) appearance in the title role. **70m/B; DVD.** *UK* Hugh Sinclair; Jean Gillie; Gordon McLeod; Clifford Evans; Wylie Watson; Dennis Arundell; Louise Hampton; **D:** Paul Stein; **W:** Leslie Arliss; Wolfgang Wilhelm; James Seymour; **C:** Robert Krasker.

St. Michael Had a Rooster *San Michele Aveva un Gallo* **1972** In 19th-century Italy, idealist anarchist Giulio Manieri (Brogi) hopes to inspire the local peasantry through armed raids. Imprisoned for his trouble, Manieri learns upon his release after 10 years that his political struggles have been forgotten and he has to make a difficult adjustment to life on the outside. Based on the Leo Tolstoy story "The Divine and the Human." Italian with subtitles. **87m/C; VHS, DVD.** *IT* Giulio Brogi; Danielle Dublino; Renato Scarpa; **D:** Paolo Taviani; Vittorio Taviani; **W:** Paolo Taviani; Vittorio Taviani; **C:** Mario Masini.

The Saint of Fort Washington 1/2 **1993 (R)** Sweetly naive and schizophrenic Matthew (Dillon) is homeless and through government screw-ups is sent to the Fort Washington Armory, which houses more than 700 homeless men. Harassed by others, Matthew is befriended by Jerry, a kindly Vietnam vet, who tries to care for him. Subject is taken seriously but slips into mawkishness; good performances by the leads. **104m/C; VHS, DVD.** Danny Glover; Matt Dillon; Rick Aviles; Nina Siemaszko; Ving Rhames; Joe Seneca; **D:** Tim Hunter; **W:** Lyle Kessler; **C:** Frederick Elmes; **M:** James Newton Howard.

St. Patrick: The Irish Legend 1/2 **2000** Unfortunately neither the impressive cast, the beautiful scenery, or the special effects can transform this costumer from being bland and boring. Patrick (who allegedly drove all the snakes out of Ireland) was the privileged son of a nobleman in 5th century Britian, who suffered through six years as a slave before finding his religious calling. Over great opposition, he's eventually appointed as the first bishop of Ireland though he must still struggle with his enemies in the Church of England. **120m/C; VHS, DVD.** Patrick Bergin; Malcolm McDowell; Alan Bates; Susannah York; Luke Griffin; Eamon Owens; Stephen Brennan; Chris McHallem; Michael Caven; **D:** Robert C. Hughes; **W:** Robert C. Hughes; Martin Duffy; **C:** James Mathers. **CABLE**

St. Patrick's Day **1999 (PG-13)** Widowed Mary McDonaugh (Laurie) is the matriarch of a dysfunctional Irish-American family. Four generations gather at her house for St. Patrick's Day where she announces she has taken the pledge and refuses to allows any whiskey in her home (which is ignored by certain members). As the day progresses, family secrets are revealed, including romantic feelings finally acknowledged, divorcing spouses, extramarital affairs, and other sexual shenanigans. **106m/C; VHS, DVD.** Piper Laurie; Joanne Baron; Jim Metzler; Julie Strain; Herta Ware; Redmond M. Gleeson; David Ault; Colleen (Ann) Fitzpatrick; Chris Valenti; Stephen O'Mahoney; **D:** Hope Perello; **W:** Hope Perello; **C:** Denise Brassard; **M:** Michael Muhlfriedel.

Saint Ralph **2004 (PG-13)** With his mother in the hospital dying, young Ralph (Adam Butcher) decides that if he can pull off the miracle of winning the Boston Marathon, his mother will benefit from the overflow. Heartfelt story, but lacks grit and emotion, leading to a rather flat end. **98m/C; DVD.** Campbell Scott; Gordon Pinsent; Jennifer Tilly; Tamara Hope; Adam Butcher; Shauna Macdonald; Michael Kanev; **C:** Rene Ohashi; **M:** Andrew Lockington.

The Saint Strikes Back **1939** Sanders debuts as the mysterious Simon Templar in this competent series. On a trip to San Francisco, the Saint aims to clear the name of a murdered man. The second in the series. **67m/B; VHS, DVD.** George Sanders; Wendy Barrie; Jonathan Hale; Jerome Cowan; Neil Hamilton; Barry Fitzgerald; Edward (Ed) Gargan; Robert Strange; **D:** John Farrow.

The Saint Takes Over **1940** More adventures with the British mystery man; this time involving racetrack gambling. An original story that wasn't based on a Leslie Charteris novel as were the others. **69m/B; VHS, DVD.** George Sanders; Jonathan Hale; Wendy Barrie; Paul Guilfoyle; Morgan Conway; Cy Kendall; **D:** Jack B. Hively.

The St. Tammany Miracle 1/2 **1994** Predictable, good-natured sports film about young coach Lootie Pfannder (Luner) who takes a job at a prep school and turns the losing girls basketball team into winners. Her broadcaster boyfriend Carl (Gosselaar) thinks she's crazy but aided by her assistant (Frye), Lootie is determined to prove everyone wrong. **90m/C; VHS, DVD.** Jamie Luner; Mark-Paul Gosselaar; Soleil Moon Frye; Jeffrey Meek; Julie McCullough; **Cameo(s):** Steve Allen; **D:** Jim McCullough, Sr.; **W:** Jim McCullough, Jr.; **M:** Jay Weigel.

St. Trinian's **2007 (PG-13)** Britcom based on the Ronald Searle cartoons and the five Ealing studio movies filmed between 1954 and 1980. Shady art dealer Carnaby Fritton (Everett) transfers his daughter Annabelle (Riley) to the girls school run by his flirty sister Camilla (Everett in drag) where chaos (and criminal behavior) rule. With the school in financial straits, minister of education Geoffrey Thwaites (Firth) is planning to close it down and sell the property as a profitable real estate venture. So some of the students decide to steal a painting from London's National Gallery while they're participating in a national quiz program there. Not as anarchical as the originals but pic has its moments. **100m/C; On Demand.** *GB* Rupert Everett; Colin Firth; Talulah Riley; Lucy Punch;

Tamsin Egerton; Aamir Khan; Chloe; Russell Brand; Lena Headey; Anna Chancellor; Celia Emrie; Toby Jones; Mischa Barton; Fenella Woolgar; Gemma Arterton; Juno Temple; Stephen Fry; *D:* Oliver Parker; Barnaby Thompson; *W:* Piers Ashworth; Nick Moorcraft; *C:* Gavin Finney; *M:* Charlie Mole.

St. Urbain's Horseman **2007** Originally shown as a two-part Canadian TV movie based on Mordecai Richter's 1971 novel. Jake grows up in the isolated Jewish Montreal community of St. Urbain with the dream of becoming a filmmaker. Maintaining the idealized memory of his heroic, adventurous cousin Joey, Jake moves to London and become a modestly successful director until a scandal threatens to derail both his career and personal lives. **180m/C; DVD.** *CA* David Julian Hirsh; Jacob Tierney; Selina Giles; Gabriel Hogan; Michael Riley; Elliott Gould; Andrea Martin; Liane Balaban; Joe Wiesenfeld; *D:* Peter Moss; *W:* Gerald Wexler; Joe Wiesenfeld; Howard Wiseman; *C:* Norayr Kasper; *M:* James Gelfand. **TV**

The St. Valentine's Day Massacre 1/2 **1967** Corman's big studio debut re-creates the events leading to one of the most violent gangland shootouts in modern history: the bloodbath between Chicago's Capone and Moran gangs on February 14, 1929. Uninspired and unremittingly violent. Watch for Jack Nicholson's bit part. **100m/C; VHS, DVD, Blu-Ray.** Jason Robards, Jr.; Ralph Meeker; Jean Hale; Joseph Campanella; Bruce Dern; Clint Ritchie; Richard Bakalyan; George Segal; Harold J. Stone; Jonathan Haze; Dick Miller; Barboura Morris; Jack Nicholson; Frank Silvera; Milton Frome; Alex Rocco; John Agar; Tom Signorelli; *D:* Roger Corman; *W:* Howard Browne; *C:* Milton Krasner; *M:* Lionel Newman.

St. Vincent 1/2 **2014 (PG-13)** Sometimes you're in the mood for a piece of crowd-pleasing cheese and Melfi's dramedy, with its great cast and likable tone, could be just right pic. It's not challenging but it's never anything less than enjoyable. Murray does his best work in years as Vincent, an irascible New Yorker whose life turns upside down when single mom Maggie (McCarthy) and her son Oliver (Lieberher) move in next door. Vincent ends up watching the kid after school and teaching him some life lessons. It's formulaic but the cast is strong enough and the script funny enough that it's easy not to care. **103m/C; DVD, Blu-Ray.** Bill Murray; Jaeden Lieberher; Melissa McCarthy; Naomi Watts; Chris O'Dowd; Terrence Howard; Donna Mitchell; *D:* Theodore Melfi; *W:* Theodore Melfi; *C:* John Lindley; *M:* Theodore Shapiro.

Saintly Sinners 1/2 **1962** Very minor crime comedy. Slim (Clements) and Duke (Bryar) rob a bank and stash the loot in the car they've stolen from ex-con Joe (Hagerthy). Before they can retrieve the money, the car is repossessed and sold to kindly parish priest Father Dan (Beddoe). More trouble's afoot and the thieves start suffering from guilty consciences. **78m/B; DVD.** Don Beddoe; Paul Bryar; Stanley Clements; Ron Hagerthy; Ellen Corby; Erin O'Donnell; Addison Richards; *D:* Jean Yarbrough; *W:* Kevin Barry; *C:* Gilbert Warrenton; *M:* Richard LaSalle.

A Saintly Switch 1/2 **1999** Aging quarterback Grier has just moved his pregnant wife Fox and their kids to a New Orleans. Mom's very unhappy and the kids are worried that their parents are going to split up—at least until they manage to mysteriously swap their parents' bodies. So now dad gets to be pregnant and mom has to learn to score touchdowns. **90m/C; VHS, DVD.** David Alan Grier; Vivica A. Fox; Rue McClanahan; Al Waxman; *D:* Peter Bogdanovich. **TV**

Saints and Sinners 1/2 **1995 (R)** Street-smart "Pooch" Puccia (Chapa) returns to his 'hood as an undercover cop to set up childhood buddy, drug dealer Big Boy Baynes (Plank), and winds up getting involved with seductive bad girl Eve (Rubin), who's also bedding Baynes. Then Pooch discovers his police contact is in the pay of the mob. Lots of macho posturing (attractive actors). **99m/C; VHS, Streaming.** Damian Chapa; Scott Plank; Jennifer Rubin; Damon Whitaker; Panchito Gomez; William Atherton; *D:* Paul Mones; *W:* Paul Mones; *C:* Michael Bonvillain.

Saints and Soldiers 1/2 **2003 (PG-13)** Ragtag group of G.I.s narrowly escapes a massacre during the Battle of the Bulge, only to find themselves stumbling around and philosophizing in No-Man's-Land. Mormon sponsored WWII film is surprisingly quiet and even-handed in dealing with big metaphysical conundrums, but pro-war theme may raise the hackles of some. **90m/C; Blu-Ray, On Demand.** Corbin Allred; Petre Asle Holden; Alexander Polinsky; Kirby Heyborne; Larry Bagby; Ethan Vincent; *D:* Ryan Little; *M:* Bart Hendrickson.

Saints and Soldiers: Airborne Creed 1/2 **2012 (PG-13)** American paratroopers try to find the way back to their side after being dropped several miles off course during 1944's Operation Dragoon. **94m/C; DVD, Blu-Ray, Streaming.** Corbin Allred; David Nibley; Jasen Wade; Virginie Fourtina Anderson; Lincoln Hoppe; *D:* Ryan Little; *W:* Lincoln Hoppe; Lamont Gray; *C:* Ryan Little; *M:* J Bateman. **VIDEO**

The Saint's Double Trouble **1940** Leslie Charteris' suave detective becomes embroiled in another mystery, this one involving jewel thieves. Sanders plays a dual role as the hero and the crook. The fourth in the series. **68m/B; VHS, DVD.** George Sanders; Helene Whitney; Jonathan Hale; Bela Lugosi; Donald MacBride; John Hamilton; *D:* Jack B. Hively.

Sal 1/2 **2011** Shoestring-budgeted indie from Franco is an impressionistic tribute to Hollywood actor Sal Mineo. After finding success as a sensitive juvie type, Mineo openly acknowledged his homosexuality, resulting in a loss of work. Mineo found something of a comeback doing theater and Franco's slight drama follows the last 24 hours of Mineo's life before his robbery-related murder in 1976. Lauren gives a fine lead performance but Franco can't resist unneccesary directorial flourishes that add nothing to the story. **92m/C; On Demand.** Val Lauren; Jim Parrack; Vince Jolivette; Stacey Miller; James Franco; *D:* James Franco; *W:* Stacey Miller; *C:* Christina Voros; *M:* Neil Benezra.

Salaam Bombay! **1988** A gritty film about a child street beggar in the slums of Bombay trying to raise enough money to return to his mother's house in the country. The boy experiences every variety of gutter life imaginable, from humiliation to love. Moving and searing. Filmed on location, with actual homeless children; Nair's first feature. In Hindi with subtitles. **114m/C; VHS, DVD, Blu-Ray.** *IN GB* Shafiq Syed; Hansa Vithal; Chanda Sharma; Nana Patekar; Aneeta Kanwar; Sarfuddin Quarassi; Raju Barnad; Raghuvir Yadav; *D:* Mira Nair; *W:* Sooni Taraporevala; *C:* Sandi Sissel; *M:* L. Subramaniam.

The Salamander 1/2 **1982 (R)** A French detective tries to find the assassin of the leaders of a neo-fascist underground movement in Italy and follows clues that lead back to WWII. Disappointing, overwrought adaptation of a Morris West novel. **101m/C; VHS, DVD, Blu-Ray.** *GB* Franco Nero; Anthony Quinn; Martin Balsam; Sybil Danning; Christopher Lee; Cleavon Little; Paul Smith; Claudia Cardinale; Eli Wallach; *D:* Peter Zinner; *M:* Jerry Goldsmith.

The Salem Witch Trials **2002** TV dramatization of the Salem Witch trials influenced by the squabbling and hate mongering of modern day politics. **191m/C; DVD, Blu-Ray.** Kirstie Alley; Henry Czerny; Jay O. Sanders; Kristin Booth; Katie Boland; *D:* Joseph Sargent; *W:* Maria Nation; *C:* Pierre Gill; *M:* Jonathan Goldsmith. **CABLE**

Salem's Lot 1/2 *Blood Thirst* **1979 (PG)** Based on Stephen King's novel about a sleepy New England village which is infiltrated by evil. A mysterious antiques dealer takes up residence in a forbidding hilltop house—and it becomes apparent that a vampire is on the loose. Generally creepy; Mason is good, but Soul only takes up space in the lead as a novelist returning home. **112m/C; VHS, DVD, Blu-Ray.** David Soul; James Mason; Lance Kerwin; Bonnie Bedelia; Lew Ayres; Ed Flanders; Elisha Cook, Jr.; Reggie Nalder; Fred Willard; Kenneth McMillan; Marie Windsor; *D:* Tobe Hooper; *W:* Paul Monash; *C:* Jules Brenner; *M:* Harry Sukman. **TV**

Salem's Lot **2004** Made-for-TNT remake of the 1979 miniseries based on Stephen King's novel, this time a bit more faithful to the book, but still using the miniseries format. Writer Ben Mears (Lowe) returns to his hometown to exorcise some personal demons, only to find a real-life demon, in the form of vampire Barlow (Hauer) taking over. Resurrects characters and subplots that the original ignored, but the pacing is too rushed to create any real atmosphere or genuine chills. Another in a long line of disappointing King adaptations. **180m/C; DVD.** Rob Lowe; Samantha Mathis; Andre Braugher; Donald Sutherland; Robert Mammone; Rutger Hauer; James Cromwell; Julia Blake; Dan Byrd; Andy Anderson; Robert Grubb; Steven Vidler; Elizabeth (Liz) Alexander; Nicholas Hammond; Tara Morice; Penny McNamee; *D:* Mikael Salomon; *W:* Peter Filardi; *C:* Ben Nott; *M:* Patrick Cassidy; Lisa Gerrard; Christopher Gordon. **TV**

The Salesman *Forushande* **2016 (PG-13)** Asghar Farhadi's Oscar winner for Best Foreign Language Film (the director's second) features a couple in turmoil during a production of "Death of a Salesman." Ranaa and Emad are evicted from their home after nearby construction left it unstable. In their new apartment, Ranaa is attacked after being mistaken for the prostitute who previously lived there. Ranaa recovers but Emad starts to unravel, feeling responsible for the attack and determined to find the attacker. A complex, challenging film that reflects the director's culture but works in any language. **124m/C; DVD, Blu-Ray, Streaming.** *FR IA* Taraneh Alidoosti; Shahab Hosseini; Babak Karimi; Farid Sajjadi Hosseini; Mina Sadati; *D:* Asghar Farhadi; *W:* Asghar Farhadi; *C:* Hossein Jafarian; *M:* Sattar Oraki. Oscars '16: Foreign Film.

Salinger 1/2 **2013 (PG-13)** Making a documentary about a notoriously elusive public figure like author J.D. Salinger seems an inherently flawed proposition. Filmed in secret for years and then promoted as a series of major revelations about its subject matter so extreme that it needed accompaniment by a 700-page book, writer/director Salerno's interview-heavy film fails to live up to expectations. Filled with more rumor and hearsay about the author of "Catcher in the Rye" than actual information, Salerno barely makes what qualifies as a TV special, much less the hype that surrounded a theatrical release. **120m/C; DVD.** *D:* Shane Salerno; *C:* Anthony Savini; Buddy Squires; *M:* Lorne Balfe.

Sallah **1963** A North African Jew takes his family to Israel in 1949 in hopes of making his fortune. He finds himself in a transit camp and runs up against the local bureaucracy in a quest for permanent housing as well as the European work ethic. Amusing and enjoyable satire. In Hebrew with English subtitles. **105m/B; VHS, DVD.** *IS* Topol; Geula Noni; Gila Almagor; Arik Einstein; Shraga Friedman; Esther Greenberg; *D:* Ephraim Kishon; *C:* Floyd Crosby. Golden Globes '65: Foreign Film.

Sally 1/2 **1929** Cinderella story finds orphaned Sally (Miller) working as a New York waitress although her dream is to dance on Broadway. Sally meets booking agent Otis Hooper (Barnes), who has her impersonate a famous Russian dancer who eloped, and this leads to Sally getting her own starring gig in the Ziegfeld Follies. The tiny Miller had a lot of natural charisma although the merits of her singing and dancing are still debated; she only made three talkies, preferring her stage career. Includes sequences in two-strip Technicolor. Based on the 1920 musical by Jerome Kern and Guy Bolton in which Miller also starred. **101m/C; DVD.** T. Roy Barnes; Joe E. Brown; Pert Kelton; Ford Sterling; Nora Lane; Marilyn Miller; Alexander Gray; Maude Turner Gordon; *D:* John Francis Dillon; *W:* Waldemar Young; *C:* Devereaux Jennings; Charles E. Schoenbaum.

Sally Hemings: An American Scandal 1/2 **2000** Soap opera-ish romance based on the relationship between widowed ambassador (and third President) Thomas Jefferson (Neill) and his young mulatto house slave Sally Hemings (Ejogo)?an affair that lasted for 38 years. (DNA proved Jefferson to be the father of one and possibly all six of Heming's children.) Sally remains dignified through the years as does Jefferson. The most excitement is Sally castigating her lover about his contradictory attitudes towards slavery. **173m/C; VHS, DVD.** Carmen Ejogo; Sam Neill; Diahann Carroll; Mare Winningham; Rene Auberjonois; Mario Van Peebles; *D:* Charles Haid; *W:* Tina Andrews; *C:* Donald M. Morgan; *M:* Joel McNeely. **TV**

Sally, Irene and Mary 1/2 **1938** Three gals want to break into showbiz but their fast-talking agent can only get them work as cigarette girls at a New York nightspot. Still, Sally (Faye) meets singer Tommy (Martin) and the duo mke sweet music until a jealous dame gets Sally fired. Luckily, Mary (Weaver) inherits an old ferry and they make it into a floating club where they can perform. Cue the happy ending for this pleasant musical comedy. **85m/B; DVD.** Alice Faye; Joan Davis; Marjorie Weaver; Tony Martin; Fred Allen; Gregory Ratoff; Gypsy Rose Lee; Jimmy Durante; *D:* William A. Seiter; *W:* Harry Tugend; Jack Yellen; *C:* J. Peverell Marley.

Sally of the Sawdust 1/2 **1925** Fields's first silent feature; he is carnival barker Professor Eustace McGargle who's the guardian of orphaned Sally (Dempster). Then Sally's wealthy grandfather (Alderson), a stern judge, becomes determined to claim her from showbiz lowlifes. Fields gets to demonstrate his talent for juggling, conning customers, and car chasing. Interesting movie caught director Griffith on the decline and Fields on the verge of stardom. Remade as a talkie in 1936 entitled "Poppy." Includes musical score. **113m/B; Silent; VHS, DVD.** W.C. Fields; Carol Dempster; Erville Alderson; *D:* D.W. Griffith; *W:* Forrest Halsey; *C:* Harry Fischbeck; H. Sintzenich.

Salmon Fishing in the Yemen 1/2 **2011 (PG-13)** A pleasant fish-out-of-water romantic comedy that's actually about fish for a change! Harriet (Blunt) is a businesswoman approached by a sheikh (Waked) who is eager to introduce the sport of salmon fishing to a desert river in his homeland of Yemen. After being pressured by a government PR flack (Scott-Thomas), fishery expert Alfred (MacGregor) reluctantly agrees to help, even though he finds it absolutely ludicrous. Although Harriet has a military boyfriend and Alfred has a wife, the two begin to grow closer and try to resist the natural urge to spawn. Based on the novel by Paul Torday. **112m/C; DVD, Blu-Ray.** *GB* Ewan McGregor; Emily Blunt; Kristin Scott Thomas; Amr Waked; Rachael Stirling; *D:* Lasse Hallstrom; *W:* Simon Beaufoy; *C:* Terry Stacey; *M:* Dario Marianelli.

Salmonberries 1/2 **1991 (R)** East German Roswitha (Zech) is devastated when her lover is killed trying to scale the Berlin Wall. She manages to escape and finds herself stuck in a remote Eskimo community in Alaska where she becomes involved with Kotzebue (lang in her film debut), who poses as a man to work on the Alaskan pipeline. The title has something to do with preserved berries—don't bother, it makes about as much sense as the entire movie. English and German with English subtitles. **94m/C; VHS, DVD.** *GE CA* Rosel Zech; k.d. lang; Chuck Connors; Jane Lind; Oscar Kawagley; Wolfgang Steinberg; Wayne Waterman; Christel Merian; *D:* Percy Adlon; *W:* Percy Adlon; Felix Adlon; *C:* Newton Thomas (Tom) Sigel.

Salo, or the 120 Days of Sodom **1975** Extremely graphic film follows 16 children (eight boys and eight girls) who are kidnapped by a group of men in Fascist Italy. On reaching a secluded villa in the woods, the children are told to follow strict rules and then subjected to incredible acts of sadomasochism, rape, violence, and mutilation. This last film of Pasolini's was taken from a novel by the Marquis de Sade. Viewers are strongly recommended to use their utmost discretion when watching this controversial film. In Italian with English subtitles. **117m/C; VHS, DVD, Blu-Ray.** *IT FR* Giorgio Cataldi; Umberto P. Quintavalle; Paolo Bonacelli; Caterina Boratto; *D:* Pier Paolo Pasolini; *W:* Pier Paolo Pasolini; Sergio Citti; *C:* Tonino Delli Colli; *M:* Ennio Morricone.

Salome **1953** An over-costumed version of Oscar Wilde's Biblical story about King Herod's lascivious stepdaughter who danced her way to stardom and tried to save the life of John the Baptist. Talented cast can't overcome hokey script. **103m/C; VHS, DVD.** Rita Hayworth; Stewart Granger; Charles Laughton; Judith Anderson; Cedric Hardwicke; Basil Sydney; Maurice Schwartz; *D:* William Dieterle; *C:* Charles B(ryant) Lang, Jr.; *M:* George Duning.

Salome's Last Dance 🦴🦴 **1988 (R)** A theatrical, set-surreal adaptation of the Wilde story. Typically flamboyant Russell. **113m/C; VHS, DVD.** Glenda Jackson; Stratford Johns; Nickolas Grace; Douglas Hodge; Imogen Millais Scott; *D:* Ken Russell; *W:* Ken Russell; *C:* Harvey Harrison.

The Salon 🦴 ½ **2005 (PG-13)** The release was delayed until 2007, which makes this stereotypical comedy even more dated (Ben Affleck/J.Lo jokes, anyone?). Lame rehash of "Barbershop" and "Beauty Shop" set in Baltimore, with Jenny (Fox) as the owner of the hair salon that's also the local meeting place filled with the usual eccentrics (both workers and customers). The shop's threatened by an urban renewal project but Jenny's determined to fight City Hall. Writer/director/producer Brown, who also produced the "Barbershop" flicks, needs to find a new thematic 'do. **92m/C; DVD.** Vivica A. Fox; Kym E. Whitley; Brooke Burns; Darrin Dewitt Henson; Terrence Howard; Dondre T. Whitfield; Garrett Morris; Monica Calhoun; Taral Hicks; Greg Germann; D'Angelo Wilson; Sheila Cutchlow; *D:* Mark Brown; *W:* Mark Brown; *C:* Brandon Trost.

Salsa 🦴🦴 **1988 (PG)** An auto repairman would rather dance in this "Dirty Dancing" clone. Rosa was formerly a member of the pop group Menudo. **97m/C; VHS, DVD.** Robby Rosa; Rodney Harvey; Magali Alvarado; Miranda Garrison; Moon Orona; Kamar De Los Reyes; *D:* Boaz Davidson; *W:* Boaz Davidson; Tomas Benitez.

Salt 🦴🦴🦴 **2010 (PG-13)** Accused of being a sleeper agent by a Russian spy, CIA officer Evelyn Salt (Jolie) goes on the run to clear her name. Along the way, she decides to single-handedly attempt to prevent a worldwide nuclear assault with a barrage of butt-kicking that trumps any idea of a logical story. Part female James Bond and donning more disguises than the Pink Panther, Jolie excels as a dangerous action babe. No stranger to the genre, director Noyce doesn't avoid the obligatory action cliches but heartily pushes them to the max. **91m/C; Blu-Ray, On Demand.** Angelina Jolie; Liev Schreiber; Chiwetel Ejiofor; Daniel Olbrychski; August Diehl; *D:* Phillip Noyce; *W:* Kurt Wimmer; Brian Helgeland; *C:* Robert Elswit; *M:* James Newton Howard.

Salt & Pepper 🦴 ½ **1968 (PG-13)** Uninspired spy comedy that's very dated '60s mod. Lawford and Davis Jr. run a London nightclub and are reluctantly recruited as spies thanks to a couple of murders at said club. MI-5 is trying to stop a crazy military officer from hijacking a nuclear sub and overthrowing the British government and think the duo can help. Followed by 1970's "One More Time." **101m/C; DVD.** *GB* Sammy Davis, Jr.; Peter Lawford; John Le Mesurier; Michael Bates; Ernest Clark; Graham Stark; Ilona Rodgers; *D:* Richard Donner; *W:* Michael Pertwee; *C:* Ken Higgins; *M:* John Dankworth.

Salt of the Earth 🦴🦴🦴 ½ **1954** Finally available in this country after being suppressed for 30 years, this controversial film was made by a group of blacklisted filmmakers during the McCarthy era. It was deemed anti-American, communist propaganda. The story deals with the anti-Hispanic racial strife that occurs in a New Mexico zinc mine when union workers organize a strike. **94m/B; VHS, DVD, Blu-Ray.** Rosaura Revueltas; Will Geer; David Wolfe; *D:* Herbert Biberman; *W:* Michael Wilson; *C:* Stanley Meredith; Leonard Stark; *M:* Sol Kaplan. Natl. Film Reg. '92.

The Salt of the Earth 🦴🦴🦴 **2014 (PG-13)** A moving tribute to one of Brazil's most celebrated photographers, Sebastião Salgado, and the legacy of his important cultural photography. Now 70, his son Juliano and famed director Wim Wenders team up to help tell his story, through news articles, intimate family details, and interviews with Salgado recounting his days photographing distraught gold-miners in the mid-80s and the nightmares he saw in Rwanda. From his early days on a farm, to the high points of his career, organizing large-scale photo projects that lured him away from his home and family for months on end, Wenders and Juliano carefully balance Salgado's career history with his personal history. **110m/C; DVD, Blu-Ray.** *FR IT* Sebastiao Salgado; *D:* Wim Wenders; Juliano Ribeiro Salgado; *W:* Wim Wenders; Juliano Ribeiro Salgado; David Rosier; *C:* Juliano Ribeiro Salgado; Hugo Barbier; *M:* Laurent Petitgand.

Salt of the Sea 🦴 ½ *Milh Hadha Al-Bahr* **2008** Heavy-handed political drama. Brooklyn-born Soraya travels to Israel to claim a bank account left behind by her exiled Palestinian grandfather in 1948. In Ramallah, she's told the money has long-been confiscated and she can't legally remain in the country because she has no connection to the present-day Occupied Territories. Increasingly frustrated, Soraya takes drastic (and stupid) action. English, Arabic, and Hebrew with subtitles. **105m/C; DVD.** *FR* Suheir Hammad; Saleh Bakri; Riyad Ideis; Shelly Goral; *D:* Annemarie Jacir; *W:* Annemarie Jacir; *C:* Benoit Chamaillard; *M:* Kamran Rastegar.

The Salton Sea 🦴🦴 **2002 (R)** Feature debut by helmer Caruso is very good at getting down into the sleaze and grime of the world of methedrine addicts, dealers, and victims. Maybe too good. The parade of degradation drowns out everything else; the performances of Kilmer as the nominal hero, and D'Onofrio as kingpin/sadist Pooh-Bear, the time-addled plot that begs for concentration, and any sense that anything good will come from viewing this film. What it does, it does well, the question is, does anyone have the stomach to see it done? **103m/C; DVD.** Val Kilmer; Vincent D'Onofrio; Adam Goldberg; Luis Guzman; Doug Hutchison; Anthony LaPaglia; Glenn Plummer; Peter Sarsgaard; Deborah Kara Unger; Chandra West; B.D. Wong; R. Lee Ermey; Shalom Harlow; *D:* D.J. Caruso; *W:* Tony Gayton; *C:* Amir M. Mokri; *M:* Thomas Newman.

Salty O'Rourke 🦴 ½ **1945** Salty (Ladd) and Smitty (Demarest) are in desperate need of some quick cash to pay bookie Doc Baxter (Cabot). They get a race horse and disbarred jockey, Johnny Cates (Clements), who fakes his identity in order to race and win the gamblers some cash. But the plan is foiled when Johnny and Salty both fall for the gorgeous Ms. Brooks (Byington), and Johnny decides to throw the race for revenge. **100m/B; DVD.** Alan Ladd; Gail Russell; William Demarest; Stanley Clements; Bruce Cabot; Spring Byington; *D:* Raoul Walsh; *W:* Milton Holmes; *C:* Theodor Sparkuhl; *M:* Robert Emmett Dolan.

Salute to the Marines 🦴🦴 ½ **1943** Technicolor ode to wartime patriotism and anti-Japanese sentiment. Sgt. Major William Bailey (Beery) retires from the Corps after 30 years serving in the Philippines but is ashamed that he never saw combat. But when the Japanese invade the islands, Bailey gets his chance by organizing the civilian withdrawal. **101m/C; DVD.** Wallace Beery; Fay Bainter; Reginald Owen; Ray Collins; Keye Luke; Marilyn Maxwell; William Lundigan; *D:* S. Sylvan Simon; *W:* George Bruce; *C:* Charles E. Schoenbaum; *M:* Lennie Hayton.

Salvador 🦴🦴🦴 ½ **1986 (R)** Photo journalist Richard Boyle's unflinching and sordid adventures in war-torn El Salvador. Boyle (Woods) must face the realities of social injustice. Belushi and Woods are hard to like, but excellent. Early critical success for director Stone. **123m/C; VHS, DVD, Blu-Ray.** James Woods; James Belushi; John Savage; Michael Murphy; Elpidia Carrillo; Cynthia Gibb; Tony Plana; Colby Chester; Will MacMillan; Jose Carlos Ruiz; Jorge Luke; Juan Fernandez; Valerie Wildman; *D:* Oliver Stone; *W:* Oliver Stone; Richard Boyle; *C:* Robert Richardson; *M:* Georges Delerue. Ind. Spirit '87: Actor (Woods).

Salvage 🦴 ½ *Gruesome* **2006** Claire (Lauren Currie Lewis) is stalked, beaten, and brutally murdered. The next day she wakes up at work only to relive the whole process, as she does every day afterwards. No matter how hard she works to find out what is happening or prevent her killer from finding her, she ends up dead every day in one of the creepiest uses of the 'Groundhog Day' premise. **79m/C; DVD, Blu-Ray.** Lauren Currie Lewis; Chris Ferry; Cody Darbe; Maureen Olander; John P. Miller; *D:* Jeff Crook; Josh Crook; *W:* Jeff Crook; Josh Crook; *C:* John Ashmore; *M:* Evan Wilson. **VIDEO**

The Salvation 🦴🦴 ½ **2014** Mikkelsen stars in this Danish take on the very American genre of the Western. It's the 1870s in America and Danish settler Jon (Mikkelsen) takes justice into his own hands and murders the man who took his family away from him, unleashing the vengeance of a notorious gang leader. Instead of standing behind this outsider, the townspeople betray Jon, leaving him alone on a quest for vengeance. This story of an outsider in the Old West is greatly enhanced by the presence of ultra-charismatic Mikkelsen and the film looks great, the kind of old-fashioned Western they don't make very often any more, at least in the States. **92m/C; DVD, Blu-Ray.** *DK* Mads Mikkelsen; Eva Green; Jeffrey Dean Morgan; Jonathan Pryce; Douglas Henshall; Mikael Persbrandt; *D:* Kristian Levring; *W:* Kristian Levring; Anders Thomas Jensen; *C:* Jens Schlosser; *M:* Kasper Winding.

Salvation Boulevard 🦴 ½ **2011 (R)** Another social satire adapted from "Wag the Dog" author Larry Beinhart. This time the target is mega-churches and blind obedience in general. Big-shot pastor Dan Day (Brosnan) accidentally shoots an atheist professor (Harris) in front of Carl (Kinnear), a born-again former stoner in his congregation. After Day attempts to pin the death on him, Carl relies on the aid of spacey security guard (Tomei) and flees to Mexico. The cast is solid, but the plot and pacing is a bit scattered and the jokes are mostly duds. **95m/C; DVD, Blu-Ray.** Pierce Brosnan; Greg Kinnear; Jennifer Connelly; Ed Harris; Jim Gaffigan; Marisa Tomei; Isabelle Fuhrman; Yul Vasquez; Howard Hesseman; *D:* George Ratliff; *W:* George Ratliff; Doug Max Stone; *C:* Tim Orr; *M:* George S. Clinton.

Sam & Janet 🦴🦴 **2002 (PG-13)** Sam (Brown) goes through a messy divorce and is reluctant to hook up again, until he meets Janet (Ferguson). What follows is a long and tedious courtship in which Janet hides her past, which includes a nasty ex-husband who causes trouble. Most of the movie is devoted to the growing relationship, which is realistic but gets boring. It's basically like seeing your most boring friends' stories about how they met played out on your TV. Should garner a strong following among the Lifetime set. **90m/C; VHS, DVD.** Gary Busey; Ryan Brown; Jennifer Ferguson; Anna Beck; Blake Wolney; George Back; *D:* Rick Walker; *W:* Rick Walker; *C:* Byron Werner; *M:* David Percefull.

Sam Whiskey 🦴🦴 ½ **1969 (PG-13)** Charming but uneven western/heist flick has widow Dickinson hire a motley group of misfits, led by Sam Whiskey (Reynolds) to retrieve her late husband's gold from the bottom of a river. Only she wants them to return it to the U.S. Mint from which he stole it. Quirky comedy has a great cast, but doesn't always equal the sum of its parts. **96m/C; DVD, Blu-Ray.** Burt Reynolds; Clint Walker; Ossie Davis; William Schallert; Angie Dickinson; Woodrow Parfrey; Anthony James; Del Reeves; William Boyett; *D:* Arnold Laven; *W:* William W. Norton, Sr.; *M:* Herschel Burke Gilbert.

Samantha 🦴🦴 ½ **1992 (PG)** Twenty-one year-old Samantha discovers she was left on her parents' doorstep in a basket and decides to find out where she came from. Good cast and high charm quotient help this film along. **101m/C; VHS, DVD.** Martha Plimpton; Dermot Mulroney; Hector Elizondo; Mary Kay Place; Ione Skye; *D:* Steven La Rocque; *W:* John Golden; Steven La Rocque.

Samar 🦴🦴 ½ **1962 (PG)** A liberal penal colony commandant rebels against his superiors by leading his prisoners through the Philippine jungles to freedom. Original action drama with an interesting premise. **89m/C; VHS, DVD.** George Montgomery; Gilbert Roland; Joan O'Brien; Ziva Rodann; *D:* George Montgomery.

Samaritan Girl 🦴🦴 *Samaria* **2004 (R)** Yeo-Jin (Ji-min Kwak) pimps out her fellow teen Jae-yeong (Yeo-reum Han) so they can buy tickets to Europe. Jae-yeong ends up in the hospital after jumping out a window and asks her friend to retrieve one of her former clients, who won't go to the hospital unless Yeo-Jin has sex with him. By the time they arrive, Jae-yeong is dead, and Yeo-Jin vows to find all her friends former clients, have sex with them, and return their money. In the meantime her father (a cop) is hunting down and sometimes killing the men sleeping with his daughter. **97m/C; DVD.** *NK* Yeo-reum Han; Ji-min Kwak; Eol Lee; In-gi Jung; *D:* Ki-Duk Kim; *W:* Ki-Duk Kim; *C:* Sun Sang-Jae; Sang-jae Seon; *M:* Park Ji; Ji-woong Park.

Samaritan: The Mitch Snyder Story 🦴🦴🦴 **1986** Effective TV drama based upon the true story of Vietnam vet Mitch Snyder (Sheen) who battles various government agencies and ultimately fasts to call national attention to his crusade against homelessness. (Snyder eventually committed suicide.) Tyson appears as a bag lady. **90m/C; VHS, DVD.** Martin Sheen; Roxanne Hart; Joe Seneca; Stan Shaw; Cicely Tyson; *D:* Richard T. Heffron. **TV**

Samba 🦴🦴 **2014 (R)** Young Senegalese immigrant (Sy) has lived in France for years on the edge of poverty, trying to make ends meet as so many do in major cities around the world. Just when you think this is going to be a tough immigrant drama with a social conscious, it surprisingly shifts gears to become a romantic comedy when Samba meets an executive named Alice (played by the delightful Gainsbourg). Each film kind of works, but the biggest problem is that the whole thing feels like two movies smashed into one. **118m/C; DVD.** *FR* Omar Sy; Charlotte Gainsbourg; Tahar Rahim; Izia Higelin; Isaka Sawadogo; Stephane Fontaine; *D:* Olivier Nakache; Eric Toledano; *W:* Olivier Nakache; Eric Toledano; *M:* Ludovico Einaudi.

Same Kind of Different as Me 🦴🦴 ½ **2017 (PG-13)** A heart-felt religious drama, based on a true story. After wealthy art dealer Ron (Kinnear) cheats on his wife Debbie (Zellweger), he interacts with people at a homeless shelter as an act of penance. There, the couple meets a violent homeless man known as Suicide, but whose real name is Denver (Hounsou). As Ron and Debbie invest time in Denver and bring him into their lives, they learn about his tragic life story and provided support when his troubles grow deeper. Hounsou's intense, soulful performance, as well as solid work by Kinnear and Zellweger, add unexpected depth to the predictable, shallow story. **119m/C; Blu-Ray, Streaming.** Greg Kinnear; Renée Zellweger; Djimon Hounsou; Jon Voight; Olivia Holt; *D:* Michael Carney; *W:* Michael Carney; Alexander Foard; Ron Hall; *C:* Don Burgess; *M:* John Paesano.

Same River Twice 🦴🦴 ½ **1997** Four men who became friends while working as river rafting guides decide to have a reunion on the same river some 13 years after the death of a friend in a rafting accident. But each man realizes that the years have brought a certain amount of caution and that they are no longer young daredevils. Likewise, their personal quirks must be overcome if they are to successfully negogiate the white water rapids ahead of them. **103m/C; VHS, DVD.** John Putch; Dwier Brown; Shea Farrell; Robert Curtis-Brown; *D:* Scott Featherstone; *W:* Scott Featherstone; *C:* Art Wilder; *M:* Bradley Smith. **VIDEO**

Same Time, Next Year 🦴🦴🦴 **1978** A chance meeting between an accountant and a housewife results in a sometimes tragic, always sentimental 25-year affair in which they meet only one weekend each year. Well-cast leads carry warm, touching story based on the Broadway play by Bernard Slade. **119m/C; VHS, DVD.** Ellen Burstyn; Alan Alda; *D:* Robert Mulligan; *C:* Robert L. Surtees; *M:* Marvin Hamlisch. Golden Globes '79: Actress--Mus./Comedy (Burstyn).

Samsara 🦴🦴 ½ **2012 (PG-13)** An untraditional documentary, director Fricke and producer Mark Magidson's film attempts to provoke a response or say something purely through imagery and music. Samsara, a word that means "the ever turning wheel of life," uses footage shot over five years and in 25 countries to explore the truthful connections in life that transcend language and the spoken word. The film is visually extraordinary and will make a beautiful showpiece to sell HDTVs but it feels a little more ultimately hollow than the best works of this unique genre. **102m/C; DVD, Blu-Ray.** *D:* Ron Fricke; *W:* Ron Fricke; Mark Magidson; *C:* Ron Fricke; *M:* Marcello De Francisci; Lisa Gerrard; Michael Stearns.

Samson 🦴 **1961** Samson attempts to

keep wits and hair about him. **90m/C; VHS, DVD.** *IT* Brad Harris; Luisella Boni; Alan Steel; Serge Gainsbourg; Mara Berni; *D:* Gianfranco Parolini.

Samson 🦴🦴 **2018 (PG-13)** A sincere, yet lacking, dramatic adaptation of the well-known Bible story. In 1170 BC, Samson (James) has been foretold to be the one to lead the Jews to freedom from their enslavers, the Philistines led by evil King Balek (Zane), using his God-given gift of superhuman strength. Despite believing there is a peaceful way for the Jews to become free, Samson fails to make a deal with Balek. When he hides with Philistine Delilah (Leahy), all is in jeopardy. Though the film pays homage to the classic Hollywood religious epics, it lacks consistent performances and a much-needed cinematic style. **110m/C; DVD.** Jackson Rathbone; Billy Zane; Taylor James; Rutger Hauer; Caitlin Leahy; *D:* Bruce Macdonald; Gabriel Sabloff; *W:* Jason Baumgardner; Galen Gilbert; Timothy Ratajczak; Zach Smith; *C:* Trevor Michael Brown; Brian Shanley; *M:* Will Musser.

Samson and Delilah 🦴🦴🦴 **1949** The biblical story of the vindictive Delilah, who after being rejected by the mighty Samson, robbed him of his strength by shearing his curls. Delivered in signature DeMille style. Wonderfully fun and engrossing. Mature is excellent. **128m/C; DVD, Blu-Ray.** Victor Mature; Hedy Lamarr; Angela Lansbury; George Sanders; Henry Wilcoxon; Olive Deering; Fay Holden; Russ Tamblyn; *D:* Cecil B. DeMille; *W:* Jesse Lasky, Jr.; *C:* George Barnes; *M:* Victor Young. Oscars '50: Art Dir./Set Dec., Color, Costume Des. (C).

Samson and Delilah 🦴🦴 **1984** TV version of the biblical romance, semi-based on DeMille's 1950 version. Original Samson (Mature) plays Samson's father. Too long but inoffensive; see the DeMille version instead. **95m/C; VHS, DVD.** Antony (Tony) Hamilton; Belinda Bauer; Max von Sydow; Jose Ferrer; Victor Mature; Maria Schell; *D:* Lee Philips; *M:* Maurice Jarre. **TV**

Samson and Delilah 🦴🦴 **1996** Another in TNT's biblical retellings, this time with Israelite shepherd Samson (Thal), who also the strongest man alive, falling for beautiful-but-treacherous Philistine Delilah (Hurley). Seems Samson is causing havoc with General Tariq's (Hopper) Philistine army and Delilah is to discover the secret of his strength. **180m/C; VHS, DVD.** Eric Thal; Elizabeth Hurley; Dennis Hopper; Michael Gambon; Diana Rigg; Ben Becker; Paul Freeman; Daniel Massey; Pinkas Braun; Debora Caprioglio; Alessandro Gassman; Mark McGann; Jonathan Rhys Meyers; *D:* Nicolas Roeg; *W:* Allan Scott; *C:* Raffaele Mertes; *M:* Marco Frisina. **CABLE**

Samson and His Mighty Challenge 🦴 ½ **1964** In this rarely seen muscle epic, Hercules, Maciste, Samson and Ursus all take part in a battle royale. **94m/C; VHS, DVD.** *IT* Alan Steel; Red Ross; *D:* Giorgio Capitani.

Samson and the 7 Miracles of the World 🦴🦴 *Maciste Alla Corte Del Gran Khan; Maciste at the Court of the Great Khan; Goliath and the Golden City* **1962** This time the hero known as Maciste (renamed Samson for Americans) is in the 13th century battling brutal Tartar warlords. The very Earth itself shakes when our hero goes into battle! **80m/C; VHS, DVD.** *FR IT* Gordon Scott; Yoko Tani; Gabriele Antonini; Leonardo Severini; Valeri Inkizhinov; Helene Chanel; *D:* Riccardo Freda; *M:* Les Baxter.

Samson in the Wax Museum 🦴 ½ *Santo en el Museo de Cera; Santo in the Wax Museum* **1963** Masked Mexican wrestling hero Santo (here called Samson) does battle with a scientist who has discovered a way to make wax monsters come to life. **92m/B; VHS, DVD.** *MX* Santo; Claudio Brook; Ruben Rojo; Norma Mora; Roxana Bellini; *D:* Alfonso Corona Blake.

Samson vs. the Vampire Women 🦴 ½ **1961** Santo (here called Samson) the masked hero and athlete, battles the forces of darkness as a horde of female vampires attempt to make an unsuspecting girl their next queen. Not bad if you're into the Mexican wrestling genre. **89m/B; VHS, DVD.** *MX* Santo; Lorena Lalazquez; Jaime Fernandez; Maria Duval; *D:* Alfonso Corona Blake.

Samurai 1: Musashi Miyamoto 🦴🦴🦴 ½ **1955** The first installment in the film version of Musashi Miyamoto's life, as he leaves his 17th century village as a warrior in a local civil war only to return beaten and disillusioned. Justly award-winning. In Japanese with English subtitles. **92m/C; VHS, DVD, Blu-Ray.** *JP* Toshiro Mifune; Kaoru Yachigusa; Rentaro Mikuni; Eiko Miyoshi; *D:* Hiroshi Inagaki; *W:* Hiroshi Inagaki; Tokuhei Wakao; *C:* Jun Yasumoto; *M:* Ikuma Dan. Oscars '55: Foreign Film.

Samurai 2: Duel at Ichijoji Temple 🦴🦴🦴 ½ **1955** Inagaki's second film depicting the life of Musashi Miyamoto, the 17th century warrior, who wandered the disheveled landscape of feudal Japan looking for glory and love. In Japanese with English subtitles. **102m/C; VHS, DVD, Blu-Ray.** *JP* Toshiro Mifune; Akihiko Hirata; Daisuke Kato; Mariko Okada; Sachio Sakai; Kaoru Yachigusa; *D:* Hiroshi Inagaki; *W:* Hiroshi Inagaki; *C:* Jun Yasumoto; *M:* Ikuma Dan.

Samurai 3: Duel at Ganryu Island 🦴🦴🦴 ½ **1956** The final film of Inagaki's trilogy, in which Musashi Miyamoto confronts his lifelong enemy in a climactic battle. Depicts Miyamoto's spiritual awakening and realization that love and hatred exist in all of us. In Japanese with English subtitles. **102m/C; VHS, DVD, Blu-Ray.** *JP* Toshiro Mifune; Koji Tsurata; Kaoru Yachigusa; Mariko Okada; *D:* Hiroshi Inagaki; *W:* Hiroshi Inagaki; Tokuhei Wakao; *C:* Kazuo Yamada; *M:* Ikuma Dan.

Samurai Banners 🦴🦴 ½ *Furin Kazan; Under the Banner of Samurai; Wind-Fire-Forest-Mountain* **1969** In the 16th century, while working to advance the cause of a united Japan, a Samurai warrior and his master both fall in love with the same woman who happens to be the daughter of a slain rival. Handsome production moves along well, balancing a complex story with grand battles and scenes of intimacy. **165m/C; VHS, DVD.** *JP* Toshiro Mifune; Yoshiko Sakuma; Kinnosuke Nakamura; Katsuo Nakamura; Masakazu Tamura; Yujiro Ishihara; Mayumi Ozora; *C:* Kazuo Yamada; *M:* Masaru Sato. **VIDEO**

Samurai Cop WOOF! **1989** A Yakuza gang is terrorizing LA, and to get help before they destroy the city, the force imports Joe 'Samurai' Marshall (Hanon) from Japan. A man raised in Japan who is suspiciously incapable of speaking the language, but given the other problems of this film that isn't really significant. The best part is probably the intro by Joe Bob Briggs. **96m/C; DVD, Blu-Ray.** Robert Z'Dar; Matt Hannon; Jannis Farley; Mark Frazer; *D:* Amir Shervan; *W:* Amir Shervan; *C:* Peter Palian; *M:* Alan DerMarderosian.

Samurai Fiction 🦴🦴🦴 *SF: Episode One* **1999** A satiric parody of old samurai films as well as being a tribute to them. Inukai is a young and foolish samurai, and when his family's sword is stolen in a misunderstanding involving a new hire, he and his friends set out to retrieve it from the thief. Said thief is actually a competent swordsman who gives them a sound thrashing. While Inukai is being nursed back to health by a beautiful young woman and her father, the thief becomes a bodyguard for an evil female gambler. Eventually they must meet again, but in the meantime some funny stuff ensues. **111m/B; DVD.** *JP* Morio Kazama; Mitsuru Fukikoshi; Mari Natsuki; Taketoshi Naito; Tomoyasu Hotei; Tamaki Ogawa; Hiroshi Kanbe; Ryo Iwamatsu; Kei Tani; Fumiya Fujii; *D:* Hiroyuki Nakano; *W:* Hiroyuki Nakano; Hiroshi Saito; *C:* Yujiro Yajima; *M:* Tomoyasu Hotei.

Samurai Rebellion 🦴🦴🦴 *Rebellion* **1967** Isaburo (Mifune) is a reknowned swordsman in 18th-century Japan who is the model of loyalty until his overlord demands the return of a former mistress, who is now Isaburo's daughter-in-law. This insult to his family forces Isaburo to take a deadly stand, which turns out to be against his best friend (Nakadai) who's trying to uphold the feudal code. Lots of swordplay. Last in Kobayashi's trilogy following "Harakiri" (1962) and "Kwaidan" (1964). Japanese with subtitles. **121m/B; VHS, DVD.** *JP* Toshiro Mifune; Tatsuya Nakadai; *D:* Masaki Kobayashi; *W:* Shinobu Hashimoto.

Samurai Reincarnation 🦴🦴 **1981** After the Shogunate government kills 18,000 Christian rioters in the revolt of 1638, and publicly beheads the leader Shiro Amakusa, Shiro reincarnates during a monstrous thunderstorm. Consumed with hatred, he discards the teachings of Jesus Christ and seeks revenge. In Japanese with English subtitles. **122m/C; VHS, DVD.** *JP* Sonny Chiba; Kenji Sawada; Akiko Kana; Ken Ogata; Hiroyuki (Henry) Sanada; *D:* Kinji Fukasaku; *W:* Kinji Fukasaku; *C:* Kiyoshi Hasegawa.

San Andreas 🦴🦴 **2015 (PG-13)** The remarkably charismatic Dwayne Johnson plays Ray, a helicopter pilot caught in the "big one" striking California. And in typical disaster movie storytelling, Ray must save his wife (Gugino) and daughter (Daddario) on the day that the San Andreas fault moves in such a way that Lex Luthor's plan to turn Nevada into a beach state looks like it might come true. Of course, the thin plot is just an excuse for set pieces in which CGI recreations of mass death serve as summer blockbuster entertainment. Fans of such fare will not be disappointed. **125m/C; DVD, Blu-Ray.** Dwayne "The Rock" Johnson; Carla Gugino; Alexandra Daddario; Colton Haynes; Ioan Gruffudd; *D:* Brad Peyton; *W:* Carlton Cuse; *C:* Steve Yedlin; *M:* Andrew Lockington.

San Antonio 🦴🦴 **1945** A bad girl working in a dance hall turns over a new leaf on meeting the good guy. Trite plot, but good production. **105m/C; VHS, DVD.** Errol Flynn; Alexis Smith; S.Z. Sakall; Victor Francen; Florence Bates; John Litel; Paul Kelly; *D:* David Butler; *W:* W.R. Burnett; *M:* Max Steiner.

San Francisco 🦴🦴🦴 ½ **1936** The San Francisco Earthquake of 1906 serves as the background for a romance between an opera singer and a Barbary Coast saloon owner. Somewhat overdone but gripping tale of passion and adventure in the West. Wonderful special effects. Finale consists of historic earthquake footage. Also available colorized. **116m/B; VHS, DVD.** Jeanette MacDonald; Clark Gable; Spencer Tracy; Jack Holt; Jessie Ralph; Al Shean; Ted Healy; Shirley Ross; Margaret Irving; Harold Huber; Edgar Kennedy; Kenneth Harlan; Roger Imhof; Russell Simpson; Bert Roach; Warren Hymer; *D:* W.S. Van Dyke; *W:* Anita Loos. Oscars '36: Sound.

The San Francisco Story 🦴🦴 ½ **1952** Solid B-western set in 1850s San Francisco. Newspaper editor Jim Martin (Stevens) asks wealthy miner Rick Nelson (McCrea) to help him oust crooked politico Andrew Cain (Blackmer) from power. Cain's girlfriend Adelaide (De Carlo) also decides she likes Rick better. The big shootout takes place on horseback with shotguns. **80m/B; DVD.** Joel McCrea; Yvonne De Carlo; Sidney Blackmer; Onslow Stevens; Richard Erdman; Florence Bates; *D:* Robert Parrish; *W:* D.D. Beauchamp; *C:* John Seitz; *M:* Paul Dunlap; Emil Newman.

San Franpsycho 2006 Serial killer. Yawn. Two San Francisco detectives, a priest, and a reporter hunt for a serial killer who has been sending the newshound letters after each slaying. **?m/CDVD.** Joe Estevez; Jose Rosette; Todd Bridges; Eleni C. Krimitsos; Chris Angelo; Victor Zaragoza; Elias Castillo; *D:* Eduardo Quiroz; Jose Quiroz; *W:* Eduardo Quiroz; Jose Quiroz; *C:* Rocky Robinson; *M:* Eduardo Quiroz. **VIDEO**

San Quentin 🦴🦴 ½ **1937** Former army officer Stephen Jameson (O'Brien) heads to San Q to try some reform work on the rowdy cons, including Red Kennedy (Bogart), who isn't buying his routine. Jameson has it bad for Red's singing sister May (Sheridan), who thinks he's okay for trying to help Red. Only Red, egged on by con Hanson (Sawyer), escapes the road gang to have it out with May. Convinced it's real love, Red surrenders and makes a plea to give Jameson's methods a chance—which Red doesn't get. Much of the melodrama was shot in and around the prison itself. **70m/B; DVD.** Pat O'Brien; Humphrey Bogart; Ann Sheridan; Barton MacLane; Joseph (Joe) Sawyer; Veda Ann Borg; Joe King; Gordon Oliver; Emmett Vogan; Garry Owen; Marc Lawrence; George Lloyd; *D:* Lloyd Bacon; *W:* John Bright; Peter Milne; Robert Tasker; *C:* Sidney Hickox; *M:* Charles Maxwell; David Raksin; Heinz Roemheld.

San Saba 2008 PI Bud (Macfadyen) is discovered unconscious next to the corpse of a corporate bigwig. Bud's the prime suspect though his amnesia about the events makes it a problem for him to find out whodunit. But Bud's first step is contacting old high school classmate Leigh (Rohm), who's related to the dead guy. **?m/CDVD.** Angus MacFadyen; Elisabeth Rohm; Sunny Mabrey; Vivica A. Fox; John Enos; Daniel Zacapa; Benton Jennings; Mehera Blum; *D:* Mike Greene; *W:* Chris Beams; *C:* Jeffrey Smith; *M:* Ron Sures. **VIDEO**

Sanctimony WOOF! **2001** It's just like "American Psycho"... only much, much worse. Director Uwe Boll steals liberally from Bret Easton Ellis and David Fincher's "Se7en" in one of the clumsiest serial killer stories ever put to film. Two cops (Pare and Rubin) suspect that stock broker Tom Merrick (Van Dien) is really the psycho murderer known as the "Monkey Maker." (Worst. Villain. Name. Ever.) So what do they do about it? Not much. Boll's screenplay is as aimless as friendly fire and just as entertaining. By the time you get to the inexplicable snuff film sequence, you'll be wondering if Boll had a stroke halfway through writing the script. **87m/C; DVD.** *GE US* Casper Van Dien; Eric Roberts; Michael Paré; Jennifer Rubin; Catherine Oxenberg; *D:* Uwe Boll; *W:* Uwe Boll; *C:* Mathias Neumann; *M:* Uwe Spies. **VIDEO**

Sanctuary 🦴🦴 **1998 (R)** A former government agent, Luke Connolly has completely changed his life by becoming a clergyman. However, when his old agency discovers his whereabouts, the deadly skills he's renounced may be all that can save him. **110m/C; VHS, DVD.** Mark Dacascos; Kylie Travis; Jaimz Woolvett; Alan Scarfe; *D:* Tibor Takacs; *W:* Michael Stokes; *M:* Norman Orenstein. **VIDEO**

The Sanctuary 🦴 ½ *Sam pan boke* **2009** In the vein of other recent Thai martial art films, foreign bad guys are looking to steal national treasures, and a local martial artist is all that stands in their way. This wouldn't be bad, had much of Tony Jaa's film career not been based on doing the very same thing, only better. **85m/C; DVD.** *TH* Michael B.; Russell Wong; Intira Jaroenpura; Patharawarin Timkul; Erik Markus Schuetz; Winston Sefu; Lak-Khet Waslikachart; *D:* Thanapon Maliwan; *W:* Thanapon Maliwan; Anuwat Kaewsopark; *C:* Arnon Chunprasert; *M:* Tuomas Kantelinen; Thai Team.

Sanctum 🦴🦴 *James Cameron's Sanctum* **2011 (R)** Underwater cave divers led by Frank (Roxburgh) and his son Josh (Wakefield) get trapped in the South Pacific's Esa-ala Caves for months when a tropical storm forces them into the caverns. The divers must look for a new way out, battling savage nature and psychological turmoil in their struggle to survive. A poorly constructed plot and lack of character depth make this fall short of the high expectations and thrilling grandeur promised by the trailer. Shot in 3D off the Gold Coast in Queensland, Australia and executive produced by Cameron. Taken from an actual 1988 diving accident in Australia in which co-writer Wight was involved. **108m/C; DVD, Blu-Ray, On Demand.** Richard Roxburgh; Rhys Wakefield; Ioan Gruffudd; Alice Parkinson; Daniel Wyllie; *D:* Alister Grierson; *W:* Andrew Wight; John Garvin; *C:* Jules O'Loughlin; *M:* David Hirschfelder.

Sand 🦴🦴 **2000** Tyler Briggs (Vartan) wants to start over—away from his violent father (Quaid) and brothers. So after his mother's death, he heads to the quiet beach town where his mom grew up. There Tyler falls for Sandy (Wuhrer) and starts to make a peaceful new life but trouble and family follow. **90m/C; VHS, DVD.** Michael Vartan; Denis Leary; Randy Quaid; Kari Wuhrer; Marshall Bell; Julie Delpy; Rodney Eastman; Bodhi (Pine) Elfman; Emilio Estevez; John Hawkes; Jon Lovitz; Norman Reedus; Peter Simmons; Harry Dean Stanton; *D:* Matt Palmieri; *W:* Matt Palmieri; *C:* John Skotchdopole.

The Sand Pebbles 🦴🦴🦴 ½ **1966** An American expatriate engineer, transferred to a gunboat on the Yangtze River in 1926, falls in love with a missionary teacher. As he becomes aware of the political climate of American imperialism, he finds himself at odds with his command structure; the treatment of this issue can be seen as commentary on the situation in Vietnam at the time of the film's release. Considered one of McQueen's best performances, blending action and romance. **193m/C; VHS, DVD, Blu-Ray.** Steve McQueen; Richard Crenna; Richard Attenborough; Candice Bergen; Marayat Andriane; Mako; Larry Gates; Gavin MacLeod; Simon Oakland; James Hong; Richard Loo; Barney (Bernard) Phillips; Tommy Lee; Ford Rainey; Walter Reed; Gus Trikonis; Joe Turkel; Glenn Wilder; ***D:*** Robert Wise; ***W:*** Robert Anderson; ***C:*** Joe MacDonald; ***M:*** Jerry Goldsmith. Golden Globes '67: Support. Actor (Attenborough).

Sand Serpents 1/2 **2009** Basic monsters vs. soldiers flick with a limited cast, cliched plot and dialogue, but decent CGI. A small force of Marines is sent into the Afghan desert but the Taliban are the least of their worries after they encounter giant, hungry prehistoric sand worms with very big teeth. **90m/C; DVD.** Jason Gedrick; Michelle Asante; Sebastian Knapp; Tamara Hope; Elias Toufexis; Chris Jarman; ***D:*** Jeff Renfroe; ***W:*** Raul Inglis; ***M:*** Pierpaolo Tiano. **CABLE**

Sanders of the River *Bosambo* **1935** A British officer in colonial Africa must work with the local chief to quell a rebellion. Tale of imperialism. Dated but still interesting and of value. Robeson is very good; superb location cinematography. **80m/B; VHS, DVD.** *GB* Paul Robeson; Leslie Banks; Robert Cochran; ***D:*** Zoltan Korda; ***C:*** Georges Perinal.

The Sandlot **1993 (PG)** Young Scotty (Guiry) moves to a new neighborhood in California in 1962 and tries to make friends despite not knowing anything about playing baseball. His scrappy teammates include the friendly Benny (Vitar), a chubby loudmouthed catcher named Ham (Renna), and Squints (Leopardi), a would-be Lothario before his time. Action revolves around Scotty's attempt to get baseball autographed by Babe Ruth out of the clutches of giant killer junkyard dog owned by Jones before dad Leary discovers it's missing. Small wonder is nostalgic without being sentimental, and tells its tale with grace and humor, supported by a period soundtrack. **101m/C; DVD, Blu-Ray.** Tom Guiry; Mike Vitar; Patrick Renna; Chauncey Leopardi; Marty York; Brandon Adams; Denis Leary; Karen Allen; James Earl Jones; Maury Wills; Art LaFleur; Marley Shelton; Brooke Adams; ***V:*** Arliss Howard; ***D:*** David Mickey Evans; ***W:*** David Mickey Evans; Robert Gunter; ***C:*** Anthony B. Richmond; ***M:*** David Newman.

The Sandlot 2 1/2 **2005 (PG)** The original came out in 1993, so this sequel basically features the same plot with a new group of baseball-playing kids. Now set in 1972, the sandlot guys team up with several softball-playing girls to take on some rivals. There's also a subplot about a rocket-loving shrimp who accidentally gets his hands on a NASA prototype and you can figure out what happens next. Innocuous fun but not destined to be a childhood classic. **97m/C; DVD.** Brett Kelly; Reece Thompson; James Earl Jones; Teryl Rothery; Greg Germann; Max Lloyd-Jones; Samantha Burton; James Willson; Cole Evan Weiss; Sean Brady; Neilen Benvegnu; Jessica King; Mckenzie Freemantle; ***D:*** David Mickey Evans; ***W:*** David Mickey Evans; ***C:*** David Pelletier; ***M:*** Laura Karpman. **VIDEO**

The Sandlot 3: Heading Home 1/2 **2007 (PG)** More of the same but with a couple of the characters from the 1993 original appearing as grown-ups: Benny Rodriguez (Nucci) is the manager of the L.A. Dodgers and pharmacy owner Squints (Leopardi) sponsors the newest sandlot team. But the story is about arrogant major-leaguer Tommy Santorelli (Perry), who gets beaned on the head and wakes up as a 12-year-old in 1976. Given a do-over, he now has the chance to choose friends and loyalty over selfish gains. **96m/C; DVD.** Luke Perry; Danny Nucci; Chauncey Leopardi; Sarah Deakins; Keanu Pires; Brandon Olds; Cole Heppell; Kai James; ***D:*** William Dear; ***W:*** Keith Mitchell; Allie Dvorin; ***C:*** Pascal Jean Provost; ***M:*** Kendall Marsh. **VIDEO**

Sandok *La montagna di luce; Temple of a Thousand Lights* **1965** Alan Foster (Harrison) is a notorious thief who has fled New York for India to lay low. At least until the Sultan asks him to steal a priceless jewel from the head of a heavily guarded statue. **87m/C; DVD.** *IT* Richard Harrison; Luciana Gilli; Wilbert Bradley; Daniele Vargas; ***D:*** Umberto Lenzi; ***W:*** Fulvio Gicca Palli; ***C:*** Angelo Lotti; ***M:*** Francesco De Masi.

Sandokan the Great 1/2 *Sandokan, the Tiger of Mompracem; Sandokan, la Tigre di Mompracem* **1963** Heroic Malay pirate Sandokan (Reeves) fights for freedom against British imperialism by kidnapping the niece of evil Brit, Lord Guillonk (Anchoriz). Mary Ann (Grad) is suitably dazzled while Sandokan has to also battle a tiger, headhunters, and a monsoon. **110m/C; DVD.** *IT SP* Steve Reeves; Genevieve Grad; Leo Anchoriz; Rik Battaglia; Maurice Poli; Andrea Bosic; ***D:*** Umberto Lenzi; ***W:*** Umberto Lenzi; Victor Andres Catena; ***C:*** Aurelio G. Larraya; ***M:*** Giovanni Fusco.

The Sandpiper **1965** Free-spirited artist Taylor falls in love with Burton, the married headmaster of her son's boarding school. Muddled melodrama offers little besides starpower. Filmed at Big Sur, California. **117m/C; VHS, DVD.** Elizabeth Taylor; Richard Burton; Charles Bronson; Eva Marie Saint; Robert Webber; Morgan Mason; ***D:*** Vincente Minnelli; ***C:*** Milton Krasner. Oscars '65: Song ("The Shadow of Your Smile").

Sands of Iwo Jima 1/2 **1949** Wayne earned his first Oscar nomination as a tough Marine sergeant, in one of his best roles. He trains a squad of rebellious recruits in New Zealand in 1943. Later they are responsible for the capture of Iwo Jima from the Japanese—one of the most difficult campaigns of the Pacific Theater. Includes striking real war footage. **109m/B; DVD, Blu-Ray.** John Wayne; Forrest Tucker; John Agar; Richard Jaeckel; Adele Mara; Wally Cassell; James Brown; Richard Webb; Arthur Franz; Julie Bishop; William Murphy; George Tyne; Hal Baylor; John McGuire; ***D:*** Allan Dwan; ***W:*** Harry Brown; James Edward Grant; ***C:*** Reggie Lanning; ***M:*** Victor Young.

Sands of the Kalahari **1965** Dr. Bondrachai charters a small plane to get him to Johannesburg when his original flight is delayed. There are a variety of other passengers, including shady big game hunter O'Brien who bribes pilot Sturdevan to head towards Capetown instead. The plane crashes in the desert with O'Brien brutally making himself the group's leader as the survivors' numbers soon dwindle. Killer baboons figure into the ending. **120m/C; DVD, Blu-Ray.** *GB* Stuart Whitman; Stanley Baker; Susannah York; Theodore Bikel; Nigel Davenport; Harry Andrews; Barry Lowe; ***D:*** Cy Endfield; ***W:*** Cy Endfield; ***C:*** Erwin Hillier; ***M:*** John Dankworth.

The Sandy Bottom Orchestra 1/2 **2000** Sandy Bottom, Wisconsin is a quaint small town that is resistant to change. Big city Ingrid (Headly), a former classical pianist, discovered this when she married local dairy farmer Norman (Irwin). Norman is also having problems—he wants to include a classical concert in the town's annual summer festival rather than the usual marching band and is meeting with opposition. Their daughter Rachel (Zima) also longs to fit in but her musical talent has outgrown the limited resources of the community and decisions must be made. **100m/C; VHS, DVD.** Glenne Headly; Tom Irwin; Madeline Zima; Jane Powell; Richard McMillan; Tamara Hope; Roger Dunn; Bradley Reid; ***D:*** Bradley Wigor; ***W:*** Joseph Maurer; ***C:*** Robert Primes; ***M:*** David Bell. **CABLE**

Sanitarium **2013** A trio of short horror stories, all telling the story of a patient at a mental institution. Dr. Stenson (McDowell), the primary physician at the hospital, introduces each patient—all new arrivals to his facility—and their stories. In one film, an artist who exhibits dolls soon starts to listen to their commands, while in another, a conflict emerges between a young boy, his mean father, a caring teacher, and a not-quite-real monster. In the trilogy's final film, a professor fully believes that Mayan prophecies related to the world's end will come true. To protect his loved ones, he constructs a bomb shelter. **108m/C; DVD, Streaming, Download.** Malcolm McDowell; John Glover; Walter Perez; Lou Diamond Phillips; Robert Englund; ***D:*** Bryan Ortiz; Bryan Ramirez; Kerry Valderrama; ***W:*** Bryan Ortiz; Bryan Ramirez; Kerry Valderrama; C.M. Bratton; Evan Boston; James Hartz; Scott Marcano; ***C:*** Philip Roy; ***M:*** Douglas Edward. **VIDEO**

Sanjuro *Tsubaki Sanjuro* **1962** In this offbeat, satiric sequel to "Yojimbo," a talented but lazy samurai comes to the aid of a group of naive young warriors. The conventional ideas of good and evil are quickly tossed aside; much less earnest than other Kurosawa Samurai outings. In Japanese with English subtitles. **96m/B; VHS, DVD, Blu-Ray.** *JP* Toshiro Mifune; Tatsuya Nakadai; Keiju Kobayashi; Yuzo Kayama; ***D:*** Akira Kurosawa; ***W:*** Akira Kurosawa; Ryuzo Kikushima; Hideo Oguni; ***C:*** Fukuzo Koizumi; Takao Saito; ***M:*** Masaru Sato.

Sans Soleil *Sunless* **1982** A female narrator reads and comments on the letters she receives from a friend, a freelance cameraman traveling through Japan, West Africa, and Iceland. The cameraman meditates on the cultural dislocation he feels and the meaning of his work and of life itself. Both narrator and cameraman remain unseen with the visuals being the cameraman's work in progress. **100m/C; VHS, DVD, Blu-Ray.** *FR* ***Nar:*** Alexandra Stewart; ***D:*** Chris Marker; ***W:*** Chris Marker.

Sanshiro Sugata **1943** Kurosawa's first film. A young man learns discipline in martial arts from a patient master. Climactic fight scene is early signature Kurosawa. In Japanese with English subtitles. **82m/B; VHS, DVD.** *JP* Susumo Fusuita; Takashi Shimura; Denjiro Okochi; Yukiko Todoroki; Ranko Hanai; Ryonosuke Tsukigata; Sugisaku Aoyama; Kokuten Kodo; ***D:*** Akira Kurosawa.

Sansho the Bailiff *The Bailiff; Sansho Dayu* **1954** A world masterpiece by Mizoguchi about feudal society in 11th century Japan. A woman and her children are sold into prostitution and slavery. As an adult, the son seeks to right the ills of his society. Powerful and tragic, and often more highly esteemed than "Ugetsu." In Japanese with English subtitles. **132m/B; VHS, DVD, Blu-Ray.** *JP* Kinuyo Tanaka; Yoshiaki Hanayagi; Kyoko Kagawa; Eitaro Shindo; Ichiro Sugai; ***D:*** Kenji Mizoguchi; ***W:*** Yoshikata Yoda; ***M:*** Fumio Hayasaka.

Santa & Me *Monster & Me* **2013** In this family film, a mean girl is creatively taught a lesson by Santa Claus. A bully from a wealthy family, Rubie (Baumeister) is disliked by everyone at her school. During the holiday season, she visits a mall Santa Claus and presents a long list of Christmas demands. Because of her attitude, the Santa tells her she does not understand the true meaning of Christmas and she tells him that he is not really Santa. Rubie's world is turned upside down on Christmas Eve and that Santa comes through her chimney. He turns Rubie into a "monster" and tells her that she must get a real present from a real friend by Christmas or she will remain in this form. **84m/C; DVD.** Athena Baumeister; David Neff; Lucas Barker; Alyssa Kennedy; Christine Springett; ***D:*** Jeff Solema; ***W:*** Koji Steven Sakai; ***C:*** Max Margolin; ***M:*** Dan Vithyavuthi. **VIDEO**

Santa and Pete **1999** Kind of a weird take on the Santa story. Grandpa Nicholas and grandson Terrence are decorating the Xmas tree and the last two ornaments are of a Santa and a Moor who Gramps says is Santa's sidekick Pete. Seems the legendary St. Nick gets arrested in Spain while making his rounds and gets thrown in jail where he meets a Muslim named Pete. They escape and begin traveling together and little pieces of the Santa legend (reindeer, red suit, etc.) get explained as they make their deliveries. **98m/C; DVD.** James Earl Jones; Hume Cronyn; Flex Alexander; Erica Gimpel; Sedrathe Gillespie; Tempestt Bledsoe; ***D:*** Duwayne Dunham; ***W:*** Greg Taylor; ***C:*** John Newby; ***M:*** Alan Williams. **TV**

Santa Baby 1/2 **2006 (PG)** Amusing comedy about finding the true spirit of Christmas. Mary (McCarthy) is a successful marketing exec who decides her dad's (Wendt) business needs to run more efficiently. And, of course, dad is Santa Claus. Mary returns to the North Pole when Santa has some heart trouble and tries to whip those elves into shape (too many cookie breaks) while rekindling a romance with ex-beau Luke (Sergei). **89m/C; DVD.** Jenny McCarthy; George Wendt; Ivan Sergei; Lynne Griffin; ***D:*** Ron Underwood; ***W:*** Garrett Frawley; Brian Turner; ***C:*** Derick Underschultz; ***M:*** Misha Segal. **CABLE**

Santa Baby 2: Santa Maybe **2009** ABC Family movie that is oriented towards the older family crowd. Corporate exec Mary, daughter of Santa Claus, has to leave Manhattan when dad suffers a crisis and wants to retire—expecting Mary to take over. Then she has to deal with both management and personal problems: the elves have labor issues and an assistant is making a power grab while Mary's boyfriend Luke clearly prefers the North Pole to living in the city. **85m/C; DVD.** Jenny McCarthy; Dean McDermott; Paul Sorvino; Kelly Stables; ***D:*** Ron Underwood; ***W:*** Garrett Frawley; Brian Turner; ***C:*** Attila Szalay; ***M:*** Misha Segal. **CABLE**

Santa Buddies 1/2 **2009 (G)** Puppy Paws (the son of Santa Paws) and the Buddies attempt to stop a holiday disaster at the North Pole when the magical Christmas icicle starts melting and everyone forgets the true meaning of the season. **88m/C; DVD, Blu-Ray.** George Wendt; Christopher Lloyd; Danny Woodburn; ***V:*** Zachary Gordon; Field Cate; Josh Flitter; Ty Panitz; ***D:*** Robert Vince; ***W:*** Robert Vince; Anna McRoberts; ***C:*** Kamal Derkaoui; ***M:*** Brahm Wenger. **VIDEO**

Santa Claus Conquers the Martians *Santa Claus Defeats the Aliens* **1964** A Martian spaceship comes to Earth and kidnaps Santa Claus and two children. Martian kids, it seems, are jealous that Earth tykes have Christmas. Features then-child star Pia Zadora. **80m/C; VHS, DVD, Blu-Ray.** John Call; Leonard Hicks; Vincent Beck; Victor Stiles; Donna Conforti; Bill McCutcheon; Christopher Month; Pia Zadora; ***D:*** Nicholas Webster; ***W:*** Glenville Mareth; ***C:*** David Quaid; ***M:*** Milton Delugg.

Santa Claus: The Movie **1985 (PG)** A big-budgeted spectacle about an elf who falls prey to an evil toy maker and almost ruins Christmas and Santa Claus. Boring, 'tis-the-season fantasy-drama meant to warm our cockles. **112m/C; VHS, DVD, Blu-Ray.** Dudley Moore; John Lithgow; David Huddleston; Judy Cornwell; Burgess Meredith; ***D:*** Jeannot Szwarc; ***W:*** David Newman; ***C:*** Arthur Ibbetson; ***M:*** Henry Mancini.

The Santa Clause 1/2 **1994 (PG)** If you like Allen, you'll enjoy this lightweight holiday comedy about divorced workaholic dad Scott Calvin and eight-year-old son Charlie (Lloyd). Seems Santa injures himself falling off the Calvin roof and dad winds up putting on Santa's suit. But as it turns out when you put on Santa's suit, you become Santa, including a noticeable weight gain, a fluffy beard, and all those reindeer and elves to deal with (but where's Mrs. Claus?). **97m/C; VHS, DVD, Blu-Ray.** Tim Allen; Eric Lloyd; Judge Reinhold; Wendy Crewson; David Krumholtz; Mary Gross; ***D:*** John Pasquin; ***W:*** Leo Benvenuti; Steve Rudnick; ***C:*** Walt Lloyd; ***M:*** Michael Convertino. Blockbuster '95: Male Newcomer, T. (Allen).

The Santa Clause 2 1/2 **2002 (G)** Sequel to the 1994 film has Santa (Allen again) facing expulsion if he doesn't find himself a Mrs. Claus. He also has to deal with the fact that his son Charlie (Lloyd) just landed on the "naughty" list. When Santa/Scott heads back to the U.S. to help Charlie, he runs afoul of the school's female principal (can you see where this is going?). Back at the Pole, the clone Santa he left in charge is staging a coup, of sorts. Funnier, with more of an edge than the original, this one gives adults plenty to smirk at while the kids are distracted by all the yuletide yahooey. **95m/C; VHS, DVD, Blu-Ray.** Tim Allen; Elizabeth Mitchell; David Krumholtz; Eric Lloyd; Judge Reinhold; Wendy Crewson; Spencer Breslin; Liliana Mumy; Art LaFleur; Kevin Pollak; Jay Thomas; Michael Dorn; Danielle Woodman; Aisha Tyler; ***D:*** Michael Lembeck; ***W:*** Don Rhymer; Cinco Paul; Ken Daurio; Edward Decter; John J. Strauss; Leo Benvenuti; ***C:*** Adam Greenberg; ***M:*** George S. Clinton.

The Santa Clause 3: The Escape Clause 1/2 **2006 (G)** Tim Allen returns to beat a dead reindeer in this pointless sequel. Reprising his role as Scott/Santa, he's faced with a pregnant Mrs. Claus (Mitchell) and an uprising by Jack Frost (Short), who wants to turn the North Pole into Upper Vegas. Forced to deal with a visit by his in-laws (Arkin, Margret) and toy sabotage by Frost, he contemplates quitting his seasonal job. The anti-commercialism message is a little hypocritical for a movie that could have been called "Beclause We Want More of your Dough." **91m/C; DVD, Blu-Ray.** Tim Allen; Elizabeth Mitchell; Martin Short; Spencer Breslin; Judge Reinhold; Wendy Crewson; Eric Lloyd; Liliana Mumy; Alan Arkin; Ann Margret; ***Cameo(s):*** Kevin Pollak; Jay Thomas; Peter Boyle; Aisha Tyler; ***D:*** Michael Lembeck; ***W:*** Edward Decter; John J. Strauss; ***C:*** Robbie Greenberg; ***M:*** George S. Clinton.

Santa Fe **1951** Action-packed western with Scott playing a Confederate soldier who heads West to take a job with the Santa Fe Railroad. However, his brothers, with their wounded rebel pride, have different ideas for forgetting the defeat. Refusing to take money from Northern businesses, they become outlaws. Based on a story by Louis Stevens and the novel by James Marshall. **89m/C; VHS, DVD.** Randolph Scott; Janis Carter; Jerome Courtland; Peter Thompson; John Archer; Warner Anderson; Roy Roberts; Billy House; ***D:*** Irving Pichel; ***W:*** Kenneth Gamet.

Santa Fe **1/2 1997 (R)** Muddled romantic drama with an appealing cast. It's taken cop Paul Thomas (Cole) eight months to recover from bullet wounds suffered in a shoot-out with a local cult. In the meantime, wife Leah's (Kelley) distanced herself from the marriage but still urges Paul into group counseling with charismatic Eleanor (Davidovich). Despite Paul's mistrust of her guru-like status, he's naturally drawn to Eleanor (and she to him). There's some tedious subplot stuff but the leads do fine. **97m/C; VHS, DVD.** Gary Cole; Lolita Davidovich; Sheila Kelley; Tina Majorino; Jere Burns; Pamela Reed; Phyllis Frelich; Mark Medoff; Tony Plana; Jeffrey Jones; ***D:*** Andrew Shea; ***W:*** Mark Medoff; Andrew Shea; ***C:*** Paul Elliott; ***M:*** Mark Governor.

Santa Fe Trail **1/2 1940** Historically inaccurate but entertaining tale about the pre-Civil War fight for "bloody Kansas." The action-adventure depicts future Civil War Generals J.E.B. Stuart (Flynn) and George Armstrong Custer (Reagan!) as they begin their military career (although Custer was really just a youth at this time). Good action scenes. Also available colorized. **110m/B; VHS, DVD, Blu-Ray.** Errol Flynn; Olivia de Havilland; Ronald Reagan; Van Heflin; Raymond Massey; Alan Hale; ***D:*** Michael Curtiz; ***W:*** Robert Buckner; ***C:*** Sol Polito; ***M:*** Max Steiner.

The Santa Incident **1/2 2010** Holiday fare from the Hallmark Channel finds overzealous Homeland Security agents Erickson and Cunningham actually having Santa's sleigh shot down when he flies into restricted military airspace. They're going to ruin the holiday as the bah-humbug duo hunt for the interloper and Santa takes refuge in a small town. A couple of Christmas-believing kids are determined to put things right. **88m/C; DVD.** Greg Germann; Sean McConaghy; James Cosmo; Ali Lyons; Scott Graham; Ione Skye; ***D:*** Yelena Lanskaya; ***W:*** Jeffrey Scott Simmons; ***C:*** Chris O'Dell; ***M:*** Ray Harman. **CABLE**

Santa Paws 2: The Santa Pups **2012 (G)** Holiday fare sequel should keep the kiddies amused. Pups Hope, Charity, Jingle, and Noble are sled stowaways when Mrs. Claus visits Pineville. The pups get into mischief granting wishes and everyone starts to lose the Christmas spirit so they must fix the mess they've made. **88m/C; DVD, Blu-Ray.** Cheryl Ladd; Pat Finn; Danny Woodburn; Obba Babatunde; George Newbern; ***V:*** Richard Kind; Tom Everett Scott; ***D:*** Robert Vince; ***W:*** Robert Vince; ***C:*** Mark Irwin; ***M:*** Brahm Wenger. **VIDEO**

Santa Sangre **1990 (R)** A circus in Mexico City, a temple devoted to a saint without arms, and a son who faithfully dotes upon his armless mother are just a few of the bizarre things in this wildly fantastic film. Fenix acts as his mother's arms, plays the piano for her, and carries out any wish she desires—including murder. Visually intoxicating but strange outing may prove too graphic for some viewers. Not as rigorous as other Jodorowsky outings. Also available in an NC-17 version. **123m/C; VHS, DVD, Blu-Ray.** *IT MX* Axel Jodorowsky; Sabrina Dennison; Guy Stockwell; Blanca Guerra; Thelma Tixou; Adan Jodorowsky; Faviola Tapia; Jesus Juarez; ***D:*** Alejandro Jodorowsky; ***W:*** Robert Leoni; Claudio Argento; Alejandro Jodorowsky; ***C:*** Danielle Nannuzzi; ***M:*** Simon Boswell.

The Santa Suit **2010** Greedy corporate mogul Drake Hunter has turned his dad's homey toy company into a shoddy mega-business. He hires a bunch of Santa's to promote the merchandise and then gets into an argument with a Santa-suited fellow who turns out to be the real deal. Santa thinks Drake needs to learn a lesson and turns him into a broke Santa-lookalike who has to work in a department store, listening to the kids, and regaining that Christmas spirit. From the Hallmark Channel. **88m/C; DVD.** Kevin Sorbo; Derry Robinson; Jason Blicker; Jodie Dowdall; Rosemary Dunsmore; Ted Atherton; ***D:*** Robert Vaughn; ***W:*** Kevin Commins; ***C:*** Russ Goozee; ***M:*** Stacey Hersh. **CABLE**

The Santa Trap **1/2 2002** Having just moved from snowy New England to the desert Southwest, it just doesn't feel like Christmas to the Emerson family. Young Judy is afraid Santa isn't real, so she sets a trap and captures a jolly intruder, who's arrested and thrown in jail. Now what'll happen to Christmas if Santa can't make his deliveries? And what about those reindeer on the Emersons' roof? **92m/C; DVD.** Shelley Long; Robert Hays; Dick Van Patten; Stacy Keach; Sierra Abel; Corbin Bernsen; Amanda Pays; Steve Monroe; ***D:*** John Shepphird; ***W:*** John Shepphird; ***C:*** Neal Brown; ***M:*** Joseph Conlan. **TV**

Santee **1973 (PG)** A father-son relationship develops between a bounty hunter and the son of a man he killed. Good, but not great, Western. **93m/C; VHS, DVD.** Glenn Ford; Dana Wynter; Jay Silverheels; John Larch; Michael Burns; ***D:*** Gary Nelson.

Santiago **1/2 1956** In 1895, cynical gunrunner Cash Adams (Ladd) and his hated rival Clay Pike (Nolan) are supposed to supply guns to the Cuban revolutionaries in their fight against colonial Spain. They also turn into romantic rivals after meeting idealistic revolutionary Isabella (Podesta). However, there's more trouble when they discover the Cubans can't actually pay for the merchandise. **92m/C; DVD.** Alan Ladd; Rossana Podesta; Lloyd Nolan; Chill Wills; L.Q. Jones; Frank De Kova; Paul Fix; Royal Dano; ***D:*** Gordon Douglas; ***W:*** John Twist; Martin Rackin; ***C:*** John Seitz; ***M:*** David Buttolph.

The Saphead **1/2 1921** Keaton's first outing as the rich playboy has him playing the none-to-bright son of a Wall Street mogul. Some great moments provide a glimpse of cinematic greatness to come from the budding comedic genius. Based on the play "The New Henrietta" by Winchell Smith and Victor Mapes. Silent. **70m/B; Silent; VHS, DVD, Blu-Ray.** William H. Crane; Buster Keaton; Carol Holloway; Edward Connelly; Irving Cummings; ***D:*** Herbert Blache; ***W:*** June Mathis; ***C:*** Harold Wenstrom.

Sapphire **1959** Two Scotland Yard detectives seek the killer of a beautiful black woman who was passing for white. Good mystery and topical social comment; remains interesting and engrossing. Superbly acted all around. **92m/C; VHS, DVD.** *GB* Nigel Patrick; Yvonne Mitchell; Michael Craig; Paul Massie; Bernard Miles; ***D:*** Basil Dearden. British Acad. '59: Film.

Saraband **1/2 2003 (R)** Bergman's final film has his "Scenes From a Marriage" (1974) characters reuniting after a 30-year separation. When Marianne (Ullman) visits Johan (Josephson) she finds he is still bitter and full of hatred, which is geared mostly toward his son Henrik (from another marriage) and granddaughter Karin who live in his guest house. When Karin is provided an opportunity to study music in Helsinki, an emotional confrontation comes to a head. Exceptional swan song. **107m/C; DVD, Blu-Ray.** *SW IT GE FI DK AT* Erland Josephson; Liv Ullmann; Borje Ahlstedt; Julia Dufvenius; Gunnel Fred; ***D:*** Ingmar Bergman; ***W:*** Ingmar Bergman; ***C:*** Raymond Wemmenlov; Sofi Stridh; P.O. Lantto.

Sarafina! **1992 (PG-13)** Part coming-of-age saga, part political drama, part musical, and all emotionally powerful. Sarafina is a young girl in a township school in Soweto, South Africa in the mid-'70s, gradually coming into a political awakening amid the Soweto riots. Khumalo recreates her stage role as the glowing and defiant Sarafina with both Goldberg and Makeba good in their roles as Sarafina's outspoken and inspirational teacher and her long-suffering mother, respectively. Adapted from Ngema's stage musical. **98m/C; VHS, DVD.** Leleti Khumalo; Whoopi Goldberg; Miriam Makeba; John Kani; Mbongeni Ngema; ***D:*** Darrell Roodt; ***W:*** Mbongeni Ngema; William Nicholson; ***M:*** Stanley Myers.

The Saragossa Manuscript **1/2** *Rekopis Znaleziony W Saragossie* **1965** Ambitious fantasy based on the 1813 novel "Sanatorium under the Hourglass" by Bruno Schultz. A romantic Belgian army officer, travelling to Spain, meets two beautiful princesses who send him on a fantastic journey to prove himself worthy of their affections. Polish with subtitles. **174m/B; VHS, DVD.** *PL* Zbigniew Cybulski; Iga Cembrzynska; Joanna Jedryka; Slawomir Lindner; ***D:*** Wojciech Has; ***W:*** Tadeusz Kwiatkowski; ***C:*** Mieczyslaw Jahoda; ***M:*** Krzysztof Penderecki.

Sarah, Plain and Tall **1991 (G)** New England school teacher (Close) travels to Kansas circa 1910 to care for the family of a widowed farmer who has advertised for a wife. Superior entertainment for the whole family. Adapted from Patricia MacLachlan's novel of the same name by MacLachlan and Carol Sobieski. Nominated for nine Emmy Awards. A "Hallmark Hall of Fame" presentation. **98m/C; VHS, DVD.** Glenn Close; Christopher Walken; Lexi (Faith) Randall; Margaret Sophie Stein; Jon (John) DeVries; Christopher Bell; ***D:*** Glenn Jordan; ***W:*** Carol Sobieski; ***C:*** Mike Fash; ***M:*** David Shire. **TV**

Sarah, Plain and Tall: Skylark **1/2** *Skylark* **1993 (G)** In a sequel to Hallmark Hall of Fame's hugely successful "Sarah, Plain and Tall," the whole Kansas crew shows up for more of their little-farm-on-the-prairie life. After two years in America's squarest state, mail-order bride Sarah (Close) loves Jacob (Walken), but not the scenery and still yearns for the lush greenery of Maine. When drought and fire threaten the farm, Jacob fears for the family's health and safety, and sends them back East for a visit. Close's "tough Yankee" expression grows a bit tiresome in a plot that is a tad predictable, yet the simplistic charm and nostalgia are unresistable and work to propel this quality Hallmark production. **98m/C; VHS, DVD.** Glenn Close; Christopher Walken; Lexi (Faith) Randall; Christopher Bell; Tresa Hughes; Lois Smith; Lee Richardson; Elizabeth Wilson; Margaret Sophie Stein; Jon (John) DeVries; James Rebhorn; Woody Watson; ***D:*** Joseph Sargent; ***W:*** Patricia MacLachlan; ***C:*** Mike Fash; ***M:*** David Shire. **TV**

Sarah, Plain and Tall: Winter's End *Winter's End* **1999 (G)** The third installation of the "Sarah" saga is set in 1918. A harsh winter is making life difficult for Sarah (Close), Jacob (Walken), and their three children. Then their lives take a strange turn when Jacob's father, John Witting (Palance), who abandoned his family when Jacob was a boy, suddenly shows up on their farm. A devastating storm proves just as paralyzing as the unresolved feelings between Jacob and John, but Sarah is determined to do what's best for her family. **99m/C; VHS, DVD.** Glenn Close; Christopher Walken; Jack Palance; Lexi (Faith) Randall; Christopher Bell; Emily Osment; ***D:*** Glenn Jordan; ***C:*** Ralf Bode; ***M:*** David Shire. **TV**

Sarah Silverman: Jesus Is Magic **1/2 2005** Stand-up show performed by delightfully potty-mouthed comedian Silverman at North Hollywood's El Portal Theater, with a couple of offstage skits thrown in. Her routine is an equal opportunity offender of race, religion, sex, and current events as Silverman hypes her Jewish American Princess attractiveness and her nice-girl-gone-naughty persona. Best left to her fans. **72m/C; DVD.** ***D:*** Liam Lynch; ***C:*** Rhet Baer; ***M:*** Sarah Silverman; Liam Lynch.

Sarah's Child **1/2 1996 (PG-13)** Sarah LaMere is devastated to learn that she can never have children. While husband Michael tries to accept, Sarah's upbringing has led her to believe that's her only purpose in life and she becomes increasingly unbalanced. Seemingly out of nowhere children's clothes and toys appear in their home and soon a strange young girl named Melissa appears, whom Sarah treats as her own child. When their landlady dies horribly after questioning Melissa, Michael is afraid the line between reality and fantasy has been breached but just how can he fight? **90m/C; VHS, DVD.** Mary Parker Williams; Michael Berger; Ruth Hale; Bryce Chamberlain; ***D:*** Ron Beckstrom; ***W:*** Muffy Mead Thomas; ***C:*** Gregg Stouffer; ***M:*** Jim Ball; Glenn Workman.

Sarah's Key *Elle S'Appelait Sarah* **2010 (PG-13)** Assured, emotional drama, based on the novel by Tatiana de Rosnay, that's part of Holocaust history the French don't want to face. American journalist Julia Jarmond (Scott Thomas) is living in Paris with her husband Bertrand Tezac (Pierrot) and investigating the roundup of Jewish families by the French police in July 1942. She learns that the apartment they live in belonged to the Starzynski family and flashbacks depict the tragedy that engulfed 10-year-old Sarah (Mayance) and the Tezac's connection to the past. Fine work can be expected from Scott Thomas but young Mayance is truly a heartbreaker. English and French with subtitles. **111m/C; DVD.** *FR* Kristin Scott Thomas; Melusine Mayance; Frederic Pierrot; Aidan Quinn; Niels Arestrup; Dominique Frot; Michel Duchaussoy; Gisele Casadesus; ***D:*** Gilles Paquest-Brenner; ***W:*** Gilles Paquest-Brenner; Serge Joncour; ***C:*** Pascal Ridao; ***M:*** Max Richter.

Saratoga **1/2 1937** Gable plays a bookie and Harlow the daughter of an impoverished horse breeder in this romantic comedy centered around the race tracks. This was the final film appearance for Harlow, who died before the film's completion. Mary Dees was chosen as her stand-in and had to finish many of the scenes. "Saratoga" was released just a month after Harlow's death and became one of the biggest moneymakers of the year. **94m/B; VHS, DVD.** Jean Harlow; Clark Gable; Lionel Barrymore; Walter Pidgeon; Frank Morgan; Una Merkel; Cliff Edwards; George Zucco; Hattie McDaniel; Jonathan Hale; ***D:*** Jack Conway; ***W:*** Anita Loos; Robert Hopkins.

Saratoga Trunk **1/2 1945** Lavish, if slow-moving, version of Edna Ferber's romance novel reteams Cooper and Bergman (who starred in "For Whom the Bell Tolls"). It's 1875 New Orleans and bitter Clio, the half-Creole illegitimate daughter of a local, is determined to marry rich. But first, she gets involved with Texas gambler Clint Maroon (Cooper). He's in a business deal with wealthy Van Steed (Warburton), about the Saratoga railroad line, and Clio decides to go after him. Of course, she really wants Clint and they go through lots of bother before ending up together. Filmed in 1943 but release was delayed because of WWII. **135m/B; VHS, DVD.** Gary Cooper; Ingrid Bergman; John Warburton; Flora Robson; Florence Bates; Jerry Austin; ***D:*** Sam Wood; ***W:*** Casey Robinson; ***C:*** Ernest Haller; ***M:*** Max Steiner.

Sartana's Here. . . Trade Your Pistol for a Coffin **1970** A soldier of fortune searches for a missing shipment of gold in the Old West. **92m/C; VHS, DVD, Blu-Ray.** *IT* George Hilton; Charles Southwood; Erika Blanc; Linda Sini; ***D:*** Giuliano Carnimeo; ***W:*** Tito Carpi; ***C:*** Stelvio Massi; ***M:*** Francesco De Masi.

Sasha **2010** Despite having lived in Germany for 20 years, the refugee Petrovic clan retains their insular Yugoslav attitudes, which is why son Sasha has been hiding the fact that he is gay. He's devastated after learning his crush-worthy piano teacher Gebhard is moving to Vienna. Fellow student Jiao urges Sasha to make his love declaration before it's too late but he doesn't know if he can overcome his family fears. German, Croatian, and Serbian with subtitles. **102m/C; DVD.** *GE* Tim Bergmann; Sascha Kekez; Yvonne Ying Hee; Predrag Bjelac; Zeljka Preksavec; Jasin Mjumjunow; Ljubisa Gruicic; Arno Kempf; ***D:*** Dennis Todorovic; ***W:*** Dennis Todorovic; ***C:*** Andreas Kohler; ***M:*** Daniel Chour.

Saskatchewan **1954** In 1877, Canadian Mountie Thomas O'Rourke (Ladd) and his Cree blood brother Cajou (Silverheels) find a burned-out wagon train with a lone survivor--saloon gal Grace (Winters). A Sioux raiding party crossed the border and commander Benton (Douglas) was ordered to move his men to reinforce a border fort, but things get messy along the way. The action sequences are tops but the story is weak and Winters over-acts. **87m/C; DVD.** Alan Ladd; Shelley Winters; J. Carrol Naish; Jay Silverheels; Robert Douglas; Hugh O'Brian; Antonio Moreno; ***D:*** Raoul Walsh; ***W:*** Gil Doud; ***C:*** John Seitz.

Sasquatch WOOF! 1976 Purported "documentary" about the mythical creature Bigfoot. Includes pictures of the "actual" monster. For those real stupid moods. **94m/C; VHS, DVD, Blu-Ray.** George Lauris; ***D:*** Ed Ragozzini.

Sasquatch 🦴🦴 **1/2** *The Untold* **2002 (R)** Mogul Harlan Knowles (Henriksen) runs a bio-tech company and is frantic when one of the company's planes crashes in the forests of the Pacific Northwest. Not only is his daughter (Parker) aboard but so is the very expensive prototype of a DNA testing machine. So Knowles assembles a rescue team and heads into the woods—only to discover the plane's crew torn to shreds. **86m/C; VHS, DVD.** *CA* Lance Henriksen; Andrea Roth; Philip Granger; Russell Ferrier; Jeremy Radick; Erica Durance; ***D:*** Jonas Quastel; ***W:*** Jonas Quastel; Chris Lanning; ***C:*** Shaun Lawless; ***M:*** Tal Bergman; Larry Seymour. **VIDEO**

The Sasquatch Gang 🦴 *The Sasquatch Dumpling Gang* **2006** Three mild-mannered loser buddies (Sumpter, Palmer, Pinkston) upset their stoner neighbor Zerk (Long) with their sword-and-fantasy fights. So he decides to play a trick by having the trio stumble over a faked Bigfoot site in the woods. Clumsy comedy. **86m/C; DVD.** Jeremy Sumpter; Justin Long; Rob Pinkston; Joey Kern; Hubbel Palmer; Addie Land; Carl Weathers; Jon(athan) Gries; Stephen Tobolowsky; Michael Mitchell; ***D:*** Tim Skousen; ***W:*** Tim Skousen; ***C:*** Munn Powell; ***M:*** John Swihart. **VIDEO**

The Satan Bug 🦴 **1/2 1965** Too much talk and not enough action. Vials of a lethal virus are stolen from a California government lab. Security agent Barrett (Maharis) is called in and quickly discovers Dr. Hoffman (Basehart) is behind the crime. Hoffman's threatening to release the virus in L.A. to prove a point about government involvement in germ warfare. Based on a novel by Alistair MacLean. **114m/C; DVD.** George Maharis; Richard Basehart; Anne Francis; Dana Andrews; Ed Asner; Simon Oakland; ***D:*** John Sturges; ***W:*** Edward Anhalt; James Clavell; ***C:*** Robert L. Surtees; ***M:*** Jerry Goldsmith.

Satan in High Heels 🦴 **1/2 1961** Sordid show-biz tale of a carnival dancer (Myles) who dreams of making it big on Broadway. First she finagles her way into a position as a nightclub singer and the mistress of a convenient millionaire. But she loses it all for love when she falls for the millionaire's misbehaving son. Flamboyant performance by Hall as the lesbian nightclub owner. **90m/B; VHS, DVD.** Meg Myles; Grayson Hall; Del Tenney; Mike Keene; Robert Yuro; Sabrina; Earl Hammond; Paul Scott; ***D:*** Jerald Intrator; ***W:*** John T. Chapman; ***C:*** Bernard Hirschenson; ***M:*** Mundell Lowe.

Satan Met a Lady 🦴🦴 **1/2 1936** A weak adaptation of Dashiell Hammett's "Maltese Falcon." This version has Davis employing a private detective to track down a mysterious woman. The hunted woman is herself searching for a valuable collectible. **74m/B; VHS, DVD.** Bette Davis; Warren William; Alison Skipworth; Arthur Treacher; Marie Wilson; Porter Hall; Olin Howlin; ***D:*** William Dieterle.

Satanic 🦴 **1/2 2015 (R)** Four friends travel California in a tour of famous crime sites linked to Satanism or the occult, and things quickly go south when they encounter a runaway girl who claims to know the local occult scene. It brings nothing new, and is the latest in a long line of horror films in which you wish the protagonists were smart enough to watch horror movies, and thus spare you this trip. **84m/C; DVD, Blu-Ray, Streaming.** Sarah Hyland; Steven Krueger; Justin Chon; Clara Mamet; Sophie Dalah; ***D:*** Jeffrey G. Hunt; ***W:*** Anthony Jaswinski; Todd Haberman; ***C:*** Mike Karasick; ***M:*** Jim Dooley. **VIDEO**

Satanic Panic 🦴🦴 **2019** On her first night on the job delivering pizzas, Samantha (Griffith) does not get a tip from a wealthy man who lives in a mansion. Angry, Samantha barges into the house and finds the occupants are a coven of satanic witches, led by Danica (Romijn), who are performing a satanic ritual. When the group learns that Samantha is a virgin, they drug her and lock her to use her for a forthcoming ritual. Though full of humor, creative special effects, and some solid performances, Stardust's directorial debut horror comedy is painfully unsteady. **85m/C; DVD.** Rebecca Romijn; Arden Myrin; Hayley Griffith; Ruby Modine; AJ Bowen; ***D:*** Chelsea Stardust; ***W:*** Grady Hendrix; ***C:*** Mark Evans; ***M:*** Wolfmen Of Mars.

The Satanic Rites of Dracula 🦴🦴 *Count Dracula and His Vampire Bride; Dracula Is Dead and Well and Living in London* **1973** Count Dracula is the leader of a satanic cult of prominent scientists and politicians who develop a gruesome plague virus capable of destroying the human race. Preceded by "Dracula A.D. 1972" and followed by "The 7 Brothers Meet Dracula." **88m/C; VHS, DVD, Blu-Ray.** *GB* Christopher Lee; Peter Cushing; Michael Coles; William Franklyn; Freddie Jones; Joanna Lumley; Richard Vernon; Patrick Barr; Barbara Yu Ling; ***D:*** Alan Gibson; ***W:*** Don Houghton; ***C:*** Brian Probyn; ***M:*** John Cacavas.

Satan's Brew 🦴🦴 *Satansbraten* **1976** Aspiring poet (Raab) murders his mistress and assumes the identity of 19th-century symbolist poet Stefan George, including his idol's homosexual tastes. Fassbinder at his most excessive. German with subtitles. **100m/C; VHS, DVD.** *GE* Kurt Raab; Margit Carstensen; Volker Spengler; Ingrid Caven; Helen Vita; ***D:*** Rainer Werner Fassbinder; ***W:*** Rainer Werner Fassbinder; ***C:*** Michael Ballhaus; ***M:*** Peer Raben.

Satan's Cheerleaders WOOF! 1977 (R) A demonic high school janitor traps a bevy of buxom cheerleaders at his Satanic altar for sacrificial purposes. The gals use all of their endowments to escape the clutches of the evil sheriff and his fat wife. Is it ever campy! **92m/C; VHS, DVD, Blu-Ray.** John Carradine; John Ireland; Yvonne De Carlo; Kerry Sherman; Jacqulin Cole; Hilary Horan; Alisa Powell; Sherry Marks; Jack Kruschen; Syd Chaplin; ***D:*** Greydon Clark; ***W:*** Greydon Clark; Alvin L. Fast; ***C:*** Dean Cundey; ***M:*** Gerald Lee.

Satan's Little Helper 🦴 **2004 (R)** On Halloween, naive Doug befriends a masked serial killer, not realizing that the carnage they leave behind is real, and takes him home to meet his family. His mom (Plummer) and sister (Winnick) must then save the family from the maniac. Terrible genre spoof is cheap, distasteful, and pointless. **99m/C; DVD.** Amanda Plummer; Alexander Brickel; Stephen Graham; Dan Ziskie; Katheryn Winnick; Joshua Annex; ***D:*** Jeff Lieberman; ***W:*** Jeff Lieberman; ***C:*** Dejan Georgevich; ***M:*** David Horowitz. **VIDEO**

Satan's Sadists 🦴 **1969 (R)** Tamblyn and his biker gang terrorize folks in the Southern California desert, including a retired cop, a Vietnam vet and a trio of vacationing coeds. Violent film will probably be best appreciated by Adamson completists. **88m/C; VHS, DVD.** Russ Tamblyn; Regina Carrol; Gary Kent; Jackie Taylor; John Cardos; Kent Taylor; Robert Dix; Scott Brady; Evelyn Frank; Greydon Clark; Bill Bonner; Bobby Clark; Yvonne Stewart; Cheryl Anne; Randee Lynn; Bambi Allen; Breck Warwick; ***D:*** Al Adamson; ***W:*** Dennis Wayne; ***C:*** Gary Graver; ***M:*** Harley Hatcher.

Satan's School for Girls 🦴 **1/2 1973** When a young woman investigates the circumstances that caused her sister's suicide, it leads her to a satanic girl's academy. Dumb and puerile made for TV "horror." **74m/C; VHS, DVD.** Pamela Franklin; Roy Thinnes; Kate Jackson; Lloyd Bochner; Jamie Smith-Jackson; Jo Van Fleet; Cheryl Ladd; Gwynne Gilford; Bing (Neil) Russell; ***D:*** David Lowell Rich; ***W:*** Arthur Ross; ***M:*** Laurence Rosenthal. **TV**

Satellite in the Sky 🦴 **1/2 1956** CinemaScope sci fi snoozer with no surprises. Commander Michael Hayden (Moore) leads the first manned space satellite, which is supposed to test out a new bomb over the Earth's atmosphere. Reporter Kim Hamilton (Maxwell) is a stowaway and everyone onboard is in trouble when the test goes wrong and the bomb attaches itself to the hull of the satellite. So it's either remove the bomb, defuse it, or go boom. **84m/C; DVD.** *GB* Kieron Moore; Lois Maxwell; Donald Wolfit; Bryan Forbes; Jimmy Hanley; Alan Gifford; Donald Gray; Barry Keegan; ***D:*** Paul Dickson; ***W:*** John C. Mather; Edith Dell; J.T. McIntosh; ***C:*** Georges Perinal; James Wilson; ***M:*** Albert Elms.

Satin 🦴 **1/2 2010** Narcissistic lounge singer Jack Satin blows his Vegas gig so he decides to head for Atlantic City. Of course, his car breaks down in a tiny desert community where he finds a mentor in jazz musician/mechanic Doc and a job (and romance) with bar owner Lauren. Too bad Jack's Vegas problems also find him. **94m/C; DVD.** Hamilton von Watts; Melissa Joan Hart; Robert Guillaume; Michael Kudlitz; Alley Mills; Jackie Debatin; ***D:*** Christopher Olness; ***W:*** Christopher Olness; ***C:*** Harris Charalambous; ***M:*** Joseph Bauer. **VIDEO**

Satin Rouge 🦴🦴 **1/2 2002** Lilia (Abbass) is a very proper widowed seamstress who lives with her in-laws and rebellious teenaged daughter Salma (El Fahem). Salma is taking belly-dancing classes and Lilia suspects the girl is flirting with musician Chokri (Kamoun), so she follows him to a club and is seduced by the exuberance of the dancers. One, Folla (Hichri), invites Lilia in and soon she is leading a double-life—grieving widow by day and costumer and part-time dancer by night. Arabic with subtitles. **95m/C; VHS, DVD.** *FR TN* Hiam Abbass; Hend El Fahem; Maher Kamoun; Monia Hichri; ***D:*** Raja Amari; ***W:*** Raja Amari; ***C:*** Diane Baratier; ***M:*** Nawfel El Manaa.

Satisfaction 🦴 **1988 (PG-13)** An all-girl, high school rock band play out the summer before college. The Keatons should have sent Bateman to her room for this stunt. **93m/C; VHS, DVD.** Justine Bateman; Trini Alvarado; Britta Phillips; Julia Roberts; Scott Coffey; Liam Neeson; Deborah Harry; ***D:*** Joan Freeman; ***W:*** Charles Purpura; ***M:*** Michel Colombier.

Saturday Night and Sunday Morning 🦴🦴🦴 **1/2 1960** This "kitchen sink" drama finds the 23-year-old Finney in star form as working-class Arthur Seaton, who's devoted to good times, spending his weekends with boozing, brawling, and willing women. He's having an affair with the older, married Brenda (Roberts) and pursuing the strictly moral Doreen (Field), who refuses to sleep with him without a commitment. Arthur thinks he's falling in love and is (eventually) ready for marriage but not without complications and not before warning Doreen that he's unlikely to completely change his carefree ways. Reisz's first feature film; Sillitoe adapted from his novel. **98m/B; DVD.** *UK* Albert Finney; Rachel Roberts; Shirley Anne Field; Bryan Pringle; Norman Rossington; Hylda Baker; Robert Cowdra; Elsie Wagstaff; Frank Pettitt; ***D:*** Karel Reisz; ***W:*** Alan Sillitoe; ***C:*** Freddie Francis; ***M:*** John Dankworth. British Acad. '60: Actress (Roberts), Film; Natl. Bd. of Review '61: Actor (Finney).

Saturday Night at the Baths 🦴🦴 **1975** A no-budget production that's a time capsule for post-Stonewall and pre-AIDS gay life. Desperately needing work, straight Michael gets a job playing piano at NYC's Continental Baths (the kind of place where Bette Midler sang and drag queens and disco boys performed). He complains to girlfriend Tracy that the manager keeps propositioning him, but then Michael stops complaining. Beware the edited version. **86m/C; DVD.** Robert Aberdeen; Don Scotti; Ellen Sheppard; Steve Ostrow; ***D:*** David Buckley; ***W:*** David Buckley; Franklin Khedouri; ***C:*** Ralf Bode.

Saturday Night Fever 🦴🦴 **1/2 1977 (R)** Brooklyn teenager (Travolta), bored with his daytime job, becomes the nighttime king of the local disco. Based on a story published in "New York Magazine" by Nik Cohn. Acclaimed for its disco dance sequences, memorable soundtrack by the Bee Gees, and carefree yet bleak script; extremely dated, although it made its mark on society in its time. Followed by the sequel "Staying Alive." Also available in a 112-minute "PG" rated version. **118m/C; VHS, DVD, Blu-Ray.** John Travolta; Karen (Lynn) Gorney; Barry Miller; Donna Pescow; Joseph Cali; Bruce Ornstein; Paul Pape; Fran Drescher; ***D:*** John Badham; ***W:*** Norman Wexler; ***C:*** Ralf Bode; ***M:*** David Shire. Natl. Bd. of Review '77: Actor (Travolta); Natl. Film Reg. '10.

Saturday Night Special 🦴 **1/2 1992 (R)** Country singer/songwriter Travis (played by Nashville stalwart Burnette) gets a job fronting the house band of Tennessee tavern owner T.J. (Dean). Travis also takes up with ambitious Darlene (Ford), who happens to be T.J.'s wife. But it's Darlene who has the brains in this unpleasant trio, she decides to get rid of hubby and sets Travis up to take the fall. It's all been done before (and better). **75m/C; VHS, DVD.** Billy Burnette; Maria Ford; Rick Dean; ***D:*** Dan Golden; ***W:*** Jonathan Banks; ***M:*** Billy Burnette; Nicholas Rivera.

Saturday the 14th 🦴 **1/2 1981 (PG)** A parody of the popular axe-wielding-maniac genre, about a family inheriting a haunted mansion. Poorly made; not funny or scary. Followed by even worse sequel: "Saturday the 14th Strikes Back." **91m/C; VHS, DVD, Blu-Ray.** Richard Benjamin; Paula Prentiss; Severn Darden; Jeffrey Tambor; Kari Michaelsen; Kevin Brando; Rosemary DeCamp; Stacy Keach; ***D:*** Howard R. Cohen; ***W:*** Howard R. Cohen; Jeff Begun; ***C:*** Daniel Lacambre; ***M:*** Parmer Fuller.

Saturday the 14th Strikes Back 🦴 **1988** Continuing the name, but not the story line, cast, or characters of the original, this one concerns the invasion of a birthday party by a vampire (Stonebrook) and her monstrous friends. The monsters decide that the birthday boy (Presson) should be their new leader. Pretty lame, even by the original's standards. **91m/C; VHS, DVD.** Ray Walston; Avery Schreiber; Patty McCormack; Julianne McNamara; Rhonda Aldrich; Daniel Will-Harris; Joseph Ruskin; Pamela Stonebrook; Phil Leeds; Jason Presson; Michael Berryman; Victoria Morsell; ***D:*** Howard R. Cohen; ***W:*** Howard R. Cohen; ***C:*** Levie Isaacks; ***M:*** Parmer Fuller.

Saturday's Children 🦴🦴 **1/2 1940** Change of pace role for Garfield who plays a bumbling, would-be inventor in this adaptation of Maxwell Anderson's Pulitzer Prize-winning play. Humble bookkeeper Henry Halevy (Rains) gets his ambitious daughter Bobby (Shirley) a job with his company, but she's soon taking her older sister Florrie's (Patrick) advice about looking for a husband rather than a career. She manages to trick Rims Rosson into marriage, but reality sets in when the young couple suffer financial problems and Bobby discovers she's pregnant just as Rims is offered a better job opportunity, sans wife, in the Philippines. **102m/B; DVD.** John Garfield; Anne Shirley; Claude Rains; Lee Patrick; Roscoe Karns; George Tobias; Dennie Moore; ***D:*** Vincent Sherman; ***W:*** Julius J. Epstein; Philip G. Epstein; ***C:*** James Wong Howe; ***M:*** Adolph Deutsch.

Saturn in Opposition 🦴🦴 **1/2** *Saturno Contro* **2007** The title is an astrological term referring to upheaval and change, which is what happens to a group of 30-somethings in this ensemble drama. Davide and his partner Lorenzo have a wonderful life with devoted friends. Then Lorenzo is rushed to the hospital, where he dies; while Davide struggles to cope, his friends' lives fall apart as well. Italian with subtitles. **110m/C; DVD.** *IT TU* Pierfrancesco Favino; Stefano Accorsi; Margherita Buy; Serra Yilmaz; Ennio Fantastichini; Luigi Diberti; Isabella Ferrari; Luca Argentero; Ambra Angiolini; Michelangelo Tommaso; Filippo Timi; Lunetta Savino; ***D:*** Ferzan Ozpetek; ***W:*** Ferzan Ozpetek; ***C:*** Gianfilippo Corticelli; ***M:*** Giovanni Pellini.

Saturn 3 🦴 **1/2 1980 (R)** Two research scientists create a futuristic Garden of Eden in an isolated sector of our solar system, but love story turns to horror story when a killer robot arrives. Sporadically promising, but ultimately lame; dumb ending. For Farrah fans only. **88m/C; VHS, DVD, Blu-Ray.** *GB* Farrah Fawcett; Kirk Douglas; Harvey Keitel; Ed Bishop; ***D:*** Stanley Donen; ***W:*** Martin Amis; ***C:*** Billy Williams; ***M:*** Elmer Bernstein.

Saul and David 🦴🦴 **1/2** *Saul e David* **1964** Beautifully filmed story of David's life with King Saul, the battle with Goliath, and the tragic end of Saul. From the "Bible" series. **120m/C; VHS, DVD.** Norman Wooland; Gianni "John" Garko; Elisa Cegani; Virgilio Teixeira; ***D:*** Marcello Baldi; ***W:*** Tonino

Guerra; *C:* Juan Ruiz Romero; Marcello Masciocchi; *M:* Teo Usuelli.

Sausage Party 🦴🦴 1/2 **2016 (R)** Rogen and Goldberg turn a pot-fueled conversation about a silly spoof of Pixar and Disney movies into a reality in this cartoon that is most definitely not for kids. The food at Shopwell's think that when customers buy their buddies that they're taken to "The Great Beyond" for an existence of bliss and happiness. Frank (Rogen), a sausage, and Brenda (Wiig), a bun, hope to finally "unite" after they're purchased together, but they learn the hard way what really happens to food. Rogen's animated comedy, the highest-grossing R-rated animated film of all time, is clever, funny, and very dirty. **89m/C; DVD, Blu-Ray.** Seth Rogen; Kristen Wiig; Jonah Hill; Bill Hader; Michael Cera; James Franco; *D:* Greg Tiernan; Conrad Vernon; *W:* Seth Rogen; Kyle Hunter; Ariel Shaffir; Evan Goldberg; *M:* Christopher Lennertz; Alan Menken.

The Savage 🦴🦴 *Le Sauvage* **1975** Unlikely adventure-comedy starring Deneuve and Montand. In Caracas, Nelly runs away from her would-be fiance Vittorio (Vannucchi), taking a valuable painting with her. She's unexpectedly aided by Vincent, who's fled his own marital and business woes by retreating to a small island. Nelly flirts with Vincent so he'll help her sell the painting. But first the duo have to deal with Vincent's enraged wife (Wynter), who has finally tracked him down, as well as Vittorio and his goons. English and French with subtitles. **110m/C; DVD.** *FR* Catherine Deneuve; Yves Montand; Luigi Vannucchi; Dana Wynter; Tony Roberts; Vernon Dobtcheff; Bobo Lewis; *D:* Jean-Paul Rappeneau; *W:* Jean-Paul Rappeneau; Elisabeth Rappeneau; Jean-Loup Dabadie; *C:* Pierre Lhomme; *M:* Michel Legrand.

Savage Abduction 🦴 **1973 (R)** Two girls visiting Los Angeles are kidnapped by a bizarre man. **84m/C; VHS, DVD.** Tom Drake; Stephen Oliver; Sean Kenney; *D:* John Lawrence.

Savage Beach 🦴 **1989 (R)** A pair of well-endowed female federal agents battle assorted buccaneers on a remote Pacific isle over a rediscovered cache of gold from WWII. Exploitative, pornographic, and degrading to watch. Sequel to "Picasso Trigger." **90m/C; VHS, DVD, Blu-Ray.** Dona Speir; Hope Marie Carlton; Bruce Penhall; Rodrigo Obregon; John Aprea; Teri Weigel; Lisa London; *D:* Andy Sidaris.

Savage Dawn 🦴 1/2 **1984 (R)** In yet another desert town, yet another pair of combat-hardened vets are confronted by yet another vicious motorcycle gang. Haven't we seen this one before? **102m/C; VHS, DVD, Blu-Ray.** George Kennedy; Karen Black; Richard Lynch; Lance Henriksen; William Forsythe; *D:* Simon Nuchtern.

Savage Drums 🦴 1/2 **1951** Sabu returns to his South Seas island to help end tribal warfare there. Dated and dumb, but fun-to-watch melodrama/action. **70m/B; VHS, DVD.** Sabu; Lita Baron; H.B. Warner; Sid Melton; Steven Geray; Margia Dean; Hugh Beaumont; *D:* William Berke; *W:* Fenton Earnshaw; *C:* Jack Greenhalgh; *M:* Darrell Calker.

Savage Fury 🦴 *The Call of the Savage* **1935** Feature-length version of the popular movie serial. **80m/B; VHS, DVD.** Noah Beery, Jr.; Dorothy Short; Harry Woods; Bryant Washburn; Fred MacKaye; *D:* Lew Landers; *C:* Richard Fryer; William Sickner.

Savage Grace 🦴 1/2 **2007** Based on the sordid true crime story of the heirs to the Bakelite plastics fortune. Insecure Brooks Baekeland (Dillane) is soon indifferent to his wife Barbara (Moore), a poseur who craves acceptance within their jet-set society. Pathologically needy for love, Barbara smothers only son Tony (Redmayne) to the point of being incestuous, which exacerbates his mental instability until he murders mommy dearest. Although it covers decades (from the mid-1940s to the early 1970s), Moore never ages, which is just one of the conundrums. **96m/C; DVD.** *US FR SP* Julianne Moore; Stephen (Dillon) Dillane; Eddie Redmayne; Hugh Dancy; Elena Anaya; *D:* Tom Kalin; *W:* Howard A. Rodman; *C:* Juanmi (Juan Miguel) Azpiroz; *M:* Fernando Velazquez.

Savage Harvest 2: October Blood 🦴 1/2 **2006** Sequel that was 13 years in the making follows low-budget horror film director Tyge Murdock (Gaa) as he returns home to reassess his life after an actor is accidentally killed on one of his sets. But home is where the nightmares are. Reuniting with his high school flame (Haack) brings back remnants of a mass murder that took place ten years earlier and the old gang quickly finds themselves trapped in a demonic gore-spattered nightmare. Script is decent enough but the cast doesn't have the chops to pull it off, Haack being the exception as the deadly-intense Ashley Lomack. **119m/C; DVD.** Benjamin Gaa; Emily Haack; Eric Stanze; David Propst; Jonathan Baker; *D:* Jason Christ; *W:* Jason Christ; *C:* Jason Christ; *M:* Shawn Donoho. **VIDEO**

Savage Is Loose WOOF! **1974 (R)** Drivel about a scientist, his wife, and their son stranded on a deserted island for 20 years. Not surprisingly, as junior matures he realizes there isn't a woman for him—or is there? Completely lacking in redeeming qualities. Absurd pseudo-Freudian claptrap produced by Scott. **114m/C; VHS, DVD.** George C. Scott; Trish Van Devere; John David Carson; Lee Montgomery; *D:* George C. Scott.

Savage Island 🦴 1/2 **1985 (R)** Women's prison in the tropics sets the scene for the usual exploitative goings-on. Blair is actually in the film only for a few minutes. Chopped-up, even worse version of "Escape From Hell." **74m/C; VHS, DVD.** *SP IT* Nicholas Beardsley; Linda Blair; Anthony Steffen; Ajita Wilson; Christina Lai; Leon Askin; *D:* Edward (Edoardo Mulargia) Muller; *W:* Nicholas Beardsley. Golden Raspberries '85: Worst Actress (Blair).

Savage Island 🦴 1/2 **2003** Wanting to escape their troubled marriage, Steven and Julie seek refuge with their baby at her parents' remote island home. The serenity is squelched when they're held responsible for a horrible accident that claims the life of one of the island's other inhabitants—the rural Savage family—who will stop at nothing to avenge their loss. **90m/C; VHS, DVD.** Winston Rekert; Brendan Beiser; Gregg Scott; Don S. Davis; Steven Man; Kristina Copeland; Beverley Breuer; Zoran Vukelic; Nahanni Arntzen; *D:* Jeffrey Scott Lando; *W:* Kevin Mosley; *C:* Geoff Rogers; *M:* Chris Nickel. **VIDEO**

Savage Journey 🦴 1/2 **1983 (PG)** A wagon train of pioneers has difficulty on its westward journey. Simple story with no real appeal. **99m/C; VHS, DVD.** Richard Moll; Maurice Grandmaison; Faith Clift; *D:* Tom McGowan.

Savage Justice 🦴 **1988** A young woman seeks revenge against leftist rebels (boo, hiss) in a Southeast Asian country who killed her parents and raped her. She hooks up with an ex-Green Beret, and they fight and love their way through the jungle. The usual nudity and violence; derivative and dumb. **90m/C; DVD.** Julia Montgomery; Steven Memel; Ken Metcalfe; *D:* Joey Romero.

Savage Land 🦴🦴 1/2 **1994 (PG)** Family western finds a young brother and sister travelling by stage to meet up with their father. The stage is robbed by some bumbling bad guys, who then pursue the kids and two other passengers across the frontier. The kids, of course, are smarter than most of the adults, and manage to get the best of the bad hombres. **91m/C; VHS, DVD.** Graham Greene; Corbin Bernsen; Vivian Schilling; Mercedes McNab; Corey Carrier; Brion James; Bo Svenson; Charlotte Ross; *D:* Dean Hamilton; *W:* Dean Hamilton; *C:* Roland Smith; *M:* Michael Conway Baker.

Savage Messiah 🦴🦴🦴 **1972 (R)** Bio of young French sculptor Henri Gaudier and his intense, though platonic, affair with a refined Polish woman 20 years his senior. Stylized drama is spared most of director Russell's noted excesses but he manages to believably show their magnetic attraction. Gaudier was killed in WWI at the age of 24. Based on the biography by H.S. Ede. **96m/C; VHS, DVD.** *GB* Scott Antony; Dorothy Tutin; Dame Helen Mirren; Lindsay Kemp; Peter Vaughan; Michael Gough; *D:* Ken Russell; *W:* Christopher Logue; *C:* Dick Bush.

Savage Messiah 🦴🦴 *Moise: L'Affaire Roch Theriault* **2002 (R)** Canadian social worker Paula Jackson (Walker) discovers that charismatic Roch Theriault (Picard), who calls himself Moses, maintains a backwoods commune/religious cult consisting of several women who think of themselves as his wives. When Paula tries to intercede on behalf of their children, she finds the women would rather give their kids up to social services than leave their leader despite their abuse at his hands. Based on a true story, which took place in Quebec. English and French with subtitles. **96m/C; VHS, DVD.** *CA* Polly Walker; Luc Picard; Isabelle Blais; Isabelle Cyr; Pascale Montpetit; Domini Blythe; Julie La Rochelle; Elizabeth Robertson; *D:* Mario Azzopardi; *W:* Sharon Riis; *C:* Serge Ladouceur; *M:* Frank Ilfman. Genie '02: Actor, Adapt. Score, Support. Actress (Montpetit).

Savage Run 🦴🦴🦴 *Run, Simon, Run* **1970** Reynolds is a Papago Indian framed and imprisoned for his brother's murder. Sprung from the pen, he heads back to the reservation to find the real killers and to avenge his brother's death. Convincing drama. Stevens's last role before her suicide. **73m/C; VHS, DVD.** Burt Reynolds; Inger Stevens; James Best; Rodolfo Acosta; Don Dubbins; Joyce Jameson; Barney (Bernard) Phillips; Eddie Little Sky; *D:* George McCowan. **TV**

Savage Sam 🦴🦴 **1963** Intended as a sequel to "Old Yeller." Sam, the offspring of the heroic dog named Old Yeller, tracks down some children kidnapped by Indians. Fun, but not fully successful. **103m/C; VHS, DVD.** Tommy Kirk; Kevin Corcoran; Brian Keith; Dewey Martin; Jeff York; Marta Kristen; *D:* Norman Tokar; *C:* Edward Colman.

Savage Sisters 🦴 **1974** AIP babes-with-guns exploitation flick. Three women team up to prevent anyone but themselves from finding a million dollars looted from the treasury of some corrupt regime on some nameless island. **89m/C; DVD.** Gloria Hendry; Cheri Caffaro; Rosanna Ortiz; John Ashley; Sid Haig; *D:* Eddie Romero; *W:* Harry Corner; *C:* Justo Paulino; *M:* Les Baxter.

Savage Streets 🦴 1/2 **1983 (R)** Blair seeks commando-style revenge on the street gang that raped her deaf sister. Extended rape scene betrays the exploitative intentions, though other bits are entertaining, in a trashy kind of way. **93m/C; VHS, DVD, Blu-Ray.** Linda Blair; John Vernon; Sal Landi; Robert Dryer; Debra Blee; Linnea Quigley; *D:* Danny Steinmann; *M:* John D'Andrea. Golden Raspberries '85: Worst Actress (Blair).

Savage Weekend WOOF! *The Killer Behind the Mask; The Upstate Murders* **1980 (R)** A killer behind a ghoulish mask stalks human prey in the boonies, of course. Astoundingly, there is one interesting role—William Sanderson's looney. Otherwise, throw this one no bones. **88m/C; VHS, DVD.** Christopher Allport; James Doerr; Marilyn Hamlin; Caitlin (Kathleen Heaney) O'Heaney; David Gale; William Sanderson; *D:* David Paulsen; John Mason Kirby; *W:* David Paulsen.

Savage Wilderness 🦴🦴 1/2 *The Last Frontier* **1955** When a trio of fur trappers lose a year's worth of skins to a band of marauding Indians, they decide to take scouting jobs at a cavalry outpost. But they find the new commander (Preston) hasn't gotten his nickname as the "Butcher of Shiloh" without reason. Adapted from the novel "The Gilded Rooster" by Richard Emery Roberts. **98m/C; VHS, DVD.** Victor Mature; Robert Preston; Guy Madison; James Whitmore; Anne Bancroft; Russell Collins; Peter Whitney; Pat Hogan; Manuel Donde; Guy Williams; *D:* Anthony Mann; *W:* Philip Yordan; Russell S. Hughes; *M:* Leigh Harline.

Savages 🦴🦴 **1972** A group of savages descend on a palatial mansion, and after living there for some time, become refined ladies and gentlemen. The moral savages and "civilized" men are really the same. **106m/C; VHS, DVD.** Lewis J. Stadlen; Anne Francine; Thayer David; Salome Jens; Susan Blakely; Kathleen Widdoes; Sam Waterston; *D:* James Ivory; *C:* Walter Lassally.

Savages 🦴🦴 1/2 **1975** Griffith as a demented nut-case stalking another man in the desert? That's right, Opie. "The Most Dangerous Game" remade-sort-of-for TV. **74m/C; VHS, DVD.** Andy Griffith; Sam Bottoms; Noah Beery, Jr.; *D:* Lee H. Katzin.

The Savages 🦴🦴🦴 1/2 **2007 (R)** The Savages are a highly dysfunctional family consisting of middle-aged siblings Wendy (Linney) and Jon (Hoffman) as well as their aging father Lenny (Bosco), who still lives in his recently deceased girlfriend's condo in Sun City, Arizona. After years of estrangement, two phone calls bring to light Lenny's advancing dementia, which reunites the three as they return Lenny to Buffalo. This task is complicated by the predictable but hilarious neuroses of the self-absorbed sibs. Writer/director Jenkins has taken the pathetic inevitability of midlife and shines a light on all of the ridiculous humor that bubbles up through the cracks. **113m/C; On Demand.** Laura Linney; Philip Seymour Hoffman; Philip Bosco; Peter Friedman; Cara Seymour; *D:* Tamara Jenkins; *W:* Tamara Jenkins; *C:* W. Mott Hupfel, III; *M:* Stephen Trask. Ind. Spirit '08: Actor (Hoffman), Screenplay.

Savages 🦴🦴 1/2 **2012 (R)** Director Stone has turned to sagas of bad people being caught by worse people before but the good news is that this displays an energy and life that has been missing of late. Buddhist Ben (Johnson) and his best friend, former Navy SEAL Chon (Kitsch), share a Laguna Beach pot-growing business and a girlfriend, Ophelia (Lively). Everything is copacetic until a Baja cartel tries to take over their operation and kidnaps O to prove they're serious. Travolta plays a DEA agent; Winslow co-scripted from his 2010 crime novel. **131m/C; DVD, Blu-Ray, Streaming.** Blake Lively; Taylor Kitsch; Aaron Taylor-Johnson; Benicio Del Toro; John Travolta; Demian Bichir; Salma Hayek; *D:* Oliver Stone; *W:* Oliver Stone; Shane Salerno; Don Winslow; *C:* Dan(iel) Mindel; *M:* Adam Peters.

Savages from Hell 🦴 *Big Enough and Old Enough* **1968 (R)** Greasy biker dude beats up a young black guy because he was flirting with the biker's woman. The biker also tries to rape a migrant farmworker's daughter because he lusts after her. Trashy exploitation film. **79m/C; VHS, DVD.** Bobbie Byers; Cyril Poitier; Diwaldo Myers; Viola Lloyd; William Kelley; *D:* Joseph Prieto; *W:* Joseph Prieto.

Savannah 🦴🦴 1/2 **2014 (PG-13)** Based on a true story, this early twentieth century drama explores the life of the romantic figure Ward Allen. Part of a Southern family with a strong plantation heritage, the grandiose, charismatic Ward (Caviezel) takes a different path when he choses to live on a river instead. Accompanied by loyal friend and freed slave Christmas Moultrie (Ejiofor), Wards hunts fowl and sells it in markets in Savannah, Georgia. Also master of words, Shakespeare, and rhetoric, Ward wins the love of a society woman who marries him in spite of her father and his condemnation of their relationship. Throughout his life, Ward repeatedly decides to reject or sidestep the social norms of the time and invest in the lives of others with whom he choses to share himself. **101m/C; DVD, Blu-Ray, Streaming, Download.** Jim Caviezel; Chiwetel Ejiofor; Jaimie Alexander; Bradley Whitford; Sam Shepard; *D:* Annette Haywood-Carter; *W:* Annette Haywood-Carter; Ken Carter; *C:* Mike Ozier; *M:* Gil Talmi.

Savannah Smiles 🦴🦴 1/2 **1982 (PG)** Poor little rich girl Anderson runs away from home, into the clutches of two ham-handed crooks. She melts their hearts, and they change their ways. Decent, sentimental family drama. **104m/C; VHS, DVD, Blu-Ray.** Bridgette Andersen; Mark Miller; Donovan Scott; Peter Graves; Chris Robinson; Michael Parks; *D:* Pierre De Moro.

Save Me 🦴 **2007** Mark (Allen) is a self-destructive, drug-addicted, multi-suicide attempt survivor who just can't come to grips with his sexuality. So he checks into Genesis House to get sexual healing via a steady dose of Christianity and heterosexuality, a promised one-two punch with unquestioned effectiveness. But getting locked in with other sexually broken men might not be the best prescription—a better one might get to his underlying drug abuse and self-hatred issues, perhaps? Anyway, Mark meets fellow 12-stepper Scott (Gant), they dig each other, and the melodrama churns away. **96m/C; DVD.** Chad Allen; Robert Gant; Judith Light; Stephen Lang; Robert Baker; *D:* Robert Cary; *W:* Craig Chester; Robert Desiderio; Alan Hines; *C:* Rodney Taylor; *M:* Jeff Cardoni.

Save the Date **2012 (R)** Insipid rom com with uninteresting characters. Sarah's sister Beth is deep into wedding plans with fiance Andrew, who's the bandmate of Sarah's boyfriend Kevi. Kevin gets wedding fever but commitment-phobe Sarah shoots down his ill-advised and public proposal, breaking up with hm instead. Then she gets involved in a rebound romance with Jonathan that could become serious. Meanwhile, Beth's pre-marital jitters increase and neither Sarah nor Andrew can be counted on to talk her down. **97m/C; DVD, Blu-Ray.** Lizzy Caplan; Alison Brie; Martin Starr; Geoffrey Arend; Mark Webber; Timothy Busfield; ***D:*** Michael Mohan; ***W:*** Michael Mohan; ***C:*** Elisha Christian; ***M:*** Hrishikesh Hirway. **VIDEO**

Save the Last Dance **1/2 2001 (PG-13)** "Fame" (or "Flashdance" or "Saturday Night Fever") meets "Romeo and Juliet" (or "West Side Story" or any trashy talk show) in this clearly not-so-original but solid teen drama. White, middle-class Sara (Stiles) adjusts to life and rediscovers her passion for dance in an all-black, inner-city Chicago high school when she must give up her dreams of attending Juilliard and move in with her down-on-his-luck father (Kinney) on the South Side. There, she befriends Chenille (Washington), who helps her get hip, and falls for her smart, ambitious brother Derek (Thomas), who helps her learn hip-hop. Stiles and Thomas turn in good performances despite somewhat stereotypical cast of characters. **112m/C; VHS, DVD.** Julia Stiles; Sean Patrick Thomas; Fredro Starr; Kerry Washington; Terry Kinney; Bianca Lawson; Garland Whitt; Vince Green; ***D:*** Thomas Carter; ***W:*** Duane Adler; Cheryl Edwards; ***C:*** Robbie Greenberg; ***M:*** Mark Isham.

Save the Last Dance 2 *Save the Last Dance 2: Stepping Up; Steppin' Up: Save the Last Dance 2* **2006 (PG-13)** Sequel to popular dance film Save the Last Dance fails to live up to the original. Though Sara (Miko) has been admitted to Julliard to become a ballerina, she finds herself drawn to hip-hop dance because of her roommate Zoe (Dollar) and guest lecturer Miles (Short). Sara works hard to meet the demanding standards of her famous ballet teacher, Monique Delacroix (Bisset), but experiences great creative and romantic passion working with Miles. When Sara is given a prominent role in a ballet performance, she questions if she should remain on the rigid road of ballet or the more raw path of hip-hop. Her choice determines her future. **92m/C; DVD.** Izabella Miko; Columbus Short; Jacqueline Bisset; Maria Brooks; Aubrey Dollar; ***D:*** David Petrarca; ***W:*** Kwame Nyanning; ***C:*** David A. Makin. **VIDEO**

Save the Tiger **1973 (R)** A basically honest middle-aged man sees no way out of his failing business except arson. The insurance settlement will let him pay off his creditors, and save face. David, as the arsonist, and Gilford, as Lemmon's business partner, are superb. Lemmon is also excellent throughout his performance. **100m/C; VHS, DVD.** Jack Lemmon; Jack Gilford; Laurie Heineman; Patricia Smith; Norman Burton; Thayer David; ***D:*** John G. Avildsen; ***M:*** Marvin Hamlisch. Oscars '73: Actor (Lemmon); Writers Guild '73: Orig. Screenplay.

Saved! **1/2 2004 (PG-13)** Uneven, subversive satire about teens at a fundamentalist Christian high school hits a lot of standard cliches and makes a plea for tolerance at the same time. Good girl Mary (Malone) finds out boyfriend Dean (Faust) is gay and has a vision of "curing" him through sex. She gets pregnant, which puts Mary clearly on the side of the sinners as far as the school's queen bee Hilary Faye (Moore) is concerned. Mary's situation engages the sympathy of sweet believer Patrick (Fugit), the son of the school's zealous principal, Pastor Skip (Donovan). Moore and Malone well play the opposing force of their characters and are ably supported by the rest of the cast. **92m/C; DVD, Blu-Ray.** Jena Malone; Mandy Moore; Macaulay Culkin; Patrick Fugit; Heather Matarazzo; Eva Amurri; Martin Donovan; Mary-Louise Parker; Chad Faust; Elizabeth Thai; ***Cameo(s):*** Valerie Bertinelli; ***D:*** Brian Dannelly; ***W:*** Brian Dannelly; Michael Urban; ***C:*** Bobby Bukowski; ***M:*** Christophe Beck.

Saving Christmas **WOOF!** *Kirk Cameron's Saving Christmas* **2014 (PG)** Cameron's misguided attempt to bring the reason for the season back to its biblical meaning is a heavy-handed family comedy that will only appeal to his fellow evangelical Christians. His bah-humbug brother-in-law Christian is ruining the family holiday by whining about its commercialism so Kirk has to give him a talking to (complete with some weird recreations, including an angry St. Nicholas). **80m/C; DVD.** Kirk Cameron; Darren Doane; Brigette Ridenour; ***D:*** Darren Doane; ***W:*** Darren Doane; ***C:*** Andy Patch. Golden Raspberries '14: Worst Actor (Cameron), Worst Picture, Worst Screenplay.

Saving Face **1/2 2004 (R)** Director/writer Alice Wu's debut effort adeptly explores some familiar, and not so familiar, mother/daughter themes with a Chinese-American backdrop. Ma (Chen) is disappointed that her up-and-coming surgeon daughter, Wilhelmina (Krusiec), or Wil, isn't married yet as Ma is in denial over Wil's lesbianism. Just when Wil begins a hot, new, and still-closeted romance, the 48-year-old Ma (who has lived with her parents since her husband died, as is custom) moves in after being kicked out once her pregnancy by an unnamed man is revealed, which forces the pair to confront their issues. **90m/C; DVD.** Michelle Krusiec; Joan Chen; Lynn Chen; Li Zhiyu; Shen Gung Lan; Jessica Hecht; Ato Essandoh; ***D:*** Alice Wu; ***W:*** Alice Wu; ***C:*** Harlan Bosmajian; ***M:*** Anton Sanko.

Saving God **1/2 2008 (PG-13)** Ex-con Armstrong Cane (Rhames) returns to the 'hood to serve as a minister in his father's old church. As he tries to stay on the right path, Cane counsels young dealer Norris (Murphy) to leave the thug life behind but Norris' boss Blaze (McDermott) isn't happy with the pastor's interference. Strong Christian themes without becoming overbearing. **101m/C; DVD.** Ving Rhames; Dwain Murphy; Dean McDermott; Kate Todd; Ricardo Chavira; Genelle Williams; ***D:*** Duane Crichton; ***W:*** Michael Jackson; ***C:*** Rudolf Blahacek; ***M:*** Eric Cadesky; Nick Dyer.

Saving Grace **1/2 2000 (R)** Widowed Blethyn finds out her late hubby has left her deeply in debt and in order to maintain her comfortable lifestyle, her gardener (Ferguson) suggests that she grow pot and sell it. Quaint comedy has the trademark quirky characters and gently bawdy humor you'd expect. Blethyn and Ferguson are fine, and it's all veddy cheerful. Low-key approach lends itself well to the small screen. **93m/C; VHS, DVD.** *GB* Brenda Blethyn; Craig Ferguson; Martin Clunes; Tcheky Karyo; Jamie Foreman; Valerie Edmond; Tristan Sturrock; ***D:*** Nigel Cole; ***W:*** Craig Ferguson; Mark Crowdy; ***C:*** John de Borman.

Saving Grace B. Jones **2009 (R)** Actress Connie Stevens made her directorial debut at age 70 in this uneven, melodramatic family drama based on an incident from her own childhood. In 1951, 10-year-old Carrie is sent by her parents from Brooklyn to small town Missouri to stay at the home of family friend Landy Bretthorst. Landy decides it's time to bring his sister Grace home from a mental asylum after many years, which isn't a good idea since no one seems to understand how devastating Grace's illness really is. Especially since it's exacerbated by the constant rain that threatens to flood the community. **116m/C; DVD.** Michael Biehn; Tatum O'Neal; Penelope Ann Miller; Joel Gretsch; Tricia Leigh Fisher; Piper Laurie; Scott Wilson; Rylee Fansler; ***D:*** Connie Stevens; ***W:*** Connie Stevens; Jeffry Elison; ***C:*** Denis Maloney; ***M:*** Peter Golub. **VIDEO**

Saving Mr. Banks **1/2 2013 (PG-13)** Walt Disney (Hanks) really wants to make a film version of Mary Poppins' book by P.L. Travers (Thompson), but the reclusive author doesn't want the infamous film pioneer to turn her very personal story into just another "mouse house" cartoon. Director Hancock's crowd-pleasing film tries to dig into the story behind one of the all-time most beloved movies. But the whitewashing done to the truth here is disappointing, especially the way Disney is made into an icon and Travers is demonized. The truth of the real story is muted but Hanks and Thompson make the final product nearly worth a look. **125m/C; DVD, Blu-Ray.** Tom Hanks; Emma Thompson; Paul Giamatti; Jason Schwartzman; B.J. Novak; Colin Farrell; Rachel Griffiths; Annie Rose Buckley; Bradley Whitford; Ruth Wilson; Kathy Baker; ***D:*** John Lee Hancock; ***W:*** Kelly Marcel; Sue Smith; ***C:*** John Schwartzman; ***M:*** Thomas Newman.

Saving Private Ryan **1998 (R)** Big-budget WWII Spielberg epic finds eight soldiers, led by army captain Hanks, forced to go behind enemy lines in order to rescue downed paratrooper James Ryan (Damon). He's the sole surviving brother of four soldier siblings and the government wants some good PR—the men pulling the duty are less than enthusiastic, however. Pick your favorite reviewer-speak word—gripping, moving, intense, masterpiece—any or all of them will work. The opening 25-minute graphic depiction of Omaha Beach on D-Day is, on its own, Oscar-worthy. Hanks and the rest of the cast (which included a few surprise cameos) are excellent. Spielberg deglamorizes war, without belittling the sacrifices made by those who fought. The actors (except Damon) went through boot camp in England in order to get the proper attitude. **175m/C; VHS, DVD, Blu-Ray.** Tom Hanks; Edward Burns; Tom Sizemore; Jeremy Davies; Giovanni Ribisi; Adam Goldberg; Barry Pepper; Vin Diesel; Matt Damon; Ted Danson; Dale Dye; Dennis Farina; Harve Presnell; Paul Giamatti; Bryan Cranston; David Wohl; Leland Orser; Joerg Stadler; Maximillian Martini; Amanda Boxer; Harrison Young; ***D:*** Steven Spielberg; ***W:*** Robert Rodat; Frank Darabont; ***C:*** Janusz Kaminski; ***M:*** John Williams. Oscars '98: Cinematog., Director (Spielberg), Film Editing, Sound, Sound FX Editing; British Acad. '98: Sound; Directors Guild '98: Director (Spielberg); Golden Globes '99: Director (Spielberg), Film—Drama; L.A. Film Critics '98: Cinematog., Director (Spielberg), Film; Natl. Film Reg. '14; N.Y. Film Critics '98: Film; Broadcast Film Critics '98: Director (Spielberg), Film, Score.

Saving Sarah Cain **1/2 2007 (PG)** Sarah (Pepper) is a struggling Portland newspaper columnist who travels back to her Pennsylvania Amish family for the funeral of her sister. Sarah learns that she is now the guardian of her sister's five children and she moves the kids back to the city with her, using their story as the topic of her columns. But Sarah soon realizes that she must choose between her own ambitions and what's best for the kids. Based on the novel "The Redemption of Sarah Cain" by Beverly Lewis. **103m/C; DVD.** Elliott Gould; Tess Harper; Soren Fulton; David Clennon; Lisa Pepper; Abigail Mason; ***D:*** Michael Landon, Jr.; ***W:*** Brian Bird; Cindy Kelley; ***C:*** Matthew Williams; ***M:*** Mark McKenzie. **CABLE**

Saving Shiloh **1/2 2006 (PG)** The last of the trilogy based on the Phyllis Reynolds Naylor novels finds adorable beagle Shiloh and his master, Marty (Dolley), believing that their troubled neighbor Judd (Wilson) is sincere about becoming a better person. Marty continues to stand by Judd even when the man is accused of thievery and worse. But Judd isn't all they have to worry about—there's also a watery rescue and some escaped convicts to deal with. Wholesome without being too sweet. **90m/C; DVD, Blu-Ray.** Scott Wilson; Gerald McRaney; Jason Dolley; Ann Dowd; Jordan Garrett; ***D:*** Sandy Tung; ***W:*** Dale Rosenbloom; ***C:*** Lex du Pont; ***M:*** Adam Gorgoni.

Saving Silverman *Evil Woman* **2001 (PG-13)** Testosterone-driven comedy has three buddies' bond threatened by ball-breaking fiancee of one of the boys. Peet is the whip-wielding control freak Judith Snodgrass-Fessbeggler, out to tame Neil Diamond-loving loser Darren (Biggs) and despised by best buds Wayne (Zahn) and J.D. (Black). The boys scheme to break up the duo by kidnaping Judith and re-acquainting Darren with his first love, now an aspiring nun. Black and Zahn provide much-needed comic relief, as do the scenes with their Diamond cover band. However, over-the-top characters and sophomoric humor mixed with increasingly gross gags ultimately not so much save but sink "Silverman." **90m/C; VHS, DVD.** Jason Biggs; Steve Zahn; Jack Black; Amanda Peet; R. Lee Ermey; Amanda Detmer; Neil Diamond; ***D:*** Dennis Dugan; ***W:*** Hank Nelken; Greg DePaul; ***C:*** Arthur Albert; ***M:*** Mike Simpson.

Saving Zoe **2019 (R)** After the suspicious death of Zoe (V. Marano), her younger sister, Echo (L. Marano), is left to fend for herself on her first day of high school in suburban Ohio. Their mother (Goin) is overmedicated while their father (Davis) has drowned himself in work. Yet Echo is the only one who can see Zoe, as Zoe gives her advice and reassurance through her day. At the same time, Echo is investigating the circumstances of Zoe's untimely demise. Based on a novel by Alyson Noel, the film was intended to be a step forward in Marano sisters' careers but is never more than basically competent. **95m/C; DVD.** Laura Marano; Vanessa Marano; Chris Tavarez; Giorgia Whigham; Michael Provost; ***D:*** Jeffrey G. Hunt; ***W:*** Brian J. Adams; LeeAnne H. Adams; ***C:*** Cory Geryak.

Savior **1998 (R)** After his wife and son are killed in a terrorist bombing, an American officer (Quaid) turns mercenary and assumes a new identity. As Guy, he's a soulless killing machine, working for the Serbs in Bosnia. At a prisoner exchange, he is told to take a pregnant young Serbian woman, Vera (Ninkovic), back to her village. Guy winds up delivering the baby and protecting Vera on their hazardous (and ultimately tragic) journey as he slowly regains flickers of his own humanity. Excellent change-of-pace performance by Quaid in a gut-wrenching film inspired by a true story. **104m/C; VHS, DVD.** Dennis Quaid; Natasa Ninkovic; Sergej Trifunovic; Stellan Skarsgard; Nastassja Kinski; ***D:*** Pedrag (Peter) Antonijevic; ***W:*** Robert Orr; ***C:*** Ian Wilson; ***M:*** David Robbins.

Saw **2004 (R)** Splatter film finds a serial killer named Jigsaw playing sadistic games with two men he's kidnapped: doctor Lawrence Gordon (Elwes) and photog Adam (co-writer Whannell). They're chained on opposite corners of a filthy bathroom with a corpse between them, several other items, a couple of hacksaws, and a time limit. They have to collaborate and figure out the clues left them in order to free themselves before the doc's wife and child (who are being held hostage) are killed. Oh, and the saws aren't strong enough to cut through metal but flesh and bone isn't a problem. Glover figures in as an obsessed ex-cop who's had previous dealings with Jigsaw. Lots of gruesome flashbacks and various cheap scares. **100m/C; DVD, Blu-Ray, UMD.** Tobin Bell; Ned Bellamy; Cary Elwes; Danny Glover; Ken Leung; Dina Meyer; Monica Potter; Shawnee Smith; Makenzie Vega; Leigh Whannell; ***D:*** James Wan; ***W:*** Leigh Whannell; ***C:*** David A. Armstrong; ***M:*** Charlie Clouser.

Saw 2 **2005 (R)** Since the sequel is just more of the same, if you liked the first one, you'll find this outing equally sadistic, disgusting, and enjoyable. Sicko Jigsaw (Bell) has trapped eight victims in a house with a number of booby traps that will force them to play his life-or-death games. One victim is the teenaged son (Knudsen) of the detective (Wahlberg) who has captured the madman. Of course, the groundwork is laid for more sequels. **93m/C; DVD, Blu-Ray, UMD.** Tobin Bell; Shawnee Smith; Donnie Wahlberg; Erik Knudsen; Franky G.; Glenn Plummer; Beverley Mitchell; Dina Meyer; Emmanuelle Vaugier; ***D:*** Darren Lynn Bousman; ***W:*** Darren Lynn Bousman; Leigh Whannell; ***C:*** David A. Armstrong; ***M:*** Charlie Clouser.

Saw 3 **1/2 2006 (R)** With death sequences so unnecessarily elaborate, even fans of the franchise may be tiring of the gore. Along with accomplice Amanda (Smith), a dying Jigsaw (Bell) kidnaps surgeon Lynn (Soomekh), with the hope that she can remove his brain tumor. A difficult procedure, especially when you're wearing an explosive neck brace that will detonate if your patient's heart rate flatlines. Distracting flashbacks supposedly offer motivations for the actions but, by now, the franchise lacks the surprise of the original. **107m/C; DVD, Blu-Ray.** Tobin Bell; Shawnee Smith; Angus MacFadyen; Dina Meyer; Bahar Soomekh; Mpho Koaho; Debra McCabe; Donnie Wahlberg; Barry Flatman; Lyriq Bent; Costas Mandylor; Betsy Russell; ***D:*** Darren Lynn Bousman; ***W:*** Leigh Whannell; ***C:*** David A. Armstrong; ***M:*** Charlie Clouser.

Saw 3D: The Final Chapter *Saw 7* **2010 (R)** The 7th and allegedly last chapter in the tedious franchise turns to 3D in an effort to deliver some shocks. Self-help guru Bobby Dagen (Flanery) is on a promotional book tour, claiming to be a survivor of Jigsaw torture. Except he was never a victim—until he winds up in a cage about to really experience what he only lied about. There are flashbacks so various characters can continue to make appearances, including Jigsaw (Bell) himself. **90m/C; DVD, Blu-Ray.** Cary Elwes; Sean Patrick Flanery; Costas Mandylor; Betsy Russell; Gina Holden; Tobin Bell; Chad E. Donella; ***D:*** Kevin Greutert; ***W:*** Marcus Dunstan; Patrick Melton; ***C:*** Brian Gedge; ***M:*** Andrew Coutts; Charlie Clouser.

Saw 4 WOOF! 2007 (R) John/Jigsaw (Bell) is at it again in this bloody mesh of soft-core porn and horror that "Saw" fans have come to expect from director Bousman, this time doling out his special brand of moral murder from the afterlife. At the autopsy, a tape recorder is found in John's stomach echoing the killer's words and setting the scene for the fourth installment as his murder-machines continue all that yucky butchering in his absence. Flashbacks are thrown in between the gore and the (ahem) plot, offering glimpses into just what made this formerly successful and previously normal guy into the film franchise he is today. Pop the corn and settle in if you must, but this "Saw" ends up being about as sharp as a butter knife. **108m/C; Blu-Ray, On Demand.** Tobin Bell; Costas Mandylor; Scott Patterson; Betsy Russell; Lyriq Bent; Athena Karkanis; Billy Otis; ***D:*** Darren Lynn Bousman; ***W:*** Patrick Melton; Marcus Dunstan; ***C:*** David A. Armstrong; ***M:*** Charlie Clouser.

Saw 5 2008 (R) Money-making horror franchises have taught us one thing. Even if dead, the killer will always return for a paycheck. Jigsaw (Bell) is back for another postmortem torture game, this time involving an FBI agent, who, after escaping death, begins to unravel the mystery behind a shady cop who survived the previous sequel. Relentless flashbacks using recycled footage, and disjointed editing makes this just another cheap, confusing notch on the blade. **92m/C; DVD, Blu-Ray.** Tobin Bell; Shawnee Smith; Costas Mandylor; Julie Benz; Scott Patterson; Meagan Good; Betsy Russell; Carlo Rota; ***D:*** David Hackl; ***W:*** Patrick Melton; Marcus Dunstan; ***C:*** David A. Armstrong; ***M:*** Charlie Clouser.

Saw 6 2009 (R) Hasn't this franchise's blade become dull yet? Because it's certainly lost its edge—even the torture scenes. Agent Strahm is really dead and Hoffman has taken over Jigsaw's (who's seen in flashbacks and recorded messages) legacy. This time the main victims are evil insurance company executives—one of whom denied Jigsaw experimental gene treatment for his cancer. **90m/C; Blu-Ray, On Demand.** Costas Mandylor; Mark Rolston; Betsy Russell; Tobin Bell; Shawnee Smith; Peter Outerbridge; Athena Karkanis; George Newbern; ***D:*** Kevin Greutert; ***W:*** Marcus Dunstan; Patrick Melton; ***C:*** David A. Armstrong; ***M:*** Charlie Clouser.

Sawdust & Tinsel *The Naked Night; Sunset of a Clown; Gycklarnas Afton* **1953** Early Bergman film detailing the grisly, humiliating experiences of a traveling circus rolling across the barren Swedish countryside. Lonely parable of human relationships. In Swedish with English subtitles. **87m/B; VHS, DVD, Blu-Ray.** *SW* Harriet Andersson; Ake Gronberg; ***D:*** Ingmar Bergman; ***W:*** Ingmar Bergman.

Say Anything 1989 (PG-13) A semi-mature, successful teen romance about an offbeat loner Lloyd Dobler (Cusack, in a winning performance), whose interested in the martial arts and going after the beautiful class brain, Diane Court (Skye), of his high school. Things are complicated when her father James (Mahoney) is suspected of embezzling by the IRS. Joan Cusack, John's real-life sister, also plays his sister in the film. Works well on the romantic level without getting too sticky. **100m/C; VHS, DVD, Blu-Ray.** John Cusack; Ione Skye; John Mahoney; Joan Cusack; Lili Taylor; Richard Portnow; Pamela Segall; Jason Gould; Loren Dean; Bebe Neuwirth; Aimee Brooks; Eric Stoltz; Chynna Phillips; Joanna Frank; Jeremy Piven; Don "The Dragon" Wilson; ***D:*** Cameron Crowe; ***W:*** Cameron Crowe; ***C:*** Laszlo Kovacs; ***M:*** Anne Dudley; Richard Gibbs; Nancy Wilson.

Say Hello to Yesterday 1/2 **1971 (PG)** A May-December romance that takes place entirely in one day. An unhappy housewife meets an exciting young traveler while both are in London. Cast and director try hard but fail to get the point across to the audience. **91m/C; VHS, DVD.** *GB* Jean Simmons; Leonard Whiting; Evelyn Laye; ***D:*** Alvin Rakoff.

Say It Isn't So 1/2 **2001 (R)** The Farrelly brothers produced this tale of boy-meets-girl, boy-gets-girl, boy-finds-out-girl-is-his-sister. Good-guy orphan Gilly (Klein) meets cute with Jo (Graham), an inept hairdresser with the most screwed-up family this side of the Mansons. Her mom (Field) decides Gilly isn't upwardly mobile enough so she makes everyone think the couple are kin. Gilly sets out to set things right amid Farrelly-approved gross-out gags and humiliations galore. First-time helmer Rogers lacks the Farrelly sense of timing and sentiment, which results in most of the jokes falling flat or not developing at all. **95m/C; DVD.** Chris Klein; Heather Graham; Orlando Jones; Sally Field; Richard Jenkins; John Rothman; Jack Plotnick; Eddie Cibrian; Mark Pellegrino; Richard Riehle; Brent Briscoe; Henry Cho; Suzanne Somers; Brent Hinkley; ***D:*** James B. Rogers; ***W:*** Peter Gaulke; Gerry Swallow; ***C:*** Mark Irwin; ***M:*** Mason Daring.

Say It With Songs 1/2 **1929** Carousing radio singer Joe Lane (Jolson) accidentally kills his boss Arthur (Thomson) after he made a sleazy pass at Joe's neglected missus Katherine (Nixon). While Joe's in prison, Katherine goes back to work as a nurse to support herself and their son (Lee) and surgeon Burnes (Bowers) falls for her. Joe gets paroled but more heartbreak follows. Jolson's first full-length, all-talkie (plus the usual singing) film. **95m/B; DVD.** Al Jolson; Davey Lee; Marion (Marian) Nixon; John Bowers; Holmes Herbert; Kenneth Thomson; ***D:*** Lloyd Bacon; ***W:*** Joseph Jackson; ***C:*** Lee Garmes.

Say Nothing 2001 (R) While on vacation by herself, unhappy Grace (Kinski) has a one-nighter with wealthy Julian (Baldwin) who becomes obsessed and wants to get her away from her unemployed husband Matt (Bochner). He even hires Matt to work at his company—much to Grace's distress. A low-budget "Fatal Attraction" minus the boiled bunny. **94m/C; VHS, DVD.** Nastassja Kinski; William Baldwin; Hart Bochner; Michelle Duquet; ***D:*** Allan Moyle; ***W:*** Madeline Sunshine; ***C:*** Walter Bal. **CABLE**

Say One for Me 1959 Generally unconvincing musical comedy. Father Conroy (Crosby) has a New York parish that caters to showbiz folk. Naive Holly (Reynolds) gets a job as a dancer in a skeevy nightclub managed by slick Tony Vincent (Wagner) and the priest warns Tony not to take advantage. Tony later insists he's serious about the girl and things come to an unlikely resolution at the charity TV show Conroy is hosting. **120m/C; DVD.** Bing Crosby; Debbie Reynolds; Robert Wagner; Ray Walston; Les Tremayne; ***D:*** Frank Tashlin; ***W:*** Robert O'Brien; ***C:*** Leo Tover; ***M:*** Lionel Newman.

Say Uncle 2005 (R) Paul (Paige) dotes excessively on his young godson and is devastated when he learns the boy and his family are moving to Japan. So he decides to take his surrogate parenting to the local park where the watchful mothers eye this man-child with suspicion, especially after he admits to mom Maggie (Najimy) that he's gay. Paul's actions may be misconstrued but he behaves stupidly as well, although Maggie is little more than a one-note hysteric. Paige's directorial debut. **91m/C; DVD.** Peter Paige; Kathy Najimy; Anthony Clark; Melanie Lynskey; Gabrielle Union; Lisa Edelstein; ***D:*** Peter Paige; ***W:*** Peter Paige; ***C:*** David Makin; ***M:*** Kurt Swinghammer.

Sayonara 1957 An Army major is assigned to a Japanese airbase during the Korean conflict at the behest of his future father-in-law. Dissatisfied with his impending marriage, he finds himself drawn to a Japanese dancer and becomes involved in the affairs of his buddy who, against official policy, marries a Japanese woman. Tragedy surrounds the themes of bigotry and interracial marriage. Based on the novel by James Michener. **147m/C; VHS, DVD, Blu-Ray.** Marlon Brando; James Garner; Ricardo Montalban; Patricia Owens; Red Buttons; Miyoshi Umeki; Martha Scott; Kent Smith; Miiko Taka; ***D:*** Joshua Logan; ***W:*** Paul Osborn; ***C:*** Ellsworth Fredericks; ***M:*** Franz Waxman. Oscars '57: Art Dir./Set Dec., Sound, Support. Actor (Buttons), Support. Actress (Umeki); Golden Globes '58: Support. Actor (Buttons).

The Scalphunters 1/2 **1968** Semi-successful, semi-funny western about an itinerant trapper (Lancaster) who is forced by Indians to trade his pelts for an educated black slave (Davis); many chases and brawls ensue. Good performances. **102m/C; VHS, DVD, Blu-Ray.** Burt Lancaster; Ossie Davis; Telly Savalas; Shelley Winters; Nick Cravat; Dabney Coleman; Paul Picerni; ***D:*** Sydney Pollack; ***W:*** William W. Norton, Sr.; ***M:*** Elmer Bernstein.

Scalps 1983 (R) Hunted Indian princess and man whose family was killed by Indians form uneasy alliance in old West. **90m/C; VHS, DVD, Blu-Ray.** Karen Wood; Alberto Farnese; Benny Cardosa; Charlie Bravo; Vassili Garis; ***D:*** Werner Knox.

The Scamp 1/2 *Strange Affection* **1957** Neglected 10-year-old Tod is victimized by his drunken father so schoolteacher Stephen Leigh and his wife Barbara try to get him moved somewhere safe. But the situation worsens and, when Tod thinks he's committed a horrible crime, he runs to the Leighs for help. **88m/B; DVD.** *GB* Richard Attenborough; Dorothy Allison; Colin Petersen; Terence Morgan; Jill Adams; ***D:*** Wolf Rilla; ***W:*** Wolf Rilla; ***C:*** Freddie Francis; ***M:*** Francis Chagrin.

Scandal *Shuban* **1950** Handsome artist (Mifune) and beautiful concert singer (Yamaguchi) become the victims of a libelous article in a gossip magazine. The artist decides to sue but, being softhearted, chooses a questionable lawyer because the man's young daughter is dying. Then the unethical lawyer accepts a bribe to prejudice the case. Japanese with subtitles. **105m/B; VHS, DVD.** *JP* Toshiro Mifune; Takashi Shimura; Yoshiko (Shirley) Yamaguchi; ***D:*** Akira Kurosawa; ***W:*** Ryuzo Kikushima; Akira Kurosawa; ***M:*** Fumio Hayasaka.

Scandal 1989 (R) A dramatization of Britain's Profumo government sex scandal of the 1960s. Hurt plays a society doctor who enjoys introducing pretty girls to his wealthy friends. One of the girls, Christine Keeler, takes as lovers both a Russian government official and a British Cabinet Minister. The resulting scandal eventually overturned an entire political party, and led to disgrace, prison, and death for some of those concerned. Also available in an unedited 115-minute version which contains more controversial language and nudity. Top-notch performances make either version well worth watching. **105m/C; VHS, DVD; Open Captioned.** *GB* John Hurt; Joanne Whalley; Ian McKellen; Bridget Fonda; Jeroen Krabbe; Britt Ekland; Roland Gift; Daniel Massey; Leslie Phillips; Richard Morant; ***D:*** Michael Caton-Jones; ***W:*** Michael Thomas; ***C:*** Mike Molloy; ***M:*** Carl Davis.

Scandal at Scourie 1953 Garson and Pidgeon team up for the ninth and final time in this family melodrama set in Ontario, Canada. Childless Victoria and Patrick McChesney decide to adopt Patsy, a young Catholic orphan, which upsets their Protestant community. Patrick is accused of currying favor with voters to advance his political career while Victoria must deal with gossip about the girl's past, especially when Patsy runs away after being accused of setting a fire. **90m/C; DVD.** Greer Garson; Walter Pidgeon; Donna Corcoran; Agnes Moorehead; Philip Ober; Arthur Shields; ***D:*** Jean Negulesco; ***W:*** Karl Tunberg; Leonard Spigelgass; Norman Corwin; ***C:*** Robert Planck; ***M:*** Daniele Amfitheatrof.

A Scandal in Paris 1/2 *Thieves Holiday* **1946** Based on the real-life escapades of 19th-century criminal Francois Eugene Vidocq. Vidocq (Sanders) escapes from prison, briefly joins Napoleon's army, and catches the eye of Therese (Hasso), whose father is an important official. Under an assumed name, Vidocq joins the Paris police force in order to perpetrate his biggest crime. Instead, thanks to Therese's love, he goes straight. Sanders does an excellent job. **100m/B; VHS, DVD.** George Sanders; Signe Hasso; Akim Tamiroff; Carole Landis; Gene Lockhart; Alan Napier; Vladimir Sokoloff; Alma Kruger; ***D:*** Douglas Sirk; ***W:*** Ellis St. Joseph; ***C:*** Guy Roe; ***M:*** Hanns Eisler; Heinz Roemheld.

Scandal Sheet 1/2 **1952** Crawford is compelling as bullying editor Mark Chapman, who turns a respected New York newspaper into a tabloid and boosts circulation through a series of stunts. Protege reporter McCleary (Derek) thinks it's great but writer gal pal Julie (Reed) finds Chapman a sleaze. Chapman's past comes back to haunt him and he's involved in a murder, which is then investigated by McCleary who turns out to be more tenacious that Chapman gave him credit for. Based on Samuel Fuller's novel "The Dark Page." **82m/B; DVD.** Broderick Crawford; John Derek; Donna Reed; Rosemary DeCamp; Henry O'Neill; Harry (Henry) Morgan; James Millican; Jonathan Hale; ***D:*** Phil Karlson; ***W:*** Ted Sherdeman; James Poe; Eugene Ling; ***C:*** Burnett Guffey; ***M:*** George Duning.

Scandalous John 1971 (G) Comedy western about a last cattle drive devised by an aging cowboy (Keith) in order to save his ranch. Keith's shrewd acting as the ornery cattle man who won't sell to developers carries this one. **113m/C; VHS, Streaming.** Brian Keith; Alfonso Arau; Michele Carey; Rick Lenz; John Ritter; Harry (Henry) Morgan; ***D:*** Robert Butler.

A Scanner Darkly 1/2 **2006 (R)** Trippy, faithful adaptation of Philip K. Dick's 1977 novel of the same name forecasts a blurry, drug-fueled world of paranoia in which the government not only listens to phone calls but watches its denizens through ambiguous undercover police whose identities are secret even to their bosses. Fred (Reeves) is one such agent, ordered to spy on his pill-popping friends (Downey Jr., Harrelson, Cochrane, and Ryder) and the owner of the house where they drop in to check out, who happens to be another incarnation of himself. Confusing? That's the point. Director Linklater utilizes a technique known as "interpolated rotoscoping," essentially digitally adding a layer of animation over footage of live actors, which effectively enhances the altered-states feel. **102m/C; DVD, Blu-Ray, HD-DVD.** Keanu Reeves; Winona Ryder; Robert Downey, Jr.; Woody Harrelson; Rory Cochrane; Melody Chase; Lisa Marie Newmyer; ***D:*** Richard Linklater; ***W:*** Richard Linklater; ***C:*** Shane Kelly; ***M:*** Graham Reynolds.

Scanners 1/2 **1981 (R)** "Scanners" are telepaths who can will people to explode. One scanner in particular harbors Hitlerian aspirations for his band of psychic gangsters. Gruesome but effective special effects. **102m/C; VHS, DVD, Blu-Ray.** *CA* Stephen Lack; Jennifer O'Neill; Patrick McGoohan; Lawrence Dane; Michael Ironside; Robert A. Silverman; ***D:*** David Cronenberg; ***W:*** David Cronenberg; ***C:*** Mark Irwin; ***M:*** Howard Shore.

Scanners: The Showdown 1/2 **1994 (R)** Carl Volkin (Kilpatrick), the "scanner" killer, has escaped jail and is stalking the streets of L.A. His ultimate target is Sam Staziak (Quinn), the scanner cop who sent him away. Since Volkin's powers grow with every kill, Staziak better get to Volkin in a hurry. **95m/C; VHS, DVD.** Patrick Kilpatrick; Daniel Quinn; Khrystyne Haje; Stephen Mendel; Brenda Swanson; Jewel Shepard; Robert Forster; ***D:*** Steve Barnett; ***W:*** Mark Sevi.

The Scapegoat 1/2 **1959** Solitary teacher John Barratt (Guinness) meets his double, Count Jacques De Gue, while on vacation. After a drunken night, De Gue vanishes, and Barratt can't convince anyone he's not the scheming Frenchman. Barratt discovers a deadly plot's been set in motion and he's been set up to be the, well the title says it all. Based on the Daphne du Maurier novel. **92m/B; DVD.** *UK* Alec Guinness; Bette Davis; Irene Worth; Nicole Maurey; Peter Bull; Pamela Brown; Geoffrey Keen; ***D:*** Robert Hamer; ***W:*** Robert Hamer; Gore Vidal; ***C:*** Paul Beeson; ***M:*** Bronislau Kaper.

The Scapegoat 1/2 **2012** Remake of the 1959 pic, based on the Daphne Du Maurier mystery, is far-fetched but compelling and benefits from its good cast. In 1953, unattached schoolteacher John Standing (Rhys) loses his job and is drowning his sorrows in a pub when he meets his double, Johnny Spence. Spence gets Standing drunk and steals his nondescript identity, so Standing decides to assume Johnny's life for a bt. He soon discovers the wastrel had made a mess, nearly ruining the family business and the family as well, so Standing decides to put things right. **107m/C; DVD.** *UK* Matthew Rhys; Eileen Atkins; Alice Orr-Ewing; Sheridan Smith; Andrew Scott; Jodhi May; Sylvie Testud; ***D:*** Charles Sturridge; ***W:*** Charles Sturridge; ***C:*** Matt Gray; ***M:*** Adrian Johnston.

The Scar ♪♪ 1/2 *Hollow Triumph* **1948** A cunning criminal robs the mob, then hides by "stealing" the identity of a lookalike psychologist. But he's overlooked one thing...or two. Farfetched film noir showcases a rare villainous role for Henreid (who also produced). Based on a novel by Murray Forbes. **83m/B; VHS, DVD, Blu-Ray.** Paul Henreid; Joan Bennett; Eduard Franz; Leslie Brooks; John Qualen; Mabel Paige; Herbert Rudley; ***D:*** Steve Sekely.

Scar WOOF! 2007 (R) Torture porn originally shot in 3D. Joan Burrows (Bettis) returns to her hometown after 16 years to see her niece Olympia (Blanton) graduate from high school. Joan left after escaping from mortician/serial killer Ernie Bishop (Cotton), although she bears more than one kind of scar from the experience. Now Olympia's classmates are becoming new victims; is it a copycat or has Ernie returned? **90m/C; DVD, Blu-Ray.** Angela Bettis; Christopher Titus; Kirby Bliss Blanton; Ben Cotton; Devon Graye; Tegan Moss; Al Sapienza; Monika Mar-Lee; ***D:*** Jed Weintrob; ***W:*** Zack Ford; ***C:*** Toshiaki Ozawa; ***M:*** Roger Neill.

The Scar of Shame ♪♪ **1927** Explores the ill-fated romance between a successful black concert pianist and the lower-class woman he marries. Gives a look at the color caste system and divisions within the black community of the era. **90m/B; Silent; DVD, Blu-Ray.** Harry Henderson; Lucia Lynn Moses; Ann Kennedy; Norman Johnstone; ***D:*** Frank Peregini.

Scaramouche ♪♪ **1923** Based on Rafael Sabatini's historical novel. Orphaned Andre-Louis Moreau (Novarro) is an outspoken opponent of the aristocracy during the French Revolution. He must flee the wrath of cruel swordsman, the Marquis de la Tour d'Azyr (Stone), who also desires Alice (Terry), the daughter of Moreau's patron. Moreau joins a traveling acting troupe, disguising himself as roguish clown Scaramouche, while he practices his swordsmanship until the inevitable showdown with the Marquis. **123m/B; Silent; DVD.** Ramon Novarro; Lewis Stone; Alice Terry; Lloyd Ingraham; Julia Swayne Gordon; George Siegmann; ***D:*** Rex Ingram; ***W:*** Willis Goldbeck; ***C:*** John Seitz.

Scaramouche ♪♪♪ 1/2 **1952** Thrilling swashbuckler about a nobleman (Granger, very well cast) searching for his family during the French Revolution. To avenge the death of a friend, he joins a theatre troupe where he learns swordplay and becomes the character "Scaramouche." Features a rousing six-and-a-half-minute sword battle. **111m/C; VHS, DVD.** Stewart Granger; Eleanor Parker; Janet Leigh; Mel Ferrer; Henry Wilcoxon; Nina Foch; Richard Anderson; Robert Coote; Lewis Stone; Elisabeth Risdon; Howard Freeman; ***D:*** George Sidney; ***C:*** Charles Rosher.

Scarecrow ♪♪ 1/2 **1973 (R)** Two homeless drifters (Hackman and Pacino) walk across America, heading toward a car wash business they never reach. An oft-neglected example of the early 70s extra-realistic subgenre initiated by "Midnight Cowboy." Engrossing until the end, when it falls flat. Filmed on location in Detroit. **112m/C; VHS, DVD, Blu-Ray.** Gene Hackman; Al Pacino; Ann Wedgeworth; Eileen Brennan; Richard Lynch; Fredric Myrow; Penelope Allen; Dorothy Tristan; Rutanya Alda; ***D:*** Jerry Schatzberg; ***W:*** Garry Michael White; ***C:*** Vilmos Zsigmond. Cannes '73: Film.

Scared Silent ♪♪ **2002** Based on a true story. Kathy Clifson (Miller) is happily married to Doug (Diamond), the police chief of Freemont, Minnesota. At least until Doug hires new deputy John McCrane (Jackson) and Kathy realizes he's the man who raped her as a teenager. He used his badge to intimidate her then and he also did it with other women who come together to get justice from a system that is protecting a fellow officer. **90m/C; DVD.** Penelope Ann Miller; Reed Edward Diamond; Andrew Jackson; Lisa Repo Martell; Shannon Lawson; Marnie McPhail; Matt Craven; ***D:*** Mike Robe; ***W:*** Richard Leder; ***C:*** Eric Van Haren Noman; ***M:*** Laura Karpman. **CABLE**

Scared Stiff ♪♪♪ **1953** Fleeing a murder charge, Martin and Lewis find gangsters and ghosts on a Caribbean island. Funny and scary, a good remake of "The Ghost Breakers," with cameos by Hope and Crosby. **108m/B; DVD.** Dean Martin; Jerry Lewis; Lizabeth Scott; Carmen Miranda; Dorothy Malone; ***Cameo(s):*** Bob Hope; Bing Crosby; ***D:*** George Marshall; ***W:*** Herbert Baker; Walter DeLeon; ***C:*** Ernest Laszlo; ***M:*** Leith Stevens.

Scared to Death ♪ **1980 (R)** A scientific experiment goes awry as a mutation begins killing off the residents of Los Angeles. **93m/C; VHS, DVD.** John Stinson; Diana Davidson; David Moses; Kermit Eller; ***D:*** William Malone; ***M:*** Tom Chase.

Scarface ♪♪♪ *Scarface: The Shame of a Nation* **1931** The violent rise and fall of 1930s Chicago crime boss Tony Camonte—magnetically played by Muni—and based on the life of notorious gangster Al Capone. Release was held back by censors due to the amount of violence and its suggestion of incest between the title character and his sister (Dvorak). Morley is ice-cold as Tony's moll Poppy. Producer Howard Hughes recut and filmed an alternate ending, without director Hawks' approval, to pacify the censors, and both versions of the film were released at the same time. Almost too violent and intense at the time. Remains brilliant and impressive. Remade in 1983. **93m/B; VHS, DVD, Blu-Ray.** Paul Muni; Ann Dvorak; Karen Morley; Osgood Perkins; George Raft; Boris Karloff; W.R. Burnett; Ben Hecht; John Lee Mahin; Seton I. Miller; ***D:*** Howard Hawks; ***W:*** Fred Pasley; ***C:*** Lee Garmes; ***M:*** Gus Arnheim; Adolph Tandler. Natl. Film Reg. '94.

Scarface ♪♪♪ **1983 (R)** Al Pacino is a Cuban refugee who becomes powerful in the drug trade until the life gets the better of him. A remake of the 1932 classic gangster film of the same name, although the first film has more plot. Extremely violent, often unpleasant, but not easily forgotten. **170m/C; VHS, DVD, Blu-Ray, UMD.** Al Pacino; Steven Bauer; Michelle Pfeiffer; Robert Loggia; F. Murray Abraham; Mary Elizabeth Mastrantonio; Harris Yulin; Paul Shenar; Oliver Stone; Pepe Serna; Mark Margolis; Richard Belzer; Victor Campos; Gregg Henry; ***D:*** Brian De Palma; ***W:*** Oliver Stone; ***C:*** John A. Alonzo; ***M:*** Giorgio Moroder.

The Scarlet & the Black ♪♪ 1/2 **1983** A priest clandestinely works within the shield of the Vatican's diplomatic immunity to shelter allied soldiers from the Nazis in occupied Rome. His efforts put him at odds with the Pope and target him for Gestapo assassination. Swashbuckling adventure at its second-best. Based on the nonfiction book "The Scarlet Pimpernel of the Vatican" by J.P. Gallagher. **145m/C; VHS, DVD.** Gregory Peck; Christopher Plummer; John Gielgud; Raf Vallone; Angelo Infanti; ***D:*** Jerry London; ***M:*** Ennio Morricone. **TV**

Scarlet Claw ♪♪♪ *Sherlock Holmes and the Scarlet Claw* **1944** Holmes and Watson solve the bloody murder of an old lady in the creepy Canadian village of Le Mort Rouge. The best and most authentic of the Sherlock Holmes series. **74m/B; VHS, DVD.** Basil Rathbone; Nigel Bruce; Miles Mander; Gerald Hamer; Kay Harding; ***D:*** Roy William Neill.

The Scarlet Clue ♪♪ **1945** A better script and faster pacing improved this Monogram entry in the Chan series. Charlie investigates a series of mysterious deaths which lead to a plot to steal secret government radar plans. **65m/B; VHS, DVD.** Sidney Toler; Benson Fong; Mantan Moreland; Robert E. Homans; Helen Devereaux; ***D:*** Phil Rosen.

The Scarlet Coat ♪♪ **1955** Revolutionary War adventure. Top secret information is recovered from a dead British spy, and American agent John Boulton (Wilde) poses as an Army deserter to find the traitor. This leads him to the commander of West Point--General Benedict Arnold (Douglas). Talky but the Technicolor cinematography and New York locations help. **101m/C; DVD.** Cornel Wilde; Michael Wilding; Anne Francis; Robert Douglas; George Sanders; John McIntire; John Dehner; ***D:*** John Sturges; ***W:*** Karl Tunberg; ***C:*** Paul Vogel; ***M:*** Conrad Salinger.

Scarlet Diva ♪♪ **2000** Writer/director/star Argento, daughter of Italian horror director Dario Argento, explores the trappings of fame in her semi-autobiographical debut. As Anna Battista, Argento is an Italian actress tired of her success and looking for love and fulfillment. Anna's mother (Argento's real life mother, Nicolodi), glimpsed in flashbacks, died of a methadone overdose, and her childhood in general has clearly left her damaged. She becomes easy prey for Hollywood vultures like the lascivious producer (Coleman) who wants to cast her in a "Cleopatra" remake opposite Robert De Niro. Back in Rome, Anna's decadent lifestyle is briefly interrupted when she falls in love with an Australian rock star (Shepherd) who promptly leaves her pregnant and devastated. Strangely watchable, but wildly formless style and digital video format matches pic's equally rambling writing and acting. In English, French, and Italian. **91m/C; VHS, DVD, Blu-Ray.** *IT* Asia Argento; Daria Nicolodi; Joe Coleman; Francesca D'Aloja; Jean Shepard; Herbert Fritsch; Gianluca Arcopinto; ***D:*** Asia Argento; ***W:*** Asia Argento; ***C:*** Frederic Fasano.

Scarlet Empress ♪♪♪ 1/2 **1934** One of Von Sternberg's greatest films tells the story of Catherine the Great and her rise to power. Dietrich stars as the beautiful royal wife who outwits her foolish husband Peter (Jaffe) to become empress of Russia. Incredibly rich decor is a visual feast for the eye, as perfectionist von Sternberg fussed over every detail. Dietrich is excellent as Catherine, and von Sternberg's mastery of lighting and camera work makes for a highly extravagant film. Based on the diary of Catherine the Great. **110m/B; VHS, DVD, Blu-Ray.** Marlene Dietrich; John Lodge; Sam Jaffe; Louise Dresser; Maria Sieber; Sir C. Aubrey Smith; Ruthelma Stevens; Olive Tell; ***D:*** Josef von Sternberg; ***W:*** Manuel Komroff; ***C:*** Bert Glennon.

The Scarlet Letter ♪♪ **1934** Unlikely comic relief provides only measure of redemption for this poorly rendered version of Hawthorne's classic novel about sin and Hester Prynne. **69m/B; VHS, DVD.** Colleen Moore; Hardie Albright; Henry B. Walthall; Alan Hale; Cora Sue Collins; Betty Blythe; ***D:*** Robert G. Vignola.

The Scarlet Letter ♪♪♪ **1973** A studied, thoughtful, international production of the Nathaniel Hawthorne classic about a woman's adultery which incites puritanical violence and hysteria in colonial America. Fine modernization by Wenders. In German with English subtitles. **90m/C; VHS, DVD.** *SP GE* Senta Berger; Lou Castel; Yella Rottlaender; William Layton; Yelena Samarina; Hans-Christian Blech; ***D:*** Wim Wenders.

The Scarlet Letter ♪♪♪ **1979** Faithful yet passionate TV adaptation of Hawthorne's classic novel of 17th-century New England. Hester Prynne (Foster) is condemned by her Puritan fellows for having a child out of wedlock and is forced to wear a scarlet letter A for adultery. Secretly sharing Hester's torment is the Rev. Arthur Dimmesdale (Heard), the baby's father, and Hester's vengeful back-from-the-dead husband, Roger Chillingsworth (Conway). **240m/C; VHS, DVD.** Meg Foster; John Heard; Kevin Conway; Josef Sommer; ***D:*** Rick Hauser; ***W:*** Allan Knee; Alvin Sapinsley; ***M:*** John Morris.

The Scarlet Letter WOOF! 1995 (R) Ewwwwww—ego-driven stinker of '95 ("Showgirls" not-withstanding). Feisty Hester Prynne (Moore) is condemned to wear the scarlet letter "A" of adultery by her 17th-century Puritan neighbors because she bore a child out of wedlock. Oldman is the lusty Reverend Arthur Dimmesdale (her partner in illicit passion) while Duvall chews scenery as Hester's wronged hubby. This "freely adapted" version of the 1850 American classic should have set author Nathaniel Hawthorne spinning in his grave as his moral saga of sin and redemption meets 20th-century moviemaking by having the passion made explicit and a happy ending tacked on. **135m/C; VHS, DVD, Blu-Ray.** Demi Moore; Gary Oldman; Robert Duvall; Robert Prosky; Edward Hardwicke; Joan Plowright; Roy Dotrice; Dana Ivey; Sheldon Peters Wolfchild; Diane Salinger; Lisa Jolliff-Andoh; Amy Wright; Tim Woodward; ***D:*** Roland Joffé; ***W:*** Douglas Day Stewart; ***C:*** Alex Thomson; ***M:*** John Barry. Golden Raspberries '95: Worst Remake/Sequel.

The Scarlet Pimpernel ♪♪♪ 1/2 **1934** Sir Percy Blakeney (Howard) is a supposed dandy of the English court who assumes the identity of "The Scarlet Pimpernel" in order to outwit the French Republicans and aid innocent aristocrats during the French Revolution. The frustrated French send sinister ambassador Chauvelin (Massey) to discover the rogue's identity and involve Blakeney's French wife, Marguerite (Oberon) in their plot. Classic rendering of Baroness Orczy's novel, full of exploits, 18th century costumes, intrigue, damsels, etc. Produced by Alexander Korda, who fired the initial director, Rowland Brown. Remade twice for TV. **95m/B; DVD.** *UK* Leslie Howard; Joan Gardner; Merle Oberon; Raymond Massey; Anthony Bushell; Nigel Bruce; Bramwell Fletcher; Walter Rilla; O.B. Clarence; Ernest Milton; Edmund Breon; Melville Cooper; Gibb McLaughlin; Morland Graham; Allan Jeayes; ***D:*** Harold Young; ***W:*** Robert Sherwood; Arthur Wimperis; Lajos Biro; ***C:*** Harold Rosson; ***M:*** Arthur Benjamin.

The Scarlet Pimpernel ♪♪♪ **1982** Remake of the classic about a British dandy who saved French aristocrats from the Reign of Terror guillotines during the French Revolution. Almost as good as the original 1935 film, with beautiful costumes and sets and good performances from Seymour and Andrews. **142m/C; VHS, DVD.** *GB* Anthony Andrews; Jane Seymour; Ian McKellen; James Villiers; Eleanor David; ***D:*** Clive Donner; ***M:*** Nick Bicat. **TV**

The Scarlet Pimpernel ♪♪ 1/2 **1999** Wealthy, foppish English aristocrat, Sir Percy Blakeney (Grant), is not the fool he seems. Indeed, he masquerades as the daring Scarlet Pimpernel, the rescuer of those persecuted by the French Revolution, and the bane of French spy Chauvelin (Shaw). Why Percy has even managed to fool his lovely French wife, Marguerite (McGovern), who was once involved with Chauvelin, and who comes to see her husband in a more heroic light. Based on the novels by Baroness Emmuska Orczy. **120m/C; VHS, DVD.** Richard E. Grant; Elizabeth McGovern; Martin Shaw; Anthony Green; Ronan Vibert; Christopher Fairbank; Jonathan Coy; Emilia Fox; Dominic Mafham; ***D:*** Patrick Lau; ***W:*** Richard Carpenter; ***C:*** Simon Kossoff; ***M:*** Michael Pavlicek. **CABLE**

The Scarlet Pimpernel 2: Mademoiselle Guillotine ♪♪ 1/2 **1999** The Scarlet Pimpernel and wife Marguerite head to France to save the daughter of a French nobleman from the clutches of Gabrielle Damiens (Black), AKA Mademoiselle Guillotine, and her band of revolutionaries. The disgraced Chauvelin is also involved and then Marguerite gets captured, so quite a lot of rescuing needs to be done. Based on the books by Baroness Emmuska Orczy. **90m/C; VHS, DVD.** Richard E. Grant; Elizabeth McGovern; Martin Shaw; Anthony Green; Ronan Vibert; Christopher Fairbank; Jonathan Coy; Denise Black; James Callis; Peter Jeffrey; Julie Cox; ***D:*** Patrick Lau; ***W:*** Richard Carpenter; ***C:*** Simon Kossoff; ***M:*** Michael Pavlicek. **CABLE**

The Scarlet Pimpernel 3: The Kidnapped King ♪♪ 1/2 **1999** France's 10-year-old Dauphin is under the control of Robespierre when he is captured by a masked figure. As Sir Percy investigates, all clues point to legendary swordsman Chevalier D'Orly. Meanwhile, Marguerite has supposedly left Sir Percy and although Robespierre isn't convinced, Chauvelin is plotting to win back his former love. Based on the books by Baroness Emmuska Orczy. **90m/C; VHS, DVD.** Richard E. Grant; Elizabeth McGovern; Martin Shaw; Anthony Green; Ronan Vibert; Christopher Fairbank; Jonathan Coy; Suzanne Bertish; Jerome Willis; Bryce Engstrom; Dalibor Sipek; ***D:*** Edward Bennett; ***W:*** Richard Carpenter; ***C:*** John Hooper; ***M:*** Michael Pavlicek. **CABLE**

Scarlet Street ♪♪♪ **1945** A mild-mannered, middle-aged cashier becomes an embezzler when he gets involved with a predatory, manipulating woman. Lang remake of Jean Renoir's "La Chienne" (1931). Set apart from later attempts on the same theme by excellent direction by Lang and acting. Also available Colorized. **95m/B; VHS, DVD.** Edward G. Robinson; Joan Bennett; Dan Duryea; Samuel S. Hinds; ***D:*** Fritz Lang; ***C:*** Milton Krasner.

The Scarlet Tunic 🦴🦴 ½ **1997** Based on the novella "The Melancholy Hussar of the German Legion" by Thomas Hardy. It's 1802 in Hardy's fictional Wessex countryside where a light cavalry regiment of bored Germans, fighting with the British against Napoleon, has an encampment on the land of retired doctor Edward Groves (Shepherd). Groves' pretty daughter Frances (Fielding) is engaged to local businessman Humphrey Gould (Sessions) but, of course, she falls for dashing German hussar Matthaus Singer (Barr). Since this is a Hardy story, don't expect any happy endings. **101m/C; VHS, Streaming.** *GB* Jean-Marc Barr; Emma Fielding; Simon Callow; John Sessions; Jack Shepherd; Andrew Tiernan; Thomas Lockyer; ***D:*** Stuart St. Paul; ***W:*** Stuart St. Paul; Mark Jenkins; Colin Clements; ***C:*** Malcolm McLean; ***M:*** John Scott. **TV**

Scarlett 🦴🦴 ½ **1994 (PG-13)** Well, fiddle-dee-dee. While purists may object to any tampering of "Gone With the Wind," this epic TV miniseries, from the Alexandra Ripley novel, manages to be good if overlong fun for those willing to sit back and relax. Scarlett tries to get back Tara and Rhett (they divorce but still battle continuously); explores her Irish family ties and even moves to Ireland; then gets involved with the wrong man and is accused of murder so Rhett can save her and everything can turn out okay (there's lots more). The big budget is up on-screen with lavish costumes and sets and a big cast—although why two Brits got the leads in this Southern melodrama is anyone's guess (Whalley and Dalton try hard). **360m/C; VHS, DVD.** Joanne Whalley; Timothy Dalton; Ann-Margret; Barbara Barrie; Sean Bean; Brian Bedford; Stephen Collins; John Gielgud; Annabeth Gish; George Grizzard; Julie Harris; Tina Kellegher; Melissa Leo; Colm Meaney; Esther Rolle; Jean Smart; Elizabeth Wilson; Paul Winfield; Betsy Blair; Peter Eyre; Pippa Guard; Ronald Pickup; Gary Raymond; Dorothy Tutin; ***D:*** John Erman; ***W:*** William Hanley; ***M:*** John Morris. **TV**

Scarred 🦴 ½ *Street Love; Red on Red* **1984 (R)** Unwed teenage mother becomes prostitute to support baby. Predictable plot and acting pull this one down. **85m/C; VHS, DVD.** Jennifer Mayo; Jackie Berryman; David Dean; ***D:*** Rosemarie Turko; ***W:*** Rosemarie Turko.

Scarred City 🦴🦴 **1998 (R)** Cliched and predictable actioner with a decent cast. Trigger-happy cop John Trace (Baldwin) is forced to join an elite crime unit, headed by Laine Devon (Palminteri), which uses any means necessary to get the job done. But Trace soon decides that his fellow cops are basically just fulfilling their own violent impulses. Then Trace saves hooker Candy (Carrere) from a mob hit and his buddies decide they'd be better off without him. **95m/C; VHS, DVD.** Chazz Palminteri; Stephen Baldwin; Tia Carrere; Gary Dourdan; Michael Rispoli; Steve Flynn; ***D:*** Ken Sanzel; ***W:*** Ken Sanzel; ***C:*** Michael Slovis; ***M:*** Anthony Marinelli.

The Scars of Dracula 🦴🦴 ½ **1970 (R)** A young couple tangles with Dracula in their search for the man's missing brother. Gory, creepy, violent, sexy tale from the dark side. Don't see it late at night. Preceded by "Taste the Blood of Dracula" and followed by "Dracula A.D. 1972." **96m/C; VHS, DVD, Blu-Ray.** *GB* Christopher Lee; Jenny Hanley; Dennis Waterman; Wendy Hamilton; Patrick Troughton; Michael Gwynn; Anouska (Anoushka) Hempel; Michael Ripper; Christopher Matthews; Delia Lindsay; ***D:*** Roy Ward Baker; ***W:*** John (Anthony Hinds) Elder; ***M:*** James Bernard.

Scary Movie 🦴 ½ **2000 (R)** If the last few Leslie Nielsen outings didn't convince you that the genre spoof was played out, this parody of "Scream" and all its progeny will. The Wayans brothers go for quantity of jokes and targets, and quality definitely suffers for it. Fart gags and gratuitous cussing (neither of which we often object to, but we have our limits) are substituted for focused satire. If you're looking for well-done genre spoofery, rent "Airplane" and "I'm Gonna Git You Sucka" and leave this one to the discount previously viewed bin. **85m/C; VHS, DVD, Blu-Ray.** Keenen Ivory Wayans; Marlon Wayans; Shawn Wayans; Carmen Electra; Jon Abrahams; Shannon Elizabeth; Lochlyn Munro; Cheri Oteri; Anna Faris; Regina Hall; Kurt Fuller; David Lander; Dave Sheridan; Dan Joffre; ***D:*** Keenen Ivory Wayans; ***W:*** Marlon Wayans; Shawn Wayans; ***C:*** Francis Kenny; ***M:*** David Kitay.

Scary Movie 2 🦴 **2001 (R)** You knew they were lying when the tagline of the first film declared "No mercy, no shame, no sequel," especially since the spoof brought in more than $144 mil worldwide. The plot, such as it is, consists of a spooky doctor (Curry) convincing the cast from the original to spend the night in a haunted house to study insomnia. Familiar, no? But it's really just an excuse for the Wayans to parody a whole new batch of movies and do a lot (and we mean A LOT) of bodily fluid and sex jokes. Unfortunately, they don't do it any better than they did the first time, and whatever freshness the original had is long gone. **82m/C; VHS, DVD.** Anna Faris; Tim Curry; Shawn Wayans; Marlon Wayans; Chris Elliott; Tori Spelling; Christopher K. Masterson; Kathleen Robertson; Regina Hall; James Woods; David Cross; Andy Richter; Natasha Lyonne; Veronica Cartwright; Richard Moll; ***V:*** Colleen (Ann) Fitzpatrick; ***D:*** Keenen Ivory Wayans; ***W:*** Shawn Wayans; Marlon Wayans; Alyson Fouse; Greg Grabianski; Dave Polsky; Michael Anthony Snowden; Craig Wayans; ***C:*** Steven Bernstein.

Scary Movie 3 🦴 ½ **2003 (PG-13)** Zucker-directed spoof pushes the limits of parody in this Wayans-created franchise with rehashed gags and strained satire. Mainly a send up of flicks "The Ring" and "Signs." TV reporter Cindy Campbell (Faris), from the previous "Srarys", ends up on the farm of Tom Logan (Sheen) and his little brother George (Rex) while tracking down a mysterious videotape portending doom to whoever watches. Machine-gun fire gags whiz by, missing most of their targets, as Zucker takes the worst of the movies he spoofs and plays them for all they're worth, which isn't very much. Blond moment between Anderson and McCarthy is a highlight, as is Latifah in a "Matrix" spoof. **90m/C; VHS, DVD.** Anna Faris; Anthony Anderson; Leslie Nielsen; Camryn Manheim; Simon Rex; George Carlin; Queen Latifah; Eddie Griffin; Denise Richards; Regina Hall; Charlie Sheen; Kevin Hart; ***Cameo(s):*** Pamela Anderson; Jenny McCarthy; Jeremy Piven; D.L. Hughley; Ja Rule; Master P; Macy Gray; Redman; Raekwon; RZA; ***D:*** Jerry Zucker; ***W:*** Craig Mazin; Pat Proft; ***C:*** Mark Irwin; ***M:*** James L. Venable.

Scary Movie 4 🦴 ½ **2006 (PG-13)** Critic-proof spoof has Zucker returning for a second director's stint and the formula staying the same. Nominal story involves Cindy (Faris) being a home care worker for an elderly woman (unbilled Leachman) and falling for divorced dad Tom (Bierko, doing that Cruise couch-jumping thing in front of a fake Oprah). Films spoofed include "Saw" (with Shaq and Dr. Phil), "The Grudge," "The Village," "War of the Worlds," and more. Some jokes hit, more miss, but the franchise made $41 million its opening weekend so it's likely to lead to a fifth go-round. **83m/C; DVD, HD-DVD.** Anna Faris; Regina Hall; Craig Bierko; Anthony Anderson; Carmen Electra; Chris Elliott; Kevin Hart; Cloris Leachman; Michael Madsen; Leslie Nielsen; Bill Pullman; Simon Rex; Charlie Sheen; Molly Shannon; Shaquille O'Neal; Bryan Callen; Dave Attell; Conchita Campbell; Debra Wilson; Patrice O'Neal; ***Nar:*** James Earl Jones; ***D:*** David Zucker; ***W:*** David Zucker; Craig Mazin; Jim Abrahams; ***C:*** Thomas Ackerman; ***M:*** James L. Venable.

Scary Movie 5 **WOOF! 2013 (PG-13)** Why bother? Seven years after this franchise was mercilessly killed, it surfaces again for no apparent reason other than to teach people how not to make a comedy. It's been long enough that the producers and writers of this sequel nobody asked for had plenty of material with which to work, including "Paranormal Activity," "Inception," and "Black Swan," but they forgot to actually write a script. The scariest thing about this pop culture wasteland is how incredibly unfunny it ended up. The lesson? Just making a reference is not writing a joke. **86m/C; DVD, Blu-Ray.** Ashley Tisdale; Simon Rex; Molly Shannon; Heather Locklear; Charlie Sheen; Lindsay Lohan; ***D:*** Malcolm Lee; ***W:*** David Zucker; Pat Proft; ***C:*** Steven Douglas Smith; ***M:*** James L. Venable.

Scary Stories to Tell in the Dark 🦴🦴 ½ **2019 (PG-13)** Around Halloween 1968 in a small Pennsylvania town, a group of teens visit an off-limits haunted mansion. While there, they take a storybook belonging to the spirit of killer Sarah Bellows (Pollard), who was locked in the basement by her cruel family. Each night, a new gruesome story appears in the book featuring a town resident and his or her worst fears, which plays out in real life. Features enough visual flair, interesting monsters, and well-told tales to appeal to the younger horror viewers who are fans of the source material, a series of anthology books. **108m/C; DVD, Blu-Ray.** Zoe Margaret Colletti; Michael Garza; Gabriel Rush; Dean Norris; Gil Bellows; ***D:*** André Ovredal; ***W:*** Dan Hageman; Kevin Hageman; Guillermo del Toro; ***C:*** Roman Osin; ***M:*** Marco Beltrami; Anna Drubich.

A Scene at Sea 🦴🦴 ½ *Ano natsu, ichiban shizukana umi* **1992** Director Takeshi Kitano tells the story of a deaf-mute garbage man who discovers a used surfboard and goes on to expand his formerly limited life by taking on competitive surfing while giving those around him insights into their own behavior. **101m/C; DVD.** *JP* Kuroudo Maki; Hiroko Oshima; Sabu Kawahara; Toshizo Fujiwara; ***D:*** Takeshi "Beat" Kitano; ***W:*** Takeshi "Beat" Kitano; ***C:*** Katsumi Yanagijima; ***M:*** Joe Hisaishi.

Scene of the Crime 🦴🦴 **1949** L.A. homicide Lt. Mike Conovan (Johnson) must prove that a plainclothes detective, murdered outside a bookie joint, was not on the take. This leads him to some thugs robbing bookies for a new syndicate and Mike trying to get info from showgirl Lili (DeHaven), while his wife Gloria (Dahl) complains at home. **94m/B; DVD.** Van Johnson; Gloria DeHaven; Arlene Dahl; Tom Drake; Leon Ames; John McIntire; Richard Benedict; ***D:*** Roy Rowland; ***W:*** Charles Schnee; ***C:*** Paul Vogel; ***M:*** Andre Previn.

Scene of the Crime 🦴🦴 ½ **1985** Three short mysteries, which the audience is asked to solve: "The Newlywed Murder," "Medium Is the Murder," and "Vote for Murder." **74m/C; VHS, DVD.** Markie Post; Alan Thicke; Ben Piazza; ***Nar:*** Orson Welles; ***D:*** Walter Grauman. **TV**

Scene of the Crime 🦴🦴🦴 **1987** Beautiful widow, trapped in small French town, is sexually awakened by escaped convict hiding out near her home. Acclaimed, but sometimes distracting camera technique and slow pace undermine the film. In French with English subtitles. **90m/C; VHS, DVD.** *FR* Catherine Deneuve; Danielle Darrieux; Wadeck Stanczak; Victor Lanoux; Nicolas Giraudi; Jean Bousquet; Claire Nebout; ***D:*** Andre Techine; ***W:*** Olivier Assayas.

Scenes from a Mall 🦴🦴 **1991 (R)** Conspicuous consumers spend 16th wedding anniversary waltzing in mall while marriage unravels with few laughs. Surprisingly superficial comedy given the depth of talent of Allen and Midler. **87m/C; VHS, DVD, Blu-Ray.** Woody Allen; Bette Midler; Bill Irwin; Daren Firestone; Rebecca Nickels; ***Cameo(s):*** Fabio; ***D:*** Paul Mazursky; ***W:*** Paul Mazursky; ***C:*** Fred Murphy.

Scenes from a Marriage 🦴🦴🦴🦴 **1973 (PG)** Originally produced in six one-hour episodes for Swedish TV, this bold and sensitive film excruciatingly portrays the painful, unpleasant, disintegration of a marriage. Ullmann is superb. Realistic and disturbing. Dubbed. **168m/C; VHS, DVD, Blu-Ray.** *SW* Liv Ullmann; Erland Josephson; Bibi Andersson; Jan Malmsjo; Anita Wall; ***D:*** Ingmar Bergman; ***W:*** Ingmar Bergman; ***C:*** Sven Nykvist. Golden Globes '75: Foreign Film; N.Y. Film Critics '74: Actress (Ullmann), Screenplay; Natl. Soc. Film Critics '74: Actress (Ullmann), Film, Screenplay, Support. Actress (Andersson).

Scenes from the Goldmine 🦴 ½ **1987 (R)** A young woman joins a rock band and falls in love with its lead singer. Realistic but bland; music not memorable (performed mostly by the actors themselves). **99m/C; VHS, Streaming.** Catherine Mary Stewart; Cameron Dye; Joe Pantoliano; John Ford Coley; Steve Railsback; Timothy B. Schmit; Jewel Shepard; Alex Rocco; Lee Ving; Lesley-Anne Down; ***D:*** Marc Rocco.

Scenes of a Sexual Nature 🦴🦴 **2006 (R)** All talk and no action, in case you were wondering about that title. The relationships of seven couples are explored during one summer afternoon on London's Hampstead Heath. There's a gay couple, a divorced couple, one on a blind date, one couple arguing and breaking up, and one meeting accidentally years after their romance, among other moments. **92m/C; DVD.** *GB* Ewan McGregor; Eileen Atkins; Hugh Bonneville; Holly Aird; Douglas Hodge; Adrian Lester; Andrew Lincoln; Tom (Thomas) Hardy; Gina McKee; Sophie Okonedo; Mark Strong; Catherine Tate; Elgantine Rembauville; Polly Walker; Benjamin Whitrow; ***D:*** Ed Blum; ***W:*** Aschlin Ditta; ***C:*** David Meadows; ***M:*** Dominik Scherrer.

Scenes of the Crime 🦴 ½ **2001 (R)** Mechanic Lenny earns extra cash by driving around local thug Rick. Rick kidnaps gangster Jimmy Berg and holds him hostage in Lenny's van. Before long Rick's dead and a scared Lenny is left negotiating with Jimmy's partner Steven. The van, which is parked on a city street, is drawing some attention while the standoff between the criminals continues. Beware—the production apparently ran out of money and time, because the pic meanders (no chance to edit?) and the ending is abrupt. **92m/C; DVD.** Jon Abrahams; Jeff Bridges; Peter Greene; Bob Gunton; Morris Chestnut; Madchen Amick; R. Lee Ermey; Henry Rollins; Dominic Purcell; Noah Wyle; ***D:*** Dominique Forma; ***W:*** Dominique Forma; Daniel Golka; ***C:*** James R. Bagdonas; ***M:*** Christopher Young.

The Scenesters 🦴 **2009** Too many gimmicks and useless humor doom this comic crime/mystery. A serial killer targets blonde chicks who are part of L.A.'s hip indie crowd. Aspiring filmmaker Wallace is videotaping crime scenes, but he and his former producer Ray think they can parlay the serial killer angle into a documentary. First, they have to convince crime clean-up guy Charlie to help them and then avoid the competition—TV reporter Jewell. **96m/C; DVD.** Todd Berger; Jeff Grace; Blaise Miller; Suzanne May; Sherilyn Fenn; Kevin Brennan; Monika Jolly; James Jolly; John Landis; ***D:*** Todd Berger; ***W:*** Todd Berger; ***C:*** Helena Wei; ***M:*** Dan Houlbrook.

Scenic Route 🦴 **2013 (R)** An exercise in tedium with a twist ending that's somewhat redeeming. Longtime pals Mitchell and Carter are driving on a little-travelled road in Death Valley when Carter's rickety truck breaks down. Naturally, they start blaming each other as resentments surface, making their survival even more unlikely. **87m/C; DVD, Blu-Ray.** Josh Duhamel; Dan Fogler; ***D:*** Kevin Goetz; Michael Goetz; ***W:*** Kyle Killen; ***C:*** Sean O'Dea; ***M:*** Michael Einziger. **VIDEO**

The Scent of a Woman 🦴🦴 ½ *Sweet Smell of Woman; Profumo di Donna* **1975** An acclaimed dark comedy that may be an acquired taste for some. A blinded military officer and his valet take a sensual tour of Italy, the sightless man seducing beautiful women on the way. But at the end of the journey awaits a shock, and the real point of the tale, based on a novel by Giovanni Arpino. In Italian with English subtitles. Remade in 1992 as "Scent of a Woman." **103m/C; VHS, DVD.** *IT* Vittorio Gassman; Alessandro Momo; Agostina Belli; Moira Orfei; Franco Ricci; ***D:*** Dino Risi; ***W:*** Dino Risi; Ruggero Maccari; ***C:*** Claudio Civillo; ***M:*** Armando Trovajoli.

Scent of a Woman 🦴🦴🦴 **1992 (R)** Pacino is a powerhouse (verging on caricature) in a story that, with anyone else in the lead, would be your run-of-the-mill, overly sentimental coming of age/redemption flick. Blind, bitter, and semi-alcoholic Pacino is a retired army colonel under the care of his married niece. He's home alone over Thanksgiving, under the watchful eye of local prep school student Charlie (O'Donnell). Pacino's abrasive (though wonderfully intuitive and romantic) colonel makes an impact on viewers that lingers like a woman's scent long after the last tango. O'Donnell is competently understated in key supporting role, while the tango lesson between Pacino and Anwar dances to the tune of "classic." Boxoffice winner is a remake of 1975 Italian film "Profumo di Donna." **157m/C; VHS, DVD, Blu-Ray, HD-DVD.** Al Pacino; Chris O'Donnell; James Rebhorn; Gabrielle Anwar; Philip Seymour Hoffman; Richard Venture; Bradley Whitford; Rochelle Oliver; Margaret Eginton; Tom Riis Farrell; Frances Conroy; Ron Eldard; ***D:*** Martin Brest; ***W:*** Bo Goldman; ***C:*** Donald E. Thorin; ***M:*** Thomas Newman. Oscars '92: Actor (Pacino); Golden Globes '93: Actor--Drama (Pacino), Film--Drama, Screenplay.

The Scent of Green Papaya 🦴🦴🦴 *Mui du du Xanh* **1993** Tranquil film, set in 1951 Vietnam, follows 10-year-old peasant girl Mui as she spends the next 10 years as a servant in a troubled family, gracefully accommodating herself to the small changes in her life. At 20, she finds a fairy-tale romance with her next employer, a young pianist. Presents a romanticized view of the stoicism of Vietnamese women but is visually beautiful. Directorial debut of Hung is based on his childhood memories of Vietnam, which he re-created on a soundstage outside Paris. In Vietnamese with English subtitles. **104m/C; VHS, DVD, Blu-Ray.** *VT* Tran Nu Yen-Khe; Lu Man San; Truong Thi Loc; Vuong Hoa Hoi; ***D:*** Tran Anh Hung; ***W:*** Tran Anh Hung; Patricia Petit; ***C:*** Benoit Delhomme; ***M:*** Ton That Tiet.

The Scent of Rain & Lightening 🦴🦴 ½ **2017 (R)** When Jody Linder (Monroe) learns that her parents' killer, Billy (Carter), has been released from prison early, she decides to confront him. Though Billy is menacing and has a violent history, Jody comes to believe he may not be guilty nor have received a fair trial as she conducts her own inquiry among her relatives, law enforcement, and Billy's family. As Jody pursues the truth, flashbacks with her parents (Chatwin, Grace) provide related context. A tension-filled adaptation of the Nancy Pickard novel. **100m/C; DVD.** Brad Carter; Maika Monroe; Will Patton; Mark Webber; Aaron Poole; ***D:*** Blake Robbins; ***W:*** Casey Twenter; Jeff Robison; ***C:*** Lyn Moncrief; ***M:*** Brooke Blair; Will Blair.

Schemes 🦴🦴 **1995 (R)** Grieving widower Paul Stewart (McCaffrey) becomes interested in Laura Pierce (Hope), a lovely young woman who said she knew his late wife. Then, Paul's business partner Evelyn (Draper) discovers Laura's not on the up and up and is really interested in Paul's substantial insurance payoff. Laura's part of a con job set up by volaile Victor (Glover), but since Evelyn's also in love with Paul, things aren't at all what they seem. **95m/C; VHS, DVD.** John Glover; Polly Draper; Leslie Hope; James McCaffrey; John de Lancie; Allison Mackie; ***D:*** Derek Westervelt; ***W:*** Derek Westervelt; ***C:*** Claudio Obregon; ***M:*** Mark Chait.

Schindler's List 🦴🦴🦴🦴 **1993 (R)** Spielberg's staggering evocation of the Holocaust finds its voice in Oscar Schindler (Neeson), womanizing German businessman and aspiring war profiteer, who cajoled, bribed, and bullied the Nazis into allowing him to employ Jews in his Polish factories during WWII. By doing so he saved over 1,000 lives. The atrocities are depicted matter of factly as a by-product of sheer Nazi evil. Shot in black and white and powered by splendid performances. Neeson uses his powerful physique as a protective buffer; Kingsley is watchful as his industrious Jewish accountant; and Fiennes personifies evil as Nazi Amon Goeth. Based on the novel by Thomas Keneally, which itself was based on survivor's memories. Filmed on location in Cracow, Poland; due to the sensitive nature of the story, sets of the Auschwitz concentration camp were reconstructed directly outside the camp after protests about filming on the actual site. A tour de force and labor of love for Spielberg, who finally garnered the attention and respect as a filmmaker he deserves. **195m/B; VHS, DVD, Blu-Ray.** Liam Neeson; Ben Kingsley; Ralph Fiennes; Embeth Davidtz; Caroline Goodall; Jonathan Sagalle; Mark Ivanir; Malgoscha Gebel; Shmulik Levy; Beatrice Macola; Andrzej Seweryn; Friedrich von Thun; Norbert Weisser; Michael Schneider; Anna Mucha; ***D:*** Steven Spielberg; ***W:*** Steven Zaillian; ***C:*** Janusz Kaminski; ***M:*** John Williams. Oscars '93: Adapt. Screenplay, Art Dir./Set Dec., Cinematog., Director (Spielberg), Film, Film Editing, Orig. Score; AFI '98: Top 100; British Acad. '93: Adapt. Screenplay, Director (Spielberg), Film, Support. Actor (Fiennes); Directors Guild '93: Director (Spielberg); Golden Globes '94: Director (Spielberg), Film--Drama, Screenplay; L.A. Film Critics '93: Cinematog., Film; Natl. Bd. of Review '93: Film; Natl. Film Reg. '04; N.Y. Film Critics '93: Cinematog., Film, Support. Actor (Fiennes); Natl. Soc. Film Critics '93: Cinematog., Director (Spielberg), Film, Support. Actor (Fiennes); Writers Guild '93: Adapt. Screenplay.

Schizo 🦴 *Amok; Blood of the Undead* **1977 (R)** Devious intentions abound as a middle-aged man is overcome by weird scenes and revelations, caused by the impending wedding of the figure skater he adores. Confusing tale of insanity, obsession, and skating. **109m/C; VHS, DVD, Blu-Ray.** *GB* Lynne Frederick; John Leyton; Stephanie Beacham; John Fraser; Jack Watson; John McEnery; ***D:*** Pete Walker; ***W:*** John M. Watson, Sr.; ***C:*** Peter Jessop.

Schizo 🦴🦴 *Shiza* **2004** Set amid the dusty and desolate bleakness of rural Kazakhstan, film follows 15 year old Mustafa (Eralibeva), who has been given the nickname Schizo because of an apparent mental disorder. His mother's boyfriend, who he idolized, is a small time gangster whose racket is setting up illegal bare-fisted boxing matches. With little else to do in his dead-end town, Mustafa gets involved by recruiting men looking for a quick buck in the ring. When one combatant dies after an especially brutal fight, Mustafa is obliged to fulfill the man's dying wish to deliver his winnings to his girlfriend. This leads to an unlikely romantic involvement, which has the uneasy feel of Mustafa stepping into another man's shoes. **86m/C; DVD.** Olzhas Nusuppaev; Eduard Tabychev; Olga Landina; Bakhytbek Baymukhanbetov; Soukhorukov; Gulnara Jeralieva; Kanagat Nurtay; ***D:*** Gulshad Omarova; ***W:*** Sergei Bodrov; Gulshad Omarova; ***C:*** Khasan Kydyraliyev.

Schizopolis 🦴🦴 **1997** Experimental, empty satire on modern spirituality and communication combines a number of weird and wacky devices that are not particularly entertaining. In an interesting premise, Soderburgh takes the lead in a dual role as Fletcher Munson, a manically neurotic employee of a self-help guru and his own lookalike, a ho-hum dentist having an affair with Fletcher's wife. Soderburgh's real-life ex, actress Brantley, plays his wife, who also has a double that shows up at the dentist. Things grow more bizarre for no apparent reason, as secondary cast members speak in other languages or just complete nonsense while strange sound effects confuse, in a film which also lists no credits (the title is shown in film on a character's t-shirt). Soderburgh, who wrote, directed and lensed this surrealist homage, shot on a super-low $250,000 budget as a way of expressing ideas not allowed in bigger budget, conventional films. To most, this just looks like expensive therapy. **96m/C; VHS, DVD.** Steven Soderbergh; Betsy Brantley; David Jensen; ***D:*** Steven Soderbergh; ***W:*** Steven Soderbergh; ***C:*** Steven Soderbergh.

Schlock 🦴🦴 *The Banana Monster* **1973 (PG)** Accurately titled horror parody is first directorial effort for Landis, who does double duty as a missing link who kills people and falls in love with blind girl. Look for cameo appearance by Forrest J. Ackerman; apemakeup by Rick Baker. **78m/C; VHS, DVD, Blu-Ray.** John Landis; Saul Kahan; Joseph Piantadosi; Eliza (Simons) Garrett; Emile Hamaty; Eric Allison; ***Cameo(s):*** Forrest J Ackerman; ***D:*** John Landis; ***W:*** John Landis; ***C:*** Robert E. (Bob) Collins; ***M:*** David Gibson.

School Daze 🦴🦴🦴 **1988 (R)** Director/writer/star Lee's second outing is a rambunctious comedy (with a message, of course) set at an African-American college in the South. Skimpy plot revolves around the college's homecoming weekend and conflict among frats and sororities and African-Americans who would lose their racial identity and others who assert it. Entertaining and thought provoking. A glimpse at Lee's "promise," fulfilled in "Do the Right Thing." **114m/C; VHS, DVD, Blu-Ray.** Spike Lee; Laurence Fishburne; Giancarlo Esposito; Tisha Campbell; Ossie Davis; Joe Seneca; Art Evans; Ellen Holly; Branford Marsalis; Bill Nunn; Kadeem Hardison; Darryl M. Bell; Joie Lee; Tyra Ferrell; Jasmine Guy; Gregg Burge; Kasi Lemmons; Samuel L. Jackson; Phyllis Hyman; James Bond, III; ***D:*** Spike Lee; ***W:*** Spike Lee; ***C:*** Ernest R. Dickerson; ***M:*** Bill Lee.

School for Scoundrels 🦴🦴🦴 **1960** Top-notch British satire finds lifelong loser Henry Palfrey (Carmichael) about to have the girl of his dreams fall into the hands of rival Raymond Delauncey (Terry-Thomas). In desperation, Henry enrolls at the College of Lifemanship, learning to one-up his competition. Observed by teacher Potter (Sim), Henry tries turning the tables on those who've taken advantage of him. Vastly preferable to the mean-spirited 2006 remake. **90m/B; DVD, Blu-Ray.** *GB* Ian Carmichael; Alastair Sim; Janette Scott; Dennis Price; Irene Handl; Terry-Thomas; ***D:*** Robert Hamer; ***W:*** Hal E. Chester; Patricia Moyes; ***C:*** Erwin Hillier; ***M:*** John Addison.

School for Scoundrels 🦴 **2006 (PG-13)** Remake of the 1960 British comedy about a student-teacher battle for the same girl. Wimp Roger (Heder) needs to man up so he signs on for a course on self-esteem taught by arrogant Dr. P (Thornton). Roger gains enough confidence to ask out pretty neighbor Amanda (Barrett), only to discover that the leering doc is after the same babe, who is too good for either of these losers. A comedy that's not at all funny drags itself from mean-spirited to mushy. **101m/C; DVD.** Billy Bob Thornton; Jon Heder; Jacinda Barrett; Michael Clarke Duncan; Ben Stiller; Luis Guzman; Horatio Sanz; Sarah Silverman; David Cross; Todd Louiso; Steve Monroe; ***D:*** Todd Phillips; ***W:*** Todd Phillips; Scot Armstrong; ***C:*** Jonathan Brown; ***M:*** Christophe Beck.

School of Life 🦴🦴 ½ **2006 (PG)** Stodgy middle school biology teacher Matt Warner (Paymer) is bent on continuing his late dad's (Astin) "Teacher of the Year" legacy but he feels challenged when a young and hip history teacher, Mr. D (Reynolds), comes along and wows everyone. A little touchy-feely at times, though Reynolds is fun to watch. **100m/C; DVD.** David Paymer; Ryan Reynolds; John Astin; Andrew Robb; Kate Vernon; ***D:*** William Dear; ***W:*** Jonathan Kahn; ***C:*** Brian Pearson; ***M:*** Ari Wise. **TV**

School of Rock 🦴🦴🦴 **2003 (PG-13)** Substitute any other actor for Jack Black and this movie becomes a direct-to-video blip, or doesn't get made at all. Black is Dewey Finn, a life-long rocker and true believer who gets tossed by his band and forced to get a job. Dewey snakes a teaching gig from his roomie, ending up at an exclusive elementary school with a stuffy principal (Cusack). There he finds a classroom full of precocious kids with musical talent and an entire spectrum of self-esteem problems. He molds them into a rock band with the intention of entering the Battle of the Bands. Some plot points are treated casually (sometimes to the point of ignoring them), but Black's wild-eyed, fully-committed performance easily carries the day, and he's ably supported by the kids, all of whom can actually play and sing, and by a savvy script that takes the music seriously. **108m/C; VHS, DVD, Blu-Ray.** Jack Black; Joan Cusack; Mike White; Sarah Silverman; Joey Gaydos; Miranda Cosgrove; Kevin Alexander Clark; Rebecca Julia Brown; Robert Tsai; Maryam Hassan; Caitlin Hale; Aleisha Allen; Brian Falduto; Zachary Infante; James Hosey; Angelo Massagli; Cole Hawkins; Nicole Afflerbach; Jordan-Claire Green; Adam Pascal; Chris Stack; Tim Hopper; Nicky Katt; Kate McGregor-Stewart; ***D:*** Richard Linklater; ***W:*** Mike White; ***C:*** Rogier Stoffers; ***M:*** Craig Wedren.

School Spirit 🦴 **1985 (R)** A hormonally motivated college student is killed during a date. He comes back as a ghost to haunt the campus, disrupt the stuffy president's affair, and fall in love. Forgettable, lame, low-grade teen sex flick. **90m/C; VHS, DVD.** Tom Nolan; Elizabeth Foxx; Larry Linville; ***D:*** Allan Holleb; ***W:*** Geoffrey Baere; ***M:*** Tom Bruner.

School Ties 🦴🦴🦴 **1992 (PG-13)** Encino man Fraser does a dramatic turn as a talented 1950s quarterback who gets a scholarship to the elite St. Matthew prep school. To conform with the closed-mindedness of the McCarthy era, both his father and coach suggest that he hide his Jewish religion. Fraser's compliance results in his big-man-on-campus status, until his rival in football and his love interest both find out that he is Jewish, creating an ugly rift in the school. What easily could have been just another teen hunk flick looks at much more than just Fraser's pretty face in successful, unflinching treatment of anti-Semitism. **110m/C; VHS, DVD.** Brendan Fraser; Matt Damon; Chris O'Donnell; Randall Batinkoff; Andrew Lowery; Cole Hauser; Ben Affleck; Anthony Rapp; Amy Locane; Peter Donat; Zeljko Ivanek; Kevin Tighe; Michael Higgins; Ed Lauter; ***D:*** Robert Mandel; ***W:*** Darryl Ponicsan; Dick Wolf; ***C:*** Freddie Francis; ***M:*** Maurice Jarre.

Schoolgirl Hitchhikers 🦴 *Jeunes filles impudiques; High School Hitch Hikers* **1973** Two female delinquents on the run break into a French chateau to discover a pair of criminals also on the run. **74m/C; Blu-Ray.** *FR* Joelle Coeur; Gilda Arancio; Marie Helene Regne; Willy Braque; Pierre Julien; ***D:*** Jean Rollin; ***M:*** Pierre Raph. **VIDEO**

Schtonk 🦴🦴 **1992** Hermann Willie is a down-and-out journalist who thinks he's come upon the find of the century when he's given what are supposedly Hitler's diaries. Based on the 1983 scandal when the German publication "Der Stern" paid $5 million and printed what turned out to be not-very-clever forgeries. Director Dietl mocks the greedy gullibility of the journal, the ingenuity of the forger, as well as the nostalgia of the ex- and neo-Nazis of the modern Germany. The title is a meaningless expletive uttered by Charlie Chaplin in "The Great Dictator." German with subtitles. **115m/C; VHS, DVD.** *GE* Goetz George; Uwe Ochsenknecht; Rolf Hoppe; ***D:*** Helmut Dietl; ***W:*** Helmut Dietl. Berlin Intl. Film Fest. '92: Actor (George), Director (Dietl), Film.

Schultze Gets the Blues 🦴🦴 ½ **2003 (PG)** Bittersweet, sentimental comedy finds hefty bachelor salt miner Schultze (Krause) pushed into early retirement and wondering what he's going to do besides play the accordion at his local polka club. One night, Schultze's world changes when he happens to catch a zydeco song on the radio. Amazed at how different an accordion can sound, he sets his familiar polkas to a zydeco beat. Schulze's friends are equally amazed and decide to take up a collection and send him to compete in a music festival in their sister city of Moulton, Texas. Adventure is just the liberating journey that shy Schultze needs. German with subtitles. **114m/C; DVD.** Horst Krause; Harald Warmbrunn; Karl-Fred Muller; Hannelore Schubert; Wolfgang Boos; Rosemarie Deibel; Wilhelmine Horschig; Anne V. Angelle; Ursula Schucht; Alozia St. Julien; ***D:*** Michael Schorr; ***W:*** Michael Schorr; ***C:*** Axel Schneppat; ***M:*** Thomas Wittenbecher.

Sci-Fighter 🦴 ½ *X-Treme Fighter* **2004** After playing a virtual reality game his grandpa designed, a teenager needs his father to join in to free him from the clutches of a vicious virus that won't let them leave without a fight. **90m/C; VHS, DVD.** Don "The Dragon" Wilson; Cynthia Rothrock; Aki Aleong; Lorenzo Lamas; Dan(eya) Mayid; Rebecca Chaney; ***D:*** Art Camacho; ***W:*** Tom Callicoat; ***C:*** Andrea V. Rossotto; ***M:*** Vince DiCola. **VIDEO**

Sci-Fighters 🦴🦴 ½ **1996 (R)** Renegade cop Cameron Grayson (Piper) is tracking rapist Adrian Dunn (Drago) in 2009 Boston and discovers that Dunn has been exposed to a deadly, mutating virus. It's actually changing the bad guy into an alien methane-breathing lifeform that, of course, wants to inhabit the earth. Appropriately gross alien makeup and some decent special effects. **94m/C; VHS, DVD.** Roddy Piper; Billy Drago; Jayne Heitmeyer; ***D:*** Peter Svatek; ***W:*** Mark Sevi; ***C:*** Barry Gravelle; ***M:*** Milan Kymlicka.

The Science of Sleep 🦴🦴 **2006 (R)** Fanciful and surreal effort will appeal most to fans of Gondry's previous work. Immature and hyper-imaginative graphic artist Stephane (Garcia Bernal) has just returned to Paris and his mother (Miou-Miou) after growing up in Mexico with his divorced dad. Maybe he's suffering from culture shock and maybe Stephane is more than a little weird but he's certainly more comfortable living in his own fantasies. Stephane chums up with artist neighbor Stephanie (Gainsbourg) but pulls back from the romantic impulses he can't handle, going back into his dream world. Visually fascinating and sometimes funny, but the perpetual parade of dream sequences never pays off. **105m/C; DVD.** *FR IT* Gael Garcia Bernal; Charlotte Gainsbourg; Alain Chabat; Miou-Miou; Pierre Vaneck; Emma de Caunes; Sacha Bourdo; Alain de Noyencourt; ***D:*** Michel Gondry; ***W:*** Michel Gondry; ***C:*** Jean-Louis Bompoint; ***M:*** Jean-Michel Bernard.

Scissors 🦴 ½ **1991 (R)** Yes, this Hitchcock imitation needs trimming. An unstable young woman contends with a rapist, devious lookalikes, birds, and a prison-like apartment, not all of which are relevant to the plot. An unsharp stab at suspense from novelist/filmmaker DeFelitta. **105m/C; VHS, Blu-Ray, Streaming.** Sharon Stone; Steve Railsback;

Michelle Phillips; Ronny Cox; Albert "Poppy" Popwell; *D:* Frank De Felitta; *W:* Frank De Felitta.

Scoob! 🦴🦴 **2020 (PG)** A friendless young Shaggy (Armitage) is hanging out at Venice Beach when he finds a stray Great Dane puppy he names Scooby Dooby Doo. Soon after, he makes three human friends. As they grow into young adults, brave Fred (Efron), smart Velma (Rodriguez), and fearless Daphne (Seyfried) solve mysteries with Shaggy (Forte) and Scooby (Welker). Their current case involves helping vain superhero Blue Falcon (Wahlberg) defeat Dick Dastardly (Isaacs) and prevent him from opening up the underworld. The animated origin story for Scooby-Doo and the gang is energetic and full of vibrant colors, but the plot is both simple and unnecessarily convoluted. **93m/C; DVD.** Will Forte; Mark Wahlberg; Jason Isaacs; Gina Rodriguez; Zac Efron; *D:* Tony Cervone; *W:* Matt Lieberman; Adam Sztykiel; Jack Donaldson; Derek Elliott; *M:* Junkie XL.

Scooby-Doo 🦴🦴 **2002 (PG)** Zoinks! Everybody's favorite cartoon Great Dane comes to life in this live action-plus-CGI summer blockbuster. Fred (Prinze) is out to debunk the apparent haunting of theme-park Spooky Island, accompanied by Daphne (Gellar), Velma (Cardellini), Shaggy (Lillard), and Scooby, of course. The plot, which is shaky to begin with, goes against the theme of the cartoon, where there are no ghosts, and meddling kids overcome mean old men in wacky costumes. The movie only takes off when the CGI Scooby (a large reason for the inflated budget) is on screen. Based on the 1969 cartoon, "Scooby-Doo, Where Are You?" **87m/C; VHS, DVD, Blu-Ray, UMD.** Freddie Prinze, Jr.; Sarah Michelle Gellar; Matthew Lillard; Linda Cardellini; Rowan Atkinson; Miguel A. Nunez, Jr.; Stephen Grives; Isla Fisher; Sam Greco; *D:* Raja Gosnell; *W:* James Gunn; Craig Titley; *C:* David Eggby; *M:* David Newman.

Scooby-Doo 2: Monsters Unleashed 🦴🦴 **2004 (PG)** Those meddling kids are at it again! During their enshrinement into the Coolsonian Criminology Museum for all their prior do-good acts, all the ghosts and goblins on display suddenly come back to life and the gang sets out to unmask the culprit responsible. Shaggy (Lillard) and the CGI Scooby do not disappoint but this second act is weighed down with special-effects action sequences that play more violently (cartoonish, but still) than its predecessor. Seth Green is fun to watch as the museum's curator and Velma's love interest. **93m/C; DVD.** Freddie Prinze, Jr.; Sarah Michelle Gellar; Linda Cardellini; Matthew Lillard; Seth Green; Peter Boyle; Tim Blake Nelson; Alicia Silverstone; *V:* Neil Fanning; Ian Abercrombie; *D:* Raja Gosnell; *W:* James Gunn; *C:* Oliver Wood; *M:* David Newman. Golden Raspberries '04: Worst Remake/Sequel.

Scoop 🦴🦴 **2006 (PG-13)** Allen's 35th directorial feature is evidence he should ease up on that yearly quota. This time the kvetching centers around a naive journalism student (Johansson) who is given the scoop of a lifetime by the ghost of a muckraking journalist (McShane), and must investigate with the help of a third-rate magician (Allen) on whose stage the ghost appeared. Feels like a patchwork collection of past Allen flicks with nothing new or interesting, including the requisite abundance of self-centered Judaic jokes. **96m/C; DVD.** Woody Allen; Scarlett Johansson; Hugh Jackman; Ian McShane; Charles Dance; Romola Garai; Fenella Woolgar; Julian Glover; Victoria Hamilton; Anthony Head; *D:* Woody Allen; *W:* Woody Allen; *C:* Remi Adefarasin.

Scorched 🦴🦴 **2002 (PG-13)** Tepid crime caper finds three disgruntled bank tellers—unbeknownst to each other—deciding to rob their bank branch on the same day. Sheila has just been dumped by bank manager/longtime boyfriend Rick (Leonard) and wants to rob the ATM so he'll lose his job. Milquetoast desert-dwelling Jason (Harrelson) decides to steal the contents of the safety deposit box of evil millionaire Mr. Merchant (Cleese), who's caused him grief. And Stuart (Costanzo) has a Vegas get-rich-quick scheme that he decides to finance by taking the bank's ready cash. **94m/C; DVD.** Alicia Silverstone; Woody Harrelson; John Cleese; Paulo Costanzo; Joshua Leonard; Rachael Leigh Cook; David Krumholtz; *D:* Gavin Grazer; *W:* Joe Wein; *C:* Bruce Douglas Johnson; *M:* John (Gianni) Frizzell.

Scorcher 🦴 ½ **2002 (R)** China sets off a series of underground nuclear explosions that cause tectonic plate shifts, earthquakes, volcanoes, and a rapid rise in global temperature. The only way to save the planet is a nuclear counterstrike—centered beneath L.A. in three days. So the city is evacuated and the usual team of misfits is assembled to do the impossible. At least this flick's fast-paced enough to run right over all those pesky plot holes. **87m/C; VHS, DVD.** Mark Dacascos; Rutger Hauer; John Rhys-Davies; Mark Rolston; G.W. Bailey; Rayne Marcus; Tamara Davies; *D:* James Seale; *W:* Steve Latshaw; Rebecca Morrison; *C:* Maximo Munzi; *M:* Bill Brown. **VIDEO**

Scorchers 🦴🦴 **1992 (R)** Back in the bayou, Splendid (Lloyd), a newlywed who won't sleep with her husband, and her cousin Talbot (Tilly), a preacher's daughter whose husband prefers the town whore Thais (Dunaway), find their lives intertwined because of their marital and sexual problems. A real "scorcher." **81m/C; VHS, DVD.** Faye Dunaway; Denholm Elliott; James Earl Jones; Emily Lloyd; Jennifer Tilly; Leland Crooke; James Wilder; Anthony Geary; *D:* David Beaird; *W:* David Beaird.

Score 🦴🦴 **1972** Swinging marrieds Jack and Elvira turn their attention to a newlywed couple in order to indulge their sexual desires. Campy, culty erotica. **89m/C; VHS, DVD.** Calvin Culver; Claire Wilbur; Lynn Lowry; Gerald Grant; Carl Parker; *D:* Radley Metzger; *W:* Jerry Douglas; *C:* Franco Vodopivec.

Score WOOF! **1995** If you've seen "Hard Boiled," "City on Fire," or "Reservoir Dogs," then you can skip this one. Chance (Ozawa) is released from prison and forced to return to work for his old crime boss. Chance recruits three other thieves to rip off a jewelry store. Following the robbery, distrust sets in amongst the crooks and a pair of hitchhikers interfere with their getaway plans. Borrows liberally from the films mentioned above and is never exciting or engaging. Instead, it's morally ambiguous and boring. Also, this film features some of the thinnest and reddest blood ever seen in a movie. **94m/C; DVD.** *JP* Hitoshi Ozawa; Osamu Ebara; Ryuuji Minakami; Kazuyoshi Ozawa; Miyuki Takano; Masahiro Yamashita; *D:* Atsushi Muroga.

The Score 🦴🦴 ½ **2001 (R)** Slow-starting crime comedy with De Niro as a semi-retired thief, living a quiet life running a Montreal jazz club, until his fence (Brando) and a wannabe thief (Norton) talk him into pulling another job in Montreal's customs house. Bassett is DeNiro's squeeze (good taste there) who wants him out of the life. Painstaking but realistic in its portrayal of the preparation and events leading to the heist, but when things finally get going, it crackles with tense "will-they-get-caught" moments and double-crosses aplenty. De Niro is solid, as always, but he seems like he may be getting too old for this stuff. Norton gets most of the screen time, and uses it well. Brando is surprisingly understated in an amusing way. **124m/C; VHS, DVD, Blu-Ray.** Robert De Niro; Edward Norton; Marlon Brando; Angela Bassett; Gary Farmer; Paul Soles; Jamie Harrold; *D:* Frank Oz; *W:* Kario Salem; Scott Marshall Smith; Lem Dobbs; *C:* Rob Hahn; *M:* Howard Shore.

A Score to Settle 🦴 ½ **2019** After nearly two decades in prison, Frank (Cage) is released because he suffers from a form of insomnia so severe that it requires medication. Meeting up with his now adult son Joey (Le Gros), Frank spends some of the money he was paid to do time for another man's crime on himself and his son. While spending big money, Frank also tracks the men who set him up with the help of former colleague Q (Bratt). The film is a showcase for Cage's particular set of acting skills but is otherwise unremarkable. **104m/C; DVD.** Nicolas Cage; Benjamin Bratt; Noah Le Gros; Mohamed Karim; Karolina Wydra; *D:* Shawn Ku; *W:* John Stuart Newman; *C:* Mark Dobrescu; *M:* John Kaefer.

Scorned 2 🦴 ½ **1996 (R)** Amanda (McClure) seems happily married to psych prof Mark—even if she is having those bad dreams. But when her hubby is tempted by a pretty coed and Amanda finds out—well this is one woman that should never be scorned. **105m/C; VHS, DVD.** Tane McClure; Wendy Schumacher; Myles O'Brien; John McCook; Andrew Stevens; Seth Jaffe; *D:* Rodney McDonald; *W:* Sean McGinley; *C:* Gary Graver; *M:* Patrick Seymour.

Scorpio 🦴🦴 ½ **1973 (PG)** Okay cat-and-mouse espionage tale about a wily, veteran CIA agent (Lancaster) who may have turned traitor. He's set-up to be killed by a CIA boss but the assassin, code-name Scorpio (Delon), has some trouble fulfilling his assignment. Cross- and double-cross abound. **114m/C; VHS, DVD, Blu-Ray.** Burt Lancaster; Alain Delon; Paul Scofield; John Colicos; Gayle Hunnicutt; J.D. Cannon; Joanne Linville; Melvin Stewart; James B. Sikking; Vladek Sheybal; William (Bill) Smithers; Celeste Yarnall; *D:* Michael Winner; *W:* David W. Rintels; Gerald Wilson.

The Scorpio Factor 🦴🦴 **1990** Murder and mayhem follow microchip heist. **87m/C; VHS, DVD.** Attila Bertalan; David Nerman; Wendy Dawn Wilson; *D:* Michel Wachniuc; *W:* Carole Sauve; June Pinheiro; *C:* Bruno Philip; *M:* Richard Gresko.

Scorpio One 🦴 ½ **1997 (R)** Scientists aboard spacestation Scorpio One have made a discovery that has cost them their lives and may now cause the destruction of earth. **92m/C; VHS, DVD.** Jeff Speakman; Robert Carradine; Robin Curtis; Steve Kanaly; George Murdock; Judith Chapman; *D:* Worth Keeler; *W:* Steve Latshaw; *C:* Doyle Smith; *M:* David Wurst; Eric Wurst.

Scorpion 🦴 **1986 (R)** A karate-master and anti-terrorist expert defuses a skyjacking and infiltrates international assassination conspiracies. Ex-real life karate champ Tulleners is a ho-hum hero, and the story is warmed over. **98m/C; VHS, DVD.** Tonny Tulleners; Allen Williams; Don Murray; *D:* William Reed.

The Scorpion King 🦴🦴 **2002 (PG-13)** Billed as a prequel to "The Mummy" series, this actioner is more in the "Sword 'n' Sandals" vein. The Rock is the title star, an assassin hired by a group of beleaguered tribes to defeat the evil warlord Memnon (Brand). The warlord is helped, somewhat unenthusiastically, by a sorceress (Hu) who can foresee the outcome of battles. Yes, it's cheesy, and downright silly at times, but it doesn't really strive for any more than that. The only motivation behind the whole endeavor seems to be to make The Rock a movie star, and if he sticks with action pics, he seems to be on his way. All the men do the requisite amount of killing, and discussing killing, and the women are all scantily clad. The target audience should be overjoyed. **94m/C; VHS, DVD, Blu-Ray, HD-DVD.** Dwayne "The Rock" Johnson; Michael Clarke Duncan; Steven Brand; Kelly Hu; Bernard Hill; Grant Heslov; Peter Facinelli; Ralph (Ralf) Moeller; Branscombe Richmond; Roger Rees; Sherri Howard; Conrad Roberts; *D:* Chuck Russell; *W:* Stephen Sommers; William Osborne; David Hayter; *C:* John R. Leonetti; *M:* John Debney.

The Scorpion King 2: Rise of a Warrior 🦴 ½ **2008 (PG-13)** A prequel to the 2002 prequel that follows the standard how-a-legend-is-born template. Young Mathayus witnesses his father's murder at the hands of evil warlord Sargon (Couture). He hones his body and fighting skills until the adult Mathayus (Copon) can get his revenge on the man, who is now king. There's also a sword-wielding, leather-clad babe (David), who takes up with our hero, and a sorceress hottie (Becker) on the bad guy's side. **109m/C; DVD, Blu-Ray.** Michael Copon; Karen Shenaz David; Randy Couture; Natalie Becker; Simon Quaterman; *D:* Russell Mulcahy; *W:* Randall McCormick; *C:* Glynn Speeckaert; *M:* Klaus Badelt. **VIDEO**

The Scorpion King 3: Battle for Redemption 🦴 ½ **2011 (PG-13)** Direct-to-video sword-and-sandal fantasy sequel. After his wife dies, Mathayus loses his kingdom and returns to being a mercenary. This pits him against evil Talus, who wants to wrest the throne from his brother Horus. Mathayus' large companion Olaf offers some laughs. **104m/C; DVD, Blu-Ray.** Victor Webster; Billy Zane; Ron Perlman; Bostin Christopher; Dave Bautista; Selina Lo; Kevin Ferguson; *D:* Roel Reine; *W:* Shane Kuhn; Brendan Cowles; *C:* Roel Reine; *M:* Trevor Morris. **VIDEO**

The Scorpion King 4: Quest for Power 🦴 ½ **2015 (PG-13)** No-brainer sword-and-sandal (and some sorcery) action that's just fun and where the plot doesn't actually matter. But if you want one: Scorpion King Mathayus is betrayed and imprisoned after being sent by King Zakkour to retrieve an artifact that will bestow immense power on those that claim it. (And other stuff happens.) **105m/C; DVD, Blu-Ray.** Victor Webster; Ellen Hollman; Barry Bostwick; Will(iam) Kemp; Rutger Hauer; Michael Biehn; Lou Ferrigno; M. Emmet Walsh; *D:* Mike Elliott; *W:* Michael D. Weiss; *C:* Trevor Michael Brown; *M:* Geoff Zanelli. **VIDEO**

Scorpion Spring 🦴🦴 **1996 (R)** Drug runner Astor (Morales) is on the lam through the desert with a beautiful hostage (Aviles) when two unsuspecting travelers (Molina and McGaw) offer the stranded duo a ride. But drug lord El Rojo (McConaughey) wants Astor dead and doesn't care who gets in his way and there's also a border patrol officer (Blades) on their trail as well. **89m/C; VHS, DVD.** Esai Morales; Alfred Molina; Patrick McGaw; Matthew McConaughey; Angel Aviles; Ruben Blades; Miguel (Michael) Sandoval; Richard Edson; John Doe; *D:* Brian Cox; *W:* Brian Cox; *C:* Nancy Schreiber; *M:* Lalo Schifrin.

Scorpion with Two Tails 🦴 **1982** In an underworld of terror, people die grotesque deaths that a woman dreams of. **99m/C; VHS, DVD.** *IT* John Saxon; Van Johnson; Paolo Malco; Claudio Cassinelli; Marilu Tolo; Elvire Audray; *D:* Sergio Martino; *W:* Ernesto Gastaldi; *C:* Giancarlo Ferrando; *M:* Fabio Frizzi.

The Scorpion's Tail 🦴 **1971** Graphic murder scenes rev up this early thriller by Martino filmed with plot twists and visual games. Dubbed in English. **90m/C; VHS, DVD.** *IT SP* Evelyn Stewart; Anita Strindberg; George Hilton; Luigi Pistilli; Janine Reynaud; *D:* Sergio Martino; *W:* Sauro Scavolini; Ernesto Gastaldi; *M:* Bruno Nicolai.

Scotland, PA 🦴🦴 ½ **2002 (R)** Shakespeare's "Macbeth" meets Mcjobs in director Morrissette's original black comedy set in 1970s rural Pennsylvania. Far from royalty, these McBeths, Slacker Mac (LeGros) and wife Pat (Tierney), are burger flippers at Duncan's, toiling away on minimum wage. At Pat's urging, they off nepotistic restaurant owner Norm Duncan (Rebhorn) after a promotion goes to his two sons. After a fryer "mishap" and a cover-up, the power-hungry couple are then free to have it their way, remodeling the restaurant and changing the name to McBeth's, complete with a (wink-wink) giant "M." However, vegetarian cop McDuff (Walken) is assigned to find Duncan's killer. Falls just short of reaching full potential, but Tierney is especially great and the black humor should prove enjoyable for both Shakespeare and non-Shakespeare fans alike. **102m/C; VHS, DVD.** Maura Tierney; James LeGros; Christopher Walken; Kevin Corrigan; James Rebhorn; Tom Guiry; Amy Smart; Andy Dick; Josh Pais; Geoff Dunsworth; *D:* Billy Morrissette; *W:* Billy Morrissette; *C:* Wally Pfister; *M:* Anton Sanko.

Scotland Yard Inspector 🦴🦴 *Lady in the Fog* **1952** An American newspaperman (Romero) in London looks for a killer. Nothing special. **73m/B; VHS, DVD.** *GB* Cesar Romero; Bernadette O'Farrell; Lois Maxwell; Geoffrey Keen; Campbell Singer; *D:* Sam Newfield; *W:* Orville H. Hampton; *C:* Walter J. (Jimmy W.) Harvey; *M:* Ivor Slaney.

Scott Joplin 🦴🦴 ½ **1977** Showbiz bio notable for its music not its accuracy about the life of black composer/piano player Scott Joplin (Williams). Joplin's syncopated music comes to the attention of white publisher John Stark (Carney) and he becomes well-known when the craze for ragtime hits. Joplin then settles in St. Louis with wife Belle (Avery) but his life is wracked by disappointment and the syphilis that ravages his body. **96m/C; DVD.** Billy Dee Williams; Clifton Davis; Art Carney; Margaret Avery; Eubie Blake; Godfrey Cambridge; Seymour Cassel; *D:* Jeremy Paul Kagan; *W:* Christopher Knopf; *C:* David M. Walsh. **TV**

Scott of the Antarctic 🦴🦴 ½ **1948** Drama of doomed British expedition of 1911 struggling to be the first group to reach the South Pole. Much of the stunning location filming was shot in the Swiss Alps. Story is authentic, but oddly uninvolving, as though seen from afar. **111m/C; VHS, DVD.** *GB* John Mills; Christopher Lee; Kenneth More; Derek Bond; ***D:*** Charles Frend; ***C:*** Geoffrey Unsworth.

Scott Pilgrim vs. the World **2010 (PG-13)** Garage band bass player Scott Pilgrim (Cera) is a 22-year-old Toronto slacker who almost has it all, especially when beautiful Ramona Flowers (Winstead) shows up. Too bad she has seven evil ex-boyfriends who want to eliminate Scott from Ramona's life through a series of stylized, potentially lethal, fights. Hyperactive adaptation of Bryan Lee O'Malley's graphic novels geared to its videogame savvy, text messaging audience. **112m/C; Blu-Ray.** Michael Cera; Mary Elizabeth Winstead; Kieran Culkin; Chris Evans; Anna Kendrick; Alison Pill; Brandon Routh; Jason Schwartzman; Mae Whitman; Brie Larson; Aubrey Plaza; Stephen Stills; Ellen Wong; Ben Lewis; ***D:*** Edgar Wright; ***W:*** Edgar Wright; Michael Bacall; ***C:*** Bill Pope.

The Scout **1994 (PG-13)** Brooks is an about-to-be-canned scout for the New York Yankees who discovers a weird, though genuine, phenom pitcher (Fraser) on a trip to Mexico. He convinces the Yankees to take the phenom on, though he's not sure whether Fraser isn't a few innings shy of a complete game. But with a 100 mph fast ball and a bat that would have made Babe Ruth envious, who cares? Film straddles sports comedy and melodrama territories, satisfying in neither. Fraser plays variation on Encino Man. Brooks rewrote part of the script, adding much needed biting humor, but not enough. Bombastic real-life team owner Steinbrenner plays himself. **101m/C; VHS, DVD.** Albert Brooks; Brendan Fraser; Dianne Wiest; Lane Smith; Michael Rapaport; Steve Garvey; Bob Costas; Roy Firestone; Anne Twomey; Tony Bennett; ***D:*** Michael Ritchie; ***W:*** Albert Brooks; Andrew Bergman; Monica Johnson; ***C:*** Laszlo Kovacs; ***M:*** Bill Conti.

Scout's Guide to the Zombie Apocalypse *Scouts v. Zombies* **2015 (R)** This awful horror comedy was originally conceived as a coming-of-age sex comedy like Superbad and then retrofitted to include a zombie element when that didn't work. The last-minute change did the film no favors. Three high school sophomores (Tye Sheridan, Logan Miller & Joey Morgan) happen to still be scouts, which makes them slightly more likely to survive the zombie apocalypse. Mostly just an excuse for dirty jokes and splattered brains. This is an oppressively bad movie, the kind of garbage for which one asks for their money or writes letters to the producers after seeing. **93m/C; DVD, Blu-Ray.** Halston Sage; Tye Sheridan; Sara Malakul Lane; Patrick Schwarzenegger; David Koechner; Logan Miller; ***D:*** Christopher Landon; ***W:*** Christopher Landon; Carrie Evans; Emi Mochizuki; ***C:*** Brandon Trost; ***M:*** Matthew Margeson.

Scout's Honor: Badge to the Bone **WOOF! 2009** Totally crappy comedy filled with stupid and/or obnoxious characters and dumb situations. Brothers David and Tim have struggled for 20 years to earn one Tiger Scout merit badge at the family-owned summer camp. Dad announces he's leaving to join the circus and the two must keep the camp from being taken over by their greedy, badge-laden brother Brandon. **90m/C; DVD.** Chris Kattan; Dave Schultz; Electra Avellan; Brian Jacob Bales; Kip King; Fred Willard; Katie Bryan; ***D:*** Jesse Bryan; ***W:*** Dave Schultz; Jesse Bryan; ***C:*** Benjamin Kasulke; ***M:*** Sam Stewart. **VIDEO**

The Scratch **2009** A wannabe hacker steals something he shouldn't have and gets kidnapped. All he can rely upon to rescue him is a rookie private eye and his bumbling friends who want the booty themselves. **92m/C; DVD.** Jason Adkins; Brian Forrest; Phil Idrissi; Kristen Nedopak; ***D:*** Jorge Suarez; ***W:*** Jorge Suarez; ***C:*** T.J. Williams, Jr.; ***M:*** Kyle Porter.

Scream **1983 (R)** Vacationers on a raft trip down the Rio Grande are terrorized by a mysterious murderer. Hopelessly dull. **86m/C; VHS, DVD, Blu-Ray.** Pepper Martin; Hank Worden; Alvy Moore; Woody Strode; John Ethan Wayne; ***D:*** Byron Quisenberry.

Scream *Scary Movie* **1996 (R)** Director Craven playfully tweaks the cliches of teen slasher pics (which he helped create with "Nightmare on Elm Street") with this tongue-in-cheek thriller. Yep, where there's a mad slasher on the loose, there must be a group of teenagers "just out for a good time." The difference is both the killer and the victims have been raised on '80s splatter movies and, therefore, know all the rules. Sexual activity and/or substance abuse? Start picking out coffins. The stalker uses his cellular phone to terrorize his victims. He also uses it to ask his prey trivia questions or offer critiques of low-grade horror movies. Campbell plays the virginal heroine in the tight sweater, with Ulrich playing opposite as the sexually frustrated boyfriend. More fun than a bucket full of Karo syrup with red dye #3. **111m/C; VHS, DVD, Blu-Ray.** Drew Barrymore; Neve Campbell; Courteney Cox; David Arquette; Skeet Ulrich; Rose McGowan; Henry Winkler; Liev Schreiber; W. Earl Brown; Jamie Kennedy; Lawrence Hecht; Matthew Lillard; ***Cameo(s):*** Wes Craven; Linda Blair; ***D:*** Wes Craven; ***W:*** Kevin Williamson; ***C:*** Mark Irwin; ***M:*** Marco Beltrami. MTV Movie Awards '97: Film.

Scream 2 *Scream Again* **1997 (R)** Sidney (Campbell) trades psychotheraphy for college, only to be harassed by a lunatic willing to duplicate her nightmares from the original. All the cast that survived the first pic are back (and some new faces, with O'Connell as Sidney's new boyfriend) including TV-tabloider Gale Weathers (Cox), who has turned a best-seller about the murders into a movie called "Stab"; lovable, huggable sheriff Dewey (Arquette); and horror film fanatic Randy (Kennedy). Director Craven and writer Williamson add more of the satirical spark that propelled its predecessor into boxoffice success. By following the rules of sequels, they increase the suspense (everyone is a suspect) and gore to tantalizing fun, making this entry to the popular franchise a hard one to top. **120m/C; VHS, DVD, Blu-Ray.** Courteney Cox; Neve Campbell; Jerry O'Connell; David Arquette; Jada Pinkett Smith; Jamie Kennedy; Liev Schreiber; Sarah Michelle Gellar; Laurie Metcalf; Elise Neal; Lewis Arquette; Duane Martin; Omar Epps; David Warner; Timothy Olyphant; Rebecca Gayheart; Portia de Rossi; Heather Graham; ***Cameo(s):*** Tori Spelling; ***D:*** Wes Craven; ***W:*** Kevin Williamson; ***C:*** Peter Deming; ***M:*** Marco Beltrami. MTV Movie Awards '98: Female Perf. (Campbell).

Scream 3 1/2 **2000 (R)** The filmmakers swear that this series is indeed only a trilogy. Good thing because, while entertaining enough, this third film is showing wear. Sidney is working as a crisis counselor and living in blessed anonymity in northern California. However, the actors involved in "Stab 3" are being offed and it ties in to her mother's mysterious past, so Sid is forced to resurface. Ambitious Gale (Cox Arquette) returns as does dopey Dewey (Arquette) and newcomer LAPD detective Kincaid (Dempsey) tries to figure out if there are any film rules that will help him catch a killer. **116m/C; VHS, DVD, Blu-Ray.** Neve Campbell; David Arquette; Courteney Cox; Patrick Dempsey; Scott Foley; Lance Henriksen; Matt Keeslar; Jenny McCarthy; Emily Mortimer; Parker Posey; Deon Richmond; Patrick Warburton; Liev Schreiber; Heather Matarazzo; Jamie Kennedy; Carrie Fisher; Kevin Smith; Jason Mewes; Roger Corman; ***D:*** Wes Craven; ***W:*** Ehren Kruger; ***C:*** Peter Deming; ***M:*** Marco Beltrami.

Scream 4 **2011 (R)** So it's not over after all. Ten years later and recovered writer Sidney Prescott's (Campbell) book tour takes her home to Woodsboro. She reunites with her family and the now-married Sheriff Dewey (Arquette) and Gale (Cox). But it isn't long before the masked Ghostface Killer revisits her. And so begins another killing spree, though this time the rules have changed. Director Craven and series creator Williamson lend their talents as the all-star cast brings this continuation of the franchise to life (and death). Fun and mindless for some—shallow and obnoxious for others. **103m/C; Blu-Ray, On Demand.** Neve Campbell; Courteney Cox; David Arquette; Emma Roberts; Hayden Panettiere; Rory Culkin; Nico Tortorella; Marley Shelton; Mary McDonnell; Adam Brody; Anthony Anderson; Anna Paquin; Kristen Bell; ***D:*** Wes Craven; ***W:*** Kevin Williamson; ***C:*** Peter Deming; ***M:*** Marco Beltrami.

Scream and Scream Again 1/2 *Screamer* **1970 (PG)** Price is a sinister doctor who tries to create a super race of people devoid of emotions. Cushing is the mastermind behind the plot. Lee is the agent investigating a series of murders. Three great horror stars, a psychadelic disco, great '60s fashions; it's all here. **95m/C; VHS, DVD, Blu-Ray.** *GB* Vincent Price; Christopher Lee; Peter Cushing; Judy Huxtable; Alfred Marks; Anthony Newlands; Uta Levka; Judi Bloom; Yutte Stensgaard; ***D:*** Gordon Hessler; ***W:*** Christopher Wicking; ***C:*** John Coquillon.

Scream, Baby, Scream *Nightmare House* **1969** An unsuccessful artist switches from sculpting clay to carving young models' faces into hideous deformed creatures. **86m/C; VHS, DVD.** Ross Harris; Eugenie Wingate; Chris Martell; Suzanne Stuart; Larry Swanson; Brad Grinter; ***D:*** Joseph Adler.

Scream Blacula Scream **1973 (R)** Blacula returns from his dusty undoing in the original movie to once again suck the blood out of greater Los Angeles. A voodoo priestess (Grier) is the only person with the power to stop him. A weak follow up to the great "Blacula," but worth a look for Marshall and Grier. **96m/C; VHS, DVD, Blu-Ray.** William Marshall; Don Mitchell; Pam Grier; Michael Conrad; Richard Lawson; Lynne Moody; Janee Michelle; Barbara Rhoades; Bernie Hamilton; ***D:*** Bob Kelljan.

Scream Bloody Murder **WOOF! 1972 (R)** A young boy grinds his father to death with a tractor but mangles his own hand trying to jump off. After receiving a steel claw and being released from a mental institution he continues his murderous ways in and around his home town. Inspiring. **90m/C; VHS, DVD.** Fred Holbert; Leigh Mitchell; Robert Knox; Suzette Hamilton; ***D:*** Robert Emery.

Scream of Fear *Taste of Fear* **1961** A wheelchair-bound young woman goes to visit her father and new stepmother only to find her father is away on business. But she believes she sees her father's corpse. Is someone trying to drive her mad? Abounds in plot twists and mistaken identities. A truly spooky film, suspenseful, and well-made. **81m/B; VHS, DVD, Blu-Ray.** *GB* Susan Strasberg; Ronald Lewis; Ann Todd; Christopher Lee; ***D:*** Seth Holt; ***W:*** Jimmy Sangster.

Scream of the Banshee 1/2 **2011 (R)** Syfy Channel flick tackles the Irish legend with some decent makeup effects and the victims deserving what they get for being so stupid. A 12th-century knight cuts off the head of the banshee and encloses it in a box that somehow winds up hidden at the university where archeologist Isla Whelan (Holly) works. Isla and several of her assistants find and open the box, the banshee screams, and that means nightmares and death. **90m/C; DVD.** Lauren Holly; Leane Cochran; Todd Haberkorn; Marcelle Baer; Lance Henriksen; Garrett Hines; Edrick Brown; ***D:*** Steven C. Miller; ***W:*** Anthony C. Ferrante; ***C:*** Andrew Strahorn; ***M:*** Ryan Dodson. **CABLE**

Scream of the Demon Lover **WOOF! 1971 (R)** A young biochemist has a busy day as she works for a reclusive Baron. She fantasizes about him, tries to track down a murderer, and eventually discovers a mutant in the cellar. About as bad as they come, but short! **75m/C; VHS, DVD.** Jennifer Hartley; Jeffrey Chase; ***D:*** Jose Luis Merino.

Scream of the Wolf **1974** Author and ex-hunter John (Graves) is called on to help the police in their investigation of a series of murders that seem to have been caused by a wolf that can walk on two legs. He turns to Byron (Walker), an old friend and obsessive hunter (think Zaroff in "The Most Dangerous Game") for help, but Byron refuses, arguing that the murders are making the people in the community feel more alive than ever. Byron involves John in a battle of brawn and hunting skill that will ultimately reveal the truth behind the killings. Passable TV movie by director Curtis feels like another attempt to create a "Kolchak: The Night Stalker"-type TV series, complete with Graves's flashy red Corvette, and a jazzy '70s "wokka-chikka" soundtrack. **74m/C; VHS, DVD.** Peter Graves; Clint Walker; JoAnn Pflug; Phil Carey; James Storm; ***D:*** Dan Curtis; ***W:*** Richard Matheson; David Case; ***C:*** Paul Lohmann; ***M:*** Robert Cobert. **TV**

Screamers *L'Isola Degli Uomini Pesce; Island of the Fishmen; Something Waits in the Dark* **1980 (R)** A mad scientist on a desert island gleefully turns escaped convicts into grotesque monstrosities. Gory and gratuitous. **83m/C; VHS, DVD, Blu-Ray.** Richard Johnson; Joseph Cotten; Barbara Bach; ***D:*** Dan T. Miller; Sergio Martino.

Screamers **1996 (R)** In the year 2078, Colonel Joe Hendricksson (Weller) and a small band of survivors fight a civil war on the radiation contaminated planet Sirius 6B. They run up against the screamers—mechanical creatures with razor-sharp claws, originally designed to protect humans. The screamers are bent on destroying all life in the universe while somehow mutating and breeding on their own. Unfortunately, director Duguay doesn't give any indication how this is taking place. Some fine stunt work and special effects redeem standard action adventure. Based on the novella "Second Variety" by Philip K. Dick ("Blade Runner"). **107m/C; DVD, Blu-Ray.** Peter Weller; Jennifer Rubin; Andrew Lauer; Charles Powell; Ron White; Michael Caloz; ***D:*** Christian Duguay; ***W:*** Dan O'Bannon; Miguel Tejada-Flores; ***C:*** Rodney Gibbons; ***M:*** Normand Corbeil.

Screamers: The Hunting 1/2 **2009 (R)** It's been 13 years since the robotic screamers destroyed the human colony on Sirius 6B. But when a distress signal is picked up from the supposedly deserted planet it attracts a rescue team. What they discover is that the screamers have evolved into mutant machine/human hybrids still out to destroy the human race. Based on the Philip K. Dick story. **95m/C; DVD.** Greg Bryk; Gina Holden; Tim Rozon; Christopher Redman; Lance Henriksen; ***D:*** Sheldon Wilson; ***W:*** Miguel Tejada-Flores; ***C:*** John Tarver; ***M:*** Benoit Grey. **VIDEO**

The Screaming Dead *Dracula vs. Frankenstein* **1972** Monsters rise from the tomb to do battle with planet Earth and each other. Not to be confused with the Al Adamson epic "Dracula vs. Frankenstein." **84m/C; VHS, DVD.** *SP* Dennis Price; Howard Vernon; Alberto Dalbes; Mary Francis; Genevieve Deloir; Josianne Gibert; Fernando Bilbao; ***D:*** Jess (Jesus) Franco.

Screaming Dead **2003 (R)** Satisfactory exploitation/horror flick has a fetish photographer, his assistant, and some models doing a shoot in an abandoned, possibly haunted hospital where hundreds of patients were tortured and killed in a basement dungeon. Not as much skin or gore as you'd expect from the set-up, and it takes a while to get going, but it's not too bad for fans of the genre. **95m/C; DVD.** Misty Mundae; Rob Monkiewicz; Joseph Farrell; Rachael Robbins; Heidi Kristoffer; ***D:*** Bret Piper; ***W:*** Bret Piper; ***M:*** Jon Greathouse. **VIDEO**

Screaming Eagles 1/2 **1956** Cheapie war pic. American paratroopers are on their way to France before D-Day to secure the bridges leading to Utah Beach. Overshooting the drop zone, the platoon must cross 20 miles of German-occupied territory to accomplish their mission. **81m/B; DVD.** Tom Tryon; Jan Merlin; Martin Milner; Alvy Moore; Robert (Bobby) Blake; Paul Burke; Mark Damon; ***D:*** Charles F. Haas; ***W:*** David Lang; Robert Presnell, Jr.; ***C:*** Harry Neumann; ***M:*** Harry Sukman.

Screaming Mimi 1/2 **1958** Unhinged, convoluted psycho-thriller starring the busty Ekberg as a stripper. Virginia is attacked in her shower by a knife-wielding madman but is rescued by stepbrother Charlie. She's traumatized and goes to shrink Greenwood but he becomes obsessed and begins controlling her life, which consists of Virginia working as an exotic dancer in a sleazy nightclub. Reporter Sweeney links Virginia's attack to a series of murders where the statue of a screaming woman is left by each female victim. **79m/B; DVD.** Anita Ekberg; Philip Carey; Harry Townes; Romney Brent; Gypsy Rose Lee; Alan Gifford; Linda Cherney; ***D:*** Gerd Oswald; ***W:*** Robert Blees; ***C:*** Burnett Guffey; ***M:*** Mischa Bakaleinikoff.

Screw Loose *Svitati* **1999 (R)** Bernardo's (Greggio) dying father (Barra) has one last request—he wants a reunion with his American WWII buddy Jake (Brooks). So being a dutiful son, Bernardo comes to America and discovers Jake is in an L.A. mental institution. Nevertheless, he breaks him out and flies Jake back to Italy with him—followed by Jake's doctor, Barbara (Condra). And it turns out maybe Jake isn't the only one with a few loose screws. Slapsticky, with a weak script. **85m/C; VHS, DVD.** *IT* Mel Brooks; Ezio Greggio; Gianfranco Barra; Julie Condra; Randi Ingerman; *D:* Ezio Greggio; *W:* Rudy DeLuca; Steve Haberman; *C:* Luca Robecchi.

Screwballs 🦴 **1983 (R)** Freewheeling group of high school boys stirs up trouble for their snooty and virginal homecoming queen. Another inept teen sex comedy with no subtlety whatsoever. Sequel: "Loose Screws." **80m/C; VHS, DVD, Blu-Ray.** Peter Keleghan; Lynda Speciale; *D:* Rafal Zielinski; *W:* Jim Wynorski.

Screwed WOOF! 2000 (PG-13) Chauffeur MacDonald tries kidnapping his mean boss's dog for ransom but things get screwed up so badly that the boss thinks it's the chauffeur that's been kidnapped. Lame physical and gross-out "comedy" ensues. Just who the title refers to is never made clear, but it seems like it's the producers, who had to pay the actors and writer/directors for this, ahem, dog. DeVito is the only one on screen who seems to know what he's doing, and Alexander and Karaszewski look to be cashing in on some far superior prior screenwriting work. **82m/C; VHS, DVD.** Norm MacDonald; Elaine Stritch; Danny DeVito; Dave Chappelle; Daniel Benzali; Sherman Hemsley; Malcolm Stewart; *D:* Scott M. Alexander; Larry Karaszewski; *W:* Scott M. Alexander; Larry Karaszewski; *C:* Robert Brinkmann; *M:* Michel Colombier.

The Scribbler 🦴 ½ **2014 (R)** With an abundance of graphic novel style but none of the budget or personality to pull it off, Cassidy stars as Suki, a girl who lives in a halfway house of mentally addled women (including Gershon, Grey, and Trachtenberg). She's a part of an experimental procedure called "The Siamese Burn," which is designed to electro-shock out the multiple personalities that have destroyed her life. But what if it leaves the wrong one standing? You won't care if it does or doesn't. **88m/C; DVD, Blu-Ray.** Katie Cassidy; Garret Dillahunt; Billy Campbell; Michael Imperioli; Eliza Dushku; Gina Gershon; Michelle Trachtenberg; *D:* John Suits; *W:* Dan Schaffer; *C:* Mark Putnam; *M:* Alec Puro.

Scrooge 🦴🦴 ½ **1970 (G)** Well done musical version of Charles Dickens' classic "A Christmas Carol," about a miserly old man who is faced with ghosts on Christmas Eve. Finney is memorable in the title role. **86m/C; VHS, DVD.** *GB* Albert Finney; Alec Guinness; Edith Evans; Kenneth More; *D:* Ronald Neame; *W:* Leslie Bricusse; *C:* Oswald Morris; *M:* Leslie Bricusse. Golden Globes '71: Actor--Mus./Comedy (Finney).

Scrooged 🦴🦴 **1988 (PG-13)** Somewhat disjointed big-budgeted version of the hallowed classic. A callous TV executive staging "A Christmas Carol" is himself visited by the three ghosts and sees the light. Kane is terrific as one of the ghosts. Film is heavy-handed, Murray too sardonic to be believable. **101m/C; VHS, DVD, Blu-Ray.** Bill Murray; Carol Kane; John Forsythe; David Johansen; Bobcat Goldthwait; Karen Allen; Michael J. Pollard; Brian Doyle-Murray; Alfre Woodard; John Glover; Robert Mitchum; Buddy Hackett; Robert Goulet; Jamie Farr; Mary Lou Retton; Lee Majors; Damon Hines; Mary Ellen Trainor; Mabel King; Wendie Malick; Joel Murray; John Houseman; Steve Kahan; Kate McGregor-Stewart; *D:* Richard Donner; *W:* Mitch Glazer; Michael O'Donoghue; *C:* Michael Chapman; *M:* Danny Elfman.

Scrubbers 🦴 **1982 (R)** Young girl is sent to reform school where she's forced to survive in a cruel and brutal environment. Low-budget "reform school" movie with no point, but lots of lesbianism. **93m/C; VHS, Streaming.** *GB* Amanda York; Chrissie Cotterill; Elizabeth Edmonds; Kate Ingram; Debbie Bishop; Dana Gillespie; *D:* Mai Zetterling.

Scruples 🦴🦴 ½ **1980** Set in the glamorous, jet-setting world of Beverly Hills, this top-rated miniseries follows the career of Billy Ikehorn (Wagner) as she weds a wealthy industrialist and opens a clothing boutique named "Scruples." She caters to high society's haute couture, and encounters unscrupulous individuals who threaten to dethrone her from her position of power and privilege. Based on the best-selling novel by Judith Krantz. **279m/C; VHS, DVD.** Lindsay Wagner; Barry Bostwick; Kim Cattrall; Gavin MacLeod; Connie Stevens; Efrem Zimbalist, Jr.; Gene Tierney; *M:* Charles Bernstein.

The Sculptress 🦴🦴 **1997** Troubled writer Rosalind Leigh (Goodall) prepares to interview convicted killer Olive Martin (Quirke), who five years before was found with the dead bodies of her mother and sister. Nicknamed "The Sculptress" for the gruesome nature of the murders, the equally troubled Olive is also a convincing liar. Although Olive says she's guilty, Roz is certain she's hiding something and becomes determined to discover the truth. Very creepy. Made for British TV; based on the novel by Minette Walters. **180m/C; VHS, DVD.** *GB* Caroline Goodall; Pauline Quirke; Christopher Fulford; Dermot Crowley; David Horovitch; Jay Villiers; Lynda Rooke; *D:* Stuart Orme; *W:* Reg Gadney; *C:* Gavin Finney; *M:* Colin Towns. **TV**

Scum 🦴🦴🦴 **1979** Adapted from Roy Minton's acclaimed play, this British production looks at the struggle among three young men in a British Borstal (a prison for young convicts.) Portrays the physical, sexual, and psychological violence committed. Horrifying and powerful. **96m/C; VHS, DVD, Blu-Ray.** *GB* Phil Daniels; Mick Ford; Ray Winstone; *D:* Alan Clarke.

Scum of the Earth 🦴 ½ **1963** Early '60s skin flick about innocent young Kim (Miles), who is cruelly tricked into posing topless for a photographer and is then blackmailed into a downward spiral of sleaze that ends in murder and suicide. The film features much of the cast and crew of director Lewis's "Blood Feast." **73m/B; DVD.** Vicki (Allison Louise Downe) Miles; Lawrence Wood; Mal Arnold; Thomas Sweetwood; Sandy Sinclair; *D:* Herschell Gordon Lewis; *W:* Herschell Gordon Lewis.

The Sea 🦴🦴 **2002** A "King Lear" variation set in Iceland and concerned with fish. Fierce patriarch Thordur (Eyolfsson) summons his three adult children to discuss the family fishery. The kids are upset because dad never modernized the business and it can't compete with the larger corporations. His unhappy progeny want to sell out, divide the profits, and get on with their lives. Everyone enjoys spreading their own particular misery and angst around. Icelandic with subtitles. **109m/C; DVD.** *IC* Gunnar Eyjolfsson; Kristbjorg Kjeld; Hilmir Snaer Gudnason; Gundrun S. Gisladottir; Sigurdur Skulason; Herdis Orvaldsdottir; *D:* Baltasar Kormakur; *W:* Baltasar Kormakur; Olafur Haukur Simonarson; *C:* Jean-Louis Vialard; *M:* Jon Asgeirsson.

Sea Beast 🦴🦴 *Troglodyte* **2008** The CGI is barely adequate but this SciFi Channel flick actually gets bloody and scary. Fisherman Will McKenna (Nemec) has one of his crew snatched by a beastie during a storm. Meanwhile, his teenaged daughter Carly (McDonald) has snuck off to an island cabin with her boyfriend (Wisler). The cabin is located in the beast's (and its babies) territory. So Will teams ups with marine biologist Arden (Sullivan) and local drunk Ben (Stait) to stop the hungry sea critters. **87m/C; DVD.** Corin "Corky" Nemec; Camille Sullivan; Miriam McDonald; Brent Stait; Daniel Wisler; Gary Hudson; Gwynyth Walsh; *D:* Paul Ziller; *W:* Paul Ziller; Gordon Williams; *C:* Mahlon Todd Williams; *M:* Chuck Cirino. **CABLE**

The Sea Change 🦴🦴 **1998** Ambitious businessman Rupert Granger has been neglecting his girlfriend Alison at the worst possible time (she's just found out she's pregnant). He goes to Barcelona to close a deal and gets stranded at the airport, which forces Rupert to share a hotel room with relaxed, working-class bloke Chas, who decides Rupert (who's always complaining) needs a personality makeover before he returns home. **92m/C; DVD.** *GB* Sean Chapman; Ray Winstone; Maryam D'Abo; Andre Bernard; *D:* Michael Bray; *W:* Michael Bray; Jill Uden; *C:* Josep Civit; *M:* Mark Thomas.

Sea Chase 🦴🦴 ½ **1955** An odd postwar sea adventure, wherein a renegade German freighter captain is pursued by British and German navies as he leaves Australia at the outbreak of WWII. A Prussian Wayne rivaled only by his infamous Genghis Khan in "The Conqueror" for strange character selection. Turner is on board as Wayne's girlfriend. **117m/C; VHS, DVD.** John Wayne; Lana Turner; Tab Hunter; James Arness; Lyle Bettger; David Farrar; Richard (Dick) Davalos; Claude Akins; John Qualen; *D:* John Farrow; *C:* William Clothier.

Sea Devils 🦴🦴 **1953** A smuggler and a beautiful spy come together during the Napoleonic Wars in this sea romance filled with intrigue and adventure. **86m/C; VHS, DVD.** *GB* Rock Hudson; Yvonne De Carlo; Maxwell Reed; *D:* Raoul Walsh.

The Sea Ghost 🦴 ½ *U-67; Phantom Submarine U-67* **1931** After a German sub sinks a passenger liner during WWI, American naval officer Greg Winters lets the sub escape to search for survivors. This leads to his court-martial for disobeying orders and he later becomes the owner of a salvage ship and encounters the German submarine captain again. **73m/B; DVD.** Alan Hale; Peter Erkelenz; Laura La Plante; Clarence Wilson; Claud Allister; *D:* William Nigh; *W:* William Nigh; Jo Van Ronbeo; *C:* Sidney Hickox.

The Sea Gull 🦴🦴 **1968** Slow-moving adaptation of the 1895 play by Anton Chekhov. Set at a Russian country estate, various self-absorbed characters deal with their would-be ambitions, including writing and acting; love, requited and otherwise; and family problems and rejections. **141m/C; DVD.** James Mason; Vanessa Redgrave; Simone Signoret; David Warner; Denholm Elliott; Harry Andrews; Kathleen Widdoes; Alfred Lynch; *D:* Sidney Lumet; *W:* Moura Budberg; *C:* Gerry Fisher.

Sea Gypsies 🦴🦴 **1978 (G)** A sailing crew of five is shipwrecked off the Aleutian Islands. They must escape before winter or learn to survive. Passable family drama. **101m/C; VHS, Streaming.** Robert F. Logan; Mikki Jamison-Olsen; Heather Rattray; Cjon Damitri; *D:* Stewart Raffill; *W:* Stewart Raffill.

The Sea Hawk 🦴🦴 **1924** Gentleman privateer Sir Oliver Tressilian (Sills) has retired to his Cornish estate and hopes to marry Rosamund Godolphin (Bennett). After Lionel (Hughes), Oliver's half-brother, kills Rosamund's brother in a duel, he blames Oliver and arranges for his kidnapping by Capt. Leigh (Beery Sr.). Leigh's ship is captured by the Spanish and Oliver is chained to the oars until the ship is besieged by Moors and Oliver joins their ranks to become the dreaded Sea Hawk. Lots of swashbuckling and a more faithful adaptation of the Rafael Sabatini novel than the 1940 Errol Flynn remake. **123m/B; Silent; DVD.** Milton Sills; Enid Bennett; Lloyd Hughes; Wallace Beery; Wallace MacDonald; Frank Currier; William "Buster" Collier, Jr.; *D:* Frank Lloyd; *W:* J.G. Hawks; *C:* Norbert Brodine.

The Sea Hawk 🦴🦴🦴 ½ **1940** An English privateer learns the Spanish are going to invade England with their Armada. After numerous adventures, he is able to aid his queen and help save his country, finding romance along the way. One of Flynn's swashbuckling best. Available colorized. **128m/B; VHS, DVD, Blu-Ray.** Errol Flynn; Claude Rains; Donald Crisp; Alan Hale; Flora Robson; Brenda Marshall; Henry Daniell; Gilbert Roland; James Stephenson; Una O'Connor; *D:* Michael Curtiz; *W:* Howard Koch.

The Sea Inside 🦴🦴🦴 *Mar Adentro* **2004 (PG-13)** Poignant, unsentimental, fact-based drama based on the life of Spanish quadriplegic Ramon Sampedro, who tried for some 30 years for the right to commit assisted suicide. Paralyzed in a diving accident, Ramon (Bardem) becomes a cause celebre as he lies bedridden, cared for by his religious family who are opposed to his decision. He builds his case with the help of his lawyer Julia (Rueda), who suffers herself from a degenerative disease. Ramon also inspires Rosa (Duenas), a neighbor who tries to convince the single-minded man to live and then falls in love with him. Bardem does an amazing job since, except for some brief flashbacks and fantasies, his movement is limited to his neck and head. The real Sampedro wrote poetry and a best-selling memoir, gave numerous interviews, and filmed his assisted suicide (in 1998) so it could be shown on TV. Spanish with subtitles. **125m/C; DVD.** Javier Bardem; Celso Bugallo; Jose(p) Maria Pou; Belen Rueda; Lola Duenas; Mabel Rivera; Clara Segura; Joan Dalmau; Alberto Jimenez; Tamar Novas; Francesc Garrido; *D:* Alejandro Amenabar; *W:* Alejandro Amenabar; Mateo Gil; *C:* Javier Aguirresarobe; *M:* Alejandro Amenabar. Oscars '04: Foreign Film; Golden Globes '05: Foreign Film; Ind. Spirit '05: Foreign Film.

The Sea is Watching 🦴🦴🦴 *Umi wa miteita; The Sea Witches* **2002 (R)** Akira Kurosawa was working on the screenplay for this film but was prevented from filming it due to his untimely death, and it was turned over to director Kei Kumai to finish. Life for women at the end of the Tokugawa period was hard, and many found prostitution to be the only means they had of putting food on the table. Here are the stories of two of them, O-Shin (Nagiko Tono), who is naive and desperately hopes to wed a man and thus escape her situation, and her more cynical friend Kikuno (Misa Shimizu). **119m/B; DVD.** *JP* Misa Shimizu; Masatoshi Nagase; Hidetaka Yoshioka; Eiji Okuda; Renji Ishibashi; Yumiko Nogawa; Yukiya Kitamura; Nagiko Tono; Miho Tsumuki; Michiko Kawai; Tenshi Kamogawa; *D:* Kei Kumai; *W:* Akira Kurosawa; Shugoro Yamamoto; *C:* Kazuo Okuhara; *M:* Teizo Matusmura.

The Sea of Grass 🦴🦴 **1947** Melodramatic Tracy/Hepburn western directed by Kazan, whose relative inexperience had his stars overacting. Lutie (Hepburn) marries New Mexico cattle baron James Brewton (Tracy) after a whirlwind courtship and then confronts his ruthless streak. He opposes homesteaders and illegally keeps them off the government-owned land he uses for grazing. Marital angst follows as Lutie leaves, gets involved with lawyer Brice Chamberlain (Douglas), returns, and has their problems follow them into the next generation. **133m/B; DVD.** Spencer Tracy; Katharine Hepburn; Melvyn Douglas; Phyllis Thaxter; Robert Walker; Edgar Buchanan; Harry Carey, Sr.; Ruth Nelson; James Bell; *D:* Elia Kazan; *W:* Marguerite Roberts; Vincent Lawrence; *C:* Harry Stradling, Sr.; *M:* Herbert Stothart.

Sea of Love 🦴🦴🦴 ½ **1989 (R)** A tough, tightly wound thriller about an alcoholic cop with a mid-life crisis. While following the track of a serial killer, he begins a torrid relationship with one of his suspects. Pacino doesn't stand a chance when Barkin heats up the screen. **113m/C; VHS, DVD, Blu-Ray, HD-DVD.** Al Pacino; Ellen Barkin; John Goodman; Michael Rooker; William Hickey; Richard Jenkins; *D:* Harold Becker; *W:* Richard Price; *C:* Ronnie Taylor; *M:* Trevor Jones.

Sea of Sand 🦴🦴 ½ *Desert Patrol* **1958** Typical actioner set in WWII finds a British desert patrol's latest mission is to blow up Rommel's fuel supply before the battle of El Alamein. Lots of heroics against the Nazis and stiff upper lips. **97m/B; VHS, DVD.** *GB* Richard Attenborough; John Gregson; Michael Craig; Vincent Ball; Ray McAnally; *D:* Guy Green; *W:* Robert Westerby; *C:* Wilkie Cooper; *M:* Clifton Parker.

The Sea of Trees 🦴 **2016 (PG-13)** Gus Van Sant reaches a career low with this schmaltzy drama about a man dealing with the tragic loss of his wife. Arthur Brennan (McConaughey) travels to the legendary Aokigahara, a forest at the base of Mt. Fuji in Japan that has become a popular locale for people to kill themselves. While working toward his final moments, he meets a man (Watanabe) lost in the forest, and the two work together to try to find their way home. It's a defiantly goofy, silly movie that piles up twists in the final act in a way that produce more laughter than tears. **110m/C; DVD, Blu-Ray.** Matthew McConaughey; Naomi Watts; Ken(saku) Watanabe; James Saito; Charles Van Eman; *D:* Gus Van Sant; *W:* Chris Sparling; *C:* Kasper Tuxen; *M:* Mason Bates.

Sea People 🦴🦴 **2000** Teen swimmer Amanda (Moss) rescues elderly John McRae (Cronyn) after he leaps from a bridge into the water. But she discovers that John wasn't trying to commit suicide and that he and his wife, Bridget (Gregson), have a very unique relationship with the sea. **92m/C; VHS, DVD.** Hume Cronyn; Tegan Moss; Joan Gregson; Ron Lea; Don McKellar; Cedric Smith; *D:* Vic Sarin. **CABLE**

Sea Wife 🦴🦴 ½ *Sea Wyf and Biscuit* **1957** Using nicknames and a newspaper's personal column to correspond, Sea Wife,

Bulldog, and Biscuit are apparently rehashing a crime committed against a fourth person that's still haunting them. A flashback reveals three men and a woman in a lifeboat after their ship has been torpedoed by the Japanese in 1942. Only three ultimately survive their ordeal. Collins plays a nun of all things, although she keeps her calling a secret from the others. Rather drab adaptation of J.M. Scott's adventure/thriller "Sea-Wyf." **82m/C; VHS, DVD.** *GB* Richard Burton; Joan Collins; Basil Sydney; Ronald Squire; Cy Grant; Joan Hickson; Lloyd Lamble; Eileen Way; ***D:*** Bob McNaught; ***W:*** George K. Burke; ***C:*** Edward (Ted) Scaife; ***M:*** Kenneth V. Jones; Leonard Salzedo.

Sea Wolf: The Pirate's Curse 🦴 1/2 *The Sea Wolf; The Pirate's Curse* **2005 (PG-13)** Jeffrey Thorpe (Griffith) fancies himself a modern-day pirate and will do any job for the right price. Soon enough he gets suckered into a scheme to find Montezuma's lost gold treasure by a pretty woman. **83m/C; DVD.** Thomas Ian Griffith; Gerit Kling; Barry Flatman; ***D:*** Mark Roper; ***W:*** Harry Alan Towers; ***C:*** Stefano Coletta; ***M:*** Norman Ornstein.

Sea Wolves 🦴🦴 1/2 **1981 (PG)** True WWII story about a commando-style operation undertaken by a group of middle-aged, retired British cavalrymen in India in 1943. Decent acting, though Peck's British accent fades in and out, with Moore as Bond. **120m/C; VHS, DVD.** *GB* Gregory Peck; Roger Moore; David Niven; Trevor Howard; Patrick Macnee; William Morgan Sheppard; Barbara Kellerman; Kenneth Griffith; Patrick Allen; ***D:*** Andrew V. McLaglen; ***W:*** Reginald Rose.

Seabiscuit 🦴🦴🦴 1/2 **2003 (PG-13)** Equine Cinderella story of the legendary Seabiscuit—a funny-looking, ill-tempered thoroughbred—and the men who shaped him into a racing legend: owner Charles Howard (Bridges); partially blind, over-sized, luck-challenged jockey Red Pollard (Maguire); and trainer "Silent" Tom Smith (Cooper) who believed in the underdog horse. The ragtag trio eventually wangles a race with the more-celebrated War Admiral, whose owner had previously refused to share a track with the far inferior Seabiscuit. Writer/director Ross delivers suitably rousing race scenes in this can't miss story of an unlikely champion who brought hope and inspiration to the Depression-era crowds and became a symbol of hope. All three leads are outstanding, as is Macy as an excitable radio announcer. Based on Laura Hillenbrand's best-seller "Seabiscuit: An American Legend." **140m/C; VHS, DVD, Blu-Ray, HD-DVD.** Tobey Maguire; Jeff Bridges; Chris Cooper; Elizabeth Banks; William H. Macy; Gary Stevens; Eddie Jones; Ed Lauter; Michael O'Neill; Royce D. Applegate; Annie Corley; Valerie Mahaffey; ***Nar:*** David McCullough; ***D:*** Gary Ross; ***W:*** Gary Ross; ***C:*** John Schwartzman; ***M:*** Randy Newman.

The Seagull 🦴🦴 1/2 **1975** Danner's sensitive performance as Nina, an aspiring actress with fragile emotions, highlights this filmed production of Chekhov's "The Seagull," originally staged by the Williamstown Theatre Festival. **117m/C; VHS, DVD.** Blythe Danner; Olympia Dukakis; Lee Grant; Frank Langella; Kevin McCarthy; Marian Mercer; William Swetland; Louis Zorich; ***D:*** John J. Desmond; Nikos Psacharopoulos; ***M:*** Arthur B. Rubinstein. **TV**

The Seagull 🦴🦴 1/2 **2018 (PG-13)** An unassuming adaptation of the classic Chekhov play. Outside of Moscow in 1904, self-absorbed actress Arkadina (Bening) and her younger boyfriend, writer Trigorin (Stoll), visit the estate of her sick brother Sorin (Dennehy). Arkadina's artistic son Konstantin (Howle), who was raised on the estate and is jealous of his mother and her lover, has his own love interest in aspiring actress Nina (Ronan). Along with a group of other guests and locals, destructive passions, artistic and amorous, are explored. Despite solid performances by the star-studded cast, the film falls short of stage versions. **98m/C; DVD.** Saoirse Ronan; Annette Bening; Corey Stoll; Elisabeth Moss; Mare Winningham; ***D:*** Michael Mayer; ***W:*** Stephen Karam; ***C:*** Matthew Lloyd; ***M:*** Nico Muhly; Anton Sanko.

Seal Team 🦴 1/2 **2008 (R)** A black ops counterterrorism team is dispatched behind enemy lines in Iraq on a covert mission days before Operation: Desert Shield is to begin. When their mission is compromised, the team must focus on surviving so they can return home. **97m/C; DVD.** Zach McGowan; Jeremy Davis; Chris Warner; Kristoffer Garrison; Ken Gamble; Neto DePaula Pimenta; ***D:*** Mark C. Andrews; ***W:*** Mark C. Andrews; ***C:*** Chia-Yu Chen; ***M:*** Matt Gates. **VIDEO**

Seal Team 8: Behind Enemy Lines 🦴 **2014 (R)** An action flick of no distinction except for the unintentional laughs. A covert team of Navy SEALs are sent to the Congo on an unsanctioned mission in order to prevent the sale of weapons-grade uranium to terrorists. **98m/C; DVD, Blu-Ray.** Lex Shrapnel; Tom Sizemore; Darron Meyer; Anthony Oseyemi; ***D:*** Roel Reine; ***W:*** Brendan Cowles; Shane Kuhn; ***C:*** Roel Reine; ***M:*** Mark Kilian. **VIDEO**

Seal Team Six: The Raid on Osama Bin Laden 🦴 1/2 **2012** Dramatic reenactment based loosely on the mission to hunt and kill Osama Bin Laden. **90m/C; DVD, Blu-Ray, Streaming.** Cam Gigandet; Anson Mount; Freddy Rodriguez; Xzibit; Kathleen Robertson; ***D:*** John Stockwell; ***W:*** Kendall Lampkin; ***C:*** John Sejdinaj; ***M:*** Paul Haslinger. **TV**

Seamless **WOOF!** **2000 (R)** Overwrought, silly and senseless story about a group of rave-happy homeless kids who are offered work and a place to live by paternalistic J.B. (charmless Kentaro Seagal, Steven's son). Things don't work out so the kids wind up back on the street, resorting to drug dealing, prostitution and the like to get by, and that's bad but not nearly as bad as this dreck. **91m/C; VHS, DVD.** Shannon Elizabeth; Peter Alexander; Melinda Scherwinski; Broc Benedict; ***D:*** Debra Lemattre; ***C:*** Denise Brassard; ***M:*** Mamoru Mochizuki. **VIDEO**

Seance 🦴 **2006 (R)** Typically dumb, low-budget teen slasher/horror flick. College student Lauren (Erickson) gets a nasty surprise when she sees the ghost of a young girl in her dorm room. Stuck on campus over Thanksgiving break, the remaining students decide to hold a seance and see if they can contact Cara, whom Lauren learned died suspiciously in their dorm. Instead, Spence (Paul) appears and they quickly discover that the former janitor was a serial killer who's not done yet. **88m/C; DVD.** Adrian Paul; Kandis Erickson; A.J. Lamas; Tori White; Chauntal Lewis; Joel Geist; Bridget Shergalis; ***D:*** Mark Smith; ***W:*** Mark Smith; ***C:*** Geoffrey Schaaf; ***M:*** Vincent Gillioz. **VIDEO**

Seance on a Wet Afternoon 🦴🦴🦴 1/2 **1964** Dark, thoughtful film about a crazed pseudo-psychic who coerces her husband into a kidnapping so she can gain recognition by divining the child's whereabouts. Directed splendidly by Forbes, and superb acting from Stanley and Attenborough, who co-produced with Forbes. **111m/B; VHS, DVD.** *GB* Kim Stanley; Richard Attenborough; Margaret Lacey; Maria Kazan; Mark Eden; Patrick Magee; ***D:*** Bryan Forbes; ***M:*** John Barry. British Acad. '64: Actor (Attenborough); Natl. Bd. of Review '64: Actress (Stanley); N.Y. Film Critics '64: Actress (Stanley).

The Search 🦴🦴🦴 1/2 **1948** Clift, an American solider stationed in post-WWII Berlin, befriends a homeless nine-year-old amnesiac boy (Jandl) and tries to find his family. Meanwhile, his mother has been searching the Displaced Persons camps for her son. Although Clift wants to adopt the boy, he steps aside, and mother and son are finally reunited. "The Search" was shot on location in the American Occupied Zone of Germany. Jandl won a special juvenile Oscar in his first (and only) film role. This was also Clift's first screen appearance, although this movie was actually filmed after his debut in "Red River," it was released first. **105m/B; VHS, DVD.** Montgomery Clift; Aline MacMahon; Ivan Jandl; Jarmila Novotna; Wendell Corey; ***D:*** Fred Zinnemann; ***W:*** Paul Jarrico. Oscars '48: Story; Golden Globes '49: Screenplay.

Search and Destroy 🦴 *Striking Back* **1981 (PG)** Deadly vendetta is begun by a Vietnamese official during the war. It is continued in the U.S. as he hunts down the American soldiers he feels betrayed him. Sub-par, forgettable war/action flick. **93m/C; VHS, DVD.** Perry King; Don Stroud; Park Jong Soo; George Kennedy; Tisa Farrow; ***D:*** William Fruet.

Search and Destroy 🦴 **1988 (R)** Sci-fi action flick about the capture of a secret biological warfare research station. Lotsa action, that's for sure—where's the plot? **87m/C; VHS, DVD.** Stuart Garrison Day; Dan Kuchuck; Peggy Jacobsen; ***D:*** J. Christian Ingvordsen; ***W:*** J. Christian Ingvordsen; ***C:*** Steven Kaman; ***M:*** Chris Burke.

Search and Destroy 🦴🦴 **1994 (R)** Complex story finds bankrupt businessman Martin Mirkheim (Dunne) trying to overcome his financial woes by making a film based on a book by self-help guru, Dr. Luther Waxling (Hopper). Of course, since Martin's broke, he first has to find someone willing to invest in his venture, and the shady duo (Walken and Turturro) he does just leave him with more problems. Tediously stagy adaptation of Howard Korders' play. Directorial debut by artist Salle at least looks great and provides some quirky moments. **91m/C; VHS, DVD.** Griffin Dunne; Dennis Hopper; Rosanna Arquette; Christopher Walken; John Turturro; Illeana Douglas; Ethan Hawke; ***Cameo(s):*** Martin Scorsese; ***D:*** David Salle; ***W:*** Michael Almereyda; ***C:*** Michael Spiller; Bobby Bukowski; ***M:*** Elmer Bernstein.

Search for Beauty 🦴🦴 **1934** American Don (Crabbe) and Brit Barbara (Lupino) are both Olympic medal winners. Being physically fit and attractive, they are offered the chance to help edit a physiques magazine, but discover the publishers are more interested in cheesecake than health and are running a scam contest to attract athletes to pose. **78m/B; DVD.** Buster Crabbe; Ida Lupino; Toby Wing; James Gleason; Robert Armstrong; Gertrude Michael; ***D:*** Erle C. Kenton; ***W:*** Frank Butler; Claude Binyon; ***C:*** Harry Fischbeck.

The Search for Bridey Murphy 🦴🦴 **1956** Long before channelers, Ramtha and New-Age profiteers, there was a Colorado housewife who under hypnosis described a previous life as an Irish girl. Her famous claim was never proven—but that didn't stop this well-acted but dull dramatization. Neither sensationalist, nor likely to persuade skeptics. Based on the book by Morey Bernstein, hypnotist in the case. **84m/B; VHS, Streaming.** Teresa Wright; Louis Hayward; Nancy Gates; Kenneth Tobey; Richard Anderson; ***D:*** Noel Langley; ***W:*** Noel Langley.

The Search for John Gissing 🦴🦴 **2001** Skillfully done corporate comedy. American Matthew Barnes (Binder) assumes he's been brought to London to consult on a business merger but he's actually a replacement for his British counterpart, John Gissing (a wonderfully supercilious Rickman). Gissing intends to make every moment of Barnes and his sharp-tongued wife Linda's (Garofalo) stay a nightmare so Matthew will go away. When he finally realizes what's going on, Matthew prepares to get even until he and John realize that they have a lot in common, including protecting themselves from corporate chicanery. **91m/C; DVD.** Mike Binder; Alan Rickman; Janeane Garofalo; Juliet Stevenson; Allan Corduner; Sonya Walger; James Lance; ***D:*** Mike Binder; ***W:*** Mike Binder; ***C:*** Sue Gibson; ***M:*** Lawrence Nash Groupe.

The Search for One-Eye Jimmy 🦴 1/2 **1994 (R)** Good-natured slice-of-life comedy about lowlife friends in the Brooklyn neighborhood of Red Hook. Film school grad Les (McCallany) returns to his old stomping grounds to make a documentary and decides missing local character Jimmy (Rockwell) will be his topic. Only no one except Jimmy's parents seem really concerned and Les' friends are such dimwits that they couldn't find a hole in the ground anyway. **80m/C; VHS, DVD, Blu-Ray.** Holt McCallany; Steve Buscemi; Nicholas Turturro; Michael Badalucco; John Turturro; Ray "Boom Boom" Mancini; Samuel L. Jackson; Anne Meara; Jennifer Beals; Sam Rockwell; ***D:*** Sam Henry Kass; ***W:*** Sam Henry Kass; ***C:*** Charles K. Levy; Charles Levey; ***M:*** William Bloom.

The Search for Santa Paws 🦴🦴 **2010 (G)** Prequel to 2009's "Santa Buddies: The Legend of Santa Paws" has more trauma than the kids might be able to handle without parental explanations. Santa and Paws head to New York after Santa learns his toy store-owning friend Mr. Huckle has left his business to his bah humbug grandson James. But circumstances separate the pair jeopardizing Christmas. **88m/C; DVD, Blu-Ray.** Richard Riehle; Kaitlyn Maher; Madison Pettis; John Ducey; Bonnie Somerville; Wendi McLendon-Covey; Danny Woodburn; ***V:*** Zachary Gordon; Richard Kind; ***D:*** Robert Vince; ***W:*** Robert Vince; Anna McRoberts; ***C:*** Kamal Derkaoui; ***M:*** Brahm Wenger. **VIDEO**

Search for Signs of Intelligent Life in the Universe 🦴🦴🦴 **1991 (PG-13)** Tomlin's brilliant one-woman show has been expanded into a wonderful film. As Tomlin's cast of 12 female and male characters meet and interact, they show every viewer his/her own humanity. **120m/C; VHS, DVD.** Lily Tomlin; ***D:*** John Bailey; ***W:*** Jane Wagner; ***M:*** Jerry Goodman.

Search for the Gods 🦴 1/2 **1975** A dig in the Southwest turns interesting when one of the archeologists comes across an exquisite ancient medallion that could answer questions about alien visitors. Pilot for a TV series that didn't make it. **100m/C; DVD.** Kurt Russell; Stephen McHattie; Ralph Bellamy; Victoria Racimo; Raymond St. Jacques; ***D:*** Jud Taylor; ***W:*** Ken Pettus; ***C:*** Matthew F. Leonetti; ***M:*** Billy Goldenberg. **TV**

The Searchers 🦴🦴🦴🦴 **1956** The classic Ford western, starring John Wayne as a hard-hearted frontiersman who spends years doggedly pursuing his niece, who was kidnapped by Indians. A simple western structure supports Ford's most moving, mysterious, complex film. Many feel this is the best western of all time. **119m/C; VHS, DVD, Blu-Ray, HD-DVD.** John Wayne; Jeffrey Hunter; Vera Miles; Natalie Wood; Ward Bond; John Qualen; Harry Carey, Jr.; Olive Carey; Antonio Moreno; Henry (Kleinbach) Brandon; Hank Worden; Lana Wood; Dorothy Jordan; Patrick Wayne; ***D:*** John Ford; ***W:*** Frank Nugent; ***C:*** Winton C. Hoch; ***M:*** Max Steiner. AFI '98: Top 100; Natl. Film Reg. '89.

Searching 🦴🦴🦴 **2018 (PG-13)** A crime drama/thriller centered on a Korean-American family that is primarily set on a computer screen. In San Jose, fortysomething widower David (Cho) spends much of his time online to keep up with his daughter Margot (La). One day, when he cannot reach her, he grows panicked after learning that she has not attended her prepaid piano lessons in six months. Though police detective Rosemary (Messing) is put on the case, David digs into his daughter's email and Facebook accounts and is disturbed by what he learns. First-time filmmaker Chaganty has created a well-constructed, striking film with a compelling narrative and strong performances. **102m/C; DVD, Blu-Ray.** John Cho; Debra Messing; Joseph Lee; Michelle La; Sara Sohn; ***D:*** Aneesh Chaganty; ***W:*** Aneesh Chaganty; ***C:*** Juan Sebastian Baron; ***M:*** Torin Borrowdale.

Searching for Bobby D 🦴 **2005 (R)** Lame wiseguy/showbiz comedy. Four bit part Brooklyn actors decide to make their own movie and, thanks to family mobster connections, wind up in Pennsylvania. There, Johnny's cousin Leo has lied to a financial backer by saying Robert De Niro is starring in their flick (they bring in a look-alike). Naturally, much stupidity follows. **105m/C; DVD.** William DeMeo; James Madio; Tyson Beckford; Louis Vanaria; Daniel Margotta; Tony Darrow; Carmen Electra; ***D:*** Paul Borghese; ***W:*** William DeMeo; Paul Borghese; ***C:*** George Mitas; ***M:*** Neil Berg.

Searching for Bobby Fischer 🦴🦴🦴 1/2 **1993 (PG)** Seven-year-old Josh Waitzkin (Pomeranc, in his debut) shows an amazing gift for chess, stunning his parents, who must then try to strike the delicate balance of developing his abilities while also allowing him a "normal" childhood. Excellent cast features Mantegna and Allen as his parents, Kingsley as demanding chess teacher Pandolfini, and Fishburne as an adept speed-chess hustler. Pomeranc is great, and his knowledge of chess (he's a ranked player) brings authenticity to his role. Title comes from Pandolfini's belief that Josh may equal the abilities of chess whiz Bobby Fischer. Underrated little gem based on a true story and adapted from the book by Waitzkin's father. **111m/C; VHS,**

DVD. Joe Mantegna; Max Pomeranc; Joan Allen; Ben Kingsley; Laurence Fishburne; Robert Stephens; David Paymer; William H. Macy; Hal Scardino; ***D:*** Steven Zaillian; ***W:*** Steven Zaillian; ***C:*** Conrad L. Hall; ***M:*** James Horner. MTV Movie Awards '94: New Filmmaker (Zaillian).

Searching for Paradise 1/2 **2002 (R)** Gilda (Pratt) is obsessed with New York actor Michael De Santis (Noth). After her father dies (and she's disillusioned by some family skeletons), Gilda decides to take up her grandmother's offer to visit her in the Big Apple—the better to stalk De Santis. Hopelessly naive and a little unhinged, Gilda eventually poses as a journalist to meet her hero. Underdeveloped drama with little character development or explantion. Writer/director Paci's debut. **88m/C; VHS, DVD.** Susan May Pratt; Chris Noth; Jeremy Davies; Mary Louise Wilson; Josef Sommer; Michele Placido; Laila Robins; ***D:*** Myra Paci; ***W:*** Myra Paci; ***C:*** Teodoro Maniaci; ***M:*** Carter Burwell.

Searching For Sugar Man 1/2 **2012 (PG-13)** Rodriguez was almost a musical urban legend. Found in a Detroit bar in the '60s, it once looked like this soul singer would be the next icon of his genre. He essentially disappeared and some thought he had killed himself. His music didn't get a lot of airplay and his story would have ended there if not for a pair of fans who set out to find out what happened to their favorite singer. Bendejelloul's stellar documentary blends music history with a startling mystery filled with plenty of twists and turns. **85m/C; DVD, Blu-Ray.** ***D:*** Malik Bendjelloul; ***W:*** Malik Bendjelloul; ***C:*** Camilla Skagerstrom. Oscars '12: Feature Doc.; British Acad. '12: Feature Doc.; Directors Guild '12: Documentary Director (Bendjelloul); Writers Guild '12: Documentary Screenplay.

Searching For Wooden Watermelons 1/2 **2001** A small-town woman with big-time dreams of becoming a television writer battles her trepidations about ditching her hum-drum life for the Hollywood hills in this poignant narrative drawn from star/co-producer/writer English's personal experiences. While the moral might be simplistic and overstated, the players are genuine. **86m/C; VHS, DVD.** Wendy English; Chad Safar; Scott M. Rudolph; Dixie Tucker; Victoria Anne LeBlanc; ***D:*** Bryan Goldsworthy; ***W:*** Wendy English; ***C:*** David M. Sammons; ***M:*** Andy Daniels. **VIDEO**

Seas Beneath **1931** Commander Bob Kingsley and his men are sent on a secret mission to sink a German U-boat. Maria, whom Kingsley loves, turns out to be a German spy whose brother is the captain of the U-boat. She tries to sabotage Kingsley's mission but is thwarted. Shot off Catalina Island, Ford received naval assistance, including the use of two submarines and a mine sweeper. **90m/B; DVD.** George O'Brien; Mona Maris; Henry Victor; John Lodge; Marion Lessing; Steve Pendleton; Larry Kent; ***D:*** John Ford; ***W:*** Dudley Nichols; ***C:*** Joseph August.

Seaside Swingers 1/2 *Every Day's a Holiday* **1965** A group of teenagers at a seaside resort work to win a talent competition on TV. But where is the talent? Dumb teen romance comedy with accidental plot. **94m/C; VHS, DVD.** *GB* Michael Sarne; Grazina Frame; John Leyton; ***D:*** James Hill.

A Season for Miracles 1/2 **1999** Because their drug-addict mother, Berry (Dern), is in jail, Alanna (Whitman) and younger brother J.T. (Sabara) are about to be placed in foster care. Instead, they go on the lam with their devoted Aunt Emilie (Gugino), whose car breaks down in the quaint community of Bethlehem (hey, it's a Christmas movie!). The family are taken under the eccentric wing of a diner waitress (Duke) and the trio warily settle in—with Emilie even drawing the romantic interest of handsome cop Nathan (Conrad). Of course, trouble comes calling when their secret is exposed. (It's Christmas—there's a happy ending.) Adapted from the book by Marilyn Papano. **90m/C; VHS, DVD.** Carla Gugino; David Conrad; Kathy Baker; Laura Dern; Patty Duke; Lynn Redgrave; Mae Whitman; Evan Sabara; Faith Prince; Mary Louise Wilson; ***D:*** Michael Pressman; ***W:*** Maria Nation; ***C:*** Shelly Johnson; ***M:*** Craig Safan. **TV**

Season of Change 1/2 **1994** Tepid coming of age saga set in rural Montana, circa 1946. Thirteen-year-old Sally Mae (Tom) notices the tensions between her Bible-bound mother (Anderson) and war vet dad (Madsen), who's worried about finding a job to support his family. Sally Mae tries to understand all these adult notions even as she herself becomes attracted to teen mechanic Bobby (Randall). Cliched script and awkward performances don't help. **93m/C; VHS, DVD.** Nicholle Tom; Michael Madsen; Jo Anderson; Hoyt Axton; Ethan (Randall) Embry; ***D:*** Robin Murray; ***W:*** Shirley Hillard.

Season of the Witch 1/2 *Hungry Wives; Jack's Wife* **1973 (R)** A frustrated housewife becomes intrigued with a neighboring witch and begins to practice witchcraft herself, through murder and seduction. Meant to be suspenseful, thrilling, and topical, it is none of these. Poorly acted at best. Originally 130 minutes! **89m/C; DVD, Blu-Ray.** Jan White; Ray Laine; Bill Thunhurst; Joedda McClain; Virginia Greenwald; Ann Muffly; Neil Fisher; Esther Lapidus; Dan Mallinger; Ken Peters; ***D:*** George A. Romero; ***W:*** George A. Romero; ***C:*** George A. Romero.

Season of the Witch **2010 (PG-13)** Two 14th-century Crusaders—Behmen (Cage) and Felson (Perlman), who abandoned the cause for moral reasons—are forced to escort a girl (Foy) suspected of spreading the Black Plague through witchcraft to a distant Hungarian monastery to be exorcised and presumably end the plague. An abundance of ineffective CGI demons and evil witches destroys any historical legitimacy and makes this nothing more than an overblown medieval buddy flick with shoddy, out-of-place, and unfunny dialogue. **95m/C; Blu-Ray, On Demand.** Nicolas Cage; Ron Perlman; Ulrich Thomsen; Claire Foy; Stephan Campbell Moore; Stephen Graham; ***D:*** Dominic Sera; ***W:*** Bragi Schut, Jr.; ***C:*** Amir M. Mokri; ***M:*** Atli Ovarsson.

A Season on the Brink 1/2 **2002 (R)** Indiana University basketball coach Bobby Knight (Dennehy) is determined that the 1985-86 season will be a winning one. But his constant tirades are beginning to negatively affect his players. Dennehy owns this role as the abusive blowhard but since there's nothing sympathetic about Knight, it's hard to get too involved. Based on the book by journalist John Feinstein. **87m/C; VHS, DVD.** Brian Dennehy; Al Thompson; James Lafferty; Michael James Johnson; James Kirk; ***D:*** Robert Mandel; ***W:*** David W. Rintels; ***C:*** Claudio Chea; ***M:*** Randy Edelman; Steve Porcaro. **CABLE**

Seattle Superstorm **2012** The title tells you all you need to know about this Syfy Channel disaster flick. The military shoots down a UFO that lands in Puget Sound and soon the weird weather is destroying the city. NASA scientist Tom Reynolds is trying to save the day but it's his almost stepdaughter, teenager Chloe, who actually comes up with a solution. The falling Space Needle is kinda cool. **88m/C; DVD.** Esai Morales; Ona Grauer; Mackenzie Porter; Jared Abrahamson; Martin Cummins; Michelle Harrison; Jay Brazeau; ***D:*** Jason Bourque; ***W:*** David Ray; Jeff Renfroe; ***C:*** Mahlon Todd Williams; ***M:*** Michael Neilson. **CABLE**

Sebastiane **1979** An audacious film version of the legend of St. Sebastian, packed with homoerotic imagery and ravishing visuals. Honest, faithful rendering of the Saint's life and refusal to obey Roman authorities. Jarman's first film, in Latin with English subtitles. **90m/C; VHS, DVD, Blu-Ray.** *GB* Leonardo Treviglio; Barney James; Neil Kennedy; Richard Warwick; Lindsay Kemp; ***D:*** Derek Jarman; Paul Humfress; ***W:*** Derek Jarman; Paul Humfress; ***C:*** Peter Middleton; ***M:*** Brian Eno.

Seberg **2019 (R)** After winning a talent contest in Marshalltown, Iowa, Jean Seberg (Stewart) moves to Hollywood to become a star. Though she suffers an accident on her first movie set, she perseveres yet success remains elusive. When Jean moves to France, she stars in the breakout French New Wave film Breathless and becomes the movement's leading star. Despite her success, Jean finds purpose in activism related to the Civil Rights movement, which leads to FBI harassment. Though based on a true story and intended to highlight Seberg's legacy, it takes a simplistic approach to her story and Stewart does not fit the role well. **103m/C; DVD.** Kristen Stewart; Yvan Attal; Gabriel Sky; Jack O'Connell; Margaret Qualley; ***D:*** Benedict Andrews; ***W:*** Joe Shrapnel; Anna Waterhouse; ***C:*** Rachel Morrison; ***M:*** Jed Kurzel.

Second Act **2018 (PG-13)** Stuck in a go-nowhere job, 43-year-old Maya (Lopez) bemoans the limited career options for middle-agers without a college degree. The son of her best friend Joan (played by Lopez's real-life bestie Remini) fudges her résumé and fakes her online presence, opening the door to a Madison Avenue position. You already know how this is going to play out, but Lopez shines in these types of roles and Remini is hilarious as her foul-mouthed sidekick. **103m/C; Blu-Ray.** Jennifer Lopez; Vanessa Anne Hudgens; Leah Remini; Treat Williams; Milo Ventimiglia; ***D:*** Peter Segal; ***W:*** Justin Zackham; Elaine Goldsmith-Thomas; ***C:*** Ueli Steiger; ***M:*** Michael Andrews.

The Second Awakening of Christa Klages *Das Zweite Erwachen der Christa Klages* **1978** Young divorced mother Christa (Engel) decides to finance her money-troubled day-care center by robbing a bank with her lover Werner (Muller-Westernhagen). Werner's killed and Christa becomes a fugitive, taking refuge with her friend Ingrid (Reize). German with subtitles. **90m/C; VHS, DVD.** *GE* Tina Engel; Sylvia Reize; Marius Muller-Westernhagen; Peter Schneider; Katharina Thalbach; ***D:*** Margarethe von Trotta; ***W:*** Margarethe von Trotta; Luisa Francia; ***C:*** Franz Rath; ***M:*** Klaus Doldinger.

Second Best **1994 (PG-13)** Quiet, intimate drama about a lonely Welsh postmaster (Hurt) who decides to adopt a son (Miles). James, the 11-year-old boy he considers adopting, comes from a troubled background and is prone to violent outbursts. Graham, the village postmaster, is dealing with emotional demons of his own, and his problems are interwoven with those of the deprived, temperamental James. Although Hurt seems miscast as a shy, middle-aged Welshman, he turns in one of the best performances of his career. Richly acted and flawlessly directed, Menges has created a convincing and effective father-son drama. Based on David Cook's novel. **105m/C; DVD, Blu-Ray.** *UK* William Hurt; Chris Cleary Miles; Keith Allen; Prunella Scales; Jane Horrocks; Alan Cumming; John Hurt; ***D:*** Chris Menges; ***W:*** David Cook; ***M:*** Simon Boswell.

Second Best **2005** In this 'guy flick' Elliot (Pantoliano) is the protagonist, emotionally dwelling a few levels below the incessant whinings of Woody Allen. Fired from a Manhattan publishing house for not producing best sellers, he now spends his days hosting a Web site for downcasts like himself and writing stories he never has the guts to submit to a publisher. When a long-time friend, now a hot shot movie producer (Gaines), returns home and treats his buddies to some greener pastures, Elliot is forced to seriously reassess his life. Directing is a bit laid back and the buddies' kvetch sessions become somewhat wearing, but it does make poignant observations amidst the wry humor. **86m/C; DVD.** Joe Pantoliano; Boyd Gaines; Jennifer Tilly; Peter Gerety; Bronson Pinchot; Polly Draper; Barbara Barrie; James Ryan; Paulina Porizkova; Matthew Arkin; Fiona Gallagher; ***D:*** Eric Weber; ***W:*** Eric Weber; ***C:*** Christopher Norr; ***M:*** Tom O'Brien; Nathaniel Wilson; John Leccese; Joe Weber.

The Second Best Exotic Marigold Hotel **2015 (PG)** This sequel no one really asked for gets the surviving members of the first film back together for more relationship and elderly humor, and throws in Richard Gere for good measure. Sonny (Patel) wants to open another hotel (given that the residents of the first one never leave) and the rest of the film offers character-driven subplots for great actors like Maggie Smith, Dench, Nighy, and more. They're all good, as always, but they are also all well above this generic material. It's a hard film to hate but it's not worth checking in for most viewers. **122m/C; DVD, Blu-Ray.** *US UK* Dev Patel; Maggie Smith; David Strathairn; Dame Judi Dench; Bill Nighy; Ronald Pickup; Celia Imrie; ***D:*** John Madden; ***W:*** Ol Parker; ***C:*** Ben Smithard; ***M:*** Thomas Newman.

The Second Chance **2006 (PG-13)** Ethan (Smith) is a young pastor preaching the faith from his dad's ministry via a protected world of TV performances to mostly rich white folks. As a lesson, he's sent to work with the troubled members of an urban black church led by Jake (Carr), a move that he initially rebuffs, but eventually Jake makes him see the error of his ways. Fans of popular Christian rock singer Smith will enjoy his first foray into film. **102m/C; DVD.** Michael W. Smith; J. Don Ferguson; Lisa Arrindell Anderson; David Alford; Jeff Obafemi Carr; Henry Haggard; Kenda Benward; Jonathan Thomas; Calvin Hobson; Bobby Daniels; Shirley Cody; Peggy Walton Walker; Vilia Steele; ***D:*** Steve Taylor; ***W:*** Steve Taylor; Henry O. Arnold; Ben Pearson; ***C:*** Ben Pearson.

Second Chances 1/2 **1998** Think a family version of "The Horse Whisperer." 10-year-old Sunny is left unable to walk without crutches after a car accident and becomes emotionally withdrawn. She and her mom move next door to former rodeo champ Ben Taylor and Sunny develops a rapport with both Ben and a crippled horse named Ginger. **107m/C; VHS.** Tom Amandes; Kelsey Mulrooney; Isabel Glasser; Stuart Whitman; Theodore Bikel; Terry Moore; Madeline Zima; ***D:*** James Fargo. **VIDEO**

Second Chorus 1/2 **1940** Rivalry of two trumpet players for a girl and a job with Artie Shaw Orchestra. Music, dance, and romance. Nothing great, but pleasant. **83m/B; VHS, DVD.** Fred Astaire; Paulette Goddard; Burgess Meredith; Artie Shaw; Charles Butterworth; ***D:*** H.C. Potter.

The Second Civil War 1/2 **1997 (R)** Political satire falls apart at the end but until then manages to provide some dark comedy. In the near future, Idaho Governor Farley (Bridges) closes his state's borders to a planeload of refugee children from a Pakistan-India nuclear war. The President (Hartman), who wants to look tough, gives Farley 72 hours to change his mind and the media, led by executive producer Mel Burgess (Hedaya), goes into a typical frenzy. **105m/C; VHS, DVD.** Beau Bridges; Phil Hartman; James Coburn; Dan Hedaya; Elizabeth Pena; Kevin Dunn; Denis Leary; James Earl Jones; Ron Perlman; Joanna Cassidy; ***D:*** Joe Dante; ***W:*** Martyn Burke; ***C:*** Mac Ahlberg; ***M:*** Hummie Mann. **CABLE**

Second Coming of Suzanne 1/2 **1980** Young actress encounters a hypnotic film director. Her role: to star in a crucifixion—which may be more real than she imagines. Winner of two international film festivals. **90m/C; VHS, DVD.** Sondra Locke; Richard Dreyfuss; Gene Barry; Paul Sand; Jared Martin; ***D:*** Dr. Michael Barry; ***W:*** Dr. Michael Barry; ***C:*** Isidore Mankofsky.

The Second Front **2005 (R)** American agent Frank Hossom (Sheffer) must make certain that German Jewish scientist Nicky Raus doesn't fall into Nazi or Russian hands. But Frank makes the mistake of getting romantically interested in Nicky's lover, Olga (Metkina), who happens to be a KGB spy. Nonsensical melodrama enlivened by a certain amount of gunfire. **87m/C; DVD.** Craig Sheffer; Ron Perlman; Svetlana Metkina; ***D:*** Dmitri Fiks; ***W:*** Cris Sterzhen; ***C:*** Goran Paviceric; ***M:*** Igor Khoroshev.

Second-Hand Hearts **1981** Pointless comedy. Dumb drifter Loyal (Blake) gets drunk and winds up married to desperate single mom/waitress Dinette (Harris). Hoping for a better life, they hit the road leaving Texas for California. But this is one trip you won't want to be on. **102m/C; DVD.** Robert (Bobby) Blake; Barbara Harris; Bert Remsen; ***D:*** Hal Ashby; ***W:*** Charles Eastman; ***C:*** Haskell Wexler; ***M:*** Willis Alan Ramsey.

Second Honeymoon 1/2 **1937** Vicki's (Young) divorced from playboy Raoul (Power) and married to successful but dull businessman Bob (Talbot). When Vicki's vacationing in Miami, she runs into Raoul and those old sparks start to re-ignite. To smother the embers, Raoul throws a party and introduces Vicki to his new girlfriend, Joy (Weaver). Misunderstandings keep occurring until Vicki decides to follow her heart. **79m/B; DVD.** Tyrone Power; Loretta Young; Lyle Talbot; Stuart Erwin; Marjorie Weaver; Claire Trevor; J. Edward Bromberg; ***D:*** Walter Lang; ***W:*** Kathryn Scola; Darrell Ware; ***C:*** Ernest Palmer; ***M:*** David Buttolph.

Second in Command 2005 (R) Military attache Sam Keenan (Van Damme) is assigned to the American embassy in a small East European country whose government is targeted by rebels. Keenan rescues the country's president and takes him to the embassy, which is now besieged by the rebel militia, leaving Keenan and a few Marines to hold their position. Routine actioner. **95m/C; DVD, Blu-Ray.** Jean-Claude Van Damme; Julie Cox; Velibor Topic; William Tapley; Alan McKenna; Serban Celea; ***D:*** Simon Fellows; ***W:*** David Corley; Jonathan Bowers; Jayson Rothwell; ***C:*** Doug Milsome; ***M:*** Mark Sayfritz. **VIDEO**

The Second Mother 2015 (R) Brazil's entry for the Oscar for Best Foreign Language Film is a deceptively simple but remarkably deep examination of class conflict and the growing divide between the haves and the have-nots. Casé plays Val, a woman who has spent her life taking care of a wealthy family after leaving her own to do so. When her estranged daughter unexpectedly arrives on the scene, Val's life is upended through her offspring's inability to understand some of the rules of this admittedly bizarre dynamic in which Val is both an employee and a family member.A very smart, memorable drama. **114m/C; DVD.** Regina Case; Michel Joelsas; Camila Mardila; Karine Teles; Lourenco Mutarelli; ***D:*** Anna Muylaert; ***W:*** Anna Muylaert; ***C:*** Barbara Alvarez; ***M:*** Vitor Araujo; Fabio Trummer.

Second Sight 1989 (PG) A detective (Larroquette) and a goofy psychic (Pinchot) set out to find a kidnapped priest. Flick is sidetracked along the way by such peculiarities as a pixieish nun for romantic, not religious, intrigue. Remember this one? No? That's because you blinked when it was released to theatres. Eminently missable. **84m/C; VHS, DVD.** John Larroquette; Bronson Pinchot; Bess Armstrong; James Tolkan; Christine Estabrook; Cornelia Guest; Stuart Pankin; William Prince; John Schuck; Dominic Chianese; ***D:*** Joel Zwick; ***W:*** Patricia Resnick; Tom Schulman.

Second Sight 1999 Hard-charging Detective Chief Inspector Ross Tanner (Owen) is called to investigate the murder of a college student who was beaten to death within yards of his family's home. But beyond the murder, Tanner has a serious personal problem—a rare eye disease is causing him to go blind. Trying to keep his condition a secret, Tanner is forced to rely on new Detective Inspector Catherine Tully (Skinner), who has her own reasons for keeping quiet. **180m/C; VHS, DVD.** *GB* Clive Owen; Claire Skinner; Stuart Wilson; Phoebe Nicholls; Tom Mullion; Louise Atkins; Eddie Marsan; Rebecca Egan; Benjamin Smith; ***D:*** Charles Beeson; ***W:*** Paula Milne; ***C:*** Rex Maidment. **TV**

Second Sight 1/2 2007 Jenny Morris (Doig) had a breakdown after psychically witnessing her friend's murder. After starting a new life, Jenny sees another murder and this time decides to use the clues in her vision to find the killer. **90m/C; DVD.** Lexa Doig; Ty Olsson; Hrothgar Mathews; Fulvio Cecere; Alan C. Peterson; Vincent Gale; ***D:*** Allan Harmon; ***W:*** Rob Gilmer; ***C:*** Randal Platt; ***M:*** Hal Beckett. **CABLE**

Second Skin *Segunda Piel* 1999 Self-centered engineer Alberto (Molla) is married to the loving Elena (Gil) but is miserable. He hates his job even though he's successful and is terrified that his wife will discover he's been unfaithful—with doctor Diego (Bardem) who doesn't know Alberto is even married. When Elena does find out, Alberto swears he's broken off the relationship but he's lying and his security continues to crumble since he won't make a choice between either of his lovers. Molla's a diappointment since it's not clear what either lover or wife sees in him but Bardem and Gil make up for his shortcomings. Spanish with subtitles. **104m/C; VHS, DVD.** *SP* Javier Bardem; Jordi Molla; Ariadna Gil; Cecilia (Celia) Roth; Javier Albala; Mercedes Sampietro; Adrian Sac; ***D:*** Gerardo Vera; ***W:*** Angeles Gonzalez-Sinde; ***C:*** Julio Madurga; ***M:*** Roque Baños.

Second Skin 1/2 2000 (R) Sam Kane (MacFayden) falls in love with Crystal (Henstridge), who's suffering from amnesia after a car crash. Sam tries to help her out and Crystal remembers that she and Sam have a previous and dangerous connection. **91m/C; VHS, DVD.** Angus MacFadyen; Natasha Henstridge; Peter Fonda; Liam Waite; ***D:*** Darrell Roodt.

Second Thoughts 1983 (PG) Frustrated woman attorney divorces her stuffy husband and takes up with an aging hippie. She comes to regret her decision when it becomes obvious that her new man has his head firmly stuck in the 60s. Comedy-drama lacking real laughs or drama. **109m/C; VHS, DVD.** Lucie Arnaz; Craig Wasson; Ken Howard; Joe Mantegna; ***D:*** Lawrence Turman; ***W:*** Steve Brown; ***M:*** Henry Mancini.

The Second Time Around 1/2 1961 Unassuming western comedy. In 1912, young widow Lucretia Rogers (Reynolds) moves with her kids to an Arizona town to start a new life. She becomes a cowgirl on Aggie's (Ritter) ranch, is romanced by both Dan (Forest) and Pat (Griffith), and gets elected sheriff. Lucretia wants to clean out the outlaw elements but this notion gets her into some trouble. **98m/C; DVD.** Debbie Reynolds; Steve Forrest; Andy Griffith; Thelma Ritter; Juliet Prowse; ***D:*** Vincent Sherman; ***W:*** Clair Huffaker; Oscar Saul; ***C:*** Ellis W. Carter; ***M:*** Gerald Fried.

Second Time Lucky 1984 The devil makes a bet with God that if the world began all over again Adam and Eve would repeat their mistake they made in the Garden of Eden. Bites off a lot, but has no teeth nor laughs. **98m/C; VHS, DVD.** *AU NZ* Diane Franklin; Roger Wilson; Robert Morley; Jon Gadsby; Bill Ewens; ***D:*** Michael Anderson, Sr.

The Second Track *Das Zweite Gleis* 1962 Brock, a train inspector, witnesses a robbery at the railyard and recognizes one of the thieves from his wartime days, though he hides the fact from the police. But Brock's daughter has become curious about her father's past and her investigation uncovers some Nazi-era secrets that the thief (and her father) want to stay hidden. German with subtitles. **80m/B; DVD.** *GE* Walter Richter; Erik S. Klein; Albert Hetterle; Annekathrin Burger; Horst Jonischkan; Helga Goring; ***D:*** Joachim Kunert; ***W:*** Joachim Kunert; Gunter Kunert; ***C:*** Rolf Sohre; ***M:*** Pavol Simai.

The Second Woman 1/2 *Here Lies Love; Twelve Miles Out* 1951 An architect, suffering from blackouts and depression, believes himself responsible for the death of his fiancee. Well-done psychodrama. **91m/B; VHS, DVD.** Robert Young; Betsy Drake; John Sutton; ***D:*** James V. Kern; ***W:*** Mort Briskin; Robert Smith; ***C:*** Hal Mohr.

Secondhand Lions 2003 (PG) Timid Walter (Osment) is left with his eccentric uncles Hub (Duvall) and Garth (Caine) by his husband-seeking flaky mom Mae (Sedgewick). Finding no TV when he arrives, Walter becomes fascinated by the uncles' tales of an adventurous past, which are told in flashback in B-action movie style. Alternately syrupy and quirky, pic tries too much to be everything to everybody, and may not appeal to younger, jaded viewers. Their parents and grandparents, nostalgic for this kind of wholesome family entertainment, will be more receptive. Duvall and Caine make up for many of the flaws, but Osment doesn't register as strongly as hoped in his first post-child star role. **107m/C; VHS, DVD, UMD.** Michael Caine; Robert Duvall; Haley Joel Osment; Nicky Katt; Kyra Sedgwick; Emmanuelle Vaugier; Christian Kane; Kevin Michael Haberer; Josh(ua) Lucas; Adrian Pasdar; ***D:*** Tim McCanlies; ***W:*** Tim McCanlies; ***C:*** Jack N. Green; ***M:*** Patrick Doyle.

Seconds 1966 (R) Aging banker Arthur Hamilton (Randolph) is frantic to escape his dead-end existence and accepts an invitation from a mysterious organization to give him a second chance at life. Through surgery, Arthur's transformed into handsome artist Tony Wilson (Hudson). Uncomfortably living in Malibu, he soons finds out all his new neighbors are also "seconds," who are afraid he'll betray their secrets. Wilson decides he wants out of his new arrangement and back to his former life but it comes at a very high price. Eerie film manages to (mostly) overcome its plot problems, with a fine performance by Hudson. Based on the novel by Donald Ely. **107m/B; VHS, DVD, Blu-Ray.** Rock Hudson; John Randolph; Salome Jens; Will Geer; Jeff Corey; Richard Anderson; Murray Hamilton; Karl Swenson; Khigh Deigh; Frances Reid; Wesley Addy; ***D:*** John Frankenheimer; ***W:*** Lewis John Carlino; ***C:*** James Wong Howe; ***M:*** Jerry Goldsmith. Natl. Film Reg. '15.

Seconds Apart 2011 (R) Telekinetic, telepathic twins Seth and Jonah use their powers in an experiment so that they're able to experience fear. They cause their classmates to have hallucinations that make them kill themselves but the mass suicides drawn the attention of Det. Lampkin. Their brotherly bond fractures over something much simpler—both are attracted to new classmate Eve and become jealous. **89m/C; DVD.** Orlando Jones; Samantha Droke; Gary Entin; Edmund Entin; Louis Herthum; Morgana Shaw; ***D:*** Jose Antonio Negret; ***W:*** George Richards; ***C:*** Yaron Levy; ***M:*** Lior Rosner. **VIDEO**

Secre of the Andes 1/2 1998 (PG) Rebellious Diana (Belle) travels to Argentina with her mother (Allen) to visit her estranged father (Keith). He's an archeologist searching for gold and Diana dabbles in the supernatural to help him out. **102m/C; VHS, DVD.** David Keith; Nancy Allen; John Rhys-Davies; Camilla Belle; Jerry Stiller; ***D:*** Alejandro Azzano.

The Secret 1/2 1993 Businessman and political candidate Mike Dunsmore (Douglas) comes to terms with his lifelong battle with dyslexia when his grandson begins to show signs of the same affliction. Set in picturesque New England fishing village. **92m/C; VHS, DVD.** Kirk Douglas; Bruce Boxleitner; Brock Peters; Laura Harrington; ***D:*** Karen Arthur.

The Secret *Si J'Etais Toi* 2007 (R) This French remake of Yojiro Takita's 1999 Japanese flick "Himitsu" is not so much horror as just weird. Hannah (Taylor) and 16-year-old daughter Samantha (Thirlby) get into a terrible car accident. Sam lives and Hannah dies but Hannah refuses to actually leave distraught husband Ben (Duchovny), so her consciousness occupies Sam's body while Sam is in some kind of limbo. Ben and Hannah try to act normally, so Sam's body goes back to high school (which is unnerving for Hannah because of the teenaged boys and stuff) but the situation gets quite frustrating (and kinda queasy with a hint of incest). **92m/C; DVD.** *FR* David Duchovny; Lili Taylor; Olivia Thirlby; Brendan Sexton, III; Corey Servier; Macha Grenon; ***D:*** Vincent Perez; ***W:*** Ann Cherkis; ***C:*** Paul Sarossy; ***M:*** Nathaniel Mechaly.

A Secret 2007 Miller's devastating look at how the past—and its secrets—cast a pall on the present. In 1985, Parisian Francois is informed that his elderly father is missing. This triggers flashbacks to 1955 when the shy, sickly youngster realizes he's a disappointment to his athletic parents Tania and Maxime. Francois invents an imaginary older brother who is better at everything and then discovers a family secret—there was an older half-brother from Maxime's first marriage to Hannah. This leads to more revelations about the family's Jewish heritage, the Nazi invasion of France, and how his family survived the occupation. French with subtitles. **105m/C; DVD.** *FR* Mathieu Amalric; Patrick Bruel; Cecile de France; Julie Depardieu; Ludivine Sagnier; Valentin Vigourt; Quentin Dubuis; Orlando Nicoletti; ***D:*** Claude Miller; ***W:*** Claude Miller; Natalie Carter; ***C:*** Gerard de Battista; ***M:*** Zbigniew Preisner.

Secret Admirer 1985 (R) A teenager's unsigned love letter keeps falling into the wrong hands. Intends to be funny, and sometimes is; too often, though, it surrenders to obviousness and predictability. **98m/C; VHS, DVD, Blu-Ray.** C. Thomas Howell; Cliff DeYoung; Kelly Preston; Dee Wallace; Lori Loughlin; Fred Ward; Casey Siemaszko; Corey Haim; Leigh Taylor-Young; ***D:*** David Greenwalt.

A Secret Affair 1/2 *Barbara Taylor Bradford's A Secret Affair* 1999 Attractive Turner stars in this schmaltzy CBS romantic drama, based on the novel by Barbara Taylor Bradford, which has equally attractive scenery courtesy of Venice and Dublin. Pampered businesswoman Vanessa (Turner) is engaged to dull Stephen (Mailhouse). She goes on a business trip to Venice and meets pushy Irish widower Bill (Fitzgerald) but their subsequent affair doesn't go so smoothly. **88m/C; DVD.** Janine Turner; Paudge Behan; Robert Mailhouse; Fionnula Flanagan; Gia Carides; Michael J. Reynolds; Sarah Bolger; Jana Sheldon; ***D:*** Bobby Roth; ***W:*** Carole Real; ***C:*** Eric Van Haren Noman; ***M:*** Stephen McKeon. **TV**

The Secret Agent 1936 Presumed dead, a British intelligence agent (Gielgud) reappears and receives a new assignment. Using his faked death to his advantage, he easily journeys to Switzerland where he is to eliminate an enemy agent. Strange Hitchcockian melange of comedy and intrigue; atypical, but worthy offering from the Master. **83m/B; VHS, DVD.** *GB* Madeleine Carroll; Peter Lorre; Robert Young; John Gielgud; Lilli Palmer; Percy Marmont; Charles Carson; Florence Kahn; ***D:*** Alfred Hitchcock; ***W:*** Charles Bennett; ***C:*** Bernard Knowles; ***M:*** Louis Levy.

The Secret Agent *Joseph Conrad's The Secret Agent* 1996 (R) Rain, rain go away. In this waterlogged adaptation of the Conrad novel, Hoskins plays Adolf Verloc, a cowardly agent provocateur who heads a group of anarchists in soggy Victorian England. His real mission, however, is to report the actions of the expatriates to the Russian government. After he is bullied into a terrorist attack on the Greenwich Observatory by his contact at the Russian embassy, the lives of Verloc, his wife Winnie (Arquette) and her mentally disabled brother Stevie (Bale) are blown to pieces (sometimes literally) by the consequences. The only spark in the otherwise dank and gloomy production is Williams (listed as George Spelvin) as the demented explosives expert known only as the Professor. Alfred Hitchcock also used a loose interpretation of Conrad's novel for "Sabotage." **95m/C; VHS, DVD.** *GB* Bob Hoskins; Patricia Arquette; Gerard Depardieu; Robin Williams; Jim Broadbent; Christian Bale; Elizabeth Spriggs; Peter Vaughan; Julian Wadham; ***D:*** Christopher Hampton; ***W:*** Christopher Hampton; ***C:*** Denis Lenoir; ***M:*** Philip Glass.

The Secret Agent Club 1/2 1996 (PG) Secret agent Ray Chase (Hogan) steals a laser gun that evil Eve (Down) is determined to sell to the highest bidder. Ray returns home and, under the pretext of his job as a toy store owner, hides the gun in the store where his son Jeremy (McCurley) assumes it's a new toy. Eve's henchmen manage to capture Ray but not before Jeremy gets the gun and plans a rescue mission with his friends. **90m/C; VHS, DVD.** Hulk Hogan; Richard Moll; Lesley-Anne Down; Mathew McCurley; Edward Albert; Lyman Ward; James Hong; Barry Bostwick; Jack Nance; ***D:*** John Murlowski; ***W:*** Rory Johnston; ***C:*** S. Douglas Smith.

Secret Agent of Japan 1942 Cynical expatriate American Roy Bonnell (Foster) is running a bar in Shanghai and has an understanding with the Japanese, though everyone is tense about the coming war. British spy Kay (Bari) steals a letter that Bonnell is holding, which contains a coded message referring to the attack on Pearl Harbor and he wants it back. Wartime propaganda pic where the pieces don't fit very well. **72m/B; DVD.** Preston Foster; Lynn Bari; Noel Madison; Victor Sen Yung; ***D:*** Irving Pichel; ***W:*** John Larkin; ***C:*** Lucien N. Andriot.

Secret Agent Super Dragon *Super Dragon* 1966 The CIA calls in the agent known as "Super Dragon" when it is discovered that a Venezuelan drug czar plans to spike U.S. gum and candy with an LSD-like drug. Less than competent production offers some unintended laughter. Ferroni used the pseudonym Calvin Jackson Padget. **95m/C; VHS, DVD.** *FR IT GE* Ray Danton; Marisa Mell; Margaret Lee; Jess Hahn; Carlo D'Angelo; Andriana Ambesi; ***D:*** Giorgio Ferroni.

Secret Ballot *Raye Makhfi* 2001 (G) Iranian road picture/comedy gets laughs and provokes thought as a macho soldier and a liberated female pollster travel around the desert. Brought together when a ballot box parachutes down from the sky and onto the desolate beach that the soldier is guarding, the two are classic opposites. The reluctant, hardened soldier (Ab) is eventually coerced by the hopeful electioneer (Abdi) into driving her to each city on her mission to collect every vote possible for the upcoming election. The journey proves useful to both as they get more than a glimpse of the other's point of view. Their radically different views are fertile soil for the ensuing comedy as well as food for thought. The personalities and culture of Iran are explored through their journey, sometimes whimsically, in the light of democracy. Charming score matches pic's equally winsome vision of the Middle East. **105m/C; VHS, DVD.** *IA* Nassim Abdi; Cyrus Abidi; ***D:*** Babak Payami; ***W:*** Babak Payami.

Secret Beyond the Door 🦴🦴 **1948** A wealthy heiress marries a widower and soon discovers that he murdered his first wife. Understandably, she wonders what plans he might have for her. Capably done chiller, but the plot is hackneyed pseudo-Hitchcock. **99m/B; DVD, Blu-Ray.** Joan Bennett; Michael Redgrave; Barbara O'Neil; Anne Revere; ***D:*** Fritz Lang; ***M:*** Miklos Rozsa.

The Secret Bride 🦴🦴 **1/2 1935** Attorney general Robert Shelton and governor's daughter Ruth Vincent secretly marry out of state and return to find that her father is accused of taking a bribe and about to be impeached. To prevent the appearance of a conflict of interest and stop a scandal, they keep the marriage a secret while Robert officially investigates and Ruth works behind the scene, certain that her father is being framed. **76m/B; DVD.** Barbara Stanwyck; Warren William; A.S. Byron; Glenda Farrell; Grant Mitchell; Henry O'Neill; Douglass Dumbrille; ***D:*** William Dieterle; ***W:*** F. Hugh Herbert; Tom Buckingham; Mary C. McCall; ***C:*** Ernest Haller.

The Secret Diaries of Miss Anne Lister 🦴🦴 **2010** Occasionally titillating BBC drama, based on the true story of Anne Lister (1791-1840), a wealthy, orphaned Englishwoman who wrote about her exploits in a coded diary. A lesbian who refused to conform to society, Anne's first love makes a marriage of convenience but Anne eventually finds her equal and they live as they please. **90m/C; DVD.** *UK* Maxine Peake; Anna Madeley; Christine Bottomley; Susan Lynch; Gemma Jones; Alan David; Michael Culkin; Dean Lennox Kelly; Tina O'Brien; ***D:*** James Kent; ***W:*** Jane English; ***C:*** Lukas Strebel; ***M:*** Avshalom Caspi. **TV**

Secret File of Hollywood 🦴 **1/2** *Secret File: Hollywood* **1962** A down-and-out private eye gets a job taking photos for a sleazy Hollywood scandal sheet and finds himself in the midst of a blackmail plot masterminded by his editor. An often childish potboiler, perhaps inspired by the once-feared Confidential Magazine. **85m/B; VHS, DVD.** Robert Clarke; Francine York; Syd Mason; Maralou Gray; John Warburton; ***D:*** Ralph Cushman.

The Secret Four 🦴 **1/2** *Four Just Men* **1939** Four successful men secretly join together as vigilantes to protect the British Empire from traitorous, appeasing Foreign Minister, Sir Hamar Ryman. Remake of the 1921 silent was particularly topical given Britain's war situation. Adapted from an Edgar Wallace novel. **85m/B; DVD.** *GB* Griffith Jones; Francis L. Sullivan; Hugh Sinclair; Frank Lawton; Alan Napier; Anna Lee; Garry Marsh; George Merritt; ***D:*** Walter Forde; ***W:*** Roland Pertwee; Angus MacPhail; ***C:*** Ronald Neame; ***M:*** Ernest Irving.

Secret Games 🦴 **1/2 1992 (R)** An unhappily married woman (Brin) is searching for relief from her restrictive marriage. At the "Afternoon Demitasse," an exclusive brothel where women are paid for fulfilling their ultimate fantasies, she meets a man (Hewitt) who pushes her beyond her sexual limits and threatens to totally possess her. **90m/C; VHS, DVD.** Martin Hewitt; Michele Brin; Delia Sheppard; Billy Drago; ***D:*** Alexander Gregory (Gregory Dark) Hippolyte; ***W:*** Georges des Esseintes; ***C:*** Wally Pfister; Thomas Denove; ***M:*** Joseph Smith.

Secret Games 3 🦴 **1/2 1994 (R)** A bored doctor's wife gets her kicks by visiting a club catering to women's fantasies. But then she meets a criminal who wants her all to himself. An unrated version is available at 91 minutes. **82m/C; VHS, DVD.** Woody Brown; Brenda Swanson; Rochelle Swanson; ***D:*** Alexander Gregory (Gregory Dark) Hippolyte; ***C:*** Wally Pfister; ***M:*** Ashley Irwin.

The Secret Garden 🦴🦴🦴 **1949** Orphaned Mary Lennox (O'Brien) is sent to live with her cold and uncaring Uncle Archibald Craven (Marshall), who has never recovered from his wife's death. He keeps his crippled son, Colin (Stockwell), a virtual prisoner in the house until Mary discovers his presence and befriends him. She also discovers a neglected hidden garden, once the pride of Mrs. Craven, which Mary secretly begins to tend. Touching tearjerker based on the novel by Frances Hodgson Burnett. O'Brien leads an outstanding cast in one of her final juvenile roles. In black and white, with Technicolor for later garden scenes. **92m/B; DVD.** Margaret O'Brien; Herbert Marshall; Dean Stockwell; Gladys Cooper; Elsa Lanchester; Brian Roper; ***D:*** Fred M. Wilcox; ***W:*** Robert Ardrey; ***C:*** Ray June; ***M:*** Bronislau Kaper.

The Secret Garden 🦴🦴 **1/2 1984** Orphaned Mary Lennox is sent to live with her mysterious uncle after her parents die. Mary is willful and spoiled and her uncle's house holds a number of secrets, including a crippled cousin. When Mary discovers a mysteriously abandoned locked garden she makes it her mission to restore the garden to life. Based on the children's classic by Frances Hodsgon Burnett. **107m/C; VHS, DVD.** *GB* Sarah Hollis Andrews; David Patterson; ***D:*** Katrina Murray. **TV**

The Secret Garden 🦴🦴🦴 **1987 (PG)** Lonely orphan Mary Lennox is sent to live with her uncle in England after her parent's deaths. Mary, who has grown up in India, is selfish and unhappy until she discovers two secrets on her uncle's estate. Class production of the children's classic by Frances Hodgson Burnett with wonderful performances; added prologue and afterword showing Mary as an adult are unnecessary, but don't detract either. Made for television as a "Hallmark Hall of Fame" special. **100m/C; VHS, DVD.** Gennie James; Barret Oliver; Jadrien Steele; Michael Hordern; Derek Jacobi; Billie Whitelaw; Lucy Gutteridge; Julian Glover; Colin Firth; Alan Grint; ***W:*** Blanche Hanalis; ***C:*** Robert Paynter; ***M:*** John Cameron. **TV**

The Secret Garden 🦴🦴 **1/2 1993 (G)** Rekindled interest in Frances Hodgon Burnett's classic tale has prompted a Broadway musical, two TV movies, and this latest big screen version. Befitting director Holland's reputation this version is beautiful but dark, with children prey to very adult anxieties. **102m/C; VHS, DVD.** Kate Maberly; Maggie Smith; Haydon Prowse; Andrew Knott; John Lynch; ***D:*** Agnieszka Holland; ***W:*** Caroline Thompson; ***C:*** Roger Deakins; ***M:*** Zbigniew Preisner. L.A. Film Critics '93: Score.

The Secret Heart 🦴🦴 **1/2 1946** Somewhat unusual family melodrama that deals with daddy issues. Unhappy Penny (Allyson) has never accepted her father's suicide and still blames stepmom Lee (Colbert) for their problems. Both Lee and Penny's brother, Chase (Sterling), are worried about her mental stability and her shrink (Barrymore) advises the family return to their former home and confront the past. This includes a closer friendship with Chris (Pidgeon), Lee's former flame, but Penny doesn't know about the relationship and falls for the older father figure. **97m/B; DVD.** Claudette Colbert; Walter Pidgeon; June Allyson; Robert Sterling; Lionel Barrymore; Marshall Thompson; Patricia Medina; Richard Derr; ***D:*** Robert Z. Leonard; ***W:*** Whitfield Cook; Anne Morrison Chapin; ***C:*** George J. Folsey; ***M:*** Bronislau Kaper.

Secret Honor 🦴🦴🦴 *Lords of Treason; Secret Honor: The Last Testament of Richard M. Nixon; Secret Honor: A Political Myth* **1985** Idiosyncratic, single-set, one-man film version adapted by Donald Freed and Arnold Stone from their stage play about Richard Nixon coping with the death of his presidency on the night he's decided to blow his brains out. Made with students at the University of Michigan, and carried by the ranting and raving of Hall as a tragic Shakespearean Nixon with plenty of darkly humorous lines. **90m/C; VHS, DVD.** Philip Baker Hall; ***D:*** Robert Altman; ***W:*** Donald Freed; Arnold Stone; ***C:*** Pierre Mignot; ***M:*** George Burt.

The Secret in Their Eyes 🦴🦴🦴 *El Secreto de Sus Ojos* **2009 (R)** Adult crime thriller that isn't afraid to use emotion as well as action to tell its compelling story. Retired criminal-court employee Benjamin decides to write a novel based on a 25-year-old rape and murder he believes was mishandled. He shares his idea with judge Irene—for whom he carries a torch—but she warns Benjamin against getting involved. Flashbacks to the 1970s show Argentina's political corruption and military dictatorship, which ties into the crime. Spanish with subtitles. **127m/C; DVD, Blu-Ray.** *AR SP* Ricardo Darin; Soledad Villamil; Guillermo Francella; Pablo Rago; Javier Godino; ***D:*** Juan J. Campanella; ***W:*** Juan J. Campanella; ***C:*** Felix Monti; ***M:*** Federico Jusid. Oscars '09: Foreign Film.

Secret in Their Eyes 🦴🦴 **2015 (PG-13)** File this one under "Remakes That Never Justify Their Existence." This one is a true headscratcher given the excellent original from which writer/director Billy Ray is working and the great cast he's assembled here. But Ray can't find the rhythm that made the first one click. Officers Ray Kasten (Ejiofor) and Jess Cooper (Roberts) are torn apart when Jess' daughter is raped and killed. Over a decade later, the case is reopened and they come back together to solve it, unearthing secrets along the way. There are some solid performances here, but you should watch the award-winning original instead. Based on the novel by Eduardo Sacheri. **111m/C; DVD, Blu-Ray.** Chiwetel Ejiofor; Nicole Kidman; Julia Roberts; Dean Norris; Alfred Molina; ***D:*** Billy Ray; ***W:*** Billy Ray; ***C:*** Daniel (Danny) Moder; ***M:*** Emilio Kauderer.

The Secret Invasion 🦴🦴 **1/2 1964** In 1943, British intelligence officer Major Richard Mace (Granger) offers pardons to five criminals (Vallone, Rooney, Byrnes, Silva, Campbell) in return for their expertise. Their mission is to rescue an Italian general who has promised that his troops will switch sides and fight for the allies. Said general is imprisoned by the Nazis in Dubrovnik, Yugoslavia. Actioner was well-done by Corman before 1967's "The Dirty Dozen." **95m/C; DVD, Blu-Ray.** Stewart Granger; Raf Vallone; Mickey Rooney; Edd Byrnes; William Campbell; Henry Silva; Spela Rozin; Helmo Kinderman; Enzo Fiermonte; Peter Coe; ***D:*** Roger Corman; ***W:*** Arthur E. Arling; ***C:*** Hugo Friedhofer.

The Secret Life of Bees 🦴🦴🦴 **2008 (PG-13)** Big screen adaptation of the wildly successful 2002 novel by Sue Monk Kidd. In 1964 South Carolina, Lily Owens (Fanning), an idealistic 14-year-old girl with no mother, helps her black housekeeper Rosaleen (Hudson) flee the homegrown racism of a small town that had her arrested for trying to vote. The two journey to Tiburon—a place Lily remembers seeing written on her mother's honey jar label—where they're taken in by beekeeper August (Latifah) and her two sisters, June (Keys) and May (Okonedo), and both Lily and Rosaleen discover the strength of womanhood that had been hidden and suppressed all their lives. Fanning truly finds herself in this role, building from the inherent mistakes in "Hounddog." Heartfelt and well-acted all around, but the book's nuances are lost in a somewhat predictable coming-of-age melodrama. **110m/C; Blu-Ray, On Demand.** Queen Latifah; Dakota Fanning; Jennifer Hudson; Sophie Okonedo; Nathaniel Parker; Hilarie Burton; Paul Bettany; Alicia Keyes; Tristan Wilds; ***D:*** Gina Prince-Bythewood; ***W:*** Gina Prince-Bythewood; ***C:*** Rogier Stoffers.

The Secret Life of Girls 🦴🦴 **1/2 1999** Fifteen-year-old Natalie (Delfino) is caught in the midst of family turmoil when her unhappy mother, Ruby (Hamilton), reveals that Natalie's college professor father, Hugh (Levy), has been fooling around with one of his students. Natalie hides out in the university library where she shyly flirts with a cute boy, but the family chaos continues when Hugh suffers the pangs of conscience. **90m/C; VHS, DVD.** Majandra Delfino; Linda Hamilton; Eugene Levy; Kate Vernon; Meagan Good; Aeryk Egan; Andrew Ducote; ***D:*** Holly Goldberg Sloan.

The Secret Life of Mrs. Beeton 🦴🦴 **1/2 2006** Beginning in the 1850s, Isabelle Beeton writes domestic advice columns for her husband Sam's various London publications. She produces a collection of recipes (though she can't cook) and household management tips that become a best-selling sensation. However, her own marriage is fraught with secrets that include financial difficulties, many personal tragedies, and her own early death at the age of 28. **90m/C; DVD.** J.J. Feild; Jim Carter; Anna Chancellor; Anna Madeley; Siobhan Hayes; Joseph Mawle; Andrea Riseborough; ***D:*** Jon Jones; ***W:*** Sarah Williams; ***C:*** Ian Moss; ***M:*** Charlie Mole. **TV**

The Secret Life of Pets 🦴🦴 **2016 (PG)** Max (voiced by Louis C.K.) is a loyal terrier whose life is turned upside down when his owner adopts another dog named Duke (Eric Stonestreet). A series of events force Max and Duke into the streets, fighting to find their way home. Illumination Entertainment's summer family hit is undeniably overcrowded, disposable, and basically just riffs on Toy Story (and other Pixar) but it's also not as abrasively awful as a lot of kiddie flicks. It's forgettable but fun, enlivened by enjoyable vocal work from Kevin Hart, Jenny Slate, and others. **87m/C; DVD, Blu-Ray.** Louis C.K.; Eric Stonestreet; Kevin Hart; Jenny Slate; Ellie Kemper; Albert Brooks; Lake Bell; Dana Carvey; ***D:*** Yarrow Cheney; Chris Renaud; ***W:*** Cinco Paul; Ken Daurio; Brian Lynch; ***M:*** Alexandre Desplat.

The Secret Life of Pets 2 🦴🦴 **1/2 2019 (PG)** Dogs Max (Oswalt) and Duke (Stonestreet) live with their owner Katie (Kemper) and their animal neighbor friends, including bunny Snowball (Hart) and Pomeranian Gidget (Slate). Max's world is turned upside down when Katie marries and has a baby boy. Though Max is protective of the child as he grows, the family's trip to the country is challenging. While they are gone, Gidget has been charged with guarding Max's favorite squeaky toy and must retrieve it from an apartment filled with cats. More thinly plotted than the first film in this animated series, the solid cast of voice actors cannot make up for the messy story. **86m/C; DVD, Blu-Ray.** Patton Oswalt; Kevin Hart; Harrison Ford; Eric Stonestreet; Jenny Slate; ***D:*** Chris Renaud; ***W:*** Brian Lynch; ***M:*** Alexandre Desplat.

The Secret Life of Walter Mitty 🦴🦴🦴 **1947** An entertaining adaptation of the James Thurber short story about a meek man (Kaye) who lives an unusual secret fantasy life. Henpecked by his fiancee and mother, oppressed at his job, he imagines himself in the midst of various heroic fantasies. While Thurber always professed to hate Kaye's characterization and the movie, it scored at the boxoffice and today stands as a comedic romp for Kaye. Available with digitally remastered stereo and original movie trailer. **110m/C; VHS, DVD.** Danny Kaye; Virginia Mayo; Boris Karloff; Ann Rutherford; Fay Bainter; Florence Bates; ***D:*** Norman Z. McLeod; ***W:*** Everett Freeman; Ken Englund; Philip Rapp; ***C:*** Lee Garmes; ***M:*** Sylvia Fine; David Raksin.

The Secret Life of Walter Mitty 🦴🦴 **2013 (PG)** Walter Mitty's (Stiller) vivid imagination tends to remove him from reality for large chunks of time and has arguably kept him from really living. His worldview is shattered when he meets a cute new girl at work (Wiig) and is forced on an international journey to track down a photographer (Penn) who reportedly has the negative to an image that Mitty needs for the final cover of "Life" magazine. Stiller, who also directed, has created an inconsistent film with a muddled message and frustrating narrative. Some of it looks good but the script lets down the talented cast. **114m/C; DVD, Blu-Ray.** Ben Stiller; Kristen Wiig; Adam Scott; Shirley MacLaine; Sean Penn; ***D:*** Ben Stiller; ***W:*** Steve Conrad; ***C:*** Stuart Dryburgh; ***M:*** Theodore Shapiro.

The Secret Lives of Dentists 🦴🦴🦴 **2002 (R)** Rudolph's funny, dead-on take on married dentists in crisis. Mild-mannered David (Scott) suspects his wife and fellow dentist Dana (Davis) may be having an affair with a member of her community opera troupe when his imagination begins to go wild. His acerbic, misogynist patient (Leary in a no-brainer bit of casting) plays devil's advocate as David begins to see him everywhere, imparting advice on how to handle the situation. As the marriage continues to decay, David's hilarious waking dreams continue unabated and he is forced to deal with the darker side of his milquetoast persona. Refreshingly realistic, original, and well-acted. Based on the novel "The Age of Grief" by Jane Smiley. **104m/C; VHS, DVD.** Campbell Scott; Hope Davis; Denis Leary; Robin Tunney; Kevin Carroll; ***D:*** Alan Rudolph; ***W:*** Craig Lucas; ***C:*** Florian Ballhaus; ***M:*** Gary DeMichele. Ind. Spirit '04: Support. Actress (Davis); N.Y. Film Critics '03: Actress (Davis).

Secret Lives of Second Wives 🦴 **2008** Since everybody behaves like imbeciles it doesn't say much for first OR second marriages. After Lynn marries divorced Jack Hughes she soon realizes the obligations of his ex-wife and kids seem to take precedent over her. When plans for their dream home fall to financial problems and the wedding of Jack's daughter, Lynn gets in a snit and turns to handsome home inspector Alex (Payne) to boost her self-esteem. **90m/C; DVD.** Andrea Roth; Brian McNamara; Dan Payne; Laura Soltis; Jull Morrison; Tracy Spiridakos; *D:* George Mendeluk; *W:* Kelli Pryor; *C:* Anthony C. Metchie; *M:* Clinton Shorter. **CABLE**

Secret Obsession ✗ **1988 (PG)** A love triangle among a father, his illegitimate son, and the woman they both love, set in North Africa in 1955. Sounds intriguing, but don't be fooled. Slow, dull, and poorly acted. **82m/C; VHS, DVD.** Julie Christie; Ben Gazzara; Patrick Bruel; Jean Carmet; *D:* Henri Vart.

The Secret of Dr. Kildare ✗✗ **1939** Badly dated but worth seeing for the era's familiar faces and the difference in medical attitudes. Grumpy Dr. Gillespie (Barrymore) is terminally ill and trying to continue his research into new treatments for pneumonia. He doesn't have time for wealthy Paul Messenger (Atwill) and his apparently neurotic debutante daughter Nancy's (Gilbert) health problems, so he sends young Dr. Kildare (Ayres) to look into the matter. The third in the MGM B-movie series. **84m/B; DVD.** Lew Ayres; Lionel Barrymore; Lionel Atwill; Helen Gilbert; Walter Kingford; Samuel S. Hinds; Emma Dunn; Nat Pendleton; Laraine Day; *D:* Harold Bucquet; *W:* Harry Ruskin; Willis Goldbeck; *C:* Alfred Gilks; *M:* David Snell.

The Secret of Hidden Lake ✗✗ ½ **2006** Maggie Dolan (Sofer) returns to her Colorado hometown when her father Frank (Rekert) dies in a hunting accident that turns out to be no accident at all. The recently retired sheriff had opposed the corporate takeover of the community and Maggie won't let his reputation be smeared even when her questions put her in danger. **90m/C; DVD.** Rena Sofer; Winston Rekert; Dean Wray; Renae Morriseau; Adam Harrington; William B. Davis; Linda Darlow; Jodelle Ferland; Bill Mondy; *D:* Penelope Buitenhuis; *W:* David Golden; *C:* Adam Sliwinski; *M:* Michael Neilson. **CABLE**

The Secret of Kells ✗✗ ½ *Brendan and the Secret of Kells* **2009** Intricately animated Irish fantasy about how the Book of Kells, an illuminated medieval manuscript, came to be. Young novice Brendan lives in the abbey of Kells, Ireland in the 9th century where he helps the monks illustrate the gospels. The abbey is in peril from Viking raiders and Brendan is not allowed outside the walls, especially not into the supposedly haunted forest. But when refugee monk Aidan needs certain berries for ink, Brendan willingly travels into the forest to fetch them and encounters various magical creatures along the way. **75m/C; DVD, Blu-Ray.** *IR BE FR V:* Brendan Gleeson; Mick (Michael) Lally; Evan McGuire; Christen Mooney; Liam Hourican; *D:* Tomm Moore; *W:* Fabrice Ziolkowski; *C:* Fabienne Alvarez-Giro; *M:* Bruno Coulais.

The Secret of Loch Ness ✗ ½ *Das Wunder von Loch Ness* **2008 (PG)** Kids' fantasy made for German TV. Young Tim is obsessed with the Loch Ness monster and sees a man who looks like his father while watching a documentary on Nessie. Since Tim's mom told him his dad was dead, he's pretty curious and runs away from Germany to Scotland where he discovers his dad never knew he existed. While hanging around, Tim falls in the loch but is rescued by a gnome who keeps a treasure in an underwater cave. **90m/C; DVD.** *AT GE* Lisa Martinek; Lukas Schust; Hans Werner Meyer; Thomas Fritsch; Karl Mekatz; *D:* Michael Rowitz; *W:* Daniel Maximilian; Thomas Pauli; *C:* Dietmar Koelzer; *M:* Andrej Melita. **TV**

The Secret of Monte Cristo ✗ ½ *The Treasure of Monte Cristo* **1961** Not terribly exciting swashbuckler. In 1815, former British Army officer Capt. Adam Corbett (Bredin) is hired to protect Wilfrid Jackson (Hunter) and his daughter Pauline (Bredin) as they go on a treasure hunt. They possess one-quarter of a map and must join with the three other map holders to find what awaits them on the island of Monte Cristo. **96m/C; DVD.** *UK* Rory Calhoun; Patricia Bredin; Ian Hunter; John Gregson; Peter Arne; Gianna Maria Canale; *D:* Monty Berman; Robert S. Baker; *W:* Leon Griffiths; *C:* Monty Berman; Robert S. Baker; *M:* Clifton Parker.

The Secret of Moonacre ✗✗ ½ **2008 (PG)** Adaptation of the 1946 Elizabeth Goudge children's book "The Little White Horse." Orphaned Maria Merryweather is sent to live with her grumpy Uncle Benjamin in isolated Moonacre Valley. There is a dangerous rivalry between the Merryweathers and the DeNoir family over some magical pearls. Maria learns some family secrets, including the fact that she only has until the next full moon to end the rivalry or a terrible tragedy will occur. **103m/C; DVD, Blu-Ray.** *GB* Dakota Blue Richards; Ioan Gruffudd; Tim Curry; Natascha (Natasha) McElhone; Juliet Stevenson; Augustus Prew; Andy Linden; *D:* Gabor Csupo; *W:* Graham Alborough; Lucy Shuttleworth; *C:* David Eggby; *M:* Christian Henson.

The Secret of My Success ✗✗ **1987 (PG-13)** Country bumpkin Fox goes to the Big Apple to make his mark. He becomes the corporate mailboy who rises meteorically to the top of his company (by impersonating an executive) in order to win the love of an icy woman executive. He spends his days running frantically between his real job in the mailroom and his fantasy position, with various sexual shenanigans with the boss's wife thrown in to keep the viewer alert. Fox is charismatic while working with a cliche-ridden script that ties up everything very neatly at the end. **110m/C; VHS, DVD.** Michael J. Fox; Helen Slater; Richard Jordan; Margaret Whitton; Fred Gwynne; *D:* Herbert Ross; *W:* Jim Cash; Jack Epps, Jr.; A.J. Carothers; *C:* Carlo Di Palma; *M:* David Foster.

The Secret of Navajo Cave ✗✗ *Legend of Cougar Canyon* **1976 (G)** Fair family adventure. Two young friends explore the mysterious Navajo cave, where one can be assured that a secret awaits. **84m/C; VHS, DVD.** Holger Kasper; Steven Benally, Jr.; Johnny Guerro; *Nar:* Rex Allen; *D:* James T. Flocker.

The Secret of NIMH ✗✗✗ **1982 (G)** Animated tale, produced by a staff of Disney-trained artists led by "American Tail's" Bluth; concerns a newly widowed mouse who discovers a secret agency of superintelligent rats (they've escaped from a science lab) who aid her in protecting her family. As is usually the case with Bluth films, the animation is superb while the socially aware plot struggles to keep pace. That aside, it's still an interesting treat for the youngsters. Adapted from Robert C. O'Brien's "Mrs. Frisby and the Rats of N.I.M.H." **84m/C; VHS, DVD, Blu-Ray.** *V:* John Carradine; Derek Jacobi; Dom DeLuise; Elizabeth Hartman; Peter Strauss; Aldo Ray; Edie McClurg; Wil Wheaton; *D:* Don Bluth; *W:* Don Bluth; *M:* Jerry Goldsmith.

The Secret of NIMH 2 ✗✗ ½ **1998 (G)** Timmy, the youngest son of heroic mouse Jonathan Brisby, is sent from Thorn Valley to study at the university. At school, Timmy meets Jenny McBride, who has escaped from NIMH (National Institute of Mental Health), and seeks Timmy's help in rescuing her family and the other animals imprisoned there. Then Timmy discovers his older brother Martin is also being held prisoner. **68m/C; VHS, DVD.** *V:* Ralph Macchio; Eric Idle; Dom DeLuise; Harvey Korman; Peter MacNichol; William H. Macy; Andrea Martin; Meshach Taylor; *D:* Dick Sebast; *W:* Sam Graham; Chris Hubbell; *M:* Lee Holdridge. **VIDEO**

The Secret of Roan Inish ✗✗✗ ½ **1994 (PG)** Irish myth comes to life in this fantasy about the importance of family and place, seen through the eyes of 10-year-old Fiona Coneelly (newcomer Courtney) who's sent to live with her grandparents in post-WWII County Donegal. Fiona's drawn to her grandfather's stories about the family's ancestral home on the island of Roan Inish and the loss of her baby brother Jamie, who was carried out to sea. Another family tale is about a Selkie—a beautiful seal/woman captured by a Coneelly fisherman who eventually returned to her ocean home. When Fiona visits Roan Inish she becomes convinced that Jamie is alive and being cared for by the island's seals. Director Sayles keeps a firm grip on the cuteness factor while cinematographer Wexler works his usual magic on the sea, sky, and land of Ireland. Based on the 1957 novel "Secret of the Ron Mor Skerry" by Rosalie K. Fry. **102m/C; VHS, DVD.** Jeni Courtney; Mick (Michael) Lally; Eileen Colgan; John Lynch; Richard Sheridan; Susan Lynch; Cillian Byrne; *D:* John Sayles; *W:* John Sayles; *C:* Haskell Wexler; *M:* Mason Daring.

The Secret of Santa Vittoria ✗✗ ½ **1969 (PG)** Italo Bambolini (Quinn) is an amiable drunk who unexpectedly becomes the mayor of his wine-making village during WWII. Hearing the Nazis are headed toward Santa Vittoria to loot their supply of vintage wines, Italo and his savvy wife, Rosa (Magnani), enlist the villagers to hide most of the bottles in a cave outside of town, leaving a token amount to satisfy suspicious German Commander Von Prum (Kruger), who tries to learn the truth. Overly long but still amusing. Based on the novel by Robert Crichton. **139m/C; VHS, DVD, Blu-Ray.** Anthony Quinn; Anna Magnani; Hardy Kruger; Virna Lisi; Renato Rascel; Giancarlo Giannini; Valentina Cortese; Sergio Franchi; *D:* Stanley Kramer; *W:* William Rose; Ben Maddow; *C:* Giuseppe Rotunno; *M:* Ernest Gold.

Secret of Stamboul ✗ ½ *The Spy in White* **1936** British take on Hollywood action films finds two soldiers thrown out of their regiment thanks to a slinky seductress (Hobson) and into a devilish rebel plot to overthrow the Turkish government. **85m/B; VHS, DVD.** Valerie Hobson; Peter Haddon; Frank Vosper; Kay Walsh; Cecil Ramage; James Mason; *D:* Andrew Marton; *W:* Laszlo Benedek; George W. Hill. **VIDEO**

Secret of the Black Trunk ✗✗ ½ **1962** Chilling Edgar Wallace story about a series of murders at a famed English hotel. Filmed in Great Britain. **96m/C; VHS, DVD.** *GE* Joachim Hansen; Senta Berger; Hans Reiser; Leonard Steckel; Peter Carsten; *D:* Werner Klingler.

Secret of the Cave ✗✗ **2006 (PG)** Fourteen-year-old American Roy Wallace is spending the summer with his aunt and uncle in the small Irish village where his father grew up. Rumors of ghosts have the villagers in a tizzy and Roy's investigations point to a nearby sea cave. Pretty scenery and a Christian message as the film was sponsored by Southern Adventist University. **89m/C; DVD.** Kevin Novotny; Joseph Kelly; Patrick Bergin; Niall O'Brien; Niamh Finn; Noelle Brown; *D:* Zach C. Gray; *W:* Aaron Adams; Scott Fog; *C:* David George; *M:* John Carta.

The Secret of the Purple Reef ✗ ½ **1960** Weak adventure story. Chamberlain makes his film debut as one of two brothers who travel to St. Kitts to find out how their father's boat went down in calm seas. The answer involves a criminal and an insurance scam. **80m/C; DVD.** Richard Chamberlain; Jeff Richards; Peter Falk; Margia Dean; *D:* William Witney; *W:* Harold Yablonsky; *C:* Kay Norton; *M:* Buddy Bregman.

The Secret of Zoey ✗ ½ **2002** Obvious teen drama about how drugs are bad. Having problems with her parents' divorce leads Zoey Carter (Whelan) to getting involved with the wrong guy, which leads to her becoming a prescription pill addict. It isn't until Zoey overdoses that her parents get a clue and send her to rehab and into therapy. **90m/C; DVD.** Mia Farrow; Julia Whelan; Cliff De Young; Andrew McCarthy; Michael Coristine; Caroline Aaron; Katharine Isabelle; *D:* Robert Mandel; *W:* Betty Goldberg; *C:* Norayr Kasper; *M:* Jeff Beall. **CABLE**

Secret Passions ✗ ½ *Haunted by the Past* **1987** A young couple are haunted by a dark, romance-novel-type secret. **99m/C; VHS, Streaming.** John James; Susan Lucci; *D:* Michael Pressman. **TV**

The Secret Policeman's Other Ball ✗✗✗ **1982 (R)** Engaging live performance by most of the Monty Python troupe and guest rock artists, staged for Amnesty International. Follows 1979's "The Secret Policeman's Ball," and followed by 1987's "The Secret Policeman's Third Ball." **101m/C; VHS, DVD.** *GB* John Cleese; Graham Chapman; Michael Palin; Terry Jones; Pete Townshend; Sting; Billy Connolly; Bob Geldof; *D:* Julien Temple; *W:* Michael Palin.

The Secret Rapture ✗✗ **1994 (R)** Two sisters clash in this family drama, adapted by Hare from his 1988 play. The bohemian Isobel (Stevenson) and her estranged sister, the forbidding Marion (Wilton), are brought together by their father's death. While Isobel grieves, Marion seeks to gain advantage in the family business, and both must deal with their young, alcoholic, and volatile stepmother Katherine (Whalley-Kilmer). Emotional intensity with good performances but abrupt shifts in tone. **96m/C; VHS, DVD.** *GB* Juliet Stevenson; Penelope Wilton; Joanne Whalley; Alan Howard; Neil Pearson; Robert Stephens; Hilton McRae; *D:* Howard Davies; *W:* David Hare; *C:* Ian Wilson; *M:* Richard Hartley.

The Secret Six ✗✗✗ **1931** Gritty, violent crime drama. Louis Scorpio (Beery) takes over the bootlegging operations of his one-time boss Johnny Franks (Bellamy in his screen debut). He muscles into the big time and draws the attention of a secret tribunal of businessmen working with reporters Luckner (Gable) and Rogers (Brown) to get the goods on the hoods and put them behind bars. Harlow--in her first pairing with Gable--plays a waitress who turns against her boss, Scorpio. **83m/B; DVD.** Wallace Beery; Clark Gable; Ralph Bellamy; Jean Harlow; Lewis Stone; Johnny Mack Brown; John Miljan; *D:* George W. Hill; *W:* Frances Marion; *C:* Harold Wenstrom.

Secret Smile ✗ ½ **2005** Would have been better if Ashfield wasn't so wooden as the heroine; and the twist ending couldn't be seen from a mile off. Miranda (Ashfield) has a fling with Brendan (Tennant) and thinks it's over when she says so. Then her younger sister Kathy (Goose) is excited to introduce her new boyfriend (guess who). When people she's close to start turning up dead, Miranda has to decide just how far she'll go to prove Brendan is the killer, especially since no one believes her. Based on the novel by Nicci French. **137m/C; DVD.** *GB* David Tennant; Kate Ashfield; Claire Goose; John Bowe; Jill Baker; Rory Kinnear; Rob Lowe; Susannah Wise; *D:* Christopher Menaul; *W:* Kate Brooke; *C:* Jake Polonsky; *M:* Edmund Butt. **TV**

Secret Society ✗✗ **2000** Pleasingly plump Daisy gets a job in a canning factory and discovers that a group of her fellow buxom female workers are secretly meeting after work to train as Sumo wrestlers. As Daisy becomes more involved with the group, her husband Ken gets suspicious and then intervenes when he witnesses Daisy in a match. He winds up in the hospital and Daisy promises to quit until the women decide to accept the challenge of going public and fighting a group of male Japanese sumo wrestlers. **89m/C; VHS, DVD.** *GB* Charlotte Brittain; Lee Ross; Annette Badland; James Wooton; *D:* Imogen Kimmel; *W:* Imogen Kimmel; Catriona McGowan; *C:* Glynn Speeckaert; *M:* Paul Heard.

Secret State ✗✗ ½ **2012** British TV political thriller. Deputy Prime Minister Tom Dawkins is already facing numerous political hurdles investigating a major industrial accident that is blamed on an American petrochemical company. The situation becomes even more of a quagmire when the Prime Minister is killed in a plane crash and Tom unexpectedly wins election to the post. Based on "A Very British Coup" by Chris Mullins; previously filmed under that title in 1988. **180m/C; DVD.** *UK* Gabriel Byrne; Rupert Graves; Gina McKee; Charles Dance; Sylvestria Le Touzel; Stephen (Dillon) Dillane; *D:* Ed Fraiman; *W:* Robert Jones; *C:* Owen McPolin; *M:* Alex Heffes. **TV**

The Secret War of Harry Frigg ✗ ½ **1968 (R)** Non-conformist WWII Private Harry Frigg is promoted to general as part of a scheme to help five Allied generals escape from the custody of the Germans. Rare Newman bomb; dismal comedy. **123m/C; VHS, DVD.** Paul Newman; Sylva Koscina; John Williams; Tom Bosley; Andrew Duggan; *D:* Jack Smight; *C:* Russell Metty.

Secret Weapons ✗ ½ *Secrets of the Red Bedroom* **1985** Sexy Russian babes are KGB-trained to get any secret from any man. Strains credibility as well as patience. Made for TV. **100m/C; VHS, DVD.** Linda Hamilton; Sally Kellerman; Hunt Block; Viveca Lindfors; Christopher Atkins; Geena Davis; James Franciscus; *D:* Don Taylor; *M:* Charles Bernstein. **TV**

Secret Window ½ **2004 (PG-13)** Wandering around with a wicked case of bed-head in a ratty old bathrobe and talking incessantly to himself, Johnny Depp cranks this ho-hum psycho-thriller up a notch with a typically quirky and subtly humorous performance as Mort Rainey, an eccentric mystery writer. After catching wife Amy (Bello) in the sack with another man (Hutton) Mort holes up in a remote lake cottage during his traumatic divorce only to be roused from his depression-induced torpor and writers block by Shooter (Turturro) a deranged hayseed in an Amish-looking hat who claims Mort stole his story. Mort, who is increasingly showing signs that he may not be playing with a full deck, is almost sure that isn't true and can prove it if he can only find the back issue of a magazine that published his story years before Shooter claims to have penned his. Adapted from a novella by Stephen King. **95m/C; VHS, DVD, Blu-Ray.** Johnny Depp; John Turturro; Maria Bello; Timothy Hutton; Charles S. Dutton; Len Cariou; John Dunn-Hill; Vlasta Vrana; ***D:*** David Koepp; ***W:*** David Koepp; ***C:*** Fred Murphy; ***M:*** Philip Glass.

Secret Witness **1988** Young Drew Blackburn (Joaquin Phoenix then going by the name Leaf) and his friend Jennie (Martin) play at amateur spies and snoop around their neighborhood. Drew sees his divorced dad, Sandy (Rasche), with another woman, who's later found murdered. And when Sandy lies to his son, Drew begins to wonder. CBS TV movie. **72m/C; DVD.** Joaquin Rafael (Leaf) Phoenix; Kellie Martin; David Rasche; Paul LeMat; Barry Corbin; ***D:*** Eric Laneuville; ***W:*** Paul Monette; Alfred Sole; ***C:*** Matthew F. Leonetti; ***M:*** Robert Drasnin. **TV**

The Secret World of Arrietty *Kari-gurashi no Arietti* **2010 (G)** Acclaimed Japanese studio, Studio Ghibli, headed by animation icon Hayao Miyazaki brings to life this good-natured fairy tale about a small family (literally) that lives under the floorboards in an old house. When Shawn (Henrie), an ill 12-year-old, discovers tiny teenager Arrietty (Mendler) after moving into his mother's childhood home for bed rest, he becomes her protector against the caretaker who wants to reveal them to the world. A sweet, gentle film that's ultimately a bit lighter than Miyazaki's best work but often enchants. Based on "The Borrowers" by Mary Norton (1952); the Japanese version was Japan's highest grossing in 2010. **94m/C; DVD, Blu-Ray.** *JP US V:* Bridgit Mendler; David Henrie; Amy Poehler; Will Arnett; Carol Burnett; Moises Arias; ***D:*** Gary Rydstrom; Hiromasa Yonebayashi; ***W:*** Karey Kirkpatrick; Hayao Miyazaki; Keiko Niwa; ***C:*** Atsushi Okui; ***M:*** Cecile Corbel.

Secretariat ½ **2010 (PG)** Based on the true story of 1973's Triple Crown winning horse Secretariat. Despite her lack of horse-racing experience, Denver housewife and mom Penny Chenery (the always-appealing Lane) takes over her ailing father's (Glenn) Virginia-based Meadow Stables. She needs to breed a champion, which means navigating through the male-dominated business, and takes a chance on eccentric trainer Lucien Laurin (Malkovich) and stubborn jockey Ronnie Turcotte (Thorwarth) as well as her own tough-minded instincts. Story is sweet as a sugar cube, as is Lane. **123m/C; Blu-Ray.** Diane Lane; John Malkovich; Dylan Walsh; Kevin Connolly; Fred Dalton Thompson; Margo Martindale; Scott Glenn; Nestor Serrano; Amanda (A.J.) Michalka; Carissa Capobianco; James Cromwell; Dylan Baker; Nelsan Ellis; Otto Thorwarth; Julie Weiss; ***D:*** Randall Wallace; ***W:*** Mike Rich; ***C:*** Dean Semler; ***M:*** Nick Glennie-Smith.

Secretary **2002 (R)** Lighter look at S&M conveniently hooks up submissive secretary Lee (Gyllenhaal, in a breakthrough role), with her obsessive perfectionist new boss, Edward. After too many misspelled words (bad secretary!), Lee discovers the dominant Edward is perfect at fulfilling her masochistic fantasies. With a sketchy (at best) romantic history, the plucky heroine tries a normal relationship with an old classmate, Peter (Davies) but still craves her kinky boss's brand of quiet discipline. Alternately poignant and funny, story is original and doesn't fall prey to cliche or pathos. Adapted from a 1988 story by Mary Gaitskill. **104m/C; VHS, DVD.** James Spader; Maggie Gyllenhaal; Lesley Ann Warren; Jeremy Davies; Patrick Bauchau; Stephen McHattie; Oz (Osgood) Perkins, II; Jessica Tuck; Amy Locane; Michael Mantell; ***D:*** Steven Shainberg; ***W:*** Erin Cressida Wilson; ***C:*** Steven Fierberg; ***M:*** Angelo Badalamenti.

Secrets ½ **1971 (R)** A wife, her husband, and her daughter each have a sexual experience which they must keep secret. Bisset's nude love scene is an eye-opener. Fast forward through the rest of this dull, overwrought drama. **86m/C; VHS, DVD.** Jacqueline Bisset; Per Oscarsson; Shirley Knight; Robert Powell; Tarka Kings; Martin C. Thurley; ***D:*** Philip Saville; ***M:*** Michael Gibbs.

Secrets **1982** British drama about the confused life of an innocent schoolgirl who's the victim of a mess of authoritative misunderstandings. One of David Puttnam's "First Love" series. **79m/C; VHS, DVD.** *GB* Helen Lindsay; Anna Campbell-Jones; Daisy Cockburn; ***D:*** Gavin Millar.

The Secrets *Ha-Sodot* **2007 (R)** Israeli Naomi (Bokstein) is raised in an ultra Orthodox community by her strict rabbi father. When her mother dies, Naomi is expected to marry her father's rabbinical prodigy. A gifted student of the Torah, Naomi persuades her father to allow her a year's study at a women's seminary where she is befriended by newly-arrived Frenchwoman, Michelle (Shtamler). Both are assigned to aid the terminally ill and tragic Anouk (Ardant), which results in Naomi and Michelle falling in love. Good performances by the three leads but the plot seems slow and overextended. French and Hebrew with subtitles. **127m/C; DVD.** *FR IS* Fanny Ardant; Dana Ivgy; Ania Bokstein; Michal Shtamler; Tali Oren; Adir Miller; Sefi Rivlin; Guri Alfi; ***D:*** Avi Nesher; ***W:*** Avi Nesher; Hadar Galron; ***C:*** Michel Abramowicz; ***M:*** Daniel Salomon; Eyal Sela.

Secrets and Lies **1995 (R)** Too-long film focusing on family and identity. The adoptive parents of black Yuppie Londoner Hortense (Jean-Baptiste) have just died and she decides it's time to seek out her birth parents. She's warned about the emotional consequences, especially upon discovering her biological mother is white—factory worker Cynthia (Blethyn), who has another daughter, Roxanne (Rushbrook), who doesn't get along with mum. Naturally, when Hortense is introduced to the rest of Cynthia's family, there's lots of dysfunction to explore. Good performances, although Hortense's character is bland, but pacing drags. **142m/C; VHS, DVD.** *GB* Brenda Blethyn; Marianne Jean-Baptiste; Timothy Spall; Claire Rushbrook; Phyllis Logan; Lee Ross; Ron Cook; Lesley Manville; ***Cameo(s):*** Alison Steadman; ***D:*** Mike Leigh; ***W:*** Mike Leigh; ***C:*** Dick Pope; ***M:*** Andrew Dickson. Australian Film Inst. '97: Foreign Film; British Acad. '96: Actress (Blethyn), Orig. Screenplay; Cannes '96: Actress (Blethyn), Film; Golden Globes '97: Actress--Drama (Blethyn); L.A. Film Critics '96: Actress (Blethyn), Director (Leigh), Film.

Secrets in the Walls ½ **2010** Family horror from the Lifetime channel. Single mom Rachel gets a new job and a too-good-to-be-true deal on a house in a nice neighborhood. She and her two daughters move in, but daughter Molly realizes that the place is haunted and something (or someone) is targeting her older sister Lizzie. **89m/C; DVD.** Jeri Ryan; Kay Panabaker; Peyton List; Ian Kahn; Marianne Jean-Baptiste; John Hawkinson; ***D:*** Christopher Leitch; ***W:*** Chris Sey; ***C:*** Kees Van Oostrum; ***M:*** Jeff Cardoni. **CABLE**

Secrets of a Married Man **1984** A married man's philandering ways are his ruination when he falls hard for a beautiful prostitute. Shatner and Shepherd contain their laughter as they make their way through this hyper-earnest family drama. **96m/C; VHS, DVD.** William Shatner; Cybill Shepherd; Michelle Phillips; Glynn Turman; ***D:*** William A. Graham.

Secrets of a Soul ½ **1925** A visually impressive presentation of Freudian psychoanalytic theory, in which a professor, wanting a child and jealous of his wife's childhood sweetheart, moves toward madness (we did say Freudian) and is cured through dream interpretation. Great dream sequences bring out the arm-chair psychoanalyst. Silent. **94m/B; Silent; VHS, DVD.** *GE* Werner Krauss; Ruth Weyher; Jack Trevor; ***D:*** G.W. Pabst.

Secrets of an Undercover Wife ½ **2007** Lisa's new husband is arrested by the FBI and convicted of embezzlement and murder. When he refuses to talk to her, Lisa decides to get to the truth on her own and discovers a mob-run money laundering scheme that could get her killed. **90m/C; DVD.** Shawnee Smith; Michael Woods; Robert Moloney; Gordon Michael Woolvett; Lori Ann Triolo; Daryl Shuttleworth; Jane Sowerby; ***D:*** George Mendeluk; ***W:*** George Mendeluk; Keith Shaw; ***C:*** George Campbell; ***M:*** Clinton Shorter. **CABLE**

The Secrets of Comfort House ½ **2006** Wendy (Lee) establishes Comfort House, a home for battered women, in a small Oregon town. When three of the women's abusive husbands are murdered, the local sheriff (Trapp) is sure Wendy is guilty while the deputy sheriff (Bisson) wants to keep investigating. **90m/C; DVD.** Sheryl Lee; John Novak; Yannick Bisson; John Tench; Jillian Fargey; Jody Thompson; Xantha Radley; ***D:*** Timothy Bond; ***W:*** Donald Martin; John Benjamin Martin; ***C:*** Anthony C. Metchie; ***M:*** Michael Richard Plowman. **CABLE**

Secrets of Eden ½ **2012** After Alice and George Hayward are the victims of an apparent murder-suicide, secrets about the 'perfect' couple begin to come out. George was abusive and, when they were separated, Alice had an affair with Pastor Stephen Drew. Detective Catherine Benicasa discovers both Haywards were murdered and Stephen becomes the prime suspect. Fifteen-year-old Kate Hayward may the only one who really knows the truth. Adapted from Chris Bohjalian's novel. A Lifetime Original movie. **96m/C; DVD.** John Stamos; Anna Gunn; Samantha Munro; Sonya Salomaa; Graham Abbey; J.P. Manoux; ***D:*** Tawnia Mckiernan; ***W:*** Anne Meredith; ***C:*** Michael Storey; ***M:*** Lawrence Shragge. **CABLE**

Secrets of the Mountain **2010** Divorced mom Dana James takes her unhappy kids to a mountain cabin she's inherited from her eccentric Uncle Henry. Only Henry isn't dead, he's just hiding out from some treasure-hunting bad guys and now the whole family gets involved. **84m/C; DVD.** Paige Turco; Barry Bostwick; Shawn Christian; Adelaide Kane; Crawford Wilson; Kayla Carlson; Andreas Apergis; ***D:*** Douglas Barr; ***W:*** Douglas Barr; ***C:*** Pierre Jodoin; ***M:*** Eric Allaman. **TV**

The Secrets of the Summer House **2008** Nikki's (Price) husband, George Wickersham (Haydn-Jones), suffers a near-fatal accident after inheriting his family's Maine island summer house, and she learns of the curse befalling the male heirs. Worried for both her husband and their unborn son, Nikki starts investigating and discovers the family's history of slavery and a vengeful spirit. Made for Lifetime. **90m/C; DVD.** Lindsay Price; David Haydn-Jones; Sadie LeBlanc; Niall Matter; Emma Stevens; Nicole Jones; Frank Schorpion; ***D:*** Jean-Claude Lord; ***W:*** John Benjamin Martin; ***C:*** Daniel Villeneuve; ***M:*** James Gelfand. **CABLE**

Secrets of Women *Kvinnors Vantan; Waiting Women* **1952** A rare Bergman comedy about three sisters-in-law who tell about their affairs and marriages as they await their husbands at a lakeside resort. His first commercial success, though it waited nine years for release (1961). In Swedish with English subtitles. **114m/B; VHS, DVD, Blu-Ray.** *SW* Anita Bjork; Karl Arne Homsten; Eva Dahlbeck; Maj-Britt Nilsson; Jarl Kulle; ***D:*** Ingmar Bergman; ***W:*** Ingmar Bergman.

Secundaria **2014** An insightful, personal feature-length documentary about ballet in Cuba. In that country, ballet is considered a high art form and the government funds a world-famous National Ballet School. Like many students at the school, Mayara loves to dance and attending the school is a way out of poverty. Though her path dramatically changes during the documentary, the film shows the power of dance and the physical and creative demands of ballet students at the school. **100m/C; DVD.** ***D:*** Mary Jane Doherty; ***C:*** Mary Jane Doherty; ***M:*** Luis D'Elias. **VIDEO**

Seduced **1985** When a rich businessman turns up dead, the ambitious politician who was involved with his wife must find the killer. Not memorable or exceptional, but not boring or offensive either. **100m/C; VHS, DVD.** Gregory Harrison; Cybill Shepherd; Jose Ferrer; Adrienne Barbeau; Michael C. Gwynne; Karmin Murcelo; Paul Stewart; ***D:*** Jerrold Freedman. **TV**

Seduced and Abandoned *Sedotta e Abbandonata* **1964** A lothario seduces his fiancee's young sister. When the girl becomes pregnant, he refuses to marry her. Family complications abound. A comic look at the Italian code of honor. In Italian with English subtitles. **118m/B; VHS, DVD.** *IT* Saro Urzi; Stefania Sandrelli; Aldo Puglisi; Leopoldo Trieste; ***D:*** Pietro Germi; ***W:*** Pietro Germi. Cannes '64: Actor (Urzi).

Seduced: Pretty When You Cry ½ *Pretty When You Cry* **2001 (R)** Albert (Kennedy) is the mild-mannered suspect in the murder of nightclub owner Frank (Cavalieri) because Albert's in love with Frank's wife Sarah (Elizabeth), who happens to be missing. Detective Black (Elliott) is investigating and learns that Frank and Sarah were into some kinky sex scenes that may have gone too far. **90m/C; VHS, DVD.** Sam Elliott; Jamie Kennedy; Carlton Elizabeth; Michael Cavalieri; Keith David; Lori Heuring; ***D:*** Jack N. Green; ***W:*** Christopher Keller; ***C:*** Jack N. Green; ***M:*** Normand Corbeil. **VIDEO**

Seducers *Death Game* **1977 (R)** Wealthy, middle-aged man unsuspectingly allows two young lesbians to use his telephone. A night of bizarre mayhem and brutal murder begins. They tease him, tear apart his house, and generally make him miserable. Why? Good question. **90m/C; VHS, DVD.** Sondra Locke; Colleen Camp; Seymour Cassel; Beth Brickell; Ruth Warshawsky; ***D:*** Peter S. Traynor; ***W:*** Anthony Overman; Michael Ronald Ross; ***C:*** David Worth; ***M:*** Jimmie Haskell.

Seducing Doctor Lewis ½ *La Grande Seduction* **2003** Dying Quebec fishing village must find a resident doctor if it is to attract new factory owners. The villagers find a possible pigeon in a young Montreal plastic surgeon (Boutin) who comes for a visit. They pretend to love everything he does, from playing cricket rather than their favored hockey to throwing a beef stroganoff festival because it's his favorite food. Very lightweight but enjoyable comedy in the style of "Waking Ned Devine." **110m/C; VHS, DVD.** *CA* David Boutin; Lucie Laurier; Benoit Briere; Bruno Blanchet; Raymond Bouchard; Pierre Collin; Rita Lafontaine; ***D:*** Jean-Francois Pouliot; ***M:*** Jean-Marie Benoit.

Seducing Maarya **1999** Maarya is an East Indian/Canadian working in a Montreal restaurant. She agrees to an arranged marriage with the restaurant owner's son, even though he's gay, and then begins a romance with the sixtysomething dad. No one seems too concerned by the situation until Maarya's violent brother turns up, exposing a family secret, and Maarya announces her pregnancy. Melodramatic. **107m/C; VHS, DVD.** *CA* Nandana Sen; Mohan Agashe; Vijay Mehta; Ryan Hollyman; Cas Anvar; ***D:*** Hunt Hoe; ***W:*** Hunt Hoe; ***C:*** Michael Wees; ***M:*** Dino Giancola; Janet Lumb.

The Seduction **1982 (R)** Superstar TV anchorwoman is harassed by a psychotic male admirer. Usual run of the mill exploitive "B" thriller with no brains behind the camera. **104m/C; VHS, DVD.** Morgan Fairchild; Michael Sarrazin; Vince Edwards; Andrew Stevens; Colleen Camp; Kevin Brophy; ***D:*** David Schmoeller; ***W:*** David Schmoeller; ***C:*** Mac Ahlberg; ***M:*** Lalo Schifrin.

The Seduction of Joe Tynan ½ **1979 (R)** Political drama about a young senator (Alda) torn between his family, his political career, and his mistress (Streep). Alda also wrote the thin screenplay, which reportedly is loosely based on the remarkable life of Ted Kennedy. Relatively shallow treatment of the meaty themes of power, hypocrisy, sex, and corruption in our nation's capital. **107m/C; VHS, DVD.** Alan Alda; Meryl Streep; Melvyn Douglas; Barbara Harris; Rip Torn; ***D:*** Jerry Schatzberg; ***W:*** Alan Alda; ***M:*** Bill Conti. L.A. Film Critics '79:

Support. Actor (Douglas), Support. Actress (Streep); Natl. Bd. of Review '79: Support. Actress (Streep); N.Y. Film Critics '79: Support. Actress (Streep); Natl. Soc. Film Critics '79: Support. Actress (Streep).

Seduction of Mimi 🦴🦴🦴 *Mimi Metallurgico Ferito Nell'Onore* **1972 (R)** Comic farce of politics and seduction about a Sicilian laborer's escapades with the Communists and the local Mafia. Giannini is wonderful as the stubborn immigrant to the big city who finds himself in trouble. One of the funniest love scenes on film. Basis for the later movie "Which Way is Up?" Italian with subtitles. **92m/C; VHS, DVD, Blu-Ray.** *IT* Giancarlo Giannini; Mariangela Melato; Turi Ferro; Agostina Belli; Elena Fiore; ***D:*** Lina Wertmuller; ***W:*** Lina Wertmuller; ***C:*** Dario Di Palma; ***M:*** Piero Piccioni.

Seduction: The Cruel Woman 🦴🦴 **1989** A curiously uninvolving look at sexual games and fantasies. Wanda is a dominatrix, who also owns a sado-masochistic gallery where her various friends and current and formers lovers act out their basest desires. Stylized, with some graphic sex. Based on the novel "Venus in Furs" by Leopold Sacher-Masoch. In German with English subtitles. **84m/C; VHS, DVD.** *GE* Mechthild Grossmann; Carola Regnier; Udo Kier; Sheila McLaughlin; ***D:*** Elfi Mikesch; Monika Treut; ***W:*** Elfi Mikesch; Monika Treut.

The Seductress 🦴 ½ **2000** Beautiful Alexis (O'Brien) is a black widow with a string of murdered wealthy husbands behind her. Kay Sanders (Hall) is a researcher obsessed with keeping tabs on each of Alexis's new identities, especially when the babe goes after Kay's boyfriend Paul (Smith). But it turns out that Kay and Alexis have a closer connection than that. The R-rated version is a mere 70 minutes. **82m/C; VHS, DVD.** Shauna O'Brien; Gabriella Hall; Jonathan Smith; ***D:*** J Edie Martin. **VIDEO**

See Here, Private Hargrove 🦴🦴 **1944** Comic screen adaptation of reporter Marion Hargrove's boot camp experiences at Fort Bragg. The bumbling Hargrove (Walker) spends most of his time on KP but when he gets some extra dough writing for his ex-editor, Hargrove comes to the attention of avaricious Mulvehill (Wynn). A scheme is easy since Hargrove is sweet on Carol (Reed) and wants a furlough to see her. Followed by "What Next, Corporal Hargrove?" **101m/B; DVD.** Robert Walker; Donna Reed; Keenan Wynn; Robert Benchley; Marta Linden; Bob Crosby; Grant Mitchell; ***D:*** Wesley Ruggles; ***W:*** Harry Kurnitz; ***C:*** Charles Lawton, Jr.; ***M:*** David Snell.

See No Evil 🦴🦴🦴 *Blind Terror* **1971 (PG)** A blind girl gradually discovers the murdered bodies of her uncle's family. Trapped in the family mansion, she finds herself pursued by the killer. Chilling and well crafted. **90m/C; VHS, DVD.** Mia Farrow; Dorothy Allison; Robin Bailey; ***D:*** Richard Fleischer; ***W:*** Brian Clemens; ***M:*** Elmer Bernstein.

See No Evil 🦴 **2006 (R)** Wrestling star Kane (7 feet tall and some 400 pounds) plays psycho Jacob Goodnight, who's living in an abandoned hotel. He's pleasantly surprised when his ex-cop nemesis (Vidler) and eight delinquents on a community service detail show up. And he welcomes them one-by-one (keeping eyeballs as souvenirs). Typically gory teen-slasher flick. **84m/C; DVD, Blu-Ray.** Michael J. Pagan; Christina Vidal; Steven Vidler; Penny McNamee; Glen "Kane" Jacobs; Samantha Noble; Luke Pegler; Rachael Taylor; Craig Horner; ***D:*** Gregory Brown; ***W:*** Dan Madigan; ***C:*** Ben Nott; ***M:*** Tyler Bates.

See No Evil, Hear No Evil 🦴🦴 **1989 (R)** Another teaming for Pryor and Wilder, in which they portray a blind man and a deaf man both sought as murder suspects. Pryor and Wilder deserve better. **103m/C; VHS, DVD, Blu-Ray.** Gene Wilder; Richard Pryor; Joan Severance; Anthony Zerbe; Kevin Spacey; ***D:*** Arthur Hiller; ***W:*** Gene Wilder; Andrew Kurtzman; Eliot Wald; Earl Barret; Arne Sultan; ***C:*** Victor Kemper; ***M:*** Stewart Copeland.

See No Evil: The Moors Murders 🦴🦴 **2006** Released on the 40th anniversary of the 1966 trial of killers Ian Brady (Harris) and Myra Hindley (Peake). In the early 1960s, 3 children and 2 teenagers are kidnapped, tortured, and murdered, with their bodies buried on Saddleworth Moor outside Manchester. When Brady tries to entice his sister's husband, David Smith (McNulty), to participate, Smith goes to the police instead and the duo is finally caught. Made with the cooperation of the victims' families, the reconstruction of trial evidence can be rather gruesome. Also released the same year was "Longford," which featured an older Hindley's attempts to get parole. **180m/C; DVD.** *GB* Sean Harris; George Costigan; John Henshaw; Maxine Peake; Matthew McNulty; Joanne Frogatt; ***D:*** Christopher Menaul; ***W:*** Neil McKay; ***C:*** Lukas Strebel; ***M:*** John Lunn. **TV**

See Spot Run WOOF! **2001 (G)** How can you not like a movie with dogs? Easy, put David Arquette in it. Spot, an FBI-trained dog, has a contract on his life after removing "one of the family jewels" of crime family boss Sonny Talia (Sorvino) and ends up in a doggie witness protection program. He lands in the possession of James (Jones), his mother (Bibb), and babysitter neighbor Gordon (Arquette). One may find the true essence of the movie in the middle of a large pile of Spot's morning business, where Gordon eventually finds himself. More scatological humor and other crass gags send "Spot" to the doghouse. Duncan is the sole high point as the dog's FBI handler. **97m/C; VHS, DVD.** David Arquette; Michael Clarke Duncan; Leslie Bibb; Angus T. Jones; Joe (Johnny) Viterelli; Paul Sorvino; Anthony Anderson; ***D:*** John Whitesell; ***W:*** George Gallo; Dan Baron; Chris Faber; ***C:*** John Bartley; ***M:*** John Debney.

See You in the Morning 🦴 ½ **1989 (PG-13)** Ill-conceived romantic comedy-drama about a divorced psychiatrist and a widow, both of whom had unhappy marriages, who meet and marry. They must cope with their respective children, family tragedies, and their own expectations, in order to make this second marriage work. **119m/C; VHS, DVD.** Jeff Bridges; Alice Krige; Farrah Fawcett; Drew Barrymore; Lukas Haas; Macaulay Culkin; David Dukes; Frances Sternhagen; Theodore Bikel; George Hearn; Linda Lavin; ***D:*** Alan J. Pakula; ***W:*** Alan J. Pakula.

See You Yesterday 🦴🦴 ½ **2019** New York teen scientist C.J. (Duncan-Smith) is working on time travel with her best friend and classmate Sebastian (Crichlow). While they work on jumping back one day, C.J.'s life is disrupted by the murder of her brother Calvin (Astro) by police. Determined to save her brother's life, she and Sebastian keep going back in time but make everything more complicated with every change they make. The debut film by filmmaker Bristol is an ambitious sci-fi drama that balances social consciousness with lighthearted adventure. **84m/C; DVD.** Eden Duncan-Smith; Dante Crichlow; Brian "Astro" Bradley; Marsha Stephanie Blake; Johnathan Nieves; ***D:*** Stefon Bristol; ***W:*** Stefon Bristol; Fredrica Bailey; ***C:*** Felipe Vara de Rey; ***M:*** Michael Abels. Ind. Spirit '20: First Screenplay. **VIDEO**

Seed WOOF! **2008** Urban legend maintains that if a criminal can withstand three 15 minute bursts of power in the electric chair and live, he has to be let go. It's complete nonsense, of course, except in the mind of Uwe Boll. Villainous serial killer Sam Seed actually survives the ordeal of electrocution, so worried authorities bury him alive. He subsequently digs himself out to revenge in the goriest, most disturbing ways possible. **90m/C; DVD.** Michael Paré; Will Sanderson; Ralph (Ralf) Moeller; Jodelle Ferland; Thea Gill; Andrew Jackson; Brad Turner; Phil Mitchell; Mike Dopud; Tyron Leitso; John Sampson; ***D:*** Uwe Boll; ***W:*** Uwe Boll; ***C:*** Mathias Neumann; ***M:*** Jessica de Rooij. **VIDEO**

Seed of Chucky 🦴 ½ **2004 (R)** The fifth in the "Child's Play" series is filled with the usual camp and carnage, and a movie-within-a-movie premise. Tilly plays herself as an actress filming a "Chucky" movie as well as the voice of Chucky's doll bride, Tiffany. Homicidal dolls Chuck (voiced by Dourif) and Tiff are on-set and are eventually reunited with long-lost offspring Glen (voiced by Boyd), who has a gender crisis due to a lack of anatomical correctness and is sometimes Glenda (a nod to Ed Wood's 1953 masterpiece). Chucky thinks it would be swell if Glen/Glenda could have a sibling, with Tilly as the mom. The actress is nothing if not game for a variety of indignities and snarky one-liners. Waters appears briefly as a pesky paparazzo. **86m/C; DVD, Blu-Ray, HD-DVD.** Jennifer Tilly; Hannah Spearritt; John Waters; Jason Flemyng; Keith-Lee Castle; Steve Lawton; Redman; Tony Gardner; ***V:*** Jennifer Tilly; Brad Dourif; Billy Boyd; ***D:*** Don Mancini; ***W:*** Don Mancini; ***C:*** Vernon Layton; ***M:*** Pino Donaggio.

Seeding of a Ghost 🦴 **1986** A cabbie picks up a sorcerer, who seems to curse him. Then a gang of thugs rapes and kills his wife. Appealing to the sorcerer to lift the curse somehow leads to him having to deal with zombie hordes. Not pleasant, unless you enjoy undead sex and insect vomiting, among some other general nastiness. **90m/C; VHS, DVD, Blu-Ray.** *CH* Philip Ko; Chuan Chi Hui; Norman Chu; Maria Jo; ***D:*** Yang Chuan.

Seedpeople 🦴🦴 ½ **1992** Mindless horror flick has bloodthirsty plants inhabiting peaceful Comet Valley after their seeds fall from outer space and germinate. These "seedpeople" possess tremendous powers and soon have the rural residents transformed into zombies. Bears an uncanny resemblance to "Invasion of the Bodysnatchers," and is so bad it's almost good. Also available with Spanish subtitles. **87m/C; VHS, DVD.** Sam Hennings; Andrea Roth; Dane Witherspoon; David Dunard; Holly Fields; Bernard Kates; Anne Betancourt; Sonny Carl Davis; ***D:*** Peter Manoogian; ***W:*** Jackson Barr; ***M:*** Bob Mithoff.

Seeds of Destruction 🦴 *The Terror Beneath; Garden of Evil* **2011 (PG-13)** A seed from the Biblical Garden of Eden sets in motion the end of the world as it quickly begins destroying the country in the Asylum's latest production. **91m/C; DVD, Blu-Ray, Streaming.** *CA US* Adrian Pasdar; Stefanie von Pfetten; Jesse Moss; Luisa D'Oliveira; James Morrison; ***D:*** Paul Ziller; ***W:*** Paul Ziller; Mike Muldoon; ***C:*** Anthony C. Metchie; ***M:*** Michael Neilson. **VIDEO**

Seeds of Evil 🦴🦴 *The Gardener* **1976 (R)** Warhol alumnus Dallesandro is a strange gardener who grows flowers that can kill. He can also turn himself into a tree and figures to seduce rich and bored housewife Houghton (niece of Katharine Hepburn) after he finishes tending her garden. Strange, quirky horror flick. **97m/C; VHS, DVD.** Katharine Houghton; Joe Dallesandro; Rita Gam; ***D:*** James H. Kay.

Seeing Other People 🦴🦴 ½ **2004 (R)** About-to-be-married couple begin seeing other people in this fun, top-notch sex comedy romp. Ed (Mohr) and Alice (Nicholson) decide to sow some wild oats before settling down into marital bliss. Initially exciting for both, the affairs spark their own lagging passion. Soon, however, the two enter more dangerous territory when conquest Donald (Davis) begins obsessing over Alice and Ed meets waitress Sandy (Ritchie) and it is clear no good can come of this hair-brained experiment. Despite a rather worn-out premise, characters have wonderful chemistry and are likeable, unique and well-drawn. Able supports include Graham, as Alice's sister, and Richter as Ed's grounded best friend. **90m/C; DVD.** Jay Mohr; Julianne Nicholson; Lauren Graham; Bryan Cranston; Josh Charles; Andy Richter; Matthew Davis; Helen Slater; Jill Ritchie; Alex Borstein; Mimi Rogers; Nicole Marie Lenz; Jonathan Davis; Mike Faiola; Sheeri Rappaport; Liz Phair; ***D:*** M. Wallace Wolodarsky; ***W:*** M. Wallace Wolodarsky; Maya Forbes; ***C:*** Mark Doering-Powell; ***M:*** Alan Elliott.

The Seeker: The Dark Is Rising 🦴 ½ **2007 (PG)** Fourteen-year-old Will (Ludwig), transplanted from America to England, wakes up one day with magical powers and an important destiny in this all-too-familiar tale that is both a lousy adaptation of a 1973 book and a rip-off of comparable, contemporary stories. McShane, as Will's mentor Merriman, does his best with the poor script, but there's no saving this mess. Needlessly simplifies and Americanizes the original story until there's not much left except a bad "Harry Potter" retread. **94m/C; On Demand.** Christopher Eccleston; Ian McShane; Frances Conroy; Wendy Crewson; Alexander Ludwig; John Benjamin Hickey; Gregory Edward Smith; James Cosmo; Jim Piddock; ***D:*** David L. Cunningham; ***W:*** John Hodge; ***C:*** Joel Ransom; ***M:*** Christophe Beck.

Seeking a Friend for the End of the World 🦴🦴 ½ **2012 (R)** Director Scafaria's directorial debut is a somewhat misguided dramedy about two neighbors who fall in love just as the world is ending. Carell overplays his schlub persona as a guy whose wife runs away when she learns that everyone is doomed. He goes about his life, even going to work, until an encounter with his flighty neighbor (Knightley) gives him some final-chapter purpose. The two head off on a wacky road trip that starts well enough but gets a little lost along the way. The leads make for an interesting couple but the gloom overwhelms them. **101m/C; DVD, Blu-Ray, Streaming.** Steve Carell; Keira Knightley; Adam Brody; Connie Britton; Rob Corddry; Melanie Lynskey; Patton Oswalt; ***D:*** Lorene Scafaria; ***W:*** Lorene Scafaria; ***C:*** Tim Orr; ***M:*** Rob Simonsen; Jonathan Sadoff.

Seeking Justice 🦴 **2012 (R)** Shockingly inert and boring given the pedigree of its cast and director, this alleged thriller gets bogged down by plot holes and a truly half-asleep performance from Cage. The hit-and-miss actor plays Will, a man who is approached by the leader (Pearce) of a vigilante group on the night that his wife (Jones) has been beaten and raped. The man can give him justice but will come to him in the future for a favor. Of course, said favor is more than Will can take and he is plunged into a nightmarish underground of vigilantism and revenge. **104m/C; DVD, Blu-Ray.** Nicolas Cage; January Jones; Guy Pearce; Harold Perrineau, Jr.; Jennifer Carpenter; Xander Berkeley; Jason Davis; Marcus Lyle Brown; Joseph Chrest; ***D:*** Roger Donaldson; ***W:*** Robert Tannen; Yuri Zeltser; ***C:*** David Tattersall; ***M:*** J. Peter Robinson.

Seems Like Old Times 🦴🦴 ½ **1980 (PG)** A sweet lawyer (Hawn) finds herself helping her ex-husband (Chase) when two robbers force him to hold up a bank. Grodin is the new spouse threatened by Chase's appearance and by the heavies he's trying to escape. Better-than-average script, with funny and appealing characters. **102m/C; VHS, DVD.** Goldie Hawn; Chevy Chase; Charles Grodin; Robert Guillaume; Harold Gould; George Grizzard; T.K. Carter; ***D:*** Jay Sandrich; ***W:*** Neil Simon; ***C:*** David M. Walsh; ***M:*** Marvin Hamlisch.

Seize the Day 🦴🦴🦴 **1986** A man approaching middle age (Williams) feels that he is a failure. Brilliant performances by all, plus a number of equally fine actors in small roles. Based on the short novel by Saul Bellow. **93m/C; VHS, DVD.** Robin Williams; Joseph Wiseman; Jerry Stiller; Glenne Headly; Tony Roberts; ***D:*** Fielder Cook.

Seizure 🦴🦴 **1974 (PG)** Three demonic creatures from a writer's dreams come to life and terrorize him and his houseguests at a weekend party. Slick but disjointed; Stone's directorial debut. Interesting cast includes Tattoo from "Fantasy Island." **93m/C; DVD, Blu-Ray.** *CA* Jonathan Frid; Herve Villechaize; Christina Pickles; Martine Beswick; Joseph Sirola; Troy Donahue; Mary Woronov; Anne Meacham; ***D:*** Oliver Stone; ***W:*** Oliver Stone; Edward Andrew (Santos Alcocer) Mann; ***C:*** Roger Racine.

Selena 🦴🦴 ½ **1996 (PG)** Lopez is appealing in the title role of the 23-year-old Tejano superstar singer who was just breaking into international prominence when she was murdered by the president of her fan club in 1995. Flashbacks show dad Abraham's (Olmos) dashed musical aspirations and he serves as a stage father to his children, recognizing his daughter Selena's exceptional voice. Film covers her marriage to guitarist Chris Perez (Seda) and her building success until the final tragedy (which isn't shown). Film concludes with concert footage of the real Selena. **127m/C; VHS, DVD, Blu-Ray.** Jennifer Lopez; Edward James Olmos; Jon Seda; Constance Marie; Jacob Vargas; Lupe Ontiveros; Jackie Guerra; Sal Lopez; Rebecca Lee Mezza; ***D:*** Gregory Nava; ***W:*** Gregory Nava; ***C:*** Edward Lachman; ***M:*** Dave Grusin.

Self/Less 🦴 ½ **2015 (PG-13)** Kingsley plays a billionaire who can't buy the medical treatment to save his dying body. A mysterious businessman/scientist comes to him with a proposition—he can transfer his soul into a new body, one grown genetically in a lab. Voila, Kingsley becomes Reynolds. Life is good for a while, but then the headaches get worse as do the hallucinations, which he learns are really flashbacks. Has he taken someone else's life? Was it against his will? Visionary director Singh is reduced to a director-for-hire in this dull action flick that looks and plays more like a failed TV pilot. **117m/C; DVD, Blu-Ray, Streaming.** Ryan Reynolds; Ben Kingsley; Natalie Martinez; Matthew Goode; Derek Luke; ***D:*** Tarsem Singh; ***W:*** David Pastor; Alex Pastor; ***C:*** Gavin Frost; ***M:*** Dudu Aram; Antonio Pinto.

Sell Out ✐✐ 1/2 **1976 (PG)** A former spy living in Jerusalem is called out of retirement; his protege, who defected to the Soviets, now wants out. **102m/C; VHS, DVD.** Richard Widmark; Oliver Reed; Gayle Hunnicutt; Sam Wanamaker; ***D:*** Peter Collinson; ***W:*** Judson Kinberg; Murray Smith; ***C:*** Arthur Ibbetson; ***M:*** Colin Frichter.

Selling Hitler ✐✐ **1991** Black comedy based on a true story. In 1981, German reporter Gerd Heidemann (Pryce) believes he can revive his floundering career when he gets a scoop about Hitler's 'lost' diaries. He convinces "Stern" magazine to pay millions to publish the material. Only they turn out to be fake. **256m/C; DVD.** *UK* Jonathan Pryce; Alexei Sayle; Barry Humphries; Tom Baker; Richard Wilson; Alison Doody; Peter Capaldi; ***D:*** Alistair Reid; ***W:*** Robert Harris; Howard Schuman; ***C:*** Clive Tickner; ***M:*** John Keane; Tim Souster. **TV**

The Sellout ✐✐ **1951** Crusading big city newspaper editor Haven Allridge (Pidgeon) goes after corrupt county sheriff Burke (Gomez) but finds himself keeping quiet after getting some disturbing info. This frustrates the state's special prosecutor Charles Johnson (Hodiak) who can't seem to get anyone to testify against the bad guy. Think justice will prevail? **83m/B; DVD.** Walter Pidgeon; John Hodiak; Thomas Gomez; Karl Malden; Cameron Mitchell; Paula Raymond; Audrey Totter; Everett Sloane; ***D:*** Gerald Mayer; ***W:*** Charles A. Palmer; ***C:*** Paul Vogel; ***M:*** David Buttolph.

The Sellout ✐ *The Sell-Out; La spia senza domain; Melimot Be-Yerushalaim; The Set-Up* **1976** The KGB and CIA decide that retired agents are a potential embarrassment to their respective organizations, and make a mutual agreement to off them all. Former agent Gabriel Lee (Reed) is on vacation in Israel and discovers he's the newest target. It probably has something to do with his defecting to the Russians, and now deciding to re-defect to America. His only hope is his old mentor Sam Lucas (Widmark) who has settled down with Gabriel's ex. **88m/C; DVD.** Oliver Reed; Richard Widmark; Gayle Hunnicutt; Sam Wanamaker; Vladek Sheybal; Ori Levy; Peter Frye; Assi Dayan; Shmuel Rodensku; ***D:*** Peter Collinson; ***W:*** Murray Smith; Judson Kinberg; ***C:*** Arthur Ibbetson; ***M:*** Colin Frechter; Mike Green.

Selma ✐✐✐ 1/2 **2014 (PG-13)** Director/writer DuVernay makes the past present in this stunning drama about the marches in Selma, Alabama, led by Martin Luther King. As played by Oyelowo, King is a masterful tactician, realizing that Lyndon B. Johnson (Wilkinson) will only be moved to do what's needed for civil rights through public pressure to do so. The marches on Selma get the attention to the cause needed to demand action. DuVernay approach is tactile—we can feel the urgency to the march and the realism to the quieter scenes between King and his wife (a great Ejogo). It's more than a biopic. It's a piece of history about a fight that's still going on. **128m/C; DVD, Blu-Ray.** David Oyelowo; Carmen Ejogo; Tom Wilkinson; Oprah Winfrey; Cuba Gooding, Jr.; Common; Andre Holland; Tessa Thompson; Lorraine Toussaint; Ruben Santiago-Hudson; Tim Roth; Dylan Baker; Martin Sheen; Nigel Thatch; ***D:*** Ava DuVernay; ***W:*** Paul Webb; ***C:*** Bradford Young; ***M:*** Jason Moran. Oscars '14: Song ("Glory"); Golden Globes '15: Song ("Glory").

Selma, Lord, Selma ✐✐ 1/2 **1999** Civil rights drama focuses on the youngest two participants in a 1965 voting-rights march from Selma to Montgomery. Preteen Sheyann Webb (Smollett) is inspired by Dr. Martin Luther King Jr.'s (Powell) message of nonviolent demonstration and becomes dedicated to the cause, along with her best friend Rachel Nelson (Peyton). Things come to a climax with the March 7th march to the Edmund Pettus Bridge in Selma, a day that became known as "Bloody Sunday" when state troopers attacked the demonstrators. Adapted from the book "Selma, Lord, Selma" by Webb-Christburg, Nelson, and Frank Sikora. **88m/C; DVD.** Jurnee Smollett; Stephanie Zandra Peyton; Clifton Powell; Yolanda King; ***D:*** Charles Burnett; ***W:*** Cynthia Whitcomb. **TV**

Semi-Pro ✐✐ **2008 (R)** Faced with low fan turnout, the failing ABA of the '70s plans to dissolve the league and incorporate four of its best teams into the NBA. Owner/player Jackie Moon (a fully-froed Ferrell) rises to the occasion, pulling out all the stops to get his lousy Flint Tropics (that's Flint, Michigan, nowhere near anything remotely tropical) on the map and into contention. He recruits aging star Ed Monix (Harrelson) and stages events like bear wrestling to get fans in the door. A funny premise that awkwardly confuses itself with an actual underdog sports drama. As with most of Ferrell's co-stars, Harrelson and Benjamin (as Coffee Black) take a backseat to the SNL alum's outrageous antics, making this little more than a scattering of Will Ferrell sketches. **90m/C; DVD, Blu-Ray.** Will Ferrell; Woody Harrelson; Andre Benjamin; Maura Tierney; Will Arnett; Andy Richter; David Koechner; Rob Corddry; Matt Walsh; Jackie Earle Haley; Andrew Daly; ***D:*** Kent Alterman; ***W:*** Scot Armstrong; ***C:*** Shane Hurlbut; ***M:*** Theodore Shapiro.

Semi-Tough ✐✐ 1/2 **1977 (R)** Likeable, still current social satire involving a couple of pro-football buddies and their mutual interest in their team owner's daughter. Romantic comedy, satire of the sports world, zany highjinks—it's all here, though not enough of any of these. Pleasant and enjoyable. Based on the novel by Dan Jenkins. **107m/C; VHS, DVD, Blu-Ray.** Burt Reynolds; Kris Kristofferson; Jill Clayburgh; Lotte Lenya; Robert Preston; Bert Convy; Richard Masur; Carl Weathers; Brian Dennehy; John Matuszak; Ron Silver; ***D:*** Michael Ritchie; ***W:*** Walter Bernstein.

Seminole ✐✐ **1953** Boetticher's efficient military drama stars Hudson as Army officer Lance Caldwell, who's assigned to a Florida fort where commanding officer Degan (Carlson) dislikes him as much as he does the local Seminole tribe. Caldwell grew up in the Everglades and renews his friendship with Seminole chief Osceola (Quinn). Tensions arise between the Army and the tribe after a murder and Caldwell is accused and on trial. **87m/C; DVD.** Rock Hudson; Anthony Quinn; Barbara Hale; Richard Carlson; Hugh O'Brien; Lee Marvin; Russell Johnson; ***D:*** Budd Boetticher; ***W:*** Charles W. Peck, Jr.; ***C:*** Russell Metty.

Seminole Uprising ✐ **1955** Stock western on a mini budget tells the familiar story of the cavalry rounding up the Indians. Lieutenant Cam Elliot (Montgomery) is charged with the delivery of terrorizing tribe leader Black Cat, who has just kidnapped Colonel Hannah's daughter and Cam's love interest Susan (Booth) and is about to trade her to renegades in return for guns. Cam's men pursue, forcing a bloody battle in typical western-style. Stock battle footage offers a confusing but not unexpected disjointed feel to this low-budget flick. **74m/C; DVD.** George Montgomery; Karin (Karen, Katharine) Booth; William "Bill" Fawcett; Steven Ritch; Ed Hinton; John Pickard; James Maloney; Rory Mallinson; Howard Wright; Rus Conklin; ***D:*** Earl Bellamy; ***W:*** Curt Brandon; Robert E. Kent.

Semper Fi ✐✐ **2019 (R)** Members of the Marine Corp Reserves, a tight-knit group of friends have been called up for combat duty. Among them is cop Cal (Courtney) and his younger brother/legal ward Oyster (Wolff). When rebellious Oyster accidentally kills someone in a bar fight, he is sentenced to 25 years in prison while the rest of the group goes to Iraq. Because Cal believes that Oyster will be killed in prison, he convinces the rest of the group to break him after they return from the war. The drama struggles after a major plot shift and includes too many ideas and characters that are left unexplored. **99m/C; DVD, Blu-Ray.** Leighton Meester; Jai Courtney; Finn Wittrock; Nat Wolff; Beau Knapp; ***D:*** Henry Alex Rubin; ***W:*** Henry Alex Rubin; Sean Mullin; ***C:*** David Devlin; ***M:*** Hanan Townshend.

Send Me No Flowers ✐✐✐ **1964** Vintage Hudson-Day comedy. Hudson plays a hypochondriac who thinks his death is imminent. He decides to provide for his family's future by finding his wife a rich husband. She thinks he's feeling guilty for having an affair. **100m/C; VHS, DVD, Blu-Ray.** Rock Hudson; Doris Day; Tony Randall; Paul Lynde; ***D:*** Norman Jewison; ***W:*** Julius J. Epstein; ***C:*** Daniel F. Fapp.

The Sender ✐✐ **1982 (R)** An amnesiac young man is studied by a psychiatrist. She discovers that her patient is a "sender," who can transmit his nightmares to other patients at a hospital. **92m/C; VHS, DVD, Blu-Ray.** *GB* Kathryn Harrold; Zeljko Ivanek; Shirley Knight; Paul Freeman; Sean Hewitt; Harry Ditson; Marsha A. Hunt; Al Matthews; Angus MacInnes; Olivier Pierre; ***D:*** Roger Christian; ***W:*** Thomas Baum; ***M:*** Trevor Jones.

The Sender ✐✐ 1/2 **1998 (R)** Naval officer Dallas Grayson (Madsen) and his daughter Lisa are possessed of a mysterious power they may have inherited from Dallas' long-missing father, a Naval pilot shot down in the '60s. Whatever they have, the government wants, and they don't care how they get it. **98m/C; VHS, DVD.** Michael Madsen; Dyan Cannon; Robert Vaughn; R. Lee Ermey; Steven Williams; Brian Bloom; Shelli Lether; ***D:*** Richard Pepin; ***W:*** Richard Preston, Jr.; Nathan Long; ***C:*** Michael Weaver.

Senior Skip Day ✐ 1/2 **2008 (R)** Average high school senior Adam (Lundy) is trying to avoid the senior skip day party because he can't stand that his dream girl Cara (Ewell) doesn't know he exists. Then Adam accidentally spills the party location to mean principal Dickwalder (Miller), who's determined to punish anyone not in class. To make amends, Adam promises to hold the bash at his house and uses a classmate's funeral as the excuse for the seniors to be out of school. Yeah, it's over-the-top and kinda offensive but about average for a teen comedy. **81m/C; DVD.** Larry Miller; Lea Thompson; Tara Reid; Clint Howard; Norm MacDonald; Gary Lundy; Kayla Ewell; ***D:*** Nick Weiss; ***W:*** Evan Wasssserstrom; ***C:*** Michael Negrin; ***M:*** Chris Boardman. **VIDEO**

Senior Trip ✐ **1981** N.Y.C. will never be the same after a bunch of rowdy Midwestern high school seniors tear up the town on their graduation trip. **96m/C; VHS, DVD.** Scott Baio; Mickey Rooney; Faye Grant; Vincent Spano; Jane Hoffman; James Carroll; ***D:*** Kenneth Johnson. **TV**

The Seniors ✐✐ **1978 (R)** A group of college students decide to open a phony sex clinic, but the joke is on them when the clinic becomes a success. Better than it sounds. Pretty good acting and much harmless goofiness. **87m/C; VHS, DVD.** Dennis Quaid; Priscilla Barnes; Jeffrey Byron; Gary Imhoff; ***D:*** Rod Amateau.

Senna ✐✐ 1/2 **2011 (PG-13)** Sports documentary follows the true story of Brazilian race car legend Ayrton Senna, who held the Formula One racing championship three times before being killed in a crash in 1994 during the San Marino race. Director Kapadia uses only archival footage, including home movies, TV coverage, and in-car mini-cams that include the accident, and highlights the increasing tension and rivalry with former teammate Alain Prost, the sport's number two driver. **106m/C; DVD, Blu-Ray.** *GB* Ayrton Senna; Richard Williams; Pierre van Vliet; Reginaldo Leme; John Bisignano; Alain Prost; Frank Williams; ***D:*** Asif Kapadia; ***W:*** Manish Pandey; ***C:*** Jake Polonsky; ***M:*** Antonio Pinto. British Acad. '11: Feature Doc., Film Editing.

Senorita Justice ✐ **2003 (R)** While this urban drama is heavily marketed as a debut of Eva Longoria, she's in the film for maybe 5 minutes. Instead viewers get a story of a Hispanic female lawyer who returns to the ghetto to get revenge on the man who killed her gangster brother. **88m/C; DVD.** Yancy Mendia; Mirtha Michelle; Eva Longoria; Tito Puente, Jr.; ***D:*** Kantz; ***W:*** Daniel Wai Chiu; ***C:*** Angel Barroeta.

Sensation ✐✐ **1994 (R)** A college co-ed agrees to participate in a professor's paranormal experiments in order to test her psychic abilities. Unfortunately what she senses is her prof involved in the unsolved sex-murder of a former student. **102m/C; VHS, Streaming.** Kari Wuhrer; Eric Roberts; Ron Perlman; Ed Begley, Jr.; Paul LeMat; Claire Stansfield; Kieran Mulroney; Tracey Needham; ***D:*** Brian Grant; ***W:*** Doug Wallace; ***M:*** Arthur Kempel.

The Sensation of Sight ✐ 1/2 **2006 (R)** An awkward and solemn story that slowly reveals its connections via flashbacks. Former English teacher Finn (Strathairn) inexplicably takes to selling encyclopedias door-to-door after some sort of tragedy that involves a loner (Somerhalder), a troubled young man (Gillies), a single mother (Adams), and a widower (Wilson). **134m/C; DVD.** David Strathairn; Ian Somerhalder; Daniel Gillies; Jane Adams; Scott Wilson; Ann Cusack; Joseph Mazzello; Elizabeth Waterston; ***D:*** Aaron J. Wiederspahn; ***W:*** Aaron J. Wiederspahn; ***C:*** Christopher Lanzenberg; ***M:*** Rupert A. Thompson.

Sensations of 1945 ✐✐ 1/2 *Sensations* **1944** A press agent turns his firm over to one of his clients, a dancer with some wild promotional ideas. Brings together numerous variety and musical acts. W. C. Fields has a cameo in his last film role. Mostly unremarkable, occasionally fun musical. **86m/B; VHS, DVD.** Eleanor Powell; Dennis O'Keefe; Sir C. Aubrey Smith; Eugene Pallette; Cab Calloway; Sophie Tucker; Woody Herman; Lyle Talbot; Marie Blake; ***Cameo(s):*** W.C. Fields; ***D:*** Andrew L. Stone.

Sense & Sensibility ✐✐ **1985** BBC miniseries adaptation of Jane Austen's first novel concerning two sisters striving for happiness in their well-ordered lives. **174m/C; VHS, DVD.** *GB* Irene Richard; Tracey Childs; ***D:*** Rodney Bennett. **TV**

Sense and Sensibility ✐✐✐ 1/2 **1995 (PG)** Thanks to the machinations of greedy relatives, the impecunious Dashwood family is forced to move to a country cottage when father dies. Sensible Elinor (Thompson) looks after the household while overly romantic Marianne (Winslet) pines for passion—ignoring the noble attentions of middle-aged neighbor Brandon (Rickman) for the far more dashing Willoughby (Wise). Elinor has her own hopes for marriage with boyishly ineffectual Edward (Grant) but all three men have secrets that could crush romantic dreams (at least temporarily). Somewhat slow-paced but witty adaptation (by Thompson) of Jane Austen's first novel, well-acted and beautifully photographed (oh, to be in the English countryside). **135m/C; VHS, DVD, Blu-Ray.** *GB* Emma Thompson; Kate Winslet; Hugh Grant; Alan Rickman; Greg Wise; Robert Hardy; Elizabeth Spriggs; Emile Francois; Gemma Jones; James Fleet; Harriet Walter; Imogen Stubbs; Imelda Staunton; Hugh Laurie; Richard Lumsden; ***D:*** Ang Lee; ***W:*** Emma Thompson; ***C:*** Michael Coulter; ***M:*** Patrick Doyle. Oscars '95: Adapt. Screenplay; British Acad. '95: Actress (Thompson), Film, Support. Actress (Winslet); Golden Globes '96: Film--Drama, Screenplay; L.A. Film Critics '95: Screenplay; Natl. Bd. of Review '95: Actress (Thompson), Director (Lee), Film; N.Y. Film Critics '95: Director (Lee); Screen Actors Guild '95: Support. Actress (Winslet); Writers Guild '95: Adapt. Screenplay; Broadcast Film Critics '95: Film, Screenplay.

Sense & Sensibility ✐✐ 1/2 **2007** When her husband dies, Mrs. Dashwood (McTeer) is forced to remove herself and her daughters Elinor (Morahan), Marianne (Wakefield), and young Margaret (Boynton) into genteel poverty at a country cottage. Impulsive, romantic Marianne is drawn to charming cad Willoughby (Cooper), despite the more suitable Colonel Brandon (Morrissey) also expressing his interest. Meanwhile, practical Elinor is quietly pining for the unassuming Edward Ferrars (Stevens) who has familial (and other) obligations that prevent him from courting her. So the Dashwood sisters' romantic hopes seem destined to be, well, dashed. Based on the novel by Jane Austen. **180m/C; DVD.** *GB* Janet McTeer; Dan Stevens; David Morrissey; Dominic Cooper; Claire Skinner; Mark Gatiss; Jean Marsh; Charity Wakefield; Hattie Morahan; Lucy Boyton; ***D:*** John Alexander; ***W:*** Andrew Davies; ***C:*** Sean Bobbitt; ***M:*** Martin Phipps. **TV**

The Sense of an Ending ✐✐ 1/2 **2017 (PG-13)** This powerful adaptation of Julian Barnes 2011 novel explores ideas of memory and aging through the life of very particular, but lonely, Tony (Broadbent). A camera shop owner in London, Tony spends most of his time with his ex-wife Margaret (Walter) and daughter (Dockery). His life is upturned when the mother (Mortimer) of his first love wills him an item that his former girlfriend refuses to give him. As he tries to track the item down, Tony shares the story of his past, including the tragic end of a college friend, with Margaret. Restrained in tone, and well-acted with a stellar cast. **108m/C; DVD.** Jim Broadbent; Charlotte Rampling; Harriet Walter; Michelle Dockery; Matthew Goode; ***D:*** Ritesh Batra; ***W:*** Nick Payne; ***C:*** Christopher Ross; ***M:*** Max Richter.

Senseless 1998 **(R)** Darryl (Wayans) is a poverty stricken college student trying to work his way through school while still supporting his family back home. He agrees to be a medical test subject for a procedure intended to heighten the senses. Unfortunately, as one sense is amplified, the others are drowned out, and Darryl becomes a flailing buffoon. Meanwhile he is in a competition against smarmy frat boy Scott (Spade, who looks about ten years late for his last Econ class) that would land him a job on Wall Street. After dealing with sounds that are too loud and smells that are too pungent, his body adjusts itself. The slapstick bits are hit and miss, but the likable Wayans and dislikable Spade prop up the movie fairly well. **93m/C; VHS, DVD.** Marlon Wayans; David Spade; Matthew Lillard; Rip Torn; Tamara Taylor; Brad Dourif; Ken Lerner; Ernie Lively; Richard McGonagle; Esther Scott; Kenya Moore; ***D:*** Penelope Spheeris; ***W:*** Greg Erb; Craig Mazin; ***C:*** Daryn Okada; ***M:*** Yello.

Senso *The Wanton Contessa* **1954** Tragic story of romance and rebellion as Italian patriots battle the Austro-Hungarian empire for independence in 1866. An Italian noblewoman betrays her marriage, and almost her country, to be with a cynical Austrian soldier in this visually stunning piece of cinematography. In Italian with English subtitles or dubbed. **125m/C; VHS, DVD, Blu-Ray.** *IT* Alida Valli; Massimo Girotti; Heinz Moog; Farley Granger; ***D:*** Luchino Visconti; ***C:*** Robert Krasker.

The Sensuous Nurse 1976 **(R)** Italian comedy about a beautiful nurse hired by the greedy, treacherous relatives of a weak-hearted count in hopes that her voluptuousness will give him a heart attack. It doesn't, and she falls in love. Mindless, but fun and sexy. Dubbed in English. **79m/C; VHS, DVD.** *IT* Ursula Andress; Mario Pisu; Duilio Del Prete; Jack Palance; ***D:*** Nello Rosatti.

The Sentinel 1976 **(R)** A model, who has moved into a New York City brownstone, encounters an aging priest and some unusual neighbors. When she investigates strange noises she finds out that the apartment building houses the doorway to hell—and that she's intended to be the next doorkeeper. Modest suspense film with a good cast and enough shock and special effects to keep the viewer interested. **92m/C; VHS, DVD.** Chris Sarandon; Christina Raines; Ava Gardner; Jose Ferrer; Sylvia Miles; John Carradine; Burgess Meredith; Tom Berenger; Beverly D'Angelo; Jeff Goldblum; Arthur Kennedy; Deborah Raffin; Eli Wallach; Christopher Walken; ***D:*** Michael Winner; ***W:*** Michael Winner; Jeffrey Konvitz; ***C:*** Richard Kratina; ***M:*** Gil Melle.

The Sentinel 1/2 **2006 (PG-13)** Veteran Secret Service agent Pete Garrison (Douglas) is in charge of guarding first lady Sarah Ballentine (Basinger), which is really convenient since they're having an affair. It's bad news though when Garrison gets blackmailed and learns that a presidential assassination is planned. Accused of treason and on the run, Garrison is pursued by his former protege-turned-enemy David Breckinridge (a grim Sutherland). Longoria provides supporting eye candy as rookie agent Jill Marin. Much like Harrison Ford, Douglas excels as a strong (ageless) man who can overcome any crisis and take on all his (younger) adversaries. **105m/C; DVD, Blu-Ray.** Michael Douglas; Kiefer Sutherland; Martin Donovan; Ritchie Coster; Eva Longoria; Kim Basinger; Blair Brown; David Rasche; Kristen Lehman; Raynor Scheine; Chuck Shamata; Paul Calderon; Clark Johnson; ***D:*** Clark Johnson; ***W:*** George Nolfi; ***C:*** Gabriel Beristain; ***M:*** Christophe Beck.

Seoul Raiders *Tokyo Raiders 2; Han Cheng Gong Lue* **2005** Silly action-comedy about a Korean counterfeiting ring in possession of plates for forging U.S. currency. Cutrate, freelancing spy Lam and ambitious thief JJ are both after the goods. Lam gets the plates only to be doublecrossed by his contact. The action is less than spectacular and the comedy is lame. Cantonese with subtitles. **99m/C; DVD.** *CH* Tony Leung Chiu-wai; Qi Shu; Richie Ren; James Kim; Jeong-jin Lee; ***D:*** Jingle Ma; ***W:*** Jingle Ma; Brian Chung; Eric Lin; ***C:*** Kwok Hung Chan; ***M:*** Tommy Wai.

Separate but Equal 1/2 **1991 (PG)** One of TV's greatest history lessons, a powerful dramatization of the 1954 Brown vs. The Board of Education case that wrung a landmark civil rights decision from the Supreme Court. Great care is taken to humanize all the participants, from the humblest schoolchild to NAACP lawyer Thurgood Marshall (Poitier). On two cassettes. **194m/C; VHS, DVD.** Sidney Poitier; Burt Lancaster; Richard Kiley; Cleavon Little; John McMartin; Graham Beckel; Lynne Thigpen; Albert Hall; ***D:*** George Stevens, Jr.; ***W:*** George Stevens, Jr.

Separate Lies 1/2 **2005 (R)** Fellowes makes his writer/director debut with a politely chilling domestic drama. Bored Anne (Watson) informs her stuffy older husband James (Wilkinson) that she is having an affair with the insufferably caddish Bill Bule(Everett). Lawyer James seems more concerned that Bill is responsible for a hit-and-run accident that killed their cleaning woman's husband. Fearful of what will be revealed, James eschews his ethical standards for a cover-up that proves costly, especially in emotional ways. Based on the novel "A Way Through the Wood" by Nigel Balchin. **87m/C; DVD.** *GB* Tom Wilkinson; Emily Watson; Rupert Everett; Linda Bassett; Dave Harwood; John Neville; Hermione Norris; ***D:*** Julian Fellowes; ***W:*** Julian Fellowes; ***C:*** Tony Pierce-Roberts; ***M:*** Stanislas Syrewicz.

Separate Lives 1/2 **1994 (R)** Psych prof Lauren Porter (Hamilton) is in need of some counseling herself. Seems she has a sexy alter ego calling herself Lena and Lauren fears she may have killed someone in her Lena persona. So she turns to her student Tom (Belushi), who happens to be an ex-cop, for help. Sketchy characters and a tired formula make this one a yawner. **101m/C; VHS, Streaming.** Linda Hamilton; James Belushi; Vera Miles; Elisabeth Moss; Drew Snyder; Mark Lindsay Chapman; Marc Poppel; Elizabeth Arlen; ***D:*** David Madden; ***W:*** Steven Pressfield; ***M:*** William Olvis.

A Separate Peace 1/2 **2004 (R)** Uninspired coming of age story based on the John Knowles novel. In 1942, bookworm Gene (Barton) transfers to the all-male Devon prep school in New England. His roomie is campus jock/rule breaker Finny (Moore), who can't wait to enlist. Finny practices his paratrooper moves by jumping from a tree into the lake below. Gene is the only one who'll jump with him and they forge a bond until a questionable accident affects their friendship. **92m/C; DVD.** J Barton; Toby Moore; Jacob Pitts; Aaron Ashmore; Danny Swerdlow; Alison Pill; Sean McCann; Hume Cronyn; ***D:*** Peter Yates; ***W:*** Wendy Kesselman; ***C:*** Checco Varese. **CABLE**

Separate Tables 1/2 **1958** Adaptation of the Terence Rattigan play about a varied cast of characters living out their personal dramas in a British seaside hotel. Guests include a matriarch and her shy daughter, a divorced couple, a spinster, and a presumed war hero. Their secrets and loves are examined in grand style. Fine acting all around. **98m/B; VHS, DVD, Blu-Ray.** Burt Lancaster; David Niven; Rita Hayworth; Deborah Kerr; Wendy Hiller; Rod Taylor; Gladys Cooper; Felix Aylmer; Cathleen Nesbitt; Audrey Dalton; May Hallatt; Priscilla Morgan; Hilda Plowright; ***D:*** Delbert Mann; ***W:*** John Gay; ***C:*** Charles B(ryant) Lang, Jr.; ***M:*** David Raksin. Oscars '58: Actor (Niven), Support. Actress (Hiller); Golden Globes '59: Actor--Drama (Niven); N.Y. Film Critics '58: Actor (Niven).

Separate Ways 1/2 **1982 (R)** Unhappily married couple involved in various affairs split up in order to deal with themselves and their marriage. Good cast; bad script wandering down Maudlin Lane. **92m/C; VHS, DVD.** Karen Black; Tony LoBianco; David Naughton; Sybil Danning; ***D:*** Howard (Hikmet) Avedis; ***C:*** Dean Cundey.

The Separation **1994** Emotions (and fine performances) rather than action move along this domestic drama. Anne (Huppert) and Pierre (Auteuil) are living together in Paris with their toddler son when Anne suddenly announces that she's involved with another man. Anne doesn't see why this this should cause any rift in their domestic arrangements but Pierre slowly falls to pieces. Adapted from the novel by Dan Franck; French with subtitles. **85m/C; VHS, DVD.** *FR* Isabelle Huppert; Daniel Auteuil; Karin Viard; Jerome Deschamps; ***D:*** Christian Vincent; ***W:*** Christian Vincent; Dan Franck; ***C:*** Denis Lenoir.

A Separation 1/2 *Nader and Simin, a Separation; Jodaeiye Nader az Simin* **2011 (PG-13)** A middle-class Tehran couple split up when Simin wants to emigrate but her husband Nader refuses to leave his Alzheimer's-stricken father. She wants there to be more choices for their 11-year-old daughter Temeh, who will carry too much on her young shoulders as the so-called adults bicker and blame. Simin and Temeh move out and Nader hires the inexperienced but desperate Razieh as a caregiver and housekeeper. She needs the money since her hot-tempered, working-class husband Hodjat is unemployed. One unexpected tragedy then leads to the courtroom. Persian with subtitles. **123m/C; DVD, Blu-Ray.** *IA* Payman Moaadi; Leila Hatami; Sarina Farhadi; Sareh Bayat; Shahab Hosseini; ***D:*** Asghar Farhadi; ***W:*** Asghar Farhadi; ***C:*** Mahmoud Kalari. Oscars '11: Foreign Film; Golden Globes '12: Foreign Film; Ind. Spirit '12: Foreign Film.

Sepia Cinderella **1947** A songwriter, who finds himself with a hit, abandons his current life and love to try high society. He finds out it's not what he wants after all. **67m/B; VHS, DVD.** Sheila Guyse; Rubel Blakely; Freddie Bartholomew; Sid Catlett; Deke Wilson; ***D:*** Arthur Leonard; ***W:*** Vincent Valentini; ***C:*** George Webber; ***M:*** Charlie Shavers.

September 1/2 **1988 (PG-13)** Woody does Bergman again with a shuttered, claustrophobic drama about six unhappy people trying to verbalize their feelings in a dark summer house in Vermont. Well-acted throughout and interesting at first, but the whining and angst attacks eventually give way to boredom. Of course, the Woodman went on to "Crimes and Misdemeanors," blending his dark and comedic sides masterfully, so the best way to look at this is as a training film. **82m/C; VHS, DVD, Blu-Ray.** Mia Farrow; Dianne Wiest; Denholm Elliott; Sam Waterston; Elaine Stritch; Jack Warden; ***D:*** Woody Allen; ***W:*** Woody Allen; ***C:*** Carlo Di Palma; ***M:*** Art Tatum.

September **1996** Showtime adaptation of the Rosamunde Pilcher novel. The Scottish Highlands village of Stratcroy holds its share of secrets. After 20 years, Pandora (Bisset) returns home and the two men she had affairs with—married army vet Archie (Fox) and wealthy businessman Edmund (York)?wonder why she's suddenly come back and what she'll reveal. The drama is pegged to the changing seasons. **178m/C; DVD.** *GB* Edward Fox; Michael York; Mariel Hemingway; Virginia McKenna; Jenny Agutter; Paul Guilfoyle; Judy Parfitt; Angela Pleasence; Jesse Birdsall; Jacqueline Bisset; ***D:*** Colin Bucksey; ***W:*** Lee Langley; ***C:*** Peter Sinclair; ***M:*** Richard Hartley. **CABLE**

September Affair 1/2 **1950** A married engineer and a classical pianist miss their plane from Naples. When the plane crashes, they're presumed dead, and they find themselves free to continue their illicit love affair. They find they cannot hide forever and must make peace with their pasts. Features the hit "September Song," recorded by Walter Huston. **104m/B; VHS, Streaming.** Joseph Cotten; Joan Fontaine; Francoise Rosay; Jessica Tandy; Robert Arthur; ***D:*** William Dieterle; ***C:*** Charles B(ryant) Lang, Jr. Golden Globes '52: Score.

September Dawn WOOF! **2007 (R)** Take a stock Old West setting, add a theme of religious intolerance, a "Romeo and Juliet" subplot, a ton of gratuitous violence, Jon Voight, and the label "based on a true story," and you have this truish fiasco about a Mormon militia massacring 120 settlers on September 11th, 1857. Bishop Jacob Samuelson (Voight) isn't pleased about a wagon train of non-Mormons and their worldy ways passing through his territory, but when his son (Ford) falls for one of the settlers (Hope), he goes berserk and decides to show them who's religion is right, after all. Mass-murder of the settlers (and the viewer's tolerance) ensues. Voight chews scenery while the movie collapses into a pit of one-dimensional characters, heavy-handed plotting, and made-for-TV level production values. Movie stirred controversy and accusations of anti-Mormon bias because of the implication that Mormon leader Brigham Young authorized the massacre. **110m/C; DVD.** *US CA* Jon Voight; Trent Ford; Taylor Handley; Tamara Hope; Jon(athan) Gries; Shaun Johnston; Lolita Davidovich; Dean Cain; Huntley Ritter; Terence Stamp; ***D:*** Christopher Cain; ***W:*** Christopher Cain; Carole Whang Schutter; ***C:*** Juan Ruiz-Anchia; ***M:*** William Ross.

The September Issue **2009 (PG-13)** Meryl Streep's character in "The Devil Wears Prada" is said to be based on Anna Wintour, "Vogue"'s icy, brusque longtime editor-in-chief. Cutler's documentary examines the fashion-publishing icon as she and her team of designers, stylists, and photographers put together "Vogue"'s influential September 2007 issue (which came in at 800 pages). **90m/C; DVD.** Sienna Miller; Anna Wintour; ***D:*** R.J. Cutler; ***C:*** Bob Richman; ***M:*** Craig Richey.

September 30, 1955 1/2 *9/30/55* **1977 (PG)** A college undergrad (Thomas) in a small Arkansas town is devastated when he learns of the death of his idol, James Dean. (The title refers to the day Dean died.) Jimmy gathers a group of friends together for a vigil which turns into a drinking-binge, resulting in police chases and, finally, tragedy. Film debut of Quaid. **107m/C; VHS, Streaming.** Richard Thomas; Lisa Blount; Deborah Benson; Tom Hulce; Dennis Christopher; Dennis Quaid; Susan Tyrrell; ***D:*** James Bridges; ***W:*** James Bridges.

Septembers of Shiraz **2016 (PG-13)** A dramatic exploration of one family's experiences during the 1979 Iranian Revolution, based on true events. As prosperous secular Jews living in Iran during the revolution, Isaac (Brody), his wife Farnez (Hayek), and their family know there are risks. But their worst nightmare occurs when Isaac is suddenly arrested and taken to a secret prison. After he is taken, his wife must figure out what happened to her husband, gain his release, and bring everyone to safety. **110m/C; DVD, Streaming, Download.** Adrien Brody; Salma Hayek; Shohreh Aghdashloo; Gabriella Wright; Alon Aboutboul; ***D:*** Wayne Blair; ***W:*** Hanna Weg; ***C:*** Warwick Thornton; ***M:*** Mark Isham.

Septic Man 1/2 **2014 (R)** A sewer worker finds himself changed by his job. Jack (Brown) is employed as a sewer worker in his city. During a water contamination crisis, Jack is determined to find answers. Jack finds himself trapped in the septic tank without food or water, and his appearance becomes hideously transformed. Jack fights to stay alive and leave the tank despite becoming Septic Man. **83m/C; DVD, Download.** Jason David Brown; Molly Dunsworth; Julian Richings; Robert Maillet; Timothy Burd; ***D:*** Jesse Thomas Cook; ***W:*** Tony Burgess; ***C:*** Brendan Uegama; ***M:*** Nate Kreiswirth.

Seraphim Falls **2006 (R)** Irishmen Neeson and Brosnan star as a couple of post-Civil War soldiers (film's set in 1868) in an old-fashioned and beautifully filmed tale of brutal revenge. Wounded Yankee Gideon (Brosnan) is being hunted by Confederate Carver (Neeson) and his four hired guns over a wartime horror, but he won't go easily. There are various showdowns as Gideon picks off the thugs while awaiting that inevitable final confrontation. **115m/C; DVD.** Liam Neeson; Pierce Brosnan; Anjelica Huston; Michael Wincott; Robert Baker; Ed Lauter; John Robinson; Tom Noonan; Kevin J. O'Connor; ***D:*** David Von Ancken; ***W:*** David Von Ancken; Abby Everett Jaques; ***C:*** John Toll; ***M:*** Harry Gregson-Williams.

Seraphine **2008** Vivid biography of French primitive painter Seraphine Louis (Moreau), a middle-aged domestic living in the small town of Senalis in pre-WWI France.

Her precious free time is spent painting fruit and flowers with the limited amount of paint she can afford supplemented with animal's blood, dirt, and other substances. German art critic Wilhelm Uhde (Tukur) is shocked by the power of her work after seeing one of her paintings and promptly becomes Seraphine's champion in the art world. They are reunited in the 1920s (Seraphine paints throughout the war) but her mental deterioration leads to an unhappy end. French and German with subtitles. **126m/C; On Demand.** *BE FR* Yolande Moreau; Ulrich Tukur; Anne Bennent; Genevieve Mnich; Adelaide Leroux; Nico Rogner; ***D:*** Martin Provost; ***W:*** Martin Provost; Marc Abdelnour; ***C:*** Laurent Brunet; ***M:*** Michael Galasso.

Serena 🦴 **1/2 2014 (R)** An absolute disaster that sat for three years while A-list stars Cooper and Lawrence got famous enough for its quiet theatrical and On Demand release. Cooper plays timber baron Pemberton; Lawrence is the titular strong-willed wife who over-embraces his business. Serena truly goes off the rails when confronted by a devastating secret from her husband's past, coupled with her own trauma. Director Bier has no grip on how to make this 1930s North Carolina period piece feel current, turning a potentially tense drama into a slo-mo melodrama that threatens to put you to sleep. Based on Ron Rash's 2008 best-selling novel. **109m/C; DVD, Blu-Ray.** Bradley Cooper; Jennifer Lawrence; Rhys Ifans; Toby Jones; David Dencik; Sean Harris; Ana Ularu; ***D:*** Suzanne (Susanne) Bier; ***W:*** Christopher Kyle; ***C:*** Morten Soborg; ***M:*** Johan Soderqvist.

Serenade 🦴 **1/2 1956** Tragic tenor Lanza's last U.S.-made pic was this extremely loose adaptation of James M. Cain's 1937 novel. Damon Vincenti is a California vineyard worker with a beautiful tenor voice that's heard by wealthy dilettante Kendall Hale (Fontaine). She helps him on his operatic path but tosses Damon aside when she gets bored, which shatters his confidence and health. He flees to Mexico where he's nursed by Juana (Montiel); eventually Kendall reenters their now-happy lives. **122m/C; DVD.** Mario Lanza; Joan Fontaine; Sara Montiel; Vincent Price; Joseph Calleia; Vince Edwards; Frank Puglia; ***D:*** Anthony Mann; ***W:*** Ben Roberts; John Twist; Ivan Goff; ***C:*** J. Peverell Marley.

Serendipity 🦴🦴 **1/2 2001 (PG-13)** Romance finds Jonathan (Cusack) and Sara (Beckinsale) falling in love one cold New York winter's night but then they part company because Sara believes if it's meant to be, fate will bring them back together. Sara's a twinkling twit. Ten years later both are engaged, but Jon and Sara also become separately convinced that they are destined to be together—if they can find each other again. Lots of near-misses and travel between New York and San Francisco until the inevitable happens. Swoony romanticism and more dippy than serendipitous but done in an expert manner. **87m/C; VHS, DVD.** John Cusack; Kate Beckinsale; Molly Shannon; John Corbett; Jeremy Piven; Bridget Moynahan; Eugene Levy; ***D:*** Peter Chelsom; ***W:*** Marc Klein; ***C:*** John de Borman; ***M:*** Alan Silvestri.

Serenity 🦴🦴🦴 **2005 (PG-13)** Failed TV shows usually make pretty crappy movies (remember "Mod Squad?"), but Joss Whedon's big-screen adaptation of his small-screen "Firefly" series is one of the coolest sci fi adventures in recent memory. Captain Mal Reynolds (Fillion) and the crew of his cargo ship, Serenity, attempt to hide River Tam (Glau), a waifishly good-natured super-assassin, from the evil government Alliance that created her. Things hit the fan when the coolly evil Operative (Ejiofor) gets on their trail, but that won't keep Mal from "aiming to misbehave." Imagine a movie based on everything you loved about Han Solo and the Millenium Falcon, and you'll get an idea of why so many fanboys worship at the altar of Whedon. **119m/C; DVD, Blu-Ray, UMD, HD-DVD.** Nathan Fillion; Gina Torres; Alan Tudyk; Adam Baldwin; Sean Maher; Ron Glass; Chiwetel Ejiofor; Morena Baccarin; Jewel Staite; Summer Glau; ***D:*** Joss Whedon; ***W:*** Joss Whedon; ***C:*** Jack N. Green; ***M:*** David Newman.

Serenity 🦴 **1/2 2019 (R)** Iraq veteran Baker Dill (McConaughey) works as the captain of a fishing boat for hire on a tropical island. Locally Baker is known for being obsessed with catching a large, elusive tuna fish he has named Justice. One day, Karen (Hathaway), Baker's ex-wife, shows up and makes him offer. She is unhappily married to Frank Zariakas (Clarke), a wealthy man who abuses her, and offers Baker $10 million to make it look like Frank has died in an accident on his boat. The neo-noir film suffers from unbelievable dialogue and plots twists as well as cliched dialogue and over-the-top performances. **106m/C; DVD.** Matthew McConaughey; Anne Hathaway; Diane Lane; Jason Clarke; Djimon Hounsou; ***D:*** Steven Knight; ***W:*** Steven Knight; ***C:*** Jess Hall; ***M:*** Benjamin Wallfisch.

The Sergeant 🦴🦴 **1968** Master Sgt. Albert Callan (Steiger) is a stern, by-the-book super soldier who is stationed in an Army camp in post-WWII France. His commanding officer (Latimore) is a lush and only too happy to let Callan take over although his undisciplined soldiers resent Callan's strict policies. Then Callan begins eyeing handsome Pvt. Swanson (Law) and all those lonely, repressed sexual urges come bubbling up. Since Callan can't openly express them, he makes Swanson's life and his own miserable until the inevitable final act. **108m/C; DVD.** Rod Steiger; John Phillip Law; Ludmila Mikael; Frank Latimore; ***D:*** John Flynn; ***W:*** Dennis Murphy; ***C:*** Henri Persin; ***M:*** Michel Magne.

Sgt. Bilko 🦴 **1/2 1995 (PG)** Popular '50s sitcom doesn't march so much as limp to the big screen with Martin leading the troops as the wise-cracking title character, crafted so brilliantly by Phil Silvers on the small screen. Martin flims and flams with frenetic energy as he tries to save his base from Washington cutbacks and the film from utter disaster. Enter Major Thorn (Hartman), Bilko's old adversary, who's plotting revenge on the con artist sergeant. Aykroyd's Bilko's naive boss, Col. Hall, but has little to do. Director Lynn finds his usual comic flair on leave this time around—too few laughs, spread too thin. Sentimental stroke has Catherine Silvers, Phil's daughter, playing Lt. Monday. **95m/C; VHS, DVD, Blu-Ray.** Steve Martin; Dan Aykroyd; Phil Hartman; Glenne Headly; Daryl (Chill) Mitchell; Max Casella; Brian Leckner; Pamela Segall; Eric Edwards; Dan Ferro; John Marshall Jones; Brian Ortiz; Dale Dye; ***D:*** Jonathan Lynn; ***W:*** Andy Breckman; ***C:*** Peter Sova; ***M:*** Alan Silvestri.

Sergeant Deadhead 🦴 **1/2 1965** Limp AIP comedy has Sgt. Deadhead (Avalon) accidentally launched into space with a chimpanzee. Somehow the trip alters his personality and Deadhead is locked in the brig to keep the mishap secret. The Air Force finds a double to take his place but Deadhead's engaged to Lucy (Walley) and intends to make it to his wedding. **89m/C; DVD.** Frankie Avalon; Deborah Walley; Cesar Romero; Fred Clark; Gale Gordon; Eve Arden; Buster Keaton; Harvey Lembeck; ***D:*** Norman Taurog; ***W:*** Louis M. Heyward; ***C:*** Floyd Crosby; ***M:*** Les Baxter.

Sgt. Kabukiman N.Y.P.D. WOOF! 1994 When New York cop Harry Griswold (Gianasi) investigates the death of a famous Japanese Kabuki actor, he suddenly finds himself in a kimono, having really bad hair-days, and vested with the powers of "Kabukiman." With the help of his beautiful teacher Lotus (Byun), he learns to channel his command of such amazing weapons as suffocating sushi rolls and lethal chopsticks into crime fighting. Stupid and insulting (deliberately so), all at the same time. A PG-13 version runs 95 minutes. **104m/C; VHS, DVD, Blu-Ray.** Rick Gianasi; Susan Byun; Brick Bronsky; Bill Weeden; Thomas Crnkovich; Larry Robinson; Noble Lee Lester; ***D:*** Lloyd Kaufman; Michael Herz; ***W:*** Lloyd Kaufman; Andrew Osborn; ***C:*** Bob Williams; ***M:*** Bob Mithoff.

Sergeant Klems 🦴 **1/2** *Il Sergente Klems* **1971** Based loosely on the story of Josef Otto Klems, a German soldier in WWI who assumes the identity of another soldier to avoid being killed for desertion and ends up becoming Chief of Staff to one of the local Arab leaders. **95m/C; DVD.** *IT SP* Peter Strauss; Tina Aumont; Howard Ross; Massimo Serato; ***D:*** Sergio Grieco; ***W:*** Sergio Grieco; ***C:*** Stelvio Massi; ***M:*** Carlo Rustichelli.

Sgt. Pepper's Lonely Hearts Club Band WOOF! 1978 (PG) "Rip-off" would be putting it kindly. A classic album by one of the greatest rock bands of all time deserves the respect of not having a star-studded extravaganza "filmization" made of it. Gratuitous, weird casting, bad acting give it a surreal feel. And the Bee Gees? Please. A nadir of '70s popular entertainment. **113m/C; VHS, DVD, Blu-Ray.** Peter Frampton; Barry Gibb; Steve Martin; Takaaki Yamashita; George Burns; Maurice Gibb; Donald Pleasence; ***D:*** Michael A. Schultz.

Sergeant Rutledge 🦴🦴🦴 **1960** The story of a court-martial, told in flashback, about a black cavalry officer on trial for rape and murder. A detailed look at overt and covert racism handled by master director Ford. It is always apparent Strode (as Rutledge) is a heroic, yet human, figure who refuses to be beaten down by circumstances. The courtroom setting is deliberately oppressive but does make the film somewhat static. Based on the novel "Captain Buffalo" by James Warner Bellah. **112m/C; VHS, DVD.** Woody Strode; Jeffrey Hunter; Constance Towers; Billie Burke; Juano Hernandez; Carleton Young; Charles Seel; Jan Styne; Mae Marsh; ***D:*** John Ford; ***W:*** Willis Goldbeck; James Warner Bellah; ***M:*** Howard Jackson.

Sergeant York 🦴🦴🦴🦴 **1941** Timely and enduring war movie based on the true story of Alvin York, the country boy from Tennessee drafted during WWI. At first a pacifist, Sergeant York (Cooper, well cast in an Oscar-winning role) finds justification for fighting and becomes one of the war's greatest heros. Gentle scenes of rural life contrast with horrific battlegrounds. York served as a consultant. **134m/B; VHS, DVD.** Gary Cooper; Joan Leslie; Walter Brennan; Dickie Moore; Ward Bond; George Tobias; Noah Beery, Jr.; June Lockhart; Stanley Ridges; Margaret Wycherly; James Anderson; David Bruce; Lane Chandler; Elisha Cook, Jr.; Erville Alderson; Howard da Silva; Donald "Don" Douglas; Frank Faylen; Pat Flaherty; Joseph Girard; Creighton Hale; Russell Hicks; George Irving; Selmer Jackson; Jack Pennick; Harvey Stephens; Kay Sutton; Clem Bevans; Charles Trowbridge; Guy Wilkerson; Gig Young; ***D:*** Howard Hawks; ***W:*** Abem Finkel; Harry Chandler; Howard Koch; John Huston; ***C:*** Sol Polito; ***M:*** Max Steiner. Oscars '41: Actor (Cooper), Film Editing; Natl. Film Reg. '08; N.Y. Film Critics '41: Actor (Cooper).

Sergeants 3 🦴 **1/2 1962** A 'Rat Pack' western with Sinatra, Martin, and Lawford as the titular brawling cavalry sergeants (Davis Jr. is the company bugler) who take on warring Native American chief Mountain Hawk (Silva). There's also a subplot about Lawford's character wanting to leave the military and his buddies for marriage to Lee. It's actually a remake of 1939's "Gunga Din" played for a few laughs and some action. Three of Bing Crosby's sons are cast as soldiers. **113m/C; DVD.** Frank Sinatra; Dean Martin; Peter Lawford; Sammy Davis, Jr.; Joey Bishop; Henry Silva; Ruta Lee; Buddy Lester; Philip Crosby; Lindsay Crosby; Dennis Crosby; ***D:*** John Sturges; ***W:*** W.R. Burnett; ***C:*** Winton C. Hoch; ***M:*** Billy May.

Sergio Lapel's Drawing Blood 🦴 *Drawing Blood* **1999** Artist/vampire Diana (Spinella) fulfills her artistic visions with blood instead of oils or watercolors. Her human slave Edmond (Wilson) supplies a constant flow of "models" until he meets homeless prostitute Dee (Smith) and decides to take control of his life. Edmond also has his hands full keeping his ever-horny dad (Palatta) out of trouble. The Troma label says it all: non-existent production values, mediocre acting, plenty of flowing red stuff, and ample female exposure (although this time there's a genuine narrative logic to all the nudity). **90m/C; DVD.** Kirk Wilson; Larry Palatta; Dawn Spinella; Leo Otero; Erin Smith; ***D:*** Sergio Lapel; ***W:*** Noel Anderson; ***C:*** Shawn Lewallen.

Serial 🦴🦴🦴 **1980 (R)** Fun spoof of hyper-trendiness—open marriage, health foods, fad religions, navel-gazing—in Marin County, the really cool place to live across the Golden Gate from San Francisco. Mull in his first lead is the oddly normal guy surrounded by fruits and nuts. Based on Cyra McFadden's novel. **90m/C; VHS, DVD, Blu-Ray.** Martin Mull; Sally Kellerman; Tuesday Weld; Tom Smothers; Bill Macy; Peter Bonerz; Barbara Rhoades; Christopher Lee; ***D:*** Bill Persky; ***W:*** Rich Eustis; Michael Elias.

Serial Bomber 🦴🦴 **1996 (R)** A would-be bomber in Seattle targets his ex-girlfriend but his plan is foiled by an FBI agent. So the bomber shifts targets. Based on the novel "Christmas Apocalypse" by Toshiyuki Tajima. **89m/C; VHS, DVD.** Jason London; Lori Petty; James LeGros; Yuki Amami; ***D:*** Keoni Waxman.

Serial Killer 🦴🦴 **1995 (R)** Selby Younger (Delaney) is able to think like a killer in order to catch them. That's how the beautiful cop captured serial killer William Lucian Morrano (Bell) who has now escaped—Selby's his ultimate target but first he wants revenge. So he uses her friends as bait and leaves the bodies for Selby to discover. **94m/C; VHS, DVD.** Kim Delaney; Gary Hudson; Tobin Bell; Pam Grier; Marco Rodriguez; Lyman Ward; Cyndi Pass; Andrew Prine; ***D:*** Pierre David; ***W:*** Mark Sevi; ***C:*** Thomas Jewett; ***M:*** Louis Febre.

Serial Killing 101 🦴🦴 *Serial Killing 4 Dummys* **2004 (R)** Outcast high-school kid Casey decides that he wants to be a serial killer when he grows up. His suicidal (and presumably equally outcast) girlfriend thinks this is a great idea. At least they won't have to sweat the SATs. When a real serial killer shows up, guess who the cops suspect. Myriad problems (besides the tasteless premise) ensure a small audience for this one. **88m/C; VHS, DVD.** Thomas Haden Church; Justin Urich; Lisa Loeb; Rick Overton; George Murdock; Barbara Niven; ***D:*** Trace Slobotkin; ***W:*** Trace Slobotkin; ***C:*** John Tarver; ***M:*** Jeffrey Alan Jones. **VIDEO**

Serial Mom 🦴🦴🦴 **1994 (R)** June Cleaver-like housewife Turner is nearly perfect, except when someone disrupts her orderly life. Didn't rewind your videotape? Chose the white shoes after Labor Day? Uh oh. Stardom reigns after she's caught and the murderer-as-celebrity phenomenon is exploited to the fullest. Darkly funny Waters satire tends toward the mainstream and isn't as perverse as earlier efforts, but still maintains a shocking edge (vital organs are good for an appearance or two). Turner's chameleonic performance as the perfect mom/crazed killer is right on target, recalling "The War of the Roses." Waterston, Lake, and Lillard are terrific as her generic suburban family. **93m/C; VHS, DVD, Blu-Ray.** Kathleen Turner; Sam Waterston; Ricki Lake; Matthew Lillard; Mink Stole; Traci Lords; Suzanne Somers; Joan Rivers; Patty (Patricia Campbell) Hearst; Mary Jo Catlett; Justin Whalin; Susan Lowe; Alan J. Wendl; Mary Vivian Pearce; ***V:*** John Waters; ***D:*** John Waters; ***W:*** John Waters; ***C:*** Robert M. Stevens; ***M:*** Basil Poledouris.

Serial Slayer 🦴 **1/2** *Claustrophobia* **2003 (R)** A serial killer hunts in the daylight. Three office workers are trapped in a suburban house trying to avoid being the next victims of the Crossbow Killer. Modestly suspenseful, although it can't avoid most of the genre's cliches. At least the three chicks don't run around screaming in their scanties (sorry, guys). **79m/C; DVD.** Melanie Lynskey; Sheeri Rappaport; Mary Lynn Rajskub; Judith O'Dea; ***D:*** Mark Tapio Kines; ***W:*** Mark Tapio Kines; ***C:*** Bevan Crothers; ***M:*** Christopher Farrell.

Series 7: The Contenders 🦴🦴 **1/2 2001 (R)** Reality TV takes to the big screen in this morbid but insightful portrayal of a fictional show called "The Contenders" in which the participants hunt each other down to their ultimate, televised, demise. Pic is presented in the form of a marathon of the show, which stars eight-months pregnant Dawn (Smith), the champ who takes on five new challengers, including an 18-year-old girl (Wever), a cancer victim and artist who was also, coincidentally, Dawn's first boyfriend (Fitzgerald). Revealing portrayals make all the contestants sympathetic, but Dawn and Jeff's unique plight is the most interesting. A scene where Dawn casually guns people down in a convenience store while bystanders look on is a highlight in this interesting social satire. **86m/C; VHS, DVD.** Brooke Smith; Glenn Fitzgerald; Merritt Wever; Michael Kaycheck; Richard Venture; Donna Hanover; Marylouise Burke; Nada Despotovich; Danton Stone; Jennifer Van Dyck; Angelina Phillips; Tanny McDonald; ***Nar:*** Will Arnett; ***D:*** Daniel Minahan; ***W:*** Daniel Minahan; ***C:*** Randy Drummond; ***M:*** Girls Against Boys.

Serious Charge 🦴🦴 **1/2 1959** Howard Phillips (Qualyle) is a single clergyman, newly-arrived at his small town parish. The progressive reverend is determined to stem the juvenile delinquent problem but has his work cut out for him, especially with psychotic troublemaker Larry (Ray), who falsely accuses Phillips of indecent assault. His lie is backed up by vindictive spurned spinster Hester (Churchill), but in order to save his reputation, Phillips must get Hester to tell the truth. Cliff Richard (in his film debut) gets to sing. Based on the Philip King play. **99m/B; DVD.** *GB* Anthony Quayle; Sarah Churchill; Andrew Ray; Irene Browne; Percy Herbert; Noel Howlett; Cliff Richard; ***D:*** Terence Young; ***W:*** Guy Elmes; Mickey Delamar; ***C:*** Georges Perinal; ***M:*** Leighton Lucas.

A Serious Man 🦴🦴🦴 **2009 (R)** A Coen brothers' film that's personal and an angst-ridden dark comedy. Problems arise for the Jewish Gropnik family in 1967 in an unnamed Minnesota city suburb. Physicist Larry's wife Judith is having an affair with his obnoxious university colleague Sy and wants a divorce. His crazy mathematician brother Larry is unemployable and living with the family, son Danny is buying pot and goes to his bar mitzvah stoned, and daughter Sarah steals money from Larry's wallet to save up for a nose job. Larry is worried he won't get tenure even as a graduate student gives him grief and his beautiful neighbor shakes his libido by sunbathing in the nude. If Larry reminds you of the biblical Job—well that's deliberate. **105m/C; Blu-Ray, On Demand.** Michael Stuhlbarg; Richard Kind; Sari Lennick; Fred Melamed; Adam Arkin; Fyvush Finkel; Aaron Wolff; Jessica McManus; ***D:*** Joel Coen; Ethan Coen; ***W:*** Joel Coen; Ethan Coen; ***C:*** Roger Deakins; ***M:*** Carter Burwell. Ind. Spirit '10: Cinematog.

Serious Moonlight 🦴 **1/2 2009** High-powered attorney Louise (Ryan) is expecting a romantic weekend getaway with hubby Ian (Hutton) only to find out he's planning on leaving her for a trip to Paris with his much-younger mistress Sara (Bell). Enraged, Louise knocks Ian out and then duct-tapes him to the toilet while haranguing him about making their marriage work. Meanwhile, Sara gets tired of waiting for Ian and shows up on their doorstep and weird gardener Todd (Long) comes along and drunkenly decides to rob the place. Unfortunately shrill marital comedy is the directorial debut for Hines, who acted with late screenwriter Shelly in the 2007 film "Waitress." **84m/C; DVD.** ***D:*** Cheryl Hines.

The Serpent and the Rainbow

WOOF! 1987 (R) A good, interesting book (by Harvard ethnobotanist Wade Davis) offering serious speculation on the possible existence and origin of zombies in Haiti was hacked and slashed into a cheap Wes Craven-ized screen semblance of itself. And a shame it is: the result is racist, disrespectful, exploitative, and superficial. **98m/C; VHS, DVD, Blu-Ray.** Bill Pullman; Cathy Tyson; Zakes Mokae; Paul Winfield; Conrad Roberts; Badja (Medu) Djola; Theresa Merritt; Brent Jennings; Michael Gough; Paul Guilfoyle; ***D:*** Wes Craven; ***W:*** Richard Maxwell; A.R. Simoun; ***C:*** John Lindley; ***M:*** Brad Fiedel.

The Serpent's Egg 🦴 **1/2** *Das Schlangenei* **1978 (R)** Big disappointment from the great Bergman in his second film in English. Ullmann is not sultry and Carradine is horrible. Big budget matched by big Bergman ego, making a big, bad parody of himself. The plot concerns a pair of Jewish trapeze artists surviving in Berlin during Hitler's rise by working in a grisly and mysterious medical clinic. **119m/C; VHS, DVD, Blu-Ray.** *GE* David Carradine; Liv Ullmann; Gert Frobe; James Whitmore; ***D:*** Ingmar Bergman; ***W:*** Ingmar Bergman; ***C:*** Sven Nykvist.

The Serpent's Kiss 🦴🦴 **1997 (R)** Great cast can't quite overcome the story's predictability. In 1699, young Dutch landscape artist Meneer Chrome (MacGregor) accepts a job at the remote English estate of Thomas Smithers (Postlethwaite) who wants a magnificent garden to present to his bored wife, Julianna (Scacchi). But Chrome is secretly employed by Juliana's scheming cousin, James Fitzmaurice (Grant), to bankrupt Smithers so that James can regain Juliana affections. Of course, Julianna casts her eyes on the handsome gardener instead, and then there's the matter of the Smithers' teenaged daughter, Thea (Chaplin). Rousselot is better known as a cinematographer (this is his first directorial effort) and the film at least looks gorgeous. **110m/C; VHS, DVD.** *GB FR* Ewan McGregor; Greta Scacchi; Pete Postlethwaite; Richard E. Grant; Carmen Chaplin; Donal McCann; Charley Boorman; ***D:*** Philippe Rousselot; ***W:*** Tim Rose Price; ***C:*** Jean-Francois Robin; ***M:*** Goran Bregovic.

Serpico 🦴🦴🦴 **1973 (R)** Based on Peter Maas's book about the true-life exploits of Frank Serpico, a New York undercover policeman who exposed corruption in the police department. Known as much for his nonconformism as for his honesty, the real Serpico eventually retired from the force and moved to Europe. South Bronx-raised Pacino gives the character reality and strength. Excellent New York location photography. **130m/C; VHS, DVD, Blu-Ray.** Al Pacino; John Randolph; Jack Kehoe; Barbara Eda-Young; Cornelia Sharpe; F. Murray Abraham; Tony Roberts; ***D:*** Sidney Lumet; ***W:*** Waldo Salt; Norman Wexler; ***C:*** Arthur Ornitz; ***M:*** Mikis Theodorakis. Golden Globes '74: Actor--Drama (Pacino); Natl. Bd. of Review '73: Actor (Pacino); Writers Guild '73: Adapt. Screenplay.

The Servant 🦴🦴🦴 **1/2 1963** A dark, intriguing examination of British class hypocrisy and the master-servant relationship. Wealthy, bored aristocratic playboy Tony (Fox) is ruined by his socially inferior but crafty and ambitious Cockney manservant Hugo (Bogarde). Playwright Harold Pinter wrote the adaptation of Robin Maugham's novel in his first collaboration with expatriate American director Losey. The best kind of British societal navel-gazing. **112m/B; VHS, DVD.** *GB* Dirk Bogarde; James Fox; Sarah Miles; Wendy Craig; Catherine Lacey; Richard Vernon; ***D:*** Joseph Losey; ***W:*** Harold Pinter; ***C:*** Douglas Slocombe; ***M:*** John Dankworth. British Acad. '63: Actor (Bogarde); N.Y. Film Critics '64: Screenplay.

Servants of Twilight 🦴🦴 **1991 (R)** Religious zealots target a small boy for assassination because their cult leader says he's the anti-Christ. Adaptation of the Dean R. Koontz novel. Packed with action, its spell on the viewer hinges on a cruel shock ending that undercuts what came before. **95m/C; VHS, DVD.** Bruce Greenwood; Belinda Bauer; Grace Zabriskie; Richard Bradford; Jarrett Lennon; Carel Struycken; Jack Kehoe; Kelli Maroney; Dale Dye; ***D:*** Jeffrey Obrow; ***W:*** Stephen Carpenter. **CABLE**

Serving in Silence: The Margarethe Cammermeyer Story 🦴🦴🦴 **1995** Army nurse Margarethe Cammermeyer (Close) has had a distinguished career for 24 years, a bronze star earned in Vietnam, and obtained the rank of colonel. During a security clearance interview, she admits to the military that she is a lesbian and finds herself reluctantly in the eye of the media storm. The TV film won 3 EMMY awards: Best Actress for Close; Best Supporting Actress for Davis (as Margarethe's lover); and Best Screenplay. **92m/C; VHS, DVD.** Glenn Close; Judy Davis; Jan Rubes; Wendy Makkena; William Converse-Roberts; Susan Barnes; Colleen Flynn; William Allen Young; ***D:*** Jeff Bleckner; ***W:*** Allison Cross. **TV**

Serving Sara 🦴 **2002 (PG-13)** Unfunny comedy stars Perry as process server Joe Tyler, who is trying to serve divorce papers on flirty Englishwoman Sara Moore (Hurley), who's married to womanizing Texas cattle baron Gordon (Campbell). But Sara turns the tables by bribing Joe to try to serve divorce papers to the elusive Gordon instead. Perry's trip to rehab during filming delayed production but the lack of laughs surely can't be laid solely at his door. **99m/C; VHS, DVD.** Matthew Perry; Elizabeth Hurley; Bruce Campbell; Vincent Pastore; Cedric the Entertainer; Amy Adams; Terry Crews; Jerry Stiller; Joe (Johnny) Viterelli; ***D:*** Reginald (Reggie) Hudlin; ***W:*** Jay Scherick; David Ronn; ***C:*** Robert Brinkmann; ***M:*** Marcus Miller.

Sesame Street Presents: Follow That Bird 🦴🦴 **1/2** *Follow That Bird* **1985 (G)** Possibly the best children's TV show in the history of the medium makes a so-so transition to the big screen. Suffering an identity crisis, a lonely Big Bird allows himself to be adopted by a family of birds. Quickly realizing that his new family is a bunch of do-dos (literally), the big guy heads back to NYC, followed by a vindictive social worker, two scheming carnival owners, and the assorted residents of Sesame Street. There are great moments (mostly involving Super-Grover and Ernie & Bert) and some fun cameos from Waylon Jennings and SCTV alumni, but it never lives up to the potential of the TV show. **92m/C; VHS, DVD.** Sandra Bernhard; John Candy; Chevy Chase; Joe Flaherty; Dave Thomas; Waylon Jennings; ***V:*** Carroll Spinney; Jim Henson; Frank Oz; ***D:*** Ken Kwapis; ***W:*** Judy Freudberg; Tony Geiss; ***C:*** Curtis Clark; ***M:*** Lennie Niehaus.

Session 9 🦴🦴 **2001 (R)** Hazardous materials contractor Gordon (Mullan) bids on a job to remove asbestos from a run-down insane asylum. He secures the contract by promising to complete the work in a week, although under ideal circumstances it should take a month. Unfortunately, "ideal circumstances" are not afoot in the creepy booby hatch. The oppressive atmosphere soon gets to Gordon and his crew, who begin turning on each other after the discovery of nine audio tapes confirming rumors of satanic rituals and torture of patients. Somewhat marred by editing that gives away the plot too early, and also by the fact that for workers under a deadline, these guys stand around getting freaked out way too much. Shot using Sony's CineAlta HD digital video cameras instead of film. **100m/C; VHS, DVD, Blu-Ray.** Peter Mullan; David Caruso; Josh(ua) Lucas; Brendan Sexton, III; Paul Guilfoyle; Stephen Gevedon; ***D:*** Brad Anderson; ***W:*** Brad Anderson; Stephen Gevedon; ***C:*** Uta Briesewitz; ***M:*** Climax Gold Twins.

A Session with The Committee 🦴🦴 **1968 (PG)** Comedy film of the seminal comedy troupe "The Committee," specialists in short, punchy satire. Dated, but of interest to comedy buffs. **88m/C; VHS, DVD.** Wolfman Jack; Howard Hesseman; Barbara Bosson; Peter Bonerz; Garry Goodrow; Carl Gottlieb; ***D:*** Jack Del.

The Sessions 🦴🦴🦴 **1/2** *The Surrogate* **2012 (R)** True account of 38-year-old writer and poet Mark O'Brien (Hawkes), as he attempts to experience sex for the first time. As a result of a severe case of childhood polio, Mark is confined to an iron lung most of the day, and lightens his sexual anxieties with jokes and open discussions with a hip Catholic priest (Macy). He mostly seeks advice on hiring a sexual surrogate, Cheryl (Hunt), not a hooker but a trained, compassionate guide to ease him into manhood. A moving depiction of fear and tenderness, with a pitch-perfect cast, especially Hawkes capturing the heart and body of a man in constant limbo. Based on O'Brien's autobiographical essay. **95m/C; DVD, Blu-Ray.** John Hawkes; Helen Hunt; William H. Macy; Moon Bloodgood; W. Earl Brown; Annika Marks; ***D:*** Ben Lewin; ***W:*** Ben Lewin; ***C:*** Geoffrey Simpson; ***M:*** Marco Beltrami. Ind. Spirit '13: Actor (Hawkes), Actress--Supporting (Hunt).

Set It Off 🦴🦴 **1/2 1996 (R)** Lethal "Waiting to Exhale," finds four female friends in Los Angeles pushed over the edge and taking up bank robbery to escape poverty and strike a blow against "the man." The felonious, funky divas of crime include Stony (Pinkett, who seems to be having fun with this role) and Latifah as Cleo, in a powerhouse performance. Butt-kicking action scenes are most entertaining combined with a soundtrack, including Seal, En Vogue, the Fugees and Brandy, to match. Melodramatic sequences, including Stony's romance with Keith (Underwood), drag. **121m/C; VHS, DVD.** Jada Pinkett Smith; Queen Latifah; Vivica A. Fox; Kimberly Elise; Blair Underwood; John C. McGinley; Anna Maria Horsford; Ella Joyce; Charles Robinson; Chaz Lamar Shepherd; Vincent Baum; Van Baum; Thomas Jefferson Byrd; Samantha MacLachlan; ***D:*** F. Gary Gray; ***W:*** Takashi Bufford; Kate Lanier; ***C:*** Marc Reshovsky; ***M:*** Christopher Young.

The Set-Up 🦴🦴🦴 **1/2 1949** Excellent, original if somewhat overwrought morality tale about integrity set in the world of boxing. Filmed as a continuous narrative covering only 72 minutes in the life of aging fighter Stoker Thompson (Ryan). His manager (Tobias) takes a gangster's bribe for Thompson to throw the fight (without informing him), never believing the washed-up boxer has a chance to win. Powerful, with fine performances, especially from Ryan in the lead. Inspired by Joseph Moncure March's narrative poem. **72m/B; VHS, DVD, Blu-Ray.** Robert Ryan; Audrey Totter; George Tobias; Alan Baxter; James Edwards; Wallace Ford; ***D:*** Robert Wise; ***W:*** Art Cohn; ***C:*** Milton Krasner.

The Set Up 🦴🦴 **1/2 1995 (R)** Electronic engineer-turned-cat burglar Charlie Thorpe (Zane) is now apparently reformed after a prison stint and works designing and installing security systems. His latest job is for Chairman Jeremiah Cole (Coburn) at Charter Trust bank where he begins romancing the beautiful Gina (Sara). But she becomes the hostage of Charlie's ex-prison buddy Kliff (Russo), who wants Charlie's help in breaking into the bank. However, there's a double-cross (or maybe even a triplecross) that has Charlie scrambling to save his life. Based on the book "My Laugh Comes Last" by James Hadley Chase. **103m/C; VHS, DVD.** Billy Zane; Mia Sara; James Coburn; James Russo; ***D:*** Strathford Hamilton; ***W:*** Michael Thoma; ***C:*** David Lewis; ***M:*** Conrad Pope.

The Settlement 🦴🦴 **1999** Con men Jerry and Pat try to make money by buying life insurance policies on the terminally ill. Unfortunately for them, their clients have been living a lot longer than anticipated. Then they meet the seriously ill Barbara and things begin to change. **92m/C; VHS, DVD.** Kelly McGillis; John C. Reilly; William Fichtner; Dan Castellaneta; David Rasche; ***D:*** Mark Steilen; ***C:*** Judy Irola; ***M:*** Brian Tyler.

Setup 🦴 **1/2 2011 (R)** Recycled crime drama with Jackson an uncharismatic lead. Friends plan a diamond heist but it turns deadly when Vincent betrays his buddies and takes off with the score. To get even, survivor Sonny goes to mobster Biggs, who'll help Sonny if Sonny agrees to steal a couple million bucks from the Russian mafia. **90m/C; DVD, Blu-Ray.** 50 Cent; Ryan Phillippe; Bruce Willis; Randy Couture; Shaun Toub; Jenna Dewan; James Remar; Will Yun Lee; ***D:*** Mike Gunther; ***W:*** Mike Gunther; ***C:*** Steve Gainer; ***M:*** The Newton Brothers. **VIDEO**

Seven 🦴🦴🦴 *Se7en* **1995 (R)** If this grim thriller can't make you jump, you're dead, and you won't be the only one. Arrogant, ignorant detective David Mills (Pitt) is newly partnered with erudite old-timer William Somerset (Freeman) and they're stuck with the bizarre case of a morbidly obese man who was forced to eat himself to death. The weary Somerset is certain it's just the beginning and he's right—the non-buddy duo are on the trail of a serial killer who uses the seven deadly sins (gluttony, greed, sloth, pride, lust, envy, and wrath) as his modus operandi. Since most of the film is shot in dark, grimy, and unrelentingly rainy circumstances, much of the grotesqueness of the murders is left to the viewer's imagination—which will be in overdrive. **127m/C; VHS, DVD, Blu-Ray.** Brad Pitt; Morgan Freeman; Gwyneth Paltrow; Kevin Spacey; R. Lee Ermey; Richard Roundtree; John C. McGinley; Julie Araskog; Reg E. Cathey; Peter Crombie; ***D:*** David Fincher; ***W:*** Andrew Kevin Walker; ***C:*** Darius Khondji; ***M:*** Howard Shore. MTV Movie Awards '96: Film, Most Desirable Male (Pitt), Villain (Spacey); Natl. Bd. of Review '95: Support. Actor (Spacey); N.Y. Film Critics '95: Support. Actor (Spacey); Broadcast Film Critics '95: Support. Actor (Spacey).

The 7 Adventures of Sinbad

WOOF! 2010 (PG-13) Bad acting, bad CGI, and a plot that defies sense. An oil tanker is deposited at the bottom of the ocean by a sea monster. The industrialist who owns the tanker, Adrian Sinbad (Muldoon), has his helicopter go down on his way to the incident and he and some other survivors wake up on some mystery island. Sinbad then meets a native girl who declares he must complete seven tasks (battling various monsters) in order to save the world. **90m/C; DVD, Blu-Ray.** Patrick Muldoon; Bo Svenson; Sarah Desage; Kelly O'leary; Dylan Jones; Berne Velasquez; ***D:*** Adam Silver; Ben Hayflick; ***W:*** Adam Silver; Ben Hayflick; ***C:*** Mikey Jechart; ***M:*** Chris Ridenhour. **VIDEO**

Seven Alone 🦴🦴 **1/2** *House Without Windows* **1975 (G)** Family adventure tale (based on Monroe Morrow's book "On to Oregon," based in turn on a true story) about seven siblings who undertake a treacherous 2000-mile journey from Missouri to Oregon, after their parents die along the way. Inspiring and all that; good family movie. **85m/C; VHS,**

DVD. Dewey Martin; Aldo Ray; Anne Collins; Dean Smith; Stewart Petersen; *D:* Earl Bellamy.

7 Angels in Eden 🦴 **2007** Two lovers who are the last people alive on Earth attempt to escape Texas, when their fears materialize as seven murderous rednecks hellbent on doing bad things. There's a bad joke in there somewhere. **78m/C; DVD, Streaming.** Marshall Mills; Kristin Sutton; *D:* Marshall Mills; *W:* Marshall Mills; *C:* Dimitar Orovcanec; *M:* Ferd Moyse. **VIDEO**

Seven Angry Men 🦴 ½ **1955** Massey stars as the very angry abolitionist John Brown, who gets his numerous sons involved in his 1859 would-be slave revolt at Harper's Ferry, Virginia. Massey previously portrayed Brown in 1940's "Santa Fe Trail." **92m/B; DVD.** Raymond Massey; Jeffrey Hunter; Debra Paget; Dennis Weaver; Guy Williams; Larry Pennell; Leo Gordon; *D:* Charles Marquis Warren; *W:* Daniel Ullman; *C:* Ellsworth Fredericks; *M:* Carl Brandt.

Seven Beauties 🦴🦴🦴🦴 *Pasqualino Settebellezze; Pasqualino: Seven Beauties* **1976** Very dark war comedy about a small-time Italian crook in Naples with seven ugly sisters to support. He survives a German prison camp and much else; unforgettably, he seduces the ugly commandant of his camp to save his own life. Good acting and tight direction. **116m/C; VHS, DVD, Blu-Ray.** *IT* Giancarlo Giannini; Fernando Rey; Shirley Stoler; Elena Fiore; Enzo Vitale; *D:* Lina Wertmuller; *W:* Lina Wertmuller; *C:* Tonino Delli Colli.

7 Below 🦴 ½ **2011 (R)** A tour bus breaks down, stranding the passengers in the middle of nowhere. Their only shelter is a home where a series of murders committed by a 10-year-old boy occurred during a 1910 hurricane. Their loner host Jack (Rhames) has his reasons for wanting his unexpected visitors to stay when terrible things start to happen. **90m/C; DVD, Blu-Ray.** Ving Rhames; Val Kilmer; Luke Goss; Bonnie Somerville; Matt Barr; Rebecca Da Costa; Brianna Lee Johnson; *D:* Kevin Carraway; *W:* Kevin Carraway; Lawrence Sara; *C:* Harris Charalambous; *M:* Jake Staley. **VIDEO**

Seven Blood-Stained Orchids 🦴 ½ *Sette Orchide Macchiate di Rosso* **1972** A serial killer is murdering women and leaving a crescent moon-shaped pendant in their hands. Giulia survives an interrupted attack but the police keep this a secret as she and her husband Mario decide to investigate the connection between the women themselves. Italian with subtitles. **88m/C; DVD, Blu-Ray.** *IT* Antonio (Tony) Sabato; Uschi Glas; Pier Paolo Capponi; Claudio Gora; Bruno Corazzari; Rossella Falk; *D:* Umberto Lenzi; *W:* Umberto Lenzi; Roberto Gianviti; *C:* Angelo Lotti; *M:* Riz Ortolani.

7 Boxes 🦴🦴🦴 *7 Cajas* **2014** Victor is a 17-year-old kid who unknowingly gets involved in a deadly game when he accepts an unusual proposal—carry seven boxes of unknown content on a delivery and he'll get $100. Delivering them proves to be much harder than poor Victor first assumes when he learns that other people want their contents badly enough to chase him. A tightly-made, streamlined action-drama with social context given Victor's lifestyle and desire to do anything, even something he doesn't understand, for money. It's a clever, well-made slice of life that doubles as a commentary on how easy it is to slide into a life of crime. Spanish with subtitles. **100m/C; On Demand.** *PG* Celso Franco; Lali Gonzalez; Victor Sosa; *D:* Juan Carlos Maneglia; Tana Schembori; *W:* Juan Carlos Maneglia; *C:* Richard Carega; *M:* Fran Villalba.

Seven Brides for Seven Brothers 🦴🦴🦴 ½ **1954** The eldest of seven fur-trapping brothers in the Oregon Territory brings home a wife. She begins to civilize the other six, who realize the merits of women and begin to look for romances of their own. Thrilling choreography by Michael Kidd—don't miss "The Barn Raising." Charming performances by Powell and Keel, both in lovely voice. Based on Stephen Vincent Benet's story. Thrills, chills, singin', dancin'?a classic Hollywood good time. **103m/C; VHS, DVD, Blu-Ray.** Howard Keel; Jane Powell; Russ Tamblyn; Julie Newmar; Jeff Richards; Tommy (Thomas) Rall; Virginia Gibson; *D:* Stanley Donen; *W:* Albert Hackett; Frances Goodrich; Dorothy Kingsley; *C:* George J. Folsey. Oscars '54: Scoring/Musical; Natl. Film Reg. '04.

Seven Cities of Gold 🦴🦴 **1955** An expedition of Spanish conquistadors and missionaries descend on 18th-century California, looking for secret Indian caches of gold. Semi-lavish costume epic. **103m/C; VHS, Streaming.** Anthony Quinn; Michael Rennie; Richard Egan; Rita Moreno; Jeffrey Hunter; Eduardo Noriega; John Doucette; *D:* Robert D. Webb.

7 Days in Entebbe 🦴🦴 *Entebbe* **2018 (PG-13)** A dramatic look at a 1976 hijacking of an Air France flight. When the flight from Tel Aviv to Paris makes a stop in Athens, pro-Palestinian activists board the plane and force the crew and 250 passengers to fly to Libya and, finally, Entebbe, Uganda. As the revolutionaries hold their captives at an abandoned airport terminal, they find themselves in an increasingly no-win situation. In Jerusalem, there is disagreement within the Israeli government over what to do: negotiate with terrorists or take action. Though the film has an authentic 1970s look, the scattered story and pacing limit its power. **106m/C; DVD, Blu-Ray.** Rosamund Pike; Daniel Brühl; Eddie Marsan; Nonso Anozie; Ben Schnetzer; *D:* Jose Padilha; *W:* Gregory Burke; *C:* Lula Carvalho; *M:* Rodrigo Amarante.

Seven Days in May 🦴🦴🦴 ½ **1964** Topical but still gripping Cold War nuclear-peril thriller. After President Jordan Lyman (March) signs a nuclear disarmament treaty with the Soviets, General James M. Scott (Lancaster), the leader of the Joint Chiefs of Staff, plans a military takeover because he considers the president's pacifism traitorous. Lyman learns of the potential coup and works to expose the plot before it's too late. Highly suspenseful, with a breathtaking climax. Based on a novel by Fletcher Knebel and Charles Waldo Bailey II. **117m/B; VHS, DVD, Blu-Ray.** Burt Lancaster; Kirk Douglas; Edmond O'Brien; Fredric March; Ava Gardner; Martin Balsam; George Macready; Whit Bissell; Hugh Marlowe; Richard Anderson; Andrew Duggan; John Houseman; *D:* John Frankenheimer; *W:* Rod Serling; *C:* Ellsworth Fredericks; *M:* Jerry Goldsmith. Golden Globes '65: Support. Actor (O'Brien).

Seven Days in Utopia 🦴🦴 **2011 (G)** A family drama about finding your true path in life. For most of his life, Luke Chisolm (Black) has focused on golf. He showed talent from an early age and now is trying to turn professional and play on a tour. Unfortunately, Luke's first big chance to shine on a public stage turns into a disaster. After this humiliation, he seeks an escape from the pressures of golf and ends up stranded in Utopia, Texas. There, Luke meets rancher Johnny Crawford (Duvall), an eccentric man with profound knowledge about life. By meeting Johnny, Luke finds himself examining his past and his future. **100m/C; DVD, Blu-Ray.** Lucas Black; Robert Duvall; Melissa Leo; Deborah Ann Woll; Brian Geraghty; *D:* Matt Russell; *W:* Matt Russell; David L. Cook; Rob Levine; Sandra Thrift; *C:* M. David Mullen; *M:* Klaus Badelt; Christopher Carmichael.

Seven Days' Leave 🦴🦴 **1942** Spunky RKO musical comedy finds Army Pvt. Johnny Grey (Mature) in line for an inheritance if he fulfills one stipulation--he must marry socialite Terry Havalok-Allen (Ball) for some silly family reasons. Johnny and Terry both happen to already be engaged and Johnny has only seven days to woo Terry before he ships off to Japan. **87m/B; DVD.** Victor Mature; Lucille Ball; Mary McGuire; Mapy Cortes; Arnold Stang; Harold (Hal) Peary; *D:* Tim Whelan; *W:* Kenneth Earl; William Bowers; *C:* Robert De Grasse.

Seven Days of Grace 🦴 **2006 (PG-13)** Despite the familiar faces in the cast, this looks like a low-budget amateur production. Struggling Hollywood actress Grace (Coyne) has inherited her father's failing Italian eatery. So she joins forces with three female friends in an effort to keep the place going until she can figure out how to duplicate the secret rib recipe he took to his grave. **90m/C; DVD.** Stephanie Beacham; Olivia Hussey; Lesley-Anne Down; Gavan O'Herlihy; Peter Evans; Ria Coyne; *D:* Don E. Fauntleroy; *C:* Don E. Fauntleroy; *M:* Michael Werckle. **VIDEO**

7 Days to Live 🦴🦴 *Seven Days to Live* **2000 (R)** A couple moves into a haunted house, and the husband ties his wife up after she tells him she keeps seeing signs she will die in seven days. An odd ripoff of "The Shining." **96m/C; VHS, DVD.** *CZ GE US* Nick Brimble; Sean Pertwee; Sean Chapman; Amanda Plummer; Gina Bellman; Amanda Walker; *D:* Sebastian Niemann; *W:* Dirk Ahner; *C:* Gerhard Schirlo; *M:* Egon Riedel. **VIDEO**

Seven Deadly Sins 🦴🦴 **2010** Two-part miniseries shown on Lifetime and based on the novels by Robin Wasserman. High school senior Harper Grace wants to get out of the small California town her once-important family controlled. However, the arrival of New Yorker Kaia causes chaos for Harper and everyone around her since the newcomer has her own destructive plans for the town. **175m/C; DVD.** *CA* Dreama Walker; Rachel Melvin; Jared Kesso; Kirsten Prout; Emma Lahana; Eric Close; *D:* Jeff Renfroe; *W:* Gary Tieche; *C:* Mathias Herndl; *M:* James Janovisch. **CABLE**

Seven Deaths in the Cat's Eye 🦴🦴 **1972** A ravenous beast slaughters people in a small Scottish village. This flick reveals a little-known fact about felines. **90m/C; VHS, DVD.** *IT* Anton Diffring; Jane Birkin; *D:* Anthony M. Dawson.

Seven Doors to Death 🦴 **1944** Young architect tries to solve a crime to avoid being placed under suspicion. The suspects are six shop owners in this low-budget attempt at a murder mystery. **70m/B; VHS, DVD.** Chick Chandler; June Clyde; George Meeker; Gregory Gay; Edgar Dearing; *D:* Elmer Clifton.

711 Ocean Drive 🦴🦴 **1950** Telephone repairman Mal Granger (O'Brien) gets involved with bookies Vince (Kelley) and Larry (Porter) when he fixes up a system to bring in results from far away tracks. When both bookies are murdered, an increasingly reprehensible Mal takes over the operation but big-timer Carl Stephens (Kruger) decides to muscle in. The climax takes place at Hoover Dam. **102m/B; DVD, Blu-Ray.** Edmond O'Brien; Otto Kruger; Joanne Dru; Don Porter; Barry Kelley; Sammy White; Dorothy Patrick; Howard St. John; *D:* Joseph M. Newman; *W:* Francis Swann; Richard English; *C:* Franz Planer; *M:* Sol Kaplan.

7 Faces of Dr. Lao 🦴🦴🦴 **1963** Dr. Lao is the proprietor of a magical circus that changes the lives of the residents of a small western town. Marvelous special effects and makeup (Randall plays seven characters) highlight this charming family film in the Pal tradition. Charles Finney adapted from his novel. **101m/C; VHS, DVD.** Tony Randall; Barbara Eden; Arthur O'Connell; Lee Patrick; Noah Beery, Jr.; John Qualen; John Ericson; Royal Dano; *D:* George Pal; *W:* Charles Beaumont; *C:* Robert J. Bronner; *M:* Leigh Harline.

Seven Girlfriends 🦴🦴 **2000 (R)** Melancholy romantic comedy has thirtysomething bachelor Jesse (Daly) so disheartened by his string of failed romances that he seeks out seven ex-girlfriends to find out what went wrong. Good cast. **100m/C; VHS, DVD.** Timothy Daly; Laura Leighton; Mimi Rogers; Olivia D'Abo; Jami Gertz; Elizabeth Pena; Melora Hardin; Arye Gross; Katy Selverstone; *D:* Paul Lazarus; *W:* Paul Lazarus; Stephen Gregg; *C:* Don E. Fauntleroy; *M:* Christopher Tyng.

7 Grand Masters 🦴🦴🦴 *Hu bao long she ying; Tiger, Leopard, Dragon, Snake, Eagle; The Grandmaster* **2004** Long considered on of the best martial arts films made, it combines two of the more classic themes of early Kung Fu films (i.e. the aging master trying to prove he still has it, and the foolish young man desperate to learn Kung Fu). Retiring Kung Fu master Shang Kaun-cheng (Jack Long) must travel China to retain his status as master by defeating the masters of other schools. Along the way he takes on novice Hsia Hsiao-ying (Yi Min Li), who is bullied by the other students, especially as he begins to surpass them. But both he and his master have secrets that are coming back to haunt them. **84m/C; DVD.** *TW* Yuet Sang Chin; Alan Chui Chung San; Yi-min Li; Jack Long; Mark Long; Fei Lung; Nancy Yen; Corey Yuen; *D:* Joseph Kuo; *W:* Joseph Kuo; Raymond To; Ching Kang Yao; *M:* Fu-liang Chow.

The Seven Hills of Rome 🦴🦴 ½ **1958** Quiet story of a TV star (Lanza) who follows his girlfriend (Castle) to Rome after a lovers' quarrel, and there falls in love with Allasio. Fantastic music makes up for a weak plot. Based on a story by Giueseppi Amato. **107m/C; VHS, DVD.** Mario Lanza; Peggy Castle; Renato Rascel; Marisa Allasio; Clelia Matania; Rosella Como; *D:* Roy Rowland; *W:* Giorgio Prosperi; Art Cohn; *M:* Georgie Stoll.

Seven Hours to Judgment 🦴🦴 **1988 (R)** When the punks who murdered his wife go free, a psychotic man (Leibman) decides to take justice into his own hands. He kidnaps the wife of the judge in charge (Bridges, who also directed) and leads him on a wild goose chase. Leibman steals the film as the psycho. Ex-Springsteen spouse Phillips plays the judge's wife. Ambitious but credulity-stretching revenge/crime drama. Screenplay written by de Souza under the pseudonym Elliot Stephens. **90m/C; VHS, DVD.** Beau Bridges; Ron Leibman; Julianne Phillips; Al Freeman, Jr.; Reggie Johnson; *D:* Beau Bridges; *W:* Steven E. de Souza; Walter Halsey Davis; *C:* Hanania Baer; *M:* John Debney.

Seven Keys to Baldpate 🦴🦴 ½ **1929** Early talkie version of the film which was based on the famous stage play of the same name by George M. Cohan and the Earl Derr Biggers novel which follows an author into a deserted Baldpate Inn on a bet that he can't finish a novel in 24 hours while in the Inn. Preceded by a 1917 silent and followed by 1935 and 1947 versions. **70m/B; DVD.** Richard Dix; Miriam Seegar; Crauford Kent; Margaret Livingston; Lucien Littlefield; *D:* Reginald Barker; *W:* Jane Murfin; *C:* Edward Cronjager.

Seven Keys to Baldpate 🦴 ½ **1935** Weak RKO mystery. Writer William Magee (Raymond) makes a bet that he can finish his new crime novel in 24 hours. So he plans on holding up in the Baldpate inn, thinking he has the only key to the place. Until others come trickling in, each with their very own key. Soon Magee is caught up in missing money and murder instead of writing. Based on a novel by Earl Derr Biggers. Preceded by 1917 and 1929 versions and followed by a 1947 film. **80m/B; DVD.** Gene Raymond; Margaret Callahan; Eric Blore; Moroni Olsen; Erin O'Brien-Moore; Grant Mitchell; Murray Alper; *D:* William Hamilton; Edward Killy; *W:* Anthony Veiller; Wallace Smith; *C:* Robert De Grasse.

The Seven Little Foys 🦴🦴🦴 **1955** Enjoyable musical biography of Eddie Foy (played ebulliantly by Hope) and his famed vaudevillian troupe. Cagney's appearance as George M. Cohan is brief, but long enough for a memorable dance duet with Hope. **95m/C; VHS, DVD.** Bob Hope; Milly Vitale; George Tobias; Angela (Clark) Clarke; James Cagney; *D:* Melville Shavelson; *W:* Melville Shavelson; Jack Rose.

7 Men From Now 🦴🦴 ½ **1956** Revenge story is the first of seven westerns from director Boetticher and star Scott. Ex-sheriff Ben Stride (Scott) is after the seven men who killed his wife during their robbery of the Wells Fargo office. Stride aids travelers John Greer (Reed) and his wife Annie (Russell) who are on their way to Flora Vista where Stride believes the bandits are hiding. They also encounter shifty outlaw Masters (Marvin), who makes it clear he wants the stolen gold for himself and believes he'll be the last man standing. **78m/C; DVD.** Randolph Scott; Walter Reed; Gail Russell; Lee Marvin; John Larch; Donald (Don "Red") Barry; John Beradino; *D:* Budd Boetticher; *W:* Burt Kennedy; *C:* William Clothier; *M:* Henry Vars.

7 Minutes 🦴🦴 **2015** This Tarantino-esque dramatic crime thriller centers on a robbery gone very, very bad. Due to life circumstances, three high school friends must commit an audacious robbery that should only take seven minutes. However, the robbery goes wrong and the stakes get higher as each minute goes by. Instead of making out with their loot, they face a life and death situation. **92m/C; DVD, Blu-Ray, Download.** Luke Mitchell; Zane Holtz; Jason Ritter; Brandon Hardesty; Kevin Gage; *D:* Jay Martin; *W:* Jay Martin; *C:* Noah Rosenthal; *M:* tomandandy.

Seven Minutes in Heaven 🦴🦴 **1986 (PG)** Sensitive love story about a 15-year-old girl who invites her platonic male friend to live in her house, and finds it disturbs her boyfriend, as these things will. Ever so tasteful (unlike most other teen comedies), with gentle comedy—but forgettable. **90m/C; VHS, DVD.** Jennifer Connelly; Byron Thames; Maddie Corman; Lauren Holly; ***D:*** Linda Feferman; ***W:*** Jane Bernstein; ***C:*** Steven Fierberg.

7 Mummies **2006** Several escaped convicts in Arizona are on the run with a hostage when they find a hidden Spanish treasure in a town full of vampires and zombies. Along the way the films creators throw in some bosoms and super ninja mummies just in case you got bored. **90m/C; DVD, Streaming.** Thadd Turner; James Intveld; Matt Schulze; Billy Wirth; Billy Drago; Andrew Bryniarski; Danny Trejo; Martin Kove; Noel Gugliemi; Max Perlich; Cerina Vincent; Adrianne Palicki; ***D:*** Nick Quested; ***W:*** Thadd Turner; ***C:*** Patrick Loungway; ***M:*** James Intveld; Michael Turner. **VIDEO**

The Seven-Per-Cent Solution **1976 (PG)** Dr. Watson (Duvall) persuades Sherlock Holmes (Williamson) to meet with Sigmund Freud (Arkin) to cure his cocaine addiction. Holmes and Freud then find themselves teaming up to solve a supposed kidnapping. Adapted by Nicholas Meyer from his own novel. One of the most charming Holmes films; well-cast, intriguing blend of mystery, drama, and fun. Title refers to the solution of cocaine Holmes injects. **113m/C; VHS, DVD, Blu-Ray.** Alan Arkin; Nicol Williamson; Laurence Olivier; Robert Duvall; Vanessa Redgrave; Joel Grey; Samantha Eggar; Jeremy Kemp; Charles Gray; Regine; ***D:*** Herbert Ross; ***W:*** Nicholas Meyer; ***C:*** Oswald Morris; ***M:*** John Addison.

Seven Pounds **1/2 2008 (PG-13)** A depressed IRS agent, Ben (Smith), kicks things off by calling a 911 operator to report his own suicide. Cue the uncertainty—and flashback scenes—behind what motivates Ben to act as he does, apparently seeking out seven individuals to assist for various reasons as part of a larger plan for his own redemption. However, things get complicated when he falls in love with one of the recipients, Emily (Dawson), who suffers from a congenital heart disorder yet sees beyond her own pain and senses Ben's. Visually bleak reteaming of Smith and director Muccino puts the star back on his superhero-esque pedestal, though he has enough charm to pull it off, as does Dawson who's more than worthy of sharing the screen with him. **123m/C; Blu-Ray, UMD, On Demand.** Will Smith; Rosario Dawson; Woody Harrelson; Michael Ealy; Barry Pepper; Bill Smitrovich; Elpidia Carrillo; Robine Lee; Tim Kelleher; Gina Hecht; Joseph A. Nunez; ***D:*** Gabriele Muccino; ***W:*** Grant Nieporte; ***C:*** Philippe Le Sourd; ***M:*** Angelo Milli.

Seven Psychopaths **2012 (R)** Martin McDonagh's follow-up to his Oscar-nominated "In Bruges" gets a little haphazard at times but often works as bloody escapism with an A-list cast. Farrell's alcoholic L.A. writer Marty works on a script with the same title as McDonagh's film. He encounters a number of lunatics along the way, including a mobster played by Harrelson, a serial killer embodied by Waits, and, possibly, his own best buddy played with infectious glee by Rockwell. Even with all the star power, Walken steals the piece as the crazy dognapper who starts all the mischief. **110m/C; DVD, Blu-Ray.** *US UK* Colin Farrell; Woody Harrelson; Sam Rockwell; Christopher Walken; Tom Waits; Abbie Cornish; Zeljko Ivanek; ***D:*** Martin McDonagh; ***W:*** Martin McDonagh; ***C:*** Ben Davis; ***M:*** Carter Burwell.

Seven Samurai *Shichinin No Samurai; The Magnificent Seven* **1954** Kurosawa's masterpiece, set in 16th-century Japan. A small farming village, beset by marauding bandits, hires seven professional soldiers to rid itself of the scourge. Wanna watch a samaurai movie? This is the one. Sweeping, complex human drama with all the ingredients: action, suspense, comedy. Available in several versions of varying length, all long—and all too short. Splendid acting. In Japanese with English subtitles. **204m/B; VHS, DVD, Blu-Ray.** *JP* Toshiro Mifune; Takashi Shimura; Yoshio Inaba; Kuninori Kodo; Isao (Ko) Kimura; Seiji Miyaguchi; Minoru Chiaki; Daisuke Kato; Bokuzen Hidari; Kamatari (Keita) Fujiwara; Yoshio Kosugi; Yoshio Tsuchiya; Jun Tatara; Sojin; Kichijiro Ueda; Jun Tazaki; Keiji Sakakida; Keiko Tsushima; Gen Shimizu; ***D:*** Akira Kurosawa; ***W:*** Akira Kurosawa; Shinobu Hashimoto; Hideo Oguni; ***C:*** Asakazu Nakai; ***M:*** Fumio Hayasaka. Venice Film Fest. '54: Silver Prize.

Seven Seas to Calais **1/2 1962** Simple swashbuckler bout British privateer Sir Francis Drake (Taylor) and his ultimate battle with the Spanish Armada to protect Queen Elizabeth I (Worth). Director Mate's final film. **102m/C; DVD.** *IT* Rod Taylor; Irene Worth; Keith Michell; Basil Dignam; Anthony Dawson; Terence Hill; Edy Vessel; ***D:*** Rudolph Mate; Primo Zeglio; ***W:*** Filippo Sanjust; ***C:*** Giulio Gianini; ***M:*** Franco Mannino.

Seven Seconds **2005 (R)** Snipes' career isn't helped by this confusing and lackluster actioner. Professional thief Jack Tolliver (Snipes) and his crew are after an armored car when a rival gang shows up to steal a Van Gogh that's also inside. During the melee, Jack gets away with the painting but most of his crew are dead, except for one who has been taken as a hostage. Now he must rescue his partner, aided or hindered by NATO cop Kelly Anders (Outhwaite). **90m/C; DVD, UMD.** Wesley Snipes; Pete Lee-Wilson; Dhobi Oparei; Georgina Rylance; Tamzin Outhwaite; Serge Soric; ***W:*** Simon Fellows; ***C:*** Michael Slovis; ***M:*** Barry Taylor. **VIDEO**

Seven Sinners *Cafe of the Seven Sinners* **1940** A South Seas cabaret singer (Dietrich) attracts sailors like flies, resulting in bar brawls, romance, and intrigue. Manly sailor Wayne falls for her. A good-natured, standard Hollywood adventure. Well cast; performed and directed with gusto. **83m/B; DVD.** Marlene Dietrich; John Wayne; Albert Dekker; Broderick Crawford; Mischa Auer; Billy Gilbert; Oscar Homolka; ***D:*** Tay Garnett; ***W:*** John Meehan; Harry Tugend; ***C:*** Rudolph Mate; ***M:*** Frank Skinner.

Seven Stages to Achieve Eternal Bliss **1/2** *Seven Stages to Achieve Eternal Bliss by Passing Through the Gateway Chosen by the Holy Storsh* **2020** Claire and Paul think they've hit the jackpot with their new, low-rent L.A. apartment, unaware that cult leader Storsh had killed himself in their tub. Worse, Storsh's disciples keep breaking in to replicate his "self murder," but they're not very good at it. Stuck where they are, the couple adopts an if-you-can't-beat-em-join-em stance and lends them a hand in offing themselves, resulting in an original, offbeat, black comedy. **93m/C; DVD.** Kate Micucci; Sam Huntington; Taika Waititi; Dan Harmon; Rhea Seehorn; ***D:*** Vivieno Caldinelli; ***W:*** Christopher Hewitson; Clayton Hewitson; Justin Jones; ***C:*** Mathew Rudenberg; ***M:*** Joe Wong.

Seven Sweethearts **1/2 1942** Backlot MGM musical. Reporter Henry Taggart (Heflin) is sent to the Dutch-settled town of Little Delft, Michigan to cover the annual tulip festival. He becomes smitten with innkeeper Papa Van Maaster's (Sakall) youngest daughter Billie (Grayson) but the two have no chance of getting serious because of Papa's old-world ways. He insists that his seven daughters (who have male names) must get married in birth order but the oldest, Reggie (Hunt), is so vain and bossy that she doesn't even have a suitor. **98m/B; DVD.** Van Heflin; Kathryn Grayson; S.Z. Sakall; Marsha Hunt; Cecilia Parker; Peggy Moran; Dorothy Morris; Frances Rafferty; Frances Raeburn; Carl Esmond; ***D:*** Frank Borzage; ***W:*** Leo Townsend; Walter Reisch; ***C:*** George J. Folsey; ***M:*** Franz Waxman.

Seven Swords **1/2** *Chat gim; Qi Jian* **2007** Adapted from a classic Chinese novel, this is the story of the beginning of the Ching Dynasty. The Ming Emperors have fallen, and the Chings have declared martial law, stating anyone disobeying their orders will be executed. Fire-Wind (Honglei Sun), a general from the previous dynasty sees this as an opportunity for wealth and sets about slaughtering the populace and taking their possessions in the name of the new rulers. Eventually he makes it to the frontier village of Bowei Fortress, where a retired executioner recruits six other men with special swords to put an end to the General's nonsense. Seven against a few hundred is pretty stiff odds though. **151m/C; DVD, Blu-Ray.** *CH CH NK* Donnie Yen; Leon Lai; Charlie Yeung; Liwu Dai; Chia-Liang Liu; Duncan Lai; Yi Lu; Jingwu Ma; Jason Pai Paio; Honglei Sun; Michael Wong; Jingchu Zhang; So-yeon Kim; ***D:*** Hark Tsui; ***W:*** Hark Tsui; Chi-Sing Cheung; Tin Chun; Yusheng Liang; ***C:*** Kwok-Man Keung; ***M:*** Kenji Kawai.

Seven Thieves **1960** Charming performances and nice direction make this tale of the perfect crime especially watchable. Robinson, getting on in years, wants one last big heist. With the help of Collins and Steiger, he gets his chance. From the Max Catto novel "Lions at the Kill." Surprisingly witty and light-hearted for this subject matter, and good still comes out ahead of evil. **102m/C; VHS, DVD.** Joan Collins; Edward G. Robinson; Eli Wallach; Rod Steiger; Alexander Scourby; Michael Dante; Berry Kroeger; Sebastian Cabot; Marcel Hillaire; John Beradino; Jonathan Kidd; ***D:*** Henry Hathaway; ***W:*** Sydney (Sidney) Boehm; ***C:*** Sam Leavitt; ***M:*** Dominic Frontiere.

7 Things to Do Before I'm 30 **2008** A month before her 30th birthday, Lori Madison (Benson) loses her job, her boyfriend, and her New York apartment. So she heads home to Colorado and moves back in with her parents. Lori finds a childhood wish list and discovers she hasn't done one thing on it, so she makes it her goal to try everything before her birthday rolls around as part of her new start. **90m/C; DVD.** Amber Benson; Christopher Jacot; John Reardon; Haig Sutherland; Julia Duffy; Tegan Moss; Lori Walsh; ***D:*** Paul Kaufman; ***W:*** Duane Poole; ***C:*** Adam Sliwinski; ***M:*** James McVay. **CABLE**

The Seven-Ups **1/2 1973 (PG)** An elite group of New York City detectives seeks to avenge the killing of a colleague and to bust crooks whose felonies are punishable by jail terms of seven years or more. Unoriginal premise portends ill; plotless cop action flick full of car chases. Scheider tries hard. Directed by the producer of "The French Connection." **109m/C; VHS, DVD, Blu-Ray.** Roy Scheider; Tony LoBianco; Larry Haines; Jerry Leon; ***D:*** Philip D'Antoni.

Seven Were Saved **1/2 1947** Dull effort despite the actual footage of the Air-Sea Rescue Service's operations. A plane goes down in the Pacific Ocean and the survivors are adrift in a life raft, awaiting rescue. Relating to the recently ended WWII: one survivor is a Japanese commander on his way to a war crimes trial and two are former POWs from a Japanese camp. **72m/B; DVD.** Richard Denning; Catherine Craig; Russell Hayden; Ann Doran; John Eldridge; Richard Loo; Don Castle; ***D:*** William H. Pine; ***W:*** Maxwell Shane; ***C:*** Jack Greenhalgh; ***M:*** Darrell Calker.

The Seven Year Hitch **1/2 2012** Hallmark Channel rom com. Jennifer has been letting her best friend Kevin stay with her for years while he tries to find himself. Jen's boyfriend Bryce asks her to marry him but wants Kevin gone. However, Kevin knows Bryce is a louse and, with some help from meddling neighbor Mr. Henderson, Kevin tells Jen that they are considerd to have a legal common law marriage. Now he has to prove to her that he's the guy to be her husband. **86m/C; DVD.** Natalie Hall; Darin Brooks; Ryan Doom; George Wendt; Frances Fisher; ***D:*** Bradford May; ***W:*** Brian Sawyer; Gregg Rossen; ***C:*** James W. Wrenn; ***M:*** Nathan Furst. **CABLE**

The Seven Year Itch **1955** Classic, sexy Monroe comedy. Stunning blonde model (who else?) moves upstairs just as happily married guy Ewell's wife leaves for a long vacation. Understandably, he gets itchy. Monroe's famous blown skirt scene is here, as well as funny situations and appealing performances. **105m/C; VHS, DVD, Blu-Ray.** Marilyn Monroe; Tom Ewell; Evelyn Keyes; Sonny Tufts; Victor Moore; Doro Merande; Robert Strauss; Oscar Homolka; Carolyn Jones; ***D:*** Billy Wilder; ***W:*** Billy Wilder; George Axelrod; ***C:*** Milton Krasner; ***M:*** Alfred Newman. Golden Globes '56: Actor--Mus./Comedy (Ewell).

Seven Years Bad Luck **1921** French comic Linder has the proverbial seven years' bad luck all in one day (!) after he breaks a mirror. Original and quite funny; full of fetching sophisticated sight gags. Silent with music score. **67m/B; Silent; VHS, DVD.** Max Linder; Thelma Percy; Alta Allen; Betty Peterson; ***D:*** Max Linder; ***W:*** Max Linder; ***C:*** Charles Van Enger.

Seven Years in Tibet **1/2 1997 (PG-13)** Big budget epic of a cold-hearted Austrian mountaineer Heinrich Harrer (Pitt) who becomes a WWII POW in a British internment camp in India. When he and fellow climber Peter Aufschnaiter (Thewlis) escape, they travel to Tibet where Harrer bonds with and becomes a tutor to the young Dalai Lama (Wangchuk). Sweeping vistas and snow-capped mountain scenery does little to aid the sluggish and unfocused narrative, which tries to cover too many subplots and doesn't really get going until halfway through. Pitt's screen presence is forceful and his performance capable but hampered by a somewhat labored Austrian accent. Based on Harrer's memoirs, film ran into numerous problems, including the revelation that Harrer had Nazi ties, China's sensitivity to the storyline, and India's refusal to allow filming. Director Annaud wound up substituting the Argentine Andes for the Himalayas. **131m/C; VHS, DVD, Blu-Ray.** Brad Pitt; David Thewlis; B.D. Wong; Jamyang Jamtsho Wangchuk; Mako; Victor Wong; Ingeborga Dapkounaite; ***D:*** Jean-Jacques Annaud; ***W:*** Becky Johnston; ***C:*** Robert Fraisse; ***M:*** John Williams.

Seventeen Again **2000** Willie (Tahj Mowry) is doing a science project involving an anti-aging formula that accidentally gets mixed into some soap that his divorced grandparents, Cat (Clarke) and Gene (Hooks), wind up using. This turns them both in 17-year-olds (Tamara Mowry as Cat and Taylor as Gene). Cat winds up going to high school with look-alike granddaughter Sydney (Tia Mowry) and has a second chance with the teenaged Gene. Meanwhile, Willie is searching for an antidote since his formula has some potentially serious flaws. That the story is silly isn't the problem—it's also incoherent. **97m/C; VHS, DVD.** Tia Mowry; Tamera Mowry; Tahj Mowry; Mark Taylor; Hope Clarke; Robert Hooks; ***D:*** Jeff Byrd; ***W:*** Stewart St. John; ***C:*** John Tarver; ***M:*** Christopher Franke; Shawm Stockman. **CABLE**

17 Again **1/2 2009 (PG-13)** Mike O'Donnell (Efron) is a star on the high school basketball team with a bright future in his grasp. Instead, he trades it to share his life with his girlfriend Scarlett (Miller) and the baby he just learned they are expecting. Almost 20 years later, Mike's (Perry) glory days are decidedly behind him—he's in a dead-end job, separated from his wife (Mann), and his own teenaged kids think he's a loser—but he's given another chance when he is miraculously transformed back to the age of 17. Unfortunately, Mike may look 17 again, but his thirtysomething outlook is totally uncool with the class of 2009. If the silly premise sounds familiar, it should, as both the original *Freaky Friday* as well as the Lindsey Lohan/Jamie Lee Curtis version are both superior to this, which says a lot. Might appeal to teen girls who simply want to stare at Efron. **102m/C; Blu-Ray, On Demand.** Matthew Perry; Zac Efron; Leslie Mann; Thomas Lennon; Michelle Trachtenberg; Sterling Knight; ***D:*** Burr Steers; ***W:*** Jason Filardi; ***C:*** Tim Suhrstedt; ***M:*** Rolfe Kent.

Seventeen and Missing **1/2 2006** Emilie Janzen (Pfeiffer) has always had psychic visions that her family have dismissed. But when 17-year-old Lori (Moss) goes missing, Emilie knows that she's been kidnapped and is trapped in an underground bunker. No one else may believe her but Emilie and husband Richard (Harrison) are going to use her visions to find their daughter. **90m/C; DVD.** Matthew Harrison; Tegan Moss; Terry David Mulligan; Victor Ayala; Dedee Pfeiffer; ***D:*** Paul Schneider; ***W:*** Kraig Wenman; ***C:*** Larry Lynn; ***M:*** Ken Williams. **CABLE**

Seventeen Years *Guo nian hui jia* **1999** Two step-sisters are driven to rivalry by their bickering parents, and one of them accidentally kills the other during an accusation of theft. After 17 years in prison she receives a New Year's furlough to visit her family, but no one is waiting for her but a sympathetic prison guard who decides to take her home to her parents himself. **85m/C; DVD.** *IT* Lin Liu; Li Bingbing; Yeding Li; Song Liang; Yun Li; ***D:*** Yuan Zhang; ***W:*** Dai Ning; Hua Yu; Wen Zhu; ***C:*** Xigui Zhang; ***M:*** Jiping Zhao.

1776 **1972 (G)** Musical comedy about America's first Continental Congress. The delegates battle the English and each other trying to establish a set of laws and the Declaration of Independence. Adapted from the Broadway hit with many members of the original cast. **141m/C; VHS, DVD, Blu-Ray.** William Daniels; Howard da Silva; Ken Howard; Donald Madden; Blythe Danner; Ronald Holgate; Virginia Vestoff; Stephen Nathan; Ralston Hill; ***D:*** Peter H. Hunt; ***C:*** Harry Stradling, Jr.

The Seventeenth Bride 🦴🦴 **1984** Set in a Czechoslovakian town; a strong-willed young woman is slowly destroyed by the insanity of war and racism. **92m/C; VHS, DVD.** Lisa Hartman Black; Rosemary Leach; ***D:*** Israeli Nadav Levitan.

Seventh Cavalry 🦴🦴 **1/2** *7th Cavalry* **1956** A somewhat different look at Custer's defeat at the Little Big Horn. A soldier who was branded a coward for not taking part in the festivities tries to assuage his guilt by heading up the burial detail. The muddled ending tries to tell us that the Indians were afraid of Custer's horse. **75m/C; VHS, DVD.** Randolph Scott; Barbara Hale; Jay C. Flippen; Jeannette Nolan; Frank Faylen; Leo Gordon; Denver Pyle; Harry Carey, Jr.; Michael Pate; Donald Curtis; Frank Wilcox; Pat Hogan; Russell Hicks; ***D:*** Joseph H. Lewis; ***C:*** Ray Rennahan.

The Seventh Coin 🦴🦴 **1/2 1992 (PG-13)** The legendary King Herod minted seven coins bearing his image which have become coin collector Emil Saber's (O'Toole) obsession. (He's a homicidal lunatic who thinks he's the reincarnation of Herod anyway.) Saber has found six of the coins but the seventh has fallen into the unsuspecting hands of Salim (Chowdhry), a pickpocket who has actually snatched it from the equally unsuspecting Ronnie (Powers), an American teenager visiting Jerusalem (good local color). The two become allies when Saber comes after them. They're an appealing couple; O'Toole camps it up shamelessly; and the movie is easygoing escapism. **92m/C; VHS, DVD.** Alexandra Powers; Navin Chowdhry; Peter O'Toole; John Rhys-Davies; Ally Walker; ***D:*** Dror Soref; ***W:*** Michael Lewis; Dror Soref; ***C:*** Avi (Avraham) Karpik.

The 7th Commandment 🦴 **1/2 1961** Unlikely melodrama about a man afflicted with amnesia following an auto accident. He becomes a successful evangelist only to be blackmailed by an old girlfriend. Don't you just hate when that happens? **82m/B; VHS, DVD.** Jonathan Kidd; Lynn Statten; ***D:*** Irvin Berwick.

The Seventh Dawn 🦴🦴 **1964** Cliched adventure romance set in Malaysia in 1945. Guerrilla fighter Ferris (Holden) decides to become a landowner and stay on with mistress Dhana (Capucine) after the war. Ferris's old buddy Ng (Tamba) takes off for Moscow and returns indoctrinated and determined to convert the country to Communism. Ng and his fighters exclude Ferris from their attacks until British governor Trumphrey (Goodliffe) accuses Dhana of treason and threatens to execute her. So Ferris has to get Ng or risk Dhana. The young York plays Candace, the governor's daughter who has a crush on Ferris and helps him out. Based on the novel "The Durian Tree" by Michael Koen. **123m/C; VHS, DVD.** *GB US* William Holden; Capucine; Susannah York; Tetsuro Tamba; Michael Goodliffe; Allan Cuthbertson; Maurice Denham; Beulah Quo; ***D:*** Lewis Gilbert; ***W:*** Karl Tunberg; ***C:*** Frederick A. (Freddie) Young; ***M:*** Riz Ortolani.

The Seventh Floor 🦴 **1/2 1993 (R)** Kate's computer-controlled apartment becomes her prison when a psycho takes charge of the system. **99m/C; VHS, DVD.** *AU* Brooke Shields; Masaya Kato; Craig Pearce; Linda Cropper; ***D:*** Ian Barry.

7th Heaven 🦴🦴 **1927** Paris sewer worker Chico (Farrell) takes pity on waif Diane (Gaynor), who's been forced into prostitution by her vicious sister (Brockwell), after some gendarmes get suspicious. He declares they are married and lets her stay in his garret. The lug doesn't realize he loves her until he's sent to the front in WWI. Diane's been told he's dead but Chico does return (although he's now blind) and they mutually admit their love. The first romantic pairing (of 12 movies) for Gaynor and Farrell. **115m/B; Silent; DVD.** Janet Gaynor; Charles Farrell; Ben Bard; David Butler; Gladys Brockwell; Marie Mosquini; ***D:*** Frank Borzage; ***W:*** Benjamin Glazer; ***C:*** Ernest Palmer. Oscars '28: Actress (Gaynor), Adapt. Screenplay, Director (Borzage).

Seventh Heaven 🦴🦴 **1998** Married Mathilde (Kiberlain) is sunk in a serious depression that only begins to lessen when she meets a mysterious doctor (Berleand) who specializes in hynosis and alternative medicine. He tells her there are seven levels of heaven—the last a sort of self-fulfilled bliss. After a successful session with the doctor, Mathilde is suddenly sexually and emotionally rejuvenated—much to the consternation of her (til then) dominating spouse, Nico (Lindon). The more Mathilde takes control, the less Nico is able to cope with their role reversals. French with subtitles. **91m/C; VHS, DVD.** *FR* Sandrine Kiberlain; Vincent Lindon; Francois Berleand; ***D:*** Benoit Jacquot; ***W:*** Benoit Jacquot; Jerome Beaujour; ***C:*** Romain Winding.

Seventh Moon 🦴 **1/2 2008 (R)** Too much shaky-cam does not a scary horror story make. Yul (Chiou) has taken his American bride Melissa (Smart) to honeymoon in China so they can meet his family. They get stranded in a remote village where a Chinese myth that ghosts rise on the seventh lunar moon during a full moon is about to come true. **87m/C; DVD, Blu-Ray.** Tim Chiou; Amy Smart; Dennis Chan; ***D:*** Eduardo Sanchez; ***W:*** Eduardo Sanchez; ***C:*** Wah-Chen Lam; ***M:*** Tony Cora; Kent Sparling. **VIDEO**

The Seventh Seal 🦴🦴🦴🦴 *Det Sjunde Inseglet* **1956** As the plague sweeps through Europe a weary knight convinces "death" to play one game of chess with him. If the knight wins, he and his wife will be spared. The game leads to a discussion of religion and the existence of God. Considered by some Bergman's masterpiece. Von Sydow is stunning as the knight. In Swedish with English subtitles. **96m/B; VHS, DVD, Blu-Ray.** *SW* Gunnar Bjornstrand; Max von Sydow; Bibi Andersson; Bengt Ekerot; Nils Poppe; Gunnel Lindblom; ***D:*** Ingmar Bergman; ***W:*** Ingmar Bergman; ***C:*** Gunnar Fischer; ***M:*** Erik Nordgren. Cannes '57: Grand Jury Prize.

The Seventh Sign 🦴🦴 **1988 (R)** A pregnant woman realizes that the mysterious stranger boarding in her house and the bizarre events that accompany him are connected to Biblical prophesy and her unborn child. Tries hard, but it's difficult to get involved in the supernatural goings-on. **105m/C; VHS, DVD.** Demi Moore; Jurgen Prochnow; Michael Biehn; John Heard; Peter Friedman; Manny Jacobs; John Taylor; Lee Garlington; Akosua Busia; ***D:*** Carl Schultz; ***W:*** W.W. Wicket; ***C:*** Juan Ruiz-Anchia; ***M:*** Jack Nitzsche.

Seventh Son 🦴 **1/2 2015 (PG-13)** Another byproduct of the YA phenomenon, "The Spook's Apprentice" by Joseph Delaney gets adapted in this inert, predictable, dull fantasy feature. Thomas Ward (Barnes) is the seventh son of a seventh son and he is a Spook, a knightly order that protects the human race from annihilation by things like dragons. The young Thomas becomes an apprentice and is put in charge of guarding the powerful Mother Malkin (Moore), who escapes under his watch and threatens to return dark forces to the land. It's standard fantasy fare—well-done but forgettable. **102m/C; DVD, Blu-Ray.** *US UK* Ben Barnes; Jeff Bridges; Julianne Moore; Alicia Vikander; Kit Harington; Olivia Williams; Jason Scott Lee; Djimon Hounsou; ***D:*** Sergei Bodrov; ***W:*** Charles Leavitt; Steven Knight; ***C:*** Newton Thomas (Tom) Sigel; ***M:*** Marco Beltrami.

The Seventh Stream 🦴🦴 **1/2 2001** Filmed on location in the west of Ireland and based on the Celtic legend of the selkies. Owen Quinn (Glenn) is a fisherman whose life is empty since the death of his wife. Then he comes to the rescue of Mairead (Burrows), a beautiful and mysterious woman with strong ties to the sea. Owen opens his heart and home to her but will Mairead vanish as easily as she appeared? **98m/C; VHS, DVD.** Scott Glenn; Saffron Burrows; John Lynch; Fiona Shaw; Eamon Morrissey; ***D:*** John Gray; ***W:*** John Gray; ***C:*** Seamus Deasy; ***M:*** Ernest Troost. **TV**

The Seventh Victim 🦴🦴🦴 **1943** Another Val Lewton-produced low-budget exercise in shadowy suggestion, dealing with a woman searching for her lost sister, who'd gotten involved with Satanists. The Hays Office's squeamishness regarding subject matter makes the film's action a bit cloudy but it remains truly eerie. **71m/B; VHS, DVD.** Kim Hunter; Tom Conway; Jean Brooks; Hugh Beaumont; Erford Gage; Isabel Jewell; Evelyn Brent; ***D:*** Mark Robson; ***W:*** Charles "Blackie" O'Neal.

The Seventh Voyage of Sinbad 🦴🦴🦴 **1958 (G)** Sinbad seeks to restore his fiancee from the midget size to which an evil magician (Thatcher) has reduced her. Ray Harryhausen works his animation magic around a well-developed plot and engaging performances by the real actors. Great score and fun, fast-moving plot. **94m/C; VHS, DVD, Blu-Ray.** Kerwin Mathews; Kathryn Grant; Torin Thatcher; Richard Eyer; Alec Mango; Danny Green; Harold Kasket; Alfred Brown; ***D:*** Nathan "Jerry" Juran; ***W:*** Kenneth Kolb; ***C:*** Wilkie Cooper; ***M:*** Bernard Herrmann. Natl. Film Reg. '08.

The '70s 🦴🦴 **1/2 2000** Follows "The '60s" miniseries with the same superficial exploration of the decade seen through the eyes of four friends and lots of music. (Disco rules!) Dexter (Torry), Byron (Rowe), Eileen (Shaw), and Christine (Smart) are all at Kent State on that fateful day with the National Guard and their lives continue through numerous hot-button issues, including Watergate, feminism, drugs, sex, the Black Panthers, the environment, and religious cults. Cast is surprisingly strong. **170m/C; VHS, DVD.** Brad Rowe; Guy Torry; Vinessa Shaw; Amy Smart; Kathryn Harrold; Graham Beckel; Tina Lifford; Chandra West; Robert Joy; Jeanetta Arnette; Michael Easton; Peggy Lipton; ***D:*** Peter Werner; ***W:*** Mitch Brian; Kevin Willmott; ***C:*** Neil Roach; ***M:*** Peter Manning Robinson. **TV**

78/52: Hitchcock's Shower Scene 🦴🦴🦴 *78/52* **2017** A documentary examining the iconic shower scene in Alfred Hitchcock's masterpiece *Psycho*, a scene that required 78 camera angles and 52 edits for a mere three minutes of finished film, and that irrevocably changed the landscape of cinema. Features archive footage of Hitchcock himself, as well as commentary by dozens of former and modern-day filmmakers. A must-see for film lovers and horror buffs. **91m/B; DVD, Blu-Ray.** Alfred Hitchcock; Jamie Lee Curtis; Guillermo del Toro; Peter Bogdanovich; Danny Elfman; ***D:*** Alexandre O. Philippe; ***W:*** Alexandre O. Philippe; ***C:*** Robert Muratore; ***M:*** Jon Hegel.

7500 🦴 **1/2 2012** Passengers aboard a transpacific flight are trapped with a supernatural force--that's going to mean an airborne disaster. **?m/CDVD.** Leslie Bibb; Ryan Kwanten; Amy Smart; Johnathon Schaech; ***D:*** Takashi Shimizu; ***W:*** Craig Rosenberg; ***C:*** David Tattersall.

'71 🦴🦴🦴 **2014 (R)** The city of Belfast in 1971 was a war zone between the Irish Republican Army and the British Army's Military Reaction Force. A soldier in the latter group named Gary (the great O'Connell) finds himself behind enemy lines when his unit is ambushed in the streets of Belfast. He has to survive long enough to get back to safety, and he's a man under threat of death in his own country. Director Demange crafts action-drama with a natural, on-the-ground approach to characters and dynamics. The result is a daring, engrossing, complex drama. **99m/C; DVD, Blu-Ray.** *UK* Jack O'Connell; Sam Reid; Richard Dormer; Sean Harris; ***D:*** Yann Demange; ***W:*** Gregory Burke; ***C:*** Tat Radcliffe; ***M:*** David Holmes.

75 Degrees 🦴🦴 **1/2** *75 Degrees in July* **2000** A family reunion leads to the reopening of old wounds in this downbeat drama. Letty Anderson (Silas) visits her family's Texas ranch to see her parents and married sister, Kay (Swedberg). Letty is a successful artist with a show at a local gallery and Kay is resentful because their manipulative mother, Jo Beth (Knight), squashed her dreams of becoming a singer. Instead, Kay takes her frustrations out on ranch foreman hubby Jed (Moses), who has his own problems with her family. Jo Beth's husband, Rick (Yulin), is neglectful and callous and treats everyone badly. Not exactly a family you'd want to spend a lot of time with, although the cast is compelling. **98m/C; DVD.** Heidi Swedberg; Harris Yulin; Shirley Knight; William R. Moses; Karen Sillas; ***D:*** Hyatt Bass; ***W:*** Hyatt Bass; ***C:*** Michael Barrett; ***M:*** Stephen (Steve) Edwards.

Severance 🦴🦴 **2006 (R)** In a team-building exercise, the sales division of an international arms manufacturer heads for a weekend retreat at a desolate chalet located in a Hungarian forest. But it seems the woods are filled with booby-traps and crazed commandos determined to see them all dead. An extreme example of how team spirit and cooperation will save your life (not to mention your job). **96m/C; DVD.** *GE GB* Tim (McInnerny) McInnery; Laura Harris; Toby Stephens; Danny Dyer; Claudie Blakley; Andy Nyman; Babou Ceesay; ***D:*** Chris Smith; ***W:*** Chris Smith; James Moran; ***C:*** Ed Wild; ***M:*** Christian Henson.

The Severed Arm WOOF! **1973 (R)** Trapped in a cave, five men are compelled to cut off the arm of a companion in order to ward off starvation. Then as luck would have it, they're rescued. Years later, one by one they meet a bloody demise. Is it the one-armed man? **89m/C; VHS, DVD, Blu-Ray.** Deborah Walley; Marvin Kaplan; Paul Carr; John Crawford; David Cannon; ***D:*** Thomas Alderman.

A Severed Head 🦴🦴 **1970** Married uppercrusty nympho Antonia (Remick) tells her husband Martin (Holm) that she's having an affair with his best friend, shrink Palmer (Attenborough). Palmer is also involved with his half-sister Honor (Bloom) and the bedroom shenanigans prove disturbing only to Martin. Adaptation of the Iris Murdoch novel. **98m/C; DVD.** *GB* Lee Remick; Ian Holm; Richard Attenborough; Claire Bloom; Jennie Linden; Clive Revill; Ann(e) Firbank; ***D:*** Dick Clement; ***W:*** Frederic Raphael; ***C:*** Austin Dempster; ***M:*** Stanley Myers.

Severed Ways 🦴 **2009** In the 11th-century, two Vikings are the only survivors of a massacre of their North American camp and must struggle to live amidst harsh conditions. Minimal, unconventional narrative with a score comprised of heavy-metal music. **107m/C; DVD.** Dave Perry; Tony Stone; Fiore Tedesco; Noelle Bailey; James Fuentes; ***D:*** Tony Stone; ***W:*** Tony Stone; ***C:*** Nathan Corbin; Damien Paris.

Sex 🦴🦴 **1/2 1920** Interesting dated relic. Morality play about a Broadway star who uses her charms to destroy a marriage only to dump her lover for richer prospects. The businessman she lands then shamelessly betrays her. What a title, especially for its time! **87m/B; Silent; VHS, DVD, Streaming.** Adrienne Renault; Louise Glaum; Irving Cummings; Peggy Pearce; Myrtle Stedman; ***D:*** Fred Niblo.

Sex and Breakfast 🦴 **1/2 2007 (R)** Having couples troubles, James (Culkin) and Heather (Dziena) and Ellis (Becker) and Renee (Dushku) experiment with group sex while trying to figure out what makes a relationship successful. But jealousy, confusion, and insecurity make things as difficult as you might expect. Not as sexual as you might expect though, despite the title and rating. **81m/C; DVD.** Macaulay Culkin; Alexis Dziena; Kuno Becker; Eliza Dushku; Joanna Miles; Eric Lively; Tracie Thoms; Jaime Ray Newman; ***D:*** Miles Brandman; ***W:*** Miles Brandman; ***C:*** Mark Schwartzband.

Sex and Death 101 🦴 **2007 (R)** Crude but stupid sex fantasy has Roderick Blank (a miscast Baker, who just comes across as too sweet) receiving an anonymous email that lists the names of the 101 women he will have sex with before he dies. The first 29 are accurate, including his fiance Fiona (Bowen), so Rod dumps her and gets busy. Then there's Ryder, playing a bizarre feminist avenger nicknamed Death Nell, who kills off high-profile sex sleazes. **117m/C; DVD, Blu-Ray.** Simon Baker; Winona Ryder; Leslie Bibb; Julie Bowen; Mindy Cohn; Robert Wisdom; Patton Oswalt; Frances Fisher; Tanc Sade; ***D:*** Daniel Waters; ***W:*** Daniel Waters; ***C:*** Daryn Okada; ***M:*** Rolfe Kent.

Sex & Drugs & Rock & Roll 🦴🦴 **2010** A maybe too stylish bio of colorful '70s British punk rock pioneer Ian Drury (Serkis), who had to deal with childhood polio (which left him partially paralyzed) to fulfill his dreams. The film dwells as much (if not more) on his chaotic family life, which includes a wife, young son, and girlfriend, as his music career and eccentric, restless personality. Drury died from cancer in 2000 although the bio ends before that. Title refers to Drury's 1977 hit song. **115m/C; On Demand.** *GB* Andy Serkis; Ray Winstone; Olivia Williams; Bill Milner; Naomie Harris; Wesley Nelson; Mackenzie Crook; Toby Jones; *D:* Mat Whitecross; *W:* Paul Viragh; *C:* Christopher Ross; *M:* Chaz Jankel.

Sex & Lies in Sin City: The Ted Binion Scandal 🦴🦴 **2008** Sleazy true story about a stripper, a Vegas casino heir, murder, and a trial. Stripper Sandy (Suvari) has it made when she shacks up with smitten casino heir/junkie Ted Binion (Modine). Ted is found dead and Sandy becomes the prime suspect, especially after her guy-on-the-side Rick (Schaech) is caught with some of Ted's property. Adapted from the book "Murder in Sin City" by Jeff German. **89m/C; DVD.** Mena Suvari; Matthew Modine; Johnathon Schaech; Marcia Gay Harden; *D:* Peter Medak; *W:* Teena Booth; *C:* Anthony B. Richmond; *M:* Ed Shearmur. **CABLE**

Sex and Lucia 🦴🦴 *Lucia y el Sexo* **2001** Sexually explicit, if confusing, story finds waitress Lucia (Vega) learning that her ex-boyfriend, writer Lorenzo (Ulloa), has supposedly died. So, she decides to revisit the island where they first met. Lucia meets scuba-diver Carlos (Freire) who lives with Elena (Nimri), who has ties to Lorenzo that Lucia never suspected. Elena's brother, Pepe (Camara), happens to be Lorenzo's best friend and introduces nanny Belen (Anaya) into the menage and it all just kinda goes 'round and 'round. Spanish with subtitles. **128m/C; DVD.** *SP* Paz Vega; Tristan Ulloa; Najwa Nimri; Daniel Freire; Elena Anaya; Silvia Llanos; Javier Camara; *D:* Julio Medem; *W:* Julio Medem; *C:* Kiko de la Rica; *M:* Alberto Iglesias.

Sex & Mrs. X 🦴🦴 ½ **2000** New York magazine journalist Joanna Scott (Hamilton) thought her marriage was as successful as her career—until husband Dale (Bick) leaves her for a younger woman. So Joanna is happy to go to Paris to interview the notorious Madame Simone (Bisset), but she winds up learning just as much about herself and how to face her new future. **91m/C; VHS, DVD.** Linda Hamilton; Jacqueline Bisset; Paolo Seganti; Stewart Bick; Peter MacNeill; Tracy Bregman; Daniel Pilon; *D:* Arthur Allan Seidelman; *W:* Elisa Bell; *C:* Don E. Fauntleroy; *M:* Joseph Conlan. **CABLE**

Sex and the City: The Movie 🦴🦴 ½ **2008 (R)** What's essentially a supersized episode of the hugely popular HBO series becomes the mother of all chick flicks. The well-heeled galpals, now over forty but still able to spend a ridiculous amount of time together, serve up more of the same as they each ponder the fate of their impossibly fabulous domestic lives. This time it's Carrie's (Parker) non-wedding to Mr. Big (Noth) that anchors the break-ups and make-ups. What the plot lacks in substance (and at times, sense), it makes up for in style. Davis's Charlotte is especially sharp amid the melodrama and silliness, but it's the witty, shameless glee of the collective sisterhood that's the real draw. **135m/C; Blu-Ray, On Demand.** Sarah Jessica Parker; Kim Cattrall; Kristin Davis; Cynthia Nixon; Chris Noth; David Eigenberg; Jason Lewis; Evan Handler; Jennifer Hudson; Willie Garson; Mario Cantone; Lynn Cohen; Candice Bergen; *D:* Michael Patrick King; *W:* Michael Patrick King; *C:* John Thomas; *M:* Aaron Zigman.

Sex and the City 2 🦴🦴 **2010 (R)** A love-it-or-hate-it reappearance by our recession-proof fab foursome is a mildly-amusing paean to lasting friendship. Carrie is bored with marriage when Big turns out to be a homebody; Charlotte finds motherhood complicated; Miranda is having work issues; and Samantha is having hot flashes. Fortunately an all-expenses-paid trip to Abu Dhabi (from an admiring sheik/client of Samantha's) shakes up their lives. They ride camels in couture, sing karaoke, and Carrie just happens to run into old flame Aidan in the local spice market. **146m/C; Blu-Ray.** Sarah Jessica Parker; Kim Cattrall; Kristin Davis; Cynthia Nixon; Chris Noth; David Eigenberg; Evan Handler; Jason Lewis; Mario Cantone; Willie Garson; Penelope Cruz; *Cameo(s):* Liza Minnelli; *D:* Michael Patrick King; *W:* Michael Patrick King; *C:* John Thomas. Golden Raspberries '10: Worst Actress (Cattrall), Worst Actress (Davis), Worst Actress (Nixon), Worst Actress (Parker), Worst Sequel/Prequel.

Sex and the Other Man 🦴🦴 *Captive* **1995 (R)** Bill's (Eldard) having this little impotence problem, which girlfriend Jessica (Wuhrer) naturally finds frustrating. So much so that she succumbs to the charms of her married boss, Arthur (Tucci). But when Bill catches them together in bed, his reaction is something none of them expected. Based on the play "Captive" by Paul Weitz. **89m/C; VHS, DVD.** Ron Eldard; Kari Wuhrer; Stanley Tucci; *D:* Karl Slovin; *W:* Karl Slovin; *C:* Frank Prinzi; *M:* Anton Sanko.

Sex and the Single Girl 🦴🦴 ½ **1964** Curtis is a reporter for a trashy magazine who intends to write an expose on "The International Institute of Advanced Marital and Pre-Marital Studies," an organization run by Wood. Curtis poses as a man having marital trouble, using his neighbor's name and marital problems, in order to get close to Wood. Things get sticky when Wood wants to meet Curtis' wife and three women show up claiming to be her. This confusing but amusing tale twists and turns until it reaches a happy ending. Loosely based on the book by Helen Gurley Brown. **114m/C; VHS, DVD.** Tony Curtis; Natalie Wood; Henry Fonda; Lauren Bacall; Mel Ferrer; Fran Jeffries; Leslie Parrish; Edward Everett Horton; Larry Storch; Count Basie; *D:* Richard Quine; *W:* David R. Schwartz; *C:* Charles B(ryant) Lang, Jr.; *M:* Neal Hefti.

Sex and the Single Mom 🦴🦴 **2003** Divorced Jess has a busy working life and is raising her 15-year-old daughter Sara. Does Jess seem like a hypocrite when she has an affair with Dr. Alex Lofton while discouraging Sara from exploring her own burgeoning sexuality? Their home life then gets more complicated when Jess gets pregnant and doesn't tell Alex in this Lifetime drama, which is followed by "More Sex and the Single Mom." **90m/C; DVD.** Gail O'Grady; Danielle Panabaker; Grant Show; Nigel Bennett; Joshua Close; Kyle Schmid; Maria Ricossa; Barbara Gordon; *D:* Don McBrearty; *W:* Judith Paige Mitchell; *C:* Rhett Morita; *M:* Alexina Louie; Alex Pauk. **CABLE**

Sex Crimes 🦴🦴 **1992** A tough female judge is brutally raped and she keeps the attack a secret. However, she does ask a friendly police detective to teach her how to use a gun. He's suspicious of her reasons and decides to trail her as she sets out for revenge on her attacker. Predictable actioner. **90m/C; VHS, DVD.** Jeffery Osterhage; Maria Richwine; Fernando Garzon; Craig Alan; Grace Morley; *D:* David Garcia.

Sex Drive 🦴🦴 **2008 (R)** Desperate 18-year-old virgin Ian (Zuckerman), tempted by online chats with "Ms. Tasty," drags his geeky buddy Lance (Clarke) on a road trip in a stolen 1969 GTO from Wisconsin to Tennessee to consummate his cyber-love. Also along for the ride (for no apparent recent other than to be grossed out by the boys' behavior) is female friend Felicia (Crew). Their trip takes them to Amish country during its annual sex orgy, of course, among other non-stop ridiculous, raunchy situations. Despite its obvious attempt to cash in on the horny teen flick revival (first re-launched by "American Pie," then done better years later by "Superbad"), this one lacks the heart of its more successful predecessors. **109m/C; DVD, Blu-Ray, On Demand.** Josh Zuckerman; Amanda Crew; Clark Duke; James Marsden; Seth Green; *D:* Sean Anders; *W:* Sean Anders; John Morris; *C:* Tim Orr; *M:* Stephen Trask.

Sex Ed 🦴🦴 ½ **2014** A comic look at a teacher trying to educate his students in a subject he is not exactly qualified to teach. Eddie Cole (Osment) is in his mid-twenties and a first time teacher at a middle school when he finds himself in charge of detention. To his surprise, his students have not received any type of sex education. Though Eddie tries to teach them, his own experiences are quite limited since he is a virgin. Eddie soon learns that his students may be able to school him on this subject. **92m/C; DVD, Streaming, Download.** Haley Joel Osment; Lorenza Izzo; Glen Powell; Laura Elena Harring; Lamorne Morris; *D:* Isaac Feder; *W:* Bill Kennedy; *C:* Brian Burgoyne; *M:* Alexander Kemp.

Sex is Comedy 🦴🦴 **2002** Breillat's plot is a fictionalized re-creation of her own difficulties filming the crucial sex scene between a 15-year-old girl (Mesquida, reprising her role) and her older boyfriend (Colin) for her 2001 film "Fat Girl." Breillat's stand-in as director is the neurotic and demanding Jeanne (Parillaud), whose troubles include lousy weather, leads who can't stand each other, and a problematic prosthetic penis. Jeanne irritates her actors and crew (and they her) and only finds a sympathetic ally in her smitten assistant Leo (Wanninger). Actors are always quick to say that filming sex scenes is not erotic and here's the proof. French with subtitles. **92m/C; DVD.** Anne Parillaud; Ashley Wanninger; Dominique Colladant; *D:* Catherine Breillat; *W:* Catherine Breillat; *C:* Laurent Machuel.

Sex Is Crazy 🦴 **1979** A melange from Italian horror director Franco containing some epic, some horror, some sex, some sitcom, and some documentary. Little green aliens touch down and impregnate earth women in one skit. In another, a gambler's girlfriend demands two thugs ravage her for the sheer sexual thrill. And in a third, a severed hand commands a heroine to martyr herself to the great god Cucufat. Spanish with English subtitles. **81m/C; VHS, DVD.** *SP* Lina Romay; Anthony (Jose, J. Antonio, J.A.) Mayans; Tony Skios; *D:* Jess (Jesus) Franco.

Sex Kittens Go to College 🦴 ½ **1960** Silly sex farce. Collins College's supercomputer Thinko picks Dr. Mathilda West (Van Doren) to head the science department, but the faculty is distracted by her va-va-va-voom curves. Meanwhile, gangsters are after Thinko because it's got a knack for pickig winning horse races and they also know a secret about Mathilda--she used to be a stripper! Hey, you have to pay for your education some how. **103m/B; DVD.** Mamie Van Doren; Tuesday Weld; Mijanou Bardot; Mickey Shaughnessy; Louis Nye; Martin Milner; Pamela Mason; John Carradine; Jackie Coogan; *D:* Albert Zugsmith; *W:* Robert Hill; *C:* Ellis W. Carter; *M:* Dean Elliott.

sex, lies and videotape 🦴🦴🦴 **1989 (R)** Acclaimed, popular independent film by first-timer Soderbergh, detailing the complex relations among a childless married couple, the wife's adulterous sister, and a mysterious college friend of the husband's obsessed with videotaping women as they talk about their sex lives. Heavily awarded, including first prize at Cannes. Confidently uses much (too much?) dialogue and slow (too slow?) pace. **101m/C; VHS, DVD, Blu-Ray.** James Spader; Andie MacDowell; Peter Gallagher; Laura San Giacomo; Ron Vawter; Steven Brill; *D:* Steven Soderbergh; *W:* Steven Soderbergh; *C:* Walt Lloyd; *M:* Cliff Martinez. Cannes '89: Actor (Spader), Film; Ind. Spirit '90: Actress (MacDowell), Director (Soderbergh), Film, Support. Actress (San Giacomo); L.A. Film Critics '89: Actress (MacDowell); Natl. Film Reg. '06; Sundance '89: Aud. Award.

The Sex Monster 🦴🦴 **1999 (R)** Unhappy husband convinces reluctant wife to get involved in a menage-a-trois. Only she's more turned on by the other woman than he is. Not very funny for a comedy, and not very sexy for a flick with the word "sex" in the title. Binder does Woody Allen without the humor, but then, so does Woody lately. **97m/C; VHS, DVD.** Mike Binder; Mariel Hemingway; Renee Humphrey; Taylor Nichols; Missy (Melissa) Crider; Stephen Baldwin; *D:* Mike Binder; *W:* Mike Binder; *C:* Keith L. Smith.

Sex on the Run WOOF! *Cassanova and Co.; Some Like It Cool* **1978 (R)** Love-starved wife of an oil-rich sheik, stimulated by the idea of having Casanova for her lover, teases her master into delivering him, but Casanova finds peace in the arms of three convent lovelies. Disgusting, amateurish, and offensive. **88m/C; VHS, DVD.** Tony Curtis; Marisa Berenson; Britt Ekland; *D:* Francosis Legrand.

Sex Positive 🦴🦴 **2009 (R)** Documentary is a belated portrait of gay activist Richard Berkovitz and his experiences in 1970s New York when he worked as an S&M hustler, giving him a front seat to the burgeoning AIDS epidemic. Berkowitz was early to espouse safe-sex practices (and was frequently discredited by the gay community among others). And, along with activist Michael Callan, he wrote the first safe sex guide although his experiences eventually led to a drug addiction. Wein has interviews with the HIV-positive Berkowitz as well as others in the community and uses various archival video from newscasts as well. **76m/C; VHS, DVD.** *D:* Daryl Wein; *C:* Alex Bergman; *M:* Michael Tremante.

Sex Tape 🦴 ½ **2014 (R)** Married couple Annie (Diaz) and Jay (Segel) are looking for a way to spice up their inert love life and so they film themselves having sex. Jay then makes the crucial mistake of uploading the video to the Cloud, where it is downloaded accidentally to all of the iPads that the couple recently gave out as gifts (yes, this is a world where rich people give iPads to their friends). The fact that this comedy is remarkably unfunny is only one of its problems--worse yet is that neither lead character is particularly likable. **94m/C; DVD, Blu-Ray.** Jason Segel; Cameron Diaz; Rob Corddry; Ellie Kemper; Rob Lowe; Nat Faxon; *D:* Jake Kasdan; *W:* Jason Segel; Kate Angelo; Nicholas Stoller; *C:* Tim Suhrstedt; *M:* Michael Andrews. Golden Raspberries '14: Worst Actress (Diaz).

The Sex Thief 🦴 ½ *Handful of Diamonds; Her Family Jewels* **1974** Unlikely comedy about a smut writer who moonlights as a thief and seduces his female victims when he's caught in the act. **89m/C; DVD, Blu-Ray, Streaming.** *UK* Jennifer Westbrook; David Warbeck; Henry Rayner; Gerald Taylor; Michael Armstrong; *D:* Martin Campbell; *W:* Michael Armstrong; *C:* Grenville Middleton; *M:* Michael Vickers. **VIDEO**

Sex Through a Window 🦴 *Extreme Close-Up* **1972 (R)** TV reporter becomes an obsessive voyeur after filing a report on high tech surveillance equipment. Flimsy premise is a yucky, lame excuse to show skin. **81m/C; VHS, DVD.** James McMullan; James A. Watson, Jr.; Kate Woodville; Bara Byrnes; Al Checco; Antony Carbone; *D:* Jeannot Szwarc; *W:* Michael Crichton.

Sextette WOOF! **1978 (PG)** Lavish film about an elderly star who is constantly interrupted by former spouses and well-wishers while on a honeymoon with her sixth husband. West unwisely came out of retirement for this last film role, based on her own play. Exquisitely embarrassing to watch. Interesting cast. **91m/C; VHS, DVD.** Mae West; Timothy Dalton; Ringo Starr; George Hamilton; Dom DeLuise; Tony Curtis; Alice Cooper; Keith Moon; George Raft; Rona Barrett; Walter Pidgeon; Regis Philbin; *D:* Ken Hughes; *W:* Herbert Baker; *C:* James A. Crabe; *M:* Artie Butler.

Sexting 🦴 ½ *Textuality* **2011** Mostly innocuous rom com uses texting and social networks to get its relationship issues across. Artist Simone is involved with a married man while pursuing other meaningless sexual encounters. Stockbroker Breslin has been dumped at the altar and decides to screw around to mend his broken heart. They meet and become romantically entangled while using devices (and not the sexual kind) to keep things moving along. **94m/C; DVD.** Jason Lewis; Carly Pope; Eric McCormack; Kris Holden-Ried; Kristen Hager; Liam Card; *D:* Warren Sonoda; *W:* Liam Card; *C:* Jeremy Benning; *M:* Craig McConnell. **VIDEO**

Sexting in Suburbia 🦴🦴 *Shattered Silence* **2012** Suburban mom Rachel thinks her teen daughter Dina tells her everything until Dina commits suicide. Rachel struggles to find a reason and learns Dina was tormented by online bullies after a nude picture she sent her boyfriend went viral. This Lifetime movie veers somewhat off-course when Rachel starts receiving threats to stop investigating. **96m/C; DVD.** Liz Vassey; Jenn Proske; Ryan Kelley; Kelli Goss; Judith Hoag; Tom Kemp; *D:* John Stimpson; *W:* John Stimpson; *C:* Brian Crane; *M:* Ed Grenga.

Sexton Blake and the Hooded Terror 🦴🦴 **1938** Sexton Blake a British private detective a la Holmes, is after "The Snake," a master criminal, and his gang The Hooded Terror. One of a series of melodramatic adventures interesting chiefly for Slaughter's performance as the gangleader. **70m/B; VHS, DVD.** *GB* Tod Slaughter; Greta Gynt; George Curzon; *D:* George King.

Sexual Malice 🦴🦴 **1993 (R)** Another erotic thriller finds a bored wife involved in an obsessive affair with a mystery man who has murder on his mind. Also available in an unrated version. **96m/C; VHS, DVD.** Diana Barton; John Laughlin; Chad McQueen; Edward Albert; Don Swayze; Kathy Shower; Samantha (Sam) Phillips; *D:* Jag Mundhra; *W:* Carl Austin; *C:* James Mathers.

Sexual Roulette 🦴 **1996 (R)** A distaff and decidedly raunchier "Indecent Proposal." Jed and Sally wind up in money trouble and get in deeper by trying to recoup their loses (and losing bigtime) in a Vegas horse race. Then a rich blonde with some kinky preferences makes Jed an offer he can't afford to refuse. The unrated version is six minutes longer. **90m/C; VHS, DVD.** Tane McClure; Tim Abell; Gabriella Hall; Richard Gabai; Myles O'Brien; G. Gordon Baer; *D:* Gary Graver; *W:* Sean McGinley; *C:* Gary Graver.

Sexy Beast 🦴🦴🦴 1/2 **2000 (R)** This British suspense/thriller is not only tense and caustically funny at times, it also has the guy who played Gandhi as a snarling, bad-ass gangster. Ben Kingsley plays Logan, who's sent to southern Spain to lure retired gangster "Gal" Dove (Winstone) back to England for the standard "one last job." When Gal refuses, Logan threatens non-non-violence on Gal's wife Deedee (Redman) and pals Aitch (Kendall, in his last role) and Jackie (White). Gal is forced into accepting after some unfortunate events, and the plot, masterminded by Logan's boss Teddy (McShane), is carried out. After the caper is done, however, Gal will have a harder time relaxing poolside with the reminders of the "sexy beast" of his criminal life all too close. Kingsley dominates the movie as the profanity-spewing Logan, but the rest of the cast also turn in outstanding performances. **88m/C; VHS, DVD, Blu-Ray.** *GB* Ray Winstone; Ben Kingsley; Ian McShane; Amanda Redman; James Fox; Robert Atiko; Julianne White; Cavan Kendall; Alvaro Monje; *D:* Jonathan Glazer; *W:* Louis Mellis; David Scinto; *C:* Ivan Bird; *M:* Roque Baños. Broadcast Film Critics '02: Support. Actor (Kingsley).

Sexy Evil Genius 🦴🦴 **2013 (R)** In this so-so comedic thriller, the title character, Nikki Franklyn, is released from prison after killing her last boyfriend. She invites all her ex-lovers (male and female) to an L.A. bar as she plays mind games and everyone tries to figure out what the nutcase is planning. **91m/C; DVD.** Katee Sackhoff; Seth Green; Michelle Trachtenberg; Harold Perrineau, Jr.; William Baldwin; Anthony Michael Hall; *D:* Shawn Piller; *W:* Scott Lew; *C:* Jules Labarthe; *M:* Patric Caird. **VIDEO**

Seymour: An Introduction 🦴🦴🦴 **2015 (PG)** Director Hawke met subject Seymour Bernstein at a dinner party and found his dining companion so fascinating that he made this documentary about him. Some of the film details this phenomenal pianist's career—and the unique decision he made to walk away fame and fortune—but much of it plays like a detailed, philosophical conversation about the very nature of art, which Hawke admits is a subject on which he has obsessed over for years. What obligation does an artist have to his fans, if any? What obligation does he have to himself? The result is a conversation-starting, unique documentary. **84m/C; DVD.** Seymour Bernstein; Jiyang Chen; Ethan Hawke; Junko Ichikawa; Marcus Ostermiller; *D:* Ethan Hawke; *C:* Ramsey Fendall; *M:* Bill Finizio.

S.F.W. 🦴🦴 **1994 (R)** Get out your cliche-o-meter for another look at Generation X. Suburban teen Cliff Spab (Dorff) unwillingly becomes a media sensation during a terrorist hostage crisis at a convenience store. The phrasemaking teen's apathetic words are adopted by his peers just as he realizes that there is something he actually cares about—fellow hostage Wendy Pfister (Witherspoon), a cheerleader who wouldn't have given him the time of day before. A somewhat heavy-handed commentary on fame in our tabloid-intensive society. Title acronym stands for "So F***ing What." Many reviewers had a similar reaction. Based on the novel by Andrew Wellman. **92m/C; VHS, DVD.** Stephen Dorff; Reese Witherspoon; Jake Busey; Joey Lauren Adams; Pamela Gidley; David Barry Gray; Jack Noseworthy; Richard Portnow; *D:* Jefery Levy; *W:* Jefery Levy; James Foley.

Sgt. Stubby: An American Hero 🦴 1/2 **2018 (PG)** A family-friendly, animated look at the true story of a Boston terrier who became a battlefield hero during World War I. In 1917, the stray dog finds his way to the training ground at Yale University for an infantry division. Dubbed Stubby, he adopts Robert (Lerman), a young private in training, as his master and joins the basic training exercises. When the division ships out to France, Stubby sneaks out with them, proves his worth in the trenches, and becomes a mascot for the soldiers on the front line. Without showing the horrors of combat, the film shows the importance of Stubby's accomplishments. **84m/C; DVD, Blu-Ray.** Helena Bonham Carter; Logan Lerman; Gerard Depardieu; Nicholas Rulon; Brian Cook; *D:* Richard Lanni; *W:* Richard Lanni; Mike Stokey; *M:* Patrick Doyle.

The Shack 🦴 1/2 **2017 (PG-13)** Mack Phillips' (a flat Worthington) daughter disappears during a camping trip and is considered the victim of a serial killer. To handle his grief, Mack is invited to a cabin where he meets a trio of strangers who teach him about forgiveness. Based on William P. Young's hit religious novel, director Hazeldine's film is a ridiculous parable about a man finding faith to overcome grief and his painful upbringing. It's not just the suggestion that being abused by a drunken father can be overcome through God that feels manipulative but the thin writing overall and weak performances that drain this piece of any emotional power. **132m/C; DVD, Blu-Ray.** Sam Worthington; Octavia Spencer; Tim McGraw; Radha Mitchell; Avraham Aviv Alush; *D:* Stuart Hazeldine; *W:* John Fusco; Andrew Lanham; Destin Daniel Cretton; *C:* Declan Quinn; *M:* Aaron Zigman.

Shack Out on 101 🦴🦴🦴 **1955** A waitress (Moore) in an isolated cafe on a busy highway notices suspicious doings among her customers. What could they be up to? Communist subversion, of course. Of-its-era anti-pinko propoganda, but with a twist: Moore uncovers commie plots, pleases her customers, and fends off unwelcome lecherous advances all in 80 minutes, on a single set! **80m/B; DVD, Blu-Ray.** Lee Marvin; Terry Moore; Keenan Wynn; Frank Lovejoy; Whit Bissell; Jess Barker; Donald Murphy; Frank De Kova; Len Lesser; Fred Gabourie; *D:* Edward Dein; *W:* Edward Dein; Mildred Dein; *C:* Floyd Crosby; *M:* Paul Dunlap; Louis Prima.

Shackleton 🦴🦴🦴 **2002** Stirring adventure about the ill-fated expedition of Sir Ernest Shackleton (Branagh) to Antarctica in 1914. His ship, the Endurance, gets trapped in ice and eventually sinks, leaving Shackleton and his crew of 27 to set up camp on a nearby island. Shackleton and two of the crew set out for help to a whaling station on South Georgia Island—an unbelievably difficult journey of survival for those travelling and those left behind. **200m/C; VHS, DVD.** Kenneth Branagh; Kevin McNally; Chris Larkin; Mark McGann; Lorcan Cranitch; Nicholas (Nick) Rowe; Pip Torrens; Shaun Dooley; Matt(hew) Day; *D:* Charles Sturridge; *W:* Charles Sturridge; *C:* Henry Braham; *M:* Adrian Johnston. **CABLE**

Shade 🦴🦴 **2003 (R)** Glamorous group of LA card sharks finds it's a very bad idea to scam the mob and need to take on ultimate legend "The Dean" (Stallone) to worm their way out of dire straits. Nieman, in his first directorial feature, shows that you can still flop with a winning hand as he leads the talent of this A-list of actors down the river. **95m/C; VHS, DVD, Blu-Ray.** Sylvester Stallone; Gabriel Byrne; Melanie Griffith; Hal Holbrook; Thandie Newton; Stuart Townsend; Dina Merrill; Bo Hopkins; Jamie Foxx; Patrick Bauchau; Louis Freese; Roger Guenveur Smith; Charles Rocket; Michael Dorn; Jack Conley; Frank Medrano; Glenn Plummer; Damien Nieman; *D:* Damien Nieman; *W:* Damien Nieman; *C:* Anthony B. Richmond; *M:* Christopher Young.

Shades of Darkness 🦴🦴 1/2 **2000 (R)** Stephen King sort of story has to do with a woman (Trebilcock) who returns to her small hometown and finds that supernatural forces are at work. **90m/C; DVD.** John Maczko; Annie Trebilcock; *D:* Christopher Johnson.

Shades of Fear 🦴🦴 *Great Moments in Aviation* **1993 (R)** Adventurous would-be aviatrix Gabriel Angel (Ayola), who's sailing from Grenada to England, is mistakenly assigned a room with Duncan (Pryce) and decides to pose as his wife to avoid a scandal. But a fellow passenger (Hurt) believes Duncan is also the art forger who ran off with his wife and caused her death. On their last night at sea, there's a final confrontation. **93m/C; VHS, DVD.** *GB* Jonathan Pryce; Rakie Ayola; John Hurt; Vanessa Redgrave; Dorothy Tutin; *D:* Beeban Kidron. **TV**

The Shadow 🦴🦴 1/2 **1994 (PG-13)** Who knows what evil lurks in the hearts of men? Why "The Shadow" of course, as is shown in this highly stylized big screen version of the '30s radio show that once starred Orson Welles. Billionaire playboy Lamont Cranston (Baldwin) is a master of illusion and defender of justice thanks to his alter ego. Aided by companion Margo Lane (Miller), da Shadow battles super-criminal Shiwan Khan (Lone), the deadliest descendant of Ghenghis Khan. Numerous and elaborate special effects provide icing on the cake for those in the mood for a journey back to the radio past or a quick superhero fix. **112m/C; VHS, DVD, Blu-Ray.** Alec Baldwin; John Lone; Penelope Ann Miller; Peter Boyle; Ian McKellen; Tim Curry; Jonathan Winters; Andre Gregory; James Hong; Joseph Maher; John Kapelos; Sab Shimono; Max Wright; Aaron Lustig; Ethan Phillips; Larry Joshua; Al Leong; Abraham Benrubi; Armin Shimerman; Steve Hytner; Kate McGregor-Stewart; *D:* Russell Mulcahy; *W:* David Koepp; *C:* Stephen Burum; *M:* Jerry Goldsmith.

Shadow 🦴🦴🦴 *Ying* **2018** Based in China's Three Kingdoms period (220-280 AD), the doppelgänger of an anti-war king is secretly charged by the military commander to wage war and stage a coup. Shot in inky tones of black and white to emphasize the vivid red of spilled blood, director Yimou Zhang delivers a stunningly epic martial arts film. **116m/C; DVD, Blu-Ray.** *CH* Chao Deng; Li Sun; Ryan Zheng; Qianyuan Wang; Jingchun Wang; *D:* Yimou Zhang; *W:* Yimou Zhang; Wei Li; *C:* Xiaoding Zhao; *M:* Loudboy.

The Shadow Conspiracy 🦴 **1996 (R)** Laughable innocent-on-the-run tale of presidential advisor Bobby Bishop (Sheen), who finds himself smack in the middle of an assassination conspiracy against the Prez (Waterston). Accused of murder, Bishop hooks up with ex-gal pal, reporter Amanda Givens (Hamilton) to get to the truth before the police and the bad guys get to them. Hunting the duo is a pro known as "The Agent" (Lang). Lang's lethal Agent comes off as one of the only believable characters here, perhaps because he has absolutely no dialogue to sabotage him. Sutherland fares better than most as Chief of Staff Conrad Jacob. Ludicrous plot twists and unconvincing performances by leads Sheen and Hamilton. **103m/C; VHS, DVD.** Charlie Sheen; Linda Hamilton; Stephen Lang; Donald Sutherland; Sam Waterston; Ben Gazzara; Nicholas Turturro; Charles Cioffi; Theodore Bikel; Stanley Anderson; Dey Young; Gore Vidal; Paul Gleason; Terry O'Quinn; *D:* George P. Cosmatos; *W:* Rick Gibbs; Wayne Beach; *C:* Buzz Feitshans, IV; *M:* Bruce Broughton.

Shadow Dancer 🦴🦴🦴 **2012 (R)** Methodically suspenseful drama set in 1993. IRA member Collette McVeigh (Riseborough), who grew up in Belfast, has a reason to hate the Brits when she plants a bomb in a London subway station. MI5 knows all about her and agent Mac (Owen) gives her a choice: 25 years in prison away from her young son or become a British mole, reporting on the activities of her own brothers, Gerry (Gillen) and Connor (Gleeson). Distrust, betrayal, and danger are high on both sides as Collette weighs self-preservation against family loyalty and Mac discovers more's going on than he knows. **101m/C; DVD, Blu-Ray, Streaming.** *IR UK* Andrea Riseborough; Clive Owen; Gillian Anderson; Aidan Gillen; Domhnall Gleeson; David Wilmot; Brid Brennan; *D:* James Marsh; *W:* Tom Bradby; *C:* Rob Hardy; *M:* Dickon Hinchliffe.

Shadow Force 🦴 1/2 **1992** Homicide detective Rick Kelly is investigating the murders of a district attorney and a police sergeant. With the help of Mary, the usual beautiful female journalist, he uncovers a plot to assassinate key law enforcement officers. **80m/C; VHS, DVD, Streaming.** Dirk Benedict; Lance LeGault; Lise Cutter; Jack Elam; Glenn Corbett; Bob Hastings; *D:* Darrell Davenport.

The Shadow in the North 🦴🦴 **2007** It's six years after Sally Lockhart's (Piper) first adventure (in "The Ruby in the Smoke") and she has become a financial consultant to her late father's shipping company in 1870s London. A client asks her to look into a mysterious ship sinking since the insurance company won't pay up until the matter is investigated. Meanwhile, beau Frederick Garland (Feild) has become a private detective and has a peculiar case with a magician claiming he's going to be murdered. Naturally, the investigations overlap. Based on the novel by Philip Pullman. **86m/C; DVD.** *GB* Billie Piper; J.J. Feild; Matt Smith; Jared Harris; Hayley Atwell; Julian Rhind-Tutt; John Standing; Dona Croll; David Harewood; *D:* John Alexander; *W:* Adrian Hodges; *C:* Adam Suschitzky; *M:* John Lunn. **TV**

The Shadow Laughs 🦴 **1933** Newspaper reporter Robin Dale starts his own investigation into a bank robbery and the murder of a bank guard when the police are stumped. Although the title makes no sense since there's no shadow, let alone laughing, involved. **67m/B; DVD.** Hal Skelly; Rose Hobart; Harry T. Morey; Walter Fenner; Robert Keith; Cesar Romero; *D:* Arthur Hoerl; *W:* Arthur Hoerl; *C:* Don Malkames.

Shadow Magic 🦴🦴 1/2 **2000 (PG)** Englishman Raymond Wallace (Harris) turns up in Peking in 1902 with a hand-cranked, black and white, soundless camera and projector, thus bringing the first moving images to China. Local photographer Liu Jinglun (Yu), intrigued by the new technolgy, bridges the cultural barriers between Raymond and the community, causing problems of loyalty with his own family and friends and even jeopardizing his marriage chances. Mandarin with subtitles. **115m/C; VHS, DVD.** *GE* Jared Harris; Xia Yu; Peiqi Liu; Liping Lu; Xing Yufei; Wang Jingming; Li Yusheng; *D:* Ann Hu; *W:* Ann Hu; Huang Dan; Tang Louyi; Kate Raisz; Bob McAndrew; *C:* Nancy Schreiber; *M:* Zhang Lida.

The Shadow Man 🦴🦴 *Street of Shadows* **1953** A casino operator in London (Romero) is accused of killing a former girlfriend and works to clear himself. Family conventional action mystery: nothing to write home about. **76m/B; VHS, DVD.** *GB FR IT* Cesar Romero; Simone Silva; Kay Kendall; John Penrose; Edward Underdown; Victor Maddern; Jacques Champreux; Ugo Pagliali; *D:* Richard Vernon; Georges Franju; *W:* Richard Vernon; Ugo Pagliali; *C:* Phil Grindrod; Guido Bertoni; *M:* Eric Spear; Georges Franju.

Shadow Man 🦴 1/2 **2006 (R)** Mediocre adventure from Seagal. Jack Foster is a retired CIA agent who is taking his daughter (Bennett) to visit Bucharest, the home of her late mother. Only she gets kidnapped because the bad guys think Foster is in possession of a bio-weapon that he knows nothing about but rogue CIA agents do. **91m/C; DVD.** Steven Seagal; Werner Daehn; Imelda Staunton; Skye Bennett; Garrick Hagon; *D:* Michael Keusch; *W:* Steven Collins; Joe Halpin; *C:* Geoffrey Hall. **VIDEO**

Shadow of a Doubt 🦴🦴🦴 1/2 **1943** Uncle Charlie has come to visit his relatives in Santa Rosa. Although he is handsome and charming, his young niece slowly comes to realize he is a wanted mass murderer—and he comes to recognize her suspicions. Hitchcock's personal favorite movie; a quietly creepy venture into Middle American menace. Good performances, especially by Cronyn. From the story by Gordon McConnell. **108m/B; VHS, DVD, Blu-Ray.** Teresa Wright; Joseph Cotten; Hume Cronyn; MacDonald Carey; Henry Travers; Wallace Ford; *D:* Alfred Hitchcock; *W:* Thornton Wilder; Sally Benson; Alma Reville; *C:* Joseph Valentine; *M:* Dimitri Tiomkin. Natl. Film Reg. '91.

Shadow of Chikara 🦴 *Thunder Mountain; The Curse of Demon Mountain* **1977 (PG)** A Confederate Army Captain and an orphan girl encounter unexpected adventures as they search for a fortune in diamonds hidden in a river in northern Arkansas. **96m/C; VHS, DVD.** Joe Don Baker; Sondra Locke; Ted Neeley; Slim Pickens; *D:* Earl E. Smith; *W:* Earl E. Smith; *C:* Jim Roberson; *M:* Jaime Mendoza-Nava.

Shadow of Chinatown 🦴 1/2 **1936** Mad scientist creates wave of murder and terror in Chinatown. Edited version of a 15-chapter serial. **70m/B; VHS, DVD.** Bela Lugosi; Bruce Bennett; Joan Barclay; Luana Walters; Maurice Liu; William Buchanan; ***D:*** Robert F. "Bob" Hill.

Shadow of Doubt 🦴 1/2 **1935** In this routine crime drama, wealthy recluse Melissa Pilson (Collier) gets involved in murder. Lothario movie producer Len Haworth is killed, and Melissa leaves her New York home for the first time in more than 20 years. Her nephew Sim (Cortez) is in love with starlet Trenna (Bruce), whose unfortunate involvement with Haworth makes them prime suspects. **74m/B; DVD.** Constance Collier; Ricardo Cortez; Virginia Bruce; Regis Toomey; Betty Furness; Isabel Jewell; ***D:*** George B. Seitz; ***W:*** Wells Root; ***C:*** Charles G. Clarke.

Shadow of Doubt 🦴🦴 1/2 **1998 (R)** L.A. defense attorney Kitt Devereux (Girffiths) likes high-profile cases. And her latest has the added tension of being prosecuted by ex-lover, Asst. D.A. Jack Campioni (Berenger). Kitt works with an investigaotr (Lewis) to prove a rapper (Dominguez) innocent of murder while being threatened by an accused rapist (Sheffer) and a prominent Senator, who's angling for a presidential nomination. How everything ties together is something Kitt will have to figure out if she wants to discover the truth. **103m/C; VHS, DVD.** Melanie Griffith; Tom Berenger; Craig Sheffer; Huey Lewis; John Ritter; Wade Dominguez; ***D:*** Randal Kleiser; ***W:*** Raymond De Felitta; Myra Byanka.

Shadow of Fear 🦴🦴 **2012** Lifetime woman-in-peril movie based on a true story. Waitress Casey Cooper (Righetti) is glad when her odd co-worker Morgan Pierce (Estes) quits his coffee shop job. Morgan, a schizophrenic who won't take his meds, starts harassing and stalking Casey and she can't get the police to help. When Morgan hurts those Casey cares about, she takes action on her own. **96m/C; DVD; Closed Captioned.** Amanda Righetti; Will Estes; Harry Hamlin; Catherine Hicks; Eric Szmanda; Christie Burson; ***D:*** Michael Lohmann; ***W:*** Stacey K. Pantazis; ***C:*** Michael Lohmann. **CABLE**

Shadow of the Eagle 🦴🦴 **1932** Former wartime flying ace Wayne is accused of being a criminal known as "The Eagle." He's using his flying skills (which include skywriting) to threaten a corporation which has stolen plans for a new invention. But can Wayne really be our villain? 12-chapter serial. **226m/B; VHS, DVD.** John Wayne; Dorothy Gulliver; Walter Miller; ***D:*** Ford Beebe.

Shadow of the Hawk 🦴 1/2 **1976** Occasionally creepy revenge horror. Medicine man Old Man Hawk (George) needs the help of his city-bred, half-native grandson Mike (Vincent) to finally defeat a witch, executed 200 years before, who placed a curse on their family. **92m/C; DVD, Blu-Ray.** *CA* Jan-Michael Vincent; Chief Dan George; Marianne Jones; Marilyn Hassett; ***D:*** George McCowan; ***W:*** Norman Thaddeus Vane; ***C:*** John Holbrook; Reginald Morris; ***M:*** Robert McMullin.

Shadow of the Thin Man 🦴🦴🦴 **1941** In the fourth "Thin Man" film, following "Another Thin Man," Nick and Nora stumble onto a murder at the racetrack. The rapport between Powell and Loy is still going strong, providing us with some wonderful entertainment. Followed by "The Thin Man Goes Home." **97m/B; VHS, DVD.** William Powell; Myrna Loy; Barry Nelson; Donna Reed; Sam Levene; Alan Baxter; Dickie Hall; Loring Smith; Joseph Anthony; Henry O'Neill; ***D:*** W.S. Van Dyke.

Shadow of the Vampire 🦴🦴🦴 **2000** Behind the scenes look at what possibly went on during the making of the silent vampire classic, 1922's "Nosferatu." Director F.W. Murnau (Malkovich) and his crew head for Czechoslovakia for location shooting on his version of "Dracula" and the first meeting of the dedicated actor who will play the title role—a very eccentric Max Schreck (Dafoe). Only Murnau has struck a devil's bargain with Schreck, who is an actual vampire—the leading man gets leading lady Greta (McCormack) as a reward—and a snack. But it seems Schreck can't wait, as the crew starts to fall mysteriously ill. A little slow going but strangely compelling and the two lead performances are outstanding. **93m/C; VHS, DVD.** *GB* John Malkovich; Willem Dafoe; Catherine McCormack; Cary Elwes; Eddie Izzard; Udo Kier; Ronan Vibert; Aden (John) Gillett; ***D:*** Edmund Elias Merhige; ***W:*** Steven Katz; ***C:*** Lou Bogue; ***M:*** Dan (Daniel) Jones. L.A. Film Critics '00: Support. Actor (Dafoe).

Shadow on the Mesa 🦴🦴 **2013** Hallmark Channel western. After his mother is murdered by outlaws, bounty Hunter Wes Rawlins sets off to find the father he never knew. However, Ray Eastman's in the middle of a land feud and his wife, Mona, has a secret that could change all their lives. **87m/C; DVD.** Wes Brown; Kevin Sorbo; Gail O'Grady; Greg Evigan; Shannon Lucio; Meredith Baxter; Barry Corbin; ***D:*** David S. Cass, Sr.; ***W:*** Lee Martin; ***C:*** Maximo Munzi; ***M:*** Brian Byrne. **CABLE**

Shadow on the Window 🦴 1/2 **1957** Young Petey is traumatized after he and his mother witness a murder by three teen delinquents who then kidnap Linda. Mute, Petey wanders off while his police officer father Tony searches for his estranged wife and son. **73m/B; DVD, Blu-Ray.** Jerry Mathers; Phil Carey; Betty Garrett; John Barrymore; Corey Allen; Gerald Sarracini; Sam Gilman; Rusty Lane; ***D:*** William Asher; ***W:*** Leo Townsend; David Harmon; ***C:*** Kit Carson; ***M:*** George Duning.

Shadow People 🦴 *The Door* **2013 (PG-13)** A fading radio talk show host becomes obsessed with the urban legends of Shadow People, mysterious shadows said to kill people at night. **88m/C; DVD, Blu-Ray, Streaming.** Dallas Roberts; Alison Eastwood; Anne Dudek; Mariah Bonner; Mattie Liptak; ***D:*** Matthew Arnold; ***W:*** Matthew Arnold; ***C:*** Matthew Heckerling; ***M:*** Corey Wallace. **VIDEO**

Shadow Puppets 🦴 **2007** Strangers wake up in some kind of dank medical facility/prison minus both their clothes (they're in their underwear) and their memories. They try to figure out what's going on but something in the shadows is out to get 'em. Generally dopey psycho-thriller. **103m/C; DVD.** James Marsters; Jolene Blalock; Tony Todd; Jonathan Hale; Marc Winnick; ***D:*** Michael Winnick; ***W:*** Michael Winnick; ***M:*** Ross Nykiforuk. **VIDEO**

The Shadow Riders 🦴🦴 *Louis L'Amour's "The Shadow Riders"* **1982 (PG)** Two brothers who fought on opposite sides during the Civil War return home to find their brother's fiancee kidnapped by a renegade Confederate officer who plans to use her as ransom in a prisoner exchange. They set out to rescue the woman. Preceded by "The Sacketts" and based on the works of Louis L'Amour. **96m/C; VHS, DVD.** Tom Selleck; Sam Elliott; Ben Johnson; Katharine Ross; Jeffery Osterhage; Gene Evans; R.G. Armstrong; Marshall Teague; Dominique Dunne; Jeanetta Arnette; ***D:*** Andrew V. McLaglen; ***W:*** Jim Byrnes; ***C:*** Jack Whitman; ***M:*** Jerrold Immel. **TV**

Shadow Warriors 🦴 1/2 **1995 (R)** Greedy security expert Connors (O'Quinn) sells computerized bodyguards that are created from human corpses, aided by doctor Natalie (Graham). Only one of the latest creations has just gone on a killing spree, so they use another "technosapien" (Lurie) to prevent further mayhem. **80m/C; VHS, DVD.** Evan Lurie; Terry O'Quinn; Russ Tertyask; Ashley Anne Graham; Timothy Patrick Cavanaugh; ***D:*** Lamar Card; ***C:*** M. David Mullen.

Shadow Warriors 🦴🦴 *Assault on Devil's Island* **1997** Navy SEALS, led by Mike McBride (Hogan), plan an assault on the island hideaway of drug lord Gallindo (Drago). Lending assistance is undercover DEA agent Hunter Wiley (being that the part is played by Tweed she's never really covered, appearing in a variety of lingerie and bikinis while kicking butt). However, when the SEALS get Gallindo, his crew retaliates. **94m/C; VHS, DVD.** Hulk Hogan; Carl Weathers; Shannon Tweed; Martin Kove; Billy Drago; Trevor Goddard; Billy Blanks; ***D:*** Jon Cassar. **CABLE**

Shadow Warriors 2: Hunt for the Death Merchant 🦴🦴 1/2 **1997 (R)** The elite commando unit of Hogan, Weathers, and Tweed return—and this time they must rescue a group of American gymnasts who are being held hostage. If you enjoyed the first movie, you'll enjoy this one since it's more of the action-filled same. **95m/C; VHS, DVD.** Hulk Hogan; Carl Weathers; Shannon Tweed; Martin Kove; ***D:*** Jon Cassar. **CABLE**

The Shadow Within 🦴🦴 **2007 (R)** Nine-year-old Maurice can see the dead, including his twin brother Jacques. He lives in a French village with his embittered mother Marie (dad is off fighting in WWII), who is suspicious of everyone, including the local doctor and her husband, Maurice's teacher. When a diphtheria epidemic claims the lives of local children, their desperate mothers want to use Maurice's abilities to contact them but the deceased kids only have one wish—for their mothers to join them. **90m/C; DVD.** *IT* Laurence Belcher; Hayley J. Williams; Beth Winslet; Rod Hallett; Bonny Ambrose; ***D:*** Silvana Zancolo; ***W:*** Silvana Zancolo; Daniel Aarons; Giovanni Eccher; ***C:*** Pier Luigi Santi; ***M:*** Paolo Marzocchi.

A Shadow You Soon Will Be 🦴🦴 *Una Sombra Ya Pronto Seras* **1994** An allegory of the emptiness of contemporary Argentinian society, following the end of military rule, and based on a 1990 novel by Soriano, who co-wrote the screenplay. A man known merely as "The Engineer" (Sola) returns from Europe where he's lived in exile during the military dictatorship. Without family or friends, he wanders through the southern pampas, briefly communicating with other eccentric travelers, and non-commitally watching the world go by. Spanish with subtitles. **105m/C; VHS, DVD.** *AR* Miguel Angel Sola; Eusebio Poncela; Pepe Soriano; Alicia Bruzzo; Luis Brandoni; Diego Torres; Gloria Carra; ***D:*** Hector Olivera; ***W:*** Hector Olivera; Osvaldo Soriano; ***C:*** Felix Monti; ***M:*** Osvaldo Montes.

Shadowboxer 🦴 1/2 **2006 (R)** Gratuitous, graphic sex and violence dominate a story about biracial assassins who are not only lovers but stepmother and stepson, played for some reason by the great Mirren and Gooding. Complications arise when a job doesn't go as planned and the odd couple find themselves on the lam with their target and her just-born infant. Add a half bone for somehow landing Oscar-caliber leads. **93m/C; DVD.** Cuba Gooding, Jr.; Dame Helen Mirren; Vanessa Ferlito; Macy Gray; Joseph Gordon-Levitt; Mo'Nique; Stephen Dorff; ***D:*** Lee Daniels; ***W:*** William Lipz; ***C:*** M. David Mullen; ***M:*** Mario Grigorov.

Shadowheart 🦴 1/2 **2009 (PG-13)** Bounty hunter James Conners (Ament) returns to Legend, New Mexico to avenge his father's death at the hands of Will Tunney (Macfadyen). When James has the chance to reunite with first love Mary Cooper (Alton) he has to decide if revenge is worth giving up his second chance. **114m/C; DVD.** Angus MacFadyen; Marnie Alton; William Sadler; Dean Alioto; Justin Ament; Michael Spears; ***D:*** Dean Alioto; ***W:*** Dean Alioto; ***C:*** Andrew Huebscher; ***M:*** Gregor Narholz. **VIDEO**

Shadowhunter 🦴🦴 **1993 (R)** Glenn stars as a burned-out big city detective who is sent to a Navajo reservation in Arizona to bring a murder suspect back to Los Angeles. When the alleged killer escapes custody Glenn must track him across forbidding desert territory and face his suspect's unusual mystical powers. **98m/C; VHS, Streaming.** Scott Glenn; ***D:*** J.S. Cardone; ***W:*** J.S. Cardone; ***C:*** Dick Bush.

Shadowlands 🦴🦴🦴 **1993 (PG)** Touching, tragic story of the late-in-life romance between celebrated author and Christian theologian C.S. Lewis (Hopkins) and brash New York divorcee Joy Gresham (Winger). Attenborough's direction is rather stately and sweeping and Winger is really too young for her role but Hopkins is excellent as (another) repressed man who finds more emotions than he can handle. Critically acclaimed adaptation of Nicholson's play will require lots of kleenex. **130m/C; VHS, DVD.** *GB* Anthony Hopkins; Debra Winger; Edward Hardwicke; Joseph Mazzello; Michael Denison; John Wood; Peter Firth; Peter Howell; ***D:*** Richard Attenborough; ***W:*** William Nicholson; ***C:*** Roger Pratt; ***M:*** George Fenton. British Acad. '93: Film; L.A. Film Critics '93: Actor (Hopkins); Natl. Bd. of Review '93: Actor (Hopkins).

Shadows 🦴🦴 **1922** A Chinese laundryman (Chaney) lives with a group of his countrymen in a New England seacoast village. All is peaceful until the local minister decides to convert the "heathen" Chinese. Ludicrous but worth seeing for Chaney's fun performance. Silent with music score. **70m/B; Silent; VHS, DVD.** Lon Chaney, Sr.; Harrison Ford; ***D:*** Tom Forman; ***W:*** Eve Unsell; Hope Loring; ***C:*** Harry Perry; ***M:*** Gaylord Carter.

Shadows 🦴🦴🦴 **1960** Director Cassavettes' first indie feature finds jazz player Hugh (Hurd) forced to play dives to support his brother Ben (Carruthers) and sister Lelia (Goldoni). Light-skinned enough to pass for white, Lelia takes on the uptown New York art crowd and gets involved with the white Tony (Ray), who leaves when he finds out her true heritage. Meanwhile, Ben drifts along with his friends who abandon him when trouble finds them. Script was improvised by cast. **87m/B; VHS, DVD, Blu-Ray.** Hugh Hurd; Lelia Goldoni; Ben Carruthers; Anthony Ray; Rupert Crosse; Tom Allen; ***D:*** John Cassavetes; ***C:*** Erich Kollmar; ***M:*** Charles Mingus; Shifi Hadi. Natl. Film Reg. '93.

The Shadows 🦴 1/2 **2007** Horror writer Stephen Grimes is being pressured by both his editor and his ex-wife to turn out another best-seller ASAP. Driving home one night, Stephen accidentally hits a young man and takes him to the hospital. Emmet just happens to share a last name with Stephen and the two are soon moving from friends to sexual partners. But Emmet isn't really as innocent as he seems and the relationship starts looking like a plot from one of Stephen's novels. **80m/C; DVD.** Joe Lia; Emmett Allen; ***D:*** Guillermo R. Rodriguez; ***W:*** Guillermo R. Rodriguez; ***C:*** Gavin Kelly; ***M:*** Patrick Kirst. **VIDEO**

Shadows and Fog 🦴🦴 **1992 (PG-13)** Offbeat, unpredictable Allen film that is little more than an exercise in expressionistic visual stylings. The action centers around a haunted, alienated clerk (Allen) who is awakened in the middle of the night to join a vigilante group searching the streets for a killer. Although reminiscent of a silent film, Carlo DiPalma's black-and-white cinematography is stunning. Several stars appear briefly throughout this extremely unfocused comedy. **85m/B; VHS, DVD, Blu-Ray.** Woody Allen; Kathy Bates; John Cusack; Mia Farrow; Jodie Foster; Fred Gwynne; Julie Kavner; Madonna; John Malkovich; Kenneth Mars; Kate Nelligan; Donald Pleasence; Lily Tomlin; Philip Bosco; Robert Joy; Wallace Shawn; Kurtwood Smith; Josef Sommer; David Ogden Stiers; Michael Kirby; Anne Lange; ***D:*** Woody Allen; ***W:*** Woody Allen; ***C:*** Carlo Di Palma.

Shadows and Lies 🦴 *William Vincent* **2010 (R)** Anania's pretentious, confusing, and heavy-handed drama wastes its cast with too much narration and excessive brooding. Petty thief William Vincent (Franco) comes to the attention of a New York gangster (Lucas), who offers him the services of prostitute Ann (Nicholson) as a work incentive. William (who actually has a legit job as an editor of nature videos) has to flee when he and Ann become too close. **108m/C; DVD, Blu-Ray.** James Franco; Julianne Nicholson; Josh(ua) Lucas; Martin Donovan; Zoe Lister-Jones; ***D:*** Jay Anania; ***W:*** Jay Anania; ***C:*** Daniel Vecchione; ***M:*** John Medeski.

Shadows of Forgotten Ancestors 🦴🦴🦴 *Tini Zabutykh Predkiv; Shadows of Our Ancestors; Shadows of Our Forgotten Ancestors; Wild Horses of Fire* **1964** Set in rural Russia in the early 20th century. Brings to expressive life the story of a man whose entire life has been overtaken by tragedy. Folk drama about a peasant who falls in with the daughter of his father's killer, then marries another woman. Strange, resonant and powerful with distinctive camera work. In Ukrainian with English subtitles. **99m/C; VHS, DVD.** *RU* Ivan Micholaichuk; Larisa Kadochnikova; ***D:*** Sergei Paradjanov.

Shadows Over Chinatown 🦴 1/2 **1946** The slapstick doings of Birmingham (Morland) and Jimmy (Sen Yung) lessen the convoluted mystery in the 35th entry in the Charlie Chan series. Charle (Toler) investigates some San Francisco murders related to insurance fraud and an escort service. **64m/B; DVD.** Sidney Toler; Victor Sen Yung; Mantan Moreland; Tanis Chandler; John Gallaudet; ***D:*** Terry Morse; ***W:*** Raymond L. Schrock; ***C:*** William Sickner.

Shadows Run Black 🦴 1/2 **1984** A police detective must save a college coed from the clutches of a maniac wielding a meat cleaver. Ordinary slash-'em-up. Bet Costner's embarrassed now about this early role—like Stallone's porno role in "The Italian Stallion." **89m/C; VHS, DVD.** William J. Kulzer; Elizabeth Trosper; Kevin Costner; ***D:*** Howard Heard.

Shadowzone **1989 (R)** As a result of NASA experiments in dream travel, an interdimensional monster invades our world in search of victims. Begins well, with slightly interesting premise, but degenerates into typical monster flick. Good special effects. **88m/C; VHS, DVD.** Louise Fletcher; David Beecroft; James Hong; Shawn Weatherly; Lu Leonard; ***D:*** J.S. Cardone; ***W:*** J.S. Cardone.

ShadowZone: The Undead Express ½ **1996 (PG-13)** Teen-aged Zach (Leopardi) winds up in New York's subway tunnels where he meets the vampire Valentine (Silver) and his fellow bloodsuckers. Based on the book by J.R. Black. **98m/C; DVD.** Chauncey Leopardi; Ron Silver; Natanya Ross; Tony T. Johnson; Ron White; ***Cameo(s):*** Wes Craven; ***D:*** Stephen Williams; ***W:*** Roy Swallows; ***C:*** Curtis Petersen; ***M:*** Reg Powell. **CABLE**

Shadrach ½ **1998 (PG-13)** The Dabneys run-down Depression Era southern farm was once a rich tobacco plantation and, as they learn, the former home to aged black man Shadrach (Sawyer) who returns in order to die on the land where he grew up. Flawed family patriarch Vernon (Keitel) gives his word to the ex-slave that he can be buried on the land, but learns otherwise from the local sheriff. Still, Vernon tries to fulfill his promise. Director Susanna Styron's lethargic adaptation of her father William's 1978 short story proves that the story should have stayed shorter than 90 minutes. Although the relatively small budget shows, the cast provides good performances. **88m/C; DVD.** Harvey Keitel; John Franklin Sawyer; Andie MacDowell; Scott Terra; Monica Bugajski; Darrell Larson; Deborah Hedwall; Daniel Treat; Edward (Eddie) Bunker; ***D:*** Susanna Styron; ***W:*** Susanna Styron; Bridget Terry; ***C:*** Hiro Narita; ***M:*** Van Dyke Parks.

Shaft **1971 (R)** A black private eye (Roundtree) is hired to find a Harlem gangster's (Gunn) kidnapped daughter. Lotsa sex and violence; suspenseful and well directed by notable "Life" photographer Parks . Great ending. Academy Award-winning theme song by Isaac Hayes, the first music award from the Academy to an African American. Adapted from the novel by Ernest Tidyman. Followed by "Shaft's Big Score" and "Shaft in Africa." **98m/C; VHS, DVD, Blu-Ray.** Richard Roundtree; Moses Gunn; Charles Cioffi; Christopher St. John; Gwen Mitchell; Lawrence Pressman; Victor Arnold; Antonio Fargas; Drew "Bundini" Brown; ***D:*** Gordon Parks; ***W:*** John D.F. Black; Ernest Tidyman; ***C:*** Urs Furrer; ***M:*** Isaac Hayes; J.J. Johnson. Oscars '71: Song ("Theme from Shaft"); Golden Globes '72: Score; Natl. Film Reg. '00.

Shaft *Shaft Returns* **2000 (R)** Singleton's updated the 1971 blaxploitation flick with Jackson starring as the nephew of the coolest private dick ever (Roundtree has a cameo in his original role). But Jackson can more than hold his own in the cool department as he tracks down rich-kid murderer Walter Wade Jr. (Bale), who's after the only witness to his crime, a scared waitress (Collette). Wade hires a Latino drug dealer (Wright, in a standout performance almost equal to Jackson's) and a couple of bad cops to find the girl and kill Shaft, setting off much gunfire and snappy dialoque. Jackson has charisma to burn, but other characters, as well as potentially interesting plot points, get short shrift. This is most likely a result of Wright's part being (deservedly) beefed up from the original screenplay (about which Singleton and Jackson were said to be not entirely happy). **98m/C; VHS, DVD, Blu-Ray.** Samuel L. Jackson; Christian Bale; Vanessa L(ynne) Williams; Jeffrey Wright; Philip Bosco; Toni Collette; Angela Pietropinto; Dan Hedaya; Josef Sommer; Richard Roundtree; Ruben Santiago-Hudson; Lynne Thigpen; Pat Hingle; Busta Rhymes; Mekhi Phifer; Zach Grenier; Catherine Kellner; Isaac Hayes; Lee Tergesen; Gloria Reuben; Gordon Parks; Daniel von Bargen; ***D:*** John Singleton; ***W:*** Richard Price; ***C:*** Stuart Dryburgh; ***M:*** Isaac Hayes; David Arnold.

The Shaft *Down* **2001 (R)** The express elevators in New York's Millennium Building start to malfunction (as in killing passengers) but no one seems to want mechanic Mark (Marshall) to fix the problem. So Mark decides to investigate, aided by nosy reporter Jennifer (Watts). **109m/C; DVD.** *US NL* James Marshall; Naomi Watts; Eric Thal; Michael Ironside; Edward Herrmann; Dan Hedaya; Ron Perlman; ***D:*** Dick Maas; ***W:*** Dick Maas; ***C:*** Marc Felperlaan.

Shaft **2019 (R)** Raised without contact with his grandfather John Shaft (Roundtree) and his father John Shaft II (Jackson), J.J. Shaft (Usher) is a highly regarded FBI data analyst. When J.J.'s longtime friend Karim (Jogia) is found dead of an overdose in a Harlem drug den, their mutual friend, Dr. Sasha (Shipp), determines that the could not have accidentally ingested the amount of heroin found in his system. J.J. seeks his father's help in finding out the truth of what happened. Though the film includes the original Shaft, it suffers from poor direction and a forgettable plot. **111m/C; DVD, Blu-Ray.** Samuel L. Jackson; Jessie T. Usher; Richard Roundtree; Regina Hall; Alexandra Shipp; ***D:*** Tim Story; ***W:*** Kenya Barris; Alex Barnow; ***C:*** Larry Blanford; ***M:*** Christopher Lennertz.

Shaft in Africa ½ **1973 (R)** Violent actioner finds detective Shaft forced into helping an African nation stop some modern-day slave trading. Second sequel, following "Shaft's Big Score." **112m/C; VHS, DVD.** Richard Roundtree; Frank Finlay; Vonetta McGee; Neda Arneric; Jacques Marin; ***D:*** John Guillermin; ***W:*** Stirling Silliphant.

Shaft's Big Score ½ **1972 (R)** This first sequel to the extremely sucessful "Shaft" has Roundtree's detective trying to mediate between several mobsters while investigating a friend's murder. Lots of action and an exciting Brooklyn chase scene involving cars, helicopters, and boats but still routine when compared to the original. Followed by "Shaft in Africa." **105m/C; VHS, DVD.** Richard Roundtree; Moses Gunn; Joseph Mascolo; Drew "Bundini" Brown; Wally Taylor; Kathy Imrie; Julius W. Harris; Rosalind Miles; Joe Santos; ***D:*** Gordon Parks; ***W:*** Ernest Tidyman; ***M:*** Gordon Parks.

Shag: The Movie **1989 (PG)** The time is 1963, the setting Myrtle Beach, South Carolina, the latest craze shaggin' when four friends hit the beach for one last weekend together. Carson (Cates) is getting ready to marry staid Harley (Power); Melaina (Fonda) wants to be discovered in Hollywood; and Pudge (Gish) and Luanne (Hannah) are off to college. They encounter lots of music, boys, and dancing in this delightful film. Not to be confused with other "teen" movies, this one boasts a good script and an above average cast. **96m/C; VHS, DVD, Blu-Ray; Open Captioned.** Phoebe Cates; Annabeth Gish; Bridget Fonda; Page Hannah; Scott Coffey; Robert Rusler; Tyrone Power, Jr.; Jeff Yagher; Carrie Hamilton; Shirley Anne Field; Leilani Sarelle Ferrer; ***D:*** Zelda Barron; ***W:*** Robin Swicord; Lanier Laney; Terry Sweeney; ***C:*** Peter Macdonald.

The Shaggy D.A. **1976 (G)** Wilby Daniels is getting a little worried about his canine alter ego as he is about to run for District Attorney. Fun sequel to "The Shaggy Dog." **90m/C; VHS, DVD.** Dean Jones; Tim Conway; Suzanne Pleshette; Keenan Wynn; Helene Winston; ***D:*** Robert Stevenson; ***M:*** Buddy (Norman Dale) Baker.

The Shaggy Dog ½ **1959 (G)** When young Wilby Daniels utters some magical words from the inscription of an ancient ring he turns into a shaggy dog, causing havoc for family and neighbors. Disney slapstick is on target at times, though it drags in places. Followed by "The Shaggy D.A." and "Return of the Shaggy Dog." **101m/B; VHS, DVD.** Fred MacMurray; Jean Hagen; Tommy Kirk; Annette Funicello; Tim Considine; Kevin Corcoran; ***D:*** Charles T. Barton; ***C:*** Edward Colman.

The Shaggy Dog **2006 (PG)** Allen goes from man to dogman after being bitten by a 300-year-old Tibetan collie with magical DNA in this remake of Disney's 1959 live-action blockbuster. Allen plays a district attorney and full-time dad now prone to loads of anthropomorphic shtick—barking, lifting his leg to pee, chasing cats, and, of course, sniffing rear-ends. Often comes across more creepy than goofy. Downey succeeds as the prototypical mad scientist villain. Strictly for the kiddies. **98m/C; DVD.** Tim Allen; Robert Downey, Jr.; Kristin Davis; Spencer Breslin; Joshua Leonard; Danny Glover; Jane Curtin; Zena Grey; Philip Baker Hall; Craig Kilborn; Annabelle Gurwitch; Bess Wohl; Shawn Pyfrom; Laura Kightlinger; Jarrad Paul; ***D:*** Brian Robbins; ***W:*** Cormac Wibberley; Marianne S. Wibberley; Geoff Rodkey; Jack Amiel; Michael Begler; ***C:*** Gabriel Beristain; ***M:*** Alan Menken.

Shaka Zulu **1983** British miniseries depicting the career of Shaka, king of the Zulus (Cele). Set in the early 19th century during British ascendency in Africa. Good, absorbing cross-cultural action drama would have been better with more inspired directing by Faure. **300m/C; VHS, DVD.** *GB* Edward Fox; Robert Powell; Trevor Howard; Christopher Lee; Fiona Fullerton; Henry Cele; ***D:*** William C. Faure. **TV**

Shaka Zulu: The Last Great Warrior *Shaka Zulu: The Citadel* **2001 (R)** This claims to be a sequel to the 1980s mini-series 'Shaka Zulu' (a series in which Shaka dies at the end) but it's basically a historically inaccurate mess in which the Zulu warrior is sold into slavery in a country he never set foot in. **179m/C; DVD.** Henry Cele; Grace Jones; James Fox; David Hasselhoff; Karen Allen; Omar Sharif; ***D:*** Joshua Sinclair; ***W:*** Joshua Sinclair; ***M:*** Mark Ryder. **TV**

Shake Hands With the Devil **2007 (R)** Streamlined but sluggishly-paced account of the Rwandan genocide. After he's appointed to lead the United Nation troops in Rwanda, Canadian Lt. Gen. Romero Dallaire witnesses the genocide of the Tutsi minority by the Hutus as it begins in 1994. Dallaire is frustrated and appalled by the bureaucracy and lack of support he encounters. Told in flashback and based on Dallaire's autobiography. **112m/C; DVD.** *CA* Roy Dupuis; Owen Sejake; James Gallanders; Tom McCamus; Jean-Hugues Anglade; Deborah Kara Unger; Robert Lalonde; ***D:*** Roger Spottiswoode; ***W:*** Michael Donovan; ***C:*** Miroslaw Baszak; ***M:*** David Hirschfelder.

Shake Hands With the Devil: The Journey of Romeo Dallaire ½ **2004** In 1992 Lt. Gen. Romeo Dallaire went to Rwanda to help save their tormented people only to find his pleas for humane intervention from the U.N., the U.S., and other world powers blatantly ignored. He was not given authority to confiscate Hutu weapons and his soldiers dwindled quickly with no replacements being sent, but he chose to remain in country, trying to save as many lives as possible. As the General returns to Rwanda a decade after the civil war slaughter of 800,000 Tutsis and moderate Hutus, his words along with archival footage give a brutal recounting of atrocities that were given but a flash in Western news reports. Deserved winner of the Audience Best Film Documentary award at Sundance. **91m/C; DVD.** ***D:*** Peter Raymont; ***C:*** John Westheuser; ***M:*** Mark Korven.

Shake, Rattle and Rock ½ **1957** A deejay wants to open a teen music club playing rock 'n' roll, which has all the conservative parents up in arms. A court case follows (which the kids win). Incidental plot to the great music by Fats Domino, Joe Turner, Annita Ray, and Tommy Charles. Songs include "Ain't It a Shame," "Honey Chile," "I'm in Love Again," "Feelin' Happy," and "Sweet Love on My Mind." **76m/C; VHS, DVD.** Mike Connors; Lisa Gaye; Sterling Holloway; Margaret Dumont; Raymond Hatton; Douglass Dumbrille; ***D:*** Edward L. Cahn; ***W:*** Lou Rusoff.

Shake, Rattle & Rock! ½ **1994 (PG-13)** Remake of the 1957 flick. Teenager Susan (Zellweger) scandalizes her uptight mom (Dunn) and the other conservative adults in town because of her love of that evil rock 'n' rock music—and bad boy Lucky (Doe). Made as part of Showtime's "Rebel Highway" series. **83m/C; VHS, DVD.** Renée Zellweger; John Doe; Nora Dunn; Howie Mandel; Patricia Childress; Mary Woronov; Max Perlich; Dick Miller; William Schallert; Paul Anka; ***D:*** Allan Arkush; ***W:*** Trish Soodik; ***C:*** Jean De Segonzac; ***M:*** Joseph (Joey) Altruda. **CABLE**

Shakedown ½ *Blue Jean Cop* **1988 (R)** Power-packed action film. An overworked attorney and an undercover cop work together to stop corruption in the N.Y.P.D. Although lacking greatly in logic or plot, the sensational stunts make this an otherwise entertaining action flick. **96m/C; VHS, DVD, Blu-Ray.** Sam Elliott; Peter Weller; Patricia Charbonneau; Antonio Fargas; Blanche Baker; Richard Brooks; Jude Ciccolella; George Loros; Tom Waits; Shirley Stoler; Rockets Redglare; Kathryn Rossetter; ***D:*** James Glickenhaus; ***W:*** James Glickenhaus; ***C:*** John Lindley; ***M:*** Jonathan Elias.

Shakedown **2002 (R)** Perlman is the leader of a doomsday cult that plans to steal a biological weapon and unleash it on the population. They take over the L.A. bank where the weapon is stored just at the same time that an earthquake hits, which traps the bad guys. When the military discovers the situation, a general (Dryer) decides to destroy the bank to prevent the virus from escaping. **92m/C; VHS, DVD.** Ron Perlman; Erika Eleniak; Fred (John F.) Dryer; Wolf Larson; Matt Westmore; ***D:*** Brian Katkin; ***W:*** Brian Katkin; ***C:*** Yoram Astrakhan; ***M:*** Chris Farrell. **VIDEO**

Shakedown on the Sunset Strip **1988** CBS TV movie. In 1948 L.A., ambitious vice cop Charles Stoker (King) wants to make a name for himself by taking on the prostitution racket, so he arrests madam Brenda Allen (Van Ark). However, Allen has a lot of famous, powerful clients and pays out hush money to cops and politicians who're afraid of what'll happen if she reveals names. Based on a true story. **93m/C; DVD.** Perry King; Joan Van Ark; Season Hubley; David Graf; ***D:*** Walter Grauman; ***W:*** Harold Gast; ***C:*** Robert Moreno; ***M:*** Lalo Schifrin. **TV**

Shaker Run ½ **1985** A stunt car driver and his mechanic transport a mysterious package. They don't know what to do'they're carrying a deadly virus that every terrorist wants! Car chases galore, and not much else. However, if you like chase scenes... **91m/C; VHS, DVD.** *NZ* Leif Garrett; Cliff Robertson; Lisa Harrow; ***D:*** Bruce Morrison.

Shakes the Clown **1992 (R)** Chronicles the rise and fall of Shakes, an alcoholic clown wandering through the all-clown town of Palukaville. Framed for the murder of his boss by his archrival, Binky, Shakes takes it on the lam in order to prove his innocence, aided by his waitress girlfriend Judy, who dreams of becoming a professional bowler. Meant as a satire of substance-abuse recovery programs and the supposed tragedies of a performer's life, the film is sometimes zany, but more often merely unpleasant and unamusing. Williams has an uncredited role as a mime. **83m/C; VHS, DVD, Blu-Ray.** Bobcat Goldthwait; Julie Brown; Blake Clark; Adam Sandler; Tom Kenny; Sydney Lassick; Paul Dooley; Tim Kazurinsky; Florence Henderson; LaWanda Page; ***Cameo(s):*** Robin Williams; ***D:*** Bobcat Goldthwait; ***W:*** Bobcat Goldthwait; ***C:*** Bobby Bukowski; Elliot Davis.

Shakespeare in Love **1998 (R)** Lively romantic comedy about a frustrated Elizabethan playwright suffering from writer's block—who just happens to be William Shakespeare (Fiennes). Will owes a comedy to bankrupt theatre manager Henslowe (Rush) but just can't come up with a suitable story. His creative (and other) juices are sparked by wealthy beauty Viola De Lesseps (Paltrow), who so loves the theatre that she disguises herself as a boy in order to act. (Women are forbidden to be seen on the stage.) But their affair is bittersweet since Viola is about to be married. Ah well, at least Will comes up with "Romeo and Juliet." Terrific script, fine performances, spectacular costumes and cinematography, and you don't have to be a Shakespeare scholar to enjoy yourself. **122m/C; VHS, DVD, Blu-Ray.** Joseph Fiennes; Gwyneth Paltrow; Ben Affleck; Geoffrey Rush; Colin Firth; Dame Judi Dench; Simon Callow; Tom Wilkinson; Imelda Staunton; Jim Carter; Rupert Everett; Martin Clunes; Anthony Sher; Joe Roberts; ***D:*** John Madden; ***W:*** Marc Norman; Tom Stoppard; ***C:*** Richard Greatrex; ***M:*** Stephen Warbeck. Oscars '98: Actress (Paltrow), Art Dir./Set Dec., Costume Des., Film, Orig. Mus./Comedy Score, Orig. Screenplay, Support. Actress (Dench); British Acad. '98: Film, Film Editing, Support. Actor (Rush), Support. Actress (Dench); Golden Globes '99: Actress--Mus./Comedy (Paltrow), Film--Mus./Comedy, Screenplay; MTV Movie Awards '99: Kiss (Joseph

Fiennes/Gwyneth Paltrow); N.Y. Film Critics '98: Screenplay; Natl. Soc. Film Critics '98: Support. Actress (Dench); Screen Actors Guild '98: Actress (Paltrow), Cast; Writers Guild '98: Orig. Screenplay; Broadcast Film Critics '98: Orig. Screenplay.

Shakespeare Wallah 🦴🦴🦴 1/2 **1965** Tender, plausible drama of romance and postcolonial relations in India. A troupe of threadbare traveling Shakespeareans quixotically tours India trying to make enough money to return to England. Wonderfully acted and exquisitely and sensitively directed by Ivory. Based in part on the real-life experiences of the theatrical Kendal family. **120m/B; VHS, DVD, Blu-Ray.** Felicity Kendal; Shashi Kapoor; Madhur Jaffrey; Geoffrey Kendal; Laura Liddell; ***D:*** James Ivory; ***W:*** James Ivory; Ruth Prawer Jhabvala; ***C:*** Subrata Mitra; ***M:*** Satyajit Ray.

Shakespeare's Merchant 🦴 1/2 **2005** In Wagar's modern retelling of "The Merchant of Venice" the story is moved to Venice, California, and there's a love thing going on between Bassanio and his friend Antonio. When Bassanio needs money Antonio can't supply, they go to harassed Jewish moneylender Shylock, who is determined to get his pound of flesh when Antonio can't repay the loan. Shylock's daughter Portia is being wooed by several suitors, including the calculating Bassanio. **80m/C; DVD.** John D. Haggerty; Donald Stewart; Lorna McNab; Bruce Cronwell; John Ernest Tracy; Richard Tatum; ***D:*** Paul Wagar; ***C:*** Paul Mayne; ***M:*** Michael Kaulkin.

The Shakiest Gun in the West 🦴🦴 1/2 **1968** Remake of Bob Hope's "Paleface" has Philadelphia dentist Jesse W. Heywood (Knotts) heading off for a new practice in the wild west of Big Springs. There he unwittingly takes on bad guys and sultry Penny (Rhoades), an undercover government agent who ropes the nervous dentist into marriage for the sake of her job. **101m/C; VHS, DVD, Blu-Ray.** Don Knotts; Barbara Rhoades; Jackie Coogan; Donald (Don "Red") Barry; Ruth McDevitt; Dub Taylor; Noriyuki "Pat" Morita; Helene Winston; ***D:*** Alan Rafkin; ***W:*** James Fritzell; Everett Greenbaum.

Shaking the Tree 🦴🦴 1/2 **1992 (PG-13)** Group of four high school buddies are still in quest of self-fulfillment ten years after high school as they grapple with problems in the real world of adulthood, seeking distraction in adventure, romance, friendship, and sex. **97m/C; VHS, DVD.** Arye Gross; Gale Hansen; Doug Savant; Steven Wilde; Courteney Cox; Christina Haag; Michael Arabian; Nathan Davis; ***D:*** Duane Clark; ***W:*** Duane Clark; ***M:*** David E. Russo.

Shakma 🦴 1/2 **1989** A group of medical researchers involved with experiments on animal and human tendencies toward aggression take a night off to play a quiet game of "Dungeons and Dragons." The horror begins when their main experimental subject comes along and turns things nasty! **101m/C; VHS, DVD, Blu-Ray.** Roddy McDowall; Christopher Atkins; Amanda Wyss; Ari Meyers; ***D:*** Hugh Parks.

Shalako 🦴🦴 **1968** Connery/Bardot pairing promises something special, but fails to deliver. European aristocrats on a hunting trip in New Mexico, circa 1880, are menaced by Apaches. U.S. Army scout tries to save captured countess Bardot. Strange British attempt at a Euro-western. Poorly directed and pointless. Based on a Louis L'Amour story. **113m/C; VHS, DVD, Blu-Ray.** Brigitte Bardot; Sean Connery; Stephen Boyd; Honor Blackman; Woody Strode; Alexander Knox; ***D:*** Edward Dmytryk; ***W:*** Scot (Scott) Finch; James J. Griffith; Hal Hopper; Clarke Reynolds; ***C:*** Ted Moore; ***M:*** Robert Farnon.

Shall We Dance 🦴🦴🦴 **1937** And shall we ever! Seventh Astaire-Rogers pairing has a famous ballet dancer and a musical-comedy star embark on a promotional romance and marriage, to boost their careers, only to find themselves truly falling in love. Score by the Gershwins includes memorable songs. Thin, lame plot—but that's okay. For fans of good singing and dancing, and especially of this immortal pair. **116m/B; VHS, DVD.** Fred Astaire; Ginger Rogers; Edward Everett Horton; Eric Blore; ***D:*** Mark Sandrich; ***M:*** George Gershwin; ***M:*** Ira Gershwin.

Shall We Dance? 🦴🦴🦴 *Shall We Dansu?* **1996** A timid Japanese businessman (Yakusyo) is lured to ballroom dancing when he glimpses a beautiful, sad-eyed teacher (Kusakari) through a window. As much commentary on controlled Japanese society as a spirited discovery of learning to live and dance. Well-drawn, quirky characters and good humor amid the observant social commentary should put this one at the top of the anyone's foreign film dance card. In Japanese with subtitles. **118m/C; VHS, DVD.** *JP* Koji Yakusho; Tamiyo Kusakari; Naoto Takenaka; Akira (Tsukamoto) Emoto; Eriko Watanabe; Yu Tokui; Hiromasa Taguchi; Reiko Kusamura; ***D:*** Masayuki Suo; ***W:*** Masayuki Suo; ***C:*** Naoke Kayano; ***M:*** Yoshikazu Suo. Natl. Bd. of Review '97: Foreign Film; Broadcast Film Critics '97: Foreign Film.

Shall We Dance? 🦴🦴 **2004 (PG-13)** Well-to-do, attractive lawyer (Gere) with a beautiful, loving wife (Sarandon) and children suddenly faces a mid-life crisis and decides to ballroom dance his way out. Inoffensive, though forgettable, remake of a much better and more logical 1996 Japanese movie of the same name. Attractive leads are fine, as are the multitude of daffy supporting characters, but it all seem flimsy and one-dimensional. **106m/C; VHS, DVD, Blu-Ray.** Richard Gere; Jennifer Lopez; Susan Sarandon; Stanley Tucci; Lisa Ann Walter; Richard Jenkins; Bobby Cannavale; Omar Benson Miller; Anita Gillette; Mya; Stark Sands; Tamara Hope; Nick Cannon; ***D:*** Peter Chelsom; ***W:*** Masayuki Suo; ***C:*** John de Borman; ***M:*** Gabriel Yared; John Altman.

Shall We Kiss? 🦴🦴 *Un Baiser S'il Vous Plait?* **2007** Wry comedy-of-manners with a framing story involving Emilie (Gayet), who refuses to (even casually) kiss new acquaintance Gabriel (Cohen) because she says every kiss can change your life. Then she tells him the story of Nicolas (Mouret) and Judith (Ledoyen), longtime friends who take the step into intimacy (despite Judith's marriage) because sad-sack Nicolas is such a wuss with women and the complications that ensue. French with subtitles. **96m/C; DVD.** *FR* Emmanuel Mouret; Virginie Ledoyen; Julie Gayet; Stefano Accorsi; Michael Cohen; Frederique Bel; ***D:*** Emmanuel Mouret; ***W:*** Emmanuel Mouret; ***C:*** Laurent Desmet.

Shallow Grave 🦴🦴 1/2 **1994 (R)** Juliet (Fox), David (Eccleston), and Alex (McGregor), three completely unlikable housemates, face a moral dilemma when their new roomie, Hugo (Allen), turns up dead of a drug overdose, leaving behind a suitcase stuffed with cash. Their decision to chop up the body, bury the bits, and keep the loot leads to a well-deserved descent into paranoia, betrayal, and dementia. Interesting character study in which the veneer of civility is totally destroyed at the first hint of temptation. Style wins out over substance as the characters are never humanized before they're demonized. **91m/C; VHS, DVD, Blu-Ray.** *GB* Kerry Fox; Christopher Eccleston; Ewan McGregor; Keith Allen; Ken Stott; Colin McCredie; John Hodge; ***D:*** Danny Boyle; ***W:*** John Hodge; ***C:*** Brian Tufano; ***M:*** Simon Boswell.

Shallow Ground 🦴 **2004 (R)** Unable to catch a serial killer, a small-town yokel sheriff is closing up shop a year later when—this just in!?a major break in the case appears on his doorstep in the form of a muted young man carrying the murder weapon and covered in the red stuff. Script, direction, music, and acting make for one bloody mess. **97m/C; DVD, On Demand.** *CA* Timothy Murphy; Stan Kirsch; Patty McCormack; Natalie Avital; Myron Natwick; John Kapelos; Lindsey Stoddart; ***D:*** Sheldon Wilson; ***W:*** Sheldon Wilson; ***C:*** John Tarver; ***M:*** Steve London. **VIDEO**

Shallow Hal 🦴🦴 **2001 (PG-13)** Dumpy loser Hal (Black), along with buddy Mauricio (Alexander), will only go after supermodel-perfect women (with predictable results), until self-help guru Tony Robbins hypnotizes him into seeing the inner beauty of the women he encounters. This leads him to meet and pursue Rosemary (Paltrow), who he sees as the physical ideal, but the rest of the world knows to be 300 pounds. The Farrellys try to have it both ways, making fat jokes while projecting the message that appearance shouldn't matter. They're only moderately and intermittently successful. Paltrow does a good job of showing Rosemary's wariness and self-acceptance, while Black at times seems to be trying a little too hard. **114m/C; VHS, DVD, Blu-Ray, UMD.** Jack Black; Gwyneth Paltrow; Jason Alexander; Joe (Johnny) Viterelli; Bruce McGill; Susan Ward; Rene Kirby; Tony Robbins; Zen Gesner; Brooke Burns; Rob Moran; Nan Martin; ***D:*** Bobby Farrelly; Peter Farrelly; ***W:*** Bobby Farrelly; Peter Farrelly; Sean Moynihan; ***C:*** Russell Carpenter.

The Shallows 🦴🦴🦴 **2016 (PG-13)** Director Collet-Serra proves that a great summer blockbuster need not be complex to be tense. His movie is gloriously simple, playing off the Man vs. Nature theme that has been a staple of storytelling since pen was put to paper. In this case, it's Surfer vs. Shark. The former is played by a spirited Lively, giving a physical, fearless performance as Nancy, a woman surfing on a secluded beach when she's attacked by a great white shark. She's stranded on a rock—only 200 yards from shore but unable to get to safety. It's tense, clever and fun. **86m/C; DVD, Blu-Ray.** Blake Lively; Oscar Jaenada; Brett Cullen; Sedona Legge; Janelle Bailey; ***D:*** Jaume Collet-Serra; ***W:*** Anthony Jaswinski; ***C:*** Flavio Martinez Labiano; ***M:*** Marco Beltrami.

Shame 🦴🦴🦴 1/2 *The Intruder; I Hate Your Guts; The Stranger* **1961** Strangely unsuccessful low-budget Corman effort, starring pre-"Star Trek" Shatner as a freelance bigot who travels around Missouri stirring up opposition to desegregation. Moralistic and topical but still powerful. Adapted from the equally excellent novel by Charles Beaumont. Uses location filming superbly to render a sense of everydayness and authenticity. **84m/B; VHS, DVD.** William Shatner; Frank Maxwell; Jeanne Cooper; Robert Emhardt; Leo Gordon; Charles Beaumont; Beverly Lunsford; William F. Nolan; George Clayton Johnson; ***D:*** Roger Corman; ***W:*** Charles Beaumont; ***C:*** Taylor Byars; ***M:*** Herman Stein.

The Shame 🦴🦴🦴 1/2 **1968 (R)** A Bergman masterpiece focusing on the struggle for dignity in the midst of war. Married concert musicians Ullmann and von Sydow flee a bloody civil war for a small island off their country's coast. Inevitably, the carnage reaches them and their lives become a struggle to endure and retain a small measure of civilized behavior as chaos overtakes them. Deeply despairing and brilliantly acted. In Swedish with English subtitles. **103m/C; VHS, DVD, Blu-Ray.** *SW* Max von Sydow; Liv Ullmann; Gunnar Bjornstrand; Sigge Furst; Birgitta Valberg; Hans Alfredson; Ingvar Kjellson; ***D:*** Ingmar Bergman; ***W:*** Ingmar Bergman; ***C:*** Sven Nykvist. Natl. Soc. Film Critics '68: Actress (Ullmann), Director (Bergman), Film.

Shame 🦴🦴🦴 **2011 (NC-17)** New Yorker Brandon (a convincing Fassbender) is a sex addict who has kept his need for porn, one-night stands, and other illicit behavior secret from his colleagues, friends, and family, including younger, estranged sister Sissy (Mulligan), who shatters his carefully-constructed world with a weekend visit. Absent from his world is love or even any real pleasure or relief from his sexual encounters. Meanwhile Sissy suffers but in the opposite extreme—she is high-strung and desperate for love but is haunted by her own demons. Expertly shot, director McQueen uses the pavement and glass of New York City in captivating ways. **101m/C; DVD, Blu-Ray.** *UK* Michael Fassbender; Carey Mulligan; James Badge Dale; Nicole Beharie; ***D:*** Steve McQueen; ***W:*** Steve McQueen; Abi Morgan; ***C:*** Sean Bobbitt; ***M:*** Harry Escott.

Shameless 🦴🦴 *Mad Dogs and Englishmen* **1994 (R)** Wealthy Antonia Dyer (Hurley) is the self-centered, drug addict daughter of aristocrat Sir Harry Dyer (Treves). Her dealer is upper-class Tony Vernon-Smith (Brett), who's involved with Sandy (Delamere), the daughter of corrupt narcotics cop Stringer (Ackland). Stringer discovers the two girls know each other and irrationally blames Antonia for his daughter's heroin habit. Meanwhile, American student Mike (Howell) has been trying to get girlfriend Antonia off the drugs. Hurley's properly snooty and manipulative while Howell seems out-of-place and uncomfortable. **99m/C; VHS, DVD.** *GB* Elizabeth Hurley; C. Thomas Howell; Joss Ackland; Jeremy Brett; Frederick Treves; Claire Bloom; Louise Delamere; Chris(topher) Adamson; ***D:*** Henry Cole; ***W:*** Tim Sewell; ***C:*** John Peters; ***M:*** Barrie Guard.

Shampoo 🦴🦴 1/2 **1975 (R)** A satire of morals (and lack thereof) set in Southern California, concerning a successful hairdresser (Beatty) and the many women in his life. A notable scene with Julie Christie is set at a 1968 presidential election-night gathering. Fisher's screen debut, only one year before "Star Wars" made her famous. Has a healthy glow in places and a perky bounce, but too many split ends. **112m/C; VHS, DVD, Blu-Ray.** Warren Beatty; Julie Christie; Goldie Hawn; Jack Warden; Lee Grant; Tony Bill; Carrie Fisher; William Castle; Howard Hesseman; ***D:*** Hal Ashby; ***W:*** Warren Beatty; Robert Towne; ***M:*** John Barry. Oscars '75: Support. Actress (Grant); Natl. Soc. Film Critics '75: Screenplay; Writers Guild '75: Orig. Screenplay.

Shamus 🦴🦴 **1973 (PG)** Private dick Reynolds investigates a smuggling ring, beds a sultry woman, gets in lotsa fights. Classic Burt vehicle meant as a send-up. Unoriginal but fun. **91m/C; VHS, DVD.** Burt Reynolds; Dyan Cannon; John P. Ryan; ***D:*** Buzz Kulik; ***W:*** Barry Beckerman; ***M:*** Jerry Goldsmith.

Shane 🦴🦴🦴🦴 **1953** A retired gunfighter, now a drifter, comes to the aid of a homestead family threatened by a land baron and his hired gun. Ladd is the mystery man who becomes the idol of the family's young son. Classic, flawless Western. Pulitzer prize-winning western novelist A.B. Guthrie Jr. adapted from the novel by Jack Schaefer. Long and stately; worth savoring. **117m/C; VHS, DVD, Blu-Ray.** Alan Ladd; Jean Arthur; Van Heflin; Brandon de Wilde; Jack Palance; Ben Johnson; Elisha Cook, Jr.; Edgar Buchanan; Emile Meyer; ***D:*** George Stevens; ***W:*** Jack Sher; ***C:*** Loyal Griggs; ***M:*** Victor Young. Oscars '53: Color Cinematog.; AFI '98: Top 100; Natl. Bd. of Review '53: Director (Stevens); Natl. Film Reg. '93.

Shanghai 🦴🦴🦴 **2009 (R)** American expat Paul Soames returns to Japanese-occupied Shanghai four months before Pearl Harbor to investigate the murder of a friend. Well-cast, solid whodunit that requires attention to plot, with shifting allegiances and betrayals. **105m/C; DVD, Blu-Ray.** John Cusack; Jeffrey Dean Morgan; Gong Li; Daniel Lapaine; Chow Yun-Fat; Nicholas (Nick) Rowe; Franka Potente; David Morse; Ken(saku) Watanabe; Hugh Bonneville; ***D:*** Mikael Hafstrom; ***W:*** Hossein Amini; ***C:*** Benoit Delhomme; ***M:*** Gabriel Yared.

Shanghai Chest 🦴 **1948** In the 41st film in the series, three murders by snakebite and a dead man's fingerprints at each crime scene bring in Charlie Chan (Winters) to unravel the mystery and catch the killer. **65m/B; DVD.** Roland Winters; Victor Sen Yung; Mantan Moreland; John Alvin; Tim Ryan; ***D:*** William Beaudine; ***W:*** Scott Darling; Samuel Newman; ***C:*** William Sickner.

Shanghai Express 🦴🦴🦴 1/2 **1932** Dietrich is at her most alluring in this mystical and exotic story that made legends out of both star and director. Dietrich plays Shanghai Lily, a woman of objectionable reputation, who has a reunion of sorts with ex-lover Brook aboard a slow-moving train through China. Remade as "Peking Express." Based on a story by Harry Hervey. **80m/B; DVD, Blu-Ray.** Marlene Dietrich; Clive Brook; Anna May Wong; Warner Oland; Eugene Pallette; Lawrence Grant; Louise Closser Hale; ***D:*** Josef von Sternberg; ***W:*** Jules Furthman; ***C:*** Lee Garmes. Oscars '32: Cinematog.

Shanghai Express 🦴🦴 *Foo gwai lit che; Fu gui lie che; Millionaire's Express; Noble's Express* **1986 (PG-13)** Multi-genre slapstick comedy pitting various would-be thieves, con men, and wild west style bandits against the cops, a train full of millionaires, a goofy outlaw, and Japanese Samurai. Much of the humor will be lost on Western audiences due to a poorly translated script, but for fans of HK cinema it is one of the few films starring a cast composed almost entirely of famous HK actors (being rounded out with foreign talent who would later become more well-known themselves). **110m/C; DVD.** *CH* Yasuaki Kurata; Baio Yeun; Sammo Hung Kam-Bo; Rosamund Kwan; ***D:*** Sammo Hung Kam-Bo; ***W:*** Sammo Hung Kam-Bo; ***C:*** Arthur Wong; ***M:*** Anders Nelsson.

The Shanghai Gesture 🦴🦴 1/2 **1942** A wildly baroque, subversive melodrama. An English financier tries to close a gambling den, only to be blackmailed by the female proprietor—who tells him not only is the man's daughter heavily indebted to her, but that she is the wife he abandoned long ago. Based on a notorious Broadway play. Von Sternberg had to make numerous changes to the script in order to get it past the Hays censors; the director's final Hollywood work, and worthy of his oeuvre, but oddly unsatisfying. **97m/B; VHS, DVD.** Walter Huston; Gene Tierney; Victor Mature; Ona Munson; Albert Bassermann; Eric Blore; Maria Ouspenskaya; Phyllis Brooks; Mike Mazurki; ***D:*** Josef von Sternberg; ***W:*** Josef von Sternberg; Jules Furthman; Geza Herczeg; Karl Vollmoller; ***C:*** Paul Ivano; ***M:*** Richard Hageman.

Shanghai Kiss **2007** Twenty-something Liam Liu (Leung) is a struggling Chinese-American actor in L.A. who befriends 16-year-old high school genius Adelaide (Panettiere). Imagine the complications when romance starts lurking, and Liam can't quite forget temptation when he decides to move to Shanghai after inheriting his grandmother's house. **106m/C; DVD.** Ken Leung; Hayden Panettiere; Kelly Hu; Joel David Moore; James Hong; Timothy Bottoms; ***D:*** Kern Konwiser; David Ren; ***W:*** David Ren; ***C:*** Alexander Buono; ***M:*** David Kitay. **VIDEO**

Shanghai Knights ½ **2003 (PG-13)** Chon Wang (Chan) and Roy (Wilson) team up again when Wang's father is killed while guarding the Imperial Seal. Wang's sister Li (Fann) has witnessed the crime and followed the culprit to London, where the duo also converge. There they find a plot by frustrated royal heirs Rathbone (Gillen) and Wu Chan (Yen) to overthrow the British and Chinese thrones. Chan and Wilson still have their great chemistry, and the script gives them plenty of opportunities to show it. Chan choreographs the fight scenes like numbers in a musical to excellent effect, paying homage to "Singin' in the Rain" as well as some of his influences such as the Keystone Kops, Harold Lloyd, Abbott and Costello, and Charlie Chaplin. Victorian-era cultural references are fun to catalogue as well. **107m/C; VHS, DVD, Blu-Ray.** Jackie Chan; Owen Wilson; Aidan Gillen; Fann Wong; Donnie Yen; Gemma Jones; Kim Chan; Aaron Taylor-Johnson; Thomas (Tom) Fisher; Oliver Cotton; ***D:*** David Dobkin; ***W:*** Alfred Gough; Miles Millar; ***C:*** Adrian Biddle; ***M:*** Randy Edelman.

Shanghai Noon ½ **2000 (PG-13)** Goofy, good-natured, western action/comedy finds Chinese imperial guard Chon Wang (Chan) in trouble for not preventing Princess Pei Pei (Liu) from running off to America (circa 1880) with her American tutor (Connery). But it all turns out to be a kidnapping scheme and Wang winds up in Nevada, helping to deliver the ransom gold. Through some unlikely events, Wang hooks up with talkative, unsuccessful outlaw Roy O'Bannon (Wilson), learns some of the west's wilder ways, and the buds set out to rescue the damsel, who's no shrinking flower herself. Chan and Wilson are both throughly ingratiating and you've got the Chan stunts to look forward to as well. **110m/C; VHS, DVD, Blu-Ray.** Jackie Chan; Lucy Liu; Owen Wilson; Roger Yuan; Xander Berkeley; Jason Connery; Henry O; Walton Goggins; Russ Badger; Rafael Baez; Brandon Merrill; ***D:*** Tom Dey; ***W:*** Alfred Gough; Miles Millar; ***C:*** Dan(iel) Mindel; ***M:*** Randy Edelman.

Shanghai Surprise ½ **1986 (PG-13)** Tie salesman Penn and missionary Madonna (yeah, right) are better than you'd think, and the story (of opium smuggling in China in the '30s) is intrepid and wildly fun, but indifferently directed and unsure of itself. Executive producer George Harrison wrote the songs and has a cameo. **90m/C; VHS, DVD.** Sean Penn; Madonna; Paul Freeman; Richard Griffiths; ***Cameo(s):*** George Harrison; ***D:*** Jim (James) Goddard; ***W:*** Robert Bentley; ***M:*** George Harrison; Michael Kamen. Golden Raspberries '86: Worst Actress (Madonna).

Shanghai Triad ½ *Yao a Yao Yao Dao Waipo Qiao* **1995 (R)** Seventh collaboration of director Yimou and star Li takes place in violent crime dynasty of 1930s Shanghai. Here, eight days are seen through the eyes of a young boy (Cuihua) initiated into the Triad to be the lackey of the mob boss's arrogant mistress (Li). The trio and some trusty associates flee to the country after things heat up with a rival mob. Yimou subtly distinguishes the dichotomy between the jaded criminals and the naive youth with the move from the city to the country and his use of color and tone while avoiding cliche. Plot twists are fresh and technical aspects impeccable. Chinese with subtitles. **108m/C; VHS, DVD.** *FR CH* Gong Li; Baotian Li; Xuejian Li; Shun Chun Shusheng; Wang Xiaoxiao Cuihua; Jiang Baoying; ***D:*** Yimou Zhang; ***W:*** Bi Feiyu; ***C:*** Lu Yue; ***M:*** Zhang Guangtain.

Shank ½ **2009** Suffers from inexperience both in front of and behind the camera (it's Pearce's directorial debut) but has some powerful moments. Eighteen-year-old Bristol gang member Cal is immersed in a world of drugs, violence, and anonymous sex as he tries to keep secret the fact that he is gay and deeply attracted to his best mate Jonno. Would-be leader Nessa is suspicious, especially when Cal is disgusted by an attempted gay bashing and allows French exchange student Olivier to escape. Incensed by Cal's betrayal, Nessa goads Jonno into a violent revenge. **89m/C; DVD.** *GB* Wayne Virgo; Marc Laurent; Tom Bott; Alice Payne; Garry Summers; ***D:*** Simon Pearce; ***W:*** Christian Martin; Darren Flaxstone; ***C:*** Simon Pearce; ***M:*** Bernaby Taylor.

Shanks **1974 (PG)** An eccentric professor (played by world famous Marcel Marceau) discovers the secret of animating dead bodies and controlling them like puppets. Upon his death his secrets pass to his deaf-mute assistant (also played by Marcel Marceau) who decides it's high time he makes life interesting for the people who have wronged him. **94m/C; DVD, Blu-Ray, Streaming.** Marcel Marceau; Tsilla Chelton; Philippe Clay; Cindy Eilbacher; Larry Bishop; ***D:*** William Castle; ***W:*** Ranald Graham; ***C:*** Joseph Biroc; ***M:*** Alex North. **VIDEO**

Shannon's Rainbow *Amazing Racer* **2009 (PG)** A family drama about finding unexpected bonds after a big loss. When Shannon Greene's (Michelle) father dies unexpectedly, she believes she is alone in the world and focuses on her own strong feelings. The family doctor soon tells Shannon that her father kept a big secret: Shannon's mother Christine (Forlani) is alive and well. Shannon's world is transformed when she meets her mother and Max, a horse trainer (Gossett Jr.). Shannon finds that caring for and racing horses helps her heal, find new friendships, and a new way of life. **92m/C; DVD, Streaming, Download.** Julianne Michelle; Claire Forlani; Jason Gedrick; Michael Madsen; Louis Gossett, Jr.; ***D:*** Frank E. Johnson; ***W:*** Linda Morris; John Mowod; Larry Richert; ***C:*** Dean Cundey; ***M:*** Charles David Denler.

Shanty Tramp **1967** Small-town tramp puts the moves on an evangelist, a motorcycle gang, and a young black man, who risks his life trying to save her from her loose morals. Another cheesy flick made for the drive-in crowd. **72m/B; VHS, DVD.** Lee Holland; Bill Rogers; Lawrence Tobin; ***D:*** Joseph Prieto. **TV**

Shaolin & Wu Tang *Shaolin Wu Tang; Shao Lin yu Wu Dang; Shaolin Temple, Part II* **1981** Often considered an early kung fu classic, the only American version of this film has fairly bad dubbing along with subtitles translated from Chinese that don't match the dubbed dialogue, leading to moments of unintended fun. A Manchu prince sets the Shaolin and Wu Tang clans against one another to learn their secrets, and two friends turn against each other as they belong to opposite sides. Eventually making up, they team up to take on the Prince in revenge. **90m/C; DVD.** *CH* Shen Chan; Adam Cheng; Hoi-Shan Kwan; Chia Hui Liu; Elvis Tsui; Lung-Wai Wang; Idy Chan; Hoi San Lee.

Shaolin Soccer ½ *Siulam Chukkau; Siu lam juk kau* **2001 (PG-13)** Wacky action-comedy about Sing (Chow), a kung fu expert and Shaolin monk, playing on a soccer team with other monks vying for Hong Kong's national championship against "Team Evil." Went on to become the highest-grossing film in Hong Kong's history. In Cantonese, with English subtitles. **87m/C; DVD, UMD.** Stephen (Chiau) Chow; Man-Tat Ng; Cecilia Cheung; Vicki Zhao; Yin (Patrick) Tse; ***D:*** Stephen (Chiau) Chow; ***W:*** Stephen (Chiau) Chow; Kan-Cheung (Sammy) Tsang; ***C:*** Ting Wo Kwong; Pak-huen Kwen; ***M:*** Lowell Lo; Raymond Wong.

The Shape of Things **2003 (R)** LaBute is back to his own skewed view of the world, taken from his 2001 play. Nebbishy Adam (Rudd) works as a guard at a college art museum. Evelyn (Weisz) is the art student who bedazzles him, and she begins to make him over into someone desirable, which angers his chauvinistic best friend Philip (Weller). But the "new" Adam sparks feelings in Philip's fiancee Jenny (Mol), who was once the object of Adam's unrequited affection. Never subtle, LaBute's intention to leave no cruelty unexplored is blatant and wears quickly. Despite the best efforts of the actors involved, the film's stage origins and LaBute's obvious direction combine to lessen the film's impact. **96m/C; VHS, DVD.** Paul Rudd; Rachel Weisz; Gretchen Mol; Frederick Weller; ***D:*** Neil LaBute; ***W:*** Neil LaBute; ***C:*** James L. Carter; ***M:*** Elvis Costello.

The Shape of Water **2017 (R)** A beautiful exploration of loneliness and love told through a fairy tale conceived by inventive filmmaker Guillermo del Toro. Working as a janitor in a Baltimore corporation in 1962, mute Elisa (Hawkins) spends her life with the talkative coworker Zelda (Spencer) and bonding with her gay neighbor Giles (Jenkins). Elisa finds an unexpected connection when Amphibian Man (Jones), a creature from the Amazon, is brought to the facility by the government. Though guarded by the sadistic Strickland (Shannon), Elisa finds ways to communicate with the creature and goes to great lengths to save him when his life is threatened. A richly envisioned dream. **123m/C; DVD, Blu-Ray.** Sally Hawkins; Michael Shannon; Richard Jenkins; Octavia Spencer; Michael Stuhlbarg; ***D:*** Guillermo del Toro; ***W:*** Guillermo del Toro; Vanessa Taylor; ***C:*** Dan Laustsen; ***M:*** Alexandre Desplat. Oscars '17: Director (del Toro), Film, Orig. Score, Production Design; British Acad. '17: Director, Director (del Toro), Orig. Score, Production Design; Directors Guild '17: Director (del Toro); Golden Globes '18: Director (del Toro), Orig. Score.

Shark! ½ *Man-Eater; Un Arma de Dos Filos* **1968 (PG)** American gun smuggler Reynolds, stranded in a tiny seaport in Africa, joins the crew of a marine biologist's boat. He soon discovers the boat's owner and his wife are trying to retrieve gold bullion that lies deep in shark-infested waters. Typical Reynoldsian action-infested dumbness. Like "Twilight Zone: The Movie," earned notoriety because of on-location tragedy: a stunt diver really was killed by a shark. Edited without the consent of Fuller, who disowned it. **92m/C; VHS, DVD, Blu-Ray.** Burt Reynolds; Barry Sullivan; Arthur Kennedy; ***D:*** Samuel Fuller; ***W:*** Samuel Fuller.

Shark Attack ½ **1999 (R)** A marine biologist investigates a rash of shark attacks terrorizing an African fishing village that have claimed the life of a friend. **95m/C; VHS, DVD.** *SA* Casper Van Dien; Ernie Hudson; Bentley Mitchum; Jenny (Jennifer) McShane; ***D:*** Bob Misiorowski; ***W:*** Scott Devine; William Hooke; ***C:*** Lawrence Sher. **VIDEO**

Shark Attack 2 ½ **2000 (R)** Biological experiment on shark goes awry causing a mutant to go on a particularly nasty tear. Yeah, some shark hunters go after the beastie but you know they're just appetizers. **93m/C; VHS, DVD.** Nikita Ager; Daniel Alexander; Thorsten Kaye; Danny Kei; ***D:*** David Worth; Yossi Wein; ***W:*** William Hooke; Scott Devine; ***M:*** Mark Morgan. **VIDEO**

Shark Attack 3: Megalodon **2002 (R)** An amusing goof of a killer sea critter flick. A company lying cable on the ocean floor wakes up a prehistoric Megalodon shark that decides to snack on vacationers at a nearby ocean resort. This is bad for business, so resort minion Ben (Barrowman) and paleontologist Cataline (McShane) hunt the beastie down. And then find out they've only killed a baby. And boy is mama mad! **94m/C; VHS, DVD.** John Barrowman; Jenny (Jennifer) McShane; Ryan Cutrona; George Stanchev; ***D:*** David Worth; ***W:*** Scott Devine; William Hooke; ***C:*** David Worth; ***M:*** Bill Wandel. **VIDEO**

Shark Hunter *Guardians of the Deep; Il Cacciatore di Squali* **1979** Shark hunter gets ensnared in the mob's net off the Mexican coast as they race for a cache of sunken millions. The usual garden-variety B-grade adventure. **95m/C; VHS, DVD.** *IT SP* Franco Nero; Jorge Luke; Mike Forrest; Werner Pochath; ***D:*** Enzo G. Castellari; ***W:*** Tito Carpi; ***C:*** R(aul) P. Cubero; ***M:*** Guido de Angelis; Maurizio de Angelis.

Shark Island *Shark Week* **2012** The Asylum continues it's longstanding tradition of shark movies with this tribute to the Discovery Channel. A pair of married, rich psychopaths kidnaps a group and puts them on an island, trapping them with land mines and sharks. **90m/C; DVD, Blu-Ray.** Yancy Butler; Patrick Bergin; Joshua Michael Allen; Bart Baggett; Erin Coker; ***D:*** Christopher Ray; ***W:*** Liz Adams; H. Perry Horton; ***C:*** Pedja Radenkovic; ***M:*** Chris Ridenhour. **CABLE**

Shark Night 3D **2011 (PG-13)** Sharks make sushi of girls in revealing swimwear and their male counterparts in this throwaway horror flick. Sara invites her college friends to her family's Louisiana Gulf Lake cabin for the weekend. Only they don't realize that the saltwater lake has been stocked with sharks until someone gets chomped. Then the comely crew is forced back into the water because of some local snuff-filmmaking rednecks. Hey, it's as good an explanation as any. But since the pic is also rated PG-13, it's missing the necessary gore and crudeness that could at least make it campy and watchable. **95m/C; DVD, Blu-Ray.** Sara Paxton; Alyssa Diaz; Dustin Milligan; Chris Carmack; Joel David Moore; Chris Zylka; Katharine McPhee; Sinqua Walls; Joshua Leonard; Donal Louge; ***D:*** Daniel R. Ellis; ***W:*** Jesse Studenberg; William Hayes; ***C:*** Gary Capo; ***M:*** Graeme Revell.

Shark Swarm ½ **2008** An over-extended TV mini without enough shark action. Greedy industrialist Hamilton Lux (Assante) has been dumping toxins into the waters of Full Moon Bay in an effort to destroy the local fishing industry so he can buy property cheap for his planned resort. It's discovered that the local shark population of Great Whites have mutated and are even deadlier since they now hunt in packs—killing anything (or anyone) occupying their waters. **164m/C; DVD.** John Schneider; Armand Assante; Daryl Hannah; Roark Critchlow; Heather McComb; F. Murray Abraham; John Enos; ***D:*** James A. Contner; ***W:*** David Rosiak; Matthew Chernov; ***C:*** Dane Peterson; ***M:*** Nathan Furst. **TV**

Shark Tale ½ **2004 (PG)** This animated underwater comedy has the faint smell of dead fish clinging to it—probably because it tries too hard. Boastful guppy Oscar (Smith) works at the mob-fronted Whale Wash and is in trouble with his boss (Scorsese), who thinks the kid should be taught a lesson. Teaching lessons is also on the mind of shark mob boss Lino (De Niro), who wants son Frankie (Imperioli) to straighten out his younger bro, Lenny (Black), a sweet schnook who's gone vegetarian. Oscar takes the credit when Frankie accidentally gets killed and then must defend his reputation as a sharkslayer, aided by a reluctant Lenny. Longtime collaborators De Niro and Scorsese have a blast spoofing wiseguys but a lot of the humor will only be understood by movie-loving adults and may prove sleep-inducing to the younger set. **92m/C; VHS, DVD, Blu-Ray.** ***V:*** Will Smith; Robert De Niro; Renée Zellweger; Jack Black; Angelina Jolie; Martin Scorsese; Peter Falk; Michael Imperioli; Vincent Pastore; Doug E. Doug; Ziggy Marley; Katie Couric; Jenifer Lewis; Lenny Venito; Phil LaMarr; ***D:*** Victoria Jenson; Bibo Bergeron; Rob Letterman; ***W:*** Michael J. Wilson; Rob Letterman; ***M:*** Hans Zimmer.

Sharknado **2013** This Syfy Channel creature feature is mind-boggling ridiculous and deliberately bad, needing to be watched as the cheesefest of crazy it is. A freak tornado in the Pacific sucks up sharks--yes, sharks!--and then rips through California, flooding the L.A. streets and depositing the man-eaters to do their worst. Of course, the waterspout continues onward, sucking up more unfortunates to become chum. But you need some humans to root for so beach bar owner Fin (Ziering) must rescue his family--and busload of stranded schoolchildren!--by getting out his trusty chainsaw to make him some shark sushi! **90m/C; DVD, Blu-Ray.** Ian Ziering; Tara Reid; John Heard; Cassie Scerbo; Jaason Simmons; Chuck Hittinger; ***D:*** Anthony C. Ferrante; ***W:*** Thunder Levin; ***C:*** Ben Demaree; ***M:*** Ramin Kousha. **CABLE**

Sharknado 2: The Second One 🦴🦴 **2014** It's so nice when the Syfy Channel doesn't even presume to have the plot make sense, knowing viewers are in it for the pure cheese effect. The action moves to New York where a Category 7 hurricane hits the city, bringing those pesky sharks along for the ride, before tornadoes threaten what's left of the Big Apple. April, Fin, and his trusty chainsaw get in on the action. **90m/C; DVD, Blu-Ray.** Ian Ziering; Tara Reid; Vivica A. Fox; Kari Wuhrer; Mark McGrath; Judah Friedlander; ***D:*** Anthony C. Ferrante; ***W:*** Thunder Levin; ***C:*** Ben Demaree; ***M:*** Chris Ridenhour. **CABLE**

Sharknado 3: Oh Hell No! 🦴🦴 **2015** Once again Fin (Ian Ziering) must save the day when a series of Sharknadoes hit the East Coast, starting in Washington and winding their way toward Orlando. It follows the successful formula of the first two movies, but cranks the level of absurdity a little too high. Although, you probably aren't watching this for anything but the absurdity anyway. **90m/C; DVD, Blu-Ray, Streaming.** Ian Ziering; Tara Reid; Cassandra Scerbo; David Hasselhoff; Bo Derek; ***D:*** Anthony C. Ferrante; ***W:*** Thunder Levin; ***C:*** Ben Demaree; Laura Beth Love; Scott Wheeler; ***M:*** Chris(topher) Cano; Chris Ridenhour. **CABLE**

Sharknado: The 4th Awakens 🦴 ½ **2016** Weather control technology has rendered Sharknadoes an impossibility, or at least it has until the moment Fin (Ian Ziering) and his family go on vacation. Sadly, this film has lost much of the goofy charm of previous films, and relies on repeating old jokes that have begun to wear thin. **90m/C; DVD, Blu-Ray, Streaming.** Ian Ziering; Tara Reid; David Hasselhoff; Ryan Newman; Gary Busey; ***D:*** Anthony C. Ferrante; ***W:*** Thunder Levin; ***C:*** Laura Beth Love; ***M:*** Chris(topher) Cano; Chris Ridenhour. **CABLE**

Sharktopus 🦴 **2010** Typically silly, low-budget creature feature from the Syfy Channel. Genetic scientist Nathan Sands (Roberts) creates a shark/octopus hybrid as a weapon for the Navy. The beastie gets loose and heads for the sun, sea, and food supply of Puerto Vallarta, Mexico, where it proceeds to munch on bikini babes, spring break tourists, and anyone else who ventures into the water. Sands hires mercenary Andy Flynn (Bursin) to capture his creature—preferably alive. Produced by Roger Corman, who also has a cameo. **89m/C; DVD, Blu-Ray.** Eric Roberts; Sara Malakul Lane; Hector Jimenez; Kerem Bursin; Brent Huff; Ralph Garman; Shandi Finnessey; ***D:*** Declan O'Brien; ***W:*** Mike MacLean; ***M:*** Tom Hiel. **CABLE**

Sharky's Machine 🦴🦴 ½ **1981 (R)** A tough undercover cop (Reynolds) is hot on the trail of a crooked crime czar. Meanwhile he falls for a high-priced hooker. Well done but overdone action, with much violence. Based on the William Diehl novel. **119m/C; VHS, DVD, Blu-Ray.** Burt Reynolds; Rachel Ward; Vittorio Gassman; Brian Keith; Charles Durning; Bernie Casey; Richard Libertini; Henry Silva; John Fiedler; Earl Holliman; ***D:*** Burt Reynolds; ***W:*** Gerald Di Pego; ***C:*** William A. Fraker.

Sharpay's Fabulous Adventure 🦴🦴 ½ **2011 (G)** For any tweener enamored with "High School Musical," it's diva Sharpay Evans' (Tisdale) turn in the spotlight. Sharpay thinks she's getting her big break when a talent scout spots her and dog Boi performing at a charity function. She goes to New York for a Broadway audition only to find out the role is for a dog and Boi has competition from a pooch named Countess. Further mishaps occur but Sharpay has a manly shoulder to lean on when she's befriended by film student Peyton (Leverett). **89m/C; DVD, Blu-Ray.** Ashley Tisdale; Austin Butler; Cameron Goodman; Bradley Steven Perry; Jessica Tuck; Jack Plotnick; Alec Mapa; ***D:*** Michael Lembeck; ***W:*** Robert Horn; ***C:*** Ousama Rawi; ***M:*** George S. Clinton. **VIDEO**

Sharpe's Battle 🦴🦴 ½ **1994** Sharpe (Bean) must prepare the Royal Irish company, led by Lord Kiely (Durr) and used to only ceremonial duties, for their first battle. Meanwhile, Kiely's wife (Byrne) goes to Sharpe for help with a personal matter and there's more trouble with the French. Based on the novel by Bernard Cornwell; made for British TV. **100m/C; VHS, DVD, Blu-Ray.** ***GB*** Sean Bean; Daragh O'Malley; Hugh Fraser; Jason Durr; Allie Byrne; ***D:*** Tom Clegg; ***W:*** Russell Lewis. **TV**

Sharpe's Challenge 🦴🦴 ½ **2006** After Waterloo, Richard Sharpe (Bean) is dispatched to India because a local Maharaja is threatening British interests. Things worsen when Sharpe discovers best friend Harper (O'Malley) is missing, a general's daughter (Brown) has been kidnapped, and the beautiful but scheming Madhuvanthi (Lakshmi) wants to use Richard to further her own ambitions. Filmed in Rajasthan, India; based on the Bernard Cornwell novels. The first new TV Sharpe adventure since 1997. **136m/C; DVD, Blu-Ray.** ***GB*** Sean Bean; Padma Lakshmi; Toby Stephens; Daragh O'Malley; Lucy Brown; Hugh Fraser; Michael Cochrane; Peter Symonds; Karan Panthaky; ***D:*** Tom Clegg; ***W:*** Russell Lewis. **TV**

Sharpe's Company 🦴🦴 ½ **1994** Sharpe (Bean) sets out to rescue Spanish lover Teresa (Serna) and his infant daughter, trapped in the French-held city of Badajoz, which is about to be stormed by British troops. To make matters worse, Sharpe must also deal with the machinations of underhanded madman Sergeant Obadiah Hakeswill (Postlethwaite), an old enemy with a grudge to settle. Based on the novel by Bernard Cornwell; made for British TV. **100m/C; VHS, DVD, Blu-Ray.** ***GB*** Sean Bean; Assumpta Serna; Daragh O'Malley; Pete Postlethwaite; Hugh Fraser; Clive Francis; Louise Germaine; ***D:*** Tom Clegg; ***W:*** Charles Wood. **TV**

Sharpe's Eagle 🦴🦴 ½ **1993** Sharpe (Bean) and his chosen band of sharpshooters are once again in the thick of battle against Napoleon's troops but this time they have the misfortune to be led by the imbecilic Sir Henry Simmerson (Cochrane). Thanks to Simmerson's cowardice, the regimental colors are captured and a heroic officer Sharpe admires is killed. Setting out for revenge, Sharpe is determined to capture the French mascot, a carved golden eagle carried into battle, and settle some personal scores. Based on the novel by Bernard Cornwell; made for British TV. **100m/C; VHS, DVD, Blu-Ray.** ***GB*** Sean Bean; Assumpta Serna; Brian Cox; David Troughton; Daragh O'Malley; Michael Cochrane; Katia Caballero; ***D:*** Tom Clegg; ***W:*** Eoghan Harris; ***C:*** Ivan Strasburg; ***M:*** Dominic Muldowney. **TV**

Sharpe's Enemy 🦴🦴 ½ **1994** Sharpe (Bean) is sent to a mountain stronghold, held by a band of deserters, to ransom Isabella (Hurley), the bride of English colonel, Sir Augustus Farthingdale (Child). But the evil Hakeswill (Postlethwaite) is leading the criminals and he refuses to make things easy for our hero'nor will the French troops leave the English soldiers in peace. Based on the novel by Bernard Cornwell; made for British TV. **100m/C; VHS, DVD, Blu-Ray.** ***GB*** Sean Bean; Assumpta Serna; Pete Postlethwaite; Daragh O'Malley; Hugh Fraser; Elizabeth Hurley; Michael Byrne; Jeremy Child; Nicholas (Nick) Rowe; ***D:*** Tom Clegg; ***W:*** Eoghan Harris. **TV**

Sharpe's Gold 🦴🦴 ½ **1994** Circa 1813 and Richard Sharpe (Bean) has now been promoted to Major—still leading his band of renegade sharpshooters. This time they're assigned to trade rifles for deserters held by the partisans and search for hidden Aztec gold, as Wellington (Fraser) prepares to push on into France. Sharpe must also protect Wellington's cousin Bess (Linehan) and her daughter Ellie (Ashbourne) as they search for Bess' missing husband. Based on the novel by Bernard Cornwell; made for British TV. **100m/C; VHS, DVD, Blu-Ray.** ***GB*** Sean Bean; Daragh O'Malley; Hugh Fraser; Rosaleen Linehan; Jayne Ashbourne; Abel Folk; Peter Eyre; ***D:*** Tom Clegg; ***W:*** Nigel Kneale. **TV**

Sharpe's Honour 🦴🦴 ½ **1994** Sharpe (Bean) becomes a pawn of French spy Pierre Ducos when he's forced to cross enemy lines, disguised as a Spanish rebel, in order to defend himself against allegations of dishonor. Sharpe's also unable to resist the attractions of the Marquesa Dorada (Krige), who's also part of Ducos' plan. Based on the novel by Bernard Cornwell; made for British TV. **100m/C; VHS, DVD, Blu-Ray.** ***GB*** Sean Bean; Daragh O'Malley; Alice Krige; Hugh Fraser; Michael Byrne; Ron Cook; ***D:*** Tom Clegg; ***W:*** Colin MacDonald. **TV**

Sharpe's Justice 🦴🦴 ½ **1997** Having cleared his name, Richard Sharpe (Bean) returns to England and is ordered north where he's to command the local militia. But Sharpe soon has to decide whether to support the local gentry or the working class in a time of social unrest. Based on the novel by Bernard Cornwell. **100m/C; VHS, DVD, Blu-Ray.** ***GB*** Sean Bean; Daragh O'Malley; Abigail Cruttenden; Alexis Denisof; Douglas Henshall; Caroline Langrishe; Philip Glenister; ***D:*** Tom Clegg. **TV**

Sharpe's Legend 🦴🦴 ½ **1997** Highlights from the British TV series detailing the life, loves, and career of 19th-century British soldier/hero Richard Sharpe (Bean). Narrated by Rifleman Cooper (Mears). **90m/C; VHS, DVD.** ***GB*** Sean Bean; Michael Mears; ***D:*** Paul Wilmshurst. **TV**

Sharpe's Mission 🦴🦴 ½ **1996** Sharpe (Bean) joins with Colonel Brand (Strong) and his men to blow up an ammunition depot as Wellington continues his invasion of France. But Brand arouses Sharpe's suspicions that the supposedly heroic Colonel is actually a French spy. Based on the novel by Bernard Cornwell. **100m/C; VHS, DVD, Blu-Ray.** ***GB*** Sean Bean; Daragh O'Malley; Hugh Fraser; James Laurenson; Mark Strong; Abigail Cruttenden; ***D:*** Tom Clegg; ***W:*** Eoghan Harris. **TV**

Sharpe's Peril 🦴🦴 ½ **2008** BBC adventure based on the Bernard Cornwell characters. On a last mission, Lt.-Colonel Richard Sharpe (Bean) and Sgt.-Major Patrick Harper (O'Malley) are crossing central India, escorting headstrong Marie-Angelique (Rosen) to meet her fiance. Their convoy encounters bandits, East India Company troops, a massacre, and lots of fighting as they try to survive to return to England. **138m/C; DVD.** Sean Bean; Daragh O'Malley; Velibor Topic; Beatrice Rosen; Steve Speirs; Luke Ward-Wilinson; Pasacal Langdale; Amit Behl; Michael Cochrane; Ulhas Tayde; ***D:*** Tom Clegg; ***W:*** Russell Lewis; ***C:*** Dominic Muldowney; ***M:*** John Tams. **TV**

Sharpe's Regiment 🦴🦴 ½ **1996** Wellington prepares for the invasion of France in June, 1813 but the South Essex batallion needs more men. So Sharpe (Bean) and Harper (O'Malley) are sent back to London for recruits and uncover corruption in high places. Based on the novel by Bernard Cornwell. **100m/C; VHS, DVD, Blu-Ray.** ***GB*** Sean Bean; Daragh O'Malley; Nicholas Farrell; Michael Cochrane; Abigail Cruttenden; Caroline Langrishe; James Laurenson; ***D:*** Tom Clegg; ***W:*** Eoghan Harris. **TV**

Sharpe's Revenge 🦴🦴 ½ **1997** The Penisular War is over but Sharpe (Bean) is accused of stealing Napoleon's treasures by old enemy Ducos. Abandoned by his wife when he's convicted of the crime, Sharpe escapes from prison and crosses postwar France in search of the truth. Based on the novel by Bernard Cornwell. **100m/C; VHS, DVD, Blu-Ray.** ***GB*** Sean Bean; Daragh O'Malley; Abigail Cruttenden; Feodor Atkine; Alexis Denisof; Cecile Paoli; Philip Whitchurch; ***D:*** Tom Clegg; ***W:*** Eoghan Harris. **TV**

Sharpe's Rifles 🦴🦴 ½ **1993** Swashbuckling heroics dominate as the Duke of Wellington's British soldiers battle Napoleon's French forces in the 1809 Penisular War (fought in Spain and Portugal). Common soldier Richard Sharpe (Bean) has just been promoted and given the unenviable task of leading a group of malcontent sharpshooters on a secret mission to aid Britain's Spanish allies. But it's not all hard times for Sharpe since the Spanish commander happens to be a very lovely woman. Adapted from the novel by Bernard Cornwall; made for British TV. **100m/C; VHS, DVD, Blu-Ray.** ***GB*** Sean Bean; Assumpta Serna; Brian Cox; David Troughton; Daragh O'Malley; Julian Fellowes; Timothy Bentinck; Simon Andreu; Michael Mears; John Tams; Jason Salkey; Paul Trussell; ***D:*** Tom Clegg; ***W:*** Eoghan Harris; ***C:*** Ivan Strasburg; ***M:*** Dominic Muldowney. **TV**

Sharpe's Siege 🦴🦴 ½ **1996** In the winter of 1813, Napoleon Bonaparte sends his best spy, Major Ducos (Atkine), to find out where Wellington plans to invade France. The newly married Sharpe (Bean) is forced to leave his ill wife, Jane (Cruttenden), and capture a French fort while preventing Ducos' treachery. Based on the novel by Bernard Cornwell. **100m/C; VHS, DVD, Blu-Ray.** ***GB*** Sean Bean; Daragh O'Malley; Hugh Fraser; Abigail Cruttenden; James Laurenson; Feodor Atkine; ***D:*** Tom Clegg; ***W:*** Eoghan Harris. **TV**

Sharpe's Sword 🦴🦴 ½ **1994** Sharpe's (Bean) sent to protect Wellington's top spy, El Mirador, and finds himself up against Napoleon's top swordsman Colonel Leroux (Fierry). When Sharpe's wounded, it's up to Lass (Mortimer), a young mute convent girl, to save our hero's life. Based on the novel by Bernard Cornwell; made for British TV. **100m/C; VHS, DVD, Blu-Ray.** ***GB*** Sean Bean; Daragh O'Malley; Patrick Fierry; Emily Mortimer; John Kavanagh; ***D:*** Tom Clegg; ***W:*** Eoghan Harris. **TV**

Sharpe's Waterloo 🦴🦴 ½ **1997** Sharpe's (Bean) making a new life with new love Lucille (Paoli) at their French chateau. But when Napoleon returns from exile, Sharpe returns to the army and the Chosen Men to organize a defense before the battle of Waterloo. Based on the novel by Bernard Cornwell. **100m/C; VHS, DVD, Blu-Ray.** ***GB*** Sean Bean; Daragh O'Malley; Hugh Fraser; Cecile Paoli; Alexis Denisof; Paul Bettany; ***D:*** Tom Clegg. **TV**

Sharpshooter 🦴 ½ **2007** Remar's really the only reason to watch this by-the-numbers thriller. Special ops sniper Dillon (Remar) is looking forward to a peaceful retirement. Then his government contact Flick (Van Peebles) persuades him to do one last mission—eliminate a terrorist who's plotting mayhem on U.S. soil. But Dillon soon has second thoughts about the validity of his assignment and wonders just who the true target is. **89m/C; DVD.** James Remar; Mario Van Peebles; Catherine Mary Stewart; Bruce Boxleitner; Al Sapienza; ***D:*** Armand Mastroianni; ***W:*** Steven H. Berman; ***C:*** Dane Peterson; ***M:*** Stephen Graziano. **TV**

Shattered 🦴🦴 **1991 (R)** An architect recovering from a serious automobile accident tries to regain the memory that he has lost. As he begins to put together the pieces of his life, some parts of the puzzle don't quite fit. For example, he recalls his now loving wife's affair as well as his own. He remembers that he hired a private detective to follow his wife and shockingly, he remembers that he once believed his wife had planned to kill him. Are these memories the real thing, or are they all part of some mad, recuperative nightmare? Who knows. **98m/C; VHS, DVD.** Tom Berenger; Bob Hoskins; Greta Scacchi; Joanne Whalley; Corbin Bernsen; Theodore Bikel; ***D:*** Wolfgang Petersen; ***W:*** Wolfgang Petersen.

Shattered 🦴🦴 *Butterfly on a Wheel* **2007 (R)** Neil (Butler) and his wife Abby (Bello) must perform a series of nearly-impossible (and criminal) tasks around Chicago in order to save their young daughter, who's been kidnapped by sociopath Ryan (Brosnan). Implausible and unsubtle (with a twist ending) but that's one cool cast. **95m/C; DVD.** ***CA*** Pierce Brosnan; Gerard Butler; Maria Bello; Claudette Mink; Callum Keith Rennie; Nicholas Lea; Samantha Ferris; ***D:*** Mike Barker; ***W:*** William Morrissey; ***C:*** Ashley Rowe; ***M:*** Robert Duncan.

Shattered City: The Halifax Explosion 🦴🦴 ½ **2003** In 1917, the city of Halifax, Nova Scotia, is a particularly bustling port due to WWI. But on December 6th, the French freighter Mont Blanc, carrying thousands of tons of TNT, collides with a Belgian relief ship in the harbor, causing a devastating explosion that nearly destroys the city and results in thousands of deaths and injuries. The city officials eventually look for someone to blame and harbor pilot Mackey may be the fall guy until Capt. Charlie Collins takes over his defense. Based on a true incident. **181m/C; DVD.** ***CA*** Tamara Hope; Shauna Macdonald; Pete Postlethwaite; Paul Doucet; Graham Greene; Richard Donat; Zachary Bennett; Leon Pownall; Vincent Walsh; Ted Dykstra; ***D:*** Bruce Pittman; ***W:*** Keith Ross Leckie; ***C:*** Rene Ohashi; ***M:*** Christopher Dedrick. **TV**

Shattered Dreams 🦴🦴 ½ **1990** TV movie about domestic violence finds Wagner as the battered wife of a prominent, high-profile government official. Based on a true story. **94m/C; VHS, DVD.** Lindsay Wagner; Michael Nouri; Georgann Johnson; James Karen; ***D:*** Robert Iscove; ***W:*** David Hill; ***C:*** John Beymer; ***M:*** Michael Convertino.

Shattered Glass 2003 (PG-13) Christensen loses the Jedi robes to take on a character lured by a less-mystical dark side. Wunderkind Stephen Glass, a young New Republic journalist, is found to have fabricated 27 of the 41 articles he'd published. He also goes to great lengths to give truth to the lies, falsifying phone numbers, creating a bogus website, keeping fake notes. First-time director Ray was in close council with the principals involved in the true tale and does a fabulous job keeping the depiction believable. Background as to what drove him to it is all that's missing in this journalist suspense story. **99m/C; VHS, DVD.** Hayden Christensen; Peter Sarsgaard; Chloë Sevigny; Rosario Dawson; Melanie Lynskey; Steve Zahn; Hank Azaria; Luke Kirby; Cas Anvar; Ted Kotcheff; Mark Blum; Simone-Elise Girard; Chad E. Donella; ***D:*** Billy Ray; ***W:*** Billy Ray; ***C:*** Mandy Walker; ***M:*** Mychael Danna. Natl. Soc. Film Critics '03: Support. Actor (Sarsgaard).

Shattered Image 1/2 **1993 (R)** Confusing thriller about the FBI's involvement in the kidnapping of the owner of a model agency, as well as plastic surgery, and a big money scam. **100m/C; VHS, DVD.** Bo Derek; Jack Scalia; John Savage; Dorian Harewood; Ramon Franco; Carol Lawrence; Michael (M.K.) Harris; David McCallum; ***D:*** Fritz Kiersch. **CABLE**

Shattered Image 1/2 **1998** Jessie (Parillaud) is either a cold-blooded hit woman dreaming she's a honeymooner, or a newlywed dreaming she's a psycho assassin. Or both. After whacking a businessman in the men's room at a Seattle restaurant, our heroine goes home to bed, and wakes up a different woman. Literally. On her way to Jamaica with her new husband (Baldwin), Jessie again nods off and she's back in Seattle on her next hit. Each reality features characters from the alternate one, although (like Jessie) each has a different personality. Ruiz fills the screen with stunning homages (Wellesian mirror shots and Hitchcockian split personalities), a truly outrageous ending, and the surrealistic feel of a dream, making for psychotic, if not completely convincing, fun. **102m/C; VHS, DVD.** Anne Parillaud; William Baldwin; Lisanne Falk; Graham Greene; Bulle Ogier; Billy Wilmott; O'Neil Peart; Leonie Forbes; ***D:*** Raul Ruiz; ***W:*** Duane Poole; ***C:*** Robby Muller; ***M:*** Jorge Arriagada.

Shattered Innocence **1987** Chronicles the tragedies that befall ambitious-but-naive small town 18-year-old Pauleen Anderson (Lee) when she decides move to Hollywood to become a model. Soon she goes from topless photos to coke-addicted porn star. Dramatization of real-life adult actress Shauna Grant. **94m/C; DVD.** Melinda Dillon; John Pleshette; Ben Frank; Dennis Howard; Kris Kamm; Richard Cox; Jonna Lee; Stephen Schnetzer; ***D:*** Sandor Stern; ***W:*** Sandor Stern; Thanet Richard; ***C:*** Michael D. Margulies; ***M:*** Richard Bellis. **TV**

Shattered Silence 1/2 *When Michael Calls* **1971** A woman is tormented by phone calls that seem to be coming from her dead son as her life is torn apart by divorce. Leaves unanswered the question: Will there be any suspense? Made for TV. Worthless and dumb. **73m/C; VHS, DVD.** Elizabeth Ashley; Ben Gazzara; Michael Douglas; Karen Pearson; ***D:*** Philip Leacock. **TV**

Shattered Spirits 1/2 **1986 (PG-13)** Quiet family man cracks and goes on a rampage through his normally peaceful suburban neighborhood. Been done before and better. **93m/C; VHS, DVD.** Martin Sheen; Melinda Dillon; Matthew Laborteaux; Roxana Zal; Lukas Haas; ***D:*** Robert Greenwald; ***W:*** Gregory Goodell; ***C:*** John R. Jensen; ***M:*** Michael Hoenig.

Shaun of the Dead **2004 (R)** Brits Wright and Pegg's flick has been referred to as a "rom zom com" or romantic zombie comedy-certainly a cinematic rarity. Slacker clerk Shaun (Pegg), who lives with dim loser chum Ed (Frost), is dumped by frustrated girlfriend Liz (Ashfield) and goes to his favorite pub to drown his sorrows. Because of his morning hangover, Shaun is unaware that London is suddenly overrun with the walking dead. It takes a zombie in the garden to get Shaun and Ed to take action—armed with a cricket bat, shovel, and unwanted vinyl discs from their record collection (the better to slice off a zombie's head). But there's an up side: the zombie crisis brings out the best in Shaun as the survivors retreat to the pub for a final stand, and more beer. **99m/C; VHS, DVD, Blu-Ray, UMD, HD-DVD.** Kate Ashfield; Penelope Wilton; Bill Nighy; Simon Pegg; Nick Frost; Lucy Davis; Dylan Moran; Nicola Cunningham; Jessica Stevenson; Peter Serafinowicz; ***D:*** Edgar Wright; ***W:*** Simon Pegg; Edgar Wright; ***C:*** David M. Dunlap; ***M:*** Daniel Mudford; Peter Woodhead.

Shaun the Sheep Movie **2015 (PG)** Shaun hates his boring life on the farm and takes a day off from work to see what life in the city is like with a few of his sheep buddies. The latest from Aardman Animation is so simple in its storytelling that it doesn't even have any dialogue. That's right—no talking sheep here. Instead, the team behind Wallace & Gromit deliver non-stop physical comedy straight out of the era of silent comedy. Most of it is absolutely brilliant, although the G-rated proceedings may not work for viewers looking for a little more meat on their movie bones than this barnyard animal provides. **85m/C; DVD, Blu-Ray.** Justin Fletcher; John Sparkes; Omid Djalili; Richard Webber; Kate Harbour; ***D:*** Mark Burton; Richard Starzak; ***W:*** Mark Burton; Richard Starzak; ***C:*** Charles Copping; David Alex Riddett; ***M:*** Ilan Eshkeri.

A Shaun the Sheep Movie: Farmageddon **2019** When a UFO crashes near the Mossy Bottom Farm, the lives of Shaun, the other sheep, and their watchdog Bitzer protect the ship's alien from the humans who are looking for her. The adorable alien, Lu-La, is toddler-like with pink coloring and small stature. To help Lu-La find her way home, the gang must help her escape sticky situations and hide in numerous disguises. The sequel to the Oscar-nominated original features the expected quirky humor, puns, expert comic timing, and slapstick. The sci-fi twist and parody homages to such films as "Alien" and "2001: A Space Odyssey" widen its appeal. **86m/C; DVD.** Justin Fletcher; John Sparkes; Chris Morrell; Andy Nyman; David Holt; ***D:*** Will Becher; Richard Phelan; ***W:*** Jon Brown; ***C:*** Charles Copping; ***M:*** Tom Howe.

The Shawshank Redemption 1/2 **1994 (R)** Bank veep Andy (Robbins) is convicted of the murder of his wife and her lover and sentenced to the "toughest prison in the Northeast." While there he forms a friendship with lifer Red (Freeman), experiences the brutality of prison life, adapts, offers financial advice to the guards, and helps the warden (Gunton) cook the prison books...all in a short 19 years. In his theatrical debut, director Darabont avoids belaboring most prison movie cliches while Robbins' talent for playing ambiguous characters is put to good use, and Freeman brings his usual grace to what could have been a thankless role. Adapted from the novella "Rita Hayworth and the Shawshank Redemption" by Stephen King. **142m/C; VHS, DVD, Blu-Ray.** Tim Robbins; Morgan Freeman; Bob Gunton; William Sadler; Clancy Brown; Mark Rolston; Gil Bellows; James Whitmore; ***D:*** Frank Darabont; ***W:*** Frank Darabont; ***C:*** Roger Deakins; ***M:*** Thomas Newman. Natl. Film Reg. '15.

Shazam! 1/2 **2019 (PG-13)** Trouble-making foster kid Billy Batson (Angel) is assigned to a new, loving foster family that includes his superhero-obsessed foster brother Freddy (Glazer). When trying to escape bullies who picked on Freddy, Billy is trying to transport to the Rock of Eternity where the aging Wizard Shazam (Hounsou) transfers his powers to Billy. Billy learns that he can transform into the powerful superhero Shazam (Levi). However, Dr. Thaddeus Sivana (Strong) has long wanted the wizard's powers and unleashes evil forces to gain them. A twist on the classic DC comic movie, the film successfully balances humor, darkness, and family relationships. **132m/C; DVD, Blu-Ray.** Zachary Levi; Mark Strong; Asher Angel; Jack Dylan Grazer; Adam Brody; ***D:*** David F. Sandberg; ***W:*** Henry Gayden; ***C:*** Maxime Alexandre; ***M:*** Benjamin Wallfisch.

She 1/2 **1925** H. Rider Haggard's famous story about the ageless Queen Ayesha, (Blythe), who renews her life force periodically by walking through a pillar of cold flame. Story and titles by Haggard. Blythe is a stirringly mean queen, and the story remains fresh and fun. Silent film with music score. **69m/B; Silent; VHS, DVD.** Betty Blythe; Carlyle Blackwell; Mary Odette; Tom Reynolds; ***D:*** Leander De Cordova; G(eorge) B(erthold) Samuelson; ***W:*** Walter Summers.

She 1/2 **1935** First sound version of H. Rider Haggard's popular 1887 adventure tale, although the film's location was changed from Africa to the frozen Arctic. Explorers Scott and Bruce are searching for a fire that preserves rather than destroys life. They are captured by a mysterious tribe and discover a living goddess—She-Who-Must-Be-Obeyed (Gahagan)?who bathed in the Flame of Life and is now eternal. She falls for Scott, who doesn't return her love, and there's trouble. Fantastic Art Deco sets and special effects. **95m/B; VHS, DVD.** Helen Gahagan; Randolph Scott; Nigel Bruce; Helen Mack; Gustav von Seyffertitz; ***D:*** Irving Pichel; Lansing C. Holden; ***W:*** Dudley Nichols; Ruth Rose; ***C:*** J. Roy Hunt; ***M:*** Max Steiner.

She **1965** Hammer Films' lavish version of the H. Rider Haggard adventure novel. In 1918, Leo Vincey (Richardson) meets slave girl Ustane (Monteras) in Jerusalem and she insists on taking him to her mistress Ayesha (Andress). Ayesha offers Leo a fortune to meet her in the legendary city of Kuma because she's convinced he's the reincarnation of the man she loved (and murdered) centuries before. Followed by 1967's "The Vengeance of She" (with Richardson but minus Andress). **104m/C; DVD.** *GB* Ursula Andress; John Richardson; Rosenda Monteros; Peter Cushing; Bernard Cribbins; Christopher Lee; ***D:*** Robert Day; ***W:*** David Chantler; James Bernard; ***C:*** Harry Waxman; ***M:*** James Bernard.

She **1983** A beautiful female warrior rules over the men in a post-holocaust world. She is kidnapped by a wealthy merchant who uses her to fight evil mutants. Utter rubbish vaguely based on the Haggard novel. **90m/C; VHS, Blu-Ray, Streaming.** Sandahl Bergman; Harrison Muller; Quin Kessler; David Goss; ***D:*** Avi Nesher.

The She-Beast 1/2 *Il Lago di Satana; The Revenge of the Blood Beast; La Sorella de Satan; The Sister of Satan* **1965** Burned at the stake in 18th-century Transylvania, a witch returns in the body of a beautiful young English woman on her honeymoon (in Transylvania?!), and once again wreaks death and destruction. Caution, Barbara Steele fans: she appears for all of 15 minutes. Sporadically funny. **74m/C; VHS, DVD, Blu-Ray.** *IT YU* Barbara Steele; Ian Ogilvy; Mel Welles; Lucretia Love; ***D:*** Michael Reeves; ***W:*** Michael Reeves; ***M:*** Ralph Ferraro.

She Came to the Valley *Texas in Flames* **1977 (PG)** A tough pioneer woman becomes embroiled in political intrigue during the Spanish-American War. Based on Cleo Dawson's book. **90m/C; VHS, DVD.** Ronee Blakley; Dean Stockwell; Scott Glenn; Freddy Fender; ***D:*** Albert Band; ***W:*** Albert Band; ***C:*** Daniel Pearl; ***M:*** Tommy Leonetti.

The She-Creature 1/2 **1956** Typical AIP creature feature. Evil hypnotist Lombardi (Morris) puts assistant Andrea (English) into a trance and regresses her to a past life that happens to be of a prehistoric sea creature that kills. Businessman Timothy Chappel (Conway) wants to promote Lombardi's act to make a buck until Andrea—aided by suspicious doctor Ted Erickson (Fuller) who's fallen in love with her—works to control the creature and take action. **77m/B; DVD.** Chester Morris; Marla English; Lance Fuller; Tom Conway; Cathy Downs; Ron Randell; Frieda Inescort; ***D:*** Edward L. Cohn; ***W:*** Lou Rusoff; ***C:*** Frederick E. West; ***M:*** Ronald Stein.

She Creature 1/2 *Mermaid Chronicles Part 1: She Creature* **2001 (R)** In 1905, carnival barker Angus Shaw (Lily) is traveling in Ireland with his girlfriend Lily (Gugino) posing as a mermaid in a sideshow attraction. They meet drunken ex-sailor Woolrich (Morris) who takes them to his home where he has his own attraction—a real live mermaid (Kilhstedt). Angus steals the mermaid and sails for America but the mermaid begins attacking crewman and Lily develops a symbiotic relationship with the creature. Very loosely based on the AIP 1956 B-movie of the same title, this was one of a series of cable remakes under the umbrella title "Creature Features." **91m/C; VHS, DVD.** Rufus Sewell; Carla Gugino; Rya Kihlstedt; Aubrey Morris; Jim Piddock; Gil Bellows; Reno Wilson; ***D:*** Sebastian Gutierrez; ***W:*** Sebastian Gutierrez; ***C:*** Thomas Callaway; ***M:*** David Reynolds. **CABLE**

She Demons **WOOF! 1958** Pleasure craft loaded with babes crashes into a remote island controlled by a mad ex-Nazi scientist who transforms pretty girls into rubber-faced Frankensteins. Incomprehensible, to say the least. **68m/B; VHS, DVD.** Irish McCalla; Tod Griffin; Victor Sen Yung; Rudolph Anders; Tod Andrews; Gene Roth; Bill Coontz; Billy Dix; ***D:*** Richard Cunha; ***W:*** Richard Cunha; H.E. Barrie; ***C:*** Meredith Nicholson; ***M:*** Nicholas Carras.

She Devil 1/2 **1957** Suffering from TB, Kyra agrees to be a guinea pig for an experimental serum that soon has her health restored but also turns her homicidal. She becomes an impervious black widow, targeting Barton Kendall for death so she can inherit his fortune. Doctors Scott and Bach try to develop an antidote that will revert Kyra back to her former self. **77m/B; DVD, Blu-Ray.** Mari Blanchard; Jack Kelly; John Archer; Albert Dekker; Fay Baker; Marie Blake; ***D:*** Kurt Neumann; ***W:*** Kurt Neumann; Carroll Young; ***C:*** Karl Struss; ***M:*** Paul Sawtell; Bert Shefter.

She-Devil 1/2 **1989 (PG-13)** A comic book version of the acidic Fay Weldon novel "The Life and Loves of a She-Devil"; a fat, dowdy suburban wife (Arnold) becomes a vengeful beast when a smarmy romance novelist steals her husband. Uneven comedic reworking of a distinctly unforgiving feminist fiction. Arnold is given too much to handle (her role requires an actual range of emotions); Streep's role is too slight, though she does great things with it. **100m/C; VHS, DVD, Blu-Ray.** Meryl Streep; Roseanne; Ed Begley, Jr.; Linda Hunt; Elizabeth Peters; Bryan Larkin; A. Martinez; Sylvia Miles; ***D:*** Susan Seidelman; ***W:*** Mark Burns; Barry Strugatz; ***C:*** Oliver Stapleton; ***M:*** Howard Shore.

She Devils in Chains *American Beauty Hostages; Ebony, Ivory, and Jade; Foxforce* **1976 (PG)** A group of traveling female athletes are kidnapped by a groups of sadists who torture and beat them. In the end, however, the girls get their revenge, and it's bloody. **82m/C; VHS, DVD.** Colleen Camp; Rosanne Katon; Sylvia Anderson; Ken Washington; Leo Martinez; ***D:*** Cirio H. Santiago; ***M:*** Eddie Nova.

She-Devils on Wheels **WOOF! 1968** Havoc erupts as an outlaw female motorcycle gang, known as "Maneaters on Motorbikes," terrorizes a town—especially the men. Really, really bad biker flick finely honed by Lewis. **83m/C; VHS, DVD.** Betty Connell; Christie Wagner; Pat Poston; Nancy Lee Noble; Ruby Tuesday; Roy Collodi; David Harris; Steve White; ***D:*** Herschell Gordon Lewis; ***W:*** Allison Louise Downe; ***C:*** Roy Collodi; ***M:*** Larry Wellington.

She Done Him Wrong **1933** Singer Lady Lou (West) fronts an 1890s Bowery saloon for her shady boss, Gus Jordan (Beery Sr.) Gus gives her diamonds but when she gets an eyeful of young Salvation Army Capt. Cummings (Grant), Lou starts to think there's other things in life worth having. West imparts the screen version of her Broadway hit "Diamond Lil" with her usual share of double entendres and racy comments. **65m/B; VHS, DVD.** Mae West; Cary Grant; Owen Moore; Noah Beery, Sr.; Gilbert Roland; Louise Beavers; Rafaela (Rafael, Raphaella) Ottiano; ***D:*** Lowell Sherman; ***W:*** Harvey Thew; John Bright; ***C:*** Charles B(ryant) Lang, Jr.; ***M:*** Ralph Rainger; David Landau. Natl. Film Reg. '96.

She Drives Me Crazy **2007** With her recently widowed conservative sister Virginia (Bridges) in a deep depression, fun-loving Blithe (Clark) pushes her into a road trip that will take them back to their hometown just in time for Virginia's high school reunion. It will also give Blithe a chance to not only reconnect with Virginia but with her ex-husband Hank (Potter) and Blithe has a reason for wanting both things to happen. **90m/C; DVD.** Melinda (Mindy) Clarke; Krista Bridges; Chris Potter; Richard Quesnel; Michael

Seater; Lynne Griffin; *D:* Eleanor Lindo; *W:* Art D'Alessandro; *C:* Alwyn Kumst. **CABLE**

She Fell Among Thieves 🦴🦴 **1978** BBC mystery based on the 1935 Dornford Yates novel. English gentleman Richard Chandos (MacDowell) is vacationing in the French Pyrenees in 1922. The villainous Vanity Fair (Atkins) will inherit millions if she can get her innocent stepdaughter, Jenny (Dotrice), to marry before she comes of age. After discovering the corpse of one of Vanity's minions, Richard is asked by the British Embassy to quietly determine what's going on. **78m/C; DVD.** *UK* Malcolm McDowell; Eileen Atkins; Karen Dotrice; Michael Jayston; Sarah Badel; Bernard Hill; *D:* Clive Donner; *W:* Tom Sharpe; *C:* Brian Tufano; *M:* John Cameron. **TV**

She-Freak 🦴 *Alley of Nightmares* **1967** Remake of Tod Brownings' "Freaks." A cynical waitress burns everyone in a circus and gets mauled by the resident freaks. Pales beside its unacknowledged, classic original. **87m/C; VHS, DVD.** Claire Brennan; Lynn Courtney; Bill McKinney; Lee Raymond; Madame Lee; Claude Smith; Ben Moore; *D:* Byron Mabe; *W:* David Friedman; *C:* William G. Troiano; *M:* William Allen Castleman.

She Hate Me 🦴 1/2 **2004 (R)** Spike Lee's latest film is about corporate whistleblowers. No wait, it's about the AIDS epidemic. Hold on a second, it's about Watergate and lesbians and fatherhood and the Mafia. Confused? So is this movie. John Henry Armstrong is a vice-president of a drug company. After blowing the whistle and getting fired, Armstrong finds a second career as a stud for lesbians who want to be impregnated. While the movie touches on some very interesting material, Lee randomly jumps from one subject to the next, creating a rather schizophrenic hodge-podge of political rants. **138m/C; VHS, DVD.** Anthony Mackie; Kerry Washington; Ellen Barkin; Monica Bellucci; Jim Brown; Ossie Davis; Jamel Debbouze; Brian Dennehy; Woody Harrelson; Bai Ling; Lonette McKee; Paula Jai Parker; Q-Tip; John Turturro; Chiwetel Ejiofor; Dania Ramirez; David Bennett; Isiah Whitlock, Jr.; Kim Director; *D:* Spike Lee; *W:* Spike Lee; Michael Genet; *C:* Matthew Libatique; *M:* Terence Blanchard.

She Played With Fire 🦴🦴 **1957** Convoluted crime drama. London insurance investigator Oliver Branwell (Hawkins) remeets his ex-girlfriend Sarah (Dahl) when he investigates a suspicious fire in which her husband died. Their own rekindled romance leads to a marriage that is marred by art fraud, blackmail, and murder. Based on the 1952 novel "Fortune Is a Woman" by Winston Graham. **95m/B; DVD, Blu-Ray.** *UK* Arlene Dahl; Jack Hawkins; Violet Farebrother; Ian Hunter; Dennis Price; Christopher Lee; Bernard Miles; *D:* Sidney Gilliat; *W:* Sidney Gilliat; Val Valentine; Frank Launder; *C:* Gerald Gibbs; *M:* William Alwyn.

She Shoulda Said No 🦴 *The Devil's Weed; Wild Weed; Marijuana the Devil's Weed* **1949** Funny smelling cigarettes ruin the lives of all who inhale. Viewers' advice: just say no. Leed's actual drug bust with Robert Mitchum got her the lead. **70m/B; VHS, DVD.** Lila Leeds; Alan Baxter; Lyle Talbot; Jack Elam; David Gorcey; *D:* Sam Newfield.

She Wore a Yellow Ribbon 🦴🦴🦴 1/2 **1949** An undermanned cavalry outpost makes a desperate attempt to repel invading Indians. Wayne shines as an officer who shuns retirement in order to help his comrades. Still fun and compelling. The second chapter in director Ford's noted cavalry trilogy, preceded by "Fort Apache" and followed by "Rio Grande." **93m/C; VHS, DVD, Blu-Ray.** John Wayne; Joanne Dru; John Agar; Ben Johnson; Harry Carey, Jr.; Victor McLaglen; Mildred Natwick; George O'Brien; Arthur Shields; Noble Johnson; Harry Woods; Michael Dugan; Jack Pennick; Paul Fix; Francis Ford; Cliff Lyons; Tom Tyler; Chief John Big Tree; *D:* John Ford; *W:* Frank Nugent; Laurence Stallings; *C:* Winton C. Hoch; Charles P. Boyle; *M:* Richard Hageman. Oscars '49: Color Cinematog.

She Wouldn't Say Yes 🦴🦴 **1945** Shrink Susan Lane (Russell) wants to prove her theory that a person can maintain a healthy mental state by strictly controlling their emotions. Cartoonist Michael Kent (Bowman), who believes in free expression, becomes her guinea pig and they fall in love despite their differences. **87m/B; DVD.** Rosalind Russell; Lee Bowman; Adele Jergens; Charles Winninger; Harry Davenport; Percy Kilbride; Sara Haden; *D:* Alexander Hall; *W:* John Jacoby; Virginia Van Upp; Sarett Tobias; *C:* Joseph Walker; *M:* Marlin Skiles.

Sheba, Baby 🦴🦴 **1975 (PG)** A female dick (Grier) heads to Louisville where someone is trying to threaten her rich father and his loan company. Oddly non-violent for action-flick vet Grier; poorly written and directed. **90m/C; VHS, DVD, Blu-Ray.** Pam Grier; Rudy Challenger; Austin Stoker; D'Urville Martin; Charles Kissinger; *D:* William Girdler; *W:* William Girdler; *C:* William Asman; *M:* Alex Brown.

The Shed 🦴🦴 **2019** Misunderstood juvenile delinquent Stan (Warren) is 17 years old and living with his abusive, domineering grandfather (Bottoms). Though the situation is difficult, Stan does all he can to avoid going back in state care. One day, he notices something is kicking and scratching inside a shed, but does not act even after the creature murders his grandfather. Nailing the shed door shut, Stan realizes it is a vicious vampire. He and his misfit friends, Roxy (Happonen) and Dommer (Kostro), consider using the creature to enact revenge. A relatively decent horror flick that capably uses its tools (pun intended). **97m/C; DVD, Blu-Ray.** Jay Jay Warren; Cody Kostro; Sofia Happonen; Frank Whaley; Timothy Bottoms; *D:* Frank Sabatella; *W:* Frank Sabatella; *C:* Matthias Schubert; *M:* Sam Ewing.

Shed No Tears 🦴 1/2 **1948** Cheap film noir wannabe. Edna Grover persuades husband Sam to fake his death so they can live in style on the insurance money. The scheme is carried out but Sam wonders where Edna and the money are. Turns out she's been cheating on him and only has plans for a new life with her lover and Sam is an inconvenience that needs dealing with. **70m/B; DVD.** Wallace Ford; June Vincent; Mark Roberts; Dick Hogan; Frank Albertson; *D:* Jean Yarbrough; *W:* Brown Holmes; *C:* Frank Redman; *M:* Raoul Kraushaar.

Sheeba 🦴🦴 *Crab Orchard* **2005** After 9/11, Kim insists on leaving New York City and taking son Clay to live with her father in her rural hometown. Clay resents leaving city life and his traumatized firefighter dad Jim behind. Kim gets Clay a dog, Sheeba, to cheer him up but Clay is continually harassed by school bully Wax, who even dognaps Sheeba as their conflict escalates. **91m/C; DVD.** Dylan Patton; Ed Asner; Ruby Handler; Kyle Tolliver; Judge Reinhold; *D:* Michael Jacobs; *W:* Robin Christian; *C:* John Luker; *M:* Alan Williams. **VIDEO**

Sheena **WOOF! 1984 (PG)** TV sportscaster aids a jungle queen in defending her kingdom from being overthrown by an evil prince. Horrid bubble-gum "action" fantasy. **117m/C; VHS, DVD, Blu-Ray.** Tanya Roberts; Ted Wass; Donovan Scott; Elizabeth Toro; *D:* John Guillermin; *W:* David Newman; *C:* Pasqualino De Santis.

The Sheep Has Five Legs 🦴🦴 1/2 **1954** Quintuplet brothers return from around the world for a reunion in their small French village. Fernandel plays the father and all five sons; otherwise, comedy is only average-to-good. In French with English subtitles. **96m/B; VHS, DVD.** *FR* Fernandel; Edouard Delmont; Louis de Funes; Paulette Dubost; *D:* Henri Verneuil.

The Sheepman 🦴🦴 1/2 **1958** Western comedy starring a deadpan Ford as gambler/ex-gunslinger Jason Sweet. Sweet wins a flock of sheep in a poker game and decides to graze them on the public land of Powder River. But the town is basically owned by cattle baron Stephen Bedford (Nielsen), who doesn't want any woolies around. Too bad Sweet recognizes Bedford as former rival gunslinger Johnny Bledsoe, who's assumed a new identity to live a new life. **86m/C; DVD.** Glenn Ford; Shirley MacLaine; Leslie Nielsen; Mickey Shaughnessy; Edgar Buchanan; Pernell Roberts; Willis Bouchey; Slim Pickens; *D:* George Marshall; *W:* William Bowers; James Edward Grant; *C:* Robert J. Bronner; *M:* Jeff Alexander.

Sheer Madness 🦴🦴🦴 **1984** Focuses on the intense friendship between a college professor and a troubled artist, both women. Engrossing and subtle exposition of a relationship. Ambiguous ending underscores film's general excellence. Subtitled. **105m/C; VHS, DVD.** *GE FR* Hanna Schygulla; Angela Winkler; *D:* Margarethe von Trotta; *W:* Margarethe von Trotta; *C:* Michael Ballhaus.

The Sheik 🦴🦴🦴 **1921** High camp Valentino has English woman fall hopelessly under the romantic spell of Arab sheik who flares his nostrils. Followed by "Son of the Sheik." **80m/B; Silent; VHS, DVD, Blu-Ray.** Agnes Ayres; Rudolph Valentino; Adolphe Menjou; Walter Long; Lucien Littlefield; George Waggner; Patsy Ruth Miller; *D:* George Melford; *W:* Monte Katterjohn; *C:* William Marshall.

Sheitan 🦴 1/2 *Satan* **2006** Beautiful Eve (Mesquida) invites a group of horny, drunken teens she met at the disco to join her at her isolated farmhouse on Christmas Eve. Strange servant Joseph (Cassel) seems to have something sinister planned. Weird and creepy rather than horror gory. French with subtitles. **94m/C; DVD.** *FR* Vincent Cassel; Roxane Mesquida; Olivier Barthelemy; Leila Bekhti; Nico Le Phat Tan; Ladj Ly; *D:* Kim Chapiron; *W:* Kim Chapiron; Christian Chapiron; *C:* Alex Lamarque; *M:* Nguyen Le.

She'll Be Wearing Pink Pajamas 🦴🦴 **1984** Eight women volunteer for a rugged survival course to test their mettle. The intense shared experience gives them all food for thought. Well acted from a pretty thin story. **90m/C; VHS, DVD.** Julie Walters; Anthony (Corlan) Higgins; *D:* John Goldschmidt; *M:* John Du Prez.

The Shell Seekers 🦴🦴 1/2 **1989 (PG)** The widowed Penelope Keeling (Lansbury) is recovering from a heart attack and her three grown children want her to take things easy. But the scare has convinced Penelope to revisit her past and the happiness she once knew. So she returns to her childhood home in Cornwall to see what she can discover. Fine cast in a heart-tugger (with some lovely scenery from Cornwall, England and the island of Ibiza). Adapted from the novel by Rosamunde Pilcher. A Hallmark Hall of Fame presentation. **94m/C; VHS, DVD.** *GB* Angela Lansbury; Sam Wanamaker; Anna Carteret; Michael Gough; Christopher Bowen; Patricia Hodge; Denis Quilley; Sophie Ward; Irene Worth; *D:* Waris Hussein; *W:* John Pielmeier. **TV**

The Shell Seekers 🦴🦴 1/2 **2006** The Hallmark Channel remakes the 1989 Hallmark Hall of Fame drama, based on the Rosamunde Pilcher novel. Recovering from a heart attack gives Penelope Keeling (Redgrave) a chance for reflection while her three children press her to sell her artist father's (Schell) paintings, which would leave them financially secure. Instead, Penelope decides to travel to Ibiza where she meets and reminisces with young Antonia (Stumph) about first love. **129m/C; DVD.** Vanessa Redgrave; Stephanie Stumph; Maximilian Schell; Alastair Mackenzie; Victoria Smurfit; Sebastian Koch; Charles Edward; Victoria Hamilton; Prunella Scales; Maisie Dimbelby; Lukas Gregorowicz; *D:* Piers Haggard; *W:* Brian Finch; *C:* Tony Imi; *M:* Richard Blackford. **CABLE**

Shelter 🦴🦴 **1998 (R)** ATF agent Martin Roberts (Allen) is set up by his commanding officer and has a bounty on his head. He takes refuge with a crime lord (Onorati), whom the bad guys feds are also after, and plans how to get even. **92m/C; VHS, DVD.** John Allen Nelson; Peter Onorati; Brenda Bakke; Costas Mandylor; Charles Durning; Linden Ashby; Kurtwood Smith; *D:* Scott Paulin; *W:* Max Strom; *C:* Eric Goldstein; *M:* David Williams.

Shelter 🦴🦴 1/2 **2007 (R)** Zach (Wright) delays his dreams of going to art school to care for his five-year-old nephew Cody (Wurth) since his manipulative single mom sister Jeanne (Holmes) is so irresponsible. Feeling stuck in San Pedro, Zack likes to go surfing and hooks up with Shaun (Rowe), the older brother of his best friend Gabe (Thomas). An L.A.-based writer, Shaun is taking an extended break and is only too happy to spend time with Zach. And he's really happy to help Zach figure out that they can be more than friends. Sweet-natured coming of age, coming out story. **97m/C; DVD.** Trevor Wright; Brad Rowe; Tina Holmes; Ross Thomas; Katie Walder; Jackson Wurth; *D:* Jonah Markowitz; *W:* Jonah Markowitz; *C:* Joseph White; *M:* J. Peter Robinson. **CABLE**

Shelter 🦴 **2015** Movies don't get much more maudlin and manipulative than actor Bettany's directorial debut. The actor directs his wife Connelly in the role of Hannah, a homeless woman who falls in love with a homeless man named Tahir (Mackie). When Bettany's film pauses to focus on the reality of finding companionship even in challenging conditions, it almost works, but it eventually dives into a hollow last act. A final tribute to the homeless couple who lived outside this multi-millionaire's apartment leaves an especially bad taste in one's mouth. **105m/C; DVD.** Anthony Mackie; Jennifer Connelly; Amy Hargreaves; Bruce Altman; Scott Johnsen; *D:* Paul Bettany; *W:* Paul Bettany; *C:* Paula Huidobro.

Shelter Island 🦴 **2003 (R)** Lou (Sheedy) was living the good life, but a brutal assault makes her and lesbian lover Alex (Kensit) run away to Lou's island digs. One dark and stormy night brings a creepy, uninvited guest (Baldwin) who gets grim with 'em when the lights go out. Familiar cast drifts aimlessly out to sea trying to create a tense erotic thriller. **83m/C; VHS, DVD.** Ally Sheedy; Patsy Kensit; Stephen Baldwin; Mimi Langeland; Christopher Penn; Joey Gironda; Kathleen York; *D:* Geoffrey Schaaf; *W:* Paul Corvino; *M:* Jeff Rona. **VIDEO**

The Sheltering Sky 🦴🦴🦴 **1990 (R)** American couple Winger and Malkovich flee the plasticity of their native land for a trip to the Sahara desert where they hope to renew their spirits and rekindle love. Accompanied by socialite acquaintance Scott with whom Winger soon has an affair, their personalities and belief systems deteriorate as they move through the grave poverty of North Africa in breathtaking heat. Based on the existential novel by American expatriate Paul Bowles who narrates and appears briefly in a bar scene. Overlong but visually stunning, with cinematography by Vittorio Storaro. **139m/C; VHS, DVD.** Debra Winger; John Malkovich; Campbell Scott; Jill Bennett; Timothy Spall; Eric Vu-An; Sotigui Koyate; Amina Annabi; Paul Bowles; *D:* Bernardo Bertolucci; *W:* Mark Peploe; Bernardo Bertolucci; *C:* Vittorio Storaro; *M:* Ryuichi Sakamoto; Richard Horowitz. Golden Globes '91: Score; N.Y. Film Critics '90: Cinematog.

Shenandoah 🦴🦴🦴 **1965** A Virginia farmer (Stewart, in a top-notch performance) who has raised six sons and a daughter, tries to remain neutral during the Civil War. War takes its toll as the daughter marries a Confederate soldier and his sons become involved in the fighting. Screen debut for Ross. **105m/C; VHS, DVD.** James Stewart; Doug McClure; Glenn Corbett; Patrick Wayne; Rosemary Forsyth; Katharine Ross; George Kennedy; Phillip Alford; James Best; Charles Robinson; James McMullan; Tim McIntire; Eugene Jackson; Paul Fix; Denver Pyle; Harry Carey, Jr.; Dabbs Greer; Strother Martin; Warren Oates; Kelly Thordsen; *D:* Andrew V. McLaglen; *W:* James Lee Barrett; *C:* William Clothier; *M:* Frank Skinner.

Shepherd 🦴🦴 **1999 (R)** Offers plenty of cheap thrills as long as you don't expect the plot to make any sense. You've got your basic futuristic nightmare world—this time ruled by rival religious cults who use guns to extend their power. Howell is a sharpshooting mercenary who decides not to follow orders anymore—and there's hell to pay. **86m/C; VHS, DVD.** C. Thomas Howell; Roddy Piper; Robert Carradine; Heidi von Palleske; *D:* Peter Hayman. **VIDEO**

The Shepherd: Border Patrol 🦴🦴 **2008 (R)** Van Damme has slowed down a kick or two but he's still got enough moves to make this action flick enjoyable. Jack Robideaux is a border patrol agent in New Mexico who's attempting to stop a rogue American Special Forces unit from smuggling heroin into the U.S. **94m/C; DVD.** Jean-Claude Van Damme; Scott Adkins; Stephen Lord; Garry McDonald; Isaac Florentine; Natalie Robb; *W:* Joe Gayton; Cade Courley; *C:* Douglas Milstone; *M:* Mark Sayfritz. **VIDEO**

The Shepherd of the Hills 🦴🦴🦴 **1941** Young Ozark mountain moonshiner Matt Matthews (Wayne) vows to one day find and kill the unknown father who deserted his family, leading to the early death of Matt's mother. His hatred is so strong that his girlfriend Sammy (Field) refuses to marry him because of it. Then a stranger, Daniel Howitt (Carey Sr.), comes to town and his kind deeds have everyone calling him "The Shepherd." Even Matt warms to the man—until he discovers that Howitt is his father. Based on the novel by Harold Bell Wright. **89m/B; DVD.** John Wayne; Harry Carey, Sr.; Betty Field; Beulah Bondi; James Barton; Marjorie Main; Ward Bond; Fuzzy Knight; ***D:*** Henry Hathaway; ***W:*** Grover Jones; Stuart Anthony; ***C:*** Charles B(ryant) Lang, Jr.; William Howard Greene; ***M:*** Gerard Carbonara.

The Sheriff of Fractured Jaw 🦴🦴 1/2 **1959** A spoof of the old west with More as a Londoner who inherits a gun company and decides to head to the Wild West to show off his wares. He is tricked into becoming the sheriff of a lawless town but never loses his British stiff-upper-lip. Mansfield is the tough-talking sharpshooter who sets out to get her man. **103m/C; VHS, DVD.** *GB* Kenneth More; Jayne Mansfield; Henry Hull; William Campbell; Charles Farrell; ***D:*** Raoul Walsh; ***W:*** Howard Dimsdale; ***C:*** Otto Heller; ***M:*** Robert Farnon.

Sherlock: Case of Evil 🦴🦴 1/2 *Case of Evil* **2002 (R)** A young Sherlock Holmes (D'Arcy) is out to make a name for himself in London where he is hired by drug lord Ben Harrington (Rodger) to discover who is killing the local dealers and introducing a new narcotic—heroin—in an effort to control the market. That will turn out to be Professor Moriarty (D'Onofrio); also in the mix is Mycroft Holmes (Grant), who here is a drug addict, and Dr. Watson (Morlidge), who is not Sherlock's confidante at this time. In fact, Holmes's assistant is actress Rebecca (Anwar), who has her own agenda. **100m/C; VHS, DVD, On Demand.** James D'Arcy; Vincent D'Onofrio; Gabrielle Anwar; Roger Morlidge; Struan Rodger; Nicholas Gecks; Richard E. Grant; ***D:*** Graham Theakston; ***W:*** Piers Ashworth; ***C:*** Lukas Strebel; ***M:*** Mike Moran. **CABLE**

Sherlock Gnomes 🦴🦴 **2018 (PG)** An animated take on the famous detective, gnome style, by the creators of Gnomeo and Juliet. Someone has stolen all the gnomes in London--including gnomes like Lord Redbrick (Caine) and Lady Blueberry (Smith)--and they must be found within 24 hours of they will all be destroyed. Sherlock (Depp) and his put-upon assistant Watson (Ejiofor) are on the case, with the help of Gnomeo (McAvoy) and Juliet (Blunt). Along the way, Holmes becomes entangled with his adversary Moriarty (Demetriou). Less playful than Gnomeo, this film uses puns and its settings well but lacks wit and an exciting sense of adventure. **86m/C; DVD, Blu-Ray.** Johnny Depp; James McAvoy; Chiwetel Ejiofor; Emily Blunt; Mary J. Blige; ***D:*** Dr. John Stevenson; ***W:*** Ben Zazove; ***M:*** Chris Bacon.

Sherlock Holmes 🦴 1/2 **1922** The screenplay is a muddle, probably because the plot was taken from several Conan Doyle stories, and Barrymore makes for a surprisingly dull Holmes. Arch-villain Moriarty is introduced through his connection to a Cambridge student scandal although Holmes and Watson take some time to make an appearance. This silent version was thought lost and the restoration is taken from various prints, although some pieces still seem to be missing. Young and Powell make their screen debuts. **85m/B; Silent; DVD.** John Barrymore; Roland Young; Gustav von Seyffertitz; William Powell; Carol Dempster; Louis Wolheim; Percy Knight; Hedda Hopper; ***D:*** Albert Parker; ***W:*** Earle Browne; Marion Farifax; ***C:*** J. Roy Hunt.

Sherlock Holmes 🦴🦴 **2009 (PG-13)** Brit director Ritchie makes Arthur Conan Doyle's Victorian-era detective into an action hero thanks to Downey's vivid (if disheveled) portrayal of a man with a frightening intellect, drug problems, few social boundaries, and fighting skills. Law is exasperated partner/confidante Dr. Watson and there's a hint of romance in McAdams' portrayal of the criminally-minded Irene Adler, although the actress really doesn't have much to do. The plot involves a satanic sort of aristo baddie (Strong) bent on destruction of the British Empire. Ritchie's can't leave well enough alone and has to overstuff his pic with too much scenery, action, and CGI though it is entertaining in a frenetic way. He (and his main character) needs to stop and have a soothing cup of tea. **128m/C; Blu-Ray, On Demand.** Robert Downey, Jr.; Jude Law; Rachel McAdams; Mark Strong; Kelly Reilly; Eddie Marsan; James Fox; Hans Matheson; Geraldine James; ***D:*** Guy Ritchie; ***W:*** Guy Ritchie; Michael R. Johnson; Anthony Peckham; Simon Kinberg; ***C:*** Philippe Rousselot; ***M:*** Hans Zimmer. Golden Globes '10: Actor--Mus./Comedy (Downey).

Sherlock Holmes 🦴 *Sir Arthur Conan Doyle's Sherlock Holmes* **2010 (PG-13)** Could have been a mildly amusing Victorian monster/detective pastiche if it wasn't for the completely miscast, mild-mannered and dull Syder in the title role. In 1882, a sea monster, a dinosaur, and a dragon (no, it's not a set-up for a pub joke) attack London and Sherlock Holmes must find a way to defeat them and discover who set the beasts loose in the first place. **90m/C; DVD.** Ben Syder; David Gareth-Lloyd; Dominic Keating; Elizabeth Arends; William Huw; Catriona McDonald; Rachael Evelyn; ***D:*** Rachel Goldenberg; ***W:*** Paul Bales; ***C:*** Adam Silver; ***M:*** Chris Ridenhour. **VIDEO**

Sherlock Holmes: A Game of Shadows 🦴🦴 **2011 (PG-13)** Holmes (Downey Jr.) and Watson (Law) are back and this time they have to track the infamous Moriarty (Harris) and stop him just in time for dear Watson to finally get married to Mary (Reilly). Typically action-filled yet hard to follow, director Ritchie wastes the potential of this concept, delivering a film that somehow feels hurried and light on plot at the same time. Downey and Law are clearly having a fun time with all their witty banter, but said enjoyment is not always translated to the audience. That said, a third installment is probable. **129m/C; DVD, Blu-Ray.** Robert Downey, Jr.; Jude Law; Eddie Marsan; Jared Harris; Stephen Fry; Noomi Rapace; Rachel McAdams; Kelly Reilly; Geraldine James; Paul Anderson; ***D:*** Guy Ritchie; ***W:*** Kieran Mulroney; Michele Mulroney; ***C:*** Philippe Rousselot; ***M:*** Hans Zimmer.

Sherlock Holmes and the Deadly Necklace 🦴🦴 1/2 *Sherlock Holmes und das Halsband des Todes; Valley of Fear* **1962** Once again, Holmes and Watson are up against their old nemesis Moriarty. This time, Moriarty wants to get his hands on a necklace stolen from Cleopatra's tomb. Not only does Scotland Yard not consider him a suspect, they seek his advice. Enter Holmes and Watson, and the game's afoot. The offbeat casting and direction help make this one of the odder versions of Conan Doyle's work. **84m/B; VHS, DVD.** *GE* Christopher Lee; Senta Berger; Hans Sohnker; Hans Nielsen; Ivan Desny; Leon Askin; Thorley Walters; ***D:*** Terence Fisher.

Sherlock Holmes and the Incident at Victoria Falls 🦴 1/2 *Incident at Victoria Falls* **1991** A substandard Holmes excursion brings the Baker Street sleuth out of retirement to transport the world's largest diamond from Africa to London. The resulting mystery involves Teddy Roosevelt, the inventor of radio, and poor plotting. **120m/C; VHS, DVD.** *GB* Christopher Lee; Patrick Macnee; Jenny Seagrove; ***D:*** Bill Corcoran.

Sherlock Holmes and the Secret Weapon 🦴🦴🦴 *Secret Weapon* **1942** Based on "The Dancing Men" by Sir Arthur Conan Doyle. Holmes battles the evil Moriarty in an effort to save the British war effort. Good Holmes mystery with gripping wartime setting. Hoey is fun as bumbling Inspector Lestrade. Available colorized. **68m/B; VHS, DVD.** Basil Rathbone; Nigel Bruce; Karen Verne; William Post, Jr.; Dennis Hoey; Holmes Herbert; Mary Gordon; Henry Victor; Philip Van Zandt; George Eldredge; Leslie Denison; James Craven; Paul Fix; Hugh Herbert; Lionel Atwill; ***D:*** Roy William Neill; ***W:*** Scott Darling; ***C:*** Lester White; ***M:*** Frank Skinner.

Sherlock Holmes and the Voice of Terror 🦴 1/2 **1942** The first of the Rathbone/Bruce movies made by Universal was updated for use as WWII propaganda. The 'Voice of Terror' broadcasts from Nazi Germany, announcing acts of sabotage that are heard via BBC radio and immediately carried out in London. Holmes is asked to stop the saboteur and turns to some underworld associates for help. **65m/B; DVD.** Basil Rathbone; Nigel Bruce; Evelyn Ankers; Reginald Denny; Henry Daniell; Thomas Gomez; Montagu Love; Mary Gordon; ***D:*** John Rawlins; ***W:*** Robert D. (Robert Hardy) Andrews; Lynn Riggs; John Bright; ***C:*** Elwood "Woody" Bredell; ***M:*** Frank Skinner.

Sherlock Holmes Faces Death 🦴🦴🦴 **1943** Dead bodies are accumulating in a mansion where the detecting duo are staying. Underground tunnels, life-size dress boards, and unanswered mysteries... Top-notch Holmes. Peter Lawford appears briefly as a sailor. Also available with "Hound of the Baskervilles" on Laser Disc. **68m/B; VHS, DVD.** Basil Rathbone; Nigel Bruce; Hillary Brooke; Milburn Stone; Halliwell Hobbes; Arthur Margetson; Gavin Muir; ***D:*** Roy William Neill.

Sherlock Holmes in Washington 🦴🦴 1/2 **1943** A top-secret agent is murdered; seems it's those blasted Nazis again! Holmes and Watson rush off to Washington, D.C. to solve the crime and to save some vitally important microfilm. Heavily flag-waving Rathbone-Bruce episode. Dr. Watson is dumbfounded by bubble gum. **71m/B; VHS, DVD.** Basil Rathbone; Nigel Bruce; Henry Daniell; George Zucco; Marjorie Lord; John Archer; ***D:*** Roy William Neill.

Sherlock: Undercover Dog 🦴🦴 1/2 **1994 (PG)** Billy (Eroen) arrives on Catalina island to spend the summer with his father, an eccentric inventor. He makes a human friend in Emma (Cameron) and a canine companion in Sherlock, a police dog who's able to talk but naturally only to the two kids. Seems Sherlock's policeman master has been kidnapped by bumbling smugglers and its up to the trio to come to the rescue. **80m/C; VHS, DVD.** Benjamin Eroen; Brynne Cameron; Anthony Simmons; Margy Moore; Barry Philips; ***D:*** Richard Harding Gardner; ***W:*** Richard Harding Gardner; ***M:*** Lou Forestieri.

Sherman's March 🦴🦴🦴 **1986** Director Ross McElwee set out to re-trace Sherman's March through Georgia and document that event's lingering effect on the modern South. Instead, after his girlfriend left him shortly before filming began, he ended up documenting how the various southern women he encountered affected him. McElwee's self-depracating manner and the interesting variety of women he meets keep things enjoyable. **157m/C; DVD. *Cameo(s):*** Burt Reynolds; ***D:*** Ross McElwee; ***W:*** Ross McElwee; ***C:*** Ross McElwee.

Sherman's Way 🦴 1/2 **2008** Uptight recent law grad Sherman Black (Shulman) finally makes an impulsive decision and goes to visit his girlfriend in Napa Valley, only to witness her reunion with an old boyfriend. When he finds himself stranded, Sherman makes a second impulsive decision and accepts a ride from eccentric Palmer (LeGros), a former Olympic skier who's down on his luck. Naturally free-spirit Palmer intends to loosen up stuffy Sherman. **98m/C; DVD.** Michael Shulman; James LeGros; Enrico Colantoni; Brooke Nevin; Donna Murphy; Thomas Ian Nicholas; Lacey Chabert; M. Emmet Walsh; ***D:*** Craig Saavedra; ***W:*** Tom Nance; ***C:*** Joaquin Sedillo; ***M:*** David Michael Frank.

Sherpa 🦴🦴🦴 **2015** When filmmaker Jennifer Peedom began making a documentary about Sherpas on Mount Everest, her intent was to explore the stresses behind the 2014 Everest climbing season from the Sherpas' point of view. A year earlier, a group of European climbers ran away from an angry group of Sherpas. While tensions continued, the worst tragedy in Everest's history struck on April 18, 2014 when a major avalanche crashed onto a major climbing route killing 16 Sherpas. Though it has the requisite awe-inspiring scenery and perhaps explores too many controversies, the very human stories make this documentary a powerful statement. **96m/C; DVD, Streaming, Download.** ***D:*** Jennifer Peedom; ***W:*** Jennifer Peedom; ***C:*** Hugh Miller; Renan Ozturk; Ken Sauls; ***M:*** Antony Partos.

Sherrybaby 🦴🦴 **2006** Gyllenhaal startles in the title role of this compelling but disturbing drama. Sherry is a needy, emotionally stunted and impulsive ex-heroin addict who has cleaned herself up and has just been paroled from prison. She desperately wants to regain custody of her young daughter Alexis (Simpkins), who's bonded with her surrogate family, Sherry's brother Bobby (Henke) and his wife Lynette (Barkan). They've got a right to be cautious of Sherry's plans since the only way she knows to get what she needs is by using her sexuality, and her temptation to slip back into her druggy ways is still strong. **95m/C; DVD.** Maggie Gyllenhaal; Brad William Henke; Danny Trejo; Giancarlo Esposito; Bridget Barkan; Ryan Simpkins; Sam Bottoms; ***D:*** Laurie Collyer; ***W:*** Laurie Collyer; ***C:*** Russell Fine; ***M:*** Jack Livesey.

She's All That 🦴🦴 **1999 (PG-13)** There are no surprises to be found in this formulaic Pygmalion-via-MTV teen comedy. Zack (Prinze Jr.) is the BMOC in yet another broadly drawn high school pecking order. After he's dumped by girlfriend Taylor (O'Keefe) for vain semi-celebrity Brock (Lillard, in an amusing send-up of MTV's "The Real World"), he accepts a bet from a pal that he can make artsy wallflower Laney (Cook) into a prom queen. The intelligent Laney suspects his motives, but proceeds with the makeover with caution. When Taylor decides she wants her man back, the stage is set for a predictable prom night showdown. **97m/C; VHS, DVD.** Rachael Leigh Cook; Freddie Prinze, Jr.; Matthew Lillard; Paul Walker; Jodi Lyn O'Keefe; Kevin Pollak; Anna Paquin; Kieran Culkin; Elden (Ratliff) Henson; Usher Raymond; Gabrielle Union; Dulé Hill; Kimberly (Lil' Kim) Jones; Milo Ventimiglia; Sarah Michelle Gellar; Tamara Mello; Clea DuVall; Tim Matheson; Debbi (Deborah) Morgan; Alexis Arquette; Dave Buzzotta; Katharine Towne; Flex Alexander; ***D:*** Robert Iscove; ***W:*** R. Lee Fleming, Jr.; ***C:*** Francis Kenny; ***M:*** Stewart Copeland.

She's Back on Broadway 🦴🦴 **1953** Movie star Catherine Terris (Mayo) is hoping to revive her fading career by returning to Broadway where it all started. She's the lead in a new musical directed by ex-lover Rick Sommers (Cochran), who's still unhappy about Catherine walking out on him and her role for Hollywood and he figures that if she's successful, she'll do it again. **95m/C; DVD.** Virginia Mayo; Steve Cochran; Gene Nelson; Frank Lovejoy; Patrice Wymore; Larry Keating; Virginia Gibson; Paul Picerni; ***D:*** Gordon Douglas; ***W:*** Orin Jannings; ***C:*** Edwin DuPar; ***M:*** Carl Sigman.

She's Dressed to Kill 🦴🦴 *Someone's Killing the World's Greatest Models* **1979** Beautiful models are turning up dead during a famous designer's comeback attempt at a mountain retreat. Who could be behind these grisly deeds? Suspenseful in a made for TV kind of way, but not memorable. **100m/C; VHS, DVD.** Eleanor Parker; Jessica Walter; John Rubinstein; Connie Sellecca; ***D:*** Gus Trikonis. **TV**

She's Funny That Way 🦴🦴 1/2 **2015 (R)** Tries and fails to be an homage to classic screwball comedies, but is a much less charming, comedy-free Woody Allen-type NYC romp. After a night spent together, Hollywood director Arnold Albertson (Wilson) helps hooker Izzy Finkelstein (Poots) achieve her goal of becoming an actress by casting her in his Broadway project. The play also stars his wife Delta (Hahn) and movie star Seth Gilbert (Ifans), who is in love with Delta and witnessed Izzy departing Arnold's hotel room. A series of coincidences and entanglements ensue as the characters manage to communicate and miscommunicate their way through the rest of the film. **93m/C; DVD.** Imogen Poots; Illeana Douglas; Owen Wilson; Rhys Ifans; Richard Lewis; ***D:*** Peter Bogdanovich; ***W:*** Peter Bogdanovich; Louise Stratten; ***C:*** Yaron Orbach; ***M:*** Ed Shearmur.

She's Got Everything 🦴 1/2 **1937** Debutante Carol Rogers is faced with lots of creditors, thanks to her late father's debts. She takes a secretarial job with coffee magnate, Fuller Partridge, but her Aunt Jane and bookie Waldo Eddington scheme to have Carol marry the boss. Their plan backfires (at least momentarily). **72m/B; DVD.** Ann Sothern; Gene Raymond; Helen Broderick; Victor Moore; Billy Gilbert; ***D:*** Joseph Santley; ***W:*** Harry Segall; Maxwell Shane; ***C:*** Jack MacKenzie; ***M:*** Roy Webb.

She's Gotta Have It 🦴🦴🦴 **1986 (R)** Lee wrote, directed, edited, produced and starred in this romantic comedy about an independent-minded black girl in Brooklyn and the three men and one woman who compete for her attention. Full of rough edges, but vigorous, confident, and hip. Filmed entirely in black and white except for one memorable scene. Put Lee on the film-making map. **84m/B; VHS, DVD.** Tracy C. Johns; Spike Lee; Tommy Redmond Hicks; Raye Dowell; John Canada Terrell; Joie Lee; S. Epatha Merkerson; Bill Lee; Cheryl Burr; Aaron Dugger; Stephanie Covington; Renata Cobbs; Cheryl Singleton; Monty Ross; Lewis Jordan; Erik Todd Dellums; Reginald (Reggie) Hudlin; Eric Payne; Marcus Turner; Gerard Brown; Ernest R. Dickerson; ***D:*** Spike Lee; ***W:*** Spike Lee; ***C:*** Ernest R. Dickerson; ***M:*** Bill Lee. Ind. Spirit '87: First Feature; Natl. Film Reg. '19.

She's Having a Baby 🦴🦴 1/2 **1988 (PG-13)** Newlyweds Bacon and McGovern tread the marital waters with some difficulty, when news of an impending baby further complicates their lives. Told from Bacon's viewpoint as the tortured young writer/husband, who wonders if the yuppie life they lead is trapping him. Hughes's first venture into the adult world isn't as satisfying as his teen angst flicks, although the charming leads help. Major drawbacks are the arguably sexist premise and dull resolution. Great soundtrack; observant viewers will notice the beemer's license plate is the title's acronym: "SHAB." **106m/C; VHS, DVD.** Kevin Bacon; Elizabeth McGovern; William Windom; Paul Gleason; Alec Baldwin; Cathryn Damon; Holland Taylor; James Ray; Isabel Lorca; Dennis Dugan; Edie McClurg; John Ashton; ***D:*** John Hughes; ***W:*** John Hughes; ***C:*** Don Peterman; ***M:*** Stewart Copeland.

She's Not Our Sister 🦴 1/2 **2011** The three Walker sisters (Vivian, Cynthia, and Deniece) are still dealing with their estranged father's death when they get some shocks at the reading of his will. They have a half-sister--Allison--from their dad's affair with a white woman and he's divided his considerable estate amongst all four of them. The catch is they will only get the money if they can all live together for six months. Oldest sister Vivian just can't cope. **90m/C; DVD.** Kellita Smith; Drew Sidora; Azur-de Johnson; Jazsmin Lewis; Clifton Powell; Tony Grant; ***D:*** Vernon Snoop Robinson; ***W:*** Johnnie Johnson; ***C:*** Timothy Vandenberg. **VIDEO**

She's Out of Control 🦴 1/2 **1989** Dad Danza goes nuts when teen daughter Dolenz (real-life daughter of Monkee Mickey Dolenz) takes the advice of Dad's girlfriend on how to attract boys. Formulaic plot could almost be an episode of "Who's the Boss?" Danza is appealing, but not enough to keep this one afloat. **95m/C; VHS, DVD.** Tony Danza; Ami Dolenz; Catherine Hicks; Wallace Shawn; Dick O'Neill; Laura Mooney; Derek McGrath; Matthew Perry; Dana Ashbrook; Todd Bridges; Robbie (Reist) Rist; ***D:*** Stan Dragoti; ***C:*** Don Peterman; ***M:*** Alan Silvestri.

She's Out of My League 🦴🦴 *Hard 10* **2010 (R)** This is another entry into the "there's no way that odd guy can date that hot girl" formula, and the outcome won't surprise anyone. Geeky airport screener Kirk (Baruchel) and hottie Molly (Eve) meet cute when he saves her from travel hassles. She asks him out, but his trio of close buds warns him against pursuing her. They rate her as a ten, and he is merely a five. Kirk proceeds to embrace his inner ten-ness, and wander through embarrassing and awkward situations with the result never in doubt. It doesn't really break any new ground, but it's pleasant enough. **106m/C; Blu-Ray.** Jay Baruchel; Alice Eve; T.J. Miller; Nate Torrence; Krysten Ritter; Geoff Stults; Lindsay Sloane; Mike Vogel; ***D:*** Jim Field Smith; ***W:*** Sean Anders; John Morris; ***C:*** Jim Denault; ***M:*** Michael Andrews.

She's So Lovely 🦴🦴 1/2 *She's De Lovely; Call It Love* **1997 (R)** Troubled young alcoholic Eddie (Penn) disappears for three days on his pregnant wife Maureen (Wright), and returns to discover that she has been brutalized by a neighbor. Retaliation costs him 10 years in a mental institution. Upon his release, Eddie decides to find his now ex-wife and the daughter he's never known. Maureen's moved on—she's happily married to Joey (Travolta), has two daughters by him, and is justifiable worried that Eddie's love (which is as strong as ever) will upset the balance of her new life. Somewhat unevenly directed by Nick Cassavetes from a screenplay written by his late father John, who had already cast Penn and was set to direct when he became ill. Film revels in the style that made the elder Cassavetes famous (or infamous), and is best appreciated as a tribute. Travolta and Penn play well off each other. **97m/C; VHS, DVD, Blu-Ray.** Sean Penn; Robin Wright; John Travolta; Harry Dean Stanton; Debi Mazar; James Gandolfini; Gena Rowlands; Kelsey Mulrooney; David Thornton; Susan Traylor; Chloe Webb; Burt Young; ***D:*** Nick Cassavetes; ***W:*** John Cassavetes; ***C:*** Thierry Arbogast; ***M:*** Joseph Vitarelli. Cannes '97: Actor (Penn).

She's the Man 🦴🦴 1/2 **2006 (PG-13)** Get past the familiar story and the fact that adorable Bynes can in no way pass for a boy, and this light-hearted teen comedy provides an amusing take on Shakespeare's "Twelfth Night." When the girls' soccer team is disbanded at her prep school, star soccer player Viola (Bynes) disguises herself as her twin brother Sebastian (Kirk) and takes his place at his new school. Her first problem (besides the cross-dressing) is falling for handsome roomie/soccer captain Duke (Tatum), who has a crush on Olivia (Ramsey) who's soon crushing on Viola—ah, Sebastian. Confusion follows. **105m/C; DVD.** Amanda Bynes; Channing Tatum; Laura Ramsey; Vinnie Jones; Robert Hoffman, III; Julie Hagerty; David Cross; Alex Breckinridge; Jonathan Sadowski; Emily Perkins; James Kirk; Clifton McCabe Murray; Brandon Jay McLaren; ***D:*** Andy Fickman; ***W:*** Karen McCullah Lutz; Kirsten Smith; Ewan Leslie; ***C:*** Greg Gardiner; ***M:*** Nathan Wang.

She's the One 🦴🦴 1/2 **1996 (R)** Another Irish family saga from Burns covering lots of the same territory as "The Brothers McMullen." Semi-slacker taxi driver Mickey Fitzpatrick (Burns) impulsively marries passenger Hope (Bahns) and their romance is contrasted with the disintegrating marriage of Mickey's younger brother, buttoned-down stockbroker Francis (McGlone) and his frustrated wife Rene (Aniston). No wonder she's frustrated, Francis is having an affair with slutty Heather (Diaz), who turns out to be Mickey's former flame. Mahoney offers a typically fine performance, along with bad marital advice as the boys' father. Again the blustering men don't have a clue about the usually smarter women. **95m/C; VHS, DVD, Blu-Ray.** Edward Burns; Mike McGlone; Jennifer Aniston; Cameron Diaz; Maxine Bahns; John Mahoney; Leslie Mann; George McCowan; Amanda Peet; Anita Gillette; Frank Vincent; ***D:*** Edward Burns; ***W:*** Edward Burns; ***C:*** Frank Prinzi; ***M:*** Tom Petty.

She's Too Young 🦴 1/2 **2004** Over-the-top portrait of the sex games that teens play. Trish Vogel's (Harden) 14-year-old daughter Hannah (Dziena) wants to be popular and succumbs to peer pressure to get sexually involved with somewhat older Nick (Erwin). When there's a syphilis outbreak reported at the high school, Trish is shocked that her 'good' daughter is involved and just what the teens have been doing. **90m/C; DVD.** Marcia Gay Harden; Alexis Dziena; Gary Hudson; Mike Erwin; Miriam McDonald; Megan Park; Deborah Odell; Rhoda Mclean; ***D:*** Tom McLoughlin; ***W:*** Richard Kletter; ***C:*** Bill Wong; ***M:*** Mark Snow. **CABLE**

She's Working Her Way Through College 🦴🦴 1/2 **1952** Loose musical remake of 1942's "The Male Animal" (from the play by James Thurber and Elliott Nugent) that focuses on Mayo's coed rather than Reagan's professor. Former burlesque dancer Angela Gardner (Mayo) enrolls at a small Midwestern college and takes writing classes from Prof. John Palmer (Reagan), who also directs the school's plays. Angela writes a musical for the students to put on, but her checkered past comes to light thanks to jealous Ivy (Wymore), whose football star boyfriend Don (Nelson) is smitten by the curvy cutie. **101m/C; DVD.** Virginia Mayo; Ronald Reagan; Gene Nelson; Patrice Wymore; Phyllis Thaxter; Don DeFore; Roland Winters; Raymond Greenlead; ***D:*** H. Bruce Humberstone; ***W:*** Peter Milne; ***C:*** Wilfred M. Cline; ***M:*** Vernon Duke.

Shifty 🦴🦴 1/2 **2008** Shifty (Ahmed) is a young British crack dealer whose life unravels when an old friend comes to visit and wants him to leave the criminal life behind. This would go so much easier if so many people didn't want them both dead. **86m/C; DVD.** *UK* Riz Ahmed; Daniel Mays; Jason Flemyng; Nitin Ganatra; Jay Simpson; Francesca Annis; ***D:*** Eran Creevy; ***W:*** Eran Creevy; ***C:*** Ed Wild; ***M:*** Molly Nyman; Harry Escott.

Shiloh 🦴🦴 1/2 **1997 (PG)** Schmaltzy but redeeming story about small town West Virginia 11-year-old Marty (Heron), who seeks to rescue and care for mistreated hunting dog Shiloh, who belongs to mean hermit Judd (Wilson). Goes beyond the typical "boy and his dog" theme with moral and ethical issues that Marty faces when he takes the dog from its owner. Frannie (who plays Shiloh) is a very cute and expressive beagle. Adapted from the Newberry award-winning novel by Phyllis Reynolds Naylor. **93m/C; VHS, DVD, Blu-Ray.** Blake Heron; Michael Moriarty; Scott Wilson; Rod Steiger; Ann Dowd; Bonnie Bartlett; ***D:*** Dale Rosenbloom; ***W:*** Dale Rosenbloom; ***C:*** Frank Byers; ***M:*** Joel Goldsmith.

Shiloh 2: Shiloh Season 🦴🦴 1/2 **1999** Low-key rural drama finds 12-year-old Marty Preston (Browne) claiming responsibility for lovable beagle Shiloh from his hard-drinking owner, Judd Travers (Wilson). But when Travers is injured in an accident, the kid has enough compassion to ask his parents to help him with the ornery cuss. Adapted from the novel by Phyllis Reynolds Naylor. **96m/C; VHS, DVD.** Zachary Browne; Scott Wilson; Michael Moriarty; Ann Dowd; Rod Steiger; Bonnie Bartlett; Joe Pichler; ***D:*** Sandy Tung; ***W:*** Dale Rosenbloom; ***C:*** Troy Smith; ***M:*** Joel Goldsmith.

Shin Godzilla 🦴🦴 1/2 *Godzilla Resurgence; Shin Gojira* **2016** The people who started it all, the men and women of Toho, return to the Godzilla franchise for the first time in years for a complete reboot of the franchise yet again. Unlike a lot of series reboots, this one works, playing off modern concerns of nuclear fallout after the incident at Fukushima. While there are a lot more modern bells and whistles in this production, it harkens back to the origins of the series, playing like the classic monster movie that a Godzilla flick needs to be to succeed. In other words, it doesn't take itself too seriously. **120m/C; DVD.** Hiroki Hasegawa; Yutaka Takenouchi; Satomi Ishihara; Ren Ohsugi; Akira (Tsukamoto) Emoto; ***D:*** Hideaki Anno; ***W:*** Hideaki Anno; ***C:*** Kosuke Yamada; ***M:*** Shiroh Sagisu.

Shin Heike Monogatari 🦴🦴🦴🦴 *New Tales of the Taira Clan* **1955** Mizoguchi's second to last film, in which a deposed Japanese emperor in 1137 endeavors to win back the throne from the current despot, who cannot handle the feudal lawlessness. Acclaimed; his second film in color. In Japanese with English subtitles. **106m/C; VHS, DVD.** *JP* Raizo Ichikawa; Ichijiro Oya; Michiyo Kogure; Eijiro Yanagi; Tatsuya Ishiguro; Yoshiko Kuga; ***D:*** Kenji Mizoguchi.

Shinbone Alley 🦴🦴 1/2 **1970 (G)** Animated musical about Archy, a free-verse poet reincarnated as a cockroach, and Mehitabel, the alley cat with a zest for life. Based on the short stories by Don Marquis. **83m/C; VHS, DVD.** ***V:*** Carol Channing; Eddie Bracken; John Carradine; Alan Reed; ***D:*** John D. Wilson.

Shine 🦴🦴🦴 1/2 **1995 (PG-13)** Astonishing true portrayal of musical genius and its cost. Teenaged pianist David Helfgott (Taylor) is a prodigy in his native Australia but is pushed to the limit by his authoritarian father Peter (Mueller-Stahl). Eventually defying his father's strictures, David accepts a scholarship to London's Royal College of Music where he triumphs under the tutelege of professor Cecil Parkes (Gielgud), but then collapses from strain. For 15 years, he is confined to psychiatric hospitals, unable to play the piano, until the now-adult David (Rush) has a chance meeting with the loving Gillian (Redgrave), whose support enables him to resume his career. Helfgott himself plays piano for his screen counterparts. **105m/C; VHS, DVD.** *AU* Geoffrey Rush; Noah Taylor; Armin Mueller-Stahl; Lynn Redgrave; John Gielgud; Googie Withers; Chris Haywood; Sonia Todd; Alex Rafalowicz; Randall Berger; ***D:*** Scott Hicks; ***W:*** Jan Sardi; ***C:*** Geoffrey Simpson; ***M:*** David Hirschfelder. Oscars '96: Actor (Rush); Australian Film Inst. '96: Actor (Rush), Cinematog., Director (Hicks), Film, Film Editing, Orig. Screenplay, Score, Sound, Support. Actor (Mueller-Stahl); British Acad. '96: Actor (Rush); Golden Globes '97: Actor--Drama (Rush); L.A. Film Critics '96: Actor (Rush); Natl. Bd. of Review '96: Film; N.Y. Film Critics '96: Actor (Rush); Screen Actors Guild '96: Actor (Rush); Broadcast Film Critics '96: Actor (Rush).

Shine a Light 🦴🦴 1/2 **2008 (PG-13)** Scorsese does the Stones. Most of the documentary is devoted to the band's 2006 performance at the Beacon Theater with some pre-performance set-up. The director also primarily focuses on lead showman Jagger (with cutaways to Watts, Wood, and Richards), and the ravages of time over their 40-year career are highlighted with some interspersed interview footage from earlier decades. Performance-wise the Stones live up to the legend, but on screen, it all seems a little forced. Guest performers include Buddy Guy, Christina Aguilera, and Jack White. **122m/C; DVD, Blu-Ray.** ***D:*** Martin Scorsese; ***C:*** Robert Richardson.

A Shine of Rainbows 🦴🦴 1/2 **2009 (PG)** Touching family drama with good performances and lovely Irish scenery. Timid 8-year-old orphan Tomas (Bell) is adopted by loving Maire O'Donnell (Nielsen), who lives with her stern husband Alec (Quinn) on Corrie Island off the Irish coast. She teaches Tomas about the local folklore, including the caves and seals, and Tomas finds an abandoned baby seal and secretly cares for it. Maire becomes ill and Tomas is fearful he will be abandoned again. **101m/C; DVD.** *CA IR* John Bell; Connie Nielsen; Aidan Quinn; Jack Gleeson; Tara Alice Scully; Niamh Shaw; ***D:*** Vic Sarin; ***W:*** Vic Sarin; Dennis Foon; Catherine Spear; ***C:*** Vic Sarin; ***M:*** Keith Power.

Shiner 🦴🦴 1/2 **2000** Caine delivers the goods as a small-time boxing promoter from London's East End on the brink of hitting it big. As Billy "Shiner" Simpson, Caine preps his son Eddie for a high-profile, possibly career-making match against an American. The match has disaster written all over it early on, however, when Billy's daughter interrupts to bring up some past legal problems, Eddie doesn't perform as expected, and murder, betrayal, and doublecrosses rear their ugly heads. A showcase for Caine's talents, unfortunately, the story around him loses it's luster after a solid first half turns disappointing. Borrows liberally from Shakespeare's "King Lear." **99m/C; VHS, DVD.** *GB* Michael Caine; Martin Landau; Matthew Marsden; Frances Barber; Frank Harper; Andy Serkis; Claire Rushbrook; Danny (Daniel) Webb; Kenneth Cranham; David Kennedy; Peter Wight; Nicola Walker; ***D:*** John Irvin; ***W:*** Scott Cherry; ***C:*** Mike Molloy; ***M:*** Paul Grabowsky.

The Shining 🦴🦴 1/2 **1980 (R)** Very loose adaptation of the Stephen King horror novel about a writer and his family, snowbound in a huge hotel, who experience various hauntings caused by either the hotel itself or the writer's dementia. Technically stunning, and pretty dang scary, but too long, pretentious and implausible. Nicholson is excellent as the failed writer gone off the deep end. **143m/C; VHS, DVD, Blu-Ray, HD-DVD.** Jack Nicholson; Shelley Duvall; Danny Lloyd; Scatman Crothers; Joe Turkel; Barry Nelson; Philip Stone; Lia Beldam; Billie Gibson; Barry Dennen; David Baxt; Lisa Burns; Alison Coleridge; Kate Phelps; Anne Jackson; Tony Burton; ***D:*** Stanley Kubrick; ***W:*** Stanley Kubrick; Diane Johnson; ***C:*** John Alcott; ***M:*** Walter (Wendy) Carlos; Rachel Elkind. Natl. Film Reg. '18.

The Shining Hour 🦴🦴 1/2 **1938** A compelling melodrama in which Crawford portrays a New York night club dancer who is pursued by the rather conservative Douglas. His brother tries to persuade him from marrying Crawford, but then he soon finds himself attracted to her. A devastating fire wipes out all problems of family dissension in this intelligent soap opera. **76m/B; VHS, DVD.** Joan Crawford; Margaret Sullavan; Melvyn Douglas; Robert Young; Fay Bainter; Allyn Joslyn; ***D:*** Frank Borzage; ***W:*** Ogden Nash; Jane Murfin; ***C:*** George J. Folsey.

Shining Star 🦴 1/2 *That's the Way of the World* **1975 (PG)** A recording company is run by the mob. Potentially interesting film is hampered by quality of sound and photography and general lack of purpose or direction. **100m/C; VHS, DVD, Blu-Ray, HD-DVD.** Harvey Keitel; Ed Nelson; Cynthia Bostick; Bert Parks; ***D:*** Sig Shore.

Shining Through 🦴🦴 1/2 **1992 (R)** Baby-voiced Griffith as a spy sent behind enemy lines without training? Douglas as a spy sent behind enemy lines without speaking German? Old-fashioned blend of romance, espionage, and derring-do where noble hero saves spunky heroine from nasty Nazis in WWII Germany works despite thin plot. Series of flash-forwards to an aged Griffith is annoying and tends to stop action cold, but everyone tries hard and period flavor is authentic. Adapted from best-selling Susan Isaacs novel, but bears little resemblance to book. **133m/C; VHS, DVD.** Michael Douglas; Melanie Griffith; Liam Neeson; Joely Richardson; John Gielgud; Francis Guinan; Patrick Winczewski; Sylvia Syms; ***D:*** David Seltzer; ***W:*** David Seltzer; ***C:*** Jan De Bont; ***M:*** Michael Kamen. Golden Raspberries '92: Worst Actress (Griffith), Worst Director (Seltzer), Worst Picture.

Shinobi ♪♪♪ *Shinobi: Heart Under Blade* **2005 (R)** Based on the novel "The Kouga Ninja Scrolls", the Iga and Koga Ninja clans are asked to live in peace after 400 years of war. But eventually the Shogun decides they are a threat to the peace and has his advisor create a plot to have them both killed in a pointless fight. When the heads of the clan die, it is discovered that the new heads are in love with each other. However, their being in love doesn't stop the many magically infused ninja fights. **91m/C; DVD.** *JP* Joe Odagiri; Kippei Shiina; Tak Sakaguchi; Houka Kinoshita; Minori Terada; Toshiya Nagasawa; Yutaka Matsushige; Renji Ishibashi; Kazuo Kitamura; Yukie Nakama; Tomoka Kurotani; Erika Sawajiri; Takeshi Masu; Mitsuki Koga; Shun Ito; Riri; Masaki Nishina; ***D:*** Ten Shimoyama; ***W:*** Kenya Hirata; Futaro Yamada; ***C:*** Masasai Chikamori; ***M:*** Taro Iwashiro.

Shinobi no Mono ♪♪♪ *Ninja 1; The Ninja; Band of Assassins* **1962** Loosely adapted on history, this is the first of eight ninja films made in the 60s, and said to be part of the inspiration for the James Bond film "You Only Live Twice." Tyrannical Lord Oda Nobunaga is waging war on all the Shinobi (ninja) clans, and they are competing to be the ones who kill him first. Considered among the most realistic of ninja films made, possibly in part because two former ninja were said to be technical advisors. **105m/C; DVD.** *JP* Raizo Ichikawa; Yunosuke Ito; Shiho Fujimura; Kyoko Kishida; Chitose Maki; Tomisaburo Wakayama; Katsuhiko Kobayashi; Reiko Fujiwara; ***D:*** Satsuo Yamamoto; ***W:*** Hajime Taikawa; ***C:*** Yasukazu Takemura; ***M:*** Michiaki Watanabe.

Shinobi no Mono 2: Vengeance ♪♪♪ *Zoku shinobi no mono; The Ninja Part II* **1963** The second of the 1960s ninja series, and the last of the eight to have actual ninjas as advisors. The Iga ninja clan has been all but destroyed by Odan Nobunaga, and he is conducting a terror campaign to find the last of them—Goemon (Raizo Ichikawa). He teams up with Hattori Hanzo (Date Saburo) to bring down Nobunaga once and for all. A bit more brutal than the first film, and definitely darker, it shows feudal Japan as a dangerous place to have lived. **93m/C; DVD.** *JP* Raizo Ichikawa; Shiho Fujimura; Mikiko Tsubouchi; Tomisaburo Wakayama; Date Saburo; ***D:*** Satsuo Yamamoto; ***W:*** Hajime Taikawa; Tomoyoshi Murayama; ***C:*** Senkichiro Takeda; ***M:*** Michiaki Watanabe.

Shinobi No Mono 3: Resurrection ♪♪ 1/2 *Shin shinobi no mono; Goemon Will Never Die; Ninja 3; The New Ninja* **2009** When last we saw Goemon (Raizo Ichikawa) he was in a bit of a predicament. Escaping it with the help of the mysterious Hattori Hanzo, he once again pursues warlord Toyotomi Hideyoshi while pretending to still be deceased. Meanwhile the villain Tokugawa Ieyasu prepares to become the one true ruler of Japan by pulling the strings behind the scenes. The third of eight films in the series, this one is more of a political drama than a martial arts or action film. **86m/B; DVD.** *JP* Raizo Ichikawa; Ayako Wakao; ***D:*** Kazuo Mori; ***W:*** Hajime Taikawa; ***C:*** Hiroshi Imai; ***M:*** Michiaki Watanabe.

Ship Ahoy ♪♪ 1/2 **1942** Songs, comedy, a spy spoof, and some patriotism thrown in for good measure. Powell plays a dancer who works with Tommy Dorsey and his orchestra. They're on their way to Puerto Rico, via ocean liner, along with her pulp fiction writer boyfriend (Skelton). Emery, posing as an FBI man, convinces Powell to smuggle a package for him but he's really a spy and the whole thing's a con which turns out to be based on one of Skelton's potboiler plots. An uncredited Frank Sinatra is the singer with the Dorsey band, along with drummer Buddy Rich and trumpeter Ziggy Elman who provide some great musical solos. **95m/B; VHS, DVD.** Eleanor Powell; Red Skelton; Bert Lahr; Virginia O'Brien; John Emery; William Post, Jr.; ***D:*** Edward Buzzell; ***W:*** Harry Kurnitz; Harry Clork; Irving Brecher.

Ship of Fools ♪♪♪ **1965** A group of passengers sailing to Germany in the '30s find mutual needs and concerns, struggle with early evidence of Nazi racism, and discover love on their voyage. Twisted story and fine acting maintain interest. Appropriate tunes written by Ernest Gold. Based on the Katherine Ann Porter novel. Leigh's last film role; she died two years later. Kramer grapples with civil rights issues in much of his work. **149m/B; VHS, DVD, Blu-Ray.** Vivien Leigh; Simone Signoret; Jose Ferrer; Lee Marvin; Oskar Werner; Michael Dunn; Elizabeth Ashley; George Segal; Jose Greco; Charles Korvin; Heinz Ruhmann; ***D:*** Stanley Kramer; ***W:*** Abby Mann; ***C:*** Ernest Laszlo; ***M:*** Ernest Gold. Oscars '65: Art Dir./Set Dec., B&W, B&W Cinematog.; Natl. Bd. of Review '65: Actor (Marvin); N.Y. Film Critics '65: Actor (Werner).

Shipmates ♪ 1/2 **1931** Early talkie is a run-of-the-mill romance that has ordinary seaman Jonesy (Montgomery) in love with admiral's daughter Kit Corbin (Jordan), but the difference in their social status is an obstacle. Jonesy tries to get into the Naval Academy but is constantly thwarted by his angry superior, McTavish (Torrence). **72m/B; DVD.** Robert Montgomery; Ernest Torrence; Dorothy Jordan; Hobart Bosworth; Cliff Edwards; George Irving; ***D:*** Harry A. Pollard; ***W:*** Delmer Daves; ***C:*** Clyde De Vinna.

Shipmates Forever ♪♪ **1935** To please his Admiral father, Dick (Powell) enters the Naval Academy even though he would rather have a singing career. He's in love with dancer June (Keeler), whose family has a long Navy tradition so she tells him he should make the effort to get through the training. Dick doesn't want to make friends with any of his fellow cadets but circumstances change in a tragic way. **109m/B; DVD.** Dick Powell; Ruby Keeler; Lewis Stone; Ross Alexander; John Arledge; Eddie Acuff; Dick Foran; ***D:*** Frank Borzage; ***W:*** Delmer Daves; ***C:*** Sol Polito.

The Shipping News ♪♪ **2001 (R)** Spacey is Quoyle, a middle-aged lifetime loser who returns to his childhood home of Newfoundland with his daughter and aunt (Dench) after his adulterous wife (Blanchett) dies. There, among the absurdly quirky citizenry, he meets Wavey (Moore) a widow who runs the day-care center and may hold the key to changing Quoyle's life around. Those who read the book (and there are many), will be deeply disappointed, and those who haven't may merely be deeply depressed. The desolate landscape is beautifully shot, but Spacey is badly miscast as the sad-sack loser, and subplots that could lead to some drama are dropped inexplicably. Blanchett and Moore distinguish themselves nicely. **120m/C; VHS, DVD, Blu-Ray.** Kevin Spacey; Dame Judi Dench; Cate Blanchett; Julianne Moore; Pete Postlethwaite; Scott Glenn; Rhys Ifans; Gordon Pinsent; Jason Behr; Larry Pine; Jeanetta Arnette; Robert Joy; Alyssa Gainer; Kaitlyn Gainer; Lauren Gainer; Marc Lawrence; ***D:*** Lasse Hallstrom; ***W:*** Robert Nelson Jacobs; ***C:*** Oliver Stapleton; ***M:*** Christopher Young. Natl. Bd. of Review '01: Support. Actress (Blanchett).

Shipwrecked ♪♪ 1/2 *Haakon Haakonsen* **1990 (PG)** Kiddie swashbuckler based on the 1873 popular novel "Haakon Haakonsen." A cabin boy is marooned on an island where he defends the hidden pirate treasure he finds by boobytrapping the island. **93m/C; VHS, DVD.** *NO* Gabriel Byrne; Stian Smestad; Louisa Haigh; Trond Munch; Bjorn Sundquist; Eva Von Hanno; Kjell Stormoen; ***D:*** Nils Gaup; ***W:*** Nils Gaup; Nick Thiel; ***M:*** Patrick Doyle.

Shirin ♪♪ **2009** This unusual drama offers an unexpected perspective on a popular 12th century Persian poem, Khosrow and Shirin. Staged by Kiarostami, the film focuses solely on the silent spectators of the theatrical production. The audience consists of 114 well-known actresses from Iranian stage and screen, as well as a French film star, Juliette Binoche. **92m/C; DVD.** Juliette Binoche; Golshifteh Farahani; Leila Hatami; Mahnaz Afshar; Taraneh Alidoosti; ***D:*** Abbas Kiarostami; ***C:*** Mahmoud Kalari.

Shirley Valentine ♪♪♪ **1989** A lively middle-aged English housewife gets a new lease on life when she travels to Greece without her husband. Collins reprises her London and Broadway stage triumph. The character frequently addresses the audience directly to explain her thoughts and feelings; her energy and spunk carry the day. Good script by Russell from his play. From the people who brought us "Educating Rita." **108m/C; DVD.** *UK* Pauline Collins; Tom Conti; Alison Steadman; Julia McKenzie; Joanna Lumley; Bernard Hill; Sylvia Syms; ***D:*** Lewis Gilbert; ***W:*** George Hadjinassios; Willy Russell; ***C:*** Alan Hume; ***M:*** Willy Russell. British Acad. '89: Actress (Collins).

Shoah ♪♪♪♪ **1985** Epic, awe-inspiring documentary that details the devastation of the Holocaust exclusively through interviews with survivors of the camps, former Nazis and native Germans who knew what was happening and stood by. A searing, significant document hailed as one of the most important documentaries in the history of film. **570m/C; VHS, DVD, Blu-Ray.** ***D:*** Claude Lanzmann; ***C:*** Dominique Chapuis; William Lubtchansky. British Acad. '87: Feature Doc.

The Shock ♪♪ 1/2 **1923** Crippled low-life Chaney becomes restored spiritually by a small-town girl and rebels against his Chinese boss. This causes an unfortunate string of melodramatic tragedies, including the San Francisco earthquake of 1906. Silent. Odd, desultory tale with bad special effects is worth seeing for Chaney's good acting. **96m/B; Silent; VHS, DVD.** Lon Chaney, Sr.; Virginia Valli; ***D:*** Lambert Hillyer.

Shock! ♪♪ **1946** A psychiatrist is called on to treat a woman on the edge of a nervous breakdown. He then discovers she saw him murder his wife, and tries to keep her from remembering it. Interesting premise handled in trite B style. Price's first starring role. **70m/B; VHS, DVD.** Vincent Price; Lynn Bari; Frank Latimore; Anabel Shaw; ***D:*** Alfred Werker.

Shock ♪♪ 1/2 *Beyond the Door 2; Shock; Suspense; Al 33 di Via Orologio fa Sempre Freddo* **1979 (R)** Better treatment of the possession theme, but this time the door is to the home of a new family: Colin (from the original) plays a boy possessed by his dead father, who seeks revenge on his widow and her new husband. Director Bava's last feature. **90m/C; VHS, DVD.** *IT* John Steiner; Daria Nicolodi; David Colin, Jr.; Ivan Rassimov; Nicola Salerno; ***D:*** Mario Bava; ***W:*** Lamberto Bava; Franco Barbieri; Dardano Sacchetti; Paolo Brigenti; ***C:*** Alberto Spagnoli.

Shock and Awe ♪♪ **2018 (R)** In the wake of 9/11, as the Bush administration scrambles for a plausible excuse to initiate war with Iraq, a team of Knight Ridder journalists suspects that the weapons of mass destruction allegedly held by Saddam Hussein don't exist. What could have been a taut account of tenacious, hard-nosed investigative journalism falls flat. Harrelson, Reiner, Jones, and Marsden deliver the goods, but the script is so pedestrian and clumsy that there's little tension or urgency, much less awe or shock. **90m/C; DVD, Blu-Ray.** Rob Reiner; Woody Harrelson; James Marsden; Tommy Lee Jones; Jessica Biel; ***D:*** Rob Reiner; ***W:*** Joey Hartstone; ***C:*** Barry Markowitz; ***M:*** Jeff Beal.

Shock Corridor ♪♪♪ **1963** A reporter, dreaming of a Pulitzer Prize, fakes mental illness and gets admitted to an asylum, where he hopes to investigate a murder. He is subjected to disturbing experiences, including shock therapy, but does manage to solve the murder. However, he suffers a mental breakdown in the process and is admitted for real. Disturbing and lurid. **101m/B; VHS, DVD.** Peter Breck; Constance Towers; Gene Evans; Hari Rhodes; James Best; Philip Ahn; Larry Tucker; Paul Dubov; ***D:*** Samuel Fuller; ***W:*** Samuel Fuller; ***C:*** Stanley Cortez; ***M:*** Paul Dunlap. Natl. Film Reg. '96.

Shock 'Em Dead ♪♪ **1990 (R)** A devil worshipper trades his life to Lucifer for a chance at rock and roll fame and beautiful Miss Lords. Sexy thriller, with a good share of violence and tension. Ironically, ex porn great Lords is one of the few starlets who doesn't disrobe in the film. **94m/C; DVD, Blu-Ray.** Traci Lords; Aldo Ray; Troy Donahue; Stephen Quadros; Tim Moffett; Gina Parks; Laurel Wiley; Tyger Sodipe; Karen Russell; ***D:*** Mark Freed; ***W:*** Mark Freed; Andrew Cross; Dave Tedder; ***C:*** Ron Chapman.

A Shock to the System ♪♪♪ **1990 (R)** Business exec. Caine is passed over for a long-deserved promotion in favor of a younger man. When he accidentally pushes a panhandler in front of a subway in a fit of rage, he realizes how easy murder is and thinks it may be the answer to all his problems. Tries to be a satire take on corporate greed, etc., but somehow loses steam. Excellent cast makes the difference; Caine adds class. Based on the novel by Simon Brett. **88m/C; VHS, DVD, Blu-Ray.** Michael Caine; Elizabeth McGovern; Peter Riegert; Swoosie Kurtz; Will Patton; Jenny Wright; John McMartin; Barbara Baxley; ***D:*** Jan Egleson; ***W:*** Andrew Klavan; ***C:*** Paul Goldsmith; ***M:*** Gary Chang.

Shock to the System ♪♪ 1/2 **2006 (R)** In the second Donald Strachey mystery (following "Third Man Out"), the Albany PI (Allen) is suspicious when client Paul Hale allegedly commits suicide. He discovers Paul's homophobic mom (Fairchild) pushed him towards a gay conversion therapy group run by the shady Dr. Cornell (Woods). So Donald decides to go undercover to investigate, which may cost him his own life. Based on the series by Richard Stevenson. **95m/C; DVD.** Chad Allen; Sebastian Spence; Michael Woods; Morgan Fairchild; Daryl Shuttleworth; Nelson Wong; Anne Marie Deluise; ***D:*** Ron Oliver; ***W:*** Ron McGee; ***C:*** C. Kim Miles; ***M:*** Peter Allen. **CABLE**

Shock Treatment ♪ 1/2 *Traitement de Choc* **1981 (PG)** Seldom-seen mediocre semi-sequel to the cult classic, "The Rocky Horror Picture Show" (1975). Brad and Janet, now married and portrayed by different leads, find themselves trapped on a TV gameshow full of weirdos. Same writers, same director, and several original cast members do make an appearance. **94m/C; VHS, DVD.** Richard O'Brien; Jessica Harper; Cliff DeYoung; Patricia Quinn; Charles Gray; Ruby Wax; Nell Campbell; Rik Mayall; Barry Humphries; Darlene Johnson; Manning Redwood; ***D:*** Jim Sharman; ***W:*** Richard O'Brien; Jim Sharman; ***C:*** Mike Molloy; ***M:*** Richard O'Brien; Richard Hartley.

Shock Waves ♪♪ *Death Corps; Almost Human* **1977 (PG)** Group of mutant-underwater-zombie-Nazi-soldiers terrorizes stranded tourists staying at a deserted motel on a small island. Cushing is the mad scientist intent on recreating the Nazi glory days with the seaweed-attired zombies. Odd B-grade, more or less standard horror flick somehow rises (slightly) above badness. Halpin's name was erroneously listed as Halprin—even on the original movie poster! **90m/C; VHS, DVD, Blu-Ray.** Peter Cushing; Brooke Adams; John Carradine; Luke Halpin; Jack Davidson; Fred Buch; ***D:*** Ken Wiederhorn; ***W:*** Ken Wiederhorn; John Kent Harrison; ***C:*** Reuben Trane; ***M:*** Richard Einhorn.

Shocker ♪♪ 1/2 **1989 (R)** Another Craven gore-fest. A condemned serial killer is transformed into a menacing electrical force after being fried in the chair. Practically a remake of Craven's original "Nightmare on Elm Street." Great special effects, a few enjoyable weird and sick moments. What's Dr. Timothy Leary doing here? **111m/C; VHS, DVD.** Michael Murphy; Peter Berg; Camille (Cami) Cooper; Mitch Pileggi; Richard Price; Timothy Leary; Heather Langenkamp; Theodore (Ted) Raimi; Richard Brooks; Sam Scarber; ***D:*** Wes Craven; ***W:*** Wes Craven; ***C:*** Jacques Haitkin; ***M:*** William Goldstein.

The Shocking Miss Pilgrim ♪♪ **1947** Minor Technicolor musical comedy. Typist Cynthia Pilgrim (Grable) is the first female employee at a Boston shipping company in1874. She intrigues her boss, John Pritchard (Haymes), but he objects to her shocking involvement with the suffrage movement and her job and their would-be romance is called into question. **87m/C; DVD.** Betty Grable; Dick Haymes; Anne Revere;

Allyn Joslyn; Gene Lockhart; ***D:*** George Seaton; ***W:*** George Seaton; ***C:*** Leon Shamroy.

Shockproof **1949** Minor noir. Tough Jenny Marsh (Knight) is paroled on a self-defense rap and parole officer Griff Marat (Wilde) gets her work caring for his blind mother after warning her against meeting up with her bad news ex-beau Harry (Baragrey). Eventually, Jenny and Griff fall for each other and Harry tries to blackmail them. Has a forced, hokey ending that was allegedly written by Deutsch not Fuller. **79m/B; DVD.** Cornel Wilde; John Baragrey; Howard St. John; Russell Collins; Patricia Knight; Esther Miniciotti; Charles Bates; ***D:*** Douglas Sirk; ***W:*** Helen Deutsch; Samuel Fuller; ***C:*** Charles Lawton, Jr.; ***M:*** George Duning.

Shockwave ½ *A.I. Assault* **2006 (R)** A plane crashes on a deserted Pacific island carrying two self-aware combat robots. The military orders the Navy SEALS to go in and contain the threat but the robots get smarter and more lethal the longer they're on. **94m/C; DVD.** Joe Lando; Lisa LoCicero; Joshua Cox; Blake Gibbons; Hudson (Heidi) Leick; ***D:*** Jim Wynorski; ***W:*** Jim Wynorski; Bill Monroe; ***C:*** Ken Blakey; ***M:*** Chuck Cirino. **CABLE**

The Shoes of the Fisherman ½ **1968 (G)** Morris West's interesting, speculative best seller about Russian Pope brought to the big screen at much expense, but with little care or thought. Siberian prison-camp vet Quinn, elected Pope, tries to arrest nuclear war. Director Anderson wasted the prodigious talents of Olivier, Gielgud, et al. Sloppy use of good cast and promising plot. **160m/C; VHS, DVD.** Anthony Quinn; Leo McKern; Laurence Olivier; John Gielgud; Vittorio De Sica; Oskar Werner; David Janssen; ***D:*** Michael Anderson, Sr.; ***M:*** Alex North. Golden Globes '69: Score; Natl. Bd. of Review '68: Support. Actor (McKern).

Shoeshine **1947** Two shoeshine boys struggling to survive in post-war Italy become involved in the black market and are eventually caught and imprisoned. Prison scenes detail the sense of abandonment and tragedy that destroys their friendship. A rich, sad achievement in neo-realistic drama. In Italian with English subtitles. **90m/B; VHS, DVD.** *IT* Franco Interlenghi; Rinaldo Smordoni; Annielo Mele; Bruno Ortensi; Pacifico Astrologo; ***D:*** Vittorio De Sica; ***W:*** Cesare Zavattini; Sergio Amidei; Adolfo Franci; C.G. Viola. Oscars '47: Foreign Film.

Shogun ½ *James Clavell's Shogun* **1980** Miniseries chronicling the saga of a shipwrecked English navigator who becomes the first Shogun, or Samurai warrior chief, from the Western world. Colorfully adapted from the James Clavell bestseller. Also released in a two-hour version, but this full-length version is infinitely better. **550m/C; VHS, DVD, Blu-Ray.** Richard Chamberlain; Toshiro Mifune; Yoko Shimada; John Rhys-Davies; Damien Thomas; William Morgan Sheppard; ***Nar:*** Orson Welles; ***D:*** Jerry London; ***M:*** Maurice Jarre. **TV**

Shogun Assassin ½ **1980 (R)** Story of a proud samurai named Lone Wolf who served his Shogun master well as the Official Decapitator, until the fateful day when the aging Shogun turned against him. Extremely violent, with record-breaking body counts. Edited from two other movies in a Japanese series called "Sword of Vengeance"; a tour de force of the cutting room. The samurai pushes his son's stroller through much of the film-sets it aside to hack and slash. **89m/C; VHS, DVD, Blu-Ray.** *JP* Tomisaburo Wakayama; Kayo Matsuo; Shin Kishida; Masahiro Tomikawa; ***D:*** Robert Houston; ***W:*** Robert Houston; David Weisman; Kazuo Koike; ***C:*** Chishi Makiura; ***M:*** W. Michael Lewis; Mark Lindsay.

Shogun Assassin 2: Lightning Swords of Death *Kozure Okami: Shinikazeni mukau ubaguruma; Baby Cart; Lone Wolf and Cub: Baby Cart to Hades* **1973** Few Japanese comics are more iconic than the Lone Wolf and Cub series, about a rogue samurai and his young son facing down an army of assassins. In the seventies they were made into six films, and these were dubbed and re-edited into Shogun Assassins for U.S. release. **89m/C; DVD, Blu-Ray.** *JP* Tomisaburo Wakayama; Yuko Hamada; Isao Yamagata; Akihiro Tomikawa; Jun Hamamura; Go Kato; Michitaro Mizushima; ***D:*** Kenji Misumi; ***W:*** Kazuo Koike; Goseki Kojima; ***C:*** Chishi Makiura; ***M:*** Hiroshi Kamayatsu; Hideaki Sakurai.

Shoot 'Em Up ½ **2007 (R)** Mystery man Smith (Owen) sees a pregnant woman being chased by a crew of thugs and decides to step in. The woman dies, but not before Smith delivers the baby and takes it under his protection, recruiting prostitute Donna (Bellucci) to help nurse it. Meanwhile he's got to fight off mercenary Hertz (Giamatti), who's determined to get the baby no matter what it takes. Inevitably, the bodies start to pile up as Smith shows that he's handled a gun or four in his past. Extraordinarily violent with a tongue-in-cheek attitude, owing much to John Woo and other Asian action directors (Davis cites "Hard Boiled" as his inspiration). It doesn't match other big guns/big explosion actioners in quality but it hits fairly often, although Davis doesn't have Woo's knack for story or breaking the tension between onslaughts of extreme violence. **87m/C; DVD, Blu-Ray.** Clive Owen; Paul Giamatti; Monica Bellucci; Daniel Pilon; Julian Richings; ***D:*** Michael Davis; ***W:*** Michael Davis; ***C:*** Peter Pau; ***M:*** Paul Haslinger.

Shoot First and Pray You Live **2008 (R)** Dull western with a duller lead. Red Pierre falls in with Jim Boone and his outlaw gang when he seeks revenge for the murder of his father by bandit Bob McGurk. **110m/C; DVD.** Jeff Hephner; John Doman; Jim Gaffigan; James Russo; Clay Wilcox; Tamara Hope; Richard Tyson; ***D:*** Lance Doty; ***W:*** Lance Doty; ***C:*** Bruce McCleery; ***M:*** Keith Patchell. **VIDEO**

Shoot First, Die Later ½ *Il poliziotto è marcio* **1974** Officer Malacarne (Luc Merenda) has a shining record that conceals his side job as part of a seemingly benign smuggling operation. When his partners switch from smuggling booze to guns, Malacarne objects and quickly sees his life deteriorate around him. **95m/C; DVD, Blu-Ray.** *FR IT* Luc Merenda; Richard Conte; Delia Boccardo; Raymond Pellegrin; Gianni Santuccio; ***D:*** Fernando Di Leo; ***W:*** Fernando Di Leo; Sergio Donati; ***C:*** Franco Villa; ***M:*** Luis Bacalov. **VIDEO**

Shoot Loud, Louder, I Don't Understand! ½ *Spara Forte, Piu Forte...Non Capisco* **1966** A sculptor who has a hard time separating reality from dreams thinks he witnessed a murder. Shenanigans follow. Meant to be a black comedy, but when not dull, it is confusing. Welch looks good, as usual, but doesn't show acting talent here. In Italian with English subtitles. **101m/C; VHS, DVD.** *IT* Marcello Mastroianni; Raquel Welch; ***D:*** Eduardo de Filippo; ***M:*** Nino Rota.

Shoot or Be Shot ½ **2002 (PG-13)** Harvey Wilkes (Shatner) is a movie-lover who bolted from the psych ward with a script of his very own. As luck would have it, he happens upon a film crew shooting in the desert and usurps the production. Shatner is in great comedic form in this otherwise stale mockery of all that is Hollywood. **90m/C; VHS, DVD.** William Shatner; Harry Hamlin; Tim Thomerson; James Healy, Jr.; Scott Rinker; ***D:*** Randy Argue; ***C:*** Ralph Linhardt; ***M:*** Joseph Alfuso. **VIDEO**

Shoot Out ½ *Shootout* **1971** Hamfisted western based on Will James' novel "The Lone Cowboy" and previously filmed in 1934. Clay Lomax (Peck) gets out a prison and wants revenge on the partner, Sam Foley (Gregory), who doublecrossed him. So Foley hires a young gunslinger (Lyons) to take care of Lomax. In addition, Lomax gets stuck with an orphaned 8-year-old girl, who's the daughter of an ex-lover (and may be Lomax's flesh-and-blood). Peck's just too nice while Lyons chews all the scenery. **94m/C; DVD.** Gregory Peck; Robert F. Lyons; Susan Tyrrell; Jeff Corey; James Gregory; Rita Gam; Pepe Serna; John Davis Chandler; Paul Fix; Arthur Hunnicutt; Nicolas Beauvy; ***D:*** Henry Hathaway; ***W:*** Marguerite Roberts; ***C:*** Earl Rath; ***M:*** Dave Grusin.

Shoot-out at Medicine Bend ½ **1957** This routine western was Scott's last for Warner Bros. Civil war vet Buck Devlin goes undercover to find out who sold faulty ammunition to the Army, resulting in his brother's death. Dickinson is his nominal love interest. **87m/B; DVD.** Randolph Scott; James Craig; Angie Dickinson; James Garner; Gordon Jones; ***D:*** Richard L. Bare; ***W:*** John Tucker Battle; D.D. Beauchamp; ***C:*** Carl Guthrie; ***M:*** Roy Webb.

Shoot the Living, Pray for the Dead *Prega il Morto e Ammazza il Vivo* **1970** While travelling through Mexico, the leader of a band of killers promises his guide half of a share in stolen gold if he can lead them to it. **90m/C; VHS, DVD.** *IT* Klaus Kinski; Victoria Zinny; Paul Sullivan; Dino Stano; ***D:*** Giuseppe Vari; ***C:*** Franco Villa; ***M:*** Mario Migliardi.

Shoot the Moon ½ **1982 (R)** A successful writer, married and with four children, finds his life unrewarding and leaves his family to take up with a younger woman. The wife must learn to deal with her resentment, the fears of her children, and her own attempt at a new love. Fine acting but a worn-out story. **124m/C; VHS, DVD.** Diane Keaton; Albert Finney; Karen Allen; Peter Weller; Dana Hill; Viveka Davis; Tracey Gold; Tina Yothers; ***D:*** Alan Parker; ***W:*** Bo Goldman.

Shoot the Piano Player *Tirez sur le Pianiste; Shoot the Pianist* **1962** Former concert pianist (Aznavour, spendidly cast) changes his name and plays piano at a low-class Paris cafe. A convoluted plot ensues; he becomes involved with gangsters, though his girlfriend wants him to try a comeback. Lots of atmosphere, character development, humor, and romance. A Truffaut masterpiece based on a pulp novel by David Goodis. In French with English subtitles. **92m/B; VHS, DVD.** *FR* Charles Aznavour; Marie DuBois; Nicole Berger; Michele Mercier; Albert Remy; ***D:*** Francois Truffaut; ***W:*** Marcel Moussey; Francois Truffaut; ***C:*** Raoul Coutard; ***M:*** Georges Delerue.

Shoot to Kill **1988 (R)** A city cop (Poitier, better than ever after 10 years off the screen) and a mountain guide (Berenger) reluctantly join forces to capture a killer who is part of a hunting party traversing the Pacific Northwest and which is being led by the guide's unsuspecting girlfriend (Alley). Poitier may be a bit old for the role, but he carries the implausible plot on the strength of his performance. Good action. **110m/C; VHS, DVD.** Sidney Poitier; Tom Berenger; Kirstie Alley; Clancy Brown; Richard Masur; Andrew (Andy) Robinson; Frederick Coffin; Kevin Scannell; ***D:*** Roger Spottiswoode; ***W:*** Michael Burton; Harv Zimmel; Daniel Petrie, Jr.; ***C:*** Michael Chapman; ***M:*** John Scott.

Shoot to Kill *Disparen a Matar* **1990** An innocent young man is murdered during a police round-up while his mother watches helplessly. The police try a whitewash—proclaiming the victim a criminal—but she launches a long campaign for justice. Spanish with subtitles. **90m/C; VHS, DVD.** *VZ* Amalia Perez Diaz; Jean Carlo Simancas; Dan Alvarado; Flor Nunez; ***D:*** Carlos Azpurua; ***W:*** David Suarez; ***C:*** Adriano Moreno; ***M:*** Waldemar D'Lima.

The Shooter ½ *Deadly Shooter* **1997** The frontier town of Kingston is being terrorized by outlaw Krantz (Smith) and his gang until gunfighter Michael Atherton (Dudikoff) becomes their reluctant defender. Modest budget but lots of action. **93m/C; VHS, DVD, Streaming.** Michael Dudikoff; Randy Travis; Andrew Stevens; William (Bill) Smith; ***D:*** Fred Olen Ray. **VIDEO**

Shooter ½ **2007 (R)** Political conspiracy action thriller, based on the novel "Point of Impact" by Stephen Hunter. Former Marine sniper Bob Lee Swagger (Wahlberg, the perfect stoic hero) is living peacefully in a Wyoming cabin when he's approached by retired colonel Isaac Johnson (Glover), who tells Swagger his expertise is needed to prevent a presidential assassination. Naturally, it's all a set-up and Swagger has to go on the run to counteract those government weasels. Pena and Mara serve as allies while Glover, Beatty, Koteas, and Sherbedgia are on the side of evil. **122m/C; DVD, Blu-Ray, HD-DVD.** Mark Wahlberg; Michael Peña; Danny Glover; Kate Mara; Elias Koteas; Rhona Mitra; Rade Serbedzija; Levon Helm; Ned Beatty; Tate Donovan; Justin Louis; ***D:*** Antoine Fuqua; ***W:*** Jonathan Lemkin; ***C:*** Peter Menzies, Jr.; ***M:*** Mark Mancina.

Shooters **2000 (R)** South London bad boy Gilly (Dempsey) is out on parole after six years. All he wants is his share from a long-ago heist with violent partner J (Howard) but J wants Gily to help him out on one last job that involves an arms dealer (Dunbar). Naturally, things go very wrong. Typical Cool Britannia crime actioner. **95m/C; VHS, DVD.** *GB* Louis Dempsey; Andrew Howard; Adrian Dunbar; Gerard Butler; Jason Hughes; Matthew Rhys; Ioan Gruffudd; Melanie Lynskey; ***D:*** Glenn Dufort; Colin Teague; ***W:*** Louis Dempsey; Andrew Howard; ***C:*** Tom Erisman; ***M:*** Kemal Ultanur.

The Shooting **1966** A mysterious woman, bent on revenge, persuades a former bounty hunter and his partner to escort her across the desert, with tragic results. Offbeat, small film filled with strong performances by Nicholson and Oates. Filmed concurrently with "Ride in the Whirlwind," with the same cast and director. Bang-up surprise ending. **82m/C; VHS, DVD, Blu-Ray.** Warren Oates; Millie Perkins; Jack Nicholson; Will Hutchins; ***D:*** Monte Hellman; ***W:*** Adrien (Carole Eastman) Joyce; ***C:*** Gregory Sandor; ***M:*** Richard Markowitz.

Shooting Dogs *Beyond the Gates* **2005 (R)** The Ecole Technique Officielle is a secondary school located in Kigali, Rwanda. Young British teacher Joe Connor (Dancy) is getting his feet wet by spending a year at the school, run by steadfast Father Christopher (Hurt). Tensions are building between the Hutu and Tutsi factions and the school eventually becomes an uncertain shelter amidst the genocide. Film comes off as well-intentioned but overly familiar, although Hurt is a highlight. **115m/C; DVD.** *GB GE* John Hurt; Hugh Dancy; Dominique Horwitz; Nicola Walker; Louis Mahoney; Steve Toussaint; ***D:*** Michael Caton-Jones; ***W:*** Richard Wolstencroft; ***C:*** Ivan Strasburg; ***M:*** Dario Marianelli.

Shooting Elizabeth ½ **1992 (PG-13)** A fed-up husband decides to shut his loudmouthed wife up—permanently. Only before he can kill her, she disappears. The police don't buy it and want to charge him with murder. Can he find his wife before things really get serious? **96m/C; VHS, DVD.** Jeff Goldblum; Mimi Rogers; ***D:*** Baz Taylor.

Shooting Fish ½ **1998 (PG)** London con-artists Dylan (Futterman) and Jez (Townsend) hire perky temp Georgie (Beckinsale) to lend an air of authenticity to one of their scams. She charms them both, while figuring out that they're not the legit businessmen they pretend to be. When one of their scams goes awry, landing them in prison, Georgie helps them out. All the whiile, she's trying to figure out a way to save her retarded brother's home from her greedy fiance. Breezy, fun comedy benefits from great chemistry between the likable leads, but suffers from plot overload near the end. **109m/C; VHS, DVD.** *GB* Dan Futterman; Stuart Townsend; Kate Beckinsale; Dominic Mafham; Claire Cox; Nickolas Grace; Peter Capaldi; Annette Crosbie; Jane Lapotaire; ***D:*** Stefan Schwartz; ***W:*** Stefan Schwartz; Richard Holmes; ***C:*** Henry Braham; ***M:*** Stanislas Syrewicz.

Shooting Livien **2005** John Livien (Behr), named after John Lennon, is a self-destructive rock singer who is about to blow his band's big chance at success with his behavior, which endears him to no one but groupie Emi (Wynter). As Livien becomes increasingly unstable, he connects ever more dangerously with Lennon's life—and death. **94m/C; DVD.** Jason Behr; Sarah Wynter; Dominic Monaghan; Joshua Leonard; Ally Sheedy; Polly Draper; Jay O. Sanders; ***D:*** Rebecca Cook; ***W:*** Rebecca Cook; ***C:*** Harlan Bosmajian.

The Shooting Party ½ **1977** Told in flashbacks, a story of a crime of passion, an innocent man, and guilty secrets. A magistrate cannot admit his love for a woodsman's daughter so she falls into a loveless marriage and a decadent affair. In a fit of passion, the magistrate kills her and then decides to prosecute her innocent husband for the crime. Based on a story by Chekhov. In Russian with English subtitles. **105m/C; VHS, DVD.** *RU* Oleg (Yankovsky) Jankowsky; Galina Belyayeva; ***D:*** Emil Loteanu.

The Shooting Party 1/2 **1985** A group of English aristocrats assemble at a nobleman's house for a bird shoot on the eve of WWI. Splendid cast crowned Mason, in his last role. Fascinating crucible class anxieties, rich with social scheming, personality conflicts, and things left unsaid. Adapted from Isabel Colegate's novel. **97m/C; VHS, DVD.** *GB* James Mason; Dorothy Tutin; Edward Fox; John Gielgud; Robert Hardy; Cheryl Campbell; Judi Bowker; ***D:*** Alan Bridges; ***W:*** Julian Bond. L.A. Film Critics '85: Support. Actor (Gielgud); Natl. Soc. Film Critics '85: Support. Actor (Gielgud).

Shooting the Past 1/2 **1999** Christopher Anderson (Cunningham) is a wealthy American developer who has just purchased an old London mansion, which he is intending to convert into a business school. The mansion presently houses the Fallon Photo Library, consisting of some 10 million historical pictures. The indifferent Anderson says the pictures must be sold or destroyed within a week. But Anderson reckons without the library's impervious employees, who will do whatever is necessary to save their library. **180m/C; VHS, DVD.** *GB* Liam Cunningham; Lindsay Duncan; Timothy Spall; Emilia Fox; ***D:*** Stephen Poliakoff; ***W:*** Stephen Poliakoff. **TV**

The Shootist 1/2 **1976 (PG)** Wayne, in a supporting last role, plays a legendary gunslinger afflicted with cancer who seeks peace and solace in his final days. Town bad guys Boone and O'Brian aren't about to let him rest and are determined to gun him down to avenge past deeds. One of Wayne's best and most dignified performances about living up to a personal code of honor. Stewart and Bacall head excellent supporting cast. Based on Glendon Swarthout's novel. **100m/C; VHS, DVD.** John Wayne; Lauren Bacall; Ron Howard; James Stewart; Richard Boone; Hugh O'Brian; Bill McKinney; Harry (Henry) Morgan; John Carradine; Sheree North; Scatman Crothers; ***D:*** Donald Siegel; ***W:*** Scott Hale; Miles Hood Swarthout; ***C:*** Bruce Surtees; ***M:*** Elmer Bernstein.

The Shop Around the Corner 1/2 **1940** A low-key romantic classic in which Stewart and Sullavan are feuding clerks in a small Budapest shop, who unknowingly fall in love via a lonely hearts club. Charming portrayal of ordinary people in ordinary situations. Adapted from the Nikolaus Laszlo's play "Parfumerie." Later made into a musical called "In the Good Old Summertime" and, on Broadway, "She Loves Me." **99m/B; VHS, DVD.** Margaret Sullavan; James Stewart; Frank Morgan; Joseph Schildkraut; Sara Haden; Felix Bressart; Charles Halton; ***D:*** Ernst Lubitsch; ***W:*** Samson Raphaelson; ***C:*** William H. Daniels; ***M:*** Werner R. Heymann. Natl. Film Reg. '99.

The Shop on Main Street *The Shop on High Street; Obch Od Na Korze* **1965** During WWII, a Slovak takes a job as an "Aryan comptroller" for a Jewish-owned button shop. The owner is an old deaf woman; they slowly build a friendship. Tragedy ensues when all of the town's Jews are to be deported. Sensitive and subtle. Surely among the most gutwrenching portrayals of human tragedy ever on screen. Exquisite plotting and direction. In Czechoslovakian with English subtitles. **111m/B; VHS, DVD.** *CZ* Ida Kaminska; Josef Kroner; Hana Slivkoua; Frantisek Holly; Martin Gregor; ***D:*** Jan Kadar; Elmar Klos; ***W:*** Jan Kadar; Elmar Klos; ***C:*** Vladimir Novotny; ***M:*** Zdenek Liska. Oscars '65: Foreign Film; N.Y. Film Critics '66: Foreign Film.

Shopgirl **2005 (R)** Writer/actor/director Steve Martin adapts his novella about a rather bland, disconnected and melancholy 20-something glove salesgirl. Mirabelle (Danes) shares an unemotional romance with older rich guy Ray Porter (Martin), then meets Jeremy (Schwartzman), who is perhaps a better (and younger) match. Martin doesn't depart from his previous films, again staying in his beloved LA. Characters are a bit flat, but Martin's flair for words and setting the scene add an artsy, high-brow element that absolutely works. **116m/C; DVD.** Steve Martin; Claire Danes; Jason Schwartzman; Bridgette Wilson-Sampras; Sam Bottoms; Frances Conroy; Rebecca Pidgeon; Samantha Shelton; Gina Doctor; Clyde Kusatsu; Romy Rosemont; Anne Marie Howard; ***D:*** Anand Tucker; ***W:*** Steve Martin; ***C:*** Peter Suschitzky; ***M:*** Barrington Pheloung.

Shoplifters *Manbiki kazoku* **2018 (R)** Osamu is the head of a family barely eking out an existence in Tokyo. While out shoplifting one evening, he finds a small, shivering, seemingly abandoned young girl, and takes her home. After finding evidence of physical abuse on her body, the family disguises her and unofficially adopts her, a jig that is threatened once the news reports of her disappearance. A quiet, beautiful exploration of love and family that packs a heartbreaking punch. **121m/C; DVD.** Riri Furanki; Sakura Andô; Mayu Matsuoka; Jyo Kairi; Miyu Sasaki; ***D:*** Hirokazu Kore-eda; ***W:*** Hirokazu Kore-eda; ***C:*** Ryûto Kondô; ***M:*** Haruomi Hosono.

Shopping **1993 (R)** A crumbling British industrial city (filmed at London's docklands) is the bleak setting for gangs of aimless youth who steal cars, crash into the windows of various shops, grab whatever comes to hand, and then lead the police on high-speed chases. Adrenaline junkie Billy (Law) is accompanied by thrill-seeking girlfriend Jo (Frost) on one such escapade while fending off rival Tommy (Pertwee), who doesn't like his burgeoning criminal empire disturbed. Tries too hard for that rebel youth feeling. **86m/C; VHS, DVD.** *GB* Jude Law; Sadie Frost; Sean Pertwee; Fraser James; Sean Bean; Marianne Faithfull; Jonathan Pryce; Daniel Newman; ***D:*** Paul W.S. Anderson; ***W:*** Paul W.S. Anderson; ***C:*** Tony Imi; ***M:*** Barrington Pheloung.

Shopworn **1932** Waitress Kitty (Stanwyck) gets engaged to wealthy college boy David (Toomey) to the horror of his snob mother Helen (Blandick). She gets a friendly judge to send Kitty to the workhouse on trumped-up charges. Kitty changes her life when she gets out and David starts hanging around, but Kitty doesn't trust him because Mommy Dearest still controls his life. **72m/B; DVD.** Barbara Stanwyck; Regis Toomey; Clara Blandick; Zasu Pitts; Lucien Littlefield; Oscar Apfel; ***D:*** Nick Grinde; ***W:*** Robert Riskin; Jo Swerling; ***C:*** Joseph Walker.

Shopworn Angel **1938** Weepy melodrama about a sophisticated actress who leads on a naive Texas soldier who's in New York prior to being shipped out for WWI duty. Later, just before she goes on stage, she learns he's been killed at the front. She rallys to sing "Pack Up your Troubles in Your Old Kit Bag and Smile, Smile, Smile." Lots of tears. Adapted from the story "Private Pettigrew's Girl" by Dana Burnet. This remake of the same-titled 1929 film considerably softened the characters. Remade again in 1959 as "That Kind of Woman." **85m/B; VHS, DVD.** Margaret Sullavan; James Stewart; Walter Pidgeon; Nat Pendleton; Alan Curtis; Sam Levene; Hattie McDaniel; Charley Grapewin; Charles D. Brown; ***D:*** H.C. Potter; ***W:*** Waldo Salt; ***C:*** Joseph Ruttenberg.

Shore Leave **1925** Dressmaker Mackaill isn't getting any younger. Tough-guy sailor Bilge Smith (Barthelmess, in top form) meets her on shore leave; little does he realize her plans for him! She owns a dry-docked ship, you see, and it (and she) will be ready for him when he comes ashore next. Lovely, fun (if rather plodding) romantic comedy. Later made into musicals twice, as "Hit the Deck" and "Follow the Fleet." **74m/B; Silent; VHS, DVD.** Richard Barthelmess; Dorothy Mackaill; ***D:*** John S. Robertson.

Short Circuit **1986 (PG)** A newly developed robot designed for the military is hit by lightning and begins to think it's alive. Sheedy and Guttenberg help it hide from the mean people at the weapons lab who want to take it home. Followed two years later, save Sheedy and Guttenberg, by the lame "Short Circuit 2." **98m/C; VHS, DVD, Blu-Ray, UMD.** Steve Guttenberg; Ally Sheedy; Austin Pendleton; Fisher Stevens; Brian McNamara; ***D:*** John Badham; ***W:*** S.S. Wilson; Brent Maddock; ***C:*** Nick McLean; ***M:*** David Shire.

Short Circuit 2 1/2 **1988 (PG)** A sequel to the first adorable-robot-outwits-bad-guys tale. The robot, Number Five, makes his way through numerous plot turns without much human assistance or much purpose. Harmless (unless you have to spend time watching it), but pointless and juvenile. Very occasional genuinely funny moments. **95m/C; VHS, DVD, Blu-Ray.** Fisher Stevens; Cynthia Gibb; Michael McKean; Jack Weston; David Hemblen; ***D:*** Kenneth Johnson; ***W:*** S.S. Wilson; Brent Maddock; ***C:*** John McPherson; ***M:*** Charles Fox.

Short Cuts 1/2 **1993 (R)** Multi-storied, fish-eyed look at American culture with some 22 characters intersecting—profoundly or fleetingly—through each other's lives. Running the emotional gamut from disturbing to humorous, Altman's portrait of the contemporary human condition is nevertheless fascinating. Based on nine stories and a prose poem by Raymond Carver. **189m/C; VHS, DVD, Blu-Ray.** Annie Ross; Lori Singer; Jennifer Jason Leigh; Tim Robbins; Madeleine Stowe; Frances McDormand; Peter Gallagher; Lily Tomlin; Tom Waits; Bruce Davison; Andie MacDowell; Jack Lemmon; Lyle Lovett; Fred Ward; Buck Henry; Huey Lewis; Matthew Modine; Anne Archer; Julianne Moore; Lili Taylor; Christopher Penn; Robert Downey, Jr.; Jarrett Lennon; Zane Cassidy; Natalie Strong; ***D:*** Robert Altman; ***W:*** Frank Barhydt; Robert Altman; ***C:*** Walt Lloyd; ***M:*** Mark Isham. Ind. Spirit '94: Director (Altman), Film, Screenplay; Natl. Soc. Film Critics '93: Support. Actress (Stowe); Venice Film Fest. '93: Film.

Short Eyes 1/2 *The Slammer* **1979 (R)** When a child molester (Davison) enters prison, the inmates act out their own form of revenge against him. Filmed on location at New York City's Men's House of Detention, nicknamed "The Tombs." Script by Manuel Pinero from his excellent play; he also acts in the film. Top-notch performances and respectful direction from Young bring unsparingly realistic prison drama to the screen. Title is prison jargon for child molester. **100m/C; VHS, DVD, Blu-Ray.** Bruce Davison; Miguel Pinero; Nathan George; Donald Blakely; Curtis Mayfield; Jose Perez; Shawn Elliott; ***D:*** Robert M. Young.

Short Grass **1950** Gunslinger-turned-drifter Steve Llewellyn returns to Willow Creek just in time to stop greedy cattle baron Hal Fenton from grabbing all the good grasslands. Steve partners with smalltime rancher Pete Lynch (Steve's sweet on his daughter) but there's a climatic showdown to settle the land matter. **90m/B; DVD.** Rod Cameron; Cathy Downs; Morris Ankrum; Stanley Andrews; Johnny Mack Brown; Alan Hale, Jr.; Raymond Walburn; ***D:*** Lesley Selander; ***W:*** Thomas W. Blackburn; ***C:*** Harry Neumann; ***M:*** Edward Kay.

A Short History of Decay **2013 (R)** Ernest, meandering family comedy-drama. Nathan Fisher (Greenberg) is a neurotic, 30-something struggling writer, living in Brooklyn, whose successful girlfriend, Erika (Chriqui), has just ended their relationship. He's already obsessing over his mom's (Lavin) early onset Alzheimer's when his older brother Jack (King) calls and says their irascible father (Yulin) has had a mild stroke. So Nathan heads to Florida to spend time with the 'rents and get his life back on track while also dealing with some sibling rivalry. **94m/C; DVD.** Bryan Greenberg; Linda Lavin; Harris Yulin; Benjamin King; Emmanuelle Chriqui; Rebecca Dayan; Kathleen Rose Perkins; ***D:*** Michael Maren; ***W:*** Michael Maren; ***C:*** Nancy Schreiber.

Short Night of Glass Dolls *Corta Notte delle Bambole di Vetro; Paralyzed; Malastrana* **1971** Journalist Gregory Moore (Sorel) is found dead in a Prague square and taken to the morgue. Only he's not dead but paralyzed—he can't move or communicate but his brain works and through flashbacks he tries to remember what's happened to him. Gregory is investigating the disappearance of his girlfriend Mira (Bach) and learns that she is only one of many girls who have gone missing. The police are no help and Gregory's snooping leads to a sinister club and a secret society. Italian with subtitles. **97m/C; DVD, Blu-Ray.** *IT* Jean Sorel; Ingrid Thulin; Mario Adorf; Barbara Bach; Fabian Sovagovic; ***D:*** Aldo Lado; ***W:*** Aldo Lado; ***C:*** Giuseppe Ruzzolini; ***M:*** Ennio Morricone.

A Short Stay in Switzerland **2009** Reaction to this British TV drama (based on a true story) will depend on the watcher's view of euthanasia. Dr. Anne Turner (Walters) has just buried her husband after caring for him through a long battle with motor neuron disease. She is diagnosed with a degenerative brain disease and, rather than become increasingly incapacitated, Anne informs her children that she is going to a Swiss clinic for an assisted suicide. Bleak drama with some gallows humor from lead Walters. **90m/C; DVD.** *GB* Julie Walters; Stephen Moore; Lyndsey Marshal; Liz White; Patrick Malahide; Michelle Fairley; ***D:*** Simon Curtis; ***W:*** Frank McGuinness; ***C:*** Ben Smithard; ***M:*** John Hale. **TV**

Short Term 12 **2013 (R)** A beautiful, gentle gem that captures that there are ways to stop the bleeding of depression and past horrors that feels so real that it hurts. It's a movie that you experience as much as watch, thanks in large part to a stunning central performance from Larson as Grace, a worker at the title facility, a location for at-risk kids who are dealing with abuse, addiction, and more while waiting for stable homes to take them. Grace has her own horrors that have brought her here, making her the kind of support figure who can identify with the kids but who also brings work home with her. **96m/C; DVD, Blu-Ray.** Brie Larson; John Gallagher, Jr.; Kaitlyn Dever; Stephanie Beatriz; Rami Malek; Lakeith Stanfield; ***D:*** Destin Daniel Cretton; ***W:*** Destin Daniel Cretton; ***C:*** Brett Pawluk; ***M:*** Joel West. Ind. Spirit '14: Film Editing.

The Shortcut 1/2 **2009 (PG-13)** Kids and dogs disappear near the old Hartley place so no one uses the shortcut through the woods until newcomers Derek and his younger brother Tobey do so on a dare. Then Derek and his new high school friends decide to find out just how weird old weirdo Hartley really is. But sometimes the past should be left alone. More creepy mystery than gory horror. **85m/C; DVD, Blu-Ray.** Andrew Seeley; Shannon Marie Woodward; Dave Franco; Katrina Bowden; Nicholas Elia; Raymond J. Barry; ***D:*** Nicholaus Goossen; ***W:*** Scott Sandler. **VIDEO**

Shorts: The Adventures of the Wishing Rock **2009 (PG)** Zippy (if deliberately disjointed) kid comedy finds 11-year-old bullied misfit Toe Thompson (Bennett) living in the company town of Black Hills where his workaholic parents (Cryer, Mann) ignore him in favor of their jobs at Black Box Industries. So naturally when Toe gets hit in the head by a rainbow-colored rock during a freak storm and said rock turns out to be able to grant wishes, Toe asks for friends. Of course, the wishes don't come true in exactly the fashion that anyone expects causing more than a little trouble. **89m/C; Blu-Ray.** Jimmy Bennett; Kat Dennings; Trevor Gagnon; Jake Short; Jolie Vanier; Leo Howard; Devon Gearhart; Rebel Rodriguez; Leslie Mann; Jon Cryer; William H. Macy; James Spader; ***D:*** Robert Rodriguez; ***W:*** Robert Rodriguez; ***C:*** Robert Rodriguez; ***M:*** Carl Thiel; George Oldziey.

Shot 1/2 *Focus* **2001 (R)** Photographer Robert (Karrer) befriends young Marcus (Gray) when he discovers the inner-city youth has a natural ability behind the lens. Robert gets drawn into the thug life but makes a big mistake when he photographs Marcus's older brother, Keith (Cameron), and his gang murdering undercover cops. **97m/C; VHS, DVD.** Brandon Karrer; Trent Cameron; Jennifer Jostyn; Bruce Weitz; ***D:*** Roger Roth; ***W:*** Roger Roth; ***C:*** Mark Woods; ***M:*** Norman Arnold. **VIDEO**

A Shot at Glory **2000 (R)** So-so Scottish soccer saga starring Duvall as McLeod, the manager of a struggling local football club. Looking to launch the lads into stardom, the team's new American owner Cameron (Keaton) hires former star McQuillan (real-life player McCoist) against the wishes of McLeod. Despite McQuillan's drinking and carousing—which has cost him his marriage to none other than McLeod's daughter Kate (Mitchell)?the Knockies soon find their way into the Scottish Cup finals, where McLeod meets up with his old nemesis Smith (Cox), manager of the opposing Glasgow Rangers. Though thin on drama, well-shot soccer action will appeal to sports fans. Duvall's high profile and manufactured brogue bog down an otherwise solid performance. **115m/C; VHS, DVD.** Robert Duvall; Michael Keaton; Brian Cox; Cole Hauser; Ally McCoist; Kirsty Mitchell; Morag Hood; Libby

Langdon; **D:** Michael Corrente; **W:** Dennis O'Neill; **C:** Alex Thomson; **M:** Mark Knopfler.

A Shot in the Dark **1935** When his son is murdered at a New England college, a distraught dad takes it on himself to investigate. Movie cowboy Starrett plays the sleuthing pop in this undistinguished mystery. **69m/B; VHS, DVD.** Charles Starrett; Robert Warwick; Edward Van Sloan; Marion Shilling; Doris Lloyd; Helen Jerome Eddy; James Bush; **D:** Charles Lamont.

A Shot in the Dark 1/2 **1964** Second and possibly the best in the classic "Inspector Clouseau-Pink Panther" series of comedies. The bumbling Inspector Clouseau (Sellers, of course) investigates the case of a parlor maid (Sommer) accused of murdering her lover. Clouseau's libido convinces him she's innocent, even though all the clues point to her. Classic gags, wonderful music. After this film, Sellers as Clouseau disappears until 1975's "Return of the Pink Panther" (Alan Arkin played him in "Inspector Clouseau," made in 1968 by different folks). **101m/C; VHS, DVD, Blu-Ray.** Peter Sellers; Elke Sommer; Herbert Lom; George Sanders; Bryan Forbes; Ann Lynn; **D:** Blake Edwards; **W:** William Peter Blatty; Blake Edwards; **C:** Christopher Challis; **M:** Henry Mancini.

Shot in the Heart **2001 (R)** In 1977, shortly after the Supreme Court reinstated capital punishment, convicted murderer Gary Gilmore (Koteas) requested execution by a Utah firing squad, becoming the first person executed in a decade. But Gilmore's brothers, Frank Jr. (Tergesen), and his younger brother, writer Mikal (Ribisi), come to Draper Prison to plead with him to change his mind. Alienated for years, the brothers' uneasy reunion brings up lots of twisted family memories. Haunting movie about internal demons and brotherly ties; based on Mikal's 1994 memoir of the same name. **98m/C; VHS, DVD.** Giovanni Ribisi; Elias Koteas; Lee Tergesen; Sam Shepard; Amy Madigan; Eric Bogosian; **D:** Agnieszka Holland; **W:** Frank Pugliese; **C:** Jacek Petrycki. **CABLE**

Shot Through the Heart **1998 (R)** Based on a true story of the ethnic conflict that tore apart the former Yugoslavia and started a civil war between 1992 and 1995. Serbian Slavko (Perez) and Croat Vlado (Roache), whose wife Maida (William) is a Muslim, are childhood friends and former teammates on the Yugoslavian target-shooting team. Slavko is drafted into the Serbian army and urges his friend to flee Sarajevo. Instead, Vlado and his family are trapped in the city and Vlado is forced to take up his rifle in defense against deadly Serbian snipers. Which leads him to a final confrontation with Slavko. Filmed in Sarajevo and Budapest. **115m/C; VHS, DVD.** Linus Roache; Vincent Perez; Lothaire Bluteau; Adam Kotz; Lia Williams; Karianne Henderson; **D:** David Attwood; **W:** Guy Hibbert; **M:** Ed Shearmur. **CABLE**

Shotgun 1/2 **1955** A sheriff on the trail of a killer is accompanied by a girl he's saved from Indians. Average western cowritten by western actor Rory Calhoun, who had hoped to star in the film, but was turned down by the studio. **81m/C; VHS, DVD.** Sterling Hayden; Zachary Scott; Yvonne De Carlo; **D:** Lesley Selander; **C:** Ellsworth Fredericks.

Shotgun Stories **2007 (PG-13)** Violence begets violence and a blood feud produces only tragedy. Son, Kid, and Boy Hayes are living hardscrabble lives in a small Arkansas town. Their dad was an abusive drunk, but after leaving the family he eventually cleaned up his act, remarried, and had four more sons who are prospering. His funeral causes a graveside fight between the half-brothers that escalates with some predictable (but watchable) results. **92m/C; DVD.** Michael Shannon; Natalie Canerday; Douglas Ligon; Barlow Jacobs; Michael Abbott, Jr.; Travis Smith; Lynsee Provence; David Rhodes; Glenda Pannell; G. Allen Wilkins; **D:** Jeff Nichols; **W:** Jeff Nichols; **C:** Adam Stone; **M:** Ben Nichols; Lucero.

Shout **1991 (PG-13)** Romance and rebellion set in a sleepy Texas town during the 1950s. Jesse Tucker's (Walters) rebellious ways land him in the Benedict Home for Boys and he seems lost until Jack Cabe (Travolta) enters town. Jack introduces Jesse and the gang to the exciting new sounds of rock 'n' roll. Been done before and better. **93m/C; VHS, DVD.** John Travolta; James Walters; Heather Graham; Richard Jordan; Linda Fiorentino; Scott Coffey; **D:** Jeffrey Hornaday; **C:** Robert Brinkmann; **M:** Randy Edelman.

The Show **1927** MGM's twisted silent melodrama of jealousy and murder from director Browning. The Palace of Illusions is a carnival that features a lurid "Dance of the Seven Veils" by Salome (Adoree) and her partner Cock Robin (Gilbert). The jealous Greek (Barrymore) intends to get rid of his rival but his plan goes awry, leaving him open to revenge. **76m/B; Silent; DVD.** John Gilbert; Renee Adoree; Lionel Barrymore; **D:** Tod Browning; **W:** Waldemar Young; **C:** John Arnold.

The Show **1995 (R)** Choppy and incoherent behind-the-scenes look at the attitude and people who make up the explosive hip-hop and rap scene. Mixes black and white concert footage and interviews with Russell Simmons, LL Cool J and Snoop Doggy Dogg, who discuss their music and fans. Will be a disappointment for those looking for a more in-depth study of the music, as this exercise merely scratches the surface. Includes an abundance of cameos from today's top hip hop artists such as Notorious B.I.G., Naughty by Nature and Wu-Tang Clan. **90m/B; VHS, DVD.** Craig Mack; Dr. Dre; Run DMC; Slick Rick; Warren G; Kurtis Blow; **D:** Brian Robbins; **C:** Larry Banks; Steven Consentino; Ericson Core; John L. (Ndiaga) Demps, Jr; Todd A. Dos Reis.

Show Boat **1936** The second of three film versions of the Jerome Kern/Oscar Hammerstein musical (based on the Edna Ferber novel), filmed previously in 1929, about a Mississippi showboat and the life and loves of its denizens. Wonderful romance, unforgettable music. Director Whale also brought the world "Frankenstein." The laser edition includes a historical audio essay by Miles Kreuger, excerpts from the 1929 version, Ziegfeld's 1932 stage revival, "Life Aboard a Real Showboat" (a vintage short), radio broadcasts, and a 300-photo essay tracing the history of showboats. Remade 15 years later. **110m/B; DVD, Blu-Ray.** Irene Dunne; Allan Jones; Paul Robeson; Helen Morgan; Hattie McDaniel; Charles Winninger; Donald Cook; Bobs Watson; **D:** James Whale; **W:** Oscar Hammerstein; **M:** Oscar Hammerstein; Jerome Kern. Natl. Film Reg. '96.

Show Boat 1/2 **1951** Third movie version of the 1927 musical about the life and loves of a Mississippi riverboat theatre troupe. Terrific musical numbers, with fun dance routines from Champion, who went on to great fame as a choreographer. Grayson is somewhat vapid, but lovely to look at and hear. Gardner didn't want to do the part of Julie, although she eventually received fabulous reviews—her singing was dubbed by Annette Warren. The 171-foot "Cotton Blossom" boat was built on the Tarzan lake on the MGM back lot at an astounding cost of $126,468. Warfield's film debut—his "Ole Man River"?was recorded in one take. excerpts from "Broadway," "Silent Film," and radio Version of "Show Boat," a documentary featuring life on a real show boat, and a commentary on the performers, the film, and the history of show boats. **115m/C; VHS, DVD.** Kathryn Grayson; Howard Keel; Ava Gardner; William Warfield; Joe E. Brown; Agnes Moorehead; Gower Champion; **D:** George Sidney; **W:** George Wells; Jack McGowan; **C:** Charles Rosher; **M:** Oscar Hammerstein.

Show Business **1944** Historically valuable film record of classic vaudeville acts, especially Cantor and Davis. A number of vaudevillians re-create their old acts for director Marin—unforgettable slapstick and songs. All this pegged on a plot that follows Cantor's rise to fame with the Ziegfeld Follies. **92m/B; VHS, DVD.** Eddie Cantor; Joan Davis; George Murphy; **D:** Edwin L. Marin.

Show Dogs **2018 (PG)** A live-action talking animal comedy about show dogs. When Rottweiler Max (Bridges), a New York City police dog, makes a mess of a sting operation centered on an endangered baby panda, he meets FBI agent Frank Mosley (Arnett). Despite a personality clash, the pair teams up at a Las Vegas dog show to save the panda. To prepare for the dog show, Max and Frank receive help from dog groomer Mattie (Lyonne). Along the way, Max gains new friends among the dog show veterans. The desperate attempts at laughter make the Hound sad. **92m/C; DVD, Blu-Ray, Streaming.** *UK US* Will Arnett; Natasha Lyonne; **V:** Chris Bridges; Stanley Tucci; Alan Cumming; **D:** Raja Gosnell; **W:** Max Botkin; Marc Hyman; **C:** David Mackie; **M:** Heitor Pereira.

Show Girl in Hollywood 1/2 **1930** Broadway chorine Dixie Dugan (White) is performing in a New York nightclub when shifty Hollywood director Frank Buelow (Miljan) offers her a movie contract. Dixie gets the leading role but then turns diva, which ruins the comeback efforts of fading silent star Donna Harris (Sweet). A desperate act by Donna causes Dixie to question the tawdry tinsel behind the glamour. White also played the same role in 1928's "Show Girl." **77m/C; DVD.** Alice White; Jack Mulhall; Blanche Sweet; John Miljan; Ford Sterling; Virginia Sale; **D:** Mervyn LeRoy; **W:** Harvey Thew; James A. Starr; **C:** Sol Polito.

Show Me 1/2 **2004 (R)** No, please don't. Sarah (Nolden) is carjacked and kidnapped by two homeless teens, Jenna (Isabelle) and Jackson (Turton), who force her to take them to her isolated cabin. Only Sarah decides to turn the tables on her captors and plays some mind games herself. Grubby and unpleasant story although Isabelle is frighteningly feral. **97m/C; DVD.** *CA* Michelle Nolden; Katharine Isabelle; Kett Turton; Gabriel Hogan; **D:** Cassandra Nicolaou; **W:** Cassandra Nicolaou; **C:** Patrick Mcgowan; **M:** Evelyne Datl.

Show Me Love **1999** Sixteen-year-old Agnes (Liljeberg) is the new girl in the boring, small Swedish town of Amal. Agnes isn't cool enough to be with the popular crowd (she's a brainy vegetarian) and she's rumored to be a lesbian as well. Agnes does have a crush on bored beauty, Elin (Dahlstrom), who goes to extremes to get her kicks, even making a bet with her sister Jessica (Carlson) about kissing Agnes. Then, shocked by her own reactions, Elin makes out with convenient Johan (Rust). But Elin's betrayal of self leads to self-discovery—for both girls. Swedish with subtitles. **89m/C; VHS, DVD.** *SW* Rebecca Liljeberg; Alexandra Dahlstrom; Mathias Rust; Erica Carlson; Stefan Horberg; Ralph Carlsson; Maria Hedborg; **D:** Lukas Moodysson; **W:** Lukas Moodysson; **C:** Ulf Brantas.

A Show of Force **1990 (R)** Reporter Irving investigates the coverup of a murder with political ramifications. Brazilian director Barreto cast (surprise!) his girlfriend in the lead; she doesn't exactly carry the day. Phillips is good, but you'll end up feeling cheated if you expect to see much of highly billed Duvall or Garcia. Based on a real incident of 1978, but hardly believable as political realism or even moralism. **93m/C; VHS, DVD.** Erik Estrada; Amy Irving; Andy Garcia; Robert Duvall; Lou Diamond Phillips; **D:** Bruno Barreto; **W:** Evan Jones; **M:** Georges Delerue.

The Show Off 1/2 **1926** Irresponsible Aubrey Piper's (Sterling) incessant boasting wrecks havoc with his wife Amy (Wilson) and their life together. Brooks has a small role as the girl-next-door. **82m/B; Silent; VHS, DVD.** Ford Sterling; Lois Wilson; Louise Brooks; Claire McDowell; C.W. Goodrich; Gregory Kelly; **D:** Malcolm St. Clair; **W:** Pierre Collins; **C:** Lee Garmes; **M:** Timothy Brock.

Show People **1928** A pretty girl from the boonies tries to make it big in Tinseltown. But as a slapstick star?! She wanted to be a leading lady! Enjoyable, fun silent comedy shows Davies's true talents. Interesting star cameos, including director Vidor at the end. **82m/B; Silent; VHS, DVD.** Marion Davies; William Haines; Dell Henderson; Paul Ralli; William S. Hart; Rod La Rocque; ***Cameo(s):*** King Vidor; **D:** King Vidor. Natl. Film Reg. '03.

The Showdown **1940** The title actually refers to a tricky poker game, the highlight of yet another Hopalong Cassidy versus hoss thieves quickie epic. Kermit Maynard is the brother of cowboy hero Ken Maynard. **65m/B; VHS, DVD.** William Boyd; Russell Hayden; Britt Wood; Morris Ankrum; Jan Clayton; Roy Barcroft; Kermit Maynard; **D:** Howard Bretherton.

Showdown 1/2 **1973 (PG)** Billy Massey (Martin) and Chuck Garvis (Hudson) had been friends since childhood, until they fell out over the attentions of the pretty Kate (Clark), whom Chuck married. Chuck became the honest town sheriff while Billy took to train robbing. Now it's up to Chuck to bring Billy to justice. Director Seaton's final film. **99m/C; DVD.** Dean Martin; Rock Hudson; Susan Clark; Donald Moffat; John McLiam; Ed Begley, Jr.; **D:** George Seaton; **W:** Theodore Taylor; **C:** Ernest Laszlo; **M:** David Shire.

Showdown *Lookin' Italian* **1994 (R)** New Yorker Vinny (Acovone) has left the family crime business and moved to California for a quieter life. But when his fast-living nephew Anthony (LeBlanc) moves in, Vinny reluctantly finds himself drawn back into violence. **90m/C; VHS, DVD.** Jay Acovone; Matt LeBlanc; Lou Rawls; John Lamotta; Stephanie Richards; Real Andrews; **D:** Guy Magar; **W:** Guy Magar; **C:** Gerry Lively; **M:** Jeff Beal.

Showdown at Area 51 *Alien vs. Alien* **2007 (R)** Cheap-looking sci-fi smackdown between two alien races who crash-land on Earth and decide to settle their differences without caring if the locals get in their way. The bad alien is after an obelisk that is capable of wiping out all life on the planet so its resources can be plundered. He's opposed by a reasonably good alien and Jake (London), a human ex-soldier who's not too bright. **96m/C; DVD.** Jason London; Christa Campbell; Lee Horsley; Gigi Edgley; Coby Bell; Jahidi White; Brock Roberts; **D:** C. Roma; **W:** Brook Durham; Kevin Moore; Ari Graham; **C:** Christopher Benson; **M:** John Dickson. **CABLE**

Showdown at Boot Hill **1958** A bounty hunter (Bronson) kills a wanted murderer but cannot collect the reward because the townspeople will not identify the victim. Rather ordinary plot is carried by Bronson's performance. **76m/B; DVD, Blu-Ray.** Charles Bronson; Robert Hutton; John Carradine; Carole Mathews; **D:** Gene Fowler, Jr.; **W:** Louis Vittes; **C:** John M. Nickolaus, Jr.; **M:** Albert Harris.

Showdown at Williams Creek 1/2 *Kootenai Brown* **1991 (R)** A graphic Canadian Western set in the old Montana territory, where an outcast settler goes on trial for killing an old man. Testimony recounts a shocking history of greed and betrayal. The dark side of the Gold Rush, generally well-acted. Inspired by an actual incident. **97m/C; VHS, DVD.** *CA* Tom Burlinson; Donnelly Rhodes; Raymond Burr; Michael Thrush; John Pyper-Ferguson; Alex Bruhanski; **D:** Allen Kroeker; **W:** John Gray; **M:** Michael Conway Baker.

Showdown in Little Tokyo **1991 (R)** Lundgren stars as a martial arts master/L.A. cop who was raised in Japan, and has all the respect in the world for his "ancestors" and heritage. Brandon Lee (son of Bruce) is Lundgren's partner, and he's a bona fide American-made, pop-culture, mall junkie. Together, they go after a crack-smuggling gang of "yakuza" (Japanese thugs). Lots of high-kicking action and the unique angle on stereotypes make this a fun martial arts film. **78m/C; VHS, DVD, Blu-Ray.** Dolph Lundgren; Brandon Lee; Tia Carrere; Cary-Hiroyuki Tagawa; **D:** Mark L. Lester; **W:** Caliope Brattlestreet; **C:** Mark Irwin; **M:** David Michael Frank.

The Showgirl Murders 1/2 **1995 (R)** Stripper Jessica (Ford) goes into management when she turns a failing Las Vegas bar into a money-maker but this femme fatale wants owner Mitch (Preston) to stop sharing the wealth with his boozy wife Carolyn (Case). Meanwhile, blackmailing DEA agent Ridley (McFarland) and hitman Joey (Alber) cause problems. **84m/C; VHS, DVD.** Maria Ford; Matt Preston; Jeff Douglas; D.S. Case; Kevin Alber; Bob McFarland; **D:** Gene Hertel; **W:** Christopher Wooden.

Showgirls WOOF! **1995 (NC-17)** Long on ridiculous dialogue and bad acting and short on costumes, coming-of-age tale follows one young woman as she nakedly climbs the ladder of success as a Vegas showgirl. Oh, the things she must do to be headliner. Berkley makes the jump from TV's

"Saved by the Bell" to portray Nomi, the young lap dancer with the gift of pelvic thrust and the will to succeed. Whether cavorting clothed or nude, Berkley is uniformly wooden, a mass of lip gloss and mascara struggling to emote. Gershon, as her sly nemesis, brings some wit and splash to her role as the jaded headliner. Eszterhas script descends below its maker's usual standards, which are not particularly high. Titanic amount of female flesh on display fails to give film even a faint hint of sexuality, proof that there is a hell. Rent it, and be prepared to fast forward (to what, we're not sure, though there is a certain camp element that might have been amusing if not imprisoned here). Also available in "R" and unrated versions. **131m/C; VHS, DVD, Blu-Ray.** Elizabeth Berkley; Gina Gershon; Kyle MacLachlan; Glenn Plummer; Alan Rachins; Robert Davi; Gina Ravera; ***D:*** Paul Verhoeven; ***W:*** Joe Eszterhas; ***C:*** Jost Vacano; ***M:*** David A. Stewart. Golden Raspberries '95: Worst Actress (Berkley), Worst Director (Verhoeven), Worst New Star (Berkley), Worst Picture, Worst Screenplay, Worst Song ("Walk into the Wind").

Showtime **2002 (PG-13)** Murphy hams and De Niro grimaces as they both plod through this lame buddy cop comedy. The odd couple are the fiery LAPD detective Preston (De Niro), who's forced to star in a reality-based TV cop show with beat cop/frustrated actor Sellars (Murphy) after Preston impulsively shoots out a network camera and must avoid a law suit. Russo is the show's producer and has little to do here. The rest of the action involves tracking down some robbers who are also the owners of a really, really big gun. Shatner briefly injects some life into the lackluster action as he coaches the boys on how to play to the camera. Although the two leads are unarguably cast correctly and easy to watch doing what they do best, the premise lets them, and the audience, down. **95m/C; VHS, DVD.** Robert De Niro; Eddie Murphy; Rene Russo; Frankie Faison; Mos Def; William Shatner; Pedro Damian; Nestor Serrano; Drena De Niro; Kadeem Hardison; TJ Cross; Judah Friedlander; ***D:*** Tom Dey; ***W:*** Alfred Gough; Keith Sharon; Miles Millar; ***C:*** Thomas Kloss; ***M:*** Alan Silvestri.

Shredderman Rules **1/2 2007** Amusing teen comedy with a few messages about responsibility snuck in. Nolan Byrd (Wekheiser) is constantly tormented by junior high bully Bubba (Caldwell). When the harassment becomes too much, Byrd uses a school computer assignment to create the Shredderman alter-ego and sets up a website filled with video of Bubba's many transgressions, which becomes a big hit with his fellow students. Then Nolan discovers Bubba's businessman dad (Roebuck) has a plan for dumping sewer waste into the town's pond, but trying to expose the plot lands him in real trouble. **91m/C; DVD.** Francia Raisa; Tim Meadows; Daniel Roebuck; Dave Coulier; Clare Carey; Curtis Armstrong; Devon Wekheiser; Andrew Caldwell; Marisa Guterman; ***D:*** Savage Steve Holland; ***W:*** Russell Marcus; ***C:*** William Barber; ***M:*** Paul Doucette. **CABLE**

Shrek **1/2 2001 (PG)** Animated tale from DreamWorks about a grumpy green ogre, Shrek (Myers), who's upset when some annoying fairy types overrun his swamp. So he makes a deal with the local hotshot, Lord Farquaad (Lithgow), to save his home by rescuing Princess Fiona (Diaz) from a tower that's guarded by your not-so-basic dragon type so Farquaad can marry her. Along as Shrek's unwelcome sidekick is a smart-mouthed donkey (Murphy), who insists on helping the ogre out. This one has some eye-popping visuals as well as inside jokes (and digs at Disney) to keep the adults amused. Based (loosely) on the children's book by William Steig. **89m/C; VHS, DVD, Blu-Ray.** ***V:*** Mike Myers; Cameron Diaz; Eddie Murphy; John Lithgow; Vincent Cassel; Kathleen Freeman; Conrad Vernon; ***D:*** Andrew Adamson; Victoria Jenson; ***W:*** Ted Elliott; Terry Rossio; Roger S.H. Schulman; Joe Stillman; ***M:*** Harry Gregson-Williams; John Powell. Oscars '01: Animated Film; British Acad. '01: Adapt. Screenplay; L.A. Film Critics '01: Animated Film; Broadcast Film Critics '01: Animated Film.

Shrek 2 **2004 (PG)** Sequel picks up with Shrek (Myers) and Princess Fiona (Diaz) returning from their honeymoon. They are invited to visit Fiona's parents in the high-falutin' Kingdom of Far, Far Away and Shrek must deal with something more dangerous than dragons or diminutive evil kings—his in-laws, King Harold (Cleese) and Queen Lillian (Andrews), who don't much care to have an ogre in the family (let alone as a daughter). In fact, there's a plot to eliminate Shrek for Fiona's old beau Prince Charming (Everett). The King hires feline assassin Puss-in-Boots (Banderas, uproariously capitalizing on his Spanish heartthrob/Zorro image). Donkey's (Murphy) along as well. The film tries a little too hard in spots, but ya still gotta love the big guy. **92m/C; DVD, Blu-Ray.** ***V:*** Mike Myers; Cameron Diaz; Eddie Murphy; John Cleese; Julie Andrews; Rupert Everett; Antonio Banderas; Jennifer Saunders; Larry King; Conrad Vernon; ***D:*** Andrew Adamson; Kelly Asbury; ***W:*** Andrew Adamson; Joe Stillman; J. David Stem; David N. Weiss; ***M:*** Harry Gregson-Williams.

Shrek Forever After **1/2 2010 (PG)** In this fourth and allegedly final installment (in 3-D), Shrek's bored and feels he's lost his ogre mojo to domesticity. So he strikes a crummy deal with Rumpelstiltskin for a 24-hour reprieve and (shades of "It's a Wonderful Life") finds out how life in Far Far Away would be if he never existed. Things are bad: Rumpelstiltskin is the vicious king, Fiona leads the ogre resistance movement, Donkey is literally a beast of burden, and Puss in Boots is an overweight pampered pet. To save the day, Shrek just has to get a disdainful Fiona to fall in love with him again. **93m/C; Blu-Ray.** ***V:*** Mike Myers; Cameron Diaz; Eddie Murphy; Antonio Banderas; Walt Dohrn; Justin Timberlake; Julie Andrews; Maya Rudolph; Eric Idle; Craig Robinson; Jon Hamm; Jane Lynch; Amy Sedaris; Ryan Seacrest; Kathy Griffin; Kirsten Schaal; Larry King; Regis Philbin; ***D:*** Mike Mitchell; ***W:*** Josh Klausner; ***C:*** Yong Duk Jhun; ***M:*** Harry Gregson-Williams.

Shrek the Third **2007 (PG)** Third time is not the charm in the latest tale of the cranky ogre. Shrek (Myers), Fiona (Diaz), and Donkey (Murphy) must find an heir by the name of Arthur (Timberlake) to replace Fiona's dying father (Cleese), prevent Prince Charming (Everett) from staging a coup, and deal with the idea of tiny baby ogres and donkey-dragon toddlers. Swashbuckling kitty Puss (Banderas) is along for the ride, as well as the standard host of fairy tale and legendary characters, old and new. Potty gags and in-jokes abound, but don't seem nearly as fresh or fun as in previous efforts. The all-star cast and some of the charm of the first two remains, but all in all the movie spends more time trying to be funny rather than actually being funny and doesn't bring anything fresh or new to the story. **92m/C; DVD, Blu-Ray, HD-DVD.** ***V:*** Mike Myers; Cameron Diaz; Eddie Murphy; Antonio Banderas; John Cleese; Julie Andrews; Justin Timberlake; Rupert Everett; Amy Sedaris; Maya Rudolph; Cheri Oteri; Amy Poehler; John Krasinski; Ian McShane; Eric Idle; Regis Philbin; Larry King; Conrad Vernon; Cody Cameron; Seth Rogen; ***D:*** Chris Miller; Raman Hui; ***W:*** Jeffrey Price; Peter S. Seaman; Jon Zack; ***M:*** Harry Gregson-Williams.

Shriek If You Know What I Did Last Friday the 13th **1/2 2000 (R)** If you're a member of the no joke is too cheap to laugh at club, you'll like this parody of parodies. There's a killer on the loose and he's targeting a group of friends who go to Bulimia High. The humor may date quickly. **86m/C; VHS, DVD.** Harley Cross; Tiffani(-Amber) Thiessen; Coolio; Tom Arnold; Julie Benz; Aimee Graham; Majandra Delfino; Shirley Jones; Rose Marie; Mink Stole; Simon Rex; Danny Strong; ***D:*** John Blanchard; ***W:*** Sue Bailey; Joe Nelms; ***C:*** David J. Miller; ***M:*** Tyler Bates. **CABLE**

Shriek of the Mutilated **WOOF! 1974 (R)** An anthropological expedition on a deserted island turns into a night of horror as a savage beast kills the members of the group one by one. **85m/C; VHS, DVD.** Alan Brock; Jennifer Stock; Michael (M.K.) Harris; Tawn Ellis; Darcy Brown; ***D:*** Michael Findlay; ***W:*** Ed Adlum; Ed Kelleher; ***C:*** Roberta Findlay.

Shrieker **1997 (R)** Six college students are squatting in an abandoned hospital that just happens to be the scene of a 50-year-old massacre. So, one gets the bright idea of conjuring up the creature that did the deed after learning that it will only kill five victims—and the sixth will become the creature's master. This one's really lame. **80m/C; VHS, DVD.** Tanya Dempsey; Jamie Gannon; Parry Shen; ***D:*** Victoria Sloan; ***W:*** Benjamin Carr.

The Shrimp on the Barbie **1/2 1990 (R)** When daddy refuses to bless her marriage to dim bulb boyfriend, Australian Samms hires L.A. low life Marin to pose as new beau. Another pseudonymous Smithee effort. **86m/C; VHS, DVD.** Richard "Cheech" Marin; Emma Samms; Vernon Wells; Bruce Spence; Carole (Raphaelle) Davis; ***D:*** Alan Smithee.

The Shrine **1/2 2010** Slow-paced and low-action horror. Aspiring journalist Carmen, her photographer boyfriend Marcus, and their colleague Sara travel to a rural Polish village to investigate the disappearance of backpacker Eric. The girls get kidnapped and Marcus discovers the locals are druids who practice human sacrifice. The Polish spoken in the film deliberately remains untranslated since the trio doesn't understand the language. **85m/C; DVD, Blu-Ray, Streaming.** *CA* Cindy Sampson; Aaron Ashmore; Meghan Heffern; Trevor Matthews; Vieslav Krystyan; Ben Lewis; ***D:*** Jon Knautz; ***W:*** Jon Knautz; Brendan Moore; ***C:*** James J. Griffith; ***M:*** Ryan Shore.

Shrink **2009 (R)** Strained and perhaps overly-insider drama about a celebrity shrink who has more problems than his patients. Depressed Henry Carter (Spacey) is still shaken by his wife's suicide and spends his time in a pot-induced stupor, even during sessions with his Hollywood patients, including an actress (Burrows) dealing with age issues, an obnoxious agent (Roberts) with extreme OCD, and an actor (Williams) who will admit to a sex addiction but not a drinking problem. Most of the characters are sketchy although Spacey and Palmer (as a young pro bono patient) know how to make the most of the scenes they're given. **110m/C; On Demand.** Kevin Spacey; Robin Williams; Saffron Burrows; Keke Palmer; Dallas Roberts; Pell James; Jack Huston; Mark Webber; Robert Loggia; Laura Ramsey; ***D:*** Jonas Pate; ***W:*** Thomas Moffett; ***C:*** Lukas Ettlin; ***M:*** Ken Andrews; Brian Reitzell.

Shrooms **2007** Slasher flick has five American college students meeting up with their Irish friend Jake to go camping. Jake picks a great spot too'a rural area with an abandoned Catholic reformatory that local legend says is haunted because the children were tortured and murdered by sadistic priests! And then they all snack on psychedelic mushrooms! Because, of course, no one will become paranoid and psycho. **85m/C; DVD.** *GB IR* Jack Huston; Max Kasch; Alice Greczyn; Lindsey Haun; Robert Hofman; Maya Hazan; ***D:*** Paddy Breathnach; ***W:*** Pearse Elliott; ***C:*** Nanu Segal; ***M:*** Dario Marianelli.

Shut-Eye **1/2 2003** Low budget drama about an urban Chicago couple who have fallen into a criminal life to survive. Things only get worse when their family steals the cash they've been storing for the Mafia. What kind of Mafia goon entrusts their safe money to a house-frau? **85m/C; DVD.** John Covert; Jenny Kern; James Aidan; Stana Katic; ***D:*** John Covert; ***W:*** John Covert; ***C:*** Adam Rehmeier; ***M:*** Bradley Parker Sparrow.

Shut In **2016 (PG-13)** Watts deserves better than this. You do too. The great actress plays Mary Portman, a psychologist who is shut off from the rest of the world during a storm and in a remote cabin, and emotionally shut in after an accident that takes the life of her husband and leaves her son paralyzed. Into this awkward set-up, add the potential of a home invasion, as Portman starts to convince herself that there's someone outside during the storm who is trying to get in. This is the Shyamalan rip-off they made a lot of after "The Sixth Sense," and they don't make that often any more. For a good reason. **91m/C; DVD, Blu-Ray.** Naomi Watts; Oliver Platt; Charlie Heaton; Jacob Tremblay; Clementine Poidatz; ***D:*** Farren Blackburn; ***W:*** Christina Hodson; ***C:*** Yves Bélanger; ***M:*** Nathaniel Mechaly.

Shut Up and Kiss Me **2005** Harmless, unremarkable romantic romp with best buds Ryan (Barnes) and Pete (Rowe) who see their 20s in the rearview mirror when true love finally catches up to them—at the same time. The serious Ryan gets plowed over—literally—by Jessica (Richardson) while Pete is in over his head with Tiara (Allen), whose protective mobster uncle (Young) isn't too keen about the surfer dude. **101m/C; DVD.** Christopher Daniel Barnes; Krista Allen; Brad Rowe; Burt Young; Kristin Richardson; John Capodice; Victoria Jackson; Frank Bonner; Yelba Osorio; Kevin Meaney; ***D:*** Gary Brockette; ***W:*** Alden "Steve" Chase; Howard Flamm; ***C:*** Jacques Haitkin; ***M:*** Andrew Gross. **VIDEO**

Shut Up Little Man! An Audio Misadventure **1/2 2011** Real-life drunk, bickering roommates Raymond Huffman and Peter Haskett became viral sensations before the phrase was created merely by virtue of having a pair of neighbors who found them endlessly entertaining. When two guys calling themselves Eddie Lee Sausage and Mitchell D. recorded their neighbors' over-the-top hostility, they had no idea how popular the tapes would become, spawning stage productions and even a film. The drunks and the two men who made them celebrities make for interesting documentary subjects, especially when the filmmakers delve a bit deeper into the moral gray area of foisting fame on people who never asked for it. **85m/C; DVD, Blu-Ray.** Bryan Mason; Mitch Deprey; Raymond Huffman; Peter Haskett; Daniel Clowes; Tony Newton; Ivan Brunetti; ***D:*** Mathew Bate; ***W:*** Mathew Bate; ***M:*** Jonny Elk Walsh.

Shutter *Shutter: They Are Around Us* **2005** This superior Thai horror film is the inspiration of the lackluster U.S. remake of the same name. While driving down a country road late at night, a photographer and his wife run down a woman who appears from nowhere, then flee the scene in a panic. But once in Bangkok the spectral woman starts appearing in the photographer's photos and in his wife's dreams. They return to the scene but discover no report of any accident and no victim to speak of. Going back to Bangkok they watch their friends die one after another while trying to figure out what has happened. The Thai version includes many things omitted from the American remake because they deal with Thai religious practices. **95m/C; DVD.** *TH* Ananda Everingham; Nattaweeranuch Thongmee; Achita Sikamana; Unnop Chanpaibool; Titikarn Tongprasearth; Sivigorn Muttamara; Kachormsak Naruepatr; Panitan Mavichak; Tanapon Chansming; Thamonwan Srinatsomsuk; ***D:*** Banjong Pisanthanakun; Parkpoom Wongpoom; ***W:*** Banjong Pisanthanakun; Parkpoom Wongpoom; Sopon Sukdapisit; ***C:*** Niramon Ross; ***M:*** Chartchai Prongpapapan.

Shutter **1/2 2008 (PG-13)** Another watered-down version of Asian horror, this time around the 2004 Thai chiller by the same name gets the Hollywood treatment. New bride Jane (Taylor) joins her photographer husband Benjamin (Jackson) on a business trip to Japan. One foggy night the couple accidentally hit a girl in the road. They assume she's okay and life goes on. However, her ghostly image begins appearing in Benjamin's photographs, tormenting the couple. Tame and tepid compared to the original, recycling the usual scare tactics now common in J-horror remakes. **85m/C; DVD, Blu-Ray.** Joshua Jackson; Rachael Taylor; Megumi Okina; David Denman; John Hensley; Maya Hazen; James Kyson Lee; ***D:*** Masayuki Ochiai; ***W:*** Luke Dawson; ***C:*** Katsumi Yanagijima; ***M:*** Nathan Barr.

Shutter Island **2009 (R)** Scorsese takes on the horror and noir genres in this moody thriller set in 1954. U.S. Marshals Teddy Daniels (DiCaprio) and Chuck Aule (Ruffalo) try to find a murderer who disappeared from a hospital for the criminally insane on remote Shutter Island. The staff, headed by Drs. Cawley (Kingsley) and Naehring (von Sydow), prove to be less than helpful. Sinister conspiracies and haunting flashbacks cause Teddy to understand less the more he discovers. The twist ending proves that nothing is as it seems in this gothic asylum. This film marks the fourth collaboration between Scorsese and DiCaprio. Based on a novel by Dennis Lehane. **148m/C; Blu-Ray, On Demand.** Leonardo DiCaprio; Mark Ruffalo; Ben Kingsley; Michelle Williams; Emily Mortimer; Max von Sydow; Jackie Earle Haley; Elias Koteas; Patricia Clarkson; ***D:*** Martin Scorsese; ***W:*** Laeta Kalogridis; ***C:*** Robert Richardson.

Shutterbug 🦴 ½ **2010** Uneven experimental low-budget indie follows photog Alex Santiago (Del Casillo) who, fed up with his fashion shoots, starts late night wanderings around New York taking pictures of whatever he likes. Alex also takes pictures of the rising sun, which damages his eyes causing blurry sight and weird visions of a phantom woman (Stoyanova). He also meets a lot of gabby street denizens with their own lines of existential bull. **90m/C; DVD, Blu-Ray.** Nando Del Castillo; Ariel Blue Sky; Doug Barron; Stanislava Stoyanova; Brett Mole; Frank Cadillac; Anna Gutto; ***D:*** Minos Papas; ***W:*** Minos Papas; ***C:*** Rosanna Rizzo; ***M:*** Tao Zervas.

Shuttle 🦴 **2009 (R)** Stranded late on a rainy night at the Boston airport, Mel (List) and Jules (Goodman) flag down exactly the wrong shuttle. Along with three male passengers, the gals soon realize that their driver is a psycho. The psycho's got the upper hand until at least the femmes start fighting back, but even with this undemanding plot there's too much that's just dumb. **106m/C; DVD.** Peyton List; Cameron Goodman; Cullen Douglas; Dave Power; James Snyder; Tony Curran; ***D:*** Edward A. Anderson; ***W:*** Edward A. Anderson; ***C:*** Michael Fimognari; ***M:*** Henning Lohner.

Siam Sunset 🦴🦴 ½ **1999** Mild fish-out-of-water comedy finds British chemist Perry (Roache), who works on devising new paint colors, caught up in every conceivable disaster while on an Australian holiday. The recent widower (his wife was crushed by a refrigerator) wins his vacation, which turns out to be a decidedly third-rate bus trip cross-country with a petty tyrant operator (Billing) and a number of Aussie eccentrics. Title refers to a particular shade of red that Perry is trying to develop. **91m/C; VHS, DVD.** *AU* Linus Roache; Danielle Cormack; Roy Billing; Alan Brough; Ian Bliss; Victoria Hill; Rebecca Hobbs; ***D:*** John Polson; ***W:*** Max Dann; Andrew Knight; ***C:*** Brian J. Breheny; ***M:*** Paul Grabowsky.

Siberia 🦴 ½ **2018 (R)** Reeves brings his trademark stoicism (and a surprising bilingualism) as Lucas, an American diamond dealer who travels to Russia to sell $50 million worth of ultra-rare blue beauties. But both his Russian partner and his diamonds disappear, and with an impatient and menacing buyer breathing down his neck, Lucas flees to Siberia, where he finds a hook-up (Katya) instead of any of the rather important items he's lost. Vacillating between romance and thriller, this flick settles on neither, landing in the Siberia of filmmaking. **104m/C; DVD, Blu-Ray.** Keanu Reeves; Molly Ringwald; Ana Ularu; Aleks Paunovic; Pasha D. Lychnikoff; ***D:*** Matthew Ross; ***W:*** Scott B. Smith; ***C:*** Eric Koretz; ***M:*** Danny Bensi; Saunder Jurriaans.

Siberiade 🦴🦴🦴 **1979** Depicts life in a Siberian village from 1909 to 1969 for a wealthy family and a peasant clan and how Soviet society affects them. Rambling narrative with strong characters. In Russian with subtitles. **190m/C; VHS, DVD.** *RU* Vladimir Samoilov; Vitaly Solomin; Nikita Mikhalkov; Lyudmila Gurchenko; Nathalia Andretchenko; ***D:*** Andrei Konchalovsky; ***W:*** Valentin Yezhov; Andrei Konchalovsky; ***M:*** Eduard Artemyev. Cannes '79: Grand Jury Prize.

Siberian Lady Macbeth 🦴🦴🦴 ½ *Fury Is a Woman; Sibirska Ledi Magbet* **1961** A Polish version of Shakespeare's Macbeth which ranks with the greatest film translations of his work. In Czarist Russia the passionate wife of a plantation owner begins an affair with a farm hand, and poisons her father-in-law when he finds them out. As her madness grows, she plots the murder of the husband and other suspicious family members. In Serbian with English subtitles. **93m/B; VHS, DVD.** *RU* Olivera Markovic; Ljuba Tadic; Kapitalina Eric; ***D:*** Andrzej Wajda; ***W:*** Sveta Lukic; ***C:*** Aleksandar Sekulovic.

The Sibling 🦴🦴 *Psycho Sisters; So Evil, My Sister* **1972 (PG)** Two sisters become involved in the accidental murder of a man who was a husband to one woman and lover to the other. Of course, one sister has just been released from the mental rehabilitation clinic. **85m/C; VHS, DVD.** Susan Strasberg; Faith Domergue; Syd Chaplin; Steve Mitchell; ***D:*** Reginald LeBorg.

Sibling Rivalry 🦴🦴 **1990 (PG-13)** Repressed doctor's wife (redundant) Alley rolls in hay with soon to be stiff stranger upon advice of footloose sister. Stranger expires from heart attack in hay and Alley discovers that the corpse is her long-lost brother-in-law. Slapstick cover-up ensues. **88m/C; VHS, DVD, Blu-Ray.** Kirstie Alley; Bill Pullman; Carrie Fisher; Sam Elliott; Jami Gertz; Ed O'Neill; Scott Bakula; Frances Sternhagen; Bill Macy; ***D:*** Carl Reiner.

Siblings 🦴🦴 **2004 (R)** Toronto teen Joe (Alex Campbell) and his stepsiblings Margaret (Gadon), Pete (Chalmers), and Danielle (Weinstein) want their evil boozy stepmom (Smits) and evil lascivious stepdad (Nicholas Campbell) dead. And then the gruesome twosome die—kinda semi-accidentally. So now the sibs have to get rid of the bodies, claim their inheritance, and watch out for each other. Polley plays the wacky, helpful girl-next-door whom Joe has a crush on. **85m/C; VHS, DVD.** *CA* Alex Campbell; Andrew Chalmers; Sarah Polley; Sonja Smits; Nicholas (Nick) Campbell; Tom McCamus; Martha Burns; Sarah Gadon; Samantha Weinstein; ***D:*** David Weaver; ***W:*** Jackie May; ***C:*** David (Robert) A. Greene; ***M:*** Ron Sures.

Sicario 🦴🦴🦴 **2015 (R)** Villeneuve's thriller is a tight, refined chronicle of the chaos that has erupted on the border between Mexico and the United States under the banner of a failed war on drugs. FBI agent Kate Macer (Blunt) sees this world firsthand when she's tasked to join a special group led by Matt Graver (Brolin) and the mysterious Alejandro (Del Toro). Who are these people with extreme authority—CIA, DEA, something else? Villeneuve, with expert cinematography by Roger Deakins, captures the insanity of fighting a losing war, and a great performance by Del Toro drives it home. **120m/C; DVD, Blu-Ray.** Emily Blunt; Benicio Del Toro; Josh Brolin; Jon Bernthal; Jeffrey Donovan; ***D:*** Denis Villeneuve; ***W:*** Taylor Sheridan; ***C:*** Roger Deakins; ***M:*** Johan Johannson.

Sicario: Day of the Soldado 🦴🦴 **2018 (R)** When Mexican drug cartels diversify into the trafficking of terrorists, U.S. federal agent Graver (Brolin) orders the mysterious Alejandro (Del Toro) to kidnap a kingpin's daughter with the aim of igniting a self-imploding war between the cartels. Without Emily Blunt's character to provide moral grounding and a good guy to root for, this testosterone-fueled action-thriller sequel subverts its beautifully sad predecessor by offering little more than grim, mindless violence from all sides. **122m/C; DVD, Blu-Ray.** Benicio Del Toro; Josh Brolin; Isabela Moner; Jeffrey Donovan; Catherine Keener; ***D:*** Stefano Sollima; ***W:*** Taylor Sheridan; ***C:*** Dariusz Wolski; ***M:*** Hildur Guonadottir.

The Sicilian 🦴 ½ **1987** Adapted from the Mario Puzo novel and based on the life of Salvatore Giuliano. Chronicles the exploits of the men who took on the government, the Catholic Church, and the Mafia in an effort to make Sicily secede from Italy and become its own nation in the 1940s. Pretentious, overdone, and confused. This long, uncut version was unseen in America, but hailed by European critics; the 115-minute, R-rated American release is also available, but isn't as good. See "Salvatore Giuliano" (Francesco Rosi, 1962) instead of either version. **146m/C; VHS, DVD, Blu-Ray.** Christopher Lambert; John Turturro; Terence Stamp; Joss Ackland; Barbara Sukowa; ***D:*** Michael Cimino; ***W:*** Steve Shagan; ***C:*** Alex Thomson; ***M:*** David Mansfield.

The Sicilian Girl 🦴 ½ **2009** Based on the true story of Rosa Atria, a teenager who testified against the Mafia in 1991. Young Rita suffers extreme trauma after finding her Mafioso father's bullet-ridden body and begins making careful notes on the gangsters' criminal activities. After her brother is murdered, now 17-year-old Rita wants revenge and approaches the special prosecutor with her evidence but she's treated like a pariah for breaking the law of omerta. Director Amenta's pic wastes its dramatic story with a lack of momentum and dull storytelling. Italian with subtitles. **110m/C; DVD.** *IT* Veronica D'Agostino; Gerard Jugnot; Marcello Mazzarello; Lucia Sardo; Mario Pupella; Primo Reggiani; Francesco Casisa; Paolo Briguglia; Miriana Faja; ***D:*** Marco Amenta; ***W:*** Marco Amenta; Sergio Donati; Gianni Romoli; ***C:*** Luca Bigazzi; ***M:*** Pasquale Catalano.

S.I.C.K. Serial Insane Clown Killer 🦴 ½ *Grim Weekend* **2003** Five unsympathetic characters travel to a remote cabin for a weekend of ghost stories and fun. Instead they find a decidedly unfunny clown, a high body count, and little dolls. Amateurish effort doesn't really have much to recommend it, unless you like evil clowns. **97m/C; VHS, DVD.** Ken Hebert; Amanda Watson; Melissa Bale; Chris Bruck; Hank Fields; ***D:*** Bob Willems; ***W:*** Ken Hebert; ***C:*** Jaroslav Vodehnal. **VIDEO**

Sicko 🦴🦴 ½ **2007 (PG-13)** Rabble-rousing Moore takes on the profit-driven U.S. health care industry. He showcases various Americans who have suffered (primarily because of being denied insurance coverage and/or claims) and looks at other countries with national health care services, including England, France, Canada—and most controversial—Cuba. It's still personal storytelling but less bombastic than Moore's usual rants, and the greed, double-dealing, and health concerns are easy for most Americans to follow. **113m/C; DVD.** ***D:*** Michael Moore; ***W:*** Michael Moore; ***M:*** Erin O'Hara.

Sid & Nancy 🦴🦴🦴 ½ *Sid & Nancy: Love Kills* **1986 (R)** The tragic, brutal, true love story of The Sex Pistols' Sid Vicious and American groupie Nancy Spungen, from the director of "Repo Man." Remarkable lead performances in a very dark story that manages to be funny at times. Depressing but engrossing; no appreciation of punk music or sympathy for the self-destructive way of life is required. Oldman and Webb are superb. Music by Joe Strummer, the Pogues, and Pray for Rain. **111m/C; VHS, DVD, Blu-Ray.** *GB* Gary Oldman; Chloe Webb; Debbie Bishop; David Hayman; Andrew Schofield; Tony London; Xander Berkeley; Biff Yeager; Courtney Love; Iggy Pop; ***D:*** Alex Cox; ***W:*** Alex Cox; Abbe Wool; ***C:*** Roger Deakins; ***M:*** The Pogues; Pray for Rain; Joe Strummer. Natl. Soc. Film Critics '86: Actress (Webb).

Siddhartha 🦴🦴 **1972** Siddhartha (Kapoor), a wealthy young Brahmin, decides to become a wandering ascetic and follow holy teachings. But after several years, Siddhartha abandons himself to hedonism and the delights of courtesan Kamala (Garewal) until his ultimate decision to return to his search for inner peace. Based on the novel by Herman Hesse. **85m/C; VHS, DVD.** Shashi Kapoor; Simi Garewal; ***D:*** Conrad Rooks; ***W:*** Conrad Rooks; ***C:*** Sven Nykvist; ***M:*** Hemant Kumar.

Side by Side 🦴🦴🦴 **2012** Narrator Reeves makes a surprisingly good tour guide through the complicated, divisive debate surrounding the impact of digital film on the movie industry, as well as on a technology that has been the past century's only way of capturing the moving image. With interview contributions from luminaries like Martin Scorsese, James Cameron, George Lucas, Robert Rodriguez, and many more, director Kenneally's documentary deftly navigates this complex issue and its effect on what is seen today and how it will be archived for years to come. A little too techie at times but it's mostly fascinating stuff. **99m/C; DVD, Blu-Ray.** Richard Linklater; Martin Scorsese; David Lynch; Steven Soderbergh; ***Nar:*** Keanu Reeves; ***D:*** Christopher Kenneally; ***W:*** Christopher Kenneally; ***C:*** Chris Cassidy; ***M:*** Billy Ryan; Brendan Ryan.

Side Effects 🦴 ½ **2005 (R)** Shrill comedy about corporate evils. Karly is a sales rep for an unscrupulous drug firm. She falls for fellow rep Zach, who wants to throw over corporate greed for country life. Karly decides to work six more months and suddenly the perks are rolling in, just as she learns about some shady dealings. So will Karly decide to listen to her conscience or her cash flow? **90m/C; DVD.** Katherine Heigl; Lucian McAfee; David Durbin; Dorian DeMichele; ***D:*** Kathleen Slattery-Moschkau; ***W:*** Kathleen Slattery-Moschkau; ***C:*** Carl F. Whitney; ***M:*** John Tanner; Ralph Bruner.

Side Effects 🦴🦴🦴 **2013 (R)** Director Soderbergh's alleged last film (he has proclaimed retirement) serves as a brilliant greatest hits for his entire career, capturing many of the themes he's worked with before into a captivating thriller. After the release of her husband (Tatum) from prison, Emily (Mara) deals with severe depression and goes on a regimen of pills from a helpful doctor (Law). What starts as a cautionary tale about the over-medicated '10s turns into something Alfred Hitchcock and Brian De Palma would love. Brilliantly conceived, incredibly clever, and perfectly acted, Soderbergh has ended his career on a high note (no pun intended). **106m/C; DVD, Blu-Ray.** Rooney Mara; Channing Tatum; Jude Law; Catherine Zeta-Jones; Vinessa Shaw; Mamie Gummer; Ann Dowd; ***D:*** Steven Soderbergh; ***W:*** Scott Z. Burns; ***C:*** Steven Soderbergh; ***M:*** Thomas Newman.

Side Out 🦴 ½ **1990 (PG-13)** The first major film about volleyball!? What a claim! What a bore. Midwestern college guy spends summer in Southern Cal. working for slumlord uncle; instead enters "the ultimate" beach volleyball touring. Bogus. Don't see it, dude. **100m/C; DVD.** C. Thomas Howell; Peter Horton; Kathy Ireland; Sinjin Smith; Randy Stoklos; Courtney Thorne-Smith; Harley Jane Kozak; Christopher Rydell; ***D:*** Peter Israelson.

Side Street 🦴🦴 **1950** Sweaty noir with young postman Joe Norson (Granger) giving into a momentary weakness and finding a world of hurt. He just wants to provide for pregnant wife Ellen (O'Connell), so when he sees a wad of cash in a lawyer's office, he takes it. But the tainted loot is part of a blackmail payoff tied to murder. Joe tries to return the dough but runs into problems and finds more trouble when the money (and the friend who was holding it for him) disappears. About this time Joe learns the greenbacks belonged to gangster Garsell (Craig). Joe has to go on the lam from Garsell and the cops, who now think the poor stooge is tied into the murder. **83m/B; DVD.** Farley Granger; Cathy O'Donnell; James Craig; Paul Kelly; Edmon Ryan; Paul Harvey; Jean Hagen; Charles McGraw; Nick Drumman; ***D:*** Anthony Mann; ***W:*** Sydney (Sidney) Boehm; ***C:*** Joseph Ruttenberg; ***M:*** Lennie Hayton.

The Sidehackers **WOOF!** *Five the Hard Way* **1969** Crap exploitation based on the brief racing sport of sidehacking (a three-wheeled motorcycle with an attached sidecar). Rommel gets into a beef with competitor J.C., whose girlfriend lies about being raped after making a play for Rommel and getting rejected. This leads to Rommel getting beaten and his fiancee Rita getting murdered by J.C. and his cronies. Naturally, Rommel wants revenge. **82m/C; DVD.** Ross Hagen; Michael Pataki; Diane McBain; Claire Polan; Dick Merrifield; Edward Parrish; Michael Graham; ***D:*** Gus Trinkonis; ***W:*** Larry Billman; Tony (Walter Anthony) Huston; ***C:*** Jon Hall; ***M:*** Michael Curb; Guy Hemric; Jerry Styner.

Sidekick 🦴 ½ **2005** Norman, a comic-book-obsessed geek, discovers his coworker Victor has telekinetic powers and trains him as a superhero so he can live out his dream of becoming a superhero sidekick and battling criminal elements. Only self-absorbed Victor isn't superhero material and wants to use his newfound ability for his own greedy enjoyment. **87m/C; DVD.** *CA* David W. Ingram; Perry Mucci; Mackenzie Lush; Daniel Baldwin; Julian Osen; ***D:*** Blake Van de Graaf; ***W:*** Michael Sparaga; ***C:*** Jordan Cushing; ***M:*** Matt Judge.

Sidekicks 🦴🦴 **1974** Unsold CBS TV pilot sequel to 1971's "Skin Game" with Hagman taking over the James Garner role. Con man Quince Drew (Hagman) travels west with his freeborn black partner Jason O'Rourke (Gossett Jr.). On the run from a posse, they're unexpectedly captured by sheriff's daughter, Purdy (Danner), who thinks they're part of an outlaw gang run by the inept Boss (Elam). Boss busts them out of jail to help him rob a bank while the partners hope to catch the bandits and claim the reward. **73m/C; DVD.** Larry Hagman; Louis Gossett, Jr.; Blythe Danner; Harry (Henry) Morgan; Jack Elam; Noah Beery, Jr.; John Beck; ***D:*** Burt Kennedy; ***W:*** William Bowers; ***C:*** Robert B. Hauser; ***M:*** David Shire. **TV**

Sidewalks of London 🦴🦴🦴 *St. Martin's Lane* **1938** Laughton's a sidewalk entertainer who takes in homeless waif Leigh and puts her in his act and in his heart. Harrison steals her away and before long she's a star in the music halls. Meanwhile, Laughton has fallen on hard times. Memorable performances. **86m/B; DVD, Blu-Ray.** *UK* Charles

Laughton; Vivien Leigh; Rex Harrison; Larry Adler; Tyrone Guthrie; Maire O'Neill; *D:* Tim Whelan; *W:* Charles Laughton; Tim Whelan; Clemence Dane; Erich Pommer; Bartlett Cormack; *C:* Jules Kruger; *M:* Arthur Johnston.

Sidewalks of New York ✌✌ ½ **1931** A hapless New York millionaire (Keaton) falls for tenement gal Page and tries to win her heart by saving her street urchin brother from joining the local gang of toughs. Keaton was a silent screen classic as a comedian but his talkie career was disappointing as he lost creative control and battled alcohol problems. **74m/B; VHS, DVD.** Buster Keaton; Anita Page; Cliff Edwards; Frank LaRue; Frank Rowan; Norman Phillips, Jr.; *D:* Jules White; Zion Myers.

Sidewalks of New York ✌✌ **2001 (R)** Burns's lightweight comedy about various New Yorkers looking for sex and/or romance suffered from post-Sept. 11 disdain for anything frivolous. But it also suffers from weak writing, obvious "borrowing" from Woody Allen when he was still funny, and too few characters the audience can connect with. Burns is recently dumped TV producer Tommy, who hooks up with recently divorced teacher Maria (Dawson), whose ex, Ben (Krumholtz), thinks they can reunite, before he meets young waitress Ashley (Murphy), who's having an affair with a dentist (Tucci), who's married to Tommy's real-estate agent (Graham), in whom he naturally becomes interested. They're all being interviewed for a documentary on love and sex in NYC. Even if it doesn't work on many levels, the performances are generally fine, with Tucci standing out in the meatiest role. **107m/C; VHS, DVD.** Edward Burns; Heather Graham; Rosario Dawson; Dennis Farina; David Krumholtz; Brittany Murphy; Stanley Tucci; Callie (Calliope) Thorne; Aida Turturro; Nadia Dajani; Michael Leydon Campbell; *D:* Edward Burns; *W:* Edward Burns; *C:* Frank Prinzi.

Sideways ✌✌✌ ½ **2004 (R)** Open a bottle of pinot noir and enjoy the darkly comedic road trip of two self-absorbed, middle-aged buddies in denial. Divorced English teacher, failed novelist, and oenophile Miles (teddy-bearish Giamatti) decides that his lothario, D-list actor pal Jack (Church) deserves a weeklong send-off in the California wine country before his marriage. Naturally, they meet two women infinitely more self-aware and honest than themselves. For Miles, it's kindly blonde waitress Maya (Madsen) while Jack figures he can indulge in a pre-wedding fling with tart-tongued wine pourer Stephanie (Payne's wife Oh). Payne's film is for adults in the best possible way: it's intelligent, amusing, exasperating, and romantic—much like the characters themselves. Great performances by all; based on the novel by Rex Pickett. **124m/C; DVD, Blu-Ray.** Paul Giamatti; Thomas Haden Church; Virginia Madsen; Sandra Oh; Marylouise Burke; Jessica Hecht; M.C. Gainey; Missy Doty; *D:* Alexander Payne; *W:* Alexander Payne; *C:* Phedon Papamichael; *M:* Rolfe Kent. Oscars '04: Adapt. Screenplay; British Acad. '04: Adapt. Screenplay; Golden Globes '05: Film--Mus./ Comedy, Screenplay; Ind. Spirit '05: Actor (Giamatti), Director (Payne), Film, Screenplay, Support. Actor (Church), Support. Actress (Madsen); Screen Actors Guild '04: Cast; Writers Guild '04: Adapt. Screenplay.

Sidewinder One ✌ **1977 (PG)** Motocross racing is the setting for a romance between a racer and an heiress. Good racing footage, but where's the plot? If you like cars a whole lot . . . **97m/C; VHS, DVD.** Michael Parks; Marjoe Gortner; Susan Howard; Alex Cord; Charlotte Rae; *D:* Earl Bellamy; *W:* Nancy Voyles Crawford.

The Siege ✌✌ ½ *Against All Enemies* **1998 (R)** Controversial political suspense/action movie caused quite a ruckus when first released. Although protested by Arab-American groups for alleged negative stereotyping, it actually points the finger at the U.S. military as the bad guys. First half centers on FBI honcho Hubbard (Washington) and his prominently Lebanese-American partner Haddad (Shaloub) as they try to stop terrorist bombings of New York. After the bombings escalate, martial law is declared in Brooklyn. Under semi-fascist Gen. Devereaux, all Constitutional rights are suspended and young Arab-Americans are rounded up and imprisoned. Hubbard forms a shaky alliance with shady CIA lady Elise Kraft to break the terrorist ring and restore freedom. Substitutes cardboard cutouts spouting political platitudes for characters. **116m/C; VHS, DVD, Blu-Ray.** Denzel Washington; Tony Shalhoub; Annette Bening; Bruce Willis; Sami Bouajila; David Proval; Jack Gwaltney; Chip Zien; Victor Slezak; Will Lyman; Dakin Matthews; John Rothman; E. Katherine Kerr; Jimmie Ray Weeks; Lance Reddick; Mark Valley; Liana Pai; Amro Salama; *D:* Edward Zwick; *W:* Edward Zwick; Menno Meyjes; Lawrence Wright; *C:* Roger Deakins; *M:* Graeme Revell. Golden Raspberries '98: Worst Actor (Willis).

Siege at Red River ✌✌ ½ **1954** In 1864, Confederates Jim Farraday and Benjy Guderman are posing as traveling medicine show salesmen and hiding a stolen Gatling gun in their wagon. They help nurse Nora when she is stranded, and the gun is later stolen by bad guy Manning. He sells it to the Shawnee, who plan to use it on the soldiers at a nearby fort. Union officer Kelso captures Farraday and he agrees to get the gun back in return for his release and a chance at a future with Nora. Action-packed finale and a good use of color cinematography. **86m/C; DVD, Streaming.** Van Johnson; Joanne Dru; Richard Boone; Milburn Stone; Jeff Morrow; Craig Hill; Rico Alaniz; *D:* Rudolph Mate; *W:* Sydney (Sidney) Boehm; *C:* Edward Cronjager; *M:* Lionel Newman.

The Siege of Firebase Gloria ✌ ½ **1989** Story of the Marines who risked their lives defending an outpost against overwhelming odds during the 1968 Tet offensive in Vietnam. Purportedly patriotic war drama made by an Australian director; lead Hauser is a disgusting sadist, and plot is hopelessly hackneyed. **95m/C; VHS, DVD, Blu-Ray.** Wings Hauser; R. Lee Ermey; Mark Neely; Gary Hershberger; Clyde Jones; Margi Gerard; Richard Kuhlman; David Anderson; Robert Arevalo; John Calvin; Albert "Poppy" Popwell; *D:* Brian Trenchard-Smith; *W:* Tony Johnston; William Nagle; *C:* Joe Batac; *M:* Paul Schutze.

The Siege of Sidney Street ✌✌ **1960** Set in London's East End in 1911 and based on a true incident. Inspector Mannering (Sinden) goes undercover to look into the activities of a gang of foreign anarchists, led by Peter the Painter (Wyngarde). Mannering befriends Sara (Berger), a lonely Russian girl who's Peter's girlfriend until she learns about their violent activities. When Mannering wants to arrest the anarchists, it turns into an armed siege at their headquarters. **93m/B; DVD.** *GB* Donald Sinden; Peter Wyngarde; Kieron Moore; Nicole Berger; T.P. McKenna; Tutte Lemkow; Godfrey Quigley; *D:* Robert S. Baker; Monty Berman; *W:* Jimmy Sangster; *C:* Robert S. Baker; Monty Berman; *M:* Stanley Black.

Siegfried ✌✌✌✌ *Siegfrieds Tod; Siegfried's Death* **1924** Half of Lang's epic masterpiece "Der Niebelungen," based on German mythology. Title hero bathes in the blood of a dragon he has slain. He marries a princess, but wicked Queen Brumhilde has him killed. Part two, in which Siegfried's widow marries Attila the Hun, is titled "Kriemheld's Revenge." These dark, brooding, archetypal tours de force were patriotic tributes, and were loved by Hitler. Silent with music score. **100m/B; Silent; VHS, DVD.** *GE* Paul Richter; Margareta Schoen; *D:* Fritz Lang.

Sierra ✌ ½ **1950** Jeff Hassard (Jagger) has been falsely accused of murder and he and his son Ring (Murphy) are hiding out in the mountains. While lawyer Riley Martin (Hendrix) gets lost, the Hassards help her and she vows to clear Jeff's name since she's now sweet on Ring as well. (Hendrix and Murphy were married at the time of filming.) **83m/C; DVD.** Dean Jagger; Audie Murphy; Wanda Hendrix; Burl Ives; Tony Curtis; Houseley Stevenson; Richard Rober; *D:* Alfred E. Green; *W:* Edna Anhalt; Milton Gunzberg; *C:* Russell Metty; *M:* Walter Scharf.

A Sierra Nevada Gunfight ✌ *The Sorrow* **2013 (R)** Casper Hazzard (Ryan Ballance) joins his father prospecting for gold in the wilderness only to watch his parent slowly devolve into complete insanity. Indians and outlaws complicate his attempts to get his father aid. **90m/C; DVD.** Kirk Harris; Ryan Ballance; Michael Madsen; John Savage; Yvonne Delarosa; Ruben Hinojosa, Jr.; *D:* Vernon E. Mortensen; *W:* Vernon E. Mortensen; Johnny Harrington; *C:* Ace Underhill; *M:* John Coda. **VIDEO**

Sightseers ✌✌ **2012** Black comedies don't get much darker than Wheatley's pitch black story of a road trip gone hysterically awry. Chris (Oram) just wants to show his girlfriend Tina (Lowe) the countryside but he keeps encountering people who aggravate him and light his short fuse. Chris doesn't hold back when he's angry. He kills. Wheatley is a very smart director, keeping the balance between the horror of what turns into a killing spree by the two and the humor of the ridiculousness. **88m/C; DVD.** *UK* Alice Lowe; Steven H. Oram; Eileen Davies; Jonathan Aris; Monica Dolan; *D:* Ben Wheatley; *W:* Alice Lowe; Steven H. Oram; *C:* Laurie Rose; *M:* Mr. Jim Williams.

The Sign of Four ✌ ½ **1983** Sherlock Holmes and the ever-faithful Watson are hired by a young woman who has been anonymously sent an enormous diamond. An inept production which looks good but that's all. **97m/C; VHS, DVD.** *GB* Ian Richardson; David Healy; Thorley Walters; Cherie Lunghi; *D:* Desmond Davis; *W:* Charles Edward Pogue; *C:* Denis Lewiston; *M:* Harry Rabinowitz.

The Sign of Four ✌✌ ½ **2001** Holmes (Frewer), Watson (Welsh), and the Baker Street Irregulars are involved in murder, poison darts, a fortune in Indian jewels, and much suspicious behavior. **120m/C; VHS, DVD.** *CA* Matt Frewer; Kenneth Welsh; Marcel Jeannin; Sophie Lorain; Edward Yankie; Michel Perron; Kevin Woodhouse; *D:* Rodney Gibbons; *W:* Joe Wiesenfeld; *C:* Eric Cayla; *M:* Marc Ouellette. **CABLE**

The Sign of the Cross ✌✌ ½ **1933** Depraved Emperor Nero (Laughton) decides he wants a new city so he burns down Rome—blaming the fire on the Christians he also wants to get rid of (preferably by the lions in the arena). Meanwhile, Marcus (March), the Roman Prefect, has fallen for the virginal Christian Mercia (Landi) and risks his life to save her. Besides Laughton's overwhelmingly hammy performance, Colbert slinks seductively as the emperor's vixenish wife, Poppaea. Again, lots of crowd scenes (DeMille's specialty). Based on the play by Wilson Barrett. **125m/B; VHS, DVD.** Fredric March; Elissa Landi; Charles Laughton; Claudette Colbert; Ian Keith; Harry Beresford; Arthur Hohl; Nat Pendleton; *D:* Cecil B. DeMille; *W:* Waldemar Young; Sidney Buchman; *M:* Rudolph Kopp.

The Sign of Zorro ✌✌ **1960** Adventures of the masked swordsman as he champions the cause of the oppressed in early California. Full-length version of the popular late-50s Disney TV series. **89m/C; VHS, Streaming.** Guy Williams; Henry Calvin; Gene Sheldon; Romney Brent; Britt Lomond; George Lewis; Lisa Gaye; *D:* Norman Foster; Lewis R. Foster.

The Signal ✌✌ **2014 (PG-13)** Three MIT students are on a road trip when they seize an opportunity to track down a hacker they've crossed paths with in the past. They follow the hacker's signal until they're kidnapped and awaken in an underground facility. Then things get weird. Eubank's sci-fi/horror film defies easy synopsis and the story loses the audience about halfway through. It deserves points for originality even if the execution leaves something to be desired. It's an original that could have a cult following but will frustrate as many as it thrills. **97m/C; DVD, Blu-Ray.** Brenton Thwaites; Beau Knapp; Olivia Cooke; Laurence Fishburne; *D:* William Eubank; *W:* William Eubank; Carlyle Eubank; *C:* David Lanzenberg.

Signal 7 ✌✌ **1983** An improvised, neoverite document of a night in the lives of two San Francisco taxi drivers. Nilsson's first major release and a notable example of his unique scriptless, tape-to-film narrative technique. **89m/C; VHS, DVD.** Bill Ackridge; Dan Leegant; *D:* Rob Nilsson; *W:* Rob Nilsson.

Signed, Sealed, Delivered for Christmas ✌✌ ½ **2014** Hallmark Channel holiday fare. Postal workers Oliver, Rita, and Norman are used to taking care of mail addressed to Santa at the holidays. But one little girl's letter is addressed to God and, with the help of mysterious volunteer Jordan, they are determined to help her with her plea. **85m/C; DVD.** Eric Mabius; Kristin Booth; Crystal Lowe; Rob(ert) Estes; *D:* Kevin Fair; *W:* Martha Williamson; *C:* Adam Silwinski; *M:* James Jandrisch. **CABLE**

Signs ✌✌✌ **2002 (PG-13)** Shyamalan takes on crop circles in this eerily potent psycho-thriller. Widowed father Gibson, a lapsed minister, lives on a farm with children Culkin and Breslin, along with younger brother Phoenix when things start to get strange. Everything seems normal, but even simple everyday actions are steeped in the brand of moodiness and unspoken dread that Shyamalan does best. By the time mysterious circles appear in the cornfields, it's clear that the question of whether or not aliens are to blame for the crop circles is secondary to how the characters will react. Quiet and intense, what doesn't happen is as important as what does in this top-notch suspenser. Film was shot in the director's native Pennsylvania. **120m/C; VHS, DVD, Blu-Ray.** Mel Gibson; Joaquin Rafael (Leaf) Phoenix; Rory Culkin; Abigail Breslin; Cherry Jones; Patricia Kalember; M. Night Shyamalan; *D:* M. Night Shyamalan; *W:* M. Night Shyamalan; *C:* Tak Fujimoto; *M:* James Newton Howard.

Signs & Wonders ✌✌ **2000** Commodities trader Alec (Skarsgard) has been living in Athens with wife Marjoire (Rampling) and their children. He begins an affair with sultry co-worker Katherine (Unger) and abandons his family to go to the States with her and then changes his mind. However, when he returns to Athens, Alec discovers Marjorie has moved on with her own lover, Andreas (Katalifos). But Alec isn't giving up and the consequences are unexpected. **108m/C; VHS, DVD.** *FR* Stellan Skarsgard; Charlotte Rampling; Deborah Kara Unger; Dimitris Katalifos; Ashley Remy; Michael Cook; *D:* Jonathan Nossiter; *W:* Jonathan Nossiter; James Lasdun; *C:* Yorgos Arvanitis; *M:* Adrian Utley.

Signs of Life ✌✌ *Lebenszeichen* **1968** German soldier Stroszek (Brogle), injured during the occupation of Crete, is sent to recuperate on the remote island of Kos. With his Greek wife Nora, Stroszek has nothing to do but guard a deserted fortress and a store of abandoned ammunition. But soon the suspicious natives and the isolation begin to drive Stroszek to madness and he decides to blow up the ammunition dump (and the island along with it). German with subtitles. **90m/B; VHS, DVD.** *GE* Peter Brogle; Wolfgang Reichmann; Athina Zacharopoulous; Wolfgang Stumpf; *D:* Werner Herzog; *W:* Werner Herzog; *C:* Thomas Mauch; *M:* Stavros Xarchakos.

Signs of Life ✌✌ ½ *One for Sorrow, Two for Joy* **1989 (PG-13)** A boat-building company in Maine closes its doors after centuries in business; the employees and families whose lives have been defined by it for generations learn to cope. Wonderful performances compensate only partly for a week script. An episode on PBS's "American Playhouse." **95m/C; VHS, Streaming.** Beau Bridges; Arthur Kennedy; Vincent D'Onofrio; Kevin J. O'Connor; Will Patton; Kate Reid; Michael Lewis; Kathy Bates; Mary-Louise Parker; Georgia Engel; *D:* John David Coles; *W:* Mark Malone; *C:* Elliot Davis; *M:* Howard Shore.

Silas Marner ✌✌✌ **1985** Superb adaptation of the 1861 George Eliot classic about an itinerant weaver subjected to criminal accusation, poverty, and exile. Wonderful detail and splendid acting. Shot on location in the Cotswold district of England. **92m/C; VHS, DVD.** *GB* Ben Kingsley; Jenny Agutter; Patrick Ryecart; Patsy Kensit; *D:* Giles Foster; *M:* Carl Davis. **TV**

The Silence ✌✌✌ *Tystnaden* **1963** A brutal, enigmatic allegory about two sisters, one a nymphomaniac, the other a violently frustrated lesbian, traveling with the former's young son to an unnamed country beset by war. Fascinating and memorable but frustrating and unsatisfying: What is it about? What is it an allegory of? Where is the narrative? The third in Bergman's crisis-of-faith trilogy following "Through a Glass Darkly" and "Winter Light." In Swedish with English subtitles or dubbed. **95m/B; VHS, DVD, Blu-Ray.** *SW* Ingrid Thulin; Gunnel Lindstrom; Birger Malmsten; *D:* Ingmar Bergman; *W:* Ingmar Bergman; *C:* Sven Nykvist.

Silence ✌✌ *Crazy Jack and the Boy* **1973 (G)** An autistic boy gets lost in the wilderness and faces an array of difficulties while his foster parents search for him. **82m/C; VHS, DVD.** Will Geer; Ellen Geer; Richard Kelton; Ian Geer Flanders; Craig G. Kelly; ***D:*** John Korty.

The Silence 1/2 **2006** Bland Aussie TV police drama. Detective Richard Treloar (Roxburgh) suffers from post-traumatic stress after an accidental shooting death so he's reassigned to curate a photographic exhibit at the Sydney police museum. While looking at 1960s-era crime scene photos, Richard becomes obsessed with May (Rothwell), a murder victim and decides to reinvestigate the unsolved case. **104m/C; DVD.** *AU* Richard Roxburgh; Essie Davis; Emily Barclay; Ellouise Rothwell; Alice McConnell; Damien de Montemas; ***D:*** Cate Shortland; ***W:*** Alice Addison; Mary Walsh; ***C:*** Robert Humphreys; ***M:*** Antony Partos. **TV**

The Silence 1/2 **2010** Two men (Ulrich Thomsen & Wotan Wilke Moehring) are involved in a horrendous crime that appears to repeat itself 23 years later when a girl goes missing in this smart German thriller that's been correctly compared to AMC's The Killing. A girl has gone missing and clues are found in the exact same place that a girl was murdered over two decades ago. Director Baran bo Odar has a brilliant touch with the atmosphere of a small town and how crime impacts not just the people directly involved but ripples out to so many others. It's a clever, intense thriller that places emphasis on character as much as the twists and turns of its very-dark story. **118m/C; DVD, Blu-Ray.** *GE* Ulrich Thomsen; Wotan Wilke Mohring; Katrin Sass; Sebastian Blomberg; Burghart Klaussner; ***D:*** Baran bo Odar; ***W:*** Baran bo Odar; ***C:*** Nikolaus Summerer; ***M:*** Michael Kamm.

Silence **2016 (R)** Scorsese delivers one of the most personal films of his career in this long-gestating adaptation of Shusaku Endo's novel about 16th century Jesuit priests captured and tortured in a Japan led by men that want nothing at all to do with their religion. Garfield and Driver play the men sent to this dangerous land to find their former mentor, played by Neeson. Scorsese's film is about keeping faith in a Godless world in which deserting your religion is regularly, albeit briefly, rewarded. It is a technical masterpiece, but its heart and passion allows it to linger. **161m/C; DVD, Blu-Ray.** Andrew Garfield; Adam Driver; Liam Neeson; Tadanobu Asano; Ciaran Hinds; ***D:*** Martin Scorsese; ***W:*** Martin Scorsese; Jay Cocks; ***C:*** Rodrigo Prieto; ***M:*** Kathryn Kluge; Kim Allen Kluge.

Silence of the Heart **1984** Mother copes with aftermath of suicide of teenage son. The teen's best friend also tries to deal with his feelings of guilt. Hartley is captivating in this gripping drama. **100m/C; VHS, DVD.** Mariette Hartley; Dana Hill; Howard Hesseman; Chad Lowe; Charlie Sheen; Alexandra Powers; Silvania Gallardo; Elizabeth Berridge; Sherilyn Fenn; Casey Siemaszko; Jaleel White; ***D:*** Richard Michaels; ***W:*** Phil Penningroth; ***M:*** Georges Delerue.

The Silence of the Lambs 1/2 **1991 (R)** Foster is FBI cadet Clarice Starling, a woman with ambition, a cum laude degree in psychology, and a traumatic childhood. When a serial killer begins his ugly rounds, the FBI wants psychological profiles from other serial killers and she's sent to collect a profile from one who's exceptionally clever—psychiatrist Hannibal Lecter, a vicious killer prone to dining on his victims. Brilliant performances from Foster and Hopkins, finely detailed supporting characterizations, and elegant pacing from Demme. Some brutal visual effects. Excellent portrayals of women who refuse to be victims. Based on the Thomas Harris novel. **118m/C; VHS, DVD, Blu-Ray.** Jodie Foster; Anthony Hopkins; Scott Glenn; Ted Levine; Brooke Smith; Charles Napier; Roger Corman; Anthony Heald; Diane Baker; Chris Isaak; Dan E. Butler; Frankie Faison; Kasi Lemmons; Kathryn Witt; Tracey Walter; Obba Babatunde; Ron Vawter; Brent Hinkley; Daniel von Bargen; ***D:*** Jonathan Demme; ***W:*** Ted Tally; ***C:*** Tak Fujimoto; ***M:*** Howard Shore. Oscars '91: Actor (Hopkins), Actress (Foster), Adapt. Screenplay, Director (Demme), Film; AFI '98: Top 100; British Acad. '91: Actor (Hopkins), Actress (Foster); Directors Guild '91: Director (Demme); Golden Globes '92: Actress--Drama (Foster); Natl. Bd. of Review '91: Director (Demme), Film, Support. Actor (Hopkins); Natl. Film Reg. '11; N.Y. Film Critics '91: Actor (Hopkins), Actress (Foster), Director (Demme), Film; Writers Guild '91: Adapt. Screenplay.

The Silencer **1992 (R)** Walden stars as Harley-riding Angel who is out to stop a slavery and prostitution ring that abuses young runaways. Video arcades hold the clues, and Angel must learn to kill without a conscience. Every time she kills, Angel seeks comfort in the arms of anonymous lovers. However, what she doesn't know is that her demented ex-boyfriend is watching. **85m/C; VHS, DVD.** Lynette Walden; Chris Mulkey; Paul Ganus; Morton Downey, Jr.; ***D:*** Amy Goldstein; ***W:*** Amy Goldstein; Scott Kraft.

The Silencer **1999 (R)** FBI agent Jason Wells (Elliott) fakes his own death in order to assume a new identity for a new assignment. Now known as Jason Black, he's an eager would-be assassin who wants to join the terrorist organization Division 5 where he can learn from master marksman Quinn Simmons (Dudikoff). But when Jason learns what's really behind his mission, things aren't so simple after all. **92m/C; VHS, DVD.** *CA* Michael Dudikoff; Brennan Elliott; Gabrielle Miller; Terence Kelly; Peter Lacroix; ***D:*** Robert Lee; ***M:*** Peter Allen. **VIDEO**

The Silencers 1/2 **1966** Rompy spy spoof is the first of Martin's Matt Helm films, made to take advantage of the James Bond craze. Sexy secret agent man Helm must save the American atomic missile system from sabotage by Big O, the organization headed by Tung-Tze (Buono). That is if Matt can stay away from the babes and the booze. Based on the novels "The Silencers" and "Death of a Citizen" by Donald Hamilton. Followed by "Murderer's Row" (1966), "The Ambushers" (1967), and "The Wrecking Crew" (1968). **103m/C; VHS, DVD.** Dean Martin; Victor Buono; Stella Stevens; Daliah Lavi; Arthur O'Connell; Beverly Adams; Robert Webber; James Gregory; Nancy Kovack; Roger C. Carmel; Cyd Charisse; Richard Devon; ***D:*** Phil Karlson; ***W:*** Oscar Saul; ***C:*** Burnett Guffey; ***M:*** Elmer Bernstein.

The Silencers 1/2 **1996 (R)** Secret Service agent Chuck Rafferty (Scalia) discovers that his latest enemies, known as the Men In Black, are actually human-appearing aliens seeking to conquer Earth. Now Rafferty's only hope is to team up with inter-galactic peace officer Condor (Christopher) to defeat this evil. **103m/C; VHS, DVD, Streaming.** Jack Scalia; Dennis Christopher; Clarence Williams, III; Carlos Lauchu; Lucinda Weist; ***D:*** Richard Pepin; ***W:*** William Applegate, Jr.; Joseph John Barmettler, Jr.; Richard Preston, Jr.; ***C:*** Ken Blakey; ***M:*** Louis Febre. **VIDEO**

Silent Cry Aloud **2016** A drama about a mother who must lose it all to gain self-awareness. Dina (White) is a single mom to a young daughter. Spending all of her energy on trying to find her estranged boyfriend, Dina ignores the emotional trauma of her daughter Star (Matthews). It is not until social services take her daughter away that Dina comes to understand hard truths about her life, her former boyfriend, and her daughter. **76m/C; DVD, Streaming, Download.** Karen Malina White; Sasha Matthews; Toni M. Youngblood; Darrin Dewitt Henson; Terry Dexter; ***D:*** Erika Rogers; ***W:*** Erika Rogers; ***C:*** Austin Nordell; ***M:*** Sheila Brown; Richard Ellis. **VIDEO**

The Silent Enemy 1/2 **1958** The true-life exploits of British frogmen battling Italian foes during WWII. Suspenseful and engrossing; good performances and good rendering of underwater action. Video release snips 20 minutes from the original and adds color. **91m/C; VHS, DVD.** *GB* Laurence Harvey; John Clements; Michael Craig; Dawn Addams; Sidney James; Alec McCowen; Nigel Stock; ***D:*** William Fairchild.

Silent Fall 1/2 **1994 (R)** Grisly double murder of his parents is witnessed by autistic nine-year-old, Tim Warden (Faulkner), and his traumatized over-protective teenaged sister Sylvie (Tyler). Retired psychiatrist Jake Rainier (Dreyfuss) is reluctant to get involved, ever since an autistic child in his care died, but when authoritarian rival Dr. Harlinger (Lithgow) is called instead, Jake changes his mind. Second half of film takes a lurid turn as Jake probes Tim's damaged psyche to discover the killer. Trite, clueless whodunnit that generally wastes the talent involved; Tyler and Faulkner make their film debuts. **101m/C; VHS, DVD.** Richard Dreyfuss; Ben Faulkner; John Lithgow; Liv Tyler; Linda Hamilton; J.T. Walsh; ***D:*** Bruce Beresford; ***W:*** Akiva Goldsman; ***C:*** Peter James; ***M:*** Stewart Copeland.

Silent Hill **2006 (R)** Visually arresting but nonsensical adaptation of a videogame. Rose (Mitchell) and husband Christopher (a wasted Bean) find their young daughter Sharon (Ferland) sleepwalking, muttering about "Silent Hill." Rose researches the name and learns it's a West Virginia mining community that's been deserted since 1974 due to a devastating fire. Nevertheless, Rose grabs Sharon and heads for the town, only to become lost in some alternate existence where she runs around looking for the vanished Sharon and encounters various ghostly freaks, creepy religious fanatics, and a helpful motorcycle cop named Cybil (Holden). **127m/C; DVD, Blu-Ray, UMD.** *CA FR* Radha Mitchell; Sean Bean; Laurie Holden; Deborah Kara Unger; Jodelle Ferland; Alice Krige; Kim Coates; Tanya Allen; ***D:*** Christophe Gans; ***W:*** Roger Avary; ***C:*** Dan Laustsen; ***M:*** Jeff Danna.

Silent Hill: Revelation 3D WOOF! **2012 (R)** A surprising chunk of time after the modestly successful original comes this incomprehensible follow-up that fails--even for the low-expectations video game adaptations genre. One problem is using a teenage girl as the heroine, a poor thing tormented by nightmarish forces. Now 18, Heather Mason (Clemens) learns she isn't who she thought she was. She and her father must return to an alternate dimension in an ash-covered town called Silent Hill to destroy an evil cult that has sought her since her last visit in the first movie. There's a difference between grotesque violence and actual fear that writer/director Bassett doesn't get. **94m/C; DVD, Blu-Ray.** *FR US CA* Adelaide Clemens; Kit Harington; Carrie-Anne Moss; Sean Bean; Radha Mitchell; Malcolm McDowell; Martin Donovan; Deborah Kara Unger; Roberto Campanella; Peter Outerbridge; Jefferson Brown; Milton Barnes; ***D:*** Michael J. Bassett; ***W:*** Michael J. Bassett; ***C:*** Maxime Alexandre; ***M:*** Jeff Danna; Akira Yamaoka.

Silent House 1/2 **2012 (R)** The remake of the well-regarded 2010 Uruguayan film has a clever one-shot gimmick but without it there's not much here. Told in one unbroken take, this quasi-horror film attempts to put viewers in the shoes of its terrified protagonist, but is more style than substance. Sarah (Olsen) is helping her father (Trese) fix up an old house to sell when he's attacked. As she tries to save her father and escape her attackers, the thrills get increasingly bizarre, even supernatural, but the lack of logic leads to a lack of honest scares. **88m/C; DVD, Blu-Ray.** Elizabeth Olsen; Adam Trese; Eric Sheffer Stevens; Julia Taylor Ross; Haley Murphy; Adam Barnett; ***D:*** Chris Kentis; Laura Lau; ***W:*** Laura Lau; ***C:*** Igor Martinovic; ***M:*** Nathan Larson.

Silent Hunter 1/2 **1994 (R)** Undercover cop Jim Paradine (O'Keeffe) retreats to a remote mountains cabin when his family is killed by a gang of bank robbers. Naturally, the thugs just happen to crash land on Paradine's mountain top with their stolen loot and he goes off to hunt them down. **97m/C; VHS, DVD.** Miles O'Keeffe; Fred Williamson; Lynne Adams; Peter Colvey; Jason Cavalier; Sabine Karsenti; ***D:*** Fred Williamson.

Silent Movie 1/2 **1976 (PG)** A has-been movie director (Brooks) is determined to make a comeback and save his studio from being taken over by a conglomerate. Hilarious at times but uneven. An original idea; not as successful as it could have been. Has music and sound effects, but only one word of spoken dialogue by famous mime Marceau. **88m/C; Silent; VHS, DVD, Blu-Ray.** Mel Brooks; Marty Feldman; Dom DeLuise; Burt Reynolds; Anne Bancroft; James Caan; Liza Minnelli; Paul Newman; Sid Caesar; Bernadette Peters; Harry Ritz; Marcel Marceau; ***D:*** Mel Brooks; ***W:*** Mel Brooks; Ron Clark; Rudy DeLuca; Barry Levinson.

Silent Night **2002** Hallmark Channel Christmas movie based on a true story. On Christmas Eve, 1944, German Elisabeth Vincken and her son Fritz have found some peace away from the war in an isolated hunting cabin. At least until three American soldiers (one wounded) stumble across them—soon followed by three German soldiers. Elisabeth forces the men to set aside their differences and share in the true meaning of the night. **90m/C; DVD.** Linda Hamilton; Matthew Harbour; Romano Orzari; Alain Goulem; Michael Elkin; Martin Neufeld; Mark Anthony Krupa; Cassian Bopp; ***D:*** Rodney Gibbons; ***W:*** Roger Aylward; ***C:*** Eric Cayla; ***M:*** James Gelfand. **CABLE**

Silent Night **2012 (R)** Sorta remake of 1984's "Silent Night, Deadly Night" has a few inventive touches amid the carnage--but it's nothing you'd want to find under your Christmas tree. A serial killer gets his jollies by dressing up in a Santa suit and going after townsfolk on Christmas Eve. The local cops have trouble identifying the sicko because the Santa Claus parade gives them a lot of possible suspects. **94m/C; DVD, Blu-Ray.** Malcolm McDowell; Jaime King; Brendan Fehr; Donal Logue; Ellen Wong; Lisa Marie; ***D:*** Steven C. Miller; ***W:*** Jayson Rothwell; ***C:*** Joseph White; ***M:*** Kevin Riepl. **VIDEO**

Silent Night, Bloody Night *Night of the Dark Full Moon; Death House* **1973 (R)** An escaped lunatic terrorizes a small New England town, particularly a mansion that was once an insane asylum. Not great, but well done by director Gershuny, with some nail-biting suspense and slick scene changes. **83m/C; VHS, DVD.** Patrick O'Neal; John Carradine; Walter Abel; Mary Woronov; Astrid Heeren; Candy Darling; ***D:*** Theodore Gershuny.

Silent Night, Deadly Night **1984 (R)** A psycho ax-murders people while dressed as jolly old St. Nick. Violent and disturbing, to say the least. Caused quite a controversy when it was released to theatres. Santa gimmick sold some tickets at the time, but resist the urge to rent it: it's completely devoid of worth, whatever the killer's outfit. As if one were not enough, we've been blessed with four sequels. **92m/C; VHS, DVD, Blu-Ray.** Lilyan Chauvin; Gilmer McCormick; Toni Nero; ***D:*** Charles E. Sellier; ***M:*** Perry Botkin.

Silent Night, Deadly Night 2 **1987 (R)** The psychotic little brother of the psychotic, Santa Claus-dressed killer from the first film exacts revenge, covering the same bloody ground as before. Almost half this sequel consists of scenes lifted whole from the original. **88m/C; VHS, DVD, Blu-Ray.** Eric Freeman; James Newman; Elizabeth Kaitan; Jean Miller; ***D:*** Lee Harry; ***W:*** Lee Harry.

Silent Night, Deadly Night 3: Better Watch Out! 1/2 **1989 (R)** The now grown-up psycho goes up against a young blind woman. Santa is no longer the bad guy, thank goodness. The least bad of the lot, with black humor—though not enough to make it worth seeing. **90m/C; VHS, DVD.** Richard Beymer; Bill Moseley; Samantha Scully; Eric (DaRe) Da Re; Laura Elena Harring; Robert Culp; ***D:*** Monte Hellman.

Silent Night, Deadly Night 4: Initiation **1990 (R)** A secret L.A. cult of she-demons use the slasher Ricky for their own ends—making for more mayhem and horror. Has virtually nothing to do with the other "sequels"?which is not to say it's very good. **90m/C; VHS, DVD.** Maud Adams; Allyce Beasley; Clint Howard; Reggie Bannister; ***D:*** Brian Yuzna.

Silent Night, Deadly Night 5: The Toymaker **1991 (R)** A young boy's Christmas is overrun by murderous Santas and viscious stuffed animals. Definitely for fans of the genre only. **90m/C; VHS, DVD.** Mickey Rooney; William Thorne; Jane Higginson; ***D:*** Martin Kitrosser; ***W:*** Martin Kitrosser; Brian Yuzna; ***C:*** James Mathers; ***M:*** Matthew Morse.

The Silent Partner **1978** A bank teller (Gould) foils a robbery, but manages to take some money for himself. The unbalanced robber (Plummer) knows it and wants the money. Good script and well directed, with emphasis on suspense and detail. Unexpectedly violent at times. Early, non-comedic role for big guy Candy. **103m/C; VHS, DVD, Blu-Ray.** *CA* Elliott Gould; Christopher

Plummer; Susannah York; John Candy; *D:* Daryl Duke; *W:* Curtis Hanson; *C:* Billy Williams.

Silent Partner 🦴 1/2 **2005 (R)** CIA desk jockey Gordon Patrick (Moran) is sent to Moscow to look into the suspicious death of a major political figure. He meets hooker Dina (Reid), who is in possession of a briefcase filled with incriminating files, which belonged to the dead man. Pop tart Reid is a natural in her role but this is a familiar story. **96m/C; DVD.** *US RU* Nick Moran; Tara Reid; Gregg Henry; Patrick Gallagher; Katrina M. Faessel; *D:* James D. Deck; *W:* James D. Deck; *C:* Mikhail Agranovich; *M:* Lawrence Brown. **VIDEO**

The Silent Passenger 🦴🦴 1/2 **1935** Amateur sleuth Lord Peter Wimsey makes cinematic debut investigating murder and blackmail on the British railway. Dorothy Sayer's character later inspired BBC mystery series. **75m/B; VHS, DVD.** *GB* John Loder; Peter Haddon; Mary Newland; Austin Trevor; Donald Wolfit; Leslie Perrins; Aubrey Mather; Ralph Truman; *D:* Reginald Denham.

Silent Predators 🦴🦴 **1999** SNAKE! Of course, not any any snake but mean hybrid rattlesnakes who slither over a small California desert town when an explosion at a construction site disturbs their home. And it's up to fire chief Hamlin to save the town! If the snakes are half as creepy as the video box art, this is one seriously scary snake movie. **91m/C; VHS, DVD.** Harry Hamlin; Shannon Sturges; Patty McCormack; Jack Scalia; David Spielberg; Beau Billingslea; *D:* Noel Nosseck; *W:* John Carpenter; Matt Dorff; *C:* John Stokes; *M:* Michael Tavera. **CABLE**

Silent Rage 🦴 **1982 (R)** Sheriff Norris of a small Texas town must destroy killer Libby who has been made indestructible through genetic engineering. Chuck Norris meets Frankenstein, sort of. Nice try, but still thoroughly stupid and boring. **100m/C; VHS, DVD, Blu-Ray.** Chuck Norris; Ron Silver; Steven Keats; Toni Kalem; Brian Libby; Stephen Furst; *D:* Michael Miller; *W:* Joseph Fraley; *C:* Robert C. Jessup; Neil Roach; *M:* Peter Bernstein.

Silent Running 🦴🦴🦴 **1971 (G)** Members of a space station orbiting Saturn care for the last vegetation of a nuclear-devastated earth. When orders come to destroy the vegetation, Dern takes matters into his own hands. Speculative sci-fi at its best. Trumbull's directorial debut; he created special effects for "2001" and "Close Encounters." Strange music enhances the alien atmosphere. **90m/C; VHS, DVD, Blu-Ray.** Bruce Dern; Cliff (Potter) Potts; Ron Rifkin; *D:* Douglas Trumbull; *W:* Michael Cimino; Deric Washburn; Steven Bochco; *C:* Charles F. Wheeler; *M:* Prof. Peter Schickele.

Silent Scream 🦴 1/2 **1980 (R)** College kids take up residence with the owners of an eerie mansion complete with obligatory murders. Obvious to the point of being gratuitous—and just plain uninteresting. **87m/C; VHS, DVD, Blu-Ray.** Rebecca Balding; Cameron Mitchell; Avery Schreiber; Barbara Steele; Steve Doubet; Brad Reardon; Yvonne De Carlo; *D:* Denny Harris; *W:* Wallace C. Bennett; Jim Wheat; Ken Wheat; *C:* Michael D. Murphy; David Shore.

Silent Tongue 🦴🦴 **1992 (PG-13)** Weird western finds the crazed Talbot Roe (Phoenix) alone in the wilderness, guarding the tree that is the burial place of his half-breed wife Awbonnie (Tousey). Roe's father (Harris) bought his son's bride from her greedy and abusive father McCree (Bates). In an effort to return Talbot to some semblance of normality, Roe offers to buy McCree's other daughter (Arredondo) for his son. But Talbot is haunted by his wife's angry ghost, who wants her spirit set free by ritual burning, and McCree himself fears the vengeance of his one-time Indian wife Silent Tongue (Cardinal). Messy, over-the-top plot with some poignant performances, especially Phoenix's. **101m/C; VHS, DVD.** River Phoenix; Sheila Tousey; Richard Harris; Alan Bates; Jeri Arredondo; Dermot Mulroney; Tantoo Cardinal; *Cameo(s):* Bill Irwin; David Shiner; *D:* Sam Shepard; *W:* Sam Shepard; *C:* Jack Conroy; *M:* Patrick O'Hearn.

Silent Trigger 🦴🦴 **1997 (R)** Special Forces commando Shooter (Lundgren) becomes a paid assassin for an undercover agency but an ill-fated mission causes him and partner Spotter (Bellman) to question the agency, who then decide the duo are expendable. Fast-paced with some eye-catching action sequences. **94m/C; VHS, DVD.** Dolph Lundgren; Gina Bellman; Conrad Dunn; *D:* Russell Mulcahy; *W:* Sergio D. Altieri; *C:* David Franco; *M:* Stefano Mainetti.

Silent Venom 🦴 *Recoil* **2008** Snakes in a sub. James O'Neill (Perry) is being forced into retirement and he's not happy about his last assignment. Using a decommissioned sub, he has to evacuate scientist Andrea Swanson (Allen) and her assistant Jake (Mandylor), plus her cargo of mutant snakes, when the military project she was working on is shut down. The sub is attacked by the Chinese and the snakes get loose and start eating the crew. **86m/C; DVD.** Luke Perry; Krista Allen; Louis Mandylor; Tom Berenger; John L. Curtis; Anthony Tyler Quinn; *D:* Fred Olen Ray; *W:* Mark Sanderson; *C:* Theo Angell; *M:* Stu Goldberg.

Silent Victim 🦴🦴 1/2 **1992 (R)** Greene stars as Bonnie Jackson, a Georgia housewife whose marriage has not only gone wrong but turned violent. She takes a drug overdose in a suicide attempt but it results only in a miscarriage. Her furious husband sues her for the murder of their unborn child while an ambitious district attorney petitions the state to charge Bonnie with committing an illegal abortion. Bonnie's torment soon becomes a media circus as she goes on trial. Based on a true story. **116m/C; VHS, Streaming.** Michele Greene; Kyle Secor; Ely Pouget; Alex Hyde-White; Dori Brenner; Leann Hunley; *D:* Menahem Golan; *W:* Nelly Adnil; Jonathan Platnick; *M:* William T. Stromberg.

Silent Waters 🦴 1/2 *Khamosh Pani* **2003** When a young Muslim makes an all-too-quick conversion from his romance-filled life to militant indoctrination, it leads his mother to confront her haunted past. Geared primarily for the Pakistani audience, the story takes for granted that Western viewers have a background understanding of the 1947 partitioning of India and Pakistan. While Kirron Kher delivers a full-dimensional performance as the mother, other characters aren't as fleshed out. Teeters between doc and Bollywood. In Punjabi with subtitles. **95m/C; DVD.** Kiron Kher; Aamir Ali Malik; Salman Shahid; Shilpa Shukla; Sarfaraz Ansari; *D:* Sabiha Sumar; *C:* Ralph Netzer; *M:* Madan Gopal Singh; Arshad Mahmud.

Silent Witness 🦴 **1985 (R)** A woman (Bertinelli) witnesses her brother-in-law and his friend rape a young woman. She must decide whether to testify against them or keep the family secret. Exploitative and weakly plotted. Rip-off of the much-discussed Massachusetts barroom rape case. **97m/C; VHS, DVD.** Valerie Bertinelli; John Savage; Chris Nash; Melissa Leo; Pat Corley; Steven Williams; Jacqueline Brookes; Alex McArthur; Katie McCombs; *D:* Michael Miller. **TV**

Silent Witness 🦴🦴 1/2 *Do Not Disturb* **1999 (R)** Walter Richmond (Hurt) and his wife Cathryn (Tilly) are in Amsterdam with their mute daughter Melissa so Walter can close a business deal. But Melissa witnesses a murder and then disappears, leaving her frantic parents to find her before the killers do. This one turns out to be more of a parody of the thriller genre than a serious example. **94m/C; VHS, DVD.** William Hurt; Jennifer Tilly; Denis Leary; Francesca Brown; Michael Chiklis; Michael Goorjian; *D:* Dick Maas.

Silicon Cowboys 🦴🦴 **2016** A feature-length documentary on Compaq and the computers wars of the early 1980s. In 1981, three friends in Dallas, Texas, come up with the idea for the Compaq portable computer at a diner. The documentary examines how their vision played out, focusing on how the trio took on IBM for supremacy. Broader issues such as how Compaq changed the future of computing and the world are considered as well. **77m/C; DVD, Blu-Ray, Streaming, Download.** *D:* Jason Cohen; *W:* Jason Cohen; Steven Leckart; *C:* Svetlana Cvetko; *M:* Ian Hultquist.

Silicon Towers 🦴 1/2 **1999 (PG-13)** Charlie Cook (Quint) is suddenly promoted to an executive position at Silicon Towers. But a mysterious e-mail warns him that the corporation is illegally accessing bank accounts worldwide and then Charlie gets accused of embezzling. **95m/C; VHS, DVD.** Jonathan Quint; Brian Dennehy; Daniel Baldwin; Robert Guillaume; Brad Dourif; *D:* Serge Rodnunsky; *W:* Serge Rodnunsky. **VIDEO**

Silk 🦴 **2007 (R)** Boring historical drama strives for epic romance but lacks appealing characters, convincing plot, or any chemistry between its leads. Herve (Pitt) leaves his wife Helene (Knightley) and their 19th-century French village for Japan to obtain silkworms for his boss (Molina), but ends up falling for a concubine (Ashina) of the warlord who provides the silkworms (Yakusho). Movie skips anything interesting about the historical period in which it's set and opts for tired cliches about love and fate while failing to build any dramatic tension. **109m/C; DVD.** *CA IT JP* Michael Pitt; Keira Knightley; Koji Yakusho; Alfred Molina; Kenneth Welsh; Sei Ashina; *D:* Francois Girard; *W:* Francois Girard; Michael Golding; *C:* Alan Dostie; *M:* Ryuichi Sakamoto.

Silk 'n' Sabotage 🦴 1/2 *Wildchild 2* **1994** Serious-minded Jamie comes up with a program for a new computer game. When it's stolen by a con artist, Jamie and her frivolous roommates team up to retrieve it. Since the roomies operate a lingerie business there's lots of pulchritude on display. Also available unrated. **70m/C; VHS, DVD.** Cherilyn Shea; Stephanie Champlin; Julie Skiru; *D:* Joe Cauley.

Silk Stockings 🦴🦴🦴 **1957** Splendid musical comedy adaptation of "Ninotchka," with Astaire as a charming American movie man, and Charisse as the cold Soviet official whose commie heart he melts. Music and lyrics by Cole Porter highlight this film adapted from George S. Kaufman's hit Broadway play. Director Mamoulian's last film. **117m/C; VHS, DVD, Blu-Ray.** Fred Astaire; Cyd Charisse; Janis Paige; Peter Lorre; George Tobias; *D:* Rouben Mamoulian; *M:* Andre Previn.

Silkwood 🦴🦴🦴 **1983 (R)** The story of Karen Silkwood, who died in a 1974 car crash under suspicious circumstances. She was a nuclear plant worker and activist who was investigating shoddy practices at the plant. Streep acts up a storm, disappearing completely into her character. Cher surprises with her fine portrayal of a lesbian co-worker, and Russell is also good. Nichols has a tough time since we already know the ending, but he brings top-notch performances from his excellent cast. **131m/C; VHS, DVD, Blu-Ray.** Meryl Streep; Kurt Russell; Cher; Diana Scarwid; Bruce McGill; Fred Ward; David Strathairn; Ron Silver; Josef Sommer; Craig T. Nelson; *D:* Mike Nichols; *W:* Nora Ephron; Alice Arlen; *C:* Miroslav Ondricek; *M:* Georges Delerue. Golden Globes '84: Support. Actress (Cher).

Silver Bullet 🦴🦴 *Stephen King's Silver Bullet* **1985 (R)** Adapted from Stephen King's "Cycle of the Werewolf," about a town whose inhabitants are being brutally murdered. It finally dawns on them the culprit is a werewolf. Action moves along at a good clip and the film has its share of suspense. **94m/C; VHS, DVD, Blu-Ray.** Corey Haim; Gary Busey; Megan Follows; Everett McGill; Robin Groves; Leon Russom; Terry O'Quinn; Bill Smitrovich; Kent Broadhurst; Lawrence Tierney; *D:* Daniel Attias; *W:* Stephen King; *C:* Armando Nannuzzi.

Silver Case 🦴 1/2 **2011** A shady producer decides to end his rival's career and his plan hinges on the contents of a silver case which is misappropriated by a pair of thugs. So begins the latest comedy about common everyday violent shenanigans in the film industry. **87m/C; DVD.** *IT US* Eric Roberts; Brian Keith Gamble; Chris Facey; Claire Falconer; Brad Light; *D:* Christian Filippella; *W:* Christian Filippella; Jason White; *C:* Christian Filippella; *M:* Cody Westheimer; Roberto Boarini.

The Silver Chalice 🦴 **1954** Newman's career somehow survived his movie debut in this bloated, turgid Biblical epic (the camp factor is huge) about the momentous events that befall a young Greek sculptor who fashions a holder for the cup that was used at the Last Supper. Newman later took out an ad in Variety to apologize for the film, in which Greene also made his debut. Based on the novel by Thomas Costain. **135m/C; DVD.** Paul Newman; Virginia Mayo; Pier Angeli; Jack Palance; Natalie Wood; Joseph Wiseman; Lorne Greene; E.G. Marshall; *D:* Victor Saville; *W:* Lesser Samuels; *C:* William V. Skall; *M:* Franz Waxman.

Silver City 🦴🦴 **2004 (R)** Surprisingly clumsy political drama finds Sayles pushing his ensemble in places they're not comfortable going. Conservative Richard "Dim Dickie" Pilager (Cooper) is the son of a U.S. senator (Murphy) and the current frontrunner in the Colorado governor's race. He's about to film a commercial on a picturesque river when he fishes out a very dead body instead of a trout. Savvy and suspicious campaign manager Chuck Raven (Dreyfuss) hires disgraced journalist-turned-PI Danny O'Brien (Huston) to investigate the three prime suspects: talk show host Castleton (Ferrer), environmental crusader Lyle (Waite), and Dickie's black sheep sister Maddy (Hannah). Disappointing tale of a conspiracy of corruption and all-too easy targets. **129m/C; DVD.** Danny Huston; Maria Bello; Billy Zane; Chris Cooper; Richard Dreyfuss; Michael Murphy; Daryl Hannah; Kris Kristofferson; Mary Kay Place; David Clennon; Miguel Ferrer; Ralph Waite; Sal Lopez; James Gammon; Tim Roth; Thora Birch; Luis Saguar; Alma Delfina; Aaron Vieyra; Hugo Carbajal; *D:* John Sayles; *W:* John Sayles; *C:* Haskell Wexler; *M:* Mason Daring.

Silver Dream Racer 🦴 1/2 **1983 (PG)** An English grease monkey wants to win the World Motorcycle Championship title away from an American biker. He's also after someone else's girlfriend. Boring, stilted, unoriginal "Big Race" flick. **103m/C; VHS, DVD.** Beau Bridges; David Essex; Christina Raines; Diane Keen; Harry H. Corbett; *D:* David Wickes; *M:* David Essex.

The Silver Fleet 🦴🦴 **1943** British war propaganda piece. Dutch shipyard owner Jaap van Leyden (Richardson) appears to cooperate with the occupying Nazis when he builds them two prototype submarines. His workers mutiny and allow the Resistance to ferry one sub to England. Gestapo leader von Schiffer (Knight) turns threatening, but van Leyden asks the Nazis to join him for a trial run on the second sub. Expect a big boom. **88m/B; DVD.** *GB* Ralph Richardson; Esmond Knight; Googie Withers; Beresford Egan; Frederick Burtwell; Joss Ambler; Willem Akkerman; *D:* Vernon Sewell; Gordon Wellesley; *W:* Vernon Sewell; Gordon Wellesley; *C:* Erwin Hillier; *M:* Allan Gray.

Silver Hawk 🦴🦴 *Fei Ying* **2004 (PG-13)** Campy kung fu superhero adventure stars Yeoh as socialite Lulu Wong, who masquerades as silver latex-wearing crimebuster Silver Hawk. Her latest rescue mission is a scientist (Chen), working on an artificial intelligence project, who has been kidnapped by her arch-enemy Wolfe (Goss). Yeoh can kick butt, which may be the best reason to see this flick. English and Cantonese with subtitles. **100m/C; DVD.** Michelle Yeoh; Luke Goss; Daoming Chen; Michael Jai White; Richie Ren; Li Bingbing; Brandon Chang; *D:* Jingle Ma; *W:* Jingle Ma; Susan Chan; *C:* Chi Ying Chan.

The Silver Horde 🦴🦴 1/2 **1930** Alaskan salmon fishery owner McCrea battles villainous competitor Gordon for both his livelihood and his ladyfriend—dancehall dame Brent. Arthur's the society gal who briefly catches McCrea's eye. Silent screen star Sweet ended her career with a brief role. Based on a novel by Rex Beach. **80m/B; VHS, DVD.** Joel McCrea; Evelyn Brent; Jean Arthur; Gavin Gordon; Louis Wolheim; Raymond Hatton; Blanche Sweet; Purnell Pratt; William B. Davidson; *D:* George Archainbaud; *W:* Wallace Smith; *C:* Leo Tover.

Silver Linings Playbook 🦴🦴🦴 1/2 **2012 (R)** Troubled Pat Solitano (a career-best Cooper) leaves a mental hospital to return to a life he doesn't really want in his parents' (Weaver, De Niro) attic. Determined to get his wife back, he runs into an equally damaged woman in the recently widowed Tiffany (a beyond-her-years amazing Lawrence) and the two form an unlikely pair. Intensely funny, intensely dramatic, intensely clever, and occasionally shocking--but in the best way possible. Sure the story gets a little muddled along the way but that matters little. As Pat would say, it's got a strategy. Based on the debut novel of the same name by Matthew Quick. **122m/C; DVD, Blu-Ray.** Bradley Cooper; Jennifer Lawrence; Robert De Niro; Jacki Weaver; Chris Tucker; Anupam Kher; John Ortiz; Shea Whigham; Julia Stiles; Dash

Mihok; *D:* David O. Russell; *W:* David O. Russell; *C:* Masanobu Takayanagi; *M:* Danny Elfman. Oscars '12: Actress (Lawrence); British Acad. '12: Adapt. Screenplay; Golden Globes '13: Actress--Mus./Comedy (Lawrence); Ind. Spirit '13: Actress (Lawrence), Director (Russell), Film, Screenplay; Screen Actors Guild '12: Actress (Lawrence).

Silver Lode 🦴🦴 1/2 **1954** A man accused of murder on his wedding day attempts to clear his name while the law launches an intensive manhunt for him. Ordinary story improved by good, energetic cast. **92m/C; VHS, DVD.** John Payne; Dan Duryea; Lizabeth Scott; Stuart Whitman; *D:* Allan Dwan.

Silver Queen 🦴🦴 **1942** A woman finds out her father has gambled away a silver mine and left her with debts. She opens a saloon, only to have her fiance use the money to hunt for more silver. **81m/B; VHS, DVD.** Priscilla Lane; George Brent; Bruce Cabot; Eugene Pallette; *D:* Lloyd Bacon.

Silver Skates 🦴 1/2 **1943** A Monogram effort to showcase their skating star Belita although the plot revolves about the romance between Claire, the debt-ridden owner of the skating revue, and crooner Danny. Star Belita is leaving to marry her boyfriend but when Danny makes a play to keep her around she mistakes his intentions and thinks Danny has proposed. **76m/B; DVD.** Patricia Morison; Kenny L. Baker; Belita; Joyce Compton; Frank Faylen; Irene Dare; Henry Wadsworth; *D:* Leslie Goodwins; *W:* Jerome Cady; *C:* Mack Stengler.

The Silver Stallion: King of the Wild Brumbies 🦴🦴 1/2 *The Silver Brumby* **1993 (G)** The adolescent Indi is enthralled as her writer-mother relates each new chapter in the saga of Thara, the amazing silver stallion. And she images each adventure as the horse triumphs over evil men, other horses, and the elements to become leader of the herd. Based on the Australian children's novel "The Silver Brumby" by Elyne Mitchell. **93m/C; VHS, DVD.** *AU* Caroline Goodall; Ami Daemion; Russell Crowe; *D:* John Tatoulis; *W:* John Tatoulis; Jon Stephens; *M:* Tassos Ioannides.

Silver Star 🦴🦴 **1955** Man elected sheriff of a western town turns down the job because he is a pacifist. He changes his mind when his defeated opponent hires a trio of killers to come after him. **73m/B; VHS, DVD.** Edgar Buchanan; Marie Windsor; Lon Chaney, Jr.; Earle Lyon; Richard Bartlett; Barton MacLane; Morris Ankrum; Edith Evanson; *D:* Richard Bartlett; *W:* Richard Bartlett; Ian MacDonald; *C:* Guy Roe; *M:* Leo Klatzkin.

The Silver Streak 🦴🦴 **1934** The sickly son of a diesel train designer needs an iron lung—pronto. A rival's super-fast locomotive is the only hope for the boy. Murders, runaway engines, and a crew that would rather walk enliven this race against time. **72m/B; VHS, DVD.** Sally Blane; Charles Starrett; Arthur Lake; Edgar Kennedy; William Farnum; *D:* Thomas Atkins.

Silver Streak 🦴🦴🦴 **1976 (PG)** Pooped exec Wilder rides a train from L.A. to Chicago, planning to enjoy a leisurely, relaxing trip. Instead he becomes involved with murder, intrigue, and a beautiful woman. Energetic Hitchcock parody features successful first pairing of Wilder and Pryor. **113m/C; VHS, DVD, Blu-Ray.** Gene Wilder; Richard Pryor; Jill Clayburgh; Patrick McGoohan; Ned Beatty; Ray Walston; Richard Kiel; Scatman Crothers; *D:* Arthur Hiller; *W:* Colin Higgins; *M:* Henry Mancini.

The Silver Whip 🦴🦴 **1953** Stagecoach guard Race Crim (Robertson) and young driver Jess Harker (Wagner) are transporting a gold shipment when they are attacked by outlaws. Race kills several bandits and goes after outlaw Slater (Kellogg). The sheriff (Calhoun) makes Jess his new deputy and they take the captured Slater to jail. But Race incites a lynch mob, leaving Jess to decide whether to protect his prisoner or turn him over. **73m/B; DVD.** Dale Robertson; Robert Wagner; Rory Calhoun; John Kellogg; *D:* Harmon Jones; *W:* Jesse Lasky, Jr.; *C:* Lloyd Ahern; *M:* Lionel Newman.

Silver Wolf 🦴🦴 1/2 **1998** Jesse (Meier) and his dad head into the mountains on a snow board trip when a sudden storm hits. Jesse's dad is killed and he is injured. But he finds a companion, a wounded young wolf he names Silver. However, when Jesse is rescued, Silver disappears and Jesse is desperate to find him. Jesse gets his chance when he's taken in by his mountain man uncle (Biehn) but their search pits them against a villainous hunter (Scheider). **97m/C; VHS, DVD.** Michael Biehn; Roy Scheider; Shane Meier; Kimberly Warnat; *D:* Peter Svatek; *W:* Michael Amo; *C:* Curtis Petersen; *M:* Robert Carli. **VIDEO**

Silverado 🦴🦴🦴 **1985 (PG-13)** Affectionate pastiche of western cliches has everything a viewer could ask for—except Indians. Straightforward plot has four virtuous cowboys rise up against a crooked lawman in a blaze of six guns. No subtlety from the first big Western in quite a while, but plenty of fun and laughs. **132m/C; VHS, DVD.** Kevin Kline; Scott Glenn; Kevin Costner; Danny Glover; Brian Dennehy; Linda Hunt; John Cleese; Jeff Goldblum; Rosanna Arquette; Jeff Fahey; *D:* Lawrence Kasdan; *W:* Lawrence Kasdan; *C:* John Bailey; *M:* Bruce Broughton.

Simba 🦴🦴🦴 *Simba: Mark of Mau Mau* **1955** A young Englishman arrives at his brother's Kenyan farm to find him murdered in a local skirmish between the Mau Maus and white settlers. Well made, thoughtful look at colonialism, racial animosity, and violence. **98m/C; VHS, DVD.** *GB* Dirk Bogarde; Donald Sinden; Virginia McKenna; Orlando Martins; *D:* Brian Desmond Hurst; *C:* Geoffrey Unsworth.

The Simian Line 🦴🦴 1/2 **1999** Uneven but affecting look at several couples trying to define their romantic relationships. Middle-aged divorcee Katharine (Redgrave) is jealously in love with her younger live-in lover, Rick (Connick), and very fond of throwing dinner parties. But Katharine's latest soiree not only includes two other couples who are also romantically questionable but an eccentric psychic (Daly), who sees two ghosts in the house (Hurt, Mathis) and makes an ominous prediction. Too many stories clutter the film, particularly since the best performances come from Redgrave and Connick (with Daly offering comedic support). **106m/C; VHS, DVD.** Lynn Redgrave; Harry Connick, Jr.; Jamey Sheridan; Cindy Crawford; Tyne Daly; Monica Keena; Dylan Bruno; Samantha Mathis; William Hurt; Eric Stoltz; *D:* Linda Yellen; *W:* Gisella Bernice; *C:* David Bridges; *M:* Patrick Seymour.

Simon 🦴🦴 1/2 **1980 (PG)** A group of bored demented scientists brainwash a college professor into believing he is an alien from a distant galaxy, whereupon he begins trying to correct the evil in America. Screwball comedy, or semi-serious satire of some kind? Hard to tell. Some terrific set pieces but the movie as a whole doesn't quite hold together. Directorial debut of Brickman, who previously worked as a scriptwriter with Woody Allen ("Sleeper," etc.). **97m/C; VHS, DVD.** Alan Arkin; Madeline Kahn; Fred Gwynne; Adolph Green; Wallace Shawn; Austin Pendleton; *D:* Marshall Brickman; *W:* Marshall Brickman; Thomas Baum.

Simon and Laura 🦴🦴 **1955** A fading acting couple maintains the facade of a perfect marriage for a new TV show supposedly based on their lives, but behind the scenes it's a constant battle. Producer David (Carmichael) expresses sympathy for Laura (Kendall) and writer Janet (Pavlow) has a crush on Simon (Finch), which further complicates matters. Soon the backstage volatility is crossing over into the live TV production. **91m/C; DVD.** *GB* Peter Finch; Kay Kendall; Ian Carmichael; Muriel Pavlow; Maurice Denham; Thora Hird; Hubert Gregg; *D:* Muriel Box; *W:* Peter Blackmore; *C:* Ernest Steward; *M:* Benjamin Frankel.

Simon and the Oaks 🦴🦴 1/2 *Simon och ekarna* **2012** Based on a novel by Marianne Fredriksson, a period drama about the impact of World War II on two families in Gothenberg, Sweden, in the mid-twentieth century. The film takes the perspective of Simon Larsson (Skarsgard). Though he was raised in a happy working class family in this city, he never feels fully a part of his family but finds more comfort in an upper class grammar school befriends a Jewish boy Isak (Linnertorp) and his book-focused family. Simon comes to understand that he was adopted and his biological father was German and Jewish. In contrast, Isak finds his place by helping Simon's father Erik (Godicke) work as a boat builder. As the war engulfs Europe, the two families grow closer in ways neither could imagine. German, Swedish, and Hebrew with subtitles. **122m/C; DVD, Streaming, Download.** Bill Skarsgård; Helen Sjoholm; Jan Josef Liefers; Stefan Godicke; Karl Linnertorp; *D:* Lisa Ohlin; *W:* Marnie Blok; *C:* Dan Laustsen; *M:* Annette Focks.

Simon Birch 🦴🦴 *A Small Miracle* **1998 (PG)** Young Simon Birch (Smith) believes he's destined to become a hero, and that his disability—dwarfism resulting from Morquio's syndrome—is actually a gift from God to facilitate his destiny. After his best friend Joe's idolized mother dies, the two decide to track down Joe's father, who hasn't been seen for years. The quest leads to the climactic disaster that is the impetus for the heroics Simon has been waiting for. Smith's on-screen presence is the main attraction, as most of the emotion and inspiration in the source material, John Irving's novel "A Prayer for Owen Meany," is absent. Irving demanded both the character name change (Meany to Birch) and a screen credit change—from "based on" to "suggested by." **110m/C; DVD.** Ian Michael Smith; Joseph Mazzello; Ashley Judd; Oliver Platt; David Strathairn; Dana Ivey; Jan Hooks; Beatrice Winde; Ceciley Carroll; Sumela-Rose Keramidopulos; Sam Morton; *Nar:* Jim Carrey; *D:* Mark Steven Johnson; *W:* Mark Steven Johnson; *C:* Aaron Schneider; *M:* Marc Shaiman.

Simon, King of the Witches 🦴🦴 1/2 **1971 (R)** An L.A. warlock who lives in a sewer drain finds himself the center of attention when his spells actually work. This interesting hippie/witchcraft entry bogs down now and then but Prine's performance is droll and lively. **90m/C; VHS, DVD, Blu-Ray.** Andrew Prine; Brenda Scott; George Paulsin; Norman Burton; Ultra Violet; *D:* Bruce Kessler; *W:* Robert Phippeny; *C:* David L. Butler.

Simon Says 🦴 1/2 **2007 (R)** Typical pic in the evil twins/slasher genre with Glover playing crazy yet again. Five college kids on a road trip pick exactly the wrong camping spot. Don't be fooled by the prominence of Blake Lively's name in the ads; her dad Ernie produced the pic and Blake and sister Lori have only small roles. **90m/C; DVD.** Crispin Glover; Greg Cipes; Carrie Finklea; Bruce Glover; Blake Lively; Margo Hershman; Kelly Vutz; Artie Baxter; Lori Lively; *D:* William Dear; *W:* William Dear; *C:* Bryan Greenberg; *M:* Ludek Drizhal.

Simon Sez 🦴 1/2 **1999 (PG-13)** Convoluted spy thriller stars basketball bad boy Dennis Rodman as Simon, an Interpol agent on the trail of effete illegal arms dealer Ashton (Pradon). He must be posing undercover as a gigantic space-age punk rock coloring book, because the nose rings, tattoos and shock treatment hair don't exactly say "inconspicuous." He is approached for help by his old friend and colleague Nick (Cook), a private eye who's in over his head on a kidnapping case. The two cases just happen to be connected, but the plot is just an excuse to show car chases and shoot 'em up action sequences. Rodman shows some decent acting skills, and he's still as bad as he wants to be. Unfortunately, the movie is a lot worse than he wants it to be. **85m/C; VHS, DVD.** Dennis Rodman; Dane Cook; Natalia Cigliuti; Filip Nikolic; John Pinette; Jerome Pradon; Ricky Harris; *D:* Kevin Elders; *W:* Andrew Miller; Andrew Lowery; *C:* Avi (Avraham) Karpik; *M:* Brian Tyler. **VIDEO**

Simone 🦴🦴 **2002 (PG-13)** Part Hollywood send-up and part child of Hollywood, pic shows pitfalls of using gimmicks to sell movies and uses the same gimmick to sell the movie itself. Perfect Tinseltown logic. Pacino is Viktor, a has-been filmmaker, who becomes a high tech Pygmalian when he creates an actress from scratch after inheriting a mad inventor's computer program. Solving his recent dilemma involving a temperamental star (Ryder), Viktor's digital thesp, Simone (short for simulated one) becomes a smash hit and revives his career in the process. Of course, the rabid tabloid press and public expect to see a real actress, not a synthespian, creating a host of publicity problems. Writer/director/producer Niccol is in familiar techno-wizardry territory here, but doesn't match his previous efforts. **117m/C; VHS, DVD.** Al Pacino; Catherine Keener; Jay Mohr; Jason Schwartzman; Pruitt Taylor Vince; Stanley Anderson; Evan Rachel Wood; Daniel von Bargen; Rachel Roberts; Elias Koteas; Rebecca Romijn; *Cameo(s):* Winona Ryder; *D:* Andrew Niccol; *W:* Andrew Niccol; *C:* Edward Lachman; *M:* Carter Burwell.

Simpatico 🦴🦴 1/2 **1999 (R)** Excellent performances and a disappointing script mark this adaptation of the Sam Shephard play. Nolte is Vinnie, who has evidence of horse breeder Carter's (Bridges) involvement in a past race fixing and blackmail scheme. Vinnie's been blackmailing Carter for years and summons him to California on the pretense of helping Vinnie out of a sexual misconduct rap. The supposed victim (Keener) of the misconduct is unaware that any took place and agrees to help Carter. Vinnie then steals Carter's I.D, car, and plane ticket and visits their old blackmail victim (Finney), and then Carter's wife Rosie (Stone), who was also in on the con. In a haze of confused motivations and implausible plot macinations, the three try to redeem their past deeds, with Vinnie and Carter seemingly switching places. **106m/C; VHS, DVD.** Nick Nolte; Sharon Stone; Jeff Bridges; Catherine Keener; Albert Finney; Shawn Hatosy; Kimberly Williams; Liam Waite; *D:* Matthew Warchus; *W:* Matthew Warchus; David Nicholls; *C:* John Toll; *M:* Stewart Copeland.

A Simple Curve 🦴🦴 **2005** Caleb is trying to keep his custom woodworking shop in business despite the contrariness of his widowed father Jim, an aging hippie and one-time draft dodger who's also his partner. When wealthy American Matthew, a former friend of Jim's, arrives in town to build a luxury lodge, Caleb sees his opportunity and secretly makes a deal, which could cost him more than he realizes. Filmed in the Slocan Valley of British Columbia. **92m/C; DVD.** *CA* Kris Lemche; Michael Hogan; Matt Craven; Pascale Hutton; Sara Lind; Kett Turton; Michael Robinson; *D:* Aubrey Nealon; *W:* Aubrey Nealon; *C:* David Geddes; *M:* Ohad Benchetrit; Justin Small.

A Simple Favor 🦴🦴🦴 **2018 (R)** Widowed single mother Stephanie Smothers (Kendrick) has a modestly successful lifestyle mommy blog and over-volunteers at her young son Miles' (Satine) school. Her world is changed forever when she meets the sophisticated Emily Nelson (Lively), whose son Nicky (Ho) is Miles' best friend. Though intimidated by Emily, Stephanie quickly regards her as a best friend as well. When Emily suddenly goes missing, Stephanie draws on her newly recognized inner strength to discover who Emily really was. Successfully balances elements of suspense and comedy while insightfully exploring the nature of women's friendships through outstanding performances by the charismatic Kendrick and Lively. **116m/C; DVD, Blu-Ray.** Anna Kendrick; Blake Lively; Henry Golding; Joshua Satine; Ian Ho; *D:* Paul Feig; *W:* Jessica Sharzer; *C:* John Schwartzman; *M:* Theodore Shapiro.

Simple Justice 🦴 1/2 **1989 (R)** Mindless, justice-in-own-hands anti-liberal hogwash. Overwrought, smug, and violent story of a young couple beaten by robbers who remain at large. **91m/C; VHS, DVD.** Cesar Romero; John Spencer; Doris Roberts; Candy McClain; *D:* Deborah Del Prete.

A Simple Life 🦴🦴🦴 *Tao jie* **2011** Ah Tao (Deannie Yip) has served her employer and his family as a maid for four generations before retiring after a stroke. The family's more successful son Roger (Andy Lau) realizes how much of a loss Ah Tao is, and returns from America to ensure she is okay. **118m/C; DVD, Blu-Ray, Streaming.** *CH* Andy Lau; Deannie Yip; *D:* Ann Hui; *W:* Susan Chan; Yan-lam Lee; *C:* Nelson Yu Lik-wai; *M:* Wing-fai Law. **VIDEO**

The Simple Life of Noah Dearborn 🦴🦴 1/2 **1999 (PG)** Simple morality tale with an affecting performance by Poitier. Noah Dearborn is a 91-year-old carpenter and farmer who refuses to sell his Georgia property to developers. So they try to declare the old man incompetent. **87m/C; VHS, DVD.** Sidney Poitier; Mary-Louise Parker; Dianne Wiest; George Newbern; *D:* Gregg Champion. **TV**

Simple Men ☊☊☊ **1992 (R)** Odd-ball brothers Bill (a petty criminal) and Dennis (a shy college student) decide to track down their missing father in this fractured comedy. Dad, a former big-league baseball player who bombed the Pentagon in the '60s, is a long-time fugitive hiding out somewhere in the wilds of Long Island. Their search leads them to two equally opposite women, the wary Kate, whom Bill immediately falls for, and the sexy Elina, who turns out to know dear old dad quite well. Deliberately deadpan and cliched, Hartley's quirky style can either irritate or illuminate via the weird turnings of his characters' lives. **105m/C; VHS, DVD.** Robert John Burke; William Sage; Karen Sillas; Elina Lowensohn; Martin Donovan; Mark Bailey; John MacKay; Jeffrey Howard; Holly Marie Combs; ***D:*** Hal Hartley; ***W:*** Hal Hartley; ***C:*** Michael Spiller; ***M:*** Hal Hartley.

A Simple Plan ☊☊☊ **1998 (R)** Hank (Paxton), his "slow" brother Jacob (Thornton), and Jacob's best bud, alcoholic Lou (Briscoe) find the wreckage of a small plane in the snowy Minnesota woods. The pilot is dead and there's a bag filled with $4 million in cash, which they decide is drug money. The trio decide to keep quiet about the find and keep the money hidden until the plane is discovered by someone else. But having all that loot brings out the greed in everyone and soon nasty things begin to happen to all those involved. Adapted from the 1993 novel by Scott Smith. **121m/C; VHS, DVD.** Bill Paxton; Billy Bob Thornton; Brent Briscoe; Bridget Fonda; Gary Cole; Becky Ann Baker; Chelcie Ross; Jack Walsh; ***D:*** Sam Raimi; ***W:*** Scott B. Smith; ***C:*** Alar Kivilo; ***M:*** Danny Elfman. L.A. Film Critics '98: Support. Actor (Thornton); Broadcast Film Critics '98: Adapt. Screenplay, Support. Actor (Thornton).

A Simple Promise ☊☊ **2007** Struggling artist Marcus and aspiring singer Madison get romantically involved and make a promise to help each other with their careers. But when one gets that longed-for big break, it causes a lot of friction and they have to figure out if their love can get them through. **95m/C; DVD.** Ella Joyce; Layla Kayleigh; Wallace Demarria; Bobby Reed; Selwyn Ward; Glen Mac; ***D:*** Earnest Harris; ***W:*** Max Lucas; ***C:*** Andrew Giannetta; Gigi Malavasi; ***M:*** Matt Hamel.

A Simple Twist of Fate ☊☊ ½ **1994 (PG-13)** Comedy drama gives Martin chance to flex serious muscles with this update of George Eliot's "Silas Marner." Adoptive father Michael McMann wants to keep his daughter Mathilda (played by the prerequisite adorable twins) in the face of demands from her biological father (Byrne), who happens to be a local politician. Then revelations brought out at the custody hearing threaten the politician's career. Cuddly dad is hardly Martin's image (in spite of "Parenthood"), though strong cast limits the sugar. **106m/C; VHS, DVD, Blu-Ray.** Steve Martin; Gabriel Byrne; Catherine O'Hara; Stephen Baldwin; Alana Austin; Alyssa Austin; Laura Linney; Anne Heche; Michael Des Barres; Byron Jennings; ***D:*** Gilles Mackinnon; ***W:*** Steve Martin; ***M:*** Cliff Eidelman.

A Simple Wish ☊☊ ½ **1997 (PG)** Equal employment opportunities now even extend to the fairy godmother realm. Anabel (Wilson) knows her dad (Pastorelli) wants to become a Broadway actor. So she wishes for a fairy godmother—and gets stuck with Murray (Short), the first affirmative-action male practitioner, who's really not very good at spellcasting. Both Anabel and Murray have bigger problems—evil fairy godmother Claudia (Turner) is after all the fairy godmothers' magic wands so she can rule the world's wishes. Short's brand of comic energy plays right into the kid audience, and Wilson lights up every scene she's in. **95m/C; VHS, DVD, Blu-Ray.** Mara Wilson; Martin Short; Kathleen Turner; Robert Pastorelli; Amanda Plummer; Teri Garr; Francis Capra; Jonathan Hadary; Alan Campbell; Ruby Dee; ***D:*** Michael Ritchie; ***W:*** Jeff Rothberg; ***C:*** Ralf Bode; ***M:*** Bruce Broughton.

Simply Irresistible ☊ **1999 (PG-13)** Romantic comedy in which failing restaurant owner/chef Amanda Shelton (Gellar) falls for exec Tom Barlett (Flanery). Thanks to the intervention of fairy-godfather O'Reilly (Durang) Amanda suddenly possesses a unique culinary ability—every emotion she's feeling goes into her food and winds up affecting her customers. Tries too hard (this kind of whimsical comedy should be lighter than a souffle) and the leads, appealing as they may be, don't generate any heat when together. The film also sounds like an Americanized version of "Like Water for Chocolate," even if no one's admitting to the notion. **95m/C; VHS, DVD, Blu-Ray.** Sarah Michelle Gellar; Sean Patrick Flanery; Patricia Clarkson; Dylan Baker; Christopher Durang; Larry (Lawrence) Gilliard, Jr.; Betty Buckley; ***D:*** Mark Tarlov; ***W:*** Judith Roberts; ***C:*** Robert M. Stevens; ***M:*** Gil Goldstein.

The Simpsons Movie ☊☊☊☊ **2007 (PG-13)** Best. Movie. Ever. Okay, maybe not, but it's pretty good. Homer's infatuation with a condemned pig sparks a near apocalyptic fate for Springfield and a cross-country trek to Alaska for the Simpson clan in their long-awaited big screen debut. All of the main characters, and many of the minor ones, get their shot in the spotlight, and the show's trademark sly humor, social commentary, and digs at popular culture are, thankfully, intact. Marge provides the voice of reason, and some surprising pathos along the way. **87m/C; DVD, Blu-Ray.** ***V:*** Dan Castellaneta; Julie Kavner; Nancy Cartwright; Yeardley Smith; Harry Shearer; Hank Azaria; Albert Brooks; Joe Mantegna; Marcia Wallace; Pamela Hayden; Tom Hanks; ***D:*** David Silverman; ***W:*** James L. Brooks; David Mirkin; Matt Groening; Mike Reiss; Al Jean; Ian Maxton-Graham; George Meyer; Mike Scully; Matt Selman; John Swartzwelder; Jon Vitti; ***M:*** Hans Zimmer.

Sin ☊ ½ **2002 (R)** Retired cop Eddie Burns (Rhames) searches for his missing sister Kassie (Washington) and discovers she's part of a twisted plot by crime boss Charlie Strom (Oldman) to get revenge on Burns for their shared past. Too many plot holes and unbelievable situations make this revenge thriller less than scintillating despite the pro work of the leads. (Okay, so Oldman chews the scenery but you expect that.) **107m/C; DVD.** Ving Rhames; Gary Oldman; Kerry Washington; Brian Cox; Alicia Coppola; William Sage; Gregg Henry; Arie Verveen; Chris Spencer; ***D:*** Michael Stevens; ***W:*** Tim Willocks; ***C:*** Zoran Popovic; ***M:*** Michael Giacchino.

Sin City ☊☊ *Frank Miller's Sin City* **2005 (R)** Rodriguez teamed with comic legend Frank Miller to co-direct this overly literal adaptation of Miller's black-and-white crime noir series. Set in the hellishly corrupt Basin City, the plot bounces between a menagerie of unsavory anti-heroes, including Marv (Rourke), a lovable thug bent on avenging a hooker's murder; Dwight (Owen), a moralistic man-with-a-past; and Hartigan (Willis), a cop who spent eight years in prison to protect a virtuous stripper (Alba). More of a slideshow than a film, you'll marvel at how closely it resembles the comic, though the directors' fundamentalist zeal for their source material tests the audience's patience throughout. Acting and pacing are ignored while Rodriguez uses cheap-looking CGI to slavishly reproduce exact panels of Miller's art. Fanboy fervor gone too far. **124m/B; DVD, Blu-Ray, UMD.** Jessica Alba; Devon Aoki; Alexis Bledel; Rosario Dawson; Benicio Del Toro; Michael Clarke Duncan; Carla Gugino; Josh Hartnett; Rutger Hauer; Jaime King; Michael Madsen; Brittany Murphy; Clive Owen; Mickey Rourke; Nick Stahl; Bruce Willis; Elijah Wood; Marley Shelton; Powers Boothe; Nicky Katt; Makenzie Vega; Arie Verveen; Tommy Nix; Jude Ciccolella; Rick Gomez; Lisa Marie Newmyer; Nick Offerman; ***D:*** Robert Rodriguez; Frank Miller; ***C:*** Robert Rodriguez; ***M:*** Robert Rodriguez; Graeme Revell; John Debney.

Sin City: A Dame to Kill For ☊☊ *Frank Miller's Sin City: A Dame to Kill For* **2014 (R)** In movie-world terms, it took forever for this sequel to the 2005 Robert Rodriguez hit to get off the ground. But this follow-up feels like an afterthought more than a proper follow-up. Much of the cast of the original is downgraded, even if Rourke and Alba do return for another go-around of stylized graphic novel action. Most of the style of the first film is lovingly recreated here, but this never comes close to matching its energy, largely because we've seen it done before. Still brutally fun, but more of a brutal disappointment for all those fanboys and girls who waited so long. **102m/B; DVD, Blu-Ray.** Mickey Rourke; Joseph Gordon-Levitt; Powers Boothe; Eva Green; Josh Brolin; Jessica Alba; Bruce Willis; Marton Csokas; Dennis Haysbert; Christopher Meloni; Rosario Dawson; ***D:*** Robert Rodriguez; Frank Miller; ***W:*** Robert Rodriguez; Frank Miller; ***C:*** Robert Rodriguez; ***M:*** Robert Rodriguez; Carl Thiel.

Sin Nombre ☊☊☊ **2009 (R)** Teenager Sayra (Gaitan) lives in Honduras but hungers for a brighter future, leading her to illegally emigrate with her estranged father into Mexico and then the United States. Meanwhile, teenager Casper, a.k.a. Willy (Flores) from Tapachula, Mexico, faces a bleak future as a member of the ultra-violent Mara Salvatrucha gang and joins the family after murdering his gang's leader. A gripping tale of the wretched circumstances that drive people from Central America into the "land of opportunity" in hopes of a better life despite the dangers and sacrifices that accompany such a harrowing journey. An excellent debut from writer/director Fukunaga. **96m/C; Blu-Ray.** Paulina Gaitan; Gerardo Taracena; Edgar Flores; Diane Garcia; Catalina Lopez; ***D:*** Cary Fukunaga; ***W:*** Cary Fukunaga; ***C:*** Adriano Goldman; ***M:*** Marcelo Zarvos.

The Sin of Harold Diddlebock ☊☊ ½ *Mad Wednesday* **1947** A man gets fired from his job, stumbles around drunk, and wins a fortune gambling. He then buys a circus and uses a lion to frighten investors into backing him. Inventive comedy, but missing the spark and timing of "The Freshman" (1925), of which it is a sequel. The final feature film for Lloyd (who did all his own stunts), made at the urging of director Sturges. **89m/B; VHS, DVD.** Harold Lloyd; Margaret Hamilton; Frances Ramsden; Edgar Kennedy; Lionel Stander; Rudy Vallee; Franklin Pangborn; ***D:*** Preston Sturges.

The Sin of Madelon Claudet ☊☊☊ *The Lullaby* **1931** Hayes plays common thief who works her way into upper crust of Parisian society only to tumble back into the street, all in the name of making a better life for her illegitimate son. Very sudsy stuff, with an outstanding performance by Hayes. **74m/B; VHS, DVD.** Helen Hayes; Lewis Stone; Neil Hamilton; Robert Young; Cliff Edwards; Jean Hersholt; Marie Prevost; Karen Morley; Charles Winninger; Alan Hale; ***D:*** Edgar Selwyn. Oscars '32: Actress (Hayes).

The Sin Seer ☊ ½ **2015** A dramatic thriller centered on a woman with special vision and secrets from her past. Rose Ricard (Arrindell Anderson) has known since childhood that she can see into someone's soul and the secrets that are held there. In adulthood, she uses her gift as a private investigator to solve the case that the police cannot. Working with an ex-con partner Grant Summit (Washington), Rose becomes involved in a case in which she sees into the soul of a murderer, leads to secrets from her past coming to light, and places her in danger. **99m/C; DVD, Streaming, Download.** Lisa Arrindell Anderson; Isaiah Washington, IV; Salli Richardson-Whitfield; Michael Ironside; Richard Brooks; ***D:*** Paul D. Hannah; ***W:*** Paul D. Hannah; ***C:*** Keith L. Smith; ***M:*** Mark Daniel Dunnett. **VIDEO**

Sin Takes a Holiday ☊☊ ½ **1930** A woman marries her boss to save him from his girl friend. On a trip to Paris, she is wooed by a refined European gentleman, but finds that she really does love her husband. By today's standards, it doesn't sound like much, but in the '30s, it was pretty sophisticated stuff. **81m/B; VHS, DVD, Blu-Ray.** Constance Bennett; Kenneth MacKenna; Basil Rathbone; Rita La Roy; Zasu Pitts; Fred Walton; Richard Carle; Helen Johnson; ***D:*** Paul Stein.

Sin You Sinners ☊ **1963** Aging stripper gets ahold of an amulet that allows her to look youthful and manipulate the lives of others. When she loses the amulet, however, bad things happen. Twisted ending. **73m/B; VHS, DVD, Blu-Ray.** June Colbourne; Dian Lloyd; Derek Murcott; Beverly Nazarow; Charles Clements; ***D:*** Anthony Farrar.

Sinatra ☊☊ ½ **1992** TV biopic chronicles the stormy life of crooner Frank Sinatra. Begins with his childhood in Hoboken, New Jersey and works its way through his big band tours, bobby soxer days, career skids, and triumphant comeback with his Oscar-winning performance in "From Here to Eternity," as well as his three marriages, "Rat Pack" friends, and mob connections. Executive Producer Tina Sinatra, Frank's daughter, doesn't gloss over her father's less savory character points and Casnoff does well with his leading role. Songs are lip-synched to classic Sinatra tunes with a few early recordings redone by actor Tom Burlinson and Frank Sinatra Jr. **245m/C; VHS, DVD.** Philip Casnoff; Olympia Dukakis; Joe Santos; Gina Gershon; Nina Siemaszko; Marcia Gay Harden; Rod Steiger; Bob Gunton; David Raynr; James F. Kelly; Matthew Posey; Jay Robinson; Robin Gammell; Todd Waring; Joris Stuyck; Danny Gans; Jeff Corey; ***D:*** James Sadwith; ***W:*** William Mastrosimone; ***C:*** Reynaldo Villalobos. **TV**

Sinbad and the Eye of the Tiger ☊☊ **1977 (G)** The swashbuckling adventures of Sinbad the Sailor as he encounters the creations of Ray Harryhausen's special effects magic. Don't see this one for the plot, which almost doesn't exist. Otherwise, mildly fun. **113m/C; VHS, DVD, Blu-Ray.** *GB* Patrick Wayne; Jane Seymour; Taryn Power; Margaret Whiting; ***D:*** Sam Wanamaker; ***W:*** Beverley Cross; ***C:*** Ted Moore; ***M:*** Roy Budd.

Sinbad and the Minotaur ☊ **2011** Syfy Channel silliness has Sinbad sneaking into the camp of sorcerer Al-Jibar on a search for gold. Instead, he finds a pirate's logs revealing where the golden head of the Colossus of Rhodes is hidden. Sinbad and his crew journey to the island of Minos, where the treasure is guarded by the minotaur. **90m/C; DVD.** Manu Bennett; Pacharo Mzembe; Steven Grives; Holly Brisley; David Vallon; Brad McMurray; ***D:*** Karl Zwicky; ***W:*** Jim Noble; ***C:*** Nino Martinetti; ***M:*** Garry McDonald. **CABLE**

Sinbad: Legend of the Seven Seas ☊☊ **2003 (PG)** Loose retelling of the "Arabian Nights" tale (so loose that it incorporates Greek and Roman legends and gods) from DreamWorks studio that's a combo of computer generated and hand-drawn animation. Sinbad the sailor/thief (voiced by Pitt) gets in trouble when Eris (Pfeiffer), the goddess of chaos, steals the Book of Peace and frames Sinbad for the crime. His best friend, Proteus (Fiennes) believes in Sinbad's innocence and stakes his life on Sinbad's return with the book. Proteus's fiancee Marina (Zeta-Jones) stows away to make sure Sinbad keeps his promises and to provide him with a foil. Jumbled story and inconsistent animation lead to ho-hum outing that the kids may enjoy, if they've tired of "Finding Nemo" after the umpteenth viewing. **86m/C; VHS, DVD, Blu-Ray.** ***V:*** Brad Pitt; Catherine Zeta-Jones; Michelle Pfeiffer; Joseph Fiennes; Dennis Haysbert; Timothy West; Adriano Giannini; ***D:*** Tim Johnson; Patrick Gilmore; ***W:*** John Logan; ***M:*** Harry Gregson-Williams.

Sinbad of the Seven Seas ☊ ½ **1989** Italian muscle epic based on the ancient legends. Ferrigno isn't green, but he's still a hulk, and he still can't act. It's poorly dubbed, which makes little difference; it would be stupid regardless. **90m/C; VHS, DVD, Blu-Ray.** *IT* Lou Ferrigno; John Steiner; Leo Gullotta; Teagan Clive; ***D:*** Enzo G. Castellari.

Sinbad, the Sailor ☊☊☊ **1947** Fairbanks fits well in his father's swashbuckling shoes, as he searches for the treasure of Alexander the Great. Self-mocking but ham-handed, and confusing if you seek the hidden plot. Still, it's all in fun, and it is fun. **117m/C; VHS, DVD.** Douglas Fairbanks, Jr.; Maureen O'Hara; Anthony Quinn; Walter Slezak; George Tobias; Jane Greer; Mike Mazurki; Sheldon Leonard; ***D:*** Richard Wallace; ***W:*** John Twist; ***C:*** George Barnes; ***M:*** Roy Webb.

Since Otar Left. . . ☊☊ *Depuis Qu'Otar est Parti* **2003** Bittersweet female-centric drama set in a rundown flat in Tblisi, in the former Soviet Republic of Georgia. Domineering matriarch Eka (90-year-old Gorintin) dotes on her son who works illegally in Paris. Meanwhile, her middle-aged daughter Marina (Khomassouridze) resents her mother's obvious preference, and her own daughter, Ada (Droukarova), tries to keep the peace between the two women. When Marina and Ada learn that Otar has been killed, they conspire to keep the truth from Eka through an elaborate ruse with unexpected consequences. Russian, Georgian and French with subtitles. **102m/C; VHS, DVD.** *FR* Esther Gorintin; Nino Khomassouridze; Dinara Droukarova; Temour Kalandadze; Roussoudan Bolkvadze; Sacha Sarichvili; Douta Skhirtladze; ***D:*** Julie Bertuccelli; ***W:*** Julie Bertuccelli; Roger Bohbot; Bernard Renucci; ***C:*** Christophe Pollock.

Since You Went Away 1/2 **1944** An American family copes with the tragedy, heartache and shortages of wartime in classic mega-tribute to the home front. Be warned: very long and bring your hankies. Colbert is superb, as is the photography. John Derek unobtrusively made his film debut, as an extra. **172m/B; VHS, DVD, Blu-Ray.** Claudette Colbert; Jennifer Jones; Shirley Temple; Joseph Cotten; Agnes Moorehead; Monty Woolley; Guy Madison; Lionel Barrymore; Robert Walker; Hattie McDaniel; Keenan Wynn; Craig Stevens; Albert Bassermann; Alla Nazimova; Lloyd Corrigan; Terry Moore; Florence Bates; Ruth Roman; Andrew V. McLaglen; Dorothy Dandridge; Rhonda Fleming; Addison Richards; Jackie Moran; ***D:*** John Cromwell; ***W:*** David O. Selznick; ***C:*** Stanley Cortez; Lee Garmes; ***M:*** Max Steiner. Oscars '44: Orig. Dramatic Score.

Since You've Been Gone *Dogwater* **1997 (R)** The Clear View High School class of 1987 has their ten-year reunion and rivalries and romance are rediscovered. Grace (Boyle) has a penchant for nasty practical jokes she's never gotten over while Marie (Hatcher) is a self-important would-be exec who insults her one-time classmates and Rob (Schwimmer) is the still-loathed class president. **95m/C; VHS, DVD.** David Schwimmer; Lara Flynn Boyle; Teri Hatcher; Joey Slotnick; Tom (Thomas E.) Hodges; Philip Rayburn Smith; Heidi Stillman; David Catlin; Laura Eason; ***Cameo(s):*** Marisa Tomei; Jon Stewart; Liev Schreiber; Molly Ringwald; Jennifer Grey; ***D:*** David Schwimmer.

Sincerely Yours WOOF! 1955 Liberace wisely stayed away from acting after inauspiciously debuting in this horrible, maudlin remake of "The Man Who Played God." He plays a pianist who loses his hearing and decides to become a philanthropist to help those less fortunate than himself. Laughably cheesy. Thirty-one musical numbers, including Liberace's inimitable arrangement of "Chopsticks." **116m/C; DVD.** Liberace; Joanne Dru; Dorothy Malone; William Demarest; Alex Nicol; Lurene Tuttle; ***D:*** Gordon Douglas; ***W:*** Irving Wallace; ***C:*** William Clothier.

Sinful Davey 1/2 **1969** In this tired Brit adventure film, young Davey wants to follow his late father's profession as a highwayman without ending up on the gallows. Davey is not very competent and is either being accused of a crime or getting caught. He's frequently rescued from his folly by lover Annie, who just wants Davey to settle down to a respectable life with her. **95m/C; DVD.** *UK* John Hurt; Pamela Franklin; Nigel Davenport; Robert Morley; Donal McCann; Ronald Fraser; ***D:*** John Huston; ***W:*** James R. Webb; ***C:*** Frederick A. (Freddie) Young; Edward (Ted) Scaife; ***M:*** Ken Thorne.

Sinful Intrigue **1995 (R)** A bunch of wealthy, lusty, and busty ladies are being attacked in their neighborhood. All fingers point to the local handyman as the main suspect. **88m/C; VHS, DVD.** Bobby Johnston; Beckie Mullen; Mark Zuelzke; Griffin (Griffen) Drew; ***D:*** Edward Holzman; ***W:*** John Nelson; ***C:*** Harris Done; ***M:*** Patrick John Scott.

A Sinful Life **1989 (R)** A strained, offbeat, B-grade comedy about an odd, infantile mother fighting to keep her unusual child from being taken away. Definitely not a must-see; can be irritating and obnoxious, depending on viewer and mood. Morris is at her oddball comedic best as the mother and former show dancer. Adult Tefkin plays her little girl. Based on the play "Just Like the Pom Pom Girls." **112m/C; VHS, Streaming.** Anita Morris; Rick Overton; Dennis Christopher; Blair Tefkin; Mark Rolston; Cynthia Szigeti; ***D:*** William Schreiner.

Sing **2016 (PG)** On one hand, the latest from Universal's Illumination Entertainment is another bland family film designed to push product more than out of any possible artistic venture. On the other hand, it has cute animals singing catchy pop songs. McConaughey voices Buster Moon, a koala, who runs a failing theater. He throws a singing competition to try to save the business and dozens of animals show up to sing dozens of songs. Again, this is not Pixar-level quality but you could do worse in the "cute" department. It's generally harmless if you don't mind that it's superficial. **108m/C; DVD, Blu-Ray.** Matthew McConaughey; Reese Witherspoon; Seth MacFarlane; Scarlett Johansson; John C. Reilly; Taron Egerton; Tori Kelly; ***D:*** Garth Jennings; ***W:*** Garth Jennings; ***M:*** Joby Talbot.

Sing, Baby, Sing 1/2 **1936** Musical comedy from 20th Century Fox. Joan's (Faye) looking to make it as a society singer in New York, but she can't catch a break until her shady agent, Nicky (Ratoff), hooks her up with drunken actor Bruce Farraday (Menjou). However, Bruce's manager, Robert (Love), thinks Joan's just another gold-digger and hustles the actor out of town before an important radio gig. The Ritz Brothers do some of their vaudeville routines and Tony Martin sings the Oscar-nominated song "When Did You Leave Heaven." **87m/B; DVD.** Alice Faye; Adolphe Menjou; Gregory Ratoff; Montagu Love; Patsy Kelly; Ted Healy; Michael Whalen; ***D:*** Sidney Lanfield; ***W:*** Harry Tugend; Milton Sperling; Jack Yellen; ***C:*** J. Peverell Marley; ***M:*** Richard A Whiting; Walter Bullock.

Sing Street **2016 (PG-13)** John Carney's third film is a glorious love letter to the power of music, the importance of individuality, and the essential ties of brotherhood. Cosmo (Walsh-Peelo) is sent to a new school, full of bullies and morons, but he's immediately interested in the mysterious girl (Boynton) who lives across the street. With the assistance of his brother Brendan (the fantastic Reynor), Cosmo starts his own band, mimicking many of the hit bands of the day (Duran Duran, The Cure, etc.) in music videos designed to impress his new love. Carney's film is joyous and beautiful. **106m/C; DVD, Blu-Ray.** Ferdia Walsh-Peelo; Aidan Gillen; Maria Doyle Kennedy; Jack Reynor; Lucy Boynton; ***D:*** John Carney; ***W:*** John Carney; ***C:*** Yaron Orbach.

Sing You Sinners 1/2 **1938** Lazy Joe Beebe (Crosby) schemes rather than works, unlike his responsible brother David (MacMurray). Their mom (Patterson) wants Joe to set a better example for their teenaged brother Mike (O'Connor) but the singer takes off for L.A. looking to get some easy dough. His family soon follows, but instead of a job Joe has bought a racehorse and is betting everything on a big race. **88m/B; DVD.** Bing Crosby; Fred MacMurray; Elizabeth Patterson; Donald O'Connor; Ellen Drew; John Gallaudet; ***D:*** Wesley Ruggles; ***W:*** Claude Binyon; ***C:*** Karl Struss.

Singham 1/2 **2011** Over the top Bollywood actioner featuring a cop/one man army against a gangster with corrupt politicians in his pocket. **144m/C; DVD.** *IN* Ajay Devgn; Kajal Agarwal; Prakash Raj; Sonali Kulkarni; Sachin Khedekar; ***D:*** Rohit Shetty; ***W:*** Yunus Sajawal; ***C:*** Dudley; ***M:*** Ajay Gogavale; Atul Gogavale; Amar Mohile.

Singin' in the Rain **1952** One of the all-time great movie musicals—an affectionate spoof of the turmoil that afflicted the motion picture industry in the late 1920s during the changeover from silent films to sound. Don Lockwood (Kelly) and Lina Lamont (Hagen) are a popular romantic silent screen team when sound comes along. To continue, temperamental Lina must have her terrible voice dubbed by aspiring actress Kathy Selden (Reynolds), whom Don falls for. O'Connor's an acrobatic marvel as Don's best pal, Cosmo Brown, and of course there's Kelly's classic much-copied title dance. Later a Broadway musical. **103m/C; VHS, DVD, Blu-Ray.** Gene Kelly; Donald O'Connor; Jean Hagen; Debbie Reynolds; Rita Moreno; King Donovan; Millard Mitchell; Cyd Charisse; Douglas Fowley; Madge Blake; Joi Lansing; ***D:*** Gene Kelly; Stanley Donen; ***W:*** Adolph Green; Betty Comden; ***C:*** Harold Rosson; ***M:*** Nacio Herb Brown; Lennie Hayton. AFI '98: Top 100; Golden Globes '53: Actor--Mus./Comedy (O'Connor); Natl. Film Reg. '89.

The Singing Blacksmith 1/2 **1938** A relic of American Yiddish cinema, adapting popular 1909 play by David Pinski. A married blacksmith is wooed by another woman and falls victim to alcoholism. Overlong, but Oysher and his rich baritone voice still shine. In Yiddish with English subtitles. **95m/B; VHS, DVD.** *PL* Miriam Riselle; Florence Weiss; Moishe Oysher; ***D:*** Edgar G. Ulmer.

The Singing Detective **1986** A musical/mystery/fantasy British miniseries, based on the work by Dennis Potter. Pulp fiction writer Phillip Marlowe (Gambon) is confined to his hospital bed, unable to move due to extreme psoriasis. In his lucid moments he tries to figure out the cause of his condition, but in his elaborate daydreams he's a detective (and big band singer) who's working to solve a series of murders. Six episodes: "Skin," "Heat," "Lovely Days," "Clues," "Pitter Patter," and "Who Done It." **420m/C; VHS, DVD.** *GB* Michael Gambon; Patrick Malahide; Janet Suzman; Joanne Whalley; ***D:*** Jon Amiel. **TV**

The Singing Detective 1/2 **2003 (R)** Dan Dark (Downey) is a pulp crime novelist who suffers from a painful debilitating disease that leaves him confined to a hospital bed. As Dark drifts in and out of reality, his imagination fuses episodes from his novels with memories of his childhood. In his fantasies, Dark imagines himself as a detective of a '50s film noir. Real personas in his life begin to play characters in his fantasy and his delusions begin to bleed into his real life. Adding to the surreality is the slew of '50s pop songs that the characters sing at the slightest provocation. Visually stunning, and a bit convoluted. Downey delivers a solid performance, as do the supporting cast, including an almost unrecognizable Mel Gibson. Based on the BBC mini-series of the same name. **109m/C; VHS, DVD, Blu-Ray.** Robert Downey, Jr.; Robin Wright; Mel Gibson; Jeremy Northam; Katie Holmes; Adrien Brody; Jon Polito; Carla Gugino; Saul Rubinek; Alfre Woodard; ***D:*** Keith Gordon; ***W:*** Dennis Potter; ***C:*** Tom Richmond.

The Singing Fool 1/2 **1928** Al Stone (Jolson) becomes a sensation as a singing waiter/songwriter turned Broadway star until his ambitious wife Molly (Dunn) gets bored, walks out, and takes their son with her to Paris. Al then goes on the skids until cigarette girl Grace (Bronson) gets him back on the right track. However, Molly's return also brings tragic news. **105m/B; DVD.** Al Jolson; Betty Bronson; Josephine Dunn; Reed Howes; Arthur Housman; Davey Lee; Edward Martindel; ***D:*** Lloyd Bacon; ***W:*** C. Graham Baker; Joseph Jackson; ***C:*** Byron Haskin.

The Singing Kid 1/2 **1936** Predictable and rather dull Jolson effort finds musical and radio star Al Jackson losing his voice and fortune. But he recovers both thanks to a Maine rest cure, finding landlady Ruth (Roberts) a romantic tonic. (Although it's charming young Sybil Jason as Ruth's niece who steals every scene.) Then Al returns to Broadway to get back on top. **85m/B; DVD.** Al Jolson; Beverly Roberts; Sybil Jason; Edward Everett Horton; Allen Jenkins; Lyle Talbot; William B. Davidson; Claire Dodd; ***D:*** William Keighley; ***W:*** Warren Duff; Pat C. Flick; ***C:*** George Barnes.

The Singing Nun **1966** The true story of a Belgian nun who takes a liking to a motherless little boy. She writes a song for him, and a kind-hearted priest talks to a record producer to see about getting the song to go somewhere. The song soon becomes an international hit, and the nun ends up on the "Ed Sullivan Show." Sentimental and sugary sweet, but a big boxoffice hit. **98m/C; VHS, DVD.** Debbie Reynolds; Ricardo Montalban; Greer Garson; Agnes Moorehead; Chad Everett; Katharine Ross; Juanita Moore; Ricky Cordell; Michael Pate; Tom Drake; ***D:*** Henry Koster; ***C:*** Milton Krasner.

The Singing Princess 1/2 *La Rosa di Bagdad; The Rose of Baghdad* **1949 (G)** Arabian Nights inspired animated tale features a pretty princess, a poor-but-honest hero, an evil sultan and a slave of the lamp. Julie Andrews made her film debut in the English released version as the voice of Princess Zeila. **76m/C; DVD.** *IT* Howard Marion-Crawford; Julie Andrews; ***D:*** Anton Gino Domenighini; ***W:*** Nina Maguire; Tony Maguire.

A Single Girl 1/2 *La Fille Seule* **1996** Follows, in real time, a young woman as she tells her boyfriend that she's pregnant, (Ledoyen) through her job handling room service at a Paris hotel, then again with her boyfriend after work. French with subtitles. Part sexual hotel fantasy, part observation of an ordinary couple going about daily life. **90m/C; VHS, DVD, Blu-Ray.** *FR* Virginie Ledoyen; Benoît Magimel; Vera Briole; Dominique Valadie; ***D:*** Benoit Jacquot; ***W:*** Benoit Jacquot; Jerome Beaujour; ***C:*** Caroline Champetier; ***M:*** Kvarteto Mesta Prahi.

A Single Man **2009 (R)** Former fashion designer Tom Ford's directorial debut is based on a 1964 novel by Christopher Isherwood that's set in L.A. in 1962 over a single day. Middle-aged Brit ex-pat college professor George (Firth) is still devastated months later by the car crash death of his longtime lover Jim (Goode) and, because of the times and his own stiff-upper-lip, George is isolated and can't acknowledge his sexuality, let alone his sorrow. Now George is planning to commit suicide. He follows his usual routine while putting his affairs in order and spends his intended last evening with longtime friend, sophisticated, brittle alcoholic Charley (Moore). Ford offers a sunlit California setting that George can only see as unimaginably bleak while Firth gives a stunningly quiet performance of a man overwhelmed by inexpressible grief. **99m/C; Blu-Ray, On Demand.** Colin Firth; Julianne Moore; Nicholas Hoult; Matthew Goode; Jon Kortajarena; Lee Pace; Paulette Lamori; Ryan Simpkins; Ginnifer Goodwin; Paul Butler; Aaron Sanders; ***V:*** Jon Hamm; ***D:*** Tom Ford; ***W:*** Tom Ford; David Scearce; ***C:*** Eduard Grau; ***M:*** Abel Korzeniowski. British Acad. '09: Actor (Firth).

Single Room Furnished 1/2 **1968** The fall of a buxom blonde from uncorrupted innocence through pregnancies to desperate prostitution. Fails to demonstrate any range of talent in Mansfield, who died before it was completed. Exploitative and pathetic. **93m/C; VHS, DVD.** Jayne Mansfield; Dorothy Keller; ***D:*** Matt Cimber; Matteo Ottaviano.

A Single Shot 1/2 **2013 (R)** Backwoods crime drama. West Virginia, trailer-living loner John Moon (Rockwell) likes to do some illegal hunting in the mountains. One misty morning, he accidentally shoots and kills a young woman. While hiding the body, Moon finds a cash-filled lockbox in her possession and takes the dough, which ultimately leads to increasing trouble since it belongs to some local thugs who want it back. Bleak and atmospheric, but the convoluted story falls flat despite novelist Jones adapting his own work. **116m/C; Blu-Ray, Streaming.** Sam Rockwell; Jeffrey Wright; William H. Macy; Kelly Reilly; Jason Isaacs; Joe Anderson; Ted Levine; ***D:*** David M. Rosenthal; ***W:*** Matthew F. Jones; ***C:*** Eduard Grau; ***M:*** Atli Ovarsson.

The Single Standard **1929** San Francisco deb Garbo flings with artsy Asther and finds out the Hayes Code is just around the corner. **93m/B; Silent; VHS, DVD.** Greta Garbo; Nils Asther; Johnny Mack Brown; Dorothy Sebastian; Lane Chandler; Zeffie Tilbury; ***D:*** John S. Robertson.

Single White Female 1/2 **1992 (R)** Psycho thriller casts Fonda as chic Manhattan computer consultant Allison Jones, who advertises for a roommate after a falling out with her boyfriend. Leigh is the frumpy, shy, bookstore clerk Hedra who answers the ad and moves into Allie's great Upper West Side apartment. They hit it off, that is until Allie notices Hedra's beginning to look and sound very familiar. Hmm. . . Derivative, though bonus points for creative murder implements and interesting performances throughout, including Friedman as Allie's gay upstairs neighbor. Based on the novel "SWF Seeks Same" by John Lutz. **107m/C; VHS, DVD, Blu-Ray.** Bridget Fonda; Jennifer Jason Leigh; Steven Weber; Peter Friedman; Stephen Tobolowsky; Frances Bay; Renee Estevez; Kenneth Tobey; Jessica Lundy; ***D:*** Barbet Schroeder; ***W:*** Don Roos; ***C:*** Luciano Tovoli; ***M:*** Howard Shore. MTV Movie Awards '93: Villain (Leigh).

Single White Female 2: The Psycho WOOF! 2005 (R) So in the first movie she wasn't a psycho? Down-on-her-luck young woman moves into an apartment and soon discovers her new roomie has become fixated on her, later turning killer. Inept rehash of the original with all the thrills (and acting ability) removed. And still it took three writers to come up with this dreck. **93m/C; DVD.** Kristen Miller; Allison Lange; Brooke Burns; Todd Babcock; Francois Giroday; Rif Hutton; ***D:*** Keith Samples; ***W:*** Andy Hurst; Ross Helford; Glenn Hobart; ***C:*** Thomas M. (Tom) Harting; ***M:*** Steven Stern. **VIDEO**

Singles 1992 (PG-13) Seattle's music scene is the background for this lighthearted look at single 20-somethings in the '90s. Hits dead on thanks to Crowe's tight script and a talented cast, and speaks straight to its intended audience—the "Generation X" crowd. Real life band Pearl Jam plays alternative band Citizen Dick and sets the tone for a great soundtrack featuring the hot Seattle sounds of Alice in Chains, Soundgarden, and Mudhoney. The video contains six extra minutes of footage after the credits that was thankfully edited out of the final cut. Look for Horton, Stoltz (as a mime), Skerritt, and Burton in cameos. **100m/C; VHS, DVD, Blu-Ray.** Matt Dillon; Bridget Fonda; Campbell Scott; Kyra Sedgwick; Sheila Kelley; Jim True-Frost; Bill Pullman; James LeGros; Ally Walker; Devon Raymond; Camillo Gallardo; Jeremy Piven; ***Cameo(s):*** Peter Horton; Eric Stoltz; Tim Burton; Tom Skerritt; ***D:*** Cameron Crowe; ***W:*** Cameron Crowe; ***C:*** Ueli Steiger; ***M:*** Paul Westerberg.

Singleton's Pluck *Laughterhouse* **1984** Touching British comedy about a determined farmer who must walk his 500 geese 100 miles to market because of a strike. He becomes a celebrity when the TV stations start covering his odyssey. **89m/C; VHS, DVD.** *GB* Ian Holm; Penelope Wilton; Bill Owen; Richard Hope; ***D:*** Richard Eyre.

Sinister 1/2 **2012 (R)** Despite being advised against it, true-crime author Ellison (Hawke) moves his family into a bargain of a house. Soon enough Ellison finds a stash of grisly super 8 home movies in the attic, revealing the sick, horrific nature of the previous owner. Obsessed with the footage, he secretly transfers the film to his computer and begins analyzing it, frame by frame. Meanwhile, he and his family fall victim to terrifying supernatural ghost trickery throughout the house. An undeniably chilling horror flick, regardless of hitting all the usual cliches and delivering a predictable ending. **110m/C; DVD, Blu-Ray.** Ethan Hawke; Vincent D'Onofrio; Claire Foley; Victoria Leigh; Juliet Rylance; ***D:*** Scott Derrickson; ***W:*** Scott Derrickson; C. Robert Cargill; ***C:*** Christopher Norr; ***M:*** Christopher Young.

Sinister 2 1/2 **2015 (R)** Look! Another horror sequel nobody asked for! The sinister spirit of Buhguul, introduced in the 2012 horror film Sinister, gathers steam and impacts the life of a single mother (Sossaon) and her young twin boys after they move to a new home in a rural area. They experience hauntings from the demon Bhughul, who convinces innocent children to kill their parents. The Deputy from the first film (Ransone) recognizes the pattern and races to stop the tragedy before it happens. The concept of children who betray their parents is ripe for horror as is the suburban legend idea of the boogeyman, but this is handled in straight-to-DVD fashion. **97m/C; DVD, Blu-Ray.** James Ransone; Shannyn Sossamon; Tate Ellington; Caden M. Fritz; Nicholas King; ***D:*** Ciaran Foy; ***W:*** Scott Derrickson; C. Robert Cargill; ***C:*** Amy Vincent; ***M:*** tomandandy.

Sinister Hands 1/2 **1932** Reviled tycoon Richard Lang is murdered during a seance at his home and police detective Devlin has numerous suspects, including Lang's wife and daughter and fake psychic Swami Yormurda. **65m/B; DVD.** Jack Mulhall; Phyllis Barrington; Mischa Auer; Lillian West; Gertrude Messinger; Phillips Smalley; Crauford Kent; James Burtis; Lloyd Ingraham; Louis Natheaux; Fletcher Norton; ***D:*** Armand Schaefer; ***W:*** Oliver Drake; ***C:*** William Nobles.

The Sinister Urge **WOOF!** *The Young and the Immortal; Hellborn* **1960** Vice cops Duncan and Moore search for the murderer of three women. Seems the disturbed slayer is unbalanced because he's been looking at pictures of naked ladies. Was this meant to be taken seriously at the time? The last film by camp director Wood, maker of the infamous "Plan 9 from Outer Space." A must see for Wood fans. **82m/B; VHS, DVD.** Kenne Duncan; Duke Moore; Jean Fontaine; Carl Anthony; Harvey B. Dunn; Dino Fantini; Reed Howes; Conrad Brooks; ***D:*** Edward D. Wood, Jr.; ***W:*** Edward D. Wood, Jr.; ***C:*** William C. Thompson.

Sink or Swim 1/2 *Hacks* **1997 (R)** TV writer/producer Brian (a suitably hangdog Rea) is suffering from creative burnout and depression. His agent, Danny (Arnold), has just landed Brian a new job writing a TV series that he's dreading. His weekly poker buddies (and fellow writers) offer possible scenarios, amidst their backstabbing, but Brian may have reignited his creative spark after witnessing a romantic encounter between two silhouetted figures in a hotel window. He thinks the woman may be Georgia (Douglas), whom he meets in a bar, and Brian wants her story—at practically any price. **93m/C; VHS, DVD.** Stephen Rea; Illeana Douglas; Tom Arnold; John Ritter; Dave Foley; Richard Kind; Ryan O'Neal; Ricky Jay; Jason Priestley; Olivia D'Abo; Bob Odenkirk; ***D:*** Gary Rosen; ***W:*** Gary Rosen; ***C:*** Ralf Bode; ***M:*** Anthony Marinelli.

Sink the Bismarck **1960** British navy sets out to locate and sink infamous German battleship during WWII. Good special effects with battle sequences in this drama based on real incidents. One of the better of the plethora of WWII movies, with stirring naval battles and stylish documentary-style direction. **97m/B; VHS, DVD.** *GB* Kenneth More; Dana Wynter; Karel Stepanek; Carl Mohner; Laurence Naismith; Geoffrey Keen; Michael Hordern; Maurice Denham; Esmond Knight; Michael Goodliffe; Jack Watling; Jack (Gwyllam) Gwillim; Mark Dignam; Ernest Clark; John Horsley; Sydney Tafler; John Stuart; Walter Hudd; Sean Barrett; Peter Burton; Edward R. Murrow; ***D:*** Lewis Gilbert; ***W:*** Edmund H. North; ***C:*** Christopher Challis; ***M:*** Clifton Parker.

The Sinking of the Laconia 1/2 **2010** Cliched BBC miniseries. When a German U-boat torpedoes the British RMS Laconia in September 1942, the ship is filled with civilians and Italian POWs. The German captain figures out the Laconia was not a warship and tries to rescue survivors by striking a temporary ceasefire. **170m/C; DVD; Closed Captioned.** *GE UK* Andrew Buchan; Ken Duken; Franka Potente; Brian Cox; Thomas Kretschmann; Lindsay Duncan; ***D:*** Uwe Janson; ***W:*** Alan Bleasdale; ***C:*** Michael Schreitel; ***M:*** Adrian Johnston. **TV**

Sinner **2007** Father Romano's faith has been tested by all the scandals in the church and his own parish is teetering on the edge of bankruptcy. Hooker/grifter Lil arrives at the church with the idea of seducing and blackmailing the priest—a con that has worked before. Instead, Father Romano offers cynical Lil sanctuary and a chance to redeem herself while his own belief is rekindled. Good performances by the leads in a strong story. **88m/C; DVD.** Georgina Cates; Nick (Nicholas) Chinlund; Michael E. Rodgers; Brad Dourif; ***D:*** Marc Benardout; ***W:*** Steven Sills; ***C:*** David Kerr; ***M:*** Pinar Toprak.

Sinners **1989** Outrageous portrait of an Italian family in the Big Apple trying to come to terms with the violence that surrounds their neighborhood. **90m/C; VHS, DVD.** Joey Travolta; Robert Gallo; Joe Palese; Lou Calvelli; Angie Daglas; Sabrina Ferrand; ***D:*** Charles Kanganis.

Sinners and Saints 1/2 **2010 (R)** New Orleans detective Sean Reilly is taking all his personal troubles out on the perps, behaving so violently even his sympathetic captain can't ignore his actions. He pairs Reilly with younger detective William Ganz, hoping to rein Reilly in, but their first investigation is a brutal murder and the evidence points to Reilly's old pal Colin. **104m/C; DVD, Blu-Ray.** Johnny Strong; Kevin Phillips; Sean Patrick Flanery; Tom Berenger; Costas Mandylor; Kim Coates; Method Man; ***D:*** William Kaufman; ***W:*** William Kaufman; ***C:*** Mark Rutledge; ***M:*** Johnny Strong. **VIDEO**

Sins 1/2 **1985** On her way up the ladder of success in the fashion industry, Helene has stepped on a few toes. Those rivals and her ever-increasing acquisition of power and money make this film an exciting drama. **336m/C; VHS, DVD.** Joan Collins; Timothy Dalton; Catherine Mary Stewart; Gene Kelly; James Farentino; ***D:*** Douglas Hickox.

Sins of Jezebel **1954** Biblical epic about Jezebel, who worships an evil god. She marries the king of Israel and brings the kingdom nothing but trouble. **74m/C; VHS, DVD.** Paulette Goddard; George Nader; John Hoyt; Eduard Franz; John Shelton; Margia Dean; Joe Besser; Ludwig Donath; ***D:*** Reginald LeBorg; ***W:*** Richard H. Landau; ***C:*** Gilbert Warrenton; ***M:*** Bert Shefter.

Sins of Our Youth 1/2 **2016 (R)** A dramatic thriller about the murder of a young boy and the gun culture in the United States. When four teenagers decide to shoot assault weapons for fun, the unexpected occurs when a young boy is accidentally killed by their gunfire. After the incident, the four teens make plans and decisions that negatively impact the case, their lives, and their futures. **93m/C; DVD, Streaming, Download.** Lucas Till; Joel Courtney; Mitchel Musso; Ally Sheedy; Bridger Zadina; ***D:*** Gary Entin; ***W:*** Edmund Entin; ***C:*** Matthew Irving; ***M:*** Lior Rosner.

The Sins of Rachel Cade **1961** Rachel Cade (Dickinson) is a missionary nurse working in the Belgian Congo at the start of World War II. She manages to win the trust of the local tribe and is smitten when injured RAF volunteer, Dr. Paul Winton (Moore), literally lands at her feet. Rachel succumbs to Paul's blandishments and discovers she's pregnant after he returns home. Belgian administrator Henri Derode (Finch), who is in love with Rachel, informs Paul and he returns but wants Rachel to lie about their previous relationship. She rejects him and realizes she'd chosen the wrong man all along. **122m/C; DVD.** Angie Dickinson; Peter Finch; Roger Moore; Juano Hernandez; Woody Strode; Scatman Crothers; Frederick O'Neal; Mary Wickes; Errol John; ***D:*** Gordon Douglas; ***W:*** Edward Anhalt; ***C:*** J. Peverell Marley; ***M:*** Max Steiner.

Sins of Rome **1954** Spartacus risks it all in a bold attempt to free his fellow slaves. Not nearly the equal of Kirk Douglas's "Spartacus," but much better than later Italian adventure epics. **75m/B; VHS, DVD.** *IT* Ludmilla Tcherina; Massimo Girotti; Gianna Maria Canale; Yves Vincent; ***D:*** Riccardo Freda.

Sins of the Father **2001** Thomas Frank Cherry (Sizemore) is a middle-aged Texan who comes to believe that his father, Bobby Frank Cherry (Jenkins), was one of four KKK members who bombed the Sixteenth Street Baptist Church in Birmingham, Alabama, in 1963. Four young black girls were killed in the explosion and the investigation dragged on and off for 38 years. When the investigation is revived once again, Tom decides to give testimony before a grand jury that casts down on his father's original alibi. Cherry was convicted of murder in 2002. **93m/C; VHS, DVD.** Tom Sizemore; Ving Rhames; Richard Jenkins; Colm Feore; ***D:*** Robert Dornhelm; ***W:*** John Pielmeier; ***C:*** Derick Underschultz; ***M:*** Harald Kloser. **CABLE**

Sinthia: The Devil's Doll **1970** A little girl is thought to be possessed by a demon after she has horrible dreams about killing her father. **78m/C; VHS, DVD.** Shula Roan; Diane Webber; ***D:*** Ray Dennis Steckler.

Sioux City 1/2 **1994 (PG-13)** Jesse Rainfeather Goldman (Phillips) is a Lakota Sioux adopted away from the reservation of his birth and raised in Beverly Hills by a Jewish family. Jesse's curious when his birth mother suddenly contacts him, but when he arrives at the Sioux City reservation, he discovers she's suddenly died under mysterious circumstances. So Jesse sticks around to find out what's going on and discovers his heritage along the way. Well-meaning but dull. **102m/C; VHS, DVD.** Lou Diamond Phillips; Salli Richardson-Whitfield; Melinda Dillon; Ralph Waite; Adam Roarke; Bill Allen; Gary Farmer; ***D:*** Lou Diamond Phillips; ***W:*** L. Virginia Browne; ***M:*** Christopher Lindsey.

Sioux City Sue **1946** Talent scouts looking to cast a western musical find Autry, then trick him into being the voice of a singing donkey in an animated production. But, the yodelin' cowboy belts out a number or two, and the poobahs give him the lead. Singin' and fancy ridin' abound in Autry's first post-WWII role. **69m/B; VHS, DVD.** Gene Autry; Lynne Roberts; Sterling Holloway; Richard Lane; Ralph Sanford; Kenneth Lundy; Pierre Watkin; ***D:*** Frank McDonald; ***W:*** Olive Cooper; ***C:*** Reggie Lanning; ***M:*** R. Dale Butts.

Christmas All Over Again **2016 (PG)** A family Christmas movie that addresses the theme of materialism with humor and a touch of fantasy. Teenage Eddie (Fox) just wants one thing for Christmas: a pair of Breezy 3000s to impress his friends. When Christmas comes, Eddie doesn't get the shoes or anything else. Instead, his family is focusing on the wedding of his elder brother and overlooked Christmas. When Eddie leaves to get over his anger about the family he sees as uncaring, he finds a new shoe store and its owner grants him one wish. When Eddie wishes to have Christmas back the way he wants it, he is given his wish. Eddie soon learns that means he must live the same Christmas day without presents over and over again until he appreciates the true meaning of the holiday. **78m/C; DVD.** Sean Ryan Fox; Joseph Lawrence; Christy Carlson Romano; Amber Montana; Armani Jackson; ***D:*** Christy Carlson Romano; ***W:*** Brendan Rooney; ***C:*** Cory Fraiman-Lott; ***M:*** Gavin James Atkins; Terrence Atkins; Brian Jackson Harris; Michael Wickstrom. **VIDEO**

Siren of the Tropics 1/2 *La Sirene des Tropiques* **1927** In love with a French businessman, West Indies native girl Papitou (Baker) sneaks back to Paris with him—despite his engagement to another woman—but finds her true calling in life as a dancer in music halls. Memorable only as the legendary Baker's film debut, showcasing her stunning dancing abilities. Silent with French soundtrack added. **86m/B; DVD.** Josephine Baker; Pierre Batcheff; Georges Melchior; Regina Dalthy; Regina Thomas; ***D:*** Mario Nalpas; Henri Etievant; ***W:*** Maurice Dekobra.

Sirens 1/2 **1994 (R)** Staid minister Anthony Campion (Grant) takes Australian artist Norman Lindsay to task for submitting scandalous works to public exhibitions. Noted by one reviewer as "Enchanted April with nipples," comedy of manners is witty but lacks plot and looks remarkably like a centerfold layout. Ample displays of nudity as the models (including supermodel MacPherson in her acting debut) frolic in the buff. Grant is terrific as the seemingly enlightened but easily shocked minister, but Neill's Lindsay is thinly written and too often takes a back seat to the vamping models. Fictionalized account of a true incident from the 1930s; Lindsay's home and some of his artworks were used. Check out writer/director Duigan as a pompous village minister. **96m/C; VHS, DVD.** *AU GB* Hugh Grant; Tara Fitzgerald; Sam Neill; Elle Macpherson; Kate Fischer; Portia de Rossi; Pamela Rabe; Ben Mendelsohn; John Polson; Mark Gerber; Julia Stone; Ellie MacCarthy; Vincent Ball; ***Cameo(s):*** John Duigan; ***D:*** John Duigan; ***W:*** John Duigan; ***C:*** Geoff Burton; ***M:*** Rachel Portman.

Sirens **2002** Detective Jay Pearson (Nardini) is investigating a London serial rapist while fending off the unwelcome advances of her boss (Glenister). But soon one of the suspects is leading too close to home—sister Ali's (Parish) shrink boyfriend Oliver (Wise) is on the list. Jay learns the motive is tied to a years-old incident that happened at Oxford and the rapist is out for revenge, which puts her in increasing danger. **180m/C; DVD.** *GB* Daniela Nardini; Greg Wise; Robert Glenister; Sarah Parish; Anthony Calf; ***D:*** Nicholas Laughland; ***W:*** Chris Lang; ***C:*** Dominic Clemence; ***M:*** John Lunn. **TV**

Sirocco 1/2 **1951** An American gunrunner (Bogart) stuck in Syria in 1925 matches wits with a French intelligence officer amid civil war and intrigue. About the underbelly of human affairs. **111m/B; VHS, DVD.** Humphrey Bogart; Lee J. Cobb; Zero Mostel; Everett Sloane; Gerald Mohr; ***D:*** Curtis Bernhardt; ***C:*** Burnett Guffey.

S.I.S. **2008** Spike TV 'guy' movie with lots of action and minimal plot. The Special Investigation Squad is an elite LAPD unit that goes after habitual violent offenders. They're supposed to be on the QT but their controversial methods have drawn the unwelcome attention of police brass. **82m/C; DVD.** Keith David; Peter Stebbings; Christina Cox; Omari Hardwick; Colleen Porch; Matthew Nable; ***D:*** John Herzfeld; ***W:*** John Herzfeld; ***M:*** J. Peter Robinson. **CABLE**

Sister 1/2 *L'Enfant d'en Haut; The Child From Above* **2012** Resolute 12-year-old Simon (Mottet Klein) looks after himself and his emotionally immature, underemployed older sister Louise (Seydoux) by stealing from the rich (vacationers) and giving to the poor (themselves). Living in a dreary apartment below a luxury Swiss ski resort, Simon travels up the mountain and siphons off anything useful and saleable that's left casually lying around by the wealthy guests. Their sense of privilege insulates them from noticing Simon's thievery until some small emotional connections change his world. French with subtitles. **97m/C; DVD.** *FR SI* Kacey Mottet Klein; Lea Seydoux; Martin Compston; Gillian Anderson; *D:* Ursula Meier; *W:* Ursula Meier; Antoine Jaccoud; *C:* Agnes Godard; *M:* John Parish.

Sister Act 🦴🦴 ½ **1992 (PG)** Surprising boxoffice hit casts Goldberg as a Reno lounge singer, Deloris, who's an inadvertent witness to a mob murder by her boyfriend Vince (Keitel). The cops hide her in a convent—where she's as comfortable in a habit as a fish is out of water. Much to the dismay of the poker-faced Mother Superior (Smith), Deloris takes over the rag-tag choir and molds them into a swinging, religious version of a '60s girls group. Stock characters and situations are deflected by some genuinely funny moments and good performances, especially by Najimy and Makkena. Coached by the very clever Shaiman, Whoopi handles her singing bits with gusto, highlight of which is "My God," sung to the tune of "My Guy." **100m/C; VHS, DVD, Blu-Ray.** Whoopi Goldberg; Maggie Smith; Harvey Keitel; Bill Nunn; Kathy Najimy; Wendy Makkena; Mary Wickes; Robert Miranda; Richard Portnow; Joseph Maher; *D:* Emile Ardolino; *W:* Joseph Howard; *C:* Adam Greenberg; *M:* Marc Shaiman.

Sister Act 2: Back in the Habit 🦴🦴 **1993 (PG)** Mediocre retread finds Goldberg once again donning her nun's habit and getting a choir rocking. Deloris has established her singing career in Vegas, but she's persuaded by her nun friends to whip the incorrigible music students at a troubled inner-city high school into shape for an all-state choral competition. The musical numbers and singing are catchy and well-done but Goldberg seems to have phoned her work in; given her reported $7, 000,000 salary, a little more life is expected. She's still sharp with the one-liners but it's all familiar ground. Geared directly towards young viewers. **107m/C; VHS, DVD, Blu-Ray.** Whoopi Goldberg; Kathy Najimy; James Coburn; Maggie Smith; Wendy Makkena; Barnard Hughes; Mary Wickes; Sheryl Lee Ralph; Michael Jeter; Robert Pastorelli; Thomas Gottschalk; Lauryn Hill; Brad Sullivan; Jennifer Love Hewitt; *D:* Bill Duke; *W:* James Orr; Jim Cruickshank; Judi Ann Mason; *C:* Oliver Wood; *M:* Miles Goodman. Blockbuster '95: Comedy Actress, V. (Goldberg).

Sister Aimee: The Aimee Semple McPherson Story 🦴🦴 **2006 (PG)** Famous L.A. evangelist Aimee Semple McPherson (Michaels), founder of the Foursquare Church, disappears from a beach one day in 1926. She reappears a month later, claiming to have been kidnapped, but her story is suspect and rumors fly that the married McPherson was having a tryst with a lover. Rossi then takes a sympathetic look at McPherson's complicated life, beginning with her growing up on a Canadian farm to her conversion and ministry and her problem-plagued personal life. **110m/C; DVD.** Rance Howard; Mimi Michaels; Chad Nadolski; Charles Hoyes; Michael Minor; Etienne Eckert; Richard Rossi; *D:* Richard Rossi; *W:* Richard Rossi; *M:* Richard Rossi. **VIDEO**

The Sister-in-Law 🦴🦴 **1974 (R)** Shady dealings, seduction, and adultery run rampant. Savage (who also wrote and sings the folk score) reluctantly agrees to deliver a package across the Canadian border for his brother. Intriguing. **80m/C; VHS, DVD.** John Savage; Anne Saxon; Will MacMillan; Meridith Baer; *D:* Joseph Rubin.

Sister My Sister 🦴🦴 **1994 (R)** True crime story that served as the inspiration for Jean Genet's play "The Maids." In a French provincial town lives the authoritarian Madame Danzard (Walters), who stifles daughter Isabelle (Thursfield), and subjects her two maids, sisters Christine (Richardson) and Lea (May), to an equally harsh discipline. The tension between the four women reaches a highstrung crescendo, leading to violence. Claustrophobic character study. **89m/C; VHS, DVD.** *GB* Julie Walters; Joely Richardson; Jodhi May; Sophie Thursfield; *D:* Nancy Meckler; *W:* Wendy Kesselman; *C:* Ashley Rowe; *M:* Stephen Warbeck.

Sister, Sister 🦴🦴 **1987 (R)** A Congressional aide on vacation in Louisiana takes a room in an old mansion. He gradually discovers the secret of the house and its resident sisters. Dark Southern gothicism, full of plot surprises, with a twisted ending. **91m/C; VHS, DVD.** Eric Stoltz; Judith Ivey; Jennifer Jason Leigh; Dennis Lipscomb; Anne Pitoniak; Natalija Nogulich; *D:* Bill Condon; *W:* Bill Condon; Joel Cohen; Ginny Cerrella; *M:* Richard Einhorn.

Sister Street Fighter 🦴 **1976** Action star Sonny Chiba takes a rest from his "Street Fighter" series in favor of protege Long, who's determined to deliver her own brand of deadly justice in this martial arts fest. **81m/C; VHS, DVD, Blu-Ray.** Etsuko (Sue) Shihomi; Sonny Chiba; *D:* Kazuhiko Yamaguchi.

Sister Street Fighter 2: Hanging by a Thread 🦴 ½ *Onna hisatsu ken: kiki ippatsu* **1974** Li-Hong Long (Shihomi) returns to rescue a kidnapped heiress and put down a band of smugglers in this uninspired sequel. **85m/C; DVD, Blu-Ray.** *JP* Etsuko (Sue) Shihomi; Tamayo Mitsukawa; Michiyo Bando; Hisayo Tanaka; *D:* Kazuhiko Yamaguchi; *W:* Masahiro Kakefuda; Noribumi Suzuki; *C:* Yoshio Nakajima.

The Sisterhood of the Traveling Pants 🦴🦴 ½ **2005 (PG)** Before heading their own way one summer, four teenage gal pals stumble upon a rare pair of jeans that fits each of them and they pledge to share the jeans via mail while they're apart. Their separate adventures and resulting life lessons are sincere and lively with just a touch of weepiness. Faithful telling of the popular coming-of-age novel by Ann Brashares is highlighted by appealing young actresses. **119m/C; DVD.** America Ferrera; Amber Tamblyn; Alexis Bledel; Jenna Boyd; Blake Lively; Bradley Whitford; Nancy Travis; Rachel Ticotin; Mike Vogel; Kyle Schmid; *D:* Ken Kwapis; *W:* Delia Ephron; Elizabeth Chandler; *C:* John Bailey; *M:* Cliff Eidelman.

The Sisterhood of the Traveling Pants 2 🦴🦴 ½ **2008 (PG-13)** Fast forward three years from the original and the four BFFs have finished up their freshman year at college and are again headed off for different summer destinations. The charm inspired by those magical jeans is starting to fade, despite the earnest girl-powered message about relationships and identity and nice turns by the leads. Not bad, just typical sequel letdown. Drawn from several novels of the Ann Brashares series. **111m/C; Blu-Ray, On Demand.** Blake Lively; Alexis Bledel; America Ferrera; Amber Tamblyn; Rachel Nichols; Shohreh Aghdashloo; Blythe Danner; Kyle MacLachlan; Jesse Williams; Tom Wisdom; Michael Rady; Ernie Lively; *D:* Sanaa Hamri; *W:* Elizabeth Chandler; *C:* Jim Denault; *M:* Rachel Portman.

The Sisters 🦴🦴🦴 **1938** Lavish film of three sisters and their marital problems in turn of the century San Francisco. Davis gives a great performance as the oldest sister with the most trouble—notably in the form of unreliable sports reporter Flynn. Look for Susan Hayward in a bit role, as well as Bogart's wife, Mayo Methot. Based on the bestselling novel by Myron Brinig. **98m/B; VHS, DVD.** Bette Davis; Errol Flynn; Anita Louise; Jane Bryan; Ian Hunter; Henry Travers; Beulah Bondi; Donald Crisp; Dick Foran; Patric Knowles; *D:* Anatole Litvak; *M:* Max Steiner.

Sisters 🦴🦴🦴 **1973 (R)** Siamese twins are separated surgically, but one doesn't survive the operation. The remaining sister is scarred physically and mentally with her personality split into bad and good. And then things really get crazy. DePalma's first ode to Hitchcock, with great music by Hitchcock's favorite composer, Bernard Herrmann. Scary and suspenseful. **93m/C; VHS, DVD.** Margot Kidder; Charles Durning; Barnard Hughes; Jennifer Salt; William Finley; Lisle Wilson; Mary Davenport; Dolph Sweet; *D:* Brian De Palma; *W:* Brian De Palma; Louisa Rose; *C:* Gregory Sandor; *M:* Bernard Herrmann.

The Sisters 🦴 ½ **2005 (R)** Alfieri adapted his play, which was inspired by Anton Chekhov's "The Three Sisters." In this contemporary update, set in a Manhattan college faculty lounge, sisters Olga (Masterson), Marsha (Bello), and Irene (Christensen) gather with their brother Andrew (Nivola) and various lovers and colleagues, most of whom are an insufferable talky bunch. Irene's birthday seems to be just the right time to bring up family secrets and play psychological roulette. Unlike Chekov, this is overwrought yet boring. **113m/C; DVD.** Maria Bello; Mary Stuart Masterson; Erika Christensen; Eric McCormack; Chris O'Donnell; Tony Goldwyn; Steven Culp; Alessandro Nivola; Elizabeth Banks; Rip Torn; *D:* Arthur Allan Seidelman; *W:* Richard Alfieri; *C:* Chuy Chavez; *M:* Thomas Morse.

Sisters 🦴🦴 *The Nest* **2015 (R)** When the home they grew up in is being put up for sale by their parents, 30-something sisters Jane Jones (Fey) and Maura Ellis (Poehler) host a wild weekend-long party there. Fey and Poehler are always good fun when they pair up, and they're the only reason to see this. Writer Pell has woefully given the BFFs some boorish material. They and the audience deserve better. **118m/C; DVD, Blu-Ray.** Tina Fey; Amy Poehler; Heather Matarazzo; Maya Rudolph; John Leguizamo; Ike Barinholtz; *D:* Jason Moore; *W:* Paula Pell; *C:* Barry Peterson; *M:* Christophe Beck.

The Sisters Brothers 🦴🦴 ½ **2018 (R)** In 1850s Oregon, Eli Sisters (Reilly) and his brother Charlie (Phoenix) are cold-blooded hit men who work for dangerous crime boss The Commodore (Haurer). As Eli questions his life, The Commodore gives them a new assignment. They are to kill Hermann Kemit Warm (Ahmed), a criminal who betrayed him. Bounty hunter Morris (Gyllenhaal) is tasked with delivering Warm to the brothers. Once the Morris and the brothers learn that Warm has a way of creating instant wealth, the situation grows more complicated. The English language debut of Audiard is a witty, absurdist take on the Western genre with stand-out performances by the lead actors. **121m/C; DVD, Blu-Ray.** John C. Reilly; Joaquin Rafael (Leaf) Phoenix; Jake Gyllenhaal; Riz Ahmed; Rebecca Root; *D:* Jacques Audiard; *W:* Jacques Audiard; Thomas Bidegain; *C:* Benoît Debie; *M:* Alexandre Desplat.

Sister's Keeper 🦴🦴 **2007 (R)** Low-budget but more than competent action-thriller. Hitman Jake Tate (Faulcon, also the writer/director) takes one last job for handler Malikai (Roberts). He's sent to a southern town to off Diane Shaw (Boutte), who mistakes him for her long-lost brother, which is tied into the disappearance of their mother 30 years before. With his conscience suddenly kicking in, Jake wonders why schoolteacher Diane is targeted even as he develops some not-so-brotherly feelings for her. **101m/C; DVD.** Kent Faulcon; Denise Boutte; Eric Roberts; David Jean Thomas; Gary Poux; Tico Wells; *C:* David Oye; *M:* Felix Byrd. **VIDEO**

Sisters of Death 🦴🦴 **1976 (PG)** Five members of a sorority gather together for a reunion in a remote California town. Little do they know, a psychopath is stalking them, one by one. Could it have something to do with the terrible secret they each keep? Good, cheap thrills and some Bicentennial fashions to boot. **87m/C; VHS, DVD.** Arthur Franz; Claudia Jennings; Cheri Howell; Sherry Boucher; Paul Carr; *D:* Joseph Mazzuca.

Sisters of the Gion 🦴🦴 *Gion No Shimai* **1936** Story follows two geisha sisters, illuminating the plight of women in Japan. Elder sister Umekichi is traditional and dependent on her patrons while her modern younger sister Omocha exploits her customers as much as possible. But no matter the difference in their attitudes, both remain trapped by circumstances. Adapted from the novel "Yama" by Alexander Ivanovich Kuprin. Japanese with subtitles. **66m/B; VHS, DVD.** *JP* Isuzu Yamada; Yoko Umemura; Eitaro Shindo; Benkei Shiganoya; *D:* Kenji Mizoguchi; *W:* Kenji Mizoguchi; Yoshikata Yoda; *C:* Minoru Miki.

Sisters of War 🦴🦴 ½ **2010** An Australian TV movie based on a true story. In 1942, the tiny Papua New Guinea mission station of Vunapope, staffed by Australian nuns and nurses, is overrun by Japanese troops. As POWs, Army nurse Lorna Whyte (Snook) and Sister Berenice Twohill (van der Boom) work together with their captors to continue to care for the wounded during great adversity. Be warned there are some disturbing episodes, including a bombing run and executions. **96m/C; DVD.** *AU* Claire Van Der Boom; Sara Snook; Khan Chittenden; Anna Volska; Susie Porter; Kentaro Hara; Gerald Lepkowski; *D:* Brendan Maher; *W:* John Misto; *C:* Ben Nott. **TV**

Sisters, Or the Balance of Happiness 🦴🦴 *Schwestern Oder die Balance des Glucks* **1979** Orderly Maria (Lampe) runs the household for her resentful, dependent sister Anna (Gabriel). Opposites in temperment, the dysfunctional duo can neither live with or without each other. When Anna commits suicide, Maria tries to makeover young typist Miriam (Fruh) to take her sister's place. German with subtitles. **97m/C; VHS, DVD.** *GE* Jutta Lampe; Gudrun Gabriel; Jessica Fruh; *D:* Margarethe von Trotta; *W:* Margarethe von Trotta; *C:* Franz Rath; *M:* Konstantin Wecker.

Sit Tight 🦴🦴 **1931** Winnie (Lightner) runs a health clinic where she and smitten employee Jojo (Brown) are training Paul (Weston) to become a championship wrestler. Unfortunately for Jojo, he's the one who gets in the ring with angry masked hulk Olaf (Hagney) who thinks Jojo is stepping out with his wife. **75m/B; DVD.** Joe E. Brown; Paul Gregory; Claudia Dell; Hobart Bosworth; Snitz Edwards; Winnie Lightner; Frank S. Hagney; *D:* Lloyd Bacon; *W:* William K. Wells; Rex Taylor; *C:* William Rees.

Sitcom 🦴🦴 **1997** Family dysfunction taken to the extreme. There's a pet rat, a new maid whose African husband seduces the son of the family, a daughter who becomes a paraplegic dominatrix, orgies, incest, and dad, who kills everyone when they throw him a surprise birthday party. Or does he? Or does it matter, anyway? French with subtitles. **80m/C; VHS, DVD.** *FR* Evelyne Dandry; Francois Marthouret; Marina de Van; Adrien de Van; Stephane Rideau; Lucia Sanchez; Jules-Emmanuel Eyoum Deido; *D:* Francois Ozon; *W:* Francois Ozon; *C:* Yorick Le Saux; *M:* Eric Neveux.

The Sitter 🦴 *While the Children Sleep* **2007** Predictable Lifetime cable movie about a pretty psycho with a shovel. After Meghan (O'Grady) decides to go back to work, eager Abby (Klaveno) becomes the Eastmans live-in babysitter. Turns out she has an unexpected tie to lawyer dad Carter (Moses) that he apparently doesn't remember. But she is really, really grateful—like "get rid of anybody who causes a problem so she can have Carter to herself" grateful. **88m/C; DVD.** William R. Moses; Gail O'Grady; Stacy Haiduk; Mariana Klaveno; *D:* Russell Mulcahy; *W:* Stephen Niver; *C:* Maximo Munzi; *M:* Elia Cmiral. **TV**

The Sitter 🦴 ½ **2011 (R)** Noah (Hill) wants to help his divorced mom have a night out and agrees to babysit her friend's kids: awkward Slater (Records), outgoing Blithe (Bender), and dangerous Rodrigo (Hernandez). The quartet ends up having a madcap adventure involving theft, explosions, and assault in New York City after Noah drags them into the Big Apple on a quest for drugs to satisfy his needy girlfriend (Graynor). Hill is as likeable an actor as they come, but isn't suited for director Green's disappointing and inconsistent second stoner comedy flick in a year's time ("Your Highness"). **81m/C; DVD, Blu-Ray.** Jonah Hill; Sam Rockwell; Ari Graynor; J.B. Smoove; Method Man; Max Records; Kevin Hernandez; Landry Bender; Bruce Altman; Jessica Hecht; *D:* David Gordon Green; *W:* Brian Gatewood; Alessandro Tanaka; *C:* Tim Orr; *M:* David Wingo; Jeff McIlwain.

Sitting Bull 🦴🦴 **1954** Thanks to Cody acting as an advisor, this take on Little Big Horn was more sympathetic to the plight of the Native Americans than the typical western. Sioux chief Sitting Bull (Naish) calls for patience while Crazy Horse (Cody) wants war against the white interlopers. Maj. Bob Parrish (Robertson) gets court-martialed for siding with the Injuns against bloodthirsty Col. Custer (Kennedy). President Grant (Hamilton) wants Parrish to pow-wow with Sitting Bull but there's more trouble coming. **105m/B; DVD.** Dale Robertson; J. Carrol Naish; Iron Eyes Cody; Mary Murphy; Douglas Kennedy; John Litel; Josh Hamilton; Joel Fluellen; William Hopper; *D:* Sidney Salkow; *W:* Sidney

Salkow; Jack DeWitt; *C:* Charles Van Enger; *M:* Raoul Kraushaar.

Sitting Ducks ✐✐✐ **1980 (R)** Mild-mannered accountant and lecherous pal rip off and then attempt to outrun the mob—all while swapping songs and confessions. Emil and Norman make it up as they go along; their hilarious repartee is largely improvised. They pick up a gorgeous lady (Townsend) and go about their way. **88m/C; VHS, DVD.** Michael Emil; Zack Norman; Patrice Townsend; Richard Romanus; Irene Forrest; Henry Jaglom; *D:* Henry Jaglom; *W:* Henry Jaglom.

Sitting On the Moon ✐ ½ **1936** Songwriter Danny leaves longtime musical partner Mike to help the fading career of movie star Polly Blair. Mike takes up with Polly's pal Mattie but is really plotting to break up the happy twosome by getting bombshell Blossom to try a little blackmail by claiming Danny married her while drunk. **76m/B; DVD.** Roger Pryor; William "Billy" Newell; Grace Bradley; Pert Kelton; Joyce Compton; Henry Kolker; Henry Wadsworth; *D:* Ralph Staub; *W:* Raymond L. Schrock; *C:* Ernest Miller.

Sitting Pretty ✐✐✐ **1948** Webb is a delight in his Oscar-nominated role as the prissy Lynn Belvedere, who takes a job as a babysitter to the three hellion sons of Harry (Young) and Tacey (O-Hara) in their typical suburban community. Mr. Belvedere has soon wrangled the family in line but there's more to the man than his superior skills. It seems he's doing research and writing on expose on life in the suburbs, which becomes a best-seller and a local scandal. Followed by "Mr. Belvedere Goes to College" and "Mr. Belvedere Rings the Bell." Based on the novel "Belvedere" by Gwen Davenport. **84m/B; DVD, Blu-Ray, Streaming.** Clifton Webb; Robert Young; Maureen O'Hara; Richard Haydn; Louise Allbritton; Randy Stuart; Ed Begley, Sr.; *D:* Walter Lang; *W:* F. Hugh Herbert; *C:* Norbert Brodine; *M:* Alfred Newman.

Sitting Target ✐✐ **1972** Fast-paced Brit pulp crime thriller. Vicious convicted killer Harry Lomart (Reed) breaks out of prison with fellow inmate Birdy Williams (McShane) to go after his unfaithful, pregnant wife Pat (St. John). They head to London where Inspector Milton (Woodward) is guarding the wayward missus. **93m/C; DVD.** *UK* Oliver Reed; Edward Woodward; Jill St. John; Ian McShane; Frank Finlay; Freddie Jones; Jill Townsend; *D:* Douglas Hickox; *W:* Alexander Jacobs; *C:* Edward (Ted) Scaife; *M:* Stanley Myers.

The Situation ✐ ½ **2006 (R)** Slack pacing and a colorless romantic triangle doom this Iraqi War story to boredom. Journalist Anna (Nielsen) is working in Baghdad. Her friend with benefits is American intelligence agent Dan (Lewis). Iraqi photographer Zaid (Hamada) is in love with her although he struggles with their cultural differences. When a close contact of Anna's is killed in an apparent political assassination, Anna and Zaid want to break the story but leads are elusive and they find themselves being manipulated by various factions—American and Iraqi. English and Arabic with subtitles. **106m/C; DVD.** Damian Lewis; Nasser Memarzia; John Slattery; Connie Neilsen; Mido Hamada; Said Amadia; Driss Roukh; *D:* Philip Haas; *W:* Wendell Steavenson; *C:* Sean Bobbitt; *M:* Jeff Beal.

6 Below: Miracle on the Mountain ✐✐ **2017 (PG-13)** A faith-based story of survival, based on true events in the life of Eric LeMarque (Hartnett). When the former pro hockey player goes snowboarding in the Sierra Nevada Mountains, he unexpectedly becomes lost when a storm hits and wanders around for eight days. As he suffers from lack of food, water, and warmth, he reflects on his problematic past, including a complicated relationship with his demanding father (Cottle) and his drug addiction. Though Eric is unsure he will make it out alive, his mother (Sorvino) takes action to save him. The lack of suspense and tedious pacing make the film less than compelling. **89m/C; DVD.** Josh Hartnett; Mira Sorvino; Sarah Dumont; Kale Culley; Jason Cottle; *D:* Scott Waugh; *W:* Madison Turner; *C:* Michael Svitak; *M:* Nathan Furst.

6 Bullets ✐✐ **2012 (R)** After his daughter is kidnapped by Russian sex traffickers, MMA fighter Andrew Fayden (Flanigan) persuades former mercenary Samson Gaul (Van Damme) to come out of retirement and get her back. Action flick with ethics doesn't completely work but Van Damme is good and takes his weight-of-the-world character seriously. **93m/C; DVD.** Jean-Claude Van Damme; Joe Flanigan; Anna-Louise Plowman; Charlotte Beaumont; Steve Nicolson; Uriel Emil Pollack; *D:* Ernie Barbarash; *W:* Chad Law; Evan Law; *C:* Phil Parmet; *M:* Neal Acree. **VIDEO**

Six Days, Seven Nights ✐✐ ½ **1998 (PG-13)** Brash magazine editor Robin Monroe (Heche) is on a tropical vacation with fiance Frank (Schwimmer) when a deadline crisis forces her to ask gruff cargo pilot Quinn Harris (Ford) for a lift to Tahiti. A plane crash strands the incompatible duo on a remote island and naturally they need each other to survive. This started out as a routine romantic comedy but the action quotient was upped as filming progressed, thanks to a storyline involving modern-day pirates that's a waste of time. Also a waste are scenes involving Frank with Quinn's bodacious babe, Angelica (Obradors). Why does the only other woman with a significant part have to be a coochie-coo Charo impersonator? Thankfully, Ford and Heche do have considerable sass between them. Filmed on location in Kauai. **101m/C; VHS, DVD.** Harrison Ford; Anne Heche; David Schwimmer; Temuera Morrison; Jacqueline Obradors; Allison Janney; Danny Trejo; *D:* Ivan Reitman; *W:* Michael Browning; *C:* Michael Chapman; *M:* Randy Edelman.

Six Days, Six Nights ✐✐ *A la Folie* **1994 (R)** Two French sisters—the older and competitive Elsa (Dalle) and the creative and evasive Alice (Parillaud)?move to New York with Alice's boxer boyfriend (Aurignac). Sex and heartbreak ensues, as it usually does. French with subtitles. **96m/C; DVD.** Anne Parillaud; Beatrice Dalle; Patrick Aurignac; *D:* Diane Kurys; *W:* Diane Kurys; Antoine Lacomblez.

6 Degrees of Hell ✐ **2012** Six random individuals are caught up by a web of coincidences when a demon is unleashed at a haunted house attraction. **92m/C; DVD, Blu-Ray, Streaming.** Corey Feldman; Jill Whelan; Brian Anthony Wilson; Nikki Bell; Brian Gallagher; *D:* Joe Raffa; *W:* Harrison Smith; *C:* Charlie Anderson; *M:* John Avarese. **VIDEO**

Six Degrees of Separation ✐✐ ½ **1993 (R)** Some believe that any two people, anywhere in the world, are connected by links to only six other people, hence the six degrees of separation. For the upper crust New Yorker Kittredges, Ouisa (Channing) and Flan (Sutherland), this becomes an issue when they encounter a charming young man (Smith) who claims to be Sidney Poitier's son and a friend of their children. The story unfolds as they realize they've been hustled—and don't understand why. Guare adapted his hit play, but what worked well there is almost too talky here. Channing, reprising her stage role, is very good as the stuffy Ouisa, with Sutherland delivering another interesting performance. Incredibly, the play was based on a true story. **112m/C; VHS, DVD.** Stockard Channing; Will Smith; Donald Sutherland; Mary Beth Hurt; Bruce Davison; Ian McKellen; Richard Masur; Anthony Michael Hall; Heather Graham; Eric Thal; Anthony Rapp; Oz (Osgood) Perkins, II; Kitty Carlisle Hart; Catherine Kellner; *D:* Fred Schepisi; *W:* John Guare; *C:* Ian Baker; *M:* Jerry Goldsmith.

6 Guns ✐ **2010 (R)** Selina asks bounty hunter Frank to teach her how to be a gunslinger so she can go after the men who killed her family. Unfortunately, there's more standing around and talking than gun action in this sub-par western. **90m/C; DVD.** Sage Mears; Barry Van Dyke; Greg Evigan; Brian Wimmer; Jonathan Nation; Carey Van Dyke; Geoff Meed; Shane Van Dyke; *D:* Shane Van Dyke; *W:* Geoff Meed; *C:* Alexander Yellen; *M:* Chris Ridenhour. **VIDEO**

600 Miles ✐✐ ½ *600 Millas* **2016 (R)** A dramatic thriller about a kidnapping turned road trip and unexpected connections. When ATF agent Hank Harris (Roth) tries to arrest Arnulfo Rubio (Ferrer), a weapons runner for a Mexican cartel, Rubio turns the tables by kidnapping him instead. Intending on bringing Harris to his superiors at the cartel, Rubio and Harris drive for 600 miles across Mexico. During the drive, the two men, who should be enemies, establish a bond of friendship. **85m/C; DVD, Streaming, Download.** Tim Roth; Kristyan Ferrer; Monica Del Carmen; Greg Lutz; Harrison Thomas; *D:* Gabriel Ripstein; *W:* Gabriel Ripstein; Issa Lopez; *C:* Alain Marcoen. **VIDEO**

633 Squadron ✐✐ ½ **1964** A skilled R.A.F. pilot attempts to lead his squadron on a mission deep into the fjords of Norway in search of a Nazi fuel plant. Robertson tries hard, as always, but is really not British officer material. Well-made war flick, based on a true story. **102m/C; VHS, DVD.** Cliff Robertson; George Chakiris; Maria Perschy; Harry Andrews; *D:* Walter Grauman; *W:* James Clavell.

Six in Paris ✐✐ ½ *Paris vu Par* **1968** Six short films by acclaimed French New Wave directors, each depicting a different Parisian neighborhood. "Saint-Germain-des-Pres" finds an American girl disillusioned by two French boys. "Gare du Nord" has a woman meeting a handsome stranger who announces he's going to kill himself. A shy dishwasher brings a prostitute to his room in the "Rue Saint-Denis." When a salesman is accosted by a derelict in the "Place de l'Etoile" he hits him with his umbrella and then thinks he's killed the man. "Montparnasse-Levallois" has a woman thinking she's mixed-up her meetings with her two lovers. "La Muette" finds a small boy buying earplugs to shut out the noise of his parents constant arguing. In French with English subtitles. **93m/C; VHS, DVD.** *FR* Barbara Wilkin; Jean-Francois Chappey; Jean-Pierre Andreani; Nadine Ballot; Barbet Schroeder; Gilles Queant; Micheline Dax; Claude Melki; Jean-Michel Rouziere; Marcel Gallon; Joanna Shimkus; Philippe Hiquilly; Serge Davri; Stephane Audran; Gilles Chusseau; Dinah Saril; Claude Chabrol; *D:* Jean Douchet; Jean Rouch; Jean-Daniel Pollet; Eric Rohmer; Jean-Luc Godard; Claude Chabrol; *W:* Jean Douchet; George Keller; Jean Rouch; Jean-Daniel Pollet; Eric Rohmer; Jean-Luc Godard; Claude Chabrol; *C:* Nestor Almendros.

Six Pack ✐ ½ **1982 (PG)** The Gambler goes auto racing. Rogers, in his theatrical debut, stars as Brewster Baker, a former stock car driver. He returns to the racing circuit with the help of six larcenous orphans (the six-pack, get it?) adept at stripping cars. Kinda cute if you're in the mood for sugar-powered race car story. **108m/C; VHS, DVD.** Kenny Rogers; Diane Lane; Erin Gray; Barry Corbin; Anthony Michael Hall; *D:* Daniel Petrie; *M:* Charles Fox.

Six-Pack Annie ✐ **1975** Cornpone AIP exploitation. Busty, blonde, hotpants-wearing hillbilly Annie (Bloom) and her sister Mary Lou (Bellan) work at their Aunt Tess' (Hansen) diner. It's going into bank foreclosure unless they can get $5,000 so the gals head for Miami where older sister Flora (Moritz) has been boasting about her wealth. Turns out she's not rich and is working as a hooker. She gets her sisters working to find a sugar daddy but neither of them seem very competent. **88m/C; DVD.** Lindsay Bloom; Jana Bellan; Louisa Moritz; Danna Hansen; Joe Higgins; Ray Danton; Bruce Boxleitner; *D:* Fred G. Thorne; *W:* Norman Winski; David Kidd; *C:* Daniel Lacambre; *M:* Raoul Kraushaar.

6 Plots ✐ ½ **2012 (R)** A thriller centered how a fear of death can affect your perspective. Brie (Darling) and her underage friends spend a night partying together. The next morning Brie wakes up alone. Her friends are missing. After she receives a mysterious phone call, she learns that their fate is in her hands and that they will lose their lives unless she can solve a series of puzzles. **87m/C; DVD, Streaming, Download.** Alice Darling; Ryan Corr; Penelope Mitchell; Joey Coley-Sowry; Emily Wheaton; *D:* Leigh Sheehan; *W:* Tim C. Patterson; *M:* Frank Strangio.

666: The Beast ✐ **2007** Think "Omen" sequels rip-off. Devil child Donald Lawson is now a Harvard grad with no memory of the horrible things he did growing up. But he soon learns that his destiny is to become the Antichrist unless a priest sent by the Vatican to L.A. can stop him. **85m/C; DVD.** Chad Mathews; Collin Brock; Makinna Ridgway; Amol Shah; Alma Saraci; Stephen Blackehart; Doug Burch; *D:* Nick Everhart; *W:* Nick Everhart; *C:* Bianca Bahena. **VIDEO**

666: The Child ✐ **2006** Yep, "Omen" wannabe. A boy named Donald is the only survivor of an airline crash but the couple who adopt him soon realize he's evil incarnate as death seems to accompany him wherever he goes. Donald even has a bad nanny named 'Lucy Fir' (think about it a moment). **81m/C; DVD.** Booboo Stewart; Adam Vincent; Sarah Lieving; Rodney Bowman; Nora Jesse; Kim Little; *D:* Jack Perez; *W:* Benjamin Henry; Austin Laurel; *C:* Lucia Diaz Sas; *M:* Mel Lewis. **VIDEO**

6 Souls ✐ *Shelter* **2013 (R)** The always-great Moore missteps in this nearly straight-to-video thriller (shot in 2009, released in 2013) that lacks the thrills for a mass audience and the smarts for a specialized one. Moore plays Cara Harding, a female forensic psychiatrist investigating the case of a patient (Rhys Meyers) who has multiple personalities. She realizes that each of the young man's individual personalities is a murder victim and questions whether he is being possessed by the recently and brutally deceased. Too many jump scares and too many twists, this is six movies in one and none of them work. **112m/C; DVD, Blu-Ray, Streaming.** Julianne Moore; Jonathan Rhys Meyers; Jeffrey DeMunn; Frances Conroy; Nathan (Nate) Corddry; Brooklynn Proulx; *D:* Mans Marlind; Bjorn Stein; *W:* Michael Cooney; *C:* Linus Sandgren; *M:* John (Gianni) Frizzell.

Six-String Samurai ✐✐ **1998 (PG-13)** In 1957 the USSR bombs and assumes control of the U.S., and Las Vegas is the only safe haven of freedom. Forty years later, a rock musician/samurai is on an odyssey across the desert to replace the recently deceased Elvis as king of the neon city; challenging his quest is another guitar-slinger, Death (Gauger), and his cronies. Our hero Buddy (played by martial artist Falcon as a cross between Buddy Holly and Yojimbo) and his sidekick The Kid (McGuire) must face all the bad guys we've come to expect in a post-apocalyptic adventure. Filled with campy dialogue and well-staged Hong Kong-style action (directed by Falcon), basically all the makings of a good midnight movie, but it doesn't quite come together. **89m/C; VHS, DVD.** Jeffrey Falcon; Justin McGuire; Stephane Gauger; John Sakisian; *D:* Lance Mungia; *W:* Jeffrey Falcon; Lance Mungia; *C:* Kristian Bernier; *M:* Brian Tyler.

Six Strong Guys ✐✐ *Luk jong si* **2004** Four stressed-out men meet on a rooftop of an office block planning to commit suicide. Agreeing to give themselves three hours to say goodbye and settle their affairs, they are surprised when two more men join them with the same self-destructive intentions. Their typical male problems (unhappy marriages, evil ex-girlfriends, stressful jobs, impotence) are exaggerated for effect. Despite the attempts at comedy, suicide isn't terribly funny, and while this film tries, it can only go so far. **107m/C; DVD.** *HK* Ekin Cheng; Hacken Lee; Andy Hui; Chapman To; *D:* Chun-Chun Wong; *W:* Chun-Chun Wong; *C:* Man Po Cheung; *M:* Ken Chan.

Six: The Mark Unleashed ✐ ½ **2004** Christian-themed flick set in a near-future where religion has been usurped by a cult-like leader who demands all his adherents wear a mark to prove their allegiance. Those that don't are thrown into prison and given a month to change their minds or be executed. Car thieves Brody and Jerry wind up in the slammer alongside Luke, who claims to talk to God, and ex-cop Tom, who has been tortured into agreeing to assassinate a Christian leader after plotting an escape with the thieves. **106m/C; DVD.** Kevin Downes; Brad Heller; Amy Moon; David A.R. White; Jeffrey Dean Morgan; Stephen Baldwin; Eric Roberts; Troy Winbush; *D:* Kevin Downes; *W:* Kevin Downes; Chipper Lowell; David A.R. White; *C:* Philip Hurn; *M:* Marc Fantini; Steffan Fantini. **VIDEO**

6 Underground ✐✐ *Six Underground* **2019 (R)** One (Reynolds) is an eccentric billionaire who faked his own death to go underground and lead a team of mercenaries, each with their own specialty, to take actions governments cannot. His team includes a CIA spook (Laurent), a hitman (Garcia-Rulfo), and a sniper with PTSD (Hawins). The team deposes the cruel dictator of Turgistan and works to replace him with a peace lover. Though the film features signature Bay action sequences and other visuals, its tone is troubling because the violence is directed at groups like children in refugee camps and it takes on complex issues, such as Middle Eastern politics, in a superficial manner. **128m/C; DVD.** Ryan Reynolds; Melanie Laurent; Manuel Garcia-Rulfo; Ben Hardy; Adria Arjona; *D:* Michael Bay; *W:* Paul Wernick; Rhett Reese; *C:* Bojan Bazelli; *M:* Lorne Balfe.

Six Ways to Sunday 🦴🦴 **1999 (R)** Weird mob drama about a hitman and his Oedipal relationship with mom. Passive, repressed teenager, Harry Odum (Reedus), lives with his domineering mother, Kate (Harry), who controls his life. That is, until Harry assists his hoodlum buddy Arnie (Brody) with a job and manages to impress Arnie's boss, Mr. Varga (Adler). Since Harry turns out to have a latent talent for violence, he's soon elevated to hit man—although mom's still a problem. Based on the 1962 novel "Portrait of a Young Man Drowning" by Charles Perry. **97m/C; VHS, DVD.** Norman Reedus; Deborah Harry; Adrien Brody; Jerry Adler; Peter Appel; Elina Lowensohn; Isaac Hayes; Anna Thomson; David Ross; *D:* Adam Bernstein; *W:* Adam Bernstein; Marc Gerald; *C:* John Inwood; *M:* Theodore Shapiro.

Six Weeks 🦴🦴 **1982 (PG)** A young girl dying of leukemia brings together her work-driven mother and an aspiring married politician. Manipulative hanky-wringer has good acting from both Moores but oddly little substance. **107m/C; VHS, Streaming.** Dudley Moore; Mary Tyler Moore; Katherine Healy; *D:* Tony Bill; *M:* Dudley Moore.

The Six Wives of Henry Lefay 🦴 **2009 (PG-13)** Completely crass comedy that wastes its familiar cast and their talents. Chronic horndog Henry (Allen) is presumed drowned during a Mexico vacation and his daughter Barbara (Cuthbert) is left to make funeral arrangements (minus a body). Unfortunately for her, Henry has a plethora of exes who all have opinions (and delusions) about their role in Henry's life and are certain only they can fulfill Henry's final wishes. **95m/C; DVD, Blu-Ray.** Tim Allen; Elisha Cuthbert; Andie MacDowell; Jenna Elfman; Paz Vega; Lindsay Sloane; Jenna Dewan; S. Epatha Merkerson; Chris Klein; Eric Christian Olsen; Barbara Barrie; Edward Herrmann; *D:* Howard Michael Gould; *W:* Howard Michael Gould; *C:* Nancy Schreiber; *M:* Stephen Barton. **VIDEO**

Six Wives of Henry VIII 🦴🦴🦴 **1971** Michell has been called the definitive Henry VIII, and this BBC Classic (shown as part of "Masterpiece Theatre" on PBS) was perhaps the most praised series on British TV. Henry's wives were: Catherine of Aragon, Anne Boleyn, Jane Seymour, Anne of Cleves, Catherine Howard, and Catherine Parr. Each episode tells of their (sometimes tragic) fates as pawns in Henry's quest for an heir, and his changes from an eager young man to aged, bitter monarch. **540m/C; VHS, DVD.** *GB* Keith Michell; Annette Crosbie; Dorothy Tutin; Anne Stallybrass; Elvi Hale; Angela Pleasence; Rosalie Crutchley; *D:* John Glenister; Naomi Capon. **TV**

Sixteen 🦴🦴 *Like a Crow on a June Bug* **1972 (R)** A naive country lass is attracted to the glitter and hum of the outside world. Her determination and optimism help her triumph. **84m/C; VHS, DVD.** Mercedes McCambridge; Parley Baer; Ford Rainey; Beverly (Hills) Powers; John Lozier; Simone Griffeth; Maidie Norman; *D:* Lawrence (Larry) Dobkin.

16 Blocks 🦴🦴🦴 **2006 (PG-13)** Willis lets himself go to seed as alcoholic NYPD detective Jack Moseley, a burnout who's been corrupted by the job and is just waiting to collect his pension. He's assigned to transport motor-mouthed witness Eddie Bunker (Mos Def) to a grand jury hearing 16 blocks from the station. Easy—until someone starts shooting at them. Jack calls for backup only to discover that Eddie is testifying about some bad cops, including Jack's ex-partner Frank Nugent (a menacing Morse), who isn't about to let that happen. Donner directed the "Lethal Weapon" series, so he knows how to keep things moving. **105m/C; DVD, Blu-Ray, HD-DVD.** Bruce Willis; Mos Def; David Morse; Cylk Cozart; Casey Sander; David Zayas; Jenna Stern; Robert Racki; *D:* Richard Donner; *W:* Richard Wenk; *C:* Glen MacPherson; *M:* Klaus Badelt.

Sixteen Candles 🦴🦴🦴 **1984 (PG)** Almost 25 years after hitting the theatres, "Sixteen Candles" is still popular—reaching near cult status among generation X-ers. Hilarious comedy of errors features the pouty Ringwald as an awkard teen who's been dreaming of her 16th birthday. But the rush of her sister's wedding causes everyone to forget, turning her birthday into her worst nightmare. Hughes may not be critically acclaimed, but his movies are so popular they nearly take on a life of their own. Ringwald and Hall are especially charming as the angst-ridden teens, encountering one trauma after another. Great soundtrack includes the title song by The Stray Cats. **93m/C; VHS, DVD, Blu-Ray.** Molly Ringwald; Justin Henry; Michael Schoeffling; Haviland (Haylie) Morris; Gedde Watanabe; Anthony Michael Hall; Paul Dooley; Carlin Glynn; Blanche Baker; Edward Andrews; Carole Cook; Max (Casey Adams) Showalter; Liane (Alexandra) Curtis; John Cusack; Joan Cusack; Brian Doyle-Murray; Jami Gertz; Cinnamon Idles; Zelda Rubinstein; Billie Bird; *D:* John Hughes; *W:* John Hughes; *C:* Bobby Byrne; *M:* Ira Newborn.

16 Wishes 🦴🦴 **2010 (G)** Disney Channel pic intended for tween girls. Abby Jensen (Ryan) has been making a sweet 16 birthday wish list since she was eight. The big day is here and Abby is given a box of 16 magical birthday candles by the mysterious Celeste (Routledge). Each candle represents a wish that comes true, but when Abby impulsively wishes to be treated as an adult that wish doesn't quite work out as she expects. **90m/C; DVD, Blu-Ray.** Debby Ryan; Jean-Luc Bilodeau; Anna Mae Wills; Karissa Tynes; Kendall Cross; Patrick Gillmore; Cainan Wiebe; *D:* Peter DeLuise; *W:* Annie DeYoung; *C:* Michael Lohmann; *M:* James Jandrisch. **CABLE**

16 Years of Alcohol 🦴🦴 **2003 (R)** Abandoned by his mother as a child and raised by an abusive, alcoholic father, Frankie grows up a drunk who leads a brutal gang in Edinburgh. But when he falls in love he decides to straighten up. Former punk rocker and first-time director Richard Jobson loosely adapts his life story. **96m/C; VHS, DVD.** *GB* Kevin McKidd; Ewen Bremner; Laura Fraser; Susan Lynch; Stuart Sinclair Blyth; Lisa May Cooper; Lewis Macleod; *D:* Richard Jobson; *W:* Richard Jobson; *C:* John Rhodes. **VIDEO**

Sixth and Main 🦴🦴 **1977** Wrier Monica (Garland) is hanging out in an L.A. slum to get inspiration for a book when she meets a man calling himself John Doe (Nielsen). Discovering he's written a number of manuscripts, she slips them to a critic, thinking she's discovered a new talent. Instead, Monica learns John's a once-successful screenwriter who deliberately left that life behind and doesn't want to be reminded of the past. **103m/C; DVD.** Leslie Nielsen; Beverly Garland; Joe Maross; Leo Penn; Roddy McDowall; *D:* Christopher Cain; *W:* Christopher Cain; *C:* Hilyard John Brown; *M:* Bob Summers.

The 6th Day 🦴🦴 ½ **2000 (PG-13)** Arnold's a family guy in the near-future who finds out a clone has taken over his life. Not only that, but the evil corporation behind the clone doesn't want the original around to muck up their nefarious plans. Typical (although somewhat toned-down) Ah-nuld type mayhem ensues. Schwarzenegger has fun with his image, and the supporting players get some fine moments, too. Thought-provoking questions about human cloning add an interesting dimension, raising this one slightly above the genre-pic/star-vehicle level. **124m/C; VHS, DVD.** Arnold Schwarzenegger; Tony Goldwyn; Sarah Wynter; Michael Rooker; Robert Duvall; Michael Rapaport; Wendy Crewson; Rodney Rowland; Ken Pogue; Wanda Cannon; Christopher Lawford; Terry Crews; Colin Cunningham; Taylor Anne Reid; Jennifer Gareis; Don McManus; Steve Bacic; *D:* Roger Spottiswoode; *W:* Cormac Wibberley; Marianne S. Wibberley; *C:* Pierre Mignot; *M:* Trevor Rabin.

The Sixth Man 🦴 ½ **1997 (PG-13)** College basketball star Antoine Tyler (Hardison) dies but returns as a ghost to help his brother (Wayans) lead their team to the NCAA finals. Basketball seems to be the sport of choice for Hollywood lately, so you'd think they'd be able to get one of these movies right. Once again, they blow the layup. The first half features the requisite flashback and tear-jerker death scene, both of which are surprisingly effective. But then the focus turns to "hilarious" on-court hijinks and the all-time sports cliche champion: the second-half rally from an impossible deficit. Hardison and Wayans are the bright spots, displaying fine comic and dramatic chemistry. **107m/C; VHS, DVD.** Kadeem Hardison; Marlon Wayans; David Paymer; Michael Michele; Kevin Dunn; Vladimir Cuk; Chris Spencer; Kirk Baily; Saundra McClain; Lorenzo Orr; Travis Ford; Harold Sylvester; *D:* Randall Miller; *W:* Christopher Reed; Cynthia Carle; *C:* Michael Ozier; *M:* Marcus Miller.

The Sixth Sense 🦴🦴🦴 **1999 (PG-13)** Creepy psycho thriller about a traumatized young boy who can communicate with the dead (this is not the film's big surprise). Failed child shrink Malcolm Crowe (Willis in an excellent subdued performance) takes on the case of 9-year-old Cole (a touching Osment, carrying the picture on frail shoulders), who's divorced mom, Lynn (Collette), is worried about her terrified son's nightmares and episodes of acting out. Well, if you saw dead people all the time, you'd be scared too. When Crowe (who's dealing with traumas of his own) finally believes Cole, it leads to a breakthrough and an unexpected twist on what's happened before. **107m/C; VHS, DVD, Blu-Ray.** Bruce Willis; Haley Joel Osment; Toni Collette; Olivia Williams; Donnie Wahlberg; Glenn Fitzgerald; Trevor Morgan; Mischa Barton; Bruce Norris; *D:* M. Night Shyamalan; *W:* M. Night Shyamalan; *C:* Tak Fujimoto; *M:* James Newton Howard. MTV Movie Awards '00: Breakthrough Perf. (Osment); Broadcast Film Critics '99: Breakthrough Perf. (Osment).

The '60s 🦴🦴 ½ **1999 (PG-13)** A quick trip through the decade of peace, love, and Vietnam, told with all the usual cliches. Film uses the parallel stories of two families to hit the high points—the white, middleclass Herlihy family of Chicago and the black Taylor family of Mississippi. You've got hippies, Black Panthers, civil rights, the war, the antiwar movement, drugs, and rock 'n' roll. The soundtrack may be the best thing the miniseries has going for it. **171m/C; VHS, DVD.** Jerry O'Connell; Josh Hamilton; Julia Stiles; Bill Smitrovich; Annie Corley; Leonard Roberts; Charles S. Dutton; Jordana Brewster; David Alan Grier; Jeremy Sisto; Cliff Gorman; Donovan Leitch; Carnie Wilson; Rosanna Arquette; *D:* Mark Piznarski; *W:* Jeffrey Alladin Fiskin; *C:* Michael D. O'Shea. **TV**

Sixty Glorious Years 🦴🦴 ½ *Queen of Destiny* **1938** Since this sequel to 1937's "Victoria the Great" covers the same material, the focus is more on Victoria's (Neagle) engagement and marriage to Prince Albert (Walbrook). Distrusted because he was a foreigner, Albert struggles to find a place for himself both publicly and privately. After Albert dies, the film moves swiftly through Victoria's widowhood until her own death in 1901. Filmed in Technicolor. **90m/C; DVD.** *GB* Anna Neagle; Anton Walbrook; Sir C. Aubrey Smith; Walter Rilla; Charles Carson; Felix Aylmer; Lewis Casson; *D:* Herbert Wilcox; *W:* Richard Vanstone; Miles Malleson; Charles de Grandcourt; *C:* Frederick A. (Freddie) Young.

61* 🦴🦴🦴 **2001** Crystal's nostalgic and meticulous telling of the 1961 home run race between Mickey Mantle (Jane) and Roger Maris (Pepper) clears the fence. Pepper and Jane are excellent as the "M & M Boys," and the rest of the solid cast is up to the task as well. The fine script mixes the baseball action with the behind the scenes material well. Crystal and writer Steinberg take great pains to show the tremendous pressure and outside distractions with which both players had to contend. With the exception of a few sportswriters (the obligatory villains), most of the characters are fleshed out nicely, instead of becoming a checklist of familiar names. Baseball geeks will find nits to pick, but for the most part, the baseball scenes and historical facts are right on the mark. Crystal's daughter plays Mrs. Maris. **128m/C; VHS, DVD, Blu-Ray.** Thomas Jane; Barry Pepper; Chris Bauer; Christopher McDonald; Anthony Michael Hall; Bob Gunton; Bruce McGill; Richard Masur; Bobby Hosea; Donald Moffat; Renee Taylor; Joe Grifasi; Michael Nouri; Paul Borghese; Jennifer Crystal Foley; Seymour Cassel; Peter Jacobson; Robert Joy; Pat(ricia) Crowley; Robert Costanzo; *D:* Billy Crystal; *W:* Hank Steinberg; *C:* Haskell Wexler; *M:* Marc Shaiman. **CABLE**

Sizzle Beach U.S.A. 🦴 *Malibu Hot Summer* **1974 (R)** Three aspiring young actresses want a shot at becoming famous and travel to Los Angeles where they spend their time at the beach with little budget and no particular purchase. Re-released and renamed in 1986 when Costner (in his film debut) became more well-known. **89m/C; VHS, DVD.** Terry Congie; Leslie Brander; Roselyn Royce; Kevin Costner; *D:* Richard Brander.

Skateboard 🦴 **1977 (PG)** A down-and-out Hollywood agent creates a pro skateboarding team and enters them in a race worth $20,000. Quickie premise executed lamely. **97m/C; VHS, DVD.** Allen Garfield; Kathleen Lloyd; Chad McQueen; Leif Garrett; Richard Van Der Wyk; Tony Alva; Antony Carbone; *W:* Dick Wolf.

The Skateboard Kid 🦴 ½ **1993 (PG)** When an outsider finds a magical talking skateboard, he suddenly becomes the envy of the in-group of skateboarding thrashers. **90m/C; VHS, DVD.** Bess Armstrong; Timothy Busfield; *V:* Dom DeLuise; *D:* Larry Swerdlove; *W:* Roger Corman.

The Skateboard Kid 2 🦴🦴 **1994 (PG)** Mystery creature helps Sammy build his dream skateboard, which turns out to have a mind of its own. **95m/C; VHS, DVD.** Trenton Knight; Dee Wallace; Bruce Davison; Andrew Stevens; *D:* Andrew Stevens.

Skateland 🦴🦴 ½ **2010 (PG-13)** Solid, nostalgic coming-of-age teen drama. It's the early 1980s in small town East Texas and 19-year-old slacker Ritchie (Fernandez) is going to lose his job when the local hangout, the Skateland roller rink, shuts down. Ritchie's college-bound girlfriend Michelle (Greene) would like to see him show some ambition while his equally drifting friends have various crises, including a car accident and divorcing parents, which mean they have to make some adult decisions. **98m/C; DVD, Blu-Ray.** Shiloh Fernandez; Ashley Greene; Heath Freeman; Taylor Handley; Haley Ramm; A.J. Buckley; James LeGros; Brett Cullen; D.W. Moffett; *D:* Anthony Burns; *W:* Heath Freeman; Anthony Burns; Brandon Freeman; *C:* Peter Simonite; *M:* Michael Penn.

Skeeter 🦴 ½ **1993 (R)** Yes, it's the attack of the killer mosquito! Not just any mosquito of course, but a new gigantic species bred on toxic waste. They're invading the quiet desert town of Mesquite—and they're out for blood! **95m/C; VHS, DVD.** Tracy Griffith; Jim Youngs; Charles Napier; Michael J. Pollard; *D:* Clark Brandon; *W:* Clark Brandon; Lanny Horn; *M:* David Lawrence.

Skeleton Coast 🦴 *Fair Trade* **1989 (R)** Borgnine plays a retired U.S. Marine colonel who organizes a Magnificent Seven-like group of tough mercenaries to go into eastern Africa to save hostages held by Angolan terrorists. Cliches abound, including a token large-breasted woman, Mulford, getting her t-shirt ripped open. No plot and a bad script. **94m/C; VHS, DVD.** Ernest Borgnine; Robert Vaughn; Oliver Reed; Herbert Lom; Daniel Greene; Nancy Mulford; Leon Isaac Kennedy; *D:* John Cardos.

Skeleton Crew 🦴 **2009** Low-budget derivative horror from Finland. In an abandoned mental hospital near the Russian border, a film crew discovers the 1970s-era screening room of a nutzo doctor who used it to stage his own snuff films (the directors incorporate torture porn footage to represent his work). Director Steven, working on his own opus, becomes obsessed and suddenly the crew is falling victim to the same old slaughter. **92m/C; DVD.** *FI* Steve Porter; David Yolen; Rita Suomalainen; Anna Alkiomaa; *D:* Tommi Lepola; Tero Molin; *W:* Tommi Lepola; Tero Molin; *C:* Tommi Lepola; Tero Molin; *M:* Tuomas Kantelinen. **VIDEO**

The Skeleton Key 🦴🦴 **2005 (PG-13)** Caroline Ellis (Hudson) is a live-in nurse for a bayou stroke victim who finds herself creeping around in her underwear at night trying to uncover the hoodoo history of the homestead and save her patient from its curses. Tight plot and just enough suspenseful garnish keep the journey engaging enough. **104m/C; DVD, Blu-Ray.** Kate Hudson; Peter Sarsgaard; Gena Rowlands; John Hurt; Joy Bryant; *D:* Iain Softley; *W:* Ehren Kruger; *C:* Dan(iel) Mindel; *M:* Ed Shearmur.

Skeleton Key 2: 667, the Neighbor of the Beast 🦴 **2008** A sequel to a 2006 direct-to-video trash horror/comedy film with the same name is a camcorder-quality parade of vampires, zombies, leprechauns, lesbians, songs about pooping yourself, and giant robots forged from bad CGI. **122m/C; DVD.** Conrad Brooks; Monique Dupree; Jay Barber; Chris J. Duncan; John Johnson; John R. Price, II; Saint; Johnny Sullivan; ***D:*** John Johnson; ***W:*** John Johnson; ***C:*** John Johnson. **VIDEO**

The Skeleton Twins **2014 (R)** Hader and Wiig do the best work of their careers as Milo and Maggie, siblings forced together when the former tries to kill himself. Maggie takes him in, thereby revealing secrets of their dark pasts. Director Johnson straddles the line between drama and comedy with brilliance, finding just the right amount of laughter and tearjerking, and he allows his stars, including Wilson, to shine in the process. The final act is a bit too neat in the way it trades off revelations and recoveries but the performances and characters are so likable that you won't care. **90m/C; DVD, Blu-Ray.** Bill Hader; Kristen Wiig; Luke Wilson; Joanna Gleason; Ty Burrell; Boyd Holbrook; ***D:*** Craig Johnson; ***W:*** Craig Johnson; ***C:*** Mark Heyman; Reed Morano; ***M:*** Nathan Larson.

Skeletons 1/2 **2010** Lackluster British comedy. Davis and Bennett are mismatched partners in a psychic business that has them helping people come to terms with buried secrets (the skeletons in their closets). They're hired by Jane to find her eight years missing husband in hopes that some closure will help their gone-mute daughter Rebecca. **96m/C; DVD.** *GB* Ed Gaughan; Andrew Buckley; Paprika Steen; Tuppence Middleton; Jason Issacs; Josef Whitfield; ***D:*** Nick Whitfield; ***W:*** Nick Whitfield; ***C:*** Zac Nicholson; ***M:*** Simon Whitfield.

Skeletons in the Closet 1/2 **2000 (R)** Seth Reed (Jackson) is more than just a rebellious teenager. A loner, he's given to violent outbursts that have his widowed father, Will (Williams), worried. Especially when a series of murders are committed in their New Hampshire town. But since Will is still suffering from the aftermath of his wife's death in a fire, maybe it's his sanity that's in question. Creepy, if sometimes cliched, thriller. **86m/C; VHS, DVD.** Treat Williams; Jonathan Jackson; Linda Hamilton; Schuyler Fisk; Gordon Clapp; ***D:*** Wayne Powers; ***W:*** Wayne Powers; Donna Powers; ***C:*** Michael Barrett; ***M:*** Christopher L. Stone. **VIDEO**

Skellig: The Owl Man **2009** Awkward preteen Michael isn't happy when his parents move into a fixer-upper in the country. In a crumbling cottage, Michael finds the odd and ill Skellig but, as Michael helps him, they forge a friendship. This comes in handy as Michael also sees that Skellig has healing powers (as well as unexplained wings), which are needed when Michael's sister is born with critical medical problems. Based on the children's novel by David Almond. **104m/C; DVD.** *GB* Tim Roth; Bill Milner; John Simm; Kelly Macdonald; Skye Bennett; Jermain Allen; Edna Dore; ***D:*** Annabel Jankel; ***W:*** Irena Brignull; ***C:*** Steve Lawes; ***M:*** Stephen Warbeck. **TV**

The Skeptic 1/2 **2009** Seems more like an old-fashioned TV movie-of-the-week than something intended for the big screen. Lawyer Bryan (Daly) inherits a creepy mansion from his late aunt and moves in to prevent break-ins (and as an excuse to separate from his wife). Soon the skeptic is subjected to spectral visions and other hauntings, leading Bryan to eventually connect things to childhood trauma. So he contacts a psychic researcher (Saldana) to rid the house of spooks. Mild scares. **89m/C; DVD.** Timothy Daly; Tom Arnold; Zoe Saldana; Edward Herrmann; Andrea Roth; Bruce Altman; Robert Prosky; ***D:*** Tennyson Blackwell; ***W:*** Tennyson Blackwell; ***C:*** Claudio Rocha; ***M:*** Brett Rosenberg.

Sketch Artist **1992 (R)** Jack Whitfield (Fahey) is a police sketch artist whose latest rendering of a murder suspect looks suspiciously like his wife. Jack decides to keep this information to himself while he does some quiet investigating but he may not have any time. The police have a new murder suspect in mind—Jack! **89m/C; VHS, Streaming.** Jeff Fahey; Sean Young; Drew Barrymore; Frank McRae; Tcheky Karyo; James Tolkan; Charlotte Lewis; ***D:*** Phedon Papamichael; ***W:*** Michael Angeli. **CABLE**

Ski Party **1965** Slight and rather lame comedy. Gal pals Deborah and Yvonne are off on a ski trip to Squaw Valley, leaving behind their clueless would-be boyfriends Frankie and Dwayne. The guys decide to follow and cross-dress, passing themselves off as a couple of English chicks to get a better understanding of the mysteries of women. This causes some confusion when Dwayne falls for their sexy Swedish ski instructor (Shaw) and Frankie gets hit on by the clueless Kincaid. Lesley Gore and James Brown and the Flames perform. **90m/C; DVD.** Frankie Avalon; Dwayne Hickman; Deborah Walley; Yvonne Craig; Bobbi Shaw; Aron Kincaid; Robert Q. Lewis; ***D:*** Alan Rafkin; ***W:*** Robert Kaufman; ***C:*** Arthur E. Arling; ***M:*** Gary Usher.

Ski Patrol **1989 (PG)** Wacky ski groupies try to stop an evil developer. Good ski action in a surprisingly plotful effort from the crazy crew that brought the world "Police Academy." **85m/C; VHS, Streaming.** Roger Rose; Yvette Nipar; T.K. Carter; Leslie Jordan; Ray Walston; Martin Mull; ***D:*** Richard Correll.

Ski School **1991 (R)** Rival ski instructors compete for jobs and babes. Brow lowering. **89m/C; VHS, DVD, Blu-Ray.** Ava Fabian; Dean Cameron; Tom Breznahan; Stuart Fratkin; ***D:*** Damian Lee.

Ski School 2 1/2 **1994 (R)** Former ski instructor Dave finds that both his job and his ex-gal have been acquired by a jerk. So Dave decides to get them both back. **92m/C; VHS, DVD.** Dean Cameron; Wendy Hamilton; Heather Campbell; Brent Sheppard; Bill Dwyer; ***D:*** David Mitchell; ***W:*** Jay Naples.

Skidoo **WOOF!** **1968** Truly awful would-be psychedelic comedy from Preminger and a host of old stars who apparently worked without a completed script. Retired San Francisco mob enforcer Tony Banks (Gleason) is forced by his former crime boss (Marx in his final role) into getting thrown into Alcatraz so he can off snitch Packard (Rooney). He accidentally ingests LSD and comes up with an escape plan involving floating garbage cans. Meanwhile, Tony's mod daughter Darlene (Hay) has fallen for hippie Stash (Law) and somehow the two stories come together in an excruciating fashion. **98m/C; DVD, Blu-Ray.** Jackie Gleason; Carol Channing; Mickey Rooney; Alexandra Hay; John Phillip Law; Groucho Marx; Frankie Avalon; Michael Constantine; Cesar Romero; George Raft; Burgess Meredith; Peter Lawford; Austin Pendleton; ***D:*** Otto Preminger; ***W:*** Doran William Cannon; ***C:*** Leon Shamroy; ***M:*** Harry Nilsson.

The Skin *La Pelle* **1981** Based on the writings of war correspondent Malaparte, played here by Mastroianni. In 1943, the Allies liberate Naples and the Americans move in, led by Gen. Mark Clark (Lancaster). The Germans might be gone, but things don't change for the residents as they trade one occupying force for another and continue to struggle to survive. Especially the women, who are still being exploited. Director Cavani throws in an erupting volcano so the film is hardly subtle. Italian with subtitles. **131m/C; DVD, Blu-Ray.** *IT FR* Marcello Mastroianni; Burt Lancaster; Claudia Cardinale; Ken Marshall; ***D:*** Liliana Cavani; ***W:*** Liliana Cavani; Robert Katz; ***C:*** Armando Nannuzzi; ***M:*** Lalo Schifrin.

Skin **2018 (R)** For years, Byron Widner (Bell) has been a member of and an authority figure in the white supremacist group Vinlanders Social Club run by Fred (Camp) and Shareen (Farmiga) Krager. Though heavily tattooed with white power and racist symbols, Byron is loyal and loving to his dog and the daughters of his girlfriend Julie (Macdonald). After connecting with activist Daryle Jenkins (Colter), Byron questions his racist beliefs and faces threats despite undergoing a painful physical transformation to leave his old life behind. Based on a true story, Bell's dynamic performance carries the drama. **120m/C; DVD, Blu-Ray.** Jamie Bell; Danielle MacDonald; Bill Camp; Louisa Krause; Zoe Margaret Colletti; ***D:*** Guy Nattiv; ***W:*** Guy Nattiv; ***C:*** Arnaud Potier; ***M:*** Dan Romer.

Skin Deep 1/2 **1989 (R)** A boyish Don Juan tries everything to win back his ex-wife. Ritter whines about his mid-life crisis and seduces women; this substitutes for plot. A few funny slapstick scenes still don't make this worth watching. **102m/C; VHS, DVD; Open Captioned.** John Ritter; Vincent Gardenia; Julianne Phillips; Alyson Reed; Nina Foch; Chelsea Field; Denise Crosby; ***D:*** Blake Edwards; ***W:*** Blake Edwards; ***M:*** Henry Mancini.

Skin Game 1/2 **1931** Two British families feud over land rights. Not thrilling; not characteristic of working with Hitchcock. Way too much talking in excruciating, drawn-out scenes. Adapted from the play of the same name. **87m/B; VHS, DVD, Blu-Ray.** *GB* Phyllis Konstam; Edmund Gwenn; Frank Lawton; C.V. France; Jill Esmond; Helen Haye; ***D:*** Alfred Hitchcock; ***W:*** Alfred Hitchcock; ***C:*** Jack Cox.

Skin Game **1971 (PG)** A fast talking con-artist (Garner) and his black partner (Gossett) travel throughout the antebellum South setting up scams—Gossett is sold to a new owner by Garner, who helps him escape. Garner and Gossett make a splendid comedy team in this different kind of buddy flick. All is well until Asner turns the tables on them. Finely acted comedy-drama. **102m/C; VHS, DVD.** James Garner; Louis Gossett, Jr.; Susan Clark; Ed Asner; Andrew Duggan; ***D:*** Paul Bogart; ***M:*** David Shire.

The Skin I Live In 1/2 *La Piel Que Habito* **2011 (R)** Legendary director Almodovar reunites with Banderas in this typically-twisted thriller about identity, appearance, and human desire to control that which is out of our reach. Plastic surgeon Robert Ledgard (Banderas) develops a synthetic skin to combat the guilt he feels over a car accident that burned his wife. In mad scientist fashion, the good doctor experiments on a captive patient (Anaya), trying to perfect his protection of the human quality of vulnerability. Acclaimed as a horror-edged departure from Almodovar's traditional romantic style, it still features his unique wit, style, and ingenuity. **117m/C; DVD, Blu-Ray.** *SP* Antonio Banderas; Marisa Paredes; Elena Anaya; Blanca Suarez; Jan Cornet; ***D:*** Pedro Almodóvar; ***W:*** Pedro Almodóvar; ***C:*** Jose Luis Alcaine; ***M:*** Alberto Iglesias. British Acad. '11: Foreign Film.

Skinned Alive **WOOF!** **1989** A woman and her children travel cross-country to sell leather goods. When a detective discovers where the leather comes from he's hot on their trail. **90m/C; VHS, DVD.** Mary Jackson; Scott Spiegel; ***D:*** Jon Killough; ***W:*** Jon Killough.

Skinned Alive 1/2 *Eat Your Heart Out* **2008 (R)** Lonely, depressed Jeffrey enjoys the company of prostitutes, and he falls for the lovely Pandora, who is into skinning people and eating them alive. Bet that costs extra. **90m/C; DVD.** Alan Rowe Kelly; Melissa Bacelar; Jack Dillon; Joshua Nelson; Jeanette Bonner; Greg Depetro; Ed Avila; ***D:*** James Tucker; ***W:*** Joshua Nelson; ***C:*** Brian Fass; ***M:*** Duane Peery. **VIDEO**

Skinner **1993 (R)** Psychopath Dennis Skinner (Raimi) more than lives up to his grisly name with his penchant for stalking hookers with carving knives and cleavers. Now he's going after his innocent landlady (Lake) and it's up to Heidi (Lords), a victim who managed to get away, to find him before he can kill again. Lords in lingerie (and nasty scars) and some really disgusting skinning scenes. **89m/C; VHS, DVD, Blu-Ray.** Theodore (Ted) Raimi; Traci Lords; Ricki Lake; ***D:*** Ivan Nagy; ***W:*** Paul Hart-Wilden; ***C:*** Greg Littlewood.

Skinner's Dress Suit 1/2 **1926** Meek, hen-pecked office clerk tells domineering wife he got a raise so she'll get off his back. She quickly insinuates them into upper crusty social circle, where the fib pays off big. Remake of the 1917 version based on Henry Irving Dodge's novel. **79m/B; Silent; VHS, DVD.** Reginald Denny; Laura La Plante; Arthur Lake; Hedda Hopper; ***D:*** William A. Seiter.

Skins 1/2 **2002 (R)** The Pine Ridge Indian Reseration in South Dakota is rife with unemployment, alcoholism, drug abuse, and violence, which native cop Rudy (Schweig) contends with on a daily basis. His older brother Mogie (Greene) is an embittered Vietnam vet and alcoholic who can't be a father to his own teenage son Herbie (Watts). While Rudy seems to have a better handle on life, in fact his frustrations lead to an act of destruction that has unexpected consequences. Based on the 1995 novel by Adrian C. Louis. **90m/C; VHS, DVD.** Eric Schweig; Graham Greene; Gary Farmer; Noah Watts; Lois Red Elk; Michelle Thrush; Nathaniel Arcand; Chaske Spencer; ***D:*** Chris Eyre; ***W:*** Jennifer D. Lyne; ***C:*** Stephen Kazmierski; ***M:*** B.C. Smith.

Skinwalker 1/2 **2002** Middle-aged Native American detective Joe Leaphorn has moved from the city to an Arizona Navajo reservation at the behest of his wife Emma (Tousey). He's finding it difficult to adjust, particularly when someone—or something—begins killing the local medicine men. His young partner, Officer Jim Chee (Beach) of the Navajo Tribal Police, thinks a skinwalker—an evil shape-shifting force—is at work but Leaphorn thinks the killer is more human than supernatural. Based on the mystery series by Tony Hillerman. **120m/C; VHS, DVD.** Wes Studi; Adam Beach; Sheila Tousey; Alex Rice; RuPaul Charles; ***D:*** Chris Eyre; ***W:*** James Redford. **TV**

Skinwalkers **2007 (PG-13)** Timothy (Knight) is about to turn thirteen when he discovers that he, like his dead father, uncle, and extended family, is a werewolf—not a bad werewolf, but a good werewolf that fights bad werewolves. Plus, there's a mysterious prophecy about him, so he and Uncle Jonas (Koteas) must go on the run to avoid bad werewolf Varek (Behr) and his crew of motorcycle-riding henchmen. Embarrassing howler (despite Koteas's decent performance) sanitizes the lycanthropic sex and violence for the adolescent set, and the results are dull and silly. **110m/C; DVD.** *US CA GE* Jason Behr; Elias Koteas; Rhona Mitra; Matthew Knight; Kim Coates; Tom Jackson; Barbara Gordon; ***D:*** James Isaac; ***W:*** James DeMonaco; James Roday; Todd Harthan; ***C:*** Adam Kane; David A. Armstrong; ***M:*** Barbara Carrera; Andrew Lockington.

Skipped Parts 1/2 **2000 (R)** Fourteen-year-old Sam Callahan (Hall) and his bad-girl mom, Lydia (Leigh), have been exiled to Wyoming in 1963 by Lydia's southern big daddy, Caspar (Ermey). Lydia promptly takes up with the wrong guy (Greyeyes) and encourages Sam in sexual experimentation with schoolmate Maurey (Barton), with unfortunate results. Based on Sandlin's coming-of-age trilogy, the film is flat and predictable. **93m/C; VHS, DVD.** Jennifer Jason Leigh; Bug Hall; Michael Greyeyes; Mischa Barton; Peggy Lipton; Brad Renfro; R. Lee Ermey; Angela Featherstone; Alison Pill; Drew Barrymore; Gerald Lenton-Young; ***D:*** Tamra Davis; ***W:*** Tim Sandlin; ***C:*** Claudio Rocha; ***M:*** Stewart Copeland.

Skirts Ahoy! **1952** Williams, Evans, and Blaine are three WAVES who have their eyes set on three handsome men. To get them, of course, they must sing and dance a lot, and Williams must perform one of her famous water ballets. **109m/C; VHS, DVD.** Esther Williams; Joan Evans; Vivian Blaine; Barry Sullivan; Keefe Brasselle; Billy Eckstine; Debbie Reynolds; ***D:*** Sidney Lanfield.

The Skull **1965** Horror abounds when Cushing gets his hands on the skull of the Marquis de Sade that has mysterious, murderous powers. Based on a story by Robert Bloch. **83m/C; VHS, DVD, Blu-Ray.** Peter Cushing; Patrick Wymark; Christopher Lee; Nigel Green; Jill Bennett; Michael Gough; George Coulouris; Patrick Magee; Peter Woodthorpe; ***D:*** Freddie Francis; ***W:*** Milton Subotsky; ***C:*** John Wilcox; ***M:*** Elisabeth Lutyens.

The Skulls 1/2 **2000 (PG-13)** Well, you just can't trust those darn secret societies. Teen star Jackson is Luke, an ambitious kid from the wrong side of the tracks at an "unnamed" Ivy League school that starts with "Y." Because he's the captain of the rowing team, he's asked to join the elite secret society the "Skulls." After the requisite hazing and initiation, Luke is showered with money and other perks. Membership has its privileges. But when his best friend Will (Harper) is found dead after snooping in Skull business, Luke supects foul play and the movie goes from laughable to ludicrous. This secret society, led by evil judge Litten Mandrake (Nelson), does a lot of its business, including duels and car chases, out in the open. Another entry using the teen-paranoia-adults-are-bad theme, which should, mercifully, help kill off the genre for a while. **106m/C; VHS, DVD, Blu-Ray.** Joshua Jackson; Paul Walker; Hill Harper; Leslie Bibb; Christopher McDonald; Steve Harris; William L. Petersen; Craig T. Nelson; ***D:*** Rob Cohen; ***W:*** John Pogue; ***C:*** Shane Hurlbut; ***M:*** Randy Edelman.

The Skulls 2 🦴🦴 **2002 (R)** College student Ryan (Dunne) becomes a member of the secret fraternity the Skulls but when he sees a girl fall off the fraternity's roof, the situation turns ugly. **100m/C; VHS, DVD.** *CA* Robin Dunne; Aaron Ashmore; Ashley Lyn Cafagna; Christopher Ralph; Nathan West; James Callanders; Lindy Booth; ***D:*** Joe Chappelle; ***W:*** Hans Rodionoff; Michele Colucci-Zieger; ***C:*** Steve Danyluk; ***M:*** Christophe Beck. **VIDEO**

Sky Captain and the World of Tomorrow 🦴🦴 ½ **2004 (PG)** More of a film experiment from first-timer Conran (it looks stunning) than a truly engaging film—notable for being the first studio feature where the actors worked against backgrounds that were entirely created digitally. In a pulp wartime melodrama, a sleek, streamlined New York is under attack from giant robots; it must be saved from destruction by the dashing Joe Sullivan (Law) better known as Sky Captain. Former flame/ace girl reporter Polly Perkins (Paltrow) goes along for the ride as she investigates the disappearance of a number of German scientists. The winsome twosome work together, aided (briefly) by eye-patch-wearing British air ace Franky (Jolie), to uncover the sinister plot of evil Dr. Totenkopf (the long-deceased Olivier creepily resurrected via digitized stock footage). **107m/C; DVD, Blu-Ray, HD-DVD.** Gwyneth Paltrow; Jude Law; Angelina Jolie; Giovanni Ribisi; Michael Gambon; Omid Djalili; Laurence Olivier; Trevor Baxter; Julian Curry; ***D:*** Kerry Conran; ***W:*** Kerry Conran; ***C:*** Eric Adkins; ***M:*** Ed Shearmur.

The Sky Crawlers 🦴🦴 *Sukai kurora* **2008** Mamoru Oshii's films are not for every audience, and this one is no exception. In the future mankind has put an end to war, yet still craves violence. So the rival corporations that look as though they pretty much run the world put on wars for entertainment, using genetically altered humans called Kildren (attractive teens who never age) using WWII equipment. Beautifully animated, subtle, and more cerebral, despite the aerial dogfights in the trailers. **122m/C; DVD, Blu-Ray.** *JP* Rinko Kikuchi; Chiaki Kuriyama; Shosuke Tanihara; ***V:*** Bryce Hitchcock; ***D:*** Mamoru Oshii; ***W:*** Hiroshi Mori; Chihiro Itou; ***C:*** Hisashi Ezura; ***M:*** Kenji Kawai.

Sky Full of Moon 🦴 ½ **1952** Minor MGM western comedy. Innocent ranch hand Harley Williams (Carpenter) comes to Vegas to participate in a rodeo but he doesn't quite have the entrance fee. He goes gambling at Al's (Wynn) smalltime casino and gets lucky, both with winning some dough and catching the eye of an interested dame in Dixie (Sterling). She gets Harley into some trouble, but then does right by the naïve cowboy. **73m/B; DVD.** Carleton Carpenter; Jan Sterling; Keenan Wynn; ***D:*** Norman Foster; ***W:*** Norman Foster; ***C:*** Ray June; ***M:*** Paul Sawtell.

Sky High 🦴 **1984** Three college students become immersed in international intrigue when the C.I.A. and the K.G.B. pursue them through Greece looking for a secret Soviet tape. **103m/C; VHS, DVD.** Daniel Hirsch; Clayton Norcross; Frank Schultz; Lauren Taylor; ***D:*** Nico Mastorakis.

Sky High 🦴🦴🦴 **2005 (PG)** Will Stronghold (Angarano) is expected to follow in the footsteps of his superhero parents the Commander (Russell) and Jetstream (Preston) by attending Sky High School to learn the tricks of the trade. He is at first deemed a sidekick, which adds to his adolescence miseries, including a showdown against nemesis Warren Peace (Strait). Carries just the right mix of action, humor and gooeyness delivered by a top notch all-ages cast. **100m/C; DVD, UMD.** Michael Angarano; Kurt Russell; Kelly Preston; Bruce Campbell; Lynda Carter; Dave Foley; Danielle Panabaker; Mary Elizabeth Winstead; Steven Strait; Kevin Heffernan; Nicholas Braun; Kevin McDonald; Cloris Leachman; Dee-Jay Daniels; Kelly Vitz; Jim Rash; Jake Sandvig; Will Harris; Malika Khadijah; ***V:*** Patrick Warburton; ***D:*** Mike Mitchell; ***W:*** Robert Schooley; Mark McCorkle; Paul Hernandez; Paul Amundson; ***C:*** Shelly Johnson; ***M:*** Michael Giacchino.

The Sky Is Falling 🦴🦴 *Il Cielo Cade* **2000** In 1944, young orphaned sisters Penny (Niccolai) and Baby (Campoli) are sent to the Tuscan countryside to live with their Aunt Katchen (Roselli) and German-Jewish Uncle Wilhelm (Krabbe). Although they have managed to survive the war so far, things worsen as the retreating German Army closes in on their small town and the family is urged to make their way to Switzerland. But Uncle Wilhelm doesn't want to leave his home. Based on the autobiographical novel by Lorenza Mazzetti. Italian with subtitles. **102m/C; VHS, DVD.** *IT* Isabella Rossellini; Jeroen Krabbe; Veronica Niccolai; Lara Campoli; ***D:*** Andrea Frazzi; ***W:*** Suso Cecchi D'Amico; ***C:*** Franco Di Giacomo; ***M:*** Luis Bacalov.

Sky Murder 🦴 ½ **1940** Detective Nick Carter (Walter Pidgeon) defends a German refugee accused of murdering a man found locked in an airplance compartment. **72m/C; DVD.** Walter Pidgeon; Donald Meek; Kaaren Verne; Edward Ashley; Joyce Compton; ***D:*** George B. Seitz; ***W:*** William R. Lipman; ***C:*** Charles Lawton, Jr.; ***M:*** David Snell. **VIDEO**

Sky Riders 🦴🦴 ½ **1976 (PG)** Hang-gliders risk it all to take on a group of political kidnappers. Fine hang-gliding footage and glorious Greek locations make up for garden-variety plot. **93m/C; VHS, DVD.** James Coburn; Susannah York; Robert Culp; Charles Aznavour; Harry Andrews; John Beck; ***D:*** Douglas Hickox; ***W:*** Jack DeWitt; Garry Michael White; ***M:*** Lalo Schifrin.

Skyfall 🦴🦴🦴 ½ **2012 (PG-13)** James Bond returns in a film that serves as a perfect bridge to his next generation of fans, perfectly capturing both the iconic nature of the spy hero who couldn't be killed and looking to the future of the franchise. Craig is back as 007 as he battles former spy-gone-bad Silva (Bardem) and tries to save M (Dench) from her own past sins. Director Mendes and cinematographer Roger Deakins brilliantly pace their action film--along with perfect technical elements bolstering a stellar ensemble--making it arguably Bond's best film outing to date. **143m/C; DVD, Blu-Ray.** *UK US* Daniel Craig; Dame Judi Dench; Javier Bardem; Ralph Fiennes; Naomie Harris; Berenice Marlohe; Ben Whishaw; Helen McCrory; ***D:*** Sam Mendes; ***W:*** Neal Purvis; Robert Wade; John Logan; ***C:*** Roger Deakins; ***M:*** Thomas Newman. Oscars '12: Song ("Skyfall"), Sound FX Editing; British Acad. '12: Orig. Score; Golden Globes '13: Song ("Skyfall").

Skyjacked 🦴🦴 *Sky Terror* **1972 (PG)** Captain Henry 'Hank' O'Hara (Heston) is conducting a routine flight when he is given messages to divert the plane to land in Anchorage instead or a bomb will be exploded. He has no idea who wrote the note, just that the bad guy is in first class. Potential first time viewers take note: this mystery covers the first third of the film, and is completely spoiled on the back of the DVD case. **100m/C; DVD.** Charlton Heston; Yvette Mimieux; James Brolin; Claude Akins; Jeanne Crain; Susan Dey; Roosevelt "Rosie" Grier; Mariette Hartley; Walter Pidgeon; Ken Swofford; Leslie Uggams; Ross Elliot; Nicholas Hammond; Mike Henry; John Hillerman; Maureen Connell; John Fiedler; Jayson Kane; Toni Clayton; Kelley Miles; ***D:*** John Guillermin; ***W:*** David Harper; Stanley R. Greenberg; ***C:*** Harry Stradling, Jr.; ***M:*** Perry Botkin.

Skyline 🦴 ½ **2010 (PG-13)** Directed by sibling special effects gurus who bill themselves as the Brothers Strause, this entry in the "aliens attack" genre steals bits of its thin plot from other recent sci-fi films. After a hard night of partying, a group of hungover LA hipsters awake to find themselves in the midst of an invasion of squid-like space invaders who use an eerie light show to mesmerize and devour the populace. Faison and Balfour do their best, but the dialogue is ridiculous. The special effects are good, especially considering that the movie was reportedly made for about $10 million. **100m/C; Blu-Ray, On Demand.** Eric Balfour; Donald Adeosun Faison; Scottie Thompson; Brittany Daniel; David Zayas; Crystal Reed; ***D:*** Greg Strause; Colin Strause; ***W:*** Joshua Cordes; Liam O'Donnell; ***C:*** Michael Watson; ***M:*** Matthew Margeson.

The Sky's No Limit 🦴🦴 ½ **1984** CBS TV movie, inspired by astronaut Sally Ride, hypes the personal melodrama between three women undergoing NASA training to become America's first woman in space aboard the Challenger space shuttle. Internist Susan Browning (Archer), mathematics professor Joanna Douglas (Gless), and physicist Maureen Harris (Wallace) have private issues that cause more impediments than anything professional. **95m/C; DVD.** Anne Archer; Sharon Gless; Dee Wallace; David Ackroyd; Barnard Hughes; Paul Menzel; ***D:*** David Lowell Rich; ***W:*** Harry S. Longstreet; Renee Longstreet; ***C:*** Mike Fash; ***M:*** Maurice Jarre. **TV**

The Sky's the Limit 🦴🦴 ½ **1943** Astaire spends his leave in Manhattan and falls in love with fetching journalist Leslie. He's in civvies, so little does she know he's a war hero. Nothing-special semi-musical, with Fred-Ginger spark missing. **89m/B; VHS, DVD.** Fred Astaire; Joan Leslie; Robert Benchley; Robert Ryan; Elizabeth Patterson; ***D:*** Edward H. Griffith.

Skyscraper 🦴 **1995 (R)** Gun-wielding helicopter pilot/heroine Carrie Wink (Smith) must battle villainous mercenaries holding hostages in an LA skyscraper. But she stills manages to find time for lots of steamy showers (to best display the only assets the film has). **96m/C; VHS, DVD, On Demand.** Anna Nicole Smith; Richard Steinmetz; ***D:*** Raymond Martino; ***W:*** William Applegate, Jr.; ***C:*** Frank Harris; ***M:*** Jim Halfpenny.

Skyscraper 🦴🦴 **2018 (PG-13)** The stakes are sky-high for Will Ford (Johnson), who's framed for a fire raging inside the world's largest building with his family trapped on the upper floors. This is Johnson doing what Johnson does best: feats of nearly superhuman strength combined with displays of tenderness for his loved ones. If you're a fan, you'll be on the edge of your seat. **102m/C; DVD, Blu-Ray.** Dwayne "The Rock" Johnson; Neve Campbell; Kevin Rankin; McKenna Roberts; Byron Mann; ***D:*** Rawson Marshall Thurber; ***W:*** Rawson Marshall Thurber; ***C:*** Robert Elswit; ***M:*** Steve Jablonsky.

Skyscraper Souls 🦴🦴🦴 **1932** William stars as David Dwight, a ruthless businessman who manipulates stock prices and double-crosses lovers in order to have complete control of a 100-story office building. He sacrifices everything and everyone in this story of big business. Based on the novel "Skyscraper" by Faith Baldwin. **98m/B; DVD.** Warren William; Maureen O'Sullivan; Gregory Ratoff; Anita Page; Verree Teasdale; Norman Foster; Jean Hersholt; Wallace Ford; ***D:*** Edgar Selwyn; ***W:*** C. Gardner Sullivan; ***C:*** William H. Daniels.

Skyway 🦴 ½ **1933** Brash aviator Flash agrees to take a boring bank clerk job to please gal Lila, daughter of the bank president. But when funds go missing, Flash gets the blame and uses his plane to go after the actual crook. **70m/B; DVD.** Ray Walker; Kathryn Crawford; Jed Prouty; Lucien Littlefield; Arthur Vinton; Tom Dugan; Claude Gillingwater; ***D:*** Lewis D. Collins; ***W:*** Albert DeMond; ***C:*** Charles E. Schoenbaum.

Slacker 🦴🦴🦴 **1991 (R)** Defines a new generation: Overwhelmed by the world and it's demands, "Slackers" react by retreating into lives of minimal expectations. Filmed as a series of improvisational stories about people living on the fringes of the working world and their reactions (or lack thereof) to the life swirling around them. First feature for writer/director Linklater on a budget of $23,000; filmed on location in Austin, Texas with a cast of primarily non-professional actors. **97m/C; VHS, DVD, Blu-Ray.** Richard Linklater; Rudy Basquez; Jean Caffeine; Jan Hockey; Stephan Hockey; Mark James; Samuel Dietert; ***D:*** Richard Linklater; ***W:*** Richard Linklater; ***C:*** Lee Daniel. Natl. Film Reg. '12.

Slackers 🦴 ½ **2002 (R)** Schwartzman is wasted as Ethan, a social outcast college student with his stalker-like eye on the prize—an intelligent college girl with model good looks (former model King). Nicknaming himself "Cool Ethan," our semi-delusional hero blackmails three of the campus's best and brightest, who have gotten that rep entirely through cheating. Ethan demands the boys use their unique methods of chicanery to get him his dream girl, or he'll get them all expelled. Leader of the gang Dave (Sawa) leads the fix-up charade but ends up falling for the cutie himself. Uninteresting, annoying characters, awkward plotting, and the requisite ton of sophomoric, sexual, and gross-out humor, including a gratuitous septugenarian sponge bath. **86m/C; VHS, DVD.** Devon Sawa; Jason Schwartzman; Jaime King; Jason Segel; Michael Maronna; Laura Prepon; Mamie Van Doren; Joe Flaherty; Leigh Taylor-Young; Sam Anderson; Cameron Diaz; ***D:*** Dewey Nicks; ***W:*** David H. Steinberg; ***C:*** James R. Bagdonas; ***M:*** Joseph (Joey) Altruda.

Slam 🦴🦴 **1998 (R)** Documentarian Levin makes his feature film debut with this part-prison, part-ghetto drama. Street-smart, low-level drug dealer Ray (Williams) is living in gang-ridden D.C. when he's busted for possession and suspicion of murdering his supplier. Jail's just as rough as the streets since two local inside gangs each want Ray's allegiance. Ray wants to keep to himself and work on his writing—the poetry he composes about what he sees in life. He manages to get bail and then has a lot of hard decisions to make. **100m/C; VHS, DVD.** Saul Williams; Sonja Sohn; Bonz Malone; ***D:*** Marc Levin; ***W:*** Marc Levin; Saul Williams; Sonja Sohn; Bonz Malone; Richard Stratton; ***C:*** Mark Benjamin. Sundance '98: Grand Jury Prize.

Slam Dunk Ernest 🦴 ½ **1995 (PG-13)** Ernest (Varney) becomes a basketball star in a city league exhibition game when the Basketball Angel (Abdul-Jabbar) loans him his magic shoes. **93m/C; VHS, DVD.** Jim Varney; Kareem Abdul-Jabbar; Jay Brazeau; ***D:*** John R. Cherry, III; ***W:*** John R. Cherry, III; Daniel Butler; ***M:*** Mark Adler.

Slamdance 🦴 ½ **1987 (R)** A struggling cartoonist is framed for the murder of a beautiful young woman while being victimized by the real killer. A complicated murder mystery with a punk beat and visual flash. But the tale is unoriginal—and where's the slamdancing? **99m/C; VHS, DVD, Blu-Ray.** Tom Hulce; Virginia Madsen; Mary Elizabeth Mastrantonio; Harry Dean Stanton; Adam Ant; John Doe; ***D:*** Wayne Wang.

Slammer Girls 🦴 **1987 (R)** In this sex-drenched, unfunny spoof on women's prison films, the inmates of Loch Ness Penitentiary try to break out using their sexual wiles. The actresses are pseudonymous porn stars. **82m/C; VHS, DVD.** Tally Brittany; Jane Hamilton; Jeff Eagle; Devon Jenkin; ***D:*** Chuck Vincent.

The Slammin' Salmon 🦴 **2009 (R)** Extremely strained and obvious comedy from the Broken Lizard troupe. Former heavyweight boxer turned Miami restaurant owner Cleon Salmon (Duncan) needs to make $20, 000 in one night to pay off a gambling debt. He threatens his waitstaff with bodily harm (and cash) so that they'll do anything necessary to make it happen. **98m/C; DVD.** Michael Clarke Duncan; Jay Chandrasekhar; Steve Lemme; Paul Soter; Erik Stolhanske; Cobie Smulders; April Bowlby; Vivica A. Fox; Lance Henriksen; Morgan Fairchild; ***D:*** Kevin Heffernan; ***W:*** Jay Chandrasekhar; Steve Lemme; Paul Soter; Erik Stolhanske; Kevin Heffernan; ***C:*** Robert Barocci; ***M:*** Nathan Barr.

The Slams 🦴 ½ **1973** Very violent crime drama. Curtis Hook stole mob money, hid it in an amusement park, and then got caught. He hears the park is about to be demolished and is anxious to break out of the slammer to get his ill-gotten gains. There are plenty who'll help him for a piece of his stash but the mob also wants Curtis dead and has a hit out on him. **91m/C; DVD.** Jim Brown; Roland Bob Harris; Frank De Kova; Ted Cassidy; Judy Pace; Quinn (K.) Redeker; ***D:*** Jonathan Kaplan; ***W:*** Richard DeLong Adams; ***C:*** Andrew Davis; ***M:*** Luther Henderson.

Slander 🦴🦴 **1957** Scandal sheet owner H.R. Manley (Cochran) needs a big story to keep his rag going. Puppeteer Scott Martin (Johnson) is the star of a kiddie TV show, but Manley threatens to expose his criminal past unless Martin gets the dirt on a childhood friend who's now a star with a squeaky clean image. Even Manley's mother (Rambeau) gets disgusted by her slimy son--and takes action. **81m/B; DVD.** Van Johnson; Steve Cochran; Ann Blyth; Marjorie Rambeau; ***D:*** Roy Rowland; ***W:*** Jerome Weidman; ***C:*** Harold Marzorati; ***M:*** Jeff Alexander.

Slap Her, She's French 🦴🦴 ½ *She Gets What She Wants* **2002 (PG-13)** Ambitious Starla (McGregor) is her high school's head cheerleader, dates the quarterback, and fully intends to become the beauty queen of the Spendora Beef Pageant. But a supposedly French exchange student named Genevieve (Perabo) is out to steal Starla's crown. **91m/C; VHS, DVD.** Piper Perabo; Jane McGregor; Jesse James; Trent Ford; Julie White; Brandon Smith; Nicki Aycox; Michael McKean; *D:* Melanie Mayron; *W:* Robert Lee King; *C:* Charles Minsky; *M:* Christophe Beck; David Michael Frank.

Slap Shot 🦴🦴🦴 **1977 (R)** Profane satire of the world of professional hockey. Over-the-hill player-coach of the third-rate Charlestown Chiefs, Reggie Dunlop (Newman), gathers an odd-ball mixture of has-beens and young players and reluctantly initiates them, using violence on the ice to make his team win. The on-ice striptease by star player Ned Braden (Ontkean) needs to be seen to be believed. Charming in its own bone-crunching way. **123m/C; VHS, DVD, Blu-Ray.** Paul Newman; Michael Ontkean; Jennifer Warren; Lindsay Crouse; Jerry Houser; Melinda Dillon; Strother Martin; Andrew Duncan; M. Emmet Walsh; Nancy Dowd; Swoosie Kurtz; Allan Nicholls; Paul D'Amato; Brad Sullivan; Stephen Mendillo; Kathryn Walker; Paul Dooley; Yvon Barrette; Jeff Carlson; Steve Carlson; Dave Hanson; Ned Dowd; *D:* George Roy Hill; *W:* Nancy Dowd; *C:* Victor Kemper; *M:* Elmer Bernstein.

Slap Shot 2: Breaking the Ice 🦴🦴 **2002 (R)** Okay, it took 25 years to make a sequel—is this a record? Rude and crude hockey comedy finds the Charlestown Chiefs being sold to media mogul Busey, who moves the team to Omaha, Nebraska. But the team is not supposed to play "real" hockey; they are only supposed to take the money and serve as comic foils to the game, which upsets the geeky Hanson brothers and team captain Baldwin. **104m/C; VHS, DVD.** Stephen Baldwin; Jeff Carlson; Steve Carlson; Dave Hanson; Gary Busey; Callum Keith Rennie; Jessica Steen; *D:* Steve Boyum; *W:* Broderick Miller; *C:* Joel Ransom. **VIDEO**

Slappy and the Stinkers 🦴🦴 1/2 **1997 (PG)** Five young misfits, known as "The Stinkers," are constantly in trouble with their stuffy school principal Morgan Brinway (Wong). On a class trip to the acquarium, the Stinkers meet Slappy the sea lion and decide to liberate him (they think he looks unhappy), stowing Slappy in Mr. Brinway's hot tub. Then the kids find out that evil animal thief Boccoli (McMurray) wants to steal the critter and sell him to a circus. Just as silly as it sounds but Slappy is really cute. **78m/C; VHS, DVD.** B.D. Wong; Bronson Pinchot; Sam McMurray; Joseph Ashton; Travis Tedford; Gary LeRoi Gray; Carl Michael Lindner; Scarlett Pomers; Jennifer Coolidge; *D:* Barnet Kellman; *W:* Michael Scott; Bob Wolterstorff.

Slash 🦴🦴 1/2 **2016** Neil (Michael Johnston) has a quiet, introverted life writing slash fanfiction online. All is well, until he meets a girl who pushes him to publish his writing, turning his world upside down by exposing him to the public eye. Not the usual teen rom-com, and some knowledge of internet culture will be helpful for potential viewers. **100m/C; DVD, Blu-Ray, Streaming. VIDEO**

Slashdance WOOF! **1989** A really pathetic thriller follows a lady cop undercover in a chorus line to find out who's been murdering the dancers. The acting is on the level of pro wrestling. Don't be fooled by the naked babes on the cassette box—there's no nudity. **83m/C; VHS, DVD.** Cindy Maranne; James Carroll Jordan; Deanna (Dee) Booher; Joel von Ornsteiner; Jay Richardson; *D:* James Shyman; *W:* James Shyman.

Slashed Dreams 🦴🦴 *Sunburst* **1974 (R)** Hippie couple travels to California wilderness in search of a friend. A pair of woodsmen assault them and rape the woman, which really messes with their heads. Retitled and packaged as slasher movie. **74m/C; VHS, DVD.** Peter Hooten; Kathrine Baumann; Ric Carrott; Anne Lockhart; Robert Englund; Rudy Vallee; James Keach; David Pritchard; Peter Brown; *D:* James Polakof; *W:* James Keach; David Pritchard.

Slattery's Hurricane 🦴🦴 **1949** Routine melodrama. Former Navy pilot Willard Slattery (Widmark) has flashbacks to his life's regrets as he flies through a hurricane. Having problems settling into postwar life, Slattery flies drug shipments for the mob, has an affair with junkie Dolores (Lake), and tries to break up his ex-girlfriend Aggie's (Darnell) marriage to a war buddy. Based on a novel by co-scripter Wouk. **83m/B; DVD.** Richard Widmark; Linda Darnell; Veronica Lake; John Russell; Gary Merrill; *D:* Andre de Toth; *W:* Richard Murphy; Herman Wouk; *C:* Charles G. Clarke; *M:* Cyril Mockridge.

Slaughter 🦴 **1972 (R)** After his parents are murdered, a former Green Beret goes after their killers. Plenty of brutality. Followed by "Slaughter's Big Ripoff." **92m/C; VHS, DVD.** Jim Brown; Stella Stevens; Rip Torn; Cameron Mitchell; Don Gordon; Marlene Clark; Robert Phillips; *D:* Jack Starrett; *W:* Mark Hanna; Don Williams; *C:* Rosalio Solano; *M:* Luchi De Jesus.

Slaughter High 🦴 **1986 (R)** A high school nerd is accidentally disfigured by a back-firing prank. Five years later, he returns to exact bloody revenge. Available in an unrated version. **90m/C; VHS, DVD, Blu-Ray.** Caroline Munro; Simon Scuddamore; Kelly Baker; *D:* George Dugdale.

Slaughter Hotel 🦴 *Asylum Erotica; La Bestia Uccide a Sangue Freddo* **1971 (R)** An asylum already inhabited by extremely bizarre characters is plagued by a series of gruesome murders. Lots of skin and lots of blood; Neri shines as a nymphomaniacal lesbian nurse. **72m/C; VHS, DVD, Blu-Ray.** Klaus Kinski; Rosalba Neri; Margaret Lee; John Ely; *D:* Fernando Di Leo.

Slaughter of the Innocents 🦴🦴 **1993 (R)** FBI agent Broderick (Glenn) is sent to Salt Lake City to investigate the murders of two children which are found to be connected to a series of bizarre killings that have occurred around Monument Valley. Unbeknownst to his associates, Broderick often uses his 11-year-old whiz-kid son Jesse's (Cameron-Glickenhaus) computer skills to aid his research. Only this time, his inquisitive son gets too close to a serial killer and unless Dad can figure things out on his own, Jesse will be the next victim. **104m/C; VHS, DVD, Blu-Ray.** Scott Glenn; Jesse Cameron-Glickenhaus; Sheila Tousey; Darlanne Fluegel; Zitto Kazann; *D:* James Glickenhaus; *W:* James Glickenhaus.

The Slaughter Rule 🦴🦴 1/2 **2001** In rural Montana, high schooler Roy Chutney (Gosling) gets cut from the football team days after his estranged dad is killed in a train accident. With his divorced mom (Lynch) unable to cope, Roy finds some unexpected diversion when he joins the six-man football squad coached by eccentric loner Gideon Ferguson (Morse). Gideon has a dark past and a somewhat unsavory local reputation but Roy needs someone he can turn to, whatever the consequences. Performances by Gosling and Morse are the reason to watch since the storytelling is uneven. **115m/C; VHS, DVD.** Ryan Gosling; David Morse; Clea DuVall; Kelly Lynch; David Cale; Eddie Spears; Amy Adams; *D:* Alex Smith; Andrew J. Smith; *W:* Alex Smith; Andrew J. Smith; *C:* Eric Alan Edwards; *M:* Jay Farrar.

Slaughterhouse WOOF! **1987 (R)** A rotund, pig-loving country boy kills, maims, and eats numerous victims. Features the requisite dumb teens and plenty of blood. **87m/C; VHS, DVD, Blu-Ray.** Joe Barton; Sherry Bendorf; Don Barrett; Bill Brinsfield; *D:* Rick Roessler; *W:* Rick Roessler; *C:* Richard Benda.

Slaughterhouse Five 🦴🦴 **1972 (R)** A suburban optometrist becomes "unstuck" in time and flits randomly through the experiences of his life, from the Dresden bombing to an extraterrestrial zoo. Noticed at Cannes but not at theatres; ambitious failure to adapt Kurt Vonnegut's odd novel. **104m/C; VHS, DVD, Blu-Ray.** Michael Sacks; Valerie Perrine; Ron Leibman; Eugene Roche; Perry King; Sharon Gans; Roberts Blossom; *D:* George Roy Hill; *W:* Stephen Geller; *C:* Miroslav Ondricek; *M:* Glenn Gould. Cannes '72: Special Jury Prize.

Slaughter's Big Ripoff 🦴 1/2 **1973 (R)** Slaughter is back battling the Mob with guns, planes and martial arts. This undistinguished sequel features McMahon as a mob boss. **92m/C; VHS, DVD.** Jim Brown; Brock Peters; Don Stroud; Ed McMahon; Art Metrano; Gloria Hendry; *D:* Gordon Douglas; *W:* Charles Johnson; *C:* Charles F. Wheeler; *M:* James Brown; Fred Wesley.

The Slave 🦴🦴 *Son of Spartacus; Il Figlio di Spartacus* **1962** Italian sword and sandals adventure from Reeves. Although Spartacus is dead, the rebellion lives. While on duty in Egypt, centurion Randus (Reeves) discovers he's actually the son of the slave hero. He rebels against the Romans and, wearing his father's helmet and wielding his sword, he carries on the family legacy. **102m/C; DVD.** *IT* Steve Reeves; Jacques Sernas; Gianna Maria Canale; Claudio Gora; Ivo Garrani; Ombretta Colli; *D:* Sergio Corbucci; *W:* Giovanni Grimaldi; Adriano Bolzoni; *C:* Enzo Barboni; *M:* Piero Piccioni.

Slave 🦴 **2009 (R)** For some stupid reason, David Dunsmore thinks he should have his fiancee Georgie meet his crude criminal dad at his Spanish villa. When the couple visits a local nightclub, Georgie is quickly drugged and sold into sexual slavery to a yacht-owning psycho who maintains his own drugged-up harem. **81m/C; DVD.** Sam Page; Natassia Malthe; David Gant; Michael Maxwell; Howard Marks; Roger Pera; *D:* Darryn Welch; *W:* Brett Goldstein; *C:* Toby Moore. **VIDEO**

Slave Girls from Beyond Infinity 🦴🦴 **1987 (R)** In this B-movie spoof, two beautiful intergalactic slave girls escape their penal colony, land on a mysterious planet, and meet a cannibalistic despot. Fun spoof of '50s "B" sci-fi movies. **80m/C; VHS, DVD, Blu-Ray.** Elizabeth Kaitan; Cindy Beal; Brinke Stevens; Don Scribner; Carl Horner; Kirk Graves; Randolph Roehbling; Bud Graves; *D:* Ken Dixon; *W:* Ken Dixon; *C:* Thomas Callaway; Kenneth Wiatrak; *M:* Carl Dante.

A Slave of Love 🦴🦴🦴 **1978** Poignant love story set in the Crimea as the Bolshevik Revolution rages around a film crew attempting to complete a project. Interesting as ideological cinema but also enjoyable romantic drama. In Russian with English subtitles. **94m/C; VHS, DVD.** *RU* Elena Solovei; Rodion Nakhapetov; Alexander Kalyagin; *D:* Nikita Mikhalkov; *M:* Eduard Artemyev.

Slave Ship 🦴 1/2 **1937** Slave trader Jim Lovett (Baxter) wants to go respectable after marrying Nancy (Allan) and orders first mate Thompson (Beery) to get rid of the crew and hire new sailors. No surprise that the men don't like that and mutiny. **90m/B; DVD.** Warner Baxter; Wallace Beery; Elizabeth Allan; Mickey Rooney; George Sanders; Joseph Schildkraut; Miles Mander; Jane Darwell; *D:* Tay Garnett; *W:* Sam Hellman; Lamar Trotti; Gladys Lehman; *C:* Ernest Palmer.

Slavers 🦴🦴 **1977 (R)** Detailed depiction of the 19th century African slave trade with a little romance thrown in. **102m/C; VHS, DVD.** *GE* Trevor Howard; Britt Ekland; Ron Ely; Cameron Mitchell; Ray Milland; *D:* Jurgen Goslar.

Slaves of Hollywood 🦴🦴 1/2 **1999** Paulette (Morgan) is filming a documentary about five aspiring Hollywood wannabe execs as they work their way up the Tinseltown ladder. Lots of stylish flourishes highlight a familiar tale of the backstabbing, schmoozing movie biz. **80m/C; VHS, DVD.** Nicholas Worth; Katherin Morgan; Amy Lyndon; Tim Duquette; Hill Harper; Andre Barron; Rob Hyland; Elliot Markman; *D:* Terry Keefe; Michael J. Wechsler; *W:* Terry Keefe; Michael J. Wechsler; *C:* David Alan Parks; *M:* Joseph (Joey) Altruda; Bradford T. Ellis.

Slaves of New York 🦴 1/2 **1989 (R)** Greenwich Village artists worry about life and love in the '80s and being artistic enough for New York. Adapted from the stories of Tama Janowitz, who also wrote the screenplay and appears as Abby. Disastrous adaptation of a popular novel. **115m/C; VHS, DVD.** Bernadette Peters; Chris Sarandon; Mary Beth Hurt; Madeleine Potter; Adam Coleman Howard; Jsu Garcia; Mercedes Ruehl; Joe Leeway; Charles McCaughan; John Harkins; Anna (Katerina) Katarina; Tama Janowitz; Michael Schoeffling; Steve Buscemi; Anthony LaPaglia; Stanley Tucci; *D:* James Ivory; *W:* Tama Janowitz; *C:* Tony Pierce-Roberts; *M:* Richard Robbins.

Slaves to the Underground 🦴 1/2 **1996 (R)** Love affair between Seattle bandmates Shelly (Gross) and Suzy (Ryan) runs into problems when Shelly's ex-boyfriend Jimmy (Bortz) re-enters the picture and some old feelings are also re-ignited. Mediocre yet abrasive, with that dated postgrunge, Seattle-is-so-over feeling. **90m/C; VHS, DVD, On Demand.** Molly Gross; Marisa Ryan; Jason Bortz; *D:* Kristine Peterson; *W:* Bill Cody; *C:* Zoran Hochstatter; *M:* Mike Martt.

The Slayer WOOF! *Nightmare Island* **1982 (R)** It's movies like this that give getting back to nature a bad name. That horrible monster is after those nice young people again! This time it's on an island off the coast of Georgia. **95m/C; VHS, DVD, Blu-Ray.** Alan McRae; Sarah Kendall; Frederick Flynn; Carol Kottenbrook; *D:* J.S. Cardone; *W:* J.S. Cardone; *C:* Karen Grossman; *M:* Robert Folk.

Slayer 🦴 1/2 **2006** Deliberately gory schlock redo of vampire myths. Major Hawk (Van Dien) and his Army unit are sent to South America to deal with vicious vamps who can come out during the day. Hawk's ex-wife, scientist Laurie Williams (O'Dell), just happens to be in the area doing research and if she needs rescuing, well, Hawk's up for the mission. Most of the budget seems to have been spent on fake blood. **88m/C; DVD.** Casper Van Dien; Danny Trejo; Lynda Carter; Alexis Cruz; Jennifer O'Dell; Kevin Grevioux; Ray Park; *D:* Kevin Van Hook; *W:* Kevin Van Hook; *C:* Matt Steinauer; *M:* Ludek Drizhal. **CABLE**

Slayground 🦴 1/2 **1984 (R)** Man, distraught at the accidental death of his daughter, hires a hitman to exact revenge. Excruciating adaptation of the novel by Richard Stark (Donald E. Westlake). **85m/C; VHS, DVD, Blu-Ray.** *GB* Peter Coyote; Mel Smith; Billie Whitelaw; Philip Sayer; Kelli Maroney; *D:* Terry Bedford; *M:* Colin Towns.

SLC Punk! 🦴🦴 **1999 (R)** Lillard is Stevo, a punk rocker rebelling against "the establishment" in mid-'80s Salt Lake City, Utah before it's time to head off to Harvard Law. He and his friends wander aimlessly from fights with rednecks and hippies to trashy clubs to various girlfriends. Nothing really funny or particularly dramatic happens in the comedy-drama, which seems like an excuse for director/writer Merendino to relive his carefree college years. **97m/C; VHS, DVD.** Matthew Lillard; Michael Goorjian; Annabeth Gish; Jennifer Lien; Christopher McDonald; Devon Sawa; James Duval; Til Schweiger; Kevin Breznahan; Jason Segel; Summer Phoenix; Adam Pascal; Chiara Barzini; *D:* James Merendino; *W:* James Merendino; *C:* Greg Littlewood; *M:* Melanie Miller.

Sledgehammer WOOF! **1983** A madman is wreaking havoc on a small town, annihilating young women with a sledgehammer. **87m/C; VHS, DVD.** Ted Prior; Doug Matley; Steven Wright; *D:* David A. Prior; *W:* David A. Prior.

Sleep Easy, Hutch Rimes 🦴🦴 **2000** Insurance agent Hutch Rimes (Weber) may be a womanizer but he knows nothing about women. When abused wife (and Hutch's squeeze) Holly (Siemaszko) decides to murder hubby Cotton (Henry), she enlists Hutch's help. The plan is botched, Holly dies, and Cotton goes to prison. Ten years later, Hutch is now seeing Olivia (O'Grady) who wants to get rid of her jealous hubby (Tobolowsky) and wants Hutch to aid her. But he's got bigger problems—Cotton is out of prison and out for revenge. Meanwhile, Hutch's faithful secretary (Kurtz) decides it's time to make her romantic feelings known to her boss. **99m/C; VHS, DVD.** Steven Weber; Swoosie Kurtz; Gail O'Grady; Gregg Henry; Gabriel Mann; Nina Siemaszko; Stephen Tobolowsky; Stacey Travis; Bonnie Somerville; Jack Johnson; *D:* Matthew Irmas; *W:* Michael O'Connell; *C:* Jerry Sidell; *M:* Alex Wurman. **CABLE**

Sleep, My Love 🦴🦴 **1948** Wealthy Alison (Colbert) wakes up on a train with no idea how she got there or why she has a gun in her purse. When she's reunited with her solicitous hubby, Richard (Ameche), he says she threatened him and convinces her to see a shrink. It's all just an evil--and increasingly absurd--plot for Richard drive Alison crazy so he can get her money and marry his negligee-clad mistress (Brooks). Film noir does have some creepy moments but it's not director Sirk's best. **97m/B; DVD, Blu-Ray.** Claudette Colbert; Don Ameche; Robert Cummings; Hazel Brooks; Rita Johnson; George Coulouris; Raymond Burr; Keye Luke; *D:* Douglas

Sirk; *W:* Leo Rosten; Cy Enfield; *C:* Joseph Valentine; *M:* Rudy Schrager.

Sleep Tight 🦴🦴 *Mientras duermes* **2011** A tense psychological thriller about torment and obsession. Cesar (Tosar) is a miserable man whose sole goal in life is to make everyone around him as unhappy as he is. Employed in an apartment building in Barcelona, he uses his position to agitate the tenants. Cesar meets his match in Clara (Etura), a generally happy woman, and goes to extreme lengths, both mental and physical, to torture her. The situation only becomes more complicated with the arrival of her boyfriend Marcos (San Juan). Spanish with subtitles., A tense psychological thriller of obsession and torment. Because Cesar (Tosar) is certain that he is unable to be happy, he lives his life in misery and makes life horrible for all around him. Employed at an apartment building in Barcelona, Cesar acts in ways that makes the tenants agitated and unhappy. Cesar meets his match in Clara (Etura), a happy woman who is not as easy to break as the rest, and he goes to extremes, both mental and physical, to torment her. The situation only grows more complicated when Clara's boyfriend Marcos (San Juan), enters the picture. Spanish with subtitles. **102m/C; DVD, Blu-Ray, Streaming.** *SP* Luis Tosar; Marta Etura; Alberto San Juan; Petra Martinez; Iris Almeida; *D:* Jaume Balaguero; *W:* Alberto Marini; *C:* Pablo Rosso; *M:* Lucas Vidal. **VIDEO**

Sleep with Me 🦴🦴 ½ **1994 (R)** What happens when love comes between friendship? Sarah (Tilly), Joseph (Stoltz), and Frank (Sheffer) are soon to find out. Sarah and Joseph are about to get married when their best friend Frank realizes he's in love with Sarah. So he sets out to seduce her and when Joseph realizes what's going on, he not only questions Frank's friendship but wonders just what signals Sarah's been giving off (although Joseph's hardly blameless). Six writers each wrote one of the social scenes detailing their triangular troubles, including a party where Tarantino does a hilarious riff on the homoerotic subtext in "Top Gun." Kelly's directorial debut. **117m/C; VHS, DVD, Blu-Ray.** Craig Sheffer; Eric Stoltz; Meg Tilly; Todd Field; Adrienne Shelly; Lewis Arquette; Susan Traylor; Tegan West; Parker Posey; Dean Cameron; Thomas Gibson; June Lockhart; Quentin Tarantino; Joey Lauren Adams; *D:* Rory Kelly; *W:* Rory Kelly; Roger Hedden; Neal Jimenez; Michael Steinberg; Duane Dell'Amico; Joe Keenan; *M:* David Lawrence.

Sleepaway Camp 🦴 **1983 (R)** Crazed killer hacks away at the inhabitants of a peaceful summer camp in this run-of-the-mill slasher. **88m/C; VHS, DVD, Blu-Ray.** Mike Kellin; Jonathan Tiersten; Felissa Rose; Christopher Collet; Robert Earl Jones; *D:* Robert Hiltzik; *W:* Robert Hiltzik; *C:* Benjamin Davis; *M:* Edward Bilous.

Sleepaway Camp 2: Unhappy Campers 🦴 ½ **1988 (R)** A beautiful camp counselor is actually a blood-thirsty, murdering madwoman. Sequel to the 1983 slasher, "Sleepaway Camp." **82m/C; VHS, DVD, Blu-Ray.** Pamela Springsteen; Renee Estevez; Walter Gotell; Brian Patrick Clarke; *D:* Michael A. Simpson.

Sleepaway Camp 3: Teenage Wasteland WOOF! **1989 (R)** This second sequel is as bad as the first two movies. Another disturbed camper hacks up another bevy of teenagers. Better luck at the Motel Six. **80m/C; VHS, DVD, Blu-Ray.** Pamela Springsteen; Tracy Griffith; Michael J. Pollard; *D:* Michael A. Simpson.

Sleeper 🦴🦴🦴 ½ **1973 (PG)** Hapless nerd Allen is revived two hundred years after an operation gone bad. Keaton portrays Allen's love interest in a futuristic land of robots and giant vegetables. He learns of the hitherto unknown health benefits of hot fudge sundaes; discovers the truth about the nation's dictator, known as The Leader; and gets involved with revolutionaries seeking to overthrow the government. Hilarious, fast-moving comedy, full of slapstick and satire. Don't miss the "orgasmatron." **88m/C; VHS, DVD, Blu-Ray.** Woody Allen; Diane Keaton; John Beck; Mary Gregory; Don Keefer; John McLiam; *D:* Woody Allen; *W:* Woody Allen; Marshall Brickman; *C:* David M. Walsh; *M:* Woody Allen.

Sleeper Cell 🦴🦴 ½ **2005** Darwyn (Ealy) is a black Muslim FBI agent posing as a disgruntled ex-con to infiltrate an LA terrorist cell. Seems there's a plot by charismatic leader Farik (Fehr) to attack various city sites. Then Darwyn gets distracted from his work by getting involved with single mom Gayle (Sagemiller). Ten-episode miniseries suffers from a saggy middle and a rather bland lead. **600m/C; DVD.** Michael Ealy; Oded Fehr; Grant Heslov; Melissa Sagemiller; Alex Nesic; James LeGros; Henri Lubatti; *D:* Clark Johnson; *W:* Cyrus Voris; Ethan Reiff; *C:* Robert Primes; *M:* Paul Haslinger. **CABLE**

Sleepers 🦴🦴 ½ **1996 (R)** Tense, gritty drama based on Lorenzo Carcaterra's book about four teenaged friends from Hell's Kitchen who get into trouble and wind up being sent to a reform school, where they're brutalized by guards. John (Eldard) and Tommy (Crudup), who grow up to be hit men, recognize their chief abuser (Bacon) years later and kill him. Their trial is prosecuted by Michael (Pitt), another of the gang, who's now the assistant DA. It's supposed to be a true story (the book is published as non-fiction) but doubt has been cast on Carcaterra's veracity (his character is the fourth member, journalist Lorenzo, played by Patric). De Niro and Hoffman excel in relatively minor, but pivotal, roles. **150m/C; VHS, DVD.** Brad Pitt; Jason Patric; Ron Eldard; Billy Crudup; Kevin Bacon; Robert De Niro; Dustin Hoffman; Vittorio Gassman; Minnie Driver; Terry Kinney; Brad Renfro; Jonathan Tucker; Joe Perrino; Geoff Wigdor; Bruno Kirby; Aida Turturro; Frank Medrano; *D:* Barry Levinson; *W:* Barry Levinson; *C:* Michael Ballhaus; *M:* John Williams.

Sleepers West 🦴🦴 ½ **1941** Ah, the romance of the sleeper train! Only Shayne's (Nolan) on the job, transporting alcoholic ex-showgirl Helen (Hughes) from Denver to San Francisco so she can give her surprise testimony in a murder trial. Also aboard are Shayne's ex-girlfriend, snoopy reporter Kay Bentley (Bari), and her lawyer fiance (Douglas). Could they have anything to do with the attempts to prevent Helen from arriving safely at the station? **74m/B; DVD.** Lloyd Nolan; Lynn Bari; Mary Beth Hughes; Donald "Don" Douglas; Louis Jean Heydt; Edward Brophy; Don Costello; Ben Carter; *D:* Eugene Forde; *W:* Lou Breslow; Stanley Rauh; *C:* J. Peverell Marley; *M:* Cyril Mockridge.

Sleeping Beauty 🦴🦴🦴 **1959 (G)** Classic Walt Disney version of the famous fairy tale is set to the music of Tchaikovsky's ballet. Lavishly produced. With the voices of Mary Costa, Bill Shirley, and Vera Vague. **75m/C; VHS, DVD, Blu-Ray.** *V:* Mary Costa; Bill (William) Shirley; Barbara Luddy; Taylor Holmes; Verna Felton; Barbara Jo Allen; Pinto Colvig; Marvin Miller; *D:* Clyde Geronimi; Eric Larson; Wolfgang Reitherman; Les Clark; *M:* George Bruns. Natl. Film Reg. '19.

Sleeping Beauty 🦴 ½ **1989** Live action version of the beloved fairy tale, with Welch in the title role. **92m/C; VHS, DVD.** Tahnee Welch; Morgan Fairchild; Nicholas Clay; Sylvia Miles; Kenny Baker.

The Sleeping Beauty 🦴🦴 *La Belle Endormie* **2010** Writer/director Breillat continues her feminist revision with the 17th-century Charles Perrault fairytale, although this time she also includes Hans Christian Andersen's "The Snow Queen" into the plot. Tomboy royal Anastasia is cursed by evil fairy Carabosse to die but her fate is modified and instead she falls asleep at six and experiences vivid dreams filled with adventure and magic. When she awakens 100 years later, a beautiful 16-year-old, she must fit into a conventional life and romance. French with subtitles. **82m/C; DVD.** *FR* Carla Besnainou; Julia Artamonov; Kieran Mayan; David Chausse; Romane Portail; Diana Rudychenko; Rosine Favey; Anne-Lise Kedres; Rhizlaine El Cohen; *D:* Catherine Breillat; *W:* Catherine Breillat; *C:* Denis Lenoir.

Sleeping Beauty 🦴 ½ **2011** Passive university student Lucy (Browning) takes a job at an older men's club at a country mansion that requires her complete submission, which is obtained by sedating her. Sex isn't the point—rather the erotic fantasies of the clients. While the viewer sees all, Lucy inevitably questions what happens during these sessions. Browning is gorgeous but director Leigh's debut is just plain blah, especially considering the provocative subject matter. **104m/C; DVD, Blu-Ray.** *AU* Emily Browning; Rachael Blake; Peter Carroll; Ewen Leslie; Chris Haywood; Hugh Keays-Byrne; *D:* Julia Leigh; *W:* Julia Leigh; *C:* Geoffrey Simpson; *M:* Ben Frost.

The Sleeping Dictionary 🦴🦴 ½ **2002 (R)** In the 1930s, young Englishman John Truscott (Dancy) is newly arrived to take up his government post in Sarawak, Malaysia (where the movie was filmed). Governor Henry Bullard (Hoskins) tells Truscott that he will only be able to educate the native Iban population by learning their language and customs, so he arranges for the beautiful half-breed Selima (Alba) to become John's tutor. But John is not suppose to fall in love with the girl. Beautiful but slow-moving and that's a body double in Alba's love scenes. **109m/C; VHS, DVD.** Hugh Dancy; Jessica Alba; Bob Hoskins; Brenda Blethyn; Emily Mortimer; Noah Taylor; *D:* Guy Jenkin; *W:* Guy Jenkin; *C:* Martin Fuhrer; *M:* Simon Boswell.

Sleeping Dogs 🦴🦴 ½ **1977** A man in near-future New Zealand finds it hard to remain neutral when he is caught between a repressive government and a violent resistance movement. The first New Zealand film ever to open in the U.S., and a fine debut for director Donaldson. **107m/C; VHS, DVD, Blu-Ray.** *NZ* Sam Neill; Ian Mune; Nevan Rowe; Dona Akersten; Warren Oates; *D:* Roger Donaldson.

Sleeping Dogs Lie 🦴🦴 *Stay* **2006 (R)** Should you be completely honest in any relationship? Goldthwait's answer is a firm "no" in this off-the-wall comedy. When she was a bored college student, Amy (Hamilton) got, uh, very friendly with her dog (it's implied, not shown). When her fiance John (Johnson) asks Amy to tell him her deepest, darkest secret, she does. He's repulsed. Unfortunately, this situation occurs during their meet-the-parents weekend and Amy is left to deal with the consequences. Hamilton's a sweetie and the low-budget indie is subversively engaging. **87m/C; DVD.** Bryce Johnson; Geoffrey Pierson; Jack Plotnick; Bonita Friedericy; Melinda Page Hamilton; Colby French; *D:* Bobcat Goldthwait; *W:* Bobcat Goldthwait; *C:* Ian S. Takahashi; *M:* Jerry Brunskill.

The Sleeping Tiger 🦴🦴 ½ **1954** A thief breaks into the home of a psychiatrist, who captures him. In exchange for his freedom, the thief agrees to become a guinea pig for the doctor's rehabilitation theories with ultimately tragic results. Director Losey was originally compelled to release the film under a pseudonym, "Victor Hanbury," because he had been blacklisted by Hollywood during the 1950s red scare. First pairing of Losey and Bogarde, who collaborated on several later films, including "Modesty Blaise" (1966) and "Accident" (1967). **89m/B; VHS, DVD.** Alexis Smith; Alexander Knox; Dirk Bogarde; Hugh Griffith; *D:* Joseph Losey; *W:* Harold Buchman; Carl Foreman; *M:* Malcolm Arnold.

Sleeping with Other People 🦴🦴 ½ **2015 (R)** Jake (Sudeikis) is a serial womanizer and Lainey (Brie) sleeps around. But when both meet up after a few years apart, they become friends instead of lovers, supporting each other in their conquests. Of course, this can't last. Writer/director Headland's romantic comedy is an obvious update of the "can men and women be friends" template of "When Harry Met Sally"... but it works because of her light directorial touch and very likable performances from the two leads. Sudeikis and Brie have striking chemistry and both should be much bigger stars. **95m/C; DVD.** Alison Brie; Jason Sudeikis; Adam Scott; Jason Mantzoukas; Katherine Waterston; Anna Margaret Hollyman; *D:* Leslye Headland; *W:* Leslye Headland; *C:* Ben Kutchins; *M:* Andrew Feltenstein; John Nau.

Sleeping with the Enemy 🦴🦴 ½ **1991 (R)** Roberts escapes from abusive husband by faking death, flees to Iowa, falls for drama professor, and, gasp, is found by psycho husband. Occasionally chilling but oft predictable thriller based on novel by Nancy Price. **99m/C; VHS, DVD, Blu-Ray.** Julia Roberts; Kevin Anderson; Patrick Bergin; Elizabeth Lawrence; Kyle Secor; Claudette Nevins; *D:* Joseph Ruben; *W:* Ronald Bass; *M:* Jerry Goldsmith.

Sleepless 🦴🦴 **2001** Argento, the master of arty gore, returns in a familiar story. Retired inspector von Sydow is called back into service when a series of murders is identical to a prostitute murder spree (committed by a dwarf!) that the inspector solved 17 years earlier. Also back is the only witness (Dionisi) from the earlier crimes. **117m/C; VHS, DVD, Blu-Ray.** *IT* Max von Sydow; Stefano Dionisi; Chiara Caselli; *D:* Dario Argento; *W:* Dario Argento; Franco Ferrini; *C:* Ronnie Taylor. **VIDEO**

Sleepless 🦴 ½ **2017 (R)** Vincent (a slumming Foxx, who can do this in his sleep, pun intended) is a Las Vegas cop, partnered with a crooked officer, who steals some drugs from a powerful kingpin. When the drug lord discovers who stole his drugs, he kidnaps Vincent's son, ordering the officer to bring the stolen drugs to the casino. What should be a tense action thriller about a tough cop doing anything to get his kid back from a criminal boss and his lackeys is remarkably slow and dry. It only occasionally explodes into the B-movie escapism it needed to be throughout. **96m/C; DVD, Blu-Ray, Streaming.** Jamie Foxx; Michelle Monaghan; Dermot Mulroney; Gabrielle Union; David Harbour; *D:* Baran bo Odar; *W:* Andrea Berloff; *C:* Mihai Malaimare, Jr.; *M:* Michael Kamm.

Sleepless in Seattle 🦴🦴🦴 ½ **1993 (PG)** Witty, sweet romantic comedy explores the differences between men and women when it comes to love and romance. When widower Sam Bladwin (Hanks) talks about his wife on a national talk show, recently engaged Annie Reed (Ryan) responds. Writer/director Ephron's humorous screenplay is brought to life by a perfectly cast ensemble; it also breathed new life into the classic weepie "An Affair to Remember," comparing it to "The Dirty Dozen" in an unforgettable scene. A movie full of fine detail, from Sven Nykvist's camera work to the graphic layout of the opening credits to the great score. Captured millions at the boxoffice, coming in as the fourth highest grossing movie of 1993. **105m/C; VHS, DVD, Blu-Ray.** Tom Hanks; Meg Ryan; Bill Pullman; Ross Malinger; Rosie O'Donnell; Gaby Hoffman; Victor Garber; Rita Wilson; Barbara Garrick; Carey Lowell; Rob Reiner; Sarah Trigger; *D:* Nora Ephron; *W:* Jeffrey Arch; Larry Atlas; David S. Ward; Nora Ephron; *C:* Sven Nykvist; *M:* Marc Shaiman.

Sleepless Night 🦴🦴🦴 *Nuit Blanche* **2011** A corrupt cop (Sisley) watches his world fall apart when a drug heist gets his son kidnapped by a nightclub-owning crime lord. The bag of cocaine he needs to get his child back goes missing and he's forced to think on his feet--and fast. Taking place mostly within the massive nightclub, it moves along at a breakneck pace that helps to elevate this French thriller. And though the plotline is concise, it suffers from a few too many plot holes. **98m/C; DVD.** *FR BE* Tomer Sisley; Serge Riaboukine; Julien Boisselier; Joey Starr; Laurent Stocker; Dominique Bettenfeld; Samy Seghir; *D:* Frederic Jardin; *W:* Frederic Jardin; Olivier Douyere; *C:* Tom Stern; *M:* Nicolas Errera.

Sleepover 🦴 ½ **2004 (PG)** Lightweight teen comedy has outsider Julie (Vega) celebrating her graduation from junior high by hosting a sleepover with friends Hannah (Boorem), Yancy (Childress), and Farah (Taylor-Compton). Julie breaks parental rules and sneaks out when challenged by popular Stacie (Paxton) to a scavenger hunt—the winner gaining social status in high school. Since these girls are about 14, some scenes—involving older men, bars, showers, and barely-there attire—are quease-inducing if not downright sleazy, although the intended audience will no doubt think all the highjinks are great fun. **90m/C; VHS, DVD, Blu-Ray.** Alexa Vega; Mika Boorem; Sam Huntington; Jane Lynch; Scout Taylor-Compton; Kallie Flynn Childress; Jeff Garlin; Sean Faris; Sara Paxton; Eileen April Boylan; Timothy Dowling; Brie Larson; *D:* Joe Nussbaum; *W:* Elisa Bell; *C:* James L. Carter; *M:* Deborah Lurie.

Sleepstalker: The Sandman's Last Rites 🦴🦴 **1994 (R)** A serial killer known as the Sandman (Harris) is executed but returns as a shape-shifting horror who can strip the flesh off his victims with whirling sand. He haunts the nightmares of a reporter (Underwood), the only survivor of one of the killer's massacres, who teams up with a photographer (Morris) to learn the creature's origins and defeat him. Good special effects. **101m/C; VHS, DVD.** Jay Underwood; Michael (M.K.) Harris; Kathryn Morris; ***D:*** Turi Meyer.

Sleepwalk with Me 1/2 **2012 (PG-13)** Up-and-coming stand-up comedian Matt Pandamiglio (Birbiglia) has some issues. First, he can't seem to commit to his longtime girlfriend Abby (Ambrose), even though she's pretty much perfect and his parents are gunning for grandkids. Second, his comedy career isn't going so great. Third, he's having some pretty crazy nightmares. When he wakes up on the hotel lawn after jumping out of a second floor window in his sleep, Matt finds some answers in a diagnosis of REM sleep-behavior disorder. Comic Mike Birbiglia plays himself in what began as a one-man off-Broadway show turned book, turned imperfectly charming and funny film. **90m/C; DVD, Blu-Ray.** Mike Birbiglia; Lauren Ambrose; James Rebhorn; Carol Kane; Cristin Milioti; ***D:*** Mike Birbiglia; Seth Barrish; ***W:*** Mike Birbiglia; Seth Barrish; Joe Birbiglia; Ira Glass; ***C:*** Adam Beckman; ***M:*** Andrew Hollander.

Sleepwalkers 1/2 *Stephen King's Sleepwalkers* **1992 (R)** When Mary and her son Charles arrive in the small town of Travis, Indiana, ugly things begin to happen. And no wonder, it seems the deadly duo are sleepwalkers—fiendish, cat-like vampire creatures who can only survive by sucking the life force out of unsuspecting virgins. Gory but not without some humor, particularly in Krige's portrayal of the sexy and too-loving mother. Not nearly as good as some of King's other horror classics. **91m/C; VHS, DVD, Blu-Ray.** Brian Krause; Madchen Amick; Alice Krige; Jim Haynie; Cindy Pickett; Lyman Ward; Ron Perlman; Stephen King; Tobe Hooper; Mark Hamill; Glenn Shadix; Joe Dante; Clive Barker; John Landis; Dan Martin; ***D:*** Mick Garris; ***W:*** Stephen King; ***C:*** Rodney Charters; ***M:*** Nicholas Pike.

Sleepwalking 1/2 **2008 (R)** Down-and-out single mom Joleen (Theron) and her tween daughter Tara (Robb) are left homeless after Joleen's boyfriend is busted for drugs. The two drop in to visit Joleen's good-natured brother James (Stahl), but mom splits that night, leaving James stuck with the girl. Soon enough James loses his job and apartment, and Tara is taken away by Social Services. James then steals Tara back and they escape to the family farm house, still occupied by James and Joleen's villainous father (Hopper). A depressing, slow-moving indie flick, appropriately titled. **101m/C; Blu-Ray.** *CA US* Charlize Theron; Nick Stahl; AnnaSophia Robb; Dennis Hopper; Woody Harrelson; Deborra-Lee Furness; ***D:*** William Maher; ***W:*** Zac Stanford; ***C:*** Juan Ruiz Anchia; ***M:*** Christopher Young.

Sleepy Hollow **1999 (R)** Gorgeous and grisly Burtonized version of Washington Irving's tale "The Legend of Sleepy Hollow." In this retelling, Ichabod Crane (Depp) is a New York constable who believes in reason and science, which won't do him much good when he's sent to the upstate hamlet of Sleepy Hollow to investigate a series of decapitation murders. Crane is housed by wealthy Balthus Van Tassel (Gambon), whose somewhat fey daughter Katrina (Ricci) falls for the quaking Crane, who refuses to believe that a ghost is committing mayhem. He's soon confronted by the graphic evidence of his own eyes. (Heads do certainly roll). Landau has a wordless cameo as the second victim. **105m/C; VHS, DVD, Blu-Ray, UMD, HD-DVD.** Johnny Depp; Christina Ricci; Miranda Richardson; Michael Gambon; Christopher Walken; Casper Van Dien; Jeffrey Jones; Richard Griffiths; Ian McDiarmid; Michael Gough; Christopher Lee; Marc Pickering; Lisa Marie; Steven Waddington; Claire Skinner; Alun Armstrong; Mark Spalding; Jessica Oyelowo; ***Cameo(s):*** Martin Landau; ***D:*** Tim Burton; ***W:*** Andrew Kevin Walker; ***C:*** Emmanuel Lubezki; ***M:*** Danny Elfman. Oscars '99: Art Dir./Set Dec.; British Acad. '99: Art Dir./Set Dec., Costume Des.

The Sleepy Time Gal **2001** Frances (Bisset), in her fifties and suffering from cancer, begins reflecting on her life and the daughter she gave up for adoption. Just about this time, her daughter, Rebecca (Plimpton) has been thinking about her birth mother. Film follows both stories by showing parallels between Frances youth and Rebecca's life. In a subplot, Frances visits old flame (and Rebecca's father) Bob, and ends up bonding with his writer wife Betty. Pic steers perilously close to TV disease-movie-of-the-week territory, but impressive performance by Bisset helps it get by. Interesting melodrama will do if the cable's out and you can't watch Lifetime. **94m/C; VHS, DVD.** Jacqueline Bisset; Martha Plimpton; Nick Stahl; Amy Madigan; Frankie Faison; Carmen Zapata; Seymour Cassel; Peggy Gormley; Kate McGregor-Stewart; ***D:*** Christopher Munch; ***W:*** Christopher Munch; ***C:*** Rob Sweeney.

Sleight 1/2 **2017 (R)** Bo (Latimore) is a street magician raising his sister (Reid) after the death of their parents. He's also working for local drug kingpin Angelo (Hill) to make ends meet. Angelo has pulled him deeper into the life than he wanted to go, and getting out is complicated by Bo's budding romance with Holly (Gabriel), who has some secrets of her own. Low-budget (in a good way) thriller-romance-family drama is satisfying on many levels: Excellent performances by all (especially lead Latimore), a sharp story with excellent characterization, and a refusal to be defined by genre norms. **89m/C; DVD, Blu-Ray.** Jacob Latimore; Seychelle Gabriel; Dulé Hill; Storm Reid; Sasheer Zamata; ***D:*** J.D. Dillard; ***W:*** J.D. Dillard; Alex Theurer; ***C:*** Ed Wu; ***M:*** Charles Scott, IV.

Slender Man **2018 (PG-13)** When four teenage friends--delicate Katie (Basso), Wren (King), Chloe (Sinclair), and Hallie (Goldani Telles)--watch a cursed video online that is intended to summon the Slender Man (Botet), they begin to see and hear strange things especially near a tree-lined area. After Katie disappears, her friends panic and believe the Slender Man, a faceless figure in a suit who steals children and demands sacrifice, is involved. To get her back, the high schoolers offer up something they love. Though based on a well-known urban legend, this update of the boogeyman myth takes few risks and is generally uninspired. **93m/C; DVD, Blu-Ray.** Joey King; Juliana Telles; Jaz Sinclair; Annalise Basso; Alex Fitzalan; ***D:*** Sylvain White; ***W:*** David Birke; ***C:*** Luca Del Puppo; ***M:*** Brandon Campbell; Ramin Djawadi.

The Slender Thread **1965** Based on a true story, Poitier plays a college student who volunteers at a crisis center and must keep would-be suicide Bancroft on the phone until the police can find her. Filmed on location in Seattle. First film for director Pollack. **98m/C; DVD, Blu-Ray.** Sidney Poitier; Anne Bancroft; Telly Savalas; Steven Hill; Ed Asner; Paul Newlan; ***D:*** Sydney Pollack; ***W:*** Stirling Silliphant; ***C:*** Loyal Griggs; ***M:*** Quincy Jones.

Sleuth 1/2 **1972 (PG)** Milo (Caine), the owner of a chain of hair salons, is invited to the home of detective novelist Andrew Wyke (Olivier), who reveals that he Milo and Wyke's wife Marguerite are lovers. He persuades Milo to assist him with a fake robbery and an insurance scam that will help them both. Of course, Shaffer's complex plot (taken from his play) results in ever shifting, elaborate, and diabolical plots against each man, complete with red herrings, traps, and tricks. Playful, cerebral mystery thriller from top director Mankiewicz. **138m/C; VHS, DVD.** Laurence Olivier; Michael Caine; John Matthews; Alec Cawthorne; Teddy Martin; ***D:*** Joseph L. Mankiewicz; ***W:*** Anthony Shaffer; ***C:*** Oswald Morris; ***M:*** John Addison. N.Y. Film Critics '72: Actor (Olivier).

Sleuth **2007 (R)** You'd think that Law would've learned his lesson after trying to fill Caine's shoes in his "Alfie" remake. But no, here he remakes the 1972 pic, tackling the Caine role while Caine himself steps into Laurence Olivier's part. Working-class upstart Milo Tindle (Law) has been boffing the wife of rich mystery writer Andrew Wyke (Caine). Andrew invites Milo to his ultramodern manor to discuss the situation and says he'll give his wife a divorce if Milo will stage a jewel robbery so Andrew can claim the insurance. Pinter ups the homoerotic subtext and trims a lot of Anthony Shaffer's original dialogue, but it's all for naught as Branagh seems lost without a crowd to direct. However, Caine is as reliable as ever. **86m/C; DVD.** *GB US* Michael Caine; Jude Law; ***D:*** Kenneth Branagh; ***W:*** Harold Pinter; ***C:*** Haris Zambarloukos; ***M:*** Patrick Doyle.

Sliding Doors 1/2 **1997 (R)** The sliding doors are those of a London subway train. If Helen (Paltrow) makes it through before they close, her life (and loves) go one way. If she's left on the platform, they go another, and the audience is let in on both options. She'll either dump or stick with cheating boyfriend Gerry (Lynch), who has been sleeping with ultra-bitchy ex-girlfriend Lydia (Tripplehorn). And she will either strike up a relationship with a charming stranger (Hannah) on the train and become fabulously successful, or end up slinging hash in a diner while pregnant with her scumbag boyfriend's baby. The concept and story of the dual possibilities is pulled off well, although it is a bit too cute at times. Will you like it? Depends on if it's already been rented when you're at the video store. If it's out, be careful what you pick, because apparently the small stuff really does matter. **98m/C; VHS, DVD, Blu-Ray.** Gwyneth Paltrow; John Lynch; John Hannah; Jeanne Tripplehorn; Virginia McKenna; Zara Turner; Douglas McFerran; Paul Brightwell; Nina Young; ***D:*** Peter Howitt; ***W:*** Peter Howitt; ***C:*** Remi Adefarasin; ***M:*** David Hirschfelder.

A Slight Case of Larceny 1/2 **1953** And a slight MGM B-movie comedy. Married Fred (Bracken) is persuaded by his ex-Army buddy Geechy (Rooney) into opening a gas station. They do okay until a big oil company opens a rival station across the street. Geechy gets the idea to siphon off gas from the competition's pipeline to start a price war, but it eventually gets the boys in big trouble. **71m/B; DVD.** Mickey Rooney; Eddie Bracken; Elaine Stewart; Marilyn Erskine; Douglas Fowley; ***D:*** Don Weis; ***W:*** Jerry Davis; ***C:*** Ray June.

A Slight Case of Murder 1/2 **1938** Robinson spoofs his own tough-guy image in this screwy comedy. Remy (Robinson) and his gang made a fortune as bootleggers selling lousy beer. Now that Prohibition is over, Remy is nearly bankrupt trying to sell the same rotgut and needs cash fast. To top off the bad news, daughter Mary (Bryan) get engaged to state trooper Dick (Parker). The family heads to their country home so Remy can think but he finds four dead gangsters and loot from a heist littering up the place while shooter Innocence (Downing) is lurking around. Oh, and company is coming. **85m/B; DVD.** Edward G. Robinson; Jane Bryan; Allen Jenkins; Ruth Donnelly; Willard Parker; John Litel; Edward Brophy; Harold Huber; Paul Harvey; Bobby Jordan; Margaret Hamilton; George E. Stone; Bert Hanlon; Betty Compson; John Harmon; Harry Tenbrook; ***D:*** Lloyd Bacon; ***W:*** Earl Baldwin; Joseph Schrank; ***C:*** Sidney Hickox; ***M:*** Adolph Deutsch; Howard Jackson; Heinz Roemheld.

A Slight Case of Murder 1/2 **1999** Cable TV critic Terry Thorpe (Macy) is in a panic after accidentally killing one of his girlfriends. Instead of confessing, Terry tries to keep the truth from the cops (Arkin, Pickens Jr.) and his surviving gal pal (Huffman). Then along comes a suspicious PI (Cromwell) with a blackmail scheme. Goofy film noir that gets too complicated. Based on the novel "A Travesty" by Donald E. Westlake. **94m/C; VHS, DVD.** William H. Macy; Adam Arkin; Felicity Huffman; James Cromwell; James Pickens, Jr.; Julia Campbell; Paul Mazursky; Vincent Pastore; ***D:*** Steven Schachter; ***W:*** William H. Macy; Steven Schachter; ***C:*** Andre Pienaar. **CABLE**

Slightly Dangerous **1943** After getting fired by boss Bob Stuart (Young), bored small town clerk Peggy Evans (Turner) heads to New York where she gets a makeover, fakes amnesia, and passes herself off as the long-lost daughter of wealthy Cornelius Burden (Brennan). Because of convoluted circumstances, Bob self-servingly follows along leading to bad consequences for the dame. **94m/B; DVD.** Lana Turner; Robert Young; Walter Brennan; Dame May Whitty; Eugene Pallette; Florence Bates; ***D:*** Wesley Ruggles; ***W:*** Charles Lederer; George Oppenheimer; ***C:*** Harold Rosson; ***M:*** Bronislau Kaper.

Slightly French 1/2 **1949** A musical comedy bon-bon from director Sirk. Egocentric director John Gayle (Ameche) drives his leading lady to a breakdown and gets fired by the film's producer. He has a chance meeting with carnival singer/dancer Mary (Lamour) and decides to turn the Brooklynite into elegant French actress Rochelle so she can take over the role and he can get his job back. Mary's willing but John's superior attitude causes problems. **81m/B; DVD.** Don Ameche; Dorothy Lamour; Janis Carter; Willard Parker; Adele Jergens; Jeanne Manet; Frank Ferguson; ***D:*** Douglas Sirk; ***W:*** Karen DeWolf; ***C:*** Charles Lawton, Jr.; ***M:*** George Duning.

Slightly Honorable 1/2 **1940** A lawyer gets involved in political scandals and becomes a murder suspect. Snappy comedy-drama with good performances but too many subplots. Based on the novel "Send Another Coffin" by F. G. Presnell. **75m/B; VHS, DVD.** Pat O'Brien; Broderick Crawford; Edward Arnold; Eve Arden; Evelyn Keyes; Phyllis Brooks; ***D:*** Tay Garnett.

A Slightly Pregnant Man **1979 (PG)** Comic complications abound as a construction worker becomes the world's first pregnant man. Surprise ending saves this simple and not very exciting film. **92m/C; VHS, DVD.** *FR IT* Catherine Deneuve; Marcello Mastroianni; Marisa Pavan; Micheline Presle; Claude Melki; Andre Falcon; Maurice Biraud; Alice Sapritch; Micheline Dax; ***D:*** Jacques Demy; ***W:*** Jacques Demy; ***C:*** Andreas Winding; ***M:*** Michel Legrand.

Slightly Scarlet 1/2 **1956** Small-time hood Payne carries out an assignment from boss DeCorsia to smear a law-and-order politico running for mayor. He falls in love with the candidate's secretary, tries to go straight, and ends up running the mob when DeCorsia flees town. A spiffy, low-budget noir crime drama based on the James M. Cain novel "Love's Lovely Counterfeit." **99m/C; VHS, DVD.** Rhonda Fleming; Arlene Dahl; John Payne; Kent Taylor; Ted de Corsia; ***D:*** Allan Dwan; ***W:*** Robert Blees; ***C:*** John Alton; ***M:*** Louis Forbes.

Slim 1/2 **1937** Melodramatic buddy flick. Farm boy Slim (Fonda) wants to be an electrical lineman for the power company and persuades veteran Red (O'Brien) to take him on. Slim's quickly trained to lay lines but he also takes an interest in Red's younger girlfriend Cally (Lindsey), who's fearful of the dangerous job. With good reason as Slim and Red face a desperate situation when they must make repairs during a blizzard. William Wister Haines adapted from his novel. Jane Wyman makes an appearance as pal Stumpy's (Erwin) girlfriend. **85m/B; DVD.** Henry Fonda; Pat O'Brien; Margaret Lindsay; Dick Purcell; Stuart Erwin; J. Farrell MacDonald; ***D:*** Ray Enright; ***W:*** William Wister Haines; ***C:*** Sidney Hickox.

Slime City **1989** The widow of an alchemist poisons her tenants so they will join her husband in the hereafter. Very low-budget; occasionally funny. **90m/C; VHS, DVD, Blu-Ray.** Robert C. Sabin; Mary Huner; T.J. Merrick; Dick Biel; ***D:*** Gregory Lamberson.

The Slime People **WOOF!** **1963** Huge prehistoric monsters are awakened from long hibernation by atomic testing in Los Angeles. They take over the city, creating the fog they need to live. Thank goodness for scientist Burton, who saves the day. Filmed in a butcher shop in Los Angeles. **76m/B; VHS, DVD.** Robert Hutton; Robert Burton; Susan Hart; William Boyce; Les Tremayne; John Close; Judee Morton; ***D:*** Robert Hutton; ***W:*** Vance Skarstedt; ***C:*** William G. Troiano.

Sling Blade 1/2 **1996 (R)** Mildly retarded killer Karl Childers (Thornton, making his feature directorial debut) is released from a mental hospital, where he was placed after killing his mother and her lover, after 25 years. Returning to his hometown, he befriends a boy (Black) with problems of his own. His mother is living with a mean, bullying drunkard (Yoakam, in a brilliant performance) who has no use for anyone, least of all mom's openly gay co-worker (Ritter). Thornton's excellent script moves at the slow pace of its hero, providing the superb cast plenty of opportunity to explore the rich characterization and dialogue. Filmed in Thornton's home state of Arkansas. **134m/C; VHS, DVD, Blu-Ray.** Billy Bob Thornton; Dwight Yoakam; John Ritter; Lucas Black; Natalie Canerday; James Hampton; Robert Duvall; J.T. Walsh; Rick Dial; Brent Briscoe; Christy Ward; Col. Bruce Hampton; Vic Chesnutt; Mickey

Jones; Jim Jarmusch; Ian Moore; *D:* Billy Bob Thornton; *W:* Billy Bob Thornton; *C:* Barry Markowitz; *M:* Daniel Lanois. Oscars '96: Adapt. Screenplay; Ind. Spirit '97: First Feature; Writers Guild '96: Adapt. Screenplay.

The Slingshot 1993 (R) Quirky coming-of-age tale, set in 1920s Stockholm, finds 12-year-old Roland (Salen) trying to survive childhood dilemmas. His mother (Frydman) is a Russian Jew (who sells condoms illegally) and his father (Skarsgard) is a zealous socialist, so Roland is subjected to unceasing bullying and prejudice. But the resourceful Roland doesn't let society get him down—he uses the contraband condoms in an inventive slingshot design that brings him an unwarranted amount of attention. Based on the novel by Roland Schutt. Swedish with subtitles. **102m/C; VHS, Streaming.** *SW* Jesper Salen; Stellan Skarsgard; Basia Frydman; Niclas Olund; Ernst-Hugo Jaregard; Jacob Leygraf; *D:* Ake Sandgren; *W:* Bjorn Isfalt; Ake Sandgren.

The Slipper and the Rose 1/2 1976 (G) Lavish musical adaptation of the fairy tale "Cinderella." Chamberlain is a very princely prince and the lovely Craven makes a fine and spunky servant girl, whom he can't help falling in love with. Besides the lively musical numbers, viewers will also enjoy the beautiful Austrian scenery. **127m/C; VHS, DVD, Blu-Ray.** *GB* Richard Chamberlain; Gemma Craven; Annette Crosbie; Edith Evans; Christopher Gable; Michael Hordern; Margaret Lockwood; Kenneth More; Julian Orchard; Lally Bowers; Sherrie Hewson; Rosalind Ayres; John Turner; Keith Skinner; Polly Williams; Norman Bird; Roy Barraclough; Peter Graves; ***Cameo(s):*** Bryan Forbes; *D:* Bryan Forbes; *W:* Bryan Forbes; Robert B. Sherman; Richard M. Sherman; *C:* Tony Imi; *M:* Robert B. Sherman; Richard M. Sherman.

Slippery Slope 1/2 2006 Unbending radical feminist Gillian (Hutchinson) has her documentary accepted at Cannes but she needs 50 thou to get it out of hock at the film lab. Desperate, she accepts a job directing porn she's re-worked from literary classics. However, since she's working out of a Long Island motel, Gillian's browbeaten hubby Hugh (True-Frost) thinks she's having an affair. Has its humorous moments but how Gillian does solve her money woes is a letdown. **81m/C; DVD.** Jim True-Frost; Laila Robins; Wes Ramsey; Leslie Lyles; Kelly Hutchinson; *D:* Sarah Schenck; *W:* Sarah Schenck; *C:* Wolfgang Held.

A Slipping Down Life 1999 (R) The often-quirky Taylor gives a quirky performance as meek and depressed Evie, who has a crummy amusement park job in a small town and nothing to look forward to. That is, until she becomes obsessed with a struggling local musician called Drumstrings Casey (laconically played by Pearce). She carves his (last) name on her forehead, which at least gets Drumstrings attention and leads to some much-needed publicity. Evie begins to blossom under his interest and he appreciates her devotion, but is that all there is? You'll also be saying that about this indie (Fans of Anne Tyler, on whose novel, her first, the film is based, may not be happy that the teenagers are now twenty-somethings). After showing at the Sundance Film Festival, litigation kept the film out of circulation for five years. **111m/C; VHS, DVD.** Lili Taylor; Guy Pearce; John Hawkes; Sara Rue; Irma P. Hall; Tom Bower; Shawnee Smith; Veronica Cartwright; Marshall Bell; Bruno Kirby; *D:* Toni Kalem; *W:* Toni Kalem; *C:* Michael Barrow; *M:* Peter Himmelman.

Slipstream 1989 (PG-13) A sci-fi adventure set on a damaged Earthscape where people seek to escape a giant jet-stream. While tracking down a bounty hunter gone bad, a futuristic cop follows his quarry into the dangerous river of wind. Ambitious "Blade Runner" clone with big names (Hamill is good) was never released theatrically in the US. **92m/C; VHS, DVD, Blu-Ray; Open Captioned.** *GB* Mark Hamill; Bill Paxton; Bob Peck; Eleanor David; Kitty Aldridge; Robbie Coltrane; Ben Kingsley; F. Murray Abraham; *D:* Steven Lisberger; *W:* Tony Kayden; *C:* Frank Tidy; *M:* Elmer Bernstein.

Slipstream 2007 (R) Hopkins is the star, writer, director, and composer of this self-indulgent, experimental fantasy. Early scenes turn out to be part of a movie script that is being rewritten by aging screenwriter Felix—a production that is falling apart because its star (Slater) has suddenly died. Characters pop in and out of Felix's imagination offering suggestions and complaints while most viewers will wonder what the heck was going on in Hopkins' head. **96m/C; DVD, Blu-Ray.** Anthony Hopkins; Christian Slater; John Turturro; Michael Clarke Duncan; S. Epatha Merkerson; Fionnula Flanagan; Jeffrey Tambor; Camryn Manheim; Gavin Grazer; Lana Antonova; *D:* Anthony Hopkins; *W:* Anthony Hopkins; *C:* Dante Spinotti; *M:* Anthony Hopkins.

Slither 1973 (PG) Caan and Boyle become wrapped up in a scheme to recover $300,000 in cash, stolen seven years previously. Along the way they pick up speed freak Kellerman, who assists them in a variety of loony ways. Frantic chase scenes are the highlight. **97m/C; VHS, DVD.** James Caan; Peter Boyle; Sally Kellerman; Louise Lasser; Allen Garfield; Richard B. Shull; Alex Rocco; *D:* Howard Zieff; *W:* W.D. Richter.

Slither 2006 (R) Slime and disfiguration abound after a meteorite crashes to Earth, allowing a nasty little alien hitchhiker to burrow into the chest of a prominent businessman. From there, things get ugly. Literally. Picture the Elephant Man covered in snot, hungry for flesh, and stripped of his dashing good looks. Done with style, intelligence, and tongue firmly in cheek, it makes for a good ol' fashioned popcorn n' mutations kind of flick. Tremendous props for ditching CGI and utilizing old-school make-up effects. These creatures pulsate and drip and shock better than any MPEG file. **95m/C; DVD, Blu-Ray, HD-DVD.** *US CA* Nathan Fillion; Elizabeth Banks; Gregg Henry; Michael Rooker; Brenda James; Don Thompson; Tania Saulnier; Jenna Fischer; *D:* James Gunn; *W:* James Gunn; *C:* Gregory Middleton; *M:* Tyler Bates.

Sliver 1/2 1993 (R) Another voyeuristic thriller starring Stone. She's Carly Norris, a lonely book editor who moves into one of Manhattan's toothpick thin buildings (the "sliver" of the title). She meets pulp novelist Jack (Berenger), whose libido is as overheated as his prose, but gets involved in a steamy affair with handsome neighbor Zeke (Baldwin), a computer whiz who also owns the building. Oh, by the way, he's installed video cameras in every unit that reveal many intimate secrets. Lots of sex and murders. Murky and underdeveloped and the ending, which was reshot, still leaves much to be desired. Lots of hype, little to recommend. **106m/C; VHS, DVD, Blu-Ray.** Sharon Stone; William Baldwin; Tom Berenger; Martin Landau; Polly Walker; Colleen Camp; CCH Pounder; Nina Foch; Keene Curtis; *D:* Phillip Noyce; *W:* Joe Eszterhas; *C:* Vilmos Zsigmond; *M:* Howard Shore. MTV Movie Awards '94: Most Desirable Male (Baldwin).

Slogan 1/2 1969 Dated French story of amour fou. Middle-aged commercial director Serge (Gainsbourg), married to the pregnant Francoise (Parisy), begins a torrid affair with British teenager Evelyne (Birkin). Evelyne presses Serge to get a divorce and they move in together, though he's still married. But then the teen's eye is caught by daredevil stuntman Dado (Millinaire). Model Birkin was actually in her early 20s and married to Gainsbourg when they made the film. French with subtitles. **90m/C; DVD.** *FR* Serge Gainsbourg; Jane Birkin; Daniel Gelin; Andrea Parisy; Gilles Millinaire; *D:* Pierre Grimblat; *W:* Pierre Grimblat; *C:* Claude Gainsbourg; *M:* Serge Gainsbourg.

Slow as Lightning 1923 Daydreaming employee Jimmie March is in love with the boss' daughter Eleanor but, after getting fired, he tries to prove he can be a self-made man by investing in the stock market. When Jimmie is successful, Eleanor's other suitor, jealous Mortimer Fenton, tries to frame him for stock fraud. **?m/B; Silent; DVD.** Kenneth McDonald; Edna Pennington; William Malan; Gordon Sackville; *D:* Grover Jones; *W:* Bud Barsky; *C:* Bert Longenecker.

Slow Burn 1/2 2000 (R) Trina (Driver) is searching for a family heirloom—a box of missing diamonds—that were lost in the Mexican desert when her grandmother died. While she hunts around, the goods have already been discovered by a couple of escaped cons (Spader and Brolin) who take Trina hostage and steal her car. But when her car is disabled, things in the desert start to steam, with Trina trying to play both men against one another so she can make off with the treasure. **97m/C; VHS, DVD.** Minnie Driver; James Spader; Josh Brolin; Stuart Wilson; *D:* Christian Ford; *W:* Christian Ford; Roger Soffer; *C:* Mark Vicente; *M:* Anthony Marinelli. **VIDEO**

Slow Burn 2005 (R) Filmed in 2003, did the festival circuit in '05, and finally saw a limited release in '07; the aging process didn't improve this confusing crime flick. DA Ford Cole (Liotta) is running for mayor but scandal threatens when ADA Nora Timmer (Blalock)?who's also Ford's occasional lover—is arrested for the death of her alleged rapist. But the case isn't so open-and-shut when Luther (LL Cool J) shows up, claiming Nora deliberately did the deed to cover up some secrets. The convoluted script just gets worse and the characters aren't interesting enough to make you care. **93m/C; DVD.** Ray Liotta; Jolene Blalock; LL Cool J; Mekhi Phifer; Bruce McGill; Chiwetel Ejiofor; Taye Diggs; *D:* Wayne Beach; *W:* Wayne Beach; *C:* Wally Pfister; *M:* Jeff Rona.

Slow West 1/2 2015 (R) A Scotsman made a film about the Old West which he shot in New Zealand. The result is a unique, foreigner's take on a very American genre, turning it more into a fairy tale or myth. Jay Cavendish (Smit-McPhee) has traveled from Scotland to Colorado, chasing the love of his life, Rose (Pistorius). Jay immediately runs into trouble, having to be rescued by a bounty hunter named Silas (Fassbender) and hunted by a gang led by Payne (Mendelsohn). Everyone treks across country to Rose in this dreamlike, beautiful genre piece. **84m/C; DVD, Blu-Ray.** Kodi Smit-McPhee; Michael Fassbender; Ben Mendelsohn; Edwin Wright; Brian Sergent; *D:* John Maclean; *W:* John Maclean; *C:* Robbie Ryan; *M:* Jed Kurzel.

The Slugger's Wife 1/2 *Neil Simon's The Slugger's Wife* 1985 (PG-13) The marriage between an Atlanta Braves outfielder and a rock singer suddenly turns sour when their individual careers force them to make some tough choices. **105m/C; VHS, DVD.** Michael O'Keefe; Rebecca De Mornay; Martin Ritt; Randy Quaid; Loudon Wainwright, III; Cleavant Derricks; Lynn Whitfield; *D:* Hal Ashby; *W:* Neil Simon; *C:* Caleb Deschanel.

Slugs WOOF! 1987 (R) A health inspector discovers that spilled toxic waste is being helpfully cleaned up by the slug population, saving Uncle Sam countless dollars. But wait! The slugs are mutating into blood-thirsty man-eaters. Is this the answer to military cut-backs? **90m/C; VHS, DVD, Blu-Ray.** Michael Garfield; Kim Terry; Philip Machale; Alicia Moro; Santiago Alvarez; Emilio Linder; Concha Cuetos; *D:* J(uan) Piquer Simon; *W:* J(uan) Piquer Simon; *C:* Julio Bragado; *M:* Tim Souster.

Slumber Party '57 1/2 1976 (R) At a slumber party, six girls get together and exchange stories of how they lost their virginity. Lots of great music by the Platters, Big Bopper, Jerry Lee Lewis, the Crewcuts, and Paul and Paula but complete schlock otherwise. **89m/C; VHS, DVD.** Noelle North; Bridget Holloman; Debra Winger; Mary Ann Appleseth; Cheryl "Rainbeaux" Smith; Janet Wood; R.L. Armstrong; Rafael Campos; Larry Gelman; Will Hutchins; Joyce Jillson; Victor Rogers; Joe E. Ross; Bill (Billy) Thurman; *D:* William A. Levey; *M:* Miles Goodman.

Slumber Party Massacre 1/2 1982 (R) A psychotic killer with a power drill terrorizes a high school girls' slumber party. Contrived and forced, but not always unfunny. **84m/C; VHS, DVD, Blu-Ray.** Michele Michaels; Robin Stille; Andre Honore; Michael Villela; Debra Deliso; Gina Mari; Brinke Stevens; Jean Vargas; Rigg Kennedy; *D:* Amy Holden Jones; *W:* Rita Mae Brown; *C:* Stephen Posey; *M:* Ralph Jones.

Slumber Party Massacre 2 WOOF! 1987 Drowsy babes in lingerie are drilled to death by a perverse madman. Another disappointing sequel. **75m/C; VHS, DVD, Blu-Ray.** Crystal Bernard; Kimberly McArthur; Juliette Cummins; Patrick Lowe; *D:* Deborah Brock; *W:* Deborah Brock; *C:* Thomas Callaway; *M:* Richard Ian Cox.

Slumber Party Massacre 3 WOOF! 1990 (R) Parents: Don't let your daughters have any slumber parties! Yes, it's a drill—for the third time. **76m/C; VHS, DVD.** Keely Christian; Brittain Frye; Michael (M.K.) Harris; David Greenle; Hope Marie Carlton; Maria Ford; *D:* Sally Mattison; *W:* Catherine Cyran; *C:* Jurgen Baum; *M:* Jaime Sheriff.

Slumdog Millionaire 1/2 2008 Poor, orphaned teenager Jamil Malik (Patel), a petty criminal who lives in a squalid slum in Mumbai, gets the opportunity to become a contestant on the Indian version of "Who Wants to Be a Millionaire." He's so successful that the police arrest Jamil just before he tries for the ultimate prize, sure that the street boy must be cheating. But as he relates the story of his life, it becomes clear that each experience leads him to a correct answer on the quiz show. Director Boyle achieves the trifecta: a thought provoking film that is also beautiful and entertaining, capturing the disparity between the haves and have-nots with beauty and grace and not a shred of pity. Excellent Indian cast is universally appealing and wonderfully represents universal dreams and ambitions. **116m/C; Blu-Ray, On Demand.** *US GB* Anil Kapoor; Irfan Khan; Dev Patel; Freida Pinto; Madhur Mittal; *D:* Danny Boyle; *W:* Simon Beaufoy; *C:* Anthony Dod Mantle; *M:* A.R. Rahman. Oscars '08: Adapt. Screenplay, Cinematog., Director (Boyle), Film, Film Editing, Orig. Score, Song ("Jai Ho"), Sound; British Acad. '08: Adapt. Screenplay, Cinematog., Director (Boyle), Film, Film Editing, Orig. Score, Sound; Directors Guild '08: Director (Boyle); Golden Globes '09: Director (Boyle), Film--Drama, Orig. Score, Screenplay; Screen Actors Guild '08: Cast; Writers Guild '08: Adapt. Screenplay.

Slums of Beverly Hills 1/2 1998 (R) Every few months, Murray Abromowitz (Arkin) packs up daughter Vivian (Lyonne) and sons Ricky (Marienthal) and Ben (Krumholtz) to sneak out of their current dumpy apartment (without paying the rent) and move on to the next one, always within Beverly Hills so the kids can stay in a good school. When cousin Rita (Tomei) escapes from a rehab center, Murray takes her in. While Murray's main concern is the kids' education, Vivian is more obsessed with the size of her breasts and exploring her adolescent sexuality. Semi-autobiographical first film for Jenkins, who scripted while at the Sundance Institute, has lots of character and charm, and just enough bite. Lyonne has no trouble being the center of attention and injects comedy into the many awkward social situations that a teenage girl must endure. **91m/C; VHS, DVD.** Natasha Lyonne; Alan Arkin; Marisa Tomei; Kevin Corrigan; David Krumholtz; Carl Reiner; Eli Marienthal; Jessica Walter; Rita Moreno; *D:* Tamara Jenkins; *W:* Tamara Jenkins; *C:* Tom Richmond; *M:* Rolfe Kent.

Small Apartments 2012 (R) Annoyingly quirky comedy that tries too hard to be an indie cult darling. Tubby Franklin Franklin (Lucas) lives in a squalid L.A. apartment where he's one among many oddballs. Franklin accidentally kills their unpleasant landlord (Stormare) and tries to figure out how to dispose of the body. Except he has the IQ of lint. **96m/C; DVD, Blu-Ray.** Matt Lucas; Peter Stormare; Juno Temple; Johnny Knoxville; James Caan; Billy Crystal; *D:* Jonas Akerlund; *W:* Chris Millis; *C:* Par M. Ekberg; *M:* Per Gessle.

The Small Back Room *Hour of Glory* 1949 A crippled WWII munitions expert leads a tormented existence and laments government bureaucracy. Powerfully presented adult storyline. **106m/B; VHS, DVD.** David Farrar; Jack Hawkins; Cyril Cusack; Kathleen Byron; Anthony Bushell; Michael Gough; Robert Morley; *D:* Michael Powell; Emeric Pressburger.

Small Change *L'Argent de Poche* 1976 (PG) Pudgy, timid Desmouceaux and scruffy, neglected Goldman lead a whole pack of heartwarming tykes. A realistically and tenderly portrayed testament to the great director's belief in childhood as a "state of grace." Criticized for sentimentality, "Small Change" followed Truffaut's gloomy "The Story of Adele H." Steven Spielberg suggested the English translation of "L'Argent de Poche." In French with English subtitles. **104m/C; VHS, DVD.** *FR* Geory Desmouceaux; Philippe Goldman; Jean-Francois Stevenin; Chantal Mercier; Claudio Deluca; Frank Deluca; Richard Golfier; Laurent Devlaeminck; Francis Devlaeminck; Sylvie Grezel; Pascale Bruchon; Nicole Felix; Francois Truffaut; ***D:*** Francois Truffaut; ***W:*** Suzanne Schiffman; Francois Truffaut; ***C:*** Pierre William Glenn; ***M:*** Maurice Jaubert.

A Small Circle of Friends 1/2 **1980 (R)** Three Harvard students struggle through their shifting relationships during their college years in the 1960s. **112m/C; VHS, DVD.** Brad Davis; Jameson Parker; Karen Allen; Shelley Long; ***D:*** Rob Cohen.

Small Island 1/2 **2009** In 1948, black teacher Hortense makes a marriage of convenience with Gilbert Joseph so she can leave Jamaica and move to London where they believe they can find better prospects. Neither is prepared for the racial prejudice they encounter, although their more liberal white landlady Queenie welcomes the couple to her Brixton boardinghouse. She has her own troubles since her husband Bernard is MIA and she is pregnant from an interracial affair. The narration is often intrusive but it's a well-cast drama that's an adaptation of Andrea Levy's novel. **168m/C; DVD.** *GB* Naomie Harris; David Oyelowo; Ruth Wilson; Benedict Cumberbatch; Ashley Walters; Niki Amuka-Bird; Shaun Parkes; Mark David; ***Nar:*** Hugh Quarshie; ***D:*** John Alexander; ***W:*** Paula Milne; Sarah Williams; ***C:*** Tony Miller; ***M:*** Martin Phipps. **TV**

Small Soldiers 1/2 **1998 (PG-13)** Why do kids today get all the really cool toys? G.I. Joe with the Kung Fu Grip never held any small Ohio towns under siege, and his fingers eventually fell off. But thanks to former defense supplier turned toy maker Globotech and its chairman Gil Mars (Leary), the residents of Winslow Corners receive a shipment of action figures called the Commando Elite. These toys are designed to interact with their owners. And do they ever—they take on a life of their own and wage war, thanks to being mistakenly implanted with military intelligence chips. Led by Chip Hazard (voice of Jones), these commandoes take on the previously quiet town in their quest to eradicate their toy rivals, the peaceful alien Gorgonites. Led by the gentle Archer (voice of Langella), the Gorgonites enlist the help of teens Alan (Smith) and Christy (Dunst) to battle this miniature menace. Combo of computer animation, Stan Winston's animatronic puppets, and live-action bring the toys to life. **110m/C; VHS, DVD.** Gregory Edward Smith; Kirsten Dunst; Phil Hartman; Ann Magnuson; Jay Mohr; Denis Leary; Kevin Dunn; Wendy Schaal; Dick Miller; David Cross; Robert Picardo; ***V:*** Tommy Lee Jones; Frank Langella; Ernest Borgnine; Jim Brown; Bruce Dern; George Kennedy; Clint Walker; Christopher Guest; Michael McKean; Harry Shearer; Sarah Michelle Gellar; Christina Ricci; ***D:*** Joe Dante; ***W:*** Gavin Scott; Adam Rifkin; Ted Elliott; Terry Rossio; ***C:*** Jamie Anderson; ***M:*** Jerry Goldsmith.

Small Time **2014 (R)** Sweetly nostalgic, coming of age comedy-drama. Used car co-owner and salesman Al Klein is stunned to learn that his teenage son Freddy wants to move in with him and join him as a salesman on the car lot. At least Al's happy until quick-learner Freddy starts using some of the shadier practices Al and partner Ash use to move those cars off the lot. **95m/C; DVD, Blu-Ray.** Christopher Meloni; Dean Norris; Devon Bostick; Bridget Moynahan; Amaury Nolasco; Xander Berkeley; Ashley Jensen; Garcelle Beauvais; ***D:*** Joel Surnow; ***W:*** Joel Surnow; ***C:*** Feliks Parnell; ***M:*** Sean Callery.

Small Time Crooks 1/2 **2000 (PG)** Ex-con dishwasher Allen and his manicurist wife Ullman decide to become rich by robbing a New York City bank. Problem is, they team up with three bumblers (Lovitz, Rapaport, Darrow) to pull off the heist. As a result of the mishaps, the couple accidentally gains fame and fortune only to find it doesn't suit them at all. Grant is a well-bred snob trying to teach the lower classes some couth. Ullman, as usual, is endearing, while Allen is hard to fathom as a blue-collar guy turned crook. Hailed by some as Allen's triumphant return to his comedy stylings of old, the comedy in "Small Time Crooks" actually just seems old and tired. **94m/C; VHS, DVD.** Woody Allen; Tracey Ullman; Hugh Grant; Jon Lovitz; Michael Rapaport; Elaine May; Tony Darrow; Elaine Stritch; George Grizzard; ***D:*** Woody Allen; ***W:*** Woody Allen; ***C:*** Fei Zhao. Natl. Soc. Film Critics '00: Support. Actress (May).

Small Town Girl 1/2 *One Horse Town* **1953** Typical romantic musical of the era, as a city slicker picked up for speeding in a hick town is pursued by the sheriff's daughter. Several Busby Berkeley blockbuster musical numbers are shoehorned incongruously into the rural doings. **93m/C; VHS, DVD.** Jane Powell; Farley Granger; Bobby Van; Ann Miller; Billie Burke; Robert Keith; S.Z. Sakall; Fay Wray; Nat King Cole; Chill Wills; ***D:*** Leslie Kardos; ***M:*** Andre Previn.

A Small Town in Texas **1976 (PG)** An ex-con returns home looking for the sheriff who framed him on a drug charge, and who has stolen his woman. Not-too-violent, predictable revenge flick. **96m/C; VHS, DVD.** Timothy Bottoms; Susan George; Bo Hopkins; ***D:*** Jack Starrett; ***W:*** William W. Norton, Sr.; ***M:*** Charles Bernstein.

Small Town Murder Songs **2010 (R)** Deliberately-paced crime drama finds smalltown cop Walter (Stormare) trying to redeem himself from a violent past by reaffirming his childhood Mennonite faith. This still doesn't mean his Ontario neighbors trust him, especially when Walter targets lowlife Steve (McIntyre) as the probable killer of a young woman since Steve just happens to be the current lover of Walter's ex-girlfriend Rita (Hennessy). **75m/C; DVD.** *CA* Peter Stormare; Jill Hennessy; Stephen McIntyre; Martha Plimpton; Ari Cohen; Jackie Burroughs; Aaron Poole; ***D:*** Ed Gass-Donnelly; ***W:*** Ed Gass-Donnelly; ***C:*** Brendan Steacy; ***M:*** Bruce Peninsula.

Small Town Santa 1/2 **2014 (PG)** Small town sheriff Rick Langston has the holiday blues when he nabs an intruder claiming to be Santa Claus. But newcomer Lucy believes and tries to get Rick to have some Christmas spirit. **85m/C; DVD.** Dean Cain; Christine Lakin; Derek Brandon; ***D:*** Joel Paul Reisig; ***W:*** David Higlen; ***C:*** Dennis Thomas; ***M:*** Todd Maki. **VIDEO**

Small Town Saturday Night **2010 (R)** Twenty-four hours in the life of small town mechanic Rhett (Pine) and various family and friends. Rhett is planning to leave and move to Nashville to try and fulfill his dream of becoming a country singer. Girlfriend Samantha (Blair) and her young daughter are supposed to come with him but Sam is having second thoughts about separating her daughter from the child's father, local sheriff Tommy Carson (Christian). There are other interconnected stories revolving around parents and children but the plots tend to meander although both the cast and flick are watchable in a low-key way. **94m/C; DVD.** Chris Pine; Bre Blair; Shawn Christian; John Hawkes; Adam Hendershott; Lin Shaye; Muse Watson; Brent Briscoe; ***D:*** Ryan Craig; ***W:*** Ryan Craig; ***C:*** Matt Kovalakides; ***M:*** Stephen Bertrand. **VIDEO**

The Smallest Show on Earth **1948** A melodramatic tale about the son of an executed murderer who becomes the object of derision in the small town where he lives. One tormentor finally attacks him, and the young man must make a split-second decision that may affect his own mortality. **90m/B; VHS, DVD.** Dane Clark; Gail Russell; Ethel Barrymore; Allyn Joslyn; Harry (Henry) Morgan; Lloyd Bridges; Selena Royle; Rex Ingram; Harry Carey, Jr.; ***D:*** Frank Borzage.

The Smallest Show on Earth *Big Time Operators* **1957** A couple inherit not only an old movie house, but the three people who work there as well. Very funny and charming, with a wonderful cast. Sellers is delightful as the soused projectionist. **80m/B; VHS, DVD.** *GB* Bill Travers; Virginia McKenna; Margaret Rutherford; Peter Sellers; Bernard Miles; Leslie Phillips; Stringer Davis; Francis De Wolff; Sidney James; June Cunningham; ***D:*** Basil Dearden; ***W:*** William Rose; John Eldridge; ***C:*** Douglas Slocombe.

Smallfoot 1/2 **2018 (PG)** In a society of yetis located near a mountaintop, free-spirited yeti Migo (Tatum) happily complies with the rules that every yeti must follow. One day, he comes across a human whose plane has crashed. Both are terrified of each other because of what they have been told. The encounter increases Migo's curiosity about the outside world. It takes him to a town at the base of the mountains where he strikes up a friendship with wildlife TV host Percy (Corden). This animated musical has an unusual subject in thinking for yourself, but the film's visuals and dialogue are more bland than its message. **109m/C; DVD, Blu-Ray.** Channing Tatum; James Corden; Zendaya; Common; LeBron James; ***D:*** Karey Kirkpatrick; ***W:*** Karey Kirkpatrick; Clare Sera; ***M:*** Heitor Pereira.

Smalltime **1996 (R)** Mobster, The Dutchman, needs to deliver a bag full of drugs to a desolate ranch and then wait for someone to pick up the goods and pay him. He decides to pass the job along to lower-level goon, Ben, who figures his two friends should be in on the caper. They get bored waiting and decide to call some girls to have a party, during which time the drugs get used up. Now, they've got nothing to switch for the money. This is going to make a lot of people unhappy. **96m/C; VHS, DVD.** Jeff Fahey; Glenn Plummer; Rae Dawn Chong; Darren McGavin; ***D:*** Jeff Reiner; ***W:*** Jeff Reiner; Pat Cupo; ***C:*** Feliks Parnell; ***M:*** Vinnie Golia.

Smart Alecks 1/2 **1942** The Bowery Boys get involved with gangsters when Jordan helps capture a crook. The usual wisecracking from Hall and Gorcey helps keep things moving. **88m/B; VHS, DVD.** Leo Gorcey; Huntz Hall; Gabriel Dell; Gale Storm; Roger Pryor, Jr.; Walter Woolf King; Herbert Rawlinson; Joe (Joseph) Kirk; Marie Windsor; ***D:*** Wallace Fox.

Smart Blonde **1937** The first (and best) in Warner Bros. nine-movie series featuring intrepid, fast-talking gal reporter Torchy Blane (Farrell). Torchy snoops into the murder of racketeer Tiny Torgensen (Crehan) and generally gets in the way of police detective Steve McBride (MacLane). Not that he really minds. **65m/B; DVD.** Glenda Farrell; Barton MacLane; Wini Shaw; Craig Reynolds; Addison Richards; Charlotte Wynters; Robert Paige; Jane Wyman; Tom Kennedy; Joseph Crehan; ***D:*** Frank McDonald; ***W:*** Don Ryan; Kenneth Gamet; ***C:*** Warren Lynch.

S.M.A.R.T. Chase 1/2 **2018** Security agent Danny (Bloom) is facing hard times. Once respected for his work safely transporting valuable art works, his reputation took a hit when a Van Gogh was stolen under his watch when his security truck was ambushed. Danny is now trying to restore his reputation by successfully transporting a valued Chinese vase out of a Shanghai musuem with the help of his team. Again, they are ambushed. Danny and the team must learn who stole the art works and why. The lackluster film has a cookie cutter quality, and lots of action movie violence without much substance. **95m/C; DVD.** Orlando Bloom; Lei Wu; Simon Yam; Hannah Quinlivan; Lynn Xiong; ***D:*** Charles Martin; ***W:*** Kevin Bernhardt; ***C:*** Philipp Blaubach; ***M:*** Mark Kilian.

Smart Cookies 1/2 **2013** The Hallmark Channel celebrates the centennial of the Girl Scouts with this charming (if predictable) flick. Workaholic realtor Julie Sterling is assigned by her boss Lola to become the leader of a struggling Girl Scout troop as a way to promote the firm in the community. Julie works to boost their annual cookie sales competition against their arch-rivals and the girls' self-esteem as well. Naturally, she learns some life lessons of her own. **87m/C; DVD.** Jessalyn Gilsig; Bailee Madison; Patricia Richardson; Ty Olsson; Samantha Ferris; ***D:*** Robert Iscove; ***W:*** Kelli Pryor; Neal Dobrofsky; Tippi Dobrofsky; ***C:*** Adam Sliwinski; ***M:*** Graeme Coleman. **CABLE**

Smart House **2000** Ben lives with his widowed dad and his younger sister in a typical suburban house. But Ben likes to enter contests and he actually wins a "Smart House," a house designed to take care of all those pesky daily choices thanks to a computer, for his family and persuades his dad to move in. But Ben's dad falls for the house's creator and the house itself gets jealous and decides to keep the family trapped inside. Although the premise has been used for horror movies, this one is strictly a comedy. **82m/C; VHS, DVD.** Ryan Merriman; Kevin Kilner; Jessica Steen; Susan Haskell; ***V:*** Katey Sagal; ***D:*** LeVar Burton. **CABLE**

Smart Money 1/2 **1931** Nick (Robinson) is a small-town barber who holds a poker game in his back room, helped by his assistant, Jack (Cagney). A consistent winner, Nick is encouraged to try his luck in a big-city game and loses everything, only to realize he's been set-up. So Nick sends for Jack and they work out their own scheme to get back at the crooked gamblers. The only time Robinson and Cagney were paired up onscreen. **90m/B; DVD.** Edward G. Robinson; James Cagney; Boris Karloff; Noel Francis; Ben Taggart; Ralf Harolde; Evalyn Knapp; ***D:*** Alfred E. Green; ***W:*** Kubec Glasmon; Lucien Hubbard; John Bright; Joseph Jackson; ***C:*** Robert B. Kurrle.

Smart Money 1/2 **1988** A wrongly jailed man enlists the help of his oddball pals to get revenge on the real thief who committed the computer fraud that put him behind bars. They get even while padding their pockets. **88m/C; VHS, DVD.** Spencer Leigh; Alexandra Pigg; Ken Campbell; ***D:*** Bernard Rose; ***W:*** Matthew Jacobs.

Smart People **2008 (R)** Who don't act like it and behave badly. Supercilious Lawrence Wetherhold (Quaid) is a widowed English-lit professor at Carnegie Mellon who's bored and contemptuous of his students. His son James (Holmes) avoids the drama by living in the dorm and teen daughter Vanessa (Page) is following too closely in dad's footsteps. An accident that forbids Lawrence from driving brings doctor (and ex-student) Janet Hartigan (Parker) into Lawrence's life as well as his ne'er-do-well adoptive brother Chuck (Church), who moves in as temporary chauffeur. Church has the most fun with his stoner free spirit while everyone else does well enough by their stereotypes. **95m/C; DVD.** Dennis Quaid; Sarah Jessica Parker; Thomas Haden Church; Ellen Page; Ashton Holmes; ***D:*** Noam Murro; ***W:*** Mark Jude Poirier; ***C:*** Toby Irwin.

The Smart Set **1928** Typical sports-themed comedy from Haines in which he plays an obnoxious jerk who gets his comeuppance and then wins the day. Wealthy, polo-playing Tommy Van Buren makes the girls swoon—except for Polly (Day) since Tommy took her father's spot on the team. Eventually, Tommy's drunken behavior gets him ousted and now he has to redeem himself to regain his both his team and romantic chances. **80m/B; Silent; DVD.** William Haines; Alice Day; Jack Holt; Hobart Bosworth; Julia Swayne Gordon; Constance Howard; Paul Nicholson; Coy Watson; ***D:*** Jack Conway; ***W:*** Byron Morgan; Ann Price; ***C:*** Oliver Marsh.

SMART: Specialized Mobile Animal Rescue Team **2016** A feature-length, award-winning documentary look at the Los Angeles-based Specialized Mobile Animal Rescue Team (SMART). The animal-loving members of this group regularly risk their lives to save animals who are in need. Organized by Armando Navarrete, the team's development of new tactics and technology to rescue and assist all types of animals is chronicled over a three-year period. Part of the city's animal shelter system, Navarrete and his team do all they can to help not only cats and dogs, but creatures as diverse as horses, mountain lions, and birds. Related ethical questions are considered in the context of animal rescue as well. **75m/C; DVD.** ***D:*** Justin Zimmerman; ***C:*** Justin Zimmerman; Torrance Maurer; ***M:*** John W. Snyder. **VIDEO**

Smart Woman **1948** Not very! Defense attorney Paula Roger's (Bennett) latest client is racketeer Frank McCoy (Sullivan) who's accused of shooting the district attorney. The special prosecutor is none other than Robert Larrimore (Aherne), who's secretly involved with Paula outside the courtroom. But beside this conflict of interest, Paula has been keeping one big secret that makes for a sensational public revelation, which could jeopardize both her personal and professional lives. **93m/B; DVD.** Constance Bennett; Brian Aherne; Barry Sullivan; Michael O'Shea; Otto Kruger; James Gleason; ***D:*** Edward Blatt; ***W:*** Alvah Bessie; Herbert Margolis; Louis Morheim; Adela Rogers St. John; ***C:*** Stanley Cortez; ***M:*** Louis Gruenberg.

Smash Palace 1/2 **1982** A compelling drama of a marriage jeopardized by his obsession with building a race car and her need for love and affection. Melodramatic, but worth watching. Robson as their young daughter is wonderful. **100m/C; VHS, DVD,**

Blu-Ray. *NZ* Bruno Lawrence; Anna Maria Monticelli; Greer Robson; Keith Aberdein; ***D:*** Roger Donaldson; ***W:*** Bruno Lawrence.

Smash-Up: The Story of a Woman 🦴🦴🦴 *A Woman Destroyed* **1947** A famous nightclub singer gives up her career for marriage and a family, only to become depressed when her husband's career soars. She turns to alcohol and her life falls apart. When her husband sues for divorce and custody of their child, she fights to recover from alcoholism. Hayward's first major role. **103m/B; VHS, DVD.** Susan Hayward; Lee Bowman; Marsha Hunt; Eddie Albert; ***D:*** Stuart Heisler; ***W:*** John Howard Lawson.

Smashed 🦴🦴 ½ **2012 (R)** Teacher Kate (Winstead) is married to Charlie (Paul) and enjoys the common life of a young couple, one filled with celebrating and drinking. When Kate's constant boozing threatens her job, she cleans up and discovers that her marriage may not be what she thought it was through the haze of a hangover. A notably candid performance from Winstead carries this effective drama about addiction and how alcohol can make connections seem more remarkable than they may otherwise be if the booze wasn't flowing. **85m/C; DVD, Blu-Ray.** Mary Elizabeth Winstead; Aaron Paul; Octavia Spencer; Nick Offerman; Megan Mullally; ***D:*** James Ponsoldt; ***W:*** James Ponsoldt; Susan Burke; ***C:*** Tobias Datum; ***M:*** Andy Cabic; Eric D. Johnson.

Smashing the Rackets 🦴 ½ **1938** FBI agent Jim Conway (Morris) is shunted into a job in the DA's office. He meets playgirl debutante Letty Lane (Johnson) and falls for her more sedate sister Susan (Mercer). Since Letty has a boyfriend (Cabot) who's involved with the mob, Jim decides to use his new position to go after racketeers. Inspired by the career of New York district attorney Thomas E. Dewey. **69m/B; VHS, DVD.** Chester Morris; Frances Mercer; Rita Johnson; Bruce Cabot; Ben Welden; ***D:*** Lew Landers; ***W:*** Lionel Houser; ***C:*** Nicholas Musuraca.

Smashing Time WOOF! **1967** Abysmal British comedy was never widely released on this side of the Atlantic and it's easy to see why. The film follows two small-town girls—Brenda (Tushingham), who's mousy and bony, and Yvonne (Redgrave), who's loud and pushy—who come to London at the swinging '60s. Unfortunately, they are two of the most unattractive comic heroines ever to hit the screen, and apparently that's a choice the filmmakers made deliberately. Moreover, their accents are difficult to understand and their voices could blister an elephant's hide. **96m/C; VHS, DVD, Blu-Ray.** *GB* Rita Tushingham; Lynn Redgrave; Michael York; Anna Quayle; Irene Handl; Ian Carmichael; ***D:*** Desmond Davis; ***W:*** George Melly; ***C:*** Manny Wynn; ***M:*** John Addison.

The Smell of Success 🦴 **2009 (PG-13)** That stench isn't success. The owner of Rose's Manure Company dies and his estranged daughter Rosemary (Leoni) doesn't know anything about running the business. She learns that a rival chemical fertilizer company is plotting a takeover and turns to the firm's best salesman, Patrick Fitzpatrick (Thornton), for help. The Polish brothers' strange, sepia-toned comedy is overflowing with excrement humor and a nonsensical drug subplot. **91m/C; DVD.** Tea Leoni; Billy Bob Thornton; Kyle MacLachlan; Ed Helms; Pruitt Taylor Vince; Frances Conroy; Richard Edson; Mark Polish; ***D:*** Michael Polish; ***W:*** Mark Polish; Michael Polish; ***C:*** M. David Mullen.

Smile 🦴🦴🦴 **1975 (PG)** Barbed, merciless send-up of small-town America focusing on a group of naive California girls who compete for the "Young American Miss" crown amid rampant commercialism, exploitation and pure middle-class idiocy. Hilarious neglected '70s-style satire. Early role for Griffith. **113m/C; VHS, DVD.** Bruce Dern; Barbara Feldon; Michael Kidd; Nicholas Pryor; Geoffrey Lewis; Colleen Camp; Joan Prather; Annette O'Toole; Melanie Griffith; Denise Nickerson; Titos Vandis; ***D:*** Michael Ritchie; ***W:*** Jerry Belson; ***C:*** Conrad L. Hall; ***M:*** Daniel Osborn; Leroy Holmes.

Smile 🦴 ½ **2005 (PG-13)** Well-off teenager Katie (Boorem) wants to find more meaning to life beyond her bickering parents and her boyfriend's sexual pressuring so she joins an international reconstructive surgery charity that sends her to China to help Ling (Ding), a girl of the same age whose disfigured face has plagued her entire life. Based on director Kramer's own daughter. Uplifting message is obscured by poor execution. **107m/C; VHS, DVD.** Sean Astin; Mika Boorem; Beau Bridges; Yi Ding; Linda Hamilton; ***D:*** Jeffrey Kramer; ***W:*** Jeffrey Kramer. **VIDEO**

A Smile as Big as the Moon 🦴🦴 **2012** Overly-earnest Hallmark Hall of Fame heart-tugger based on the true story of Mike Kersjes (Corbett), a high school football coach and special ed teacher in 1988. Despite a disruptive visit to the planetarium, Mike discovers his kids are interested in attending NASA's Space Camp, which is a program for gifted science students. They have to work for months to overcome skepticism about their abilities, as well as raise funds, and then show they have 'the right stuff' at the Huntsville, Alabama camp. **90m/C; DVD.** John Corbett; Cynthia Watros; Moira Kelly; Robynn McKinney; Logan Huffman; Jimmy Bellinger; Kesun Loder; Breezy Eslin; E. Roger Mitchell; Bruce McKinnon; Peter Ten Brink; Abigail Corrigan; ***D:*** James Sadwith; ***W:*** Thomas (Tom) Rickman; ***C:*** Roy Wagner; ***M:*** Mark Adler. **TV**

Smile Jenny, You're Dead 🦴🦴 ½ **1974** Harry Orwell (Janssen) had to retire from the police force after being shot so he turns private sleuth. His latest case is finding the killer of a friend's son-in-law, but Harry thinks the dead man's wife, Jenny, is the most likely suspect. TV pilot for Janssen's series "Harry O." **90m/C; DVD.** David Janssen; Andrea Marcovicci; Zalman King; Tim McIntire; Clu Gulager; Howard da Silva; Jodie Foster; ***D:*** Jerry Thorpe; ***W:*** Howard Rodman; ***C:*** Jack Woolf; ***M:*** Billy Goldenberg. **TV**

A Smile Like Yours 🦴 ½ **1996 (R)** Too-cute yuppie couple Danny and Jennifer (Kinnear and Holly) decide to start a family, only to discover that Danny's "boys" can't swim. Many formulaic and predictable gags about masturbation and the possiblilty of infidelity ensue. Unfortunately, laughs do not. Kinnear comes off as amiable enough, while Holly turns in an aggravatingly over-the-top performance. Thomas and Cusack, as the couple's best friends, fare better than anyone, with the possible exception of scene-stealer Meullerleile as the cranky clinic nurse. Writer/director Samples is the former head of now-defuct Rysher Entertainment (flick's producing company). Coincidence? We think not. **99m/C; DVD.** Greg Kinnear; Lauren Holly; Jill(ian) Hennessey; Christopher McDonald; Joan Cusack; Jay Thomas; Donald Moffat; France Nuyen; Marianne Muellerleile; ***Cameo(s):*** Shirley MacLaine; ***D:*** Keith Samples; ***W:*** Keith Samples; Kevin Meyer; ***C:*** Richard Bowen; ***M:*** William Ross.

Smiles of a Summer Night 🦴🦴🦴 ½ *Sommarnattens Leende* **1955** The best known of Bergman's rare comedies; sharp satire about eight Swedish aristocrats who become romantically and comically intertwined over a single weekend. Inspired Sondheim's successful Broadway musical "A Little Night Music," and Woody Allen's "A Midsummer Night's Sex Comedy." In Swedish with English subtitles. **110m/B; VHS, DVD, Blu-Ray.** *SW* Gunnar Bjornstrand; Harriet Andersson; Ulla Jacobsson; Eva Dahlbeck; Jarl Kulle; Margit Carlquist; ***D:*** Ingmar Bergman; ***W:*** Ingmar Bergman.

Smiley 🦴 ½ **2012** Ashley (Gerard) is the damsel in distress who becomes caught up in the urban legend of Smiley, a masked killer who stabs people on a chat-roulette service and becomes a viral sensation in the process. Some of director Gallagher's ideas are interesting, and the film flirts with becoming a look at paranoia and insanity as Ashley starts to wonder if she's actually losing it. But the pic is way too talky, choosing more often to discuss the impact of evil and the Internet instead of embodying it. **90m/C; DVD.** Caitlin Gerard; Melanie Papalia; Shane Dawson; Andrew James Allen; Roger Bart; Michael Traynor; ***D:*** Michael J. Gallagher; ***W:*** Michael J. Gallagher; Glasgow Phillips; ***C:*** Nicola Marsh; ***M:*** Dave Porter.

Smiley Face 🦴 **2007 (R)** Lame reefer comedy. Wannabe actress and chronic stoner Jane (Faris) starts off her day eating some pot-laced cupcakes baked by her roommate and then runs mundane errands like going to an audition, visiting her dentist, and paying off her drug dealer while experiencing life in a very high and happy place. However, it's not a place a viewer will care to experience with her unless they're in the same drug-induced state. **88m/C; DVD.** Anna Faris; John Krasinski; Danny Masterson; Adam Brody; Ben Falcone; ***D:*** Gregg Araki; ***W:*** Dylan Haggerty; ***C:*** Shawn Kim; ***M:*** David Kitay.

Smiley's People 🦴🦴 ½ **1982** George Smiley (Guinness) is once again retired from British Intelligence when he learns that the murder of a former colleague is linked to their Soviet spy rival, Karla (Stewart). Smiley doggedly pursues his information, despite opposition, while Karla seeks to cover his tracks. Based on the novel by John Le Carre; the sequel to "Tinker, Tailor, Soldier, Spy." **324m/C; VHS, DVD, Blu-Ray.** *GB* Alec Guinness; Barry Foster; Patrick Stewart; Bernard Hepton; Eileen Atkins; Anthony Bate; Michael Byrne; Sian Phillips; Beryl Reid; Michael Gough; Curt Jurgens; Rosalie Crutchley; ***D:*** Simon Langton; ***W:*** John Hopkins; ***C:*** Kenneth Macmillan; ***M:*** Patrick Gowers. **TV**

Smilin' Through 🦴🦴🦴 **1932** First sound version of this melodrama/romance which Franklin had directed as a silent in 1922. Shearer is set to marry Howard when jealous rival March shows up armed at the wedding and accidentally kills the bride. March escapes and Howard spends his years as a recluse until his young niece, the image of his dead fiance (naturally, since she's also played by Shearer) arrives to live with him. She meets a young man who turns out to be March's son (played again by March) and they fall in love. Pure sentiment done with high gloss. Remade in 1941. **97m/B; DVD.** Norma Shearer; Fredric March; Leslie Howard; O.P. Heggie; Ralph Forbes; Beryl Mercer; Margaret Seddon; ***D:*** Sidney Franklin; ***C:*** Lee Garmes.

Smilin' Through 🦴🦴 ½ **1941** Third filming, second with sound, first in color, of a popular melodrama. An embittered man whose wife was murdered on their wedding day raises an orphaned niece, only to have her fall in love with the son of her aunt's murderer. Songs include title tune and "A Little Love, a Little Kiss." **101m/C; VHS, DVD.** Jeanette MacDonald; Brian Aherne; Gene Raymond; Ian Hunter; Frances Robinson; ***D:*** Frank Borzage.

Smiling Fish & Goat on Fire 🦴🦴 ½ **1999 (R)** Title refers to the childhood nicknames that Chris Remi (Derick Martini) and his brother Tony (Steven Martini) were given by their Native American/Italian grandma. Accountant Chris and aspiring actor Tony share a house in L.A. and have trouble with women. Their current relationships are falling apart, but new ones are looming, and the confused bros get some sage advice from their elderly friend, Clive (Henderson). Low-budget, wry slice-of-life. **90m/C; VHS, DVD.** Steven Martini; Derick Martini; Bill Henderson; Christa Miller; Amy Hathaway; Rosemarie Addeo; Heather Jae Marie; Nicole Rae; Wesley Thompson; ***D:*** Kevin Jordan; ***W:*** Steven Martini; Derick Martini; Kevin Jordan; ***C:*** Fred Iannone; ***M:*** Chris Horvath.

The Smiling Ghost 🦴 ½ **1941** Lively comic mystery. Grandmother Bentley hires down-on-his-luck 'Lucky' Downing to become her heiress granddaughter Elinor's fake fiance. Elinor's previous three engagements ended in death or serious injury to the gentlemen involved, which seems suspicious. Lucky investigates, along with intrepid reporter Lil, at the Bentley's allegedly haunted mansion. **71m/B; DVD.** Wayne Morris; Alexis Smith; Brenda Marshall; Helen Westley; Alan Hale; Lee Patrick; Roland Drew; Willie Best; Charles Halton; David Bruce; ***D:*** Lewis Seiler; ***W:*** Kenneth Gamet; Stuart Palmer; ***C:*** Arthur L. Todd.

The Smiling Lieutenant 🦴🦴 ½ **1931** Flirting at the wrong time/wrong place can get a guy into big trouble. Niki (Chevalier), an officer with Vienna's Royal Guards, is romancing violinist Franzi (Colbert). During a visit by King Adolf (Barbier), his plain daughter Princess Anna (Hopkins) mistakes a smile meant for Franzi to mean that Niki is interested in her. Duty-bound, Niki is forced into a royal marriage. So the worldly Franzi decides to help Anna win her reluctant new hubby's love by turning her into a knockout. **102m/B; DVD.** Maurice Chevalier; Claudette Colbert; Miriam Hopkins; George Barbier; Charlie Ruggles; Robert Strange; Hugh O'Connell; ***D:*** Ernst Lubitsch; ***W:*** Ernst Lubitsch; Ernest Vajda; Samson Raphaelson; ***C:*** George J. Folsey; ***M:*** Oscar Straus.

Smilla's Sense of Snow 🦴🦴 **1996 (R)** Thriller starts off well but fails to sustain the suspense of the Peter Hoeg mystery on which it is based. Solitary scientist Smilla Jasperson (Ormond) is a half-Inuit, half-American (Danish in the book) resident of Copenhagen who's an expert on snow and ice. Born and raised in Greenland, Smilla is drawn back to her home when the body of six-year-old Isaiah (Miano), whom she's grudgingly befriended, is discovered at their apartment building. Smilla believes the boy was murdered and when she begins investigating it leads to the Greenland mining company where Isaiah's late father worked and which is run by the suspicious Tork (Harris). Location cinematography is particularly impressive. **121m/C; VHS, DVD.** *GE DK SW* Julia Ormond; Gabriel Byrne; Richard Harris; Vanessa Redgrave; Robert Loggia; Jim Broadbent; Mario Adorf; Bob Peck; Tom Wilkinson; Peter Capaldi; Clipper Miano; Emma Croft; ***D:*** Bille August; ***W:*** Ann Biderman; ***C:*** Jorgen Persson; ***M:*** Hans Zimmer; Harry Gregson-Williams.

Smith! 🦴🦴 ½ **1969 (G)** Naive but well intentioned look at present-day treatment of Native Americans. Rancher Ford becomes embroiled in the trial of murder suspect Ramirez. Based on Paul St. Pierre's novel "Breaking Smith's Quarter Horse." **101m/C; VHS, DVD.** Glenn Ford; Frank Ramirez; Keenan Wynn; ***D:*** Michael O'Herlihy; ***W:*** Louis Pelletier; ***M:*** Robert F. Brunner.

Smithereens 🦴🦴 ½ **1982 (R)** Working-class girl leaves home for New York's music scene. Rugged, hip character study. Director Seidleman's first feature. **90m/C; VHS, DVD, Blu-Ray.** Susan Berman; Brad Rijn; Richard Hell; Chris Noth; ***D:*** Susan Seidelman; ***W:*** Ron Nyswaner; Peter Askin.

Smoke 🦴🦴 **1993** Three days in the life of Michael, as he travels between fantasy and reality, past and present, searching for love with the perfect older man. **90m/C; VHS, DVD.** Mark D'Aruia; Nick Discenza; Barbara Andrews; ***D:*** Mark D'Aruia; ***M:*** Arnold Bieber.

Smoke 🦴🦴 **1995 (R)** Brooklyn slice of life centers around the local cigar store run by Auggie Wren (Keitel). An ensemble piece, divided into five chapters, which includes such characters as down-on-his luck novelist Paul (Hurt), troubled black teenager Rashid (Perrineau Jr.), Augie's ex-wife Ruby (Channing) and supposed daughter (Judd), and many more (some of whom get lost in the shuffle). Wonderfully acted but the stories tend to disappear in a wisp of smoke. Based on a story by Auster. Wang and Auster also made an impromptu companion film "Blue in the Face." **112m/C; VHS, DVD.** Harvey Keitel; William Hurt; Stockard Channing; Forest Whitaker; Harold Perrineau, Jr.; Ashley Judd; Mary Ward; Victor Argo; Jared Harris; Giancarlo Esposito; Mel Gorham; Stephen Gevedon; Erica Gimpel; Malik Yoba; Jose Zuniga; RuPaul Charles; ***D:*** Wayne Wang; ***W:*** Paul Auster; ***C:*** Adam Holender; ***M:*** Rachel Portman.

Smoke Jumpers 🦴 ½ *Trial by Fire* **2008** Firefighter Kristen is blamed for a colleague's death and branded as unqualified. To prove her detractors wrong, Kristen is determined to join the dangerous ranks of smoke jumpers. Just after her training, Kristen gets the chance to prove herself when she's sent to assist at a forest fire that's gone out of control. **93m/C; DVD.** Brooke Burns; Rick Ravanello; Winston Rekert; Erin Karpluk; Robert Molorey; ***D:*** John Terlesky; ***W:*** Jeff Stephenson; ***C:*** C. Kim Miles. **CABLE**

Smoke Screen 🦴 ½ *Sandra Brown's Smoke Screen* **2010** Unlikely Lifetime thriller. Journalist Britt Shelley (Pressley) is working on exposing a cover-up murder involving the police and the D.A.'s office. Britt's framed when she awakens next to a murdered cop and the detectives assigned to the case just assume she's guilty. Based on the novel by Sandra Brown. **87m/C; DVD.** Jaime Pressly; Currie Graham; Garwin Sanford; Blu Mankuma; Zak Santiago; Martin Cummins; ***D:*** Gary Yates; ***W:*** Karen Stillman; ***C:*** C. Kim Miles; ***M:*** Jonathan Goldsmith. **CABLE**

Smoke Signals 1998 (PG-13) Serious themes are treated in a deceptively simple and humorous manner, based on stories from Alexie's book "The Lone Ranger and Tonto Fistfight in Heaven." Geeky, orphaned Thomas (Adams) lives on the Coeur d'Alene reservation in Idaho where he's reluctantly looked after by stoic Victor (Beach), whose long-gone father Arnold (Farmer) saved Thomas from the fire that killed his parents. When Victor learns of Arnold's death in Phoenix, Thomas says he'll pay the expenses of the trip if he can accompany Victor. The young men reach an understanding during their travels, while Victor struggles to deal with his complicated feelings about his father and the past. **88m/C; VHS, DVD.** Adam Beach; Evan Adams; Irene Bedard; Gary Farmer; Tantoo Cardinal; Michelle St. John; Robert Miano; Molly Cheek; Elaine Miles; Michael Greyeyes; Chief Leonard George; John Trudell; Tom Skerritt; Cody Lightning; Cynthia Geary; Simon Baker; ***D:*** Chris Eyre; ***W:*** Sherman Alexie; ***C:*** Brian Capener; ***M:*** B.C. Smith. Ind. Spirit '99: Debut Perf. (Adams); Natl. Film Reg. '18; Sundance '98: Aud. Award, Filmmakers Trophy.

The Smokers 2000 (R) Bleech—this would-be revenge comedy is guaranteed to leave a bad taste in your mouth with its unappealing characters and storyline. Boarding school friends Jefferson (Swain), Karen (Philipps), and Lisa (Pratt) are sick of boys treating them wrong. So with a stolen gun, they are determined to have the miscreants make amends. **97m/C; VHS, DVD.** Dominique Swain; Keri Lynn Pratt; Busy Philipps; Oliver Hudson; Ryan Browning; Joel West; Thora Birch; Nicholas M. Loeb; ***D:*** Christina Peters; ***W:*** Christina Peters; Kenny Golde; ***C:*** J.B. Letchinger; ***M:*** Lawrence Gingold.

Smokey and the Bandit 1/2 1977 (PG) The first and best of the series about bootlegger Reynolds is one long car chase. Reynolds makes a wager that he can deliver a truckload of Coors beer—once unavailable east of Texas—to Atlanta from Texas in 28 hours. Gleason is a riot as the "smokey" who tries to stop him. Field is the hitchhiker Reynolds picks up along the way. Great stunts; director Needham was a top stunt man. **96m/C; VHS, DVD, Blu-Ray.** Burt Reynolds; Sally Field; Jackie Gleason; Jerry Reed; Mike Henry; Paul Williams; Pat McCormick; Susan McIver; John Schneider; Hank Worden; Sonny Shroyer; ***D:*** Hal Needham; ***W:*** Hal Needham; Charles Shyer; ***C:*** Bobby Byrne; ***M:*** Jerry Reed; Bill Justis.

Smokey and the Bandit 2 *Smokey and the Bandit Ride Again* 1980 (PG) Pathetic sequel to "Smokey and the Bandit" proved a boxoffice winner, grossing $40 million. The Bandit is hired to transport a pregnant elephant from Miami to the Republican convention in Dallas. Sheriff Buford T. Justice and family are in hot pursuit. **101m/C; VHS, DVD, Blu-Ray.** Burt Reynolds; Sally Field; Jackie Gleason; Jerry Reed; Mike Henry; Dom DeLuise; Pat McCormick; Paul Williams; John Anderson; Brenda Lee; Mel Tillis; David Huddleston; ***Cameo(s):*** Joe "Mean Joe" Greene; Don Williams; Terry Bradshaw; ***D:*** Hal Needham; ***W:*** Jerry Belson; Michael Kane; Brock Yates; ***C:*** Michael C. Butler.

Smokey and the Bandit, Part 3 1983 (PG) You thought the second one was bad? Another mega car chase, this time sans Reynolds and director Needham. **88m/C; VHS, DVD, Blu-Ray.** Jackie Gleason; Jerry Reed; Paul Williams; Pat McCormick; Mike Henry; Colleen Camp; ***Cameo(s):*** Burt Reynolds; ***D:*** Dick Lowry; ***W:*** Stuart Birnbaum; David Dashev.

Smokey & the Judge 1980 (PG) Police officer has his hands full with a trio of lovely ladies. **90m/C; VHS, DVD.** Gene Price; Wayde Preston; Juanita Curiel; Rory Calhoun; ***D:*** Dan Seeger; ***W:*** Harry Hope; Dan Seeger; ***C:*** Misha (Mikhail) Suslov; ***M:*** Bruce Stewart.

Smokey Bites the Dust 1981 (PG) Car-smashing gag-fest about a sheriff's daughter kidnapped by her smitten beau. Near-plotless and literally unoriginal: lifted footage from several other Corman-produced flicks, a technique that can aptly be called garbage picking. **87m/C; VHS, DVD.** Janet (Johnson) Julian; Jimmy (James Vincent) McNichol; Patrick Campbell; Kari Lizer; John Drew (Blythe) Barrymore, Jr.; Kedrick Wolfe; ***D:*** Charles B. Griffith; ***W:*** Max Apple; ***C:*** Gary Graver; ***M:*** Bent Myggen.

Smokin' Aces 2007 (R) Exhaustingly convoluted guy flick from Carnahan has sleazy nightclub magician Buddy "Aces" Israel (Piven) willing to turn FBI snitch on the Nevada mob. Naturally, the head gangster puts out a hit, attracting all sorts of other violent lowlifes, while the feds ineffectually protect Buddy in a sleazy Lake Tahoe penthouse suite. Lots of flash—lots of violence—no payoff (or maybe one too many). Like its location, it's stylish but empty. **109m/C; DVD, Blu-Ray, HD-DVD.** Jeremy Piven; Ben Affleck; Andy Garcia; Ray Liotta; Alicia Keys; Ryan Reynolds; Peter Berg; Taraji P. Henson; Martin Henderson; Chris Pine; Jason Bateman; Joseph Ruskin; Davenia McFadden; Nestor Carbonell; Tommy Flanagan; Alex Rocco; Vladimir Kulich; David Proval; Joel Edgerton; Matthew Fox; Common; Mike Falkow; Kevin Durand; Maury Sterling; Christopher Egan; ***D:*** Joe Carnahan; ***W:*** Joe Carnahan; ***C:*** Mauro Fiore; ***M:*** Clint Mansell.

Smokin' Aces 2: Assassins' Ball 1/2 2010 (R) Direct-to-video sequel with lots of violence and killers but not much else to connect it the 2007 flick. Low-level FBI desk jockey Walter Weed is confused upon discovering he's the target of a group of crazy assassins, thanks to a mystery man who's offered a high bounty for his death. **86m/C; DVD.** Tom Berenger; Vinnie Jones; Ernie Hudson; Autumn Reeser; Michael Parks; Tommy Flanagan; Clayne Crawford; ***D:*** P.J. Pesce; ***W:*** P.J. Pesce; ***C:*** David Geddes; ***M:*** Timothy S. (Tim) Jones. **VIDEO**

Smooch 1/2 2011 In this Hallmark Channel rom com, young, fairytale-loving Zoe can't bear to dissect her class frog and sets it free in the park after giving it a little kiss (ewww). Zoe wants her widowed mom Gwen to find a new husband and is more than happy to take amnesiac stranger Percy home when she finds him in the park--thinking he's the frog prince. And he actually IS a prince. Well, it's Valentine Day so just go with it. **92m/C; DVD.** Kiernan Shipka; Kellie Martin; Simon Kassianides; ***D:*** Ron Oliver; ***W:*** Howard Burkons; ***C:*** Kees Van Oostrum; ***M:*** Claude Foisy. **CABLE**

Smooth Talk 1985 (PG-13) An innocent, flirtatious teenager catches the eye of a shady character, played by Williams. Disturbing and thought-provoking film that caused some controversy when it opened. Dern gives a brilliant performance as the shy, sheltered girl. Based on the Joyce Carol Oates story "Where Are You Going, Where Have You Been?" Made for PBS' "American Playhouse" series. **92m/C; VHS, DVD, Blu-Ray.** Laura Dern; Treat Williams; Mary Kay Place; Levon Helm; William Ragsdale; Margaret Welsh; Sarah Inglis; ***D:*** Joyce Chopra; ***W:*** Tom Cole; ***C:*** James Glennon. Sundance '86: Grand Jury Prize. **TV**

Smother 1/2 2008 (PG-13) Shrill family comedy. Noah's (Shepard) just been fired, his wife (Tyler) is pressing him to have a baby, his wife's weird cousin (White) is sleeping on their couch, and the last thing he needs is his needy, manipulative mother (Keaton) moving in with her five dogs. But that's what happens and naturally mom can't resist interfering. **92m/C; DVD.** Dax Shepard; Diane Keaton; Liv Tyler; Mike White; Ken Howard; Selma Stern; Sarah Lancaster; Tim Rasmussen; Donnie Booker; ***D:*** Vince Di Meglio; ***W:*** Vince Di Meglio; ***C:*** Julio Macat; ***M:*** Manish Raval; Tom Wolfe.

Smouldering Fires 1/2 1925 A tough businesswoman falls in love with an ambitious young employee, who is 15 years her junior. After they marry, problems arise in the form of the wife's attractive younger sister. Surprisingly subtle melodrama, if that's not an oxymoron. **100m/B; Silent; VHS, DVD.** Pauline Frederick; Laura La Plante; Tully Marshall; Malcolm McGregor; Wanda (Petit) Hawley; Helen Lynch; George Cooper; Bert Roach; ***D:*** Clarence Brown.

Smugglers *Lover of the Great Bear* 1975 Opportunistic smugglers take advantage of the Russian Revolution to sack the land and make a bundle. **110m/C; VHS, DVD.** *IT* Senta Berger; Giuliano Gemma; ***D:*** Valintino Orsini.

The Smurfs 1/2 2011 (PG) In this benignly mediocre live-action/3D animated combo, the tiny blue Smurfs are sucked out of their magical world and fall straight into New York City's Central Park, pursued by evil wizard Gargamel (Azaria) and his cat companion Azrael. Coming to the aid of the bewildered blue visitors are ad man Patrick (Harris) and his pregnant wife Grace (Mays). Belgian artist Peyo's 1950s comics and the 1981-89 NBC animated series provide the basis for self-aware humor for the nostalgia buffs, and noisy comic misadventures (with a few family-value lessons) for the kiddie set. **103m/C; DVD, Blu-Ray.** Neil Patrick Harris; Jayma Mays; Gary Basaraba; Tim Gunn; ***V:*** Jonathan Winters; Alan Cumming; George Lopez; Fred Armisen; Anton Yelchin; Hank Azaria; Sofia Vergara; Katy Perry; Paul (Pee-wee Herman) Reubens; Frank Welker; Kenan Thompson; Jeff Foxworthy; ***Nar:*** Tom Kane; ***D:*** Raja Gosnell; ***W:*** J. David Stern; David N. Weiss; Jay Scherick; David Ronn; ***C:*** Phil Meheux; ***M:*** Heitor Pereira.

The Smurfs 2 2013 (PG) This recycled sequel again has Smurfette (Perry) kidnapped by the Great Gargamel (Azaria), this time taken to Paris along with his two artificial underlings Vexy (Ricci) and Hackus (Smoove). The Smurf village makes the trek to rescue their beloved female companion, helped along by married human couple Patrick (Harris) and Grace (Mays). As heartfelt and fun as it may be, this dopey rehashing of gags is little more than a box-office cash-in, strictly for the kiddies. **105m/C; DVD, Blu-Ray.** Jayma Mays; Brendan Gleeson; Sofia Vergara; Neil Patrick Harris; ***V:*** Hank Azaria; Katy Perry; Jonathan Winters; Anton Yelchin; Alan Cumming; Christina Ricci; J.B. Smoove; ***D:*** Raja Gosnell; ***W:*** David Ronn; David N. Weiss; ***C:*** Phil Meheux; ***M:*** Heitor Pereira.

Smurfs: The Lost Village 2017 (PG) Smurfette, Brainy, Clumsy, and Hefty Smurf find a map and go off looking for a lost village in the Forbidden Forest, trying to outrace Gargamel. The law of diminishing returns is in full effect for this 90-minute babysitter of a movie. None but the very young and undiscriminating or hardcore Smurf aficionados will get any enjoyment out of it. **90m/C; DVD, Blu-Ray.** ***V:*** Demi Lovato; Rainn Wilson; Joe Manganiello; Jack McBrayer; Danny Pudi; ***D:*** Kelly Asbury; ***W:*** Stacey Harman; Pamela Ribon; ***M:*** Christopher Lennertz.

Snake & Mongoose 1/2 2013 (PG-13) Straightforward sports bio of the friendship and rivalry between drag racing legends Don "The Snake" Prudhomme and Tom "The Mongoose" McEwen in Southern California. In order to actually make some money to continue racing, the two approach the Mattel toy company in 1969 and arrange to promote their Hot Wheels line and the first corporate sponsorship becomes a reality. **102m/C; DVD, Blu-Ray.** Jesse Williams; Richard Blake; Noah Wyle; Ashley Hinshaw; Ian Ziering; Tim Blake Nelson; John Heard; ***D:*** Wayne Holloway; ***W:*** Wayne Holloway; Alan Paradise; ***C:*** John Bailey; ***M:*** Gary Barlough.

Snake Eyes 1/2 1998 (R) Stylish thriller with Nick Cage at his wild-eyed best. Cage is corrupt Atlantic City cop Rick Santoro, investigating the bold assassination of Secretary of Defense Kirkland (Fabiani) during a heavyweight boxing match. The first half of the film packs a visual punch, with De Palma's trademark jazzy camera work, but shortly after Santoro partners with his Navy officer pal Kevin Dunne (Sinise), and realizes nothing is what it seems, story is ko'd with a combination of implausibility and a lackluster climax. De Palma's first film since directing the b.o. smash "Mission Impossible." Shot exclusively in a Montreal skating arena. **99m/C; VHS, DVD, Blu-Ray.** Nicolas Cage; Gary Sinise; Carla Gugino; John Heard; Stan Shaw; Kevin Dunn; Michael Rispoli; Joel Fabiani; Luis Guzman; Tamara Tunie; ***D:*** Brian De Palma; ***W:*** David Koepp; ***C:*** Stephen Burum; ***M:*** Ryuichi Sakamoto.

The Snake People *Isle of the Snake People; Cult of the Dead; La Muerte Viviente; Isle of the Living Dead* 1968 A police captain investigates a small island littered with LSD-experimenting scientists, snake-worshippers, and voodoo. One of the infamous quartet of Karloff's final films, all made in Mexico. **90m/C; VHS, DVD.** *MX* Boris Karloff; Julissa; Carlos East; ***D:*** Enrique Vergara.

The Snake Pit 1/2 1948 One of the first films to compassionately explore mental illness and its treatment. Following an emotional collapse Virginia (de Havilland) is placed in a mental institution by her husband, Robert (Stevens). The severity of her depression causes her sympathetic doctor (Genn) to try such treatments as electric shock, hydrotherapy, and drugs, along with the psychoanalysis which gradually allows her to accept her fears and make her recovery. Tour-de-force performance by de Havilland. Based on the novel by Mary Jane Ward. **108m/B; VHS, DVD, Blu-Ray.** Olivia de Havilland; Mark Stevens; Leo Genn; Celeste Holm; Glenn Langan; Helen Craig; Leif Erickson; Beulah Bondi; ***D:*** Anatole Litvak; ***W:*** Frank Partos; Millen Brand; ***C:*** Leo Tover; ***M:*** Alfred Newman. Oscars '48: Sound; N.Y. Film Critics '48: Actress (de Havilland).

The Snake Woman 1961 A herpetologist working in a small English village during the 1890s is conducting strange experiments to try to cure his wife's madness. He tries injecting his pregnant wife with snake venom and she gives birth to a cold-blooded daughter, who, when she grows up, has the ability to change herself into a deadly snake. She promptly begins killing the local male populace until Scotland Yard is called in to investigate. The curvy Travers is appropriately snakey but this movie is dull. **68m/C; VHS, DVD.** *GB* John P. McCarthy; Susan Travers; Arnold Marle; ***D:*** Sidney J. Furie.

Snakehead Terror 2004 A small northeastern fishing community had a problem with invasive snakehead fish in the local lake. So they dumped a bunch of chemicals in to kill the fishies but instead they turned them into mutants capable of walking on land and eating the local populace. The finale is remarkably gore-soaked yet campy. A Sci-Fi Channel original. **88m/C; DVD.** Bruce Boxleitner; Carol Alt; Chelan Simmons; Juliana Wimbles; Ryan McDonell; William B. Davis; ***D:*** Paul Ziller; ***W:*** A.G. Lawrence; ***C:*** Mark Dobrescu; ***M:*** Ken William. **CABLE**

Snakeman **WOOF!** *The Snake King* 2005 Sci-Fi channel cheesefest with lousy CGI. A group of scientists are tramping through the Amazon jungle and encounter a gigantic, multi-headed snake that sees them as chow and a snake-worshiping tribe that would be happy to sacrifice the interlopers. **96m/C; DVD.** Stephen Baldwin; Jayne Heitmeyer; Larry Day; Gary Hudson; ***D:*** Allan Goldstein; ***W:*** Allan Goldstein; Declan O'Brien; ***C:*** Eric Moynier; ***M:*** Claude Doisy. **CABLE**

Snakes on a Plane 2006 (R) And the title says it all. An Internet fan-phenom long before its opening, the studio was so taken by the buzz that they had director Ellis do some re-shoots to make the popcorn flick scarier (more snakes, more gore). FBI agent Neville Flynn (Jackson) is escorting a witness on a commercial flight from Hawaii to L.A. When the plane is halfway over the ocean, some 400 deadly snakes are let loose from a time-release crate into the cabin in an effort to eliminate the witness and apparently everyone else. Unfortunately, the flick doesn't live up to the buzz, failing to supply the gleeful camp and wink that the title suggests, and that the audience expects. **105m/C; DVD, Blu-Ray.** Samuel L. Jackson; Julianna Margulies; Kenan Thompson; Nathan Phillips; Flex Alexander; Bobby Cannavale; David Koechner; Sunny Mabrey; Todd Louiso; Lin Shaye; Terry Chen; Elsa Pataky; Taylor Kitsch; Samantha McLeod; Byron Lawson; Rachel Blanchard; ***D:*** David R. Ellis; ***W:*** Sebastian Gutierrez; John Heffernan; ***C:*** Adam Greenberg; ***M:*** Trevor Rabin.

Snap Decision 1/2 2001 Widowed mom Jen (Winningham) allows her friend Carrie (Huffman), a professional photographer, to take candid pictures of her three children when Carrie visits. But the owner of a photo-developing shop gets flustered by what she sees and contacts the police about the "obscene" material. The kids are taken away from Jen and she faces prison time for child pornography in this true story that is every parent's nightmare. **92m/C; VHS, DVD.** Mare Winningham; Felicity Huffman; Chelcie Ross; Chuck Shamata; Megan Fahlenbock; Ronn Sarosiak; Robert Bockstael; Don Allison; ***D:*** Alan Metzger; ***W:*** Ara Watson; Sam Blackwell; ***C:*** Rhett Morita; ***M:*** James McVay. **CABLE**

Snapdragon ✓✓ **1993 (R)** Police psychologist is led astray by his libido while investigating a luscious amnesiac. His sensible vice cop girlfriend then discovers the sexpot is actually a psycho serial killer calling herself the Snapdragon but will her boyfriend even care? **96m/C; VHS, DVD.** Steven Bauer; Pamela Anderson; Chelsea Field; ***D:*** Worth Keeter; ***W:*** Gene Church; ***C:*** James Mathers; ***M:*** Michael Linn.

The Snapper ✓✓✓ ½ **1993 (R)** Originally made for BBC TV, Frears creates a small comic gem based on the second novel of Doyle's Barrytown trilogy. Set in Dublin, 20-year-old Sharon Curley (Kellegher) finds herself unexpectedly pregnant and refuses to name the father. Family and friends are understanding—until they discover the man's identity. Affecting performances, particularly from Meaney as Sharon's dad who takes a much greater interest in the birth of his grandchild than he ever did with his own children. Cheerful semi-sequel to "The Commitments" serves up domestic upheavals graced with humor and a strong sense of family loyalty. **95m/C; VHS, DVD.** *IR* Tina Kellegher; Colm Meaney; Ruth McCabe; Colm O'Byrne; Pat Laffan; Eanna MacLiam; Ciara Duffy; ***D:*** Stephen Frears; ***W:*** Roddy Doyle. **TV**

Snapshot ✓ *Sweeter Song* **1977 (R)** Typical grade Z sex comedy; a free-lance photographer ogles lots of variously dishabilled young women through his lens. **84m/C; VHS, DVD.** Jim Henshaw; Susan Petrie; ***D:*** Allan Eastman; ***W:*** Allan Eastman; ***C:*** Robert Brooks.

Snapshots ✓✓ ½ **2002 (R)** Aging Larry (Reynolds) has been an American expatriate in Amsterdam for the last 30 years. He runs a used bookstore and is attracted to young, free-spirited Aisha (Chaplin) when she comes into the shop. Eventually, Larry finds out that the girl is the daughter of his long-lost love Narma (Christie), whom he remembers from his visit to Morocco (shown in flashbacks), when circumstances bring them back together. **93m/C; VHS, DVD.** Burt Reynolds; Carmen Chaplin; Julie Christie; Eric Michael Cole; Jemima Rooper; ***D:*** Rudolf Van Den Berg; ***W:*** Rudolf Van Den Berg; Michael O'Loughlin; ***C:*** Gabor Szabo.

Snatch ✓✓✓ **2000 (R)** A la "Lock, Stock and 2 Smoking Barrels," director Ritchie's second film is another well-populated and disorganized crime caper, this time with descriptively named lowlifes trying to heist a stolen 84-carat diamond. Leading the mayhem are Turkish (Statham) and Tommy (Graham), two boxing promoters who sign Mickey (Pitt), an Irish Gypsy, to take a dive. Meanwhile, Franky Four Fingers (Del Toro) transports the red-hot rock to London and his boss Avi (Farina), where it promptly gets lifted. Enter Bullet Tooth Tony (Jones) to find missing Franky and a host of others whose seemingly unrelated subplots eventually meet. Casting, lots of action, and Ritchie's dialogue are spot on. Ritchie's usual use of heavy Cockney accents are upstaged by Pitt's Gypsy pugilist and his much talked about thick-as-Guinness brogue which even the other characters can't decipher. The elaborate and sometimes confusing plotlines are aided by titles and narration and effective use of Ritchie's usual slo-mo, fast cutting, and split-screen. **104m/C; VHS, DVD, Blu-Ray, UMD.** *GB* Benicio Del Toro; Dennis Farina; Brad Pitt; Vinnie Jones; Rade Serbedzija; Jason Statham; Lennie James; Ewen Bremner; Alan Ford; Mike Reid; Robbie Gee; Jason Flemyng; Sorcha Cusack; Stephen Graham; ***D:*** Guy Ritchie; ***W:*** Guy Ritchie; ***C:*** Tim Maurice-Jones; ***M:*** John Murphy.

Snatched ✓ **2017 (R)** On the eve of an exotic jungle vacation, Emily (Schumer) gets dumped by her boyfriend. She then persuades her mom (Hawn) to join her. Shenanigans and chaos ensue as mom and daughter try to work through their clichéd dynamic while being kidnapped in a small village. Schumer and Hawn are sabotaged by bad writing and poor direction at every turn, but manage to elicit a few laughs here and there. Unfortunately, not enough to make it worth the time. These two ladies deserved better. **90m/C; DVD, Blu-Ray.** Amy Schumer; Goldie Hawn; Joan Cusack; Ike Barinholtz; Wanda Sykes; ***D:*** Jonathan Levine; ***W:*** Katie Dippold; ***C:*** Florian Ballhaus; ***M:*** Chris Bacon; Theodore Shapiro.

Sneakerheadz ✓✓ ½ **2015** A feature-length documentary look at the sneaker collecting subculture worldwide. Considering the wide social impact of sneakers, the documentary explores why collectors go to extreme lengths to purchase unique sneakers and why they want to wear the art they buy. How sneakers became such valued objects is considered as well. **70m/C; DVD, Blu-Ray, Streaming, Download.** ***D:*** David T. Friendly; Mick Partridge; ***C:*** Paul de Lumen.

Sneakers ✓✓ ½ **1992 (PG-13)** Competent thriller about five computer hackers with questionable pasts and an equally questionable government job. Of course, nothing is as it seems. Rather slow-going considering the talents and suspense involved but includes enough turns to keep a viewer's interest. **125m/C; VHS, DVD, Blu-Ray.** Robert Redford; Sidney Poitier; River Phoenix; Dan Aykroyd; Ben Kingsley; David Strathairn; Mary McDonnell; Timothy Busfield; George Hearn; Eddie Jones; James Earl Jones; Stephen Tobolowsky; Donal Logue; ***D:*** Phil Alden Robinson; ***W:*** Lawrence Lasker; Walter F. Parkes; Phil Alden Robinson; ***C:*** John Lindley; ***M:*** James Horner; Branford Marsalis.

The Sniper ✓✓ **1952** Interesting time capsule of San Francisco in the early '50s as well as a psychological study of a mentally-ill killer. Miller (Franz) knows he's unstable so he seeks help for his compulsion to kill women. Treated with indifference by the medical community, he takes to a rooftop with a rifle and starts picking off women who've rejected him. Lt. Kafka (Menjou) is assigned the politically hot case and eventually gets a lead into the psychosis compelling Miller to kill. **87m/B; DVD.** Adolphe Menjou; Arthur Franz; Gerald Mohr; Richard Kiley; Marie Windsor; Frank Faylen; ***D:*** Edward Dmytryk; ***W:*** Harry Brown; ***C:*** Burnett Guffey; ***M:*** George Antheil.

Sniper ✓✓✓ *The Deadly Tower* **1975** Suspenseful drama based on true story of Charles Whitman, who shot at University of Texas students from Texas Tower on a summer day in 1966. Disney alumunus Russell breaks type as mass killer, with fine support by Yniguez as a police officer on the scene and Beatty as the passerby who lends a hand. Finely crafted re-creation of disturbing, true event. **85m/C; VHS, DVD.** Kurt Russell; Richard Yniguez; John Forsythe; Ned Beatty; Pernell Roberts; Clifton James; Paul Carr; Alan Vint; Pepe Serna; ***D:*** Jerry Jameson. **TV**

Sniper ✓ ½ **1992 (R)** Less than compelling shoot-'em-up set in Panama. Lead characters include Sgt. Beckett (Berenger), a seasoned assassin who gets a rush from killing. Also assigned to the case is Richard Miller (Zane), a newcomer who knows his guns but not his jungles. Together they go in search of their target, a politician planning a coup with the help of a druglord. Action is poorly choreographed and plot is cursory at best. **99m/C; VHS, DVD.** Tom Berenger; Billy Zane; J.T. Walsh; Aden Young; Ken Radley; Reinaldo Arenas; Carlos Alvarez; Roy Edmonds; Dale Dye; ***D:*** Luis Llosa; ***W:*** Michael Frost Beckner; Crash Leyland; ***C:*** Bill Butler; ***M:*** Gary Chang.

Sniper 2 ✓ ½ **2002 (R)** This sequel comes some 10 years after the first "Sniper" and you wonder why anyone would bother with such a familiar story. Marine sniper Beckett (Berenger) is called on for one last mission: to kill a Serbian general who's committing atrocities on the Muslim population. Beckett is teamed with soldier Cole (Woodbine), who's on death row and has a chance to earn his freedom if he survives. **91m/C; VHS, DVD.** Tom Berenger; Bokeem Woodbine; Dan E. Butler; Erika Marozsan; Linden Ashby; ***D:*** Craig R. Baxley; ***W:*** Ron Mita; Jim McClain; ***C:*** David Connell; ***M:*** Gary Chang. **VIDEO**

Sniper 3 ✓ **2004 (R)** An assassin's work is never done, so yet again, Beckett dusts off the old hardware to rub out a supposed terrorist for his new employer, the National Security Agency. Things go haywire, seeing as his prey is an old chum and so his aim turns to tracking down the truth. **90m/C; VHS, DVD.** Tom Berenger; Byron Mann; John Doman; Denis Arndt; Troy Winbush; Jeanetta Arnette; William Duffy; ***D:*** P.J. Pesce; ***W:*** J.S. Cardone; Ross Helford; ***C:*** Michael Bonvillain; ***M:*** Timothy S. (Tim) Jones. **VIDEO**

Sniper: Ghost Shooter ✓✓ **2016 (R)** An action-packed war drama focused on elite snipers. While on assignment in the Middle East, snipers Brandon Beckett (Collins) and Miller (Zane) are shifted to a new mission by their superior, the Colonel (Haysbert). Charged with protecting a gas pipeline that runs from the Republic of Georgia to Western Europe from terrorists, Beckett and Miller soon find themselves engaging with an enemy that seems to know where the American snipers are located. Believing that this could be linked a breach in a security, accusations come to light including the enemy having access to inside information and perhaps even the Colonel undermining the operation. Beckett and Miller do all they can to uncover the truth and take all necessary action. **89m/C; DVD, Streaming, Download.** Billy Zane; Chad Michael Collins; Dennis Haysbert; Enoch Frost; Stephanie Vogt; ***D:*** Don Michael Paul; ***W:*** Chris Hauty. **VIDEO**

Sniper: Legacy ✓ **2014 (R)** Fifth film in the series is light on the action that made the franchise and Berenger's role is little more than an extended cameo. Sniper Brandon Beckett is lead to believe his father was killed by an assassin targeting the military. Only it's a ruse to use him to lure out the perp. **95m/C; DVD.** Chad Michael Collins; Tom Berenger; Dennis Haysbert; ***D:*** Don Michael Paul; ***W:*** Don Michael Paul; John Fasano; ***C:*** Martin Chichov; ***M:*** Frederik Wiedmann. **VIDEO**

Sniper Reloaded ✓ ½ **2011 (R)** Predictable action. Marine Sgt. Brandon Beckett is the only survivor when he and his men are ambushed by a sniper during a mission. Brandon turns to sniper instructor Richard Miller, his late father's protege, for help in finding the assassin who wants to finish the job. **91m/C; DVD, Blu-Ray.** Chad Michael Collins; Billy Zane; Annabel Wright; Richard Sammel; ***D:*** Claudio Fah; ***W:*** John Fasano; ***C:*** Lorenzo Senatore; ***M:*** Marcus Trump; Mark Sayfritz. **VIDEO**

Sniper: Special Ops ✓ ½ **2016 (R)** Afghanistan-set Steven Seagal action hero flick. During a mission to rescue an American Congressman held by the Taliban in a remote Afghan village, a special ops force succeeds in their goal but several soldiers are separated from the main group. A soldier is injured during the mission, and expert sniper Sergeant Jake Chandler (Seagal) remains with him to render aid. Defying the orders of his superior to go on a new mission to retrieve munitions instead of rescuing their cohorts, the squad's leader, Sergeant Vic Mosby (Abell), returns to the village with his team prepared to do all it takes to extract their fellow soldiers despite being outnumbered. **84m/C; DVD, Streaming, Download.** Steven Seagal; Rob van Dam; Tim Abell; Dale Dye; Jason-Shane Scott; ***D:*** Fred Olen Ray; ***W:*** Fred Olen Ray; ***C:*** Stuart Brereton; ***M:*** Nick Soole. **VIDEO**

Snipes ✓✓ ½ **2001 (R)** Snipes are the posters you see plastered to walls and lamp-posts—in this case they're of up-and-coming Philly rapper Prolifik (Nelly), who's got a gangsta background and a shady record deal. The record label owner, Bobby Starr (Winters), is in hock to local mobster Johnnie Maradino (Vincent). When Prolifik gets kidnapped and the master tape of his recordings is also stolen, Starr, for some unknown reason, thinks that gofer/fan Erik (Jones) is somehow mixed up in the mess. Actually, there's a lot that's unclear since first-timer Murray overstuffs the plot. **113m/C; VHS, DVD.** Sam Jones, III; Dean Winters; Mpho Koaho; Nelly; Zoe Saldana; Frank Vincent; ***D:*** Rich Murray; ***W:*** Rich Murray; Rob Wiser; ***C:*** Alexander Buono.

Snitch ✓✓ ½ **2013 (PG-13)** Johnson, the actor formerly known as The Rock, gets his meatiest role to date in this surprisingly effective action drama. He plays a man whose son is wrongly accused of being a drug dealer, and he enters into a deal with the government to work as an undercover informant and get the right parties to pay for their crimes. Parts are a bit muddled between action and drama, but Johnson does well at presenting a man willing to go to the edge of the criminal underworld to do what's right. **112m/C; DVD, Blu-Ray.** Dwayne "The Rock" Johnson; Susan Sarandon; Benjamin Bratt; Barry Pepper; Jon Bernthal; Harold Perrineau, Jr.; Michael K(enneth) Williams; Melina Kanakaredes; Rafi Gavron; ***D:*** Ric Roman Waugh; ***W:*** Ric Roman Waugh; Justin Haythe; ***C:*** Dana Gonzales; ***M:*** Antonio Pinto.

The Snorkel ✓✓ **1958** The perfect crime never is. Paul (Van Eyck) murders his wife Madge but sets it up to look like a suicide. He seals up the room, turns on the gas, and then hides under the floorboards, taking in fresh air through his scuba mask until her body is discovered and removed. The police are fooled but not his teenaged stepdaughter Candy (Miller) who knows Paul is a sicko and just has to prove it though everyone else thinks she's crazed by grief. **74m/B; DVD.** *GB* Peter Van Eyck; Mandy Miller; Betta St. John; Gregoire Aslan; William Franklyn; ***D:*** Guy Green; ***W:*** Jimmy Sangster; Peter Myers; ***C:*** Jack Asher; ***M:*** Francis Chagrin.

Snow ✓✓ ½ **2004** Handsome, single Nick Snowden (Cavanagh) is training to take over the family business (as Santa Claus' successor) when, three days before Christmas, his favorite reindeer Buddy is kidnapped by evil hunter Buck (Fabian). Buddy winds up in the zoo in San Ernesto, California, where Nick meets single zookeeper Sandy (Williams), whom he thinks would make a swell Mrs. Claus. So Nick moves into Sandy's boarding house and, with the help of street smart young Hector (Thompson), comes up with a plan to rescue Buddy and get the girl (oh, and save Christmas). ABC Family movie. **90m/C; DVD.** Tom Cavanagh; Ashley Williams; Patrick Fabian; Jackie Burroughs; Bobb'e J. Thompson; ***D:*** Alex Zamm; ***W:*** Rich Burns; ***C:*** Jim Westenbrink; ***M:*** David Lawrence. **CABLE**

Snow 2: Brain Freeze ✓✓ **2008** ABC Family channel sequel to 2004's "Snow." Nick Snowden (Cavanagh) has followed his late father into the family business (he's Santa Claus) but his new wife Sandy (Williams) is still overwhelmed by the intensity of the holiday workload. Then Nick has an accident, develops amnesia, and walks away at the most inopportune time. So Sandy goes looking for Nick and runs into her former beau Buck (Fabian), who's so eager to 'help.' **87m/C; DVD.** Tom Cavanagh; Ashley Williams; Patrick Fabian; Alexander Conti; Hal Williams; ***D:*** Mark Rosman; ***W:*** Rich Burns; ***M:*** Kenneth Burgomaster. **CABLE**

Snow Angels ✓✓✓ **2007 (R)** Tragedy tolls with the sound of distant gunfire as a high school marching band rehearses on the football field, stunning the students into silence. Flash back several weeks to a dreary, snowy northwest small town, where newly divorced waitress (Annie) and her on-the-edge ex (Rockwell) navigate a tense relationship and share custody of their four-year-old child. Annie's sleeping with a co-worker's (Sedaris) husband, while another young co-worker Arthur (Angarano), who she used to babysit, is in the apprehensive beginning stages of a high school romance with Lila (Thirlby). Director Green likes to dump you into his films and let you figure out your emotions along with the characters, which sometimes makes for uncomfortable viewing, but the tactic works in this study of love and loss in a claustrophobic town. **106m/C; DVD.** Kate Beckinsale; Sam Rockwell; Michael Angarano; Jeanetta Arnette; Griffin Dunne; Nicky Katt; Olivia Thirlby; Amy Sedaris; Tom Noonan; Connor Paolo; Hudson Grace; ***D:*** David Gordon Green; ***W:*** David Gordon Green; ***C:*** Tim Orr; ***M:*** Jeff McIlwain.

Snow Buddies ✓✓ ½ **2008 (G)** Big on the awwwww factor since those "Air Bud" pups are as cute as ever. Budderball gets locked into an ice cream truck and when his four siblings try to rescue him, they all wind up in Alaska. (Right, like the plot should make sense.) They're befriended by a couple of sled dogs and before you know it, our cuties are mushing the trail in an effort to get home. **87m/C; DVD.** Molly Shannon; Richard Karn; Cynthia Stevenson; ***V:*** Dylan Sprouse; James Belushi; Kris Kristofferson; Josh Flitter; Jimmy Bennett; Liliana Mumy; Skyler Gisondo; Lothaire Bluteau; Henry Hodges; ***D:*** Robert Vince; ***W:*** Robert Vince; Anna McRoberts; ***M:*** Brahm Wenger. **VIDEO**

Snow Cake ✓✓ **2006** Middle-aged Brit Alex (Rickman) is driving through Ontario and reluctantly offers a ride to hitchhiking teen Vivienne (Hampshire). She's killed in a crash and uninjured Alex decides he must convey his condolences to her mother, only to discover that Linda (Weaver) is autistic and doesn't process emotions. Alan decides to stay for the funeral and meets Linda's secretive neighbor Maggie (Moss), who offers her own personal brand of sympathy. Moss is best as a small-town femme but Rickman and Weaver are chilly and constricted. **112m/C; DVD.** *GB CA* Sigourney Weaver; Alan Rickman; Carrie-Anne Moss; James Allodi; Emily Hampshire; ***D:*** Marc Evans; ***W:*** Angela Pell; ***C:*** Steve Cosens; ***M:*** Broken Social Scene.

The Snow Creature WOOF! 1954 Stupid troop of explorers bring back a snow creature from the Himalayas. Critter escapes in L.A. and terrorizes all in its path before blending in with club crowd. Very bad monster epic (the first about a snow monster) that strains credibility frame by frame. Occasionally, depending upon camera angle, light, and viewer mood, monster appears to be something other than guy in bad suit sweating. Directed by Billy Wilder's brother and another argument against genetic consistency. **72m/B; VHS, DVD.** Paul Langton; Leslie Denison; ***D:*** W. Lee Wilder.

Snow Day 🦴 1/2 2000 (PG) Goofy, innocuous family comedy may provide a distraction for the little monsters if you're stuck with a snow day of your own. Tom (Chase) is the hapless weatherman who's as surprised as anyone when the white stuff falls. Meanwhile, the neighborhood kids seek to foil the efforts of the evil Snowplowman (Elliott) who is out to destroy their dream of having more than one day off from school. **89m/C; VHS, DVD.** Chevy Chase; Chris Elliott; Mark Webber; Jean Smart; Schuyler Fisk; Iggy Pop; Pam Grier; John Schneider; Emmanuelle Chriqui; ***D:*** Chris Koch; ***W:*** Will McRobb; Chris Viscardi; ***C:*** Robbie Greenberg; ***M:*** Steve Bartek.

The Snow Devils 🦴 *I Diavoli Dello Spazio; The Space Devils* **1967** Dubbed, shoestring Italian sci-fi. An expedition is sent to the Himalayas when a weather station is destroyed, but instead of finding the Abominable Snowman, Gamma I commander Jackson discovers evil aliens. They want to cause ecological havoc for humans by melting the polar ice caps so they can make Earth their new home. May be good for some campy laughs. **78m/B; DVD.** *IT* Giacomo "Jack" Rossi-Stuart; Goffredo "Freddy" Unger; Ombretta Colli; Renato Baldini; ***D:*** Anthony M. Dawson; ***W:*** Renato Moretti; Ivan Reiner; ***C:*** Riccardo (Pallton) Pallottini; ***M:*** Angelo Francesco Lavagnino.

Snow Dogs 🦴🦴 2002 (PG) Gooding leads this kid flick as Ted Brooks, a dentist who only finds out about his adoption after his biological mom's death in Alaska. Aside from a rather dilapidated house, mom's estate included a team of frisky Siberian husky sled dogs. Displaced city boy Ted, who's from Miami, hates the cold and the dogs but stays to take care of the estate, seek out his real father, and get better acquainted with friendly local bar owner Barb (Bacalso). Meanwhile, the grizzled Thunder Jack (Coburn) is on Ted's tail, trying to get him to sell the dogs. The expected Iditarod-type dog race ensues. Gooding mugs amiably and the good natured physical humor and action should amuse the young and undiscrimination. **99m/C; VHS, DVD, Blu-Ray.** Cuba Gooding, Jr.; James Coburn; Sisqo; Nichelle Nichols; M. Emmet Walsh; Graham Greene; Brian Doyle-Murray; Joanna Bascalso; Michael Bolton; ***D:*** Brian Levant; ***W:*** Jim Kouf; Tommy Swerdlow; Michael Goldberg; Mark Gibson; Philip Halprin; ***C:*** Thomas Ackerman; ***M:*** John Debney.

Snow Falling on Cedars 🦴🦴 1999 (PG-13) Visually beautiful but remarkably dull adaptation of David Guterson's novel. In 1954, journalist and WWII vet, the portentiously named Ishmael Chambers (Hawke), confronts his past when he's assigned to report on the trial of Japanese-American Kazuo Miyamoto (Yune), who's accused of murdering a fellow fisherman (Thal) in a small community north of Puget Sound. Kazuo just happens to be married to Ishmael's former flame, Hatsue (Kudoh)?their romance having been thwarted by the prejudicial times. Lots of impressionistic flashbacks complicate matters while the story meanders along, not helped by Hawke's blank-faced performance. **128m/C; VHS, DVD, Blu-Ray.** Ethan Hawke; Youki Kudoh; Rick Yune; Sam Shepard; Max von Sydow; James Cromwell; James Rebhorn; Richard Jenkins; Eric Thal; Celia Weston; Max Wright; ***D:*** Scott Hicks; ***W:*** Scott Hicks; Ronald Bass; ***C:*** Robert Richardson; ***M:*** James Newton Howard.

Snow Flower and the Secret Fan 🦴 1/2 2011 (PG-13) Overly sentimental story of female friendship, class issues, and women's roles. In 1829 China, Snow Flower and Lily are paired together as children to become best friends, secretly communicating via messages written in the folds of a white silk fan. In present-day Shanghai, their descendants, Nina and Sophia, were once close but when Sophia is left in a coma after an accident, Nina rushes to her hospital room. She discovers Sophia was working on a novel about their ancestors and her reading of the manuscript leads to many flashbacks showing the obvious parallels in their lives. Loosely based on the book by Lisa See. **120m/C; DVD, Blu-Ray.**

A Snow Globe Christmas 🦴🦴 2013 How about some bah-humbug with the usual Christmas cheer in this Lifetime drama. Jaded TV exec Meg (Witt) takes her frustrations out on a snow globe that's a Christmas TV movie prop and knocks herself out. She wakes up to find herself inside the bubble in an alternate reality where she's married with kids in a picturesque small town--all of which she refuses to have anything to do with. **90m/C; DVD.** Alicia Witt; Donald Adeosun Faison; Christina Milian; Trevor Donovan; Art LaFleur; ***D:*** Jodi Binstock; ***W:*** Naomi L. Selfman; ***C:*** Warren Yeager; ***M:*** Chris Ridenhour. **CABLE**

Snow in August 🦴🦴 1/2 2001 In the summer of 1947, young Michael Devlin's (Tambakis) friendship with immigrant Czech Rabbi Hirsch (Rea) brings on the wrath of the local Irish street gang. Michael witnesses the beating of a Jewish shopkeeper, loses his friends, and decides to turn to an ancient Jewish text to summon the protection of a Golem. Based on the novel by Pete Hamill. **104m/C; VHS, DVD.** Peter Tambakis; Stephen Rea; Lolita Davidovich; ***D:*** Richard Friedenberg; ***W:*** Richard Friedenberg. **CABLE**

The Snow Queen 🦴🦴 1/2 2002 An updated reworking of the Hans Christian Andersen fairytale is visually splendid but overly long. Gerda (Hobbs) lives with her bitter father (Wisden) in a remote hotel in the snowy north country. She's attracted to bellboy Kai (Guilbat), who disappears after a beautiful but sinister guest (Fonda) also leaves. So Gerda decides to track them down and save Kai from the evil Snow Queen. **172m/C; VHS, DVD.** Bridget Fonda; Robert Wisden; Jeremy Guilbaut; Chelsea Hobbs; ***D:*** David Wu; ***W:*** Simon Moore; ***C:*** Gregory Middleton; ***M:*** Lawrence Shragge. **CABLE**

Snow Shark 🦴 *Snow Shark: Ancient Snow Beast* **2011 (R)** A scientific expedition awakens a prehistoric shark that swims in snow. It's obviously an attempt at making an intentionally campy B film, but is sadly sabotaged by the department store mannequins they brought to life to use as actors. **79m/C; DVD.** Sam Qualiana; Michael O'Hear; Jackey Hall; C.J. Qualiana; Kathy Murphy; ***D:*** Sam Qualiana; ***W:*** Sam Qualiana; ***C:*** Sam Qualiana. **VIDEO**

The Snow Walker 🦴🦴 1/2 2003 (PG) A pilot and his Inuit passenger struggle to conquer the elements and their cultural differences after they crash-land in the bitterly cold Canadian Arctic—if they want to survive. Drawn from Farley Mowat's short story "Walk Well My Brother." **109m/C; VHS, DVD.** Barry Pepper; Annabella Piugattuk; James Cromwell; Kiersten Warren; Jon(athan) Gries; Robin Dunne; Greg Spottiswood; Samson Jorah; Michael Buble; ***D:*** Charles Martin Smith; ***W:*** Charles Martin Smith; ***C:*** David Connell; Jon Joffin; Paul Sarossy; ***M:*** Mychael Danna. **VIDEO**

Snow White 🦴🦴 1989 The incomparable Rigg stars in this witty retelling of the beautiful girl and her seven little friends. **85m/C; VHS, DVD.** Diana Rigg; Sarah Patterson; Billy Barty; ***D:*** Michael Berz.

Snow White: A Deadly Summer WOOF! 2012 (PG-13) You really have to stretch to find any fairytale comparisons in this no-budget, no-brains teen horror. Snow White starts acting out when her father remarries and she and her stepmother Linda hate each other. Linda sends Snow away to a wilderness camp where the teen learns the camp has a bad history since a camper was murdered and the suspect escaped into the woods and was never seen again. No surprise when the present crop of campers start getting killed. **90m/C; DVD.** Shanley Caswell; Maureen McCormick; Eric Roberts; Tim Abell; Chase Bennett; ***D:*** David DeCoteau; ***W:*** Barbara Kymlicka; ***C:*** David DeCoteau; ***M:*** Harry Manfredini. **VIDEO**

Snow White: A Tale of Terror 🦴🦴 1/2 *Snow White in the Black Forest; Grimm Brothers' Snow White* **1997 (R)** This definitely puts the grim in the Grimm Brothers version of the fairy tale. In medieval Austria, beautiful Claudia (Weaver) marries widowed Frederick who, unfortunately, has an even-more beautiful daughter, Lilli (Keena), who's put out by this rival for her father's affections. The stepmom/stepdaughter battle increases when Claudia's own long-awaited baby is still-born and the wrathful and unbalanced Claudia orders Lilli's death. Only she's rescued by seven outcasts (only one of whom is a dwarf) living in the forest. The witchy Claudia does still like to talk to her mirror, however. Filmed in the Czech Republic. **101m/C; VHS, DVD.** Sigourney Weaver; Sam Neill; Monica Keena; Gil Bellows; Taryn Davis; ***D:*** Michael Cohn; ***W:*** Thomas Szollosi; Deborah Serra; ***C:*** Mike Southon; ***M:*** John Ottman.

Snow White and the Huntsman 🦴🦴 1/2 2012 (PG-13) Stewart ably brings her sullen pout to the title role in this revisionist version of the fairytale and this time she's no shy princess but an action royal. Her evil stepmother, Queen Ravenna (Theron), has imprisoned her rival but Snow escapes into the Dark Forest where the Queen's magic can't find her. Ravenna sends her Huntsman (hunky Hemsworth) off into the woods, but instead of killing the princess he becomes her protector as Snow White decides to overthrow the Queen's rule. Even the dwarves are tough guys. Theron seems to be having the most fun and her costumes (by Colleen Atwood) are notable. **128m/C; DVD, Blu-Ray.** Kristen Stewart; Charlize Theron; Chris Hemsworth; Sam Claflin; Ian McShane; Bob Hoskins; Ray Winstone; Nick Frost; Eddie Marsan; Toby Jones; Sam Spruell; ***D:*** Rupert Sanders; ***W:*** Hossein Amini; Evan Daugherty; John Lee Hancock; ***C:*** Greig Fraser; ***M:*** James Newton Howard. Golden Raspberries '12: Worst Actress (Stewart).

Snow White and the Seven Dwarfs 🦴🦴🦴🦴 1937 (G) Classic adaptation of the Grimm Brothers fairy tale about the fairest of them all. Beautiful animation, memorable characters, and wonderful songs mark this as the definitive "Snow White." Set the stage for other animated features after Walt Disney took an unprecedented gamble by attempting the first animated feature-length film, a project which took over two years to create and $1.5 million to make, and made believers out of those who laughed at the concept. Lifelike animation was based on real stars; Margery Belcher (later Champion) posed for Snow, Louis Hightower was the Prince, and Lucille LaVerne gave the Queen her nasty look. **83m/C; VHS, DVD, Blu-Ray.** ***V:*** Adriana Caselotti; Harry Stockwell; Lucille LaVerne; Moroni Olsen; Billy Gilbert; Pinto Colvig; Otis Harlan; Scotty Matraw; Roy Atwell; Stuart Buchanan; Marion Darlington; Jim Macdonald; ***D:*** David Hand; ***W:*** Ted Sears; Otto Englander; Earl Hurd; Dorothy Blank; Richard Creedon; Dick Richard; Merrill De Maris; Webb Smith; ***M:*** Frank Churchill; Paul J. Smith; Larry Morey; Leigh Harline. AFI '98: Top 100; Natl. Film Reg. '89.

Snow White and the Three Stooges 🦴 *Snow White and the Three Clowns* **1961** The Stooges fill in for the Seven Dwarfs when they go off prospecting in King Solomon's mines. Alas, see any Stooge movie but this one. **107m/C; VHS, DVD.** Moe Howard; Larry Fine; Joe DeRita; Carol Heiss; Patricia Medina; Edson Stroll; ***D:*** Walter Lang; ***W:*** Noel Langley; Elwood Ullman; ***C:*** Leon Shamroy; ***M:*** Lyn Murray.

Snow White: The Fairest of Them All 🦴🦴 2002 Kreuk certainly looks the title part and Richardson makes a fine wicked stepmother and queen but this version of the fairy tale is lame. Snow's mother dies when she's a baby and her father (Irwin) unwittingly places his daughter under a curse when he marries the witchy Elspeth (Richardson). Oh, and the dwarves are rainbow-colored and named after the days of the week. But Snow still gets stuck in that glass coffin until the prince comes along. **90m/C; VHS, DVD.** Kristin Kreuk; Miranda Richardson; Tom Irwin; Vera Farmiga; Vincent Schiavelli; Warwick Davis; Michael J. Anderson; Clancy Brown; Tyron Leitso; ***D:*** Caroline Thompson; ***W:*** Caroline Thompson; Julie Hickson; ***C:*** Jon Joffin; ***M:*** Michael Covertino. **TV**

Snowball Express 🦴🦴 1972 (G) When a New York City accountant inherits a hotel in the Rocky Mountains, he decides to move his family west to attempt to make a go of the defunct ski resort, only to find that the place is falling apart. Run-of-the-mill Disney comedy, based on the novel "Chateau Bon Vivant" by Frankie and John O'Rear. **120m/C; VHS, DVD.** Dean Jones; Nancy Olson; Harry (Henry) Morgan; Keenan Wynn; ***D:*** Norman Tokar; ***M:*** Robert F. Brunner.

Snowballin' 🦴 *Apres-Ski* **1971** A ski instructor gives private lessons to a bunch of snow bunnies. **90m/C; VHS, DVD.** *CA* Seline Lomez; Daniel Pilon; Mariette Levesque; Robert Arcand; ***D:*** Roger Cardinal; ***W:*** Roger Cardinal; ***C:*** Roger Racine; ***M:*** Mark Hamilton.

Snowballing 🦴 1985 (PG) Part of the polluted wave of teen-sex flicks of the 1980s, this is very mild for the genre but still no prize. Lusty high schoolers at a skiing competition look for action on and off the slopes, end up exposing a resort fraud. **96m/C; VHS, DVD.** Mary (Elizabeth) McDonough; Bob Hastings; ***D:*** Charles E. Sellier; ***W:*** Thomas Chapman; ***C:*** Henning Schellerup; ***M:*** Larry Whitley.

Snowbeast 🦴 1/2 1977 The residents of a ski resort are being terrorized by a half-human, half-animal beast leaving a path of dead bodies in its wake. "Jaws" hits the slopes. Not scary or even funny. Made for TV. **96m/C; VHS, DVD, Blu-Ray.** Bo Svenson; Yvette Mimieux; Sylvia Sidney; Clint Walker; Robert F. Logan; ***D:*** Herb Wallerstein. **TV**

Snowblind 🦴🦴 *Ski Lift to Death* **1978** Two ski gondolas derail, placing the passengers in jeopardy. Among the passengers is a mobster being pursued by an assassin. **98m/C; VHS, DVD.** Deborah Raffin; Charles Frank; Howard Duff; Don Galloway; Gail Strickland; Don Johnson; Veronica Hamel; Clu Gulager; Lisa Reeves; Suzy Chaffee; ***D:*** William Wiard.

Snowboard Academy 🦴 1/2 1996 (PG) Chris Barry (Haim), the younger son of a ski resort owner, gets into trouble when his crazy snowboarder pals take over the slopes. Chris' older brother challenges him to start a school that will turn the bumblers into racers in just two weeks. Filmed at Le Chantecler resort in the Laurentian Mountains near Montreal. **89m/C; VHS, DVD.** Corey Haim; Jim Varney; Brigitte Nielsen; Joe Flaherty; Paul Hopkins; ***D:*** John Shepphird; ***W:*** Rudy Rupak; James Salisko; ***C:*** Bruno Philip; ***M:*** Ross Vannelli.

Snowbound: The Jim and Jennifer Stolpa Story 🦴🦴 1/2 1994 Based on a true story, this TV drama finds Jim (Harris) Stolpa, his wife Jennifer (Williams), and their 5-month-old baby fighting for survival when they're trapped in the open by a Nevada snowstorm for eight days. **120m/C; VHS, DVD.** Neil Patrick Harris; Kelli Williams; Susan Clark; Michael Gross; Richard Cox; ***D:*** Christian Duguay; ***W:*** Jonathan Rintels; ***C:*** Peter Woeste; ***M:*** Lou Natale. **TV**

Snowden 🦴🦴 1/2 2016 (R) If Edward Snowden wasn't a real person, Oliver Stone might have invented him. The whistleblower who revealed the scope and depth of our national security agency's invasions of worldwide privacy is the subject of the notoriously political filmmaker's latest drama. The force behind this true story flick is Joseph Gordon-Levitt's excellent performance as the title character. He captures the dilemma in the heart of a man who once fought for his country but felt betrayed by it. A valiant effort by Stone but greatness eludes him. **134m/C; DVD.** Joseph Gordon-Levitt; Shailene Woodley; Melissa Leo; Zachary Quinto; Tom Wilkinson;

Nicolas Cage; *D:* Oliver Stone; *W:* Oliver Stone; Kieran Fitzgerald; *C:* Anthony Dod Mantle; *M:* Craig Armstrong; Adam Peters.

Snowglobe ½ **2007** Angela (Milian) feels overwhelmed by her family. She lives in the same apartment building, works at the family deli, and her mother Rose (Bracco) picks out the guys she dates. If only Angela could have a perfect Christmas just like the one in the antique snowglobe she inherited from her grandmother. She has a dream about entering that world and discovers how to make her own holidays special. An ABC Family original. **90m/C; DVD.** Christina Milian; Lorraine Bracco; Matt Keeslar; Josh Cooke; Ron Canada; *D:* Ron Lagomarsino; *W:* Garrett Frawley; Brian Turner; *C:* Derick Underschultz. **CABLE**

The Snowman **2017 (R)** A futuristic mystery-thriller of a Norwegian police detective, based on the best-selling novel by Jo Nesbo. In 2075, detective Henry Hole (Fassbender) is recognized as a genius by his colleagues but he has a messy personal life that includes alcoholism and an ex-girlfriend Rakel (Gainsbourg). When a serial killer with a memorable personal signature begins killing people in Hole's city, the detective is aided in his investigation by Katrine Bratt (Ferguson). Despite the first-rate talent involved in the film, its plot is simplistic and full of obvious coincidences. **119m/C; DVD, Blu-Ray.** *SW UK US* Michael Fassbender; Rebecca Ferguson; Charlotte Gainsbourg; Val Kilmer; J.K. Simmons; *D:* Tomas Alfredson; *W:* Peter Straughan; Hossein Amini; Soren Sveistrup; *C:* Dion Beebe; *M:* Marco Beltrami.

Snowmen ½ **2010 (PG)** Ten-year-old Billy is diagnosed with cancer and becomes determined to get into the Guinness Book of World Records. Aided by his pals, Jason and Howard, the Colorado trio set out to make the most snowmen created in one day despite schoolyard bullies and concerned dads. A frozen corpse and a cemetery caretaker also figure into the boys' adventures. **87m/C; DVD.** Bobby Coleman; Josh Flitter; Bobb'e J. Thompson; Ray Liotta; Doug E. Doug; Christopher Lloyd; *D:* Robert Kirbyson; *W:* Robert Kirbyson; *C:* Geno Salvatori; *M:* John Debney. **VIDEO**

Snowpiercer **2014 (R)** Bong's very loose adaptation of the hit French graphic novel details a future in which a global tragedy led to the near annihilation of the entire human race. The only people that remain are on a never-stopping train that circles the globe for eternity, cutting through the snow that covers the Earth. A class system immediately formed on the Snowpiercer, with the lowest class left to rot and die in the back while the upper class eats sushi and parties in the front. Bong's brilliant film details the collapse of that system. Smart, fun, and action-packed, this is the kind of sci-fi they don't make that often any more. **126m/C; DVD, Blu-Ray.** *SK US FR* Chris Evans; Tilda Swinton; John Hurt; Jamie Bell; Octavia Spencer; Kang-ho Song; Ah-sung Ko; Ed Harris; Ewen Bremner; *D:* Joon-ho Bong; *W:* Joon-ho Bong; Kelly Masterson; *C:* Kyung-Pyo Hong; *M:* Marco Beltrami.

The Snows of Kilimanjaro **1952** Called by Hemingway "The Snows of Zanuck," in reference to the great producer, this film is actually an artful pastiche of several Hemingway short stories and novels. The main story, "The Snows of Kilimanjaro," acts as a framing device, in which the life of a successful writer is seen through his fevered flashbacks as he and his rich wife, while on safari, await a doctor to save his gangrenous leg. **117m/C; VHS, DVD.** Gregory Peck; Susan Hayward; Ava Gardner; Hildegarde Knef; Leo G. Carroll; Torin Thatcher; Ava Norring; Helene Stanley; Marcel Dalio; Vincente Gomez; Richard Allen; Leonard Carey; *D:* Henry King; *W:* Casey Robinson; *C:* Leon Shamroy; *M:* Bernard Herrmann.

The Snowtown Murders **2012** This unflinching, brutal docudrama about a series of murders that took place in Australia in the 1990s is sometimes very hard to watch, but director Kurzel (making his debut) refrains from the often-used film technique that places serial killers on a pedestal and makes an uncompromising work in the process. Teenager Jamie Vlassakis (Pittaway) is growing up in a horrible blue collar community, surrounded by criminals and without a father figure. He finds the worst kind in John Bunting (Henshall), a man with no sense of morality who essentially teaches Jamie to help him kill. **119m/C; DVD, Blu-Ray.** *AU* Lucas Pittaway; Daniel Henshall; Louise Harris; Anthony Grove; Aaron Viergever; Richard Green; Beau Gosling; *D:* Justin Kurzel; *W:* Shaun Grant; *C:* Adam Arkapaw; *M:* Jed Kurzel.

Snuffy Smith, Yard Bird ½ *Private Snuffy Smith; Snuffy Smith* **1942** The pint-sized moonshiner finds himself in the Army, clashing with his sergeant. Followed by "Hillbilly Blitzkrieg" later the same year. Duncan is perfect for the part, and Kennedy is right on as his foil. **67m/B; VHS, DVD.** Bud Duncan; Edgar Kennedy; Sarah Padden; Doris Linden; J. Farrell MacDonald; Frank Austin; Jimmie Dodd; *D:* Edward F. (Eddie) Cline.

So B. It ½ **2017 (PG-13)** A coming of age drama based on the novel by Sarah Weeks. When Heidi (Bateman) was a baby 12 years ago, she and her intellectually disabled mother, known as SO B. IT (Collins), found themselves on the doorstep of Bernadette (Woodard). Though Bernadette did not know where they came from, she has helped take care of them and homeschooled Heidi because Bernadette suffers from agoraphobia. When a sudden discovery changes their lives, Heidi goes on a far-away journey to discover who she is and where she came from. A sympathetic handling of complex issues like disability, isolation, and death add depth to the uplifting film. **98m/C; DVD.** Talitha Bateman; Jessica Collins; Alfre Woodard; John Heard; Jacinda Barrett; *D:* Stephen Gyllenhaal; *W:* Garry Williams; *C:* Patrick Murguia; *M:* Nick Urata.

So Close ½ *Chik yeung tin si* **2002 (R)** Lynn (Qi Shu) and Sue (Wei Zhao) are sisters who have become assassins after their father developed a surveillance device that would let its user see through any video camera in the world. Predictably, after fulfilling a contract their former client tries to have them killed, and an obsessive cop begins tailing them as well. **110m/C; DVD.** *CH GB* Qi Shu; Karen Mok; Josie Ho; Tats Lau; Wei Zhao; Seung-heon Song; Michael Wai; Siu-Lun Wan; Sau Sek; Ki Yan Lam; Sheung Mo Lam; May Kwong; So Pik Wong; Ben Lam; Ricardo Mamood-Vega; *D:* Corey Yuen; *W:* Jeff Lau; *C:* Kwok-Man Keung; *M:* Sam Kao; Kenji Tan.

So Dark the Night **1946** Low-budget backlot film noir. Renowed Paris detective Henri Cassin takes a country vacation, staying at the inn run by the Michauds. He immediately falls for daughter Nanette and she agrees to marry him (for his money) but then runs off with her actual fiance, farmer Leon Achaurd. They're found murdered and Cassin is obsessed with solving the crime, but there's a sinister twist. **70m/B; DVD, Blu-Ray.** Steven Geray; Micheline Cheirel; Eugene Borden; Ann Codee; Paul Marion; Egon Brecher; *D:* Joseph H. Lewis; *W:* Martin Berkeley; Aubrey Wisberg; *C:* Burnett Guffey; *M:* Hugo Friedhofer.

So Dear to My Heart ½ **1949** A farm boy and his misfit black sheep wreak havoc at the county fair. Several sequences combine live action with animation. Heartwarming and charming; straightforward and likeable but never sentimental. Wonderful, vintage Disney. **82m/C; VHS, DVD.** Bobby Driscoll; Burl Ives; Beulah Bondi; Harry Carey, Sr.; Luana Patten; *D:* Harold Schuster.

So Ends Our Night **1941** German scorns Nazi ideology, flees Austria, and meets young Jewish couple seeking asylum. Fine adaptation of Erich Maria Remarque's novel "Flotsam," with splendid performances from Sullavan (on loan from Universal) and young Ford. **117m/B; VHS, DVD.** Fredric March; Margaret Sullavan; Frances Dee; Glenn Ford; Anna Sten; Erich von Stroheim; *D:* John Cromwell; *C:* William H. Daniels.

So Fine ½ **1981 (R)** Absent-minded English professor O'Neal tries to rescue his father's clothing business from going bottom-up. He accidentally invents peek-a-boo bottomed jeans, which become an immediate hit and make him rich. Comedy smorgasbord, setting outing from sometime novelist Bergman, hits and misses. O'Neal is memorable, as is the ubiquitous Warden and his sidekick. **91m/C; VHS, DVD.** Ryan O'Neal; Jack Warden; Mariangela Melato; Richard Kiel; *D:* Andrew Bergman; *W:* Andrew Bergman; *M:* Ennio Morricone.

So Goes My Love **1946** Cozy biography of 19th-century inventor Hiram Stevens Maxim, based on his son's memoir "A Genius in the Family." Jane (Loy) is after a wealthy husband but instead falls in love and marries struggling Hiram (Ameche). He becomes a success thanks to his stable domestic life and the relationship with both his wife and eldest son (Driscoll). **88m/B; DVD.** Don Ameche; Myrna Loy; Bobby Driscoll; Rhys Williams; Richard Gaines; Molly Lamont; *D:* Frank Ryan; *W:* Bruce Manning; Clifton James; *C:* Joseph Valentine; *M:* Hans J. Salter.

So I Married an Axe Murderer ½ **1993 (PG-13)** Combination comedy/romance/thriller. Charlie is a hip bookstore owner with a commitment problem. When he finally falls in love with a butcher, he comes to suspect she's a serial killer and he's in line as her next victim. "Saturday Night Live" star Myers has a dual role: as Charlie and as Scottish dad Stuart, allowing him to be fanatically Scottish as Stuart and somewhat more restrained as the angst-ridden Charlie. One-gag movie counted on Myers' "Wayne's World" popularity, which didn't pan out at the boxoffice. Best appreciated by Myers' fans, this one is better on the small screen. **92m/C; VHS, DVD, Blu-Ray.** Mike Myers; Nancy Travis; Anthony LaPaglia; Amanda Plummer; Brenda Fricker; Matt Doherty; ***Cameo(s):*** Charles Grodin; Phil Hartman; Steven Wright; Alan Arkin; Michael Richards; *D:* Thomas Schlamme; *W:* Mike Myers; Robbie Fox; *M:* Bruce Broughton.

So Proudly We Hail **1943** True story of the lives of three war-front nurses and their heroism under fire during WWII. Colbert is Lt. Davidson in charge of nine Red Cross Army nurses serving in the Pacific. Lake and Goddard play the other leads. With the popularity of its stars and the patriotic spirit of the film, the picture hit boxoffice gold. Critics praised its authenticity, as the film never fell victim to the usual standards of Hollywood glamour. Fans of Lake beware: she has short hair, as the government requested that she not appear with her famous peek-a-boo hair style because female factory workers were getting their long Lake-inspired hair caught in the machinery. **126m/B; VHS, DVD.** Claudette Colbert; Paulette Goddard; Veronica Lake; George Reeves; Barbara Britton; Walter Abel; Sonny Tufts; John Litel; Mary Servoss; Ted Hecht; Mary Treen; Helen Lynd; Adrian Booth; Dorothy Adams; Ann Doran; Jean Willes; Jan Wiley; Lynn Walker; Joan Tours; Kitty Kelly; James Bell; Dick Hogan; Bill Goodwin; James Flavin; *D:* Mark Sandrich; *W:* Allan Scott; *C:* Charles B(ryant) Lang, Jr.; *M:* Miklos Rozsa.

So This Is College **1929** Eddie (Nugent) and Biff (Montgomery) are USC football teammates and frat brothers who are both unwittingly dating flirty, fickle coed Babs (Starr). Naturally when the boys find out, it causes problems off and on the field, including the day of the big game. Uses footage from the 1928 USC/Stanford matchup (although the film alters the outcome). **97m/B; DVD.** Robert Montgomery; Elliott Nugent; Sally Starr; Cliff Edwards; Phyllis Crane; Lee Shumway; Polly Moran; *D:* Sam Wood; *W:* Delmer Daves; Al Boasberg; Joe Farnham; *C:* Leonard Smith.

So This Is Love ½ **1953** Technicolor musical bio of American soprano Grace Moore with an adequate performance by Grayson (a better singer than actress) that demonstrates little of the real Moore's charisma. Heading to New York from her Tennessee hometown, Moore makes ends meet by nightclub singing and Broadway musicals before finding success (and 28 curtain calls) with her Met Opera House performance of Mimi in "La Boheme." Moore was killed in a plane crash in 1947. **100m/C; DVD.** Kathryn Grayson; Merv Griffin; Joan Weldon; Walter Abel; Rosemary DeCamp; *D:* Gordon Douglas; *W:* John Monks, Jr.; *C:* Robert Burks; *M:* Max Steiner.

So This Is New York **1948** Radio comedian Morgan makes his film debut in this adaptation of Ring Lardner's novel "The Big Town." Midwesterner Ernie Finch reluctantly accompanies wife Ella and single sister-in-law Kate to New York City after Ella inherits some dough. She wants her sister to meet a higher class of men than she thinks their small town can provide, but the trio are soon bewildered by the city slickers. **78m/B; DVD, Blu-Ray.** Henry Morgan; Virginia Grey; Dona Drake; Rudy Vallee; Bill Goodwin; Leo Gorcey; *D:* Richard Fleischer; *W:* Herbert Baker; Carl Foreman; *C:* John L. Russell; *M:* Dimitri Tiomkin.

So This Is Washington ½ *Remove Lum & Abner* **1943** The comedy team go to Washington with wacky inventions to help the war effort. Turns out there's too entirely too much nonsense going around, and the boys give 'em a piece of their mind. Fun, featherweight wartime comedy. **70m/B; VHS, DVD.** Chester Lauck; Norris Goff; Alan Mowbray; Mildred Coles; *D:* Ray McCarey; *W:* Leonard Praskins; Roswell Rogers; *C:* Harry Wild.

So Undercover ½ **2013 (PG-13)** Amiable but cliched comedy though pop music star Cyrus isn't much of an actress. Molly Morris (Cyrus) assists her dad Sam (O'Malley) with his PI business. She's approached by FBI agent Armon Rand (Piven) since she's the right age to go undercover to protect Taylor (Knapp), the daughter of a witness testifying against the mob. This means living in a college sorority where Molly is completely out of her element. **94m/C; DVD, Blu-Ray.** Miley Cyrus; Alexis Knapp; Jeremy Piven; Joshua Bowman; Mike O'Malley; Autumn Reeser; Kelly Osbourne; *D:* Tom Vaughan; *W:* Allan Loeb; Steven Pearl; *C:* Denis Lenoir. **VIDEO**

So Well Remembered ½ **1947** Hilton narrates from his own novel in this slow-moving British drama, which starts on the day celebrating the end of WWII and then uses flashbacks. Small town newspaper editor George (Mills) takes the side of the working man and his constant selflessness aggravates his ambitious wife Olivia (Scott). She divorces him, moves away and remarries, but eventually returns with her son Charles (Carlson) who falls for the adopted daughter (Roc) of the local doctor (Howard). However, Olivia tries to interfere. **114m/B; DVD.** *GB* John Mills; Martha Scott; Trevor Howard; Richard Carlson; Patricia Roc; ***Nar:*** James Hilton; *D:* Edward Dmytryk; *W:* John Paxton; *C:* Frederick A. (Freddie) Young; *M:* Hanns Eisler.

Soapdish **1991 (PG-13)** The back stage lives of a daytime soap opera, "The Sun Also Sets," and its cast. When the soap's ratings fall, a character written out of series via decapitation is brought back to give things a lift. While the writer struggles to make the reincarnation believable, the cast juggles old and new romances, and professional jealousies abound. Some genuinely funny moments as film actors spoof the genre that gave many of them a start. **97m/C; VHS, DVD.** Sally Field; Kevin Kline; Robert Downey, Jr.; Cathy Moriarty; Whoopi Goldberg; Elisabeth Shue; Carrie Fisher; Garry Marshall; Teri Hatcher; Paul Johansson; Costas Mandylor; Stephen Nichols; Leeza Gibbons; John Tesh; Kathy Najimy; Sheila Kelley; Finola Hughes; *D:* Michael Hoffman; *W:* Andrew Bergman; Robert Harling; *C:* Ueli Steiger; *M:* Alan Silvestri.

S.O.B. ½ **1981 (R)** Blake Edwards' bitter farce about Hollywood and the film industry wheelers and dealers who inhabit it. When a multi-million dollar picture bombs at the boxoffice, the director turns suicidal, until he envisions re-shooting it with a steamy, "X"-rated scene starring his wife, a star with a goody-two-shoes image. Edwards used his real-life wife, Julie ("Mary Poppins") Andrews, for the scene in which she bared her breasts. Oft-inspired, but oft-terrible. Zestfully vengeful. William Holden's last film. **121m/C; VHS, DVD, Blu-Ray.** William Holden; Robert Preston; Richard Mulligan; Julie Andrews; Robert Webber; Shelley Winters; Robert Vaughn; Larry Hagman; Stuart Margolin; Loretta Swit; Craig Stevens; Larry Storch; Jennifer Edwards; Robert Loggia; Rosanna Arquette; Marisa Berenson; *D:* Blake Edwards; *W:* Blake Edwards; *C:* Harry Stradling, Jr.; *M:* Henry Mancini. Natl. Soc. Film Critics '81: Support. Actor (Preston).

Soccer Dog: The Movie ½ **1998 (PG)** Clay Newlin (Foley) discovers the small town he's just moved to doesn't seem very friendly. His joins the local soccer team but isn't having much luck and Clay's only friend is stray dog Lincoln, who likes to watch the games. Then, when the team is short a player and in danger of forfeiting, the coach drafts Lincoln and the team actually wins. If you've watched the "Air Bud" movies, you've seen this before. **98m/C; VHS, DVD.** Jeremy Foley; James Marshall; Olivia D'Abo; ***D:*** Tony Giglio; ***W:*** Daniel Forman. **VIDEO**

Soccer Mom **2008** When Becca's (Osment) losing soccer team needs a new coach, her crazy mother Wendy (Pyle) decides to masquerade as a famous (male) Italian player and takes the job. The girls start winning and are on their way to the regional finals but how much longer can Wendy and Becca keep up the unraveling charade? **92m/C; DVD.** Emily Osment; Missi Pyle; Dan Cortese; Master P; Victoria Jackson; Kristen Wilson; Cassie Scerbo; Jennifer Sciole; ***D:*** Gregory McClatchy; ***W:*** Frederick Ayeroff; ***C:*** Jeff Venditti; ***M:*** Jerry Brunskill. **VIDEO**

Social Intercourse **WOOF! 2001** Waste of celluloid concerning the social reclamation of cyber geek Todd (Taylor, who also edited, produced, directed, and coscripted) at a friend's blow-out bash. If horny hijinks, tough-talking chicks, and a water-balloon sniper constituted good plot elements, then "Social Intercourse" would be the "Citizen Kane" of party films. **88m/C; DVD.** Steve Taylor; Lee Abbott; Kim Little; Ashley Davis; Steve Grabowsky; ***D:*** Steve Taylor; ***W:*** Steve Taylor; Roger Kristian Jones; ***C:*** Armand Gazarian.

Social Misfits **2000** Twelve troubled teenagers, including our narrator Skylar (co-writer Tann), are sent to Camp Resurrection outside Fresno for a weekend of "reeducation." The film claims to be based on events that took place on March 14, 1997, but this alternative boot-camp seems to consist mostly of unsupervised psycho-drama as each of the kids tells his or her story. The whole thing is produced with more enthusiasm than experience or talent. (Note the visible camera shadows.) Production values are minimal but adequate to the subject matter. **91m/C; DVD.** Boris Cabrera; Le'Mark Cruise; Gabriel Damon; Isait de la Fuente; Ryan Francis; Bev Land; Eric Gray; Paul Gleason; Tyronne Tann; ***D:*** Rene Villar-Rios; ***W:*** Le'Mark Cruise; Tyronne Tann; ***C:*** Eric Leach; ***M:*** William Richter.

The Social Network **2010 (PG-13)** Ego and greed dominate this version of the 2004 founding of ubiquitous social networking site Facebook by Harvard sophomore Mark Zuckerberg (Eisenberg) and others. Mark is a geek genius but also a socially insecure braggart whose partnership with confident friend Eduardo Saverin (Garfield) turns them into successes. Their site draws the attention of entrepreneur Sean Parker (Timberlake) and leads to the usual betrayals and lawsuits, although no one comes across as innocent or blameless. Viewers will click "like" for director Fincher's gripping though uncharacteristic flick, as well as the excellent performances and whip-smart screenplay by Sorkin. Adapted from Ben Mezrich's "The Accidental Billionaires." **120m/C; Blu-Ray, On Demand.** Jesse Eisenberg; Justin Timberlake; Andrew Garfield; Joseph Mazzello; Rashida Jones; Brenda Song; Max Minghella; Armie Hammer; Bryan Barter; Rooney Mara; Patrick Mapel; David Selby; Wallace (Wally) Langham; ***D:*** David Fincher; ***W:*** Aaron Sorkin; ***C:*** Jeff Cronenweth; ***M:*** Trent Reznor; Atticus Ross. Oscars '10: Adapt. Screenplay, Film Editing, Orig. Score; British Acad. '10: Adapt. Screenplay, Director (Fincher), Film Editing; Golden Globes '11: Director (Fincher), Film--Drama, Orig. Score, Screenplay; Writers Guild '10: Adapt. Screenplay.

Society **1992 (R)** A teenager wonders if his visions are real or hallucinations when he believes his family, and everyone else around him, are flesh-eating predators. The puzzle isn't much but wait for the special-effects ladened ending to get your fill of gore. **99m/C; VHS, DVD, Blu-Ray.** Billy Warlock; Devin Devasquez; Evan Richards; ***D:*** Brian Yuzna.

Society Lawyer **1/2 1939** Lawyer Christopher Durant (Pidgeon) wins a case for gangster Tony Gazotti (Carillo), who says he owes him. Durant must claim his favor when a friend is set-up for murder by Gazotti's crime rival Crelliman (Ciannelli). Several femmes are involved, including nightclub singer Pat Abbott (Bruce) who knows a lot about Crelliman's illegal activities. Remake of 1933's more risque "Penthouse." **78m/B; DVD.** Walter Pidgeon; Virginia Bruce; Leo Carillo; Eduardo Ciannelli; Lee Bowman; Frances Mercer; Ann Morriss; ***D:*** Edwin L. Marin; ***W:*** Albert Hackett; Frances Goodrich; ***C:*** George J. Folsey; ***M:*** Edward Ward.

Socrates **2018** After the unexpected death of his mother, 15-year-old Socrates (Malheiros) takes her place at her janitorial job, claiming she is ill, but her boss will not pay him and his rent is past due. Socrates gets a sympathetic social worker but has few options and his age limits his employment opportunities. He eventually gets a job at a junkyard, where he meets the handsome Maicon (Ordakji). Though the pair become involved, the relationship adds new complications to Socrates' already difficult life. Gritty and intimate, the debut feature by Moratto features outstanding overall filmmaking and performances by the lead actors. Portuguese with subtitles. **71m/C; DVD.** Christian Malheiros; Tales Ordakji; Caio Martinez Pacheco; Rosane Paulo; Jayme Rodrigues; ***D:*** Alexandre Moratto; ***W:*** Alexandre Moratto; Thayna Mantesso; ***C:*** João Gabriel de Queiroz.

Soda Springs **2011** Eden Jackson (Pickett) gets out of prison and returns to his Idaho hometown where he's greeted with suspicion. He slowly gets his second chance as the truth comes out about the accident that sent him to the joint. **114m/C; DVD.** Jay Pickett; Victoria Pratt; Tom Skerritt; Michael Bowen; Henry Darrow; Patty McCormack; ***D:*** Michael Feifer; ***W:*** Jay Pickett; Michael Feifer; ***C:*** Jeffrey D. Smith; ***M:*** Steve Mark Fulton. **VIDEO**

Sodom and Gomorrah *Sodome et Gomorrhe; The Last Days of Sodom and Gomorrah* **1962** The Italian-made, internationally produced epic about Lot, the Hebrews and the destruction of the two sinful biblical cities. Moderately entertaining—but ponderous, to say the least, and very long. **154m/C; DVD.** *IT* Stewart Granger; Stanley Baker; Pier Angeli; Anouk Aimee; Rossana Podesta; ***D:*** Robert Aldrich; ***W:*** Hugo Butler; ***C:*** Cyril Knowles; Mario Montuori; Silvano Ippoliti; ***M:*** Miklos Rozsa.

Sofie **1/2 1992** Sweet family melodrama about a late 19th Jewish family in Denmark. Sofie (Mynster) is the unmarried 28-year-old daughter of loving, protective parents. She has fallen in love with a gentile artist (Christensen) but gives him up to marry within her faith. Unsuited, Sofie and Jonas (Zeller) lead melancholy lives, which Sofie redeems through her joy in her son. Self-effacing drama is Ullmann's directorial debut. Adapted from the novel "Mendel Philipsen & Son" by Henri Nathansen. In Swedish with English subtitles. **145m/C; VHS, DVD.** *SW* Karen-Lise Mynster; Ghita Norby; Erland Josephson; Jesper Christensen; Henning Moritzen; Torben Zeller; Stig Hoffmeyer; Kirsten Rolffes; Lotte Herman; ***D:*** Liv Ullmann; ***W:*** Liv Ullmann; Peter Poulsen.

Soft for Digging **1/2 2001** Something evil is happening in the Maryland woods. Virgil (Mercier) is a hermit-like old man who believes he sees a man strangle a young girl (Ingerson) in the forest. Of course, when the cops arrive there's no body and nothing to indicate a crime happened. But Virgil knows it did—since the little girl is haunting him, demanding justice. Film is nearly without dialogue and title cards divide the scenes. It's an interesting but generally amateurish experiment. **78m/C; DVD.** Edmond Mercier; Sarah Ingerson; Andrew Hewitt; David Husko; Joshua Billings; ***D:*** J.T. Petty; ***W:*** J.T. Petty; ***C:*** Patrick McGraw; ***M:*** James L. Wolcott.

The Soft Kill **1994 (R)** LA private eye Jack Ramsey (Bernsen) becomes the prime murder suspect when his girlfriend is strangled. Can he prove his innocence before more bodies pile up and the cops catch him? **95m/C; VHS, DVD.** Corbin Bernsen; Brion James; Matt McCoy; Michael (M.K.) Harris; Kim Morgan Greene; Carrie-Anne Moss; ***D:*** Eli Cohen.

The Soft Skin *Le Peau Douce; Silken Skin* **1964** A classic portrayal of marital infidelity by the master director. A writer and lecturer has an affair with a stewardess. After the affair ends, his wife confronts him, with tragic results. Cliche plot is forgivable; acted and directed to perfection. Frequent Truffaut star Jean-Pierre Leaud served here as an apprentice director. In French with English subtitles. **120m/B; VHS, DVD, Blu-Ray.** *FR* Jean Desailly; Nelly Benedetti; Francoise Dorleac; Daniel Ceccaldi; ***D:*** Francois Truffaut; ***W:*** Francois Truffaut; Jean-Louis Richard; ***C:*** Raoul Coutard; ***M:*** Georges Delerue.

Soggy Bottom U.S.A. **1984 (PG)** A sheriff has his hands full trying to keep the law enforced in a small Southern town. Quite-good cast keeps the plot from disappearing altogether. **90m/C; VHS, DVD.** Don Johnson; Ben Johnson; Dub Taylor; Ann Wedgeworth; Lois Nettleton; Anthony Zerbe; ***D:*** Theodore J. Flicker.

Soho Square **1/2 2000 (R)** Meandering, low-budget, first-time effort from Rafn. A nameless detective (Biggs) is assigned to a serial killer case where the killer preys on young women in London's Soho district, setting them on fire. This detective may not have been the best choice since he's drinking too much and seeing visions of his dead wife. Then he meets Julia (Davenport), a woman who could be his dead wife's doppelganger, and she may be the big break in the case. **90m/C; DVD.** *GB* Lucy Davenport; Anthony Biggs; Livy Armstrong; Emma Poole; Sasha Lowenthal; Amanda Haberland; William Wilde; ***D:*** Jamie Rafn; ***W:*** Jamie Rafn; ***C:*** Brendan McGinty; ***M:*** Chris Read.

Sol Goode **1/2 2001 (R)** Sol Goode (Getty) is a familiar character—a 20something wannabe actor who uses his looks and charm to bed the babes. But his best pal Chloe (Towne) knows there's a decent guy lurking somewhere underneath the hipster facade. When a series of minor misfortunes find Sol examining his life, he realizes that Chloe is the woman of his dreams—now he just has to convince her that he's sincere. **100m/C; VHS, DVD.** Balthazar Getty; Katharine Towne; Jamie Kennedy; Natasha Gregson Wagner; Tori Spelling; Cheri Oteri; Robert Wagner; Danny Comden; Carmen Electra; Johnathon Schaech; Christina Pickles; Max Perlich; Jason Bateman; China Chow; ***D:*** Danny Comden; ***W:*** Danny Comden; ***C:*** Chris Walling.

Solace **1/2 2016 (R)** An overwrought serial killer thriller. Befuddled by a series of killings with victims who lack any connection, FBI agents Joe Merriweather (Morgan) and Katherine Cowles (Cornish) consult John Clancy (Hopkins). The world-weary Clancy is a genius psychic and a former colleague of Merriweather's who now lives as a recluse after a personal tragedy. Just by touching someone, Clancy can see their multiple possible futures. With Clancy's help, the agents put together pieces of the puzzle about the killer and learn the dark secret that connects the victims. Fun for its twists and effective, if not predicable fare. **101m/C; DVD.** Anthony Hopkins; Jeffrey Dean Morgan; Abbie Cornish; Colin Farrell; Matt Gerald; ***D:*** Afonso Poyart; ***W:*** Sean Bailey; Ted Griffin; ***C:*** Brendan Galvin; ***M:*** BT.

Solar Attack *Solar Strike* **2006 (PG)** Scientists try to figure out how to prevent a coronal mass ejection by the sun from igniting pockets of methane in the Earth's atmosphere and causing mass extinction. Nonsensical, but you're not getting your science facts from a cheesy TV movie, are you? **91m/C; DVD.** *CA* Mark Dacascos; Joanne Kelly; Kevin Jubinville; Sugith Varughese; Craig Eldridge; ***D:*** Paul Ziller; ***W:*** Michael Konyves; Miguel Tejada-Flores; ***C:*** Robert Saad; Kit Whitmore; ***M:*** Chuck Cirino. **TV**

Solar Crisis **1/2 1992 (PG-13)** Eye-popping special effects highlight this Earth-on-the-edge-of-destruction sci-fier. In 2050 the sun has gone on self-destruct and begins throwing off giant solar flares which turn the Earth extra-crispy. A space team is sent to divert the flares but the mission may become a victim of sabotage. Director Sarafian actually forgoes credit for the standard Smithee pseudonym. **111m/C; VHS, DVD.** Tim Matheson; Charlton Heston; Peter Boyle; Annabel Schofield; Jack Palance; Corin "Corky" Nemec; ***D:*** Richard Sarafian; Alan Smithee; ***W:*** Joe Gannon; Tedi Sarafian; ***C:*** Russell Carpenter; ***M:*** Maurice Jarre.

Solar Force **1994 (R)** Cop (Pare), stationed on the moon, is sent to earth to find a stolen chemical that is capable of restoring a destroyed environment. But there are secrets behind the assignment which could cost him his life. **91m/C; VHS, DVD.** Michael Paré; Billy Drago; Walker Brandt; ***D:*** Boaz Davidson; ***W:*** Terrence Pare; ***C:*** Avi (Avraham) Karpik; ***M:*** Don Peake.

Solarbabies **1986 (PG-13)** Roller-skating youths in a drought-stricken future vie for a mysterious power that will replenish the Earth's water. Shades of every sci-fi movie you've ever seen, from "Mad Max" to "Ice Pirates." Pathetic. **95m/C; VHS, DVD, Blu-Ray.** Richard Jordan; Sarah Douglas; Charles Durning; Lukas Haas; Jami Gertz; Jason Patric; ***D:*** Alan Johnson; ***W:*** Walon Green; ***M:*** Maurice Jarre.

Solaris *Solyaris* **1972** With this the USSR tried to eclipse "2001: A Space Odyssey" in terms of cerebral science-fiction. Some critics thought they succeeded. You may disagree now that the lumbering effort is available. Adapted from a Stanislaw Lem novel, it depicts a dilapidated space lab orbiting the planet Solaris, whose ocean, a vast fluid "brain," materializes the stir-crazy cosmonauts' obsessions—usually morose ex-girlfriends. Talk, talk, talk, minimal special effects. In Russian with English subtitles. **167m/C; VHS, DVD, Blu-Ray.** *RU* Donatas Banionis; Natalya Bondarchuk; Juri Jarvet; Vladislav Dvorzhetsky; Nikolai Grinko; Anatoli (Otto) Solonitzin; Sos Sarkisyan; ***D:*** Andrei Tarkovsky; ***W:*** Andrei Tarkovsky; ***C:*** Vadim Yusov; ***M:*** Eduard Artemyev. Cannes '72: Grand Jury Prize.

Solaris **1/2 2002 (R)** In the midst of grieving over his dead wife Rheya (McElhone), psychologist Chris Kelvin (Clooney) is summoned to help bring back the survivors of a failed mission aboard a space station orbiting the planet Solaris. Once there, he finds the commander dead and the remaining crewmembers in the grip of some planet-induced paranoia. He also finds his supposedly-dead wife in bed with him the next morning. Soderburgh's moody, claustrophobic, deliberately-paced space oddity offers up existential dread, regret, and search for redemption as the main foes for his characters, rather than some malevolent outside force. This will definitely put off those looking for "Star Wars/Alien" type thrills, but will satisfy those looking for a more cerebral exercise. **99m/C; VHS, DVD.** George Clooney; Natascha (Natasha) McElhone; Jeremy Davies; Viola Davis; Ulrich Tukur; Morgan Rusler; ***D:*** Steven Soderbergh; ***W:*** Steven Soderbergh; ***C:*** Steven Soderbergh; ***M:*** Cliff Martinez.

Soldier **1998 (R)** Steals trite scenes from other post-apolyptic sci-fi shoot-'em-ups just to prove that 47-year-old Kurt Russell had been working out. Genetically engineered soldier Russell is discarded as obsolete on a garbage dump planet inhabited by a freedom-loving survivalist (Pertwee) and his band of human flotsam. When a force led by next-generation soldier Jason Scott Lee invades the planet, Russell helps save the skanky-looking group of squatters. Robbed of his Snake Plissken smirk, Russell delivers a hollow character who is hard to like. The garbage planet set recycles props used in "Demolition Man," "Executive Decision," and "Event Horizon." The movie recycles ideas from every other sci-fi flick. **99m/C; VHS, DVD.** Kurt Russell; Jason Scott Lee; Gary Busey; Michael Chiklis; Sean Pertwee; Jason Isaacs; Connie Nielsen; Brenda Wehle; Mark Bringleson; K.K. Dodds; ***D:*** Paul W.S. Anderson; ***W:*** David Peoples; ***C:*** David Tattersall; ***M:*** Joel McNeely.

Soldier Blue **1970 (R)** Two survivors of an Indian attack make their way back to an army outpost. The cavalry then seeks revenge on the Cheyenne tribe accused of the attack. Gratuitously violent Vietnam-era western hits hard on racial themes. Based on the novel "Arrow in the Sun" by Theodore V. Olsen on the Sand Creek Indian massacre. **109m/C; VHS, DVD.** Candice Bergen; Peter Strauss; Donald Pleasence; Dana Elcar; Jorge (George) Rivero; ***D:*** Ralph Nelson; ***W:*** John Gay; ***C:*** Robert B. Hauser.

Soldier in the Rain **1/2 1963** An unusual friendship develops between career sergeant Gleason and wheeler-dealer Mc-

Queen. Gleason is in good form, but McQueen is listless, and the story (set in a Southern army camp) is unsatisfying. Weld is the comely teen who makes for an intriguing love triangle. From the novel by William Goldman. **88m/B; VHS, DVD.** Steve McQueen; Jackie Gleason; Tuesday Weld; Tony Bill; Tom Poston; Ed Nelson; *D:* Ralph Nelson; *W:* Blake Edwards; *M:* Henry Mancini.

Soldier Love Story 𝒮𝒮 1/2 *Meet My Mom* **2010** A Hallmark Channel original movie. Recently divorced Dana (Loughlin) and her young son Jared (Wyson) start a new life by moving in with Dana's mom Louise (Powers), 1600 miles from their old home. Jared's dad makes empty promises to stay in touch so the lonely boy is glad for his 4th-grade school assignment to write letters to soldiers stationed overseas. Sgt. Vince Carrera (Messner) responds, becoming a long-distance mentor. Vince makes a surprise visit when he gets leave and Jared encourages a romance with his mom. Then Vince gets the unexpected news that he'll be redeployed in 10 days. **88m/C; DVD.** Lori Loughlin; Johnny Messner; Charles Henry Wyson; Stefanie Powers; *D:* Harvey Frost; *W:* Pamela Wallace; *C:* James W. Wrenn; *M:* Stephen Graziano. **CABLE**

Soldier of Fortune 𝒮𝒮 1/2 **1955** A woman (Hayward) enlists mercenaries to help find her lost husband in Red China. Late Gable vehicle with the formula beginning to feel the post-war strain and the star looking a trifle long in the tooth. Still, a fun adventure from a top star. Hayward had been among the myriad starlets vying for the Scarlett O'Hara roles nearly two decades earlier. **96m/C; VHS, DVD.** Clark Gable; Susan Hayward; Gene Barry; Alexander D'Arcy; Michael Rennie; Tom Tully; Anna Sten; Russell Collins; Leo Gordon; Jack Kruschen; Robert Quarry; *D:* Edward Dmytryk; *W:* Ernest K. Gann; *C:* Leo Tover; *M:* Hugo Friedhofer.

Soldier of Orange 𝒮𝒮𝒮 *Soldaat van Oranje* **1978** The lives of six Dutch students are forever changed by the WWII invasion of Holland by the Nazis. Based on the true-life exploits of Dutch resistance leader Erik Hazelhoff. Exciting and suspenseful; cerebral; carefully made and well acted. Made Rutger Hauer an international star. **144m/C; VHS, DVD.** *NL* Rutger Hauer; Jeroen Krabbe; Edward Fox; Susan Penhaligon; Derek de Lint; *D:* Paul Verhoeven; *W:* Paul Verhoeven; Gerard Soeteman; Kees Holierhoek; *C:* Jan De Bont; *M:* Roger van Otterloo. L.A. Film Critics '79: Foreign Film.

A Soldier's Daughter Never Cries 𝒮𝒮 1/2 **1998 (R)** American novelist and WWII vet Bill Willis (Kristofferson) lives in 1960s Paris with his sexy, free-thinking and -drinking wife Marcella (Hershey), their adopted French son Billy (Gruen), and teenage daughter Channe, the center of the story. Her relationships with her brother and a rude (yet likable) classmate (Costanzo) provide much of the film's emotional punch. Bill develops heart problems and takes the family home to the States. Against the backdrop of social and political turmoil, Bill's core values help the family through their own challenges. Ivory and Merchant make an admirable leap into the 20th century. Unfortunately, the film's episodic jumps are too confusing to make it a complete success. Based on the 1990 book by Kaylie Jones, daughter of novelist James Jones. **128m/C; VHS, DVD.** Kris Kristofferson; Barbara Hershey; Leelee Sobieski; Jesse Bradford; Anthony Roth Costanzo; Dominique Blanc; Jane Birkin; Virginie Ledoyen; Isaach de Bankole; Samuel Gruen; Luisa Conlon; *D:* James Ivory; *W:* James Ivory; Ruth Prawer Jhabvala; *C:* Jean-Marc Fabre; *M:* Richard Robbins.

Soldier's Girl 𝒮𝒮𝒮 **2003** First-rate drama takes some time to find its pace but boasts superior performances and a strong final act. Unsophisticated Army Pvt. Barry Winchell (Garity) is dragged as a joke to a gay bar in Nashville where he sees Calpernia Addams (Pace), a transgendered nightclub performer, who is taken with Barry's gentlemanly manners. They begin a tentative courtship that progresses from curiosity to love, which threatens the relationship between Barry and his unstable roommate Fisher (Hatosy), who begins spreading rumors about a gay soldier on base. The manipulative Fisher engineers a confrontation between Barry and a young Oklahoma redneck recruit that explodes into stunning violence. Based on the 1999 murder of a G.I. at a Kentucky military base. **112m/C; VHS, DVD.** Troy Garity; Lee Pace; Andre Braugher; Shawn Hatosy; Philip Eddolls; *D:* Frank Pierson; *W:* Ron Nyswaner; *C:* Paul Sarossy; *M:* Jan A.P. Kaczmarek. **CABLE**

Soldiers of Change 𝒮𝒮 *The Painting* **2006 (PG-13)** Follows the life of a young white man, Randy (Freeman), who grows up during the social turmoil that was 1960s America. He falls for a young black woman, Hallie (Dash), faces criticism from both families prior to heading off to the Vietnam War, and endures the struggles of a novice soldier. Bland, though subject matter is treated with respect by the able cast. **95m/C; DVD.** Clifton Davis; Charles Shaughnessy; Stacey Dash; Heath Freeman; *D:* Peter Manoogian; Joshua D. Rose; *W:* J. Marina Muhlfriedel. **VIDEO**

Soldier's Revenge 𝒮𝒮 *Vengeance of a Soldier* **1984** A Vietnam vet has a hard time adjusting to life at home. **92m/C; VHS, DVD.** John Savage; Maria Socas; Paul Lambert; Edgardo Moreira; Francisco Cano; *D:* David Worth; *W:* David Worth; Lee Stull; *C:* Leonardo Solis; *M:* Gary Reast.

A Soldier's Story 𝒮𝒮𝒮 **1984 (PG)** A black army attorney is sent to a Southern base to investigate the murder of an unpopular sergeant. Features WWII, Louisiana, jazz and blues, and racism in and outside the corps. From the Pulitzer-prize winning play by Charles Fuller, with most of the Broadway cast. Fine performances from Washington and Caesar. **101m/C; VHS, DVD.** Howard E. Rollins, Jr.; Adolph Caesar; Denzel Washington; Patti LaBelle; Robert Townsend; Scott Paulin; Wings Hauser; Art Evans; Larry Riley; David Alan Grier; *D:* Norman Jewison; *W:* Charles Fuller; *C:* Russell Boyd; *M:* Herbie Hancock. L.A. Film Critics '84: Support. Actor (Caesar).

A Soldier's Tale 𝒮𝒮 **1991 (R)** During WWII, a menage-a-trois develops that can only lead to tragedy, yet the participants find themselves unable to resist. **96m/C; VHS, DVD.** Gabriel Byrne; Marianne Basler; Judge Reinhold; Paul Wyett; *D:* Larry Parr; *W:* Larry Parr; *C:* Alun Bollinger; *M:* John Charles.

Sole Survivor 𝒮 1/2 **1984 (R)** A group of zombies are searching for a beautiful advertising executive who was the sole survivor of a plane crash. **85m/C; VHS, DVD, Blu-Ray.** Anita Skinner; Kurt Johnson; Caren Larkey; Brinke Stevens; Leon Robinson; *D:* Thom Eberhardt; *C:* Russell Carpenter.

Solid Gold Cadillac 𝒮𝒮𝒮 **1956** Holliday is a winning lead as Laura Patridge, an idealistic, small-time stockholder who discovers that the corporate board of directors are crooked. She makes waves at a stockholders meeting, gets noticed by the press, finds romance with former CEO Edward McKeever (Douglas), and works to oust the scalawags from power. The title comes from Laura's fervent desire to own a—you guessed it—solid gold cadillac. Based on the Broadway play by George S. Kaufman and Howard Teichmann. **99m/B; VHS, DVD.** Judy Holliday; Paul Douglas; Fred Clark; Neva Patterson; Arthur O'Connell; Ray Collins; *Nar:* George Burns; *D:* Richard Quine; *W:* Abe Burrows; *C:* Charles B(ryant) Lang, Jr.; *M:* Cyril Mockridge. Oscars '56: Costume Des. (B&W).

Solid State 𝒮 1/2 **2012** A sci-fi action drama on the strange effects linked to a meteor. When a large meteor nears Earth, a missile is launched that seems to destroy it before it can cause problems. However, a small piece of the meteor lands in a remote area of Europe. When an American rock band touring in the region nears the meteor, their van breaks down. They soon notice that no one is living in the area despite evidence that people were there. The band members soon figure out that the meteor is affecting them in odd, if not deadly, ways. **90m/C; DVD, Blu-Ray, Streaming, Download.** Debbie Rochon; Vivica A. Fox; Ava Brunini; Suzi Lorraine; Diego Casale; *D:* Stefano Milla; *W:* Gero Giglio; *C:* Fabrizio Meynardi; *M:* Dominic Capuano. **VIDEO**

Solitary Man 𝒮𝒮𝒮 **2010 (R)** Coming-of-old-age dark comedy that plays more like a biopic of the star himself. Possibly facing some serious health issues, former used car dealer Ben Kalmen (Douglas) sets out to recapture the hedonism of his youth, including divorcing his wife (Sarandon) followed by shacking up with a younger woman (Parker). Everyone around him is appalled, especially his daughter Susan (Fischer) who gets hit up for rent money. An experienced cast turns in excellent performances for writer/director Koppelman, who gives Douglas the best material he's had in 10 years. **90m/C; Blu-Ray, On Demand.** Michael Douglas; Susan Sarandon; Danny DeVito; Mary-Louise Parker; Jesse Eisenberg; Richard Schiff; Jenna Fischer; *D:* Brian Koppelman; *W:* Brian Koppelman; David Levien; *C:* Alwin Kuchler; *M:* Michael Penn.

Solo 𝒮𝒮 **1996 (PG-13)** Fast-paced actioner stars Van Peebles as Solo, an android assassin with a heart of gold. It seems the muscle-bound, computerized killer is programmed with not only amazing fighting skills but the ability to think and learn. Solo who, being naughty in the sight of one-dimensional government bigwigs, is scheduled for replacement by a fighting machine that won't be so fickle when it comes to pulling the trigger. The chase is on when Solo learns of their plot and takes to the jungles of Central America, where together with the local peasants, the rebellious robot fights to preserve his humanity and his life. Poor man's "Terminator" is sprinkled with the kind of glib one-liners usually reserved for Schwarzenegger, although Van Peebles' performance hikes this rehashed premise up a notch. Adapted from Robert Mason's novel "Weapon." **106m/C; VHS, DVD.** Mario Van Peebles; William Sadler; Seidy Lopez; Barry Corbin; Adrien Brody; Abraham Verduzo; Jaime Gomez; Demian Bechir; Joaquin Garrido; *D:* Norberto Barba; *W:* David Corley; *C:* Chris Walling; *M:* Christopher Franke.

Solo 𝒮𝒮 **2006** World-weary Sydney killer Jack Barrett (Friels) is a 30-year man in the mob and he wants to retire. While selling his gun collection at a pawn shop, he meets university student Billie (Novakovic), who's writing her thesis on local criminals. Jack talks just enough to make his bosses nervous and they decide that his last hit will be Billie. Good performance by Friels brings this crime story up a notch. **96m/C; DVD.** *AU* Colin Friels; Bojana Novakovic; Linal Haft; Angie Milliken; Vince Colosimo; Bruce Spence; Tony Barry; Chris Heywood; *D:* Morgan O'Neill; *W:* Morgan O'Neill; *C:* Hugh Miller; *M:* Martyn Love; Damian DeBoos-Smith.

Solo: A Star Wars Story 𝒮𝒮 1/2 **2018 (PG-13)** The origin story of Han Solo and his life pre-Star Wars. To escape a forced labor camp on a mining planet, young Han (Ehrenreich) signs up for the Imperial military and takes part in pointless military campaigns. Han does meet his future smuggling partners Val (Newton) and Tobias (Harrelson). As the trio grifts, Han shows off his flying chops, meets Chewbacca (Suotamo), and wins the Millennium Falcon from a young Lando Calrissian (Glover). Though the film has great humor and lively performances, especially from the scene-stealing Glover, it feels like a checklist of expectations has been met and nothing daring occurs. **135m/C; Blu-Ray, Streaming.** Alden Ehrenreich; Joonas Suotamo; Woody Harrelson; Emilia Clarke; Donald Glover; Thandie Newton; *D:* Ron Howard; *W:* Jonathan Kasdan; Lawrence Kasdan; *C:* Bradford Young; *M:* John Powell.

The Soloist 𝒮𝒮 1/2 **2009 (PG-13)** Downey Jr. and Foxx do right by their characters in this compassionate, albeit romanticized, version of a true story. Los Angeles Times columnist Steve Lopez is researching a story when he hears homeless Nathaniel Ayers playing violin on the streets. He learns that the classically-trained musical prodigy's life fell apart when he became schizophrenic and vows to help him. Steve learns the hardest lesson when he realizes that he can only do so much for Nathaniel and that there is no conventional happy ending for his situation. **105m/C; Blu-Ray, On Demand.** Robert Downey, Jr.; Jamie Foxx; Stephen (Steve) Root; Tom Holland; Lisa Gay Hamilton; Catherine Keener; Lorraine Toussaint; *D:* Joe Wright; *W:* Susannah Grant; *C:* Seamus McGarvey; *M:* Dario Marianelli.

Solomon 𝒮𝒮 1/2 **1998** Solomon is crowned King of Israel and vows to build a temple to house the Ark of the Covenant. In return, he is granted the gift of widom, which he doesn't seem to make much use of. He falls deeply in love with the Queen of Sheba but when she is forced to return to her homeland, Solomon falls into such a depression that he neglects his kingdom and allows corruption to spread. **172m/C; VHS, DVD.** Ben Cross; Vivica A. Fox; Anouk Aimee; Max von Sydow; Maria Grazia Cucinotta; Stefania Rocca; David Suchet; Richard Dillane; *D:* Roger Young. **CABLE**

Solomon and Gaenor 𝒮𝒮 **1998 (R)** Around 1911, a young Jewish peddler named Solomon (Gruffudd) meets Gaenor (Roberts), the daughter of Welsh mineworkers. Hiding his Orthodox Jewish origins, Solomon calls himself Sam and the young duo are soon in love. Gaenor winds up pregnant and her family wants to send her away and force her to give up the baby. She finally tracks down Solomon's family but they are equally upset that their son is involved with a gentile. Amidst all this family turmoil, is a violent dispute between the workers and the mine owners. Conventional tear-stained period piece. **103m/C; VHS, DVD.** *GB* Ioan Gruffudd; Nia Roberts; Mark Lewis Jones; William Thomas; Maureen Lipman; David Horovitch; *D:* Paul Morrison; *W:* Paul Morrison; *C:* Nina Kellgren; *M:* Ilona Sekacz.

Solomon and Sheba 𝒮𝒮 **1959** King Solomon's brother and the Egyptian Pharaoh send the Queen of Sheba to Israel to seduce King Solomon so they may gain his throne. Tyrone Power had filmed most of the lead role in this silly, overwrought epic when he died of a heart attack. The role was reshot, with Brynner (with a full head of hair) replacing him. Director Vidor's unfortunate last film. Shot on location in Spain. **139m/C; VHS, DVD, Blu-Ray.** Yul Brynner; Gina Lollobrigida; Marisa Pavan; George Sanders; Alejandro Rey; *D:* King Vidor; *C:* Frederick A. (Freddie) Young; *M:* Malcolm Arnold.

Some Came Running 𝒮𝒮𝒮 **1958** James Jones's follow-up novel to "From Here to Eternity" does not translate nearly as well to the screen. Overlong and with little plot, the action centers around a would-be writer, his floozy girl friend, and the holier-than-thou characters which populate the town in which he grew up and to which he has now returned. Strong performances by all. **136m/C; VHS, DVD.** Frank Sinatra; Dean Martin; Shirley MacLaine; Martha Hyer; Arthur Kennedy; Nancy Gates; *D:* Vincente Minnelli; *C:* William H. Daniels; *M:* Elmer Bernstein.

Some Days Are Better Than Others 𝒮 **2010** Pretentious indie drama populated by lonely sad sacks, who are linked in the most unlikely ways. There's Eli with his series of temp jobs, Katrina's work for an animal shelter, Camille's thrift store clerk, and Eli's retiree friend, Otis. **93m/C; DVD, Blu-Ray.** Carrie Brownstein; James Mercer; Renee Roman Nose; David Wodehouse; *D:* Matt McCormick; *W:* Matt McCormick; *C:* Greg Schmidt; *M:* Matt McCormick; Matthew Cooper.

Some Girls 𝒮𝒮 1/2 *Sisters* **1988 (R)** A man goes to Quebec to see his college girlfriend who informs him that she is not in love with him anymore. But she has two sisters ready to comfort him! Strange black comedy; Gregory as the girl's father elevates so-so story. **104m/C; VHS, DVD.** Patrick Dempsey; Andre Gregory; Lila Kedrova; Florinda Bolkan; Jennifer Connelly; Sheila Kelley; *D:* Michael Hoffman; *M:* James Newton Howard.

Some Girl(s) 𝒮 1/2 **2013** A nameless 30-something college professor/author decides he needs to take a cross-country trip before his wedding and revisit some former flames to explain his past (bad) behavior. The reunions occur in real time in various hotel rooms and it's quickly revealed that the guy is still a self-deluded narcissist and the women have a very different take on things. Since LaBute adapted from his play, this isn't a revelation as the story darkens considerably. **90m/C; DVD.** Adam Brody; Jennifer (Jenny) Morrison; Mia Maestro; Emily Watson; Zoe Kazan; Kristen Bell; *D:* Daisy von Scherler Mayer; *W:* Neil LaBute; *C:* Rachel Morrison; *M:* David Carbonara.

Some Kind of Beautiful 𝒮𝒮 *How to Make Love Like an Englishman* **2015 (R)** In this comedy, a poetry professor suffers from a complicated romantic life. Respected English professor Richard Haig (Brosnan) teaches poetry at Trinity College, and finds romance among young undergraduates. Finally ready for a more meaningful relationship, he is pleased when his 25-year-old American girlfriend Kate (Alba) becomes pregnant and he looks forward to a settled fatherhood. The situation has a complication, however. Richard has been in love with Kate's sister Olivia (Hayek) from the moment he saw her. Three years later, Kate leaves Richard for someone else but sends Olivia to check on Richard and the quality of his care of their son. Olivia soon gains complicated feelings of her own for the formerly irresponsible playboy. **99m/C; DVD, Blu-Ray, Streaming, Download.** Pierce Brosnan; Salma Hayek; Jessica Alba; Malcolm McDowell; Duncan Joiner; *D:* Tom Vaughan; *W:* Matthew Newman; *C:* David Tattersall; *M:* Stephen Endelman.

Some Kind of Hate **2015** A horror exploration of the acts of a vengeful spirit. After years of relentless bullying, teenager Lincoln Taggert (Rubinstein) is sent to a remote reform school for troubled teens. There, Lincoln again is bullied. However, he unintentionally conjures the spirit of a girl, Moira (McCormick), who had been bullied in life and eventually committed suicide. Moira takes bloody revenge for the teen on those who have tormented him. **82m/C; DVD, Blu-Ray, Streaming, Download.** Ronen Rubinstein; Sierra McCormick; Spencer Breslin; Grace Phipps; Andrew Bryniarski; *D:* Adam Egypt Mortimer; *W:* Adam Egypt Mortimer; *C:* Benji Bakshi; *M:* Robert Allaire. **VIDEO**

Some Kind of Hero **1982 (R)** A Vietnam prisoner of war returns home to a changed world. Pryor tries hard, but can't get above this poorly written, unevenly directed film. **97m/C; VHS, DVD.** Richard Pryor; Margot Kidder; Ray Sharkey; Ronny Cox; Lynne Moody; Olivia Cole; Paul Benjamin; Peter Jason; Tim Thomerson; *D:* Michael Pressman; *W:* Robert Boris; *C:* King Baggot; *M:* Patrick Williams.

Some Kind of Wonderful **1987 (PG-13)** A high-school tomboy has a crush on a guy who also happens to be her best friend. Her feelings go unrequited as he falls for a rich girl with snobbish friends. In the end, true love wins out. Deutch also directed (and John Hughes also produced) the teen flick "Pretty in Pink," which had much the same plot, with the rich/outcast characters reversed by gender. OK, but completely predictable. **93m/C; VHS, DVD.** Eric Stoltz; Lea Thompson; Mary Stuart Masterson; Craig Sheffer; John Ashton; Elias Koteas; Molly Hagan; *D:* Howard Deutch; *W:* John Hughes.

Some Like It Hot **1959** Two unemployed musicians witness the St. Valentine's Day massacre in Chicago. They disguise themselves as women and join an all-girl band headed for Miami to escape the gangsters' retaliation. Flawless cast includes a fetching Monroe at her best; hilarious script. Curtis does his Cary Grant impression. Classic scenes between Lemmon in drag and Joe E. Brown as a smitten suitor. Brown also has the film's famous closing punchline. Monroe sings "I Wanna Be Loved By You," "Running Wild," and "I'm Through With Love." One of the very funniest movies of all time. **120m/B; VHS, DVD, Blu-Ray.** Marilyn Monroe; Tony Curtis; Jack Lemmon; George Raft; Pat O'Brien; Nehemiah Persoff; Joe E. Brown; Joan Shawlee; Mike Mazurki; *D:* Billy Wilder; *W:* Billy Wilder; I.A.L. Diamond; *C:* Charles B(ryant) Lang, Jr.; *M:* Adolph Deutsch. Oscars '59: Costume Des. (B&W); AFI '98: Top 100; British Acad. '59: Actor (Lemmon); Golden Globes '60: Actor--Mus./Comedy (Lemmon), Actress--Mus./Comedy (Monroe), Film--Mus./Comedy; Natl. Film Reg. '89.

Some Mother's Son *Sons and Warriors* **1996 (R)** Young IRA members Gerard Quigley (Gillen) and Frank Higgins (O'Hara) are sentenced to long prison terms after an attack on the British army. Tough, politically active Annie Higgins (Flanagan) has already lost one son to "The Troubles" and is willing to support Frank in whatever he does. But her son Gerard's involvement takes apolitical schoolteacher Kathleen (Mirren) completely by surprise. When their sons join in a prison hunger strike, the two mothers must face the choice of supporting their sons' possible deaths by starvation or allowing the prison's officials to force-feed them. The leads give tough, terrific performances in a heartwrenching story. **112m/C; VHS, DVD, Streaming.** *IR GB* Dame Helen Mirren; Fionnula Flanagan; Aidan Gillen; David O'Hara; John Lynch; Tim Woodward; Ciaran Hinds; Gerard McSorley; Geraldine O'Rawe; *D:* Terry George; *W:* Jim Sheridan; Terry George; *C:* Geoffrey Simpson; *M:* Bill Whelan.

Some Prefer Cake **1997** Best friends Kira (Fontaine) and Sydney (Howley) are also roomies in San Francisco. Kira's stage fright prevents her from pursuing a career as a stand-up comedian and she's resentful when the material she wrote for her sister (Gonzalez) makes her a success. Kira's also got problems with a one-night stand turned stalker (Saito). Meanwhile, Syd is insisting everything is fine but she has career and boyfriend problems. Both women struggle with their co-dependency until realizing that the only way to move forward is to do it without clinging to each other. **95m/C; DVD.** Kathleen Fantaine; Tara Howley; Mimi Gonzalez; Machiko Saito; Desi del Valle; Leon Acord; *D:* Heidi Arnesen; *W:* Jeannie Kahaney; *C:* Matt Siegel.

Some Velvet Morning 1/2 **2013 (R)** Playwright Neil LaBute returns to the dark dramas that made him a star with this intimate character piece that essentially plays like a filmed play with its limited cast and setting. Fred (Tucci) has something he wants to talk about with his former mistress, a lovely woman named Velvet (Eve). The two trade barbs and secrets for the film's brief running time, and LaBute's cynical view of humanity and romance makes for an interesting affair even if the film isn't quite consistent. But thankfully Tucci gets a meaty role after so many years in relatively thankless supporting work. **82m/C; DVD.** Alice Eve; Stanley Tucci; *D:* Neil LaBute; *W:* Neil LaBute; *C:* Rogier Stoffers.

Somebody Has to Shoot the Picture **1990 (R)** Photographer Scheider is hired by a convicted man to take a picture of his execution. Hours before the event, Scheider uncovers evidence that leads him to believe the man is innocent. He then embarks in a race against time to save him. Adapted by Doug Magee from his book "Slow Coming Dark." Unpretentious, tough drama. **104m/C; VHS, DVD.** Roy Scheider; Bonnie Bedelia; Robert Carradine; Andre Braugher; Arliss Howard; *D:* Frank Pierson; *W:* Doug Magee; *C:* Bojan Bazelli; *M:* James Newton Howard. **CABLE**

Somebody to Love 1/2 **1994 (R)** Spunky taxi dancer Mercedes (Perez) wants to be an actress despite the bad luck actor/boyfriend Harry (a subdued Keitel) has. One of her clients is the bumpious Ernesto (De Lorenzo), who quickly becomes infatuated by Mercedes and, to impress her, takes a job with local racketeer Emillio (Quinn). Ernesto even decides to take a contract hit to get the money Mercedes needs to help out Harry, leading to tragedy. Confusing look at the fringes of the L.A. showbiz scene, with lots of missed chances though Perez gets some flashy diva scenes. **103m/C; VHS, DVD.** Rosie Perez; Harvey Keitel; Michael Delorenzo; Anthony Quinn; Steve Buscemi; Stanley Tucci; Gerardo Mejia; Paul Herman; Edward (Eddie) Bunker; *Cameo(s):* Angel Aviles; Quentin Tarantino; *D:* Alexandre Rockwell; *W:* Alexandre Rockwell; Sergei Bodrov.

Somebody Up There Likes Me **1956** Story of Rocky Graziano's (Newman) gritty battle from his poor, street-wise childhood to his prison term (where he developed his boxing skills) and his eventual success as the middleweight boxing champion of the world. Adapted from Graziano's autobiography. Superior performance by Newman (in his third screen role, after the miserable "The Silver Chalice" and forgettable "The Rack"); screen debuts for McQueen and Loggia. **113m/B; VHS, DVD.** Paul Newman; Pier Angeli; Everett Sloane; Eileen Heckart; Sal Mineo; Robert Loggia; Steve McQueen; *D:* Robert Wise; *W:* Ernest Lehman; *C:* Joseph Ruttenberg; *M:* Bronislau Kaper. Oscars '56: Art Dir./Set Dec., B&W, B&W Cinematog.

Somebody Up There Likes Me **2012** Bob Byington's absurd comedy plays like a lost Wes Anderson movie from early in his career although even the divisive director of "Moonrise Kingdom" might call this strange flick pretentious. Unlikable protagonist Max (Poulson) approaches the world with such apathy that the writer/director doesn't even bother aging him as the film stretches out over decades. He's in eternal adolescence. Max hangs out with buddy Sal (Offerman), gets married (to the always-great Weixler), and generally shrugs off all major occurrences. Only some of the jokes connect. **76m/C; Streaming.** Keith Poulson; Jess Weixler; Nick Offerman; Stephanie Hunt; Marshall Bell; *D:* Bob Byington; *W:* Bob Byington; *C:* Sean Price Williams; *M:* Chris Baio.

Someday This Pain Will Be Useful to You 1/2 **2011** Director/writer Faenza's drama does nothing to distinguish itself from countless others in the teen angst/dysfunctional family categories. Troubled 17-year-old New Yorker James (Rego) has issues with his divorced parents, his older sister, and the direction of his life in general. Since he doesn't cooperate with his mother Marjorie's (Harden) plans for him, she sends him to life coach Rowena (Liu), who offers James the sounding board he needs to express his confusion. No big revelations here. **99m/C; DVD.** *US IT* Toby Rego; Marcia Gay Harden; Peter Gallagher; Deborah Ann Woll; Ellen Burstyn; Lucy Liu; *D:* Roberto Faenza; *W:* Roberto Faenza; Dahlia Heyman; *C:* Maurizio Calvesi; *M:* Andrea Guerra.

Someone Behind the Door 1/2 *Two Minds for Murder; Quelqu' Un Derriere la Porte* **1971 (PG)** Evil brain surgeon Perkins implants murderous suggestions into psychopathic amnesia victim Bronson's mind, then instructs him to kill the surgeon's wife and her lover. **97m/C; VHS, DVD, Blu-Ray.** Charles Bronson; Anthony Perkins; Jill Ireland; Henri Garcin; *D:* Nicolas Gessner; *W:* Nicolas Gessner; Marc Behm; *C:* Pierre Lhomme; *M:* Georges Garvarentz.

Someone Great 1/2 **2019 (R)** When music journalist Jenny (Rodriguez) lands her dream job at a publication in California, her happiness hits a roadblock when her already struggling relationship with her long-term boyfriend Nate (Stanfield) ends. Though Jenny cries when they break up, she calls on her old friends Blair (Snow) and Erin (Wise) to help her get through it. As the trio experiences a fun day in New York City involving alcohol, drugs, and a concert, they also examine the state of each of their lives. The lively comedy is an effective debut feature from filmmaker Robinson and succeeds primarily because of the chemistry among the three leads. **92m/C; DVD.** Gina Rodriguez; Lakeith Stanfield; Brittany Snow; DeWanda Wise; Michelle Buteau; *D:* Jennifer Kaytin Robinson; *W:* Jennifer Kaytin Robinson; *C:* Autumn Eakin; *M:* Germaine Franco. **VIDEO**

Someone I Touched 1/2 **1975** Wayoverdone melodrama starring Leachman as a finally pregnant woman who learns her husband and a teenager he slept with have venereal disease. **74m/C; VHS, Streaming.** Cloris Leachman; James Olson; Glynnis O'Connor; Andrew (Andy) Robinson; Allyn Ann McLerie; *D:* Lou Antonio.

Someone Like You 1/2 **2001 (PG-13)** New Yorker Jane (Judd) is a talk-show talent booker who falls for the program's new exec, Ray (Kinnear), who seems to be very serious about her too. In fact, Jane gives up her apartment expecting to move in with Ray, then is suddenly dumped. Homeless, Jane agrees to temporarily share the loft of coworker Eddie (Jackman), a one-night only stud. Well, it does give Jane a chance to test her theory comparing men to bulls, who aren't interested in a cow (or girlfriend) they've had before. Gets by because the cast is so darn cute. Based on the novel "Animal Husbandry" by Laura Zigman. **97m/C; VHS, DVD.** Ashley Judd; Hugh Jackman; Greg Kinnear; Marisa Tomei; Ellen Barkin; Peter Friedman; Catherine Dent; Laura Regan; *D:* Tony Goldwyn; *W:* Elizabeth Chandler; *C:* Anthony B. Richmond; *M:* Rolfe Kent.

Someone Marry Barry **2012** A raunchy comedy that seems to exist for no reason other than to be raunchy, Pearlstein's boring rom com again wastes the talents of the funny Labine in a movie that can't figure out how to make the bad behavior of its protagonist actually funny. Labine plays the socially inappropriate Barry, a gent who defies dating life even as his friends are coupling up and getting hitched. And so they try to set him up, finding the only girlfriend (Punch) as obnoxious as he is. Watch two mostly horrible people fall in love! Or don't. Please don't. **87m/C; On Demand.** Tyler Labine; Lucy Punch; Damon Wayans, Jr.; Thomas Middleditch; Hayes Macarthur; Frances Shaw; *D:* Rob Pearlstein; *W:* Rob Pearlstein; *C:* Marten Tedin; *M:* Joey Katsaros.

Someone to Love **1987 (R)** Rootless filmmaker gathers all his single friends together and interviews them about their failed love lives. Welles's last film as an actor. Wildly uneven, interesting experiment. **110m/C; VHS, DVD.** Henry Jaglom; Orson Welles; Sally Kellerman; Andrea Marcovicci; Michael Emil; Oja Kodar; Stephen Bishop; Ronee Blakley; Kathryn Harrold; Monte Hellman; *D:* Henry Jaglom; *W:* Henry Jaglom; *C:* Hanania Baer.

Someone to Watch Over Me **1987 (R)** After witnessing the murder of a close friend, beautiful and very wealthy Claire Gregory (Rogers) must be protected from the killer. Working-class New York detective Mike Keegan (Berenger), who's assigned the duty, is more than taken with her, despite the fact that he has both a wife (a knowing Bracco) and son at home. A highly watchable, stylish romantic crime thriller. **106m/C; VHS, DVD, Blu-Ray.** Tom Berenger; Mimi Rogers; Lorraine Bracco; Jerry Orbach; Andreas Katsulas; Tony DiBenedetto; James Moriarty; John Rubinstein; *D:* Ridley Scott; *W:* Howard Franklin; *C:* Steven Poster; *M:* Michael Kamen.

Somersault **2004** Troubled Heidi (Cornish) is a luscious, 16-year-old blonde testing her sexuality on her mother's boyfriend, which gets her kicked out of the house. She travels to the ski resort town of Jindabyne, where she casually trades sex for a place to stay. Eventually Heidi lands a job at a convenience store and persuades motel owner Irene (Curran) to rent her a room. She also finds sparks with 20-something Joe (Worthington), the son of a wealthy local farmer, but he's got problems too, and her neediness frightens him off. Debut feature for Shortland skimps on the character details but Cornish is a real heartbreaker. **106m/C; DVD.** *AU* Sam Worthington; Lynette Curran; Leah Purcell; Nathaniel Dean; Abbie Cornish; Erik Thomson; Hollie Andrew; Olivia Pigeot; Blake Pittman; *D:* Cate Shortland; *W:* Cate Shortland; *C:* Robert Humphreys.

Something About Sex *Denial* **1998 (R)** Acerbic bachelor Art (Alexander) broaches the subject of marital fidelity with three couples at a dinner party. All the couples publicly denounce flings while privately not practicing what they preach. **92m/C; VHS, DVD.** Patrick Dempsey; Jonathan Silverman; Christine Taylor; Amy Yasbeck; Jason Alexander; Leah Lail; Ryan Alosio; Jessica Lundy; Charles Shaughnessy; Angie Everhart; Hudson (Heidi) Leick; Nicholas Worth; Jessica Capshaw; Steve Schirripa; *Cameo(s):* Adam Rifkin; *D:* Adam Rifkin; *W:* Adam Rifkin; *C:* Francis Kenny.

Something Beneath **2007** Something beneath dumb and awful actually. In this Sci-Fi Channel original, biologist Dr. Walter Connelly (Beiser) warns that a new resort/conference center is built on toxic ground. An oily black slime starts oozing everywhere and is discovered to be an intelligent organism that causes hallucinations of the nightmarish kind (well, more the hokey kind). Sorbo is the heroic Episcopalian priest who saves the day (and he still gets to flirt with the pretty girl). **93m/C; DVD.** Kevin Sorbo; Brendan Beiser; Peter MacNeill; Gordon Tanner; Natalie Brown; Brittany Scobie; *D:* David Winning; *W:* Mark Mullin; Ethlie Ann Vare; *C:* Brenton Spencer; *M:* Michael Richard Plowman. **CABLE**

Something Borrowed **2011 (PG-13)** Rachel's (Goodwin) a single and successful New York lawyer who's a little gunshy when it comes to love. But her unrequited law school crush on Dex (Egglesfield) leads to a night together after she gets drunk at her 30th birthday bash. Problem is, Dex is her bubbly best friend Darcy's (Hudson) fiance and Rachel finds herself torn. No new twists on this all-too-common story. Dull and insufferable with unlikeable lead characters—not even the charming Krasinski (who plays Rachel's confidante, Ethan) can spare this one. Based on the 2005 novel by Emily Giffin. **112m/C; Blu-Ray, On Demand.** Ginnifer Goodwin; Kate Hudson; Colin Egglesfield; John Krasinski; Steve Howey; Ashley Williams; ***D:*** Luke Greenfield; ***W:*** Jennie Snyder Urman; ***C:*** Charles Minsky; ***M:*** Alex Wurman.

Something for the Birds 🦴🦴 **1952** Environmentalist Anne Richards (Mature) goes to DC to lobby for protection for the nearly-extinct California Condor by establishing a sanctuary on land coveted by an oil company. Thanks to expert party crasher Johnnie Adams (Gwenn), Anne meets opposition lobbyist Steve Bennett (Mature) and becomes determined to get him over to her side. **81m/B; DVD.** Victor Mature; Patricia Neal; Edmund Gwenn; Larry Keating; ***D:*** Robert Wise; ***W:*** Boris Ingster; I.A.L. Diamond; ***C:*** Joseph LaShelle; ***M:*** Sol Kaplan.

Something for the Boys 🦴🦴 **1944** Chiquita (Miranda), Blossom (Blaine), and Harry (Silvers) are distant cousins who inherit a run-down southern plantation. Army Sgt. Rocky Fulton (O'Shea), who's stationed nearby, convinces them to turn the place into a hotel for military wives and to raise the money needed for restoration, they decide to put on a show. Como's debut as a singing soldier. **87m/C; DVD.** Carmen Miranda; Vivian Blaine; Phil Silvers; Michael O'Shea; Sheila Ryan; Perry Como; Glenn Langan; Thurston Hall; Clarence (C. William) Kolb; ***D:*** Lewis Seiler; ***W:*** Robert Ellis; Helen Logan; Frank Gabrielson; ***C:*** Ernest Palmer; ***M:*** Jimmy McHugh.

Something in the Air 🦴🦴 ½ *Après mai* **2013** As the political revolution winds down in early 1970's Paris, Gilles (a dynamic Metayer in his debut performance) is a young, idealistic artist who's enamored with the beautiful girl (Laure) as well as the confrontation going on around him. He loses the girl but finds another (Creton) when he throws himself into the remains of the fracas. A respectable effort from director/writer Assayas, who drew from his own life's experiences as a high-schooler during the era. French, with subtitles. **122m/C; DVD.** Clement Metayer; Lola Creton; Felix Armand; Carole Combes; India Menuez; ***D:*** Olivier Assayas; ***W:*** Olivier Assayas; ***C:*** Eric Gautier.

Something in the Wind 🦴🦴 ½ **1947** Mary Collins (Durbin) is a DJ having a sort of romance with Donald Read (Dall), who gets the mistaken idea that she was once his wealthy Uncle Chester's (Winninger) mistress and is still after the family money. O'Connor gets to steal the show as Durbin's ally, Charlie. **89m/B; VHS, DVD.** Deanna Durbin; Donald O'Connor; John Dall; Charles Winninger; Helena Carter; Margaret Wycherly; ***D:*** Irving Pichel; ***W:*** William Bowers; Harry Kurnitz; ***C:*** Milton Krasner; ***M:*** Johnny Green.

Something Like Happiness 🦴🦴 *Stesti* **2005** Monika, Tonik, and Dasha have been friends since childhood but their adult lives are less than fulfilled. Monika's boyfriend Jiri is finding his fortune in America without her; Tonik has left his conservative family to live with his eccentric aunt in a ramshackle farmhouse; and Dasha, a single mother of two boys, has a married lover and mental problems. When Dasha winds up institutionalized, Monika looks after her children and Tonik offers them all a place to stay at the farmhouse. Czech with subtitles. **102m/C; DVD.** Pavel Liska; Anna Geislerova; Marek Daniel; Tatiana Vilhelmova; Zuzana Kronerova; David Dolnik; ***D:*** Bohdan Slama; ***W:*** Bohdan Slama; ***C:*** Divis Marek; ***M:*** Leonid Soybelman.

Something More 🦴🦴 **1999 (R)** Sam (Gooojian), the romantic loser, and best bud Jim (Lovgren), the obnoxious womanizer, both fall for Kelly (West). The usual romantic complications abound as do all the usual romantic cliches. Cute cast. **97m/C; VHS, DVD.** Michael Goorjian; Chandra West; David Lovgren; Jennifer Beals; Tom Cavanagh; ***D:*** Rob King; ***W:*** Peter Bryant; ***C:*** Jon Kranhouse; ***M:*** Rob Bryanton.

Something New 🦴🦴 ½ **2006 (PG-13)** Interracial romance with two completely delectable leads. Kenya (Lathan) is a successful African-American accountant who's too busy for romance. She does agree to a blind date, only to discover it's with the very white Brian (Baker), an affable landscape architect. She rejects him as boyfriend material but hires him to redo her pathetic backyard. Kenya then tries to resist his wooing, especially when her upscale family and friends don't approve. Then IBM (Ideal Black Man) Mark (Underwood) enters the picture and Kenya must decide if she can get past her own prejudices and find that happy ending. **100m/C; DVD, Blu-Ray.** Sanaa Lathan; Simon Baker; Mike Epps; Donald Adeosun Faison; Blair Underwood; Wendy Raquel Robinson; Golden Brooks; Taraji P. Henson; Earl Billings; Katharine Towne; Alfre Woodard; ***D:*** Sanaa Hamri; ***W:*** Kristopher Turner; ***C:*** Shane Hurlbut; ***M:*** Wendy Melvoin; Lisa Coleman; Paul Anthony Stewart.

Something of Value 🦴🦴🦴 **1957** Good ensemble performances in a serious colonial story about the Mau Mau rebellion in Kenya. Hudson and Poitier are torn between their friendship and their opposing loyalties. Drama solidly grounded in fact from the book by Robert Ruark. **113m/B; VHS, DVD.** Rock Hudson; Sidney Poitier; Wendy Hiller; Dana Wynter; Juano Hernandez; ***D:*** Richard Brooks; ***W:*** Richard Brooks; ***M:*** Miklos Rozsa.

Something Short of Paradise 🦴 ½ **1979 (PG)** The owner of a Manhattan movie theatre has an on again/off again romance with a magazine writer. Would-be Allenesque romantic comedy is too talky and pretentious. **87m/C; VHS, DVD.** David Steinberg; Susan Sarandon; Jean-Pierre Aumont; Marilyn Sokol; ***D:*** David Helpern; ***W:*** Fred Barron.

Something the Lord Made 🦴🦴 **2004** HBO drama based on a true story. In 1941, Dr. Alfred Blalock is offered the position of Chief of Surgery at Johns Hopkins University and he brings along his African-American lab assistant Vivien Thomas. Blalock is a pioneer in open-heart procedures but he owes a lot of his technical success to Thomas. The era's racism divides them outside of the operating room and Thomas is not given the same recognition (or compensation) as Blalock for their work. **110m/C; DVD.** Alan Rickman; Mos Def; Kyra Sedgwick; Gabrielle Union; Mary Stuart Masterson; Charles S. Dutton; ***D:*** Joseph Sargent; ***W:*** Peter Silverman; Robert Caswell; ***C:*** Donald M. Morgan; ***M:*** Christopher Young. **CABLE**

Something to Live For 🦴🦴 **1952** Surprisingly obscure Paramount release considering the cast and director. Actress Jenny Carey (Fontaine) drinks to help her with her stage fright but it's gotten out of control. Thanks to a third-party call to an AA hotline, recovering alcoholic Alan Miller (Milland) shows up to encourage Jenny to quit the booze. The two don't expect to become romantically involved but since Alan is married-with-kids, they know letting their emotions take over is wrong. **89m/B; DVD, Blu-Ray.** Joan Fontaine; Ray Milland; Teresa Wright; Richard Derr; ***D:*** George Stevens; ***W:*** Dwight Taylor; ***C:*** George Barnes; ***M:*** Victor Young.

Something to Sing About 🦴🦴 *Battling Hoofer* **1936** Musical melodrama about a New York bandleader's attempt to make it big in Hollywood. Allows Cagney the opportunity to demonstrate his dancing talents; he also sings. Rereleased in 1947. Also available colorized. Frawley was Fred on "I Love Lucy." **84m/B; VHS, DVD.** James Cagney; William Frawley; Evelyn Daw; Gene Lockhart; ***D:*** Victor Schertzinger.

Something to Talk About 🦴🦴 ½ *Grace Under Pressure* **1995 (R)** Romantic comedy/drama finds Grace (Roberts) running her overbearing father Wyly's (Duvall) horsebreeding operation and learning that her husband Eddie (the ever-charming Quaid) is tomcatting around. So Grace tosses him out and makes a temporary move with daughter Caroline (Aull) back home. Tart-tongued sister Emma Rae (Sedgwick) is sympathetic but long-suffering mama Georgia (Rowlands) thinks Grace should make the best of things (the way she's done). Naturally, Eddie wants his family back but the frazzled Grace is just coming to terms with what she wants out of life. Star appeal from both leads lends this familiar plot some spark. **106m/C; VHS, DVD.** Julia Roberts; Dennis Quaid; Robert Duvall; Gena Rowlands; Kyra Sedgwick; Brett Cullen; Haley Aull; Muse Watson; Anne Shropshire; ***D:*** Lasse Hallstrom; ***W:*** Callie Khouri; ***C:*** Sven Nykvist; ***M:*** Hans Zimmer.

Something Weird **WOOF!** **1968** McCabe is disfigured horribly in an electrical accident. A seemingly beautiful witch fixes his face, on condition that he be her lover. The accident also gave him ESP—and it gets cheesier from there. **80m/C; VHS, DVD.** Tony McCabe; Elizabeth Lee; William Brooker; Mudite Arums; Ted Heil; Lawrence Wood; Larry Wellington; Roy Collodi; Jeffrey Allen; Stan Dale; Richard Nilsson; Carolyn Smith; Norm Lenet; Louis Newman; Dick Gaffield; Janet Charlton; Lee Ahsmann; Roger Papsch; Daniel Carrington; ***D:*** Herschell Gordon Lewis; ***W:*** James F. Hurley; ***C:*** Herschell Gordon Lewis; Andy Romanoff.

Something Wicked This Way Comes 🦴🦴 **1983 (PG)** Two young boys discover the evil secret of a mysterious traveling carnival that visits their town. Bradbury wrote the screenplay for this much-anticipated, expensive adaptation of his own novel. Good special effects, but disappointing. **94m/C; VHS, DVD.** Jason Robards, Jr.; Jonathan Pryce; Diane Ladd; Pam Grier; Richard (Dick) Davalos; James Stacy; Royal Dano; Vidal Peterson; Shawn Carson; ***D:*** Jack Clayton; ***W:*** Ray Bradbury; ***C:*** Stephen Burum; ***M:*** James Horner.

Something Wild 🦴 **1961** Perverse, psycho-babble melodrama. College student Mary Ann (Baker) keeps the fact she was raped from her mother and stepfather but her life falls apart and she leaves home to move into a seedy apartment. Her depression gets to be too much causing her to attempt suicide, but is saved by troubled alcoholic mechanic Mike (Meeker). He becomes obsessive about Mary Ann and locks her in his apartment, pleading with her to 'save' him by accepting his marriage proposal. **112m/B; DVD, Blu-Ray.** Carroll Baker; Ralph Meeker; Mildred Dunnock; Charles Watts; Jean Stapleton; Martin Kosleck; Clifton James; ***D:*** Jack Garfein; ***W:*** Jack Garfein; Alex Karmel; ***C:*** Eugene Schuftan; ***M:*** Aaron Copland.

Something Wild 🦴🦴 ½ **1986 (R)** Mild-mannered business exec Daniels is picked up by an impossibly free-living vamp with a Louise Brooks hairdo, and taken for the ride of his up-till-then staid life, eventually leading to explosive violence. A sharp-edged comedy with numerous changes of pace. Too-happy ending wrecks it, but it's great until then. Look for cameos from filmmakers John Waters and John Sayles. **113m/C; VHS, DVD, Blu-Ray.** Jeff Daniels; Melanie Griffith; Ray Liotta; Margaret Colin; Tracey Walter; Dana Peru; Jack Gilpin; Su Tissue; Kenneth Utt; Sr. Carol East; John Sayles; John Waters; Charles Napier; ***D:*** Jonathan Demme; ***W:*** E. Max Frye; ***C:*** Tak Fujimoto; ***M:*** Rosemary Paul; John Cale; Laurie Anderson; David Byrne.

Something's Gotta Give 🦴🦴🦴 **2003 (PG-13)** The title's bland but the film is anything but (particularly for the woman of a certain age). Harry Sanborn (Nicholson) is a legendary womanizer. Now 60-something, he's notorious for dating only much-younger chicks. Harry's current squeeze is Marin (Peet), who takes Harry to her mom's Hamptons beach house to consummate the relationship. Turns out mom, successful (if neurotic) divorced playwright Erica Barry (Keaton), and her sister, feminist professor Zoe (McDormand), are there as well. Harry has a mild heart attack and his doctor, Julian Mercer (Reeves), says Harry can't travel, leading to changing ideas, beds, and relationships. It's Keaton's film all the way (she's a natural wonder) and even scene-stealer Nicholson concedes to her charm; McDormand provides some droll asides and Reeves is relaxed. **124m/C; DVD.** Diane Keaton; Jack Nicholson; Keanu Reeves; Amanda Peet; Frances McDormand; Rachel Ticotin; Paul Michael Glaser; Jon Favreau; KaDee Strickland; ***D:*** Nancy Meyers; ***W:*** Nancy Meyers; ***C:*** Michael Ballhaus; ***M:*** Hans Zimmer. Golden Globes '04: Actress--Mus./Comedy (Keaton); Natl. Bd. of Review '03: Actress (Keaton).

Sometimes a Great Notion 🦴🦴🦴 *Never Give an Inch* **1971 (PG)** Trouble erupts in a small Oregon town when a family of loggers decide to honor a contract when the other loggers go on strike. Newman's second stint in the director's chair; Fonda's first role as an old man. Based on the novel by Ken Kesey. **115m/C; VHS, DVD, Blu-Ray.** Paul Newman; Henry Fonda; Lee Remick; Richard Jaeckel; Michael Sarrazin; ***D:*** Paul Newman; ***W:*** John Gay; ***M:*** Henry Mancini.

Sometimes Always Never 🦴🦴 ½ *Sometimes Always Never (Triple Word Score)* **2019 (PG-13)** In northwestern England, well-dressed tailor Alan (Nighy) is a passionate Scrabble player who mostly plays with strangers online. A widower, he has an awkward relationship with his sign painter son Peter (Riley). Alan believes he may have found his long lost son Michael when he plays an online opponent who uses words and strategy like Michael, who disappeared after an argument over the game. At the same time, Alan tries to improve his relationship with Peter, Peter's wife Sue (Lowe), and his adolescent grandson Jack (Healy). The comedy-drama has a wistful feel, an amusing though sometimes random story, and strong work from the cast. **91m/C; DVD.** Bill Nighy; Sam Riley; Alice Lowe; Jenny Agutter; Tim McInnerny; ***D:*** Carl Hunter; ***W:*** Frank Cottrell Boyce; ***C:*** Richard Stoddard; ***M:*** Edwyn Collins; Sean Read.

Sometimes in April 🦴🦴🦴 **2005** In 1994 almost one million citizens of Rwanda were massacred in 100 days. Focusing on two brothers, one a Rwandan Army officer and one a broadcaster at an extremist radio station, the film gives the country's genocide perspective and human faces. In the same vein as "Hotel Rwanda," filmed in Rwanda using the locals as extras. Paints a powerful picture of a genocide that may have otherwise gone unnoticed by most of the Western world. **140m/C; DVD.** Idris Elba; Debra Winger; Noah Emmerich; Oris Erhuero; Carole Karemara; Pamela Nomvete; ***D:*** Raoul Peck; ***W:*** Raoul Peck; ***C:*** Eric Gurchard; ***M:*** Bruno Coulais. **TV**

Sometimes They Come Back 🦴🦴 **1991 (R)** Another Stephen King tale of terror. Matheson plays a man haunted by the tragedy in his past. A witness to his brother's death, he also witnesses the fiery crash of his brother's killers. Only now the killers have returned from the dead, to take their revenge on him. **97m/C; VHS, DVD, Blu-Ray.** Tim Matheson; Brooke Adams; Robert Rusler; William Sanderson; ***D:*** Tom McLoughlin; ***W:*** Mark Rosenthal; Larry Konner; ***C:*** Bryan England; ***M:*** Terry Plumeri. **TV**

Sometimes They Come Back. . . Again 🦴 ½ **1996 (R)** Psychologist John Porter (Gross) and his teenaged daughter (Swank) return to Porter's hometown after his mother's mysterious death. He should know you can never go home again since they're both soon threatened by a young man (Arquette) involved in the ritualistic murder of Porter's sister years before. Gruesome special effects are the highlight. **98m/C; VHS, DVD.** Michael Gross; Hilary Swank; Alexis Arquette; Jennifer Elise Cox; William Morgan Sheppard; ***D:*** Adam Grossman; ***W:*** Adam Grossman; ***C:*** Christopher Baffa; ***M:*** Peter Manning Robinson.

Sometimes They Come Back. . . For More 🦴🦴 **1999 (R)** Two military officers investigate the disappearances of crew members at a government outpost in Antarctica. **89m/C; VHS, DVD.** Clayton Rohner; Chase Masterson; Faith Ford; Max Perlich; Damian Chapa; ***D:*** Daniel Berk.

A Somewhat Gentle Man 🦴🦴 **2010** Recently released from prison, Ulrik isn't so much gentle as indifferent. The only thing that really matters to him is reuniting with his now-adult son Geir. Ulrik needs a job so he goes back to his crazy boss Jensen, who wants Ulrik to kill a snitch. Norwegian with subtitles. **105m/C; DVD.** *NO* Stellan Skarsgard; Bjorn Floberg; Gard B. Eidsvold; Jan Gunnar Roise; Jorunn Kjellsby; Kjersti Holmen; Julia Bache-Wiig; Jannike Kruse; ***D:*** Hans Petter Moland; ***W:*** Kim Fupz Aaekson; ***C:*** Philip Ogaard; ***M:*** Halfdan E.

Somewhere 🦴🦴 ½ **2010 (R)** Frequent tabloid fodder, actor Johnny Marco (Dorff) lives an aimless and hedonistic life at the legendary Hollywood hotel, the Chateau Marmont. When his 11-year-old daughter Cleo (Fanning) unexpectedly comes to stay, Johnny is forced to re-examine his life choices. Strong, charming performances from Dorff and Fanning but Coppola's thoughtful, slow-paced directing can test the patience of modern audience members accustomed to fast-paced action. It's a matter of taste whether this is engaging and poignant versus tedious and trite. Winner of the Golden Lion Award for Best Picture at the 2010 Venice International Film Festival. **98m/C; Blu-Ray.** Stephen Dorff; Elle Fanning; Chris Pontius; Michelle Monaghan; ***D:*** Sofia Coppola; ***W:*** Sofia Coppola; ***C:*** Harris Savides; ***M:*** Phoenix.

Somewhere I'll Find You **1942** Clark and Turner heat up the screen as correspondents running all over the war-torn world in their second film together. ("Honky Tonk" was their first.) Notable mainly because Gable's beloved wife, Carole Lombard, was killed in a plane crash only three days into production. Gable forced himself to finish the film and it became one of the studio's biggest hits. Although critics applauded his determination to complete the film, many felt his performance was subdued and strained. Film debut of Wynn. Based on a story by Charles Hoffman. **108m/B; VHS, DVD.** Clark Gable; Lana Turner; Robert Sterling; Reginald Owen; Lee Patrick; Charles Dingle; Tamara Shayne; Leonid Kinskey; Diana Lewis; Molly Lamont; Patricia Dane; Sara Haden; Keenan Wynn; ***D:*** Wesley Ruggles; ***W:*** Walter Reisch; Marguerite Roberts.

Somewhere in the City 1/2 **1997** Covers the screwy lives of six tenants of a Lower East Side New York apartment building. Betty (a subdued Bernhard) is an unlucky-in-love therapist who's still neurotically trying. She agrees to help out Chinese exchange student Lu Lu (Ling) who's desperately seeking a green card marriage. Then there's unhappy wife Marta (Muti), whose upstairs lover, Frankie (Burke), is a completely incompetent crook. There's also gay actor Graham (Stormare), who's disappointed personally and professionally, and basement-dwelling Che (Stewart), a trust-fund baby who wants to be a radical revolutionary. Sporadically amusing with a talented cast. **93m/C; VHS, DVD.** Sandra Bernhard; Bai Ling; Ornella Muti; Robert John Burke; Peter Stormare; Paul Anthony Stewart; Bulle Ogier; ***Cameo(s):*** Edward I. Koch; ***D:*** Ramin Niami; ***W:*** Ramin Niami; Patrick Dillon; ***C:*** Igor Sunara; ***M:*** John Cale.

Somewhere in the Night **1946** Marine George Taylor (Hodiak) wakes up in a hospital with a reconstructed face and amnesia, and the only clues to his past are a Dear John letter and an L.A. address. This leads him to a letter of credit signed by someone named Larry Cravat, nightclub owner Mel Phillips (Conte), and songbird Christy Smith (Guild). Is Taylor actually Cravat, who's not only a murder suspect but involved in laundering Nazi cash? Detective Kendall (Nolan) is sure Taylor will figure things out. Noir with convoluted subplots and weak leads, especially debuting starlet Guild. **108m/B; DVD.** John Hodiak; Nancy Guild; Lloyd Nolan; Richard Conte; Fritz Kortner; Margo Woode; Josephine Hutchinson; Sheldon Leonard; Houseley Stevenson; ***D:*** Joseph L. Mankiewicz; ***W:*** Joseph L. Mankiewicz; Howard Dimsdale; ***C:*** Norbert Brodine; ***M:*** David Buttolph.

Somewhere in Time 1/2 **1980 (PG)** Playwright Reeve (in his first post-Clark Kent role) falls in love with a beautiful woman in an old portrait. Through self-hypnosis he goes back in time to 1912 to discover what their relationship might have been. The film made a star of the Grand Hotel, located on Mackinac Island in Michigan, where it was shot. Adapted by Richard Matheson from his own novel. Knowing that, you'd think it'd be better. Reeve is horrible; Seymour is underused. All in all, rather wretched. **103m/C; VHS, DVD, Blu-Ray.** Christopher Reeve; Jane Seymour; Christopher Plummer; Teresa Wright; Bill Erwin; George Voskovec; Susan French; William H. Macy; George Wendt; Tim Kazurinsky; ***D:*** Jeannot Szwarc; ***W:*** Richard Matheson; ***C:*** Isidore Mankofsky; ***M:*** John Barry.

Somewhere Slow **2014** Recently fired 40-something professional midlife-crisis candidate Anna (Gilsig) witnesses a gas-station robbery gone bad and decides to take the money and run. She hops a bus to Maine and encounters a mysterious teenage drifter (Martin), whose easy-going attitude covers up his own damaged past. Together, the two try to sort out their lives. Low-budget indie has its strong points but does little to distinguish itself from other films about people turning to youth for inspiration during a midlife crisis. **96m/C; On Demand.** Jessalyn Gilsig; Graham Patrick Martin; David Costabile; Lindsay Crouse; Wallace (Wally) Langham; Robert Forster; ***D:*** Jeremy O'Keefe; ***W:*** Jeremy O'Keefe; ***C:*** Justin Talley; ***M:*** Barry J. Neely.

Somewhere Tomorrow 1/2 **1985 (PG)** A lonely, fatherless teenage girl is befriended by the ghost of a young man killed in a plane crash. Charming and moving, if not perfect. **91m/C; VHS, DVD.** Sarah Jessica Parker; Nancy Addison; Tom Shea; ***D:*** Robert Wiemer.

Somm **2013** Director Wise's documentary about the men (exclusively men, which is interesting but never explored) who choose to become master sommeliers starts with an intriguing idea--exploring the world of the people who love wine and obsess over knowing everything about it--but goes nowhere with it. The biggest problem with the film lies in the lack of likability of its subjects, people who come off as egocentric and annoying. To work, we need to root for these people as the film captures their efforts to rise to the top of their profession. Instead, it just makes The Hound want a drink. **93m/C; DVD, Blu-Ray.** ***D:*** Jason Wise; ***W:*** Jason Wise; ***C:*** Jackson Myers; ***M:*** Brian Carmody.

Sommersby 1/2 **1993 (PG-13)** A too-good-to-be-true period romance based on the film "The Return of Martin Guerre." A Civil War veteran (Gere) returns to his wife's (Foster) less-than-open arms. She soon warms up to his kind, sensitive and caring manner, but can't quite believe the change that the war has wrought. Neither can the neighbors, especially the one (Pullman) who had his own eye on Laurel Sommersby. So is he really Jack Sommersby or an all too clever imposter? Lots of hankies needed for the tender-hearted. Strong performance by Foster. Filmed in Virginia (passing for the state of Tennessee.) **114m/C; VHS, DVD, Blu-Ray.** Richard Gere; Jodie Foster; Bill Pullman; James Earl Jones; William Windom; Brett Kelley; Richard Hamilton; Maury Chaykin; Lanny Flaherty; Frankie Faison; Wendell Wellman; Clarice Taylor; R. Lee Ermey; ***D:*** Jon Amiel; ***W:*** Nicholas Meyer; Sarah Kernochan; ***C:*** Philippe Rousselot; ***M:*** Danny Elfman.

Son-in-Law 1/2 **1993 (PG-13)** Surfer-dude comic Shore's a laconic fish out of water as a city-boy rock 'n' roller who falls in love with a country beauty, marries her, and visits the family farm to meet the new in-laws. Once there, he weirds out family and neighbors before showing everyone how to live, Pauly style. Silly entertainment best appreciated by Shore fans. **95m/C; VHS, DVD.** Pauly Shore; Carla Gugino; Lane Smith; Cindy Pickett; Mason Adams; Patrick Renna; Dennis Burkley; Dan Gauthier; Tiffani(-Amber) Thiessen; ***D:*** Steve Rash; ***W:*** Shawn Schepps; Fax Bahr; Adam Small; ***C:*** Peter Deming; ***M:*** Richard Gibbs.

Son of a Gun 1/2 **2014 (R)** Many movies rolled into one, writer/director Avery's crime drama features some strong performances buried by over-plotting and overdirection. New star Brenton Thwaites leads the cast as 19-year-old JR, the latest inmate at the facility that happens to house Australia's public enemy no. 1 Brendan Lynch (McGregor). After a few incidents at the prison, JR is taken under Lynch's wing as a criminal protégé, which might be enough for one movie but then it shifts gears into heist-movie territory, becoming more like a Michael Mann work about strong men with big guns. Everyone's good, movie's a hot mess. **108m/C; Blu-Ray, Streaming.** ***AU*** Brenton Thwaites; Ewan McGregor; Alicia Vikander; Matthew Nable; Jacek Koman; ***D:*** Julius Avery; ***W:*** Julius Avery; ***C:*** Nigel Bluck; ***M:*** Jed Kurzel.

Son of a Gunfighter **1965** Mediocre western with Tamblyn not particularly believable as a gunslinger. A stagecoach robbery is prevented by Johnny, who next tries to prevent Mexican bandits from attacking the ranch owned by his girlfriend's father. Johnny's estranged outlaw dad comes to his aid. **92m/C; DVD.** Russ Tamblyn; James Philbrook; Aldo Sambrell; Kieron Moore; Fernando Rey; Maria Granada; ***D:*** Paul Landres; ***W:*** Clarke Reynolds; ***C:*** Manuel Berenguer.

Son of Ali Baba **1952** Kashma Baba, son of Ali Baba, enters the military academy to learn to withstand adversity. He has other ideas however, until he must suddenly fill his father's shoes and fight the evil Caliph. He fights bravely with the help of his childhood friend, a beautiful princess, in this swashbuckler. **85m/C; DVD.** Tony Curtis; Piper Laurie; Susan Cabot; Victor Jory; Hugh O'Brian; William Reynolds; Gerald Mohr; ***D:*** Ross Hunter.

Son of Billy the Kid 1/2 **1949** In this revisionist western, Billy is never killed by Pat Garrett and lives to become a respectable banker (Baxter). His bank is threatened when outlaws trying robbing the stage of a gold shipment but are stopped by Pat's son Jack Garrett (LaRue). They then try to rob the bank itself but are thwarted by Billy's son (James). But the bad guys just don't want to give up. **65m/B; DVD.** Lash LaRue; George Baxter; John James; Al "Fuzzy" St. John; June Carr; Marion Colby; Terry Frost; ***D:*** Ray Taylor; ***W:*** Ira Webb; Ron Ormond; ***C:*** Ernest Miller; ***M:*** Walter Greene.

Son of Dracula ***Young Dracula*** **1943** In this late-coming sequel to the Universal classic, a stranger named Alucard is invited to America by a Southern belle obsessed with eternal life. It is actually Dracula himself, not his son, who wreaks havoc in this spine-tingling chiller. **80m/B; VHS, DVD, Blu-Ray.** Lon Chaney, Jr.; Evelyn Ankers; Frank Craven; Robert Paige; Louise Allbritton; J. Edward Bromberg; Samuel S. Hinds; ***D:*** Robert Siodmak; ***W:*** Eric Taylor; ***C:*** George Robinson.

Son of Flubber 1/2 **1963** Sequel to "The Absent Minded Professor" finds Fred MacMurray still toying with his prodigious invention, Flubber, now in the form of Flubbergas, which causes those who inhale it to float away. Disney's first-ever sequel is high family wackiness. **96m/C; VHS, DVD, Blu-Ray.** Fred MacMurray; Nancy Olson; Tommy Kirk; Leon Ames; Joanna Moore; Keenan Wynn; Charlie Ruggles; Paul Lynde; ***D:*** Robert Stevenson; ***C:*** Edward Colman; ***M:*** George Bruns.

Son of Frankenstein **1939** The second sequel (after "The Bride of Frankenstein") to the 1931 version of the horror classic. The good doctor's skeptical son returns to the family manse and becomes obsessed with his father's work and with reviving the creature. Full of memorable characters and brooding ambience. Karloff's last appearance as the monster. **99m/C; VHS, DVD, Blu-Ray.** Basil Rathbone; Bela Lugosi; Boris Karloff; Lionel Atwill; Josephine Hutchinson; Donnie Dunagan; Emma Dunn; Edgar Norton; Lawrence Grant; Lionel Belmore; ***D:*** Rowland V. Lee; ***W:*** Willis Cooper; ***C:*** George Robinson.

Son of Fury **1942** Dashing Ben Blake (Power) is left penniless when his sinister uncle (Sanders) wrongfully takes the family fortune. Ben escapes to sea and then to an island paradise—all the while plotting his revenge. But he still finds time to fall for the beautous Tierney. Fine 18th-century costumer done in grand style. Based on the novel "Benjamin Blake" by Edison Marshall. **98m/C; VHS, DVD.** Tyrone Power; Gene Tierney; George Sanders; Frances Farmer; Roddy McDowall; John Carradine; Elsa Lanchester; Harry Davenport; Kay Johnson; Dudley Digges; Halliwell Hobbes; Marten Lamont; Arthur Hohl; Pedro de Cordoba; Dennis Hoey; Heather Thatcher; ***D:*** John Cromwell; ***W:*** Philip Dunne; ***M:*** Alfred Newman.

Son of Gascogne 1/2 ***Les Fils de Gascogne*** **1995** Offbeat comedy about identity, romance, and wish fullfillment. Gawky Harvey (Colin) is serving as a travel guide to a group of Georgian folksingers who are giving concerts in Paris. Harvey falls for their pretty teenaged interpreter, Dinara (Droukarova), who reciprocates. The duo meets Marco (Dreyfus), a chauffeur/con man, who insists that Harvey is the son of the late legendary director Gascogne (Harvey doesn't know who his father is) and insists on introducing him to his dad's cinematic colleagues (thus supplying cameos of numerous French cinema greats). French with subtitles. **106m/C; VHS, DVD.** ***FR*** Gregoire Colin; Jean-Claude Dreyfus; Dinara Drukarova; Bernadette LaFont; Alexandra Stewart; Stephane Audran; Jean-Claude Brialy; Bulle Ogier; Marie-France Pisier; Anemone; Patrice Leconte; Marina Vlady; ***D:*** Pascal Aubier; ***W:*** Pascal Aubier; Patrick Modiano; ***C:*** Jean-Jacques Flori; ***M:*** Angelo Zurzulo.

Son of God 1/2 **2014 (PG-13)** The miniseries production of "The Bible" was such a hit that someone had the brilliant idea to cut it down to theatrical-size, focusing on the 'Jesus Years' and releasing it at the multiplex. Directly targeting faith-based groups, this dull affair stars Morgado in the title role as Spencer's film chronicles Jesus' birth, teachings, crucifixion and resurrection. Overly familiar, sanitized to death, and featuring the smiling, waving Jesus of TV moviedom, it's as boring as a Sunday School class. **138m/C; DVD, Blu-Ray.** Diogo Morgado; Greg Hicks; Adrian Schiller; Roma Downey; Sebastian Knapp; Darwin Shaw; ***D:*** Christopher Spencer; ***W:*** Christopher Spencer; Richard Bedser; Colin Swash; ***C:*** Rob Goldie; ***M:*** Hans Zimmer; Lorne Balfe.

Son of Godzilla ***Gojira no Musuko; Monster Island's Decisive Battle: Godzilla's Son*** **1966** Dad and junior protect beauty Maeda from giant spiders on a remote island ruled by a mad scientist. Fun monster flick with decent special effects. **86m/C; VHS, DVD, Blu-Ray.** ***JP*** Akira Kubo; Beverly (Bibari) Maeda; Tadao Takashima; Akihiko Hirata; Kenji Sahara; ***D:*** Jun Fukuda; ***W:*** Shinichi Sekizawa; Kazue Shiba; ***C:*** Kazuo Yamada; ***M:*** Masaru Sato.

Son of Hercules in the Land of Darkness **1963** Argolis (Vadis) must rescue prisoners trapped in an underground city. **74m/B; VHS, DVD.** ***IT*** Dan Vadis; Carol Brown; Spela Rozin; ***D:*** Alvaro Mancori; ***W:*** Alvaro Mancori; ***C:*** Claude Haroy; ***M:*** Francesco De Masi.

Son of Ingagi 1/2 **1940** Lonely ape-man kidnaps woman in search of romance. Early all-black horror film stars Williams of "Amos 'n' Andy." **70m/B; VHS, DVD.** Zack Williams; Laura Bowman; Alfred Grant; Spencer Williams, Jr.; Daisy Bufford; Arthur Ray; ***D:*** Richard C. Kahn; ***W:*** Spencer Williams, Jr.; ***C:*** Roland Price; Herman Schopp.

Son of Kong 1/2 **1933** King Kong's descendant is discovered on an island amid prehistoric creatures in this often humorous sequel to RKO's immensely popular "King Kong." Hoping to capitalize on the enormous success of its predecessor, director Schoedsack quickly threw this together. As a result, its success at the boxoffice did not match the original's, and didn't deserve to, but it's fun. Nifty special effects from Willis O'Brien, the man who brought them to us the first time. **70m/B; VHS, DVD, Blu-Ray.** Robert Armstrong; Helen Mack; ***D:*** Ernest B. Schoedsack; ***M:*** Max Steiner.

Son of Lassie 1/2 **1945 (G)** It seems that Lassie's son Laddie just isn't quite as smart as his mother. After the dog sneaks onto his master's plane during WWII, the plane gets shot down, and Lawford parachutes out with Laddie in his arms. The dog goes to get help because Lawford is hurt, but he brings back two Nazis! A sequel to "Lassie Come Home." **102m/C; VHS, DVD.** Peter Lawford; Donald Crisp; June Lockhart; Nigel Bruce; William Severn; Leon Ames; Donald Curtis; Nils Asther; Robert Lewis; ***D:*** S. Sylvan Simon.

The Son of Monte Cristo 1/2 **1940** Illegitimate offspring of the great swashbuckler with Robert Donat proves they made pathetic, pointless sequels even back then. **102m/B; VHS, DVD.** Louis Hayward; Joan Bennett; George Sanders; Florence Bates; Montagu Love; Ralph Byrd; Clayton Moore; ***D:*** Rowland V. Lee; ***W:*** George Bruce; ***C:*** George Robinson; ***M:*** Edward Ward.

Son of Morning **2011 (R)** Limp, would-be satire with little humor and annoying characters. A solar catastrophe threatens the planet and young Phillip Katz is mistaken for the next messiah thanks to a sensationalistic story by ambitious reporter Josephine Tuttle. Phillip gets exploited by the devout as well as politicians and the media. **80m/C; DVD.** Joseph Cross; Heather Graham; Danny Glover; Jamie-Lynn Sigler; Stephen (Steve) Root; Jesse Bradford; Jon Polito; Steven Weber; ***D:*** Yaniv Raz; ***W:*** Yaniv Raz; ***C:*** Jonathan Wenstrup; ***M:*** Jonathan Zalben. **VIDEO**

The Son of No One 2011 (R) A misguided police drama, director Montiel's third film with Tatum is a disastrously melodramatic and nonsensical examination of the secret lives hidden behind the badge. The very concept that a journalist (Binoche) would be looking into two unexplained deaths from fifteen years earlier in a New York project doesn't hold up. It turns out that the deaths were both accidentally caused by a now-cop (Tatum) and both the previous police chief (Pacino) and current one (Liotta) get caught up in the cover-up. **95m/C; DVD, Blu-Ray.** Channing Tatum; Al Pacino; Juliette Binoche; Ray Liotta; Jake Cherry; Katie Holmes; Tracy Morgan; Brian Gilbert; Ursula Parker; James Ransone; ***D:*** Dito Montiel; ***W:*** Dito Montiel; ***C:*** Benoit Delhomme; ***M:*** Dave Wittman; Jonathan Elias.

Son of Paleface 1/2 1952 Hilarious sequel to the original Hope gag-fest, with the Harvard-educated son of the original character (again played by Hope) heading west to claim an inheritance. Hope runs away with every cowboy cliche and even manages to wind up with the girl. Songs include "Buttons and Bows" (reprised from the original), "There's a Cloud in My Valley of Sunshine," and "Four-legged Friend." **95m/C; VHS, DVD, Blu-Ray.** Bob Hope; Jane Russell; Roy Rogers; Douglass Dumbrille; Iron Eyes Cody; Bill Williams; Harry von Zell; ***D:*** Frank Tashlin; ***W:*** Frank Tashlin; Joseph Quillan; Robert L. Welch; ***C:*** Harry Wild.

Son of Rambow 1/2 2007 (PG-13) Quirky coming-of-age flick centering around two young boys away at summer camp in early '80s England. Sheltered from the corrupt influence of television, movies, and pop music, scrawny little Will Proudfoot spends most of his time inside his imagination, sketching and doodling. Soon, he strikes up an unlikely friendship with school bully Lee, who's got a video camera and a passion for making movies. Will's tiny world suddenly gets much bigger after Lee introduces him to "First Blood," and the two set out to shoot their own Rambo adventure. Its offbeat flair owes just as much to Wes Anderson as it does Jon Hughes. Unfortunately, a massive wave of sappy sentimentality takes over the second half when a French foreign exchange student is introduced and spoils the fun. **96m/C; Blu-Ray, On Demand.** *GB* Jessica Stevenson; Neil Dudgeon; Bill Milner; Will Poulter; Jules Sitruk; Ed Westwick; ***D:*** Garth Jennings; ***W:*** Garth Jennings; ***C:*** Jess Hall; ***M:*** Joby Talbot.

Son of Sam 2008 (R) German horror director Lommel tackles another serial killer story in this boring low-budget retelling. Via flashbacks after his arrest in 1977, David Berkowitz (Joshi) blames a satanic cult and the voices he hears for making him kill people. **80m/C; DVD.** Elissa Dowling; Yogi Joshi; Jamie Bernadette; ***D:*** Ulli Lommel; ***W:*** Ulli Lommel; ***C:*** Bianco Pacelli; ***M:*** Green River Band. **VIDEO**

Son of Samson 1/2 *Le Geant de la Vallee Das Rois* 1962 Man with large pectoral muscles puts an end to the evil Queen of Egypt's reign of terror **89m/C; VHS, DVD.** *FR IT YU* Mark Forest; Chelo Alonso; Angelo Zanolli; Vira (Vera) Silenti; Frederica Ranchi; ***D:*** Carlo Campogalliani.

Son of Saul *Saul fia* 2015 (R) Saul (Rohrig) is a Sonderkommando, the men tasked with helping the Nazis in concentration camps with tasks such as cleaning out the gas chambers and burning bodies. Near the end of World War II, in Auschwitz, Saul witnesses a child who briefly survives a gas chamber. He becomes convinced the boy is his son, and he must now get him the right burial. Nemes' masterpiece only allows us to see what Saul sees, focusing mostly on his face in a tight, 4:3 frame. The result is a terrifying experience, one that forces us to look at the Holocaust in a new way. **107m/C; DVD, Blu-Ray.** Geza Rohrig; Levente Molnar; Urs Rechn; Todd Charmont; Jerzy Walczak; ***D:*** László Nemes; ***W:*** László Nemes; Clara Royer; ***C:*** Mátyás Erdély; ***M:*** László Melis. Oscars '15: Foreign Film; British Acad. '15: Foreign Film; Golden Globes '16: Foreign Film; Ind. Spirit '16: Foreign Film.

The Son of the Bride 1/2 *El Hijo de la Novia* 2001 (R) Middle-aged Rafael Belvedere (Darin) manages the Buenos Aires restaurant started by his father Nino (Alterio) and mother Norma (Aleandro). Rafael's workaholic behavior has cost him his marriage and estranged him from his daughter and his girlfriend Naty (Verbeke). After suffering a mild heart attack, Rafael is forced to slow down and take more of an interest in domestic matters, including Nino's decision to remarry his wife in the church service they never had, even though Norma is living in a nursing home because she suffers from Alzheimer's and is frequently unaware of what is going on around her. Spanish with subtitles. **123m/C; DVD.** *AR* Ricardo Darin; Hector Alterio; Norma Aleandro; Natalia Verbeke; Eduardo Blanco; Gimena Nobile; Claudia Fontan; ***D:*** Juan J. Campanella; ***W:*** Juan J. Campanella; Fernando Castets; ***C:*** Daniel Shulman; ***M:*** Angel Illaramendi.

Son of the Gods 1/2 1930 Dated story of prejudice with a still-shocking scene of violence and an unbelievable personal and romantic outcome. Chinese-American Sam Lee (Barthelmess), the son of a successful businessman, is tired of the racial prejudice he encounters. He decides to travel to Europe, where he's taken for white, and falls for socialite Allana (Bennett), who reacts violently when she discovers Sam's heritage. **90m/B; DVD.** Richard Barthelmess; Constance Bennett; E. Alyn (Fred) Warren; Barbara Leonard; Claude King; Frank Albertson; Anders Randolph; King Hou Chang; ***D:*** Frank Lloyd; ***W:*** Bradley King; ***C:*** Ernest Haller.

Son of the Mask 2005 (PG) Ill-conceived sequel has Tim Avery (Kennedy), a low-level cartoonist who yearns to advance beyond his current position at an animation company, finding the magical mask in time for his company's Halloween party. Of course he puts it on and gets transformed. Before the night is over, Avery gets a promotion and impregnates his wife (how's that for multi-tasking?). Soon after their son Alvey is born they realize that he's not like other kids. He has mask-like powers and the ability to warp into a freakish tornado of cartoon characters. Flick wilts under the weight of the digital effects, which on a baby seem creepily misplaced. **86m/C; DVD.** Jamie Kennedy; Alan Cumming; Traylor Howard; Steven Wright; Liam Falconer; Ryan Falconer; Kal Penn; Bob Hoskins; ***D:*** Lawrence (Larry) Guterman; ***W:*** Lance Khazei; ***C:*** Greg Gardiner; ***M:*** Randy Edelman. Golden Raspberries '05: Worst Remake/Sequel.

Son of the Pink Panther 1/2 *Blake Edwards' Son of the Pink Panther* 1993 (PG) Lame leftover from the formerly popular comedy series. Director Edwards has chosen not to resurrect Inspector Clouseau, instead opting for his son (Benigni), who turns out to be just as much of a bumbling idiot as his father. Commissioner Dreyfus (Lom), the twitching, mouth-foaming former supervisor of the original Clouseau is looking for a kidnapped princess (Farentino) along with Clouseau, Jr., who himself does not know he is the illegitimate son of his partner's dead nemesis. Many of the sketches have been recycled from previous series entrants. Rather than being funny, they seem used and shopworn like a threadbare rug. **115m/C; VHS, DVD, Blu-Ray.** Roberto Benigni; Herbert Lom; Robert Davi; Debrah Farentino; Claudia Cardinale; Burt Kwouk; Shabana Azmi; ***D:*** Blake Edwards; ***W:*** Blake Edwards; ***C:*** Dick Bush; ***M:*** Henry Mancini.

Sonatine 1996 (R) Middle-age Yakuza mobster Murakama (director Kitano, using his screen name Beat Takeshi) wishes to retire but is instead sent to mediate a low-level gang war. Upon arrival, an attempt is made on his life, so he and his men hole up at a beach house. The young punks of the gang engage in horseplay and antics that indicate their violent natures and signal that all will not remain calm for long. Kitano's performance, writing, and direction are superb, understating the violence while not glamorizing it, and showing the effect it has on the man who carries it out. The relatively tranquil setting of the hideout allows some humor and character development, as well as preventing the cliches that usually pop up in this type of movie. Ever on the prowl for Far East gangster chic, Tarantino's Rolling Thunder brought this one to U.S. shores. Japanese with subtitles. **93m/C; VHS, DVD.** *JP* Takeshi "Beat" Kitano; Aya Kokumai; Tetsu Watanabe; Masanobu Katsumura; Susumu Terashima; Ren Osugi; Tonbo Zushi; Eiji Minakata; Kenichi Yajima; ***D:*** Takeshi "Beat" Kitano; ***W:*** Takeshi "Beat" Kitano; ***C:*** Katsumi Yanagishima; ***M:*** Jo Hasaishi.

A Song for Martin 1/2 *En Sang for Martin* 2001 (PG-13) Love found and lost but not in the usual way. Martin (Wolter) is a famous conductor/composer and Barbara (Seldahl) is his first violinist. Both are past middle-age and married but that doesn't stop them from falling deliriously in love, divorcing their spouses, and marrying each other. But Martin's memory soon begins to give him trouble and he is diagnosed with Alzheimer's, which causes him to push Barbara away. Swedish with subtitles. **118m/C; VHS, DVD.** *DK SW* Sven Wollter; Viveka Seldahl; Reine Brynolfsson; Linda Kallgren; Lisa Werlinder; ***D:*** Bille August; ***W:*** Bille August; ***C:*** Jorgen Persson; ***M:*** Stefan Nilsson.

A Song From the Heart 1/2 1999 CBS TV movie marked the acting debut of singer Amy Grant. Blind cellist Maryann (Grant) teaches at the local high school where famous pianist Gregory Pavan (Moffett) is working with her youth orchestra on a special concert. Despite their differences, Maryann and Greg start dating and he encourages her to undergo a cornea transplant that could restore her sight. Maryann is unaware that she has a more suitable suitor closer than she knows. **96m/C; DVD.** Amy Grant; D.W. Moffett; Keith Carradine; Alexandra Purvis; Charles Siegel; ***D:*** Marcus Cole; ***W:*** Giorgio Serafini; ***C:*** Attila Szalay; ***M:*** Patrick Williams. **TV**

A Song Is Born 1948 A group of music professors try to trace the history of music. Kaye is in charge of a U.S. music foundation whose research has led him up to ragtime. He is soon, however, thrust into the sometimes seedy world of jazz joints and night spots, all in the name of research. Enter love interest Mayo, a woman on the run from her gangster boyfriend who hides out at the foundation. Not one of Kaye's funniest or best, but if you enjoy big band music, you'll love this. Includes music by Louis Armstrong and his orchestra, Tommy Dorsey and his orchestra, and Charlie Barnet and his orchestra. This was Kaye's last film for Goldwyn. Part of the 'MGM Movie Collection: 10 Musicals' collection. **113m/B; DVD.** Danny Kaye; Virginia Mayo; Benny Goodman; Hugh Herbert; Steve Cochran; J. Edward Bromberg; Felix Bressart; ***D:*** Howard Hawks; ***W:*** Billy Wilder; Thomas Monroe; ***C:*** Gregg Toland; ***M:*** Hugo Friedhofer; Emil Newman.

Song o' My Heart 1930 Not so much a movie as an excuse for popular Irish tenor McCormack to perform some 11 songs. The singer makes his film debut as Sean O'Callaghan, who's in love with Mary (Joyce), a young lass forced into marriage with a wastrel who eventually leaves her with two kiddies. Sean unselfishly steps in to help out and then raises the tykes after Mary dies. **85m/B; DVD.** John McCormack; Alice Joyce; Maureen O'Sullivan; Tommy Clifford; John Garrick; J.M. Kerrigan; J. Farrell MacDonald; ***D:*** Frank Borzage; ***W:*** Sonya Levien; ***C:*** J.O. Taylor; Chester Lyons; Al Brick.

The Song of Bernadette 1943 Depicts the true story of a peasant girl who sees a vision of the Virgin Mary in a grotto at Lourdes in 1858. The girl is directed to dig at the grotto for water that will heal those who believe in its powers, much to the astonishment and concern of the townspeople. Based on Franz Werfel's novel. Directed with tenderness and carefully cast, and appealing to religious and sentimental susceptibilities, it was a boxoffice smash. **156m/B; VHS, DVD, Blu-Ray.** Charles Bickford; Lee J. Cobb; Jennifer Jones; Vincent Price; Anne Revere; Gladys Cooper; ***D:*** Henry King; ***C:*** Arthur C. Miller; ***M:*** Alfred Newman. Oscars '43: Actress (Jones), B&W Cinematog., Orig. Dramatic Score; Golden Globes '44: Actress--Drama (Jones), Director (King), Film--Drama.

Song of Freedom 1/2 1936 John Zinga (Robeson) is a British-born black dockworker whose voal gifts are discovered by an opera impresario. After realizing a career as a concert performer, Zinga ventures to Africa to investigate his ancestry and finds he has royal roots, and that his tribe have fallen under the grip of corrupt spiritualists. Robeson turns in a fine performance in what is otherwise an average film. **80m/B; VHS, DVD.** *GB* Paul Robeson; Elisabeth Welch; George Mozart; ***D:*** J. Elder Wills; ***W:*** Ingram D'Abbes; Fenn Sherie; ***C:*** Eric Cross; Harry Rose.

The Song of Hiawatha 1997 (PG) This Hallmark Channel movie is based on the epic poem by Henry Wadsworth Longfellow. Hiawatha is the legendary leader of the Ojibway and both French trader Bertrand and priest Marcel want a meeting to further their own ends with the natives. Their guide O Kagh leads them to Hiawatha's grandmother Nokomis and his mentor Iagoo, who are happy to share stories about his exploits but does Hiawatha still live? **120m/C; DVD.** *CA* Litefoot; Graham Greene; Michael Rooker; David Strathairn; Irene Bedard; Sheila Tousey; Gordon Tootoosis; Adam Beach; Russell Means; ***D:*** Jeffrey Shore; ***W:*** Earl W. Wallace; ***C:*** Curtis Petersen; ***M:*** Reg Powell. **CABLE**

A Song of Innocence *La Ravisseuse* 2005 In 1877, ambitious architect Julien (Colin) hires peasant girl Angele-Marie (Le Besco) to come to his country chateau as the wet nurse to his newborn daughter. His convent-bred wife Charlotte (Dequenne) is happy to forgo child-rearing and sex with her husband who wants a son and heir as soon as possible. Bored Charlotte, a teenager like Angele-Marie, soon begins to bond with her supposed servant, much to Julien's displeasure. French with subtitles. **90m/C; DVD.** *FR* Gregoire Colin; Islid Le Besco; Emilie Dequenne; Anemone; Frederic Pierrot; Bernard Blancan; ***D:*** Antoine Santana; ***W:*** Antoine Santana; ***C:*** Giorgos Arvanitis; ***M:*** Louis Sclavis.

Song of Love *A Love Story* 1947 Hepburn gracefully depicts the gifted 19th-century concert pianist Clara Wieck Schumann, who set aside her talents to be the wife of composer Robert Schumann and care for their seven children, which she did by herself after his untimely death in a mental facility. Clara shunned a marriage proposal from her deceased husband's star pupil, Johannes Brahms, who had long been infatuated with her, in order to dedicate her life to performing Schumann's works. **121m/B; VHS, DVD.** Katharine Hepburn; Paul Henreid; Robert Walker; Henry Daniell; Leo G. Carroll; Gigi Perreau; Ann Carter; Jimmy Hunt; Elsa (Else) Janssen; Janine Perreau; Eilene Janssen; Roman Bohnen; Ludwig Stossel; Tala Birell; Konstantin Shayne; Henry Stephenson; ***D:*** Clarence Brown; ***W:*** Robert Ardrey; Ivan Tors; Allen Vincent; ***C:*** Harry Stradling, Sr.

The Song of Names 2019 (PG-13) Before World War II breaks out, a young Jewish musical prodigy Dovidl (Doyle) is left in the care of the father of young Martin (Hindley). As Martin's father molds the violinist for a musical career, the boys become close friends.The evening that young adult Dovidl (Hauer-King) is supposed to appear in an important London performance, he disappears. Thirty years later, adult Martin (Roth), a music teacher, auditions a student that reminds him of Dovidl, compelling him to look for his long-lost friend. Based on a novel, it poignantly explores complex issues and features an outstanding performance by Roth. **113m/C; DVD, Blu-Ray.** Clive Owen; Tim Roth; Catherine McCormack; Jonah Hauer-King; Saul Rubinek; ***D:*** Francois Girard; ***W:*** Jeffrey Caine; ***C:*** David Franco; ***M:*** Howard Shore.

The Song of Songs 1/2 1933 Orphaned Lily (Dietrich) is living with her elderly Aunt Rasmussen (Skipworth) in Berlin and falling for sculptor, Richard (Aherne). He wants her to pose for a nude statue, based on the Song of Solomon, after getting a gander at Lily's legs. However, wealthy Baron von Merzbach (Atwill), who's Richard's art patron, eventually persuades both Aunt and Richard that Lily needs a better life than either can offer. Their marriage has the Baron making Lily over, so she'll socially be a worthy Baroness, but these situations never work out as anticipated. Based on the novel by Hermann Sudermann and the play by Edward Sheldon. **89m/B; DVD, Blu-Ray.** Marlene Dietrich; Brian Aherne; Lionel Atwill; Alison Skipworth; Hardie Albright; Helen Freeman; ***D:*** Rouben Mamoulian; ***W:*** Samuel Hoffenstein; Leo Birinski; ***C:*** Victor Milner; ***M:*** Karl Hajos; Milan Roder.

The Song of Sparrows 1/2 2008 Iranian slice of life. Rural ostrich wrangler Karim is fired after one of the birds escapes.

When his eldest daughter breaks her hearing aid, Karim is forced to go into Tehran for a replacement and suddenly finds himself working as a motorcycle taxi driver and succumbing to the lure of materialism. His wife strongly disapproves of the changes to his character and it takes a tragedy for Karim to realize what's important to his family. Farsi with subtitles. **96m/C; DVD.** *IA* Mohammad Reza Naji; Maryam Akbari; Shabnam Akhlaghi; Hamed Aghazi; ***D:*** Majid Majidi; ***W:*** Majid Majidi; Mehran Kashani; ***C:*** Tooraj Mansoouri; ***M:*** Hossein Alizadeh.

The Song of Sway Lake 1/2 **2018 (R)** In 1992, young Ollie Sway (Culkin) makes a plan to break into the lakehouse of his wealthy family to steal a rare recording of "The Song of Sway Lake" with the help of Russian friend Nikolai (Sheehan). Though they believe home is empty, they find some attractive locals on the property when they get there. The situation grows more complicated when Ollie's grandmother Charlie (Peil) and housekeeper Marlena (Pena) arrive a short time later. Writer/director Gold's ode to record collecting is an unfocused coming of age story but includes attractive scenery and a distinguished last performance by Pena. **100m/C; DVD.** Rory Culkin; Robert Sheehan; Isabelle McNally; Mary Beth Peil; Elizabeth Pena; ***D:*** Ari Gold; ***W:*** Ari Gold; Elizabeth Bull; ***C:*** Eric Lin; ***M:*** Ethan Gold.

The Song of the Lark 1/2 **2001** Thea Kronborg (Elliott) is a minister's daughter in 1890s Colorado who is encouraged by local doctor Howard Archie (Howard) to pursue her musical dreams. At first, Thea travels to Chicago to study piano but her teacher (Hules) realizes that Thea's true gift is her voice. Handsome brewery heir Fred Ottenburg (Goldwyn) offers to sponsor her career but their romance is rocky and Thea must eventually make her own way. Based on the novel by Willa Cather. **120m/C; VHS, DVD.** Alison Elliott; Arliss Howard; Tony Goldwyn; Maximilian Schell; Norman Lloyd; Robert Floyd; Endre Hules; Nan Martin; Christian Meoli; ***D:*** Karen Arthur; ***W:*** Joseph Maurer; ***M:*** Charles Fox. **TV**

Song of the Thin Man 1/2 **1947** The sixth and final "Thin Man" mystery. This time Nick and Nora Charles (Powell and Loy) investigate the murder of a bandleader. Somewhat more sophisticated than its predecessor, due in part to its setting in the jazz music world. Sequel to "The Thin Man Goes Home." **86m/B; VHS, DVD.** William Powell; Myrna Loy; Keenan Wynn; Dean Stockwell; Phillip Reed; Patricia Morison; Gloria Grahame; Jayne Meadows; Don Taylor; Leon Ames; Ralph Morgan; Warner Anderson; ***D:*** Edward Buzzell; ***C:*** Charles Rosher.

A Song to Remember **1945** With music performed by Jose Iturbi, this film depicts the last years of the great pianist and composer Frederic Chopin, including his affair with famous author George Sand, the most renowned French woman of her day. Typically mangled film biography. **112m/C; VHS, DVD, Streaming.** Cornel Wilde; Paul Muni; Merle Oberon; Nina Foch; George Coulouris; ***D:*** Charles Vidor; ***C:*** Gaetano Antonio "Tony" Gaudio; ***M:*** Miklos Rozsa.

Song to Song 1/2 **2017 (R)** Mara, Gosling, Fassbender, and Portman star in this love story between two entangled couples set in Austin, Texas, one of the indie music/film capitals of the world. Once an elusive filmmaker, Malick has become one of our most prolific, releasing a new film almost every year. This effort is just as divisive as you'd expect from a filmmaker getting less interested in traditional plotting as he gets older. Malick's style is more improvisational, defying anyone looking for clear themes or even a traditional plot, but he remains mesmerizing for those on his wavelength. **129m/C; DVD, Blu-Ray.** Ryan Gosling; Rooney Mara; Michael Fassbender; Natalie Portman; Cate Blanchett; ***D:*** Terrence Malick; ***W:*** Terrence Malick; ***C:*** Emmanuel Lubezki.

Song Without End 1/2 **1960** This musical biography of 19th century Hungarian pianist/composer Franz Lizst is given the Hollywood treatment. The lavish production emphasizes Liszt's scandalous exploits with married women and his life among the royal courts of Europe rather than his musical talents. Features music from several composers including Handel, Beethoven, Bach and Schumann. This film marked the debut of Capucine. Director Vidor died during filming and Cukor stepped in, so there is a noticeable change in style. Although there is much to criticize in the story, the music is beautiful. **130m/C; VHS, DVD.** Dirk Bogarde; Capucine; Genevieve Page; Patricia Morison; Ivan Desny; Martita Hunt; Lou Jacobi; ***D:*** Charles Vidor; George Cukor; ***C:*** James Wong Howe; ***M:*** Morris Stoloff; Harry Sukman. Oscars '60: Scoring/Musical; Golden Globes '61: Film--Mus./Comedy.

Songcatcher **1999** Turn-of-the-century musicologist Dr. Lily Penleric (McTeer) heads for Appalachia in a huff after the all-male review board of the East Coast university where she teaches refuses to grant her tenure. She begins teaching at her sister Elna's (Adams) mountain school, harboring a superior attitude toward the rubes she's teaching. She discovers to her amazement that the songs the rustic people sing, dance and live to are barely altered from the time they were brought over from Europe. She rushes to record the native folk music, but meets resistance from local Tom (Quinn) who feels that if the hillbillies have something civilized folk want, they should be payed for it. Excellent performances and visuals throughout. **113m/C; VHS, DVD.** Janet McTeer; Aidan Quinn; Pat Carroll; Jane Adams; Emmy Rossum; Mike Harding; Iris DeMent; Greg Cook; David Patrick Kelly; E. Katherine Kerr; Taj Mahal; Muse Watson; Stephanie Ross; ***D:*** Maggie Greenwald; ***W:*** Maggie Greenwald; ***C:*** Enrique Chediak; ***M:*** David Mansfield.

Songs My Brother Taught Me **2015** The unexpected death of Johnny's absentee father compels the young adult to make plans to leave his home on the reservation, his single mother, and his beloved sister Jashuan for a new life in Los Angeles. **98m/C; DVD.** John Reddy; Jashaun St. John; Irene Bedard; Kevin Hunter; Taysha Fuller; ***D:*** Chloé Zhao; ***W:*** Chloé Zhao; ***C:*** Joshua James Richards; ***M:*** Peter Golub.

Songwriter 1/2 **1984 (R)** A high-falutin' look at the lives and music of two popular country singers with, aptly, plenty of country tunes written and performed by the stars. Singer-businessman Nelson needs Kristofferson's help keeping a greedy investor at bay. Never mind the plot; plenty of good music. **94m/C; VHS, DVD, Blu-Ray.** Willie Nelson; Kris Kristofferson; Rip Torn; Melinda Dillon; Lesley Ann Warren; ***D:*** Alan Rudolph.

Sonic Impact 1/2 **1999 (R)** Nutjob hijacks an airliner and threatens to crash it into the nearest large city. So a group of commandoes led by Nick Halton (Russo) makes plans to stop him. **94m/C; VHS, DVD.** James Russo; Ice-T; Mel Harris; ***D:*** Rodney McDonald. **VIDEO**

Sonic the Hedgehog 1/2 **2020 (PG)** Sonic, a super-speedy blue hedgehog from another planet, befriends Tom (Marsden), and the duo must stay one step ahead of evil scientist Dr. Robotnik (Carrey), who wants to capture Sonic and harness his powers for world domination. The live action/animation combination is fun enough for the kiddos, even if they're not familiar with its videogame inspiration, and Jim Carrey's classic wackiness is a pleasure for all ages to behold. **99m/C; DVD, Blu-Ray.** *CA JP US* James Marsden; Jim Carrey; Tika Sumpter; Natasha Rothwell; ***V:*** Ben Schwartz; ***D:*** Jeff Fowler; ***W:*** Patrick Casey; Josh Miller; ***C:*** Stephen F. Windon; ***M:*** Junkie XL.

Sonny **2002 (R)** Cage's directorial debut is about one man's frustrated attempts at leaving a life of crime. In 1981 New Orleans, Sonny (Franco) is fresh out of the Army and hopeful about working in his buddy's Texas bookstore. His corrupt pimp mother Jewel (Blethyn) would rather him reenter the family business and attempts to fix him up with Carol (Suvari), one of her new "girls." The two fall in love and, after a disastrous encounter with the "straight" world, Sonny descends back into the life he once dreamed of leaving for good. Stanton is in his element, underplaying the good-hearted, drunk boyfriend of Jewel while Cage makes an amusing appearance as Acid Yellow, a gay pimp. Heavy handed and overly emotional (the hysterical Blethyn is practically unwatchable), with an uneven rhythm and not a lot of explanation. Cage falls victim to first-time indulgence, but respectable narrative manages to make its point. **105m/C; VHS, DVD.** James Franco; Mena Suvari; Brenda Blethyn; Harry Dean Stanton; Nicolas Cage; Seymour Cassel; Brenda Vaccaro; Scott Caan; ***D:*** Nicolas Cage; ***W:*** John Carlen; ***C:*** Barry Markowitz; ***M:*** Clint Mansell.

Sonny and Jed *La Banda J.&S. Cronaca Criminale del Far West* **1973 (R)** An escaped convict and a free-spirited woman travel across Mexico pillaging freely, followed determinedly by shiny-headed lawman Savalas. Lame rip-off of the Bonnie and Clyde legend. **85m/C; VHS, DVD.** *IT* Tomas Milian; Telly Savalas; Susan George; Rosanna Janni; Laura Betti; ***D:*** Sergio Corbucci; ***M:*** Ennio Morricone.

Sons and Lovers **1960** Character-driven, fairly faithful adaptation of the 1913 D.H. Lawrence novel set in the coal mining town of Nottinghamshire. Sensitive Paul Morel (Stockwell) wishes to become an artist in London, something his hard-drinking miner father, Walter (Howard), doesn't understand though his ambitious yet possessive mother Gertrude (Hiller) encourages him. Paul dallies with religious farm girl Miriam (Sears) and has an affair with suffragette Clara (Ure) while trying to loosen his mother's grasp. Stockwell, the only American in the cast, is somewhat out of his depth, but his callowness is lessened by the British actors. **102m/B; DVD.** *UK* Dean Stockwell; Mary Ure; Trevor Howard; Wendy Hiller; Heather Sears; Conrad Phillips; ***D:*** Jack Cardiff; ***W:*** Gavin Lambert; T.E.B. Clarke; ***C:*** Freddie Francis; ***M:*** Mario Nascimbene. Oscars '60: Cinematog. (Francis).

Sons of Katie Elder **1965** After their mother's death, four brothers are reunited. Wayne is a gunman; Anderson is a college graduate; silent Holliman is a killer; and Martin is a gambler. When they learn that her death might have been linked to their father's murder, they come together to devise a way to seek revenge on the killer. The town bullies complicate matters; the sheriff tells them to lay off. Especially strong screen presence by Wayne, in his first role following cancer surgery. One of the Duke's most popular movies of the '60s. **122m/C; VHS, DVD.** John Wayne; Dean Martin; Earl Holliman; Michael Anderson, Jr.; Martha Hyer; George Kennedy; Dennis Hopper; Paul Fix; James Gregory; ***D:*** Henry Hathaway; ***W:*** Harry Essex; Allan Weiss; William Wright; ***C:*** Lucien Ballard; ***M:*** Elmer Bernstein.

Sons of the Desert *Sons of the Legion; Convention City; Fraternally Yours* **1933** Laurel and Hardy in their best-written film. The boys try to fool their wives by pretending to go to Hawaii to cure Ollie of a bad cold when in fact, they are attending their lodge convention in Chicago. Also includes a 1935 Thelma Todd/Patsy Kelly short, "Top Flat." **73m/B; VHS, DVD.** Stan Laurel; Oliver Hardy; Mae Busch; Charley Chase; Dorothy Christy; ***D:*** William A. Seiter; ***W:*** Frank Craven; ***C:*** Kenneth Peach, Sr. Natl. Film Reg. '12.

Sons of Trinity **1995 (PG)** The two sons, Bambino (Neubert) and Trinity (Kizzier), of legendary cowpokes first meet when Bambino is about to be hung for horse thieving in the town of San Clementino. When Trinity gets his new friend off, they wind up as sheriff and deputy of the same town. Lots of physical comedy. **90m/C; VHS, DVD.** Heath Kizzier; Keith Neubert; Ronald Nitschke; Siegfried Rauch; ***D:*** E.B. (Enzo Barboni) Clucher; ***C:*** Juan Amoros; ***M:*** Stefano Mainetti.

The Son's Room *La Stanza del Figlio* **2000** Giovanni (Moretti) is a psychiatrist in a provincial seaside town, with a wife, Paola (Morante), and two teenage children—Irene (Trinca) and Andrea (Sanfelice). Their average lives are suddenly shattered when Andrea dies in a diving accident. The family falls apart and begins to distance themselves from each other and their grief. By accident, Arianna (Vigliar), a casual girlfriend of Andrea's who doesn't know about his death, contacts the family and surprisingly becomes a link to help heal. Italian with subtitles. **99m/C; VHS, DVD.** *IT FR* Nanni Moretti; Laura Morante; Giuseppe Sanfelice; Jasmine Trinca; Stefano Accorsi; Sofia Vigliar; Silvio Orlando; Claudia Della Seta; ***D:*** Nanni Moretti; ***W:*** Nanni Moretti; Linda Ferri; Heidrun Schleef; ***C:*** Giuseppe Lanci; ***M:*** Nicola Piovani. Cannes '01: Film.

Sooner or Later 1/2 **1978** 13-year-old girl passes herself off as 16 with a local rock idol and must decide whether to go all the way. **100m/C; VHS, DVD.** Rex Smith; Judd Hirsch; Denise Miller; Morey Amsterdam; Lynn Redgrave; ***D:*** Bruce Hart. **TV**

Sophie Scholl: The Final Days *Sophie Scholl: Die Letzten Tage* **2005** Documentary traces the five days prior to the killing of University of Munich students Sophie Scholl (Jentsch) and her brother Hans (Hinrichs) in 1943 by German Nazis for their rebellious behavior in distributing anti-war literature at the school. Powerful interrogation scenes between Sophie and General Alexander Held (Mohr), as her quiet determination affects the general. Whatever empathy he feels can't change her inevitable fate. **117m/C; DVD.** Julia Jentsch; Alexander Held; Fabian Hinrichs; Joanna Gastdorf; Andre Hennicke; Florian Stetter; ***D:*** Marc Rothemund; ***W:*** Fred Breinersdorfer; ***C:*** Martin Langer; ***M:*** Johnny Klimek; Reinhold Heil.

Sophie's Choice 1/2 **1982 (R)** A haunting modern tragedy about Sophie Zawistowska, a beautiful Polish Auschwitz survivor settled in Brooklyn after WWII. She has intense relationships with a schizophrenic genius and an aspiring Southern writer. An artful, immaculately performed and resonant drama, with an astonishing, commanding performance by the versatile Streep; a chilling portrayal of the banality of evil. From the best-selling, autobiographical novel by William Styron. **157m/C; VHS, DVD, Blu-Ray.** Meryl Streep; Kevin Kline; Peter MacNichol; Rita Karin; Stephen D. Newman; Josh Mostel; ***D:*** Alan J. Pakula; ***W:*** Alan J. Pakula; ***C:*** Nestor Almendros; ***M:*** Marvin Hamlisch. Oscars '82: Actress (Streep); Golden Globes '83: Actress--Drama (Streep); L.A. Film Critics '82: Actress (Streep); Natl. Bd. of Review '82: Actress (Streep); N.Y. Film Critics '82: Actress (Streep), Cinematog.; Natl. Soc. Film Critics '82: Actress (Streep).

Sorcerer 1/2 *Wages of Fear* **1977 (PG)** To put out an oil fire, four men on the run in South America agree to try to buy their freedom by driving trucks loaded with nitroglycerin over dangerous terrain--with many natural and man-made obstacles to get in their way. Remake of "The Wages of Fear" is nowhere as good as the classic original, but has exciting moments. Puzzlingly retitled, which may have contributed to the boxoffice failure, and the near demise of Friedkin's directing career. **121m/C; VHS, DVD, Blu-Ray.** Roy Scheider; Bruno Cremer; Francisco Rabal; Soudad Amidou; Ramon Bieri; ***D:*** William Friedkin; ***W:*** Walon Green; ***C:*** Dick Bush; John Stephens; ***M:*** Tangerine Dream.

The Sorcerer and the White Snake 1/2 *Bai She Chuan Shuo* **2013 (PG-13)** Sorcerer Abott Fahai (Li) discovers that a thousand-year-old White Snake is masquerading as a beautiful woman (Huang). As she attempts to trap an unsuspecting herbalist who's smitten with her, the sorcerer is the only one who stands in her way. More wire-fu action, more CGI backgrounds, the whole thing just gets kind of silly for anyone not completely devoted to seeing all of the martial arts fantasy flicks ever made. As for Li, it only reminds the viewer of better Li flicks they could be watching. **100m/C; DVD, Blu-Ray.** *CH HK* Jet Li; Eva Huang; Raymond Lam; Charlene (Cheuk-Yin) Choi; ***D:*** Siu-Tung Ching; ***W:*** Tan Zhang; ***C:*** Kwok-Man Keung; ***M:*** Mark Lui.

The Sorcerers **1967** Low-budget Brit cult horror. Elderly hypnotist Marcus Monserrat (Karloff) invents a mind control machine that allows the user to experience the sensations of the subject. He lures bored, young Mike Roscoe (Ogilvy) to be his guinea pig but Monserrat's crazy wife Estelle (lacey) doesn't care about the potential scientific benefits. She uses Mike as a pawn to commit crimes while he experiences blackouts. **87m/C; DVD.** *UK* Boris Karloff; Ian Ogilvy; Catherine Lacey; Elizabeth Ercy; Victor Henry; Susan George; ***D:*** Michael Reeves; ***W:*** Michael Reeves; ***C:*** Stanley Long; ***M:*** Paul Ferris.

The Sorcerer's Apprentice 1/2 **2010 (PG)** Disney's modern-day tale of master sorcerer Balthazar Blake (Cage) striving to defend Manhattan from an apocalyptic war with archenemy Maxim Horvath (Molina). Balthazar recruits hapless and reluctant 10-year-old Dave (Baruchel) as his apprentice and gives him a crash course in magic. Cut to a now 20-year-old Dave coming of age with sorcery and in love with his childhood crush Becky (Palmer). Cage plays up his standard high-spirited neurotic schtick but Baruchel mostly annoys. Big and explosive, like most Bruckheimer efforts, but falls flat once the special effects take over. Takes many of its cues from the Mickey Mouse "Fantasia" segment. **111m/C; Blu-Ray.** Nicolas Cage; Jay Baruchel; Alfred Molina; Monica Bellucci; Toby Kebbell; ***D:*** Jon Turteltaub; ***W:*** Matt Lopez; Doug Miro; Carlo Bernard; ***C:*** Bojan Bazelli; ***M:*** Trevor Rabin.

Sorceress *Le Moine et la Sorciere* **1988** A friar in medieval Europe feels insecure in his religious beliefs after encountering a woman who heals through ancient practices. Historically authentic and interestingly moody. Written, produced, and directed by two women: an art history professor and a collaborator of Francois Truffaut's. In French with English subtitles or dubbed. **98m/C; VHS, DVD.** *FR* Tcheky Karyo; Christine Boisson; Jean Carmet; Raoul Billerey; Catherine Frot; Feodor Atkine; ***D:*** Suzanne Schiffman; ***W:*** Pamela Berger; Suzanne Schiffman; ***C:*** Patrick Blossier.

Sorceress 1/2 **1994 (R)** Larry Barnes (Poindexter) is on his way to a partnership at his law firm, especially since his wife Erica (Strain) eliminates his competition—permanently. But Erica goes after the wrong guy when she comes up against Howard Reynolds (Albert). Seems Howard's loving spouse Amelia (Blair) happens to be a witch and she has her own evil spells to cast. **93m/C; VHS, DVD, Blu-Ray.** Julie Strain; Larry Poindexter; Linda Blair; Edward Albert; ***D:*** Jim Wynorski; ***W:*** Mark Thomas McGee; ***C:*** Gary Graver; ***M:*** Chuck Cirino; Darryl Way.

Sordid Lives **2000** Shores adapted his play but the comedy goes flat before the finale. Texas matriarch Peggy dies (under scandalous circumstances) and her dysfunctional family goes into hyperdrive. There's proper daughter Latrelle (Bedelia) who can't accept that her actor son Ty (Geiger) is gay, probably because her own brother—known only as Brother Boy (Jordan)?is a drag queen confined to a mental institution. But brassy sister LaVonda (Walker) still thinks he should come to the funeral. And there's Aunt Sissy (Grant) and G.W. (Bridges), who was having an affair with Peggy, and his wife Noleta (Burke), who's LaVonda's best friend and...it just kinda goes on and on. **111m/C; VHS, DVD, Blu-Ray.** Bonnie Bedelia; Beth Grant; Delta Burke; Ann Walker; Leslie Jordan; Beau Bridges; Kirk Giger; Rosemary Alexander; Olivia Newton-John; ***D:*** Del Shores; ***W:*** Del Shores; ***C:*** Max CiVon; ***M:*** George S. Clinton.

Sorority Babes in the Slimeball Bowl-A-Rama *The Imp* **1987 (R)** An ancient gremlin-type creature is released from a bowling alley, and the great-looking sorority babes have to battle it at the mall, with the help of a wacky crew of nerds. Horrible horror spoof shows plenty of skin. **80m/C; DVD, Blu-Ray.** Linnea Quigley; Brinke Stevens; Andras Jones; John Wildman; Robin Rochelle; Michelle (McClellan) Bauer; George "Buck" Flower; ***V:*** Michael Sonye; ***D:*** David DeCoteau; ***W:*** Sergei Hasenecz; ***C:*** Scott Ressler; Stephen Blake; ***M:*** Guy Moon.

Sorority Boys **2002 (R)** Three frat boys (Williams, Rosenbaum and Watson) become bosom buddies when they don girlish garb to pass as sorority sisters in this contrived campus comedy. After being accused of a theft in their frat house, the badly disguised trio head to the notorious loser Delta Omega Gamma (DOG) house to stay in school. The boys teeter in their high heels, can't find dresses big enough for their ample "cabooses," and generally begin to understand the drag of being a gal while the film continues to serve up a kegful of gross-out and misogynist humor. Another in a string of misguided homages to "Animal House," with alums Daughton, Metcalf, Furst, and Vernon showing up for paychecks. Although Williams is considered to be the best of the three leads, all are terrible. Tepid romantic subplot with DOG house president doesn't help matters any. **93m/C; VHS, DVD.** Barry Watson; Michael Rosenbaum; Harland Williams; Melissa Sagemiller; Tony Denman; Brad Beyer; Heather Matarazzo; Kathryn Stockwood; Yvonne Scio; ***D:*** M. Wallace Wolodarsky; ***W:*** Joe Jarvis; Greg Coolidge; ***C:*** Michael D. O'Shea; ***M:*** Mark Mothersbaugh.

Sorority House Massacre WOOF! 1986 (R) A knife-wielding maniac stalks a sorority girl while her more elite sisters are away for the weekend. Yawn—haven't we seen this one before? Unfortunately for us we'll see it again because this one's followed by a sequel. **74m/C; VHS, DVD.** Angela O'Neill; Wendy Martel; Pamela Ross; Nicole Rio; ***D:*** Carol Frank; ***W:*** Carol Frank; ***C:*** Marc Reshovsky; ***M:*** Michael Wetherwax.

Sorority House Massacre 2: Nighty Nightmare WOOF! 1992 Another no-brainer with a different cast and director. This time around three lingerie-clad lovelies are subjected to the terrors of a killer their first night in their new sorority house. College just keeps getting tougher all the time. **80m/C; VHS, DVD.** Melissa Moore; Robin Harris; Stacia Zhivago; Dana Bentley; Shannon Wilsey; ***D:*** Jim Wynorski; ***W:*** James B. Rogers; Bob Sheridan; ***M:*** Chuck Cirino.

Sorority House Vampires 1/2 **1995** Sexy college coed Buffy fights to save her man and her sorority from Natalia, Queen of Darkness, and Count Vlad. **90m/C; VHS, DVD.** Eugenie Bondurant; Robert Bucholz; Kathy Presgrave; ***D:*** Geoffrey De Vallois. **VIDEO**

Sorority Row *The House on Sorority Row* **2009 (R)** A group of Theta Pi seniors try to teach their sister Megan's (Partridge) cheating boyfriend (Lanter) a lesson during pledge week through an elaborate hoax in which Megan's death is staged. Naturally the hoax goes horribly wrong when the freaked out boyfriend plunges a tire iron into her chest. Now with a body to deal with, frosty head sister Jessica (Pipes) invokes the sorority value of secrecy. But eight months later as graduation nears, one by one the sisters are dealt retribution for their ghastly scheme. Carrie Fisher as housemother Mrs. Crenshaw is a treat, but this remake of the 1983 slasher falls short, wobbling between gags and horrors. In the end it seems the boobs were on both sides of the camera. **101m/C; Blu-Ray, On Demand.** Briana Evigan; Rumer Willis; Julian Morris; Leah Pipes; Margo Harshman; Jamie Chung; Audrina Patridge; Carrie Fisher; ***D:*** Stewart Hendler; ***W:*** Peter Goldfinger; Josh Stolberg; Mark Rosman; ***C:*** Ken Seng; ***M:*** Lucian Piane.

Sorority Wars 1/2 **2009** Predictable and sporadically amusing mom-and-daughter Lifetime flick. Katie (Hale) is expected to pledge the Delta sorority, which her overly-involved mom Lutie (Thorne-Smith) helped found. But Katie, dismayed by mean girl Gwen's (Schull) house domination, pledges rival Kappa instead, which places strains in her relationships at home and at college. **90m/C; DVD.** Lucy Kate Hale; Courtney Thorne-Smith; Amanda Schull; Faith Ford; Phoebe Strole; Kristen Hager; ***D:*** James Hayman; ***W:*** Michelle A. Lovretta; ***C:*** Neil Roach; ***M:*** Danny Luz. **CABLE**

The Sorrow and the Pity 1/2 **1971** A classic documentary depicting the life of a small French town and its resistance during the Nazi occupation. Lengthy, but totally compelling. A great documentary that brings home the atrocities of war. In French with English narration. **265m/B; VHS, DVD.** *FR* Pierre Mendes-France; Sir Anthony Eden; Dr. Claude Levy; Denis Rake; Louis Grave; Maurice Chevalier; ***D:*** Marcel Ophuls; ***C:*** Mandre Gazut; Jurgen Thieme.

Sorrowful Jones **1949** A "Little Miss Marker" remake, in which bookie Hope inherits a little girl as collateral for an unpaid bet. Good for a few yuks, but the original is much better. **88m/B; VHS, DVD.** Bob Hope; Lucille Ball; William Demarest; Bruce Cabot; Thomas Gomez; Mary Jane Saunders; ***D:*** Sidney Lanfield; ***W:*** Jack Rose; Melville Shavelson; ***C:*** Daniel F. Fapp.

Sorry, Haters **2005** Behaving erratically, New York cable TV executive Phoebe (Wright Penn) hops into a cab driven by Ashade (Kechiche) to head to her ex-husband's house in Jersey seeking to get even with him for remarrying and taking everything. A chemist in his homeland, Ashade is suffering too, as the Syrian Muslim's brother is being unjustly held at Guantanamo, unable to enter the country. But his compassion for her and belief that she could help him are horribly misguided. Wright Penn and Kechiche are solid in this uneven look at post-9/11 culture and attitudes. **83m/C; DVD.** Robin Wright; Abdellatif Kechiche; Sandra Oh; Elodie Bouchez; Aasif Mandvi; Remy K. Selma; Fred Durst; ***D:*** Jeff Stanzler; ***W:*** Jeff Stanzler; ***C:*** Mauricio Rubinstein; ***M:*** Raz Mesinai.

Sorry to Bother You 1/2 **2018 (R)** A social satire/comedy/fantasy exploration of identity politics focused on a young African-American trying to make his mark. Cassius "Cash" Green (Stanfield) longs to do something important, but cannot even pay his rent. Taking a telemarketing job, Cash finds success when he follows the advice of fellow telemarketer Langston (Glover) to use his "white voice." As Cash becomes more successful, he abandons his unionizing coworkers and loses his artist girlfriend Detroit (Thompson) as he comes under the Faustian grip of company owner Steve Lift (Hammer). The film is a brilliant exploration of racial and social issues, tinged with magic realism, and featuring pitch perfect performances. **105m/C; DVD, Blu-Ray.** Lakeith Stanfield; Tessa Thompson; Armie Hammer; Terry Crews; Steven Yeun; ***D:*** Boots Riley; ***W:*** Boots Riley; ***C:*** Doug Emmett; ***M:*** Boots Riley; Tune-Yards; Merrill Garbus; The Coup.

Sorry We Missed You **2020** This drama, its title taken from those attempted delivery notes left on doors, is a heartfelt account of a family struggling financially in England. In a shiny new van, Ricky (Hitchen) ventures out as a self-employed delivery man, while his wife Abbie (Honeywood) toils thanklessly as a homecare provider. This commentary on the plight of ordinary workers doesn't pull any punches; its rage and emotion are dolled out in equal measure. **101m/C; DVD.** Kris Hitchen; Debbie Honeywood; Rhys Stone; Katie Proctor; Ross Brewster; ***D:*** Ken Loach; ***W:*** Paul Laverty; ***C:*** Robbie Ryan; ***M:*** George Fenton.

Sorry, Wrong Number 1/2 **1948** A wealthy, bedridden wife overhears two men plotting a murder on a crossed telephone line, and begins to suspect that one of the voices is her husband's. A classic tale of paranoia and suspense. Based on a radio drama by Louise Fletcher, who also wrote the screenplay. Remade for TV in 1989. **89m/B; VHS, DVD.** Barbara Stanwyck; Burt Lancaster; Ann Richards; Wendell Corey; Harold Vermilyea; Ed Begley, Sr.; ***D:*** Anatole Litvak; ***W:*** Lucille Fletcher; ***C:*** Sol Polito; ***M:*** Franz Waxman.

Sorted 1/2 **2004** Compelled by his brother's odd drowning death in London, Carl noses around only to become consumed with the same wild party scene that could lead him to a similar demise. **105m/C; VHS, DVD.** Matthew Rhys; Sienna Guillory; Fay Masterson; Tim Curry; Jason Donovan; Stephen Marcus; ***D:*** Alexander Jovy; ***W:*** Malcolm Campbell; Alexander Jovy; Christian Spurrier; Nick Villiers; ***C:*** Mike Southon; ***M:*** Guy Farley. **VIDEO**

S.O.S. Coast Guard 1/2 **1937** A fiendish scientist creates a disintegrating gas and the U.S. Coast Guard must stop him from turning it over to unfriendly foreigners. Loads of action in this 12-part serial. **224m/B; VHS, DVD.** Ralph Byrd; Bela Lugosi; Maxine Doyle; Richard Alexander; Lawrence Grant; Thomas Carr; Lee Ford; John Picorri; George Chesebro; ***D:*** Alan James; William Witney; ***W:*** Frank (Franklyn) Adreon; Winston Miller; Barry Shipman; ***C:*** William Nobles.

S.O.S. Iceberg *S.O.S. Eisberg* **1933** A note that washes up on a piece of jetsam asks for rescue for an exploratory team thought long dead near Greenland. Their rescue team soon winds up in trouble itself. It's most notable for being an American/German co-production before WWII and for co-starring Riefenstahl, who would infamously direct Nazi propaganda films. **90m/B; DVD.** Rod La Rocque; Leni Riefenstahl; Sepp Rist; Gibson Gowland; ***D:*** Tay Garnett; ***W:*** Tom Reed; ***C:*** Richard Angst; ***M:*** Paul Dessau.

S.O.S. Pacific **1960** A seaplane crashes on a nuclear-test island and the survivors find that they have only five hours before they get nuked. Even though there is plenty of the usual action one would expect from such a film, the story really revolves around the characters. The British and U.S. versions have different endings. **91m/B; VHS, DVD.** *GB* Eddie Constantine; Pier Angeli; Richard Attenborough; John Gregson; Eva Bartok; ***D:*** Guy Green.

S.O.S. Titanic 1/2 **1979** The story of the Titanic disaster, recounted in flashback, in docu-drama style. James Costigan's teleplay of the familiar story focuses on the courage that accompanied the horror and tragedy. Thoroughly professional, absorbing TV drama. **102m/C; VHS, DVD.** *GB* David Janssen; Cloris Leachman; Susan St. James; David Warner; Ian Holm; Dame Helen Mirren; Harry Andrews; David Battley; Ed Bishop; Peter Bourke; Shevaun Briars; Nick Brimble; Jacob Brooke; Catherine Byrne; Tony Caunter; Warren Clarke; Nicholas Davies; Deborah Fallender; Beverly Ross; ***D:*** William (Billy) Hale; ***W:*** James Costigan; ***C:*** Christopher Challis; ***M:*** Howard Blake. **TV**

Soul Assassin **2001 (R)** Kevin Burke (Ulrich) works for the security branch of an international investment bank in Rotterdam. He's been mentored by the bank's managing director, Karl Jorgensen (de Lint), much to the disgust of Jorgensen own son, Karl, Jr. (Kamerling). When Kevin's fiancee Rosalind (Lang) is assassinated, Kevin discovers he didn't know her as well as he thought. Seems she was involved in money laundering and corporate espionage. While Kevin seeks the truth, mystery woman Tessa (Swanson) is shadowing him—is she friend or foe? **97m/C; VHS, DVD.** *NL* Skeet Ulrich; Kristy Swanson; Derek de Lint; Antoine Kamerling; Rena Owen; Serge-Henri Valcke; Thom Hoffman; Katherine Lang; Pierre Allard; ***D:*** Laurence Malkin; ***W:*** Laurence Malkin; Chad Thurman; ***C:*** Lex Wertwijn; ***M:*** Alan Williams.

Soul Food 1/2 **1997 (R)** In between the mouth watering servings of fried-chicken, collard greens and catfish unfolds the lives of sisters Williams, Fox, and Long. They struggle to hold their family together by keeping up their mother's Sunday dinner tradition after she becomes ill. As mom's health deteriorates, so do the sisters' relationships with their significant others, turning things a bit soapy and predictable. Unfulfilling appetizer for those looking for a stark urban drama, but with an attractive ensemble cast which brings to life truthful characters, it's a hearty feast for those hungry for a heartwarming, contemporary tale. Warmth and humor won over audiences across color lines. Boasts many promising debuts, including director/writer Tillman and young narrator Hammond. Produced by music producer Kenneth (Babyface) Edmonds. **114m/C; VHS, DVD.** Vanessa L(ynne) Williams; Vivica A. Fox; Nia Long; Michael Beach; Mekhi Phifer; Irma P. Hall; Jeffrey D. Sams; Gina Ravera; Brandon Hammond; Carl Wright; Mel Jackson; Morgan Michelle Smith; John M. Watson, Sr.; ***D:*** George Tillman, Jr.; ***W:*** George Tillman, Jr.; ***C:*** Paul Elliott; ***M:*** Wendy Melvoin; Lisa Coleman.

The Soul Guardians 1/2 *Toemarok* **1998** In a bizarre religious mix from Korea, a satanic cult commits suicide during a raid while one of their members gives birth to a girl before dying. The girl grows up to be a telepathic car mechanic before being told she was intended to be possessed by Satan who needs her body to successfully reincarnate. Defending her are a fallen priest, a video-gamer with magical powers, and a warrior whose knife has a mind of its own. Not quite as bad as it sounds but no classic of the genre. **96m/C; DVD.** *NK* Hyeon-jun Shin; Sang-mi Choo; Sung-kee Ahn; Hyun-chul Oh; ***D:*** Kwang-chun Park; ***W:*** K.C. Park; Kwang-chun Park; Woo-hyouk Lee; ***C:*** Hyeon-cheol Park; ***M:*** Dong-jun Lee.

Soul Hustler WOOF! 1976 (PG) A con man becomes rich and famous as a tent-show evangelist. Pathetic drivel. **81m/C; VHS, DVD.** Fabian; Casey Kasem; Larry Bishop; Nai Bonet; ***D:*** Burt Topper.

Soul Man **1986 (PG-13)** Denied the funds he expected for his Harvard tuition, a young white student (Howell) masquerades as a black in order to get a minority scholarship. As a black student at Harvard, Howell learns about racism and bigotry. Pleasant lightweight comedy with romance thrown in (Chong is the black girl he falls for), and with pretensions to social satire that it never achieves. **112m/C; VHS, DVD.** C. Thomas Howell; Rae Dawn Chong; James Earl Jones; Leslie Nielsen; Arye Gross; ***D:*** Steve Miner; ***W:*** Carol Black; ***C:*** Jeffrey Jur; ***M:*** Tom Scott.

Soul Men ½ **2008 (R)** Louis Hinds (Jackson) and Floyd Henderson (Mac) are former backup singers for a 1970s soul act whose lead singer left them for a solo career. Fast-forward to present and their former bandmate has just died, prompting a tribute concert. Louis and Floyd agree to drive cross-country to participate in the concert after more than 20 years of estrangement, which might have something to do with a stolen girlfriend. Basically on a road trip, the two stop to perform along the way as they alternately blow-up and make-up. Much of the plot and gags are pure formula, but Jackson and Mac rise above the predictability to deliver memorable performances. Not the best movie but worth a viewing to see the much-missed Bernie Mac in a performance filmed just months before his untimely death. **100m/C; Blu-Ray, On Demand.** Samuel L. Jackson; Bernie Mac; Isaac Hayes; Sharon Leal; Adam Herschman; Sean P. Hayes; Johnny (Martin Margulies) Legend; Jennifer Coolidge; Mike Epps; Affion Crockett; ***D:*** Malcolm Lee; ***W:*** Robert Ramsey; Matthew Stone; ***C:*** Matthew F. Leonetti; ***M:*** Stanley Clarke.

Soul of the Beast ½ **1923** An elephant repeatedly saves Bellamy from the villainous Beery. Silent with original organ score. **77m/B; Silent; VHS, DVD.** Madge Bellamy; Cullen Landis; Noah Beery, Sr.; ***D:*** John Griffith Wray; ***W:*** Ralph Dixon; ***C:*** Henry Sharp.

Soul of the Game **1996 (PG-13)** Cable movie follows the lives of three talented players in the Negro League during the 1945 season as they await the potential integration of baseball. Brooklyn Dodgers general manager Branch Rickey (Herrmann) has his scouts focusing on three men in particular: flashy, aging pitcher Satchel Paige (Lindo), mentally unstable catcher Josh Gibson (Williamson), and the young, college-educated Jackie Robinson (Underwood). Manages to resist melodrama through terrific performances. **105m/C; VHS, DVD.** Delroy Lindo; Mykelti Williamson; Blair Underwood; Edward Herrmann; R. Lee Ermey; Gina Ravera; Salli Richardson-Whitfield; Obba Babatunde; Brent Jennings; Edwin Morrow; Richard Riehle; ***D:*** Kevin Rodney Sullivan; ***W:*** David Himmelstein; ***C:*** Sandi Sissel; ***M:*** Lee Holdridge. **CABLE**

Soul Patrol **1980 (R)** Black newspaper reporter clashes with the all-white police department in a racist city. **90m/C; VHS, DVD.** Nigel Davenport; Ken Gampu; Peter Dyneley; ***D:*** Christopher Rowley.

Soul Plane **2004 (R)** Nashawn Wade (Hart) wins a $100 million settlement after a near-disastrous flight and promptly creates a new airline for the "urban traveler." With a pimped out plane, lusty security officer (Mo'Nique) and a pilot (Snoop Dogg) who likes to get high, this one's doomed before the plane even takes off. What it lacks in entertainment, it more than makes up for in raunchiness, over-the-top stereotypes and sleazy sex jokes, making it a sure-fire cable and late-night Comedy Central hit. Tom Arnold also makes an appearance as the token white guy. **86m/C; VHS, DVD, Blu-Ray.** Kevin Hart; Tom Arnold; Method Man; Snoop Dogg; K.D. Aubert; Brian Hooks; D.L. Hughley; Mo'Nique; Godfrey; Arielle Kebbel; Loni Love; Missi Pyle; Stacey Travis; ***D:*** Jessy Terrero; ***W:*** Bo Zenga; Chuck Wilson; ***C:*** Jonathan Sela; ***M:*** RZA.

Soul Power **2008 (PG-13)** Levy-Hinte, who worked on the 1995 documentary "When We Were Kings" about the 1974 Muhammad Ali-George Foreman fight in Kinshasa, Zaire, gathered unedited backstage and concert performances to put together footage of the three-day concert that preceded the boxing match. Includes on-site preparations, interviews, and some 14 musical numbers from James Brown, The Spinners, Celia Cruz, and others. **93m/C; DVD.** James Brown; Celia Cruz; Miriam Makeba; Don King; B.B. King; Muhammad Ali; George Plimpton; ***D:*** Jeffrey Levy-Hinte; ***C:*** Paul Goldsmith; Kevin Keating; Albert Maysles; Roderick Young.

Soul Surfer ½ **2011 (PG)** Based of the true story of one-armed teenage champion surfer Bethany Hamilton (Robb) who lost her arm after a tiger shark attacked her in 2003 as she surfed at her home in Kauai, Hawaii. An inspiring story of determination and the importance of faith and familial support as Bethany pursued her dream of competing in the surfing championship again. Ironically, the story floats on the surface at times, susceptible to awkward cheerfulness and motivational catchphrases. Country musician Underwood makes her big screen debut. **105m/C; Blu-Ray, On Demand.** AnnaSophia Robb; Dennis Quaid; Helen Hunt; Carrie Underwood; Lorraine Nicholson; Kevin Sorbo; Craig T. Nelson; Sonya Balmores; Ross Thomas; ***D:*** Sean McNamara; ***W:*** Sean McNamara; Michael Berk; Deborah Schwartz; Douglas Schwartz; ***C:*** John R. Leonetti; ***M:*** Marco Beltrami.

Soul Survivor ½ **1995 (PG-13)** Set in Toronto's Jamaican community, this urban drama focuses on twentysomething Tyrone (Williams) who's stuck in a custodial job and looking to make some easy money. He goes to work making collections for local gangster Winston (Harris), who tries to reassure his protege that money buys respect. But when Tyrone falls for straight-living social worker Annie (Scott), he begins to see the potholes in the path he's on. **89m/C; VHS, DVD.** ***CA*** Peter Williams; George Harris; Judith Scott; Clark Johnson; Dave Smith; ***D:*** Stephen Williams; ***W:*** Stephen Williams; ***C:*** David Franco; ***M:*** John McCarthy.

Soul Survivors WOOF! 2001 (R) Perhaps the worst slash and burn editing job in the history of film was used to chop this muddled horror flick from an R to a PG-13 rating. Cassie (Sagemiller) and her boyfriend Sean (Affleck) go to one last party with their friends Annabel (Dushku) and Matt (Bentley). The party is a nasty Goth rave held in a cathedral, seemingly run by juvenile delinquent vampires. Sean gets upset when he misinterprets an innocent kiss between Cassie and Matt, who is also her ex. On the way home, a distracted Cassie crashes the car while trying to iron things out with Sean, killing him. Or not, as the case may be, because Cassie keeps seeing her dead boyfriend wherever she goes. Also, she keeps being chased by creepy Goth skanks. So is Cassie crazy? Is Sean alive? Frankly, you won't care even if you make it to the end of this contorted mess. **85m/C; VHS, DVD.** Melissa Sagemiller; Wes Bentley; Casey Affleck; Eliza Dushku; Luke Wilson; ***D:*** Stephen Carpenter; ***W:*** Stephen Carpenter; ***C:*** Fred Murphy; ***M:*** Daniel Licht.

Soul Vengeance *Welcome Home Brother Charles* **1975** Black man is jailed and brutalized for crime he didn't commit and wants revenge when he's released. Many afros and platform shoes. Vintage blaxploitation. **91m/C; VHS, DVD, Blu-Ray.** Marlo Monte; Reatha Grey; Stan Kamber; Tiffany Peters; Ven Bigelow; Jake Carter; ***D:*** Jamaa Fanaka; ***W:*** Jamaa Fanaka.

The Souler Opposite **1997 (R)** Buddies Barry (Meloni) and Robert (Busfield) haven't grown up—especially where women are concerned. Most of struggling comic Barry's material is about his failed relationships while complacent, married Robert learns that his wife has decided she's a lesbian. Then sexist Barry meets feminist Thea (Moloney) and sparks fly—but can "souler" opposites really come together? First-time writer/director Kalmenson knows the territory since he's a stand-up comedian himself. **104m/C; DVD.** Christopher Meloni; Timothy Busfield; Janel Moloney; Allison Mackie; John Putch; Rutanya Alda; Steve Landesberg; ***D:*** Bill Kalmenson; ***W:*** Bill Kalmenson; ***C:*** Amit Bhattacharya; ***M:*** Peter Himmelman.

Souls at Sea ½ **1937** Good buddy work by Cooper and Raft highlight this complicated seafaring yarn. In the 1840s sailor and abolitionist Nuggin Taylor (Cooper) is secretly sabotaging slave ships, working undercover for the British Navy. With loyal friend Powdah (Raft), Taylor tries to gather evidence against British officer Tarryton (Wilcoxon) even though he's fallen for Tarryton's sister Margaret (Dee). But after a sea disaster, Taylor's accused of murder and brought to trial. Will the truth come out in time to save him? **93m/B; DVD.** Gary Cooper; George Raft; Henry Wilcoxon; Frances Dee; Olympe Bradna; George Zucco; Harry Carey, Sr.; Robert Cummings; Porter Hall; Joseph Schildkraut; ***D:*** Henry Hathaway; ***W:*** Dale Van Every; Grover Jones; ***C:*** Charles B(ryant) Lang, Jr.

Souls for Sale **1923** Offers a fascinating glimpse into the world of silent film-making with cameos by a number of stars and directors of the era. Remember 'Mem' Steddon (Boardman) impulsively marries Owen Scudder (Cody), who turns out to be a wife-murdering con man. On their honeymoon train trip, Mem gets suspicious and hops off at a water stop in the middle of the California desert. She stumbles onto a movie location shoot where she's befriended by director Frank Claymore (Dix). Mem eventually goes to Hollywood, studies acting, and Frank makes her a star. But her success brings Scudder back into Mem's life. **89m/B; Silent; DVD.** Eleanor Boardman; Lew Cody; Richard Dix; Frank Mayo; Barbara La Marr; Mae Busch; William Haines; Snitz Edwards; Forrest Robinson; ***D:*** Rupert Hughes; ***W:*** Rupert Hughes.

Soul's Midnight ½ **2006 (R)** So how do you feel about bloody cults in Texas? Charles (Floyd) and his pregnant wife Alicia (Bennett) have come home for his dad's funeral. The town is big on celebrating the feast of St. George and the defeat of that pesky dragon, which was fond of human sacrifices. Charles is supposed to be a descendant of St. George and Alicia has weird dreams that hotel owner Simon (Assante) wants their unborn child to carry on the sacrificial ritual. **87m/C; DVD.** Armand Assante; Robert Floyd; Elizabeth Bennett; Miguel Perez; Lucila Sola; Joe Nipote; ***D:*** Harry Basil; ***W:*** Brian Cleveland; Jason Cleveland; ***C:*** Keith J. Duggan; ***M:*** Cieri Torjussen. **VIDEO**

Soultaker ½ **1990 (R)** The title spirit is after a young couple's souls, and they have just an hour to reunite with their bodies after a car crash. Meanwhile, they're in limbo (literally) between heaven and earth. The ending's OK, if you can make it that far. **94m/C; VHS, DVD.** Joe Estevez; Vivian Schilling; Gregg Thomsen; David "Shark" Fralick; Jean Reiner; Chuck Williams; Robert Z'Dar; ***D:*** Michael Rissi; ***W:*** Vivian Schilling; ***C:*** James Rosenthal; ***M:*** Jon McCallum.

The Sound Barrier ½ **1952** RAF pilot Tony Garthwaite (Patrick) marries Sue (Todd), the daughter of wealthy airplane designer John Ridgefield (Richardson). Ridgefield is obsessed with designing a jet that can break the sound barrier and Sue is worried about her father's reckless disregard for the lives of the test pilots, which soon include her husband. Film ignores the fact that American test pilot Chuck Yeager had already accomplished the goal, with Lean filming in a semi-documentary style complete with aerial footage of actual jets. **110m/B; DVD, Blu-Ray.** ***GB*** Ralph Richardson; Ann Todd; Nigel Patrick; John Justin; Dinah Sheridan; Joseph Tomelty; Denholm Elliott; ***D:*** Nigel Patrick; David Lean; ***W:*** Terence Rattigan; ***C:*** Jack Hildyard; ***M:*** Malcolm Arnold.

Sound City **2013** Nirvana and Foo Fighters' Grohl directs this love letter to one of the most influential and unheralded studios in the world, the legendary Sound City in the San Fernando Valley. The recording studio served as the home for artists as diverse as Metallica, Tom Petty, Fleetwood Mac, and Nirvana, and many of the key players who recorded there return for the documentary to celebrate the creativity it helped produce. Grohl's film smartly is not an elegy to a bygone era of rock but a call to the artists who strive to make music that sounds human in an increasingly digital world. **108m/C; Blu-Ray, Streaming.** ***D:*** Dave Grohl; ***W:*** Mark Monroe; ***C:*** Kenny Stoff.

Sound of Horror ½ *El Sonido de la Muerte; Sound From a Million Years Ago; The Prehistoric Sound* **1964** The Hound usually admires creative efforts to keep budgets down, but this is too much (or too little). A dinosaur egg hatches, and out lashes an invisible predator. Yes, you'll have to use your imagination as archaeologists are slashed to bits by the no-show terror. **85m/B; VHS, DVD.** ***SP*** James Philbrook; Arturo Fernandez; Soledad Miranda; Ingrid Pitt; ***D:*** Jose Antonio Nieves-Conde.

The Sound of Music **1965** The classic film version of the Rodgers and Hammerstein musical based on the true story of the singing von Trapp family of Austria and their escape from the Nazis just before WWII. Beautiful Salzburg, Austria location photography and an excellent cast. Andrews, fresh from her Oscar for "Mary Poppins," is effervescent, in beautiful voice, but occasionally too good to be true. Not Rodgers & Hammerstein's most innovative score, but lovely to hear and see. Plummer's singing was dubbed by Bill Lee. Marni Nixon, behind-the-scenes songstress for "West Side Story" and "My Fair Lady," makes her on-screen debut as one of the nuns. **174m/C; VHS, DVD, Blu-Ray.** Julie Andrews; Christopher Plummer; Eleanor Parker; Peggy Wood; Charmian Carr; Heather Menzies; Marni Nixon; Richard Haydn; Anna Lee; Norma Varden; Nicholas Hammond; Angela Cartwright; Portia Nelson; Duane Chase; Debbie Turner; Kym Karath; ***D:*** Robert Wise; ***W:*** Ernest Lehman; ***C:*** Ted D. McCord. Oscars '65: Adapt. Score, Director (Wise), Film, Film Editing, Sound; AFI '98: Top 100; Directors Guild '65: Director (Wise); Golden Globes '66: Actress--Mus./Comedy (Andrews), Film--Mus./Comedy; Natl. Film Reg. '01.

Sound of My Voice **2011 (R)** Uneasy, low-budget drama divided into 10 sections. Documentary filmmakers Peter and Lorna are clandestinely investigating a potential L.A. cult lead by beautiful 20-something Maggie, who claims to be from the future. Part cheerleader, part shrink, Maggie's compelling presence puts Peter in an uncomfortable spot as she forces her adherents to open up emotionally and tests their loyalty. **86m/C; DVD, Blu-Ray.** Christopher Denham; Nicole Vicius; Brit Marling; ***D:*** Zal Batmanglij; ***W:*** Brit Marling; Zal Batmanglij; ***C:*** Rachel Morrison; ***M:*** Rostam Batmanglij.

The Sound of Silence **2019** A room tuner, Peter Lucian (Saarsgard) helps wealthy New Yorkers who are struggling to understand why they feel uneasy or can't sleep. Using tuning forks and old audio equipment, Peter enters their spaces to find what elements are out of tune and replaces them so the inhabitant can rest again. When Ellen (Jones) hires him, Peter is stumped by the acoustics in her space. At the same time, Peter's work has attracted the unwanted attention of a corporation that wants him to sell out. The comedy-drama lives up to its offbeat concept, due in large part to Saarsgard. **85m/C; DVD.** Peter Sarsgaard; Rashida Jones; Tony Revolori; Austin Pendleton; Bruce Altman; ***D:*** Michael Tyburski; ***W:*** Michael Tyburski; Ben Nabors; ***C:*** Eric Lin; ***M:*** Will Bates.

A Sound of Thunder **2005 (PG-13)** Not much more needs to be said other than this is a summer flick, a time-traveling adventure, very loosely based on a Ray Bradbury story. The setting is 2055 Chicago, where folks with deep pockets get the opportunity to run with (okay, hunt) the dinosaurs, courtesy of a greedy entrepreneur (Kingsley). A snafu threatens to change the future, reverting Chicago (and the rest of the planet) back to prehistoric times. Loads and loads of special effects and, well, that's about it. "The Simpsons" fleshed out this premise with more success a few years ago. **102m/C; DVD.** ***GE US CZ*** Edward Burns; Catherine McCormack; Ben Kingsley; Jemima Rooper; August Zirner; Corey Johnson; David Oyelowo; Wilfried Hochholdinger; ***D:*** Peter Hyams; ***W:*** Thomas Dean Donnelly; Joshua Oppenheimer; Gregory Poirier; ***C:*** Peter Hyams; ***M:*** Nick Glennie-Smith.

Sounder **1972 (G)** The struggles of a family of black sharecroppers in rural Louisiana during the Depression. When the father is sentenced to jail for stealing in order to feed his family, they must pull together even more, and one son finds education to be his way out of poverty. Tyson brings strength and style to her role, with fine help from Winfield. Moving and well made, with little sentimentality and superb acting from a great cast. Adapted from the novel by William Armstrong. **105m/C; VHS, DVD.** Paul Winfield; Cicely Tyson; Kevin Hooks; Taj Mahal; Carmen Mathews; James Best; Janet MacLachlan; ***D:*** Martin Ritt; ***W:*** Lonnie Elder, III; ***C:***

John A. Alonzo; *M:* Taj Mahal. Natl. Bd. of Review '72: Actress (Tyson); Natl. Soc. Film Critics '72: Actress (Tyson).

Soundman 1/2 **1999** Very black showbiz comedy about obsessive sound engineer Igby Walters (Pere) who manages to piss off anyone with any clout on his current movie job. As his life just gets worse, Igby's behavior becomes increasingly violent, including his arranging a musical audition for his violin-playing next-door neighbor (Chappuis)?at gunpoint. **105m/C; VHS, DVD.** Wayne Pere; William Forsythe; Wes Studi; Eliane Chappuis; Nick Stahl; Tamlyn Tomita; Danny Trejo; John Koyama; *D:* Steven Ho; *W:* Steven Ho; *C:* David Aubrey.

Sour Grapes **1998 (R)** "Seinfeld" co-creator David's feature directorial debut has cousins Evan and Richie (Weber and Bierko) feuding over an Atlantic City slot machine jackpot. Evan, a successful neurosurgeon lends Richie, an extroverted loser, two quarters for one last pull on the slots. Of course, Richie wins $400,000. Escalating revenge schemes, petty greed, and quirky small talk scream sitcom episode, as do the TV quality production values, and lighting. The dialogue is biting and clever, but on the whole there's not enough here to justify 90 minutes of screen time. Robyn Peterman, the real-life daughter of J. Peterman, plays Richie's girlfriend. If you liked "Seinfeld," this flick's for you. **91m/C; VHS, DVD.** Steven Weber; Craig Bierko; Karen Sillas; Matt Keeslar; Robyn Peterman; Jennifer Leigh Warren; Richard Gant; James MacDonald; Philip Baker Hall; Ann Guilbert; Jack Kehler; *D:* Larry David; *W:* Larry David; *C:* Victor Hammer.

Source Code **2011 (PG-13)** Captain Colter Stevens (Gyllenhaal) becomes part of a government experiment in which he can enter the last eight minutes of another human's life. Stevens must figure out who bombed a Chicago commuter train, the mastermind behind it, and where the next attack will be—but only by returning to that same moment again and again. With each new clue Stevens works to prevent an attack threatening to kill millions in downtown Chicago. An intelligent, suspenseful ride by skillful director Jones (son of David Bowie) with strong lead performances and an edge-of-your-seat plot. **94m/C; Blu-Ray, On Demand.** Jake Gyllenhaal; Michelle Monaghan; Vera Farmiga; Jeffrey Wright; Michael Arden; *D:* Duncan Jones; *W:* Ben Ripley; *C:* Don Burgess; *M:* Chris P. Bacon.

The Source Family **2013** In the early '70s, Father Yod (aka Ya Ho Wa aka James Edward Baker) became one of the more notable cult leaders in the United States. Wille and Demopoulous' documentary tracks his ascendance, groovy times, and then the dissolving of his group, known as The Source Family. Yod funds the group, moves them into a house in L.A., and basically hangs out with his 13 wives, doing drugs and playing music. It was hippie heaven until the authorities came calling. Never mocking its subjects, the directors present a seemingly simpler time that naturally had to come to an end. **98m/C; DVD.** *D:* Maria Demopoulos; Jodi Wille; *C:* John Tanzer.

South Beach **1992 (R)** Two ex-football players turned private eyes are living the good life and partying it up in Miami Beach. However, their leisurely lifestyles are soon disrupted when they accept a mysterious challenge from the beautiful Vanity. **93m/C; VHS, DVD.** Fred Williamson; Gary Busey; Vanity; Peter Fonda; *D:* Fred Williamson; *W:* Mark Montgomery; *M:* Joe Renzetti.

South Beach Academy **1996 (R)** Eye candy focusing on a beach school that specializes in surfing, swimming, and volleyball rather than the usual academics. Maybe that's why the school's about to close—unless the lightly clad student body can come up with a plan to save their alma mater. **91m/C; VHS, DVD.** Corey Feldman; Al Lewis; James Hong; Elizabeth Kaitan; *D:* Joe Esposito.

South Bronx Heroes 1/2 *The Runaways; Revenge of the Innocents* **1985 (R)** A police officer helps two children when they discover their foster home is the headquarters for a pornography ring. **105m/C; VHS, DVD.** Brendan Ward; Mario Van Peebles; Megan Van Peebles; Melissa Esposito; Martin Zurla; Jordan Abeles; *D:* William Szarka; *W:* William Szarka; Don Shiffrin; *C:* Eric Schmitz; *M:* Al Zima.

South Central **1992 (R)** A low-budget urban drama set in a gang-infested L.A. neighborhood. Bobby is a young black man, and former gang leader, who has spent ten years in prison for murder. His wife has become a drug addict and his young son Jimmie has begun running with his dad's old gang. Now paroled, Bobby hopes to re-establish the bond with his son—enough to protect him from following in his nowhere-to-go-but-down footsteps. Worthy effort with an emotional ending. Feature debut of director Anderson. Based on the novel "Crips" by Donald Bakeer. **99m/C; VHS, DVD.** Glenn Plummer; Carl Lumbly; Christian Coleman; LaRita Shelby; Byron Keith Minns; *D:* Steve (Stephen M.) Anderson; *W:* Steve (Stephen M.) Anderson; *C:* Charlie Lieberman; *M:* Tim Truman.

South of Heaven, West of Hell 1/2 **2000 (R)** A marshal (Yoakam), who once ran with an outlaw clan, must deal with his past when the bandits show up to terrorize the Arizona town he's sworn to protect. Yoakam's not much of a leading man and there's a lot of brutal violence to contend with. **133m/C; VHS, DVD.** Dwight Yoakam; Bridget Fonda; Vince Vaughn; Billy Bob Thornton; Peter Fonda; Bud Cort; Michael Jeter; Paul (Pee-wee Herman) Reubens; *D:* Dwight Yoakam; *W:* Dwight Yoakam; *C:* James Glennon; *M:* Dwight Yoakam.

South of Panama 1/2 *Panama Menace* **1941** Knowing she's being followed by enemy agents, Jan Martin leads them away from her government chemist brother Paul by pretending stranger Mike is her sibling. He goes along with the ruse and then tries to help Jan foil a spy plot. **68m/B; DVD.** Roger Pryor; Virginia Vale; Lionel Royce; Lucien Prival; Hugh Beaumont; Jack Ingram; Warren Jackson; Duncan Renaldo; *D:* Jean Yarbrough; *W:* Ben Roberts; Sidney Sheldon; *C:* Mack Stengler.

South of Pico **2007 (R)** Ensemble drama. The lives of a chauffeur, waitress, doctor, and teenaged boy all change when they witness the same tragedy on L.A.'s Pico Boulevard, and their disparate characters bond over their shared moment. **106m/C; DVD.** Kip Pardue; Henry Simmons; Gina Torres; Soren Fulton; Paul Hipp; Jimmy Bennett; Christina Hendricks; *D:* Ernst Gossner; *W:* Ernst Gossner; *C:* Richard Marcus; *M:* John Swihart.

South of St. Louis 1/2 **1948** A peaceful cattle rancher turns renegade gunrunner during the Civil War when his stock is destroyed by Union guerrillas. Overplotted but exciting and action-packed western, with Smith dazzling in a plethora of costumes. **88m/C; DVD, Blu-Ray.** Joel McCrea; Zachary Scott; Victor Jory; Douglas Kennedy; Alexis Smith; Alan Hale; Dorothy Malone; *D:* Ray Enright; *C:* Karl Freund; *M:* Max Steiner.

South of the Border **1939** Autry and Burnette are government agents sent to Mexico to investigate a possible revolution instigated by foreign agents. Propaganda-heavy singing western appeared just before the U.S. entered WWII; did well at the boxoffice and boosted Autry's career. **70m/B; VHS, DVD.** Gene Autry; Smiley Burnette; June Storey; Lupita Tovar; Mary Lee; Duncan Renaldo; William Farnum; Frank Reicher; *D:* George Sherman; *W:* Betty Burbridge; Gerald Geraghty; *C:* William Nobles.

South of the Border **2009** Stone's polemic documentary about South American leftism and socialism begins when he goes to Venezuela to interview President Hugo Chavez about how he is depicted in the U.S. media. Stone then goes on to interview seven other presidents in the region: Evo Morales of Bolivia; Lula da Silva of Brazil; Fernando Lugo of Paraguay; Rafael Correa of Ecuador; Cristina Kirchner of Argentina and her husband and ex-President Nestor Kirchner; and then Raul Castro of Cuba. English, Spanish, and Portuguese with subtitles. **78m/C; Blu-Ray, On Demand.** *Nar:* Oliver Stone; *D:* Oliver Stone; *W:* Oliver Stone; Tariq Ali; *C:* Albert Maysles; Carlos Marcovich; Lucas Fuica; *M:* Adam Peters.

South Pacific 1/2 **1958** A young American Navy nurse and a Frenchman fall in love during WWII. Expensive production included much location shooting in Hawaii. Based on Rodgers and Hammerstein's musical; not as good as the play, but pretty darn good still. The play in turn was based on James Michener's novel "Tales of the South Pacific." **167m/C; VHS, DVD, Blu-Ray.** Mitzi Gaynor; Rossano Brazzi; Ray Walston; France Nuyen; John Kerr; Juanita Hall; Tom Laughlin; *V:* Giorgio Tozzi; *D:* Joshua Logan; *W:* Paul Osborn; *C:* Leon Shamroy; *M:* Richard Rodgers; Oscar Hammerstein. Oscars '58: Sound.

South Park: Bigger, Longer and Uncut 1/2 **1999 (R)** The most unlikely critical darling of the summer of 1999 caught everyone's attention with it's MPAA-baiting language and sexual subject matter, and made audiences laugh—a lot—along the way. Stan, Kenny, Cartman, and Kyle sneak into an R-rated movie and shock their families with what they learn. So, concerned South Park parents form a censorship board to take on Canada (which results in a war, with enough bloody violence to make Sam Peckinpah sick, but didn't faze the MPAA), and the kids decide to fight back. Like most TV shows adapted for the big screen, this one flags at times, but has enough inspired comic moments to (mostly) justify the hype. The easily offended should definitely pass. **80m/C; VHS, DVD, Blu-Ray.** *V:* Trey Parker; Matt Stone; Isaac Hayes; George Clooney; Minnie Driver; Mike Judge; Eric Idle; Mary Kay Bergman; Brent Spiner; Nick Rhodes; Stewart Copeland; *D:* Trey Parker; *W:* Trey Parker; Matt Stone; Pam Brady; *M:* Marc Shaiman; *M:* Trey Parker.

South Riding **2011** Convoluted BBC adaptation of the Winifred Holtby novel finds Sarah Burton (Maxwell Martin) returning to her provincial Yorkshire hometown as the new headmistress at the local girls' school. It's the 1930s and the time is rife with economic and political upheaval with Sarah representing a more progressive attitude in contrast to moody, hidebound married landowner Robert Carne (Morrissey). Various romantic sparks are still struck. **180m/C; DVD.** *GB* Anna Maxwell Martin; David Morrissey; Penelope Wilton; Katherine McGolpin; Charlie Clark; Douglas Henshall; Peter Firth; Lydia Wilson; Ian Bartholomew; Shaun Dooley; Jennifer Hennessy; *D:* Diarmuid Lawrence; *W:* Andrew Davies; *C:* Alan Almond; *M:* Robert (Rob) Lane. **TV**

South Sea Woman 1/2 **1953** Nightclub tootsie Ginger Martin (Mayo) testifies at the court-martial of Marine Sgt. James O'Hearn (Lancaster). Seems he and buddy Pvt. Davy White (Connors) met the stranded Ginger in Shanghai just before Pearl Harbor. O'Hearn tries to prevent the impulsive White from marrying her and the trio wind up on the Vichy French island of Namou, where O'Hearn discovers some Nazis plotting evil. There's derring-do and various heroics but O'Hearn doesn't make it back to his unit in time and gets accused of desertion—hence the trial. Good action and a light touch—there's more comedy than angst. **99m/B; DVD.** Burt Lancaster; Virginia Mayo; Chuck Connors; Barry Kelley; Hayden Rorke; Bob Sweeney; Leon Askin; *D:* Arthur Lubin; *W:* Earl Baldwin; Edwin Blum; Stanley Shapiro; *C:* Ted D. McCord; *M:* David Buttolph.

Southbound 1/2 **2016** Since the arthouse success of V/H/S and The ABCs of Death, anthology horror has returned in a big way, and this may be the best of the modern bunch. Five stories are woven around one of those desolate stretches of highway in the middle of nowhere it which it feels like something truly dangerous could be lurking over the next horizon. Men run from something supernatural, a group of women stumble on a cult, and a businessman tries to save the girl he hit with his car to no avail in the best three. It's smart, fun, and has a way higher batting average than its brethren. **89m/C; DVD.** Chad Villella; Matt Bettinelli-Olpin; Kristina Pesic; Fabianne Therese; Hannah Marks; *D:* Roxanne Benjamin; David Bruckner; Patrick Horvath; Radio Silence; *W:* Matt Bettinelli-Olpin; Roxanne Benjamin; David Bruckner; Patrick Horvath; Susan Burke; Dallas Richard Hallam; *C:* Tarin Anderson; Tyler Gillett; Alexandre Naufel; Andrew Shulkind; *M:* The Gifted.

Southern Belles **2005 (R)** Hare-brained-but-likeable trailer park chicks Bell (Breckenridge) and Belle (Faris) want to escape their dull lives in rural Georgia to start anew in the "big city" of Atlanta. But they need some quick cash to get there so they concoct a half-baked plan that is interrupted by Bell's affections toward a policeman named Rhett Butler (Chambers). **90m/C; DVD.** Anna Faris; Justin Chambers; Frederick Weller; Heather Goldenhersch; Laura Breckenridge; *D:* Paul S. Myers; Brennan Shroff; *W:* Paul S. Myers; Brennan Shroff. **VIDEO**

Southern Comfort **1981 (R)** A group of National Guardsmen are on weekend maneuvers in the swamps of Louisiana. They run afoul of some of the local Cajuns, and are marked for death in this exciting and disturbing thriller. Boothe is excellent in a rare exploration of a little-understood way of life. Lots of blood. If you belong to the National Guard, this could make you queasy. **106m/C; VHS, DVD, Blu-Ray.** Powers Boothe; Keith Carradine; Fred Ward; Franklyn Seales; Brion James; T.K. Carter; Peter Coyote; Ned Dowd; Lewis Smith; Les Lannom; Alan Autry; Sonny Landham; *D:* Walter Hill; *W:* Walter Hill; David Giler; Michael Kane; *C:* Andrew Laszlo; *M:* Ry Cooder.

Southern Man **1999** Turgid, undernourished drama revolves around an actor (Withers) who goes back to Nashville from Los Angeles to work out childhood problems involving sexual abuse. **104m/C; DVD.** Mark Withers; Ellia Vierling; Jesse Head; Leigh Rose; Jack Betts; *D:* Rick Rosenberg; *W:* Rick Rosenberg; Robert Northup; *C:* Ken Glassing; *M:* Matthew Ferrado.

The Southern Star **1969** Crime adventure/comedy based on a Jules Verne novel. Broke American geologist Dan is working in Africa when he and his partner Matakit are hired by businessman Kramer to get him the Southern Star diamond. Dan succeeds, but Matakit then steals the gem and Dan is also blamed. He has to get the diamond back to clear his name while being pursued by a number of crooks. **104m/C; DVD.** *GB* George Segal; Ursula Andress; Harry Andrews; Johnny Sekka; Ian Hendry; Orson Welles; *D:* Sidney Hayes; *W:* David Pursall; Jack Seddon; *C:* Raoul Coutard; *M:* Georges Garvarentz.

A Southern Yankee 1/2 *My Hero* **1948** Skelton plays a bumbling bellboy who ends up as a Union spy during the Civil War. Enjoyable comedy, thanks largely to the off-screen input of Buster Keaton. **90m/B; VHS, DVD.** Red Skelton; Brian Donlevy; Arlene Dahl; George Coulouris; Lloyd Gough; John Ireland; Minor Watson; Charles Dingle; Art Baker; Reed Hadley; Arthur Space; Addison Richards; Joyce Compton; Paul Harvey; Jeff Corey; *D:* Edward Sedgwick.

The Southerner **1945** A man used to working for others is given some land by an uncle and decides to pack up his family and try farming for himself. They find hardships as they struggle to support themselves. A superb, naturalistic celebration of a family's fight to survive amid all the elements. From the story "Hold Autumn in Your Hand," by George Sessions Perry. Novelist Faulkner had an uncredited hand in the script. He thought Renoir the best contemporary director, and later said "The Southerner" gave him more pleasure than any of his other Hollywood work (though this is faint praise; Faulkner is said to have hated Hollywood). **91m/B; VHS, DVD, Blu-Ray.** Zachary Scott; Betty Field; Beulah Bondi; Norman Lloyd; Bunny Sunshine; Jay Gilpin; Estelle Taylor; Blanche Yurka; Percy Kilbride; J. Carrol Naish; *D:* Jean Renoir; *W:* Jean Renoir; Hugo Butler; William Faulkner; *C:* Lucien N. Andriot; *M:* Werner Janssen. Natl. Bd. of Review '45: Director (Renoir); Venice Film Fest. '46: Film.

Southie **1998 (R)** Another return of the native son drama offers some decent performances but nothing much that is new. Danny Quinn (Wahlberg) is a South Boston bad boy returning to home turf after a sojourn in New York. Danny's pals are tied up with one Irish gangster crew while his own family is involved with oldtimer Colie (Tierney) and Danny himself has a score to settle with longtime rival, Joey (Cummings). **95m/C; VHS, DVD, On Demand.** Donnie Wahlberg; Rose McGowan; Lawrence Tierney; James (Jimmy) Cummings; Anne Meara; Amanda Peet; John Shea; *D:* John Shea; *W:* James (Jimmy) Cummings; John Shea; Dave McLaughlin; *C:* Allen Baker; *M:* Wayne Sharp.

Southland Tales 1/2 **2006 (R)** The U.S. is now monitored by a Big Brother-esque agency called US-IDENT, but revolutionaries in World War III-era Los Angeles are plotting to turn popular opinion against the government. Meanwhile, right-wing action star Boxer Santaros (Johnson) has lost his memory and has started an affair with porn actress-turned-talk show host Krysta Now (Gellar), which is somehow connected to the anti-government plot and the presidential election, in which his father-in-law (Osborne) is the Republican vice presidential candidate. Oh, and Justin Timberlake guards a pier against terrorist invaders while (mis)quoting T.S. Eliot and Revelations. Kelly's twisted, convoluted sci-fi black comedy is, at best, difficult to follow, with far more questions than it answers. When the movie works, it's an entertaining, absurdist post-9/11 farce; when it doesn't, it verges on incomprehensible. Kelly trimmed 19 minutes after the film was booed at Cannes. **144m/C; Blu-Ray, On Demand.** Dwayne "The Rock" Johnson; Sarah Michelle Gellar; Seann William Scott; Curtis Armstrong; Nora Dunn; Wood Harris; John Larroquette; Mandy Moore; Holmes Osborne; Miranda Richardson; Justin Timberlake; ***D:*** Richard Kelly; ***W:*** Richard Kelly; ***C:*** Steven Poster; ***M:*** Moby.

Southpaw 1/2 **2015 (R)** Gyllenhaal transforms himself once again into a boxer near the end of his career. He's been putting off a big fight for fear that he might lose it when his wife (McAdams) is shot and killed in an altercation, sending him in a suicidal spiral. When his daughter is taken away from him, he has to start over, training for the fight of his life with an inner city trainer (Whitaker) who doesn't care that he used to be a celebrity. Sure, this melodrama's themes are no more refined than boxing dramas of the '40s, but the execution is entertaining enough. **123m/C; DVD, Blu-Ray, Streaming.** Jake Gyllenhaal; Forest Whitaker; Rachel McAdams; Naomie Harris; 50 Cent; Victoria Ortiz; ***D:*** Antoine Fuqua; ***W:*** Kurt Sutter; ***C:*** Mauro Fiore; ***M:*** James Horner.

Southside 1-1000 **1950** Imprisoned counterfeiter Eugene Deane (Ankrum) manages to smuggle his plates out of his San Quentin cell and funny money is everywhere. The Treasury Department sends agent John Riggs (affable Defore) undercover, and he follows the bills to a L.A. hotel, managed by icy film noir femme Nora Craig (King). **79m/B; DVD.** Don DeFore; Andrea King; Morris Ankrum; George Tobias; Barry Kelley; ***D:*** Boris Ingster; ***W:*** Boris Ingster; Leo Townsend; ***C:*** Russell Harlan; ***M:*** Paul Sawtell.

Southside with You **2016 (PG-13)** This excellent romantic dramedy tells the story of a wonderful first date that gains added meaning due to what the two people at its center would go on to accomplish. In Chicago in 1989, Michelle Robinson (Sumpter) was a young lawyer who agreed to go to a meeting with a young associate named Barack Obama (Sawyers). They spent the day together, even seeing "Do the Right Thing," and sharing a first kiss. This dialogue-heavy film is delightful, smart, sweet and even moving. And both performers have great charisma, mirroring the people they portray. **84m/C; DVD, Blu-Ray.** Tika Sumpter; Parker Sawyers; Vanessa Bell Calloway; Phillip Edward Van Lear; Taylar Fondren; ***D:*** Richard Tanne; ***W:*** Richard Tanne; ***C:*** Patrick Scola; ***M:*** Stephen James Taylor.

Southwest Passage 1/2 **1954** A standard western, despite the use of camels rather than horses, originally filmed in 3D. Edward Beale is hired by the Army to test the viability of using camels in desert terrain. He's joined by Clint McDonald, a bank robber posing as a doctor, McDonald's gal Lilly, and grumbling mule skinner Carrol among others. The group faces multiple hardships, including a scarcity of water and attacks by Apache raiding parties. **75m/C; DVD.** Rod Cameron; John Ireland; Joanne Dru; John Dehner; Guinn "Big Boy" Williams; Darryl Hickman; Morris Ankrum; ***D:*** Ray Nazarro; ***W:*** Harry Essex; Daniel Mainwaring; ***C:*** Sam Leavitt; ***M:*** Arthur Lange.

Souvenir **1988 (R)** A German soldier returns to France after WWII to find the woman he left behind and the daughter he never saw. Might have been good, but too melodramatic and overwrought, with lukewarm acting. **93m/C; VHS, DVD.** Christopher Plummer; Catherine Hicks; Christopher Cazenove; Michael (Michel) Lonsdale; ***D:*** Geoffrey Reeve.

The Souvenir **2019 (R)** Raised in a life of privilege, Julie (Swinton Byrne) is an aspiring film student who meets a mysterious man at a party. Tom (Burke) is older and works in the Foreign Office. Tom takes an interest in Julie, taking her out for fancy dinners and sending her romantic letters. They soon move into together. One night, the situation began to change when Julie notices bruises on his arm. Tom's behavior grows more concerning, challenging the very core of their relationship. A semi-autobiographical film from writer/director Hogg, the film features remarkable performances by Swinton Byrne and Burke. **120m/C; DVD, Blu-Ray.** Honor Swinton Byrne; Tom Burke; Tilda Swinton; Tosin Cole; Jack McMullen; ***D:*** Joanna Hogg; ***W:*** Joanna Hogg; ***C:*** David Raedeker.

Soylent Green 1/2 **1973 (PG)** In the 21st Century, hard-boiled police detective Heston investigates a murder and discovers what soylent green—the people's principal food—is made of. Robinson's final film is a disappointing end to a great career. Its view of the future and of human nature is relentlessly dark. Don't watch it with kids. **95m/C; VHS, DVD, Blu-Ray.** Charlton Heston; Leigh Taylor-Young; Chuck Connors; Joseph Cotten; Brock Peters; Paula Kelly; Edward G. Robinson; Stephen Young; Whit Bissell; Dick Van Patten; ***D:*** Richard Fleischer; ***W:*** Stanley R. Greenberg; ***C:*** Richard H. Kline; ***M:*** Fredric Myrow.

The Space Between **2010** Ten-year-old New Yorker Omar (Keyvan) is a Pakistani Muslim whose academic excellence means sending him to an Islamic boarding school in L.A. Cranky, middle-aged flight attendant Montine (Leo) should be watching the unaccompanied minor but Omar hides himself in the lavatory and doesn't come out until the plane lands. Montine takes Omar into the terminal where everyone is distraught: the date is September 11, 2001. Omar wants to return home but with no planes going anywhere, an impulsive Montine buys them bus tickets with some unexpected stops along the way. **90m/C; DVD.** Melissa Leo; Anthony Keyvan; Brad William Henke; AnnaSophia Robb; Phillip Rhys; Hunter Parrish; ***D:*** Travis Fine; ***W:*** Travis Fine; ***C:*** Marc Sharp; Marc Shap; ***M:*** Joey Newman.

The Space Between Us **2017 (PG)** Gardner Elliot (a bland Butterfield) is the first human born on a newly colonized Mars. Gardner doesn't have many friends—there aren't a lot of people on Mars yet—so he forms an online friendship with a Earth girl named Tulsa (a way too-old-for-this Robertson), and he longs to see her in person. Of course, he's given the chance to go to Earth, where he not only finds love but gets a chance to find his father. And, of course, his organs can't withstand the planet's atmosphere, adding a life or death element to all this silliness. **120m/C; DVD, Blu-Ray.** Gary Oldman; Asa Butterfield; Carla Gugino; Britt Robertson; B.D. Wong; ***D:*** Peter Chelsom; ***W:*** Allan Loeb; ***C:*** Barry Peterson; ***M:*** Andrew Lockington.

Space Buddies **2008 (G)** The never-ending franchise now finds those awww-so-cute golden retriever pups stuck aboard a spaceship and they're smart enough to realize that something about the mission isn't quite right. **84m/C; DVD, Blu-Ray.** Diedrich Bader; Kevin Weisman; ***V:*** Jason Earles; Bill Fagerbakke; Ali Hillis; Lochlyn Munro; Field Cate; ***D:*** Robert Vince; ***W:*** Robert Vince; Anna McRoberts; ***C:*** Kamal Derkaoui; ***M:*** Brahm Wenger. **VIDEO**

The Space Children 1/2 **1958** In this anti-nukes sci-fier, the children of nuclear scientists, who are living on a California Air Force base, start receiving telepathic messages after seeing a strange light in the sky. The kids go to a cave on the beach where they find a giant alien brain who wants the youngsters to talk to their parents about the dangers of sending a hydrogen bomb into space. When the adults won't listen, the alien uses the kiddies to take more direct action. **70m/B; DVD, Blu-Ray.** Adam Williams; Peggy Webber; Michel Ray; Johnny Crawford; Jackie Coogan; Sandy Descher; Richard Shannon; Johnny Washbrook; Russell Johnson; ***D:*** Jack Arnold; ***W:*** Bernard C. Schoenfeld; ***C:*** Ernest Laszlo; ***M:*** Nathan Van Cleave.

Space Chimps 1/2 **2008 (G)** Circus chimp and slacker Ham III (Samberg)?grandson of first chimp in space, Ham I—is unwittingly recruited to retrieve a space probe that's gone AWOL. Accompanied by "real" astro-chimps Luna (Hines) and commander Titan (Warburton), the trio land on alien Zartog's (Daniels) planet looking to retrieve their probe, but that's not going to be so easy since Zartog has found a rather unique use for it. The trio embark on all sorts of madcap adventures on the alien planet, even while back on Earth there's talk of disbanding the space program entirely. The CGI chimps are kinda creepy, and the gags are just plain cheap. Even so, it's a relatively benign 81 minutes that at least the kiddies will enjoy. **81m/C; Blu-Ray, On Demand.** ***V:*** Andy Samberg; Cheryl Hines; Patrick Warburton; Jeff Daniels; Stanley Tucci; Kristin Chenoweth; Kenan Thompson; Omid Abtahi; Patrick Breen; Kath Soucie; Jane Lynch; Zack Shada; ***D:*** Kirk De Micco; ***W:*** Kirk De Micco; Rob Moreland; ***C:*** Jerrica Cleland; ***M:*** David A. Stewart; Chris P. Bacon.

Space Cowboys **2000 (PG-13)** Eastwood, starring and directing again, plays a retired Air Force pilot who was passed over for the astronaut training program in the late 1950s. However, now NASA needs his expertise when an ailing 1960s satellite poses a threat if it crashes to Earth. He agrees to go into space and repair it only if he can bring his equally codgerly buddies, Sutherland, Jones, and Garner, to assist. Hey, if John Glenn can go back into space at age 77, why not Eastwood? Fun ensemble piece that successfully weaves some action and thrills into the final act. **123m/C; VHS, DVD, Blu-Ray, HD-DVD.** Clint Eastwood; Tommy Lee Jones; James Garner; James Cromwell; Donald Sutherland; Marcia Gay Harden; Loren Dean; William Devane; Rade Serbedzija; Courtney B. Vance; Barbara Babcock; Blair Brown; ***D:*** Clint Eastwood; ***W:*** Ken Kaufman; Howard Klausner; ***C:*** Jack N. Green; ***M:*** Lennie Niehaus.

Space Jam 1/2 **1996 (PG)** Expensive live action-animation combo finds basketball great Jordan forced to play ball against evil intergalatic invaders who are out to capture Bugs Bunny and the rest of the Looney Tunes characters. It's all fairly silly but the kids will enjoy it. **87m/C; VHS, DVD, Blu-Ray.** Michael Jordan; Bill Murray; Wayne Knight; Theresa Randle; ***V:*** Danny DeVito; ***D:*** Joe Pytka; ***W:*** Leo Benvenuti; ***C:*** Michael Chapman; ***M:*** James Newton Howard.

Space Master X-7 *Blood Rust* **1958** Space satellite "Space Master X-7" returns to earth carrying a Martian fungus, which, in a lab mishap, reveals a creepy penchant for human blood. Tasting human blood and tissue, the "space rust" grows into a blubbery glob of oozing slime, claiming a lab scientist as its first victim just after the scientist and his ex have a nasty confrontation. On her way home to Honolulu, the ex sees a headline announcing the scientist's death—now she's on the lam, but she's also unwittingly spreading the deadly rust. **71m/B; DVD.** Bill Williams; Lyn Thomas; Robert Ellis; Paul Frees; ***D:*** Edward L. Bernds; ***W:*** George Worthing Yates; Daniel Mainwaring; ***C:*** Brydon Baker; ***M:*** Josef Zimanich.

Space Mutiny **1988 (PG)** Spaceship falls under the attack of the mutinous Kalgan. To keep everyone from being sold into slavery, a small band of loyal passengers strike back. Will they be successful in thwarting the attack? Who cares? **93m/C; VHS, DVD.** Reb Brown; James Ryan; John Phillip Law; Cameron Mitchell; ***D:*** David Winters; ***W:*** Maria Dante.

Space Station 76 1/2 **2014 (R)** Deadpan indie sci-fi comedy, set aboard the Omega 76 Space Station, which has a deliberate 1970s soap opera feel. Repressed Capt. Glenn alternates between glum and hostile, especially when his new second-in-command, Jessica Marlowe, turns out to be an authoritative female. Pot-smoking, frustrated Ted likes that authority just fine, especially since his self-absorbed wife Misty avoids sex--at least with him since she having an affair with Steve, who's just had a baby with overly-cheerful wife Donna. Tensions rise. **93m/C; DVD.** Patrick Wilson; Liv Tyler; Matt Bomer; Marisa Coughlan; Jerry O'Connell; Kali Rocha; Kylie Rogers; ***D:*** Jack Plotnick; ***W:*** Kali Rocha; Jack Plotnick; Jennifer Elise Cox; ***C:*** Robert Brinkmann; ***M:*** Steffan Fantini; Marc Fantini.

Space Truckers **1997 (PG-13)** Sci-fi spoof about space haulage-truckers in the 21st century. Veteran hauler John Canyon (Hopper) accepts a dangerous assignment when he agrees to transport some sealed containers to Earth—no questions asked. Canyon, girlfriend Cindy (Mazar), and newbie driver Mike (Dorff) have their ship boarded by space pirates, led by Capt. Macaunudo (Dance), who's part-machine. The cargo turns out to be murderous androids, sent to conquer Earth. Canyon and his crew must perform various heroics to save the planet! Lots of campy bad taste. **97m/C; VHS, DVD.** ***IR*** Dennis Hopper; Stephen Dorff; Charles Dance; Debi Mazar; George Wendt; Shane Rimmer; Vernon Wells; Barbara Crampton; ***D:*** Stuart Gordon; ***W:*** Ted Mann; ***C:*** Mac Ahlberg; ***M:*** Colin Towns.

Space Warriors 1/2 **2013 (PG)** Hallmark Channel adventure. Jimmy Hawkins, the son of retired astronaut Andy Hawkins, lives astrophysics. This earns him a place at a space camp where Jimmy and his team compete against some strong rivals. When a crises unfolds aboard the International Space Station, the teens get the chance to test their abilities in a real life-and-death situation. **88m/C; DVD, Blu-Ray.** Thomas Horn; Josh(ua) Lucas; Danny Glover; Dermot Mulroney; Mira Sorvino; Booboo Stewart; Ryan Simpkins; Grayson Russell; ***D:*** Sean McNamara; ***W:*** Sean McNamara; Jeff Phillips; ***C:*** Robert Hayes; ***M:*** Larry Brown. **CABLE**

Spaceballs 1/2 **1987 (PG)** A humorous Brooks parody of recent science fiction pictures, mostly notably "Star Wars," with references to "Alien," the "Star Trek series," and "The Planet of the Apes." Disappointingly tame and tentative, but chuckle-laden enough for Brooks fans. The great man himself appears in two roles, including puny wise man/wise guy Yogurt. **96m/C; VHS, DVD, Blu-Ray.** Mel Brooks; Rick Moranis; John Candy; Bill Pullman; Daphne Zuniga; Dick Van Patten; John Hurt; George Wyner; Joan Rivers; Lorene Yarnell; Sal Viscuso; Stephen Tobolowsky; Dom DeLuise; Michael Winslow; ***D:*** Mel Brooks; ***W:*** Mel Brooks; Ronny Graham; Thomas Meehan; ***M:*** John Morris.

SpaceCamp **1986 (PG)** Gang o'teens and their instructor at the U.S. Space Camp are accidentally launched on a space shuttle, and then must find a way to return to Earth. Hokey plot, subpar special effects; why bother? Well, it is "inspirational." **115m/C; VHS, DVD, Blu-Ray.** Kate Capshaw; Tate Donovan; Joaquin Rafael (Leaf) Phoenix; Kelly Preston; Larry B. Scott; Tom Skerritt; Lea Thompson; Terry O'Quinn; ***D:*** Harry Winer; ***M:*** John Williams.

Spaced Invaders 1/2 **1990 (PG)** Five ultra-cool aliens crash-land in a small midwestern town at Halloween. Local denizens mistake them for trick-or-treaters. Poorly made and a waste of time. **102m/C; VHS, DVD.** Douglas Barr; Royal Dano; Ariana Richards; Kevin Thompson; Jimmy Briscoe; Tony Cox; Debbie Lee Carrington; Tommy Madden; ***D:*** Patrick Read Johnson; ***W:*** Scott Lawrence Alexander; ***C:*** James L. Carter.

Spaced Out **WOOF!** *Outer Reach* **1980 (R)** Naughty sci-fi sex comedy that parodies everything from "Star Wars" to "2001," though not very well. The sultry female aliens are visually pleasing, though. Watch this one with the sound turned off. **85m/C; VHS, DVD.** Barry Stokes; Glory Annen; ***D:*** Norman J. Warren.

Spacehunter: Adventures in the Forbidden Zone 1/2 **1983 (PG)** Galactic bounty hunter agrees to rescue three damsels held captive by a cyborg. Strauss ain't no Harrison Ford. Filmed in 3-D, but who cares? **90m/C; VHS, DVD, Blu-Ray.** ***CA*** Peter Strauss; Molly Ringwald; Michael Ironside; Ernie Hudson; Andrea Marcovicci; ***D:*** Lamont Johnson; ***W:*** Len Blum; ***C:*** Frank Tidy; ***M:*** Elmer Bernstein.

Spacejacked 1/2 **1998 (R)** In the future, the wealthy take pleasure trips to the Moon. Only greedy Barnes (Bernsen) sabotages the ship in order to extort money from the passengers—promising them a safe passage home in the escape pod. Of course, Barnes tries to double-cross everyone. Filled with low-budget cliches. **89m/C; VHS, DVD.** Corbin Bernsen; Amanda Pays; Steve Bond; ***D:*** Jeremiah Cullinane; ***W:*** Brendan Broderick; Daniella Purcell; ***C:*** Laurence Manly; ***M:*** Siobhan Cleary.

Spaceship 🦴 ½ *The Creature Wasn't Nice; Naked Space* **1981 (PG)** Misguided attempt to spoof creature-features. Mad scientist tries to protect kindly monster from crazed crew. Not very funny, with the exception of the song-and-dance routine by the monster. **88m/C; VHS, DVD.** Cindy Williams; Bruce Kimmel; Leslie Nielsen; Gerrit Graham; Patrick Macnee; Ron Kurowski; Paul Brinegar; Cheri(e) Steinkellner; ***D:*** Bruce Kimmel; ***W:*** Bruce Kimmel; ***C:*** Denny Lavil; ***M:*** Bruce Kimmel; David Spear. **VIDEO**

Spaceways 🦴 ½ **1953** Scientist Duff is beset by all sorts of troubles: his experimental rockets explode, his wife has an affair with an ambitious scientist, and when they disappear together, he's accused of killing them and placing their bodies in the exploded rocket. All in all, a pretty bad (and long) day for our hero. Why should we suffer through it with him? **76m/B; VHS, DVD.** Howard Duff; Eva Bartok; Ceclie Cheyreau; Andrew Osborn; ***D:*** Terence Fisher; ***W:*** Richard H. Landau; Paul Tabori; ***C:*** Reg Wyer; ***M:*** Ivor Stanley.

Spanglish 🦴 ½ **2004 (PG-13)** Sandler plays a sweetheart of a hubby in Brooks's problematic social comedy. As celebrity chef John Clasky, he's loving and supportive despite the complete self-absorption of his disturbingly unpleasant wife, Deborah (Leoni). Even Deborah's live-in lush of a mother (Leachman) knows what a horror her daughter is. Into this unhappy household comes lovely Flor (Vega), a Mexican illegal (who doesn't yet speak English) who takes the job as housekeeper because it will offer a better life for her own daughter, Cristina (Bruce). Given John's marital circumstances, is it any wonder that he and Flor become increasingly simpatico? Sandler's sincere and Leoni is nothing if not gutsy but it hardly seems worth the effort. **129m/C; VHS, DVD, Blu-Ray.** Adam Sandler; Tea Leoni; Paz Vega; Cloris Leachman; Thomas Haden Church; Shelbie Bruce; Sarah Steele; Ian Hyland; Victoria Luna; ***D:*** James L. Brooks; ***W:*** James L. Brooks; ***C:*** John Seale; ***M:*** Hans Zimmer.

The Spaniard's Curse 🦴🦴 ½ **1958** When a man is convicted for a murder he did not commit, he puts a curse on the judge and jury responsible. Mysteriously, the marked people begin dying. Is he responsible? Then he dies and the mystery thickens. Intriguing but sloppy murder mystery. **80m/B; VHS, DVD.** ***GB*** Tony Wright; Lee Patterson; Michael Hordern; Ralph Truman; Henry Oscar; ***D:*** Ralph Kemplen.

The Spanish Gardener 🦴🦴🦴 **1957** A boy in a prominent family spends more time with the gentle gardner than with the domineering father, so dad arranges for his rival to be framed and sent to prison. An affecting British adaptation of the A.J. Cronin novel, turned into a showcase for Bogarde in the title role. **95m/C; DVD.** ***UK*** Dirk Bogarde; Jon Whiteley; Michael Hordern; Cyril Cusack; Maureen Swanson; Lyndon Brook; Josephine Griffin; Bernard Lee; ***D:*** Philip Leacock; ***W:*** John Bryan; Mabel Margaret Clark; ***C:*** Christopher Challis; ***M:*** John Veale.

Spanish Judges 🦴 ½ **1999 (R)** Boring crime drama set in L.A. finds three criminals—muscle Max (D'Onofrio), brains Jack (Lillard), and vamp Jamie (Golino)?looking to steal a couple of valuable Spanish pistols. Yes, it does sound roughly like the plot to "The Mexican" but this film is much worse. **98m/C; VHS, DVD.** Vincent D'Onofrio; Matthew Lillard; Valeria Golino; Sam Hiona; ***D:*** Oz Scott; ***W:*** William Rehor; ***C:*** Stephen McNutt.

The Spanish Main 🦴🦴 ½ **1945** Typical, gusto-laden swashbuckler, RKO's first in Technicolor. Evil Spanish governor Slezak captures Dutch crew led by Henreid. They escape and kidnap his fiancee (O'Hara) off a ship coming from Mexico. Henreid forces her to marry him, but his crew uses the might of the armada and returns O'Hara to Slezak behind Henreid's back. Wow! **100m/C; DVD.** Paul Henreid; Maureen O'Hara; Walter Slezak; Binnie Barnes; John Emery; Barton MacLane; ***D:*** Frank Borzage; ***C:*** George Barnes.

The Spanish Prisoner 🦴🦴🦴 **1997 (PG)** Playwright-filmmaker Mamet goes Hitchcockian in thriller involving an elaborate con game. Naive inventor Joe Ross (Scott) develops a formula for something called "the Process" and soon finds himself a victim of industrial espionage. In a bit of stunt casting that works, Martin plays a sinister, wealthy businessman who befriends Joe and advises him about his coroprate employers. No one is what they appear to be (if they were, it wouldn't be much of a thriller) in this unpredictable and seductive puzzle. Although the staccato dialogue is grating at times, and the emotional payoff is slight, there's enough twists throughout to keep you intrigued. Title comes from an old scam that feeds on the greed and lust of the mark. **112m/C; VHS, DVD, Blu-Ray.** Campbell Scott; Steve Martin; Rebecca Pidgeon; Ben Gazzara; Ricky Jay; Felicity Huffman; Ed O'Neill; ***D:*** David Mamet; ***W:*** David Mamet; ***C:*** Gabriel Beristain; ***M:*** Carter Burwell.

Spanking the Monkey 🦴🦴🦴 **1994 (R)** "What'd ya do on your summer vacation?" Ray Aibelli (Davies) has an interesting answer in this dark comedy about family dysfunction, sexual politics, incest and masturbation, topics which guarantee it a special place on the video shelf. Returning from his freshman year at M.I.T., Ray learns he must give up a prestigious internship to care for his bedridden mother (Watson) while Dad goes on an extended "business" trip. Much sexual and emotional confusion follows. Mom, it seems, is rather attractive, controlling, and in need of hands-on assistance. Black comedy is understated and sensitive, focusing attention on the story and characters rather than the delicate subject matter, but you'll be aware of the delicate subject matter, nonetheless. Sharp directorial debut by Russell features fine performances by mostly unknown cast, elevating low-budget feel. See it with a relative. **99m/C; VHS, DVD.** Jeremy Davies; Alberta Watson; Benjamin Hendrickson; Carla Gallo; Matthew Puckett; ***D:*** David O. Russell; ***W:*** David O. Russell; ***C:*** Mike Mayers. Ind. Spirit '95: First Feature, First Screenplay; Sundance '94: Aud. Award.

Spare Parts **WOOF! 1979** Guests at a remote hotel discover that it is run by black marketeers who kill guests and sell the body parts. Of course, they don't bother signing out. **108m/C; VHS, DVD.** ***GE*** Judith Speidel; Wolf Roth; ***D:*** Rainer Erler; ***W:*** Rainer Erler; ***C:*** Wolfgang Grasshoff; ***M:*** Eugen Thomass.

Spare Parts 🦴🦴 **2015 (PG-13)** Based on a true story about a group of high school students who compete in an underwater robotics competition, this drama was adapted from an article in Wired Magazine...further proving that movies shouldn't be adapted from articles in Wired Magazine. In 2004, four Carl Hayden High School students won first place in a national robotics competition over M.I.T. How did they do it, especially with a meager $800 budget and a bunch of used car parts? Add to the heartwarming true story that all were undocumented Mexican immigrants, it's amazing that it took Hollywood a decade to come calling. **114m/C; DVD.** George Lopez; Carlos Pena; Jose Julian; David Del Rio; Oscar Gutierrez; Alexa Vega; Jamie Lee Curtis; Esai Morales; Marisa Tomei; ***D:*** Sean McNamara; ***W:*** Elissa Matsueda; ***C:*** Richard Wong; ***M:*** Andres Levin.

Spark 🦴 ½ **1998** Quarreling lovers Byron and Nina are stranded when their car breaks down in nowheresville. Stuck in a redneck dump while their ride is being fixed, the couple learns too many ugly local secrets. **102m/C; DVD.** Terrence Howard; Nicole Ari Parker; Brendan Sexton, III; Sandra Ellis Lafferty; Timothy McNeil; ***D:*** Garret Williams; ***W:*** Garret Williams; ***C:*** Samuel Ameen; ***M:*** Marc Anthony Thompson.

Spark: A Space Tail **WOOF! 2017 (PG)** In this uninspired animated outing, Spark is a teen living with his friends on an abandoned planet, hanging out and doing what Hollywood animation writers imagine teens on abandoned planets do. He finds out that the evil General Zhong, who destroyed his planet and killed his parents, plans to DESTROY THE UNIVERSE! With a space Kraken. Yeah, it's just as silly as it sounds. Despite a good voice cast, nothing about it works, with a lame script filled with bad puns, dismal computer-generated animation, and unlikeable characters. **91m/C; DVD.** ***V:*** Jace Norman; Jessica Biel; Susan Sarandon; Patrick Stewart; Hilary Swank; ***D:*** Aaron Woodley; ***W:*** Aaron Woodley; ***M:*** Robert Duncan.

Sparkle 🦴🦴 ½ **1976 (PG)** The saga of three singing sisters struggling to rise to the top of the charts in the 1950s. Sound familiar? Well done but cliched fictional version of the Supremes' career. McKee shines. Alcohol, drugs, and mobsters get in the way. Excellent musical score. **98m/C; VHS, DVD, Blu-Ray.** Irene Cara; Lonette McKee; Dwan Smith; Philip Michael Thomas; Mary Alice; Dorian Harewood; Tony King; ***D:*** Sam O'Steen; ***W:*** Joel Schumacher; ***M:*** Curtis Mayfield.

Sparkle 🦴🦴 **2007** Ambitious, charming, 22-year-old Sam (Evans) moves to London but is appalled when his single mom Jill (Manville) insists on joining him to further her singing career. Sam manages to win over much-older public relations exec Sheila (Channing) in the office and the bedroom, but then gets involved with young Kate (Ryan) as well. However, this romantic triangle has more than one obvious problem. **104m/C; DVD.** Shaun Evans; Stockard Channing; Amanda Ryan; Lesley Manville; Bob Hoskins; Anthony Head; John Schrapnel; ***D:*** Tom Hunsinger; Neil Hunter; ***W:*** Tom Hunsinger; Neil Hunter; ***C:*** Sean Van Hales; ***M:*** Adrian Johnston.

Sparkle 🦴🦴 ½ **2012 (PG-13)** Houston's final film, a remake of the 1976 pic, features some striking musical numbers for both the former superstar and Sparks but the the plot never reaches above melodrama and remains too old-fashioned to be memorable. The title refers to Sparks' character, a musical rising star who has to leave behind her single mother (Houston) as she finds love (with Luke) and tries to form a trio with her sisters (Ejogo, Sumpter). Sparks is a charismatic lead but the film is too familiar. **116m/C; DVD, Blu-Ray.** Jordin Sparks; Carmen Ejogo; Tika Sumpter; Whitney Houston; Mike Epps; Derek Luke; Michael Beach; ***D:*** Salim Akil; ***W:*** Mara Brock Akil; ***C:*** Anastas Michos; ***M:*** Salaam Remi.

Sparkler 🦴🦴 ½ **1999 (R)** Effervescemt Melba May (Overall) is a trailer-park wife, living just off the highway to Vegas. She leaves husband, Flint (Harvey), for cheating on her and eventually winds up in Vegas with three young men she just met and her old high-school buddy Dottie (Cartwright), who's now a stripper. And everybody gets an education of sorts. Doesn't have a consistent tone, with Overall and Cartwright providing the best performances. **96m/C; VHS, DVD.** Park Overall; Veronica Cartwright; Jamie Kennedy; Steven Petrarca; Freddie Prinze, Jr.; Don Harvey; Grace Zabriskie; Sandy Martin; ***D:*** Darren Stein; ***W:*** Darren Stein; Catherine Eads; ***C:*** Rodney Taylor; ***M:*** David E. Russo.

Sparks 🦴🦴 **2013** A comic book action film based on a graphic novel series created by Christopher Folino. When a radioactive meteor hits Earth, a group of people are genetically altered and gain superpowers in the process. Ian Sparks (Williamson) is one of the group, known as the Rochester 13. It is not until his parents die that he uses his powers to fight crime in New York City. His partner in fighting crime is Lady Heavenly (Bell), with whom he falls in love. Together, they defeat the criminal element in the city with ease, but find themselves without enough strength to defeat the most evil villain in the United States. After Sparks loses it all, including Bell, he seeks vengeance that results in changes in him and the world. **90m/C; DVD, Blu-Ray, Streaming, Download.** Chase Williamson; Ashley Bell; Clancy Brown; Jake Busey; William Katt; ***D:*** Todd Burrows; Christopher Folino; ***W:*** Christopher Folino; ***C:*** Josh Fritts; Jackson Myers; ***M:*** Jacob Shea.

Sparrows 🦴🦴🦴 **1926** Hidden in a southern swamp, the evil Grimes (von Seyffertz) runs a baby farm, where unwanted children are sent and used a slave labor. The eldest, nicknamed Mama Mollie (Pickford), tries to protect the others from Grimes's cruelty. They eventually plan their escape but must cross treacherous quicksand with Grimes in pursuit. Silent melodrama features a notable performance by Pickford. **109m/B; Silent; VHS, DVD, Blu-Ray.** Mary Pickford; Gustav von Seyffertitz; Charlotte Mineau; Roy Stewart; Mary Louise Miller; "Spec" (Walter) O'Donnell; Mary Frances McLean; Cammilla Johnson; Seesel Ann Johnson; ***D:*** William Beaudine; ***W:*** C. Gardner Sullivan; Winifred Dunn; ***C:*** Charles Rosher; Karl Struss; Hal Mohr; ***M:*** William Perry.

Spartacus 🦴🦴🦴🦴 **1960 (PG-13)** The true story of a gladiator who leads other slaves in a rebellion against the power of Rome in 73 B.C. The rebellion is put down and the rebels are crucified. Douglas, whose political leanings are amply on display herein, also served as executive producer, surrounding himself with the best talent available. Magnificent climactic battle scene features 8,000 real, live Spanish soldiers to stunning effect. A version featuring Kubrick's "director's cut" is also available, featuring a restored, controversial homoerotic bath scene with Olivier and Curtis. Anthony Mann is uncredited as co-director. A boxoffice triumph that gave Kubrick much-desired financial independence. **196m/C; VHS, DVD, Blu-Ray, HD-DVD.** Kirk Douglas; Laurence Olivier; Jean Simmons; Tony Curtis; Charles Laughton; Herbert Lom; Nina Foch; Woody Strode; Peter Ustinov; John Gavin; John Ireland; Charles McGraw; Joanna Barnes; Vinton (Hayworth) Haworth; ***D:*** Stanley Kubrick; ***W:*** Dalton Trumbo; ***C:*** Russell Metty; ***M:*** Alex North. Oscars '60: Art Dir./Set Dec., Color, Color Cinematog., Costume Des. (C), Support. Actor (Ustinov); Golden Globes '61: Film--Drama; Natl. Film Reg. '17.

Spartan 🦴🦴🦴 **2004 (R)** The president's daughter has been kidnapped—possibly by a Middle Eastern group of woman slave traders—and cagey special ops agent Robert Scott (Kilmer) is entrusted with the task of bringing her home. But, as with any Mamet venture, what seems to be the reality might not be and the deeper Scott gets into the job the less he can be certain of. His dilemma and the questions that swirl around make for high-octane action-thriller fun...until it sadly runs out of gas toward the end. Kilmer seizes the character along with the fundamentals of the smart, fast-paced language; Luke has a good turn (as Scott's trainee) as do perpetual Mamet performers Macy and O'Neill. **107m/C; DVD.** Val Kilmer; Derek Luke; Tia Texada; Kristen Bell; Johnny Messner; Lionel Mark Smith; Tony Mamet; Clark Gregg; Steven Culp; Aaron Stanford; Geoffrey Pierson; William H. Macy; Ed O'Neill; Andrew Davoli; Said Taghmaoui; Matt Malloy; Kick (Christopher) Gurry; David Paymer; ***D:*** David Mamet; ***W:*** David Mamet; ***C:*** Juan Ruiz-Anchia; ***M:*** Mark Isham.

Spawn 🦴🦴🦴 **1997 (PG-13)** Government agent Al Simmons (White) returns to earth, six years after being murdered, in the form of Spawn, a hell-born creature with supernatural powers. He wants to avenge his death and also save his loved ones from the evil Violator (Leguizamo). With green eyes and a friendship with Satan, Spawn's more of a lethal weapon and way more sinister looking than the villain. An unrecognizable Leguizamo and sleazy Sheen team up as adequate adversaries. Extravagant special effects, and a complex, dark story put a unique spin on the over-exposed superhero premise. Adapted from the best-selling comic book. An R-rated director's cut, which includes a "making of" feature and an interview with Todd McFarlane, is also available. **97m/C; VHS, DVD, Blu-Ray.** Michael Jai White; John Leguizamo; Martin Sheen; Theresa Randle; D.B. Sweeney; Nicol Williamson; Melinda (Mindy) Clarke; Miko Hughes; Michael (Mike) Papajohn; ***D:*** Mark Dippe; ***W:*** Alan B. McElroy; ***C:*** Guillermo Navarro; ***M:*** Graeme Revell.

Spawn of the North 🦴🦴 ½ **1938** Alaska's the final frontier in the early 1900s as fisherman Jim Kimmerlee (Fonda) tries to earn an honest buck. But former friend Tyler Dawson (Raft) has joined a group of Russian pirates who plunder the nets of others and the two men are forced into a deadly confrontation. Solid cast, weak script, and a special Oscar for photographic and sound effects (a glacier's involved). Based on the novel by Barrett Willoughby; remade in 1954 as "Alaska Seas." **110m/B; VHS, DVD.** Henry Fonda; George Raft; Dorothy Lamour; John Barrymore; Akim Tamiroff; Louise Platt; Fuzzy Knight; Duncan Renaldo; ***D:*** Henry Hathaway; ***W:*** Jules Furthman; Talbot Jennings; ***C:*** Charles B(ryant) Lang, Jr.; ***M:*** Dimitri Tiomkin.

Speak 2004 (PG-13) Stewart gives an amazingly touching performance as Melinda Sordino, a high school freshman who has retreated into selective mutism after being raped at a summer party. Having called the cops on a popular senior, Melinda is now a social pariah, with her parents (Perkins, Sweeney) too preoccupied to recognize her anguish. But over the school year, her unconventional art teacher, Mr. Freeman (Zahn), shows Melinda that expressing herself is a way to confront her experience. Based on the novel by Laurie Halse Anderson. **93m/C; DVD.** Kristen Stewart; Steve Zahn; Elizabeth Perkins; D.B. Sweeney; Hallee Hirsh; Eric Lively; Michael Angarano; Robert John Burke; Allison Siko; ***D:*** Jessica Sharzer; ***W:*** Jessica Sharzer; Annie Young; ***C:*** Andrij Parekh. **CABLE**

Speak Easily 1/2 1932 Keaton is bored with his dull life as a college professor. Durante tries to spice things up with a phony inheritance letter, and Keaton decides to spend his supposed money backing a stage show. Keaton is the star, but Durante steals the show. Great supporting cast. **82m/B; VHS, DVD.** Buster Keaton; Jimmy Durante; Ruth Selwyn; Thelma Todd; Hedda Hopper; Sidney Toler; Lawrence Grant; Henry Armetta; Edward Brophy; ***D:*** Edward Sedgwick.

Speaking Parts 1989 VCR-obsessed laundry worker and another woman battle for the attention of bit-part actor McManus who works in ritzy hotel. A telling picture of the inextricable nature of modern technology. **92m/C; VHS, DVD.** *CA* Michael McManus; Arsinee Khanjian; David Hemblen; Gabrielle Rose; Tony Nardi; Patricia Collins; Gerard Parkes; ***D:*** Atom Egoyan; ***W:*** Atom Egoyan; ***C:*** Paul Sarossy; ***M:*** Mychael Danna.

Special 1/2 2006 (R) Comic book fan Les (Rapaport) is a completely average L.A. working guy. He's accepted into an experimental drug program designed to overcome depression but the side effects have Les believing he's turned into a vigilante superhero. Now delusional, Les is not only a danger to himself but to others. **82m/C; DVD.** Michael Rapaport; Paul Blackthorne; Josh Peck; Robert Baker; Jack Kehoe; Alexandra Holden; Ian Bohen; ***D:*** Hal Haberman; Jeremy Passmore; ***W:*** Hal Haberman; Jeremy Passmore; ***C:*** Nelson Craig; ***M:*** Tom Wolfe; Manish Raval.

Special Bulletin 1983 A pacifistic terrorist threatens to blow up Charleston, South Carolina, with a nuclear warhead. Done quite well in docu-drama style as a TV news bulletin. Interesting examination of the media's treatment of dramatic events. Top-notch made-for-TV fare. **105m/C; VHS, DVD.** Ed Flanders; Christopher Allport; Kathryn Walker; Roxanne Hart; ***D:*** Edward Zwick; ***W:*** Marshall Herskovitz; Edward Zwick. **TV**

A Special Day *Una Giornata Speciale; The Great Day* 1977 The day of a huge rally celebrating Hitler's visit to Rome in 1939 serves as the backdrop for an affair between weary housewife Loren and lonely, unhappy homosexual radio announcer Mastroianni. Good performances from two thorough pros make a depressing film well worth watching. In Italian with English subtitles or dubbed. **105m/C; VHS, DVD, Blu-Ray.** *IT* Sophia Loren; Marcello Mastroianni; John Vernon; Francoise Berd; ***D:*** Ettore Scola; ***W:*** Ettore Scola; Ruggero Maccari; Maurizio Costanzo; ***C:*** Pasqualino De Santis; ***M:*** Armando Trovajoli. Golden Globes '78: Foreign Film.

Special Delivery 1/2 2008 Courier Maxine Carter (Edelstein) works in the Pacific Rim and her latest job is to escort bratty teenager Alice Cantwell (Song) from Macau to Maui. The daughter of a wealthy businessman living in China, Alice has been the object of a bitter custody battle. However, when Max discovers that Alice's father is in trouble with the Chinese government, her delivery gets a lot more dangerous. There's more bonding than action but both leads are good. **90m/C; DVD.** Lisa Edelstein; Brenda Song; Robert Gant; Ned Van Zandt; Michael Cowell; Stan(ford) Egi; Dann Seki; ***D:*** Michael Scott; ***W:*** Matt Dearborn; ***C:*** Stuart Asbjornsen; ***M:*** Philip Griffin. **CABLE**

Special Effects 1985 (R) A desperate movie director murders a young actress, then makes a movie about her death. Solid, creepy premise sinks in the mire of flawed execution; a good film about Hollywood ego trips and obsession is lurking inside overdone script. **103m/C; VHS, DVD, Blu-Ray.** *GB* Zoe Tamerlis; Eric Bogosian; Kevin J. O'Connor; Brad Rijn; Bill Oland; Richard Greene; ***D:*** Larry Cohen; ***W:*** Larry Cohen.

Special Forces *Hell in Normandy* 1968 Eight specially trained soldiers drop behind enemy lines to rescue prisoners of war in WWII. **90m/C; VHS, DVD.** *IT* Peter Lee Lawrence; Guy Madison; Erika Blanc; Tony Norton; ***D:*** Alfonso Brescia; ***W:*** Maurice De Vries; Lorenzo Gicca Palli; ***C:*** Fausto Rossi; ***M:*** Italo Fischetti.

Special Forces 1/2 2003 (R) American photojournalist Wendy Teller (Deutscher) stumbles across war crimes in a fictitious Eastern European country and is held hostage. A team of Army commandos is sent in to rescue her and their leader (Teague) happens to have a past with the head bad guy (Danker). **96m/C; DVD.** Marshall Teague; Tim Abell; Eli Danker; Scott Adkins; Daniella Deutscher; Danny Lee Clark; ***D:*** Isaac Florentine; ***W:*** David N. White; ***C:*** Gideon Porath; ***M:*** Stephen (Steve) Edwards. **VIDEO**

Special Forces *Forces Spéciales* 2011 (R) When a french reporter is kidnapped by the Taliban, her government sends a special forces team to rescue her. **109m/C; DVD, Blu-Ray, Streaming.** *FR* Diane Kruger; Djimon Hounsou; Benoît Magimel; Denis Menochet; Raphael Personnaz; ***D:*** Stephane Rybojad; ***W:*** Stephane Rybojad; Michael Cooper; Emmanuelle Collomp; ***C:*** David Jankowski; ***M:*** Xavier Berthelot.

The Special Relationship 2010 The third film from writer Morgan about British Prime Minister Tony Blair (following "The Deal" and "The Queen") focuses on the friendship and political support that develops between Blair and President Bill Clinton from 1996-2000. Then the Monica Lewinsky scandal sidetracks Clinton domestically while Blair increasingly plays a larger hand in world events, especially in Kosovo. **93m/C; DVD.** Michael Sheen; Dennis Quaid; Hope Davis; Helen McCrory; Marc Rioufol; Mark Bazeley; Adam Godfrey; ***D:*** Richard Loncraine; ***W:*** Peter Morgan; ***C:*** Barry Ackroyd; ***M:*** Alexandre Desplat. **CABLE**

Special Treatment 1/2 *Sans Queue ni Tete* 2010 Subdued and remarkably bland French drama. Forty-something, high-priced Parisian prostitute Alice (Huppert) has a new client in depressed psychoanalyst Xavier (Lanners). Finding similarities between their two careers, Alice decides to seek his professional help in finally quitting her occupation, which now bores her. French with subtitles. **95m/C; DVD.** *FR* Isabelle Huppert; Bouli Lanners; Mathieu Carrere; Richard Debuisne; ***D:*** Jeanne Labrune; ***W:*** Richard Debuisne; Jeanne Labrune; ***C:*** Virginie Saint-Martin; ***M:*** Andre Mergenthaler.

The Specialist 1/2 1975 (R) Lawyer West thinks he has seduced stunning Capri, but she has lured him into her clutches—she's been hired to kill him. Campy crud. It's old home week for '60s TV alums: West was Batman; bailiff Moore was Mr. Kimbell on Green Acres. **93m/C; VHS, DVD.** Adam West; John Anderson; Ahna Capri; Alvy Moore; ***D:*** Howard (Hikmet) Avedis; ***W:*** Howard (Hikmet) Avedis; Marlene Schmidt; Ralph B. Potts; ***C:*** Massoud Joseph; ***M:*** Shorty Rogers.

The Specialist 1/2 1994 (R) Buffed bods do not a movie make—at least not in this mechanical actioner featuring Stone as the revenge-minded May Munro. Seems May's parents were killed by Cuban gangsters, led by father/son thugs Joe (Steiger) and Tomas Leon (Roberts), and she decides ex-CIA bomb specialist Ray Quick (Stallone) is just the man she needs to settle the score. But Quick has his own reasons for accepting—his ex-partner is nutball Ned Trent (Woods), who's now working for the Leons. Things blow up a lot, the two leads show off their toned flesh (but not much acting), and Woods gets to steal the movie with his amusing scenery chewing. **110m/C; VHS, DVD, Blu-Ray.** Sylvester Stallone; Sharon Stone; James Woods; Eric Roberts; Rod Steiger; ***D:*** Luis Llosa; ***W:*** Alexandra Seros; ***C:*** Jeffrey L. Kimball; ***M:*** John Barry. Golden Raspberries '94: Worst Actress (Stone).

The Specials 2000 This is the movie that "Mystery Men" wanted to be. It's a smart comic book spoof that depends on good acting and well-written characters. The Specials are the sixth or seventh greatest team of superheroes in the business. Headquarters is a suburban house in Silver Lake. Their immediate goal—if they can quit bickering among themselves—it to get a line of action figures on the market. **89m/C; DVD.** Rob Lowe; Jamie Kennedy; Thomas Haden Church; Paget Brewster; Judy Greer; James Gunn; Sean Gunn; Jordan Ladd; Kelly Coffield; ***D:*** Craig Mazin; ***W:*** James Gunn; ***C:*** Eliot Rockett; ***M:*** Brian Langsbard; Spring Aspers.

Species 1/2 1995 (R) A "friendly" galactic message containing a recipe on how to combine extraterrestrial DNA with human DNA is sent to scientists on Earth. The scientists, led by Fitch (Kingsley), whip up a batch of genetic material resulting in a sexy half alien, half human procreating/killing machine named Sil (model Henstridge's film debut). Naturally, Sil escapes from the lab, leaving the scientists with the unenviable task of catching her/it. All-star special effects team, including "Alien" designer H. R. Giger, create over-the-top, stomach-churning thrills. Dips liberally into the tricks of many sci-fi classics. For avid gore-meisters only. **108m/C; VHS, DVD, Blu-Ray, UMD.** Ben Kingsley; Michael Madsen; Alfred Molina; Forest Whitaker; Marg Helgenberger; Natasha Henstridge; Michelle Williams; ***D:*** Roger Donaldson; ***W:*** Dennis Feldman; ***C:*** Andrzej Bartkowiak; ***M:*** Christopher Young. MTV Movie Awards '96: Kiss (Natasha Henstridge/Anthony Guidera).

Species 2 1/2 1998 (R) Genetic scientists, in their quest to see an actual babe who will talk to genetic scientists, create a clone named Eve (Henstridge) from the monster in the original movie. Meanwhile, the U.S. has managed to successfully put an underwear model who can't act on Mars. Astronaut Patrick Ross (Lazard) has been infected with spores of alien DNA. Soon Ross' urge to procreate takes over and nasty alien babies are exploding out of screaming women all over town Government assassin Press Lennox (Madsen) and Dr. Laura Baker (Helgenberger) are once again called in to help track down the new species, with the help of Eve. Can they stop Ross and his brood before they mature? Can they stop Eve and Ross from making the beast with several scaly slimy multi-appendaged backs? Can they please stop making this movie again? **95m/C; VHS, DVD, Blu-Ray.** Natasha Henstridge; Justin Lazard; Michael Madsen; Marg Helgenberger; Mykelti Williamson; George Dzundza; James Cromwell; Myriam Cyr; Baxter Harris; ***D:*** Peter Medak; ***W:*** Chris Brancato; ***C:*** Matthew F. Leonetti; ***M:*** Ed Shearmur.

Species 3 2004 (R) Eve has a daughter as she's dying and that girl, Sara (Mabrey), a genetically superior specimen, is out to mate with humans to propogate her species. She is pursued by a military team, a group of half-breed aliens with a fatal defect, and the professor who wants to experiment on her DNA. Lots of female nudity is supposed to make up for an extremely low budget and convoluted story. Surprisingly, it doesn't. **112m/C; DVD, Blu-Ray.** Natasha Henstridge; Sunny Mabrey; Robert Knepper; Robin Dunne; Amelia Cooke; Michael Warren; Christopher Neame; John Paul (J.P.) Pitoc. **VIDEO**

Species 4: The Awakening 2007 Same old, same old. Miranda (Mattsson) discovers she's been cloned from both human and alien DNA. She awakens from a blackout and learns she's probably a murderer after her alien side goes on the hunt for a mate. **103m/C; DVD, Blu-Ray.** Ben Cross; Dominic Keating; Helena Mattsson; Marco Bacuzzi; ***D:*** Nick Lyon; ***W:*** Ben Ripley; ***C:*** Jaime Reynoso; ***M:*** Paul Cristo; Kevin Haskins. **VIDEO**

Specimen 1/2 1997 (R) Twenty-four years ago, aliens impregnated Carol Hillary and she gave birth to a son, Mark. Now, the aliens have returned to claim him, only he doesn't want to go. **85m/C; VHS, DVD.** *CA* Mark-Paul Gosselaar; Doug O'Keefe; Michelle Johnson; Andrew Jackson; ***D:*** John Bradshaw; ***W:*** Damian Lee; Sheldon Inkol; ***C:*** Gerald R. Goozie; ***M:*** Terence Gowan.

The Speckled Band 1931 Set in 1930, this early talkie is a Sherlock Holmes adventure wherein the great detective must solve the mysterious death of a young woman. Massey makes his screen debut as Holmes, making the sleuth cynical, unhappy and pessimistic. Interesting prototypical Holmes case, faithful to the like-titled Conan Doyle story. **84m/B; VHS, DVD.** Raymond Massey; Lyn Harding; Athole Stewart; Angela Baddeley; Nancy Price; ***D:*** Jack Raymond; ***C:*** Frederick A. (Freddie) Young.

Spectacular 2009 (G) In this Nickelodeon teen musical, rebellious rocker Nikko (Funk) needs cash to make a demo. So he agrees to partner with uptight high school singer Courtney (Sursok) who leads a choir that is trying to win the $10,000 first prize in a singing contest. Squeaky-clean similarities to Disney's "High School Musical" franchise are, no doubt, intentional. **93m/C; DVD.** Tammin Sursok; Greg Germann; Brittney Irvin; Nolan Gerard Funk; Victoria Justice; ***D:*** Robert Iscove; ***W:*** James Krieg; ***C:*** David Moxness. **CABLE**

The Spectacular Now 2013 (R) Sutter Keely (a magnificent Teller) is that high school senior who's the hit at every party but has no idea where he's going. He lives in the now--hence the title--and ignores the future but can't avoid it when his new girlfriend Aimee (Woodley) forces him to ask some serious questions about his direction in life. Smart, romantic, and moving, director Ponsoldt's film makes most other teen dramas pale in comparison just by being real and not schmaltzy. Adapted from Tim Tharp's 2008 novel. **95m/C; DVD, Blu-Ray.** Shailene Woodley; Miles Teller; Mary Elizabeth Winstead; Brie Larson; Jennifer Jason Leigh; Kyle Chandler; Andre Royo; Bob Odenkirk; ***D:*** James Ponsoldt; ***W:*** Scott Neustadter; Michael H. Weber; ***C:*** Jess Hall; ***M:*** Rob Simonsen.

The Spectator *La Spettatrice* 2004 Lonely 20-something Valeria (Bobulova), a translator in Turin, becomes obsessed with her middle-aged neighbor Massimo (Renzi), a doctor whose work she translates. When he moves to Rome, Valeria follows, only to discover he has a companion, Flavia (Catillon). After befriending Flavia, Valeria discovers that Massimo is now also interested in her. Romantic tribulations ensue. Italian with subtitles. **98m/C; DVD.** *IT* Barbara Bobulova; Andrea Renzi; Brigitte Catillon; ***D:*** Paolo Franchi; ***W:*** Paolo Franchi; ***C:*** Giuseppe Lanci; Stefano Paradiso; ***M:*** Carlo Crivelli.

Spectre *House of the Damned; Roger Corman Presents: House of the Damned* 1996 (R) Maura South (Paul) is the heiress to a old mansion in Ireland and when she, husband Will (Evigan), and their young daughter Aubrey (played by Evigan's daughter Briana) move in they discover it's haunted by the vengeful spirit of a young girl. When they discover the girl's body, the family hope a proper burial will set her spirit to rest but the ghost has other ideas. Filmed in Ireland. **82m/C; VHS, DVD.** Greg Evigan; Alexandra Paul; Briana Evigan; Eamon Draper; Dick Donaghue; ***D:*** Scott Levy; ***W:*** Brendan Broderick; ***C:*** Christopher Baffa; ***M:*** Christopher Lennertz. **CABLE**

Spectre 1/2 2015 (PG-13) Bond will always be Bond with his bravado, action-packed sequences, dashing suits, his way with the ladies, and all the toys. This 24th installment of Ian Fleming's superspy finds Bond (Craig) traveling the globe seeking information about an evil group known as Spectre. Meanwhile, M (Fiennes) works to ensure the viability of the secret service, which is threatened with disbandment in favor of electronics. Director Mendes' continues exposing Bonds' darker, brooding side rather than the campy fun of old. Which will suffice for those longtime fans. And regardless it's a lively jaunt in some beautiful places. **148m/C; DVD, Blu-Ray.** Dave Bautista; Monica Bellucci; Daniel Craig; Lea Seydoux; Ralph Fiennes; ***D:*** Sam Mendes; ***W:*** Neal Purvis; John Logan; Robert Wade; Jez Butterworth; ***C:*** Hoyte Van Hoytema; ***M:*** Thomas Newman. Oscars '15: Song ("Writing's on the Wall"); Golden Globes '16: Song ("Writing's on the Wall").

Speechless 1/2 1994 (PG-13) Cute romantic comedy about sparring speechwriters who fall in love, and then briefly turn enemies when they discover they're working at professional odds. Davis is the idealistic liberal working for senatorial candidate Wannamaker, while Keaton is a TV sitcom writer doing a one-shot deal for a millionaire businessman, Republican Garvin. Both stars do a likable job; the supporting cast fares better with Reeve as an egotistical TV reporter, as well as Davis's fiance, and Bedelia as Keaton's ex-wife/campaign press secretary. Although the film parallels the real-life romance of rival Bush-Clinton spin doctors Mary Matalin and James Carville, it was written prior to the last presidential race. **99m/C; VHS, DVD, Blu-Ray.** Michael Keaton; Geena Davis; Christopher Reeve; Bonnie Bedelia; Ernie Hudson; Charles Martin Smith; Gailard Sartain; Ray Baker; Mitchell Ryan; ***D:*** Ron Underwood; ***W:*** Robert King; ***C:*** Don Peterman; ***M:*** Marc Shaiman.

Speed 1/2 **1936** Routine MGM 'B' pic that's of interest more for its auto racing footage than plot. Terry Martin (Stewart) is a test driver and inventor at Emory Motors, working on a new carburetor. He wants it ready for the Indy 500, which means working with engineer Frank (Heyburn). Martin's reluctant--and not just because they're both interested in publicist Jane (Barrie). **70m/B; DVD.** James Stewart; Wendy Barrie; Weldon Heyburn; Una Merkel; Ted Healy; Ralph Morgan; ***D:*** Edwin L. Marin; ***W:*** Michael Fessier; ***C:*** Lester White; ***M:*** Edward Ward.

Speed 1/2 **1994 (R)** Excellent dude Reeves has grown up (and bulked up) as Los Angeles SWAT cop Jack Traven, up against bomb expert Howard Payne (Hopper, more maniacal than usual), who's after major ransom money. First it's a rigged elevator in a very tall building. Then it's a rigged bus—if it slows, it will blow, bad enough any day, but a nightmare in LA traffic. And that's still not the end. Terrific directorial debut for cinematographer De Bont, who certainly knows how to keep the adrenaline pumping. Fine support work by Daniels, Bullock, and Morton and enough wit in Yost's script to keep you chuckling. Great nonstop actioner from the "Die Hard" school. **115m/C; VHS, DVD, Blu-Ray, UMD.** Keanu Reeves; Dennis Hopper; Sandra Bullock; Joe Morton; Jeff Daniels; Alan Ruck; Glenn Plummer; Richard Lineback; Beth Grant; Hawthorne James; David Kriegel; Carlos Carrasco; Natsuko Ohama; Daniel Villarreal; ***D:*** Jan De Bont; ***W:*** Graham Yost; ***C:*** Andrzej Bartkowiak; ***M:*** Mark Mancina. Oscars '94: Sound; MTV Movie Awards '95: Action Seq., Female Perf. (Bullock), Most Desirable Female (Bullock), On-Screen Duo (Keanu Reeves/Sandra Bullock), Villain (Hopper); Blockbuster '95: Action Actress, T. (Bullock), Action Actress, V. (Bullock), Movie, V.

Speed 2: Cruise Control **1997 (PG-13)** Bigger's certainly not better in this lame sequel. Annie's (Bullock) got a new beau, hot-headed cop Alex (Patric), and the twosome decide to go on a Caribbean cruise for a little romance. Annie's luck with transportation holds as the ship is taken over by villainous computer geek-with-a-grudge John Giger (a particularly wild-eyed Dafoe), who sends the liner on a collision course with an oil tanker. Since Alex is off performing heroics, there's not much togetherness and Annie's left to get taken hostage (again). De Bont spent $25 mil on the ship's endless crash into a Caribbean island, which still manages to look fake and only elicits "you've got to be kidding me" disappointment. Bullock's feisty but powerless to save the flick. Patric's bland, and Dafoe is never menancing enough to create any thrills. This sea disaster crashes against the rocks of high expectations and poor execution. **123m/C; VHS, DVD, Blu-Ray.** Sandra Bullock; Jason Patric; Willem Dafoe; Temuera Morrison; Brian McCardie; Glenn Plummer; Royale Watkins; Colleen Camp; Lois Chiles; Michael G. (Mike) Hagerty; Kimmy Robertson; Christine Firkins; Bo Svenson; Patrika Darbo; Richard Speight, Jr.; Joe Morton; Enrique Murciano; ***Cameo(s):*** Tim Conway; ***D:*** Jan De Bont; ***W:*** Jan De Bont; Jeff Nathanson; Randall McCormick; ***C:*** Jack N. Green; ***M:*** Mark Mancina. Golden Raspberries '97: Worst Remake/Sequel.

Speed Dating 1/2 **2007 (R)** Uneven Irish romcom finds wealthy, lonesome loser James (O'Conor) deciding to try speed dating to find the woman of his dreams. He becomes attracted to a mysterious femme in a bar, gets caught up in a murder mystery, winds up with amnesia, and is cared for by pretty nurse Emma (King). **85m/C; DVD.** *IR* Hugh O'Conor; Emma Choy; Don Wycherley; Luke Griffin; David Hayman; Paul Ronan; Charlotte Bradley; Gerry O'Brien; ***D:*** Tony Herbert; ***W:*** Tony Herbert; ***C:*** John Conroy.

Speed-Dating **2010 (R)** Wannabe comedy about three losers you don't want to spend any time with. Bachelor buddies Dog, Beaver, and Too Cool are always futilely scheming their way to becoming rich and getting women. Two have a failing nightclub where the third sets up a speed dating business but nothing goes as planned. **90m/C; DVD.** Chico Benymon; Leonard Robinson; Wesley Jonathan; Holly Robinson Peete; Vanessa Simmons; Chris Elliott; Mekita Faiye; Clint Howard; Nick (Nicholas) Chinlund; ***D:*** Joseph A. Elmore, Jr.; ***W:*** Joseph A. Elmore, Jr.; ***C:*** David Daniel; ***M:*** Evan Scot Hornsby. **VIDEO**

Speed Kills **2018 (R)** In early 1960s New Jersey, Ben Aronoff (Travolta) flees to Miami after mobster Meyer Lansky (Remar) threatens his construction business. There, Aronoff falls in love with speedboats. Not only does become a successful racer, he also begins to sell them. Because Lansky gave him money, Aronoff agrees to use his boat business as a front for Lansky's drug business. This activity eventually attracts the attention of the DEA. Aronoff also faces family problems including the severe injury of his estranged son (Gillespie). Based on a true story, it's an un-entertaining, amateur quality film. **102m/C; DVD, Blu-Ray.** John Travolta; Katheryn Winnick; Jennifer Esposito; Michael Weston; Jordi Molla; ***D:*** Jodi Scurfield; ***W:*** David Aaron Cohen; John Luessenhop; ***C:*** Andrzej Sekula; ***M:*** Geronimo Mercado.

The Speed Lovers **1968** Stock car driver Lorenzen plays himself as an inspiration to a young man to join the auto racing circuit. More of a pat on the industry's back than a serious drama. Features footage from a number of race tracks around the country although shot principally in Atlanta. **102m/C; VHS, DVD.** Fred Lorenzen; William F. McGaha; Peggy O'Hara; David Marcus; Carol Street; Glenda Brunson; ***D:*** William F. McGaha; ***W:*** William F. McGaha; Elaine Wilkerson; Fred Tuch.

Speed of Life 1/2 *Saturn* **1999 (R)** Although Drew (Caan) loves his father (Burmester), he would prefer to be doing anything else instead of having the emotional and physical burden of caring for the terminally-ill man. Meeting drug-addicted Sarah (Kirshner) only heightens his desire to flee. Slow-moving and shallow. **95m/C; VHS, DVD.** Scott Caan; Mia Kirshner; Leo Burmester; Anthony Michael Ruivivar; ***D:*** Rob Schmidt; ***W:*** Rob Schmidt; ***C:*** Matthew Libatique; ***M:*** Ryeland Allison. **VIDEO**

The Speed of Thought 1/2 **2011** Predictable sci-fi thriller. Telepath Joshua Lazarus has been trained by the NSA to use his skills for government purposes. According to his handler, all telepaths in the program go nuts and chose euthanasia at the age of 29. Since Josh is 28 this is a major issue, especially since he's fallen in love with Anna. But what if it's all a lie? **93m/C; DVD.** Nick Stahl; Mia Maestro; Taryn Manning; Wallace Shawn; Blair Brown; Erik Palladino; ***D:*** Evan Oppenheimer; ***W:*** Evan Oppenheimer; ***C:*** Luke Geissbuhler; ***M:*** Andrew Gross.

Speed Racer 1/2 **2008 (PG)** It's a dizzying FX retro ride with Speed Racer (Hirsch) and his racing family, including Pops (Goodman), Mom (Sarandon), Spritle (Litt), and pet chimp Chim-Chim as they fight against corporate overlord Royalton's nasty plan for world domination, with a little help from the mysterious Racer X (Fox), who might just be Rex, Speed's older brother thought to have bought it in a crash. Also on hand is Trixie (Ricci), the girlfriend Speed might have if he weren't so busy righting wrongs behind the wheel of his car, the Mach 5. The story is flat, moody, and weird, but the racing is wild and the visuals are wilder—kids will dig it, as will fans of the original Japanese anime rendering. **129m/C; DVD, Blu-Ray, On Demand.** Emile Hirsch; Christina Ricci; Matthew Fox; John Goodman; Susan Sarandon; Roger Allam; Hiroyuki (Henry) Sanada; Richard Roundtree; Paulie (Litowsky) Litt; Benno Furmann; Scott Porter; Christian Oliver; ***D:*** Lilly Wachowski; Lana Wachowski; ***W:*** Lilly Wachowski; Lana Wachowski; ***C:*** David Tattersall; ***M:*** Michael Giacchino.

Speedway **1929** Brash mechanic Bill (Haines) is seemingly happy working for old racecar driver Jim MacDonald (Torrence) although he takes more than his fair share of credit for their success. He tries to impress Patricia (Page) but has no luck until he rescues her from a plane crash, which gets him publicity. Lee Renny (Miljan) offers Bill the chance to drive in the Indy 500 but it's all a ploy to get Bill to fine-tune his racecar so Renny can then dump Bill and drive a winner. **82m/B; Silent; DVD.** William Haines; Anita Page; Ernest Torrence; John Miljan; Eugenie Besserer; Karl (Daen) Dane; ***D:*** Harry Beaumont; ***W:*** Joe Farnham; ***C:*** Henry Sharp.

Speedway **1968 (G)** Elvis the stock car driver finds himself being chased by Nancy the IRS agent during an important race. Will Sinatra keep to the business at hand? Or will the King melt her heart? Some cameos by real-life auto racers. Watch for a young Garr. Movie number 27 for Elvis. **90m/C; VHS, DVD.** Elvis Presley; Nancy Sinatra; Bill Bixby; Gale Gordon; William Schallert; Carl Ballantine; Ross Hagen; ***Cameo(s):*** Richard Petty; Cale Yarborough; Teri Garr; ***D:*** Norman Taurog; ***C:*** Joseph Ruttenberg.

Speedway Junky 1/2 **1999** Army brat Johnny (Bradford) dreams of being an auto racing champion. So he runs away from his home in California determined to make it to North Carolina and get a job with driver Richard Petty's crew. At a stop in Vegas, naive Johnny gets robbed and comes to the attention of seasoned hustler Eric (Brower) who offers to teach Johnny the ropes. Johnny agrees but will only deal with women clients—while the gay Eric falls in love with the new kid in town. **105m/C; VHS, DVD.** Jesse Bradford; Jordan Brower; Jonathan Taylor Thomas; Daryl Hannah; Patsy Kensit; Tiffani(-Amber) Thiessen; ***D:*** Nickolas Perry; ***W:*** Nickolas Perry; ***C:*** Steve Adcock; ***M:*** Stan Ridgway.

Speedy **1928** Lloyd comes to the rescue when the last horse car in NYC, operated by his fiance's grandfather, is stolen by a gang. Thoroughly phoney, fun pursuit/action comedy shot on location. Look for a brief appearance by Babe Ruth. **72m/B; VHS, DVD, Blu-Ray.** Harold Lloyd; Bert Woodruff; Ann Christy; ***D:*** Ted Wilde.

Speedy Death *The Mrs. Bradley Mysteries: Speedy Death* **1999** Gladys Mitchell wrote some 66 mysteries starring the witty and clever Mrs. Adela Bradley (Rigg). A wealthy divorcee, Mrs. Bradley has a knack for investigations and a helpful chauffeur, George Moody (Dudgeon). In 1929, Adela is invited to the country estate of friends to celebrate Eleanor Bing's (Fielding) engagement. Only her fiance is murdered and then doesn't turn out to be what he seemed. But then, neither does anyone else. **90m/C; VHS, DVD.** *GB* Diana Rigg; Neil Dudgeon; John Alderton; Emma Fielding; Tristan Gemmill; Tom Butcher; Sue Devaney; John Conroy; Michael Troughton; ***D:*** Audrey Cooke; ***W:*** Simon Booker. **TV**

The Spell **1977** An obese 15-year-old girl has the power to inflict illness and death on the people she hates. Necessarily mean-spirited, if we're being asked to sympathize with the main character. Therein lies the rub. Made for TV. **86m/C; VHS, Blu-Ray, Streaming.** Lee Grant; James Olson; Susan Myers; Barbara Bostock; Lelia Goldoni; Helen Hunt; ***D:*** Lee Philips. **TV**

Spellbinder 1/2 **1988 (R)** L.A. lawyer Daly falls in love with a woman he saves from an attacker, then discovers she's a fugitive from a satanic cult that wants her back. Unoriginal, but slickly made. **96m/C; VHS, DVD, Blu-Ray.** Timothy Daly; Kelly Preston; Rick Rossovich; Audra Lindley; M.C. Gainey; ***D:*** Janet Greek; ***W:*** Tracy Torme; ***M:*** Basil Poledouris.

Spellbound *The Spell of Amy Nugent* **1941** Broken-hearted over dead girlfriend, young college student attempts to contact her through spiritualism, succeeds, and suffers nervous breakdown. **75m/B; VHS, DVD.** *GB* Derek Farr; Vera Lindsay; Frederick Leister; Hay Petrie; Felix Aylmer; ***D:*** John Harlow.

Spellbound 1/2 **1945** Peck plays an amnesia victim accused of murder. Bergman plays the psychiatrist who uncovers his past through Freudian analysis and ends up falling in love with him. One of Hitchcock's finest films of the 1940s, with a riveting dream sequence designed by Salvador Dali. Full of classic Hitchcock plot twists and Freudian imagery. Based on Francis Beeding's novel "The House of Dr. Edwardes." **111m/B; VHS, DVD, Blu-Ray.** Ingrid Bergman; Gregory Peck; Leo G. Carroll; Michael Chekhov; Wallace Ford; Rhonda Fleming; Regis Toomey; ***D:*** Alfred Hitchcock; ***W:*** Ben Hecht; ***C:*** George Barnes; ***M:*** Miklos Rozsa. Oscars '45: Orig. Dramatic Score; N.Y. Film Critics '45: Actress (Bergman).

Spellbound **2002 (G)** Excellent documentary follows a group of teenagers and their families as they compete in the 1999 National Spelling Bee. Shows the preparation and competition the students go through to make it to the Nationals. **97m/C; VHS, DVD.** ***D:*** Jeffrey Blitz; ***C:*** Jeffrey Blitz; ***M:*** Daniel Hulsizer.

Spencer's Mountain 1/2 **1963** Fonda plays the larger-then-life patriarch of nine (with O'Hara as his wife), who's inherited the Wyoming mountain land claimed by his father. Fonda's dream is to build a new house large enough to contain his brood but something always gets in his way. This time it's eldest son MacArthur's dream of a college education. Sentimental family fare based on a novel by Earl Hamner Jr., which also became the basis for the TV series "The Waltons." **118m/C; VHS, DVD, Blu-Ray.** Henry Fonda; Maureen O'Hara; James MacArthur; Donald Crisp; Wally Cox; Mimsy Farmer; Virginia Gregg; Lillian Bronson; Whit Bissell; Hayden Rorke; Dub Taylor; Victor French; Veronica Cartwright; ***D:*** Delmer Daves; ***W:*** Delmer Daves; ***M:*** Max Steiner.

Spenser: A Savage Place 1/2 **1994** PI Spenser (Urich) is lured to Toronto by an old flame who wants him to help her expose a racketeering scam in the city's film industry. **91m/C; VHS, DVD.** Robert Urich; Cynthia Dale; Avery Brooks; Ross Petty; Wendy Crewson; ***D:*** Joseph L. Scanlan; ***W:*** Donald Martin; ***C:*** Vic Sarin; ***M:*** Brad MacDonald.

Spenser: Ceremony 1/2 **1993** Urich resumes his role as Robert B. Parker's Boston PI, which he played in the TV series "Spenser: For Hire." This time around Spenser is searching for a troubled runaway who's gotten involved in prostitution. But her suburban dad, who has political aspirations, seems reluctant to have her found. Brooks returns as Spenser's menacing associate Hawk. Toronto stands in for Boston. Based on Parker's novel "Ceremony." **95m/C; VHS, DVD.** Robert Urich; Avery Brooks; Barbara Williams; Tanya Allen; David Nichols; Lynne Cormack; ***D:*** Paul Lynch; ***W:*** Joan H. Parker; Robert B. Parker. **CABLE**

Spenser Confidential 1/2 **2020 (R)** When Spenser (Wahlberg) gets released from prison after being framed, dirty cops and drug cartels want him gone permanently. He teams up with his boxer roommate Hawk (Duke) and his unhinged ex-girlfriend Cissy (Shlesinger) to bring the bad guys to justice. A fairly routine yet overall entertaining buddy cop/action/comedy flick. Inspired by *Robert B. Parker's Wonderland*, 42nd in the Spenser series of novels by Ace Atkins. **111m/C; DVD, Streaming.** Mark Wahlberg; Winston Duke; Alan Arkin; Iliza Shlesinger; Michael Gaston; ***D:*** Peter Berg; ***W:*** Sean O'Keefe; Brian Helgeland; ***C:*** Tobias A. Schliessler; ***M:*** Steve Jablonsky.

Spenser: Pale Kings & Princes 1/2 **1994** Spenser's (Urich) new case involves the murder of a reporter who was investigating a drug-ridden small New England town. But was the journalist killed for what he found out about a Colombian cocaine connection or did his womanizing have deadly consequences? Adapted from Robert B. Parker's novel. **95m/C; VHS, DVD.** Robert Urich; Avery Brooks; Barbara Williams; ***D:*** Vic Sarin; ***W:*** Joan H. Parker; Robert P. Parker; ***C:*** Vic Sarin; ***M:*** Paul Zaza. **CABLE**

Spenser: The Judas Goat 1/2 **1994** Boston PI Spenser (Urich) is hired by billionaire mining exec Hugh Dixon (Pownall) and sent to Ottawa, Canada to investigate the deadly car bombing that killed his wife and children. Seems black African political leader Boyko (Bess) was the true target and the assassin hasn't given up. Adapted from the Robert B. Parker novel; made for cable TV. **95m/C; VHS, DVD.** Robert Urich; Avery Brooks; Leon Pownall; Ardon Bess; Geordie Johnson; Natalie Radford; Wendy Crewson; ***D:*** Joseph L. Scanlan. **CABLE**

Spent 🦴🦴 1/2 **2000** Gambling addict/occassional actor Max (London) has a girlfriend, Brigette (Spradling), who has a drinking problem, and a roommate, Grant (Park), who won't admit he's gay although his crush on Max seems pretty obvious. In fact, any communication is a big problem, since no one really wants to see their lives for what they are. Film coasts along without much happening. **90m/C; VHS, DVD.** Jason London; Charlie Spradling; James Parks; Phill Lewis; Richmond Arquette; Barbara Barrie; Gilbert Cates; Rain Phoenix; Margaret Cho; ***D:*** Gil Cates, Jr.; ***W:*** Gil Cates, Jr.; ***C:*** Robert D. Tomer; ***M:*** Stan Ridgway.

Spetters 🦴🦴 1/2 **1980 (R)** Four Dutch teenagers follow the motorcycle racing circuit and motocross champ Hauer. Misdirected youth film with a spicy performance from Soutendijk. Plenty of violence, sex, and gripping photography. Verhoeven went on to direct "Robocop" and "Total Recall." **108m/C; VHS, DVD, Blu-Ray.** *NL* Rutger Hauer; Renee Soutendijk; ***D:*** Paul Verhoeven; ***C:*** Jan De Bont.

Sphere 🦴 1/2 **1997 (PG-13)** It must've looked good on paper, but bringing Michael Crichton's decade-old novel to the screen turned out to be a big mistake for all involved. Hoffman, Jackson, and Stone are a team of researchers sent underwater to investigate a mysterious 300-year-old space ship. After realizing the ship has American origins, they stumble across a huge liquid metal sphere that can make their deepest fears come true, in the form of huge squids and sea snakes. Never lives up to the promising premise or high-class looks. Despite three mega-stars and an A-list director, it's a hollow excursion low on thrills and originality, but there's plenty of existential ramblings about the power of the mind. **152m/C; VHS, DVD.** Dustin Hoffman; Sharon Stone; Samuel L. Jackson; Peter Coyote; Queen Latifah; Liev Schreiber; ***D:*** Barry Levinson; ***W:*** Paul Attanasio; Stephen Hauser; ***C:*** Adam Greenberg; ***M:*** Elliot Goldenthal.

Sphinx **WOOF!** **1981 (PG)** Woman archaeologist searches for hidden riches in the tomb of an Egyptian king. The scenery is impressive, but otherwise, don't bother. Based on the novel by Robin Cook. **117m/C; VHS, DVD.** Lesley-Anne Down; Frank Langella; John Gielgud; Maurice Ronet; John Rhys-Davies; ***D:*** Franklin J. Schaffner; ***W:*** John Byrum.

Spice World: The Movie 🦴 1/2 **1997 (PG)** Clear some space on the video rack next to "Cool as Ice," the Spice Girls made a movie! Stretching their acting ability, the pop group plays a band of marginally talented singers who are inexplicably thrown to the top of the charts by a bitter twist of pop culture fate. What passes for the plot is stolen from "A Hard Day's Night," by the Beatles, depicting five days before a sellout concert at Albert Hall. The courageous champions of girl power do battle with the hassles of fame, bossy managers, and the media in their quest to get to the show. They find the time to visit a pregnant ex-Spice, change their clothes a kajillion times, and generally poke fun at themselves along the way. Unfortunately (at least for those over 13) they're not poked with anything really sharp. Loads of celebrity cameos (Elton John, Elvis Costello, Bob Hoskins), some of whom run off screen faster than if they were on fire. **92m/C; VHS, DVD.** *GB* Emma (Baby Spice) Bunton; Geri (Ginger Spice) Halliwell; Victoria (Posh Spice) Beckham; Melanie (Sporty Spice) Chisholm; Melanie (Scary Spice) Brown; Richard E. Grant; Alan Cumming; George Wendt; Claire Rushbrook; Mark McKinney; Richard O'Brien; Roger Moore; Barry Humphries; Jason Flemyng; Meat Loaf Aday; Bill Paterson; Stephen Fry; Richard Briers; Michael Barrymore; Naoko Mori; Hugh Laurie; Jennifer Saunders; ***Cameo(s):*** Elvis Costello; Bob Geldof; Bob Hoskins; Sir Elton John; ***D:*** Bob Spiers; ***W:*** Kim Fuller; Jamie Curtis; ***C:*** Clive Tickner; ***M:*** Paul Newcastle. Golden Raspberries '98: Worst Actress (Beckham), Worst Actress (Brown), Worst Actress (Bunton), Worst Actress (Chisholm), Worst Actress (Halliwell).

Spider 🦴🦴🦴🦴 **2002 (R)** Gripping and well-directed psychodrama tells the story of Spider, a paranoid-schizophrenic, as he tries to resolve his convoluted memories and emotions. After being released from a mental hospital, Spider (Ralph Fiennes) lives in an eerie halfway house for mental patients. There he recounts the events of his life that led to his tortured state of mind. Yet, since the film is told entirely from Spider's perspective it's impossible to distinguish between reality and the blurred fiction of a madman, making the entire film both illusionary and fascinatingly real. Stellar performances from Fiennes, Miranda Richardson, Gabriel Byrne, and Bradley Hall in an amazing turn as the young Spider. Cronenberg's most polished drama to date shows that he's successfully outgrown the moniker of Canada's "baron of blood." **98m/C; VHS, DVD.** *CA GB* Ralph Fiennes; Miranda Richardson; Gabriel Byrne; Bradley Hall; Lynn Redgrave; John Neville; Gary Reineke; Sara Stockbridge; Philip Craig; ***D:*** David Cronenberg; ***W:*** Patrick McGrath; ***C:*** Peter Suschitzky; ***M:*** Howard Shore. Genie '02: Director (Cronenberg).

Spider Baby 🦴 *The Liver Eaters; Spider Baby, or the Maddest Story Ever Told; Cannibal Orgy, or the Maddest Story Ever Told* **1964** A tasteless horror-comedy about a chauffeur who takes care of a psychotic family. Theme song sung by Lon Chaney. **86m/B; VHS, DVD, Blu-Ray.** Lon Chaney, Jr.; Mantan Moreland; Carol Ohmart; Sid Haig; Beverly Washburn; Jill Banner; Quinn (K.) Redeker; Mary Mitchell; ***D:*** Jack Hill; ***W:*** Jack Hill; ***C:*** Alfred Taylor; ***M:*** Ronald Stein.

Spider-Man 🦴🦴🦴 **2002 (PG-13)** Raimi does a little 21st-century updating of the Marvel comic hero, who first made his appearance back in 1962, but remembers to keep the heart along with the action. Peter Parker (Maguire) is a nerdy teenager who gets tongue-tied every time he's around the babe of his dreams—Mary Jane Watson (Dunst). His life changes—not necessarily for the better—when he gets bitten by a genetically altered spider and takes on weird arachnid traits, such as strength, agility, wall crawling, web shooting, and swinging. After a family tragedy, the newly monickered Spider-Man becomes a crime fighter. His nemesis is, of course, the Green Goblin (Dafoe), who himself has a dual identity. **121m/C; VHS, DVD, Blu-Ray.** Tobey Maguire; Willem Dafoe; Kirsten Dunst; James Franco; Cliff Robertson; Rosemary Harris; J.K. Simmons; Gerry Becker; Bill Nunn; Jack Betts; Joe Manganiello; Stanley Anderson; Ron Perkins; Theodore (Ted) Raimi; Larry Joshua; Michael (Mike) Papajohn; Joseph (Joe) D'Onofrio; ***Cameo(s):*** Bruce Campbell; Lucy Lawless; ***D:*** Sam Raimi; ***W:*** David Koepp; ***C:*** Don Burgess; ***M:*** Danny Elfman.

Spider-Man 2 🦴🦴🦴 1/2 **2004 (PG-13)** Spidey's back, with more to worry about than ever. Mary Jane's engaged, Harry Osborne is out to avenge the death of his father (Green Goblin), and there's a new villain in town: Doctor Octopus (Molina). Raimi's first installment was the best comic book adaptation in a while, and he's managed to top it here. Peter Parker's angst over Spidey's affect on his life, romantic conflict over MJ, and guilt over his uncle's death provide more depth than any comic book character has previously been granted on screen. Even Doc Ock is three dimensional and somewhat sympathetic, in no small part because of Molina's portrayal. The effects are again top-notch and non-intrusive. Raimi shows enough humor to remind everybody why they're called comic books. **127m/C; DVD, Blu-Ray, UMD.** Tobey Maguire; Kirsten Dunst; Alfred Molina; James Franco; Elizabeth Banks; Rosemary Harris; J.K. Simmons; Vanessa Ferlito; Bill Nunn; Theodore (Ted) Raimi; Dylan Baker; Donna Murphy; Bruce Campbell; Aasif Mandvi; Willem Dafoe; Cliff Robertson; Daniel Gillies; Daniel Dae Kim; Reed Edward Diamond; Emily Deschanel; ***D:*** Sam Raimi; ***W:*** Alvin Sargent; Alfred Gough; Miles Millar; Michael Chabon; ***C:*** Bill Pope; ***M:*** Danny Elfman. Oscars '04: Visual FX.

Spider-Man 3 🦴🦴 1/2 **2007 (PG-13)** Raimi's sublime superhero series falters in this third chapter, thanks largely to the director's cheeseball sensibilities. Spider-Man (Maguire) is enjoying a brief period of popularity, which only makes things worse with his fading star girlfriend MJ (Dunst) and his vengeance-minded pal Harry (Franco). Adding to the mix is a nasty rival photographer (Grace), the powerful ex-con Sandman (Church), and Venom, an evil alien parasite that gives Spidey a black suit and makes him act like a jerk. There's a lot of blockbuster fun, but you'll spend half the movie rolling your eyes at the unconvincing love quadrangle and Raimi's attempts to turn Spidey into the messiah of New York. Still, much better than the third chapters of the X-Men, Superman, or Batman franchises. **139m/C; DVD, Blu-Ray.** Tobey Maguire; Kirsten Dunst; James Franco; Thomas Haden Church; Topher Grace; Bryce Dallas Howard; James Cromwell; Rosemary Harris; J.K. Simmons; Dylan Baker; Bill Nunn; Theresa Russell; Theodore (Ted) Raimi; Cliff Robertson; Elizabeth Banks; Perla Haney-Jardine; Michael (Mike) Papajohn; Joe Manganiello; Lucy Gordon; Bruce Campbell; Daniel Gillies; ***D:*** Sam Raimi; ***W:*** Sam Raimi; Alvin Sargent; Ivan Raimi; ***C:*** Bill Pope; ***M:*** Christopher Young.

Spider-Man: Far from Home 🦴🦴🦴 **2019 (PG-13)** Five years after part of Earth's population disappeared and returned, Peter Parker/Spider-Man (Holland) is still in high school while the world faces another super villain threat. As Peter prepares for a class trip to Europe, a new hero emerges, Mysterio (Gyllenhaal), who dispatches the villains with ease. As Peter travels and romantically pursues MJ (Zendaya), Nick Fury (Jackson) tracks down the reluctant Peter to help fight the threats and again save the world. Part high school comedy and part comic book action-adventure, the film struggles at times to reconcile its two sides but has an appealing cast and numerous humorous moments. **129m/C; DVD, Blu-Ray.** Tom Holland; Samuel L. Jackson; Jake Gyllenhaal; Marisa Tomei; Jon Favreau; ***D:*** Jon Watts; ***W:*** Chris(topher) McKenna; Erik Sommers; ***C:*** Matthew J. Lloyd; ***M:*** Michael Giacchino.

Spider-Man: Homecoming 🦴🦴🦴 **2017 (PG-13)** Tom Holland brings delightful earnestness to the super character in this enjoyable reboot. Exhilarated by his brief adventure alongside the Avengers in "Captain America: Civil War," high schooler Peter Parker is eager to test out his spider suit's gadgetry to fight real crime, not just the lightweight neighborhood stuff he squelches after school. His mentor Tony Stark (Downey) is reluctant to take the training wheels of-f...until the Vulture (Keaton) starts throwing his weight around, and Spider-Man is given the test of his young life. **133m/C; DVD, Blu-Ray.** Tom Holland; Michael Keaton; Robert Downey, Jr.; Marisa Tomei; Jon Favreau; Gwyneth Paltrow; ***D:*** Jon Watts; ***W:*** Jon Watts; Jonathan M. Goldstein; John Francis Daley; Christopher Ford; Chris McKenna; Erik Sommers; ***C:*** Salvatore Totino; ***M:*** Michael Giacchino.

Spider-Man: Into the Spider-Verse 🦴🦴🦴 1/2 **2018 (PG)** A gloriously animated feature that restores the superhero to his roots, the comic book. Brooklyn teen Miles Morales, a Spider-Man wannabe, is mentored by the former legend himself. The duo is soon joined by Spidies from parallel dimensions--Gwen Stacy, Spider-Man Noir, Peni Parker, and Spider-Ham (a Porky Pig-type character)--to vanquish a common foe. A humorous, action-packed coming-of-age tale (with a terrific soundtrack) that will help undo damage to the superhero's legacy caused by countless recent live-action flicks. **117m/C; DVD, Blu-Ray, Streaming.** ***V:*** Shameik Moore; Jake Johnson; Hailee Steinfeld; Mahershala Ali; Brian Tyree Henry; ***D:*** Bob Persichetti; Peter Ramsey; Rodney Rothman; ***W:*** Rodney Rothman; Phil Lord; ***M:*** Daniel Pemberton. Oscars '18: Animated Film; British Acad. '18: Animated Film; Golden Globes '19: Animated Film.

The Spider Returns 🦴 1/2 **1941** Number 14 of the 15-part serial, The Spider Returns offers the typical good-guy sleuth versus criminal mastermind and his band of witless henchmen. The Spider (Hull) routinely undercuts Police Commissioner Kirk (Girard) as he squares off against master criminal "the Gargoyle." The plot is a little thin but the action is where it's at. **300m/B; DVD.** Warren Hull; Mary Ainslee; Dave O'Brien; Joseph Girard; Kenne Duncan; Corbet Morris; Bryant Washburn; Charles F. Miller; Anthony Warde; Harry Harvey; ***D:*** James W. Horne; ***W:*** Morgan Cox; Lawrence Taylor.

Spiders 🦴🦴🦴 **1918** One of the earliest surviving films by director Lang, and predates Indiana Jones by almost 60 years. In these first two chapters ("The Golden Lake" and "The Diamond Ship") of an unfinished 4-part thriller, Carl deVogt battles with the evil Spider cult for a mystically powerful Incan diamond. Restored version has original color-tinted scenes. Silent with organ score. **137m/B; Silent; VHS, DVD, Blu-Ray.** *GE* Lil Dagover; ***D:*** Fritz Lang; ***M:*** Gaylord Carter.

Spiders 🦴 *Spiders 3D* **2013 (PG-13)** When a russian satellite crashes into New York, it isn't long before aliens resembling giant spiders begin over-running the city. **89m/C; DVD, Blu-Ray, Streaming.** Christa Campbell; Patrick Muldoon; William Hope; Shelly Varod; Sydney Sweeney; ***D:*** Tibor Takacs; ***W:*** Tibor Takacs; Joseph Farruggia; ***C:*** Lorenzo Senatore; ***M:*** Joseph Conlan. **VIDEO**

Spiders 🦴🦴 1/2 **2000 (R)** Throwback to the "big bug" sci-fi horrors of the 1950s also borrows heavily from "The X-Files." College reporter Marci (Parrilla) and a couple of her pals sneak into a desert military base in time to witness the secret landing of a space shuttle. On board is a spider that has been injected with alien DNA and is doing absolutely disgusting things. It all ends with an arachnid attack on Phoenix! Can the city be saved? **93m/C; VHS, DVD, Blu-Ray.** David Carpenter; Lana Parrilla; ***D:*** Gary Jones. **VIDEO**

Spiders 2: Breeding Ground 🦴 1/2 **2001 (R)** Alexandra (Niznik) and hubby Jason (Cromer) are enjoying a boating holiday when a storm capsizes their craft and they are rescued by freighter captain Bigelow (Quinn). The ship's doctor, Gabac (Moll), gives Jason a shot of "antibiotics," which give him hallucinations about giant spiders that incubate in human bodies. Alex thinks this is nuts until she finds some spiders and realizes that Jason has been infected. She then proceeds to kicks butt 'cause nobody messes with her man! **96m/C; VHS, DVD, Blu-Ray.** Stephanie Niznik; Daniel Quinn; Richard Moll; Greg Cromer; ***D:*** Sam Firstenberg; ***W:*** Stephen Brooks; ***C:*** Peter Belcher; Plamen Somov; ***M:*** Serge Colbert. **VIDEO**

The Spider's Web 🦴 1/2 **1938** Crime-fighting Spider (Hull) leads his loyal men including Blinky McQuade (Hull) and Ram Singh (Duncan) against the villainous masked underlord Octopus, who is bent on global destruction. Shootouts galore help this story click along with energy to spare showing the class of the serial genre. **300m/B; DVD.** Warren Hull; Iris Meredith; Richard Fiske; Kenne Duncan; Forbes Murray; Donald "Don" Douglas; Marc Lawrence; Charles C. Wilson; ***D:*** James W. Horne; Ray Taylor; ***W:*** Robert E. Kent; George Plympton; ***C:*** Allen Siegler.

Spider's Web 🦴🦴 **2001 (R)** Investment banker Baldwin is seduced into stealing $40 million from his politically connected father but betrayal follows. **87m/C; VHS, DVD.** Stephen Baldwin; Kari Wuhrer; Michael Gregory; George Lazenby; Benjamin King; Scott Williamson; George Murdock; ***D:*** Paul Levine; ***W:*** D. Alvelo; David Lloyd; Robert Stift; ***M:*** Michael Cohen. **VIDEO**

The Spiderwick Chronicles 🦴🦴🦴 **2008 (PG)** Jared (Highmore), his twin Simon, and sister Mallory (Bolger) move into a rural mansion with their mom (Parker) and discover that their new home is a gateway into a world of magical creatures, some of which aren't so nice. Evil Mulgarath (Nolte) wants a magic book written by Jared's ancestor, and it's up to Jared to protect it while convincing his siblings that the charmed world outside their door is real. Well-written, ably directed adaptation of the bestselling children's series. **97m/C; DVD, Blu-Ray.** Freddie Highmore; Sarah Bolger; Mary-Louise Parker; David Strathairn; Joan Plowright; Andrew McCarthy; ***V:*** Nick Nolte; Seth Rogen; Martin Short; ***D:*** Mark S. Waters; ***W:*** Karey Kirkpatrick; David Berenbaum; John Sayles; ***C:*** Caleb Deschanel; ***M:*** James Horner.

Spies 🦴🦴🦴 1/2 *Spione* **1928** A sly criminal poses as a famous banker to steal government information and create chaos in the world in this silent Lang masterpiece. Excellent entertainment, tight plotting and pacing, fine performances. Absolutely relentless intrigue and tension. **88m/B; Silent; VHS, DVD, Blu-Ray.** *GE* Rudolf Klein-Rogge; Lupu Pick; Fritz Rasp; Gerda Maurus; Willy Fritsch; ***D:*** Fritz Lang.

Spies in Disguise 🦴🦴 1/2 **2019 (PG)** Young science genius Walter Beckett (Holland) works for a national spy agency creating innovative gadgets that follow his "first do no harm" policy. An outsider among his peers, he is framed for treason and goes on the run. When cynical super secret agent Lance Sterling (Smith) gets entangled in Walter's situation, he uses Walter's untested formula to turn himself into a pigeon to escape a difficult situation, spy on his enemies, and save both himself and Walter. The animated film is a fun yet intelligent espionage adventure with a well-crafted story and solid voicing by Smith and Holland. **101m/C; DVD, Blu-Ray.** Will Smith; Tom Holland; Reba McEntire; Masi Oka; Rashida Jones; ***D:*** Nick Bruno; Troy Quane; ***W:*** Brad Copeland; Lloyd Taylor; ***M:*** Theodore Shapiro.

Spies, Lies and Naked Thighs 1/2 **1991** A pair of crackpot CIA agents find themselves in a whirlpool of comedic madness when they are assigned to track down a deadly assassin. The problem? The assassin happens to be the ex-wife of one of the guys. Can he go another round with her and this time come out on top? Who cares? **90m/C; VHS, DVD.** Harry Anderson; Ed Begley, Jr.; Rachel Ticotin; Linda Purl; Wendy Crewson; ***D:*** James Frawley.

Spies Like Us 1/2 **1985 (PG)** Chase and Aykroyd meet while taking the CIA entry exam. Caught cheating on the test, they seem the perfect pair for a special mission. Pursued by the Soviet government, they nearly start WWIII. Silly, fun homage to the Bing Crosby-Bob Hope "Road" movies that doesn't capture those classics' quota of guffaws, but comes moderately close. Look for several cameos by film directors. **103m/C; VHS, DVD.** Chevy Chase; Dan Aykroyd; Steve Forrest; Bruce Davison; William Prince; Bernie Casey; Tom Hatton; Donna Dixon; Frank Oz; Michael Apted; Constantin Costa-Gavras; Terry Gilliam; Ray Harryhausen; Joel Coen; Martin Brest; Bob Swaim; ***D:*** John Landis; ***W:*** Dan Aykroyd; Lowell Ganz; Babaloo Mandel; ***C:*** Robert Paynter; ***M:*** Elmer Bernstein.

Spies of Warsaw 1/2 **2013** Generally straightforward Brit spy drama based on the 2008 Alan Furst novel. In 1937, Jean-Francois Mercier (Tennant) is a widowed Army officer serving as a military attache in Warsaw, who must convince his skeptical Paris superiors that Hitler is a serious threat. Mercier runs a small group of informants and agents while attending diplomatic functions, which is how he meets beautiful League of Nations lawyer Anna Skarbek (Montgomery). The Nazis know Mercier is working against them even as German tanks get closer to the Polish border. **180m/C; DVD, Blu-Ray.** *UK* David Tennant; Janet Montgomery; Burn Gorman; Julian Glover; Piotr Baumann; Ludger Pistor; ***D:*** Coky Giedroyc; ***W:*** Dick Clement; Ian La Frenais; ***C:*** Wojciech Szepel; ***M:*** Rob Lane. **TV**

The Spikes Gang **1974** Wounded outlaw Harry Spikes (Marvin) is found by three teenaged farm boys—Will (Grimes), Les (Howard), and Tod (Smith)?who nurse him back to health and are dazzled by his exploits. They decide to run away from home and become outlaws, eventually robbing banks with leader Spikes. But when the reward money gets large enough, there's a betrayal. **96m/C; DVD, Blu-Ray.** Lee Marvin; Gary Grimes; Ron Howard; Charles Martin Smith; Arthur Hunnicutt; Noah Beery, Jr.; ***D:*** Richard Fleischer; ***W:*** Irving Ravetch; Harriet Frank, Jr.; ***C:*** Brian West; ***M:*** Fred Karlin.

Spin **2004 (PG-13)** Orphaned by his parents' deaths, young Eddie's cold uncle passes him off to one of his Hispanic ranch hands and his wife who, despite their best efforts, have difficulty keeping the teenager on the right track. Based on Donald Everett Axinn's novel. **107m/C; VHS, DVD.** Ryan Merriman; Stanley Tucci; Dana Delany; Paula Garces; Ruben Blades; ***D:*** James Redford; ***W:*** James Redford; ***C:*** Dr. Paul Ryan; ***M:*** Todd Boekelheide. **VIDEO**

Spin 1/2 *You Are Here* **2007** Predictable ensemble drama set over one night in an L.A. nightclub. Ryan is the house DJ at the momentary hotspot where he wants waitress/actress Cassie to become more than just his friend. The busy night also sees a number of patrons looking for sex, drugs, or industry contacts (hey, it's Hollywood). **78m/C; DVD.** Patrick Flueger; Lauren German; Michael Biehn; Chris Lowell; Adam Campbell; Bijou Phillips; Katie Cassidy; Amber Heard; ***D:*** Henry Pincus; ***W:*** Henry Pincus; ***C:*** Steve Gainer; ***M:*** B.C. Smith.

Spin a Dark Web **1956** Derivative crime melodrama. Femme fatale Bella Francesci (Domergue) likes to indulge herself with her Soho gangster brother Rico's (Benson) prizefighters. Jim (Patterson) wants to get rich and his talent extends outside the ring to his electronics expertise, which Rico decides to use in an off-track betting scheme. Bella's the incentive to get Jim to stick around though he definitely comes to regret it. **77m/B; DVD, Blu-Ray.** *UK* Faith Domergue; Lee Patterson; Martin Benson; Joss Ambler; Rona Anderson; ***D:*** Vernon Sewell; ***W:*** Ian Stuart Black; ***C:*** Basil Emmott; ***M:*** Robert Sharples.

Spin the Bottle **1997** Jonah (Graham) invites four childhood friends, whom he hasn't seen in 10 years, for a weekend reunion at his Vermont lakefront summer house, which leads to sexual hijinks and sweet revenge. Yerkes's debut feature. **83m/C; VHS, DVD.** Holter Graham; Jessica Faller; Mitchell Riggs; Kim Winter; Heather Goldenhersch; ***D:*** Jamie Yerkes; ***W:*** Amy Sohn; ***C:*** Harlan Bosmajian.

Spinning Man **2018 (R)** A ho-hum mystery thriller of a professor accused of involvement in a teenager's disappearance, based on a novel by George Harrar. When high schooler Joyce Bonner (Rush) disappears at a local lake, philosophy professor Evan Birch (Pearce) becomes the prime suspect for police detective Malloy (Brosnan). Evan previously left a teaching job after being involved with a student and evidence shows he was near the lake at that time. Though the professor talks to Malloy about philosophy, he becomes increasingly hostile and evasive as the investigation continues. **100m/C; DVD, Blu-Ray, Streaming.** *IR SW US* Pierce Brosnan; Minnie Driver; Guy Pearce; Alexandra Shipp; Odeya Rush; ***D:*** Simon Kaijser; ***W:*** Matthew Aldrich; ***C:*** Polly Morgan; ***M:*** Jean-Paul Wall. **VIDEO**

Spinout *California Holiday* **1966** A pouty traveling singer decides to drive an experimental race car in a rally. Usual Elvis fare with the King being pursued by an assortment of beauties. **93m/C; VHS, DVD.** Elvis Presley; Shelley Fabares; Carl Betz; Diane McBain; Cecil Kellaway; Jack Mullaney; Deborah Walley; Una Merkel; Warren Berlinger; Will Hutchins; Dodie Marshall; ***D:*** Norman Taurog.

Spiral **2007** Pathologically shy and delusional, artist Mason (Moore) gets a job at an insurance company, thanks to his only friend Berkeley (Levi). Fellow new employee Amber (Tamblyn) bonds with Mason over their work and she agrees to pose for a portrait. And then the trouble really begins. **91m/C; DVD, Blu-Ray.** Joel David Moore; Amber Tamblyn; Zachary Levi; Tricia Helfer; David Muller; Annie Neal; ***D:*** Adam Green; Joel David Moore; ***W:*** Joel David Moore; Jeremy Danial Boreing; ***C:*** Will Barratt; ***M:*** Todd Baldwell; Michael "Fish" Herring.

The Spiral Staircase **1946** A mute servant, working in a creepy Gothic mansion, may be the next victim of a murderer preying on women afflicted with deformities, especially when the next murder occurs in the mansion itself. Great performance by McGuire as the terrified victim. Remade for TV in 1975. **83m/B; VHS, DVD, Blu-Ray.** Dorothy McGuire; George Brent; Ethel Barrymore; Kent Smith; Rhonda Fleming; Gordon Oliver; Elsa Lanchester; Sara Allgood; ***D:*** Robert Siodmak; ***W:*** Mel Dinelli; ***C:*** Nicholas Musuraca; ***M:*** Roy Webb.

Spiral Staircase 1/2 **1975** Mild TV remake of the 1946 classic about a mute servant who is menaced by a psychopathic killer. Why didn't they just show the original? **99m/C; VHS, DVD.** *GB* Jacqueline Bisset; Christopher Plummer; John Phillip Law; Mildred Dunnock; Sam Wanamaker; Gayle Hunnicutt; ***D:*** Peter Collinson; ***W:*** Allan Scott; Chris Bryant.

The Spirit 1/2 **1987** The Will Eisner 1940s comic book gets updated to the 1980s in this tongue-in-cheek ABC TV movie. Poice detective Denny Colt gets shot and lets everyone believe he's dead. Instead, he dons a blue suit and a mask to fight crime in Central City. This time he's out to bust an art forgery ring, aided by his girl, Ellen Dolan, and her police commissioner father. **74m/C; DVD.** Sam Jones; Nana Visitor; Garry Walberg; Laura Robinson; Bumper Robinson; Philip Baker Hall; ***D:*** Michael A. Schultz; ***W:*** Steven E. de Souza; ***C:*** Frank Thackery; ***M:*** Barry Goldberg. **TV**

The Spirit WOOF! **2008 (PG-13)** A rookie cop is murdered but comes back to life as The Spirit (Macht), an immortal crime-fighting sort of superhero, who (naturally) is stalked by an obligatory nemesis, The Octopus (Jackson). The so-called story is drawn from Will Eisner's comic book series though unfortunately none of his ironic wit makes it to the screen. Toss in a couple of poorly named vixens that alternate between lover and assailant and, well, there you have it. The essential lesson here is that not every graphic novel can become a worthwhile feature film, even with eye candy like Mendes and Johansson. If you can't pass on style over substance or off-the-chart camp, go ahead and indulge in this guilty pleasure, but don't say The Hound didn't warn you. **102m/C; Blu-Ray, On Demand.** Gabriel Macht; Samuel L. Jackson; Scarlett Johansson; Eva Mendes; Jaime King; Paz Vega; Sarah Paulson; Stana Katic; Eric Balfour; Dan Lauria; ***D:*** Frank Miller; ***W:*** Frank Miller; ***C:*** Bill Pope; ***M:*** David Newman.

Spirit Bear: The Simon Jackson Story 1/2 **2005** Canadian TV movie shows how one person can follow their heart and make a difference. After teenager Simon Jackson has an encounter with an extremely rare white Kermode bear, he learns the endangered species is threatened further by the forestry industry. The bears occupy a very small territory in British Columbia, which may be subjected to clearcut logging. Simon becomes an activist against business and the provincial government in a land protection battle. **90m/C; DVD.** *CA* Mark Rendall; Graham Greene; Katie Stuart; Ed Begley, Jr.; Jonathan Potts; ***D:*** Stefan Scaini; ***W:*** Kent Staines; ***C:*** Michael Storey; ***M:*** Gary Koftinoff. **TV**

Spirit Lost **1996 (R)** John (Leon) and wife Willy (Taylor) move to an old seaside home, where he hopes to find artistic inpiration. Instead, he finds an attractive ghost, Arabella (Williams), who has been hanging around for 200 years after her lover's betrayal. And the jealous Arabella wants to get her new lover's wife out of the way. Yes, ghosts CAN do it. Based on the book by Nancy Thayer. **90m/C; VHS, DVD.** Leon; Regina Taylor; Cynda Williams; James Avery; Juanita Jennings; ***D:*** Neema Barnette; ***W:*** Joyce Renee Lewis; ***C:*** Yuri Neyman; ***M:*** Lionel Cole.

Spirit of St. Louis **1957** A lavish Hollywood biography of famous aviator Charles Lindbergh and his historic transatlantic flight from New York to Paris in 1927, based on his autobiography. Intelligent; Stewart shines as the intrepid airman. Inexplicably, it flopped at the boxoffice. **137m/C; VHS, DVD.** James Stewart; Patricia Smith; Murray Hamilton; Marc Connelly; ***D:*** Billy Wilder; ***W:*** Billy Wilder; Wendell Mayes; ***C:*** Robert Burks; ***M:*** Franz Waxman.

Spirit of '76 1/2 **1991 (PG-13)** In the 22nd century, the Earth faces certain disaster as a magnetic storm wipes out all of American culture. Now time travellers must return to 1776 to reacquire the Constitution to fix things up. But when their computer goes on the blink, the do-gooders land, not in 1776, but in 1976 at the beginning of disco fever! **82m/C; VHS, DVD.** David Cassidy; Olivia D'Abo; Leif Garrett; Geoff Hoyle; Jeff (Jeffrey) McDonald; Steve McDonald; Liam O'Brien; Barbara Bain; Julie Brown; Thomas Chong; Iron Eyes Cody; Don Novello; Carl Reiner; Rob Reiner; Moon Zappa; Mark Mothersbaugh; Lucas Reiner; ***D:*** Lucas Reiner; ***W:*** Lucas Reiner; ***C:*** Stephen Lighthill; ***M:*** David Nichtern.

Spirit of the Beehive *El Espiritu de la Colmena* **1973** An acclaimed and haunting film about a young Spanish girl enthralled by the 1931 "Frankenstein," embarking on a journey to find the creature in the Spanish countryside. One of the best films about children's inner life; in Spanish with subtitles. **95m/C; VHS, DVD.** *SP* Fernando Fernan-Gomez; Teresa Gimpera; Ana Torrent; Isabel Telleria; Laly Soldevilla; ***D:*** Victor Erice; ***W:*** Victor Erice; ***C:*** Luis Cuadrado; ***M:*** Luis De Pablo.

Spirit of the Eagle **1990 (PG)** Man and young son wander in mountains and make friends with feathered creature. Then boy is kidnapped, creating problems for dad. Somnolent family fare. **93m/C; VHS, DVD.** Dan Haggerty; William (Bill) Smith; Don Shanks; Jeri Arredondo; Trever Yarrish; ***D:*** Boon Collins; ***W:*** Boon Collins; ***C:*** Lew V. Adams; ***M:*** Parmer Fuller.

The Spirit of Youth **1937** Joe Louis supports his family with menial jobs until he shows his knack as a fighter. When he's knocked down, his gal appears at ringside to inspire him, and does. **70m/B; VHS, DVD.** Joe Louis; Mantan Moreland; Clarence Muse; Edna Mae Harris; Mae Turner; Cleo Desmond; Jewel Smith; Jesse Lee Brooks; ***D:*** Harry Fraser; ***W:*** Arthur Hoerl; ***C:*** Robert E. Cline; ***M:*** Clarence Muse; Elliot Carpenter.

Spirit Rider **1993** Jesse Threebears is a sullen 16-year-old Ojibway who has been shuttled from foster homes since the age of six. Repatriated to his family's Canadian reservation, he's left in the care of his grandfather, Joe Moon. The entire community works to make Jesse's return successful but there are Jesse's resentments and some family tragedies to be overcome first. Based on the novel "Winners" by Mary-Ellen Lang Collura. **120m/C; VHS, DVD.** *CA* Herbie Barnes; Adam Beach; Graham Greene; Tantoo Cardinal; Gordon Tootoosis; Tom Jackson; Michelle St. John; ***D:*** Michael Scott; ***W:*** Jean Stawarz.

Spirit: Stallion of the Cimarron **2002 (G)** Spirit is a wild stallion and leader of his herd, who is captured and treated badly by a Cavalry Colonel (Cromwell) until he escapes with the help of a young Lakota brave, Little Creek (Studi). Action sequences are impressive, even breathtaking, but the simplistic story and constant musical clues to the moods expressed on screen wear quickly. Combination of traditional 2-D and computer-generated 3-D elements doesn't always work, either. On the other hand, the animals don't speak (except for some of Spirit's thoughts in a voiceover provided by Damon), and there are no wacky sidekicks to clutter what is a pretty serious story for an animated feature. **85m/C; VHS, DVD, Blu-Ray.** ***V:*** Matt Damon; James Cromwell; Daniel Studi; ***D:*** Kelly Asbury; Lorna Cook; ***W:*** John Fusco; ***M:*** Hans Zimmer; ***M:*** Bryan Adams.

Spirited Away 1/2 *Miyazaki's Spirited Away; Sen to Chihiro'No Kamikakushi* **2001 (PG)** Bratty 10-year-old Chihiro (voiced by Chase) is upset that her family is moving. What's worse is when they get lost and discover what appears to be an abandoned Japanese theme park. Her greedy parents get turned into pigs and Chihiro is trapped inside the park's palace. She learns that it is a resting place for millions of spirits and is run by a sorceress who makes Chihiro work for her and wants the girl to renounce her identity and never return to the human world. Also available in the original Japanese language version. **124m/C; VHS, DVD, Blu-Ray.** *JP* ***V:*** Daveigh Chase; Suzanne Pleshette; Jason Marsden; Susan Egan; David Ogden Stiers; Lauren Holly; Michael Chiklis; John Ratzenberger; Tara Strong; ***D:*** Hayao Miyazaki; ***W:*** Hayao Miyazaki; ***M:*** Joe Hisaishi. Oscars '02: Animated Film.

Spirits of the Dead *Histoires Extraordinaires; Tre Passi nel Delirio; Tales of Mystery; Tales of Mystery and Imagination; Trois Histoires Extraordinaires d'Edgar Poe* **1968 (R)** Three Edgar Allan Poe stories adapted for the screen and directed by three of Europe's finest. "Metzengerstein," directed by Roger Vadim stars the Fonda siblings in a tale of incestuous lust. "William Wilson" finds Louis Malle directing Delon and Bardot in the story of a vicious Austrian army officer haunted by a murder victim. Finally, Fellini directs "Never Bet the Devil Your Head" or "Toby Dammit" in which Stamp plays a drunken British film star who has a gruesome date with destiny. Although Fellini's segment is generally considered the best (and was released on its own) all three provide an interesting, atmospheric vision of Poe. French and Italian with subtitles. **117m/C; VHS, DVD.** *IT FR* Jane Fonda; Peter Fonda; Carla Marlier; Francoise Prevost; James Robertson Justice; Brigitte Bardot; Alain Delon; Katia Christine; Terence Stamp; Salvo Randone; ***Nar:*** Vincent Price; Clement Biddle Wood; ***D:*** Roger

Vadim; Louis Malle; Federico Fellini; *W:* Roger Vadim; Louis Malle; Federico Fellini; Daniel Boulanger; Bernardino Zapponi; *C:* Tonino Delli Colli; Claude Renoir; Giuseppe Rotunno; *M:* Nino Rota; Diego Masson.

Spite Marriage **1929** When Sebastian's lover dumps her like yesterday's garbage, she marries Keaton out of spite. Much postnuptual levity follows. Keaton's final silent. **82m/B; Silent; VHS, DVD.** Buster Keaton; Dorothy Sebastian; Edward Earle; Leila Hyams; William Bechtel; Hank Mann; *D:* Edward Sedgwick.

Spitfire **1934** Sentimental comedy-drama starring Hepburn as a hillbilly faith healer from the Ozarks who falls into a love triangle. One in a string of early boxoffice flops for Hepburn. She wanted to play a role other than patrician Eastern Seaboard, and did, but audiences didn't buy it. **90m/B; VHS, DVD.** Katharine Hepburn; Robert Young; Ralph Bellamy; Sidney Toler; Martha Sleeper; Sara Haden; Virginia Howell; Will Geer; *D:* John Cromwell; *W:* Jane Murfin; *C:* William Cronjager; *M:* Max Steiner.

Spitfire *The First of the Few* **1942** True story of Reginald J. Mitchell, who designed "The Spitfire" fighter plane, which greatly assisted the Allies during WWII. Howard's last film. Heavily propagandist but enjoyable and uncomplicated biography, with a splendid score. **88m/B; VHS, DVD.** *GB* Leslie Howard; David Niven; Rosamund John; Roland Culver; David Horne; J.H. Roberts; Patricia Medina; *D:* Leslie Howard; *C:* Georges Perinal; *M:* William Walton.

The Spitfire Grill 1/2 *Care of the Spitfire Grill* **1995 (PG-13)** Newly released from prison, Perry Talbott (Elliott) moves to smalltown Gilead, Maine, and gets a waitressing job at the Spitfire Grill, run by the cranky Hannah (Burstyn). Perry's upfront about her jail time, which doesn't endear her to the suspicious locals. Particularly censorious is businessman Nahum Goddard (Patton), who sends his downtrodden wife Shelby (Harden) to keep an eye on Perry. There are a number of personal dilemmas that take their toll in this familiar setting—redeemed by strong performances. **117m/C; DVD.** Alison Elliott; Ellen Burstyn; Marcia Gay Harden; Will Patton; Kieran Mulroney; Gailard Sartain; Louise De Cormier; John M. Jackson; *D:* Lee David Zlotoff; *W:* Lee David Zlotoff; *C:* Rob Draper; *M:* James Horner. Sundance '96: Aud. Award.

Splash 1/2 **1984 (PG)** A beautiful mermaid ventures into New York City in search of a man she's rescued twice when he's fallen overboard. Now it's her turn to fall—in love. Charming performances by Hanks and Hannah. Well-paced direction from Howard, with just enough slapstick. Don't miss the lobster scene. **109m/C; VHS, DVD.** Tom Hanks; Daryl Hannah; Eugene Levy; John Candy; Dody Goodman; Shecky Greene; Richard B. Shull; Bobby DiCicco; Howard Morris; *D:* Ron Howard; *W:* Babaloo Mandel; Lowell Ganz; *C:* Don Peterman; *M:* Lee Holdridge. Natl. Soc. Film Critics '84: Screenplay.

Splatter University **WOOF!** **1984** A deranged killer escapes from an asylum and begins to slaughter and mutilate comely coeds at a local college. Abysmally motiveless killing and gratuitous sex. Also available in a 78-minute "R" rated version. **79m/C; VHS, DVD, Blu-Ray.** Francine Forbes; Dick Biel; Cathy Lacommaro; Ric Randing; Dan Eaton; Denise Texeira; Mary Ellen David; Joanna Mihalakis; *D:* Richard W. Haines; *W:* Richard W. Haines; John Michaels; Michael Cunningham; *M:* Chris Burke.

Splendor 1/2 **1999 (R)** A '90s screwball comedy about an unconventional sexual arrangement. Veronica (Robertson) is an aspiring L.A. actress who enjoys her sexual exploits and who falls for two men on the opposite ends of the romantic spectrum. Abel (Schaech) is a freelance music critic who's intelligent and handsome while punk rock drummer Zed (Keeslar) is dumb but really sexy. Veronica refuses to choose between the two, so both move in with her (and prove to be more immature than the lady herself). Then Veronica meets successful and wealthy TV director, Ernest (Mabius), and wonders if it's time for a real adult relatonship. Surprisingly sweet and stylish fluff from Araki. **93m/C; VHS, DVD.** Kathleen Robertson; Johnathon Schaech; Matt Keeslar; Eric Mabius; Kelly Macdonald; *D:* Gregg Araki; *W:* Gregg Araki; *C:* Jim Fealy; *M:* Daniel Licht.

Splendor in the Grass **1961** A drama set in rural Kansas in 1925, concerning a teenage couple who try to keep their love on a strictly intellectual plane and the sexual and family pressures that tear them apart. After suffering a mental breakdown and being institutionalized, the girl returns years later in order to settle her life. Film debuts of Beatty, Dennis, and Diller. Inge wrote the screenplay specifically with Beatty in mind, after the actor appeared in one of Inge's stage plays. Filmed not in Kansas, but on Staten Island and in upstate New York. **124m/C; VHS, DVD.** Natalie Wood; Warren Beatty; Audrey Christie; Barbara Loden; Zohra Lampert; Phyllis Diller; Sandy Dennis; *D:* Elia Kazan; *W:* William Inge; *C:* Charles Durnham; *M:* David Amram. Oscars '61: Story & Screenplay.

Splice **2010 (R)** Geneticists Clive (Body) and Elsa (Polley) set ethics aside to take their DNA recombinations a step further by adding human DNA into their animal mix. The hybrid gestation is rapid and the two are confronted by Dren, a weirdly-beautiful mutant with strong physical abilities and intelligence. And the emotional Dren doesn't like to be confined to the lab. **107m/C; DVD, Blu-Ray.** Adrien Brody; Sarah Polley; David Hewlett; Delphine Chaneac; Brandon McGibbon; Simona Maicanescu; Abigail Chu; *D:* Vincenzo Natali; *W:* Vincenzo Natali; Doug Taylor; Antoinette Terry Bryant; *C:* Tetsuo Nagata; *M:* Cyrille Aufort.

Spliced 1/2 **2003 (R)** Slick slasher that may be derivative but still manages some shudders. High school senior Mary Ryan (Balaban) is obsessed with horror movies and much too suggestible. She becomes convinced that the mad slasher character in one of her faves is not only real but offing her classmates. School doctor Morgan Campbell (Silver) first thinks Mary is merely crazy but then comes to change his mind. **86m/C; VHS, DVD.** Liane Balaban; Ron Silver; Sin Baruc; Drew Lachey; *D:* Gavin Wilding; *W:* Ellen Cook. **VIDEO**

Splinter **2006 (R)** L.A. gangbanger brothers Dreamer (Almeida) and Dusty (Guglielmi) are looking for their older brother's killer. Someone is also torturing and killing fellow gang members, which brings in rookie detective Gramm (Atis), who's teamed up with corrupt, unstable veteran Cunningham (Sizemore, perhaps typecast). Maybe someone just wants to expand their turf or maybe a serial killer is targeting the gangs. Olmos plays a police captain and yeah, that's his kid helming this familiar pic. **90m/C; DVD.** Tom Sizemore; Edward James Olmos; Noel Guglielmi; Resmine Atis; Enrique Almeida; Dallas Page; *D:* Michael D. Olmos; *W:* Michael D. Olmos; *C:* Bridger Nielson; *M:* Jae Chong. **VIDEO**

Splinterheads 1/2 **2009 (R)** Aimless slacker Justin falls for con woman Galaxy who scams him when the carnival she's working for shows up in town. He's at least a nice guy, unlike her carny boyfriend, so Galaxy starts paying him a little attention. A little attention is all the movie deserves as well since it's kind of a yawner. **94m/C; DVD.** Thomas Middleditch; Rachael Taylor; Christopher McDonald; Lea Thompson; Jason Rogel; Edmund Lyndeck; Dean Winters; Frankie Faison; *D:* Brant Sersen; *W:* Brant Sersen; *C:* Michael Simmonds; *M:* John Swihart.

The Split **1968** In this routine heist flick, adapted from the Donald E. Westlake novel "The Seventh," McClain and his crew target the L.A. Coliseum during a football game. The heist goes as planned and McClain hides the loot in his ex-wife's apartment. She gets killed, the money is stolen, and McClain's crew think it's a doublecross. The crime gets more complicated when crooked cop Brill gets involved. **90m/C; DVD.** Jim Brown; Gene Hackman; Julie Harris; Diahann Carroll; Ernest Borgnine; Donald Sutherland; Jack Klugman; James Whitmore; Warren Oates; *D:* Gordon Flemyng; *W:* Robert Sabaroff; *C:* Burnett Guffey; *M:* Quincy Jones.

Split 1/2 **2016 (PG-13)** Shyamalan returns to the twisty thriller genre that he helped define with this well-directed genre piece, carried by two great leads. The first comes from McAvoy, who gives his all to a man with 23 distinct personalities. After he kidnaps a trio of girls (Richardson, Sula, and the incredible Taylor-Joy), they are forced to figure out which personality can help them escape. Shyamalan brilliantly ups the tension bit by bit, but it's McAvoy and Taylor-Joy's totally believable and in-the-moment performances that fuse this together. **234m/C; DVD, Blu-Ray, Streaming.** James McAvoy; Anya Taylor-Joy; Betty Buckley; Haley Lu Richardson; Jessica Sula; *D:* M. Night Shyamalan; *W:* M. Night Shyamalan; *C:* Mike Gioulakis; *M:* West Dylan Thordson.

Split Decisions **1988 (R)** An Irish family of boxers, dad and his two sons, slug it out emotionally and physically, as they come to terms with career choices and each other. Good scenes in the ring but the drama leans toward melodrama. Decent family drama, but somewhat of a "Rocky" rip-off. **95m/C; VHS, DVD.** Gene Hackman; Craig Sheffer; Jeff Fahey; Jennifer Beals; John McLiam; Eddie Velez; Carmine Caridi; James Tolkan; *D:* Dr. David Drury; *W:* David Fallon; *M:* Basil Poledouris.

Split Second 1/2 **1953** An escaped prisoner holds hostages in a Nevada atomic bomb testing area. McNally's excellent performance as the kidnapper, in addition to strong supporting performances, enhance a solid plot. Powell's directorial debut. **85m/B; VHS, DVD.** Paul Kelly; Richard Egan; Jan Sterling; Alexis Smith; Stephen McNally; *D:* Dick Powell; *W:* William Bowers; Irving Wallace.

Split Second 1/2 **1992 (R)** Hauer is a futuristic cop tracking down a vicious alien serial killer in London in the year 2008. The monster rips out the hearts of his victims and then eats them in what appears to be a satanic ritual in this blood-soaked thriller wanna-be. Hauer gives a listless performance and overall, the action is quite dull. The music soundtrack also manages to annoy with the Moody Blues song "Nights in White Satin" playing at the most inappropriate times. A British/American co-production. **91m/C; VHS, DVD.** *GB* Rutger Hauer; Kim Cattrall; Neil Duncan; Michael J. Pollard; Alun Armstrong; Pete Postlethwaite; Ian Dury; Roberta Eaton; *D:* Tony Maylam; *W:* Gary Scott Thompson; *C:* Clive Tickner; *M:* Francis Haines; Stephen Parsons.

Split Second **1999** Corporate lawyer Michael Anderson (Owen) is fed up with both his work and home lives. A road rage incident leaves a cyclist dead and Michael fleeing the scene. He tries to repress the incident but it only leads to further angst and anger. Owen is a champion brooder but this is a routine diversion. **90m/C; DVD.** *GB* Clive Owen; Helen McCrory; John Bowe; James Cosmo; Tony Curran; *D:* David Blair. **TV**

Splitting Heirs 1/2 **1993 (PG-13)** Idle stars as the offspring of titled parents who is accidentally abandoned in a restaurant as an infant and raised by poor Pakistanis. (His mother winds up claiming the wrong abandoned baby.) When he discovers he's actually the 15th Duke of Bournemouth he plots, ineffectually, to kill off the present unknowing imposter, a nitwit American (Moranis). Cleese pops in as a shabby lawyer hired by Idle to help him claim the title with Hershey as Idle's real mother, the addlebrained and sex-starved Duchess. Convoluted plot, bland comedy. **87m/C; VHS, DVD.** Eric Idle; Rick Moranis; Barbara Hershey; John Cleese; Catherine Zeta-Jones; Sadie Frost; Stratford Johns; Brenda Bruce; William Franklyn; Jeremy Clyde; David Ross; *D:* Robert M. Young; *W:* Eric Idle; *M:* Michael Kamen.

Splitz **WOOF!** **1984 (PG-13)** An all-girl rock band agrees to help out a sorority house by participating in a series of sporting events. **89m/C; VHS, DVD.** Robin Johnson; Patti Lee; Shirley Stoler; Raymond Serra; *D:* Domonic Paris.

Spoiler 1/2 **1998** Wrongly convicted Daniels is stuck in a sadistic 21st-century prison with just one aim—to escape and reunite with his young daughter. **100m/C; VHS, DVD.** Gary Daniels; Meg Foster; Bryan Genesse; Jeffrey Combs; Arye Gross; Duane Whitaker; David Groh; *D:* Carmen Von Daacke; *W:* Michael Kalesniko; *C:* Philip Lee. **VIDEO**

The Spoilers **1942** Two adventurers in the Yukon are swindled out of their gold mine and set out to even the score. A trademark scene of all versions of the movie (and there are many) is the climactic fistfight, in this case between hero Wayne and badguy Scott. One of the better films adapted from the novel by Rex Beach. William Farnum, who starred in both the 1914 and the 1930 versions, has a small part. **88m/B; VHS, DVD, Blu-Ray.** John Wayne; Randolph Scott; Marlene Dietrich; Margaret Lindsay; Harry Carey, Sr.; Richard Barthelmess; Charles Halton; *D:* Ray Enright; *C:* Milton Krasner.

Spoilers of the North **1947** Conniving Alaska salmon fisherman Matt Garraway persuades girlfriend Laura to put up the money for his cannery. Then he dumps her to take up with half-breed Jane so she'll persuade her Native American friends to do some illegal fishing for him. Jane's brother Pete realizes Matt is no good and decides to bring him down. Made cringe-worthy by the blatantly racist attitudes of the day. **66m/B; DVD.** Paul Kelly; Evelyn Ankers; Adrian Booth; Francis McDonald; James Millican; Roy Barcroft; *D:* Richard Sale; *W:* Milton Raison; *C:* Alfred S. Keller.

The SpongeBob Movie: Sponge Out of Water **2015 (PG)** The Nickelodeon character makes another film appearance, this time in a live-action/3-D animation hybrid that is kinda entertaining and kinda creepy. A pirate named Burger Beard (Banderas) steals the formula for the Krabby Patty, sending all of Bikini Bottom into total chaos. Spongebob (Kenny) and Sandy (Lawrence) have to go above ground to retrieve it, at which point the 2-D animation turns to 3-D and these beloved characters interact with the real world, essentially turning into superheroes along the way. As with most Spongebob properties, the hyperactivity gets overwhelming at times, even if some of the jokes are admittedly clever. **92m/C; DVD, Blu-Ray.** Antonio Banderas; *V:* Tom Kenny; Bill Fagerbakke; Rodger Bumpass; Clancy Brown; *D:* Paul Tibbitt; *W:* Glenn Berger; Jonathan Aibel; *C:* Phil Meheux; *M:* John Debney.

The SpongeBob SquarePants Movie 1/2 **2004 (PG)** Nickelodeon's animated series (equally popular with kiddies, college students, and wannabe hipsters) makes its debut on the big screen with all its bright colored frivolity intact. Our peppy yellow sea sponge and his dim-witted best pal, starfish Patrick, must save their home of Bikini Bottom from the evil Plankton, who steals the crown of King Neptune. You weren't honestly expecting more of a plot, were you? Hasselhoff appears in all his "Baywatch" glory to save our watery heroes from a desperate dry land fate. **90m/C; VHS, DVD, Blu-Ray, UMD.** ***Cameo(s):*** David Hasselhoff; *V:* Tom Kenny; Bill Fagerbakke; Clancy Brown; Rodger Bumpass; Alec Baldwin; Scarlett Johansson; Jeffrey Tambor; Carolyn Lawrence; Mary Jo Catlett; Mr. Lawrence; Jill Talley; *D:* Stephen Hillenburg; *W:* Derek Drymon; Tim Hill; Paul Tibbett; *C:* Jerzy Zielinski; *M:* Gregor Nabholz.

Spontaneous Combustion **1989 (R)** A grisly horror film detailing the travails of a hapless guy who has the power to inflict the title phenomenon on other people. **97m/C; VHS, DVD, Blu-Ray; Open Captioned.** Brad Dourif; Jon Cypher; Melinda Dillon; Cynthia Bain; William Prince; Dey Young; Dick Butkus; John Landis; Dale Dye; *D:* Tobe Hooper; *W:* Tobe Hooper; Howard Goldberg; *C:* Levie Isaacks; *M:* Graeme Revell.

The Spook Who Sat by the Door 1/2 **1973 (PG)** A black CIA agent organizes an army of inner-city youths and launches a revolution. Based on the novel by Sam Greenlee. **95m/C; VHS, DVD.** Lawrence Cook; Paula Kelly; J.A. Preston; *D:* Ivan Dixon; *M:* Herbie Hancock. Natl. Film Reg. '12.

Spooky Buddies 1/2 **2011 (G)** A Fernfield legend has Warwick the Warlock and the Halloween Hound needing the souls of five dogs of the same bloodline to allow spirits to escape the underworld. The talking pups stumble into the middle of the evil plan and must save the day. **88m/C; DVD, Blu-Ray.** Harland Williams; Tucker Albrizzi; Elisa

Donovan; *V:* Nico Ghisi; Skyler Gisondo; G. Hannelius; Ty Panitz; Charles Henry Wyson; Diedrich Bader; Frankie Jonas; Debra Jo Rupp; Tim Conway; *D:* Robert Vince; *W:* Anna McRoberts; *C:* Mike Southon; *M:* Brahm Wenger. **VIDEO**

Spooky Encounters 🦴🦴 1/2 *Encounters of the Spooky Kind* **1980** Writer/director/star Samo Hung is Cheung, a simple-minded braggart who takes a bet to spend one night in a haunted temple. But it's a set-up. His unfaithful wife's lover hires an evil sorcerer to raise the dead. The film covers practically the entire palette of Chinese horror, including hopping vampires and flesh-eating zombies, along with flying undead and plenty of black magic. Samo pulls the film off easily, using his trademark humor to soften the horrific edge. **94m/C; DVD.** *CH* Sammo Hung; Chung Fat; *D:* Sammo Hung; *W:* Sammo Hung.

Spooky Stakeout 🦴🦴 1/2 **2016** A family-friendly mystery-solving adventure in the vein of Scooby-Doo and Goosebumps. Four young teens are good at solving mysteries, having figured out what happened in an abandoned school building and a run-down hotel. Team Spooky then land a job to solve a mystery related to an ancient haunted castle. The four friends soon discover that there is a common element to all three mysteries and it could be a real ghost! **89m/C; DVD, Streaming, Download.** Alix Bailey; Darragh Barron; Harry Behan; Evan Colgan; Zena Donnelly; *D:* Ruth Treacy; *W:* Matthew Roche; *C:* Julianne Forde.

Spooner 🦴 1/2 **2008 (R)** Man-child Herman Spooner is finally forced to grow up on his 30th birthday. That's the deadline his parents gave the socially awkward used car salesman to move out of the house and they're sticking to it. At the same time, Herman's boss threatens to fire him for poor sales numbers. His situation isn't completely bleak since it's love at first sight for Herman and lively Rose—until she tells him she's moving to the Philippines. **84m/C; DVD.** Mathew Lillard; Nora Zehetner; Christopher McDonald; Kate Burton; Shea Whigham; Wendi McLendon-Covey; *D:* Drake Doremus; *W:* Lindsay Stidham; *C:* John Guleserian; *M:* Bobby Johnston.

Spork 🦴🦴 **2010** Odd-but-sweet first feature from Ghuman with a notable hook (and a lot of presumably deliberate racial and social stereotypes). A spork is neither a spoon nor a fork and hermaphrodite high schooler Spork (Stehlin) is neither male nor female. Spork lives in trailer park squalor with her older brother Spit (Eastman) and his girlfriend Felicia (Hendrix). A school scapegoat, oppressed by blonde Becky Byotch (Fox) and her harridans, Spork finds inspiration from her wise friend Chunk (Chung). She also has no-nonsense newcomer Tootsie Roll (Park) encouraging Spork to learn breakdancing for that big dance competition finale. **86m/C; DVD.** Savannah Stehlin; Sydney Park; Kevin Chung; Rachel G. Fox; Rodney Eastman; Elaine Hendrix; Oana Gregory; Michael William Arnold; Chad Allen; *D:* J.B. Ghuman, Jr.; *W:* J.B. Ghuman, Jr.; *C:* Bradley Stonesifer; *M:* Casey James.

Sporting Blood 🦴🦴 **1931** Convoluted horse racing story in which the non-equine stars take their time to make an appearance. Thoroughbred Tommy Boy is sold to crooked Tip Scanlon (Cody) who drugs and abuses the animal to fix races. Tip eventually sells the horse to casino dealer Ruby (Evans), who wants to restore Tommy Boy to health, while mobbed-up gambler Rid Riddell (Gable minus his moustache) has other ideas—despite his romancing Ruby. It all ends at the Kentucky Derby. **82m/B; DVD.** Madge Evans; Clark Gable; Lew Cody; Ernest Torrence; Marie Prevost; Hallam Cooley; J. Farrell MacDonald; John Larkin; *D:* Charles Brabin; *W:* Charles Brabin; Willard Mack; Wanda Tuchock; *C:* Harold Rosson.

Spotlight 🦴🦴🦴 **2015 (R)** McCarthy proves to be the perfect writer/director for this true story of how the writers on the "Spotlight Team" of The Boston Globe unearthed the massive conspiracy within the church to hide pedophile priests. He tackles the subject from a procedural standpoint, presenting these great journalists doing what they do best—challenging authority and digging to get the story. Keaton leads the team, ably supported by a cast that includes Ruffalo, McAdams, Slattery, Schreiber, Tucci, and more. There's not a weak player on the team. This is one of those great dramas that plays more like a thriller, even though we know how it ends. **128m/C; DVD, Blu-Ray.** Mark Ruffalo; Michael Keaton; Rachel McAdams; Liev Schreiber; John Slattery; *D:* Tom McCarthy; *W:* Tom McCarthy; Josh Singer; *C:* Masanobu Takayanagi; *M:* Howard Shore. Oscars '15: Film, Orig. Screenplay; British Acad. '15: Orig. Screenplay; Ind. Spirit '16: Director (McCarthy), Film, Film Editing, Screenplay; Screen Actors Guild '15: Cast; Writers Guild '15: Orig. Screenplay.

Spotlight Scandals 🦴🦴 *Spotlight Revue; Spotlight on Scandal* **1943** A barber and a vaudevillian team up and endure the ups and downs of showbiz life in this low-budget musical from prolific B-movie director Beaudine. **79m/B; VHS, DVD.** Billy Gilbert; Frank Fay; Bonnie Baker; *D:* William Beaudine; *W:* Beryl Sachs; *C:* Mack Stengler.

Spread 🦴 1/2 **2009 (R)** Just a gigolo? Kutcher stars as Nicki, a handsome, probably as dumb-as-he-appears Hollywood hustler who specializes in being the kept boy toy of a successful older woman. His latest mark is well-toned, 40-something lawyer Samantha (Heche) who's all about the continuous sex. When she's in New York for a few days, he throws a party at her fabulous home and gets involved with Heather (Levieva), the distaff version of himself. Actually, Heather is a lot better at the sex game since Nicki doesn't have anything tangible to show for his efforts and he can't keep his eye on the prize when he begins suddenly suffering from some vague moral qualms. **97m/C; DVD.** Ashton Kutcher; Anne Heche; Margarita Levieva; Sebastian Stan; Rachel Blanchard; Maria Conchita Alonso; Hart Bochner; *D:* David Mackenzie; *W:* Jason Dean Hall; *C:* Steven Poster; *M:* John Swihart.

Spree 🦴 *Survival Run* **1979 (R)** . A car full of partying teenagers get stranded in the desert and they meet up with drug dealers while hiking back to civilization. It's no surprise what happens next. Somewhere between a mainstream flick and brutal exploitation. **90m/C; DVD.** *MX US* Peter Graves; Ray Milland; Vincent Van Patten; Pedro Armendariz, Jr.; *D:* Larry Spiegel; *W:* Larry Spiegel; *C:* Alex Phillips, Jr.; *M:* Gary William Friedman.

Spriggan 🦴🦴 1/2 **1998 (R)** Based on the comic of the same name, and directed by Katsuhiro Otomo ("Akira"), it's "Raiders of the Lost Ark" on steroids. A super-secret group called Arkam is attempting to find Noah's Ark in order to protect humanity from its power, but a rival American organization wants to use it to rule the world. So the Americans send a team of superhuman assassins codenamed Fatman and Little Boy (subtle!) to off the protagonist before he can find the Ark himself. Beautifully animated and lots of action, but the plot is muddled by trying to squeeze several years of comic storyline into an hour and a half. **90m/C; DVD.** *JP* *V:* Chris Patton; Kevin Corn; Ted Pfister; Andy McAvin; Kelly Manison; Mike Kleinhenz; Spike Spencer; John Paul Shephard; John Swasey; *D:* Hirotsugu Kawasaki; *W:* Hirotsugu Kawasaki; Yasutaka Ito; *M:* Kuniaki Haishima.

The Spring 🦴🦴 1/2 **2000 (PG-13)** Widower Dennis Conway (MacLachlan) and his son Nick (Cross) stop in the small town of Springville when travelling and Nick has an accident. The kid has to spend some time in the hospital where Dennis becomes involved with his son's doctor, Sophie Weston (Eastwood). But the town hides a secret—the local spring is a modern-day fountain of youth, the residents are much older than they appear, and none can ever leave. Based on the novel by Clifford Irving. **90m/C; VHS, DVD.** Kyle MacLachlan; Alison Eastwood; Joseph Cross; George Eads; Zachary Ansley; Aaron Pearl; *D:* David Jackson; *W:* J.B. White. **TV**

Spring 🦴🦴🦴 **2015** Evan (Taylor Pucci) goes off the grid after the death of his mother, packing up his bags to backpack around Europe. He ends up in Italy, noticing a beautiful woman one night and summons the courage to talk to her. Her name is Louise (Hilker) and the two have instant, amazing chemistry. But Louise masks a deep, dark, supernatural secret. Benson and Moorhead's striking horror film is surprisingly tender while also being daringly original. **109m/C; DVD, Blu-Ray.** Lou Taylor Pucci; Nadia Hilker; Vanessa Bednar; Shane Brady; Francesco Carnelutti; *D:* Justin Benson; *W:* Justin Benson; Aaron Moorhead; *C:* Aaron Moorhead; *M:* Jimmy Lavalley.

Spring 1941 🦴🦴 **2008 (R)** As the Nazis occupy Poland, the Jewish Planck family flee Warsaw and find refuge with acquaintance Emilia at her farm. With her husband away fighting, Emilia is happy to have Artur around to help out but then they have an affair and she gets pregnant. Artur is afraid if he rejects Emilia now she'll betray them to the authorities, but the tensions continue to grow. **97m/C; DVD.** *IS PL* Joseph Fiennes; Neve McIntosh; Kelly Harrison; *D:* Uri Barbash; *W:* Matti Lerner; *C:* Ryszard Lenczewski; *M:* Misha Segal.

Spring Break 🦴 **1983 (R)** Four college students go to Fort Lauderdale on their spring vacation and have a wilder time that they bargained for, though viewer is deprived of excitement. **101m/C; VHS, DVD, Blu-Ray.** Perry Lang; David Knell; Steve Bassett; Paul Land; Jayne Modean; Corinne Alphen; *D:* Sean S. Cunningham.

Spring Breakdown 🦴🦴 **2008 (R)** Three 40ish women, who have been friends since their staid college days, vacation on South Padre Island in Texas, which is known as a spring break haven for co-eds. Becky (Posey) has been sent by her senator boss (Lynch) to secretly keep an eye on her daughter Ashley (Tamblyn) while Gayle (Poehler) and Judi (Dratch) decide to indulge in everything they didn't do in their youth, including drunken debauchery with frat boys. **84m/C; DVD.** Parker Posey; Amy Poehler; Rachel Dratch; Amber Tamblyn; Seth Meyers; Sophie Monk; Jonathan Sadowski; Missi Pyle; Jane Lynch; Mae Whitman; *D:* Ryan Shiraki; *W:* Ryan Shiraki; *C:* Frank DeMarco; *M:* Deborah Lurie.

Spring Breakers 🦴🦴🦴 **2013 (R)** Writer/director Korine's dubstep-infused journey into the world of sun and sin that calls itself spring break is an inspired satire of people unable to know when the party's over and features a mesmerizing James Franco (believe it!). Brit (Benson), Candy (Hudgens), Cotty (Korine), and Faith (Gomez) don't have the money to make it to spring break, so they rob the Chicken Shack. It's just the first questionable decision of many that push them past the norms of society and into the world of rapper/gangster Alien (Franco). Unpredictable, unforgettable, and just a little bit insane. **94m/C; DVD, Blu-Ray.** Selena Gomez; Vanessa Anne Hudgens; Ashley Benson; Rachel Korine; James Franco; *D:* Harmony Korine; *W:* Harmony Korine; *C:* Benoît Debie; *M:* Cliff Martinez.

Spring Fever 🦴🦴 **1927** Jack Kelly (Haines) may be a lowly shipping clerk but he is a natural golfer who, in return for helping boss Mr. Waters (Fawcett) with his swing, is given a two-week membership to a fancy country club. There he meets (and falls for) wealthy Allie Monte (Crawford) as well as becoming the club's representative in a championship tournament. But will Allie still love him when she discovers Jack's poor? Adapted from a play by Vincent Lawrence. Remade as 1930's "Love in the Rough." **78m/B; Silent; DVD.** William Haines; Joan Crawford; George Fawcett; Eileen Percy; Bert Woodruff; George K. Arthur; *D:* Edward Sedgwick; *W:* Frank Davis; Albert Lewin; *C:* Ira Morgan.

Spring Forward 🦴🦴 1/2 **1999 (R)** Playwright and director Gilroy's debut stays close to his stage roots in this fastidious character drama involving the budding relationship of two men who work for the parks department in a small New England town. Regular joes Murph (Beatty), a world-weary senior close to retirement, and Paul (Schreiber), a feisty ex-con who wants a second chance, are seeming opposites who bond over the course of numerous events on the job, ranging from the death of Murph's gay son to a chance encounter with a vixen with the hots for Paul. Dead-on dialogue and restrained style, along with pitch perfect performances shine even when drama gets stagnant. Filmed mostly sequentially over the course of a year, seasons and character changes are laudably real. **111m/C; VHS, DVD.** Ned Beatty; Liev Schreiber; Campbell Scott; Ian Hart; Peri Gilpin; Bill Raymond; Catherine Kellner; Hallee Hirsh; *D:* Tom Gilroy; *W:* Tom Gilroy; *C:* Terry Stacey; *M:* Hahn Rowe.

Spring in Park Lane 🦴🦴 1/2 **1948** Charmingly light drawing-room comedy. Temporarily without funds, aristocratic Richard (Wilding) hides his identity to take a job as a footman for weathy art collector Joshua Howard (Walls). Howard's niece Judy (Neagle), who serves as her uncle's secretary, becomes suspicious of Richard's obvious sophistication but this doesn't stop them from falling in love. **91m/B; DVD.** *UK* Michael Wilding; Anna Neagle; Tom Walls; Peter Graves; Marjorie Fielding; Nicholas Phipps; *D:* Herbert Wilcox; *W:* Nicholas Phipps; *C:* Mutz Greenbaum; *M:* Robert Farnon.

Spring Parade 🦴🦴 1/2 **1940** Typically lighthearted musical starring Durbin in a Viennese setting. Ilona (Durbin) goes to a fair and buys a card from a gypsy fortune teller promising she'll meet someone important and have a happy marriage. She gets a job as a baker's assistant and meets army drummer Harry (Cummings), who secretly composes music. Ilona includes sheet music for one of Harry's waltzes in the pastry order going to the Austrian Emperor and it paves the way for the gypsy's predictions to come true. **89m/B; DVD.** Deanna Durbin; Robert Cummings; Mischa Auer; Henry Stephenson; S.Z. Sakall; Edward (Ed) Gargan; Anne Gwynne; Peggy Moran; Reginald Denny; Franklin Pangborn; Allyn Joslyn; *D:* Henry Koster; *W:* Felix Jackson; Bruce Manning; *C:* Joseph Valentine; *M:* Charles Previn.

Spring, Summer, Fall, Winter. . . and Spring 🦴🦴🦴 *Bom Yeorum Gaeul Gyeoul Geurigo. . .Bom* **2003 (R)** Telling his tale in five segments as the title suggests, writer-director-actor Ki-Duk departs from his typically violent fare and poignantly walks through the life of a young Buddhist monk—from his beginnings as a mischievous boy to a troubled adult running from the law and his demons—and his relationship with an older monk serving as his mentor. All scenes take place in a floating monastery (created specifically for the film) in a breathtaking Korean lake that truly reflects the drama's elegance and stark simplicity. In Korean, with English subtitles. **102m/C; VHS, DVD.** *NK* Oh Young Soo; Kim Ki Duk; Kim Young Min; Seo Jae Kyung; Ha Yeo Jin; Kim Jong Ho; Kim Jung Young; Ji Dae Han; Choi Min; Park Ji A; Song Min Young; *D:* Kim Ki Duk; *C:* Baek Dong Hyun; *M:* Bark Jee Wong.

Spring Symphony 🦴🦴 1/2 *Fruhlingssinfonie* **1986 (PG-13)** A moody, fairy-tale biography of composer Robert Schumann, concentrating on his rhapsodic love affair with pianist Clara Weick. Kinski is very good as the rebellious daughter, while the music is even better. Reasonably accurate in terms of history; dubbed. **102m/C; VHS, DVD.** *GE* Nastassja Kinski; Rolf Hoppe; Herbert Gronemeyer; *D:* Peter Schamoni; *W:* Peter Schamoni; *C:* Gerard Vandenburg.

Springfield Rifle 🦴🦴 1/2 **1952** Based on the real-life story of Major Les Kearney, who joined forces with outlaws to catch the thief stealing government weapons. Average. **93m/C; VHS, DVD.** Gary Cooper; Phyllis Thaxter; David Brian; Lon Chaney, Jr.; Paul Kelly; Phil Carey; Guinn "Big Boy" Williams; *D:* Andre de Toth; *M:* Max Steiner.

Springsteen & I 🦴🦴🦴 **2013** Bruce Springsteen has served as a rock-and-roll icon for many decades and continues his legendary worldwide tours with the E Street Band as well as produces new material. Over the years he has amassed a fan base that is second to none, and this documentary allows his followers to share their love and admiration for the artist as well as divulge the impact he's had on their lives via videos they submitted. Clearly intended for those who regularly attend the House of Bruce, it features 77 minutes of those videos along with about 45 minutes of his band's 2012 performance in London's Hyde Park. **124m/C; DVD, Blu-Ray.** Bruce Springsteen; *D:* Baillie Walsh; *C:* Marco Tomaselli.

Springtime in the Rockies 🦴🦴 1/2 **1942** A Broadway duo Vicky (Grable) and Dan (Payne) just can't get along despite being in love with each other. So Vicky decides to partner up with Victor (Romero) while Dan tries to make Vicky jealous by dating his Brazilian secretary Rosita (Miranda). Top-notch musical, with a touch of romantic tension and comedy. Beautifully filmed in the Canadian Rockies. **91m/C; VHS, DVD.** Betty Grable; John Payne; Carmen Miranda; Cesar Romero; Charlotte Greenwood; Edward Everett Horton; Jackie Gleason; ***D:*** Irving Cummings; ***W:*** Ken Englund; Walter Bullock; ***C:*** Ernest Palmer.

Sprung 🦴🦴 **1996 (R)** The dating scene among four young African Americans is examined in this well-intended, yet unfocused romantic comedy. Couple A are Brandy (Campbell) and Montel (Cundieff) who realize that they have a chance at true love. Couple B are their friends Adina (Parker) and Clyde (Torry) who try to sabatoge Brandy and Montel's happiness in order to save them from being "sprung" (in love) with each other. The camaraderie between the couples is funny, some of the time, but the humor often turns from vulgar to juvenile and scenes drag on a bit. Cundieff and Campbell are too bland to carry over the used plot but Torry is a comedic find who makes the film tolerable. **105m/C; VHS, DVD.** Tisha Campbell; Paula Jai Parker; Rusty Cundieff; Joe Torry; John Witherspoon; Clarence Williams, III; ***D:*** Rusty Cundieff; ***W:*** Rusty Cundieff; Darin Scott; ***C:*** Joao Fernandes; ***M:*** Stanley Clarke.

Spun 🦴 **2002** A bleached-out, grunge look at meth heads. Ross (Schwartzman) is on a three-day crystal binge, thanks to hooking up with dealer Spider Mike (Leguizamo). Film lurches along from supplier to dealer to addict and from one disgusting scene to another. Who cares. **96m/C; VHS, DVD, Blu-Ray.** Jason Schwartzman; John Leguizamo; Mena Suvari; Patrick Fugit; Brittany Murphy; Mickey Rourke; Peter Stormare; Alexis Arquette; Eric Roberts; ***D:*** Jonas Akerlund; ***W:*** Will De Los Santos; Creighton Vero; ***C:*** Eric Broms; ***M:*** Billy Corgan.

Spy 🦴🦴🦴 **2015 (R)** Sending up the typically alpha-male dominated genre, McCarthy comes into her own, as secret governmental pencil pusher Susan Cooper forced into active duty to track down a deadly nuclear arms dealer. Luckily, she's got a killer supporting cast on her side, including Jude Law's suave Brit agent, Statham's boneheaded macho agent, and Byrne deconstructing the usual Bond girl. Surprisingly intelligent action comedy, allowing McCarthy to run buck wild the entire time, under director Feig's careful control, expertly goofing on James Bond tropes the entire time without ever veering into spoof territory. **117m/C; DVD, Blu-Ray, Streaming.** Melissa McCarthy; Jason Statham; Rose Byrne; Bobby Cannavale; Jude Law; Allison Janney; ***D:*** Paul Feig; ***W:*** Paul Feig; ***C:*** Robert Yeoman; ***M:*** Theodore Shapiro.

Spy Game 🦴🦴 **1/2 2001 (R)** It's 1991, and cagey veteran spy Nathan Muir (Redford) is on the verge of retirement, when he discovers that former protege Tom Bishop (Pitt) is to be executed in a Chinese prison for espionage. Muir has 24 hours to rescue Bishop, and to do it, he must first outwit his CIA superiors, who would rather lose the rogue agent than risk damaging an international trade agreement. Story's core is implausible but script is dense with information and drama, and the ultra-brisk editing leaves little time to consider the inadequacies. The use of geopolitical atrocities to add weight to a romantic subplot between Bishop and a British foreign-aid worker (McCormack) feels forced and, at times, insensitive. But Redford's cool and sarcastic performance, recalling his role in "Three Days of the Condor," makes up for some deficiencies and anchors the film nicely. **127m/C; VHS, DVD, Blu-Ray, HD-DVD.** Robert Redford; Brad Pitt; Catherine McCormack; Stephen (Dillon) Dillane; Larry Bryggman; Michael Paul Chan; Marianne Jean-Baptiste; David Hemmings; Matthew Marsh; Todd Boyce; Charlotte Rampling; ***D:*** Tony Scott; ***W:*** Michael Frost Beckner; David Arata; ***C:*** Dan(iel) Mindel; ***M:*** Harry Gregson-Williams.

Spy Games 🦴 **1/2** *History is Made at Night* **1999** CIA agent Harry (Pullman) and Russian SVR agent Natasha (Jacob) dash around Helsinki chasing a videotape that contains U.S. satellite codes and spatting romantically. Old-fashioned and lame. **94m/C; VHS, DVD.** *GB* Bill Pullman; Irene Jacob; Bruno Kirby; Glenn Plummer; Udo Kier; Andre Oumansky; Feodor Atkine; ***D:*** Ilkka Jarvilaturi; ***W:*** Patrick Amos; ***C:*** Michel Amathieu; ***M:*** Courtney Pine.

Spy Hard 🦴 **1996 (PG-13)** Nielsen does yet another genre spoof—this time a combo of "Die Hard" meets James Bond. Agent Dick Steele aka WD40 (Nielsen) is brought out of retirement to thwart the plans of crazed General Rancor (Griffith) for world domination. Not much else plotwise, which ropes Nielsen along in domino fashion through the myriad of unimaginative spoofs on such films as "Speed" and "Pulp Fiction." Minus the charm and pace of parody pioneers Zucker/Abrahams/Zucker, this latest entry should retire the whole genre. Directorial debut of Friedberg. **80m/C; VHS, DVD.** Leslie Nielsen; Nicolette Sheridan; Andy Griffith; Charles Durning; Marcia Gay Harden; Barry Bostwick; ***D:*** Rick Friedberg; ***W:*** Rick Friedberg; Dick Chudnow; Jason Friedberg; Aaron Seltzer; ***C:*** John R. Leonetti; ***M:*** Bill Conti.

Spy in Black 🦴🦴🦴 *U-Boat 29* **1939** A German submarine captain returns from duty at sea during WWI and is assigned to infiltrate one of the Orkney Islands and obtain confidential British information. Known in the U.S. as "U-Boat 29," this film is based on a J. Storer Clouston novel. This was the first teaming of director Powell and writer Pressburger, who followed with "Contraband" in 1940. Part of the 'Valerie Hobson Collection'. **82m/B; VHS, DVD.** *GB* Conrad Veidt; Valerie Hobson; Sebastian Shaw; Marius Goring; June Duprez; Helen Haye; Cyril Raymond; Hay Petrie; ***D:*** Michael Powell; ***M:*** Miklos Rozsa.

Spy in the Sky 🦴 **1958** Agent Cabot travels to Vienna in search of a missing rocket scientist that a communist spy ring is coercing into building a spy satellite. **75m/B; DVD.** Steve Brodie; George Coulouris; Sandra Francis; Hans Tiemeyer; Andrea Domburg; Bob De Lange; ***D:*** W. Lee Wilder; ***W:*** Myles Wilder; ***C:*** Walter J. (Jimmy W.) Harvey; ***M:*** Hugo de Groot.

Spy Kids 🦴🦴🦴 **2001 (PG)** Rare live-action kid's movie that doesn't talk down to its target audience has pre-teens Carmen (Vega)and Juni Cortez (Sabara) bemoaning their boring life and dealing with troublesome bullies until their parents disappear. It seems that Mom (Gugino) and Dad (Banderas) are retired superspies who get kidnapped while on one last mission. It's up to the kids, along with perennial sidekick Marin, to save their folks (and the world) from evil kid-show host Fegan Floop (Cumming, bidding for the title of world's busiest screen villian) and Minion (Shalhoub). Director/writer/editor/composer Rodriquez makes a concerted effort to provide family entertainment with zero objectionable material but plenty of gee-whiz gadgetry, fanciful set design, and exciting action. He said he wanted to make a movie that he'd be proud to show his children and his parents. He has succeeded. **88m/C; VHS, DVD, Blu-Ray.** Alexa Vega; Daryl Sabara; Antonio Banderas; Carla Gugino; Alan Cumming; Tony Shalhoub; Teri Hatcher; Richard "Cheech" Marin; Robert Patrick; Danny Trejo; George Clooney; ***D:*** Robert Rodriguez; ***W:*** Robert Rodriguez; ***C:*** Guillermo Navarro; ***M:*** Robert Rodriguez; Danny Elfman; John Debney.

Spy Kids 2: The Island of Lost Dreams 🦴🦴🦴 **2002 (PG)** Worthy sequel finds Carmen (Vega) and Juni (Sabara) fighting rival spy kids when they take on a mystery man and his creatures on a distant island. Vexing blond siblings Gary and Gerti Giggles (O'Leary and Osment) take credit for the Cortez's super-sleuthing at every turn. Meanwhile Cortez patriarch Gregorio (Banderas) has his own problems with the Giggles' dad Donnagon (Judge), as they battle for OSS leadership. Life in a spy family isn't always easy. All that aside, the newly minted Junior OSS agents must do their thing and save the day, traveling to the mutant-animal-populated island of mad scientist Buscemi. Nearly as good as the original. Montalban and Taylor as mom Ingrid's disapproving folks are a highlight. **86m/C; VHS, DVD, Blu-Ray.** Antonio Banderas; Carla Gugino; Alexa Vega; Daryl Sabara; Mike Judge; Steve Buscemi; Danny Trejo; Richard "Cheech" Marin; Ricardo Montalban; Holland Taylor; Matt O'Leary; Emily Osment; ***D:*** Robert Rodriguez; ***W:*** Robert Rodriguez; ***C:*** Robert Rodriguez; ***M:*** John Debney.

Spy Kids 3-D: Game Over 🦴🦴 **2003 (PG)** Yes, in order to watch the film, you need the funny glasses. Despite that bit of amusing nostalgia, George Clooney as the President of the United States and Sylvester Stallone in four different roles, this third and latest addition to director Rodriguez's "Spy Kids" franchise still doesn't manage to make much of an impression. The evil villain Toymaker (Stallone) and his three quirky alter ego henchmen (also Stallone) make a dangerous virtual reality video game which traps returning adolescent super-spies Juni (Sabara) and Carmen (Vega) inside. So it's parents (Banderas, Gugino) and grandpa (Montalban) to the rescue. With a tired plot, lackluster pacing, unimaginative visuals, and wooden acting, even the plethora of high-profile cameos can't save this chapter from virtual obscurity. **85m/C; VHS, DVD, Blu-Ray.** Antonio Banderas; Carla Gugino; Daryl Sabara; Alexa Vega; Ricardo Montalban; Sylvester Stallone; Holland Taylor; Danny Trejo; Mike Judge; Emily Osment; Matt O'Leary; Salma Hayek; Richard "Cheech" Marin; Bobby Edner; Courtney Jines; Alan Cumming; Tony Shalhoub; Steve Buscemi; Bill Paxton; George Clooney; Elijah Wood; ***D:*** Robert Rodriguez; ***W:*** Robert Rodriguez; ***M:*** Robert Rodriguez. Golden Raspberries '03: Worst Support. Actor (Stallone).

Spy Kids 4: All the Time in the World 🦴 **1/2 2011 (PG)** Since the original spy kids have grown-up, writer/director Rodriguez gets a new team as retired spy and new mom Marissa Cortez Wilson (Alba) is called back into action. Resented by her stepkids Cecil (Cook) and Rebecca (Blanchard), Marissa is suddenly cool when she recruits them to help her defeat the villainous Timekeeper (Piven) as part of the reactivated Spy Kids Division of the OSS. Besides being the fourth flick in the franchise, Rodriguez used '4-D' scratch-and-sniff aroma cards to give a boost to the gimmicky, predictable adventure. **89m/C; DVD, Blu-Ray.** Jessica Alba; Jeremy Piven; Joel McHale; Alexa Vega; Daryl Sabara; Danny Trejo; Mason Cook; Rowan Blanchard; Antonio Banderas; ***V:*** Ricky Gervais; ***D:*** Robert Rodriguez; ***W:*** Robert Rodriguez; ***C:*** Jimmy Lindsey; ***M:*** Carl Thiel.

The Spy Next Door 🦴 **1/2 2010 (PG)** Chop-socky legend Chan must have been suffering from post-concussion syndrome when he agreed to star in this formulaic action/comedy for the kiddies. He plays Bob Ho, a mild mannered salesman who's also an international super-spy. After retiring, he just wants to settle down with sweetheart-next-door Gillian (Valetta) and her three children, all of whom think Bob is a bore. After a plot device sends their mom out of town, the kids are foisted on Bob with alleged domestic hilarity ensuing. When geeky son Ian accidentally downloads classified material to his iPod, a pair of cartoonish Russian spies come after him. It's up to Bob to save the day and win the admiration of the children. Okay for young kids or fans of Chan's stunts, but predictable for everyone else. **94m/C; DVD, Blu-Ray, On Demand.** Jackie Chan; Madeline Carroll; Alina Foley; Will Shadley; George Lopez; Billy Ray Cyrus; Amber Valletta; Katherine Boecher; ***D:*** Brian Levant; ***W:*** Jonathan Bernstein; James Greer; ***C:*** Dean Cundey; ***M:*** David Newman.

Spy School 🦴🦴 *Doubting Thomas* **2008 (PG)** Thomas has been caught telling too many tall tales so no one believes him when he says there's a plot to kidnap the president's daughter. So Thomas is forced to come up with a plan to save her himself. **88m/C; DVD.** Forrest Landis; AnnaSophia Robb; Rider Strong; Lea Thompson; D.L. Hughley; Roger Bart; ***D:*** Mark Blutman; ***W:*** Mark Blutman; David BuBos; ***C:*** Paul Elliott. **VIDEO**

The Spy Who Came in from the Cold 🦴🦴🦴 **1/2 1965** The acclaimed adaptation of the John Le Carre novel about an aging British spy who attempts to infiltrate the East German agency. Prototypical Cold War thriller, with emphasis on de-glamorizing espionage. Gritty and superbly realistic with a documentary style which hampered it at the boxoffice. **110m/B; VHS, DVD, Blu-Ray.** Richard Burton; Oskar Werner; Claire Bloom; Sam Wanamaker; Peter Van Eyck; Cyril Cusack; Rupert Davies; Michael Hordern; ***D:*** Martin Ritt; ***W:*** Paul Dehn; Guy Trosper; ***C:*** Oswald Morris; ***M:*** Sol Kaplan. British Acad. '66: Film; Golden Globes '66: Support. Actor (Werner).

The Spy Who Dumped Me 🦴🦴 **2018 (R)** An action-comedy about best friends and their unexpected globetrotting misadventures. Cashier Audrey (Kunis) and out-of-work actress Morgan (McKinnon) live together in a small Los Angeles apartment. After Audrey's boyfriend Drew (Theroux) breaks up with her, the friends learn that he was secretly a spy. The situation grows more complicated when armed home invaders kill Drew. The pair decides to carry out Drew's mission and deliver what he has been protecting to the right person. As they travel through Europe, they quickly learn how to survive dangerous situations. While the leads have chemistry, the film does not balance extreme violence and comedy well. **117m/C; DVD, Blu-Ray.** Mila Kunis; Kate McKinnon; Justin Theroux; Sam Heughan; Hasan Minhaj; ***D:*** Susanna Fogel; ***W:*** Susanna Fogel; David Iserson; ***C:*** Barry Peterson; ***M:*** Tyler Bates.

The Spy Who Loved Me 🦴🦴 **1977 (PG)** James Bond teams up with female Russian Agent XXX to squash a villain's plan to use captured American and Russian atomic submarines in a plot to destroy the world. The villain's henchman, 7'2" Kiel, is the steel-toothed Jaws. Carly Simon sings the memorable, Marvin Hamlisch theme song, "Nobody Does It Better." **136m/C; VHS, DVD, Blu-Ray.** *GB* Roger Moore; Barbara Bach; Curt Jurgens; Richard Kiel; Caroline Munro; Walter Gotell; Geoffrey Keen; Valerie Leon; Bernard Lee; Lois Maxwell; Desmond Llewelyn; ***D:*** Lewis Gilbert; ***W:*** Christopher Wood; Richard Maibaum; ***C:*** Claude Renoir; Lamar Boren; ***M:*** Marvin Hamlisch; Paul Buckmaster.

The Spy Within 🦴🦴 *Flight of the Dove* **1994 (R)** Spy Alex (Russell) is working undercover as a call girl and Will (Glenn) is an explosives expert on the run from his past. The two share more than a mutual attraction since a covert organization wants them both dead. Confusing plot but fast-paced action. Railsback's directorial debut. **92m/C; VHS, DVD.** Theresa Russell; Scott Glenn; Lane Smith; Terence Knox; Katherine Helmond; Alex Rocco; Joe Pantoliano; Rudy Ramos; ***D:*** Steve Railsback; ***W:*** Lewis Green.

S*P*Y*S 🦴 **1974 (PG)** An attempt to cash in on the success of "M*A*S*H," this unfunny spy spoof details the adventures of two bumbling CIA men who botch a Russian defection, and get both sides after them. Usually competent director Kershner had a bad day. **87m/C; VHS, DVD.** Donald Sutherland; Elliott Gould; Joss Ackland; Zouzou; Shane Rimmer; Vladek Sheybal; Nigel Hawthorne; ***D:*** Irvin Kershner; ***W:*** Malcolm Marmorstein; Lawrence J. Cohen; ***M:*** Jerry Goldsmith.

The Squall 🦴 **1929** Director Korda's stilted melodrama was based on the Jean Bart play. Loy plays another exotic vixen, in this case Hungarian gypsy Nubi who seeks refuge during a storm with the prosperous Lajos family. She stays on, claiming she's afraid of an abusive lover, and repays their hospitality by seducing every man in the household and causing jealousy and discord. Loy's pidgin dialogue ("Nubi not bad!") is particularly egregious. **104m/B; DVD.** Myrna Loy; Richard Tucker; Alice Joyce; Carroll Nye; Loretta Young; Zasu Pitts; Harry Cording; ***D:*** Alexander Korda; ***W:*** Bradley King; ***C:*** John Seitz.

Squanto: A Warrior's Tale 🦴🦴🦴 **1994 (PG)** Family adventure fare about 17th-century Massachusetts brave Squanto (Beach), who's captured by English traders and taken to Plymouth, England for display as a "savage." He manages to escape, eventually hiding aboard a trading vessel bound for America, and on returning home even brings about a peace between fearful Pilgrims and a neighboring tribe (which culminates in the first Thanksgiving feast). It may be history lite but it's also a thoughtful, adventurous saga with good performances, and fine location filming in Nova Scotia and Cape Breton, Canada. **101m/C; VHS, DVD.** Adam Beach; Mandy Patinkin; Michael Gambon; Nathaniel Parker; Eric Schweig; Donal Donnelly; Stuart Pankin; Alex Norton; Irene Bedard; ***D:*** Xavier Koller; ***W:*** Darlene Craviotto; ***M:*** Joel McNeely.

The Square 🦴🦴 **2008 (R)** Confident contemporary Aussie noir about a pair of married lovers who try to take the (ill-gotten) money and run. Construction foreman Ray (Roberts) is trysting with much-younger Carla (van der Boom) whose thuggish husband Smithy (Hayes) has criminal ties. When Carla finds a bag of money hidden by Smithy, she badgers Ray to hire an arsonist to torch her house, thus hiding the theft. The plan goes awry, resulting in blackmail and death. **105m/C; Blu-Ray, On Demand.** *AU* David Roberts; Joel Edgerton; Anthony Hayes; Kieran Darcy-Smith; Peter Phelps; Bill Hunter; Claire Van Der Boom; Lucy Bell; Brendan Donoghue; Darshan Kitare; Luke Doolan; ***D:*** Nash Edgerton; ***W:*** Joel Edgerton; Matthew Dabner; ***C:*** Brad Shield; ***M:*** Francois (Frank) Tetaz.

The Square 🦴🦴 *Al midan* **2013** Title refers to Cairo's Tahrir Square and the demonstrations that first toppled President Hosni Mubarak in 2011 and later President Mohamed Morsi and the Muslim Brotherhood. Director Noujaim focuses on various participants who are united only by their fervor as they must contend with the violence of the Egyptian army against the demonstrations as well as conflicting political aims for the country. Arabic with subtitles. **95m/C; DVD, Blu-Ray.** *US EG* ***D:*** Jehane Noujaim; ***C:*** Muhammad Hamdy; ***M:*** Jonas Colstrup; H. Scott Salinas. Directors Guild '13: Documentary Director (Noujaim).

The Square 🦴🦴 **2017 (R)** A meandering, somewhat plotless social satire about modern life told through the experiences of the curator of a Stockholm-based contemporary art museum. Christian (Bang) struggles to publicize a new exhibit called The Square, a small space defined by a white light strip representing a communal safe space. While managing this and other professional difficulties, he is robbed of wallet, phone, and cufflinks, and the actions he takes with his subordinate Michael (Laesso) to get them back have unintended consequences. Christian also has an unusual one-night stand with an American journalist (Moss), which illustrates the comedy-drama's lack of depth. English, Danish, and Swedish with subtitles. **142m/C; DVD.** Claes Bang; Elisabeth Moss; Dominic West; Terry Notary; Christopher Laesso; ***D:*** Ruben Ostlund; ***W:*** Ruben Ostlund; ***C:*** Fredrik Wenzel.

Square Dance 🦴🦴 ½ *Home is Where the Heart Is* **1987 (PG-13)** A Texas teenager leaves the farm where she's been raised by her grandfather to live in the city with her promiscuous mother (Alexander, cast against type) where she befriends a retarded young man (yes, it's Lowe, also cast against type). Too slow, but helped by good acting. **118m/C; VHS, DVD.** Jane Alexander; Jason Robards, Jr.; Rob Lowe; Winona Ryder; Deborah Richter; Guich Koock; Elbert Lewis; ***D:*** Daniel Petrie; ***W:*** Alan Hines; ***M:*** Bruce Broughton.

Square Dance Jubilee 🦴 ½ **1951** TV scouts hit Prairie City in search of cowboy stars, and stumble onto cattle rustlers; 21 C&W tunes support a near-invisible plot, suitable for fridge runs. **78m/B; VHS, DVD.** Mary Beth Hughes; Donald (Don "Red") Barry; Wally Vernon; John Eldridge; ***D:*** Paul Landres; ***W:*** William Nolte; Ron Ormond; Daniel Ullman; ***C:*** Ernest Miller; ***M:*** Walter Greene.

The Square Peg 🦴🦴 **1958** Norman Pitkin (Wisdom) is a civilian worker during WWII who causes continual problems by digging up a road outside an army barracks. Fed-up, the commander has Norman and his colleague Grimsdale (Chapman) conscripted and sent to repair roads in France. Grimsdale is captured by German soldiers and Norman comes to the attention of the French Resistance because he just happens to look exactly like a Nazi general, and they wish to put his presence to good use. Much mistaken bumbling ensues as Norman tries to free British prisoners without getting caught himself. **88m/B; DVD.** *GB* Norman Wisdom; Edward Chapman; Honor Blackman; Campbell Singer; Hattie Jacques; Brian Worth; Terence Alexander; ***D:*** Jack Paddy Carstairs; ***W:*** Henry Blyth; Jack Davies; Eddie Leslie; ***C:*** Jack Cox; ***M:*** Philip Green.

The Squaw Man 🦴🦴 **1914** Cecil B. DeMille's first directorial feature, with mentor Oscar Apfel listed as co-director. Englishman James Wynnegate takes the blame for his embezzling cousin Sir Henry and decides to start over on a Wyoming cattle ranch. He soon marries native girl Nat-U-Ritch after she saves his life from evil Cash Hawkins. His cousin's wife, Lady Diana, eventually finds James and tells him that Henry has confessed to his crimes before dying and making James the new Earl. DeMille remade the film in 1918 and 1931. **74m/B; Silent; DVD.** Dustin Farnum; Winifred Kingston; Monroe Salisbury; Red Wing; William Elmer; Foster Knox; ***D:*** Cecil B. DeMille; Oscar Apfel; ***W:*** Cecil B. DeMille; Oscar Apfel; ***C:*** Alfred Gandolfi.

The Squaw Man 🦴🦴 **1931** DeMille's second remake of his 1914 and 1918 silents. The plot hasn't changed much but DeMille is a better filmmaker. Englishman James Wingate takes the blame for his cousin Henry's crimes and moves to America after buying a cattle ranch. He marries native girl Naturich and runs afoul of local bad guy Cash Hawkins. The early talkie melodrama goes on from there. **107m/B; DVD.** Warner Baxter; Eleanor Boardman; Lupe Velez; Charles Bickford; Paul Cavanagh; Roland Young; DeWitt Jennings; Dickie Moore; J. Farrell MacDonald; ***D:*** Cecil B. DeMille; ***W:*** Lenore Coffee; Lucien Hubbard; ***C:*** Harold Rosson.

The Squeaker 🦴🦴 ½ **1965** Complicated but interesting thriller about the underworld goings-on after a big-time diamond heist. German remake of an early (1930) British talkie, also done in 1937, based on the Edgar Wallace novel. **95m/B; VHS, DVD.** *GE* Heinz Drache; Eddi Arent; Klaus Kinski; Barbara Rutting; ***D:*** Alfred Vohrer.

The Squeeze 🦴🦴 **1977 (R)** Scotland Yard detective Keach, fired for drunkeness, gets a chance to reinstate himself when his ex-wife is caught up in a brutal kidnapping scheme. Slim script gives good cast uphill work. Ordinary thriller. Available with Spanish subtitles. **106m/C; VHS, DVD.** Stacy Keach; Carol White; David Hemmings; Edward Fox; Stephen Boyd; Angelo Infanti; ***D:*** Michael Apted.

The Squeeze 🦴 ½ *Diamond Thieves; The Heist; Rip-Off* **1980** An aging safecracker is hired for a final job, but learns that his cohorts plan to kill him when the heist is finished. Blah revenge thriller. **93m/C; VHS, DVD.** *IT* Lee Van Cleef; Karen Black; Edward Albert; Lionel Stander; Robert Alda; ***D:*** Anthony M. Dawson; ***W:*** Paul Costello; ***C:*** Sergio d'Offizi; ***M:*** Paolo Vasile.

The Squeeze WOOF! 1987 (PG-13) Keaton is wasted in this attempt at a comedy about a small-time con artist who discovers a Mafia plan to fix a lottery electromagnetically. **101m/C; VHS, DVD, Blu-Ray.** Michael Keaton; Rae Dawn Chong; John Davidson; Ric Abernathy; Bobby Bass; Joe Pantoliano; Meat Loaf Aday; Paul Herman; ***D:*** Roger Young; ***C:*** Arthur Albert; ***M:*** Miles Goodman.

Squeeze 🦴🦴 **1997 (R)** Self-conscious but not unappealing first effort made on a shoestring budget, with a director who teaches acting at a Boston youth center and who wrote his script based on the lives of his three teeanged lead actors. Tyson (Burton), Hector (Cutanda) and Boa (Duong) lead aimless lives on Boston's meaner streets where trouble finds them despite their efforts to stay (more-or-less) clear. **96m/C; VHS, DVD.** Tyrone Burton; Eddie Cutanda; Phuong Duong; Geoffrey Rhue; Russell Jones; Leigh Williams; ***D:*** Robert Patton-Spruill; ***W:*** Robert Patton-Spruill; ***C:*** Richard Moos; ***M:*** Bruce Flowers.

The Squeeze 🦴🦴 ½ **2015 (PG-13)** A naive but seriously skilled golf player becomes involved in high stakes golf matches in this sports comedy-drama. Living in rural Texas, Augie Baccus (Sumpter) is a talented golf phenom and uses his skills to provide for his mother and sister. One day, Riverboat (McDonald), a flashy gambler, arrives in town and Augie believes he has found an answer to his money problems. Teaming with Riverboat, the pair become golf hustlers between Texas and Vegas. Augie soon realizes that he is in over his head and that he might lose more even if he wins. With the help of his friends from Texas, he tries to pull of a sting and outwit the gamblers and their game. **95m/C; DVD, Streaming, Download.** Jillian Murray; Jeremy Sumpter; Katherine LaNasa; Christopher McDonald; Jason Dohring; ***D:*** Terry Jastrow; ***W:*** Terry Jastrow; ***C:*** Taron Lexton; ***M:*** Michael D. Simon.

Squeeze Play WOOF! 1979 Group of young women start a softball team and challenge the boyfriends to a game. Standard battle of the sexes takes places, with a wet T-shirt contest thrown in for good measure. Cheap, plotless, offensive trash from Troma. **92m/C; VHS, DVD.** Al Corley; Jennifer Hetrick; Jim Metzler; Jim Harris; Rick Gitlin; Helen Campitelli; Rick Kahn; Diana Valentien; ***D:*** Lloyd Kaufman; ***W:*** Charles Kaufman; Haim Pekelis; ***C:*** Lloyd Kaufman.

The Squid and the Whale 🦴🦴🦴 **2005 (R)** Writer-director Baumbach's semi-autobiographical tale of two adolescent brothers struggling to cope with their self-centered parents' divorce. Set in Brooklyn in 1986, Walt (Eisenberg) and Frank (Kline) are the progeny of pompous writer Bernard (Daniels), whose career is faltering, and unfaithful writer Joan (Linney), whose career is on the rise. The title refers to a popular exhibit at the Natural History Museum and its significance gradually becomes clear. Expert acting by all concerned; newcomer Kline is the son of actors Kevin Kline and Phoebe Cates. **88m/C; DVD, Blu-Ray.** Jeff Daniels; Laura Linney; Jesse Eisenberg; Owen Kline; Anna Paquin; William Baldwin; Halley Feiffer; David Benger; ***D:*** Noah Baumbach; ***W:*** Noah Baumbach; ***C:*** Robert Yeoman; ***M:*** Britta Phillips; Dean Wareham. L.A. Film Critics '05: Screenplay; Natl. Bd. of Review '05: Screenplay; N.Y. Film Critics '05: Screenplay; Natl. Soc. Film Critics '05: Screenplay.

Squirm 🦴🦴 **1976 (R)** Storm disrupts a highly charged power cable, electrifying a host of garden-variety worms. The worms then turn themselves into giant monsters that terrorize a small town in Georgia. The opening credits claim it's based on an actual 1975 incident. Yeah, right. Okay entry in the giant worm genre. **92m/C; VHS, DVD, Blu-Ray.** Don Scardino; Patricia Pearcy; Jean Sullivan; ***D:*** Jeff Lieberman; ***W:*** Jeff Lieberman.

Sssssss 🦴🦴 ½ **1973 (PG-13)** Campy, creepy story of snake expert Carl Stoner (Strother Martin) who's developed a serum from cobra venom that just happens to turn human beings into snakes. His latest unwitting guinea pig is reasearch assistant David Blake (Benedict). Cool makeup effects. **99m/C; VHS, DVD, Blu-Ray.** Strother Martin; Dirk Benedict; Heather Menzies; Richard B. Shull; Tim O'Connor; Jack Ging; ***D:*** Bernard L. Kowalski; ***W:*** Hal Dresner; ***C:*** Gerald Perry Finnerman; ***M:*** Patrick Williams.

Stacy's Knights 🦴🦴 *Double Down* **1983 (PG)** A seemingly shy girl happens to have an uncanny knack for blackjack. With the odds against her and an unlikely group of "knights" to aid her, she sets up an implausible "sting" operation. Blah TV fodder for the big screen. **95m/C; VHS, DVD.** Kevin Costner; Andra Millian; ***D:*** Jim Wilson; ***W:*** Michael Blake.

Stag 🦴🦴 **1997 (R)** Bachelor party goes out of control and it's every guy for himself. Best man Michael (Van Peebles) surprises groom-to-be Victor (Stockwell) by inviting guys to his bachelor party that he hasn't seen in years—for good reason—such as drug dealer Pete (McCarthy). But when stripper Kelly (McShane) is accidentally killed, Pete's the only one to keep his cool and lay out their options. And this group is a lot more interested in self-preservation than in doing the right thing. **92m/C; VHS, DVD.** Mario Van Peebles; Andrew McCarthy; John Stockwell; Kevin Dillon; Taylor Dane; William McNamara; Jerry Stiller; Ben Gazzara; John Henson; Jenny (Jennifer) McShane; ***D:*** Gavin Wilding; ***W:*** Evan Tylor; ***C:*** Maryse Alberti; ***M:*** Paul Zaza.

Stag Night 🦴 **2008 (R)** Gory recycled horror. Tony harasses two strippers he and his three equally drunk buddies met while celebrating Mike's bachelor party and the six are forced off their NY subway train at an abandoned underground station. Naturally, it's not deserted but the home of cannibal tunnel dwellers that begin to hunt the group as they try to make their way to the surface. **83m/C; DVD.** Kip Pardue; Breckin Meyer; Scott Adkins; Karl Geary; Sarah Barrand; Vinessa Shaw; ***D:*** Peter A. Dowling; ***W:*** Peter A. Dowling; ***C:*** Toby Moore; ***M:*** Benedikt Brydern. **VIDEO**

Stage Beauty 🦴🦴 ½ **2004 (R)** Set in London during the 1660s, this entertaining but sometimes stiff drama centers on gender identity. Actor Ned Kynaston (Crudup) is renowned for his female roles (his Desdemona is legendary) at a time when women were banned from the stage. But that does not stop his devoted dresser Maria (Danes) from appearing in the same part in an illegal production that comes to the attention of flamboyant King Charles II (Everett), who is then persuaded that only women should now play female parts. This turn of events makes Ned's life a misery since he doesn't know how to play the man—either on or off the stage. Danes is somewhat mediocre playing a mediocre actress but Crudup is eye-catching as he plays vain, charming, desperate, and, finally, resilient. Adapted by Hatcher from his play "Compleat Female Stage Beauty." **105m/C; DVD.** *GE GB US* Billy Crudup; Claire Danes; Rupert Everett; Tom Wilkinson; Ben Chaplin; Edward Fox; Zoe Tapper; ***D:*** Richard Eyre; ***W:*** Jeffrey Hatcher; ***C:*** Andrew Dunn; ***M:*** George Fenton.

Stage Door 🦴🦴🦴 ½ **1937** An energetic ensemble peek at the women of the theatre. A boarding house for potential actresses houses a wide variety of talents and dreams. Patrician Hepburn and wisecracking Rogers make a good team in a talent-packed ensemble. Realistic look at the sub-world of Broadway aspirations includes dialogue taken from idle chat among the actresses between takes. Based on the play by Edna Ferber and George S. Kaufman, who suggested in jest a title change to "Screen Door," since so much had been changed. Watch for young stars-to-be like Ball, Arden, and Miller. **92m/B; VHS, DVD.** Katharine Hepburn; Ginger Rogers; Lucille Ball; Eve Arden; Andrea Leeds; Jack Carson; Adolphe Menjou; Gail Patrick; ***D:*** Gregory La Cava. N.Y. Film Critics '37: Director (La Cava).

Stage Door Canteen 🦴🦴 ½ **1943** The Stage Door Canteens were operated by the American Theatre Wing during WWII for servicemen on leave. They were staffed by some of the biggest stars of the day, 65 of whom are featured here. The slight, hokey plot concerns three soldiers who fall for canteen workers while on furlough in NYC. Many musical numbers, cameos, and walk-ons by a plethora of stars. **135m/B; VHS, DVD.** Cheryl Walker; William Terry; Marjorie (Reardon) Riordan; Lon (Bud) McCallister; Sunset Carson; Tallulah Bankhead; Merle Oberon; Katharine Hepburn; Paul Muni; Ethel Waters; Judith Anderson; Ray Bolger; Helen Hayes; Harpo Marx; Gertrude Lawrence; Ethel Merman; Edgar Bergen; George Raft; Benny Goodman; Peggy Lee; Count Basie; Kay Kyser; Guy Lombardo; Xavier Cugat; Johnny Weissmuller; ***D:*** Frank Borzage; ***W:*** Delmer Daves; ***C:*** Harry Wild; ***M:*** Al Dubin; Freddie Rich.

Stage Fright 🦴🦴🦴 **1950** Wyman will stop at nothing to clear her old boyfriend, who has been accused of murdering the husband of his mistress, an actress (Dietrich). Disguised as a maid, she falls in love with the investigating detective. Dietrich sings "The Laziest Gal in Town." The Master's last film made in England until "Frenzy" (1971). **110m/B; VHS, DVD.** *GB* Jane Wyman; Marlene Dietrich; Alastair Sim; Sybil Thorndike; Michael Wilding; Kay Walsh; ***D:*** Alfred Hitchcock.

Stage Fright 🦴🦴 ½ **2014 (R)** A slasher is targeting kids at a musical theatre camp, and the murders may be related to the slicing and dicing of a potential superstar (Driver) whose daughter (MacDonald) now plans to take on the same role as mommy was playing when she died. Meat Loaf also stars, which should tell you something. Director Sable's genre oddity goes full loony, staging elaborate musical numbers in between the decapitations, and one wishes both the singing and horror elements were more accomplished but gives a LOT of points for originality. **89m/C; DVD, Blu-Ray.** Allie MacDonald; Douglas Smith; Meat Loaf Aday; Brandon Uranowitz; Minnie Driver; ***D:*** Jerome Sable; ***W:*** Jerome Sable; ***C:*** Bruce Chun; ***M:*** Jerome Sable; Eli Batalion.

Stage Struck 🦴🦴 **1948** Solid B-movie noir from Monogram. A Broadway hopeful is murdered in gangster Nick Mantee's nightclub and her sister Nancy signs on with the same talent agency (that's a front for some shady doings) so she can do some sleuthing. But will she interfere with the detectives who are working the case? **84m/B; DVD.** Conrad Nagel; Ralph Byrd; Audrey Long; Kane Richmond; John Gallaudet; Anthony Warde; ***D:*** William Nigh; ***W:*** George Wallace Sayre; Agnes Christine Johnston; ***C:*** Harry Neumann.

Stagecoach 🦴🦴🦴🦴 **1939** Varied group of characters with nothing in common are stuck together inside a coach besieged by bandits and Indians. Considered structurally perfect, with excellent direction by Ford, it's the film that made Wayne a star as the Ringo Kid, an outlaw looking to avenge the murder of his brother and father. The first pairing of Ford and Wayne changed the course of the modern western. Stunning photography by Bert Glennon and Ray Binger captured the mythical air of Monument Valley, a site that Ford was often to revisit. Based on the story "Stage to Lordsburg" by Ernest Haycox. Remade miserably with in 1966 and again—why??as a TV movie in 1986. **100m/B; VHS, DVD.** John Wayne; Claire Trevor; Thomas Mitchell; George Bancroft; John Carradine; Andy Devine; Donald Meek; Louise Platt; Berton Churchill; Tim Holt; Tom Tyler; Chris-Pin (Ethier Crispin Martini) Martin; Francis Ford; Jack Pennick; ***D:*** John Ford; ***W:*** Dudley Nichols; ***C:*** Bert Glennon; Ray Binger. Oscars '39: Score, Support. Actor (Mitchell); AFI '98: Top 100; Natl. Film Reg. '95; N.Y. Film Critics '39: Director (Ford).

Stagecoach 🦴🦴 ½ **1966** Made-for-TV remake of the John Ford/John Wayne classic manages to stand on its own as solid entertainment. This variety of stagecoach-riding, emperiled characters is well-played by some of the popular entertainers of the day, including Bing Crosby and Ann-Margret. **114m/C; DVD, Blu-Ray, Streaming.** Alex Cord; Ann-Margret; Bing Crosby; Red Buttons; Mike Connors; Robert Cummings; Van Heflin; Slim Pickens; Keenan Wynn; Stefanie Powers; ***D:*** Gordon Douglas; ***W:*** Joseph Landon; ***C:*** William Clothier; ***M:*** Jerry Goldsmith.

Stagecoach 🦴 **1986** A forgettable remake of the classic 1939 western about a motley crew of characters in a cross-country coach beset by thieves and Indians. **95m/C; VHS, DVD, Blu-Ray.** Willie Nelson; Waylon Jennings; Johnny Cash; Kris Kristofferson; John Schneider; Elizabeth Ashley; Mary Crosby; Anthony Newley; Anthony (Tony) Franciosa; ***D:*** Ted Post; ***M:*** Willie Nelson. **TV**

Stagecoach: The Texas Jack Story 🦴🦴 **2016** This western centers on a U.S. marshal seeking vengeance from a former stagecoach robber who seeks redemption. Nathaniel Lee (Adkins) was once a gunslinging outlaw known as Texas Jack, but is now retired and a ranch owner with family. His world is turned upside down when he learns that Woody Calhoun (Coates), whom he maimed during a stagecoach robber, is now a U.S. marshal. After a violent shootout, Lee again becomes Jack and looks for second chances while being chased by a bounty hunter. **90m/C; DVD, Blu-Ray, Streaming, Download.** Trace Adkins; Kim Coates; Judd Nelson; Michelle Harrison; Helena Marie; ***D:*** Terry Miles; ***W:*** Dan Benamor; Matt Williams; ***C:*** Jan Klompje; ***M:*** Sam Levin.

Stagefright 🦴 **1987** A maniacal serial killer tries to cover his trail by joining the cast of a play about mass murder. The other actors soon have more to worry about than remembering their lines. Typical low-grade horror. **95m/C; VHS, DVD, Blu-Ray.** David Brandon; Barbara Cupisti; Robert Gligorov; ***D:*** Michele (Michael) Soavi; ***W:*** Luigi Montefiore.

Stairway to Heaven 🦴🦴🦴 ½ *A Matter of Life and Death* **1946 (PG)** Wonderful romantic fantasy features Niven as RAF pilot Peter D. Carter, who falls in love with American WAC June (Hunter). Forced to bail out during a mission, Peter is rescued and must undergo a risky operation. What's riskier is an angel (Goring) has made a mistake and realizes that Peter should have died. While on the operating table, Peter's spirit travels to Heaven and pleads his case for life against a harsh prosecutor (Massey) and a group of judges. Terrific work by cinematographer Cardiff. **104m/C; VHS, DVD, Blu-Ray.** *GB* David Niven; Kim Hunter; Marius Goring; Raymond Massey; Roger Livesey; Robert Coote; Kathleen Byron; Richard Attenborough; ***D:*** Michael Powell; Emeric Pressburger; ***W:*** Michael Powell; Emeric Pressburger; ***C:*** Jack Cardiff; ***M:*** Allan Gray.

Stake Land 🦴🦴 **2010 (R)** Low-budget but well-executed (pun intended) horror. It's your basic post-apocalyptic nightmare America, but with an epidemic of vampirism that has brought down society. Teenager Martin (Paolo) is rescued from becoming an unwilling meal by grizzled hunter Mister (Damici), who teaches him how to stake the zombie-like bloodsuckers. The two then hit the road in a Chevy convertible to safety in vampire-free (they hope) Canada. **98m/C; DVD, Blu-Ray.** Connor Paolo; Nick Damici; Danielle Harris; Kelly McGillis; Sean Nelson; Michael Ceveris; ***D:*** Jim Mickle; ***W:*** Nick Damici; Jim Mickle; ***C:*** Ryan Samul; ***M:*** Jeff Grace.

Stakeout 🦴🦴 **1962** An ex-con tries to start life anew, but every time he finds a good job, his past catches up with him. A return to the life of crime looks tempting. Predictable and familiar plot, but performances are sincere. **81m/B; VHS, Streaming.** Bing (Neil) Russell; Billy Hughes; Bill Hale; Jack Harris; Eve Brent; ***D:*** James Landis; ***W:*** James Landis.

Stakeout 🦴🦴 ½ **1987 (R)** A sometimes violent comedy-thriller about a pair of detectives who stake out a beautiful woman's apartment, hoping for a clue to the whereabouts of her psycho boyfriend who has broken out of prison. One of them (Dreyfuss) then begins to fall in love with her. Natural charm among Estevez, Dreyfuss, and Stowe that adds to the proceedings, which are palpably implausible and silly. Slapstick sequel "Another Stakeout" followed in 1993. **117m/C; VHS, DVD.** Richard Dreyfuss; Emilio Estevez; Madeleine Stowe; Aidan Quinn; Forest Whitaker; Dan Lauria; Earl Billings; ***D:*** John Badham; ***W:*** Jim Kouf; ***M:*** Arthur B. Rubinstein.

Stalag 17 🦴🦴🦴🦴 **1953** A group of American G.I.s in a German POW camp during WWII suspects the opportunistic Sefton (Holden) of being the spy in their midst. One of the very best American movies of the 1950s, adapted from the play by Donald Bevan and Edmund Trzcinski. Wilder, so good at comedy, proved himself equally adept at drama, and brought a top-drawer performance out of Holden. Features superb photography from Ernest Laszlo, and a wonderful score. **120m/B; VHS, DVD, Blu-Ray.** William Holden; Don Taylor; Peter Graves; Otto Preminger; Harvey Lembeck; Robert Strauss; Sig Rumann; Richard Erdman; Neville Brand; Gil Stratton; Robinson Stone; Robert Shawley; Jay Lawrence; ***D:*** Billy Wilder; ***W:*** Billy Wilder; Edwin Blum; ***C:*** Ernest Laszlo; ***M:*** Franz Waxman. Oscars '53: Actor (Holden).

Stalag Luft 🦴🦴 **1993** Senior British officer James Forrester (Fry) is regarded by fellow POWs as a first-class idiot, since he has a record 23 escapes and re-captures. But he's determined to break all 327 prisoners out of their Nazi camp while the nervous German Kommandant keeps one eye on the advancing Allied army and the other on his prisoners. **103m/C; VHS, DVD.** *GB* Stephen Fry; Geoffrey Palmer; Nicholas Lyndhurst; David Bamber; Hugh Bonneville; ***D:*** Adrian Shergold. **TV**

Stalingrad 🦴🦴 **1994** Group of German stormtroopers fall victim to the brutal war of attrition over Stalingrad in 1942 and 1943. Realistic depiction of war is not for the faint-hearted. Originally a TV miniseries; German with subtitles. **150m/C; VHS, DVD, Blu-Ray.** *GE* Dominique Horwitz; Thomas Kretschmann; Jochen Nickel; ***D:*** Joseph Vilsmaier; ***W:*** Joseph Vilsmaier; ***C:*** Joseph Vilsmaier; ***M:*** Norbert J. Schneider.

Stalked WOOF! **1999** Macedonian transplant Aleksandr (Ognenovski) wakes up to an American nightmare, finding himself the target of a small town's wrath when framed for murder. Mayhem ensues, but not without those forced moments of pathos, romance, and testosterone-infused male bonding. Writer/director/star Ognenovski retreads the formula from early Stallone, Schwarzenegger, and Van Damme films: an outsider trapped in a hostile environment with only his wits and a few hundred rounds to protect him. Here, the cliches pile up faster than the body count. Add abysmal dialog, casting misfires (like the actor with a thick Russian accent playing the mayor of a small American town), and fight scenes rife with punches that don't connect, and we are in the presence of a potential Ed Wood for the action crowd. Sublime schlock, any way you slice it. **93m/C; DVD.** Jorgo Ognenovski; Meto Jovanovski; Lisa Marie Wilson; ***D:*** Jorgo Ognenovski; ***W:*** Jorgo Ognenovski; Mary Quijano; ***C:*** Ricardo Jacques Gale.

Stalked at 17 🦴 ½ **2012** One-note Lifetime teen drama. Naive high school student Angela is flattered when college boy Chad takes an interest. He soon crosses the line, turning psycho stalker, and the situation worsens when he finds out Angela is pregnant. **90m/C; DVD.** Taylor Spreitler; Chuck Hittinger; Amy Pietz; Brian Krause; Linda Purl; Jamie Luner; ***D:*** Doug Campbell; ***W:*** Christine Conradt; ***C:*** Akis Konstantakopoulos; ***M:*** Steve Gurevitch. **CABLE**

Stalker 🦴🦴🦴 **1979** A meteorite, crashing to Earth, has caused a wasteland area known as the Zone. The Zone is forbidden to anyone except special guides called Stalkers. Three Stalkers enter the region searching for its center, which contains a room that supposedly reveals fantasies. From the Soviet team that made "Solaris." Filmed with both color and black-and-white sequences. Suspenseful atmosphere due to the director's use of long takes, movement, and color. In Russian with English subtitles. **160m/C; VHS, DVD, Blu-Ray.** *RU* Alexander Kaidanovsky; Nikolai Grinko; Anatoli (Otto) Solonitzin; Alice Freindlikh; ***D:*** Andrei Tarkovsky; ***M:*** Eduard Artemyev.

Stalker 🦴 ½ *Fatal Affair* **1998 (R)** And what a very dumb, psychopathic stalker he is too. Family man Mack Maddox (Howell) is selected for jury duty and realizes that the murder victim is a woman with whom he had an affair. What's worse is the accused killer (Underwood) finds out that Maddox was involved with his wife and begins, well, stalking him and his family, even though Maddox has confessed his involvement to his wife and the cops. The plot never does make any sense and the flat performances don't help either. **93m/C; VHS, DVD.** *CA* C. Thomas Howell; Jay Underwood; Mark Camacho; Maxim Roy; Bryn McAuley; ***D:*** Marc S. Grenier; ***W:*** Michael Rauch; ***C:*** Georges Archambault; ***M:*** Normand Corbeil. **VIDEO**

Stalking Danger 🦴 ½ *C.A.T. Squad* **1986 (PG)** A secret government group must terminate an assassination plot by a terrorist organization. **97m/C; VHS, DVD.** Joe Cortese; Steve James; Patricia Charbonneau; Jack Youngblood; ***D:*** William Friedkin; ***M:*** Ennio Morricone.

Stalking Laura 🦴 ½ *I Can Make You Love Me* **1993** Laura Black (Shields) has just landed her first job at a California engineering firm where she meets co-worker Richard Farley (Thomas). He asks her out—she turns him down—he starts harassing her. Laura reports it to the company, who eventually fire Farley, and obtains a restraining order. He goes on a murderous rampage. Fact-based TV movie with Thomas effective as the dangerous obsessive. **90m/C; VHS, DVD.** Brooke Shields; Richard Thomas; Viveka Davis; William Allen Young; Richard Yniguez; Scott Bryce; ***D:*** Michael Switzer; ***W:*** Frank Abatemarco; ***C:*** Rob Draper; Sylvester Levay.

The Stalking Moon 🦴 ½ **1969 (G)** Indian scout Peck, ready to retire, meets a woman and her half-breed son who have been captives of the Apaches for 10 years. He agrees to help them escape but learns that the woman's Indian husband is hunting them down. Skeletal plot with little meat on it; great scenery but you wouldn't know it. **109m/C; VHS, DVD, Blu-Ray.** Gregory Peck; Eva Marie Saint; Robert Forster; Noland Clay; ***D:*** Robert Mulligan; ***W:*** Alvin Sargent.

Stallion Road 🦴🦴 **1947** Veterinarian Larry Hanrahan (Reagan) earns the gratitude of horse breeder Rory Teller (Smith) when he saves her prize stallion. An anthrax epidemic strikes a herd of cattle and the noble vet is too busy to be at Rory's beck-and-call. Rory's unhappy but things get worse. A side story with Larry's writer buddy Stephen (Scott) deciding to romance Rory is just a distraction. **97m/B; DVD.** Ronald Reagan; Alexis Smith; Zachary Scott; Peggy Knudsen; Patti Brady; Harry Davenport; Lloyd Corrigan; ***D:*** James V. Kern; ***W:*** Stephen Longstreet; ***C:*** Arthur Edeson; ***M:*** Frederick "Friedrich" Hollander.

Stampede 🦴 ½ **1949** Arizona cattleman Mike McCall resists ruthless land developers who then cause a stampede, sending Mike's herd over a cliff in an effort to get him to sell out. Instead, gunfights follow. **77m/B; DVD.** Rod Cameron; Johnny Mack Brown; Gale Storm; Donald Curtis; John Eldredge; Don Castle; ***D:*** Lesley Selander; ***W:*** Blake Edwards; John C. Champion; Edward Kay; ***C:*** Harry Neumann.

Stan & Ollie 🦴🦴🦴 **2018 (PG)** A loving tribute to the 1930s Hollywood comedy duo, Stan Laurel and Oliver Hardy. In an attempt to reignite their film career, the pair embarks on a 1953 variety hall tour of England. Coogan (Laurel) and Reilly (Hardy) absolutely embody their characters, giving us a glimpse into their craft, the toll it took on their health and friendship, and the bond that superseded all challenges. **97m/C; DVD, Blu-Ray.** Steve Coogan; John C. Reilly; Nina Arianda; Shirley Henderson; Danny Huston; ***D:*** Jon S. Baird; ***W:*** Jeff Pope; ***C:*** Laurie Rose; ***M:*** Rolfe Kent.

Stan Helsing 🦴 **2009 (R)** Inept and unfunny parody of horror cliches. On Halloween, video store clerk Stan Helsing and three friends are on their way to a Halloween party when they detour into a ghost town inhabited by such familiar icons as Freddy Kreuger, Pinhead, Leatherface, and Jason. And a cross-dressing Leslie Nielsen. **90m/C; DVD.** Steve Howey; Diora Baird; Kenan Thompson; Desi Lydic; Leslie Nielsen; ***D:*** Bo Zenga; ***W:*** Bo Zenga; ***C:*** Robert New; ***M:*** Ryan Shore. **VIDEO**

Stand and Deliver 🦴🦴🦴 **1988 (PG)** A tough teacher inspires students in an East L.A. barrio to take the Advanced Placement Test in calculus. A superb, inspirational true story, with a wonderful performance from Olmos. **105m/C; VHS, DVD.** Edward James Olmos; Lou Diamond Phillips; Rosanna Desoto; Andy Garcia; Will Gotay; Ingrid Oliu; Virginia Paris; Mark Eliot; Eugene Robert Glazer; ***D:*** Ramon Menendez; ***W:*** Ramon Menendez; Tom Musca; ***C:*** Tom Richmond; ***M:*** Craig Safan. Ind. Spirit '89: Actor (Olmos), Director (Menendez), Film, Screenplay, Support. Actor (Phillips), Support. Actress (Desoto); Natl. Film Reg. '11.

Stand by for Action 🦴🦴 ½ **1942** A drydocked WWI destroyer is recommissioned for action after the bombing of Pearl Harbor. Cocky Lt. Masterman (Taylor) scoffs and is assigned as the executive officer under vet Martin Roberts (Donlevy). The destroyer joins a convoy and rescues a group of women and babies from a torpedoed ship but the convoy has been targeted by the Japanese. The film earned an Oscar for special effects. **109m/B; DVD.** Robert Taylor; Brian Donlevy; Charles Laughton; Walter Brennan; Henry O'Neill; Douglass Dumbrille; Chill Wills; Marilyn Maxwell; Marta Linden; ***D:*** Robert Z. Leonard; ***W:*** Herman J. Mankiewicz; George Bruce; John Lloyd Balderston; ***C:*** Charles Rosher; ***M:*** Lennie Hayton.

Stand by Me 🦴🦴🦴 **1986 (R)** A sentimental, observant adaptation of the Stephen King novella "The Body." Four 12-year-olds trek into the Oregon wilderness to find the body of a missing boy, learning about death and personal courage. Told as a reminiscence by narrator "author" Dreyfuss with solid performances from all four child actors. Too much gratuitous obscenity, but a very good, gratifying film from can't-miss director Reiner. **87m/C; VHS, DVD, Blu-Ray.** River Phoenix; Wil Wheaton; Jerry O'Connell; Corey Feldman; Kiefer Sutherland; Richard Dreyfuss; Casey Siemaszko; John Cusack; ***D:*** Rob Reiner; ***W:*** Raynold Gideon; ***C:*** Thomas Del Ruth; ***M:*** Jack Nitzsche.

Stand Clear of the Closing Doors 🦴🦴🦴 **2013** A cross-cutting urban wilderness saga fashioned out of the grim realities of modern day New York City. A family panics after the disappearance of their autistic 13-year-old son, Ricky (Sanchez-Velez), slowly unraveling into an angry domestic blame game. But outside the house, Ricky simply wanders the subways, struggling to find his way, relying on the kindness of a homeless man for food and direction. Shot almost like a hallucinogenic day dream, Ricky's journey takes him through the worst of the city and right into the aftermath of Hurricane Sandy. A surprisingly suspenseful drama, built around the concern for someone who simply can't help himself. **102m/C; DVD.** Jesus Sanchez-Velez; Andrea Suarez Paz; Azul Zorrilla; Tenoch Huerta; Marsha Stephanie Blake; ***D:*** Sam Fleischner; ***W:*** Rose Lichter-Marck; Micah Bloomberg; ***C:*** Adam Jandrup; Ethan Palmer.

Stand-In 🦴🦴🦴 **1937** When a Hollywood studio is threatened with bankruptcy, the bank sends in timid efficiency expert Howard to save it. Satire of studio executives and big-budget movie making. Bogart is interestingly cast and effective in his first comedy role, playing a drunken producer in love with star Shelton. **91m/B; VHS, DVD, Blu-Ray.** Humphrey Bogart; Joan Blondell; Leslie Howard; Alan Mowbray; Marla Shelton; Jack Carson; ***D:*** Tay Garnett.

Stand-In **1985** A strange comedy-action film that takes a behind-the-scenes look at sleaze films and organized crime. **87m/C; VHS, DVD.** Danny Glover; ***D:*** Robert Zagone.

Stand-Ins ½ **1997** Would-be actresses in pre-WWII Hollywood find themselves looking for fame and unwillingly settling for stand-in status. The girls all hang out at Jack's (Mandylor) bar, where Greta Garbo-double, druggie Shirley (Zuniga), battles with cynical Bette Davis stand-in, Monica (Ladd), as they celebrate the birthday of Jean Harlowish Martha Anne (Davis), along with Mae West clone Peggy (Chatton) and Marlene Dietrich stand-in Rhonda (Crider). This desperate gang are bitchy and frustrated and, of course, theatrical. Based on Kelleher's one-act play. **89m/C; VHS, DVD, On Demand.** Daphne Zuniga; Jordan Ladd; Sammi Davis; Missy (Melissa) Crider; Charlotte Chatton; Costas Mandylor; Katherine Heigl; ***D:*** Harvey Keith; ***W:*** Harvey Keith; Ed Kelleher; ***C:*** Andrzej Sekula; ***M:*** Bill Elliott.

Stand Off ½ *Whole Lotta Sole* **2011 (R)** Jimbo (McCann) is in serious debt to the mob, so to protect his family he robs a fish market to get the money he needs. Unfortunately the market belongs to the same mobster he owes, and the police quickly corner him in a curio shop where he takes hostages. The hostages are pretty sympathetic and do their best to think of a way out for poor Jimbo. **89m/B; DVD, Blu-Ray.** *UK* Martin McCann; Colm Meaney; Brendan Fraser; Yaya Alafia; David O'Hara; ***D:*** Terry George; ***W:*** Terry George; Thomas Gallagher; ***C:*** Des Whelan.

Stand Up and Cheer ½ **1934 (PG)** The new federal Secretary of Entertainment organizes a huge show to raise the country's depressed spirits. Near-invisible plot, fantastic premise are an excuse for lots of imagery, dancing, and comedy, including four-year-old Temple singing "Baby Take a Bow." Also available colorized. **80m/B; VHS, DVD.** Shirley Temple; Warner Baxter; Madge Evans; Nigel Bruce; Stepin Fetchit; Frank Melton; Lila Lee; James Dunn; John Boles; Scotty Beckett; ***D:*** Hamilton MacFadden; ***W:*** Will Rogers; Ralph Spence; ***C:*** Ernest Palmer.

Stand Up and Fight ½ **1939** In 1844 Maryland, stagecoach line overseer Boss Starkey (Beery) is losing business to the newfangled steam locomotive. Blake Cantrell (Taylor) went bankrupt and was forced to sell his plantation (and his slaves) and now works for the railroad. Cantrell becomes suspicious that Starkey's making up his losses by capturing fugitive slaves for the reward money, but Starkey turns out to be a patsy for a couple of real villians. Came out the same year as "Gone With the Wind" but shows a very different view of slave life. **91m/B; DVD.** Robert Taylor; Wallace Beery; Florence Rice; Helen Broderick; Charles Bickford; Barton MacLane; ***D:*** W.S. Van Dyke; ***W:*** James M. Cain; Jane Murfin; Harvey Fergusson; ***C:*** Leonard Smith; ***M:*** William Axt.

A Stand Up Guy **2016** A comedy centered on a man who finds his life in jeopardy because of stand-up comedy. Lovable loser Sammy Lagucci (Abeckaser) takes action when he learns that gangsters are planning to kill him. To protect his beloved daughter, he and his family enter the Witness Protection program. Sammy experiences culture shock when he is moved from New York City to a small community in Wisconsin. Sammy seems to find his niche on a dare when he does a stand-up comedy routine. He puts himself and his family in danger when his act goes viral and the mob begin to look for him again. **90m/C; DVD, Streaming, Download.** Danny A. Abeckaser; Annie Heise; Nick Cordero; Luke Robertson; Jay R. Ferguson; ***D:*** Mike Young; ***W:*** Mike Young; ***C:*** Daniele Napolitano; ***M:*** MJ Mynarski.

Stand Up Guys **2012 (R)** After 28 years in the slammer, old gangster Val (Pacino) is finally set free. Doc (Walken) is there for his former partner in crime and the two reconnect with another elderly bad guy named Hirsch (Arkin). They presume it's just good friends catching up but past behavior intrudes and the trio gets involved in criminal activity once again. Director Stevens leads an all-star cast to nowhere in this humdrum comedy with more talent on the screen than smarts in the script. But the boys seem to be having a good time, which might be a good enough reason to watch. **95m/C; DVD, Blu-Ray.** Al Pacino; Christopher Walken; Alan Arkin; Julianna Margulies; Mark Margolis; Lucy Punch; Vanessa Ferlito; Katheryn Winnick; ***D:*** Fisher Stevens; ***W:*** Noah Haidie; ***C:*** Michael Grady; ***M:*** Lyle Workman.

Standard Operating Procedure ½ **2008 (R)** Morris's extremely disturbing and morose documentary examines the story behind the infamous photographs out of Abu Ghraib, which portrayed U.S. guards torturing and degrading Iraqi prisoners by posing them in humiliating sexual positions, dressing them up in costumes, and inflicting other indignities. Descriptions by members of the prison's MP squad and reenactments serve to reveal the motivation behind these bizarre acts, which play out as chillingly as any contemporary thriller. **116m/C; DVD.** ***D:*** Errol Morris; ***W:*** Errol Morris; ***C:*** Robert Chappell; Robert Richardson; ***M:*** Danny Elfman.

Stander ½ **2003 (R)** Set in 1976 in South Africa, the volatile antihero of the title (played with bravado by Jane) is the youngest police captain in Johannesburg and is in charge of the riot patrol during a Soweto protest march that quickly turns violent. Guilt-stricken after killing an unarmed black youth, Andre Stander realizes that the police are so busy enforcing apartheid that a white criminal can get away with anything. To test his theory, he robs a bank, and then another bank, and then more. Eventually arrested, Stander, along with mates McCall (Fletcher) and Heyl (O'Hara), breaks out of prison and goes on another bank-robbing spree and into the annals of folk hero notoriety. Loosely based on a true story. **111m/C; DVD.** *GB CA SA GE* Thomas Jane; Dexter Fletcher; Deborah Kara Unger; Marius Weyers; David O'Hara; Ashley Taylor; ***D:*** Bronwen Hughes; ***W:*** Bronwen Hughes; Bima Stagg; ***C:*** Jess Hall; ***M:*** David Holmes; Steve Hilton.

Standing in the Shadows of Motown **2002 (PG)** Director Justman and writer Slutsky (who wrote the book of the same name) reveal the behind-the-scenes story of the "Funk Brothers," the musicians who backed-up Motown's best and were unknown to anyone but their peers and music fanatics. There's archival footage, interviews with the remaining "Brothers," and a concert performance with contemporary singers doing the Motown standards accompanied by these living legends. **108m/C; VHS, DVD.** ***D:*** Paul Justman; ***W:*** Ntozake Shange; Walter Dallas; ***C:*** Doug Milsome; Lon Stratton. N.Y. Film Critics '02: Feature Doc.

Standing on Fishes **1999 (R)** With their relationship already on the rocks, Caleb, an aspiring sculptor, pushes Erica's feminist ideals to the limit by taking an odd job of designing a fake vagina for a film. So when an adoring kindred soul makes moves on him, he's more than tempted. Writing/directing team Tatum and Scott Lynn also star in the lead roles. **89m/C; VHS, DVD.** Bradford Tatum; Meredith Scott Lynn; Jason Priestley; Lauren Fox; Kelsey Grammer; Pamela Reed; James Black; ***D:*** Bradford Tatum; Meredith Scott Lynn; ***W:*** Bradford Tatum; ***C:*** Mark Mervis; ***M:*** Juliet Prater. **VIDEO**

Standing Still **2005 (R)** Talented cast is wasted in an all-too-familiar story about a post-collegiate reunion of 20-somethings who find adulthood a generally bewildering trial. Los Angeles couple Michael (Garcia) and Elise (Adams) gather their friends together for their wedding. Among them are best man Rich (Stanford) and his girlfriend Samantha (Sagemiller), sarcastic Lana (Suvari) and oddball Pockets (Abrahams), movie star Simon (Van Der Beek), agent Quentin (Hanks), and outspoken lesbian Jennifer (German), who has issues with the bride, who's not the only one keeping secrets. **90m/C; DVD.** Adam Garcia; Amy Adams; Aaron Stanford; Melissa Sagemiller; Mena Suvari; Jon Abrahams; Xander Berkeley; Lauren German; Colin Hanks; Roger Avary; Ethan (Randall) Embry; James Van Der Beek; ***D:*** Michael Cole Weiss; ***W:*** Timm Sharp; Matthew Perniciaro; ***C:*** Robert Brinkmann; ***M:*** B.C. Smith.

Standing Up ½ **2013 (PG)** Based on the popular young adult novel of the same name, this drama explores what happens when two bullied kids make the best of their situation. At summer camp, 11-year-old Howie (Canterbury) and 12-year-old Grace (Basso) find themselves the outsiders among their peers. Bullied, the pair is the subject of an extremely mean prank: being stripped naked and left together on an island in lake. Instead of returning to camp humiliated, the pair go on the run together and have a three-day adventure of self-discovery. **93m/C; DVD, Streaming, Download.** Chandler Canterbury; Annalise Basso; Radha Mitchell; Val Kilmer; Kate Maberly; ***D:*** D.J. Caruso; ***W:*** D.J. Caruso; ***C:*** Alex Nepomniaschy; ***M:*** Brian Tyler.

Standoff **2016 (R)** An intense dramatic thriller about the lengths one man goes to protect a little girl to gain personal redemption. Twelve-year-old Bird (Ballentine) is the only eyewitness to a murder. Because of her knowledge, a deadly assassin, Sade (Fishburne), has been charged with finding and silencing her. A veteran with deep issues of his own, Carter (Jane) takes charge of protecting Bird, putting himself at extreme personal risk. Carter's only protection is a single shell in a shotgun, so the focus of his fight for her life lie in battles both physical and psychological with the relentless Sade. **86m/C; DVD, Blu-Ray, Streaming, Download.** Thomas Jane; Laurence Fishburne; Ella Ballentine; Joanna Douglas; Jim Watson; ***D:*** Adam Alleca; ***W:*** Adam Alleca; ***C:*** Zoran Popovic; ***M:*** Austin Wintory.

The Standoff at Sparrow Creek ½ **2019** After leaving the police force, Gannon (Dale) joins a militia group in Michigan because he feels betrayed by the government. After a police officer's funeral, someone enters the cemetery from the woods, opens fire with an AR-15, and kills more officers. The leaders of the militia group figure out that one of them is responsible, and Gannon takes charges of the investigation. As he questions the other members to figure out who is the killer, the situation grows more angry, tense, and fearful. The film features strong performances from Dale and others in the ensemble cast as well as a taunt, riveting script. **88m/C; DVD.** James Badge Dale; Brian Geraghty; Patrick Fischler; Happy Anderson; Robert Aramayo; ***D:*** Henry Dunham; ***W:*** Henry Dunham; ***C:*** Jackson Hunt.

The Stanford Prison Experiment ½ **2015 (R)** One of the most legendary behavioral experiments of all time is chronicled in this fictional recreation of what happens when you give young men power over other people. At Stanford University, a Professor (Crudup) got the idea to test aggression and control by having subjects submit to a fake prison setting for a few days. Some would be made guards, others prisoners. They couldn't commit acts of violence, but the prisoners had to listen to the guards. Things got bad on night one, and progressed from there, until the experiment had to be ended early. The cast is good, but the movie is shallow. **122m/C; DVD, Blu-Ray, Streaming.** Billy Crudup; Michael Angarano; Ezra Miller; Tye Sheridan; Johnny Simmons; ***D:*** Kyle Patrick Alvarez; ***W:*** Tim Talbott; ***C:*** Jas Shelton; ***M:*** Andrew Hewitt.

Stanley ½ **1972 (PG)** Seminole Vietnam veteran Robinson uses rattlesnakes as his personal weapon of revenge against most of mankind. Thoroughly wretched effort in the gross-pets vein of "Willard" and "Ben." **108m/C; VHS, DVD.** Chris Robinson; Alex Rocco; Susan Carroll; ***D:*** William Grefe.

Stanley and Iris ½ **1990 (PG-13)** Blue collar recent widow Fonda meets co-worker De Niro, whose illiteracy she helps remedy. Romance follows, inevitably but excruciatingly. Leads' strong presence helps along a very slow, underdeveloped plot. **107m/C; VHS, DVD, Blu-Ray.** Jane Fonda; Robert De Niro; Swoosie Kurtz; Martha Plimpton; Harley Cross; Jamey Sheridan; Feodor Chaliapin, Jr.; Zohra Lampert; Loretta Devine; Julie Garfield; ***D:*** Martin Ritt; ***W:*** Harriet Frank, Jr.; Irving Ravetch; ***M:*** John Williams.

The Star **1952** A washed-up and self-destructive former Hollywood star (Davis, who allegedly took the role to lampoon rival Joan Crawford) gets, and blows, one last chance at a comeback and finds love with a former protege (Hayden) who gave up stardom for the simple life. To the chagrin of both him and her daughter (Wood), she can't quite give up the siren song of her past glory and continues to sabotage what could be a happy life. Gut-wrenching and squirmy for the scenes in which Davis's character, for which she received an Oscar nomination, debases herself personally and professionally. **89m/B; VHS, DVD.** Bette Davis; Sterling Hayden; Natalie Wood; Warner Anderson; Minor Watson; June Travis; Paul Frees; Robert Warwick; Barbara Lawrence; Fay Baker; Herb Vigran; Stuart Heisler; ***W:*** Katherine Albert; Dale Eunson; ***C:*** Ernest Laszlo; ***M:*** Victor Young.

Star! *Those Were the Happy Times* **1968** Campy showbiz extravaganza based on the life of famed musical comedy performer Gertrude Lawrence (Andrews), star of the London and Broadway stage. Film follows Lawrence's adventures from the British music halls to her fateful meeting with Noel Coward (Massey), who would not only become her dearest friend but perform with and write for her as well. A tumultuous private life is also on display. 17 lavishly staged musical numbers helped boost the cost of the film to $14 million—big bucks in '68. Movie was a colossal flop on opening and was recut, deleting 50 minutes, but still didn't recoup its losses. Has gained a cult following. **172m/C; VHS, DVD.** Julie Andrews; Daniel Massey; Richard Crenna; Michael Craig; Robert Reed; Bruce Forsyth; Beryl Reid; John Collin; Alan Oppenheimer; Anthony Eisley; Jenny Agutter; J. Pat O'Malley; Richard Karlan; Lynley Laurence; Harvey Jason; Elizabeth St. Clair; ***D:*** Robert Wise; ***W:*** William Fairchild; ***C:*** Ernest Laszlo.

The Star **2017 (PG)** A family-friendly animated re-telling of the Nativity story primarily from the animals' point of view. Though the film gives the back story of how Mary (Rodriguez) came to carry the Christ child and her marriage to Joseph (Levi), it spends more time giving voice to the mostly wise-cracking animals. Bo the donkey (Yeun) and Dave the dove (Key) find a home with Mary and Joseph, while the three kings' camels (Perry, Morgan, and Winfrey) witness the actions of their riders with Herod (Plummer). Diversity in casting is found in the animals at the stable as well, adding to the film's distinctive personality. **86m/C; DVD, Blu-Ray.** Steven Yeun; Keegan Michael Key; Aidy Bryant; Gina Rodriguez; Zachary Levi; ***D:*** Timothy Reckart; ***W:*** Carlos Kotkin; ***M:*** John Paesano.

The Star Chamber **1983 (R)** A conscientious judge (Douglas) sees criminals freed on legal technicalities and wonders if he should take justice into his own hands. He finds a secret society that administers justice extra-legally. Implausible yet predictable. **109m/C; VHS, DVD, Blu-Ray.** Michael Douglas; Hal Holbrook; Yaphet Kotto; Sharon Gless; James B. Sikking; ***D:*** Peter Hyams; ***W:*** Peter Hyams; Roderick Taylor.

Star Crash ½ *Stella Star* **1978 (PG)** Trio of adventurers (woman, man, and robot) sent by emperor Plummer square off against interstellar evil (Spinell) by using their wits and technological wizardry. Semi-funny and cheesy sci-fi, done with style beyond its limited budget. **92m/C; VHS, DVD.** *IT* Caroline Munro; Marjoe Gortner; Christopher Plummer; David Hasselhoff; Robert Tessier; Joe Spinell; Nadia Cassini; Judd Hamilton; ***D:*** Luigi Cozzi; ***W:*** Luigi Cozzi; ***M:*** John Barry.

Star Crystal **1985 (R)** Aboard a spaceship, an indestructible alien hunts down the human crew. Cheap imitation of "Alien." **93m/C; VHS, DVD, Blu-Ray.** C. Jutson Campbell; Faye Bolt; John W. Smith; ***D:*** Lance Lindsay.

Star Dust **1940** Carolyn Sayres (Darnell) is determined to become a movie star when a studio agent comes around looking for new talent. She's turned down for a contract by studio head Dane Wharton (Gargan) but is persuaded to preserve by football player Bud (Payne), who's also starting out, and drama coach Lola (Greenwood), who believes in her. Allegedly based on Darnell's own experiences with Darryl Zanuck and 20th Century Fox. **90m/B; DVD.** Linda Darnell; John Payne; Charlotte Greenwood; William Gargan; Roland Young; Mary Healy; Donald Meek; *D:* Walter Lang; *W:* Helen Logan; Robert Ellis; *C:* J. Peverell Marley; *M:* David Buttolph.

Star 80 1/2 **1983 (R)** Based on the true-life tragedy of Playmate of the Year Dorothy Stratten and her manager-husband Paul Snider as they battle for control of her body, her mind, and her money, with gruesome results. Roberts is overpowering as the vile Snider, but the movie is generally unpleasant. Fosse's last film. **104m/C; DVD.** Mariel Hemingway; Eric Roberts; Cliff Robertson; David Clennon; Josh Mostel; Roger Rees; Carroll Baker; *D:* Bob Fosse; *W:* Bob Fosse; *C:* Sven Nykvist; *M:* Ralph Burns.

A Star for Christmas 1/2 **2012** TV movie that's tooth-achingly sweet even for a Christmas romance. Lovelorn Cassie is a cupcake baker who's apparently so unaware of what's happening in her hometown that she doesn't recognize action star Alex, who's doing location shooting, when he comes into her shop. But can their whirlwind romance survive exes jealousies and what happens when filming ends? **88m/C; DVD.** Briana Evigan; Corey Sevier; Brooke Burns; Travis Van Winkle; Jeremy Howard; *D:* Michael Feifer; *W:* Amy Heidish; *C:* Hank Baumert, Jr.; *M:* Brandon Jarrett. **TV**

Star Hunter 1/2 **1995 (R)** When a bus filled with football players and cheerleaders takes a wrong turn, it winds up in an intergalatic hunting ground where the humans become the prey. Lots of lame chase and would-be action scenes. **80m/C; VHS, DVD.** Roddy McDowall; Stella Stevens; Ken Stott; Zack (Zach) Ward; Wendy Schumacher; *D:* Cole McKay.

A Star Is Born 1/2 **1937** A movie star declining in popularity marries a shy girl and helps her become a star. Her fame eclipses his and tragic consequences follow. Shows Hollywood-behind-the-scenes machinations. Stunning ending is based on the real-life tragedy of silent film star Wallace Reid, who died of a morphine overdose in 1923 at age 31. Remade twice, in 1954 and 1976. **111m/C; VHS, DVD, Blu-Ray.** Janet Gaynor; Fredric March; Adolphe Menjou; May Robson; Andy Devine; Lionel Stander; Franklin Pangborn; *D:* William A. Wellman; *W:* William A. Wellman; David O. Selznick; Dorothy Parker; *C:* William Howard Greene; *M:* Max Steiner. Oscars '37: Color Cinematog., Story.

A Star Is Born 1/2 **1954 (PG)** Aging actor helps a young actress to fame. She becomes his wife, but alcoholism and failure are too much for him. She honors his memory. Remake of the 1937 classic was Garland's triumph, a superb and varied performance. Newly restored version reinstates over 20 minutes of long-missing footage, including three Garland musical numbers. **175m/C; VHS, DVD, Blu-Ray.** Judy Garland; James Mason; Jack Carson; Tommy Noonan; Charles Bickford; Emerson Treacy; Charles Halton; *D:* George Cukor; *W:* Moss Hart; *C:* Sam Leavitt; *M:* Harold Arlen; Ira Gershwin. Golden Globes '55: Actor--Mus./Comedy (Mason), Actress--Mus./Comedy (Garland); Natl. Film Reg. '00.

A Star Is Born **1976 (R)** Miserable update of the 1937 and 1954 classics permitting Ms. Streisand to showcase her hit song "Evergreen." The tragic story of one rock star (the relentlessly un-hip Streisand) on her way to the top and another (good old boy Kristofferson) whose career is in decline. Kristofferson is miscast, Streisand eventually numbing, but film may interest those looking into big-budget, big-star misfires. **140m/C; VHS, DVD, Blu-Ray.** Barbra Streisand; Kris Kristofferson; Paul Mazursky; Gary Busey; Sally Kirkland; Oliver Clark; Marta Heflin; Robert Englund; *D:* Frank Pierson; *W:* Frank Pierson; Joan Didion; John Gregory Dunne; *C:* Robert L. Surtees; *M:* Paul Williams. Oscars '76: Song ("Evergreen"); Golden Globes '77: Actor--Mus./Comedy (Kristofferson), Actress--Mus./Comedy (Streisand), Film--Mus./Comedy, Score, Song ("Evergreen").

A Star Is Born **2018 (R)** When superstar country singer Jackson Maine (Cooper) meets talented waitress Ally (Lady Gaga), he is immediately attracted to her and her singing and songwriting talent. The pair becomes more involved, and he helps launch her musical career. As Ally's fame rises as a pop singer, Jackson's alcohol and drug issues negatively affect his career and their relationship. A remake of the classic film about the highs and lows of musical stardom, the film has unexpected depth and chemistry between the lead actors. It also highlights the unexpected musical talent of Cooper and acting chops of Lady Gaga. **136m/C; DVD, Blu-Ray.** Lady Gaga; Bradley Cooper; Sam Elliott; Andrew Dice Clay; Dave Chappelle; *D:* Bradley Cooper; *W:* Bradley Cooper; Eric Roth; Will Fetters; *C:* Matthew Libatique. Oscars '18: Song ("Shallow"); British Acad. '18: Orig. Score; Golden Globes '19: Song ("Shallow").

Star Kid *The Warrior of Waverly Street* **1997 (PG)** Twelve-year-old Spencer Griffith (Mazzello) is the new wimp in town, with a face that immediately attracts the fists of the biggest bully around, Turbo Bradley (Simmrin). On the run from Turbo, Spencer encounters Cy, an experimental cyber-battle-suit built by cutesy good aliens to save themselves from reptilian bad aliens. After inserting himself into Cy, and solving a few problems common to boy-inside-alien relationships, Spencer takes his first awkward steps, gets some humorous revenge on Turbo, and learns some lessons about confronting one's fears and accepting responsibility. Film delivers enough action and effects to keep everyone happy. **101m/C; VHS, DVD.** Joseph Mazzello; Alex Daniels; Richard Gilliland; Joey Simmrin; Brian Simpson; Danny Masterson; Corinne Bohrer; Arthur Burghardt; Ashlee Levitch; Heidi Lotito; *D:* Manny Coto; *W:* Manny Coto; *C:* Ronn Schmidt; *M:* Nicholas Pike.

Star Knight *Starknight* **1985 (PG-13)** Weird combo of sci fi and medieval romance. A spaceship lands near a European castle and the local princess falls for one of the visitors—much to her daddy's dismay. Very silly. **92m/C; VHS, DVD.** *SP* Harvey Keitel; Klaus Kinski; Fernando Rey; *D:* Fernando Colomo.

The Star Maker *The Star Man; L'Uomo delle Stelle* **1995 (R)** Con man Joe Morelli (Castellitto) travels through the villages of 1950s Sicily claiming to be a movie talent scout. For a fee, he offers the locals a chance to shoot a screen test, which reveals various bits and pieces of their lives. There's a brief romance and Joe's scam eventually comes to light but the story's more nostalgia than narrative. Italian with subtitles. **107m/C; VHS, DVD.** *IT* Sergio Castellitto; Tiziana Lodato; *D:* Giuseppe Tornatore; *W:* Giuseppe Tornatore; Fabio Rinaudo; *C:* Dante Spinotti; *M:* Ennio Morricone.

Star Maps **1997 (R)** Ambitious and ambiguous effort from first-time director Arteta has boyish Carlos (Spain) chase his dreams of movie stardom on the streets of Hollywood. Pimped by his manipulative and brutal father Pepe (Figueroa), Carlos sells "maps of the stars' homes" as a cover for his real job, male prostitute. Dad's hooker mistress (Murphy) mentors him in the family business. Add in a mother (Velez) "recovering" from a nervous breakdown by talking to long-dead Mexican comedy star Cantinflas, and a brother (Chandler) who acts out scenes from Mexican wrestling movies, and it's a wonder he doesn't make his screen debut on Jerry Springer. Despite fine performances and a solid debut effort from Arteta, the tragic elements don't fit well with the attempted comic tone of the rest of the movie. **80m/C; VHS, Streaming.** Douglas Spain; Efrain Figueroa; Lysa Flores; Kandeyce Jensen; Martha Velez; Annette Murphy; Vincent Chandler; Al Vincente; Herbert Siguenza; Robin Thomas; Jeff Michalski; *D:* Miguel Arteta; *W:* Miguel Arteta; *C:* Chuy Chavez; *M:* Lysa Flores.

Star of Midnight **1935** A lawyer/detective becomes involved in the disappearance of the leading lady in a Broadway show and the murder of a columnist. Powell and Rogers take on characters similar to Nick and Nora Charles, but the pizazz of the "Thin Man" series is missing. **90m/B; VHS, DVD.** Ginger Rogers; William Powell; Paul Kelly; *D:* Stephen Roberts.

Star Quest 1/2 **1994 (R)** Eight astronauts, suspended in a cryogenic sleep for nearly 100 years, awaken to find the human race has been destroyed by a nuclear holocaust. **95m/C; VHS, DVD.** Steven Bauer; Emma Samms; Alan Rachins; Brenda Bakke; Ming Na; Gregory McKinney; Cliff DeYoung; *D:* Rick Jacobson.

Star Slammer 1/2 **1987 (R)** A beautiful woman is unjustly sentenced to a brutal intergalactic prison ship. She leads the convicts to escape amid zany situations. Unevenly funny sci-fi comedy. **85m/C; VHS, DVD, Blu-Ray.** Ross Hagen; John Carradine; Sandy Brooke; Aldo Ray; *D:* Fred Olen Ray; *W:* Michael Sonye; *C:* Paul Elliot; *M:* Anthony Harris.

Star Spangled Girl 1/2 **1971 (G)** One of Neil Simon's lesser plays, one of his least movies. A pert, patriotic young lady captures the hearts of two left-wing alternative-newspaperguys next door; their political conflicts never rise above bland sitcom level. **94m/C; VHS, DVD.** Sandy Duncan; Tony Roberts; Todd Susman; Elizabeth Allen; *D:* Jerry Paris; *W:* Neil Simon; *C:* Sam Leavitt; *M:* Charles Fox.

Star Spangled Rhythm **1942** Movie studio guard (Moore) has told his son (Bracken), a sailor, that he's actually the head of the studio in this WW2 musical/comedy. When he learns his son and his pals are coming for a visit, he enlists the aid of a friendly studio switchboard operator (Hutton) to pull a fast one. (Luckily, the real studio boss is out of town). Plot doesn't matter anyway since its just an excuse for a lot of studio stars to show up and perform. **99m/B; DVD.** Betty Hutton; Eddie Bracken; Victor Moore; Bing Crosby; Ray Milland; Bob Hope; Veronica Lake; Dorothy Lamour; Susan Hayward; Dick Powell; Mary Martin; Alan Ladd; Paulette Goddard; Cecil B. DeMille; Arthur Treacher; Preston Sturges; Eddie Anderson; William Bendix; *D:* George Marshall; *W:* Melvin Frank; George S. Kaufman; Norman Panama; Arthur Ross; Harry Tugend; *C:* Theodor Sparkuhl; Leo Tover.

Star Trek *Star Trek: The Future Begins* **2009 (PG-13)** Director Abrams boldly takes the Starfleet crew where it hasn't been in a long time--on a lively, eventful, action-charged voyage that introduces the old familiar gang literally from the beginning, in James T. Kirk's (Pine) case when he is born amidst amazingly vibrant and explosive chaos. Spock's Vulcan race becomes the target of baffling vengeance by an angry Romulan, Nero (Bana), thereby threatening the Enterprise and every Federation planet. The new set of actors each holds some fantastical similarity to the original '60s cast but each makes it their own without lampooning. Pine has the right amount of bravado playing well off of Urban's Bones and Quinto's Spock. Adding to the nostalgia is Nimoy's return as elder Spock, who makes a meaningful space-time-continuum appearance. No doubt the crew will live long and prosper--in a sequel or two. **127m/C; Blu-Ray, On Demand.** Chris Pine; Zachary Quinto; Simon Pegg; Karl Urban; John Cho; Zoe Saldana; Anton Yelchin; Eric Bana; Winona Ryder; Bruce Greenwood; Ben Cross; Leonard Nimoy; Jennifer (Jenny) Morrison; Rachel Nichols; Tyler Perry; Clifton (Gonzalez) Collins, Jr.; Faran Tahir; Deep Roy; Chris Hemsworth; *V:* Greg Grunberg; Majel Barrett; *D:* J.J. (Jeffrey) Abrams; *W:* Roberto Orci; Alex Kurtzman; *C:* Dan(iel) Mindel. Oscars '09: Makeup.

Star Trek: The Motion Picture 1/2 **1979 (PG)** The Enterprise fights a strange alien force that threatens Earth in this first film adaptation of the famous TV series. Shatner's Kirk has been promoted to admiral and is called to take command of the vessel. He gets his old crew to tag along as well. Underrated at its theatrical release, but has benefitted from time, re-evaluation, and a director's cut. **136m/C; VHS, DVD, Blu-Ray.** William Shatner; Leonard Nimoy; DeForest Kelley; James Doohan; Stephen Collins; Persis Khambatta; Nichelle Nichols; Walter Koenig; George Takei; Majel Barrett; Mark Lenard; Grace Lee Whitney; *D:* Robert Wise; *W:* Harold Livingston; *C:* Richard H. Kline; *M:* Jerry Goldsmith.

Star Trek 2: The Wrath of Khan **1982 (PG)** Picking up from the 1967 Star Trek episode "Space Seed," Admiral James T. Kirk and the crew of the Enterprise must battle Khan, an old foe out for revenge. Warm and comradly in the nostalgic mode of its successors. Introduced Kirk's former lover and unknown son to the series plot, as well as Mr. Spock's "death," which led to the next sequel (1984's "The Search for Spock"). **113m/C; VHS, DVD, Blu-Ray.** William Shatner; Leonard Nimoy; Ricardo Montalban; DeForest Kelley; Nichelle Nichols; James Doohan; George Takei; Walter Koenig; Kirstie Alley; Merritt Butrick; Paul Winfield; Bibi Besch; *D:* Nicholas Meyer; *W:* Jack Sowards; *C:* Gayne Rescher; *M:* James Horner.

Star Trek 3: The Search for Spock 1/2 **1984 (PG)** Captain Kirk hijacks the USS Enterprise and commands the aging crew to go on a mission to the Genesis Planet to discover whether Mr. Spock still lives (supposedly he died in the last movie). Klingons threaten, as usual. Somewhat slow and humorless, but intriguing. Third in the series. **105m/C; VHS, DVD, Blu-Ray.** William Shatner; Leonard Nimoy; DeForest Kelley; James Doohan; George Takei; Walter Koenig; Mark Lenard; Robin Curtis; Merritt Butrick; Christopher Lloyd; Judith Anderson; John Larroquette; James B. Sikking; Nichelle Nichols; Cathie Shirriff; Miguel Ferrer; Grace Lee Whitney; *D:* Leonard Nimoy; *W:* Harve Bennett; *C:* Charles Correll; *M:* James Horner.

Star Trek 4: The Voyage Home **1986 (PG)** Kirk and the gang go back in time (to the 1980s, conveniently) to save the Earth of the future from destruction. Filled with hilarious moments and exhilarating action; great special effects enhance the timely conservation theme. Watch for the stunning going-back-in-time sequence. Spock is particularly funny as he tries to fit in and learn the '80s lingo! Also available as part of Paramount's "director's series," in which Nimoy discusses various special effects aspects in the making of the film. One of the best in the series. **119m/C; VHS, DVD, Blu-Ray.** William Shatner; DeForest Kelley; Catherine Hicks; James Doohan; Nichelle Nichols; George Takei; Walter Koenig; Mark Lenard; Leonard Nimoy; Michael Berryman; Majel Barrett; Brock Peters; John Schuck; Jane Wyatt; *D:* Leonard Nimoy; *W:* Nicholas Meyer; Harve Bennett; Peter Krikes; Steve Meerson; *C:* Don Peterman; *M:* Leonard Rosenman.

Star Trek 5: The Final Frontier 1/2 **1989 (PG)** A renegade Vulcan kidnaps the Enterprise and takes it on a journey to the mythic center of the universe. Shatner's big-action directorial debut (he also co-wrote the script) is a poor follow-up to the Nimoy-directed fourth entry in the series. Heavy-handed and pretentiously pseudo-theological. **107m/C; VHS, DVD, Blu-Ray.** William Shatner; Leonard Nimoy; DeForest Kelley; James Doohan; Laurence Luckinbill; Walter Koenig; George Takei; Nichelle Nichols; David Warner; Melanie Shatner; Harve Bennett; *D:* William Shatner; *W:* William Shatner; David Loughery; *C:* Andrew Laszlo; *M:* Jerry Goldsmith. Golden Raspberries '89: Worst Actor (Shatner), Worst Director (Shatner), Worst Picture.

Star Trek 6: The Undiscovered Country 1/2 **1991 (PG)** The final chapter in the long running Star Trek series to feature the original crew of the Enterprise. The Federation and the Klingon Empire are preparing a much-needed peace summit but Captain Kirk has his doubts about the true intentions of the Federation's longtime enemies. When a Klingon ship is attacked, Kirk and the crew of the Enterprise, who are accused of the misdeed, must try to find the real perpetrator. Has an exciting, climactic ending. As is typical of the series, the film highlights current events—glasnost—in its plotlines. Meyer also directed th e second Star Trek movie ("The Wrath of Khan") and wrote the screenplay for the fourth ("The Voyage Home"). **110m/C; VHS, DVD, Blu-Ray.** William Shatner; Leonard Nimoy; DeForest Kelley; James Doohan; George Takei; Walter Koenig; Nichelle Nichols; Christopher Plummer; Kim Cattrall; Iman; David Warner; Mark Lenard; Grace Lee Whitney; Brock Peters; Kurtwood Smith; Rosanna Desoto; John Schuck; Michael Dorn; Christian Slater; *D:* Nicholas Meyer; *W:* Nicholas Meyer; Denny Martin Flinn; *C:* Hiro Narita; *M:* Cliff Eidelman.

Star Trek: Beyond **2016 (PG-13)** While the last two J.J. Abrams-helmed Star Trek films felt weighed down by expectations and homages to the original series, this one plays more like an extended episode, for better and worse. On the former side, the entire cast seems to be having more fun, engaged by director Justin Lin's skill with action sequences and breakneck pacing. On the latter side, this is a remarkably forgettable film in the series. Still, it's nice to see a major franchise film that doesn't feel bloated and self-important, and one that remembers that this series can and should still be fun more than anything else. **122m/C; DVD, Blu-Ray.** Chris Pine; Zachary Quinto; Karl Urban; Zoe Saldana; Simon Pegg; John Cho; Anton Yelchin; Idris Elba; ***D:*** Justin Lin; ***W:*** Simon Pegg; Doug Jung; ***C:*** Stephen F. Windon; ***M:*** Michael Giacchino.

Star Trek: First Contact 🦴🦴🦴 **1996 (PG-13)** The eighth big-screen Trek saga is firmly in the hands of the "Next Generation" cast as Picard and the Enterprise cross paths with the Borg and their sinister Queen. It's hard to tell whether the cry "Resistance is Futile" is coming from the Borg, or the Trek franchise itself, as this installment may well bring in new "Trekkers" with its "less techobabble, more action" approach and the fact that this crew can act. The Borg attempt to change history by travelling back in time (to 2063) to prevent scientist Cromwell from inventing warp drive. While the less-interesting members of the crew stay on Earth to help out with the launch, the battle for the Enterprise rages on up in space. Trademark effects, humor, and idealism are in abundant supply and should please the long-time fan as well as the neophyte. **111m/C; VHS, DVD, Blu-Ray.** Patrick Stewart; Jonathan Frakes; Brent Spiner; LeVar Burton; Michael Dorn; Marina Sirtis; Gates (Cheryl) McFadden; Alfre Woodard; James Cromwell; Alice Krige; Neal McDonough; Robert Picardo; Dwight Schultz; ***D:*** Jonathan Frakes; ***W:*** Brannon Braga; Ronald D. Moore; ***C:*** Matthew F. Leonetti; ***M:*** Jerry Goldsmith.

Star Trek: Generations 🦴🦴🦴 **1994 (PG)** The sci-fi phenomena continues with the first film spun off from the recently departed "Star Trek: The Next Generation" TV series and the seventh following the adventures of the Enterprise crew. Captain Kirk is propelled into the future thanks to an explosion and manages to hook up with current starship captain, Picard. Of course, just in time to save the galaxy from the latest space loon, the villainous Dr. Soren (McDowell), renegade Klingons, and your basic mysterious space entity. For comic relief, android Data gets an emotion chip. Terrific special effects (courtesy of Industrial Light and Magic) and yes, the heroic Kirk receives his mandatory grandiose death scene. Other original characters making a brief appearance are Scotty and Chekov. An entertaining romp through time and space. **117m/C; VHS, DVD, Blu-Ray.** William Shatner; Patrick Stewart; Malcolm McDowell; Whoopi Goldberg; Jonathan Frakes; Brent Spiner; LeVar Burton; Michael Dorn; Gates (Cheryl) McFadden; Marina Sirtis; James Doohan; Walter Koenig; Alan Ruck; ***V:*** Majel Barrett; ***D:*** David Carson; ***W:*** Ronald D. Moore; Brannon Braga; ***C:*** John A. Alonzo; ***M:*** Dennis McCarthy.

Star Trek: Insurrection 🦴🦴 1/2 **1998 (PG)** In the ninth film, Captain Picard (Stewart) goes to Data's (Spiner) rescue when the android seemingly goes berserk while on a scientific mission to investigate the non-techno culture of the peaceful Ba'ku. What Picard discovers is a planet that's virtually a fountain of youth and a dastardly plan by the Federation and the evil Son'a, led by bitter Ru'afro (Abraham), to gain the secret even though it means destroying the planet to do so. More humor and romance than usual done in the typical professional manner of the franchise. **100m/C; VHS, DVD, Blu-Ray.** Patrick Stewart; Brent Spiner; Donna Murphy; F. Murray Abraham; Jonathan Frakes; LeVar Burton; Michael Dorn; Anthony Zerbe; Gates (Cheryl) McFadden; Marina Sirtis; Gregg Henry; Daniel Hugh-Kelly; Claudette Nevins; ***D:*** Jonathan Frakes; ***W:*** Michael Piller; ***C:*** Matthew F. Leonetti; ***M:*** Jerry Goldsmith.

Star Trek: Into Darkness 🦴🦴🦴 **2013 (PG-13)** Abrams' follows up his 2009 reboot with this dynamic adventure. After massively violent attacks back on Earth, Kirk (Pine) leads the crew of the Enterprise on a hunt for a mysterious terrorist (an imposing Cumberbatch) with 72 prototype photon torpedoes in tow courtesy of Admiral Marcus (Weller), against regulations. As the mission's covert purpose takes an unexpected turn, Kirk struggles with his own beliefs about who the real enemy is. For Trekkies, there are many throwback moments that are cause for euphoria; for the rest, a solid story and some exhilarating out-of-this-world action sequences make for super-galactic entertainment. **129m/C; DVD, Blu-Ray.** Chris Pine; Zachary Quinto; Zoe Saldana; Karl Urban; John Cho; Anton Yelchin; Benedict Cumberbatch; Simon Pegg; Bruce Greenwood; Alice Eve; Peter Weller; ***D:*** J.J. (Jeffrey) Abrams; ***W:*** Roberto Orci; Alex Kurtzman; Damon Lindelof; ***C:*** Dan(iel) Mindel; ***M:*** Michael Giacchino.

Star Trek: Nemesis 🦴🦴 **2002 (PG-13)** The venerable (some may say dusty) franchise ends(?) its "Next Generation" incarnation with this disappointing outing. After crew members Riker and Troi get hitched, the Enterprise heads to her homeworld for a celebration, but is sidetracked by the discovery of a dismantled prototype of Data. Picard then receives word of the Romulans' intention to negotiate a peace with the Federation. He smells a rat, and he's right. The leader of the Romulans is actually from Romulus's sister planet Remus, he's a clone of Picard, and he's mad. MAD, I TELL YOU!! Stewart brings his usual gravitas to the role of Picard, even he can't save this snooze-fest that even tried the patience of hard-core Trekkers. **116m/C; VHS, DVD, Blu-Ray, UMD.** Patrick Stewart; Jonathan Frakes; Brent Spiner; LeVar Burton; Michael Dorn; Marina Sirtis; Gates (Cheryl) McFadden; Tom (Thomas) Hardy; Ron Perlman; Shannon Cochran; Dina Meyer; Jude Ciccolella; Kate Mulgrew; Wil Wheaton; ***V:*** Majel Barrett; ***D:*** Stuart Baird; ***W:*** John Logan; ***C:*** Jeffrey L. Kimball; ***M:*** Jerry Goldsmith.

Star Wars 🦴🦴🦴🦴 *Star Wars: Episode 4—A New Hope* **1977 (PG)** First entry in Lucas's "Star Wars" trilogy proved to be one of the biggest boxoffice hits of all time. A young hero, a captured princess, a hot-shot pilot, cute robots, a vile villain, and a heroic and mysterious Jedi knight blend together with marvelous special effects in a fantasy tale about rebel forces engaged in a life or death struggle with the tyrant leaders of the Galactic Empire. Set a new cinematic standard for realistic special effects, making many pre-"Star Wars" effects seem almost laughable in retrospect. Followed by "The Empire Strikes Back" (1980) and "Return of the Jedi" (1983). **121m/C; VHS, DVD, Blu-Ray.** Mark Hamill; Carrie Fisher; Harrison Ford; Alec Guinness; Peter Cushing; Kenny Baker; James Earl Jones; David Prowse; Anthony Daniels; Peter Mayhew; ***D:*** George Lucas; ***W:*** George Lucas; ***C:*** Gilbert Taylor; ***M:*** John Williams. Oscars '77: Art Dir./Set Dec., Costume Des., Film Editing, Orig. Score, Sound, Visual FX; AFI '98: Top 100; Golden Globes '78: Score; L.A. Film Critics '77: Film; Natl. Film Reg. '89.

Star Wars: Episode 1—The Phantom Menace 🦴🦴🦴 **1999 (PG)** Lucas's first "Star Wars" film in 16 years is also the beginning of his prequel trilogy. Jedi Master Qui-Gon Jinn (Neeson) and rebellious apprentice Obi-Wan Kenobi (McGregor) are sent to the peaceful planet Naboo to aid young Queen Amidala (Portman), who is being forced to sign a Trade Federation treaty. When the Jedis escape to Tatooine with Amidala, they encounter a slave boy, Anakin (Lloyd), whom Jinn realizes is empowered by the Force, and are pursued by the Federation and evil Dark Lord, Darth Maul (Park). The special effects are all they're cracked up to be (practically the whole thing is computer generated, but doesn't look it), and the action scenes have the zip and excitement you'd expect. The characters and story may aim a little more at kids than some would like, but those kids will be the teenagers that flock to see the next two. Some plot holes, but that's to be expected in the first installment of a trilogy. **130m/C; VHS, DVD, Blu-Ray.** Liam Neeson; Ewan McGregor; Natalie Portman; Jake Lloyd; Ian McDiarmid; Samuel L. Jackson; Ray Park; Pernilla August; Terence Stamp; Brian Blessed; Oliver Ford Davies; Hugh Quarshie; Ralph Brown; Sofia Coppola; ***V:*** Ahmed Best; Frank Oz; ***D:*** George Lucas; ***W:*** George Lucas; ***C:*** David Tattersall; ***M:*** John Williams. MTV Movie Awards '00: Action Seq.

Star Wars: Episode 2—Attack of the Clones 🦴🦴🦴 **2002 (PG)** Ambitious Jedi knight Anakin (Christensen) goes further on his journey to the dark side while Obi-Wan (McGregor) tries to rein him in. He and Amidala (Portman), who's now a senator, have a forbidden romance, and the Republic continues to be plagued by enemies from within and without. The romance angle, so touted in the pre-release hype, seems forced due to a lack of chemistry (and some ridiculous dialogue) between the two leads, but everything else is spectacular. The exposition is handled much better that in Episode 1, (and really whets the appetite for Episode 3) and the action set pieces are (as expected) well done, and superbly choreographed. Christensen shows brief flashes of the personality changes to come in Anakin, but his performance is uneven. Jackson finally gets to show what he's got as the baddest Jedi this side of Yoda. **124m/C; VHS, DVD, Blu-Ray.** Ewan McGregor; Hayden Christensen; Natalie Portman; Ian McDiarmid; Temuera Morrison; Samuel L. Jackson; Christopher Lee; Pernilla August; Jimmy Smits; Jack Thompson; Rose Byrne; Oliver Ford Davies; Leanna (Leeanna) Walsman; Anthony Daniels; Kenny Baker; Ronald Falk; David Bowers; ***V:*** Frank Oz; Ahmed Best; Andrew Secombe; ***D:*** George Lucas; ***W:*** George Lucas; Jonathan Hales; ***C:*** David Tattersall; ***M:*** John Williams. Golden Raspberries '02: Worst Support. Actor (Christensen).

Star Wars: Episode 3—Revenge of the Sith 🦴🦴🦴 **2005 (PG-13)** After three years of fighting, the Clone Wars are finally ending; the Jedi dispatch Obi-Wan (McGregor) to bring General Grievous to justice; Supreme Chancellor Palpatine (McDiarmid) seeks to consolidate power and bring Anakin Skywalker (Christensen) to the dark side (thus turning him into Darth Vader); the Republic is transformed into the Galactic Empire and the last of the Jedi go into hiding. The end chapter of Lucas' prequel trilogy is appropriately dark, with Lucas's trademark great battle scenes (especially Anakin and Obi-Wan going at it) and at times laughable dialogue and direction. Wraps some elements up neatly, but leaves some major logic holes as well. **140m/C; DVD, Blu-Ray.** Ewan McGregor; Hayden Christensen; Natalie Portman; Samuel L. Jackson; Ian McDiarmid; Peter Mayhew; Jimmy Smits; Kenny Baker; Anthony Daniels; Christopher Lee; Ahmed Best; Oliver Ford Davies; Temuera Morrison; Keisha Castle-Hughes; Bruce Spence; Silas Carson; Jay Laga'aia; Wayne Pygram; David Bowers; ***V:*** Frank Oz; James Earl Jones; Matthew Wood; ***D:*** George Lucas; ***W:*** George Lucas; ***C:*** David Tattersall; ***M:*** John Williams. Golden Raspberries '05: Worst Support. Actor (Christensen).

Star Wars: The Clone Wars 🦴 1/2 **2008 (PG)** Fairly unnecessary computer-animated "Star Wars" spin-off, bridging the gap between "The Clone Wars" and "Revenge of the Sith." During the epic Clone War between the Republic and Separatists, the Jedi are blamed for the kidnapping of Jabba the Hutt's baby (no joke). Anakin Skywalker and his new Padawan learner Ahsoka Tano are sent off to rescue the Huttlet and clear the Jedi name, while Obi-Wan and Yoda hang back to fight the war. George Lucas is only partly to blame for this stinker, as he places his once-imaginative vision in the hands of video game and cartoon veterans, allowing the franchise to slowly degenerate into tame Saturday morning bantha fodder. **98m/C; Blu-Ray.** ***V:*** Matt Lanter; Tom Kane; Ian Abercrombie; Kevin M. Richardson; Ashley Eckstein; James Arnold Taylor; Samuel L. Jackson; Anthony Daniels; Christopher Lee; Corey Burton; ***D:*** Dave Filoni; ***W:*** Henry Gilroy; Steven Melching; Scott Murphy; ***M:*** Kevin Kiner.

Star Wars: The Force Awakens 🦴🦴🦴 1/2 *Star Wars: Episode VII—The Force Awakens* **2015 (PG-13)** It may be little more than fan service, but what glorious fan service! Nostalgia reigns in J.J. Abrams' update of the biggest franchise of all time, which picks up a few decades after episode 6, introducing us to two new protagonists, reluctant Stormtrooper Finn (Boyega) and a young lady named Rey (Ridley) who finds herself a major player in the latest battle against a newly formed Empire led by the malevolent Kylo Ren (Driver). Han, Leia, Chewie, even C-3P0 are all back; the effects are fantastic; the pacing is perfect. In the end, it's just what the prequels never were: fun. **136m/C; DVD, Blu-Ray.** Harrison Ford; Mark Hamill; Carrie Fisher; Adam Driver; Daisy Ridley; John Boyega; Oscar Isaac; Domhnall Gleeson; ***D:*** J.J. (Jeffrey) Abrams; ***W:*** J.J. (Jeffrey) Abrams; Lawrence Kasdan; ***C:*** Dan(iel) Mindel; ***M:*** John Williams. British Acad. '15: Visual FX.

Star Wars: The Last Jedi 🦴🦴🦴 1/2 *Star Wars: Episode VIII—The Last Jedi* **2017 (PG-13)** The eighth installment of the legendary saga gloriously picks up where "The Force Awakens" left off. Rey (Ridley) seeks help from an unwilling Luke Skywalker (Hamill), who is tormented by his failure with Ben Solo, aka Kylo Ren (Driver) of the Dark Side's First Order. Meanwhile, Rey's strong connection to Kylo Ren both terrifies and emboldens her. Other favorites return including General Organa (Fisher, making her final Star Wars performance) as well as Finn (Boyega) and Poe (Isaac). Writer/director Johnson's new vision of the Star Wars' universe is both bold and captivating. **152m/C; DVD, Blu-Ray.** Mark Hamill; Carrie Fisher; Adam Driver; Daisy Ridley; John Boyega; ***D:*** Rian Johnson; ***W:*** Rian Johnson; ***C:*** Steve Yedlin; ***M:*** John Williams.

Star Wars: The Rise of Skywalker 🦴🦴 1/2 *Star Wars: Episode IX—The Rise of Skywalker* **2019 (PG-13)** Despite ever decreasing hope and numbers, Rey (Ridley) and the Resistance have continued to fight. Their cause becomes more desperate when they learn that Emperor Palpatine (McDiarmid) is still alive and organizing a return of the Sith and the Empire. As the Resistance prepares to fight Palpatine's massive fleet, Rey must find the Sith Wayfinder and battle Palpatine's disciple, Kylo Ren (Driver). With strong performances, well-executed action sequences, and incomparable set design, the nostalgic conclusion to the Star Wars saga tries to tie up all the story threads in a way that pleases everyone instead of carving its own identity. **142m/C; DVD, Blu-Ray.** Mark Hamill; Adam Driver; Daisy Ridley; John Boyega; Oscar Isaac; Carrie Fisher; ***D:*** J.J. (Jeffrey) Abrams; ***W:*** J.J. (Jeffrey) Abrams; Chris Terrio; ***C:*** Dan(iel) Mindel; ***M:*** John Williams.

Starchaser: The Legend of Orin 🦴🦴 1/2 **1985 (PG)** Animated fantasy about a boy who must save the world of the future from malevolent hordes. **107m/C; VHS, DVD, Blu-Ray.** ***V:*** Joe Colligan; Carmen Argenziano; Anthony DeLongis; Tyke Caravelli; Dennis Alwood; Daryl Bartley; ***D:*** Steven Hahn; ***W:*** Jeffrey Scott; ***M:*** Andrew Belling.

Stardom 🦴🦴 1/2 **2000 (R)** Price of fame, media-obsessed drama set in the world of modeling. Sultry teen Tina (Pare) is playing on a women's hockey team in smalltown Ontario when she's discovered. French photog Philippe (Berling) puts her on the road to stardom, American manager Renny (Gibson) moves her career forward, but her success causes trouble for the older man she becomes involved with—celebrity restaurateur Barry Levine (Aykroyd) until Tina moves on. All the while she's part of the disposable, instant celeb culture but you're never too sure who's doing the manipulating and how much Tina is complicit in her own exploitation. **102m/C; VHS, DVD.** *FR CA* Jessica Pare; Dan Aykroyd; Thomas Gibson; Charles Berling; Frank Langella; Robert Lepage; ***D:*** Denys Arcand; ***W:*** Denys Arcand; Jacob Potashnik; ***C:*** Guy Dufaux; ***M:*** Francois Dompierre.

Stardust 🦴🦴🦴 **2007 (PG-13)** Tristan (Cox) wants to win the love of cold-hearted Victoria (Miller) by promising that he'll retrieve a star that's fallen into the magical realm bordering their village. But he discovers that the star has transformed into the lovely Yvaine (Danes)?and Tristan isn't the only one who wants the prize. Among the others are Lamia the witch (Pfeiffer) and cross-dressing pirate Shakespeare (De Niro). The mix of epic magical fable, swashbuckling adventure, romance, and "Princess Bride"-style irreverence doesn't always mesh, but eventually settles into an involving and satisfying tale. Based on the novel by Neil Gaiman. **128m/C; DVD, Blu-Ray, HD-DVD.** *GB US* Charlie Cox; Claire Danes; Robert De Niro; Sienna Miller; Michelle Pfeiffer; Peter O'Toole; Jason Flemyng; Rupert Everett; Mark Strong; Henry Cavill; Ricky Gervais; Nathaniel Parker; David Walliams; Kate Magowan; David Kelly; Sarah Alexander; ***Nar:*** Ian McKellen; ***D:*** Matthew Vaughn; ***W:*** Matthew Vaughn; Jane Goldman; ***C:*** Benjamin Davis; ***M:*** Ilan Eshkeri.

Stardust Memories 1/2 **1980 (PG)** Allen's "8 1/2." A comic filmmaker is plagued with creative blocks, relationships, modern fears and fanatical fans. The last film in Allen's varying self-analysis, with explicit references to Fellini and Antonioni. **88m/B; VHS, DVD, Blu-Ray.** Woody Allen; Charlotte Rampling; Jessica Harper; Marie-Christine Barrault; Tony Roberts; Helen Hanft; Cynthia Gibb; Amy Wright; Daniel Stern; ***D:*** Woody Allen; ***W:*** Woody Allen; ***C:*** Gordon Willis.

Starfish 1/2 **2019** On the day of the funeral of Aubrey's (an exceptional Gardner) best friend Grace (Masterson), Earth is attacked by creatures from another dimension. By that time, Aubrey has made her way to Grace's old apartment, where she spends time alone in her pain and sadness. After it snows and the aliens arrive her in small town, Aubrey tries to save the world using cassette tapes Grace has placed around the town that have signals that will stop the aliens. An exploration of grief, the atmospheric film effectively uses its sci-fi elements to enhance Aubrey's story. **99m/C; DVD.** Virginia Gardner; Christina Masterson; Eric Beecroft; Natalie Mitchell; Shannon Hollander; ***D:*** Al White; ***W:*** Al White; ***C:*** Alberto Banares; ***M:*** Al White.

Stargate **1994 (PG-13)** U.S. military probe of a ring-shaped ancient Egyptian artifact (your tax dollars at work) sends he-man colonel Russell and geeky Egyptologist Spader into a parallel universe. There they meet the builders of the pyramids who are enslaved by an evil despot (Davidson) posing as a sun god. Ambitious premise zapped from prepubescent imaginations gets an A for effort, but a silly plot that jumbles biblical epic panoramas and space odyssey special effects with otherworldly mysticism and needless emotional hang-ups trade shlock for style. Spader's shaggy scholar is neurotically fun, Russell's jarhead a bore, and Davidson's vampy villain an unintended hoot. **119m/C; VHS, DVD, Blu-Ray, UMD.** Kurt Russell; James Spader; Jaye Davidson; Viveca Lindfors; Alexis Cruz; Leon Rippy; John Diehl; Erik Avari; Mili Avital; ***D:*** Roland Emmerich; ***W:*** Dean Devlin; Roland Emmerich; ***C:*** Jeff Okun; ***M:*** David Arnold.

Stargate: Continuum **2008** In this stand-alone DTV effort from the "Stargate:SG-1" TV series, the team—plus Jack O'Neill (Anderson)?are offworld to witness the execution of the evil Ba'al (Simon). Of course the bad guy has a plan to survive that involves time-travelling back to 1939 Earth to prevent the Stargate project from ever getting started so that he can eventually conquer the planet. This changes the timeline and makes for sticky situations for Mitchell (Browder), Carter (Tapping), and Jackson (Shanks). The plot jumps around a lot (there's even an Arctic adventure) but if you liked the series, this is like catching up with old friends. **98m/C; DVD, Blu-Ray.** Ben Browder; Michael Shanks; Amanda Topping; Richard Dean Anderson; Christopher Judge; Beau Bridges; Claudia Black; William Devane; Cliff Simon; Dona S. Davis; ***D:*** Martin Wood; ***W:*** Brad Wright; ***C:*** Peter Woeste; ***M:*** Joel Goldsmith. **VIDEO**

Stargate: The Ark of Truth 1/2 **2008** Direct-to-video movie finishes off most of the story left dangling when "Stargate: SG-1" ended its 10th TV season. In this adventure (think "Raiders of the Lost Ark" with some "Terminator" thrown in), Daniel Jackson, Teal'c, and Vala are continuing their planetary search for the Merlin weapon that will defeat the fanatical Ori before they have a chance to attack Earth. Meanwhile, Mitchell and Sam are aboard the Odyssey dealing with a double-crossing official, Ori motherships, and a lot of replicators. A nice bonus for fans of the series. **102m/C; DVD, Blu-Ray.** Ben Browder; Amanda Topping; Christopher Judge; Michael Shanks; Claudia Black; Beau Bridges; Currie Graham; Tim Guinee; Morena Baccarin; Sarah Strange; Julian Sands; Michael Beach; Spencer Maybee; ***D:*** Robert Cooper; ***W:*** Robert Cooper; ***C:*** Peter Woeste; ***M:*** Jeff Goldsmith. **VIDEO**

Stark Raving Mad 1/2 **2002 (R)** Likeable hood Ben (Scott) inherits a big debt to gangster Mr. Gregory (Phillips) after his brother is murdered. His chance to clear it is by stealing a valuable statue from a bank vault located next to a Chinese nightclub that will be hosting a loud and crowded rave. Of course there's all kinds of complicatons, including a potential double-cross, a local Triad member who wants the statue for himself, and a couple of feds working a drug operation on the club. Scott maintains his goofy charm and adds some physical action to the mix but there's nothing new about this tired plot. **98m/C; DVD.** Seann William Scott; Lou Diamond Phillips; Patrick Breen; Terry Chen; Monet Mazur; Suzy Nakamura; Timm Sharp; John Crye; Adam Arkin; Dave Foley; Kavan Smith; ***D:*** David Schneider; Drew Drywalt; ***W:*** David Schneider; Drew Drywalt; ***C:*** Chuck Cohen; ***M:*** John Digweed; Nick Muir.

Starkweather 1/2 **2004 (R)** Humdrum retelling of 19-year-old Charlie Starkweather's (Taylor) 1958 murder spree across Nebraska in the company of his 14-year-old sweetie Caril-Ann Fugate (Lucio). See "Badlands" instead. **90m/C; DVD.** Lance Henriksen; Jerry Kroll; Brent Taylor; Shannon Lucio; ***D:*** Byron Werner; ***W:*** Stephen Johnston; ***C:*** Byron Werner. **VIDEO**

Starlet **2012** A unique friendship across multiple generations serves as the foundation for Baker's interesting drama, a tale of guilt and youthful indiscretion that works best as a character study even if its final act is disappointingly thin. Jane (stunning newcomer Hemingway) is a leggy blonde porn star who forms a friendship with octogenarian Sadie (first-time actress Johnson) after she finds a large amount of cash in a vase she buys at the old lady's yard sale. Hemingway and Johnson sketch fascinating characters and the film works best in their smaller moments, allowing for the realism of what could have been a very-contrived buddy comedy. **103m/C; DVD, Blu-Ray.** Dree Hemingway; Besedka Johnson; James Ransone; ***D:*** Sean Baker; ***W:*** Sean Baker; Chris Bergoch; ***C:*** Radium Cheung.

Starlift **1951** Basically a variety showcase for Warner Bros. stars that was intended as a patriotic salute to Korean War GIs. The flimsy plot finds starlet Nell (Rule) visiting the troops at San Francisco's Travis Air Force Base and soldier Rick (Hagerthy) falling for her. Doris Day, Gordon MacRae, Virginia Mayo, and James Cagney are among those making an appearance (to a greater or lesser extent). **103m/B; DVD.** Janice Rule; Ron Hagerthy; Dick Wessel; Richard Webb; Doris Day; Gordon MacRae; ***D:*** Roy Del Ruth; ***W:*** John Klorer; ***C:*** Ted D. McCord.

Starman **1984 (PG)** An alien from an advanced civilization lands in Wisconsin. He hides beneath the guise of a grieving young widow's recently deceased husband. He then makes her drive him across country to rendezvous with his spacecraft so he can return home. Well-acted, interesting twist on the "Stranger in a Strange Land" theme. Bridges is fun as the likeable starman; Allen is lovely and earthy in her worthy follow-up to "Raiders of the Lost Ark." **115m/C; VHS, DVD, Blu-Ray.** Jeff Bridges; Karen Allen; Charles Martin Smith; Richard Jaeckel; Dirk Blocker; M.C. Gainey; ***D:*** John Carpenter; ***W:*** Bruce A. Evans; Raynold Gideon; ***C:*** Donald M. Morgan; ***M:*** Jack Nitzsche.

Starred Up **2013** Eric Love (O'Connell) is an inmate graduating from the juvenile system to the adult prison system where he joins a facility already run to a certain extent by his estranged father Neville (the fantastic Mendelsohn). Neville's biological father figure is balanced by a behavioral one in counselor Oliver Baumer (Friend). Neither man can really save Eric from his own demons. A fierce drama of the stark reality of prison life by director Mackenzie, which also features the stunning and charismatic debut by O'Connell. **106m/C; Streaming.** *UK* Jack O'Connell; Ben Mendelsohn; Rupert Friend; Sam Spruell; ***D:*** David Mackenzie; ***W:*** Jonathan Asser; ***C:*** Michael McDonough.

Starry Night 1/2 **1999 (PG-13)** So what would artist Vincent Van Gogh do if he suddenly found himself alive (a century after his death) in modern-day Los Angeles and discovered that his paintings, which were considered ugly and worthless in his lifetime, were collected by the wealthy and worth a fortune? Well, he might decide to steal them back, sell them himself, and give the money to other struggling artists. And he might also find himself falling in love with a pretty art student who inspires him to paint new masterpieces. **98m/C; VHS, DVD.** Abbott Alexander; Lisa Waltz; Sally Kirkland; Lou Wagner; ***D:*** Paul Davids; ***W:*** Paul Davids; ***C:*** David W. Smith; ***M:*** Brad Warnaar.

Stars and Stripes Forever *Marching Along* **1952** Sumptious, Hollywoodized bio of composer John Phillip Sousa, based on his memoir "Marching Along," but more concerned with the romantic endeavors of young protege Wagner. Accuracy aside, it's solid entertainment even if you're not mad about march music. **89m/C; VHS, DVD, Blu-Ray.** Clifton Webb; Debra Paget; Robert Wagner; Ruth Hussey; Finlay Currie; ***D:*** Henry Koster.

The Stars Fell on Henrietta 1/2 **1994 (PG)** Down-on-his-luck wildcatter Mr. Cox (Duvall) searches for oil and redemption. He's looking for it on the failing farm of couple Don and Cora Day (Quinn and Fisher) in the middle of the 1930s Texas dustbowl with the reluctant backing of more successful oil man (Dennehy). Quiet character study of an obsessed wheeler-dealer playing with his last poker chip verges on the romantic in its quest for black gold, true to its message about never giving up hope. Directorial debut for Keach is led by typically excellent portrayals by Duvall and Dennehy, but Quinn and Fisher are given little to work with. Marks the first movie Clint Eastwood's Malpaso company has produced in which he didn't star or direct since "Ratboy." **110m/C; VHS, DVD.** Robert Duvall; Aidan Quinn; Frances Fisher; Brian Dennehy; Lexi (Faith) Randall; Kaytlyn Knowles; Francesca Ruth Eastwood; ***D:*** James Keach; ***W:*** Philip Railsback; ***C:*** Bruce Surtees; ***M:*** David Benoit.

Stars in My Crown **1950** McCrea provides a moving performance as the pistol-wielding preacher who helps the residents of a 19th-century small town battle a typhoid epidemic and KKK terrorism. Adapted from the novel by Joe David Brown. **89m/B; VHS, DVD.** Joel McCrea; Ellen Drew; Dean Stockwell; Alan Hale; Lewis Stone; Amanda Blake; Juano Hernandez; Charles Kemper; Connie Gilchrist; Ed Begley, Sr.; James Arness; Jack Lambert; Arthur Hunnicutt; ***Nar:*** Marshall Thompson; ***D:*** Jacques Tourneur; ***W:*** Margaret Fitts; ***M:*** Adolph Deutsch.

The Stars Look Down **1939** A mine owner forces miners to work in unsafe conditions in a Welsh town and disaster strikes. Redgrave is a miner's son running for office, hoping to improve conditions, and to escape the hard life. Forceful, well-directed effort suffered at the boxoffice, in competition with John Ford's similar classic "How Green Was My Valley." From the novel by A.J. Cronin. The original British version was released at 110 minutes. **96m/B; VHS, DVD.** *GB* Michael Redgrave; Margaret Lockwood; Emlyn Williams; Cecil Parker; ***D:*** Carol Reed.

Starship Troopers **1997 (R)** As Bugs Bunny would say, "Of course you know, this means war!" Giant arachnids prove to be an invincible opponent with zero tolerance for things with less than four legs in Verhoeven's comic-book styled, epic slaughter fest. The futuristic, fascist, co-ed Moblie Infantry, led by renegade Commander Rasczak (Ironside), does battle with the sinister arthropods, usually resulting in much human bloodshed. The high body count includes many young actors, but unlike Verhoeven's "Showgirls," their careers should remain relatively unscathed. The acting is straight out of a Mattel toy factory, but the action and confrontations with the enemy insects are a thrill thanks to computer animated special effects. Cheesy, bloody good fun, if you can ignore the fact that fascists are portrayed as the good guys. Based on the 1959 novel by Robert A. Heinlein. **129m/C; VHS, DVD, UMD.** Casper Van Dien; Michael Ironside; Neil Patrick Harris; Clancy Brown; Denise Richards; Dina Meyer; Jake Busey; Patrick Muldoon; Seth Gilliam; Rue McClanahan; Marshall Bell; Eric Bruskotter; Blake Lindsley; Anthony Michael Ruivivar; Dean Norris; Dale Dye; Amy Smart; ***D:*** Paul Verhoeven; ***W:*** Edward Neumeier; ***C:*** Jost Vacano; ***M:*** Basil Poledouris.

Starship Troopers 2: Hero of the Federation WOOF! **2004 (R)** You'll really want the bugs to win in this would-be sequel that's all kinds of bad. A platoon of Federation soldiers are stranded on a bug-infested planet and take refuge in an abandoned outpost while they await rescue. Three stray soldiers show up and soon the grunts are acting weird because a new breed of bugs now uses human hosts. Tippett is an award-winning special effects guy making his directorial debut but he needs to rethink the career move. **92m/C; DVD.** Richard Burgi; Colleen Porch; Ed Lauter; Edward Quinn; Brenda Strong; Kelly Carlson; Lawrence Monson; ***D:*** Phil Tippett; ***W:*** Edward Neumeier; ***C:*** Christian Sebaldt; ***M:*** William T. Stromberg; John Morgan. **VIDEO**

Starship Troopers 3: Marauder 1/2 **2008 (R)** Well anything would be an improvement over the first sequel and at least Van Dien is back (from the original) to save the day. After a Federation ship crash lands on planet OM-1, Johnny Rico (Van Dien), who's in the brig at the time, is released so he can lead a rescue mission. His unit is armed with the latest advanced weapon, called the Marauder, but the low-budget means you really don't get to see it in action that much. Neumeier, who wrote the first two space adventures, takes on directorial duties this time as well. **105m/C; DVD.** Casper Van Dien; Jolene Blalock; Amanda Donohoe; Boris Kodjoe; Stephen Hogan; ***D:*** Edward Neumeier; ***W:*** Edward Neumeier; ***C:*** Lorenzo Senatore; ***M:*** Klaus Badelt. **VIDEO**

Starsky & Hutch 1/2 **2004 (PG-13)** The big-screen adaptation with Ben Stiller (as Starsky) and Owen Wilson (as Hutch) spoofs everything the TV show took so seriously, and to good effect. In this outing, we find out how the duo became partners, and why. It seems both are misfits, with the opposing personality traits of the originals exaggerated to an almost-impossible level, giving them a very high-energy odd-couple buddy vibe as they chase aspiring drug kingpin Reese Feldman (Vaughn). Of course, Huggy Bear is there to assist (in the person of Snoop Dogg, who is spot-on). Stiller and Wilson have this act down, and they never linger on a gag too long. One of the better '70s show spoofs (which may seem like damning with faint praise). Paul Michael Glaser and David Soul have a quick cameo near the end. **97m/C; VHS, DVD, Blu-Ray.** Ben Stiller; Owen Wilson; Snoop Dogg; Fred Williamson; Vince Vaughn; Juliette Lewis; Amy Smart; Carmen Electra; Jason Bateman; Will Ferrell; Christopher Penn; Richard Edson; George Kee Cheung; Jeffrey Lorenzo; Molly Sims; Patton Oswalt; ***Cameo(s):*** Paul Michael Glaser; David Soul; ***D:*** Todd Phillips; ***W:*** Todd Phillips; John O'Brien; Scot Armstrong; ***C:*** Barry Peterson; ***M:*** Theodore Shapiro.

Starstruck 1/2 **1982 (PG)** Fun-loving folly about a teen who tries to help his talented cousin make it as a singer. Playfully tweeks Hollywood musicals. Enjoyable and fun. **95m/C; VHS, DVD.** *AU* Jo Kennedy; Ross O'Donovan; Pat Evison; ***D:*** Gillian Armstrong; ***C:*** Russell Boyd.

StarStruck 1/2 **2010 (G)** Bland Disney Channel teen musical. Jessica and her older sister Sara are with their parents on a family vacation to L.A. to visit their grandmother. Sara is thrilled because she's determined to meet her idol, teen pop star Christopher Wilde. It's the unimpressed Jessica who meets cute with the paparazzi-plagued star, who denies their subsequent romance for the sake of his career and their privacy. **85m/C; DVD, Blu-Ray.** Danielle Campbell; Sterling Knight; Maggie Castle; Chelsea Kane; Matt Winston; Beth Littleford; Dan O'Connor; Alice Hirson; ***D:*** Michael Grossman; ***W:*** Barbara Johns; Annie DeYoung; ***C:*** Horacio Marquinez; ***M:*** David Lawrence. **CABLE**

Start the Revolution without Me **1970 (PG)** Hilarious, Moliere-esque farce about two sets of identical twins (Wilder and Sutherland) separated at birth, who meet 30 years later, just before the French Revolution. About as hammy as they come; Wilder is unforgettable. Neglected when released, but now deservedly a cult favorite. **91m/C; VHS, DVD.** Gene Wilder; Donald Sutherland; Orson Welles; Hugh Griffith; Jack MacGowran; Billie Whitelaw; Victor Spinetti; Ewa Aulin; Denise Coffey; Helen Fraser; Murray Melvin; ***D:*** Bud Yorkin; ***W:*** Lawrence J. Cohen; Fred Freeman; ***C:*** Jean Tournier; ***M:*** John Addison.

Starter for 10 1/2 **2006 (PG-13)** Title refers to the number of points given for starter questions on popular Brit TV quiz show "University Challenge." In 1985, working-class Brian (McAvoy) crosses the social barrier when he's accepted at Bristol University and meets posh blonde Alice (Eve) while trying out for the quiz team. Appealingly geeky, Brian is too starry-eyed to realize he's better suited to firebrand Rebecca (Hall) as he tries to reconcile his past with the potential of his future. **96m/C; DVD, Blu-Ray.** *US GB UK* James McAvoy; Rebecca Hall; Dominic Cooper; Charles Dance; Alice Eve; Catherine Tate; Benedict Cumberbatch; Mark Gatiss; Lindsay Duncan; ***D:*** Tom Vaughan; ***W:*** David Nicholls; ***C:*** Ashley Rowe; ***M:*** Blake Neely.

The Starter Wife 🦴🦴 1/2 **2007** Hollywood wife Molly Kagan (Messing) gets discarded by her studio honcho louse of a hubby, Kenny (Jacobson), for an ambitious younger bimbo. Her status suddenly gone, Molly is given the loan of boozy buddy Joan's (Davis) beach house where she can lick her wounds and plan for her future. Which may just include suave but depressed movie mogul Lou (Mantegna) or hunky, secretive beach bum Sam (Moyer). Showbiz fluff based on the insider novel by Gigi Levangie Grazer. **276m/C; DVD.** Debra Messing; Judy Davis; Stephen Moyer; Peter Jacobson; Lou Mantegna; Miranda Otto; Anika Noni Rose; Aden Young; Chris Diamantopoulos; ***D:*** Jon Avnet; ***W:*** Josann McGibbon; Sara Parriott; ***C:*** Geoffrey Simpson; ***M:*** Ed Shearmur. **CABLE**

Starting Out in the Evening 🦴🦴 1/2 **2007 (PG-13)** Leonard Schiller (Langella) is a 70-year-old, still-respected writer whose books are out of print and who has been working on his latest novel for more than 10 years. Ambitious grad student Heather Wolfe (Ambrose) insists on making Leonard the subject of her master's thesis and also hopes to inspire him to complete his book. She wants to shake up his life; he insists on maintaining his dignity. Meanwhile, Ambrose tries to hold her own against a riveting performance by Langella. **111m/C; DVD.** Frank Langella; Lauren Ambrose; Lili Taylor; Adrian Lester; Jessica Hecht; ***D:*** Andrew Wagner; ***W:*** Andrew Wagner; Fred Parnes; ***C:*** Harlan Bosmajian; ***M:*** Adam Gorgoni.

Starting Over 🦴🦴🦴 **1979 (R)** His life racked by divorce, Phil Potter learns what it's like to be single, self-sufficient, and lonely once again. When a blind date grows into a serious affair, the romance is temporarily halted by his hang-up for his ex-wife. Enjoyable love-triangle comedy loses direction after a while, but Reynolds is subtle and charming, and Bergen good as his ex, a very bad songwriter. Based on a novel by Dan Wakefield. **106m/C; VHS, DVD.** Burt Reynolds; Jill Clayburgh; Candice Bergen; Frances Sternhagen; Austin Pendleton; Mary Kay Place; Kevin Bacon; Daniel Stern; ***D:*** Alan J. Pakula; ***W:*** James L. Brooks; ***C:*** Sven Nykvist; ***M:*** Marvin Hamlisch.

Starved 🦴🦴 **1997** Monica (Beaman) thinks she's found a terrific guy in Scott Dawson (Adams). He gives her flowers, writes her romantic notes, and offers her candle lit dinners. So naturally, Monica falls in love. Too bad, Scott's a sociopath. He takes her prisoner, keeps her in his basement, and uses mind games and starvation to try and break Monica's will. Monica's best friend Jane (Zobel) continues to search for her, even after the police have let the case go. But can she find her in time? Based on a true story. **90m/C; VHS, DVD.** Lee Ann Beaman; Hal Adams; Toni Zobel; ***D:*** Guy Crawford; Yvette Hoffman.

The Starving Games 🦴 1/2 **2013 (PG-13)** A satire that targets the popular teen-focused franchise The Hunger Games, while also winking at Harry Potter, The Avengers, and Sherlock Holmes. In a dark, post-apocalyptic future, heroine Kantmiss Evershot (Walsh) volunteers to take her sister's place in the 75th annual Starving Games. The decision affects her love life—she leaves behind her friend Dale (Daugherty) and teams up with geek Peter Malarkey (Christian)—but could positively impact her future as she could win such delights as an old ham, a pickle that is only partially eaten, or a coupon for sub sandwich! **83m/C; DVD, Blu-Ray, Streaming, Download.** Maiara Walsh; Cody Christian; Brant Daugherty; Diedrich Bader; Ross Wyngaarden; ***D:*** Jason Friedberg; Aaron Seltzer; ***W:*** Jason Friedberg; Aaron Seltzer; ***C:*** Shawn Maurer; ***M:*** Tim Wynn.

Stash House 🦴 1/2 **2012 (R)** Labored home invasion thriller with Lundgren as a 'one last job' bad guy. David and Emma buy a house in a government foreclosure and notice it has an extensive and expensive security system. That's because there's a fortune in drugs stashed there. The drug cartel hires two enforcers to retrieve its merchandise and get rid of any witnesses. **99m/C; DVD.** Sean Faris; Briana Evigan; Dolph Lundgren; Jon Huertas; ***D:*** Eduardo Rodriguez; ***W:*** Gary Spinelli; ***C:*** Matthew Irving; ***M:*** Luis Ascanio. **VIDEO**

State and Main 🦴🦴🦴 **2000 (R)** Hollywood filmmakers descend on a small New England town, which promptly becomes dazzled by all the showbiz glitter. Much of the story rotates around Hoffman, who plays the down-to-earth writer forced to rewrite his script entitled "The Old Mill" after the crew discovers the town's mill burned down years ago. Meanwhile, he becomes concerned when he realizes the film's star (Baldwin) has become involved with a local teenaged girl. Macy and LuPone, Mamet regulars, also enliven the cast. Entertaining, satirical look at Hollywood egos bumping up against middle America. Not too many guffaws, but nice to see Mamet lighten things up with a comedy. **90m/C; VHS, DVD.** Alec Baldwin; Philip Seymour Hoffman; William H. Macy; Julia Stiles; David Paymer; Rebecca Pidgeon; Sarah Jessica Parker; Charles Durning; Patti LuPone; ***D:*** David Mamet; ***W:*** David Mamet; ***C:*** Oliver Stapleton; ***M:*** Theodore Shapiro.

State Department File 649 🦴 1/2 **1949** Insipid spy drama set in northern China. Mongolian rebels hold U.S. agent Lundigan captive; he hopes to capture a Chinese warlord. **87m/C; VHS, DVD.** Virginia Bruce; William Lundigan; ***D:*** Sam Newfield.

State Fair 🦴🦴🦴 *It Happened One Summer* **1945** The second version of the glossy slice of Americana about a family at the Iowa State Fair, featuring plenty of great songs by Rodgers and Hammerstein. Adapted from the 1933 screen version of Phil Stong's novel. Remade again in 1962. **100m/C; VHS, DVD.** Charles Winninger; Jeanne Crain; Dana Andrews; Vivian Blaine; Dick Haymes; Fay Bainter; Frank McHugh; Percy Kilbride; Donald Meek; William Marshall; Harry (Henry) Morgan; ***D:*** Walter Lang; ***W:*** Oscar Hammerstein; ***C:*** Leon Shamroy; ***M:*** Richard Rodgers; Oscar Hammerstein. Oscars '45: Song ("It Might as Well Be Spring").

State Fair 🦴🦴 **1962** The third film version of the story of a farm family who travel to their yearly state fair and experience life. The original songs are still there, but otherwise this is a letdown. Texas setting required dropping the song "All I Owe Iowa." **118m/C; VHS, DVD, Blu-Ray.** Pat Boone; Ann-Margret; Bobby Darin; Tom Ewell; Alice Faye; Pamela Tiffin; Wally Cox; ***D:*** Jose Ferrer; ***C:*** William Mellor.

State of Emergency 🦴🦴 1/2 **1994 (R)** John Novelli (Mantegna) is a cynical, overworked emergency-room doctor for an overcrowded, underequipped big-city hospital. His latest casualty is a head trauma case the hospital is ill-prepared to handle and as the patient's condition worsens both doctor and hospital are put at risk. **97m/C; VHS, DVD.** Joe Mantegna; Lynn Whitfield; Paul Dooley; ***D:*** Leslie Linka Glatter; ***W:*** Susan Black; Lance Gentile. **TV**

State of Grace 🦴🦴🦴 **1990 (R)** Irish hood Penn returns to old NYC neighborhood as undercover cop and becomes involved with an Irish Westies mob in a fight for survival as urban renewal encroaches on their Hell's Kitchen turf. Shrinking client base for shakedown schemes and protection rackets forces them to become contract killers for the Italian mafia. Fine performances, with Penn tense but restrained, gang honcho Harris intense, and Oldman chewing up gritty urban scenery as psycho brother of Harris, but the story is long and meandering. Well-choreographed violence. **134m/C; VHS, DVD, Blu-Ray.** Sean Penn; Ed Harris; Gary Oldman; Robin Wright; John Turturro; Burgess Meredith; John C. Reilly; Joe (Johnny) Viterelli; ***D:*** Phil Joanou; ***W:*** Dennis McIntyre; ***C:*** Jordan Cronenweth; ***M:*** Ennio Morricone.

State of Play 🦴🦴🦴 **2003** Ambitious MP Stephen Collins (Morrissey) learns that his research assistant Sonia has died in a suspicious accident. Could her death be in any way connected to the execution-style murder of a teenaged thief and drug dealer? Newspaper editor Cameron Foster (Nighy) assigns reporters Cal (Simm), Della (Macdonald), and Dan (MacAvoy) to chase leads and soon dirty secrets, political and private, start spilling out. Complex miniseries with notable performances. **350m/C; DVD.** *GB* David Morrissey; Bill Nighy; Kelly Macdonald; James McAvoy; John Simm; Polly Walker; Amelia Bullmore; Philip Glenister; Marc Warren; Benedict Wong; ***D:*** David Yates; ***W:*** Paul Abbott; ***C:*** Chris Seager; ***M:*** Nicholas Hooper. **TV**

State of Play 🦴🦴🦴 **2009 (PG-13)** A rising congressman, Stephen Collins (Affleck), and a D.C. investigative journalist, Cal McCaffrey (Crowe) are old friends who become embroiled in a case of seemingly unrelated, brutal murders. When Stephen's research assistant (and secret mistress) is killed, Cal and his partner Della (McAdams) are assigned by their ruthless boss (Mirren) to get the story. An engrossing political conspiracy thriller/murder mystery, even if it lacks a bit in character development. Also serves as a commentary on the limitations of journalism in the face of the D.C. political machine. Adapted from the complicated 2003 BBC miniseries, which was better-suited to explore plot twists and the players involved. **127m/C; Blu-Ray, On Demand.** Russell Crowe; Ben Affleck; Rachel McAdams; Dame Helen Mirren; Jason Bateman; Robin Wright; Viola Davis; Jeff Daniels; Katy Mixon; ***D:*** Kevin MacDonald; ***W:*** Matthew Carnahan; Tony Gilroy; Billy Ray; ***C:*** Rodrigo Prieto; ***M:*** Alex Heffes.

State of the Union 🦴🦴🦴 1/2 *The World and His Wife* **1948** Liberal multimillionaire Tracy is seeking the Republican presidential nomination. His estranged wife (Hepburn) is asked to return so they can masquerade as a loving couple for the sake of his political career. Hepburn tries to help Tracy, as the backstage political machinations erode his personal convictions. Adapted from a highly successful, topical Broadway play; the writers changed dialogue constantly to reflect the news. Capra and his partners at Liberty Pictures originally hoped to cast Gary Cooper and Claudette Colbert. Hepburn and Menjou were at odds politically (over communist witch hunts in Hollywood) but are fine together onscreen. **124m/B; VHS, DVD.** Spencer Tracy; Katharine Hepburn; Angela Lansbury; Van Johnson; Adolphe Menjou; Lewis Stone; Howard Smith; ***D:*** Frank Capra; ***C:*** George J. Folsey.

State Property 2 **WOOF!** **2005 (R)** Rappers who think they can act glamorize their world of drugs and violence in a most reprehensible way. Jail time, scores to settle, double- and triple-crossing, homicidal fantasies and plenty of actual death. Everything you don't want your kids to see. Come to think of it, you probably don't want to see it either. **94m/C; DVD.** Beanie Sigel; Michael Bentt; Victor NORE Santiago; Damon Dash; Omillio Sparks; Oschino; ***D:*** Damon Dash; ***W:*** Adam Moreno; ***C:*** Tom Houghton; ***M:*** Kerry Muzzey.

The State Within 🦴🦴 1/2 **2006** A very complicated political conspiracy entangles British ambassador to the U.S., Sir Mark Brydon (Isaacs), with terrorists, corporate hijinks, and the tough-talking U.S. secretary of defense (Gless). When a British airliner is blown up over D.C., the bomb is traced to a British Muslim suicide bomber with apparent ties to a Central Asian nation in political turmoil. Then there's British national Luke Gardner (James), who's on Florida's death row, and is tied into the players in unexpected ways. Isaacs and Gless are outstanding, but the story has too many shadowy characters and subplots for its own good. **360m/C; DVD.** *GB* Jason Isaacs; Sharon Gless; Ben Daniels; Eva Birthistle; Lennie James; Neil Pearson; Alex Jennings; Noam Jenkins; Genevieve O'Reilly; Nigel Bennett; ***D:*** Daniel Percival; ***W:*** Elizabeth (Lizzie) Mickery; ***C:*** David Perrault; ***M:*** Jennie Muskett. **CABLE**

Stateline Motel 🦴 1/2 *Last Chance For a Born Loser* **1975 (R)** Cheap Italian ripoff of "The Postman Always Rings Twice," with a surprise ending but little of great interest. **86m/C; VHS, DVD.** *IT* Eli Wallach; Ursula Andress; Fabio Testi; Barbara Bach; ***D:*** Maurizio Lucidi.

The Statement 🦴🦴 **2003 (R)** Michael Caine plays Pierre Brossard, a Frenchman who helped the Nazis in the execution of several Jews during World War II. As a wanted war criminal, Brossard has been eluding authorities for years with the help of arch-conservative extremists within the Catholic church. While an interesting story, the movie is schizophrenic and leaves a lot of questions unanswered. Adapted from the novel by Brian Moore, it is actually based on the true story of Paul Touvier. **120m/C; VHS, DVD.** *CA GB FR* Michael Caine; Tilda Swinton; Jeremy Northam; Alan Bates; Charlotte Rampling; John Neville; Ciaran Hinds; Frank Finlay; William Hutt; Matt Craven; Noam Jenkins; Peter Wight; Colin Salmon; David de Keyser; ***D:*** Norman Jewison; ***W:*** Ronald Harwood; ***C:*** Kevin Jewison; ***M:*** Normand Corbeil.

Staten Island 🦴🦴 **2009 (R)** Absurdist nonlinear crime comedy. Staten Island mobster Parmie (D'Onofrio) survives a hit and takes refuge in a treehouse in a wildlife area that's part of a protest against a developer. Dim bulb Sully (Hawke) needs money for an experimental in-vitro operation for his unborn son and robs the house of Parmie's mother (big mistake). Deaf-mute deli owner Jasper (Cassel) has Sully and Parmie for customers but, in Parmie's case, Jasper provides a body disposal service as well. Hawke's character is the least interesting, D'Onofrio's mother-loving mobster is beyond odd, and Cassell steals the movie. **96m/C; DVD.** Ethan Hawke; Vincent D'Onofrio; Seymour Cassel; Julianne Nicholson; Rosemary De Angelis; ***D:*** James DeMonaco; ***W:*** James DeMonaco; ***C:*** Christopher Norr; ***M:*** Frederic Verrieres.

State's Attorney 🦴🦴 1/2 *Cardigan's Last Case* **1931** Mob attorney Barrymore finds trouble after his boss sets him up as District Attorney and he decides to go after his old cronies. His ex-prostitute lover gets caught in the middle after he dumps her for a powerful politico's daughter. Contrived, improbable story succumbs to star-quality lead acting from Barrymore. Remade in 1937 with Lee Tracy as "Criminal Lawyer." **79m/B; VHS, DVD.** John Barrymore; Jill Esmond; William "Stage" Boyd; Helen Twelvetrees; Mary Duncan; Ralph Ince; Albert Conti; C. Henry Gordon; Leon Ames; ***D:*** George Archainbaud; ***W:*** Gene Fowler, Sr.; Rowland Brown; ***C:*** Leo Tover; ***M:*** Max Steiner.

States of Control 🦴🦴 1/2 **1998** Penetrating, disturbing character study follows Lisa (Van Dyck) as she transforms herself from secure Manhattan wife into something much different and difficult to define. **84m/C; DVD.** Jennifer Van Dyck; Stephen Bogardus; John Cunningham; Ellen Greene; Jennie Moreau; Nancy Giles; ***D:*** Zack Winestine; ***W:*** Zack Winestine; ***C:*** Susan Starr; ***M:*** Richard Termini.

Stateside 🦴🦴 **2004 (R)** Romantic soap opera that writer/director Anselmo says is based on a true story. The movie starts in 1984 with hospitalized Marine Mark (Tucker) flashing back to 1980. While drunk, high schooler Mark gets into a serious car accident that his wealthy dad (Mantegna) fixes by having Mark enlist in the Corps rather than doing jail time. On leave, Mark visits gal pal Sue (Bruckner) in a mental hospital and meets her schizophrenic ex-actress/singer roomie Dori (Cook). They immediately fall for each other and the drama ensues. Tucker fares best as his character matures from boy to man under Kilmer's tough drill instructor, while Cook is playing standard Hollywood-crazy. Movie might have benefited from a longer run time since the overstuffed plot doesn't have time to develop. Penny Marshall has an uncredited cameo as a nurse. **96m/C; VHS, DVD.** *US GE* Rachael Leigh Cook; Jonathan Tucker; Agnes Bruckner; Val Kilmer; Joe Mantegna; Carrie Fisher; Diane Venora; Ed Begley, Jr.; Michael Goduti; Daniel Franzese; Penny Marshall; ***D:*** Reverge Anselmo; ***W:*** Reverge Anselmo; ***C:*** Adam Holender; ***M:*** Joel McNeely.

Static 🦴🦴 1/2 **1987 (PG-13)** A strange, disquieting independent film about an eccentric youth who claims to have built a machine through which one can see heaven. Uneven, with some dull stretches. **89m/C; VHS, Streaming.** Keith Gordon; Amanda Plummer; Bob Gunton; Jane Hoffman; Barton Heyman; Lily Knight; ***D:*** Mark Romanek; ***W:*** Keith Gordon; Mark Romanek.

The Station Agent 2003 (R) Reclusive train enthusiast dwarf, Fibar McBride (Dinklage) takes up residence in an abandoned rural New Jersey train station he inherited in writer/director McCarthy's funny and poignant first film. Finbar's seemingly happy solitude is intruded upon by incurably outgoing local coffee cart owner Joe (Cannavale) who is fascinated by the strange newcomer. Among the other lonely locals is the downtrodden Olivia (Clarkson) who is dealing with the death of her child and a divorce. Finbar's passion for trains soon takes a back seat to some regular human contact. Dinklage is a standout in the title role, while Clarkson, Williams and Cannavale are equally excellent in this well-crafted dramedy. **88m/C; VHS, DVD.** Peter Dinklage; Patricia Clarkson; Bobby Cannavale; Raven Goodwin; Paul Benjamin; Michelle Williams; ***D:*** Thomas (Tom) McCarthy; ***W:*** Thomas (Tom) McCarthy; ***C:*** Oliver Bokelberg; ***M:*** Stephen Trask. British Acad. '03: Orig. Screenplay; Ind. Spirit '04: First Screenplay; Natl. Bd. of Review '03: Support. Actress (Clarkson); Natl. Soc. Film Critics '03: Support. Actress (Clarkson).

Station Jim 1/2 2001 In the 1890s, a performing circus dog escapes its abusive master and is found by railway station porter Bob (Creed-Miles), who names the terrier Jim. Jim becomes a favorite of the kiddies at the local orphanage, especially young Henry (Sangster). Jim and Bob soon find themselves in a battle to save the orphanage from closure, even as the pooch helps Bob with romancing schoolteacher Harriet (Fraser) and thwarts a plot to kill Queen Victoria. **87m/C; DVD.** *GB* Charlie Creed-Miles; George Cole; Laura Fraser; Thomas Brodie-Sangster; Frank Finlay; David Haig; Celia Imrie; Prunella Scales; Timothy West; David Ross; ***D:*** John Roberts; ***W:*** Mark Wallington; ***C:*** Vernon Layton. **TV**

The Stationmaster's Wife 1/2 1977 In Germay's Weimar Republic a provincial stationmaster's wife expresses her boredom with her pleasant ineffectual husband by having numerous meaningless affairs. Meant to invoke postwar German dread and the fake bourgeois morality which covered political and social resentments. Originally shown as a 200-minute miniseries for German TV; subtitled. **111m/C; VHS, DVD.** *GE* Elisabeth Trissenaar; Kurt Raab; Gustal Bayrhammer; Bernard Helfrich; Udo Kier; Volker Spengler; ***D:*** Rainer Werner Fassbinder; ***W:*** Rainer Werner Fassbinder; ***C:*** Michael Ballhaus; ***M:*** Peer Raben. **TV**

Stavisky 1974 Sumptuously lensed story of Serge Stavisky, a con-artist and bon-vivant whose machinations almost brought down the French government when his corruption was exposed in 1934. Belmondo makes as charismatic an antihero as you could find. Excellent score complements the visuals. In French with English subtitles. **117m/C; VHS, DVD.** Jean-Paul Belmondo; Anny (Annie Legras) Duperey; Charles Boyer; Francois Perier; Gerard Depardieu; ***D:*** Alain Resnais; ***W:*** Jorge Semprun; ***C:*** Sacha Vierny; ***M:*** Stephen Sondheim. N.Y. Film Critics '74: Support. Actor (Boyer).

Stay 1/2 2005 (R) Confusing psychological thriller finds compassionate shrink Sam Foster (McGregor) trying to prevent his patient Henry (Gosling) from committing suicide. Distracting and oblique things happen and Sam begins to question whether what he sees is real or part of a nightmare. ou probably won't be able to understand what you're seeing either. Good cast, good director, but too artsy by far. **99m/C; DVD.** Ewan McGregor; Naomi Watts; Ryan Gosling; Janeane Garofalo; B.D. Wong; Bob Hoskins; Kate Burton; Michael Gaston; Mark Margolis; Elizabeth Reaser; Amy Sedaris; Isaach de Bankole; ***D:*** Marc Forster; ***W:*** David Benioff; ***C:*** Roberto Schaefer; ***M:*** Thad Spencer.

Stay 1/2 2013 Ponderous romantic drama has May-December couple Dermot and Abby settling in to life in a rural Irish village. Dermot's content but Abby's restless and her unintended pregnancy causes a severe rift and has her fleeing back to Montreal to visit her dad. Dermot's unwillingness to be a father is rooted in a secret that's easy to figure out even as he bonds with a couple of young locals, including a young, unwed mother. **99m/C; DVD.** *CA* Aidan Quinn; Taylor Schilling; Michael Ironside; Barry Keoghan; Nika McGuigan; ***D:*** Wiebke von Carolsfeld; ***W:*** Wiebke von Carolsfeld; ***C:*** Ronald Plante; ***M:*** Robert Marcel Lepage.

Stay Alive 2006 (PG-13) Hackneyed horror. The title refers to a videogame that was being tested by players who subsequently died. The game is then passed on to Hutch (Foster). When he and his fellow gamers play, more teens die and Hutch finally realizes that when a player dies in the game, they die exactly the same way in real life. Their nemesis (for no good reason) turns out to be sadistic, blood-bathing 16th-century Hungarian countess Elizabeth Bathory, who is now occupying a Louisiana plantation. Apparently the deaths keep her young and beautiful. Makes about as much sense as it sounds like it would. **85m/C; DVD.** Jon Foster; Samaire Armstrong; Frankie Muniz; Jimmi Simpson; Wendell Pierce; Sophia Bush; Adam Goldberg; ***D:*** William Brent Bell; ***W:*** William Brent Bell; Matthew Peterman; ***C:*** Alejandro Martinez; ***M:*** John (Gianni) Frizzell.

Stay Awake 1987 (R) A demon stalks, haunts and tortures eight young girls sleeping together at a secluded Catholic school. Title might be addressed to the viewer, who will be tempted to snooze. **90m/C; VHS, DVD.** *SA* Shirley Jane Harris; Tanya Gordon; Jayne Hutton; Heath Porter; ***D:*** John Bernard.

Stay Away, Joe 1968 (PG) The King is a singing half-breed rodeo star who returns to his reservation where he finds love and trouble. Utterly cliche, embarrassing, and stupid even by Elvis-movie standards. **98m/C; VHS, DVD.** Elvis Presley; Burgess Meredith; Joan Blondell; Thomas Gomez; L.Q. Jones; Katy Jurado; Henry Jones; ***D:*** Peter Tewkesbury.

Stay Cool 2009 (PG-13) Tepid, painfully underdeveloped rom com filled with caricatures. Author Henry McCarthy (Polish) returns to his hometown to give the commencement address at his high school. Henry finds he hasn't quite left old times behind when he reunites with his one-time crush Scarlett (Ryder) and some buddies who haven't exactly moved on. Duff plays a high school senior who gets her own crush on Henry and invites him to the prom. **94m/C; DVD.** Mark Polish; Winona Ryder; Sean Astin; Josh Holloway; Hilary Duff; Chevy Chase; Jon Cryer; Marc Blucas; ***D:*** Michael Polish; ***W:*** Mark Polish; ***C:*** M. David Mullen; ***M:*** Ryan Franks.

Stay Hungry 1976 (R) A wealthy southerner (Bridges) is involved in a real estate deal which depends on the sale of a gym where a number of body builders hang out. He becomes immersed in their world and finds himself in love with the working-class Field. Big Arnold's first speaking role in his own inimitable accent (his first role in "Hercules in New York" was dubbed.) Offbeat and occasionally uneven comedy-drama based on a novel by Charles Gaines is a sleeper. **102m/C; VHS, DVD, Blu-Ray.** Jeff Bridges; Sally Field; Arnold Schwarzenegger; Robert Englund; Scatman Crothers; ***D:*** Bob Rafelson; ***W:*** Bob Rafelson.

Stay Tuned 1992 (PG-13) Suburban yuppie couple buys a large-screen TV and satellite dish from Hellvision salesman, are sucked into their dish, and wind up starring in hellish TV shows such as "Wayne's Underworld," "Northern Overexposure," "Sadistic Home Videos," and "My Three Sons of Bitches." If they can survive for 24 hours, they'll be able to return to their normal lives. Clever idea for a film is wasted as this one never really gets off the ground; viewers may not want to stay tuned to the low comedy and frantic sucks. **90m/C; VHS, DVD, Blu-Ray.** John Ritter; Pam Dawber; Jeffrey Jones; Eugene Levy; David Tom; Heather McComb; ***D:*** Peter Hyams; ***W:*** Tom S. Parker; ***C:*** Peter Hyams; ***M:*** Bruce Broughton.

Staying Alive 1/2 1983 (PG) "Saturday Night Fever" was the ultimate cheesy '70s musical, hence likeable in a dorky way. This pathetic sequel (directed by Stallone from a Rocky-esque script about beating the odds, etc.) is utterly predictable and forgettable. Set six years after the first film, the sequel finds Tony Manero (Travolta) working as a waiter while trying to break into the big lights of Broadway. Music mostly by Frank Stallone, the great heir to Rodgers and Hammerstein. **96m/C; VHS, DVD.** John Travolta; Cynthia Rhodes; Finola Hughes; Norma Donaldson; ***D:*** Sylvester Stallone; ***W:*** Sylvester Stallone; ***M:*** Frank Stallone.

Staying On 1/2 1980 Based on the Paul Scott novel, this English drama follows the life of a post-colonial British colonel and his wife who chose to remain in India. **87m/C; VHS, DVD.** *GB* Trevor Howard; Celia Johnson; ***D:*** Irene Shubik.

Staying Together 1/2 1989 (R) Three midwestern brothers go into a panic when their father decides to sell the restaurant they've worked at all their adult lives. Somehow they manage the transition and learn about life. Sloppy comedy-drama with way too many unresolved subplots. **91m/C; VHS, DVD; Open Captioned.** Dermot Mulroney; Tim Quill; Sean Astin; Stockard Channing; Melinda Dillon; Daphne Zuniga; ***D:*** Lee Grant; ***W:*** Monte Merrick; ***C:*** Dick Bush; ***M:*** Miles Goodman.

Staying Vertical 1/2 *Rester Vertical* 2016 Leo (Bonnard) is a formerly vibrant filmmaker who has lost his way as he approaches middle age. While in France looking for inspiration for another film, he has an affair with a shepherdess (Hair), who then leaves the filmmaker with the resultant baby. Confronted with raising the child on his own, he refuses to let the situation destroy his creative impulses. Writer/director Guiraudie's latest isn't his most daring film but it's unpredictable and strange, creating an uniquely intense journey. **100m/C; DVD.** *FR* India Hair; Damien Bonnard; Raphaël Thiéry; Laure Calamy; Christian Bouillette; ***D:*** Alain Guiradie; ***W:*** Alain Guiradie; ***C:*** Claire Mathon.

Steal Big, Steal Little 1995 (PG-13) Twins Robby and Reuben Martinez (Garcia) battle over the California ranch land left to Reuben by their mother. Evil, manipulative Robby, all fancy suits and slicked-back hair, wants to build condos while gentle, less-fashionable Reuben must fight to fulfill his dream of building a home for the migrant workers he employs. Yawn. Writer/director Davis' flashy action movie technique doesn't fit into the dramatic social commentary—it's too fast and forced to work. Garcia's radical character changes are impressive though. Arkin provides comic relief as the good-hearted used-car dealer who tries to save the day, if not the film. **130m/C; VHS, DVD.** Andy Garcia; Alan Arkin; Rachel Ticotin; Joe Pantoliano; David Ogden Stiers; Charles Rocket; Holland Taylor; ***D:*** Andrew Davis; ***W:*** Lee Blessing; Jeanne Blake; Terry Kahn; Andrew Davis; ***C:*** Frank Tidy; ***M:*** William Olvis.

Steal the Sky 1988 Israeli agent Hemingway seduces Iraqi pilot Cross and persuades him to steal a Soviet MIG jet and defect to Israel. Unlikely plot but swell flying scenes. Hemingway is poorly cast, as she often is. **110m/C; VHS, DVD.** Mariel Hemingway; Ben Cross; Etta Ankri; ***D:*** John Hancock. **CABLE**

Steal This Movie! *Abbie* 2000 (R) Bio of anti-war activist and Yippie founder Abbie Hoffman tries to explore the counterculture of the 60s but bites off more than it can chew. Film's fragmented by its structure of using the flashback recollections of Abbie's (D'Onofrio) first wife Anita (Garofalo) and lawyer Gerry Lefcourt (Pollak) to explain the manic and charismatic Hoffman, who wound up spending most of the 70s an underground fugitive and who died a suicide. Garity, who's the son of Tom Hayden and Jane Fonda, plays his activist dad. **111m/C; VHS, DVD.** Vincent D'Onofrio; Janeane Garofalo; Jeanne Tripplehorn; Donal Logue; Kevin Pollak; Kevin Corrigan; Troy Garity; Alan Van Sprang; ***D:*** Robert Greenwald; ***W:*** Bruce Graham; ***C:*** Denis Lenoir; ***M:*** Mader.

Stealing Beauty 1/2 1996 (R) The film's main asset, besides the beautiful Tuscan scenery, is the coltish charm of Tyler, who stars as virginal teenager Lucy Harmon. An innocent abroad, she's spending the summer with family friends after her mother's suicide. Ostensibly artist Ian Grayson (McCann) is doing her portrait but Lucy's more interested in finding romance with neighbor lad Niccolo (Zibetti), who bestowed her first kiss on a previous visit. Lucy's sunny appeal doesn't go unnoticed by the villa's other inhabitants, including dying playwright Alex (Irons), but it seems Lucy's growing up won't be easy on anyone (not even herself). **118m/C; VHS, DVD.** *IT GB FR* Liv Tyler; Jeremy Irons; Donal McCann; Sinead Cusack; Jean Marais; D.W. Moffett; Stefania Sandrelli; Carlo Cecchi; Roberto Zibetti; Joseph Fiennes; Jason Flemyng; Leonardo Treviglio; Rachel Weisz; ***D:*** Bernardo Bertolucci; ***W:*** Bernardo Bertolucci; Susan Minot; ***C:*** Darius Khondji; ***M:*** Richard Hartley.

Stealing Candy 2004 (R) Two ex-cons and a computer whiz team up to kidnap a movie star Candi (Lano) so they can stage a pay-per-view internet sex session with her. Predictable thriller piles on the nonstop action and plays on the promise of sex. **83m/C; VHS, DVD.** Jenya Lano; Daniel Baldwin; Coolio; Alex McArthur; Julie St. Claire; ***D:*** Mark L. Lester; ***W:*** C. Courtney Joyner. **VIDEO**

Stealing Cars 2016 (R) A moving drama about self-discovery. Because of his troubled past and rebellious actions, promising teen Billy Wyatt (Cohen) is sent to the Bernville Camp for Boys. Though he must deal with an unjust system, cruel staff, and dangerous inmates, Billy also comes to understand himself and inspire others along the way. **94m/C; DVD, Streaming, Download.** Emory Cohen; William H. Macy; John Leguizamo; Paul Sparks; Heather Lind; ***D:*** Bradley Kaplan; ***W:*** Will Aldis; Steve Mackall.

Stealing Harvard 2002 (PG-13) Prince of low-brow Green adds another tarnished jewel to his crown with this tired, inane crime caper comedy. As Duff, Green is teamed with Jason Lee as John, who needs to raise $30,000 to finance the Harvard education he promised his neice. That should take care of her first semester. His fiancee (Mann), also wants John to bankroll their future together, and won't marry him until he has the exact amount in the bank. What follows are the disastrous duo's clumsy attempts to steal the money. Largely unfunny, with small chunks of mild humor. **83m/C; VHS, DVD, Blu-Ray.** Tom Green; Jason Lee; Leslie Mann; Megan Mullally; Dennis Farina; Richard Jenkins; John C. McGinley; Christopher Penn; Tammy Blanchard; Seymour Cassel; ***D:*** Bruce McCulloch; ***W:*** Peter Tolan; ***C:*** Ueli Steiger; ***M:*** Christophe Beck.

Stealing Home 1/2 1988 (PG-13) A washed-up baseball player learns his former babysitter (who was also his first love and inspiration), has committed suicide. Their bittersweet relationship is told through flashbacks. Foster's superb performance steals the show in this quiet sleeper. **98m/C; VHS, DVD.** Mark Harmon; Jodie Foster; William McNamara; Blair Brown; Harold Ramis; Jonathan Silverman; John Shea; Helen Hunt; Richard Jenkins; Ted Ross; Thatcher Goodwin; Yvette Croskey; ***D:*** Steven Kampmann; Will Aldis; ***W:*** Steven Kampmann; Will Aldis; ***C:*** Bobby Byrne; ***M:*** David Foster.

Stealing Las Vegas 2012 An amateurish, low-budget heist flick--with Roger Corman as an executive producer--that's overly-complicated and ultimately silly. Sleazy, greedy casino owner Alex (Roberts, the only reason to watch) steals 20 million from his employees' health and pension funds. When electrician Nick (Landry) discovers the theft, he rallies some other workers to steal the money back. **87m/C; DVD.** Eric Roberts; Ethan Landry; Antonio Fargas; Eloy Mendez; Anabella Casanova; ***D:*** Francisco Menendez; ***W:*** Francisco Menendez; Warren D. Cobb; ***C:*** Alex Salahi; ***M:*** Justin Raines. **VIDEO**

Stealing Sinatra 1/2 2004 (R) Telling of the screwy but true details behind the 1963 botched kidnapping of Frank Sinatra, Jr. by three amateurs trying to score some quick dough from his renowned father. **95m/C; VHS, DVD.** David Arquette; William H. Macy; Ryan Browning; Sam McMurray; Thomas Ian Nicholas; Gillian Barber; Colin Cunningham; Brandy Heidrick; Catherine Barroll; Matthew Bennett; Johnathan Brownlee; Ron Chartier; Michael Coristine; ***D:*** Ron Underwood; ***W:*** Howard Korder; ***C:*** Brian Pearson; ***M:*** John Powell; James McKee Smith. **TV**

Stealth 1/2 2005 (PG-13) Dumb, loud, special effects-heavy action flick falls into the mindless entertainment category. Three elite Navy pilots (Lucas, Biel, Foxx)--who all look really good in their dress whites—are chosen to test the latest stealth aircraft, with a fourth jet as wingman. This is a pilot-less craft controlled by an artificial intelligence known as EDI. Naturally, EDI goes haywire and must be stopped by those puny humans. Director Cohen likes action, and the actors are just along for the ride. **121m/C; DVD, Blu-Ray, UMD.** Josh(ua) Lucas; Jamie Foxx; Jessica Biel; Sam Shepard; Joe Morton; Richard Roxburgh; Ian Bliss; Nicholas Hammond; ***V:*** Wentworth Miller; ***D:*** Rob Cohen; ***W:*** W.D. Richter; ***C:*** Dean Semler; ***M:*** BT (Brian Transeau).

Stealth Fighter 🦴 ½ **1999 (R)** Naval pilot Owen Turner (Ice-T) fakes his own death and goes to work for the bad guys in South America. Then he steals a stealth fighter from a U.S. military base and starts bombing foreign military installations. So naval officer Ryan Mitchell (Mandylor) is sent to stop him. Wynorski directed under the pseudonym "Jay Andrews." **87m/C; VHS, DVD.** Ice-T; Costas Mandylor; Ernie Hudson; Erika Eleniak; Andrew Divoff; John Enos; Steve Eastin; ***D:*** Jim Wynorski; ***W:*** Lenny Juliano; ***C:*** J.E. Bash; ***M:*** K. Alexander (Alex) Wilkinson. **VIDEO**

Steam: A Turkish Bath 🦴🦴🦴 *Hamam: Il Bagno Turco* **1996** Francesco (Gassman) is a young Italian businessman married to the equally busy Marta (d'Aloja) and living a fashionable life in Rome. When he learns an aunt has left him a building in Istanbul, he leaves to check out his inheritance. What Francesco discovers is that he now possesses a traditional Turkish bath and that the family his aunt lived with and employed is eager for him to stay. Mysterious Istanbul begins to work its magic as does Francesco's unexpected (and mutual) growing attraction to the family's son, Mehmet (Gunsur). Of course, Marta does eventually show up. Italian and Turkish with subtitles. **96m/C; VHS, DVD.** *TU IT SP* Alessandro Gassman; Francesca D'Aloja; Carlo Cecchi; Mehmet Gunsur; Serif Sezer; Basak Koklukaya; Halil Ergun; Alberto Molinari; ***D:*** Ferzan Ozpetek; ***W:*** Ferzan Ozpetek; Stefano Tummolini; ***C:*** Pasquale Mari; ***M:*** Aldo De Scalzi.

Steamboat Bill, Jr. 🦴🦴🦴 ½ **1928** City-educated student returns to his small home-town and his father's Mississippi river boat, where he's an embarrassment to dad. But bond they do, to ward off the owner of a rival riverboat, whose daughter Keaton falls for. Engaging look at small-town life and the usual wonderful Keaton antics, including braving the big tornado. **75m/B; Silent; VHS, DVD, Blu-Ray.** Buster Keaton; Ernest Torrence; Marion Byron; Tom Lewis; ***D:*** Charles Reisner; ***W:*** Carl Harbaugh; ***C:*** Bert Haines; Devereaux Jennings. Natl. Film Reg. '16.

Steamboat Round the Bend 🦴🦴 ½ **1935** Snake oil salesman Dr. John Pearly (Rogers) is traveling to meet his nephew Duke (McGuire) so they can go into the riverboat business together. But Duke has been falsely convicted of murder and will hang unless Pearly and Duke's girlfriend Fleety Belle (Shirley) can find the only witness to the crime. A big steamboat race is part of the plot. The last film that Rogers shot, although "In Old Kentucky" was released after. **81m/B; DVD.** Will Rogers; Anne Shirley; John McGuire; Eugene Pallette; Berton Churchill; Stepin Fetchit; Francis Ford; Irvin S. Cobb; Roger Imhof; Hobart Bosworth; Raymond Hatton; ***D:*** John Ford; ***W:*** Lamar Trotti; Dudley Nicholas; ***C:*** George Schneiderman; ***M:*** Samuel Kaylin.

Steamboy 🦴🦴 **2005 (PG-13)** Generational conflict explodes into epic machine war above the streets of an alternate Victorian London. It all revolves around something called the steamball, a dangerous revolutionary new form of power created by a father-son pair of mad scientists (Stewart and Molina) who battle for the loyalty of a grandson (Paquin) and the proper use of their invention. Overwrought, over-thought anime spectacle with some absolutely mind-blowing visuals from the mind of "Akira" creator Otomo. Could have benefited from some wise surgical editing. Original and English language versions available. **126m/C; DVD, Blu-Ray, UMD.** ***V:*** Anne Suzuki; Masane Tsukayama; Katsuo Nakamura; Manami Konishi; Kiyoshi Kodama; Ikki Sawamura; Susumu Terajima; Anna Paquin; Alfred Molina; Patrick Stewart; Kari Wahlgren; Robin Atkin Downes; David Lee; ***D:*** Katsuhiro Otomo; ***W:*** Katsuhiro Otomo; Sadayuki Murai; ***M:*** Steve Jablonsky.

Steel 🦴 ½ **1997 (PG-13)** Metal specialist John Henry Irons (O'Neal) has designed a top-secret military weapon that falls into the hands of a street gang. Donning a suit of armor he designed, he become super hero Steel and sets out to end the reign of terror of former colleague turned super villian Burke (Nelson). Adaptation of popular DC comic keeps target audience in mind with lots of action and plenty of humor. Shaq proves once again that as an actor he's a pretty good basketball player. **97m/C; VHS, DVD.** Shaquille O'Neal; Judd Nelson; Annabeth Gish; Richard Roundtree; Irma P. Hall; Charles Napier; Kerrie Keane; Hill Harper; Thom Barry; ***D:*** Kenneth Johnson; ***W:*** Kenneth Johnson; ***C:*** Mark Irwin; ***M:*** Mervyn Warren.

Steel City 🦴🦴 **2006 (R)** Blue-collar angst and family dysfunction in a low-key drama. Alcoholic Carl (Heard) abandoned his family long ago and is presently jailed for vehicular homicide. Younger son PJ (Guiry) is trying to man up but he's scared and confused and tends to make bad choices while his repentant father offers advice during prison visits and conceals a secret. Debut feature from Jun was shot in his Alton, Illinois, hometown. **95m/C; DVD.** John Heard; Tom Guiry; America Ferrera; Clayne Crawford; James McDaniel; Laurie Metcalf; Heather McComb; Raymond J. Barry; ***D:*** Brian Jun; ***W:*** Brian Jun; ***C:*** Ryan Samul; ***M:*** Mark Geary.

The Steel Claw 🦴🦴 **1961** One-handed ex-Marine Montgomery organizes guerilla forces against the Japanese in the Philippines in WWII. Good location shooting and plenty of action. **95m/C; VHS, DVD.** George Montgomery; Charito Luna; Mario Barri; ***D:*** George Montgomery.

Steel Dawn 🦴 ½ **1987 (R)** Another "Mad Max" clone: A leather-clad warrior wields his sword over lots of presumably post-apocalyptic desert terrain. Swayze stars with his real-life wife Niemi in unfortunate follow-up to "Dirty Dancing." **90m/C; VHS, DVD.** Patrick Swayze; Lisa Niemi; Christopher Neame; Brett Hool; Brion James; Anthony Zerbe; Arnold Vosloo; ***D:*** Lance Hool; ***W:*** Doug Lefler; ***C:*** Jiri (George) Tirl; ***M:*** Brian May.

Steel Frontier 🦴 ½ **1994 (R)** Post-apocalypse actioner finds a group of survivors trying to make a new life in a town they call New Hope. But then a group of bandit soldiers take over—until a lone hero comes along to save the day. **94m/C; VHS, DVD, On Demand.** Joe Lara; Brion James; Bo Svenson; Stacie Foster; ***D:*** Paul G. Volk; Jacobsen Hart; ***W:*** Jacobsen Hart.

The Steel Helmet 🦴🦴🦴 ½ **1951** Hurriedly made Korean War drama stands as a top-notch war film. Brooding and dark, GIs don't save the world for democracy or rescue POWs; they simply do their best to survive a horrifying situation. Pointless death, confused loyalties and cynicism abound in writer-director Fuller's scathing comment on the madness of war. **84m/B; VHS, DVD.** Gene Evans; Robert Hutton; Steve Brodie; William Chun; James Edwards; Richard Loo; Harold Fong; Neyle Morrow; Sid Melton; Richard Monahan; Lynn Stalmaster; ***D:*** Samuel Fuller; ***W:*** Samuel Fuller; ***C:*** Ernest Miller; ***M:*** Paul Dunlap.

The Steel Lady 🦴🦴 **1953** Four oilmen survive a plane crash in the Sahara and stumble across a buried WWII German tank. They manage to repair the vehicle so they can drive to the safety of a French Foreign Legion fort. However, they run into trouble with a Bedouin tribe, who's certain the men have also found a fortune in stolen jewels hidden since the war. **84m/C; DVD.** Rod Cameron; Tab Hunter; John Dehner; Richard Erdman; John Abbott; Frank Puglia; Anthony Caruso; ***D:*** Ewald Andre Dupont; ***W:*** Richard Schayer; ***C:*** Floyd Crosby; ***M:*** Arthur Lange; Emil Newman.

Steel Magnolias 🦴🦴🦴 **1989 (PG)** Shelby Eatenton (Roberts) is a young woman stricken with severe diabetes who chooses to live her life to the fullest despite her bad health. Much of the action centers around a Louisiana beauty shop (run by Parton) where the women get together to discuss the goings-on of their lives. Screenplay by R. Harling, based on his partially autobiographical play. Sweet, poignant, and often hilarious, yet just as often overwrought. MacLaine is funny as a bitter divorcee; Parton is sexy and fun as the hairdresser; but Field and Roberts (as mother and daughter) go off the deep end and make it all entirely too weepy. **118m/C; VHS, DVD, Blu-Ray.** Sally Field; Dolly Parton; Shirley MacLaine; Daryl Hannah; Olympia Dukakis; Julia Roberts; Tom Skerritt; Sam Shepard; Dylan McDermott; Kevin J. O'Connor; Bill McCutcheon; Ann Wedgeworth; Janine Turner; ***D:*** Herbert Ross; ***W:*** Robert Harling; ***C:*** John A. Alonzo; ***M:*** Georges Delerue. Golden Globes '90: Support. Actress (Roberts).

Steel Magnolias 🦴🦴🦴 **2012** Lifetime remake of the 1989 women's weepie with a fine African-American cast. The story remains the same and is centered around Truvy's (Scott) hair salon where these friends gather in good times and bad. M'Lynn (Queen Latifah) worries about newlywed daughter Shelby (Condola Rashad), who's determined to have a baby despite diabetes and a kidney condition. M'Lynn gathers strength from Clairee (Phylicia Rashad), cranky Ouiser (Woodard), Truvy, and even the young Annelle (Oduye), whom Truvy has taken in. **90m/C; DVD.** Queen Latifah; Alfre Woodard; Phylicia Rashad; Jill Scott; Condola Rashad; Adepero Oduye; Tory Kittles; ***D:*** Kenny Leon; ***W:*** Sally Robinson; ***C:*** Francis Kenny; ***M:*** William Ross. **CABLE**

Steel Sharks 🦴🦴 **1997 (R)** A military coup in Iran finds chemical weapons expert Dr. Van Tasset (Livingston) kidnapped by revolutionaries. Members of an elite squad of Navy SEALs are sent to rescue him, aided by a U.S. sub. But the good guys wind up prisoners on an Iranian sub and a deadly game of underwater hide-and-seek follows. **94m/C; VHS, DVD.** Billy Dee Williams; Gary Busey; Tim Lounibos; Barry Livingston; Billy Warlock; Larry Poindexter; Tim Abell; Robert Miranda; David Roberson; Matthew St. Patrick; ***D:*** Rodney McDonald; ***W:*** Rodney McDonald; William C. Martell; ***C:*** Bryan Greenberg; ***M:*** David Lawrence. **VIDEO**

Steel Toes 🦴🦴 **2006 (R)** Jewish liberal lawyer Danny Dunkleman (Strathairn) becomes the court-appointed attorney for skinhead Michael Downey (Walker), who's confessed to murdering an East Indian immigrant in a Montreal alley. Danny is trying to find Michael a defense and make him confront what he has done, without much cooperation. Lots of jailhouse talk; gets an extra half a bone for Straithairn's compelling performance. **90m/C; DVD.** *CA* David Strathairn; Andrew W. Walker; Marina Orsini; Ivan Smith; ***D:*** David Gow; Mark Adam; ***W:*** David Gow; ***C:*** Mark Adam; ***M:*** Benoit Groulx.

The Steel Trap 🦴🦴 **1952** L.A. assistant bank manager James Osborne (Cotten) comes up with a daring heist: rob the vault during Friday afternoon business hours and then fly to Brazil, which doesn't have an extradition treaty with the U.S., before the money is discovered missing on Monday. He's successful until his beloved wife Laurie (Wright) learns why they're suddenly going on vacation and she leaves him. If James wants Laurie back, he has to return the money before Monday morning. **85m/B; DVD.** Joseph Cotten; Teresa Wright; Jonathan Hale; Aline Towne; Eddie Marr; ***D:*** Andrew L. Stone; ***W:*** Andrew L. Stone; ***C:*** Ernest Laszlo; ***M:*** Dimitri Tiomkin.

Steele Justice 🦴 **1987 (R)** A tough 'Nam vet takes on the whole Vietnamese Mafia in Southern California after his friend is murdered. One of those head-scratchers: Should I laugh, or be offended? **96m/C; VHS, Blu-Ray, Streaming.** Martin Kove; Sela Ward; Ronny Cox; Bernie Casey; Joseph Campanella; Sarah Douglas; ***D:*** Robert Boris; ***W:*** Robert Boris.

Steele's Law 🦴🦴 **1991 (R)** A loner cop is forced to take the law into his own hands in order to track down an insane international assassin. **90m/C; VHS, DVD.** Fred Williamson; Bo Svenson; Doran Ingham; Phyllis Cicero; ***D:*** Fred Williamson; ***W:*** Charles Eric Johnson; ***C:*** David Blood; ***M:*** Mike Logan.

Steelyard Blues 🦴🦴 ½ *The Final Crash* **1973 (PG)** A motley-crew comedy about a wacky gang that tries to steal an abandoned WW II airplane. Zany pranks abound. Technically flawed direction from Myerson mars a potentially hilarious story. **93m/C; DVD.** Jane Fonda; Donald Sutherland; Peter Boyle; Howard Hesseman; John Savage; Garry Goodrow; ***D:*** Alan Myerson; ***W:*** David S. Ward; ***M:*** David Shire.

Stella 🦴🦴 ½ **1955** Mercouri's film debut has her as a free-spirited bar singer who gets involved in a tragic romantic triangle with a middle-class writer and a local football hero. Melodramatic but Mercouri's earthy joie de vivre is already apparent. In Greek with English subtitles. **94m/B; VHS, DVD.** *GR* Melina Mercouri; Yiorgo Fountas; Aiekos Alexandrikis; Sophia Vembo; ***D:*** Michael Cacoyannis; ***W:*** Michael Cacoyannis; ***C:*** Costa Theodorides; ***M:*** Manos Hadjidakis.

Stella 🦴 ½ **1989 (PG-13)** Anachronistic remake update of "Stella Dallas" casts Midler as a single mother who sacrifices everything to give her daughter a better life. Barbara Stanwyck did it much better in 1937. Based on Olive Higgins Prouty's novel. **109m/C; VHS, DVD, Blu-Ray.** Bette Midler; John Goodman; Stephen Collins; Eileen Brennan; Ben Stiller; Trini Alvarado; Marsha Mason; ***D:*** John Erman; ***W:*** Robert Getchell; ***C:*** Billy Williams.

Stella Dallas 🦴🦴🦴 **1937** Uneducated Stella (Stanwyck) lets go of the daughter (Shirley) she loves when she realizes her ex-husband (Boles) can give the girl more advantages. What could be sentimental turns out believable and worthwhile under Vidor's steady hand. Stanwyck never makes a wrong step. From a 1923 novel by Olive Higgins Prouty. Remade in 1989 as "Stella," starring Bette Midler. **106m/B; VHS, DVD.** Barbara Stanwyck; Anne Shirley; John Boles; Alan Hale; Marjorie Main; Barbara O'Neil; Tim Holt; ***D:*** King Vidor; ***W:*** Sarah Y. Mason; Victor Heerman; ***C:*** Rudolph Mate; ***M:*** Alfred Newman.

Stella Days 🦴🦴 ½ **2012** Subdued drama about faith set in 1950s rural Ireland and based on Michael Doorley's memoir. Father Daniel Barry (Sheen) brings his flock together to raise money to build a local cinema rather than an unnecessary new church. His modernistic ways are at odds with the oppressive control both the church and the local prudes want to maintain on the community's morals. It leads to Father Barry having a crisis of conscience over what's best for both himself and his parishioners. **90m/C; DVD.** *IR* Martin Sheen; Stephen Rea; Trystan Ravelle; Marcella Plunkett; ***D:*** Thaddeus O'Sullivan; ***W:*** Antoine O'Flatharta; ***C:*** John Christian Roselund; ***M:*** Nicholas Hooper.

Stella Does Tricks 🦴🦴 **1996** Stella (Macdonald) is a teen runaway, working as a prostitute in London for pimp Mr. Peters (Bolam). She was abused by her dad (Stewart) and has revenge fantasies—some of which she takes out on clients, which leads to punishment by her boss. She briefly gets free of Peters and gets a legit job, but Stella has also become involved with junkie Eddie (Matheson) and his drug needs have him betraying Stella. No Cinderella stories here—Stella's life is bleak and violent, with Macdonald giving a powerhouse performance. **97m/C; VHS, DVD.** *GB* Kelly Macdonald; James Bolam; Ewan Stewart; Hans Matheson; Andy Serkis; Paul Chahidi; ***D:*** Coky Giedroyc; ***W:*** A.L. Kennedy; ***C:*** Barry Ackroyd; ***M:*** Nick Bicat.

Stella Maris 🦴🦴🦴 **1918** Pickford inspiringly plays two difficult roles. As Stella Maris, she's a wealthy orphaned cripple who's in love with the married John Risca (Tearle), whose wife, Louise (Ankewich), is an abusive alcoholic. John eventually leaves her and Louise takes out her anger on homely servant Unity Blake (Pickford's second role). When Unity is eventually rescued by John, she also falls in love with him. Brimming with the tragic consequences of love. **100m/B; Silent; VHS, DVD.** Mary Pickford; Conway Tearle; Camille Ankewich; Ida Waterman; Herbert Standing; ***D:*** Marshall Neilan; ***W:*** Frances Marion; ***C:*** Walter Stradling.

The Stendahl Syndrome 🦴🦴 *La Sindrome di Stendhal* **1995** Psycho serial-killer thriller about a Rome police detective, Anna (Argento), who has an extreme hallucinatory reaction to artwork (the title syndrome). While visiting an art gallery, she collapses and is assisted by Alfredo (Kretschmann), who turns out to be the very rapist-killer whom she's hunting. Anna escapes from him once (after being tortured) but is captured again. However, she manages to fight back in ways squeamish viewers may want to avoid watching. Inspired by Graziella Magherini's novel "La Sindrome di Stendhal." **118m/C; VHS, DVD, Blu-Ray.** *IT* Asia Argento; Thomas Kretschmann; Marco Leonardi; Luigi Diberti; Paolo Bonacelli; John Quentin; ***D:*** Dario Argento; ***W:*** Dario Argento; ***C:*** Giuseppe Rotunno; ***M:*** Ennio Morricone.

Step 1/2 **2017 (PG)** A meaningful, inspirational documentary of the Lethal Ladies step team at the Baltimore Leadership School for Young Women. The film follows three members of the charter school's first graduating class as they face challenges in their personal, family, and academic lives. Though step is part of their development, the school's goal is to get each senior into college, ensure that any scholastic and financial needs are met, and overcome all barriers to enrollment. Filmed in Baltimore in 2015, the Freddie Gray case and the Black Lives Matter movement serve as a backdrop to the film's deft, moving exploration of race-related issues. **84m/C; DVD.** ***D:*** Amanda Lipitz; ***C:*** Casey Regan; ***M:*** Laura Karpman; Raphael Saadiq.

Step Brothers **2008 (R)** When Brennan's (Ferrell) mom Nancy (Steenburgen) and Dale's (Reilly) dad Robert (Jenkins) get married, the 40ish living-at-home losers find themselves sharing a bedroom, making for some serious sibling rivalry until the men/boys bond over their shared John Stamos crushes and their contempt for Brennan's brother Derek (Scott), an egotistical corporate suit. Ferrell and Reilly masterfully channel their inner brats while maxing out their knack for getting laughs from gross-out gags (like it or not) all the way up to the happy sappy ending. **95m/C; Blu-Ray, UMD, On Demand.** Will Ferrell; John C. Reilly; Mary Steenburgen; Richard Jenkins; Adam Scott; Kathryn Hahn; Andrea Savage; ***D:*** Adam McKay; ***W:*** Will Ferrell; Adam McKay; ***C:*** Oliver Wood; ***M:*** Jon Brion.

Step Dogs **2013** This family comedy explores what happens when a couple forms a blended dog family. Cassie (Wilson) is a small, pampered city dog, while Meatball (Tockar) has spent his life in the country living a carefree life. After their owners marry, the humans, their children, and the dogs move to the rural north. Though Cassie and Meatball struggle to get along, they come together when two, not-so-bright thieves break into their new home and put their new family at risk. Can opposites appreciate each other after all? **82m/C; DVD, Blu-Ray, Streaming, Download.** Lee Tockar; Brittney Wilson; Joris Jarsky; Ryan Belleville; Emilie Ullerup; ***D:*** Geoff Anderson; ***W:*** Willem Wennekers; ***C:*** Mark Dobrescu; ***M:*** Ben Lumsden. **VIDEO**

Step Into Liquid **2003** Brown is the son of surf-documentary pioneer Bruce "Endless Summer" Brown, so he knows his way around visuals. Brown takes on the positive energy of surfing around the world with the sport's top competitors, including Laird Hamilton, Kelly Slater, and Taj Burrow, as well as a number of ordinary folks who just like to catch the wave. **87m/C; DVD, Blu-Ray.** ***Nar:*** Dana Brown; ***D:*** Dana Brown; ***W:*** Dana Brown; ***C:*** John-Paul Beeghly; ***M:*** Richard Gibbs.

Step Lively 1/2 **1944** A convoluted plot doesn't slow down the enjoyment of this musical comedy. Naive Glen (Sinatra) writes a dramatic play and sends it—along with his life savings—to slick NY producer Miller (Murphy). When he shows up to see how things are progressing, Glen learns that Miller has used his dough to help finance a new musical, so Miller has showgirl Christine (DeHaven) keep Glen occupied. But the show is in trouble without a male lead—and then Miller hears Glen sing. And the rest is showbiz, folks. **88m/B; DVD.** Frank Sinatra; George Murphy; Adolphe Menjou; Walter Slezak; Anne Jeffreys; Eugene Pallette; Gloria DeHaven; ***D:*** Tim Whelan; ***W:*** Peter Milne; Warren Duff; ***C:*** Robert De Grasse.

A Step Out of Line **1971** CBS TV movie. Three aging, debt-ridden Korean War buddies plan a bank heist to ease their financial woes. However, things go wrong (naturally) and they wind up in worse trouble. **96m/C; DVD.** Peter Falk; Peter Lawford; Vic Morrow; John Randolph; JoAnn Pflug; Tom Bosley; Lynn Carlin; ***D:*** Bernard McEveety; ***W:*** S.S. Schweitzer; ***C:*** James A. Crabe; ***M:*** Jerry Goldsmith. **TV**

Step Up 1/2 **2006 (PG-13)** Tyler Gage (Tatum) is from the wrong side of the Baltimore line. He's assigned to do community service at the elite Maryland School of the Arts after he helps trash their auditorium. Beautiful ballet dancer Nora (Dewan) needs a partner for an important recital and, with her encouragement, Ty discovers his inner Fred Astaire. Dance sequences are excellent, and the cast is appropriately beautiful, but you've seen the rest of the plot before, especially if you've seen writer Adler's "Save the Last Dance." **98m/C; DVD, Blu-Ray.** Channing Tatum; Rachel Griffiths; Damaine Radcliff; Jenna Dewan; Dwight "Heavy D" Myers; De'Shawn Washington; Josh Henderson; Deirdre Lovejoy; ***D:*** Anne Fletcher; ***W:*** Duane Adler; Melissa Rosenberg; ***C:*** Michael Seresin; ***M:*** Aaron Zigman.

Step Up 3D 1/2 **2010 (PG-13)** In this third franchise effort, a tight-knit group of Brooklyn street dancers team up with college freshmen Moose and Camille in a high-stakes showdown against the best breakdancers worldwide. Elaborate dance sequences actually make good use of 3D technology but there's nothing new about the tired plot. **106m/C; Blu-Ray.** Adam G. Sevani; Rick Malambri; Sharni Vinson; Harry Shum, Jr.; Ally Maki; Alyson Stoner; Joe Slaughter; ***D:*** Jon M. Chu; ***W:*** Amy Andelson; Emily Meyer; ***C:*** Ken Seng; ***M:*** Bear McCreary.

Step Up: All In **2014 (PG-13)** The fifth film in the Step Up franchise proves nothing other than that this series just won't die as long as they keep producing eye-popping 3D dance sequences. The plots are entirely disposable. All that matters is if the beat kicks in and the athletic specimens on screen get their dance on at regular intervals. This one actually brings back more characters from the previous films for a dance battle in Las Vegas called The Vortex. It'd almost be better if all dialogue and plot were removed. **112m/C; DVD, Blu-Ray.** Ryan Guzman; Briana Evigan; Adam G. Sevani; Alyson Stoner; ***D:*** Trish Sie; ***W:*** John Swetnam; ***C:*** Brian Pearson; ***M:*** Jeff Cardoni.

Step Up Revolution 1/2 *Step Up 4* **2012 (PG-13)** Fourth in the formula-driven dance franchise series. Emily (McCormick) comes to Miami to dance professionally and falls for Sean (Guzman), who leads a dance flash mob crew that's angling for a major sponsorship. Emily's dad is, of course, a greedy businessman whose latest development project will destroy Sean's neighborhood. **99m/C; DVD, Blu-Ray, Streaming.** Ryan Guzman; Stephen Boss; Megan Boone; Kathryn McCormick; Chadd Smith; ***D:*** Scott Speer; ***W:*** Duane Adler; Amanda Brody; ***C:*** Karsten Gopinath; ***M:*** Aaron Zigman.

Step Up 2 the Streets **2008 (PG-13)** Andie (Evigan) is kicked out of her crew of street dancers when she's admitted to the prestigious Maryland School of the Arts. She responds by starting her own crew with classmate Chase and demands a chance to compete in a dance contest at a local club. Weak plot is undercut further by movie's fumbling of the race and class issues it raises with its fake-inspirational message, which seems to be, "We're all equal when we dance, especially the white kids who go to the nice high school." **98m/C; DVD, Blu-Ray.** Briana Evigan; Robert Hoffman; Will(iam) Kemp; Sonja Sohn; Channing Tatum; Adam G. Sevani; Cassie Ventura; ***D:*** Jon M. Chu; ***W:*** Toni Johnson; Karen Barna; ***C:*** Max Malkin; ***M:*** Aaron Zigman.

The Stepdaughter 1/2 **2000 (R)** After years of abuse in foster homes, Susan (Roth) wants to strike back at the birth mother who abandoned her. She tracks down the now happily married woman (Pickett), gets a job on the ranch where she lives, and plans her next deadly move. **92m/C; VHS, DVD.** Andrea Roth; Lisa Dean Ryan; Jaimz Woolvett; Cindy Pickett; Gary Hudson; Gil Gerard; Matt Farnsworth; Lee Dawson; ***D:*** Peter Paul Liapis; ***W:*** Richard Dana; ***C:*** Maximo Munzi. **VIDEO**

The Stepfather 1/2 **2009 (PG-13)** Lazy, clumsy remake of the 1987 flick (based on a screenplay by Donald E. Westlake) that starred Terry O'Quinn in the title role. This time it's Walsh as the psycho whose new wife (Ward) and stepsons don't live up to his perfect family ideals. So he decides to kill them and try again even as troubled teenager Michael (Badgley) gets very suspicious. Walsh plays his character as a smug creep no one with any brains would trust, so the premise is a loser from the beginning. However, Badgley and Heard (as his girlfriend) do provide eye candy with Heard frequently shown scantily clad. **101m/C; DVD, Blu-Ray.** Dylan Walsh; Sela Ward; Penn Badgley; Amber Heard; Jon Tenney; Sherry Stringfield; Braeden Lemasters; Paige Turco; ***D:*** Nelson McCormick; ***W:*** J.S. Cardone; ***C:*** Patrick Cady; ***M:*** Charlie Clouser.

The Stepfather **1987 (R)** Creepy thriller about a seemingly ordinary stepfather who is actually a homicidal maniac searching for the "perfect family." An independently produced sleeper tightly directed and well written. Followed by two inferior sequels. **89m/C; VHS, DVD, Blu-Ray.** Terry O'Quinn; Shelley Hack; Jill Schoelen; Stephen Shellen; Charles Lanyer; Stephen E. Miller; ***D:*** Joseph Ruben; ***W:*** Donald E. Westlake; ***C:*** John Lindley; ***M:*** Patrick Moraz.

Stepfather 2: Make Room for Daddy 1/2 **1989 (R)** A poor sequel to the suspenseful sleeper, wherein the psychotic family man escapes from an asylum and woos another suburban family, murdering anyone who may suspect his true identity. Followed by yet another sequel. **93m/C; VHS, DVD; Open Captioned.** Terry O'Quinn; Meg Foster; Caroline Williams; Jonathan Brandis; Henry Brown; Mitchell Laurance; ***D:*** Jeff Burr; ***W:*** John P. Auerbach; ***C:*** Jacek Laskus.

Stepfather 3: Father's Day **1992 (R)** The father from Hell is back! Escaping from the loony bin with a surgically altered face, the stepfather settles in a small town and gets a job at a nursery (the plant kind, not the children kind). His favorite gardening tool fast becomes the mulch machine, and soon locals are fertilizing the garden. Well below the original, but it may please fans of this genre. **110m/C; VHS, DVD, Streaming.** Robert Wightman; Priscilla Barnes; Season Hubley; ***D:*** Guy Magar; ***C:*** Alan Caso.

The Stepford Wives **1975** Joanna (Ross) and husband Walter (Masterson) move from bustling Manhattan to the supposedly idyllic Connecticut town of Stepford. Joanna gets suspicious when she notices all the wives are strangely content and subservient and when she meets fellow newcomer, Bobby (Prentiss), they decide to investigate. Creepy adaptation of the Ira Levin novel. **115m/C; VHS, DVD.** Katharine Ross; Paula Prentiss; Peter Masterson; Nanette Newman; Patrick O'Neal; Tina Louise; Dee Wallace; William Prince; Mary Stuart Masterson; Carol Rossen; ***D:*** Bryan Forbes; ***W:*** William Goldman; ***C:*** Owen Roizman; ***M:*** Michael Small.

The Stepford Wives 1/2 **2004 (PG-13)** Remake of the spooky 70's classic. Joanna Eberhart (Kidman) is a successful television network executive fired after a reality show disaster. Joanna, her husband Walter (Broderick) and their family move to the seemingly perfect Connecticut town of Stepford. Strangely enough, the impeccably perfect bombshell women of Stepford have no other interests than housecleaning and making their rather nerdy-looking husbands happy. Trades eerie suspense of the original for campy comedy. While there are some well placed barbs and one-liners, plot holds no surprises and loses the satirical edge of the source material. Walken, as the community leader who holds the secret to Stepford, and Midler as a fellow outsider, do well in their respective roles. **93m/C; DVD.** Nicole Kidman; Matthew Broderick; Christopher Walken; Glenn Close; Bette Midler; Jon Lovitz; Roger Bart; David Marshall Grant; Faith Hill; ***D:*** Frank Oz; ***W:*** Paul Rudnick; ***C:*** Rob Hahn; ***M:*** David Arnold.

Stephanie Daley **2006 (R)** Disturbing talky drama with flashbacks depicting what happened to a pregnant teen. 16-year-old Stephanie (Tamblyn) gives birth on a school ski trip and is brought up on criminal charges when the baby is found dead. She claims not to have known she was pregnant and that the infant was stillborn. Forensic psychologist Lydie Crane (Swinton) is called in to examine Stephanie, but the situation may be too close for Lydie to be objective. She is pregnant again after suffering a stillbirth herself and both Lydie and Stephanie have a lot of unresolved feelings. Strong performances by both leads in a story with no easy answers. **91m/C; DVD.** Amber Tamblyn; Tilda Swinton; Timothy Hutton; Denis O'Hare; Jim Gaffigan; Deirdre O'Connell; Melissa Leo; Halley Feiffer; Kel O'Neill; ***D:*** Hilary Brougher; ***W:*** Hilary Brougher; ***C:*** David Rush Morrison; ***M:*** David Mansfield.

Stephen King's Golden Years 1/2 *Golden Years* **1991** Stephen King creates a chilling vision of scientific progress gone awry in this shocking techno-thriller. After being accidentally exposed to exotic chemicals in a lab explosion, an aging janitor undergoes an extraordinary transformation and the government will sacrifice anything to learn more about it. **232m/C; VHS, DVD.** Keith Szarabajka; Frances Sternhagen; Ed Lauter; R.D. Call; Stephen King; Felicity Huffman; Stephen (Steve) Root; ***D:*** Kenneth Fink; Stephen Tolkin; Allen Coulter; Michael G. Gerrick; ***W:*** Stephen King; Josef Anderson. **TV**

Stephen King's It 1/2 **1990** A group of small town children, who were terrorized by an evil force in their youth, are traumatized again some 30 years later, when they learn a new series of child murders occurred in their Eastern home town. The adults, who now all have successful and diverse careers, must come to terms with the terrible secret they share, as "IT" has returned to wreak havoc in their New England home town. Based on horror master King's bestselling novel of the same name. **193m/C; VHS, DVD, Blu-Ray.** Tim Reid; Richard Thomas; John Ritter; Annette O'Toole; Richard Masur; Dennis Christopher; Harry Anderson; Olivia Hussey; Tim Curry; Jonathan Brandis; Michael Cole; ***D:*** Tommy Lee Wallace; ***W:*** Stephen King; ***M:*** Richard Bellis. **TV**

Stephen King's Rose Red *Rose Red* **2002 (PG-13)** The fictional memoir "The Diary of Ellen Rimbauer" was released shortly before the miniseries aired, rather than the movie being based on an already successful novel. The "Diary's" editor, Dr. Joyce Reardon (Travis), is a college professor looking for the supernatural inside Rose Red, a decaying mansion known for its strange history. She gathers together various paranormals, including autistic teenager Annie (Brown) who has strong telekinetic powers. The house begins to feed off Annie's energy and all hell breaks loose. Last role for Dukes (as Joyce's nemesis Professor Miller) who died during filming. **254m/C; VHS, DVD.** Nancy Travis; Kimberly J. Brown; Matt Keeslar; David Dukes; Julian Sands; Judith Ivey; Melanie Lynskey; Matt Ross; Kevin Tighe; Julia Campbell; Jimmi Simpson; ***D:*** Craig R. Baxley; ***W:*** Stephen King; ***C:*** David Connell; ***M:*** Gary Chang. **TV**

Stephen King's The Langoliers 1/2 *The Langoliers* **1995 (PG-13)** Bloated variation of "Ten Little Indians" finds 10 airline passengers dozing off on their L.A.-to-Boston flight and awakening to find their fellow passengers and the crew have vanished. Of course, one passenger (Morse) is a pilot and he gets them to Bangor, Maine (where the miniseries was filmed), only to discover the airport is deserted and very weird things are going on. Oh yeah, the "langoliers" look like flying cannonballs with piranha teeth and have something to do with neurotic Pinchot's character. Not that you'll care much. **180m/C; VHS, DVD.** David Morse; Bronson Pinchot; Patricia Wettig; Dean Stockwell; Kate Maberly; Christopher Collet; Kimber Riddle; Mark Lindsay Chapman; Frankie Faison; Baxter Harris; Stephen King; Tom Holland; ***D:*** Tom Holland; ***W:*** Tom Holland; ***C:*** Paul Maibaum; ***M:*** Vladimir Horunzhy. **TV**

Stephen King's The Night Flier *The Night Flier* **1996 (R)** Portrays blood-sucking beings that prey upon the weakness of mortal men in order to survive. And besides tabloid journalists, there's vampires in it, too! Richard Dees (Ferrer) is a reporter/photographer for a National Enquirer-like paper who is not above staging lurid photos to grab Page One. His editor pits him in a contest with rookie paparazzo Katherine (Entwistle) for a story about a murderer who wears a black cape and tricorn hat, flies into small airports in a sinister black plane and drains his victims' blood. Dees follows the killer's trail in his own plane, stopping to ruthlessly grill survivors and doctor up a few pictures. Genuinely spooky showdown will leave only one monster standing. Who is it? Inquiring minds want to know. **97m/C; VHS, DVD.** Michael H. Moss; Miguel Ferrer; Julie Entwisle; Dan Monahan; John Bennes; Beverly Skinner; Rob Wilds; Richard Olsen; Elizabeth McCormick; ***D:*** Mark Pavia; ***W:*** Mark Pavia; Jack O'Donnell; ***C:*** David Connell; ***M:*** Brian Keane. **CABLE**

Stephen King's The Stand 1/2 *The Stand* **1994** Ghoulish made for TV adaptation of the King novel about a superflu/plague that decimates the U.S. population. The few survivors are soon divided into two camps—those dreaming of a godly old black woman known as Mother Abigail and others of the satanic Randall Flagg, the Walkin' Dude. Boulder, Colorado (where King was living when he wrote the novel) serves as headquarters for Abigail's brood while Las Vegas (where else) is Flagg territory. It all comes down to a battle of good vs. evil, with the future of mankind at stake. Religious allegory can get tedious but it's a varied cast with some scenes not for those with queasy stomachs. On four cassettes. **360m/C; VHS, DVD, Blu-Ray.** Jamey Sheridan; Ruby Dee; Gary Sinise; Molly Ringwald; Miguel Ferrer; Laura San Giacomo; Rob Lowe; Adam Storke; Matt Frewer; Corin "Corky" Nemec; Ray Walston; Bill Fagerbakke; Ossie Davis; Shawnee Smith; Rick Aviles; John (Joe Bob Briggs) Bloom; Michael (Mike) Lookinland; Ed Harris; Kathy Bates; Kareem Abdul-Jabbar; Stephen King; Sam Raimi; ***D:*** Mick Garris; ***W:*** Stephen King; ***C:*** Edward Pei; ***M:*** W.G. Snuffy Walden. **TV**

Stephen King's The Storm of the Century 1/2 *Storm of the Century* **1999 (PG-13)** Little Tall Island, Maine, is under siege—and not just from the most ferocious storm the island has seen in years. No, there's madness and murder afoot in the form of demonic stranger Andre Linoge (Feore). He seems to know everyone's secrets but what he wants is anybody's guess. Now it's up to amiable constable Michael Anderson (Daly) to control the rising hysteria and come up with a solution. **247m/C; VHS, DVD.** Colm Feore; Timothy Daly; Debrah Farentino; Casey Siemaszko; Jeffrey DeMunn; Richard Blackburn; ***D:*** Craig R. Baxley; ***W:*** Stephen King; ***C:*** David Connell; ***M:*** Gary Chang. **TV**

Stephen King's The Tommyknockers 1/2 *The Tommyknockers* **1993 (R)** Another of King's creepy tales, adapted for TV. Bobbi (Helgenberger) and Gard (Smits) live in the small town of Haven, Maine (actually filmed on New Zealand's North Island). She's an aspiring writer; he's a fading poet with a drinking problem and a metal plate in his head (this is important). Walking in the woods, Bobbi stumbles over a long-buried spaceship which begins to take possession of the townspeople—their eyes shine green, their teeth fall out, and they act out their (often violent) fantasies—all but Gard. The whole thing's more silly than scary. The title comes from an old children's rhyme. **120m/C; VHS, DVD.** Jimmy Smits; Marg Helgenberger; Joanna Cassidy; E.G. Marshall; Traci Lords; John Ashton; Allyce Beasley; Cliff DeYoung; Robert Carradine; Leon Woods; Paul McIver; ***D:*** John Power; ***W:*** Lawrence D. Cohen; ***M:*** Christopher Franke. **TV**

Stephen King's Thinner *Thinner* **1996 (R)** Holland takes all the meat out of this supernatural horror by turning it into a formulaic pursuit-of-justice bore. Porcine lawyer Billy Halleck (Burke) accidentally hits a gypsy with his car and is cursed with a case of perpetual weight loss. Conveniently for Billy, the client he has just gotten an acquittal for is local mobster Richie "The Hammer" Ginelli (Mantegna) who is now determined to save him. Ponderous plot and lackluster-looking latex is redeemed by decent acting. King makes his requisite cameo as Dr. Bangor (get it, Maine?) Originally published in 1984 under King's pseudonym Richard Bachman. **92m/C; DVD, Blu-Ray.** Robert John Burke; Joe Mantegna; Lucinda Jenney; Michael Constantine; Kari Wuhrer; John Horton; Sam Freed; Daniel von Bargen; Elizabeth Franz; Joy Lentz; Jeff Ware; ***Cameo(s):*** Stephen King; ***D:*** Tom Holland; ***W:*** Michael McDowell; Tom Holland; ***C:*** Kees Van Oostrum; ***M:*** Daniel Licht.

Stepmom **1998 (PG-13)** The opening scenes make it look like a comedic catfight-filled ride. Harris is a divorced dad with two kids, a supermom ex-wife (Sarandon), and a glamorous new girlfriend (Roberts), whose career seems more important than the kids. Jibes and glares are traded by the two women until mom is stricken with some form of untreatable terminal cancer. This changes the story from broad comedy to emotional drama as Sarandon must train the younger woman to be the new mom. Columbus seems comfortable with the shift, and manages to keep everything upbeat. The script, penned by five writers, becomes more cliched as the film goes on, but stays just this side of chick-flick. **124m/C; VHS, DVD, Blu-Ray.** Julia Roberts; Susan Sarandon; Ed Harris; Jena Malone; Liam Aiken; Lynn Whitfield; Darrell Larson; Mary Louise Wilson; ***D:*** Chris Columbus; ***W:*** Jessie Nelson; Steven Rogers; Ronald Bass; Gigi Levangie; Karen Leigh Hopkins; ***C:*** Donald McAlpine; ***M:*** John Williams. Natl. Bd. of Review '98: Support. Actor (Harris).

Stepmonster 1/2 **1992 (PG-13)** A boy tries to convince his father that his new stepmother is a monster—literally. Doesn't work any better than "My Stepmother Is an Alien." **85m/C; VHS, DVD.** Alan Thicke; Robin Riker; Corey Feldman; John Astin; Ami Dolenz; George Gaynes; ***D:*** Jeremy Stanford.

The Stepmother 1/2 **1971** Yet another Hitchcock ripoff story involving an evil stepmother. Rey is passable, but there's not much else to recommend this dredge. **100m/C; VHS, DVD.** Alejandro Rey; John Anderson; Katherine Justice; John David Garfield; Marlene Schmidt; Claudia Jennings; Larry Linville; ***D:*** Howard (Hikmet) Avedis.

Steppenwolf 1/2 **1974 (PG)** Static, enigmatic film version of the famous Herman Hesse novel about a brooding writer searching for meaning and self-worth. Interesting to watch, but the offbeat novel doesn't translate to the screen; leaves you flat. **105m/C; VHS, DVD.** *SI* Max von Sydow; Dominique Sanda; Pierre Clementi; Carla Romanelli; Roy Bosier; ***D:*** Fred Haines; ***W:*** Fred Haines; ***C:*** Tomislav Pinter; ***M:*** George Gruntz.

Stepping Out **1931** Naughty Pre-Code marital comedy.Sally and Eve set out on vacation hoping their busy Hollywood movie producer husbands will miss them. Instead, Tom and Tubby invite a couple of starlets over to 'audition.' Their wives unexpectedly catch them, and the women make plans to get even. **73m/B; DVD.** Charlotte Greenwood; Leila Hyams; Reginald Denny; Harry Stubbs; Cliff Edwards; Kane Richmond; Lilian Bond; Merna Kennedy; ***D:*** Charles Reisner; ***W:*** Elmer Harris; Robert Hopkins; ***C:*** Leonard Smith.

Stepsisters **WOOF!** *Hands of Blood; Texas Hill Killings* **1974** Murderous double-crosses occur among a pilot, his wife, and her sister. **75m/C; VHS, DVD.** Hal Fletcher; Sharyn Talbert; Bond Gideon; ***D:*** Perry Tong; ***W:*** Perry Tong; ***M:*** Sandy Pinkard.

The Sterile Cuckoo *Pookie* **1969 (PG)** An aggressive co-ed pursues a shy freshman who seems to embody her romantic ideal. Minnelli's performance is outstanding; Burton as the naive young man is also fine. Pakula's splendid first directing job. **108m/C; DVD, Blu-Ray.** Liza Minnelli; Wendell Burton; Tim McIntire; ***D:*** Alan J. Pakula; ***W:*** Alvin Sargent; ***C:*** Milton Krasner.

Steve Jobs **2015 (R)** Michael Fassbender is riveting as the title character in Aaron Sorkin's adaptation of Walter Isaacson's book, directed with trademark flair by Oscar-winner Danny Boyle. Sorkin brings all of his typical wit to this story of a man driven to succeed who fails so many of those around him, including his own daughter. The script is cleverly divided into three acts, all of which center around the unveiling of a key product by Jobs' Apple. So, most of the film takes place behind the scenes, detailing its characters as they worry and work to keep Jobs happy. The whole cast shines but it's Fassbender's movie and he nails it. **122m/C; DVD, Blu-Ray, Streaming.** Michael Fassbender; Seth Rogen; Kate Winslet; Sarah Snook; Jeff Daniels; ***D:*** Danny Boyle; ***W:*** Aaron Sorkin; ***C:*** Alwin Kuchler; ***M:*** Daniel Pemberton. British Acad. '15: Actress--Supporting (Winslet); Golden Globes '16: Actor--Supporting (Winslet), Screenplay.

Steve Jobs: The Man in the Machine 1/2 **2015 (R)** Hard-working documentarian Gibney pulls down the curtain around The Wizard of Apple in this informative and engaging documentary about a mysterious man who has been made into an icon. Gibney starts from an interesting piace—why did the world mourn so much when Jobs died? What did he tap into in the international consciousness? He then pulls back to reveal the man behind the genius image, one who was notoriously hard to work with and reportedly abandoned his own family in the pursuit of financial and technological gain. The doc is sometimes a bit too much like a TV special instead of a film but Gibney keeps it moving. **128m/C; DVD, Blu-Ray.** ***D:*** Alex Gibney; ***C:*** Samuel Painter; Yutaka Yamazaki; ***M:*** Will Bates.

Steve Martini's The Judge 1/2 *The Judge* **2001** Notorious Baltimore judge Armando Acosti (Olmos) is arrested for soliciting a hooker who's actually an undercover cop. When the woman is murdered, Acosti is the prime suspect. He wants defense attorney Paul Madriani (Noth) to take his case but Paul despises the judge. Still, the case is a challenge, especially since it involves a hostile client, police corruption, and threats on his own life. **180m/C; DVD.** Edward James Olmos; Chris Noth; Lolita Davidovich; Charles Durning; Sonia Braga; John Terry; Heidi Mark; Mark Blum; Peter MacNeill; ***D:*** Mick Garris; ***W:*** Christopher Lofton; ***C:*** Edward Pei; ***M:*** Nicholas Pike. **TV**

Steve Martini's Undue Influence 1/2 *Undue Influence* **1996** Widowed defense lawyer Paul Madriani (Dennehy) is struggling to care for his daughter as well as working with his sister-in-law Laurel (Richardson) on a bitter custody dispute with her ex-husband Jack (Masur) over their teenage son. After Jack's new wife Melanie is murdered, Laurel is arrested. As Paul investigates, his life is threatened, and he runs afoul of the witness protection program, a federal corruption case, and a secret Laurel is keeping. **180m/C; DVD.** Brian Dennehy; Patricia Richardson; Jean Smart; Alan Rosenberg; Richard Masur; Allison Mackie; Eric Michael Cole; Joe Grifasi; Donna Goodhand; ***D:*** Bruce Pittman; ***W:*** Philip Rosenberg; ***C:*** Michael Storey; ***M:*** Jeff Beal. **TV**

Stick 1/2 **1985 (R)** Ex-con Stick (Reynolds, directing himself) wants to start a new life for himself in Miami. Lots of drug dealers and guns don't help the interest level in this dull underworld tale. Based upon the Elmore Leonard novel. **109m/C; VHS, DVD, Blu-Ray.** Burt Reynolds; Candice Bergen; George Segal; Charles Durning; Dar Robinson; ***D:*** Burt Reynolds; ***W:*** Elmore Leonard; ***M:*** Steve Dorff.

Stick It **2006 (PG-13)** Teenager Haley (Peregrym) walked away from a promising gymnastics career and into trouble. Thanks to her latest run-in with the law, Haley is sentenced to attend a gymnastics academy run by gruff coach Burt Vickerman (Bridges). The other girls dislike her attitude, but training and competition bring them closer as Haley foments rebellion against the sport's conformity and nitpicky rules. Writer/director Bendinger did the similarly girl-powered cheerleading comedy "Bring It On." **105m/C; DVD.** Missy Peregrym; Jeff Bridges; Vanessa Lengies; John Patrick Amedori; Nikki SooHoo; Maddy Curley; Kellan Lutz; Svetlana Efremova; Mio Dzakula; Jon(athan) Gries; Gia Carides; Polly Holliday; Julie Warner; John Kapelos; Tarah Paige; ***Cameo(s):*** Bart Conner; ***D:*** Jessica Bendinger; ***W:*** Jessica Bendinger; ***C:*** Daryn Okada; ***M:*** Mike Simpson.

Stickmen 1/2 **2001** Bar owner Dave talks three regulars into entering a pool tournament to get him out of debt. The three pals are more than willing, but their relationship problems keep popping up. Not especially original concept is helped by the chemistry of the buddies and some amusingly quirky subplots. **94m/C; VHS, DVD.** *NZ* Paolo Rotondo; Robbie Magasiva; Scott Wills; Anne Nordhaus; John Leigh; Simone Kessell; Emma Nooyen; Luann Gordon; Kirk Torrance; ***D:*** Hamish Rothwell; ***W:*** Nick Ward; ***C:*** Nigel Bluck.

Sticks **1998 (R)** Who knew cigars could cause so much trouble? Lenny (Brancato) discovers that an illicit shipment of Cuban cigars, the special private label of Castro himself, have been stolen. Maria (Machado) wants to swap the cigars for weapons to help liberate Cuba while her boyfriend Mark (Brunsmann) just wants some cold hard cash by selling the merchandise to a private Hollywood club frequented by high rollers. And Lenny sees a chance to make his own score. Too bad the mob and the feds have their own ideas. **94m/C; VHS, DVD.** Lillo Brancato; Leo Rossi; Justina Machado; Keith Brunsmann; ***D:*** Brett Mayer; ***W:*** Brett Mayer; ***C:*** Nils Erickson; ***M:*** Bill Elliott. **VIDEO**

Sticks and Stones 1/2 **2008 (PG)** During a visit to Canada shortly after the start of the Iraq War, a youth hockey team from Boston is booed by anti-war protestors. Appalled by such behavior, the coach of the opposing team organizes a rematch to make amends and demonstrate good sportsmanship. **90m/C; DVD.** *CA* David Sutcliffe; Alexander De Jordy; Daniel Magder; John Robinson; Richard Fitzpatrick; Debra McCabe; ***D:*** George Mihalka; ***W:*** Sharon Buckingham; Andrew Wreggitt; ***C:*** Daniel Vincelette. **TV**

The Stickup **2001 (R)** Burned-out cop Parker (Spader) travels to a small resort town and promptly gets involved with the wrong woman (Stefanson), a bank robbery, and the feds. This one is trickier than it seems at first. **97m/C; VHS, DVD.** James Spader; Leslie Stefanson; David Keith; John Livingston; Robert Miano; Alf Humphreys; ***D:*** Rowdy Herrington; ***W:*** Rowdy Herrington; ***C:*** Chris Manley; ***M:*** David Kitay. **VIDEO**

Sticky Fingers **1988 (PG-13)** Two female musicians, asked to watch nearly a million bucks in drug money, go on a mega shopping spree. Completely incredible, unlikeable and mean-spirited attempt at zany comedy. **89m/C; VHS, Streaming; Open Captioned.** Melanie Mayron; Helen Slater; Eileen Brennan; Carol Kane; Christopher Guest; Danitra Vance; Gwen Welles; Stephen McHattie; Shirley Stoler; ***D:*** Catlin Adams; ***W:*** Melanie Mayron; Catlin Adams; ***C:*** Gary Thieltges; ***M:*** Gary Chang.

The Sticky Fingers of Time **1997** New York writer Tucker (Matthews) is not having your average day. She goes out for coffee in 1953 and winds up in 1997 (thanks to some kind of atom-bomb mutation in her DNA). Turns out she's not the only time traveller, according to fellow freak, Isaac (Urbaniak). In fact, Isaac was responsible for bringing Tucker into the future so she wouldn't be murdered. Tucker (who's a pulp novelist) takes everything that happens with chain-smoking aplomb. **81m/B; VHS, DVD.** Terumi Matthews; James Urbaniak; Belinda Becker; Nicole Zaray; Samantha Buck; ***D:*** Hilary Brougher; ***W:*** Hilary Brougher; ***C:*** Ethan Mass; ***M:*** Miki Navazio.

Stiff Upper Lips 1/2 **1996** Spoof of all the upper-crusty British costume dramas replete with sexual innuendoes and enlightening travel to hot climes. Twitish Edward (West) tries to pair off best chum Cedric (Portal) with his virgin sister, Emily (Cates). Only Emily prefers hearty servant, George (Pertwee). Snooty Aunt Agnes (Scales) decides everyone should take a restorative trip to Italy and later to India, where Aunt Agnes herself is subjected to a leering tea-planter, Horace (Ustinov). Meanwhile, Edward and Cedric are exploring their own "strange feelings" for one another. As with any film in this genre some gags work better than others. **85m/C; VHS, DVD.** *GB* Samuel West; Robert Portal; Georgina Cates; Sean Pertwee; Prunella Scales; Peter Ustinov; Brian Glover; Frank Finlay; ***D:*** Gary Sinyor; ***W:*** Gary Sinyor; Paul Simpkin; ***C:*** Simon Archer; ***M:*** David A. Hughes; John Murphy.

Stiffs **2006 (R)** Ladies man Frank Tramontana is the most popular hearse-driving employee at Felix Ragucci's Boston funeral home. When he discovers the business is in trouble, he recruits fellow workers John and Nino to save their jobs through some shady means. **104m/C; DVD.** Danny Aiello; Jon Polito; Louis Vanaria; Joseph R. Sicari; Heather Tom; Frank Bongiorno; Lesley Ann Warren; Eddie Malavarca; ***D:*** Frank Ciota; ***W:*** Joseph Ciota; ***C:*** Giulio Pietromarch; ***M:*** Giuliano Taviani; Carmelo Travia.

Stigma 1/2 **1973** "Miami Vice" star Thomas (then 23; later to restore his middle name, Michael) is a young doctor who treats a syphilis epidemic in a small town. He's indistinguishable, but better than anything else here. Ever seen close-ups of advanced syphilis? Here's your chance—but it's not pretty. **93m/C; DVD.** Philip Michael Thomas; Harlan Cary Poe; *D:* David E. Durston.

Stigmata 1/2 **1999 (R)** Disappointing horror flick that's campy instead of creepy. Airhead Pittsburgh beautician Frankie (Arquette) doesn't even believe in God, so why is she suddenly afflicted with visions and seizures that leave her with Christ-like wounds? Could it have anything to do with the rosary her vacationing mom sent her from Brazil? When the media picks up the story, the Vatican decides to send Father Kiernan (Byrne, who makes a very sexy priest) to check things out. Lots of hokey mumbo-jumbo ensues. **103m/C; VHS, DVD, Blu-Ray.** Patricia Arquette; Gabriel Byrne; Jonathan Pryce; Portia de Rossi; Patrick Muldoon; Nia Long; Thomas Kopache; Rade Serbedzija; Enrico Colantoni; Dick Latessa; Ann Cusack; *D:* Rupert Wainwright; *W:* Rick Ramage; Tom Lazarus; *C:* Jeffrey L. Kimball; *M:* Elia Cmiral.

Stiletto **2008 (R)** Decent cast although the story is nothing special. Femme assassin Raina (Katic) is out to destroy the criminal organization of mobster Virgil Vadalos (Berenger) despite the fact that she used to be his gal. (Her reasons take awhile to surface.) When Virgil discovers who's after him, he hires crooked detective Beck (Sloan) to take care of Raina first. **99m/C; DVD.** Stana Katic; Tom Berenger; Michael Biehn; William Forsythe; Paul Sloan; James Russo; Tom Sizemore; Diane Venora; Kelly Hu; Amanda Brooks; Dominique Swain; D.B. Sweeney; *D:* Nick Vallelonga; *C:* Jeffrey Mygatt; *M:* Cliff Martinez.

Stiletto Dance 1/2 **2001 (R)** Anton (Doyle) is the head of the Russian mob in Buffalo, NY, who plans to sell a nuclear device to the Albanians. Undercover cop Kit Adrian (Roberts) has other ideas—before he makes the mistake of falling for a mob enforcer's wife (Laurier). **97m/C; VHS, DVD.** Eric Roberts; Shawn Doyle; Brett Porter; Romano Orzari; Lucie Laurier; Yaphet Kotto; Mark Camacho; Justin Louis; *D:* Mario Azzopardi; *W:* Alfonse Ruggiero; *C:* Pierre Jodoin. **CABLE**

Still Alice **2014 (PG-13)** Distinguished linguistics Columbia University professor, Alice Howland (Moore), is the last to believe that she's in the early stages of Alzheimer's. With the support of her husband (Baldwin), and three grown children, she tries to live an uninterrupted life, teaching, continuing research projects, jogging through the park. Moore brings an elegance to Alice, maintaining a sense of wit as she confuses her sense of direction, or loses her train of thought mid-lecture. A gripping exploration of a startling disease, that remains faithful to Lisa Genova's best-selling novel. **101m/C; DVD, Blu-Ray.** Julianne Moore; Kristen Stewart; Kate (Catherine) Bosworth; Hunter Parrish; Alec Baldwin; Seth Gilliam; *D:* Richard Glatzer; Wash Westmoreland; *W:* Richard Glatzer; Wash Westmoreland; *C:* Denis Lenoir; *M:* Ilan Eshkeri. Oscars '14: Actress (Moore); British Acad. '14: Actress (Moore); Golden Globes '15: Actress--Drama (Moore); Ind. Spirit '15: Actress (Moore); Screen Actors Guild '14: Actress (Moore).

Still Breathing 1/2 **1997 (PG-13)** Romance with elements of the fantastical. Fletcher (Fraser) is an eccentric street performer in San Antonio, who dreams of a woman he knows will become his wife (it's a family thing). This turns out to be tough L.A. con woman Rosalyn (Going), whose next sting just happens to involve a Texan. When Fletcher flies to L.A. to find his would-be lady love, they meet cute and have a lot of mistaken assumptions before things come out right. Fraser's character may be wide-eyed but he's no fool and Going displays a needed touch of vulnerability for her manipulative bad girl. **109m/C; VHS, DVD.** Brendan Fraser; Joanna Going; Ann Magnuson; Celeste Holm; Lou Rawls; Angus MacFadyen; Paolo Seganti; *D:* James F. Robinson; *W:* James F. Robinson; *C:* John Thomas; *M:* Paul Mills.

Still Crazy 1/2 **1998 (R)** Twenty years after the breakup of his band Strange Fruit, Tony (Rea) is ready to give it a go again. With the Wisbech rock festival beckoning, he rounds up the others: lead singer Ray (Nighy), still a musician living in a mansion; drummer Beano (Spall), a gardener on the run from the tax collector; and singer-bassist Les (Nail), who runs a roofing business. One glitch: lead guitarist Brian (Robinson), the most popular band member, is supposedly dead. Luckily, love of the music (and money) forces the band to get it together. Inspired by a reunion tour of the Animals, but has more "Full Monty" fun and heart than "Spinal Tap" parody to it. The cast is superb and the actual concert makes you want to stand up and cheer, when you're done laughing. **96m/C; VHS, DVD.** *GB* Stephen Rea; Billy Connolly; Jimmy Nail; Timothy Spall; Bill Nighy; Juliet Aubrey; Helena Bergstrom; Bruce Robinson; Hans Matheson; Rachael Stirling; Phil Daniels; Frances Barber; Philip Davis; *D:* Brian Gibson; *W:* Dick Clement; Ian La Frenais; *C:* Ashley Rowe; *M:* Clive Langer.

Still Green **2007** Ten teens rent a Florida beach house for a week before separating for college but sun and surf doesn't lessen their need for their emotional baggage to come spilling out, including various family traumas, sexual attractions, and insecurities. **87m/C; DVD.** Sarah Jones; Ryan Kelley; Douglas Spain; Noah Segan; Paul Costa; Brandon Meyer; Ashleigh Snyder; Michael Strynkowski; Nicole Komendat; Gricel Castineira; *D:* Jon Artigo; *W:* Georgia Menides; *C:* Brian Crane.

The Still Life **2007** Julian Lamont (Barry) is a reclusive, alcoholic artist who developed a new art genre called destructionism that brings surprising commercial success, which he has not handled well. Struggling to regain his identity, once past the self-loathing and deep-rooted inner-hatred, he comes to realize taking responsibility for his actions is the first step. Too much angst, not enough substance. **155m/C; DVD.** Jason Barry; Rachel Miner; Terry Moore; Don S. Davis; Robert Miano; *D:* Joel Miller; *W:* Joel Miller; *C:* Richard Barbadillo.

Still Mine **2013 (PG-13)** The always-great Cromwell anchors this Canadian true story of a man who wanted to create one final, lasting testament to the love of his life (the still-luminous Bujold) before age-influenced dementia took her away from him. As he started to build a cottage on his own property, Craig Morrison was stymied by red tape and bureaucracy that took him all the way to a courtroom. Cromwell injects Morrison with his typical square-jawed everyman personality but he allows more emotion than usual, making for a truly moving film that works despite its more blatant melodramatic clichés. **102m/C; DVD, Blu-Ray.** James Cromwell; Genevieve Bujold; Campbell Scott; *D:* Michael McGowan; *W:* Michael McGowan; *C:* Brendan Steacy; *M:* Hugh Marsh.

Still of the Night **1982 (PG)** A Hitchcock-style thriller about a psychiatrist infatuated with a mysterious woman who may or may not be a killer. **91m/C; VHS, DVD, Streaming.** Meryl Streep; Roy Scheider; Jessica Tandy; Joe Grifasi; Sara Botsford; Josef Sommer; *D:* Robert Benton; *W:* Robert Benton; David Newman; *C:* Nestor Almendros.

Still Small Voices 1/2 **2007** 911 operator Michael Summer (Bell) starts getting calls for help from a young girl who actually died 30 years before as an alleged drowning victim. She is drawn to the girl's hometown and begins her own investigation, which leads to a pedophile and a kidnap/murder as well as some revelations from Michael's own murky past. Bell gives a good performance and the twist is rather unexpected. **90m/C; DVD.** Catherine Bell; Mark Humphrey; Damir Andrei; George Buza; Deborah Grover; Charles Martin Smith; Mimi Kuyzk; Eugene Clark; Lawrence Dane; Barbara Gordon; *D:* Mario Azzopardi; *W:* Jolene Rice; *C:* Michael Storey; *M:* Stacey Hersh. **CABLE**

Still Waiting **2008 (R)** Lame-o sequel to 2005's equally crude "Waiting." The Shenaniganz restaurant is in trouble because of competition from Ta-Ta's Wing Shack next door. The waitresses have left because skimpier uniforms mean bigger tips and the customers are following. But Shenaniganz isn't going down with a (food) fight. **88m/C; DVD.** Justin Long; John Michael Higgins; Steve Howey; Andy Milonakis; Rob Benedict; Alanna Ubach; Danneel Harris; Luis Guzman; Vanessa Lengies; Tania Raymonde; *D:* Jeff Balis; *W:* Rob McKittrick; *C:* Thomas Callaway. **VIDEO**

The Sting 1/2 **1973 (PG)** Newman and Redford together again in this sparkling story of a pair of con artists in 1930s Chicago. They set out to fleece a big-time racketeer, pitting brain against brawn and pistol. Very inventive, excellent acting, Scott Joplin's wonderful ragtime music adapted by Marvin Hamlisch. The same directorial and acting team from "Butch Cassidy and the Sundance Kid" triumphs again. **129m/C; VHS, DVD, Blu-Ray, HD-DVD.** Paul Newman; Robert Redford; Robert Shaw; Charles Durning; Eileen Brennan; Harold Gould; Ray Walston; Dana Elcar; Jack Kehoe; Dimitra Arliss; Robert Earl Jones; Sally Kirkland; *D:* George Roy Hill; *W:* David S. Ward; *C:* Robert L. Surtees; *M:* Marvin Hamlisch. Oscars '73: Art Dir./Set Dec., Costume Des., Director (Hill), Film, Film Editing, Orig. Song Score and/or Adapt., Story & Screenplay; Directors Guild '73: Director (Hill); Natl. Film Reg. '05.

The Sting 2 1/2 **1983 (PG)** Complicated comic plot concludes with the final con game, involving a fixed boxing match where the stakes top $1 million and the payoff could be murder. Lame sequel to "The Sting" (1973). **102m/C; VHS, DVD, Blu-Ray.** Jackie Gleason; Mac Davis; Teri Garr; Karl Malden; Oliver Reed; Tony Giorgio; *D:* Jeremy Paul Kagan; *W:* David S. Ward; *C:* Bill Butler; *M:* Lalo Schifrin.

Stingaree 1/2 **1934** A strange musical western. Australian bandit Stingaree (Dix) likes to steal for fun and writes songs in his spare time. He's enamored of would-be opera singer Hilda (Dunne) and kidnaps her, though Hilda doesn't protest too much. Stingaree winds up in jail and she goes to Europe with composer Julian Kent (Tearle) to further her career but the lovers will meet again. Based on the novel by E.W. Hornung. **76m/B; DVD, Blu-Ray.** Richard Dix; Irene Dunne; Conway Tearle; Mary Boland; Henry Stephenson; Andy Devine; Una O'Connor; *D:* William A. Wellman; *W:* Becky Gardiner; *C:* James Van Trees.

Stingray 1/2 **1978 (PG)** Two guys buy a Corvette, not knowing it's loaded with stolen heroin. Gangsters with an interest in the dope come after them, and the chase is on. Very violent and not all that funny. **105m/C; VHS, DVD.** Chris Mitchum; Sherry Jackson; Les Lannom; *D:* Richard Taylor.

Stir Crazy 1/2 **1980 (R)** Two down-on-their luck losers find themselves convicted of a robbery they didn't commit and sentenced to 120 years behind bars with a mean assortment of inmates. Wilder and Pryor's second teaming isn't quite as successful as the first go-round, but still provides plenty of laughs. **111m/C; VHS, DVD, Blu-Ray.** Richard Pryor; Gene Wilder; Nicolas Coster; Lee Purcell; Craig T. Nelson; JoBeth Williams; Erland van Lidth; Georg Stanford Brown; Barry Corbin; Charles Weldon; Grand L. Bush; *D:* Sidney Poitier; *W:* Bruce Jay Friedman; *C:* Fred Schuler; *M:* Tom Scott; Michael Masser.

Stir of Echoes 1/2 **1999 (R)** The kid in "The Sixth Sense" isn't the only one seeing dead people, although blue-collar Tom Witzky (Bacon) really doesn't have a clue as to what's happening to him. After being hypnotized at a party by his witchy sister-in-law, Lisa (Douglas), Tom winds up with some very scary clairvoyant abilities, which link him to a neighborhood teenaged girl who's presumed missing but has, in fact, been murdered. Naturally, Tom's visions and obsessions lead to some problems with his family and friends. Based on the novel by Richard Matheson. **110m/C; VHS, DVD, Blu-Ray.** Kevin Bacon; Illeana Douglas; Kathryn Erbe; Liza Weil; Kevin Dunn; Conor O'Farrell; Zachary David Cope; Jennifer (Jenny) Morrison; Eddie Bo Smith, Jr.; *D:* David Koepp; *W:* David Koepp; *C:* Fred Murphy; *M:* James Newton Howard.

Stir of Echoes 2: The Homecoming 1/2 **2007 (R)** Another of those mostly-in-name-only sequels. Army Captain Ted Cogan (Lowe) and his unit erroneously fire upon a van of civilians (who die) in Iraq, which leads to an insurgent attack that wounds Cogan. After coming out of his coma, Cogan is discharged and returns home to Chicago, where his wife and kid are having their own problems. Cogan starts suffering disturbing flashbacks that include ghosts who seemingly are trying to communicate with him. **89m/C; DVD.** Rob Lowe; Marnie McPhail; Katya Gardner; Zachary Bennett; Ben Lewis; *D:* Ernie Barbarash; *W:* Ernie Barbarash; *C:* Francois Dagenais; *M:* Norman Orenstein. **CABLE**

Stitches 1/2 **2012 (R)** A group of rude kids accidentally kill the clown asked to perform at their birthday party. Decades later, as they are about to become adults, the clown decides he's had enough of being dead and that it's time he gave them their comeuppance. **87m/C; DVD, Blu-Ray, Streaming.** *IR* Ross Noble; Tommy Knight; Shane Murray-Corcoran; Gemma-Leah Devereux; Thommas Kane Byrnes; *D:* Conor McMahon; *W:* Conor McMahon; David O'Brien; *C:* Patrick Jordan; *M:* Paul McDonnell; Marcello De Francisci. **VIDEO**

Stoker 1/2 **2013 (R)** After Richard (Mulroney) dies in a car accident, his impossibly cool world-traveling brother Charles Stoker (Goode) makes his first visit to an 18-year-old niece he'd never met, India (Wasikowska), and Richard's seductive--if flaky--wife Evelyn (Kidman). From here, Uncle Charlie strikes a bizarre affair with both women, one nearly supernatural and the other burning with lust. A creepy and tense thriller, riddled with Dracula references and existing in a dark world all its own. English-language debut of acclaimed Korean director Park. **99m/C; DVD, Blu-Ray.** Mia Wasikowska; Matthew Goode; Nicole Kidman; Dermot Mulroney; Jacki Weaver; Alden Ehrenreich; Lucas Till; *D:* Chan-wook Park; *W:* Wentworth Miller; *C:* Chung-hoon Chung; *M:* Clint Mansell.

Stolen 1/2 *Stolen Lives* **2009 (R)** Uninspired thriller. Detective Tom Adkins' (Hamm) 10-year-old son went missing in 2000. A boy's body is excavated from a construction site but the body dates from 1958 and flashbacks show struggling single dad Matthew (Lucas) trying to care for his handicapped son John (Bennett), who is kidnapped from Matthew's car. As Tom investigates, he becomes obsessed with the parallels between the two cases. **90m/C; DVD.** Jon Hamm; Josh(ua) Lucas; Jimmy Bennett; Rhona Mitra; James Van Der Beek; Jessica Chastain; Beth Grant; Morena Baccarin; Joanna Cassidy; *D:* Anders T. Anderson; *W:* Glenn Taranto; *C:* Andy Steinman; *M:* Trevor Morris.

Stolen **2012 (R)** Ex-con Will (Cage) must rescue his kidnapped daughter from his ex-partner Vincent (Lucas), who has her locked in the trunk of a taxi. Vincent wants the money from the last job they did together, and is "action-movie villain" crazy, so Will knows there's a double-cross coming. Ridiculousness abounds, as it tends to do in a Nic Cage action flick, but at least it moves along at a brisk pace. **96m/C; DVD, Blu-Ray.** Nicolas Cage; Josh(ua) Lucas; Malin Akerman; Danny Huston; Sami Gayle; Edrick Browne; Mark Valley; Barry (Shabaka) Henley; M.C. Gainey; J.D. Evermore; *D:* Simon West; *W:* David Guggenheim; *C:* Jim Whitaker; *M:* Mark Isham.

The Stolen Children 1/2 *Il Ladro di Bambini* **1992** Highly acclaimed Italian neo-realist film that tells the story of a shy carabiniere and two children who have been placed in his care. They are an emotionally battered 11-year-old girl who was forced into prostitution by her mother and her sullen 9-year-old brother. As they journey from Milan to Sicily and gradually get to know each other, all three of the characters undergo a slight transformation. Gracefully executed, this haunting masterpiece explores the overriding themes of guilt and innocence and keeps you thinking about them long after the movie's over. Italian with subtitles. **108m/C; VHS, DVD.** *IT* Enrico Lo Verso; Valentina Scalici; Giuseppe Ieracitano; Florence Darel; Marina Golovine; Fabio Alessandrini; *D:* Gianni Amelio; *W:* Gianni Amelio; Sandro Petraglia; Stefano Rulli; *M:* Franco Piersanti. Cannes '92: Grand Jury Prize.

A Stolen Face **1952** Creepy, implausible drama of a plastic surgeon, spurned by a beautiful concert pianist, who transforms a female convict to look just like her. The convict runs away, but perhaps there's hope in the future with the pianist. **71m/B; VHS, DVD.** *GB* Paul Henreid; Lizabeth Scott; Andre Morell; Susan Stephen; Everley Gregg; Cyril Smith; *D:* Terence Fisher; *W:* Martin Berkeley; Richard H. Landau; *C:* Walter J. (Jimmy W.) Harvey; *M:* Malcolm Arnold.

Stolen Face **1952** Film noir from Hammer Films. Plastic surgeon Philip Ritter (Henreid) and concert pianist Alice Brent

(Scott) fall in love, but she decides to stick with her manager/fiancé (Morell). Distraught, Philip lends his services to the local women's prison and makes over disfigured career criminal Lily (Mackenzie) into Alice's image and then marries Lily when she's paroled. Only the ex-con isn't going straight and humiliates Philip with her criminal ways. Then, when Alice comes back wanting a second chance, Lily refuses to give Philip a divorce. This isn't going to end well for someone. **72m/B; DVD.** *UK* Paul Henreid; Lizabeth Scott; Mary MacKenzie; Andre Morell; John Wood; ***D:*** Terence Fisher; ***W:*** Martin Berkeley; Richard H. Landau; ***C:*** Walter J. (Jimmy W.) Harvey; ***M:*** Malcolm Arnold.

Stolen Hearts 🦴 *Two If By Sea* **1995 (R)** Instead of reporting con man Brandon Keyes (Finiani) to the cops after he takes her money, bar owner Dana Andrews (Aletonis) hires PI Justin Gibbons (Dale) to get back her savings. Justin happens to work with a psychic, Tess (Hall), and the twosome have a mutual attraction. They find the sleaze and get back the dough. Very boring. **82m/C; VHS, DVD.** Landon Hall; Vincent Dale; Jim Finiani; Paula Aletonis; ***D:*** Ralph Portillo.

Stolen Holiday 🦴🦴 **1937** Based on a true crime scandal that nearly brought down the French government in the early 1930s. Suave swindler Stefan Orloff moves in the top social and financial circles and is protected lest his contacts be accused of complicity. Ambitious model Nicole marries Stefan but is quickly disillusioned despite the wealth it brings her. But Stefan's crimes can't go on forever. **84m/B; DVD.** Kay Francis; Claude Rains; Ian Hunter; Alison Skipworth; Alexander D'Arcy; ***D:*** Michael Curtiz; ***W:*** Casey Robinson; ***C:*** Sidney Hickox.

Stolen Hours 🦴🦴 ½ **1963** Inferior remake of Bette Davis's "Dark Victory" casts Hayward as an oil-rich heiress who learns she has a fatal illness. Bring the tissues for this tearjerker. Based on the play "Dark Victory" by George Emerson Brewer Jr. and Bertram Block. **100m/C; VHS, DVD.** Susan Hayward; Michael Craig; Diane Baker; Edward Judd; Paul Rogers; ***D:*** Daniel Petrie; ***W:*** Jessamyn West; Joseph Hayes.

Stolen Kisses 🦴🦴🦴 ½ *Baisers Voles* **1968** Sequel to "The 400 Blows," the story of Antoine Doinel: his unsuccessful career prospects as a detective in Paris, and his initially awkward but finally successful adventures with women. Made during Truffaut's involvement in a political crisis involving the sack of Cinematique Francais director Henri Langlois. Truffaut dedicated the film to Langlois and the Cinematique, but it is a thoroughly apolitical, small-scale, charming (some say too charming) romantic comedy, Truffaut-style. Followed by "Bed and Board." **90m/C; VHS, DVD.** *FR* Jean-Pierre Leaud; Delphine Seyrig; Michael (Michel) Lonsdale; Claude Jade; ***D:*** Francois Truffaut; ***W:*** Francois Truffaut; Claude de Givray; ***C:*** Denys Clerval; ***M:*** Antoine Duhamel. Natl. Soc. Film Critics '69: Director (Truffaut).

A Stolen Life 🦴🦴 **1946** Remake of 1939 film of the same title starring Elisabeth Bergner. Oddly, Davis chose this as her first and last producing effort. Implausible tale of an evil twin (Davis) who takes her sister's (Davis) place so she can have the man they both love. Davis pulls it off as both twins; Ford is good as the hapless hubby. **107m/B; VHS, DVD.** Bette Davis; Glenn Ford; Dane Clark; Walter Brennan; Charlie Ruggles; Bruce Bennett; Esther Dale; Peggy Knudsen; ***D:*** Curtis Bernhardt; ***M:*** Max Steiner.

Stolen Summer 🦴🦴 *Project Greenlight's Stolen Summer* **2002 (PG)** The background of the film (first-timer Jones won a national competition sponsored by Ben Affleck and Matt Damon) may be more interesting than this decidedly old-fashioned story. It's a Chicago summer in 1976 with young Irish Catholic Pete O'Malley (Stein) deciding that, in order to get to heaven, he needs to convert his Jewish friend Danny Jacobsen (Weinberg). Danny's father (Pollak), who happens to be a rabbi, takes the news benignly while Pete's dad, Joe (Quinn), has some trouble believing that his family is not being condescended to. The performances are appealing and there's a good lesson about the acceptance of another's religion. **95m/C; VHS, DVD.** Adi Stein; Mike Weinberg; Aidan Quinn; Kevin Pollak; Bonnie Hunt; Eddie Kaye Thomas; Brian Dennehy; ***D:*** Pete Jones; ***W:*** Pete Jones; ***C:*** Pete Biagi; ***M:*** Danny Lux.

Stolen Women, Captured Hearts 🦴🦴 ½ **1997** CBS TV movie. In 1868, Anna and Sarah are traveling to Fort Hays where Anna has made an arranged marriage to farmer Daniel Morgan. The wagon train is attacked by the Sioux but warrior Tokalah allows the two women to live. However, after her marriage, Anna and Sarah are taken captive by the same tribe with Anna and Tokalah falling in love. When they are eventually rescued by General Custer, Anna must choose between her heart and the conventions of her former life. **87m/C; DVD.** Janine Turner; Michael Greyeyes; Patrick Bergin; Jean Louisa Kelly; William Shockley; Dennis Weaver; ***D:*** Jerry London; ***W:*** Richard Fielder; ***C:*** Frank Prinzi; ***M:*** Dana Kaproff. **TV**

Stomp the Yard 🦴🦴 ½ **2007 (PG-13)** The yard in question would be a highly competitive step dancing war between two rival black fraternities. L.A. teen DJ (Short) gets into a major beef and is shipped off to his Uncle Nate (Lennix) in Atlanta to be enrolled at historic Truth University. The brash freshman immediately pisses off Mu Gamma Xi hotshot Grant (Henson), but his street moves win DJ a place at rival frat Theta Nu Theta. They want to win that national championship (yes, there's a dance-off). Oh so predictable plot but the dancing is impressive. **114m/C; DVD, Blu-Ray.** Columbus Short; Meagan Good; Brian White; Laz Alonso; Ne-Yo; Yun Qu; Valarie Pettiford; Harry J. Lennix; Allan Louis; ***D:*** Sylvain White; ***W:*** Robert Adetuyi; ***C:*** Scott Kevan; ***M:*** Sam Retzer; Tim Boland.

Stomp the Yard 2: Homecoming 🦴🦴 **2010 (PG-13)** Chance is a new pledge at Theta Nu frat at Atlanta's Truth University. He believes his team has a strong chance to win an important step competition against a rival fraternity but his concentration is divided. Chance's dad needs help with the family diner, his girlfriend is unhappy, and he owes a debt to some very impatient street thugs. **88m/C; DVD.** Collins Pennie; Keith David; Columbus Short; David Banner; Tika Sumpter; Kiely Williams; Pooch Hall; ***D:*** Rob Hardy; ***W:*** Meena Payne; Albert Leon; ***C:*** Maz Makani; ***M:*** Todd Bozung. **VIDEO**

Stonados 🦴 **2013** Goofy Syfy Channel disaster pic that has a tornado hitting Boston. Only it's not the ordinary kind since the storm contains exploding boulders. Stones plus tornados--stonados. Naturally, the oh-so-serious main weather scientist has to explain what's happening while trying to rescue his trapped kids from the storm. **88m/C; DVD.** Paul Johansson; Sebastian Spence; Miranda Frigon; Thea Gill; William B. Davis; ***D:*** Jason Bourque; ***W:*** Rafael Jordan. **CABLE**

Stone 🦴🦴 ½ **2010 (R)** Retiring parole officer Jack Maybury's (De Niro) longtime loveless marriage to Madylyn (Conroy) figures into this prison drama that finds convicted arsonist Gerald 'Stone' Creeson (Norton, in cornrows and street attitude) willing to do whatever it takes to get an early release. He looks to manipulate Maybury by getting his sexy wife Lucetta (Jovovich) to vamp the older man but you begin to wonder who's working whom. De Niro and Norton are reliably good, but Jovovich adds some much-needed spark to the tale that's a little too complex for its own good. **105m/C; Blu-Ray.** Edward Norton; Robert De Niro; Milla Jovovich; Frances Conroy; Enver Gjokaj; Pepper Binkley; ***D:*** John Curran; ***W:*** Angus MacLachlan; ***C:*** Maryse Alberti; ***M:*** Jon Brion; Selena Arizanovic.

The Stone Angel 🦴🦴 **2007 (R)** Adaptation of Margaret Laurence's 1964 novel. Hagar Shipley (Burstyn) may be 90 but she has no intention of letting her son Marvin (Baker) shuffle her into a nursing home. At least not until she can travel through Manitoba to revisit some of her old haunts and relive her past, including her difficult marriage to reckless Bram. **115m/C; DVD.** Ellen Burstyn; Wings Hauser; Cole Hauser; Dylan Baker; Christine Horne; Kevin Zegers; Sheila McCarthy; Ellen Page; Aaron Ashmore; Ted Atherton; Luke Kirby; ***D:*** Keri Skogland; ***C:*** Bobby Bukowski; ***M:*** John McCarthy.

The Stone Boy 🦴🦴🦴 ½ **1984 (PG)** A boy accidentally kills his older brother on their family's Montana farm. The family is torn apart by sadness and guilt. Sensitive look at variety of reactions during a crisis, with an excellent cast led by Duvall's crystal-clear performance. **93m/C; VHS, DVD.** Glenn Close; Robert Duvall; Jason Presson; Frederic Forrest; Wilford Brimley; Linda Hamilton; Mary Ellen Trainor; ***D:*** Christopher Cain; ***W:*** Gina Berriault; ***C:*** Juan Ruiz-Anchia; ***M:*** James Horner; John Beal.

Stone Cold WOOF! **1991 (R)** Flamboyant footballer Bosworth made his acting debut in this sensitive human document, playing the usual musclebound, one-punk-army terminator cop, out to infiltrate a sadistic band of fascist biker barbarians engaged in drug running and priest shooting. Profane, lewd, gory, self-deifying; a crash course (accent on crashes) in everything despicable about modern action pics. **91m/C; VHS, DVD, Blu-Ray.** Brian Bosworth; Lance Henriksen; William Forsythe; Arabella Holzbog; Sam McMurray; ***D:*** Craig R. Baxley; ***W:*** Walter Doniger; ***C:*** Alexander Grusynski; ***M:*** Sylvester Levay.

The Stone Killer 🦴🦴 ½ **1973 (R)** Bronson stars as a tough plainclothes cop in this action-packed drama about a Mafia plot to use Vietnam vets in a mass killing. Violent but tense and action-packed revenge adventure set in the underworlds of New York and Los Angeles. **95m/C; VHS, DVD, Blu-Ray, Streaming.** Charles Bronson; Martin Balsam; Norman Fell; Ralph Waite; John Ritter; ***D:*** Michael Winner.

The Stone Merchant 🦴 ½ *Il Mercante di Pietre* **2006** Unhappy Leda (March) works for Alitalia airlines and is married to Alceo (Molla), who is a paraplegic because of a terrorist attack. She falls for gemstone merchant Ludivico (Keitel), a convert to Islam, who turns out to be an Al-Qaeda operative who is planning to use Leda to transport some bomb-making material. Grim and obvious. **122m/C; DVD.** *GB IT* Harvey Keitel; Jane March; Jordi Molla; F. Murray Abraham; ***D:*** Renzo Martinelli; ***W:*** Renzo Martinelli; Fabio Campus; ***C:*** Blasco Giurato; ***M:*** Aldo de Scalzi Pivio.

Stone Reader 🦴🦴🦴 **2002 (PG-13)** Mark Moskowitz searches for "The Stones of Summer" author Dow Mossman. He also interviews critic Leslie Fiedler and editor Robert Gottleib, who edited "Catch 22." **128m/C; VHS, DVD.** ***D:*** Mark Moskowitz; ***W:*** Mark Moskowitz; ***C:*** Mark Moskowitz; Joseph Vandergast; Jeffrey Confer; ***M:*** Michael Mandrell.

Stonebrook 🦴🦴 **1998 (PG-13)** Two college roommates at a private university gamble to make their tuition money and wind up drawing the attention of a detective who wants to use their illegal activities to incriminate the mob. **90m/C; VHS, DVD.** Seth Green; Brad Rowe; Zoe McLellan; William Mesnik; Stanley Kamel; ***D:*** Byron W. Thompson; ***W:*** Steven Robert Morris; ***C:*** John Tarver; ***M:*** Dean Grinsfelder.

Stoned 🦴🦴 **2005** A muddled and unenlightening account of the final months of drug addicted Rolling Stones guitarist Brian Jones (Gregory), who was found dead in his swimming pool in 1969. Although "death by misadventure" is the official cause, a 1994 deathbed confession by Jones' contractor/whipping boy Frank Thorogood (Considine) allegedly reveals that Frank admitted drowning Jones. Flashbacks linger on the guitarist's hedonistic lifestyle while, before his death, Jones lethargically stirs himself to torment those around him. Woolley's directorial debut. **102m/C; DVD.** *GB* Leo Gregory; Paddy Considine; David Morrissey; Ben Whishaw; Amelia Warner; Monet Mazur; David Walliams; Tuva Novotny; Luke De Woolfson; Melanie Ramsay; Ruediger Rudolph; ***D:*** Stephen Woolley; ***W:*** Robert Wade; Neal Purvis; ***C:*** John Mathieson; ***M:*** David Arnold.

The Stoned Age 🦴 **1994 (R)** Buddies look to get wasted and find some chicks. Set in the '70s. **90m/C; VHS, DVD.** Michael Kopelow; China Kantner; Renee Griffen; ***D:*** James Melkonian.

Stoned Bros. 🦴 ½ *Stone Bros.* **2009** A pair of Australian natives go on a spiritual quest to fulfill a family promise, only to encounter deadly spiders, demonically possessed dogs, cross dressers, and enough marijuana to make Cleveland high along the way. **93m/C; DVD, Streaming.** *AU* Luke Carroll; Leon Burchill; Valentino del Toro; David Page; Luke Hewitt; ***D:*** Richard Frankland; ***W:*** Richard Frankland; William Bainbridge; ***C:*** Joseph Pickering; ***M:*** Shane O'Mara. **VIDEO**

Stonehearst Asylum 🦴🦴 *Eliza Graves* **2013 (PG-13)** Anderson adapts a Poe short in this star-studded disappointment. Dr. Edward Newgate (Sturgess) comes to the titular establishment in the middle of the night and immediately discerns something isn't quite right. He meets Dr. Silas Lamb (Kingsley) and falls in love with a woman named Eliza Graves (Beckinsale). Then he finds the doctors (including Caine) locked in the basement. It turns out the inmates truly have taken over the asylum. Sadly, it doesn't quite work. There's no danger, no dread, and no atmosphere. The great cast helps, but it's more boring than terrifying. **112m/C; DVD, Blu-Ray, Streaming.** Kate Beckinsale; Jim Sturgess; Ben Kingsley; Michael Caine; Brendan Gleeson; David Thewlis; Jason Flemyng; ***D:*** Brad Anderson; ***W:*** Joesph Gangemi; ***C:*** Thomas Yatsko; ***M:*** John Debney.

Stonehenge Apocalypse 🦴 **2010 (PG-13)** Doomsday thriller from the Syfy Channel with one of those elaborate plots that make no sense whatsoever. Stonehenge turns out to be some weird machine sitting on an electromagnetic field. When the stones start moving, increasingly violent natural disasters follow. Fringe scientist Jacob Blazer has some crackpot ideas to save the planet, including using an ancient artifact that promptly gets stolen. **90m/C; DVD.** Misha Collins; Torri Higginson; Hill Harper; Michael Kopsa; Peter Wingfield; Brent Stait; ***D:*** Paul Ziller; ***W:*** Paul Ziller; ***C:*** Anthony C. Metchie; ***M:*** Michael Neilson. **CABLE**

Stoner Express 🦴🦴 *AmStarDam* **2016** A stoner comedy. When Jack (Readwin) travels to Amsterdam, his primary goal is to find his father. He soon learns that his dad owns a failing marijuana coffee shop there. When Jack has an unexpected encounter, he discovers a way to turn around his father's business. **105m/C; DVD, Streaming, Download.** Jonathan Readwin; Sean Power; Eline Powell; Eric Lampaert; Kenneth Collard; ***D:*** Lee Lennox; Wayne Lennox; ***W:*** Lee Lennox; Wayne Lennox; ***C:*** Andy Parsons; ***M:*** Paul Arnold; Andrew Barnabas. **VIDEO**

Stonewall 🦴🦴🦴 **1995 (R)** Fictional account of the June, 1969 police raid on Greenwich Village gay bar the Stonewall Inn, which is considered to have launched the modern gay rights movement. White-bread, midwestern activist Matty Dean (Weller) arrives in New York and gets thrown in jail for defending streetwise drag queen LaMiranda (Diaz) from harassing cops. They become lovers but Matty is also involved with conservative prepster Ethan (Corbalis), who thinks the flamboyant queens give the gay movement a bad name. Meanwhile, the drag queens at the mob-backed Stonewall are getting fed up with police raids and brutal treatment. Adapted from Martin Duberman's social history "Stonewall." Director Finch died during the final editing stages of the film. **93m/C; VHS, DVD.** Frederick Weller; Guillermo Diaz; Brendan Corbalis; Bruce MacVittie; Duane Boutte; Peter Ratray; Luis Guzman; ***D:*** Nigel Finch; ***W:*** Rikki Beadle Blair; ***C:*** Chris Seager; ***M:*** Michael Kamen.

Stonewall 🦴 **2015 (R)** Emmerich stretches his wings from the CGI-blockbuster genre and falls flat on his face with this insulting, awful rendering of the fight for gay rights that picked up steam at the Stonewall Riots in 1969. The battle for self-expression that led to violence outside the Stonewall Inn can be told in so many ways that Emmerich's decision to tell it through the eyes of a young white man named Danny (Irvine) is baffling. Completely ignoring minority involvement in a film about equal rights is almost too insulting to fathom, and yet here we are. **129m/C; DVD.** Jonathan Rhys Meyers; Ron Perlman; Caleb Landry Jones; Jeremy Irvine; Joey King; ***D:*** Roland Emmerich; ***W:*** Jon Robin Baitz; ***C:*** Markus Forderer; ***M:*** Rob Simonsen.

The Stoning of Soraya M. 🦴🦴 **2008 (R)** Blunt and brutal drama (based on a true story) that takes place in flashbacks. French-Iranian journalist Feredoune Sahebjam's (Caviezel) car breaks down in an Iranian village. While he waits for it to be fixed, distraught Zahra (Aghdashloo) tells him about the murder of her niece, Soraya

(Marno). Unhappy in an arranged marriage, she refuses to divorce her husband because he is her only means of support. Because he wants to marry a more-compliant teenager, he accuses Soraya of adultery and persuades the local mullah to issue the ultimate medieval punishment—death by stoning. English and Farsi with subtitles. **114m/C; Blu-Ray, On Demand.** Shohreh Aghdashloo; James (Jim) Caviezel; Mozhan Marno; Navid Negahban; Vida Ghahremani; David Diaan; Ali Pourtash; Parviz Sayyad; ***D:*** Cyrus Nowrasteh; ***W:*** Cyrus Nowrasteh; Betsy Giffen Nowrasteh; ***C:*** Joel Ransom; ***M:*** John Debney.

Stony Island **1977** Shot on Chicago's south side, director Davis' low-budget first film is a musical drama. Richie Bloom, the only white kid on the block, forms a band called Stony Island with his best black friend Kevin. With the help of their mentor, aging sax legend Percy, the blues/jazz/rock musicians survive hard times to show off their talent. **95m/C; DVD.** Richard Davis; Edward Stoney Robinson; Gene Barge; George Englund; Ronnie Barron; Rae Dawn Chong; ***D:*** Andrew Davis; ***W:*** Andrew Davis; Tamar Simon Hoffs; ***C:*** Tak Fujimoto; ***M:*** David M. Matthews.

The Stooge **1/2 1951** Singer Bill Miller (Martin) asks the antic Ted Rogers (Lewis) to join him in his vaudeville act, where Rogers' clowning has them on the road to success. But then Miller decides he wants to go solo. Sounds more than a little autobiographical. **100m/B; DVD.** Dean Martin; Jerry Lewis; Polly Bergen; Marion Marshall; Eddie Mayehoff; Richard Erdman; Frances Bavier; ***D:*** Norman Taurog; ***W:*** Martin Rackin; Fred Finklehoffe; Elwood Ullman; ***C:*** Daniel F. Fapp.

Stop-Loss **1/2 2008 (R)** Fresh from duty in Iraq, Sgt. Brandon King (Phillippe) and his buddy Sgt. Steve Shriver (Tatum) return home to Texas only to struggle with assimilation and strained relationships due to the war experiences. Suddenly, Brandon is ordered to return to Iraq (the title refers to the military term for extending a soldier's enlistment contract without consent or even a heads-up), setting off a bomb of emotion and leading to an AWOL escape that puts him, his friends, and his family in jeopardy. Director and co-writer Kimberly Pierce, whose brother had been stop-lossed by the army, brings honesty and humanity to a subject close to her heart, and the lead performances are grippingly spot-on. **112m/C; DVD, Blu-Ray.** Ryan Phillippe; Abbie Cornish; Channing Tatum; Joseph Gordon-Levitt; Ciaran Hinds; Timothy Olyphant; Josef Sommer; Victor Rasuk; Rob Brown; Mamie Gummer; ***D:*** Kimberly Peirce; ***W:*** Kimberly Peirce; Mark Richard; ***C:*** Chris Menges; ***M:*** John Powell.

Stop Making Sense **1/2 1984** The Talking Heads perform 18 of their best songs in this concert filmed in Los Angeles. Considered by many to be the best concert movie ever made. The band plays with incredible energy and imagination, and Demme's direction and camera work is appropriately frenzied and original. Features such Talking Heads songs as "Burning Down the House," "Psycho Killer," and "Once in a Lifetime." Band member Tina Weymouth's Tom Tom Club also performs for the audience. **99m/C; VHS, DVD, Blu-Ray.** ***D:*** Jonathan Demme; ***C:*** Jordan Cronenweth.

Stop Me Before I Kill! **1960** Race car driver Alan (Lewis) is seriously injured on his wedding day, leaving him mentally unstable. Since he tries to strangle his bride Denise (Cilento) every time they get romantic, he decides to consult shrink Dr. Prade (Dauphin). Alan's suspicions are aroused when he sees the doc and his new missus apparently getting cozy, but is that really what's going on or is Alan suffering from hallucinations, as Prade insists? **93m/B; DVD.** ***GB*** Ronald Lewis; Diane Cilento; Claude Dauphin; Franciose Rosary; ***D:*** Val Guest; ***W:*** Val Guest; Ronald Scott Thorn; ***C:*** Gilbert Taylor; ***M:*** Stanley Black.

Stop! or My Mom Will Shoot **1992 (PG-13)** Getty is an overbearing mother paying a visit to her cop son (Stallone) in Los Angeles. When mom witnesses a crime she has to stay in town longer than intended, which gives her time to meddle in her son's work and romantic lives. If Stallone wants to change his image this so-called comedy isn't the way to do it—because the joke is only on him. Viewers who rent this may find the joke is on them. **87m/C; VHS, DVD.** Sylvester Stallone; Estelle Getty; JoBeth Williams; Roger Rees; Martin Ferrero; Gailard Sartain; Dennis Burkley; ***D:*** Roger Spottiswoode; ***W:*** William Osborne; William Davies; Blake Snyder; ***M:*** Alan Silvestri. Golden Raspberries '92: Worst Actor (Stallone), Worst Screenplay, Worst Support. Actress (Getty).

Stopover Tokyo **1957** An American intelligence agent uncovers a plot to assassinate the American ambassador while on leave in Japan. Nice location shooting and scenery; limp story and characters. Based on a novel by John P. Marquand. **100m/C; VHS, DVD.** Robert Wagner; Joan Collins; Edmond O'Brien; Ken Scott; Larry Keating; Sarah Selby; Reiko Oyama; Solly Nakamura; H. Okhawa; K.J. Seijto; Denmei Suzuki; ***D:*** Richard L. Breen; ***W:*** Richard L. Breen; Walter Reisch; Charles G. Clarke; ***M:*** Paul Sawtell.

Storage 24 **2012 (R)** A military cargo plane crashes, spewing its classified cargo across London. The city goes into lockdown while a Charlie, Shelley and their friends are emptying out a storage locker. When the power goes out, they soon become the prey to something not of this world. **87m/C; DVD, Blu-Ray.** ***UK*** Noel Clarke; Antonia Campbell-Hughes; Colin O'Donoghue; Laura Haddock; ***D:*** Johannes Roberts; ***W:*** Noel Clarke; Davie Fairbanks; ***C:*** Tim Schell; ***M:*** Christian Henson.

The Stork Club **1945** A little song, a little dance, will Betty Hutton find romance? The actors manage to rise above the script in this silly, overdone fable. Hutton stars as the poor but spunky hatcheck girl who unwittingly saves the life of a cynical billionaire. His expressions of gratitude are less than appreciated by her G.I. beau. Done mainly as a vehicle for Hutton's promotion, so Betty's die-hard fans may find it to their liking. **98m/B; VHS, DVD.** Betty Hutton; Barry Fitzgerald; Don DeFore; Robert Benchley; Bill Goodwin; Iris Adrian; Noel Neill; Andy Russell; ***D:*** Hal Walker.

Storks **2016 (PG)** In this clever-but-disposable animated comedy, storks have moved on from delivering babies to delivering packages. Junior (voiced by Samberg) is the company's top delivery stork, but he accidentally activates the defunct Baby Making Machine, producing a real, live baby girl. Now, Junior has to do what his kind did for generations, deliver the baby, with the help of the only human on Stork Mountain, a girl named Tulip (Crown). The voice cast, which also includes Jennifer Aniston and Kelsey Grammer, keeps it fun and light. **87m/C; DVD, Blu-Ray.** Andy Samberg; Katie Crown; Kelsey Grammer; Jennifer Aniston; Ty Burrell; ***D:*** Nicholas Stoller; Doug Sweetland; ***W:*** Nicholas Stoller; ***C:*** Simon Dunsdon; ***M:*** Jeff Danna; Mychael Danna.

Storm **2005** A Swedish hardcore action thriller bringing together comedy, science fiction, and psychological horror. After journalist Donny "DD" Davidson (Ericson) randomly meets a woman in a cab, his life changes forever. The odd Lova (Rose) once had a box that desperate criminals will do anything to retrieve. Not only is Donny accused of murder because of this woman, he becomes part of a series of horrible events, must go on the run, and face the truth about his own life. Swedish with subtitles. **110m/C; DVD, Streaming, Download.** Eric Ericson; Eva Rose; Lina Englund; Jacqueline Ramel; Matias Varela; ***D:*** Mans Marlind; Bjorn Stein; ***W:*** Mans Marlind; ***C:*** Linus Sandgren; ***M:*** Carl-Michael Herlofsson. **VIDEO**

The Storm **1/2 2009** Silly disaster flick finds scientist Kirk Hafner (Van Der Beek) working on a device that allows researchers to manipulate weather systems. He intends good things but General Braxton (Elliott) wants to weaponize the technology and industrialist Robert Terrell (Williams) also has nefarious intentions. Kirk tries to turn whistleblower and ends up on the run. Originally shown as a two-part NBC miniseries. **170m/C; DVD.** James Van Der Beek; Teri Polo; Treat Williams; David James Elliott; Marisol Nichols; John Larroquette; Luke Perry; ***D:*** Bradford May; ***W:*** Dennis A. Pratt; David Abramowitz; ***C:*** Maximo Munzi; ***M:*** Jonathan Snipes. **TV**

Storm and Sorrow **1990** Molly Higgins is known as the "Spiderwoman of the Rockies" for her legendary mountain climbing abilities. Then she joins a team looking to scale the 24,000-foot peaks of Russia's Pamir Mountains. The group meets deadly hazards—both natural and those caused by the ego-driven rivalries of the group's members. A fact-based drama based on the novel by Richard Craig. **96m/C; VHS, DVD.** Lori Singer; Todd Allen; Steve (Stephen M.) Anderson; Jay Baker; ***W:*** Leigh Chapman.

Storm Boy **1/2 (PG)** Michael Kingley (Rush) is the director of a company he founded that is now run by his son-in-law Malcolm (Thomson). When Michael attends an important board vote on leasing farmland in Western Australia to a mining company, he shares his memories of 1950s coastal South Australia with his granddaughter Maddy (Davis). There, pre-teen Michael (Little) raises three pelican chicks after their mother is killed by a hunter with the help of reclusive Aboriginal man Fingerbone Bill (Jamieson). An adaptation of a classic Australian children's book by Colin Thiele, the film is heartfelt but the added modern context detracts from the story. **98m/C; DVD.** Jai Courtney; Geoffrey Rush; Finn Little; David Gulpilil; Erik Thompson; ***D:*** Shawn Seet; ***W:*** Justin Monjo; ***C:*** Bruce Young; ***M:*** Alan John.

Storm Catcher **1999 (R)** Air Force pilot Jack Holloway (Lundgren) is falsely convicted of stealing a prototype military aircraft. He manages to escape in order to find the real culprits, which also puts Hollway's family in danger. **95m/C; VHS, DVD.** Dolph Lundgren; Mystro Clark; Yvonne Zima; Kylie Bax; ***D:*** Anthony Hickox; ***W:*** Bill Gucwa; Eric Masterson. **VIDEO**

Storm Cell **1/2 2008 (PG-13)** After an Oklahoma twister kills her parents, April Saunders (Rogers) grows up to study and track tornadoes. While visiting her brother (Moloney) in Seattle with her surly teen daughter Dana (Levesque), April realizes a supercell is building that could destroy the city. Combo of disaster flick and family drama courtesy of the Lifetime channel. **92m/C; DVD.** Mimi Rogers; Robert Moloney; Andrew Airlie; Michael Ironside; Ryan Kennedy; Elyse Levesque; ***D:*** Stephen R. Monroe; ***W:*** Graham Ludlow; Michael Konyves; ***C:*** C. Kim Miles; ***M:*** Corey A. Jackson. **CABLE**

Storm Center **1956** Widow Alicia Hull (Davis) is the longtime librarian in a small town who encourages the local kids, especially young Freddie (Coughlin). Red scare hysteria looms and Alicia loses her job for refusing to give into censorship and then is shunned after accusations of being a communist by politically ambitious Paul Duncan (Keith). An increasingly upset Freddie takes drastic action to bring the grownups to their senses. **86m/B; DVD.** Bette Davis; Brian Keith; Kim Hunter; Paul Kelly; Kevin Coughlin; Joe Mantell; Sally Brophy; Howard Wierum; ***D:*** Daniel Taradash; ***W:*** Daniel Taradash; Elick Moll; ***C:*** Burnett Guffey; ***M:*** George Duning.

Storm Chasers: Revenge of the Twister **1/2 1998** Having lost her husband in a plane crash, "storm chaser" Jaime (McGillis) throws herself into her work. Sent to Colorado to investigate a tornado, she hooks up with hunky FEMA coordinator, Will (Larson). There are some severe disturbances in the atmosphere causing problems—and disturbances on a more personal level as well. Dull and dumb. **96m/C; VHS, DVD.** Kelly McGillis; Wolf Larson; Liz Torres; Adrian Zmed; James MacArthur; ***D:*** Mark Sobel. **VIDEO**

Storm in a Teacup **1/2 1937** A reporter starts a campaign to save a sheepdog that the town magistrate has ordered killed because the owner, an old woman, is unable to pay the license tax. As the dog's fate hangs in the balance, this often humorous film provides an interesting look at British society of the 1930s. **80m/B; DVD, Blu-Ray.** ***UK*** Vivien Leigh; Rex Harrison; Cecil Parker; Sara Allgood; ***D:*** Victor Saville; Ian Dalrymple; ***W:*** Ian Dalrymple; Donald Bull; ***C:*** Mutz Greenbaum; ***M:*** Frederick Lewis.

Storm over Asia *The Heir to Genghis Khan* **1928** A Mongolian trapper is discovered to be descended from Genghis Khan and is made puppet emperor of a Soviet province. Beautiful and evocative. Silent masterpiece. **70m/B; Silent; VHS, DVD, Blu-Ray.** ***RU*** I. Inkizhinov; Valeri Inkizhinov; Alexander Chistyakov; A. Dedinstev; V. Tzoppi; Paulina Belinskaya; ***D:*** Vsevolod Pudovkin; ***C:*** Anatoli Golovnya.

Storm Over the Nile **1/2 1955** Steel makes for a dull hero in this remake of 1939's "The Four Feathers." Harry resigns his military commission just before his unit is sent to the Sudan causing three fellow officers and Harry's fiancee Mary to give him feathers of cowardice. Harry later decides to follow in disguise and prove his bravery after all. **107m/C; DVD.** ***UK*** Anthony Steel; Laurence Harvey; Ronald Lewis; Ian Carmichael; Mary Ure; James Robertson Justice; Michael Hordern; Christopher Lee; ***D:*** Zoltan Korda; Terence Young; ***W:*** R.C. Sherriff; ***C:*** Edward (Ted) Scaife; ***M:*** Benjamin Frankel.

Storm Rider **1957** A gunman hired to protect a group of ranchers from a powerful rancher falls in love with a local widow. After his job is done, however, he leaves her behind. Typical western fare. **70m/B; VHS, DVD.** Scott Brady; Mala Powers; Bill Williams; Olin Howlin; William "Bill" Fawcett; John Goddard; ***D:*** Edward L. Bernds; ***W:*** Edward L. Bernds; ***M:*** Les Baxter.

Storm Rider **1/2 2013 (PG)** In this touching family film, 18-year-old Dani Fielding has to leave her upscale city life behind when he father Mitch is sent to prison for fraud and her icy stepmother Vanessa takes off. Dani goes to live in the country with her gruff bachelor uncle, Sam, and has a hard time adjusting until she finds an orphaned colt. A championship rider, Dani fosters and trains Stormy, giving her a sense of purpose and belonging. **90m/C; DVD.** Danielle Chuchran; Kevin Sorbo; Kristy Swanson; C. Thomas Howell; Sam Jenkins; ***D:*** Craig Clyde; ***W:*** Craig Clyde; ***C:*** Brandon Christensen; ***M:*** Russ Whitelock. **VIDEO**

Storm Seekers **2008** Boring disaster pic. Meteorologist Leah's (Hannah) parents were killed during a hurricane when she was a child, leading to an excessive amount of flashbacks during her therapy sessions (yawn). Leah agrees to fly with reporter Ryan (Neal) on a routine storm-seeking story only to recognize that a hurricane developing off the Florida coast is turning into monster storm. Too bad the boss of the National Storm Center isn't heeding their warnings. **88m/C; DVD.** Daryl Hannah; Dylan Neal; Barclay Hope; Terry Chen; Gwynyth Walsh; Sean Bell; MacKenzie Gray; ***D:*** George Mendeluk; ***W:*** Kyle Hart; ***C:*** Anthony C. Metchie; ***M:*** Peter Allen. **TV**

Storm Tracker **1/2** *Storm* **1999 (PG-13)** Meteorologist Ron Young (Perry) develops a method of manipulating the path of deadly storms and is recruited by General Roberts (Sheen) to perfect his storm-tracking system for government use. Naturally, this isn't altruistic, the General wants to turn the violent storms on his enemies. **90m/C; VHS, DVD.** Luke Perry; Martin Sheen; Alexandra Powers; David Moses; Renee Estevez; ***D:*** Harris Done. **CABLE**

Storm Trooper **1/2 1998** Abused wife Grace Tolson (Alt) is just cleaning up after killing her husband when the mysterious Stark (Laughlin) shows up at her back door. Closely following are a group of armed men who manage to wound the stranger, exposing wires and circuitry. Stark the cyborg gets Grace into a lot of danger but she's got a gun and she's not gonna take it anymore. **89m/C; VHS, DVD.** Carol Alt; John Laughlin; Zach Galligan; Corey Feldman; Richard (Rick) Hill; Kool Moe Dee; ***D:*** Jim Wynorski; ***W:*** T.L. Lankford; ***C:*** J.E. Bash; ***M:*** Terry Plumeri. **VIDEO**

Storm Warning **1951** New York model Martha (Rogers) visits her sister Lucy (Day, in a non-singing role), who's living in a small southern town. She's barely off the bus before Martha witnesses a murder committed by the KKK. She's hiding and sees two men's faces and when she does get to Lucy's, Martha sees that her brutish brother-in-law Hank (Cochran) was one of the killers and the other is his boss, Charlie (Sanders). When prosecutor Burt Rainey (Reagan) learns that Martha was a witness, he tries to get her to testify but she clams up. But her silence doesn't do her any good. Hard-hitting for its time although there are no black characters in the story; the dead man is a white reporter writing an expose. Film was shot in Corona, California and an occasional palm tree incongruously appears. **93m/B; DVD.** Ronald Reagan; Ginger Rogers; Doris Day; Steve Cochran; Hugh Sanders; Raymond Greenleaf; Lloyd Gough; ***D:*** Stuart Heisler; ***W:*** Richard Brooks; Daniel Fuchs; ***C:*** Carl Guthrie; ***M:*** Daniele Amfitheatrof.

Stormswept 🦴 1/2 **1995** Actress Brianna (Hughes) rents a haunted Louisiana mansion housing the spirit of a slave master. When a storm strands Brianna and friends, the spirit causes everyone to get up to all sorts of sexual escapades. **94m/C; VHS, DVD.** Julie Hughes; Melissa Moore; Kathleen Kinmont; Justin Carroll; Lorissa McComas; Ed Wasser; Kim Kopf; Hunt Scarritt; ***D:*** David Marsh; ***W:*** David Marsh.

Stormy Monday 🦴🦴 1/2 **1988 (R)** An American developer conspires to strike it rich in Newcastle, England real estate by resorting to violence and political manipulations. Sting plays the jazz club owner who opposes him. Slow plot, but acted and directed well; interesting photography. **108m/C; VHS, DVD, Blu-Ray.** *GB* Melanie Griffith; Tommy Lee Jones; Sting; Sean Bean; James Cosmo; Mark Long; Brian Lewis; ***D:*** Mike Figgis; ***W:*** Mike Figgis; ***C:*** Roger Deakins; ***M:*** Mike Figgis.

Stormy Weather 🦴🦴 1/2 **1943** In this cavalcade of black entertainment, the plot takes a back seat to the nearly non-stop array of musical numbers, showcasing this stellar cast at their performing peak. **77m/B; VHS, DVD, Blu-Ray.** Lena Horne; Bill Robinson; Fats Waller; Dooley Wilson; Cab Calloway; ***D:*** Andrew L. Stone; ***C:*** Leon Shamroy. Natl. Film Reg. '01.

The Story Lady 🦴🦴 1/2 **1993** A retiree uses her story-telling abilities as a hostess on a public-access children's program. She becomes so popular that two network execs want to exploit her as a spokesperson for a toy company. Only a young girl can help her find a way to resist going commercial. **120m/C; VHS, DVD.** Jessica Tandy; Lisa Jakub; Ed Begley, Jr.; Charles Durning; Stephanie Zimbalist; ***D:*** Larry Elikann; ***M:*** Lee Holdridge. **TV**

The Story of a Cheat 🦴🦴🦴 **1936** The hero of the film discovers at an early age that dishonesty is probably the best policy and he sets out to put his theory into use. Director/writer Guitry also turns in a great performance as the central character. Guitry was a major influence on such different directors as Welles, Resnais and Truffaut. Based on Guitry's novel "Memoires d'Un Tricheur." In French with English subtitles. **83m/B; VHS, DVD.** *FR* Sacha Guitry; ***D:*** Sacha Guitry; ***W:*** Sacha Guitry.

Story of a Love Affair 🦴🦴 *Cronaca di un Amore* **1950** Paola (Bose) is the young wife of wealthy industrialist Enrico (Sarmi), who swiftly married her during the war. Now curious about her unknown past, Enrico hires a detective (Rossi) to investigate. This results in reuniting Paola with her ex-lover Guido (Girotti). Both are afraid that questions will be raised about the suspicious death of Guido's fiancee and, as the two rekindle their involvement, they consider getting rid of Enrico to preserve their secrets. Antonioni's first dramatic feature; Italian with subtitles. **98m/B; DVD.** *IT* Lucia Bose; Massimo Girotti; Gino Rossi; ***D:*** Michelangelo Antonioni; ***W:*** Michelangelo Antonioni; Francesco Maselli; Daniele D'Anza; Silvio Giovannetti; ***C:*** Enzo Serafin; ***M:*** Giovanni Fusco.

The Story of a Three Day Pass 🦴🦴 1/2 *La Permission* **1968** A black American GI falls in love with a white French girl he meets in peacetime Paris. Based on Van Peebles book "La Permission." With English subtitles. Made on a low budget and flawed, but poignant and impressive. **87m/B; VHS, DVD.** Harry Baird; Nicole Berger; Pierre Doris; ***D:*** Melvin Van Peebles; ***W:*** Melvin Van Peebles.

The Story of Adele H. 🦴🦴🦴 *L'Histoire d'Adele H.* **1975 (PG)** The story of Adele Hugo, daughter of Victor Hugo, whose love for an English soldier leads to obsession and finally to madness after he rejects her. Sensitive and gentle unfolding of characters and story. Beautiful photography. In French with English subtitles. **97m/C; VHS, DVD, Blu-Ray.** *FR* Isabelle Adjani; Bruce Robinson; Sylvia Marriott; ***D:*** Francois Truffaut; ***W:*** Suzanne Schiffman; Jean Gruault; ***C:*** Nestor Almendros; ***M:*** Maurice Jaubert. Natl. Bd. of Review '75: Actress (Adjani); N.Y. Film Critics '75: Actress (Adjani), Screenplay; Natl. Soc. Film Critics '75: Actress (Adjani).

The Story of Alexander Graham Bell 🦴🦴🦴 **1939** Lavish Fox biography on the inventor of the telephone provided Ameche with his most popular role. He's a serious Scot who comes to Boston to teach speech to the deaf and falls in love with the rich, beautiful and hearing impaired Young (whose three sisters, Georgianna, Polly Ann, and Sally are also in the film). Thanks to Young's rich daddy (Coburn), Bell gets the money to work on his invention, aided by enthusiastic assistant Watson (Fonda). No, it's not an entirely accurate retelling but it's well-done. **97m/B; DVD.** Don Ameche; Loretta Young; Henry Fonda; Charles Coburn; Spring Byington; Gene Lockhart; Sally Blane; Polly Ann Young; Georgianna Young; Bobs Watson; Jonathan Hale; Harry Davenport; ***D:*** Irving Cummings; ***W:*** Lamar Trotti; ***C:*** Leon Shamroy.

The Story of an African Farm 🦴🦴 1/2 *Bustin' Bonaparte: The Story of an African Farm* **2004 (PG)** Grant stars as a gleeful villain named Bonaparte Benkins, who invades the lives of young cousins Em (Weidemann) and Lydall (Kropinski). It's 1870, and the two orphaned girls are stuck on the remote African farm of their strict Aunt Sannie (Van der Laag), whom drifter Bonaparte proceeds to charm into letting him stay. The children are plucky and the adults are generally foolish but the experience is only mildly entertaining. Based on the 1883 children's book by South African Olive Schreiner. **97m/C; DVD.** *SA* Richard E. Grant; Armin Mueller-Stahl; Kasha Kropinski; Anneke Weidemann; Karin van der Laag; Luke Gallant; ***D:*** David Lister; ***W:*** Bonnie Rodini; Thandi Brewer; Peter Tischhauser; ***M:*** J.B. Arthur.

The Story of David 🦴🦴🦴 **1976 (PG)** Well-done Old Testament Bible drama about the shepherd boy who slew Goliath, overcame the Philistines, and united Israel. Then, as King David, he winds up involved in an illicit love affair with Bathsheba that threatens to destroy his kingdom. Fine acting and a literate script highlight this TV production. **192m/C; VHS, DVD.** Timothy Bottoms; Anthony Quayle; Jane Seymour; Keith Michell; Susan Hampshire; ***D:*** Alex Segal; ***W:*** Ernest Kinoy. **TV**

The Story of G.I. Joe 🦴🦴🦴 1/2 **1945** Grunt's-eye-view of the European theatre in WWII, based on the columns of war correspondent Ernie Pyle. Follows an infantry unit through Italy and concentrates on the everyday experiences of the soldiers, registering genuine emotion and realism. Mitchum's breakthrough role. Most of the actual unit played themselves. Pyle was killed by a sniper shortly before the film's release. **109m/B; VHS, DVD.** Burgess Meredith; Robert Mitchum; Wally Cassell; William Benedict; William Murphy; Jimmy Lloyd; Freddie (Fred) Steele; William (Bill) Self; Jack Reilly; Tito Renaldo; Hal Boyle; Chris Cunningham; Jack Foisie; George Lah; Bob Landry; Clete Roberts; Robert Rueben; Don Whitehead; ***D:*** William A. Wellman; ***W:*** Leopold Atlas; Guy Endore; Philip Stevenson; Ernie Pyle; ***C:*** Russell Metty; ***M:*** Louis Applebaum; Ann Ronell. Natl. Film Reg. '09.

The Story of Jacob & Joseph 🦴🦴🦴 **1974 (R)** Fine biblical drama finds brothers Jacob and Esau fighting over their birthright, tearing apart their family for 20 years. When the brothers finally reconcile, it's only to cast an envious eye on youngest brother Joseph, whom they sell into slavery. Taken to Egypt Joseph uses his talents to become the Pharoah's chief advisor but he can never forget his family or what was done to him. All-around good acting, directing, and writing. **96m/C; VHS, DVD.** Keith Michell; Tony LoBianco; Julian Glover; Colleen Dewhurst; Herschel Bernardi; Harry Andrews; ***Nar:*** Alan Bates; ***D:*** Michael Cacoyannis; ***W:*** Ernest Kinoy; ***M:*** Mikis Theodorakis. **TV**

Story of Mankind 🦴 **1957** Producer, director, and co-writer Irwin Allen made an unintended disaster(ous) flick in this terrible Technicolor fantasy that was Ronald Colman's last film. He serves as the speaker for mankind before a celestial tribunal that has convened to determine Man's fate. The heavenly court is upset that humans have discovered the hydrogen bomb too soon in our evolution and has to be convinced that we should survive. Opposing council is portrayed by the ever-suave Price as Mr. Scratch (AKA the Devil), who enjoys pointing out man's inhumanity to man. Viewers will enjoy pointing out the often-miscast actors briefly portraying historical figures. **100m/C; DVD.** Ronald Colman; Vincent Price; Cedric Hardwicke; Hedy Lamarr; Groucho Marx; Harpo Marx; Virginia Mayo; Agnes Moorehead; Peter Lorre; Dennis Hopper; ***D:*** Irwin Allen; ***W:*** Irwin Allen; Charles Bennett; ***C:*** Nicholas Musuraca; ***M:*** Paul Sawtell.

The Story of Marie and Julien 🦴🦴 *Histoire de Marie et Julien* **2003** Moody clockmaker Julien (Radziwilowicz) indulges his memories of a brief affair with Marie (Beart), who suddenly re-enters his life. She immediately moves in with him, begging Julien not to ask about her past, but he can't resist. Something supernatural is apparently going on but the entire situation is confusing rather than intriguing and solemn rather than enlightening. Beart's beauty is at least one reason to watch. French with subtitles. **150m/C; DVD.** *FR* Emmanuelle Beart; Jerzy Radziwilowicz; Anne Brochet; ***D:*** Jacques Rivette; ***W:*** Jacques Rivette; Christine Laurent; Pascal Bonitzer; ***C:*** William Lubtchansky.

The Story of O 🦴🦴 **1975 (NC-17)** A young woman's love for one man moves her to surrender herself to many men, in order to please him. Soft-core porn with bondage and S&M beautified by camera work. Based on the classic Freudian-erotic novel by Pauline Reage. **105m/C; VHS, DVD.** Corinne Clery; Anthony Steel; Udo Kier; Jean Gaven; Christiane Minazzoli; Martine Kelly; Nadine Perles; ***D:*** Just Jaeckin; ***W:*** Sebastien Japrisot; ***C:*** Robert Fraisse; Yves Rodallec; ***M:*** Pierre Bachelet.

The Story of O, Part 2 🦴 **1987** A sort-of sequel to the erotic classic, in which the somewhat soiled vixen takes over an American conglomerate by seducing everyone in it. **107m/C; DVD.** *FR* Sandra Wey; Carole James; ***D:*** Eric Rochat; ***W:*** Eric Rochat; ***C:*** Andres Berenguer; ***M:*** Hans Zimmer.

The Story of Qiu Ju 🦴🦴🦴 *Qiu Ju Da Guansi* **1991 (PG)** A simple story, beautifully directed and acted, about a peasant woman's search for justice. The pregnant Qiu Ju's husband is assaulted and injured by the head of their village. Outraged, Qui Ju slowly climbs the Chinese administrative ladder from official to higher official as she insistently seeks redress. Presents a close observance of daily life and customs with a strong female lead. Adapted from the novel "The Wan Family's Lawsuit" by Chen Yuan Bin. In Mandarin Chinese with English subtitles. **100m/C; VHS, DVD.** *CH* Gong Li; Lei Lao Sheng; Liu Pei Qu; Ge Zhi Jun; Ye Jun; Yang Liu Xia; Zhu Qanging; Cui Luowen; Yank Huiqin; Wang Jianfa; Lin Zi; ***D:*** Yimou Zhang; ***W:*** Liu Heng; ***C:*** Chi Xiaonin; Yu Xaioqun; ***M:*** Jiping Zhao. Natl. Soc. Film Critics '93: Foreign Film; Venice Film Fest. '92: Actress (Li), Film.

The Story of Robin Hood & His Merrie Men 🦴🦴🦴 *The Story of Robin Hood* **1952** Well-made swashbuckler based on the English legend was Disney's second live action feature. Almost, but not quite, as memorable as the 1938 Michael Curtiz "Adventures of Robin Hood." Curtiz's version had Errol Flynn, after all. **83m/C; VHS, DVD.** Richard Todd; Joan Rice; Peter Finch; Martita Hunt; ***D:*** Ken Annakin.

The Story of Ruth 🦴🦴 **1960** Biblical saga of adventures of Ruth as she denounces her pagan gods and flees to Israel. Typically "epic" with overwrought performances. Alternately not too bad to downright boring. **132m/C; VHS, DVD.** Elana Eden; Viveca Lindfors; Peggy Wood; Tom Tryon; Stuart Whitman; Jeff Morrow; Thayer David; Eduard Franz; ***D:*** Henry Koster.

The Story of Seabiscuit 🦴🦴 1/2 *Pride of Kentucky* **1949** The famous racing winner Seabiscuit is featured in a fluffy story of a racetrack romance. Temple is in love with a jockey (McCallister) but wants him to give up racing. Her uncle (Fitzgerald), who is Seabiscuit's trainer, has other things in mind. **93m/C; VHS, DVD.** Shirley Temple; Barry Fitzgerald; Lon (Bud) McCallister; Rosemary DeCamp; ***D:*** David Butler.

The Story of the Weeping Camel 🦴🦴🦴 *Die Geschichte vom Weinenden Kamel* **2003 (PG)** Tale of animal estrangement and reconciliation combining reality sequences with re-creations of authentic situations. Follows a family tribe of shepherds through the camel's birthing season, a way of life that is slowly being eliminated. When one camel mother rejects her white calf, a musician from the village is sent to perform a musical ceremony using a two-stringed, boxlike violin and soothing, hypnotic, melodies to reunite calf and mother. Some may argue the re-created sequences are out of balance or perhaps unnecessary but the story is presented in a thoughtful, honest manner. In Mongolian with English subtitles. **90m/C; DVD.** *GE* Odgerel Ayush; Ikhbayar Amgaabazar; Enkhbulgan Ikhbayar; Uuganbaadar Ikhbayar; Chimed Ohin; Janchiv Ayurzana; Amgaabazar Gonzon; Zeveljamz Nyam; Guntbaatar Ikhbayar; Munkhbayar; Ariun'jargal Adiya; Dago Roljav; Chuluunzezeg Gur; ***D:*** Byambasuren Davaa; Luigi Falorni; ***W:*** Byambasuren Davaa; Luigi Falorni; ***C:*** Luigi Falorni; ***M:*** Marcel Leniz. Directors Guild '04: Documentary Director (Falorni).

The Story of Three Loves 🦴🦴 1/2 **1953** Three passengers aboard an ocean liner dwell on romance. Ballet impresario Charles Coudray (Mason) is enchanted seeing ballerina Paula Woodward (Shearer) privately perform one of his dances and insists on making a new ballet for her, which leads to tragedy. French governess Mademoiselle (Caron) is exasperated by her young American charge Tommy (Nelson), who asks witch Mrs. Pennicott (Barrymore) to make him older. But like Cinderella his wish—which turns him into the adult Thomas (Granger-)?has a strict time limit. Daredevil trapeze artist Pierre Narval (Douglas) retired after his female partner died in an accident. After saving guilt-ridden Nina (Angelia) from a suicide attempt, Pierre decides to train her for a new act but when they fall in love, he worries history will repeat itself. **122m/C; DVD.** James Mason; Moira Shearer; Agnes Moorehead; Leslie Caron; Ethel Barrymore; Farley Granger; Ricky Nelson; Kirk Douglas; Pier Angeli; Richard Anderson; ***D:*** Gottfried Reinhardt; Vincente Minnelli; ***W:*** George Froeschel; Jan Lustig; ***C:*** Charles Rosher; Harold Rosson; ***M:*** Miklos Rozsa.

The Story of Us 🦴🦴 1/2 **1999 (R)** Hey attraction is easy but sustaining a relationship is hard—particularly after 15 years in a marriage of opposites. Crossword puzzle editor Katie (Pfeiffer) is a planner and organizer while hubby Ben (Willis), a TV comedy writer, is a spontaneous free-spirit. The kids are away at summer camp when the constantly bickering duo decide on a trial separation as they wonder what went wrong. Appealing leads but story is repetitive and sentimental. **98m/C; VHS, DVD.** Bruce Willis; Michelle Pfeiffer; Rita Wilson; Paul Reiser; Rob Reiner; Tim Matheson; Julie Hagerty; Jayne Meadows; Tom Poston; Betty White; Red Buttons; ***D:*** Rob Reiner; ***W:*** Alan Zweibel; Jessie Nelson; ***C:*** Michael Chapman; ***M:*** Eric Clapton; Marc Shaiman.

The Story of Vernon and Irene Castle 🦴🦴🦴 **1939** In this, their last film together for RKO, Astaire and Rogers portray the internationally successful ballroom dancers who achieved popularity in the early 1900s. Irene Castle served as technical advisor for the film and exasperated everyone on the set by insisting that Rogers be a brunette. Still fun, vintage Fred and Ginger. **93m/B; VHS, DVD.** Fred Astaire; Ginger Rogers; Edna May Oliver; Lew Fields; Jack Perrin; Walter Brennan; ***D:*** H.C. Potter.

The Story of Will Rogers 🦴🦴 1/2 **1952** Folksy if undemanding Warner Bros. bio with Will Rogers Jr. starring as his dad in a movie based on his mom Betty's recollections (she's played in the film by Wyman). Includes Roger's Oklahoma childhood, his time as a rodeo performer, as the homespun philosopher/star of the Ziegfeld Follies, and as a newspaper columnist and radio and film personality. Viewers will still tear up when

Rogers takes his final 1935 plane trip with friend Wiley Post (Beery Jr.). **109m/C; DVD.** Will Rogers, Jr.; Jane Wyman; Slim Pickens; Carl Benton Reid; James Gleason; Noah Beery, Jr.; William Forrest; Eva Muller; Mary Wickes; Jay Silverheels; *D:* Michael Curtiz; *W:* Stanley Roberts; John Moffitt; Frank Davis; *C:* Wilfred M. Cline; *M:* Victor Young.

The Story of Women *Une Affaire de Femmes* **1988** Riveting factual account of a woman (Huppert) who was guillotined for performing abortions in Nazi-occupied France. In French with English subtitles. **110m/C; VHS, DVD.** *FR* Isabelle Huppert; Francois Cluzet; Marie Trintignant; Nils (Niels) Tavernier; Louis Ducreux; *D:* Claude Chabrol; *W:* Claude Chabrol; Colo Tavernier O'Hagan; *C:* Jean Rabier; *M:* Matthieu Chabrol. L.A. Film Critics '89: Foreign Film; N.Y. Film Critics '89: Foreign Film; Venice Film Fest. '88: Actress (Huppert).

Storybook ½ **1995 (G)** Eight-year-old Brandon finds a magic storybook and enters into a realm of fantasy. He discovers the only way to return home from Storyland is to save the kingdom from the rule of Queen Evilia and along with Woody the Woodsman, Pouch the Boxing Kangaroo, and Hoot the Wise Owl, Brandon just may succeed. **88m/C; VHS, DVD.** Sean Fitzgerald; William McNamara; Swoosie Kurtz; Robert Costanzo; James Doohan; Brenda Epperson; Gary Morgan; Richard Moll; Jack Scalia; Milton Berle; *D:* Lorenzo Doumani; *W:* Lorenzo Doumani; Susan Bowen.

Storytelling **2001 (R)** Anthology explores the roles that sex and dysfunction play in creativity. First story, "Fiction" explores the complex relationship of writing student Vi (Blair) and her boyfriend Marcus (Fitzpatrick), who has cerebral palsy. The two are using each other for different ends, most notably to read each other's writing. Vi moves on to an intense one-night stand with her formidable black writing professor (Wisdom). Shaken, Vi weaves the graphic, brutal, but fascinating encounter into a story of her own. In "Nonfiction," feature documentarian Toby (Giamatti) goes to the burbs to document the life of a teen, his extremely dysfunctional family, and their Salvadoran maid. Solondz's characteristic black humor and social satire offers a range of hot topics, including homosexuality, political correctness, social stereotypes, the Holocaust, race, poverty, and the disabled. **87m/C; VHS, DVD.** Selma Blair; Leo Fitzpatrick; Aleksa Palladino; Robert Wisdom; Noah Fleiss; Paul Giamatti; John Goodman; Julie Hagerty; Lupe Ontiveros; Franka Potente; Mike Schank; Mark Webber; Jonathan Osser; *D:* Todd Solondz; *W:* Todd Solondz; *M:* Belle & Sebastian; Nathan Larson.

Storyville **1992 (R)** Southern Gothic tale set in New Orleans about a feckless young lawyer running for a local congressional seat. Neither Cray nor his family are strong candidates for the family values vote. Cray is separated from his wife and willingly indulges in an affair with a beautiful and mysterious young woman. This leads to a blackmail plot when he finds out his lover has been videotaping their antics. There's also a murder investigation and a host of family skeletons rattling around. Robards is fine as the crafty uncle but Spader's low-key attitude works against the story. Directorial debut of Frost. **112m/C; VHS, DVD.** James Spader; Joanne Whalley; Jason Robards, Jr.; Charlotte Lewis; Michael Warren; Piper Laurie; Michael Parks; Chuck McCann; Woody Strode; Charles Haid; *D:* Mark Frost; *W:* Mark Frost; Lee Reynolds; *M:* Carter Burwell.

Stowaway **1936 (G)** After her missionary parents are killed in a Chinese revolution, Shirley stows away on a San Francisco-bound liner and plays cupid to a bickering couple who adopt her. **86m/B; VHS, DVD.** Shirley Temple; Robert Young; Alice Faye; Eugene Pallette; Helen Westley; Arthur Treacher; Astrid Allwyn; *D:* William A. Seiter; *C:* Arthur C. Miller.

Straight A's ½ **2013 (R)** A drug addict is told by his mother's ghost to return to his family, where he discovers his former lover has married his brother. **88m/C; DVD, Blu-Ray, Streaming.** Ryan Phillippe; Anna Paquin; Luke Wilson; Christa Campbell; Riley Thomas Stewart; *D:* James Cox; *W:* Dave Cole; *C:* Shawn Kim; *M:* Joe Purdy. **VIDEO**

Straight from the Heart **2003** In this Hallmark Channel romantic drama, New York photographer Jordan Donovan (Polo) is depressed by her commitment-phobe boyfriend Edward (Evigan) and agrees to a matchmaking ad written by her pal Carla (Tucci). Jordan feels obligated when there's a set-up with widowed Wyoming rancher Tyler Ross (McCarthy). Despite the city/country mismatch, the two grow closer but their pasts cause problems. **88m/C; DVD.** Teri Polo; Andrew McCarthy; Patricia Kalember; Greg Evigan; Christine Tucci; *D:* David S. Cass, Sr.; *W:* Pamela Wallace; *C:* James W. Wrenn. **CABLE**

Straight into Darkness ½ **2004 (R)** Privates Losey (Francis) and Deming (MacDonald) go AWOL in Nazi-occupied France, eventually finding shelter at an abandoned hotel. The hotel also houses Deacon (Warner), Maria (Thorson), and a brood of orphans who have been trained to fight. The numerous flashbacks are confusing and the fate of the child soldiers is disturbing. **94m/C; DVD.** Ryan Francis; Scott MacDonald; David Warner; Linda Thorson; James LeGros; Daniel Roebuck; *D:* Jeff Burr; *W:* Jeff Burr; *C:* Viorel Sergovici, Jr.; *M:* Michael Convertino.

Straight out of Brooklyn **1991 (R)** A bleak, nearly hopeless look at a struggling black family in a Brooklyn housing project. The son seeks escape through crime, his father in booze. An up-close and raw look at part of society seldom shown in mainstream film, its undeniable power is sapped by ragged production values and a loose narrative prone to melodrama. Rich (seen in a supporting role) was only 19 years old when he completed this, funded partly by PBS-TV's "American Playhouse." **91m/C; VHS, DVD.** George T. Odom; Ann D. Sanders; Larry (Lawrence) Gilliard, Jr.; Mark Malone; Reana E. Drummond; Barbara Sanon; Matty Rich; *D:* Matty Rich; *W:* Matty Rich; *C:* John Rosnell; *M:* Harold Wheeler. Ind. Spirit '92: First Feature; Sundance '91: Special Jury Prize.

Straight out of Compton **1999** Stereotype-riddled saga of a tough Compton local, Henry "Hen" Alabaster, and his plan to score some big time cash and start his own record company. He targets a racist politician named Drake Norelli who's made a fortune laundering mob money. The whole thing seems to want to deliver the meaningful message that "you can't escape your past," but it's lost amidst a mess of cliches and offensive stereotypes. **?m/CDVD.** Ryan Combs; Johnny DeaRenzo; Jules Dupree; Sean Epps; *D:* Ryan Combs; *W:* Ryan Combs; *C:* Eric M. Green.

Straight Outta Compton **2015 (R)** It is the mid-'80s and life on the streets of Compton is brutal for five young men looking for a way to express themselves. What would come out of this nightmarish, gang-ridden part of the country is music that would change the world. F. Gary Gray deftly chronicles the rise and fall of N.W.A., capturing their importance to an entire cultural movement and social revolution, but not delivering a film that feels overly righteous. Sure, some of the darker elements of N.W.A. are ignored too easily, but this is a fun, clever, well-made music biopic. **147m/C; DVD, Blu-Ray.** O'Shea Jackson, Jr.; Corey Hawkins; Jason Mitchell; Neil Brown, Jr.; Aldis Hodge; *D:* F. Gary Gray; *W:* Jonathan Herman; Andrea Berloff; *C:* Matthew Libatique; *M:* Joseph Trapanese.

Straight Shooter **1999 (R)** Former Foreign Legionnaire Volker Bretz (Ferch) seeks revenge for his daughter's death by killing the politicians he thinks are responsible. Frank Hector (Hopper), his former trainer, may be the only one who can stop him but will he? Hopper's the only English-speaking actor in this German thriller—the other actors are dubbed. **98m/C; VHS, DVD.** *GE* Dennis Hopper; Heino Ferch; Ulrich Muhe; *D:* Thomas Bohn.

The Straight Story ½ **1999 (G)** Surprisingly sweet true story from the generally eccentric Lynch. Septugenarian Alvin Straight (Farnsworth), who lives in Iowa, is determined to visit his ailing, estranged brother Lyle (Stanton) even though he can no longer drive a car. So, he hitches a small trailer to his riding mower and heads off at a stately 6 miles per hour—to Wisconsin (a 300 mile trip). Alvin realizes this is his last chance at both freedom and family and he's determined to make the most of it. Farnsworth plays Straight as a gruff, straight-talking old geezer and there's little or no sentimentality involved. **111m/C; VHS, DVD.** Richard Farnsworth; Harry Dean Stanton; Sissy Spacek; *D:* David Lynch; *W:* John Roach; *C:* Freddie Francis; *M:* Angelo Badalamenti. Ind. Spirit '00: Actor (Farnsworth); N.Y. Film Critics '99: Actor (Farnsworth), Cinematog.

Straight Talk ½ **1992 (PG)** Shirlee (Parton), a down-home gal from Arkansas, heads for Chicago to start life anew. She finds a job as a receptionist at WNDY radio, but is mistaken for the new radio psychologist. Her homespun advice ("Get off the cross. Somebody needs the wood.") becomes hugely popular and soon "Dr." Shirlee is the toast of the town. Parton's advice is the funniest part of this flimsy movie, but she is helped immensely by Dunne and Orbach. Woods, however, is not in his element in a romantic comedy, and holds the movie down. **91m/C; VHS, DVD, Blu-Ray.** Dolly Parton; James Woods; Griffin Dunne; Michael Madsen; Deirdre O'Connell; John Sayles; Teri Hatcher; Spalding Gray; Jerry Orbach; Philip Bosco; Charles Fleischer; Jay Thomas; *D:* Barnet Kellman; *W:* Craig Bolotin; Patricia Resnick; *M:* Brad Fiedel.

Straight Time **1978 (R)** Ex-con Hoffman hits the streets for the first time in six years and finds himself again falling into a life of crime. Well-told, sobering story flopped at the boxoffice and has never received the recognition it deserved. Convincing, realistic portrayal of a criminal. Hoffman was the original director, but gave the reins to Grosbard. Based on the novel "No Beast So Fierce" by Edward Bunker. **114m/C; VHS, DVD.** Dustin Hoffman; Harry Dean Stanton; Gary Busey; Theresa Russell; M. Emmet Walsh; Kathy Bates; Edward (Eddie) Bunker; *D:* Ulu Grosbard; *W:* Jeffrey Boam; Alvin Sargent; Edward (Eddie) Bunker; *C:* Owen Roizman; *M:* David Shire.

Straight to Hell ½ **1987 (R)** A wildly senseless, anachronistic western spoof about a motley, inept gang of frontier thieves. An overplayed, indiscriminating punk spaghetti oat-opera. **86m/C; VHS, DVD, Blu-Ray.** Dennis Hopper; Joe Strummer; Elvis Costello; Grace Jones; Jim Jarmusch; Dick Rude; Courtney Love; Sy Richardson; Biff Yeager; Xander Berkeley; Shane McGowan; *D:* Alex Cox; *W:* Dick Rude; Alex Cox; *C:* Tom Richmond; *M:* The Pogues; Pray for Rain.

Strait-Jacket ½ **1964** After Crawford is released from an insane asylum where she was sent 20 years for axing her husband and his mistress, mysterious axe murders begin to occur in the neighborhood. Coincidence? Aging axist Crawford is the prime suspect, and even she cannot say for sure who's doing it. Daughter Baker is there to help her adjust. Moderately creepy grade B+ slasher is lifted somewhat by Crawford. Written by Robert Bloch ("Psycho"). Never one to miss a gimmick, director Castle arranged for the distribution of cardboard "bloody axes" to all theatre patrons attending the movie. **89m/B; VHS, DVD, Blu-Ray.** Joan Crawford; Leif Erickson; Diane Baker; George Kennedy; Howard St. John; Rochelle Hudson; Edith Atwater; Lee Majors; John Anthony Hayes; Mitchell Cox; Lee Yeary; Patricia Krest; *D:* William Castle; *W:* Robert Bloch; *C:* Arthur E. Arling; *M:* Van Alexander.

Stranded **1935** Lynn Palmer (Francis) works for the San Francisco Traveler's Aid Society. She falls for Mack Hale (Brent), the chief construction foreman on the Golden Gate Bridge. Their romance is slow to proceed because of their busy schedules and Mack expects Lynn to become a traditional housewife if they get married, but Lynn refuses to give up her job. The most interesting thing about the melodrama is the newsreel footage of the bridge's construction. **76m/B; DVD.** Kay Francis; George Brent; Patricia Ellis; Donald Woods; Barton MacLane; Robert Barrat; *D:* Frank Borzage; *W:* Delmer Daves; *C:* Sidney Hickox.

Stranded ½ **2006** Bride-to-be Carina (Durance) and her bridesmaids are having her bachelorette blowout at a San Carlos resort but they decide to spend a day sunning on a nearby deserted island. Only their sleazy charter boat captain doesn't return and they are forced to spend the night. However, two of the women have disappeared by the next morning so the island isn't so deserted after all. Lots of revealing swimwear in a mindlessly cheesy thriller. **90m/C; DVD.** Erica Durance; Bree De Beau; Michelle Jones; Vane Millon; Jessica Lauren; Ashley Totin; Jack Hartnett; Carlos Ponce; *D:* Kern Konwiser; *W:* Matt Dorff; Brian Hurwitz; *C:* P.J. Lopez; *M:* Andrew Keresztes. **CABLE**

Stranded **2013** Drab, low-budget scifier is assembled via one cliche from column A and another from column B. A meteor shower severely damages the Ark moon base and also contaminates the air supply. Suddenly, astronaut Ava is preggers with an alien spawn that rapidly mutates after birth and causes terror. **88m/C; DVD, Blu-Ray.** *CA UK* Christian Slater; Amy Matysio; Brendan Fehr; Michael Thierrault; *D:* Roger Christian; *W:* Roger Christian; Christian Piers Betley; *C:* Mark Dobrescu; *M:* Todd Bryanton. **VIDEO**

Strange Affair ½ **1944** Comic mystery shtick. Bill Harrison (Joslyn), the artist of a detective comic strip, turns sleuth after the poisoning death of a doctor. Bill is suspicious of the man's beautiful widow but the real detectives on the case wish he would quit poking around. **79m/B; DVD.** Allyn Joslyn; Edgar Buchanan; Frank Jenks; Marguerite Chapman; Evelyn Keyes; Nina Foch; Hugo Haas; Shemp Howard; *D:* Alfred E. Green; *W:* Eve Greene; Jerome Odlum; Oscar Saul; *C:* Franz Planer; *M:* Marlin Skiles.

The Strange Affair of Uncle Harry ½ *Uncle Harry* **1945** Small-town gothic with fine acting by Sanders, an aging bachelor who plots murder when his romance is threatened by a jealous sister. A title card asks you not to reveal the 'surprise' ending—a hackneyed twist that appeased the censors but made producer Joan Harrison resign in protest. Based on a play by Robert Job. Tape suffers from poor film-video transfer. **80m/B; VHS, Blu-Ray, Streaming.** George Sanders; Geraldine Fitzgerald; Ella Raines; Sara Allgood; Moyna MacGill; Samuel S. Hinds; Harry von Zell; *D:* Robert Siodmak.

Strange Awakening **1958** Traveling in France while recuperating from amnesia, Barker is trapped in a plot of fraud and theft. Confused and contrived. **75m/B; VHS, Streaming.** *GB* Lex Barker; Carole Mathews; Nora Swinburne; Richard Molinos; Peter Dyneley; *D:* Montgomery Tully.

Strange Bedfellows ½ **1965** Within 24 hours of Carter Hudson (Hudson) arriving to work in London, he's met and married eccentric Italian Toni Vincenti (Lollobrigida). Complete opposites, the marriage is soon over and Carter returns to the States. Seven years later, he's back in London, ready to officially divorce Toni but learns from company PR whiz Dick Bramwell (Young) that his big promotion is contingent on his happy marriage. Carter courts Toni again, and tries to support her liberal causes and friends, but it turns out her latest stunt is aimed at his firm. Supposedly a check of the closing credits shows the film was shot on a Universal back lot and not on location. **104m/C; VHS, DVD, Blu-Ray.** Rock Hudson; Gina Lollobrigida; Gig Young; Edward Judd; Howard St. John; Nancy Kulp; Bernard Fox; Terry-Thomas; *D:* Melvin Frank; *W:* Melvin Frank; Michael Pertwee; *C:* Leo Tover; *M:* Leigh Harline.

Strange Bedfellows ½ **2004 (R)** Because of financial problems, lifelong buddies Vince (Hogan) and Ralph (Caton) pose as a gay couple to get a newly-enacted tax break. But suspicious auditor Russell McKenzie (Postlethwaite) comes to their small town to check out their story. Surprisingly charming, though predictable, comedy plays up the outrageous aspects of the deception while still maintaining its heart. **100m/C; VHS, DVD.** *AU* Paul Hogan; Michael Caton; Pete Postlethwaite; Alan Cassell; Kestie Morassi; Roy Billing; Glynn Nicholas; Amanda Monroe; Stewart Faichney; *D:* Dean Murphy; *W:* Dean Murphy; Stewart Faichney; *C:* Roger Lanser; *M:* Dale Cornelius.

Strange Behavior *Dead Kids; Small Town Massacre* **1981 (R)** In a small Midwestern town, the police chief follows the clues from a series of murders to the experimental lab of the local college. Seems there's a mad scientist involved. Grisly and creepy, but unduly ballyhooed when it appeared. Shot on location in New Zealand. **105m/C; VHS, DVD, Blu-Ray.** Michael Murphy; Louise Fletcher; Dan Shor; Fiona Lewis; Arthur Dignam; Marc McClure; Scott Brady; Dey Young; Charles Lane; *D:* Michael Laughlin; *W:* Michael Laughlin; Bill Condon; *C:* Louis Horvath.

Strange Brew 🦴🦴 ½ **1983 (PG)** The screen debut of the SCTV alumni's characters Doug & Bob MacKenzie, the Great White North duo. They do battle with a powerful, megalomaniacal brew master over—what else??a case of beer. Dumb, but what did you expect? Watch it, or be a hoser. **91m/C; VHS, DVD, Blu-Ray.** *CA* Rick Moranis; Dave Thomas; Max von Sydow; Paul Dooley; Lynne Griffin; Angus MacInnes; *V:* Mel Blanc; *D:* Rick Moranis; Dave Thomas; *W:* Rick Moranis; Dave Thomas; Steve DeJarnatt; *C:* Steven Poster; *M:* Charles Fox.

Strange But True 🦴🦴 **2019 (PG-13)** Five years after the death of her boyfriend Ronnie (Jessup) in a car wreck on prom night, Melissa Moody (Qualley) returns home claiming to be pregnant with Ronnie's child. Her re-appearance unsettles Ronnie's brother Philip (Robinson) and his mother Charlene (Ryan), who divorced her husband Richard (Kinnear) after the accident. Philip and Charlene conduct their own investigations to learn the truth about Melissa's pregnancy. Based on a John Seares novel, the psychological thriller is an unbelievable suburban drama whose story mistreats the able cast. **96m/C; DVD.** Nick Robinson; Amy Ryan; Greg Kinnear; Brian Cox; Margaret Qualley; *D:* Rowan Athale; *W:* Eric Garcia; *C:* Stuart Bentley; *M:* Neil Athale.

Strange Cargo 🦴🦴 ½ **1940** Convicts escaping from Devil's Island are mystically entranced by a Christ-like fugitive en route to freedom. An odd, pretentious Hollywood fable waiting for a cult following. Gable and Crawford's eighth and final pairing. Adapted by Anita Loos from the book "Not Too Narrow...Not Too Deep" by Richard Sale. **105m/B; VHS, DVD.** Clark Gable; Joan Crawford; Ian Hunter; Peter Lorre; Paul Lukas; Albert Dekker; J. Edward Bromberg; Eduardo Ciannelli; Frederick Worlock; *D:* Frank Borzage; *W:* Lesser Samuels; *C:* Robert Planck; *M:* Franz Waxman.

The Strange Case of Angelica 🦴🦴 *O Estranho Caso de Angelica* **2010** A magical drama by respected filmmaker Manoel de Oliveira that focuses on one photographer's obsession with a subject he can never truly have. Young photographer Isaac (Trepa) is called to take a job late one night by a family of means. Daughter Angelica (Lopez de Ayala) was a young bride and has died suddenly. Taking the last photographs of Angelica for the family, Isaac falls in love her and she seems to come to life when he looks through his camera lens. In his dreams and in his waking hours, Isaac becomes haunted by the vision of Angelica. Portuguese with subtitles. **97m/C; DVD, Blu-Ray.** Ricardo Trepa; Pilar Lopez de Ayala; Leonor Silveira; Isabel Ruth; Filipe Vargas; *D:* Manoel de Oliveira; *W:* Manoel de Oliveira; *C:* Sabine Lancelin.

Strange Case of Dr. Jekyll & Mr. Hyde 🦴🦴 **1968** An adaptation of the classic Robert Louis Stevenson book about a scientist who conducts experiments on himself to separate good from evil. Palance is oddly but appealingly cast; Jarrott's bad direction wrecks it. Made for TV. **128m/C; VHS, DVD.** Jack Palance; Leo Genn; Oscar Homolka; Billie Whitelaw; Denholm Elliott; *D:* Charles Jarrott; *M:* Robert Cobert. **TV**

The Strange Case of Dr. Jekyll and Mr. Hyde 🦴 **2006 (R)** The umpteenth adaptation of the Robert Louis Stevenson story is an illogical and uninteresting waste of time. In this modern update, Dr. Jekyll (Todd) works at a big lab studying heart problems. He injects himself with a serum intended to cure his own heart defect and unleashes Edward Hyde, a hairy guy with fangs everyone at work not only sees but treats like a new and unpleasant employee. Edward likes to go out and eviscerate college coeds and Jekyll finally figures out what he's become. **79m/C; DVD.** Tony Todd; Tracy Scoggins; Vernon Wells; Tim Thomerson; Peter Jason; Stephen Wastell; *D:* John Carl Buechler; *W:* John Carl Buechler; *C:* James M. LeGoy.

The Strange Case of Dr. Rx 🦴 **1942** What's strange is how boring this Universal flick truly is, probably because it focuses on the dull PI and his personal life more than the crimes. A killer kills killers who were acquitted thanks to a crooked lawyer, leaving a label with the Rx symbol on his victims. PI Jerry Church (Knowles) investigates and thinks his best suspect is sinister Dr. Fish (Atwill with a very brief screen time). And yep, that's "Three Stooges" Howard offering some comic relief. **66m/B; DVD, Blu-Ray.** Patric Knowles; Anne Gwynne; Lionel Atwill; Samuel S. Hinds; Mona Barrie; Shemp Howard; Edmund MacDonald; Mantan Moreland; Paul Cavanagh; *D:* William Nigh; *W:* Clarence Upson Young; *C:* Elwood "Woody" Bredell.

Strange Days 🦴🦴🦴 **1995 (R)** It's 1999 in volatile L.A. and vice cop-turned-street-hustler Lenny Nero (Fiennes) is plying his SQUID trade—discs that offer the wearer the chance to experience any vice. The seedily likeable Lenny draws the line at peddling snuff clips until one capturing the murder of his friend, hooker Iris (Bako), shows up. Lenny's in way over his head and turns to self-sufficient security agent Mace (Bassett) to save him. The phenomenal Bassett heats up the screen (and kicks major butt) while the generally cerebral Fiennes shows why someone could care about his desperate lowlife. Bigelow's an action expert and struts on the film's dark visuals while offering some emotional impact with her society-on-the-eve-of-destruction saga. **145m/C; VHS, DVD.** Ralph Fiennes; Angela Bassett; Juliette Lewis; Tom Sizemore; Michael Wincott; Brigitte Bako; Vincent D'Onofrio; William Fichtner; Richard Edson; Glenn Plummer; Josef Sommer; Kelly Hu; Michael Jace; *D:* Kathryn Bigelow; *W:* James Cameron; Jay Cocks; *C:* Matthew F. Leonetti; *M:* Graeme Revell.

The Strange Door 🦴 ½ **1951** Laughton hams it up as the evil Alan de Maletroit (Laughton), who's imprisoned his brother Edmond (Cavanagh) for the crime of marrying Alan's one love. Now Maletroit wants to destroy his niece Blanche (Forrest) as well. But Edmond's faithful retainer Voltan (Karloff) is determined to stop the evil. Low-budget hokum adapted from the Robert Louis Stevenson story "The Sire de Maletroits's Door." **81m/B; VHS, DVD, Blu-Ray.** Charles Laughton; Boris Karloff; Paul Cavanagh; Sally Forrest; Richard Stapley; Michael Pate; Alan Napier; *D:* Joseph Pevney; *W:* Jerry Sackheim; *C:* Irving Glassberg.

Strange Fits of Passion 🦴🦴 ½ **1999** Low-budget comedy/drama is McCredie's directorial debut. A nameless overly romantic young woman (Noonan) is convinced that she has just let the perfect man (Finsterer) slip away and she becomes obsessive about finding him again. Her search does not stop her, however, from having some alternative romantic prospects in mind. **83m/C; VHS, DVD.** *AU* Michela Noonan; Mitchell Butel; Samuel Johnson; Steve Adams; Anni Finsterer; Jack Finsterer; *D:* Elise McCredie; *W:* Elise McCredie; *C:* Jaems Grant; *M:* Cezary Skubiszewski.

Strange Frequency 2 🦴🦴 **2001 (R)** Anthology consisting of four episodes from the title TV series: "Soul Man," "Instant Karma," "Cold Turkey," and "Don't Stop Believing." They each have a musical premise and a frequently supernatural twist about the price of fame and success. **84m/C; DVD.** Roger Daltrey; Jason Gedrick; Patsy Kensit; Wendie Malick; James Marsters; Peter Strauss; *D:* Jeff Woolnough. **TV**

Strange Fruit 🦴🦴 **2004** Intriguing premise is done in by a sluggish production (although the performances are generally strong). Gay black lawyer William Boyals (Faulcon) reluctantly leaves New York to return to the Louisiana bayou town he left years before after an old friend is found lynched. He needs to conduct his own investigation since the local sheriff (Jones) is a homophobic bigot. **115m/C; DVD.** Sam Jones; Cecile Johnson; Kent Faulcon; Berlinda Tolbert; David Raibon; *D:* Kyle Schickner; *W:* Kyle Schickner; *C:* David Oye; *M:* Sidney James.

Strange Illusion 🦴🦴 ½ *Out of the Night* **1945** Unbalanced teen Lydon believes his mother, about to remarry, was responsible for his father's death. He feigns insanity in a plan to catch her, but is sent to an asylum, where he nearly goes insane for real. Slow and implausible, but creepy enough to hold your interest. **87m/B; VHS, DVD.** Jimmy Lydon; Warren William; Sally Eilers; Regis Toomey; Charles Arnt; George Reed; Jayne Hazard; *D:* Edgar G. Ulmer; *W:* Adele Comandini; *C:* Philip Tannura; *M:* Leo Erdody.

Strange Impersonation 🦴🦴 ½ **1946** Dreamy noir has chemist Nora Goodrich (Marshall) injecting herself in order to test a new anesthetic she's developing. (This is never a good idea.) Then her life goes nuts when she can't separate reality from her dreams. **68m/B; VHS, DVD.** Brenda Marshall; William Gargan; Hillary Brooke; George Chandler; Ruth Ford; H.B. Warner; Lyle Talbot; Mary Treen; *D:* Anthony Mann; *W:* Mindret Lord; *C:* Robert Pittack.

Strange Interlude 🦴🦴🦴 *Strange Interval* **1932** Shearer is at her best in screen adaptation of talky Eugene O'Neill play in which she portrays a young wife who wants a child, but discovers that insanity runs in her husband's family. Doing the only sensible thing, she decides to have a child by another man (Gable). Interesting because the characters' thoughts are revealed to the audience through voice-overs. **110m/B; VHS, DVD.** Norma Shearer; Clark Gable; May Robson; Ralph Morgan; Robert Young; Mary Alden; Maureen O'Sullivan; Henry B. Walthall; *D:* Robert Z. Leonard; *C:* Lee Garmes.

Strange Invaders 🦴🦴🦴 **1983 (PG)** Body-snatchers-from-space sci-fi with an attitude—fun spoof of '50s alien flicks. Space folks had taken over a midwestern town in the '50s, assuming the locals' appearance and attire before returning to their ship. Seems one of them married an earthling—but divorced and moved with her half-breed daughter to New York City. So the hicksters from space arrive in Gotham wearing overalls. . . **94m/C; VHS, DVD, Blu-Ray.** Paul LeMat; Nancy Allen; Diana Scarwid; Michael Lerner; Louise Fletcher; Wallace Shawn; Fiona Lewis; Kenneth Tobey; June Lockhart; Charles Lane; Dey Young; Mark Goddard; Jack Kehler; *D:* Michael Laughlin; *W:* Bill Condon; *C:* Louis Horvath; *M:* John Addison.

Strange Lady in Town 🦴🦴 **1955** Garson's only western is a tame affair. In 1879, Boston doctor Julia Garth heads west to set up her medical practice in Santa Fe where her brother David is stationed in the army. She struggles to win acceptance because she's a woman and also has new-fangled ideas. Julia's befriended by tomboy Spurs O'Brien, whose dad is the established doctor in town. Rourke then falls for Julia despite his sexist attitude towards her medical skills. **112m/C; DVD.** Greer Garson; Dana Andrews; Cameron Mitchell; Lois Smith; *D:* Mervyn LeRoy; *W:* Frank Butler; *C:* Harold Rosson; *M:* Dimitri Tiomkin.

The Strange Love of Martha Ivers 🦴🦴🦴 **1946** Douglas is good in his screen debut as the wimpy spouse of unscrupulous Stanwyck. Stanwyck shines as the woman who must stay with Douglas because of a crime she committed long ago... Tough, dark melodrama; classic film noir. **117m/B; VHS, DVD, Blu-Ray.** Barbara Stanwyck; Van Heflin; Kirk Douglas; Lizabeth Scott; Judith Anderson; *D:* Lewis Milestone; *W:* Robert Rossen; *C:* Victor Milner; *M:* Miklos Rozsa.

The Strange Love of Molly Louvain 🦴 ½ *Molly Louvain* **1932** Unwed mother Dvorak finds herself in hiding after her criminal beau fatally shoots a police officer. She falls in love with the unsuspecting newsman (Tracy) hot on her trail. Good performance from Dvorak but the film in general lacks sparkle. Adapted from the play "Tinsel Girl" by Maurine Watkins. **70m/B; DVD.** Ann Dvorak; Lee Tracy; Richard Cromwell; Guy Kibbee; Leslie Fenton; Frank McHugh; Evalyn Knapp; Charles Middleton; Mary Doran; C. Henry Gordon; *D:* Michael Curtiz; *W:* Erwin Gelsey; Brown Holmes; *C:* Robert B. Kurrle; *M:* Bernhard Kaun.

Strange Magic 🦴 **2015 (PG)** Produced by George Lucas, this is one of those early-year animated films that comes and goes mostly unnoticed by American kids. This truly bizarre and grating Disney musical-comedy is a variation on Shakespeare's "A Midsummer Night's Dream," complete with pop and rock hits from the last several decades like "I Wanna Dance with Somebody (Who Loves Me)" and "Wild Thing." If the karaoke soundtrack wasn't traumatic enough, the awful characters, boring visuals, and lackluster story would be. It's only notable for having one of the worst opening weekends for a wide release in movie history. Nothing magical here. **99m/C; Streaming.** *V:* Evan Rachel Wood; Meredith Anne Bull; Alan Cumming; Elijah Kelley; Kristin Chenoweth; Maya Rudolph; Sam Palladio; Peter Stormare; *D:* Gary Rydstrom; *W:* Gary Rydstrom; David Berenbaum; Irene Mecchi; *M:* Marius De Vries.

Strange New World 🦴 **1975** Unsuccessful TV pilot movie about three astronauts who spend 180 years in suspended animation. When they finally return to Earth they discover it has been decimated by asteroid strikes and is populated by clones and other strange creatures. Poor Saxon gets to spend most of his time wearing a pink toga/skirt. Based on a Gene Roddenberry project that was previously tried as "Genesis 2" (1973) and "Planet Earth" (1974) although Roddenberry wasn't directly involved in this third attempt. **97m/C; DVD.** John Saxon; Kathleen Miller; Keene Curtis; Martine Beswick; James Olson; Catherine Bach; Richard Farnsworth; Ford Rainey; *D:* Robert Butler. **TV**

The Strange One 🦴🦴 ½ **1957** Appropriate title for this dank drama based on Willingham's novel and play "End As a Man." Jacko De Paris (Gazzara) is the student leader at a Southern military school, who uses his power to intimidate and brutalize fellow cadets, aided by minions Knoble (Hingle) and Gatt (Olson). Finally a group of younger students, led by Marquales (Peppard, in his film debut) go after the tyrant. Also filmed as 1957's "Sorority Girl." **100m/B; VHS, DVD.** Ben Gazzara; Pat Hingle; James Olson; George Peppard; Peter Mark Richman; Larry Gates; Clifton James; Arthur Storch; *D:* Jack Garfein; *W:* Calder Willingham; *C:* Burnett Guffey; *M:* Kenyon Hopkins.

Strange Planet 🦴🦴 ½ **1999** Romantic comedy that follows six characters (three young women who share a house and three male buddies) from one New Year's Eve to the next. They have affairs, fall in love, break-up, and get together with different partners over the span of time. It's not new but it's sweet and Watts, Karvan, and Williamson are standouts. **95m/C; VHS, DVD.** *AU* Claudia Karvan; Naomi Watts; Alice Garner; Tom Long; Hugo Weaving; Marshall Napier; Aaron Jeffrey; Felix Williamson; *D:* Emma-Kate Croghan; *W:* Emma-Kate Croghan; Stavros Kazantzidis; *C:* Justin Brickle.

Strange Relations 🦴🦴 **2002** New York shrink Jerry Lipman (Reiser) is diagnosed with leukemia and needs a bone marrow transplant. His mother Esther (Dukakis) finally confesses that Jerry was adopted in England and he heads to Liverpool to find his biological mother. That would be tough-talking, working class Sheila (Walters), who has a soft heart and is eager to welcome Jerry into the family. Jerry keeps his cancer a secret—not wanting to admit that's why he sought out his new relatives, especially as he gets closer to them. Walters is the one to watch but Reiser's sarcasm does help to keep the sentiment at bay. **107m/C; VHS, DVD.** Paul Reiser; Julie Walters; George Wendt; Olympia Dukakis; Amy Robbins; Tony Maudsley; Suzanne Hitchmough; Ian Puleston-Davies; *D:* Paul Seed; *W:* Tim Kazurinsky; *C:* Lawrence Jones; *M:* Rupert Gregson-Williams. **CABLE**

Strange Wilderness 🦴 **2008 (R)** Peter Gaulke (Zahn) takes over as host of his dead father's popular wildlife show, but his inept stoner on-air persona pushes it to the brink of cancellation. Desperate, Peter and his loyal soundman Fred Wolf (Covert; note that the writers named the two main characters after themselves) hatch a plan to showcase their search for Bigfoot in Ecuador, with their merry band of dudes in tow. Lots of herbally enhanced gags and goof-ups ensue, none of them particularly amusing (unless you're equally medicated). Given the funny-guy cast, what could have been a clever send-up of nature documentaries is all but wasted (in more ways than one) by the dopey script. **85m/C; Blu-Ray, On Demand.** Steve Zahn;

Allen Covert; Jonah Hill; Kevin Heffernan; Ashley Scott; Justin Long; Peter Dante; Harry Hamlin; Robert Patrick; Joe Don Baker; Jeff Garlin; Ernest Borgnine; *D:* Fred Wolf; *W:* Fred Wolf; Peter Gaulke; *C:* David Hennings; *M:* Waddy Wachtel.

The Strange Woman 🦴🦴 **1946** Uneventful Hollywood costume drama. Lamarr stalks man after man, but never creates much excitement in spite of Ulmer's fancy camera work and intense pace. **100m/B; DVD.** Hedy Lamarr; George Sanders; Louis Hayward; Gene Lockhart; Hillary Brooke; June Storey; *D:* Edgar G. Ulmer; *W:* Herb Meadow; *C:* Lucien N. Andriot; *M:* Carmen Dragon.

The Stranger 🦴🦴🦴 1/2 **1946** Notably conventional for Welles, but swell entertainment nonetheless. War crimes tribunal sets Nazi thug Shayne free hoping he'll lead them to his superior, Welles. Robinson trails Shayne through Europe and South America to a small town in Connecticut. Tight suspense made on a tight budget saved Welles's directorial career. **95m/B; DVD, Blu-Ray.** Edward G. Robinson; Loretta Young; Martha Wentworth; Konstantin Shayne; Richard Long; Orson Welles; *D:* Orson Welles; *W:* Victor Trivas; *C:* Russell Metty; *M:* Bronislau Kaper.

The Stranger 🦴🦴🦴 **1987 (R)** Amnesiac car-wreck victim Bedelia begins regaining her memory, and realizes she witnessed several grisly murders. Is her shrink (Riegert) helping her remember, or keeping something from her? Good, neglected thriller. **93m/C; VHS, Streaming.** *AR* Bonnie Bedelia; Peter Riegert; Barry Primus; David Spielberg; Julio de Grazia; Cecilia (Celia) Roth; Marcus Woinski; *D:* Adolfo Aristarain; *W:* Dan Gurskis; *M:* Craig Safan.

The Stranger 🦴 **2010 (R)** An apparent victim (along with his family) of Russian mobsters and Mexican drug cartels, an amnesiac tries to regain his memories with the help of a shrink and an FBI agent. Too many flashbacks, double-crossing distractions, and not as much action as you might expect. **99m/C; DVD, Blu-Ray.** Steve Austin; Erica Cerra; Adam Beach; Ron Lea; Stephen Dimopoulos; Viv Leacock; Jason Schombing; *D:* Robert Lieberman; *W:* Quinn Scott; *C:* Peter Woeste; *M:* Peter Allen. **VIDEO**

The Stranger 🦴 *Eli Roth Presents: The Stranger; La Maldición* **2015** Eli Roth presents (which means he puts his name on, not directs) this incredibly stupid horror movie, one that has a strong visual language for about five minutes until you realize it's a load of nonsense. Essentially, this is a vampire movie crossed with a revenge flick like "Death Wish." Martin returns home to a small Canadian town to look for his wife Ana, quickly discovering that she's dead. He's soon harassed and left for dead himself. Vengeance awaits. The film is awash in style—most scenes are so darkly lit you can't tell what's happening—but it's at the service of nothing new. **92m/C; DVD, Blu-Ray, Streaming.** *CL* Christobal Tapia Montt; Lorenza Izzo; Luis Gnecco; Ariel Levy; Aaron Burns; *D:* Guillermo Amoedo; *W:* Guillermo Amoedo; *C:* Chechu Graf; *M:* Manuel Riveiro. **VIDEO**

A Stranger Among Us 🦴🦴 **1992 (PG-13)** A missing jeweler turns up dead and more than $1 million in diamonds has disappeared. NYPD Detective Emily Eden (Griffith) is called in to solve the case, and she decides she must go undercover in a community of Hasidic Jews to find the perpetrator. She not only finds the criminal, but she also falls in love with one of the group's most devout residents. Griffith is out of her element as a tough cop with her baby voice and cutesy style, but other actors, including Thal (in his movie debut) and Sara, perform splendidly, even though they're held back by a cumbersome script with many similarities to "Witness." **109m/C; VHS, DVD, Blu-Ray.** Melanie Griffith; Eric Thal; John Pankow; Tracy Pollan; Lee Richardson; Mia Sara; Jamey Sheridan; James Gandolfini; *D:* Sidney Lumet; *W:* Robert J. Avrech; *C:* Andrzej Bartkowiak; *M:* Jerry Bock. Golden Raspberries '92: Worst Actress (Griffith).

Stranger by Night 🦴🦴 **1994 (R)** Detective Bobby Corcoran and his partner are hunting a mutilating serial killer. Since Corcoran suffers from black-outs and fits of rage the evidence begins pointing very close to home. **96m/C; VHS, DVD.** Steven Bauer; William Katt; Jennifer Rubin; Michael Parks; Michele Greene; J.J. Johnston; *D:* Gregory Brown; *W:* Daryl Haney; *C:* Wally Pfister; *M:* Ashley Irwin.

Stranger by the Lake 🦴🦴🦴 *L'inconnu du lac* **2013** This winner of the Best Director Award at the 2013 Cannes Film Festival is a darkly humorous, very sexually explicit commentary on how sexual desire can force one to ignore personal safety. Taking place entirely around a lake that's a cruising ground for casual sex between gay males, Guiraudie's film hides nothing in its portrayal of a community driven by pleasure. Franck (Deladonchamps) seems like a normal, everyday guy just looking for some fun, but he becomes drawn to a man named Michel (Paou), who turns out to be dangerous. French with subtitles. **97m/C; DVD, Blu-Ray.** *FR* Pierre Deladonchamps; Christophe Paou; Patrick D'Assumcao; Francois Labarthe; *D:* Alain Guiraudie; *W:* Alain Guiraudie; *C:* Claire Mathon. Cannes '13: Director.

Stranger from Venus WOOF! *Immediate Disaster; The Venusian* **1954** "The Day the Earth Stood Still" warmed over. Venusian Dantine tells earth lady Neal he's worried about the future of her planet. Real low budget. Includes previews of coming attractions from classic sci-fi. **78m/B; VHS, DVD.** Patricia Neal; Helmut Dantine; Derek Bond; *D:* Burt Balaban; *W:* Hans Jacoby; *C:* Ken Talbot; *M:* Eric Spear.

The Stranger Game 🦴 1/2 **2006** Completely predictable psycho-thriller. After they move to a new home in the country, working parents Joanne (Rogers) and Paul (Hope) need someone to help look after their 9-year-old son Sam (Dubois). Joanne hires the seemingly perfect Charlie (Orth) who soon wants to assume Paul's role as head of the family. **90m/C; DVD.** Mimi Rogers; David Orth; Barclay Hope; Casey Dubois; Sonya Salomaa; Liam Ranger; *D:* Terry Ingram; *W:* Judy Skelton; Cynthia Weil; *C:* David Pelletier; *M:* Michael Richard Plowman. **CABLE**

Stranger in My Bed 🦴 **2005** Sara (Luner) fakes her death to escape her abusive husband Ryan (Chris) and starts a new life in Portland, Oregon. But Ryan easily tracks her down because Sara is such a dumb bunny and doesn't cover her tracks very well, so she must reveal her past to new boyfriend Brad (Cermak) if she intends to stay alive. **90m/C; DVD.** Jamie Luner; Chris Kramer; Ivan Cermak; Barbara Fixx; Alistair Abell; Barbara Niven; *D:* George Erschbamer; *W:* George Erschbamer; Jeff Barmash; *C:* C. Kim Miles; *M:* John Sereda. **CABLE**

A Stranger in the Kingdom 🦴🦴 **1998 (R)** Walt Andrews (Hudson) has been hired sight unseen to be the new minister in a small Vermont community in the '50s. The unseen part is a problem since the townspeople are shocked when Walt turns out to be black. Then Walt gets arrested for the murder of a young housekeeper, Claire (Bayne), whom he was sheltering from her abusive employer and the town seems determined to make him the scapegoat. Based on a Howard Frank Mosher novel. **111m/C; VHS, DVD.** Ernie Hudson; David Lansbury; Jean Louisa Kelly; Martin Sheen; Sean Nelson; Jordan Bayne; Bill Raymond; Henry Gibson; Larry Pine; Tom Aldredge; Carrie Snodgress; *D:* Jay Craven; *W:* Jay Craven; Don Bredes; *C:* Philip Holahan.

A Stranger in Town 🦴🦴 1/2 **1995** Single mom Kay Tarses (Smart) has relocated to a small, quiet town with her infant son. But her peace is disturbed by menacing Barnes (Hines), a stranger who seems to know Kay has been lying about her past—and her child. When he seems determined to take her child, Kay has to decide whether to run, accept her fate, or fight. **93m/C; VHS, DVD.** Jean Smart; Gregory Hines; Jeffrey Nordling; Lucinda Jenney; Richard Riehle; *D:* Peter Levin; *M:* Mark Snow. **TV**

A Stranger Is Watching 🦴 1/2 **1982 (R)** Rapist-murderer Torn holds his victim's 10-year-old daughter hostage, along with a New York TV anchorwoman. Complicated and distasteful. **92m/C; VHS, DVD.** Rip Torn; Kate Mulgrew; James Naughton; *D:* Sean S. Cunningham. **TV**

Stranger on Horseback 🦴🦴 **1955** Circuit Court Judge Richard Thorne (McCrea) is determined to bring suspected killer Tom Bannerman (McCarthy) to trial even though Bannerman's cattle baron father (McIntire) controls the town. But the judge isn't above using his six-shooters to make that happen. Based on a story by Louis L'Amour. **66m/C; DVD.** Joel McCrea; Kevin McCarthy; John McIntire; Miroslava Stern; John Carradine; Nancy Gates; Emile Meyer; *D:* Jacques Tourneur; *W:* Don Martin; Herb Meadow; *C:* Ray Rennahan; *M:* Paul Dunlap.

Stranger on the Prowl 🦴🦴 **1952** A blacklisted Losey used a postwar Italy for his melodrama about a nameless vagrant (Muni) who wants to get out of the country to make a new life. He tries to sell his one possession--a gun--to get the money to ship out on a freighter, but bad luck results in a killing witnessed by young Giacomo. The old man and the boy then go on the lam from the police and are briefly sheltered by a lonely maid. It doesn't end well. **82m/B; DVD, Blu-Ray.** *IT* Paul Muni; Vittorio Manunta; Joan Lorring; *D:* Joseph Losey; *W:* Ben Barzman; *C:* Henri Alekan; *M:* Giulio Cesare Sonzogno.

Stranger than Fiction 🦴 1/2 **1999 (R)** Would-be horror thriller wastes its talented cast. Jared (Astin) arrives, hysterical and bloody, at the home of his best friend, Austin (Field), with some confusing tale about a murder in his apartment. Austin, Jared and their friends Emma (Meyer) and Violet (Wagner) return to the scene of the crime, only to discover that Jared has been less than honest with them. **100m/C; VHS, DVD, Blu-Ray.** MacKenzie Astin; Todd Field; Dina Meyer; Natasha Gregson Wagner; *D:* Eric Bross; *W:* Tim Garrick; Scott Russell; *C:* Horacio Marquinez; *M:* Larry Seymour.

Stranger Than Fiction 🦴🦴 1/2 **2006 (PG-13)** Ferrell stars as milquetoast everyman Harold Crick, a Chicago IRS agent living a tiny little life, which he suddenly starts hearing his life narrated by a British-accented woman. Harold appears to be a character in writer Kay Eiffel's (Thompson) latest book in which that character is supposed to die. Except neurotic Kay has terrible writer's block and can't think of an appropriate way to kill him. Harold, real or imaginary, doesn't want to die and seeks the services of literature professor Jules Hilbert (Hoffman), who advises Harold to do what he's always wanted to do, prompting Harold to turn to feisty baker Ana (Gyllenhaal). Good move, Harold. Cast is first-rate but, remember, Ferrell is supposed to be low-key. **113m/C; DVD, Blu-Ray.** Will Ferrell; Maggie Gyllenhaal; Dustin Hoffman; Emma Thompson; Queen Latifah; Tony Hale; Tom Hulce; Linda Hunt; *D:* Marc Forster; *W:* Zach Helm; *C:* Roberto Schaefer; *M:* Brian Reitzell; Britt Daniel.

Stranger than Paradise 🦴🦴🦴 **1984 (R)** Would-be New York hipster Willie (Lurie) is a Hungarian emigre who is asked to look after his newly arrived teenaged cousin Eva (Balint). They develop a weird affectionate relationship before Eva heads to Cleveland to live with an aunt (Stark). When Willie realizes he misses her, he and buddy Eddie (Edson) drive to visit her and the threesome then decide to head to Florida for some fun in the sun. The thinking person's mindless flick. Inventive, independent comedy made on quite a low budget was acclaimed at Cannes. **90m/B; VHS, DVD, Blu-Ray.** *GE* John Lurie; Eszter Balint; Richard Edson; Sara Driver; Cecillia Stark; Danny Rosen; *D:* Jim Jarmusch; *W:* Jim Jarmusch; *C:* Tom DiCillo; *M:* John Lurie. Natl. Film Reg. '02; Natl. Soc. Film Critics '84: Film.

The Stranger Within 🦴 1/2 **1974** Made-for-TV "Rosemary's Baby" rip-off. Eden is in a family way, though hubby Grizzard is impotent. The stranger within begins commanding her to do its bidding, just as if she were a genie. **74m/C; VHS, DVD.** Barbara Eden; George Grizzard; Joyce Van Patten; Nehemiah Persoff; *D:* Lee Philips; *M:* Charles Fox. **TV**

The Stranger Within 🦴 1/2 **2013 (R)** After suffering a trauma, actress Emily (Warren) and her shrink husband, Robert (Baldwin), get away to a remote Mediterrean island for some R&R. However, their vacation is disturbed by the hysterical Sarah (Butler), who shows up bloodied, saying her boyfriend has been killed in a hiking accident. They take her in, but Emily regrets their kindness when she comes to believe Sarah is a threat. **90m/C; DVD.** *DK* Estella Warren; William Baldwin; Sarah Butler; *D:* Adam Neutzsky-Wulff; *W:* Adam Neutzsky-Wulff; *C:* Michael Sauer Christensen; *M:* Soren Hyldgaard. **VIDEO**

The Stranger Wore a Gun 🦴🦴 **1953** Hoping to remove a black mark against his name, Jeff Travis (Scott) goes to Arizona and ends up foiling a stagecoach robbery. Features a great action sequence in a burning saloon. Originally shot in 3-D, this is based on the novel "Yankee Gold" by John M. Cunningham. **83m/C; VHS, DVD.** Randolph Scott; Claire Trevor; Joan Weldon; George Macready; Alfonso Bedoya; Lee Marvin; Ernest Borgnine; Pierre Watkin; Joseph (Joe) Vitale; *D:* Andre de Toth.

Strangerland 🦴 **2015 (R)** Kidman does her best opposite a truly awful Fiennes in this Australian melodrama about regret and unforgiven sins, but she can't save it from being almost torturous to sit through. They play the parents of two children in a family that recently moved to a small Outback town after a scandal. One night, the kids simply walk out the front door and disappear. The search for them tears their parents apart and reveals a seedy underbelly in this remote locale. Farrant cannot figure out the tone of this film, resulting in an absolute mess of overdone symbolism and overcooked sexuality. **112m/C; DVD, Blu-Ray, Streaming.** *AU IR* Nicole Kidman; Joseph Fiennes; Hugo Weaving; Meyne Wyatt; Nicholas Hamilton; *D:* Kim Farrant; *W:* Michael Kinirons; Fiona Seres; *C:* P. J. Dillon; *M:* Keefus Ciancia.

The Strangers 🦴 **1998** Seems Trent doesn't know as much about his lover Jade as he thinks—until she turns him into a werewolf. He gets away and hides out in the small town of Pine Fork, even beginning to fall in love. Then Jade shows up with her new boyfriend—looking for revenge and fresh meat. **90m/C; VHS, DVD.** Richard Bent; Shanna Betz; Victoria Hunter; Jennifer Marks; Matt Martin; Jimmy Lord; J.J. Denton; Joe Durrenberger; Charles Solomon, Jr.; *D:* Sergei Ivanov; *W:* Sergei Ivanov; Steven Weller; *C:* Anthony Moncado. **VIDEO**

The Strangers 🦴🦴 **2008 (R)** Young couple James (Speedman) and Kristen (Tyler) retreat to the family cabin after attending an emotionally draining wedding, but they soon discover that they're not alone. A trio of creepy masked psychos quietly stalk the cabin, eventually inflicting utter horror upon the couple. Nearly every slasher flick convention is on display, as expected, but without the cheese, thanks to the patient and skillful execution of rookie director Bertino, who winds the suspense and fear into what we see as well as what we don't. Nevertheless, it still borders on snuff. **90m/C; DVD, Blu-Ray.** Liv Tyler; Scott Speedman; Glenn Howerton; Gemma Ward; Kip Weeks; Laura Margolis; *D:* Bryan Bertino; *W:* Bryan Bertino; *C:* Peter Sova; *M:* tomandandy.

A Stranger's Heart 🦴 1/2 **2007** A sappy yet faintly disturbing story. Callie's (Mathis) parents died when she was a child and she was raised by relatives. She's always been sickly and now needs a new heart. She meets fellow patient Jasper (Dobson) in the hospital and both receive successful transplants. As their feelings for each other grow stronger during their recoveries, the two are also drawn to young Cricket (Mouser), who turns out to be the now-orphaned daughter of their donors. **85m/C; DVD.** Samantha Mathis; Peter Dobson; Kevin Kilner; June Squibb; Thomas Kopache; Raynor Scheine; Marilyn Matilyn Mouser; Gina Hecht; *D:* Andy Wolk; *W:* Kelli Pryor; *C:* Maximo Munzi; *M:* Lawrence Shragge. **CABLE**

Strangers in Good Company 🦴🦴🦴 *The Company of Strangers* **1991 (PG)** A loving metaphor to growing older. Director Scott uses non-actors for every role in this quiet little film about a bus-load of elderly women lost in the Canadian wilderness. They wait for rescue without hystrionics, using the opportunity instead to get to know each other and nature. Beautifully made, intelligent, uncommon and worthwhile. **101m/C; VHS, DVD.** *CA* Alice Diabo; Mary Meigs; Cissy Meddings; Beth Webber; Winifred Holden; Constance Garneau; Catherine Roche; Michelle Sweeney; *D:* Cynthia Scott; *W:*

Cynthia Scott; David Wilson; Gloria Demers; Sally Bochner; ***M:*** Marie Bernard.

Strangers in the City **1962** Puerto Ricans newly arrived in New York try to make their way. Serious but slightly overwrought immigrant-family melodrama. **80m/B; VHS, DVD.** Robert Gentile; Camilo Delgado; Rosita De Triana; ***D:*** Rick Carrier.

Strangers May Kiss 1/2 **1931** A Pre-Code melodrama with an unpleasant double standard and a cad of a romantic lead. Lisbeth (Shearer) is obsessed by her love for newsman Alan (Hamilton), who leaves her repeatedly for work (and, oh yeah, forgets to tell her he has a wife in Paris). She eventually dallies with various men and contemplates marrying charming, drunken longtime pal, Steve (Montgomery). Then Alan reappears and has the nerve to be upset about how she's spent her time since he's finally gotten a divorce and wants to make an honest woman of her. **85m/B; DVD.** Norma Shearer; Robert Montgomery; Neil Hamilton; Marjorie Rambeau; ***D:*** George Fitzmaurice; ***W:*** John Meehan; ***C:*** William H. Daniels.

Strangers of the Evening **1932** In its day this dark comedy/mystery caught flak for its gruesomeness. There's been a mixup at the undertaker's, and the wrong body was buried—possibly alive. Good photography and acting make the humor work, intentionally or not. Based on the novel "The Illustrious Corpse," by Tiffany Thayer. **70m/B; VHS, DVD.** Zasu Pitts; Eugene Pallette; Lucien Littlefield; Tully Marshall; Miriam Seegar; Theodore von Eltz; ***D:*** H. Bruce Humberstone.

Strangers on a Train **1951** Long before there was "Throw Momma from the Train," there was this Hitchcock superthriller about two passengers who accidentally meet and plan to "trade" murders. Amoral Walker wants the exchange and the money he'll inherit by his father's death; Granger would love to end his stifling marriage and wed Roman, a senator's daughter, but finds the idea ultimately sickening. What happens is pure Hitchcock. Screenplay co-written by murder-mystery great Chandler. Patricia Hitchcock, the director's only child, plays Roman's sister. The concluding "carousel" scene is a masterpiece. From the novel by Patricia Highsmith. **101m/B; VHS, DVD, Blu-Ray.** Farley Granger; Robert Walker; Ruth Roman; Leo G. Carroll; Patricia Hitchcock; Marion Lorne; ***D:*** Alfred Hitchcock; ***W:*** Raymond Chandler; ***C:*** Robert Burks; ***M:*** Dimitri Tiomkin.

The Strangers: Prey at Night **2018 (R)** This sequel to 2008's creepy psycho-thriller follows the same format: secluded house inhabited by fresh meat, three masked lunatics with blades, and Tamara's still not home. Because this is familiar ground, the tension isn't as taut as the original, but the energy is higher and the potential victim count is doubled. Bertino pulled back on his responsibilities for this follow-up, co-writing it but turning the director's reins over to Roberts. **85m/C; DVD, Blu-Ray.** Christina Hendricks; Bailee Madison; Emma Bellomy; Martin Henderson; Lewis Pullman; ***D:*** Johannes Roberts; ***W:*** Bryan Bertino; Ben Ketai; ***C:*** Ryan Samul; ***M:*** Adrian Johnston.

Strangers When We Meet 1/2 **1960** A married architect and his equally married neighbor begin an affair. Their lives become a series of deceptions. Lavish but uninvolving soaper. Written by Evan Hunter and based on his novel. **117m/B; VHS, DVD.** Kirk Douglas; Kim Novak; Ernie Kovacs; Walter Matthau; Barbara Rush; Virginia Bruce; Kent Smith; ***D:*** Richard Quine; ***C:*** Charles B(ryant) Lang, Jr.

Strangers with Candy **2006 (R)** Sedaris takes her Comedy Central series to the big screen with all its crude tackiness on display. Jerri is a middle-aged ex-junkie, ex-hooker, ex-con who goes back to high school and wants to win the science fair to make her comatose dad proud. Calling her dim-witted would be kind. But she's in good company because mostly everyone around her falls into freak territory. It's one over-extended sketch with a lead you don't really want to spend time with unless you're already a fan. **97m/C; DVD.** Amy Sedaris; Paul Dinello; Stephen Colbert; Deborah Rush; Greg Hollimon; Dan Hedaya; Allison Janney; Philip Seymour Hoffman; Kristen Johnston; Justin Theroux; Matthew Broderick; Sarah Jessica Parker; Ian Holm; Carlo Alban; Maria Thayer; Elisabeth Harnois; Chris Pratt; Joseph Cross; David Pasquesi; Alicia Ashley; Ryan Donowho; ***D:*** Paul Dinello; ***W:*** Amy Sedaris; Paul Dinello; Stephen Colbert; ***C:*** Oliver Bokelberg.

Stranglehold 1/2 **1994 (R)** Cooper (Trimble) is the executive assistant of Congresswoman Fillmore (McWhirter), who becomes the hostage of a nerve gas holding nutcase (Wells). Cooper manages to evade the nutcase's thugs while using his martial arts prowess to rescue his boss. **73m/C; VHS, DVD.** *AU* Jerry Trimble; Jillian McWhirter; Vernon Wells; ***D:*** Cirio H. Santiago.

The Strangler 1/2 **1964** A confused, mother-fixated psychopath strangles young women. Made at the time the Boston Strangler was terrorizing Beantown. The film slayer strangles ten lasses before his love of dolls gives him away. **89m/B; VHS, DVD.** Victor Buono; David McLean; Diane Sayer; Ellen Corby; Jeanne Bates; James B. Sikking; ***D:*** Burt Topper.

Strangler of Blackmoor Castle **1963** Someone is murdering people at an old English castle and Scotland Yard sends an investigator to track down the killer. **87m/B; VHS, DVD.** *GE* Karin Dor; Ingmar Zeisberg; Harry Riebauer; Rudolf Fernau; Hans Nielsen; Dieter Eppler; ***D:*** Harald Reinl; ***W:*** Ladislas Fodor; ***C:*** Ernst W. Kalinke; ***M:*** Oskar Sala.

The Stranglers of Bombay **1960** Lurid low-budget Hammer production. Captain Lewis (Rolfe) works for the East India Company in the 1820s. His superiors refuse to listen when he tells them about all the people who have gone missing in the area so he continues his investigation on his own. Lewis discovers that followers of Kali, a blood-thirsty cult known as the Stranglers, are behind the mayhem and he resolves to put a stop to their terror. **80m/B; DVD.** *GB* Guy Rolfe; Allan Cuthbertson; George Pastell; Marne Maitland; Jan Holden; John Harvey; Andrew Cruickshank; Paul Stassino; Michael Nightngale; ***D:*** Terence Fisher; ***W:*** David Zelag Goodman; James Bernard; ***C:*** Arthur Grant; ***M:*** James Bernard.

Strapless 1/2 **1990 (R)** Just-turned-40 American doctor Brown lives and works in London. She has just ended a long-term romance, and takes up with suave foreigner Ganz. Her young sister Fonda, arrives for a visit. Good, interesting if sometimes plodding story of adult relationships. **99m/C; VHS, DVD.** *GB* Blair Brown; Bridget Fonda; Bruno Ganz; Alan Howard; Michael Gough; Hugh Laurie; Suzanne Burden; Camille Coduri; Alexandra Pigg; Billy Roch; Gary O'Brien; ***D:*** David Hare; ***W:*** David Hare; ***C:*** Andrew Dunn; ***M:*** Nick Bicat.

Strapped 1/2 **1993** Earnest urban drama about a young man who needs quick cash and turns to selling guns to get it. ("Strapped" in street lingo means both carrying a gun and needing money.) Diquan's (Woodbine) pregnant girlfriend is in jail for selling crack and he doesn't have the bail money. So he and a partner begin selling guns but it turns out Diquan has also cut a deal with the cops and the deal doesn't stay a secret for long. Whitaker's directorial debut. **102m/C; VHS, DVD.** Bokeem Woodbine; Kia Joy Goodwin; Fred "Fredro" Scruggs; Michael Biehn; Craig Wasson; ***D:*** Forest Whitaker; ***W:*** Dena Kleiman. **CABLE**

Strategic Air Command 1/2 **1955** A classic post-WWII chunk of Air Force patriotism. Veteran third baseman Stewart is recalled to flight duty at the hint of a nuclear war. He's already put in his time in the Big One and thinks he's being singled out now, but he answers his Uncle Sam's call. Allyson plays Stewart's wife for the third time. **114m/C; VHS, Blu-Ray, Streaming.** James Stewart; June Allyson; Frank Lovejoy; Barry Sullivan; John McKee; ***D:*** Anthony Mann; ***C:*** William H. Daniels.

The Stratton Story **1949** Stewart and Allyson teamed up for the first of the three pictures they'd make together in this true story of Monty Stratton, the Chicago White Sox pitcher. A baseball phenom, Stratton suffers a devastating hunting accident which leads to the amputation of one leg. Learning to walk with an artificial limb, Stratton also struggles to resume his baseball career. Stewart's fine as always, with Allyson lending noble support as the loving wife. Chisox manager Jimmy Dykes played himself as did pitcher Gene Bearden, lending further authenticity to an excellent production. **106m/B; VHS, DVD.** James Stewart; June Allyson; Frank Morgan; Agnes Moorehead; Bill Williams; Bruce Cowling; ***D:*** Sam Wood; ***W:*** Guy Trosper; Douglas S. Morrow. Oscars '49: Story.

The Strauss Family 1/2 **1973** British miniseries covers the drama and scandal surrounding 85 years in the lives of the musical Strauss family of 19th-century Vienna. Woolfe is patriarch Johann Strauss, whose son Schanni (Wilson) will exclipse his egotistical father's talents. Music performed by the London Symphony Orchestra. On 4 cassettes. **390m/C; VHS, DVD.** *GB* Eric Woolfe; Stuart Wilson; Anne Stallybrass; Derek Jacobi; Jane Seymour; ***D:*** David Giles; Peter Potter; David Reid; ***W:*** David Butler; David Reid; Anthony Skene. **TV**

Straw Dogs **1972 (R)** An American mathematician, disturbed by the predominance of violence in American society, moves with his wife to an isolated Cornish village. He finds that primitive savagery exists beneath the most peaceful surface. After his wife is raped, Hoffman's character seeks revenge. Hoffman is good, a little too wimpy at times. A violent, frightening film reaction to the violence of the 1960s. **118m/C; VHS, DVD, Blu-Ray.** *GB* Dustin Hoffman; Susan George; Peter Vaughan; T.P. McKenna; David Warner; Sally Thomsett; Colin Welland; Peter Arne; ***D:*** Sam Peckinpah; ***W:*** Sam Peckinpah; David Zelag Goodman; ***C:*** John Coquillon; ***M:*** Jerry Fielding.

Straw Dogs 1/2 **2011 (R)** Needless remake of the violent and provocative 1971 Sam Peckinpah pic. Hollywood screenwriter David Sumner (Marsden), an emasculated modern male, and his bitchy actress wife Amy (Bosworth) return to her deep South hometown after her father's death. Marital strife and past conflicts surface, including problems with Amy's ex-beau, hunky good ole boy Charlie (Skarsgard), and his crude and violent buddies. When Amy's obvious charms get her in trouble, David has to find his inner-macho man and protect his woman from redneck home invaders. **110m/C; DVD, Blu-Ray.** James Marsden; Kate (Catherine) Bosworth; Alexander Skarsgård; Dominic Purcell; Laz Alonso; Walton Goggins; Anson Mount; Willa Holland; James Woods; Billy Lush; ***D:*** Rod Lurie; ***W:*** Rod Lurie; ***C:*** Alik Sakharov; ***M:*** Lawrence Nash Groupe.

Strawberry and Chocolate *Fresa y Chocolate* **1993 (R)** Sex, politics, and friendship set in 1979 Havana. University student David (Cruz) is sitting morosely in a cafe eating chocolate ice cream when he's spotted by older, educated, gay, strawberry-eating Diego (Perugorria), who manages to persuade David to visit him at his apartment. Resolutely hetero (and communist), David is appalled not only by Diego's sexuality but by his subversive politics. But gradually David's seduced by Diego's ideas and friendship into questioning the regime's harsh policies (and homophobia). Satiric and sympathetic—not only to the characters but to Cuba itself. Ill with cancer, Gutierrez Alea finished the film with the aid of Tabio. From the short story "The Wolf, the Forest and the New Man" by sceenwriter Paz. Spanish with subtitles. **110m/C; VHS, DVD.** *CU* Jorge Perugorria; Vladimir Cruz; Mirta Ibarra; Francisco Gattorno; Jorge Angelino; Marilyn Solaya; ***D:*** Tomas Gutierrez Alea; Juan Carlos Tabio; ***W:*** Tomas Gutierrez Alea; Senel Paz; ***C:*** Mario Garcia Joya; ***M:*** Jose Maria Vitier.

Strawberry Blonde **1941** A romantic comedy set in the 1890s, with Cagney as a would-be dentist infatuated with money-grubbing Hayworth (the strawberry blonde of the title), who wonders years later whether he married the right woman (chestnut brunette de Havilland). Attractive period piece remade from 1933's "One Sunday Afternoon," and revived yet again in 1948 by Raoul Walsh. **100m/B; VHS, DVD.** James Cagney; Olivia de Havilland; Rita Hayworth; Alan Hale; George Tobias; Jack Carson; Una O'Connor; George Reeves; ***D:*** Raoul Walsh; ***W:*** Julius J. Epstein; Philip G. Epstein; ***C:*** James Wong Howe.

Strawberry Fields **1997** Rebellious teenaged Japanese-American Irene (Nakamura) takes off on a road trip of self-discovery with her boyfriend, whom she soon dumps to spend quality time alone in the Arizona desert figuring out life. **86m/C; VHS, DVD.** Suzy Nakamura; James Sie; Chris Tashima; Marilyn Tokuda; Reiko Mathieu; Peter Yoshida; Heather Yoshimura; Takayo Fischer; ***D:*** Rea Tajiri; ***W:*** Rea Tajiri; Kerri Sakamoto; ***C:*** Zack Winestine; ***M:*** Bundy Brown.

The Strawberry Statement **1970 (R)** Dated message film about a campus radical who persuades a college student to take part in the student strikes on campus during the '60s. Ambitious anti-violence message is lost in too many subplots. Soundtrack features songs by Crosby, Stills, Nash and Young and John Lennon. **109m/C; VHS, Streaming.** Kim Darby; Bruce Davison; Bud Cort; James Coco; Kristina Holland; Bob Balaban; David Dukes; Jeannie Berlin; ***D:*** Stuart Hagmann; ***W:*** Israel Horovitz. Cannes '70: Special Jury Prize.

Strawberry Summer 1/2 **2012** Hallmark Channel romantic drama. High school music teacher Beth Landon invites her favorite country singer, Jason Keith, to headline her town's Strawberry Festival. Jason's career is faltering and, despite his need for some good publicity, his ego is bigger than his hat. Beth tries to convince him that he could win back his audience, but Jason may be more interested in winning Beth's heart. **86m/C; DVD.** Julie Mond; Trevor Donovan; Shelley Long; Cindy Williams; Barry Van Dyke; ***D:*** Kevin Connor; ***W:*** Jim Head; Gary Goldstein; ***C:*** James W. Wrenn; ***M:*** Nathan Furst. **CABLE**

The Stray **2000 (R)** When Vonna Grayson (Everhart) accidentally hits a homeless man (Lysenko) when she's driving home, she insists on having him recover at her ranch. Soon the relationship becomes romantic, but her "stray" has a hidden agenda and Vonna winds up in danger. **98m/C; VHS, DVD, On Demand.** Angie Everhart; Stefan Lysenko; Michael Madsen; Frank Zagarino; Seidy Lopez; ***D:*** Kevin Mock; ***W:*** Terry Cunningham; ***C:*** Ken Blakey; ***M:*** John Sponsler. **VIDEO**

The Stray **2017 (PG)** The true tale of a dog named Pluto who rescues a family from itself. One workaholic father + one put-upon wife + one friendless child + one bolt of lightning (literally) + one stray dog = an uninspired, faith-based melodrama about the importance of family and God. Writer/director Mitch Davis tries too hard to pull at the heartstrings (perhaps because the story is based on his life), resulting in a family drama that strays into over-sweetness. **92m/C; DVD, Blu-Ray.** Michael Cassidy; Sarah Lancaster; Connor Corum; Jacque Gray; Scott Christopher; ***D:*** Mitch Davis; ***W:*** Mitch Davis; Parker Davis; ***C:*** T.C. Christensen; ***M:*** Christian Davis.

Stray **2019** During the investigation of the murder of a middle-aged woman found burned to death, female homicide detective Murphy (Woods) learns from forensics that the corpse has been dead for 1,000 years and was petrified. This scenario does not make sense since the victim was seen with her mother (Fischer) and adolescent daughter Nori (Fukuhara) the previous day. As Murphy digs deeper, she learns that Nori has supernatural powers that come out when she is stressed. The directorial debut of Sill brings together generic concepts from multiple genres somewhat effectively. **89m/C; DVD.** Karen Fukuhara; Christine Woods; Miyavi; Ross Partridge; Takayo Fischer; ***D:*** Joel Sill; ***W:*** J.D. Dillard; Alex Theurer; ***C:*** Greg Cotten; ***M:*** Trevor Doherty.

Stray Dog **1949** A tense, early genre piece by Kurosawa, about a police detective who has his revolver picked from his pocket on a bus, and realizes soon after it's being used in a series of murders. Technically somewhat flawed, but tense and intense. Mifune's pursuit of the criminal with his gun becomes metaphorically compelling. In Japanese with English subtitles. **122m/B;**

VHS, DVD. *JP* Toshiro Mifune; Takashi Shimura; Isao Kimura; ***D:*** Akira Kurosawa.

Stray Dog *Stray Dogs; Stray Dog: Kerberos Panzer Cops; Jigoku no banken: kerubersu* **1991** Second film in Mamoru Oshii's Kerberos Panzer Corps saga is the prequel of "The Red Spectacles," and the sequel to the last film "Jin-Roh." Begins with the Kerberos armored police unit making a last stand against the military after being told to disband. Three of them flee via helicopter, and the lone witness is imprisoned for three years, until he is sprung by a group seeking the escaped Kerberos, so he goes off to find his former coworkers. **95m/C; DVD.** Shigeru Chiba; Takashi Matsuyama; Yoshikazu Fujiki; Eaching Sue; ***D:*** Mamoru Oshii; ***W:*** Mamoru Oshii; ***C:*** Yousuke Mamiya; ***M:*** Kenji Kawai.

Stray Dogs *Jiao You* **2013** The almost nonexistent story here is a sketch of people who live on the edge of society. They are a homeless family in Taipei: he twirls a sign outside a store, they seek shelter from the elements, and forage for food in an urban jungle. You'll either fall asleep from boredom or be mesmerized. Director Tsai's films require remarkable patience by the viewer--this pic features such simplistic storytelling that the last half-hour consists of two—count'em—just two, shots. Neither with a line of dialogue. Yet what it lacks in visuals is made up in emotions. Mandarin Chinese with subtitles. **138m/C; DVD, Blu-Ray.** *TW FR* Kang-sheng Lee; ***D:*** Ming-liang Tsai; ***W:*** Ming-liang Tsai; Cheng-yu Tung; Peng-fei Song; ***C:*** Pen-jung Liao; Woon-Chong Shong.

Strayed *Les Egares* **2003** Set in the chaotic summer of 1940, when the Germans invaded France. Film follows the flight of recently widowed schoolteacher Odile (Beart) and her children, 13-year-old Philippe (Leprince-Ringuet) and 7-year-old Cathy (Meyer), out of Paris. Part of a stream of refugees heading south, the family is forced into the countryside when German planes strafe the roads; there they meet 17-year-old Yvan (Ulliel), who's illiterate but skilled at survival. Stumbling across an abandoned villa, the foursome set aside their uncertainties to manage a precarious semblance of family life as the sexual tension between Odile and Yvan grows. Since Techine specializes in character studies, this is a story about conflict and desire, civilization versus savagery. Based on the 1983 novel, "The Boy With Grey Eyes," by Gilles Perrault; French with subtitles. **95m/C; VHS, DVD.** *FR* Emmanuelle Beart; Samuel Labarthe; Gaspard Ulliel; Gregoire Leprince-Ringuet; Clemence Meyer; Jean Fornerod; ***D:*** Andre Techine; ***W:*** Andre Techine; Gilles Taurand; ***C:*** Agnes Godard; ***M:*** Philippe Sarde.

Streamers **1983 (R)** Six young soldiers in a claustrophobic army barracks tensely await the orders that will send them to Vietnam. Written by Rabe from his play. Well acted but downbeat and drawn out. **118m/C; VHS, DVD.** Matthew Modine; Michael Wright; Mitchell Lichtenstein; George Dzundza; Bill Allen; ***D:*** Robert Altman; ***W:*** David Rabe.

Street Angel **1928** Silent melodrama. Neapolitan waif Angela (Gaynor) makes an unsuccessful attempt at street walking (hence the title) and then stealing to get money for her sick mama. Hiding out from the cops, Angela meets artist Gino (Farrell), who paints a portrait of her as the Madonna. She's finally caught and jailed, but on her release reunites with Gino, who's been struggling to get over Angela's checkered past. **102m/B; Silent; DVD.** Janet Gaynor; Charles Farrell; Henry Armetta; Guido Conti; Louis Liggett; ***D:*** Frank Borzage; ***W:*** Marion Orth; Philip Klein; Robert Symonds; ***C:*** Ernest Palmer. Oscars '28: Actress (Gaynor).

Street Boss 1/2 **2009 (R)** Standard-fare, based on the true crime story of how FBI agent Philip Kerby worked to bring down Detroit crime boss Anthony Joseph 'Tony Jack' Giacalone in the 1970s. **98m/C; DVD.** Robert Gallo; Mark Bierlein; Nicholas Turturro; Edward Carnevale; Vincent Pastore; Carmen Argenziano; ***D:*** Lance Kawas; ***C:*** Wayne Murphy; ***M:*** Misha Segal. **VIDEO**

A Street Cat Named Bob 1/2 **2016** Based on a best-selling memoir about a street musician whose life is saved by an orange cat. In London, homeless James Bowen (Treadaway) struggles to find shelter. After overdosing on heroin, his life turns around with the help of drug counselor Val (Froggatt) who gets him on methadone and finds him a small apartment. One day, James finds a ginger cat stealing food in his kitchen. The cat, named Bob, adopts him and gives his life purpose as man and cat care for each other. Though the film has heart, a few cliched moments undercut its appeal. **103m/C; DVD.** Luke Treadaway; Bob the Cat; Ruta Gedmintas; Joanne Froggatt; Anthony Head; ***D:*** Roger Spottiswoode; ***W:*** Tim John; Maria Nation; ***C:*** Peter Wunstorf; ***M:*** David Hirschfelder.

Street Corner Justice **1996** Typical vigilante action movie features ex-cop Mike Justus (Singer), who's possessed of a short fuse and a strong sense of justice. He inherits a house in a crime-ridden L.A. neighborhood and finds himself coming to the aid of merchants who are being terrorized by the local drug-dealing gangs. **102m/C; VHS, DVD.** Marc Singer; Steve Railsback; Kim Lankford; Willie Gee; ***D:*** Charles "Chuck" Bail; ***W:*** Charles "Chuck" Bail; Gary Kent; Stan Berkowitz; ***C:*** Doug O'Neons; David Golia; ***M:*** K. Alexander (Alex) Wilkinson.

Street Crimes **1992 (R)** A streetwise cop convinces gang members to put down their weapons and settle their grudges in the boxing ring. But when a gang leader starts shooting down the police and civilians, the cop and his young partner must work together to keep the neighborhood safe. **93m/C; VHS, DVD.** Dennis Farina; Max Gail; Mike Worth; ***D:*** Stephen Smoke; ***W:*** Stephen Smoke; ***M:*** John Gonzalez.

The Street Fighter 1/2 *Satsujin-ken* **1974** Fast-paced martial arts action finds freelance fighter Terry Tsuguri (Chiba) hired to spring a convicted killer from prison. But after he succeeds, his employers renege on their payment. Big mistake. Dubbed from Japanese. Three sequels: "Return of the Street Fighter," "The Street Fighter's Last Revenge," and "Sister Street Fighter." **91m/C; VHS, DVD, Blu-Ray.** *JP* Sonny Chiba; Gerald (Waichi) Yamada; Tony Cetera; Doris (Yutaka) Nakajima; ***D:*** Shigehiro (Sakae) Ozawa; ***W:*** Motohiro Torii; Koji Takada; ***C:*** Ken Tsukakoshi; ***M:*** Toshiaki Tsushima.

Street Fighter 1/2 **1994 (PG-13)** Yes, it's a movie based on a popular video game (guess no one worried about the colossal flop of "Super Mario Bros"). Van Damme is action-minded Colonel Guile who is assigned to defeat crazed dictator General Bison (Julia in one of his last roles) in order to rescue kidnapped relief workers. Yes, there's lots of cartoon action but the game's more exciting (and even makes more sense). Shot on location in Australia and Bangkok. **101m/C; VHS, DVD, Blu-Ray.** Jean-Claude Van Damme; Raul Julia; Wes Studi; Ming Na; Damian Chapa; Simon Callow; Roshan Seth; Kylie Minogue; Byron Mann; ***D:*** Steven E. de Souza; ***W:*** Steven E. de Souza; ***C:*** William A. Fraker; ***M:*** Graeme Revell.

Street Fighter: The Legend of Chun-Li 1/2 **2009 (PG-13)** Mindless, action-filled adaptation of the videogame. Brooding, wealthy, and orphaned—thanks to crime boss Bison (McDonough)?beautiful Chun-Li (Kreuk) has turned herself into a revenge-seeking martial arts weapon working for the dispossessed on the Bangkok streets. **96m/C; DVD, Blu-Ray, On Demand.** Kristin Kreuk; Michael Clarke Duncan; Neal McDonough; Moon Bloodgood; Chris Klein; Robin Shou; Josie Ho; Taboo; ***D:*** Andrzej Bartkowiak; ***W:*** Justin Marks; ***C:*** Geoff Boyle; ***M:*** Stephen Endelman.

The Street Fighter's Last Revenge *Revenge! The Killing Fist; Street Fighter Counterattacks* **1974** Third in the martial arts series finds Terry Tsuguri (Chiba) hired by a mob boss to do some dirty work and then getting doublecrossed—resulting in the death of Terry's girl. So, Terry hunts the miscreants down one by one. Lots of action, not much acting. Followed by "Sister Street Fighter." **79m/C; VHS, DVD, Blu-Ray.** *JP* Sonny Chiba; Etsuko (Sue) Shihomi; ***D:*** Teru Ishii.

Street Girls **1975 (R)** A father enters the world of urban drugs and prostitution to find his runaway daughter. **77m/C; VHS, DVD.** Carol Case; Christine Souder; Paul Pompian; ***D:*** Michael Miller.

Street Gun **1996** Small-time hood Joe Webster (Pagel) pines for some sense of accomplishment in his life. A tip from his hustler-friend lands Joe in the good graces of the local crime boss. As he ingratiates himself into his new malevolent world, the shadows yield betrayal, murder, and no place to hide. Potentially interesting premise is botched, with cowriter/director Milloy aping John Woo gun pyrotechnics and "Reservoir Dogs" attitude (a Woo rip-off once removed). There is also the thorny dilemma of rooting for a hero who aspires to be an exceptional thug. **92m/C; DVD.** Justin Pagel; Scott Cooke; Michael Egan; ***D:*** Travis Milloy; ***W:*** Travis Milloy; Timothy Lee; ***C:*** Joel King.

The Street King 1/2 *King Rikki* **2002 (R)** Rikki Ortega (Seda) wants to be top dog on the gang-ravaged streets of East L.A. And the one man to oppose him is his childhood buddy turned cop, Juan Vallejo (Lopez). It's alleged to be a modern reworking of Shakespeare's "Richard III." **90m/C; VHS, DVD, On Demand.** Jon Seda; Mario Lopez; Timothy Paul Perez; Jill-Michele Melean; ***D:*** James Gavin Bedford; ***W:*** Jesse Graham; ***C:*** Rob Sweeney.

Street Kings **2008 (R)** Ellroy had a hand in the script (adapted from his novel) but this over-the-top violent melodrama more closely resembles what director Ayers did as a writer with the equally preposterous "Training Day." Widowed vice cop Tom Ludlow (Reeves) drinks on the job and is possibly more violent than the L.A. criminals he's after. Ludlow's commanding officer Wander (Whitaker, practically pop-eyed and frothing) seems to have his back until Tom's ex-partner Washington (Crews) is gunned down after he talks to Internal Affairs, which puts a bullseye on Ludlow's back. **109m/C; DVD.** Keanu Reeves; Forest Whitaker; Hugh Laurie; Chris Evans; Jay Mohr; John Corbett; Amaury Nolasco; Cedric the Entertainer; Terry Crews; Naomie Harris; Common; The Game; Martha Higareda; ***D:*** David Ayer; James Moss; ***W:*** Kurt Wimmer; James Ellroy; ***C:*** Gabriel Beristain; ***M:*** Graeme Revell.

Street Kings 2: Motor City 1/2 **2011 (R)** Has no ties with the original flick except for its crooked cops storyline. Veteran Detroit narcotics detective Marty Kingston (Liotta) was involved in a deal that went bad. Now someone is murdering any of the cops who survived and Marty and his ambitious new partner Dan Sullivan (Hatosy) are assigned to the case. **120m/C; DVD, Blu-Ray.** Ray Liotta; Shawn Hatosy; Linda Boston; Kevin Chapman; Stephanie Cotton; ***D:*** Chris Fisher; ***W:*** Ed Gonzalez; Jeremy Haft; ***C:*** Marvin V. Rush; ***M:*** Jonathan Sadoff. **VIDEO**

Street Law *The Citizen Rebels; Il Cittadino si Ribella* **1974 (R)** Vivid and violent study of one man's frustrated war on crime. **77m/C; VHS, DVD, Blu-Ray.** *IT* Franco Nero; Barbara Bach; Renzo Palmer; Giancarlo Prete; ***D:*** Enzo G. Castellari; ***W:*** Massimo De Rita; Arduino (Dino) Maiuri; ***C:*** Carlo Carlini; ***M:*** Guido de Angelis; Maurizio de Angelis.

Street Law **1995 (R)** John Ryan (Wincott) is a down-on-his-luck trial lawyer whose childhood buddy Luis Calderone (Prieto) is willing to lend a helping hand. Too bad Luis is an ex-con who hasn't left his dangerous street ways behind him and now John is caught up in some unsavory action. **98m/C; VHS, DVD.** Jeff Wincott; Paco Christian Prieto; Christina Cox; ***D:*** Damian Lee; ***W:*** Damian Lee; ***C:*** Gerald R. Goozie; ***M:*** Ronald J. Weiss.

Street of Shame 1/2 *Red-Light District; Akasen Chitai* **1956** A portrayal of the abused lives of six Tokyo prostitutes. Typically sensitive to the roles and needs of women and critical of the society that exploits them, Mizoguchi creates a quiet, inclusive coda to his life's work in world cinema. Kyo is splendid as a hardened hooker and has a memorable scene with her father. Kogure is also good. The great director's last finished work was instrumental in the outlawing of prostitution in Japan. In Japanese with English subtitles. **88m/B; VHS, DVD.** *JP* Machiko Kyo; Aiko Mimasu; Michiyo Kogure; ***D:*** Kenji Mizoguchi.

Street of Women **1932** Talky and complicated romantic drama. Larry Baldwin has a mistress—Natalie—whose brother Clarke falls in love with Larry's daughter Doris. Larry wants a divorce from his wife Lois but she doesn't. A series of unfortunate events changes things though. This is a Pre-Code flick so Larry doesn't suffer the consequences of being a two-timer. **70m/B; DVD.** Alan Dinehart; Kay Francis; Marjorie Gateson; Gloria Stuart; Allen Vincent; Roland Young; Adrienne Dore; ***D:*** Archie Mayo; ***W:*** Mary C. McCall; Brown Holmes; Charles Kenyon; ***C:*** Ernest Haller.

Street People **WOOF!** **1976 (R)** Gratuitous car chases and violence do not a movie make, as in this case in point. Utter woofer has Brit Moore cast as a mafiosa. Yeah, right. **92m/C; VHS, Blu-Ray, Streaming.** Roger Moore; Stacy Keach; Ivo Garrani; Ettore Manni; ***D:*** Maurizio Lucidi.

Street Scene **1931** Life in a grimy New York tenement district, circa 1930. Audiences nationwide ate it up when Elmer Rice adapted his own Pulitzer Prize-winning play and top helmsman Vidor gave it direction. **80m/B; VHS, DVD.** Sylvia Sidney; William "Buster" Collier, Jr.; Estelle Taylor; Beulah Bondi; David Landau; ***D:*** King Vidor; ***W:*** Elmer Rice; ***C:*** George Barnes; ***M:*** Alfred Newman.

Street Smart 1/2 **1987 (R)** Reeve was blah as Superman (let's be frank), and he's blah here as a desperate New York freelance writer who fakes a dramatic story about prostitution. When his deception returns to haunt him, he's in trouble with pimps and murderers, as well as the D.A. Freeman and Baker are both superb. Based on screenwriter David Freeman's own experience with "New York" magazine. **97m/C; VHS, DVD, Blu-Ray.** Christopher Reeve; Morgan Freeman; Kathy Baker; Mimi Rogers; Andre Gregory; Jay Patterson; Anna Maria Horsford; ***D:*** Jerry Schatzberg; ***W:*** David Freeman; ***C:*** Adam Holender; ***M:*** Miles Davis. Ind. Spirit '88: Support. Actor (Freeman); L.A. Film Critics '87: Support. Actor (Freeman); N.Y. Film Critics '87: Support. Actor (Freeman); Natl. Soc. Film Critics '87: Support. Actor (Freeman), Support. Actress (Baker).

Street Trash **WOOF!** **1987** In Brooklyn, a strange poisonous liquor is being sold cheap to bums, making them melt and explode. A gross, cheap, tongue-in-cheek shocker. **91m/C; VHS, DVD, Blu-Ray.** Vic Noto; Mike Lackey; Bill Chepil; R.L. Ryan; James Lorinz; Miriam Zucker; ***D:*** J.(James) Michael Muro; ***W:*** Roy Frumkes; ***C:*** David Sperling.

Street Vengeance **WOOF!** **1995** Drug lord seeks vengeance against cop for death of brother. No-budget shot-on-video flick is atrocious in every way. **85m/C; DVD.** Mari Blackwell; Michael Eugene; ***D:*** Rene Migliaccio; ***W:*** Michael Farakash.

Street War *Paura in citta* **1976** A cop pursues the Mob in the name of revenge as well as duty. **90m/C; VHS, DVD.** *IT* James Mason; Cyril Cusack; Raymond Pellegrin; Maurizio Merli; Silvia Dionisio; Fausto Tozzi; ***D:*** Giuseppe Rosati; ***W:*** Giuseppe Rosati; Giuseppe Pulieri; ***C:*** Giuseppe Bernardini; ***M:*** Gianpaolo Chiti.

Street Wars 1/2 **1991 (R)** Violent low-budgeter about 17-year-old Sugarpop, who takes over older brother Frank's Los Angeles drug operation, after Frank is murdered, and finds himself battling a rival gang. **90m/C; VHS, DVD.** Alan Joseph; Bryan O'Dell; Clifford Shegog; Jean Pace; Vaughn Cromwell; Cardella Demilo; ***D:*** Jamaa Fanaka; ***W:*** Jamaa Fanaka; ***C:*** John L. (Ndiaga) Demps, Jr.; ***M:*** Michael Dunlap; Yves Chicha.

The Street with No Name **1948** In his follow-up to "Kiss of Death," Widmark confirms his rep as one disturbed guy playing psychotic career criminal whose life is a grisly trail of murder and brutality. **93m/B; VHS, DVD.** Mark Stevens; Richard Widmark; Lloyd Nolan; Barbara Lawrence; Ed Begley, Sr.; Donald Buka; Joseph Pevney; ***D:*** William Keighley.

A Streetcar Named Desire **1951 (PG)** Powerful film version of Tennessee Williams' play about a neurotic southern belle with a hidden past who comes to visit her sister and is abused and driven mad by her brutal brother-in-law. Grim New Orleans setting for terrific performances by all, with

Malden, Leigh, and Hunter winning Oscars, and Brando making highest impact on audiences. Brando disliked the role, despite the great impact it had on his career. **122m/B; VHS, DVD, Blu-Ray.** Vivien Leigh; Marlon Brando; Kim Hunter; Karl Malden; ***D:*** Elia Kazan; ***W:*** Tennessee Williams; ***C:*** Harry Stradling, Sr.; ***M:*** Alex North. Oscars '51: Actress (Leigh), Art Dir./Set Dec., B&W, Support. Actor (Malden), Support. Actress (Hunter); AFI '98: Top 100; British Acad. '52: Actress (Leigh); Golden Globes '52: Support. Actress (Hunter); Natl. Film Reg. '99; N.Y. Film Critics '51: Actress (Leigh), Director (Kazan), Film.

A Streetcar Named Desire 𝒮𝒮 1/2 **1995** Baldwin and Lange recreate their 1992 stage roles of brutal Stanley Kowalski and fragile Southern belle Blanche DuBois from the Broadway revival of Tennessee Williams 1947 Pulitzer Prize-winning play. This TV version is truer to the dialogue and situations of the original production than the censored '51 film. **156m/C; VHS, DVD.** Jessica Lange; Alec Baldwin; Diane Lane; John Goodman; Frederick Coffin; ***D:*** Glenn Jordan; ***C:*** Ralf Bode; ***M:*** David Mansfield.

Streetfight 𝒮 1/2 *Coonskin* **1975 (R)** Semi-animated racist exploitation from the creator of "Fritz the Cat." Features some superb animation. Sold under the title 'Coonskin'. **89m/C; VHS, DVD.** Philip Michael Thomas; Scatman Crothers; Barry White; Charles Gordone; ***D:*** Ralph Bakshi; ***W:*** Ralph Bakshi; ***C:*** William A. Fraker; ***M:*** Chico Hamilton.

Streets 𝒮𝒮 **1990 (R)** Applegate (of Fox TV's "Married...With Children") is believable as an illiterate runaway teen. Good drama set in Venice, California about life on the streets is flawed by near-gratuitous pairing with story of a crazy prostitute-killing cop. **90m/C; VHS, DVD.** Christina Applegate; David Mendenhall; Eb Lottimer; ***D:*** Katt Shea; Andy Ruben; ***W:*** Andy Ruben.

Streets of Blood 𝒮 1/2 **2009 (R)** Six months after Hurricane Katrina, veteran detective Andy Devereaux (Kilmer) comes to suspect that his late partner didn't drown in the disaster but was murdered. And it seems his new partner Stan (Jackson) is also hiding something while police shrink Nina (Stone) knows more than she's telling too. **95m/C; DVD.** Val Kilmer; 50 Cent; Sharon Stone; Michael Biehn; Shirly Brener; Jose Pablo Cantillo; ***D:*** Charles Winkler; ***W:*** Eugene Hess; ***C:*** Roy Wagner; ***M:*** Stephen Endelman. **VIDEO**

Streets of Fire 𝒮𝒮 1/2 **1984** A soldier of fortune rescues his ex-girlfriend, now a famous rock singer, after she's been kidnapped by a malicious motorcycle gang. Violently energetic in its insistent barrage of imagery. Director Hill's never-never land establishes a retro-futuristic feel and is beautifully photographed, however vacuous the ending may be. **93m/C; VHS, DVD, Blu-Ray, HD-DVD.** Michael Paré; Diane Lane; Rick Moranis; Amy Madigan; Willem Dafoe; Deborah Van Valkenburgh; Richard Lawson; Rick Rossovich; Bill Paxton; Lee Ving; Stoney Jackson; Robert Townsend; Grand L. Bush; Mykelti Williamson; Elizabeth Daily; Lynne Thigpen; Marine Jahan; Ed Begley, Jr.; John Dennis Johnston; Olivia Brown; ***D:*** Walter Hill; ***W:*** Walter Hill; Larry Gross; ***C:*** Andrew Laszlo; ***M:*** Ry Cooder.

The Streets of San Francisco 𝒮𝒮𝒮 **1972** The pilot that spawned the popular TV series. A streetwise old cop and his young college-boy partner (who else but Malden and Douglas as Stone and Keller) investigate the murder of a young woman. Adapted from "Poor, Poor Ophelia" by Carolyn Weston. **120m/C; VHS, DVD.** Karl Malden; Robert Wagner; Michael Douglas; Andrew Duggan; Tom Bosley; Kim Darby; Mako; ***D:*** Walter Grauman. **TV**

Streets of Sin 𝒮𝒮 1/2 *Not Wanted* **1949** Written and produced by movie star Lupino (who also took over directing when credited director Clifton became ill), this morality play tells the story of a naive girl's tribulations when she becomes infatuated with a musician and then becomes pregnant by him. Shunned by the musician, she enters a home for unwed mothers to sort out her life and feelings for a crippled veteran who wants to marry her. **91m/B; VHS, DVD, Blu-Ray.** Sally Forrest; Keefe Brasselle; Leonard Penn; Dorothy Adams; Rita Lupino; ***D:*** Elmer Clifton; ***W:*** Ida Lupino.

Streetwalkin' 𝒮 **1985 (R)** Life in the Big Apple isn't always rosy for a brother and sister who must contend with prostitutes, drug dealers, and tough cops. She turns to prostitution to get by. Miserable, exploitative trash somewhat improved by the performance of Leo. **86m/C; VHS, DVD.** Melissa Leo; Dale Midkiff; Leon Robinson; Julie Newmar; Randall Batinkoff; Annie Golden; Antonio Fargas; Khandi Alexander; Deborah Offner; Greg Germann; Kirk Taylor; ***D:*** Joan Freeman; ***W:*** Joan Freeman; Robert Alden; ***C:*** Steven Fierberg.

Stricken 𝒮𝒮 **1998 (R)** Six college buddies become obesessed with practical jokes that becomes more and more vicious—all of which are orchestrated by Guffy (Gunn). The butt of most of the gags, Banyon (Kennedy), has certainly had enough and helps play one last joke on Guffy that leads to his accidental death. Everyone but Banyon begins to panic and turn on each other but Banyon sees his chance to get back at everyone who humiliated him. Offers low-budget tension. **90m/C; VHS, DVD.** Jamie Kennedy; Sean Gunn; Judy Green; Tait Smith; Kevin Patrick Walls; ***D:*** Paul Chilsen; ***W:*** William W. Vought; ***C:*** Maida Sussman; ***M:*** Todd Scales.

Strictly Ballroom 𝒮𝒮𝒮 1/2 **1992 (PG)** Offbeat, cheerfully tacky dance/romance amusingly turns every movie cliche slightly askew. Scott (Mercurio) has been in training for the Pan-Pacific ballroom championships since the age of six. While talented, he also refuses to follow convention and scandalizes the stuffy dance establishment with his new steps. When his longtime partner leaves him, Scott takes up with a love-struck beginner (Morice), with some surprises of her own. Ballet dancer Mercurio (in his film debut) is appropriately arrogant yet vulnerable, with Morice as the plain Jane turned steel butterfly. Wonderful supporting cast; great debut for director Luhrmann. **94m/C; VHS, DVD, Blu-Ray.** *AU* Paul Mercurio; Tara Morice; Bill Hunter; Pat Thomsen; Barry Otto; Gia Carides; Peter Whitford; John Hannan; Sonia Kruger-Tayler; Kris McQuade; Pip Mushin; Leonie Page; Antonio Vargas; Armonia Benedito; ***D:*** Baz Luhrmann; ***W:*** Baz Luhrmann; Craig Pearce; ***C:*** Steve Mason; ***M:*** David Hirschfelder. Australian Film Inst. '92: Costume Des., Director (Luhrmann), Film, Film Editing, Screenplay, Support. Actor (Otto), Support. Actress (Thomsen).

Strictly Business 𝒮 1/2 **1991 (PG-13)** An upwardly mobile black broker has his career aspirations in order until he meets a beautiful club promoter who finds him square and boring. Wanting to impress her he asks the advice of a young man who works in the mail room for the proper way to dress and talk. A low-rent Pygmalion story. **83m/C; VHS, DVD.** Halle Berry; Tommy Davidson; Joseph C. Phillips; ***D:*** Kevin Hooks; ***M:*** Michel Colombier.

Strictly Dynamite 𝒮 1/2 **1934** A little shtick goes a long way in this send-up of radio shows. Popular comedian Moxie Slaight needs a new gag writer to liven up his show and unsuccessful poet Nick Montgomery gets the job. Nick becomes a success but this leads to some problems between Nick, his wife Sylvia, and Moxie's lively co-star Vera. **71m/B; DVD.** Jimmy Durante; Lupe Velez; Norman Foster; Marion (Marian) Nixon; Eugene Pallette; William Gargan; Sterling Holloway; Minna Gombell; Franklin Pangborn; Berton Churchill; ***D:*** Elliott Nugent; ***W:*** Maurine Watkins; Ralph Spence; ***C:*** Edward Cronjager.

Strictly Sexual 𝒮𝒮 **2008 (R)** Donna and her best friend Christi Ann are bored trying to find relationships in L.A. and decide to go for straight sex. They meet Stanny and Joe at a bar and think they're hustlers so they take them home for the night. The gals discover the guys are actually unemployed construction workers looking for jobs so they make them an offer: they can stay in the pool house in exchange for no-strings booty calls. Naturally, things don't work out that way. **99m/C; DVD.** Amber Benson; Kristen Kerr; Johann Urb; Steve Long; ***D:*** Joel Viertel; ***C:*** Andreas Burgess; ***M:*** H. Scott Salinas.

Strictly Sinatra 𝒮𝒮 1/2 *Cocozza's Way* **2001 (R)** Sinatra cover song act Toni Cocozza (Hart) plys his trade in the local pubs of Glasgow, dreaming about making it as big as Old Blue Eyes himself. The Scottish-Italian crooner's tiny faction of fans under 65 includes some local mobsters. When one claims he met Sinatra himself in Vegas, Toni, who's only truly comfortable on-stage, finds himself intrigued and drawn in to their gang, who shower him with the attention and respect he craves. Underworld mayhem complicates a potentially interesting comedy/thriller that doesn't fully live up to either. Technically adroit, with top-notch songs and arrangements and a stunning performance by Hart. **97m/C; VHS, DVD.** *GB* Ian Hart; Kelly Macdonald; Brian Cox; Alun Armstrong; Tommy Flanagan; Iain Cuthbertson; Jimmy Chisholm; Jimmy Yuill; ***Cameo(s):*** Richard E. Grant; ***D:*** Peter Capaldi; ***W:*** Peter Capaldi; ***C:*** Stephen Blackman; ***M:*** Stanislas Syrewicz.

Strike 𝒮𝒮𝒮 1/2 **1924** Eisenstein's debut, and a silent classic. Stirring look at a 1912 clash between striking factory workers and Czarist troops. **94m/B; Silent; VHS, DVD, Blu-Ray.** *RU* Alexander Antonov; Yudif Glizer; Ivan Klyukvin; Grigori Aleksandrov; ***D:*** Sergei Eisenstein; ***W:*** Sergei Eisenstein; Grigori Aleksandrov; ***C:*** Eduard Tisse.

Strike WOOF! *7-10 Split* **2007** Raunchy, witless smarm with an utterly terrible performance by lead actor/writer Patterson. Struggling actor Ross takes out his frustrations at the bowling alley where he's spotted by PBA recruiter Buddy (Wise), who offers him a chance at a pro career. Packing up his balls, best bud (Crawford), and girlfriend (Reid), Ross travels cross-country working on his game before challenging top bowler Jerry (Huebel) but soon Ross' ego is landing him in the gutter. And yes, that is Tara's brother who's nominally directing. **90m/C; DVD.** Ross Patterson; Tara Reid; Clayne Crawford; Ray Wise; Rob Huebel; Vinnie Jones; Robin (Robyn) Lively; Rachel Hunter; ***D:*** Tommy Reid; ***W:*** Ross Patterson; ***C:*** Massimo Zeri; ***M:*** Greg Morgenstein.

The Strike 𝒮𝒮 **2016** A comedy-drama about the lengths three actors will go to have careers. Living in New York City, three thirty-something actors do not have much talent but keep trying to make it. They have missed chances, endured harsh criticism, and made horrible first impressions. To finally get their big chance, the desperate trio come up with a plan to stage a siege at a yoga studio prove their acting skills to a top notch talent agent. **90m/C; DVD, Blu-Ray, Streaming, Download.** Bronson Pinchot; Paul Calderon; Katie Morrison; Guillermo Ivan; Erin Fogel; ***D:*** Guillermo Ivan; ***W:*** Guillermo Ivan; ***C:*** Joshua Dixon. **VIDEO**

Strike a Pose 𝒮 1/2 **1993 (R)** Erotic thriller finds international model-turned-fashion photographer Miranda Cross, her boyfriend LAPD detective Nick Carter, and Miranda's model friends stalked by a revenge-minded killer. Also available in an unrated version. **75m/C; VHS, DVD.** Margie Peterson; Robert Eastwick; Michelle LaMothe; ***D:*** Dean Hamilton.

Strike Force 𝒮 *Crack* **1975** A New York City cop, a Federal agent and a state trooper work together to battle a large drug ring. Failed made-for-TV pilot. Early Gere appearance; not related to later Robert Stack film with the same title. **74m/C; VHS, DVD.** Cliff Gorman; Richard Gere; Donald Blakely; ***D:*** Barry Shear. **TV**

Strike It Rich 𝒮 1/2 *Loser Take All* **1990 (PG)** A honeymooning couple find themselves resorting to the Monte Carlo gambling tables in order to raise money for the ride home. Lightweight fluff unfortunately adapted from Graham Greene's short novel "Loser Takes All." Only for hard-core Gielgudites. **86m/C; VHS, DVD; Open Captioned.** Molly Ringwald; Robert Lindsay; John Gielgud; Max Wall; Simon de la Brosse; ***D:*** James Scott; ***W:*** James Scott; ***C:*** Robert Paynter; ***M:*** Cliff Eidelman.

Strike Up the Band 𝒮𝒮 1/2 **1940** A high school band turns to hot swing music and enters a national radio contest. Rooney and Garland display their usual charm in this high-energy stroll down memory lane. **120m/B; VHS, DVD.** Judy Garland; Mickey Rooney; Paul Whiteman; William Tracy; June Preisser; ***D:*** Busby Berkeley. Oscars '40: Sound.

Striking Distance 𝒮𝒮 1/2 **1993 (R)** Tom Hardy (Willis) is a hard-nosed fifth-generation Pittsburgh homicide cop whose police detective father (Mahoney) is killed, apparently by a serial killer. Hardy insists the perp was really a fellow cop and winds up on the River Rescue squad (at least his partner is the fetching Parker). When the serial killer starts striking at women with some connection to Hardy, he finds scant support from his fellow cops. High action quotient backed by a fine cast, but the killer's identity won't be any surprise. **101m/C; VHS, DVD.** Bruce Willis; Sarah Jessica Parker; Dennis Farina; Tom Sizemore; Brion James; Robert Pastorelli; Timothy Busfield; John Mahoney; Andre Braugher; ***D:*** Rowdy Herrington; ***W:*** Marty Kaplan; Rowdy Herrington; ***C:*** Mac Ahlberg; ***M:*** Brad Fiedel.

The String 𝒮𝒮 *Le Fil; The Son* **2009** After spending years in Paris, Malik is forced to return to Tunisia after the death of his father. His longtime anxiety attacks increase when he realizes his wealthy mother Sara expects Malik to stay home and finally get married. Malik has never revealed to her that he's gay, but then he falls for hunky handyman Bilal. Now he has to decide if he can cut those maternal apron strings. French and Arabic with subtitles. **92m/C; DVD.** *FR* Antonin Stahly-Vishwanadan; Claudia Cardinale; Salim Kechiouche; Lotfi Dziri; ***D:*** Mehdi Ben Attia; ***W:*** Mehdi Ben Attia; Olivier Laneurie; ***C:*** Sofian El Fani; ***M:*** Karol Beffa.

Strip Search 𝒮 1/2 **1997 (R)** Police detective Robby (Pare) gets seduced by easy money and sex when he gets involved with sex clubs and underworld gangs. **90m/C; VHS, DVD.** *CA* Michael Paré; Pam Grier; Caroline Neron; Lucie Laurier; Maury Chaykin; Heidi von Palleske; MacKenzie Gray; ***D:*** Rod Hewitt.

Stripes 𝒮𝒮 1/2 **1981 (R)** Feeling like losers and looking to straighten out their lives, two friends enlist in the Army under the mistaken impression that military life is something like a summer camp for grown-ups. A boxoffice success (despite a weak script) due in large part to Murray's charm and his verbal and sometimes physical sparring with Oates, who is good as the gruff-tempered platoon sergeant. Features humorous stints from various "Second City" players, including Candy, whom Murray turns into a "lean, mean fighting machine." **105m/C; VHS, DVD, Blu-Ray, UMD.** Bill Murray; Harold Ramis; P.J. Soles; Warren Oates; John Candy; John Larroquette; Judge Reinhold; Sean Young; Dave Thomas; Joe Flaherty; Lance LeGault; ***D:*** Ivan Reitman; ***W:*** Harold Ramis; Len Blum; ***C:*** Bill Butler; ***M:*** Elmer Bernstein.

Stripped to Kill 𝒮𝒮 **1987 (R)** A female cop goes undercover to lure a psycho killing strippers. Not-bad entry from Corman and cohorts. Followed by—you guessed it—?"Stripped to Kill II." **88m/C; VHS, DVD, Blu-Ray.** Kay Lenz; Greg Evigan; Norman Fell; Pia Kamakahi; Tracy Crowder; Deborah Ann Nassar; Lucia Nagy Lexington; Carlye Byron; Athena Worthy; Michelle Foreman; Diana Bellamy; ***D:*** Katt Shea; ***W:*** Katt Shea; Andy Ruben; ***C:*** John LeBlanc; ***M:*** John O'Kennedy.

Stripped to Kill 2: Live Girls 𝒮 **1989** A young woman with extra-sensory powers dreams of murders which she discovers are all too real. A weak sequel, despite the interesting premise. **83m/C; VHS, DVD.** Maria Ford; Eb Lottimer; Karen Mayo-Chandler; Marjean Holden; Birke Tan; Debra Lamb; ***D:*** Katt Shea; ***W:*** Katt Shea.

Stripshow 𝒮 **1995 (R)** Veteran Vegas stripper shows the ropes to newcomer and then must vie with the upstart for her boyfriend's interest. **96m/C; VHS, DVD.** Monique Parent; Tane McClure; Steven Tietsort; ***D:*** Gary Orona; ***W:*** Gary Orona.

Striptease 𝒮𝒮 1/2 **1996 (R)** Single mom Erin Grant (Moore) loses custody of her daughter Angela (Moore's real-life offspring, Rumer) to her lowlife ex, Darrell (Patrick). In order to raise the money for an appeal, she dances at a Miami strip club, where she runs across politician David Dilbeck (Reynolds), who has a thing for both vaseline and Erin. Unlike "Showgirls," this one's intentionally funny and features some fine script work and performances, which got overlooked amidst all the hype, including Moore's record-setting (for an actress) $12 million paycheck, 4 mil of which reportedly was for agreeing to dance nude. Based on the novel by Carl Hiaasen. **115m/C; VHS, DVD.** Demi Moore; Armand Assante; Ving Rhames; Robert Patrick; Burt Reynolds; Rumer Willis; Paul Guilfoyle; Dina Spybey; *D:* Andrew Bergman; *W:* Andrew Bergman; *C:* Stephen Goldblatt; *M:* Howard Shore. Golden Raspberries '96: Worst Actress (Moore), Worst Director (Bergman), Worst Picture, Worst Screenplay, Worst Song ("Pussy, Pussy, Pussy (Whose Kitty Cat Are You?)").

Stripteaser 𝄞 1/2 **1995 (R)** Sicko psycho Dean holds dancers and patrons hostage in an L.A. strip joint where he provides various humiliations for his captives. Ford's the beautiful ecdysiast whose been the object of the fellow's secret obsessions. Also available unrated. **82m/C; VHS, DVD.** Rick Dean; Maria Ford; Lance August; *D:* Dan Golden.

Stroker Ace WOOF! 1983 (PG) Flamboyant stock car driver tries to break an iron-clad promotional contract signed with a greedy fried-chicken magnate. Off duty, he ogles blondes as dopey as he is. One of the worst from Reynolds—and that's saying something. **96m/C; VHS, DVD.** Burt Reynolds; Ned Beatty; Jim Nabors; Parker Stevenson; Loni Anderson; Bubba Smith; *D:* Hal Needham; *W:* Hal Needham; Hugh Wilson; *C:* Nick McLean; *M:* Al Capps. Golden Raspberries '83: Worst Support. Actor (Nabors).

Strong Island 𝄞𝄞𝄞 **2017** A moving exploration of the effect of a murder on the victim's family. The film's director, Yance Ford, addresses the camera directly as he discusses his brother's murder and how it destroyed their family over two decades. He also explains how his African American parents came to live in New York City, and the perspective of his mother on events. Additionally, the film looks at the seemingly cold-blooded murder itself and the subsequent police investigation. Drawing on his formidable skills as a documentarian, Ford effectively frames and uses backgrounds to emphasize the story he has crafted from the tragedy. **107m/C; DVD.** *DK US D:* Yance Ford; *C:* Alan Jacobsen; *M:* Craig Sutherland; Hildur Guonadottir. **VIDEO**

Strong Man 𝄞𝄞𝄞 **1926** A WWI veteran, passing himself off as an unlikely circus strongman, searches an American city for the girl whose letters gave him hope during the war. Perhaps Langdon's best full-length film. **78m/B; VHS, DVD.** Harry Langdon; Gertrude Astor; Tay Garnett; *D:* Frank Capra. Natl. Film Reg. '07.

Stronger 𝄞𝄞𝄞 **2017 (R)** Gyllenhall delivers a top-shelf performance in his portrayal of Jeff Bauman, the bystander who had his legs blown off in the 2013 Boston Marathon bombing, and who became a symbol of resilience, strength, and patriotism. Equally strong turns from the entire cast, particularly Maslany as his girlfriend, lift this powerful story above clichéd melodramas. Based on Bauman's autobiography of the same name. **119m/C; DVD, Blu-Ray.** Jake Gyllenhaal; Tatiana Maslany; Miranda Richardson; Clancy Brown; Frankie Shaw; *D:* David Gordon Green; *W:* John Pollono; *C:* Sean Bobbitt; *M:* Michael Brook.

Stronger Than Desire 𝄞 1/2 **1939** Married to workaholic lawyer Tyler Flagg (Pidgeon), Elizabeth (Bruce) dallies with Michael McLain (Bowman) for fun until he tries blackmailing her. She shoots him (no secret there) but then McLain's wife Eva (Dvorak) is accused and a guilty Elizabeth gets her husband to defend the innocent woman. Remake of 1934's "Evelyn Prentice." **80m/B; DVD.** Walter Pidgeon; Virginia Bruce; Lee Bowman; Ann Dvorak; Ann Todd; Ilka Chase; Rita Johnson; Richard Lane; *D:* Leslie Fenton; *W:* William Ludwig; David Hertz; *C:* William H. Daniels; *M:* Edward Ward; David Snell.

The Strongest Man in the World 𝄞𝄞 1/2 **1975 (G)** Another crazy mix-up involves Dexter Riley (Russell) and his friends at Medfield College in wacky adventures. One of their experiment gets mixed up with one of the students' breakfast cereal and turns out to give humans super-strength for a short time. The dean makes a deal with the local cereal company, and crooks hired by a rival company try to steal the formula. Typically enjoyable Disney live-action fare from the '70s may provide fun for the young 'uns, and will definitely bring back fond memories for their parents. **92m/C; VHS, DVD, Blu-Ray.** Kurt Russell; Joe Flynn; Eve Arden; Cesar Romero; Phil Silvers; Dick Van Patten; Harold Gould; Richard Bakalyan; Michael McGreevey; William Schallert; Benson Fong; James Gregory; Don Carter; John Debney; Fritz Feld; Roy Roberts; Kathleen Freeman; *W:* Joseph L. McEveety; Herman Groves; *C:* Andrew Jackson; *M:* Robert F. Brunner.

Stroszek 𝄞𝄞𝄞 **1977** Three German misfits—a singer, a prostitute and an old man—tour the U.S. in search of their dreams. Touching, hilarious comedy-drama with a difference and an attitude. One of Herzog's easiest and also best films. In English and German with English subtitles. **108m/C; VHS, DVD, Blu-Ray.** *GE* Eva Mattes; Bruno S; Clemens Scheitz; Wilhelm von Homburg; *D:* Werner Herzog; *W:* Werner Herzog; *C:* Thomas Mauch; *M:* Chet Atkins; Tom Paxton.

Struck by Lightning 𝄞 1/2 **2012** A series of flashbacks focuses on high school misfit, Carson (Colfer), who's zapped and killed by lightning in the opening moments. The dead Carson recounts the bullying from thugs who didn't understand his literary ambitions, the burden of having a boozed-up divorced mom, and other teen melodrama with a heavy dose of zaniness on the side. First-time writer and star Colfer makes his Carson into the coolest kid in school--above jocks, cheerleaders, nerds, closeted gay kids, and just about any other stereotype needed to fill the cliche quota. It aims for edgy and provocative but there's nothing shocking here. **90m/C; Blu-Ray, Streaming.** Christina Hendricks; Chris Colfer; Rebel Wilson; Allison Janney; Dermot Mulroney; Sarah Hyland; *D:* Brian Dannelly; *W:* Chris Colfer; *C:* Bobby Bukowski; *M:* Jake Monaco.

Struggle 𝄞 **1931** Unfortunately, Griffith's final directorial effort is a ludicrous melodrama about the evils of alcohol. Because of Prohibition, working man Jimmie Wilson (Skelly) takes to illegal hootch, which turns out to be tainted, causing Jimmie to abuse his wife and daughter and destroy their formerly happy home. **87m/B; VHS, DVD.** Hal Skelly; Zita Johann; Evelyn Baldwin; Charlotte Wynters; Helen Mack; Kate Bruce; Jackson Halliday; Edna Hagan; Claude Cooper; Arthur Lipson; Charles Richman; Scott Moore; Dave Manley; *D:* D.W. Griffith; *W:* D.W. Griffith; Anita Loos; John Emerson; *C:* Joseph Ruttenberg; *M:* D.W. Griffith; Philip A. Scheib.

Stryker 𝄞 1/2 **2004** Just your typical Canadian gangster and transvestite flick. Stryker is a speechless 14-year-old boy on the lam after burning down a church near his Indian reservation. He hops a train and finds himself a blank observer, wandering the seedy underbelly Winnipeg. After witnessing a mob throwdown between the warring Indian Posse and the Asian Bomb Squad, he finds protection in a home of transvestite prostitutes and then under the wing of the police. Low budget flair that tries to be quirky and fresh, but suffers from stiff performances and amateur theatrics. Fans of early John Waters may be amused. **93m/C; DVD.** Kyle Henry; Ryan Black; Deena Fontaine; Joseph Mesiano; Nick Oullette; Nancy Sanderson; *D:* Noam Gonick; *W:* Noam Gonick; David MacIntosh; *C:* Edward Lachman; *M:* Karmen Omeosoos.

Stuart Bliss 𝄞𝄞 **1998** Curious little comedy mixes elements of "The X-Files" and "The Truman Show." Stuart Bliss (Zelnicker) is an ordinary guy who slowly succumbs to paranoia and apocalyptic religious visions. Of course, the question is: Is he crazy or well-informed? **88m/C; VHS, DVD.** Michael Zelniker; Dea Lawrence; Derek McGrath; Ania Suli; Mark Fite; *D:* Neil Grieve; *W:* Michael Zelniker; Neil Grieve; *C:* Jens Sturup.

Stuart Little 𝄞𝄞 1/2 **1999 (PG)** This bigscreen adaptation of E.B. White's 1945 children's classic is hardly faithful but has its own charms. Mr. (Laurie) and Mrs. (Davis) Little decide to expand their family through adoption and wind up with a tiny, talking, clothes-wearing white mouse named Stuart (Fox). Their son George (Lipnicki) has a hard time thinking of a mouse as his little brother and family cat Snowbell (Lane) thinks the rodent is snack food. When his attempt to eat Stuart fails, Snowbell turns to kidnapping. The array of digital effects is amazing. **92m/C; VHS, DVD, UMD.** Geena Davis; Hugh Laurie; Jonathan Lipnicki; Brian Doyle-Murray; Estelle Getty; Julia Sweeney; Dabney Coleman; *V:* Michael J. Fox; Nathan Lane; Chazz Palminteri; Steve Zahn; Bruno Kirby; Jennifer Tilly; David Alan Grier; Jim Doughan; *D:* Rob Minkoff; *W:* M. Night Shyamalan; Greg Booker; *C:* Guillermo Navarro; *M:* Alan Silvestri.

Stuart Little 2 𝄞𝄞𝄞 **2002 (PG-13)** Amazingly good sequel finds Stuart tooling around Manhattan in his miniature red sport car with a new, similar-sized friend: a cute, yellow bird named Margalo (Griffith). Stuart is smitten with his fine-feathered friend, taking her on a very PG date to a drive-in movie (his car parked in front of the TV set). Unbeknownst to Stuart, Margalo is actually in cahoots with a scheming Falcon (Woods) which sets off numerous adventures out in the big city for Stuart and a reluctant and even snarkier Snowbell (Lane). New York looks just as idyllic and the animation blended with live-action is even better than the original. More faithful adaptation of E.B. White's 1945 children's classic, on which both films were based. **78m/C; VHS, DVD, UMD.** Geena Davis; Hugh Laurie; Jonathan Lipnicki; Brad Garrett; *V:* Michael J. Fox; Nathan Lane; Melanie Griffith; James Woods; Steve Zahn; *D:* Rob Minkoff; *W:* Bruce Joel Rubin; *C:* Steven Poster; *M:* Alan Silvestri.

Stuart Little 3: Call of the Wild 𝄞 1/2 **2006 (G)** The Little family spends the summer at a lakeside cottage and mouse Stuart wants to join the Lake Scouts. When he's separated from his group, skunk Reeko comes to Stuart's rescue. **72m/C; DVD.** Peter MacNichol; *V:* Michael J. Fox; Geena Davis; Hugh Laurie; Wayne Brady; Virginia Madsen; *D:* Audu Paden. **VIDEO**

Stuart Saves His Family 𝄞𝄞 **1994 (PG-13)** Fired from his self-help TV show on a Chicago public-access station, New-Age advice guru Smalley (Franken) returns home to help his pathetically dysfunctional family sort out their problems and an inheritance, a nonplot that gives Smalley a chance to do his 12-step shtick. And that's. . .O.K. A tolerable installment in the endless parade of mediocre "Saturday Night Live" sketches stretched for the big screen that takes a few surprisingly maudlin turns. Based on Franken's book of Smalley's "daily affirmations," "I'm Good Enough, I'm Smart Enough, and Doggone It, People Like Me!" **97m/C; DVD.** Al Franken; Laura San Giacomo; Vincent D'Onofrio; Shirley Knight; Harris Yulin; Julia Sweeney; Aaron Lustig; Darrell Larson; Camille Saviola; Gerrit Graham; Theodore (Ted) Raimi; Joe Flaherty; *D:* Harold Ramis; *W:* Al Franken; *C:* Lauro Escorel; *M:* Marc Shaiman.

Stuber 𝄞𝄞 **2019 (R)** On the day that tough, job-obsessed cop Vic (Bautista) has Lasik surgery, he learns that may finally be able to arrest the drug runner that killed his partner a year ago. Unable to drive or move well, he uses the Uber app his adult artist daughter Nicole (Morales) put on his phone to arrange a ride. Vic gets Stu (Nanjiani) as his driver. To preserve his five star rating, Stu does his best to help Vic though the cop makes unreasonable demands on him. Nanjiani and Bautista have chemistry, but the action-comedy lacks a plot that lives up to their talents. **105m/C; DVD, Blu-Ray.** Dave Bautista; Kumail Nanjiani; Mira Sorvino; Natalie Morales; Iko Uwais; *D:* Michael Dowse; *W:* Tripper Clancy; *C:* Bobby Shore; *M:* Joseph Trapanese.

Stuck 𝄞𝄞 **2007 (R)** Sardonic black comedy disturbingly based on a true story. Tom (Rea) has lost his job and become homeless but his life gets infinitely worse when hard-partying Brandi (Suvari) slams into him and Tom is stuck in her windshield. She drives home, parks in the garage, and leaves him there—apparently not realizing (or maybe caring) that he's alive. Next day, Brandi asks her drug-dealing boyfriend Rashid (Hornsby) to dispose of the body. Except Tom's still not dead, but now he's mondo ticked, struggling to get free, and out for payback. **94m/C; DVD, Blu-Ray.** Mena Suvari; Stephen Rea; Russell Hornsby; *D:* Stuart Gordon; *W:* John Strysik; *C:* Denis Maloney; *M:* Bobby Johnson.

Stuck Between Stations 𝄞 1/2 **2011 (R)** Casper is on leave from duty in Iraq to attend his dad's funeral in Minneapolis. He goes to a bar and unexpectedly reconnects with crush Becky, the pretty girl who didn't know he existed in high school, whose own life is damaged by a sexual peccadillo. They start wandering around, talking, and getting involved in odd situations, but it's neither as dull nor as pretentious as you might fear. **84m/C; DVD.** Sam Rosen; Zoe Lister-Jones; Michael Imperioli; Josh Hartnett; *D:* Brady Kiernan; *W:* Sam Rosen; Nat Bennett; *C:* Bo Hakala; *M:* Grant Cutler.

Stuck in Love 𝄞𝄞 **2012 (R)** The turbulent plot lines from a family of writers doesn't quite match the storm clouds of their actual love lives, as they each struggle to stay afloat. Divorced father Borgens (Kinnear) and mother Erica (Connelly) try to steer their daughter Samantha (Collins) into making the right decisions with her newly published novel, while navigating their son's (Wolff) frustration with not being able to finish his own. Bogged down by pseudo-intellectualism and a lack of bite, the proceedings of this so-called troubled family play out more like a Stephen King novel without the horror and less like the Woody Allen homage it aspires to be. **97m/C; DVD, Blu-Ray.** Greg Kinnear; Jennifer Connelly; Lily Collins; Nat Wolff; Logan Lerman; Liana Liberato; Kristen Bell; *D:* Josh Boone; *W:* Josh Boone; *C:* Tim Orr; *M:* Mike Mogis; Nate Walcott.

Stuck on You 𝄞 **1984 (R)** Couple engaged in a palimony suit takes their case to a judge to work out their differences. Wing-clipped angel Gabriel (Corey) comes to earth to help them patch it up. Never mind. **90m/C; VHS, DVD.** Prof. Irwin Corey; Virginia Penta; Mark Mikulski; *D:* Lloyd Kaufman; Michael Herz; *W:* Lloyd Kaufman; Michael Herz; *C:* Lloyd Kaufman.

Stuck On You 𝄞𝄞 1/2 **2003 (PG-13)** Surprisingly sentimental movie for the Farrelly brothers. Damon and Kinnear play conjoined twins Bob and Walt Tenor who've adapted to their rather unusual living arrangement with ease. Walt, however, has caught the acting bug and wants to make it big in Hollywood. As fate would have it, Walt becomes an unlikely star. While the movie borders on being a one-joke premise, it does have its sincere moments. **118m/C; VHS, DVD, Blu-Ray.** Matt Damon; Greg Kinnear; Eva Mendes; Wen Yann Shih; Pat Crawford Brown; Jean-Pierre Cassel; Cher; Ray "Rocket" Valliere; *Cameo(s):* Jay Leno; *D:* Bobby Farrelly; Peter Farrelly; *W:* Bobby Farrelly; Peter Farrelly; *C:* Dan(iel) Mindel.

The Stud WOOF! 1978 (R) Owner of a fashionable "after hours" dance spot hires a young, handsome stud to manage the club and attend to her personal needs. Low-budget look and seemingly scriptless. Faithfully adapted by sister Jackie Collins from her novel. **90m/C; VHS, DVD.** *GB* Joan Collins; Oliver Tobias; *D:* Quentin Masters; *W:* Jackie Collins.

Student Bodies WOOF! 1981 (R) A "Halloween"-style spoof of high-school horror films, except it's not funny. And what's so funny about bloody murder anyway? When the on-the-set problems and strife arose (which they did), why didn't everyone just cut their losses and go home? **86m/C; VHS, DVD, Blu-Ray.** Kristen Riter; Matthew Goldsby; Richard Belzer; Joe Flood; Joe Talarowski; Mimi Weddell; *D:* Mickey Rose; *W:* Mickey Rose.

Student Confidential 𝄞 **1987 (R)** A Troma-produced spoof of seedy high school youth movies, new and old, involving four students who are led into the world of adult vices by a mysterious millionaire. Badly made and dull. Douglas and Jackson both have brothers named Michael. **99m/C; VHS, DVD.** Eric Douglas; Marlon Jackson; Susie Scott; Ronee Blakley; Elizabeth Singer; *D:* Richard Horian.

The Student Nurses 𝄞𝄞 **1970 (R)** The adventures, amourous and otherwise, of four last-year nursing students. Followed by four sequels: "Private Duty Nurses," "Night Call Nurses," "The Young Nurses," and "Candy Stripe Nurses." Better than average exploitation fare. First release from Roger Corman's New World studios; it goes down hill from there. **89m/C; VHS, DVD.** Elaine Giftos; Karen Carlson; Brioni Farrell; Barbara Leigh; Reni Santoni; Richard Rust; Lawrence Casey; Darrell Larson; Paul Camen; Richard Stahl; Scottie MacGregor; Pepe Serna; *D:* Stephanie Rothman; ***W:*** Don Spencer; ***C:*** Stevan Larner.

The Student Prince 🦴🦴 **1954** Delightful rendition of Sigmund Romberg's famous operetta in which Purdom stars as the Prince of Heidelberg who falls for barmaid Blyth. Lanza recorded the soundtrack, but could not star in this film because of his weight problem. Previously filmed in 1919 and 1927 without music. **107m/C; VHS, DVD.** Ann Blyth; Edmund Purdom; John Ericson; Louis Calhern; Edmund Gwenn; S.Z. Sakall; Betta St. John; ***D:*** Richard Thorpe; ***C:*** Paul Vogel.

Student Seduction 🦴 ½ **2003** Lifetime drama based on a true story. Married high school chemistry teacher Christie Dawson (Berkley) is young and attractive and troubled, failing student Josh Gaines (Sevier) reads more into her offer to tutor him. He attacks Christie in her home but when she reports the crime, Josh's wealthy family go on the attack and Josh accuses her of molesting him. **96m/C; DVD.** Elizabeth Berkley; Corey Sevier; Karen Robinson; Rick Roberts; Sarah Smyth; ***D:*** Peter Svatek; ***W:*** Edithe Swensen; ***C:*** Serge Ladouceur; ***M:*** James Gelfand. **CABLE**

The Student Teachers 🦴 ½ **1973** Yet another soft-core Corman product. Three student teachers sleep around, on screen. **79m/C; VHS, DVD.** Susan Damante-Shaw; Brooke Mills; Bob Harris; John Cramer; Chuck Norris; ***D:*** Jonathan Kaplan.

Studs Lonigan 🦴🦴 **1960** Drifting, too artsy rendering a James T. Farrell's trilogy about an Irish drifter growing up in Chicago in the '20s. Good period detail, but oddly off-kilter and implausible as history. **96m/B; VHS, DVD.** Christopher Knight; Frank Gorshin; Jack Nicholson; Jay C. Flippen; Katherine Squire; Dick Foran; Carolyn Craig; ***D:*** Irving Lerner; ***W:*** Philip Yordan; ***C:*** Haskell Wexler; ***M:*** Jerry Goldsmith.

A Study in Scarlet 🦴🦴 **1933** Owen played Watson the previous year in "Sherlock Holmes"; here he's miscast as Holmes, and the plot differs from the Doyle story of the same title. **77m/B; VHS, DVD.** Reginald Owen; Alan Mowbray; Anna May Wong; June Clyde; Alan Dinehart; ***D:*** Edwin L. Marin; ***W:*** Reginald Owen.

A Study in Terror 🦴🦴🦴 *Sherlock Holmes Grosster Fall; Fog* **1966** A well-appointed Sherlock Holmes thriller, and the second one in color. Premise has a young, athletic Holmes in pursuit of an educated Jack the Ripper in 1880s London. **94m/C; VHS, DVD, Blu-Ray.** *GE GB* John Neville; Donald Houston; Dame Judi Dench; Anthony Quayle; Robert Morley; Frank Finlay; Cecil Parker; ***D:*** James Hill.

The Stuff 🦴 ½ **1985 (R)** Surreal horror semi-spoof about an ice cream mogul and a hamburger king who discover that the new, fast-selling confection in town zombifies its partakers. Forced, lame satire from producer/director/writer Cohen. **93m/C; VHS, DVD, Blu-Ray.** Michael Moriarty; Andrea Marcovicci; Garrett Morris; Paul Sorvino; Danny Aiello; Brooke Adams; Patrick O'Neal; Alexander Scourby; Scott Bloom; James Dixon; Tammy Grimes; Clara Peller; Abe Vigoda; ***D:*** Larry Cohen; ***W:*** Larry Cohen; ***C:*** Paul Glickman; ***M:*** Anthony Guefen.

Stuff Stephanie in the Incinerator 🦴 *In Deadly Heat* **1989 (PG-13)** A Troma gagfest about wealthy cretins who torture and kill young women. "Funny" title betrays utter, exploitive mindlessness. **97m/C; VHS, DVD.** Catherine Dee; William Dame; M.R. Murphy; Dennis Cunningham; ***D:*** Don Nardo.

The Stunt Man 🦴🦴🦴🦴 **1980 (R)** A marvelous and unique exercise in meta-cinematic manipulation. O'Toole, in one of his very best roles, is a power-crazed movie director; Railsback is a fugitive sheltered by him from sherrif Rocco. When a stunt man is killed in an accident, O'Toole prevails on Railsback to replace him, leading Railsback to wonder if O'Toole wants him dead. A labor of love for director-producer Rush, who spent nine years working on it, and waited two years to see it released, by Fox. Based on the novel by Paul Brodeur. **129m/C; VHS, DVD, Blu-Ray.** Peter O'Toole; Steve Railsback; Barbara Hershey; Charles "Chuck" Bail; Alex Rocco; Allen Garfield; Adam Roarke; Sharon Farrell; Philip Bruns; ***D:*** Richard Rush; ***W:*** Richard Rush; Lawrence B. Marcus; ***C:*** Mario Tosi; ***M:*** Dominic Frontiere. Golden Globes '81: Score; Montreal World Film Fest. '80: Film; Natl. Soc. Film Critics '80: Actor (O'Toole).

Stuntmen 🦴 ½ **2009 (R)** A crazy documentary filmmaker reignites the rivalry between the two leading stuntmen in the industry, who have both been nominated for the Stuntman of the Year award. When Steve tries to uncover what's behind the riff, he learns some secrets that could ruin the stunt community. **90m/C; DVD.** Marc Blucas; Ross Patterson; Chris Tarantino; Brandon Routh; Dominique Swain; Carly Pope; Zachary Levi; Ray Wise; ***D:*** Eric Amadio; ***W:*** Eric Amadio; ***C:*** Todd Hickey. **VIDEO**

Stunts 🦴🦴 *Who Is Killing the Stuntman* **1977 (PG)** See "The Stunt Man" instead. OK script hides near-invisible plot; stunt man engages in derring-do. **90m/C; VHS, DVD.** Robert Forster; Fiona Lewis; Joanna Cassidy; Darrell Fetty; Bruce Glover; James Luisi; ***D:*** Mark L. Lester; ***M:*** Michael Kamen.

Stuntwoman 🦴 ½ **1981** Welch plays a stuntwoman whose death-defying job interferes with her love life. What ever shall she do? **95m/C; VHS, DVD.** Raquel Welch; Jean-Paul Belmondo; ***D:*** Claude Zidi.

The Stupids 🦴 ½ **1995 (PG)** In the tradition of "Dumb and Dumber," the aptly named Stupids—dad Stanley (Arnold), mom Joan (Lundy), brother Buster (Hall), and sis Petunia (McKenna)?blunder unwittingly into and out of dangerous adventures involving their garbage. Landing Arnold for the lead seems like the casting coup of the decade but the movie itself is shaky and uninspired. Based on the children's best-selling books. Keep a lookout for Captain Kangaroo (Keeshan) and numerous other cameos. **93m/C; VHS, DVD.** Tom Arnold; Jessica Lundy; Bug Hall; Alex McKenna; Mark Metcalf; Matt Keeslar; Frankie Faison; Christopher Lee; Bob Keeshan; ***Cameo(s):*** Robert Wise; Norman Jewison; Constantin Costa-Gavras; David Cronenberg; Atom Egoyan; Gillo Pontecorvo; ***D:*** John Landis; ***W:*** Brent Forrester; ***C:*** Manfred Guthe; ***M:*** Christopher L. Stone. Golden Raspberries '96: Worst Actor (Arnold).

Styx 🦴🦴 ½ **2000 (R)** Nelson (Weller) decides to get out of the safecracking trade after his brother Mike (MacFadyen) rescues him from a botched bank heist that leaves several accomplices unaccounted for. Nelson tries to go straight but Mike is a losing gambler with a big debt to some loan sharks. Nelson agrees to do a diamond heist only to learn that his not-so-missing partner Art (Brown) is the mastermind and Art just may be holding a grudge. Pro cast and fast-paced action take this above the usual heist flicks. **94m/C; VHS, DVD.** Peter Weller; Bryan Brown; Angus MacFadyen; Adrienne Pierce; Anthony Bishop; Nan Hamilton; Shane Howarth; Gerard Rudolf; ***D:*** Alexander Wright; ***W:*** George Ferris; ***C:*** Russell Lyster; ***M:*** Roy Hay.

Sub Down 🦴 **1997 (PG-13)** Silly underwater saga about a submarine trapped under the polar ice cap in the Bering Strait. Scientists Baldwin, Conti, and Anwar are aboard the USS Portland when it manages to collide with a Russian sub and sink. So they're running out of air and have to figure out a way to survive. Director Gregg Champion took his name off, so be warned. **91m/C; VHS, DVD.** Stephen Baldwin; Gabrielle Anwar; Tom Conti; Chris Mulkey; Tony Plana; Joel Thomas Traywick; Doug McKeon; ***D:*** Alan Smithee; ***W:*** Howard Chesley; ***C:*** Hiro Narita; ***M:*** Stefano Mainetti. **CABLE**

Subhuman 🦴 *Shelf Life* **2004 (R)** Psycho bounty hunter Martin (McDonald) is going around decapitating people when he's accidentally run over by Ben (McLaughlin) and Julie (Kramer). He convinces them not to take him to a hospital; instead they take him to their home (because they're really stupid). Martin tells them he's hunting blood-sucking parasites that can only be destroyed by decapitating the host, which turns out to be true as the couple soon finds out. **90m/C; DVD.** *CA* William McDonald; Earl Pastko; Bryce McLaughlin; Courtney Kramer; ***D:*** Mark Tuit; ***W:*** Mark Tuit; ***C:*** Craig Powell; ***M:*** Stephen Bukat; Jeff Tymoschuk.

Subject Two 🦴 ½ **2006 (R)** A claustrophobic "Frankenstein" variation. In a remote Rocky Mountain cabin, scientist Dr. Vick (Stapleton) uses his new assistant, Adam (Oliver), as a guinea pig in his controversial research on death and resurrection. He kills Adam and revives him, over and over again. **93m/C; DVD.** Dean Stapleton; Christian Oliver; Courtney Mace; Jurgen Jones; ***D:*** Philip Chidel; ***W:*** Philip Chidel; ***C:*** Rich Confalone; ***M:*** Erik Godal.

The Subject Was Roses 🦴🦴🦴 ½ **1968** Outstanding story of family dysfunction and love based on Gilroy's Pulitzer Prize-winning play. Timmy Cleary (Sheen) returns from WWII to find that his parents' marriage has disintegrated into open hostility. Formerly mom Nettie's (Neal) fave, Timmy finally starts to learn about blustery dad John (Albertson) and attempts to moderate between the rancorous duo. But he quickly discovers that each of his parents will use him against the other and Timmy decides the best thing for everyone would be if he strikes out on his own. First film for Neal after her recovery from a series of strokes. **107m/C; VHS, DVD.** Martin Sheen; Patricia Neal; Jack Albertson; ***D:*** Ulu Grosbard; ***W:*** Frank D. Gilroy; ***C:*** Jack Priestley; ***M:*** Lee Pockriss. Oscars '68: Support. Actor (Albertson).

Sublime 🦴 ½ **2007 (R)** George Grieves (Cavanagh) goes to the hospital for a routine procedure and doctors mistakenly perform a different surgery that results in George contracting a flesh-eating bacteria. This results in more surgeries and a series of flashbacks concerning George's anxieties, including his health care concerns (guess he was right about that). **113m/C; DVD.** Tom Cavanagh; Kathleen York; Lawrence-Hilton Jacobs; Kyle Gallner; Katherine Cunningham-Eves; Paget Brewster; Shanna Collins; ***D:*** Tony Krantz; ***W:*** Erik Jendresen; ***C:*** Dermott Downs; ***M:*** Peter Golub. **VIDEO**

Submarine 🦴🦴🦴 **2010 (R)** Coming of age comedy follows 15-year-old Oliver Tate's (Roberts) quest to lose his virginity before his sixteenth birthday—ideally, with his classmate, the quirky pyromaniac Jordana (Paige). But even more important is his mission to protect his parents' marriage after his mother's ex-lover returns to her life. Adapted from Joe Dunthorpe's novel, writer/director Ayoade's debut is a well-written, poignant, and bittersweet family drama. The highlight is the refreshing view of a teenage boy: Oliver is awkward, caring, funny, deeply flawed and deeply human. **96m/C; DVD, Blu-Ray, On Demand.** *GB* Craig Roberts; Yasmin Paige; Noah Taylor; Sally Hawkins; Paddy Considine; ***D:*** Richard Ayoade; ***W:*** Richard Ayoade; ***C:*** Erik Wilson; ***M:*** Andrew Hewitt.

Submarine Attack 🦴🦴 *Torpedo Zone; The Great Hope; La Grande Speranza* **1954** Unconventional war story posits an Italian submarine captain (Baldini) who decides to rescue the survivors of a Danish freighter that he has sunk. **92m/B; VHS, DVD.** *IT* Renato Baldini; Lois Maxwell; Folco Lulli; Carlo Bellini; Earl Cameron; ***D:*** Duilio Coletti; ***C:*** Leonida Barboni; ***M:*** Nino Rota.

Submarine Base 🦴 ½ **1943** Gangster Joe Morgan has left New York for an island off South America. He rescues merchant seaman Jim Taggert from a ship torpedoed by the Germans but Jim (an ex-cop) is suspicious and thinks Joe is re-supplying German U-boat commanders. But the situation isn't that simple. **65m/B; DVD.** Alan Baxter; John Litel; Fifi d'Orsay; Eric Blore; Iris Adrian; George Metaxa; Lucien Prival; Luis Alberni; ***D:*** Albert Kelley; ***W:*** George M. Merrick; Arthur St. Claire; ***C:*** Marcel Le Picard; ***M:*** Charles Dant.

Submarino 🦴 ½ **2010** Dark, drab Danish drama finds two estranged brothers forever damaged by their pasts. Neglected by their drunken, abusive mother, Nick became a boozer who's just out of prison and living in a shelter. His younger (nameless) brother is a junkie with a neglected young son of his own. Vinterberg follows each of them around for awhile before they finally reconnect. Danish with subtitles. **110m/C; DVD.** *DK* Jacob Cedergren; Peter Plaugborg; Gustave Fischer; ***D:*** Thomas Vinterberg; ***W:*** Thomas Vinterberg; Tobias Lindholm; ***C:*** Charlotte Bruus Christensen; ***M:*** Thomas Blachmann.

Submerged 🦴🦴 **2000 (R)** Terrorists hijack a commerical airliner carrying a computer decoder that controls a national defense satellite capable of launching nuclear weapons. The hijackers deliberately plunge the plane into the Pacific Ocean and while the passengers struggle to survive, a team of Nacy SEALS attempt a rescue mission and a strike against the bad guys. **95m/C; VHS, DVD.** Coolio; Nicole Eggert; Fred Williamson; Dennis Weaver; Maxwell Caulfield; Brent Huff; Tim Thomerson; Stacey Travis; Yvette Nipar; ***D:*** Fred Olen Ray; ***W:*** Steve Latshaw; ***C:*** Thomas Callaway. **VIDEO**

Submerged 🦴 **2005 (R)** Cookie-cutter Steven Seagal action flick has the fading star as a notorious "freelance" anti-terrorist agent sprung from prison to help end a US government conspiracy and fight terrorists aboard a nuclear sub. **96m/C; DVD.** Steven Seagal; Vinnie Jones; Nick Brimble; William Hope; Christine Adams; ***D:*** Anthony Hickox; ***W:*** Anthony Hickox; Paul DeSouza; ***C:*** David Bridges; ***M:*** Guy Farley. **VIDEO**

Submergence 🦴 **2018** After their meet-cute in Normandy, British secret agent (McAvoy) and deep-sea scientist (Vikander) go their separate directions, her to the depths of the ocean and him to a jihadist jail cell in Somalia, but distance only makes their love grow. Despite having the whole ocean at his disposal, Wenders delivers a story as dull as dishwater. The script is pure saccharine, and the overly frequent flashbacks drain what little life there is from their romance. Based on J.M. Ledgard's novel of the same name. **112m/C; DVD, Blu-Ray.** James McAvoy; Alicia Vikander; Celyn Jones; Alexander Siddig; Reda Kateb; ***D:*** Wim Wenders; ***W:*** Erin Dignam; ***C:*** Benoît Debie; ***M:*** Fernando Velazquez.

Subspecies 🦴 ½ **1990 (R)** New improved vampire demons descend on earth. The first full-length feature film shot on location in Transylvania. For horror buffs only. **90m/C; VHS, DVD, Blu-Ray.** Laura Tate; Michael Watson; Anders (Tofting) Hove; Michelle McBride; Irina Movila; Angus Scrimm; ***D:*** Ted Nicolaou.

The Substance of Fire 🦴🦴 **1996 (R)** Publisher Isaac Geldhart (Rifkin) is an autocrat in both his business and his personal life, which may be why he's having so much trouble with both. A Holocaust survivor, Geldhart's obsessive about publishing a lavish four-volume history of Nazi medical experiments that will bankrupt the family firm. So his children wind up ousting him from the company and Isaac slowly slips over the edge into madness. Very King Lear, with an astonishing performance by Rifkin who also played the character in Baitz's 1991 Off-Broadway play. **100m/C; VHS, DVD.** Ron Rifkin; Tony Goldwyn; Timothy Hutton; Sarah Jessica Parker; Ronny Graham; Elizabeth Franz; Gil Bellows; ***D:*** Daniel Sullivan; ***W:*** Jon Robin Baitz; ***C:*** Robert Yeoman; ***M:*** Joseph Vitarelli.

The Substitute 🦴🦴 **1993 (R)** Donohue plays a sexy high-school substitute teacher who turns out to have homicidal tendencies, which she decides to take out on her students. Film debut for rapper/underwear model Mark. **86m/C; VHS, DVD, Streaming.** Amanda Donohoe; Dalton James; Natasha Gregson Wagner; Eugene Robert Glazer; Mark Wahlberg; ***D:*** Martin Donovan; ***W:*** Cynthia Verlaine; ***M:*** Gerald Gouriet.

The Substitute 🦴 **1996 (R)** Berenger plays a Vietnam vet mercenary who poses as a substitute teacher to uncover a drug ring after his girlfriend (Venora) is roughed up by the gang. At one point, he displays his unique teaching style by throwing some unruly students out of the second floor window. Hmm. . .wonder if that was on the test. Being a concerned teacher, he decides to uncover the kingpin of the unruly drug gang. Being an unruly drug gang, they decide to shoot at him. . .a lot. Unless you're a fan of heavy weaponry, banal one liners or yelling at the screen in frustration, substitute another movie for this one. **114m/C; VHS, DVD.** Tom Berenger; Ernie Hudson; Diane Venora; Marc Anthony; Glenn Plummer; Cliff DeYoung; William Forsythe; Raymond Cruz; Sharron Corley; Richard Brooks; Rodney A. Grant; Luis Guzman; ***D:*** Robert Mandel; ***W:*** Alan Ormsby; Roy Frumkes;

Rocco Simonelli; *C:* Bruce Surtees; *M:* Gary Chang.

The Substitute 2: School's Out 🦴🦴 **1997 (R)** Mercenary Carl Thomasson (Williams) poses as a high school substitute teacher to hunt down the New York gang bangers who murdered his brother during a carjacking. But his plans for revenge put innocent schoolchildren at risk as well. **90m/C; VHS, DVD.** Treat Williams; B.D. Wong; Angel David; Michael Michele; Larry (Lawrence) Gilliard, Jr.; *D:* Steven Pearl; *W:* Roy Frumkes; Rocco Simonelli; *C:* Larry Banks; *M:* Joe Delia. **VIDEO**

The Substitute 3: Winner Takes All 🦴🦴 **1/2 1999 (R)** Mercenary Karl Thomasson (Williams) visits Nicole, the daughter of a dead friend who's a teacher at an eastern college. After Nicole is badly beaten, Karl takes over as a substitute and has his fellow mercenaries investigate. They discover members of the football team are on steroids, thanks to an in with the son of the local crime boss, so Karl and his buddies decide to clean things up. **90m/C; VHS, DVD.** Treat Williams; Rebecca Staab; Claudia Christian; James Black; Richard Portnow; *D:* Robert Radler; *W:* Roy Frumkes; Rocco Simonelli; *C:* Barry M. Wilson; *M:* Tor Hyams. **VIDEO**

The Substitute 4: Failure is Not an Option 🦴 **1/2 2000 (R)** Undercover cop Karl Thomaason (Williams) poses as a teacher at a military academy and discovers a group of neo-Nazi cadets whose aims are supported by members of the staff. The more sequels, the less steam this series has—this one is definitely running on low. **91m/C; VHS, DVD.** Treat Williams; Angie Everhart; Bill Nunn; Tim Abell; Simon Rhee; Patrick Kilpatrick; Michael Weatherly; Grayson Fricke; *D:* Robert Radler; *W:* Dan Gurskis; *C:* Richard M. Rawlings, Jr.; *M:* Stephen (Steve) Edwards. **VIDEO**

The Substitute Wife 🦴🦴 **1/2 1994 (PG-13)** Dying Nebraska frontier woman Amy Hightower (Thompson) decides to find her husband Martin (Weller) a new wife to help on the farm and look after their four children. But women are so scarce (and the farm is so isolated) that the only one willing to give it a try is prostitute Pearl (Fawcett), who's fed up with her profession but isn't exactly the motherly type (at least not at first). Amusing relationships develop between the two women and the bewildered husband. Made for TV. **92m/C; VHS, DVD.** Farrah Fawcett; Lea Thompson; Peter Weller; *D:* Peter Werner; *W:* Stan Daniels; *C:* Neil Roach; *M:* Mark Snow. **TV**

Subterano 🦴 **2001 (R)** The low-budget defeats this sci-fier. In a totalitarian future society (yawn), rebel leader Conrad (Dimitriades) and fellow dissdent Stone (Walton) get chased by the feds into an underground parking garage. But they (and others trapped with them) have bigger problems—a crazy videogame designer uses the garage as a set-up for the life-size version of his virtual reality game Subterano and they've just become his new players. **95m/C; VHS, DVD.** *AU* Alex Dimitriades; Tasma Walton; Alison Whyte; Kate Sherman; Jason Stojanovski; *D:* Esben Storm; *W:* Esben Storm; *C:* Graeme Wood.

Subterfuge 🦴🦴 **1998 (R)** When a plane explodes over the Black Sea, the CIA, Russian spies, and drug runners are all after the black box. **95m/C; VHS, DVD.** Matt McColm; Amanda Pays; Glynn Turman; Jason Gould; Richard Brake; Ben Hammer; *D:* Herb Freed; *W:* Marion Segal; *C:* Irek Hartowicz; *M:* Jim Halfpenny.

Suburban Commando 🦴🦴 **1991 (PG)** A goofy, muscular alien mistakenly lands on Earth while on vacation. He does his best to remain inconspicuous, resulting in numerous hilarious situations. Eventually he is forced to confront his arch, interstellar nemesis in order to defend the family who befriended him. A harmless, sometimes cute vehicle for wrestler Hogan, which will certainly entertain his younger fans. **88m/C; VHS, DVD.** Hulk Hogan; Christopher Lloyd; Shelley Duvall; Larry Miller; William Ball; JoAnn Dearing; Jack Elam; Roy Dotrice; Christopher Neame; Tony Longo; *D:* Burt Kennedy; *W:* Frank Cappello.

Suburban Girl 🦴🦴 **2007 (PG-13)** Naive NYC associate book editor Brett (Gellar) is overwhelmed by her new job. Then she meets lecherous star publisher Archie Knox (Baldwin), who offers to show her how to fit in. The mismatched love affair works kinda well, basically because Baldwin knows how to sell his somewhat smarmy charm. Gellar seems a little out of her depth. Based on two stories from "The Girls' Guide to Hunting and Fishing" by Melissa Grant. **97m/C; DVD, Blu-Ray.** Sarah Michelle Gellar; Alec Baldwin; James Naughton; Maggie Grace; Chris Carmack; *D:* Marc Klein; *W:* Marc Klein; *C:* Steven Fierberg; *M:* Hector Pereira.

Suburban Roulette 🦴 **1967** "Adults only" feature from splattermaster Lewis caters to the prurient. Groovy themes like wife swapping and other very daring subjects. Totally '60s. Presented as part of Joe Bob Brigg's "Sleaziest Movies in the History of the World" series. **91m/C; VHS, DVD.** Elizabeth Wilkinson; Ben Moore; Tony McCabe; Debbie Grant; *D:* Herschell Gordon Lewis; *W:* Herschell Gordon Lewis; *C:* Roy Collodi.

The Suburbans 🦴 **1/2 1999 (R)** Bland and not very funny ensemble comedy. The Suburbans were an '80s one-hit wonder band who reunite 18 years later at member Gil's (Ferrell) wedding. Their impromptu reunion draws the attention of unlikely record company talent scout Kate (Hewitt), who decides she wants to resurrect their would-be music careers. The music satire is funny but the domestic angst is boring. **81m/C; VHS, DVD.** Jennifer Love Hewitt; Will Ferrell; Donal Lardner Ward; Craig Bierko; Amy Brenneman; Bridgette Wilson-Sampras; Tony Guma; Robert Loggia; Antonio Fargas; Ben Stiller; Jerry Stiller; *D:* Donal Lardner Ward; *W:* Donal Lardner Ward; Tony Guma; *C:* Michael Barrett; *M:* Robbie Kondor.

Suburbia 🦴 *The Wild Side* **1983 (R)** When a group of punk rockers move into a condemned suburban development, they become the targets of a vigilante group. Low budget, needless violent remake of anyone of many '50s rebellion flicks that tries to have a "message." **99m/C; VHS, DVD, Blu-Ray.** Chris Pederson; Bill Coyne; Jennifer Clay; Timothy Eric O'Brien; Andrew Pece; Don Allen; *D:* Penelope Spheeris; *W:* Penelope Spheeris; *C:* Tim Suhrstedt; *M:* Alex Gibson.

Suburbicon 🦴🦴 **2017 (R)** A mixed bag of stories exploring the dark side of American suburbia in 1957 that does not gel into a cohesive whole. One storyline centers on a black family moving into the all-white community and the racist response of their new neighbors. The family includes a boy, Andy (Espinosa), who becomes friends with his next door neighbor, Nicky (Jupe), whose father Gardner (Damon) has his own deadly secrets. Not clearly a dark comedy nor an inspirational survival story, the film also lacks memorable performances and characters outside of Oscar Isaac's Roger (Isaac). **105m/C; DVD, Blu-Ray.** Matt Damon; Julianne Moore; Noah Jupe; Glenn Fleshler; Jack Conley; *D:* George Clooney; *W:* George Clooney; Joel Coen; Ethan Coen; Grant Heslov; *C:* Robert Elswit; *M:* Alexandre Desplat.

Subversion 🦴🦴 **1979** An absurdist political fantasy-drama by acclaimed filmmaker Stanislav Stanojevic. An allegory that explores political repression, the plot centers on a president who is both blind and paralyzed but with a heightened sense of hearing. He uses his hearing, his relentless nature, and his very corrupt daughter to keep his small (fictitcious) country in line. However, his daughter has her own agenda, which includes equality with men. To that end, she names herself chief of firefighters but commits acts of arson to ensure she is needed. **95m/C; DVD.** Sacha (Sascha) Pitoeff; Nathalie Nell; Florence Giorgetti; Jean-Pierre Bouvier; Daniel Emilfork; *D:* Stanislav Stanojevic; *W:* Stanislav Stanojevic; *C:* Paul Bonis; *M:* Benito Merlino. **VIDEO**

Subway 🦴 **1/2 1985 (R)** Surreal, MTV-esque vision of French fringe life from the director of "Le Dernier Combat." A spike-haired renegade escapes the law by plunging into the Parisian subway system. Once there, he encounters a bizarre subculture living under the city. Plenty of angry-youth attitude, but where's the point? And frankly, too much bad New Wave music. **103m/C; VHS, DVD.** *FR* Christopher Lambert; Isabelle Adjani; Jean-Hugues Anglade; Jean Reno; Richard Bohringer; Michel Galabru; Éric Serra; Arthur Simms; *D:* Luc Besson; *W:* Luc Besson; Pierre Jolivet; Alain Le Henry; Marc Perrier; Sophie Schmit; *C:* Carlo Varini; *M:* Éric Serra; Rickie Lee Jones. Cesar '86: Actor (Lambert), Art Dir./Set Dec., Sound.

Subway Stories 🦴🦴 **1997 (R)** Ten short films based on actual experiences on the New York subway system featuring such topics as harassment, flirtation, sex, food, and money. **82m/C; VHS, DVD.** Bill Irwin; Kris Parker; Denis Leary; Christine Lahti; Steve Zahn; Jerry Stiller; Bonnie Hunt; Lili Taylor; Michael Rapaport; Mercedes Ruehl; Sarita Choudhury; Taral Hicks; Danny Hoch; Mike McGlone; Rosie Perez; Gregory Hines; Anne Heche; *D:* Ted (Edward) Demme; Abel Ferrara; Jonathan Demme; Julie Dash; Seth Zvi Rosenfeld; Bob Balaban; Alison Maclean; Lucas Platt; Patricia Benoit; Craig McKay; *W:* Danny Hoch; John Guare; Adam Brooks; Julie Dash; Lynn Grossman; Marla Hanson; Seth Zvi Rosenfeld; Joe Viola; Albert Innaurato; Angela Todd; *C:* Ken Kelsch; Adam Kimmel; Tom Hurwitz; Anthony C. "Tony" Jannelli.

Success Is the Best Revenge 🦴🦴 **1984 (R)** Ambitious Polish stage director Alex Rodak (York) and his family are living in exile in London because of Poland's martial law. He's working on a stage production about the subject and turns to a questionable businessman (Hurt) for financing, which displeases his unhappy wife. Also disillusioned is Rodak's teen son Adam (Lyndon), who has made his own arrangements to return to Warsaw. **88m/C; DVD.** *GB FR* Michael York; Michael Lyndon; John Hurt; Anouk Aimee; Janna Szerzerbic; Jerry Skal; *D:* Jerzy Skolimowski; *W:* Jerzy Skolimowski; *C:* Mike Fash; *M:* Stanley Myers; Hans Zimmer.

A Successful Calamity 🦴🦴 **1932** Domestic comedy finds wealthy Henry Wilton disturbed by his family's selfish attitudes. So he announces that he's lost his fortune and they will all have to adapt to being poor. However, Henry is surprised by everyone's response to the crisis. **72m/B; DVD.** George Arliss; Mary Astor; Evalyn Knapp; William Janney; Hardie Albright; Randolph Scott; Grant Mitchell; David Torrence; *D:* John G. Adolfi; *W:* Austin Parker; Julien Josephson; Maude Howell; *C:* James Van Trees.

Such a Long Journey 🦴🦴🦴 **1998** Bank clerk Gustad Noble has a modest life that is beginning to fall apart. First his young daughter becomes very ill and then his son defies Gustad's ambitions for him. Finally, he receives a letter from an old friend asking for his help and Gustad finds himself caught up in unexpected danger and deception. Set in Bombay in 1971, as India prepares for war, and based on the novel by Rohinton Mistry. **110m/C; VHS, DVD.** *CA GB* Roshan Seth; Om Puri; Kurush Deboo; Naseeruddin Shah; Ranjit Chowdhari; *D:* Sturla Gunnarsson; *W:* Sooni Taraporevala; *C:* Jan Kiesser. Genie '98: Actor (Seth), Film Editing.

Such Good Friends 🦴 **1/2 1971** Unpleasant people betray each other in this caustic adaptation of Lois Gould's novel. Conventional New York housewife Julie's (Cannon) self-centered husband Richard (Luckinbill) goes into a coma after some minor surgery goes wrong. She finds his little black book and learns he was chronically unfaithful, including dallying with her friends, so she decides to get even as he gets worse. **101m/C; DVD, Blu-Ray.** Dyan Cannon; Laurence Luckinbill; James Coco; Jennifer O'Neill; Ken Howard; Louise Lasser; Nina Foch; Burgess Meredith; Sam Levene; *D:* Otto Preminger; *W:* Elaine May; *C:* Gayne Rescher; *M:* Thomas Shepard.

Suck 🦴🦴 **2009 (R)** Joey's (Stefaniuk) 10-year-old indie band is still going nowhere when bassist Jen (Pare) goes home with a weird fan and gets turned into a vampire. She converts the other members and they can suddenly mesmerize their audiences while also being pursued by vamp hunter Eddie Van Helsing (McDowell). **90m/C; DVD.** *CA* Rob Stefaniuk; Jessica Pare; Malcolm McDowell; Paul Anthony; Mike Lobel; Chris Ratz; Dave Foley; Henry Rollins; Iggy Pop; Alice Cooper; Alex Lifeson; Moby; Dimitri Coats; *D:* Rob Stefaniuk; *W:* Rob Stefaniuk; Dave Foley; *C:* D. Gregor Hagey; *M:* John Kastner.

Sucker Free City 🦴🦴🦴 **2005** Three young men of different ethnicities turn to crime as the answer to surviving their rough lives in San Francisco'Nick (Crowley) steals credit card data at his office mailroom job; K-Luv (Mackie) is part of a black gang but wants out; and Chinese mafia member Lincoln (Leung) is moving up the ranks. Eventually tensions arise and an explosive showdown unfolds. Showtime original movie was directed by Spike Lee as a series pilot, though it wasn't picked up. **116m/C; DVD.** Ken Leung; Anthony Mackie; Darris Love; Laura Allen; Ben Crowley; Kathy Baker; *D:* Spike Lee; *W:* Alex Tse. **CABLE**

Sucker Punch 🦴 **2011 (PG-13)** Mish-mash of pop culture references and provocative young women in fetish wear goes nowhere in Snyder's looks-like-a-videogame dreck. Abused Babydoll (Browning) is locked away in a mental institution by her evil stepfather and is scheduled for a lobotomy. So she creates her own alternate reality (which happens to be a sleazy brothel) complete with a quartet of fellow inmates as they escape into various CGI fantasies that allegedly give Babydoll new inner strength. The PG13 rating is also a bad joke, though the flick seems intended only for horny guys of all ages. **109m/C; Blu-Ray, On Demand.** Emily Browning; Jena Malone; Vanessa Anne Hudgens; Jamie Chung; Abbie Cornish; Oscar Isaac; Carla Gugino; Jon Hamm; Scott Glenn; *D:* Zack Snyder; *W:* Zack Snyder; Steve Shibuya; *C:* Larry Fong; *M:* Tyler Bates; Marius De Vries.

Suckerfish 🦴🦴 **1999** Veteran pet supply salesmen Alan (Donovan) and Dick (Orr) resent that a retiring colleague's lucrative territory is being given to ambitious newbie Ken (Bodden). So they set out to sabotage him. When Ken finds out why he's not making any sales, he plans revenge—starting with the knowledge that Dick's wife Elizabeth (Lawlor) is having an affair with Alan. **88m/C; VHS, DVD.** Dan Donovan; Tim Orr; Kurt Bodden; Gerri Lawler; *D:* Brien Burroughs; *C:* Christopher Braun; *M:* Joshua Raoul Brody.

Sudden Death 🦴 **1977 (R)** Two professional violence merchants put themselves up for hire. **84m/C; VHS, DVD.** Robert Conrad; Felton Perry; Don Stroud; Bill Raymond; Ron Vawter; Harry Roskolenko; *D:* Richard Foreman.

Sudden Death 🦴🦴 **1995 (R)** Terrorists invade a hockey arena where the Vice President and 17,000 fans, including Fire Marshal Jean-Claude and his kids, are watching the seventh game of the Stanley Cup Finals. The latest in the "Die Hard in a. . ." genre covers the territory with the now-standard lack of characterization, family member in peril, and ever-increasing body count. Boothe (playing Alan Rickman playing a bad guy) does most of the talking while Van Damme kicks people in the head and plays goalie. Producer Howard Baldwin owns the Pittsburgh Penguins, coincidentally one of the teams on the ice for the second pairing of "Timecop" vets Hyams and Van Damme. **110m/C; VHS, DVD, Blu-Ray.** Jean-Claude Van Damme; Powers Boothe; Ross Malinger; Whittni Wright; Raymond J. Barry; Dorian Harewood; Kate McNeil; Audra Lindley; *D:* Peter Hyams; *W:* Gene Quintano; *C:* Peter Hyams; *M:* John Debney.

Sudden Fear 🦴🦴🦴 **1952** Successful playwright/heiress Myra Hudson (Crawford) has a whirlwind romance, leading to marriage, with oh-so-charming actor Lester Blaine (Palance). But Les is more interested in Myra's money and gets together with former flame Irene (always the bad girl Grahame) to get rid of his new bride and inherit her fortune. But Myra finds out about the plot and puts her writing talent to work in coming up with a new scenario. Good suspenser with fine performances. Adapted from the book by Edna Sherry. **111m/B; VHS, DVD, Blu-Ray.** Joan Crawford; Jack Palance; Gloria Grahame; Bruce Bennett; Virginia Huston; Mike Connors; *D:* David Miller; *W:* Lenore Coffee; Robert Smith; *C:* Charles B(ryant) Lang, Jr.; *M:* Elmer Bernstein.

Sudden Impact 🦴🦴 **1/2 1983 (R)** Eastwood directs himself in this formula thriller, the fourth "Dirty Harry" entry. This time "Dirty Harry" Callahan tracks down a revenge-obsessed murderess and finds he has more in common with her than he expected. Meanwhile, local mobsters come gunning for him. This is the one where he says, "Go ahead.

Make my day." Followed by "The Dead Pool." **117m/C; VHS, DVD, Blu-Ray.** Clint Eastwood; Sondra Locke; Pat Hingle; Bradford Dillman; Albert "Poppy" Popwell; Jack Thibeau; Michael Currie; Kevyn Major Howard; Bette Ford; Nancy Parsons; Michael V. Gazzo; Camryn Manheim; ***D:*** Clint Eastwood; ***W:*** Joseph C. Stinson; ***C:*** Bruce Surtees; ***M:*** Lalo Schifrin.

Sudden Manhattan **1996** Unemployed single Donna (Shelly) thinks she witnesses a murder—over and over again. Of course, no one believes her and she tries to figure out the truth. Shelly's directorial debut. **80m/C; VHS, DVD.** Adrienne Shelly; Tim Guinee; Roger Rees; Louise Lasser; Hynden Walch; ***D:*** Adrienne Shelly; ***W:*** Adrienne Shelly; ***C:*** Jim Denault; ***M:*** Pat Irwin.

Suddenly **1/2 1954** Crazed gunman John Baron (Sinatra) holds a family hostage in the hick town of Suddenly, California, as part of a plot to kill the president, who's stopping at the local train station. As things begin to go wrong, Baron begins to unravel. Tense thriller is a good display for Sinatra's acting talent. Unfortunately hard to find because Sinatra forced United Artists to take it out of distribution after hearing that Kennedy assassin Lee Harvey Oswald had watched "Suddenly" only days before November 22, 1963. Really, Ol' Blue Eyes should have stuck with making top-notch thrillers like this one, instead of degenerating into the world's greatest lounge singer. **75m/B; VHS, DVD, Blu-Ray.** Frank Sinatra; Sterling Hayden; James Gleason; Nancy Gates; Paul Frees; Willis Bouchey; Kim Charney; Christopher Dark; ***D:*** Lewis Allen; ***W:*** Richard Sale; ***C:*** Charles G. Clarke; ***M:*** David Raksin.

Suddenly, Last Summer **1/2 1959** Brain surgeon is summoned to the mansion of a rich New Orleans matron who wishes him to perform a lobotomy on her niece, supposedly suffering from a mental breakdown. Based on the play by Tennessee Williams. Softened for the censors, though the themes of homosexuality, insanity, and murder, characterizations of evil, and unusual settings presage many movies of the next two decades. Extremely fine performances from Hepburn and Taylor. Clift never completely recovered from his auto accident two years before and does not come across with the strength of purpose really necessary in his character. Still, fine viewing. **114m/B; VHS, DVD, Blu-Ray.** Elizabeth Taylor; Katharine Hepburn; Montgomery Clift; Mercedes McCambridge; Albert Dekker; ***D:*** Joseph L. Mankiewicz; ***W:*** Gore Vidal; ***C:*** Jack Hildyard; ***M:*** Malcolm Arnold. Golden Globes '60: Actress—Drama (Taylor).

Sudie & Simpson **1990** Heart-tugging tale of friendship set in rural 1940s Georgia. Twelve-year-old white Sudie's forbidden friendship with the adult black Simpson provides a lot of talk in their small town. Racial barriers finally cause Simpson to be accused of child molestation and the odds of his survival, despite his innocence, don't seem great. Based on Sara Flanigan Carter's autobiographical novel. **95m/C; VHS, DVD.** Sara Gilbert; Louis Gossett, Jr.; Frances Fisher; John M. Jackson; Paige Danahy; Ken Strong; ***D:*** Joan Tewkesbury; ***W:*** Sara Flanigan Carter; Ken Koser; ***C:*** Mario DiLeo; ***M:*** Michel Colombier. **CABLE**

Suds **1/2 1920** Pickford is tragic laundress with major crush on a guy who left his shirt at the laundry. **75m/B; Silent; VHS, DVD.** Mary Pickford; William Austin; Harold Goodwin; Madam Rose (Dion) Dione; Theodore Roberts; ***D:*** John Francis Dillon.

Sueno **2005 (PG-13)** Simple rags-to-riches musical saga follows Antonio (Leguizamo), a Mexican-born singer-musician who moves to LA to find success in the city's Latino music scene. He's got big dreams that may come true if he can overcome some predictable hardships. Pena is a delightful surprise as Mirabela, a recently divorced mother who regains her confidence when she begins singing with Antonio. **108m/C; DVD.** John Leguizamo; Ana Claudia Talancon; Elizabeth Pena; Nestor Serrano; Jsu Garcia; Jose Maria Yazpik; ***D:*** Renee Chabria; ***W:*** Renee Chabria; ***C:*** Eric Moynier; ***M:*** Joselo Rangel.

Suez **1938** Hollywood version of the 1850 building of the Suez Canal, which is actually secondary to the romantic trials of diplomat Ferdinand de Lesseps (Power). He falls for the same woman, Countess Eugenie (Young), desired by Louis Napoleon (Ames), who sends his rival off to Egypt. After coming up with his canal idea, Ferdinand is tricked by Napoleon, who gives him financial backing in exchange for unwittingly betraying the political opposition so Louis can declare himself emperor. Ferdinand slinks back to Egypt where more trouble awaits. **104m/B; DVD.** Tyrone Power; Loretta Young; Leon Ames; Annabella; J. Edward Bromberg; Henry Stephenson; Joseph Schildkraut; Miles Mander; ***D:*** Allan Dwan; ***W:*** Philip Dunne; Julien Josephson; ***C:*** J. Peverell Marley; ***M:*** Louis Silvers.

Sufat Chol *Sand Storm* **2016** In a Bedouin village in Southern Israel, two women are at very different points in their lives. Jalila (Ruba Blal) is in the awkward position of hosting a celebration for her husband's second wife (the culture allows multiple) while her daughter Layla (Lamis Ammar) is having a forbidden love affair with a man named Anuar. When Jalila discovers the affair, events are set in motion that tear the entire family apart and threaten the women's survival. Elite Zexer writes and directs this confident drama about gender roles in a part of the world in which they seem to be constantly evolving. **87m/C; DVD.** Lamis Ammar; Ruba Blal; Hitham Omari; Khadija Al Akel; Jalal Masrwa; ***D:*** Elite Zexer; ***W:*** Elite Zexer; ***C:*** Shai Peleg; ***M:*** Ran Bagno.

Suffragette **1/2 2015 (PG-13)** Sarah Gavron makes a stunning misstep by telling the story of the woman's suffragette movement in the United Kingdom through the eyes of the wrong character, a fictional one that the true story doesn't really need. Carey Mulligan, great even in bad films, plays Maud Watts, a laundry worker who gets drawn into the quest for woman's voting rights by her co-workers. While her husband Sonny (Ben Whishaw) looks on disapprovingly, Maud marches and protests, putting her own freedom and her family at risk. Everything here is well-intentioned but Maud is clearly a fictional character. Everyone around her is more interesting. **106m/C; DVD, Blu-Ray.** Carey Mulligan; Helena Bonham Carter; Meryl Streep; Brendan Gleeson; Anne-Marie Duff; ***D:*** Sarah Gavron; ***W:*** Abi Morgan; ***C:*** Eduard Grau; ***M:*** Alexandre Desplat.

Sugar **1/2 2009 (R)** Miguel 'Sugar' Santos (Soto) is a hot-shot pitching phenom from the baseball hotbed of San Pedro de Macoris, Dominican Republic. Once summoned to the American minor leagues, he experiences isolation, loneliness, bigotry, and a career-threatening injury, as well as the pressure of other talented prospects coming up behind him. He also has to deal with the expectations of his family. Complex drama surprises those expecting a by-the-book, "underdog-beats-the-odds" story by finding bigger ideas, and smaller, more personal moments. **120m/C; Blu-Ray.** Algenis Perez Soto; Rayniel Rufino; Andre Holland; Ann Whitney; Ellary Porterfield; Jamie Tirelli; Michael Gaston; Richard Bull; ***D:*** Anna Boden; Ryan Fleck; ***W:*** Anna Boden; Ryan Fleck; ***C:*** Andrij Parekh; ***M:*** Michael Brook.

Sugar & Spice **2001 (PG-13)** If there is such a thing as a smart cheerleader teen pic, this is it. Satire of offbeat pep squadders who cheer by day and rob banks by night includes Suvari's rebellious Kansas and Shelton's permanently upbeat Diane. Diane meets Jack (Marsden), and two American kids do the best they can when they learn Diane is pregnant. They decide to marry, move into a seedy apartment, and take up work at a local fast food joint. After losing said employment, the motivation becomes clear for the girls' ensuing illegal capers. Littered with pop culture references: the girls rent "Reservoir Dogs" to prepare for the heist, rob the banks in "Betty" masks, and deal with one of the girls' hots for Conan O'Brien. **81m/C; VHS, DVD.** Marley Shelton; James Marsden; Mena Suvari; Marla Sokoloff; Rachel Blanchard; Melissa George; Alexandra Holden; Sara Marsh; Sean Young; ***D:*** Francine McDougall; ***W:*** Mandy Nelson; ***C:*** Robert Brinkmann; ***M:*** Mark Mothersbaugh.

Sugar Cane Alley *Rue Cases Negres* **1983 (PG)** After the loss of his parents, an 11-year-old orphan boy goes to work with his grandmother on a sugar plantation. She realizes that her young ward's only hope is an education. Set in Martinique in the 1930s among black workers. Poignant and memorable. French with subtitles. **106m/C; VHS, DVD.** *FR* Garry Cadenat; Darling Legitimus; Douta Seck; ***D:*** Euzhan Palcy; ***W:*** Euzhan Palcy; ***C:*** Dominique Chapuis.

Sugar Cookies **WOOF! 1977 (R)** Erotic horror story in which young women are the pawns as a satanic satyr and an impassioned lesbian play out a bizarre game of vengeance, love, and death. **89m/C; VHS, DVD, Blu-Ray.** Mary Woronov; Lynn Lowry; Monique Van Vooren; ***D:*** Michael Herz.

Sugar Hill *Voodoo Girl; Zombies of Sugar Hill* **1974** AIP studio blaxploitation horror. Sugar Hill's boyfriend Langston is murdered by white gangsters and she turns to local voodoo priestess Mama Maitresse for help. Sugar makes a deal with the undead Baron Samedi to sell her soul in exchange for a group of ex-slave zombies to help her get her revenge in appropriately gruesome ways. **91m/C; DVD, Blu-Ray.** Marki Bey; Don Pedro Colley; Zara Cully; Robert Quarry; Charles Robinson; Richard Lawson; Betty Anne Rees; ***D:*** Paul Maslansky; ***W:*** Tim Kelly; ***C:*** Robert C. Jessup.

Sugar Hill **1994 (R)** Two brothers (Wright & Snipes) are heroin dealers who have built their own crime empire in the Sugar Hill section of Harlem. Snipes is moved to reconsider his career options when he falls for an aspiring actress (Randle). Jarring editing sequence recaps the seminal event in the brothers' upbringing and serves to explain how the wide-eyed boys became cold-blooded pushers. Good performances by all, but formulaic plot will leave viewers asking themselves if they haven't seen it before and why it was they saw it then. **123m/C; VHS, DVD.** Wesley Snipes; Michael Wright; Theresa Randle; Clarence Williams, III; Abe Vigoda; Ernie Hudson; Larry Joshua; Leslie Uggams; Khandi Alexander; Raymond Serra; Joe Dallesandro; Vondie Curtis-Hall; Steve Harris; Kimberly Russell; Dulé Hill; Donald Adeosun Faison; Nick(y) Corello; ***D:*** Leon Ichaso; ***W:*** Barry Michael Cooper; ***C:*** Bojan Bazelli; ***M:*** Terence Blanchard.

Sugar Kisses *Besos de Azucar* **2013** A coming-of-age story set against violence in Mexico. Thirteen-year-old Nacho (Kancino) is the son of a corrupt agent who makes money selling pirated music in the market neighborhood of Tepito. He falls in love with Mayra (Arce), the daughter of the market's most powerful owner. Both Nacho and Mayra are experiencing love for the first time, but issues like corruption, poverty, and discrimination threaten to derail their young relationship. Spanish with subtitles. **85m/C; DVD, Streaming, Download.** Cesar Kancino; Daniela Arce; Hector Jimenez; Veronica Falcon; Paloma Arredondo; ***D:*** Carlos Cuaron; ***W:*** Carlos Cuaron; ***C:*** Kenji Katori. **VIDEO**

Sugar Sweet **1/2 2002** Amusing, if slight, Japanese lesbian romantic comedy. Struggling filmmaker Naomi is trying to pay the bills by shooting lesbian porn but the producers protest that she's being too "arty." Frazzled, Naomi confides her troubles to an online friend named Sugar. Then, Naomi gets the chance to direct a girl-meets-girl matchmaking TV show and casts her pal Azusa and an exotic dancer named Miki to play the romantic couple. Azusa is willing but Miki turns out to be more interest in romancing Naomi. Japanese with subtitles. **67m/C; VHS, DVD.** *JP* Saori Kitagawa; Saki; C Snatch Z; ***D:*** Desiree Lim; ***W:*** Desiree Lim; Carole Hisasue; ***C:*** Natsuyo Nakamura; ***M:*** Masan Tahara; Katsuharu Imano.

Sugar Town **1999 (R)** Ambitions collide in this saga of the L.A. music scene. Savvy and unscrupulous young singer Gwen (Gordon) is determined to land a recording contract while a group of middle age rock stars (Taylor, Des Barres, and Kemp) want to recapture their fame—with music producer Burt (Klein) as their catalyst. There's also struggling studio musician Carl (Doe) and his woes with Latina singer, Rosio (Cavazos) and various other subplots—none of which hang together terribly well. **92m/C; VHS, DVD.** Michael Des Barres; Jade Gordon; John Taylor; Martin Kemp; Larry Klein; John Doe; Lumi Cavazos; Lucinda Jenney; Rosanna Arquette; Ally Sheedy; Beverly D'Angelo; Richmond Arquette; Jeff (Jeffrey) McDonald; Vincent Berry; Polly Platt; Chris Mulkey; ***D:*** Allison Anders; Kurt Voss; ***W:*** Allison Anders; Kurt Voss; ***C:*** Kristian Bernier; ***M:*** Larry Klein.

Sugarhouse **1/2 2007 (R)** Middle-class London accountant Tom (Mackintosh) wants to kill his wife's lover so he purchases a gun from crackhead D (Walters). Unfortunately, the gun was stolen from psychotic drug lord Hoodwink (Serkis) who wants it back because it ties him to a murder. Violent, but not much more. Based on the 2003 play "Collision" by Dominic Leyton, who also wrote the screenplay. **94m/C; DVD.** *GB* Steven Mackintosh; Ashley Walters; Andy Serkis; Tolga Safer; ***D:*** Gary Love; ***W:*** Dominic Leyton; ***C:*** Michael Price; Dan Bronks.

The Sugarland Express **1974 (PG)** To save her son from adoption, a young woman helps her husband break out of prison. In their flight to freedom, they hijack a police car, holding the policeman hostage. Spielberg's first feature film is a moving portrait of a couple's desperation. Based on a true story, adapted by Hal Barwood and Matthew Robbins. **109m/C; VHS, DVD, Blu-Ray.** Goldie Hawn; Ben Johnson; Michael Sacks; William Atherton; ***D:*** Steven Spielberg; ***W:*** Steven Spielberg; Matthew Robbins; Hal Barwood; ***C:*** Vilmos Zsigmond; ***M:*** John Williams.

Sugartime **1/2 1995 (R)** Based on the true-life romance of '60s Chicago mobster Sam Giacana (Turturro) and song bird Phyllis Maguire (Parker), one of the wholesome Maguire Sisters. Naturally, getting involved with a crime boss did little for her image and Maguire's career hit the skids while Giacana's volatile jealousy brought unwanted attention from both fellow gangsters and the feds. (He was murdered in 1975 but had broken off with Phyllis before that). The real Maguire denounced the inaccuracy of the TV production. Suggested by William F. Roemer, Jr.'s book "Roemer: Man Against the Mob." **108m/C; VHS, DVD.** John Turturro; Mary-Louise Parker; Elias Koteas; Maury Chaykin; Louis Del Grande; Richard Blackburn; ***D:*** John N. Smith; ***W:*** Martyn Burke; ***C:*** Pierre Letarte.

Suicide Club *Jisatsu Sakuru* **2002** Fifty-four high school girls join hands and leap to their deaths from a subway platform into the path of an oncoming train. Police detective Kuroda (Ishibashi) receives a message from a mystery girl who informs him of a website that predicts the deaths even before they happen. With a continuing rash of suicides in Tokyo, the police are baffled—are the jumpers part of a cult and does a teen-girl pop group have some strange influence? Very bloody, very surreal, and a wicked social critique of disaffected Japanese youth. Japanese with subtitles. **92m/C; VHS, DVD.** *JP* Ryo Ishibashi; Takashi Nomura; Masatoshi Nagase; Tamao Sato; Mai Housyou; ***D:*** Sono Sion; ***W:*** Sono Sion; ***C:*** Kazuto Sato.

Suicide Fleet **1931** When three playboy sailors aren't fighting German U-boats aboard a decoy ship they're fighting to win the affections of a young woman (Rogers) working on the Coney Island midway. Some great shots of WWI vessels but a poor overall effort. **87m/B; VHS, DVD.** William Boyd; Robert Armstrong; James Gleason; Ginger Rogers; ***D:*** Albert Rogell; ***W:*** Herbert A. Jones; Lew Lipton. **VIDEO**

Suicide Kings **1997 (R)** When the sister of one of four prep school friends is kidnapped, the guys decide to take retired mobster Charlie Barrett (Walken) hostage so he'll help them. The wanna-be "Reservoir Pups" lose control almost as soon as the caper begins, and the savvy Barrett takes advantage to turn his captors against each other with news that the girl's abduction may have been an inside job. Maze of a plot, which wanders into "Usual Suspects" is-this-all-real? territory, does nothing to help any of the young actors, who are clearly overmatched by Walken. Not much here for anyone except fans of Walken's patented Gangster Cool. **106m/C; VHS, DVD.** Henry Thomas; Sean Patrick Flanery; Jay Mohr; Christopher Walken; Denis Leary; Jeremy Sisto; Johnny Galecki; Cliff DeYoung; Laura San Giacomo; Laura Harris; Louis Lombardi; Brad Garrett; Nina Siemaszko; Frank Medrano; Lisanne Falk; Sean M. Whalen; ***D:*** Peter O'Fallon; ***W:*** Josh McKinney; Gina Goldman; Wayne Rice; ***C:***

Christopher Baffa; ***M:*** Graeme Revell; Tim Simonec.

Suicide Squad 🦴🦴 **2016 (PG-13)** U.S. Intelligence Officer Amanda Waller (Davis) has a plan—to assemble the city's greatest supervillains to use on missions that the heroes won't even bother to try. The Suicide Squad, which includes Deadshot (Smith), Harley Quinn (Robbie), El Diablo, Captain Boomerang, Killer Croc, and Slipknot, will be expendable tools of the government. Meanwhile, The Joker (Leto) has some plans of his own. WB/DC's attempt to create their own "Guardians of the Galaxy" is a cluttered, loud, annoying mess, despite good work from Robbie and Leto, who got a ton of advance press but is barely in the movie. **123m/C; DVD, Blu-Ray.** Will Smith; Jared Leto; Margot Robbie; Joel Kinnaman; Viola Davis; ***D:*** David Ayer; ***W:*** David Ayer; ***C:*** Roman Vasyanov; ***M:*** Steven Price. Oscars '16: Makeup.

Suite 16 🦴 **1994 (R)** A penthouse suite in a French Riviera hotel is occupied by rich, manipulative, wheelchair-bound Glover (Postlethwaite). Young gigolo/thief Chris (Kamerling), who believes he's killed his latest trick, is given refuge by Glover in exchange for allowing the aging voyeur to watch Chris (via camera) perform with a succession of prostitutes. Finally, Chris wants to leave but Glover offers him a huge amount of money for one final vicarious—and deadly—thrill. Eurotrash, with corny dialogue, but Postlethwaite's chillingly creepy. Also available in an R-rated version. **93m/C; VHS, DVD.** *BE GB* Pete Postlethwaite; Antoine Kamerling; Geraldine Pailhas; Thom Jansen; ***D:*** Dominique Deruddere; ***W:*** Charles Higson; Lise Mayer; ***C:*** Jean-Francois Robin; ***M:*** Walter Hus.

The Suitors 🦴 **1988** When a group of Iranians decide to sacrifice a lamb in their apartment, the New York police send in SWAT team assuming they're terrorists. First time effort by Ebrahimian, in Farsi with English subtitles. **106m/C; VHS, DVD.** Pouran Esrafily; Assurbanipal Babila; Shahab Navab; Ali Azizian; ***D:*** Ghasem Ebrahimian; ***W:*** Ghasem Ebrahimian; ***C:*** Manfred Reiff.

Sukiyaki Western Django 🦴 **1/2 2008 (R)** Best appreciated by fans of director Miike or those who don't mind a genre homage in this Japanese combo samurai/spaghetti western. In the late 1880s, two clans battle over a fortune hidden in a desolate mountain town. A nameless gunman rides in and plans to pick over what's left until he joins in a saloon gal's revenge plot. Subtitled, heavily-accented English dialogue sounds like it was learned phonetically. **121m/C; DVD, Blu-Ray.** *JP* Hideaki Ito; Yoshino Kimura; Koichi Sato; Mansanobu Ando; Yusuke Iseya; Takaaki Ishibashi; Kaori Momoi; Teruyuki Kagawa; Ruka Uchida; Quentin Tarantino; ***D:*** Takashi Miike; ***W:*** Takashi Miike; Masaru Nakamura; ***C:*** Toyomichi Kurita; ***M:*** Koji Endo.

Sullivan's Travels 🦴🦴🦴🦴 **1941** Sturges' masterpiece is a sardonic, whip-quick romp about a Hollywood director tired of making comedies who decides to make a serious, socially responsible film and hits the road masquerading as a hobo in order to know hardship and poverty. Beautifully sustained, inspired satire that mercilessly mocked the ambitions of Depression-era social cinema. Gets a little over-dark near the end before the happy ending; Sturges insisted on 20-year-old Lake as The Girl; her pregnancy forced him to rewrite scenes and design new costumes for her. As ever, she is stunning. **90m/B; VHS, DVD, Blu-Ray.** Joel McCrea; Veronica Lake; William Demarest; Robert Warwick; Franklin Pangborn; Porter Hall; Eric Blore; Byron Foulger; Robert Greig; Torben Meyer; Jimmy Conlin; Margaret (Maggie) Hayes; Chester Conklin; Alan Bridge; ***D:*** Preston Sturges; ***W:*** Preston Sturges; ***C:*** John Seitz; ***M:*** Leo Shuken. Natl. Film Reg. '90.

Sully 🦴🦴 **1/2 2016 (PG-13)** In 2009 Chesley "Sully" Sullenberger (Hanks) was the pilot of a commercial airline who became a household name when he piloted his damaged plane to a landing in the middle of the Hudson River, saving the entire crew and all 155 of its passengers. As directed by Eastwood, the actual water landing is a feat of filmmaking, but to say there's not quite enough story here to justify a film drama would be an understatement. So much so that the writers had to fabricate key elements, including the film's version of an NTSB investigation into what really happened that day. **96m/C; DVD, Blu-Ray.** Tom Hanks; Aaron Eckhart; Laura Linney; Sam Huntington; Valerie Mahaffey; ***D:*** Clint Eastwood; ***W:*** Todd Komarnicki; ***C:*** Tom Stern; ***M:*** Christian Jacob; Tierney Sutton Band.

The Sum of All Fears 🦴🦴 **1/2 2002 (PG-13)** Affleck takes over as Jack Ryan, who is now just an analyst, and has a girlfriend (Moynihan) who's a young doctor (hmmm...), but the film is still set in the present-day. That's just the first confusing element of this complicated spy thriller. The first half is spent on set pieces that seem to have no connection, until a climactic event (which takes place an hour in). Ryan is trying to prevent a nuclear war between the U.S. and Russia. Neo-Nazis are the baddies who put the world on the brink, and give the audience a safe, cartoony villian to make up for the now all-too-possible nuclear scenario. Affleck shows signs of growing into the role if the franchise continues, but he's not there yet. Pic is at its best when in the conference rooms of the White House and Kremlin, with each leader's advisors pressing their agendas. **118m/C; VHS, DVD, Blu-Ray.** Ben Affleck; Morgan Freeman; James Cromwell; Bridget Moynahan; Liev Schreiber; Ron Rifkin; Alan Bates; Ciaran Hinds; Philip Baker Hall; Bruce McGill; Colm Feore; Josef Sommer; Ken Jenkins; Michael Byrne; John Beasley; Jamie Harrold; Richard Marner; Lee Garlington; Eugene (Yevgeny) Lazarev; Sven-Ole Thorsen; Lisa Gay Hamilton; Lisa Bronwyn Moore; ***D:*** Phil Alden Robinson; ***W:*** Paul Attanasio; Daniel Pyne; ***C:*** John Lindley; ***M:*** Jerry Goldsmith.

The Sum of Us 🦴🦴🦴 **1994 (R)** Sweet and faithful adaptation of David Stevens' stage play about a father and his gay son. Widowed Harry Mitchell (Thompson) shares his house with son Jeff (Crowe), who's never made a secret of his sexual orientation. Affable Harry only wants what's best for his boy, including his over-enthusiastic welcome to Jeff's potential new boyfriend (Polson). Too bad Harry's not so lucky in love—his new woman friend Joyce (Kennedy) has problems with Jeff's sexuality. Well, she just has to adjust. Pervasive feel-good message may leave less well-adjusted viewer addled. Sensitive performances, though the film's antecedents as a play are highlighted by having the main characters talk directly to the camera. Aussie slang provides a challenge. **99m/C; VHS, DVD, Blu-Ray.** *AU* Jack Thompson; Russell Crowe; John Polson; Deborah Kennedy; Mitch Mathews; Julie Herbert; Joss Moroney; Rebekah Elmaloglou; ***D:*** Kevin Dowling; Geoff Burton; ***W:*** David Stevens; ***C:*** Geoff Burton; ***M:*** Dave Faulkner. Australian Film Inst. '94: Adapt. Screenplay; Montreal World Film Fest. '94: Screenplay.

Summer 🦴🦴🦴 **1/2** *Le Rayon Vert; The Green Ray* **1986 (R)** The fifth and among the best of Rohmer's "Comedies and Proverbs" series. A romantic but glum young French girl finds herself stuck in Paris during the tourist season searching for true romantic love. Takes time and patience to seize the viewer; moving ending makes it all worthwhile. In French with English subtitles. **98m/C; VHS, DVD.** *FR* Marie Riviere; Lisa Heredia; Beatrice Romand; Eric Hamm; Rosette; Isabelle Riviere; ***D:*** Eric Rohmer; ***W:*** Eric Rohmer; ***C:*** Sophie Maintigneux; ***M:*** Jean-Louis Valero.

Summer '03 🦴🦴 **1/2 2018** In the summer of 2003, the life of teen Jamie (King) changes forever when her anti-Semitic grandmother Dotty (Squibb) is dying. Dottie makes a series of deathbed confessions, including the fact that Jamie's father Ned (Scheer) never knew his biological father. Dottie also reveals that she secretly baptized Jamie, who is Jewish. This leads Jamie to seek advice from a priest and become involved with a conflicted seminary student Luke (Kilmer). Jamie makes a series of bad choices but eventually has confessions of her own. This coming of age dark comedy deftly explores the nature of the teen psyche with a satiric touch. **95m/C; DVD.** Joey King; Andrea Savage; Paul Scheer; Logan Medina; Jack Kilmer; ***D:*** Becca Gleason; ***W:*** Becca Gleason; ***C:*** Ben Hardwicke; ***M:*** Nathan Mathew David.

Summer 1993 🦴🦴🦴 *Estiu 1993* **2017** An emotional autobiographical drama from filmmaker Simon told from the perspective of a six-year-old girl. After the recent death of her parents from AIDS-related illnesses, young Frida (Artigas) is moved from Barcelona to a small rural village to live with her aunt Marga (Cusi), uncle Esteve (Verdaguer), and cousin Anna (Robles). As Frida experiences the carefree joys of childhood with Anna, she processes her loss, how she came to be the ward of her aunt, and the complex emotions she feels. The filmmaker uses such tools as camerawork and point of view to tell her story. Catalan with subtitles. **97m/C; DVD, Blu-Ray.** *SP* Laia Artigas; Paula Blanco; Etna Campillo; Bruna Cusi; Paula Robles; ***D:*** Carla Simón; ***W:*** Carla Simón; ***C:*** Santiago Racaj; ***M:*** Pau Boigues; Ernest Pipó.

Summer and Smoke 🦴🦴 **1/2 1961** Repressed, unhappy Page falls for handsome doctor Harvey. A tour de force for Page, but that's all; adapted clumsily from the overwrought Tennessee Williams play. **118m/C; VHS, DVD, Blu-Ray.** Laurence Harvey; Geraldine Page; Rita Moreno; Una Merkel; John McIntire; Thomas Gomez; Pamela Tiffin; Lee Patrick; Max (Casey Adams) Showalter; Earl Holliman; Harry Shannon; Pattee Chapman; ***D:*** Peter Glenville; ***C:*** Charles B(ryant) Lang, Jr.; ***M:*** Elmer Bernstein. Golden Globes '62: Actress--Drama (Page); Natl. Bd. of Review '61: Actress (Page).

Summer Camp 🦴🦴 **2016 (R)** A horror-thriller set a summer camp in Spain. When four young Americans go to Europe to work as camp counselors, they think they will have a summer of of fun. What they do not know is that a disease is spreading throughout the camp that turns people in raging, demon-like creatures. Though the counselors try to escape, they are out in the wilderness without phones and no means of transportation. Will they make it before the disease spreads further? **81m/C; DVD, Streaming, Download.** Diego Boneta; Jocelin Donahue; Maiara Walsh; Andres Velencoso; Alex Monner; ***D:*** Alberto Marini; ***W:*** Alberto Marini; Danielle Schleif; ***C:*** Pablo Rosso; ***M:*** Arnau Bataller.

Summer Catch 🦴 **1/2 2001 (PG-13)** Freddie Prinze, Jr. is really gonna have to learn to shake off some of the signs his agent is giving him. In this rip-off of every baseball movie of the last decade, Prinze plays underdog pitcher Ryan, on his last chance in his hometown Cape Cod league. Complicating matters are his flamboyant rival Eric (Pearson) and upperclass babe Tenley (Biel), who he falls for while cutting lawns for his irascible father (Ward). Can Ryan make it to the big leagues with help from grizzled manager Schiffner (Dennehy)? Will he win the bodacious babe despite protests from her blue-blood father (Davison)? Will Lillard make another appearance in a Freddie Prinze, Jr. movie? If you don't know the answers to those questions, you deserve to watch this bush-league flick. **108m/C; DVD.** Freddie Prinze, Jr.; Jessica Biel; Matthew Lillard; Bruce Davison; Brian Dennehy; Fred Ward; Jason Gedrick; Brittany Murphy; Marc Blucas; ***D:*** Mike Tollin; ***W:*** Kevin Falls; John Gatins; ***C:*** Tim Suhrstedt; ***M:*** George Fenton.

Summer City 🦴 **1/2** *Coast of Terror* **1977** Fun-and-sun surfing movie complete with romance, hot rods, murder and great shots of the sea features Gibson in his debut. Ever wonder what Australian surf bums do on weekends? The same as their California counterparts—except they talk funny. **83m/C; VHS, DVD.** *AU* Mel Gibson; Phillip Avalon; John Jarratt; Christopher Fraser; ***C:*** Jerry Marek; ***M:*** Phil Butkis.

Summer Eleven 🦴🦴 **1/2 2010 (PG)** Four 11-year-old best friends vow to have an adventurous summer before their big move into middle school. Wannabe actress Vanessa prepares for a film audition; Lizzie welcomes home her war vet brother who's now in a wheelchair; Jess tries to deal with her parents' separation; and Peri is keeping a major secret. **93m/C; DVD.** Alice Ziolkowski; Meaghan Hughes; Sarah Butterworth; Sydney Fox; Adam Arkin; Valerie Mahaffey; ***D:*** Joseph Kell; ***W:*** Joseph Kell; ***C:*** Cameron Cannon; ***M:*** Dave Christensen. **VIDEO**

Summer Heat 🦴 **1/2 1987 (R)** In rural, mid-Depression North Carolina, a young, lonely wife and mother is seduced by a drifter and together they plot murder. Her husband neglects her, and you should neglect to see this utter yawner. Based on a Louise Shivers novel. **80m/C; VHS, DVD.** Lori Singer; Anthony Edwards; Bruce Abbott; Kathy Bates; ***D:*** Michie Gleason; ***C:*** Elliot Davis.

Summer Holiday 🦴🦴 **1/2 1948** Rooney comes of age with a vengeance during summer vacation in musical rendition of "Ah, Wilderness." Undistinguished musical numbers, inferior to the original, but jazzy Technicolor cinematography. Ended up in the red by over $1.5 million, lotsa money back then. **92m/C; VHS, DVD.** Mickey Rooney; Gloria De Haven; Walter Huston; Frank Morgan; Jackie "Butch" Jenkins; Marilyn Maxwell; Agnes Moorehead; Selena Royle; Anne Francis; ***D:*** Rouben Mamoulian.

Summer Hours 🦴🦴 **1/2** *L'Heure d'Ete* **2008** Assayas' not-too-nostalgic look at the family ties that bind and how to handle a legacy in the present. Helene Berthier (Scob) is celebrating her 75th birthday at her country house with her two sons Frederic (Bering) and Jeremie (Renier), their wives and kids, and her daughter Adrienne (Binoche). They rarely get together (everyone's SO busy) so Helene takes the opportunity to discreetly tell responsible Frederic how she would like everything handled after she's gone. The house is filled with priceless art collected by Helene's Uncle Paul and she would like the collection kept intact for a museum but doesn't want the house and its other contents turned into a shrine. Complicating matters is the fact that Adrienne lives in New York, Jeremie is moving to Shanghai, and Frederic is the only one who wants to keep the past preserved. English and French with subtitles. **103m/C; Blu-Ray, On Demand.** *FR* Juliette Binoche; Charles Berling; Jeremie Renier; Edith Scob; Dominique Reymond; Valerie Bonneton; Isabelle Sadoyan; ***D:*** Olivier Assayas; ***W:*** Olivier Assayas; ***C:*** Eric Gautier.

Summer in February 🦴 **1/2 2013** A pretty but unconvincing romantic melodrama based on actual events. In 1913, a bohemian artist colony in Cornwall includes arrogant artist Alfred James Munnings (Cooper). His best friend is restrained land agent Gilbert Evans (Stevens) and both men fall for a newcomer--would-be artist Florence (Browning). Florence impulsively marries Munnings, then attempts suicide when she realizes she's made a terrible mistake. Gilbert tries to help her, but the situation remains unhappy. **100m/C; DVD.** *UK* Dominic Cooper; Dan Stevens; Emily Browning; Hattie Marahan; Shaun Dingwall; ***D:*** Christopher Menaul; ***W:*** Jonathan Smith; ***C:*** Andrew Dunn; ***M:*** Benjamin Wallfisch.

A Summer in Genoa 🦴 **1/2** *Genova* **2008 (R)** Episodic family drama of moving past grief is attractive but ordinary. Seeking a fresh start after the death of his wife Marianne in a car accident, Joe accepts a visiting professorship in Genoa and makes the move with his daughters Mary and Kelly. Teenager Kelly turns rebellious while young Mary feels guilty and believes she sees Marianne's ghost. Joe gets the romantic eye from a flirtatious student and an old friend. **93m/C; DVD, Blu-Ray.** *GB* Colin Firth; Willa Holland; Perla Haney-Jardine; Hope Davis; Catherine Keener; Margherita Romeo; Alessandro Guggioli; Dante Ciari; ***D:*** Michael Winterbottom; ***W:*** Michael Winterbottom; Laurence Coriat; ***C:*** Marcel Zyskind; ***M:*** Melissa Parmenter.

Summer Interlude 🦴🦴🦴 **1/2** *Illicit Interlude; Summerplay; Sommarlek* **1950** A ballerina recalls a romantic summer spent with an innocent boy, who was later tragically killed. Bergman's 10th film contains many earmarks and visual ideas of later masterpieces. In Swedish with English subtitles. **95m/B; DVD, Blu-Ray.** *SW* Maj-Britt Nilsson; Birger Malmsten; Alf Kjellin; ***D:*** Ingmar Bergman; ***W:*** Ingmar Bergman; Herbert Grevenius; ***C:*** Gunnar Fischer; ***M:*** Erik Nordgren.

Summer Lover 🦴 *Sappho* **2008** Pretty-but-dumb, and badly acted, romantic triangle, set in 1926. Wealthy, beautiful Sappho Lovell and her artist husband Phil come to the Greek isle of Lesbos for their honeymoon. Both are soon beguiled by Russian Helene and a friendship turns into a menage a trois. As Sappho delves into her namesake's erotic poetry, she learns about thwarted desire and tragedy. **86m/C; DVD.** Avalon Barrie; Todd Soley; Lyudmila Shiryaeva; Bogdan Stupka; ***D:*** Robert Crombie; ***W:*** Robert Crombie; ***C:*** Bagir Rafiyev; ***M:*** Maro Theodorakis.

Summer Lovers 1982 (R) Summer vacation finds young couple traveling to the exotic Greek island of Santorini. They meet up with a fun-loving woman and discover three-way sexual tension, but little in the way of plot, dialogue, or acting. From the director of "Grease" and "Blue Lagoon" and best watched late at night while half conscious. **98m/C; VHS, DVD, Blu-Ray.** Peter Gallagher; Daryl Hannah; Valerie Quennessen; *D:* Randal Kleiser; *M:* Basil Poledouris.

Summer Magic 1963 An impecunious recent widow is forced to leave Boston and settle her family in a small town in Maine. Typical, forgettable Disney drama; early Mills vehicle. A remake of "Mother Carey's Chickens." **116m/C; VHS, DVD.** Hayley Mills; Burl Ives; Dorothy McGuire; Deborah Walley; Una Merkel; Eddie Hodges; *D:* James Neilson; *M:* Buddy (Norman Dale) Baker.

Summer Night with Greek Profile, Almond Eyes & Scent of Basil 1987 (R) A wealthy woman tycoon hires an ex-CIA man to kidnap a high-priced, professional terrorist and hold him for ransom. An ironic battle of the sexes follows. In Italian with English subtitles. **94m/C; VHS, DVD, Blu-Ray.** *IT* Mariangela Melato; Michele Placido; Roberto Herlitzka; Massimo Wertmuller; *D:* Lina Wertmuller; *W:* Lina Wertmuller.

Summer of '04 1/2 *Sommer '04* **2006** Considering the subject matter, this is a frequently dull affair. Forty-year-old Miriam (Gedeck) spends summer vacation at a country house with her husband Andre (Davor), 15-year-old son Niels (Kotaranin), and his younger girlfriend Livia (Lohde), who's testing her sexual boundaries. Niels lets Livia go sailing alone with 30-something neighbor Bill (Seeliger), which worries Miriam. She confronts Bill about what might be happening, only to be drawn unexpectedly into a torrid affair. An end twist is unsatisfying. German with subtitles. **97m/C; DVD.** *GE* Martina Gedeck; Svea Lohde; Robert Seeliger; Peter Davor; Lucas Kotaranin; *D:* Stefan Krohmer; *W:* Daniel Nocke; *C:* Patrick Orth; *M:* Ellen McIlwaine.

Summer of 84 2018 Though young suburban teen Davey Armstrong (Verchere) spends most of this time with his three male friends in their clubhouse talking about girls and movies, he is also interested in a local mystery involving the disappearance of three boys close to his age. Davey and friends investigate the mystery themselves, and get his former babysitter-and current crush- involved. Davey suspects his loner cop neighbor McKay (Sommer) is the culprit, but the truth is unexpected. Full of potential and featuring a thoughtful performance from Sommer, this suspense drama is otherwise too superficial. **105m/C; DVD, Blu-Ray.** Graham Verchere; Judah Lewis; Caleb Emery; Cory Gruter-Andrew; Tiera Skovbye; *D:* Francois Simard; Anouk Whissell; Yoann-Karl Whissell; *W:* Matt Leslie; Stephen J. Smith; *C:* Jean-Philippe Bernier; *M:* Jean-Philippe Bernier; Jean-Nicolas Leupi Le Matos.

The Summer of Aviya *Kayitz Shel Aviya* **1988** Ten-year-old Aviya has spent most of her life in orphanages as her partisan Jewish mother fought the Nazis. Now, Aviya faces the prospect of returning to a home and woman she doesn't really know, one who is also balanced on the edge of madness. Based on the memoirs of Almagor. Hebrew with subtitles. Followed by "Under the Domim Tree." **95m/C; VHS, DVD.** *IS* Kaipo Cohen; Gila Almagor; *D:* Eli Cohen; *W:* Gila Almagor; Eli Cohen.

Summer of Fear *Stranger in Our House* **1978** A happy young woman (Blair) must overcome evil forces when her cousin (a teenage witch not akin to Sabrina) comes to live with—and control—her family. Based on a novel by Lois Duncan, who also wrote the source novel for 1997's "I Know What You Did Last Summer." Pretty scary if ordinary, made-for-TV horror from later-famous Craven. **94m/C; VHS, DVD, Blu-Ray.** Linda Blair; Lee Purcell; Jeremy Slate; Carol Lawrence; MacDonald Carey; Jeff McCracken; Jeff East; Fran Drescher; *D:* Wes Craven; *M:* Tom D'Andrea. **TV**

Summer of '42 1971 (R) Touching if sentimental story about 15-year-old Hermie's (Grimes) sexual coming of age during his summer vacation on an island off New England. While his friends are fumbling with girls their own age, he falls in love with a beautiful 22-year-old woman (O'Neill) whose husband is off fighting in the war. **102m/C; VHS, DVD, Blu-Ray.** Jennifer O'Neill; Gary Grimes; Jerry Houser; Oliver Conant; *Nar:* Robert Mulligan; *D:* Robert Mulligan; *W:* Herman Raucher; *C:* Robert L. Surtees; *M:* Michel Legrand. Oscars '71: Orig. Dramatic Score.

Summer of Sam 1/2 1999 (R) Spike Lee's take on the summer of 1977, when serial killer Son of Sam traumatized New York City. The plot does not center on the actual crimes of David Berkowitz, but on the repercussions they had in the neighborhoods of New York. Leguizamo and Sorvino play a married Bronx couple who grow to question pal Ritchie (Brody), a newly converted punk rocker who leads a double life as a gay dancer. As the killer's attacks continue, fear begins to rise along with the temperature, and the neighborhood begins to tear itself apart. Lee's film drew highly publicized protests from the families of Berkowitz's victims. **142m/C; VHS, DVD, Blu-Ray.** Adrien Brody; John Leguizamo; Spike Lee; Mira Sorvino; Jennifer Esposito; Michael Badalucco; Anthony LaPaglia; Patti LuPone; Ben Gazzara; Bebe Neuwirth; John Savage; Roger Guenveur Smith; Michael Rispoli; *D:* Spike Lee; *W:* Spike Lee; *C:* Ellen Kuras; *M:* Terence Blanchard.

Summer of the Monkeys 1/2 1998 (G) Fairly sappy family pic set in rural America. John Lee (Ontkean) is a hard-working farmer with a caring wife, Sara (Hope), precocious son Jay Berry (Sevier), and a crippled daughter, Daisy (Stuart). Gramps (Brimley) runs the local general store and Jay works there, hoping to save money to buy Daisy a pony. When a nearby train wreck leads to the escape of a foursome of circus monkeys, Jay aims to find them first and get the reward for their return. **101m/C; VHS, DVD.** *CA* Michael Ontkean; Leslie Hope; Corey Sevier; Katie Stuart; Wilford Brimley; Don Francks; B.J. McLellan; *D:* Michael Anderson, Sr.; *W:* Greg Taylor; Jim Strain; *C:* Michael Storey; *M:* George Blondheim.

Summer Palace *Yihe Yuan* **2006** The lives of Yu Hong (Hao) and her lover Zhou Wei (Guo)are traced from their enrollment in Bejing University in 1988 and subsequently involvement in the demonstrations in Tiananmen Square, into adulthood, which never seems to match the promise of their youth. Frank and explicit in both its sexuality and its examination of the changes China has undergone since 1989. Director Ye was banned from filmmaking for five years by the Chinese government after showing this at Cannes without permission. **140m/C; DVD.** *CH FR* Lei Hao; Xiaodong Guo; Ling Hu; Xianmin Zhang; *D:* Ye Lou; *W:* Ye Lou; Mei Feng; The Range Busters; *C:* Qing Hua; *M:* Peyman Yazdanian.

A Summer Place 1959 Melodrama about summer liaisons amid the young and middle-aged rich on an island off the coast of Maine. Too slick; romantic drama is little more than skin-deep, and dialogue is excruciating. Donahue's first starring role. Based on the novel by Sloan Wilson. Featuring "Theme from a Summer Place," which was a number-one hit in 1959. **130m/C; VHS, DVD.** Troy Donahue; Richard Egan; Sandra Dee; Dorothy McGuire; Arthur Kennedy; Constance Ford; Beulah Bondi; *D:* Delmer Daves; *W:* Delmer Daves; *C:* Harry Stradling, Sr.; *M:* Max Steiner.

Summer Rental 1985 (PG) That John Candy just can't win, can he? Here, as a hopeless, harried air traffic controller, he tries to have a few days to relax in sunny Florida. Enter mean rich guy Crenna. Candy can add something hefty to the limpest of plots, and does so here. Watch the first hour for yuks, then rewind. **87m/C; VHS, DVD.** John Candy; Rip Torn; Richard Crenna; Joseph Lawrence; Karen Austin; Kerri Green; John Larroquette; Pierrino Mascarino; *D:* Carl Reiner; *W:* Mark Reisman; Jeremy Stevens; *C:* Ric Waite; *M:* Alan Silvestri.

Summer School 1977 (R) A teenaged boy's girlfriend will stop at nothing to prevent him from going out with the pretty new girl in town. **80m/C; VHS, DVD.** John McLaughlin; Steve Rose; Phoebe Schmidt; *D:* Bethel Buckalew; *W:* Bethel Buckalew; *C:* William E. Hines; *M:* Bill Schereck.

Summer School 1/2 1987 (PG-13) A high-school teacher's vacation plans are ruined when he gets stuck teaching remedial English in summer school. It seems all these students are interested in is re-enacting scenes from "The Texas Chainsaw Massacre," learning to drive, and surfing. Actually, one of the better films of this genre, thanks mostly to Harmon's likeability. **98m/C; VHS, DVD.** Mark Harmon; Kirstie Alley; Courtney Thorne-Smith; Shawnee Smith; Robin Thomas; Dean Cameron; Gary Riley; Kelly Jo Minter; Fabiana Udenio; Beau Starr; Ken Olandt; Lucy Lee Flippin; Nels Van Patten; *Cameo(s):* Carl Reiner; *D:* Carl Reiner; *W:* Jeff Franklin; *C:* David M. Walsh; *M:* Danny Elfman.

Summer School Teachers WOOF! 1975 (R) Three sultry femmes bounce about Los Angeles high school and make the collective student body happy. Typical Corman doings; sequel to "The Students Teachers." **87m/C; VHS, DVD.** Candice Rialson; Pat Anderson; Rhonda Leigh Hopkins; Christopher Wales; *D:* Barbara Peeters.

Summer Solstice 1/2 1981 Fonda and Loy are splendid as a couple married half a century who revisit the beach where they first met. Fonda especially shines, as a crusty old artist. Yes, it is an awful lot like "On Golden Pond." **75m/C; VHS, DVD.** Henry Fonda; Myrna Loy; Lindsay Crouse; Stephen Collins; *D:* Ralph Rosenblum. **TV**

Summer Stock *If You Feel Like Singing* **1950** Garland plays farm owner Jane Falbury whose sister, Abigail (DeHaven) arrives with a summer stock troupe, led by Joe Ross (Kelly), to rehearse a show in the family barn. Jane agrees, if the troupe will help her with the farm's harvest. When Abigail decamps for New York, leaving the leading lady role open, guess who steps into the breach. Slim plot papered over with many fun song-and-dance numbers. Also features Garland's first MGM short, "Every Sunday," made in 1936 with Deanna Durbin. **109m/C; VHS, DVD, Blu-Ray.** Judy Garland; Gene Kelly; Gloria De Haven; Carleton Carpenter; Eddie Bracken; Phil Silvers; Hans Conried; Marjorie Main; Ray Collins; *D:* Charles Walters; *W:* George Wells; Sy Gomberg.

Summer Storm 1/2 1944 Based on the Anton Chekhov story "The Shooting Party." In 1912, beautiful and ambitious Russian peasant Olga (Darnell) marries farmer Anton Urbenin (Haas) but is soon having a series of affairs with wealthy men. This includes cynical, aristocratic judge Fedor Petroff (Sanders), who becomes obsessed with Olga, leading to deadly consequences. Not quite as over-the-top as Sirk's best work but still quite the melodrama. **106m/B; DVD.** Linda Darnell; George Sanders; Hugo Haas; Anna Lee; Edward Everett Horton; Sig Rumann; Lori Lahner; *D:* Gregg Tallas; *W:* Robert Thoeren; Rowland Leigh; *C:* Eugene Schuftan; Archie Stout; *M:* Karl Hajos.

A Summer Story 1988 (PG-13) Superbly acted, typically British period drama about beautiful farm girl Stubbs and city lawyer Wilby, who fall in love. But can they overcome difference of social class? From the story "The Apple Tree" by John Galsworthy. **97m/C; DVD, Blu-Ray, Streaming.** *UK* James Wilby; Imogen Stubbs; Susannah York; Sophie Ward; Kenneth Colley; Jerome Flynn; *D:* Piers Haggard; *W:* Penelope Mortimer; *C:* Kenneth Macmillan; *M:* Georges Delerue.

A Summer to Remember *Seryozha* **1961** A five-year-old boy spends a summer with his stepfather on a Soviet collective farm. The two become deeply attached. Scenes of collective life will be of more interest to Westerners than the near-sentimental story. Star Bondarchuk later directed the epic, award-winning "War and Peace." **80m/B; VHS, DVD.** *RU* Borya Barkhazov; Sergei Bondarchuk; Irana Skobtseva; *D:* Igor Talankin; Georgi Daneliya; *W:* Igor Talankin; Georgi Daneliya; *C:* Anatoli Nitochkin; *M:* Boris Chaikovsky.

A Summer to Remember 1/2 1984 (PG) A deaf boy (played by Gerlis, himself deaf since birth) develops a friendship with an orangutan through sign language. Bad guys abduct the friendly ape—but all is right in the end. Nice, innocuous family viewing. Based on a story by Scott Swanton and Robert Lloyd Lewis. **93m/C; VHS, DVD.** Tess Harper; James Farentino; Burt Young; Louise Fletcher; Sean Gerlis; Bridgette Andersen; *D:* Robert Lewis; *C:* Stephen W. Gray; *M:* Charles Fox. **TV**

Summer Wars *Sama uozu* **2009** (PG) While on summer vacation, a young math whiz must put aside his dreams of the girl he loves to save the internet and possibly the world. **120m/C; DVD, Blu-Ray, Streaming.** *JP V:* Michael Sinterniklaas; Brina Palencia; Pam Dougherty; Todd Haberkorn; J. Michael Tatum; *D:* Mamoru Hosoda; *W:* Mamoru Hosoda; Satoko Okadera; *M:* Akihiko Matsumoto. **VIDEO**

Summer Wishes, Winter Dreams 1973 (PG) Woodward and Balsam are a materially prosperous middle-aged couple with little but tedium in their lives—a tedium accurately replicated, in what feels like real life, in this slow, dull film. The two leads and Sidney—in her first screen role in 17 years—are all excellent, but the story of regret and present unhappiness wears the viewer down. **95m/C; VHS, DVD.** Joanne Woodward; Martin Balsam; Sylvia Sidney; Dori Brenner; Ron Richards; *D:* Gilbert Cates; *W:* Stewart Stern. British Acad. '74: Actress (Woodward); Natl. Bd. of Review '73: Support. Actress (Sidney); N.Y. Film Critics '73: Actress (Woodward).

Summer With Monica *Sommaren Med Monika* **1953** The first of nine films Bergman did with Andersson. Reckless teen Monika (Andersson) and naive Harry (Ekborg) are both from unhappy working-class families in Stockholm. They run away to spend the summer on a secluded beach but must face reality when their money runs out and Monika becomes pregnant. Swedish with subtitles. **97m/B; DVD, Blu-Ray.** *SW* Harriet Andersson; Lars Ekborg; Ake Fridell; *D:* Ingmar Bergman; *W:* Ingmar Bergman; Per Anders Fogelstrom; *C:* Gunnar Fischer; *M:* Erik Nordgren.

Summer's End 1/2 1999 In 1983, physician William Blakely (Jones) decides to retire to the small Georgia town where he grew up. But the lakeside community is lily-white and hostile (Blakely's family was originally driven out by racial violence). However, fatherless 12-year-old Jamie (LeDoux) and the doc become friends, despite pressures on the boy to toe the racist line. **101m/C; VHS, DVD.** James Earl Jones; Wendy Crewson; Brendan Fletcher; Jake LeDoux; *D:* Helen Shaver. **CABLE**

Summer's Moon *Summer's Blood* **2009** (R) Horror drivel. Teenager Summer is road tripping in search of her estranged daddy and heads to some backwoods burg where she's hassled by the local cop and rescued by cute handyman Tom. Tom invites Summer to spend the night at the family home but won't let her leave the next morning. Seems the family is a bunch of murderous crazies who want Summer to join their clan. **92m/C; DVD.** *CA* Ashley Greene; Barbara Niven; Stephen McHattie; Peter Mooney; *D:* Lee Demarbre; *W:* Christine Conradt; Sean Hogan; *C:* Ioana Vasile; *M:* Steve Gurevitch. **VIDEO**

A Summer's Tale 1/2 *Conte d'Ete* **1996** Talky and slow-moving vacation comedy is the third in Rohmer's "Tales of the Four Seasons" series. Young Gaspard (Poupaud) is spending a month in a borrowed flat in the seaside resort of Dinard. He becomes friendly with waitress Margot (Langlet) while he waits for his girlfriend Lena (Nolin) to join him, but is also introduced to Margot's friend Solene (Simon), who's interested in a quick fling with Gaspard. When all three women agree to accompany him on a sightseeing trip, he's got more a than a little maneuvering to do. French with subtitles. **133m/C; VHS, DVD.** *FR* Melvil Poupaud; Amanda Langlet; Aurelia Nolin; Gwenaelle Simon; *D:* Eric Rohmer; *W:* Eric Rohmer; *C:* Diane Baratier; *M:* Sebastien Erms; Philippe Eidel.

Summertime 1/2 *Summer Madness* **1955** Spinster Hepburn vacations in Venice and falls in love with Brazzi. She is hurt when inadvertently she learns he is married, but her life has been so bleak she is not about to end her one great romance. Moving, funny, richly photographed in a beautiful Old World city. From Arthur Laurents' play "The Time of the Cuckoo." **98m/C; VHS, DVD.** Katharine Hepburn; Rossano Brazzi; Isa Miranda; Darren McGavin; Mari Aldon; MacDonald Parke; Jeremy Spenser; ***D:*** David Lean; ***W:*** David Lean; H.E. Bates; ***C:*** Jack Hildyard; ***M:*** Alessandro Cicognini. N.Y. Film Critics '55: Director (Lean).

Summertime *La Belle Saison* **2016** A sensual romantic drama set in 1971 about first loves and difficult choices. Living in Paris, Carole (De France) and Delphine (Higelin) fall deeply in love while taking part in the women's movement. When Delphine is asked to come and help her family at their farm in the countryside after her father has a stroke, she must make a choice between them and her life with Carole in Paris. While Delphine is considering her choices, Carole cannot tolerate the estrangement and joins Delphine at the farm. However, living together in the countryside in this era may not lead to long-term happiness. French with subtitles. **105m/C; DVD, Streaming, Download.** Cecile de France; Izia Higelin; Noemie Lvovsky; Jean-Henri Compere; Kévin Azaïs; ***D:*** Catherine Corsini; ***W:*** Catherine Corsini; Laurette Polmanss; ***C:*** Jeanne Lapoirie; ***M:*** Gregoire Hetzel.

Summertree **1971 (PG)** Douglas stars as a young musician in the 1960s trying to avoid the draft and the wrath of his parents. Contrived and heavy-handed. Produced by Douglas pere, Kirk. Adapted from the play by Ron Cower. **88m/C; VHS, DVD.** Michael Douglas; Jack Warden; Brenda Vaccaro; Barbara Bel Geddes; Kirk Calloway; Bill Vint; ***D:*** Anthony Newley; ***M:*** David Shire.

The Summit **1/2 2008** Maria Puerto (Maestro) watches her son die from a tainted vaccine and loses her lawsuit against the international pharmaceutical company who made it. Carrying a vial of her son's poisoned blood, Maria travels from Colombia to the G8 summit to protest but the drug company wants her stopped at all costs. However, when people start dying, Maria joins with bio-terrorism expert Thom Lightstone (Purefoy) to find an antidote even while the government ministers deny everything. **180m/C; DVD.** *CA* Mia Maestro; James Purefoy; Bruce Greenwood; Christopher Plummer; Rachelle Lefevre; Stephen McHattie; Wendy Crewson; Nigel Bennett; ***D:*** Nick Copus; ***W:*** John Krizanc; ***C:*** Alwyn Kumst; ***M:*** Tom Third. **TV**

The Summit **1/2 2013 (R)** What happened on that frigid day in August of 2008 when 22 climbers began the ascent to the summit of K2, the deadliest mountain in the world, but only 11 came home? Nick Ryan's documentary interviews most of the major players in that awful climb, getting close to the answers about what went wrong. He even tries to address the deeper questions of why people continue to climb a mountain that takes one out of every four lives of those who challenge it. It's ultimately a bit familiar, but it's well-made and historically informative about its specific incident. **95m/C; DVD.** ***D:*** Nick Ryan; ***W:*** Mark Monroe; ***C:*** Robbie Ryan; ***M:*** Nick Seymour.

The Sun *Solntse* **2005** Sokurov's unhurried narrative begins a few days before the official end of WWII as Japan's Emperor Hirohito (Ogata) prepares to officially surrender to an arrogant General MacArthur (Dawson), which also means renouncing his divine status. Daily life in the palace, with its ubiquitous servants, is shown in contrast to the brusque treatment the cloistered Emperor initially receives from the American occupiers. English and Japanese with subtitles. **110m/C; DVD.** *RU* Issey Ogata; Shiro Sano; Kaori Momoi; Robert Dawson; ***D:*** Alexander Sokurov; ***W:*** Yuri Arabov; ***C:*** Alexander Sokurov; ***M:*** Andrei Sigle.

The Sun Also Rises **1/2 1957** Dull adaptation of Ernest Hemingway's 1926 novel about the Lost Generation, with all the leading actors too old for their roles. American expat Jake Barnes (Power) and British aristocrat/promiscuous divorcee Lady Brett Ashley (Gardner) are in love but cynical Jake is impotent from a war wound and knows their romance wouldn't work. He and buddy Bill (Albert) decide to leave Paris to see the running of the bulls in Pamplona, Spain, but find Brett and her latest coterie of men there as well, which causes trouble. **130m/C; DVD.** Tyrone Power; Ava Gardner; Errol Flynn; Mel Ferrer; Gregory Ratoff; Eddie Albert; Juliette Greco; Robert Evans; ***D:*** Henry King; ***W:*** Peter Viertel; ***C:*** Leo Tover; ***M:*** Hugo Friedhofer.

Sun Choke **1/2 2016** Ben Cresciman's disturbing horror film is the kind that doesn't offer many explanations as to what's even happening. We meet a young woman (a fearless performance by Hagen) who needs a caretaker (Crampton) but it's unclear why. Is she ill? In rehab? Just on a health kick? It becomes clear that the caretaker is abusive and possibly insane, pushing our heroine to the edge of mental and physical well-being. Then this young woman becomes obsessed with someone in her neighborhood, and things go very badly. It's a surreal, terrifying movie that reminds one of David Lynch. **83m/C; DVD, Blu-Ray.** Sarah Hagan; Barbara Crampton; Sara Malakul Lane; Jim Boeven; Joe Nieves; ***D:*** Ben Cresciman; ***W:*** Ben Cresciman; ***C:*** Mathew Rudenberg; ***M:*** Bryan Hollon.

The Sun Comes Up **1949** MacDonald, in her last screen appearance, plays a bitter widow whose life is changed by an orphan's love for a collie. Songbird MacDonald manages to sing a number of songs, some of them backed by a chorus of "orphans." Based on short stories by Marjorie Kinnan Rawlings. **93m/C; DVD.** Jeanette MacDonald; Lloyd Nolan; Claude Jarman, Jr.; Lewis Stone; Dwayne Hickman; ***D:*** Richard Thorpe; ***W:*** William Ludwig; ***C:*** Ray June; ***M:*** Andre Previn.

Sun Don't Shine **2012** Intense, unsettling indie has irrational married mom Crystal and her boyfriend Leo driving across steamy central Florida on their way to the Gulf Coast. Reasons for their flight are slow to become clear and Leo starts to crack under Crystal's ever-increasing hysterical accusations after they stop at his friend Teri's home. Ultimately, Seimetz's feature film debut is more about atmosphere than coherent narrative. **80m/C; Streaming.** Kate Lyn Sheil; Kentucker Audley; Kit Gwin; ***D:*** Amy Seimetz; ***W:*** Amy Seimetz; ***C:*** Jay Keitel; ***M:*** Ben Lovett; John Garland.

The Sun Is Also a Star **2019 (PG-13)** In New York City, Natasha (Shahidi) is the daughter of Jamaican immigrants and her whole family is facing deportation after an ICE raid. One day, she literally runs into Daniel (Melton), the son of Korean immigrants, on the sidewalk as he is on his way to a college interview. Though they are opposites in interests and views on love, Daniel bets Natasha that he can make her fall in love with him by the end of the day. Based on a young adult novel by Nicola Yoon, the film explores big issues in an appealing package but ends in an unexpected, ineffective way. **100m/C; DVD.** Yara Shahidi; Charles Melton; John Leguizamo; Gbenga Akinnagbe; Miriam A. Hyman; ***D:*** Ry Russo-Young; ***W:*** Tracy Oliver; Nicola Yoon; ***C:*** Autumn Cheyenne Durald; ***M:*** Herdis Stefánsdóttir.

The Sun Sets at Dawn **1/2 1950** Oddball, low-rent allegory with religious overtones. A young man on death row will be the first to die in the state's new electric chair so the story is drawing a lot of attention. Reporters are hanging out at a nearby greasy spoon, speculating about the convict who's still proclaiming his innocence. Various threads come together that lend credence to his claims, but will they be enough to stop the execution? Most of the characters are nameless and what's that supposed to be about? **71m/B; DVD.** Patrick Waltz; Walter Reed; Howard St. John; Sally Parr; Houseley Stevenson; Lee Frederick; ***D:*** Paul Sloane; ***W:*** Paul Sloane; ***C:*** Lionel Lindon; ***M:*** Leith Stevens.

The Sun Shines Bright **1953** Heavily stereotyped, contrived tale of a Southern judge with a heart of gold who does so many good deeds (defending a black man accused of rape; helping a desperate prostitute) that he jeopardizes his re-election. Set during Reconstruction. An unfortunate remake of Ford's own 1934 "Judge Priest," starring Will Rogers. **92m/B; DVD, Blu-Ray.** Charles Winninger; Arleen Whelan; John Russell; Stepin Fetchit; Milburn Stone; Russell Simpson; ***D:*** John Ford; ***W:*** Laurence Stallings; ***C:*** Archie Stout; ***M:*** Victor Young.

Sunchaser **1/2 1996 (R)** Mishmash of medicine and mysticism focuses on yuppie UCLA oncologist Dr. Michael Reynolds (Harrelson) who's kidnapped by 16-year-old patient, Brandon "Blue" Monroe (Seda). Blue is a half-Navajo gangbanger whose cancer is inoperable and he needs the doc to drive him to a reservation in Arizona where he feels a medicine man and the waters of a supposedly magical lake can cure him. Reynolds naturally discovers some humanity on the trip and decides to help his truculent patient. Leads give sincere performances but film is half-baked at best. **123m/C; VHS, DVD, Blu-Ray.** Woody Harrelson; Jon Seda; Anne Bancroft; Alexandra Tydings; Matt Mulhern; Talisa Soto; Lawrence Pressman; Michael O'Neill; Harry Carey, Jr.; ***D:*** Michael Cimino; ***W:*** Charles Leavitt; ***C:*** Doug Milsome; ***M:*** Maurice Jarre.

Sundance and the Kid *Sundance Cassidy and Butch the Kid; Vivi O, Prefeibilmente, Morti* **1969 (PG)** Slapstick spaghetti western has two estranged brothers trying to collect an inheritance by living together for six months. Hilarity fails to ensue. **84m/C; VHS, DVD.** *IT* Giuliano Gemma; Sydne Rome; Nino Benvenuti; ***D:*** Duccio Tessari; ***W:*** Ennio Flaiano; ***C:*** Cesare Allione; ***M:*** Gianni Ferrio.

Sunday **1996** Basically a two-character study of mistaken identity among lonely, middleaged people. On a winter's Sunday morning in Queens, depressed Oliver (Suchet) is greeted by failing British actress Madeleine (Harrow), who mistakes him for a director she once met. She invites him to lunch and Oliver, who's actually a homeless former accountant, struggles to maintain the charade. The unstable Madeleine's bitter when she discovers his deception but is also unwillingly to let the connection between them die. **93m/C; VHS, DVD.** David Suchet; Lisa Harrow; Larry Pine; Jared Harris; Joe Grifasi; ***D:*** Jonathan Nossiter; ***W:*** Jonathan Nossiter; James Lasdun; ***C:*** Michael Barrow; John Foster; ***M:*** Jonathan Nossiter. Sundance '97: Grand Jury Prize, Screenplay.

Sunday, Bloody Sunday **1971 (R)** Adult drama centers around the intertwined love affairs of the homosexual Finch, the heterosexual Jackson, and self-centered bisexual artist Head, desired by both. Fully drawn characters brought to life by excellent acting make this difficult story well worth watching—though Head's central character is sadly rather dull. Day-Lewis makes his first (brief) screen appearance as a car vandalizing teenager. Powerful, sincere, and sensitive. **110m/C; VHS, DVD.** *GB* Glenda Jackson; Peter Finch; Murray Head; Peggy Ashcroft; Tony Britton; Maurice Denham; Vivian Pickles; Bessie Love; Daniel Day-Lewis; ***D:*** John Schlesinger; ***W:*** Penelope Gilliatt; ***C:*** Billy Williams; ***M:*** Ron Geesin. British Acad. '71: Actor (Finch), Actress (Jackson), Director (Schlesinger), Film; Golden Globes '72: Foreign Film; N.Y. Film Critics '71: Screenplay; Natl. Soc. Film Critics '71: Actor (Finch), Screenplay; Writers Guild '71: Orig. Screenplay.

Sunday Dinner for a Soldier **1/2 1944** Sweet wartime morale booster. Grandpa Osborne (Winninger) looks after his orphaned grandchildren aboard a ramshackle houseboat in Florida. They're poor, but they save up to provide a special dinner for a soldier and Sgt. Eric Moore (Hodiak) accidentally makes it to their door. He's smitten by eldest Osborne, Tessa (Baxter), and the warmth of the family. **85m/B; DVD.** Anne Baxter; John Hodiak; Charles Winninger; Anne Revere; Connie Marshall; Bobby Driscoll; Chill Wills; Jane Darwell; ***D:*** Lloyd Bacon; ***W:*** Wanda Tuchock; Melvin Levy; ***C:*** Joseph Macdonald; ***M:*** Alfred Newman.

Sunday in New York **1/2 1963** Distraught Eileen (Fonda) heads to New York to seek counsel from her airline pilot brother Adam (Robertson) after she breaks up with fiance Russ (Culp). Adam is in the middle of setting up a much-interrupted date with sometime-girlfriend Mona, so Eileen wanders around NYC. Soon she meets cute with suave fella Mike on the bus. Romantic comedy complications follow as Russ comes back into the picture. Amusing look at the changing sexual mores of the time must've seemed mildly shocking then, but now seems quaint. Robertson stands out among great cast. **105m/C; VHS, DVD, Blu-Ray.** Rod Taylor; Jane Fonda; Cliff Robertson; Robert Culp; Jo Morrow; Jim Backus; Rayford Barnes; Jim Hutton; ***Cameo(s):*** Peter Nero; ***D:*** Peter Tewkesbury; ***W:*** Norman Krasna; ***C:*** Leo Tover; ***M:*** Peter Nero.

A Sunday in the Country **1/2** *Un Dimanche a la Campagne* **1984 (G)** A lush, distinctively French affirmation of nature and family life. This character study with a minimal plot takes place during a single summer day in 1910 France. An elderly impressionist painter-patriarch is visited at his country home by his family. Highly acclaimed, though the pace may be too slow for some. Beautiful location photography. In French with English subtitles. **94m/C; VHS, DVD, Blu-Ray.** *FR* Louis Ducreux; Sabine Azema; Michel Aumont; ***D:*** Bertrand Tavernier; ***W:*** Bertrand Tavernier; Colo Tavernier O'Hagan; ***C:*** Bruno de Keyzer. Cannes '84: Director (Tavernier); Cesar '85: Actress (Azema), Cinematog., Writing; Natl. Bd. of Review '84: Support. Actress (Azema); N.Y. Film Critics '84: Foreign Film.

Sunday in the Park with George **1986** Taped theatrical performance of the Tony, Grammy, and Pulitzer Prize-winning musical play, which is based upon impressionist Georges Seurat's painting "A Sunday Afternoon on the Island of Grande Jatte." Features a celebrated music score by Sondheim. **120m/C; VHS, DVD.** Mandy Patinkin; Bernadette Peters; Barbara Byrne; Charles Kimbrough; ***D:*** James Lapine; ***M:*** Stephen Sondheim.

Sunday School Musical **2008** Low-budget but lively teen musical. Zachary is a talented choir member at an urban school but must transfer to a competing suburban high where he's welcome by Savannah. The two have been rivals for a big choir competition but when Zach learns his former school will be closing because of money trouble the two choirs decide to band together and win. **90m/C; DVD.** Chris Chatman; Candise Lakota; Krystle Connor; Robert Acinapura; Amy Ganser; Millena Gay; Dustin Fitzsimons; Mark Hengst; ***D:*** Rachel Goldenberg; ***W:*** Rachel Goldenberg; Ashley Holloway; ***C:*** Gabriel Diniz; ***M:*** Don Raymond. **VIDEO**

Sundays at Tiffany's **2010** Control freak Jane Clermont (Milano) manages her mother Vivian's (Channing) New York theater and is engaged to vain actor Hugh (Sergei). Maybe being perfect has finally gotten to her since Jane's imaginary childhood friend (and possible guardian angel) Michael (Winter) reappears for the first time since she was 10. Jane may be questioning her sanity but she's finally discovering what it means to have some fun. Adapted from the James Patterson/Gabrielle Charbonnet bestseller. **87m/C; DVD.** Alyssa Milano; Eric Winter; Ivan Sergei; Stockard Channing; Emily Alyn Lind; Gage Munroe; ***D:*** Mark Piznarski; ***W:*** Jennifer Heath; Nancey Silvers; ***C:*** Adam Swica; ***M:*** Mateo Messina. **CABLE**

Sundown **1/2 1941** In Africa at the beginning of WWII, a local girl aids the British against a German plot to run guns to the natives and start a rebellion. Engaging performances and efficient direction keep it above the usual cliches. Also available in a colorized version. **91m/B; VHS, DVD.** Gene Tierney; Bruce Cabot; George Sanders; Harry Carey, Sr.; Cedric Hardwicke; Joseph Calleia; Dorothy Dandridge; Reginald Gardiner; ***D:*** Henry Hathaway; ***C:*** Charles B(ryant) Lang, Jr.; ***M:*** Miklos Rozsa.

Sundown **1/2 1991 (R)** An ambitious shot at a vampire western fails because it drains almost all vampire lore and winds up resembling a standard oater. Carradine plays a reformed vampire king (guess who) running a desert clinic that weans bloodsuckers away from preying on humans. But undead renegades attack using sixguns and wooden bullets. The climax may outrage horror purists. **104m/C; VHS, DVD.** David Carradine; Bruce Campbell; Deborah Foreman; Maxwell Caulfield; Morgan Brittany; ***D:*** Anthony Hickox.

Sundown **1/2 2016 (R)** A spring break comedy. When high school seniors Logan (Werkheiser) and Blake (Marquette) go to Puerto Vallarta, Mexico, for spring break, their goal is spend quality time with their high school crushes. Hitting the clubs, they see many beautiful women. After Logan spends the night with a beautiful local named Gaby (Belle), he finds that his grandfather's Rolex watch is missing. As they try to get the valuable family heirloom back, they learn that a gangster has it and wants triple its value before he will give it back. The more Logan and Blake try to solve their problem, the worse it gets. **103m/C; DVD, Streaming, Download.** Devon Werkheiser; Sean Marquette; Silverio Palacios; Camilla Belle; Teri Hatcher; *D:* Fernando Lebrija; *W:* Fernando Lebrija; Miguel Tejada-Flores; *C:* Gerardo Madrazo; Pietro Zuercher; *M:* Edward Rogers.

Sundown: The Vampire in Retreat **2008 (R)** A group of vampires live the quiet life in a small western town, drinking synthetic blood made at a nearby factory. When the factory begins to malfunction, a scientist is brought in to fix it, and some of the vampires who want to go back to preying on people for the real thing decide to stage a coup. They have guns with wooden bullets and they aren't afraid to use them. Notable for starring Campbell as a descendant of Van Helsing whose devotion to killing vampires goes out the window the second he meets a hot blonde dead girl. **104m/C; DVD.** David Carradine; Morgan Brittany; Bruce Campbell; Jim Metzler; Maxwell Caulfield; Deborah Foreman; M. Emmet Walsh; John Ireland, Jr.; Dana Ashbrook; John Hancock; Dabbs Greer; Bert Remsen; Marion Eaton; Elizabeth (Ward) Gracen; Christopher Bradley; George "Buck" Flower; Sunshine Parker; Helena Carroll; Kathy MacQuarrie Martin; Jack Eiseman; Brendan Hughes; Gerardo Mejia; Erin Gourlay; Vanessa Pierson; Mike Najjar; Phillip Simon; Chris Caputo; Phillip Esposito; *D:* Anthony Hickox; *W:* Anthony Hickox; John Burgess; *C:* Levie Isaacks; *M:* Richard Stone. **VIDEO**

The Sundowners 1/2 **1960** Slow, beautiful, and often moving epic drama about a family of Irish sheepherders in Australia during the 1920s who must continually uproot themselves and migrate. They struggle to save enough money to buy their own farm and wind up training a horse they hope will be a money-winner in racing. Well-acted by all, with Johns and Ustinov providing some humorous moments. Adapted from the novel by Jon Cleary. Filmed in Australia and London studios. **133m/C; VHS, DVD.** Deborah Kerr; Robert Mitchum; Peter Ustinov; Glynis Johns; Dina Merrill; Chips Rafferty; Michael Anderson, Jr.; Lola Brooks; Wylie Watson; *D:* Fred Zinnemann; *C:* Jack Hildyard; *M:* Dimitri Tiomkin. Natl. Bd. of Review '60: Actor (Mitchum); N.Y. Film Critics '60: Actress (Kerr).

Sunlight Jr. **2013** Downbeat drama finds Melissa Winters earning minimum wage as a convenience store cashier in Florida while her paraplegic boyfriend Richie spends most of his disability check drinking with his buddies at the local bar. However, they are tenderly in love and happy when Melissa learns she's pregnant until they get evicted from their motel home and are forced to move in with Melissa's alcoholic mother. To add to their problems, Melissa's being stalked by her violent ex. **95m/C; On Demand.** Naomi Watts; Matt Dillon; Norman Reedus; Tess Harper; *D:* Laurie Collyer; *W:* Laurie Collyer; *C:* Igor Martinovic.

Sunny **1930** Marsh reprised her 1925 Broadway musical hit as an English circus bareback rider who poses as a boy to stowaway on an ocean liner to New York. She's avoiding a marriage arranged by her father so she can be with the man she does love—Tom Warren (Gray). She's discovered but it works to Sunny's advantage until she has to marry amiable fellow passenger Jim (Donahue) so she can legally enter the United States. They agree to a quickie divorce but the situation gets more complicated. **78m/B; DVD.** Marilyn Miller; Lawrence Gray; Joe Donahue; Inez Courtney; O.P. Heggie; Mackenzie Ward; Barbara Bedford; Judith Vosselli; *D:* William A. Seiter; *W:* Humphrey Pearson; Henry McCarty; *C:* Ernest Haller; *M:* LeRoy Stone.

Sunny **1941** Another glossed-over, love-conquers-all musical with Neagle as a circus star who falls for a wealthy car maker's son. Dad and crew disapprove, putting a damper on the romance. In spite of the weak storyline and flat direction, Kerns' music and Bolger's dancing make it enjoyable. **98m/B; VHS, DVD.** Anna Neagle; Ray Bolger; John Carroll; Edward Everett Horton; Frieda Inescort; Helen Westley; Benny Rubin; Richard Lane; Martha Tilton; *D:* Herbert Wilcox.

Sunny Skies **1930** Bargain-basement retread has Lease donating a pint of blood. **75m/B; VHS, DVD.** Benny Rubin; Marceline Day; Rex Lease; Marjorie "Babe" Kane; Wesley Barry; *D:* Norman Taurog.

Sunrise *Sunrise—A Song of Two Humans* **1927** Magnificent silent story of a simple country boy who, prodded by an alluring city woman, tries to murder his wife. Production values wear their age well. Gaynor won an Oscar for her stunning performance. Remade in Germany as "The Journey to Tilsit." Based on a story by Hermann Suderman. **110m/B; Silent; VHS, DVD, Blu-Ray.** George O'Brien; Janet Gaynor; Bodil Rosing; Margaret Livingston; J. Farrell MacDonald; Carl Mayer; *D:* F.W. Murnau; *C:* Charles Rosher; Karl Struss. Oscars '28: Actress (Gaynor), Cinematog., Film; Natl. Film Reg. '89.

Sunrise at Campobello **1960** A successful adaptation of the Tony award-winning play by Schary, who wrote the screenplay and also produced the film. In 1921, the Roosevelt family is vacationing at Campbello when Franklin (Bellamy, re-creating his stage role) becomes ill with what turns out to be polio. His formidable mother Sara (Shoemaker) wants her paralyzed son to give up his political aspirations but politico pal Louis Howe (Cronyn) insists Franklin get on with living, aided by the strength of wife Eleanor (an excellent performance by Garson). **143m/C; VHS, DVD.** Ralph Bellamy; Greer Garson; Hume Cronyn; Jean Hagen; Jack Perrin; Lyle Talbot; Ann Shoemaker; Tim Considine; Zena Bethune; Pat Close; *D:* Vincent J. Donehue; *W:* Dore Schary; *C:* Russell Harlan; *M:* Franz Waxman. Golden Globes '61: Actress--Drama (Garson); Natl. Bd. of Review '60: Actress (Garson).

Sunset **1988 (R)** Edwards wanders the range in this soft-centered farce about a couple of Western legends out to solve a mystery. On the backlots of Hollywood, silent screen star Tom Mix (Willis) meets aging marshal Wyatt Earp (Garner) and participates in a time-warp western circa 1927. They encounter a series of misadventures while trying to finger a murderer. Garner ambles enjoyably, lifting him a level above the rest of the cast. **101m/C; VHS, DVD.** Bruce Willis; James Garner; Mariel Hemingway; Darren McGavin; Jennifer Edwards; Malcolm McDowell; Kathleen Quinlan; M. Emmet Walsh; Patricia Hodge; Richard Bradford; Joe Dallesandro; Dermot Mulroney; *D:* Blake Edwards; *W:* Blake Edwards; Rod Amateau; *C:* Anthony B. Richmond; *M:* Henry Mancini. Golden Raspberries '88: Worst Director (Edwards).

Sunset 1/2 *Napszállta* **2018 (R)** In Budapest in 1913, Irisz Leiter (Jakab) is a young woman whose family was part of high society. Her parents died under mysterious circumstances, and she is estranged from her remaining family. When she goes to the department store once owned by her parents in search of employment, she is pushed aside by the relatives, Brill (Ivanov) and Zelma (Dobos), who run it. Though everyone, including Brill and Zelma, tells Irisz to stop asking questions, especially about the past, she persists no matter what the consequences. A costume drama, the film is a carefully crafted character study centered on Jakab's moving performance. **142m/C; DVD.** Vlad Ivanov; Susanne Wuest; Evelin Dobos; Björn Freiberg; Juli Jakab; *D:* László Nemes; *W:* László Nemes; *C:* Mátyás Erdély; *M:* László Melis.

Sunset Boulevard 1/2 **1950** Famed tale of Norma Desmond (Swanson), aging silent film queen, who refuses to accept that stardom has ended for her and hires young down-on-his-luck screenwriter Joe Gillis (Holden) to help engineer her movie comeback. The screenwriter, who becomes the actress' kept man, assumes he can manipulate her, but finds out otherwise. Reality was almost too close for comfort, as Swanson, von Stroheim (as her major domo Max), and others very nearly play themselves. A darkly humorous look at the legacy and loss of fame with witty dialog, stellar performances, and some now-classic scenes. Based on the story "A Can of Beans" by Brackett and Wilder. **100m/B; VHS, DVD, Blu-Ray.** Gloria Swanson; William Holden; Erich von Stroheim; Nancy Olson; Buster Keaton; Jack Webb; Cecil B. DeMille; Fred Clark; *D:* Billy Wilder; *W:* Billy Wilder; Charles Brackett; D.M. Marshman, Jr.; *C:* John Seitz; *M:* Franz Waxman. Oscars '50: Art Dir./Set Dec., B&W, Orig. Dramatic Score, Story & Screenplay; AFI '98: Top 100; Golden Globes '51: Actress--Drama (Swanson), Director (Wilder), Film--Drama, Score; Natl. Film Reg. '89.

Sunset Grill **1992 (R)** While investigating his wife's murder, detective Ryder Hart (Weller) discovers a pattern of grisly killings. Sexy singer Loren Duquesne (Singer) leads him south of the border to her boss and his bloody money-making scheme. Unrated version also available. **103m/C; VHS, DVD.** Peter Weller; Lori Singer; Alexandra Paul; John Rhys-Davies; Michael Anderson, Jr.; Stacy Keach; *D:* Kevin Connor.

The Sunset Limited **2011** HBO adaptation of the two-character 2006 play by Cormac McCarthy. God-fearing ex-con Black (Jackson) saves a would-be subway jumper, college professor White (Jones), and they retire to his New York apartment to debate the existence of God, the meaning of life, and the absurdity of humanity among other heavy topics. McCarthy can be florid so the actors underplay, which isn't such a bad thing. **91m/C; DVD.** Samuel L. Jackson; Tommy Lee Jones; *D:* Tommy Lee Jones; *W:* Cormac McCarthy; *C:* Paul Elliot; *M:* Marco Beltrami.

Sunset Limousine 1/2 **1983** An out-of-work stand-up comic gets thrown out by his girlfriend, then takes a job as a chauffeur. Standard vehicle with occasional bursts of speed. **92m/C; VHS, DVD.** John Ritter; Martin Short; Susan Dey; Paul Reiser; Audrie Neehan; Lainie Kazan; Charles Lane; *D:* Terry Hughes.

Sunset Park **1996 (R)** Brooklyn phys ed teacher Phyllis Saroka (Perlman) becomes the coach of a high school basketball team that, despite her total lack of knowledge about the game, makes it to the city championships. The cast's excellent performances hold interest, even though the predictable storyline gives away all of its moves before it gets near the hoop. Starr (of the rap group Onyx) is outstanding as the most talented (and most troubled) member of the team. **100m/C; VHS, DVD.** Rhea Perlman; Carol Kane; Terrence Howard; Camille Saviola; Fredro Starr; James Harris; Antwon Tanner; Shawn Michael Howard; De'Aundre Bonds; *D:* Steve Gomer; *W:* Seth Zvi Rosenfeld; Kathleen McGhee-Anderson; *C:* Robbie Greenberg; *M:* Kay Gee; Miles Goodman.

Sunset Rock 1/2 **2016** An indie romantic coming-of-age drama centered on the YouTube scene in Los Angeles and the celebrities it creates. Midwestern college student Jasey Rae (Baim) is using her enthusiasm for online fandom in her social media thesis. To do research, she travels to Hollywood to meet and study a YouTube star known as Lincoln (Nowak). The pair unexpectedly have a connection and develop a new web series together. As their romantic bond grows stronger, they consider how they project their image online and the way they see each other. **96m/C; DVD.** Andrew Nowak; Megan Baim; Marc Wilkinson; Mike Lopez; Amy Bury; *D:* Marc Wilkinson; *W:* Marc Wilkinson; *C:* Marc Wilkinson; *M:* Tyler Koontz. **VIDEO**

Sunset Song 1/2 **2016 (R)** Director/writer Davies returns to the past of his country in this adaptation of Lewis Grassic Gibbon's novel, a beloved book in the United Kingdom. Deyn plays Chris Guthrie, a farm girl in Aberdeen, who we follow through several trials and tribulations and even generations. It starts when she's young, before World War I, and forced to deal with an abusive father (Mullan). Later in life, she meets and marries a young man (Guthrie) with whom she falls in love, but he goes to war and returns a different person. Davies has a beautiful grasp on how people and countries change with conflict and development. **135m/C; DVD.** Peter Mullan; Agyness Deyn; Mark Bonnar; Stuart Bowman; Ron Donachie; *D:* Terence Davies; *W:* Terence Davies; *C:* Michael McDonough; *M:* Gast Waltzing.

Sunset Strip WOOF! **1991 (R)** A young dancer finds a job in a strip club and competes against the other women there to find the man of her dreams. The women take their jobs very seriously—even attending ballet classes to improve their performances. However, the viewer probably won't take this movie very seriously since it is just another excuse to show women in as little clothing as possible. **95m/C; VHS, DVD.** Jeff Conaway; Michelle Foreman; Shelley Michelle; *D:* Paul G. Volk; *M:* John Gonzalez.

Sunset Strip **1999 (R)** Slice of L.A. music biz life looks at the infamous eponymous strip in the '70s. Several music-industry wannabes try to make it in the industry and with each other in an interconnected storyline and intertwined lives kind of way. Good cast is wasted on a slight script that tries to cover too much ground and seems derivative of better rock and roll movies. **90m/C; VHS, DVD.** Jared Leto; Adam Goldberg; Anna Friel; Nick Stahl; Simon Baker; Rory Cochrane; Tommy Flanagan; Darren E. Burrows; John Randolph; Stephanie Romanov; Mary Lynn Rajskub; Krista Allen; Judy Greer; *D:* Adam Collis; *W:* Russell DeGrazier; Randall Johnson; *C:* Ron Fortunato; *M:* Stewart Copeland.

Sunshine **1999 (R)** Sprawling look at four generations of an assimilated Hungarian-Jewish family covers a lot of time at the expense of cohesiveness and character. Title refers to the health tonic that makes the family fortune and is a pun on the family's original name, Sonnenschein. Fiennes turns up in three roles as the family prospers in Budapest by changing their name to avoid the anti-Semitic society—eventually converting to Catholicism. It will not protect them, however, from the Nazi holocaust and the turbulent postwar period that leads to the Hungarian Revolution of 1956. **180m/C; VHS, DVD.** *CA HU* Ralph Fiennes; Rosemary Harris; Rachel Weisz; Jennifer Ehle; Molly Parker; Deborah Kara Unger; James Frain; William Hurt; John Neville; Miriam Margolyes; Mark Strong; *D:* Istvan Szabo; *W:* Istvan Szabo; Israel Horovitz; *C:* Lajos Koltai; *M:* Maurice Jarre. Genie '99: Film.

Sunshine 1/2 **2007 (R)** The year is 2057, and the sun is dying. A previous mission to reignite it has failed, and the pluckiest, prettiest crew of scientists ever assembled is sent with a massive nuclear bomb to do the job. Of course, technical and human calamities seemingly cobbled from other big-screen space odysseys ensue. Stunning visuals and lots of claustrophobic suspense mix with metaphysical spookiness, but even sci-fi fans who can forgive the deja vu will be tested by the "what-planet-are-you-on?" ending. **107m/C; DVD, Blu-Ray.** *GB US* Cillian Murphy; Chris Evans; Rose Byrne; Michelle Yeoh; Hiroyuki (Henry) Sanada; Clifford Curtis; Troy Garity; Benedict Wong; Mark Strong; *D:* Danny Boyle; *W:* Alex Garland; *C:* Alwin Kuchler; *M:* John Murphy.

The Sunshine Boys **1975 (PG)** Two veteran vaudeville partners, who have shared a love-hate relationship for decades, reunite for a TV special. Adapted by Neil Simon from his play. Matthau was a replacement for Jack Benny, who died before the start of filming. Burns, for his first starring role since "Honolulu" in 1939, won an Oscar. **111m/C; VHS, DVD, Blu-Ray.** George Burns; Walter Matthau; Richard Benjamin; Lee Meredith; F. Murray Abraham; Carol Arthur; Howard Hesseman; *D:* Herbert Ross; *W:* Neil Simon. Oscars '75: Support. Actor (Burns); Golden Globes '76: Actor--Mus./Comedy (Matthau), Film--Mus./Comedy, Support. Actor (Benjamin); Writers Guild '75: Adapt. Screenplay.

The Sunshine Boys **1995** TV version of the Neil Simon play about two old vaudevillians is updated, not necessarily for the better. The feuding duo are a formerly popular 50s TV comedy team whose breakup was not amicable (Think Lewis and Martin. Go ask your folks, we'll wait). They are persuaded to reunite for a special appearance, but the old grudges come back. Suffers by comparison to the original, with Allen and Falk unable to duplicate the chemistry of Burns and Matthau. **90m/C; VHS, DVD.** Woody Allen; Peter Falk; Sarah Jessica Parker; Michael McKean; Liev Schreiber; Edie Falco; Kirk Acevedo; Michael Badalucco; Jennifer Esposito; Whoopi Goldberg; *D:* John Erman; *W:* Neil Simon. **TV**

Sunshine Cleaning 1/2 **2009 (R)** Single mom Rose (Adams) wants a better life for herself and her troubled 7-year-old son

Oscar (Spevack) but poor choices, lousy circumstances, and lousier wages have kept her stuck. That is, till cop Mac (Zhan)?her son's father, now married, and with whom she's having a secret affair—tips her off to the profitability of cleaning up murder and suicide investigation scenes. Rose opens Sunshine Cleaning, enlisting her hapless sister Norah (Blunt) as her partner in not the sunniest of new adventures. They make the most of it while addressing the untidy aspects of their own lives as they scrub up the unspeakable messes. Their father Joe (Arkin) lightens the mood with familiar crusty old man wisecracks, while the quirky interplay between Rose and Norah almost distracts from the gruesome nature of their work. **102m/C; Blu-Ray, On Demand.** Amy Adams; Emily Blunt; Alan Arkin; Jason Spevack; Steve Zahn; Mary Lynn Rajskub; Clifton (Gonzalez) Collins, Jr.; Eric Christian Olsen; Kevin Chapman; ***D:*** Christine Jeffs; ***W:*** Megan Holly; ***C:*** John Toon; ***M:*** Michael Penn.

Sunshine State **2002 (PG-13)** Sayles returns with a tale of developers invading a northern Florida resort island and the effect on the locals. Of the excellent ensemble, a superb Falco is the unsatisfied Marly, who runs a fleabag motel/restaurant, inherited from her blind, retired father (Waite). The Sea-Vue was her parents' dream but not hers. With a few failed relationships and many shots of tequila under her belt, Marly meets architect Jack (Hutton), one of the pack of real estate sharks after her property. Bassett is Desiree, who returns to her neighboring hometown in an attempt to reconcile with her mother (Alice), whose own island dream home was a nightmare for Desiree growing up. Not so much big biz vs. the little people as a coming to terms with life, family and the past. **141m/C; VHS, DVD.** Edie Falco; Angela Bassett; Timothy Hutton; James McDaniel; Mary Steenburgen; Marc Blucas; Jane Alexander; Ralph Waite; Mary Alice; Bill Cobbs; Alex Lewis; Gordon Clapp; Richard Edson; Tom Wright; Perry Lang; Miguel Ferrer; Michael Greyeyes; Alan King; Charlaine Woodard; ***D:*** John Sayles; ***W:*** John Sayles; ***C:*** Patrick Cady; ***M:*** Mason Daring. L.A. Film Critics '02: Support. Actress (Falco).

Sunstorm **2001** Four sisters who've never met unite to find out who killed their father (Keach), who was an important general. When the same people come after the sisters, the stage is set for a ridiculously confused plot and plenty of fight scenes between the sisters and numerous henchmen. Sets out as exploitation, but plays it too seriously and even disappoints in the eye candy department. **94m/C; VHS, DVD.** Stacy Keach; Bo Derek; Geoffrey Lewis; Margaret Scarborough; Ray Raglin; Ron Hale; Rebecca Stauber; Michael Manasseri; ***D:*** Mike Marvin; ***C:*** Steve (Steven) Shaw. **VIDEO**

The Super **1/2 1991 (R)** Pesci stars as a slumlord who faces a prison sentence thanks to his terminal neglect. The option given to him is to live in his own rat hole until he provides reasonable living conditions. This he does, and predictably learns a thing or two about his own greed and the people who suffer as a result of it. Pesci as always gives an animated performance but poor scripting laden with stereotypes and cliches successfully restricts effort. **86m/C; VHS, DVD.** Joe Pesci; Vincent Gardenia; Madolyn Smith; Ruben Blades; Stacey Travis; ***D:*** Rod Daniel; ***C:*** Bruce Surtees.

Super **2010** In writer/director Gunn's dark comedy, everyman Frank D'Arbo (Wilson) becomes an unlikely costumed vigilante, The Crimson Bolt, after his wife (Tyler) falls under the influence of sleazy drug dealer Jacques (Bacon). Frank takes inspiration from TV superhero The Holy Avenger (Fillion) and even acquires his own sidekick, comic book store clerk Libby (Page) a.k.a. Boltie. Things turn violent as Crimson Bolt, with the best intentions if not the skills, fights to save his wife. Wilson and Page shine but the tone and humor are uneven. Wacky, dark, and violent but more of a mere-mortal than superhero result. **96m/C; Blu-Ray, On Demand.** Rainn Wilson; Ellen Page; Liv Tyler; Kevin Bacon; Nathan Fillion; Gregg Henry; Michael Rooker; Andre Royo; William Katt; ***V:*** Rob Zombie; ***D:*** James Gunn; ***W:*** James Gunn; ***C:*** Steve Gainer; ***M:*** Tyler Bates.

Super Bitch **1/2** ***Mafia Junction*** **1973** Nasty, cold, and uncaring woman uses men to keep up her expensive habits, then ruthlessly tosses them aside when she is done. She purposely entangles them in her drug trade and thinks nothing of their deaths. Proving once again that you get what you pay for. **90m/C; VHS, DVD.** Stephanie Beacham; Patricia Hayes; Gareth Thomas; ***D:*** Massimo Dallamano.

Super Buddies **1/2 2013 (G)** Budderball, Mudbud, and the other buddies turn into superheroes for this adventure after they find some mysterious alien rings that give each pup a special power. But a shape-shifting alien bully is after the rings and threatens the planet! **81m/C; DVD, Blu-Ray.** John Ratzenberger; Jason Earles; Trey Loney; ***V:*** Cooper Roth; Jeremy Shinder; Ty Panitz; Colin Hanks; Tim Conway; ***D:*** Robert Vince; ***W:*** Robert Vince; ***M:*** Brahm Wenger. **VIDEO**

Super Capers **WOOF! 2009 (PG)** Excruciatingly juvenile spoof of superhero flicks. Deluded Ed Gruberman is sentenced to a halfway house/training academy for dysfunctional minor superheroes. An evil plot is discovered (it may involve the script) and the wannabes go to work. **98m/C; DVD.** Justin Whalin; Danielle Harris; Michael Rooker; Christine Lakin; Adam West; Ryan McPartlin; Samuel Lloyd; Ray Griggs; ***C:*** Martin Rodenberg; ***M:*** Nathan Lanier.

The Super Cops **1974** Loosely based on the exploits of unorthodox New York City cop partners David Greenberg (Leibman) and Robert Hantz (Selby), nicknamed Batman and Robin, who were successful in taking down drug dealers and other criminals in the Bedford-Stuyvesant ghetto. Fast-paced, deliberately cartoon-like, yet edgy. **93m/C; DVD.** Ron Leibman; David Selby; Sheila Frazier; Pat Hingle; Dan Frazer; Joseph Sirola; ***D:*** Gordon Parks; ***W:*** Lorenzo Semple, Jr.; ***C:*** Richard Kratina; ***M:*** Jerry Fielding.

Super Dark Times **1/2 2017** A moody, dramatic look at how a violent act impacts the lives of teens in the early 1990s New England. Best friends and latchkey kids Zach (Campbell) and Josh (Tahan) spend their time talking about girls, sex, and swearing. They also hang out with classmate Darryl (Talisman) and middle schooler Charlie (Barth). The plot turns dark when they smoke pot for the first time and play with a sword taken from Josh's brother. The resulting tragic death leads to self-destructive emotional fallout. The debut feature by Kevin Phillips deftly explores the vulnerable adolescent male psyche with realism and an unnerving eye. **100m/C; DVD.** Owen Campbell; Charlie Tahan; Elizabeth Cappuccino; Max Talisman; Sawyer Barth; ***D:*** Kevin Phillips; ***W:*** Ben Collins; Luke Piotrowski; ***C:*** Eli Born; ***M:*** Ben Frost.

Super 8 **1/2 2011 (PG-13)** Writer/director Abrams pays homage to executive producer Steven Spielberg's early sci fi films. Set in 1979, a group of middle school boys led by Joe Lamb (Courtney) along with new girl/love interest Alice Dainard (Fanning) are making a Super 8 zombie movie when a train gets derailed (in spectacular special-effects fashion) releasing some unusual freight. Suddenly all manner of oddities ensue about town, most disturbing is the disappearance of people and animals. The group is forced to unravel the mystery before it consumes the entire community. There's a lot to like here but it doesn't make you fall in love. Definitely stick around for the kids' humorous zombie video during the end credits. **112m/C; DVD, Blu-Ray.** Kyle Chandler; Elle Fanning; Ron Eldard; Noah Emmerich; Amanda (A.J.) Michalka; Riley Griffiths; Joel Courtney; ***D:*** J.J. (Jeffrey) Abrams; ***W:*** J.J. (Jeffrey) Abrams; ***C:*** Larry Fong; ***M:*** Michael Giacchino.

Super Eruption **WOOF! 2011** A super-sized volcano lying dormant under Yellowstone National Park suddenly becomes active, spewing lava and causing increasing destruction unless volcanologist Dr. Kate Brooks and ranger Charlie Young can stop it. But Kate's plan involves a plot point that's even more ridiculous (and less fun) than is usual in even a Syfy Channel flick. **89m/C; DVD.** Juliet Aubrey; Richard Burgi; MyAnna Buring; Emma Davies; ***D:*** Matt Codd; ***W:*** Rafael Jordan; ***C:*** Martin Chichov; ***M:*** Joseph Conlan. **CABLE**

Super Fuzz **1/2** ***Supersnooper*** **1981 (PG)** Rookie policeman develops super powers after being accidentally exposed to radiation. Somewhat ineptly, he uses his abilities to combat crime. Somewhat ineptly acted, written, and directed as well. **97m/C; VHS, DVD.** Terence Hill; Joanne Dru; Ernest Borgnine; ***D:*** Sergio Corbucci; ***W:*** Sergio Corbucci.

Super Hybrid **1/2** ***Hybrid*** **2010 (PG-13)** Killer car. A car is brought into a Chicago police impound garage after an accident and the mechanics on-duty are the first to discover that it can outwit and outrun the locals. And then eat them. **94m/C; DVD, Blu-Ray.** Oded Fehr; Ryan Kennedy; Shannon Beckner; Melanie Papalia; Adrien Dorval; ***D:*** Eric Valette; ***W:*** Benjamin Carr; ***C:*** John R. Leonetti; ***M:*** Martin Tillman; Thomas Schobel.

Super Mario Bros. **1/2 1993 (PG)** $42 million adventure fantasy based on the popular Nintendo video game. The brothers are in hot pursuit of the Princess Daisy who's been kidnapped by evil slimebucket Hopper and taken to Dinohattan, a fungi-infested, garbage-strewn, rat-hole version of Manhattan. Hopper will amuse the adults, doing a gleeful reptilian version of Frank Booth from "Blue Velvet." Hoskins and Leguizamo act gamely in broad Nintendo style, enthusiastically partaking in high-tech wizardry and the many gags. Hits bullseye of target audience—elementary and junior high kids—with frenetic pace, gaudy special effects, oversized sets, and animatronic monsters. **104m/C; VHS, DVD.** Bob Hoskins; John Leguizamo; Samantha Mathis; Fisher Stevens; Richard Edson; Dana Kaminsky; Dennis Hopper; Fiona Shaw; Mojo Nixon; Lance Henriksen; ***D:*** Rocky Morton; Annabel Jankel; ***W:*** Edward Solomon; Parker Bennett; Terry Runte; ***M:*** Alan Silvestri.

Super Size Me **2004** Director Spurlock becomes a human guinea pig in his cautionary tale/experiment into the apparently very dangerous world of fast food. Vowing to eat three meals a day at McDonald's for a full 30 days, Spurlock also had a strict "always say yes" policy when asked by a Mickey D's employee if he wanted to super size. The result was a 30-pound weight gain, severely declining health, and a film so controversial it caused McDonald's to stop their super size promotion months after the film debuted at the Sundance Film Festival. Gross-out doc mixes comedy with concern. Watching this one might even have die hard fast food freaks munching salad. Includes interviews with ice cream heir John Robbins, former surgeon general David Sacher, and Subway poster-boy Jared. **98m/C; DVD.** ***D:*** Morgan Spurlock; ***W:*** Morgan Spurlock; ***C:*** Scott Ambrozy; ***M:*** Steve Horowitz; Michael Parrish.

Super Size Me 2: Holy Chicken! **1/2 2019 (PG-13)** The sequel to the fast food documentary finds director-star Spurlock looking at the chicken sandwich industry. Instead of subjecting himself to a fast food diet as in the original, Spurlock chronicles his plans for opening his own chicken-themed fast food franchise. Totally transparent about ingredients and intentions, Spurlock not only explores the fast food chicken industry and the related chicken farming industry but also issues of human behavior related to marketing manipulation and consumption such as the words used to sell food to people. A capable follow-up even with the unsettling content. **93m/C; DVD.** Morgan Spurlock; ***D:*** Morgan Spurlock; Jeremy Chilnick; ***W:*** Morgan Spurlock; ***C:*** David Vlasits; ***M:*** Jeff Meegan; David Tobin.

Super Storm **WOOF!** ***Mega Cyclone; Space Twister*** **2012** No matter what it's called, this is a stinky, generic SyFy Channel disaster flick. Changes on the planet Jupiter are about to cause Earth's annihilation because of mega-cyclones and electrical storms. But instead of some super-scientist coming to the rescue, a couple of small town teens (and a rocket-building dad) are our planet's only hope! **89m/C; DVD, Blu-Ray.** David Sutcliffe; Mitch Pileggi; Brett Dier; Luisa D'Oliveira; Leah Cairns; Erica Cerra; ***D:*** Sheldon Wilson; ***W:*** David Ray; ***C:*** Neil Cervin; ***M:*** Michael Neilson. **CABLE**

Super Sucker **2003 (R)** Daniels wrote, directed, and starred in this sometimes sleazy and intermittently funny comedy. Fred Barlow (Daniels) works for Johnson City Super Sucker Vacuums as a salesman, only his career is in trouble. The company has launched a sales contest to see (essentially) who will remain employed and who will get the boot. Fred is despondent until he discovers his wife using one of the vacuum's attachments for personal satisfaction that has nothing to do with household cleaning. Suddenly Fred has the proper gimmick to sell the vacuum to the city's lonely housewives. **95m/C; VHS, DVD.** Jeff Daniels; Matt Letscher; Harve Presnell; Guy Sanville; Sandra Birch; John Seibert; Kate Peckham; Dawn Wells; ***D:*** Jeff Daniels; ***W:*** Jeff Daniels; ***C:*** Richard Brauer.

Super Troopers **1/2** ***Broken Lizard's Super Troopers*** **2001 (R)** Vermont is the setting for this snobs vs. slobs comedy that pits wacky state troopers facing a budget-forced shutdown against the local cops, who curry favor with the politicians. Plot involving a jurisdictional fight over a murder and a drug bust only occassionally interferes with the drug, sex, and gross-out humor that carries the pic to a satisfying conclusion. Cox is hilarious as the barely-in-control commander of the station, while Von Bargen does a great job as his nemesis. **100m/C; VHS, DVD, Blu-Ray, UMD.** Jay Chandrasekhar; Kevin Heffernan; Steve Lemme; Paul Soter; Erik Stolhanske; Brian Cox; Daniel von Bargen; Marisa Coughlan; Michael Weaver; Jim Gaffigan; John Bedford Lloyd; Lynda Carter; ***D:*** Jay Chandrasekhar; ***W:*** Jay Chandrasekhar; Kevin Heffernan; Steve Lemme; Paul Soter; Erik Stolhanske; ***C:*** Joaquin Baca-Asay.

Super Troopers 2 ***Broken Lizard's Super Troopers 2*** **2018 (R)** The unfocused, mostly unfunny sequel to the popular Broken Lizard film that essentially rehashes the first film's plot, punchlines, and dynamics. In southern Canada, two law enforcements teams—a set of American state troopers and three Canadian Mounties—duel to see who can break up a mysterious local smuggling ring. Along the way, the officers are involved in escapades involving traffic stops and stand-offs. Former rookie Rabbit (Stolhanske) also seems to find love with sultry Canadian Genevieve (Chirqui). While the original was goofy and this film has its humorous moments, the follow-up lacks charm and is generally less appealing. **99m/C; DVD, Blu-Ray, Streaming.** Jay Chandrasekhar; Kevin Heffernan; Steve Lemme; Paul Soter; Erik Stolhanske; ***D:*** Jay Chandrasekhar; ***W:*** Jay Chandrasekhar; Kevin Heffernan; Steve Lemme; Paul Soter; Erik Stolhanske; ***C:*** Joe Collins; ***M:*** Eagles of Death Metal.

Superargo ***Il Re Dei Criminali; Superargo the Giant; The King of Criminals*** **1967** A wrestler becomes a superhero with psychic powers and a bulletproof leotard, fighting a madman who is turning athletes into robots. Successful Italian hero who wouldn't last two minutes in the ring with Batman. **95m/C; VHS, DVD.** ***IT SP*** Guy Madison; Ken Wood; Liz Barrett; Diana Loris; ***D:*** Paul Maxwell.

Superbabies: Baby Geniuses 2 **WOOF! 2004 (PG)** A super stupid waste of time. The who cares follow-up to the 1999 release pits evil German media mogul Biscane (Oscar-winner Voight, who once had a real career) against four toddlers who have a super ability to communicate with each other via really bad dubbing and Kahuna (the Fitzgerald triplets), who only looks like a 7-year-old (don't ask). Biscane's diabolical plan is to control the minds of children by brainwashing them via subliminal messages through the TV. Wait, hasn't that already been done? Baio and Angel pop in as the owners of an L.A. daycare center. **90m/C; VHS, DVD.** ***GE GB*** Jon Voight; Scott Baio; Vanessa Angel; Peter Wingfield; Justin Chatwin; Gerry Fitzgerald; Leo Fitzgerald; Myles Fitzgerald; Skyler Shaye; Max Iles; Michael Iles; Jared Scheideman; Jordan Scheideman; Maia Bastidas; Keana Bastidas; Joshua Lockhart; Maxwell Lockhart; ***D:*** Bob (Benjamin) Clark; ***W:*** Gregory Poppen; ***C:*** Maher Maleh; ***M:*** Paul Zaza; Helmut Zerlett.

Superbad **1/2 2007 (R)** Seth (Hill) and Evan (Cera) are crude, socially inept, and sex-obsessed, like most teenage boys. When the girls they have crushes on ask them to buy booze for a graduation party, Seth sees this as their last chance to woo their beloveds the best way he knows how—by getting them drunk. Roping their fake-ID wielding friend Fogell (Mintz-Plasse) into Seth's scheme, their night becomes an odyssey of cops, robbers, crazed bums, cokeheads, violent thugs, party-crashing losers, vomit, and facing fears about their futures. Unapologetically teems with both raunch and heart. Hill and Cera shine as the hapless leads (named after writers Rogan and Goldberg, who penned the original version of the project while in junior high), but newcomer Mintz-Plasse steals every scene as the hopeless geek who re-names himself "McLovin." **112m/C; DVD, Blu-Ray.** Jonah Hill; Michael Cera; Bill Hader; Seth Rogen; Christopher Mintz-Plasse; Aviva; Stacy Edwards; Kevin Corrigan; Emma Stone; Martha MacIsaac; ***D:*** Greg Mottola; ***W:*** Seth Rogen; Greg Mottola; Evan Goldberg; ***C:*** Russ T. Alsobrook; ***M:*** Lyle Workman.

Superbug Super Agent 1/2 **1976** Dodo, the wonder car puts the brakes on crime in this silly action-adventure tale. A lemon in a lot full of Herbies. **90m/C; VHS, DVD.** *GE* Robert Mark; Heidi Hansen; George Goodman; ***D:*** Rudolf Zehetgruber; ***W:*** Rudolf Zehetgruber; ***C:*** Hannes Staudinger; ***M:*** Jurgen Elert.

Superchick WOOF! 1971 (R) Mild-mannered stewardess by day, sexy blonde with karate blackbelt by night. In addition to stopping a skyjacking she regularly makes love to men around the world. A superbomb that never gets off the ground. **94m/C; VHS, DVD.** Joyce Jillson; Louis Quinn; Thomas Reardon; Uschi Digart; ***D:*** Ed Forsyth; ***W:*** Gary Crutcher; ***C:*** Paul Hipp; ***M:*** Allan Alper.

Supercop 1/2 *Police Story 3: Supercop* **1992 (R)** Super Hong Kong cop Kevin Chan (Chan) heads to China to assist the authorities in cracking an international drug ring. He's partnered with disciplined-but-beautiful Director Yang (Yeoh), who's also a terrific fighter, and the duo go undercover (as a married couple) to infiltrate the operation, which takes them to a Malaysian resort. Then Chan's girlfriend shows up, blowing their cover. Lots of action-packed fighting and wild chases. The 1996 American release loses about a half-hour of run time from the original. Dubbed from Cantonese. **93m/C; VHS, DVD, Blu-Ray.** *CH* Jackie Chan; Michelle Yeoh; Maggie Cheung; Kenneth Tsang; Yuen Wah; ***D:*** Stanley Tong; ***W:*** Edward Tang; Fibe Ma; Lee Wai Yee; ***C:*** Ardy Lam; ***M:*** Joel McNeely.

Supercop 2 *Police Story 3, Part 2* **1993 (R)** Rising star Inspector Jessica Yang (Yeoh) has her life disrupted when her boyfriend David is dishonorably discharged from the police force and leaves town. Several months later, Jessica is assigned to stop a crime ring that turns out to be headed by David. Chan has a brief cameo (in drag). **94m/C; VHS, DVD.** *CH* Michelle Yeoh; Yukari Oshima; Eric Tsang; Rongguang Yu; Athene Chu; Siu-wong Fan; Jackie Chan; Emile Chau; Chu Yan; ***D:*** Stanley Tong; ***W:*** Stanley Tong; Mok Tang Han; Sui Lai Kang.

Supercross: The Movie 1/2 **2005 (PG-13)** In case you are unaware, supercross is an offshoot of motocross racing but is held on indoor tracks equipped with gravity-defying jumps. Brothers KC (Howey) and Trip (Vogel) want to become champs but, for now, they are underdogs. KC has to play second bike to corporate sponsor star Rowdy (Tatum), so Trip decides he'd be better off going it alone and gets his own sponsor, Earl Cole (Patrick, the only one with actual acting ability). Richardson and Bush are the chicks the brothers get involved with. The plot may be clunky but director Boyum cranks up the racing thrills and noise level. **98m/C; DVD, Blu-Ray.** Mike Vogel; Channing Tatum; J.D. Pardo; Robert Carradine; Steve Howey; Cameron Richardson; Sophia Buh; Aaron Carter; Carolina Garcia; Ryan Locke; ***D:*** Steve Boyum; ***W:*** Ken Solarz; Bart Baker; ***C:*** William Wages.

Superdad **1973 (G)** A middle-aged parent is determined to bridge the generation gap by trying his hand at various teenage activities. Disney family fare that's about as complicated as a TV commercial. The adolescents are two-dimensional throwbacks to the fun-loving '50s. **94m/C; VHS, DVD, Streaming.** Bob Crane; Kurt Russell; Joe Flynn; Barbara Rush; Kathleen (Kathy) Cody; Dick Van Patten; ***D:*** Vincent McEveety; ***M:*** Buddy (Norman Dale) Baker.

SuperFire 1/2 **2002 (PG-13)** Hackneyed heroes story. Jim Merrick (Sweeney) is a disgraced fire-fighter tanker pilot whose mistakes cost the lives of 12 smokejumpers. So no one is ready to listen when Jim says an enormous superfire is forming that will obliterate the local community. Then the wildfire gets out of control and it's up to Jim to save the day. **99m/C; VHS, DVD.** D.B. Sweeney; Wes Studi; Chad E. Donella; Diane Farr; Ellen Muth; Katrina Hobbs; ***D:*** Steven Quale; ***W:*** Michael Vickerman; ***C:*** William Wages. **TV**

Superfly 1/2 **1972 (R)** Controversial upon release, pioneering blaxploitation has Harlem dope dealer finding trouble with gangs and police as he attempts to establish retirement fund from one last deal. Excellent period tunes by Curtis Mayfield. Two lesser sequels. **98m/C; VHS, DVD, Blu-Ray.** Ron O'Neal; Carl Lee; Sheila Frazier; Julius W. Harris; Charles McGregor; ***D:*** Gordon Parks, Jr.; ***W:*** Phillip Fenty; ***C:*** James Signorelli; ***M:*** Curtis Mayfield.

SuperFly **2018 (R)** In this remake of the 1972 Blaxploitation flick, Youngblood Priest and his gang plan to pull off one last heist against a Mexican cartel. With more flash than substance, it feels more like a music video than a crime drama, much less any sort of social statement. But if you don't mind a tired plot and a disjointed narrative as long as the sets and people are stylish, you'll be entertained. **116m/C; DVD, Blu-Ray.** Trevor Jackson; Jason Mitchell; Michael K(enneth) Williams; Lex Scott Davis; Jennifer (Jenny) Morrison; ***D:*** Director X.; ***W:*** Alex Tse; ***C:*** Amir M. Mokri; ***M:*** Josh Atchley.

Supergirl 1/2 **1984 (PG)** Big-budget bomb in which Slater made her debut and nearly killed her career, with the help of Kryptonite. Unexciting and unsophisticated story of a young woman, cousin to Superman, with super powers, based on the comic book series. She's in pursuit of a magic paperweight, but an evil sorceress wants it too. Dunaway is a terrifically vile villainess with awesome black magic powers. Slater is great to look at, but is much better in almost any other film. **114m/C; VHS, DVD, Blu-Ray.** *GB* Faye Dunaway; Helen Slater; Peter O'Toole; Mia Farrow; Brenda Vaccaro; Marc McClure; Simon Ward; Hart Bochner; Maureen Teefy; David Healy; Matt Frewer; ***D:*** Jeannot Szwarc; ***W:*** David Odell; ***C:*** Alan Hume; ***M:*** Jerry Goldsmith.

SuperGuy: Behind the Cape 1/2 **2002** Leaping into a thin plot with a single bound, this comic-book farce exposes the increasingly mortal superhero SuperGuy who fights having his super-image tarnished as humanlike weaknesses are revealed and his once-adoring fans afford him no pity. **74m/C; VHS, DVD.** Charles Dierkop; Katherine Victor; Mark Teague; Jan Garrett; Christopher Fey; Elizabeth Jaeger-Rydall; Marcello Paz-Pullam; Tim Peyton; Peter Stacker; David Anthony Hernandez; ***D:*** Bill Lae; ***C:*** Mike Ziemkowski. **VIDEO**

Superhero Movie **2008 (PG-13)** Holy send-up, Batman! In this swing at blockbuster superhero flicks, weakling Rick Riker (likable teen dream Bell) is bitten by a genetically altered dragonfly and transforms into a dragonfly superhero, possessing all manner of super powers—except he can't fly. Dragonfly then has a showdown with power-crazed CEO-turned-villainous-arch enemy Hourglass (McDonald). Strings together the usual lazy jabs at pop-culture targets and D-list cameos, the irony of which will be lost on the target teenybopper audience. Another waste of time and effort. **86m/C; DVD, Blu-Ray.** Drake Bell; Marion Ross; Sara Paxton; Christopher McDonald; Leslie Nielsen; Ryan Hansen; ***C:*** Thomas Ackerman; ***M:*** James L. Venable.

Superheroes **2007** Suffering from post-traumatic stress disorder, Iraqi War vet Ben Patchett (Mihok) can no longer cope with his family and self-medicates as he struggles to get through each day. Young and earnest videographer Nick Jones (Clark) is taping a VA outpatient group Ben is attending. They form a tentative friendship and Nick agrees to accompany Ben on a change-of-pace country retreat the vet hopes will offer him a little peace. **87m/C; DVD.** Dash Mihok; Spencer Treat Clark; Nancy Giles; Margo Martindale; Kelly McAndrew; ***D:*** Alan Brown; ***W:*** Alan Brown; ***C:*** Derek McKane; ***M:*** Paul Cantelon.

Superman: The Movie 1/2 **1978 (PG)** The DC Comics legend comes alive in this wonderfully entertaining saga of Superman's life from a baby on the doomed planet Krypton (with Brando as Supe's dad) to Earth's own Man of Steel (a chiseled Reeve). Hackman and Beatty pair marvelously as super criminal Lex Luthor and his bumbling sidekick Otis, while Kidder is an intelligent Lois Lane. Award-winning special effects and a script that doesn't take itself too seriously make this great fun. Followed by three sequels. **152m/C; VHS, DVD, Blu-Ray, HD-DVD.** Christopher Reeve; Margot Kidder; Marlon Brando; Gene Hackman; Glenn Ford; Susannah York; Ned Beatty; Valerie Perrine; Jackie Cooper; Marc McClure; Trevor Howard; Sarah Douglas; Terence Stamp; Jack O'Halloran; Phyllis Thaxter; ***D:*** Richard Donner; ***W:*** Mario Puzo; Robert Benton; David Newman; ***C:*** Geoffrey Unsworth; ***M:*** John Williams. Oscars '78: Visual FX; Natl. Film Reg. '17.

Superman 2 **1980 (PG)** The sequel to "the movie" about the Man of Steel. This time, he has his hands full with three super-powered villains from his home planet of Krypton. The romance between reporter Lois Lane and our superhero is made believable and the story line has more pace to it than the original. A sequel that often equals the first film—leave it to Superman to pull off the impossible. **128m/C; VHS, DVD, Blu-Ray, HD-DVD.** Christopher Reeve; Margot Kidder; Gene Hackman; Ned Beatty; Jackie Cooper; Sarah Douglas; Jack O'Halloran; Susannah York; Marc McClure; Terence Stamp; Valerie Perrine; E.G. Marshall; ***D:*** Richard Lester; ***W:*** Mario Puzo; David Newman; ***C:*** Robert Paynter; ***M:*** John Williams.

Superman 3 **1983 (PG)** Villainous businessman Ross Webster (Vaughn) tries to conquer Superman (Reeve) via the expertise of bumbling computer expert Gus Gorman (Pryor) and the judicious use of an artificial form of Kryptonite. Superman explores his darker side after undergoing transformation into sleaze ball. Promising satiric start ultimately defeated by uneven story and direction and boring physical comedy. Notable is the absence of Lois Lane as a main character, instead the big guy takes up with former flame Lana Lang (O'Toole). Followed by "Superman 4." **123m/C; VHS, DVD.** Christopher Reeve; Richard Pryor; Pamela Stephenson; Annette O'Toole; Jackie Cooper; Margot Kidder; Marc McClure; Annie Ross; Robert Vaughn; ***D:*** Richard Lester; ***W:*** David Newman; ***C:*** Robert Paynter; ***M:*** John Williams.

Superman 4: The Quest for Peace **1987 (PG)** The third sequel, in which the Man of Steel endeavors to rid the world of nuclear weapons, thereby pitting himself against nuclear-entrepreneur Lex Luthor and his superpowered creation, Nuclear Man. Special effects are dime-store quality and it appears that someone may have walked off with parts of the plot. Reeve deserves credit for remaining true to character through four films. **90m/C; VHS, DVD.** Christopher Reeve; Gene Hackman; Jon Cryer; Marc McClure; Margot Kidder; Mariel Hemingway; Sam Wanamaker; ***V:*** Susannah York; ***D:*** Sidney J. Furie; ***W:*** Mark Rosenthal; ***M:*** John Williams.

Superman Returns 1/2 **2006 (PG-13)** Over-hyped and overlong return of the Man of Steel, last seen on the big screen in 1987's "Superman IV." Christopher Reeve look-alike Routh fills out the spandex but lacks a certain superhero charm as Supes returns to Earth five years after the events of "Superman 2" (like everyone else, they pretend that "III" and "IV" never happened). Clark Kent heads back to the "Daily Planet" where he discovers that Lois (a shallow Bosworth) is on an anti-Superman rant and also has a son and a fiance. Lex Luthor (Spacey) wants to take over the world—again. Superman comes to the rescue—again. Singer plays the story straight and there's not a lot of gee-whiz joy to be found. **140m/C; DVD, Blu-Ray, HD-DVD.** Brandon Routh; Kate (Catherine) Bosworth; Kevin Spacey; James Marsden; Eva Marie Saint; Parker Posey; Frank Langella; Sam Huntington; Kal Penn; Noel Neill; Jack Larson; Marlon Brando; Tristan Lake Leabu; David Fabrizio; ***D:*** Bryan Singer; ***W:*** Bryan Singer; Michael Dougherty; Daniel P. "Dan" Harris; ***C:*** Newton Thomas (Tom) Sigel; ***M:*** John Ottman.

Superman: Unbound **2013 (PG-13)** Animated adaptation of the 'Superman: Brainiac' graphic novel in which Brainiac kidnaps the city of Kandor. **75m/C; DVD, Blu-Ray, Streaming.** Diedrich Bader; ***V:*** Matt Bomer; Stana Katic; John Noble; Molly C. Quinn; ***D:*** James Tucker; ***W:*** Bob Goodman; ***M:*** Kevin Kliesch. **VIDEO**

Supernatural 1/2 **1933** Roma (Lombard) falls prey to a phony medium (Dinehart) who promises to call up the spirit of her recently murdered twin brother. At the same moment of the seance a murderess dies in the electric chair and her body is used in Dr. Houston's (Warner) life-after-death experiment. Too bad Roma becomes possessed by the woman's evil spirit. Now the doctor and Roma's fiance (Scott) must undo the curse. A hokey B-grade movie disliked by Lombard. **78m/B; DVD, Blu-Ray.** Carole Lombard; Randolph Scott; H.B. Warner; Alan Dinehart; Vivienne Osborne; Beryl Mercer; William Farnum; Willard Robertson; ***D:*** Victor Halperin; ***W:*** Harvey Thew; Brian Marlow; ***C:*** Arthur Martinelli.

Supernova 1/2 **1999 (PG-13)** This one got stuck on the studio shelf for awhile and didn't improve with age. In fact, director Walter Hill was so incensed over studio re-editing that he removed his name, leaving the pseud. "Thomas Lee" to grace this space mishmash. Nick Vanzant (Spader) is stuck piloting a 22nd-century medical vessel after the captain (Forster) is killed. The craft receives a distress call and makes the mistake of rescuing Karl (Facinelli), an odd duck who proves to be very dangerous. You'll wonder what got left on the cutting-room floor. **91m/C; VHS, DVD, Blu-Ray.** James Spader; Angela Bassett; Robin Tunney; Peter Facinelli; Lou Diamond Phillips; Wilson Cruz; Robert Forster; ***D:*** Walter Hill; ***W:*** David Campbell Wilson; ***C:*** Lloyd Ahern, II; ***M:*** David Williams.

Supernova **2005** Ill-conceived cable sci-fi disaster movie about an astrophysicist who discovers the sun will shortly be using the Earth for target practice with fireballs. It's a common cliche that low-budget sci-fi movies have horribly inaccurate science, but few take it to the lows this one does. **172m/C; DVD, Blu-Ray.** *SA US* Luke Perry; Tia Carrere; Peter Fonda; Clemency Burton-Hill; Emma Samms; ***D:*** John Harrison; ***W:*** Steven H. Berman; Don Opper; ***C:*** Frank Perl; Michael Swan; ***M:*** Irwin Fisch. **CABLE**

Supernova WOOF! *2012: Supernova* **2009** You don't really expect scientific accuracy in a cheesy sci-fi flick, but c'mon! Fires in the vacuum of outer space?! And that's just some of the egregious crapola foisted on unsuspecting viewers in this cheapie that suffers from lame plot, acting, and CGI. An exploding star is going to destroy the Earth unless an astrophysicist and two fellow scientists can come up with a way to save the planet. **90m/C; DVD.** Brian Krause; Heather McComb; Najarra Townsend; Londale Theus; ***D:*** Anthony Fankhauser; ***W:*** Anthony Fankhauser; Jon Macy; ***C:*** Mark Atkins; ***M:*** Chris Ridenhour. **VIDEO**

Supersonic Man WOOF! 1978 (PG) Incoherent shoestring-budget Superman spoof with a masked hero fighting to save the world from the evil intentions of a mad scientist. **85m/C; VHS, DVD.** *SP* Michael Coby; Cameron Mitchell; Diana Polakov; ***D:*** J(uan) Piquer Simon.

Superstar **1999 (PG-13)** Yet another SNL skit tries to stretch to feature film length and remain funny. Don't these people ever give up?! What's next? "Weekend Update: The Movie?" This time producer Lorne Michaels showcases klutzy Catholic schoolgirl Mary Katherine Gallagher (Shannon) as she tries to win a school talent contest and a kiss from the campus hunk (Ferrell). Of course, it's really about her strange armpit sniffing technique and panty-flashing behavior. The material doesn't translate well to movie length (shocking!), and the "teenagers" look like they're about 20 years late for homeroom. There are some funny bits, however, and if you like the character on the show you'll probably like the movie. Warning: There are scenes where Ms. Gallagher french kisses a tree, which sounds a lot funnier than it actually is. **82m/C; VHS, DVD.** Molly Shannon; Will Ferrell; Elaine Hendrix; Glynis Johns; Mark McKinney; Harland Williams; Emmy Laybourne; ***D:*** Bruce McCulloch; ***W:*** Steve Koren; ***C:*** Walt Lloyd; ***M:*** Michael Gore.

Superstar: The Life and Times of Andy Warhol **1990** Even if you didn't grok Andy's 'pop' artwork and self-created celebrity persona, this ironic, kinetic, oft-rollicking documentary paints a vivid picture of the wild era he inspired and exploited. Interviewees range from Warhol cohorts like Dennis Hopper to proud executives at the Campbell Soup plant. One highlight: a Warhol guest shot on "The Love Boat." **87m/C; VHS, DVD.** Tom Wolfe; Sylvia Miles; David Hockney; Taylor Mead; Dennis Hopper; Viva; Allen Ginsberg; Ultra Violet; Paul Morrissey; Sally Kirkland; Fran Lebowitz; Lou Reed; Shelley Winters; Holly Woodlawn; ***D:*** Chuck Workman; ***W:*** Chuck Workman; ***C:*** Burleigh Wartes.

Superstition 1/2 *The Witch* **1982** A reverend and his family move into a vacant house despite warnings about a curse from the townsfolk. Some people never learn. **85m/C; VHS, DVD, Blu-Ray.** James Houghton; Albert Salmi; Lynn Carlin; ***D:*** James Robertson.

Supervixens *Russ Meyer's SuperVixens; SuperVixens Eruption; Vixens* **1975** True to Meyer's low-rent exploitation film canon, this wild tale is filled with characteristic Amazons, sex and violence. A gas station attendant is framed for the grisly murder of his girlfriend and hustles out of town, meeting a succession of well-endowed women during his travels. As if it needed further problems, it's hampered by a tasteless storyline and incoherent writing. **105m/C; VHS, DVD.** Shari Eubank; Charles Napier; Uschi Digart; Charles Pitts; Henry Rowland; Sharon Kelly; Haji; ***D:*** Russ Meyer; ***W:*** Russ Meyer; ***C:*** Russ Meyer; ***M:*** William Loose.

Support the Girls 1/2 **2018 (R)** Regina Hall won the New York Film Critics Circle award for best actress as the general manager of a Chili's-meets-Hooters restaurant. It's funny, yes, but not in a cheap, slapstick, boob-centric way. Taking place over a single day, this hidden gem showcases Hall's character as a professional, intelligent, and protective woman at the end of her rope, a leader dealing with the everyday headaches of work and of working within the patriarchy. **93m/C; DVD, Blu-Ray.** Regina Hall; Haley Lu Richardson; Dylan Gelula; Zoe Graham; Ann McCaskey; ***D:*** Andrew Bujalski; ***W:*** Andrew Bujalski; ***C:*** Matthias Grunsky.

Support Your Local Gunfighter **1971 (G)** Garner plays a western con man with his tongue firmly in his cheek. He comes to the small town of Purgatory and is thought to be a notorious gunfighter. He decides to go with the mistaken identity and use it to his profitable advantage. Elam is his bumbling sidekick and Pleshette the love interest. A delightful, deliberately cliche-filled western. A follow-up, not a sequel, to "Support Your Local Sheriff" (1969). **92m/C; VHS, DVD, Blu-Ray.** James Garner; Jack Elam; Suzanne Pleshette; Harry (Henry) Morgan; Dub Taylor; John Dehner; Joan Blondell; Ellen Corby; Henry Jones; ***D:*** Burt Kennedy; ***W:*** James Edward Grant; ***C:*** Harry Stradling, Jr.; ***M:*** Jack Elliott; Allyn Ferguson.

Support Your Local Sheriff 1/2 **1969 (G)** Amiable, irreverent western spoof with more than its fair share of laughs. When a stranger stumbles into a gold rush town, he winds up becoming sheriff. Garner is perfect as the deadpan sheriff, particularly in the scene where he convinces Dern to remain in jail, in spite of the lack of bars. Neatly subverts every western cliche it encounters, yet keeps respect for formula western. Followed by "Support Your Local Gunfighter." **92m/C; VHS, DVD, Blu-Ray.** James Garner; Joan Hackett; Walter Brennan; Bruce Dern; Jack Elam; Harry (Henry) Morgan; ***D:*** Burt Kennedy; ***W:*** William Bowers; ***C:*** Harry Stradling, Jr.

Supporting Characters 1/2 **2013** Nick (Karpovsky) and Darryl (Lowe, who also co-wrote) are best friends who also work together, a recipe for indie movie disaster. The New York City editors are hired to rescue a director's (Corrigan) failed project as he's thrown in the towel. The project threatens to take both men down, damaging their friendship and even impacting their relationships. Nick is tempted to leave his fiancée (Takal) for the film's ingénue (Kebbel) and Darryl struggles with his girlfriend (Diaz). The cast is engaging and likeable, offering a clever, funny take on modern life for twenty-somethings in the Big Apple. **87m/C; Streaming.** Alex Karpovsky; Tarik Lowe; Arielle Kebbel; Melonie Diaz; Kevin Corrigan; Lena Dunham; ***D:*** Daniel Schechter; ***W:*** Tarik Lowe; Daniel Schechter; ***C:*** Richard P. Ulivella; ***M:*** Jordan Galland.

Suppose They Gave a War and Nobody Came? 1/2 *War Games* **1970 (G)** A small Southern town battles with a local army base in this entertaining but wandering satire. The different acting styles used as the producers wavered on making this a comedy or drama were more at war with one another than the characters involved. **113m/C; VHS, DVD, Blu-Ray.** Tony Curtis; Brian Keith; Ernest Borgnine; Suzanne Pleshette; Ivan Dixon; Bradford Dillman; Don Ameche; ***D:*** Hy Averback; ***W:*** Don McGuire.

Supreme Sanction **1999 (R)** An assassin (Swanson) working for a covert government agency decides not to kill the journalist who's threatening to expose the corrupt organization that trained her. This doesn't please her bosses and they mark her for death. **95m/C; VHS, DVD.** Michael Madsen; Kristy Swanson; David Dukes; Donald Adeosun Faison; Tommy (Tiny) Lister; Ron Perlman; ***D:*** John Terlesky; ***W:*** John Terlesky. **VIDEO**

Sure Fire **1990** Wes (Blair) is a mercurial entrepreneur who thinks he has found the financial ticket to paradise with his vacation home scheme. Much to the chagrin of his wife Ellen (Dezina), he refuses to let anything stand in the way of his sure-fire fortune, even his family. Wes develops a little self-control as he realizes he's beginning to flake out, but it may be too late. Director Jost has put together a surprisingly unpretentious film with a virtually no-name cast, its plot speaking volumes on the American condition while unfolding in the bleak Utah desert. **86m/C; VHS, DVD.** Tom Blair; Kristi Hager; Robert Ernst; Kate Dezina; Phillip R. Brown; ***D:*** Jon Jost; ***W:*** Jon Jost.

The Sure Thing **1985 (PG-13)** College students who don't like each other end up travelling to California together, and of course, falling in love. Charming performances make up for predictability. Can't-miss director (and ex-Meathead) Reiner's second direct hit at the boxoffice. **94m/C; VHS, DVD, Blu-Ray.** John Cusack; Daphne Zuniga; Anthony Edwards; Boyd Gaines; Lisa Jane Persky; Viveca Lindfors; Nicolette Sheridan; Tim Robbins; ***D:*** Rob Reiner; ***W:*** Jonathan Roberts; Steven L. Bloom; ***C:*** Robert Elswit; ***M:*** Tom Scott.

Surf Nazis Must Die **1987** A piece of deliberate camp in the Troma mold, about a group of psychotic neo-Nazi surfers taking over the beaches of California in the wake of a devastating earthquake. Tongue-in-cheek, tasteless and cheap, but intentionally so. **83m/C; VHS, DVD.** Barry Brenner; Gail Neely; Michael Sonye; Dawn Wildsmith; Tom Shell; Bobbie Bresee; ***D:*** Peter George; ***W:*** John Ayre; ***C:*** Rolf Kestermann; ***M:*** Jon McCallum.

Surf Ninjas 1/2 *Surf Warriors* **1993 (PG)** Action comedy for the kiddies finds two young surfer dudes who are actually the long-lost crown princes of the obscure nation of Patu San. The country's incompetent (what a surprise, it's Nielsen) warlord wants the boys to stay lost. Lame jokes and tame martial arts sequences. **87m/C; VHS, DVD.** Ernie Reyes, Jr.; Nick Cowen; Leslie Nielsen; Tone Loc; Rob Schneider; John Karlen; Ernie Reyes, Sr.; Kelly Hu; ***D:*** Neal Israel; ***W:*** Dan Gordon; ***C:*** Arthur Albert; ***M:*** David Kitay.

Surfacing 1/2 *Wet Bum* **2014** A rather dark dramatic look at the impact of teenage loneliness and awkwardness through the life of one girl. Living in the a small northern Canadian town, Sam (Stone) is 14 years old and feels discomfort at the changes she is experiencing. Though the beginning of spring term should mean new classes and new possibilities for many students, Sam does not share her friends' enthusiasms for boys, drug experimentation, and other steps forward in adolescence. Instead, Sam cannot even bring herself to take off her swimsuit in front of other girls after swim lessons. Sam's perspective changes after her mother punishes a transgression by making her work as a cleaner in the retirement home she manages. Sam bonds with two of the residents who give her a new perspective on life changes. **98m/C; DVD, Streaming, Download.** Julia Sarah Stone; Kenneth Welsh; Craig Arnold; Leah K. Pinsent; Diana Leblanc; ***D:*** Lindsay Mackay; ***W:*** Lindsay Mackay; ***C:*** Guy Godfree; ***M:*** Ohad Benchetrit; Brendan Canning. **VIDEO**

Surfer, Dude **2008 (R)** Seems to be a very lame excuse to get McConaughey shirtless and frolicking in the Malibu surf and sun. He nominally stars as long-board surfer Steve Addington, who returns from his travels happy but broke. A slick endorsement sponsor wants Steve to participate in a reality TV show while Steve is more worried about the lack of wave action. Although babes and weed are a lot easier to find. **88m/C; DVD, Blu-Ray.** Matthew McConaughey; Jeffrey Nordling; Woody Harrelson; Ramon Rodriguez; Willie Nelson; Alexie Gilmore; ***D:*** S. R. Bindler; ***W:*** S. R. Bindler; Cory Van Dyke; George Mays; Mark Gustawes; ***C:*** Elliot Davis; ***M:*** Matthew McConaughey; Blake Neely; Xavier Rudd.

Surf's Up 1/2 **2007 (PG)** Dude! Penguins march, tap dance, and now they surf. Young Cody Maverick (LaBeouf) is an outcast among his peers with his surfer dreams. He follows a scout to the tropical Pen Gu Island, the home of a championship contest, and finds a mentor in laid-back legend Big Z (Bridges). Cody even gets a much more competent potential love interest in lifeguard Lani (Deschanel). Sidekick Chicken Joe (Heder) provides some diversion. Not ground-breaking in the animation department (although the look of the waves is impressive), but the story is fun and the vocal work just right. **85m/C; DVD, Blu-Ray, HD-DVD.** ***V:*** Shia LaBeouf; Jeff Bridges; Zooey Deschanel; Jon Heder; James Woods; Diedrich Bader; Mario Cantone; Jane Krakowski; Brian Benben; Michael McKean; Dana Belben; ***D:*** Chris Buck; Ash Brannon; ***W:*** Lisa Addario; Joe Syracuse; Christian Darren; Don Rhymer; ***M:*** Mychael Danna.

Surfwise **2007 (R)** Less a surfing documentary, and more a glimpse into the world of the nomadic Paskowitz family, dubbed "the first family of surfing." After graduating from Stanford's med school, Dorian "Doc" Paskowitz, twice-divorced, sold all his possession and traveled the world, introducing the sport of surfing to Israel and meeting his soon-to-be-wife, Juliette, along the way. The two raised eight children in a 24-foot camper, cruising the coasts, substituting a standard education for a crash course in the zen of the wave, creating a gap that some of the children grew to resent. At 85, the surfing bohemian and his wife reunite with their children to hash out the family differences. Insightful and unbiased, always allowing its subjects to tell the story. **93m/C; DVD.** ***D:*** Doug Pray; ***C:*** Dave Homcy; ***M:*** Joh Dragonetti.

Surge of Power: The Stuff of Heroes **2004** Campy, low-budge satire in which hapless gay lawyer Gavin likes to debate the merits of superheroes and their powers with his equally comic book-obsessed geeky friends. Gavin gets the chance to live his dream and become a superhero after a lab accident--and he has his very own super-villain to defeat! Targeted towards pop culture fans, with many comic book in-jokes and cameos by numerous stars of TV Sci Fi and fantasy series. **99m/C; DVD.** Vincent J. Roth; John Venturini; Robert Hurt; Seth Harrington; Harry Cassidy; ***D:*** Mike Donahue; ***W:*** Vincent J. Roth; ***C:*** Matt Mcfarland; ***M:*** Ken Fix. **VIDEO**

The Surgeon *Exquisite Tenderness* **1994 (R)** Routine hospital horror finds Dr. Theresa McCann (Glasser) caught up in murder when patients and doctors become poison victims. Aided by toxicologist Benjamin Hendricks (Remar), McCann finds a lollipop left behind and realizes the killer is ex-boyfriend/doctor Julian Matar (Haberle), whose unlawful experiments in tissue regeneration got him suspended. Now he's hiding out in the hospital and killing to get the pituitary glands necessary for his miracle serum. Film's original title "Exquisite Tenderness" is a term for the point when pain becomes so extreme it turns to pleasure—the film merely turns grisly. **100m/C; VHS, DVD.** ***GE*** Isabel Glasser; James Remar; Sean Haberle; Charles Dance; Peter Boyle; Malcolm McDowell; Charles Bailey-Gates; Gregory West; Mother Love; ***D:*** Carl Schenkel; ***W:*** Patrick Cirillo; ***C:*** Thomas Burstyn; ***M:*** Christopher Franke.

Surprise, Surprise **2009** Closeted TV star Den lives in a secluded Hollywood Hills home with his younger lover Colin, a dancer who's now confined to a wheelchair. Their changing relationship becomes more complicated when Den's previously unknown 16-year-old son David shows up and turns out to be a troubled homophobe. **85m/C; DVD.** Travis Michael Holder; John Brotherton; Luke Eberl; Mary Jo Catlett; Deborah Shelton; Jesse C. Boyd; ***D:*** Jerry Turner; ***W:*** Travis Michael Holder; Jerry Turner; ***C:*** Cooper Dunn; ***M:*** Bryan Jay.

Surrender Dorothy 1/2 **1998** Weird psychosexual drama focuses on 26-year-old sexually confused Trevor (Pryor), who's afraid of women. He offers drugs and a place to crash to heroin addict Lahn (Di Novis) but their arrangement soons turn bizarre when Trevor desires Lahn to cross-dress as Dorothy, his concept of the ideal girlfriend, and then wants to take his obsession even farther. **97m/B; VHS, DVD.** Kevin Di Novis; Peter Pryor; Jason Centeno; Elizabeth Casey; ***D:*** Kevin Di Novis; ***W:*** Kevin Di Novis; ***C:*** Jonathan Kovel; ***M:*** Christopher Matarazzo.

The Surrogate **2013** Silly and unpleasant Lifetime drama. Jacob and Allison Kelly are having trouble conceiving so they decide to use a surrogate. College prof Jacob has attracted a psycho admirer, Kate, who manages to become their baby mama. She wants the daddy-to-be for herself and tries to push Allison into giving Jacob a divorce. **90m/C; DVD.** Cameron Mathison; Annie Wersching; Amy Scott; Eve Mauro; Diane Baker; ***D:*** Doug Campbell; ***W:*** Doug Campbell; Barbara Kymlicka; ***C:*** Robert Ballo; ***M:*** Steve Gurevitch. **CABLE**

Surrogates **2009 (PG-13)** In the near future, humans live isolated and safe in their homes while lookalike robotic surrogates manage their lives outside. After a series of murders, Agent Greer (Willis) discovers he'll actually have to leave his house for the first time in years if he expects to solve the crimes. His investigation leads him to an underground band of rebel humans, called The Dreads, revolting against the robotic surrogate world, lead by The Prophet (Rhames). What could've been an intriguing allegorical sci-fi mystery quickly turns into a cut-and-paste action flick. Based on the graphic novel series. **88m/C; Blu-Ray.** Bruce Willis; Radha Mitchell; Rosamund Pike; Boris Kodjoe; James Francis Ginty; James Cromwell; Ving Rhames; Jack Noseworthy; Michael Cudlitz; Devin Ratray; Helena Mattsson; Jeffrey De Serrano; ***D:*** Jonathan Mostow; ***W:*** Michael Ferris; John Brancato; ***C:*** Oliver Wood; ***M:*** Richard (Rick) Marvin.

Surveillance **2008 (R)** What on earth would draw actors the caliber of Ormond and Pullman (who both overact to compensate) to this graphically tasteless mediocrity? Two masked serial killers attack a married couple in a desert community. Then there's a mass highway shooting that brings in FBI agents Anderson (Ormond) and Hallaway (Pullman) and some unprofessional (and lying) cops interrogating witnesses. **97m/C; DVD.** Julia Ormond; Bill Pullman; Pell James; Ryan Simpkins; Cheri Oteri; Hugh Dillon; Michael Ironside; French Stewart; Gill Gayle; Kent Harper; ***W:*** Kent Harper; ***M:*** Todd Bryanton.

Surveillance 24/7 **2007** Low-budget thriller that doesn't quite hang together. Gay teacher Adam heads off to London to party and get laid. He picks up Jake and his life goes to hell, especially when Jake turns up dead. Why? Well, although Adam was unaware, Jake gave him some evidence that a British royal is involved in a gay affair and no one wants the truth to come out. **87m/C; DVD.** ***GB*** Simon Callow; Tom Harper; Dawn Steele; Sean Brosnan; ***D:*** Paul Oremland; ***W:*** Kevin Sampson; ***C:*** Alistair Cameron; ***M:*** Helen Jane Long.

Survival Island *Demon Island; The Pinata: Survival Island* **2002 (R)** Kinda cheesy horror fun. Group of college students are on a Cinco de Mayo treasure hunt on a tropical island when something evil turns up—a killer pinata! Actually, it's a demon hidden inside the pinata that starts picking off the clueless one by gory one. What a way to get voted off the island. **90m/C; VHS, DVD.** Nicholas Brendon; Jaime Pressly; Garrett Wang; Eugene Byrd; Daphne Lynn Duplaix; ***D:*** David Hillenbrand; Scott Hillenbrand; ***W:*** David Hillenbrand; Scott Hillenbrand; ***C:*** Philip D. Schwartz; ***M:*** David Hillenbrand. **VIDEO**

Survival of the Dead 🦴 ½ *George A. Romero's Survival of the Dead* **2009 (R)** In this routine sixth installment, plague-ridden zombies are causing havoc on Plum Island and the two main island families are feuding over how to deal with the problem. The Muldoons want to quarantine the undead and the O'Flynns want to kill. When the O'Flynns are forced off the island, they team up with Sarge and his mercenaries, return, and find the island overrun. Let the bloody battle begin! **88m/C; DVD, Blu-Ray.** *CA* Alan Van Spang; Eric Woolfe; Kenneth Welsh; Richard Fitzpatrick; Kathleen Munroe; Stefano di Matteo; Joris Jarsky; ***D:*** George A. Romero; ***W:*** George A. Romero; ***C:*** Adam Swica; ***M:*** Robert Carli.

Survival Quest 🦴 ½ **1989 (R)** Students in a Rocky Mountain survival course cross paths with a band of bloodthirsty mercenaries-in-training. A battle to the death ensues; you'll wish they'd all put each other out of their misery a lot sooner. **90m/C; VHS, DVD.** Lance Henriksen; Dermot Mulroney; Mark Rolston; Steve Antin; Paul Provenza; Ben Hammer; Traci Lind; Catherine Keener; Reggie Bannister; ***D:*** Don A. Coscarelli; ***W:*** Don A. Coscarelli; ***M:*** Christopher L. Stone.

Surviving Christmas 🦴 **2004 (PG-13)** Affleck finds himself stuck in another boxoffice disaster as wealthy yuppie Drew, who gets dumped by snooty girlfriend Missy (Morrison) right before the holidays. Following some bad advice from his shrink, Drew decides to reconnect with his past by visiting his boyhood home. The house is now occupied by working-class grump Tom Valcos (Gandolfini), his frustrated wife Christine (O'Hara), their porn-obsessed teen son Brian (Zuckerman) and serious daughter Alicia (Applegate). For $250,000, the Valcos agree to be Drew's rented relatives and indulge his Christmas dreams. Comedic embarrassment follows resulting in a few, brief, reluctant chuckles. **92m/C; VHS, DVD, Blu-Ray.** Ben Affleck; James Gandolfini; Christina Applegate; Catherine O'Hara; Josh Zuckerman; Bill Macy; Jennifer (Jenny) Morrison; Stephen (Steve) Root; ***D:*** Mike Mitchell; ***W:*** Deborah Kaplan; Harry Elfont; Jeffrey Ventimilia; Joshua Sternin; ***C:*** Peter Collinson; Tom Priestley; ***M:*** Randy Edelman.

Surviving Desire 🦴🦴🦴 **1991** Donovan plays Jude, a neurotic, romantic English professor who falls madly in love with an independently minded student, Sophie. Unfortunately, Sophie is more interested in how the seduction will advance her writing than how it will affect her life. The lovers explore their brief affair by analyzing every emotion and motive in a series of quirky conversations. Intelligent, amusing, and stylized film from director Hartley. The tape also includes two Hartley shorts: "Theory of Achievement" and "Ambition." **86m/C; VHS, DVD.** Martin Donovan; Mary B. Ward; Matt Malloy; Rebecca Nelson; ***D:*** Hal Hartley; ***C:*** Michael Spiller.

Surviving Picasso 🦴🦴 ½ **1996 (R)** Merchant-Ivory team takes time off from bodice-rippers to tear into the personal life of the Cubist legend, Pablo Picasso. Takes an unglamourous look at the mythically famous artist, focusing on the rocky ten-year affair with Francoise Gilot (newcomer McElhone), who met the artist in Nazi-occupied Paris when she was 22 and he was 62. Hopkins is well-cast as the insufferable senior and adds a strong dose of charm to soften his portrayal. Scores high tech credits, especially picture's sumptuous look, compliments of production designer and frequent collaborator Luciana Arrighi. Unfortunately adapted from the decidedly one-sided biography "Picasso: Creator and Destroyer" by controversial author Arianna Huffington. Denied use of the artist's works by his estate, the filmmakers settled for some "work in progress" replicas. **126m/C; VHS, DVD.** Anthony Hopkins; Natascha (Natasha) McElhone; Julianne Moore; Joss Ackland; Joan Plowright; Diane Venora; Peter Eyre; Jane Lapotaire; Joseph Maher; Bob Peck; ***D:*** James Ivory; ***W:*** Ruth Prawer Jhabvala; ***C:*** Tony Pierce-Roberts; ***M:*** Richard Robbins.

Surviving the Game 🦴 **1994 (R)** Poorly made hunt-the-human story. Homeless Ice-T is hired by a group of men to assist them on their annual hunt. But wait, he's the prey. Unbelievable premise pits the streetwise, down and out Ice-T against the savvy and weapons rich group—and he beats them at their own game. Few high-impact action sequences. The violence, although there isn't as much as might be expected, is graphic. **94m/C; VHS, DVD.** Rutger Hauer; Ice-T; F. Murray Abraham; Gary Busey; Charles S. Dutton; John C. McGinley; William McNamara; Jeff Corey; ***D:*** Ernest R. Dickerson; ***W:*** Eric Bernt; ***C:*** Bojan Bazelli; ***M:*** Stewart Copeland.

Survivor 🦴 **1980** A jetliner crashes, leaving but one survivor, the pilot, who is then plagued by visions, tragedies, and ghosts of dead passengers. Viewers also suffer. **91m/C; VHS, DVD, Blu-Ray.** *AU* Robert Powell; Jenny Agutter; Joseph Cotten; Angela Punch McGregor; ***D:*** David Hemmings; ***W:*** David Ambrose; ***M:*** Brian May.

Survivors 🦴🦴 **1983 (R)** Two unemployed men find themselves the target of a hit man, whom they have identified in a robbery attempt. One of the men goes gun-crazy protecting himself. Uneven comedy with wild Williams and laid-back Matthau. **102m/C; VHS, DVD.** Robin Williams; Walter Matthau; Jerry Reed; John Goodman; James Wainwright; Kristen Vigard; ***D:*** Michael Ritchie; ***W:*** Michael Leeson; ***C:*** Billy Williams; ***M:*** Paul Chihara.

Susan and God 🦴🦴🦴 *The Gay Mrs. Trexel* **1940** A selfish socialite returns from Europe and starts practicing a new religion, much to the dismay of her friends and family. Despite her preaching, her own domestic life is falling apart and she realizes that her preoccupation and selfish ways have caused a strain on her marriage and her relationship with her daughter. An excellent script and a fine performance from Crawford make this a highly satisfying film. **115m/B; VHS, DVD.** Joan Crawford; Fredric March; Ruth Hussey; John Carroll; Rita Hayworth; Nigel Bruce; Bruce Cabot; Rose Hobart; Rita Quigley; Marjorie Main; Gloria De Haven; ***D:*** George Cukor; ***W:*** Anita Loos.

Susan Lenox: Her Fall and Rise 🦴🦴 ½ *The Rise of Helga; Rising to Fame* **1931** Garbo, the daughter of an abusive farmer, falls into the arms of the handsome Gable to escape an arranged marriage. Both stars are miscast, but the well-paced direction keeps the melodrama moving. **84m/B; VHS, DVD.** Greta Garbo; Clark Gable; Jean Hersholt; John Miljan; Alan Hale; Hale Hamilton; ***D:*** Robert Z. Leonard; ***C:*** William H. Daniels.

Susan Slade 🦴🦴 ½ **1961** A glossy soap with pretty leads. Teenaged Susan (Stevens) gets pregnant by her boyfriend who inconveniently dies. An extended trip out of the country has mom Leah (McGuire) deciding they can pass off the baby as her own after they return. Susan eventually gets marriage proposals from wealthy but dull Wells Corbett (Convy) and sullen would-be writer Hoyt Brecker (Donahue). But when Susan's "little brother" is injured in a fire, the truth comes out and only one of the two guys is willing to stand by her. **116m/C; DVD.** Connie Stevens; Troy Donahue; Dorothy McGuire; Lloyd Nolan; Bert Convy; Brian Aherne; Natalie Schafer; Grant Williams; ***D:*** Delmer Daves; ***W:*** Delmer Daves; ***C:*** Lucien Ballard; ***M:*** Max Steiner.

Susan Slept Here 🦴🦴 ½ **1954** While researching a movie on juvenile delinquents, a Hollywood script writer (Powell) is given custody of a spunky 17-year-old delinquent girl (Reynolds) during the Christmas holidays. Cute sex comedy. Based on the play "Susan," by Alex Gottlieb and Steve Fisher. **98m/C; VHS, DVD, Blu-Ray.** Dick Powell; Debbie Reynolds; Anne Francis; ***D:*** Frank Tashlin.

Susana 🦴🦴🦴 **1951** Minor though still interesting Bunuel, in which a sexy delinquent young girl is rescued from vagrancy by a Spanish family, and how she subsequently undermines the family's structure through sexual allurement and intimidation. In Spanish with English subtitles. **87m/B; VHS, Streaming.** *MX* Rosita Quintana; Fernando Soler; Victor Manuel Mendoza; Matilde Palou; ***D:*** Luis Bunuel.

Susanna Pass 🦴🦴 **1949** Oil deposits underneath a fish hatchery lake attract bad guys. They set off explosions to destroy the fishery, but game warden Rogers investigates. Minor outing for Roy. **67m/C; VHS, DVD.** Roy Rogers; Dale Evans; Estelita Rodriguez; Martin Garralaga; Robert Emmett Keane; Lucien Littlefield; Douglas Fowley; ***D:*** William Witney.

Susannah of the Mounties 🦴🦴 ½ **1939 (PG)** An adorable young girl is left orphaned after a wagon train massacre and is adopted by a Mountie. An Indian squabble gives Shirley a chance to play little peacemaker and teach Scott how to tap dance, too. Could she be any cuter? Available colorized. **78m/B; VHS, DVD.** Shirley Temple; Randolph Scott; Margaret Lockwood; J. Farrell MacDonald; Moroni Olsen; Victor Jory; ***D:*** William A. Seiter; ***C:*** Arthur C. Miller.

Sushi Girl 🦴🦴 **2012 (R)** Fish (Noah Hathaway) has been imprisoned for 6 years and upon release his former partners throw him a party, complete with sushi being served on a nude woman in a creepy, isolated building. **99m/C; DVD, Blu-Ray, Streaming.** Tony Todd; Noah Hathaway; James Duval; Andy Mackenzie; Mark Hamill; Sonny Chiba; ***D:*** Kern Saxton; ***W:*** Kern Saxton; Destin Pfaff; ***C:*** Aaron Meister; ***M:*** Fritz Myers. **VIDEO**

Suspect 🦴🦴 ½ **1987 (R)** An overworked Washington, DC, public defender (Cher) is assigned to a controversial murder case in which her client is a deaf-mute, skid-row bum. A cynical lobbyist on the jury illegally researches the case himself. They work together to uncover a far-reaching conspiracy. Unrealistic plot, helped along by good performances and tight direction. **101m/C; VHS, DVD, Blu-Ray.** Dennis Quaid; Cher; Liam Neeson; E. Katherine Kerr; Joe Mantegna; John Mahoney; Philip Bosco; ***D:*** Peter Yates; ***W:*** Eric Roth; ***C:*** Billy Williams; ***M:*** Michael Kamen.

The Suspect 🦴 ½ **2005** Lawyer Paul James' murder shocks the community and his second wife Beth (Luner) is arrested after some evidence conveniently comes to light. Ex-cop turned insurance investigator Jerry Calhoun (Bocher) thinks the police investigation was sloppy and soon figures out that Paul was not the model citizen everyone assumed. **90m/C; DVD.** Jamie Luner; Christian Bocher; Adrian Hough; Belinda Metz; Taylor Anne Reid; Alf Humphreys; John Tench; ***D:*** Keoni Waxman; ***W:*** Richard Leder; ***C:*** Eric Goldstein; ***M:*** Jerry Lambert; Harry Manfredini. **CABLE**

The Suspect 🦴🦴 ½ **2014** A dramatic thriller about a social science experiment gone very wrong. Two African-American men (Phifer and Brown) are social scientists who want to better understand racial issues in law enforcement in small town white America. To do so, they pose as bank robbers. When the first armed bank robbery takes place in one community, they try to link the crime to one of the men. When he refuses to cooperate, the experiment goes awry unexpectedly, leading to the loss of life. **98m/C; DVD, Blu-Ray, Streaming, Download.** Mekhi Phifer; Sterling K. Brown; William Sadler; Derek Roche; James McCaffrey; ***D:*** Stuart Connelly; ***W:*** Stuart Connelly; ***C:*** Eric Giovon; ***M:*** Stephen Coates.

Suspect Zero 🦴 ½ **2004 (R)** Maverick FBI agent Thomas Mackelway (Eckhart) has been demoted to a backwater bureau just in time to discover a serial killer whose M.O. is that he kills other serial killers and likes to taunt the fed via fax. Soon, Mackelway is joined by no-nonsense former partner/lover Fran Kulok (Moss in a thankless role). Eckhart's generally wasted as the standard troubled good guy (he works better in edgier roles) while Kingsley does what a professional does—make the most of an absurd movie sociopath. Merhige apparently prefers to set an artistic moodiness rather than worry about pace, plot, or coherence. **99m/C; DVD.** Aaron Eckhart; Ben Kingsley; Carrie-Anne Moss; Harry J. Lennix; William Mapother; Ellen Blake; Chloe Russell; Kevin Chamberlin; ***D:*** Edmund Elias Merhige; ***W:*** Zak Penn; Billy Ray; ***C:*** Michael Chapman; ***M:*** Clint Mansell.

Suspended Animation 🦴🦴 **2002** Animator Thomas Kempton (McArthur) takes a break from his work to go snowmobiling with some buddies. He gets separated from the group and taken captive by a couple of crazy sisters who have a hatred of men and a love of cannibalism. Menacing and engaging script mixes the "Misery" with comic spatterings. Hancock goes old-school but fails to overcome structural flaws. **114m/C; DVD.** Alex McArthur; Sage Allen; Rebecca Harrell; Laura Esterman; Maria Cina; ***D:*** John Hancock; ***W:*** Dorothy Tristan; ***C:*** Misha (Mikhail) Suslov; ***M:*** Angelo Badalamenti.

Suspense 🦴🦴 **1946** Adultery, betrayal, and murder all set around an ice skating show and starring attractive pro skater Belita. L.A. ice show queen Roberta cheats on hubby Frank (Dekker) with his ambitious new employee Joe (Sullivan). Frank goes missing, Joe takes over the business, and Roberta starts getting very, very nervous. **100m/B; DVD.** Belita; Barry Sullivan; Albert Dekker; Bonita Granville; Eugene Pallette; ***D:*** Frank Tuttle; ***W:*** Philip Yourdan; ***C:*** Karl Struss; ***M:*** Daniele Amfitheatrof.

Suspicion 🦴🦴🦴 ½ **1941** Alfred Hitchcock's suspense thriller about a woman who gradually realizes she is married to a killer and may be next on his list. An excellent production unravels at the end due to RKO's insistence that Grant retain his "attractive" image. This forced the writers to leave his guilt or innocence undetermined. Available colorized. **99m/B; VHS, DVD, Blu-Ray.** Cary Grant; Joan Fontaine; Cedric Hardwicke; Nigel Bruce; May Whitty; Leo G. Carroll; Heather Angel; ***D:*** Alfred Hitchcock; ***C:*** Harry Stradling, Sr.; ***M:*** Franz Waxman. Oscars '41: Actress (Fontaine); N.Y. Film Critics '41: Actress (Fontaine).

Suspicion 🦴🦴 **2003** Carol Finnegan (Redman) is celebrating her 20th wedding anniversary to husband Mark (Dunbar) when she begins receiving a series of anonymous emails accusing Mark of having an affair with his secretary. She tells Mark, who dismisses them as the work of a disgruntled ex-employee, but Carol's suspicions grow. Then the secretary is murdered and it's Carol who is accused of the crime. **150m/C; DVD.** *GB* Amanda Redman; Adrian Dunbar; Saskia Reeves; Adam Kotz; ***D:*** Jamie Payne; ***W:*** Peter Whalley; ***C:*** Chris Seager; ***M:*** Nick Bicat. **TV**

Suspicious Minds 🦴🦴 ½ **1996 (R)** PI Jack Ramsey (Bergin) is hired to get the goods on Isabelle's (Heitmeyer) alleged infidelities. But Jack winds up in an affair with the femme, whose other lover has just been murdered. **97m/C; VHS, Streaming.** Patrick Bergin; Jayne Heitmeyer; Gary Busey; Daniel Pilon; ***D:*** Alain Zaloum.

Suspicious River 🦴 **2000** Leila's answer to a stale marriage and the small-town blues? Start hooking with guests at her seedy motel job of course! And wait for that very special lunatic to come along and steal her heart and beat her up a time or two. **92m/C; VHS, DVD.** Molly Parker; Callum Keith Rennie; Mary Kate Welsh; Joel Bissonnette; Deanna Milligan; Sarah Jane Redmond; Norman Armour; Byron Lucas; Michael Shanks; Don S. Davis; Jay Brazeau; Gillian Barber; Paul Jarrett; Bruno Verdoni; Ingrid Tesch; Bill Dow; ***D:*** Lynne Stopkewich; ***W:*** Lynne Stopkewich; ***C:*** Gregory Middleton; ***M:*** Don MacDonald. **VIDEO**

Suspiria 🦴🦴🦴 **1977 (R)** An American dancer enters a weird European ballet academy and finds they teach more than movement as bodies begin piling up. Sometimes weak plot is aided by great-but-gory special effects, fine photography, good music, and a chilling opening sequence. Also available in unrated version. **99m/C; VHS, DVD, Blu-Ray.** *IT* Jessica Harper; Joan Bennett; Alida Valli; Udo Kier; Stefania Casini; Flavio Bucci; Barbara Magnolfi; Rudolf Schuendler; ***D:*** Dario Argento; ***W:*** Dario Argento; Daria Nicolodi; ***C:*** Luciano Tovoli; ***M:*** Dario Argento.

Suspiria 🦴🦴 **2018 (R)** A remake of the 1977 dance/horror film, this one taking place in 1970s divided Berlin. Dakota Johnson enthralls as the wide-eyed dancer new to the school, naïve to the grotesque underworkings by the school's coven of witches. Throw in a missing dancer, themes of guilt, and a grieving psychotherapist (one of two roles played by Swinton), and you've got a weird, bloody, and atmospheric horror flick. **152m/C; DVD, Blu-Ray.** Dakota Johnson; Tilda Swinton; Mia Goth; Sylvie Testud; Jessica Harper; Chloë Grace Moretz; ***D:*** Luca Guadagnino; ***W:*** David Kajganich; ***C:*** Sayombhu Mukdeeprom; ***M:*** Thom Yorke. Ind. Spirit '19: Cinematog.

Suture **1993** Quirky thriller is a homage to late '50s melodramas with its strange tale of mistaken identity. Vincent wants to hide his unsavory past by assuming the identity of his estranged half-brother, Clay, which should be difficult since Vincent is white and Clay is black but the movie's premise is that everyone confuses the two. Vincent tries to kill Clay in an explosion but he survives—with amnesia and with everyone in the hospital assuming he's Vincent. Shifting points of view as he struggles to piece together his memory offer disorientation not just for Clay but the viewer as well. Feature film debut for the directors. **96m/B; VHS, DVD, Blu-Ray.** Dennis Haysbert; Sab Shimono; Mel Harris; Michael (M.K.) Harris; Dina Merrill; David Graf; Fran Ryan; ***D:*** Scott McGehee; David Siegel; ***W:*** Scott McGehee; David Siegel; ***C:*** Greg Gardiner; ***M:*** Cary Berger. Sundance '94: Cinematog.

Suzy 1/2 **1936** Harlow's fourth film and her only one with Grant is a mixture of romance, action, and comedy set during WWI. Grant plays a French flier who falls in love with Harlow, although she is married to Tone. Excellent air footage and some good funny scenes keep this film moving right along. Even has Grant singing hit song, "Did I Remember?" **99m/B; VHS, DVD.** Jean Harlow; Franchot Tone; Cary Grant; Benita Hume; Lewis Stone; Inez Courtney; ***D:*** George Fitzmaurice.

Svengali **1931** A music teacher uses his hypnotic abilities to manipulate one of his singing students and make her a star. Soon the young woman is singing for sell-out crowds, but only if her teacher is present. Barrymore in a hypnotic performance. Adapted from "Trilby" by George Du Maurier. Remade in 1955 and 1983. **76m/B; VHS, DVD, Blu-Ray.** John Barrymore; Marian Marsh; Donald Crisp; ***D:*** Archie Mayo; ***W:*** J. Grubb Alexander; ***C:*** Barney McGill.

Svengali 1/2 **1955** Limp remake of the 1931 film about Trilby, an artist's model, falling under the mesmerizing spell of the title character, who is determined to make her into a famous singer. Chiefly notable for its visuals which were based on the illustrations from the original novel "Trilby" by George du Maurier. **82m/C; VHS, DVD.** *GB* Hildegarde Knef; Donald Wolfit; Terence Morgan; Derek Bond; Paul Rogers; David Kossoff; ***D:*** Noel Langley; ***W:*** Noel Langley.

Svengali 1/2 **1983** Flamboyant but faded music star O'Toole mentors Foster, a young pop singer looking for stardom. Boring remake of the Barrymore classic. **96m/C; VHS, DVD.** Peter O'Toole; Jodie Foster; Elizabeth Ashley; Larry Joshua; Pamela Blair; Barbara Byrne; Holly Hunter; ***D:*** Anthony Harvey; ***M:*** John Barry. **TV**

Swallow 1/2 **2020 (R)** Facing mounting pressures over her pregnancy and attempts to please her seemingly perfect husband and in-laws, Hunter develops pica, an eating disorder involving the consumption of non-food items. Haley Bennett delivers an outstanding portrayal of a woman so desperate for control that she harms herself. This psychological thriller is not for the squeamish. **94m/C; DVD.** Haley Bennett; Austin Stowell; Denis O'Hare; Elizabeth Marvel; David Rasche; ***D:*** Carlo Mirabella-Davis; ***W:*** Carlo Mirabella-Davis; ***C:*** Katelin Arizmendi; ***M:*** Nathan Halpern.

Swamp Devil 1/2 **2008** SciFi Channel creation where the twists are obvious and the only reason to watch is Dern. Sheriff turned swamp hermit Howard Blaime (Dern) is accused of murdering a teenaged girl, which brings his estranged daughter Melanie (Sampson) back to their small town. A local walking compost pile (the titular devil) is apparently the real culprit. **90m/C; DVD.** Bruce Dern; Cindy Sampson; Nicholas Wright; Robert Higden; Allison Graham; James Kidnie; ***D:*** David Winning; ***W:*** Gary Dauberman; Ethlie Ann Vare; ***C:*** Daniel Vincelette; ***M:*** James Gelfand. **CABLE**

Swamp Fire 1/2 **1946** Mississippi riverboat captain Weissmuller, wrestles alligators and battles with Crabbe for the woman he loves in this turgid drama. Look for Janssen in an early screen performance. **69m/B; VHS, DVD.** Johnny Weissmuller; Virginia Grey; Buster Crabbe; Carol Thurston; Edwin Maxwell; Pedro de Cordoba; Pierre Watkin; David Janssen; ***D:*** William H. Pine; ***W:*** Daniel Mainwaring; ***C:*** Fred H. Jackman, Jr.; ***M:*** Rudolph (Rudy) Schrager.

Swamp Shark 1/2 **2011 (R)** Creature feature from the Syfy Channel with the usual silly story and questionable CGI. The title shark escapes when a critter-smuggling operation goes wrong and it finds a swimming hole in a Louisiana backwater. It starts eating anything edible, including customers at Rachel Bouchard's (Swanson) diner, and she decides to hunt the shark down before it can ruin the annual Gator Festival. **93m/C; DVD.** Kristy Swanson; D.B. Sweeney; Robert Davi; Sophie Sinise; Jeffrey Chase; ***D:*** Griff Furst; ***W:*** Charles Bolon; ***C:*** Lorenzo Senatore; ***M:*** Andrew Morgan Smith. **CABLE**

Swamp Thing 1/2 **1982 (PG)** Overlooked camp drama about scientist accidentally turned into tragic half-vegetable, half-man swamp creature, with government agent Barbeau caught in the middle, occasionally while topless. A vegetarian nightmare or ecology propaganda? You be the judge. Adapted from the comic book by Craven. **91m/C; VHS, DVD, Blu-Ray.** Adrienne Barbeau; Louis Jourdan; Ray Wise; Dick Durock; ***D:*** Wes Craven; ***W:*** Wes Craven; ***C:*** Robbie Greenberg; ***M:*** Harry Manfredini.

Swamp Women *Swamp Diamonds; Cruel Swamp* **1955** Four escaped women convicts, known as the "Nardo Gang," chase after a stash of diamonds in this super cheap, super bad action adventure from cult director Corman. **73m/C; VHS, DVD.** Mike Connors; Marie Windsor; Beverly Garland; Carole Mathews; Susan Cummings; Jonathan Haze; Jill Jarmyn; Ed Nelson; Lou Place; ***D:*** Roger Corman; ***W:*** David Stern; ***M:*** Bill Holman.

The Swan **1956** A twist on the Cinderella story with Kelly (in her last film before her marriage) as the charming beauty waiting for her prince. Both Guinness, as the crown prince, and Jourdan, as her poor tutor, want her hand (and the rest of her). Attractive cast, but story gets slow from time to time. Remake of a 1925 silent film. **112m/C; VHS, DVD.** Grace Kelly; Louis Jourdan; Alec Guinness; Jessie Royce Landis; Brian Aherne; Estelle Winwood; ***D:*** Charles Vidor; ***C:*** Joseph Ruttenberg; Robert L. Surtees.

The Swan Princess 1/2 **1994 (G)** Formulaic prince-and-princess love story based loosely on "Swan Lake" takes a modern twist: Princess Odette, offended by the emphasis her intended, Prince Derek, places on her beauty, flees the kingdom. She's kidnapped by the evil Rothbart, an enchanter who turns her into a swan able to take human form only when touched by moonlight. A snappy trio of animal characters eventually helps Odette reunite with her newly P.C. love, with lots of zesty musical numbers and various Disney-inspired plot points along the way. Adults may yawn, but kiddies will be charmed just the same. **90m/C; VHS, DVD, Blu-Ray.** ***V:*** Jack Palance; Michelle Nicastro; Howard McGillin; Liz Callaway; John Cleese; Steven Wright; Steve Vinovich; Dakin Matthews; Sandy Duncan; Mark Harelik; James Arrington; Davis Gaines; Joel McKinnon Miller; ***D:*** Richard Rich; ***W:*** Richard Rich; Brian Nissen; ***M:*** Lex de Azevedo.

The Swan Princess 2: Escape from Castle Mountain 1/2 **1997 (G)** Heroine Odette changes back into a swan to help husband Derek defeat evil magician Clavius. Some humor, some action, some nice tunes, and decent animation should keep the kids happy. **75m/C; VHS, DVD.** ***V:*** Michelle Nicastro; Douglas Sills; Jake Williamson; Christy Landers; ***D:*** Richard Rich; ***W:*** Brian Nissen; ***M:*** Lex de Azevedo.

Swanee River **1939** Generally sanitized Technicolor bio of songwriter Stephen Foster (Ameche). Foster's work is inspired by the south and he gains recognition when famous minstrel man, E.P. Christy (Jolson), performs the title song. Foster is accused of being a Southern sympathizer during the Civil War, and he and his family flee to New York where Foster turns to drink. **88m/C; DVD.** Don Ameche; Andrea Leeds; Al Jolson; Felix Bressart; Chick Chandler; ***D:*** Sidney Lanfield; ***W:*** John Taintor Foote; Philip Dunne; ***C:*** Bert Glennon; ***M:*** Louis Silvers.

Swann in Love 1/2 *Un Amour De Swann* **1984 (R)** A handsome, wealthy French aristocrat makes a fool of himself over a beautiful courtesan who cares nothing for him. Elegant production lacks spark. Based upon a section of Marcel Proust's "Remembrance of Things Past." In French with English subtitles or an English language version. **110m/C; VHS, DVD.** *FR GE* Jeremy Irons; Ornella Muti; Alain Delon; Fanny Ardant; Marie-Christine Barrault; ***D:*** Volker Schlondorff; ***W:*** Peter Brook; Jean-Claude Carriere; ***C:*** Sven Nykvist. Cesar '85: Art Dir./Set Dec., Costume Des.

The Swap 1/2 *Sam's Song* **1971 (R)** Ex-con searches for his brother's killer. Muddled story uses clips from early De Niro film "Sam's Song." **120m/C; VHS, DVD.** Robert De Niro; Jered Mickey; Jennifer Warren; Terrayne Crawford; Martin Kelley; ***D:*** Jordan Leondopoulos; ***C:*** Alex Phillips, Jr.; ***M:*** Gershon Kingsley.

The Swarm **1978 (PG)** Low-brow insect contest as scientist Caine fends off a swarm of killer bees when they attack metro Houston. The bees are really just black spots painted on the film. And the acting is terrible. "B" movie on bees, but it's still better than "The Bees." **116m/C; DVD, Blu-Ray.** Michael Caine; Katharine Ross; Richard Widmark; Lee Grant; Richard Chamberlain; Olivia de Havilland; Henry Fonda; Fred MacMurray; Patty Duke; Ben Johnson; Jose Ferrer; Slim Pickens; Bradford Dillman; Cameron Mitchell; ***D:*** Irwin Allen; ***W:*** Stirling Silliphant; ***C:*** Fred W. Koenekamp; ***M:*** Jerry Goldsmith; John Williams.

Swashbuckler *Scarlet Buccaneer* **1976 (PG)** Jaunty pirate returns from sea to find his friends held captive by dastardly dictator for their political views. He rescues them, and helps them overthrow the erstwhile despot. **101m/C; VHS, DVD.** Robert Shaw; James Earl Jones; Peter Boyle; Genevieve Bujold; Beau Bridges; Geoffrey Holder; ***D:*** James Goldstone; ***W:*** Jeffrey Bloom; ***C:*** Philip H. Lathrop; ***M:*** John Addison.

S.W.A.T. 1/2 **2003 (PG-13)** Hondo (Jackson) is the leader of the elite LAPD Special Weapons and Tactics unit. He and his crew have to guard captured drug lord Alex (Martinez) and move him into federal custody. Only Alex has an open offer of $100 mil to anyone who can free him. Above-average big screen version of the mid-seventies TV series provides the correct summer blockbuster mix of action, stunts, and humor, with just enough character development to make you care about the outcome, but not so much that you get bored. **111m/C; VHS, DVD, Blu-Ray, UMD.** Samuel L. Jackson; Colin Farrell; LL Cool J; Josh Charles; Michelle Rodriguez; Olivier Martinez; Jeremy Renner; Brian Van Holt; Reg E. Cathey; Larry Poindexter; Domenick Lombardozzi; Lucinda Jenney; Reed Edward Diamond; ***Cameo(s):*** Clark Johnson; Steve Forrest; ***D:*** Clark Johnson; ***W:*** David Ayer; David McKenna; ***C:*** Gabriel Beristain; ***M:*** Elliot Goldenthal.

S.W.A.T.: Firefight 1/2 **2011 (R)** Cheap, slick DTV sequel to the 2003 actioner. L.A. Lt. Paul Cutler (Macht) is sent to train the Detroit S.W.A.T. team on advanced homeland security methods. He doesn't get a very warm welcome from his new team, except for cop shrink Kim Byers (Pope). The team must quickly pull together when they're targeted by vengeful, ex-government agent Walter Hatch (Patrick). **89m/C; DVD, Blu-Ray.** Gabriel Macht; Robert Patrick; Carly Pope; Giancarlo Esposito; Nicholas Gonzalez; Kristanna Loken; ***D:*** Benny Boom; ***W:*** Reed Steiner; ***C:*** Don Davis; ***M:*** John Paesano. **VIDEO**

SWAT: Unit 887 1/2 *24 Hours* **2015** The city of Los Angeles faces destruction in this problematic action thriller. When a domestic terrorist takes hostages in LA, the city's elite SWAT team is called into action. It soon becomes clear that the terrorists not only want to kill their hostages. With only 24 hours to stop the threat, the members of the team must draw on all their skills, knowledge, and instincts to neutralize the threat and save their city. **96m/C; DVD, Streaming, Download.** Tom Sizemore; Mischa Barton; Timothy Woodward, Jr.; Michael Paré; Marlon Young; ***D:*** Timothy Woodward, Jr.; ***W:*** Lauren De Normandie; ***C:*** Geoff Browne; ***M:*** Sid De La Cruz. **VIDEO**

Sway 1/2 *Yureru* **2006** A celebrity photographer visits home for his mother's funeral, and the rivalry between him and his brother appears once again over a woman they both want. When she dies, one of them is blamed, and the other is the only witness to testify on the other's behalf. **119m/C; DVD.** *JP* Joe Odagiri; Teruyuki Kagawa; Masato Ibu; Hirofumi Arai; Yoko Maki; ***D:*** Miwa Nishikawa; ***W:*** Miwa Nishikawa; ***C:*** Hiroshi Takase; ***M:*** Cauliflowers.

Swedish Auto **2006** The auto in question is a 1967 Volvo and the trusted mechanic is shy loner Carter (Haas), who likes to follow violinist Ann (Davis) around just so he can hear her play. He doesn't seem to realize that timid waitress Darla (Jones)?who has more domestic violence issues than the flick can support—actually likes him. **97m/C; DVD.** Lukas Haas; January Jones; Brianne Davis; Lee Weaver; Chris(topher) Williams; Tim DeZarn; Mary Mara; ***D:*** Derek Sieg; ***W:*** Derek Sieg; ***C:*** Richard Lopez; ***M:*** Josh Robertson.

The Sweeney 1/2 **2012 (R)** British cops and robbers flick following the exploits of hard-nosed London officer Jack Regan (Winstone). Regan leads a special arm of London's metropolitan police that specializes in armed robberies, called the Flying Squad. His job and the team's practices are scrutinized after an innocent woman is executed during a jewelry heist. Luckily, the generic cop talk and bland crime procedurals are interjected with some wild car chases and tense, hard-boiled stakeouts. Based on the 1970's British TV series of the same name. **112m/C; DVD, Blu-Ray, Streaming.** *UK* Ray Winstone; Ben Drew; Hayley Atwell; Steven Mackintosh; Damian Lewis; Steven Waddington; Paul Anderson; ***D:*** Nick Love; ***W:*** Nick Love; John Hodge; ***C:*** Simon Dennis; ***M:*** Lorne Balfe.

Sweeney Todd: The Demon Barber of Fleet Street 1/2 **1984** A filmed performance of Sondheim's Tony-winning Broadway musical. Creepy thriller about a demon barber, his razor, and his wife's meatpies. **139m/C; VHS, DVD.** *GB* Angela Lansbury; George Hearn; ***D:*** Harold Prince; ***M:*** Stephen Sondheim.

Sweeney Todd: The Demon Barber of Fleet Street **2007 (R)** Some critics seemed to think that this adaptation of the Stephen Sondheim Broadway musical was too gory. Well, it's true, it's a lot harder to deal with buckets of blood onstage than in the movies, and Burton does seem to revel in his subject matter, which happens to be a singing, throat-slitting serial killer whose victims get turned into meat pies in dank, 19th-century London. A real toe-tapper that is. Sweeney (Depp) was unfairly transported to Australia when corrupt judge Turpin (Rickman) coveted his wife and daughter. Now years later, barber Sweeney has returned (unrecognizable) to exact his revenge, partnered in crime by his equally corpse-like (and ever-loving) landlady Mrs. Lovett (Bonham Carter). Not a direct adaptation (Burton omits and abridges songs and does some reshaping) and neither Depp nor Bonham Carter are singers, but you have to admire the sheer chutzpah. **117m/C; Blu-Ray, On Demand.** Johnny Depp; Helena Bonham Carter; Alan Rickman; Timothy Spall; Sacha Baron Cohen; Jayne Wisner; Jamie Campbell Bower; Edward Sanders; ***D:*** Tim Burton; ***W:*** John Logan; ***C:*** Dariusz Wolski; ***M:*** Stephen Sondheim. Oscars '07: Art Dir./Set Dec.; Golden Globes '08: Actor--Mus./Comedy (Depp), Film--Mus./Comedy.

The Sweeper 1/2 **1995 (R)** LA cop Mark Goddard (Howell) has a problem—his suspects have a bad habit of dying in his custody. Then he's recruited by a secret police organization whose aim is to dispense their own brand of deadly justice and Mark discovers a key to his troubled past and the murder of his cop father (Fahey). **101m/C; VHS, DVD.** C. Thomas Howell; Ed Lauter; Cynda Williams; Jeff Fahey; ***D:*** Joseph Merhi; ***W:***

William Applegate, Jr.; *C:* Ken Blakey; *M:* K. Alexander (Alex) Wilkinson.

Sweepers 1999 (R) Former land mine sweeper Christian Erickson (Lundgren) is called out of retirement to help bomb expert Michelle Flynn (Stansfield) uncover a terrorist plot to plant landmines in the U.S. **96m/C; VHS, DVD.** Dolph Lundgren; Claire Stansfield; Bruce Payne; *D:* Darby Black; *W:* Darby Black; Kevin Bernhardt; *C:* Yossi Wein. **VIDEO**

Sweepings 1/2 1933 After the Chicago fire, self-made Daniel Pardway (Barrymore) builds a department store into a great success over the years. He believes that one of his four children will take over the business as a family legacy, but they've grown up ungrateful and spoiled by their dad's hard-earned wealth. Remade in 1939 as "Three Sons." **80m/B; DVD.** Lionel Barrymore; Alan Dinehart; William Gargan; Eric Linden; Gloria Stuart; Gregory Ratoff; *D:* John Cromwell; *W:* Lester Cohen; *C:* Edward Cronjager; *M:* Max Steiner.

Sweepstake Annie 1/2 1935 Hollywood script girl Annie wins a lot of dough in the lottery but her boyfriend Bill gets upset when she uses it to help out her lazy family. However, he comes through when Annie is threatened by lowlifes who want her money. **81m/B; DVD.** Marion (Marian) Nixon; Tom Brown; Inez Courtney; Lucien Littlefield; Wera Engels; Ivan Lebedeff; *D:* William Nigh; *W:* Scott Darling; *C:* Harry Neumann.

Sweet and Low-Down 1/2 1944 Music saves this showbiz fluff as Benny Goodman and his band swing. Young trombonist Johnny Birch (Cardwell) gets his big break when Goodman hires him. Johnny falls for New York debutante Trudy Wilson (Darnell), but thinks she's out of his league even after he gets a swelled head and leaves the band to start his own group. Johnny fails miserably, learns his lesson, and Goodman even gives him a second chance. **75m/B; DVD.** James B. Cardwell; Linda Darnell; Benny Goodman; Lynn Bari; Jack Oakie; Allyn Joslyn; *D:* Archie Mayo; *W:* Richard English; *C:* Lucien Ballard.

Sweet and Lowdown 1/2 1999 (PG-13) Slight jazzy comedy, set in the '30s, traces the up-and-down career of fictional musician Emmet Ray (Penn), who's haunted by the fact that he's the second-best jazz guitarist in the world (Django Reinhardt is the first). However talented Emmet is musically, he's scum as a human being, abandoning Hattie (Morton), the mute laundress who turns out to be the love of his life in favor of wealthy writer Blanche (Thurman). Fine cast, good look, great music. **95m/C; VHS, DVD.** Sean Penn; Samantha Morton; Uma Thurman; Brian Markinson; Anthony LaPaglia; Gretchen Mol; Vincent Guastaferro; John Waters; James Urbaniak; Constance Shulman; Kellie Overbey; Michael Sprague; Woody Allen; *D:* Woody Allen; *W:* Woody Allen; *C:* Fei Zhao; *M:* Dick Hyman.

Sweet Bird of Youth 1962 An acclaimed adaptation of the Tennessee Williams play about Chance Wayne, a handsome drifter who travels with an aging movie queen to his small Florida hometown, hoping she'll get him started in a movie career. However, coming home turns into a big mistake, as the town boss wants revenge on Chance for seducing his daughter, Heavenly. Williams's original stage ending was cleaned up, providing a conventional "happy" movie ending for the censors. Remade for TV in 1989 with Elizabeth Taylor and Mark Harmon in the lead roles. **120m/C; VHS, DVD, Blu-Ray; Open Captioned.** Paul Newman; Geraldine Page; Ed Begley, Sr.; Mildred Dunnock; Rip Torn; Shirley Knight; Madeline Sherwood; Kelly Thordsen; *D:* Richard Brooks; *W:* Richard Brooks; *C:* Milton Krasner. Oscars '62: Support. Actor (Begley); Golden Globes '63: Actress—Drama (Page).

Sweet Bird of Youth 1989 (R) TV remake of the Tennessee Williams's play, which was filmed for the big screen in 1962, with Harmon and Taylor having the unenviable task of following in the roles played by Paul Newman and Geraldine Page. She is an egotistical, has-been movie star and he is her ambitious gigolo who wants a movie career of his own. Unfortunately, the trouble that drove him from his Florida hometown is still there when he reappears, actress in tow. Things don't bode well. The TV production uses Williams's original ending, which was cleaned up for a "happier" version in the '62 film. **95m/C; VHS, DVD.** Elizabeth Taylor; Mark Harmon; Rip Torn; Valerie Perrine; Ruta Lee; Seymour Cassel; Kevin Geer; Michael Wilding, Jr.; *D:* Nicolas Roeg; *W:* Gavin Lambert; *M:* Ralph Burns. **TV**

Sweet Charity 1969 An ever-optimistic dime-a-dance girl has a hard time finding a classy guy to marry. MacLaine is appealing in this big-budget version of the popular Broadway musical by Neil Simon (derived from Fellini's "Notti di Cabiria"). Fosse's debut as film director. Watch for Cort as a flower child. **148m/C; VHS, DVD, Blu-Ray.** Shirley MacLaine; Chita Rivera; John McMartin; Paula Kelly; Sammy Davis, Jr.; Ricardo Montalban; Bud Cort; *D:* Bob Fosse; *C:* Robert L. Surtees; *M:* Cy Coleman.

Sweet Country Road 1/2 1983 A rock singer journeys to Nashville to try to cross over into country music. **95m/C; VHS, DVD.** Buddy Knox; Kary Lynn; Gordy Trapp; Johnny Paycheck; Jeanne Pruett; *D:* Jack McCallum; *W:* Gordy Trapp; *C:* Cyrus Black.

Sweet Dreams 1/2 1985 (PG-13) Biography of country singer Patsy Cline (Lange), who is struggling until her recording of "Walking After Midnight" becomes a hit. Her second marriage to fan Charlie Dick (Harris) begins to unravel as his drinking and her success both increase and Charlie turns abusive. Patsy's rise to stardom ended in an early death. Fine performances thoughout, with Lange lip-synching to Cline's original recordings. **115m/C; VHS, DVD.** Jessica Lange; Ed Harris; Ann Wedgeworth; David Clennon; John Goodman; James Staley; Gary Basaraba; P.J. Soles; *D:* Karel Reisz; *W:* Robert Getchell; *C:* Robbie Greenberg; *M:* Charles Gross.

Sweet Ecstasy 1/2 *Douce Violence; Sweet Violence* 1962 Wealthy shenanigans on the French Riviera. Olivier (Pezy) is the upright young man who can't sleep with anyone unless he's in love, much to sex bomb Elke's (Sommer) dismay. **75m/B; VHS, DVD.** *FR* Elke Sommer; Pierre Brice; Christian Pezy; Claire Maurier; *D:* Max Pecas; *M:* Charles Aznavour.

Sweet Evil 1/2 1995 (R) Naomi and Mike seek the help of a surrogate after a number of failed fertility treatments. Jenny seems to be perfect but after she moves into their home, they learn Jenny's got a nasty secret. **92m/C; VHS, DVD.** Bridgette Wilson-Sampras; Peter Boyle; Scott Cohen; Eiko Matsuda; Claudette Nevins; *D:* Rene Eram. **VIDEO**

Sweet Evil 1998 Anthony Thurman is the owner of a club that specializes in exotic dancers and sometimes the married Anthony gets a little too involved with the entertainment. His wife knows about his habits and doesn't mind until one of Anthony's affairs uncovers an old secret that was better left hidden. **87m/C; VHS, DVD.** Al Sapienza; Andrea Riave; Douglas De Marco; *D:* Michael Paul Girard; *W:* Michael Paul Girard; *C:* Luis Escobar; *M:* Michael Paul Girard. **VIDEO**

Sweet 15 1990 A young Hispanic girl learns that there is more to growing up than parties when she learns her father is an illegal alien. Originally aired on PBS as part of the "Wonderworks" family movie series. **120m/C; VHS, DVD.** Karla Montana; Panchito Gomez; Tony Plana; Jenny Gago; Susan Ruttan; *D:* Victoria Hochberg.

Sweet Georgia 1972 Soft-core star Jordan is a lusty wife whose husband is an alcoholic, so she has a roll in the hay with almost every other cast member. Lots of action, too, including a pitchfork fight. Ride 'em cowboy. **80m/C; VHS, DVD.** Marsha Jordan; Barbara Mills; Gene Drew; Chuck Lawson; *D:* Edward Boles; *W:* Ron Hennessy; *M:* Hal Southern.

Sweet Hearts Dance 1988 (R) Parallel love stories follow two long-time friends, one just falling in love, the other struggling to keep his marriage together. Charming performances from all, but a slow pace undermines the film. **95m/C; VHS, DVD.** Don Johnson; Jeff Daniels; Susan Sarandon; Elizabeth Perkins; Justin Henry; Holly Marie Combs; *D:* Robert Greenwald; *W:* Ernest Thompson; *C:* Tak Fujimoto; *M:* Richard Gibbs.

The Sweet Hereafter 1/2 1996 (R) A schoolbus crash kills 14 children in the small town of Sam Dent, British Columbia. Big city lawyer Mitchell Stephens (Holm) arrives to persuade the townspeople to begin a class-action suit targeting city authorities and the bus manufacturer, while struggling to deal with his drug-addicted daughter Zoe (Banks). Paralyzed teenaged survivor Nicole Burnell (Polley) tries to cope with the aftermath of the tragedy as does widower Billy Ansell (Greenwood), whose two children died in the crash. But the case soon begins to tear the reeling town apart as everyone struggles with loss and fate. Egoyan's intimate, lyrical adaptation of the novel by Russell Banks, is filled with wonderful performances, particularly by Polley. **110m/C; VHS, DVD.** *CA* Ian Holm; Sarah Polley; Bruce Greenwood; Tom McCamus; Arsinee Khanjian; Alberta Watson; Gabrielle Rose; Maury Chaykin; David Hemblen; Earl Pastko; Peter Donaldson; Caerthan Banks; Brook Johnson; Stephanie Morgenstern; *D:* Atom Egoyan; *W:* Atom Egoyan; *C:* Paul Sarossy; *M:* Mychael Danna. Cannes '97: Grand Jury Prize; Genie '97: Actor (Holm), Cinematog., Director (Egoyan), Film, Film Editing, Score, Sound; Ind. Spirit '98: Foreign Film; Toronto-City '97: Canadian Feature Film.

Sweet Home Alabama 1/2 2002 (PG-13) Rich hot city guy or hot poor country guy? That's the choice NYC fashion designer Melanie (Witherspoon) has to make in this amiable romantic comedy. The dueling beaus are Andrew (Dempsey), son of NYC mayor Bergen, and Jake (Lucas), Melanie's high school sweetheart (and current husband) back home in Alabama who still has the hots for her. When Andrew pops the question in high style, Melanie accepts and then races off to Alabama to finish matters with Jake, who hasn't given her a divorce. Complications abound when sparks fly with Jake and Mel's snooty city friends discover her well-hidden, trailer-trash upbringing. Witherspoon plays her trademark plucky act well, elevating a so-so vehicle. **105m/C; VHS, DVD, Blu-Ray.** Reese Witherspoon; Josh(ua) Lucas; Patrick Dempsey; Candice Bergen; Mary Kay Place; Fred Ward; Jean Smart; Ethan (Randall) Embry; Melanie Lynskey; Courtney Gains; Rhona Mitra; Mary Lynn Rajskub; Nathan Lee Graham; Dakota Fanning; Michelle Krusiec; *D:* Andy Tennant; *W:* C. Jay Cox; *C:* Andrew Dunn; *M:* George Fenton.

Sweet Hostage 1/2 1975 Escaped mental patient kidnaps uneducated farm girl and holds her captive in a remote cabin. Blair and Sheen turn in good performances. Adaptation of Nathaniel Benchley's "Welcome to Xanadu." **93m/C; VHS, DVD.** Linda Blair; Martin Sheen; Jeanne Cooper; Lee DeBroux; Dehl Berti; Bert Remsen; *D:* Lee Philips. **TV**

Sweet Insanity WOOF! 2006 (R) Despite being troubled by nightmares (no doubt caused by a series of local murders), high schooler Stacey (Hoyle) invites strange transfer student Christina (Firgens) to her party when her parents go out of town for the weekend. Boring and stupid even by teen slasher standards. **87m/C; DVD.** Rebekah Hoyle; MacKenzie Firgens; David Fine; Josh McRae; *D:* Daniel Hess; *W:* Daniel Hess; Adam Weis; *C:* Kenn Ferro; Virgil Harper; *M:* Jesper Kyd.

Sweet Jane 1/2 1998 Teenaged Tony (Gordon-Levitt) has AIDS and no family. He becomes infatuated with HIV-positive heroin addict Jane (Mathis), whom he sees in the hospital, and follows her into a dangerous street life. Although Jane treats him badly, Tony sticks around to "protect" her and they slowly establish a mutally dependent relationship that offers surrogate family ties and solace for them both. **83m/C; VHS, DVD.** Samantha Mathis; Joseph Gordon-Levitt; Bud Cort; William McNamara; Mary Woronov; *D:* Joe Gayton; *W:* Joe Gayton; *C:* Greg Littlewood; *M:* Walter Werzowa.

Sweet Justice 1/2 1992 (R) This time its the women who get to be commandos, have all the adventures, and get revenge on various scum. The nominal plotline has Sunny Justice (Carter) and her group of gal-warriors avenging the sadistic murder of a friend. Martial arts, weapons, and action galore. **92m/C; VHS, DVD.** Finn Carter; Kathleen Kinmont; Marc Singer; Frank Gorshin; Mickey Rooney; *D:* Allen Plone; *W:* Allen Plone; Jim Tabilio.

Sweet Killing 1993 (R) A banker murders his shrewish wife to be with another woman. He thinks he has the perfect alibi, but then his fictitious excuse comes to life when a mysterious stranger begins stalking him. Based on the novel "Qualthrough" by Agnes Hall. **87m/C; VHS, DVD.** Anthony (Corlan) Higgins; F. Murray Abraham; Leslie Hope; Michael Ironside; Andrea Ferreol; *D:* Eddy Matalon; *W:* Eddy Matalon.

Sweet Land 1/2 2005 (PG) Inge Ottenberg (Reaser) becomes a mail-order bride for Norwegian-American farmer Olaf (Guinee) in Minnesota just after WWI. But the fact that she is German (and knows minimal English) causes strong feelings within the community and the local minister (Heard) refuses to marry them. Olaf moves into the barn to preserve decorum while Inge tries to settle in and they fall in love. Sweet story, told in flashbacks. **110m/C; DVD.** Elizabeth Reaser; Tim Guinee; Alan Cumming; John Heard; Alex Kingston; Ned Beatty; Lois Smith; Paul Sand; *D:* Ali Selim; *W:* Ali Selim; *C:* David Tumblety; *M:* Mark Orton.

Sweet Liberty 1986 (PG) Alda's hometown is overwhelmed by Hollywood chaos during the filming of a movie version of his novel about the American Revolution. Pleasant but predictable. **107m/C; VHS, DVD.** Alan Alda; Michael Caine; Michelle Pfeiffer; Bob Hoskins; Lillian Gish; *D:* Alan Alda; *W:* Alan Alda; *M:* Bruce Broughton.

Sweet Lies 1/2 1988 (R) An insurance investigator tracking a scam artist in Paris is preyed upon by a group of single women betting one another that any man can be seduced. Slow comedy. **86m/C; VHS, Streaming.** Treat Williams; Joanna Pacula; Julianne Phillips; Laura Manszky; Norbert Weisser; Marilyn Dodds Frank; *D:* Nathalie Delon; *M:* Trevor Jones.

The Sweet Life 1/2 2003 Nothing's very sweet in this letdown romantic comedy that turns into a story of sibling rivalry and the emotional bullying of the objection of their would-be affections. Shy Michael envies the ease with which his shallow older brother Frankie deals with women. Frankie puts the moves on sexy bartender Lila while Michael is given an unlikely fix-up with Lila's biker roommate Sherry. After Frankie dumps Lila, she and Michael take an interest in each other, which means Frankie has to get her back at any cost. **86m/C; DVD.** James Lorinz; Robert Mobley; Barbara Sicuranza; Joan Jett; *D:* Rocco Simonelli; *W:* Rocco Simonelli; Roy Frumkes; *C:* James Carmen; *M:* Kenny Laguna.

Sweet Lorraine 1987 (PG-13) A bittersweet, nostalgic comedy about the staff and clientele of a deteriorating Catskills hotel on the eve of its closing. **91m/C; VHS, DVD.** Maureen Stapleton; Lee Richardson; Trini Alvarado; Freddie Roman; John Bedford Lloyd; Giancarlo Esposito; Edie Falco; Todd Graff; Evan Handler; *D:* Steve Gomer; *W:* Michael Zettler; Shelly Altman; *M:* Richard Robbins.

Sweet Movie 1975 A provocative cult classic concerning a South African tycoon who purchases a virgin bride and then exploits her sexually. In English and French with subtitles. **120m/C; VHS, DVD.** *CA FR GE* Carole Laure; Pierre Clementi; Sami Frey; Anna Prucnal; Jane Mallet; John Vernon; *D:* Dusan Makavejev; *W:* Dusan Makavejev; *C:* Pierre Lhomme; *M:* Manos Hadjidakis.

Sweet Nothing in My Ear 2008 This Hallmark Hall of Fame production leaves itself with an unresolved ending after an often dramatic and contentious situation. Dan (Daniels), who can hear, is married to Laura (Matlin), who is deaf. Their eight-year-old son Adam (Valencia) lost his own hearing at age five and a doctor is now recommending Adam as a candidate for cochlear implants that could restore some of his hearing. This alarms Laura and irritates her activist deaf parents, who don't think their grandson needs to be fixed. The situation gets so bad that the Millers separate and begin a custody battle for Adam. Voiceovers are used to translate the sign language. Adapted by

Sachs from his play. **98m/C; DVD.** Jeff Daniels; Marlee Matlin; Sonya Walger; Phyllis Frelich; David Oyelowo; Rosemary Forsyth; Bradford English; Noah Valencia; Ed Waterstreet; *D:* Joseph Sargent; *W:* Stephen Sachs; *C:* Donald M. Morgan; *M:* Charles Bernstein. **TV**

Sweet November 1968 Tearjerker stars Dennis as Sara Deever, a terminally ill woman who shares her apartment with a different lover each month. She helps the guy with his particular hang-up and he helps her, well, live. That is until Mr. November (Newley) refuses to leave when his month is up because he's fallen in love. Remade in 2001. **113m/C; VHS, DVD.** Sandy Dennis; Anthony Newley; Theodore Bikel; Burr de Benning; Sandy Baron; Marj Dusay; Martin West; Virginia Vincent; King Moody; *D:* Robert Ellis Miller; *W:* Herman Raucher; *C:* Daniel F. Fapp; *M:* Michel Legrand.

Sweet November 1/2 **2001 (PG-13)** Stale and contrived remake of the 1968 film stars Theron as a kooky, carefree boho looking to rehabilitate uptight businessmen one month at a time, until her inevitable demise from a mysterious illness. Nelson Moss (Reeves) is Mr. November, who is invited to live with Sara in exchange for losing his cell phone, monkeysuit, and too-tense attitude for a day at the beach (literally). As the November holiday looms and Sara's secret is sappily revealed, we can give thanks that the movie is almost over. Improbable story with decent performance by Theron, while Reeves's is less so, shocking no one. **114m/C; VHS, DVD.** Keanu Reeves; Charlize Theron; Jason Isaacs; Greg Germann; Liam Aiken; Lauren Graham; Michael Rosenbaum; Robert Joy; Jason Kravits; Frank Langella; *D:* Pat O'Connor; *W:* Kurt Voelker; *C:* Edward Lachman; *M:* Christopher Young.

Sweet Perfection *The Perfect Model* **1990 (R)** Jackson plans a big promotion for her beauty contest. Who will be voted the "Perfect Woman?" Tired premise, but it has its moments. **90m/C; VHS, DVD.** Stoney Jackson; Anthony Norman McKay; Catero Colbert; Liza Crusat; Reggie Theus; Tatiana Tumbtzen; *D:* Daryll Roberts; *C:* Sam Sako.

Sweet Revenge *Dandy, the All-American Girl* **1976** Qirky crime comedy. A young woman--call her Dandy or maybe Vurrla--has as many identities as the cars she steals and that's a lot. This serial car thief is saving up to buy a rare Ferrari Dino 246, but public defender Le Clerq tries to steer the headstrong young woman down the straight and narrow instead. **90m/C; DVD.** Stockard Channing; Sam Waterston; Franklin Ajaye; Richard Doughty; Norman Matlock; *D:* Jerry Schatzberg; *W:* Marilyn Goldin; *C:* Vilmos Zsigmond; *M:* Paul Chihara.

Sweet Revenge **1987 (R)** TV journalist kidnapped by a white slavery ring in the Asian jungles. After escaping, she returns for vegeance. Meek drama. **79m/C; VHS, Streaming.** Ted Shackleford; Nancy Allen; Martin Landau; *D:* Mark Sobel.

Sweet Revenge **1990** When a judge tells a divorced couple that the woman must pay the man alimony, she hires an actress to marry her ex. The tables are turned in this way-out marriage flick, reminiscent of the screwball comedies of the 1940s. **89m/C; VHS, Streaming.** Rosanna Arquette; Carrie Fisher; John Sessions; *D:* Charlotte Brandstrom; *W:* Janet Brownell; *M:* Hubert Bougis.

Sweet Revenge 1/2 *The Revengers' Comedies* **1998** Even this professional cast can't rescue this predictable black comedy that is condensed from two 1991 Alan Ayckbourn plays, "The Revengers' Comedies." After saving each other from committing suicide, depressed businessman Henry Bell (Neill) and orphaned aristocrat Karen Knightly (Bonham Carter) agree on reciprocal revenge plots. Karen will punish the guy (Coogan) who stole Henry's job while Henry will destroy the neurotic wife (Scott Thomas) whose husband was once Karen's lover. Then Henry discovers Karen hasn't been telling him the truth. Too much seems to be lost from the original source. **82m/C; VHS, DVD.** *GB FR* Sam Neill; Helena Bonham Carter; Kristin Scott Thomas; Martin Clunes; Rupert Graves; Steve Coogan; John Wood; Liz Smith; Charlotte Coleman; *D:* Malcolm Mowbray; *W:* Malcolm Mowbray; *C:* Romain Winding; *M:* Alexandre Desplat. **CABLE**

The Sweet Ride **1968** Dumb '60s flick has tennis pro Collie (Franciosa), surfer Denny (Sarrazin), and musician Choo-Choo (Denver) sharing a Malibu bachelor beach pad. Denny falls for sexy starlet Vickie (Bisset), who has a problematic past. She gets into trouble with a violent biker and Denny can't save her. **110m/C; DVD.** Anthony (Tony) Franciosa; Michael Sarrazin; Bob Denver; Jacqueline Bisset; Michael Wilding; Warren Stevens; Charles Dierkop; *D:* Harvey Hart; *W:* Tom Mankiewicz; *C:* Robert B. Hauser; *M:* Pete Rugolo.

Sweet Sixteen **2002 (R)** Compston is exceptional in his debut role of teenaged Liam, who lives in Greenock, Scotland where unemployment and violence are rampant. Liam's one wish is to buy a trailer he can move his mother Jean (Coulter) into when she's released from prison in time for his 16th birthday. In order to get the money, petty criminal Martin and his friend Pinball (Ruane) steal the heroin stash of Jean's dealer boyfriend Stan (McCormack). Selling it puts the boys in opposition to local gangster Tony (McCardie), who decides to hire Martin himself. Then things go from bad to worse. Film is melancholy, humorous, tender, and subtitled because of the thick Scottish accents. **106m/C; VHS, DVD.** *GB GE SP* Martin Compston; William Ruane; Annmarie Fulton; Michelle Coulter; Gary McCormack; Martin McCardie; Michelle Abercromby; Tommy McKee; *D:* Ken Loach; *W:* Paul Laverty; *C:* Barry Ackroyd; *M:* George Fenton. Cannes '03: Screenplay.

Sweet Smell of Success 1/2 **1957** Powerful and ruthless New York City gossip columnist J.J. Hunsecker (Lancaster) writes a syndicated newspaper column that pandering press agent Sidney Falco (Curtis) is desperate to have his clients be a part of. Hunsecker only cares about the welfare of his younger sister, Susan (Harrison), and is outraged over her budding romance with jazz musician Steve Dalls (Milner). So he strong arms Falco into breaking up the relationship, with unexpected consequences. Engrossing performances, great dialogue. **96m/C; VHS, DVD.** Burt Lancaster; Tony Curtis; Martin Milner; Barbara Nichols; Sam Levene; Susan Harrison; *D:* Alexander MacKendrick; *W:* Ernest Lehman; Clifford Odets; *C:* James Wong Howe; *M:* Elmer Bernstein. Natl. Film Reg. '93.

Sweet Spirits **WOOF!** *The Red Headed Corpse* **1971** Soft-sell European fluff about a modern mannequin having a raucous affair with an artist. **87m/C; VHS, DVD.** *IT* Erika Blanc; Farley Granger; *D:* Renzo Russo; *W:* Renzo Russo.

Sweet Sugar 1/2 *Chaingang Girls; Captive Women 3: Sweet Sugar* **1972 (R)** Slave girls try to escape from a Costa Rican sugar cane plantation and its cruel owner. Needless to say, vulgar exploitation runs hither and yon in this film. **90m/C; VHS, DVD, Blu-Ray, Streaming.** Phyllis E. Davis; Ella Edwards; Pamela Collins; Cliff Osmond; Timothy Brown; *D:* Michel Levesque.

Sweet Sweetback's Baadasssss Song **1971** A black pimp kills two policemen who beat up a black militant. He uses his street-wise survival skills to elude his pursuers and escape to Mexico. A thriller, but racist, sexist, and violent. **97m/C; VHS, DVD, Blu-Ray.** Melvin Van Peebles; Simon Chuckster; Hubert Scales; John Dullaghan; Rhetta Hughes; John Amos; West Gale; Niva Rochelle; Nick Ferrari; Mario Van Peebles; Megan Van Peebles; *D:* Melvin Van Peebles; *W:* Melvin Van Peebles; *C:* Robert Maxwell; *M:* Melvin Van Peebles.

Sweet Talker 1/2 **1991 (PG)** Following his release from prison, a charming con man shows up in a small coastal village, thinking the townsfolk will be ripe for the picking. What he doesn't know is they can do some sweet talking of their own, and he soon finds himself caring for a pretty widow and her son. Enjoyable light comedy works thanks to likable leads. **91m/C; VHS, DVD.** *AU* Bryan Brown; Karen Allen; Chris Haywood; Bill Kerr; Bruce Spence; Bruce Myles; Paul Chubb; Peter Hehir; Justin Rosniak; *D:* Michael Jenkins; *W:* Tony Morphett; *C:* Russell Boyd; *M:* Richard Thompson; Peter Filleul.

Sweet Thing **2000 (R)** Well-constructed tale concerning a troubled young artist, Sean Fields (Fox), who begins a potentially meteoric rise with a series of controversial paintings. His abusive stepfather, Ray Fields (Lunning), a district judge, has announced his intention to run for U.S. Congress and his campaign success is mirrored by the growing popularity of Sean's work, although the graphic nature of the paintings sparks a warped media frenzy. **115m/C; DVD.** Jeremy Fox; Amalia Stifter; Ev Lunning, Jr.; *D:* Mark David; *W:* Mark David; Mark Spacek; *C:* Mark David; Levy Castleberry; Marc Wiskemann.

Sweet Virginia 1/2 **2017 (R)** An Alaska-set indie thriller that incorporates aspects of neo-noir and westerns. In an isolated, small town, ex-rodeo champ Sam Rossi (Benthal) runs a cheap motel that serves other drifters. One night, Elwood (Abbott) checks into the motel after killing three men at a local bar. The crime was done for Lila McCabe (Poots), who ended years of marital misery by having her husband killed. However, she did not count on the outfall, including the pain of a friend (DeWitt) whose husband was killed there as well. The tense character-driven film is unsettling, and features a strong cast and effective script. **93m/C; DVD, Blu-Ray.** Jon Bernthal; Imogen Poots; Christopher Abbott; Rosemarie DeWitt; Jared Abrahamson; *D:* Jamie M. Dagg; *W:* Benjamin China; Paul China; *C:* Jessica Lee Gagne; *M:* Brooke Blair; Will Blair.

Sweet William **1979 (R)** A philandering and seemingly irresistible young man finds that one sensitive woman hasn't the patience or time for his escapades. Adult comedy concerned with sex without displaying any on the screen. **88m/C; VHS, DVD.** *GB* Sam Waterston; Jenny Agutter; Anna Massey; Arthur Lowe; *D:* Claude Whatham; *W:* Beryl Bainbridge.

The Sweeter Side of Life 1/2 **2013** Hallmark Channel family comedy. Pampered Manhattan doctor's wife, Desiree Harper (Morris), is dumped by her hubby for his young acupuncturist. Losing big thanks to her pre-nup, Desiree takes her business degree and goes back to Jersey to help her dad (Best) save their failing family bakery. Soon, Desiree finds that cupcakes aren't the only sweet things around. **81m/C; DVD.** Kathryn Morris; James Best; Jane March; Alastair Mackenzie; Stephen Hogan; *D:* Michael Damian; *W:* Michael Damian; Janeen Damian; *C:* Viorel Sergovici, Jr.; *M:* Mark Thomas. **CABLE**

The Sweetest Thing **2002 (R)** Girls can be just as sex-obsessed and disgusting as boys as this raunchy comedy sets out to prove. San Francisco party girl Christina Walters (Diaz) isn't looking for Mr. Right—just Mr. Right Now. And she thinks she's met him when Christina and gal pal Courtney (Applegate) take the third of their Musketeer trio'the just-dumped Jane (Blair-)?out to a dance club to drink and flirt. Christina meets cute with Peter (Jane) but doesn't follow through. After getting ragged on by Courtney, the babe duo decide to track him down at the oh-so-genteel wedding he's attending. Havoc ensues. Film's both giddy and sleazy but if you like Diaz at her daffiest, you'll sit through the tacky situations. **84m/C; VHS, DVD.** Cameron Diaz; Christina Applegate; Thomas Jane; Selma Blair; Jason Bateman; Parker Posey; *D:* Roger Kumble; *W:* Nancy M. Pimenthal; *C:* Anthony B. Richmond; *M:* Ed Shearmur.

Sweetgrass 1/2 **2009** Unsentimental documentary about the last sheep drive (in 2003) granted on a federal grazing permit to the summer pasture up into Montana's Absaroka-Beartooth Mountains and the vanishing tradition it represents. It's a months-long drive of some 3,000 sheep that leaves just two men to look after the herd once they reach the highlands: quiet veteran shepherd John Ahem and younger Pat Connelly, who becomes increasingly frustrated by their isolated conditions. The married filmmakers are Harvard University anthropologists and ethnographers. **101m/C; DVD.** *D:* Lucien Castaing-Taylor; Ilisa Barbash; *C:* Lucien Castaing-Taylor.

Sweethearts **1938** MacDonald and Eddy star as married stage actors trying to get some time off from their hectic schedule in this show-within-a-show. Trouble ensues when their conniving producer begs, pleads and tricks them into staying. Lots of well-staged musical numbers. **114m/C; VHS, DVD.** Jeanette MacDonald; Nelson Eddy; Frank Morgan; Florence Rice; Ray Bolger; Mischa Auer; *D:* W.S. Van Dyke. Oscars '38: Color Cinematog.

Sweethearts 1/2 **1997 (R)** Manic-depressive Jasmine (Garofalo) responds to a personal ad placed by Arliss (Rouse), so she'll have a date for her 31st birthday. When the experience goes badly, Jasmine prevents Arliss from leaving by pulling a gun on him. Offbeat and downbeat. **85m/C; VHS, DVD.** Janeane Garofalo; Mitch Rouse; Margaret Cho; Bobcat Goldthwait; *D:* Aleks Horvat; *W:* Aleks Horvat; *C:* John Peters; *M:* Carl Schurtz.

Sweetie **1989 (R)** Bizarre, expressive Australian tragicomedy about a pair of sisters—one a withdrawn, paranoid Plain Jane, the other a dangerously extroverted, overweight sociopath who re-enters her family's life and turns it upside down. Campion's first feature. **97m/C; VHS, DVD; Open Captioned.** *AU* Genevieve Lemon; Karen Colston; Tom Lycos; Jon Darling; Dorothy Barry; Michael Lake; Andre Pataczek; *D:* Jane Campion; *W:* Gerard Lee; Jane Campion; *M:* Martin Armiger.

Sweetwater 1/2 *Sweet Vengeance* **2013 (R)** Fiery ex-prostitute, Sarah (Jones), seeks revenge against a religious nut (Isaacs) who murdered her Mexican husband, stopping at nothing along the way. She'll even bait two horny henchmen by bathing in the river, then gunning them down, au natural. Meanwhile, the local sheriff (Harris) is hot on everyone's trail, intervening just in time for the obligatory standoff. Too well-photographed and dramatic for a B-movie and too zany to be taken seriously. **95m/C; DVD, Blu-Ray.** January Jones; Ed Harris; Jason Isaacs; Eduardo Noriega; Stephen (Steve) Root; Jason Aldean; Vic Browder; *D:* Logan Miller; *W:* Logan Miller; Noah Miller; *C:* Brad Shield; *M:* Martin Davich.

Swelter **2014 (R)** Dumb, too-familiar heist/revenge flick. Five men hit a Las Vegas casino, but four are quickly captured. They break out of prison after 10 years and track down their accomplice to get their share of the money only to find him a small town sheriff who claims to have amnesia and not a clue as to who they are or where the money is. They don't believe him. **83m/C; DVD, Blu-Ray.** Lennie James; Grant Bowler; Josh Henderson; Alfred Molina; Jean-Claude Van Damme; Catalina Sandino Moreno; *D:* Keith Parmer; *W:* Keith Parmer; *C:* Michael Mayers; *M:* Tree Adams. **VIDEO**

Swept Away. . . *Swept Away. . .By an Unusual Destiny in the Blue Sea of August* **1975 (R)** A rich and beautiful Milanese woman is shipwrecked on a desolate island with a swarthy Sicilian deck hand, who also happens to be a dedicated communist. Isolated, the two switch roles, with the wealthy woman dominated by the crude proletarian. Sexy and provocative. Italian with subtitles. **116m/C; VHS, DVD, Blu-Ray.** *IT* Giancarlo Giannini; Mariangela Melato; *D:* Lina Wertmuller; *W:* Lina Wertmuller; *C:* Julio Battiferri; *M:* Piero Piccioni.

Swept Away **2002 (R)** Guy Ritchie directs his wife Madonna in this ill-advised remake of Lina Wertmuller's politically charged romantic comedy. Amber (Madonna) arrives with her husband (Greenwood) as part of a group of ugly Americans taking a tour of the Greek islands on a yacht. A demanding prima (Ma)donna, she is especially rude to first mate Giuseppe (Giannini), whom she calls either "Guido" or "Pee Pee." Amber demands that Guiseppe take her out in the dinghy and they run out of gas and are forced to drift. They end up on a deserted island where Giuseppe now has the upper hand and begins to dominate Amber. Despite the fact that these actors fail at chemistry worse than remedial students, we're supposed to believe that they fall in love. "Gilligan's Island" is more believable, with more romantic sparks. Adriano Giannini reprises the role his father Giancarlo played in the original. **93m/C; VHS, DVD.** Madonna; Adriano Giannini; Jeanne Tripplehorn; Bruce Greenwood; David Thornton; Yorgo Voyagis; Elizabeth Banks; Michael Beattie; *D:* Guy Ritchie; *W:* Guy Ritchie; *C:* Alex Barber; *M:* Michel Colombier. Golden Raspberries '02: Worst Actress (Madonna), Worst Director (Ritchie), Worst Picture.

Swept from the Sea 1/2 *Amy Foster* **1997 (PG-13)** Shipwrecked foreigner (Perez) and ostracized servant girl (Weisz) are star-crossed lovers in 19th century Cornwall. Told in flashback by Dr. Kennedy (McKellen) to Kathy Bates' invalid Miss Swaffer, he recalls how the native Ukrainian Yanko, who could speak no English, was thought to be an idiot by all in town, except the kind and gentle Amy, who found him washed up on the shore. Kennedy and Yanko bond through a game of chess, and the kindly doctor teaches him English. Armed with the native words of love, Yanko goes a'courtin' Miss Amy. Definitely for die-hard romantics, the films throws in all the melodrama it can muster and then some, but performances are worthy (especially McKellen's). Based on a short story by Joseph Conrad. **115m/C; VHS, DVD.** *GB* Vincent Perez; Rachel Weisz; Kathy Bates; Ian McKellen; Joss Ackland; Tom Bell; Zoe Wanamaker; Tony Haygarth; Fiona Victory; ***D:*** Beeban Kidron; ***W:*** Tim Willocks; ***C:*** Dick Pope; ***M:*** John Barry.

Swimfan 1/2 **2002 (PG-13)** Watered down, teen "Fatal Attraction." Ben Cronin (Bradford) is a suburban NYC high school swimming star, and Madison Bell (Christensen) a new girl in town who hooks the studly jock and reels him in. Otherwise involved, the promising athlete allows Madison to seduce him in the pool on one occasion, which automatically sets off her crazy mechanism. She immediately begins to run the well-worn stalker playbook. Ben's life begins to unravel due to Madison's devious designs and after a face-off with his psycho one-night-stand, he's forced to fight back with the help of her cousin, the class nerd. Mildly thrilling pic suffers from editing and continuity gaffes. **93m/C; VHS, DVD.** Erika Christensen; Jesse Bradford; Shiri Appleby; Kate Burton; Clayne Crawford; Jason Ritter; Kia Joy Goodwin; Dan Hedaya; Michael Higgins; Nick Sandow; James DeBello; Pamela Isaacs; Phyllis Somerville; ***D:*** John Polson; ***W:*** Charles F. Bohl; Phillip Schneider; ***C:*** Giles Nuttgens; ***M:*** Louis Febre.

The Swimmer 1/2 **1968 (PG)** A lonely suburbanite swims an existential swath through the pools of his neighborhood landscape in an effort at self-discovery. A surreal, strangely compelling work based on a story by John Cheever. **94m/C; VHS, DVD, Blu-Ray.** Burt Lancaster; Janice Rule; Janet Landgard; Marge Champion; Kim Hunter; Rose Gregorio; John David Garfield; ***D:*** Frank Perry; ***M:*** Marvin Hamlisch.

Swimming 1/2 **2000** Teenaged tomboy Frankie (Ambrose) works in the family diner in the resort town of Myrtle Beach, S.C., alongside her older brother Neil (Pais). Her best friend is extroverted body piercer Nicola (Dundas Lowe), who is somewhat overprotective of the inexperienced Frankie. This shows when Neil hires slinky, confident Josee (Carter) as a waitress and Josee makes a pass at Frankie, who doesn't know how to react. Frankie also catches the eye of newcomer Heath (Harrold) to whom she is drawn, although he makes her no romantic promises. Coming-of-ager with an appealing performance by Ambrose. **98m/C; VHS, DVD.** Lauren Ambrose; Joelle Carter; Jennifer (Jennie) Dundas Lowe; Jamie Harrold; Josh Pais; Anthony Michael Ruivivar; ***D:*** Robert Siegel; ***W:*** Robert Siegel; Liza Bazadona; Grace Woodard; ***C:*** John Leuba; ***M:*** Mark Wike.

Swimming Pool 1/2 **1970 (PG)** Two men and two women spend a weekend in a villa on the French Riviera, manipulating each other, playing sexual games, and changing partners. Their escapades end in murder. Romantic melodrama is sensuous if slow-moving. French film dubbed in English. **85m/C; VHS, Streaming.** *FR* Romy Schneider; Alain Delon; Maurice Ronet; Jane Birkin; ***D:*** Jacques Deray.

Swimming Pool **2003 (R)** Sophisticated, tricky thriller stars Rampling as successful British crime writer Sarah Morton—who's suffering from writer's block. Sarah complains to her publisher, John (Dance), and he offers her his summer house in the South of France. She accepts, thinking a change of scene will be inspiring and hoping John will visit. Instead, Sarah's quiet vacation is rudely interrupted by the arrival of John's uninhibited French daughter from his first marriage, Julie (Sagnier). The neglected teen moves in, flaunts her sexuality (and body) in front of the repressed Englishwoman, and brings home a series of one-night stands. Sarah surreptitiously watches Julie and begins a novel about her. Then, when one of Julie's lovers disappears, Sarah fantasizes that something deadly has occurred. A surprise denouncement may leave viewers frustrated but there's an uneasy seduction to the the film, with both actresses giving their roles edge and vulnerability. **102m/C; VHS, DVD.** *FR GB* Charlotte Rampling; Ludivine Sagnier; Charles Dance; Marc Fayolle; Jean-Marie Lamour; ***D:*** Francois Ozon; ***W:*** Francois Ozon; Emmanuele Bernheim; ***C:*** Yorick Le Saux; ***M:*** Philippe Rombi.

Swimming to Cambodia **1987** Gray tells the story of his bit part in "The Killing Fields," filmed in Cambodia, and makes ironic observations about modern life. It works. **87m/C; DVD.** Spalding Gray; ***D:*** Jonathan Demme; ***C:*** John Bailey; ***M:*** Laurie Anderson.

Swimming Upstream **2003 (PG-13)** Dysfunctional family drama with a sports twist based on a true story. Screenwriter/exec producer Anthony Fingleton fictionalizes his own story of competitive swimming during the 50s and 60s in Brisbane, Australia. His career did not reach true heights due to an overbearing and increasingly violent alcoholic father. Perhaps this poorly executed film had a more cathartic effect on the creator than it does on an audience. **113m/C; DVD.** Geoffrey Rush; Judy Davis; Jesse Spencer; Deborah Kennedy; Mark Hembrow; Melissa Thomas; Tim Draxl; David Hoflin; Craig Horner; Brittany Byrnes; Mitchell Dellevergin; Thomas Davidson; Kain O'Keefe; Robert Quinn; Keeara Byrnes; Des Drury; Dawn Fraser; Remi Broadway; Murray Rose; ***D:*** Russell Mulcahy; ***W:*** Anthony Fingleton; ***C:*** Martin McGrath; ***M:*** Reinhold Heil; Johnny Klimek.

Swimming with Sharks *The Buddy Factor* **1994 (R)** Budding screenwriter Guy (Whaley) goes to work for notoriously insulting movie producer Buddy (Spacey). Soon, Guy grows tired of his boss's demeaning treatment and cruel means of communication and devises a scheme which would even the score. Hollywood satire has more bite than "The Player," and a devious climax, but it's mostly an opportunity for Spacey to hang his hams, which he does with glee. Debut for director Huang, who based his script on his experience as a production assistant. See it with your boss. **93m/C; VHS, DVD.** Kevin Spacey; Frank Whaley; Michelle Forbes; Benicio Del Toro; ***D:*** George Huang; ***W:*** George Huang; ***C:*** Steven Finestone; ***M:*** Tom Heil. N.Y. Film Critics '95: Support. Actor (Spacey).

Swimsuit 1/2 **1989** A young ad executive decides to revitalize a swimsuit company's failing business by sponsoring a contest for the perfect swimsuit model in this TV fluff. **100m/C; VHS, DVD.** William Katt; Catherine Oxenberg; Cyd Charisse; Nia Peeples; Tom Villard; Cheryl Pollak; Billy Warlock; Jack Wagner; ***D:*** Chris Thomson; ***W:*** Robert Schiff; ***C:*** Laszlo George; ***M:*** John D'Andrea. **TV**

The Swindle *Rien ne va plus* **1997** Chabrol's 50th film deals with femme fatale con woman Betty (Huppert) and her older partner, Victor (Serrault). Their modus operandi is for Betty to pick up a businessman, go to his hotel room, and after he passes out from the mickey she's put in his drink, Betty and Victor steal just enough to make it worth their time without raising immediate suspicions. But Betty wants to go for higher stakes and works her own scam with shady Maurice (Cluzet), which has unexpected consequences for the trio. French with subtitles. **105m/C; VHS, DVD.** *FR* Isabelle Huppert; Michel Serrault; Francois Cluzet; Jean-Francois Balmer; ***D:*** Claude Chabrol; ***W:*** Claude Chabrol; ***C:*** Eduardo Serra; ***M:*** Matthieu Chabrol.

Swindle 1/2 **2002 (R)** One-dimensional heist flick. Seth George (Sizemore) is a New York undercover cop who's maybe been undercover a little too long. He's investigating a crime syndicate run by nightclub owner Sophie (Fenn), who's planning a bank heist using Seth as muscle. Since his superiors decide Seth is untrustworthy, they try to shut down his operation, but, having fallen for Sophie, Seth is determined to see her plans through. **93m/C; VHS, DVD.** Tom Sizemore; Sherilyn Fenn; Dave Foley; Conrad Pla; ***D:*** K.C. Bascombe; ***W:*** K.C. Bascombe; ***C:*** Bruce Chun.

Swindled *Incautos* **2004** Young con man Ernesto (Altiero) partners up with older Manco (Alexandre) and the fabled Federico (Luppi) for a potentially lucrative real estate swindle. However, they need the help of sexy Pilar (Abril), a former lover of Federico's who has double-crossed him before. Can they trust each other enough to work together? Or will the temptation of the con be too much for the shady partners? Spanish with subtitles. **107m/C; DVD.** *SP* Ernesto Alterio; Victoria Abril; Federico Luppi; Manuel Alexandre; ***D:*** Miguel Bardem; ***W:*** Miguel Bardem; Carlos Martin; ***C:*** Thierry Arbogast; ***M:*** Juan Bardem.

Swing Fever 1/2 **1943** Bandleader Kyser takes his only shot at playing someone other than himself in this minor MGM musical. Composer Lowell Blackford (Kyser) has inherited a talent for hypnosis. He meets torch singer Ginger Gray (Maxwell) and her boxing promoter fiance, Waltzy Malone (Gargan), who think this unusual ability will come in handy for fixing a fight. Waltzy gets Lowell a nightclub job to sweeten the deal and it all just goes on from there. Harry James and Tommy Dorsey have cameos, Ava Gardner has a bit part, and Lena Horne shows up at the club to sing a song. **80m/B; DVD.** Kay Kyser; Marilyn Maxwell; William Gargan; Nat Pendleton; Curt Bois; Morris Ankrum; Maxie "Slapsie" Rosenbloom; ***D:*** Tim Whelan; ***W:*** Nat Perrin; Warren Wilson; ***C:*** Charles Rosher.

Swing High, Swing Low 1/2 **1937** A trumpet player fights the bottle and the dice to become a hit in the jazz world and marry the woman he loves. Solid drama. From the stage play "Burlesque." Made first as "The Dance of Life," then as "When My Baby Smiles At Me." **95m/B; VHS, DVD.** Carole Lombard; Fred MacMurray; Charles Butterworth; Dorothy Lamour; ***D:*** Mitchell Leisen.

Swing Hostess 1/2 **1944** Judy Alvin (Tilton) gets a room at a theatrical boarding house and pursues her singing career while taking a job at a jukebox company. There's a case of mistaken singing identity when Judy and her untalented rival Phoebe (Brodel) both audition for a band leader's new show and the audition recordings get mixed up. Tilton sang with Benny Goodman's big band. **76m/B; DVD.** Martha Tilton; Betty Brodel; Iris Adrian; Charles Collins; Harry Holman; Emmett Lynn; ***D:*** Sam Newfield; ***W:*** Gail Davenport; Louise Rousseau; ***C:*** Jack Greenhalgh.

Swing Kids **1993 (PG-13)** In 1939 in Germany, big band or "swing" music is the instrument used by a group of young people to rebel against the conformity demanded by Hitler. Highlights the politics of the era, but concentrates mainly on three teenagers and the strains that Nazi power put on their friendship. Although the premise is based in historic fact, there is still something disturbingly silly about the entire production. Dance sequences are lively and well-choreographed. Branagh (in an uncredited role) plays a smooth-talking Gestapo chief. Filmed on location in Prague, Czechoslovakia (as a substitute for Hamburg, Germany). **114m/C; VHS, DVD.** Robert Sean Leonard; Christian Bale; Frank Whaley; Barbara Hershey; Tushka Bergen; David Tom; Kenneth Branagh; Noah Wyle; ***D:*** Thomas Carter; ***W:*** Jonathan Marc Feldman; ***C:*** Jerzy Zielinski; ***M:*** James Horner.

Swing Parade of 1946 1/2 **1946** One of the multitude of 1940s musicals. Young songwriter falls in love with club owner. Highlights include an appearance by the Three Stooges. **74m/B; VHS, DVD, Streaming.** Gale Storm; Phil Regan; Moe Howard; Edward Brophy; Connee Boswell; ***D:*** Phil Karlson.

Swing Shift 1/2 **1984 (PG)** When Hawn takes a job at an aircraft plant after her husband goes off to war, she learns more than riveting. Lahti steals the film as her friend and co-worker. A detailed reminiscence of the American home front during WWII that never seems to gel. Produced by Hawn. **100m/C; DVD.** Goldie Hawn; Kurt Russell; Ed Harris; Christine Lahti; Holly Hunter; Chris Lemmon; Belinda Carlisle; Fred Ward; Roger Corman; Lisa Pelikan; ***D:*** Jonathan Demme; ***W:*** Ron Nyswaner; Bo Goldman; ***C:*** Tak Fujimoto. N.Y. Film Critics '84: Support. Actress (Lahti).

Swing Shift Maisie **1943** Since it's wartime, Maisie (Sothern) gives up her uncertain showbiz career for steady work in an airplane factory. She falls for test pilot Breezy McLaughlin (Craig) only to have the big dope bamboozled by her conniving roommate Iris (Rogers). Maisie threatens to tell the flyboy about Iris' loose morals, and Iris accuses Maisie of being a spy! Seventh in the MGM series. **87m/B; DVD.** Ann Sothern; James Craig; Jean Rogers; Connie Gilchrist; John Qualen; Kay Medford; ***D:*** Norman Z. McLeod; ***W:*** Mary C. McCall; Robert Halff; ***C:*** Harry Stradling, Sr.; ***M:*** Lennie Hayton.

Swing Time **1936** Astaire, a dancer who can't resist gambling, is engaged to marry another woman, until he meets Ginger. One of the team's best efforts. **103m/B; VHS, DVD, Blu-Ray.** Fred Astaire; Ginger Rogers; Helen Broderick; Betty Furness; Eric Blore; Victor Moore; ***D:*** George Stevens; ***M:*** Jerome Kern; Dorothy Fields. Oscars '36: Song ("The Way You Look Tonight"); Natl. Film Reg. '04.

Swing Vote **1999** Provocative TV movie with a bit too much speechifying. When Roe vs. Wade is overturned by the Supreme Court, individual states can make their own laws. Alabama outlaws abortion and convicts Virginia Mapes (Hamilton) of first-degree murder. Her case eventually goes before the Supreme Court and newly-appointed Justice Joseph Kirkland (Garcia) has to cast the deciding vote since the other Justices are evenly split. **90m/C; DVD.** Andy Garcia; Lisa Gay Hamilton; Margaret Colin; Harry Belafonte; Ray Walston; James Whitmore; Kate Nelligan; Milo O'Shea; Albert Hall; Bob Balaban; John Aylward; Robert Prosky; ***D:*** David Anspaugh; ***W:*** Ronald Bass; Jane Rusconi; ***C:*** Johnny E. Jensen; ***M:*** Harry Gregson-Williams. **TV**

Swing Vote 1/2 **2008 (PG-13)** Panicked, butt-kissing presidential campaigns swarm to a New Mexico trailer park when news breaks that the results of the election rest in the hands of one man's final vote. Bud Johnson (Costner), a hung-over lovable-loser and affectionate father, turns out to be the lucky voter who's whisked away by both Republican (Grammer) and Democratic (Hopper) candidates in hopes of winning his vote. A Capra-esque human comedy that pits the Everyday Guy up against The Man, and somehow almost spins the entire far-fetched scenario into something logical. **119m/C; Blu-Ray.** Kevin Costner; Madeline Carroll; Paula Patton; Kelsey Grammer; Dennis Hopper; Nathan Lane; Stanley Tucci; George Lopez; Judge Reinhold; Mare Winningham; Nana Visitor; Mark Moses; Floyd "Red Crow" Westerman; ***D:*** Joshua Michael Stern; ***W:*** Joshua Michael Stern; Jason Richman; ***C:*** Shane Hurlbut; ***M:*** John Debney.

Swing Your Lady 1/2 **1938** Corny hillbilly comedy, adapted from a Broadway comedy, stars an unlikely Bogart as wrestling promoter Ed Hatch. Stranded in Kentucky, Hatch comes up with a publicity stunt to pit his meathead wrestler against the town's female blacksmith. But the wrestler falls for the lady and refuses to go through with the show. **77m/B; DVD.** Humphrey Bogart; Nat Pendleton; Louise Fazenda; Frank McHugh; Penny Singleton; Allen Jenkins; ***D:*** Ray Enright; ***W:*** Maurice Leo; Joseph Schrank; ***C:*** Arthur Edeson; ***M:*** Adolph Deutsch.

Swingers **1996 (R)** Hip, hilarious, and highly entertaining low-budget comedy features five young showbiz wanna-bes on the prowl for career breaks and beautiful "babies" in the Hollywood retro club scene. Mike (screenwriter Favreau) is a struggling actor/comedian from New York who's having trouble getting over his ex. His slick, handsome friend Trent (Vaughn, in a star-making turn) and the rest of his neo-Rat Pack buddies try to get him back in the game with nightly parties and lounge-hopping. Witty script and clever camera work make this one "money, baby, money!" **96m/C; VHS, DVD, Blu-Ray, UMD.** Jon Favreau; Vince Vaughn; Ron Livingston; Patrick Van Horn; Alex Desert; Brooke Langton; Heather Graham; Deena Martin; Katherine Kendall; Blake Lindsley; ***D:*** Doug Liman; ***W:*** Jon Favreau; ***C:*** Doug Liman; ***M:***

Justin Reinhardt. MTV Movie Awards '97: New Filmmaker (Liman).

The Swinging Cheerleaders ½ **1974 (PG)** A group of amorous cheerleaders turn on the entire campus in this typical sexploiter. **90m/C; VHS, DVD, Blu-Ray.** Cheryl "Rainbeaux" Smith; Colleen Camp; Rosanne Katon; Jo Johnston; Mae Mercer; Bob Minor; George D. Wallace; *D:* Jack Hill; *W:* Betty Conklin; *C:* Alfred Taylor; *M:* William Allen Castleman; William Loose.

Swinging Safari ½ **2019 (R)** In a small seaside town in Australia in 1975, 14-year-old Jeff Marsh (Robb) is a budding filmmaker with a Super-8 camera and a growing relationship with neighbor Melly Jones (Wilson). As the community struggles with the issues created by washed up giant whale on the beach, Jeff's home life grows complicated when Melly's parents invite Jeff's parents and another couple to a swingers party and the event does not go as planned. Based loosely on the filmmaker's childhood, the film successfully captures a time when teens were less supervised but is more meaningful when it explores the lives of the adults. **97m/C; DVD.** Guy Pearce; Kylie Minogue; Jesse Denyer; Kotan Jacob; Alex Kotan; *D:* Stephan Elliott; *W:* Stephan Elliott; *C:* Brad Shield; *M:* Guy Gross.

Swinging With the Finkels **2011 (R)** Dumb and decidedly not funny rom com. American Ellie Finkel (Moore) and her Brit hubby Alvin (Freeman) are bored in the bedroom. After trying out a few new toys and roles, which don't help, they find a couple willing to swap partners. **82m/C; DVD.** *UK* Mandy Moore; Martin Freeman; Angus Deayton; Daisy Beaumont; Jonathan Silverman; Melissa George; Jerry Stiller; *D:* Jonathan Newman; *W:* Jonathan Newman; *C:* Dirk Nel; *M:* Mark Thomas.

Swiss Army Man ½ **2016 (R)** The most controversial film at Sundance 2016 was also its most original, a daring, even moving fantasy tale of a man who becomes best friends with a talking corpse. Hank (Dano) is a lonely man on a deserted island, about to hang himself and end it all when Manny (Radcliffe) washes ashore. First, Hank discovers that Manny's post-death flatulence can be used as a propeller to get him off the island. Then he starts talking. And it turns out this odd friendship is as much about what Hank needs in the real world as it is a supernatural occurrence. **97m/C; DVD, Blu-Ray.** Paul Dano; Daniel Radcliffe; Mary Elizabeth Winstead; Antonia Ribero; Richard Gross; *D:* Dan Kwan; Daniel Scheinert; *W:* Dan Kwan; Daniel Scheinert; *C:* Larkin Seiple; *M:* Andy Hull; Robert McDowell.

Swiss Conspiracy *Per Saldo Mord* **1977 (PG)** Against the opulent background of the world's richest financial capital and playground of the wealthy, one man battles to stop a daring and sophisticated blackmailer preying on the secret bank account set. Fast-paced, if sometimes confusing. **92m/C; VHS, DVD.** *GE* David Janssen; Senta Berger; John Saxon; Ray Milland; Elke Sommer; *D:* Jack Arnold; *W:* Norman Klenman; Philip Saltzman; Michael Stanley; *M:* Klaus Doldinger.

The Swiss Family Robinson **1960** A family, seeking to escape Napoleon's war in Europe, sets sail for New Guinea, but shipwrecks on a deserted tropical island. There they build an idyllic life, only to be confronted by a band of pirates. Lots of adventure for family viewing. Filmed on location on the island of Tobago. Based on the novel by Johann Wyss. **126m/C; VHS, DVD, Blu-Ray.** John Mills; Dorothy McGuire; James MacArthur; Tommy Kirk; Janet Munro; Sessue Hayakawa; Kevin Corcoran; *D:* Ken Annakin; *W:* Lowell S. Hawley; *C:* Harry Waxman; *M:* William Alwyn.

Swiss Miss ½ **1938** Stan and Ollie are mousetrap salesmen on the job in Switzerland. Highlights include Stan's tuba serenade and the gorilla-on-the-bridge episode. Also included on this tape is a 1935 Thelma Todd/Patsy Kelly short, "Hot Money." **97m/B; VHS, DVD.** Stan Laurel; Oliver Hardy; Della Lind; Walter Woolf King; Eric Blore; Patsy Kelly; *D:* John Blystone.

The Switch *The Con Artists; Bluff Storia di Truffe e di Imbroglioni* **1976 (R)** An escaped convict takes the place of a talented conman and chaos ensues. **105m/C; VHS, DVD.** *IT* Anthony Quinn; Adriano Celentano; Capucine; Corinne Clery; *D:* Sergio Corbucci; *W:* Massimo De Rita; *C:* Marcello Gatti; *M:* Lelio Luttazzi.

Switch **1991 (R)** A chauvinist louse, slain by the girlfriends he misused, is sent back to Earth as an alluring female to learn the other side's point of view. The plot may lack urgency, but this is a sparkling adult comedy that scores as it pursues the gimmicky concept to a logical, outrageous and touching conclusion. Barkin's act as swaggering male stuck in a woman's body is a masterwork of physical humor. **104m/C; VHS, DVD.** Ellen Barkin; Jimmy Smits; JoBeth Williams; Lorraine Bracco; Perry King; Bruce Payne; Tony Roberts; *D:* Blake Edwards; *W:* Blake Edwards; *C:* Dick Bush; *M:* Henry Mancini.

The Switch ½ *The Baster* **2010 (PG-13)** The father-son bonding turns out to be the strongest part of this predictable Gordon/Speck comedy. Neurotic Wally (Bateman) learns best friend Kassie (Aniston) is using artificial insemination to have a baby. So he drunkenly substitutes his own swimmers and then slowly figures out he's a dad when Kassie, who finally returns to New York, introduces her six-year-old son Sebastian (Robinson), a mini-me version of Wally. Adapted from the Jeffrey Eugenides' short story. **101m/C; Blu-Ray.** Jennifer Aniston; Jason Bateman; Patrick Wilson; Scott Elrod; Jeff Goldblum; Thomas Robinson; Juliette Lewis; *D:* Will Speck; Josh Gordon; *W:* Allan Loeb; *C:* Jess Hall; *M:* Alex Wurman.

Switchback *Going West in America* **1997 (R)** FBI agent Frank Lacrosse (Quaid) pursues the serial killer who kidnapped his son. Against the backdrop of a Texas sheriff's election and a Colorado snowstorm, the killer, who may or may not be a former rail worker (Glover) or the hitchhiking ex-doctor (Leto) he picked up, leads Lacrosse on a convoluted cat-and-mouse game with no apparent logic or motive. First-time director Stuart, who wrote "Die Hard" and "The Fugitive," wrote this one in film school, and it shows. Connect-the-dots set pieces and plot twists only provide Quaid more time to perfect his Harrison Ford impression and Glover more scenery and dialogue to chew. Ermey is impressive as the put-upon small-town sheriff. Stunt work is well done and the Colorado countryside looks great. **120m/C; VHS, DVD.** Dennis Quaid; Danny Glover; Jared Leto; R. Lee Ermey; William Fichtner; Ted Levine; Leo Burmester; Merle Kennedy; Julio Oscar Mechoso; *D:* Jeb Stuart; *W:* Jeb Stuart; *C:* Oliver Wood; *M:* Basil Poledouris.

Switching Channels ½ **1988 (PG)** A modernized remake of "His Girl Friday," and therefore the fourth version of "The Front Page." Beautiful TV anchorwoman (Turner) wants to marry handsome tycoon (Reeve), but her scheming ex-husband (Reynolds) gets in the way. Weak performances from everyone but Beatty and lackluster direction render this off-told story less funny than usual. **108m/C; VHS, DVD, Streaming.** Burt Reynolds; Kathleen Turner; Christopher Reeve; Ned Beatty; Henry Gibson; George Newbern; Al Waxman; Ken James; Joe Silver; Charles Kimbrough; Tony Rosato; *D:* Ted Kotcheff; *W:* Jonathan Reynolds; *M:* Michel Legrand.

Swoon **1991** Kalin's directorial debut is a stylish rendering of the sensational 1924 kidnapping and murder of Bobby Franks by Richard Loeb and Nathan Leopold Jr. and their subsequent trial and imprisonment. Core elements of the case remain but Kalin imposes contemporary styles and morals on the past, particularly his protest against the homophobic attitudes influencing the trial while acknowledging the jaded and dispassionate behavior of the two young men. Previous cinematic versions of the murder case include "Rope" and "Compulsion" but Kalin graphically portrays the characters homosexuality, which was only hinted at in the earlier films. **95m/B; VHS, DVD.** Daniel Schlachet; Craig Chester; Ron Vawter; Michael Kirby; Michael Stumm; Valda Z. Drabla; Natalie Stanford; *D:* Tom Kalin; *W:* Tom Kalin; *C:* Ellen Kuras; *M:* James Bennett. Sundance '92: Cinematog.

The Sword & the Rose ½ *When Knighthood Was in Flower* **1953** Mary Tudor, sister of King Henry VIII, shuns the advances of a nobleman for the love of a commoner. Johns is an obstinate princess; Justice, a fine king. Based on the book "When Knighthood Was in Flower." **91m/C; VHS, Streaming.** Richard Todd; Glynis Johns; Michael Gough; Jane Barrett; James Robertson Justice; *D:* Ken Annakin; *C:* Geoffrey Unsworth.

Sword & the Sorcerer ½ **1982 (R)** Young prince strives to regain control of his kingdom, now ruled by an evil knight and a powerful magician. Mediocre script and acting is enhanced by decent special effects. **100m/C; VHS, DVD.** Lee Horsley; Kathleen Beller; George Maharis; Simon MacCorkindale; Richard Lynch; Richard Moll; Robert Tessier; Nina Van Pallandt; Anna Bjorn; Jeff Corey; *D:* Albert Pyun; *W:* Albert Pyun; *C:* Joseph Mangine; *M:* David Whitaker.

The Sword in the Stone **1963 (G)** The Disney version of the first volume of T.H. White's "The Once and Future King" wherein King Arthur, as a boy, is instructed in the ways of the world by Merlin and Archimedes the owl. Although not in the Disney masterpiece fold, boasts the usual superior animation and a gripping mythological tale. **79m/C; VHS, DVD, Blu-Ray.** *V:* Ricky Sorenson; Sebastian Cabot; Karl Swenson; Junius Matthews; Alan Napier; Norman Alden; Martha Wentworth; Barbara Jo Allen; *D:* Wolfgang Reitherman; *W:* Bill Peet; *M:* George Bruns.

Sword Masters: Brothers Five ½ *Wu hu tu long; Ng fu tiu lung; Brothers Five* **1970** Yen Hsing-Kung (Pei-pei Ching) has vowed revenge on the usual all powerful villain, and is on a quest to unite the five brothers of the Gao family to aid her. Like most revenge martial arts films, it's a little light on story and heavy on fights. In this case more so than usual as at least two thirds of the film is fight scenes—though at least they are pretty well done. **90m/C; DVD.** *CH* Pei Pei Cheng; Han Chin; Yi Chang; Yuen Kao; Hua Yueh; Lieh Lo; Feng Tien; Feng Ku; *D:* Wei Lo; *W:* Wei Lo; Kuang Ni; *C:* Cho-Hua Wu; *M:* Fu-ling Wang.

Sword Masters: The Battle Wizard *Tian long ba bu; Tin lung bat bou; Battle Wizard* **1977** Less a martial arts film than a bizarre fantasy movie, loosely based on an old Chinese novel. Tuan Yu (Danny Lee) is a scholar pursuing the magical red python, which can grant superhuman strength and power. Standing in his way are a kung fu gorilla and a fire breathing wizard with metal chicken legs. **73m/C; DVD.** *CH* Danny Lee; Ni Tien; Chen Chi Lin; *D:* Hsueh Li Pao; *W:* Louis Cha; Kuang Ni; *C:* Ting Pan Yuan; *M:* Yung-Yu Chen.

Sword Masters: Two Champions of Shaolin *Shao Lin yu Wu Dang; Two Champions of Shaolin; Two Champions of Death* **1980** Tung Chien-Chen (Meng Lo) is accepted into the Shaolin temple despite being a despised Manchu because his family has been murdered by the Manchu. Upon ending his apprenticeship in Kung Fu, he is told to keep his head low as the Manchurians and the Wu Tang clan are after the Shaolin temple, and while he tries to hide his rage it's inevitable he gets into a fight with a knife fighter from the Wu Tang looking for revenge on the Shaolin for an act of revenge they committed earlier. Basically everyone wants revenge on someone else. **105m/C; DVD.** *CH* Tat-wah Cho; Yu Hsiao; Chung Kwan; Chien Sun; Siu-hou Chin; Ying Tan; Hsueh-erh Wen; Ching-Ching Yeung; Tai Ping Yu; *D:* Cheh Chang; *W:* Kuang Ni; *C:* Hui-chi Tsao.

Sword Masters: Web of Death **WOOF!** *The Web of Death; Wu du tian luo* **1976** The Master of one of the five Venom Clans wants to reunite them once again, so he attempts to seduce one of the other clan leaders while tracking down a legendary weapon: A spider that roars like an elephant and vomits smoke and fireworks that turn into poisonous webbing. Obviously supernatural spiders are a traditional Kung Fu weapon. **87m/C; DVD, Blu-Ray.** *HK* Feng Ku; Lieh Lo; Hsieh Wang; Hua Yueh; Li Ching; *D:* Yuen Chor; *W:* Kuang Ni; *C:* Chieh Huang; *M:* Yung-Yu Chen.

Sword of Doom *Daibosatsu Toge* **1967** A rousing samurai epic detailing the training of an impulsive, bloodlusting warrior by an elder expert. In Japanese with English subtitles. **120m/B; VHS, DVD, Blu-Ray.** *JP* Tatsuya Nakadai; Toshiro Mifune; *D:* Kihachi Okamoto.

Sword of Gideon ½ **1986** An action-packed and suspenseful TV film about an elite commando group who set out to avenge the Munich Olympic killings of 1972. Adapted from "Vengeance" by George Jonas. **148m/C; VHS, DVD.** Steven Bauer; Michael York; Rod Steiger; Colleen Dewhurst; Robert Joy; Laurent Malet; Lino Ventura; Leslie Hope; *D:* Michael Anderson, Sr.; *W:* Chris Bryant; *M:* Georges Delerue. **TV**

Sword of Honor ½ **1994 (R)** Undercover cop and martial arts expert Johnny Lee (Leigh) investigates his partner's mysterious death amidst the tawdry glamor of Vegas. **97m/C; VHS, DVD.** Steven Leigh; Sophia Crawford; Angelo Tiffe; Jerry Tiffe; Jeff Pruitt; Debbie Scofield; *D:* Robert Tiffe; *W:* Robert Tiffe; Clay Ayers; *M:* David Rubinstein. **VIDEO**

Sword of Honour **2001** After a divorce, 35-year-old Guy Crouchback (Craig) finds new resolve by joining up (although his unit is composed of misfits) and battling the Nazis—until the absurdities of war cause cracks in his idealism. Based on Evelyn Waugh's WWII trilogy. **200m/C; DVD.** *GB* Daniel Craig; Katrin Cartlidge; Megan Dodds; Robert Pugh; Guy Henry; Nicholas Boulton; *D:* Bill Anderson; *W:* William Boyd; *C:* Daf Hobson; *M:* Nina Humphreys. **TV**

Sword of Lancelot ½ *Lancelot and Guinevere* **1963** A costume version of the Arthur-Lancelot-Guinevere triangle, with plenty of swordplay and a sincere respect for the old legend. **115m/C; VHS, DVD.** *GB* Cornel Wilde; Jean Wallace; Brian Aherne; George Baker; *D:* Cornel Wilde.

Sword of Sherwood Forest ½ **1960** The Earl of Newark plots the murder of the Archbishop of Canterbury in yet another rendition of the Robin Hood legend. Cushing is truly evil as the villain. **80m/C; VHS, DVD, Blu-Ray.** *GB* Richard Greene; Peter Cushing; Niall MacGinnis; Richard Pasco; Jack (Gwyllam) Gwillim; Sarah Branch; Nigel Green; Oliver Reed; *D:* Terence Fisher.

Sword of the Beast *Kedamono no Ken; Samurai Gold Seekers* **1965** Gennosuke (Hira) kills a minister of his own clan in a plot to bring about government reform, and flees after being betrayed. Hounded by former comrades he takes shelter in a lonely mountain, which doesn't remain lonely for long once gold is discovered on it. **85m/B; DVD.** *JP* Mikijiro Hira; Go Kato; Shima Iwashita; Toshie Kimura; *D:* Hideo Gosha; *W:* Hideo Gosha; *C:* Toshitada Tsuchiya; *M:* Toshiaki Tsushima.

Sword of the Valiant **1983 (PG)** The Green Knight arrives in Camelot to challenge Gawain. Remake of "Gawain And The Green Knight." Connery adds zest to a minor epic. **102m/C; VHS, DVD.** *GB* Sean Connery; Miles O'Keeffe; Cyrielle Claire; Leigh Lawson; Trevor Howard; Peter Cushing; Wilfrid Brambell; Lila Kedrova; John Rhys-Davies; *D:* Stephen Weeks; *W:* Philip M. Breen; *C:* Frederick A. (Freddie) Young.

Sword of Trust ½ **2019 (R)** When Cynthia (Bell) inherits an antique Civil Warera sword and letter from her grandfather, she and her wife Mary (Watkins) bring it to a Birmingham, Alabama, pawn shop owned by Mel (Maron). With his unfocused assistant Nathaniel (Bass), the four take a convoluted road trip to try to sell the piece. Their first stop is Hog Jaws (Huss), a member of a cult that believes in fringe theories. As they get deeper into their commercial journey, they encounter numerous scary, even dangerous, people. The character-driven indie comedy-drama has memorable moments but also has uninspired wackiness and many repeated comic bits. **88m/C; DVD.** Marc Maron; Jon Bass; Michaela Watkins; Jillian Bell; Toby Huss; *D:* Lynn Shelton; *W:* Lynn Shelton; Michael Patrick O'Brien; *C:* Jason Oldak.

Sword of Venus *Island of Monte Cristo* **1953** Uninspired production finds the son of the Count of Monte Cristo the victim in a scheme to deprive him of his wealth.

73m/B; VHS, DVD. Robert Clarke; Catherine McLeod; Dan O'Herlihy; William Schallert; *D:* Harold Daniels.

Sword of War ½ *Barbarossa* **2009 (R)** Twelfth-century German emperor Frederick I (Hauer), nicknamed Barbarossa for his red beard, wants to revive Charlemagne's Holly Roman Empire by conquering his neighbors. A rebellion led by Alberto da Giussano (Degan) and his Company of Death oppose the emperor's Italian campaign. **123m/C; DVD.** *IT* Rutger Hauer; Raz Degan; Kasia Smutniak; F. Murray Abraham; Christo Jivkov; Antonio Cupo; Cecile Cassel; *D:* Renzo Martinelli; *W:* Renzo Martinelli; Anna Samueli; Giorgio Schottler; *C:* Fabio Cianchetti; *M:* Aldo De Scalzi.

Swordfish **2001 (R)** CIA operative Gabriel Shear (Travolta) uses associate Ginger (Berry) to coerce a computer hacker (Jackman), who's just been released from prison, to steal nine billion dollars from a DEA slush fund. In return, the hacker gets a fresh start with his wife and daughter. The plot goes on from there, but it's too convoluted and pointless to bother with. As is usually the case with anything directed by Sena or produced by Joel Silver, the emphasis is on flash, high-energy action set pieces, and collateral damage, all of which is well done, if eventually repetitive, here. Travolta is an expert at playing the smirking supervillain, but it does wear. Jackman and Cheadle give better performances than the flick deserves, and Berry has fun with her obligatory femme fatale role. **99m/C; VHS, DVD, Blu-Ray, UMD, HD-DVD.** John Travolta; Hugh Jackman; Halle Berry; Don Cheadle; Vinnie Jones; Sam Shepard; Zach Grenier; Camryn Grimes; Rudolf Martin; Drea De Matteo; *D:* Dominic Sena; *W:* Skip Woods; *C:* Paul Cameron; *M:* Christopher Young.

The Swordsman ½ **1947** Technicolor swashbuckler. In 18th-century Scotland the MacArden and Glowan clans are feuding so naturally Alexander MacArden and Barbara Glowan fall in love. Alexander tries to maintain a truce so he and Barbara can get married despite some opposition. **81m/C; DVD.** Larry Parks; Ellen Drew; George Macready; Edgar Buchanan; Ray Collins; Marc Platt; *D:* Joseph H. Lewis; *W:* Wilfred Pettitt; *C:* William E. Snyder; *M:* Hugo Friedhofer.

The Swordsman ½ **1992 (R)** The quest to return the stolen sword of the legendary Alexander the Great to a museum is muscular detective Lamas' assignment. Turns out the detective and his evil millionaire antagonist have been chasing each other through time in their endless quest for revenge and power. **98m/C; VHS, DVD.** Lorenzo Lamas; Claire Stansfield; Michael Champion; *D:* Michael Kennedy; *W:* Michael Kennedy.

Swordsman of Siena ½ **1962** Siena's famous horse race is used as a cover for a rebellion in this predictable but fun swashbuckler. English mercenary Thomas Stanwood (Granger) is hired by the town's brutal Spanish overlord Don Carlos (Garrone) to guard his reluctant fiancee, Lady Orietta (Koscina). Evil schemes cause Thomas to get involved in the rebels' plotting. **96m/C; DVD.** *IT* Stewart Granger; Sylva Koscina; Riccardo Garrone; Christine Kaufmann; Fausto Tozzi; *D:* Etienne Perier; *W:* Michael Kanin; Alec Coppel; *C:* Tonino Delli Colli; *M:* Mario Nascimbene.

Swordsmen in Double Flag Town ½ **1991** Stylized martial arts flick best-appreciated by aficionados. Young Hei Ge (Gao) enters the village of Double Flag Town to claim his promised bride. He kills a man trying to rape his intended and provokes the wrath of the man's brother, a well-known killer called the Lethal Swordsman. Naturally, there's the Chinese equivalent of a showdown at high noon. Mandarin with subtitles. **90m/C; DVD.** *CH* Wei Gao; Mana Zhao; Jiang Chang; Haiying Sun; Gang Wang; *D:* Ping He; *W:* Ping He; Zhangguang Yang; *C:* Deling Ma; *M:* Long Tao.

Sworn Enemies ½ **1996 (R)** Clifton Santier (Greene) goes on a killing spree in a small town where the local sheriff turns out to be his ex-partner, Pershing Quinn (Pare). Now the two enemies decide that only death will settle their old (and new) scores. **101m/C; VHS, DVD.** *CA* Peter Greene; Michael Paré; Macha Grenon; *D:* Shimon Dotan; *W:* Rod Hewitt; *C:* Sylvain Brault; *M:* Walter Christian Rothe; Richard Anthony Boast.

Sworn to Justice ½ **1997 (R)** Psychologist Jana Dane (Rothrock) wakes up with psychic powers after sustaining a serious head injury from the burglars who killed her sister and nephew. Jana then decides to put her new abilities to work for her by becoming a night time avenger. **90m/C; VHS, DVD.** Cynthia Rothrock; Kurt McKinney; Tony LoBianco; Brad Dourif; Mako; Kenn Scott; *D:* Paul Maslak; *W:* Robert Easter; *C:* Richard Benda; *M:* John Coda.

Sybil **1976** Fact-based story of a woman who developed 16 distinct personalities, and the supportive psychiatrist who helped her put the pieces of her ego together. Excellent production featuring Field's Emmy-winning performance. **122m/C; VHS, DVD.** Sally Field; Joanne Woodward; Brad Davis; Martine Bartlett; Jane Hoffman; *D:* Daniel Petrie. **TV**

Sydney White **2007 (PG-13)** Hi ho, hi ho, it's off to college we go. Shut out of her dead mother's sorority, Sydney (Bynes) ends up living with seven, ahem, dorks and must find a way to defeat "fairest-of-them-all" sorority president Rachel (Paxton), win the heart of dreamy Tyler Prince (Long), and teach the entire campus to appreciate the diverse assortment of nerds she calls sidekicks. Bynes has ample charm and talent, but that can't overcome the failings of this modern-day retelling of the Snow White story, whose message is undercut by the fact that it mocks a lot of the characters as much as it uplifts them. **105m/C; DVD, Blu-Ray.** Amanda Bynes; Matt Long; Sara Paxton; John Schneider; Crystal Hunt; Jack Carpenter; Jeremy Howard; *D:* Joe Nussbaum; *W:* Chad Gomez Creasy; *C:* Mark Irwin; *M:* Deborah Lurie.

Sylvester **1985 (PG)** A 16-year-old girl and a cranky stockyard boss team up to train a battered horse named Sylvester for the National Equestrian trials. Nice riding sequences and good performances can't overcome familiar plot, but the kids will enjoy this one. **104m/C; VHS, DVD.** Melissa Gilbert; Richard Farnsworth; Michael Schoeffling; Constance Towers; *D:* Tim Hunter.

Sylvia ½ **2003 (R)** Paltrow gamely takes on the life of the talented but tortured American poet Sylvia Plath in Jeff's bummer biopic. Following Plath's seven-year marriage to English poet Ted Hughes (Craig) until her 1963 suicide in London at 30, pic deals impartially with the details of the affair that caused Plath to jettison Hughes. Also explores her mental illness and long-time grief over her father's death, as well as her conflicted feelings over the dueling roles of artist and wife/mother, and icon for budding feminist issues. Thoughtfully directed, although Paltrow doesn't quite get her teeth into the challenging role. **110m/C; VHS, DVD.** *GB* Gwyneth Paltrow; Daniel Craig; Jared Harris; Amira Casar; Andrew Havill; Sam Troughton; Anthony Strachan; Lucy Davenport; Blythe Danner; Michael Gambon; David Birkin; Michael Mears; *D:* Christine Jeffs; *W:* John Brownlow; *C:* John Toon; *M:* Gabriel Yared.

Sylvia Scarlett ½ **1935** An odd comedy/drama about a woman who masquerades as a boy while on the run with her father, who causes all kinds of instinctive confusion in the men she meets. **94m/B; VHS, DVD.** Katharine Hepburn; Cary Grant; Brian Aherne; Edmund Gwenn; Natalie Paley; Dennie Moore; Lennox Pawle; Daisy Belmore; Nola Luxford; *D:* George Cukor; *W:* John Collier; Gladys Unger; Mortimer Offner; *C:* Russell Metty.

Sympathy for Delicious **2010 (R)** Offbeat, ambitious directorial debut for actor Ruffalo. A once-hot L.A. DJ known as Delicious D, Dean O'Dwyer (Thornton) hasn't gotten a gig since he became paralyzed and wheelchair-bound. Do-gooder priest Father Joe (Ruffalo) encourages embittered Dean, who suddenly develops faith-healing powers (although he can't heal himself). Dean only wants to get back into music so he allows himself to be exploited for money and publicity by an up-and-coming band before there's a moral crisis. **103m/C; DVD, Blu-Ray.** Mark Ruffalo; Juliette Lewis; Orlando Bloom; Christopher Thornton; Laura Linney; Noah Emmerich; James Karen; *D:* Mark Ruffalo; *W:* Christopher Thornton; *C:* Christopher Norr.

Sympathy for Mr. Vengeance *Boksuneun naui geot* **2002 (R)** The first and most brutal of director Park Chan-wook's Vengeance trilogy. A young deaf-mute works in a factory to gain money for his ailing sister's kidney transplant. After being laid off he manages to get a $10k loan from a bank to buy her a kidney from the black market. Instead he is beaten unconscious and robbed, and one of his kidneys is removed, sparking an increasingly disturbing cycle of retribution and violence, which manages to actually further the story (as opposed to being merely gratuitous). **121m/C; DVD, Blu-Ray.** *JP* Kang-ho Song; Du-na Bae; Dae-yeon Lee; Ha-Kyun Shin; Bo-bae Han; *D:* Chan-wook Park; *W:* Jae-sun Lee; Mu-yeong Lee; Yong-jong Lee; *C:* Byeong-il Kim.

Sympathy for the Devil *One Plus One* **1970** Rolling Stones provide music for confused, revolutionary documentary. Episodic jumble is odd, sometimes fascinating. **110m/C; VHS, DVD, Blu-Ray.** *FR* Mick Jagger; Rolling Stones; *D:* Jean-Luc Godard.

Symphony of Six Million **1932** Jewish doctor Felix Klauber (Cortez) is pushed by his family to leave behind the tenements of New York's Lower East Side to make it as a Park Avenue surgeon. However, Felix distances himself from his slum roots and his relatives until several tragedies make him realize what he's truly lost. Dunne is miscast as his crippled former girlfriend Jessica. Adaptation of the Fannie Hurst novel. **94m/B; DVD.** Ricardo Cortez; Irene Dunne; Gregory Ratoff; Anna Appel; Noel Madison; Lita Chevret; John St. Polis; *D:* Gregory La Cava; *W:* J. Walter Ruben; Bernard Schubert; *C:* Leo Tover; *M:* Max Steiner.

Synanon ½ **1965** Reformed alcoholic Chuck Dederich (O'Brien) opens Synanon House in Santa Barbara to help all kinds of addicts. Ex-con druggie Zankie (Cord) gets involved with Joaney (Stevens), who's supposed to be monitoring his progress. When Zankie can't follow the rules, the two leave rehab but run into trouble on the outside. **107m/B; DVD.** Edmond O'Brien; Alex Cord; Stella Stevens; Chuck Connors; Eartha Kitt; Richard Conte; Barbara Luna; Alejandro Rey; *D:* Richard Quine; *W:* Ian Bernard; S. Lee Pogostin; *C:* Harry Stradling, Jr.; *M:* Neal Hefti.

Synapse **1995 (R)** Black-marketeer Andre (Makepeace) is doublecrossed by a partner and arrested by Life Corp., which runs this futuristic civilization. As an experimental punishment, his mind is implanted into the body of Celeste (Duffy), who manages to escape and join up with a band of revolutionaries determined to destroy the evil corporation. Fast-paced story and good special effects. **89m/C; VHS, DVD.** Karen Duffy; Saul Rubinek; Matt McCoy; Chris Makepeace; *D:* Allan Goldstein.

Synchronicity **2016 (R)** Physicist Jim Beale (McKnight) has invented a time machine. Suspicious of a woman he meets named Abby (Davis), he sends himself back in time to learn more about her. Clearly inspired by other sci-fi noirs, Gentry's debut works well within its low budget but it doesn't quite stick the landing. Like a lot of time travel films, the movie makes less and less sense as it goes along and collapses under the weight of its high concept. Still, this is one of those projects that people like to call "promising." **101m/C; DVD, Blu-Ray.** Chad McKnight; Brianne Davis; AJ Bowen; Scott Poythress; Michael Ironside; *D:* Jacob Gentry; *W:* Jacob Gentry; *C:* Eric Maddison; *M:* Ben Lovett.

Syncopation **1942** Chicago trumpeter falls for New Orleans piano-playing babe as pic celebrates the roots of jazz from ragtime through swing. The band's more important than the plot since it features Benny Goodman, Gene Krupa, Harry James, and Charlie Barnet among others. **88m/B; DVD, Blu-Ray.** Jackie Cooper; Bonita Granville; Adolphe Menjou; Walter Catlett; George Bancroft; Robert Benchley; *D:* William Dieterle; *W:* Frank Cavett; Philip Yordan; *C:* J. Roy Hunt.

Synecdoche, New York **2008 (R)** A genius in his own mind, stage director Caden Cotard (Hoffman), who suffers from a variety of ailments, goes off the deep end to conceive his grand opus: a replication of Manhattan in a warehouse and a re-enactment of his life-is-art philosophy. Oscar-winning writer Kaufmann shows he has as much talent behind the camera in his directorial debut. Hoffman delivers another Oscar-worthy performance and anchors the occasionally meandering, existential script, which showcases Kaufmann's unique voice and ability to portray melancholy with such depth and wit as to avoid his material being utterly depressing. **124m/C; Blu-Ray, On Demand.** Philip Seymour Hoffman; Samantha Morton; Michelle Williams; Catherine Keener; Emily Watson; Dianne Wiest; Jennifer Jason Leigh; Hope Davis; Tom Noonan; *D:* Charlie Kaufman; *W:* Charlie Kaufman; *C:* Fred Elmes; *M:* Jon Brion. Ind. Spirit '09: First Feature.

Syngenor ½ **1990 (R)** Syngenor stands for Synthesized Genetic Organism, to differentiate it from all other organisms. Created by science, it escapes, and a crack team of scientists and gung-ho military types are mobilized to track it down. **98m/C; VHS, DVD.** Starr Andreeff; Mitchell Laurance; David Gale; Charles Lucia; Riva Spier; Jeff Doucette; Bill Gratton; Lewis Arquette; Jon Korkes; Melanie Shatner; *D:* George Elanjian, Jr.; *M:* Tom Chase; Steve Rucker.

Syriana ½ **2005 (R)** Gaghan once again uses multiple storylines to tackle a major social issue (after his excellent "Traffic"). This time he studies the interactions of foreign and U.S. governments, Wall Street, the CIA, energy companies, ordinary workers, and lawyers that control the flow of oil to consumers. Dense narrative follows a displaced oil field worker, corporate trouble-shooting lawyer (Wright), an energy analyst (Damon) who suffers a tragic loss, a betrayed CIA operative (Clooney), an oil-rich prince (Siddiq), and a behind-the-scenes power broker (Plummer) as they maneuver to, intentionally or not, affect who controls the energy market, through backroom deals, terrorism (or the threat of it), and even less-pleasant methods. Well-done, if confusing film will generate discussion and reflection. **126m/C; DVD, Blu-Ray, HD-DVD.** George Clooney; Matt Damon; Jeffrey Wright; Chris Cooper; William Hurt; Tim Blake Nelson; Amanda Peet; Christopher Plummer; Alexander Siddig; Akbar Kurtha; Max Minghella; David Clennon; Robert Foxworth; Mark Strong; Mazhar Munir; Khan Shadid Ahmed; William C. Mitchell; Dadral Sonnell; *D:* Stephen Gaghan; *W:* Stephen Gaghan; *C:* Robert Elswit; *M:* Alexandre Desplat; Cynthia Weil. Oscars '05: Support. Actor (Clooney); Golden Globes '06: Support. Actor (Clooney); Natl. Bd. of Review '05: Adapt. Screenplay.

Syrup ½ **2013 (R)** Hotshot ad exec Scat (Fernandez) is desperate to get his new energy drink FUKK on the market before his conniving roommate Sneaky (Lutz) steals his idea. He brings in sexy ad consultant Six (Heard) to use her God-given assets in the name of capitalism. Not surprisingly, Scat and Six eventually fall for each other in their attempt to overcome the brand-snatching villain. The entire affair comes off as clownish and flat, while shooting for clever and layered. An unnecessary and obvious satire as witless at the product being sold - FUKK doesn't stand for anything, and just tries its best to look good on the shelf. **90m/C; DVD, Blu-Ray.** Shiloh Fernandez; Kellan Lutz; Amber Heard; Brittany Snow; Josh Pais; *D:* Aram Rappaport; *W:* Aram Rappaport; Max Barry; *C:* Julio Macat; *M:* Peter Bateman.

The System **1953** Crime drama with some unexpected twists. Bookie John Merrick (Lovejoy) is targeted by a reporter investigating organized crime. Then the politicians get involved when John is called before a crime commission. He pleads the Fifth but soon realizes his fellow crooks don't trust him to keep quiet. **90m/B; DVD.** Frank Lovejoy; Joan Weldon; Paul Picerni; Don Beddoe; Robert Arthur; Fay Roope; Jerome Cowan; *D:* Lewis Seiler; *W:* Jo Eisinger; *C:* Edwin DuPar; *M:* David Buttolph.

The System *The Girl-Getters* **1964** Souvenir photographer Tinker (Reed) and his pals like to take advantage of the pretty female tourists visiting their seaside town. Tinker makes a play for London fashion model Nicola (Merrow), who's onto his game, although Tinker's very surprised when he thinks he's in love. **90m/B; DVD.** *GB* Oliver Reed; Jane Merrow; Barbara Ferris; Julia Foster; Harry Andrews; ***D:*** Michael Winner; ***W:*** Peter Draper; ***C:*** Nicolas Roeg; ***M:*** Stanley Black.

T-Bird Gang ½ **1959** A high school student goes undercover to infiltrate a teen gang. When his cover is blown, things get hairy. Laughable sleazebag production. **75m/B; VHS, DVD.** Ed Nelson; John Brinkley; Pat George; Beach Dickerson; Tony Miller; ***D:*** Richard Harbinger; ***M:*** Shelley Manne.

T-Force ½ **1994 (R)** T-Force is a successful cybernetic law enforcement team set up in the year 2007. But when innocent people get caught in the T-Force crossfire, a team shutdown is ordered, causing the members to turn renegade and fight for their survival instead. The plot rarely gets in the way of the hard-hitting action. **101m/C; VHS, DVD.** Jack Scalia; Erin Gray; Evan Lurie; Daron McBee; ***D:*** Richard Pepin.

T-Men **1947** Treasury Department agents Dennis O'Brien (O'Keefe) and Tony Genaro (Ryder) infiltrate a mob counterfeiting gang. Filmed in semi-documentary style, exciting tale serves also as an effective commentary on the similarities between the agents and those they pursue. Mann and cinematographer Alton do especially fine work here. **96m/B; VHS, DVD, Blu-Ray.** Alfred Ryder; Dennis O'Keefe; June Lockhart; Mary Meade; Wallace Ford; Charles McGraw; ***D:*** Anthony Mann; ***W:*** John C. Higgins; ***C:*** John Alton; ***M:*** Paul Sawtell.

T2 Trainspotting ½ **2017 (R)** The law of diminishing returns impacts Danny Boyle's long-delayed return to the cast of characters that made Trainspotting one of the most beloved films of the '90s. Renton (McGregor) returns to Edinburgh for the first time since fleeing his heroin-addicted buddies with the money he stole two decades earlier. He's reunited with a few friends happy to see him, and an old enemy who wants revenge in the maniacal Begbie (Carlyle). Boyle's nostalgic sequel has some of the energy of the original but never feels anywhere near as breakthrough, leading one to wonder if it was necessary to revisit Renton at all. **117m/C; DVD, Blu-Ray.** Ewan McGregor; Ewen Bremner; Jonny Lee Miller; Robert Carlyle; Kelly Macdonald; ***D:*** Danny Boyle; ***W:*** John Hodge; ***C:*** Anthony Dod Mantle.

Table for Five ½ **1983 (PG)** A divorced father takes his children on a Mediterranean cruise and while sailing, he learns that his ex-wife has died. The father and his ex-wife's husband struggle over who should raise the children. Sentimental and well-acted. **120m/C; VHS, DVD, Blu-Ray.** Jon Voight; Millie Perkins; Richard Crenna; Robbie Kiger; Roxana Zal; Son Hoang Bui; Marie-Christine Barrault; Kevin Costner; ***D:*** Robert Lieberman; ***W:*** David Seltzer; ***M:*** Miles Goodman.

Table for Three **2009 (R)** After Scott's (Routh) girlfriend dumps him and his roommate moves away, he meets seemingly perfect couple Mary (Bush) and Ryan (Bradford) and they move in. Without any concept of personal boundaries, the duo are soon taking over Scott's life, which becomes a big problem when he falls for Leslie (Morrison). Mary and Ryan don't want any interference in their perfect arrangement, which complements their dysfunctional relationship, and try to sabotage the romance (in a funny, not horrific way). **93m/C; DVD.** Brandon Routh; Sophia Bush; Jesse Bradford; Jennifer (Jenny) Morrison; Johnny Galecki; ***D:*** Michael Samonek; ***W:*** Michael Samonek; ***C:*** Matthew Irving; ***M:*** Philip Griffin.

Table 19 ½ **2017 (PG-13)** Imagine the most annoying wedding reception you've been to became a movie. And so here it is in this generally pointless ensemble comedy that squanders its talented group. Eloise (Kendrick) is a once-bridesmaid demoted to one of the worst tables at a wedding reception, a motley crew of people that the bride kind of hoped wouldn't even show up. The idea of a table of lovable losers driving a comedy isn't a horrible one but the writing is atrocious, spared only slightly by the capable cast, which also includes Craig Robinson, Stephen Merchant, and Lisa Kudrow. **87m/C; DVD, Blu-Ray.** Anna Kendrick; Craig Robinson; June Squibb; Lisa Kudrow; Stephen Merchant; Tony Revolori; ***D:*** Jeffrey Blitz; ***W:*** Jay Duplass; Mark Duplass; ***C:*** Ben Richardson; ***M:*** John Swihart.

Table One ½ **2000 (R)** Mildly amusing but too familiar comedy finds Norman (Herman) and his buddies deciding to open a restaurant/bar in Manhattan so they can meet chicks. But they can't quite raise enough money, so Norman gets a local mobster to become a partner, only the mobster sends along his right-hand man Jimmy (Baldwin) to keep an eye on his investment. **84m/C; VHS, DVD.** David Herman; Stephen Baldwin; Michael Rooker; Luis Guzman; Burt Young; Ben Shenkman; ***D:*** Michael Scott Bregman; ***W:*** Michael Scott Bregman.

Tabloid **2010 (R)** In 1977, former beauty queen Joyce McKinney falls for Mormon Kirk Anderson, who is sent to London to do his missionary work. The obsessed McKinney follows him, allegedly kidnaps Anderson, and holds him captive in a Devon cottage for a weekend of kinky sex. British tabloids provided constant coverage and salacious details at the time and director Morris updates the story by interviewing the now middle-aged McKinney, among others (Anderson declined to participate). **88m/C; DVD.** Joyce McKinney; ***D:*** Errol Morris; ***C:*** Robert Chappell; ***M:*** John Kusiak.

Taboo *Gohatto* **1999** In 1865 in Kyoto, the Shogunate is crumbling and Japanese politics are turbulent. Two new recruits join a strict samurai academy—the rugged Tashiro (Asano) and a delicate teenager named Kano (Matsuda). Kano soon proves his worth to the militia commander, Kondo (Sai), and Captain Hijikata (Kitano) but his androgynous beauty begins to cause dissension—leading Kondo to forbid any relations between his men. Japanese with subtitles. **100m/C; VHS, DVD.** *JP* Takeshi "Beat" Kitano; Ryuhei Matsuda; Shinji Takeda; Tadanobu Asano; ***D:*** Nagisa Oshima; ***W:*** Nagisa Oshima; ***C:*** Toyomichi Kurita; ***M:*** Ryuichi Sakamoto.

Taboo **2002 (R)** Mish-mash horror/psycho-thriller flick. Six college friends gather at a remote mansion to play a provocative game of "Taboo" involving a sex question. The following New Year's Eve they gather again and each receives an anonymous note condemning their previous answer. Then the killings start. **80m/C; VHS, DVD.** Nick Stahl; Eddie Kaye Thomas; January Jones; Lori Heuring; Derek Hamilton; Amber Benson; ***D:*** Max Makowski; ***W:*** Chris Fisher; ***M:*** Ryan Beveridge.

Tabu: A Story of the South Seas ½ **1931** Fascinating docudrama about a young pearl diver's ill-fated romance. The gods have declared the young woman he desires "taboo" to all men. Filmed on location in Tahiti. Authored and produced by Murnau and Flaherty. Flaherty left in mid-production due to artistic differences with Murnau, who was later killed in an auto accident one week before the premiere of film. **81m/B; Silent; VHS, DVD, Blu-Ray.** ***D:*** Robert Flaherty; F.W. Murnau; ***C:*** Floyd Crosby. Oscars '31: Cinematog.; Natl. Film Reg. '94.

Tactical Assault ½ **1999 (R)** During the Gulf War, Air Force pilot John Holiday (Hauer) loses it under pressure and nearly shoots down an unarmed passenger jet. Pilot Lee Banning (Patrick) is forced to shoot down Holiday's plane instead to save the situation. But Holiday doesn't see things that way and decides to get revenge on Lee. Good action in what's really a revenge thriller. **89m/C; VHS, DVD.** Rutger Hauer; Robert Patrick; Isabel Glasser; Ken Howard; ***D:*** Mark Griffiths. **VIDEO**

Tactical Force ½ **2011 (R)** Predictable actioner. Three members of an L.A. SWAT team are on a training mission in an abandoned hangar when they are unexpectedly trapped by two rival gangs after the same merchandise. **90m/C; DVD, Blu-Ray.** Steve Austin; Michael Jai White; Lexa Doig; Steve Bacic; Michael Shanks; ***D:*** Adamo P. Cultraro; ***W:*** Adamo P. Cultraro; ***C:*** Bruce Chun; ***M:*** Michael Richard Plowman. **VIDEO**

Tadpole ½ **2002 (PG-13)** You know you've hit a chord when your movie's title has been adopted as a verb (tadpoling) for the trend of older women cruising younger men. Precocious, prep-schooler Oscar Grubman (Stanford) comes home to Manhattan to spend the holidays with his remarried dad (Ritter) and his new stepmom (Weaver), on whom he promptly develops a crush. Soon the unrequited love for his new mum, the aptly named Eve, is soothed instead by her cradle-robbing best friend (a show-stealing Neuwirth). Stanford shines, even through the drab digital camerawork, in this witty, new millennium "Graduate." **77m/C; VHS, DVD.** Aaron Stanford; Sigourney Weaver; John Ritter; Bebe Neuwirth; Robert Iler; Peter Appel; Adam LeFevre; ***D:*** Gary Winick; ***W:*** Heather McGowan; Niels Mueller; ***C:*** Hubert Taczanowski.

Taffin ½ **1988 (R)** An Irish bill collector battles a group of corrupt businessmen who want to replace the local soccer field with a hazardous chemical plant. Pretty dull fare, overall, with Brosnan much less charismatic than usual. **96m/C; VHS, DVD.** *GB* Pierce Brosnan; Ray McAnally; Alison Doody; Patrick Bergin; ***D:*** Francis Megahy; ***W:*** David Ambrose.

Tag **2018 (R)** For the last 30 years, a group of friends has devoted the month of May to a no-holds-barred game of tag. When the only undefeated player (Renner) announces his impending retirement from the game, the other players pull out all the stops on their last chance to tag him "it." The inherent silliness of the concept is manifest on screen, but there's also a healthy dose of emotion over the bonds of friendship. Two tidbits make the flick more interesting: it's based on a true story, and Renner's arms are CGIed in many scenes because he broke them both on the third day of filming. **100m/C; DVD, Blu-Ray.** Ed Helms; Jake Johnson; Jeremy Renner; Hannibal Buress; Isla Fisher; ***D:*** Jeff Tomsic; ***W:*** Rob McKittrick; Mark Steilen; ***C:*** Larry Blanford; ***M:*** Germaine Franco.

Tai-Pan ½ **1986 (R)** A 19th century Scottish trader and his beautiful Chinese mistress are the main characters in this confusing attempt to dramatize the story of Hong Kong's development into a thriving trading port. Too many subplots and characters are introduced in a short time to do justice to James Clavell's novel of the same name, the basis for the movie. The first American production completely filmed in China. **130m/C; VHS, DVD.** Bryan Brown; Joan Chen; John Stanton; Kyra Sedgwick; Tim Guinee; Russell Wong; Bert Remsen; ***D:*** Daryl Duke; ***W:*** John Briley; ***C:*** Jack Cardiff; ***M:*** Maurice Jarre.

Tail Lights Fade **1999 (R)** Angie (Allen) is living in Toronto when she learns her marijuana-dealing brother has been busted. So she convinces boyfriend Cole (Meyer) that they should drive to Vancouver in order to destroy his greenhouse crop before the cops discover it. And for some reason, Cole decides this would be a perfect opportunity to convince their friends Bruce (Busey) and Wendy (Richards) that they should indulge in a cross-country relay race. Dumb. Title comes from a Buffalo Tom song. **87m/C; VHS, DVD.** *CA* Tanya Allen; Breckin Meyer; Jake Busey; Denise Richards; Lisa Marie; Elizabeth Berkley; Jaimz Woolvett; ***D:*** Malcolm Ingram; ***W:*** Matthew Gissing; ***C:*** Brian Pearson.

Tail Spin **1939** Trixie Lee (Faye) is determined to succeed flying in cross-country races. Her main competition--in the air and in the romance department--is wealthy Gerry Lester (Bennett), whom the other fliers don't much like. Lots of crashes and not everyone makes it out alive. **84m/B; DVD.** Alice Faye; Constance Bennett; Nancy Kelly; Joan Davis; Jane Wyman; Charles Farrell; Kane Richmond; ***D:*** Roy Del Ruth; ***W:*** Frank Wead; ***C:*** Karl Freund.

The Tailor of Panama ½ **2000 (R)** British spy Andrew Osnard (Brosnan) threatens to expose the shady past of society tailor Harry Pendel (Rush) unless Harry passes on information about the political situation in Panama. But since Harry doesn't really know anything, he just makes up plausible lies. Le Carre and Boorman create a smart, cynical film from Le Carre's 1996 novel, utilizing Brosnan to treak his famous alter-ego and expose the corruption of post-Cold War espionage and Western foreign affairs. Well-written, with believable characterizations and subtle, consistent plotting, and as an added bonus, the performances match the high standards of the writing. **109m/C; VHS, DVD, Blu-Ray.** *US IR* Pierce Brosnan; Geoffrey Rush; Jamie Lee Curtis; Brendan Gleeson; Catherine McCormack; Leonor Varela; Harold Pinter; Daniel Radcliffe; David Hayman; Mark Margolis; Martin Ferrero; John Fortune; ***D:*** John Boorman; ***W:*** John Boorman; Andrew Davies; John Le Carre; ***C:*** Philippe Rousselot; ***M:*** Shaun Davey.

Tailspin Tommy **1934** Features 12 chapters of the great action serial. Intrepid pilot helps a small airline win a mail contract then must battle an unscrupulous rival to keep it. **248m/B; VHS, DVD.** Maurice Murphy; Noah Beery, Jr.; Walter Miller; Patricia Farr; Grant Withers; John Davidson; William Desmond; Charles A. Browne; ***D:*** Lew Landers.

The Taint ½ **2010** A town's local water supply is contaminated with a form of super viagra that causes men to become obsessed with killing women, preferably by crushing their heads. **75m/C; DVD, Blu-Ray.** Drew Bolduc; Colleen Walsh; Cody Crenshaw; Kenneth Hall; Gabriella Herzberg; ***D:*** Drew Bolduc; Dan Nelson; ***W:*** Drew Bolduc; ***C:*** Dan Nelson; ***M:*** Drew Bolduc. **VIDEO**

Tainted ½ **1988** Small-town woman tries to endure after being raped. Both her husband and the attacker are killed, and she is forced to conceal their deaths. Poorly scripted. **90m/C; VHS, DVD.** Shari Shattuck; Park Overall; Gene Tootle; Magilla Schaus; Blaque Fowler; ***D:*** Orestes Matacena.

Tainted ½ **1998** Ever wonder what would happen if the guys from "Clerks" fell in with a bunch of vampires? Well, lucky you. Now you can find out. Video clerks Ryan and J.T. hitch a ride to the midnight movie with their new co-worker Alex, who just happens to be a vampire whose ex is shacking up with the new vamp in town, who wants to taint the city's blood supply with undead blood. Script has many laughs, lots of attitude, and plenty of pop-culture knowledge, but gets a bit windy at times. Sometimes the actors seem to to trying a little too hard, but it doesn't detract from the story. Filmed in Detroit with lots of excellent local product placement. **106m/C; VHS, DVD.** Dusan "Dean" Cechvala; Greg James; Sean Farley; Jason Brouwer; Tina Kapousis; Edward Zeimis; Robert St. Mary; Brian Evans; ***D:*** Brian Evans; ***W:*** Sean Farley; ***C:*** Brian Evans; ***M:*** Jessie McClear. **VIDEO**

The Take ½ **1974** Cop Terry Sneed (Williams) is brought in to stop a crime wave plaguing Paloma, New Mexico. The corrupt police captain is on the payroll of local crime boss Victor Manso (Morrow) but it turns out Sneed is running his own bribery racket in this quasi-blaxploitation flick. **92m/C; DVD, Blu-Ray.** Billy Dee Williams; Vic Morrow; Albert Salmi; Eddie Albert; Sorrell Brooke; Frankie Avalon; Tracy Reed; A. Martinez; James Luisi; ***D:*** Robert Hartford-Davis; ***W:*** Franklin Coen; Del Reisman; ***C:*** Duke Callaghan; Kirk Axtell; ***M:*** Fred Karlin.

The Take **2009** Violent Brit crime miniseries based on the novel by Martina Cole. In 1984, London gangster Freddie Jackson (Hardy) gets out of prison after four years of hard time and heads straight back to business. As a protege of incarcerated crime boss Ozzy (Cox), Freddie figures he's on his way to the top rung of the criminal ladder until his smarter cousin Jimmy (Evans) comes along. This doesn't sit well with Freddie, who has a lot of other family issues he can't deal with either. **180m/C; DVD.** *UK* Tom (Thomas) Hardy; Shaun Evans; Brian Cox; Charlotte Riley; Kierston Wareing; ***D:*** Dr. David Drury; ***W:*** Neil Biswas; ***C:*** Owen McPolin; ***M:*** Ruth Barrett. **TV**

The Take ½ *Bastille Day* **2016 (R)** A British spy thriller centered on self-absorbed CIA Agent Briar (Elba), the only one who can stop a terrorist group ready to wreak havoc in Paris. In the French city, the terrorists work in the shadows and manipulate working class protestors to create diversions for their crimes. One of Briar's partners in Paris is Zoe Naville (Le Bon), a protestor who reluctantly becomes a terrorist. Briar uses any means necessary to being the terrorists down, including punching Zoe after disarming her. Briar's brutal, unapologetic ugly American stereotype is but one problem in this film, saved only by Elba's magnetic presence. **92m/C; DVD, Blu-Ray.** Idris Elba; Richard Madden; Charlotte Le Bon; Kelly Reilly; Jose Garcia; ***D:*** James Watkins; ***W:*** James Watkins; Andrew Baldwin; ***C:*** Tim Maurice-Jones; ***M:*** Alex Heffes.

Take a Giant Step **1959** Spencer Scott (played by pop singer Nash) struggles to find an identity as the only black student in a white suburban high school. His middle-class family bows to the racist times, except for his outspoken Grandma Martin, who's the only one to understand how alienated Spencer feels. **99m/B; DVD.** Johnny Nash; Estelle Hemsley; Ruby Dee; Frederick O'Neal; Beah Richards; Ellen Holly; Paulene Myers; ***D:*** Philip Leacock; ***W:*** Julius J. Epstein; Lou Peterson; ***C:*** Arthur E. Arling; ***M:*** Jack Marshall.

Take a Girl Like You 1/2 **1970** Dated Brit sex comedy adapted from a novel by Kingsley Amis. Virginal Jenny takes a job in London as a schoolteacher and soon attracts the attention of art teacher Patrick, who thinks he's irresistible to women. Jenny resists, but changes her mind about Patrick's sincerity until she's informed that Patrick is not the marrying kind. **98m/C; DVD, Blu-Ray.** *UK* Hayley Mills; Oliver Reed; Noel Harrison; Sheila Hancock; Ronald Lacey; ***D:*** Jonathan Miller; ***W:*** George Melly; ***C:*** Dick Bush; ***M:*** Stanley Myers.

Take a Hard Ride 1/2 **1975 (R)** Dull spaghetti western about a cowboy transporting money to Mexico, evading bandits and bounty hunters. **103m/C; VHS, DVD, Blu-Ray.** *IT* Jim Brown; Lee Van Cleef; Fred Williamson; Jim Kelly; Barry Sullivan; ***D:*** Anthony M. Dawson; ***M:*** Jerry Goldsmith.

Take Care of My Cat 1/2 *Goyangileul butaghae* **2001** Five girlfriends graduate from a port city in Korea and try to make lives for themselves after high school, with varying degrees of success. The girls try to arrange for reunions to remain together despite their distance. Uses the same bleaching method as "Seven" to achieve a kind of odd color palette for the film. **112m/C; DVD.** *NK* Du-na Bae; Yu-won Lee; Ji-young Ok; Eung-sil Lee; ***D:*** Jae-eun Jeong; ***W:*** Jae-eun Jeong; ***C:*** Yeong-hwon Choi.

Take Down 1/2 *Deliver Them from Evil: The Taking of Alta View* **1992 (PG-13)** Rick Worthington (Hamlin) takes hostages in a Utah hospital maternity ward, seeking revenge on the doctors who sterilized his wife. He threatens to detonate a bomb even as a hostage negogiator (O'Quinn) tries to defuse the situation. **96m/C; VHS, DVD.** Harry Hamlin; Teri Garr; Terry O'Quinn; Gary Frank; Keith Coulouris; ***D:*** Peter Levin; ***W:*** John Miglis; ***C:*** Ronald Orieux; ***M:*** Mark Snow. **TV**

Take Her, She's Mine 1/2 **1963** In this befuddled dad comedy, respectable Frank Michaelson (Stewart) is sent into a frenzy of embarrassment by the rebellious antics of his daughter Mollie (Dee). Overprotective Frank even goes to Paris when the art student falls for avart-garde artist Henri (Forquet), with Dad bedevilled by cultural misunderstandings. Based on the Phoebe and Henry Ephron play. **98m/C; DVD.** James Stewart; Sandra Dee; Audrey Meadows; Philippe Forquet; Robert Morley; John McGiver; Bob Denver; ***D:*** Henry Koster; ***W:*** Nunnally Johnson; ***C:*** Lucien Ballard; ***M:*** Jerry Goldsmith.

Take It to the Limit 1/2 **2000** Troubled teen Rick (Fitzpatrick) is sent to stay with his uncle (Marlo) in hopes that it'll straighten him out. But that happens when Jill (Roenfeldt), a cute girl, introduces him to rock climbing. This is a pretty good movie for kids. It's a bit obvious, but it treats the characters seriously. **87m/C; DVD.** Leo Fitzpatrick; John Marlo; Gretel Roenfeldt; Jason Bortz; Christin Couto; ***D:*** Sam Kieth; ***W:*** Arthur Jeon; ***C:*** Michael Anderson; ***M:*** Louis Gabriel Cowan.

Take Me 1/2 **2001** Jack and Kay Chambers move to a new community in hopes of saving their marriage but all their neighbors are wife-swappers and the Chambers' are soon joining in. Then there's a problem with a murder and the dull overextended sexcapades turn into a dull overextended thriller. **300m/C; DVD.** *GB* Robson Green; Beth Goddard; Danny (Daniel) Webb; Keith Barron; Olga Sosnovska; ***D:*** Alex Pillai; ***W:*** Caleb Ranson; ***C:*** Simon Maggs; ***M:*** John Harle. **TV**

Take Me Home 1/2 **2011 (PG-13)** Thom (Sam Jaeger) is driving an illegal cab in New York when he picks up a distraught Claire (Amber Jaeger). She's just discovered her husband in flagrante when she finds out her estranged father has had a heart attack. She tells him to drive--all the way to California where her dad lives. Their impulsive road trip doesn't go smoothly but the leads are appealing and the pic's upbeat. **97m/C; DVD.** Sam Jaeger; Amber Jaeger; Victor Garber; Christine Rose; Lin Shaye; Brennan Elliott; Bree Turner; ***D:*** Sam Jaeger; ***W:*** Sam Jaeger; ***C:*** Jesse Feldman.

Take Me Home: The John Denver Story **2000** Biopic of the 70s country-folk crooner hits the high points and explores the lows, but it's typical TV movie fare, made quickly after Denver's death in a plane crash. Although he bares no physical resemblance to the the singer, Lowe does a fine job. Based on the autobiography Denver co-wrote with Arthur Tobier. **90m/C; VHS, DVD.** Chad Lowe; Kristin Davis; Gerald McRaney; Brian Markinson; Susan Hogan; Garry Chalk; ***D:*** Jerry London; ***W:*** Stephen Harrigan; ***C:*** Mike Fash; ***M:*** Lee Holdridge. **TV**

Take Me Home Tonight 1/2 *Kids in America* **2011 (R)** Familiar pop-culture, up-all-night comedy-drama. In 1988, aimless MIT grad Matt takes a job as a video store clerk and awkwardly tries to impress dream girl Tori at a Labor Day blowout. Meanwhile, Matt, his bright twin sister Wendy (who's involved with party-throwing doofus jock Kyle), and his tubby, unhip best bud Barry try to figure out what to do with their lives. **98m/C; DVD, Blu-Ray.** Topher Grace; Anna Faris; Dan Fogler; Teresa Palmer; Chris Pratt; Michael Biehn; Michelle Trachtenberg; Michael Ian Black; Lucy Punch; Demetri Martin; Angie Everhart; ***D:*** Michael Dowse; ***W:*** Michael Dowse; Jackie Filgo; Jeff Filgo; ***C:*** Terry Stacey; ***M:*** Trevor Horn.

Take Me Out to the Ball Game 1/2 *Everybody's Cheering* **1949** Williams manages a baseball team, locks horns with players Sinatra and Kelly, and wins them over with song. Naturally, there's a water ballet scene. Contrived and forced, but enjoyable. **93m/C; VHS, DVD.** Frank Sinatra; Gene Kelly; Esther Williams; Jules Munshin; Betty Garrett; Edward Arnold; Tom Dugan; Richard Lane; ***D:*** Busby Berkeley; ***W:*** Harry Tugend; George Wells; ***C:*** George J. Folsey; ***M:*** Roger Edens.

Take My Advice: The Ann & Abby Story 1/2 **1999** Lifetime drama with a good period look and work from Malick in the title roles. Twin sisters Esther and Pauline Friedman become fierce syndicated rivals when they both become advice columnists: Esther as Ann Landers and Pauline as Abigail Van Buren. Covers a four decade period from the 1950s through the late 1990s, involving their personal and professional feuds. **90m/C; DVD.** Wendie Malick; Robert Desiderio; David Groh; Kenneth Gilman; Joann Johnson; Michelle Duffy; ***D:*** Alan Metzger; ***W:*** Howard Burkons; Adam Gilad; ***C:*** Eric Van Haren Noman; ***M:*** Patrick Williams. **CABLE**

Take My Eyes *Te Day Mis Ojos* **2003** Pilar takes her young son Juan and hides out at her sister Ana's to escape violent husband Antonio. He, of course, can't understand what he did wrong and insists Pilar come back, but Ana has gotten her a job that gives her a little independence and self-esteem. When Antonio goes into counseling, Pilar reluctantly agrees to return but things are soon back to their nasty routine. Spanish with subtitles. **106m/C; DVD.** *SP* Laia Marull; Luis Tosar; Candela Pena; Rosa Maria Sarda; Sergi Calleja; ***D:*** Iciar Bollain; ***W:*** Iciar Bollain; Alicia Luna; ***C:*** Carlos Gusi; ***M:*** Alberto Iglesias.

Take Shelter **2011 (R)** Shannon gives a captivating performance as Curtis, an average Ohio construction worker with a happy family life who may be the only one to know that the apocalypse is imminent. Terrifying nightmares of the end of the world have rattled him so hard that they make him physically ill and he decides to build a shelter. Shannon is nothing less than spectacular, assisted ably by the great Chastain as his wife. A dark, mesmerizing tale of a man who realizes that he is either a prophet or a psychopath. **124m/C; DVD, Blu-Ray.** Michael Shannon; Jessica Chastain; Shea Whigham; Katy Mixon; Ray McKinnon; Lisa Gay Hamilton; Robert Longstreet; Kathy Baker; Tova Stewart; ***D:*** Jeff Nichols; ***W:*** Jeff Nichols; ***C:*** Adam Stone; ***M:*** David Wingo.

Take the Lead 1/2 **2006 (PG-13)** Charming Banderas dances with happy feet in this cliched, inspirational saga based on a true story. The instructor/owner of a Manhattan ballroom dance academy, Pierre Dulaine offers his services to Principal James (Woodard) in an effort to teach her South Bronx high school detention students some discipline and manners. The kids are reluctantly impressed by a smoldering tango, and Dulaine is equally intrigued when they add their hip-hop moves to his formal steps. Everyone is gradually won over and, yes, it all leads up to a big "I've had the time of my life" dance competition. **117m/C; DVD.** John Ortiz; Antonio Banderas; Alfre Woodard; Jenna Dewan; Dante Basco; Rob Brown; Yaya DaCosta; Lauren Collins; Brandon D. Andrews; ***D:*** Liz Friedlander; ***W:*** Dianne Houston; ***C:*** Alex Nepomniaschy; ***M:*** Aaron Zigman.

Take the Money and Run **1969 (PG)** Allen's directing debut; he also co-wrote and starred. "Documentary" follows a timid, would-be bank robber who can't get his career off the ground and keeps landing in jail. Little plot, but who cares? Nonstop one-liners and slapstick. **85m/C; VHS, DVD, Blu-Ray.** Woody Allen; Janet Margolin; Marcel Hillaire; Louise Lasser; Jacquelyn Hyde; Lonny (Lonnie) Chapman; Jan Merlin; James Anderson; Jackson Beck; Howard Storm; ***D:*** Woody Allen; ***W:*** Woody Allen; Mickey Rose; ***C:*** Lester Shorr; ***M:*** Marvin Hamlisch.

Take This Job & Shove It **1981 (PG)** The Johnny Paycheck song inspired this story of a hot-shot efficiency expert who returns to his hometown to streamline the local brewery. Encounters with old pals inspire self-questioning. Alternately inspired and hackneyed. Cameos by Paycheck and other country stars. **100m/C; VHS, DVD.** Robert Hays; Art Carney; Barbara Hershey; David Keith; Martin Mull; Eddie Albert; Penelope Milford; ***Cameo(s):*** Johnny Paycheck; David Allan Coe; Charlie Rich; Lacy J. Dalton; ***D:*** Gus Trikonis; ***W:*** Barry Schneider.

Take This Waltz 1/2 *Take this Waltz: Une histoire d'amour* **2011 (R)** Toronto freelance writer Margot (Williams) loves her good-hearted cookbook writer husband, Lou (Rogen), but has become faintly dissatisfied with their marriage and her life. She needs a spark and suddenly finds it in her would-be artist neighbor Daniel (Kirby) and their will-they-or-won't-they encounters. Maybe the intensity just lies in the temptation. Williams doesn't disappoint as a woman struggling to come to terms with the crossroads she finds herself at. **116m/C; DVD, Blu-Ray, Streaming.** *CA JP SP* Michelle Williams; Seth Rogen; Luke Kirby; Sarah Silverman; Jennifer Podemski; ***D:*** Sarah Polley; ***W:*** Sarah Polley; ***C:*** Luc Montpellier; ***M:*** Jonathan Goldsmith.

Takedown 1/2 *Transparency* **2010 (R)** Security guard David is a former cop whose daughter was raped and murdered. So he's looking for retribution when he finds out that the Serbian girl hiding in a truck ran away from Russian human traffickers. **97m/C; DVD.** Lou Diamond Phillips; Estella Warren; Deborah Kara Unger; Aaron Pearl; Jordana Largy; Kendall Cross; Michael Kropsa; ***D:*** Raul Inglis; ***W:*** Raul Inglis; ***C:*** Michael Blundell; ***M:*** Chris Nickel. **VIDEO**

Taken 1/2 **1999 (R)** Businessman Coleman gets kidnapped only both his wife and business partners see a financial opportunity and decide not to pay the ransom. When he realizes this, Coleman thinks it prudent to befriend kidnapper Boutsikaris and hope that something can be worked out. **96m/C; VHS, DVD.** *CA* Dabney Coleman; Dennis Boutsikaris; Linda Smith; Dorothee Berryman; Carl Alacchi; ***D:*** Max Fischer; ***W:*** Pierre Lapointe.

Taken 1/2 *Steven Spielberg Presents: Taken* **2002** There was nothing "mini" about this 10-part series shown on the Sci Fi Channel. It's a classic saga of alien abductions over 60 years and three generations, beginning in 1947. Series is narrated by 10-year-old Allie Keys (Fanning), the granddaughter of WWII fighter pilot Russell (Burton), who is taken by mysterious blue lights. There's also that Roswell incident and contact with aliens and strange powers and, well, a lot. **900m/C; DVD.** Steve (Stephen) Burton; Julie Benz; Joel Gretsch; Michael Moriarty; Tina Holmes; Catherine Dent; Eric Close; Ryan Hurst; Chad Morgan; Willie Garson; Matt Frewer; James McDaniel; Emily Bergl; Dakota Fanning; ***Nar:*** Dakota Fanning; ***D:*** Tobe Hooper; Bryan Spicer; Felix Alcala; Thomas J. Wright; Jeremy Paul Kagan; Jeff Woolnough; John Fawcett; Breck Eisner; Sergio Mimica-Gezzan; Michael Katleman; ***W:*** Leslie Bohem; ***C:*** Jonathan Freeman; Joel Ransom; ***M:*** Laura Karpman. **CABLE**

Taken 1/2 **2008 (PG-13)** Ex-spy and estranged dad Bryan Mills (Neeson) moves to L.A. to be nearer 17-year-old daughter Kim, his ex-wife (Janssen), and her moneyed second husband to atone for his years of absence—but Kim's off to Paris for the summer. His concerns for her safety dismissed, Kim goes and is almost immediately abducted, although she makes one desperate phone call to dad who sets retirement aside and springs into action. With help from former colleagues and a lifetime of experience facing bad guys, Mills has mere hours to sort out ruthless Albanian kidnappers, perverse Arab sheiks, and assorted nasty evil-doers to spare Kim from a violent career as a sex slave. Typical action thriller, but Neeson is imposing in the midst of a pretty implausible narrative. **93m/C; Blu-Ray, On Demand.** *FR* Liam Neeson; Maggie Grace; Famke Janssen; Xander Berkeley; Katie Cassidy; Olivier Rabourdin; Leland Orser; Jon(athan) Gries; Gerard Watkins; Arben Bajraktaraj; ***D:*** Pierre Morel; ***W:*** Luc Besson; Robert Mark Kamen; ***C:*** Michel Abramowicz; ***M:*** Nathaniel Mechaly.

Taken 2 **2012 (PG-13)** A truly horrendous sequel that misses everything that worked about the surprise hit about a father (Neeson) with a certain set of skills. Grace and Janssen return as Bryan Mills' daughter and ex-wife, who are kidnapped by the father of one of the men he killed in the first film. Whereas the first film played off both youth fears of being far away from home and parental fears of letting children go, the follow-up has no such relatable foundation, becoming little more than a series of poorly directed action scenes. **92m/C; DVD, Blu-Ray.** *US FR* Liam Neeson; Famke Janssen; Maggie Grace; Rade Serbedzija; Leland Orser; Jon(athan) Gries; D.B. Sweeney; Luke Grimes; ***D:*** Olivier Megaton; ***W:*** Luc Besson; Robert Mark Kamen; ***C:*** Romain Lacourbas; ***M:*** Nathaniel Mechaly.

Taken 3 *Tak3n* **2015 (PG-13)** Dropping not only the European vacation paranoia for a more familiar stateside romp, the entire "taken" bit has been cast aside. This time around, Bryan Mills (Neeson), everyone's favorite dad-with-a-particular-set-of-skills, is framed for murder and must elude a bloodthirsty police squad led by clever inspector Franck Dotzler (Whitaker) and an assembly line of nameless goons in a destructive barrage through the streets of Los Angeles. Sure, there is fun in watching the gonzo car chases and inventive hand-to-hand combats, but by this point, it borders on comedy thriller, rather than action thriller. **109m/C; DVD, Blu-Ray.** *FR US* Liam Neeson; Maggie Grace; Forest Whitaker; Dougray Scott; Sam Spruell; Famke Janssen; Jon(athan) Gries; Leland Orser; ***D:*** Olivier Megaton; ***W:*** Luc Besson; Robert Mark Kamen; ***C:*** Eric Kress; ***M:*** Nathaniel Mechaly.

Taken for Ransom *Final Recourse* **2013** Typical woman-in-peril Lifetime drama takes an unbelievable turn that does the suspenser no favors. Wealthy Brooke turns to alcohol and drugs after blaming herself for the death of her son. She gets kidnapped and it's implied that even if her husband pays the ransom, Brooke isn't getting out alive. That's where the twists come in. **90m/C; DVD.** Teri Polo; Chazz Palminteri; Tia Carrere; Matt Socia; Luke Eberl; ***D:*** Barbara Stepansky; ***W:*** Steven Edell; Harvey S. Fisher; ***C:*** Jayson Crothers; ***M:*** Dana Niu. **CABLE**

Taken From Me: The Tiffany Rubin Story 1/2 **2010** African-American Tiffany Rubin is locked in a custody battle with her young son Kobe's father. When Chris Rubin takes Kobe from his New York home to Seoul, South Korea, Tiffany works with a child advocacy organization and comes up with a daring rescue plan to get her son back in this true story from the Lifetime channel. **94m/C; DVD.** Taraji P. Henson; Drew Davis; David Haydn-Jones; Sean Baek; Terry O'Quinn; Beverly Todd; ***D:*** Gary Harvey; ***W:*** Michael Bortman; ***C:*** Mathias Herndl; ***M:*** James Gelfand. **CABLE**

Taken in Broad Daylight **2009** True crime story from Lifetime. Teenager Anne Sluti (Canning) is kidnapped from a mall parking lot by survivalist Tony Zappa (Van Der Beek), apparently because the maladjusted career criminal is lonely. As she endures a six-day ordeal across multiple state lines, Anne struggles to manipulate and outwit her captor to survive. **83m/C; DVD.** Sara Canning; James Van Der Beek; LeVar Burton; Diana Reis; Tom Anniko; Brian Roach; Alexandra Castillo; ***D:*** Gary Yates; ***W:*** Kim Delgado; Charlene Blaine; ***C:*** Brenton Spencer; ***M:*** Jeff Toyne. **CABLE**

Takers ♪♪ **2010 (PG-13)** A gang of L.A. criminals, led by the ever-cool Gordon Cozier (Elba), pulls off a series of perfectly-executed bank robberies and then enjoy themselves between jobs. When they attempt a high stakes armored-car heist, obsessed police detective Welles (Dillon) is determined to finally bring them down. The familiar plot is slickly-executed but instantly forgettable as well. **107m/C; Blu-Ray, On Demand.** Matt Dillon; Paul Walker; Idris Elba; Jay Hernandez; Tip "T.I." Harris; Michael Ealy; Chris Brown; Johnathon Schaech; Hayden Christensen; Zoe Saldana; ***D:*** John Luessenhop; ***W:*** John Luessenhop; Peter Allen; Gabriel Casseus; Avery Duff; ***C:*** Michael Barrett; ***M:*** Paul Haslinger.

Taking Care of Business ♪ ½ *Filofax* **1990 (R)** Too familiar tale of switched identity has crazed Cubs fan Belushi find Grodin's Filofax, allowing him to pose as businessman. Old jokes and a story full of holes. **108m/C; VHS, DVD, Blu-Ray.** James Belushi; Charles Grodin; Anne DeSalvo; Loryn Locklin; Veronica Hamel; Hector Elizondo; Mako; Gates (Cheryl) McFadden; Stephen Elliott; ***D:*** Arthur Hiller; ***W:*** J.J. (Jeffrey) Abrams; ***C:*** David M. Walsh; ***M:*** Stewart Copeland.

Taking Chance ♪♪ ½ **2009** Based on the experiences of Lt. Col. Michael Strobl (an overly stoic Bacon), a Desert Storm vet, who volunteers to accompany the body of an Iraq War soldier back to his Wyoming hometown. The film details the lengths the military goes to in honoring its dead through the ritual of military escort and Strobl's random encounters with ordinary citizens on his journey. **77m/C; DVD.** Kevin Bacon; Tom Wopat; Ann Dowd; Paige Turco; ***D:*** Ross Katz; ***W:*** Ross Katz; Michael Strobl; ***C:*** Alar Kivilo; ***M:*** Marcelo Zarvos. **CABLE**

Taking Chances ♪♪ **2009 (R)** Geeky Chase Revere (Long) joins with babe Lucy Shanks (Chriqui) when he learns an Indian casino is going to be built on their small town's ignored Revolutionary War-era battlefield. Since the community needs the income and jobs the casino will offer, no one else is happy about their interference. **99m/C; DVD.** Justin Long; Emmanuelle Chriqui; Keir O'Donnell; Rob Corddry; Missi Pyle; Nick Offerman; Phil Reeves; Robert Beltran; ***D:*** Talmage Cooley; ***W:*** Annie Nocenti; ***C:*** Steve Gainer; ***M:*** Scott Glasgow. **VIDEO**

Taking Lives ♪♪ **2004 (R)** Illeana Scott (Jolie), a sexy FBI profiler with an affinity for the macabre, is called in by the Montreal police to use her "special" skills to track down a serial killer who assumes the identity of his victims. Since the heroine cannot be without a love interest, along comes art gallery owner James Costa (Hawke) who, naturally, is a witness...no, wait, he's a suspect...oh, now he's a target. Keep your scorecards handy, folks. Caruso strives to craftily overwhelm his audience with loads of gruesome gore, and perhaps if the plot weren't as mangled as the victims it would have succeeded. Sutherland does little more than play the convenient scapegoat while Rowlands masters the role of the alleged slayer's surly mother. Adapted from Michael Pye's novel where, interestingly, Jolie's character didn't exist. **103m/C; VHS, DVD, Blu-Ray.** Angelina Jolie; Ethan Hawke; Kiefer Sutherland; Gena Rowlands; Olivier Martinez; Tcheky Karyo; Jean-Hugues Anglade; Paul Dano; Justin Chatwin; ***D:*** D.J. Caruso; ***W:*** Jon Bokenkamp; ***C:*** Amir M. Mokri; ***M:*** Philip Glass.

The Taking of Pelham One Two Three ♪♪♪ **1974 (R)** A hijack team, lead by the ruthless Shaw, seizes a NYC subway car and holds the 17 passengers for $1 million ransom. Fine pacing keeps things on the edge. New cinematic techniques used by cameraman Owen Roizman defines shadowy areas like never before. **105m/C; VHS, DVD, Blu-Ray.** Robert Shaw; Walter Matthau; Martin Balsam; Hector Elizondo; James Broderick; Earl Hindman; Dick O'Neill; Jerry Stiller; Tony Roberts; Doris Roberts; Kenneth McMillan; Julius W. Harris; Sal Viscuso; ***D:*** Joseph Sargent; ***W:*** Peter Stone; ***C:*** Owen Roizman; ***M:*** David Shire.

The Taking of Pelham 123 ♪♪ ½ **2009 (R)** New York subway dispatcher Walter Garber's (Washington) shift isn't starting well after a subway train is hijacked by homicidal nutjob Ryder (Travolta) and his armed crew. They threaten to execute passengers one-by-one until a large ransom is paid, but how exactly do they then plan to escape? Remake of the 1974 thriller (that starred Walter Matthau and Robert Shaw) is filled with Scott's swooping, fast-paced images; Washington's workmanlike, compromised, reluctant hero; Travolta's over-the-top, tattooed baddie; and a visually interesting comparison of a post 9/11 Big Apple vs. the grungy city of the 1970s. **106m/C; Blu-Ray.** Denzel Washington; John Travolta; Luis Guzman; John Turturro; James Gandolfini; Michael Rispoli; ***D:*** Tony Scott; ***W:*** Brian Helgeland; ***C:*** Tobias Schliessler; ***M:*** Harry Gregson-Williams.

Taking Sides ♪♪♪ ½ *Der Fall Furtwangler* **2001** Szabo again looks at Nazi-era Germany, this time in the story of famed conductor Wilhelm Furtwangler, who stayed in Germany as conductor of the Berlin Philharmonic under the Nazis. The film concentrates on Furtwangler's (Skaarsgaard) pretrial interrogation by American Denazification Committee officer Steve Arnold (Keitel), whose aides, both of German and Jewish decscent, have some sympathy for Furtwangler. Arnold is caustic and unrelenting in his mission to get to the bottom of the conductor's collaboration, while Furtwangler refuses to believe he has anything to apologize for, invoking his allegiance to his art, and his professed belief that he was making a difference. Both performances are magnificent and aid greatly in Szabo and Harwood's ability to let you know where they stand, yet be balanced in their portrayal of both views of the man. **105m/C; DVD.** *FR GE GB AT* Harvey Keitel; Stellan Skarsgard; Moritz Bleibtreu; Birgit Minichmayr; Oleg Tabakov; Ulrich Tukur; Hanns Zischler; August Zirner; R. Lee Ermey; Robin Renucci; ***D:*** Istvan Szabo; ***W:*** Ronald Harwood; ***C:*** Lajos Koltai.

Taking Woodstock ♪♪ **2009 (R)** Laid-back and unstructured adaptation of Elliot Tiber's memoir of the festival and his becoming its unexpected host while trying to drum up business for his family's failing Catskills motel. The uptight 34-year-old businessman hears that a music festival has lost its permit so Elliot (Martin) agrees to help promoter Michael Lang (Goff) find a new location, which turns out to be Max Yasgur's (Levy) farm. Peace-and-love help loosen Elliot up but this is strictly a back- and off-stage view. **110m/C; DVD, On Demand.** Imelda Staunton; Liev Schreiber; Eugene Levy; Emile Hirsch; Kelli Garner; Paul Dano; Jeffrey Dean Morgan; Demetri Martin; Dan Fogler; Henry Goodman; Mamie Gummer; Jonathan Groff; Richard Thomas; ***D:*** Ang Lee; ***W:*** James Schamus; ***C:*** Eric Gautier; ***M:*** Danny Elfman.

The Tale ♪♪♪ **2018** The life of documentary filmmaker Jennifer (an impeccable Dern) is turned upside down after her elderly mother Nettie (Burstyn) finds a box of Jennifer's from middle school and realizes that she had been raped by her running coach, Bill (Ritter). When she was 13, Jennifer spent a summer at horseback riding camp with Mrs. G (Debicki), who helped groom her. Though Jennifer initially remembers having a romantic relationship with Bill, she sifts through her memories to understand what really happened. Based on the filmmaker's own life, the debut narrative feature from documentarian Fox provides an agonizing and personal view into the way storytelling and memory affects people's perceptions about their lives. **114m/C; Silent; DVD.** Elizabeth Debicki; Laura Dern; Jason Ritter; Ellen Burstyn; Common; ***D:*** Jennifer Fox; ***W:*** Jennifer Fox; ***C:*** Denis Lenoir; Ivan Strasburg; ***M:*** Ariel Marx. **VIDEO**

Tale of a Vampire ♪♪ ½ **1992 (R)** In present day London, ageless vampire Alex (Sands) still mourns his long-lost vampiric love, Virginia, when he meets Anne (Hamilton) (who resembles Virginia). Alex doesn't know he's being stalked by Virginia's husband, Edgar (Cranham), also a vampire. Edgar decides to use Anne (with whom Alex has fallen in love) as bait, in a revenge plot. A tiny budget and slow pacing mar the film's fine visual style and good work by the two male leads. Film debut for director Sato. **93m/C; VHS, Streaming.** *GB* Julian Sands; Kenneth Cranham; Suzanna Hamilton; ***D:*** Shimako Sato; ***W:*** Jane Corbett; Shimako Sato; ***M:*** Julian Joseph.

The Tale of Despereaux ♪ ½ **2008 (G)** Universal's computer-animated feature is less of a hip, frantic, wise-cracking modern legacy Pixar and more of a somber older Disney cartoon. Castle mouse Despereaux (Broderick), a misfit rodent content with reading books, dreams of adventures outside the dreary castle walls. Desperaeux's tale mixes with the stories of two other unhappy residents—grumpy rat Roscuro (Hoffman) and frumpy girl Miggery Sow (Ullman), who believes she's destined to be a princess. Based on Kate DiCamillo's Newberry Award-winning children's book, the uneven script may be too slow and confusing for most kids. **93m/C; Blu-Ray.** ***V:*** Matthew Broderick; Dustin Hoffman; Emma Watson; Tracey Ullman; Christopher Lloyd; Kevin Kline; William H. Macy; Stanley Tucci; Robbie Coltrane; Ciaran Hinds; Tony Hale; Frances Conroy; Richard Jenkins; Frank Langella; Charles Shaughnessy; ***Nar:*** Sigourney Weaver; ***D:*** Sam Fell; Robert Stevenhagen; ***W:*** Gary Ross; ***C:*** Brad Blackbourn; ***M:*** William Ross.

A Tale of Love and Darkness ♪♪ ½ **2016 (PG-13)** The film directing debut of actress Natalie Portman is a bleak adaptation of Amos Oz's memoir of his childhood in Jerusalem as the free state of Israel emerged in the late 1940s. Told through flashbacks, Oz's mother Fania (Portland) encourages her pre-teen son (Tessler) to make up stories to cope with their difficult circumstances. Fania is married to a dull librarian/author Arieh (Kahana), with whom she has little in common and whose family kills her dreamy spirit. Young Amos internalizes his mother's lessons on diplomacy and storytelling, which helps his interactions with his peers. Small, wonderful moments demonstrate Portman's developing artistic vision. Hebrew with subtitles. **95m/C; DVD.** Natalie Portman; Gilad Kahana; Amir Tessler; Moni Moshonov; Ohad Knoller; ***D:*** Natalie Portman; ***W:*** Natalie Portman; ***C:*** Slawomir Idziak; ***M:*** Nicholas Britell.

A Tale of Springtime ♪♪ ½ **1989 (PG)** Comedy-romance is the first film in Rohmer's planned new series, the "Tales of the Four Seasons," not to be confused with his "Six Moral Tales" or his "Comedies and Proverbs." Centers around Jeanne, a high school philosophy teacher; Natacha, a young student; and Igor, Natacha's father. As characteristic of Rohmer films, texture and character largely overshadow linear plots and social messages. However, the efficiency and directness of his camera work make it a pleasure to watch. **107m/C; VHS, DVD.** *FR* Anne Teyssedre; Hugues Quester; Florence Darel; Eloise Bennett; Sophie Robin; ***D:*** Eric Rohmer; ***W:*** Eric Rohmer; ***C:*** Luc Pages; ***M:*** Robert Schumann.

Tale of Tales ♪♪ ½ *Il racconto dei racconti* **2015** This is Matteo Garrone's first film in English, and the conflict of languages has a notable impact on the overall product as this piece lacks the wit and spark of this brilliant Italian filmmaker's best. It's certainly not predictable though. Based on a collection of short stories by Giambattista Basile that includes early versions of classic fables like Rapunzel and Sleeping Beauty, Garrone's film is a surreal journey to a fantasy land, starring Hayek, Reilly, Cassel, and many more. It's a visual treat that never bores, but it also doesn't quite come together to be much more than that. **133m/C; DVD, Blu-Ray.** Salma Hayek; Vincent Cassel; Toby Jones; John C. Reilly; Shirley Henderson; ***D:*** Matteo Garrone; ***W:*** Matteo Garrone; Edoardo Albinati; Ugo Chiti; Massimo Gaudioso; ***C:*** Peter Suschitzky; ***M:*** Alexandre Desplat.

The Tale of the Princess Kaguya ♪♪♪ **2013 (PG)** The legendary Isao Takahata returns to Studio Ghibli for his first film in years with this delicate, touching adaptation of a classic Japanese fable. With nearly incomplete pencil strokes that invoke mood more than detail, it's truly beautiful, although suffers a bit by virtue of its remarkable length. A bamboo cutter finds a tiny girl in a random stalk, who then grows quickly into a girl, a woman, and then a princess. As a father is quickly forced to deal with letting his daughter go, Takahata brilliantly balances the emotional connections within the story with its more fantastical elements. **137m/C; DVD, Blu-Ray.** *JP* ***V:*** Chloë Grace Moretz; James Caan; Mary Steenburgen; Darren Criss; Lucy Liu; Beau Bridges; James Marsden; Dean Cain; ***D:*** Isao Takahata; ***W:*** Isao Takahata; Riko Sakaguchi; ***M:*** Joe Hisaishi.

A Tale of Two Cities ♪♪♪♪ **1936** Lavish production of the Dickens' classic set during the French Revolution, about two men who bear a remarkable resemblance to each other, both in love with the same girl. Carefree lawyer Sydney Carton (Colman) roused to responsibility, makes the ultimate sacrifice. A memorable Madame DeFarge from stage star Yurka in her film debut, with assistance from other Dickens' film stars Rathbone, Oliver, and Walthall. **128m/B; VHS, DVD.** Ronald Colman; Elizabeth Allan; Edna May Oliver; Reginald Owen; Isabel Jewell; Walter Catlett; H.B. Warner; Donald Woods; Basil Rathbone; Blanche Yurka; Henry B. Walthall; ***D:*** Jack Conway; ***W:*** W.P. Lipscomb; S.N. Behrman; ***M:*** Herbert Stothart.

A Tale of Two Cities ♪♪♪ **1958** A well-done British version of the Dickens' classic about a lawyer who sacrifices himself to save another man from the guillotine during the French Reign of Terror. The sixth remake of the tale. **117m/B; DVD.** *UK* Dirk Bogarde; Dorothy Tutin; Christopher Lee; Donald Pleasence; Ian Bannen; Cecil Parker; ***D:*** Ralph Thomas.

A Tale of Two Cities ♪♪ ½ **1980** Impressive looking but bloodless adaptation of the Dickens novel set in the French Revolution. Saradon takes on the dual role of sacrificing English lawyer Carton and French nobleman Darnay, with Krige as the lovely woman caught between the two. **156m/C; DVD, Blu-Ray.** Chris Sarandon; Alice Krige; Peter Cushing; Kenneth More; Barry Morse; Flora Robson; Billie Whitelaw; ***D:*** Jim (James) Goddard; ***W:*** John Gay. **TV**

A Tale of Two Cities ♪♪♪ **1989** Masterpiece Theatre production of the classic Dickens tale. The French revolution was a time of revenge and brutality, but also provided the proving ground for a love greater than life. Terrific cast and perfectly detailed production. **240m/C; DVD.** James Wilby; Serena Gordon; John Mills; Jean-Pierre Aumont; Anna Massey; ***D:*** Philippe Monnier; ***W:*** Arthur Hopcraft; ***M:*** Serge Franklin.

A Tale of Two Pizzas ♪ ½ **2003 (PG)** Predictable family comedy with some charm. Rival Yonkers pizzeria owners Vito (Pastore) and Frank (Vincent) are constantly at odds over whose secret recipe is best. However, their kids, Angela (Paul) and Tony (Dubin), have more than sauce and crust on their minds. **82m/C; DVD.** Vincent Pastore; Frank Vincent; Conor Dubin; Patti D'Arbanville; Robin Paul; Angela Pietropinto; Louis Guss; ***D:*** Vincent Sassone; ***W:*** Vincent Sassone; ***C:*** Peter Nelson; ***M:*** Peter Fish.

Tale of Two Sisters ♪♪ ½ **1989** Sheen narrates sensual drama about two beautiful, ambitious sisters. **90m/C; VHS, DVD.** Valerie Breiman; Claudia Christian; Sydney Lassick; Jeff Conaway; Peter Berg; ***Nar:*** Charlie Sheen; ***D:*** Adam Rifkin; ***W:*** Charlie Sheen; ***C:*** John Parenteau; ***M:*** Marc David Decker.

Talent for the Game ♪♪ ½ **1991 (PG)** A slight but handsomely produced baseball pleasantry about a talent scout who recruits a phenomenonal young pitcher, then sees the kid exploited by the team owner. More like an anecdote than a story, with an ending that aims a little too hard to please. Good for sports fans and family audiences. **91m/C; VHS, DVD.** Edward James Olmos; Lorraine Bracco; Jeff Corbett; Jamey Sheridan; Terry Kinney; ***D:*** Robert M. Young; ***W:*** David Himmelstein; Thomas Michael Donnelly; Larry Ferguson; ***M:*** David Newman.

The Talent Given Us ♪♪♪ **2004** Writer/director/producer Andrew Wagner gives this road trip story a quasi-reality twist by casting his father Allen, mother Judy and sisters Emily and Maggie as, well, themselves. The Wagners have not seen their elusive son Andrew (Wagner) in several years, and embark on a cross-country drive from Manhattan to Los Angeles to catch up with him, picking up family friend Bumby (Dixon) en route. The miles are filled with unfiltered and sometimes unflattering discussion of everything from driving habits to sex to prescription drugs to thoughts of infidelity. The unnerving fascination with the line between real life and fantasy is a major draw. **97m/C; DVD.** Billy Wirth; Judy Wagner; Allen Wagner; Emily Wagner; Maggie Wagner; Judy Dixon; ***D:*** Andrew Wagner; ***W:*** Andrew Wagner; ***C:*** Andrew Wagner; ***M:*** David Dyas.

The Talented Mr. Ripley 🦴🦴 1/2 **1999 (R)** Beautiful but ultimately hollow adaptation of Patricia Highsmith's chiller, which was previously filmed as 1960's "Purple Noon." This time around Damon takes on the title role as a poor nobody who is sent to Italy in 1958 to persuade rich playboy, Dickie Greenleaf (Law), to return to the bosom of his family in New York. Only the more the emotionally needy Ripley sees of Dickie's sybaritic lifestyle—the more he wants it for himself, even if it means killing Dickie and literally assuming his identity. Law is the draw and the movie suffers a letdown after his death. **139m/C; VHS, DVD, Blu-Ray.** Matt Damon; Jude Law; Gwyneth Paltrow; Cate Blanchett; Philip Seymour Hoffman; Jack Davenport; James Rebhorn; Sergio Rubini; Philip Baker Hall; Lisa Eichhorn; Stefania Rocca; ***D:*** Anthony Minghella; ***W:*** Anthony Minghella; ***C:*** John Seale; ***M:*** Gabriel Yared. British Acad. '99: Support. Actor (Law); Natl. Bd. of Review '99: Director (Minghella), Support. Actor (Hoffman).

Tales from the Crypt 🦴🦴🦴 **1972 (PG)** A collection of five scary stories from the classic EC comics that bear the movie's title. Richardson tells the future to each of five people gathered in a cave, each tale involving misfortune and, of course, gore. **92m/C; VHS, DVD, Blu-Ray.** *GB* Ralph Richardson; Joan Collins; Peter Cushing; Richard Greene; Ian Hendry; ***D:*** Freddie Francis.

Tales from the Crypt Presents Bordello of Blood 🦴🦴 *Bordello of Blood* **1996 (R)** Detective Rafe Guttman (Miller) is on the case of a Bible thumper's (Eleniak) missing brother (Feldman). The trail leads him to a unique establishment, a brothel presided over by vampire queen Lilith (Everhart), whose clients all wind up dead (but probably with smiles on their faces), and the strange Reverend Current (Sarandon, who made a fine vampire himself in "Fright Night"). Crypt Keeper's second big screen outing showcases Miller's slant on the leading man gig and serves up campy fun with the blood. **87m/C; VHS, DVD, Blu-Ray.** Dennis Miller; Angie Everhart; Chris Sarandon; Corey Feldman; Erika Eleniak; ***D:*** Gilbert Adler; ***W:*** Gilbert Adler; A.L. Katz; ***C:*** Tom Priestley; ***M:*** Chris Boardman.

Tales from the Crypt Presents Demon Knight 🦴🦴 *Demon Knight; Demon Keeper* **1994 (R)** Gruesomely garish big-screen version of the TV series that was inspired by the lurid 1950s E.C. comics. Horrormeister Crypt Keeper offers his usual pun-filled introduction to a tale set in a seedy boarding-house. Brayker (Sadler) is the guardian of an ancient key that keeps the forces of darkness from overwhelming mankind, a key desired by the charismatic Collector (Zane), who unleashes a disgusting mix of demons against the house's inhabitants. Curious hybrid of spoof/splatter pic that doesn't quite work in either genre. **93m/C; VHS, DVD, Blu-Ray.** Billy Zane; William Sadler; Jada Pinkett Smith; Brenda Bakke; CCH Pounder; Dick Miller; Thomas Haden Church; John Schuck; Gary Farmer; Charles Fleischer; ***V:*** John Kassir; ***D:*** Ernest R. Dickerson; ***W:*** Ethan Reiff; Cyrus Voris; Mark Bishop; ***C:*** Rick Bota; ***M:*** Ed Shearmur.

Tales from the Crypt Presents Ritual 🦴 1/2 *Ritual; Tales from the Crypt Presents Revelation* **2002 (R)** Remake of 'I Walked with a Zombie' featuring a young doctor with a suspended license who travels to Jamaica after being offered a job to care for a young man targeted by a voodoo cult. **99m/C; DVD, Blu-Ray.** Jennifer Grey; Craig Sheffer; Daniel Lapaine; Kristen Wilson; Gabriel Casseus; ***D:*** Avi Nesher; ***W:*** Avi Nesher; Rob Cohen; ***C:*** David A. Armstrong; Douglas Milsome; ***M:*** Shirley Walker. **VIDEO**

Tales from the Darkside: The Movie 🦴🦴 **1990 (R)** Three short stories in the tradition of the ghoulish TV show are brought to the big screen, with mixed results. The plot centers around a boy who is being held captive by a cannibal. In order to prolong his life, he tells her horror stories. The tales were written by Sir Arthur Conan Doyle, Stephen King, and Michael McDowell. **93m/C; VHS, DVD.** Deborah Harry; Christian Slater; David Johansen; William Hickey; James Remar; Rae Dawn Chong; Julianne Moore; Robert Klein; Steve Buscemi; Matthew Lawrence; ***D:*** John Harrison; ***W:*** George A. Romero; Michael McDowell; ***C:*** Rob Draper.

Tales from the Gimli Hospital 🦴🦴 **1988** A smallpox outbreak at the turn of the century finds Einar and Gunnar sharing a hospital room. They begin telling each other increasingly bizarre personal secrets and develop a serious rivalry. Sharp dialogue with some equally grotesque imagery. Director Maddin's first feature film. **68m/B; VHS, DVD.** *CA* Kyle McCulloch; Michael Gottli; Angela Heck; Margaret Anne McLeod; ***D:*** Guy Maddin; ***W:*** Guy Maddin; ***C:*** Guy Maddin.

Tales from the Hood 🦴🦴 **1995 (R)** Horror anthology with that urban twist. Three young thugs search for lost drugs inside a funeral parlor run by creepy Mr. Simms (Williams III) and instead walk into a world of four chilling and funny stories of fright dealing with racism and black on black crime. Tales aren't very original and are often too preachy for true enjoyment, but its nice to see someone attempt to breath life into an old and familiar genre. Williams III, with his pop-eyed stares and Don King coif, is fitting as the eerie storyteller. **97m/C; VHS, DVD, Blu-Ray.** Clarence Williams, III; Corbin Bernsen; David Alan Grier; Wings Hauser; Rosalind Cash; Rusty Cundieff; Joe Torry; Anthony Griffith; Lamont Bentley; Darin Scott; De'Aundre Bonds; Tom Wright; Michael Massee; Duane Whitaker; Brandon Hammond; Paula Jai Parker; Roger Guenveur Smith; Art Evans; ***D:*** Rusty Cundieff; ***W:*** Rusty Cundieff; Darin Scott; ***C:*** Anthony B. Richmond; ***M:*** Christopher Young.

Tales of an Ancient Empire WOOF! **2011 (R)** A very long-in-coming sequel to 1982's "The Sword and the Sorcerer" that's shoddy, incoherent, and boring. Demonic sorceress Xia threatens the kingdom of Abelar with her vampires. Queen Ma-at sends Princess Tanis out to reunite her previously unknown half-siblings, who are all mercenaries, with their father Oda, the only warrior to have ever defeated Xia. **89m/C; DVD.** Kevin Sorbo; Michael Paré; Melissa Ordway; Whitney Able; Jennifer Siebel (Newsom); Sarah Ann Schultz; Lee Horsley; ***D:*** Albert Pyun; ***W:*** Cynthia Curnan; ***C:*** Philip Alan Waters; ***M:*** Tony Riparetti. **VIDEO**

Tales of Erotica 🦴🦴 *Die Erotische Geschichten* **1993 (R)** Four stories made for German TV. "The Dutch Master" finds New Yorker Teresa (Sorvino) becoming obsessed with a Vermeer-style painting at a museum. She begins to dress like the lively characters and eventually disappears into the picture itself. "The Insatiable Mrs. Kirsch" finds a vacationing writer (Shepherd) becoming fascinated by a fellow guest (Baynes), who seems to be hiding something. In "Vroom Vroom Vroom" luckless Leroy (Barboza) asks a voodoo doctor for help with the girls and winds up with a motorcycle that transforms itself into a beautiful woman when ridden. "Wet" has bathroom-fixture salesman Bruce (Howard) enticed by persistent customer Davida (Williams), who insists they both try out the showroom hot tub before she'll consider buying. **104m/C; VHS, DVD.** *GE* Mira Sorvino; Aida Turturro; Simon Shepherd; Hetty Baynes; Ken Russell; Richard Barboza; Arliss Howard; Cynda Williams; ***D:*** Ken Russell; Susan Seidelman; Melvin Van Peebles; Bob Rafelson; ***W:*** Susan Seidelman; Melvin Van Peebles; Bob Rafelson; Jonathan Brett; ***C:*** Maryse Alberti; Hong Manley; Igor Sunara; ***M:*** Melvin Van Peebles; Wendy Blackstone; David McHugh. **TV**

Tales of Halloween 🦴🦴 1/2 **2015 (R)** Horror anthology films are often only sporadically entertaining, but this ten-story series of adventures set on Halloween works far more often than it does not and ends with such a strong run of short films that it's easier to forgive its missteps. Highlights include Mike Mendez's incredible "Friday the 31st" (about a Jason Voorhees-esque character interrupted in his killing spree by an alien invasion) and John Skipp's hysterical "This Means War" (about neighbors whose competing Halloween lawn displays get out of control). Neil Marshall ends the anthology with a piece that ties it all together in a way that's likely to leave horror hounds happy. **97m/C; Blu-Ray, Streaming.** Booboo Stewart; Grace Phipps; Keir Gilchrist; Greg Grunberg; Adrienne Barbeau; ***D:*** Darren Lynn Bousman; Axelle Carolyn; Adam Gierasch; Andrew Kasch; Neil Marshall; Lucky McKee; Mike Mendez; Dave Parker; Ryan Schifrin; John Skipp; Paul Solet; ***W:*** Axelle Carolyn; Andrew Kasch; Neil Marshall; Lucky McKee; Mike Mendez; Dave Parker; Ryan Schifrin; John Skipp; Clint Sears; ***C:*** Jan-Michael Losada; Zoran Popovic; David Tayar; Alex Vendler; Richard J. Vialet; Joseph White; Scott Wing; ***M:*** Joseph Bishara; Michael Sean Colin; Christopher Drake; Christian Henson; Bobby Johnston; Lalo Schifrin; Sean Spillane; Edwin Wendler; Austin Wintory.

The Tales of Hoffmann 🦴🦴 1/2 **1951** A ballet-opera consisting of three stories by Jacques Offenbach covering romance, magic and mystery arising out of a poet's misadventures in love. Lavishly designed and highly stylized. **138m/C; VHS, DVD.** Robert Rounseville; Robert Helpmann; Moira Shearer; ***D:*** Michael Powell; Emeric Pressburger.

Tales of Manhattan 🦴🦴🦴 **1942** Star-studded anthology about a tailor who curses a tailcoat that then travels, with varying degrees of good and bad fortune, from owner to owner. There's a love triangle, a love match, a concert appearance, a down-on-his-luck lawyer, a swanky party, a crook, and a windfall for some sharecroppers. Fields' party episode (he wears the coat to give a lecture and winds up wreaking havoc) was cut out of the original theatrical release. **118m/C; DVD.** Charles Boyer; Rita Hayworth; Thomas Mitchell; Ginger Rogers; Henry Fonda; Cesar Romero; Elsa Lanchester; Charles Laughton; Edward G. Robinson; George Sanders; James Gleason; J. Carrol Naish; Paul Robeson; Ethel Waters; Eddie Anderson; W.C. Fields; Margaret Dumont; ***D:*** Julien Duvivier; ***W:*** Ben Hecht; Donald Ogden Stewart; Samuel Hoffenstein; Ferenc Molnar; Alan Campbell; ***C:*** Joseph Walker; ***M:*** Sol Kaplan.

Tales of Ordinary Madness 🦴 **1983** Gazzara as a poet who drinks and sleeps with assorted women. Based on the stories of Charles Bukowski. Pretentious and dull. **107m/C; VHS, DVD.** Ben Gazzara; Ornella Muti; Susan Tyrrell; Tanya Lopert; Roy Brocksmith; Katya Berger; ***D:*** Marco Ferreri; ***W:*** Marco Ferreri; Sergio Amidei; Anthony Foutz; ***C:*** Tonino Delli Colli; ***M:*** Philippe Sarde.

Tales of Terror 🦴🦴 *Poe's Tales of Terror* **1962** Three tales of terror based on stories by Edgar Allan Poe: "Morella," "The Black Cat," and the "The Case of M. Valdemar." Price stars in all three segments and is excellent as the bitter and resentful husband in "Morella." **90m/C; VHS, DVD, Blu-Ray.** Vincent Price; Peter Lorre; Basil Rathbone; Debra Paget; Joyce Jameson; Maggie Pierce; Leona Gage; Edmund Cobb; ***D:*** Roger Corman; ***W:*** Richard Matheson; ***C:*** Floyd Crosby; ***M:*** Les Baxter.

Tales of the Kama Sutra 2: Monsoon 🦴 **1998** Naval officer Kenneth Blake (Tyson) and his fiancee Sally (McShane) travel to the island of Goa, off the coast of India, to enjoy a resort vacation. But Blake is drawn into an affair with Leela (Brodie), who tells him that they are the reincarnation of legendary lovers who leaped to their death from the island's lighthouse 500 years before. It's one way to get a man interested. **96m/C; VHS, DVD.** Richard Tyson; Helen Brodie; Jenny (Jennifer) McShane; Matt McCoy; Doug Jeffery; Gulshan Grover; ***D:*** Jag Mundhra. **VIDEO**

Tales of the Kama Sutra: The Perfumed Garden 🦴 *The Perfumed Garden* **1998 (R)** Not particularly erotic story centers on Americans Michael and Lisa, who have a rocky romantic relationship. Lisa follows Michael to India where he is helping to restore the erotic sculptures of Khajuraho. However, Michael's lust is aroused by a mysterious Indian woman (Kumar), who happens to resemble the statue he's repairing, which leads to a retelling of one Kama Sutra story about a royal courtesan set 1000 years earlier. **104m/C; VHS, DVD.** Pravesh Kumar; Ivan Baccarat; Amy Lindsey; Rajeshwari Sachdev; Bhupinder Singh; Nasser; ***D:*** Jag Mundhra.

Tales of the Unexpected 🦴🦴 1/2 **1991** Four tales designed to startle the senses and provoke the imagination. Episodes include "People Don't Do Such Things," about a marriage gone awry, "Youth from Vienna," about a weird fountain of youth, "Skeleton in the Cupboard," which tells of a man desperately trying to hide some strange secret and finally, "Bird of Prey," in which a pet parrot leaves its owners an enormous egg before dying. **101m/C; VHS, DVD.** Arthur Hill; Samantha Eggar; Don Johnson; Dick Smothers; Sharon Gless; James Carroll Jordan; Charles Dance; Zoe Wanamaker; Sondra Locke; Frank Converse; ***D:*** Gordon Hessler; Norman Lloyd; Paul Annett; Ray Danton.

Tales That Witness Madness 🦴🦴 1/2 **1973 (R)** An asylum is the setting for four tales of horror, as a doctor tells a visitor how four patients ended up in his clinic. Stories are "Mr. Tiger," "Penny Farthing," "Mel" and "Luau." At the time this was Novak's first film appearance in four years. **90m/C; VHS, DVD, Blu-Ray.** *GB* Jack Hawkins; Donald Pleasence; Suzy Kendall; Joan Collins; Kim Novak; Mary Tamm; Georgia Brown; Donald Houston; David Wood; Peter McEnery; ***D:*** Freddie Francis.

Talhotblond 🦴🦴 *Tall Hot Blonde* **2012** Lifetime movie inspired by true events. Blue-collar, middle-aged, married father of two Thomas (Dillahunt) starts playing online poker with some buddies. He ends up in an Internet chat room and his soon-compulsive online involvement with 18-year-old Katie (Hinshaw) begins. His wife Carol (San Giacomo) eventually finds out, Katie tells Thomas she's dating one of his co-workers, and the entire situation goes bad. **89m/C; DVD.** Garret Dillahunt; Laura San Giacomo; Ashley Hinshaw; Brando Eaton; Molly Hagan; Courteney Cox; ***D:*** Courteney Cox; ***W:*** Trent Haaga; ***C:*** Doug Emmett; ***M:*** Erran Baron Cohen. **CABLE**

Talisman 🦴 1/2 **1998 (R)** Theriel, the Black Angel, has been fused to an ancient Talisman for centuries. Summoned from his rest, he must offer seven human sacrifices to complete an evil ritual that will open the gates of hell and usher in the end of the world. Two teenagers are chosen to help Theriel but they've got other things in mind. Director DeCoteau used the pseud "Victoria Sloan" for this venture. **90m/C; VHS, DVD.** Walter Jones; Jason Adelman; Billy Parish; Ilinca Goia; ***D:*** David DeCoteau; ***W:*** Benjamin Carr. **VIDEO**

Talk of Angels 🦴🦴 **1996 (PG-13)** Young Irish aristocrat Mary (Walker) leaves her homeland for Spain to serve as governess for a wealthy family, just as the country is about to erupt into civil war. She ignites passion in everyone she encounters, especially her married employer and his married son. This forbidden relationship serves as the crux of the story. Unfortunately, good looks alone (which both stars have) don't create chemistry, and Walker and Perez simply fizzle on screen. The film and its leads are certainly nice to look at, but there's something missing: an interesting story. With several obvious thefts from the ultimate wartime love story, "Gone With the Wind" (including a blatant rip-off of the famous scene where Scarlett walks among the sea of dead soldiers), the story is hardly original. **97m/C; VHS, DVD.** Polly Walker; Vincent Perez; Frances McDormand; Franco Nero; Marisa Paredes; Penelope Cruz; Ruth McCabe; Francisco Rabal; Ariadna Gil; Rossy de Palma; ***D:*** Nick Hamm; ***W:*** Ann Guedes; Frank McGuinness; ***C:*** Alexei Rodionov; ***M:*** Trevor Jones.

Talk of the Town 🦴🦴🦴 **1942** A brilliantly cast, strange mixture of screwball comedy and lynch-mob melodramatics. An accused arsonist, a Supreme Court judge and the girl they both love try to clear the former's name and evade the cops. **118m/B; VHS, DVD.** Ronald Colman; Cary Grant; Jean Arthur; Edgar Buchanan; Glenda Farrell; Rex Ingram; Emma Dunn; ***D:*** George Stevens.

Talk Radio 🦴🦴🦴 **1988** Riveting Stone adaptation of Bogosian's one-man play. An acidic talk radio host confronts America's evil side and his own past over the airwaves. The main character is loosely based on the life of Alan Berg, a Denver talk show host who was murdered by white supremacists. **110m/C; VHS, DVD, Blu-Ray.** Eric Bogosian; Alec Baldwin; Ellen Greene; John Pankow; John C. McGinley; Michael Wincott; Leslie Hope; ***D:*** Oliver Stone; ***W:*** Eric Bogosian; Oliver Stone; ***C:*** Robert Richardson; ***M:*** Stewart Copeland.

Talk to Her 🦴🦴🦴½ *Hable con Ella* **2002 (R)** Powerful entry from director Almodovar about the bond of two men caring for comatose women. Marco (Grandinetti), a travel writer, in the early stages of dating Spain's most famous female bullfighter Lydia (Flores), finds himself looking after her after she is gored by a bull. Benigno (Camara) is a male nurse who looks after the comatose Alicia (Watling), a ballerina he has only seen from afar but loves. The two men meet in the hospital and, sharing similar experiences, come to know one another in their grief. While both men are truly caring during their bedside vigils, a slightly disturbing, kinky undercurrent is also at work, and strange and shocking events will occur before film fully unspools. Refusing to judge these actions, however, Almodovar artfully offers some alternate motivations for his characters' seemingly antisocial behaviors and takes material that could have easily been a soap opera in lesser hands, and elevates it to a new level. Silent fantasy sequence depicts director's signature sexual exploration. **112m/C; VHS, DVD.** *SP* Javier Camara; Dario Grandinetti; Rosario Flores; Leonor Watling; Geraldine Chaplin; ***D:*** Pedro Almodóvar; ***W:*** Pedro Almodóvar; ***C:*** Javier Aguirresarobe; ***M:*** Alberto Iglesias. Oscars '02: Orig. Screenplay; British Acad. '02: Foreign Film, Orig. Screenplay; Golden Globes '03: Foreign Film; L.A. Film Critics '02: Director (Almodóvar); Natl. Bd. of Review '02: Foreign Film.

Talk to Me 🦴🦴½ **2007 (R)** Back when radio personalities had, well, personality, excon turned DJ Ralph Waldo "Petey" Greene Jr. (Cheadle) used his outlandish on- and off-air presence to lend a voice to the simmering racial and social unrest in 1960s Washington DC. Cheadle is magnetic as Greene battles both his uptight station director (the excellent Ejifor) and his own personal demons during his tumultuous flash of fame. Director Lemmons explores both the hilarity and gravity of Greene's complex story, resisting the need to tie it up with a neat, triumphant bow. **118m/C; DVD, Blu-Ray, HD-DVD.** Don Cheadle; Chiwetel Ejiofor; Martin Sheen; Taraji P. Henson; Cedric the Entertainer; Elle Downs; Mike Epps; Vondie Curtis-Hall; ***D:*** Kasi Lemmons; ***W:*** Michael Genet; Rick Famuyiwa; ***C:*** Stephane Fontaine; ***M:*** Terence Blanchard. Ind. Spirit '08: Support. Actor (Ejiofor).

Talkin' Dirty after Dark 🦴🦴 **1991 (R)** Sexy comedy starring Lawrence as a suave comedian who will do anything to get a late-night spot at Dukie's comedy club. **89m/C; VHS, DVD.** Martin Lawrence; Jedda Jones; Phyllis Stickney; Darryl Sivad; ***D:*** Topper Carew; ***W:*** Topper Carew.

Talking to Heaven 🦴🦴½ *Living With the Dead* **2002 (PG-13)** James Van Praagh (Danson) has suppressed the visions he's had since childhood in an effort to lead a normal life. That becomes impossible after James sees young boys who have disappeared, apparently the work of a longtime serial killer. He draws the attention of Detective Karen Condrin (Steenburgen) since the latest young victim may still be alive. **175m/C; DVD.** Ted Danson; Mary Steenburgen; Diane Ladd; Queen Latifah; Jack Palance; Kavan Smith; Michael Moriarty; Reece Thompson; James Kirk; ***D:*** Stephen Gyllenhaal; ***W:*** John Pielmeier; ***C:*** Jeffrey Jur; ***M:*** Normand Corbeil. **TV**

The Tall Blond Man with One Black Shoe 🦴🦴🦴 *Le Grand Blond avec une Chassure Noire* **1972 (PG)** A violinist is completely unaware that rival spies mistakenly think he is also a spy, and that he is the center of a plot to booby-trap an overly ambitious agent at the French Secret Service. A sequel followed called "Return of the Tall Blond Man with One Black Shoe" which was followed by a disappointing American remake, "The Man with One Red Shoe." In French with English subtitles or dubbed. **90m/C; VHS, DVD, Blu-Ray.** *FR* Pierre Richard; Bernard Blier; Jean Rochefort; Mireille Darc; Jean Carmet; ***D:*** Yves Robert; ***W:*** Francis Veber; ***M:*** Vladimir Cosma.

Tall, Dark and Handsome 🦴🦴½ **1941** Title role is a natural for Romero as 1929 Chicago gangster Shep Morrison who's (mistakenly) known for his ruthlessness. Then he meets good girl Judy and Shep decides he wants to go straight. Berle provides comic relief. Remade as 1950's "Love That Brute." **78m/B; DVD.** Cesar Romero; Virginia Gilmore; Milton Berle; Charlotte Greenwood; Sheldon Leonard; ***D:*** H. Bruce Humberstone; ***W:*** Darrell Ware; Karl Tunberg; ***C:*** Ernest Palmer.

The Tall Guy 🦴🦴🦴 **1989 (R)** Goldblum is a too-tall actor who tries the scene in London and lands the lead in a musical version of 'The Elephant Man,' becoming an overnight success. Not consistently funny, but good British comedy, including an interesting sex scene. **92m/C; VHS, DVD.** Jeff Goldblum; Emma Thompson; Rowan Atkinson; Geraldine James; Kim Thomson; Anna Massey; ***D:*** Mel Smith; ***W:*** Richard Curtis; ***C:*** Adrian Biddle; ***M:*** Peter Brewis.

Tall in the Saddle 🦴🦴½ **1944** A misogynist foreman (Wayne) finds himself accused of murder. Meanwhile, he falls in love with his female boss's niece. An inoffensive and memorable western. **79m/B; VHS, DVD.** John Wayne; Ella Raines; George "Gabby" Hayes; Ward Bond; ***D:*** Edwin L. Marin.

Tall Lie 🦴🦴 *For Men Only* **1953** A student quits a fraternity hazing exercise. He's pursued by a psychotic bunch of his fraternity brothers and is killed in a smash-up. A local doctor goes onto an anti-hazing campaign in the aftermath. **93m/B; DVD.** Paul Henreid; Robert Sherman; Russell Johnson; Margaret Field; Vera Miles; ***D:*** Paul Henreid; ***W:*** Louis Morheim; ***C:*** Paul Ivano; ***M:*** Hoyt Curtin.

The Tall Man 🦴½ **2012 (R)** Not a conventional horror pic although the sense of dread and questionable morality are horrifying enough (as are the numerous plot twists). Cold Rock is an isolated, economically depressed mining town in Washington. Widowed nurse Julia Denning (Biel) has always scoffed at the local legend of 'The Tall Man,' who kidnaps children who are never seen again. At least she does until her own son David disappears. **106m/C; DVD, Blu-Ray.** Jessica Biel; Jodelle Ferland; William B. Davis; Stephen McHattie; Jakob Davies; ***D:*** Pascal Laugier; ***W:*** Pascal Laugier; ***C:*** Kamal Derkaoui; ***M:*** Todd Bryanton. **VIDEO**

The Tall Men 🦴🦴 **1955** Standard western features frontier hands on a rough cattle drive confronting Indians, outlaws, and the wilderness while vying with each other for the love of Russell. **122m/C; VHS, DVD, Blu-Ray.** Clark Gable; Jane Russell; Robert Ryan; Cameron Mitchell; Mae Marsh; ***D:*** Raoul Walsh; ***W:*** Sydney (Sidney) Boehm; Frank Nugent; ***C:*** Leo Tover; ***M:*** Victor Young.

Tall Story 🦴🦴 **1960** Perkins is a star basketball player who must pass a crucial test in order to continue to play the game. In addition to the pressure of the exam, he is being pressured by gamblers to throw a game against the Russians. Fonda makes her screen debut as a cheerleader who is so awe-struck by Perkins that she takes the same classes just to be close to him. Based on the play by Howard Lindsay and Russel Crouse, and the novel "The Homecoming Game" by Howard Nemerov. **91m/C; VHS, DVD, On Demand.** Anthony Perkins; Jane Fonda; Ray Walston; Marc Connelly; Anne Jackson; Tom Laughlin; Gary Lockwood; Elizabeth Patterson; Barbara Darrow; ***D:*** Joshua Logan; ***W:*** Julius J. Epstein; ***C:*** Ellsworth Fredericks; ***M:*** Cyril Mockridge.

The Tall T 🦴🦴½ **1957** A veteran rancher (Pat) stumbles onto big trouble when by chance he catches a stage coach that is eventually overrun by an evil band of cutthroats. After killing everyone on the coach except Pat and the daughter of a wealthy copper mine owner (Doretta), the renegades decide to leave the scene with the unfortunate two as hostages. Pat and Doretta, although in dire straits, find time to fall in love and devise an intricate plan for their escape. Regarded in certain western-lover circles as a cult classic. **77m/B; VHS, DVD.** Randolph Scott; Richard Boone; Maureen O'Sullivan; Arthur Hunnicutt; Skip Homeier; Henry Silva; Robert Burton; Robert Anderson; ***D:*** Budd Boetticher; ***W:*** Burt Kennedy. Natl. Film Reg. '00.

Tall Tale: The Unbelievable Adventures of Pecos Bill 🦴 **1995 (PG)** Having trouble with greedy land owners out for his pa's land, Daniel Hackett (Stahl) summons the help of three Old West legends: Pecos Bill (Swayze), John Henry (Brown), and Paul Bunyan (Platt) to face off with the evil industrialist J.P. Stiles (Glenn). Disney's variation on the "Wizard of Oz" is riddled with cartoonish characters and sleep-inducing dialogue. It would truly be a tall tale if it were said that this movie was any good. **98m/C; VHS, Streaming.** Patrick Swayze; Oliver Platt; Roger Aaron Brown; Nick Stahl; Scott Glenn; Stephen Lang; Jared Harris; Catherine O'Hara; ***D:*** Jeremiah S. Chechik; ***W:*** Steven L. Bloom; Robert Rodat; ***C:*** Janusz Kaminski.

The Tall Target 🦴🦴½ **1951** Based on an actual assassination plot to kill President-elect Abraham Lincoln. In 1861, New York police Sgt. John Kennedy (Powell), briefly a Lincoln bodyguard, learns of a plot to kill Lincoln during a Baltimore stopover. When his suspicions are dismissed, Kennedy resigns and boards a Washington-bound train to thwart the plotters who are part of the train's numerous suspicious passengers. **78m/B; DVD.** Dick Powell; Adolphe Menjou; Paula Raymond; Marshall Thompson; Ruby Dee; Will Geer; Florence Bates; Leif Erickson; ***D:*** Anthony Mann; ***W:*** Art Cohn; George Worthing Yates; ***C:*** Paul Vogel.

Tall Texan 🦴🦴½ **1953** A motley crew seeks gold in an Indian burial ground in the desert. Flawed but interesting and suspenseful. Greed, lust, Indians and desert heat. **82m/B; VHS, DVD.** Lloyd Bridges; Lee J. Cobb; Marie Windsor; George Steele; ***D:*** Elmo Williams; ***C:*** Joseph Biroc.

Talladega Nights: The Ballad of Ricky Bobby 🦴🦴 **2006 (PG-13)** It's a no-brainer concept—Will Ferrell as a NASCAR driver—but Ferrell's talented enough that he could probably make "Will Ferrell as a stamp collector" pretty entertaining. Race car legend Ricky Bobby is the oblivious king of his racing circuit until French Formula-1 driver Jean Girard (Baron Cohen) bests him and ruins Ricky's confidence. There are lots of laughs as Ricky claws his way back on top, but the scenario is so similar to Ferrell and director Adam McKay's previous effort, "Anchorman", that the whole affair has a "been there, done that" vibe. McKay's inability to ever yell "cut" during Ferrell's increasingly tedious tangents doesn't help either. **108m/C; DVD, Blu-Ray, UMD.** Will Ferrell; John C. Reilly; Sacha Baron Cohen; Michael Clarke Duncan; Leslie Bibb; Amy Adams; Gary Cole; Molly Shannon; Jane Lynch; Andy Richter; Houston Tumlin; Grayson Russell; ***D:*** Adam McKay; ***W:*** Will Ferrell; Adam McKay; ***C:*** Oliver Wood; ***M:*** Alex Wurman.

Talons of the Eagle 🦴🦴 **1992 (R)** Martial arts adventure centers around three undercover agents who go up against crimelord Mr. Li (Hong). To impress Li, martial arts champion Tyler Wilson (Blanks) and vice detective Michael Reeds (Merhi) enter a deadly martial arts tournament. They later hook up with beautiful agent Cassandra Hubbard (Barnes), who has already investigated Li's drug, gambling, and prostitution rings. Features the most advanced fighting techniques ever filmed. **96m/C; VHS, DVD.** Billy Blanks; Jalal Merhi; James Hong; Priscilla Barnes; Matthias Hues; ***D:*** Michael Kennedy; ***W:*** J. Stephen Maunder.

Tamara 🦴 **2005 (R)** Low-budget horror retread. Weird high school wallflower Tamara (Dewan) is mercilessly tormented by her cooler classmates until a prank results in her death. Tamara, who practiced witchcraft while alive, gets resurrected as a sexpot ready for revenge. **98m/C; DVD.** Jeffrey Reddick; Jenna Dewan; Katie Stuart; Chad Faust; Bryan Clark; Melissa Elias; Matthew Marsden; Claudette Mink; Gil Hacohen; Marc Devigne; Chris Sigurdson; Sarah Blondin; Magally Zelaya; Ernesto Griffith; Brian Davisson; Brandy Jaques; ***D:*** Jeremy Haft; ***W:*** Jeffrey Reddick; ***C:*** Scott Kevan; ***M:*** Michael Suby.

Tamara Drewe 🦴🦴½ **2010 (R)** Posy Simmonds based her graphic novel on Thomas Hardy's "Far From the Madding Crowd" and turned it into a contemporary social comedy, which director Frears follows in his adaptation. Now a sexy newspaper columnist, formerly gawky Tamara (Arterton) returns to her home village to fix up and sell the family home and stuns much of the local male population, including a vain adulterous writer, a preening rock musician, and her stoic ex-teenage flame. The ensemble cast is as vivid and delightful as the England backdrop. **110m/C; Blu-Ray, On Demand.** *GB* Gemma Arterton; Roger Allam; Dominic Cooper; Luke Evans; Tamsin Greig; Jessica Barden; Charlotte Christie; Susan Woolridge; Bronagh Gallagher; Bill Camp; ***D:*** Stephen Frears; ***W:*** Moira Buffini; ***C:*** Benjamin Davis; ***M:*** Alexandre Desplat.

The Tamarind Seed 🦴½ **1974** Andrews and Sharif are star-crossed lovers kept apart by Cold War espionage. Dated, dull and desultory. **123m/C; VHS, Streaming.** Julie Andrews; Omar Sharif; Anthony Quayle; Dan O'Herlihy; Sylvia Syms; ***D:*** Blake Edwards; ***W:*** Blake Edwards; ***C:*** Frederick A. (Freddie) Young; ***M:*** John Barry.

The T.A.M.I. Show 🦴🦴🦴½ **1964** The Santa Monica Civic Auditorium was the site, the Teenage Awards Music International was the show featuring Rock and R&B performances by such greats as Smokey Robinson and the Miracles, Jan and Dean, Marvin Gaye, Chuck Berry, the Supremes and the Rolling Stones. Young Teri Garr is a go-go dancer. Legendary show was a long time in coming to DVD. **100m/B; DVD.** ***D:*** Steve Binder; ***W:*** Steve Binder. Natl. Film Reg. '06.

Taming Andrew 🦴🦴 *When Andrew Came Home* **2000** Lifetime family drama based on a true story. Gail institutes a search for her young son Andrew after he is kidnapped in a parental custody dispute by her ex-husband. When the ex sends the boy home after five years, Andrew is embittered and distrustful after being abused, so Gail must convince her son he is safe and loved. **92m/C; DVD.** Park Overall; Seth Adkins; Jason Beghe; Lynne Deragon; Carl Marotte; Craig Eldridge; ***D:*** Artie Mandelberg; ***W:*** Susan Rice; ***C:*** Malcolm Cross; ***M:*** Jay Ferguson. **CABLE**

The Taming of the Shrew 🦴🦴½ **1929** Historically interesting early talkie featuring sole (if perhaps unfortunate) pairing of Pickford and Fairbanks. Features the legendary credit line "By William Shakespeare, with additional dialogue by Sam Taylor." Re-edited in 1966; 1967 Zeffirelli remake featured Taylor and Burton. **66m/B; VHS, DVD.** Mary Pickford; Douglas Fairbanks, Sr.; Edwin Maxwell; Joseph Cawthorn; ***D:*** Sam Taylor; ***C:*** Karl Struss.

The Taming of the Shrew 🦴🦴🦴½ **1967** A lavish screen version of the classic Shakespearean comedy. Burton and Taylor are violently physical and perfectly cast as the battling Katherine and Petruchio. At the time the film was made, Burton and Taylor were having their own marital problems, which not only added an inner fire to their performances, but sent the interested moviegoers to the theatres in droves. **122m/C; VHS, DVD.** *IT* Elizabeth Taylor; Richard Burton; Michael York; Michael Hordern; Cyril Cusack; ***D:*** Franco Zeffirelli; ***W:*** Franco Zeffirelli; ***C:*** Oswald Morris; ***M:*** Nino Rota.

Tammy 🦴½ **2014 (R)** McCarthy continues to waste the goodwill earned by her breakthrough in "Bridesmaids" by starring as another abrasive, unlikable character built around her larger-than-life personality. She plays the title character, who gets fired from her fast food restaurant job only to find her husband with another woman. She goes off the rails, grabs her grandma (Sarandon), and heads on a road trip. To say that the two stars are better than the material is an understatement—they find moments that other actresses wouldn't but it's not enough. **97m/C; DVD, Blu-Ray.** Melissa McCarthy; Susan Sarandon; Kathy Bates; Sandra Oh; Gary Cole; Mark Duplass; Nat Faxon; Toni Collette; Allison Janney; Dan Aykroyd; Ben Falcone; ***D:*** Ben Falcone; ***W:*** Melissa McCarthy; Ben Falcone; ***C:*** Russ T. Alsobrook; ***M:*** Michael Andrews.

Tammy and the Bachelor 🦴🦴½ **1957** A backwoods Southern girl becomes involved with a romantic pilot and his snobbish family. They don't quite know what to make of her but she wins them over with her down-home philosophy. Features the hit tune, "Tammy." Charming performance by Reynolds. **89m/C; VHS, DVD, Blu-Ray.** Debbie Reynolds; Leslie Nielsen; Walter Brennan; Fay Wray; Sidney Blackmer; Mildred Natwick; Louise Beavers; ***D:*** Joseph Pevney; ***W:*** Oscar Brodney.

Tammy and the Doctor 🦴🦴 **1963** Sandra Dee reprises Debbie Reynolds's backwoods gal ("Tammy and the Bachelor"). Dee becomes a nurse's aide and is wooed by doctor Fonda, in his film debut. **88m/C; VHS, DVD.** Sandra Dee; Peter Fonda; MacDonald Carey; ***D:*** Harry Keller; ***W:*** Oscar Brodney.

Tammy Tell Me True 🦴🦴 **1/2 1961** In this sequel to the 1957 comedy, Sandra Dee takes over the role (from Debbie Reynolds) of backwoods gal Tammy Tyree. She decides to better herself by enrolling in college and becomes the paid companion of wealthy, elderly Annie McCall (Bondi). This dismays Annie's greedy niece Suzanne (Meade), who has her aunt brought up on a sanity hearing. Tammy manages to find romance with speech professor Tom Freeman (Gavin). Followed by "Tammy and the Doctor" (1963). **97m/C; DVD.** Sandra Dee; John Gavin; Beulah Bondi; Julia Meade; Edgar Buchanan; Virginia Grey; Cecil Kellaway; ***D:*** Harry Keller; ***W:*** Oscar Brodney; ***C:*** Clifford Stine; ***M:*** Percy Faith.

Tampico 🦴 **1/2 1944** Not very believable wartime drama. Oil tanker captain, Bart Manson (Robinson), rescues survivors of a ship torpedoed in the Gulf of Mexico, despite first mate Adamson's (Mature) objections. The captain is taken by young and lovely Kathy Hall (Bari), but when his own ship is sunk, she is accused of being a German spy. Manson sets out to prove her innocence. **75m/B; DVD.** Edward G. Robinson; Lynn Bari; Victor McLaglen; Robert Bailey; Marc Lawrence; ***D:*** Lothar Mendes; ***W:*** Fred Niblo, Jr.; Kenneth Gamet; ***C:*** Charles G. Clarke; ***M:*** David Raskin.

Tampopo 🦴🦴🦴 *Dandelion* **1986** A hilarious, episodic Japanese comedy. Young restaurant hostess Tampopo (Miyamoto) is coached by 10 gallon-hatted stranger Goro (Yamazaki) in how to make the perfect noodle so she can open her own successful shop. There's also a food-loving gangster (Yakusho) who serves as an occasional narrator and gourmet. Popular, free-form hit that established Itami in the West. Japanese with subtitles. **114m/C; VHS, DVD, Blu-Ray.** *JP* Ken(saku) Watanabe; Tsutomu Yamazaki; Nobuko Miyamoto; Koji Yakusho; Rikiya Yasuoka; Kinzo Sakura; Hideji Otaki; ***D:*** Juzo Itami; ***W:*** Juzo Itami; ***C:*** Masaki Tamura; ***M:*** Kunihiko Murai.

Tangerine 🦴🦴 **1/2 2015 (R)** Shot entirely on an iPhone, Baker's dramedy pulses with the energy of the world it captures. Sin-Dee Rella (Rodriguez) is a trans sex worker just out of a brief prison term. She meets up with her best friend Alexandra (Taylor), also a trans sex worker, who tells her that her pimp boyfriend Chester (Ransone) has been cheating on her with a cis white woman. This will not do. Sin-Dee scours Los Angeles for the man who done her wrong while Alexandra prepares for a stage show. Baker uses new technology to capture a world not really see on film before. **88m/C; DVD, Blu-Ray, Streaming.** Kitana Kiki Rodriquez; Mya Taylor; Karren Karagulian; James Ransone; Alla Tumanian; ***D:*** Sean Baker; ***W:*** Sean Baker; Chris Bergoch; ***C:*** Sean Baker; Radium Cheung. Ind. Spirit '16: Actress--Supporting (Taylor).

Tangled 🦴🦴 **1/2 2001 (R)** After being found on a country road badly beaten, David (Hatosy) struggles to remember and explain what happened to a detective (Bracco) who is also investigating the disappearance of David's friend Jenny (Cook). Jenny was swept off her feet by David's old roommate Alan (Rhys-Meyers), who was strictly bad news. When Alan gets into trouble for drug posession, he blames David and Jenny and is determined to get revenge. Too tangled for its own good. **89m/C; VHS, DVD.** Shawn Hatosy; Rachael Leigh Cook; Jonathan Rhys Meyers; Lorraine Bracco; Estella Warren; ***D:*** Jay Lowi; ***W:*** Jeffrey Lieber; ***C:*** Bobby Bukowski; ***M:*** Reinhold Heil; Johnny Klimek.

Tangled 🦴🦴🦴 *Rapunzel* **2010 (PG)** Disney's musical take on the classic Rapunzel tale, brought to life in 3D computer animation. Princess Rapunzel (voiced by Moore) has been stolen from her parents and locked up by her evil adopted mother (Murphy) in a tower accessible to no one, allowing her magical golden locks to flow 70 feet long. Confused, and co-dependent on her mother (it's a new millennium, after all) she enlists the help of a smug thief (Levi) to break her out of this private prison. Despite straying from the original Grimm's fairy tale, the musical numbers never get too gooey, still retaining a sense of dread. As with the cartoons of Disney's golden age, adults can connect just as easily as the kids. **100m/C; Blu-Ray.** Ron Perlman; ***V:*** Mandy Moore; Zachary Levi; Donna Murphy; Brad Garrett; Jeffrey Tambor; ***D:*** Byron Howard; Nathan Greno; ***W:*** Dan Fogelman; ***M:*** Alan Menken.

Tango 🦴🦴 **1998 (PG-13)** There's not much plot and it's not really needed when cinematographer Storaro so stunningly lenses Saura's semi-documentary look at Argentina's national dance. Middleaged Buenos Aires director Mario Suarez (Sola) is depressed after being abandoned by his wife, Laura (Narova), and decides to throw himself into making a movie about the tango. The film's shady investor, Angelo Larroca (Galiardo), insists Mario hire his young dancer mistress, Elena (Maestro), with whom Mario unwisely starts to fall in love. Spanish with subtitles. **115m/C; VHS, DVD.** *SP* Miguel Angel Sola; Juan Luis Galiardo; Mia Maestro; Cecilia Narova; ***D:*** Carlos Saura; ***W:*** Carlos Saura; ***C:*** Vittorio Storaro; ***M:*** Lalo Schifrin.

Tango and Cash 🦴🦴 **1989 (R)** Stallone and Russell are L.A. cops with something in common: they both think they are the best in the city. Forced to work together to beat drug lord Palance, they flex their muscles a lot. Directing completed by Albert Magnoli, after Andrei Konchalovsky left in a huff. **104m/C; VHS, DVD, Blu-Ray.** Sylvester Stallone; Kurt Russell; Jack Palance; Brion James; Teri Hatcher; Michael J. Pollard; James Hong; Marc Alaimo; Robert Z'Dar; Edward (Eddie) Bunker; Clint Howard; Lewis Arquette; Michael Jeter; Glenn Morshower; Geoffrey Lewis; ***D:*** Andrei Konchalovsky; ***W:*** Randy Feldman; ***C:*** Donald E. Thorin; ***M:*** Harold Faltermeyer.

The Tango Lesson 🦴🦴 **1/2 1997 (PG)** Semiautobiographical tale of director/star/writer and former dancer Potter ("Orlando" director), as Sally, who finds love and the meaning of life in the tango while living in Paris. While penning a noncommercial script called "Rage" about a paraplegic designer who stalks leggy models, Sally meets a tango instructor (Pablo) without a partner, and soon the two are doing more than just the tango. Sally grooms Pablo to star in her upcoming pic as long as he allows the headstrong director to take the lead while they dance. Occasionally departs from the story to the "Rage" script, played out in color. While light on their toes, performances by the real-life director and real-life tango instructor are as heavy and stilted as some of the dialogue. Using dance as the metaphor for control and power in relationships, Potter falls flat in a pretentious "Lesson." **101m/B; VHS, DVD.** *GB* Sally Potter; Pablo Veron; Gustavo Naveira; Fabian Salas; David Toole; Carolina Iotti; Carlos Copello; Peter Eyre; Heathcote Williams; ***D:*** Sally Potter; ***W:*** Sally Potter; ***C:*** Robby Muller; ***M:*** Sally Potter; Fred Frith.

Tank 🦴 **1/2 1983 (PG)** Retired Army officer Garner's son is thrown into jail on a trumped-up charge by a small town sheriff. Dad comes to the rescue with his restored Sherman tank. Trite and unrealistic portrayal of good versus bad made palatable by Garner's performance. **113m/C; VHS, DVD.** James Garner; Shirley Jones; C. Thomas Howell; Mark Herrier; Sandy Ward; Jenilee Harrison; Dorian Harewood; G.D. Spradlin; ***D:*** Marvin J. Chomsky; ***W:*** Dan Gordon; ***C:*** Donald Birnkrant; ***M:*** Lalo Schifrin.

Tank Girl 🦴 **1/2 1994 (R)** Big-budget adaption of the underground British comic book about a brash punker chick (Petty), her mutant friends, and the evil establishment in the post-apocalyptic future. The heavily armed pixie battles the tyrannical Department of Water and Power, run by evil Dr. Kesslee (McDowell), for control of the world's water supply in the year 2033. Straying a bit too far from the source comic, the plot (such as it is) is crammed into a rigid action-movie structure that lacks excitement. Plays like a cheap Gen-X marketing ploy with its bizarre mixture of pop culture references and a hipper-than-thou soundtrack coordinated by Courtney Love. **104m/C; VHS, DVD, Blu-Ray.** Lori Petty; Malcolm McDowell; Ice-T; Naomi Watts; Jeff Kober; Reg E. Cathey; Scott Coffey; Ann Cusack; Don Harvey; Brian Wimmer; Stacey Linn Ramsower; Iggy Pop; Ann Magnuson; ***D:*** Rachel Talalay; ***W:*** Tedi Sarafian; ***C:*** Gale Tattersall; ***M:*** Graeme Revell.

The Tanks Are Coming 🦴🦴 **1951** The title basically tells you everything you need to know. Sgt. Sullivan (Cochran) is forced to take over command of the Third Armored Division as the tanks push across France towards the Siegfried Line in 1944. Based on a story by Samuel Fuller. **90m/B; DVD.** Steve Cochran; Phil Carey; Paul Picerni; Harry Bellaver; James Dobson; George O'Hanlon; John McIntire; Mari Aldon; ***D:*** Lewis Seiler; David Ross Lederman; ***W:*** Robert D. (Robert Hardy) Andrews; ***C:*** Edwin DuPar; Warren Lynch; ***M:*** William Lava.

Tanner '88 🦴🦴🦴 *Tanner: A Political Fable* **1988** Murphy is excellent as a longshot politician on the trail of the Democratic presidential nomination. Precise political satire from a story by Gary "Doonesbury" Trudeau. **120m/C; VHS, DVD.** Michael Murphy; Pamela Reed; Cynthia Nixon; ***D:*** Robert Altman. **CABLE**

Tanner Hall 🦴 **1/2 2009 (R)** Too-familiar plot about shallow teen girls at boarding school. Queen Bee Fernanda doesn't want to share senior-year glory with manipulative childhood acquaintance Victoria, who's a newcomer at their private school. There are a few subplots of the sexual variety but the flick can't decide where it wants to go so it goes nowhere. **95m/C; DVD, Blu-Ray.** Rooney Mara; Georgia King; Brie Larson; Amy Ferguson; Tom Everett Scott; Chris Kattan; Amy Sedaris; ***D:*** Francesca Gregorini; Tatiana von Furstenberg; ***W:*** Francesca Gregorini; Tatiana von Furstenberg; ***C:*** Brian Rigney Hubbard; ***M:*** Roger Neill. **VIDEO**

Tanner on Tanner 🦴🦴 **2004** Trudeau's Tanner (Murphy) returns sixteen years later with Alex (Nixon) struggling to make a documentary of her dad's dashed presidential dreams while her own life is unraveling. Meanwhile, he's busily inflating his prominence within the party during the national convention. **120m/C; VHS, DVD.** Michael Murphy; Cynthia Nixon; Pamela Reed; Matt Malloy; Ilana Levine; Jim Fyfe; Avery Clyde; ***Cameo(s):*** Tom Brokaw; Steve Buscemi; Mario Cuomo; Howard Dean; Michael Dukakis; ***D:*** Robert Altman; ***W:*** Garry Trudeau; ***C:*** Robert Altman; Tom Richmond. **TV**

Tanya's Island 🦴🦴 **1/2 1981 (R)** Abused girlfriend fantasizes about life on deserted island and romance with an ape. Vanity billed as D.D. Winters. **100m/C; VHS, DVD.** Vanity; Dick Sargent; Mariette Levesque; Don McCleod; ***D:*** Alfred Sole.

The Tao of Steve 🦴🦴🦴 **2000 (R)** Overweight, intelligent kindergarten teacher Dex (Logue) is a hit with the ladies, but feels a vague sense of wanting something more. The title of the film comes from Dex's personal philosophy of cool, which he takes from the images of such icons as Steve McQueen, Steve McGarrett, and Steve Austin—but is also tossed with equal parts Kierkegaard and Aquinas. He's ripe for some growing up, and only needs to find the perfect mate, who comes along in the form of Syd (played by Greer Goodman, sister of the director and one of the film's three screenwriters), one of Dex's one-night stands. A sweet romantic comedy that can thank Logue for much of its charm. **87m/C; VHS, DVD.** Donal Logue; Greer Goodman; Kimo Wills; Ayelet Kaznelson; David Aaron Baker; Nina Jaroslaw; ***D:*** Jenniphr Goodman; ***W:*** Greer Goodman; Jenniphr Goodman; Duncan North; ***C:*** Teodoro Maniaci; ***M:*** Joe Delia.

Tap 🦴🦴 **1/2 1989 (PG-13)** The son of a famous tap dancer, a dancer himself, decides to try to get away from his former life of crime by helping an aging hoofer revitalize the art of tap dancing. Fun to watch for the wonderful dancing scenes. Davis' last big screen appearance. Hines is sincere in this old-fashioned story, and dances up a storm. Captures some never-before filmed old hoofers. **106m/C; VHS, DVD.** Gregory Hines; Sammy Davis, Jr.; Suzzanne Douglass; Joe Morton; Terrance McNally; Steve Condos; Jimmy Slyde; Harold Nicholas; Etta James; Savion Glover; Dick Anthony Williams; Howard "Sandman" Sims; Bunny Briggs; Pat Rico; Arthur Duncan; ***D:*** Nick Castle; ***W:*** Nick Castle; ***M:*** James Newton Howard.

Tape 🦴🦴🦴 **2001 (R)** Director Linklater makes digital technology an asset in this intriguing, claustrophobic character study based on a play by Stephen Belber. Johnny (Leonard) pays a visit to high school chum Vince (Hawke), who's working as a low-level drug dealer. Their casual conversation becomes increasingly hostile as Vince begins making accusations involving Johnny and his first love, Amy (Thurman), who soon pays a visit herself. Despite a tiny cast and only one location, story stays stimulating throughout, as the script deftly shifts viewer allegiance between characters and explores interesting themes of memory, subjectivity and ownership of one's past. Linklater's use of high-definition video gives the film a vitality and spontaneous feel that suits the material. **86m/C; VHS, DVD.** Ethan Hawke; Robert Sean Leonard; Uma Thurman; ***D:*** Richard Linklater; ***W:*** Stephen Belber; ***C:*** Maryse Alberti.

Tapeheads 🦴🦴 **1/2 1989 (R)** Silly, sophomoric, sexy comedy starring Cusack and Robbins as young wanna-be rock-video producers who get mixed up with perverted politicos, conniving music-industry types, and asinine bands looking for MTV stardom before they eventually strike it big helping their childhood idols, The Swanky Modes. Many big-name music industry cameos and a great soundtrack help keep things lively when the plot goes out of control. Sam Moore and Junior Walker are the Sam & Dave-esque Modes. **93m/C; VHS, DVD.** John Cusack; Tim Robbins; Mary Crosby; Connie Stevens; Susan Tyrrell; Lyle Alzado; Don Cornelius; Katy Boyer; Doug McClure; Clu Gulager; Jessica Walter; Stiv Bators; Sam Moore; Junior Walker; Martha Quinn; Ted Nugent; Weird Al Yankovic; Bobcat Goldthwait; Michael Nesmith; Xander Berkeley; Bojan Bazelli; Courtney Love; Ebbe Roe Smith; Lee Arenberg; Rocky Giordani; John Marshall Jones; John Durbin; Milton Selzer; Zander Schloss; Jo Harvey Allen; Sy Richardson; Coati Mundi; John Fleck; ***D:*** Bill Fishman; ***W:*** Bill Fishman; Peter McCarthy; ***C:*** Bojan Bazelli.

Tapped Out 🦴 **1/2 2003 (R)** Aspiring rap musicians steal a song from another singer, and unexpectedly it becomes a massive hit for them. Equally as unexpected he doesn't sue them, but tries to put a bullet in their heads instead. **95m/C; DVD.** Coolio; Clifton Powell; Kelly Jo Minter; Kasan Butcher; Georgio; ***D:*** Georgio; ***W:*** Georgio; ***C:*** Kirk Douglas; ***M:*** Georgio.

Taps 🦴🦴 **1/2 1981 (PG)** Military academy students led by Hutton are so true to their school they lay siege to it to keep it from being closed. An antiwar morality play about excesses of zeal and patriotism. Predictable but impressive. **126m/C; VHS, DVD.** Timothy Hutton; George C. Scott; Ronny Cox; Sean Penn; Tom Cruise; Giancarlo Esposito; Evan Handler; Brendan Ward; John P. Navin, Jr.; Earl Hindman; ***D:*** Harold Becker; ***W:*** Darryl Ponicsan; Robert Mark Kamen; ***C:*** Owen Roizman; ***M:*** Maurice Jarre.

Tar 🦴🦴 **1997** Female cop Prescott and crook Thigpen were high school sweethearts who went their separate ways. But they're reunited when Thigpen hijacks a squad car that just happens to be driven by guess who. There's also a story involving a group of black nationalists who kidnap white businessman and cover them in—you guessed it—tar. Likeable leads, improbable characters. **90m/C; VHS, DVD.** Kevin Thigpen; Nicole Prescott; Seth Gilliam; Ron Brice; Frank Minucci; ***D:*** Goetz Grossmann; ***W:*** Goetz Grossmann; ***C:*** Lloyd Handwerker; ***M:*** John Hill.

Tara Road 🦴 **1/2 2005 (PG)** American Marilyn's (MacDowell) son dies in an accident and she can't recover from her grief, while Irish Ria (Williams) is told by her husband (Glen) that he's leaving her to marry his pregnant girlfriend. Through a series of coincidences, the unhappy women decide to switch houses for two months and see if it will change their lives. Bland adaptation of the novel by Maeve Binchy. **97m/C; DVD.** *IR* Andie MacDowell; Olivia Williams; Iain Glen; Stephen Rea; Brenda Fricker; Jean-Marc Barr; ***D:*** Gilles Mackinnon; ***W:*** Shane Connaughton; ***C:*** John de Borman; ***M:*** John Keane.

Tarantella 🦴🦴 ½ **1995** Aspiring New York photographer Diane DiSorella (Sorvino) gets a shock when her mother dies suddenly. After returning to the New Jersey home and Italian-American community she rejected, Diane is given a journal her mother secretly kept by old family friend Pina (Gregorio). Small-scale story with Diane's big change being learning to accept where she came from. **84m/C; VHS, DVD.** Mira Sorvino; Rose Gregorio; Stephen Spinella; Matthew Lillard; Antonia Rey; Frank Pellegrino; ***D:*** Helen DeMichiel; ***W:*** Helen DeMichiel; Richard Hoblock; ***C:*** Teodoro Maniaci; ***M:*** Norman Moll.

Tarantula 🦴🦴🦴 **1955** If you're into gigantic killer insect movies this is one of the best with nifty special effects and some good action. Carroll plays a scientist working on a growth formula which he's testing on a spider when it accidentally gets loose. This eight-legged horror grows to 100 feet high and causes havoc in the Arizona desert until the Air Force napalms the sucker. Look for Eastwood in the final sequence as an Air Force pilot. **81m/B; VHS, DVD, Blu-Ray.** Leo G. Carroll; John Agar; Mara Corday; Nestor Paiva; Ross Elliott; Clint Eastwood; ***D:*** Jack Arnold; ***W:*** Robert M. Fresco; Martin Berkeley; Jack Arnold.

Tarantulas: The Deadly Cargo 🦴 **1977** Eek! Hairy spiders terrorizing our sleepy town and destroying our orange crop! Made-for-TV cheapie not creepy; will make you sleepy. **100m/C; VHS, DVD.** Claude Akins; Charles Frank; Deborah Winters; Pat Hingle; Sandy McPeak; Bert Remsen; Howard Hesseman; Tom Atkins; Charles Siebert; Mathew Laborteaux; Pepe Serna; ***D:*** Stuart Hagmann; ***W:*** Guerdon (Gordon) Trueblood; ***C:*** Robert L. Morrison; ***M:*** Mundell Lowe. **TV**

Taras Bulba 🦴🦴 ½ **1962** Well-photographed costume epic on the 16th century Polish revolution. Brynner as the fabled Cossack; Curtis plays his vengeful son. Good score. Shot on location in Argentina. Based on the novel by Nikolai Gogol. **122m/C; VHS, DVD, Blu-Ray.** Tony Curtis; Yul Brynner; Christine Kaufmann; Sam Wanamaker; George Macready; Vladimir Sokoloff; Perry Lopez; ***D:*** J. Lee Thompson.

Tarawa Beachhead 🦴🦴 **1958** Cynical WWII pic finds Marine sergeant Tom Sloan (Mathews) witnessing his lieutenant, Joel Brady (Danton), kill a cowardly soldier in a combat situation on Guadalcanal. Sloan keeps quiet, assuming he won't be believed, but tensions ratchet up since the men are constantly serving together. **77m/B; DVD.** Kerwin Mathews; Ray Danton; Julie Adams; Karen Sharpe; John Baer; Onslow Stevens; Russ Thorson; Eddie Ryder; ***D:*** Paul Wendkos; ***W:*** Richard Alan Simmons; ***C:*** Henry Freulich.

Target 🦴🦴 **1985 (R)** Normal dad/hubby Hackman slips into a figurative phone booth and emerges as former CIA when his better half is kidnapped in Paris. Good action scenes, but poorly scripted and too long. **117m/C; VHS, DVD.** Gene Hackman; Matt Dillon; Gayle Hunnicutt; Josef Sommer; ***D:*** Arthur Penn; ***W:*** Howard Berk.

The Target 🦴 ½ *The Piano Player* **2002 (R)** Mercenary Alex Laney (Lambert) goes to South Africa to protect wealthy businessman Robert Nile (Hopper) from the crime boss (Majiba) who's now in jail thanks to Nile's promised testimony. But those who attempt to testify soon wind up dead, so after some near-misses, Niles, his daughter (Kruger), and Laney wind up in a small town with the bad guy (freed from prison) still on their trail. Typical "B" movie action. **94m/C; VHS, DVD.** Christopher Lambert; Dennis Hopper; James Faulkner; Diane Kruger; Simon Majiba; ***D:*** Jean-Pierre Roux; ***W:*** Brad Mirman; ***C:*** Larry Smith.

The Target 🦴🦴 *Pyojeok* **2015 (R)** A dramatic action thriller about a doctor's effort to save his wife and expose corruption. After saving one of his patients—a suspect in a murder case—from an attempt on his life by an assassin, an emergency room doctor suffers a horrific loss when his pregnant wife is kidnapped soon after. As it becomes clear that the events are linked and a conspiracy is involved, the doctor and his patient form an alliance to save the woman and reveal the depth and length of the corruption. Korean with subtitles. **98m/C; DVD, Blu-Ray, Streaming, Download.** Ryu Seung-Ryong; Joon-sang Yoo; Jin-Wook Lee; Seong-ryeong Kim; Eun-ji Jo; ***D:*** Chang; ***W:*** Cheol-Hong Jeon; Seong-Geol Jo; ***M:*** Ja wan Koo; In-young Park. **VIDEO**

Target for Killing 🦴🦴 **1966** Mediocre thriller about a secret agent who must protect a young heiress from a Lebanese syndicate that's out to kill her. **93m/C; VHS, DVD.** Stewart Granger; Curt Jurgens; Molly Peters; Adolfo Celi; Klaus Kinski; Rupert Davies; ***D:*** Manfred Kohler.

Target of Opportunity 🦴🦴 ½ **2004 (R)** Rousing action tale hits the mark. Jim Jacobs (Cochran) is a former CIA guy who heads to Eastern Europe to rescue childhood buddy Nick Carlton (Jensen), an agent jailed for being on the wrong side of some spy games. But in the process Jim finds himself on his old employer's most wanted list. **91m/C; VHS, DVD.** Todd Jensen; Hristo Naumov Shopov; Dean Cochran; Nadia Konakchieva; Bashar Rahal; ***D:*** Dan Lerner; ***W:*** Les Weldon. **VIDEO**

Target Zero 🦴 ½ **1955** In 1952, GIs are making their way back to their company while stuck behind enemy lines in Korea. They pick up part of a British tank unit that has gotten lost and a stranded UN biochemist, but then the squad is rerouted and told to hold an outpost against the enemy. **92m/B; DVD.** Richard Conte; Charles Bronson; Chuck Connors; L.Q. Jones; Abel Fernandez; Richard Park; Richard Stapley; Peggie Castle; ***D:*** Harmon Jones; ***W:*** Sam Rolfe; ***C:*** Edwin DuPar; ***M:*** David Buttolph.

Targets 🦴🦴🦴 **1968 (PG)** Bogdanovich's suspenseful directorial debut. An aging horror film star (Karloff) plans his retirement, convinced that real life is too scary for his films to have an audience. A mad sniper at a drive-in movie seems to prove he's right. Some prints still have anti-gun prologue, which was added after Robert Kennedy's assassination. **90m/C; DVD.** Boris Karloff; James Brown; Tim O'Kelly; Monte Landis; Mary Jackson; Sandy Baron; Tanya Morgan; Arthur Peterson; Nancy Hsueh; Peter Bogdanovich; ***D:*** Peter Bogdanovich; ***W:*** Peter Bogdanovich; ***C:*** Laszlo Kovacs.

Tarnation 🦴🦴 ½ **2003** Feature debut of Caouette is an experimental documentary constructed from home movies, photographs, letters, phone messages, and created video footage that Caouette edited on his home computer and layered with appropriate songs. It follows the emotional journey of Caouette and his mentally ill mother from a Texas childhood legacy of abuse, neglect, and an escape into a self-created fantasy world, to their lives 20-odd years later. **88m/C; DVD.** ***D:*** Jonathan Caouette; ***W:*** Jonathan Caouette; ***C:*** Jonathan Caouette; ***M:*** John Califra; Max Lichtenstein.

Tarnished Angels 🦴🦴🦴 **1957** Reporter Burke Devlin (Hudson) is writing a story for the local New Orleans paper about a tormented trio of air circus barnstormers. A former WWI ace, Roger Shumann (Stack) cares more about flying than he does his sizzling wife Laverne (Malone), who's loved-from-afar by loyal mechanic Jiggs (Carson). When Roger's plane cracks up, he uses his wife to obtain use of an experimental aircraft in order to win a race—and brings disaster crashing around them all. Good action, fine cast. Based on William Faulkner's 1930 novel "Pylon." **91m/B; VHS, DVD, Blu-Ray.** Rock Hudson; Robert Stack; Dorothy Malone; Jack Carson; Robert Middleton; Troy Donahue; Alan Reed; Robert J. Wilke; William Schallert; ***D:*** Douglas Sirk; ***W:*** George Zuckerman; ***C:*** Irving Glassberg; ***M:*** Frank Skinner.

Tart 🦴🦴 **2001 (R)** Cat Storm (Swain) is desperate to belong to the in-crowd at her New York prep school even if it means dumping her best friend, Delilah (Phillips). But privilege has its price. **94m/C; VHS, DVD.** Dominique Swain; Brad Renfro; Bijou Phillips; Mischa Barton; Lacey Chabert; Alberta Watson; Myles Jeffrey; Scott Thompson; Melanie Griffith; ***D:*** Christina Wayne; ***W:*** Christina Wayne; ***C:*** Stephen Kazmierski; ***M:*** Jeehun Hwang.

The Tartars **WOOF!** **1961** Unintentionally humorous costume adventure that Welles and Mature must have been doing for the money since it stinks. Viking chief Oleg (Mature) slays a Russian Tartar leader and holds a Tartar maiden captive. Tartar overlord Burundai (Welles) retaliates and captures Oleg's wife. The two sides become embroiled in an all-out war. **83m/C; DVD.** *IT* Victor Mature; Orson Welles; Liana Orfei; Bella Cortez; Arnoldo Foa; Luciano Marin; ***D:*** Richard Thorpe; ***W:*** Ferdinando Baldi; Ambrogio Molteni; ***C:*** Amerigo Gengarelli; ***M:*** Renzo Rossellini.

Tartuffe 🦴🦴 *Herr Tartuff* **1925** Murnau's film-within-a-film adaptation of Moliere's play. A greedy housekeeper (Valetti) wants to profit from her elderly employer's (Picha) will so she tells him that his actor grandson (Mattoni) is a wastrel. The grandson disguises himself as a traveling film projectionist and shows his grandfather the film about Tartuffe (Jannings), which parallels their own story of greed and hypocrisy. **74m/B; Silent; DVD, Blu-Ray.** *GE* Emil Jannings; Lil Dagover; Werner Krauss; Rosa Valetti; Andre Mattoni; Hermann Picha; ***D:*** F.W. Murnau; ***W:*** Carl Mayer; ***C:*** Karl Freund.

Tarzan 🦴🦴🦴 **1999 (G)** Disney animated film finds baby Tarzan lost in the jungle and raised by a gorilla family—patriarch Kerchak (Henriksen), nurturing mom Kala (Close), and bossy big sister Terk (O'Donnell). But, years later, a now grownup Tarzan's (Goldwyn) life is thrown into chaos when he first encounters humans—and realizes he is one. Eccentric gorilla scientist Professor Porter (Hawthorne) and his lovely daughter Jane (Driver) are willing to help, but jungle guide Clayton (Blessed) is the villain on the scene. Disney's animation is even more amazing than usual thanks to some new computer software that gives the jungle background unbelievable depth and Tarzan glides, surfs, and jumps in a wow! look! manner. **88m/C; VHS, DVD, Blu-Ray.** ***V:*** Tony Goldwyn; Minnie Driver; Rosie O'Donnell; Glenn Close; Lance Henriksen; Wayne Knight; Brian Blessed; Nigel Hawthorne; Alex D. Linz; ***D:*** Kevin Lima; Chris Buck; ***W:*** Tab Murphy; Bob Tzudiker; Noni White; ***M:*** Phil Collins. Oscars '99: Song ("You'll Be In My Heart"); Golden Globes '00: Song ("You'll Be In My Heart").

Tarzan 2 🦴🦴 ½ **2005** Animated prequel to the 2004 Disney flick finds young Tarzan (Chad) upset that he's not as strong or as fast as his ape foster family. When his human weakness puts his mom's (Close) life in danger, Tarzan leaves the tribe and seeks out a cranky, old hermit ape (Carlin) for advice. Lots of fun for the pee-wee set (and their parents will enjoy the Carlin humor). **72m/C; DVD.** ***V:*** Harrison Chad; Glenn Close; George Carlin; Brad Garrett; Lance Henriksen; Ron Perlman; Estelle Harris; ***D:*** Brian J. Smith; ***W:*** Bob Tzudiker; Noni White; ***M:*** Mark Mancina. **VIDEO**

Tarzan and His Mate 🦴🦴🦴 **1934** Second entry in the lavishly produced MGM Tarzan series. Weissmuller and O'Sullivan cohabit in unmarried bliss before the Hays Code moved them to a tree house with twin beds. Many angry elephants, nasty white hunters, and hungry lions. **93m/B; VHS, DVD.** Johnny Weissmuller; Maureen O'Sullivan; Neil Hamilton; Paul Cavanagh; ***D:*** Jack Conway; ***W:*** Leon Gordon; James Kevin McGuinness; Howard Emmett Rogers; ***C:*** Clyde De Vinna; Charles G. Clarke; ***M:*** William Axt. Natl. Film Reg. '03.

Tarzan and the Amazons 🦴 ½ **1945** In this ninth adventure, Tarzan and Boy reunite with Jane (now played by Joyce) and Tarzan helps out an injured Amazon tribeswoman, thus learning the location of their gold-rich hidden city. Boy secretly follows and later innocently shows the way to a greedy group of archeologists after Tarzan turns them down. Boy gets into big trouble and has to be rescued. **76m/B; DVD.** Johnny Weissmuller; Brenda Joyce; John(ny) Sheffield; Henry Stephenson; Barton MacLane; Maria Ouspenskaya; Shirley O'Hara; Donald "Don" Douglas; Steven Geray; ***D:*** Kurt Neumann; ***W:*** Hans Jacoby; Marjorie L. Pfaelzer; ***C:*** Archie Stout; ***M:*** Paul Sawtell.

Tarzan and the Great River 🦴 ½ **1967** In Henry's 2nd Tarzan film, he's summoned to Brazil by an old friend when the cult of the Leopard Men, led by Barcuna (Johnson), try to start a tribal uprising. **88m/C; DVD.** Mike Henry; Jan Murray; Rafer Johnson; Manuel Padilla, Jr.; Diana Millay; ***D:*** Robert Day; ***W:*** Bob Barbash; ***C:*** Irving Lippman; ***M:*** William Loose.

Tarzan and the Green Goddess 🦴 ½ *New Adventures of Tarzan* **1938** Tarzan searches for a statue that could prove dangerous if in the wrong hands. **72m/B; VHS, DVD.** Bruce Bennett; Ula Holt; Frank Baker; ***D:*** Edward Kull.

Tarzan and the Huntress 🦴 ½ **1947** Weissmuller's eleventh Tarzan appearance and 16-year-old Sheffield's last. Tarzan comes to the rescue of his animal friends when Tanya leads a trapping expedition, intending to ship the beasts to zoos. The group takes more animals than allotted from King Farrod's lands because Tanya's evil partner Paul Weir has teamed up with Farrod's evil nephew Ozira to help him take over the throne. Tarzan's elephants once again play a big role in defeating the bad guys. **72m/B; DVD.** Johnny Weissmuller; Brenda Joyce; John(ny) Sheffield; Patricia Morison; Barton MacLane; John Warburton; Charles Trowbridge; Maurice Tauzin; Ted Hecht; ***D:*** Kurt Neumann; ***W:*** Rowland Leigh; Jerry Gruskin; ***C:*** Archie Stout; ***M:*** Paul Sawtell.

Tarzan and the Jungle Boy 🦴 ½ **1968** Tarzan helps journalist Myrna (Gur) track a lost boy who survived a plane crash that killed his father. Evil Nagambi (Johnson) knows where young Eric (Bond) is, but since Tarzan foiled his plan to take over his tribe, he plans to kill the boy. Henry's third and final effort in the role. **99m/C; DVD.** Mike Henry; Rafer Johnson; Alizia Gur; Steve Bond; Ronald Gans; Ed Johnson; ***D:*** Robert Gordon; ***W:*** Stephen Lord; ***C:*** Ozen Sermet; ***M:*** William Loose.

Tarzan and the Leopard Woman 🦴 ½ **1946** In this tenth adventure, caravans are being attacked, allegedly by leopards. Though it's really members of a leopard cult, led by Queen Lea, who also sends her young brother Kimba to spy on Tarzan. The cult capture Tarzan, Jane, and Boy, and it's ultimately Cheeta who rescues them. **72m/B; DVD.** Johnny Weissmuller; Brenda Joyce; John(ny) Sheffield; Acquanetta; Tommy Cook; Edgar Barrier; Anthony Caruso; Dennis Hoey; ***D:*** Kurt Neumann; ***W:*** Carroll Young; ***C:*** Karl Struss; ***M:*** Paul Sawtell.

Tarzan and the Lost City 🦴🦴 ½ *Tarzan and Jane; Greystoke 2: Tarzan and Jane* **1998 (PG)** Gorgeous locations in South Africa are a decided plus in this routine hero/adventure story. Lord Greystoke, AKA Tarzan (Van Dien), returns to Africa from England in order to save his home from mercenaries hunting the lost city of Opar. Spunky fiance Jane (March) heads to the jungle after her Ape Man and gets into (and out of) trouble with bad guy Nigel Ravens (Waddington). Not very convincing special effects but Van Dien looks good in his loincloth and has the action moves down cold. **84m/C; VHS, DVD.** Casper Van Dien; Jane March; Steven Waddington; Winston Ntshona; Rapulana Seiphemo; Ian Roberts; ***D:*** Carl Schenkel; ***W:*** Bayard Johnson; J. Anderson Black; ***C:*** Paul Gilpin; ***M:*** Christopher Franke.

Tarzan and the Lost Safari 🦴 ½ **1957** Scott's second film as Tarzan has him leading the survivors of a plane crash to safety. But hunter Tusker Hawkins (Beatty) has made a deal with the natives to give the survivors to them as human sacrifices in return for lots of ivory. Shot in CinemaScope on location in Africa. **84m/C; DVD.** *GB* Gordon Scott; Robert Beatty; Yolande Donlan; Betta St. John; Peter Arne; Wilfrid Hyde-White; George Coulouris; ***D:*** H. Bruce Humberstone; ***W:*** Montgomery Pittman; Lillie Hayward; ***C:*** C.M. Pennington-Richards; Miki Carter; ***M:*** Clifton Parker.

Tarzan and the Mermaids 🦴 ½ **1948** Weissmuller's twelfth and last appearance in the Tarzan series was filmed on location in Mexico. The mermaids are actually a seaside tribe of pearl divers. Evil trader Varga pretends to be their god Balu, both to get the pearls and pretty diver Mara, who's offered up by high priest Palanth. Tarzan has to defeat an octopus as well as the bad guys to set things right. **68m/B; DVD.** Johnny Weissmuller; Brenda Joyce; Linda Christian; Fernando Wagner; George Zucco; Gustavo Rojo; Edward Ashley; Andrea Palma; John Laurenz; ***D:*** Robert Florey; ***W:*** Carroll Young; ***C:*** Jack Draper; ***M:*** Dimitri Tiomkin.

Tarzan and the She-Devil 1/2
1953 Barker makes his fifth and final appearance as Tarzan in the RKO series. Greedy Lyra (Van Vooren) and her minions are ivory-poachers, which means killing elephants. Lyra imprisons Tarzan, who doesn't try hard to escape since he thinks they've killed Jane. When he realizes that Jane is alive, he calls his elephants to stampede. **76m/B; DVD.** Lex Barker; Monique Van Vooren; Raymond Burr; Tom Conway; Joyce MacKenzie; Michael Granger; ***D:*** Kurt Neumann; ***W:*** Karl Kamb; Carroll Young; ***C:*** Karl Struss; ***M:*** Paul Sawtell.

Tarzan and the Slave Girl 1/2
1950 Or would-be slave girls anyway as Jane (Brown) and nurse Lola (Darcel) are kidnapped by a lion-worshipping tribe dying from a mysterious plague. Their ruler thinks they need some new blood to repopulate his people but it's Tarzan (Barker's second appearance) to the rescue. **74m/B; DVD.** Lex Barker; Vanessa Brown; Hurd Hatfield; Denise Darcel; Robert Alda; Robert Warwick; Arthur Shields; ***D:*** Lee Sholem; ***W:*** Arnold Belgard; Hans Jacoby; ***C:*** Russell Harlan; ***M:*** Paul Sawtell.

Tarzan and the Trappers 1/2 **1958** Bad-guy trappers and would-be treasure-seekers wish they hadn't messed with the ape man. **70m/B; VHS, DVD.** Gordon Scott; Eve Brent; Ricky Sorenson; Maurice Marsac; ***D:*** Charles F. Haas; H. Bruce Humberstone; Sandy Howard.

Tarzan and the Valley of Gold 1/2
1965 Mike Henry took over the role of Tarzan from Jock Mahoney for three movies. In this first adventure, he rescues young Ramel (Padilla Jr.) from wealthy, gold-mad Vinaro (Opatoshu) who thinks the boy can lead him to some legendary gold mines. **90m/C; DVD.** Mike Henry; David Opatoshu; Manuel Padilla, Jr.; Nancy Kovack; Don Megowan; Enrique Lucero; Eduardo Noriega; ***D:*** Robert Day; ***W:*** Clair Huffaker; ***C:*** Irving Lippman; ***M:*** Van Alexander.

Tarzan Escapes **1936** Jane is tricked by evil hunters into abandoning her fairy tale life with Tarzan, so the Ape Man sets out to reunite with his one true love. The third entry in MGM's Weissmuller/O'Sullivan series is still among the better Tarzan movies thanks to the leads, but the Hays Office made sure Jane was wearing a lot more clothes this time around. **95m/B; VHS, DVD.** Johnny Weissmuller; Maureen O'Sullivan; John Buckler; Benita Hume; William Henry; ***D:*** Richard Thorpe.

Tarzan Finds a Son **1939** Weissmuller and O'Sullivan returned to their roles after three years with the addition of the five-year-old Sheffield as Boy. He's an orphan whose awful relatives hope he stays lost so they can collect an inheritance. Jane and Tarzan fight to adopt the tyke and when the new family are captured by a wicked tribe only an elephant stampede can save them! **90m/B; VHS, DVD.** Johnny Weissmuller; Maureen O'Sullivan; John(ny) Sheffield; Ian Hunter; Henry Stephenson; Frieda Inescort; Henry Wilcoxon; ***D:*** Richard Thorpe.

Tarzan Goes to India 1/2 **1962** Princess Kumara (Garewal) contacts Tarzan (Mahoney) to come to India and save a herd of elephants whose habitat will be destroyed upon completion of a dam. Tarzan has problems with both the engineer of the project and a bunch of foreign elephants who don't realize he's king of the jungle and aren't very willing to obey his commands. **87m/C; DVD, Blu-Ray.** Jock Mahoney; Leo Gordon; Simi Garewal; Mark Dana; Feroz Khan; ***D:*** John Guillermin; ***W:*** John Guillermin; Robert D. (Robert Hardy) Andrews; ***C:*** Paul Beeson; ***M:*** Ravi Shankar; Kenneth V. Jones.

Tarzan, the Ape Man **1932** The definitive Tarzan movie; the first Tarzan talkie; the original of the long series starring Weissmuller. Dubiously faithful to the Edgar Rice Burroughs story, but recent attempts to remake, update or improve it (notably the pretentious 1984 Greystoke) have failed to near the original's entertainment value or even its technical quality. O'Sullivan as Jane and Weissmuller bring style and wit to their classic roles. **99m/B; VHS, DVD.** Johnny Weissmuller; Maureen O'Sullivan; Neil Hamilton; ***D:*** W.S. Van Dyke; ***C:*** Clyde De Vinna.

Tarzan, the Ape Man WOOF! **1981 (R)** Plodding, perverted excuse to see Derek cavort nude in jungle. So bad not even hard-core Tarzan fans should bother. **112m/C; VHS, DVD.** Bo Derek; Richard Harris; John Phillip Law; Miles O'Keeffe; Wilfrid Hyde-White; Akushula Selayah; Steven Strong; Laurie Main; Harold Ayer; ***D:*** John Derek; ***W:*** Gary Goddard; ***C:*** John Derek; ***M:*** Perry Botkin. Golden Raspberries '81: Worst Actress (Derek).

Tarzan the Fearless 1/2 **1933** Tarzan (Crabbe) helps a young girl find her missing father. **84m/B; VHS, DVD.** Buster Crabbe; Julie Bishop; E. Alyn (Fred) Warren; Edward (Eddie) Woods; Philo (Philip, P.H., P.M.) McCullough; Matthew Betz; ***D:*** Robert F. "Bob" Hill; ***W:*** Walter Anthony; ***C:*** Joseph Brotherton; Harry Neumann.

Tarzan the Magnificent 1/2 **1960** Scott's sixth and final Tarzan movie was a cheap, dull effort that had the loinclothed hero leading criminal Coy Banton (Mahoney) through the jungle to the authorities with various problems accompanying them. Mahoney would succeed Scott in the Tarzan role while Scott himself went to Italy to make Hercules flicks. **82m/C; DVD.** *GB* Gordon Scott; Jock Mahoney; John Carradine; Betta St. John; Lionel Jeffries; Alexandra Stewart; ***D:*** Robert Day; ***W:*** Robert Day; Berne Giler; ***C:*** Edward (Ted) Scaife; ***M:*** Ken Jones.

Tarzan the Tiger **1929** Series of 15 chapters is loosely based on the Edgar Rice Burroughs novel entitled "Tarzan and the Jewels of Opar." These chapters were filmed as silent pieces, and were later released with a musical score and synchronized sound effects. Here Merrill is the first to sound the cry of the bull ape, Tarzan's trademark. **266m/B; Silent; VHS, DVD.** Frank Merrill; Natalie Kingston; Lilian Worth; Al Ferguson; ***D:*** Henry MacRae.

Tarzan Triumphs 1/2 **1943** The isolated Tarzan is only vaguely aware of what's happening outside his jungle until German paratroopers take over Palandrya and enslave its people. Boy is kidnapped and Tarzan finally offers his help to Princess Zandra and brings his attack elephants. Cheeta wields a machine gun and is mistaken for the voice of Adolf Hitler when he uses the Germans' short wave radio! The seventh film in the series and the first (of 6) made by RKO. **76m/B; DVD.** Johnny Weissmuller; John(ny) Sheffield; Frances Gifford; Stanley Ridges; Sig Rumann; Philip Van Zandt; Rex Williams; ***D:*** Wilhelm Thiele; ***W:*** Carroll Young; Roy Chanslor; ***C:*** Harry Wild; ***M:*** Paul Sawtell.

Tarzan's Desert Mystery 1/2 **1943** In the eighth Weissmuller/Tarzan jungle adventure, an unseen Jane (who's in London working for the war effort) sends Tarzan a letter asking him to find some rare herbs to help Allied troops fight off malaria. While Tarzan and Boy head into the Saharan desert, they meet American showgirl Connie Bryce and battle Nazis, Arabs, a giant spider and dinosaurs! **70m/B; DVD.** Johnny Weissmuller; John(ny) Sheffield; Nancy Kelly; Otto Kruger; Lloyd Corrigan; Robert Lowery; Philip Van Zandt; Joe Sawyer; ***D:*** Wilhelm Thiele; ***W:*** Edward T. Lowe; ***C:*** Russell Harlan; Harry Wild; ***M:*** Paul Sawtell.

Tarzan's Fight for Life 1/2 **1958** Jane (Brent) finally shows up in Scott's third outing, which finds our jungle man trying to convince a superstitious tribe to give Dr. Sturdy's (Reid) modern methods a try over their witch doctor Futa's (Edwards) efforts. This results in Tarzan's being captured since Futa wants to use his heart in a tribal ceremony. **86m/C; DVD.** Gordon Scott; Eve Brent; Jill Jarmyn; Carl Benton Reid; James Edwards; Ricky Sorenson; Woody Strode; Harry Lauter; ***D:*** H. Bruce Humberstone; ***W:*** Thomas Hal Phillips; ***C:*** William E. Snyder; Mike Carter; ***M:*** Ernest Gold.

Tarzan's Greatest Adventure
1959 Scott's fifth outing is a surprisingly violent (and well-done) revenge story. Ruthless diamond smuggler Slade (Quayle) is more interested in killing Tarzan (who once put him in jail) than his ill-gotten goods. Tarzan has other ideas. **88m/C; DVD, Blu-Ray.** *GB* Gordon Scott; Anthony Quayle; Sara Shane; Sean Connery; Niall MacGinnis; Al Mulock; Scilla Gabel; ***D:*** John Guillermin; ***W:*** John Guillermin; Berne Giler; ***C:*** Edward (Ted) Scaife; ***M:*** Douglas Gamley.

Tarzan's Hidden Jungle 1/2 **1955** Beefcake Scott's first (of six) Tarzan films was the last made in black and white and the last from the RKO studio. Tarzan and his elephants go after evil hunters who have involved a local doctor and nurse in a plot that upsets the natives. **73m/B; DVD.** Gordon Scott; Robert Beatty; Yolande Donlan; Betta St. John; Peter Arne; Wilfrid Hyde-White; George Coulouris; ***D:*** H. Bruce Humberstone; ***W:*** Montgomery Pittman; Lillie Hayward; ***C:*** C.M. Pennington-Richards; Miki Carter; ***M:*** Clifton Parker.

Tarzan's Magic Fountain 1/2 **1948** Barker takes over from Weissmuller in the first of his five appearances as Tarzan in this RKO series. Jane (Joyce) is an aviatrix who crashes in the jungle and finds the fountain of youth in a hidden valley. Tarzan eventually comes along to lead her back to civilization but not before some nosy hunters try to find the valley themselves. **73m/B; DVD.** Lex Barker; Brenda Joyce; Evelyn Ankers; Alan Napier; Albert Dekker; Charles Drake; ***D:*** Lee Sholem; ***W:*** Curt Siodmak; Harry Chandlee; ***C:*** Karl Struss; ***M:*** Alexander Laszlo.

Tarzan's New York Adventure 1/2 **1942** O'Sullivan's final appearance as Jane is a so-so adventure with some humorous moments when Tarzan meets the big city. When Boy is kidnapped by an evil circus owner, Tarzan, Jane, and Cheta head out to rescue him. Tarzan shows off his jungle prowess by climbing skyscrapers and diving off the Brooklyn Bridge into the East River. Lincoln, the screen's first Tarzan, has a cameo. **70m/B; VHS, DVD.** Johnny Weissmuller; Maureen O'Sullivan; John(ny) Sheffield; Virginia Grey; Charles Bickford; Paul Kelly; Chill Wills; Russell Hicks; Cy Kendall; ***Cameo(s):*** Elmo Lincoln; ***D:*** Richard Thorpe.

Tarzan's Peril 1/2 **1951** Gunrunners are willing to trade for jewels with King Bulam (O'Neal) so that his Yorango tribe can attack the peaceful Ashubas, led by Queen Melmendi (Dandridge). (The King is peeved that the Queen rejected him.) But Tarzan (Barker) isn't going to stand for that. Barker's third appearance in the title role. **79m/B; DVD.** Virginia Huston; Frederick O'Neal; Dorothy Dandridge; Douglas Fowley; Lex Barker; George Macready; Glenn Anders; Alan Napier; ***D:*** Byron Haskin; ***W:*** Francis Swann; Samuel Newman; ***C:*** Karl Struss; ***M:*** Michel Michelet.

Tarzan's Revenge **1938** Morris is a better Olympic runner than actor; Holm is horrible. Only for serious Tarzan fans. **70m/B; VHS, DVD.** Glenn Morris; Eleanor Holm; Hedda Hopper; ***D:*** David Ross Lederman.

Tarzan's Savage Fury 1/2 **1952** Tarzan (Barker in No. 4) is approached by two British agents who need a guide into the diamond-rich Wazuri region. But imagine his fury when Tarzan discovers he's been duped and the men are thieves! **79m/B; DVD.** Lex Barker; Dorothy Hart; Patric Knowles; Charles Korvin; Tommy Carlton; ***D:*** Cy Enfield; ***W:*** Hans Jacoby; Cyril Hume; Shirley White; ***C:*** Karl Struss; ***M:*** Paul Sawtell.

Tarzan's Secret Treasure 1/2
1941 Tarzan saves an expedition from a savage tribe only to be repaid by having the greedy hunters hold Jane and Boy hostage. They want Tarzan's help in finding a secret cache of gold. But Tarzan doesn't take kindly to threats to his family and teaches those evil-doers a lesson! **81m/B; VHS, DVD.** Johnny Weissmuller; Maureen O'Sullivan; John(ny) Sheffield; Reginald Owen; Barry Fitzgerald; Tom Conway; Philip Dorn; ***D:*** Richard Thorpe.

Tarzan's Three Challenges 1/2
1963 Mahoney's last time in the role finds Tarzan traveling to Thailand to ensure that the young heir to the crown doesn't fall victim to his evil Uncle Khan's (Strode) machinations. So Tarzan must best Khan in three tests of strength and daring. In place of Cheetah there's a baby elephant named Hungry. **100m/C; DVD, Blu-Ray.** Jock Mahoney; Woody Strode; Ricky Der; Tsuruko Kobayashi; Earl Cameron; Salah Jamal; ***D:*** Robert Day; ***W:*** Robert Day; Berne Giler; ***C:*** Edward (Ted) Scaife; ***M:*** Joseph Horovitz.

Tarzeena: Queen of Kong Island
WOOF! *Tarzeena: Jiggle in the Jungle* **2008** Horrible Tarzan spoof about a couple standing to inherit a fortune if they can prove the owner (and his daughter) who crashed on a jungle island years ago are dead. Arriving they find the daughter was raised by apes and the island has a mad scientist hoping to use a mind control device to brainwash her into becoming his love slave. If only it were nearly as good as that description made it sound. **80m/C; DVD.** Christine Nguyen; Evan Stone; Michael Gaglio; ***D:*** Fred Olen Ray; ***W:*** Cyrus Nickleby; ***C:*** Molly McClintock.

Task Force 1/2 **1949** History of naval aviation and the development of the aircraft carrier highlighted by actual WWII combat footage (in color). Cooper and his naval buddies try to convince the brass that planes can be landed on the decks of ships. Slowly the Navy goes ahead and when Pearl Harbor is attacked, Cooper is given command of his own aircraft carrier. The use of the carriers proved very effective in Pacific battles and Cooper is finally vindicated. **116m/B; VHS, DVD.** Gary Cooper; Jane Wyatt; Wayne Morris; Walter Brennan; Julie London; Bruce Bennett; Jack Holt; Stanley Ridges; John Ridgely; Richard Rober; Art Baker; Moroni Olsen; ***D:*** Delmer Daves; ***W:*** Delmer Daves.

A Taste for Killing **1992 (R)** Two boys, both from well-to-do families, decide to take summer jobs on an offshore Texas oil rig. The best friends think a summer of adventure awaits them; however, their lives are made miserable by their blue-collar boss, who is resentful of their high society background. Then they meet Bo Landry, who befriends them and helps them survive. Unfortunately, Bo turns out to be anything but a friend as he reveals himself as a deadly con-artist in this intense psychological thriller. **87m/C; VHS, DVD.** Jason Bateman; Henry Thomas; Michael Biehn; Edward "Blue" Deckert; Helen Cates; ***D:*** Lou Antonio; ***W:*** Dan Bronson.

A Taste of Blood 1/2 **1967** Goremeister Lewis's vampire film is actually fairly restrained when compared to "2000 Maniacs" and "Blood Feast." When John Stone (Rogers) drinks brandy containing the blood of Count Dracula, he turns into a green-faced killer bent on revenge against the ancestors of...oh, never mind. **118m/C; DVD.** Bill Rogers; Elizabeth Wilkinson; William Kerwin; Lawrence Tobin; ***D:*** Herschell Gordon Lewis; ***W:*** Donald Stanford; ***C:*** Andy Romanoff.

The Taste of Cherry *Ta'm e Guilass; Taste of Cherries* **1996** Despairing, middle-aged Mr. Badii (Ershadi) is contemplating suicide and looking for someone who will bury his corpse discreetly. (He's already dug his own shallow grave in the countryside.) He drives through the streets and picks up several different men—all of whom remind him that suicide goes against the teachings of Islam. Finally, one old Turkish man relates his own story of attempted suicide and seemingly persuades Badii to rethink his actions. **95m/C; VHS, DVD.** *IA* Homayon Ershadi; Abdolrahma Bagheri; Afshin Bakhtiari; ***D:*** Abbas Kiarostami; ***W:*** Abbas Kiarostami; ***C:*** Homayun Payvar. Cannes '97: Film; Natl. Soc. Film Critics '98: Foreign Film.

Taste of Death *Quanto Costa Morire; Cost of Dying* **1968** A youth discovers his courage within when he stands up to the bandits invading his village. **90m/C; VHS, DVD.** *IT* John Ireland; Raymond Pellegrin; Bruno Corazzari; Andrea Giordana; ***D:*** Sergio Merolle; ***W:*** Biagio Proietti; ***C:*** Benito Frattari; ***M:*** Francesco De Masi.

The Taste of Money *Do-Nui Mat* **2012** Korean director Soo continues his examination of complex lives behind outwardly happy domestic facades with this odd piece of work. One of South Korea's richest families lives on the outskirts of town and they partake in the kind of immoral and illegal activities that's been witnessed before in countless other movies. Of course, their delicate house of cards collapse (there'd be no movie otherwise) and Soo brings to the proceedings his typical visual flair but the story feels overly familiar. **115m/C; Streaming.** *SK* Kang-Woo Kim; Yun-sik Baek; Yeo-jung Yoon; Hyo-jin Kim; Maui Taylor; ***D:*** Sang-soo Im; ***W:*** Sang-soo Im; ***C:*** Woo-hyung Kim.

The Taste of Others *Le Gout des Autres* **2000** This classy import is a hard sell to American audiences; first, it's in French, and second, it begins as if the first reel is missing—the low-key action opens with two banal conversations at separate tables. Actress/writer Jaoui, in her directorial debut, takes time in sorting out relationships. Eventually it becomes clear that married, boorish businessman Castella (Bacri) is falling for 40-year-old actress Clara (Alvaro), who's fretting about aging and her uncertain prospects, and who has been hired to teach Castella English. He pursues, she resists—at first. Meanwhile, Castella's tough bodyguard Moreno (Lanvin) is involved with Clara's friend, free-spirited barmaid Manie (Jaoui). For fans of Rohmer, it works. The characters are engagingly different and interesting. The film looks as sharp and polished as a comparable Hollywood ensemble comedy. French with subtitles. **112m/C; DVD.** *FR* Jean-Pierre Bacri; Christiane Millet; Agnes Jaoui; Anne Alvaro; Gerard Lanvin; Wladimir Yordanoff; Brigitte Catillon; Xavier De Guillebon; Alain Chabat; Raphael Defour; ***D:*** Agnes Jaoui; ***W:*** Jean-Pierre Bacri; Agnes Jaoui; ***C:*** Laurent Dailland; ***M:*** Jean-Charles Jarrell.

A Taste of Romance 1/2 **2012** Hallmark channel rom com. Widowed firefighter Gill Callahan opens up a diner with some buddies that's next to the fancy French restaurant chef Sara Westbrook is trying to make a success. The two are soon clashing, but then Gill's daughter Hannah and Sara become friends, although the two adults protest (too much) that a romance between them would never work. **87m/C; DVD.** Teri Polo; James Patrick Stuart; Bailee Madison; Rockmond Dunbar; Romy Rosemont; Jack Conley; ***D:*** Lee Rose; ***W:*** Jennifer Notas; ***C:*** Maximo Munzi. **CABLE**

Taste the Blood of Dracula 1/2 **1970 (PG)** Lee's Dracula only makes a brief appearance in this Hammer horror film which has three children taking over from the bloodsucker. Three Victorian dandies have killed the wizard who revived Dracula and he seeks their deaths by using their own children as the means of his revenge. Not enough Lee but still creepy. Preceded by "Dracula Has Risen from the Grave" and followed by "Scars of Dracula." **91m/C; VHS, DVD, Blu-Ray.** *GB* Christopher Lee; Ralph Bates; Geoffrey Keen; Gwen Watford; Linda Hayden; John Carson; Peter Sallis; Isla Blair; Martin Jarvis; Roy Kinnear; Anthony (Corlan) Higgins; Michael Ripper; ***D:*** Peter Sasdy; ***W:*** John (Anthony Hinds) Elder; ***C:*** Arthur Grant; ***M:*** James Bernard.

The Tattered Web **1971** A police sergeant confronts and accidently kills the woman with whom his son-in-law has been cheating. He's then assigned the case. When he tries to frame a wino for the murder, things get more and more messy. Fine performances. **74m/C; VHS, DVD.** Lloyd Bridges; Frank Converse; Broderick Crawford; Murray Hamilton; Sallie Shockley; ***D:*** Paul Wendkos; ***M:*** Robert Drasnin. **TV**

Tattoo, a Love Story 1/2 **2002** Sara's perfectly planned future crumbles when she's dumped by her groom-to-be, but the elementary school teacher lets loose after "not-her-type" tattoo artist Virgil pops in for show-and-tell. Predictable yet pleasing indie romance. **95m/C; VHS, DVD.** Megan Edwards; Stephen Davies; India Allen; Virgil Mignanelli; Benjamin Burdick; Kathryn Cherasaro; Gordon Reinhart; Stitch Marker; Stacey Bean; Nick Garcia; Tom Willmorth; Ben Larned; Tyler Maier; Christina Lang; E.J. Pettinger; Travis Swartz; Sara Bruner; Gene Bickley; Amy Krengal; Jim Agenbroad; Eryn Spaeth; Ariel Spaeth; Gus Pollio; Phil Atlakson; Flint Weisser; Mark Salow; Kate Gorney; Jacelyn Anderson; Michelle Waddell; Grant Lawley; Jessyca Harrold; Angie Lachapelle; Nick Halfrich; Curtis Stigers; Dave Yasuda; Carlie Powell; Walker Ragan; Jordan Gore; Joel Hawkins; ***D:*** Richard W. Bean; ***W:*** Richard W. Bean; Gregg Sacon; ***C:*** David Klein; ***M:*** Pete Droge. **VIDEO**

The Tattooist **2007 (R)** Tedious horror. American tattooist Jake Sawyer (Behr) goes to Singapore for an exhibition and meets New Zealand native Sina (Blake) while exploring a display of Samoan cultural tattooing. Jake steals one of the traditional tools (cutting himself in the process) and then decides to head for Auckland to learn Samoan tattooing. Too bad that Jake's stolen tool contains a now-released evil spirit and when he starts using it, the tattoos he inks take over their wearers' bodies and kill them. Sina's in a lot of trouble unless Jake can find a solution. **91m/C; DVD.** *NZ* Jason Behr; Robbie Magasiva; Michael Hurst; Mia Blake; David Fane; Caroline Cheong; ***D:*** Peter Burger; ***W:*** Jonathan King; Matthew Grainger; ***C:*** Leon Narbey; ***M:*** Peter Scholes. **VIDEO**

The Tavern **2000** Ronnie (Dye) is a bartender who wants to buy a Manhattan watering hole from its alleged Florida-bound owner, Kevin (Zittel). He borrows the money from a number of people, including his best friend Dave (Geer), who becomes his partner. But they're underfinanced and beset by competition and numerous other problems soon surface threatening their business survival. Unsentimental and downbeat. **88m/C; VHS, DVD.** Cameron Dye; Kevin Geer; Margaret Cho; Greg Zittel; Nancy Ticotin; Steven Marcus; Carlo Alban; Kym Austin; Gary Perez; ***D:*** Walter Foote; ***W:*** Walter Foote; ***C:*** Kurt Lennig; ***M:*** Bill Lacey; Loren Toolajian.

Taxi! **1932** Independent, hot-tempered New York cabbie Matt Nolan (Cagney) has trouble with gangsters who are using the big firms to squeeze out the little guys. Matt's brother Danny (Cooke) gets killed and he vows revenge at any cost even though his wife Sue (Young) tries to restrain him. George Raft briefly appears as a hoofer who gets on the wrong side of Cagney in a dance contest. **69m/B; DVD.** James Cagney; Loretta Young; Guy Kibbee; David Landau; Ray Cooke; George E. Stone; Leila Bennett; Dorothy Burgess; ***D:*** Roy Del Ruth; ***W:*** John Bright; Kubec Glasmon; ***C:*** James Van Trees.

Taxi 1/2 **2004 (PG-13)** Nowhere comedy loosely based on director Luc Besson's 1998 French film. Stripped of his driver's license, inept New York cop Andy Washburn (Fallon, a negligible screen presence) enlists the aid of dynamo cabbie Belle Williams (Queen Latifah) to drive him to the scene of a bank robbery. The heist turns out to have been committed by a quartet of gorgeous Brazilian gals who are also supermodels (led by Bundchen in her, um, acting debut). Ann-Margaret lends support in a wincing comic turn as Andy's lush of a mother. The Queen, as always, is an irrepressible delight and the only reason to spend any time with this hack. **97m/C; VHS, DVD.** Jimmy Fallon; Jennifer Esposito; Ann-Margret; Henry Simmons; Christian Kane; Queen Latifah; Gisele Bundchen; Ana Christine de Oliveira; Ingrid Vandebosch; Magali Amadei; ***D:*** Tim Story; ***W:*** Robert Ben Garant; Thomas Lennon; Jim Kouf; ***C:*** Vance Burberry; ***M:*** Christophe Beck.

Taxi Blues 1/2 **1990** A political allegory with the two protagonists representing the new and old Soviet Union. A hard-working, narrow-minded cabdriver keeps the saxophone of a westernized, Jewish, jazz-loving musician who doesn't have his fare. The two strike up a wary friendship as each tries to explain his view of life to the other. Good look at the street life of Moscow populated by drunks, punks, and black marketeers. Directorial debut of Lounguine. In Russian with English subtitles. **110m/C; VHS, DVD.** *RU* Piotr Mamonov; Piotr Zaitchenko; Natalia Koliakanova; Vladimir Kachpour; ***D:*** Pavel (Lungin) Lounguine; ***W:*** Pavel (Lungin) Lounguine. Cannes '90: Director (Lounguine).

Taxi Driver **1976 (R)** A psychotic NYC taxi driver tries to save a child prostitute and becomes infatuated with an educated political campaigner. He goes on a violent rampage when his dreams don't work out. Repellant, frightening vision of alienation. On-target performances from Foster and De Niro. **112m/C; VHS, DVD, Blu-Ray.** Robert De Niro; Jodie Foster; Harvey Keitel; Cybill Shepherd; Peter Boyle; Albert Brooks; Leonard Harris; Joe Spinell; Martin Scorsese; ***D:*** Martin Scorsese; ***W:*** Paul Schrader; ***C:*** Michael Chapman; ***M:*** Bernard Herrmann. AFI '98: Top 100; British Acad. '76: Support. Actress (Foster); Cannes '76: Film; L.A. Film Critics '76: Actor (De Niro); Natl. Film Reg. '94; N.Y. Film Critics '76: Actor (De Niro); Natl. Soc. Film Critics '76: Actor (De Niro), Director (Scorsese), Support. Actress (Foster).

A Taxi Driver *Taeksi Woonjunsa* **2017** Based on true events, this historical drama focuses on violently suppressed student protests in rural Gwangju, South Korea, in 1980. Depressed cab driver Sa-bok Kim (Song) shuttles German journalist Jurgen "Peter" Hinzpeter (Kretschmann) to and from Gwangju so that he can cover these events. Because of their conversations during the long trip, Sa-bok, a cheapskate widower and indifferent father of Eun-sung (Eun-mi), becomes politically and morally awakened. To return to his daughter, Sa-bok must help Peter get incriminating footage to show what happened. Song's strong performance does not compensate for the script's deficiencies, especially the lack of character development. Korean with subtitles. **137m/C; DVD, Blu-Ray.** Kang-ho Song; Thomas Kretschmann; Hae-jin Yoo; Jun-yeol Ryu; Hyuk-kwon Park; ***D:*** Hun Jang; ***W:*** Yu-na Eom.

Taxi for Tobruk **1960** Shifting attitudes and some twists highlight this French actioner set in Libya in 1942. A French commando unit destroys a German gas depot but the four survivors find themselves lost in the desert when they spot a German armored car. With one German prisoner, the men try to reach the Allied forces at El Alamein but this means they must cooperate to survive. French with subtitles. **95m/B; DVD, Blu-Ray.** *FR* Lino Ventura; Charles Aznavour; Hardy Kruger; German Cobos; Maurice Biraud; ***D:*** Denys de la Patelliere; ***W:*** Denys de la Patelliere; Michel Audiard; ***C:*** Marcel Grignon; ***M:*** Georges Garvarentz.

Taxi zum Klo **1981** An autobiographical semi-documentary about the filmmaker's aimless existence and attempts at homosexual affairs after being fired from his job as a teacher. Explicit. In German with English subtitles. Sordid sexual situations. **98m/C; VHS, DVD.** *GE* Bernd Broaderup; Frank Ripploh; ***D:*** Frank Ripploh.

A Taxing Woman 1/2 *Marusa No Onna* **1987** Satiric Japanese comedy about a woman tax collector in pursuit of a crafty millionaire tax cheater. Followed by the equally hilarious "A Taxing Woman's Return." In Japanese with English subtitles. **127m/C; VHS, DVD.** *JP* Nobuko Miyamoto; Tsutomu Yamazaki; Hideo Murota; Shuji Otaki; ***D:*** Juzo Itami; ***W:*** Juzo Itami; ***C:*** Yonezo Maeda; ***M:*** Toshiyuki Honda.

The Taxman **1998 (R)** Al Benjamin (Pantoliano) is an obsessive New York State tax investigator who stumbles across six dead bodies in a Brighton Beach gasoline company while on the job. He teams up with a pain-in-the-butt cop, Joseph Romero (Dominguez), who's proficient in Russian—a necessity in the immigrant community. Their sleuthing leads them to the Russian mob, a scam involving gasoline taxes, and a lot of violence. **95m/C; VHS, DVD.** Joe Pantoliano; Wade Dominguez; Elizabeth Berkley; Michael Chiklis; Robert Townsend; ***D:*** Avi Nesher; ***W:*** Avi Nesher; Roger Berger; ***C:*** Jim Denault; ***M:*** Roger Neill.

Taza, Son of Cochise **1954** In Sirk's only western, originally shot and shown in 3-D, muscle-bound Hudson stars as Apache warrior Taza who promises his dying father Cochise (Chandler) that he will maintain the peace with the Army and the settlers. However, his brother Naiche (Reason) has other ideas and wants to unite the tribe with warring Geronimo (MacDonald) rather than live on the reservation. **79m/C; DVD, Blu-Ray.** Barbara Rush; Rex Reason; Ian MacDonald; Gregg (Hunter) Palmer; Morris Ankrum; Jeff Chandler; ***D:*** Douglas Sirk; ***W:*** George Zuckerman; Gerald Drayson Adams; ***C:*** Russell Metty; ***M:*** Frank Skinner.

Tea and Sympathy **1956** A young prep school student, confused about his sexuality, has an affair with an older woman, his teacher's wife. The three leads recreate their Broadway roles in this tame adaption of the Robert Anderson play which dealt more openly with the story's homosexual elements. **122m/C; VHS, DVD.** Deborah Kerr; John Kerr; Leif Erickson; Edward Andrews; Darryl Hickman; Norma Crane; Dean Jones; ***D:*** Vincente Minnelli; ***W:*** Robert Anderson; ***C:*** John Alton.

Tea for Two **1950** This take-off on the Broadway play "No, No, Nanette" features Day as an actress who takes a bet that she can answer "no" to every question for 24 hours (life was less complex back then). If she can, she gets to finance and star in her own Broadway musical. **98m/C; VHS, DVD.** Doris Day; Gordon MacRae; Gene Nelson; Patrice Wymore; Eve Arden; Billy DeWolfe; S.Z. Sakall; Bill Goodwin; Virginia Gibson; Crauford Kent; Harry Harvey; ***D:*** David Butler.

Tea with Mussolini **1999 (PG)** Semiautobiographical account of director Zeffirelli's own childhood in fascist Italy. In 1935, young Luca (Lucas) is abandoned by his mother and his neglectful father is happy when the boy is taken in by a group of middleaged, eccentric Englishwomen, including Mary (Plowright), Lady Hester (Smith), and Arabella (Dench). Soon, their group is joined by flamboyantly wealthy (and Jewish) American Elsa (Cher). But as Mussolini consolidates his power and WWII begins, Luca is sent away to school, and the women find themselves unwelcome foreigners. **116m/C; VHS, DVD.** *IT GB* Joan Plowright; Maggie Smith; Dame Judi Dench; Cher; Baird Wallace; Charlie Lucas; Lily Tomlin; Paolo Seganti; Massimo Ghini; Claudio Spadaro; ***D:*** Franco Zeffirelli; ***W:*** Franco Zeffirelli; John Mortimer; ***C:*** David Watkin; ***M:*** Alessio Vlad; Stefano Arnaldi. British Acad. '99: Support. Actress (Smith).

Tea with the Dames 1/2 *Nothing Like a Dame* **2018** A delightful documentary that centers on a conversation between four major British actresses. Set at the home of Joan Plowright, the circle includes longtime friends Maggie Smith, Eileen Atkins, and Judi Dench. The four women share stories of their years on the British stage and screen, such as stories involving Plowright's late husband Laurence Olivier who was the head of the Royal National Theatre and often appeared with Smith. Their conversation also includes gentle ribbing of each other and discussions of such varied topics as death, reviews, and their work. The often humorous film allows viewers to gain new insights into these acting icons. **84m/C; DVD, Blu-Ray.** Eileen Atkins; Dame Judi Dench; Joan Plowright; Maggie Smith; ***D:*** Roger Michell; ***C:*** Eben Bolter.

Teach Me **1997 (R)** Erotic romance novelist Sara Kane gets a story idea from observing a troubled couple at a restaurant. Janine's got some sexual fears that are causing problems in her marriage but Sara's willing to intercede and help ease her tensions. **90m/C; VHS, DVD.** Shannon Leahy; Raasa Leela Shields; Greg Provance; ***D:*** Gary Delfiner. **VIDEO**

The Teacher *The Seductress* **1974 (R)** TV's "Dennis the Menace" (North) has an affair with his high school teacher; the pair is menaced by a deranged killer. Cheap but enjoyable. **97m/C; VHS, DVD.** Angel Tompkins; Jay North; Anthony James; ***D:*** Howard (Hikmet) Avedis.

Teachers **1984 (R)** A lawsuit is brought against a high school for awarding a diploma to an illiterate student. Comedy-drama starts slowly and seems to condemn the school system, never picking up strength or resolving any issues, though Nolte is fairly intense. Shot in Columbus, Ohio. **106m/C; VHS, DVD, Blu-Ray.** Nick Nolte; JoBeth Williams; Lee Grant; Judd Hirsch; Ralph Macchio; Richard Mulligan; Royal Dano; Morgan Freeman; Laura Dern; Crispin Glover; Madeline Sherwood; Zohra Lampert; ***D:*** Arthur Hiller.

Teacher's Pet **1958** Cynical newspaper editor Jim Gannon (Gable) enrolls in a night college journalism course, believing that it won't teach anything of substance. But that's before he gets an eyeful of teacher Erica Stone (Day). Gannon decides to continue to pose as a student but watch the sparks fly when Erica finds out about his deception. Charming comedy with a well-written script and a superb comic performance by Young as Day's lovelorn suitor. **120m/B; VHS, DVD.** Clark Gable; Doris Day; Mamie Van Doren; Gig Young; Nick Adams; Marion Ross; Jack Albertson; Charles Lane; ***D:*** George Seaton; ***W:*** Fay Kanin; Michael Kanin; ***C:*** Haskell Boggs; ***M:*** Roy Webb.

Teaching Mrs. Tingle *Killing Mrs. Tingle* **1999 (PG-13)** Williamson delivers a disappointing directorial debut in this teen horror/comedy adapted from one of his first scripts. Wrong-side-of-the-tracks Leigh Ann (Holmes) is anticipating being high school valedictorian until her sadistic English teacher Mrs. Tingle (Mirren) mistakenly accuses her of cheating. Leigh Ann and friends Jo Lynn (Coughlan) and Luke (Watson) go to Mrs. Tingle's house to plead their case and beg for mercy, but the heartless old hag refuses to listen to them. During an argument, Mrs. Tingle is knocked unconscious and the teens decide to tie her up and exact their revenge. **96m/C; VHS, DVD, Blu-Ray.** Katie Holmes; Dame Helen Mirren; Liz Stauber; Barry Watson; Jeffrey Tambor; Vivica A. Fox; Marisa Coughlan; Molly Ringwald; Michael McKean; ***D:*** Kevin Williamson; ***W:*** Kevin Williamson; ***C:*** Jerzy Zielinski; ***M:*** John (Gianni) Frizzell.

The Teahouse of the August Moon 🦴🦴 1/2 **1956** An adaptation of the John Patrick play. Post-war American troops are assigned to bring civilization to a small village in Okinawa and instead fall for Okinawan culture and romance. Lively cast keeps it generally working, but assessments of Brando's comedic performance vary widely. **123m/C; VHS, DVD.** Glenn Ford; Marlon Brando; Eddie Albert; Paul Ford; Machiko Kyo; Harry (Henry) Morgan; ***D:*** Daniel Mann; ***C:*** John Alton.

Team America: World Police 🦴🦴🦴 **2004 (R)** The guys behind "South Park" take on Osama Bin Laden, Kim Jong Il, America's "bull-in-a-china-shop" foreign relations, the Hollywood Left, the Far Right, Jerry Bruckheimer movies, and especially the MPAA with...puppets (marionettes, to be exact). With a truly heroic commitment to over-the-top satire, they tell the story of America's elite anti-terrorist force, the World Police, a gung-ho, if collateral damage-intensive band of action flick archetypes. New member Gary is recruited for his acting ability and goes through the usual conflicts before battling terrorists, the aforementioned North Korean dictator, and actor/activists such as Alec Baldwin. It's all pretty ridiculous, but that's the point. Add or subtract bones depending on your tolerance for puppet sex, vomit, and intentionally horrible dialogue. **98m/C; DVD, Blu-Ray, UMD.** ***V:*** Trey Parker; Matt Stone; Masasa; Maurice LaMarche; Kristen Miller; Daran Norris; Phil Hendrie; ***D:*** Trey Parker; ***W:*** Trey Parker; Matt Stone; Pam Brady; ***C:*** Bill Pope; ***M:*** Harry Gregson-Williams.

Teamster Boss: The Jackie Presser Story 🦴🦴🦴 **1992 (R)** Well-done cable movie powered by a riveting performance by Dennehy. Presser followed Jimmy Hoffa as president of the Teamsters and was equally caught between the mob and the government as he tried to do what he considered best for the union. **111m/C; VHS, DVD.** Brian Dennehy; Jeff Daniels; Maria Conchita Alonso; Eli Wallach; Robert Prosky; Donald Moffat; Tony LoBianco; Kate Reid; Henderson Forsythe; Al Waxman; ***D:*** Alastair Reid. **CABLE**

Tears in the Rain 🦴🦴 **1988** Casey Cantrell (Stone) travels to London to deliver a deathbed letter from her mother to Lord Richard Bredon. While in England, she is pursued by two men, an heir to the Bredon fortune, and his wealthy friend. After she finds a love which is forbidden, she makes a bizarre discovery that changes her life forever. **100m/C; VHS, DVD.** *GB* Sharon Stone; Christopher Cazenove; Leigh Lawson; Paul Daneman; ***D:*** Don Sharp. **TV**

Tears of the Sun 🦴🦴 1/2 **2003 (R)** Navy SEAL team, led by Lt. Waters (Willis), is sent into the middle of a Nigerian civil war to rescue Americans at a missionary hospital. When they get there, the doctor (Bellucci) refuses to go without the people she's been treating, who will surely be slaughtered by the rebels in the area. Waters defies orders to lead them all on a hazerdous journey out of the country. Fuqua follows up "Training Day" with this visually stunning, almost thoughtful battle picture. Until the film degenerates into standard action fare at the end, it aspires to answer questions about the difficulty of America's role as world cop and what makes a hero. Fuqua is aided immensely by Willis's stoic performance and the work of editor Conrad Bluff. **121m/C; VHS, DVD, Blu-Ray.** Bruce Willis; Monica Bellucci; Cole Hauser; Tom Skerritt; Eamonn Walker; Nick (Nicholas) Chinlund; Fionnula Flanagan; Malick Bowens; Paul Francis; Johnny Messner; Akosua Busia; Peter Mensah; Chad Smith; Charles Ingram; ***D:*** Antoine Fuqua; ***W:*** Alex Lasker; Patrick Cirillo; ***C:*** Mauro Fiore; ***M:*** Hans Zimmer.

Ted 🦴🦴🦴 **2012 (R)** Seth MacFarlane wrote, directed, and gives voice to the title character--a Teddy Bear. Ted, a Christmas gift that came to life, is still at the side of his now-adult owner, John (Wahlberg), after a childhood wish came true. Ted and John have settled into a slacker existence after a brief taste of celebrity, and both try the patience of John's girlfried (Kunis). Eventually the strained dynamic comes to a head. "Family Guy" creator MacFarlane brings the same subversive sense of humor and pop culture blender sensibility to his feature debut. So if you like his TV gig, you'll love this. **106m/C; DVD, Blu-Ray, Streaming.** Mark Wahlberg; Mila Kunis; Seth McFarlane; Joel McHale; Giovanni Ribisi; Patrick Warburton; Laura Vandervoort; ***V:*** Seth McFarlane; ***D:*** Seth McFarlane; ***W:*** Seth McFarlane; Alec Sulkin; Wellesley Wild; ***C:*** Michael Barrett; ***M:*** Walter Murphy.

Ted 2 🦴🦴 **2015 (R)** What's less funny than being told the same joke again after you already know the punchline? The track record for comedy sequels continues as the follow-up to the MacFarlane's breakthrough film proves the law of diminishing returns. Talking teddy bear Ted (voiced by MacFarlane) wants to have a baby with his new wife Tami-Lynn but he has to prove he's a person in a court of law to do so legally. The "plot" is merely an excuse for more of MacFarlane's brand of raunchy dude-bro humor, half of which is pretty funny, half of which is not. **120m/C; DVD, Blu-Ray, Streaming.** Mark Wahlberg; Amanda Seyfried; Jessica Barth; Morgan Freeman; ***V:*** Seth MacFarlane; ***D:*** Seth MacFarlane; ***W:*** Seth MacFarlane; Alec Sulkin; Wellesley Wild; ***C:*** Michael Barrett; ***M:*** Walter Murphy.

Ted & Venus 🦴🦴 1/2 **1993 (R)** Cort plays Ted, an oddball cult poet in love with Linda, a beach beauty who finds him repulsive. The more she rejects him, the more obsessed about her Ted gets, especially when his equally oddball friends offer him romantic advice. **100m/C; VHS, DVD.** Bud Cort; Kim Adams; Rhea Perlman; James Brolin; Carol Kane; ***Cameo(s):*** Gena Rowlands; Martin Mull; Woody Harrelson; Andrea Martin; Timothy Leary; Cassandra Peterson; ***D:*** Bud Cort; ***W:*** Bud Cort; Paul Ciotti.

Teen Beach Movie 🦴🦴 1/2 **2013** Likeable musical fluff from Disney is a nod to the beach party films of yore. Modern-day teens Brady and Mckenzie are sweethearts who are magically transported back to an over-the-top 1962 beach flick where it's surfers versus bikers. Only the newbies inadvertantly change the plot, so it' not all fun in the sun, especially when Mckenzie's modern attitude clashes with some old-fashioned gender roles. **91m/C; DVD.** Ross Lynch; Maia Mitchell; Garrett Clayton; Grace Phipps; John DeLuca; Chrissie Fit; ***D:*** Jeffrey Hornaday; ***W:*** Robert Horn; Vince Marcello; Mark Landry; ***C:*** Mark Irwin. **CABLE**

Teen Spirit 🦴🦴 1/2 **2011** ABC Family movie. Mean-spirited high school queen bee Amber Pollock (Scerbo) finally achieves her goal of becoming prom queen only to die in a freak accident while being crowned. Despite her bad earthly behavior, Amber's given a chance to earn her angel wings if she can transform completely awkward Lisa (Shaw) into her prom successor in just one week. **82m/C; DVD.** Cassie Scerbo; Lindsey Shaw; Chris Zylka; Rhoda Griffis; Elena Varela; ***D:*** Gil Junger; ***W:*** David Kendall; ***C:*** Dave Perkal. **CABLE**

Teen Spirit 🦴🦴 1/2 **2018 (PG-13)** Polish teen Violet lives on the Isle of Wight with her mother and seems to hate her life. However, when she sings at open mics, she reveals that she has a beautiful voice. One day, retired opera singer Vlad (Buric) hears her sing and recognizes her talent. With his help, Violet enters a television singing competition and makes it to the live broadcast in London, where her fate will be decided by viewers. Though the debut film by Minghella explores the power of pop, features a rich soundtrack, and displays Fanning's considerable singing talents, the generic story does not encourage investment in Violet's fate. **93m/C; DVD, Blu-Ray.** Elle Fanning; Agnieszka Grochowska; Archie Madekwe; Zlatko Buric; Millie Brady; ***D:*** Max Minghella; ***W:*** Max Minghella; ***C:*** Autumn Cheyenne Durald; ***M:*** Marius De Vries.

Teen Titans Go! To the Movies 🦴🦴 1/2 **2018 (PG)** In the first feature based on the popular Cartoon Network animated series, Teen Titan leader Robin (Menville) is jealous that just about every other superhero has gotten a movie except for him. After seeing previews for films like "Alfred" and "Utility Belt," he comes up with a plan to get his own movie. To get the attention of a well-known director, Robin convinces the rest of the Teen Titans that they need a nemesis. They battle the mental manipulation master Slade (Arnett) to achieve their goal. Goofy yet clever, the family friendly film provides an interesting take on superhero culture. **84m/C; DVD, Blu-Ray.** ***V:*** Greg Cipes; Scott Menville; Khary Payton; Tara Strong; Hynden Walch; ***D:*** Aaron Horvath; Peter Rida Michail; ***W:*** Aaron Horvath; Michael Jelenic; ***M:*** Jared Faber.

Teen Witch 🦴🦴 **1989 (PG-13)** A demure high schooler uses black magic to woo the most popular guy in school. **94m/C; VHS, DVD, Blu-Ray.** Robin (Robyn) Lively; Zelda Rubinstein; Dan Gauthier; Joshua John Miller; Dick Sargent; ***D:*** Dorian Walker; ***W:*** Robin Menken.

Teen Wolf 🦴🦴 1/2 **1985 (PG)** A nice, average teenage basketball player begins to show werewolf tendencies which suddenly make him popular at school when he leads the team to victory. The underlying message is to be yourself, regardless of how much hair you have on your body. Lighthearted comedy carried by the Fox charm; followed by subpar "Teen Wolf Too." **92m/C; VHS, DVD, Blu-Ray.** Michael J. Fox; James Hampton; Scott Paulin; Susan Ursitti; ***D:*** Rod Daniel; ***M:*** Miles Goodman.

Teen Wolf Too 🦴🦴 **1987 (PG)** The sequel to "Teen Wolf" in which the Teen Wolf's cousin goes to college on a boxing scholarship. More evidence that the sequel is rarely as good as the original. **95m/C; VHS, DVD, Blu-Ray.** Jason Bateman; Kim Darby; John Astin; Paul Sand; ***D:*** Christopher Leitch; ***W:*** Timothy King.

Teenage Bad Girl 🦴🦴 1/2 *Bad Girl; My Teenage Daughter* **1959** A woman who edits a magazine for teenagers can't control her own daughter. The kid does time in the pen after staying out all night and generally running around with the wrong crowd. Syms first lead performance is memorable in an otherwise routine teensploitation flick. **100m/B; VHS, DVD.** Anna Neagle; Sylvia Syms; Norman Wooland; Wilfrid Hyde-White; Kenneth Haigh; Julia Lockwood; ***D:*** Herbert Wilcox.

Teenage Catgirls in Heat 🦴🦴 **2000** On their lighthearted commentary track, the filmmakers admit that they had originally titled this Texas-produced horror simply "Catgirls." It was the good folks at Troma who came up with the modifiers that turns it into an inspired piece of exploitation. If the film doesn't quite live up (or down) to it, that's not too surprising. It is a nice, silly little horror and nobody involved takes it very seriously. **90m/C; DVD.** Gary Graves; Carrie Vanston; Dave Cox; ***D:*** Scott Perry; ***W:*** Scott Perry; Grace Smith; ***C:*** Thad Halcli; ***M:*** Randy Buck; Nenad Vugrinec.

Teenage Caveman 🦴🦴 *Out of the Darkness; Prehistoric World* **1958** A teenage boy living in a post-apocalypse yet prehistoric world journeys across the river, even though he was warned against it, and finds an old man who owns a book about past civilizations in the 20th Century. Schlocky, and one of the better bad films around. The dinosaur shots were picked up from the film "One Million B.C." **66m/B; VHS, DVD.** Robert Vaughn; Darrah Marshall; Leslie Bradley; Frank De Kova; Jonathan Haze; Beach Dickerson; Marshall Bradford; Robert Shayne; Joseph H. Hamilton; June Jocelyn; Charles P. Thompson; ***D:*** Roger Corman; ***W:*** Robert W(right) Campbell; ***C:*** Floyd Crosby; ***M:*** Albert Glasser.

Teenage Caveman 🦴🦴 **2001 (R)** Post-apocalyptic nightmare world has a small group of cave dwellers, led by elders who ban sex to keep the population down. But teenage hormones will win out and David leads girlfriend Sarah and a group of friends into the wilderness where they meet Neil and Judith, who are the result of genetic experimentation that has some unpleasant side effects for our little band of survivors (think sex). A "Creature Features" remake of the 1958 movie. **100m/C; VHS, DVD.** Andrew Keegan; Tara Subkoff; Richard Hillman; Shan Elliot; Tiffany Limos; Stephen Jasso; Crystal Grant; Hayley Keenan; Paul Hipp; ***D:*** Larry Clark; ***W:*** Christos N. Gage; ***C:*** Steve Gainer; ***M:*** Zoe Poledouris. **CABLE**

Teenage Devil Dolls 🦴 **1953** A cheap exploitation teenage flick wherein an innocent girl is turned on to reefer and goofballs, and eventually ends up on the street. **70m/C; VHS, DVD.** Barbara Marks; Bramlef L. Price, Jr.; ***D:*** B. Lawrence Price.

Teenage Doll 🦴🦴 **1957** Good old Corman teen exploitation pic features a good girl who's tired of being good and gets mixed up with some street punks. She even manages to set off a gang war by accidentally kiling a beat girl from a rival group. **71m/B; VHS, DVD.** Fay Spain; John Brinkley; June Kenney; Collette Jackson; Barbara Wilson; Ed Nelson; Richard Devon; Ziva Rodann; Barboura Morris; Bruno VeSota; ***D:*** Roger Corman; ***W:*** Charles B. Griffith; ***C:*** Floyd Crosby; ***M:*** Walter Greene.

Teenage Exorcist 🦴 1/2 **1993** Tired horror spoof finds the prim Diane (Stevens) renting a creepy house from an equally creepy real estate agent (Berryman). After she moves in, Diane begins having horrible nightmares and calls her family for help. When they arrive Diane has turned into a chainsaw-wielding seductress. The family is so distressed that they misdial the phone and wind up with a pizza delivery geek (Deezen) instead of the exorcist they need. **90m/C; VHS, DVD.** Brinke Stevens; Eddie Deezen; Michael Berryman; Robert Quarry; Jay Richardson; Tom Shell; Elena Sahagun; ***D:*** Grant Austin Waldman; ***W:*** Brinke Stevens.

Teenage Gang Debs 🦴 **1966** These chicks throw a sleazy coming out party the likes of which defy description. Simply the most important social function of 1966. **77m/B; VHS, DVD.** Diana Conti; Linda Gale; Eileen Scott; Sandra Kane; Robin Nolan; Linda Cambi; Sue McManus; Geri Tyler; Joey Naudic; John Batis; Tom Yourk; Thomas Andrisano; George Winship; Doug Mitchell; Tom Eldred; Frank Spinella; Alec Primrose; Gene Marrin; Lyn Kennedy; Janet Banzet; ***D:*** Sande N. Johnsen; ***W:*** Hy Cahl; ***C:*** Harry Petricek; ***M:*** Steve Karmen.

Teenage Mother WOOF! **1967** A Swedish sex education teacher comes to town and poisons the minds of the local high school kids. Naturally one becomes pregnant and has to try to trick the father into marrying her. More awful stuff from the director of "Girl On a Chain Gang." **78m/C; VHS, DVD, Streaming.** Arlene Sue Farber; Frederick Riccio; Julie Ange; Howard Le May; George Peters; ***D:*** Jerry Gross; ***W:*** Jerry Gross; ***C:*** Richard Brooks; ***M:*** Steve Karmen.

Teenage Mutant Ninja Turtles 🦴🦴 **2014 (PG-13)** Everything old is new again, and so it was only a matter of time before someone rebooted TMNT, this time not as animation but a CGI-heavy action film. The result is a mixed bag, not really sure of its target audience--is this for kids, teens, or thirtysomethings who remember the original? The plot is totally secondary to the cartoonish action but here goes: Shredder is taking over New York City; the Teenage Mutant Ninja Turtles come out of the sewers to help with April O'Neil (Fox as action eye candy yet again) at their side. Mediocre but not horrendous. **101m/C; DVD, Blu-Ray.** Alan Ritchson; Noel Fisher; Pete Ploszek; Jeremy Howard; Megan Fox; Danny Woodburn; Will Arnett; William Fichtner; Tohoru Masamune; Whoopi Goldberg; ***D:*** Jonathan Liebesman; ***W:*** Josh Applebaum; André Nemec; Evan Daugherty; ***C:*** Lula Carvalho; ***M:*** Brian Tyler. Golden Raspberries '14: Worst Support. Actress (Fox).

Teenage Mutant Ninja Turtles: The Movie 🦴🦴 1/2 **1990 (PG)** Four sewer-dwelling turtles that have turned into warrior ninja mutants due to radiation exposure take it upon themselves to rid the city of crime and pizza. Aided by a television reporter and their ninja master, Splinter the Rat, the turtles encounter several obstacles, including the evil warlord Shredder. A most excellent live-action version of the popular comic book characters which will hold the kids' interest. Much head-kicking and rib-crunching action as Leonardo, Donatello, Raphael, and Michelangelo fight for the rights of pre-adolescents everywhere. Combines real actors with Jim Henson creatures. **95m/C; VHS, DVD, Blu-Ray.** Judith Hoag; Elias Koteas; ***V:*** Robbie

(Reist) Rist; Corey Feldman; Brian Tochi; Kevin Clash; David McCharen; ***D:*** Steven Barron; ***W:*** Todd W. Langen; ***C:*** John Fenner; ***M:*** John Du Prez.

Teenage Mutant Ninja Turtles 2: The Secret of the Ooze 🦴🦴 **1991 (PG)** Amphibious pizza-devouring mutants search for the toxic waste that turned them into marketable martial artist ecologically correct kid idols. Same formula as the first go-round with some new characters tossed in. Animatronic characters from the laboratory of Jim Henson, first screen appearance by rapper Vanilla Ice. Marked end of pre-teen turtle craze. **88m/C; VHS, DVD, Blu-Ray.** Francois Chau; David Warner; Paige Turco; Ernie Reyes, Jr.; Vanilla Ice; ***D:*** Michael Pressman.

Teenage Mutant Ninja Turtles 3 🦴🦴 **1993 (PG)** Check it out dudes; the Teenage Mutant Ninja Turtles hit 17th century Japan to rescue loyal friend, reporter April O'Neil. Plenty of smoothly executed, blood-free martial arts moves keep the pace rolling, while the turtles battle an evil lord and English pirates. Seeing the TMNT's use a little more of their reptilian grey matter, and snarf a little less pizza should contribute to a relatively high adult tolerance level (considering the genre), and loads of good clean fun for the kiddies. **95m/C; VHS, DVD, Blu-Ray.** Elias Koteas; Paige Turco; Stuart Wilson; Sab Shimono; Vivian Wu; ***V:*** Randi Mayem Singer; Matt Hill; Jim Raposa; David Fraser; ***D:*** Stuart Gillard; ***W:*** Stuart Gillard; ***M:*** John Du Prez.

Teenage Mutant Ninja Turtles: Out of the Shadows 🦴 ½ *TMNT 2* **2016 (PG-13)** Another adventure for the anthropomorphic turtles with ninja powers, another CGI-heavy extravaganza that can't really find its audience. The turtles reunite with April O'Neil (Fox) after the intrepid journalists learns that a respected scientist is working for the evil Shredder (Brian Tee) and unwittingly unleashes the dimensional power of a creature named Krang (voiced by Brad Garrett). Can the Turtles defeat the old enemies from the cartoon—Shredder, Krang, Rock Steady and Bebop? It's a little more chaotic and eager to please than the last TMNT movie but it's a minor upgrade. **112m/C; DVD, Blu-Ray.** Megan Fox; Will Arnett; Laura Linney; Stephen Amell; Noel Fisher; Jeremy Howard; Pete Ploszek; Alan Ritchson; ***D:*** Dave Green; ***W:*** Josh Appelbaum; André Nemec; ***C:*** Lula Carvalho; ***M:*** Steve Jablonsky.

Teenage Rebel 🦴🦴 **1956** Thanks to custody issues, Dorothy (Keim) grew up with her divorced dad, Eric (Stephenson). Then her mother Nancy (Rogers) remarries and wants her rebellious daughter to live with her. Eric okays the arrangement since he wnats to remarry himself and start over without parental burdens. This leaves an insecure Dorothy unwilling to accept her new family. Keim married co-star Berlinger (who plays a sympathetic neighbor) in 1959 and quit acting. **94m/B; DVD.** Betty Lou Keim; Ginger Rogers; Michael Rennie; John Stephenson; Mildred Natwick; Warren Berlinger; ***D:*** Edmund Goulding; ***W:*** Charles Brackett; Walter Reisch; ***C:*** Joseph Macdonald; ***M:*** Leigh Harline.

Teenage Space Vampires 🦴 *Darkness: The Teen Space Vampire Saga; Darkness Comes* **1999 (PG)** A teenage boy tries to stop an alien vampire from shielding the Earth from the Sun so it's stops shining and his people can take over. Which is flawed thinking because if he succeeds we die and he has nothing to eat. **90m/C; DVD.** *CA RO US* Robin Dunne; Mac Fyfe; James Kee; Lindy Booth; Jessie Nilsson; ***D:*** Martin Wood; ***W:*** Martin Wood; ***C:*** Gabriel Kosuth; ***M:*** Orest Hrynewich; Jack Lenz; Stephen Skratt. **VIDEO**

Teenage Zombies **WOOF!** **1958** Mad scientist on remote island kidnaps teenagers and uses her secret chemical formula to turn them into zombies as part of her plan to enslave the world. Not as good as it sounds. **71m/B; VHS, DVD.** Don Sullivan; Katherine Victor; Chuck Niles; ***D:*** Jerry Warren; ***W:*** Jerry Warren; ***C:*** Allen Chandler.

Teenager 🦴 **1974 (R)** Three desperate, reckless individuals, all caught up in making a low budget movie, interact and eventually self-destruct. **91m/C; VHS, DVD.** Andrea Cagan; Reid Smith; Susan Bernard; ***D:*** Gerald Seth Sindell.

Teenagers from Outer Space **WOOF!** *The Gargon Terror* **1959** Low-budget sci-fi effort finds extraterrestrial youngsters visiting earth to conquer it and find food for their "monstrous pets" (they're really lobster shadows.) So cheaply made and melodramatic that it just may be good for a laugh. **86m/B; VHS, DVD, Blu-Ray.** Tom Graeff; Dawn Anderson; Harvey B. Dunn; Bryant Grant; Thomas Lockyer; King Moody; Bob Williams; ***D:*** Tom Graeff; ***W:*** Tom Graeff; ***C:*** Tom Graeff.

Teeth and Blood 🦴🦴 **2015** A vampire horror flick in which more humanity's survival is at stake! During the filming of the horror film "Chapel Blood," a demanding actress is murdered. Before her body can make it to the coroner's office, it disappears. At the same time, much the donated blood in the city has gone missing as well. Two police detectives, Mike Hung (Hutchinson) and Sasha Colfax (Van Der Water), are assigned to the case. While conducting an undercover investigation at the movie studio, they find themselves in the middle of a battle between two vampire covens who have been battling for the ages. Survival becomes perilous for both the detectives and the rest of the humans on Earth. **96m/C; DVD, Streaming, Download.** Glenn Plummer; Michelle Van Der Water; Sean Christopher; Danielle Vega; King Kedar; ***D:*** Al Franklin; ***W:*** Al Franklin; ***C:*** Bruce Ando; Jack Garrett; ***M:*** Steve Holtman.

TekWar 🦴🦴 ½ **1994** It's 2044 and society is plagued by "Tek," an illegal, addictive drug-like computer disk that creates powerful but destructive virtual-reality fantasies. Jake Cardigan (Evigan) is an cop framed on drug and murder charges, fresh out of prison, who's trying to both clear his name and find out what happened to his now ex-wife and son. Shatner, who wrote the Tek novels, guests as Walter Bascom, the head of a detective agency who promises to help Cardigan if Jake helps find a missing scientist. Made for TV. **92m/C; VHS, DVD.** Greg Evigan; Eugene Clark; Torri Higginson; William Shatner; ***D:*** William Shatner. **TV**

Telefon 🦴🦴 **1977 (PG)** Suspenseful, slick spy tale. Soviet agents battle a lunatic comrade who tries to use hypnotized Americans to commit sabotage. Daly, later of TV's "Cagney and Lacey," is memorable. **102m/C; VHS, DVD.** Charles Bronson; Lee Remick; Donald Pleasence; Tyne Daly; Patrick Magee; Sheree North; ***D:*** Donald Siegel; ***W:*** Stirling Silliphant; Peter Hyams; ***M:*** Lalo Schifrin.

The Telephone Book 🦴🦴 ½ **1971** A sex comedy about a young woman who is searching for the obscene phone caller she has fallen in love with. Considered ground breaking and obscene enough in it's day to be rated an adult film, it comes across as fairly mild by modern standards. **87m/B; DVD, Blu-Ray.** Sarah Kennedy; Norman Rose; James Harder; Jill Clayburgh; ***Nar:*** Ondine; ***D:*** Nelson Lyon; ***W:*** Nelson Lyon; ***C:*** Leon Perera; ***M:*** Nathan Sassover. **VIDEO**

Tell It to the Bees 🦴🦴 ½ **2019** An earnest, if contrived, adaptation of the novel by Fiona Shaw. In a small, English town in the 1950s, Jean Markham (Paquin), a doctor and beekeeper, begins a clandestine relationship with the mother (Grainger) of her young patient Charlie (Selkirk). But secrets don't stay hidden for long in a small town, and the women soon endure a backlash ranging from scorn to threats of violence. The acting of the three principals is superb, with Selkirk doing as fine a job as his elder thespians. **108m/C; Streaming.** *UK* Anna Paquin; Holliday Grainger; Gregor Selkirk; Emun Elliott; Lauren Lyle; ***D:*** Annabel Jankel; ***W:*** Henrietta Ashworth; Jessica Ashworth; ***C:*** Bartosz Nalazek; ***M:*** Claire M. Singer.

Tell It to the Judge 🦴🦴 ½ **1949** Russell plays the exuberant ex-wife of lawyer Cummings. They repeatedly try reconciling but ditzy blonde McDonald always manages to catch Cummings' eye. Fed up Russell takes off for a holiday in the mountains where she meets Young. When her ex-hubby follows her, she decides to try and make him jealous using Young as the bait. **87m/B; VHS, DVD, Streaming.** Rosalind Russell; Robert Cummings; Gig Young; Marie McDonald; Harry Davenport; Louise Beavers; ***D:*** Norman Foster.

Tell It to the Marines 🦴🦴 ½ **1926** An unexpected role for Chaney (sans any makeup) proved to be a popular choice in this military comedy/drama. A blustering Marine drill sergeant, O'Hara (Chaney) turns callow youths into respectable soldiers, including reluctant recruit Skeet Burns (Haines). Both fall for Navy nurse Norma (Boardman) but the romantic rivals must set aside their differences when they are sent to China to rescue Norma and the other nurses from a bandit leader. **103m/B; Silent; DVD.** Lon Chaney, Sr.; William Haines; Eleanor Boardman; Carmel Myers; Warner Oland; Eddie Gribbon; ***D:*** George W. Hill; ***W:*** Richard Schayer; ***C:*** Ira Morgan.

Tell Me a Riddle 🦴🦴 ½ **1980 (PG)** A dying woman attempts to reconcile with her family in this poignant drama about an elderly couple rediscovering their mutual love after 47 years of marriage. Fine acting; Grant's directorial debut. **94m/C; VHS, DVD.** Melvyn Douglas; Lila Kedrova; Brooke Adams; Peter Coyote; ***D:*** Lee Grant; ***W:*** Joyce Eliason.

Tell Me No Lies 🦴 ½ **2007** Rebellious teen Samantha Cooper (Prout) seems to be constantly getting into trouble but what she witnesses at a frat party could be deadly. Sam's knowledge leads to her being jailed and to numerous threats, but she still refuses to tell her frustrated mother Laura (Rutherford) what's going on until it's nearly too late. **90m/C; DVD.** Kelly Rutherford; Kirsten Prout; James Moss; Eric Keenleyside; Jesse Haddock; Andrew Francis; David Pearson; Andrea Whitburn; Samantha Ferris; Stephen Spender; Aidan Kahn; ***D:*** Michael Scott; ***W:*** Rick Drew; ***C:*** Adam Sliwinski; ***M:*** Peter Allen. **CABLE**

Tell No One 🦴🦴🦴 ½ *Ne le Dis a Personne* **2006** Pediatrician Alexandre Beck (Cluzet) struggles to piece together the events of a mysterious day at the lake eight years earlier when his wife was murdered and he was struck on the head, rendering the details fuzzy. When two more bodies are found buried at the murder site, police once again suspect Beck and inquire about possible evidence that turns up in his apartment. The airtight plot spirals out of control when Beck begins receiving cryptic emails regarding the day in question and he is forced to flee the cops. A perplexing thriller that will reward only those willing to trust the material and not second-guess the outcome. **125m/C; Blu-Ray, On Demand.** *CA* Francois Cluzet; Andre Dussollier; Marie Josee Croze; Kristin Scott Thomas; Nathalie Baye; Francois Berleand; Jean Rochefort; Marina Hands; Guillaume Canet; Gilles Lellouche; ***D:*** Guillaume Canet; ***W:*** Guillaume Canet; Philippe Lefebvre; ***C:*** Christophe Offenstein; ***M:*** Mathieu Chedid.

The Tell-Tale Heart 🦴🦴 ½ *The Hidden Room of 1,000 Horrors* **1960** Daydreaming author fantasizes about falling for major babe and killing his best friend for her. Adapted Poe tale. **78m/B; VHS, DVD.** *GB* Laurence Payne; Adrienne Corri; Dermot Walsh; Selma Vaz Dias; John Scott; David Lander; Annette Carell; ***D:*** Ernest Morris; ***W:*** Brian Clemens.

Tell Them Who You Are 🦴🦴 **2005 (R)** Mark Wexler's documentary about his cinematographer father Haskell Wexler is not so much about the man's award-winning movie work as it is an expose of their father-son relationship. Acknowledged for his work and political endeavors, Haskell is undeniably witty, egotistical and outspokenly blunt. "I don't think there's a movie that I've been on that I wasn't sure I could direct better," he says at one point, and that includes his son's. **95m/C; DVD.** ***D:*** Mark S. Wexler; ***W:*** Mark S. Wexler; Robert DeMaio; ***C:*** Mark S. Wexler.

Tell Them Willie Boy Is Here 🦴🦴🦴 **1969 (PG)** Western drama set in 1909 California about a Paiute Indian named Willie Boy and his white bride. They become the objects of a manhunt (led by the reluctant local sheriff, Redford) after Willie kills his wife's father in self-defense. This was once-blacklisted Polonsky's first film in 21 years. **98m/C; VHS, DVD, Blu-Ray.** Robert Redford; Katharine Ross; Robert (Bobby) Blake; Susan Clark; Barry Sullivan; John Vernon; Charles McGraw; ***D:*** Abraham Polonsky; ***W:*** Abraham Polonsky; ***C:*** Conrad L. Hall; ***M:*** Dave Grusin.

Telling Lies 🦴🦴 **2006 (R)** Troubled Faith (Harrison) returns to her private school to discover her boyfriend Derek (Di Angelo) is hooking up with her BFF Portia (Lipskis). Faith starts acting out and gets more self-destructive after meeting bad girl Eve (Stables), who convinces Faith to invent a boyfriend (they call him Vincent) to make Derek jealous. Only a real Vincent is murdered and evidence points to Faith's involvement, especially since Eve has mysteriously vanished. However, Det. Maggie Thomas (Brown) doesn't think the case against Faith is so cut-and-dried. **81m/C; DVD.** *GB* Kelly Stables; Melanie (Scary Spice) Brown; Jason Flemyng; Jenna Harrison; Matt Di Angelo; Algina Lipskis; ***D:*** Antara Bhardwai; ***W:*** Carl Austin; Michael Kramer; ***C:*** Ravi Yadav; ***M:*** Pravin Mani.

Telling Lies in America 🦴🦴 **1996 (PG-13)** Semiautobiographical Esterhaus-penned coming-of-ager allies a star-struck and naive Hungarian immigrant teen with dirty deejay on the take in early 60s Cleveland. Karchy Jones (Renfro) worships the slick polyester prince of the airwaves Billy Magic (Bacon), and through a contest at school, wins a chance to become his eager-beaver lackey. The twisted rock-n-roll mentor shows Karchy his own, highly cynical version of attaining the American Dream which, naturally, leads to trouble. Universally acclaimed performance by Bacon, who takes a one-dimensional persona and runs with it. Flockhart plays the "it" girl of Karchy's dreams. Smoothly told story suffers from a few of the usual cliches, but makes up for in heart. **101m/C; VHS, DVD, Blu-Ray.** Kevin Bacon; Brad Renfro; Maximilian Schell; Calista Flockhart; Paul Dooley; Jonathan Rhys Meyers; Luke Wilson; ***D:*** Guy Ferland; ***W:*** Joe Eszterhas; ***C:*** Reynaldo Villalobos; ***M:*** Nicholas Pike.

Telling You 🦴🦴 ½ **1998 (R)** Buddies Phil (Facinelli) and Dennis (Mihok) work at the local pizzeria and try to score but don't have much success since they're, basically, amiable losers. Fluff and Hewitt's role is small as Phil's ex-girlfriend. **94m/C; VHS, DVD.** Peter Facinelli; Dash Mihok; Matthew Lillard; Jennifer Love Hewitt; Richard Libertini; Robert DeFranco; Frank Medrano; Jennifer Jostyn; Rick Rossovich; Jennie Garth; ***D:*** Robert DeFranco; ***W:*** Robert DeFranco; Marc Palmieri; ***C:*** Mark Doering-Powell; ***M:*** Russ Landau.

Telstar: The Joe Meek Story 🦴🦴 **2008 (R)** British showbiz bio of do-it-yourself producer-composer Joe Meek (O'Neill) set in London's early '60s pop scene. The eccentric Meek, working from his home studio, gets an instrumental megahit with 'Telstar' in 1962 but pinballs between enjoying his outsider status and wanting acceptance in the legit music business. His life turns tragic. Adapted from the 2005 play "Telstar." **119m/C; DVD.** *UK* Con O'Neill; Tom Burke; Pam Ferris; Kevin Spacey; J.J. Feild; James Corden; ***D:*** Nick Moran; ***W:*** Nick Moran; James Hicks; ***C:*** Peter Wignall; ***M:*** Ilan Eshkeri.

The Temp **WOOF!** **1993 (R)** Unbelievably bad attempt at office horror. Beautiful, mysterious Kris temps for Hutton, a junior exec at the Mrs. Appleby baked goods company. She's almost too good to be true with unbelievable organizational skills and her dead serious ambition to climb the corporate ladder. Pyscho-drama has pyscho, but lacks drama, direction, plot development, intelligent dialogue, and anything resembling motive. While Hutton is tolerable, we nominate ex-Twin Peaker Boyle for the bad acting hall of shame as the conniving psycho. **99m/C; VHS, DVD.** Timothy Hutton; Lara Flynn Boyle; Faye Dunaway; Dwight Schultz; Oliver Platt; Steven Weber; Scott Coffey; Colleen Flynn; Dakin Matthews; Maura Tierney; ***D:*** Tom Holland; ***W:*** Kevin Falls; ***C:*** Steve Yaconelli; ***M:*** Frederic Talgorn. Golden Raspberries '93: Worst Support. Actress (Dunaway).

Tempest 🦴🦴 **1928** This must have been particularly intriguing at the time since the events it depicts were still so historically fresh. Russian peasant Markov (Barrymore) rises in the ranks of the Czar's army although his lowly birth causes him to be insulted by Princess Tamara (Horn). It's because of her that Markov is imprisoned, although the Russian Revolution frees him and he then switches sides to become a rising Party member. Tamara is now jailed and threatened with execution but Markov (who loves her) tries to come to her rescue. **111m/B;**

Silent; DVD. John Barrymore; Camilla Horn; Louis Wolheim; George Fawcett; Boris DeFas; Ullrich Haupt; ***D:*** Sam Taylor; ***W:*** C. Gardner Sullivan; ***C:*** Charles Rosher. Oscars '28: Art Dir./Set Dec.

The Tempest 🦴🦴🦴 **1982 (PG)** New York architect Phillip (Cassavettes), fed up with city living, chucks it all and brings his daughter Miranda (Ringwald in her screen debut), and singer Aretha (Sarandon) to live with him on a barren Greek island where they encounter a hermit named Kalibanos (Julia). Then, thanks to a shipwreck, all the other people in Phillip's life, including his unfaithful wife Antonia (Rowland), show up to complicate his midlife crisis. Loosley based on the Shakespeare play of the same name. Well-written, thoughtfully acted, and beautifully filmed. **140m/C; VHS, DVD.** John Cassavetes; Gena Rowlands; Susan Sarandon; Vittorio Gassman; Molly Ringwald; Paul Stewart; Sam Robards; Raul Julia; ***D:*** Paul Mazursky; ***W:*** Paul Mazursky; Leon Capetanos; ***C:*** Donald McAlpine; ***M:*** Stomu Yamashta.

The Tempest 🦴🦴 **2010 (PG-13)** Furious retelling of Shakepeare's final play, with the lead character no longer a Duke named Prospero, but a woman accused of witchcraft named Prospera (Mirren). Usurped by her brother Caliban (Hounsou) for dabbling in alchemy, Prospera, along with her daughter Miranda, find themselves shipwrecked on a mysterious island filled with strange creatures, anarchy, and dark magic. Even while exiled, Prospera must engage in a power struggle with her relentless brother, while coping with life as a single mom. The experienced cast, especially Mirren, is at top form, but the performances are overshadowed by loud, frantic storytelling. Unfortunately writer/director Taymor trumps the original's poetry and symbolism with too many thunderous special effects and exploding animals. **110m/C; Blu-Ray, On Demand.** Dame Helen Mirren; Felicity Jones; Djimon Hounsou; Ben Whishaw; Reeve Carney; Alan Cumming; Russell Brand; David Strathairn; Alfred Molina; Tom Conti; Chris Cooper; ***D:*** Julie Taymor; ***W:*** Julie Taymor; ***C:*** Stuart Dryburgh; ***M:*** Elliot Goldenthal.

Temple Grandin 🦴🦴🦴 **2010** Inspirational—without being sentimental—true story of Temple Grandin (Danes), who is diagnosed with autism in the 1950s when doctors recommended institutionalization. Instead, Temple's mother Eustacia (Ormond) is determined that she will be mainstreamed, including going to college. Temple, who thinks visually, becomes fascinated by cattle and earns a Ph.D in animal science while dealing with various cruelties (including sexism). Danes gives a stirring performance without resorting to caricature behavior. **109m/C; DVD.** Claire Danes; Catherine O'Hara; Julia Ormond; David Strathairn; ***D:*** Mick Jackson; ***W:*** Christopher Monger; William Merritt Johnson; ***C:*** Ivan Strasburg; ***M:*** Alex Wurman. **CABLE**

Tempo 🦴 ½ **2003 (R)** Sarah (Griffith) is an American expatriate living in Paris and supporting her expensive lifestyle by smuggling for criminals. All goes well until her kept lover falls in love with a younger woman and her life begins to fall apart. **83m/C; DVD.** *GB FR CA LU* Melanie Griffith; Rachael Leigh Cook; Hugh Dancy; Malcolm McDowell; Art Malik; ***D:*** Eric Styles; ***W:*** L.M. Kit Carson; Jennifer Salt; ***C:*** Robert Fraisse; ***M:*** John McCarthy.

Temptation of a Monk 🦴🦴 **1994** Costume drama about China's 7th-century Tang Dynasty finds General Shi (Hsin-kuo) duped into an assassination plot against the crown prince. After a massacre, the General flees and finds sanctuary with a group of Buddhist monks at a remote temple. There's also the General's sometime lover and a mystery woman (both played by Chen). Sometimes slow-moving and confusing but with exotic visuals. Based on a novel by Lilian Lee; Mandarin with subtitles. **118m/C; VHS, DVD.** *CH* Wu Hsin-kuo; Joan Chen; Fengyi Zhang; Michael Lee; ***D:*** Clara Law; ***W:*** Eddie Ling-Ching Fong; ***C:*** Andrew Lesnie; ***M:*** Tats Lau.

The Temptations 🦴🦴 ½ **1998** Miniseries bio of the Motown group from its high school beginnings in 1958 (under various names) through a meeting with Motown founder Berry Gordy (Babatunde) and major success in the '60s. Told from the viewpoint of the last original Temp, Otis Williams (Whitfield), as he and buddies Melvin Franklin (Woodside) and Paul Williams (Payton) hook up with first lead singer Eddie Kendricks (Brooks). When Kendricks goes solo it's the turn of David Ruffin (Leon) but the group suffers various ego traumas and tragedies. Naturally, the music's the real highlight. **150m/C; VHS, DVD.** Charles Malik Whitfield; DB Woodside; Terron Brooks; Christian Payton; Leon; Alan Rosenberg; Obba Babatunde; Charles Ley; Tina Lifford; Gina Ravera; Vanessa Bell Calloway; Chaz Lamar Shepherd; ***D:*** Allan Arkush; ***W:*** Kevin Arkadie; Robert P. Johnson; ***C:*** Jamie Anderson. **TV**

Tempted 🦴🦴 **2001 (R)** Wealthy builder Charlie LeBlanc (Reynolds) hires college student Jimmy Mulante (Facinelli) to do some carpentry work—and test the fidelity of his beautiful young wife Lilly (Burrows). Charlie heads out of town after offering Jimmy mucho bucks to seduce Lilly but Jimmy confesses the scheme to her instead and she decides to use the stud for her own purposes. **95m/C; VHS, DVD.** Burt Reynolds; Peter Facinelli; Saffron Burrows; Mike Starr; George DiCenzo; Eric Mabius; ***D:*** Bill Bennett; ***W:*** Bill Bennett; ***C:*** Tony Clark; ***M:*** David Bridie.

Tempted 🦴🦴 **2003** Ah, paradise. Unhappily married mom Emma Burke (Madsen) travels from Boston to Kauai, Hawaii for the funeral of Lily, her one-time nanny and surrogate mom. She embraces more than the island's relaxed attitude and sunshine when she gets involved with Lily's nephew Kala (Momoa) but that's before Emma learns a secret Lily had been keeping for a very long time. **90m/C; DVD.** Virginia Madsen; Jason Momoa; Lainie Kazan; Kieu Chinh; Andrew McFarlane; ***D:*** Maggie Greenwald; ***W:*** Vivienne Radkoff; ***C:*** Nino Martinetti; ***M:*** David Mansfield. **CABLE**

The Temptress 🦴🦴 **1926** Garbo plays a femme fatale, who is the cause of her own unhappiness. Parisian Elena falls in love with Argentine engineer Manuel and neglects to tell him she's married to his friend the Marquis (he finds out). The couple visit Manuel in Argentina where Elena vamps every man around, including bandit Duras, which leads to a shocking bullwhip duel between the two men. **90m/B; Silent; DVD.** Greta Garbo; Antonio Moreno; Roy D'Arcy; Marc McDermott; Armand Kaliz; Lionel Barrymore; Robert Anderson; ***D:*** Fred Niblo; ***W:*** Dorothy Farnum; ***C:*** William H. Daniels; Gaetano Antonio "Tony" Gaudio.

Temptress Moon 🦴🦴 *Feng Yue* **1996 (R)** 1920s Shanghai is displayed in all its decadence with opium-addicted Ruyi (Li) forced to officially head the Pang family after the death of her father. Power actually lies with distant male cousin Duanwen (Lin), who manages the household and is drawn to his cold relative. Ruyi's childhood playmate and fellow addict, Zhongliang (Cheung), is now a professional gigolo and blackmailer, working for a gangster (Tian) who wants him to seduce Ruyi and steal the Pang fortune. What happens is an obsessive affair between two beautiful manipulators. Chilly high-style soap opera. Mandarin with subtitles. **113m/C; VHS, DVD.** *CH* Gong Li; Leslie Cheung; Kevin Lin; Xie Tian; Zhou Jie; Saifei He; ***D:*** Chen Kaige; ***W:*** Shu Kei; ***C:*** Christopher Doyle; ***M:*** Jiping Zhao.

10 🦴🦴 ½ **1979 (R)** A successful songwriter who has everything finds his life is incomplete without the woman of his dreams, the 10 on his girl-watching scale. His pursuit brings surprising results. Also popularizes Ravel's "Bolero." **121m/C; VHS, DVD.** Dudley Moore; Julie Andrews; Bo Derek; Dee Wallace; Brian Dennehy; Robert Webber; ***D:*** Blake Edwards; ***W:*** Blake Edwards; ***C:*** Frank Stanley; ***M:*** Henry Mancini.

The Ten 🦴🦴 **2007 (R)** Number eleven must be "thou shalt be funny," because the lack of laughs in this collection of ten irreverent sketch-style short films based on the Ten Commandments is surely a sin of omission. Rudd plays the tablet-toting narrator who introduces each vignette, played out by a bevy of Hollywood B-listers. Yeah, a "thou shalt not steal" tale starring Winona Ryder is kinda clever, but the rest of the warped jokes have narrow appeal—some hit, others miss, and most are too smug to gauge when a gag has gone on too long. **93m/C; DVD.** Paul Rudd; Jessica Alba; Adam Brody; Bobby Cannavale; Famke Janssen; Gretchen Mol; Justin Theroux; Winona Ryder; Rob Corddry; Oliver Platt; Ron Silver; Ken Marino; ***D:*** David Wain; ***W:*** Ken Marino; David Wain; ***C:*** Yaron Orbach; ***M:*** Craig Wedren.

Ten Benny 🦴🦴 *Nothing to Lose* **1998 (R)** Frustrated New Jersey shoe salesman Ray (Brody) borrows $10,000 from a local wiseguy in order to win enough money at the track to set himself up in business. Bad idea. As his luck continues a downward spiral, he abuses his wife (Temchen) into the arms of his buddy (Gallagher) and becomes more desparate to climb out of the hole he's dug for himself. First-time director Bross has obviously studied the Scorsese school of filmmaking, but must've skipped the classes on originality, subtlety, and characterization. Not much going on here that hasn't been done (better) somewhere else, but Brody turns in a fine performance. **98m/C; VHS, DVD.** Adrien Brody; Sybil Temchen; Michael Gallagher; Tony Gillan; James Moriarty; Frank Vincent; ***D:*** Eric Bross; ***W:*** Eric Bross; Tom Cudworth; ***C:*** Horacio Marquinez; ***M:*** Chris Hajian.

Ten Canoes 🦴🦴 ½ **2006** Minygululu (Peter Minygululu) fears his younger brother is up to no good and tells him a long moral fable to keep him out of trouble. Noteworthy for being the first film shot entirely in the Australian aboriginal language. **92m/B; DVD.** *AU* Crusoe Kurrdal; Jamie Gulpilil; Richard Birrinbirrin; Peter Minygululu; Frances Djulibing; ***D:*** Rolf de Heer; Peter Djigirr; ***W:*** Rolf de Heer; ***C:*** Ian Jones; ***M:*** Billy Black.

Ten Cents a Dance 🦴🦴 **1931** Taxi dancer Barbara (Stanwyck) rejects the romantic overtures of wealthy Bradley Carlon (Cortez) in favor of fellow boarding house resident Eddie (Owsley), whom she marries. Not surprisingly Eddie turns out to be a lazy louse and Barbara turns to Bradley for help. Lucky for her he's still carrying a romantic torch. **75m/B; DVD.** Barbara Stanwyck; Ricardo Cortez; Monroe Owsley; Sally Blane; Blanche Frederici; ***D:*** Lionel Barrymore; ***W:*** Jo Swerling; ***C:*** Ernest Haller; Gilbert Warrenton.

10 Cloverfield Lane 🦴🦴🦴 **2016 (PG-13)** Producer J.J. Abrams and debut director Trachtenberg filmed this clever thriller, a quasi-sequel to Cloverfield, completely in secret, revealing it to the world in a trailer mere weeks before it premiered. The film itself is a fun three-character piece in which a young woman (Winstead) finds herself the prisoner of a suspicious man (Goodman)...or has the world really ended and this survivalist is her savior? Trachtenberg allows his two leads to do the heavy lifting and they are sensational. The finale is a little silly, but the movie has worked well enough by then not to care. **103m/C; DVD, Blu-Ray, Streaming.** John Goodman; Mary Elizabeth Winstead; John Gallagher, Jr.; ***V:*** Bradley Cooper; ***D:*** Dan Trachtenberg; ***W:*** Josh Campbell; Matthew Stuecken; Damien Chazelle; ***C:*** Jeff Cutter; ***M:*** Bear McCreary.

The Ten Commandments 🦴🦴 ½ **1923** The silent epic that established DeMille as a popular directorial force and which he remade 35 years later as an even bigger epic with sound. Follows Moses' adventures in Egypt, plus a modern story of brotherly love and corruption. Features a new musical score by Gaylord Carter. Remade in 1956. **146m/B; Silent; VHS, DVD, Blu-Ray.** Theodore Roberts; Richard Dix; Rod La Rocque; Edythe Chapman; Nita Naldi; ***D:*** Cecil B. DeMille; ***C:*** Archie Stout; ***M:*** Gaylord Carter.

The Ten Commandments 🦴🦴🦴 **1956 (G)** DeMille's remake of his 1923 silent classic (and his last film) is a lavish Biblical epic that tells the life story of Moses, who turned his back on a privileged life to lead his people to freedom outside of Egypt. Exceptional cast, with Fraser Heston (son of Charlton) as the baby Moses. Parting of Red Sea rivals any modern special effects. A 35th Anniversary Collector's Edition is available uncut at 245 minutes, in widescreen format and Dolby Surround stereo, and 1,000 copies of an Autographed Limited Edition that includes an engraved bronze plaque and an imprinted card written and personally signed by Charlton Heston are also available. **219m/C; VHS, DVD, Blu-Ray.** Charlton Heston; Yul Brynner; Anne Baxter; Yvonne De Carlo; Nina Foch; John Derek; H.B. Warner; Henry Wilcoxon; Judith Anderson; John Carradine; Douglass Dumbrille; Cedric Hardwicke; Martha Scott; Vincent Price; Debra Paget; ***D:*** Cecil B. DeMille; ***W:*** Aeneas MacKenzie; Jesse Lasky, Jr.; Frederic M. Frank; Jack Gariss; ***C:*** Loyal Griggs; ***M:*** Elmer Bernstein. Natl. Film Reg. '99.

Ten Days That Shook the World 🦴🦴🦴 ½ *October; Oktyabr* **1927** Silent masterpiece based on American author John Reed's book of the same name. Eisenstein, commissioned by the Soviet government, spared no expense to chronicle the Bolshevik Revolution of 1917 (in a flattering Communist light, of course). He was later forced to cut his portrayal of Leon Trotsky, who was then an enemy of the state. Includes rare footage of the Czar's Winter Palace in Leningrad. Haunting score, combined with some of Eisenstein's most striking work. See Warren Beatty's "Reds" for a fictional look at Reed and the Russian Revolution. **104m/B; Silent; VHS, DVD.** *RU* Nikandrov; N. Popov; Boris Livanov; ***D:*** Sergei Eisenstein; Grigori Alexandrov; ***W:*** Sergei Eisenstein; Grigori Alexandrov; ***C:*** Vladimir Popov; Eduard Tisse; ***M:*** Edmund Meisel.

Ten Days Wonder 🦴🦴 ½ *La Decade Prodigieuse* **1972 (PG)** Mystery/drama focuses on the patriarch of a wealthy family (Welles), his young wife, and his adopted son (Perkins), who is having an affair with his stepmother. It also turns out that Perkins is certifiable and is trying to break all of the Ten Commandments, which he succeeds in doing before killing himself (gruesomely). Based on the mystery novel by Ellery Queen. **101m/C; VHS, DVD.** *FR* Orson Welles; Anthony Perkins; Marlene Jobert; Michel Piccoli; Guido Alberti; ***D:*** Claude Chabrol.

Ten Inch Hero 🦴 ½ **2007 (R)** Piper (Harnois) moves to Santa Cruz to search for the daughter she gave up for adoption and gets a job at a quirky sandwich shop with a quirky boss (Doe) and quirky employees who all have issues revolving around self-esteem and sex. Meanwhile, Piper believes young Julia is her offspring so she gets friendly with the tyke and her dad Noah (Flanery). **102m/C; DVD.** Elisabeth Harnois; John Doe; Sean Patrick Flanery; Adair Tishler; Danneel Harris; Clea DuVall; Jensen Ackles; Alice Krige; Jordan Belfi; ***D:*** David Mackay; ***W:*** Betsy Morris; ***C:*** Gordon Verheul; ***M:*** Don Davis. **VIDEO**

10 Items or Less 🦴🦴 **2006 (R)** Minimalist flick that focuses on a nameless big-time actor (Freeman) venturing into method territory. He travels outside LA in order to spend time at a local downscale grocery store to study how his store-manager character would behave, but instead observes all-business checkout clerk Scarlet (Vega) at work. When he's left stranded, Scarlet agrees to drive him home and he offers to help her prepare for a secretarial job interview the way he would prep for an audition. You can't deny the warmth of either Freeman or Vega but even for an indie this is slight material. **81m/C; DVD.** Morgan Freeman; Paz Vega; Bobby Cannavale; Anne Dudek; Jonah Hill; Danny DeVito; Rhea Perlman; ***D:*** Brad Silberling; ***W:*** Brad Silberling; ***C:*** Phedon Papamichael; ***M:*** Antonio Pinto.

Ten Laps to Go 🦴 ½ **1936** Champion race car driver Larry Evans is deliberately injured on the track by his rival Eddie DeSylvia. After being released from the hospital, Larry realizes he's lost his nerve until he discovers his replacement driver Barney Smith is actually working for Eddie and plans to throw the big race. **67m/B; DVD.** Rex Lease; Duncan Renaldo; Muriel Evans; Tom Moore; Yakima Canutt; Marie Prevost; Charles Delaney; ***D:*** Elmer Clifton; ***W:*** Charles Condon; ***C:*** Arthur Martinelli.

Ten Little Indians 🦴🦴 ½ *And Then There Were None* **1975 (PG)** Ten people are gathered in an isolated inn under mysterious circumstances. One by one they are murdered, each according to a verse from a children's nursery rhyme. British adaptation of the novel and stage play by Agatha Christie. **98m/C; VHS, DVD, Blu-Ray.** *GB* Herbert Lom; Richard Attenborough; Oliver Reed; Elke Sommer; Charles Aznavour; Stephane Audran; Gert Frobe; Adolfo Celi; Orson Welles; ***D:*** Peter Collinson.

10 Minutes Gone 🦴 ½ **2019 (R)** Rex (Willis) carefully selects crews to rob banks for anonymous clients while keeping his distance from all involved. He hires five men, including safecracker Frank (Chiklis), to extract a metal case from an underground bank vault. After the heist goes bad, Frank is ambushed in a back alley trying to leave and wakes up with amnesia. As Frank hunts for the case on Rex's orders, he struggles to remember what happened. A haplessly forgettable plot for two Hollywood action icons. **88m/C; DVD.** Bruce Willis; Michael Chiklis; Meadow Williams; Kyle Schmid; Texas Battle; ***D:*** Brian A. Miller; ***W:*** Kelvin Mao; Jeff Jingle; ***M:*** Josh Atchley.

Ten Nights in a Barroom 🦴🦴 **1913** The evils of alcohol are dramatized when they ruin a man's life. One of many propaganda films about alcohol and the problems that it caused that were made during the prohibition era. Silent, with a musical score. Remade in 1931. **68m/B; Silent; VHS, DVD, Streaming.** Robert Lawrence; Marie Trado; Gladys Egan; Violet Horner; Jack Regan; ***D:*** Lee Beggs; ***W:*** Lee Beggs.

10 Rillington Place 🦴🦴🦴 **1971 (PG)** A grimy, upsetting British film about the famed serial killer John Christie and the man wrongly hanged for his crimes, the incident that led to the end of capital punishment in England. Impeccably acted. One of Hurt's earliest films. **111m/C; VHS, DVD, Blu-Ray.** *GB* Richard Attenborough; John Hurt; Judy Geeson; Gabrielle Daye; Andre Morell; Bernard Lee; Isobel Black; Pat Heywood; ***D:*** Richard Fleischer; ***W:*** Clive Exton; ***C:*** Denys Coop; ***M:*** John Dankworth.

10 Rules for Sleeping Around WOOF! 2013 (R) Should have been titled "10 Rules for How Not to Make a Movie." A sex comedy that has little of either and is poorly written and directed by Greif who leaves the actors floundering. Married Vince and Cameron allegedly have an open relationship as long as they follow the aforementioned rules. They urge engaged friends, Ben and Kate, to loosen up and join them for a raucous Hamptons weekend, but the hijinks result in nothing that hasn't been seen before--even the nudity is overdone. **94m/C; DVD, Blu-Ray.** Jesse Bradford; Virginia Williams; Christopher Marquette; Tammin Sursok; Wendi McLendon-Covey; Bryan Callen; Michael McKean; ***D:*** Leslie Greif; ***W:*** Leslie Greif; ***C:*** Tom Priestley, Jr.

Ten Things I Hate about You 🦴🦴🦴 **1999 (PG-13)** This Bill Shakespeare guy must be raking in the royalties, dude! The Bard is once again adapted for teens in this update of his very un-PC comedy "The Taming of the Shrew." Obstetrician and single dad Walter (Miller) has seen enough teen pregnancies to fear all adolescent boys who show up with flowers. He decrees that his ultra-popular daughter Bianca (Oleynik) cannot date before her man-hating sister Kat (Stiles) does. Two lovesick suitors, vain Joey (Keegan) and sensitive guy Cameron (Gordon-Levitt), bribe new-kid-in-town Patrick (Ledger) to make advances on Kat in order to play "jumpeth the maiden" with Bianca. Kat and Patrick then engage in a duel of verbal thrusts and parries, gradually falling for each other. Incorporates some of Shakespeare's dialogue, but glosses over the more chauvinistic elements of his play. **97m/C; VHS, DVD.** Julia Stiles; Heath Ledger; Larisa Oleynik; Joseph Gordon-Levitt; Andrew Keegan; David Krumholtz; Larry Miller; Susan May Pratt; Daryl (Chill) Mitchell; Allison Janney; David Leisure; Gabrielle Union; ***D:*** Gil Junger; ***W:*** Karen McCullah Lutz; Kirsten Smith; ***C:*** Mark Irwin; ***M:*** Richard Gibbs. MTV Movie Awards '00: Breakthrough Perf. (Stiles).

10,000 A.D.: The Legend of the Black Pearl 🦴 **2008 (PG-13)** A few thousand years after WWIII, humanity is represented by two warring tribes who complain through the movie about the horrifying drought conditions caused by the war while standing in a forest next to a river. A mysterious Evil known as the Sinasu begins hunting both tribes, and the hunt is on for the one man who can stop it. Massively cliched and full of plot holes, it is quite beautifully filmed for an indie. **86m/C; DVD.** *IT* Raul Gasteazoro; Julian Perez; Russ Russo; Lilly Husbands; Chyna Layne; Joaquin Perez; Loukas Papas; Nevin Millan; Edgar Feliciano; Nina Carney; Celina Murk; ***D:*** Raul Gasteazoro; Giovanni Messner; ***W:*** Raul Gasteazoro; ***C:*** Giovanni Messner; ***M:*** Jed Smith.

10,000 B.C. 🦴 **2008 (PG-13)** In some prior "mythical age" on earth, tribal peoples (who all speak different languages; lucky for us, one of them is English) live on a land ruled by nature and spirits. D'Leh (Strait), a young hunter, and Evolet (Belle), the blue-eyed beauty, are lovers in a remote mountain tribe. Evolet is kidnapped by a band of raiders and D'Leh heads out to save her. D'Leh and his small crew meet up with other civilizations along the way and soon there's an army behind him. Good thing, as it turns out that his mission isn't just to save Evolet, but civilization, too. All of which sounds okay in theory, but on screen it falls especially flat in all its cheesy computer-generated glory. The special effects are cheap, the supposedly prehistoric actors too gorgeous, and the whole thing doesn't even try to make sense, with woolly mammoths trotting about at the same time pyramids are being erected. Stick with "The Flintstones." **109m/C; DVD, Blu-Ray.** Steven Strait; Camilla Belle; Clifford Curtis; Joel Virgel; Ben Badra; ***Nar:*** Omar Sharif; ***D:*** Roland Emmerich; ***W:*** Roland Emmerich; Harald Kloser; ***C:*** Ueli Steiger; ***M:*** Harald Kloser; Thomas Wander.

Ten Thousand Bedrooms 🦴 ½ **1957** After splitting with partner Lewis, this dull MGM musical nearly ended Martin's solo film career. Hotel magnate Ray Hunter heads to Rome to check on his latest investment and gets entangled with the four marriageable daughters of Vittorio Martelli (Slezak). **114m/C; DVD.** Dean Martin; Anna Maria Alberghetti; Eva Bartok; Dewey Martin; Walter Slezak; Lisa Montell; Lisa Gaye; Jules Munshin; Paul Henreid; ***D:*** Richard Thorpe; ***W:*** Leonard Spigelgass; Art Cohn; Laszlo Vadnay; William Ludwig; ***C:*** Robert J. Bronner.

10,000 Black Men Named George 🦴🦴 ½ **2002 (R)** Showtime drama concerns the founding of the first black union in 1925--the Brotherood of Sleeping Car Porters. Despite threats, union activist Asa Philip Randolph (Braugher) and porter Ashley Totten (Van Peebles) sought the signatures of 10,000 black men who were generally all referred to as 'George' after George Pullman, who first hired emacipated slaves to work on the trains. **95m/C; DVD.** Andre Braugher; Mario Van Peebles; Charles S. Dutton; Kenneth McGregor; Carla Brothers; Brock Peters; Ellen Holly; ***D:*** Robert Townsend; ***W:*** Cyrus Nowrasteh; ***C:*** Edward Pei; ***M:*** Stephen James Taylor. **CABLE**

Ten Thousand Saints 🦴🦴 **2015 (R)** Well-meaning but ultimately familiar and forgettable coming-of-age story set in '80s NYC. Awkward teen Jude's (Butterfield) life forever changes when his buddy Teddy (Jogia) has a one-night stand with Eliza (Steinfeld) before dying in a freak accident. Jude wants to be there for his buddy's kid and for Eliza, which takes him to New York and back into the world of his dad Les (Hawke), whom his mother divorced years ago. He also ends up befriending Teddy's brother Johnny (Hirsch), who wants to raise the kid. **113m/C; DVD.** Henry Kelemen; Julianne Nicholson; Ethan Hawke; Asa Butterfield; Avan Jogia; Elisabeth Vastola; ***D:*** Shari Springer Berman; Robert Pulcini; ***W:*** Shari Springer Berman; Robert Pulcini; ***C:*** Ben Kutchins; ***M:*** Garth Stevenson.

Ten 'Til Noon 🦴🦴 **2006 (R)** Low-budget but ingenious thriller that shows a ten-minute period (11:50 to noon) from several different viewpoints. Tech tycoon Larry Taylor (Wasserman) is rudely awakened by hitman Mr. Jay (Freeman) and his associate (Lano), who announce his murder. Maybe his unfaithful wife (Guest) has something to do with it, maybe it's the ruthless Mr. Duke (Kopache), or maybe someone else is pulling the strings. **88m/C; DVD.** Jenya Lano; Dylan Kussman; Thomas Kopache; Daniel Nathan Spector; Rick D. Wasserman; Alfonso Freeman; Rayne Guest; Jason Hamer; Daniel Hagen; George Williams; ***D:*** Scott Storm; ***W:*** Paul Osborne; ***C:*** Alice Brooks; ***M:*** Joe Kraemer.

Ten to Midnight 🦴🦴 **1983 (R)** Vigilante Bronson is on the prowl again, this time as a police officer after a kinky serial murderer. The psychotic killer stalks his daughter and Dad's gonna stop him at any cost. **101m/C; VHS, DVD, Blu-Ray.** Charles Bronson; Wilford Brimley; Lisa Eilbacher; Andrew Stevens; ***D:*** J. Lee Thompson; ***W:*** William Roberts.

10 Violent Women WOOF! 1979 (R) Ten women who take part in a million dollar jewelry heist are tossed into a women's prison where brutal lesbian guards subject them to degradation and brutality. **97m/C; VHS, DVD.** Sherri Vernon; Dixie Lauren; Sally Gamble; ***D:*** Ted V. Mikels; ***W:*** Ted V. Mikels; ***C:*** Yuval Shousterman; ***M:*** Nicholas Carras.

Ten Wanted Men 🦴 **1954** A successful cattle baron is confronted by a pistol-wielding landowner determined to ruin him. Standard fare, with better than average performances from Scott and Boone. **80m/C; VHS, DVD.** Randolph Scott; Jocelyn Brando; Richard Boone; Skip Homeier; Leo Gordon; Jack Perrin; Donna Martell; ***D:*** H. Bruce Humberstone; ***W:*** Harriet Frank, Jr; Irving Ravetch.

Ten Who Dared 🦴🦴 **1960** Ten Civil War heroes brave the Colorado River in an effort to chart its course. Although it's based on an actual historic event, the film is poorly paced and lacks suspense. **92m/C; VHS, DVD.** Brian Keith; John Beal; James Drury; ***D:*** William Beaudine.

10 Years 🦴🦴 ½ **2012 (PG-13)** High school reunion comedy stars Tatum as Jake, a guy who has no problems with his increasingly serious relationship with Jess (real-life wife Dewan-Tatum) until he crosses paths again with his high school sweetheart Mary (Dawson). A cast of likeable stars, including Graynor, Long, and Mara, goes a long way to help a script and entire production that doesn't really add anything to the subgenre of beautiful people who try to come to terms with life at their reunion. **100m/C; DVD, Blu-Ray.** Channing Tatum; Jenna Dewan-Tatum; Rosario Dawson; Justin Long; Max Minghella; Oscar Isaac; Chris Pratt; Ari Graynor; Kate Mara; Lynn Collins; Brian Geraghty; Aubrey Plaza; ***D:*** Jamie Linden; ***W:*** Jamie Linden; ***C:*** Steven Fierberg; ***M:*** Chad Fischer.

Tenacious D in the Pick of Destiny 🦴🦴 ½ **2006 (R)** Big screen story of one guitar pick, two rockers and quite a bit of mind-altering substances. JB (Black) and KG (Gass) are Tenacious D, the hard-rockin' duo that simultaneously pays tribute to and pokes fun at the cliches of the world of hard rock. This hit-and-miss comedy traces the origins of the band and their experiences with talking Dio posters, Sasquatch and a musical duel with the Devil (Grohl). A must-see for fans of the band (however, it does not have powers comparable to Wonderboy), it is also entertaining for others. Raise your Goblet of Rock and lower your cognitive capacity for this one. **93m/C; DVD.** Jack Black; Kyle Gass; Troy Gentile; Ben Stiller; Jason (JR) Reed; Tim Robbins; Meat Loaf Aday; Amy Poehler; Paul F. Tompkins; David Grohl; Colin Hanks; Amy Adams; David Krumholtz; John C. Reilly; Fred Armisen; Ned Bellamy; ***D:*** Liam Lynch; ***W:*** Jack Black; Kyle Gass; Liam Lynch; ***C:*** Robert Brinkmann; ***M:*** Tenacious D.

The Tenant 🦴🦴🦴 ½ ***Le Locataire*** **1976 (R)** Disturbing story of a hapless office worker who moves into a spooky Paris apartment house. Once lodged inside its walls, he becomes obsessed with the previous occupant, who committed suicide, and the belief that his neighbors are trying to kill him. Based on a novel by Roland Topor. **126m/C; VHS, DVD.** *FR* Roman Polanski; Isabelle Adjani; Melvyn Douglas; Jo Van Fleet; Bernard Fresson; Shelley Winters; Lila Kedrova; Claude Dauphin; Michel Blanc; ***D:*** Roman Polanski; ***W:*** Roman Polanski; Gerard Brach; ***C:*** Sven Nykvist; ***M:*** Philippe Sarde.

The Tenant of Wildfell Hall 🦴🦴 ½ **1996** Anne Bronte gets her turn in the spotlight with this TV adaptation of her 1848 novel. When the mysterious Helen Graham (Fitzgerald) and her young son become the new tenants of decaying Wildfell Hall, they naturally elicit lots of gossip in their rural community. Then young farmer Gilbert Markham (Stephens) becomes romantically interested in Helen and she's eventually forced to reveal her secret—she's run away from her alcoholic and abusive husband Arthur Huntingdon (Graves), who has now kidnapped their son to force Helen to return. **180m/C; VHS, DVD.** *GB CA* Tara Fitzgerald; Toby Stephens; Rupert Graves; Beatie Edney; James Purefoy; Jonathan Cake; Kenneth Cranham; Janet Dale; ***D:*** Mike Barker; ***W:*** Janet Barron; David Nokes; ***C:*** Daf Hobson; ***M:*** Richard G. Mitchell. **TV**

The Tenants 🦴 ½ **2006 (R)** Adaptation of Bernard Malamud's 1972 novel, helmed by first-time director Green, is a small, grim drama about the failure to bridge racial and ethnic divides. Landlord Levenspiel (Cassel) is trying to force Harry (McDermott), his last legal tenant, to vacate his crumbling Brooklyn tenement so it can be torn down. But the obsessive writer refuses to go until he can finish his third novel; squatter Willie (Snoop Dogg) is an unpublished writer also working on his opus. The two meet, but racial tensions and mistrust eventually erupt. Snoop is convincing (in a stereotypical role) but the movie isn't. **97m/C; DVD.** Dylan McDermott; Snoop Dogg; Rose Byrne; Seymour Cassel; Niki J. Crawford; Laz Alonso; ***D:*** Danny Green; ***W:*** David Diamond; Danny Green; ***C:*** David W. Dubois; ***M:*** Leigh Gorman.

Tender Flesh WOOF! 1997 Unashamed exercise in sleaze from the prolific Jess Franco is worth noting for only one scene wherein a woman urinates on camera. Beyond that dubious distinction, it's yet another unfocused variation on "The Most Dangerous Game." **90m/C; DVD.** *SP* Lina Romay; Amber Newman; Monique Parent; ***D:*** Jess (Jesus) Franco; ***W:*** Jess (Jesus) Franco; ***M:*** Jess (Jesus) Franco.

Tender Is the Night 🦴 ½ **1962** F. Scott Fitzgerald's novel about American ex-pats in post-WWI Europe turns into an over-long, syrupy meldorama. Wealthy Nicole (Jones) has mental problems and is under the care of shrink Dick Diver (Robards). They marry and live a society life on the French Riviera but as Nicole becomes stronger, Dick drinks too much, lets his professional skills lapse, and becomes emotionally and financially dependent on his wife. **146m/C; DVD.** Jennifer Jones; Jason Robards, Jr.; Joan Fontaine; Tom Ewell; Cesare Danova; Jill St. John; Paul Lukas; ***D:*** Henry King; ***W:*** Ivan Moffat; ***C:*** Leon Shamroy; ***M:*** Bernard Herrmann.

Tender Loving Care 🦴 **1973** Three nurses dispense hefty doses of T.L.C. in their hospital, and the patients aren't the only ones on the receiving end. **72m/C; VHS, DVD.** Donna Desmond; Leah Simon; Anita King; ***D:*** Don Edmonds.

Tender Mercies 🦴🦴🦴 **1983 (PG)** Down-and-out country singer Mac Sledge (Duvall) gets roaring drunk after breaking up with his wife Dixie (Buckley) andfinds himself waking up at a motel/gas station run by religious widow, Rosa Lee (Harper). mac sticks arounds and finds his life redeemed by the love of a good woman and he also decides to attempt a comeback. Aided by Horton Foote's script, Duvall, Harper, and Barkin (as Mac's daughter Sue Anne) keep this from being simplistic and sentimental. Duvall wrote as well as performed the songs in his Oscar-winning performance. Wonderful, life-affirming flick. **88m/C; VHS, DVD.** Robert Duvall; Tess Harper; Betty Buckley; Ellen Barkin; Wilford Brimley; Lenny Von Dohlen; Allan Hubbard; ***D:*** Bruce Beresford; ***W:*** Horton Foote; ***C:*** Russell Boyd; ***M:*** George Dreyfus. Oscars '83: Actor (Duvall), Orig. Screenplay; Golden Globes '83: Actor--Drama (Duvall); L.A. Film Critics '83: Actor (Duvall); N.Y. Film Critics '83: Actor (Duvall); Writers Guild '83: Orig. Screenplay.

The Tender Trap 🦴🦴 ½ **1955** Charlie Reader (Sinatra) is a bachelor not content with the many women in his life. He meets the innocent Julie Gillis (Reynolds) and falls head over heels for her. He then torments himself over a marriage proposal, unwilling to let go of his freedom. **111m/C; VHS, DVD.** Frank Sinatra; Debbie Reynolds; Celeste Holm; David Wayne; Carolyn Jones; Lola Albright; Tom Helmore; Howard St. John; Willard Sage; James Drury; Benny Rubin; Frank Sully; David White; ***D:*** Charles Walters; ***W:*** Julius J. Epstein; ***C:*** Paul Vogel.

The Tenderfoot 🦴🦴 ½ **1932** Wealthy Texan Calvin Jones (Brown) heads to the Big Apple to invest in a Broadway show and nearly gets scammed by producer Joe Lehman (Cody) who knows his musical is a loser. Lew's secretary Ruth (Rogers) likes Calvin enough to warn him and Calvin likes Ruth enough to give her the lead in a revised production and the rest is standard showbiz comedy material (complete with gangsters). **70m/B; DVD.** Joe E. Brown; Ginger Rogers; Lew Cody; Vivien Oakland; Robert Greig; Ralph Ince; ***D:*** Ray Enright; ***W:*** Earl Baldwin; Montague (Monty) Banks; Arthur Caesar; ***C:*** Gregg Toland.

Tenderness 🦴 ½ **2008 (R)** Despite the cast, this is a static crime drama with no particular payoff. Eighteen-year-old Eric Poole (Foster) moves in with his aunt (Dern) after being released from a juvenile detention center where he was incarcerated for murdering his parents. Troubled teen Lori (Traub) is obsessed with the crime and ingratiates herself into Eric's life. Eric is also being tracked by Detective Cristofuoro (Crowe) who doesn't believe Eric has been rehabilitated at all. Based on the Robert Cormier novel. **101m/C; DVD.** *AU* Jon Foster; Russell Crowe; Sophie Traub; Laura Dern; Alexis Dziena; ***D:*** John Polson; ***W:*** Emil Stern; ***C:*** Tom Stern; ***M:*** Jonathan Goldsmith.

Tenderness of the Wolves 🦴🦴 *Die Zartlichkeit der Wolfe* **1973** Inspired by Fritz Lang's film "M" but sticking closer to its source material, the case of real-life mass murderer Peter Kurten, known as the Dusseldorf Vampire. Lommel's film is also given the "Fassbinder" spin (he's in the cast as well as the producer and editor). In 1925, black marketeer Fritz Haarmann (Raab) lures young runaway boys with the promise of a job, only to seduce and murder them—and sell their remains as meat. Raab rather resembles the Peter Lorre character but his Hartmann is all surface quiet and seething madness underneath. Very chilling. German with subtitles. **86m/C; VHS, DVD, Blu-Ray.** *GE* Kurt Raab; Jeff Roden; Margit Carstensen; Rainer Werner Fassbinder; Wolfgang Schenck; Brigitte Mira; Ingrid Caven; Jurgen Prochnow; ***D:*** Ulli Lommel; ***W:*** Kurt Raab; ***C:*** Jurgen Jurges; ***M:*** Peer Raben.

Tennessee 🦴🦴 **2008 (R)** Familiar brotherly love, road trip story. Years ago, Carter Armstrong (Rothenberg) left home with his younger brother Ellis to escape their abusive, alcoholic father Roy (Sage). Carter himself has turned into a bitter, hard-drinking cab driver still looking after the sweet-natured Ellis (Peck). Ellis has been diagnosed with leukemia, so Carter reluctantly agrees to return to Tennessee to see if Roy is a bone-marrow match. When their car breaks down, waitress Krystal (Carey), who's in an abusive marriage to state trooper Frank (Reddick), helps them out and then runs away to join them on the road, with Frank in pursuit. Then the movie really gets sentimental. Rothenberg offers the strongest performance although Carey has a modest appeal. **99m/C; On Demand.** Adam Rothenberg; Mariah Carey; Lance Reddick; Bill Sage; Michelle Harris; Ethan Peck; ***D:*** Aaron Woodley; ***W:*** Russell Schaumburg; ***C:*** David (Robert) A. Greene; ***M:*** Mario Grigorov.

Tennessee's Partner 🦴🦴 **1955** Enjoyable, unexceptional buddy Western. Reagan intervenes in an argument and becomes Payne's pal. Adapted from a story by Bret Harte. **87m/C; VHS, DVD.** Ronald Reagan; Rhonda Fleming; John Payne; ***D:*** Allan Dwan; ***W:*** D.D. Beauchamp; Milton Krims; Teddi Sherman; G. Graham Baker; ***C:*** John Alton; ***M:*** Louis Forbes.

Tension 🦴🦴 **1950** Nice guy Warren Quimby (Basehart) has modest ambitions: a steady job, a house, and a loving wife. Well, two out of three...seems sultry Mrs. Q (Totter) is bored, so she finds a wealthy beachboy brute (Gough) to satisfy her itch. When Warren finds out, he plots to assume a new identity, kill the interloper, and get the missus back. But things don't work out as intended—putting Warren in the crosshairs of cynical detective Bonnabel (Sullivan). **95m/B; DVD.** Richard Basehart; Audrey Totter; Barry Sullivan; Cyd Charisse; Lloyd Gough; William Conrad; ***D:*** John Berry; ***W:*** Allen Rivkin; ***C:*** Harry Stradling, Sr.; ***M:*** Andre Previn.

Tentacles **WOOF!** *Tentacoli* **1977 (PG)** Cheesy Italian version of "Jaws" lacking only the suspense and cogent storytelling. Huston slums as the investigator charged with finding the octopus gone mad, while Fonda collects check and makes a quick exit. Hopkins is in charge of the killer whales that save the day. You'll cheer when Winters is devoured by sea pest. From the director of an "Exorcist" rip-off, "Beyond the Door" (that's not a recommendation). **90m/C; VHS, DVD, Blu-Ray.** *IT* John Huston; Shelley Winters; Bo Hopkins; Henry Fonda; Cesare Danova; Delia Boccardo; Alan Boyd; Claude Akins; ***D:*** Ovidio G. Assonitis; ***W:*** Steven W. Carabatsos; Tito Carpi; Sonia Molteni; ***C:*** Roberto D'Ettorre Piazzoli; ***M:*** Stelvio Cipriani.

10th & Wolf 🦴🦴 **2006 (R)** In 1991, ex-Marine Tommy Santoro (Marsden) returns to his Pittsburgh 'hood, and finds out that his cousin Joey (Ribisi) and younger bro Vincent (Renfro) are heavily involved in the family's mob business. Tommy cuts a deal with FBI agent Horvath (Dennehy) to wear a wire and get the goods on the deal between Joey and the drug lord who's moving into their territory. Lots of gangland cliches. **107m/C; DVD.** James Marsden; Giovanni Ribisi; Brad Renfro; Brian Dennehy; Piper Perabo; Lesley Ann Warren; Dash Mihok; Dennis Hopper; Francesco Salvi; Tommy Lee; Val Kilmer; ***D:*** Robert Moresco; ***W:*** Robert Moresco; ***C:*** Alex Nepomniaschy; ***M:*** Aaron Zigman.

Tenth Avenue Angel 🦴🦴 ½ **1947** Depression-set family drama with O'Brien shoulderig the title role. Young Flavia Mills, who lives in a tenement along New York's Tenth Avenue, tries to brighten the lives of her hard-luck neighbors. Her trusting nature is shaken when she learns her family was telling white lies about the whereabouts of Steve, her Aunt Susan's fiance, who wasn't on a long trip but in prison, and who's now trying to go straight. Other troubles follow, but the Christmas ending should set things right. **74m/B; DVD.** Margaret O'Brien; Angela Lansbury; George Murphy; Phyllis Thaxter; Warner Anderson; ***D:*** Roy Rowland; ***W:*** Harry Ruskin; Eleanore Griffin; ***C:*** Robert L. Surtees; ***M:*** Rudolph Kopp.

The Tenth Circle 🦴🦴 **2008** Lifetime cable movie based on the Jodi Picoult novel, the title of which refers to Dante's circles of hell. College lit professor Laura Stone (Preston) and her husband Daniel (Eldard) are caught in a nightmare when their lovesick 14-year-old daughter Trixie (Robertson) gets jilted by her boyfriend (Johnston). She then says that he date raped her—with her accusation throwing their small town and all their lives into chaos. **89m/C; DVD.** Kelly Preston; Ron Eldard; Brittany Robertson; Michael Riley; Jamie Johnston; ***D:*** Peter Markle; ***W:*** Maria Nation; ***C:*** Joel Ransom; ***M:*** Velton Ray Bunch. **CABLE**

The 10th Kingdom 🦴🦴 ½ **2000** Overly long but visually impressive fairytale extravganza. New Yorkers Virginia (Williams) and her father Tony (Larroquette) find themselves magically transported into an alternate universe that consists of nine kingdoms filled with trolls, evil queens, human/beast hybrids, and all sorts of adventures. Their quest to return home (to what they learn is their own tenth kingdom) is consistently thwarted until they clear up a little good vs. evil battle that's raging. **350m/C; VHS, DVD, Blu-Ray.** Kimberly Williams; John Larroquette; Scott Cohen; Ann-Margret; Rutger Hauer; Camryn Manheim; Ed O'Neill; Dianne Wiest; Daniel Lapaine; Dawnn Lewis; Jimmy Nail; Warwick Davis; Timothy Bateson; Robert Hardy; Aden (John) Gillett; Moira Lister; ***D:*** David Carson; Herbert Wise; ***C:*** Lawrence Jones; Chris Howard; ***M:*** Anne Dudley. **TV**

The Tenth Man 🦴🦴 ½ **1988** Hopkins stars as a wealthy French lawyer, captured by the Nazis and sentenced to death. He discovers a fellow prisoner who is willing to take his place in exchange for Hopkins's wealth going to support the man's family. After his release, Hopkins returns to his old home, now occupied by the dead man's family, but doesn't reveal his true identity. When an imposter appears, claiming to be Hopkins, another twist is added. Slow-going but the usual excellent performances by Hopkins and Jacobi. Based on a novella by Graham Greene. **99m/C; VHS, DVD.** Anthony Hopkins; Kristin Scott Thomas; Derek Jacobi; Cyril Cusack; Brenda Bruce; Paul Rogers; ***D:*** Jack Gold. **TV**

10th Victim 🦴🦴🦴 *La Decima Vittima; La Dixieme Victime* **1965** Sci-fi cult film set in the 21st century has Mastroianni and Andress pursuing one another in a futuristic society where legalized murder is used as the means of population control. Intriguing movie where Andress kills with a double-barreled bra, the characters hang out at the Club Masoch, and comic books are considered literature. Based on "The Seventh Victim" by Robert Sheckley. **92m/C; VHS, DVD, Blu-Ray.** *IT* Ursula Andress; Marcello Mastroianni; Elsa Martinelli; Salvo Randone; Massimo Serato; ***D:*** Elio Petri; ***W:*** Elio Petri; Tonino Guerra; Ennio Flaiano; Giorgio Salvioni; ***C:*** Gianni Di Venanzo; ***M:*** Piero Piccioni.

10,000 Km 🦴🦴 ½ **2014 (R)** Alexandra and Sergi are a happy couple in Barcelona, Spain, planning the next phase of their life. Sergi gets offered a year-long residency in Los Angeles, but Alexandra can't go with him. Modern technology, like Skype, allows for more long-distance connectivity, but the difficulties of the distance (the source of the film's title) prove more relationship-damaging than they predicted. Writer/director Marques-Marcet's romantic drama focuses solely on these two characters and their honest pain in maintaining love across two sides of the planet. **98m/C; DVD, Streaming.** *SP* Natalia Tena; David Verdaguer; ***D:*** Carlos Marques-Marcet; ***W:*** Carlos Marques-Marcet; ***C:*** Dagmar Weaver-Madsen.

Tenure 🦴🦴 **2009 (R)** English professor Charlie Thurber (Wilson) is a nice guy and good teacher but he's suddenly upstaged for a tenure position by bright new hire Elaine Grasso (Mol), who actually publishes (a big university deal). Charlie's also dealing with his cantankerous father William (Gunton), a retired Yale University prof who gives his son an inferiority complex despite his own deteriorating mental health. Comfy film but you can easily figure out where the plot is headed. **89m/C; DVD.** Rosemarie DeWitt; Luke Wilson; Gretchen Mol; Bob Gunton; David Koechner; Sasha Alexander; Michael Cudlitz; William Bogert; ***D:*** Mark Million; ***W:*** Mark Million; ***C:*** Steve Yedlin; ***M:*** John Frizzell.

Teorema 🦴🦴 **1968** Scathing condemnation of bourgeois complacency. Stamp, either a devil or a god, mysteriously appears and enters into the life of a well-to-do Milanese family and raises each member's spirituality by sleeping with them. Ultimately, the experience leads to tragedy. In Italian with English subtitles. **98m/C; VHS, DVD, Blu-Ray.** *IT* Terence Stamp; Silvana Mangano; Massimo Girotti; Anna Wiazemsky; Laura Betti; Andres Jose Cruz; ***D:*** Pier Paolo Pasolini; ***M:*** Ennio Morricone.

Tequila Body Shots 🦴 **1999 (R)** Low-budget nightmare is suffered not just by the portentously named main character, Johnny Orpheus (Lawrence). Johnny is convinced by some buddies to attend a Day of the Dead party held on a Mexican beach where he imbibes some whacked Tequila that enables him to read women's thoughts and experience some afterlife horrors, courtesy of evil spirit Hector (Moreno). Turns out Hector is after his reincarnated wife who just happens to be the girl (Mouser) that Johnny is interested in. Oh yeah, and its all played for laughs (but you won't be). **94m/C; VHS, DVD.** Joseph Lawrence; Dru Mouser; Rene L. Moreno; Nathan Anderson; Josh Marchette; Jennifer Lyons; Henry Darrow; ***D:*** Tony Shyu; ***W:*** Tony Shyu; ***C:*** Lawrence Schweich; ***M:*** Shayne Fair; Larry Herbstritt.

Tequila Sunrise 🦴🦴 ½ **1988 (R)** Towne's twisting film about two lifelong friends and a beautiful woman. Gibson is a (supposedly) retired drug dealer afraid of losing custody of his son to his nagging ex-wife. Russell is the cop and old friend who's trying to get the lowdown on a drug shipment coming in from Mexico. Pfeiffer runs the poshest restaurant on the coast and is actively pursued by both men. Questions cloud the plot and confuse the viewer; loaded with double-crosses, intrigue and surprises around every corner, still the photogenic leads are pleasant to watch. Steamy love scene between Pfeiffer and Gibson. **116m/C; VHS, DVD, Blu-Ray.** Mel Gibson; Kurt Russell; Michelle Pfeiffer; Raul Julia; Arliss Howard; Arye Gross; J.T. Walsh; Ann Magnuson; ***D:*** Robert Towne; ***W:*** Robert Towne; ***C:*** Conrad L. Hall; ***M:*** Dave Grusin.

Term Life 🦴 **2016 (R)** The downward trajectory of Vince Vaughn's career appears to have no bottom as evidenced by this horrendous thriller, directed by his buddy Peter Billingsley. With a laughable hairpiece, Vaughn plays tough guy Nick Barrow, who arranges heists. When one of his deals goes horrendously wrong, several groups have it out for Nick, leading this wannabe thug to buy a life insurance policy to help provide for his daughter Cate (Steinfeld). Now he just has to survive long enough for it to go into effect. And you have to stay awake through the entire movie. Good luck. Based on the graphic novel by Nick Thornborrow. **93m/C; DVD, Blu-Ray.** Hailee Steinfeld; Bill Paxton; Jon Favreau; Taraji P. Henson; Vince Vaughn; ***D:*** Peter Billingsley; ***W:*** A.J. Lieberman; ***C:*** Roberto Schaefer; ***M:*** Dave Porter.

Term of Trial 🦴🦴 **1963** Typical '60s Brit 'kitchen sink' drama stars a miscast Olivier who is too dynamic an actor to convincingly play a milquetoast character. Alcoholic schoolteacher Graham Weir is married to contemptuous Anna (Signoret), who constantly taunts him for his lack of backbone. He teaches at a tough inner-city school in Northern England where he's harassed by school tough Mitchell (Stamp) and teenaged student Shirley (Miles) has a crush on him. Humiliated when Graham rejects her advances, Shirley tells her parents Graham assaulted her and he goes to trial. Miles and Stamp make their film debuts. **113m/B; DVD.** *GB* Laurence Olivier; Simone Signoret; Sarah Miles; Hugh Griffith; Terence Stamp; Roland Culver; Thora Hird; Norman Bird; Dudley Foster; ***D:*** Peter Glenville; ***W:*** Peter Glenville; James Barlow; Oswald Morris; ***M:*** Jean-Michel Demase.

The Terminal 🦴🦴 **2004 (PG-13)** Viktor Navorski (Hanks), traveling to New York, must stay in the airport's international zone because his home country has fallen into civil war and technically no longer exists. With plucky resolve Navorski creates a makeshift life for himself while winning allies among the terminal's workforce. Central players are good: Tucci as cruel airport overseer; Zeta-Jones as love interest; and Hanks always appealing as the confused but intrepid traveler. Often clever, but basically cotton candy: sweet, but way too fluffy. Based on the true story of an Iranian immigrant who got stuck in Charles de Gaulle Airport in Paris. **128m/C; VHS, DVD, Blu-Ray.** Tom Hanks; Catherine Zeta-Jones; Stanley Tucci; Chi McBride; Diego Luna; Barry (Shabaka) Henley; Zoe Saldana; Eddie Jones; Michael Nouri; Kumar Pallana; Jude Ciccolella; Corey Reynolds; Guillermo Diaz; Rini Bell; Stephen Mendel; Valery (Valeri Nikolayev) Nikolaev; ***D:*** Steven Spielberg; ***W:*** Andrew Niccol; Jeff Nathanson; Sacha Gervasi; ***C:*** Janusz Kaminski; ***M:*** John Williams.

Terminal 🦴🦴 **2018** Diner waitress-stripper-assassin Annie (Robbie) promises the mysterious Mr. Franklin (Myers) that she will kill his hitmen so she can work for him. Two of Franklin's finest, Vince (Fletcher) and Alfred (Irons), wait for a job to take place nearby, and she manipulates them both at the diner and the strip club. Annie also becomes entangled with English professor Bill (Pegg) after his suicide plan fails. When Bill visits Annie's diner, she promises to help him end his life. Soulless, overly complicated debut from director/writer Stein. **95m/C; DVD, Blu-Ray, Streaming.** *IR UK US HU CH* Margot Robbie; Simon Pegg; Mike Myers; Dexter Fletcher; Max Irons; ***D:*** Vaughn Stein; ***W:*** Vaughn Stein; ***C:*** Christopher Ross; ***M:*** Tony Clarke; Rupert Gregson-Williams.

Terminal Error 🦴 *Peace Virus* **2002 (PG-13)** Disgruntled businessman cripples his old company with a computer virus to settle the score but the bug happens to spill out into the city and spells doom unless the CEO and his smarty-pants son can stop it. **90m/C; VHS, DVD.** Robert Casey; Marina Sirtis; Michael Nouri; Timothy Busfield; ***D:*** John Murlowski; ***C:*** Philip Lee; ***M:*** James T. Sale. **VIDEO**

Terminal Force 🦴 *Rescue Force* **1988 (R)** Stupid, poorly executed story of kidnapping and the mob. So bad it never saw the inside of a theatre; went straight to video. **83m/C; VHS, DVD.** Troy Donahue; Richard Harrison; Dawn Wildsmith; ***D:*** Fred Olen Ray. **VIDEO**

Terminal Impact 🦴🦴 **1995 (R)** Bounty hunters Saint (Zagarino) and Max (Genesse) agree to a high-paying assignment at Delta Tech Labs without asking any questions. They discover that the lab's chairman Sheen

(Roberts) is messing around with DNA and has been implanting insect DNA into unwilling human subjects, which turns them into killer cyborgs as well. **94m/C; VHS, DVD.** Bryan Genesse; Frank Zagarino; Jenny (Jennifer) McShane; Ian Roberts; ***D:*** Yossi Wein; ***W:*** Jeff Albert; Dennis Dimster-Denk; ***C:*** Rod Stewart.

Terminal Invasion **2002 (R)** Cheeseball fun courtesy of the Sci-Fi Channel and Bruce Campbell, who doesn't take himself or the material seriously. Anxious passengers are stuck at a rural airport with no outside communications because of a blizzard. Then two guards show up with convicted murderer Jack Edwards (Campbell) after their transport van is in an accident. But the real problem is that some of the passengers aren't really what they seem (as in human). **84m/C; DVD.** Bruce Campbell; Chase Masterson; C. David Johnson; Sarah Lafleur; Andrew Tarbet; Kedar Brown; ***D:*** Sean S. Cunningham; ***W:*** Lewis Abernathy; John Jarrell; ***C:*** Rudolf Blahacek; ***M:*** Harry Mandredini. **CABLE**

Terminal Island ½ **1973 (R)** Tough southern California penal colony is crowded with inmates from death row. When prison becomes coed, violence breaks out. Exploitative and unappealing. **88m/C; VHS, DVD.** Phyllis E. Davis; Tom Selleck; Don Marshall; Ena Hartman; Marta Kristen; ***D:*** Stephanie Rothman.

Terminal Justice: Cybertech P.D. ½ **1995 (R)** Cop Bobby Chase (Lamas) is assigned to protect VR sex babe, Pamela Travis (Wuhrer). Turns out wealthy VR game manufacturer, Reginald Matthews (Sarandon) has teamed up with sicko doctor, Deacon (Vivyan), to clone beautiful women so they can be used in snuff films. And Matthews wants Pam's DNA to begin the process. **95m/C; VHS, DVD.** Lorenzo Lamas; Chris Sarandon; Kari Wuhrer; Peter Coyote; ***D:*** Rick King; ***W:*** Frederick Bailey; ***C:*** Chris Holmes, Jr.; ***M:*** Michael Hoenig. **VIDEO**

The Terminal Man ½ **1974 (R)** A slick, visually compelling adaptation of the Michael Crichton novel. A scientist plagued by violent mental disorders has a computer-controlled regulator implanted in his brain. The computer malfunctions and he starts a murdering spree. Futuristic vision of man-machine symbiosis gone awry. Well acted, but still falls short of the novel. **107m/C; VHS, DVD.** George Segal; Joan Hackett; Jill Clayburgh; Richard Dysart; James B. Sikking; Norman Burton; ***D:*** Mike Hodges; ***W:*** Mike Hodges.

Terminal Rush **1996 (R)** Army Ranger Johnny Price (Wilson) is thrown out of the service after being framed for a crime. But when terrorists (led by Piper) take over Hoover Dam, Price is the one person with the necessary skills to thwart this vindictive madman. **94m/C; VHS, DVD.** Don "The Dragon" Wilson; Roddy Piper; ***D:*** Damian Lee. **VIDEO**

Terminal Velocity **1994 (PG-13)** Skydiving instructor Ditch Brodie (Sheen) thinks he sees student Chris Morrow (Kinski) plummet to her death, only it turns out she's not dead and certainly not a beginner. Upon further investigation, he finds the usual web of international intrigue descending upon him, and that the KGB definitely wants him to mind his own business. Still, he pushes on. Another no-brainer actioner with few surprises satisfies the guilty pleasures of action addicts only. **132m/C; VHS, DVD, Blu-Ray.** Charlie Sheen; Nastassja Kinski; James Gandolfini; Christopher McDonald; Melvin Van Peebles; ***D:*** Deran Sarafian; ***W:*** David N. Twohy; ***C:*** Oliver Wood; ***M:*** Joel McNeely.

Termination Man **1997 (R)** Serbian terrorist blackmails NATO and the United Nations with a nerve gas threat and genetically enhanced agent Dylan Pope (Railsback), who may be immune to the gas, must lead a covert squad to save the day. Action by the numbers. **92m/C; VHS, DVD.** Steve Railsback; Athena Massey; James Farentino; Eb Lottimer; ***D:*** Fred Gallo; ***W:*** Fred Gallo; Charles Philip Moore; ***C:*** Eugeny Guslinsky; ***M:*** Deddy Tzur. **VIDEO**

Termination Point **2007 (PG-13)** The military has been working on a secret time travel project but head scientist Dr. Daniel Winter (Phillips) becomes convinced the technology is too dangerous to entrust to them. So he steals it, and Special Agent Caleb Smith (Priestley) is set to track him down before Winter can alter the course of history. **89m/C; DVD.** Jason Priestley; Lou Diamond Phillips; Garwin Sanford; Gary Hudson; Stefanie von Pfetten; Michael Eklund; ***D:*** Jason Bourque; ***W:*** Peter Sullivan; ***C:*** C. Kim Miles; ***M:*** Kyle Kenneth Batter; Gregory Tripi. **VIDEO**

The Terminator **1984 (R)** Futuristic cyborg (Schwarzenegger, suitably robotic and menacing) is sent to present-day Earth. His job: kill the woman, Sarah Connor (Hamilton), who will conceive the child destined to become the great liberator and archenemy of the Earth's future rulers. The cyborg is also pursued by another futuristic visitor, Kyle Reese (Biehn), who falls in love with the intended victim. Cameron's pacing is just right in this exhilarating, explosive thriller which displays Arnie as one cold-blooded villain who utters a now famous line: "I'll be back." Followed by "Terminator 2: Judgment Day." **108m/C; VHS, DVD, Blu-Ray.** Arnold Schwarzenegger; Michael Biehn; Linda Hamilton; Paul Winfield; Lance Henriksen; Bill Paxton; Rick Rossovich; Dick Miller; Earl Boen; ***D:*** James Cameron; ***W:*** James Cameron; ***M:*** Brad Fiedel. Natl. Film Reg. '08.

Terminator 2: Judgment Day ½ **1991 (R)** He said he'd be back and he is, programmed to protect the boy who will be mankind's post-nuke resistance leader. But the T-1000, a shape-changing, ultimate killing machine, is also on the boy's trail. Twice the mayhem, five times the special effects, ten times the budget of the first, but without Arnold it'd be half the movie. The word hasn't been invented to describe the special effects, particularly THE scariest nuclear holocaust scene yet. Worldwide megahit, but the $100 million budget nearly ruined the studio; Arnold accepted his $12 million in the form of a jet. **139m/C; VHS, DVD, Blu-Ray.** Arnold Schwarzenegger; Linda Hamilton; Edward Furlong; Robert Patrick; Earl Boen; Joe Morton; ***D:*** James Cameron; ***W:*** James Cameron; ***C:*** Adam Greenberg; ***M:*** Brad Fiedel. Oscars '91: Makeup, Sound, Sound FX Editing, Visual FX; MTV Movie Awards '92: Action Seq., Breakthrough Perf. (Furlong), Female Perf. (Hamilton), Film, Male Perf. (Schwarzenegger), Most Desirable Female (Hamilton).

Terminator 3: Rise of the Machines **2003 (R)** Satisfying third chapter does not suffer from the absence of James Cameron or Linda Hamilton. This time around, the new bad Terminator is the female T-X (Loken) but the job is the same—kill future resistance leader John Connor (Stahl). Arnold's again sent back to protect him, as well as future cohort Kate (Danes). Solid script provides plenty of action, some inside humor, and (perhaps most importantly) a logical progression from the first two movies. Stahl does a good job as Connor, and Arnold proves he's still got the goods after a few disappointing outings. The special effects are, thankfully, seamless enough not to distract from the action at hand. **110m/C; VHS, DVD, Blu-Ray, UMD, HD-DVD.** Arnold Schwarzenegger; Nick Stahl; Claire Danes; Kristanna Loken; David Andrews; Mark Famiglietti; ***D:*** Jonathan Mostow; ***W:*** John Brancato; Michael Ferris; ***C:*** Don Burgess; ***M:*** Marco Beltrami.

Terminator: Dark Fate ½ **2019 (R)** Sarah Connor (Hamilton) makes her glorious return in this final installment of the Terminator franchise. Taking place 27 years after the second movie, Connor teams up with a hybrid cyborg-human (Davis) and her old frenemy T-800 (Schwarzenegger) to save Dani Ramos from the next-generation baddie REV-9. The plot is familiar, but the nostalgia factor elevates the flick as a satisfactory conclusion to the franchise. Hasta la vista, er...adios, baby. **128m/C; DVD, Blu-Ray.** *CH US* Linda Hamilton; Arnold Schwarzenegger; Mackenzie Davis; Natalia Reyes; Gabriel Luna; ***D:*** Tim Miller; ***W:*** David S. Goyer; Justin Rhodes; Billy Ray; ***C:*** Ken Seng; ***M:*** Junkie XL.

Terminator Genisys **2015 (PG-13)** Another failed reboot of James Cameron's hit franchise sees the return of Ah-nuld to a franchise that has lost all of its magic. John Connor (Clarke) sends Kyle Reese (Courtney) back to 1984 to protect Sarah Connor (Clarke), just as in the first film, but created an alternate timeline in the process, totally changing the future and turning Schwarzenegger's character into a Guardian, while also producing new enemies. Someone should have terminated this film for what it does to the legacy of the first two films. **119m/C; DVD, Blu-Ray, Streaming.** Emilia Clarke; Jason Clarke; Jai Courtney; Arnold Schwarzenegger; J.K. Simmons; ***D:*** Alan Taylor; ***W:*** Patrick Lussier; Laeta Kalogridis; ***C:*** Kramer Morgenthau; ***M:*** Lorne Balfe.

Terminator Salvation **2009 (PG-13)** Yeah, we know that a PG-13 rating is more 'family' accessible but the studio should have gone for an 'R' and really made this 4th installment a Terminator movie. Bale goes from brooding Batman to brooding John Connor and is once again upstaged by a supporting performer. In this case, it's Worthington. Set in a post-apocalyptic 2018, Skynet has just about completed its quest to get rid of the human population. Connor has to make sure to protect Kyle Reese (Yelchin)?well if you don't already know who and how things fit together, this isn't the time for explanations. Director McG manages that metallic rubble look and can stage the prerequisite chases, crashes, and explosions with intensity. **115m/C; Blu-Ray, On Demand.** Christian Bale; Sam Worthington; Anton Yelchin; Bryce Dallas Howard; Moon Bloodgood; Common; Helena Bonham Carter; Michael Ironside; Jane Alexander; Jadagrace; ***D:*** McG; ***W:*** Michael Ferris; John Brancato; ***C:*** Shane Hurlbut; ***M:*** Danny Elfman.

The Terminators **2009** Worth a chuckle for Asylum studio's blatant rip-off of "The Terminator" and its various sequels. A computerized military system on an orbiting space station goes haywire, nukes some cities, and then the cyborgs meant to aid and defend humans instead start eliminating them. A group of survivors decide to somehow get to the space station so they can reset the system. **90m/C; DVD.** A. Martinez; Jeremy London; Paul Logan; Lauren Walsh; Stephen Blackehart; Sara Tomko; Krystle Connor; Dustin Harnish; ***D:*** Xavier Puslowski; ***W:*** David Michael Latt; Jose Prendes; ***C:*** Mark Atkins; ***M:*** Chris Ridenhour. **VIDEO**

Terminus ½ **2016 (R)** A science fiction drama centered on the power of belief and one man's quest to save humankind. One day, David Chamberlain (Koutrae) is driving when the light from a falling meteor blinds him and causes him to have a massive car accident. As he goes missing for two days, he discovers an organism from out of this world that may include the secret to human life. Reported missing by his family, David is unharmed when found by his daughter Annabelle (Appleton), who questions her father's state of mind. After his return, David believes he now has a new, alien-influenced purposed to his life, though his daughter and federal authorities believe otherwise. Driven by dark visions, David focuses on convincing his daughter of his sanity and finishing his purpose before stopped by federal agents and the destruction of the world. **94m/C; DVD, Streaming, Download.** Jai Koutrae; Kendra Appleton; Todd Lasance; Bren Foster; William Emmons; ***D:*** Marc Furmie; ***W:*** Marc Furmie; Shiyan Zheng; Gabriel Dowrick; ***C:*** Kieran Fowler; ***M:*** Brian Cachia.

Terms of Endearment **1983 (PG)** A weeper following the changing relationship between a young woman and her mother, over a 30-year period. Beginning as a comedy, turning serious as the years go by, this was Brooks' debut as screenwriter and director. Superb supporting cast headed by Nicholson's slyly charming neighbor/astronaut, with stunning performances by Winger and MacLaine as the two women who often know and love each other too well. Adapted from Larry McMurtry's novel. **132m/C; VHS, DVD, Blu-Ray.** Shirley MacLaine; Jack Nicholson; Debra Winger; John Lithgow; Jeff Daniels; Danny DeVito; ***D:*** James L. Brooks; ***W:*** James L. Brooks; ***C:*** Andrzej Bartkowiak; ***M:*** Michael Gore. Oscars '83: Actress (MacLaine), Adapt. Screenplay, Director (Brooks), Film, Support. Actor (Nicholson); Directors Guild '83: Director (Brooks); Golden Globes '84: Actress--Drama (MacLaine), Film--Drama, Screenplay, Support. Actor (Nicholson); L.A. Film Critics '83: Actress (MacLaine), Director (Brooks), Film, Screenplay, Support. Actor (Nicholson); Natl. Bd. of Review '83: Actress (MacLaine), Director (Brooks), Support. Actor (Nicholson); N.Y. Film Critics '83: Actress (MacLaine), Film, Support. Actor (Nicholson); Natl. Soc. Film Critics '83: Actress (Winger), Support. Actor (Nicholson); Writers Guild '83: Adapt. Screenplay.

Terranova **1991** Six characters in search of themselves, with the profound changes in their lives coming through an unlikely friendship. Rosetta is the poor matriarch of an Italian immigrant family while wealthy Noemi is an artistocratic landowner. But they share similiar frustrations and the desire to change their lives. Set in a rural Venezuelan town in the 1950s; Spanish with subtitles. **96m/C; VHS, DVD.** *IT* Marisa Laurito; Mimi Lazo; Antonio Banderas; Patrick Bauchau; Massimo Bonetti; Nathalia Martinez; ***D:*** Calogero Salvo.

Terri **2011 (R)** Gentle and quirky coming of age teen drama. Terri (Wysocki) is a large, socially awkward teen misfit/loner, living with his ailing Uncle James (Bratton), who's taken to showing up at high school in pajamas. Recognizing a troubled soul, vice principal Mr. Fitzgerald (Reilly) arranges for counseling sessions but, more importantly, takes Terri under his own odd-man-out wing. Director Jacobs doesn't push but lets the constantly-in-flux emotions of his characters carry the movie along. **105m/C; DVD, Blu-Ray.** John C. Reilly; Jacob Wysocki; Creed Bratton; Olivia Crocicchia; Bridger Zadina; ***D:*** Azazel Jacobs; ***W:*** Patrick DeWitt; ***C:*** Tobias Datum; ***M:*** Mandy Hoffman.

Terrified ½ **1994 (R)** Erotic thriller about a nympho being stalked by a mystery assailant. Genuinely creepy. **90m/C; VHS, DVD.** Heather Graham; Lisa Zane; Rustam Branaman; Tom Breznahan; Max Perlich; Balthazar Getty; Richard Lynch; Don Calfa; ***D:*** James Merendino; ***W:*** James Merendino; Megan Heath.

The Terror *Lady of the Shadows* **1963** A lieutenant in Napoleon's army chases a lovely maiden and finds himself trapped in a creepy castle by a mad baron. Movie legend has it Corman directed the movie in three days as the sets (from his previous movie "The Raven") were being torn down around them. **81m/C; VHS, DVD, Blu-Ray.** Boris Karloff; Jack Nicholson; Sandra Knight; Dick Miller; Dorothy Neumann; Jonathan Haze; ***D:*** Jack Nicholson; Roger Corman; Jack Hill; Francis Ford Coppola; Monte Hellman; Dennis Jacob; ***W:*** Roger Corman; Leo Gordon; Jack Hill; ***C:*** John M. Nickolaus, Jr.; ***M:*** Ronald Stein.

The Terror WOOF! **1979 (R)** After 100 years, a man reveals in a film that his family killed a witch. Friends who see the film are attacked by supernatural forces. Originally double-billed with "Dracula's Dog." **86m/C; VHS, DVD, Blu-Ray.** John Nolan; Carolyn Courage; James Aubrey; Glynis Barber; Sarah Keller; Tricia Walsh; ***D:*** Norman J. Warren; ***W:*** Lester Young; David McGillivray; ***C:*** Lester Young; ***M:*** Ivor Slaney.

Terror Among Us ½ **1981** Newly-paroled serial rapist Delbert Ramsey (Shackleford) is determined to track down and punish the five women who testified against him. Police Sgt. Tom Stockwell (Meredith) and parole officer Connie Paxton (Salt) want to get to Delbert before any violence occurs. **95m/C; DVD.** Don Meredith; Ted Shackleford; Jennifer Salt; Jane Badler; Tracy Reed; Sarah Purcell; Pat Klous; Kim Lankford; Sharon Spelman; ***D:*** Paul Krasny; ***W:*** Dallas Barnes; Joanne Barnes; ***C:*** Robert B. Hauser; ***M:*** Allyn Ferguson. **TV**

Terror at Red Wolf Inn *Club Dead; Terror House; The Folks at Red Wolf Inn* **1972 (R)** Young woman wins a vacation; finds she's been invited for dinner, so to speak. Not campy enough to overcome stupidity. **90m/C; VHS, DVD.** Linda Gillin; Arthur Space; John Neilson; Mary Jackson; Janet Wood; Margaret Avery; ***D:*** Bud Townsend; ***W:*** Allen Actor.

Terror at Tenkiller **1986** Two girls vacationing in the mountains are seemingly surrounded by a rash of mysterious murders. **87m/C; VHS, DVD.** Mike Wiles; Stacey Logan; ***D:*** Ken Meyer; ***W:*** Claudia Meyer; ***C:*** Steven Wacks; ***M:*** Robert Farrar. **VIDEO**

Terror Beneath the Sea ½ *Kaitei Daisenso; Water Cyborgs* **1966** A mad scientist wants to rule the world with his cyborgs. American and Japanese scientists unite to fight him. Fine special effects, especially the transformation from human to monster. **85m/C; VHS, DVD.** *JP* Sonny Chiba; Peggy Neal; Franz Gruber; Gunther Braun; Andrew Hughes; Mike Daneen; ***D:*** Hajime Sato.

Terror Creatures from the Grave ♂ **1966** Husband summons medieval plague victims to rise from the grave to drop in on his unfaithful wife. Should've been better. **85m/C; VHS, DVD.** *IT* Barbara Steele; Riccardo Garrone; Walter Brandi; ***D:*** Ralph Zucker.

Terror House WOOF! **1997** There's this creepy house, see, that's got an ugly family secret—in this case it's half-human and lives on warm blood. So these three college students think they have a chance at some big money if they can stay in the house, and they have visions of this beautiful woman, and night's coming, and the thing in the basement is hungry. You get the idea. **80m/C; VHS, DVD.** Jon McBride; Mark Alan Polonia; Bob Daniels; Clyde Burroughs; Holly Harrington; ***D:*** Jon McBride; Mark Alan Polonia; John Polonia; ***W:*** Mark Alan Polonia; ***C:*** Arthur Daniels.

Terror in a Texas Town ♂♂ ½ **1958** George Hansen (Hayden) is a Swedish seaman who returns home to discover his farmer father has been gunned down by the greedy Johnny Crale (Young), who's after the land so he can drill for oil. So Hansen's out for revenge. There's a final showdown that not only includes six-shooters but a harpoon. **120m/B; VHS, DVD, Blu-Ray.** Sterling Hayden; Nedrick Young; Sebastian Cabot; Victor Millan; ***D:*** Joseph H. Lewis; ***W:*** Dalton Trumbo; ***C:*** Ray Rennahan; ***M:*** Gerald Fried.

Terror in the Haunted House ♂♂ ½ *My World Dies Screaming* **1958** Newlyweds move into an old house. The bride remembers it from her nightmares. First release featured the first use of Psychorama, a technique in which scary words or advertising messages were flashed on the screen for a fraction of a second—just long enough to cause subliminal response. The technique was banned later in the year. **90m/C; VHS, DVD.** Gerald Mohr; Cathy O'Donnell; William Ching; John Qualen; Barry Bernard; ***D:*** Harold Daniels; ***W:*** Robert C. Dennis; ***C:*** Frederick E. West; ***M:*** Darrell Calker.

Terror in the Jungle ♂ **1968 (PG)** Plane crashes in Peruvian wilds and young boy survivor meets Jivaro Indians who think he's a god. Much struggling to survive and battling with horrible script. **95m/C; VHS, DVD.** Jimmy Angle; Fawn Silver; ***D:*** Tom De Simone; ***M:*** Les Baxter.

Terror in the Mall ♂ **1998** Predictable and cheesy TV disaster flick. A desperate bank-robber killer is trapped along with some shoppers during the pre-opening of a new shopping mall. Torrential rains have burst the Pine Valley Dam sending walls of water cascading through the buildings (and naturally the flood and the killer aren't the only things to worry about). **90m/C; DVD.** Rob(ert) Estes; Shannon Sturges; Kai Wiesinger; David Soul; Angeline Ball; Terence Maynard; Danny (Daniel) Webb; George Anton; ***D:*** Norberto Barba; ***W:*** Dan Gordon; John Mandel; ***C:*** Cristiano Pogany; ***M:*** Christopher Franke. **TV**

Terror Inside WOOF! **2008** Grade-Z wannabe horror. Well driller Joe has been hired to excavate mystical mud from an ancient burial mound in a backwater Florida burg. Anyone the mud (which contains a virus) oozes on becomes addicted to pain and the townspeople start doing really icky things to get that pain high. Feldman is boring as a government wonk in love with a local waitress who's an early victim. **90m/C; DVD.** Corey Feldman; Tanya Memme; Joe Abby; Susie Feldman; ***D:*** Joe G. Lender; ***W:*** Joe G. Lender; ***C:*** Flip Minott; ***M:*** Jason Solowsky. **VIDEO**

Terror Is a Man ♂♂ *Blood Creature* **1959** A mad scientist attempts to turn a panther into a man on a secluded island. Early Filipino horror attempt inspired by H.G. Wells' "The Island of Doctor Moreau." **89m/B; VHS, DVD, Blu-Ray.** *PH* Francis Lederer; Greta Thyssen; Richard Derr; Oscar Keesee; ***D:*** Gerardo (Gerry) De Leon; ***W:*** Harry Paul Harber; ***C:*** Emmanuel I. Rojas; ***M:*** Ariston Auelino.

Terror of Mechagodzilla ♂ ½ *Monsters from the Unknown Planet; The Escape of Megagodzilla; Mekagojira No Gyakushu* **1978 (G)** It's monster vs. machine in the heavyweight battle of the universe as a huge mechanical Godzilla built by aliens is pitted against the real thing. The last Godzilla movie made until "Godzilla 1985." **79m/C; VHS, DVD, Blu-Ray.** *JP* Katsuhiko Sasakai; Tomoko Al; ***D:*** Inoshiro Honda; ***W:*** Yukiko Takayama; ***C:*** Mototaka Tomioka; ***M:*** Akira Ifukube.

The Terror of the Tongs ♂♂ *Terror of the Hatchet Men* **1961** Chung King (Lee) is the leader of Hong Kong's Red Dragon Tong, a band of drug and slave traders. When Captain Jackson Sale (Toone) tries to stop them, they murder his daughter and want to publicly execute him as a warning to others not to defy them. But Sale teams up with former slave Lee (Monlaur) to incite a riot to destroy the tong. **80m/C; DVD.** *GB* Christopher Lee; Geoffrey Toone; Yvonne Monlaur; Marne Maitland; Brian Worth; Barbara Brown; Richard Leech; Charles Lloyd-Pack; Burt Kwouk; Ewen Solon; Marie Burke; ***D:*** Anthony Bushnell; ***W:*** Jimmy Sangster; ***C:*** Arthur Grant; ***M:*** James Bernard.

Terror on a Train ♂ ½ *Time Bomb* **1953** Authorities are alerted that a saboteur has placed a timing device aboard a freight train carrying militar explosives. The train is diverted to a siding and former WWII bomb disposal expert Peter Lyncourt (Ford) is called in to find the timer and defuse it. Vernon plays his anxious wife. **72m/C; DVD.** *UK* Glenn Ford; Anne Vernon; Maurice Denham; Victor Maddern; ***D:*** Ted Tetzlaff; ***W:*** Kem Bennett; ***C:*** Frederick A. (Freddie) Young; ***M:*** John Addison.

Terror on the 40th Floor ♂ **1974** Seven people make an attempt to escape from the 40th floor of an inflamed skyscraper. Poorly done re-hash of "Towering Inferno." Uninspired. **98m/C; VHS, DVD.** John Forsythe; Anjanette Comer; Don Meredith; Joseph Campanella; ***D:*** Jerry Jameson.

Terror Out of the Sky ♂ ½ *Revenge of the Savage Bees* **1978** A scientist must disguise himself as one of the insects to divert the attention of a horde of killing bees from a busload of elementary children. Subpar sequel to "The Savage Bees." **95m/C; VHS, DVD.** Efrem Zimbalist, Jr.; Dan Haggerty; Tovah Feldshuh; Lonny (Lonnie) Chapman; Ike Eisenmann; Steve Franken; Bruce French; Richard Herd; Philip Baker Hall; ***D:*** Lee H. Katzin; ***W:*** Guerdon (Gordon) Trueblood; ***C:*** Michel Hugo; ***M:*** William Goldstein. **TV**

Terror Peak ♂♂ **2003** Volcanologist Janet Fraser and her new hubby Kevin travel to New Zealand for their honeymoon accompanied by Janet's disapproving daughter Melanie. Travel agent Kevin wants to check out an adventure camp located at the base of a long dormant volcano that Janet discovers is actually about to erupt. **96m/C; DVD.** Lynda Carter; Parker Stevenson; Emily Barclay; Anthony Starr; Peter S. Elliot; Paki Cherrington; ***D:*** Dale G. Bradley; ***W:*** Dale G. Bradley; Kyle Southam; Rebecca Southam; ***C:*** Renaud Maire; ***M:*** Bruce Lynch. **CABLE**

Terror Ship ♂♂ **1954** Three people find an abandoned yacht which they believe was used for smuggling. While searching it, they find that it was used to transport stolen uranium. Before the police can arrive, the thieves show up. Not a very good handling of what was actually an interesting idea. Released as "Dangerous Voyage" in Great Britain. **72m/B; VHS, DVD.** *GB* William Lundigan; Naomi Chance; Vincent Ball; Jean Lodge; Richard Stewart; ***D:*** Vernon Sewell.

Terror Street ♂ *36 Hours* **1954** An Air Force pilot's wife is murdered. He has 36 hours to clear his name and find the killer. **84m/B; DVD.** Dan Duryea; Elsy Albiin; Ann Gudrun; Eric Pohlmann; Marianne Stone; ***D:*** Montgomery Tully; ***W:*** Steve Fisher; ***C:*** Walter J. (Jimmy W.) Harvey; ***M:*** Ivor Slaney.

Terror Tract ♂♂ **2000 (R)** Real estate agent Bob (Ritter) takes newlyweds Allen (DeLuise) and Mary Ann (Smith) to each of three homes he has for sale. But each home was the site of some horrible evil: in one a wife kills her abusive husband, only to fear he's not really dead; in the second, a father tries to stop the mischief caused by his daughter's evil pet monkey; and in the third house, a teenager finds himself psychically linked to a killer who blames the teen for his crimes. Comfortably scary fun. **97m/C; VHS, DVD, Blu-Ray.** John Ritter; Marcus Bagwell; Bryan Cranston; Will Estes; Brenda Strong; Rachel York; Allison Smith; Carmine D. Giovinazzo; David DeLuise; Wade Andrew Williams; Frederic Lehne; ***D:*** Geoffrey Wright; Lance Dreesen; Clint Hutchison; ***W:*** Clint Hutchison; ***C:*** Ken Blakey; ***M:*** Brian Tyler. **VIDEO**

Terror Train ♂♂ *Train of Terror* **1980 (R)** A masquerade party is held on a chartered train. But someone has more than mask-wearing in mind as a series of dead bodies begin to appear. Copperfield provides magic, Curtis provides screams in this semi-scary slasher movie. **97m/C; VHS, DVD, Blu-Ray.** Jamie Lee Curtis; Ben Johnson; Hart Bochner; David Copperfield; Vanity; Howard Busgang; Michael Shanks; Amanda Tapping; Troy Kennedy-Martin; Anthony Sherwood; Timothy Webber; ***D:*** Roger Spottiswoode; ***W:*** Alec Curtis; ***C:*** John Alcott.

Terror Trap ♂ **2010 (R)** Familiar horror plot and action excites little interest. Bickering Don and Nancy are stranded on a Louisiana back road after another car hits theirs (not so accidentally). Creepy local sheriff Taylor directs the couple to the local rundown motel with its equally creepy owner Carter. Don and Nancy realize that the place is wired for a live feed of the slaughter to come unless they can save themselves. **94m/C; DVD, Blu-Ray.** Michael Madsen; David James Elliott; Heather Marie Marsden; Jeff Fahey; ***D:*** Dan Garcia; ***W:*** Dan Garcia; ***C:*** John Lands. **VIDEO**

The Terror Within ♂ **1988 (R)** Reptilian mutants hit the streets searching for human women to breed with. Have the Teenage Mutant Ninja Turtles grown up? **90m/C; VHS, DVD.** George Kennedy; Andrew Stevens; Starr Andreeff; Terri Treas; ***D:*** Thierry Notz; ***W:*** Thomas McKelvey Cleaver; ***C:*** Ronn Schmidt; ***M:*** Rick Conrad.

The Terrorist ♂♂ *Malli* **1998** Malli (Dharkar) is a 19-year-old terrorist trained to kill from an early age and to die if necessary. She lives with her fellow militants in a camp and is chosen to kill a politician by detonating a bomb that will be strapped to her waist. But when Malli is forced to wait in the city for her victim, she begins to question her mission and her cause. Inspired by the 1991 assassination of Indian prime minister Rajiv Gandhi although the film itself never mentions country, group, or politics specifically. **95m/C; VHS, DVD.** *IN* Ayesha Dharker; ***D:*** Santosh Sivan; ***W:*** Santosh Sivan; ***C:*** Santosh Sivan; ***M:*** Sonu Sisupal.

The Terrorist Next Door ♂♂ **2008 (PG-13)** Canadian telepic tells the true crime story of Muslim extremist Ahmed Ressam (Hundal) who smuggled a bomb into the U.S. with the intention of blowing up the L.A. International Airport on New Year's Eve in 1999. Director Ciccoritti does a good job maintaining suspense, especially since you know the plot failed. **92m/C; DVD.** *CA* Chenier Hundal; Kathleen Robertson; Chris William Martin; Michael Ironside; Reda Guerinik; Paul Doucet; Joseph Antaki; ***D:*** Jerry Ciccoritti; ***W:*** Suzette Couture; ***C:*** Norayr Kasper; ***M:*** Robert Carli. **TV**

The Terrorists ♂ ½ **1974 (PG)** Just as later he was a Scottish Lithuanian sub-commander in "The Hunt for Red October" (1990), here Connery is a Scottish Norwegian security chief. Good cinematography and premise are wasted; generic title betrays sloppy execution. **89m/C; VHS, DVD, Blu-Ray.** Sean Connery; Ian McShane; John Quentin; ***D:*** Casper Wrede; ***M:*** Jerry Goldsmith.

Terrorvision WOOF! **1986 (R)** OUR TV GAVE BIRTH TO SPACE ALIENS! It's amazing what modern technology can do: Suburban family buys a fancy satellite dish; bad black comedy and gory special effects result. **84m/C; VHS, Blu-Ray, Streaming.** Gerrit Graham; Mary Woronov; Diane Franklin; Bert Remsen; Alejandro Rey; ***D:*** Ted Nicolaou; ***W:*** Ted Nicolaou; ***M:*** Richard Band.

Tess ♂♂♂ **1979 (PG)** Sumptuous adaptation of the Thomas Hardy novel "Tess of the D'Urbervilles." Kinski is wonderful as an innocent farm girl who is seduced by the young aristocrat she works for and then finds marriage to a man of her own class only brings more grief. Polanski's direction is faithful and artful. Nearly three hours long, but worth every minute. **170m/C; VHS, DVD, Blu-Ray.** *GB FR* Nastassja Kinski; Peter Firth; Leigh Lawson; John Collin; ***D:*** Roman Polanski; ***W:*** Roman Polanski; Gerard Brach; ***C:*** Ghislan Cloquet; Geoffrey Unsworth. Oscars '80: Art Dir./Set Dec., Cinematog., Costume Des.; Cesar '80: Cinematog., Director (Polanski), Film; Golden Globes '81: Foreign Film; L.A. Film Critics '80: Cinematog., Director (Polanski); N.Y. Film Critics '80: Cinematog.

Tess of the D'Urbervilles ♂♂ ½ **1998** Thomas Hardy's rural Victorian England is the setting for romantic tragedy. Tess Durbeyfield (Waddell) is a poor, naive 16-year-old who's unwillingly sent to work for the wealthy D'Urbervilles, whom her family believes are distant relatives. There, Tess becomes the target of wastrel Alec's (Flemyng) desires and he takes advantage of her. Several years later, Tess is now working as a dairymaid and falls in true love with Angel Clare (Milburn), but he can't accept her soiled past even though they've married. Heartbroken Tess falls deeper into hardship until Alec suddenly reappears in her life—and so does Angel. **180m/C; VHS, DVD.** *GB* Justine Waddell; Jason Flemyng; Oliver Milburn; John McEnery; Lesley Dunlop; Gerald James; Debbie Chazen; ***D:*** Ian Sharp; ***W:*** Ted Whitehead; ***C:*** Richard Greatrex; ***M:*** Alan Lisk. **TV**

Tess of the D'Urbervilles ♂♂ **2008** Typically tragic (and drawn-out) retelling of Thomas Hardy's 1891 novel. Innocent teenager Tess Durbeyfield (Arterton) is dispatched by her hardscrabble family to claim kin with the wealthier D'Urbervilles and is soon seduced by her 'cousin' Alec (Matheson). A disgraced Tess flees and eventually takes a job on a farm where she meets the priggishly noble Angel Clare (Redmayne). Things go from bad to worse for poor Tess when Angel abandons the lovelorn girl after discovering her sordid past and an obsessed Alec finds her again. **240m/C; DVD.** *GB* Gemma Arterton; Eddie Redmayne; Hans Matheson; Anna Massey; Christopher Fairbank; Jodie Whitaker; Kenneth Cranham; Ian Puleston-Davies; Ruth Jones; Rebekah Station; Jo Woodcock; ***D:*** David Blair; ***W:*** David Nicholls; ***C:*** Wojciech Szepel; ***M:*** Robert (Rob) Lane. **TV**

Tess of the Storm Country ♂♂ ½ **1922** Pickford remade her own 1914 film for the better, starring as poor Tessibel Skinner, who takes in her lover Frederick Graves' (Hughes) pregnant sister, Teola (Hope), and then says the child is hers to protect the unwed mom from her ruthless father (Torrence). Tessibel temporarily loses Frederick until the truth comes out. **120m/B; Silent; VHS, DVD.** Mary Pickford; Lloyd Hughes; David Torrence; Gloria Hope; Jean Hersholt; ***D:*** John S. Robertson; ***W:*** Elmer Harris; ***C:*** Charles Rosher; Paul Eagler; ***M:*** Jeffrey Mark Silverman.

The Tesseract ♂ ½ **2003 (R)** The lives of four folks—a psychologist, drug gopher, female assassin, and bellboy—each of whom has their own thing going on, collide at the same ratty Bangkok hotel. Wanders around in a "hopefully hip" kind of way. Based on Alex Garland's novel. **96m/C; VHS, DVD.** Jonathan Rhys Meyers; Saskia Reeves; Carlo Monni; Alexander Rendel; Lene Christensen; Veradis Vinyarath; ***D:*** Oxide Pang Chun; ***W:*** Alex Garland; Oxide Pang Chun; ***C:*** Decha Srimantra. **VIDEO**

Test Pilot ♂♂♂ ½ **1938** Gable and Spencer star as daring test pilot and devoted mechanic respectively. When Gable has to land his experimental craft in a Kansas cornfield, he meets and falls in love with farm girl Loy. The two marry and raise a family, all the while she worries over his dangerous profession. When the Air Force asks him to test their new B-17 bomber, she refuses to watch, thinking the test will end in tragedy. Superb aviation drama featuring excellent cast. **118m/B; DVD.** Clark Gable; Myrna Loy; Spencer Tracy; Lionel Barrymore; Samuel S. Hinds; ***D:*** Victor Fleming; ***W:*** Vincent Lawrence; Waldemar Young; ***C:*** Ray June; ***M:*** Franz Waxman.

Test Tube Babies WOOF! *Sins of Love; The Pill* **1948** A married couple's morals begin to deteriorate as they mourn the fact they can't have a child. The day is saved, however, when they learn about the new artificial insemination process. Amusing, campy propaganda in the vein of "Reefer Madness." Rereleased in 1967 as "The Pill" with extra scenes featuring Monica Davis and John Maitland. **83m/B; VHS, DVD.** Dorothy Dube; Timothy Farrell; William Thomason; ***D:*** W. Merle Connell; ***W:*** Richard McMahan.

Test Tube Teens from the Year 2000 🦴 *Virgin Hunters* **1993 (R)** When sex is banned in the year 2000, horny teenagers are left with no choice but to travel through time for some action. **74m/C; VHS, DVD.** Morgan Fairchild; Ian Abercrombie; Brian Bremer; Christopher Wolf; Michelle Matheson; Sara Suzanne Brown; Don Dowe; Chuck Borden; Robin Joi Brown; Conrad Brooks; ***D:*** David DeCoteau; ***W:*** Kenneth J. Hall; ***M:*** Reg Powell.

Testament 🦴🦴🦴 **1983 (PG)** Well-made and thought-provoking story of the residents of a small California town struggling to survive after a nuclear bombing. Focuses on one family who tries to accept the reality of post-holocaust life. We see the devastation but it never sinks into sensationalism. An exceptional performance from Alexander. **90m/C; DVD.** Jane Alexander; William Devane; Rossie (Ross) Harris; Roxana Zal; Kevin Costner; Rebecca De Mornay; Lukas Haas; Mako; Philip Anglim; Lilia Skala; ***D:*** Lynne Littman; ***W:*** John Sacret Young; ***C:*** Steven Poster; ***M:*** James Horner.

The Testament of Dr. Cordelier 🦴🦴🦴 *Testament in Evil; Le Testament du Docteur Cordelier* **1959** A strange, experimental fantasy about a Jekyll and Hyde-type lunatic stalking the streets and alleys of Paris. Originally conceived as a TV play, Renoir attempted to create a new mise-en-scene, using multiple cameras covering the sequences as they were performed whole. French with English subtitles. **95m/C; VHS, DVD.** *FR* Jean-Louis Barrault; Michel Vitold; Teddy Billis; Jean Topart; Micheline Gary; ***D:*** Jean Renoir; ***W:*** Jean Renoir; ***C:*** Georges Leclerc; ***M:*** Joseph Kosma.

Testament of Dr. Mabuse 🦴🦴 ½ *The Crimes of Dr. Mabuse; The Last Will of Dr. Mabuse* **1962** The director of an asylum is controlled by the evil genius, Dr. Mabuse, who hypnotizes him in this well-done remake of Lang's 1933 classic. **88m/B; VHS, DVD.** Gert Frobe; Wolfgang Preiss; Senta Berger; ***D:*** Werner Klingler; ***W:*** Ladislas Fodor; Robert A. Stemmle; ***C:*** Albert Benitz; ***M:*** Raimund Rosenberger.

The Testament of Orpheus 🦴🦴🦴 ½ *Le Testament D'Orphee* **1959** Superb, personal surrealism; writer-director Cocteau's last film. Hallucinogenic, autobiographical dream-journey through time. Difficult to follow, but rewarding final installment in a trilogy including "The Blood of the Poet" and "Orpheus." In French with English subtitles. **80m/B; VHS, DVD.** *FR* Jean Cocteau; Edouard Dermithe; Maria Casares; Francois Perier; Yul Brynner; Jean-Pierre Leaud; Daniel Gelin; Jean Marais; Pablo Picasso; Charles Aznavour; ***D:*** Jean Cocteau; ***W:*** Jean Cocteau; ***C:*** Roland Pointoizeau; ***M:*** Georges Auric.

Testament of Youth 🦴🦴 ½ **1979** Based on the autobiography of British feminist, author, and pacifist Vera Brittain (Campbell). Vera is enjoying herself at Oxford University in 1913 until war is declared. Vera then becomes a nurse on the frontlines in France and her experiences eventually shatter her, leading her to painfully change her life. **200m/C; VHS, DVD.** *GB* Cheryl Campbell; Rupert Frazer; Emrys James; Rosalie Crutchley; Joanna McCallum; Michael Troughton; Peter Woodward; ***D:*** Moira Armstrong; ***W:*** Elaine Morgan. **TV**

Testament of Youth 🦴🦴🦴 **2015 (PG-13)** It's hard to believe that there are still stories to tell about World War I but this female take on the conflict proves that there are, thanks mostly to a great performance by soon-to-be star Alicia Vikander. Based on the memoir by Vera Brittain, Vikander plays Brittain as she is forced to abandon her studies at Oxford in 1914 and become a war nurse for the cause. Brittain's brother, fiancé, and friends were all sent to serve, and James Kent's film emotionally captures the human cost of war. It's a beautiful, delicate film anchored by the believable performance by Vikander. **130m/C; DVD, Blu-Ray, Streaming.** *UK* Alicia Vikander; Taron Egerton; Dominic West; Emily Brittain; Kit Harington; ***D:*** James Kent; ***W:*** Juliette Towhidi; ***C:*** Robert Hardy; ***M:*** Max Richter.

Testimony of Two Men 🦴 ½ **1977** Convoluted miniseries adapted from Taylor Caldwell's lengthy 1968 bestseller. Dr. Martin Eaton (Forrest) returns from the Civil War to discover his love has married rival Adrian Ferrier (Shatner). The two families continue to be entwined with Adrian's son, Jonathan (Birney), becoming an idealistic doctor. There's various troubled romances and family disputes along the way. **287m/C; DVD.** Steve Forrest; David Birney; Barbara Parkins; Ralph Bellamy; Linda Purl; David Huffman; William Shatner; Tom Bosley; Theodore Bikel; ***D:*** Leo Penn; ***W:*** Larry Yust; William Hanley; ***C:*** Isidore Mankofsky; ***M:*** Gerald Fried. **TV**

Testosterone 🦴🦴 **2003** Lurid black comedy about unrequited love, obsession, and revenge. When Pablo (Sabato) leaves Dean (Sutcliffe) without explanation after a torrid affair, Dean follows him to Argentina. There he gets mixed up with Pablo's intense circle of family and admirers. Some help, some hinder Dean in his attempt to confront his errant lover. Wicked take on gay romance with some tasty over-the-top performances, especially Braga as Pablo's mother. **105m/C; DVD.** *US AR* David Sutcliffe; Jennifer Coolidge; Sonia Braga; Celia Font; Antonio Sabato, Jr.; Leonardo Brezicki; Dario Dukah; ***D:*** David Moreton; ***W:*** David Moreton; Dennis Hensley; ***C:*** Ken Kelsch; ***M:*** Marco d'Ambrosio.

Tetro 🦴🦴 **2009** Coppola's visually striking B&W (with some color flashbacks) family drama about fathers, sons, and brothers. Teenaged Bennie (Ehrenreich) works a cruise ship to Buenos Aires to track down the much-older brother (Gallo) he idolized as a child but hasn't seen in years. The self-named Tetro is a failed writer and malcontent, seemingly overwhelmed by resentment towards their successful father (Brandauer), an internationally-successful conductor and terrible human being. Tetro's generous girlfriend Miranda (Verdu) welcomes Bennie as family secrets are gradually revealed, although the revelations won't be much of a surprise. Gallo's acting isn't much of a surprise either; fortunately newcomer Ehrenreich is the one to watch. **127m/B; Blu-Ray, On Demand.** *US AR IT SP* Vincent Gallo; Maribel Verdu; Klaus Maria Brandauer; Carmen Maura; Alden Ehrenreich; ***D:*** Francis Ford Coppola; ***W:*** Francis Ford Coppola; ***C:*** Mihai Malaimare, Jr.; ***M:*** Osvaldo Golijov.

Tetsuo: The Iron Man 🦴🦴 *The Iron-man* **1992** A weird live-action science-fiction cartoon about a white-collar Japanese worker who finds himself being gradually transformed into a walking metal collection of cables, drills, wires, and gears. The newly formed metal creature then faces off with an equally bizarre metals fetishist (played by the director). In Japanese with English subtitles. **67m/B; VHS, DVD, Blu-Ray.** *JP* Tomorowo Taguchi; Kei Fujiwara; Shinya Tsukamoto; ***D:*** Shinya Tsukamoto; ***W:*** Shinya Tsukamoto; ***C:*** Shinya Tsukamoto; ***M:*** Chu Ishikawa.

Tetsuo 2: Body Hammer 🦴🦴 **1997** Taniguchi (Yaguchi) strikes back at the cyborgs who kidnapped and killed his young son by transforming himself into a killer robotic machine man. Japanese with subtitles. **83m/C; VHS, DVD, Blu-Ray.** *JP* Tomorowo Taguchi; ***D:*** Shinya Tsukamoto; ***W:*** Shinya Tsukamoto; ***C:*** Shinya Tsukamoto.

Tex 🦴🦴 ½ **1982 (PG)** Fatherless brothers in Oklahoma come of age. Dillon is excellent. Based on the novel by S.E. Hinton. **103m/C; VHS, DVD.** Matt Dillon; Jim Metzler; Meg Tilly; Bill McKinney; Frances Lee McCain; Ben Johnson; Emilio Estevez; Charles S. Haas; ***D:*** Tim Hunter; ***W:*** Tim Hunter; Charles S. Haas; ***C:*** Ric Waite; ***M:*** Pino Donaggio.

The Texans 🦴🦴 ½ **1938** Ex-Confederate soldier Kirk Jordan (Scott) struggles to make a new life for himself as a trail boss, aiming to get 10,000 head of cattle to the railroad in Abilene. But there's temptation in the form of Ivy Preston (Bennett) and a scheme to reignite the war. Remake of 1924 silent "North of '36." **93m/B; VHS, DVD.** Randolph Scott; Joan Bennett; Walter Brennan; May Robson; Robert Cummings; Raymond Hatton; Robert Barrat; Harvey Stephens; Chris-Pin (Ethier Crispin Martini) Martin; Francis Ford; ***D:*** James Hogan; ***W:*** Bertram Millhauser; Paul Sloane; William Wister Haines.

Texas 🦴🦴🦴 **1941** Two friends wander through the West after the Civil War getting into scrapes with the law and eventually drifting apart. Ford takes a job on a cattle ranch run by Trevor and discovers Holden has joined a gang of rustlers aiming to steal her herd. The two men vie for Trevor's affections. Although friends, a professional rivalry also existed between the two leading actors and they competed against each other, doing their own stunts during filming. Well-acted, funny, and enthusiastic Western. **94m/B; VHS, DVD.** William Holden; Glenn Ford; Claire Trevor; Edgar Buchanan; George Bancroft; ***D:*** George Marshall.

Texas 🦴🦴 ½ *James A. Michener's Texas* **1994** Stephen Austin (Duffy) sets up a colony in 1821 Texas, with Mexican law requiring the settlers to become Mexican citizens. Eventually, calls for statehood begin and Austin's initial resistance is overturned by rebellion and prodding from Sam Houston (Keach) and Jim Bowie (Keith). Lots of action amidst the history, including the battle for the Alamo, but it's a routine extravaganza. Made for TV miniseries adapted from Michener's novel. Filmed on location in Del Rio, Texas. **180m/C; DVD.** Patrick Duffy; Stacy Keach; David Keith; Maria Conchita Alonso; Anthony Michael Hall; Rick Schroder; Benjamin Bratt; Chelsea Field; John Schneider; Grant Show; Randy Travis; Woody Watson; ***D:*** Richard Lang; ***W:*** Sean Meredith; ***M:*** Lee Holdridge. **TV**

Texas Across the River 🦴🦴 ½ **1966** Sam Hollis (Martin) is a wise-cracking gun runner who, along with Indian sidekick Kronk (Bishop), is recruiting men to help him ship guns through hostile Comanche territory. Don Andrea, a Spanish nobleman (played by Frenchman Delon) wrongly accused of murder, joins up and much comic misadventure ensues. **101m/C; DVD.** Dean Martin; Alain Delon; Joey Bishop; Rosemary Forsyth; Tina Aumont; Peter Graves; Michael Ansara; Linden Chiles; Andrew Prine; Richard Farnsworth; Kelly Thordsen; ***D:*** Michael Gordon; ***W:*** Ben Starr; Wells Root; Harold Greene; ***C:*** Russell Metty.

Texas, Adios 🦴🦴 ½ *The Avenger* **1966** Curious spaghetti western stars Franco Nero as a sheriff who goes to Texas with his kid brother Jim (Dell'Acqua) to get the man who murdered their father. The action has all of the affectations of this rarified branch of the genre, and that makes it lots of fun for fans and virtually unwatchable for everyone else. **92m/C; DVD, Blu-Ray.** *IT* Franco Nero; Alberto Dell'Acqua; Cole Kitosch; Elisa Montes; Jose Suarez; ***D:*** Ferdinando Baldi; ***W:*** Ferdinando Baldi; ***C:*** Enzo Barboni.

Texas Carnival 🦴🦴 **1951** Williams and Skelton star as carnival performers who operate the dunk tank. When Skelton is mistaken for an oil tycoon, he lives high on the hog until the mistake is discovered. Believe it or not, this musical has only one water ballet sequence. Songs include "It's Dynamite," "Whoa! Emma," and "Young Folks Should Get Married." **77m/C; VHS, DVD.** Esther Williams; Red Skelton; Howard Keel; Ann Miller; Paula Raymond; Keenan Wynn; Tom Tully; ***D:*** Charles Walters.

Texas Chainsaw 3D 🦴 ½ **2013 (R)** Touted as a direct sequel to the 1974 horror classic, this 3D reboot is just a thinly-veiled rehash that picks up where the original left off, but quickly cheats a transition to modern day. Heir to a Texas estate, Heather (Daddario) packs her young, nubile friends in a van and heads to south. She uncovers dark family secrets and, surprise surprise, a chainsaw-wielding psycho who goes by Leatherface. As with previous "Chainsaw" entries, the failure begins as soon as a glossy, big-budget version competes with a grimy, handmade classic. Digital blood can never replace pig's blood. **92m/C; DVD, Blu-Ray.** Alexandra Daddario; Dan Yeager; Trey Songz; Scott Eastwood; Tania Raymonde; Richard Riehle; Bill Moseley; ***D:*** John Luessenhop; ***W:*** Adam Marcus; Debra Sullivan; Kirsten Elms; ***C:*** Anastas Michos; ***M:*** John (Gianni) Frizzell.

The Texas Chainsaw Massacre 🦴🦴 ½ **1974 (R)** The movie that put the "power" in power tools. An idyllic summer afternoon drive becomes a nightmare for a group of young people pursued by a chainsaw-wielding maniac. Made with tongue firmly in cheek, this is nevertheless a mesmerizing saga of gore, flesh, mayhem, and violence. **86m/C; VHS, DVD, Blu-Ray.** Marilyn Burns; Allen Danzinger; Paul A. Partain; William Vail; Teri McMinn; Edwin Neal; Jim Siedow; Gunnar Hansen; John Dugan; Jerry Lorenz; ***Nar:*** John Larroquette; ***D:*** Tobe Hooper; ***W:*** Tobe Hooper; Kim Henkel; ***C:*** Daniel Pearl; ***M:*** Tobe Hooper; Wayne Bell.

The Texas Chainsaw Massacre 🦴 **2003 (R)** Rancid remake of Hooper's 1974 classic horror original stars Biel and much more blood and gore than actual chills. Once again, five teenagers take a journey across Texas and pick up a mysterious hitchhiker who blows her brains out in their van after uttering a prophetic warning that they will all die. Enter Leatherface (Bryniarski) and his famously phallic chainsaw hacking up the horny teens to his evil heart's delight. Gruesome highlight as Leatherface has a literal face-off with Biel. Director Nispel, weaned on music videos, has a slicker looking product than the micro-budget original but far less of the palpable tension and shocking originality of its predecessor. **98m/C; VHS, DVD, UMD.** Jessica Biel; Jonathan Tucker; Erica Leerhsen; Mike Vogel; Andrew Bryniarski; R. Lee Ermey; David Dorfman; Eric Balfour; Terrence Evans; ***Nar:*** John Larroquette; ***D:*** Marcus Nispel; ***W:*** Scott Kosar; ***C:*** Daniel Pearl; ***M:*** Steve Jablonsky.

The Texas Chainsaw Massacre 2 WOOF! **1986 (R)** A tasteless, magnified sequel to the notorious blood-bucket extravaganza, about a certain family in southern Texas who kill and eat passing travelers. Followed by "Leatherface: The Texas Chainsaw Massacre 3." **90m/C; VHS, DVD, Blu-Ray.** Dennis Hopper; Caroline Williams; Bill Johnson; Jim Siedow; Bill Moseley; Lou Perry; John (Joe Bob Briggs) Bloom; ***D:*** Tobe Hooper; ***W:*** L.M. Kit Carson; ***C:*** Richard Kooris; ***M:*** Tobe Hooper.

The Texas Chainsaw Massacre 4: The Next Generation 🦴🦴 *Return of the Texas Chainsaw Massacre* **1995 (R)** Heroine Jenny (Zellweger) and her three friends take a wrong turn down a dark country road and wind up in the nightmare clutches of homicidal tow-truck driver Vilmer (McConaughey), his accomplice Darla (Perenski), and the infamous Leatherface (Jacks). No restraint here—as the borderline sadism and tension builds to, unfortunately, something of a letdown. Feature debut for Henkel, who co-wrote Tobe Hooper's 1977 horror classic. Film finally got a release in 1997 after both McConaughey and Zellweger became stars in more mainstream films. Pay attention to "Love Theme from Texas Chainsaw Massacre," sung by Debbie Harry and Leatherface himself. **94m/C; VHS, DVD, Blu-Ray.** Renée Zellweger; Matthew McConaughey; Robert Jacks; Tony Perenski; Lisa Marie Newmyer; John Dugan; Marilyn Burns; ***D:*** Kim Henkel; ***W:*** Kim Henkel; ***C:*** Levie Isaacks; ***M:*** Wayne Bell.

The Texas Chainsaw Massacre: The Beginning WOOF! **2006 (R)** Ugly is okay, ugly and dull is not. Contrary to what the title suggests, this is a prequel to the 2003 remake, although it provides flashbacks to Leatherface's origins, which include being born, hideously deformed, in a slaughterhouse. Ermey reprises his role as psycho cop/cannibal Hoyt, who becomes proud papa to his newly adopted gutter-child. As usual, a group of over-sexed teens are offered up for bloody sacrifice. With its unrelenting gore and sadism, flick's not for the squeamish. **84m/C; DVD, Blu-Ray.** Jordana Brewster; R. Lee Ermey; Andrew Bryniarski; Diora Baird; Taylor Handley; Matt Bomer; Lee Tergesen; Lew Temple; ***D:*** Jonathan Liebesman; ***W:*** Sheldon Turner; ***C:*** Lukas Ettlin; ***M:*** Steve Jablonsky.

A Texas Funeral 🦴🦴 **1999 (R)** Sheen is a Texas patriarch, seen only in flashbacks since it's his funeral that's being attended by his crazy family, which has a long tradition of dysfunction. Set in the late-'60s. **98m/C; VHS, DVD.** Martin Sheen; Robert Patrick; Jane Adams; Chris Noth; Isaiah Washington, IV; Joanne Whalley; Grace Zabriskie; Olivia D'Abo; Quinton Jones; ***D:*** W(illiam) Blake Herron; ***W:***

W(illiam) Blake Herron; ***C:*** Michael Bonvillain; ***M:*** James Legg.

Texas Guns *Once Upon a Texas Train* **1990 (PG)** A gritty western about an old-time gunman (Nelson) and his quest for one last robbery, killing those who stand in his way and some just for fun. Also watch for Cassidy's comeback. **96m/C; VHS, DVD.** Willie Nelson; Richard Widmark; Shaun Cassidy; Angie Dickinson; Kevin McCarthy; Royal Dano; Chuck Connors; Ken Curtis; Dub Taylor; ***D:*** Burt Kennedy; ***W:*** Burt Kennedy; ***C:*** Ken Lamkin; ***M:*** Arthur B. Rubinstein.

Texas Killing Fields ½ **2011 (R)** Sloppy but fitfully interesting crime drama. Detectives Mike Souder (Worthington) and Brian Heigh (Morgan) are investigating the murder of a teen prostitute when Souder's ex-wife Pam (Chastain), who's a detective in a neighboring county, asks for help in locating a young woman who's probably been dumped in the nearby swamps. Heigh's obsessed with solving the longtime killing fields murders, especially after local Little Anne (Moretz) goes missing. **105m/C; DVD, Blu-Ray.** Sam Worthington; Jeffrey Dean Morgan; Chloë Grace Moretz; Jessica Chastain; Sheryl Lee; James Herbert; Annabeth Gish; Stephen Graham; Jason Clarke; ***D:*** Ami Canaan Mann; ***W:*** Donald F. Ferrarone; ***C:*** Stuart Dryburgh; ***M:*** Dickon Hinchliffe.

Texas Lady **1956** When a woman wins $50,000 gambling, she buys a Texas newspaper on the stipulation that she can edit it in this standard fare western. Good vehicle for Colbert to look beautiful, but the plot and script are average and uninspired. **86m/C; VHS, Streaming.** Claudette Colbert; Barry Sullivan; Gregory Walcott; ***D:*** Tim Whelan.

Texas Legionnaires *Man from Music Mountain* **1943** Roy comes back to his home town and gets caught between feuding cattle and sheep herders. **71m/B; VHS, DVD.** Roy Rogers; Ruth Terry; Paul Kelly; Ann Gillis; George Cleveland; Pat Brady; ***D:*** Joseph Kane; ***W:*** Betty Burbridge; Lucille Ward; ***C:*** Jack Marta.

Texas Lightning ½ **1981 (R)** Innocuous B-grade touching movie about a father and son and their family woes. **93m/C; VHS, DVD.** Cameron Mitchell; Channing Mitchell; Maureen McCormick; Peter Jason; ***D:*** Gary Graver; ***W:*** Gary Graver; ***C:*** Gary Graver; ***M:*** Tommy Vig.

The Texas Rangers ½ **1936** Banditos Jim Hawkins (MacMurray) and Wahoo Jones (Oakie) roam the Texas frontier until the Rangers come in, establishing order. So, they switch over to the good guys but are then told to bring in their old partner-in-crime Sam McGee (Nolan). Lots of confronting villains and battling varmints. Based on the book by Walter Prescott Webb. Followed by "The Texas Rangers Ride Again" and remade as "The Streets of Laredo" (1949). **99m/B; VHS, DVD.** Fred MacMurray; Jack Oakie; Lloyd Nolan; Jean Parker; Edward Ellis; Fred Kohler, Sr.; George "Gabby" Hayes; ***D:*** King Vidor; ***W:*** Louis Stevens.

Texas Rangers **2001 (PG-13)** Western featuring Van Der Beek and Kucher (they're dreamy!) as greenhorns who volunteer to fight bandits along the Rio Grande in 1875 Texas. McDermott's Ranger McNelly of the famous Texas Rangers is their demanding mentor who teaches them a'ropin' and a'shootin'. All are robbed of their families by the bad guys, and there's a passel o' gunfights, but taming the West takes a backseat to the real drama centered mostly around the ailing McNelly's fate in this revenge actioner. Cast is good but hindered by a weak script and direction. After sitting on the shelf for two years, yella-bellied studio execs denied the stale oater an advance screening, well aware of its weak appeal. **90m/C; VHS, DVD, Blu-Ray.** James Van Der Beek; Dylan McDermott; Ashton Kutcher; Usher Raymond; Robert Patrick; Rachael Leigh Cook; Leonor Varela; Randy Travis; Jon Abrahams; Matt Keeslar; Vincent Spano; Marco Leonardi; Oded Fehr; Joe Spano; Tom Skerritt; Alfred Molina; ***D:*** Steve Miner; ***W:*** Scott Busby; Martin Copeland; ***C:*** Daryn Okada; ***M:*** Trevor Rabin.

Texas Rein ½ **2016** A family drama in which second chances result in one woman gaining the unexpected in her life. A former rodeo queen and current single mom, Cassie Roberts (Gouhtro) returns to the family she left behind when her father, Marvin (Hartman), becomes seriously ill. Once home, Cassie's plan to stay only until her father regains his health changes once she sees his impressive horse, Splash. Cassie forms a plan to have the horse compete and hires Chase Eversoll (Perrow) to oversee the training. Cassie and Chase soon grow close, and with Chase's support, Cassie truly begins to forgive and finds new connections in her family and her life. **102m/C; DVD, Streaming, Download.** Beth Gouthro; Don Hartman; Greg Perrow; Erin Bethea; Ben Davies; ***D:*** Durrell Nelson; ***W:*** Rebecca Rogers; ***C:*** Douglas Miller; ***M:*** Will Musser. **VIDEO**

The Texas Streak **1926** Unusual silent western takes advantage of its behind-the-scenes movie plot. Chad Pennington (Gibson) is working as a location extra but winds up stranded and bluffs his way into a job as a security guard for surveyors caught in a water feud between a development company and the local ranchers. Pennington helps overcome the bad guys (thanks to some movie tricks) and is then given a chance to star in his own western film series. **70m/B; Silent; DVD.** Hoot Gibson; Blanche Mehaffey; Alan Roscoe; James A. Marcus; Jack Murphy; Jacqueline Curtiss; Slim Summerville; Les Bates; ***D:*** Lynn F. Reynolds; ***W:*** Lynn F. Reynolds; ***C:*** Edward Newman.

Texasville ½ **1990 (R)** Sequel to "The Last Picture Show" finds the characters still struggling after 30 years, with financial woes from the energy crisis, mental illness inspired by the Korean War, and various personal tragedies. Lacks the melancholy sensitivity of its predecessor, but has some of the wit and wisdom that comes with age. Based again on a Larry McMurtry novel. Not well received during its theatrical release. **120m/C; VHS, DVD.** Timothy Bottoms; Jeff Bridges; Annie Potts; Cloris Leachman; Eileen Brennan; Randy Quaid; Cybill Shepherd; William McNamara; ***D:*** Peter Bogdanovich; ***W:*** Peter Bogdanovich.

The Texican ½ **1966** Former sheriff Jess Carlin (Murphy) is living in Mexico but must return to the Texas town of Rim Rock when his newspaperman brother is murdered. Town boss Luke Starr (Crawford) is behind the crime but the townspeople are too scared to help Carlin out—except for saloon gal Kit (Lorys). **86m/C; VHS, DVD.** Audie Murphy; Broderick Crawford; Diana Lorys; Aldo Sambrell; Antonio Casas; ***D:*** Lesley Selander; ***W:*** John C. Champion; ***C:*** Francis Marin.

Thank God It's Friday ½ **1978 (PG)** Episodic and desultory disco-dancing vehicle which won the Best Song Oscar for Donna Summer's rendition. Life is irony. Co-produced by Motown. **100m/C; VHS, DVD, Blu-Ray.** Valerie Landsburg; Teri Nunn; Chick Vennera; Jeff Goldblum; Debra Winger; ***D:*** Robert Klane; ***W:*** Armyan Bernstein. Oscars '78: Song ("Last Dance").

Thank You for Smoking ½ **2006 (R)** Smooth satire, based on the novel by Christopher Buckley, where no one onscreen is actually shown smoking. But if they wanted to, they have that right, which is what slick tobacco lobbyist Nick Naylor (Eckhart) is all about. No surprise that his friends are fellow "Merchants of Death," alcohol lobbyist Polly Bailey (Bello) and firearms lobbyist Bobby Jay Bliss (Koechner). Divorced Nick would like to be a good guy—he tries hard to be a concerned dad—but the game is just too enticing, even when it means bribing former cowboy icon (think Marlboro Man) Lorne Lutch (Elliott), who's dying of lung cancer, to stop attacking cigarette smoking. His opponents don't stand a chance and Eckhart plays Nick with outlandish, glib charm and confidence. **92m/C; DVD.** Aaron Eckhart; Maria Bello; Cameron Bright; Adam Brody; Sam Elliott; David Koechner; Katie Holmes; Rob Lowe; William H. Macy; J.K. Simmons; Robert Duvall; Kim Dickens; Connie Ray; Todd Louiso; ***D:*** Jason Reitman; ***W:*** Jason Reitman; ***C:*** Jim Whitaker; ***M:*** Rolfe Kent. Ind. Spirit '07: Screenplay.

Thank You for Your Service **2017 (R)** A moving, intimate look at the lingering effects of Iraq War on soldiers and their partners, based on a non-fiction book by David Finkel. Each soldier suffers from PTSD, and their families deeply feel its effects in their emotional volatility, physical actions, and anxiety after they return home. Though the film shows their combat experiences, it primarily focuses on the aftermath and how each man processes this burden. The idea that veterans are treated as props by the government when convenient is also subtly explored. **109m/C; DVD, Blu-Ray.** Haley Bennett; Joe Cole; Miles Teller; Keisha Castle-Hughes; Amy Schumer; ***D:*** Jason Hall; ***W:*** Jason Hall; ***C:*** Roman Vasyanov; ***M:*** Thomas Newman.

Thank you, Mr. Moto **1937** A series of Chinese scrolls reveal the hidden location of the treasure-laden tomb of Genghis Khan. Mr. Moto (Lorre) and his friend, Prince Chung (Ahn), are determined to protect the tomb from treasure hunters. 2nd in the series. **67m/B; DVD.** Peter Lorre; Thomas Beck; Philip Ahn; Pauline Frederick; Jayne Regan; Sidney Blackmer; John Carradine; Sig Rumann; ***D:*** Norman Foster; ***W:*** Norman Foster; Willis Cooper; ***C:*** Virgil Miller; ***M:*** Samuel Kaylin.

Thank Your Lucky Stars **1943** A lavish, slap-dash wartime musical that emptied out the Warner's lot for an array of uncharacteristic celebrity turns. Features Shore in her movie debut. **127m/B; VHS, DVD, Blu-Ray.** Eddie Cantor; Dinah Shore; Joan Leslie; Errol Flynn; Bette Davis; Edward Everett Horton; Humphrey Bogart; John Garfield; Alan Hale; Ann Sheridan; Ida Lupino; Jack Carson; Dennis Morgan; Olivia de Havilland; ***D:*** David Butler; ***W:*** Norman Panama.

Thanks a Million ½ **1935** Entertaining musical satire on politics. A travelling show mkes a stopover during a political rally for the Pennsylvania governor's race. The candidate is drunk and inept so the show's leading man, Eric (Powell), fills in. He's such a charming success that the party decides to back him instead. But his politicking ruins his romance with Sally (Dvorak) and then Eric finds out his backers are crooks, so he wants to quit. Remade as "If I'm Lucky" (1946). **86m/B; DVD.** Dick Powell; Ann Dvorak; Fred Allen; Patsy Kelly; Raymond Walburn; ***D:*** Roy Del Ruth; ***W:*** Nunnally Johnson; ***C:*** J. Peverell Marley.

Thanks for Sharing **2013 (R)** Three successful men (Ruffalo, Robbins, and Gad) are otherwise struggling with personal demons--sex addictions--that make having successful relationships with the women in their lives (Paltrow, Richardson, and Moore--aka, Pink) an almost impossible challenge. Writer Blumberg's first directorial venture is surely grateful for the talented group of actors for which he and co-writer Winston gave a sincere, yet by-the-book story, to play out. As it wobbles awkwardly between drama and comedy, it feels like it could use its own self-help, 12-step program. **112m/C; DVD, Blu-Ray.** Mark Ruffalo; Tim Robbins; Gwyneth Paltrow; Josh Gad; Joely Richardson; Patrick Fugit; Alecia Moore; Carol Kane; ***D:*** Stuart Blumberg; ***W:*** Stuart Blumberg; Matt Winston; ***C:*** Yaron Orbach; ***M:*** Christopher Lennertz.

Thanks for the Memory **1938** After Hope and Ross sang "Thanks for the Memory" in "The Big Boradcast of 1938," Paramount decided to capitalize on its popularity in this lame comedy. Steve Merrick (Hope) tends to the house while trying to write a novel. Meanwhile, wife Anne (Ross) is working as a model to support the couple. Steve rebels against being a "kept man" and their marriage enters shaky ground until they come to their senses. **79m/B; VHS, DVD.** Bob Hope; Shirley Ross; Charles Butterworth; Otto Kruger; Hedda Hopper; Laura Hope Crews; Eddie Anderson; ***D:*** George Archainbaud; ***W:*** Lynn Starling; ***C:*** Karl Struss.

That Awkward Moment *Are We Officially Dating?* **2014 (R)** Another "bromantic" comedy; this one centering on three guys in various stages of romantic cliché crisis that suffers from the same old sitcom-level writing that sinks so many of these films. Efron, Teller, and Jordan play Jason, Daniel, and Mikey, respectively—three gentleman at the title time, which is, the film alleges, when a relationship turns to the question, "So...where is this going?" In fact, the awkward moment for at least Jordan and Teller has to be when other films recently made them big enough stars that their involvement here looked like a step back. **94m/C; DVD, Blu-Ray.** Zac Efron; Miles Teller; Michael B. Jordan; Imogen Poots; Mackenzie Davis; Jessica Lucas; Addison Timlin; Josh Pais; ***D:*** Tom Gormican; ***W:*** Tom Gormican; ***C:*** Brandon Trost; ***M:*** David Torn.

That Beautiful Somewhere ½ **2006 (R)** Two lost souls bond in this dreary thriller. Troubled Ontario police detective Conk Adams (Dupuis) gets help from equally unhappy forensic archeologist Catherine Nyland (McGregor) when a body is found in a bog. Catherine must determine if the corpse is new or old but the bog is thought to have special curative properties by members of the local native tribe, and they don't want it disturbed. **93m/C; DVD.** *CA* Roy Dupuis; Jane McGregor; Gordon Tootoosis; David Fox; ***D:*** Robert Budreau; ***W:*** Robert Budreau; ***C:*** Andrew Watt; ***M:*** Steve London.

That Brennan Girl ½ **1946** A maudlin soap opera about how a girl's upbringing by an inconsiderate mother makes her a devious little wench. Fortunately her second husband had a better mom, and redemption is at hand. **95m/B; VHS, DVD.** James Dunn; Mona Freeman; William Marshall; June Duprez; Frank Jenks; Charles Arnt; ***D:*** Alfred Santell.

That Certain Age ½ **1938** Alice (Durbin) is charmed by her newspaper-owning father's houseguest, older and sophisticated journalist Vincent Bullitt (Douglas). She gets a big crush and dumps boyfriend Ken (Cooper), causing much consternation to all. **101m/B; DVD.** Deanna Durbin; Melvyn Douglas; Jackie Cooper; John Halliday; Irene Rich; Nancy Carroll; Jackie Searl; Charles Coleman; ***D:*** Edward Ludwig; ***W:*** Bruce Manning; ***C:*** Joseph Valentine.

That Certain Thing ½ **1928** Very early silent Capra comedy about a bachelor with a silver spoon in his mouth who loses his inheritance when he marries for love. It's got that certain Capra screwball feeling. **65m/B; Silent; VHS, DVD.** Viola Dana; Ralph Graves; Burr McIntosh; Aggie Herring; Syd Crossley; ***D:*** Frank Capra.

That Certain Woman ½ **1937** Sentimental drama with Davis portraying a gangster's widow who wants to make a new life for herself. Fonda plays the rich playboy with whom she falls in love. Because of Davis' star power, she demanded that Fonda play opposite her. It seems Davis had a real life crush on him when they were both players in a stock company several years earlier. Remake of Goulding's "The Trespasser" which starred Gloria Swanson. **91m/B; VHS, DVD.** Bette Davis; Henry Fonda; Ian Hunter; Anita Louise; Donald Crisp; Katherine Alexander; Minor Watson; ***D:*** Edmund Goulding; ***W:*** Edmund Goulding; ***M:*** Max Steiner.

That Championship Season **1982 (R)** Long-dormant animosities surface at the reunion of a championship basketball team. Unfortunate remake of Miller's Pulitzer-prize winning play, with none of the fire which made it a Broadway hit. **110m/C; VHS, DVD.** Martin Sheen; Bruce Dern; Stacy Keach; Robert Mitchum; Paul Sorvino; Jason Miller; ***D:*** Jason Miller; ***C:*** John Bailey; ***M:*** Bill Conti.

That Championship Season **1999 (R)** Tom Daley (Sinise) returns to his hometown for the 20th anniversary of his high-school basketball team's championship victory. A night of nostalgia with Daley, his brother (Kinney), some friends (Shalhoub, D'Onofrio), and their coach (Sorvino, who directed this remake), turns into a drunken rehash of old grievances and the airing of some dirty laundry. Miller adapted his 1973 Pulitzer Prize-winning play, which he also directed for the big screen in 1982. **126m/C; VHS, DVD.** Gary Sinise; Terry Kinney; Vincent D'Onofrio; Tony Shalhoub; Paul Sorvino; ***D:*** Paul Sorvino; ***W:*** Jason Miller; ***C:*** Bruce Surtees; ***M:*** Larry Blank. **CABLE**

That Cold Day in the Park ½ **1969 (R)** Early Altman. An unhappy woman takes in a homeless young man from the park near her home. The woman (Dennis) is obsessive and odd; so is the film. Dennis is excellent. Reminiscent of "The Collector." **91m/C; DVD, Blu-Ray.** Sandy Dennis; Michael Burns; Susanne Benton; Michael Murphy; John David Garfield; ***D:*** Robert Altman; ***W:*** Gillian Freeman; ***C:*** Laszlo Kovacs; ***M:*** Johnny Mandel.

That Darn Cat 1/2 **1965 (G)** Vintage Disney comedy about a Siamese cat that helps FBI Agent Jones thwart kidnappers. Could be shorter, but suspenseful and funny with characteristic Disney slapstick. Based on the book "Undercover Cat" by The Gordons. **115m/C; VHS, DVD.** Hayley Mills; Dean Jones; Dorothy Provine; Neville Brand; Elsa Lanchester; Frank Gorshin; Roddy McDowall; ***D:*** Robert Stevenson; ***C:*** Edward Colman; ***M:*** Robert F. Brunner.

That Darn Cat 1/2 **1996 (PG)** Innocuous Disney remake of the 1965 Disney comedy falls into the "why bother" category. Bored 16-year-old Patti (Ricci) finds some unexpected excitement when her alley-wandering cat D.C. (for Darned Cat) returns home from a prowl with a wristwatch around his neck. Turns out it's a clue in a bungled kidnapping and Patti manages to convince rookie FBI agent Zeke (Doug) to investigate. Jones, who played the FBI agent in the original, is the wealthy husband of would-be kidnap victim Cannon. Ricci's appealing as the sarcastic teen and Elvis the cat has a certain scrappy charm as well. Based on the novel "Undercover Cat" by Mildred and Gordon Gordon. **89m/C; VHS, DVD.** Christina Ricci; Doug E. Doug; Dean Jones; George Dzundza; Peter Boyle; Michael McKean; Bess Armstrong; Dyan Cannon; John Ratzenberger; Estelle Parsons; Rebecca Schull; Thomas F. Wilson; Brian Haley; Mark Christopher Lawrence; ***D:*** Bob Spiers; ***W:*** Scott M. Alexander; Larry Karaszewski; ***C:*** Jerzy Zielinski; ***M:*** Richard Gibbs.

That Evening Sun **2009 (PG-13)** Stubborn, cantankerous 80-year-old widowed Tennessee farmer Abner Meecham (Holbrook) has walked away from the retirement home his lawyer son Paul (Goggins) stuck him in. Abner returns homes to discover that the place has been rented to redneck ne'er-do-well Lonzo Choat (McKinnon) and his family. The old man knows that Choat (whom he calls 'white trash') won't be able to afford the purchase option so he moves into the farm's tenant shack prepared to wait Choat out—going mano-a-mano with the increasingly desperate and violent younger man. Choat's despicable (he's a drunk who beats his teenaged daughter) but McKinnon also makes him understandable and Holbrook's unsentimental performance is simply superb. Filmed in and around Knoxville, Tennessee. Adapted from William Gay's short story "I Hate to See the Evening Sun Go Down." **110m/C; Blu-Ray, On Demand.** Hal Holbrook; Ray McKinnon; Mia Wasikowska; Walton Goggins; Carrie Preston; Barry Corbin; Dixie Carter; ***D:*** Scott Teems; ***W:*** Scott Teems; ***C:*** Rodney Taylor; ***M:*** Michael Penn.

That Forsyte Woman *The Forsyte Saga* **1950** Based on the novel "A Man of Property" by John Galsworthy, a married Victorian woman falls for an architect engaged to be wed. Remade later (and better) for BBC-TV as "The Forsythe Saga." **112m/C; VHS, DVD.** Errol Flynn; Greer Garson; Walter Pidgeon; Robert Young; Janet Leigh; Harry Davenport; Stanley Logan; Lumsden Hare; Aubrey Mather; Matt Moore; ***D:*** Compton Bennett; ***C:*** Joseph Ruttenberg.

That Funny Feeling **1965** Lightweight romantic comedy has freelance maid Joan (Dee) meeting and falling for businessman Tom (Darin). Instead of bringing him to her small apartment, which she shares with a roommate, she takes him to a client's place, unaware that it's Tom's. He goes along since he wants to get to know her better. Humor ensues as she tries to keep up appearances by keeping the place clean. **93m/C; DVD.** Sandra Dee; Bobby Darin; Donald O'Connor; Nita Talbot; Larry Storch; Leo G. Carroll; James Westerfield; Robert Strauss; Arte Johnson; Kathleen Freeman; Ben Lessy; ***D:*** Richard Thorpe; ***W:*** David R. Schwartz; ***C:*** Clifford Stine; ***M:*** Bobby Darin.

That Hagen Girl **1947** Soapy, unconvincing melodrama with an even worse romantic angle. After 18 years, Tom Bates (Reagan) returns to Jordan, Ohio, and relgnites rumors that he fathered illegitimate Mary Hagen (Temple). Subjected to small-town gossip, and with her mother dead, the adopted Mary asks Tom for the truth. **83m/B; DVD.** Ronald Reagan; Shirley Temple; Lois Maxwell; Rory Calhoun; Dorothy Peterson; Charles Kemper; ***D:*** Peter Godfrey; ***W:*** Charles Hoffman; ***C:*** Karl Freund; ***M:*** Franz Waxman.

That Hamilton Woman *Lady Hamilton* **1941** Screen biography of the tragic 18th-century love affair between British naval hero Lord Nelson and Lady Hamilton. Korda exaggerated the film's historical distortions in order to pass the censor's production code about adultery. Winston Churchill's favorite film which paralleled Britain's heroic struggles in WWII. **125m/B; VHS, DVD.** Laurence Olivier; Vivien Leigh; Gladys Cooper; Alan Mowbray; Sara Allgood; Henry Wilcoxon; ***D:*** Alexander Korda; ***M:*** Miklos Rozsa. Oscars '41: Sound.

That Man Bolt **1973** Jefferson Bolt (Williamson) is a kung fu expert who agrees to carry $1 million from Hong Kong to Mexico City while being pursued by a government agent. Typical blaxpoitation feature. **102m/C; VHS, DVD.** Fred Williamson; Teresa Graves; Byron Webster; Miko Mayama; Satoshi Nakamura; Jack Ging; Vassili Lambrinos; John Orchard; ***D:*** Henry Levin; David Lowell Rich; ***W:*** Quentin Werty; ***C:*** Gerald Perry Finnerman; ***M:*** Charles Bernstein.

That Midnight Kiss 1/2 **1949** Glossy production of a musical romance featuring Lanza in his film debut. Thin plot has Lanza starring as a singing truck driver who is discovered by opera diva Grayson. **96m/C; VHS, DVD.** Kathryn Grayson; Jose Iturbi; Ethel Barrymore; Mario Lanza; Keenan Wynn; J. Carrol Naish; Jules Munshin; ***D:*** Norman Taurog; ***C:*** Robert L. Surtees.

That Naughty Girl *Mam'zelle Pigalle; Naughty Girl* **1958** The bored daughter of a nightclub owner decides to experience all life has to offer. **77m/C; VHS, DVD.** *FR* Brigitte Bardot; Jean Bretonniere; Francoise Fabian; Bernard Lancret; ***D:*** Michel Boisrond.

That Night 1/2 **1993 (PG-13)** A view of romance through the eyes of a young girl, circa 1961. Ten-year-old Alice (Dushku) is the confidant of rebellious 17-year-old neighbor Cheryl (Lewis), who enlists the young girl's aid as a go-between with her wrong-side-of-the tracks boyfriend Rick (Howell). 21 soundtrack oldies are featured. Directorial debut for screenwriter Bolotin. Based on a novel by Alice McDermott. **89m/C; VHS, Blu-Ray, Streaming.** C. Thomas Howell; Juliette Lewis; Eliza Dushku; Helen Shaver; John Dossett; ***D:*** Craig Bolotin; ***W:*** Craig Bolotin.

That Night in Rio 1/2 **1941** Ameche plays a dual role as entertainer Larry Martin and wealthy Baron Duarte, who's in financial trouble because of his failing airline. Needing to discreetly leave town to take care of business, the Baron asks Larry to step in, but he can't fool Duarte's wife, Cecilia (Faye), while Larry's singer girlfriend Carmen (Miranda) doesn't know what's going on. Remake of 1935's "Folies Bergere." **91m/C; DVD.** Don Ameche; Alice Faye; Carmen Miranda; S.Z. Sakall; J. Carrol Naish; Curt Bois; Leonid Kinskey; ***D:*** Irving Cummings; ***W:*** Bess Meredyth; George Seaton; Hal Long; ***C:*** Ray Rennahan; Leon Shamroy; ***M:*** Mack Gordon; Harry Warren.

That Obscure Object of Desire 1/2 *Cet Obscur Objet du Desir* **1977 (R)** Bunuel's last film, a comic nightmare of sexual frustration. A rich Spaniard obtains a beautiful girlfriend who, while changing physical identities, refuses to sleep with him. Based on a novel by Pierre Louys, which has been used as the premise for several other films, including "The Devil is a Woman," "La Femme et le Pantin," and "The Female." Available with subtitles or dubbed. **100m/C; VHS, DVD, Blu-Ray.** *SP* Fernando Rey; Carole Bouquet; Angela Molina; Julien Bertheau; ***D:*** Luis Bunuel; ***W:*** Luis Bunuel; Jean-Claude Carriere; ***C:*** Edmond Richard. L.A. Film Critics '77: Foreign Film; Natl. Bd. of Review '77: Director (Bunuel); Natl. Soc. Film Critics '77: Director (Bunuel).

That Old Feeling **1996 (PG-13)** Bitter ex-spouses Lilly (Midler) and Dan (Farina) are reunited at the wedding of their daughter and things turn ugly. They cause a scene and are sent out of the reception to cool down. Instead, their old passion flares up and they're found reeling in that old feeling in the back seat of a Porshe. After leaving to see where their whirlwind of romance takes them, they are trailed by their daughter (Marshall), her weenie husband (Denton), and their respective current spousal units Rowena (O'Grady) and Alan (Rasche). Fluffy romantic comedy carried mostly by the performances of Midler and Farina. **105m/C; VHS, DVD.** Bette Midler; Dennis Farina; Danny Nucci; Paula Marshall; Gail O'Grady; David Rasche; Jayne (Jane) Eastwood; ***D:*** Carl Reiner; ***W:*** Leslie Dixon; ***C:*** Steve Mason; ***M:*** Patrick Williams.

That Russell Girl **2008** Sarah Russell (Tamblyn) left her hometown and loved ones behind after a tragedy for which she still blames herself. Having been diagnosed with leukemia, Sarah decides to return home to tell her family, only to find that the past will not leave her alone when she gets an antagonistic reception from depressed neighbor Lorraine (Ehle). Instead of making the story about Sarah's illness, the TV pic focuses on her past trauma and how to forgive, with mixed results. **98m/C; DVD.** Amber Tamblyn; Jennifer Ehle; Mary Elizabeth Mastrantonio; Tim DeKay; Henry Czerny; Paul Wesley; Max Morrow; Daniel Clark; Richard Leacock; Ben Lewis; ***D:*** Jeff Bleckner; ***W:*** Jill Blotevogel; ***C:*** Charles Minsky; ***M:*** Jeff Beal. **TV**

That Sinking Feeling **1979 (PG)** A group of bored Scot teenagers decide to steal 90 sinks from a plumber's warehouse. Well received early film from Forsyth is genuinely funny as the boys try to get rid of the sinks and turn a profit. **82m/C; VHS, Streaming.** *GB* Robert Buchanan; John Hughes; Billy Greenlees; Alan Love; ***D:*** Bill Forsyth; ***W:*** Bill Forsyth; ***C:*** Michael Coulter.

That Thing You Do! **1996 (PG)** The Wonders, a small-town foursome, hit the big time in 1964 after a substitute drummer (like that could ever happen) adds some kick to the band's new song and sets the local kids a-fruggin'. Developed by freshman director/screenwriter Hanks (who also plays the band's Svengali-like record exec) as a diversion from Oscar hype, it's nostalgic and uncomplicated to a fault, but engaging nonetheless. Hanks clone Scott puts the beat into the charmingly wholesome quartet, while the underused Tyler is disarming as the put-upon girlfriend. Look quick or you'll miss bosom buddy Scolari as a TV host. Can't-get-it-out-of-your-head title track (played 11 times in the film) was selected from over 300 submissions after Hanks put out the call to music publishers. **110m/C; VHS, DVD.** Johnathon Schaech; Tom Hanks; Liv Tyler; Tom Everett Scott; Steve Zahn; Ethan (Randall) Embry; Obba Babatunde; Charlize Theron; Peter Scolari; Alex Rocco; Bill Cobbs; Rita Wilson; Chris Isaak; Kevin Pollak; Giovanni Ribisi; Bryan Cranston; Holmes Osborne; Dawn Maxey; Sean M. Whalen; Clint Howard; Kathleen Kinmont; Barry Sobel; Gedde Watanabe; Jonathan Demme; Marc McClure; Colin Hanks; ***D:*** Tom Hanks; ***W:*** Tom Hanks; ***C:*** Tak Fujimoto; ***M:*** Howard Shore.

That Touch of Mink 1/2 **1962** In New York City, an unemployed secretary finds herself involved with a business tycoon. On a trip to Bermuda, both parties get an education as they play their game of "cat and mouse." Enjoyable romantic comedy. **99m/C; VHS, DVD, Blu-Ray.** Cary Grant; Doris Day; Gig Young; Audrey Meadows; John Astin; Dick Sargent; ***D:*** Delbert Mann; ***W:*** Stanley Shapiro; Nate Monaster; ***C:*** Russell Metty; ***M:*** George Duning. Golden Globes '63: Film--Mus./Comedy.

That Uncertain Feeling 1/2 **1941** Light comedy about a couple's marital problems increasing when she develops the hiccups and a friendship with a flaky piano player. A remake of the earlier Lubitsch silent film, "Kiss Me Again." Available colorized. **86m/B; VHS, DVD.** Merle Oberon; Melvyn Douglas; Burgess Meredith; Alan Mowbray; Eve Arden; Sig Rumann; Harry Davenport; ***D:*** Ernst Lubitsch; ***W:*** Donald Ogden Stewart; Walter Reisch; ***C:*** George Barnes; ***M:*** Werner R. Heymann.

That Was Then. . . This Is Now **1985 (R)** Lame adaptation of S.E. Hinton teen novel about a surly kid who is attached to his adoptive brother and becomes jealous when the brother gets a girlfriend. **102m/C; VHS, DVD.** Emilio Estevez; Craig Sheffer; Kim Delaney; Jill Schoelen; Barbara Babcock; Frank Howard; Larry B. Scott; Morgan Freeman; ***D:*** Christopher Cain; ***W:*** Emilio Estevez.

That Wonderful Urge **1948** Powers remade his own 1937 film "Love Is News," although some of the sparkle is gone. He's again a newspaperman writing about a scandal-plagued heiress (Tierney instead of Loretta Young). Sara finds out Tom has been deceiving her and kicks him to the curb—but not before ruining his career. They both try to one-up each other by pretending to be married but that really gets them into trouble. A more mature Power plays a more mature character and the beautiful Tierney turns out to be a sprightly comedienne. **82m/B; DVD.** Tyrone Power; Gene Tierney; Gene Lockhart; Lucile Watson; Reginald Gardner; Arleen Wheelan; Lloyd Gough; Chill Wills; ***D:*** Robert B. Sinclair; ***W:*** Jay Dratler; ***C:*** Charles G. Clarke; ***M:*** Cyril Mockridge.

That'll Be the Day 1/2 **1973 (PG)** The early rock 'n' roll of the 1950s is the only outlet for a frustrated young working-class Brit. Prequel to "Stardust." Good, meticulous realism; engrossing story. **91m/C; VHS, DVD.** Ringo Starr; Keith Moon; David Essex; Rosemary Leach; James Booth; Billy Fury; Rosalind Ayres; Robert Lindsay; Brenda Bruce; Verna Harvey; James Ottaway; Deborah Watling; Beth Morris; Daphne Oxenford; Kim Braden; Ron Hackett; Johnny Shannon; Susan Holderness; Debonairs; ***D:*** Claude Whatham; ***W:*** Ray Connolly; ***C:*** Peter Suschitzky.

That's Dancing! **1985 (G)** This anthology features some of film's finest moments in dance from classical ballet to break-dancing. **104m/C; VHS, DVD.** Fred Astaire; Ginger Rogers; Ruby Keeler; Cyd Charisse; Gene Kelly; Shirley MacLaine; Liza Minnelli; Sammy Davis, Jr.; Mikhail Baryshnikov; Ray Bolger; Jennifer Beals; Dean Martin; ***D:*** Jack Haley, Jr.; ***M:*** Henry Mancini.

That's Entertainment **1974 (G)** A compilation of scenes from the classic MGM musicals beginning with "The Broadway Melody" (1929) and ending with "Gigi" (1958). Great fun, especially for movie buffs. **132m/C; VHS, DVD, Blu-Ray.** Judy Garland; Fred Astaire; Frank Sinatra; Gene Kelly; Esther Williams; Bing Crosby; ***D:*** Jack Haley, Jr.; ***M:*** Henry Mancini.

That's Entertainment, Part 2 1/2 **1976 (G)** A cavalcade of great musical and comedy sequences from MGM movies of the past. Also stars Jeanette MacDonald, Nelson Eddy, the Marx Brothers, Laurel and Hardy, Jack Buchanan, Ann Miller, Mickey Rooney, Louis Armstrong, Oscar Levant, Cyd Charisse, Elizabeth Taylor, Maurice Chavalier, Bing Crosby, Jimmy Durante, Clark Gable, and the Barrymores. Not as unified as its predecessor, but priceless nonetheless. **129m/C; VHS, DVD, Blu-Ray.** ***Nar:*** Fred Astaire; Gene Kelly; ***D:*** Gene Kelly; ***W:*** Leonard Gershe; ***C:*** George J. Folsey; ***M:*** Nelson Riddle.

That's Entertainment, Part 3 **1993 (G)** Third volume contains 62 MGM musical numbers from over 100 films, hosted by nine of the original stars, and is based on outtakes and unfinished numbers from studio archives. One new technique used here is a split-screen showing both the actual film with a behind-the-scenes shot that includes cameramen, set designers, and dancers scurrying around. Although it has its moments, TE3 doesn't generate the same reverence for Hollywood's Golden Age that its predecessors managed to do. That 18-year gap between sequels may say something about what the studio execs thought of their film vault's remainders. **113m/C; VHS, DVD, Blu-Ray.** ***D:*** Bud Friedgen; Michael J. Sheridan; ***W:*** Bud Friedgen; Michael J. Sheridan; ***M:*** Marc Shaiman.

That's Life! **1986 (PG-13)** A lackluster semi-home movie starring Edwards' family and friends. A single weekend in the lives of a writer who's turning 60, his singer wife who has been diagnosed with cancer, and their family. **102m/C; VHS, DVD.** Jack Lemmon; Julie Andrews; Sally Kellerman; Chris Lemmon; Emma Walton; Robert Knepper; Robert Loggia; Jennifer Edwards; ***D:*** Blake Edwards; ***W:*** Blake Edwards; ***M:*** Henry Mancini.

That's My Baby! 1/2 **1944** A number of (then-)popular musical performers (Peppy and Peanuts, Gene Rodgers, Mitchell & Lytell) as well as animated cartoons from Dave Fleisher pop up in this oddball combo of music and drama from Republic Pictures. Betty Moody (Drew) and her boyfriend Tim (Arlen) try to snap her wealthy father R.P. (Watson) out of his melancholia by having every performer they know from the clubs do their act and make him smile. Nothing works until Mrs. Moody remembers that R.P. once wanted to be a cartoonist, which brings in Fleischer's efforts. Doesn't make any sense but it's nostalgic fun. **68m/B; DVD.** Richard Arlen; Ellen Drew; Minor Watson; Leonid Kinskey; Richard Bailey; Madeline Grey; Marjorie Manners; ***D:*** William Berke; ***W:*** William Tunberg; Nicholas T. Barrows; ***C:*** Robert Pittack.

That's My Boy 1/2 **1951** Shtick-heavy comedy from Martin & Lewis. Junior Jackson is the clumsy, weakling son of a wealthy college football hero who wants his boy to play for his alma mater. Dad hires current player Bill Baker to whip the kid into shape. **98m/B; DVD.** Jerry Lewis; Dean Martin; Eddie Mayehoff; Ruth Hussey; Polly Bergen; Hugh Sanders; ***D:*** Hal Walker; ***W:*** Cy Howard; ***C:*** Lee Garmes; ***M:*** Leigh Harline.

That's My Boy *I Hate You, Dad; Donny's Boy* **2012 (R)** The biggest bomb of Sandler's career may finally be the proof that audiences have tired of his schtick. Sandler plays a man-child (the only role he really knows) who forces himself back into his son Todd's (Samberg) life, who he had at a very young age. Thing is Todd doesn't want him around. Still, he moves into Todd's house just as he's about to get married and promptly starts feuding with his daughter-in-law to be. Other than a bit more edge--it's Sandler's only R-rated film--this is stale material and had the poor box office returns to prove it. **116m/C; DVD, Blu-Ray, Streaming.** Adam Sandler; Andy Samberg; Leighton Meester; James Caan; Milo Ventimiglia; Blake Clark; Vanilla Ice; ***D:*** Sean Anders; ***W:*** David Caspe; ***C:*** Brandon Trost; ***M:*** Rupert Gregson-Williams. Golden Raspberries '12: Worst Actor (Sandler), Worst Screenplay.

That's My Man 1/2 **1947** Gambling-addicted bookkeeper Joe Grange (Ameche) bets his marriage when he uses their savings to buy a sickly colt he intends to make into a prize-winning race horse. However, even when the horse wins big, it's not enough to convince neglected, fed-up wife Ronnie (McLeod) to stick around. Can Joe win back his family too? **99m/B; DVD, Blu-Ray.** Don Ameche; Catherine McLeod; Roscoe Karns; John Ridgely; ***D:*** Frank Borzage; ***W:*** Steve Fisher; Bradley King; ***C:*** Tony Gaudio; ***M:*** Hans J. Salter.

That's Not Us 1/2 **2015** An intimate romantic comedy-drama about a weekend trip for three couples that becomes less about fun and more about the stability of long-term relationships. To enjoy the last days of summer, three committed couples (gay, straight, and lesbian) travel together to a beach house. Though the trip was intended to be fun, the couples soon find their relationships tested and tensions rising between and within each pair. As each individual grapples with questions about sex and commitment, everyone considers if love can last. **97m/C; DVD.** Mark Berger; Elizabeth Gray; Tommy Nelms; Nicole Pursell; David Rysdahl; ***D:*** William Sullivan; ***W:*** William Sullivan; ***C:*** Derek Dodge; ***M:*** Xander Singh.

That's the Way I Like It 1/2 **1999 (PG-13)** Homage to disco but set in the East rather than the West. It's 1977 and Sinapore clerk Hock (Pang) wants to win a disco tournament so he can buy a motorcycle. He drops his usual partner (Tang) for the flashier Julie (Francis) and the rivalry between the dance teams gets intense. But Hock just happens to have the spirit of the legendary "Saturday Night Fever" studster himself, Tony Manero (Pace), to give him that extra dance fever. **92m/C; VHS, DVD.** Adrian Pang; Anna Belle Francis; Dominic Pace; Madeline Tang; Caleb Goh; ***D:*** Glen Goei; ***W:*** Glen Goei; ***C:*** Brian J. Breheny; ***M:*** Guy Gross.

That's What I Am 1/2 **2011 (PG)** Earnest family film that tries a little too hard. In the 1960s, middle schooler Andy (Ellison) finds himself dealing with moral dilemmas. His dedicated teacher Mr. Simon (Harris) pairs him with the class pariah (Walters), who's just a nice, misunderstood kid, for a project and soon out-of-control rumors and bullying hurt not only the two students but the widowed Mr. Simon as well. **100m/C; DVD, Blu-Ray.** Ed Harris; Chase Ellison; Alexander Walters; Amy Madigan; Molly Parker; Daniel Roebuck; ***D:*** Michael Pavone; ***W:*** Michael Pavone; ***C:*** Kenneth Zunder; ***M:*** James Raymond.

That's What She Said WOOF! **2012 (R)** Truly awful female-centric comedic raunch looking for a plot. Insecure, overweight Bebe (DeBonis) and her BFF, loud and obnoxious Dee Dee (Heche), wander around New York attempting to prepare Bebe for the first date she's had in ages. Someow they're joined by the younger Clementine (Shawkat) who's in hysterics because of boyfriend issues. There's a lot of inappropriate talk and behavior in public that would have any normal person avoiding this trio like a plague. **84m/C; DVD.** Marcia DeBonis; Anne Heche; Alia Shawkat; Kellie Overbey; ***D:*** Carrie Preston; ***W:*** Kellie Overbey; ***C:*** William Klayer; ***M:*** Tim Adams; Mike Viola.

The Thaw **2009 (R)** Environmentalist David Kruipen chooses three college students to work at his Arctic base where they are joined by Kruipen's bitter daughter Evelyn. The station contains a decaying wooly mammoth infested by a parasite that bites several of the newcomers, causing a violent reaction. An eco-doomsday scenario that's both moderately gross and suspenseful. **94m/C; DVD, Blu-Ray.** Val Kilmer; Martha MacIsaac; Kyle Schmid; Steph Song; Aaron Ashmore; Anne Marie Deluise; William B. Davis; ***D:*** Mark Lewis; ***W:*** Mark Lewis; ***C:*** Jan Kiesser; ***M:*** Michael Neilson. **VIDEO**

Theatre of Blood *Much Ado about Murder* **1973 (R)** Shakespearean ham actor Edward Lionheart (Price) committed suicide after losing an award and being ridiculed by the critics. Now those same critics are being murdered in bizarre ways—in fact, their deaths parallel those in the plays of the Bard. Well, it's no big surprise to discover that Lionheart is indeed alive and committing the inventive crimes with the assistance of his lovely daughter, Edwina (Rigg). Top drawer comedy noir with a great supporting cast of Britain's best (and quite a bit of gore). **104m/C; VHS, DVD, Blu-Ray.** *GB* Vincent Price; Diana Rigg; Ian Hendry; Robert Morley; Dennis Price; Diana Dors; Milo O'Shea; Harry Andrews; Coral Browne; Robert Coote; Jack Hawkins; Michael Hordern; Arthur Lowe; ***D:*** Douglas Hickox; ***W:*** Anthony Greville-Bell; ***C:*** Wolfgang Suschitzky; ***M:*** Michael Lewis.

Theatre of Death 1/2 *Blood Fiend; Female Fiend* **1967** Horror master Lee is back, this time as a theatre director in Paris. Meanwhile, police are baffled by a series of mysterious murders, each bearing a trace of vampirism. Well-plotted suspense. A racy voodoo dance sequence, often cut, is available on some video versions. **90m/C; VHS, DVD.** Christopher Lee; Lelia Goldoni; Julian Glover; Evelyn Laye; Jenny Till; Ivor Dean; ***D:*** Samuel Gallu; ***W:*** Ellis Kadison; Roger Marshall; ***C:*** Gilbert Taylor.

Theeb **2015** During World War I, a Bedouin youth living in the Ottoman province of Hijaz serves as a guide to a British officer who needs to reach an important locale across the desert and comes of age as a result of experience. Arabic with subtitles. **100m/C; DVD.** Jacir Eid Al-Hwietat; Hussein Salameh Al-Sweilhiyeen; Hassan Mutlag Al-Maraiyeh; Jack Fox; ***D:*** Naji Abu Nowar; ***W:*** Naji Abu Nowar; Bassel Ghandour; ***C:*** Wolfgang Thaler; ***M:*** Jerry Lane.

Their Finest **2017 (R)** An enticing comedy-drama by director Scherfig on the efforts to make a feature film amidst the bombing of London during World War II. After the displaced Catrin Cole (Arterton) lands a job creating women's dialogue for British propaganda films, she shows talent as a writer, teams up with former writing rival Tom (Claflin), and helps craft a fictional take on the civilian Dunkirk rescue efforts. With a cast led by pithy aging matinee idol Ambrose Hilliard (Nighy), the filming proves problematic as confident Catrin manages a romantic triangle and the constant presence of death. **117m/C; DVD.** Gemma Arterton; Sam Claflin; Bill Nighy; Jack Huston; Paul Ritter; ***D:*** Lone Scherfig; ***W:*** Gaby Chiappe; ***C:*** Sebastian Blenkov; ***M:*** Rachel Portman.

Their Own Desire **1929** Debutante Lally's (Shearer) father Henry (Stone) is having an affair with Beth (Millard) so Lally persuades her devastated mother Harriet (Bennett) to go with her on a mountain resort vacation. Lally falls in love with persistent John Cheever (Montgomery) until she learns he's Beth's son but a near-tragedy has everyone taking a second look at their messy lives. **65m/B; DVD.** Norma Shearer; Lewis Stone; Belle Bennett; Robert Montgomery; Helen Millard; ***D:*** E. Mason Hopper; ***W:*** Frances Marion; ***C:*** William H. Daniels.

Thelma 1/2 **2017** Raised in isolation as a devout Christian, first-year college student Thelma (a fearless Harboe) has left home but remains tied to her parents, Trond (Rafaelsen) and Unni (Petersen). They call constantly and know her every action. After meeting Anja (Wilkins), Thelma experiences feelings she has never before, including dancing and sexual awakening. Yet a feeling of dread prevails as Thelma tries to come to terms with herself and her childhood. Norwegian with subtitles. **116m/C; DVD.** Eili Harboe; Kaya Wilkins; Henrik Rafaelsen; Ellen Dorrit Petersen; Grethe Eltervag; ***D:*** Joachim Trier; ***W:*** Joachim Trier; Eskil Vogt; ***C:*** Jakob Ihre; ***M:*** Ola Flottum.

Thelma & Louise **1991 (R)** Hailed as the first "feminist-buddy" movie, Sarandon and Davis bust out as best friends who head directly into one of the better movies of the year. Davis is the ditzy Thelma, a housewife rebelling against her dominating, unfaithful, abusive husband (who, rather than being disturbing, provides some of the best comic relief in the film). Sarandon is Louise, a hardened and world-weary waitress in the midst of an unsatisfactory relationship. They hit the road for a respite from their mundane lives, only to find violence and a part of themselves they never knew existed. Outstanding performances from Davis and especially Sarandon, with Pitt notable as the stud who gets Davis' motor revved. Director Scott has a fine eye for set details. **130m/C; VHS, DVD, Blu-Ray.** Susan Sarandon; Geena Davis; Harvey Keitel; Christopher McDonald; Michael Madsen; Brad Pitt; Timothy Carhart; Stephen Tobolowsky; Lucinda Jenney; ***D:*** Ridley Scott; ***W:*** Callie Khouri; ***C:*** Adrian Biddle; ***M:*** Hans Zimmer. Oscars '91: Orig. Screenplay; Natl. Bd. of Review '91: Actress (Davis), Actress (Sarandon); Natl. Film Reg. '16; Natl. Soc. Film Critics '91: Support. Actor (Keitel); Writers Guild '91: Orig. Screenplay.

Them! **1954** A group of mutated giant ants wreak havoc on a southwestern town. The first of the big-bug movies, and far surpassing the rest, this is a classic fun flick. See how many names you can spot among the supporting cast. **93m/B; VHS, DVD, Blu-Ray.** James Whitmore; Edmund Gwenn; Fess Parker; James Arness; Onslow Stevens; Jack Perrin; Joan Weldon; Sean McClory; Sandy Descher; Dub Taylor; William Schallert; Leonard Nimoy; Richard Deacon; ***D:*** Gordon Douglas; ***W:*** Ted Sherdeman; ***C:*** Sidney Hickox; ***M:*** Bronislau Kaper.

Them That Follow 1/2 **2019 (R)** In a deeply religious community, troubled Mara (Emgelbert) is the daughter of Lemuel (Goggins), the head pastor of a congregation of Pentecostal snake handlers. Because of her recent sexual encounter with Augie (Mann), Mara is pregnant but afraid to tell anyone because she could be exiled. She is also supposed to marry the ernest Garret (Pullman). Further complicating the situation is Augie's previous drifting from the group and the prominent role his mother Hope (Colman) plays in the community. Though the subject matter is interesting and many of the actors give outstanding performances, it often strays into melodrama. **98m/C; DVD.** Kaitlyn Dever; Walton Goggins; Olivia Colman; Lewis Pullman; Thomas Mann; ***D:*** Britt Poulton; Dan Madison Savage; ***W:*** Britt Poulton; Dan Madison Savage; ***C:*** Brett Jutkiewicz; ***M:*** Garth Stevenson.

Then Came Bronson 1/2 **1968** Pilot TV movie for the 1969-70 TV series. Parks stars as ambitious journalist James Bronson who hits the road on his Harley Roadster after his best friend (Sheen) commits suicide. Bronson travels up and down the California coast finding adventure, including a runaway bride and a hippie campsite. **90m/C; DVD.** Michael Parks; Bonnie Bedelia; Akim Tamiroff; Gary Merrill; Sheree North; Martin Sheen; Bert Freed; ***D:*** William A. Graham; ***W:*** Denne Petticlerc; ***C:*** Ray Flin; ***M:*** George Duning. **TV**

Then She Found Me **2007 (R)** In her directorial debut, Hunt (who also co-scripted) lets all actress vanity fall by the wayside as the tense, frazzled lead. Schoolteacher April is stunned by the sudden end to her brief marriage to mama's boy Ben (Broderick). This is on top of caring for her ill adoptive mother Trudy (Cohen) and finding out her birth mother is the brassy, self-absorbed Bernice (Midler). Recently divorced Frank (Firth), the father of one of April's pupils, offers advice and a manly shoulder although he's not too stable himself. Oh, and April finds out she's pregnant from her marital break-up sex. Self-deprecating comedy that's a little too anxious—much like April herself. Based on the novel by Elinor Lipman. **100m/C; Blu-Ray, On Demand.** Helen Hunt; Colin Firth; Bette Midler; Matthew Broderick; Ben Shenkman; Lynn Cohen; Salman Rushdie; John Benjamin; ***D:*** Helen Hunt; ***W:*** Helen Hunt; Alice Arlen; Victor Levin; ***C:*** Peter Donahue; ***M:*** David Mansfield.

Theodora Goes Wild **1936** Tiny, priggish Lynnfield, Connecticut is shocked to discover that a scandalous best seller about smalltown life has been written pseudonymously by their very own Theodora Lynn (Dunne). When Theodora gets a chance to meet sophisticated New Yorker Michael Grant (Douglas), who did the illustrations for her book, she falls for him. But both must throw aside their own (and everyone else's) expectations and limitations for them to be happy. Dunne's first comedic lead role. **94m/B; VHS, DVD.** Irene Dunne; Melvyn Douglas; Thomas Mitchell; Thurston Hall; Rosalind Keith; Spring Byington; Elisabeth Risdon; Margaret McWade; ***D:*** Richard Boleslawski; ***W:*** Sidney Buchman; ***C:*** Joseph Walker; ***M:*** Morris Stoloff.

Theodore Rex 1/2 **1995 (PG)** Futuristic comedy finds cynical, seasoned cop Katie Coltrane (Goldberg) furious at being teamed with Teddy, who just happens to be an eight-foot-tall, three-ton, returned-from-extinction Tyrannosaurus Rex (who has a taste for cookies). And Teddy's not exactly the brightest dinosaur on the block, which makes Katie's job all the harder when they stumble across a major crime caper. **92m/C; VHS, DVD.** Whoopi Goldberg; Armin Mueller-Stahl; Richard Roundtree; Juliet Landau; ***D:*** Jonathan Betuel; ***W:*** Jonathan Betuel; ***C:*** David Tattersall; ***M:*** Robert Folk.

The Theory of Everything 1/2 **2014 (PG-13)** Stephen Hawking changed the way we look at the world, history, and the Big Bang before (and after) succumbing to a horrendous neurological disorder that left him not only severely handicapped but told he didn't have long to live. Director Marsh certainly means well with this biopic of the legendary physicist, and Redmayne does an admirable job with the physical challenges of such a leading role (while Jones deftly handles the emotional struggles of his wife). But a strong start descends into such stale, flat biopic clichés that it becomes unforgivably dull, especially given the importance of its subject matter. **123m/C; DVD, Blu-Ray.** *UK* Eddie Redmayne; Felicity Jones; Charlie Cox; Maxine Peake; David Thewlis; Simon McBurney; Emily Watson; ***D:*** James Marsh; ***W:*** Anthony McCarten; ***C:*** Benoit Delhomme; ***M:*** Johan Johannsson. Oscars '14: Actor (Redmayne); British Acad. '14: Actor (Redmayne), Adapt. Screenplay; Golden Globes '15: Actor--Drama (Redmayne), Orig. Score; Screen Actors Guild '14: Actor (Redmayne).

The Theory of the Leisure Class **2001** Kids on a field trip discover the murdered bodies of some children, missing from a small western community. City reporter Callie (Knight) shows up and begins snooping around, uncovering the town's secrets. Based on a true story. **108m/C; VHS, DVD.** Tuesday Knight; Michael Massee; Christopher McDonald; Brad Renfro; ***D:*** Gabriel Bologna; ***W:*** Amber Benson; Gabriel Bologna; ***C:*** Christopher Tufty; ***M:*** Howard Drossin.

There Be Dragons 1/2 **2011 (PG-13)** During a trip to Spain to research a book about the founder of Opus Dei, Josemaria Escriva (Cox), journalist Robert Torres (Scott) learns that his estranged, dying father Manolo (Bentley) and Josemaria were childhood friends until a dark secret divided them after Josemaria chose the priesthood and Manolo became involved in the Spanish Civil War. Liked by audiences and lambasted by critics, it's more of a messy mystery with a story touted as "inspired by actual events" that is better in theory than execution. Unrealistic and exaggerated in its treatment of religion, it has lots of ambition but little sense. **122m/C; DVD, Blu-Ray.** Dougray Scott; Charlie Cox; Wes Bentley; Olga Kurylenko; Rodrigo Santoro; Ana Torrent; Unax Ugalde; Jordi Molla; Geraldine Chaplin; Charles Dance; Derek Jacobi; ***D:*** Roland Joffé; ***W:*** Roland Joffé; ***C:*** Gabriel Beristain; ***M:*** Stephen Warbeck.

There Goes My Baby 1/2 **1992 (R)** Eight California high school grads confront their futures on two nights in '65 (as the Watts riots ignite). There are Vietnam protests, flower children, would-be rock stars, friendships, and romantic complications. Yes, it sounds a lot like "American Graffiti" but the cast are winning and there's a good deal of affection without sinking to mawkishness. **99m/C; VHS, DVD.** Dermot Mulroney; Rick Schroder; Kelli Williams; Jill Schoelen; Noah Wyle; Kristin Minter; Lucy Deakins; Kenny Ransom; Seymour Cassel; Paul Gleason; Frederick Coffin; Andrew (Andy) Robinson; Shon Greenblatt; J.E. Freeman; ***D:*** Floyd Mutrux; ***W:*** Floyd Mutrux.

There Goes the Bride 1/2 **1932** Annette (Matthews) runs away from an arranged marriage and gets on a Paris-bound train where she's of victim of theft. Penniless, she meets dashing, wealthy Max (Nares) who helps her out although it seems he's engaged as well. Annette is tracked down and returned home, but Max soon follows. **80m/B; DVD.** *UK* Jessie Matthews; Owen Nares; Charles Carson; Barbara Everest; Basil Radford; Carol Goodner; ***D:*** Albert de Courville; ***W:*** W.P. Lipscomb; ***C:*** Alex Bryce; ***M:*** Louis Levy.

There Goes the Neighborhood 1/2 **1992 (PG-13)** A dying convict tells prison psychiatrist Daniels where he has buried $8.5 million—under the home of neighbor O'Hara. Daniels and O'Hara try to discreetly dig up the fortune but when the neighborhood finds out everyone wants a chance at the cash. **88m/C; VHS, Streaming.** Jeff Daniels; Catherine O'Hara; Dabney Coleman; Hector Elizondo; Judith Ivey; Rhea Perlman; Harris Yulin; Jonathan Banks; Chazz Palminteri; Mary Gross; ***D:*** Bill (William) Phillips; ***M:*** David Bell.

There Was a Crooked Man 1/2 **1970 (R)** An Arizona town gets some new ideas about law and order when an incorruptible and innovative warden takes over the town's prison. The warden finds he's got his hands full with one inmate determined to escape. Offbeat western black comedy supported by an excellent and entertaining production, with fine acting all around. **123m/C; VHS, DVD.** Kirk Douglas; Henry Fonda; Warren Oates; Hume Cronyn; Burgess Meredith; John Randolph; Arthur O'Connell; Alan Hale, Jr.; Lee Grant; ***D:*** Joseph L. Mankiewicz; ***W:*** Robert Benton; David Newman; ***C:*** Harry Stradling, Jr.

There Will Be Blood 1/2 **2007 (R)** Director Anderson ventures from the contemporary to a saga that covers some 30 years (from 1898 to the 1920s) following the fortunes of silver prospector turned oil magnate Daniel Planview (Day-Lewis). Misanthrope Planview wheels, deals, and cheats his way to a fortune, dogged by evangelical preacher Eli Sunday (Dano), whose family Plainview took advantage of to get his oil derricks gushing. Plainview's one human contact is the orphan H.W. (Freasier), whom he adopts (and later dismisses) in his obsessive quest for power and wealth. Foreboding, with a powerful performance from Day-Lewis as an egotist driven mad by his ambitions. Loosely based on Upton Sinclair's 1927 novel, "Oil!" **158m/C; Blu-Ray, On Demand.** Daniel Day-Lewis; Paul Dano; Kevin J. O'Connor; Ciaran Hinds; Dave Willis; Dillon Freasier; Russell Harvard; Sydney McCallister; Colleen Foy; ***D:*** Paul Thomas Anderson; ***W:*** Paul Thomas Anderson; ***C:*** Robert Elswit; ***M:*** Johnny Greenwood. Oscars '07: Actor (Day-Lewis), Cinematog.; British Acad. '07: Actor (Day-Lewis); Golden Globes '08: Actor--Drama (Day-Lewis); Screen Actors Guild '07: Actor (Day-Lewis).

Theremin: An Electronic Odyssey **1995 (PG)** Profiles the life of Russian scientist Leon Theremin (who died in 1993), founder of electronic music, and his revolutionary musical invention, the Theremin. Martin located the 95-year-old Theremin in Moscow in 1991, interviewed him on camera, then brought him back to the U.S. to film reunions with friends and colleages he hadn't seen in 50 years. Martin's focus is on the impact of the Theremin on Hollywood movie scores heard in '50s sci-fi and thriller classics ("The Day the Earth Stood Still") and in popular music (The Beach Boys' "Good Vibrations" is commented on by Brian Wilson). Theremin's life proves as curious as his instrument, with his controversial interracial marriage to a ballet star, abduction by Russian agents, and imprisonment in a Soviet mental hospital. "Theremin" provides a fascinating and heartfelt tribute to the man's work and life. **84m/C; VHS, DVD.** ***D:*** Steven M. Martin; ***W:*** Steven M. Martin; ***C:*** Robert Stone; Edward Lachman; Chris Lombardi; ***M:*** Hal Willner.

There's a Girl in My Soup **1970 (R)** Sellers is a gourmet who moonlights as a self-styled Casanova. Early post "Laugh-In" Hawn is the young girl who takes refuge at his London love nest when her boyfriend dumps her. Lust ensues. Has its funny parts, but not a highlight of anyone's career. Based on the hit play. **95m/C; VHS, DVD.** *GB* Peter Sellers; Goldie Hawn; Diana Dors; ***D:*** Roy Boulting.

There's Always Tomorrow **1956** Sirk's depressingly bleak look at conformist suburban life. Middle-aged, middle-class toy manufacturer Clifford Groves (MacMurray) lives a suffocating life in suburbia with his wife Marion (Bennett) and their three self-absorbed kids, who all take him for granted. No wonder he's so happy about an unexpected reunion with ex-flame Norma (Stanwyck), a divorced New York fashion designer. Clifford starts entertaining thoughts of having a second chance but there's heavy symbolism involved since his latest toy design is a robot. **84m/B; DVD.** Barbara Stanwyck; Fred MacMurray; Joan Bennett; William Reynolds; Gigi Perreau; Judy Nugent; Pat Crowley; Jane Darwell; ***D:*** Douglas Sirk; ***W:*** Bernard C. Schoenfeld; ***C:*** Russell Metty; ***M:*** Heinz Roemheld; Herman Stein.

There's No Business Like Show Business **1954** A top husband and wife vaudevillian act make it a family affair. Filmed in CinemaScope, allowing for full and lavish musical numbers. Good performances and Berlin's music make this an enjoyable film. **117m/C; VHS, DVD, Blu-Ray.** Ethel Merman; Donald O'Connor; Marilyn Monroe; Dan Dailey; Johnny Ray; Mitzi Gaynor; Frank McHugh; Hugh O'Brian; Charlotte Austin; ***D:*** Walter Lang; ***W:*** Phoebe Ephron; Henry Ephron; ***C:*** Leon Shamroy; ***M:*** Irving Berlin; Lionel Newman; Alfred Newman.

There's Nothing out There **1990** A group of seven teenagers spends Spring Break at a secluded mountain cabin. It sounds wonderful, but one of the boys (who claims to have seen every horror movie on video) knows the signs of a horror movie just waiting to happen. **91m/C; VHS, DVD, Blu-Ray.** Craig Peck; Wendy Bednarz; Mark Collver; Bonnie Bowers; John Carhart, III; Claudia Flores; Jeff Dachis; Lisa Grant; ***D:*** Rolfe Kanefsky; ***W:*** Rolfe Kanefsky; ***C:*** Ed Hershberger; ***M:*** Christopher Thomas.

There's Something About a Soldier 1/2 **1943** Conventional, low-budget wartime drama has a group of non-commissioned officers entering Officer Candidate School. Cocky newcomer Wally isn't willing to help out his fellow recruits, including combat vet Frank Molloy. Well, they do have a romantic rivalry going over Carol, who works at the camp. **81m/B; DVD.** Tom Neal; Evelyn Keyes; Bruce Bennett; John Hubbard; Jeff Donnell; ***D:*** Alfred E. Green; ***W:*** Horace McCoy; Barry Trivers; ***C:*** George Meehan, Jr.

There's Something about Mary **1998 (R)** Outrageously funny comedy that only veers from the gutter when it feels like taking a dip in the sewer. Set in 1985, the prologue introduces us to geeky Ted (Stiller), who gets a prom date with class knockout Mary (Diaz) after sticking up for her retarded brother Warren (Brown). The big date is not to be, however, for a vicious tuxedo zipper to the privates incapacitate Ted. Thirteen years later, Ted is still depressed over the incident, and still carries a torch for Mary. He hires Pat (Dillon), an oily detective with enormous choppers, to find her. Unfortunately for Ted, Pat is instantly smitten with Mary and lies. Ted learns the truth and heads to Miami to find her himself. Merely looking at the plot does not do justice to this lowbrow masterpiece. **118m/C; VHS, DVD, Blu-Ray, UMD.** Ben Stiller; Matt Dillon; Cameron Diaz; Chris Elliott; Lee Evans; Lin Shaye; Jeffrey Tambor; Markie Post; Keith David; Jonathan Richman; W. Earl Brown; Khandi Alexander; Richard Tyson; Rob Moran; Lenny Clarke; Zen Gesner; Harland Williams; Richard Jenkins; ***Cameo(s):*** Brett Favre; ***D:*** Bobby Farrelly; Peter Farrelly; ***W:*** Bobby Farrelly; Peter Farrelly; Edward Decter; John J. Strauss; ***C:*** Mark Irwin; ***M:*** Jonathan Richman. MTV Movie Awards '99: Female Perf. (Diaz), Fight, Film, Villain (Dillon); N.Y. Film Critics '98: Actress (Diaz).

Therese **1986** Stylish biography of a young French nun and her devotion to Christ bordering on romantic love. Explores convent life. Real-life Therese died of TB and was made a saint. A directorial tour de force for Cavalier. In French with English subtitles. **90m/C; VHS, DVD.** *FR* Catherine Mouchet; Aurore Prieto; Sylvie Habault; Ghislaine Mona; ***D:*** Alain Cavalier; ***W:*** Alain Cavalier; ***C:*** Isabelle Dedieu. Cannes '86: Special Jury Prize; Cesar '87: Cinematog., Director (Cavalier), Film, Writing.

Therese 1/2 **2012** Serviceable adaptation of Francois Mauriac's 1927 novel, "Therese Desqueyroux." An independent beauty, Therese makes a family sanctioned marriage of convenience to dull-but-wealthy landowner, Bernard, the brother of her best friend, Anne. She's soon wallowing in marital boredom, exacerbated by Anne's lively, inappropriate affair with Jewish Jean. Therese's moodiness is tiring and the character's last rash action still doesn't make her sympathetic. The costume drama was director Miller's final film. French with subtitles. **110m/C; DVD.** *FR* Audrey Tautou; Gilles Lellouche; Anais Demoustier; Stanley Weber; ***D:*** Claude Miller; ***W:*** Claude Miller; Natalie Carter; ***C:*** Gerard de Battista.

Therese & Isabelle 1/2 **1967** Story of growing love and physical attraction between two French schoolgirls. On holiday together, they confront their mutual desires. Richly photographed soft porn based on the novel by Violet Leduc. Not vulgar, but certainly for adults. French with subtitles. **118m/B; VHS, DVD.** Essy Persson; Anna Gael; Barbara Laage; Anne Vernon; ***D:*** Radley Metzger; ***W:*** Jesse Vogel; ***C:*** Hans Jura; ***M:*** Georges Auric.

Therese Raquin 1/2 **1980** Therese Raquin (Nelligan)is a young woman unhappily married to mama's boy Camille (Cranham). She has an affair with Laurent (Cox) and the lovers do away with the inconvenient spouse. But their guilt turns to loathing for each other and haunts them into further acts of betrayal and violence. Based on the novel by Emile Zola. **173m/C; VHS, DVD.** *GB* Kate Nelligan; Brian Cox; Mona Washbourne; Kenneth Cranham; Alan Rickman; Richard Pearson; ***D:*** Simon Langton; ***W:*** Philip Mackie; ***M:*** Patrick Gowers. **TV**

Therese: The Story of Saint Therese of Lisieux **2004** Therese is born into a privileged French family but begs to follow her older sister into a Carmelite convent though she has self-doubts, which she describes in her journals. She becomes more and more of an ascetic, following a life of simplicity, humility, and compassion, which is revealed when her writings are published after her early death. **90m/C; DVD.** Linda Hayden; Lindsay Younce; Samantha Kramer; Judith Kaplan; Leonardo Defilippis; ***D:*** Leonardo Defilippis; ***W:*** Patti Defilippis; ***C:*** Lourdes Ambrose; ***M:*** Sr. Marie Therese Sokol.

These Are the Damned **1963** Hammer sci fi. American Simon (Carey) falls for English Joan (Field) while on a seaside vacation but gets beaten and robbed by her psycho biker brother King (Reed). He finds refuge with scientist Bernard (Knox) and, when Simon and Joan are reunited, they discover a nearby cave is filled with strange children who are the results of experiments to have humans survive an atomic blast. However, the kiddies are highly radioactive and soon infect the couple, who try to free them from military control. **77m/B; DVD.** *GB* MacDonald Carey; Shirley Anne Field; Alexander Knox; Viveca Lindfors; Oliver Reed; Walter Gotell; James Villiers; ***D:*** Joseph Losey; ***W:*** Evan Jones; ***C:*** Arthur Grant; ***M:*** James Bernard.

These Foolish Things 1/2 **2006** A sentimental and predictable wisp of a melodrama set in 1930s London. The orphaned daughter of a stage star, Diana (Tapper) decides to follow her mother's profession. She falls in love with ambitious playwright Robin (Leon), whose new play stars Douglas (Umbers), who wants to personally work with Robin offstage as well. Stamp's an all-knowing butler, Huston's the American financing the play, and Bacall plays another star. Based on the novel by Noel Langley. **107m/C; DVD.** Zoe Tapper; David Leon; Mark Umbers; Lauren Bacall; Anjelica Huston; Terence Stamp; Joss Ackland; Andrew Lincoln; Julia McKenzie; ***D:*** Julia Taylor-Stanley; ***W:*** Julia Taylor-Stanley; ***C:*** Gavin Finney; ***M:*** Ian Lynn.

These Girls **2005 (R)** Best teen friends Keira (Dhavernas), Lisa (Lewis), and Glory (Walsh) all have a crush on married 30-year-old pot dealer Keith (Boreanaz). After discovering that Glory is already having a fling with Keith, her gal pals decide they should share the unwilling stud equally, using blackmail about Glory's underage tryst as leverage. Since none of the attractive actresses can remotely pass for teenagers, this slight comedy is already at a disadvantage. Based on a play by Vivienne Laxdal. **92m/C; DVD.** *CA* Caroline Dhavernas; David Boreanaz; Holly Lewis; Amanda Walsh; ***D:*** John Hazlett; ***W:*** John Hazlett; ***C:*** Alex Vendler; ***M:*** Ned Bouhalassa. **VIDEO**

These Old Broads 1/2 **2001** Three actresses—Addie Holden (Collins), Kate Westbourne (MacLaine), and Piper Grayson (Reynolds)?starred in a '60s musical that over the years has become a cult hit. A TV exec (Carbonell) wants to engineer a TV reunion special but the trio hate each other. Maybe the agent (Taylor) they all share can persuade them. **95m/C; VHS, DVD.** Debbie Reynolds; Joan Collins; Shirley MacLaine; Elizabeth Taylor; Jonathan Silverman; Peter Graves; Gene Barry; Pat Harrington, Jr.; ***D:*** Matthew Diamond; ***W:*** Carrie Fisher; Elaine Pope; ***C:*** Eric Van Haren Noman; ***M:*** Guy Moon; Steve Tyrell. **TV**

These Wilder Years **1956** Sudsy melodrama gets a rise from pros Cagney and Stanwyck. Steel magnate Steve Bradford (Cagney) returns to his hometown to find the son he fathered as a teenager. Orphanage director Ann Dempster (Stanwyck) refuses to let him see the adoption records and he tries to get the info through the courts. o get Steve to see the situation from someone else's viewpoint, Ann introduces him to pregnant, unwed teen Suzie (Keim). **91m/B; DVD.** James Cagney; Barbara Stanwyck; Betty Lou Keim; Walter Pidgeon; Edward Andrews; ***D:*** Roy Rowland; ***W:*** Frank Fenton; ***C:*** George J. Folsey; ***M:*** Jeff Alexander.

They *Invasion from Inner Earth; Hell Fire* **1977** Beings from beneath the earth's crust take their first trip to the surface. **88m/C; VHS, DVD.** Paul Dentzer; Debbie Pick; Nick Holt; ***D:*** Ito Rebane.

They All Laughed **1981 (PG)** Three detectives become romantically involved with the women they were hired to investigate. Essentially light-hearted fluff with little or no script. Further undermined by the real-life murder of Stratten before the film's release. **115m/C; VHS, DVD.** Ben Gazzara; John Ritter; Audrey Hepburn; Colleen Camp; Patti Hansen; Dorothy Stratten; Elizabeth Pena; ***D:*** Peter Bogdanovich; ***W:*** Peter Bogdanovich.

They Are Among Us 1/2 **2004 (R)** Alien parasites take over a small town and convert the locals to their cause by infecting them. If you've seen any of the several dozen takes on "Invasion of the Body Snatchers" you can pretty much predict how this Sci-Fi Channel flick goes. **99m/C; DVD.** Alison Eastwood; Corbin Bernsen; Bruce Boxleitner; Amy Bruckner; Nana Visitor; ***D:*** Jeffrey Obrow; ***W:*** Jeffrey Obrow; Lars Haugile; ***C:*** Mateo Londono. **CABLE**

They Call It Murder 🦴🦴 **1971** D.A. Doug Selby (Hutton) investigates the matter of a corpse found floating in a swimming pool. The characters are based on Erle Stanley Gardner. **120m/C; DVD.** Jim Hutton; Lloyd Bochner; Jessica Walter; Leslie Nielsen; JoAnn Pflug; Nita Talbot; William (Bill) Elliott; Vic Tayback; ***D:*** Walter Grauman; ***W:*** Sam Rolfe; ***M:*** Robert Drasnin. **TV**

They Call It Sin 🦴🦴 *The Way of Life* **1932** Often told story of a young country girl heading to the Big Apple in search of her big break and "Mr. Right." Young is a chorus line girl romantically involved with her married producer (Calhern) while faithful admirer Brent waits nearby. Predictable plot adapted from the novel by Alberta Stedman Eagan. **68m/B; VHS, DVD.** Loretta Young; George Brent; David Manners; Louis Calhern; Una Merkel; Joseph Cawthorn; Helen Vinson; ***D:*** Thornton Freeland; ***W:*** Lillie Hayward; Howard J. Green.

They Call Me Mr. Tibbs! 🦴🦴 **1970 (R)** Lieutenant Virgil Tibbs (Poitier) investigates the murder of a prostitute. The prime suspect is his friend, the Reverend Logan Sharpe (Landau). He is torn between his duty as a policeman, his concern for the reverend, and the turmoil of his domestic life. Less tense, less compelling sequel to "In the Heat of the Night." **108m/C; VHS, DVD, Blu-Ray.** Sidney Poitier; Barbara McNair; Martin Landau; Juano Hernandez; Anthony Zerbe; Ed Asner; Norma Crane; Jeff Corey; ***D:*** Gordon Douglas; ***W:*** Alan R. Trustman; ***C:*** Gerald Perry Finnerman; ***M:*** Quincy Jones.

They Call Me Sirr 🦴🦴 1/2 **2000** Based on the true story of Sirr Parker (Scott), a talented but poverty-stricken high school football player in South Central L.A. After Sirr and his younger brother are abandoned by their mother, Sirr struggles to look after his family (including an ailing grandmother) while keeping his place on the team. But the teen is finally forced to turn to his coach (Duncan) for help. **97m/C; VHS, DVD.** Kente Scott; Michael Clarke Duncan; ***D:*** Robert Munic; ***W:*** Robert Munic; ***C:*** David Perrault; ***M:*** Sharon Farber. **CABLE**

They Call Me Trinity 🦴🦴 1/2 *Lo Chiamavano Trinita* **1972 (G)** Lazy drifter-gunslinger and his outlaw brother join forces with Mormon farmers to rout bullying outlaws. Spoofs every western cliche with relentless comedy, parodying "The Magnificent Seven" and gibing the spaghetti western. Followed by "Trinity is Still My Name." Dubbed. **110m/C; VHS, DVD, Blu-Ray.** *IT* Terence Hill; Bud Spencer; Farley Granger; Steffen Zacharias; ***D:*** E.B. (Enzo Barboni) Clucher.

They Came Back 🦴🦴 1/2 *Les Revenants* **2004** Warning: this is not your normal zombie-eats-people movie. Instead, thousands of the dead have shuffled back to their small French village to just live their dull old lives. Sort of. As the living must work to deal with the sudden population explosion, the now-dimwitted undead have been holding secret nightly meetings. First-time director Campillo goes for a quiet look at society's reaction to the walking dead's return rather than a gorefest, a la George Romero. In French with English subtitles. **102m/C; VHS, DVD.** *FR* Geraldine Pailhas; Jonathan Zaccai; Frederic Pierrot; Victor Garrivier; Catherine Samie; ***D:*** Robin Campillo; ***W:*** Robin Campillo; Brigitte Tijou; ***C:*** Jeanne Lapoirie; ***M:*** Martin Wheeler. **VIDEO**

They Came from Beyond Space 🦴 **1967** Aliens invade the earth and possess the brains of humans. They only want a few slaves to help them repair their ship which crashed on the moon. The only person able to stop them is a scientist with a steel plate in his head. Silly and forgettable. **86m/C; VHS, DVD, Blu-Ray.** *GB* Robert Hutton; Michael Gough; ***D:*** Freddie Francis.

They Came from Within 🦴🦴 1/2 *Shivers; The Parasite Murders; Frissons* **1975 (R)** The occupants of a high-rise building go on a sex and violence spree when stricken by an aphrodisiac parasite. Queasy, sleazy, and weird. First major film by Cronenberg. **87m/C; VHS, DVD.** *CA* Paul Hampton; Joe Silver; Lynn Lowry; Barbara Steele; Susan Petrie; Allan Migicovsky; Ronald Mlodzik; ***D:*** David Cronenberg; ***W:*** David Cronenberg; ***C:*** Robert Saad; ***M:*** Ivan Reitman.

They Came to Blow Up America 🦴🦴 **1943** Entertaining wartime thriller finds Carl Steelman (Sanders) asked by the FBI to infiltrate the German-American Bund, which supports Nazi Germany. He's sent to Berlin, using the identity of a dead spy, to get info on U-boat targets before his cover is blown by the dead man's wife (Sten). There's also a little time for a dangerous romance with his anti-Nazi contact, Helga (Dur). **73m/B; DVD.** George Sanders; Anna Sten; Poldi Dur; Ward Bond; Dennis Hoey; Sig Rumann; Ludwig Stossel; Robert Barrat; ***D:*** Edward Ludwig; ***W:*** Aubrey Wisberg; ***C:*** Lucien N. Andriot; ***M:*** Hugo Friedhofer.

They Came to Cordura 🦴🦴 1/2 **1959** Mexico, 1916: a woman and six American soldiers—five heroes and one who has been branded a coward—begin a journey to the military headquarters in Cordura. Slow journey brings out personalities. Look for "Bewitched" hubby Dick York. Based on Glendon Swarthout's best-seller. **123m/C; VHS, DVD, Blu-Ray.** Gary Cooper; Rita Hayworth; Van Heflin; Tab Hunter; Dick York; Richard Conte; ***D:*** Robert Rossen; ***W:*** Ivan Moffat.

They Came to Rob Las Vegas 🦴 1/2 **1968** Offers some slight twists on the crime doesn't pay genre. Tony (Lockwood) plans to heist the cargo of an armored car during its Vegas to L.A. run. The company is owned by Steve Skorsky (Cobb) and Tony's gal Ann (Sommer) is Skorsky's secretary. But the cargo has mob ties and the company is under surveillance by Treasury Agent Douglas (Palance), who's not happy. **129m/C; DVD.** Gary Lockwood; Elke Sommer; Lee J. Cobb; Jack Palance; Jean Servais; ***D:*** Antonio (Isasi-Isasmendi) Isasi; ***W:*** Antonio (Isasi-Isasmendi) Isasi; Jorge Illa; Lluis Comeron; Jo Eisinger; ***C:*** Juan Gelpi; ***M:*** Georges Garvarentz.

They Came Together 🦴🦴 1/2 **2014 (R)** Wain, of "Wet Hot American Summer" fame, delivers the laughs with this all-out parody of the romantic comedy genre. Working from the "Airplane" school of comedy in which there are multiple jokes a minute, Wain takes on many of the rom-coms of the last two decades and produces a better movie than most of them in the process. Rudd and Poehler lead a great cast, including many of Wain's standard collaborators from TV and film. It's not perfect but if one joke doesn't work, you only have to wait a few second for one that does. **83m/C; DVD, Blu-Ray.** Amy Poehler; Paul Rudd; Bill Hader; Ellie Kemper; Cobie Smulders; Christopher Meloni; Max Greenfield; Ed Helms; Melanie Lynskey; ***D:*** David Wain; ***W:*** David Wain; Michael Showalter; ***C:*** Tom Houghton; ***M:*** Craig Werden; Matt Novack.

They Come Back 🦴 1/2 **2007** Psychologist Faith Hardy (Kirshner) is feeling vulnerable after a patient disappears, and is reluctant to take on the case of young Marley (Wilson), whose parents were killed in the car accident she survived. But after a series of strange events, Faith is sure Marley is being menaced by something evil. **90m/C; DVD.** Mia Kirshner; Niamh Wilson; Jonathan Watton; Rosemary Dunsmore; Charlotte Arnold; Christy Bruce; ***D:*** John Bradshaw; ***W:*** Gary Boulton-Brown; ***C:*** John Dyer; ***M:*** Stacey Hersh. **CABLE**

They Crawl 🦴🦴 *Crawlers* **2001 (R)** More complicated than usual for the creepy crawlie genre. Ted Gage (Cosgrove) learns his biophysicist brother has been electrocuted and all his organs removed. Ted teams up with cop Gina (Davies) to figure out what's going on and finds connections between the murder, a homicidal cult, and lethal cockroaches linked to a government surveillance project. Everybody looks convinced that this makes some kind of sense. **93m/C; VHS, DVD.** Daniel Cosgrove; Dennis Boutsikaris; Tim Thomerson; Tamara Davis; Tone Loc; Mickey Rourke; Grace Zabriskie; ***D:*** John Allardice; ***W:*** Curtis Joseph; David Mason; ***C:*** Maximo Munzi; ***M:*** Neal Acree. **VIDEO**

They Died with Their Boots On 🦴🦴🦴 **1941** The Battle of Little Big Horn is re-created Hollywood style. Takes liberties with historical fact, but still an exciting portrayal of General Custer's last stand. The movie also marks the last time de Havilland worked with Flynn. Also available colorized. **141m/B; VHS, DVD.** Errol Flynn; Sydney Greenstreet; Anthony Quinn; Hattie McDaniel; Arthur Kennedy; Gene Lockhart; Regis Toomey; Olivia de Havilland; Charley Grapewin; G.P. (Tim) Huntley, Jr.; Frank Wilcox; Joseph (Joe) Sawyer; Eddie Acuff; Minor Watson; Tod Andrews; Stanley Ridges; John Litel; Walter Hampden; Joseph Crehan; Selmer Jackson; Gig Young; Dick Wessel; ***D:*** Raoul Walsh; ***W:*** Aeneas MacKenzie; ***C:*** Bert Glennon; ***M:*** Max Steiner.

They Drive by Night 🦴🦴🦴 1/2 *The Road to Frisco* **1940** Two truck-driving brothers break away from a large company and begin independent operations. After an accident to Bogart, Raft is forced to go back to the company where Lupino, the boss's wife, becomes obsessed with him and kills her husband to gain the company and win Raft. When he rejects her, she accuses him of the murder. Well-plotted film with great dialogue. Excellent cast gives it their all. **97m/B; VHS, DVD.** Humphrey Bogart; Ann Sheridan; George Raft; Ida Lupino; Alan Hale; Gale Page; Roscoe Karns; Charles Halton; ***D:*** Raoul Walsh.

They Gave Him a Gun 🦴 1/2 **1937** Weak MGM crime drama. Fred (Tracy) looks after Jimmy (Tone) in the WWI trenches where Jimmy turns into a medal-winning marksman. Fred is MIA and nurse Rose (George) agrees to marry Jimmy instead. Postwar, a very much alive Fred, who now manages a circus, runs into Jimmy in New York and he and Rose finally figure out that Jimmy has been working as a mob hitman. There's law and romantic trouble. **94m/B; DVD.** Spencer Tracy; Franchot Tone; Gladys George; Edgar Dearing; Mary Treen; ***D:*** W.S. Van Dyke; ***W:*** Cyril Hume; Maurice Rapf; ***C:*** Harold Rosson; ***M:*** Sigmund Romberg.

They Got Me Covered 🦴🦴 **1943** Two WWII-era journalists get involved in a comic web of murder, kidnapping and romance. Hope is very funny and carries the rest of the cast. Look for Doris Day in a bit part and listen for Bing Crosby singing whenever Hope opens his cigarette case. **95m/B; VHS, DVD.** Bob Hope; Dorothy Lamour; Otto Preminger; Eduardo Ciannelli; Donald Meek; Walter Catlett; Doris Day; ***V:*** Bing Crosby; ***D:*** David Butler; ***W:*** Harry Kurnitz; ***C:*** Rudolph Mate; ***M:*** Leigh Harline.

They Had to See Paris 🦴🦴 **1929** The first sound film to feature humorist Rogers. Pike Peters (Rogers) is a simple Oklahoman who becomes rich when oil is discovered on his property. His wife Idy (Rich) insists the family go to Paris for some culture and they rent a chateau where Idy is happy to indulge herself in society. But Pike would much rather be at home. **96m/B; DVD.** Will Rogers; Irene Rich; Marguerite Churchill; Owen Davis, Jr.; Fifi d'Orsay; Ivan Lebedeff; Rex Bell; Marcelle Corday; ***D:*** Frank Borzage; ***W:*** Sonya Levien; ***C:*** Chester Lyons.

They Live 🦴🦴 1/2 *Creepers* **1988 (R)** A semi-serious science-fiction spoof about a drifter who discovers an alien conspiracy. They're taking over the country under the guise of Reaganism, capitalism and yuppiedom. Screenplay written by Carpenter under a pseudonym. Starts out fun, deteriorates into cliches and bad special effects makeup. **88m/C; VHS, DVD, Blu-Ray.** Roddy Piper; Keith David; Meg Foster; George "Buck" Flower; Peter Jason; Raymond St. Jacques; John Lawrence; Sy Richardson; Jason Robards, III; Larry Franco; Wendy Brainard; Dana Bratton; ***D:*** John Carpenter; ***W:*** John Carpenter; Frank Armitage; ***C:*** Gary B. Kibbe; ***M:*** John Carpenter; Alan Howarth.

They Live by Night 🦴🦴🦴 1/2 *The Twisted Road; Your Red Wagon* **1949** Bowie (Granger) is a naive young criminal who joins a prison break with hardened cons Chickamaw (da Silva) and T-Dub (Flippen) who then use him as an extra pair of hands in a bank heist. Bowie tries to go straight by marrying young Keechie (O'Donnell) but gets sucked back in by his criminal compatriots and winds up a fugitive with no hope. Classic film noir was Ray's first attempt at directing. Based on Edward Anderson's novel "Thieves Like Us," under which title it was remade in 1974. Compelling and suspenseful. **95m/B; VHS, DVD, Blu-Ray.** Cathy O'Donnell; Farley Granger; Howard da Silva; Jay C. Flippen; Helen Craig; Will Wright; ***D:*** Nicholas Ray; ***W:*** Nicholas Ray; Charles Schnee; ***C:*** George E. Diskant; ***M:*** Leigh Harline.

They Made Me a Criminal 🦴🦴 1/2 *I Became a Criminal; They Made Me a Fugitive* **1939** A champion prizefighter, believing he murdered a man in a drunken brawl, runs away. He finds refuge in the West with the Dead End Kids. Remake of "The Life of Jimmy Dolan." Berkeley was best-known for directing and choreographing musicals and surprisingly did very well with this movie. **92m/B; VHS, DVD.** John Garfield; Ann Sheridan; Claude Rains; Leo Gorcey; Huntz Hall; Gabriel Dell; Bobby Jordan; Billy Halop; ***D:*** Busby Berkeley; ***W:*** Sid Herzig; ***C:*** James Wong Howe; ***M:*** Max Steiner.

They Made Me a Fugitive 🦴🦴 1/2 *I Became a Criminal; They Made Me a Criminal* **1947** Former RAF officer Clem Morgan (Howard) gets drawn into the excitement of the black market after the war but then is framed by his gang boss Narcey (Jones) when Morgan won't deal drugs. After he gets out of jail, Morgan heads back to Soho to get his revenge. Based on the novel "A Convict Has Escaped" by Jackson Budd. **96m/B; VHS, DVD, Blu-Ray.** *GB* Trevor Howard; Griffith Jones; Sally Gray; Rene Ray; Mary Merrall; Vida Hope; Charles Farrell; Ballard Berkeley; ***D:*** Alberto Cavalcanti; ***W:*** Noel Langley; ***C:*** Otto Heller; ***M:*** Marius Francois Gaillard.

They Met in Bombay 🦴🦴 1/2 **1941** Two jewel thieves team up in this romantic action-comedy, complete with exotic locations and two big boxoffice stars. A Japanese invasion makes Russell reconsider her life of crime and gives Gable a chance to play hero. Look for Alan Ladd in a bit part in his pre-"This Gun for Hire" days. Based on a story by John Kafka. **86m/B; VHS, DVD.** Clark Gable; Rosalind Russell; Peter Lorre; Jessie Ralph; Reginald Owen; Eduardo Ciannelli; Alan Ladd; ***D:*** Clarence Brown; ***W:*** Anita Loos; Edwin Justus Mayer; Leon Gordon.

They Might Be Giants 🦴🦴🦴 **1971 (G)** Woodward is a woman shrink named Watson who treats retired judge Scott for delusions that he is Sherlock Holmes. Scott's brother wants him committed so the family loot will come to him. Very funny in places; Woodward and Scott highlight a solid cast. **98m/C; VHS, DVD, Blu-Ray.** George C. Scott; Joanne Woodward; Jack Gilford; Eugene Roche; Kitty Winn; F. Murray Abraham; M. Emmet Walsh; ***D:*** Anthony Harvey; ***W:*** James Goldman; ***C:*** Victor Kemper; ***M:*** John Barry.

They Only Kill Their Masters 🦴🦴 1/2 **1972 (PG)** Garner plays a California police chief investigating the death of a wild beach town resident, supposedly killed by her doberman pinscher. He discovers the woman was actually drowned and there are any number of secrets to uncover. Mild whodunit. **98m/C; VHS, DVD.** James Garner; Katharine Ross; June Allyson; Hal Holbrook; Harry Guardino; Christopher Connelly; Tom Ewell; Peter Lawford; Edmond O'Brien; Arthur O'Connell; Ann Rutherford; Art Metrano; ***D:*** James Goldstone; ***M:*** Perry Botkin.

They Saved Hitler's Brain WOOF! *Madmen of Mandoras; The Return of Mr. H.* **1964** Fanatical survivors of the Nazi holocaust gave eternal life to the brain of their leader in the last hours of the war. Now it's on a Caribbean island giving orders again. One of the truly great "bad" movies. Shot in pieces in the U.S., the Philippines, and elsewhere, with chunks of other films stuck in to hold the "story" together. **91m/B; VHS, DVD.** Walter Stocker; Audrey Caire; Nestor Paiva; Carlos Rivas; Dani Lynn; Bill Freed; John Holland; Scott Peters; Marshall Reed; ***D:*** David Bradley; ***W:*** Richard Miles; Steve Bennett; ***C:*** Stanley Cortez; ***M:*** Don Hulette.

They Shall Have Music 🦴🦴 *Melody of Youth; Ragged Angels* **1939** A poverty-stricken child hears a concert by violinist Heifetz and decides to become a musician. He joins Brennan's nearly bankrupt music school and persuades Heifetz to play at a benefit concert. Hokey but enjoyable Goldwyn effort to bring classical music to the big screen. **101m/B; DVD.** Walter Brennan; Joel McCrea; Gene Reynolds; Jascha Heifetz; Marjorie Main; Porter Hall; Andrea Leeds; Terence (Terry) Kilburn; *D:* Archie Mayo; *W:* Robert Presnell, Sr.; *C:* Gregg Toland; *M:* Alfred Newman.

They Shall Not Grow Old 1/2 **2019 (R)** Released during the anniversary of the armistice that ended World War I, this striking documentary by lauded director Jackson focuses on the experiences of the many thousands who fought in the massive conflict. Taking the British perspective on the war, the documentary considers the whole of the conflict, from its beginning to its end, especially the destructive nature of combat. The film's power comes from the digital enhancement of old footage, including adding color to black and white images, as well as using archived voice recordings of the war's veterans and sound effects to make its many horrors relatable for a modern audience. **99m/C; DVD, Blu-Ray.** *D:* Peter Jackson.

They Shoot Horses, Don't They? 1/2 **1969 (R)** Powerful period piece depicting the desperation of the Depression Era. Contestants enter a dance marathon in the hopes of winning a cash prize, not realizing that they will be driven to exhaustion. Fascinating and tragic. **121m/C; VHS, DVD, Blu-Ray.** Jane Fonda; Michael Sarrazin; Susannah York; Gig Young; Red Buttons; Bonnie Bedelia; Bruce Dern; Allyn Ann McLerie; Severn Darden; Al Lewis; *D:* Sydney Pollack; *W:* Robert E. Thompson; James Poe; *C:* Philip H. Lathrop; *M:* Johnny Green. Oscars '69: Support. Actor (Young); British Acad. '70: Support. Actress (York); Golden Globes '70: Support. Actor (Young); N.Y. Film Critics '69: Actress (Fonda).

They Went That-a-Way & That-a-Way WOOF! **1978 (PG)** Two bumbling deputies pose as convicts in this madcap prison caper. Terrible re-hash of Laurel-and-Hardy has nothing going for it. **96m/C; VHS, DVD.** Tim Conway; Richard Kiel; Chuck McCann; Sonny Shroyer; Lenny Montana; *D:* Edward Montagne; *W:* Tim Conway.

They Were Expendable 1/2 **1945** Two American captains pit their PT boats against the Japanese fleet. Based on the true story of a PT boat squadron based in the Philippines during the early days of WWII. One of the best (and most underrated) WWII films. Also available in a colorized version. **135m/B; VHS, DVD, Blu-Ray.** Robert Montgomery; John Wayne; Donna Reed; Jack Holt; Ward Bond; Cameron Mitchell; Leon Ames; Marshall Thompson; Paul Langton; Donald Curtis; Jeff York; Murray Alper; Jack Pennick; Alex Havier; Charles Trowbridge; Robert Barrat; Bruce Kellogg; Louis Jean Heydt; Russell Simpson; Philip Ahn; Betty Blythe; William B. Davidson; Pedro de Cordoba; Arthur Walsh; Harry Tenbrook; Tim Murdock; Vernon Steele; *D:* John Ford; *W:* Frank Wead; *C:* Joseph August; *M:* Herbert Stothart; Eric Zeisl.

They Were So Young 1/2 **1955** European models become the pawns of wealthy Brazilian magnates when they are sent to South America. They are threatened with death if they do not cooperate. The scenes were shot in Italy and Berlin. Well acted and believable, although rather grim story. **78m/B; VHS, DVD.** *GE* Scott Brady; Johanna (Hannerl) Matz; Raymond Burr; *D:* Kurt Neumann.

They Will Have to Kill Us First: Malian Music in Exile 1/2 **2015** This feature-length documentary focuses on the impact of an Islamic extremist policy that bans music in the areas of Mali that they control. Citing shira law, the jihadists that control northern Mali have enforced this ban by torturing and killing musicians, destroying radio stations, and burning instruments. A number of Malian musicians managed to escape and live in hiding or exile, where they continue to make music, work to preserve their cultural identities, and fight for their country and its heritage. **105m/C; DVD, Download.** **VIDEO**

They Won't Believe Me **1947** A man plots to kill his wife, but before he does, she commits suicide. He ends up on trial for her "murder." Interesting acting by Young and Hayward against type. Surprising, ironic ending. **95m/B; VHS, DVD, Streaming.** Robert Young; Susan Hayward; Rita Johnson; Jane Greer; *D:* Irving Pichel.

They Won't Forget 1/2 **1937** When a young girl is murdered in a southern town, personal interests take precedence over justice. Turner is excellent in her first billed role, as are the other actors. Superb script, and expert direction by LeRoy pulls it all together. Based on Ward Greene's "Death in the Deep South." **95m/B; VHS, DVD.** Claude Rains; Otto Kruger; Lana Turner; Allyn Joslyn; Elisha Cook, Jr.; Edward Norris; Gloria Dickson; Frank Faylen; *D:* Mervyn LeRoy; *W:* Robert Rossen; Aben Kandel.

They're Playing with Fire WOOF! **1984 (R)** An English teacher seduces a student and gets him involved in a murder plot to gain an inheritance. Turns out someone else is beating them to the punch. Sleazy semi-pornographic slasher. **96m/C; VHS, DVD, Blu-Ray.** Sybil Danning; Eric Brown; Andrew Prine; Paul Clemens; K.T. Stevens; Alvy Moore; *D:* Howard (Hikmet) Avedis; *W:* Howard (Hikmet) Avedis.

They're Watching **2016** A comedy horror about the unexpected adventures of an American television show in Eastern Europe. When the crew members of a U.S.-based home improvement television show travel to a remote village in Eastern Europe to renovate an old house, they are concerned that their biggest challenges will be the lack of free wifi and other Western comforts. However, the filming of the show unintentionally interrupts a private, sacred religious ritual of the superstitious villagers. They take their revenge on the interrupting Americans in violent ways that leaves the crew fighting for their lives. **95m/C; DVD, Streaming, Download.** David Alpay; Brigid Brannagh; Carrie Genzel; Kris Lemche; Dimitri Diatchenko; *D:* Jay Lender; Micah Wright; *W:* Jay Lender; Micah Wright; *M:* Jonathan Wandag.

Thick as Thieves 1/2 **1999 (R)** Master thief Mackin (Baldwin) likes to get the job done and then return to his quietly sophisticated private life. Pointy (White) is the arrogant up-and-comer, with mob ties, who wants to eliminate the competition by setting Mackin up for a crime. The dual between the duo upsets mob boss Sal Capetti (Byrd) and has police officer Petrone (DeMornay) also very interested. **93m/C; VHS, DVD.** Alec Baldwin; Michael Jai White; Rebecca De Mornay; Andre Braugher; Bruce Greenwood; David Byrd; Richard Edson; Khandi Alexander; Robert Miano; Janeane Garofalo; Julia Sweeney; Ricky Harris; Michael Jace; *D:* Scott Sanders; *W:* Scott Sanders; Arthur Krystal; *C:* Chris Walling; *M:* Christophe Beck. **CABLE**

Thicker Than Water **1993** Eerie psychological thriller exploring the relationship between identical twins. Sam Crawford (Pryce) is a successful doctor, happily married to Jo (Russell), whose sister Debbie (Russell again) is completely different in temperament. The two share a strong psychic bond, however, and when Jo dies in a suspicious hit-and-run accident Debbie feels compelled to make Sam her own. Based on the novel by Dylan Jones. **150m/C; VHS, DVD.** *GB* Theresa Russell; Jonathan Pryce; Robert Pugh; *D:* Marc Evans; *W:* Trevor Preston.

Thicker than Water 1/2 **1999 (R)** Typical urban gangsta flick. Two rival LA gang leaders, DJ and Lonzo, want to get into the music biz. They decide to put their rivalries aside and get the money for their venture by organizing their homeboys and pushing product for drug kingpin Gator. But just when the money starts rolling in, Gator pulls a doublecross and the gang rivalries explode again. **90m/C; DVD.** Mack-10; Fat Joe; Ice Cube; Kidada Jones; CJ Mac; MC Eight; Louis Freese; Flesh N Bone; Big Pun; *D:* Richard Cummings, Jr.; *W:* Ernest Nyle Brown; *C:* Robert Benavides; *M:* Tyler Bates; Quincey Jones, III.

The Thief **1952** An American commits treason and is overcome by guilt. Novel because there is not one word of dialogue, though the gimmmick can't sustain the ordinary story. A product of the Communist scare of the 1950s, it tends to be pretentious and melodramatic. **84m/B; VHS, DVD.** Ray Milland; Rita Gam; Martin Gabel; Harry Bronson; John McKutcheon; *D:* Russell Rouse; *W:* Russell Rouse; Clarence Greene; *C:* Sam Leavitt; *M:* Herschel Burke Gilbert.

Thief *Violent Streets* **1981 (R)** A big-time professional thief likes working solo, but decides to sign up with the mob in order to make one more big score and retire. He finds out it's not that easy. Taut and atmospheric thriller is director Mann's feature film debut. **126m/C; VHS, DVD, Blu-Ray.** James Caan; Tuesday Weld; Willie Nelson; James Belushi; Elizabeth Pena; Robert Prosky; Dennis Farina; *D:* Michael Mann; *W:* Michael Mann; *C:* Donald E. Thorin; *M:* Tangerine Dream.

The Thief *Vor* **1997 (R)** Postwar Russian drama set in 1952. Katya (Rednikova) is a young widow with a six year-old son, Sanya (Philipchuk). She's traveling by train when a soldier named Tolyan (Mashkov) enters their compartment. But the end of the trip, Katya's decided to go off with Tolyan and the threesome become a family. But Tolyan harbors a violent streak and Katya also discovers that Tolyan is an imposter—he's not a soldier but a thief. Still, she loves him and soon becomes his accomplice. Russian with subtitles. **92m/C; VHS, DVD.** *RU* Vladimir Mashkov; Yekaterina Rednikova; Misha Philipchuk; *D:* Pavel Chukhrai; *W:* Pavel Chukhrai; *C:* Vladimir Klimov; *M:* Vladimir Dashkevich.

The Thief and the Cobbler 1/2 **1996 (G)** Musically animated fairy tale about Tack, a humble cobbler (Broderick) who aids the clever and beautiful Princess Yum Yum (Beals) when their town's golden treasures are stolen. Legendary villain Price lends his voice as the evil Zig Zag. Three time Oscar winning director Williams (of "Who Framed Roger Rabbit?" fame), and a team of animators led by Harris (part of the team that created Bugs Bunny) created sophisticated optical illusions that the team dubbed "two and a half dimensional." Incorporating intricate lighting, shadows and smooth motion, the project took almost three decades to complete. Soundtrack performed by the London Symphony Orchestra. **72m/C; VHS, DVD.** *V:* Vincent Price; Matthew Broderick; Jennifer Beals; Eric Bogosian; Toni Collette; Jonathan Winters; Clive Revill; Kenneth Williams; Clinton Sundberg; Thick Wilson; *D:* Richard Williams; *W:* Richard Williams; *C:* John Leatherbarrow; *M:* Robert Folk.

The Thief Lord **2006 (PG)** Fantasy is based on a popular children's book by Cornelia Fulke, and the Venice setting is gorgeous, but it's best seen by undemanding kiddies who won't mind its contrivances. Orphaned brothers Prosper and Bo are befriended by teenaged Scipio, the self-proclaimed Thief Lord, who cares for a group of child thieves living in an abandoned cinema. Scipio is hired by a greedy dealer to find a mysterious antique that can allegedly reverse time and the brothers get caught up in the adventure. **98m/C; DVD.** *GB GE LU* Aaron Taylor-Johnson; Rollo Weeks; Jim Carter; Caroline Goodall; Jasper Harris; Alexei Sayle; Richard Bathurst; *D:* Richard Claus; *W:* Richard Claus; Daniel Musgrave; *C:* David Slama; *M:* Nigel Clarke; Michael Csanyi-Wills.

The Thief of Bagdad 1/2 **1940** A wily young thief enlists the aid of a powerful genie to outwit the Grand Vizier of Baghdad. An Arabian Nights spectacular with lush photography, fine special effects, and striking score. Outstanding performance by Ingram as the genie. **106m/C; VHS, DVD.** *GB* Sabu; Conrad Veidt; June Duprez; Rex Ingram; John Justin; Miles Malleson; Morton Selten; Mary Morris; *D:* Tim Whelan; Michael Powell; Ludwig Berger; Alexander Korda; Zoltan Korda; William Cameron Menzies; *W:* Miles Malleson; Lajos Biro; *C:* Georges Perinal; *M:* Miklos Rozsa. Oscars '40: Color Cinematog.

The Thief of Baghdad **1924** The classic silent crowd-pleaser, about a roguish thief who uses a genie's magic to outwit Baghdad's evil Caliph. With famous special effects in a newly struck print, and a new score by Davis based on Rimsky-Korsakov's "Scheherezade." Remade many times. **153m/B; Silent; DVD, Blu-Ray.** Douglas Fairbanks, Sr.; Snitz Edwards; Charles Belcher; Anna May Wong; Etta Lee; Brandon Hurst; Sojin; Julanne Johnston; *D:* Raoul Walsh; *M:* Carl Davis. Natl. Film Reg. '96.

The Thief of Baghdad 1/2 **1978 (G)** A fantasy-adventure about a genie, a prince, beautiful maidens, a happy-go-lucky thief, and magic. Easy to take, but not an extraordinary version of this oft-told tale. Ustinov is fun as he tries to marry off his daughter. **101m/C; VHS, DVD.** Peter Ustinov; Roddy McDowall; Terence Stamp; Frank Finlay; Ian Holm; *D:* Clive Donner. **TV**

Thief of Hearts **1984 (R)** A thief steals a woman's diary when he's ransacking her house. He then pursues the woman, using his secret knowledge. Slick, but too creepy. Re-edited with soft porn scenes in some video versions. Stewart's first film. **101m/C; DVD.** Steven Bauer; Barbara Williams; John Getz; Christine Ebersole; George Wendt; *D:* Douglas Day Stewart; *W:* Douglas Day Stewart; *C:* Andrew Laszlo; *M:* Harold Faltermeyer.

The Thief of Paris 1/2 *Le Voleur* **1967** Gentle study of a 19th-century burglar, Georges (Belmondo), who enters his profession out of necessity but stays because of obsession, is one of the most unjustly overlooked films of Louis Malle's career. There are many light moments, but at heart it's a gloomy and melancholy tale of a man lost in the details of his job?-his work means everything to him, and he's willing to give everything up for it. The downbeat tone didn't go over in the U.S. Visually stunning, delicate, and surprisingly affecting. **120m/C; DVD.** *FR* Jean-Paul Belmondo; Genevieve Bujold; Marie DuBois; Julien Guiomar; Francoise Fabian; Marlene Jobert; Bernadette LaFont; Martine Sarcey; Roger Crouzet; Charles Denner; Paul Le Person; Christian Lude; *D:* Louis Malle; *W:* Louis Malle; Jean-Claude Carriere; Georges Darien; *C:* Henri Decae.

A Thief of Time 1/2 **2004** Navaho tribal policemen Joe Leaphorn and Jim Chee suspect a missing anthropologist was selling Anasazi pottery on the black market. This leads them to rival colleagues, poachers, and shady collectors, as well as dead bodies. Based on the novel by Tony Hillerman. **95m/C; DVD.** Wes Studi; Adam Beach; Gary Farmer; Graham Greene; Sheila Toussey; Peter Fonda; Lee Tergesen; James Pollard; *D:* Chris Eyre; *W:* Alice Arden; *C:* Roy Wagner; *M:* B.C. Smith. **TV**

Thieves Like Us 1/2 **1974 (R)** Story of doomed lovers during the Depression is thoughtfully told by Altman. Older criminals Remsen and Schuck escape from jail with young killer Carradine. They only know one way to make a living—robbing banks—and it isn't long before they're once more working at their trade. They get a lot of press but they have a distinct problem. They're not really very good at what they do. Cops on their trail, the gang tries, unsuccessfully, to survive. Fletcher's film debut as Remsen's sister-in-law. Good period atmosphere and strong characters. Based on the novel by Edward Anderson and previously filmed as "They Live by Night." **123m/C; VHS, DVD, Blu-Ray.** Keith Carradine; Shelley Duvall; Bert Remsen; John Schuck; Louise Fletcher; Anne Latham; Tom Skerritt; *D:* Robert Altman; *W:* Joan Tewkesbury; Calder Willingham; Robert Altman.

Thieves of Fortune WOOF! **1989 (R)** Former Miss Universe stars as a contestant in a high stakes fortune hunt that spans half the globe. She meets with more than her share of action-packed encounters among the ruffians who compete for the $28 million purse. Implausible; horrible script; cliched. **100m/C; VHS, DVD.** Michael Nouri; Lee Van Cleef; Shawn Weatherly; *D:* Michael Maccarone; *W:* Michael Maccarone; *C:* James Robb.

Thin Air *Robert B. Parker's Thin Air* **2000** Frank Belson (Ferry) didn't know much about his pretty new wife Lisa (Butler) before he married her. So when she suddenly disappears, he hires Spenser (Mantegna) to locate her and the PI also uncovers some secrets from her past. Based on the novel by Robert B. Parker. **90m/C; DVD.** Joe Mantegna; Marcia Gay Harden; David Ferry; Yancy Butler; Luis Guzman; Jon Seda; Miguel (Michael) Sandoval; *D:* Robert Mandel; *W:* Robert B. Parker; *C:* Robert L. Surtees; *M:* David Shire. **CABLE**

The Thin Blue Lie 1/2 **2000 (R)** Based on a real-life police corruption scandal that took place in the '70s in Philadelphia. Jonathan Neumann (Morrow) takes over the court beat for the Philadelphia Examiner and is soon wallowing in cases of police abuse, which he promptly documents in print. He's soon threatened by the cops and gets on the bad side of blustery mayor, Frank Rizzo (Sorvino). Docudrama's kinda blustery itself. **97m/C; VHS, DVD.** Rob Morrow; Randy Quaid; Paul Sorvino; Cynthia (Cyndy, Cindy) Preston; G.W. Bailey; Al Waxman; Beau Starr; Chuck Shamata; *D:* Roger Young; *W:* Daniel Helfgott; *C:* Donald M. Morgan; *M:* Patrick Williams. **CABLE**

The Thin Blue Line 1/2 **1988** The acclaimed docudrama about the 1977 shooting of a cop in Dallas County, and the incorrect conviction of Randall Adams for the crime. A riveting, spellbinding experience. Due to the film's impact and continued lobbying by Morris, Adams is now free. **101m/C; VHS, DVD, Blu-Ray.** *D:* Errol Morris; *W:* Errol Morris; *C:* Robert Chappell; Stefan Czapsky; *M:* Philip Glass. Natl. Film Reg. '01.

Thin Ice **1937** Successful musical romance featuring European prince Power falling for commoner Henie. A fine score, solid script, and Henie's excellent ice skating routines make this her best film. Based on the play "Der Komet" by Attila Obok. **78m/B; DVD.** Sonja Henie; Tyrone Power; Arthur Treacher; Raymond Walburn; Joan Davis; Alan Hale; Sig Rumann; Melville Cooper; Maurice Cass; George Givot; Torben Meyer; *D:* Sidney Lanfield; *W:* Boris Ingster; Milton Sperling.

Thin Ice 1/2 *The Convincer* **2012 (R)** Reportedly heavily mangled in post-production, director/writer Sprecher's first film in a decade never quite comes together into the Fargo-esque black comedy that it should have been. Mickey (an inspiring Kinnear) is a sleazy insurance salesman who always goes for the up-sell. He tries to squeeze every dime out of hoarder Gorvy (Arkin) and stumbles into an increasingly complicated situation involving a violin that may be worth a tidy sum. Arkin, Kinnear, and Crudup (as an outrageous locksmith) have perfect comic timing but the piece goes awry, especially in the final act. **114m/C; DVD, Blu-Ray.** Greg Kinnear; Alan Arkin; Billy Crudup; Lea Thompson; David Harbour; Bob Balaban; *D:* Jill Sprecher; *W:* Jill Sprecher; Karen Sprecher; *C:* Dick Pope; *M:* Jeff Danna.

A Thin Line Between Love and Hate **1996 (R)** Writer/director/star Lawrence shows that there's no line between a crude, foulmouthed ego trip and an unfunny, unsuspenseful film. Darnell Wright is a smooth talker constantly on the lookout for women to conquer and discard. Eventually, he meets the wrong lady (Whitfield), a classic movie psycho who turns his life upside down. Drawing heavily from "Fatal Attraction," this halfhearted effort offers bad pacing, a weak script, and totally unsympathetic characters, which could almost be overlooked if it was at all funny. Whitfield holds the flick's only redeeming value as the femme fatale. **106m/C; VHS, DVD.** Martin Lawrence; Lynn Whitfield; Regina King; Bobby Brown; Della Reese; Roger E. Mosley; Malinda Williams; Daryl (Chill) Mitchell; Simbi Khali; Tracy Morgan; *D:* Martin Lawrence; *W:* Martin Lawrence; Bentley Kyle Evans; Kenny Buford; Kim Bass; *C:* Francis Kenny; *M:* Roger Troutman.

The Thin Man 1/2 **1934** Married sleuths Nick (Powell) and Nora (Loy) Charles investigate the mysterious disappearance of a wealthy inventor. Charming and sophisticated, this was the model for all husband-and-wife detective teams that followed. Don't miss Asta, their wire-hair terrier. Based on the novel by Dashiell Hammett. Its enormous popularity triggered five sequels, starting with "After the Thin Man." **90m/B; VHS, DVD, Blu-Ray.** William Powell; Myrna Loy; Maureen O'Sullivan; Cesar Romero; Porter Hall; Nat Pendleton; Minna Gombell; Natalie Moorhead; Edward Ellis; *D:* W.S. Van Dyke; *W:* Albert Hackett; Frances Goodrich; *C:* James Wong Howe. Natl. Film Reg. '97.

The Thin Man Goes Home 1/2 **1944** Married sleuths Nick and Nora Charles solve a mystery with Nick's disapproving parents looking on in the fifth film from the "Thin Man" series. Despite a three-year gap and slightly less chemistry between Powell and Loy, audiences welcomed the skinny guy. Sequel to "Shadow of the Thin Man"; followed by "Song of the Thin Man." **100m/B; VHS, DVD.** William Powell; Myrna Loy; Lucile Watson; Gloria De Haven; Anne Revere; Harry Davenport; Helen Vinson; Lloyd Corrigan; Donald Meek; Edward Brophy; Charles Halton; *D:* Richard Thorpe.

The Thin Red Line 1/2 **1964** First adaptation of the James Jones novel about the fight for Guadalcanal focuses on the relationship between Sgt. Welsh (Warden) and Pvt. Doll (Dullea). As battle experience hardens Doll, the mutual hatred the two have changes to a grudging respect. Effectively portrays the dehumanizing psychological effects of war. **99m/B; VHS, DVD, Blu-Ray.** Keir Dullea; Jack Warden; James Philbrook; Kieron Moore; Ray Daley; Merlyn Yordan; Bob Kanter; Stephen Levy; *D:* Andrew Marton; *W:* Bernard Gordon; *C:* Manuel Berenguer; *M:* Malcolm Arnold.

The Thin Red Line **1998 (R)** After a long hiatus, director Malick returns in this epic WWII saga about a rifle company fighting at Guadalcanal. Visually stunning and focused on the inner thoughts, feelings, and philosophical leanings of the soldiers, the film sacrifices plot and continuity to study the questions of Man vs. Nature and the Origin of Evil. Plot difficulties are highlighted by the physical similarities of relative newcomers Chaplin and Caviezel. Combat scenes are, naturally, beautifully shot and effective, while the relationship between Penn and Caviezel makes the biggest impression among the many subplots (some of which go nowhere) and the star-laden, large cast. Based on the 1962 novel by James Jones. **170m/C; VHS, DVD, Blu-Ray.** James (Jim) Caviezel; Adrien Brody; Sean Penn; Nick Nolte; John Cusack; George Clooney; Woody Harrelson; Ben Chaplin; Elias Koteas; Jared Leto; John Travolta; Tim Blake Nelson; John C. Reilly; John Savage; Arie Verveen; David Harrod; Thomas Jane; Paul Gleason; Penelope Allen; Don Harvey; Shawn Hatosy; Donal Logue; Dash Mihok; Larry Romano; Kirk Acevedo; Miranda Otto; Nick Stahl; *D:* Terrence Malick; *W:* Terrence Malick; *C:* John Toll; *M:* Hans Zimmer. N.Y. Film Critics '98: Director (Malick); Natl. Soc. Film Critics '98: Cinematog.

The Thing 1/2 *The Thing from Another World* **1951** One of the best of the Cold War allegories and a potent lesson to those who won't eat their vegetables. Sci fi classic about an alien craft and creature (Arness in monster drag), discovered by an Arctic research team. The critter is accidentally thawed and then wreaks havoc, sucking the blood from sled dog and scientist alike. It's a giant seed-dispersing vegetable run amuck, unaffected by missing body parts, bullets, or cold. In other words, Big Trouble. Excellent direction, assisted substantially by producer Hawks, and supported by strong performances. Available colorized; remade in 1982. Loosely based on "Who Goes There?" by John Campbell. **87m/B; VHS, DVD, Blu-Ray.** James Arness; Kenneth Tobey; Margaret Sheridan; Dewey Martin; Robert Cornthwaite; Douglas Spencer; James L. Young; Robert Nichols; William (Bill) Self; Eduard Franz; Sally Creighton; John Dierkes; George Fenneman; *D:* Christian Nyby; Howard Hawks; *W:* Charles Lederer; Ben Hecht; *C:* Russell Harlan; *M:* Dimitri Tiomkin. Natl. Film Reg. '01.

The Thing 1/2 **1982 (R)** A team of scientists at a remote Antarctic outpost discover a buried spaceship with an unwelcome alien survivor still alive. Bombastic special effects overwhelm the suspense and the solid cast. Less a remake of the 1951 science fiction classic than a more faithful version of John Campbell's short story "Who Goes There?," since the seeds/spores take on human shapes. **109m/C; VHS, DVD, Blu-Ray.** Kurt Russell; Wilford Brimley; T.K. Carter; Richard Masur; Keith David; Richard Dysart; David Clennon; Donald Moffat; Thomas G. Waites; Charles Hallahan; *D:* John Carpenter; *W:* Bill Lancaster; *C:* Dean Cundey; *M:* Ennio Morricone.

The Thing **2011 (R)** After 40 minutes of exposition, a mostly interchangeable cast of Norwegians and an American scientist excavate a shapeshifting alien from the Antarctic before it begins to murder them all for the crime of appearing in a sub-standard prequel to the 1982 John Carpenter film. All in all, the monster is like a metaphor for the movie itself. It makes an imperfect copy of its target that doesn't stand up to serious scrutiny. Much of what made the original special is gone. **103m/C; DVD, Blu-Ray.** Mary Elizabeth Winstead; Joel Edgerton; Adewale Akinnuoye-Agbaje; Eric Christian Olsen; Ulrich Thomsen; *D:* Matthijs van Heijningen, Jr.; *W:* Eric Heisserer; *C:* Michel Abramowicz; *M:* Marco Beltrami.

The Thing About My Folks 1/2 **2005 (PG-13)** What happens when an old man on the brink of a divorce drops into his adult son's life? You get a vehicle for Peter Falk's patented crusty lovability. Sam Kleinman (Falk), after a lifetime spent buried in his work, is alone and unfulfilled after his wife Muriel (Dukakis) walks out. Son Ben (Reiser), a successful New York professional who is happily married to Rachel (Perkins), is considering a move to the country. Ben takes his father to inspect a property and the two are plunged into an adventure which includes a classic car, a billiard hall and a fishing trip, all of which serve as a framework for unraveling the meaning of life. Totally worth seeing Falk's magic. **96m/C; DVD.** Paul Reiser; Peter Falk; Olympia Dukakis; Elizabeth Perkins; Mackenzie Connolly; Lydia Grace Jordan; Ann Dowd; Claire Beckman; Mimi Lieber; *D:* Raymond De Felitta; *W:* Paul Reiser; *C:* Dan Gillham; *M:* Steven Argila.

The Thing Called Love 1/2 **1993 (PG-13)** Take last year's surprise hit "Singles" and replace grunge rock and Seattle with Country/Western and Nashville for this unsentimental tale of four 20-something singles trying to make their mark in the world of country music. The idea for the plot comes from the real-life Bluebird Cafe—the place where all aspiring singers and songwriters want to perform. Phoenix, Mathis, Mulroney, and Bullock did their own singing; look for Oslin as the Cafe owner. Phoenix's last completed film role. **116m/C; VHS, DVD.** River Phoenix; Samantha Mathis; Sandra Bullock; Dermot Mulroney; K.T. Oslin; Anthony Clark; Webb Wilder; ***Cameo(s):*** Trisha Yearwood; *D:* Peter Bogdanovich; *W:* Allan Moyle; Carol Heikkinen; *C:* Peter James.

The Thing with Two Heads 1/2 **1972 (PG)** The inspired box copy says it all: "They share the same body...but hate each other's guts!" Max Kirshner (Milland), a white racist surgeon, plans to cheat death by having his head attached to another body. Imagine his surprise when he finds his noggin stitched onto black Jack Moss (Grier), right next to the original head. Nobody involved is taking the material too seriously. **93m/C; DVD, Blu-Ray.** Ray Milland; Roosevelt "Rosie" Grier; Don Marshall; Roger Perry; Kathrine Baumann; Lee Frost; Wes Bishop; Rick Baker; *D:* Lee Frost; *W:* James Gordon White; *C:* Jack Steely; *M:* Robert O. Ragland.

Things **1989** A man creates a monster during his freakish experiments with artificial insemination. The monster returns to his house seeking revenge, and the man's visiting brother and a friend disappear, probably a clever move given their lackluster circumstances. **90m/C; VHS, DVD.** Barry Gillis; Amber Lynn; Doug Bunston; Bruce Roach; *D:* Andrew Jordan; *W:* Andrew Jordan; *C:* Dan Riggs; *M:* Jack Procher.

Things 1/2 **1993** Two horror tales told by a jilted wife who's holding her husband's mistress hostage. "The Box" finds evil Mayor Black (Delama) incensed about a newly opened brothel in his hick Nevada town. So he decides to teach the hookers a lesson with the help of a bizarre, boxed creature that's with him at all times. "Thing in a Jar" finds an abusive husband and his mistress plotting to kill his mousy wife. Only the murder victim comes back to haunt the deadly duo'at least parts of her do. Nicely grotesque special effects courtesy of Mike Tristano. **85m/C; VHS, DVD.** Neil Delama; Trey Howard; Debra Stevens; Courtney Lercara; Kinder Hunt; ***Cameo(s):*** Jeff Burr; *D:* Dennis Devine; Jay Woelfel; *W:* Dennis Devine; Steve Jarvis; Mike Bowler.

Things Behind the Sun 1/2 **2001 (R)** Writer/director Anders partially takes on her own traumatic past to tell a story of rape and its long aftermath. Troubled singer-songwriter Sherry McGrale (Dickens) has a radio hit with a song about being raped as a girl in her Florida hometown. Music reporter Owen (Mann) gets the assignment to interview Sherry after revealing that he and Sherry were friends in school and he knows who raped her. When Owen finally meets Sherry again, the circumstances of the past are revealed to them both. **117m/C; VHS, DVD.** Kim Dickens; Gabriel Mann; Don Cheadle; Eric Stoltz; Elizabeth Pena; Rosanna Arquette; Alison Folland; Patsy Kensit; CCH Pounder; *D:* Allison Anders; *W:* Allison Anders; Kurt Voss; *C:* Terry Stacey.

Things Change **1988 (PG)** An old Italian shoeshine guy agrees, for a fee, to be a fall guy for the Mafia. A lower-echelon mob hood, assigned to watch over him, decides to give the old guy a weekend of fun in Vegas before going to jail. Director Mamet co-wrote the screenplay with Silverstein, best-known for his children's books ("Where the Sidewalk Ends," "The Giving Tree"). Combines charm and menace with terrific performances, especially from Ameche and Mantegna. **114m/C; VHS, DVD.** Joe Mantegna; Don Ameche; Robert Prosky; J.J. Johnston; Ricky Jay; Mike Nussbaum; Jack Wallace; Dan Conway; J.T. Walsh; William H. Macy; *D:* David Mamet; *W:* David Mamet; Shel Silverstein; *M:* Alaric Jans. Venice Film Fest. '80: Actor (Ameche); Venice Film Fest. '88: Actor (Mantegna).

Things Happen at Night **1948** Scientist and insurance investigator determine that friendly ghost has possessed a family's youngest daughter. Not much happens. **79m/B; VHS, DVD.** *GB* Gordon Harker; Alfred Drayton; Robertson Hare; Olga Lindo; Wylie Watson; *D:* Francis Searle.

Things I Left in Havana *Cosas que deje en La Habana* **1997** A Spanish comedy-drama exploring romance tied to Cuban immigrants abroad. On a plane to Spain, three sisters have left Havana for Madrid to stay with their aunt and work in her fur shop though they lack papers. Also on the plane is Barbaro (Garcia) who lodges with Igor (Perugorria), a poor but streetwise man seeking upward mobility. Through the efforts of a matchmaker and proximity, the groups intermingle and create romantic sparks. Spanish with subtitles. **110m/C; DVD.** Jorge Perugorria; Luis Alberto Garcia; Violeta Rodriguez; Kiti Manver; Broseliande Hernandez; *D:* Manuel Gutierrez Aragon; *W:* Manuel Gutierrez Aragon; *C:* Teodoro Escamilla.

Things I Never Told You **1996** Over-educated clerk Ann's (Taylor) just been dumped long-distance by her boyfriend. After a half-hearted suicide attempt, she calls a hot line and is connected to Don (McCarthy), who's equally depressed about the way his life is going. He discovers who Ann is and tentatively begins to court her, without revealing his true identity. The entire movie is tentative (including most of the performances). **93m/C; VHS, DVD.** Lili Taylor; Andrew McCarthy; Debi Mazar; Alexis Arquette; Leslie Mann; Richard Edson; Seymour Cassel; *D:* Isabel Coixet; *W:* Isabel Coixet; *C:* Teresa Medina; *M:* Alfonso Vilallonga.

Things to Come 1/2 **1936** Using technology, scientists aim to rebuild the world after a lengthy war, followed by a plague and other unfortunate events. Massey and Scott each play two roles, in different generations. Startling picture of the world to come, with fine sets and good acting. Based on an H.G. Wells story, "The Shape of Things to Come." **92m/B; VHS, DVD, Blu-Ray.** *GB* Raymond Massey; Margaretta Scott; Ralph Richardson; Cedric Hardwicke; Derrick DeMarney; Maurice Braddell; *D:* William Cameron Menzies; *W:* H.G. Wells; *C:* Georges Perinal; *M:* Arthur Bliss.

Things to Come *L'avenir* **2016 (PG-13)** One of two fantastic performances in 2016 by Huppert (the other being her Oscar nomination for "Elle") comes in this simple but effective drama by Mia Hansen-Love. Nathalie (Huppert) is a high school philosophy teacher in Paris. One day, completely unexpectedly, her husband announces that he's leaving her for another woman. She also has to deal with the death of her mother and getting fired from her job, and yet this is no weepie melodrama. It's about the unpredictability of life and dealing with things as they come while also recognizing that life changes for us all as we get older. **102m/C; DVD.** Isabelle Huppert; Andre Marcon; Roman Kolinka; Edith Scob; Sarah Le Picard; *D:* Mia Hansen-Love; *W:* Mia Hansen-Love; *C:* Denis Lenoir.

Things to Do 2006 Dissatisfied 25-year-old Adam (Stansko) quits his office job and moves back home for the summer. He comes up with a list of things he's always wanted to do and decides to see what he can accomplish before ultimately returning to adult responsibility. He enlists eccentric high-school buddy Mac (Wilson) to help him out. Of course, things don't always work out as expected. **85m/C; DVD.** *CA* Daniel G. Wilson; Michael Stansko; Amy Ballantyne; Pat McManus; Joanne Oke; Santo D'Asaro; ***D:*** Theodore Bezaire; ***W:*** Michael Stansko; Theodore Bezaire; ***C:*** Eric Schiller; ***M:*** Michael Stansko.

Things to Do in Denver When You're Dead 1995 (R) Jimmy the Saint (Garcia) is an ex-mobster gone straight who is called upon by his former boss, the Man With the Plan (Walken), to do one last easy-money job. Jimmy agrees and rounds up his old gang, a colorfully off-color group which includes Pieces (Lloyd), a porn movie projectionist and Critical Bill (Williams), a hair-trigger psycho who works in a funeral parlor. The job goes awry and the group becomes a target of hitman Mr. Shhh (Buscemi). Hipster dialogue, crime-gone-wrong formula, and the presence of Buscemi instantly scream Tarantino rip-off, but the performances make it a worthwhile genre entry. **115m/C; VHS, DVD.** Andy Garcia; Christopher Lloyd; William Forsythe; Bill Nunn; Treat Williams; Jack Warden; Steve Buscemi; Fairuza Balk; Gabrielle Anwar; Christopher Walken; Glenn Plummer; Don Cheadle; Bill Cobbs; Josh Charles; Michael Nicolosi; Marshall Bell; Sarah Trigger; Jenny McCarthy; Tommy (Tiny) Lister; ***D:*** Gary Fleder; ***W:*** Scott Rosenberg; ***C:*** Elliot Davis; ***M:*** Michael Convertino.

Things We Lost in the Fire ½ 2007 (R) Audrey Burke (Berry) is the widow of murdered husband Brian (Duchovny—who, for a dead character has a lot of screen time). Although she's left financially sound, she is now a grieving single mother to two young children. Audrey invites Brian's best friend, heroin addict Jerry Sunborne (Del Toro), to the funeral and something makes the two of them put aside their obvious and seemingly overwhelming differences to cling together in their grief. What works is the emotional interplay between the two, as Jerry struggles to kick his habit and Audrey struggles to rebuild a new life for herself and her children; both Del Toro and Berry shine. What doesn't is that too many elements—the differing ethnic backgrounds, Jerry's addiction, Audrey's acceptance of Jerry—simply beg questions, and at times the study of grief overpowers and feels manufactured. **118m/C; DVD, Blu-Ray.** Halle Berry; Benicio Del Toro; David Duchovny; Alison Lohman; Omar Benson Miller; John Carroll Lynch; Robin Weigert; Alexis Llewellyn; Micah Berry; Paula Newsome; ***D:*** Suzanne (Susanne) Bier; ***W:*** Allan Loeb; ***C:*** Tom Stern; ***M:*** Johan Soderqvist.

Things You Can Tell Just by Looking at Her ½ 2000 (PG-13) Ensemble female cast tells five stories that intersect in odd ways. Dr. Keener (Close) gets unhappy romantic news from tarot card reader Christine (Flockhart), whose own lover, Lilly (Golino), is terminally ill. Meanwhile, Rebecca (Hunter) has an abortion (performed by Dr. Keener) and then has an emotional breakdown. Then there's single mother Rose (Baker), who becomes intrigued by her new neighbor—a dwarf (Woodburn), and finally staid Kathy (Brenneman) and her exhuberantly sexy blind sister Carol (Diaz). **106m/C; VHS, DVD.** Cameron Diaz; Glenn Close; Calista Flockhart; Holly Hunter; Amy Brenneman; Kathy Baker; Valeria Golino; Matt Craven; Gregory Hines; Noah Fleiss; Miguel (Michael) Sandoval; Danny Woodburn; Roma Maffia; ***D:*** Rodrigo Garcia; ***W:*** Rodrigo Garcia; ***C:*** Emmanuel Lubezki; ***M:*** Ed Shearmur.

Think Fast, Mr. Moto ½ 1937 Japanese sleuth Mr. Moto (Lorre) is trailing diamond smugglers and boards a ship bound for Shanghai. He befriends Robert Hitchings (Beck), the son of the ship's owner. Robert has fallen for singer Gloria (Field) who's tied in with the smugglers and, upon their arrival, Moto must sort out the criminals from the patsies. More action-packed than the Charlie Chan mysteries although Mr. Moto is equally inscrutable. Based on the J.P. Marquand novels. First in the series. **66m/B; DVD.** Peter Lorre; Thomas Beck; Virginia Field; Lee Phelps; Sig Rumann; John Rogers; Murray Kinnell; ***D:*** Norman Foster; ***W:*** Norman Foster; Charles Kenyon; Howard E. Smith; ***C:*** Harry Jackson; ***M:*** Samuel Kaylin.

Think Like a Dog 2020 (PG) Oliver (Bateman) is a technology-saavy 13 year old who attends a school for the gifted. For his school's science fair, he has been working on a telepathy machine. The first time his machine powers up, it creates a power surge. Before long, Oliver realizes he can communicate with his pet dog Henry (Stashwick). Because his parents are focused on their failing marriage, Oliver must deal with the interest of an FBI cyber security unit and an eccentric tech billionaire (Nayyar). The kid-friendly adventure film features a solid performance by Bateman, but the plot shifts unexpectedly from science to the sentimental. **91m/C; DVD.** Gabriel Bateman; Josh Duhamel; Megan Fox; Madison Horcher; Minghao Hou; ***D:*** Gil Junger; ***W:*** Gil Junger; ***C:*** Giles Nuttgens; ***M:*** Jake Monaco. **VIDEO**

Think Like a Man ½ 2012 (PG-13) Loosely based on the self-help book "Act Like a Lady, Think Like a Man" from radio host/comedian Steve Harvey, director Story's ensemble comedy is a typical one with some subplots that work better than others. Four women follow Harvey's advice but their men think try to use it to their advantage. A surprisingly effective relationship comedy that coasts on the easy-going charm, chemistry, and likeability of its talented cast. In particular, Hart, Malco, Ealy, and Henson stand out in this battle of the sexes that doesn't demonize women or turn men into dopes--even if it's 20 minutes too long. **122m/C; DVD, Blu-Ray.** Michael Ealy; Jerry Ferrara; Meagan Good; Regina Hall; Kevin Hart; Taraji P. Henson; Gabrielle Union; Arielle Kebbel; Steve Harvey; ***D:*** Tim Story; ***W:*** Keith Merryman; David Newman; ***C:*** Larry Blanford; ***M:*** Christopher Lennertz.

Think Like a Man Too ½ 2014 (PG-13) The law of diminishing returns proves itself again with this sequel to the surprisingly funny hit comedy that turned Kevin Hart into a movie star. Thinking more is more, the writers of the follow-up take the heartfelt characters from the previous film and send them to Las Vegas to run wild, act silly, and do things that real human beings don't really do. The cast is still incredibly likable but Hart works best in small doses and his over-the-top schtick gets tired here as the whole film feels like a turned up to eleven version of the last movie. **106m/C; DVD, Blu-Ray.** Terrence Jenkins; Regina Hall; Meagan Good; Romany Malco; Jerry Ferrara; Gabrielle Union; Michael Ealy; Taraji P. Henson; Kevin Hart; Jenifer Lewis; Dennis Haysbert; ***D:*** Tim Story; ***W:*** Keith Merryman; David A. Newman; ***C:*** Christopher Duskin; ***M:*** Christopher Lennertz.

Think of Me ½ 2011 Contrived indie drama about an irresponsible, struggling divorcee and her young daughter in Las Vegas. Angela (Ambrose) blithely ignores the realities of her precarious situation and her neglect of 8-year-old daughter Sunny. The sister of a colleague makes a financial offer that tempts Angela into making another bad decision. **103m/C; DVD.** Lauren Ambrose; Audrey P. Scott; Dylan Baker; David Conrad; Adina Porter; Craig Gray; Penelope Ann Miller; ***D:*** Bryan Wizemann; ***W:*** Bryan Wizemann; ***C:*** Mark Schwartzband; ***M:*** Jeff Grace.

Think Tank ½ 2006 (PG) Four 20-something uber-nerds are horrified when their favorite hang-out—the local pool hall—is in danger of closing. So they use their smarts to come up with a solution. Goofy and gross-free dumb comedy. **90m/C; DVD.** Tina Majorino; Eric Artell; Keith Paugh; Greg Neil; Michael Miranda; Gordon Goodman; Brian Petersen; ***D:*** Brian Petersen; ***W:*** Brian Petersen; ***C:*** Michael Fimognari; ***M:*** John Swihart. **VIDEO**

The Third Clue ½ 1934 Mark Clayton is murdered for possessing jewels stolen from an East Indian idol. He gives a dying clue to his brother Rupert but all Rupert can figure out is that the gems are hidden somewhere in the family mansion. But Rupert isn't the only one searching. **72m/B; DVD.** *GB* Alfred Sangster; Basil Sydney; Molly Lamont; Robert Cochran; C.M. Hallard; Ian Fleming; ***D:*** Albert Parker; Michael Barringer; ***W:*** Frank Atkinson; ***C:*** Alex Bryce.

The Third Day ½ 1965 Has some okay thrills but also plays like minor faux-Hitchcock. A car goes through a guardrail and into a river and driver Steve Mallory (Peppard) has amnesia from the accident. The police find the drowned body of married cocktail waitress Holly (Kellerman) and arrest Steve for manslaughter. Which is just one of his problems since his wife Alexandra (Ashley) was leaving him, his cousin Oliver (McDowall) expects Steve to sell him the family business, and Holly's husband Lester (Johnson) wants revenge. **119m/C; DVD.** George Peppard; Elizabeth Ashley; Roddy McDowall; Arte Johnson; Sally Kellerman; Mona Washbourne; Herbert Marshall; Arthur O'Connell; Robert Webber; Charles Drake; ***D:*** Jack Smight; ***W:*** Burton Wohl; Robert Presnell, Jr.; ***C:*** Robert L. Surtees; ***M:*** Percy Faith.

Third Finger, Left Hand ½ 1940 Single fashion magazine editor Margot Sherwood Merrick (Loy) wears a wedding ring to fend off the advances of her male colleagues and clients. When smitten artist Jeff Thompson (Douglas) discovers Margot's secret he pretends to be her long-lost husband, causing all sorts of complications. **96m/B; DVD.** Myrna Loy; Melvyn Douglas; Raymond Walburn; Lee Bowman; Bonita Granville; Sidney Blackmer; Felix Bressart; Donald Meeks; ***D:*** Robert Z. Leonard; ***W:*** Lionel Houser; ***C:*** George J. Folsey; ***M:*** David Snell.

The Third Girl from the Left 1973 ABC TV movie. Longtime New York chorus girl Gloria Joyce (Novak) is having personal and professional problems. She's aging, the club she works in is going topless, and her equally longtime boyfriend, nightclub performer Joey (Curtis), won't marry her. Joyce finds comfort with young hunk David (Brandon), but she needs to make some serious decisions about her future. **93m/C; DVD.** Kim Novak; Tony Curtis; Michael Brandon; George Furth; Barbi Benton; ***D:*** Peter Medak; ***W:*** Dory Previn; ***C:*** Gayne Rescher; ***M:*** Dory Previn. **TV**

The Third Man 1949 An American writer of pulp westerns (Cotten) arrives in post-war Vienna to take a job with an old friend, but discovers he has been murdered. Or has he? Based on Graham Greene's mystery, this classic film noir thriller plays on national loyalties during the Cold War. Welles is top-notch as the manipulative Harry Lime, blackmarket drug dealer extraordinare. The underground sewer sequence is not to be missed. With a haunting (sometimes irritating) theme by Anton Karas on unaccompanied zither. **104m/B; VHS, DVD, Blu-Ray.** *GB* Joseph Cotten; Orson Welles; Alida Valli; Trevor Howard; Bernard Lee; Wilfrid Hyde-White; Ernst Deutsch; Erich Ponto; Siegfried Breuer; Hedwig Bleibtreu; Paul Hoerbiger; Herbert Halbik; Frederick Schreicker; Jenny Werner; Nelly Arno; Alexis Chesnakov; Leo Bieber; Paul Hardtmuth; Geoffrey Keen; Annie Rosar; ***D:*** Carol Reed; ***W:*** Graham Greene; ***C:*** Robert Krasker; ***M:*** Anton Karas. Oscars '50: B&W Cinematog.; AFI '98: Top 100; British Acad. '49: Film; Cannes '49: Film; Directors Guild '49: Director (Reed).

Third Man on the Mountain ½ *Banner in the Sky* 1959 (G) A family epic about mountain climbing, shot in Switzerland and based on James Ramsey Ullman's "Banner in the Sky." A young man is determined to climb the "Citadel" as his ancestors have. He finds there's more to climbing than he imagined. Look for Helen Hayes (MacArthur's mother) in a cameo. Standard Disney adventure drama. **106m/C; VHS, DVD.** James MacArthur; Michael Rennie; Janet Munro; James Donald; Herbert Lom; Laurence Naismith; ***Cameo(s):*** Helen Hayes; ***D:*** Ken Annakin.

Third Man Out: A Donald Strachey Mystery ½ 2005 Donald Stachey (Allen) is a semi-successful gay PI who works in Albany, New York and lives with his politico lover, Tim Callahan (Spence). Donald reluctantly takes the case of hectoring gay activist John Rutka (Wetherall), whose tabloid outings have made him a target for violence. When Rutka winds up dead, Donald has a long list of suspects but things aren't always what they appear to be. Adapted from Richard Stevenson's 1992 mystery. **98m/C; DVD.** Chad Allen; Sebastian Spence; Jack Wetherall; Sean Young; Woody Jeffreys; ***D:*** Ron Oliver; ***W:*** Mark Saltzman. **CABLE**

The Third Miracle ½ 1999 (R) Harris makes for one sexy and dynamic priest. He's Father Frank Shore who is struggling with his faith and is in a kind of voluntary retirement. However, he's summoned by power player, Bishop Cahill (Haid), to investigate the purported miracles of the late Helen O'Regan (Sukowa). A cult is growing up around her memory and the mention of sainthood (which requires three proven miracles) has the church wary. Film is set in Chicago in 1979 and based on the book by Richard Vetere. **119m/C; VHS, DVD.** Ed Harris; Anne Heche; Charles Haid; Armin Mueller-Stahl; Michael Rispoli; Jean-Louis Roux; Ken James; James Gallanders; Barbara Sukowa; ***D:*** Agnieszka Holland; ***W:*** John Romano; Richard Vetere; ***C:*** Jerzy Zielinski; ***M:*** Jan A.P. Kaczmarek.

Third Person ½ 2013 (R) Writer/director Haggis (of "Crash" fame) pulls his interlocking stories routine again without the same dramatic success. Michael (Neeson), trying to finish his latest book in Paris, has left his wife and is having an affair. Scott (Brody) is in Italy stealing fashion designs when he crosses paths with a beautiful woman. Finally, in New York, Julia (Kunis) is a failed actress trying to win back custody of her child. Unfortunately, you won't care about any of them. It's easy to read self-commentary into a film about people trying to find inspiration after success, but that's about all that makes this interesting. **137m/C; DVD, Blu-Ray.** *BE* Liam Neeson; Olivia Wilde; Kim Basinger; Adrien Brody; Moran Atias; Mila Kunis; James Franco; Maria Bello; ***D:*** Paul Haggis; ***W:*** Paul Haggis; ***C:*** Gian Filippo Corticelli; ***M:*** Dario Marianelli.

The Third Wheel 2002 (PG-13) Shy businessman Stanley finally gets up the nerve to ask out coworker Diana (Richards) after pining for her for a year. The night of the date, he hits a homeless guy Phil (screenwriter Lacopo) with his car, so Phil tags along. Stan also has to deal with a bunch of co-workers who've wagered on the outcome of the date, and are secretly monitoring the proceedings. Damon and Affleck's planned follow-up to "Good Will Hunting" sat on a shelf at Miramax for over two years, probably because of the inconsistent laughs and direction. Good cast does what it can with what it has to work with. **90m/C; DVD.** Luke Wilson; Denise Richards; Ben Affleck; Jay Lacopo; Matt Damon; Meredith Salenger; Bobby Slayton; Lauren Graham; Nicole Sullivan; ***D:*** Jordan Brady; ***W:*** Jay Lacopo; ***C:*** Jonathan Brown; ***M:*** Lisa Coleman; Wendy Melvoin. **VIDEO**

Third World Cop 1999 (R) Detective Capone (Campbell) returns to his childhood home in Kingston and discovers that his best bud Ratty (Danvers) is the right-hand man for local crime boss One Hand (Bradshaw). Their friendship leaves the gangsters suspicious that Ratty is a police informer but even when he finally agrees to help Capone, things go wrong. Straight-ahead crime story does have the advantage of the Jamaican settings to take it out of the norm. **98m/C; VHS, DVD.** *JM* Paul Campbell; Carl Bradshaw; Mark Danvers; Audrey Reid; ***D:*** Christopher Browne; ***W:*** Christopher Browne; Suzanne Fenn; Chris Salewicz; ***C:*** Richard Lannaman; ***M:*** Sly Dunbar; Robbie Shakespeare.

Thirst 1979 (R) A girl is abducted by a secret society that wants her to become their new leader. There is just one catch: she has to learn to like the taste of human blood. Chilling but weakly plotted. **96m/C; VHS, DVD, Blu-Ray.** David Hemmings; Henry Silva; Chantal Contouri; ***D:*** Rod Hardy.

The Thirst ½ 2006 Since Lisa (Kramer) has terminal cancer, she doesn't ask a lot of questions when Mariel (Scott Thomas) offers a chance at life—even if it's the undead kind. Naturally, ex-beau Maxx (Keeslar) is confused to see her out clubbing, but Lisa soon turns him and they join Eurotrash Darius (Sisto and his wandering accent) and his blood crew. Eventually the reunited lovebirds find out they don't really enjoy swilling human red. **88m/C; DVD.** Matt Keeslar; Clare Kramer; Jeremy Sisto; Serena Scott Thomas; Neil Jackson; Adam Baldwin; Erik

Palladino; Charlotte Ayanna; *D:* Jeremy Kasten; *W:* Jeremy Kasten; *C:* Raymond N. Stella; *M:* Joe Kraemer. **VIDEO**

Thirst *Bakjwi* **2009 (R)** Long, operatic, and carnal horror melodrama from South Korea. A priest becomes a volunteer in a hospital project to discover a vaccine for an emerging virus. Instead, a tainted blood transfusion leads to Sang-hyeon (Song) becoming a vampire with a lot of lust (and not just for blood). He begins an affair with bored housewife Tae-ju (Kim), the wife of his childhood friend, which soon turns very deadly. Korean with subtitles. **133m/C; Blu-Ray, On Demand.** *US NK* Kang-ho Song; Ok-vin Kim; Ha-Kyun Shin; Hae-sook Kim; *D:* Chan-wook Park; *W:* Chan-wook Park; Seo-gyeong Jeong; *C:* Jeong-hun Jeong; *M:* Yeong-wook Jo.

Thirst Street 1/2 **2017** After her lover's death, grieving flight attendant Gina (Burdge) spends a passionate night with charming bartender Jerome (Bonnard) in Paris. Though Jerome tries to distance himself from Gina, she decides that she must be in his life. Leaving her job, she moves to an apartment near his in Paris and gets hired at his club. As she invades his life seeking grand romance, he continues to be kind but pushes her away. The situation grows more tense when Clemence (Garrel), Jerome's ex-girlfriend, appears. An empathetic romantic drama about obsession and desire. **83m/C; DVD.** Anjelica Huston; Damien Bonnard; Lindsay Burdge; Esther Garrel; Lola Bessis; *D:* Nathan Silver; *W:* Nathan Silver; C. Mason Wells; *C:* Sean Price Williams; *M:* Paul Grimstad.

The Thirsty Dead WOOF! *The Blood Cult of Shangri-La; Blood Hunt* **1974 (PG)** Maybe they could learn to like Gatorade. An eternally young jungle king is looking for a wife. She can be young forever too, if she's not above vampirism and sacrificing virgins. In spite of the jungle vampire slant, this Filipino-made movie is a woofer. **90m/C; VHS, DVD.** *PH* John Considine; Jennifer Billingsley; Judith McConnell; Fredricka Meyers; Tani Phelps Guthrie; *D:* Terry Becker.

Thirteen **2003 (R)** Genuinely original indie probes the transformation of Tracy (Wood) a well-behaved, slightly nerdy, L.A. teen who, practically overnight, becomes a ragingly rebellious, boy-crazy shoplifter, thanks to psychologically scarred but savvy schoolmate Evie (co-writer Reed), who invites Tracy into her world of popularity, piercings, and partying. As Tracy's mom Melanie, a recovering alcoholic, frets over Tracy's disturbing personality makeover, Evie begins to bond with her. Performances are uniformly sparkling. Spot-on characters and all-too-real details come from director/co-writer Hardwicke's collaboration with the then 13-year-old Reed—whom she met while dating Reed's father—the real-life good girl of the story. **95m/C; VHS, DVD.** Evan Rachel Wood; Nikki Reed; Holly Hunter; Jeremy Sisto; Deborah Kara Unger; Kip Pardue; Brady Corbet; Sarah Clarke; D.W. Moffett; Vanessa Anne Hudgens; *D:* Catherine Hardwicke; *W:* Nikki Reed; Catherine Hardwicke; *C:* Elliot Davis; *M:* Mark Mothersbaugh. Ind. Spirit '04: Debut Perf. (Reed); Sundance '03: Director (Hardwicke).

XIII **2008 (R)** Convoluted political conspiracies reign when the U.S. president is assassinated and an amnesiac agent—known as XIII (Dorff) because of his tattoo's blamed for the crime. He's hunted by a lot of unsavory types who want him dead so he can take the fall without the truth becoming known. Based on a series of French-Belgian comic books. Originally shown as an NBC miniseries; the DVD is the unedited release. **180m/C; DVD.** *CA FR* Val Kilmer; Stephen McHattie; Jessalyn Gilsig; Ted Atherton; Stephen Dorff; John Bourgeois; Lucinda Davis; Caterina Murino; Mimi Suzyk; Greg Bryk; *D:* Duane Clark; *W:* David Wolkove; Philippe Lyon; *C:* David Greene; *M:* Nicolas Errera. **TV**

13 1/2 **2010 (R)** Babluani remakes his own 2005 French thriller "13 Tzameti" to little effect. Vince's family is desperate for money and when he overhears a man boasting of making a fortune in one day, and that man is suddenly dead, Vince follows his instructions to an isolated mansion. He becomes a player in a high-stakes game of Russian roulette with too many flashbacks showing how the other players came to be participants. **90m/C; DVD, Blu-Ray.** Sam Riley; Ray Winstone; Jason Statham; 50 Cent; Mickey Rourke; Michael Shannon; Ben Gazzara; David Zayas; Alexander Skarsgård; Emmanuelle Chriqui; Gaby Hoffman; *D:* Gala Babuliani; *W:* Gala Babuliani; Greg Pruss; *C:* Michael McDonough; *M:* Alexander Van Bubenheim.

13 Assassins *Jusan-nin No Shikaku* **2010 (R)** Miike's big budget samurai action/drama, a remake of the 1963 film by Eichi Kudo, is set in 1844 in the twilight of feudal Japan and the shogunate. Shogun official Sir Doi hires warrior Shinzaemon Shimada when the sadistic, lustful urges of the Shogun's evil half-brother, Lord Naritsugu Matsudaira, go too far. Shinzaemon gathers 13 assassins to kill Nartisugu and his large retinue, with everything leading up to one big, long, and bloody showdown in a rural town. The film was released in Japan at 141 minutes. Japanese with subtitles. **126m/C; DVD, Blu-Ray, Download.** *JP GB* Koji Yakusho; Goro Inagaki; Mikijiro Hira; Masachika Ichimura; Takayuki Yamada; Tsuyoski Ihara; Arata Furuta; Yusuke Iseya; *D:* Takashi Miike; *W:* Daisuke Tengan; *C:* Nobuyasu Kita; *M:* Koji Endo.

Thirteen Conversations About One Thing 1/2 **2001 (R)** "We plan, God laughs," as the saying goes. Smart, literary indie offers a fresh take on the familiar theme of destiny and the forms it takes. Focuses on the intersecting lives of five New Yorkers: college physics professor Turturro wants to change his boring life; housewife Irving confronts her hubby about his infidelity; lawyer McConaughey's life suddenly takes a wrong turn; housekeeper DuVall waits for something wonderful to happen; and cynical businessman Arkin is disturbed by his relentlessly upbeat coworker. Director Jill Sprecher and her sister, cowriter Karen, illustrates (in 13 sections), how even the smallest actions can have enormous consequences. Detailed omens arise everywhere, foreshadowing events to come in this karma chameleon of a movie. Well acted, deftly directed and smartly written. **104m/C; VHS, DVD.** Matthew McConaughey; Alan Arkin; John Turturro; Clea DuVall; Amy Irving; Barbara Sukowa; Tia Texada; Frankie Faison; William Wise; Shawn Elliott; David Connolly; Alex Burns; *D:* Jill Sprecher; *W:* Jill Sprecher; Karen Sprecher; *C:* Dick Pope; *M:* Alex Wurman.

Thirteen Days 1/2 **2000 (PG-13)** The Cuban Missile Crisis seen through the eyes of President JFK, Attorney General Robert Kennedy, and presidential aide Kenny O'Donnell (Costner). Director Donaldson wisely opts not to over-dramatize what was clearly a suspenseful story to begin with (and realizes, as well, that we know the outcome). The few sacrifices of historical accuracy made in the name of dramatic license are basically harmless. Greenwood and Culp ably handle the often difficult task of portraying the brothers Kennedy, and Costner is solid as the brothers' trusted confidante. Donaldson and Costner notably worked together on 1987's "No Way Out." **145m/C; VHS, DVD, Blu-Ray.** Kevin Costner; Bruce Greenwood; Steven Culp; Dylan Baker; Michael Fairman; Kevin Conway; Tim Kelleher; Len Cariou; Bill Smitrovich; Dakin Matthews; Madison Mason; Christopher Lawford; Ed Lauter; Elya Baskin; Boris Krutonog; Peter White; James Karen; Tim Jerome; Olek Krupa; Lucinda Jenney; Henry Strozier; Frank Wood; Stephanie Romanov; *D:* Roger Donaldson; *W:* David Self; *C:* Andrzej Bartkowiak; *M:* Trevor Jones.

13 Frightened Girls **1963** They were probably frightened of working for a schlock director in this silly spy adventure. Teenager Candace Hull is a diplomat's daughter who travels from her Swiss boarding school to a vacation in London. She has a crush on much-older spy Wally and when Candy stumbles over a political murder at the Chinese embassy, she secretly reveals it to him to further his career. Giving herself the codename 'Kitten,' she then uses her friendships with all the other diplomats' daughters to go snooping and gets into trouble. **89m/C; DVD, Blu-Ray.** Kathy Dunn; Murray Hamilton; Hugh Marlowe; Norma Varden; *D:* William Castle; *W:* Robert Dillon; *C:* Gordon Avil; *M:* Van Alexander.

13 Gantry Row 1/2 **1998 (R)** A couple moves into a new place with a haunted past and their romantic life subsequently goes into the crapper due to interference from angry ghosts. Not your usual love story. **90m/C; DVD.** *AU* John Adam; Mark Gerber; Rebecca Gibney; *D:* Catherine Millar; *W:* Tony Morphett; *C:* Mark Wareham; *M:* Chris Neal. **TV**

13 Ghosts 1/2 **1960** A dozen ghosts need another member to round out their ranks. They have four likely candidates to choose from when a family moves into the house inhabited by the ghoulish group. Originally viewed with "Illusion-O," a technology much like 3-D, which allowed the viewing of the ghosts only through a special pair of glasses. **88m/C; VHS, DVD, Blu-Ray.** Charles Herbert; Jo Morrow; Martin Milner; Rosemary DeCamp; Donald Woods; Margaret Hamilton; John van Dreelen; *D:* William Castle; *W:* Robb White; *C:* Joseph Biroc; *M:* Von Dexter.

13 Ghosts **2001 (R)** Another attempt to meld humor and horror in a William Castle remake ala "House on Haunted Hill" misfires in this flashy screamfest. Arthur (Shalhoub) inherits a weird glass mansion from his shadowy Uncle Cyrus (Abraham). He moves into the house with his kids Kathy (Elizabeth) and Bobby (Roberts) and their nanny Maggie (Digga). Along for kicks is spastic psychic Rafkin (Lillard), which is good, because the mansion ends up being a gigantic infernal contraption powered by ghosts complete with whirling gears and sliding glass panels that attack the inhabitants. It seems that crazy Uncle Cyrus built the house to open the Eye of Hell and it's up to Arthur to stop it. The special effects are above average, but the plot is clearly not. **91m/C; VHS, DVD.** Tony Shalhoub; Embeth Davidtz; Matthew Lillard; Shannon Elizabeth; Alec Roberts; Rah Digga; J.R. Bourne; F. Murray Abraham; *D:* Steve Beck; *W:* Richard D'Ovidio; Neal Marshall Stevens; *C:* Gale Tattersall; *M:* John (Gianni) Frizzell.

13 Going on 30 1/2 **2004 (PG-13)** Broadly appealing Garner makes the successful leap to bona fide big screen lead in this harmless body-switch comedy. Jenna (Allen) is an insecure 13-year-old who magically becomes the "30, flirty, and thriving" fashion magazine editor played by Garner. Comedy ensues when she is forced to deal with adult concerns foreign to a 13-year-old, including work at the magazine; her new, mature body; and her hockey player boyfriend, all of which she does with an endearing childlike zeal. Along with the perks, Jenna's transformation has also alienated her former best friend Matt (Marquette), once a chubby nerd who is now, 17 years later, a handsome and engaged hunk (Ruffalo). Of course, Jenna would like to get reacquainted. Garner and Ruffalo elevate a so-so vehicle into an appealing romantic comedy. **97m/C; DVD, Blu-Ray.** Jennifer Garner; Mark Ruffalo; Judy Greer; Andy Serkis; Christa B. Allen; Kathy Baker; Phil Reeves; Joe Grifasi; Courtney Chase; Maz Jobrani; Robine Lee; Jim Gaffigan; Sean Marquette; Alex Black; Alexandra Kyle; Renee Olstead; *D:* Gary Winick; *W:* Josh Goldsmith; Cathy Yuspa; *C:* Don Burgess; *M:* Theodore Shapiro.

13 Hours: The Secret Soldiers of Benghazi 1/2 **2016 (R)** Michael Bay brings his bombastic, overheated style to one of the more controversial international events of recent years, the attack on the diplomatic compound in Benghazi, Libya in 2012. The tagline—"When everything went wrong six men had the courage to do what was right"—pretty much says it all. Even ignoring the political aspects of conflicting reports about what happened that day and who knew what when in terms of U.S. officials, Bay's film is a loud, uber-patriotic war movie. It's undeniably technically accomplished, but it turns real tragedy and heroism into blockbuster fodder that looks more like a video game than reality. **144m/C; DVD, Blu-Ray.** John Krasinski; James Badge Dale; Pablo Schreiber; David Denman; Dominic Fumusa; *D:* Michael Bay; *W:* Chuck Hogan; *C:* Dion Beebe; *M:* Lorne Balfe.

13 Minutes 1/2 *Elser* **2017 (R)** An exploration of events surrounding a 1939 assassination attempt on Adolf Hitler. As World War II begins, disgruntled Georg Elser (Friedel) sets off a bomb in a packed beer hall time to go off on November 8, the anniversary of Hitler's failed Beer Hall Putsch. Hitler leaves 13 minutes before the bomb goes off, but many others die or suffer injury. Much of the film focuses on the Nazi torture-filled interrogation of Georg as he recounts his life and motivation for the bombing. An illuminating, if unsubtle, look at the nature of resistance to the Third Reich. German with subtitles. **114m/C; DVD.** Christian Friedel; Katharina Schuttler; Burghart Klaussner; Felix Eitner; David Zimmerschied; *D:* Oliver Hirschbiegel; *W:* Leonie-Claire Breinersdorfer; Fred Breinersdorfer; *C:* Judith Kaufmann; *M:* David Holmes.

13 Moons **2002 (R)** Only a full moon in Los Angeles could pull together several intertwining yet divergent storylines to tell what really is a simple tale of a man, Mo (Proval), whose son, Timmy (Wolff), will die without a kidney transplant. Problem is the donor is a drug addict who flees the hospital. Along with a rag-tag group of other-wise-afflicted folks (including a fired TV clown, a stripper, and a rap executive), Mo must find him...and fast! While the performances evoke a sense of sincerity, the backbone is too weak to support them. **94m/C; VHS, DVD.** Steve Buscemi; Karyn Parsons; Peter Dinklage; David Proval; Austin Wolff; Daryl (Chill) Mitchell; Rose Rollins; Peter Stormare; Pruitt Taylor Vince; Gareth Williams; Francesco Messina; Jennifer Beals; Elizabeth Bracco; Matthew Sussman; Michael Badalucco; Danny Trejo; *D:* Alexandre Rockwell; *W:* Alexandre Rockwell; *C:* Phil Parmet; *M:* Kevin Salem. **VIDEO**

13 Rue Madeleine **1946** Cagney plays a WWII spy who infiltrates Gestapo headquarters in Paris in order to find the location of a German missile site. Actual OSS footage is used in this fast-paced early post-war espionage propaganda piece. Rex Harrison rejected the part taken by Cagney. **95m/B; VHS, DVD.** James Cagney; Annabella; Richard Conte; Frank Latimore; Walter Abel; Sam Jaffe; Melville Cooper; E.G. Marshall; Karl Malden; Red Buttons; Blanche Yurka; Peter Von Zerneck; Marcel Rousseau; Dick Gordon; Alfred Linder; *D:* Henry Hathaway; *W:* Sy Bartlett; John Monks, Jr.; *C:* Norbert Brodine; *M:* David Buttolph.

13 Seconds **2003 (R)** Indie horror film about a band trying to make a video in a crumbling school, which is apparently haunted by bad stuff that intends to kill them for their acting performance. Okay, maybe it's just killing them because they're available, but they really should be killed for the acting job. **93m/C; DVD.** Danny Patrelli; Kevin Kuras; April Cole; *D:* Jeff Thomas; *W:* Jeff Thomas; *C:* Zachary Angel; *M:* Jay Sunde; Michael Poland; Dan Kuras; Russ Hayes; B.D. Daknit Blake. **VIDEO**

13 Sins 1/2 **2013 (R)** Writer/director Stamm remakes the Thai horror film "13: Game of Death" with mixed results. Elliot (Webber) gets a phone call and hears that he's basically on an existential game show. The caller can see him, knows of his recent economic woes, and knows that he's about to get married--and that he's desperate. The 13 challenges start slow—eat that fly and win some money—and get increasingly morbid. Stamm keeps a darkly humorous streak running despite the implausible events. It's a fun horror flick that may stretch suspension of disbelief but only if you look too closely. **88m/C; DVD, Blu-Ray.** Mark Webber; Rutina Wesley; Ron Perlman; Pruitt Taylor Vince; Devon Graye; Tom Bower; *D:* Daniel Stamm; *W:* Daniel Stamm; David Birke; *C:* Zoltan Honti; *M:* Michael Wandmacher.

13 West Street 1/2 **1962** After Walt Sherill (Ladd) is brutally beaten by a gang of wealthy teen punks, he feels Det. Sgt. Koleski (Steiger) isn't moving fast enough to arrest the delinquents. Walt decides to take matters into his own hands while the gang keeps retaliating against Walt and his family. Walt finally confronts leader Chuck (Callan) and realizes he's become as violent as his assailants. Ladd's not at his best and the plot hits all the cliches. **79m/B; DVD.** Alan Ladd; Rod Steiger; Michael Callan; Dolores Dorn; Margaret (Maggie) Hayes; Kenneth MacKenna; Chris Robinson; Jeanne Cooper; *D:* Philip Leacock; *W:* Bernard C. Schoenfeld; Robert Presnell, Jr.; *C:* Charles Lawton, Jr.; *M:* George Duning.

13th Child: Legend of the Jersey Devil *13th Child* **2002 (R)** Based vaguely on an incoherent re-interpretation of the Jersey Devil legend. A district attorney orders an investigator to track the rubber-suited monster. The real monster would be offended by this rubbish. **99m/C; DVD.** Christopher Atkins; Robert Guillaume; Cliff Robertson;

Lesley-Anne Down; *D:* Thomas Ashley; Steven Stockage; *W:* Cliff Robertson; Michael Maryk; *C:* Howard Krupa; *M:* Peter Calandra. **VIDEO**

The 13th Floor ½ **1988 (R)** A young girl fuses with the spirit of a young boy her father ruthlessly killed years before, and together they wreak havoc. **86m/C; VHS, DVD.** Lisa Hensley; Tim McKenzie; Miranda Otto; *D:* Chris Roach.

The Thirteenth Floor ½ **1999 (R)** Silly sci-fier with a confusing virtual-reality plot and a lot of visual effects. An investigation into the mysterious death of tycoon Hannon Fuller (Mueller-Stahl) leads to the realization that he lived in parallel worlds—one in the present and one in 1937. Exec Douglas Hall (Bierko) stands to inherit, which raises the suspicious of cop McBain (Haysbert), while mysterious femme Jane (Mol) shows up, claiming to be Fuller's daughter. And then there's Hall's colleague Whitney (D'Onofrio), who also exists in the 1937 as a barkeep with a very important letter. Not that any of this turns out to be particularly interesting. **100m/C; VHS, DVD.** Craig Bierko; Vincent D'Onofrio; Armin Mueller-Stahl; Gretchen Mol; Dennis Haysbert; Steven Schub; Jeremy Roberts; Tia Texada; Alison Lohman; *D:* Josef Rusnak; *W:* Josef Rusnak; *C:* Wedigo von Schultzendorff; *M:* Harald Kloser.

13th Guest *Lady Beware* **1932** Two people try to solve a murder that occurred at a dinner party. An incredibly creaky early talkie melodrama that created some of the cliches of the genre. **70m/B; VHS, DVD.** Ginger Rogers; Lyle Talbot; J. Farrell MacDonald; Paul Hurst; *D:* Albert Ray.

The 13th Warrior *Eaters of the Dead* **1999 (R)** Banderas stars as Ahmed Ibn Fahdlan, a sophisticated Arabian poet and lover-turned-reluctant-warrior, who gets exiled from his homeland and caught up in a quest with a bunch of uncouth, slaughter-loving Vikings. Based on the 1976 book by Michael Crichton, this one has been sitting on the shelf a while after a rocky filming history. However, if you like bloody, action-packed epics it will satisfy your cravings. **103m/C; VHS, DVD.** Antonio Banderas; Vladimir Kulich; Clive Russell; Omar Sharif; Diane Venora; Sven Wollter; Dennis Storhoi; Anders T. Anderson; Richard Bremmer; Neil Maffin; Tony Curran; Mischa Hausserman; Asbjorn Riis; Daniel Southern; Oliver Sveinall; Albie Woodington; *D:* Michael Crichton; John McTiernan; *W:* Michael Crichton; *C:* Peter Menzies, Jr.; *M:* Jerry Goldsmith.

30 **1959** Managing editor Sam Gatlin (Webb, who also directed) works to get out the next morning edition of the L.A. paper and the newsroom has a run of overlapping personal and professional stories. Longtime rewrite editor Bernice Valentine's (Lorimer) grandson is among the missing Air Force pilots who were out to set a flying record and a little girl, lost in the city's storm drains, has Gatlin reflecting on his wife Peggy's (Blake) desire for them to adopt a child. Film is much like Webb's "Dragnet" 'just the facts' work. **96m/B; DVD.** Jack Webb; William Conrad; Louise Lorimer; David Nelson; Whitney Blake; James Bell; Joe Flynn; *D:* Jack Webb; *W:* William Bowers; *C:* Edward Colman; *M:* Ray Heindorf.

Thirty Day Princess ½ **1934** Princess Catterina (Sidney) comes to New York, immediately gets sick, and is unable to fulfill her royal obligations. Banker Richard Gresham (Arnolds), who has a lot financially invested in the visit, finds a double in struggling actress Nancy (Sidney again). But newspaper publisher Porter Madison (Grant) gets suspicious, despite falling for the dame. There are a few more comedic plot points but Sidney and Grant carry through the familiarity with loads of charm. **74m/B; DVD.** Cary Grant; Sylvia Sidney; Edward Arnold; Vince Barnett; Henry Stephenson; Edgar Norton; *D:* Marion Gering; *W:* Preston Sturges; Frank Partos; Sam Hellman; Edwin Justus Mayer; *C:* Leon Shamroy.

30 Days of Night ½ **2007 (R)** Vampires have discovered that Barrow, Alaska, offers the perfect combination of human flesh and 30-day absence of sunlight, so they descend upon the town like the darkness they require, devouring all but a small number of survivors, among them two sheriffs, Eban Oleson (Hartnett) and his estranged wife Stella (George). The story, based on a graphic novel series, unfolds as a horrible game of hide-and-seek, with the town's surviving inhabitants eventually discovering how to rid themselves of the bloodthirsty pestilence. The biggest problem is the predictability and repetition of the storyline, but with no shortage of stylized violent horror for those with an unquenchable thirst for such things. A great twist on the classic vampire story not to be missed by admirers of the genre. **113m/C; DVD, Blu-Ray.** Josh Hartnett; Melissa George; Danny Huston; Ben Foster; Mark Boone, Jr.; Mark Rendall; *D:* David Slade; *W:* Stuart Beattie; Steve Niles; Brian Nelson; *C:* Jo Willems; *M:* Brian Reitzell.

30 Days of Night: Dark Days **2010 (R)** A year after the events in Barrow, Alaska, and Stella is still dealing with her husband's death and that whole 'vampires are real' problem. Then she's invited to get her revenge by joining a group of vampire hunters in L.A. for the chance to kill vampire queen Lilith. Based on the second book in the graphic novel series by Steve Niles and Ben Templesmith. **92m/C; DVD.** Kiele Sanchez; Mia Kirshner; Rhys Coiro; Ben Cotton; Diora Baird; Harold Perrineau, Jr.; *D:* Ben Ketai; *W:* Ben Ketai; Steve Niles; *C:* Eric Maddison; *M:* Andres Boulton. **VIDEO**

35 and Ticking **2010 (R)** Zenobia and Clevon are single and want to be married with kids while Victoria's husband doesn't want children (she does) and Phil's wife can't be bothered to be a mom to the child they have. The four friends try to deal with the reality of their situations while figuring out what they really want and how to get it. **104m/C; DVD, Blu-Ray.** Nicole Ari Parker; Tamala Jones; Kevin Hart; Keith D. Robinson; Wendy Raquel Robinson; Meagan Good; Clifton Powell; *D:* Russ (Russell Dean) Parr; *W:* Russ (Russell Dean) Parr; *C:* Jeff Bollman; *M:* Kenneth Lampl. **VIDEO**

The 30-Foot Bride of Candy Rock **1959** A junk dealer invents a robot, catapults into space and causes his girlfriend to grow to 30 feet in height. Lightweight, whimsical fantasy was Costello's only solo starring film, and his last before his untimely death. **73m/B; VHS, DVD.** Lou Costello; Dorothy Provine; Gale Gordon; *D:* Sidney Miller.

30 Minutes or Less **2011 (R)** Two pathetic aspiring criminals (McBride and Swardson) kidnap Nick (Eisenberg), a young man in a dead-end job, strap a bomb to him, and demand that he rob a bank in 30 minutes or less. Desperate, Nick reunites with his former best friend Chet (Ansari) to help him strategize, rob the bank, and try to save his life. Too crude to be likeable and too superficial to be satisfying. Eisenberg and Ansari have unique charms but the story is weak and the attempt at humor fizzles. **83m/C; Blu-Ray.** Jesse Eisenberg; Danny McBride; Nick Swardson; Aziz Ansari; Bianca Kajlich; Michael Peña; Dilshad Vadsaria; *D:* Ruben Fleischer; *W:* Michael Diliberti; Matthew Sullivan; *C:* Jess Hall; *M:* Ludwig Göransson.

30 Nights of Paranormal Activity with the Devil Inside the Girl with the Dragon Tattoo **2012 (R)** A spoof of popular films "Paranormal Activity," "The Devil Inside," and "The Girl With the Dragon Tattoo." **80m/C; DVD, Blu-Ray, Streaming.** Kathryn Fiore; Flip Schultz; Olivia Alexander; Danny Woodburn; French Stewart; *D:* Craig Moss; *W:* Craig Moss; *C:* Rudy Harbon; *M:* Todd Haberman. **VIDEO**

31 **2016 (R)** Rob Zombie's latest effort is a half-hearted mix of things he's done before. Set in 1976 merely because Zombie likes the fashion of the day, this ode to grindhouse features a group of carnie workers (led by the auteur's talentless wife Sheri Moon Zombie) kidnapped by a trio of aristocratically dressed people who then basically send them through a house of horrors occupied by lunatic serial killers as a "game" to see who can survive. The structure plays to Zombie's worst aspects as a filmmaker in that it requires no characters or narrative—just scene after scene of incoherent carnage. **102m/C; DVD, Blu-Ray.** Sheri Moon Zombie; Jeffrey Daniel Phillips; Lawrence Hilton-Jacobs; Meg Foster; Kevin Jackson; *D:* Rob Zombie; *W:* Rob Zombie; *C:* David Daniel; *M:* Rob Zombie; Chris Harris; John 5; Bob Marlette.

31 North 62 East ½ **2009 (R)** Blustery, venal British Prime Minister John Hammond, who's up for re-election, reveals an SAS unit's position in Afghanistan in exchange for angry Saudi royalty not cancelling an arms deal. Capt. Jill Mandelson is the only survivor and she's a hostage until French intelligence arranges her rescue. However, her return to Britain means a lot of trouble for Hammond and his government cover-up. **100m/C; DVD.** *GB* John Rhys-Davies; Heather Peace; Marina Sirtis; Craig Fairbrass; Kammy Darweish; Omar Mostafa; Mimi Ferrer; *D:* Tristan Loraine; *W:* Tristan Loraine; Leofwine Lorine; *C:* Sue Gibson; *M:* Paul Garbutt. **VIDEO**

Thirty Seconds Over Tokyo **1944** Dated but still interesting classic wartime flagwaver details the conception and execution of the first bombing raids on Tokyo by Lt. Col. James Doolittle and his men. Look for Blake Edwards, as well as Steve Brodie in his first screen appearance. Based on a true story. **138m/B; VHS, DVD.** Spencer Tracy; Van Johnson; Robert Walker; Robert Mitchum; Phyllis Thaxter; Scott McKay; Stephen McNally; Louis Jean Heydt; Leon Ames; Paul Langton; Don DeFore; Tim Murdock; Alan Napier; Dorothy Morris; Jacqueline White; Selena Royle; Bill (William) Phillips; Donald Curtis; Gordon McDonald; John R. Reilly; Douglas Cowan; Ann Shoemaker; Steve Brodie; *D:* Mervyn LeRoy; *W:* Dalton Trumbo; *C:* Robert L. Surtees; Harold Rosson; *M:* Herbert Stothart.

The 36th Precinct *36 Quai des Orfevres* **2004** Moody, dark and violent crime drama with excellent performances by the two leads. Workaholic rivals Leo Vrinks (Auteuil) and Denis Klein (Depardieu) both lead plainclothes divisions in Paris. Their boss is about to retire and whoever nails a gang attacking armored cars will get the promotion to commissioner. Klein's obsessed with power and willing to commit any betrayal to get the job. French with subtitles. **111m/C; DVD.** *FR* Daniel Auteuil; Gerard Depardieu; Andre Dussollier; Roschdy Zem; Valeria Golino; Daniel Duval; Anne Consigny; Catherine Marchal; Francis Renaud; *D:* Olivier Marchal; *W:* Olivier Marchal; *C:* Denis Rouden; *M:* Erwann Kermorvant; Axelle Renoir.

30,000 Leagues Under the Sea **2007** Another mockbuster by Asylum, this is a modern re-telling of the classic story of Captain Nemo (Lawlor) and his megalomaniacal quest. **85m/C; DVD, Blu-Ray.** Lorenzo Lamas; Sean Lawlor; Natalie Stone; Kim Little; Victor Springer; *D:* Gabriel Bologna; *W:* Eric Forsberg; *C:* Mark Atkins; *M:* David Raiklen. **VIDEO**

3022 *Thirty Twenty-Two* **2019 (R)** In the year 2190, the space station Pangea is on a ten-year mission. Though the crew members, Captain John Lane (Epps), Jackie (Walsh), Richard (Macfadyen), and Lisa (Cosgrove), are enthusiastic at first, their emotional struggles jeopardize the mission half way through. Before it can be called off, an explosion that may have ended all life on Earth hits the space station, affecting all aboard and resulting in the addition of refugees from other space stations. A decent low-budget sci-fi thriller that looks good with some solid performances. **91m/C; DVD.** Omar Epps; Kate Walsh; Miranda Cosgrove; Enver Gjokaj; Haaz Sleiman; *D:* John Suits; *W:* Ryan Binaco; *C:* William Stone; *M:* Jimmy LaValle.

30 Years to Life **2001 (R)** Six friends try to cope with the reality of turning 30, and the re-evaluation of their lives that the milestone brings. Natalie, a Wall Street success, pretends to be domesticated to attract a conservative doctor. Commitment-averse Leland is forced to propose to his live-in girl Joy because of a jewelry shop mix-up; Troy, a stand-up comedian wonders if he'll get that big break; Stephanie has liposuction to change her outlook and prospects; and Malik quits his job to become a model. It all has a very sitcomy feel, but the writing is good enough to make the various lessons learned more palatable. **110m/C; VHS, DVD.** Erika Alexander; Melissa De Sousa; Tracy Morgan; Kadeem Hardison; Paula Jai Parker; Allen Payne; T.E. Russell; Eddie Brill; Janet Hubert-Whitten; Jim Gaffigan; *D:* Vanessa Middleton; *W:* Vanessa Middleton; *C:* Cliff Charles; *M:* Timbaland. **VIDEO**

32 Short Films about Glenn Gould **1993** Perceptive docudrama about the iconoclastic Canadian classical pianist who secluded himself in the studio, forsaking live performances for much of his career. A combination of dramatic recreation, archival material, and interviews depict the biographical details of the driven artist who died at the age of 50. Feore is memorable in the title role, especially since he's never actually shown playing the piano. Title and film structure refer to Bach's "Goldberg" Variations, a recording which made Gould's reputation. **94m/C; VHS, DVD.** *CA* Colm Feore; Gale Garnett; David Hughes; Katya Ladan; Gerry Quigley; Carlo Rota; Peter Millard; Yehudi Menuhin; Bruno Monsaingeon; *D:* Francois Girard; *W:* Don McKellar; Francois Girard; *C:* Alan Dostie. Genie '93: Cinematog., Director (Girard), Film, Film Editing.

The 33 **2015 (PG-13)** In 2010, a mine collapsed in San Jose, Chile, trapping 33 miners underground for over two months. Hundreds of people worked night and day to rescue the miners from their subterranean trap, and the story became an international one. Director Riggen can't quite figure out the story here. Part of it plays like a social drama about hard-working people caught in a system that didn't protect them enough, but it too often also resembles a disaster flick, turning this harrowing true story into an action movie. Ultimately, it's the kind of thing that won't bore you on cable but not something you should seek out. **127m/C; DVD, Blu-Ray.** Antonio Banderas; Rodrigo Santoro; Juliette Binoche; James Brolin; Lou Diamond Phillips; *D:* Patricia Riggen; *W:* Mikko Alanne; Craig Borten; Michael Thomas; *C:* Checco Varese; *M:* James Horner.

33 Postcards ½ **2011** Unbelievable crime drama that can't even be saved by the talented Pearce. 16-year-old Chinese orphan Mei Mei (Zhu) has been sponsored for the past 10 years by Aussie Dean Randall (Pearce). When the orphanage choir travels to Sydney for a competition, Mei Mei sneaks off to find Randall using the postcards he's sent her. Except everything Randall's written is a lie and he's actually a longtime convict. Mei Mei gets into trouble, thanks to Randall's sleazy brother (Muldoon), and Randall works to get his parole in time to rescue her. **97m/C; DVD.** *AU CH* Guy Pearce; Lin Zhu; Rhys Muldoon; Claudia Karvan; Lincoln Lewis; *D:* Pauline Chan; *W:* Pauline Chan; Philip Dalkin; *C:* Toby Oliver; *M:* Antony Partos.

35 Shots of Rum ½ *35 Rhums* **2008** Warm family drama from Denis about letting go of restrictive-but-loving familial ties finds college student Josephine (Diop) devotedly living with her widowed, train conductor father Lionel (Descas). Happy in their routine, change still comes when Lionel's longtime colleague Rene (Toussaint) retires, leaving the middle-aged man feeling adrift. But Dad isn't too self-absorbed to notice that family friend Noe's (Colin) attraction to Josephine is not only mutual but heating up. French with subtitles. **99m/C; DVD.** *FR GE* Alex Descas; Gregoire Colin; Mati Diop; Nicole Dogue; Julieth Mars Toussaint; *D:* Claire Denis; *W:* Claire Denis; Jean-Pol Fargeau; *C:* Agnes Godard; *M:* Tindersticks.

36 Fillete **1988** Lili, an intellectually precocious 14-year-old French girl who's literally bursting out of her children's dress size 36 fillete, discovers her sexuality. So while on vacation with her family she becomes determined to see if she can seduce a middle-aged playboy. In French with English subtitles. **88m/C; VHS, DVD.** *FR* Delphine Zentout; Etienne Chicot; Oliver Parniere; Jean-Pierre Leaud; *D:* Catherine Breillat; *W:* Catherine Breillat; Roger Salloch; *C:* Laurent Dailland.

36 Hours **1964** Maj. Pike (Garner) is a high-ranking WWII Army officer with knowledge of top secret invasion plans who wakes up in an Army hospital with amnesia, a wife (Saint) he didn't know he had, and a shrink telling him that the war's been over for some time. But Pike's not sure what's real and what isn't, especially when the doc asks him to explain, in great detail, what happened just before he lost his memory. Are they telling the truth, or is this an elaborate hoax? Tight, suspenseful plot, and fine performances all around make this an enjoyable thriller even after that question is answered. Remade for TV in 1989 with Corbin Bernsen in the Garner role. **115m/B; VHS, DVD, Blu-Ray.** James Garner; Eva Marie Saint; Rod Taylor; Werner Peters; John Banner; Russ Thorson; Alan Napier; Oscar Beregi; Edmund Gilbert; Sig Rumann; Celia Lovsky; Karl Held; Marjorie Bennett; Martin Kosleck; Henry Rowland; Hilda Plowright; Joseph Mell; Rudolph Anders; James Doohan; ***D:*** George Seaton; ***W:*** George Seaton; Roald Dahl; Carl K. Hittleman; ***C:*** Philip H. Lathrop; ***M:*** Dimitri Tiomkin.

The 36th Chamber of Shaolin 🦴🦴🦴 1/2 *Shao Lin shan shi liu fang; Shaolin Master Killer; 36th Chamber; The Master Killer* **1978 (R)** Often called "the greatest Kung Fu movie of all time" (aren't there several movies that say that?), this Shaw Brothers film from the 1970s is definitely one of the most recognizable. Liu (Gordon Lau) is an ethics scholar whose friends and family are murdered by the Manchu government. Vowing revenge, he travels to the Shaolin temple to learn kung fu. After a bad start he proves to be the temple's best student, mastering in a mere five years what takes most a lifetime. Cast out for wanting to teach kung fu to the masses, he assembles a team of fighters and goes after the general responsible for the massacre of his town. **109m/C; DVD.** *CH* Chia Hui Liu; Lieh Lo; Norman Chu; Chia Yung Liu; ***D:*** Chia-Liang Liu; ***W:*** Kuang Ni; ***C:*** Yeh-tai Huang; Arthur Wong; ***M:*** Yung-Yu Chen.

The 39 Steps 🦴🦴🦴🦴 **1935** The classic Hitchcock mistaken-man-caught-in-intrigue thriller, featuring some of his most often copied set-pieces and the surest visual flair of his pre-war British period. Remade twice, in 1959 and 1979. **81m/B; VHS, DVD, Blu-Ray.** *GB* Robert Donat; Madeleine Carroll; Godfrey Tearle; Lucie Mannheim; Peggy Ashcroft; John Laurie; Wylie Watson; Helen Haye; Frank Cellier; Gus McNaughton; Jerry Verno; Peggy Simpson; Hilda Trevelyan; John Turnbull; Elizabeth Inglis; Wilfrid Brambell; ***D:*** Alfred Hitchcock; ***W:*** Charles Bennett; Alma Reville; Ian Hay; ***C:*** Bernard Knowles; ***M:*** Louis Levy.

The Thirty-Nine Steps 🦴🦴 1/2 **1979** Hitchcock remake is a visually interesting, but mostly uninvolving, mystery. Powell is the man suspected of stealing plans to begin WWI. Above average, but not by much. **98m/C; VHS, DVD.** *GB* Robert Powell; David Warner; Eric Porter; Karen Dotrice; John Mills; Andrew Keir; ***D:*** Don Sharp.

The 39 Steps 🦴🦴 1/2 **2009** In 1914, debonair former intelligence officer Richard Hanny (Penry-Jones) suddenly finds himself in possession of a coded notebook wanted by German agents and accused of murdering English spy Scudder. Pursued by the police (and the Germans), Hannay heads towards Scotland to locate the spy ring and is unexpectedly aided by suffragette Victoria Sinclair (Leonard), who seems to be keeping some secrets of her own. Based on the thriller by John Buchan that was notably filmed by Alfred Hitchcock in 1935. **90m/C; DVD.** *GB* Rupert Penry-Jones; Lydia Leonard; David Haig; Patrick Malahide; Patrick Kennedy; Alex Jennings; Eddie Marsan; Werner Daehn; Peter Stark; Steven Elder; ***D:*** James Hawes; ***W:*** Elizabeth (Lizzie) Mickery; ***C:*** James Aspinall; ***M:*** Robert (Rob) Lane. **TV**

This Above All 🦴🦴 **1942** Her distinguished family is upset when Prudence Cathaway (Fontaine) decides to join the WAAFs as a private and learn from the bottom up. She agrees to a blind date with troubled Clive Briggs (Power), a working-class man wounded at Dunkirk. He's bitterly opposed to the British aristocracy so Prudence keeps their class differences a secret until she learns that Clive has decided to go AWOL. Degenerates into flag-waving propaganda (hardly surprising since it's a wartime film), but Fontaine is lovely and sincere and Power does well in an early serious role. **110m/B; DVD.** Tyrone Power; Joan Fontaine; Philip Merivale; Thomas Mitchell; Henry Stephenson; Nigel Bruce; Gladys Cooper; ***D:*** Anatole Litvak; ***W:*** R.C. Sherriff; ***C:*** Arthur C. Miller; ***M:*** Alfred Newman. Oscars '43: Art Dir./Set Dec., B&W.

This Boy's Life 🦴🦴🦴 **1993 (R)** In 1957, Carolyn (Barkin) and her teenage son Toby (DiCaprio) are in search of a new life, far from her abusive ex-boyfriend. In the town of Concrete, just outside Seattle, she meets ex-military man Dwight (De Niro), a slick but none too suave mechanic who might be the answer to her dreams, but then again, he might not. Nicely crafted performances from all, but keep your eye on DiCaprio (great in his first major role) as the confused and abused teen divided between dreams of prep school and the allure of the going-nowhere crowd. Based on the memoirs of Tobias Wolff; director Caton-Jones sensitively illustrates the skewed understanding of masculinity in the 1950s. Vintage soundtrack takes you back. **115m/C; VHS, DVD.** Robert De Niro; Ellen Barkin; Leonardo DiCaprio; Jonah Blechman; Eliza Dushku; Chris Cooper; Carla Gugino; Zachary Ansley; Tracey Ellis; Kathy Kinney; Gerrit Graham; ***D:*** Michael Caton-Jones; ***W:*** Robert Getchell; ***C:*** David Watkin; ***M:*** Carter Burwell.

This Christmas 🦴🦴 **2007 (PG-13)** After several years apart, the Whitfields are reunited for the holidays at the solidly upper-middle-class family home in L.A. Ma'Dere (Devine) is the matriarch of this African American family whose members include the military son Claude (Short), the musician son Quentin (Elba), oldest daughter Lisa (King), workaholic Kelli (Leal), college student Mel (London), and Baby (Brown), who announces his plan to follow their long-absent father into the jazz world. His is not the only bombshell to fall as everyone has a turn having his or her buttons pushed. Ma'Dere's long-time boyfriend Joe (Lindo) does a great job of holding everyone together long enough for them to realize what a treasure they have in each other. A tad overdone and over the top but still a fun holiday romp. **117m/C; Blu-Ray.** Delroy Lindo; Idris Elba; Loretta Devine; Sharon Leal; Lauren London; Reina King; Chris Brown; Keith D. Robinson; Laz Alonso; Columbus Short; Mekhi Phifer; ***D:*** Preston A. Whitmore, II; ***W:*** Preston A. Whitmore, II; ***C:*** Alexander Grusynski.

This Day and Age 🦴 **1933** Unlikely DeMille gangster quickie filled with hokum and melodrama. A group of high school students decide on vigilante justice when adults let a gangland boss get away with murdering a friend. **86m/B; DVD.** Charles Bickford; Judith Allen; Edward J. Nugent; Richard Cromwell; Ben Alexander; ***D:*** Cecil B. DeMille; ***W:*** Bartlett Cormack; ***C:*** J. Peverell Marley.

This Film Is Not Yet Rated 🦴🦴 **2006** Veteran filmmaker Kirby Dick tackles the secrecy surrounding the MPAA ratings board, with Dick out to illustrate their nonsensical approach to the process. Created in 1968, its anonymous panel (which Dick aims to identify) is frequently accused of being lenient towards violence and uptight about sex. Filmmakers generally have no way of knowing just what the board objects to since they don't offer specific criticism because that would be censorship. Kirby uses some questionable methods to get board members on camera and he has no particular suggestions about reform, but if you're interested in filmmaking, the documentary and its revealing interviews makes for compelling viewing. **97m/C; DVD.** ***D:*** Kirby Dick; ***C:*** Shana Hagan; Kirsten Johnson; Amy Vincent.

This Girl's Life 🦴🦴 **2003 (R)** Moon (knockout Marquis in her film debut) is a forthright beauty who likes sex and makes her living in the porn industry. Film is matter-of-fact about her life, which includes caring for her Pops (Woods), who has Parkinson's, worrying about an AIDS scare, and wondering about a budding relationship with a non-industry boyfriend (Pardue). Kudos to director/writer Ash for making a flick that's compelling without being violent or exploitative despite its subject matter. **101m/C; On Demand.** James Woods; Kip Pardue; Tomas Arana; Michael Rapaport; Juliette Marquis; Rosario Dawson; Ioan Gruffudd; Isaiah Washington, IV; Cheyenne Silver; Kam Heskin; Natalie Taylor; ***D:*** Ash; ***W:*** Ash; ***C:*** Alessandro Zezza; ***M:*** Agartha Halou.

This Gun for Hire 🦴🦴🦴 1/2 **1942** In his first major film role, Ladd plays a hired gun seeking retribution from a client who betrays him. Preston is the cop pursuing him and hostage Lake. Ladd's performance as the cold-blooded killer with a soft spot for cats is stunning; his train-yard scene is an emotional powerhouse. Based on Graham Greene's novel "A Gun for Sale." Remade as "Short Cut to Hell." The first of several films using the Ladd-Lake team, but the only one in which Ladd played a villain. **81m/B; VHS, DVD, Blu-Ray.** Alan Ladd; Veronica Lake; Robert Preston; Laird Cregar; Tully Marshall; Marc Lawrence; Yvonne De Carlo; ***D:*** Frank Tuttle; ***W:*** Albert (John B. Sherry) Maltz; W.R. Burnett; ***C:*** John Seitz; ***M:*** David Buttolph.

This Gun for Hire 🦴🦴 **1990 (R)** A professional assassin finds that he has been duped into killing a powerful political figure, whom he was told was a New Orleans mobster. Now on the run, he takes a nightclub performer hostage, unaware that she is the fiance of the FBI agent who is after him. All odds are against him, but the special relationship he forms with the woman may just be his ticket out. Adapted from novel by Graham Greene. **89m/C; VHS, DVD.** Robert Wagner; Nancy Everhard; Frederic Lehne; John Harkins; ***D:*** Lou Antonio.

This Happy Breed 🦴🦴🦴 1/2 **1947** A celebrated film version of Noel Coward's classic play depicts the changing fortunes of a large family in England between the world wars. Happiness, hardships, triumph and tragedy mix a series of memorable episodes, including some of the most cherished moments in popular British cinema, though its appeal is universal. Currently only available as part of a collection titled 'David Lean Directs Noel Coward.' **114m/C; VHS, DVD, Blu-Ray.** *GB* Robert Newton; Celia Johnson; John Mills; Kay Walsh; Stanley Holloway; Amy Veness; Alison Leggatt; Eileen Erskine; John Blythe; Guy Verney; Betty Fleetwood; Merle Tottenham; ***Nar:*** Laurence Olivier; ***D:*** David Lean; ***W:*** David Lean; Noel Coward; Ronald Neame; ***C:*** Ronald Neame; ***M:*** Noel Coward; Muir Mathieson.

This Is Elvis 🦴🦴 **1981 (PG)** The life of Elvis, combining documentary footage with dramatizations of events in his life. Includes more than three dozen songs. Generally seen as an attempt to cash in on the myth, but was well-received by his fans. **144m/C; VHS, DVD.** Elvis Presley; ***D:*** Malcolm Leo; Andrew Solt; ***W:*** Malcolm Leo; Andrew Solt; ***C:*** Gil Hubbs.

This Is England 🦴🦴 **2006** Meadows' autobiographical film about a lonely 12-year-old who is befriended by local skinheads in 1983 Britain. Shaun (non-pro Turgoose), whose soldier dad was killed in the Falklands, lives with his mum in a rundown community. He stands up to the teasing of the (essentially harmless) neighborhood gang and earns the respect of young leader Woody (Gilgun). Things change when older Combo (Graham) gets out of prison. A supporter of the National Front, Combo's racist rhetoric causes a split, but Shaun sticks with him since he sees Combo as a surrogate dad. **98m/C; DVD.** *GB* Stephen Graham; Thomas Turgoose; Joe Gilgun; Vicky McClure; Andrew Shim; Jo Hartley; ***D:*** Shane Meadows; ***W:*** Shane Meadows; ***C:*** Danny Cohen; ***M:*** Ludovico Einaudi.

This Is 40 🦴🦴 **2012 (R)** Judd Apatow delivers yet another bloated comedy in this disappointing misfire, a flick that has moments that work but they're connected by cliché and contrivance that frustrates more than entertains. Rudd & Mann play the same characters they did in "Knocked Up" as they deal with their pending mid-life crises. The supporting cast, particularly Brooks and Lithgow as the pair's parents, is notably strong and Apatow still has a gift with dialogue but the secrets being held by this couple (she's pregnant, he's spending all their money) are the trade of lesser romantic comedy scribes than Apatow. **134m/C; DVD, Blu-Ray.** Paul Rudd; Leslie Mann; Maude Apatow; Iris Apatow; Jason Segel; Megan Fox; John Lithgow; ***D:*** Judd Apatow; ***W:*** Judd Apatow; ***C:*** Phedon Papamichael; ***M:*** Jon Brion.

This is Martin Bonner 🦴🦴 1/2 **2013 (R)** Hartigan's drama captures how good deeds can be defined by more than practical needs through a character study of two men. Martin Bonner (Eenhorn) has just moved to Nevada and works with newly-released prisoners as they try to assimilate back into the world. His latest assignment is Travis Holloway (Arquette), a gentle man trying to find his way again. Avoiding all clichés, Hartigan's script keeps it refreshingly simple and sincere, and with excellent performances. **83m/C; DVD.** Paul Eenhoorn; Richmond Arquette; Sam Buchanan; Robert Longstreet; ***D:*** Chad Hartigan; ***W:*** Chad Hartigan; ***C:*** Sean McElwee; ***M:*** Keegan DeWitt.

This Is My Father 🦴🦴 1/2 **1999 (R)** Teacher Kieran Johnson (Caan) decides to research his Irish roots after discovering a photo of his mother with a mystery man who may have been his father. Told in flashback, it portraits the class differences in rural Ireland in the '30s and the doomed romance between wealthy, teenaged Fiona Flynn (Farrelly) and Kieran O'Dea (Quinn), a poor tenant farmer who works for the Flynn family. Affecting role for Aidan Quinn, who worked with brothers Paul and Declan. Script is based on a story Theresa Quinn told her children. **120m/C; VHS, DVD.** Aidan Quinn; James Caan; Stephen Rea; Moya Farrelly; John Cusack; Jacob Tierney; Colm Meaney; Donal Donnelly; Brendan Gleeson; ***D:*** Paul Quinn; ***W:*** Paul Quinn; ***C:*** Declan Quinn; ***M:*** Donal Lunny.

This Is My Life 🦴🦴 **1992 (PG-13)** The story of a working mother torn between her skyrocketing career as a stand-up comic and her two daughters. Kavner plays the divorced mom who is determined to chuck her cosmetic sales job for comic success. Her career starts to really take off; she hires an agent and makes appearances on talk shows. As offers pour in, she eventually realizes that her girls are suffering as a result of her success. Good performances highlight an otherwise average drama. **105m/C; DVD.** Julie Kavner; Samantha Mathis; Carrie Fisher; Dan Aykroyd; Gaby Hoffman; ***D:*** Nora Ephron; ***W:*** Nora Ephron; Delia Ephron.

This is Not a Film 🦴🦴🦴 *In film nist* **2010** The paradoxical title of this documentary refers to its creator and subject, Iranian filmmaker Jafar Panahi, being under house arrest and banned from making films by his government for supporting a 2009 uprising. Footage of him preparing for his appeals was shot using digital cameras and smartphones, not film. Facing a 20-year ban from making movies and a six year prison term, the poignancy of Jafar "not" making his film, yet remaining creative is a sly political commentary that wryly says "No comment." Adding to the intrigue, it was reportedly snuck out of Iran in a cake and made its unannounced debut at the 2011 Cannes Film Festival. In Persian, with subtitles. **75m/C; DVD, Blu-Ray.** *IA* Mojtaba Mirtahmasb; Jafar Panahi; ***D:*** Mojtaba Mirtahmasb; Jafar Panahi; ***W:*** Jafar Panahi.

This Is Not a Love Song 🦴🦴 **2002** Petty criminal Heaton (Glenaan) has just picked up his pal Spike (Colgan) who was doing a short stint in a Glasgow prison. When their car runs out of gas on a lonely country road, they hike to the nearest farm in search of help. Too bad the farmer thinks these ruffians are there to rob the place. In the ensuing confusion, Spike accidentally shoots and kills the farmer's daughter. Now the two friends take off across the moors—pursued not only by the police but by a vigilante group of locals. Title is taken from the Public Image Ltd. song that is heard in various versions. **92m/C; VHS, DVD.** *GB* Michael Colgan; Kenny Glenaan; David Bradley; John Henshaw; ***D:*** Bille Eltringham; ***W:*** Simon Beaufoy; ***C:*** Robbie Ryan; ***M:*** Adrian Johnston; Mark Rutherford.

This Is Not a Test 🦴🦴 **1962** When news comes of an impending nuclear attack, a state trooper at a roadblock offers sanctuary to passing travellers. The effectiveness of the film's social commentary is hindered by its small budget. **72m/B; VHS, DVD.** Seamon Glass; Mary Morlass; Thayer Roberts; Aubrey Martin; ***D:*** Frederic Gadette; ***W:*** Frederic Gadette; Peter Abenheim; Betty Laskey; ***C:*** Brick Marquard; ***M:*** Greig McRitchie.

This Is Spinal Tap 🦴🦴🦴 1/2 *Spinal Tap* **1984 (R)** Pseudo-rockumentary about heavy-metal band Spinal Tap, profiling their career from "England's loudest band" to an entry in the "where are they now file." Hilarious satire, featuring music performed by Guest, McKean, Shearer, and others. Included are Spinal Tap's music video "Hell Hole," and an ad for their greatest hits album, "Heavy Metal Memories." Features great cameos, particularly David Letterman's Paul Shaffer as a record promoter and Billy Crystal as a surly mime. First feature for Reiner

(Meathead on "All in the Family"). Followed by "The Return of Spinal Tap." **82m/C; VHS, DVD, Blu-Ray.** Michael McKean; Christopher Guest; Harry Shearer; Tony Hendra; Bruno Kirby; Rob Reiner; June Chadwick; Howard Hesseman; Billy Crystal; Dana Carvey; Ed Begley, Jr.; Patrick Macnee; Fran Drescher; Paul Shaffer; Anjelica Huston; Fred Willard; Paul Benedict; Archie Hahn; ***D:*** Rob Reiner; ***W:*** Michael McKean; Christopher Guest; Harry Shearer; Rob Reiner; ***C:*** Peter Smokler; ***M:*** Michael McKean; Christopher Guest; Harry Shearer; Rob Reiner. Natl. Film Reg. '02.

This Is the Army 1/2 **1943** A robust tribute to the American soldier of WWII based on the hit play by Irving Berlin. Murphy, who later was a senator from California, played Reagan's father. **105m/C; VHS, DVD.** George Murphy; Joan Leslie; Ronald Reagan; Alan Hale; Kate Smith; George Tobias; Irving Berlin; Joe Louis; ***D:*** Michael Curtiz; ***M:*** Max Steiner. Oscars '43: Scoring/Musical.

This Is the End **2013 (R)** Rogen and Goldberg turned their teen years into comedy gold in "Superbad" and they hit the funny bone again with this meta take on end of the world movies. Rogen is forced to survive the apocalypse with buddies James Franco, Jay Baruchel, Jonah Hill, Craig Robinson, and Danny McBride. Playing exaggerated versions of themselves, the man-children prove to be totally incapable of surviving the rapture. Filled with more weed and penis jokes than a Cheech & Chong movie, Rogen's directorial debut can get a bit jerky but it's also undeniably hilarious. **107m/C; DVD, Blu-Ray.** Seth Rogen; James Franco; Jonah Hill; Jay Baruchel; Danny McBride; Craig Robinson; Michael Cera; Emma Watson; ***D:*** Seth Rogen; Evan Goldberg; ***W:*** Seth Rogen; Evan Goldberg; ***C:*** Brandon Trost; ***M:*** Henry Jackman.

This Is the Night 1/2 **1932** Pre-Code romantic comedy, adapted from the 1925 play "Naughty Cinderella," marked the debut of Cary Grant as Stephen Mathewson, an Olympic javelin thrower married to Claire (Todd). She's shocked when Stephen joins her in Paris since she's involved herself with playboy Gerald Gray (Young)..Gerald passes himself off as married and invites the Mathewsons to accompany him and his wife to Venice. Gerald has to find a woman willing to play the part and Germaine (Damita) needs the dough. **78m/B; DVD.** Lili Damita; Roland Young; Thelma Todd; Cary Grant; Charlie Ruggles; Irving Bacon; Claire Dodd; ***D:*** Frank Tuttle; ***W:*** George Marion, Jr.; ***C:*** Victor Milner.

This Is Where I Leave You 1/2 **2014 (R)** The death of a patriarch brings together four siblings, forcing them to return to their childhood home to live under the same roof together for a week. Of course, each comes not only with an assortment of significant others but life problems that can be neatly resolved in about 100 minutes. Way too tidy to be believable, it approaches sitcom qualities. But the cast is remarkably assembled to include likable stars like Bateman, Fey, Stoll, and Driver, with Fonda as their inappropriate matriarch. They make the family tripe easier to digest. Based on the book of the same name by Jonathan Tropper. **103m/C; DVD, Blu-Ray.** Jason Bateman; Tina Fey; Corey Stoll; Adam Driver; Jane Fonda; Kathryn Hahn; Connie Britton; Rose Byrne; Timothy Olyphant; Dax Shepard; Abigail Spencer; ***D:*** Shawn Levy; ***W:*** Jonathan Tropper; ***C:*** Terry Stacey; ***M:*** Michael Giacchino.

This Island Earth 1/2 **1955** The planet Metaluna is in desperate need of uranium to power its defense against enemy invaders. A nuclear scientist and a nuclear fission expert from Earth are kidnapped to help out. The first serious movie about interplanetary escapades. Bud Westmore created pulsating cranium special effects make-up. **86m/C; VHS, DVD, Blu-Ray.** Jeff Morrow; Faith Domergue; Rex Reason; Russell Johnson; ***D:*** Joseph M. Newman; ***M:*** Herman Stein.

This Land Is Mine **1943** A timid French schoolteacher gathers enough courage to defy the Nazis when they attempt to occupy his town. Laughton's characterization is effective as the meek fellow who discovers the hero within himself in this patriotic wartime flick. The second American film for an exiled Renoir. **103m/B; DVD.** Charles Laughton; Maureen O'Hara; George Sanders; Walter Slezak; George Coulouris; Una O'Connor; Kent Smith; ***D:*** Jean Renoir; ***W:*** Dudley Nichols; ***C:*** Frank Redman; ***M:*** Lothar Perl. Oscars '43: Sound.

This Man Must Die 1/2 *Que La Bete Meure; Uccidero Un Uomo; Killer!* **1970 (PG)** A man searches relentlessly for the driver who killed his young son in a hit-and-run. When found, the driver engages him in a complex cat-and-mouse chase. Another stunning crime and punishment tale from Chabrol. **112m/C; VHS, DVD.** *FR* Michel Duchaussoy; Caroline Cellier; Jean Yanne; Anouk Ferjac; Maurice Pialat; ***D:*** Claude Chabrol; ***W:*** Paul Gegauff; ***C:*** Jean Rabier.

This Matter of Marriage 1/2 **1998** Hallie Mitchell (Hope) and Donnalee Crawford (Miller) are best friends and struggling business partners who have sacrificed their personal lives for their careers as architects. Guy-next-door Steve (Peters) is interested in Hallie but she thinks he's a lunkhead. She'll change her mind. From the Harlequin Romance Series; adapted from the Debbie Macomber novel. **95m/C; DVD.** *CA* Leslie Hope; Rick Peters; Sherry Miller; Michael Nouri; Karl Pruner; Carl Marotte; Natasha Greenblatt; ***D:*** Brad Turner; ***W:*** Peter Lauterman; ***C:*** John Berrie; ***M:*** Christopher Dedrick. **TV**

This May Be the Last Time **2014** Harjo's grandfather disappeared mysteriously in Sasakwa, Oklahoma in 1962. The Seminole community of which he was a part searched for him and sang ancient songs of faith and hope in the process. Harjo seeks to find answers about what happened to his grandfather, but also to look at the way music, religion, and hymns are such an important part of the Seminole people, a tradition that traces back to Scotland, Appalachia, and the experiences of enslaved African Americas. Harjo's film is interesting but thin. **90m/C; DVD.** ***D:*** Sterlin Harjo; ***W:*** Sterlin Harjo; ***C:*** Sterlin Harjo; Matt Leach; Shane Brown; ***M:*** Ryan Beveridge.

This Means War **2012 (R)** Two covert CIA guys, playboy FDR (Pine) and romantic Tuck (Hardy), inadvertently both fall for Lauren (Witherspoon) and the boys decide they'll be gentlemen about it and see who she picks. She is none-the-wiser as they don't stick to their rules and employ a slew of high-tech spying and dirty tricks at their disposal. Certainly nothing new here in the rom-com-action genre, but Pine and Hardy make for a fun guy tandem while Handler throws out some really raunchy lines as she lives vicariously as Lauren's gal pal Trish. **97m/C; DVD, Blu-Ray.** Reese Witherspoon; Chris Pine; Tom (Thomas) Hardy; Chelsea Handler; Til Schweiger; Abigail Spencer; Angela Bassett; John Paul Ruttan; ***D:*** McG; ***W:*** Timothy Dowling; Simon Kinberg; ***C:*** Russell Carpenter; ***M:*** Christophe Beck.

This Modern Age **1931** Moralistic melodrama starring a very blonde Crawford. After being raised by her divorced (now deceased) father, Valentine (Crawford) heads to Paris to reunite with her mother, Diane (Frederick), who's hiding the fact that she's the mistress of married Frenchman Andre (Conti). Val gets caught up in the fast life with wealthy drunk Tony (Owsley), which leads to her unexpectedly meeting swell Harvard grad Bob (Hamilton). But Bob's very conservative parents object. **76m/B; DVD.** Joan Crawford; Pauline Frederick; Neil Hamilton; Monroe Owsley; Albert Conti; Hobart Bosworth; Emma Dunn; ***D:*** Nick Grinde; ***W:*** Frank Butler; Sylvia Thalberg; ***C:*** Charles Rosher.

This Must Be the Place **2012 (R)** Fading, middle-aged rock star Cheyenne (Penn) lives in the shadow of his old glory in Dublin--Goth look and all. When his estranged father dies, he returns to New York to find that the Holocaust survivor had a hidden vendetta—to exact revenge against an officer who tortured him in Auschwitz. Taking on his father's search to find the man, Cheyenne journeys across the country and through a cast of kooky characters. A bit rambly, but such is the journey to self-discovery. **118m/C; DVD, Blu-Ray.** Sean Penn; Frances McDormand; Judd Hirsch; Eve Hewson; Kerry Condon; Harry Dean Stanton; Joyce Van Patten; David Byrne; Shea Wigham; Liron Levo; Simon Delaney; ***D:*** Paolo Sorrentino; ***W:*** Paolo Sorrentino; Umberto Contarello; ***C:*** Luca Bigazzi; ***M:*** David Byrne; William Oldham.

This Property Is Condemned **1966** It's a hot time down south once again in this adaptation of the Tennessee Williams play. Wood is the overly flirtatious southern charmer who takes a shine to the latest tenant of her loathsome mama's boarding-house. And since it's Redford, who can blame her. Things steam up when he returns her interest but there's trouble a'brewin'. Both leads are lovely but the film itself is overly southern-fried. Williams was reportedly unhappy with the script and wanted his name removed from the film. **109m/C; DVD.** Robert Redford; Natalie Wood; Charles Bronson; Kate Reid; Mary Badham; Jon(athan) Provost; Robert (Bobby) Blake; John Harding; ***D:*** Sydney Pollack; ***W:*** Francis Ford Coppola; Edith Sommer; Fred Coe.

This Revolution **2005** An action-addict network TV reporter (Crooker) covers the street protests that preceded the NYC-GOP convention. The blending of real footage with fictional is most effective and difficult to distinguish. Gives a relatively interesting twist on a topic covered in documentaries like "Fahrenheit 9/11" and "Bush's Brain." Movie became part of the story when Dawson was arrested at one of the rallies being filmed. **95m/C; DVD.** Nathan Crooker; Rosario Dawson; Amy Redford; Brendan Sexton, III; Brett DelBuono; ***D:*** Stephen Marshall; ***W:*** Stephen Marshall; ***C:*** Brian Jackson.

This Side of the Law 1/2 **1950** Crooked lawyer Philip Cagle (Douglas) persuades poverty-stricken David Cummins (Smith) to impersonate a missing millionaire who's about to be declared legally dead. Cagle doesn't want that to happen and all his manipulations lead to family troubles, greed, and murder. **74m/B; DVD.** Robert Douglas; Kent Smith; Viveca Lindfors; Janis Paige; John Alvin; Monte Blue; ***D:*** Richard Bare; ***W:*** Russell S. Hughes; ***C:*** Carl Guthrie; ***M:*** William Lava.

This Sporting Life **1963** A gritty, depressing portrait of former coal miner Frank Machin (Harris), who breaks into the violent world of professional rugby, and whose inability to handle social differences causes problems. He begins an affair with widow Mrs. Hammond (Roberts), from whom he rents a room, but finds they are capable of only a physical attachment. One of the best of the British early '60s working-class angry young man melodramas. **134m/B; VHS, DVD.** *GB* Richard Harris; Rachel Roberts; Alan Badel; William Hartnell; Colin Blakely; Vanda Godsell; Arthur Lowe; ***D:*** Lindsay Anderson; ***W:*** David Storey; ***C:*** Denys Coop; ***M:*** Roberto Gerhard. British Acad. '63: Actress (Roberts); Cannes '63: Actor (Harris).

This Stuff'll Kill Ya! **WOOF!** **1971 (PG)** A backwoods preacher who believes in free love and moonshining runs into trouble with the locals when a series of gruesome religious murders are committed. Southern drive-in material from one of the genre's masters. Holt's last film. **100m/C; VHS, DVD.** Jeffrey Allen; Tim Holt; Gloria King; Ray Sager; Eric Bradly; Terence McCarthy; Larry Drake; ***D:*** Herschell Gordon Lewis; ***W:*** Herschell Gordon Lewis; ***C:*** Alex Ameri; ***M:*** Herschell Gordon Lewis.

This Thing of Ours **2003** Lame wiseguy movie hits all the cliches as broadly as possible. Ambitious hood Nick Santini (Provenzano) wants to impress the old New Jersey mobsters so he schemes with some pals to use computers to siphon off money from bank accounts worldwide and stash the cash offshore. Provenzano went to prison for tax evasion and racketeering so you'd think his experience would make the flick more compelling—no dice. **100m/C; DVD.** Christian Maelen; Louis Vanaria; Frank Vincent; James Caan; Danny Provenzano; Vincent Pastore; ***D:*** Danny Provenzano; ***W:*** Danny Provenzano; Tewd A. Bohus.

This Time for Keeps **1947** Glossy if rather dull (thanks to a bland leading man) MGM musical with Williams the star of an aquatic show on Michigan's Mackinac Island. Opera singer Richard (Melchior) and his singing son Dick (Johnston) are on vacation and Dick, who met Nora (Williams) during the war, reintroduces himself to the bathing beauty. However, neither of their families approve of their burgeoning romance. Durante provides comic relief and gets to sing "Inka Dinka Doo" while future director Stanley Donen did the choreography. **105m/C; DVD.** Esther Williams; Lauritz Melchior; Johnny Johnston; Jimmy Durante; Dame May Whitty; Xavier Cugat; ***D:*** Richard Thorpe; ***W:*** Gladys Lehman; ***C:*** Karl Freund.

This Woman Is Dangerous 1/2 **1952** Crawford's last role under her Warner Bros. contract finds her portraying a gangster's moll with a criminal record of her own. Beth Austin is loved by jealous killer Matt Jackson (Brian). After another heist, Beth learns she's going blind and goes into the hospital for eye surgery, performed by Dr. Ben Halleck (Morgan). The two fall in love while Matt is in hiding and the FBI is tracking them down. When Matt learns his gal loves another, he decides to eliminate the competition. **97m/B; DVD.** Joan Crawford; Dennis Morgan; David Brian; Richard Webb; Mari Aldon; Phil Carey; Ian MacDonald; ***D:*** Felix Feist; ***W:*** Daniel Mainwaring; George Worthing Yates; ***C:*** Ted D. McCord; ***M:*** David Buttolph.

Thomas and the Magic Railroad **2000 (G)** Thomas, a spunky blue steam engine, is bullied by big bad engine, Diesel, and aided by Mr. Conductor (Baldwin), as well as young Lily (Wilson) and her train-loving grandad (Fonda) who also come to Thomas' rescue. Part live-action, part animation adaptation of the British children's series will be fine for the kidlets but parents will overdose on the whimsy factor. **84m/C; VHS, DVD.** Mara Wilson; Alec Baldwin; Peter Fonda; Didi Conn; ***D:*** Britt Allcroft; ***W:*** Britt Allcroft; ***C:*** Dr. Paul Ryan; ***M:*** Hummie Mann.

The Thomas Crown Affair *Thomas Crown and Company; The Crown Caper* **1968 (R)** A multi-millionaire (McQueen) decides to plot and execute the perfect theft, a daring daylight robbery of a bank. Dunaway is the gorgeous and efficient insurance investigator determined to nab him. One of the best visual scenes is the chess match between the two as they begin to fall in love. Strong production with Oscar-winning theme "The Windmills of Your Mind." **102m/C; VHS, DVD, Blu-Ray.** Steve McQueen; Faye Dunaway; Jack Weston; Yaphet Kotto; Gordon Pinsent; ***D:*** Norman Jewison; ***W:*** Alan R. Trustman; ***C:*** Haskell Wexler. Oscars '68: Song ("The Windmills of Your Mind"); Golden Globes '69: Song ("The Windmills of Your Mind").

The Thomas Crown Affair **1999 (R)** Slick, lavish, updated, and loose adaptation of the 1968 Steve McQueen/Faye Dunaway caper. Thomas Crown (Brosnan) is a self-made New York billionaire, who just can't resist pulling off the perfect crime by stealing a Monet from the Metropolitan Museum of Art. Catherine Banning (Russo) is the gorgeous insurance investigator on his trail, who can't help falling for the very charming criminal. The fortysomething duo sizzle (how fantastic to see two age-appropriate lovers for a change) and if the ending has a tacked-on feel, it doesn't really matter. Dunaway makes a cameo appearance as Crown's therapist. **111m/C; VHS, DVD.** Pierce Brosnan; Rene Russo; Denis Leary; Frankie Faison; Ben Gazzara; Fritz Weaver; Charles Keating; Mark Margolis; Faye Dunaway; Esther Canadas; ***D:*** John McTiernan; ***W:*** Leslie Dixon; Kurt Wimmer; ***C:*** Tom Priestley; ***M:*** Bill Conti.

The Thompsons 1/2 **2012 (R)** In this gory sequel to 'The Hamiltons', the titular family of vampires has changed their name and fled to Europe to discover their roots. Alas, their roots are none too happy to see them. **83m/C; DVD, Blu-Ray, Streaming.** *UK US* Cory Knauf; Samuel Child; MacKenzie Firgens; Joseph McKelheer; Ryan Hartwig; ***D:*** Mitchell Altieri; Phil Flores; ***W:*** Cory Knauf; Mitchell Altieri; Phil Flores; Adam Weis; ***C:*** Matthew Cooke; David Rom; ***M:*** Kevin Kerrigan. **VIDEO**

Thompson's Last Run 1/2 **1990** Boyhood friends grow up on either side of the law. They come face-to-face, though, when one is assigned to transport the other to prison. **95m/C; VHS, DVD.** Robert Mitchum; Wilford Brimley; Kathleen York; Susan Tyrrell; ***D:*** Jerrold Freedman; ***M:*** Miles Goodman. **TV**

Thor **2011 (PG-13)** Thor (Hemsworth, a fitting choice), the son of Norse god Odin (Hopkins), is a mighty warrior whose reckless actions reignite a war. Because of his arrogance, Odin banishes Thor from Asgard and sends him to Earth—minus his superpowers—to learn some humility. However, an Asgard enemy threatens not only Thor's home planet but also the people of Earth, including Jane Foster (Portman), a scientist who tries to help. The intergalactic scenery is amazingly created and the introduction of an Avenger makes for a thrilling adventure. Part two is on the way. Adapted from Marvel Comics. **115m/C; DVD, Blu-Ray, On Demand.** Chris Hemsworth; Natalie Portman; Anthony Hopkins; Stellan Skarsgard; Kat Dennings; Rene Russo; Ray Stevenson; Idris Elba; Tom Hiddleston; Colm Feore; Clark Gregg; ***D:*** Kenneth Branagh; ***W:*** Zack Stentz; Ashley Edward Miller; Don Payne; ***C:*** Haris Zambarloukos; ***M:*** Patrick Doyle.

Thor and the Amazon Women 🦴 *Women Gladiators* **1960** The mighty Thor leads his enslaved men on an attack against the evil Queen Nera and her female-dominated Amazon society. **85m/C; VHS, DVD.** *IT* Joe Robinson; Susy Andersen; Harry Baird; Maria Fiore; Claudia Capone; Alberto Cerenini; Antonio Leonviola; Jannin Hendy; ***W:*** Fabio Piccioni; ***C:*** Guglielmo Mancori; ***M:*** Roberto Nicolosi.

Thor: Ragnarok 🦴🦴🦴 **2017 (PG-13)** An exuberantly wry entry in the Marvel movie universe that shows Hemsworth's comic range and charisma. Asgard, Thor's (Hemsworth) homeworld, is under threat of destruction in fulfillment of a prophesied apocalypse. His long lost, war-mongering sister Hela (Blanchett) seeks power in the vacuum left after their father Odin (Hopkins) has gone. Thor is initially limited in his ability to act because he is a fire demon's prisoner. Later trapped on Sakaar, he becomes part of gladiator competition run by the planet's petty yet droll Grandmaster (Goldblum). Just sit back and enjoy the God of Thunder! **130m/C; DVD, Blu-Ray.** Chris Hemsworth; Tom Hiddleston; Cate Blanchett; Idris Elba; Jeff Goldblum; ***D:*** Taika Waititi; ***W:*** Eric Pearson; Craig Kyle; Christopher Yost; ***C:*** Javier Aguirresarobe; ***M:*** Mark Mothersbaugh.

Thor the Conqueror 🦴 *Thor il conquistatore* **1983** Thor (Minniti) returns for revenge on the murderers of his parents after spending his youth being trained in combat by a Goddess. As usual for 80's Italian sword and sorcery films, this one plays loose with its source material as it claims the barbarians are Vikings despite their complete lack of resemblance to anything Viking other than the titular character's name. Italian with subtitles. **90m/C; DVD.** *IT* Bruno Minniti; Mario Romano; Luigi Mezzanotte; Raf Baldassarre; ***D:*** Tonino Ricci; ***W:*** Tito Carpi; ***C:*** Giovanni Bergamini; ***M:*** Francesco De Masi.

Thor: The Dark World 🦴🦴 **2013 (PG-13)** Thor returns to put the hammer down in this CGI blockbuster An ancient race of elves, enemies to the stability of the universe, return, leading Thor (Hemsworth) on a quest to save humanity. His adventure forces him to work with the nefarious (and movie-stealing) Loki (Hiddleston) yet again and brings back with his human love interest, Jane (Portman). **112m/C; DVD, Blu-Ray.** Chris Hemsworth; Natalie Portman; Tom Hiddleston; Anthony Hopkins; Christopher Eccleston; Rene Russo; Kat Dennings; Stellan Skarsgard; Idris Elba; ***D:*** Alan Taylor; ***W:*** Chris Yost; Christopher Markus; Stephen McFeely; ***C:*** Kramer Morgenthau; ***M:*** Brian Tyler.

The Thorn Birds 🦴🦴🦴 **1983** Pioneers find danger and romance in the Australian outback as they struggle to begin a dynasty. Charismatic priest sometimes hurts, sometimes helps them. One of Stanwyck's last performances; Ward's American TV debut. Originally a ten-hour TV miniseries based on Colleen McCullough novel. Emmy nominations for actor Chamberlain, supporting actors Brown and Plummer, supporting actress Laurie, direction, photography, music, costume design, and editing. **486m/C; VHS, DVD.** Rachel Ward; Richard Chamberlain; Jean Simmons; Ken Howard; Mare Winningham; Richard Kiley; Piper Laurie; Bryan Brown; Christopher Plummer; Barbara Stanwyck; ***D:*** Daryl Duke; ***C:*** Bill Butler; ***M:*** Henry Mancini. **TV**

The Thorn Birds: The Missing Years 🦴🦴🦴 **1996** Follow-up to the critically acclaimed miniseries "The Thorn Birds." Fills in the 19-year gap since the original romantic melodrama aired. **178m/C; DVD.** Richard Chamberlain; Amanda Donohoe; Julia Blake; Olivia Burnette; Michael Caton; Zach English; Peter Ford; Jonathan Hardy; Ingrid Mason; Maximilian Schell; Jack Thompson; Simon Westaway; Paul Bertram; Rob Doran; Christopher Gabardi; Adam Grossetti; John Heywood; Phillip Hinton; Enrico Mammarella; Marijke Mann; Todd Schulberg; ***D:*** Kevin James Dobson; ***W:*** David Stevens; Colleen McCullough; ***C:*** Ross Berryman; ***M:*** Garry McDonald; Lawrence Stone. **TV**

Thoroughbreds 🦴🦴 ½ **2017 (R)** Soon after rich high-schooler Lily (Taylor-Joy) reconnects with Amanda (Cooke), a childhood friend with sociopathic tendencies, the pair concoct a plan to kill Lily's stepfather. Originally conceived of as a play, Finley's script is dialogue-driven and witty, offering a dark-humored commentary on privilege and human nature. The action, when it finally arrives, is dark and twisted, and the score is so superb it should be credited as a character. Anton Yelchin, who plays their underworld crony Tim, died in a freak accident nearly two years before this film's release. **92m/C; DVD, Blu-Ray.** Olivia Cooke; Anya Taylor-Joy; Anton Yelchin; Paul Sparks; Kaili Vernoff; ***D:*** Cory Finley; ***W:*** Cory Finley; ***C:*** Lyle Vincent; ***M:*** Erika Friedlander.

Thoroughbreds Don't Cry 🦴🦴 ½ **1937** Rooney plays a jockey who throws a race so his no-good father can win enough money to pay for his supposed medical problems. The owner of the horse then drops dead from a heart attack. Rooney feels guilty, so he asks his father to loan the owner's grandson $1,000 to run in another race. His father says no, so Rooney steals the money from him, and when the father finds out he tells the track officials that Rooney threw the race. Garland is Rooney's best friend and moral support, and she sings a few songs too! A fairly good horse racing story. **80m/B; VHS, DVD.** Judy Garland; Mickey Rooney; Sophie Tucker; Sir C. Aubrey Smith; Ronald Sinclair; Forrester Harvey; ***D:*** Alfred E. Green.

Thoroughly Modern Millie 🦴🦴 ½ **1967 (G)** Andrews is a young woman who comes to New York in the early 1920s where she meets another newcomer, the innocent Moore. Andrews decides to upgrade her image to that of a "modern" woman, a flapper, and sets out to realize her ambition, to become a stenographer and marry the boss. Meanwhile, Moore has become an object of interest to Lillie, who just happens to run a white-slavery ring. Lots of frantic moments and big production numbers in this campy film. Channing and Lillie are exceptional fun. **138m/C; VHS, DVD.** Julie Andrews; Carol Channing; Mary Tyler Moore; John Gavin; Beatrice Lillie; James Fox; Noriyuki "Pat" Morita; ***D:*** George Roy Hill; ***W:*** Richard Morris; ***C:*** Russell Metty; ***M:*** Elmer Bernstein. Oscars '67: Orig. Score; Golden Globes '68: Support. Actress (Channing).

Those Calloways 🦴🦴 ½ **1965 (PG)** A small town family attempts to establish a sanctuary for the flocks of wild geese who fly over the woods of Swiftwater, Maine. Fine Disney family fare, with good cast. Based on Paul Annixter's novel "Swiftwater." **131m/C; VHS, DVD.** Brian Keith; Vera Miles; Brandon de Wilde; Walter Brennan; Ed Wynn; John Qualen; Linda Evans; ***D:*** Norman Tokar; ***W:*** Louis Pelletier; ***C:*** Edward Colman; ***M:*** Max Steiner.

Those Daring Young Men in Their Jaunty Jalopies 🦴🦴 *Monte Carlo or Bust; Quei Temerari Sulle Loro Pazze, Scatenate, Scalcinate Carriole* **1969 (G)** Daring young men in noisy slow cars trek 1500 miles across country in the 1920s and call it a race. **125m/C; VHS, DVD, Blu-Ray.** *GB* Tony Curtis; Susan Hampshire; Terry-Thomas; Eric Sykes; Gert Frobe; Peter Cook; Dudley Moore; Jack Hawkins; ***D:*** Ken Annakin; ***W:*** Ken Annakin; Jack Davies; ***C:*** Gabor Pogany; ***M:*** Ronald Goodwin.

Those Fantastic Flying Fools 🦴🦴 ½ *Blast-Off; Jules Verne's Rocket to the Moon* **1967** A mad race to be the first on the moon brings hilarious results. Loosely based on a Jules Verne story. **95m/C; VHS, DVD, Blu-Ray.** *GB* Burl Ives; Troy Donahue; Gert Frobe; Terry-Thomas; Hermione Gingold; Daliah Lavi; Lionel Jeffries; ***D:*** Don Sharp.

Those Glamour Girls 🦴🦴 ½ **1939** Ivy League college boy Philip (Ayres) drunkenly invites dancehall beauty Jane (Turner) up to school for a weekend party. She arrives but he's forgotten the invite and tells Jane the debutantes and snobs will make her stay a misery, but Jane knows how to handle a bunch of college kids. **78m/B; DVD.** Lew Ayres; Lana Turner; Jane Bryan; Anita Louise; Marsha Hunt; Mary Beth Hughes; Ann Rutherford; Thomas Brown; Richard Carlson; ***D:*** S. Sylvan Simon; ***W:*** Marion Parsonnet; ***C:*** Alfred Gilks; ***M:*** David Snell; Edward Ward.

Those Glory, Glory Days 🦴 ½ **1983** An English woman, secure in her position as an outstanding sports journalist, reminisces about the days when she and her friends idolized the boys on the soccer team. Nothing extraordinary, but nicely made. **92m/C; VHS, DVD.** *GB* Zoe Nathenson; Liz Campion; Cathy Murphy; ***D:*** Philip Saville; ***M:*** Trevor Jones.

Those Lips, Those Eyes 🦴🦴 ½ **1980 (R)** A pre-med student takes a job as a prop boy in a summer stock company and winds up falling in love with the company's lead dancer. Sub-plot about aging actor is more interesting, better played by Langella. O'Connor is appropriately lovely. Nicely made, charming sleeper of a film. **106m/C; VHS, DVD.** Frank Langella; Tom Hulce; Glynnis O'Connor; Jerry Stiller; Kevin McCarthy; ***D:*** Michael Pressman.

Those Magnificent Men in Their Flying Machines 🦴🦴🦴 **1965** In 1910, a wealthy British newspaper publisher is persuaded to sponsor an air race from London to Paris. Contestants come from all over the world and shenanigans, hijinks, double-crosses, and romance are found along the route. Skelton has fun in prologue, while Terry-Thomas is great as the villain. Fun from start to finish. **138m/C; VHS, DVD, Blu-Ray.** *GB* Stuart Whitman; Sarah Miles; Robert Morley; Alberto Sordi; James Fox; Gert Frobe; Jean-Pierre Cassel; Flora Robson; Sam Wanamaker; Terry-Thomas; Irina Demick; Benny Hill; Gordon Jackson; Millicent Martin; Red Skelton; ***D:*** Ken Annakin; ***W:*** Ken Annakin; Jack Davies.

Those People Next Door 🦴 ½ **1952** Class-conscious family drama, based on the play by Zelda Davees, remains static and stagebound. Working-class Anne Twigg (Cufts) falls in love with WWII RAF officer Victor Stevens (Forbes-Robertson) to the dismay of both sets of parents. However, when Victor goes missing in action after being shot down, it brings everyone together. **77m/B; DVD.** *GB* Patricia Cufts; Peter Forbes-Robertson; Jack Warner; Marjorie Rhodes; Garry Marsh; Anthony Newley; Gladys Henson; Charles Victor; ***D:*** Anthony Newley; John Harlow; ***W:*** John Harlow; ***C:*** Roy Fogwell.

Those We Love 🦴🦴 **1932** Writer Fred (MacKenna) marries fan May (Astor) and they live happily with their son Ricky (Conlon) until unhappily married neighbor Valerie (Tashman) tries to tempt Fred to stray. May has her suspicions and so does Ricky. **72m/B; DVD.** Kenneth MacKenna; Mary Astor; Tommy Conlon; Lilyan Tashman; Hale Hamilton; ***D:*** Robert Florey; ***W:*** F. Hugh Herbert; ***C:*** Arthur Edeson.

Those Who Love Me Can Take the Train 🦴🦴 *Ceux Qui M'Aiment Predront le Train* **1998** Bisexual artist Jean-Baptiste Emmerich (Trintignant) has died in Paris but wished to be buried in his hometown of Limoges—a four-hour train trip for his motley group of mourners, which include friends, relatives, and former lovers of both sexes. Things don't calm down at the cemetery where yet more relatives await, including the artist's estranged twin brother. Rather than bonding in grief, the trip and funeral succeed in bringing out old hurts and rivalries and causing the shakeup of more than one relationship. French with subtitles. **122m/C; VHS, DVD.** *FR* Jean-Louis Trintignant; Pascal Greggory; Charles Berling; Bruno Todeschini; Valeria Bruni-Tedeschi; Vincent Perez; Dominique Blanc; Sylvain Jacques; Marie Daems; ***D:*** Patrice Chereau; ***W:*** Patrice Chereau; Daniele Thompson; Pierre Trividic; ***C:*** Eric Gautier. Cesar '99: Cinematog., Director (Chereau), Support. Actress (Blanc).

Thou Shalt Not Kill. . .Except 🦴 ½ *Stryker's War* **1987** A Vietnam vet seeks revenge on the violent cult who kidnapped his girlfriend. **84m/C; VHS, DVD, Blu-Ray.** Brian Schulz; Robert Rickman; John Manfredi; Tim Quill; Cheryl Hansen; Sam Raimi; Perry Mallette; Theodore (Ted) Raimi; Glenn Barr; Scott Spiegel; Bruce Campbell; Paul Grabke; ***D:*** Josh Becker; ***W:*** Scott Spiegel; Josh Becker; ***C:*** Josh Becker; ***M:*** Joseph LoDuca.

Though None Go With Me 🦴🦴 **2006** While Elizabeth (Grabow) is growing up during the 1950s, she devotes herself to a life of service to God. But over the years, the many hardships that follow have her questioning her faith even when she's courted by both Ben (Rowe) and Will (Narona). Ladd plays the older Elizabeth who recounts her story to her granddaughter. Based on the inspirational novel by Jerry B. Jenkins. **100m/C; DVD.** Cheryl Ladd; Brad Rowe; Denise Grayson; Christopher Allport; Amy Grabow; David Norona; ***D:*** Armand Mastroianni; ***W:*** Pamela Wallace; ***C:*** Amit Bhattacharya; ***M:*** Nathan Furst. **CABLE**

A Thousand Acres 🦴🦴 **1997 (R)** Based on Jane Smiley's Pulitzer Prize-winning novel, it's "King Lear" set on an Iowa farm. Sisters (Pfeiffer, Lange, and Leigh) discover that their father has decided to divide the family's thousand-acre farm amongst the three of them. Then stranger Firth comes to town and divides Pfeiffer and Lange even further by showing an interest in both of them. Melodramatic and contrived, with every hot-button women's issue imaginable thrown into the mix. Director Moorhouse purportedly considered removing her name from the picture. **105m/C; VHS, DVD, Blu-Ray.** Jessica Lange; Michelle Pfeiffer; Jennifer Jason Leigh; Colin Firth; Jason Robards, Jr.; Keith Carradine; Pat Hingle; Kevin Anderson; John Carroll Lynch; Anne Pitoniak; Vyto Ruginis; Michelle Williams; Elisabeth Moss; ***D:*** Jocelyn Moorhouse; ***W:*** Laura Jones; ***C:*** Tak Fujimoto; ***M:*** Richard Hartley.

A Thousand Clowns 🦴🦴🦴 **1965** A nonconformist has resigned from his job as chief writer for an obnoxious kiddie show in order to enjoy life. But his independence comes under fire when he becomes guardian for his young nephew and social workers take a dim view of his lifestyle. Balsam won an Oscar for his role as Robard's agent brother. Adapted from Herb Gardner's Broadway comedy. **118m/B; VHS, DVD, Blu-Ray.** Jason Robards, Jr.; Barry J. Gordon; William Daniels; Barbara Harris; Gene Saks; Martin Balsam; ***D:*** Fred Coe; ***W:*** Herb Gardner; ***C:*** Arthur Ornitz. Oscars '65: Support. Actor (Balsam).

A Thousand Cuts 🦴 ½ **2012** Lance (Michael A. Newcomer) is a successful horror film director who has the misfortune to meet a man whose daughter was murdered in a manner highly similar to a scene in one of Lance's films. **85m/C; DVD, Blu-Ray.** Michael O'Keefe; Olesya Rulin; Michael A. Newcomer; James Van Patten; David Naughton; ***D:*** Charles Evered; ***W:*** Charles Evered; Eric Barr; Marty James; ***C:*** Shawn Dufraine; ***M:*** William Seegers; Kevin Saunders Hayes. **VIDEO**

The Thousand Eyes of Dr. Mabuse 🦴🦴 ½ *The Secret of Dr. Mabuse; The Diabolical Dr. Mabuse; The Shadow Versus the Thousand Eyes of Dr. Mabuse; Die Tausend Augen des Dr. Mabuse* **1960** Lang's last film is a return to his pre-war German character, the evil Dr. Mabuse. A series of strange murders occur in a Berlin hotel and police believe the killer thinks he's a reincarnation of the doctor. Disorienting chiller. German with subtitles. **103m/B; VHS, DVD.** *GE* Dawn Addams; Peter Van Eyck; Gert Frobe; Wolfgang Preiss; ***D:*** Fritz Lang; ***W:*** Fritz Lang; Jan Fethke; Heinz Oskar Wuttig; ***C:*** Karl Lob; ***M:*** Gerhard Becker; Bert Grund.

A Thousand Kisses Deep 🦴 ½ **2011** Disjointed and hackneyed drama about a life-changing do-over. Mia witnesses the suicide of an elderly woman and finds the woman clutching a photo of Mia's former lover, Ludwig. When caretaker Max lets Mia into the woman's flat, she realizes the dead woman is herself after a lifetime of bad choices. The building elevator (and Max) allow Mia to travel back in time to her troubled childhood and equally troubled romantic relationship and make different choices. It's all claptrap with some truly awful dialogue and Ludwig is too unlikeable and abusive unless Mia's a masochist. **84m/C; DVD.** *UK US* Jodie Whittaker; Dougray Scott; David Warner; Emilia Fox; Jonathan Slinger; Allan Corduner; ***D:*** Dana Lustig; ***W:*** Alex Kustanovich; ***C:*** George Richmond; ***M:*** Sandy McLelland.

A Thousand Words WOOF! **2012 (PG-13)** One of the most critically-reviled comedies of all time, this disaster sat on the shelf since 2008 before landing with a thud in theaters. Murphy plays a fast-talking literary agent who finds his fate tied to a magical Bodhi tree. For every word he speaks, a leaf falls. When the leaves are gone, he will die. The potential for soul-searching drama is completely destroyed by lame jokes, awkward physical comedy, and manipulative melodrama. Murphy has been a critical target in the past for poor career decisions, but this one left even his defenders speechless. **91m/C; DVD, Blu-Ray.** Eddie Murphy; Kerry Washington; Emanuel Ragsdale; Clark Duke; Allison Janney; Clifford Curtis; Ruby Dee; ***D:*** Brian Robbins; ***W:*** Steve Koren; ***C:*** Clark Mathis; ***M:*** John Debney.

A Thousand Years of Good Prayers 🦴🦴 **2007** After his wife dies, Mr. Shi decides to travel to America and visit his estranged daughter Yilan in Spokane. However, Yilan barely acknowledges his presence as she continues to go on with her usual pursuits. Despite cultural shock and his limited English, Mr. Shi walks around the city, striking up conversations with strangers while struggling at home to reconnect with Yilan. English and Chinese with subtitles. **83m/C; DVD.** Henry O; Feihong Yu; Vida Ghahremani; Pavel Lychnikoff; ***D:*** Wayne Wang; ***W:*** Yiyun Lee; ***C:*** Patrick Lindenmaier; ***M:*** Lesley Barber.

Thousands Cheer 🦴🦴 1/2 **1943** A flag-waving wartime musical about a tap-dancing Army private who falls in love with the colonel's daughter, culminating with an all-star (MGM) USO show. Songs include "Honeysuckle Rose," sung by Horne, and "The Joint Is Really Jumping Down at Carnegie Hall," sung by Garland. **126m/C; VHS, DVD.** Gene Kelly; Kathryn Grayson; Judy Garland; Mickey Rooney; Mary Astor; John Boles; Lucille Ball; Eleanor Powell; Virginia O'Brien; Margaret O'Brien; Red Skelton; Lionel Barrymore; June Allyson; Frank Morgan; Kay Kyser; Bob Crosby; Lena Horne; Donna Reed; ***D:*** George Sidney; ***W:*** Paul Jarrico; ***C:*** George J. Folsey.

Thrashin' 🦴 **1986 (PG-13)** A new-to-L.A. teen must prove himself to a tough gang on skateboards by skateboarding a certain treacherous race. For skateboarding fans only. **93m/C; VHS, DVD, Blu-Ray.** Josh Brolin; Pamela Gidley; Robert Rusler; Chuck McCann; ***D:*** David Winters; ***W:*** Paul Bown; ***M:*** Barry Goldberg.

Threat of Exposure 🦴 1/2 **2002 (R)** Hypnotherapist Dr. Daryl Sheleigh (Young) is having a problem with her patients—they keep disappearing. Cop Badger Welldon (Schaub) goes undercover as a patient to investigate since one of the missing is his younger brother. But disturbing secrets emerge from Badger's past, including an abusive childhood and his own violent nature, and evidence begins to point to Daryl as the prime suspect. It's all too easy to see where this wannabe thriller is headed. **90m/C; DVD.** Sean Young; William Devane; Will Schaub; D. Paul Thomas; Sara Crawford; ***D:*** Tom Whitus; ***W:*** Frederick Bailey; Jeno Hodl; ***C:*** Fred Paddock; ***M:*** Jamie Howarth; Kinny Landrum. **VIDEO**

Thr3e 🦴 1/2 **2007 (PG-13)** Plodding Christian psycho-thriller features Seattle seminary student Kevin Parsons (Blucas) being targeted by a serial bomber known as the Riddle Killer. He calls his victims, accuses them of getting away with a crime, and then threatens to set off a bomb unless they confess. Except RK doesn't even play by his own rules. Adapted from the book by Ted Dekker. **101m/C; DVD.** Marc Blucas; Justine Waddell; Max Ryan; Priscilla Barnes; Laura Jordan; Tom Bower; Bill Moseley; Jeff Hollis; Philip Dunbar; ***D:*** Robby Henson; ***W:*** Alan B. McElroy; ***C:*** Sebastian Milaszewski; ***M:*** David Bergeaud.

3 🦴 1/2 **2010** A would-be romance begins between a successful 40-something Berlin couple, whose relationship is in a rut, and an enigmatic younger man. Hanna and Simon separately keep meeting Adam, who becomes the lover of them both--though none are at first aware of this sexual sharing. Tykwer's film doesn't work as well as expected with too many coincidences and an unsatisfying ending. German with subtitles. **119m/C; DVD.** *GE* Sophie Rois; Sebastian Schipper; David Striesow; ***D:*** Tom Tykwer; ***W:*** Tom Tykwer; ***C:*** Frank Griebe; ***M:*** Johnny Klimek; Reinhold Heil.

3 A.M. 🦴🦴🦴 **2001** Slice-of-life ensemble drama traces the doings of NYC cabbies over 36 hours. The struggling cab company, run by the owner's daughter Box (Choudhury), is on the verge of bankruptcy and her drivers are spooked by a serial killer targeting cabbies. Meawhile, Hershey (Glover) is stretching the patience of girlfriend George (Grier); Latina Salgado (Rodriguez) is tired of being sexually harassed; Bosian refugee Rasha (Tifunovic) is on the brink of being fired; and ambitious Jose (Cannavale) finds a briefcase of stolen money. **92m/C; VHS, DVD.** Danny Glover; Pam Grier; Michelle Rodriguez; Sarita Choudhury; Sergej Trifunovic; Bobby Cannavale; Isaach de Bankole; Mike Starr; Paul Calderon; ***D:*** Lee Davis; ***W:*** Lee Davis; ***C:*** Enrique Chediak; ***M:*** Branford Marsalis. **CABLE**

Three Amigos 🦴🦴 **1986 (PG)** Three out-of-work silent screen stars are asked to defend a Mexican town from bandits; they think it's a public appearance stint. Spoof of Three Stooges and Mexican bandito movies that at times falls short, given the enormous amount of comedic talent involved. Generally enjoyable with some very funny scenes. Co-written by former "Saturday Night Live" producer Michaels. Short's first major film appearance. **105m/C; VHS, DVD.** Chevy Chase; Steve Martin; Martin Short; Joe Mantegna; Patrice Martinez; Jon Lovitz; Phil Hartman; Randy Newman; Alfonso Arau; ***D:*** John Landis; ***W:*** Steve Martin; Randy Newman; Lorne Michaels; ***C:*** Ronald W. Browne; ***M:*** Elmer Bernstein.

Three and Out 🦴 1/2 *A Deal Is a Deal* **2008 (R)** Underwhelming British comedy with an unpleasant premise. Unhappy Paul Callow is a train driver for the London Underground. Two people die on the tracks in front of his train over a two-week period and Paul learns that a third fatal accident will actually result in his forced retirement with a 10-year salary severance package. So Paul tries to find someone suicidal enough to take the leap. **108m/C; DVD.** *GB* Mackenzie Crook; Colm Meaney; Imelda Staunton; Gemma Arterton; Antony Sher; ***D:*** Jonathan Gershfield; ***W:*** Steve Lewis; Tony Owen; ***C:*** Richard Greatrex; ***M:*** Trevor Jones.

Three Avengers 🦴 *Gli Invincibili Tre* **1964** Typical Italian sword-and-sandals flick with Ciani (AKA Alan Steel) and his buddies fighting against the usual tyrants. Italian with subtitles. **97m/C; DVD.** *IT* Sergio Ciani; Mimmo Palmara; Carlo Tamberlani; Gianni Rizzo; Lisa Gastoni; Rosalba Neri; ***D:*** Gianfranco Parolini; ***W:*** Gianfranco Parolini; ***C:*** Francesco Izzarelli; ***M:*** Angelo Francesco Lavagnino.

3 Backyards 🦴 1/2 **2010 (R)** Three stories about emotional constipation and secrets set in the Long Island 'burbs. John and his wife are in deep marital trouble and when his business trip is cancelled, he hides out in a nearby airport hotel room rather than go home. Prying homemaker Peggy makes herself available to her new neighbor, a famous actress suffering from depression. But Peggy doesn't take it well when the woman won't confide in her. Young Christina misses her school bus and decides to take a shortcut through the woods where she witnesses a neighbor's kinky sex games. **88m/C; DVD.** Elias Koteas; Kathryn Erbe; Edie Falco; Embeth Davidtz; Rachel Resheff; Wesley Broulik; Danai Gurira; ***D:*** Eric Mendelsohn; ***W:*** Eric Mendelsohn; ***C:*** Kasper Tuxen; ***M:*** Michael Nicholas.

Three Bad Men 🦴 **2005 (PG-13)** Dull, incompetent western. Three bank robbers are heading for the Colorado border when they come across a dying man whose wife has been kidnapped. He begs them to rescue his missus and the outlaws must decide whether to risk their own lives or keep on riding. **118m/C; DVD.** Mike Moroff; George Kennedy; Peter Brown; John Dixon; Chris Gann; ***D:*** Jeff Hathcock; ***W:*** Jeff Hathcock; ***M:*** Tom Crosby.

Three Bad Sisters 🦴 **1956** After their wealthy father dies, vicious Valerie (Hughes) wants the inheritance for herself. She disfigures nympho sister Vicki (English), who kills herself, and plots with Jim (Bromfield) to drive virtuous sibling Lorna (Shane) crazy. Instead, Jim falls for and marries Lorna. Valerie tells her sis that she and Jim are hitting the sheets. The actresses try but there's not much heat generated by the dull script and direction although some of it goes over-the-top trashy. **73m/B; DVD.** Kathleen Hughes; Sara Shane; Marla English; John Bromfield; Jess Barker; Madge Kennedy; ***D:*** Gilbert Kay; ***W:*** Gerald Drayson Adams; ***C:*** Lester Shorr; ***M:*** Paul Dunlap.

Three Billboards Outside Ebbing, Missouri 🦴🦴🦴 1/2 **2017 (R)** Sometimes, law enforcers needs a kick in the rump to do their job, and McDormand may be just the woman to do it. In this dark comedy, a mother plasters billboards with taunts against the local police, who've left her daughter's rape and murder go unanswered. Her quick wit, willingness to get physical, and acid tongue covers her anguish, which McDormand expertly gives us peeks of between barbs and blows. Sheriff Willoughby (Harrelson) and Officer Dixon (Rockwell) are worthy adversaries, the latter stealing scenes as a stupid, racist, bullying mama's boy. **115m/C; DVD, Blu-Ray.** Frances McDormand; Woody Harrelson; Sam Rockwell; Abbie Cornish; Lucas Hedges; ***D:*** Martin McDonagh; ***W:*** Martin McDonagh; ***C:*** Ben Davis; ***M:*** Carter Burwell. Oscars '17: Actor--Supporting (Rockwell), Actress (McDormand); British Acad. '17: Actor--Supporting (Rockwell), Actress (McDormand), Film, Orig. Screenplay; Golden Globes '18: Actor--Supporting (Rockwell), Actress--Drama (McDormand), Film--Drama, Screenplay; Ind. Spirit '18: Actor--Supporting (Rockwell), Actress (McDormand); Screen Actors Guild '17: Actor--Supporting (Rockwell), Actress (McDormand), Cast.

Three Blind Mice 🦴🦴 1/2 **1938** Charming rom com finds the three Charters sisters taking their small inheritance and moving from Kansas to California to find rich husbands. Pamela (Young) poses as a socialite and falls for handsome Van Dam Smith (McCrea), but it turns out she's not the only one playing a part. Meanwhile, sisters Moira (Weaver) and Elizabeth (Moore) also meet a couple of swell fellas who aren't quite what they seem. Remade as "Moon Over Miami" (1941) and "Three Little Girls In Blue" (1946). **75m/B; DVD.** Loretta Young; Joel McCrea; Marjorie Weaver; David Niven; Pauline Moore; Stuart Erwin; Binnie Barnes; Jane Darwell; ***D:*** William A. Seiter; ***W:*** Brown Holmes; Lynn Starling; ***C:*** Ernest Palmer.

Three Blind Mice 🦴 1/2 **2002 (R)** Hacker Thomas Cross (Furlong) is obsessed with Internet webcam sites. One night, he witnesses a grisly murder at his favorite website, but when he contacts the police, Thomas realizes he doesn't know the victim's real name or address. He's soon involved in the investigation by cop Claire (Fox). Mild and implausible thriller wannabe. **92m/C; VHS, DVD.** *FR GB* Edward Furlong; Emilia Fox; Chiwetel Ejiofor; Ben Miles; Elsa Zylberstein; James Laurenson; ***D:*** Mathias Ledoux; ***W:*** Mikael Ollivier; ***C:*** Stephane Le Parc; ***M:*** Eric Neveux.

Three Blondes in His Life 🦴🦴 **1961** Looks like a pulp detective novel brought to big-screen life. Insurance investigator Duke Wallace (Mahoney) is looking into the disappearance of a fellow agent who's implicated in a jewel theft. The agent (who's been murdered) had affairs with three married blondes whom Wallace now has to question. It's a tough job. **81m/B; DVD.** Jock Mahoney; Greta Thyssen; Anthony Dexter; Jesse White; Elaine Edwards; Valerie Porter; ***D:*** Leon Chooluck; ***W:*** George Moskov; ***C:*** Ernest Haller.

Three Brave Men 🦴 1/2 **1957** Heavy-handed red scare drama. Longtime civilian Naval employee Bernie Goldsmith (Borgnine) is fired as a security risk after some youthful, minor Communist affiliations are discovered. Ostracized, Bernie hires lawyer Joe DiMarco (Milland) to clear his name. Based on a true story. **88m/B; DVD.** Ernest Borgnine; Ray Milland; Dean Jagger; Frank Lovejoy; Nina Foch; Virginia Christine; ***D:*** Philip Dunne; ***W:*** Philip Dunne; ***C:*** Charles G. Clarke.

Three Broadway Girls 🦴🦴🦴 *The Greeks Had a Word for Them* **1932** Three gold-diggers go husband-hunting. Well-paced, very funny telling of this old story. Remade many times, including "How to Marry a Millionaire," "Three Blind Mice," "Moon Over Miami," and "Three Little Girls in Blue." **78m/B; VHS, DVD.** Joan Blondell; Ina Claire; Madge Evans; David Manners; Lowell Sherman; ***D:*** Lowell Sherman.

Three Brothers 🦴🦴🦴 *Tre Fratelli* **1980 (PG)** An acclaimed Italian film by veteran Rosi about three brothers summoned to their small Italian village by a telegram saying their mother is dead. Sensitive and compassionate. In Italian with English subtitles. Adapted from Platonov's story "The Third Son." **113m/C; VHS, DVD, Blu-Ray.** *IT* Philippe Noiret; Charles Vanel; Michele Placido; Vittorio Mezzogiorno; Andrea Ferreol; Simonetta Stefanelli; ***D:*** Francesco Rosi; ***W:*** Francesco Rosi; ***C:*** Pasqualino De Santis; ***M:*** Piero Piccioni.

The Three Burials of Melquiades Estrada 🦴🦴🦴🦴 **2005 (R)** Powerful meditation on the brutality of the U.S.-Mexico border region. Rancher Pete Perkins (Jones) forces Mike Norton (Pepper) to carry the body of Pete's friend Melquiades Estrada (Cedillo) from their dusty Texas border town to the dead man's home in Mexico for burial in his family cemetery. But the bigger story is how their journey acts as a metaphor for the all-too human boundaries of wealth, sex, race, and religion. Norton, a racist patrol officer (and Estrada's murderer) is transformed from a thug with a badge into a man who must seek redemption after his eyes are opened to the weight of his actions. Amazing performances are buoyed by Arriaga's knowing script. **120m/C; DVD, Blu-Ray.** Tommy Lee Jones; Barry Pepper; Dwight Yoakam; January Jones; Melissa Leo; Levon Helm; Vanessa Bauche; Julio Cesar Cedillo; Mel Rodriguez; Cecilia Suarez; Ignacio Guadalupe; ***D:*** Tommy Lee Jones; ***W:*** Guillermo Arriaga; ***C:*** Chris Menges; ***M:*** Marco Beltrami.

The Three Caballeros 🦴🦴 1/2 **1945 (G)** Donald Duck stars in this journey through Latin America. Full of music, variety, and live-action/animation segments. Stories include "Pablo the Penguin," "Little Gauchito," and adventures with Joe Carioca, who was first introduced in Disney's "Saludos Amigos." Today this film stands as one of the very best pieces of animation ever created. Great family fare. **71m/C; VHS, DVD, Blu-Ray.** ***V:*** Sterling Holloway; Aurora Miranda; ***D:*** Norman Ferguson.

Three Came Home 🦴🦴🦴 **1950** Colbert is an American married to a British administrator in the Far East during WWII. Conquering Japanese throw the whole family into a brutal POW concentration camp, and their confinement is recounted in harrowing and unsparing detail. Superior drama, also laudable for a fairly even-handed portrayal of the enemy captors. Based on an autobiographical book by Agnes Newton-Keith. **106m/B; VHS, DVD.** Claudette Colbert; Patric Knowles; Sessue Hayakawa; Florence Desmond; Sylvia Andrew; Mark Keuning; Phyllis Morris; Howard Chuman; ***D:*** Jean Negulesco; ***W:*** Nunnally Johnson; ***C:*** William H. Daniels; Milton Krasner; ***M:*** Hugo Friedhofer.

Three Came to Kill 🦴 1/2 **1961** Formulaic hostage thriller. Pro killer Marty Brill and his crew take the family of flight controller Hal Parker hostage so he'll cooperate in the assassination of a visiting Middle Eastern dignitary. Brill needs Parker to tell him which plane the man is flying out on from the L.A. airport. **71m/B; DVD.** Cameron Mitchell; John Lupton; Lyn Thomas; Steve Brodie; Logan Field; ***D:*** Edward L. Cahn; ***W:*** Robert E. Kent; ***C:*** Maury Gertsman; ***M:*** Paul Sawtell; Bert Shefter.

Three Can Play That Game 🦴 1/2 **2007 (R)** In this sequel to "Two Can Play That Game," relationship expert Shante (Fox) moves to Atlanta and continues to offer advice on how to bring your man to heel. Byron's (George) the winner of a TV game show offering a job opportunity with manager Carla (Smith), who promptly makes a play for the looker. Of course this is witnessed by Byron's girlfriend Tiffany (Lewis), who won't believe that nothing happened. She turns to Shante for some questionable help while Byron's best friend Gizzard (Rock) offers his own opinions. The women are manipulative shrews, which isn't very appealing (though they are attractive). **91m/C; DVD.** Vivica A. Fox; Jason Winston George; Jazsmin Lewis; Tony Rock; Kellita Smith; Terri J. Vaughn; Melyssa Ford; Rashin Ali; *D:* Mody Mod; *W:* Mark Brown; *C:* Tommy Maddox-Upshaw; *M:* Kenyatta Beasley.

Three Coins in the Fountain 🦴🦴 1/2 **1954** Three women throw money into fountain and get romantically involved with Italian men. Outstanding CinemaScope photography captures beauty of Italian setting. Sammy Cahn theme song sung by Frank Sinatra. **102m/C; VHS, DVD, Blu-Ray.** Clifton Webb; Dorothy McGuire; Jean Peters; Louis Jourdan; Maggie McNamara; Rossano Brazzi; *D:* Jean Negulesco; *C:* Milton Krasner. Oscars '54: Color Cinematog., Song ("Three Coins in the Fountain").

Three Comrades 🦴🦴🦴 **1938** Taylor, Tone, and Young are three friends, reunited in bleak, post-WWI Germany, who meet and befriend Sullavan, a tubercular beauty. Reluctant to marry because of her health, she's finally persuaded to wed Taylor, amidst the country's increasing unrest. Tragedy strikes Sullavan and the politicized Young and the two remaining comrades face an uncertain future. Bleak but forceful and passionate drama. Sullavan's performance is superb. Based on the novel by Erich Maria Remarque. Fitzgerald's script was heavily rewritten because both Sullavan and producer Mankiewicz found his approach too literary with unspeakable dialogue. **99m/B; VHS, DVD.** Robert Taylor; Margaret Sullavan; Robert Young; Franchot Tone; Lionel Atwill; Guy Kibbee; Henry Hull; George Zucco; Monty Woolley; Charley Grapewin; Spencer Charters; Sarah Padden; *D:* Frank Borzage; *W:* F. Scott Fitzgerald; Edward Paramore; *C:* Joseph Ruttenberg; *M:* Franz Waxman. N.Y. Film Critics '38: Actress (Sullavan).

Three-Cornered Moon 🦴🦴 1/2 **1933** The stock market crash affects the Rimplegar family when ditzy mom Nellie (Boland) loses all their money on worthless mining stock (the movie title refers to the stock company's name). Unable to sell their Brooklyn house, the adult Rimplegar siblings are forced to look for work with daughter Elizabeth (Colbert) eventually realizing that she should pay attention to family friend, and doctor, Alan Stevens (Arlen). **77m/B; DVD.** Claudette Colbert; Richard Arlen; Mary Boland; Wallace Ford; Tom Brown; William "Billy" Bakewell; Hardie Albright; Joan Marsh; Lyda Roberti; *D:* Elliott Nugent; *W:* Ray Harris; S.K. Lauren; *C:* Leon Shamroy.

Three Daring Daughters 🦴🦴 1/2 **1948** When her husband leaves her and she almost misses her daughter's graduation due to a fainting spell, MacDonald takes hiatus on a cruise ship where she meets and marries pianist Iturbi. Unknowing, the three daughters at home conspire to get Dad back in the family. Enraged when Mom returns with new-found hubby, the threesome do all in their power to make the newlyweds as miserable as possible. Happily ended musical-comedy is chock full of memorable tunes. Based on the play "The Bees and the Flowers" by Kohner and Albert Manning. **115m/C; DVD.** Jeanette MacDonald; Jose Iturbi; Jane Powell; Edward Arnold; Harry Davenport; Moyna MacGill; Elinor Donahue; Ann E. Todd; *D:* Fred M. Wilcox; *W:* Sonya Levien; John Meehan; Albert Mannheimer; Frederick Kohner.

3 Days Gone 🦴 1/2 **2008** After somehow surviving being buried alive for three days, a man wakes up to find out his friend is dead, and the local cops and mob both want him put back in the ground. Fortunately his complete and total amnesia will help him navigate this dangerous time. **92m/C; DVD.** Oliver Coltress; Charles Wesley; Chris Backus; Patrick J. Adams; Richard Tyson; Michelle Stafford; Sarah Bastian; *D:* Scott McCullough; *W:* Oliver Coltress; Charles Wesley; *C:* Grisha Alasadi; *M:* Markus Kmitta. **VIDEO**

Three Days of Rain 🦴 1/2 **2002** Based on six loosely-connected short stories by Chekov, and set in Cleveland under a brooding rain. Director Michael Meredith attempts to highlight the small ways in which people reveal both cruelty and kindness. A wife's indifference toward a homeless person's hunger triggers a man's reevaluation of his life. A taxi driver has just lost his son, but his passenger (Danner) cannot muster an ounce of sympathy. The other stories are equally troubling, with a boozing father who takes advantage of everyone including his son, and a supervisor plotting to eliminate a mentally challenged janitor. Unfortunately these stories are no different than what you can see most days by walking out your own front door. **94m/C; DVD.** Peter Falk; Don Meredith; Merle Kennedy; Erik Avari; Maggie Walker; Joy Bilow; Michael Santoro; Penny Allen; Heather Kafka; Bill Stockton; *D:* Michael Meredith; *C:* Cynthia Pusheck; *M:* Bob Belden.

Three Days of the Condor 🦴🦴🦴 **1975 (R)** CIA researcher Joe Turner (Redford) leaves the office to get some lunch and returns to find all his colleagues murdered. He calls for help but learns his own organization is responsible for the slaughter. So Joe goes on the run until he can expose the conspiracy. Good performance by Dunaway as photographer Kathy Hale, who is forced by Joe to help him but then becomes a willing accomplice. A post-Watergate tale of paranoia and suspense. Based on "Six Days of the Condor" by James Grady. **118m/C; VHS, DVD, Blu-Ray.** Robert Redford; Faye Dunaway; Cliff Robertson; Max von Sydow; John Houseman; *D:* Sydney Pollack; *W:* David Rayfiel; *C:* Owen Roizman; *M:* Dave Grusin.

3 Days to Kill 🦴🦴 **2014 (PG-13)** CIA agent Ethan Renner (Costner) has brain cancer and needs to complete one final assignment, hunting down the world's most ruthless terrorist, while trying to reconnect with his estranged teen daughter (Steinfeld). About four movies in one, director McG's flick doesn't really work as action movie or drama, but Costner brings an adequate world-weariness to the role that makes it more entertaining than it otherwise would be. **117m/C; DVD, Blu-Ray.** *US FR* Kevin Costner; Hailee Steinfeld; Amber Heard; Connie Nielsen; Tomas Lemarquis; Richard Sammel; Eriq Ebouaney; *D:* McG; *W:* Luc Besson; Adi Hasak; *C:* Thierry Arbogast; *M:* Guillaume Roussel.

Three Days to Vegas 🦴🦴 **2007 (PG-13)** Old pros having fun. Gus (Falk) is enjoying his Florida retirement, swapping stories with golf buddies Joe (Torn), Marvin (Cobbs), and Dominic (Segal). Gus's daughter Elizabeth (Young) announces she's rushing off to Vegas to marry her foreign friend Laurent (Diamantopoulos) because he has visa problems. Gus disapproves and hauls his friends and Elizabeth's ex-beau Billy (Burke) aboard a luxury tour bus for a cross-country jaunt to stop the nuptials. 'Cause flying would mean they couldn't get into silly situations along the way. **120m/C; DVD.** Peter Falk; Rip Torn; Bill Cobbs; George Segal; Billy Burke; Chris Diamantopoulos; Coolio; Mario Cantone; Taylor Negron; Nancy Young; *D:* Charlie Picerni; *W:* Charlie Picerni; *C:* Tom Priestley. **VIDEO**

Three Desperate Men 🦴🦴 **1950** Three brothers accused of murder become outlaws. Not innovative, but satisfactory tale of the Old West. **71m/B; VHS, DVD.** Preston Foster; Virginia Grey; Jim Davis; *D:* Sam Newfield.

Three . . . Extremes 🦴🦴 **2004 (R)** Twisted horror trilogy from Hong Kong, Korea, and Japan. Chan's truncated "Dumplings" (also a 90-minute feature) finds a vain former actress (Yeung), desperate to keep her looks and husband, partaking of the titular food prepared by Mei (Ling) with a secret ingredient and serious side effects. Park's "Cut" centers on the revenge taken on horror director Ryu (Lee) and his wife (Gang) by a resentful extra (Lim). Miike's "Box" has successful novelist Kyoko (Hasegawa) haunted by the death of her twin sister in childhood and forced to continually relive her part in the tragedy. Japanese, Cantonese, and Korean with subtitles. **126m/C; DVD.** Bai Ling; Tony Leung Ka-Fai; Pauline Lau; Meme Tian; Miraim Yeung Chin Wah; Sum-Yeung Wong; Wai-Man Wu; Chak-Man Ho; Miki Yeung; So-Fun Wong; *D:* Fruit Chan; Takashi Miike; Chan-wook Park; *W:* Chan-wook Park; Haruko Fukushima; Lilian Lee; Bun Saikou; *C:* Jeong-hun Jeong; Christopher Doyle; Koichi Kawakami; *M:* Kwong Wing Chan; Koji Endo.

Three Faces East 🦴🦴 **1930** Slinky agent Z-1 infiltrates the home of Sir Winston Chamberlain, the First Sea Lord of the British Admiralty. Is she secretly working with butler Valdar, an alleged Belgian WWI hero, in a scheme to discover Allied troop movements? Based on a 1918 play by Anthony Paul Kelly. **71m/B; DVD.** Constance Bennett; Erich von Stroheim; William Holden; Anthony Bushnell; William Courtenay; Crauford Kent; Charlotte Walker; *D:* Roy Del Ruth; *W:* Oliver H.P. Garrett; Arthur Caesar; *C:* Barney McGill.

The Three Faces of Eve 🦴🦴 1/2 **1957** Emotionally disturbed Eve (Woodward) seeks the help of psychiatrist Dr. Luther (Cobb), who eventually discovers she has three distinct personalities: a downtrodden housewife, a party girl, and a well-educated, well-balanced woman. So Luther decides to integrate all three into one Eve. Although Woodward gives a powerful performance, the film has dated badly, particularly the narration by Cooke, which gives the film a now-stilted air. Although the film is fact-based, the story was deemed too implausible for the public to believe at the time without the assurances of the narrator. **91m/B; VHS, DVD, Blu-Ray.** Joanne Woodward; David Wayne; Lee J. Cobb; Nancy Kulp; Edwin Jerome; Vince Edwards; *Nar:* Alistair Cooke; *D:* Nunnally Johnson; *W:* Nunnally Johnson; *C:* Stanley Cortez; *M:* Robert Emmett Dolan. Oscars '57: Actress (Woodward); Golden Globes '58: Actress--Drama (Woodward).

Three Faces West 🦴🦴 *The Refugee* **1940** A dust bowl community is helped by a Viennese doctor who left Europe to avoid Nazi capture. He's aided by the Duke in this odd combination of Western frontier saga and anti-Nazi propaganda. Works only part of the time. **79m/B; VHS, DVD, Blu-Ray.** John Wayne; Charles Coburn; Sigrid Gurie; Sonny Bupp; Russell Simpson; *D:* Bernard Vorhaus.

3:15: The Moment of Truth 🦴🦴 **1986 (R)** A vicious high school gang is confronted by an angry ex-member in this so-so teen delinquent film. **86m/C; VHS, Streaming.** Adam Baldwin; Deborah Foreman; Rene Auberjonois; Danny De La Paz; *D:* Larry Gross; *W:* Sam Bernard; *M:* Gary Chang.

Three for the Show 🦴🦴 1/2 **1955** Julie (Grable) is a song-and-dance queen whose husband, Marty (Lemmon), was presumed dead in WWII. After she marries his songwriting partner, Vernon (Champion), Marty naturally shows up. Because she loves both men, Julie decides to set-up a household threesome until she can make up her mind. Champion's real-life spouse and dance partner, Marge, plays Grable's best friend. Some good dance numbers don't make up for the weak script. Based on the W. Somerset Maugham play "Too Many Husbands" and filmed under that title in 1940. **93m/C; VHS, DVD.** Betty Grable; Jack Lemmon; Gower Champion; Marge Champion; Myron McCormick; Paul Harvey; *D:* H.C. Potter; *W:* Leonard Stern; Edward Hope; *C:* Arthur E. Arling; *M:* George Duning.

3 from Hell 🦴🦴 **2019 (R)** After being imprisoned for murder and given life sentences, a trio of family members plans their escape. Though Captain Spaulding (Haig) dies from health issues a few years into his sentence, Otis (Moseley) taps his cousin Winslow (Brake) to help. After the pair escape, they hold the wife of the prison warden hostage until the warden releases Baby (S. Zombie) and the trio can seek their own form of justice. The subversive horror film by metal star Rob Zombie is a sequel to his first two films and showcases his attention to detail, creative fearlessness, and outstanding casting of character actors. **111m/C; DVD.** Sheri Moon Zombie; Bill Moseley; Sid Haig; Jeffrey Daniel Phillips; Richard Brake; *D:* Rob Zombie; *W:* Rob Zombie; *C:* David Daniel; *M:* Zeuss.

Three Fugitives 🦴🦴 **1989 (PG-13)** An ex-con holdup man (Nolte) determined to go straight is taken hostage by a bungling first-time bank robber, who is only attempting the holdup in order to support his withdrawn young daughter. Nolte winds up on the lam with the would-be robber and his daughter. The comedy is fun, the sentimental moments too sweet and slow. Remake of French "Les Fugitifs." **96m/C; VHS, DVD.** Nick Nolte; Martin Short; James Earl Jones; Kenneth McMillan; Sarah Rowland Doroff; Alan Ruck; Bruce McGill; Sy Richardson; Larry Miller; Lee Garlington; John Aylward; Kathy Kinney; *D:* Francis Veber; *W:* Francis Veber; *C:* Haskell Wexler; *M:* David McHugh.

3 Generations 🦴🦴 *About Ray* **2017 (PG-13)** In this overstuffed and overwrought melodrama, Ray (Fanning) is a teenager transitioning from female to male, and dealing with all the complications and problems that entails, including the fact that his absent father (Donovan) has to approve the necessary hormone treatments. Ray's mom (Watts) and lesbian grandmother (Sarandon) want to be supportive but both have major reservations. What could have been a compelling, personal look at a hot-button topic gets lost in contrived scenarios, TV-movie clichés, and lack of focus. Originally titled "About Ray," the film was shelved since its debut at 2015 Toronto Film Festival. **92m/C; DVD, Blu-Ray.** Elle Fanning; Naomi Watts; Susan Sarandon; Tate Donovan; Linda Emond; *D:* Gaby Dellal; *W:* Gaby Dellal; Nikole Beckwith; *C:* David Johnson; *M:* West Dylan Thordson.

Three Godfathers 🦴🦴 **1936** Another version of the Peter B. Kyne novel (see also 1930's "Hell's Heroes") about three bank robbers, a newborn, a promise to its dying mother, a desert trek, and a Christmas miracle. There's more fleshing out of the outlaws' characters in this version and some subplots but it's still much grittier than the 1948 remake. Filmed on location in the Mojave Desert and at Red Rock Canyon. **82m/B; DVD.** Chester Morris; Walter Brennan; Lewis Stone; Irene Hervey; Robert "Bob" Livingston; Sidney Toler; Dorothy Tree; *D:* Richard Boleslawski; *W:* Edward Paramore; *C:* Joseph Ruttenberg.

Three Godfathers 🦴🦴🦴 **1948** A sweet and sentimental western has three half-hearted outlaws on the run, taking with them an infant they find in the desert. Dedicated to western star and Ford alumni Harry Carey Sr. (whose son is one of the outlaws in the film), who died of cancer the year before. Ford had first filmed the tale with Carey Sr. as "Marked Men" in 1919. **82m/C; VHS, DVD.** John Wayne; Pedro Armendariz, Sr.; Harry Carey, Jr.; Ward Bond; Mae Marsh; Jane Darwell; Ben Johnson; Mildred Natwick; Guy Kibbee; *D:* John Ford; *C:* Winton C. Hoch.

Three Guys Named Mike 🦴🦴 **1951** Wyman plays an overly enthusiastic airline stewardess who finds herself the object of affection from three guys named Mike, including an airline pilot, an advertising man, and a scientist. A cute comedy. **89m/B; VHS, DVD.** Jane Wyman; Van Johnson; Barry Sullivan; Howard Keel; Phyllis Kirk; Jeff Donnell; *D:* Charles Walters; *W:* Sidney Sheldon.

Three Hours to Kill 🦴🦴 1/2 **1954** Cowboy Jim Guthrie escaped lynch mob justice after he's wrongly accused of murdering his former fiancee Laurie's brother. Guthrie eventually returns to town to prove his innocence but the sheriff only gives him three hours to clear his name before he'll be arrested. **77m/C; DVD.** Dana Andrews; Donna Reed; Stephen Elliott; Dianne Foster; Richard Webb; Richard Coogan; *D:* Alfred Werker; *W:* Maxwell Shane; Roy Huggins; Richard Alan Simmons; *C:* Charles Lawton, Jr.; *M:* Paul Sawtell.

300 🦴🦴 **2007 (R)** Blood, brutality, and buff bodies with the stylized action all done against bluescreen. Adaptation of Frank Miller's graphic novel follows the historical Battle of Thermopylae in 480 B.C. Sparta's King Leonidas (Butler) refuses to bow to the rule of the Persians and takes 300 of his best warriors to battle bejeweled and multi-pierced Xerxes (Santoro) and his hordes. Meanwhile, back at Sparta, the unfortunately-named Queen Gorgo (Headey) is battling sniveling politicos to get her hubby some reinforcements. This time Internet fanboy enthusiasm translated into blockbuster boxoffice bucks. **116m/C; DVD, Blu-Ray, HD-DVD.** Gerard Butler; Lena Headey; Dominic West; David Wenham; Rodrigo Santoro; Andrew Tiernan; Tom Wisdom; Vincent Regan; Michael Fassbender; Stephen McHattie; *D:* Zack Snyder; *W:* Zack Snyder; Kurt Johnstad; Michael B. Gordon; *C:* Larry Fong; *M:* Tyler Bates.

300: Rise of an Empire 🦴🦴 **2013 (R)** A bloodthirsty spectacle that serves as a companion piece to 2007's "300." This time it's the small Athenian navy battling Persian king Xerxes' (Santoro) overwhelming forces, which are commanded by ruthless beauty, Artemisia (Green). She's more than a match for he-man Greek general Themistocles (Stapleton), even in their rough sex scene. Lots of hacked-off limbs, spurting blood, and wartime chaos (all in 3D), but director Murro keeps control of most of the slaughter-filled action. Adapted from Frank Miller's graphic novel "Xerxes." **102m/C; DVD, Blu-Ray.** Sullivan Stapleton; Eva Green; Rodrigo Santoro;

Lena Headey; Hans Matheson; Jack O'Connell; David Wenham; Andrew Tiernan; Callan Mulvey; Igal Naor; *D:* Noam Murro; *W:* Zack Snyder; Kurt Johnstad; *C:* Simon Duggan; *M:* Junkie XL.

365 Nights in Hollywood **1934** With stars in her eyes, Alice (Faye) comes to Hollywood to work in the movies but is snookered into attending a fraudulent acting school run by Delmar (Mitchell) and his partner Almont (Bradford). Delmar persuades wealthy Frank Young (Medford) to bankroll a film starring Alice, intending to sabotage the production and pocket the cash. Only desperate director Jimmy Dale (Dunn) is determined to make the most of his last opportunity and make Alice a star. **86m/B; DVD.** Alice Faye; James Dunn; Grant Mitchell; Frank Mitchell; John Bradford; Frank Melton; Jack Durant; John Qualen; *D:* George Marshall; *W:* William Conselman; Harry Jackson; Henry Johnson; *M:* Samuel Kaylin.

The 300 Spartans 1/2 **1962** Typical sword-and-sandal epic (surprisingly not of the Italian muscleman variety) that's big on battles and small on character development. Sparta's King Leonidis (Egan) and his band of 300 warriors defend the mountain pass at Thermopylae against the much larger force of effete Persian king Xerxes (Farrar) in 480 B.C. Richardson is dignified as an Athenian military advisor but Egan is as stiff as the brush in that Spartan helmet. **108m/C; DVD, Blu-Ray.** Richard Egan; Ralph Richardson; David Farrar; Barry Coe; Diane Baker; Kieron Moore; *D:* Rudolph Mate; *W:* George St. George; *C:* Geoffrey Unsworth; *M:* Manos Hadjidakis.

Three Husbands 1/2 **1950** A deceased playboy leaves letters for the title characters incriminating their wives in extramarital affairs. The men's reactions are pure farce—even though this same concept was played straight with a sex change in the earlier "A Letter to Three Wives." **79m/B; VHS, DVD.** Eve Arden; Ruth Warrick; Vanessa Brown; Howard da Silva; Shepperd Strudwick; Jane Darwell; *D:* Irving Reis.

Three Identical Strangers **2018 (PG-13)** The incredible story of three identical triplets, separated at birth and adopted by different families, who miraculously find each other as young adults. But that's just the beginning of the surprises. As the exuberant and charming brothers hunt for answers, they uncover a secret that defies reason and expectations, and addresses the issue of nature versus nurture. **96m/C; DVD.** Eddy Galland; David Kellman; Robert Shafran; Natasha Josefowitz; Andrew Lovesey; *D:* Tim Wardle; *C:* Tim Cragg; *M:* Paul Saunderson. Directors Guild '18: Documentary Director (Wardle).

Three Kingdoms: Resurrection of the Dragon **2008 (R)** Historical epic set in 228 AD during the last days of China's Han Empire when the country is divided into three rival kingdoms and constantly at war. Zhao Zilong is a soldier with the Shu forces, fighting for warlord Lui Bei. He gets promoted to general for his heroism but the war is still raging after 20 years. Now late rival Cao Cao's troops are led by his granddaughter Cao Ying, who is determined to defeat the so-far undefeated Zhao. Mandarin with subtitles. **102m/C; DVD.** *CH NK* Andy Lau; Sammo Hung; Maggie Q; Damian Lau; Hua Yueh; Vanessa Wu; Andy On; Rongguang Yu; *D:* Sammo Hung; Daniel Lee; *W:* Daniel Lee; Ho Leung Lau; *C:* Tony Cheung; *M:* Henry Lai.

Three Kings **1999 (R)** Director Russell turns the war movie genre on its ear with his subversive, chaotic, and ultimately satisfying studio film debut. At the end of the Gulf War, Special Forces Major Gates (Clooney) recruits three Army reservists to join him on an illegal mission to steal gold bullion which Hussein's troops had stolen from Kuwait. They wind up learning too much about U.S. policies and broken promises in the Middle East. Clooney is perfect as the pragmatic Gates, and Russell supplies the right mix of cynicism, dark humor, and action-movie heroism. **115m/C; VHS, DVD, Blu-Ray.** George Clooney; Mark Wahlberg; Ice Cube; Spike Jonze; Nora Dunn; Jamie Kennedy; Mykelti Williamson; Clifford Curtis; Said Taghmaoui; Judy Greer; Liz Stauber; Holt McCallany; *D:* David O. Russell; *W:* David O. Russell; *C:* Newton Thomas (Tom) Sigel; *M:* Carter Burwell. Broadcast Film Critics '99: Breakthrough Perf. (Jonze).

Three Little Girls In Blue **1946** Musical reworking of the 1938 pic "Three Blind Mice." Three midwestern sisters leave the farm after receiving an inheritance and head to Atlantic City hoping to snare rich husbands. Well-worn plot maintains some charm thanks to its cast. **100m/C; DVD.** June Haver; Vivian Blaine; Vera-Ellen; George Montgomery; Frank Latimore; Charles Smith; Celeste Holm; *D:* H. Bruce Humberstone; *W:* Valentine Davies; Brown Holmes; *C:* Ernest Palmer.

Three Little Words 1/2 **1950** A musical biography of songwriting team Harry Ruby and Bert Kalmar, filled with Kalmar-Ruby numbers. Helen Kane (famous for her boop-boop-de-boops) dubbed "I Wanna Be Loved By You" for Reynolds. A musical in the best MGM tradition. **102m/C; VHS, DVD.** Fred Astaire; Red Skelton; Vera-Ellen; Arlene Dahl; Keenan Wynn; Gloria De Haven; Debbie Reynolds; Gale Robbins; *D:* Richard Thorpe; *M:* Andre Previn. Golden Globes '51: Actor--Mus./Comedy (Astaire).

The Three Lives of Thomasina **1963 (PG)** In turn-of-the-century Scotland, a veterinarian orders his daughter's beloved cat destroyed when the pet is diagnosed with tetanus. After the cat's death (with scenes of kitty heaven), a beautiful and mysterious healer from the woods is able to bring the animal back to life and restore the animal to the little girl. Lovely Disney fairy tale with good performances by all. **95m/C; VHS, DVD.** Patrick McGoohan; Susan Hampshire; Karen Dotrice; Matthew Garber; *V:* Elspeth March; *D:* Don Chaffey.

Three Loves Has Nancy **1938** Screwball comedy. After smalltown gal Nancy Briggs (Gaynor) is jilted at the altar, she heads to the city to track down her missing fiance George (Sutton). Instead, she gets noticed by debonair writer Malcolm (Montgomery) and his equally sophisticated pal Robert (Tone). George finds her, and Nancy has a triple romantic whammy on her hands. **70m/B; DVD.** Janet Gaynor; Robert Montgomery; Franchot Tone; Grady Sutton; Guy Kibbee; Charley Grapewin; Claire Dodd; Cora Witherspoon; Emma Dunn; Reginald Owen; *D:* Richard Thorpe; *W:* Bella Spewack; Samuel Spewack; George Oppenheimer; David Hertz; *C:* William H. Daniels; *M:* William Axt.

The 3 Marias 1/2 *As Tres Marias* **2003** Three decades after Filomena (Severo) dumped Guerra (Vereza) and married his rival, Guerra murders her husband and sons in cold blood. Things get messy when Filomena conspires with her three daughters—all named Maria—to avenge the deaths. Common bloody revenge tale includes bits of dark humor. In Portuguese, with English subtitles. **90m/C; VHS, DVD.** *PT* Maria Luisa Mendonca; Marieta Severo; Julia Lemmertz; Luiza Mariani; Carlos Vereza; *D:* Aluisio Abranches; *W:* Heitor Dhalia; Wilson Friere; *C:* Marcelo Durst. **VIDEO**

Three Men and a Baby **1987 (PG)** The arrival of a young baby forever changes the lives of three sworn bachelors living in New York. Well-paced, charming and fun, with good acting from all. A remake of the French movie "Three Men and a Cradle." **102m/C; VHS, DVD.** Tom Selleck; Steve Guttenberg; Ted Danson; Margaret Colin; Nancy Travis; Philip Bosco; Celeste Holm; Derek de Lint; Cynthia Harris; Lisa Blair; Michelle Blair; Paul Guilfoyle; *D:* Leonard Nimoy; *W:* James Orr; Jim Cruickshank; *C:* Adam Greenberg; *M:* Marvin Hamlisch.

Three Men and a Cradle 1/2 *Trois Hommes et un Couffin* **1985 (PG-13)** Three carefree bachelors, Jacques (Dussollier), Pierre (Giraud), and Michel (Boujenah), find a baby girl in a basket outside the door of the home they share. One is the father—although none of the men are sure which one it is. After the initial shock of learning how to take care of a child, they fall in love with her and won't let her go. There's a strange subplot about Jacques hiding heroin in the baby's diapers that gets them all involved with drug dealers. Still, everything is played for laughs and the film has heaps of charm. French with subtitles. Remade in 1987 as "Three Men and a Baby." **100m/C; VHS, DVD.** *FR* Roland Giraud; Michel Boujenah; Andre Dussollier; Philippe LeRoy; Marthe Villalonga; Dominque Lavanant; *D:* Coline Serreau; *W:* Coline Serreau; *C:* Jean-Yves Escoffier. Cesar '86: Film, Support. Actor (Boujenah), Writing.

Three Men and a Little Lady 1/2 **1990 (PG)** In this sequel to "Three Men and a Baby," the mother of the once abandonded infant decides that her child needs a father. Although she wants Selleck, he doesn't get the message and so she chooses a snooty British director. The rest of the movie features various semi-comic attempts to rectify the situation. **100m/C; VHS, DVD.** Tom Selleck; Steve Guttenberg; Ted Danson; Nancy Travis; Robin Weisman; Christopher Cazenove; Fiona Shaw; Sheila Hancock; John Boswall; Jonathan Lynn; Sydney Walsh; *D:* Emile Ardolino; *W:* Charlie Peters; Sara Parriott; Josann McGibbon; *C:* Adam Greenberg; *M:* James Newton Howard.

Three Men in a Boat **1956** Harris, J, and George decide to escape daily drudgery and romantic complications by taking a boating trip up the Thames to Oxford. But their male bonding is interrupted when they cross paths with the lovely Sophie, Primrose, and Bluebell, and the trip ends in chaos at a cricket match. Victorian-era comic nostalgia based on the Jerome K. Jerome novel. **84m/C; DVD.** *GB* Jimmy Edwards; Laurence Harvey; David Tomlinson; Shirley Eaton; Lisa Gastoni; Jill Ireland; Adrienne Corri; Martita Hunt; *D:* Ken Annakin; *W:* Vernon Harris; Hubert Gregg; *C:* Eric Cross; *M:* John Addison.

Three Men in White **1944** Fourth in the series; followed by "Between Two Women." Dr. Gillespie once again challenges his would-be assistants Red and Lee with diagnosing difficult cases. Lee must figure out why a child is allergic to sugar while Red draws a two-fer: why does Jean Brown appear drunk without actually drinking alcohol and why does her mother's arthritic condition confine her to a wheelchair? **85m/B; DVD.** Lionel Barrymore; Van Johnson; Keye Luke; Ava Gardner; Barbara Brown; Marilyn Maxwell; Alma Kruger; Rags Ragland; *D:* Willis Goldbeck; *W:* Harry Ruskin; Martin Berkeley; *C:* Ray June; *M:* Nathaniel Shilkert.

The Three Musketeers 1/2 **1921** D'Artagnan swashbuckles silently amid stylish sets, scores of extras and exquisite costumes. Relatively faithful adaptation of Alexandre Dumas novel, slightly altered in favor of D'Artagnan's lover. Classic Fairbanks, who also produced. **120m/B; Silent; VHS, DVD.** Douglas Fairbanks, Sr.; Leon Bary; George Siegmann; Eugene Pallette; Boyd Irwin; Thomas Holding; Sidney Franklin; Charles Stevens; Nigel de Brulier; Willis Robards; Mary MaClaren; *D:* Fred Niblo; *W:* Douglas Fairbanks, Sr.; Lotta Woods; *C:* Arthur Edeson; *M:* Louis F. Gottschalk.

The Three Musketeers 1/2 **1933** Modern adaptation of the classic tale by Alexander Dumas depicts the three friends as members of the Foreign Legion. Weakest of Wayne serials, in 12 parts. **215m/B; VHS, DVD.** Jack Mulhall; Raymond Hatton; Lon Chaney, Jr.; John Wayne; Francis X. Bushman; Ruth Hall; Noah Beery, Jr.; Al Ferguson; *D:* Colbert Clark; Armand Schaefer; *W:* Colbert Clark; Bennett Cohen; Wyndham Gittens; Norman S. Hall; *C:* Tom Galligan; Ernest Miller.

The Three Musketeers 1/2 *The Singing Musketeer* **1939** Musical-comedy version of the famed Alexandre Dumas swashbuckling saga. Ameche is a singing D'Artagnan and the three Ritz brothers are the inept and cowardly Musketeers (who turn out to be phonies, after all). Silly fun. **73m/B; VHS, DVD.** Don Ameche; Al Ritz; Harry Ritz; Jimmy Ritz; Binnie Barnes; Lionel Atwill; Miles Mander; Gloria Stuart; Pauline Moore; Joseph Schildkraut; John Carradine; Douglass Dumbrille; *D:* Allan Dwan; *W:* M.M. Musselman; William A. Drake; Sam Hellman.

The Three Musketeers 1/2 **1948** The three musketeers who are "all for one and one for all" join forces with D'Artagnan to battle the evil Cardinal Richelieu in this rambunctious adaptation of the classic tale by Alexander Dumas. Good performances by the cast, who combined drama and comedy well. Turner's first color film. **126m/C; VHS, DVD.** Lana Turner; Gene Kelly; June Allyson; Gig Young; Angela Lansbury; Van Heflin; Keenan Wynn; Robert Coote; Reginald Owen; Frank Morgan; Vincent Price; Patricia Medina; *D:* George Sidney.

The Three Musketeers 1/2 **1974 (PG)** Extravagant and funny version of the Dumas classic. Three swashbucklers (Reed, Chamberlain, Finlay) and their country cohort (York), who wishes to join the Musketeers, set out to save the honor of the French Queen (Chaplin). To do so they must oppose the evil cardinal (Heston) who has his eyes on the power behind the throne and who is aided by cohort Milady (Dunaway). Welch is amusing as clumsy lady-in-waiting Constance. A strong cast leads this winning combination of slapstick and high adventure. Followed by "The Four Musketeers" and "The Return of the Musketeers." **105m/C; VHS, DVD.** Richard Chamberlain; Oliver Reed; Michael York; Raquel Welch; Frank Finlay; Christopher Lee; Faye Dunaway; Charlton Heston; Geraldine Chaplin; Simon Ward; Jean-Pierre Cassel; William Hobbs; *D:* Richard Lester; *W:* George MacDonald Fraser; *C:* David Watkin; *M:* Michel Legrand. Golden Globes '75: Actress--Mus./Comedy (Welch).

The Three Musketeers 1/2 **1993 (PG)** Yet another version of the classic swashbuckler with Porthos, Athos, Aramis, and the innocent D'Artanan banding together against the evil Cardinal Richelieu and the tempting Milady DeWinter to save France. Cute stars, a little swordplay, a few jokes, and cartoon bad guys. Okay for the younger crowd. **105m/C; VHS, DVD, Blu-Ray.** Kiefer Sutherland; Charlie Sheen; Chris O'Donnell; Oliver Platt; Rebecca De Mornay; Tim Curry; Gabrielle Anwar; Julie Delpy; Michael Wincott; *D:* Stephen Herek; *W:* David Loughery; *C:* Dean Semler; *M:* Michael Kamen.

The Three Musketeers **2011 (PG-13)** Only loosely based on the legendary Dumas novel, this 3D interpretation is so deadly dull that it could give its classic source material a bad name. The title characters (MacFadyen as Aramis, Evans as Athos, and Stevenson as Porthos) have never been so boring and D'Artagnan (Lerman) might win the least engaging lead of 2011 award. The central quartet of heroes are forced to duel against far-more-entertaining villains such as the Duke of Buckingham (Bloom), Cardinal Richelieu (Waltz), Rochefort (Mikkelson), and Milady (Jovovich). Director Anderson is clearly more enraptured by the bad guys, who steal the show from the half-asleep heroes. **110m/C; DVD, Blu-Ray.** Logan Lerman; Matthew Macfadyen; Ray Stevenson; Luke Evans; Christoph Waltz; Milla Jovovich; Orlando Bloom; Juno Temple; Til Schweiger; Mads Mikkelsen; *D:* Paul W.S. Anderson; *W:* Andrew Davies; Alex Litvak; *C:* Glen MacPherson; *M:* Paul Haslinger.

3 Ninjas 1/2 **1992 (PG)** Lively kid's actioner about three brothers who are trained as ninjas by their grandpa. When a group of bad guys tries to kidnap the boys, they're in for trouble. Sort of a cross between "The Karate Kid" and "Home Alone" that is suitable for family viewing. Followed by "3 Ninjas Kick Back." **84m/C; VHS, DVD.** Victor Wong; Michael Treanor; Max Elliott Slade; Chad Power; Rand Kingsley; Alan McRae; Margarita Franco; Toru Tanaka; Patrick Laborteaux; *D:* Jon Turteltaub; *W:* Edward Emanuel; *M:* Richard (Rick) Marvin.

3 Ninjas: High Noon at Mega Mountain *Three Ninjas: Showdown at Mega Mountain* **1997 (PG)** Fourth installment of the kid-fantasy franchise finds brothers Rocky (Botuchis), Colt (O'Laskey), and Tum-Tum (Roeske) in the middle of a takeover at an amusement park. The ninja trained brothers, along with a computer-whiz neighbor (Earlywine) and retiring action hero Dave Dragon (Hogan) must save the day when Medusa (Anderson) and her henchmen ransom the park and its guests. Typically, the adults are incompetent when they're not busy being nasty. Pre-pubescent kids are the only ones likely to find this entertaining—if they're not too discriminating. The "action" is somewhere between cartoon and pro wrestling. Varney stands out as Medusa's lead henchman. **93m/C; VHS, DVD.** Hulk Hogan; Loni Anderson; Jim Varney; Victor Wong; Mathew Botuchis; Michael J.

O'Laskey, II; J.P. Roeske, II; Chelsey Earlywine; Alan McRae; Margarita Franco; Kirk Baily; ***D:*** Sean McNamara; ***W:*** Sean McNamara; Jeff Phillips; ***C:*** Blake T. Evans; ***M:*** John Coda.

3 Ninjas Kick Back 🦴🦴 ½ **1994 (PG)** Sequel to the popular "3 Ninjas." Three brothers help their grandfather protect a ceremonial knife won in a ninja tournament in Japan 50 years earlier. Gramps' ancient adversary in that tournament, now an evil tycoon, wants the sword back and he's willing to enlist the aid of his three American grandchildren, members of garage band Teenage Vomit, to get it. The showdown eventually heads to Japan, where "Kick Back," unlike predecessors, dispenses with the Japan-bashing. High-spirited action fare that kids will enjoy. **95m/C; VHS, DVD.** Victor Wong; Max Elliott Slade; Sean Fox; Evan Bonifant; Sab Shimono; Dustin Nguyen; Jason Schombing; Caroline Junko King; Angelo Tiffe; ***D:*** Charles Kanganis; ***W:*** Mark Saltzman; ***C:*** Christopher Faloona; ***M:*** Richard (Rick) Marvin.

3 Ninjas Knuckle Up 🦴🦴 ½ **1995 (PG-13)** Brothers Rocky (Treanor), Tum Tum (Power), and Colt (Slade) spend their summer vacation with ever-wise Grandpa Mori (Wong) and get to practice their martial arts skills on a variety of villains. Seems a waste management company has been illegally dumping toxins onto the nearby Indian reservation where the boys' friend Jo (Lightning) lives and have even kidnapped her dad (Shanks) to keep him silent. So it's our pint-sized heroes to the rescue. Filmed in '92 but released after "3 Ninjas Kick Back," which explains why Treanor and Power are missing from the second film. **94m/C; VHS, DVD.** Victor Wong; Michael Treanor; Chad Power; Max Elliott Slade; Crystle Lightning; Patrick Kilpatrick; Don Shanks; Charles Napier; Nick Ramus; Vincent Schiavelli; ***D:*** Simon S. Sheen; ***W:*** Alex S. Kim; ***C:*** Eugene Shlugleit; ***M:*** Gary Stevan Scott.

Three Nuts in Search of a Bolt 🦴 ½ **1964 (R)** Three neurotics send a surrogate to a comely psychiatrist for help, but the shrink thinks the surrogate's a three-way multiple personality. Raunchy monkey-shines ensue. Includes Van Doren's infamous beer bath scene. **78m/C; VHS, DVD.** Mamie Van Doren; Tommy Noonan; Paul Gilbert; Alvy Moore; ***D:*** Tommy Noonan.

Three O'Clock High 🦴🦴 ½ **1987 (PG)** A nerdy high school journalist is assigned a profile of the new kid in school, who turns out to be the biggest bully, too. He approaches his task with great unease. Silly teenage farce is given souped-up direction by Spielberg protege Joanou. Features decent work by the young cast. **97m/C; VHS, DVD, Blu-Ray.** Casey Siemaszko; Anne Ryan; Stacey Glick; Jonathan Wise; Richard Tyson; Jeffrey Tambor; Philip Baker Hall; John P. Ryan; ***D:*** Phil Joanou; ***W:*** Richard Christian Matheson; Thomas Szollosi; ***M:*** Tangerine Dream.

Three of Hearts 🦴 ½ **1993 (R)** Slick look at love in contemporary downtown New York. The triangle consists of Connie (Lynch), just dumped by bisexual girlfriend Ellen (Fenn), who is in turn seduced by hired escort Joe (Baldwin), who will break her heart, causing her to turn back to the sympathetic Connie. But guess what happens. Hiply superficial plot is transparent although the three leads are likeable, especially Lynch as the lanky lovelorn Connie. Don't read further if you don't want to know what happens since the film was shot with two endings. The U.S. release pairs Joe and Ellen for a typically American happy ending; the European release doesn't. **102m/C; VHS, DVD.** Kelly Lynch; William Baldwin; Sherilyn Fenn; Joe Pantoliano; Gail Strickland; Cec Verrell; Claire Callaway; Tony Amendola; ***D:*** Yurek Bogayevicz; ***W:*** Adam Greenman; ***M:*** Richard Gibbs.

Three on a Meathook WOOF! **1972** When a young man and his father living on an isolated farm receive female visitors, bloodshed is quick to follow. Essentially a remake of "Psycho," and very loosely based on the crimes of Ed Gein. Filmed in Louisville, Kentucky. **85m/C; VHS, DVD.** Charles Kissinger; James Pickett; Sherry Steiner; Carolyn Thompson; ***D:*** William Girdler; ***W:*** William Girdler; ***C:*** William Asman; ***M:*** William Girdler.

Three Peaks 🦴🦴 ½ **2019** French woman Lea (Bejo) goes on vacation in a remote cabin in the mountains with her long-time German boyfriend Aaron (Fehling) and young son Tristan (Montgomery). The three have strong relationships with each other, and Aaron dotes on Tristan as the pair bond over hikes and bedtime stories. When Tristan's biological father calls his son on a cell phone his mother did not know he had, the anxiety Lea and Aaron feel about their little family grows deeper and more unsettled. Though the story is a bit thin, it includes thoughtful moments and solid acting. **94m/C; DVD.** Alexander Fehling; Berenice Bejo; Arian Montgomery; ***D:*** Jan Zabeil; ***W:*** Jan Zabeil; ***C:*** Axel Schneppat.

Three Priests 🦴 ½ **2008** Jacob Sands (Parks) has a ranch in Montana that he runs with his wife Rachel (Hussey) and dutiful son Joe (Duffey). His other son, Dustin (Martin), is a troublemaker who follows the rodeo circuit and has an eye for the ladies. When Dustin comes home for a visit, sibling rivalry breaks out when he starts eyeing local beauty Abby (Jones) whom Joe is sweet on. **90m/C; DVD.** Michael Parks; Olivia Hussey; Julia Jones; Wes Studi; Alexander Martin; Aaron Duffey; ***D:*** Jim Comas Cole; ***W:*** Jim Comas Cole; ***C:*** Guy Pieres; ***M:*** Daniel Cole. **VIDEO**

Three Sailors and a Girl 🦴🦴 ½ **1953** Good tunes (by Sammy Fain and Sammy Cahn), usual silly musical plot (that's supposedly based on the George S. Kaufman play "The Butter and Egg Man"). Three submarine sailors (MacRae, Nelson, Leonard) dock in New York and are introduced to struggling singer Penny (Powell). They agree to invest in shady producer Joe Woods' (Levene) show with Penny as the lead and manage to turn the previous flop into a hit. **95m/C; DVD.** Jane Powell; Gordon MacRae; Gene Nelson; Jack E. Leonard; Sam Levene; George Givot; Veda Ann Borg; Burt Lancaster; ***D:*** Roy Del Ruth; ***W:*** Roland Kibbee; Devery Freeman; ***C:*** Carl Guthrie.

Three Secrets 🦴🦴 ½ **1950** A plane crashes and the only survivor is a five-year-old boy. Three women, each with a secret, seek to claim him as the child each gave up for adoption five years before. Tearjerker with good cast. **98m/B; DVD, Blu-Ray.** Eleanor Parker; Patricia Neal; Ruth Roman; Frank Lovejoy; Leif Erickson; ***D:*** Robert Wise; ***W:*** Gina Kaus; Martin Rackin; ***C:*** Sidney Hickox; ***M:*** David Buttolph.

360 🦴 ½ **2012 (R)** Rarely has so high a pedigree resulted in such a disappointing drama. Writer Morgan (an Oscar winner), acclaimed director Meirelles, and a dream cast of A-list actors like Weisz, Hopkins, Law, and many more get sucked into a morass of flimsy connections and false melodrama. With numerous intersecting stories (Law & Weisz play a married couple in London, Foster plays a convict in Denver, Debbouze is a Parisian dentist, etc.), the film never gains any dramatic tension and seems to purposefully turn bland to tie together its various plot arcs. **115m/C; DVD, Blu-Ray.** *UK AT FR BR* Jude Law; Rachel Weisz; Anthony Hopkins; Ben Foster; Johannes Krisch; Jamel Debbouze; Dinara Drukarova; ***D:*** Fernando Meirelles; ***W:*** Peter Morgan; ***C:*** Adriano Goldman.

Three Smart Girls 🦴🦴🦴 ½ **1936** Fast-moving musical features three high-spirited sisters who attempt to bring their divorced parents back together. Their plan is thwarted when they learn of their father's plan to marry a gold digger. 15-year-old singing sensation Durbin made her debut in this film. Based on a story by Commandini. Followed by "Three Smart Girls Grow Up." **84m/B; VHS, DVD.** Deanna Durbin; Binnie Barnes; Alice Brady; Ray Milland; Charles Winninger; Mischa Auer; Nan Grey; Barbara Read; ***D:*** Henry Koster; ***W:*** Adele Comandini; Austin Parker; ***C:*** Joseph Valentine.

Three Smart Girls Grow Up 🦴🦴🦴 **1939** Durbin once again plays matchmaker, this time for her two older sisters and their fellas. A delightful mix of comedy and song, this lighthearted sequel turned out to be one of the top-grossing films of the year. Durbin sings "Because," which became one of her biggest hits. **88m/B; DVD.** Deanna Durbin; Charles Winninger; Nan Grey; Helen Parrish; Robert Cummings; William Lundigan; Ernest Cossart; ***D:*** Henry Koster; ***W:*** Felix Jackson; Bruce Manning.

Three Sovereigns for Sarah 🦴🦴 ½ **1985** Witch-hunters tortured and toasted Sarah's two sisters for practicing witchcraft in the past. Now, accused of witchery herself, she struggles to prove the family's innocence. Excellent, made-for-PBS. Fine performances from all, especially Redgrave. **152m/C; VHS, DVD.** Vanessa Redgrave; Phyllis Thaxter; Patrick McGoohan; ***D:*** Philip Leacock.

Three Steps North 🦴 ½ **1951** American G.I. Frank Keeler ran a black-market business while stationed in Amalfi, Italy and hid his ill-gotten loot before being convicted and thrown in prison. When he's released, Keeler finds the dough is gone and there are several likely suspects. **85m/B; DVD.** Lloyd Bridges; Lea Padovani; Aldo Fabrizi; William Tubbs; Dino Galvani; ***D:*** W. Lee Wilder; ***W:*** Lester Fuller; ***C:*** Aldo Giordani; ***M:*** Roman Vlad.

The Three Stooges 🦴 ½ **2012 (PG)** When the Farrelly brothers' reboot of the classic comedy trio stays loyal to the simplicity of its source, it works really well--jokes that could have come straight from an old Stooges skit. The brothers try to save their childhood orphanage, stumble onto a murder plot, and star in a reality TV show. The three new players--Hayes, Diamantopoulos, Sasso--take the route of impersonation instead of reimagining the boys and their impressions are strong. What fails is the amount of modern pop culture references, including a nauseating amount of time spent with the cast of Jersey Shore. **92m/C; DVD, Blu-Ray, Streaming.** Sean P. Hayes; Will Sasso; Chris Diamantopoulos; Jane Lynch; Sofia Vergara; Jennifer Hudson; Stephen Collins; Larry David; ***D:*** Bobby Farrelly; Peter Farrelly; ***W:*** Bobby Farrelly; Peter Farrelly; Mike Cerrone; ***C:*** Matthew F. Leonetti; ***M:*** John Debney.

Three Stooges in Orbit 🦴🦴 ½ **1962** Three TV performers (you know who) looking for a shtick and a place to live, encounter a crazy scientist with a rocket-like invention. In a shocking plot twist, the boys accidently launch the rocket and must battle Martians to save the world and their TV career. **87m/B; VHS, DVD.** Moe Howard; Larry Fine; Joe DeRita; Emil Sitka; Carol Christensen; Edson Stroll; ***D:*** Edward L. Bernds.

The Three Stooges Meet Hercules 🦴🦴 ½ **1961** The Three Stooges are transported back to ancient Ithaca by a time machine with a young scientist and his girlfriend. When the girl is captured, they enlist the help of Hercules to rescue her. **80m/B; VHS, DVD.** Moe Howard; Larry Fine; Joe DeRita; Vicki Trickett; Quinn (K.) Redeker; Samson Burke; Lewis Charles; Marlin McKeever; Michael McKeever; John Cliff; George Neise; ***D:*** Edward L. Bernds; ***W:*** Elwood Ullman; ***C:*** Charles S. Welbourne; ***M:*** Paul Dunlap.

Three Strange Loves 🦴🦴🦴 *Thirst* **1949** Men and women struggle with loneliness, old age, and sterility. Sometimes disjointed, but for the most part, well-made. Finely acted. In Swedish with English subtitles. **88m/B; VHS, DVD, Blu-Ray.** *SW* Eva Henning; Brigit Tengroth; Birger Malmsten; ***D:*** Ingmar Bergman.

Three Strangers 🦴🦴 **1946** Overly-complicated and implausible plot mars director Negulesco's film noir effort. On the eve of the Chinese New Year in 1938 London, Crystal (Fitzgerald), Jerome (Greenstreet), and Johnny (Lorre) gather before the statue of Kwan Yin. According to legend if three strangers make a wish before the idol at the same time, it will be granted. Crystal wants revenge against the husband who left her; shady lawyer Jerome needs money to cover his embezzlement of a client's assets; and thief Johnny would like his sweepstakes ticket to be a winner. But be careful what you wish for. **93m/B; DVD.** Geraldine Fitzgerald; Sydney Greenstreet; Peter Lorre; Alan Napier; Joan Lorring; Robert Shayne; Marjorie (Reardon) Riordan; Rosalind Ivan; Peter Whitney; ***D:*** Jean Negulesco; ***W:*** John Huston; Howard Koch; ***C:*** Arthur Edeson; ***M:*** Adolph Deutsch.

Three Strikes WOOF! **2000 (R)** Two-time loser Rob is released from jail determined to stay straight and thus avoid the harsh sentencing of California's "Three Strikes" law. But as luck, and a lame script filled with fart jokes and little esle would have it, his buddy picks him up from jail in a stolen car and promptly gets in a gunfight with the cops. On the run from the police and gang members, Rob tries to find a way to clear himself and get home. There's not much to redeem this disaster of a flick, unless you find embarrassingly stereotypical characters and "In Living Color" refect jokes amusing. **83m/C; VHS, DVD.** Brian Hooks; N'Bushe Wright; Faizon Love; Starletta DuPois; David Alan Grier; Dean Norris; Meagan Good; De'Aundre Bonds; Antonio Fargas; Vincent Schiavelli; David Leisure; Gerald S. O'Loughlin; George Wallace; E40; Barima McNight; Mo'Nique; Shawn Fonteno; ***D:*** DJ Pooh; ***W:*** DJ Pooh; ***C:*** Johnny (John W.) Simmons; ***M:*** Aaron Anderson; Andrew Slack.

Three Stripes in the Sun 🦴🦴 **1955** Based on a true story. In 1949, Sgt. Hugh O'Reilly (Ray) is assigned to the occupation forces in postwar Japan. At first he's deeply resentful of having to work with former enemies until O'Reilly gets involved helping at a rundown orphanage and falls in love with his Japanese translator Yuko (Kimura). **93m/B; DVD.** Aldo Ray; Mitsuko Kimura; Phil Carey; Dick York; Chuck Connors; Camille Janclaire; Tatsuo Saito; ***D:*** Richard Murphy; ***W:*** Richard Murphy; Albert Duffy; ***C:*** Burnett Guffey; ***M:*** George Duning.

3:10 to Yuma 🦴🦴🦴 ½ **1957** In order to collect $200 he desperately needs, a poor cattle rancher (Heflin) has to hold a dangerous killer at bay while waiting to turn the outlaw (Ford) over to the authorities arriving on the 3:10 train to Yuma. Stuck in a hotel room with the outlaw's gang gathering outside, the question arises as to who is the prisoner. Heflin is continually worked on by the outlaw Ford, in a movie with more than its share of great dialogue. The two leads are exceptional, with Ford making the most of his character's cunning charm. Suspenseful, well-made action western adapted from an Elmore Leonard story. **92m/B; VHS, DVD.** Glenn Ford; Van Heflin; Felicia Farr; Richard Jaeckel; Leora Dana; Robert Emhardt; Henry Jones; Ford Rainey; ***D:*** Delmer Daves; ***W:*** Halsted Welles; ***C:*** Charles Lawton, Jr.; ***M:*** George Duning. Natl. Film Reg. '12.

3:10 to Yuma 🦴🦴🦴 ½ **2007 (R)** Remake of the 1957 classic western pits legendary outlaw Ben Wade (Crowe) against rancher Dan Evans (Bale) in a battle that's as much about psychology as it is gunplay. Crippled by war injury and battling a drought, Evans struggles to keep his ranch and the respect of his wife (Mol) and son (Lerman). When Wade is captured mid-crime spree, Evans joins the posse that will transport him to the titular train. Wade quickly recognizes the weaknesses of the men guarding him and turns them to his advantage, leaving Evans to defend himself and his son against Wade's madman second-in command Charlie Prince (Foster, in a career-making role). Masterfully explores the grey area between good and bad, and Mangold infuses the genre with a level of energy and excitement that hasn't been seen in a western in a while. **120m/C; DVD, Blu-Ray.** Russell Crowe; Christian Bale; Ben Foster; Logan Lerman; Peter Fonda; Gretchen Mol; Dallas Roberts; Alan Tudyk; Vinessa Shaw; Kevin Durand; Johnny Whitworth; ***D:*** James Mangold; ***W:*** Halsted Welles; Michael Brandt; Derek Haas; ***C:*** Phedon Papamichael; ***M:*** Marco Beltrami.

Three the Hard Way 🦴🦴 ½ **1974 (R)** An insane white supremacist has a plan to eliminate blacks by contaminating water supplies. A big blaxploitation money maker and the first to team Brown, Williamson, and Kelly, who would go on to make several more pictures together. **93m/C; VHS, DVD.** Jim Brown; Fred Williamson; Jim Kelly; Sheila Frazier; Jay Robinson; Alex Rocco; ***D:*** Gordon Parks.

3000 Miles to Graceland 🦴 ½ **2001 (R)** Shockingly original pic sets Elvis impersonators in Vegas, only these Presleys wanna rob, not rock. Ex-cellmates Russell and Costner are the lead Kings, Michael and Murphy, who team up with Arquette, Slater, and Woodbine, and head to the quaint desert burg to relieve its wagering establishments of some extra cash. After a strong opening segment, only moments of comic relief are scattered throughout, highlighted by the Elvii strutting through town in a "Reservoir Dogs" homage. Gratuitous violence and cliched action doesn't help movie's one-note appeal but the look is slick and the boys drive cool cars. **125m/C; VHS, DVD, Blu-Ray.** Kevin Costner; Kurt Russell; Christian Slater; Bokeem Woodbine; David Arquette; Courteney Cox; Kevin Pollak; Jon Lovitz; Howie Long; Thomas Haden Church; Ice-T; David Kaye; Louis Lombardi; ***D:*** Demian Lichtenstein; ***W:*** Demian Lichtenstein; Richard Recco; ***C:*** David Franco; ***M:*** George S. Clinton.

Three to Tango 🦴 1/2 **1999 (PG-13)** Dopey would-be romantic comedy only demonstrates that actors who make it big in TV series should think about sticking to the small screen. (Or being more careful about their big screen choices.) Married tycoon Charles Newman (McDermott) has it in his power to award a lucrative contract to struggling architect Oscar Novak (Perry) and his partner, Peter Steinberg (Peter). Somehow, Newman gets the impression that Oscar is gay and would be the perfect guy to spy on Newman's young mistress, Amy (Campbell), whom he fears is about to wander. Naturally, Oscar falls for the girl and then must work around all the mistaken assumptions. Yawn. **98m/C; VHS, DVD.** Dylan McDermott; Neve Campbell; Matthew Perry; Oliver Platt; Cylk Cozart; John C. McGinley; Bob Balaban; Kelly Rowan; Deborah Rush; Patrick Van Horn; ***D:*** Damon Santostefano; ***W:*** Rodney Vaccaro; Aline Brosh McKenna; ***C:*** Walt Lloyd; ***M:*** Graeme Revell.

3, 2, 1...Frankie Go Boom 🦴🦴 *Frankie Go Boom* **2012** Frankie's (Hunnam) the meeker brother of Bruce (O'Dowd), an alpha jerk who has often filmed his brother in embarrassing situations and made them Internet fodder. Frankie brings home a sweet girl named Lassie (Caplan) but has trouble performing with her. Bruce thinks he may have his next video but plans change when the brothers learn that Lassie's father (Noth) is an unstable and violent TV star. The charisma of the ensemble allows one to forgive some of the horrendous screenplay...to a point. A mediocre production of sibling rivalry taken to wacky extremes. **89m/C; Blu-Ray, Streaming.** Charlie Hunnam; Chris O'Dowd; Lizzy Caplan; Chris Noth; Ron Perlman; Nora Dunn; Whitney Cummings; ***D:*** Jordan Roberts; ***W:*** Jordan Roberts; ***C:*** Matias Troelstrup; ***M:*** Mateo Messina.

Three Violent People 🦴🦴 **1957** Family feud set in post-Civil War Old West features Heston and Baxter impulsively marrying and returning to run the family ranch. Heston's brother (Tryon) wants to sell the ranch in order to get his share of the inheritance and then Heston finds out Baxter was once a prostitute. In this case family squabbles don't make for an exciting film. **100m/C; VHS, DVD.** Charlton Heston; Anne Baxter; Gilbert Roland; Tom Tryon; Forrest Tucker; Elaine Stritch; Bruce Bennett; Barton MacLane; ***D:*** Rudolph Mate; ***W:*** James Edward Grant; ***C:*** Loyal Griggs; ***M:*** Walter Scharf.

Three Warriors 🦴 1/2 **1977** Young Native American boy is forced to leave the city and return to the reservation, where his contempt for the traditions of his ancestors slowly turns to appreciation and love. **100m/C; VHS, Streaming.** Charles White Eagle; Lois Red Elk; McKee "Kiko" Red Wing; Randy Quaid; Christopher Lloyd; Trey Wilson; ***D:*** Keith Merrill; ***W:*** Sy Gomberg; ***C:*** Bruce Surtees; ***M:*** Merrill Jenson.

3-Way 🦴🦴 *Three Way Split* **2004 (R)** Sure it can be fun to watch the pretty people double-cross each other in this adaptation of Gil Brewer's 1963 novel "Wild to Possess" but even that wears thin. A philandering hubby and his girlfriend plot to kidnap his rich wife (Gershon) then bump her off after they get the ransom. Enter Lew (Purcell)?a troubled soul (with a heart)?who overhears the scheme and sees an easy score; however a blackmailer (Yoakam) arrives just in time to foul things up. Too few degrees of separation among the players make for far-fetched scenarios that deflate potentially intriguing plot twists. **88m/C; VHS, DVD.** Joy Bryant; Gina Gershon; Dwight Yoakam; Desmond Harrington; Ali Larter; Dominic Purcell; ***D:*** Scott Ziehl; ***W:*** Russell P. Marleau; ***C:*** Antonio Calvache; ***M:*** Christopher Hoag. **VIDEO**

3 Weeks to Daytona 🦴 **2011** Low-budget, cliched drama from actors best-known for their TV work. Chuck Weber's (Cohen) passion is NASCAR racing but he hasn't won in years and is working as an airport limo driver. He and his pit crew chief girlfriend, Cheryl (Fox), have no money to continue trying to get back on the track but, naturally, Chuck gets his one last chance. **82m/C; DVD.** Scott Cohen; Jorja Fox; Rip Torn; Robert Leeshock; ***D:*** Bret Stern; ***W:*** Bret Stern; ***C:*** William M. Miller; ***M:*** David Bateman. **VIDEO**

The Three Weird Sisters 🦴🦴 **1948** The three weird sisters from "Macbeth" strive to maintain their life of luxury by plotting to kill their half-brother for the inheritance. Not a bad effort for Birt's first time out as director; script co-written by his wife, Louise and poet Thomas. **82m/B; VHS, DVD.** *GB* Nancy Price; Mary Clare; ***D:*** Daniel Birt; ***W:*** Dylan Thomas; Louise Birt.

Three Wise Girls 🦴🦴 **1932** Only two of the girls turn out to be wise--at least when it comes to romance. Cassie (Harlow) leaves her small town to become a model in New York like her pal Gladys (Clarke), only to learn that Gladys is actually the mistress of a married man. Cassie falls for Jerry (Byron) but he's married, although he tells her he's getting a divorce. Cassie's roommate Dot (Prevost) has fallen for nice guy chauffeur Jimmy (Devine). Harlow's final film for Columbia Pictures. **70m/B; DVD.** Jean Harlow; Mae Clarke; Marie Prevost; Walter Byron; Jameson Thomas; Natalie Moorhead; Andy Devine; ***D:*** William Beaudine; ***W:*** Robert Riskin; Agnes Christine Johnston; ***C:*** Ted Tetzlaff.

Three Wise Women 🦴🦴 **2011** Despite the title, this Hallmark Channel movie comes across as another version of "A Christmas Carol" although Liz is certainly no Scrooge. Instead, she's a 30-something doctor who's settling for a man who's not her soulmate when she gets engaged. Her guardian angel gets a teenage Ellie and an elderly Beth to help Liz realize she's making a mistake. **88m/C; DVD.** Amy Huberman; Fionnula Flanagan; Lauren Coe; Hugh O'Conor; John Rhys-Davies; Brendan Patricks; ***D:*** Declan Recks; ***W:*** Abby Ajayi; ***C:*** Ciaran Tanham; ***M:*** Stephen McKeon. **CABLE**

Three Wishes 🦴🦴 **1995 (PG)** Mysterious—and perhaps mystical—stranger Jack (Swayze) moves into the lives of a 1950s suburban widow (Mastrantonio) and her kids (Mazzello and Mumy) after she hits him with her car. Jack proceeds to use Zen philosophy, stories of a genie disguised as a dog, and nude sunbathing to help the kids' Little League team, make a boy fly, and scandalize the neighborhood. Adults will recognize the beatnik, Kerouac-influenced philosophy of nonconformity. They'll also recognize the sellout of that ideal with the sickeningly sappy ending. Mumy is the son of former "Lost in Space" child star Billy Mumy. **115m/C; VHS, DVD.** Patrick Swayze; Mary Elizabeth Mastrantonio; Joseph Mazzello; David Marshall Grant; Michael O'Keefe; John Diehl; Jay O. Sanders; Diane Venora; Seth Mumy; ***D:*** Martha Coolidge; ***W:*** Elizabeth Anderson; ***C:*** Johnny E. Jensen; ***M:*** Cynthia Millar.

3 Women 🦴🦴🦴 **1977 (PG)** Altman creates a surreal, dreamlike, sometimes creepy tale of women's relationships with each other. Shy reserved Pinky (Spacek) gets a job in a senior care center where she meets Millie (Duvall), a therapist who doesn't seem to acknowledge her invisibility. She immediately idolizes and moves in with Millie, following in Millie's wannabe modern woman footsteps, and slowly begins to take over her life. The two are friends with Willie (Rule), the morose, pregnant artist wife of their landlord who paints frightening figures in the bottom of the building's pool. Admittedly influenced by Ingmar Bergman, Altman deftly handles tragedy, questions of identity, and our dreams' relationship to our waking lives. **124m/C; DVD, Blu-Ray.** Shelley Duvall; Sissy Spacek; Janice Rule; Robert Fortier; Ruth Nelson; John Cromwell; Sierra Pecheur; Craig Richard Nelson; Maysie Hoy; Dennis Christopher; ***D:*** Robert Altman; ***W:*** Robert Altman; Patricia Resnick; ***C:*** Charles Rosher, Jr.

Three Word Brand 🦴🦴 **1921** Hart plays three roles in this film, a homesteader who is killed by Indians and his twin sons, who are separated after their father's death and reunited many years later. Silent with musical score. **75m/B; Silent; VHS, DVD.** William S. Hart; Jane Novak; S.J. Bingham; ***D:*** Lambert Hillyer.

The Three Worlds of Gulliver 🦴🦴 1/2 *The Worlds of Gulliver* **1959** A colorful family version of the Jonathan Swift classic about an Englishman who discovers a fantasy land of small and giant people. Visual effects by Ray Harryhausen. **100m/C; VHS, DVD.** Kerwin Mathews; Jo Morrow; Basil Sydney; Mary Ellis; ***D:*** Jack Sher; ***W:*** Jack Sher; Arthur Ross; ***C:*** Wilkie Cooper; ***M:*** Bernard Herrmann.

The 3 Worlds of Gulliver 🦴🦴 **1960** Drastically shortened version of the novel "Gulliver's Travels" that has been made acceptable for children, focusing more on Ray Harryhausen's special effects than Swift's biting satire. **98m/C; DVD, Blu-Ray.** Kerwin Mathews; Jo Morrow; June Thorburn; Lee Patterson; Gregoire Aslan; ***D:*** Jack Sher; ***W:*** Jack Sher; Arthur Ross; ***C:*** Wilkie Cooper; ***M:*** Bernard Herrmann.

The Threepenny Opera 🦴🦴 *Die Dreigroschenoper; L'Opera De Quat'Sous; Beggars' Opera* **1931** A musical about the exploits of gangster Mack the Knife. Adapted from Bertolt Brecht's play and John Gay's "The Beggar's Opera." In German with English subtitles. **107m/B; VHS, DVD.** Rudolph Forster; Lotte Lenya; Carola Neher; Reinhold Schunzel; Fritz Rasp; Valeska Gert; Ernst Busch; ***D:*** G.W. Pabst; ***W:*** Ladislao Vajda; Bela Balazs; Leo Lania; ***C:*** Fritz Arno Wagner; ***M:*** Kurt Weill.

Threesome **WOOF!** **1994 (R)** Another Generation X movie that tries hard to be hip, but fails miserably. Due to a college administrative error, Alex (Boyle) winds up sharing a suite with two male roommates, Eddy (Charles) and Stuart (Baldwin). Despite having completely different personalities, they soon become best friends and form one cozy little group, with cozy being the key word. Sexual tension abounds—Alex wants Eddy who wants Stuart who wants Alex. Filled with pathetic dialogue (most of it relating to bodily functions and body parts) and shallow, obnoxious characters, this menage a trois film is a flop. **93m/C; VHS, DVD.** Lara Flynn Boyle; Stephen Baldwin; Josh Charles; Alexis Arquette; Mark Arnold; Martha Gehman; Michelle Matheson; ***D:*** Andrew Fleming; ***W:*** Andrew Fleming; ***C:*** Alexander Grusynski; ***M:*** Thomas Newman.

Threshold 🦴 **2003** A Sci-Fi Channel original, which means it's low-budget and bad in numerous ways. Space shuttle Oklahoma suffered meteorite damage on its last mission and an astronaut turns out to have been infected with insectoid-like aliens that need new hosts for each stage of their development. Drs. Horne and Bailey have been given 48 hours to find a way to stop the critters or Houston will be destroyed to contain the outbreak. **85m/C; DVD.** Nicholas Lea; Jamie Luner; Stephen J. Cannell; Steve Bacic; David Lipper; Teryl Rothery; Karl Pruner; ***D:*** Chuck Bowman; ***W:*** Kim LeMasters; ***C:*** Richard Wincent; ***M:*** Richard John Baker. **CABLE**

The Thrill Killers **WOOF!** *The Monsters Are Loose; The Maniacs Are Loose* **1965** Young murderous thugs rampage through Los Angeles suburbs, killing indiscriminately. Pretentious and exploitative. Sometimes shown with Hallucinogenic Hypo-Vision—a prologue announcing the special effect would be shown before the film, and on cue, hooded ushers would run through the theatre with cardboard axes. Weird. **82m/C; VHS, DVD.** Ray Dennis Steckler; Liz Renay; Ron Haydock; Atlas King; Gary Kent; Carolyn Brandt; Herb Robins; Ron Burr; George Morgan; Arch (Archie) Hall, Sr.; ***D:*** Ray Dennis Steckler; ***W:*** Ray Dennis Steckler; Gene Pollock; ***C:*** Joseph Mascelli; ***M:*** Andre Brummer.

Thrill of a Romance 🦴🦴 **1945** Johnson, an Army hero, meets Williams, a swimming instructor of all things, at a resort in the Sierra Nevadas. The only problem is that she's married. Typical swim-romance vehicle. **105m/C; VHS, DVD.** Esther Williams; Van Johnson; Frances Gifford; Henry Travers; Spring Byington; Lauritz Melchior; ***D:*** Richard Thorpe.

The Thrill of It All! 🦴🦴 1/2 **1963** An average housewife becomes a star of TV commercials, to the dismay of her chauvinist husband, a gynecologist. Fast and funny, with numerous acidic jokes about television sponsors and programs. **108m/C; VHS, DVD, Blu-Ray.** James Garner; Doris Day; Arlene Francis; Edward Andrews; Carl Reiner; Elliott Reid; Reginald Owen; Zasu Pitts; ***D:*** Norman Jewison; ***W:*** Carl Reiner; ***C:*** Russell Metty.

Thrill of the Kill 🦴 1/2 **2006** Kelly Holden (Appleby) asks crime novelist Graydon Jennings (Potter) to help find her sister's killer since the murder resembles the plot of one of his books. Kelly reads her sister's diary and learns that Alison (Di Blasi) was having an affair with a powerful married man who certainly didn't want his extramarital behavior revealed. Made for Lifetime. **96m/C; DVD.** Shiri Appleby; Chris Potter; Matt Cooke; Pina Di Blasi; Paul Hopkins; Kathleen Fee; ***D:*** Richard Roy; ***W:*** John Benjamin Martin; ***C:*** Daniel Villeneuve; ***M:*** James Gelfand. **CABLE**

Thrill Seekers 🦴🦴 1/2 *The Timeshifters* **1999 (PG-13)** Fast-pace helps overcome the plot holes in this sci-fi thriller. Merrick (Van Dien) is a tabloid reporter who is researching great past catastrophes. He discovers that aliens are traveling back in time (to earth's present) to take part in disasters of their own contrivance. Trying to prevent an arena fire, Merrick teams up with another reporter, Elizabeth (Bell), and they run into a couple of alien assassins (Saldana, Outerbridge). **92m/C; VHS, DVD.** Casper Van Dien; Catherine Bell; Peter Outerbridge; Theresa Saldana; Martin Sheen; Mimi Kuzyk; Lawrence Dane; Catherine Van Dien; ***D:*** Mario Azzopardi; ***W:*** Kurt Inderbitzin; Gay Walch; ***C:*** Derick Underschultz; ***M:*** Fred Mollin. **CABLE**

Thrilled to Death 🦴 1/2 **1988 (R)** An utterly naive husband and wife get caught in the middle of a lethal game when they befriend a scheming couple. **90m/C; VHS, DVD.** Blake Bahner; Krista Lane; Richard Maris; Christine Moore; ***D:*** Chuck Vincent.

Throne of Blood 🦴🦴🦴🦴 *Kumonosujo, Kumonosu-djo; Cobweb Castle; The Castle of the Spider's Web* **1957** Kurosawa's masterful adaptation of "Macbeth" transports the story to medieval Japan and the world of the samurai. Mifune and Chiaki are warriors who have put down a rebellion and are to be rewarded by their overlord. On their way to his castle they meet a mysterious old woman who prophesizes that Mifune will soon rule—but his reign will be short. She is dismissed as crazy but her prophesies come to pass. So steeped in Japanese style that it bears little resemblance to the Shakespearean original, this film is an incredibly detailed vision in its own right. In Japanese with English subtitles. **105m/B; VHS, DVD, Blu-Ray.** *JP* Toshiro Mifune; Isuzu Yamada; Takashi Shimura; Minoru Chiaki; Akira Kubo; ***D:*** Akira Kurosawa; ***W:*** Hideo Oguni; Shinobu Hashimoto; Ryuzo Kikushima; Akira Kurosawa; ***C:*** Asakazu Nakai; ***M:*** Masaru Sato.

Through a Glass Darkly 🦴🦴🦴 *Sasom I En Spegel* **1961** Oppressive interactions within a family sharing a holiday on a secluded island: a woman recovering from schizophrenia, her husband, younger brother, and her psychologist father. One of Bergman's most mysterious, upsetting and powerful films. In Swedish with English subtitles. Part of Bergman's Silence-of-God trilogy followed by "Winter Light" and "The Silence." **91m/B; VHS, DVD, Blu-Ray.** *SW* Harriet Andersson; Max von Sydow; Gunnar Bjornstrand; Lars Passgard; ***D:*** Ingmar Bergman; ***W:*** Ingmar Bergman; ***C:*** Sven Nykvist. Oscars '61: Foreign Film.

Through Naked Eyes 🦴🦴 1/2 **1987** Thriller about two people who spy on each other. They witness a murder and realize that someone else is watching them. What a coincidence. **91m/C; VHS, Streaming.** David Soul; Pam Dawber; ***D:*** John Llewellyn Moxey. **TV**

Through the Back Door 🦴🦴 1/2 **1921** After Jeanne's widowed mother marries a rich New Yorker, she leaves her daughter behind in Belgium in the care of her devoted nanny, who later lies that Jeanne has died so she can raise the girl. When WWI breaks out, the nanny sends the teenager to America for her own safety but Jeanne (Pickford) fears no one will believe her true identity. She takes a job as a maid on her stepfather's estate to be close to her mother

(Astor). **88m/B; Silent; DVD.** Mary Pickford; Gertrude Astor; Wilfred Lucas; Adolphe Menjou; Elinor Fair; ***D:*** Alfred E. Green; Jack Pickford; ***W:*** Gerald C. Duffy; Marion Fairfax; ***C:*** Charles Rosher.

Through the Fire 🦴🦴🦴 **2005** In a sort of mini-"Hoop Dreams," director Hock engagingly follows 18-year-old basketball player Sebastian Telfair during his senior year at Coney Island's Lincoln High School. A surprisingly level-headed Telfair debates whether to play college ball or risk jumping into the uncertainties of the NBA draft as his brother unsuccessfully did a few years before. But his path becomes clear when violence erupts at his family's projects and their chance to escape rests on him. **103m/C; DVD.** ***D:*** Jonathan Hock; ***C:*** Alastair Christopher; ***M:*** Duncan Sheik; Pete Miser.

Throw Down 🦴 **2000** Ex-Marine martial artist Max Finister (Wingster) comes home to find that drug pushers have taken over the neighborhood. The rest of the story follows the familiar formula. This is an unusually inept action picture. The fights (directed by Wingster) tend to be slow and director Cyrus Beyzavi tends to cut people's heads off. **90m/C; DVD.** La'Mard J. Wingster; Mark G. Young; Maribel Velez; Wendy Fajardo; John "Kato" Hollis; Patrick "Gun" Ryan; ***D:*** Cyrus Beyzavi; ***C:*** Mike Dolgetta.

Throw Momma from the Train 🦴🦴🦴 **1987 (PG-13)** DeVito plays a man, henpecked by his horrific mother, who tries to persuade his writing professor (Crystal) to exchange murders. DeVito will kill Crystal's ex-wife and Crystal will kill DeVito's mother. Only mama isn't going to be that easy to get rid of. Fast-paced and entertaining black comedy. Ramsey steals the film. Inspired by Hitchcock's "Strangers on a Train." **88m/C; VHS, DVD.** Danny DeVito; Billy Crystal; Anne Ramsey; Kate Mulgrew; Kim Greist; Branford Marsalis; Rob Reiner; Bruce Kirby; ***D:*** Danny DeVito; ***W:*** Stu Silver; ***C:*** Barry Sonnenfeld; ***M:*** David Newman.

A Throw of Dice 🦴🦴🦴 *Prapancha Pash; Throw of the Dice* **1929** Two rival gambling addicts, who happen to be kings, fall in love with the same woman and one loses both her and his kingdom when his rival cheats using loaded dice. Fairly epic for a silent film in that it has a "cast of thousands," including a great many elephants. **75m/B; DVD.** *GB* Seeta Devi; Himansu Rai; Charu Roy; Sarada Gupta; ***D:*** Franz Osten; ***C:*** Emil Schunemann.

Thugs 🦴 1/2 *Street Gun* **1996 (R)** A young criminal, looking to move up in the mob, agrees to take a job for a crime lord to rob his rival, only to find out he's been set up. With his friends dead and killers on his tail his only option left is to confront his former employer and settle things before he dies. **92m/C; DVD.** Justin Pagel; Michael Egan; Scott Cooke; ***D:*** Travis Milloy; ***W:*** Travis Milloy; ***C:*** Joel King; ***M:*** Michael Wandmacher.

Thugz WOOF! *Urban Killaz: Thugz* **2004 (R)** Sorry excuse for a urban gangsta flick with a typical story of rival drug gangs who invade each other's turf in a war when one of their members goes on a killing spree. **75m/C; DVD.** Zero Denero; Pikahsso Jones; Gugu G. Michaels; ***D:*** Gugu G. Michaels; ***W:*** Gugu G. Michaels.

Thumb Tripping 🦴🦴 **1972 (R)** A dated '60s/hippie film. Two flower children hitchhike and encounter all kinds of other strange people in their travels on the far-out roads. **94m/C; VHS, DVD.** Meg Foster; Michael Burns; Bruce Dern; Marianna Hill; Michael Conrad; Joyce Van Patten; ***D:*** Quentin Masters.

Thumbelina 🦴🦴 1/2 *Hans Christian Andersen's Thumbelina* **1994 (G)** Ornery little girl named Mia gets magically sucked into the pages of the "Thumbelina" storybook she's reading and finds all sorts of adventures. Loose adaptation of Hans Christian Andersen fairy tale from Bluth is lackluster, with acceptable songs. Not up to the level of recent Disney animated features, but pleasant enough for the kids. **86m/C; DVD, Blu-Ray.** ***V:*** Jodi Benson; Gary Imhoff; Charo; Gilbert Gottfried; Carol Channing; John Hurt; Will Ryan; June Foray; Kenneth Mars; ***D:*** Don Bluth; Gary Goldman; ***W:*** Don Bluth; ***M:*** William Ross; Barry Manilow; ***M:*** Barry Manilow; Jack Feldman; Bruce Sussman. Golden Raspberries '94: Worst Song ("Marry the Mole").

Thumbsucker 🦴🦴🦴 **2005 (R)** Seventeen year old Justin's (Pucci) underachieving, unfulfilled parents Mike (D'Onofrio) and Audrey (Swinton), saddled with their own baggage, are incapable of dealing with their son's embarrassing thumb-sucking habit. Justin's habit lands him in the office of the orthodontist/new-age guru Dr. Perry Lyman (Reeves), who uses hypnosis to break Justin's habit. But now without a coping mechanism Justin suffers from ADD. Newly armed with Ritalin and a pharmaceutically enhanced self-confidence, he becomes an arrogant, bullying monster. The beauty of this film is in the way Justin relates to the adults around him—all of whom range from eccentric to obscure and are played to perfection. **97m/C; DVD.** Lou Taylor Pucci; Tilda Swinton; Vince Vaughn; Vincent D'Onofrio; Keanu Reeves; Benjamin Bratt; Kelli Garner; Chase Offerle; ***D:*** Mike Mills; ***W:*** Mike Mills; ***C:*** Joaquin Baca-Asay.

Thunder Alley 🦴🦴 1/2 **1967** Annette teams up with Fabian again in this AIP stock car story. Daytona driver Fabian has a blackout during a race and causes a fatal crash. He and girlfriend McBain go on a thrill driving circuit, run by Murray. Annette is Murray's daughter and a swell stunt driver herself. To ingratiate himself with Annette, Fabian agrees to teach her boyfriend (Berlinger) how to be a pro racer and they become rivals. Annette's last role for AIP was a bit more mature than what she'd previously done and the flick overall is geared more towards action than boy/girl fun in the sun. **90m/C; DVD.** Fabian; Annette Funicello; Diane McBain; Warren Berlinger; Jan Murray; Stanley Adams; ***D:*** Richard Rush; ***W:*** Sy Salkowitz; ***C:*** Monroe Askins; ***M:*** Michael Curb.

Thunder and Lightning 🦴🦴 **1977 (PG)** A mismatched young couple chase a truckload of poisoned moonshine. Action-packed chases ensue. Nice chemistry between Carradine and Jackson. **94m/C; VHS, DVD.** David Carradine; Kate Jackson; Roger C. Carmel; Sterling Holloway; Eddie Barth; ***D:*** Corey Allen.

Thunder at the Border WOOF! **1966** Truly awful German-Yugoslavian co-production that's part of a western series based on the novels of Karl May. Old Firehand and his Apache friend Winnetou come to the rescue of a Mexican village that's besieged by bandits. A weak, rip-off plot with equally weak acting; dubbed into English. **98m/C; DVD.** *GE* Rod Cameron; Pierre Brice; Marie Versini; Todd Armstrong; Harald Leipnitz; ***D:*** Alfred Vohrer; ***W:*** Harald G. Petersson; ***C:*** Karl Lob; ***M:*** Peter Thomas.

Thunder Bay 🦴🦴🦴 **1953** Stewart and Duryea are a pair of Louisiana wildcat oil drillers who believe there is oil at the bottom of the Gulf of Mexico off the coast of the town of Port Felicity. They decide to construct an oil platform which the shrimp fisherman of the town believe will interfere with their livelihoods. Tensions rise between the two groups and violence seems likely. Action packed, with timely storyline as modern oil drillers fight to drill in waters that have historically been off-limits. **82m/C; VHS, DVD, Blu-Ray.** James Stewart; Joanne Dru; Dan Duryea; Gilbert Roland; Marcia Henderson; ***D:*** Anthony Mann; ***W:*** John Michael Hayes; ***C:*** William H. Daniels.

Thunder Birds 🦴🦴 1/2 **1942** Combat flight instructor Steve Britt (Foster) trains Brit cadet Stackhouse (Sutton) to become an ace fighter pilot in spite of the fact that they love the same women (Tierney). Fine performances and an intersting story keep this from being just another WW2-era flag-waver. **78m/C; DVD.** Gene Tierney; Preston Foster; John Sutton; Jack Holt; May Whitty; George Barbier; Richard Haydn; Reginald Denny; Ted North; C. Montague Shaw; Peter Lawford; ***D:*** William A. Wellman; ***W:*** Lamar Trotti; ***C:*** Ernest Palmer; ***M:*** David Buttolph.

Thunder County 🦴 1/2 *Cell Block Girls; Swamp Fever* **1974** Federal agents and drug runners are after a group of four convicts who have just escaped from prison. **78m/C; VHS, DVD.** Mickey Rooney; Ted Cassidy; Chris Robinson; Carol Locatell; Anya Ormsby; Phyllis Robinson; ***D:*** Chris Robinson; ***C:*** Jack Beckett; ***M:*** Jaime Mendoza-Nava.

Thunder in Carolina 🦴🦴 1/2 **1960** Stock car racer Mitch Cooper (Calhoun) is forced to take some time off after a bad crash. Bored, Mitch decides to teach eager young mechanic Les York (Gentry) how to drive and Les becomes obsessed with the track, neglecting his wife Rene (Hines). When Mitch and Rene start eyeballing each other, Les gets jealous and decides to rival Mitch in the big race. Features lots of footage of the Darlington, South Carolina Southern 500. **92m/C; DVD.** Rory Calhoun; Race Gentry; Damon Hines; Alan Hale; Ed McGrath; ***D:*** Paul Helmick; ***W:*** Alexander Richards; ***C:*** Joseph Brun; ***M:*** Walter Greene.

Thunder in Dixie 🦴🦴 **1965** Mickey (Millard) and Ticker (Bradford) are the best of friends until Ticker decides to take away Mickey's wife in revenge for the accidental death of his own girlfriend. After that their unofficial rivalry on the race car track heats up and becomes a little nasty. **76m/C; DVD.** Harry Millard; Mike Bradford; Judy Lewis; Nancy Berg; ***D:*** William T. Naud; ***W:*** George L. Baxt; ***C:*** Thomas E. Spalding; ***M:*** Elliot Lawrence.

Thunder in Paradise 🦴🦴 1/2 **1993 (PG-13)** R.J. Hurricane Spencer (Hogan) is a soldier of fortune who heads into Cuba to help a woman and child escape political imprisonment, using his high-tech, weapon-filled speedboat. He has to fight off a small army and manages to find a buried treasure as well. Simple-minded TV pilot. **104m/C; VHS, DVD.** Hulk Hogan; Robin Weisman; Chris Lemmon; Carol Alt; Patrick Macnee; Sam Jones; Charlotte Rae; ***D:*** Douglas Schwartz. **TV**

Thunder in Paradise 2 🦴 1/2 **1994 (PG)** Damsel sends up a distress signal and it's the Hulkster and his pal to the rescue. Unfortunately, their commando raid fails and now they need an escape plan. From the syndicated TV series. **90m/C; VHS, DVD.** Hulk Hogan; Chris Lemmon; Carol Alt; Patrick Macnee; ***D:*** Douglas Schwartz.

Thunder in Paradise 3 🦴 1/2 **1994 (PG-13)** Hogan is on a top secret mission to capture a drug lord who's holding his daughter hostage. **88m/C; VHS, DVD.** Hulk Hogan; Chris Lemmon; Carol Alt; Ashley Gorrell; ***D:*** Douglas Schwartz; ***W:*** Deborah Schwartz.

Thunder in the City 🦴🦴🦴 **1937** Robinson is an intense American promoter in the sales game who is sent to London by his employers to learn a more subdued way of doing business. Instead, he meets a pair of down-on-their-luck artistocrats whose only asset is an apparently worthless Rhodesian mine. Robinson, however, comes up with a way to promote the mine and get enough capital together to make it profitable. Good satire with Robinson well cast. Robinson wasn't taken with the script in its original form and persuaded his friend, playwright Robert Sherwood, to re-write it. **85m/B; VHS, DVD.** *GB* Edward G. Robinson; Nigel Bruce; Ralph Richardson; Constance Collier; ***D:*** Marion Gering; ***M:*** Miklos Rozsa.

Thunder In the Valley 🦴🦴 1/2 *Bob, Son of Battle* **1947** David MacAdam comes in second to his crusty father Adam's regard for his nasty but prize-winning herding dog, Red Wool. So David helps train the dog's chief rival, Bob, for a chance at a coveted trophy, setting up a father/son confrontation. Some beautiful Scottish highlands scenery. Loosely based on the Alfred Ollivant novel. **103m/C; DVD.** Lon (Bud) McCallister; Edmund Gwenn; Peggy Ann Garner; Reginald Owen; ***D:*** Louis King; ***W:*** Jerome Cady; ***C:*** Charles G. Clarke; ***M:*** Cyril Mockridge.

A Thunder of Drums 🦴🦴 **1961** Naive new cavalry officer Lt. McQuade (Hamilton) doesn't impress tough Capt. Maddocks (Boone) at their isolated Arizona outpost. A tragedy has McQuade volunteering to become a decoy in Maddocks' plan to bring a band of marauding Apaches out into the open. A grim, brutal western although lightweight Hamilton is miscast. **97m/C; DVD.** Richard Boone; George Hamilton; Luana Patten; Arthur O'Connell; Charles Bronson; Richard Chamberlain; Duane Eddy; Slim Pickens; James Douglas; ***D:*** Joseph M. Newman; ***W:*** James Warner Bellah; ***C:*** William W. Spencer; ***M:*** Harry Sukman.

Thunder on the Hill 🦴🦴 1/2 **1951** A rainstorm and flood means a stopover for convicted local murderess Valerie Carns (Blyth) and her guards at a rural English convent hospital. Sister Mary Bonaventure (Colbert) becomes convinced that Valerie is innocent and she can find the real killer, who may be closer than the nun knows. **84m/B; DVD, Blu-Ray.** Claudette Colbert; Ann Blyth; Anne Crawford; Philip Friend; Gladys Cooper; Connie Gilchrist; Michael Pate; Gavin Muir; Norma Varden; ***D:*** Douglas Sirk; ***W:*** Andrew Solt; Oscar Saul; ***C:*** William H. Daniels; ***M:*** Hans J. Salter.

Thunder Road 🦴🦴🦴 **1958 (PG)** Luke Doolin (Mitchum) comes home to Tennessee from Korea and takes over the family moonshine business, fighting both mobsters and federal agents. An exciting chase between Luke and the feds ends the movie with the appropriate bang. Robert Mitchum not only produced, wrote and starred in this best of the moonshine-running films, but also wrote the theme song "Whippoorwill" (which later became a radio hit). Mitchum's teenaged son, James, made his film debut as brother Robin Doolin and later starred in a similar movie "Moonrunners." A cult favorite. **92m/B; VHS, DVD, Blu-Ray.** Robert Mitchum; Jacques Aubuchon; Gene Barry; Keely Smith; Trevor Bardette; Sandra Knight; Jim Mitchum; Betsy Holt; Frances Koon; Mitchell Ryan; Peter Breck; ***D:*** Arthur Ripley; ***W:*** Robert Mitchum; Walter Wise; ***C:*** Alan Stensvold; ***M:*** Jack Marshall.

Thunder Soul 🦴🦴 1/2 **2010** Uplifting documentary that reunites a predominantly black inner-city Houston high school's award-winning stage band. Formed in the 1970s by mentor/bandleader Conrad O. Johnson Sr., whose idea was to have his Kashmere High School students play Top 40 hits and his own compositions (including the hit 'Texas Thunder Soul') rather than big band standards in regional and national competitions. Includes archival material and a 2008 reunion concert performed at the high school. **83m/C; DVD, Blu-Ray.** ***D:*** Mark Landsman; ***C:*** Sandra Chandler; ***M:*** Conrad O. Johnson, Sr.

Thunderball 🦴🦴 1/2 **1965 (PG)** The fourth installment in Ian Fleming's James Bond series finds 007 on a mission to thwart SPECTRE, which has threatened to blow up Miami by atomic bomb if 100 million pounds in ransom is not paid. One of the more tedious Bond entries but a big boxoffice success. Tom Jones sang the title song. Remade as "Never Say Never Again" in 1983 with Connery reprising his role as Bond after a 12-year absence. **125m/C; VHS, DVD, Blu-Ray.** *GB* Sean Connery; Claudine Auger; Adolfo Celi; Luciana Paluzzi; Rik van Nutter; Martine Beswick; Molly Peters; Guy Doleman; Bernard Lee; Lois Maxwell; Desmond Llewelyn; ***D:*** Terence Young; ***W:*** John Hopkins; Richard Maibaum; ***C:*** Ted Moore; ***M:*** John Barry. Oscars '65: Visual FX.

Thunderbirds 🦴 1/2 **2004 (PG)** Thunderbirds are go! Nobody's really sure why, since it's a 40-year-old British TV show about creepy puppets (remember "Supermarionation"?) rescuing other, equally creepy puppets. This version is live-action but it's still wooden. Billionaire ex-astronaut Jeff Tracy (Paxton) lives on an island in the South Pacific with his five sons (all named after astronauts) and five specially designed aircraft. He uses the Thunderbirds to run International Rescue. Telekinetic evil guy, The Hood (Kingsley), is bent on world domination (what else?) and strands Dad and the four older boys on their orbiting space station, leaving youngest wannabe Thunderbird Alan (Corbett) and a couple of his pals to save the day. The 10-and-under crowd may be persuaded to sit through this harmless but lackluster adventure. **94m/C; DVD, Blu-Ray.** Bill Paxton; Brady Corbet; Ben Kingsley; Anthony Edwards; Sophia Myles; Ron Cook; Genie Francis; Lou Hirsch; Nicola Walker; Johannes Zadrozny; Soren Fulton; Vanessa Anne Hudgens; Philip Winchester; Dhobi Oparei; Kyle Herbert; Dominic Colenso; Ben Torgersen; Lex Shrapnel; ***D:*** Jonathan Frakes; ***W:*** Peter Hewitt; William Osborne; Michael McCullers; ***C:*** Brendan Galvin; ***M:*** Hans Zimmer.

Thunderbolt & Lightfoot 🦴🦴🦴 **1974 (R)** Eastwood is an ex-thief on the run from his former partners (Kennedy and Lewis) who believe he's made off with the loot from their last job, the robbery of a government vault. He joins up with drifter Bridges, who helps him to escape. Later, Eastwood manages to convince Kennedy he doesn't know where the money is. Bridges then persuades the men that they should plan the same heist and rob the same government vault all over again, which they do. But their getaway doesn't go exactly as planned. All-around fine acting; notable is Bridges' scene dressed in drag. First film for director Cimino. **115m/C; VHS, DVD, Blu-Ray.** Clint Eastwood; Jeff Bridges; George Kennedy; Geoffrey Lewis; Gary Busey; ***D:*** Michael Cimino; ***W:*** Michael Cimino; ***C:*** Frank Stanley; ***M:*** Dee Barton.

Thunderheart **1992 (R)** Young FBI agent Kilmer is sent to an Oglala Sioux reservation to investigate a murder. He is himself part Sioux, but resents being chosen for the assignment because of it. Aided by a veteran partner (Shepard), Ray learns, professionally and personally, from a shrewd tribal police officer (well played by Greene). Set in the late '70s, the film is loosely based on actual events plaguing the violence-torn Native American community at that time. Great cinematography by Roger Deakins. Filmed on the Pine Ridge Reservation in South Dakota. Director Apted deals with the actual incidents this film is based on in his documentary about Leonard Peltier, "Incident at Oglala." **118m/C; VHS, DVD.** Val Kilmer; Sam Shepard; Graham Greene; Fred Ward; Fred Dalton Thompson; Sheila Tousey; Chief Ted Thin Elk; John Trudell; Dennis Banks; David Crosby; ***D:*** Michael Apted; ***W:*** John Fusco; ***C:*** Roger Deakins; ***M:*** James Horner.

Thunderhoof 1/2 **1948** Although the title sounds like a typical low-budget, kid-friendly western this is more adult fare with jealousy and betrayal (and a horse). Aging Texas rancher Scotty Mason wants to start his herd with a wild pinto stallion. He pursues the horse into Mexico, reluctantly accompanied by his young wife, Margarita, and a ranch hand who has other ideas about what he wants to capture. The triangle causes increasing tensions. **77m/B; DVD.** Preston Foster; Mary Stuart; William Bishop; ***D:*** Phil Karlson; ***W:*** Harold Jacob Smith; ***C:*** Henry Freulich; ***M:*** Mischa Bakaleinikoff.

Thundering Gunslingers **1944** A group of gunmen terrorizing townspeople finally meet their match in this Western. **91m/B; VHS, DVD.** Buster Crabbe; Al "Fuzzy" St. John; Frances Gladwin; Charles "Blackie" King; Jack Ingram; Kermit Maynard; Karl Hackett; ***D:*** Sam Newfield; ***W:*** Fred Myton; ***C:*** Robert Cline.

Thunderstruck **2012 (PG)** Kevin Durant plays himself in this predictable sports comedy in which he magically trades basketball skills with a fan who can't play to save his life. **94m/C; DVD, Blu-Ray, Streaming.** Kevin Durant; Taylor Gray; James Belushi; Brandon T. Jackson; Larramie Doc Shaw; ***D:*** John Whitesell; ***W:*** Eric Champnella; Jeff Farley; ***C:*** Shawn Maurer; ***M:*** Ali Dee. **VIDEO**

Thurgood **2011** Laurence Fishburne stars in a one-man stage play, written by George Stevens Jr., based on the life of civil rights lawyer/pioneer Thurgood Marshall, which was filmed live at the Eisenhower Theater at the Kennedy Center. Among his accomplishments, Marshall was the chief counsel for the N.A.A.C.P. and the first black justice of the Supreme Court. A compelling Fishburne brings out Marshall's enjoyment of life and his skills as a raconteur through the anecdotes he tells. **105m/C; DVD, Blu-Ray.** Laurence Fishburne; ***D:*** Michael Stevens; ***W:*** George Stevens, Jr.; ***M:*** Rob Mathes. **CABLE**

Thursday's Child **1943** A child's success in films causes trouble for her family. Melodramatic and sappy, but Howes, as the kid, is excellent. One of Granger's early supporting roles. **95m/B; VHS, DVD.** *GB* Stewart Granger; Sally Ann Howes; Wilfred Lawson; Kathleen O'Regan; Eileen Bennett; Marianne Davis; Gerhard Kempinski; Felix Aylmer; Margaret Yarde; Vera Bogetti; Percy Walsh; Ronald Shiner; ***D:*** Rodney Ackland; ***W:*** Rodney Ackland; Donald Macardle; ***C:*** Desmond Dickinson.

THX 1138 **1971 (PG)** In the dehumanized world of the future, people live in underground cities run by computer, are force-fed drugs to keep them passive, and no longer have names—just letter/number combinations (Duvall is THX 1138). Emotion is also outlawed and when the computer-matched couple THX 1138 and LUH 3417 discover love, they must battle the computer system to escape. George Lucas' first film, which was inspired by a student film he did at USC. **88m/C; VHS, DVD.** Robert Duvall; Donald Pleasence; Maggie McOmie; ***D:*** George Lucas; ***W:*** George Lucas; ***M:*** Lalo Schifrin.

Tiara Tahiti **1962** Intrigue, double-cross, romance, and violence ensue when two old army acquaintances clash in Tahiti. Very fine performances from the two leading men. **100m/C; VHS, DVD.** James Mason; John Mills; Claude Dauphin; Rosenda Monteros; Herbert Lom; ***D:*** Ted Kotcheff.

The Tic Code 1/2 **1999 (R)** Twelve-year-old Miles (Marquette) aspires to be a jazz pianist but must practice at the local bar because his single mom Laura (Draper) can't afford a piano. But Miles has a bigger problem—he suffers from the misunderstood Tourette's syndrome, which brings him close to his idol, sax player Tyrone (Hines), who is similarly afflicted. Soon Tyrone is also playing some sweet music with Laura but the trio are on shaky ground since Tyrone can't deal with his illness. **91m/C; VHS, DVD.** Gregory Hines; Polly Draper; James McCaffrey; Christopher Marquette; Carol Kane; Bill Nunn; Tony Shalhoub; Desmond Robertson; Fisher Stevens; Camryn Manheim; David Johansen; ***D:*** Gary Winick; ***W:*** Polly Draper; ***C:*** Wolfgang Held; ***M:*** Michael Wolff.

Tick... Tick... Tick 1/2 **1970** Jimmy Price is the newly-elected black sheriff in a Southern town that is distinctly divided into two communities by race. Price plays no favorites and gets into trouble when he arrests a young white man on manslaughter charges. The young man's father then decides to organize a mob to break his son out of jail and Price has to depend on some reluctant locals for help. **97m/C; DVD.** Jim Brown; George Kennedy; Fredric March; Lynn Carlin; Don Stroud; Janet MacLachlan; Bernie Casey; Mills Watson; ***D:*** Ralph Nelson; ***W:*** James Lee Barrett; ***C:*** Loyal Griggs; ***M:*** Jerry Styner.

Tick Tock **2000 (R)** In Bakersfield, California, trophy wife Rachel (Ward) and her pal Carla (Minter) plot to get rid of wealthy hubby (Dukes). That's only the beginning of a plot that stacks trick upon trick, double-cross upon double-cross. Think "Blood Simple" lite. It's a delightful guilty pleasure made all the more enjoyable by polished production values. **93m/C; DVD.** Megan Ward; Kristin Minter; Linden Ashby; John Ratzenberger; David Dukes; ***D:*** Kevin S. Tenney; ***W:*** Kevin S. Tenney; ***C:*** Jack Conroy; ***M:*** Dennis Michael Tenney.

Tick Tock Lullaby **2007** Sasha (Gornick) and her girlfriend Maya (Cassidy) are serious about having a baby but they want to conceive the old-fashioned way, which means one of them has to find a heterosexual sex partner. But their problems aren't much different from those of their straight friends as the road to parenthood is paved with obstacles and questionable intentions. The brief run-time keeps the plot moving. **73m/C; DVD.** *GB* Lisa Gornick; Raquel Cassidy; Sarah Patterson; Joanna Bending; William Bowry; ***D:*** Lisa Gornick; ***W:*** Lisa Gornick; ***C:*** Inge Blackman; ***M:*** Mat Davidson.

Ticker 1/2 **2001 (R)** San Francisco detective Sizemore is tracking mad bomber Hopper (reprising his "Speed" role to little effect) aided by bomb squad leader Seagal. Nothing that hasn't been done a zillion times before (and much better). **92m/C; VHS, DVD.** Tom Sizemore; Steven Seagal; Nasir Jones; Jaime Pressly; Dennis Hopper; Chilli; Peter Greene; ***Cameo(s):*** Ice-T; ***D:*** Albert Pyun; ***W:*** Paul B. Margolis. **VIDEO**

The Ticket 1/2 **2017** One day, James (Stevens) wakes up with his vision unexpectedly restored and it becomes clear that wife Sam (Akerman) has been hiding things, such as the fact that son Jonah (Gaertner) is being bullied. At the office, James finds co-worker Jessica (Bishe) attractive. She shares the feeling as he becomes more successful by essentially conning people to sell their real estate. In all he does, James shows a superficiality that may have increased after becoming sighted again. Stevens' shines but the story is dim. **97m/C; DVD.** Dan Stevens; Malin Akerman; Ekaterina Samsonov; Kerry Bishe; Oliver Platt; ***D:*** Ido Fluk; ***W:*** Ido Fluk; ***C:*** Zack Galler; ***M:*** Danny Bensi; Saunder Jurriaans.

Ticket of Leave Man **1937** London's most dangerous killer fronts a charitable organization designed to help reform criminals. It actually steers them into a crime syndicate that cheats philanthropists out of their fortunes. **71m/B; VHS, DVD.** *GB* Tod Slaughter; John Warwick; Marjorie Taylor; Robert Adair; Peter Gawthorne; Jenny Lynn; Norman Pierce; ***D:*** George King; ***W:*** H.F. Maltby; A.R. Rawlinson; ***C:*** Hone Glendinning; ***M:*** Jack Beaver.

Ticket to Heaven **1981 (PG)** A young man, trying to deal with the painful breakup of a love affair, falls under the spell of a quasi-religious order. His friends and family, worried about the cult's influence, have him kidnapped in order for him to be de-programmed. Mancuso is excellent, as are his supporting players Rubinek and Thomson. **109m/C; VHS, DVD.** *CA* Nick Mancuso; Meg Foster; Kim Cattrall; Saul Rubinek; R.H. Thomson; Jennifer Dale; Guy Boyd; Paul Soles; ***D:*** Ralph L. (R.L.) Thomas; ***W:*** Anne Cameron; ***C:*** Richard Leiterman; ***M:*** Micky Erbe. Genie '82: Actor (Mancuso), Film, Support. Actor (Rubinek).

Ticking Clock **2010 (R)** Investigative reporter Lewis Hicks gets involved in a serial killer case after his girlfriend is murdered and he becomes a suspect. He finds the killer and takes his journal, which ties all the dead women to orphaned James. Then a time travel twist jars the thriller into foolishness. **101m/C; DVD.** Cuba Gooding, Jr.; Neal McDonough; Austin Abrams; Yancey Arias; Dane Rhodes; Danielle Nicolet; Veronica Berry; ***D:*** Ernie Barbarash; ***W:*** John Turman; ***C:*** Phil Parmet; ***M:*** Richard Friedman. **VIDEO**

Tickle Me 1/2 **1965** An unemployed rodeo star finds work at an all-girl health spa and dude ranch. He falls in love with a young lady who has a treasure map and keeps her safe from the evil men who want her fortune. For die-hard Elvis fans only. **90m/C; VHS, DVD.** Elvis Presley; Julie Adams; Jack Mullaney; ***D:*** Norman Taurog.

Tickled **2016 (R)** David Farrier had no idea what he stumbled into when investigating the company behind a series of online shorts billed as "competitive tickling" videos. Simple inquiries into their origins spurred homophobic, lawsuit-threatening responses. Naturally, Farrier wanted to dig even deeper, discovering that this company used these tactics before, threatening to shame and legally destroy anyone who dared criticize them. The behavior has even continued in the wake of this often-fascinating documentary. The idea that something as simple as videos of men being tickled online could lead to such drama makes for one of the most interesting non-fiction films stories of 2016. **92m/C; DVD.** David Farrier; Dylan Reeve; ***D:*** David Farrier; Dylan Reeve; ***C:*** Dominic Fryer; ***M:*** Rodi Kirkcaldy; Florian Zwietnig.

Ticks 1/2 *Infested* **1993 (R)** Mammoth mutant killer insects terrorize a Northern California campground! The predatory woodticks are the victims of steroids dumped in the water supply and a group of unwary teen campers fall prey to their deadly venom! And if that's not bad enough, a forest fire breaks out, trapping the teens! **85m/C; DVD, Blu-Ray.** Ami Dolenz; Rosalind Allen; Alfonso Ribeiro; Peter Scolari; ***D:*** Tony Randel; ***W:*** Brent Friedman; ***C:*** Steve Grass; ***M:*** Christopher L. Stone.

Tide of Empire 1/2 **1929** Convoluted, melodramatic silent. 1840s California is a land of Spanish grandees, ranchos, and missions until the 1848 Gold Rush brings gringo prospectors flooding in. Dermot D'Arcy (Keene) wins the Guerrero rancho in a horse race and then tries to win the hand of Josephita (Adoree), the daughter of its former owner. She objects and Dermot nobly gives her back the deed to return to the gold fields but they'll meet again when her brother is falsely accused of gold robbery. **72m/B; Silent; DVD.** Tom Keene; Renee Adoree; George Fawcett; William "Buster" Collier, Jr.; Fred Kohler, Sr.; Paul Hurst; James Bradbury, Sr.; ***D:*** Allan Dwan; ***W:*** Joe Farnham; Waldemar Young; ***C:*** Merritt B. Gerstad.

Tideland **2005 (R)** First 10-year-old Jeliza-Rose's (Ferland) junkie mom (Tilly) overdoses in L.A., prompting her junkie dad (Bridges) to drag her to a middle-of-nowhere Texas farmhouse where he, of course, overdoses, leaving the girl to retreat into a not-so-pleasant fantasy world with dear-old-dead-dad's corpse nearby. When not conversing with her headless dolls, she wanders the grassy fields near the train tracks, where she runs into some odd neighbors—a taxidermist who, um, helps Jeliza-Rose with the dead dad problem, and the woman's brother, a mentally-challenged man-child whose relationship with the young Jeliza-Rose gets a little creepy. Ferland's excellent performance stands out in what is otherwise an unredeemable mess. Based on Mitch Cullin's 2005 novel. **122m/C; DVD, Blu-Ray.** *CA GB* Jodelle Ferland; Janet McTeer; Brendan Fletcher; Jeff Bridges; Jennifer Tilly; ***D:*** Terry Gilliam; ***W:*** Terry Gilliam; Tony Grisoni; ***C:*** Nicola Pecorini; ***M:*** Mychael Danna; Jeff Danna.

Tie Me Up! Tie Me Down! 1/2 *Atame!* **1990 (NC-17)** A young psychiatric patient kidnaps a former porno actress he has always had a crush on, and holds her captive, certain that he can convince her to love him. Black comedy features a fine cast and is well directed. At least one fairly explicit sex scene and the bondage theme caused the film to be X-rated, although it was originally released unrated by the distributor. In Spanish with English subtitles. **105m/C; VHS, DVD, Blu-Ray.** *SP* Victoria Abril; Antonio Banderas; Loles Leon; Francisco Rabal; Julieta Serrano; Maria Barranco; Rossy de Palma; ***D:*** Pedro Almodóvar; ***W:*** Pedro Almodóvar; ***C:*** Jose Luis Alcaine; ***M:*** Ennio Morricone.

The Tie That Binds **1995 (R)** Insipid thriller is a cheap imitation of its cousin, "The Hand that Rocks the Cradle" (made by the same producers), but what the former movie did to the nanny business, this flick does to a whole genre. Leanne and John Netherwood (Hannah and Carradine) are psycho parents out to reclaim their daughter from the lame-brain yuppie couple (Spano and Kelly) who adopted her. Out of all the children there, they choose the one who likes to sleep with a butcher knife under her pillow. Duh! Every "family in danger from psychotic" cliche is employed in a vain attempt to build suspense for the silly conclusion. Dismal directorial debut of screenwriter Strick. **98m/C; VHS, DVD, Blu-Ray.** Daryl Hannah; Keith Carradine; Moira Kelly; Vincent Spano; Julia Devin; Ray Reinhardt; Cynda Williams; ***D:*** Wesley Strick; ***W:*** Michael Auerbach; ***C:*** Bobby Bukowski; ***M:*** Graeme Revell.

Tiefland 1/2 **1944** Melodrama based on the libretto for D'Abert's opera about a gypsy dancer and her loves. Unreleased until 1954, this film is the last of Riefenstahl's career; she subsequently turned to still photography. In German with English subtitles. **98m/B; VHS, DVD.** *GE* Leni Riefenstahl; Franz Eichberger; Bernard Minetti; Maria Koppenhofer; Luise Rainer; ***D:*** Leni Riefenstahl.

Tierra *Earth* **1995** Metaphysical messiness. Mystery exterminator Angel (Gomez) comes to Aragon, a land of red soil and lightning strikes, to fumigate the woodlice infesting the vineyards. He recruits some locals and gypsies to help him out while becoming involved with a couple of women—shy Angela (Suarez) and hot Mari (Klein). But Angel is also literally haunted by an alter ego'a situation that no doubt has some deep meaning that is never very clear. But neither is the rest of the movie. Spanish with subtitles. **122m/C; VHS, DVD, Blu-Ray.** *SP* Carmelo Gomez; Emma Suarez; Silke Klein; Karra Elejalde; Nancho Novo; Txema Blasco; ***D:*** Julio Medem; ***W:*** Julio Medem; ***C:*** Javier Aguirresarobe; ***M:*** Alberto Iglesias.

Ties That Bind **2006** Tacky thriller with "Fatal Attraction" overtones. A married couple rent out the guest house on their newly-purchased property but their tenant is soon making obvious plays for the hubby and won't take no for an answer. **90m/C; DVD.** Nicole de Boer; Brian Krause; Sonya Salomaa; Francoise Robertson; Dean Marshall; John Maclaren; ***D:*** Terry Ingram; ***W:*** Andy Callahan; ***M:*** Clinton Shorter. **CABLE**

Tieta of Agreste **1996** After many years, wealthy Tieta (Braga) returns to her village with her stepdaughter and immediately causes havoc for her greedy family. Based on a novel by Jorge Amado. Portuguese with subtitles. **140m/C; VHS, DVD.** *BR* Sonia Braga; Marilia Pera; Zeze Motta; Jorge Amado; ***D:*** Carlos Diegues; ***W:*** Carlos Diegues; ***C:*** Edgar Moura; ***M:*** Caetano Veloso.

Tiger and the Pussycat 1/2 *Il Tigre* **1967 (R)** A successful Italian businessman's infatuation with an attractive American art student leads him to marital and financial woes. **110m/C; VHS, DVD.** Ann-Margret; Vittorio Gassman; Eleanor Parker; ***D:*** Dino Risi.

The Tiger and the Snow 1/2 *La Tigre e la Neve* **2005** First it was the Holocaust and now Benigni uses the backdrop of the war in Iraq, circa 2003, for his absurdist tragicomedy romance. Exuberant Roman poet Attilio (Benigni) passes himself off as an aid worker and heads to Baghdad when he discovers Vittoria (Brachi), the woman he loves, has been seriously injured in a bombing. Italian with subtitles. **110m/C; DVD.** *IT* Roberto Benigni; Nicoletta Braschi; Jean Reno; Tom Waits; Emilia Fox; ***D:*** Roberto Benigni; ***W:*** Roberto Benigni; Vincenzo Cerami; ***C:*** Fabio Cianchetti; ***M:*** Nicola Povani.

Tiger Bay 1/2 **1933** Liu Chang runs a nightclub in some nameless South American country where she defies the local protection racket run by Olaf. Young visiting Brit Michael falls for Liu's English ward Letty, who's being threatened by Olaf. **70m/B; DVD.** *GB* Anna May Wong; Henry Victor; Victor Garland; Rene Ray; Margaret Yarde; Lawrence Grossmith; ***D:*** J. Elder Wills; ***W:*** John Quin; ***C:*** Robert Martin.

Tiger Bay **1959** A young Polish sailor, on leave in Cardiff, murders his unfaithful girlfriend. Lonely ten-year-old Gillie sees the crime and takes the murder weapon, thinking it will make her more popular with her peers. Confronted by a police detective, she convincingly lies but eventually the sailor finds Gillie and kidnaps her, hoping to keep her quiet until he can get aboard his ship. A delicate relationship evolves between the child and the killer as she tries to help him escape and the police close in. Marks Hayley Mills' first major role and one of her finest performances. **107m/B; VHS, DVD.** *GB* John Mills; Horst Buchholz; Hayley Mills; Yvonne Mitchell; Megs Jenkins; Anthony Dawson; Kenneth Griffith; Michael Anderson, Jr.; ***D:*** J. Lee Thompson; ***W:*** John Hawkesworth; ***C:*** John Hawkesworth; ***M:*** Laurie Johnson.

Tiger Claws 1/2 **1991 (R)** The pretty, petite Rothrock has been called the female Bruce Lee. Perhaps, but at least he got a good script every once in a while. This time Rothrock's a kung-fu cop investigating the strange ritual-murders of martial-arts champions. **93m/C; VHS, DVD.** Cynthia Rothrock; Bolo Yeung; Jalal Merhi; ***D:*** Kelly Markin; ***W:*** J. Stephen Maunder; ***C:*** Curtis Petersen; Mark Willis.

Tiger Eyes 1/2 **2013 (PG-13)** Low-key teen drama adapted by Blume from her 1981 novel along with her son, Lawrence, who also directed. When her husband is killed in a robbery, distraught Gwen (Johnson) moves to New Mexico to stay with her sister along with young son Jason and 17-year-old daughter, Davey (Holland). With her mother lost to grief and depression, Davey's own struggles are only recognized by enigmatic Native American Wolf (Means, son of Russell) as the two begin a friendship and tentative flirtation. Script is connect-the-dots, but the performances are solid and sometimes heartbreaking. **93m/C; On Demand.** Willa Holland; Tatanka Means; Amy Jo Johnson; Cynthia Stevenson; Elise Eberle; Russell Means; Lucien Dale; Forrest Frye; ***D:*** Lawrence Blume; ***W:*** Lawrence Blume; Judy Blume; ***C:*** Seamus Tierney; ***M:*** Nathan Larson.

Tiger Heart 1/2 **1996 (PG-13)** Teenaged karate champ Eric Chase (Roberts) is looking forward to a lazy summer with girlfriend Stephanie (Lyons) before heading off to college. But when his neighborhood comes under attack from an unscrupulous developer and Stephanie runs afoul of his goons, Eric decides to take action. **90m/C; DVD, On Demand.** Ted Jan Roberts; Jennifer Lyons; Robert LaSardo; Carol Potter; Timothy Williams; ***D:*** Georges Chamchoum; ***W:*** William Applegate, Jr.; ***M:*** John Gonzalez.

The Tiger Hunter 1/2 **2017** A likable immigration comedy centered on an Indian man's hope to build a better life in 1979 America. Though Sami Malik (Pudi) has an engineering degree, he cannot get a real job in his village. Accepting a job offer in Chicago, Sami's original position falls through after he gets there. Landing an entry-level job, he tries to fit in with higher level engineers like Kenneth (Page) so he can work on important projects. Through his work, Sami also hopes to impress the woman he has long been in love with. This lighthearted comedy succeeds in transcending stereotypes but is equally predictable. **94m/C; DVD, Blu-Ray.** Danny Pudi; Rizwan Manji; Jon Heder; Karen David; Kevin Pollak; ***D:*** Lena Khan; ***W:*** Lena Khan; Sameer Asad Gardezi; ***C:*** Patrice Lucien Cochet; ***M:*** Amy Correia; Paul Masvidal.

Tiger of the Seven Seas **1962** A female pirate takes over her father's command and embarks on adventures on the high seas. Generous portions of action, intrigue, and romance. Sequel to "Queen of the Pirates." **90m/C; VHS, DVD.** *IT FR* Gianna Maria Canale; Anthony Steel; Maria Grazia Spina; Ernesto Calindri; ***D:*** Luigi Capuano.

Tiger Shark **1932** San Diego tuna fisherman Mike (Robinson) saves best pal Pipes (Arlen) but loses his hand to a shark and it's replaced by a hook. When another friend is killed at sea, Mike asks the man's impoverished daughter Quita (Johann) to marry him (though she doesn't love him) so he can look after her. Quita and Pipes find themselves attracted to each other and Mike gets jealous and vengeful. But Mike has really bad luck with sharks. **80m/B; DVD.** Edward G. Robinson; Richard Arlen; Zita Johann; J. Carrol Naish; Leila Bennett; William Ricciardi; ***D:*** Howard Hawks; ***W:*** Wells Root; ***C:*** Gaetano Antonio "Tony" Gaudio.

Tiger Town 1/2 **1983 (G)** A baseball player, ending an illustrious career with the Detroit Tigers, sees his chance of winning a pennant slipping away. A young fan, however, proves helpful in chasing that elusive championship. **76m/C; VHS, DVD.** Roy Scheider; Justin Henry; Ron McLarty; Bethany Carpenter; Noah Moazezi; ***D:*** Alan Shapiro; ***C:*** Robert Elswit. **CABLE**

A Tiger Walks 1/2 **1964** A savage tiger escapes from a circus and local children start a nationwide campaign to save its life. Notable for its unflattering portrayal of America's heartland and small town dynamics. Radical departure from most Disney films of the period. **88m/C; VHS, DVD.** Sabu; Pamela Franklin; Brian Keith; Vera Miles; Kevin Corcoran; Peter Brown; Una Merkel; Frank McHugh; Edward Andrews; ***D:*** Norman Tokar; ***M:*** Buddy (Norman Dale) Baker.

Tiger Warsaw 1/2 *The Tiger* **1987 (R)** A young man returns to the town where he once lived, before he shot his father. He hopes to sort out his life and repair family problems. Muddled and sappy. **92m/C; VHS, DVD.** Patrick Swayze; Barbara Williams; Piper Laurie; Bobby DiCicco; Kaye Ballard; Lee Richardson; Mary McDonnell; ***D:*** Amin Qamar Chaudhri.

The Tiger Woods Story 1/2 **1998 (PG-13)** Kain stars as the young man who, at 21, became the youngest player ever to win the Masters Golf Tournament. Based on the book "Tiger" by John Strege. **103m/C; VHS, Streaming.** Khalil Kain; Keith David; Freda Foh Shen; ***D:*** LeVar Burton; ***W:*** Takashi Bufford. **CABLE**

Tigerland **2000 (R)** Irish newcomer Farrell made a big (and deserved) splash as Army draftee Roland Bozz, one of a group of grunts at the final stage of infantry training at Fort Polk, Louisiana in 1971. The title refers to the wilderness area designed for jungle combat simulation before the newbies are shipped out to Nam. But the rebellious, cynical Bozz gets away with defying every rule thrown at him to the disbelief of the others in the platoon. Familiar story but the ensemble cast is right on the mark and director Schumacher keeps tight control in this old-fashioned low-budget drama. **101m/C; VHS, DVD.** Colin Farrell; Matthew Davis; Clifton (Gonzalez) Collins, Jr.; Tom Guiry; Russell Richardson; Cole Hauser; Shea Whigham; ***D:*** Joel Schumacher; ***W:*** Ross Klaven; Michael McGruther; ***C:*** Matthew Libatique; ***M:*** Nathan Larson.

Tigers Are Not Afraid *Vuelven* **2019** In a contemporary Mexican city decimated by drug wars, a group of orphaned young boys lives on a rooftop and survives by stealing supplies. Led by angry Shine (Lopez), they become entangled in local crime politics when he steals thug Caco's (Guerrero) phone. Soon after, young Estrella (Lara) comes home from school to find her mother is missing. Holding three wishes and followed by something in the shadows, Estrella joins the boys as the group struggles to stay alive. A great mesh of fantasy, the supernatural, and harsh reality, the film expresses the horrors of the Mexican drug war through its outstanding young cast. **83m/C; DVD, Blu-Ray.** Paola Lara; Juan Ramon Lopez; Hanssel Casillas; Ianis Guerrero; Tenoch Huerta; ***D:*** Issa Lopez; ***W:*** Issa Lopez; ***C:*** Juan Jose Saravia; ***M:*** Vince Pope.

The Tiger's Claw *Der Tiger Akbar* **1951** Bizarre romance in which a man must compete for the affections of a circus performer with the jealous tiger she's raised from a cub. Apparently kitty doesn't want a rival for hugs and is becoming increasingly dangerous to people, but his owner is blind to it. **80m/B; DVD.** *GE* Harry Piel; Friedl Hardt; ***D:*** Harry Piel; ***W:*** Harry Piel; ***C:*** Bruno Timm; ***M:*** Fritz Wenneis.

The Tiger's Tale **2006 (R)** Liam O'Leary (Gleeson) has risen from humble beginnings to become a wealthy property owner in Dublin with a big house, a trophy wife (Cattrall), and a rebellious teen son (played by Gleeson's own son). Liam starts seeing a sinister doppelganger (though no one believes him) who takes over his life. Liam winds up at a homeless shelter while the double comes up against the realities of a bankrupt business. The answers to the mystery turn out to be mundane. Title refers to the 'celtic tiger' term coined to describe Ireland's economic boom. **107m/C; DVD.** *IR* Brendan Gleeson; Kim Cattrall; Sinead Cusack; Ciaran Hinds; Brian Gleeson; Sean McGinley; ***D:*** John Boorman; ***W:*** John Boorman; ***C:*** Seamus Deasy; ***M:*** Stephen McKeon.

Tightrope **1984 (R)** Police inspector Wes Block pursues a killer of prostitutes in New Orleans' French Quarter. The film is notable both as a thriller and as a fascinating vehicle for Eastwood, who experiments with a disturbing portrait of a cop with some peculiarities of his own. **115m/C; VHS, DVD, Blu-Ray.** Clint Eastwood; Genevieve Bujold; Dan Hedaya; Jennifer Beck; Alison Eastwood; Randi Brooks; Regina Richardson; Jamie Rose; ***D:*** Richard Tuggle; ***C:*** Bruce Surtees; ***M:*** Lennie Niehaus.

The Tigress 1/2 **1993 (R)** In 1920s Berlin two con artists set out to scam a rich American using sex as a lure. Things don't go as planned. Also available in an unrated version. **89m/C; VHS, DVD.** *GE* Valentina Vargas; James Remar; George Peppard; ***D:*** Karin Howard; ***W:*** Karin Howard.

Til There Was You 1/2 **1996 (PG-13)** You know what most great romance movies have in common? The couples actually meet each other before the end of the movie. Not here. That's one of the reasons this one isn't even good. Ghostwriter Gwen (Tripplehorn) and architect Nick (McDermott), although seemingly destined for one another, have more near-misses than a drunken, near-sighted airline pilot. They're shown in the same room, in adjoining rooms, leaving a room as soon as the other enters, etc., etc. Meanwhile, minor characters appear, speak some ham-fisted dialogue and then disappear. This happens for 20 years. Then they meet and the movie is (thankfully) over. Parker, however, does an excellent job as a rehab-addicted former child star who has ties to both characters. Feature directorial debut for Winant. **113m/C; VHS, DVD.** Dylan McDermott; Sarah Jessica Parker; Jeanne Tripplehorn; Jennifer Aniston; Ken Olin; Craig Bierko; Nina Foch; Alice Drummond; Christine Ebersole; Michael Tucker; Patrick Malahide; Kasi Lemmons; Karen Allen; ***D:*** Scott Winant; ***W:*** Winnie Holzman; ***C:*** Bobby Bukowski; ***M:*** Miles Goodman; Terence Blanchard.

Till Death Do Us Part 1/2 **1972 (PG)** Three married couples spend a weekend at a counseling retreat, unaware that the proprietor is a murderous maniac. **77m/C; VHS, DVD.** James Keach; Claude Jutra; Matt Craven; ***D:*** Timothy Brand.

Till Human Voices Wake Us 1/2 **2002 (R)** Confusing romantic drama about memory. Psych professor Sam Franks (Pearce) is going home for his dad's funeral. He has an odd encounter with Ruby (Bonham Carter), rescues her from a suicide leap off a bridge, and discovers she has amnesia. Efforts to unlock Ruby's memories help Sam with his own teenaged tragedy that revolves around his girlfriend drowning. However, the story never does make much sense. **97m/C; VHS, DVD.** *AU* Guy Pearce; Helena Bonham Carter; Frank Gallacher; Lindley Joyner; Brooke Harmon; Peter Curtin; Margot Knight; Anthony Martin; Dawn Klingberg; ***D:*** Michael Petroni; ***W:*** Michael Petroni; ***C:*** Roger Lanser; ***M:*** Dale Cornelius.

Till Murder Do Us Part 1/2 *A Woman Scorned: The Betty Broderick Story* **1992 (PG-13)** Based on the true story of Betty Broderick, an obsessively devoted wife and mother whose husband leaves her for another woman. Even after a bitter divorce, Betty refuses to let go. Until she commits murder. **95m/C; VHS, DVD.** Meredith Baxter; Stephen Collins; Michelle Johnson; Kelli Williams; Stephen (Steve) Root; ***D:*** Dick Lowry. **TV**

Till the Clouds Roll By 1/2 **1946** An all-star, high-gloss musical biography of songwriter Jerome Kern, that, in typical Hollywood fashion, bears little resemblance to the composer's life. Filled with wonderful songs from his Broadway hit. **137m/C; VHS, DVD.** Robert Walker; Van Heflin; Judy Garland; Frank Sinatra; Lucille Bremer; Kathryn Grayson; June Allyson; Dinah Shore; Lena Horne; Virginia O'Brien; Tony Martin; ***D:*** Richard Whorf; ***W:*** Myles Connolly; Jean Holloway; ***C:*** Harry Stradling, Sr.; ***M:*** Conrad Salinger; Roger Edens; Lennie Hayton.

Till the End of Time 1/2 **1946** Three GIs have trouble adjusting to civilian life in their home town after WWII. Fine performances and excellent pacing. Popular title song. Adapted from "They Dream of Home" by Niven Busch. **105m/C; DVD.** Robert Mitchum; Guy Madison; Bill Williams; Dorothy McGuire; William Gargan; Tom Tully; ***D:*** Edward Dmytryk; ***W:*** Allen Rivkin; ***C:*** Harry Wild; ***M:*** Leigh Harline.

Tillie's Punctured Romance **1914** The silent comedy which established Chaplin and Dressler as comedians. Chaplin, out of his Tramp character, is the city slicker trying to put one over on farm girl Dressler, who pursues revenge. First feature length comedy film. Followed by "Tillie's Tomato Surprise" and "Tillie Wakes Up," which starred Dressler but not Chaplin. **73m/B; Silent; VHS, DVD.** Charlie Chaplin; Marie Dressler; Mabel Normand; Mack Swain; Chester Conklin; ***D:*** Mack Sennett; ***W:*** Hampton Del Ruth; ***C:*** Frank D. Williams.

The Tillman Story **2010 (R)** Explores the public lies and cover-ups surrounding the death of Pat Tillman in Afghanistan. The football pro left his career after 9/11 to join the Army Rangers and was killed on his second tour of duty. His family became suspicious of the Army's official explanation of his death, eventually leading to an investigation and a Congressional hearing as well as military, political, and media exploitation. **94m/C; Blu-Ray, On Demand.** ***Nar:*** Josh Brolin; ***D:*** Amir Bar-Lev; ***W:*** Amir Bar-Lev; Mark Monroe; Joe Bini; ***C:*** Sean Kirby; Igor Martinovic; ***M:*** Philip Sheppard.

Tim 1/2 **1979** Follows the relationship between a handsome, mentally retarded young man and an attractive older businesswoman. Sappy story line is redeemed by Gibson's fine performance in one of his first roles. Based on Colleen McCullough's first novel. **94m/C; VHS, DVD.** *AU* Mel Gibson; Piper Laurie; Peter Gwynne; Alwyn Kurts; Pat Evison; ***D:*** Michael Pate; ***W:*** Michael Pate; ***C:*** Paul Onorato; ***M:*** Eric Jupp. Australian Film Inst. '79: Actor (Gibson).

Tim and Eric's Billion Dollar Movie 1/2 **2012 (R)** Tim Heidecker and Eric Wareheim court the open hostility of the mainstream in this unfunny comedy aimed at those already squarely in their TV cult following. After blowing a billion dollars making a three-minute movie, Tim and Eric hightail it to a surreal mall to pay back the hot-headed investor (Loggia) who fronted them the money. The mall is a decrepit barn full of stores that sell used toilet paper and swords, but the two must revive it to earn the big bucks offered by the sketchy owner (Ferrell). Rife with celebrity cameos, this intentionally weird and twisted mess won't appeal to the uninitiated. **94m/C; DVD, Blu-Ray.** Tim Heidecker; Eric Wareheim; William Atherton; Robert Loggia; Jeff Goldblum; Ray Wise; ***D:*** Tim Heidecker; Eric Wareheim; ***W:*** Tim Heidecker; Eric Wareheim; ***C:*** Rachel Morrison; ***M:*** David Wood.

Tim Burton's Corpse Bride *Corpse Bride* **2005 (PG)** The magnificent visual aesthetic of Burton's animation and a lead character voiced by Johnny Depp. What more could you want? Well what you get is a sweet story of love lost with a nether-worldly twist or two. Victor Van Dort (Depp) is set to marry Victoria Everglat (Watson) in a parentally-arranged union. Nervous and awkward, Victor retreats to the nearby graveyard, practicing the vows he has struggled to memorize, where he accidentally slips the ring on the finger (which he takes for a twig) of the long dead Corpse Bride (Carter). She comes to life and insists she is now his wife, and he is then plunged into the much brighter world of the dead. **75m/C; DVD, Blu-Ray, HD-DVD.** *GB US* ***V:*** Johnny Depp; Helena Bonham Carter; Emily Watson; Tracey Ullman; Joanna Lumley; Albert Finney; Richard E. Grant; Michael Gough; Christopher Lee; Jane Horrocks; Deep Roy; Danny Elfman; Paul Whitehouse; Enn Reitel; Stephen Ballantyne; Lisa Kay; ***D:*** Michael Johnson; Tim Burton; ***W:*** John August; Caroline Thompson; Pamela Pettler; ***C:*** Pete Kozachik; ***M:*** Danny Elfman. Natl. Bd. of Review '05: Animated Film.

Tim Tyler's Luck **1937** Lost but not forgotten serial in its 12-chapter entirety. The fearless Tim Tyler uses whatever he can to do battle with the sinister Spider Web gang. **235m/B; VHS, DVD.** Frankie Thomas, Jr.; Frances Robinson; Al Shean; Norman Willis; Earl Douglas; Jack Mulhall; Frank Mayo; Pat J. O'Brien; ***D:*** Ford Beebe; Wyndham Gittens.

Timbuktu ½ **1959** Stereotypical desert adventure flick. Col. Dufort and his wife Natalie arrive in the French Sudan in 1940 so he can assume command of the garrison. The soldiers are regularly attacked by Tuareg nomads, allegedly influenced by holy man Mohamet Adani. Dufort uses American gunrunner Mike Conway to broker a truce, but Conway is not supposed to get involved with the unhappy Natalie. **92m/B; DVD.** Victor Mature; Yvonne De Carlo; George Dolenz; Leonard Mudie; John Dehner; James Fox; ***D:*** Jacques Tourneur; ***W:*** Anthony Veiller; Paul Dudley; ***C:*** Maury Gertsman; ***M:*** Gerald Fried.

Timbuktu **2015 (PG-13)** Deeply moving, humanistic exploration of the impact of Islamic fundamentalism imposed on a local population in western Africa. Filmmaker Abderrahmane Sissako condemns intolerance and the killing of diversity through a story set in northern Mali in 2012. As jihadists take over the region, a multicultural community suffers through the adjustments demanded by these outsiders. Bans on music, soccer, most social activity, and women without covered heads are imposed, and local residents are punished for transgressions. Despite the threat of violence, individuals hold onto their pride and humanity as much as possible. The visually stunning film is enhanced by mesmerizing performances. In Arabic, Bambara, French, Songhay, and Tamasheq with subtitles. **97m/C; DVD.** Ibrahim Ahmed; Abel Jafri; Toulou Kiki; Layla Walet Mohamed; Mehdi A.G. Mohamed; ***D:*** Abderrahmane Sissako; ***W:*** Abderrahmane Sissako; Kessen Tall; ***C:*** Sofian El Fani; ***M:*** Amin Bouhafa.

Time *Shi gan* **2006** After two years, pathologically jealous She-hee believes her lover Ji-woo no longer finds her attractive, so she disappears for six months. After undergoing extensive plastic surgery, she returns with a new identity to woo him again, only to find she's competing with the memory of herself. Korean with subtitles. **97m/C; DVD.** *JP NK* Heyon-a Seong; Jung-woo Ha; Ji-yeon Park; ***D:*** Ki-Duk Kim; ***W:*** Ki-Duk Kim; ***C:*** Jong-mu Seong; ***M:*** Hyeong-woo Noh.

Time After Time **1979 (PG)** In Victorian London, circa 1893, H.G. Wells is experimenting with his time machine. He discovers the machine has been used by an associate, who turns out to be Jack the Ripper, to travel to San Francisco in 1979. Wells follows to stop any further murders and the ensuing battle of wits is both entertaining and imaginative. McDowell is charming as Wells and Steenburgen is equally fine as Well's modern American love interest. **112m/C; VHS, DVD, Blu-Ray.** Malcolm McDowell; David Warner; Mary Steenburgen; Patti D'Arbanville; Charles Cioffi; ***D:*** Nicholas Meyer; ***W:*** Nicholas Meyer; ***M:*** Miklos Rozsa.

Time and Again ½ **2007** Twisty time travel plot. Anne Malone (Burns) is surprised to inherit her Great Aunt Helena's house. She finds an old music box, but opening the box and hearing the tune seems to change the world around her. Handyman Billy (Anthony) warns Anne that the music box is cursed and will drive her crazy but Anne is mourning the deaths of her husband and daughter in a car crash and hopes she can time travel to prevent the accident. **90m/C; DVD.** Brooke Burns; Paul Anthony; Beau Starr; Morgan Brayton; David W. Ingram; Erika-Shaye Gair; David Franco; Scott Hylands; ***D:*** Penelope Buitenhuis; ***W:*** David Golden; ***C:*** Brian Johnson. **CABLE**

Time and Tide *Seunlau Ngaklau* **2000 (R)** Non-stop action from Hark with the usual convoluted plot. Tyler (Tse) is working as a bodyguard for a client who turns out to be a Triad boss. Tyler's friend Jack (Bai) is an ex-mercenary whose pregnant wife, Hui (Lo), is the criminal's estranged daughter. And then Jack's former South American colleagues show up in Hong Kong with a plan to assassinate the Triad boss, among other gun battles. Oh, and Tyler is also about to become a father, courtesy of a one-night stand who doesn't want anything to do with him. Chinese with subtitles. **113m/C; VHS, DVD.** *CH* Nicholas Tse; Wu Bai; Anthony Wong; Candy Lo; Cathy Chui; Joventino Couto Remotigue; ***D:*** Tsui Hark; ***W:*** Tsui Hark; Koan Hui; ***C:*** Herman Yau; Ko Chiu-lam; ***M:*** Tommy Wai.

Time Bandits ½ **1981 (PG)** A group of dwarves help a young boy to travel through time and space with the likes of Robin Hood, Napoleon, Agamemnon, and other time-warp playmates. Epic fantasy from Monty Python alumni. **110m/C; VHS, DVD, Blu-Ray, UMD.** *GB* John Cleese; Sean Connery; Shelley Duvall; Katherine Helmond; Ian Holm; Michael Palin; Ralph Richardson; Kenny Baker; Peter Vaughan; David Warner; Craig Warnock; ***D:*** Terry Gilliam; ***W:*** Michael Palin; Terry Gilliam; ***C:*** Peter Biziou; ***M:*** Mike Moran; George Harrison.

Time Barbarians **1990** A barbarian king pursues an evil wizard through time to modern Los Angeles to get revenge for the murder of his wife. Not enjoyably super cheesy. **90m/C; DVD.** Deron McBee; Joann Ayers; Daniel Martine; Ingrid Vold; ***D:*** Joseph John Barmettler, Jr.; ***W:*** Joseph John Barmettler, Jr.; ***C:*** Kevin Morrisey; ***M:*** Miriam Cutler.

The Time Being ½ **2012** Worth as look if you're a Langella fan, but Bentley proves to be something of a blank as struggling L.A. artist Daniel, who's summoned to the home of wealthy recluse Warner Dax. Daniel hopes it means a commission, but Dax wants him to do very precise video surveillance and Daniel soon figures out that all of his footage contains images of the same woman. The two men have more in common than artistic pretensions, but the revelations about art and family don't make it interesting. **85m/C; DVD.** Wes Bentley; Frank Langella; Sarah Paulson; Ahna O'Reilly; Corey Stoll; ***D:*** Nenad Cicin-Sain; ***W:*** Nenad Cicin-Sain; Richard N. Gladstein; ***C:*** Mihai Malaimare, Jr.; ***M:*** Jan A.P. Kaczmarek.

Time Bomb ½ **2008** Iraq vet Jason Philby (Busey) is deeply troubled by his battlefield experience and the death of his young son. The images haunting his dreams spill over into his daytime hours until he doesn't know what's real. But when Jason learns he may have been infected with a virus designed to create soldier/suicide bombers, he's determined to find out if the military done him wrong. **87m/C; DVD.** Jake Busey; Robert Bockstael; Deborah Odell; Daniel Cook; David Haydn-Jones; ***D:*** Erin Berry; ***W:*** Erin Berry; David Plusauskas; ***C:*** Simon Shohet; ***M:*** Alphonse Lanza. **VIDEO**

Time Chasers **1995** Nick Miller (Burch) invents a device that permits his airplane to travel through time. But, after selling his invention, he soon discovers that it has turned the future into a desolate wasteland. Now Nick must try to regain control and put things back to normal. **90m/C; VHS, DVD.** Matthew Burch; Bonnie Pritchard; Peter Harrington; ***D:*** David Giancola.

Time Code *Timecode* **2000 (R)** Figgis shot his film in one day, using four digital video cameras and 28 actors to tell four separate (though inter-connected) stories that were shown simultaneously onscreen in four rectangular quadrants. The stories center around a film production company headed by producer Alex Green (Skarsgard), whose wife Emma (Burrows) plans to leave him because he is having an affair with actress Rose (Hayek), whose own relationship with Lauren (Tripplehorn) is falling apart. Then there's various producers, directors, and actors pitching ideas or auditioning for parts. It's not as confusing as might be imagined although how it will play on video is a challenge. **97m/C; VHS, DVD.** Stellan Skarsgard; Saffron Burrows; Salma Hayek; Jeanne Tripplehorn; Richard Edson; Julian Sands; Xander Berkeley; Glenne Headly; Holly Hunter; Danny Huston; Kyle MacLachlan; Alessandro Nivola; Steven Weber; Viveka Davis; Aimee Graham; Andrew Heckler; Daphna Kastner; Leslie Mann; Mia Maestro; ***D:*** Mike Figgis; ***W:*** Mike Figgis; ***C:*** Patrick Alexander Stewart; ***M:*** Mike Figgis; Anthony Marinelli.

A Time for Dancing **2000 (PG-13)** Jules and Sam grew up best friends and shared a love for dancing that was to lead the girls to Juilliard College. When Jules learns that she has late-stage cancer, their life plans take a tragic shift. **94m/C; VHS, DVD.** Larisa Oleynik; Shiri Appleby; Peter Coyote; Amy Madigan; Shane West; Lynn Whitfield; Patricia Kalember; Anton Yelchin; ***D:*** Peter Gilbert; ***W:*** Kara Lindstrom; ***C:*** Alex Nepomniaschy. **TV**

A Time for Miracles ½ **1980** Dramatic biography of the first native-born American saint, Elizabeth Bayley Seton, who was canonized in 1975. **97m/C; VHS, DVD.** Kate Mulgrew; Lorne Greene; Rossano Brazzi; John Forsythe; Jean-Pierre Aumont; Milo O'Shea; ***D:*** Michael O'Herlihy. **TV**

Time Freak **2018 (PG-13)** Young physics genius Stillman (Butterfield) has made a time machine that he can use from his smartphone. It allows him to relive whatever events he would like over and over again. Stillman obsessively time travels, often with stoner best friend Evan (Gisondo), to try to prevent his girlfriend Debbie (Turner) from breaking up with him. Though Stillman tries to correct all his missteps with Debbie and Evan gains knowledge to improve his life, their actions create more and more problems. Ambitious, it relies too heavily on well-worn ideas from romantic comedies. **104m/C; DVD.** Asa Butterfield; Sophie Turner; Skyler Gisondo; Will Peltz; Aubrey Reynolds; ***D:*** Andrew Bowler; ***W:*** Andrew Bowler; ***C:*** Luke Geissbuhler; ***M:*** Andrew Lockington.

Time Indefinite **1993** Cinema verite effort once again follows filmmaker McElwee who returns to his Southern roots to confront personal tragedy by recording every moment on film. It is an emotional journey in which he discovers that his camera may not be enough to protect him from his own feelings. Moving, with occasional lapses into self-absorption. Companion film to McElwee's "Sherman's March." **117m/C; VHS, DVD.** ***D:*** Ross McElwee; ***W:*** Ross McElwee.

Time Lapse **2001 (PG-13)** Agent Clay Pierce (McNamara) is a member of a U.S. antiterrorist unit who unknowingly prevents an attempt to sell a nuclear device to the Iraquis. Too bad Clay is the only one who makes it back alive (more or less). He's got a lot of questions for his boss LaNova (Scheider), who turns out to be a double-dealer. And he deals with Clay by giving him an experimental drug that causes amnesia—so Clay is really confused about why people keep trying to kill him. **88m/C; VHS, DVD, Blu-Ray.** Roy Scheider; William McNamara; Dina Meyer; Henry Rollins; ***D:*** David Worth. **VIDEO**

Time Limit ½ **1957** Army Major Harry Cargill readily admits his guilt during a court-martial investigation on charges of collaborating with the enemy when he was a POW in Korea. Military investigator William Edwards is suspicious of his motives, which come to light during questioning and offer a moral dilemma about right vs. duty. Compelling, though somewhat stilted, drama was actor Malden's only directorial effort. **96m/B; DVD, Blu-Ray.** Richard Widmark; Richard Basehart; Rip Torn; Carl Benton Reid; Martin Balsam; June Lockhart; Dolores Michaels; ***D:*** Karl Malden; ***W:*** Henry Denker; ***C:*** Sam Leavitt; ***M:*** Fred Steiner.

Time Lock **1957** An expert safecracker races against time to save a child who is trapped inside a bank's pre-set time-locked vault. Canada is the setting, although the film was actually made in England. Based on a play by Arthur Hailey. **73m/B; VHS, DVD.** *GB* Robert Beatty; Betty McDowall; Vincent Winter; Lee Patterson; Sandra Francis; Alan Gifford; Robert Ayres; Victor Wood; Peter Mannering; Gordon Tanner; Larry Cross; Sean Connery; Jack Cunningham; ***D:*** Gerald Thomas; ***W:*** Peter Rogers; ***C:*** Peter Hennessy; ***M:*** Stanley Black.

The Time Machine **1960** English scientist living near the end of the 19th century invents time travel machine and uses it to travel into various periods of the future. Rollicking version of H.G. Wells' classic cautionary tale boasts Oscar-winning special effects. Remade in 1978. **103m/C; VHS, DVD, Blu-Ray.** Rod Taylor; Yvette Mimieux; Whit Bissell; Sebastian Cabot; Alan Young; Paul Frees; Bob Barran; Doris Lloyd; ***D:*** George Pal; ***W:*** David Duncan; ***C:*** Paul Vogel; ***M:*** Russell Garcia.

The Time Machine **2002 (PG-13)** Well, the special effects are pretty cool but this sci-fi adventure has little to do with H.G. Wells' 1894 novel. Eccentric scientist Alexander Hartdegen (an anorexic-looking Pearce) lives in New York, circa 1900. He's devastated when his fiance Emma (Guillory) is killed and is determined to change fate by building a time machine. But going back in time changes nothing so Hartdegen goes forward to discover why he can't change things. He accidentally winds up in 800,000 when the Earth is once again pastoral and its inhabitants are divided into the gentle surface-dwelling Elois and the monstrous, cannibalistic subterranean Morlocks. Irish singer Mumba debuts as Mara, whom Hartdegen falls for, and a heavily made-up Irons is the Uber-Morlock. Unfortunately, the story is dull rather than what it should be—rousing in a who-cares-about-logic, B-movie way. **96m/C; VHS, DVD.** Guy Pearce; Samantha Mumba; Mark Addy; Sienna Guillory; Omera Mumba; Jeremy Irons; Orlando Jones; Phyllida Law; Yancey Arias; ***Cameo(s):*** Alan Young; ***D:*** Simon Wells; ***W:*** John Logan; ***C:*** Donald McAlpine; ***M:*** Klaus Badelt.

Time of Favor **2000** Military commander Meanchem (Avni) and best friend Pini (Alterman) have a falling out over Michal (Tinkerbell), the disillusioned daughter of radical Orthodox Rabbi Meltzer (Dayan), whom the men follow. But when Pini is rejected, he decides to channel his frustrations by committing an act of terrorism. Hebrew with subtitles. **98m/C; DVD.** *IS* Aki Avni; Tinkerbell; Edan Alterman; Assi Dayan; Micha Selektar; Amnon Volf; ***D:*** Joseph Cedar; ***W:*** Joseph Cedar; ***C:*** Ofer Inov; ***M:*** Jonathan Bar-Girora.

The Time of His Life ½ **1955** Bumbling Charles Pastry (Hearne) is an ex-con who has been released into the care of his snooty socialite daughter Lady Florence (Pollock). She is so embarrassed by him that she first tries to have him emigrate to Australia (that doesn't work) and then locks him in the attic so he won't ruin his granddaughter's birthday party. He gets loose of course, causing well-meant havoc. **74m/B; DVD.** *GB* Richard Hearne; Ellen Pollock; Frederick Leister; Richard Wattis; Robert Moreton; ***D:*** Leslie Hiscott; ***W:*** Leslie Hiscott; ***C:*** Ken Talbot.

Time of the Gypsies *Dom Za Vesanje* **1990 (R)** Acclaimed Yugoslavian saga about a homely, unlucky Gypsy boy who sets out to steal his way to a dowry large enough to marry the girl of his dreams.

Beautifully filmed, magical, and very long. In the Gypsy language, Romany, it's the first feature film made in the Gypsy tongue. **136m/C; VHS, Streaming.** *YU* Davor Dujmovic; Sinolicka Trpkova; Ljubica Adzovic; Husnija Hasimovic; Bora Todorovic; ***D:*** Emir Kusturica. Cannes '89: Director (Kusturica).

Time of the Wolf 🦴🦴🦴 *Le Temps du Loup* **2003 (R)** City family on a weekend outing to their country home discover it occupied by squatters after an unspecified widespread disaster. Dad (Duval) tries to dispel any potential violence but is shot dead for his trouble, with the rest of the family escaping to find a suddenly very different, very dangerous outside world. They set out on a nightmarish journey across desolate and unfamiliar landscape where survival is never certain. Harsh apocalyptic vision is reminiscent of "Night of the Living Dead" and Godard's "Weekend." Austrian director Haneke is great at creating a very realistic and claustrophobic atmosphere. **113m/C; DVD.** *FR AT GE* Isabelle Huppert; Maurice Benichou; Lucas Biscombe; Patrice Chereau; Beatrice Dalle; Daniel Duval; Olivier Gourmet; Rona Hartner; Anais Demoustier; Maryline Even; Brigitte Rouan; Florence Loiret-Caille; ***D:*** Michael Haneke; ***W:*** Michael Haneke; ***C:*** Jurgen Jurges.

The Time of Their Lives 🦴🦴 ½ *The Ghost Steps Out* **1946** A pair of Revolutionary War-era ghosts haunt a modern country estate. One of the best A & C comedies. **82m/B; VHS, DVD.** Bud Abbott; Lou Costello; Marjorie Reynolds; Binnie Barnes; Gale Sondergaard; John Shelton; ***D:*** Charles T. Barton.

The Time of Your Life 🦴🦴🦴 ½ **1948** The only Cagney film that ever lost money. A simple but engaging story of people trying to live their dreams. Cagney is delightful as a barroom philosopher who controls the world around him from his seat in the tavern. Although it was not very popular with audiences at the time, the critics hailed it as an artistic achievement. Based on William Saroyan's play. **109m/B; VHS, DVD.** James Cagney; William Bendix; Jeanne Cagney; Broderick Crawford; Ward Bond; James Barton; Paul Draper; Natalie Schafer; ***D:*** H.C. Potter.

Time Out 🦴🦴 *L'Emploi du Temps* **2001 (PG-13)** Vincent (Recoing) can't admit to his family and friends that he's lost his job so he fabricates a new position working for the U.N. in Switzerland and takes to the road, driving aimlessly in his car. He uses an investment scam in order to pay his bills and then tries working for a trafficker in bogus designer goods, all the while sinking deeper into his life of lies. Very loosely based on a true story. French with subtitles. **132m/C; VHS, DVD.** *FR* Aurelien Recoing; Karin Viard; Serge Livrozet; Nicolas Kalsch; Jean-Pierre Mangeot; Monique Mangeot; Maxime Sassier; ***D:*** Laurent Cantet; ***W:*** Laurent Cantet; Robin Campillo; ***C:*** Pierre Milon; ***M:*** Jocelyn Pook.

Time Out for Rhythm 🦴🦴 **1941** In this Columbia Pictures musical, theatrical booker Mike (Lane) and his partner Daniel (Vallee) split over promoting their latest discoveries. Mike wants to feature his singer ex, Frances (Lane), and Daniel wants to give her maid, Kitty (Miller), the star treatment. They both get their chance when Mike opens a nightclub. The Three Stooges also do some routines. **75m/B; DVD.** Richard Lane; Rosemary Lane; Rudy Vallee; Ann Miller; Allen Jenkins; ***D:*** Sidney Salkow; ***W:*** Edmund L. Hartmann; Bert Lawrence; ***C:*** Franz Planer.

Time Out of Mind 🦴🦴 ½ **2014** Gere shines in Moverman's formally daring rendering of life as a homeless man in modern New York City. Moverman shot the film on an incredibly low budget and often from an extreme distance, basically putting Gere in the streets of NYC as life went on around him. The result is a drama that really gets at how easy it is to ignore human suffering even when it's right in front of our faces. The film falters a bit when the narrative element is interjected—such as in an ineffective subplot involving the man's daughter played by Malone—but there's still food for thought here. **117m/C; DVD, Blu-Ray.** Jena Malone; Richard Gere; Kyra Sedgwick; Brian d'Arcy James; Steve Buscemi; ***D:*** Oren Moverman; ***W:*** Oren Moverman; ***C:*** Bobby Bukowski.

Time Regained 🦴🦴 ½ *Le Temps Retrouve* **1999 (R)** Based on Marcel Proust's final volume of "Remembrance of Things Past," this ambitious adaptation is a sweeping and sometimes surreal saga of an elderly man's life and memories. Concentrating on turn of the century Paris, period piece time travels around the world inhabited by Marcel (Mazzarella), based on the author himself, who mingles with the wealthy and beautiful. Legendary French beauties litter the screen in supporting roles, including Deneuve, as Odette, who used her looks to get ahead and Beart, as Gilberte, her stepdaughter trapped in an unhappy marriage. Greggory is Saint-Loup, Gilberte's philandering, bisexual husband who cheats on her with Zylberstein and Perez, while Malkovich does a turn as his even more depraved uncle. Worthy performance from Proust look-alike Mazzarella. In French with subtitles. **165m/C; VHS, DVD, Blu-Ray.** *FR IT* Marcello Mazzarello; Catherine Deneuve; Emmanuelle Beart; Vincent Perez; John Malkovich; Pascal Greggory; Marie-France Pisier; Chiara Mastroianni; Arielle Dombasle; Edith Scob; Elsa Zylberstein; Philippe Morier-Genoud; Melvil Poupaud; Mathilde Seigner; Jacques Pieller; Laurence Fevrier; Jean-Francois Balmer; Jerome Prieur; ***V:*** Patrice Chereau; ***D:*** Raul Ruiz; ***W:*** Raul Ruiz; Gilles Taurand; ***C:*** Ricardo Aronovich; ***M:*** Jorge Arriagada.

Time Runner 🦴🦴 **1992 (R)** It's 2022 and the Earth is being used as target practice by alien invaders. Space captain Hamill manages to find a hole in time and slip back to 1992 where he can battle the first of the alien infiltrators and maybe change Earth's destiny. The time-travel theme (including Hamill watching his own birth) is fun and the special effects are well done. **90m/C; VHS, Streaming.** Mark Hamill; Brion James; Rae Dawn Chong; ***D:*** Michael Mazo.

Time to Choose 🦴🦴🦴 **2016** Documentarian Ferguson's latest work is urgent but, unlike a lot of "environmental warning docs," it's also hopeful. Instead of just documenting the misery rampant in communities dominated by coal mining or the impact of how much land is being used on the planet just to keep cattle alive, Ferguson and his team spend just as much time on the men and women trying to fix the problem. So many documentaries serve as cautionary tales, sometimes ending with a website URL to get more information about what can be done next, but this one excels by highlighting those making the right choices. **100m/C; DVD.** Oscar Isaac; ***D:*** Charles Ferguson; ***W:*** Charles Ferguson; Chad Beck; ***C:*** Lula Cerri; Yuanchen Liu; Kalyanee Mam; Heloisa Passos; Lucian Read; Jerry Risius.

Time to Die 🦴 ½ *Seven Graves for Rogan* **1983 (R)** WWII victim of heinous war crimes, obsessed with revenge, stalks his prey for a final confrontation, while eluding U.S. intelligence. Disappointing despite good cast working with Mario Puzo story. **89m/C; VHS, DVD.** Edward Albert; Rex Harrison; Rod Taylor; Raf Vallone; ***D:*** Matt Cimber; ***M:*** Ennio Morricone.

A Time to Die 🦴 ½ **1991 (R)** Lords plays a police photographer who, well, photographs the police. But her camera catches one in the act of murder. Routine crime thriller. **93m/C; VHS, DVD.** Traci Lords; Jeff Conaway; Richard Roundtree; Bradford Bancroft; Nitchie Barrett; ***D:*** Charles Kanganis; ***W:*** Charles Kanganis; ***M:*** Ennio Morricone.

Time to Kill 🦴🦴 *Tempo di Uccidere* **1989 (R)** A young soldier in Africa wanders away from his camp and meets a woman whom he rapes and kills. But when he returns to his outfit he finds he can't escape his tormenting conscience. **110m/C; VHS, DVD.** Nicolas Cage; Giancarlo Giannini; Robert Liensol; ***D:*** Guiliano Montaldo; ***W:*** Furio Scarpelli; ***M:*** Ennio Morricone.

A Time to Kill 🦴🦴🦴 ½ **1996 (R)** Powerful story of revenge, racism, and the question of justice in the "new south." John Grisham had a lot of clout when he finally sold his first and favorite novel to the movies, including veto power over the leading man—director Schumacher was for Woody Harrelson, Grisham was opposed but both finally agreed on newcomer McConaughey. He's outstanding as idealistic smalltown Mississippi lawyer Jake Brigance, called to defend anguished father Carl Lee Hailey (Jackson), who's accused of killing the rednecks who raped his young daughter. Jake's assisted by former mentor Lucien Wilbanks (Sutherland) and ambitious northern law student Ellen Roark (Bullock) against ruthless prosecutor Rufus Buckley (Spacey). Is it emotionally manipulative? You betcha. But Grisham's done well on screen and Schumacher (who also did "The Client") knows how to get the most from his cast and script. **150m/C; VHS, DVD, Blu-Ray.** Matthew McConaughey; Samuel L. Jackson; Sandra Bullock; Kevin Spacey; Donald Sutherland; Brenda Fricker; Oliver Platt; Charles S. Dutton; Kiefer Sutherland; Chris Cooper; Ashley Judd; Patrick McGoohan; Rae'ven (Alyia Larrymore) Kelly; John Diehl; Tonea Stewart; M. Emmet Walsh; Anthony Heald; Kurtwood Smith; ***D:*** Joel Schumacher; ***W:*** Akiva Goldsman; ***C:*** Peter Menzies, Jr.; ***M:*** Elliot Goldenthal. MTV Movie Awards '97: Breakthrough Perf. (McConaughey).

Time to Leave 🦴🦴🦴 *Les Temps Qui Reste* **2005** French flick takes an unflinching look at death and dying from the perspective of a narcissistic young photographer who learns that he has terminal cancer and reacts in a very realistic, un-Hollywood way. First he has sex with his live-in lover and then immediately kicks him out; he insults and further alienates his single-mother sister during a family dinner while telling no one about his illness except for his outcast grandmother "because you're like me, you'll be dying soon," he bluntly tells her. An absence of melodrama and an interesting subplot involving a childless waitress followed by a genuinely moving end makes for a fine French import. **85m/C; DVD.** *FR* Melvil Poupaud; Jeanne Moreau; Valeria Bruni-Tedeschi; Daniel Duval; Marie Riviere; Christian Sengewald; Louise-Anne Hippeau; Walter Pagano; Ugo Soussan Trabelsi; ***D:*** Francois Ozon; ***W:*** Francois Ozon; ***C:*** Jeanne Lapoirie.

A Time to Remember 🦴🦴 ½ **2003** Maggie (Roberts) has been diagnosed with Alzheimer's. A family Thanksgiving reunites her with her very different daughters, Valetta (Gallagher) and Brit (Delaney), who must learn to forgive old hurts in order to deal with the present. **88m/C; DVD.** Doris Roberts; Megan Gallagher; Louise Fletcher; Rosemary Forsyth; Dana Delaney; ***D:*** John Putch; ***W:*** William Sims Myers; ***C:*** James W. Wrenn; ***M:*** Joe Kraemer. **CABLE**

Time Trap 🦴🦴 ½ **2017** A group of students follow their archaeology professor into a deep cave, where time passes much more slowly than on the surface. This modest sci-fi film is surprisingly entertaining, delivering creativity, a clever script, and solid acting by an ensemble cast. **87m/C; DVD, Blu-Ray, Streaming.** Andrew Wilson; Cassidy Gifford; Brianne Howey; Reiley McClendon; Olivia Draguicevich; ***V:*** Mark Dennis; ***D:*** Mark Dennis; Ben Foster; ***C:*** Mike Simpson; ***M:*** Xiaotian Shi.

The Time Traveler's Wife 🦴🦴 ½ **2009 (PG-13)** Wistful romantic fantasy adapted from Audrey Niffenegger's 2004 novel. A rare genetic anomaly causes Henry DeTamble (Bana) to time travel uncontrollably through the past, present, and future of his own life, which includes Henry's perennial romance with Clare (McAdams). The two aren't always in sync so a (naked) adult Henry confronting a six-year-old Clare about their friendship is only one unsettling circumstance. And, as you might imagine, the plot gets rather confusing. Fortunately, Bana and McAdams make you believe. **107m/C; DVD, Blu-Ray.** Eric Bana; Rachel McAdams; Ron Livingston; Stephen Tobolowsky; Arliss Howard; Michelle Nolden; ***D:*** Robert Schwentke; ***W:*** Bruce Joel Rubin; ***C:*** Florian Ballhaus; ***M:*** Mychael Danna.

Time Walker 🦴 **1982 (PG)** An archaeologist unearths King Tut's coffin in California. An alien living inside is unleashed and terrorizes the public. **86m/C; VHS, DVD, Blu-Ray.** Ben Murphy; Nina Axelrod; Kevin Brophy; James Karen; Austin Stoker; ***D:*** Tom Kennedy; ***W:*** Tom Friedman; Karen Levitt; ***M:*** Richard Band.

Time Warp 🦴 ½ **1981** Campy low budget TV movie about the plight of an astronaut who goes through a temporal disturbance on his way back to Earth and arrives both invisible and in the future. Bummer. **88m/C; DVD.** Chip Johnson; Adam West; Gretchen Corbett; Barry J. Gordon; ***D:*** Robert Emenegger; Allan Sandler; ***W:*** Anne Spielberg; ***C:*** Jose Luis Mignone; ***M:*** Robert Emenegger. **TV**

Time Without Pity 🦴🦴 ½ **1957** Anti-capital punishment plea finds desperate alcoholic David Graham (Redgrave) discovering that his son Alec (McCowen) is about to be executed for murder. But David doesn't believe in the boy's guilt and has 24 hours to find the real killer. The audience knows Alec is innocent from the get-go, making for a certain suspense. Based on the play "Someone Waiting" by Emlyn Williams. **88m/B; VHS, DVD.** *GB* Michael Redgrave; Alec McCowen; Ann Todd; Leo McKern; Peter Cushing; Renee Houston; Paul Daneman; Lois Maxwell; Richard Wordsworth; George Devine; Joan Plowright; ***D:*** Joseph Losey; ***W:*** Ben Barzman; ***C:*** Freddie Francis; ***M:*** Tristram Cary.

Timebomb 🦴🦴 ½ **1991 (R)** When someone attempts to kill Biehn, he turns to a beautiful psychiatrist for help. She triggers flashbacks that send her hunted patient on a dangerous, perhaps deadly, journey into his past. **96m/C; VHS, DVD, Blu-Ray.** Michael Biehn; Patsy Kensit; Tracy Scoggins; Robert Culp; Richard Jordan; Raymond St. Jacques; Jim Maniaci; Billy Blanks; Ray "Boom Boom" Mancini; Steven J. Oliver; ***D:*** Avi Nesher; ***W:*** Avi Nesher; ***M:*** Patrick Leonard.

Timecop 🦴🦴 ½ **1994 (R)** "Terminator" rip-off is fodder for Van Damme followers with lots of action and special effects (you weren't expecting acting too). 2004 policeman Max Walker (Van Damme) must travel back in time to prevent corrupt politician Aaron McComb (Silver) from altering history for personal gain. It's also Walker's chance to alter his personal history since his wife Melissa (Sara) was killed in an explosion he can now prevent. Futuristic thriller based on a Dark Horse comic. **98m/C; VHS, DVD, Blu-Ray.** Jean-Claude Van Damme; Ron Silver; Mia Sara; Bruce McGill; Scott Lawrence; Kenneth Welsh; Gabrielle Rose; Duncan Fraser; Ian Tracey; Gloria Reuben; Scott Bellis; Jason Schombing; Kevin McNulty; Sean O'Byrne; Malcolm Stewart; Alfonso Quijada; Glen Roald; Theodore Thomas; ***D:*** Peter Hyams; ***W:*** Mark Verheiden; Gary De Vore; ***C:*** Peter Hyams; ***M:*** Mark Isham.

Timecop 2: The Berlin Decision 🦴 ½ **2003 (R)** Convoluted, confusing actioner. Timecop Ryan Chang (Lee) is sent to 1940s Germany where colleague Miller Branson (Griffith) is about to alter history by killing Hitler. While stopping Branson, Chang inadvertently kills Branson's wife, which means the guy wants revenge. Branson keeps on hopping through time trying to change situations for his own benefit and Chang keeps following him to fix things. You won't really care—best to stick with the Van Damme original if you like this sort of thing. **81m/C; VHS, DVD.** Jason Scott Lee; Thomas Ian Griffith; Mary Page Keller; John Beck; Tava Smiley; ***D:*** Steve Boyum; ***W:*** Gary Scott Thompson; ***C:*** Crescenzo G.P. Notarile; ***M:*** Andy Gray. **VIDEO**

Timekeeper 🦴 ½ *Clockmaker* **1998 (PG)** Three kids snoop around their neighbor's apartment and find out he has a time machine by accidentally sending a computer manual back in time and turning the world into a fascist state. Surprisingly they take responsibility for their actions and try to fix things. **90m/C; DVD.** *RO US* Anthony Medwetz; Katie Johnston; Zachary McLemore; Pierrino Mascarino; Daisy Nystul; ***D:*** Christopher Remy; ***W:*** Benjamin Carr; ***C:*** Gabriel Kosuth; ***M:*** Jim Fox. **VIDEO**

Timeless 🦴🦴 ½ **1996** Hart's experimental feature debut uses Super-8, 16mm, and 35mm formats to tell a familiar story. Eighteen-year-old Terry (Bryne) hangs out on the streets of Queens doing various odd jobs for a variety of small-time gamblers, dealers, and mobsters. He falls for Lyrica (Duge) and gets her away from her abusive lover and the teen twosome head out of town, hoping for a better life. **90m/C; VHS, DVD.** Peter Byrne; Michael Griffiths; Melissa Duge; ***D:*** Chris Hart; ***W:*** Chris Hart.

Timeline 🦴 ½ **2003 (PG-13)** Weak big screen adaption of Michael Cricton's novel of the same name. Archaeologists travel back in time to medieval France to rescue a colleague. Features some of the most wooden performances since Pinnochio. While it's easy to blame the actors for their lackluster performance, a decent script would have helped them out a lot. **116m/C; VHS, DVD.** Paul Walker; Frances O'Connor; Gerard Butler; Billy Connolly; David Thewlis; Anna Friel; Neal McDonough; Matt Craven; Ethan (Randall) Embry; Michael Sheen; Lambert Wilson; Marton

Csokas; *D:* Richard Donner; *W:* Jeff Maguire; George Nolfi; *C:* Caleb Deschanel; *M:* Brian Tyler.

Timelock ♪♪ **1999** In the 23rd century, asteroid Alpha 4 serves as a maximum security prison for the most dangerous criminals. However, the inmates have now gained controlled and its up to the reluctant heroics of a petty thief and a shuttle pilot to get the bad guys back in their cages. **100m/C; VHS, DVD.** Maryam D'Abo; Arye Gross; Jeff Speakman; Jeffrey Meek; Martin Kove; *D:* Robert Munic; *W:* Joseph John Barmettler, Jr.; *C:* Steve Adcock. **VIDEO**

Timemaster ♪♪ ½ **1995 (PG-13)** The orphaned 12-year-old Jesse (Cameron-Glickenhaus) dreams his parents are alive in another time, so he asks inventor Isaiah (Morita) for help. The duo discover Jesse's parents are being held hostage by a galactic dictator (Dorn), who's using them in sinister virtual-reality games and Jesse must time-travel to rescue them. **100m/C; VHS, DVD.** Jesse Cameron-Glickenhaus; Noriyuki "Pat" Morita; Joanna Pacula; Michael Dorn; Duncan Regehr; Michelle Williams; *D:* James Glickenhaus; *W:* James Glickenhaus.

Timer ♪♪ ½ **2009 (R)** Cute rom com debut from writer/director Schaeffer. In the near future an implanted wrist unit serves as a timer that will identify when you'll meet your soulmate (as long as they're implanted with a timer as well). Love obsessed 30-year-old Oona's (Caulfield) timer is blank while her stepsister Steph (Borth) is upset that she'll have to wait some 18 years (until she's 43) to find the one. So Steph sleeps around before meeting nice guy Dan (Harrington) and Oona falls for younger guy Mikey (Amedori). Maybe the timers are just flat out wrong. **99m/C; DVD.** Emma Caulfield; Michelle Borth; John Patrick Amedori; Desmond Harrington; JoBeth Williams; Kali Rocha; *D:* Jac Schaeffer; *W:* Jac Schaeffer; *C:* Harris Charalambous; *M:* Andrew Kaiser. **VIDEO**

Timerider ♪ ½ *The Adventure of Lyle Swan* **1983 (PG)** Motorcyclist riding through the California desert is accidentally thrown back in time to 1877, the result of a scientific experiment that went awry. There he finds no gas stations and lots of cowboys. Co-written and co-produced by Michael Nesmith, best known for his days with the rock group "The Monkees." **93m/C; VHS, DVD, Blu-Ray.** Fred Ward; Belinda Bauer; Peter Coyote; Richard Masur; Ed Lauter; L.Q. Jones; Tracey Walter; *D:* William Dear; *W:* William Dear; Michael Nesmith; *C:* Larry Pizer; *M:* Michael Nesmith.

Times Have Been Better ♪♪ ½ *La Ciel Sur la Tete* **2006** Successful Jeremy is his parents' golden first-born, much to the dismay of younger brother Robin, who's the only one to know that Jeremy is gay. That changes when Jeremy announces that he's moved in with his boyfriend. Seems his mom and dad aren't as liberal or progressive as they imagined when they decide to figure out what when "wrong" with their son. French with subtitles. **90m/C; DVD.** *FR* Bernard Le Coq; Amaud Binard; Olivier Gueritee; Charlotte de Truckheim; Stephane Boucher; Thierry Desroses; Pierre Deny; *D:* Regis Musset; *W:* Nicolas Mercier. **TV**

Times of Harvey Milk ♪♪♪ ½ **1983** A powerful and moving documentary about the life and career of San Francisco supervisor and gay activist Harvey Milk. The film documents the assassination of Milk and Mayor George Moscone by Milk's fellow supervisor, Dan White. Highly acclaimed by both critics and audiences, the film gives an honest and direct look at the murder and people's reactions. News footage of the murders and White's trial is included. **90m/C; VHS, DVD, Blu-Ray.** *D:* Robert Epstein. Oscars '84: Feature Doc.; Natl. Film Reg. '12.

Times Square ♪ ½ **1980 (R)** A 13-year-old girl learns about life on her own when she teams up with a defiant, anti-social child of the streets. Unappealing and unrealistic, the film features a New Wave music score. **111m/C; VHS, DVD.** Tim Curry; Trini Alvarado; Robin Johnson; Peter Coffield; Elizabeth Pena; Anna Maria Horsford; *D:* Allan Moyle; *W:* Jacob Brackman; *C:* James A. Contner.

Timestalkers ♪♪ ½ **1987** A college professor's infatuation with a young woman is complicated by their pursuit of a criminal from the 26th century into the past. Mildly entertaining adventure. Tucker's last film. **100m/C; VHS, Streaming.** William Devane; Lauren Hutton; Klaus Kinski; John Ratzenberger; Forrest Tucker; Gail Youngs; *D:* Michael A. Schultz. **TV**

Timmy Failure: Mistakes Were Made ♪♪ ½ **2020 (PG)** Fifth grader Timmy (Fegley) lives with his single mother Patty (Lovibond) in Portland, Oregon, and runs the city's most successful detective agency with the help of a polar bear. Though most of Timmy's cases involve problems like missing backpacks, he faces a major challenge when the Failure Mobile, a Segway that his mother told him not use, disappears. While he looks for it, he must avoid his adversary Mrs. Crocus (Shawn) and deal with his feelings about Patty's new boyfriend (Bornheimer). Based on a popular youth book series by Stephen Patis, the film is slight but fun with enjoyable performances and witty dialogue. **99m/C; DVD.** Winslow Fegley; Ophelia Lovibond; Wallace Shawn; Craig Robinson; Kyle Bornheimer; *D:* Tom McCarthy; *W:* Tom McCarthy; Stephan Pastis; *C:* Masanobu Takayanagi; *M:* Rolfe Kent. **VIDEO**

Tim's Vermeer ♪♪♪ **2013 (PG-13)** Teller, of magical duo Penn & Teller fame, directs this unique documentary that has enough commitment and madness to make it something truly special. Tim Jenison is a Texas-based inventor who tries something that has probably never been tried before—to recreate a painting of 17th century Dutch master Johannes Vermeer down to the finest detail. Jenison doesn't just create a forgery, he attempts to duplicate the very conditions in which the photo-realistic painter operated, including using the same painting tools and materials that Vermeer would have had hundreds of years earlier. **80m/C; DVD, Blu-Ray.** Tim Jenison; Penn Jillette; *D:* Teller; *C:* Shane F. Kelly; *M:* Conrad Pope.

Tin Cup ♪♪♪ **1996 (R)** You've got your romantic triangle, you've got your sports, you've got Costner reteamed with Shelton. "Bull Durham" on a golf course? Can lightening strike twice? Ron "Tin Cup" McAvoy (Costner) is a West Texas golf hustler who has the ability but not the steadiness to be on the pro tour. When McAvoy decides on a last-ditch effort to qualify for the U.S. Open, he turns to psychologist Dr. Molly Griswold (Russo) to get his game together. And the fact that Molly is the girlfriend of McAvoy's longtime rival—and successful PGA player—Don Simms (Johnson), well Tin Cup isn't adverse to playing for the lady's affections either. The U.S. Open scenes were filmed at Houston's Kingwood Country Club and the actors do hit their own shots. **133m/C; DVD, Blu-Ray.** Kevin Costner; Don Johnson; Rene Russo; Richard "Cheech" Marin; Linda Hart; Dennis Burkley; Rex Linn; Lou Myers; Richard Lineback; Mickey Jones; *D:* Ron Shelton; *W:* Ron Shelton; John Norville; *C:* Russell Boyd; *M:* William Ross.

The Tin Drum ♪♪♪♪ *Die Blechtrommel* **1979 (R)** German child in the 1920s wills himself to stop growing in response to the increasing Nazi presence in Germany. He communicates his anger and fear by pounding on a tin drum. Memorable scenes, excellent cast. In German with English subtitles. Adapted from the novel by Gunter Grass. **141m/C; VHS, DVD, Blu-Ray.** *GE* David Bennent; Mario Adorf; Angela Winkler; Daniel Olbrychski; Katharina Thalbach; Heinz Bennent; Andrea Ferreol; Charles Aznavour; *D:* Volker Schlondorff; *W:* Jean-Claude Carriere; Volker Schlondorff; *C:* Igor Luther; *M:* Maurice Jarre. Oscars '79: Foreign Film; Cannes '79: Film; L.A. Film Critics '80: Foreign Film.

Tin Man ♪♪ ½ **1983** Garage mechanic born totally deaf designs and builds a computer that can both hear and speak for him. His world is complicated, however, when a young speech therapist introduces him to new and wonderful sounds and unscrupulous and exploitative computer salesmen. Interesting premise and nice performances. **95m/C; VHS, DVD.** Timothy Bottoms; Deana Jurgens; Troy Donahue; Will MacMillan; *D:* John G. Thomas.

Tin Man ♪♪ **2007** Surreal use of L. Frank Baum's "The Wizard of Oz" that can't really offer much in the way of heart or brain. The Outer Zone (or O.Z.) is an alternative universe ruled by evil sorceress Azkadellia (Robertson) and her heaving bosom. Our Dorothy is glowering tomboy D.G. (Deschanel), who still arrives by tornado, and meets her posse: Glitch (Cumming), whose brain has been removed; psychic beastie Raw (Trujillo); shape-shifting Toto (Mankuma); and grieving Wyatt Cain (McDonough), who's called a "tin man" because he was a cop. And they have to find some emerald that will free O.Z. from Azkadellia's rule. And yes, there's a sorta druggie wizard/magician (Drefuss). A Sci-Fi Channel miniseries. **360m/C; DVD, Blu-Ray.** Zooey Deschanel; Neal McDonough; Kathleen Robertson; Alan Cumming; Raoul Trujillo; Blu Mankuma; Richard Dreyfuss; Callum Keith Rennie; Nick Willing; Anna Galvin; *W:* Steve Mitchell; Craig W. Van Sickle; *C:* Thomas Burstyn; *M:* Simon Boswell.

Tin Men ♪♪ ½ **1987 (R)** Set in Baltimore in the 1960s, this bitter comedy begins with two aluminum-siding salesmen colliding in a minor car accident. They play increasingly savage pranks on each other until one seduces the wife of the other, ruining his marriage. Like "Diner," the movie is full of Levinson's idiosyncratic local Baltimore color. **112m/C; VHS, DVD.** Richard Dreyfuss; Danny DeVito; Barbara Hershey; John Mahoney; Jackie Gayle; Stan Brock; Seymour Cassel; Bruno Kirby; J.T. Walsh; Michael Tucker; *D:* Barry Levinson; *W:* Barry Levinson; *C:* Peter Sova; *M:* David Steele.

The Tin Star ♪♪♪ **1957** Perkins is the young sheriff who persuades veteran bounty hunter Fonda to help him rid the town of outlaws. Excellent Mann western balances humor and suspense. **93m/B; DVD.** Henry Fonda; Anthony Perkins; Betsy Palmer; Neville Brand; Lee Van Cleef; John McIntire; Michel Ray; *D:* Anthony Mann; *W:* Dudley Nichols; *C:* Loyal Griggs; *M:* Elmer Bernstein.

The Tingler ♪♪♪ **1959** Coroner Price discovers that a creepy creature is capable of growing on the human spine and increasing in size through fear. The only way to get rid of it is through constant screaming. Price takes what is probably the screen's first LSD trip and a partial color sequence fights nice red blood pouring from a faucet. One of Castle's cheesy best that originally wowed movie audiences in "Percepto" format, which consisted of installing electric buzzers under the seats for that true tingling sensation. **82m/B; VHS, DVD, Blu-Ray.** Vincent Price; Darryl Hickman; Judith Evelyn; Philip Coolidge; Patricia Cutts; Pamela Lincoln; *D:* William Castle; *W:* Robb White; *C:* Wilfred M. Kline; *M:* Von Dexter.

Tinker, Tailor, Soldier, Spy ♪♪♪ **1980** Guinness is brilliant as world-weary spy master George Smiley, who has been somewhat forcibly retired from British Intelligence, better known as "The Circus," after a change at the top. But when a mole is discovered operating at the very highest levels, Smiley is approached on the quiet to root him out without giving the game away. Complex and sometimes confusing espionage drama based on the novel by John Le Carre. Followed by "Smiley's People." **324m/C; VHS, DVD.** *GB* Alec Guinness; Michael Aldridge; Ian Bannen; Bernard Hepton; Ian Richardson; Terence Rigby; Anthony Bate; Hywel Bennett; Michael Jayston; Joss Ackland; Warren Clarke; Beryl Reid; Sian Phillips; Patrick Stewart; *D:* John Irvin; *W:* Arthur Hopcraft; *C:* Tony Pierce-Roberts; *M:* Geoffrey Burgon. **TV**

Tinker Tailor Soldier Spy ♪♪♪ **2011 (R)** Working from John le Carre's 1974 dense Cold War spy thriller, director Alfredson creates an espionage-driven character study of a man forced out of retirement in one last effort to catch the Russian counterpart that got away. Set in 1973, George Smiley (Oldman, giving arguably a career-best performance) is the only one who can help MI6 uncover the mole in their ranks, who could possibly lead them to a legendary Russian spy. Brilliantly done, but struggles as it's clearly a truncated, condensed version of a much-longer story and comes off a bit too cold at times. **127m/C; DVD, Blu-Ray.** *GB* Gary Oldman; Colin Firth; Ciaran Hinds; Tom (Thomas) Hardy; Mark Strong; Benedict Cumberbatch; Toby Jones; John Hurt; Simon McBurney; Stephen Graham; Katrina Vasilieva; David Dencik; Kathy Burke; *D:* Tomas Alfredson; *W:* Bridget O'Connor; Peter Straughan; *C:* Hoyte Van Hoytema; *M:* Alberto Inglesias. British Acad. '11: Adapt. Screenplay.

Tiny Furniture ♪♪♪ **2010** Thinly veiled autobiographical debut of writer/director/star Lena Dunham, who filmed many of the scenes in her parents' Tribeca apartment. She plays post-college grad film student Aura, who returns to her family in New York while trying to emerge from their shadow. Her successful photo artist mother (Simmons) and award-winning poet sister (Grace Dunham) take turns supporting her and tearing her down as she deals with dead end jobs and deadbeat boyfriends. Helping convey the complexity of the relationship is the fact that the two supporting actresses actually are her mother and sister. Although it's not laugh-out-loud funny, the self-deprecating wit of Dunham is very appealing. **98m/C; DVD, Blu-Ray.** Lena Dunham; Laurie Simmons; Grace Dunham; Alex Karpovsky; David Call; Amy Seimetz; Merritt Wever; Jemima Kirke; *D:* Lena Dunham; *W:* Lena Dunham; *C:* Jody Lee Lipes; *M:* Teddy Blanks. Ind. Spirit '11: First Feature, First Screenplay.

Tip On a Dead Jockey ♪♪ **1957** Competent but not particularly memorable adaptation of the Irwin Shaw short story. Former Air Force pilot Lloyd Tredman (Taylor) refuses to fly after suffering postwar trauma from his Korean War experiences. An ex-pat living in Madrid, Lloyd's broke after a rigged horse race and agrees to get back in the air to smuggle contraband currency. Except he discovers his cargo also includes heroin and Interpol is hot on his trail. **98m/B; DVD.** Robert Taylor; Dorothy Malone; Marcel Dalio; Martin Gabel; Jack Lord; Gia Scala; *D:* Richard Thorpe; *W:* Charles Lederer; *C:* George J. Folsey; *M:* Miklos Rozsa.

The Tipping Point ♪ ½ **2007** Hospital med tech Nina Patterson (Winnick) suffers from schizophrenia so she makes the perfect patsy in an elaborate scheme to get the dough of wealthy industrialist Michael Cooper (Sprung). She knows he didn't die from a brain tumor but can't get anyone to believe her when she says he was murdered. **90m/C; DVD.** Katheryn Winnick; Nicolas Wright; Chuck Shamata; Karl Pruner; Claudia Besso; Guy Sprung; *D:* Michel Poulette; *W:* Steve Wilson; *C:* Stephen Reizes. **CABLE**

Tipping the Velvet ♪♪ ½ **2002** Provocative miniseries based on the Sarah Waters novel. Set in the 1890s, it takes a look at the unconventional life of male impersonator and music hall star Nan Astley (Stirling), who takes up her profession after becoming infatuated with cross-dressing performer Kitty Butler (Hawes). Hired as Kitty's assistant, Nan eventually reveals her love and the duo become partners on and off the London stage. But Nan's life takes a turn for the dark side when she turns to prostitution, gets involved with dominating aristocrat, Diana (Chancellor), and seeks help from potential new love, Florence (May). **180m/C; DVD.** *GB* Rachael Stirling; Keeley Hawes; Anna Chancellor; Jodhi May; Hugh Bonneville; Alexei Sayle; John Bowe; Sally Hawkins; *D:* Geoffrey Sax; *W:* Andrew Davies; *C:* Cinders Forshaw; *M:* Adrian Johnston. **TV**

Tiptoes ♪♪ **2003 (R)** Rolfe (Oldman) and Steven (McConaughey) are brothers. Rolfe is a dwarf, and Steven isn't, which causes some worry for Steven's girlfriend Carol (Beckinsale) when she becomes pregnant and worries that her child will get the dwarf gene. In a twist, she falls for Rolfe, and comedy, drama, and romance ensues. Director Bright had a falling out with the producers and was fired during the shoot, resulting in an uneven film and Bright issuing a scathing monologue against the producers at the film's debut at the Sundance Film Festival. Performances are good but can't save film from falling flat. **90m/C; DVD.** Gary Oldman; Matthew McConaughey; Kate Beckinsale; Peter Dinklage; Patricia Arquette; Debbie Lee Carrington; *W:* Bill Weiner; *C:* Sonja Rom. **VIDEO**

'Tis a Pity She's a Whore ♪♪ ½ *Addio, Fratello, Crudele* **1973 (R)** A brother and sister engage in an incestuous affair. She becomes pregnant and is married off. Her husband, however, becomes infuriated when he learns of his wife's pregnancy. Photography is by Vittorio Storaro in this highly stylized drama set in Renaissance Italy. **102m/C; VHS, DVD.** *IT* Charlotte Rampling;

Oliver Tobias; Fabio Testi; Antonio Falsi; Rick (Rik) Battaglia; Angela Luce; Rino Imperio; ***D:*** Giuseppe Patroni-Griffi; ***M:*** Ennio Morricone.

Tish 🦴🦴 **1942** Elderly busybody spinster Tish (Main) and her two cronies make a matchmaking muddle and wind up caring for the baby boy that results. They think the infant is an illegitimate orphan since his mom, Cora (Peters), died in childbirth without revealing the father's identity. Or they suppose. Based on the Tish stories by Mary Roberts Rinehart. **84m/B; DVD.** Marjorie Main; Zasu Pitts; Aline MacMahon; Lee Bowman; Susan Peters; Guy Kibbee; Richard Quine; Virginia Grey; ***D:*** S. Sylvan Simon; ***W:*** Harry Ruskin; ***C:*** Paul Vogel; ***M:*** David Snell.

Titan A.E. 🦴🦴 **1/2 2000 (PG)** Animated adventure set after Earth is destroyed by aliens. Young Cale begins a journey through space to find a legendary lost ship—The Titan—that holds the secret to mankind's salvation. Visuals—both computer-generated and traditionally drawn—are breathtaking, but the script is earthbound. Dialogue too often falls flat, and the story, aimed at teen boys, never lives up to the epic visual dazzle. **95m/C; VHS, DVD.** ***V:*** Matt Damon; Drew Barrymore; Bill Pullman; Nathan Lane; Janeane Garofalo; John Leguizamo; Tone Loc; Ron Perlman; Alex D. Linz; Jim Breuer; ***D:*** Don Bluth; Gary Goldman; ***W:*** Ben Edlund; John August; Joss Whedon; ***M:*** Graeme Revell.

Titanic 🦴🦴🦴 **1953** Hollywoodized version of the 1912 sinking of the famous luxury liner sets the scene for the personal drama of a mother (Stanwyck) who wants to flee her husband (Webb) for a new life in America. Story gets a little too melodramatic, but it's not a bad retelling of the sea tragedy. Film is quite effective in conveying the panic and the calm of the actual sinking. A 20-foot-long model of the ship was built for the re-creation of that fateful moment when the "Titanic" hit the inevitable iceberg. **98m/B; VHS, DVD, Blu-Ray.** Clifton Webb; Barbara Stanwyck; Robert Wagner; Richard Basehart; Audrey Dalton; Thelma Ritter; Brian Aherne; ***D:*** Jean Negulesco; ***W:*** Charles Brackett; Walter Reisch; Richard L. Breen. Oscars '53: Story & Screenplay.

Titanic 🦴 **1/2 1996 (PG-13)** Dull and draggy TV version of the 1912 tragedy between the luxury liner and an iceberg that resulted in the deaths of more than 1000 passengers. There are the usual romantic subplots, villains, and heroes, and Scott is properly noble as the veteran captain making his last voyage before retirement. Otherwise you've seen this many times before. **165m/C; VHS, DVD.** George C. Scott; Peter Gallagher; Catherine Zeta-Jones; Eva Marie Saint; Tim Curry; Roger Rees; Harley Jane Kozak; Marilu Henner; Felicity Waterman; Scott Hylands; Kevin McNulty; Malcolm Stewart; ***D:*** Robert Lieberman; ***W:*** Ross LaManna; Joyce Eliason; ***C:*** David Hennings; ***M:*** Lennie Niehaus.

Titanic 🦴🦴🦴 **1997 (PG-13)** Skipper Cameron's mega-budget three-hour tour had its own brushes with disaster with a mammoth budget and delays. A love story that happens to have the sinking of the historic ship as a backdrop, real and fictional characters are blended for a detailed re-enactment of the luxury liner's only voyage. The two lovebirds, Jack Dawson (DiCaprio) and debutante Rose Bukater (Winslet) are from different ends of the economic and social ladder. DiCaprio and Winslet are dynamic and make the running time less of a chore. The special effects are impressive, with a life-size version of the ship built just for this film. Cameron's prowess as a storyteller keeps the outcome of the ship suspenseful and tense even though the ending is no secret. **197m/C; VHS, DVD, Blu-Ray.** Kate Winslet; Leonardo DiCaprio; Billy Zane; Kathy Bates; Frances Fisher; Gloria Stuart; Jonathan Hyde; Danny Nucci; David Warner; Bill Paxton; Bernard Hill; Victor Garber; Suzy Amis; Bernard Fox; ***D:*** James Cameron; ***W:*** James Cameron; ***C:*** Russell Carpenter; ***M:*** James Horner. Oscars '97: Art Dir./Set Dec., Cinematog., Costume Des., Director (Cameron), Film, Film Editing, Orig. Score, Song ("My Heart Will Go On"), Sound, Sound FX Editing, Visual FX; Directors Guild '97: Director (Cameron); Golden Globes '98: Director (Cameron), Film--Drama, Score, Song ("My Heart Will Go On"); MTV Movie Awards '98: Film, Male Perf. (DiCaprio); Natl. Film Reg. '17; Screen Actors Guild '97: Support. Actress (Stuart); Broadcast Film Critics '97: Director (Cameron).

Titanic 🦴 **1/2 2012** Good-looking but convoluted and rather dull miniseries version (shown on ABC) of the 1912 disaster. You never really get to know the multitude of characters of various classes so there's not much emotion invested in their fates even if it's told from their perspectives. **184m/C; DVD, Blu-Ray.** *UK US* Linus Roache; Geraldine Somerville; Toby Jones; Maria Doyle Kennedy; David Calder; Steven Waddington; Brian McCardie; Perdita Weeks; ***D:*** Jon Jones; ***W:*** Julian Fellowes; ***C:*** Adam Suschitzky; ***M:*** Jonathan Goldsmith. **TV**

Titanic 2 🦴 **2010** On the 100th anniversary of the original voyage, a modern luxury liner follows the path of its namesake. Straight into another disaster since a piece of ice shelf has broken off and is directly in the ship's path. **90m/C; DVD.** Bruce Davison; Brooke Burns; Marie Westbrook; D.C. Douglas; Myles Cranford; Shane Van Dyke; ***D:*** Shane Van Dyke; ***W:*** Shane Van Dyke; ***C:*** Alexander Yellen. **VIDEO**

Tito and Me 🦴🦴🦴 *Tito i Ja; Tito and I* **1992** Ten-year-old Zoran lives in 1954 Belgrade and is fascinated by Yugoslavian leader Marshall Tito. Crowded into a flat with his extended family, Zoran learns about volatility firsthand. Then there's romance—he has a crush on a classmate who breaks up with him when she is chosen as one of Tito's Young Pioneers, which means a two-week trip to the country. Political indoctrination means nothing but love—ahh. Debut role for the young Vojnov, who carries the weight of the movie with perfect aplomb. In Serbo-Croation with English subtitles. **104m/C; VHS, DVD.** *YU* Dimitrie Vojnov; Lazar Ristovski; Anica Dobra; Miki (Predrag) Manojlovic; Olivera Markovic; ***D:*** Goran Markovic; ***W:*** Goran Markovic; ***C:*** Radoslav Vladic; ***M:*** Zoran Simjanovic.

Titus 🦴🦴 **1999 (R)** Flashy version of a lesser-known early Shakespeare play, the gory "Titus Andronicus." Theatrical director Taymor makes her film debut with verve and a wild mixture of styles. Victorius Roman general Titus (Hopkins) has just defeated the Goths and has captured Tamora (Lange), the Goth Queen and her sons, one of whom Titus promptly sacrifices to appease the gods. Decadent Emperor Saturninus (Cumming) claims Tamora for his queen; Titus's daughter Lavinia (Fraser) suffers a fate worse than death; Tamora wants revenge; Titus wants revenge; there's a villainous Moor, Aaron (Lennix), and a lot of campy fantasy and blood. **162m/C; VHS, DVD, Blu-Ray.** Anthony Hopkins; Jessica Lange; Alan Cumming; Harry J. Lennix; Colm Feore; Laura Fraser; James Frain; Angus MacFadyen; Jonathan Rhys Meyers; Geraldine McEwan; Matthew Rhys; Bruno Bilotta; ***D:*** Julie Taymor; ***W:*** Julie Taymor; ***C:*** Luciano Tovoli; ***M:*** Elliot Goldenthal.

TKO 🦴 **1/2** *Blow Back* **2006 (R)** A fighter gets drawn into illegal fights-to-the-death run by the local criminal underworld. Unoriginal and not well done. **91m/C; DVD, Blu-Ray.** Daz Crawford; Andre McCoy; Anthony Ray Parker; Fernando Chien; ***D:*** Declan Mulvey; ***W:*** Declan Mulvey; ***C:*** Chris Lytwyn.

TMNT: Teenage Mutant Ninja Turtles 🦴🦴 **2007 (PG)** Our hard-shelled heroes haven't hit the big screen since 1993; maybe the producers are hoping to entice a new generation with improved CGI and (basically) the same old story. Well, not quite, since bad guy Shredder isn't around and the turtle quartet spend more time squabbling among themselves than being a team. That is until evil cosmic forces align to destroy mankind, like they do. There's a few jokes and a few fights and not enough pizza. **86m/C; DVD, Blu-Ray, HD-DVD.** *US CH* ***V:*** Mitchell Whitfield; James Taylor; Mako; Patrick Stewart; Mikey Kelley; Nolan North; Chris Evans; Sarah Michelle Gellar; ***D:*** Kevin Munroe; ***W:*** Kevin Munroe; ***C:*** Steve Lumley; ***M:*** Klaus Badelt.

T.N.T. 🦴🦴 **1998 (R)** Gruner's managed to extricate himself from a covert fighting force but now they're threatening his family unless he does what he's told. **87m/C; VHS, DVD.** Olivier Gruner; Eric Roberts; Randy Travis; Sam Jones; Rebecca Staab; ***D:*** Robert Radler; ***C:*** Bryan Duggan; ***M:*** Stephen (Steve) Edwards. **VIDEO**

TNT Jackson WOOF! **1975 (R)** A kung fu mama searches for her brother while everyone in Hong Kong tries to kick her out of town. **73m/C; VHS, DVD.** Jeannie Bell; Stan Shaw; Pat Anderson; Ken Metcalfe; ***D:*** Cirio H. Santiago; ***W:*** Ken Metcalfe; Dick Miller; ***C:*** Felipe Sacdalan.

To All My Friends on Shore 🦴🦴🦴 **1971** Drama about a father dealing with his young son's sickle cell anemia. Fine performances, realistic script make this an excellent outing. **74m/C; VHS, DVD.** Bill Cosby; Gloria Foster; Dennis Hines; ***D:*** Gilbert Cates. **TV**

To All the Boys: P.S. I Still Love You 🦴🦴 **1/2 2020** Because Lara Jean (Condor) has never had a relationship before, she wants to be a good girlfriend to Peter (Centineo). She tries hard, even changing herself for him, even though the more experienced Peter does not do much special for her. As her relationship with Peter develops, Lara Jean's sixth grade crush, John Ambrose (Fisher), shows interest in her, including appearances at her retirement home volunteer gig and sharing bonding memories with her. Condor brings heart to this likeable teen romantic comedy follow-up. **101m/C; DVD.** Lana Condor; Noah Centineo; Jordan Fisher; Anna Cathcart; Janel Parrish; ***D:*** Michael Fimognari; ***W:*** Sofia Alvarez; J. Mills Goodloe; ***C:*** Michael Fimognari; ***M:*** Joe Wong. **VIDEO**

To All the Boys I've Loved Before 🦴🦴 **1/2 2018** High school junior Lara Jean (Convey) is a romantic who writes and then closets away love letters to her crushes. When those secret letters mysteriously get mailed, she begins fake-dating überpopular Peter (Centineo) to appear nonchalant about the whole nightmare. Everyone can see where this is headed, but it's an absolute joy to ride along. Convey is charming as all get-out, and Centineo is a modern-day Jake, the dreamy hunk from *Sixteen Candles,* both of whom make Lara Jean swoon. A better-than-average teen rom-com, based on Jenny Han's novel. **99m/C; Streaming.** Lana Condor; Noah Centineo; Janel Parrish; Anna Cathcart; Andrew Bachelor; ***D:*** Susan Johnson; ***W:*** Sofia Alvarez; ***C:*** Michael Fimognari; ***M:*** Joe Wong. **VIDEO**

To Be Fat Like Me 🦴🦴 **1/2 2007** Popular high school senior/athlete Alyson (Cuoco) is hoping her softball prowess will get her a college scholarship but her dreams are dashed when she's injured. Her mother and brother have weight-related health and self-esteem issues that Alyson has always dismissed as self-indulgence but she learns differently after entering a documentary film contest. Alyson puts on a fat suit and goes to summer school at a rival high school to prove that looks don't matter but boy is she wrong. **89m/C; DVD.** Kaley Cuoco; Caroline Rhea; Brandon Olds; Rachael Cairns; Carlo Marks; Melissa Halstrom; Adrienne Carter; ***D:*** Douglas Barr; ***W:*** Michelle A. Lovretta; ***C:*** Peter Benison; ***M:*** Hal Beckett. **CABLE**

To Be or Not to Be 🦴🦴🦴 **1/2 1942** Sophisticated black comedy set in wartime Poland. Lombard and Benny are Maria and Josef Tura, the Barrymores of the Polish stage, who use the talents of their acting troupe to protect the Warsaw Resistance against the invading Nazis. The opening sequence is regarded as a cinema classic. One of Benny's finest film performances, the movie marks Lombard's final screen appearance—she was killed in a plane crash druing a war bond drive shortly after completing the film. Classic Lubitsch. Remade in 1983 with Mel Brooks and Anne Bancroft. **102m/B; VHS, DVD, Blu-Ray.** Carole Lombard; Jack Benny; Robert Stack; Sig Rumann; Lionel Atwill; Felix Bressart; Helmut Dantine; Tom Dugan; Charles Halton; Stanley Ridges; George Lynn; Halliwell Hobbes; Miles Mander; Henry Victor; Leslie Denison; Frank Reicher; John Kellogg; James Finlayson; Roland Varno; ***D:*** Ernst Lubitsch; ***W:*** Ernst Lubitsch; Edwin Justus Mayer; Melchior Lengyel; ***C:*** Rudolph Mate; ***M:*** Werner R. Heymann; Miklos Rozsa. Natl. Film Reg. '96.

To Be or Not to Be 🦴🦴 **1/2 1983 (PG)** In this remake of the 1942 film, Bancroft and Brooks are actors in Poland during WWII. They accidently become involved with the Polish Resistance and work to thwart the Nazis. Lots of laughs, although at times there's a little too much slapstick. **108m/C; VHS, DVD, Blu-Ray.** Mel Brooks; Anne Bancroft; Charles Durning; Jose Ferrer; Tim Matheson; Christopher Lloyd; ***D:*** Alan Johnson; ***W:*** Ronny Graham.

To Be Takei 🦴🦴 **1/2 2014** This feature-length biographical documentary looks at the life, career, and cultural influence of actor George Takei. Taking an entertaining tone, the film looks at the many roles of the actor, including his long stint as Sulu on Star Trek. Also considered are his early years in a Japanese American internment camp and his emergence as a pop culture icon in the early twenty-first century. **94m/C; DVD, Streaming, Download.** ***D:*** Jennifer M. Kroot; ***C:*** Christopher Million; ***M:*** Michael Hearst.

To Be the Best 🦴 **1/2 1993 (R)** Eric, a member of the U.S. Kickboxing Team, lets his love for the beautiful Cheryl and his hot temper get the best of him. When a ruthless gambler threatens to kill Cheryl if Eric doesn't throw his big match, he joins with his family, fellow teammates, and most feared opponent, to set things right. **99m/C; VHS, DVD.** Mike Worth; Martin Kove; Phillip Troy; Brittney Powell; Alex Cord; Steven Leigh; ***D:*** Joseph Merhi; ***W:*** Michael January.

To Beat the Band 🦴 **1/2 1935** Cornball RKO musical comedy with the usual crazy story although this one is a little darker than most. In order to inherit his eccentric aunt's estate, Hugo must quickly marry a widow. He wants to marry never-married Rowena, so suicidal Larry offers to wed her first, kill himself, and problem solved! The Art Deco sets are more notable than the plot. **70m/B; DVD.** Hugh Herbert; Helen Broderick; Roger Pryor; Phyllis Brooks; Eric Blore; Fred Keating; ***D:*** Ben Stoloff; ***W:*** Rian James; ***C:*** Nicholas Musuraca.

To Catch a Killer 🦴🦴🦴 **1992** A chilling performance by Dennehy highlights this true-crime tale of a detective's relentless pursuit of serial killer John Wayne Gacy, who preyed on young men and hid the bodies in his home. Made for television. **95m/C; VHS, DVD.** Brian Dennehy; Michael Riley; Margot Kidder; Meg Foster; ***D:*** Eric Till; ***W:*** Judson Kinberg; ***C:*** Rene Ohashi; ***M:*** Paul Zaza. **TV**

To Catch a King 🦴🦴 **1984** Garr is a singer working in Wagner's nightclub in 1940s' Lisbon. The pair becomes involved in trying to foil the Nazi plot to kidnap the vacationing Duke and Duchess of Windsor. Average cable fare. **120m/C; VHS, DVD.** Robert Wagner; Teri Garr; Horst Janson; Barbara Parkins; John Standing; ***D:*** Clive Donner; ***M:*** Nick Bicat. **CABLE**

To Catch a Thief 🦴🦴🦴 **1955** On the French Riviera, a reformed jewel thief falls for a wealthy American woman, who suspects he's up to his old tricks when a rash of jewel thefts occur. Oscar-winning photography by Robert Burks, a notable fireworks scene, and snappy dialogue. A change of pace for Hitchcock, this charming comedy-thriller proved to be as popular as his other efforts. Based on the novel by David Dodge. Kelly met future husband Prince Rainier during a photo shoot while she was attending the Cannes Film Festival. **103m/C; VHS, DVD, Blu-Ray.** Cary Grant; Grace Kelly; Jessie Royce Landis; John Williams; Charles Vanel; Brigitte Auber; ***D:*** Alfred Hitchcock; ***W:*** John Michael Hayes; ***C:*** Robert Burks. Oscars '55: Color Cinematog.

To Commit a Murder 🦴 **1/2** *Peau d—Espion* **1967** Writer Charles is seduced into helping Sandra stop her husband from getting involved in the kidnapping of a nuclear scientist and turning him over to the communist Chinese. French with subtitles. **93m/C; DVD.** *FR* Louis Jourdan; Senta Berger; Bernard Blier; Edmond O'Brien; Fabrizio Capucci; Maurice Garrel; ***D:*** Edouard Molinaro; ***W:*** Edouard Molinaro; ***C:*** Raymond Lemoigne; ***M:*** Jose Berghmans.

To Cross the Rubicon 🦴🦴 **1/2 1991** Romantic comedy finds Kendall (Royce) getting dumped by David (Souther), her boyfriend of eight years, who then reconciles with former flame, Claire (Devon). Meanwhile, Kendall involves herself with James (Burke), a young musician, and becomes new best friends with—you guessed it—Claire. But will David and Kendall's previous relationship cause friction? **120m/C; VHS, DVD.** Patricia Royce; J.D. Souther; Lorraine Devon; Billy Burke; *D:* Barry Caillier; *W:* Patricia Royce; Lorraine Devon; *C:* Christopher Tufty; *M:* Paul Speer; David Lanz.

To Dance with the White Dog ½ **1993 (PG)** Robert Samuel Peek (Cronyn) is a pecan-tree grower from rural Georgia who has been married to Cora (Tandy) for 57 years. Then she dies and their fussing daughters (Baranski and Wright) wonder how their father will survive. But Sam's increasing loneliness is checked when he befriends a stray white dog that it seems no one else can see. Based on the novel by Terry Kay. **98m/C; VHS, DVD.** Hume Cronyn; Jessica Tandy; Christine Baranski; Amy Wright; Esther Rolle; Harley Cross; Frank Whaley; Terry Beaver; Dan Albright; David Dwyer; *D:* Glenn Jordan; *W:* Susan Cooper; *C:* Neil Roach. **TV**

To Die For ½ *Dracula: The Love Story* **1989 (R)** A vampire stalks, woos, and snacks on a young real estate woman. **99m/C; VHS, DVD.** Brendan Hughes; Scott Jacoby; Duane Jones; Steve Bond; Sydney Walsh; Amanda Wyss; Ava Fabian; *D:* Deran Sarafian; *W:* Leslie King; *C:* Jacques Haitkin; *M:* Cliff Eidelman.

To Die For **1995 (R)** Beauteous, manipulative Suzanne Stone (Kidman) wants to be somebody—preferably a big TV personality—and nothing will stop her. She recruits a scruffy threesome to help her ice sweet-but-dim hubby, Larry (Dillon), even if it does means seducing aimless teenager Jimmy (Phoenix). Black comedy, loosely based on the Pamela Smart murder case and adapted from the novel by Joyce Maynard, takes on the media-obsessed culture with a wicked grin. Van Sant retains his fresh and hip storytelling in his first film for a major studio. Backed by Henry's zesty script, all the actors shine—with standout performances from Kidman as the monstrous Suzanne and Phoenix (River's younger brother) as the lost/horny Jimmy. Shot entirely in Canada. **103m/C; VHS, DVD.** Nicole Kidman; Matt Dillon; Joaquin Rafael (Leaf) Phoenix; Casey Affleck; Alison Folland; Illeana Douglas; Dan Hedaya; Wayne Knight; Kurtwood Smith; Holland Taylor; Maria Tucci; Susan Traylor; ***Cameo(s):*** George Segal; Buck Henry; *D:* Gus Van Sant; *W:* Buck Henry; Johnny Burne; *C:* Eric Alan Edwards; *M:* Danny Elfman. Golden Globes '96: Actress--Mus./Comedy (Kidman); Broadcast Film Critics '95: Actress (Kidman).

To Die, Or Not ½ *Morir* **1999** It begins with a director and his wife arguing about his new film, then seven short stories that result in the death of the main character in various ways are shown. The wife rejects these depressing endings so the stories are then retold with her suggestions. Spanish with subtitles. **92m/C; DVD.** *SP* Roger Coma; Carmen Elias; Ana Azcona; Lluis Hmar; Carlotta Bantula; *D:* Ventura Pons; *W:* Ventura Pons; *C:* Jesus Escosa; *M:* Carles Cases.

The To Do List **2013 (R)** In this silly, distaff teen raunch comedy, set in 1993, good girl overachiever Brandy wants to change her image--and her virgin status--before starting college. She sets up a to-do list of sexual experiences to try over the summer, including the guys she'll be using for her experiments. Naturally, Brandy learns some emotional lessons as well as sexual ones, but the sex lessons are fairly funny. **104m/C; DVD, Blu-Ray.** Aubrey Plaza; Alia Shawkat; Sarah Steele; Johnny Simmons; Scott Porter; Bill Hader; Christopher Mintz-Plasse; Rachel Bilson; Connie Britton; Clark Gregg; *D:* Maggie Carey; *W:* Maggie Carey; *C:* Doug Emmett; *M:* Raney Shockne.

To Dust ½ **2019 (R)** After the recent death of his wife from cancer, Hasidic Jew Shmuel (Rohrig) has become tormented by thoughts of her decaying body and the idea that she might be in pain. His religion beliefs hold that a piece of the soul remains in the body of the deceased until it becomes dust. To come to terms with his feelings and grief, Shmuel turns to community college biology professor Albert (Broderick). With hapless Albert's help and experiences including burying a deceased pig, Shmuel gains a new perspective on the nature of death. This thoughtful comedy explores these deep ideas through complex, interesting characters. **92m/C; DVD.** Geza Rohrig; Matthew Broderick; Sammy Voit; Bern Cohen; Marceline Hugot; *D:* Shawn Synder; *W:* Shawn Synder; Jason Begue; *C:* Xavi Gimenez; *M:* Ariel Marx.

To End All Wars **2001 (R)** Based on Ernest Gordon's autobiographical 1962 novel "Through the Valley of the Kwai," bares the horrors that a group of WWII Allied soldiers suffered at the hands of their Japanese captors who torture the POWs during the erecting of the so-called "Railway of Death" in the nasty Burmese jungle. Related to events depicted in "The Bridge of the River Kwai" but not nearly so well imitated. **117m/C; VHS, DVD.** Robert Carlyle; Kiefer Sutherland; Ciaran McMenamin; Mark Strong; Masayuki Yui; James Cosmo; John Gregg; Pip Torrens; Sakae Kimura; Shu Nakajima; Yugo Saso; Greg Ellis; Adam Sinclair; Winton Nicholson; James McCarthy; Brendan Cowell; Duff Armour; Sergio Jones; Christopher White; Jeremy Pippin; Robert Jobe; ***Cameo(s):*** Ernest Gordon; Takashi Nagase; *C:* Greg Gardiner; *M:* John Cameron; Maire Brennan. **VIDEO**

To Gillian on Her 37th Birthday **1996 (PG-13)** Overly sentimental weeper explores the effects of a mother's death on the ones she's left behind. Gillian's been dead for two years but widower David Lewis (Gallagher) hasn't been able to let her spirit go and daughter Rachel (Danes) is having trouble growing up with a father who spends more time on the beach with his dead wife's ghost than with her. Enter nosy sister-in-law Esther (Baker) and annoying husband (Altman) who try to set him up on the anniversary of Gillian's death and you've got a mental family breakdown coming. Pfeiffer appears as Gillian in this script by husband Kelley, based on the play by Michael Brady. **92m/C; VHS, DVD.** Peter Gallagher; Claire Danes; Kathy Baker; Wendy Crewson; Bruce Altman; Michelle Pfeiffer; Freddie Prinze, Jr.; *D:* Michael Pressman; *W:* David E. Kelley; *C:* Tim Suhrstedt; *M:* James Horner.

To Grandmother's House We Go ½ **1994** The Olsen twins want to give mom a restful Christmas vacation so they decide to visit Grandma (on their own) and wind up in the hands of a pair of bumbling kidnappers. Made for TV movie. **89m/C; VHS, DVD.** Ashley (Fuller) Olsen; Mary-Kate Olsen; Cynthia Geary; Rhea Perlman; J. Eddie Peck; Stuart Margolin; ***Cameo(s):*** Bob Saget; Lori Loughlin; *D:* Jeff Franklin; *W:* Jeff Franklin. **TV**

To Have & Have Not ½ **1944** Martinique charter boat operator gets mixed up with beautiful woman and French resistance fighters during WWII. Top-notch production in every respect. Classic dialogue and fiery romantic bouts between Bogart and Bacall. Bacall's first film. Based on a story by Ernest Hemingway. Remade in 1950 as "The Breaking Point" and in 1958 as "The Gun Runners." **100m/B; VHS, DVD, Blu-Ray.** Humphrey Bogart; Lauren Bacall; Walter Brennan; Hoagy Carmichael; Marcel Dalio; Dolores Moran; Sheldon Leonard; Dan Seymour; *D:* Howard Hawks; *W:* Jules Furthman; William Faulkner.

To Have and to Hold ½ **2006** There's serious trouble when Tom has an affair with Lisa who goes psycho when he dumps her. She wants her criminal ex-boyfriend Stevie to help her get revenge, but when Tom's wife Meg accidentally kills the muscle hired to intimidate them the situation goes totally out of control. **90m/C; DVD.** Justine Bateman; Sebastian Spence; Jessica Lowndes; Derek Hamilton; William Macdonald; Colin Lawrence; *D:* Terry Ingram; *W:* Joseph Lawlor; Robert Sax; *C:* Michael Balfry; *M:* Walter Klenhard; John Sereda. **CABLE**

To Hell and Back ½ **1955** Adaptation of Audie Murphy's autobiography. Murphy plays himself, from his upbringing as the son of Texas sharecroppers to his Army career in WWII, where he was the most-decorated American soldier. Murphy won more than 20 medals, including the Congressional Medal of Honor. Features realistic battle sequences punctuated with grand heroics. **106m/C; VHS, DVD.** Audie Murphy; Marshall Thompson; Jack Kelly; Charles Drake; Gregg (Hunter) Palmer; Paul Picerni; David Janssen; Bruce Cowling; Paul Langton; Art Aragon; Felix Noriego; Denver Pyle; Brett Halsey; Susan Kohner; Anabel Shaw; Mary Field; Gordon Gebert; Rand Brooks; Richard Castle; Gen. Walter Bedell Smith; *D:* Jesse Hibbs; *W:* Gil Doud; *C:* Maury Gertsman; *M:* Henry Mancini.

To Joy *Till Gladje* **1950** The rocky marriage of a violinist and his wife illuminate the problems of the young in Swedish society. Early Bergman. In Swedish with English subtitles or dubbed. **90m/B; VHS, DVD, Blu-Ray.** *SW* Maj-Britt Nilsson; Birger Malmsten; Margit Carlquist; Stig Olin; John Ekman; Victor Sjostrom; *D:* Ingmar Bergman; *W:* Ingmar Bergman; *C:* Gunnar Fischer.

To Kill a King ½ **2003** Historical drama set during Britain's 17th-century civil war. Sir Thomas Fairfax (Scott) joins with his friend, General Oliver Cromwell (Roth), to dethrone (and eventually behead) King Charles I (Everett). But the two allies are soon at odds as Cromwell is resentful of Fairfax's aristocratic background and public popularity and Fairfax is increasingly disturbed by Cromwell's puritanical ruthlessness. **102m/C; DVD.** *GB* Dougray Scott; Tim Roth; Rupert Everett; Olivia Williams; James Bolam; Corin Redgrave; Finbar Lynch; Julian Rhind-Tutt; *D:* Mike Barker; *W:* Jenny Mayhew; *C:* Eigil Bryld; *M:* Richard G. Mitchell.

To Kill a Mockingbird **1962** Faithful adaptation of powerful Harper Lee novel, both an evocative portrayal of childhood innocence and a denunciation of bigotry. Peck's performance as southern lawyer Atticus Finch defending black Tom Robinson (Peters), who's accused of raping a white woman, is flawless. Duvall debuted as the dim-witted Boo Radley. Lee based her characterization of "Dill," the Finch children's "goin' on seven" friend, on Truman Capote, her own childhood friend. **129m/B; VHS, DVD, Blu-Ray.** Gregory Peck; Brock Peters; Phillip Alford; Mary Badham; Robert Duvall; Rosemary Murphy; William Windom; Alice Ghostley; John Megna; Frank Overton; Paul Fix; Collin Wilcox-Paxton; ***Nar:*** Kim Stanley; *D:* Robert Mulligan; *W:* Horton Foote; *C:* Russell Harlan; *M:* Elmer Bernstein. Oscars '62: Actor (Peck), Adapt. Screenplay, Art Dir./Set Dec., B&W; AFI '98: Top 100; Golden Globes '63: Actor--Drama (Peck), Score; Natl. Film Reg. '95.

To Kill a Priest **1989 (R)** Based on the true story of Father Jerzy Popieluszko, a young priest in 1984 Poland who defies his church and speaks out publicly on Solidarity. He is killed by the government as a result. Harris is good as the menacing police official. **110m/C; VHS, DVD, Streaming.** Christopher Lambert; Ed Harris; David Suchet; Tim Roth; Joanne Whalley; Pete Postlethwaite; Cherie Lunghi; Joss Ackland; *D:* Agnieszka Holland; *W:* Agnieszka Holland; *C:* Adam Holender; *M:* Georges Delerue.

To Kill a Stranger **1984** A beautiful pop singer is stranded in a storm, and then victimized by a mad rapist/murderer. **100m/C; VHS, DVD.** *MX* Donald Pleasence; Dean Stockwell; Angelica Maria; Aldo Ray; Sergio Aragones; *D:* Juan Lopez Moctezuma; *W:* Juan Lopez Moctezuma; *C:* Alex Phillips, Jr.; *M:* Mort Garson.

To Live *Huozhe* **1994** Superb drama follows the lives of one family—weak but adaptable Fugui (You), his strong-willed wife Jiazhen (Li), and their young daughter and son—from prerevolutionary China in the 1940s through the '60s Cultural Revolution. Fugui loses the family fortune in the gambling houses, actually a blessing when the Communists come to power, and the family must struggle to survive financial and increasingly difficult political changes, where fate can change on a whim. Subtle saga about ordinary human lives reacting to terrifying conditions boasts extraordinary performances and evocative imagery. Adapted from the novel "Lifetimes" by Yu Hua. Chinese with subtitles. **130m/C; VHS, DVD.** *CH* Ge You; Gong Li; Niu Ben; Guo Tao; Jiang Wu; *D:* Yimou Zhang; *W:* Lu Wei; Yu Hua; *C:* Lu Yue; *M:* Jiping Zhao. British Acad. '94: Foreign Film; Cannes '94: Actor (You), Grand Jury Prize.

To Live & Die in L.A. **1985 (R)** Fast-paced, morally ambivalent tale of cops and counterfeiters in L.A. After his partner is killed shortly before his retirement, a secret service agent sets out to track down his ruthless killer. Lots of violence; some nudity. Notable both for a riveting car chase and its dearth of sympathetic characters. **114m/C; VHS, DVD, Blu-Ray, UMD.** William L. Petersen; Willem Dafoe; John Pankow; Dean Stockwell; Debra Feuer; John Turturro; Darlanne Fluegel; Robert Downey; *D:* William Friedkin; *W:* William Friedkin.

To Paris with Love ½ **1955** A British man and his son fall in love with a shop girl and her boss while on vacation in Paris. Charming and humorous, with a witty performance from Guinness. **75m/C; VHS, DVD, Streaming.** Alec Guinness; Odile Versois; Vernon Gray; *D:* Robert Hamer; *M:* Edwin Astley.

To Play or to Die **1991** The introverted Kees attends an all-boy school where powerful bullies and sadomasochistic games are the rule. Kees is fascinated by the handsome Charel, the bullies leader. He invites Charel to his home, intending to turn the tables on his tormentor, but nothing goes as planned. Intense and controversial look at gay teens. Directorial debut of Krom. In Dutch with English subtitles. **150m/C; VHS, DVD.** *NL* Geert Hunaerts; Tjebbo Gerritsma; *D:* Frank Krom; *W:* Anne Van De Putte; Frank Krom; *C:* Nils Post; *M:* Kim Hayworth; Ferdinand Bakker.

To Play the King **1993** Sequel to "The House of Cards" finds Francis Urquhart (Richardson), having murdered his way to the Prime Ministery, now bored with his political situation. But things may be changing—the Queen has been succeeded by her liberal son (Kitchen) and Francis, goaded by his equally vicious wife (Fletcher), plots treachery to bring down the monarchy. Followed by "The Final Cut"; adapted from the novel by Michael Dobbs. **212m/C; VHS, DVD.** *GB* Ian Richardson; Michael Kitchen; Diane Fletcher; Kitty Aldridge; Bernice Stegers; Colin Jeavons; Rowena King; Erika Hoffman; Nicholas Farrell; *D:* Paul Seed; *W:* Andrew Davies.

To Please a Lady ½ *Red Hot Wheels* **1950** Romantic comedy-drama about race car driver Gable and reporter Stanwyck. Although leads do their best with the script, they're unable to generate any sparks. However, race track scenes are excellent. Filmed at the Indianapolis Speedway, the spectacular racing footage makes up for overall average film. **91m/B; VHS, DVD.** Clark Gable; Barbara Stanwyck; Adolphe Menjou; Will Geer; Roland Winters; *D:* Clarence Brown; *W:* Barre Lyndon; Marge Decker.

To Protect and Serve **1992 (R)** When crooked cops start getting killed, two young cops are assigned to investigate. Suspicion points to a rookie (Howell), who just may have decided to clean things up his own way. **93m/C; VHS, Streaming.** C. Thomas Howell; Lezlie (Dean) Deane; Richard Romanus; Joe Cortese; *D:* Eric Weston.

To Rome with Love **2012 (R)** Woody Allen seems incapable of making two critically beloved films in a row and so he naturally follows up his Best Picture-nominated "Midnight in Paris" with another step down in a career of peaks and valleys. Allen, once solely a New York filmmaker, continues his European journey of the last decade by moving to Italy and telling a relatively inconsequential ensemble story of love, Italian style. Allen, as always, assembles a notable cast (including Cruz, Baldwin, Eisenberg, and Benigni) and the film is far from his worst but the trip is surprisingly forgettable. **112m/C; DVD, Blu-Ray; Closed Captioned.** *IT US* Woody Allen; Judy Davis; Alec Baldwin; Roberto Benigni; Jesse Eisenberg; Ellen Page; Greta Gerwig; Penelope Cruz; Alison Pill; Flavio Parenti; Alessandro Tiberi; Alessandra Mastronardi; Fabio Armiliato; Antonio Albanese; *D:* Woody Allen; *W:* Woody Allen; *C:* Darius Khondji.

To Save a Life ½ *How to Save a Life* **2010 (PG-13)** In this unsubtle, religious teen drama, all-star athlete Jake Taylor (Wayne) is shaken by the gun suicide of his childhood friend and decides he must change his own life to save the lives of others. It's too bad his spiritual quest comes straight from political talking points, as Jake must endure rejection from his Christianity-hating peers and prevent his girlfriend from getting an abortion. Movie toys with hard questions but all it serves up is easy answers as it devolves into a poorly camouflaged after-school special for evangelical youth groups. Panders to believers and won't convert anyone who isn't. **120m/C; Blu-Ray, On Demand.** Randy Wayne; Sean Michael Afable; Robert Bailey, Jr.; Deja Kreutzberg; Kim Hidalgo; Joshua Weigel; Steve Crowder; Bubba Lewis; D. David Morin; ***D:*** Brian Baugh; ***W:*** Jim Britts; ***C:*** C. Clifford Jones; ***M:*** Christopher Lennertz; Tim Wynn.

To Sir, with Love 1/2 **1967** Teacher in London's tough East End tosses books in the wastebasket and proceeds to teach his class about life. Skillful and warm performance by Poitier as idealistic teacher; supporting cast also performs nicely. Based on the novel by E.R. Braithwaite. LuLu's title song was a big hit in 1967-68. **105m/C; VHS, DVD, Blu-Ray.** *GB* Sidney Poitier; Lulu; Judy Geeson; Christian Roberts; Suzy Kendall; Faith Brook; ***D:*** James Clavell; ***W:*** James Clavell; ***C:*** Paul Beeson; ***M:*** Ron Grainer.

To Sir, With Love 2 **1996** The nearly 70-year-old Poitier reprised his role of dedicated teacher Mark Thackery is this TV sequel to the 1967 film. American-born Thackeray is forced into mandatory retirement after spending 30 years teaching in a tough East End London neighborhood. Returning to Chicago, he can't stay retired and takes a teaching position working with the troublemakers at a South Side school. **92m/C; DVD.** Sidney Poitier; Daniel J. Travanti; Christian Payton; Christopher Birt; Cheryl Lynn Bruce; ***D:*** Peter Bogdanovich; ***W:*** Philip Rosenberg; ***C:*** William Birch; ***M:*** Trevor Lawrence. **TV**

To Sleep with a Vampire **1992 (R)** A Los Angeles bloodsucker is tired of his violent existence and craves the one thing he can't have—daylight. As he stalks his latest victim, a stripper, he decides to take her home and have her tell him about living in daytime. When she realizes what's going on, the intended victim decides to fight for her life. Action and eroticism raises this one above the norm. Remake of "Dance of the Damned." **90m/C; VHS, DVD.** Scott Valentine; Charlie Spradling; Richard Zobel; Ingrid Vold; Stephanie Hardy; ***D:*** Adam Friedman; ***W:*** Patricia Harrington.

To Sleep with Anger 1/2 **1990 (PG)** At first a comic, introspective look at a black middle-class family going about their business in the heart of Los Angeles. Sly charmer Glover shows up and enthralls the entire family with his slightly sinister storytelling and a gnawing doom gradually permeates the household. Insightful look into the conflicting values of Black America. Glover's best performance. **105m/C; VHS, Blu-Ray, Streaming.** Danny Glover; Mary Alice; Paul Butler; Richard Brooks; Carl Lumbly; Vonetta McGee; Sheryl Lee Ralph; ***D:*** Charles Burnett; ***W:*** Charles Burnett; ***C:*** Walt Lloyd. Ind. Spirit '91: Actor (Glover), Director (Burnett), Screenplay, Support. Actress (Ralph); Natl. Film Reg. '17; Natl. Soc. Film Critics '90: Screenplay; Sundance '90: Special Jury Prize.

To the Devil, a Daughter *Child of Satan* **1976 (R)** A nun is put under a spell by a priest who has been possessed by Satan. She is to bear his child. A writer on the occult intervenes. Based on the novel by Dennis Wheatley. One of Kinski's early films. **93m/C; VHS, DVD, Blu-Ray.** Richard Widmark; Christopher Lee; Nastassja Kinski; Honor Blackman; Denholm Elliott; Michael Goodliffe; ***D:*** Peter Sykes; ***W:*** Christopher Wicking; ***C:*** David Watkin.

To the Last Man **1933** An early Scott sagebrush epic, about two feuding families. Temple is seen in a small role. Based on Zane Grey's novel of the same name. **70m/B; VHS, DVD.** Randolph Scott; Esther Ralston; Jack La Rue; Noah Beery, Sr.; Buster Crabbe; Gail Patrick; Barton MacLane; Fuzzy Knight; John Carradine; Jay Ward; Shirley Temple; ***D:*** Henry Hathaway.

To the Lighthouse **1983** The Ramsay family's annual proper British holiday at their Cornwall home turns into a summer of disillusionment in this adaptation of the Virginia Woolf novel. Made for British TV. **115m/C; VHS, DVD.** Rosemary Harris; Michael Gough; Suzanne Bertish; Lynsey Baxter; T.P. McKenna; Kenneth Branagh; ***D:*** Colin Gregg. **TV**

To the Limit **1995 (R)** Actioner finds the pulchritudinous Colette (Smith) revealing to mobster Frank (Travolta) that she's a CIA agent (and if you believe that I have a bridge in Brooklyn to sell you) and that they are the targets of a rogue agent (Richmond). No, Smith can't act but since she takes lots of showers and is supported by some professionals who can, this gets by on trash value alone. **96m/C; VHS, DVD, On Demand.** Anna Nicole Smith; Joey Travolta; Michael Nouri; Branscombe Richmond; John Aprea; Kathy Shower; Rebecca Ferratti; David Proval; ***D:*** Raymond Martino; ***W:*** Joey Travolta; Raymond Martino; ***C:*** Henryk Cymerman; ***M:*** Jim Halfpenny.

To the Shores of Tripoli **1942** Wartime propaganda in the guise of drama, in which a smarmy playboy is transformed into a Marine in boot camp. **82m/C; VHS, DVD.** John Payne; Maureen O'Hara; Randolph Scott; Nancy Kelly; Harry (Henry) Morgan; Maxie "Slapsie" Rosenbloom; William Tracy; Minor Watson; Alan Hale, Jr.; Hugh Beaumont; Hillary Brooke; ***D:*** H. Bruce Humberstone.

To the Stars **2020** In the 1960s, feisty high schooler Maggie (Liberato) moves with her family to a small, conservative town in Oklahoma. There, Maggie connects with the reclusive Iris (Hayward), considered an outsider by her peers, when she saves Iris from a bullying incident involving a group of boys on a deserted country road. The pair build a friendship as Maggie deals with an abusive father (Hale) who blames his daughter's homosexuality on life in the big city. The coming of age story is patiently told, though sometimes predictable. **109m/C; DVD.** Kara Hayward; Jordana Spiro; Tina Parker; Shea Whigham; Lucas Jade Zumann; ***D:*** Martha Stephens; ***W:*** Shannon Bradley-Colleary; ***C:*** Andrew Reed; ***M:*** Heather McIntosh. **VIDEO**

To the Wonder **2012 (R)** Director/writer Malick's "Tree of Life" was accused of being too confusing and hard to follow. It looks downright straightforward compared to his quick (especially for him) follow-up, a drama about a love triangle that once again displays Malick's emphasis on poetry over prose. Affleck plays Neil, a young man who falls in love with Marina (Kurylenko), moving her to Oklahoma from France. While there, the two grow distant as Neil gets closer to a childhood sweetheart (McAdams). Too emotionally distant to be effective, it still has a lyrical style that couldn't be mistaken for anyone else's. **112m/C; DVD, Blu-Ray.** Ben Affleck; Olga Kurylenko; Rachel McAdams; Javier Bardem; ***D:*** Terrence Malick; ***W:*** Terrence Malick; ***C:*** Emmanuel Lubezki; ***M:*** Hanan Townshend.

To Walk with Lions 1/2 **1999 (PG)** Continues the story of lion expert George Adamson, told previously in "Born Free" and "Living Free." Tony Fitzjohn (Michie) takes what he thinks will be a temporary job with Adamson (Harris) and his brother Terence (Bannen) in Kenya in the 1980s. The brothers are running a private wildlife preserve that rehabilitates zoo lions for life in the wild. Tony is naturally wary of his new employment and his curmudgeonly new employers but comes to value them all, even falling in love with anthropologist Lucy (Fox) who's working with the local tribes. Has some disturbing violence (both animal and human). **108m/C; VHS, DVD.** *CA GB* Richard Harris; Ian Bannen; Kerry Fox; John Michie; Hugh Quarshie; Honor Blackman; Geraldine Chaplin; ***D:*** Carl Schultz; ***W:*** Keith Ross Leckie; ***C:*** Jean Lepine; ***M:*** Alan Reeves.

To Wong Foo, Thanks for Everything, Julie Newmar 1/2 **1995 (PG-13)** Hot on the high heels of "The Adventures of Priscilla, Queen of the Desert," comes the sanitized for your protection Yankee version. And its all about hanging on to your dreams and how we're all the same inside, with politically correct gay drag queens doing the sermonizing. Yes, this is the feel-good drag road movie for the 90s. Den mother Vida (Swayze), tough beauty queen Noxeema (Snipes), and hot-blooded Chi Chi (Leguizamo doing his best Rosie Perez) head to Hollywood in a 1967 Cadillac convertible that inconveniently breaks down in a tiny Nebraska town. The "girls" work their magic, and presumably the people of this uncultured, anachronistic backwater will never be the same. One-dimensional characters, flat direction, and inconsistent script undercut exceptional efforts by Swayze and Leguizamo. **108m/C; VHS, DVD, Blu-Ray.** Wesley Snipes; Patrick Swayze; John Leguizamo; Stockard Channing; Blythe Danner; Melinda Dillon; Arliss Howard; Jason London; Christopher Penn; RuPaul Charles; ***Cameo(s):*** Julie Newmar; Robin Williams; ***D:*** Beeban Kidron; ***W:*** Douglas Carter Beane; ***M:*** Rachel Portman.

To Write Love On Her Arms 1/2 **2014 (PG-13)** Based on a true story. Nineteen-year-old Renee struggles with addiction, depression, and self-abuse. She finally turns to friends for help and gets into rehab. New acquaintance Jamie starts a blog detailing her efforts in order to help others struggling with addiction, but Renee finds the attention overwhelming and threatening to her own recovery. **118m/C; DVD.** Kat Dennings; Chad Michael Murray; Rupert Friend; Mark Saul; Juliana Harkavy; ***D:*** Nathan Frankowski; ***W:*** Kate King Lynch; ***C:*** Stephen Campbell; ***M:*** Andy Hunter. **VIDEO**

Toast 1/2 **2010** In this British, made-for-TV, 60s-set family drama, Nigel is a foodie from a young age although, after his mother dies, he and his dad live on toast until 'common' Joan is hired. She turns out to be a tremendous cook who starts instructing Nigel despite his snobbish dislike of her, which doesn't waver even after she becomes his stepmother. Joan's practical training—and home economics at school—lead Nigel to some startling discoveries. Adapted from Nigel Slater's memoir "Toast: The Story of a Boy's Hunger." **96m/C; DVD.** *UK* Freddie Highmore; Oscar Kennedy; Helena Bonham Carter; Ken Stott; Victoria Hamilton; Matthew McNulty; ***D:*** S.J. Clarkson; ***W:*** Lee Hall; ***C:*** Balasz Bolygo; ***M:*** Ruth Barrett. **TV**

The Toast of New Orleans 1/2 **1950** A poor fisherman rises to stardom as an opera singer. Likable, though fluffy production features a plethora of musical numbers. **97m/C; VHS, DVD.** Kathryn Grayson; Mario Lanza; David Niven; Rita Moreno; J. Carrol Naish; ***D:*** Norman Taurog.

Toast of New York **1937** Arnold plays Jim Fisk, a New England peddler who rises to become one of the first Wall Street giants of industry. Atypical Grant performance. **109m/B; VHS, DVD.** Edward Arnold; Cary Grant; Frances Farmer; Jack Oakie; Donald Meek; Billy Gilbert; ***D:*** Rowland V. Lee.

Tobacco Road 1/2 **1941** Loosely based on the Erskine Caldwell novel. The shiftless, backwoods Lester family is struggling to hold onto their last bit of unworkable Georgia farm land but the bank is fixin' to foreclose. Patriarch Jeeter keeps scheming but the Lesters are a dumb bunch and director Ford does an indulgent, questionable southern parody (intended or not) that plays very broadly. **84m/B; DVD.** Charley Grapewin; Elizabeth Patterson; William Tracy; Gene Tierney; Zeffie Tilbury; Dana Andrews; Slim Summerville; Ward Bond; ***D:*** John Ford; ***W:*** Nunnally Johnson; ***C:*** Arthur C. Miller; ***M:*** David Buttolph.

Tobor the Great 1/2 **1954** Sentimental and poorly executed, this film tells the tale of a boy, his grandfather, and Tobor the robot. Villainous communists attempt to make evil use of Tobor, only to be thwarted in the end. **77m/B; VHS, DVD, Blu-Ray.** Charles Drake; Billy Chapin; Karin (Karen, Katharine) Booth; Taylor Holmes; Joan Gerber; Steven Geray; Helen Winston; ***D:*** Lee Sholem.

Tobruk **1966** American GI's endeavor to knock out the guns of Tobruk, to clear the way for a bombing attack on German fuel supply depots of North Africa in this WWII actioner. **110m/C; DVD, Blu-Ray.** Rock Hudson; George Peppard; Guy Stockwell; Nigel Green; ***D:*** Arthur Hiller; ***W:*** Leo Gordon; ***C:*** Russell Harlan; ***M:*** Bronislau Kaper.

Toby McTeague **1987 (PG)** A story about an Alaskan family that breeds Siberian Huskies. When his father is injured, the youngest son tries to replace him in the regional dog-sled race. **94m/C; VHS, DVD.** Winston Rekert; Wannick Bisson; Timothy Webber; ***D:*** Jean-Claude Lord; ***W:*** Djordje Milicevic; Jamie Brown.

Toby Tyler **1959 (G)** A boy runs off to join the circus, and teams up with a chimpanzee. A timeless and enjoyable Disney film that still appeals to youngsters. Good family-fare. **93m/C; VHS, DVD.** Kevin Corcoran; Henry Calvin; Gene Sheldon; Bob Sweeney; ***D:*** Charles T. Barton.

Today We Kill, Tomorrow We Die **1971 (PG)** A rancher is unjustly sent to prison; when his sentence is over he hires a gang to relentlessly track down the culprit who framed him. **95m/C; VHS, DVD.** Montgomery Ford; Bud Spencer; William Berger; Tatsuya Nakadai; Wayde Preston; ***D:*** Tonino Cervi.

Today We Live 1/2 **1933** Triangle love story set in WWI. Crawford is a hedonistic Brit having a fling with her naval brother's (Tone) friend (Young). When American flyer Cooper appears she sets her sights on him but soon he's off to combat in France where he's reported killed. Crawford returns to Young but, naturally, reports of Cooper's death have been greatly exaggerated and the two eventually reunite. Faulkner coscripted from his story "Turn About" which had no female character and concerned the rivalry between naval officers and fly boys. **113m/B; VHS, DVD.** Gary Cooper; Joan Crawford; Franchot Tone; Robert Young; Roscoe Karns; Louise Closser Hale; ***D:*** Howard Hawks; ***W:*** Dwight Taylor; William Faulkner; Edith Fitzgerald.

Today You Die 1/2 **2005 (R)** Harlan Banks (Seagal) is a criminal looking to retire from the bad life and seems genuinely surprised when his boss frames him for a crime and sends him to prison. Escaping with the help of a well-connected gangsta he goes out for the predictable bout of revenge. **90m/C; DVD.** Steven Seagal; Treach; Sarah Buxton; Nick Mancuso; Robert Miano; Kevin Tighe; ***D:*** Don E. Fauntleroy; ***W:*** Kevin Moore; ***C:*** Don E. Fauntleroy; ***M:*** Stephen (Steve) Edwards.

Today's Special **2009 (R)** Second-generation Indian-American Samir (Mandvi) is a talented sous chef at an upmarket Manhattan restaurant. Passed up for the top spot at his employer's newest restaurant, he walks out and visits his disapproving parents at their Queens restaurant, Tandoori Palace, to tell them he's moving to Paris. Dad (Petel) literally has a heart attack, forcing Samir to step in. Having never cooked Indian food, Samir finds help from cabby Akbar (Shah), who claims to have cooked for India's celebrities in the old country. Samir discovers true passion, his own culture, and love in this little gem. Great for artsies, foodies, and romantics alike. **99m/C; Blu-Ray.** Aasif Mandvi; Jess Weixler; Dean Winters; Madhur Jaffrey; Harish Patel; Kevin Corrigan; Naseeruddin Shah; ***D:*** David Kaplan; ***W:*** Aasif Mandvi; Jonathan Bines; ***C:*** David Tumblety; ***M:*** Stephane Wremble.

The Todd Killings 1/2 *A Dangerous Friend; Skipper* **1971 (R)** A psychotic young man commits a series of murders involving young women. Sleazy, forgettable picture wastes a talented cast. **93m/C; VHS, DVD.** Robert F. Lyons; Richard Thomas; Barbara Bel Geddes; Ed Asner; Sherry Miles; Gloria Grahame; Belinda J. Montgomery; ***D:*** Barry Shear; ***W:*** Joel Oliansky.

Todd McFarlane's Spawn *Spawn* **1997** McFarlane's comic book creation makes his cable TV animated debut. Hellspawn was once human CIA assassin Al Simmons, murdered in the line of duty, who sold his soul to see his wife one last time. When he comes back from the grave with superhuman powers it's again as a killer with attitude, who leaves a high body count. A PG-13 version clocks in at 90 minutes. **147m/C; VHS, DVD, UMD.** ***V:*** Keith David; Richard Dysart; Ronny Cox; ***D:*** Eric Radomski; ***W:*** Alan B. McElroy; Gary Hardwick. **CABLE**

Tod@s Caen **2019** Adan (Chaparro) is a seductive conqueror of women who follows his own rules of seduction with much success. Because of his prowess, he is willing to share all he knows with his friends. At the same time, producer Mia (Higareda) wants to launch her own dating show. She wants to use the show, Todos Caen, to teach women how to land a man and have him bend to your will. When the pair meet in a bar one night, a battle of seduction begins. Certainly an unoriginal romantic comedy but the duo's charisma overcomes what the plot lacks. Spanish with subtitles. **120m/C; DVD.** Martha Higareda; Omar Chaparro; Tiare Scanda; Edgar Vivar; Eugenio Siller; *D:* Ariel Winograd; *W:* Martha Higareda; Cory Brusseau; *C:* Juan Jose Saravia; *M:* Milo Coello; Joselo Higareda.

The Toe Tactic **2008** Odd mix of animation and live action that isn't comedy or kid-oriented for a change. When Mona's (Rabe) father passes away, she succumbs to her grief and depression. This attracts the attention of sympathetic cosmic entities in the form of cartoon doodles who influence her life in hopes it will turn around. **84m/C; DVD.** Lily Rabe; Mary Kay Place; Xander Berkeley; Richard Cox; Kevin Corrigan; *D:* Emily Hubley; *W:* Emily Hubley; *C:* Andrij Parekh.

Toe to Toe **2009** Teen girl drama about friendship, race, wealth, and sex. Disciplined African-American Tosha (Martin) is determined to leave her life in the DC projects behind and get a scholarship to Princeton. Her opposite is wealthy white chick Jesse (Krause), who acts out her every self-destructive impulse (including promiscuity). They're seniors and friendly lacrosse teammates at the same prep school until the cliche of liking the same boy comes between them. Director/writer Abt piles on the teen conflicts but has two worthy young actresses to handle the melodrama. **104m/C; DVD.** Louisa Krause; Sonequa Martin; Silvestre Rasuk; Gaius Charles; Leslie Uggams; Ally Walker; *D:* Emily Abt; *W:* Emily Abt; *C:* Alan Jacobsen; *M:* Force Theory.

Toga Party *Pelvis; Disco Madness* **1977 (R)** Fraternity house throws a wild toga party in this raunchy low-rent depiction of college life. **82m/C; VHS, DVD.** Luther Bud Whaney; Mary Mitchell; *D:* Robert T. Megginson; *W:* Straw Weisman; *C:* Lloyd Freidus.

Together ½ *He Ni Zaiyiqi* **2002 (PG)** Sentimental story about a musical prodigy, his dad, and the "new" China. With many of the restrictions of the Cultural Revolution a thing of the past, Western classical music is once more taught and performed. Violin prodigy Liu Xiaochun (Tang, who does his own playing) is 13 and his father Li Cheng (Liu) is determined to make the most of the boy's talents though the family is poor. Cheng and Xiaochun head to Beijing for an important musical competition and the boy makes an impressive showing. So much so, that his father is able to persuade a crancky but talent teacher (Wang) to mentor Xiaochun. While in the big city, the lad also becomes infatuated with beautiful new neighbor Lili (Chen), a model with a consumer-oriented lifestyle from whom he receives important lessons about sacrifice and friendship. Mandarin with subtitles. **116m/C; VHS, DVD.** *CH NK* Yun Tang; Peiqi Liu; Zhiwen Wang; Hong Chen; Chen Kaige; *D:* Chen Kaige; *W:* Chen Kaige; Xiaolu Xue; *C:* Hyung-koo Kim; *M:* Lin Zhao.

Together Again ½ **1943** Anne Crandall (Dunne) inherited the position of mayor of a small Vermont town after her husband's death. Father-in-law Jonathan (Coburn) wants Anne to remarry and when a statue of Anne's husband is damaged, he sends her to New York to meet with sculptor Corday (Boyer), who mistakes Anne for his new (nude) model. Further mistaken impressions and romantic complications ensue when Corday follows Anne back to Vermont. **93m/B; DVD.** Irene Dunne; Charles Boyer; Charles Coburn; Mona Freeman; Jerome Courtland; *D:* King Vidor; *W:* F. Hugh Herbert; Virginia Van Upp; *C:* Joseph Walker; *M:* Werner R. Heymann.

Together Again for the First Time ½ **2008** The Wolders-Frobisher clan are a reluctantly blended family who haven't spent any time together since their parents' marriage seven years before. Now circumstances have reunited them on Christmas Eve, which results in them struggling to get along and exposing some family secrets. **85m/C; DVD.** David Ogden Stiers; Julia Duffy; Larisa Oleynik; Joseph Lawrence; Kirby Heyborne; Blake Bashoff; Kelly Stables; Lauren Storm; Michelle Page; *D:* Jeff Parkin; *W:* Jeff Parkin; Reed McColm; *C:* Brandon Christensen; *M:* Michael Cohen. **VIDEO**

Togo **2019 (PG)** Alaskan sled master Seppala (Dafoe) has trained many dogs but puppy Togo is persistent and challenging. Though curmudgeon Seppala considers getting rid of clever Togo, his wife Constance (Nicholson) disagrees with the idea because of the dog's potential. Within a few years, Togo has become the leader on Seppala's sled team. Togo's skills are put to the test when Seppala and his dogs must make a perilous journey to bring a serum to their community to save dying children. The family friendly drama features an inspiring story, appropriate humor, and well-shot action sequences, all while showing a love for animals. **113m/C; DVD.** Willem Dafoe; Julianne Nicholson; Christopher Heyerdahl; Richard Dormer; Michael Greyeyes; *D:* Ericson Core; *W:* Tom Flynn; *C:* Ericson Core; *M:* Mark Isham. **VIDEO**

The Toilers and the Wayfarers **1997** New Ulm, Minnesota is an ultraconservative German-American community where the teenaged Dieter (Klemp) is the object of affection for best friend Phillip (Woodhouse). Although Dieter thinks he might be gay, he rejects Phillip, who soon takes off for Minneapolis. This leaves Dieter open to the attentions of slightly older, free-spirited Udo (Schirg). Dieter's father strongly disapproves and the young man leaves to join Phillip in the big bad city, with Udo in tow. But since none of the boys have any money, they're soon working the streets to survive. English and German with subtitles. **85m/C; VHS, DVD.** Matt Klemp; Ralf Schirg; Andrew Woodhouse; *D:* Keith Froelich; *W:* Keith Froelich; *C:* Jim Tittle; *M:* Chan Poling.

Tokyo! **2009** Directors Gondry, Carax, and Bong tell three separate stories set in Japan's capitol city of Tokyo. Instead of a love letter type tribute to the metropolis' hustle and bustle, a la "New York Stories," the setting is more of a convenience for its title. Gondry's segment features a couple feeling lost and isolated as they move to Tokyo with "Eraserhead"-esque filmmaking dreams. Bong's story is about a shut-in who hordes pizza boxes and eventually falls in love with a pizza delivery girl. Finally, Carax brings a sewer-dwelling gnome out into sunlit Tokyo for an urban adventure. Strange, but uneven and mismatched short films that say little about anything, and unfortunately aren't as engaging as they may sound. Japanese and French with subtitles. **112m/C; Blu-Ray.** *JP FR* Ayako Fujitani; Ryo Kase; Ayumi Ito; Jean-Francois Balmer; Denis Levant; Yu Aoi; Teruyuki Kagaway; *D:* Michel Gondry; Leos Carax; Joon-ho Bong; *W:* Michel Gondry; Leos Carax; Joon-ho Bong; Gabrielle Bell; *C:* Caroline Champetier; Jun Fukumoto; Masami Inomoto; *M:* Etienne Charry; Lee Byung Woo.

Tokyo Cowboy **1994** Tokyo burger flipper No Ogawa (Ida) dreams of the wild west and becoming a cowboy, inspired by the letters of his childhood pen pal, Kate (Hirt). So he decides to head for Kate's small Canadian hometown and realize his fantasies. Kate's meddling mom makes him welcome but Kate herself, only recently returned home, is hiding the fact that her friend Shelly (Mortil) is also her lover. Both have some unrealistic expectations to overcome in their quest for happiness. **94m/C; VHS, DVD.** Hiromoto Ida; Christianne Hirt; Janne Mortil; Anna Ferguson; Michael Ironside; *D:* Kathy Garneau; *W:* Caroline Adderson; *C:* Kenneth Hewlett; *M:* Ari Wise.

Tokyo-Ga ½ **1985** Impelled by his love for the films of Yasujiro Ozu, Wenders traveled to Tokyo and fashioned a caring document of both the city and of Ozu's career, using images that recall and comment on Ozu's visual motifs. **92m/C; VHS, DVD.** *D:* Wim Wenders; *W:* Wim Wenders.

Tokyo Joe ½ **1949** A war hero/nightclub owner returns to Tokyo and becomes ensnared in blackmail and smuggling while searching for his missing wife and child. Slow-moving tale has never been considered one of Bogart's better movies. **88m/B; VHS, DVD.** Humphrey Bogart; Florence Marly; Alexander Knox; Sessue Hayakawa; Jerome Courtland; Lore Lee Michel; *D:* Stuart Heisler.

Tokyo Olympiad **1966** A monumental sports documentary about the 1964 Olympic Games in its entirety. Never before available for home viewing. Letterboxed with digital sound. In Japanese with English subtitles. **170m/C; VHS, DVD.** *JP* *D:* Kon Ichikawa; *W:* Kon Ichikawa; *C:* Kazuo Miyagawa.

Tokyo Raiders **2000 (PG-13)** Remarkably stylish Hong Kong action flick. Director Jingle Ma brings a music video sensibility to the proceedings. The plot concerns a detective (Tony Leung) and his hunt for a gangster, but that's a negligible excuse for a series of cleverly choreographed action scenes. The physical violence is carefully modulated for a young audience, and many gadgets are employed. **100m/C; DVD.** *CH* Tony Leung Chiu-Wai; Ekin Cheng; Toru Nakamura; Hiroshi Abe; Kelly Chen; Kumiko Endo; Minami Shirakawa; Majyu Ozawa; Cecilia Cheung; *D:* Jingle Ma; *W:* Susan Chan; Felix Chong; *C:* Jingle Ma; Chan Chi Ying; *M:* Peter Kam.

Tokyo Sonata ½ **2009 (PG-13)** A Japanese businessman, husband, and father of two unexpectedly loses his job. Unable to break the news to his devoted wife, he dresses up every morning and pretends to go to work, instead wasting the days away with a former classmate who is also unemployed. Although unaware, his family begins to disobey him—his teenage son enlists in the Army to fight for the United States, while his adolescent son goes behind his back to take piano lessons. Known for creepy neo-horror flicks, director Kurosawa (not *that* Kurosawa) effectively portrays the horror of a disintegrating family in the wake of a global recession that translates to any culture, with just enough well-timed humor to keep it from being morose. **119m/C; Blu-Ray.** *JP CH* Teruyuki Kagawa; Kyoko Koizumi; Yukimi Koyanagi; Kanji Tsuda; Koji Yakusho; Inowaki Kai; Haruka Igawa; Kazuya Kojima; *D:* Kiyoshi Kurosawa; *W:* Kiyoshi Kurosawa; Max Mannix; Sachiko Tanaka; *C:* Akiko Ahsizawa; *M:* Kazumasa Hashimoto.

Tokyo Story *Tokyo Monogatari* **1953** Poignant story of elderly couple's journey to Tokyo where they receive little time and less respect from their grown children. Masterful cinematography, and sensitive treatment of universally appealing story. In Japanese with English subtitles. **134m/B; VHS, DVD, Blu-Ray.** *JP* Chishu Ryu; Chieko Higashiyama; So Yamamura; Haruko Sugimura; Setsuko Hara; *D:* Yasujiro Ozu; *W:* Yasujiro Ozu; *C:* Yuuharu Atsuta; *M:* Kojun Saito.

Tokyo Tribe ½ **2015** The line between music video and feature film is defiantly crossed in Sion Sono's ridiculous gangster epic, told almost entirely in hip-hop. Recapping the plot is nearly impossible, but you've never seen anything like this film that's kind of like The Warriors meets a Hype Williams music video. Most of the characters rap their lines directly to the screen and Sono never stops moving his camera, circling these Tokyo gang members as they fight and kill for territory and respect. The movie gets a little exhausting before it's even half over but one has to admire Sono's commitment to his insane concept. **116m/C; DVD, Blu-Ray, Streaming.** *JP* Ryohei Suzuki; Shota Sometani; Riki Takeuchi; Nana Seino; *D:* Shion Sono; *W:* Shion Sono; *C:* Daisuke Soma.

Tol'able David **1921** A simple tale of mountain folk, done in the tradition of Mark Twain stories. A family of hillbillies is embroiled in a feud with a clan of outlaws. When the community's mail is stolen by the troublesome ruffians, the family's youngest member, who harbors dreams of becoming a mail driver, comes to the rescue. Silent film. **91m/B; Silent; DVD.** Richard Barthelmess; Gladys Hulette; Ernest Torrence; *D:* Henry King; *W:* Henry King; Edmund Goulding; *C:* Henry Cronjager. Natl. Film Reg. '07.

Tolkien ½ **2019 (PG-13)** Young Ronald (Gilby) gains a love of mythology from his mother Mabel (Donnelly). After her early death, Ronald is orphaned, becomes a ward of a priest, and is sent to a boarding school for such children. There, Ronald becomes close friends with three other creative boys, and they remain friends as they grow and attend college. Older Ronald (Hoult) fights in World War I with these friends, but the experience changes him in unexpected ways. A biopic of iconic author J.R.R. Tolkien, the film explores his life with reverence but focuses on ideas that are hard to translate into a film story. **112m/C; DVD, Blu-Ray.** Nicholas Hoult; Colm Meaney; Laura Donnelly; Nia Gwynne; Pam Ferris; *D:* Dome Karukoski; *W:* David Gleeson; Stephen Beresford; *C:* Lasse Frank Johannessen; *M:* Thomas Newman.

The Toll Gate ½ **1920** Quick on the draw outlaw Black Deering (Hart) is betrayed by one of his own men but manages to escape the authorities. He heads into the wilderness and finds shelter with an abandoned young mother (Nilsson). But the law is on his trail. **73m/B; Silent; VHS, DVD.** William S. Hart; Anna Q. Nilsson; Jack (H.) Richardson; Joseph Singleton; *D:* Lambert Hillyer; *W:* Lambert Hillyer; *C:* Joseph August.

The Tollbooth **2004** Ernest, cliched comedy follows 22-year-old Sarabeth Cohen (Sokoloff) as she tries to escape what she sees as her smothering Brooklyn Jewish family for the life of a rebellious artist in Manhattan. She even gets a sweet goy boyfriend, Simon (McElhenney), but familial problems interfere while Sarabeth decides where her life should truly be going. **85m/C; DVD.** Marla Sokoloff; Liz Stauber; Rob McElhenney; Idina Menzel; Jayce Bartok; Ronald Guttman; Tovah Feldshuh; *D:* Debra Kirschner; *W:* Debra Kirschner; *C:* Stefan Forbes; *M:* David Shire.

Tom and Francie ½ **2005** Spinal Tap meets Sesame Street in this fabulous spoof on low-budget TV kids' shows. Twelve years after Tom and Francie's children show "The Flower Shop" is cancelled, they plan a comeback with their new show "Accepting Everyone Through Music." They are joined by a prop master who expresses his hostility through his puppets and a lawyer who smells a post-Barney gravy train. Apple-cheeked Golden is a standout as kid-show trouper Francie. **85m/C; DVD.** Annie Golden; Chris Fields; Steven Skybell; Tara O'Boyle; *D:* Patrick Michael Denny; *W:* Patrick Michael Denny; *C:* Patrick Michael Denny; *M:* Annie Golden; Chris Fields; Patrick Michael Denny. **VIDEO**

Tom and Huck **1995 (PG)** Tom Sawyer and pal Huck Finn are the only witnesses to a murder. Tom's friend Muff is framed for the crime and the boys are being tracked by the real killer, Injun Joe. They must decide to come forward, expose the true fiend, and risk their own hides or run away and let an innocent man hang. True to the Twain story, Thomas plays a mischievious Tom to Renfro's troublemaking Huck. Film was shot in Mooresville, Alabama, population 69, just down the road a piece from the Hannibal, Missouri of Twain fame. **91m/C; VHS, DVD.** Jonathan Taylor Thomas; Brad Renfro; Eric Schweig; Charles Rocket; Amy Wright; Michael McShane; Marian Seldes; Rachael Leigh Cook; Lanny Flaherty; Courtland Mead; Peter M. MacKenzie; Heath Lamberts; *D:* Peter Hewitt; *W:* Stephen Sommers; David Loughery; *C:* Bobby Bukowski; *M:* Stephen Endelman.

Tom and Jerry: The Movie **1993 (G)** Everybody's favorite animated cat/mouse duo (who began life in a 1940 MGM short "Puss Gets the Boot") hit the big screen, this time talking (unlike their animated shorts). Rather than cartoon mayhem our two protagonists are goody-two-shoes (with songs yet!) but still retain their charm. Kids will like it, but true "Tom and Jerry" fans should probably stick to the original cartoons. **84m/C; VHS, DVD.** *V:* Richard Kind; Dana Hill; Charlotte Rae; Henry Gibson; Rip Taylor; Howard Morris; Edmund Gilbert; David Lander; *D:* Phil Roman; *W:* Dennis Marks; *M:* Henry Mancini; *M:* Leslie Bricusse.

Tom & Thomas ½ **2002 (PG)** Lonely nine-year-old Thomas (Johnson) lives with his father Paul (Bean) in London. He starts having dreams about a boy who looks like him and discovers he was adopted—and his twin brother Tom grew up in an orphanage straight out of "Oliver Twist." Then the two boys find each other and trouble as well. Adventurous and not as grim as the plot may sound, although it does have disturbing elements. **110m/C; DVD.** *GB* Aaron Taylor-Johnson; Sean Bean; Bill Stewart; Inday Ba; Sean Harris; Geraldine James; Derek de Lint; *D:* Esme Lammers; *W:* Esme Lammers; *C:* Marc Felperlaan; *M:* Paul M. van Brugge.

Tom & Viv **1994 (PG-13)** American T.S. Eliot (Dafoe) is an Oxford student in 1914 when he meets the moody, monied Vivien Haigh-Wood (Richardson). After a whirlwind courtship, they marry—disastrously. Eliot begins to establish himself as a poet, while Vivien serves as muse/typist and unsuccessfully battles her misdiagnosed illnesses with too much drinking and drugs, as well as embarrassing public scenes. As Eliot gains success, he increasingly distances himself from the unhappy Viv, until finally committing her to an asylum. Dafoe is fine as the chilly, withdrawn poet but Richardson steals the film as his flamboyant, lost wife. Based on the play by Michael Hastings, who co-wrote the screenplay. **115m/C; VHS, DVD.** *GB* Willem Dafoe; Miranda Richardson; Rosemary Harris; Tim Dutton; Nickolas Grace; Philip Locke; Clare Holman; Joanna McCallum; ***D:*** Brian Gilbert; ***W:*** Michael Hastings; Adrian Hodges; ***M:*** Debbie Wiseman. Natl. Bd. of Review '94: Actress (Richardson), Support. Actress (Harris).

Tom Brown's School Days 1/2 *Adventures at Rugby* **1940** Depicts life among the boys in an English school during the Victorian era. Based on the classic novel by Thomas Hughes. Remade in 1951. **86m/B; VHS, DVD.** *GB* Cedric Hardwicke; Jimmy Lydon; Freddie Bartholomew; ***D:*** Robert Stevenson.

Tom Brown's School Days **1951** Tom enrolls at Rugby and is beset by bullies in classic tale of English school life. British remake of the 1940 version. Based on the novel by Thomas Hughes. **93m/B; VHS, DVD.** *GB* Robert Newton; John Howard Davies; James Hayter; ***D:*** Gordon Parry.

Tom Clancy's Netforce *Netforce* **1998 (R)** In 2005, technology has become so advanced that a special unit of the FBI, known as Netforce, has been established to police the Internet. Alex Michaels (Bakula) heads the unit after the murder of predecessor Steve Day (Kristofferson), leading Michaels to believe that criminals are trying to cause a global computer crash. Michael's two prime suspects are computer mogul Will Stiles (Reinhold) and crime boss Leong Cheng (Tagawa). Based on a story co-written by Clancy. **90m/C; VHS, DVD.** Scott Bakula; Joanna Going; Brian Dennehy; Kris Kristofferson; Judge Reinhold; Cary-Hiroyuki Tagawa; CCH Pounder; Paul Hewitt; Chelsea Field; Frank Vincent; Alexa Vega; Victor Raider-Wexler; ***D:*** Robert Lieberman; ***W:*** Lionel Chetwynd; ***C:*** David Hennings; ***M:*** Jeff Rona. **TV**

Tom, Dick, and Harry 1/2 **1941** Dreamy girl is engaged to three men and unable to decide which to marry. It all depends on a kiss. Remade as "The Girl Most Likely." **86m/B; VHS, DVD.** Ginger Rogers; George Murphy; Burgess Meredith; Alan Marshal; Phil Silvers; ***D:*** Garson Kanin; ***W:*** Paul Jarrico.

Tom Horn **1980 (R)** The final days of one of the Old West's legends. Gunman Tom Horn, hired by Wyoming ranchers to stop cattle rustlers, goes about his job with a zeal that soon proves embarrassing to his employers. Beautifully photographed and authentic in its attention to details of the period, the film nonetheless takes liberties with the facts of Horn's life and is lacking in other aspects of production. **98m/C; VHS, DVD.** Steve McQueen; Linda Evans; Richard Farnsworth; Billy Green Bush; Slim Pickens; ***D:*** William Wiard; ***W:*** Thomas McGuane; ***C:*** John A. Alonzo; ***M:*** Ernest Gold.

Tom Jones **1963** Bawdy comedy based on Henry Fielding's novel about a rustic playboy's wild life in 18th century England. Hilarious and clever with a grand performance by Finney. One of the sexiest eating scenes ever. Redgrave's debut. Theatrically released at 129 minutes, the film was recut by the director, who decided it needed tightening before its 1992 re-release on video. **121m/C; VHS, DVD, Blu-Ray.** *UK* Albert Finney; Susannah York; Hugh Griffith; Edith Evans; Joan Greenwood; Diane Cilento; George Devine; David Tomlinson; Joyce Redman; Lynn Redgrave; Julian Glover; Peter Bull; David Warner; ***D:*** Tony Richardson; ***W:*** John Osborne; ***C:*** Walter Lassally; ***M:*** John Addison. Oscars '63: Adapt. Screenplay, Director (Richardson), Film, Orig. Score; British Acad. '63: Film, Screenplay; Directors Guild '63: Director (Richardson); Golden Globes '64: Film--Mus./Comedy, Foreign Film; Natl. Bd. of Review '63: Director (Richardson); N.Y. Film Critics '63: Actor (Finney), Director (Richardson), Film.

Tom Jones **1998** Miniseries based on the Henry Fielding novel goes further than the hit 1963 movie by including Fielding (Sessions) as the narrator of Tom's bawdy adventures. Tom (Beesley) is an 18th-century orphan with a heart of gold, an affinity for trouble, and an eye for the ladies. His true love is Sophie (Morton), the daughter of the boisterous Squire Western (Blessed). But of course, the path of true love never runs smooth. Lavish adaptation and lots of fun. **300m/C; VHS, DVD.** *UK* Max Beesley; Samantha Morton; Brian Blessed; John Sessions; Benjamin Whitrow; Frances de la Tour; ***D:*** Metin Huseyin; ***W:*** Simon Burke. **CABLE**

Tom Sawyer 1/2 **1973 (G)** Musical version of the Mark Twain tale of the boisterous Tom, his friend Becky Thatcher, and various adventures, including the fence whitewashing. Amusing kid fare shot on location in Missouri. **104m/C; VHS, DVD, Blu-Ray.** Johnny Whitaker; Jodie Foster; Celeste Holm; Warren Oates; Jeff East; ***D:*** Don Taylor; ***M:*** John Williams.

Tom Thumb **1958** Diminutive boy saves village treasury from bad guys. Adapted from classic Grimm fairy tale. Special effects combine live actors, animation, and puppets. **92m/C; VHS, DVD.** *GB* Russ Tamblyn; Peter Sellers; Terry-Thomas; ***D:*** George Pal; ***W:*** Ladislas Fodor; ***C:*** Georges Perinal; ***M:*** Douglas Gamley.

Tomahawk 1/2 **1951** Indian sympathizer Jim Bridger (Heflin) is a local scout who anticipates trouble when the government decides to build a wagon route straight through Sioux hunting grounds in order to reach Montana's gold mines. The touchy situation is made worse by cavalry officer Dancy (Nicol) who thinks the only good Indian is a dead one. **82m/C; DVD.** Van Heflin; Preston Foster; Yvonne De Carlo; Alex Nicol; Jack Oakie; Tom Tully; Rock Hudson; Ann Doran; ***D:*** George Sherman; ***W:*** Maurice Geraghty; Silvia Richards; ***C:*** Charles P. Boyle; ***M:*** Hans J. Salter.

The Tomb 1/2 **2009 (R)** Haphazard horror that's a loose adaptation of the Poe short story "Ligeia." Prof Jonathan Merrick suddenly marries sultry Russian grad student Ligeia and they move into her childhood home in the Ukraine. Jon discovers she's terminally ill and Ligeia is turning to sorcery in a bid for immortality that relies on the extraction of human souls. **90m/C; DVD.** Wes Bentley; Sofya Skya; Eric Roberts; Mackenzie Rosman; Kaitlin Doubleday; Michael Madsen; Cary-Hiroyuki Tagawa; ***D:*** Michael Staininger; ***W:*** John Shirley; ***C:*** Christopher Benson; ***M:*** Patrick Cassidy. **VIDEO**

Tomb of Ligeia *Tomb of the Cat* **1964** The ghost of a man's first wife expresses her displeasure when groom and new little missus return to manor. One of the better Corman adaptations of Poe. Also available with "The Conqueror Worm" on Laser Disc. **82m/C; VHS, DVD, Blu-Ray.** *GB* Vincent Price; Elizabeth Shepherd; John Westbrook; Oliver Johnston; Richard Johnson; Derek Francis; Richard Vernon; Ronald Adam; Frank Thornton; Penelope Lee; Denis Gilmore; ***D:*** Roger Corman; ***W:*** Robert Towne; ***C:*** Arthur Grant; ***M:*** Kenneth V. Jones.

Tomb Raider 1/2 **2018 (PG-13)** A throwback action film based on a video game. Though Lara's (Vikander) archaeologist father has long been missing and is presumed dead, she worships him, yet still feels pain caused by his long absences during her childhood. Traveling to the supposed location of ancient cursed tomb of Himiko, a Japanese shaman queen, that her father had studied, Lara makes an ally, Lu Ren (Wu) and encounters a desperate corporate mercenary Mathias Vogel (Goggins). To find and gain entry to the tomb, she must, fight, kill, and solve puzzles. Thrilling action sequences and a strong female heroine add to this film's unexpected appeal. **118m/C; DVD, Blu-Ray.** Alicia Vikander; Dominic West; Walton Goggins; Daniel Wu; Kristin Scott Thomas; ***D:*** Roar Uthaug; ***W:*** Geneva Robertson-Dworet; Alastair Siddons; ***C:*** George Richmond; ***M:*** Junkie XL.

Tomboy **1940** Shy country boy and a not-so-shy city girl meet, fall in love, and overcome obstacles that stand in their path. **70m/B; VHS, DVD.** Jackie Moran; Marcia Mae Jones; Grant Withers; Charlotte Wynters; George Cleveland; Clara Blandick; ***D:*** Robert McGowan; ***W:*** Dorothy Davenport Reid; Marion Orth; ***C:*** Harry Neumann; ***M:*** Edward Kay.

Tomboy WOOF! **1985 (R)** A pretty auto mechanic is determined to win not only the race but the love and respect of a superstar auto racer. **91m/C; VHS, DVD, Blu-Ray.** Betsy Russell; Eric Douglas; Jerry Dinome; Kristi Somers; Richard Erdman; Toby Iland; ***D:*** Herb Freed.

Tombstone **1993 (R)** Saga of Wyatt Earp and his band of law-abiding large moustaches beat the Kasdan/Costner vehicle to the big screen by several months. Legendary lawman Wyatt (Russell) moves to Tombstone, Arizona, aiming to start a new life with his brothers, but alas, that's not to be. The infamous gunfight at the OK Corral is here, and so is best buddy Doc Holliday, gunslinger and philosopher, a role designed for scenery chewing (Kilmer excels). Romance is supplied by actress Josephine, though Delany lacks the necessary romantic spark. Russell spends a lot of time looking troubled by the violence while adding to the body count. Too self-conscious, suffers from '90s western revisionism, but blessed with a high energy level thanks to despicable villains Lang, Biehn, and Boothe. **130m/C; VHS, DVD.** Kurt Russell; Val Kilmer; Michael Biehn; Sam Elliott; Dana Delany; Bill Paxton; Powers Boothe; Stephen Lang; Jason Priestley; Dana Wheeler-Nicholson; Billy Zane; Thomas Haden Church; Joanna Pacula; Michael Rooker; Harry Carey, Jr.; Billy Bob Thornton; Charlton Heston; Robert John Burke; John Corbett; Buck Taylor; Terry O'Quinn; Pedro Armendariz, Jr.; Chris Mitchum; Jon Tenney; ***Nar:*** Robert Mitchum; ***D:*** George P. Cosmatos; ***W:*** Kevin Jarre; ***C:*** William A. Fraker; ***M:*** Bruce Broughton.

Tomcats WOOF! **2001 (R)** Writer/director Pourier takes a half-step down from his previous occupation of porn screenwriter with this steaming pile of misogyny. Michael (O'Connell) is a basically decent guy up to his ethics in gambling debt. The only way out is to marry off his last single friend, Kyle (Busey), in order to win a bet made with their other buddies. He tracks down Natalie (Elizabeth), the only one of Kyle's conquests that he regrets dumping, who agrees, for half the dough and a measure of revenge, but soon the plotters fall in love. Every woman here is depicted as some form of evil, and humiliated accordingly. This isn't new, but it wouuld help if something was at least chuckle-worthy. There's no such relief here, unless you find renegade cancerous sex organs amusing. **92m/C; VHS, DVD, UMD.** Jerry O'Connell; Shannon Elizabeth; Jake Busey; Jaime Pressly; Bernie Casey; David Ogden Stiers; Travis Fine; Heather Stephens; Horatio Sanz; Julia Schultz; ***D:*** Gregory Poirier; ***W:*** Gregory Poirier; ***C:*** Charles Minsky; ***M:*** David Kitay.

Tomie 1/2 **1999** Originally an episodic manga by Japanese horror writer Junji Ito, later made into a series of films generally regarded as not quite as scary as the comics they were based on (though to be blunt the comics are so violent it's doubtful they could be released as a film if they were absolutely true to the source material). All of the stories feature an immortal high school girl named Tomie. She inspires jealous rage and obsession in all the men (and some women) around her, causing them to commit acts of violence in brief bursts of rage. Inevitably she is always killed, but regenerates regardless of what is done to her. **95m/C; DVD.** *JP* Miho Kanno; Tomorowo Taguchi; Rumi; Ikko Suzuki; Mami Nakamura; Yoriko Douguchi; Kouta Kusano; Kenji Mizhuhashi; ***D:*** Ataru Oikawa; ***W:*** Ataru Oikawa; Junji Ito; ***C:*** Akira Sakoh; Kazuhiro Suzuki.

Tommy *The Who's Tommy* **1975 (PG)** Peter Townsend's rock opera as visualized in the usual hyper-Russell style about the deaf, dumb, and blind boy who becomes a celebrity due to his amazing skill at the pinball machines. A parade of rock musicians perform throughout the affair, with varying degrees of success. Despite some good moments, the film ultimately falls prey to ill-conceived production concepts and miscasting. **108m/C; VHS, DVD, Blu-Ray.** *GB* Ann-Margret; Sir Elton John; Oliver Reed; Tina Turner; Roger Daltrey; Eric Clapton; Keith Moon; Pete Townshend; Jack Nicholson; Robert Powell; Paul Nicholas; Barry Winch; Victoria Russell; Ben Aris; Mary Holland; Jennifer Baker; Susan Baker; Arthur Brown; John Entwhistle; ***D:*** Ken Russell; ***W:*** Keith Moon; Ken Russell; John Entwhistle; ***C:*** Ronnie Taylor; Dick Bush; ***M:*** Pete Townshend; John Entwhistle. Golden Globes '76: Actress--Mus./Comedy (Ann-Margret).

Tommy and the Cool Mule 1/2 **2009 (PG)** Cliche story of a young boy trying to save his family farm from bank foreclosure with the help of a talking mule. **94m/C; DVD.** Grant Barker; Siri Baruc; Kevin Sorbo; Jordan Reynolds; ***V:*** Ice-T; ***D:*** Andrew Stevens; ***W:*** Andrew Stevens; ***C:*** Ken Blakey; ***M:*** Eric Wurst; David Wurst.

Tommy Boy **1995 (PG-13)** Not-too-bright rich kid Tommy (Farley) teams up with snide, officious accountant Richard (Spade) to save the family auto parts business after dad (Dennehy) buys the farm. Tommy and Richard must deal with a conniving stepmom and stepbrother (Derek and Lowe), a ruthless rival (Aykroyd), and a road trip from hell to drum up some new business. Not as bad as it sounds, but inconsistent direction and too-familiar characters offset the amusing chemistry between Farley and Spade. **98m/C; VHS, DVD, Blu-Ray.** Chris Farley; David Spade; Brian Dennehy; Bo Derek; Dan Aykroyd; Julie Warner; Rob Lowe; ***D:*** Peter Segal; ***W:*** Bonnie Turner; Terry Turner; ***C:*** Victor Kemper; ***M:*** David Newman. MTV Movie Awards '96: On-Screen Duo (Chris Farley/ David Spade).

Tommy's Honour 1/2 **2017 (PG)** A heartfelt feature that explains how golf became a modern, professional sport. In nineteenth century Scotland, Tom Morris (Mullen) works as a caddy and groundskeeper at the Royal and Ancient Golf Club of St. Andrews. Though Tom plays, it is his son Tommy (Lowden) who has more talent. The pair plays together successfully but must challenge class norms and gain financial concessions from the head of the golf club, Alexander Boothby (Neill). Tommy also upends romantic norms by becoming involved with an older woman, Meg Drinnen (Lovibond). Not just for golf fans because of the complex portrayal of the father-son relationship. **112m/C; DVD.** Sam Neill; Peter Mullan; Ophelia Lovibond; Jack Lowden; Max Deacon; ***D:*** Jason Connery; ***W:*** Pamela Martin; Kevin Cook; ***C:*** Gary Shaw; ***M:*** Christian Henson.

Tomorrow **1972 (PG)** Powerful tale of the love of two lonely people. Outstanding performance by Duvall as lumber mill worker who falls for a pregnant woman. Based on the neglected Faulkner story. **102m/B; VHS, DVD, Blu-Ray.** Robert Duvall; Olga Bellin; Sudie Bond; ***D:*** Joseph Anthony; ***W:*** Horton Foote.

Tomorrow Is Another Day **1951** Bill (Cochran) was in prison since he was a kid so the man/child is easily taken advantage by dime-a-dance gal Catherine (Roman) after his release. She's got a cop/ pimp beau, there's an accidental shooting Bill doesn't remember, but it leads to Bill and Catherine going on the lam. Warner Bros. fooled with the ending, making it even more contrived than intended, but Roman is worth watching as the floozy who discovers her heart. **90m/B; DVD.** Steve Cochran; Ruth Roman; Hugh Sanders; Lurene Tuttle; Ray Teal; Morris Ankrum; John Kellogg; ***D:*** Felix Feist; ***W:*** Guy Endore; Art Cohn; ***C:*** Robert Burks; ***M:*** Daniele Amfitheatrof.

Tomorrow Is Forever 1/2 **1946** Welles and Colbert marry shortly before he goes off to fight in WWI. Badly wounded and disfigured, he decides to stay in Europe while Colbert, believing Welles dead, eventually marries Brent. Fast forward to WWII when Brent, a chemical manufacturer, hires a new scientist to work for him in the war effort (guess who). This slow-moving melodrama wastes a good cast. Six-year-old Wood debuts as Welles' adopted daughter. **105m/B; VHS, DVD, Blu-Ray.** Claudette Colbert; Orson Welles; George Brent; Lucile Watson; Richard Long; Natalie Wood; ***D:*** Irving Pichel; ***C:*** Joseph Valentine; ***M:*** Max Steiner.

The Tomorrow Man **2001 (R)** Just go with the flow, cause this time travel adventure yarn doesn't make a whole lot of sense. Larry Mackey (Bernsen) is your average joe, living an average life in the 1970s with his son Bryon. Then Mackey's son is kidnapped by notorious criminal Mac (Rusler) who happens to have time-traveled from 30 years in the future. Larry gets together with a time cop (Kennedy) to get the kid back and discovers that Byron actually grows up to be Mac—and dad needs to figure out why. **95m/C; VHS, DVD.** Corbin Bernsen; Zach Galligan; Beth Kennedy; Morgan Rusler; Adam Sutton; ***D:*** Doug Campbell. **VIDEO**

The Tomorrow Man 🦴🦴 **2019 (PG-13)** A former systems analyst at a factory, Ed (Lithgow) focuses his obsession with order in preparing for the apocalypse he believes is coming. Spending most of his time on message boards and stockpiling certain items, he meets an older woman named Ronnie (Danner) in the grocery store they both frequent and mistakenly believes she is also a doomsday prepper. He asks her out, and they become romantically involved though the relationship is challenged by their personal fears and Ed's chaotic family life. A bit unfocused at times, it efficiently delves into human experiences like loneliness with meaningful performances. **94m/C; DVD.** John Lithgow; Blythe Danner; Derek Cecil; Katie (Kathryn) Aselton; Sophie Thatcher; ***D:*** Noble Lincoln Jones; ***W:*** Noble Lincoln Jones; ***C:*** Noble Lincoln Jones; ***M:*** Paul Leonard-Morgan.

Tomorrow Never Comes 🦴 1/2 **1977** When he discovers his girlfriend has been unfaithful, a guy goes berserk and eventually finds himself in a stand-off with the police. Violent. **109m/C; VHS, DVD.** Oliver Reed; Susan George; Raymond Burr; John Ireland; Stephen McHattie; Donald Pleasence; ***D:*** Peter Collinson.

Tomorrow Never Dies 🦴🦴 **1997 (PG-13)** 18th installment of the James Bond series is all style and little else packaged in a tedious action adventure. Our villain is a media mogul (Pryce) who plans to start WWIII in order to increase his newspaper revenues. (Rupert Murdoch, start your lawyers!) In between the blantant product placements (from Heineken to Visa), our secret agent Bond (Brosnan, who seems bored with the role in his second appearance) sets out to foil the nutty plans. Bond gets help from Hong Kong action queen Yeoh as a Chinese agent, and a bevy of toys from the antiquated Q, including a BMW controlled by remote. Direction and flow is on autopilot after the opening scene and despite Yeoh's energetic high-kicks and the sleek techno toys, it can't revitalize what has become a third-class imitator of its predecessors. **119m/C; VHS, DVD, Blu-Ray.** Pierce Brosnan; Jonathan Pryce; Michelle Yeoh; Teri Hatcher; Dame Judi Dench; Colin Salmon; Samantha Bond; Desmond Llewelyn; Joe Don Baker; Ricky Jay; Vincent Schiavelli; Geoffrey Palmer; ***D:*** Roger Spottiswoode; ***W:*** Bruce Feirstein; ***C:*** Robert Elswit; ***M:*** David Arnold.

Tomorrow the World 🦴🦴 **1944** This bizarre little wartime drama is dated in almost every respect. Emil Bruckner (Homeier) is a Hitler Youth who's sent to live with his uncle (March) in America. The conflict between a fascist mindset and liberal tolerance is painted with very broad strokes. Both acting and writing have an extravagant quality that contemporary audiences will have trouble accepting. **86m/B; DVD.** Fredric March; Betty Field; Agnes Moorehead; Skip Homeier; Joan Carroll; Boots Brown; Edit Angold; Rudy Wiesler; Marvin Davis; Patsy Ann Thompson; Mary Newton; Tom Fadden; ***D:*** Leslie Fenton; ***W:*** Ring Lardner, Jr.; Leopold Atlas; ***C:*** Henry Sharp.

Tomorrow We Disappear 🦴🦴 1/2 **2014** A feature-length documentary following the last days of the Kathputi Colony in New Dehli, India. When the land is sold to real estate developers, the magicians, puppeteers, and circus performers that live in this slum must prepare for eviction. As decisions are being made about how they can stay together or if they should splinter forever, the documentary follows a puppeteer, a magician, and an acrobat as they look to the future. As they anticipate what is to come, issues such India's history and the importance of preservation of folk culture are considered as well. **80m/C; DVD, Streaming, Download.** ***D:*** Jim Goldblum; Adam M. Weber; ***C:*** Will Basanta; ***M:*** Dan Romer. **VIDEO**

Tomorrow We Live 🦴 1/2 **1942** A crazy criminal, who calls himself The Ghost, blackmails Pop Bronson, who owes a desert cafe, because he knows the old man is an escaped con. The Ghost forces Pop to store stolen tires to sell on the black market, which Pop's daughter Julie discovers. The Ghost wants Julie for himself so she uses her Army beau Bob to try and get rid of the creep but The Ghost has bigger problems with a rival gang. **66m/B; DVD.** Ricardo Cortez; Emmett Lynn; Jean Parker; William Marshall; Rose Anne Stevens; Frank S. Hagney; ***D:*** Edgar G. Ulmer; ***W:*** Barty Lytton; ***C:*** Jack Greenhalgh; ***M:*** Leo Erdody.

Tomorrow You're Gone 🦴 **2012** An ex-con goes on a road trip to fulfill his prison mentor's request for revenge by killing a man he has never met. **92m/C; DVD, Blu-Ray, Streaming.** Stephen Dorff; Michelle Monaghan; Willem Dafoe; Robert LaSardo; Kerry Rossall; ***D:*** David Jacobson; ***W:*** Matthew F. Jones; ***C:*** Michael Fimognari; ***M:*** Peter Salett. **VIDEO**

Tomorrowland 🦴🦴 1/2 **2015 (PG)** Casey Newton (Robertson) has always felt a little bit different, like she didn't belong. When she runs into a former inventor named Frank Walker (Clooney), she figures out why. Like all Disney heroes and heroines, Casey is special, and she and Frank jet off to Tomorrowland, a place where anything is possible. Brad Bird makes his first misstep with this CGI-heavy, bloated adventure film that constantly reminds the viewer about the importance of creativity and a sense of adventure but rarely provides it. There are great ideas aplenty but it's just nowhere near as fun as it should be. **107m/C; DVD, Blu-Ray.** George Clooney; Hugh Laurie; Britt Robertson; Raffey Cassidy; Tim McGraw; ***D:*** Brad Bird; ***W:*** Brad Bird; Damon Lindelof; ***C:*** Claudio Miranda; ***M:*** Michael Giacchino.

Tone-Deaf 🦴🦴 **2019 (R)** Los Angeles-based millennial Olive (Crew) believes herself to be a talented pianist though she cannot play coherently. One day, the self-absorbed Olive is fired from her job and her live-in boyfriend walks out. Convinced to take a weekend vacation in the country, she stays at an impressive rental home owned by elderly widower Harvey (Patrick). As Olive enjoys her vacation, Harvey becomes more unhinged as he expresses hatred for modern life and young people and takes violent action. Thought-provoking at times, the murky satiric film moves between dark comedy and horror as it explores ideas related to intergenerational conflict. **87m/C; DVD, Blu-Ray.** Amanda Crew; Robert Patrick; Hayley Marie Norman; Johnny Pemberton; Nancy Linehan Charles; ***D:*** Richard Bates, Jr.; Yvonne Valdez; ***W:*** Richard Bates, Jr.; ***C:*** Ed Wu; ***M:*** Michl Britsch.

Toni Erdmann 🦴🦴🦴 **2016 (R)** Winfried Conradi (Simonischek) travels to Bucharest, Romania to essentially harass his daughter Ines (an amazing Huller), who is there working on a project. She's a workaholic and Winfried is a free-wheeling jokester, who takes on the alter ego of Toni Erdmann, complete with a wig and fake teeth when he really feels like being goofy. He teaches Ines to let go a little bit, including a hysterical climax involving a clothing-optional party. Warning: Writer/director Ade's epic comedy is nearly three hours. **162m/C; DVD, Blu-Ray.** Sandra Hüller; Peter Simonischek; Michael Wittenborn; Thomas Loibl; Trystan Pütter; ***D:*** Maren Ade; ***W:*** Maren Ade; ***C:*** Patrick Orth. Ind. Spirit '17: Foreign Film.

Toni Morrison: The Pieces I Am 🦴🦴🦴 **2019 (PG-13)** A lively and captivating look at the life, work, challenges, and influence of Nobel Prize-winning author Toni Morrison, featuring interviews with her, her friends, scholars, and critics. Documentarian Greenfield-Sanders explores Morrison's childhood, including her early realizations about race and the power of words, the barriers she faced early in her career, her behind-the-scenes struggles, and her pursuit of the craft. Interviews with people like Random House editor Angela Davis reveal how Morrison helped other black authors. Released just before her death in 2019, this serves as a fitting remembrance to a literary legend. **120m/C; DVD.** Toni Morrison; Oprah Winfrey; ***D:*** Timothy Greenfield-Sanders; ***C:*** Graham Willoughby; ***M:*** Kathryn Bostic.

Tonight and Every Night 🦴🦴 1/2 **1945** Cabaret singer and RAF pilot fall in love during WWII. Her music hall post puts her in the midst of Nazi bombing, and her dedication to her song and dance career puts a strain on the romance. Imaginative production numbers outweigh pedestrian storyline. **92m/C; VHS, DVD.** Rita Hayworth; Lee Bowman; Janet Blair; Marc Platt; Leslie Brooks; ***D:*** Victor Saville.

Tonight or Never 🦴🦴 **1931** Nella (Swanson) is a young opera singer whose Venice debut is criticized for her lack of passion. So she spends the night with a nameless handsome admirer (Douglas), which does the trick. Nella is suddenly offered a contract with the Metropolitan Opera and learns that her new lover is a talent scout who arranged the whole thing and everything works out just peachy. Film is adapted from a play by Lili Hatvany, in which Douglas also starred. **80m/B; VHS, DVD.** Gloria Swanson; Melvyn Douglas; Ferdinand Gottschalk; Alison Skipworth; Boris Karloff; Robert Greig; ***D:*** Mervyn LeRoy; ***W:*** Ernest Vajda; Frederic Hatton; Fanny Hatton; ***C:*** Gregg Toland; ***M:*** Alfred Newman.

Tonight We Raid Calais 🦴🦴 **1943** Quickie propaganda effort has French-speaking British Intelligence agent Carter (Sutton) sent into Nazi-occupied France to pin point a munitions plant for an RAF bombing run. He poses as the son of patriotic farmer Bonnard (Cobb), much to the dismay of the man's daughter Odette (Annabelle), who fears Nazi reprisals. **70m/B; DVD.** John Sutton; Annabella; Lee J. Cobb; Beulah Bondi; Blanche Yurka; Howard da Silva; Marcel Dalio; ***D:*** John Brahm; ***W:*** Waldo Salt; ***C:*** Lucien Ballard; ***M:*** Emil Newman; Cyril Mockridge.

Tonight You're Mine 🦴🦴 1/2 *You Instead* **2011 (R)** Brit rom com is a lively rock 'n' roll trifle. Adam and his bandmate Tyko are headlining a big outdoor music festival in Scotland. He gets into an argument with Morello, the lead singer of a riot grrl band, and they are suddenly and inexplicably handcuffed together by some crazy religious dude preaching peace, love, and understanding. They're attracted to one another but still have to bicker and fuss (and perform) before the happy ending. Pic was shot on location during the actual T in the Park festival, which is an atmospheric plus. **80m/C; DVD, Streaming.** *UK* Luke Treadaway; Mathew Baynton; Natalia Tena; Gavin Mitchell; Joseph Mydell; Ruta Gedmintas; Alastair Mackenzie; ***D:*** David Mackenzie; ***W:*** Thomas Leveritt; ***C:*** Giles Nuttgens; ***M:*** Brian M. McAlpine.

Tonio Kroger 🦴🦴 **1965** A young writer travels through Europe in search of intellectual and sensual relationships and a home that will suit him. He must balance freedom and responsibility. Works best if one is familiar with the Thomas Mann novel on which film is based. In German with English subtitles. **92m/B; VHS, DVD.** *GE* Jean-Claude Brialy; Nadja Tiller; Gert Frobe; ***D:*** Rolf Thiele.

Tonka 🦴🦴 1/2 *A Horse Named Comanche* **1958** A children's story about a wild horse tamed by a young Indian, only to have it recruited for the Battle of Little Bighorn. Mineo is fine as the Indian brave determined to be reunited with his steed. The film also makes a laudable effort to portray the Indians as a dignified race. The movie, however, stumbles at its conclusion and is contrived throughout. **97m/C; VHS, DVD, Streaming.** Sal Mineo; Phil Carey; Jerome Courtland; ***D:*** Lewis R. Foster.

Tony Draws a Horse 🦴🦴 1/2 **1951** An eight-year-old draws an anatomically correct horse on the door of his father's office, leading to a rift between the parents as they argue how to handle the heartbreak of precociousness. Somewhat uneven but engaging comedy, based on a play by Lesley Storm. **90m/B; VHS, DVD.** Cecil Parker; Anne Crawford; Derek Bond; Barbara Murray; Mervyn Johns; Barbara Everest; David Hurst; ***D:*** Jack Paddy Carstairs.

Tony n' Tina's Wedding 🦴 1/2 **2007 (R)** Adaptation of the long-running off-Broadway comedy (and filmed in 2004) hits every broad cliche possible. Tony (McIntyre) and Tina (Kunis) are a young Italian-American couple from Queens whose wedding and reception prove to be tests of their love. Obstacles include her mother (Lopez) and his father (Fiore), who hate each other and refuse to stop fighting; Tina's drunken ex-boyfriend (Grenier), who causes trouble; the flamboyant videographer (Diaz); Tony's pot-smoking groomsmen; and general tackiness and mayhem. **105m/C; DVD.** Mila Kunis; Adrian Grenier; Priscilla Lopez; John Fiore; Guillermo Diaz; Krista Allen; Dean Edwards; Kim Director; Richard Portnow; ***D:*** Roger Paradiso; ***W:*** Roger Paradiso; ***C:*** Giselle Chamma.

Tony Rome 🦴🦴 1/2 **1967** Tony Rome (Sinatra) is a P.I. living the good life on his boat in Miami. He's hired by wealthy builder Rudolph Kosterman (Oakland) to keep an eye on his erratic daughter, Diana (Lyons). Turns out there's organized crime and blackmail involved as well—oh, and a babe named Ann (St. John). An entertaining diversion based on the novel "Miami Mayhem" by Marvin H. Albert. Followed by "The Lady in Cement" (1968). **110m/C; VHS, DVD, Blu-Ray.** Frank Sinatra; Jill St. John; Simon Oakland; Gena Rowlands; Richard Conte; Lloyd Bochner; Jeffrey Lynn; Sue Lyon; ***D:*** Gordon Douglas; ***W:*** Richard L. Breen; ***C:*** Joseph Biroc; ***M:*** Billy May.

Too Bad She's Bad 🦴🦴 1/2 *Peccato Che Sia una Canaglia* **1954** Wide-eyed cab driver Paolo (Mastroianni) can't help but desire sexy Lina (Loren with a blonde 'do) despite her attempt to swipe his ride. Later he realizes that thievery is her family's business and believes marrying her will turn her around. First of thirteen films starring the Italian acting legends. In Italian, with subtitles. **96m/B; VHS, DVD.** Vittorio De Sica; Sophia Loren; Marcello Mastroianni; Memmo Carotenuto; Giorgio Sanna; Michael Simone; Margherita Bagni; Wanda Benedetti; Maria Britneva; Manlio Busoni; Giulio Cali; Carloni Pietro; Giullo Paradisi; Cella Marga; Pasquale Cennamo; Nino Dal Fabbro; Giacomo Furia; Enrico Leurini; Marcella Melnati; Amalia Pellegrini; Giuseppe Ricagno; Giulio Tomasini; John Stacy; Walter Bartoletti; Mauro Sacripante; ***D:*** Alessandro Blasetti; ***W:*** Suso Cecchi D'Amico; Alessandro Continenza; Ennio Flaiano; Alberto Moravia; ***C:*** Aldo Giordani; ***M:*** Alessandro Cicognini.

Too Beautiful for You 🦴🦴 *Trop Belle pour Toi* **1988 (R)** A successful car salesman, married for years to an extraordinarily beautiful woman, finds himself head over heels for his frumpy secretary. Depardieu plays the regular guy who finds he's never believed in the love and fidelity of a woman he thinks is too beautiful for him. In French with English subtitles. **91m/C; VHS, DVD.** *FR* Gerard Depardieu; Josiane Balasko; Carole Bouquet; Roland Blanche; Francois Cluzet; ***D:*** Bertrand Blier; ***W:*** Bertrand Blier; ***C:*** Philippe Rousselot. Cannes '89: Grand Jury Prize; Cesar '90: Actress (Bouquet), Director (Blier), Film, Writing.

Too Big to Fail 🦴🦴 **2011** Dry but not completely unentertaining depiction of the 2008 financial crisis and the government bailout of the industry as seen through the eyes of Treasury Secretary Henry Paulson (Hurt) and a lot of bankers and policy wonks. Wall Street insiders come across as either greedy, clueless as to the severity of the problem, or both. Based on the book by Andrew Ross Sorkin. **98m/C; DVD, Blu-Ray.** William Hurt; Ed Asner; Billy Crudup; Paul Giamatti; Topher Grace; Matthew Modine; Bill Pullman; James Woods; ***D:*** Curtis Hanson; ***W:*** Peter Gould; ***C:*** Kramer Morgenthau; ***M:*** Marcelo Zarvos. **CABLE**

Too Busy to Work 🦴🦴 1/2 **1932** Hobo Jubilo (Rogers) has been searching for the man who ran off with his wife and daughter long ago. He becomes a reluctant handyman at Judge Hardy's (Burton) and discovers his daughter Rose (Nixon) is happy and living the good life and that his wife has died. Jublio decides to keep his identity a secret and encourages Rose's romance with Dan (Powell). Rogers remade his 1919 silent "Jubilo." **70m/B; DVD.** Will Rogers; Marion (Marian) Nixon; Dick Powell; Frederick Burton; Daniel Cosgrove; Louise Beavers; Charles Middleton; Bert Hanlon; Constantine Romanoff; ***D:*** John Blystone; ***W:*** Barry Connors; Philip Klein; ***C:*** Charles G. Clarke.

Too Cool for Christmas 🦴🦴 *A Very Cool Christmas* **2004** Forbidden to go on a ski trip with her friends, disdainful 16-year-old Lindsay (Nevin) doesn't want to hang with her family so she heads to the mall. Santa Claus (Hamilton) wants a makeover to impress Mrs. Claus (Mills) and rewards Lindsay's efforts by taking her along on his Christmas Eve run, which brings home the true meaning of the holidays. In this version, Lindsay has two dads; in the alternate "A Very Cool Christmas," they were replaced by a mom/dad combo. **91m/C; DVD.** Brooke Nevin; George Hamilton; Donna Mills; Barclay Hope; Adam Harrington; Jodelle Ferland; ***D:*** Sam Irvin; ***W:*** Michael Gelbart; ***C:*** Anthony C. Metchie; ***M:*** Peter Allen. **CABLE**

Too Far to Go 🦴🦴🦴 **1979** Terrific TV adaptation of a series of John Updike stories focusing on the rocky longtime marriage of not-so-proper New Englanders Danner and Moriarty. **98m/C; VHS, DVD.** Blythe Danner; Michael Moriarty; Glenn Close; Ken Kercheval; ***W:*** William Hanley.

Too Hot to Handle 🦴🦴🦴 **1938** Two rival photographers searching for a beautiful lady-pilot's missing brother wind up in Brazil, where they encounter a dangerous tribe of voodoo types. Amusing, if exaggerated, picture of the lengths to which reporters will go to for a story. Classic Gable. **105m/B; VHS, DVD.** Clark Gable; Myrna Loy; Walter Pidgeon; Walter Connolly; Leo Carrillo; Virginia Weidler; ***D:*** Jack Conway.

Too Late Blues 🦴🦴 **1961** Moody drama was the second film--and first studio production--for Cassavetes. Arrogant L.A. jazz pianist Ghost Wakefield (Darin) resists going commercial with his combo until his agent Benny (Chambers) introduces him to wannabe singer Jess (Stevens). He offers her a job and Ghost winds up playing alone in cocktail lounges until he takes a hard look at what his life's become. **103m/B; DVD, Blu-Ray.** Bobby Darin; Stella Stevens; Everett Chambers; Marilyn Clark; Seymour Cassel; Vince Edwards; Nick Dennis; Richard Chambers; ***D:*** John Cassavetes; ***W:*** John Cassavetes; Richard Carr; ***C:*** Lionel Lindon; ***M:*** David Raskin.

Too Late for Tears 🦴🦴🦴 *Killer Bait* **1949** An honest husband and his not so honest wife stumble on a load of mob-stolen cash and become entangled in a web of deceit and murder as the wife resorts to increasingly desperate measures to keep her newfound fortune. Atmospheric and entertaining film noir albeit sometimes confusing. **99m/B; VHS, DVD, Blu-Ray.** Lizabeth Scott; Don DeFore; Dan Duryea; Arthur Kennedy; Kristine Miller; Barry Kelley; Denver Pyle; Jimmy Ames; Billy Halop; Jimmie Dodd; ***D:*** Byron Haskin; ***W:*** Roy Huggins; ***C:*** William Mellor; ***M:*** R. Dale Butts.

Too Late the Hero 🦴🦴🦴 *Suicide Run* **1970 (PG)** Unlikely band of allied soldiers battle Japanese force entrenched in the Pacific during WWII. Rousing adventure, fine cast. **133m/C; VHS, DVD.** Michael Caine; Cliff Robertson; Henry Fonda; Ian Bannen; Harry Andrews; Denholm Elliott; William Beckley; Ronald Fraser; Percy Herbert; Patrick Jordan; Harvey Jason; Sam Kydd; Ken Takakura; ***D:*** Robert Aldrich; ***W:*** Robert Aldrich; Lois Heller; ***C:*** Joseph Biroc; ***M:*** Gerald Fried.

Too Many Crooks 🦴🦴 **1959** A British spoof of crime syndicate films. Crooks try to extort, but bungle the job. Terry-Thomas is fun, as always. **85m/B; VHS, DVD.** *GB* Terry-Thomas; Brenda de Banzie; George Cole; ***D:*** Mario Zampi.

Too Many Girls 🦴🦴 1/2 **1940** Beautiful heiress goes to a small New Mexico college to escape from a cadre of gold-digging suitors. Passable adaptation of the successful Rodgers and Hart Broadway show, with many original cast members and the original stage director. Lucy and Desi met while making this film, and married shortly after. **85m/B; VHS, DVD.** Lucille Ball; Richard Carlson; Eddie Bracken; Ann Miller; Desi Arnaz, Sr.; Hal LeRoy; Libby Bennett; Frances Langford; Van Johnson; ***D:*** George Abbott; ***M:*** George Bassman; Richard Rodgers; ***M:*** Lorenz Hart.

Too Many Husbands 🦴🦴 **1940** Vicky (Arthur) is told that adventurer husband Bill (MacMurray) drowned during a shipwreck so eventually she marries Henry (Douglas), Bill's best friend and business partner. Then Bill is rescued from an island and returns to his wife—who isn't anymore. The men vie for Vicky's affections and she likes the attention since both neglected her the first go-round. However, they get tired of her indecision. **84m/B; DVD.** Jean Arthur; Fred MacMurray; Melvyn Douglas; Harry Davenport; Dorothy Peterson; Melville Cooper; Edgar Buchanan; ***D:*** Wesley Ruggles; ***W:*** Claude Binyon; ***C:*** Joseph Walker; ***M:*** Frederick "Friedrich" Hollander.

Too Much Sun 🦴 1/2 **1990 (R)** A dying man can prevent his fortune from falling into the hands of a corrupt priest simply by having one of his two children produce an heir. The problem is, they're both gay! **97m/C; VHS, Streaming.** Robert Downey, Jr.; Ralph Macchio; Eric Idle; Andrea Martin; Laura Ernst; Jim Haynie; ***D:*** Robert Downey.

Too Much, Too Soon 🦴🦴 **1958** Soap opera showbiz drama based on the autobiography of Diana Barrymore. The daughter of alcoholic former matinee idol John Barrymore, Diana (Malone) can't get daddy's love and bitter mommy Blanche (Patterson), who writes poetry as Michael Strange, is also neglectful. So the young actress goes into her own self-destructive spiral of booze, men, and suicide attempts. The equally hard-drinking Errol Flynn took on the role of his old buddy Barrymore. **121m/B; DVD.** Dorothy Malone; Errol Flynn; Neva Patterson; Efrem Zimbalist, Jr.; Ray Danton; Murray Hamilton; Martin Milner; ***D:*** Art Napoleon; ***W:*** Art Napoleon; ***C:*** Carl Guthrie; ***M:*** Ernest Gold.

Too Smooth 🦴🦴 *Hairshirt* **1998 (R)** Danny (Paras) is a smooth-talking actor wannabe who lies to every woman he knows—until he meets naive Corey (Wright), whom he thinks is the girl of his dreams. But when his vindictive starlet ex (Campbell) learns about Corey's new romance, she becomes determined to expose him for the lying dog she's sure he remains. **91m/C; VHS, DVD.** Dean Paras; Neve Campbell; Katie Wright; Rebecca Gayheart; Christian Campbell; David DeLuise; Stefan Brogren; Adam Carolla; Marley Shelton; ***D:*** Dean Paras; ***W:*** Dean Paras; ***M:*** Nathan Barr.

Too Soon to Love 🦴 **1960** Teen exploitation melodrama. Bad guy Buddy (Nicholson) tries to attack Cathy (West) at the drive-in and then beats up Jim (Evans), who comes to her rescue. Cathy is a little too grateful to Jim and gets pregnant, which leads to a sleazy abortion doctor and more trouble. **85m/B; DVD.** Jennifer West; Richard Evans; Jack Nicholson; Ralph Manza; Warren Parker; ***D:*** Richard Rush; ***W:*** Richard Rush; Laszlo Gorog; ***C:*** William C. Thompson; ***M:*** Ronald Stein.

Too Young to Be a Dad 🦴🦴 *A Family's Decision* **2002** When 15-year-old honor student Matt Freeman's (Dano) equally young girlfriend Francesca (Stuart) gets pregnant, her family wants to put the baby up for adoption. Matt initially agrees but when his parents (Baker, Davison) continue to offer their support, he starts to have his doubts about giving his daughter up. Told from the teen father's perspective. **90m/C; DVD.** Paul Dano; Kathy Baker; Bruce Davison; Katie Stuart; Nigel Bennett; Sherry Miller; Terra Vnesa; ***D:*** Eva Gardos; ***W:*** Edithe Swensen; ***C:*** Ronald Orieux; ***M:*** Jonathan Goldsmith. **CABLE**

Too Young to Die 🦴🦴 **1990 (R)** Teenager Amanda (Lewis) hooks up with the wrong guy in sleazy Billy (Pitt), who hooks her on drugs and turns her into a prostitute. She meets nice guy Mike (O'Keefe), who briefly takes her away from the life but when their relationship falls apart, Amanda goes back to Billy. Billy eggs her on to get revenge for being dumped and Amanda winds up on trial for murder. Fact-based TV movie. **92m/C; VHS, DVD, Blu-Ray.** Juliette Lewis; Brad Pitt; Michael Tucker; Michael O'Keefe; Emily Longstreth; Alan Fudge; ***D:*** Robert Markowitz; ***W:*** David Hill; ***C:*** Eric Van Haren Noman; ***M:*** Charles Bernstein.

Too Young to Kiss 🦴🦴 1/2 **1951** Struggling pianist Cynthia Potter (Allyson) can't get an audition with impresario Eric Wainwright (Johnson) until she hears he's looking for young prodigies to make up a children's concert tour. So she passes herself off as a 14-year-old bobby-soxer and gets the job. This eventually causes problems since Cynthia falls for Eric and he worries over her precociousness. **91m/B; DVD.** June Allyson; Van Johnson; Gig Young; Rita (Paula) Corday; Hans Conried; Larry Keating; ***D:*** Robert Z. Leonard; ***W:*** Albert Hackett; Frances Goodrich; ***C:*** Joseph Ruttenberg.

Too Young to Marry 🦴 1/2 **2007** Predictable teen drama. Over the objections of their families, high schoolers Max (Casey) and Jessica (Dobrev) get married after graduation. Jessica starts her freshman year at Harvard but when Max's enrollment is deferred, he takes a construction job. The time apart puts their marriage in jeopardy. **90m/C; DVD.** Nina Dobrev; Dillon Casey; Trevor Blumas; Anna Hopkins; Polly Draper; Frank Schorpion; ***D:*** Michel Poulette; ***W:*** Elle Triedman; ***C:*** Stephen Reizes; ***M:*** Luc St. Pierre. **CABLE**

The Toolbox Murders 🦴 **1978 (R)** Unknown psychotic murderer brutally claims victims one at a time, leaving police mystified and townsfolk terrified. Sick and exploitative, with predictably poor production values. **93m/C; VHS, DVD, Blu-Ray.** Cameron Mitchell; Pamelyn Ferdin; Wesley Eure; Nicolas Beauvy; Aneta Corsaut; Tim Donnelly; Evelyn Guerrero; ***D:*** Dennis Donnelly; ***W:*** Robert Easter; Ann Kindberg; ***C:*** Gary Graver.

Tooth and Nail 🦴 **2007 (R)** You've got your post-apocalyptic world, you've got your struggle to survive, you've got cannibals, and it's still boring. Civilization collapses and chaos rules when the world runs out of oil. One struggling group has taken over an abandoned hospital, working together to stay alive, which is hard enough—and it only gets worse when a gang of marauding cannibals comes along, looking for their next meal. **94m/C; DVD.** Rachel Miner; Rider Strong; Michael Kelly; Robert Carradine; Vinnie Jones; Michael Madsen; Gregg Easterbrook; ***D:*** Mark H. Young; ***W:*** Mark H. Young; ***C:*** Elia Cmiral.

The Tooth Fairy 🦴 **2006** Peter (Munro) is renovating an old house, and his girlfriend Darcy (West) and her 12-year-old daughter Pamela (Munoz) come to help out. While looking around, Pam meets young Emma (Ballard), who tells her that the house was owned by an old woman named Elizabeth Craven (Konoval), who lured neighborhood kids inside with the promise of presents if they would give her their baby teeth. Instead, she killed them. Apparently, renovating the house has stirred up "The Tooth Fairy" and when Pam's last baby tooth happens to fall out, the horrors begin again. Silly rather than scary. **89m/C; DVD.** Lochlyn Munro; Chandra West; Karin Konoval; P.J. Soles; Steve Bacic; Nicole Munoz; Jianna Ballard; ***D:*** Chuck Bowman; ***W:*** Stephen J. Cannell; Corey Strode; Cookie Rae Brown; ***C:*** David Pelletier; ***M:*** Richard John Baker; Jon Lee. **VIDEO**

Tooth Fairy 🦴🦴 **2010 (PG)** Minor league hockey player Derek Thompson (Johnson) has earned his nickname because his opponents have lost a lot of their teeth in games. When Derek tells his girlfriend Carly's (Judd) six-year-old Tess (Whitlock) that the tooth fairy isn't real, the angry tooth fairy shows up and makes Derek substitute for him for two weeks—complete with tutu, wings, and magic wand. Also strained, in typical fashion, is his relationship with Carly's teenage son Randy (Ellison). And, naturally, just as things seem to turn around for Derek he whiffs on his shot, literally. Despite the cliches, a likeable Johnson is entertaining for kids of all ages and the rest of the cast—including Lily, the tooth fairy godmother (Andrews), and Jerry, the fairy gadget guy (Crystal)?helps an otherwise lackluster flick take flight. **101m/C; DVD, Blu-Ray.** Dwayne "The Rock" Johnson; Julie Andrews; Destiny Whitlock; Stephen Merchant; Ryan Sheckler; Ashley Judd; Billy Crystal; Seth MacFarlane; Chase Ellison; ***D:*** Michael Lembeck; ***W:*** Lowell Ganz; Babaloo Mandell; Joshua Sternin; Jeffrey Ventimilia; Randi Mayem Singer; ***C:*** David Tattersall; ***M:*** George S. Clinton.

Tooth Fairy 2 🦴 **2012 (PG)** Direct-to-video sequel to 2010's "Tooth Fairy." Larry wants to win over would-be girlfriend Brooke but instead he upsets a boy in her afterschool program by denying the existence of the Tooth Fairy. Larry's punished by having to assume the role--complete with wings and lots of pink clothing. Young children may find it mildly amusing. **86m/C; DVD, Blu-Ray.** Larry the Cable Guy; Erin Beute; David Mackey; Brady Reiter; ***D:*** Alex Zamm; ***W:*** Ben Zazove; ***C:*** Levie Isaacks; ***M:*** Chris Hajian. **VIDEO**

Toothless 🦴🦴 1/2 **1997** Katherine Lewis (Alley) is a work-obsessed dentist who is struck by a car and wakes up in Limbo Land (yes, she's dead). The supervisor, Ms. Rogers (Redgrave), informs Katherine that because she had no emotional connections in life her entry into heaven will have to wait—and she's going to do her time as the Tooth Fairy. Katherine is not supposed to intervene with her charges but this sarcastic lady, who doesn't much care for her princess-like Tooth Fairy attire, does get involved with 12-year-old Bobby (Malinger) and his widowed dad (Midkiff). **85m/C; VHS, DVD.** Kirstie Alley; Ross Malinger; Dale Midkiff; Lynn Redgrave; Daryl (Chill) Mitchell; Melanie Mayron; Kimberly Scott; Helen Slater; ***W:*** Mark S. Kaufman. **TV**

Tootsie 🦴🦴🦴🦴 **1982 (PG)** Stubborn, unemployed actor Michael Dorsey (Hoffman) disguises himself as a woman named Dorothy Michaels to secure a part on a soap opera. As his popularity on TV mounts, his love life becomes increasingly soap operatic. Hoffman is delightful, as is the rest of the stellar cast, especially Lange as the cast member he falls in love with. Debut of Davis; Murray's performance was unbilled. Director Pollack plays Michael's put-upon agent, George Fields. **110m/C; VHS, DVD, Blu-Ray.** Dustin Hoffman; Jessica Lange; Teri Garr; Dabney Coleman; Bill Murray; Charles Durning; Geena Davis; George Gaynes; Estelle Getty; Christine Ebersole; Sydney Pollack; ***D:*** Sydney Pollack; ***W:*** Larry Gelbart; Murray Schisgal; Don McGuire; ***C:*** Owen Roizman; ***M:*** Dave Grusin. Oscars '82: Support. Actress (Lange); AFI '98: Top 100; British Acad. '83: Actor (Hoffman); Golden Globes '83: Actor--Mus./Comedy (Hoffman), Film--Mus./Comedy, Support. Actress (Lange); L.A. Film Critics '82: Screenplay; Natl. Film Reg. '98; N.Y. Film Critics '82: Director (Pollack), Screenplay, Support. Actress (Lange); Natl. Soc. Film Critics '82: Actor (Hoffman), Film, Screenplay, Support. Actress (Lange); Writers Guild '82: Orig. Screenplay.

Top Banana 🦴🦴 **1954** Truncated version (filmed on a Los Angeles stage) of Phil Silvers' 1951 Broadway musical comedy featuring various popular comics of the era doing their bits. The plot—such as it is—has egotistical TV star Jerry Biffle forced to hire a couple of youngsters to boost his program's falling ratings. Jerry then makes the mistake of getting interested in Sally, who's in love with fellow newcomer Cliff. Johnny Mercer wrote the music and lyrics. **84m/C; DVD.** Phil Silvers; Jack Albertson; Judy Lynn; Danny Scholl; Rose Marie; Bradford Hatton; ***D:*** Alfred E. Green; Terry Morse; ***W:*** Gene Towne; ***C:*** William Bradford; ***M:*** Johnny Mercer.

Top Dog 🦴 1/2 **1995 (PG-13)** Another cop-and-dog-team-up-to-get-the-bad-guys flick. This one, however, is meant to appeal to the kids who liked "Sidekicks." That raises a problem with the unfortunately topical right-wing-hate group-bombing plot. Jake Wilder (Norris), a beer-swillin' karate-choppin' loner cop, teams up with canine Reno, whose ex-partner was killed by the neo-Nazi terrorists. Weak script and erratic storyline can't find a comfortable balance between the too-cute pooch scenes and the (admittedly toned-down) violence. Reno steals every scene he's in, and provides the flick's few redeeming moments. **93m/C; VHS, DVD.** Chuck Norris; Clyde Kusatsu; Michele Lamar Richards; Carmine Caridi; Peter Savard Moore; Erik von Detten; Herta Ware; Kai Wulff; Francesco Quinn; Timothy Bottoms; ***D:*** Aaron Norris; ***W:*** Ron Swanson; ***C:*** Joao Fernandes.

Top Five 🦴🦴🦴 **2014 (R)** Rock delivers his best film to date by going personal, telling the story of Andre Allen (played by Rock), a film star and comedian looking back at his career in ways that Rock clearly does himself. Andre is interviewed by a reporter (Dawson) in this episodic romance that recalls the films of Woody Allen in its easy-going, conversational manner. The result is the first film that lets Rock really be himself, bringing that energy from his stage show to the screen instead of feeling forced into a part. Consequently, the film is funny and smart, hampered only a bit by cliché. **101m/C; DVD, Blu-Ray.** Chris Rock; Rosario Dawson; Gabrielle Union; Kevin Hart; Cedric the Entertainer; Tracy Morgan; J.B. Smoove; ***D:*** Chris Rock; ***W:*** Chris Rock; ***C:*** Manuel Alberto Claro; ***M:*** Ludwig Göransson.

Top Gun 🦴 1/2 **1955** B-western with a familiar plot that still proves to be entertaining. Gunslinger Rick Martin returns to his hometown of Casper, Wyoming after his mother's questionable death so he can also warn the townsfolk of an upcoming raid by Tom Quentin and his gang. Corrupt landowner Canby Judd persuades the locals to disregard his warning and his ex-girlfriend Laura is one of the few who come to Rick's aid when the gang arrives. Last role for character actor Millican, who plays the local marshal. **75m/B; DVD.** Sterling Hayden; Karin (Karen, Katharine) Booth; William Bishop; John Dehner; James Millican; Rod Taylor; Regis Toomey; Denver Pyle; ***D:*** Ray Nazarro; ***W:*** Steve Fisher; Richard Schayer; ***C:*** Lester White; ***M:*** Irving Gertz.

Top Gun 🦴🦴 ½ **1986 (PG)** Young Navy pilots compete against one another on the ground and in the air at the elite Fighter Weapons School. Cruise isn't bad as a maverick who comes of age in Ray Bans, but Edwards shines as his buddy. Awesome aerial photography and high-cal beefcake divert from the contrived plot and stock characters. The Navy subsequently noticed an increased interest in fighter pilots. Features Berlin's Oscar-winning song "Take My Breath Away." **109m/C; VHS, DVD, Blu-Ray, HD-DVD.** Tom Cruise; Kelly McGillis; Val Kilmer; Tom Skerritt; Anthony Edwards; Meg Ryan; Rick Rossovich; Michael Ironside; Barry Tubb; Whip Hubley; John Stockwell; Tim Robbins; Adrian Pasdar; ***D:*** Tony Scott; ***W:*** Jim Cash; Jack Epps, Jr.; ***C:*** Jeffrey L. Kimball; ***M:*** Harold Faltermeyer. Oscars '86: Song ("Take My Breath Away"); Golden Globes '87: Song ("Take My Breath Away"); Natl. Film Reg. '15.

Top Hat 🦴🦴🦴🦴 **1935** Ginger isn't impressed by Fred's amorous attentions since she's mistaken him for a friend's other half. Many believe it to be the duo's best film together. Choreography by Astaire and score by Berlin makes this one a classic Hollywood musical. Look for a young Lucille Ball as a clerk in a flower shop. **97m/B; VHS, DVD.** Fred Astaire; Ginger Rogers; Erik Rhodes; Helen Broderick; Edward Everett Horton; Eric Blore; Lucille Ball; ***D:*** Mark Sandrich; ***W:*** Dwight Taylor; Allan Scott; ***M:*** Irving Berlin; Max Steiner. Natl. Film Reg. '90.

Top of the Lake 🦴🦴🦴 **2013** Moody miniseries set in the isolated, rural New Zealand town of Laketop. Twelve-year-old Tui is five months pregnant when she disappears. Det. Robin Griffin (Moss), who grew up in the community, is called in to investigate, causing her to relive her own traumatic childhood. Tui's father Matt (Mullan) is a brutal drug lord who seemingly owns the town, except for a ramshackle community of damaged women, led by eccentric GJ (Hunter). Evocative story seethes with secrets and violence as well as some notable performances. **360m/C; DVD.** *AU UK* Elisabeth Moss; Holly Hunter; Peter Mullan; David Wenham; Robyn Nevin; Thomas M. Wright; ***D:*** Jane Campion; Garth Davis; ***W:*** Jane Campion; Gerard Lee; ***C:*** Adam Arkapaw; ***M:*** Mark Bradshaw. **CABLE**

Top of the World 🦴 ½ **1997 (R)** Newly released con Ray Mercer (Weller) travels to Vegas with his estranged wife, Rebecca (Carrere), who wants a quickie divorce. She's got a new boyfriend, casino manager Steve Atlas (Hopper). But Ray just happens to get caught in the middle of a heist planned by Atlas to cover up his embezzling at the casino. Sounds like it should be entertaining but it's not. **98m/C; VHS, DVD.** Peter Weller; Tia Carrere; Dennis Hopper; Joe Pantoliano; Martin Kove; Peter Coyote; David Alan Grier; Cary-Hiroyuki Tagawa; ***D:*** Sidney J. Furie; ***W:*** Bart Madison; ***C:*** Alan Caso; ***M:*** Robert O. Ragland.

Top Secret! 🦴🦴🦴 **1984 (PG)** Unlikely musical farce parodies spy movies and Elvis Presley films. Young American rock star Nick Rivers goes to Europe on goodwill tour and becomes involved with Nazis, the French Resistance, an American refugee, and more. Sophisticated it isn't. From the creators of "Airplane!" **90m/C; VHS, DVD.** Val Kilmer; Lucy Gutteridge; Christopher Villiers; Omar Sharif; Peter Cushing; Jeremy Kemp; Michael Gough; Billy Mitchell; ***D:*** Jim Abrahams; Jerry Zucker; David Zucker; ***W:*** Jim Abrahams; Jerry Zucker; David Zucker; Martyn Burke; ***C:*** Christopher Challis; ***M:*** Maurice Jarre.

Top Secret Affair 🦴🦴 ½ **1957** Dottie Peale (Hayward), who runs a publishing empire, supports a civilian for an important diplomatic post. She's incensed when Army Major General Melville Goodwin (Douglas) gets the job instead and is determined to discredit him. Of course they fall in love but misunderstandings lead Dottie to print an unflattering article that lands Melville in front of a Senate committee. Based on the novel by John P. Marquand. **100m/B; DVD.** Kirk Douglas; Susan Hayward; Paul Stewart; Jim Backus; John Cromwell; Roland Winters; ***D:*** H.C. Potter; ***W:*** Allan Scott; Roland Kibbee; ***C:*** Stanley Cortez; ***M:*** Roy Webb.

Topaz 🦴🦴🦴 **1969 (PG)** American CIA agent and French intelligence agent combine forces to find information about Russian espionage in Cuba. Cerebral and intriguing, but not classic Hitchcock. Based on the novel by Leon Uris. **126m/C; VHS, DVD, Blu-Ray.** John Forsythe; Frederick Stafford; Philippe Noiret; Karin Dor; Michel Piccoli; ***D:*** Alfred Hitchcock; ***W:*** Samuel A. Taylor; ***C:*** Jack Hildyard; ***M:*** Maurice Jarre. Natl. Bd. of Review '69: Director (Hitchcock), Support. Actor (Noiret).

Topkapi 🦴🦴🦴 **1964** An international bevy of thieves can't resist the treasures of the famed Topkapi Palace Museum, an impregnable fortress filled with wealth and splendor. Comic thriller based on Eric Ambler's "The Light of Day." **122m/C; VHS, DVD, Blu-Ray.** Melina Mercouri; Maximilian Schell; Peter Ustinov; Robert Morley; Akim Tamiroff; Jess Hahn; Gilles Segal; ***D:*** Jules Dassin; ***W:*** Monja Danischewsky; ***C:*** Henri Alekan; ***M:*** Manos Hadjidakis. Oscars '64: Support. Actor (Ustinov).

Topper 🦴🦴🦴 ½ **1937** Wealthy, madcap George (Grant) and Marion (Bennett) Kerby return as ghosts after a fatal car accident, determined to assist their morose banker pal Cosmo Topper (Young) to enjoy life. Of course, since Cosmo is the only one who can see the ghostly Kerbys his life becomes very complicated. Immensely popular at the boxoffice; followed by "Topper Takes a Trip" (1939) and "Topper Returns" (1941). The series uses trick photography and special effects to complement the comedic scripts. Based on Thorne Smith's novel, "The Jovial Ghosts." Inspired a TV series and remade in 1979 as TV movie. **97m/B; VHS, DVD, Blu-Ray.** Cary Grant; Roland Young; Constance Bennett; Billie Burke; Eugene Pallette; Hoagy Carmichael; ***D:*** Norman Z. McLeod.

Topper Returns 🦴🦴🦴 **1941** Cosmo Topper helps ghost find the man who mistakenly murdered her and warns her friend, the intended victim. Humorous conclusion to the trilogy preceded by "Topper" and "Topper Takes a Trip." Followed by a TV series. **87m/B; VHS, DVD, Blu-Ray.** Roland Young; Joan Blondell; Dennis O'Keefe; Carole Landis; Eddie Anderson; H.B. Warner; Billie Burke; ***D:*** Roy Del Ruth; ***W:*** Gordon Douglas; Jonathan Latimer; ***C:*** Norbert Brodine.

Topsy Turvy 🦴🦴🦴 ½ **1999 (R)** The very contemporary Leigh takes a pass at Victorian England for his very long and chatty look at life in the theatre. His focus is on the comic-opera partnership of irascible lyricist W.S. Gilbert (Broadbent) and pleasure-loving composer, Sir Arthur Sullivan (Corduner). Their latest creation (after 10 hits) is a flop, causing a serious rift but Gilbert, after a visit to a Japanese art exhibit, is inspired to write "The Mikado" and pulls Sullivan back in. The film then follows the production of the opera from rehearsal to the 1885 premiere with all its difficulties and triumphs. **160m/C; VHS, DVD, Blu-Ray.** *GB* Jim Broadbent; Allan Corduner; Lesley Manville; Eleanor David; Ron Cook; Timothy Spall; Kevin McKidd; Mark Benton; Shirley Henderson; Martin Savage; Jessie Bond; ***D:*** Mike Leigh; ***W:*** Mike Leigh; ***C:*** Dick Pope; ***M:*** Carl Davis. Oscars '99: Costume Des., Makeup; British Acad. '99: Makeup; N.Y. Film Critics '99: Director (Leigh), Film; Natl. Soc. Film Critics '99: Director (Leigh), Film.

Tora! Tora! Tora! 🦴🦴 **1970 (G)** The story of events leading up to December 7, 1941, is retold by three directors from both Japanese and American viewpoints in this tense, large-scale production. Well-documented and realistic treatment of the Japanese attack on Pearl Harbor that brought the U.S. into WWII; notable for its good photography but lacks a story line equal to its epic intentions. **144m/C; VHS, DVD, Blu-Ray.** Martin Balsam; So Yamamura; Joseph Cotten; E.G. Marshall; Tatsuya Mihashi; Wesley Addy; Jason Robards, Jr.; James Whitmore; Leon Ames; George Macready; Takahiro Tamura; Eijiro Tono; Shogo Shimada; Koreya Senda; Jun Usami; Richard Anderson; Kazuo Kitamura; Keith Andes; Edward Andrews; Neville Brand; Leora Dana; Walter Brooke; Norman Alden; Ron Masak; Edmon Ryan; Asao Uchida; Frank Aletter; Jerry Fogel; ***D:*** Richard Fleischer; Toshio Masuda; Kinji Fukasaku; ***W:*** Ryuzo Kikushima; Hideo Oguni; Larry Forrester; ***C:*** Sinsaku Himeda; Charles F. Wheeler; Osamu Furuya; ***M:*** Jerry Goldsmith. Oscars '70: Visual FX.

The Torch 🦴🦴 ½ **1950** Mexican revolutionary restores law and order when he captures a small town but then finds himself in turmoil as he falls for an aristocratic young woman. **90m/C; VHS, DVD.** *MX* Gilbert Roland; Paulette Goddard; Pedro Armendariz, Sr.; Walter Reed; ***D:*** Emilio Fernandez.

Torch Singer 🦴🦴 **1933** Sally Trent (Colbert) discovers she's preggers after beau Michael (Manners) leaves for China to make his fortune. Unable to support herself and the baby, Sally gives her daughter up for adoption and changes her name to Mimi Benton, becoming a successful nightclub singer. When she unexpectedly gets a part hosting a kiddie radio show, Sally/Mimi figures she might be able to find her tyke again using her on-air success. Meanwhile, Michael has returned and is trying to find Sally. **70m/B; DVD.** Claudette Colbert; David Manners; Ricardo Cortez; Lyda Roberti; Florence Roberts; Charley Grapewin; ***D:*** Alexander Hall; George Somnes; ***W:*** Lenore Coffee; Lynn Starling; ***C:*** Karl Stuss.

Torch Song 🦴🦴 **1953** In this muddled melodrama, a tough, demanding Broadway actress meets her match when she is offered true love by a blind pianist. Contains a couple of notoriously inept musical numbers. Made to show off Crawford's figure at age 50. Crawford's singing in the movie is dubbed. **90m/C; VHS, DVD.** Joan Crawford; Michael Wilding; Marjorie Rambeau; Gig Young; Harry (Henry) Morgan; Dorothy Patrick; Benny Rubin; Nancy Gates; ***D:*** Charles Walters.

Torch Song Trilogy 🦴🦴 ½ **1988 (R)** Adapted from Fierstein's hit Broadway play about a gay man who "just wants to be loved." Still effective, but the rewritten material loses something in the translation to the screen. Bancroft heads a strong cast with a finely shaded performance as Fierstein's mother. **126m/C; VHS, DVD.** Anne Bancroft; Matthew Broderick; Harvey Fierstein; Brian Kerwin; Karen Young; Charles Pierce; ***D:*** Paul Bogart; ***W:*** Harvey Fierstein; ***C:*** Mikael Salomon; ***M:*** Peter Matz.

Torchlight 🦴 **1985 (R)** A young couple's life begins to crumble when a wealthy art dealer teaches them how to free base cocaine. Heavy-handed treatment of a subject that's been tackled with more skill elsewhere. **90m/C; VHS, DVD.** Pamela Sue Martin; Steve Railsback; Ian McShane; Al Corley; Rita Taggart; ***D:*** Thomas J. Wright.

Torment 🦴🦴🦴 *Hets; Frenzy* **1944** Tragic triangle has young woman in love with fellow student and murdered by sadistic teacher. Atmospheric tale hailed by many as Sjoberg's finest film. Ingmar Bergman's first filmed script. In Swedish with English subtitles. **90m/B; VHS, DVD.** *SW* Alf Kjellin; Mai Zetterling; Stig Jarrel; Olof Winnerstrand; Gunnar Bjornstrand; ***D:*** Alf Sjoberg; ***W:*** Ingmar Bergman; ***C:*** Martin Bodin; ***M:*** Hilding Rosenberg.

Tormented 🦴 ½ **1960** Man pushes his mistress out of a lighthouse, killing her. Her ethereal body parts return to haunt him. **75m/B; DVD, Blu-Ray.** Richard Carlson; Susan Gordon; Juli Reding; ***D:*** Bert I. Gordon; ***W:*** Bert I. Gordon; George Worthing Yates; ***C:*** Ernest Laszlo; ***M:*** Albert Glasser; Calvin Jackson.

Tormented 🦴 ½ **2009** Predictable Brit teen horror comedy. When he can no longer stand being bullied by his classmates, Darren Mullett commits suicide. Then he returns from the dead to get his revenge and starts gruesomely picking off his tormentors. **91m/C; DVD.** *GB* Calvin Dean; Tuppence Middleton; Demitri Leonidas; Alex Pettyfer; April Pearson; Georgia King; James Floyd; Olly Alexander; Mary Nighy; ***D:*** Jon Wright; ***W:*** Stephen Prentice; ***C:*** Trevor Forrest; ***M:*** Paul Hartnoll.

The Tormentors **WOOF!** **1971 (R)** Vaguely neo-Nazi gangs rape and murder a man's family, and he kills them all in revenge. **78m/C; VHS, DVD.** James Craig; Anthony Eisley; Chris Noel; William Dooley; Bruce Kemp; Inga Wede; James Gordon White; ***D:*** Boris Eagle; ***W:*** James Gordon White.

Torn Apart 🦴🦴 **1989 (R)** Traditional Middle East hatreds undermine the love affair between two young people. Excellent performances from the principals highlight this drama. Adapted from the Chayin Zeldis novel "A Forbidden Love." **95m/C; VHS, DVD.** Adrian Pasdar; Cecilia Peck; Machram Huri; Arnon Zadok; Barry Primus; ***D:*** Jack Fisher; ***M:*** Peter Arnow.

Torn Apart 🦴 ½ **2004** A devastated father kidnaps the husband and daughter of surgeon Vicki Weston. Then he gives her 48 hours to choose which hostage lives because she could not save his own child. **90m/C; DVD.** Tia Carrere; Dale Midkiff; Richard Burgi; Zoe Gaffin; ***D:*** Stuart Alexander; ***W:*** Stuart Alexander; ***C:*** Mark Mervis; ***M:*** Harry Manfredini. **CABLE**

Torn Between Two Lovers 🦴🦴 **1979** A beautiful married woman has an affair with an architect while on a trip. Remick is enjoyable to watch, but it's a fairly predictable yarn. **100m/C; VHS, DVD.** Lee Remick; Joseph Bologna; George Peppard; Giorgio Tozzi; ***D:*** Delbert Mann. **TV**

Torn Curtain 🦴🦴 ½ **1966** American scientist poses as a defector to East Germany in order to uncover details of the Soviet missile program. He and his fiancee, who follows him behind the Iron Curtain, attempt to escape to freedom. Derivative and uninvolving. **125m/C; VHS, DVD, Blu-Ray.** Paul Newman; Julie Andrews; Lila Kedrova; David Opatoshu; ***D:*** Alfred Hitchcock; ***W:*** Brian Moore; ***C:*** John F. Warren; ***M:*** John Addison.

Tornado 🦴 ½ **1943** Coal miner Pete (Morris) marries ambitious showgirl Victory (Kelly) and when she inherits some land, he decides to start his own mining company. She reacts to their tough times by stepping out with his mining rival Linden (Conway) before that titular tornado comes along. **83m/B; DVD.** Chester Morris; Nancy Kelly; Morgan Conway; William Henry; Joseph (Joe) Sawyer; Gwen Kenyon; Marie McDonald; ***D:*** William Berke; ***W:*** Maxwell Shane; ***C:*** Fred H. Jackman, Jr.

Tornado! 🦴 ½ **1996 (PG)** TV movie with cheesy special effects chronicles a week with tornado chaser Campbell, meteorologist Hudson, and government accountant Sturges who wants to stop funding for Hudson's new storm-warning device. Lame attempt to capture some of the "Twister" audience fails miserably. **90m/C; VHS, DVD; Closed Captioned.** Bruce Campbell; Ernie Hudson; Shannon Sturges; L.Q. Jones; Bo Eason; ***D:*** Noel Nosseck; ***W:*** John Logan; ***C:*** Paul Maibaum; ***M:*** Garry Schyman.

Tornado Valley 🦴 **2009** Really lousy CGI and almost no disaster action in this wannabe disaster flick. Liz (Monroe) survived a tornado when she was a child although she saw her mother killed. Twenty-five years later, the tornado expert/meteorologist has a young daughter (Pattee) and a storm-chaser estranged husband (Bancroft). Then a megatornado threatens their Mississippi home. **88m/C; DVD.** Meredith Monroe; Cameron Bancroft; Rachel Pattee; Pascale Hutton; Duncan Fraser; Garry Chalk; Ashley Michaels; ***D:*** Andrew C. Erin; ***W:*** Andrew C. Erin; Aaron Kim Johnston; ***C:*** Mahlon Todd Williams; ***M:*** Kevin Blumenfeld. **VIDEO**

Torpedo Run 🦴🦴 **1958** Standard submarine melodramatics, about a U.S. sub that must torpedo a Japanese aircraft carrier which holds some of the crew's family members. Sometimes slow, generally worthwhile. **98m/C; DVD.** Glenn Ford; Ernest Borgnine; Dean Jones; Diane Brewster; L.Q. Jones; ***D:*** Joseph Pevney; ***W:*** Richard Sale; William Wister Haines; ***C:*** George J. Folsey.

Torque 🦴🦴 **2004 (PG-13)** "The Fast and the Furious" on crotch rockets. Cary Ford (Henderson) is a tough-guy rider who's looking to patch things up with his girlfriend (Mazur) while trying to dodge the wrath of local gang leader Trey Wallace (Ice Cube). Turns out, Cary's been framed for the murder of Trey's brother by evil crimelord Henry James (Schulze), who's mad at Cary over the loss of a couple bikes full of crystal meth. Sounds confusing? Doesn't matter. Music video director Joseph Kahn's first feature is jam-packed with videogame action and lots of CGI effects, but the screenplay is mostly brainless with only occasional funny moments (like Ice Cube quoting his own song) to break up what's basically an 81 minute chase scene. **81m/C; DVD, Blu-Ray.** Martin Henderson; Ice Cube; Monet Mazur; Adam Scott; Matt Schulze; Jaime Pressly; Jay Hernandez; Will Yun Lee; Fredro Starr; Justina Machado; John Doe; Faizon Love; ***D:*** Joseph Kahn; ***W:*** Matt Johnson; ***C:*** Peter Levy; ***M:*** Trevor Rabin.

Torremolinos 73 🦴🦴 ½ **2003** Alfredo (Camara) is a struggling encyclopedia salesman in Spain during the waning days of Franco's puritanical regime. Desperate for money, he and his wife Carmen (Pena) are initially reluctant partners in his boss, Don Carlos' (Diego), latest scheme: producing "educational" Super-8 sex films for the Scandinavian market. They turn out to be naturals, with Alfredo directing and Carmen starring. Then Alfredo gets ambitious and decides he wants to be the new Ingmar Bergman, writing a script (the movie's title) and persuading a disillusioned Carmen to go along with his idea. Spanish and Danish with subtitles. **91m/C; DVD.** Javier Camara; Candela Pena; Juan Diego; Malena Alterio; Fernando Tejero; ***D:*** Pablo Berger; ***W:*** Pablo Berger; ***C:*** Kiko de la Rica.

Torrent 🦴🦴 **1926** American film debut of Garbo. Lorena, daughter of peasant tenant farmers, is loved by Spanish aristocrat Don Rafael Brull. His overbearing mother is appalled and forces the family out, so Lorena heads to Paris and becomes an opera star. Rafael eventually marries, though he and Lorena can't ignore their love. **88m/B; Silent; DVD.** Greta Garbo; Ricardo Cortez; Martha Mattox; Gertrude (Olmstead) Olmsted; Mack Swain; Edward Connelly; Lucy Beaumont; Lucien Littlefield; Tully Marshall; ***D:*** Monta Bell; ***W:*** Dorothy Farnum; ***C:*** William H. Daniels.

Torrents of Spring 🦴🦴 **1990 (PG-13)** Based on an Ivan Turgenev story, this lavishly filmed and costumed drama concerns a young Russian aristocrat circa 1840 who is torn between two women. Predictably, one is a good-hearted innocent, the other a scheming seductress. **102m/C; VHS, DVD; Open Captioned.** Timothy Hutton; Nastassja Kinski; Valeria Golino; William Forsythe; Urbano Barberini; Francesca De Sapio; Jacques Herlin; ***D:*** Jerzy Skolimowski.

Torrid Zone 🦴🦴 **1940** Nick (Cagney) is the former manager of a Central America banana plantation (set up on Warner's back lot) who's about to head for Chicago and a new job. But owner Steve Case (O'Brien) is in a bind since he thinks new manager Anderson (Cowan) is incompetent and a local revolutionary (Tobias) wants to take back the plantation's land. Throw in saloon singer Lee (Sheridan), who clashes with Nick, and Anderson's hot to trot wife Gloria (Vinson), and Nick's got his fair share of trouble. Sounds kinda like 1932's "Red Dust." **88m/B; DVD.** James Cagney; Ann Sheridan; Pat O'Brien; Helen Vinson; Andy Devine; Jerome Cowan; George Reeves; George Tobias; ***D:*** William Keighley; ***W:*** Richard Macaulay; Jerry Wald; ***C:*** James Wong Howe; ***M:*** Adolph Deutsch.

Torso WOOF! *I Corpi Presentano Tracce Di Violenza Carnale; Bodres Bear Traces of Carnal Violence* **1973 (R)** Crazed psychosexual killer stalks beautiful women and dismembers them. Fairly bloodless and uninteresting, in spite of lovely Kendall. Italian title translates: The Bodies Showed Signs of Carnal Violence—quite an understatement for people missing arms and legs. **91m/C; VHS, DVD, Blu-Ray.** *IT* Suzy Kendall; Tina Aumont; John Richardson; ***D:*** Sergio Martino; ***W:*** Sergio Martino; Ernesto Gastaldi; ***C:*** Giancarlo Ferrando; ***M:*** Maurizio de Angelis; Guido de Angelis.

Torso 🦴🦴 *Torso: The Evelyn Dick Story* **2002 (R)** Based on the true crime story of Canadian 'Black Widow' Evelyn Dick. Only the torso of her Hamilton, Ontario, streetcar conductor husband is found in 1946 but Evelyn (Robertson) becomes the prime suspect and is put on trial for his murder. An unsympathetic defendant, Evelyn is convicted and sentenced to hang until defense attorney J.J. Robinette (Garber) appeals the case. But the story doesn't end there. **90m/C; DVD.** *CA* Victor Garber; Brenda Fricker; Callum Keith Rennie; Ken James; Jonathan Potts; Tom McCamus; Kathleen Robertson; Jim Boeven; ***D:*** Alex Chapple; ***W:*** Dennis Foon; ***C:*** Nikos Evdemon; ***M:*** Christopher Dedrick. **TV**

Tortilla Flat 🦴🦴🦴 **1942** Based on the John Steinbeck novel of the same name, two buddies, Tracy and Garfield, struggle to make their way on the wrong side of the tracks in California. Garfield gets a break by inheriting a couple of houses, Tracy schemes to rip-off a rich, but eccentric, dog owner. In the meantime, both fall for the same girl, Lamarr, in perhaps the finest role of her career. Great performances from all, especially Morgan. **105m/B; VHS, DVD.** Spencer Tracy; Hedy Lamarr; John Garfield; Frank Morgan; Akim Tamiroff; Sheldon Leonard; John Qualen; Donald Meek; Connie Gilchrist; ***D:*** Victor Fleming; ***C:*** Karl Freund.

Tortilla Heaven 🦴🦴 **2007 (PG-13)** A tiny border town in New Mexico is propelled into the national spotlight when the face of Jesus appears on a tortilla at Isidor's modest restaurant. Soon worshippers are appearing from all over and Isidor is making a tidy profit charging admission. But city-slicker Gil Garcia tells Isidor he could be making a lot more by capitalizing on his notoriety and soon greed divides the community. **97m/C; DVD.** Jose Zuniga; Miguel (Michael) Sandoval; Olivia Hussey; George Lopez; Marcelo Tubert; Irene Bedard; Lupe Ontiveros; Alexis Cruz; Ana Ortiz; ***D:*** Judy Hecht Dumontet; ***W:*** Judy Hecht Dumontet; Julius Robinson; ***C:*** John Bedford Lloyd; ***M:*** Christopher Lennertz.

Tortilla Soup 🦴🦴 ½ **2001 (PG-13)** Widower Martin Naranjo (Elizondo) is a Mexican-American patriarch trying to control the lives of his three grown daughters. Schoolteacher Leticia (Pena) fears love has passed her by; successful Carmen (Obradors) questions her career choice; and Maribel (Mello) has graduated from high school and is just eager to leave home. Meanwhile, Martin is a chef who's lost his sense of taste and smell and is being pursued by divorced Hortensia (Welch). Food and family dinners bring the various crises out in the open. And yes, the film is the American version of the 1994 Taiwanese film "Eat, Drink, Man, Woman" with an equally engaging cast. **102m/C; VHS, DVD.** Hector Elizondo; Jacqueline Obradors; Elizabeth Pena; Tamara Mello; Nikolai Kinski; Raquel Welch; Paul Rodriguez; Joel Joan; Constance Marie; ***D:*** Maria Ripoli; ***W:*** Tom Musca; Ramon Menendez; Vera Blasi; ***C:*** Xavier Perez Grobet; ***M:*** Bill Conti.

Torture Chamber of Baron Blood 🦴🦴 ½ *Baron Blood; Gli Orrori del Castello di Norimberga; The Blood Baron; Chamber of Tortures; The Thirst of Baron Blood* **1972 (PG)** Baron with gorgeous thirst for the red stuff is reanimated and lots of innocent bystanders meet a grisly fate in this spaghetti gorefest. Familiar story has that certain Bava feel. **90m/C; VHS, DVD, Blu-Ray.** *IT* Joseph Cotten; Elke Sommer; Massimo Girotti; Rada Rassimov; Antonio Cantafora; ***D:*** Mario Bava; ***W:*** Vincent Fotre; William Bairn; ***M:*** Les Baxter.

The Torture Chamber of Dr. Sadism 🦴🦴 ½ *Blood Demon; Castle of the Walking Dead; Die Schlangengrube und das Pendel* **1969** Decapitated and drawn and quartered for sacrificing 12 virgins, the evil Count Regula is pieced together 40 years later to continue his wicked ways. Great fun, terrific art direction. Very loosely based on Poe's "The Pit and the Pendulum." Beware of the heavily edited video version. **120m/C; VHS, DVD.** *GE* Christopher Lee; Karin Dor; Lex Barker; Carl Lange; Vladimir Medar; Christiane Rucker; Dieter Eppler; ***D:*** Harald Reinl.

Torture Dungeon 🦴 **1970 (R)** Director Milligan tortures audience with more mindless medieval pain infliction from Staten Island. **80m/C; VHS, DVD.** Jeremy Brooks; Susan Cassidy; ***D:*** Andy Milligan.

Torture Garden 🦴🦴 **1967** A sinister man presides over an unusual sideshow where people can see what is in store if they allow the evil side of their personalities to take over. Written by Bloch ("Psycho") and based on four of his short stories. **93m/C; VHS, DVD.** *GB* Jack Palance; Burgess Meredith; Peter Cushing; Beverly Adams; ***D:*** Freddie Francis; ***W:*** Robert Bloch; ***M:*** Don Banks; James Bernard.

Tortured 🦴🦴 **2008 (R)** Hauser is an FBI agent who has gone undercover in a major organized crime syndicate, spending his time performing minor errands for an unseen person known only as Ziggy, who he intends to bring down. He is asked to spend a week torturing an accountant for information on $10 million dollars of Ziggy's money that's gone missing, and the feds tell him to go ahead with it rather than break cover. Somewhere in all the harm he does, he begins to notice events are taking a certain pattern, and he begins to realize all is not as it seems. **107m/C; DVD.** Cole Hauser; Laurence Fishburne; James Cromwell; Emmanuelle Chriqui; Jon Cryer; James Denton; ***D:*** Nolan Lebovitz; ***W:*** Nolan Lebovitz; ***C:*** Steven Bernstein; ***M:*** Nathan Barr. **VIDEO**

Total Dhamaal 🦴 **2019** When small-time thief Guddu (Devgn) gets a hold of an illegal booty, he is double-crossed by Pintu (Pahwa) who takes the money and hides it. Working with his sidekick Johnny (Misra), Guddu learns that Pintu has given information about the booty to three other groups before Guddu can locate him. Though Guddu offers to share the money with the others, they decline, setting up a contest to see who can reach it first. The Bollywood adventure-comedy caper is the third in a series directed by Kumar. Though it borders on illogical, the film features some amusing, energetic moments and major Hindi acting stars. Hindi with subtitles. **130m/C; DVD.** Ajay Devgn; Madhuri Dixit; Anil Kapoor; Riteish Deshmukh; Arshad Warsi; ***D:*** Indra Kumar; ***W:*** Paritosh Painter; Ved Prakash; Bunty Rathore; ***C:*** Keiko Nakahara; ***M:*** Gourav Roshan.

Total Eclipse 🦴 **1995 (R)** Unfortunate look at the mutually destructive relationship between 19th-century French poets Arthur Rimbaud (DiCaprio) and Paul Verlaine (Thewlis). Rimbaud was a 16-year-old Parisian sensation for his iconoclastic work but what's presented is an obnoxious showoff, while the older, married Verlaine is a drunken lout who abuses his teenaged wife Mathilde (Bohringer). There's lots of dissolute, violent behavior and absolutely no insight into their work (which is the only reason to care). Ugly film wastes a lot of talent. **111m/C; VHS, DVD.** Leonardo DiCaprio; David Thewlis; Romane Bohringer; Dominique Blanc; ***D:*** Agnieszka Holland; ***W:*** Christopher Hampton; ***C:*** Yorgos Arvanitis; ***M:*** Jan A.P. Kaczmarek.

Total Reality 🦴 ½ **1997 (R)** In order to escape execution, disgraced soldier Anthony Rand (Bradley) undertakes to follow renegade general Tunis (Kretschmann) back through time and prevent the destruction of the universe. **97m/C; VHS, DVD.** David Bradley; Thomas Kretschmann; Ely Pouget; Bill Shaw; Misa Koprova; ***D:*** Phillip J. Roth; ***W:*** Phillip J. Roth; Robert Tossberg; ***C:*** Andres Garreton. **VIDEO**

Total Recall 🦴🦴🦴 **1990 (R)** Mind-bending sci-fi movie set in the 21st century. Construction worker Quaid (Schwarzenegger) dreams every night about the colonization of Mars, so he decides to visit a travel service that specializes in implanting vacation memories into its clients' brains and buy a memory trip to the planet. Only during the implant, Quaid discovers his memories have been artificially altered and he must find out just what's real and what's not. Intriguing plot and spectacular special effects. Laced with graphic violence. Based on Phillip K. Dick's "We Can Remember It for You Wholesale." **113m/C; VHS, DVD, Blu-Ray, UMD.** Arnold Schwarzenegger; Rachel Ticotin; Sharon Stone; Michael Ironside; Ronny Cox; Roy Brocksmith; Marshall Bell; Mel Johnson, Jr.; ***D:*** Paul Verhoeven; ***W:*** Gary Goldman; Dan O'Bannon; ***C:*** Jan De Bont; ***M:*** Jerry Goldsmith. Oscars '90: Visual FX.

Total Recall 🦴 ½ **2012 (PG-13)** Director Wiseman's dull redo of the 1990 Paul Verhoeven film fails the primary test of any remake--it never justifies its existence. Frustrated factory worker Quaid (Farrell) gets more than he intended when the implanted memories of his mind-tripping vacation go awry. Yes, the special effects have been updated and the story has been slightly tweaked but the piece has also been drained of all of its personality. Despite the best efforts by Farrell, it plays like a video game tie-in to the original that you don't actually get to play. **121m/C; DVD, Blu-Ray.** Colin Farrell; Bryan Cranston; Jessica Biel; Kate Beckinsale; Bill Nighy; John Cho; Bokeem Woodbine; Currie Graham; Will Yun Lee; ***D:*** Len Wiseman; ***W:*** Kurt Wimmer; Mark Bomback; ***C:*** Paul Cameron; ***M:*** Harry Gregson-Williams.

Total Recall 2070: Machine Dreams 🦴🦴 **1999 (R)** Pilot movie for the brief series that had only a tentative connection to the Ah-nuld movie and the short stories of Philip K. Dick. David Hume (Easton) is a 21st century cop who is supposed to keep an eye on the Consortium, the group of private companies that unofficially now run the world. They create mayhem and he tries to clean it up. Hume must battle rogue androids and solve the murders that occurred at the virtual reality vacation agency, Total Rekall. **83m/C; VHS, DVD.** Michael Easton; Karl Pruner; Cynthia (Cyndy, Cindy) Preston; Judith Krant; Nick Mancuso; ***D:*** Mario Azzopardi; ***C:*** Peter Wunstorf. **CABLE**

Total Western 🦴🦴 **2000** Rochant's homage to the spaghetti western set in modern-day France. Gerard agrees to help his boss' nephew carry out a drug deal with associates of mobster Ludo Daes. Unfortunately there's a shootout and only Gerard gets out alive—with a bag of Daes' money. He hides out on a farm where a group of juvenile delinquents are participating in a reform school program, but Daes' thugs come after him. So Gerard and the teenaged toughs come up with a plan. French with subtitles. **84m/C; DVD.** *FR* Samuel Le Bihan; Jean-Pierre Kalfon; Jean-Francois Stevenin; Kahena Saighi; ***D:*** Eric Rochant; ***W:*** Eric Rochant; Laurent Chalumeau; ***C:*** Vincenzo Marano; Yves Agostini; ***M:*** Marco Prince.

Totally Blonde 🦴🦴 **2001 (PG-13)** Brunette Meg (Allen) is having trouble finding Mr. Right, so she decides to hit the peroxide bottle and see if blondes really do have more fun. Of course, club owner Van (Buble) already thinks Meg is hot but she's been looking at him as just a friend. Instead, Meg hooks up with mister hot (and rich) body Brad (Hutzler). Funny thing, Meg gets green-eyed when her pal Liv (Quinlan) decides to go after Van for herself. **98m/C; VHS, DVD.** Krista Allen; Maeve Quinlan; Michael Buble; Brody Hutzler; Mindy Sterling; Charlene Tilton; ***D:*** Andrew Van Slee; ***W:*** Andrew Van Slee; ***C:*** Jim Orr; ***M:*** Andrew Van Slee; Miles Hill; Ian Putz. **VIDEO**

Totally F*ed Up** 🦴🦴 **1994** The first of director Araki's teen trilogy, followed by "The Doom Generation" and "Nowhere," concerns itself with the teen angst experienced by a loose group of friends—four gays and a lesbian couple. In short chapters, they meet, talk, and wander through a soulless L.A. as one of their group, film school student Steven (Luna), makes a video documentary about their situation (footage of which in intercut throughout the film). **80m/C; VHS, DVD.** James Duval; Gilbert Luna; Lance May; Roko Belic; Susan Behshid; Jenee Gill; Alan Boyce; ***D:*** Gregg Araki; ***W:*** Gregg Araki; ***C:*** Gregg Araki.

Toto le Heros 🦴🦴🦴 *Toto the Hero* **1991 (PG-13)** Bitter old man, who as a child fantasized that he was a secret agent named Toto, harbors deep resentment over not living the life he's convinced he should have had. He maintains a childhood fantasy that he and his rich neighbor were switched at birth in the confusion of a fire at the hospital. Series of flashbacks and fast forwards show glimpses of his life, not necessarily as it was, but how he perceived it. Sounds complex, but it's actually very clear and fluid. Mix of comedy and tragedy, with lots of ironic twists, and precise visuals. In French with English subtitles. **90m/C; VHS, DVD.** *FR* Michel Bouquet; Jo De Backer; Thomas Godet; Mireille Perrier; Sandrine Blancke; Didier Ferney; Hugo Harold-Harrison; Gisela Uhlen; Peter Bohlke; ***D:*** Jaco Van Dormael; ***W:*** Jaco Van Dormael; ***C:*** Walther Vanden Ende; ***M:*** Pierre Van Dormael. Cesar '91: Foreign Film.

Touch 🦴🦴 ½ **1996 (R)** Sleazebags, fundamentalists, and a maybe saint would seem to make for a surefire success in this easy-going adaptation of the offbeat Elmore Leonard novel. And while individual scenes and performances shine, the film doesn't completely hang together. Young Juvenal (Ulrich) is a former monk, now working at an L.A. alcohol rehab center, who possesses the stigmata and seems to have an authentic gift for healing. Naturally, this brings the crazies and the scammers out of the woodwork, including former preacher Bill Hill (Walken), whose partner (Fonda) falls for the lad, and paramilitary religious fanatic August Murray (Arnold). **96m/C; VHS, DVD.** Skeet Ulrich; Bridget Fonda; Christopher Walken; Tom Arnold; Gina Gershon; Lolita Davidovich; Paul Mazursky; Janeane Garofalo; John Doe; Conchata Ferrell; Mason Adams; Breckin Meyer; Anthony Zerbe; ***D:*** Paul Schrader; ***W:*** Paul Schrader; ***C:*** Edward Lachman; ***M:*** David Grohl.

Touch and Go 1/2 **1986 (R)** Sentimental drama about a self-interested hockey pro who learns about love and giving through a young delinquent and his attractive mother. **101m/C; VHS, Streaming.** Michael Keaton; Maria Conchita Alonso; Ajay Naidu; Maria Tucci; Max Wright; John C. Reilly; ***D:*** Robert Mandel; ***W:*** Harry Colomby.

Touch Me Not *The Hunted* **1974 (PG)** A neurotic secretary is used by an industrial spy to gain information on her boss. Weak thriller. **84m/C; VHS, DVD.** *GB* Lee Remick; Michael Hinz; Ivan Desny; Ingrid Garbo; ***D:*** Douglas Fifthian.

A Touch of Class **1973 (PG)** Married American insurance adjustor working in London plans quick and uncommitted affair but finds his heart doesn't obey the rules. Jackson and Segal create sparkling record of a growing relationship. **105m/C; VHS, DVD, Blu-Ray.** George Segal; Glenda Jackson; Paul Sorvino; Hildegard(e) Neil; K. Callan; Mary Barclay; Cec Linder; ***D:*** Melvin Frank; ***W:*** Jack Rose; ***C:*** Austin Dempster; ***M:*** John Cameron. Oscars '73: Actress (Jackson); Golden Globes '74: Actor--Mus./Comedy (Segal), Actress--Mus./Comedy (Jackson); Writers Guild '73: Orig. Screenplay.

Touch of Evil **1958 (PG-13)** Stark, perverse story of murder, kidnapping, and police corruption in Mexican border town. Welles portrays a police chief who invents evidence to convict the guilty. Filled with innovative photography reminiscent of "Citizen Kane," as filmed by Russell Metty. In 1998, Walter Murch restored the film working from Welles's notes, re-editing the work to what Welles had originally envisioned before studio intervention; this version is 101 minutes and is unrated. **108m/B; VHS, DVD, Blu-Ray.** Charlton Heston; Orson Welles; Janet Leigh; Joseph Calleia; Akim Tamiroff; Marlene Dietrich; Valentin de Vargas; Dennis Weaver; Joanna Moore; Mort Mills; Victor Millan; Ray Collins; ***Cameo(s):*** Joi Lansing; Zsa Zsa Gabor; Mercedes McCambridge; Joseph Cotten; ***D:*** Orson Welles; ***W:*** Orson Welles; ***C:*** Russell Metty; ***M:*** Henry Mancini. Natl. Film Reg. '93.

Touch of Pink **2004 (R)** Kyle MacLachlan plays the ghost of Cary Grant as he advises Alim (Mistry), a gay Pakistani film studio photographer. It seems Alim needs the advice, as his conservative mother (Mathew), whom he has yet to tell of his sexual orientation, is coming to visit him. Of course, Alim, who lives with his British lover Giles (Holden-Ried), decides to hide the fact with a fake fiancee. The usual hijinx occur. Mostly unremarkable except for a great performance by MacLachlan. **92m/C; VHS, DVD.** Jimi Mistry; Kyle MacLachlan; Kris Holden-Ried; Brian George; Lisa Repo Martell; Suleka Mathew; Veena Sood; Raoul Bhaneja; ***D:*** Ian Iqbal Rashid; ***W:*** Ian Iqbal Rashid; ***C:*** David Makin; ***M:*** Andrew Lockington.

The Touch of Satan *The Touch of Melissa; Night of the Demon; Curse of Melissa* **1970 (PG)** Lost on the road, a young man meets a lovely young woman and is persuaded to stay at her nearby farmhouse. Things there are not as they seem, including the young woman—who turns out to be a very old witch. **90m/C; VHS, DVD.** Michael Berry; Emby Mallay; Lee Amber; Yvonne Wilson; Jeanne Gerson; ***D:*** Don Henderson.

A Touch of Sin *Tian zhu ding* **2013** Filmmaker Jia Zhangke tackles the undercurrent of violence simmering in modern China by pulling four stories from the headlines and reenacting them. Taking place all across this vast country, the dark tales all feature the growing chasm between the haves and the have-nots that threaten to topple many parts of the world. In one, a man lashes out at the government official that he believes lied to his working class. In another, a woman mistaken for a sex worker protects herself. Mesmerizing drama not for the faint of heart. English and Chinese (Cantonese, Mandarin, and various dialects) with subtitles. **113m/C; DVD, Blu-Ray.** *CH* Wu Jiang; Lanshan Luo; Baoqiang Wang; Tao Zhao; ***D:*** Jia Zhangke; ***W:*** Jia Zhangke; ***C:*** Yu Likwai; ***M:*** Giong Lim.

Touch the Top of the World 1/2 **2006** Well-done inspirational pic based on the autobiography of Erik Weihenmayer. As a child, Erik (Facinelli) is diagnosed with a rare eye disease that leads to blindness. His parents (Campbell, Greenhouse) challenge him to make any dream a reality and Erik becomes an expert ice and rock climber with the ultimate goal of being the first blind person to reach the top of Mount Everest. **89m/C; DVD.** Peter Facinelli; Bruce Campbell; Kate Greenhouse; Sarah Manninen; Robert Moloney; Saxon DeCocq; ***D:*** Peter Winther; ***W:*** Peter Silverman; ***C:*** Attila Szalay; ***M:*** Joseph LoDuca. **CABLE**

Touchback 1/2 **2011 (PG-13)** Lightweight, preachy sports drama. Scott Murphy was a smalltown Ohio football star when he blew out his knee in the final game and ended his college/NFL chances. Instead, 20 years later, Scott's a struggling farmer who attempts suicide and wakes up in 1991 with a chance to relive the week leading up to that life-changing event. But if Scott changes his football destiny, he apparently loses the girl he would have married. **120m/C; DVD.** Brian Presley; Melanie Lynskey; Marc Blucas; Kurt Russell; Christine Lahti; Sarah Wright; ***D:*** Don Handfield; ***W:*** Don Handfield; ***C:*** David Rush Morrison; ***M:*** William Ross. **VIDEO**

Touched **2005 (R)** A terrible car accident claims the life of Scott Davis' (Batinkoff) young son and leaves Scott in a coma for two years. He awakens in a long-term care facility under the supervision of nurse Angela Martin (Elfman). Scott's wealthy parents (Venora, Davidson) decide to bring him home but since it appears that Scott has lost his sense of touch and is suffering hallucinations, they hire Angela as a live-in nurse. Scott and Angela fall in love. It's not quite as sappy as it sounds and it's refreshing to see the sunny Elfman try her talents in a drama. **90m/C; DVD.** Jenna Elfman; Randall Batinkoff; Samantha Mathis; Diane Venora; Frederick Koehler; Mina Badie; Bruce Davidson; ***D:*** Timothy Scott Bogart; ***W:*** Timothy Scott Bogart; ***C:*** Irv Goodnoff. **VIDEO**

Touched With Fire 1/2 *Mania Days* **2016 (R)** Holmes elevates a pretty standard indie drama courtesy of writer/director Dalio. Holmes stars as Carla, a bipolar woman who meets Marco (Kirby) during a stay at a psychiatric hospital. Dalio has a respectful, gentle touch when it comes to portraying mental illness. In fact, few films have captured the ups and downs of bipolar disorder without turning it into a plot device as much as this one does. The main reason for that is how completely Holmes gets under the skin of this character, turning her into a three-dimensional person with wants and needs outside of her illness. **106m/C; DVD, Blu-Ray.** Katie Holmes; Luke Kirby; Christine Lahti; Griffin Dunne; Bruce Altman; ***D:*** Paul Dalio; ***W:*** Paul Dalio; ***C:*** Kristina Nikolova; Alexander Stanishev; ***M:*** Paul Dalio.

Touching Evil **1997** London police detective Dave Creegan (Green) and his fellow cops at the (fictional) Organized and Serial Crime Unit investigate three creepy cases in this three-tape series. The first concerns the kidnapping of three small boys; the second involves patients being drugged and killed while in hospital; and the third involves corpses, university students, and the Internet. The detectives are a fine, flawed unit and make for some interesting company. Followed by two sequels. **360m/C; VHS, DVD.** *GB* Robson Green; Ian McDiarmid; Nicola Walker; Michael Feast; Adam Kotz; Kenneth MacDonald; Antony Byrne; Shaun Dingwall; ***D:*** Julian Jarrold; Marc Munden; ***W:*** Paul Abbott; Russell T. Davies; ***C:*** David Odd; ***M:*** Adrian Johnston. **TV**

Touching Home **2008 (PG-13)** Identical twins Logan and Noah Miller make their acting/writing/directing debuts in a solid--if predictable--family drama. Lane and Clint are forced to return to their California hometown after suffering setbacks to their baseball career dreams. Living with their grandmother and uncle, the twins find work at the gravel pit that also employs their father, Charlie (the dominating Harris). He's a longtime alcoholic and gambler, now living in his truck, and while Lane would like to reconnect, brother Clint is still bitter over Charlie constantly letting them down. **108m/C; DVD.** Logan Miller; Noah Miller; Ed Harris; Brad Dourif; Lee Meriwether; Robert Forster; Ishiah Benben; ***D:*** Logan Miller; Noah Miller; ***W:*** Logan Miller; Noah Miller; ***C:*** Ricardo Jacques Gale; ***M:*** Martin Davich.

Touching the Void **2003** Documentarian Macdonald turns to reenactments to provide a dramatic narrative for this saga of two British climbers whose adventure in the Peruvian Andes in 1985 goes horribly wrong. Simpson (Mackey) and Yates (Aaron), both in their early twenties, decide to test their abilities on the previously unclimbed west face of Siula Grande. They make it to the top but are beset by a storm during their descent when Simpson breaks his leg. Yates attempts to lower his partner down the mountain but Simpson goes into a crevasse. Uncertain if Simpson is still alive, Yates must then decide whether to cut the rope binding them together and make his way alone back to base camp or risk dying himself. How they both survive constitutes the rest of this harrowing story of survival. Simpson and Yates provide their own narration; based on the book by Simpson. **106m/C; VHS, DVD.** Brendan Mackey; Nicholas Aaron; ***D:*** Kevin MacDonald; ***C:*** Mike Eley; ***M:*** Alex Heffes.

Tough Enough **1983 (PG)** A country-western singer and songwriter decides to finance his fledgling singing career by entering amateur boxing matches. Insipid and predictable, with fine cast wasted. **107m/C; VHS, DVD, Blu-Ray.** Dennis Quaid; Charlene Watkins; Warren Oates; Pam Grier; Stan Shaw; Bruce McGill; Wilford Brimley; Bob Watson; ***D:*** Richard Fleischer.

Tough Guy *The Slasher* **1953** Based on the play by Bruce Walker, a London hood carouses, mugs, breaks hearts and personifies his generation's anxiety. ALso sold under the title 'The Slasher'. **73m/B; VHS, DVD.** *GB* James Kenney; Hermione Gingold; Joan Collins; ***D:*** Lewis Gilbert.

Tough Guys 1/2 **1986 (PG)** Two aging ex-cons, who staged America's last train robbery in 1961, try to come to terms with modern life after many years in prison. Amazed and hurt by the treatment of the elderly in the 1980s, frustrated with their inability to find something worthwhile to do, they begin to plan one last heist. Tailor-made for Lancaster and Douglas, who are wonderful. Script becomes cliched at end. **103m/C; VHS, Beta, Streaming.** Burt Lancaster; Kirk Douglas; Charles Durning; Eli Wallach; Jake Steinfeld; Dana Carvey; Alexis Smith; Darlanne Fluegel; Billy Barty; Monty Ash; ***D:*** Jeff Kanew; ***W:*** James Orr; Jim Cruickshank; ***M:*** James Newton Howard.

Tough Guys Don't Dance 1/2 **1987 (R)** Mailer directed this self-satiric mystery thriller from his own novel. A writer may have committed murder—but he can't remember. So he searches for the truth among various friends, enemies, lovers, and cohorts. **110m/C; VHS, DVD.** Ryan O'Neal; Isabella Rossellini; Wings Hauser; Debra Sandlund; John Bedford Lloyd; Lawrence Tierney; Clarence Williams, III; Penn Jillette; Frances Fisher; ***D:*** Norman Mailer; ***W:*** Norman Mailer; ***C:*** John Bailey; ***M:*** Angelo Badalamenti. Golden Raspberries '87: Worst Director (Mailer).

Tour of Duty 1/2 **1987** Follows the trials that the members of an American platoon face daily during the Vietnam war. Pilot for the TV series. **93m/C; VHS, DVD.** Terence Knox; Stephen Caffrey; Joshua Maurer; Ramon Franco; ***D:*** Bill W.L. Norton. **TV**

The Tourist 1/2 **2010 (PG-13)** Well, it certainly looks pretty—and we're not just talking about the stars, though Depp and Jolie put the glam back in glamour. Unfortunately, they're let down by a convoluted and unconvincing wannabe noir plot that's a remake of the 2005 French flick "Anthony Zimmer." On a Paris train, femme fatale Elise (Jolie) starts the set-up of American tourist Frank (Depp), who looks like her thief/lover Alexander Pearce. Since Pearce is wanted by bad guys, Interpol, and Scotland Yard, he needs a fall guy. **103m/C; DVD, Blu-Ray.** Johnny Depp; Angelina Jolie; Paul Bettany; Timothy Dalton; Rufus Sewell; Steven Berkoff; Christian de Sica; Raoul Bova; ***D:*** Florian Henskel von Donnersmarck; ***W:*** Florian Henskel von Donnersmarck; Christopher McQuarrie; Julian Fellowes; ***C:*** John Seale; ***M:*** James Newton Howard.

Tourist Trap **1979 (PG)** While traveling through the desert, a couple's car has a flat. A woman's voice lures the man into an abandoned gas station, where he discovers that the voice belongs to a mannequin. Or is it? Not very interesting or suspenseful. **90m/C; VHS, DVD.** Tanya Roberts; Chuck Connors; Robin Sherwood; Jocelyn Jones; Jon Van Ness; Dawn Jeffory; Keith McDermott; ***D:*** David Schmoeller; ***W:*** David Schmoeller; ***C:*** Nicholas Josef von Sternberg; ***M:*** Pino Donaggio.

The Tournament **2009 (R)** Every 10 years, 30 of the world's best killers face off in a winner-take-all contest where the last assassin standing gets a very big payoff. This time the killing field is a small Scottish town and the local clergyman (Carlyle) may not be exactly what he seems. Meanwhile, gamblers watch and bet on the outcome via closed-circuit TV. Offers undemanding, fast-paced action. **95m/C; DVD, Blu-Ray.** *GB* Ving Rhames; Robert Carlyle; Kelly Hu; Ian Somerhalder; Scott Adkins; Liam Cunningham; ***D:*** Scott Mann; ***W:*** Jonathan Frank; Nick Rowntree; ***C:*** Gary Young; ***M:*** Emil Topuzov; Laura Karpman. **VIDEO**

Tous les Matins du Monde *All the Mornings of the World* **1992** Haunting tale of two 17th century French baroque composers and their relationship with each other and their music. Gerard Depardieu plays Marin Marais who eventually becomes a court composer at Versailles. As a young man, he studies under Sainte Colombe, a private and soulful musician, about whom little is known even today. Depardieu's son Guillaume (in his film debut) plays the young Marais, who startles the quiet Sainte Colombe home and has an affair with one of his daughters (Brochet). Filmmaker Corneau lends a quiet austere tone which parallels the life and music of Sainte Colombe. In French with English subtitles. **114m/C; VHS, DVD.** *FR* Gerard Depardieu; Guillaume Depardieu; Jean-Pierre Marielle; Anne Brochet; Caroline Sihol; Carole Richert; Violaine Lacroix; Nadege Teron; Myriam Boyer; Michel Bouquet; ***D:*** Alain Corneau; ***W:*** Pascal Quignard; Alain Corneau; ***C:*** Yves Angelo; ***M:*** Jordi Savall. Cesar '92: Cinematog., Director (Corneau), Film, Score, Support. Actress (Brochet).

Toward the Terra **1980** In the distant future mankind is forced to evacuate Earth and settles on the planet Atarakusha. Society ruthlessly suppresses anything which could destabalize it in an effort to prevent the mistakes which destroyed the Earth. The most destablizing presence is the MU, a new race with incredible mental powers, who are ruthlessly hunted and eliminated. But the leader of the MU reaches out to a human with his own inexplicable powers to aid in establishing a new world. In Japanese with subtitles. **112m/C; VHS, DVD.** *JP* ***V:*** Toru Furuya; Yasuo Hisamatsu; Taro Shigaki; Masako Ikeda; ***D:*** Hideo Onchi; ***W:*** Hideo Onchi; ***M:*** Masaru Sato.

Toward the Unknown 1/2 **1956** Major Lincoln Bond (Holden) was tortured into breaking as a Korean War POW and now he needs to prove himself at his new posting at Edwards Air Force Base. Brig. Gen. Banner (Nolan) is afraid Bond will crack again and doesn't want to give him a test pilot trial of the experimental Bell X-2 rocket. Bell Aircraft made an X-2 mockup especially for the film, adding to its authenticity. **115m/C; DVD.** William Holden; Lloyd Nolan; Virginia Leith; Charles McGraw; Murray Hamilton; Paul Fix; James Garner; ***D:*** Mervyn LeRoy; ***W:*** Beirne Lay, Jr.; ***C:*** Harold Rosson; ***M:*** Paul Baron.

Towards Darkness *Hacia la Oscuridad* **2007 (R)** Jose Gutierrez has just returned home to Colombia when he's kidnapped. Since kidnapping is a big business in the country, the Gutierrez family thought they were prepared but their insurance won't pay the ransom after all. With the kidnappers getting impatient, the family brings in a team of hostage negotiators but time is running out. Colombian-born Negret knows the situation but he overstuffs his story with a number of subplots that lessen the tension. English and Spanish with subtitles. **92m/C; DVD.** Tony Plana; David Sutcliffe; William Atherton; America Ferrera; Cameron Daddo; Carlos Valencia; Alonso Arias; Fernando Solorzano; Roberto Urbina; ***D:*** Jose Antonio Negret; ***W:*** Jose Antonio Negret; ***C:*** John Ealer; ***M:*** Chris(topher) Westlake.

Towards Zero 2 1/2 *L'Heure Zero* **2007** A comic mystery based on Agatha Christie's 1944 novel. An extended (and greedy) family gathers for a reunion at the mansion of wealthy dowager Camilla (Darrieux). Naturally, murder occurs and the local cop who investigates just happens to have his uncle, Superintendent Bataille (Morel), visiting nearby to help solve the case. French with subtitles. **107m/C; DVD.** *FR* Francois Morel; Danielle Darrieux; Melvil Poupaud; Laura Smet; Chiara Mastroianni; Clement Thomas; Xavier Thiam; Alessandra Martines; Carmen Durand; Jacques Sereys; ***D:*** Pascal Thomas; ***W:*** Francois Caviglioli; Nathalie Lafaurie; Clamence de Bieville; Roland Duval; ***C:*** Renan Polles; ***M:*** Reinhardt Wagner.

Towelhead 2 *Nothing is Private* **2007 (R)** Jasira (Bishil), a 13-year-old Lebanese-American girl living with her mother in Syracuse, New York, obsesses over her newly discovered sexuality to the point that her mother fears for the girl's safety and ships her off to live with her father in Houston. Dad seems nice, but explodes with rage, violence, and even racism when confronting Jasira's womanhood—slapping her for wearing a t-shirt, forbidding her to use tampons, and keeping her away from the black teenage boy next door. Good thing he doesn't know about the father of the kid she babysits, who takes a sick liking to the girl. An overtly melodramatic button-pusher from experienced suburban nightmare writer Ball ("American Beauty"), who lays it on too thick. Based on the 2005 novel by Alicia Erian. **124m/C; DVD.** Summer Bishil; Aaron Eckhart; Maria Bello; Toni Collette; Peter Macdissi; Matt Letscher; Chris Messina; Carrie Preston; Chase Ellison; Shari Headley; Lynn Collins; Gemmenne de la Pena; Eugene Jones, III; ***D:*** Alan Ball; ***W:*** Alan Ball; ***C:*** Newton Thomas (Tom) Sigel; ***M:*** Thomas Newman.

Tower 3 **2016** Keith Maitland's documentary tells the story of a shooting five decades ago but feels as urgent as ever, especially with the current stories that support a case for stricter gun control. On August 1, 1966, a student went to the top floor of a tower that overlooked the square at the University of Texas, and he started shooting students and other people crossing the square. To keep the story current, Maitland mostly uses animation, making this an event and its people somewhat trapped in time. He also makes sure to focus the film on the victims and survivors, not the murderer. **96m/C; DVD.** Blair Jackson; Chris Doubek; ***D:*** Keith Maitland; ***C:*** Keith Maitland; Sarah Wilson; ***M:*** Osei Essed.

Tower Heist 1/2 **2011 (PG-13)** Disgruntled employees of a luxurious condo building in New York hatch a plan to steal a solid gold Ferrari from their boss, and building owner, Arthur Shaw (Alda) who's Ponzi scheme duped them out of their pensions and livelihoods. Problem is, the Ferrari sits in Shaw's penthouse suite. The amateur crooks are led by building manager Josh (Stiller), who enlists the help of doorman Lester (Henderson), evicted tenant Mr. Fitzhugh (Broderick), and neighborhood blowhard Slide (Murphy). Somehow, the script is even clumsier than the bumbling thieves. Flashy direction and an all star cast, but all that glitters isn't good. **104m/C; DVD, Blu-Ray.** Ben Stiller; Eddie Murphy; Alan Alda; Matthew Broderick; Tea Leoni; Gabourney "Gabby" Sidibe; Casey Affleck; Michael Peña; Judd Hirsch; Stephen Henderson; ***D:*** Brett Ratner; ***W:*** Ted Griffin; Jeff Nathanson; ***C:*** Dante Spinotti; ***M:*** Christophe Beck.

Tower of Evil **WOOF!** *Horror on Snape Island; Beyond the Fog* **1972 (R)** Anthropologists and treasure hunters unite in search of Phoenician hoard on Snape Island. Suddenly, inanimate bodies materialize. Seems the island's single inhabitant liked it quiet. Cult favorite despite uneven performances. So bad it's not bad. **86m/C; VHS, DVD, Blu-Ray.** *GB* Bryant Haliday; Jill Haworth; Jack Watson; Mark Edwards; George Coulouris; ***D:*** James O'Connolly; ***W:*** James O'Connolly; ***C:*** Desmond Dickinson; ***M:*** Kenneth V. Jones.

The Tower of London 2 1/2 **1939** Tells the story of Richard III (Rathbone), the English monarch who brutally executed the people who tried to get in his way to the throne. This melodrama was considered extremely graphic for its time, and some of the torture scenes had to be cut before it was released. **93m/B; VHS, DVD, Blu-Ray.** Basil Rathbone; Boris Karloff; Barbara O'Neil; Ian Hunter; Vincent Price; Nan Grey; John Sutton; Leo G. Carroll; Miles Mander; ***D:*** Rowland V. Lee; ***W:*** Robert N. Lee; ***C:*** George Robinson; ***M:*** Hans J. Salter; Frank Skinner.

Tower of London 2 **1962** A deranged lord (Price) murdering his way to the throne of England is eventually crowned Richard III. Sophisticated and well-made Poe-like thriller. More interesting as historic melodrama than as horror film. A remake of the 1939 version starring Basil Rathbone, in which Price played a supporting role. **79m/B; VHS, DVD, Blu-Ray.** Vincent Price; Michael Pate; Joan Freeman; Robert Brown; Sandra Knight; Justice Watson; ***D:*** Roger Corman; ***W:*** Leo Gordon; F. Amos Powell; James B. Gordon; ***C:*** Arch R. Dalzell; ***M:*** Michael Anderson.

Tower of Terror 2 1/2 **1997** This Disney TV movie really isn't very scary and is related to the thrill ride located at Disney World. Disgraced reporter Buzzy (Guttenberg) and his niece (Dunst) investigate the 60-year-old murder of the family of a popular 1930s child star in a supposedly haunted hotel. **89m/C; VHS, DVD.** Steve Guttenberg; Kirsten Dunst; Nia Peeples; ***D:*** D.J. MacHale. **TV**

Tower of the Firstborn 1 *I Guardiani del Cielo* **1998 (PG-13)** Archeologist Diane goes searching the Sahara desert for her missing father, whom she believes discovered the legendary ancient tower of the title, which contains vast knowledge of the universe. Or something like that because this tedious production never makes much sense. Originally broadcast as a miniseries on Italian TV. **180m/C; DVD.** *IT* Ione Skye; Peter Weller; Ben Cross; Guy Lankester; Heino Ferch; Marco Bonini; ***D:*** Alberto Negrin; ***W:*** Alberto Negrin; George Eastman; ***M:*** Ennio Morricone. **TV**

The Towering Inferno 2 **1974 (PG)** Raging blaze engulfs the world's tallest skyscraper on the night of its glamorous dedication ceremonies. Allen had invented the disaster du jour genre two years earlier with "The Poseidon Adventure." Features a new but equally noteworthy cast. **165m/C; VHS, DVD, Blu-Ray.** Steve McQueen; Paul Newman; William Holden; Faye Dunaway; Fred Astaire; Jennifer Jones; Richard Chamberlain; Susan Blakely; O.J. Simpson; Robert Vaughn; Robert Wagner; ***D:*** John Guillermin; Irwin Allen; ***W:*** Stirling Silliphant; ***C:*** Joseph Biroc; Fred W. Koenekamp; ***M:*** John Williams. Oscars '74: Cinematog., Film Editing, Song ("We May Never Love Like This Again"); British Acad. '75: Support. Actor (Astaire); Golden Globes '75: Support. Actor (Astaire).

The Town 3 **2010 (R)** Affleck co-writes, directs, and stars in this moody crime drama based on Chuck Hogan's novel "Prince of Thieves." Doug MacRay leads a gang of Charlestown bank robbers who pride themselves on getting the job done fast and clean. Only this last time, manager Claire Keesey briefly became a hostage and all too aware that the crooks know her identity. What she doesn't know is that Doug has taken a personal interest in her and now wants to ditch his criminal life. Affleck further enhances his reputation in front of and behind the camera, with help from a number of excellent performances. **125m/C; Blu-Ray, On Demand.** Ben Affleck; Rebecca Hall; Jon Hamm; Jeremy Renner; Blake Lively; Titus Welliver; Pete Postlethwaite; Chris Cooper; Slaine; Owen Burke; Corena Chase; Dennis Mclaughlin; ***D:*** Ben Affleck; ***W:*** Ben Affleck; Aaron Stockard; Peter Craig; ***C:*** Robert Elswit; ***M:*** Harry Gregson-Williams; David Buckley.

Town and Country 1 **2001 (R)** Yep, it's as bad as you've heard. The oft-delayed and much-discussed romantic-comedy features characters you don't care about (rich Manhattanites with more money than they need) in situations that've been done to death (bed-hopping amidst middle age angst and closet-hiding). Shandling and Beatty are the cad husbands who decide to risk 25-year marriages in the name of fighting boredom. Keaton and Hawn are the revenge-fueled wives. All are upstaged by Heston and Seldes as the gun-toting, foul-mouthed parents of one of Beatty's dalliances (McDowell). **104m/C; VHS, DVD.** Warren Beatty; Diane Keaton; Goldie Hawn; Andie MacDowell; Jenna Elfman; Garry Shandling; Charlton Heston; Marian Seldes; Tricia Vessey; Josh Hartnett; Nastassja Kinski; Katharine Towne; Buck Henry; ***D:*** Peter Chelsom; ***W:*** Buck Henry; Michael Laughlin; ***C:*** William A. Fraker; ***M:*** Rolfe Kent.

A Town Called Hell 1 *A Town Called Bastard* **1972 (R)** Two men hold an entire town hostage while looking for "Aguila," the Mexican revolutionary. Greed, evil, and violence take over. Shot in Spain. Whatever you call it, just stay out of it. **95m/C; VHS, DVD, Blu-Ray.** *GB SP* Robert Shaw; Stella Stevens; Martin Landau; Telly Savalas; Fernando Rey; ***D:*** Robert Parrish.

A Town Has Turned to Dust 1/2 **1998** Lame remake of a 1958 Rod Serling script for "Playhouse 90." Serling's story was set in the old west; this version goes for sci-fi and a futuristic desert town called Carbon run by mob boss Perlman who controls the water supply and the main industry, which is mining. But when Perlman hangs an innocent man, he finally provoking drunken sheriff Lang to take action. **91m/C; VHS, DVD.** Ron Perlman; Stephen Lang; Gabriel Olds; Judy Collins; ***W:*** Rod Serling. **CABLE**

The Town Is Quiet 2 1/2 *La Ville Est Tranquille* **2000** This town isn't quiet at all. Michele (Ascaride) works in a Marseilles fish market and then returns to her dingy apartment to care for her junkie prostitute daughter Fiona (Parmetier), the latter's baby daughter, and her own alcoholic husband (Banderet). Taxi driver Paul (Darroussin) pays Michele for sex so she can buy drugs for her daughter from her former lover Gerard (Meylan). There's several subplots, murders, and a suicide. Don't watch if you're prone to depression. French with subtitles. **132m/C; VHS, DVD.** *FR* Ariane Ascaride; Gerard Meylan; Julie-Marie Parmentier; Pierre Banderet; Jean-Pierre Darroussin; Jacques Boudet; Pascale Roberts; Jacques Pieller; Christine Brucher; Alexandre Ogou; ***D:*** Robert Guediguian; ***W:*** Robert Guediguian; Jean-Louis Milesi; ***C:*** Bernard Cavalie.

A Town Like Alice 2 **1956** Given its subject matter, this is a well-done but naturally depressing war romance. In 1941, the Japanese capture British Malaya and send the men to labor camps. The women and children are forced to march through the countryside for months to a women's camp. The group meet a couple of Aussie POWs and Joe (Finch) takes an immediate fancy to Jean (McKenna) and tells her about his hometown of Alice Springs. When the war is over, she makes a pilgrimage to his home to find him. Based on the novel by Nevil Shute (based on a true story); remade as a 1981 miniseries. **107m/B; DVD.** *GB* Virginia McKenna; Peter Finch; Tran Van Khe; Jean Anderson; Marie Lohr; Maureen Swanson; Renee Houston; Kenji Takaki; ***D:*** Jack Lee; ***W:*** W.P. Lipscomb; Richard Mason; ***C:*** Geoffrey Unsworth; ***M:*** Matyas Seiber.

The Town That Banned Christmas 2 1/2 *A Merry Little Christmas* **2006** Christmas is banned in Greenlawn when the town's annual decorating contest turns ruthless, all because of new resident Norbert Bridges (McCoy). Bridges is writing a book on human behavior and goads his neighbors into a must-win mentality so he can study what happens. But when he realizes he's ruined the holiday, Bridges tries to restore the true Christmas spirit. **85m/C; DVD.** Matt McCoy; Jane Sibbett; Adam Ferrara; Carol Alt; Christa B. Allen; Anne Ramsay; ***D:*** John Dowling, Jr.; ***W:*** P. J. McIlvaine; ***C:*** Robe Haley; ***M:*** Jeff Denlea; Peter Mazzeo.

The Town That Dreaded Sundown 2 **2014 (R)** In 1946, Texarkana was terrorized by a serial killer, which was then memorialized by the original "The Town That Dreaded Sundown" in the 70s. That film was a fictionalized account of the serial killer's return, which is also what the remake/sequel hybrid is about. Texarkana is once again haunted by a serial killer and everyone is watching the first film in an effort to guess who he is. **87m/C; Blu-Ray, Streaming.** Addison Timlin; Veronica Cartwright; Anthony Anderson; Travis Tope; Joshua Leonard; Andy Abele; Gary Cole; Edward Herrmann; Ed Lauter; Denis O'Hare; ***D:*** Alfonso Gomez-Rejon; ***W:*** Roberto Aguirre-Sacasa; ***C:*** Michael Goi; ***M:*** Ludwig Göransson.

Town without Pity 2 1/2 *Stadt ohne Mitleid* **1961** Though the subject of this courtroom drama remains far too timely, its treatment is dated in some key scenes. Of course, being 40 years old will do that to a movie. In 1960, four American GIs (Blake, Jaeckel, Sutton, Sondock) stationed in Germany are accused of raping a local girl, Karin (Kaufmann). Lawyer Steve Garrett (Douglas) is brought in to defend them and elects to put the young woman on trial and on the stand. Gripping courtroom tale never fails to deliver dramatic punch. Based on the Manfred Gregor novel "The Verdict." Gene Pitney had his biggest hit with the Academy Award-nominated title song. **103m/B; VHS, DVD.** *GE* Kirk Douglas; E.G. Marshall; Robert (Bobby) Blake; Richard Jaeckel; Frank Sutton; Alan Gifford; Barbara Rutting; Christine Kaufmann; Mal Sondock; ***D:*** Gottfried Reinhardt; ***W:*** Silvia Reinhardt; Georg Hurdalek; ***C:*** Kurt Hasse; ***M:*** Dimitri Tiomkin. Golden Globes '61: Song ("Town without Pity").

Toxic 2 **2007 (R)** An unstable psychotic escapes from a mental ward and her own father puts a hit on her, provoking her into a killing spree. **97m/C; DVD.** Charity Shea; Tom Sizemore; Corey Large; Susan Ward; Master P; Bai Ling; ***D:*** Alan Pao; ***W:*** Alan Pao; ***C:*** Roger Chingirian; ***M:*** Scott Glasgow.

The Toxic Avenger 1/2 **1986 (R)** Tongue-in-cheek, cult fave has 98-pound weakling Melvin (Torgl) fall into barrel of toxic waste to emerge as Toxie (Cohen), a lumbering, bloodthirsty hulk of sludge and mire. He falls for blind babe Sara (Maranda) and sets out to do good (and get revenge). Set in the legendary city of TromaVille. Billed as "The first Super-Hero from New Jersey." Followed by: "The Toxic Avenger, Part 2;" "The Toxic Avenger, Part 3: The Last Temptation of Toxie;" and "Citizen Toxie: The Toxic Avenger, Part 4." **90m/C; VHS, DVD, Blu-Ray, UMD.** Mitchell Cohen; Andree Maranda; Jennifer Baptist; Robert Prichard; Cindy Manion; Mark Torgl; David Weiss; ***D:*** Michael Herz; Lloyd Kaufman; ***W:*** Joe Ritter; ***C:*** James London.

The Toxic Avenger, Part 2 1/2 **1989 (R)** Sequel to "Toxic Avenger." Hulky slimer targets Japanese corporations that built toxic chemical dump in Tromaville. Followed by "The Toxic Avenger, Part 3: The Last Temptation of Toxie." **90m/C; VHS, DVD, Blu-Ray.** Ron Fazio; Phoebe Legere; Rick Collins; John Altamura; Rikiya Yasuoka; Lisa Gaye; Mayako Katsuragi; ***D:*** Michael Herz; Lloyd Kaufman; ***W:*** Lloyd Kaufman; Gay Partington Terry; ***C:*** James London; ***M:*** Barrie Guard.

The Toxic Avenger, Part 3: The Last Temptation of Toxie 1/2 **1989 (R)** Unemployed superhero is tempted to sell out to greedy capitalists when his cutie Claire needs an eye operation. Also available in an unrated version. **102m/C; VHS, DVD, Blu-Ray.** Ron Fazio; Phoebe Legere; John Altamura; Rick Collins; Lisa Gaye; Jessica Dublin; ***D:*** Michael Herz; Lloyd Kaufman; ***W:*** Lloyd Kaufman; Gay Partington Terry; ***C:*** James London; ***M:*** Christopher De Marco.

Toxic Skies 1/2 **2008** Virologist Tess Martin (Heche) has to figure out the cause of a mysterious, rapidly moving disease that's spreading across the country killing people. The usual corporate greed figures in since jet fuels leaving chemical trails are the apparent culprit. Instead of being your basic, low-budget disaster flick, it goes melodrama by delving into Tess' tragic past to little purpose. **90m/C; DVD.** Anne Heche; James Tupper; Barclay Hope; Daniel Bacon; ***D:*** Andrew Christopher; ***W:*** Kyle Hart; Andrew Christopher; ***C:*** Mahlon Todd Williams; ***M:*** Kevin Blumenfeld. **VIDEO**

The Toy 1/2 **1982 (PG)** Penniless reporter finds himself the new "toy" of the spoiled son of a multimillionaire oil man.

Unfortunate casting of Pryor as the toy owned by Gleason, with heavy-handed lecturing about earning friends. Slow and terrible remake of the Pierre Richard comedy "Le Jouet." **102m/C; VHS, DVD, Blu-Ray.** Richard Pryor; Jackie Gleason; Ned Beatty; Wilfrid Hyde-White; Scott Schwartz; ***D:*** Richard Donner; ***W:*** Carol Sobieski; ***C:*** Laszlo Kovacs; ***M:*** Patrick Williams.

Toy Soldiers 1/2 **1984 (R)** A group of college students are held for ransom in a war-torn Central American country. When they escape, they join forces with a seasoned mercenary who leads them as a vigilante force. **85m/C; VHS, DVD.** Cleavon Little; Jason Miller; Tim Robbins; Tracy Scoggins; ***D:*** David Fisher.

Toy Soldiers **1991 (R)** This unlikely action tale stops short of being laughable but still has a fair share of silliness. South American narco-terrorists seize an exclusive boys' school. The mischievous students turn their talent for practical jokes to resistance-fighting. Orbach has an uncredited cameo. Based on a novel by William P. Kennedy. **104m/C; VHS, DVD, Blu-Ray.** Sean Astin; Wil Wheaton; Keith Coogan; Andrew Divoff; Denholm Elliott; Louis Gossett, Jr.; Shawn (Michael) Phelan; ***Cameo(s):*** Jerry Orbach; ***D:*** Daniel Petrie, Jr.; ***W:*** Daniel Petrie, Jr.; ***C:*** Thomas Burstyn; ***M:*** Robert Folk.

Toy Story **1995 (G)** First feature length, wholly computer animated film confirms what we suspected all along—toys do have lives of their own when we're not around. Pull-string cowboy Woody (Hanks), as favorite toy, presides over his fellow playthings in Andy's room. Enter new toy on the block, Buzz Lightyear (Allen), a space ranger action figure who thinks he's real. Jealous Woody and his delusional, high-tech companion soon find themselves in the outside world, where they must join forces to survive. Funny, intelligent script and voice characterizations that rival many live-action movies in depth and emotion. All this, and Don Rickles berating an actual hockey puck. **84m/C; DVD, Blu-Ray.** ***V:*** Tom Hanks; Tim Allen; Annie Potts; John Ratzenberger; Wallace Shawn; Jim Varney; Don Rickles; John Morris; R. Lee Ermey; Laurie Metcalf; Erik von Detten; ***D:*** John Lasseter; ***W:*** Joss Whedon; Joel Cohen; Alec Sokolow; ***M:*** Randy Newman. Natl. Film Reg. '05.

Toy Story 2 **1999 (G)** Woody is kidnapped by a greedy toy collector and finds out that he was the star of a popular '50s children's show (think Howdy Doody) with a posse of his own. Buzz and the other denizens of Andy's room set out to save him, and in the process meet up with Buzz's archnemesis Emperor Zurg. All of the original cast members return to their now-classic characters, and the plentiful new characters, in-jokes, and tributes to other movies keep this installment just as entertaining for kids and adults as the original. This one actually has more depth than the first, dealing with issues such as mortality and the meaning of (a toy's) life. **92m/C; DVD, Blu-Ray.** ***V:*** Tom Hanks; Tim Allen; Joan Cusack; Don Rickles; John Ratzenberger; Annie Potts; Wayne Knight; Laurie Metcalf; Jim Varney; Estelle Harris; Kelsey Grammer; Wallace Shawn; John Morris; R. Lee Ermey; Jodi Benson; Jonathan Harris; Joe Ranft; Andrew Stanton; Robert Goulet; ***D:*** John Lasseter; Lee Unkrich; Ash Bannon; ***W:*** Andrew Stanton; Ash Bannon; Rita Hsiao; Doug Chamberlin; Chris Webb; ***M:*** Randy Newman. Golden Globes '00: Film--Mus./Comedy.

Toy Story 3 **2010 (G)** Andy is college-bound, so Buzz, Woody and the rest of the toy box crowd are donated to a daycare center, which launches some unexpected adventures. Heartwarming and funny in the best Pixar tradition, this one blows away the "third in the trilogy" curse with genuine thrills and real emotion. Parents with kids leaving the nest are warned: you WILL tear up. In 3-D. **103m/C; Blu-Ray.** ***V:*** Tom Hanks; Tim Allen; Joan Cusack; Wallace Shawn; John Ratzenberger; Don Rickles; Estelle Harris; Blake Clark; R. Lee Ermey; Michael Keaton; Jodi Benson; Ned Beatty; Timothy Dalton; Laurie Metcalf; John Morris; Bonnie Hunt; Jeff Garlin; Kirsten Schaal; Lou Romano; Richard "Cheech" Marin; Whoopi Goldberg; Frank Welker; Beatrice Miller; Lee Unkrich; Richard Kind; Teddy Newton; Javier Fernandez Pena; Emily Hahn; ***D:*** Lee Unkrich; ***W:*** Michael Arndt; ***M:*** Randy Newman. Oscars '10: Animated Film, Song ("We Belong Together"); British Acad. '10: Animated Film; Golden Globes '11: Animated Film.

Toy Story 4 1/2 **2019 (G)** As five-year-old Bonnie (McGraw) has grown up, her playtime does not always include toys she inherited, including Woody (Hanks). However, Woody still watches out for her, and when she struggles at her kindergarten orientation, he supplies the materials she needs to make a new toy, Forky (Hale). Bonnie's love of Forky creates a crisis when she and her parents take an RV trip and Forky gets separated from Bonnie. At the same time, Woody must consider his purpose in his owner's life. Though superficially appealing to children, this gem also explores themes related to aging, new friends, and new adventures in humorous, meaningful fashion. **100m/C; DVD, Blu-Ray.** Tom Hanks; Tim Allen; Annie Potts; Tony Hale; Keegan Michael Key; ***D:*** Josh Cooley; ***W:*** Andrew Stanton; Stephany Folsom; ***M:*** Randy Newman. Oscars '19: Animated Film.

The Toy Wife **1938** Sixteen-year-old southern belle Gilberte is being courted by Andre but she's more interested in her older sister Louise's fiancé George. She steals him away and they marry and have a son but Gilberte is ill-equipped for both motherhood and looking after George's plantation. So Louise comes to help while Gilberte takes up with Andre again and runs away to New York. Their return is followed by tragedy. **95m/B; DVD.** Luise Rainer; Melvyn Douglas; Robert Young; Barbara O'Neil; H.B. Warner; Alma Kruger; ***D:*** Richard Thorpe; ***W:*** Zoë Akins; ***C:*** Oliver Marsh; ***M:*** Edward Ward.

The ToyBox 1/2 **2018** Though Steve (Denton) is estranged from his family, he and his wife Jennifer (Richards) agree to go on a summer road trip in a used RV. On the highway, they pick up a woman, Samantha (Barton), and her brother (Mercer) because their car is broken down. In the middle of nowhere, the RV takes control of itself, drives them into the desert, and crashes. As they struggle for survival in the harsh environment, they fear that the RV has horrible secrets of its own. This B-movie-quality horror/thriller is predictable and, worse, not particularly scary. **95m/C; DVD.** Denise Richards; Mischa Barton; Jeff Denton; Brian Nagel; Greg Violand; ***D:*** Tom Nagel; ***W:*** Jeff Denton; ***C:*** Ken Stachnik; ***M:*** Holly Amber Church.

Toys 1/2 **1992 (PG-13)** Diappointingly earnest comedy about Leslie (Williams), the whimsical son of a toy manufacturer who must fight to keep the playful spirit of the factory alive after it passes into the hands of his deranged uncle (Gambon). This uncle is a general who attempts to transform the factory into an armaments plant. Leslie receives assistance in this battle from his sister Alsatia (Cusack) and his cousin Patrick (L.L. Cool J). Flat characters; generally falls short by trying too hard to send a message to viewers about the folly of war. Does have extremely vivid and intriguing visuals and special effects. **121m/C; VHS, DVD.** Robin Williams; Joan Cusack; Michael Gambon; LL Cool J; Robin Wright; Donald O'Connor; ***D:*** Barry Levinson; ***W:*** Valerie Curtin; Barry Levinson; ***C:*** Adam Greenberg.

Toys in the Attic 1/2 **1963** A man returns to his home in New Orleans with his child bride, where they will live with his two impoverished, spinster sisters. Toned-down version of the Lillian Hellman play. **88m/B; VHS, DVD.** Dean Martin; Geraldine Page; Yvette Mimieux; Wendy Hiller; Gene Tierney; Nan Martin; Larry Gates; Frank Silvera; ***D:*** George Roy Hill; ***W:*** James Poe; ***C:*** Joseph Biroc.

Tracers **2015 (PG-13)** A fast-paced action crime drama centered on a bike messenger who becomes involved with organized crime. Working as a bike messenger in New York City, Cam (Lautner) is in a difficult position. Not only is he being pursued by the Chinese mafia, he is struggling in other areas of his life despite his generous nature. Cam thinks he has found kindred spirits in parkour, after meeting Nikki (Avgeropoulos) and her parkour group. However, Cam finds himself further mired in criminal activity when they convince Cam to make money by using his parkour skills in illegal ways with them. As their parkour-driven heists become increasingly dangerous and gang members still seek him out, Cam wonders how he will stay alive. **94m/C; DVD, Blu-Ray, Streaming, Download.** Taylor Lautner; Marie Avgeropoulos; Adam Rayner; Rafi Gavron; Johnny Wu; ***D:*** Daniel Benmayor; ***W:*** Matt Johnson; ***C:*** Nelson Cragg; ***M:*** Lucas Vidal.

Traces of Red **1992 (R)** Set in affluent Palm Beach, and filled with dead bodies, colorful suspects, and red herrings. The complex plot, often so serious it's funny, leads viewers through a convoluted series of events. Cop Jack Dobson (Belushi) is found dead in the opening scene; in homage to "Sunset Boulevard," his corpse acts as the narrator, a vehicle which unfortunately doesn't work as well here. He promises to recount the events leading up to his death which circle around a series of murders, and the people in his life who are possible suspects. Although Belushi's performance is average, Goldwyn, as Dobson's partner, shows off the talent he displayed in "Ghost." **105m/C; VHS, DVD.** James Belushi; Lorraine Bracco; Tony Goldwyn; William Russ; Michelle Joyner; Joe Lisi; Jim Piddock; ***D:*** Andy Wolk; ***W:*** Jim Piddock; ***C:*** Tim Suhrstedt; ***M:*** Graeme Revell.

The Tracey Fragments 1/2 **2007** McDonald uses a number of visual tricks (including split screens) to take us into the teen angst of 15-year-old Tracey Berkowitz (Page), but his disjointed storytelling proves more annoying than enlightening. Tracey uses fantasy to deal with the loneliness and frustration of her dysfunctional world. But her reality takes a hit when Tracey's young brother Sonny (Souwand) disappears while in her care and Tracey has to find him. Medved adapted from her novel. **77m/C; DVD.** *CA* Ellen Page; Ari Cohen; Julian Richings; Zie Souwand; Erin McMurtry; Max Maccabe-Lokos; ***D:*** Bruce McDonald; ***W:*** Maureen Medved; ***C:*** Steve Cosens; ***M:*** Broken Social Scene.

Track of the Cat **1954** Allegorical western from Wellman. The dysfunctional Bridges family is snowbound on their ranch and beset by an unseen (and legendary) black panther that's killing their cattle. Controlling Ma Bridges (Bondi) is contemptuous of both husband and children and has turned self-proclaimed heir apparent Curt (Mitchum) into a bully. Curt's obsession with hunting the cat proves a lesson in hubris. **102m/C; DVD.** Robert Mitchum; Beulah Bondi; Tab Hunter; Teresa Wright; William Hopper; Philip Tonge; Diana Lynn; Carl "Alfalfa" Switzer; ***D:*** William A. Wellman; ***W:*** A(lbert) I(saac) Bezzerides; ***C:*** William Clothier; ***M:*** Roy Webb.

Track of the Moonbeast **1976** An American Indian uses mythology to capture the Moonbeast, a lizard-like creature that is roaming the deserts of New Mexico. **90m/C; VHS, DVD.** Chase Cordell; Donna Leigh Drake; ***D:*** Richard Ashe.

Track of the Vampire 1/2 *Blood Bath* **1966** Half an hour of leftover footage from a Yugoslavian vampire movie stuck into the story of a California painter who kills his models. Gripping and atmospheric, but disjointed. **80m/B; VHS, DVD, Blu-Ray.** *YU* William Campbell; Jonathan Haze; Sid Haig; Marissa Mathes; Lori Saunders; Sandra Knight; ***D:*** Stephanie Rothman; Jack Hill.

Track 16 1/2 **2002** Paul, the lead singer of a small-town rock band, gets mistakenly mixed up in the investigation of a murdered woman. Now the real killer is out for Paul's blood. Not cool, especially when he's got a gig the next night! Dopey rock soundtrack goes great with a lot of dopey action, reaching its embarrassing (ahem) climax with a song called "Sex with Someone You Love," during, yup, a sex scene. Mini-budget thriller that looks and sounds more like a demo tape. **90m/C; DVD.** Billy Frank; Bobbi Ashton; Alan Pratt; ***D:*** Michael (Mick) McCleery; ***W:*** Michael (Mick) McCleery; ***C:*** Michael (Mick) McCleery; ***M:*** Billy Frank. **VIDEO**

Track the Man Down 1/2 **1955** Low-budget Brit crime drama. Hoodlum Rick robs a dog-racing track, passes the money off to his girlfriend, Pat, who passes it off to her sister, June. June boards a bus to take the satchel to a supposedly safe location, only she's unwittingly being trailed by reporter Don. **75m/B; DVD, Blu-Ray.** *UK* Kent Taylor; Petula Clark; Renee Houston; George Rose; Ursula Howells; Kenneth Griffith; ***D:*** R.G. Springsteen; ***W:*** Kenneth Hayles; Paul Erickson; ***C:*** Basil Emmott; ***M:*** Lambert Williamson.

Track 29 1/2 **1988 (R)** A confusing black comedy about a lonely woman, her husband who has a model train fetish, and a stranger who claims to be her son. Filmed in North Carolina. **90m/C; VHS, DVD, Streaming.** Theresa Russell; Gary Oldman; Christopher Lloyd; Colleen Camp; Sandra Bernhard; Seymour Cassel; Leon Rippy; Vance Colvig; ***D:*** Nicolas Roeg; ***W:*** Dennis Potter.

Tracked *Dogboys* **1998** Prisoner Julian Taylor (Cain) is sent to the patrol-dog training detail and discovers that the twisted department head (Brown) "rents" out his dogs and prisoners to hunters who want human prey. Carrere is the beautiful D.A. who investigates the rash of inmate deaths and discovers Julian is the next quarry. **92m/C; VHS, DVD.** Bryan Brown; Dean Cain; Tia Carrere; Ken James; Von Flores; Richard Chevolleau; Sean McCann; ***D:*** Ken Russell; ***W:*** David Taylor; ***C:*** Jamie Thompson; ***M:*** John Altman. **CABLE**

The Tracker 1/2 *Dead or Alive* **1988** HBO western about a retired gunman/tracker who must again take up arms. His college-educated son joins him as he searches for a murdering religious fanatic. Fairly decent for the genre. **102m/C; VHS, DVD.** Kris Kristofferson; Scott Wilson; Mark Moses; David Huddleston; John Quade; Don Swayze; Brynn Thayer; ***D:*** John Guillermin; ***M:*** Sylvester Levay. **CABLE**

Tracker **2010 (R)** Afrikaner Boer War vet Arjan van Diemen (Winstone) immigrates to New Zealand and is forcibly hired by British Major Carlysle (Reeves) to track Maori Kereama (Morrison) who's accused of killing a soldier. He does his job but when Arjan captures Kereama, he learns he's been falsely accused. Since both men have a beef against the Brits, Arjen has to decide what to do next. Cinematography by Harvey Harrison is especially notable. **102m/C; DVD, Blu-Ray.** *GB NZ* Ray Winstone; Temuera Morrison; Gareth Reeves; Mark Mitchinson; Daniel Musgrove; Mick Rose; ***D:*** Ian Sharp; ***W:*** Nicolas van Pallandt; ***C:*** Harvey Harrison; ***M:*** David Burns.

Tracks 1/2 **1976 (R)** Vietnam veteran accompanies the body of a buddy on a long train ride home. He starts suffering flashbacks from the war and begins to think some of the passengers are out to get him. **90m/C; VHS, DVD.** Dennis Hopper; Dean Stockwell; Taryn Power; Zack Norman; Michael Emil; Barbara Flood; ***D:*** Henry Jaglom; ***W:*** Henry Jaglom; ***C:*** Paul Glickman.

Tracks 1/2 **2005 (R)** Dull prison flick based on a true story. Fifteen-year-old Peter Madigan and his buds get wasted along some New Jersey train tracks and come up with a dumb prank that results in the derailing of a commuter train, killing the conductor. Peter and his pals become the first juveniles in New Jersey history to be sentenced to an adult maximum security facility. Follows Peter's adjustment to prison life as corrections officer Clark (Ice-T) takes a concerned interest in the young man, although Peter stays a pretty unsympathetic character. **92m/C; DVD.** Ice-T; John Heard; Chris Gunn; Barbara Christie; ***D:*** Peter Wade; ***W:*** Peter Wade; ***C:*** Jesse Weathington. **CABLE**

Tracks 1/2 **2014 (PG-13)** In her mid-twenties and stuck in a rut, Aussie Robyn Davidson (Wasikowska) forgoes the usual European backpack adventure and instead departs on a 1,700-mile journey across the desert. In a quest for isolation, she's joined only by four camels and a dog. Occasionally, American photographer Rick Smolan (Driver) tags along to document her blistering skin and the endurance of her ever-faithful companions. Based on the popular 1980 travel memoir, this interpretation is intentionally as slow-going as Robyn's trek, and at times feels almost as rewarding. A stunning portrait of a deadly landscape conquered by a resolve to find meaning in a mad, mad world. **112m/C; DVD.** *AU UK* Mia Wasikowska; Adam Driver; Rolley Mintuma; ***D:*** John Curran; ***W:*** Marion Nelson; ***C:*** Mandy Walker; ***M:*** Gareth Stevenson.

The Trade 🦴 1/2 **2003** Unsuccessful tale of ambitious Wall Street stockbroker Wayne Garrett (Mills), who finally realizes he's become morally bankrupt and seeks to change his sleazy ways by bringing down his firm and their ill-gotten gains. **90m/C; DVD.** Eddie Mills; Elizabeth Banks; James Rebhorn; Sascha Knopf; Judah Friedlander; ***D:*** Thomas Halikias; ***W:*** Thomas Halikias; ***C:*** Leland Krane; ***M:*** Didier Rachou. **VIDEO**

Trade 🦴 **2007 (R)** Truth-based expose of human slave trafficking is more lurid and sleazy than illuminating. Thirteen-year-old Adriana (Gaitan) is kidnapped and taken from Mexico to New Jersey to be sold into sex slavery on the internet. Her brother Jorge (Ramos) and investigator Ray (Kline) pursue, then infiltrate the operation. Director Kreuzpaintner cranks up every sleazy detail, dwelling extensively on the abuse heaped on Adriana and her fellow victims by cruel captor Manuelo (Perez). The result is more sensational than condemning, however, and it's topped off with a cop-out happy ending to make you feel less icky for watching it. **119m/C; DVD.** Kevin Kline; Cesar Ramos; Alicja Bachleda-Curus; Paulina Gaitan; Marco Perez; ***D:*** Marco Kreuzpaintner; ***W:*** Jose Rivera; ***C:*** Daniel Gottschalk; ***M:*** Jacob Lieberman; Leonardo Heiblum.

Trade of Innocents 🦴 **2012** A screed against child sex trafficking more than an actual movie. After their daughter is murdered, Alex and Claire Becker vow to protect other children. He becomes an investigator in Cambodia, pursuing sleazy pimps, while she counsels the rescued children. It's very noble but it's basically a public service announcement. English and Thai with subtitles. **91m/C; DVD.** Dermot Mulroney; Mira Sorvino; Trieu Tran; John Billingsley; ***D:*** Christopher Bessette; ***W:*** Christopher Bessette; ***C:*** Philip Hurn; ***M:*** Timothy Hosman. **VIDEO**

Traded 🦴🦴 1/2 **2016** A Western sent in 1880s Kansas centered on one man's quest to rescue his daughter. Clay Travis (Pare) was once a sharpshooter but has built a peaceful as a rancher with a family. After his son tragically dies and his daughter disappears, Clay leaves the ranch to track an evil brothel owner, LaVoie (Sizemore), with the assistance of Billy (Kristofferson). The pair go to extraordinary lengths to find Clay's daughter and destroy LaVoie and his henchmen. **98m/C; DVD, Blu-Ray, Streaming, Download.** Michael Paré; Kris Kristofferson; Tom Sizemore; Trace Adkins; Martin Kove; ***D:*** Timothy Woodward, Jr.; ***W:*** Mark Esslinger; ***C:*** Pablo Diez; ***M:*** Samuel Joseph Smythe.

Trading Mom 🦴🦴 1/2 **1994 (PG)** Harried single parent Spacek is erased from the lives of her three kids, who decide they want a parent who's more fun. So, thanks to some magic, they head off to the Mommy Mart to try out a trio of bizarre choices. This gives Spacek a chance at three more roles before the kids come to their senses. Based on "The Mommy Market" by Nancy Brelis; directorial debut for daughter Tia. **82m/C; VHS, Streaming.** Sissy Spacek; Anna Chlumsky; Aaron Michael Metchik; Asher Metchik; Maureen Stapleton; ***D:*** Tia Brelis; ***W:*** Tia Brelis; ***M:*** David Kitay.

Trading Paint 🦴 **2019 (R)** At a car race at Talladega, young Cam Munroe (Sebastian) races veteran Bob Linsky (Madsen), but loses because of the poor quality of his car's engine. The situation is more complicated because Cam's father Sam (Travolta) is the track's manager and once Bob's most bitter rival but gave up racing after a serious car accident. To improve his chances as a driver, Cam jumps at Bob's offer to drive for him, which upsets his father. In response, Sam returns to racing himself and finds himself competing against both Bob and Cam. Shallow and predictable. **88m/C; DVD.** John Travolta; Michael Madsen; Rosabell Laurenti Sellers; Barry Corbin; Toby Sebastian; ***D:*** Karzan Kader; ***W:*** Gary Gerani; Craig R. Welch; ***C:*** Jose David Montero; ***M:*** Victor Reyes. Golden Raspberries '19: Worst Actor (Travolta).

Trading Places 🦴🦴 1/2 **1983 (R)** Two elderly businessmen wager that environment is more important than heredity in creating a successful life, using a rich nephew and an unemployed street hustler as guinea pigs. Curtis is winning as a hooker-with-a-heart-of-gold who helps the hapless Aykroyd. Oft-told tale succeeds thanks to strong cast. Murphy's second screen appearance. **118m/C; VHS, DVD, Blu-Ray, HD-DVD.** Eddie Murphy; Dan Aykroyd; Jamie Lee Curtis; Ralph Bellamy; Don Ameche; Denholm Elliott; Paul Gleason; James Belushi; Al Franken; Tom Davis; Giancarlo Esposito; Kristin Holby; Stephen Stucker; Nicholas Guest; Robert Earl Jones; Bill Cobbs; ***D:*** John Landis; ***W:*** Herschel Weingrod; Timothy Harris; ***M:*** Elmer Bernstein. British Acad. '83: Support. Actor (Elliott), Support. Actress (Curtis).

Traffic 🦴🦴 1/2 **1971** Eccentric auto designer Monsieur Hulot tries to transport his latest contraption from Paris to Amsterdam for an international auto show. As usual, everything goes wrong. Tati's last feature film and his fifth to feature Hulot. French with subtitles. **89m/C; VHS, DVD, Blu-Ray.** *FR* Jacques Tati; Maria Kimberly; Marcel Fraval; ***D:*** Jacques Tati; ***W:*** Jacques Tati; Jacques Lagrange; ***C:*** Eddy van der Enden; Marcel Weiss; ***M:*** Charles Dumont.

Traffic 🦴🦴🦴 1/2 **2000 (R)** Based on the 1990 British miniseries "Traffik," Soderbergh's film has three loosely intertwined stories about the drug trade: Federal judge Douglas is appointed as head of the National Drug Task Force but learns his own daughter is a heroin addict; San Diego socialite wife Zeta-Jones learns the drug trade when her drug lord hubby gets busted; and Mexican border cop Del Toro works on his power base. Soderbergh takes on a large, complex subject with a large, complex film populated by a large, uniformly excellent cast. The outcomes of the various storylines may not end happily or neatly (just like in real life), but the characters and ideas explored along the way are compelling. **147m/C; VHS, DVD, Blu-Ray, HD-DVD.** Michael Douglas; Catherine Zeta-Jones; Benicio Del Toro; Dennis Quaid; Benjamin Bratt; Albert Finney; Amy Irving; Don Cheadle; Luis Guzman; Steven Bauer; James Brolin; Erika Christensen; Clifton (Gonzalez) Collins, Jr.; Miguel Ferrer; Tomas Milian; D.W. Moffett; Marisol Padilla Sanchez; Peter Riegert; Jacob Vargas; Rena Sofer; Stacey Travis; Salma Hayek; Topher Grace; Beau Holden; Enrique Murciano; Jsu Garcia; ***D:*** Steven Soderbergh; ***W:*** Stephen Gaghan; ***C:*** Steven Soderbergh; ***M:*** Cliff Martinez. Oscars '00: Adapt. Screenplay, Director (Soderbergh), Film Editing, Support. Actor (Del Toro); British Acad. '00: Adapt. Screenplay, Support. Actor (Del Toro); Golden Globes '01: Screenplay, Support. Actor (Del Toro); L.A. Film Critics '00: Director (Soderbergh); Natl. Bd. of Review '00: Director (Soderbergh); N.Y. Film Critics '00: Director (Soderbergh), Film, Support. Actor (Del Toro); Natl. Soc. Film Critics '00: Director (Soderbergh), Support. Actor (Del Toro); Screen Actors Guild '00: Actor (Del Toro), Cast; Writers Guild '00: Adapt. Screenplay; Broadcast Film Critics '00: Adapt. Screenplay, Director (Soderbergh).

Traffic in Souls 🦴🦴🦴 **1913** Silent melodrama dealing with white slavery. Immigrants and gullible country girls are lured into brothels where they are trapped with no hope of escape until, in a hail of bullets, the police raid the dens of vice and rescue them. **74m/B; Silent; VHS, DVD.** Matt Moore; Jane Gail; William Welsh; ***D:*** George Tucker. Natl. Film Reg. '06.

Traffik 🦴🦴🦴 **1990** A tense, unnerving look at the international world of heroin smuggling. The British drama follows the lives of three men involved in the drug trade: a farmer in the poppy fields of Pakistan, a drug smuggler in Hamburg, and a Tory cabinet minister who heads his government's anti-drug cabinet and then comes to realize his own daughter is an addict. The basis for Steven Soderbergh's much-lauded 2000 film "Traffic." **360m/C; VHS, DVD.** *GB* Lindsay Duncan; Bill Paterson; Jamal Shah; Talat Hussain; Fritz Muller-Scherz; Julia Ormond; Knut Hinz; Feryal Gauhar Shah; Peter Lakenmacher; Vincenzo Benestante; ***D:*** Alastair Reid; ***W:*** Simon Moore; ***C:*** Clive Tickner; ***M:*** Tim Souster. **TV**

Traffik 🦴🦴 **2018 (R)** After losing her reporting job, Brea (Patton) spends a romantic birthday weekend with her boyfriend John (Epps). At the swank pad, they are visited by John's friend Darren (Alonzo) and his girlfriend. While everyone argues and secrets are revealed, Brea finds a phone that contains images of trafficked women. Hoping to use the phone to restart her career, Brea refuses to give it back and finds herself increasingly involved in trafficking-related violence. A failed, unfocused thriller that purports to shine a light on human trafficking. **96m/C; DVD, Blu-Ray.** Paula Patton; Missi Pyle; William Fichtner; Roselyn Sanchez; Dawn Olivieri; ***D:*** Deon Taylor; ***W:*** Deon Taylor; ***C:*** Dante Spinotti; ***M:*** Geoff Zanelli.

Tragedy Girls 🦴🦴🦴 **2017 (R)** It's *Heathers* for the cyberage. Desperate to boost the popularity of their true-crime blog, McKayla and Sadie capture a serial killer, hold him hostage as a murder consultant, and use his techniques to terrorize their community and become Internet sensations. On paper, these self-absorbed, sociopathic cheerleaders sound unappealing, but Shipp and Hildebrand bring such humor and charm to their characters that you'll undoubtedly "like" them. **98m/C; DVD, Blu-Ray.** Alexandra Shipp; Brianna Hildebrand; Josh Hutcherson; Craig Robinson; Kevin Durand; ***D:*** Tyler MacIntyre; ***W:*** Tyler MacIntyre; Chris Lee Hill; ***C:*** Pawel Pogorzelski; ***M:*** Russ Howard, III.

The Trail of '98 🦴🦴 **1928** During the Klondike gold rush, a motley assortment of would-be fortune hunters is traveling by ship from San Francisco to Skagway. Among them are hired help Berna (Del Rio) and would-be prospector Larry (Forbes), who fall in love. The hard trip to the gold fields of Dawson City involves blizzards, fires, starvation, claim jumpers, and many other trials. **90m/B; Silent; DVD.** Dolores Del Rio; Ralph Forbes; Harry Carey, Sr.; Karl (Daen) Dane; Tully Marshall; George Cooper; Tenen Holtz; Emily Fitzroy; ***D:*** Clarence Brown; ***W:*** Benjamin Glazer; ***C:*** John Seitz.

Trail of a Serial Killer 🦴🦴 **1998 (R)** FBI agent Jason Enola (Penn) and detective Brad Abraham (Madsen) team up to find a serial killer leaving a trail of dismembered corpses. **95m/C; VHS, DVD.** Christopher Penn; Michael Madsen; Jennifer Dale; Chad McQueen; ***D:*** Damian Lee. **VIDEO**

Trail of Robin Hood 🦴🦴 1/2 **1950** Rogers sees to it that poor families get Christmas trees, in spite of the fact that a big business wants to raise the prices. Features a number of western stars, including Holt playing himself. **67m/C; VHS, DVD.** Roy Rogers; Penny Edwards; Gordon Jones; Jack Holt; Emory Parnell; Rex Allen; Allan "Rocky" Lane; Clifton Young; Monte Hale; Kermit Maynard; Tom Keene; Ray Corrigan; William Farnum; ***D:*** William Witney.

The Trail of the Lonesome Pine 🦴🦴🦴 **1936** The first outdoor film to be shot in three-color Technicolor. Two backwoods Kentucky clans, the Tolliver and the Falins, have been feuding so long no one remembers what started the fuss. But young engineer Jack Hale (MacMurray) gets stuck in the middle when he comes to build a railroad through the Blue Ridge Mountains. Hale saves the life of Dave Tolliver (Fonda) but Dave's not happy when the city slicker starts mooning over Dave's sister, June (Sidney). And the Falins aren't happy about the railroad, which leads to even more fighting. Based on the novel by John Fox Jr. and previously filmed in 1916 and 1923. **102m/C; VHS, DVD.** Henry Fonda; Fred MacMurray; Sylvia Sidney; Robert Barrat; Fred Stone; Nigel Bruce; Beulah Bondi; George "Spanky" McFarland; Fuzzy Knight; ***D:*** Henry Hathaway; ***W:*** Grover Jones; Horace McCoy; Harvey Thew; ***C:*** William Howard Greene; Robert C. Bruce.

Trail of the Pink Panther 🦴🦴 **1982 (PG)** The sixth in Sellers' "Pink Panther" series. Inspector Clouseau disappears while he is searching for the diamond known as the Pink Panther. Notable because it was released after Sellers' death, using clips from previous movies to fill in gaps. Followed by "Curse of the Pink Panther." **97m/C; VHS, DVD, Blu-Ray.** Peter Sellers; David Niven; Herbert Lom; Capucine; Burt Kwouk; Robert Wagner; Robert Loggia; ***D:*** Blake Edwards; ***W:*** Blake Edwards; Frank Waldman; ***C:*** Dick Bush; ***M:*** Henry Mancini.

Trail Street 🦴 1/2 **1947** Scott is Bat Masterson, the western hero. He aids the struggle of Kansans as they conquer the land and local ranchers. **84m/B; VHS, DVD.** Randolph Scott; Robert Ryan; Anne Jeffreys; George "Gabby" Hayes; Madge Meredith; Jason Robards, Sr.; ***D:*** Ray Enright.

The Trail to Hope Rose 🦴🦴 **2004** Hallmark Channel western. Half-Indian gunslinger Keenan Deerfield (Phillips) gets out of prison and takes a job in a small mining town under the control of tough Samuel Drigger (Stevens). When Deerfield falls for someone else's girl, the gunslinger plans to get them out of town--after he robs the mining payroll. **89m/C; DVD; Closed Captioned.** Lou Diamond Phillips; Warren Stevens; Richard Tyson; Marina Black; Ernest Borgnine; Lee Majors; ***D:*** David S. Cass, Sr.; ***W:*** Kevin Cutts; ***C:*** Amit Bhattacharya; ***M:*** Joe Kraemer. **CABLE**

Trailer, the Movie 🦴🦴 **1999** Goofy experimental comedy combines elements of "Last Action Hero" and "Purple Rose of Cairo." In a black-and-white introduction, two lonely guys (McCrudden and Pope) sneak into a theatre one night and fall in love with two actresses (Hicks and Crigler) they see in a trailer. After the guys are tossed out, they wish their way into a color world where the rules of movies apply. Unfortunately, this well-meaning independent production lacks the wit to make full use of the engaging premise. **101m/C; DVD.** Ian McCrudden; Will Pope; Miranda Hicks; Marjorie Crigler; ***D:*** Ian McCrudden; ***C:*** Matthew Uhry.

The Train 🦴🦴🦴🦴 *Le Train; Il Treno* **1965** During the German occupation of Paris in 1944, a German colonel (Scofield) is ordered to ransack the city of its art treasures and put them on a train bound for Germany. Word gets to the French Resistance who then persuade the train inspector (Lancaster) to sabotage the train. A battle of wills ensues between Scofield and Lancaster as each becomes increasingly obsessed in outwitting the other—though the cost to all turns out to be as irreplaceable as the art itself. Filmed on location in France. Frankenheimer used real locomotives, rather than models, throughout the film, even in the spectacular crash sequences. **133m/C; VHS, DVD, Blu-Ray.** *FR IT* Burt Lancaster; Paul Scofield; Jeanne Moreau; Michel Simon; Suzanne Flon; Wolfgang Preiss; Albert Remy; Charles Millot; Jacques Marin; Donald O'Brien; Jean-Pierre Zola; Arthur Brauss; Howard Vernon; Richard Munch; Paul Bonifas; Jean-Claude Bercq; ***D:*** John Frankenheimer; ***W:*** Frank Davis; Walter Bernstein; Franklin Coen; ***C:*** Jean Tournier; Walter Wottitz; ***M:*** Maurice Jarre.

Train **WOOF! 2008 (R)** Worthless torture porn. Alex is touring Eastern Europe with her college wrestling team when she and her teammates party too hard and miss their train. The athletes are given accommodations on an alternate connection that turns out to be a moving organ harvesting hospital where they are about to become unwilling donors. **94m/C; DVD.** Thora Birch; Gideon Emery; Derek Magyar; Todd Jensen; Kavan Reece; Gloria Votsis; Vladimir Vladimirov; Konya Ruseva; ***D:*** Gideon Raff; ***W:*** Gideon Raff; ***C:*** Martina Radwan; ***M:*** Michael Wandmacher. **VIDEO**

The Train Killer 🦴 **1983** A mad Hungarian is bent on destroying the Orient Express. **90m/C; VHS, DVD.** Michael Sarrazin; ***D:*** Sandor Simo.

Train Robbers 🦴🦴 **1973 (PG)** A widow employs the services of three cowboys to help her recover some stolen gold in order to clear her late husband's name. At least that's what she says. **92m/C; VHS, DVD, Blu-Ray.** John Wayne; Ann-Margret; Rod Taylor; Ben Johnson; Christopher George; Ricardo Montalban; Bobby Vinton; Jerry Gatlin; ***D:*** Burt Kennedy; ***W:*** Burt Kennedy; ***C:*** William Clothier.

Train Station Pickups 🦴 **1979** Trashy film about young girls who hook at a local train depot, until something goes wrong. **96m/C; VHS, DVD, Streaming.** Marco Knoger; Katja Carrol; Ingeborg Steinbach; Benjamin Carwath; ***D:*** Walter Boos.

Trained to Kill, U.S.A. 🦴 1/2 *The No Mercy Man* **1975 (R)** Vietnam veteran relives his war experiences when a gang of terrorists threaten his hometown. **88m/C; VHS, DVD.** Stephen Sander; Heidi Vaughn; Rockne Tarkington; Richard X. Slattery; ***D:*** Daniel Vance; ***W:*** Daniel Vance; ***C:*** Dean Cundey.

Training Day 🦴🦴 1/2 **2001 (R)** Until the script finally goes completely off the rails, this cop corruption tale is worth watching for the ferocious performance of Washington alone. He's veteran undercover narc Alonzo Harris, who's been the big dog on the L.A. streets for so long, he's become morally bankrupt and works on the might makes right theory of justice. Opposing him is rookie Jake Hoyt (Hawke), who first wants to be a part of Harris's team and then learns just what it will cost him. Fuqua shot on location so you can definitely feel the grit. **120m/C; VHS, DVD, Blu-Ray, UMD, HD-DVD.** Denzel Washington; Ethan Hawke; Scott Glenn; Clifford Curtis; Dr. Dre; Snoop Dogg; Tom Berenger; Harris Yulin; Raymond J. Barry; Charlotte Ayanna; Macy Gray; Eva Mendes; Nick (Nicholas) Chinlund; Jaime Gomez; Raymond Cruz; ***D:*** Antoine Fuqua; ***W:*** David Ayer; ***C:*** Mauro Fiore; ***M:*** Mark Mancina. Oscars '01: Actor (Washington); L.A. Film Critics '01: Actor (Washington).

Trainspotting **1995 (R)** From the same team who offered the violently comedic "Shallow Grave," comes an equally destructive look at a group of Edinburgh junkies and losers. Heroin-user Mark Renton (McGregor) once again decides to get off junk but to do so he has to get away from his friends: knife-wielding psycho Begbie (Carlyle), Sick Boy (Miller), Spud (Bremner), and Tommy (McKidd). He heads for a semi-respectable life in London but Begbie and Spud wind up involving him in a serious money drug deal that spells trouble. Strong fantasy visuals depict drug highs and lows while heavy Scottish accents (and humor) may prove difficult. Based on the 1993 cult novel by Irvine Welsh. Film drew much controversy for supposingly being pro-heroin but the junkie's life is hardly portrayed as being attractive in any way. **94m/C; VHS, DVD, Blu-Ray.** *GB* Ewan McGregor; Ewen Bremner; Jonny Lee Miller; Robert Carlyle; Kevin McKidd; Kelly Macdonald; Shirley Henderson; Pauline Lynch; ***D:*** Danny Boyle; ***W:*** John Hodge; ***C:*** Brian Tufano. British Acad. '95: Adapt. Screenplay.

Trainwreck **2015 (R)** Amy Schumer bursts into the world of film with a truly impressive leading lady comedy debut at the front of a script she wrote herself and Judd Apatow liked so much he asked to direct. Schumer plays Amy, a woman taught by her father (Quinn) that monogamy is not viable, and so she sleeps around and never settles down. Her worldview is challenged when she meets a sports doctor (the charming Hader) who wants more than just a one-night stand. As Apatow often does, he fills out the supporting cast brilliantly as well, including a scene-stealing turn by LeBron James. **122m/C; DVD, Blu-Ray, Streaming.** Amy Schumer; Bill Hader; Colin Quinn; Brie Larson; Mike Birbiglia; ***D:*** Judd Apatow; ***W:*** Amy Schumer; ***C:*** Jody Lee Lipes; ***M:*** Jon Brion.

Traitor **½ 2008 (PG-13)** Worthy entry in the post-9/11 espionage thriller subgenre puts a fairly interesting spin on an otherwise formulaic plot, showcasing the always solid Cheadle as Samir Horn, a Sudanese-American who is either a spy working for the U.S. or a converted terrorist who has embraced Muslim extremism. Pic keeps the secret well as Cheadle deftly plays both sides, and is further enhanced by strong performances by Pearce as an open-minded FBI agent and an underutilized Daniels as an intelligence bureaucrat who seems to know the truth. Stereotypes and convoluted manufactured plot twists bog things down a bit, but ultimately it's Cheadle's subtle and nuanced performance, which never tips his character's hand, that makes it worthwhile. **113m/C; Blu-Ray, On Demand.** Don Cheadle; Guy Pearce; Neal McDonough; Said Taghmaoui; Archie Panjabi; Jeff Daniels; Mozhan Marno; ***D:*** Jeffrey Nachmanoff; ***W:*** Jeffrey Nachmanoff; ***C:*** J.(James) Michael Muro; ***M:*** Mark Kilian.

Tramp, Tramp, Tramp **½ 1926** Langdon's first feature-length comedy, produced by his own company, features the silent star as the hapless son of a shoemaker who is facing bankruptcy. Wealthy shoe manufacturer John Burton (Davis) has offered substantial prize money for a coast-to-coast walking race and Harry is persuaded to enter the contest in order to save the family business. Naturally, there are many obstacles to overcome—he almost falls from a precipice, must escape from a chain gang, and is nearly killed by a cyclone. The plot is merely a series of sketches but Langdon is cheery and fearless; Crawford has an early role as his girlfriend. Langdon used numerous (uncredited) gag men for his film, including Frank Capra. The DVD also includes the Langdon short, "All Night Long." **84m/B; Silent; VHS, DVD.** Harry Langdon; Joan Crawford; Alec B. Francis; Edwards Davis; ***D:*** Harry Edwards; ***C:*** Elgin Lessley.

Trance **2013 (R)** Genre-bending director Danny Boyle takes on the heist flick, pairing London auctioneer Simon (McAvoy) with art thief Franck (Cassel) as the two plot to swipe a prized 1798 Goya masterpiece. Problems arise after a knock on the head renders Simon's memory blank, thus forgetting where he hid the painting. The two employ hypnotherapist Elizabeth (Dawson) to trigger his subconscious, but the mind-trip goes awry. An often-confusing psycho thriller, filled with double-crossing twists and cerebrals turns. Luckily, the trippy voyage is made believable by Dawson's charismatic performance. **101m/C; DVD, Blu-Ray.** *UK* James McAvoy; Vincent Cassel; Rosario Dawson; ***D:*** Danny Boyle; ***W:*** John Hodge; Joe Ahearne; ***C:*** Anthony Dod Mantle; ***M:*** Rick Smith.

Trancers *Future Cop* **1984 (PG-13)** A time-traveling cult from the future goes back in time to 1985 to meddle with fate. Only Jack Deth, defender of justice, can save mankind. Low-budget "Blade Runner." Followed by two sequels. **76m/C; VHS, DVD, Blu-Ray.** Tim Thomerson; Michael Stefoni; Helen Hunt; Art LaFleur; Telma Hopkins; ***D:*** Charles Band; ***W:*** Danny Bilson.

Trancers 2: The Return of Jack Deth **1990 (R)** Retro cop is back from the future again, but seems to have lost his wit and nerve in between sequels. Ward is miscast and the pacing undermines whatever suspense that might have been. **85m/C; VHS, DVD, Blu-Ray.** Tim Thomerson; Helen Hunt; Megan Ward; Biff Manard; Martine Beswick; Jeffrey Combs; Barbara Crampton; Richard Lynch; ***D:*** Charles Band.

Trancers 3: Deth Lives **½ 1992 (R)** In the third film of the "Trancers" series, time-traveling cop Jack Deth fights the deadliest form of government-sponsored Trancer yet—it has a brain. **83m/C; VHS, DVD, Blu-Ray.** Tim Thomerson; Melanie Smith; Andrew (Andy) Robinson; Tony Pierce; Dawn Ann Billings; Helen Hunt; Megan Ward; Stephen Macht; Telma Hopkins; ***D:*** C. Courtney Joyner; ***W:*** C. Courtney Joyner; ***M:*** Richard Band.

Trancers 4: Jack of Swords **½ 1993 (R)** Time-traveling cop Jack Deth finds himself in a mystical new dimension where the blooksucking Trancers have enslaved the local population as feeders. If Jack expects to conquer he'll first need to survive an ancient wizard's prophecy of death. Filmed on location in Romania. **74m/C; VHS, DVD.** Tim Thomerson; Stacie Randall; Ty Miller; Terri Ivens; Mark Arnold; Clabe Hartley; Alan Oppenheimer; Stephen Macht; David Nutter; ***W:*** Peter David; ***M:*** Gary Fry.

Trancers 5: Sudden Deth **½ 1994 (R)** Irreverant time-travelling cop Jack Deth (Thomerson) returns to help the Tunnel Rats occupy the castle of Caliban. But the evil Lord Caliban is resurrected and his only desire is to destroy Jack. This is supposedly the final chapter of Deth's saga. **73m/C; VHS, DVD.** Tim Thomerson; Stacie Randall; Ty Miller; Terri Ivens; Mark Arnold; Clabe Hartley; Alan Oppenheimer; Jeff Moldovan; Lochlyn Munro; Stephen Macht; ***D:*** David Nutter; ***W:*** Peter David; ***M:*** Gary Fry.

Trancers 6: Life After Deth *Trancers 6* **2002** Once again Jack Deth travels through time to put down the malevolent Trancers. He occupies the body of his own daughter that he didn't realize he had. Kind of makes for inappropriately incestuous time travel--icky! **88m/C; DVD.** Zette Sullivan; Jennifer Capo; Robert Donavan; Timothy Prindle; Jere Jon; ***D:*** Jay Woelfel; ***W:*** Danny Bilson; Paul De Meo; C. Courtney Joyner; ***C:*** Paul Deng; ***M:*** Jon Greathouse. **VIDEO**

Transamerica **2005 (R)** Bree (Huffman) is a transsexual formerly known as Stanley on the brink of completing her male to female transformation through gender reassignment surgery. (S)he lives in Los Angeles, but just prior to her long-awaited surgery she receives a call from New York street hustler Toby (Zegers). Toby is looking for Stanley, who, as a result of a brief affair with his late mother, he believes to be his father. Because her therapist insists she must come to terms with this before her surgery, Bree heads to New York. From this point the film becomes a funny and touching road trip flick, as Bree and Toby drive back to L.A. learning about each other. **104m/C; DVD.** Felicity Huffman; Kevin Zegers; Fionnula Flanagan; Elizabeth Pena; Graham Greene; Burt Young; Carrie Preston; ***D:*** Duncan Tucker; ***W:*** Duncan Tucker; ***C:*** Stephen Kazmierski; ***M:*** David Mansfield. Golden Globes '06: Actress--Drama (Huffman); Ind. Spirit '06: Actress (Huffman), First Screenplay; Natl. Bd. of Review '05: Actress (Huffman).

Transatlantic Tunnel **½** *The Tunnel* **1935** An undersea tunnel from England to America is attempted, despite financial trickery and undersea disasters. Made with futuristic sets which were advanced for their time. **94m/B; VHS, DVD.** *GB* Richard Dix; Leslie Banks; Madge Evans; Helen Vinson; Sir C. Aubrey Smith; George Arliss; Walter Huston; ***D:*** Maurice Elvey.

Transcendence **2014 (PG-13)** Legendary cinematographer Pfister makes his directorial debut with this flat piece of sci-fi nonsense that starts with a few interesting ideas but devolves into goofy mumbo-jumbo. Dr. Will Caster (Depp) is the foremost researcher in the field of Artificial Intelligence, which comes in particularly handy when he transcends himself from the physical world to the digital one. Can AI truly replicate the human experience and what might happen if a man as smart as the good doctor has the unlimited power of the technological world with which to play? **119m/C; DVD, Blu-Ray.** Johnny Depp; Rebecca Hall; Paul Bettany; Kate Mara; Morgan Freeman; Cillian Murphy; Cole Hauser; Clifton (Gonzalez) Collins, Jr.; ***D:*** Wally Pfister; ***W:*** Jack Paglen; ***C:*** Jess Hall; ***M:*** Mychael Danna.

Transfixed **½** *Bad Genres; Mauvais Genres* **2001** A whodunnit set in the seamy side of Brussels. Cross-dressing Bo (Stevenin) sees police inspector Paul Huysmans (Bohringer) arrest his father for pedophilia. Does this crime tie into a serial killer who's going after the local tranvestites and prostitutes? Muddled wannabe Hitchcock, although Stevenin gives a stellar performance. Based on the novel "Transfixions" by Brigitte Aubert. French with subtitles. **109m/C; DVD.** *BE FR* Robinson Stevenin; Richard Bohringer; Micheline Presle; Stephane Metzger; ***D:*** Francis Girod; ***W:*** Francis Girod; Philippe Cougrand; ***C:*** Thierry Jault; ***M:*** Alexandre Desplat.

Transformed **2005** Forgettable crime drama in which an inner city pastor assembles a team of martial artists and reformed criminals to take out a group of drug dealers when the police prove to be too incompetent to do so themselves. **91m/C; DVD.** Fred Williamson; Ken Moreno; Shirlee Knudson; Leo Fong; ***D:*** Leo Fong; ***W:*** Leo Fong; ***C:*** Leo Fong; ***M:*** Leo Fong.

Transformers **2007 (PG-13)** The Autobots wage their battle to destroy the evil forces of... heck, if you were alive during the 1980s, you know how the song goes. Bombast specialist Bay brings the successful toy and TV show franchise to the big screen, with this tale of transforming robots from outer space who travel to Earth in search of the mythical Allspark cube. There's lots of rock 'em-sock-'em action, but the whole movie isn't nearly as big, dumb, or fun as it should be, though LaBeouf's "boy and his robot" storyline is the best of the multiple plotlines. **140m/C; DVD, Blu-Ray, HD-DVD.** Shia LaBeouf; Megan Fox; Josh Duhamel; Tyrese Gibson; Anthony Anderson; John Turturro; Jon Voight; Rachael Taylor; Glenn Morshower; Bernie Mac; Amaury Nolasco; Kevin Dunn; Zack (Zach) Ward; Michael O'Neill; Julie White; Travis Van Winkle; Peter Jacobson; William Morgan Sheppard; John Robinson; Chris Ellis; Samantha Smith; Rick Gomez; ***V:*** Peter Cullen; Hugo Weaving; Keith David; Robert Foxworth; Reno Wilson; Darius McCrary; Mark Ryan; ***D:*** Michael Bay; ***W:*** Alex Kurtzman; Roberto Orci; ***C:*** Mitchell Amundsen; ***M:*** Steve Jablonsky.

Transformers: Age of Extinction **½** *Transformers 4* **2014 (PG-13)** Bam. Crash. Boom. Another bit of eye candy from Bay in this franchise of increasingly hollow and increasingly boring CGI orgies. You may have thought it was over when they leveled Chicago but this fourth film sort of reboots the series by ditching the cast of the first three films and upgrading to Wahlberg. He stars as Cade Yeager, a mechanic who stumbles upon Optimus Prime and gets caught up in the latest battle for interstellar domination. Whatever plot exists is merely an excuse for nearly three hours of eye-popping visual effects and a complete lack of storytelling. **165m/C; DVD, Blu-Ray.** Mark Wahlberg; Nicola Peltz; Kelsey Grammer; Stanley Tucci; Jack Reynor; Li Bingbing; T.J. Miller; ***V:*** Peter Cullen; Robert Foxworth; John Goodman; Ken(saku) Watanabe; Frank Welker; ***D:*** Michael Bay; ***W:*** Ehren Kruger; ***C:*** Amir M. Mokri; ***M:*** Steve Jablonsky. Golden Raspberries '14: Worst Director (Bay), Worst Support. Actor (Grammer).

Transformers: Dark of the Moon **½ 2011 (PG-13)** Bay's third in the Hasbro toy/movie franchise is a testosterone-fueled, CGI spectacle whose long runtime includes destroying most of Chicago, which is where the Decepticons have set up their headquarters. Sam (LeBeouf), still a reluctant ally of Optimus Prime, is working in DC and gets involved (along with the government) when the Autobots discover a Cybertronian ship hidden on the dark side of the moon. Not that the plot really matters, nor does the believability of the overblown action scenes. Disappointing for its lack of focus on the actual stars—the Transformers. Model Rosie Huntington-Whiteley takes over as babe eye candy. **157m/C; DVD, Blu-Ray, On Demand.** Shia LaBeouf; Josh Duhamel; Tyrese Gibson; Kevin Dunn; Frances McDormand; Patrick Dempsey; Alan Tudyk; John Turturro; Julie White; Rosie Huntington-Whiteley; Ken Jeong; John Malkovich; ***V:*** Hugo Weaving; Peter Cullen; James Avery; Frank Welker; Robert Foxworth; James Remar; Francesco Quinn; Leonard Nimoy; ***D:*** Michael Bay; ***W:*** Ehren Kruger; ***C:*** Amir M. Mokri; ***M:*** Steve Jablonsky.

Transformers: Revenge of the Fallen **2009 (PG-13)** In part both prequel and sequel, tells of when mankind actually first met the Transformers and of their current status quo on Earth. In this second chapter the Autobots are working with the government to track down any remaining Decepticons, and their human liaison Sam (LaBeouf) is off to college trying to live a normal life. With the discovery of a piece of the Allspark, an ancient map, and the return of Megatron aided by a new foe, the heroes are again brought together to save mankind and possibly the universe itself. Raunchier and darker than the original but with the same heart-pounding CGI action. **147m/C; DVD, Blu-Ray.** Megan Fox; John Turturro; Josh Duhamel; Tyrese Gibson; Shia LaBeouf; Kevin Dunn; Julie White; Rainn Wilson; Deep Roy; Glenn Morshower; ***V:*** Charles Adler; Peter Cullen; Robert Foxworth; Hugo Weaving; Tony Todd; Michael York; ***D:*** Michael Bay; ***W:*** Ehren Kruger; Alex Kurtzman; Roberto Orci; ***C:*** Ben Seresin; ***M:*** Steve Jablonsky. Golden Raspberries '09: Worst Director (Bay), Worst Picture, Worst Screenplay.

Transformers: The Last Knight **½** *Transformers 5* **2017 (PG-13)** Just when you think the franchise can't wage any greater assault on the eyes and ears, Michael Bay tops himself. In addition to being just plain noisy and CGI'd to within an inch of its life, the fifth installment overdoes plot. Optimus Prime returns to his dying planet, which can be saved only by sacrificing Earth. Standard intergalactic sci fi fare, but it doesn't stop there--Stonehenge and King Arthur (yes, that King Arthur) factor in as well. Bay has declared that this will be the last of the saga that he'll direct. If only he'd promised that two movies ago. **149m/C; DVD.** Mark Wahlberg; Anthony Hopkins; Josh Duhamel; Laura Haddock; Santiago Cabrera; ***D:*** Michael Bay; ***W:*** Art Marcum; Matt Holloway; Ken Nolan; ***C:*** Jonathan Sela; ***M:*** Steve Jablonsky.

Transformers: The Movie **1986 (G)** A full-length animated film featuring the universe-defending robots fighting the powers of evil. These robots began life as real toys, so there's some marketing going on. **85m/C; VHS, DVD, Blu-Ray.** ***V:*** Orson Welles; Eric Idle; Judd Nelson; Leonard Nimoy; Robert Stack; ***D:*** Nelson Shin; ***M:*** Vince DiCola.

Transit 🦴🦴 **2012 (R)** Ferocious, completely illogical action-thriller. Ex-con Nate Sidwell (Caviezel) wants to start over by taking his family on a camping trip in Louisiana. To get around a road block, four bank robbers stash their loot in the family's car at a rest stop but trying to retrieve the money isn't so easy. **90m/C; DVD.** James (Jim) Caviezel; Elisabeth Rohm; Diora Baird; James Frain; Harold Perrineau, Jr.; Ryan Donowho; Sterling Knight; Jake Cherry; ***D:*** Antonio Negret; ***W:*** Michael Gilvary; ***C:*** Yaron Levy; ***M:*** Chris(topher) Westlake. **VIDEO**

Transit 🦴🦴 ½ **2018** During a period of tension and violence, Georg (Rogowski) is living in Paris and has been asked to deliver two pieces of correspondence to writer Weidel. George finds that Weidel has committed suicide in his hotel room, takes the writer's belongings, and jumps a train with an injured man named Heinz. The pair hope to get to Marseilles and on a boat to Mexico, when tragedy strikes. While trying to escape, Georg considers the life that could have been. The last entry in Petzold's trilogy is complex, introspective, and visually stunning. **101m/C; DVD, Blu-Ray.** *GE FR* Franz Rogowski; Paula Beer; Godehard Giese; Lilien Batman; Maryam Zaree; ***D:*** Christian Petzold; ***W:*** Christian Petzold; ***C:*** Hans Fromm; ***M:*** Stefan Will.

Transmorphers 🦴 **2007** Be careful when you check out the title because this bargain-basement production (and its prequel/sequel) are Asylum studio rip-offs of "Transformers" and various other action/sci fi flicks. A race of alien robots conquer Earth and force the remaining humans underground. After several hundred years, a small group have finally developed a plan to defeat the invaders. **90m/C; DVD.** Matthew Wolf; Griff Furst; Eliza Swenson; Amy Weber; Sarah Hall; Shaley Scott; ***D:*** Leigh Scott; ***W:*** Leigh Scott; ***C:*** Steven Parker; ***M:*** Victoria Mazze; Chris Ridenhour. **VIDEO**

Transmorphers: Fall of Man 🦴 **2009 (R)** This sequel to the equally bad 2007 flick has a prequel plot concerning how the robots invaded and conquered the planet. There's something about a 1950s UFO crash in Roswell and how technological devices transform into robots. And how the resistance fighters go underground until they can come up with a plan to save mankind. Really, it's not worth the effort to try and figure it out. **90m/C; DVD.** Bruce Boxleitner; Jennifer Rubin; Shane Van Dyke; Alana DiMaria; Russ Kingston; ***D:*** Scott Wheeler; ***W:*** Shane Van Dyke; ***C:*** Mark Atkins; ***M:*** Chris(topher) Cano; Chris Ridenhour. **VIDEO**

Transpecos 🦴🦴 ½ **2016** A thriller centered on the unexpected discovery made by three border patrol agents. The trio—the weary veteran Hobbs (Collins), the experienced Flores (Luna), and rookie Davis (Simmons)—work on a checkpoint located on a remote highway. During one seemingly routine stop, the contents they find in one car turns their world upside down. They learn dark secrets, the depth of corruption, and the ever moving line between right and wrong. **86m/C; DVD, Streaming, Download.** Johnny Simmons; Gabriel Luna; Clifton (Gonzalez) Collins, Jr.; David Acord; Oscar Avila; ***D:*** Greg Kwedar; ***W:*** Greg Kwedar; Clint Bentley; ***C:*** Jeffrey Waldron; ***M:*** Aaron Dessner; Bryce Dessner.

The Transporter 🦴🦴 **2002 (PG-13)** Short on plot but long on action, this product of the Luc Besson action factory is yet another of the producer's efforts to bring kung-fu fightin' to France. Mercenary "delivery man" Frank Martin (Statham) lives by three simple rules: Never change the deal, never exchange names and never look in the package. When one of his packages starts squirming, however, he breaks one of his rules. He opens a duffel bag and discovers beautiful Taiwanese girl Lai (Qi Shu), who reveals a plot involving smuggled Asians used as slave labor. This angers the bad guys, an evil American known as Wall Street (Schulze) and Lai's creepy father Kwai (Young). They send countless henchmen after the heroes, and Martin delivers large amounts of bullets and kicks to the head without once asking anyone to sign for them. Directed by veteran Hong Kong fight choreographer Corey Yuen. **92m/C; VHS, DVD, Blu-Ray, UMD.** Jason Statham; Shu Qi; Francois Berleand; Matt Schulze; Ric Young; ***D:*** Corey Yuen; ***W:*** Luc Besson; Robert Mark Kamen; ***C:*** Pierre Morel; ***M:*** Stanley Clarke.

Transporter 2 🦴 ½ **2005 (PG-13)** Second in what appears will be a series. This time Frank (Statham) is in Miami, working as a driver for one very wealthy family's young son, Jack (Clary). Jack is kidnapped in a sinister plot to bilk his parents out of beaucoup bucks. Powerful dad (Modine) and distraught mom (Valletta) are really just along for the ride. Even hard-core action fans might balk at some of the implausible scenes (one involving a jet ski on a highway is particularly goofy), though the commitment to jam-packing action into the film is impressive. Plot is eerily similar to "Man on Fire" although the execution is not. **88m/C; DVD, Blu-Ray, UMD.** *US FR* Jason Statham; Alessandro Gassman; Amber Valletta; Matthew Modine; Jason Flemyng; Keith David; Kate Nauta; Francois Berleand; Jeffrey Chase; Hunter Clary; ***D:*** Louis Leterrier; ***W:*** Luc Besson; Robert Mark Kamen; ***C:*** Mitchell Amundsen; ***M:*** Alexandre Azaria.

Transporter 3 🦴 ½ **2008 (PG-13)** Frank Martin has relocated to Paris to continue his business of delivering high-risk packages on time and with no questions asked. This time the "package" is the beautiful daughter of a criminal kingpin and Frank doesn't have a choice in the matter, as he is rigged with explosives set to detonate if he fails to deliver. The third try at what started out promisingly as Besson's working-man's James Bond has become a parody of itself, simply rehashing the same impossible, over-the-top action and fight sequences and jazzing them up with copious amounts of explosions and Statham's bare, chiseled torso. More of the same mindless indulgence, just not as good as its own predecessors. **105m/C; Blu-Ray, On Demand.** *FR* Jason Statham; Francois Berleand; Robert Knepper; Jeroen Krabbe; Natalya Rudakova; David Atrakchi; ***D:*** Olivier Megaton; ***W:*** Luc Besson; Robert Mark Kamen; ***C:*** Giovanni Fiore Coltellacci; ***M:*** Alexandre Azaria.

The Transporter Refueled 🦴 **2015 (PG-13)** When Jason Statham turned down a Transporter sequel, they really should have just called it a day on the franchise. Instead, they downgraded the whole thing with a new Frank Martin, played by the stunningly dull Skrein. Frank's father (Stevenson) comes to visit a retired Martin in the South of France, but things get dangerous when a femme fatale (Chabanol) crosses paths with cinema's notorious driver. Before you know it, Frank is driving really fast, again and again. Seriously, the plot here is such garbage it's not worth a pit stop. **96m/C; DVD, Blu-Ray.** Ed Skrein; Ray Stevenson; Loan Chabanol; Gabriella Wright; Lenn Kudrjawizki; Tatiana Pajkovic; ***D:*** Camille Delamarre; ***W:*** Adam Cooper; Bill Collage; Luc Besson; ***C:*** Christophe Collette; ***M:*** Alexandre Azaria.

Transsiberian 🦴🦴🦴 **2008 (R)** After wrapping up their Christian-based work in China, married Americans Roy (Harrelson) and Jessie (a dynamic Mortimer) embark on a week-long train ride from Beijing to Moscow, where they are joined by Spaniard Carlos (Noriega) and his younger American girlfriend Abby (Mara). The chance encounter proves disastrous after Roy is separated from the group and Carlos' pursuit of the once-troubled Jessie—unnoticed by the naive Roy—takes a tragic turn that leaves Jessie the unknowing possessor of illegal drugs. Enter possibly-suspect Russian detective Grinko (the reliable Kingsley) whose suspicions are piqued. Murder-mystery tumbles into an action-mishap. **111m/C; Blu-Ray, On Demand.** *SP GE GB LI* Emily Mortimer; Woody Harrelson; Ben Kingsley; Kate Mara; Eduardo Noriega; Thomas Kretschmann; ***D:*** Brad Anderson; ***W:*** Will Conroy; ***C:*** Xavi Gimenez; ***M:*** Alfonso de Villalonga.

Transylmania 🦴 **2009 (R)** Crude and obvious spoof of dumb American college students who get entangled with vampires. Rusty (Skoog) convinces his friends to join him in a study-abroad trip to Romania where the college is located in a castle allegedly belonging to his lookalike—vampire Radu. There's a crazy, Frankenstein-like doctor, a vampire huntress, various bloodsuckers, and a sorceress whose spirit possesses student Lynne (Lyons). This is actually the third installment of the Hillenbrand brothers' previously direct-to-DVD "National Lampoon's Dorm Daze" series. **95m/C; On Demand.** Paul H. Kim; Oren Skoog; Irena A. Hoffman; Natalie Garza; Nicole Garza; Patrick Cavanaugh; James DeBello; Tony Denman; Jennifer Lyons; David Steinberg; Musetta Vander; ***D:*** David Hillenbrand; Scott Hillenbrand; ***W:*** Patrick Casey; Worm Miller; ***C:*** Viorel Sergovici, Jr.

Transylvania 6-5000 🦴 **1985 (PG)** Agreeably stupid horror spoof about two klutzy reporters who stumble into modern-day Transylvania and encounter an array of comedic creatures. Shot in Yugoslavia. **93m/C; VHS, DVD, Blu-Ray.** Jeff Goldblum; Joseph Bologna; Ed Begley, Jr.; Carol Kane; John Byner; Geena Davis; Jeffrey Jones; Norman Fell; Michael Richards; ***D:*** Rudy DeLuca; ***W:*** Rudy DeLuca; ***C:*** Tomislav Pinter; ***M:*** Lee Holdridge.

Transylvania Twist 🦴 ½ **1989 (PG-13)** Moronic comedy about vampires, teenage vampire hunters and half-naked babes. **90m/C; VHS, DVD.** Robert Vaughn; Teri Copley; Steve Altman; Ace Mask; Angus Scrimm; Jay Robinson; Brinke Stevens; ***D:*** Jim Wynorski; ***W:*** R.J. Robertson.

The Trap **1922** Chaney kidnaps the son of a man he's sent to prison on false charges. Rather than give up the kid when the man is released, he plans a trap. **?m/B; Silent; VHS, DVD.** Lon Chaney, Sr.; Alan Hale; Irene Rich; ***D:*** Robert Thornby; ***W:*** George C. Hall; ***C:*** Virgil Miller.

The Trap 🦴 **1946** The 40th film in the Charlie Chan series was Toler's last as he died of cancer in 1947 and was noticably ill during this production, which affected his abilities in the role. The murder of showgirls who're renting a Malibu beach house is tied into blackmail. Chan has now retired from the Honolulu Police Department and is investigating as a private detective. **68m/B; DVD.** Sidney Toler; Victor Sen Yung; Mantan Moreland; Tanis Chandler; Rita Quigley; Larry J. Blake; Kirk Alyn; ***D:*** Howard Bretherton; ***W:*** Miriam Kissinger; ***C:*** James S. Brown, Jr.

The Trap 🦴🦴 ½ *The Baited Trap* **1959** In trying to escape justice, a ruthless crime syndicate boss holds a small desert town in a grip of fear. **84m/C; DVD, Blu-Ray, Streaming.** Richard Widmark; Tina Louise; Lee J. Cobb; Earl Holliman; Lorne Greene; Carl Benton Reid; ***D:*** Norman Panama; ***W:*** Norman Panama; ***C:*** Daniel F. Fapp.

Trap for Cinderella 🦴 ½ **2013** Psycho-thriller adapted from Sebastien Japrisot's 1963 novel. London party girl Micky suffers amnesia after a fire and struggles to regain her memory. She has flashbacks of reuniting with childhood friend Do (who was killed in the fire), a meek young woman who turns jealous and obsessive about Micky and her life. **100m/C; DVD.** *UK* Tuppence Middleton; Alexandra Roach; Aneurin Barnard; Kerry Fox; Frances de la Tour; ***D:*** Iain Softley; ***W:*** Iain Softley; ***C:*** Alex Barber; ***M:*** Christian Henson.

Trapeze 🦴🦴🦴 **1956** Lancaster is a former trapeze artist, now lame from a triple somersault accident. Curtis, the son of an old friend, wants Lancaster to teach him the routine. Lollobrigida, an aerial acrobat, is interested in both men. Exquisite European locations, fine camera work. The actors perform their own stunts. **105m/C; VHS, DVD, Blu-Ray.** Burt Lancaster; Tony Curtis; Gina Lollobrigida; Katy Jurado; Thomas Gomez; ***D:*** Carol Reed; ***C:*** Robert Krasker; ***M:*** Malcolm Arnold.

Trapped 🦴🦴 ½ **1949** Semi-documentary crime drama shows in semi-documentary style how the feds hunt down a gang of counterfeiters by springing one of their comrades from prison. Well-paced, suspenseful and believable. **78m/B; VHS, DVD, Blu-Ray.** Lloyd Bridges; Barbara Payton; John Hoyt; James Todd; ***D:*** Richard Fleischer.

Trapped 🦴 ½ *24 Hours* **2002 (R)** Heavy on torture, light on revenge thriller tears a perfect family's lives apart when serial kidnappers snatch their only child. Trapped in different cities at the time, parents Will (Townsend) and Karen (Theron) Jennings are at the mercy of extortionists Bacon, Love and Vince. Vince babysits the child; Love takes on the out-of-town Townsend; while Bacon terrorizes mom at their picturesque seaside home. To make matters worse, it is revealed the child is a severe asthmatic. Bacon's efforts to seduce Theron don't help matters. Overly sadistic, pointless, and painfully unwatchable despite slick production values and creepily winning performance by vet Bacon. Based upon Iles's novel "24 Hours." **105m/C; VHS, DVD, Blu-Ray.** Stuart Townsend; Charlize Theron; Kevin Bacon; Courtney Love; Pruitt Taylor Vince; Dakota Fanning; Colleen Camp; ***D:*** Luis Mandoki; ***W:*** Greg Iles; ***C:*** Frederick Elmes; Piotr Sobocinski; ***M:*** John Ottman.

Trapped 🦴 *Dangerous Isolation* **2006** Lame thriller with eyeball-rolling acting. Internet security expert Samantha (Paul) is struggling to have a love life and raise her bratty 16-year-old daughter Gwen (Maslany). Mom and daughter are kidnapped by Adrien (Christopher), who wants Sam to hack into the FBI's database and find the whereabouts of a woman in the Witness Protection Program or Gwen is a goner. **88m/C; DVD.** Alexandra Paul; Dennis Christopher; Nicholas Turturro; Tatiana Maslany; Barbara Bain; Michelle Wolf; ***D:*** Rex Piano; ***W:*** Peter Sullivan; Jason Preston; ***C:*** Mark Melville; ***M:*** Chris Anderson. **CABLE**

Trapped: Buried Alive 🦴 ½ *Danger: Avalanche* **2002** Ski resort management ignores the usual dire warnings of avalanche, and an architect must pursue a rescue mission when the hotel his family is staying in is completely buried. **95m/C; DVD.** Jack Wagner; Gabrielle Carteris; Mark Lindsay Chapman; Aubrey Dollar; Morgan Rusler; ***D:*** Doug Campbell; ***W:*** Tim McKay; ***C:*** James Mathers.

Trapped by the Mormons 🦴🦴 *The Mormon Peril* **1922** Mormons seduce innocent young girls to add to their harems. An interesting piece of paranoid propaganda. Silent with original organ music. **97m/B; Silent; VHS, DVD.** Evelyn Brent; Lewis Willoughby; Olive Sloane; Ward McAllister; Olaf Hytten; George Wynn; ***D:*** H.B. Parkinson; ***W:*** Frank Miller.

Trapped in Paradise 🦴 ½ **1994 (PG-13)** Three bungling brothers make off with a bundle of cash from the Paradise—the town, not the afterlife—bank on Christmas Eve. The locals, naive refugees from a Rockwell painting, don't recognize the buffoons as criminals, and reward their crime with hospitality that would make Frank Capra proud. Chase scenes and subplots abound as the boys spend what seems an eternity trying to make their getaway. Routine, humdrum comedy is hampered by an obvious plot. Watchable only because of Carvey, Lovitz, and Cage. **111m/C; VHS, DVD.** Nicolas Cage; Jon Lovitz; Dana Carvey; John Ashton; Madchen Amick; Donald Moffat; Richard Jenkins; Florence Stanley; Angela Paton; Vic Manni; Frank Pesce; Sean McCann; Kathryn Witt; Richard B. Shull; ***D:*** George Gallo; ***W:*** George Gallo; ***M:*** Robert Folk.

Trapped in Silence 🦴🦴 **1986** Young Sutherland, abused since childhood, stops speaking to protect himself mentally and physically. Psychologist Mason is determined to break down the walls to help him confront his pain. Interesting cameo by Silver as a gay counselor forced out of his job when his sexual preference is discovered. Mildly melodramatic made-for-TV message drama. **94m/C; VHS, DVD.** Marsha Mason; Kiefer Sutherland; John Mahoney; Amy Wright; ***Cameo(s):*** Ron Silver; ***D:*** Michael Tuchner.

Trapper County War 🦴 **1989 (R)** A city boy and a Vietnam vet band together to rescue a young woman held captive by a backwoods clan. **98m/C; VHS, DVD.** Rob(ert) Estes; Bo Hopkins; Ernie Hudson; Betsy Russell; Don Swayze; Noah Blake; ***D:*** Worth Keeter; ***W:*** Russell V. Manzatt; ***C:*** Irl Dixon; ***M:*** Shuki Levy.

Trash 🦴🦴 **1970** Andy Warhol's profile of a depraved couple (Warhol-veteran Dallesandro and female impersonator Woodlawn) living in a lower east side basement and scouting the streets for food and drugs. Not for those easily offended by nymphomaniacs, junkies, lice, and the like; a must for fans of underground film and the cinema verite style. **110m/C; VHS, DVD.** Joe Dallesandro; Holly Woodlawn; Jane Forth; Michael Sklar; Geri Miller; Bruce Pecheur; Andrea Feldman; ***D:*** Paul Morrissey; ***W:*** Paul Morrissey; ***C:*** Paul Morrissey.

Trash 🦴🦴 **2014** Three slum-dwelling teens in Rio are looking in a garbage dump for trash they can sell when they find a wallet.

Suspicious when the cops come around and--in a rather complicated turn of events--they discover that some information from the wallet could lead to exposing bribery and corruption in the local government and police department. The young non-pro leads do well but the plot is mired in clichés. English and Portuguese with subtitles. **114m/C; DVD, Blu-Ray.** *UK BR* Rickson Tevez; Eduardo Luis; Gabriel Weinstein; Selton Mello; Martin Sheen; Rooney Mara; Stepan Nercessian; Wagner Moura; ***D:*** Stephen Daldry; ***W:*** Richard Curtis; ***C:*** Adriano Goldman; ***M:*** Antonio Pinto.

Trash Fire 🦴🦴 ½ **2016 (R)** A dark comedy centered on dysfunctional family relationships. Owen (Grenier) has had a difficult life. Not only did he survive a fire that killed his parents as a child, but his family blamed him for the blaze. After a childhood spent in the home of his hateful grandmother Violet (Flanagan), Owen left home, went in to therapy, and built a new life. Now seriously involved with Isabel (Trimbur), Owen has been given an ultimatum by his pregnant girlfriend. Among her demands is that Owen reunites with his family, despite the fact that both sides do not really want to see each other. As Owen faces his family, he and Isabel become enmeshed in a series of lies and crimes. **91m/C; DVD, Streaming, Download.** Adrian Grenier; Angela Trimbur; Fionnula Flanagan; Ezra Buzzington; Alexa Hamilton; ***D:*** Richard Bates, Jr.; ***W:*** Richard Bates, Jr.; ***C:*** Shane Daly; ***M:*** Michl Britsch.

Trauma 🦴 ½ **1962** A girl suffers amnesia after the trauma of witnessing her aunt's murder. She returns to the mansion years later to piece together what happened. A sometimes tedious psychological thriller. **93m/C; VHS, DVD.** John Conte; Lynn Bari; Lorrie Richards; David Garner; Warren Kemmerling; William Bissell; Bond Blackman; William Justine; ***D:*** Robert M. Young.

Trauma 🦴 ½ **2004 (R)** Style trumps plot. Londoner Ben (Firth) awakens from a coma and learns his wife Elisa (Harris) was killed in the same car accident that injured him. Devastated and trying to make a fresh start, Ben moves into a new place and is befriended by neighbor Charlotte (Suvari). Things aren't going so well though since Ben keeps having visions of his dead wife and a police detective (Cranham) also suspects him of involvement in the murder of a pop singer. **96m/C; DVD.** *GB* Colin Firth; Mena Suvari; Naomie Harris; Kenneth Cranham; Tommy Flanagan; Sean Harris; Brenda Fricker; ***D:*** Marc Evans; ***W:*** Richard Curson Smith; ***C:*** John Mathieson; ***M:*** Alex Heffes.

The Traveler 🦴 **2010 (R)** Kilmer sleepwalks through this too predictable, going nowhere horror flick. A drifter comes into a small town police station on Christmas Eve and informs the cops on duty that he's killed six people. Actually, he's about to kill six people since he's seeking revenge for the torture death of a drifter held in custody the year before. **91m/C; DVD.** Val Kilmer; Dylan Neal; Paul McGillion; Camille Sullivan; Nels Lennarson; John Cassini; Chris Gauthier; ***D:*** Michael Oblowitz; ***W:*** Joseph C. Muscat; ***C:*** Neil Cervin; ***M:*** Ross Vannelli. **VIDEO**

Traveling Companion 🦴🦴 *Compagna di Viaggio* **1996** Cora (Argento) is a somewhat unstable teenager who makes a living with a variety of jobs, including dog-walking. One of her clients, Ada (Cohen), hires Cora to follow Ada's elderly father, Cosimo (Piccoli). A retired professor, Cosimo has become forgetful and gets lost while wandering around Rome. When Cosimo gets on a train, Cora follows and embarks on a series of encounters that lead to a journey of self-discovery. Italian with subtitles. **104m/C; VHS, DVD.** *IT* Asia Argento; Michel Piccoli; Lino Capolicchio; Silvia Cohen; Max Malatesta; ***D:*** Peter Del Monte; ***W:*** Gloria Malatesta; Peter Del Monte; Claudia Sbarigia; ***C:*** Giuseppe Lanci; ***M:*** Dario Lucantoni.

The Traveling Executioner 🦴 ½ **1970** In 1918, Jonas Candide (Keach) is a hired executioner who travels the south with his assistant Jimmy (Cort) and his own electric chair. He's hired to execute a brother/sister duo in Alabama, but Gundred (Hill) uses her sexual wiles to get Jonas to fake her death. He pays a steep price for his obsession. Disjointed low-budget black comedy. **95m/C; DVD.** Stacy Keach; Marianna Hill; Bud Cort; Graham Jarvis; Stefan Gierasch; M. Emmet Walsh; Ford Rainey; ***D:*** Jack Smight; ***W:*** Garrie Bateson; ***C:*** Philip H. Lathrop; ***M:*** Jerry Goldsmith.

Traveling Man 🦴🦴 **1989** Drama about a veteran traveling salesman who's assigned an eager young apprentice when his sales go down. Lithgow gives a great performance as the burnt-out traveling salesman. **105m/C; VHS, DVD; Open Captioned.** John Lithgow; Jonathan Silverman; Margaret Colin; John Glover; ***D:*** Irvin Kershner; ***M:*** Miles Goodman. **CABLE**

Traveller 🦴🦴🦴 **1996 (R)** Deriving its name from the real-life group of wily Irish-American con men who prowl the Southeast, this view into the lives and clannish ways of its members may have you checking that brand-spankin' new driveway sealant. Their basic philosophy is: if you're not one of us, we're allowed to take all of your money. Bokky (Paxton) is the jack-of-all-tricks who takes the younger Pat (Wahlberg) under his wing after the boy is shunned by the rest of the group. Pat's father married outside the clan, and that's not allowed. Bokky falls into the same trap, however, when a beautiful bartender (Margulies), who he has just fleeced, steals his heart. Rather violent ending dims the good feeling that builds and may leave you feeling...well, cheated. Directorial debut of long-time Clint Eastwood cinematographer Jack Green, who also shot "Twister" with Paxton. **100m/C; VHS, DVD, Blu-Ray.** Bill Paxton; Mark Wahlberg; Julianna Margulies; James Gammon; Luke Askew; Michael Shaner; Nikki Deloach; Danielle Wiener; ***D:*** Jack N. Green; ***W:*** Jim McGlynn; ***C:*** Jack N. Green; ***M:*** Andy Paley.

Travels with My Aunt 🦴🦴 ½ **1972 (PG)** A banker leading a mundane life is taken on a wild, whirlwind tour of Europe by an eccentric woman claiming to be his aunt. Uneven but pleasant film was meant as a vehicle for Katharine Hepburn. Based on Graham Greene's best-selling novel. **109m/C; DVD.** Maggie Smith; Alec McCowen; Louis Gossett, Jr.; Robert Stephens; Cindy Williams; Robert Flemyng; ***D:*** George Cukor; ***W:*** Jay Presson Allen. Oscars '72: Costume Des.

Tre 🦴🦴 **2006** In this sequel to "Charlotte Sometimes," lives of three people are changed forever with the arrival of Tre (Cariaga), a slacker who just broke up with his girlfriend. He asks his friends, engaged couple Gabe (McDowell) and Kakela (Wolter), if he can stay with them. Nearby lives Nina (Kormozay), an actress/waitress separated from her husband because he kissed another woman for ten seconds. The inevitable affair commences. Issues such as fidelity, love, work, lies, and corruption are explored in the drama. **87m/C; DVD, Streaming, Download.** Daniel Cariaga; Kimberly-Rose Wolter; Erik McDowell; Alix Koromzay; Teddy Chen Culver; ***D:*** Erik Byler; ***W:*** Kimberly-Rose Wolter; Erik Byler; ***C:*** Robert Humphreys. **VIDEO**

Treacherous Beauties 🦴🦴 **1994** Photojournalist Anne Marie Kerr's (Samms) brother Alan (Rutledge) has supposedly been killed in a hunting accident. Suspicious, Anne Marie assumes a new identity and gets a job at Hollister Farms to investigate. She realizes the horse farm has big financial problems and someone doesn't want Anne Marie snooping around either. From the Harlequin Romance Series; adapted from the Cheryl Emerson novel. **91m/C; DVD.** *CA* Emma Samms; Mark Humphrey; Bruce Greenwood; Tippi Hedren; Catherine Oxenberg; Ron White; Paul Rutledge; ***D:*** Charles Jarrott; ***W:*** Jim Henshaw; Naomi Janzen; ***C:*** Malcolm Cross; ***M:*** Jack Lenz. **TV**

Tread Softly Stranger 🦴🦴 ½ **1958** British blonde bombshell Dors is the catalyst for trouble in this crime drama. Gambler Johnny Mansell (Baker) flees his London debts to return to his Rawborough hometown. He moves in with his clerk brother Dave (Morgan), who has a girlfriend, nightclub dancer Calico (Dors), with expensive tastes. Dave has turned to embezzlement to buy her presents and Johnny tries to win money at the track before Dave's light fingers are discovered. Urged on by Calico, Dave goes ahead with a plan to rob the payroll office, but things go wrong. **90m/B; DVD.** *GB* George Baker; Terence Morgan; Diana Dors; Patrick Allen; Jane Griffiths; Maureen Delaney; ***D:*** Gordon Parry; ***W:*** George Minter; Denis O'Dell; ***C:*** Douglas Slocombe; ***M:*** Tristram Cary.

Treasure Buddies 🦴 ½ **2012 (G)** You can't expect too much from this doggie franchise but this is not a very good Disney effort. The buddies travel to Egypt to search for treasure, which means finding a secret location in some ruins before their evil cat rival finds the riches first. **93m/C; DVD, Blu-Ray.** Richard Riehle; Tygh Runyan; Lochlyn Munro; Edward Herrmann; ***V:*** Tucker Albrizzi; Skyler Gisondo; G. Hannelius; Charles Henry Wyson; Ty Panitz; Tim Conway; Elaine Hendrix; Bonnie Somerville; ***D:*** Robert Vince; ***W:*** Robert Vince; Anna McRoberts; ***C:*** Kamal Derkaoui; ***M:*** Brahm Wenger. **VIDEO**

Treasure Guards 🦴 ½ **2011** Derivative adventure pic made for German TV. Archeologist Victoria Carter is working on excavating a temple ruin in the Jordanian desert when she discovers a parchment pointing to the location of the Seal of Solomon. She's not the only one interested in getting the artifact--so is another archeologist, her estranged father, Teddy. **93m/C; DVD.** *GE* Anna Friel; Raoul Bova; Volker Bruch; Andre Jacobs; David Sherwood; ***D:*** Iain B. MacDonald; ***W:*** Bev Doyle; Richard Kurti; ***C:*** Trevor Michael Brown; ***M:*** Michael Richard Plowman. **TV**

Treasure Island 🦴🦴🦴 ½ **1934** Fleming's adaptation of Robert Louis Stevenson's 18th-century English pirate tale of Long John Silver is a classic. Beery is great as the pirate; Cooper has trouble playing the boy. Also available colorized. Multitudinous remakes. **102m/B; DVD.** Wallace Beery; Jackie Cooper; Lionel Barrymore; Lewis Stone; Otto Kruger; Douglass Dumbrille; Charles "Chic" Sale; Nigel Bruce; ***D:*** Victor Fleming; ***C:*** Clyde De Vinna.

Treasure Island 🦴🦴🦴 ½ **1950 (PG)** Spine-tingling Robert Louis Stevenson tale of pirates and buried treasure, in which young cabin boy Jim Hawkins matches wits with Long John Silver. Some editions excise extra violence. Stevenson's ending is revised. Full Disney treatment, excellent casting. **96m/C; VHS, DVD, Blu-Ray.** Bobby Driscoll; Robert Newton; Basil Sydney; Walter Fitzgerald; Denis O'Dea; Ralph Truman; Finlay Currie; ***D:*** Byron Haskin; ***C:*** Frederick A. (Freddie) Young.

Treasure Island 🦴🦴 *La Isla Del Tersoro* **1972 (G)** Unexceptional British reheat of familiar pirate tale. Welles' interpretation of Long John Silver may be truer to Stevenson, but it's one heckuva blustering binge. **94m/C; VHS, DVD.** *GB* Orson Welles; Kim Burfield; Walter Slezak; Lionel Stander; ***D:*** John Hough; ***W:*** Orson Welles.

Treasure Island 🦴🦴 ½ **1989** Excellent cable version of the classic Robert Louis Stevenson pirate tale with Heston as Long John Silver. Written, produced, and directed by Fraser Heston, son of Charlton. **131m/C; VHS, DVD.** Charlton Heston; Christian Bale; Julian Glover; Richard Johnson; Oliver Reed; Christopher Lee; Clive Wood; Nicholas Amer; Michael Halsey; ***D:*** Fraser Heston; ***W:*** Fraser Heston. **CABLE**

Treasure Island 🦴🦴 ½ **1999** Near the end of WWII, two officers of the fictional intelligence compound called "Treasure Island" are given a dead body and a covert assignment: construct a fake "backstory." When dumped in the ocean, it is hoped that the false information will send the Japanese in the wrong direction. The two officers find themselves consumed by visions of the body, which seems to show up everywhere. Challenging and ambitious puzzle of a film which is filled with coded messages, encrypted dialogue, and implied meanings. Certainly not for all audiences, but a funny and fascinating exercise in style and cinematic invention. **83m/B; DVD.** Lance Baker; Nick Offerman; Jonah Blechman; ***D:*** Scott King; ***W:*** Scott King; ***C:*** Scott King; Phillip Glau; ***M:*** Chris Anderson.

Treasure Island 🦴🦴 ½ **1999 (PG)** Appropriately adventurous version of Robert L. Stevenson's often-filmed tale of young Jim Hawkins, who has a treasure map and a boatload of pirates eager for the riches hidden on Treasure Island! Palance is notably snarly as peg-legged Long John Silver. **95m/C; VHS, DVD.** *CA* Jack Palance; Kevin Zegers; Patrick Bergin; ***D:*** Peter Rowe; ***W:*** Peter Rowe; ***C:*** Marc Charlebois.

Treasure Island 🦴 ½ **2012** The best thing about this Syfy Channel version of the familiar story is Eddie Izzard's performance as Long John Silver. Otherwise it's an adequate retelling of pirates, buried treasure, and young Jim Hawkins' (Regbo) seafaring adventures, although writer Stewart Harcourt takes some needless liberties with the Robert Louis Stevenson novel. **183m/C; DVD, Blu-Ray.** Eddie Izzard; Toby Regbo; Elijah Wood; Donald Sutherland; Rupert Penry-Jones; Daniel Mays; Philip Glenister; Shirley Henderson; ***D:*** Steven Barron; ***W:*** Stewart Harcourt; ***C:*** Ulf Brantas; ***M:*** Martin Slattery. **CABLE**

Treasure of Arne 🦴🦴 ½ **1919** A 16th century Scottish mercenary kills and loots the estate of rich, well-to-do property owner Sir Arne. Famous early Swedish silent that established Stiller as a director. **78m/B; Silent; VHS, DVD.** *SW* Erik Stocklassa; Bror Berger; Richard Lund; Axel Nilsson; Hjalmar Selander; ***D:*** Mauritz Stiller; ***W:*** Mauritz Stiller; Gustaf Molander; ***C:*** Julius Jaenzon.

Treasure of Fear 🦴 ½ *Scared Stiff* **1945** A bungling newspaper reporter gets involved with four jade chessmen once owned by Kubla Khan. A few laughs in this contrived haunted house story. **66m/B; VHS, DVD.** Jack Haley; Barton MacLane; Ann Savage; Veda Ann Borg; Arthur Aylesworth; Lucien Littlefield; George E. Stone; Paul Hurst; Robert Emmett Keane; Eily Malyon; ***D:*** Frank McDonald; ***W:*** Maxwell Shane; Daniel Mainwaring; ***C:*** Fred H. Jackman, Jr.

The Treasure of Jamaica Reef 🦴 ½ **1974 (PG)** Adventurers battle sharks and other nasty fish as they seek a sunken Spanish galleon and its cache of golden treasure. **96m/C; VHS, DVD.** Cheryl Ladd; Stephen Boyd; Roosevelt "Rosie" Grier; David Ladd; Darby Hinton; ***D:*** Virginia Lively Stone.

The Treasure of Matecumbe 🦴🦴 **1976 (G)** A motley crew of adventurers led by a young boy search for buried treasure as they are pursued by Indians and other foes. Filmed in the Florida Key Islands. **107m/C; VHS, DVD.** Billy Attmore; Robert Foxworth; Joan Hackett; Peter Ustinov; Vic Morrow; ***D:*** Vincent McEveety; ***M:*** Buddy (Norman Dale) Baker.

Treasure of Monte Cristo 🦴🦴 **1950** A woman marries a seaman said to be an ancestor of the Count for his inheritance. Instead, she finds love and mystery. **78m/B; VHS, DVD.** *GB* Adele Jergens; Steve Brodie; Glenn Langan; ***D:*** William Berke.

The Treasure of the Amazon 🦴🦴 *El tesoro del Amazonas; Greed* **1985** In this gory low-budget rip-off of 'Indiana Jones,' two groups of people venture into the Amazon looking for lost gold (one a group on modern Nazis hoping to reestablish the Third Reich). A third group of oil surveyors stumbles on a cave full of giant diamonds guarded by headhunters, and suddenly everyone decides to go after it instead. Expect large doses of profanity, naked native women, gore, and people being killed by crabs. Yes, crabs...and they aren't even giant crabs. **105m/C; VHS, DVD.** *MX* Stuart Whitman; Donald Pleasence; Ann Sydney; Bradford Dillman; John Ireland; Pedro Armendariz, Jr.; Sonia Infante; Emilio Fernandez; Jorge Luke; Clark Jarrett; ***D:*** Rene Cardona, Jr.; ***W:*** Rene Cardona, Jr.; Jacques Wilson; ***C:*** Daniel Lopez; ***M:*** Mort Garson.

Treasure of the Sierra Madre 🦴🦴🦴🦴 **1948** Three prospectors in search of gold in Mexico find suspicion, treachery and greed. Bogart is superbly believable as the paranoid, and ultimately homicidal, Fred C. Dobbs. Huston directed his father and wrote the screenplay, based on a B. Traven story. **126m/B; VHS, DVD, Blu-Ray.** Humphrey Bogart; Walter Huston; Tim Holt; Bruce Bennett; Barton MacLane; Robert (Bobby) Blake; Alfonso Bedoya; ***D:*** John Huston; ***W:*** John Huston; ***C:*** Ted D. McCord; ***M:*** Max Steiner. Oscars '48: Director (Huston), Screenplay, Support. Actor (Huston); AFI '98: Top 100; Golden Globes '49: Director (Huston), Film--Drama, Support. Actor (Huston); Natl. Bd. of Review '48: Actor (Huston); Natl. Film Reg.

'90; N.Y. Film Critics '48: Director (Huston), Film.

Treasure of the Yankee Zephyr 🦴🦴 *Race for the Yankee Zephyr* **1983 (PG)** Trio joins in the quest for a plane that has been missing for 40 years...with a cargo of $50 million. They have competition in the form of Peppard and cronies. Decent cast muddles through the predictable plotting. **108m/C; VHS, DVD, Blu-Ray.** *AU NZ* Ken Wahl; George Peppard; Donald Pleasence; Lesley Ann Warren; Bruno Lawrence; Grant Tilly; ***D:*** David Hemmings; ***M:*** Brian May.

Treasure Planet 🦴🦴 1/2 **2002 (PG)** Futuristic fairy tale has pirate ships in space gracing this awkwardly mod animated update of Robert Louis Stevenson's classic "Treasure Island." Jim Hawkins (voiced by Gordon-Levitt, with singing voice of Rzeznik), the troubled teen hero, and a trio of irritating sidekicks take to the skies in their souped-up space galleon to find buried treasure on (where else?) Treasure Planet. Mutiny and other problems, including a looming black hole and space storms just as scary as the ones at sea, show up to threaten the mission. Innovative mix of hand drawn and computer animation is visually rich, even magical, at times but fails to fully delight. **95m/C; VHS, DVD, Blu-Ray.** ***V:*** Joseph Gordon-Levitt; Brian Murray; Emma Thompson; David Hyde Pierce; Michael Wincott; Martin Short; Laurie Metcalf; Patrick McGoohan; Roscoe Lee Browne; Corey Burton; Michael McShane; Dane A. Davis; Austin Majors; ***Nar:*** Tony Jay; ***D:*** John Musker; Ron Clements; ***W:*** John Musker; Ron Clements; Rob Edwards; ***M:*** James Newton Howard.

Treasure Raiders 🦴 **2007 (PG-13)** An American professor who finances his activities by winning illegal midnight street races is forced to team up with a Russian biker to find an ancient treasure. Horribly unbelievable storyline. **92m/C; DVD.** *RU* Stephen Brand; Alexander Nevsky; David Carradine; Sherilyn Fenn; Andrew Divoff; ***D:*** Brent Huff; ***W:*** Alexander Izotov; ***C:*** Rudy Harbon; ***M:*** Scott Greer.

The Treat 🦴 **1998 (R)** Smalltown prostitutes get invited to work the mayor's birthday party where a disaster leaves them struggling to get out alive. **87m/C; VHS, DVD.** Julie Delpy; Georgina Cates; Pamela Gidley; Daniel Baldwin; Patrick Dempsey; Seymour Cassel; Vincent Perez; Alfred Molina; Michael York; Yancy Butler; Mark Boone, Jr.; Richmond Arquette; Larry Drake; ***D:*** Jonathan Gems; ***W:*** Jonathan Gems; ***C:*** Joey Forsyte; ***M:*** Stephen Croes.

The Treatment 🦴🦴 1/2 **2006** Slight romantic comedy set mainly in New York's Upper West Side finds angst-ridden English teacher Jake (Eigeman) trying to deal with his romantic travails in his weekly sessions with demanding Freudian shrink, Dr. Morales (Holm). When Jake becomes interested in wealthy and recently widowed Allegra (Janssen), Morales encourages a fling but no deep involvement, advice Jake promptly ignores. A generally smart take on NY neuroses, with performances and a script to match. Adapted from Daniel Menaker's 1998 novel. **86m/C; DVD.** Christopher Eigeman; Famke Janssen; Harris Yulin; Stephanie March; Blair Brown; Roger Rees; Stephen Lang; ***D:*** Oren Rudavsky; ***W:*** Oren Rudavsky; Daniel Housman; ***C:*** Andrij Parekh; ***M:*** John Zorn.

The Tree 🦴🦴 **2010** The O'Neils live on a ramshackle farm in Queensland, Australia where their home is protected by an huge Moreton Bay fig tree. Peter O'Neil suddenly dies and his wife Dawn and their four children are shattered, particularly 8-year-old daddy's girl Simone, who's convinced her father's spirit is now living in the tree. The tree's ever-spreading roots are causing problems and it may have to be cut down. **100m/C; DVD.** *AU FR* Charlotte Gainsbourg; Morgana Davies; Marton Csokas; Christian Bayers; Tom Russell; Gabriel Gotting; Aden Young; ***D:*** Julie Bertuccelli; ***W:*** Julie Bertuccelli; ***C:*** Nigel Bluck; ***M:*** Gregoire Hetzel.

A Tree Grows in Brooklyn 🦴🦴🦴 1/2 **1945 (PG)** Sensitive young Irish lass growing up in turn-of-the-century Brooklyn tries to rise above her tenement existence. Based on the novel by Betty Smith. Kazan's directorial debut. **128m/B; VHS, DVD.** Peggy Ann Garner; James Dunn; Dorothy McGuire; Joan Blondell; Lloyd Nolan; Ted Donaldson; James Gleason; John Alexander; Charles Halton; ***D:*** Elia Kazan; ***C:*** Leon Shamroy; ***M:*** Alfred Newman. Oscars '45: Support. Actor (Dunn); Natl. Film Reg. '10.

The Tree of Life 🦴🦴🦴 **2011 (PG-13)** Growing up in suburban Texas in the simpler, happier 1950s, young Jack O'Brien (Penn) seems to bask in it as the eldest of three boys. He struggles with his caring-yet-authoritarian father (Pitt) and when tragedy hits the family adult Jack appears to still suffer beneath its weight. Bouncing from past to present and back again gets a bit bewildering with a slow and labored pace. But it's visually beautiful with a talented ensemble telling the vivid and inviting tale of adult Jack's search for life's meaning. Marks only the fifth feature in four decades for director Malick. **138m/C; Blu-Ray, On Demand.** Brad Pitt; Sean Penn; Jessica Chastain; Jackson Hurst; Fiona Shaw; Joanna Going; Kari Machett; ***D:*** Terrence Malick; ***W:*** Terrence Malick; ***C:*** Emmanuel Lubezki; ***M:*** Alexandre Desplat.

The Tree of Wooden Clogs 🦴🦴🦴 1/2 *L'Albero Degli Zoccoli* **1978** Epic view of the lives of four peasant families working on an estate in turn of the century Northern Italy. The title comes from the shoes the peasants wear. When a young boy breaks a shoe, his father risks punishment by cutting down one of his landlord's trees to make a new pair of clogs. Slow moving and beautiful, from former industrial filmmaker Olmi. In Italian with English subtitles. **185m/C; VHS, DVD, Blu-Ray.** *IT* Luigi Ornaghi; Francesca Moriggi; Omar Brignoll; Antonio Ferrari; ***D:*** Ermanno Olmi; ***W:*** Ermanno Olmi; ***C:*** Ermanno Olmi. Cannes '78: Film; N.Y. Film Critics '79: Foreign Film.

Treed Murray 🦴🦴 *Get Down* **2001** Yuppie ad exec Murray Roberts gets lost taking a shortcut through a secluded area of a Toronto park. He's confronted by a young punk who wants money to give him directions. Murray refuses, leading to a confrontation with the punk's friends. Murray flees and decides to hide in a large tree but he's soon found. He refuses to climb down and there's a standoff between Murray and the teens as they try to psych each other out. **90m/C; DVD.** *CA* David Hewlett; Cle Bennett; Kevin Duhaney; Jessica Greco; Aaron Ashmore; Carter Hayden; ***D:*** William Phillips; ***W:*** William Phillips; ***C:*** John Holosko; ***M:*** James McGrath.

Treehouse Hostage 🦴🦴 1/2 **1999 (PG)** Timmy needs a reat current-events project if he doesn't want to get stuck in summer school. Fortunately, he and some friends manage to capture an escaped counterfeiter, Banks (Varney), and turn him in for a grade. Only it turns out that the school principal is actually the head of the counterfeiting ring. **90m/C; VHS, DVD.** Jim Varney; Joey Zimmerman; Richard Kline; Todd Bosley; Mark Moses; Debbie Boone; Jack McGee; Aria Noelle Curzon; Vincent Schiavelli; ***D:*** Sean McNamara; ***W:*** Jeff Phillips; ***C:*** Mark Doering-Powell; ***M:*** John Coda.

Treeless Mountain 🦴🦴 **2008** Desperate Seoul mom dumps her two young daughters on her alcoholic sister-in-law when she decides to look for her absent husband. The young girls are bewildered and their aunt is indifferent to them so the sisters' plight can only get better when they are later sent on to their grandparents farm in the country. Korean with subtitles. **89m/C; DVD.** *NK* Heeyeon Kim; Song-hee Kim; Soo-ah Lee; Mi-hyang Kim; Park-boon Tak; ***D:*** So Yong Kim; ***W:*** So Yong Kim; ***C:*** Anne Misawa; ***M:*** Asobi Seksu.

Tree's Lounge 🦴🦴 1/2 **1996 (R)** First time director/writer Buscemi takes a look at the downward spiraling life of Tommy Basilio (Buscemi), a working-class misfit who loses his job and then spends most of his time hanging out at the dreary local bar. He finally winds up driving an ice cream truck, only leading to more trouble when his teenaged helper, Debbie (Sevigny), develops a crush on him—a situation her hot-headed father Jerry (Baldwin) takes exception to. And the irresponsible Tommy is finally forced to realize that his ill-concerned actions have consequences. **94m/C; VHS, DVD.** Steve Buscemi; Chloë Sevigny; Daniel Baldwin; Elizabeth Bracco; Anthony LaPaglia; Debi Mazar; Carol Kane; Seymour Cassel; Mark Boone, Jr.; Eszter Balint; Mimi Rogers; Kevin Corrigan; Samuel L. Jackson; ***D:*** Steve Buscemi; ***W:*** Steve Buscemi; ***C:*** Lisa Rinzler; ***M:*** Evan Lurie.

Tremors 🦴🦴 1/2 **1989 (PG-13)** A tiny desert town is attacked by giant man-eating worm-creatures. Bacon and Ward are the handymen trying to save the town. Amusing, with good special effects. **96m/C; VHS, DVD, Blu-Ray, HD-DVD.** Kevin Bacon; Fred Ward; Finn Carter; Michael Gross; Reba McEntire; Bibi Besch; Bobby Jacoby; Charlotte Stewart; Victor Wong; Tony Genaros; Ariana Richards; ***D:*** Ron Underwood; ***W:*** S.S. Wilson; Brent Maddock; ***C:*** Alexander Grusynski; ***M:*** Ernest Troost.

Tremors 2: Aftershocks 🦴🦴 1/2 **1996 (PG-13)** They're baaaaack! The Graboids have resurfaced to eat their way through Mexican oil fields and it's up to tough guys Earl Bassett (Ward) and Burt Gummer (Gross) to get rid of the toothy worms once and for all. Same mix of tongue-in-cheek humor and special effects as the first film. **100m/C; VHS, DVD, Blu-Ray.** Fred Ward; Michael Gross; Helen Shaver; Christopher Gartin; Marcelo Tubert; ***D:*** S.S. Wilson; ***W:*** S.S. Wilson; Brent Maddock; ***C:*** Virgil Harper; ***M:*** Jay Ferguson.

Tremors 3: Back to Perfection 🦴🦴 **2001 (PG-13)** Gross returns to his hometown of Perfection, Nevada, and sees a cheesy theme park based on the Graboids has opened. Then real Graboids return to wreck havoc again. **104m/C; VHS, DVD, Blu-Ray.** Michael Gross; Charlotte Stewart; Shawn Christian; Ariana Richards; Susan Chung; Helen Shaver; Christopher Gartin; ***D:*** Brent Maddock; ***W:*** John Whelpley; ***C:*** Virgil Harper; ***M:*** Kevin Kiner. **VIDEO**

Tremors 4: The Legend Begins 🦴🦴 **2004 (PG-13)** The fourth entry in the Tremors series explains the origins of the creatures. In the 1880s, the mining town of Rejection, Nevada, becomes prey to mysterious creatures who live below the surface. Called dirt dragons by the residents, they are the original graboids. After several deaths, no one will work in the silver mine and put their lives at risk. The mine's owner, Hiram Gummer (Gross), hires a mercenary to get rid of the creatures so he does not lose his mine and his profits. **101m/C; DVD, Blu-Ray, Download.** Michael Gross; Sara Botsford; Billy Drago; Brent Roam; August Schellenberg; ***D:*** S.S. Wilson; ***W:*** Scott Buck; ***C:*** Virgil Harper; ***M:*** Jay Ferguson.

Tremors 5: Bloodlines 🦴🦴 **2015 (PG-13)** The fifth entry in the Tremors franchise finds the monsters evolving into more lethal creatures. Survivalist Burt Gummer (Gross) is hired to capture the Ass-blasters and Graboids terrorizing South Africa with the help of sidekick Travis Welker (Kennedy). The pair must battle for survival against the creatures, who have become more terrifying and powerful than ever. **99m/C; DVD, Blu-Ray, Streaming, Download.** Michael Gross; Jamie Kennedy; Brandon Auret; Natalie Becker; Daniel Janks; ***D:*** Don Michael Paul; ***W:*** William Truesmith; M.A. Deuce; John Whelpley; ***C:*** Michael Swan; ***M:*** Frederick Wiedmann.

The Trench 🦴🦴 1/2 **1999** A sober look at the two-day buildup to the catastrophic Battle of the Somme in 1916 from the point of view of teenaged British Army soldier Billy Macfarlane (Nicholls). His tough sargeant, Telford Winter (Craig), tries to prepare the raw recruits for battle as they hunker down in their damp, vermin-infested trench but nothing can prepare them for the senseless carnage to come. Familiar cliches abound but the performances are strong. **90m/C; DVD.** *UK* Paul Nicholls; Daniel Craig; Julian Rhind-Tutt; Danny Dyer; James D'Arcy; Ciaran McMenamin; Tam Williams; Anthony Strachan; ***D:*** William Boyd; ***W:*** William Boyd; ***C:*** Tony Pierce-Roberts; ***M:*** Evelyn Glennie; Greg Malcangi.

Trenchcoat 🦴 1/2 **1983** Aspiring mystery writer travels to Malta to research her new novel and is drawn into a real-life conspiracy. Silly and contrived spoof of the detective genre. **95m/C; VHS, Streaming.** Margot Kidder; Robert Hays; ***D:*** Michael Tuchner; ***W:*** Jeffrey Price; Peter S. Seaman; ***M:*** Charles Fox.

Trespass 🦴🦴 *Looters* **1992 (R)** Violent crime tale set in East St. Louis, Illinois. Two redneck firemen learn about stolen gold artifacts supposedly hidden in an abandoned building and go on a treasure hunt. When they witness a murder they also get involved in a battle between two crime lords—who want these interlopers dead. What follows is a deadly game of cat-and-mouse. Lots of action but it's all fairly routine. Original release date of summer 1992 was delayed until the winter because of unfortunate similarities to the L.A. riots. **104m/C; VHS, DVD, Blu-Ray.** Ice Cube; Ice-T; William Sadler; Bill Paxton; Art Evans; ***D:*** Walter Hill; ***W:*** Robert Zemeckis; Bob Gale; ***C:*** Lloyd Ahern, II; ***M:*** Ry Cooder.

Trespass 🦴🦴 **2011 (R)** Efficient, if overwrought, home invasion flick. Kyle (Cage), Sarah (Kidman), and their teen daughter Avery (Liberato) are held hostage in their secluded home by four violent criminals looking for diamond dealer Kyle's stash. Only Kyle is desperate and in debt so the crime doesn't go as planned as Kyle tries to do a deal to save himself and—maybe—his family. **91m/C; DVD, Blu-Ray.** Nicolas Cage; Nicole Kidman; Cam Gigandet; Liana Liberato; Nico Tortorella; Ben Mendelsohn; Jordana Spiro; Dash Mihok; Emily Meade; ***D:*** Joel Schumacher; ***W:*** Karl Gajdusek; ***C:*** Andrzej Bartkowiak; ***M:*** David Buckley.

Trespass Against Us 🦴🦴 1/2 **2016 (R)** The great Fassbender and Gleeson play Chad and Colby Cutler, respectively, part of a family of criminals living on the edge of town and beyond the law. Chad's wife (Marshal) and children keep pushing him toward normal domesticity, but dad won't let him leave the clan all that easily. Much of this action-drama is in a thick British accent, so thick that you may not understand what's being said, but Fassbender and Gleeson ably convey the intense emotions of a son and father at a crossroads. **100m/C; DVD, Blu-Ray, Streaming.** *UK* Michael Fassbender; Brendan Gleeson; Lyndsey Marshal; Rory Kinnear; Sean Harris; ***D:*** Adam Smith; ***W:*** Alastair Siddons; ***C:*** Eduard Grau; ***M:*** The Chemical Brothers. **VIDEO**

Triage 🦴🦴 **2009 (R)** Earnest wartime drama begins in late 1980s Kurdistan and then takes its trauma home to Dublin. Best friends Mark (Farrell) and David (Sives) are longtime war photographers but David opts out of this latest conflict to return home. When a wounded Mark returns sometime later, unable to talk about his experiences, David has not made it back. Mark's worried wife, Elena (Vega), calls on her psychiatrist grandfather Joaquin (Lee) to get Mark to open up in an all-too predictable manner. **99m/C; DVD.** *IR SP* Colin Farrell; Paz Vega; Christopher Lee; Jamie Sives; Kelly Reilly; Branko Djuric; Juliet Stevenson; ***D:*** Danis Tanovic; ***W:*** Danis Tanovic; ***C:*** Seamus Deasy; ***M:*** Lucio Godoy.

Trial 🦴🦴 1/2 **1955** Suspenseful, if dated, courtroom drama. Law prof David Blake (Ford) must get courtroom experience to keep his teaching job. Underhanded attorney Barney Castle (Kennedy) hires Blake to represent 17-year-old Mexican, Angel Chavez (Campos), who's accused of killing a white girl. Blake knows race will plague the case and has a tough time with a would-be lynch mob and a prejudicial jury. Then Castle turns out to be a Communist who expects Angel to be convicted so he can use the case to the Party's advantage. Mankiewicz adapted from his novel. **109m/B; DVD.** Glenn Ford; Arthur Kennedy; Dorothy McGuire; Rafael Campos; Katy Jurado; John Hodiak; Juano Hernandez; ***D:*** Mark Robson; ***W:*** Don Mankiewicz; ***C:*** Robert L. Surtees; ***M:*** Daniele Amfitheatrof.

The Trial 🦴🦴🦴 *Le Proces; Der Prozess; Il Processo* **1963** Expressionistic Welles adaptation of classic Kafka novella about an innocent man accused, tried, and convicted of an unknown crime in an unnamed exaggeratedly bureaucratic country. Another Welles project that met with constant disaster in production, with many lapses in continuity. **118m/B; VHS, DVD.** *FR* Anthony Perkins; Jeanne Moreau; Orson Welles; Romy Schneider; Akim Tamiroff; Elsa Martinelli; ***D:*** Orson Welles; ***W:*** Orson Welles; ***C:*** Edmond Richard; ***M:*** Jean Ledrut.

The Trial 🦴🦴 **1993** Spare adaptation of Franz Kafka's novel finds Prague bank clerk Joseph K (MacLachlan) arrested on unknown charges. His increasing guilt and paranoia fit well into a world where the most illogical things happen in the most matter of fact way. Good visuals. **120m/C; VHS, DVD.** Kyle MacLachlan; Anthony Hopkins; Jason Robards, Jr.; Polly Walker; Juliet Stevenson; Alfred Molina; ***D:*** David Hugh Jones; ***W:*** Harold Pinter; ***C:*** Phil Meheux; ***M:*** Carl Davis.

The Trial ½ **2010 (PG-13)** Melodramatic courtroom drama finds suicidal small town Georgia attorney Ken McClain, whose family was killed, assigned to a capital punishment case involving a young man accused of murder. **90m/C; DVD.** Matthew Modine; Randy Wayne; Robert Forster; Bob Gunton; Rance Howard; Larry Bagby; Clare Carey; Nikki Deloach; ***D:*** Gary Wheeler; ***W:*** Gary Wheeler; Mark Freiburger; Robert Whitlow; ***C:*** Tom Priestly, Jr.; ***M:*** Rob Pottorf. **VIDEO**

Trial & Error ½ *The Dock Brief* **1962** Comedic satire, based on the play by John Mortimer, finds hapless lawyer Morgenhall (Sellers) thinking he's finally got his big chance when he defends wife murderer Fowle (Attenborough). Fowle wants to plead guilty but Morgenhall dreams of being a court star and insists on pleading his client innocent. It's a disaster just waiting to happen. **78m/B; VHS, DVD.** *GB* Peter Sellers; Richard Attenborough; Beryl Reid; David Lodge; Frank Pettingell; Eric Woodburn; ***D:*** James Hill; ***W:*** Pierre Rouve; ***C:*** Edward (Ted) Scaife; ***M:*** Ron Grainer.

Trial and Error ½ **1996 (PG-13)** Courtroom comedy may remind you of another law oriented movie. No, not "Kramer vs. Kramer." It's "My Cousin Vinny," also directed by Lynn. Both feature fake lawyers defending hopeless clients in small towns. In this case, lawyer Charles Tuttle (Daniels) is too messed up from his bachelor party to make it to court for a case in which the defendent Benny (Torn), a relative of Chuck's big-wig future father-in-law, is accused of selling mail-order "commemorative copper Lincoln engravings" which are actually pennies. His best bud Richard (Richards), an actor, decides to stand in for him, and the legal slip-and-pratfalls ensue. Richards as the physical comedian and Daniels as the white bread straight man have great comic chemistry, but the plot won't surprise you much. **98m/C; VHS, DVD.** Michael Richards; Jeff Daniels; Rip Torn; Charlize Theron; Jessica Steen; Austin Pendleton; Alexandra Wentworth; Lawrence Pressman; Dale Dye; Max Casella; Jennifer Coolidge; ***D:*** Jonathan Lynn; ***W:*** Sarah Bernstein; Gregory Bernstein; ***C:*** Gabriel Beristain; ***M:*** Phil Marshall.

The Trial Begins *L'Ora di Punta; Rush Hour* **2007** Ambitious Filippo Costa (Lastella) is with Rome's tax police, supposedly investigating tax evasion and customs fraud. Instead he increases his own bank account by taking bribes to look the other way. Filippo meets widowed art gallery owner Caterina (Ardant) while on the job and her social connections lead him to invest in equally suspect property development schemes that will eventually cause the crooked cop trouble. Italian with subtitles. **98m/C; DVD.** *FR IT* Michele Lastella; Fanny Ardant; Giulia Bevilacqua; Augusto Zucchi; Antonio Gerardi; ***D:*** Vincenzo Marra; ***W:*** Vincenzo Marra; ***C:*** Luca Bigazzi.

Trial by Fire ½ **2018 (R)** In a small Texas town, Cameron Todd Willingham (O'Connell) is known for his drinking, fighting, and volatile relationship with wife Stacy (Meade). When their house catches on fire, their three children die. Accused of setting the blaze, Cameron lacks the money for a good defense and is found guilty despite many uncertainties in the case. Given the death penalty, he gains an advocate in Elizabeth Gilbert (Dern) who meets him through a prison outreach program. Based on a real case, the actors do well but the movie tries too hard as it, rightfully, exudes anger at the miscarriage of justice. **127m/C; DVD.** Jack O'Connell; Jade Pettyjohn; Laura Dern; Emily Meade; Jeff(rey) Perry; ***D:*** Edward Zwick; ***W:*** Geoffrey Fletcher; ***C:*** John Guleserian; ***M:*** Henry Jackman.

Trial by Jury ½ **1994 (R)** Strong cast, lame script. Idealistic single mother Valerie Alston (Whalley-Kilmer) winds up on the jury trying notorious mobster Rusty Pirone (Assante). Rusty's henchman, Tommy Vesey (Hurt), lets Valerie know that her son is in mortal danger if she doesn't find his boss innocent. Of course DA Daniel Graham (Byrne) is equally adamant about a conviction and is willing to use Valerie any way he has to. **107m/C; VHS, DVD, Blu-Ray.** Joanne Whalley; William Hurt; Gabriel Byrne; Armand Assante; Kathleen Quinlan; Stuart Whitman; Margaret Whitton; Ed Lauter; Joe Santos; Richard Portnow; Beau Starr; Mike Starr; John Capodice; Lisa Arrindell Anderson; ***D:*** Heywood Gould; ***W:*** Heywood Gould; Jordan Katz; ***C:*** Frederick Elmes; ***M:*** Terence Blanchard.

Trial by Media ½ *An American Daughter* **2000** Lyssa Dent Hughes (Lahti) is a prominent D.C. doctor (and senator's daughter) who has been nominated to become surgeon general. But thanks to media scrutiny, and some careless remarks, she becomes a target and her nomination is in jeopardy. Wasserstein scripted from her 1997 play "American Daughter." **92m/C; VHS, DVD.** Christine Lahti; Tom Skerritt; Jay Thomas; Mark Feuerstein; Lynne Thigpen; Stanley Anderson; Blake Lindsley; ***D:*** Sheldon Larry; ***W:*** Wendy Wasserstein; ***C:*** Albert J. Dunk; ***M:*** Phil Marshall. **CABLE**

The Trial of Billy Jack WOOF! **1974 (PG)** Billy Jack takes on the feds and beats the hell out of a lot of people to prove that the world can live in peace. Awful, pretentious film. **175m/C; VHS, DVD.** Tom Laughlin; Delores Taylor; Victor Izay; Teresa Laughlin; William Wellman, Jr.; Russell Lane; Michelle Wilson; Geo Ann Sosa; George Aguilar; Sacheen Little Feather; ***D:*** Tom Laughlin; Frank Laughlin; ***W:*** Tom Laughlin; Delores Taylor; ***C:*** Jack Marta; ***M:*** Elmer Bernstein.

The Trial of Lee Harvey Oswald **1977** What would've happened if Jack Ruby had not shot Oswald. Oswald's trial and its likely results are painstakingly created. **192m/C; DVD.** Ben Gazzara; Lorne Greene; John Pleshette; Lawrence Pressman; ***D:*** Gordon Davidson; ***W:*** Robert E. Thompson. **TV**

The Trial of Old Drum ½ **2000 (PG)** Set in 1955 and based on a true story. 11-year-old Charlie (Edner) lives in a small farming community with his widowed father Charles (Perlman). His best friend is his golden retriever Drum, who was trained by his late mother to protect the boy. The duo's problems lie with his surly maternal Uncle Lon (Schuck), who dislikes the dog and says Drum is a sheep-killer. Lon shoots the dog for being on his property and the sheriff sends poor Drum to the pound before his case goes to court. Charlie and his father enlist the services of lawyer George Graham Vest (Bakula) and Drum's trial is both humorous and touching. **88m/C; VHS, DVD.** Bobby Edner; Ron Perlman; John Schuck; Scott Bakula; Randy Travis; David Graf; Dick Martin; Alia Shawkat; ***D:*** Sean McNamara; ***W:*** Ralph Gaby Wilson; ***C:*** Mark Doering-Powell.

The Trial of the Incredible Hulk **1989** The Hulk returns to battle organized crime and is aided by his blind superhero/lawyer friend Daredevil. Followed by "The Death of the Incredible Hulk." **96m/C; VHS, DVD.** Bill Bixby; Lou Ferrigno; Rex Smith; John Rhys-Davies; Marta DuBois; Nancy Everhard; Nicholas Hormann; ***D:*** Bill Bixby. **TV**

The Trials of Cate McCall **2013** Defense attorney Cate McCall ruined her career and marriage and lost custody of her daughter because of her alcoholism. Now out of rehab, Cate is trying to redeem herself by working in the public defender's office, but the pro bono case she's assigned she believes is a non-starter: imprisoned murderer Lacey claims she was wrongly convicted. This one gets the guilty verdict for stupidity. **89m/C; DVD.** Kate Beckinsale; Nick Nolte; Anna Anissimova; James Cromwell; Isaiah Washington, IV; Clancy Brown; Taye Diggs; Brendan Sexton, III; ***D:*** Karen Moncrieff; ***W:*** Karen Moncrieff; ***C:*** Antonio Calvache; ***M:*** Peter Nashel. **VIDEO**

The Trials of Muhammad Ali **2013** Siegel's documentary chronicles the outside-of-the-ring fight for religious equality led by Muhammad Ali when he converted to the Nation of Islam. He refused to go to Vietnam on the basis of his new religion, claiming status as a conscientious objector. Stripped of his boxing title and banned from the sport, his case went all the way to the Supreme Court, by which point it had become a referendum on not just Ali's specific situation but Vietnam and religious freedom altogether. Using a vast array of archival footage, the film makes the case that Ali was not just an important athlete but an important leader for civil rights as well. **86m/C; DVD, Blu-Ray.** ***D:*** Bill Siegel; ***M:*** Joshua Abrams.

The Trials of Oscar Wilde *The Man with the Green Carnation; The Green Carnation* **1960** Finch is the highlight as playwright/wit Wilde, who ill-advisedly sues the Marquis of Queensbury (Jeffries) for libel when the peer accuses him of being a sodomite. Wilde is, in fact, having an affair with the Marquis' son, Lord Alfred Douglas (Fraser), which eventually leads to Wilde's imprisonment and the destruction of his life. Based on the play "The Stringed Lute" by John Furnell and the book "The Trials of Oscar Wilde" by Montgomery Hyde. **123m/C; VHS, DVD, Streaming.** *GB* Peter Finch; John Fraser; Lionel Jeffries; Nigel Patrick; James Mason; Yvonne Mitchell; Maxine Audley; James Booth; Paul Rogers; Ian Fleming; Laurence Naismith; ***D:*** Ken Hughes; ***W:*** Ken Hughes; ***C:*** Ted Moore; ***M:*** Ronald Goodwin.

The Triangle **2001** This triangle is the Bermuda kind as friends charter a boat for their annual Caribbean fishing trip and instead discover the Queen of Scots, a ghostly luxury liner that has been missing for 60 years. Boarding the ship turns out to be a big mistake since the tragedy that overtook the lives of the passengers and crew lingers and begins to affect the present. **92m/C; VHS, DVD.** Luke Perry; Dan Cortese; Olivia D'Abo; Dorian Harewood; Polly Shannon; David Hewlett; ***D:*** Lewis Teague; ***W:*** Ted Humphrey; ***C:*** Ric Waite; ***M:*** Lawrence Shragge. **CABLE**

The Triangle **2005** BBC miniseries shown on the Sci-Fi Channel. After his boats keep disappearing in the Bermuda Triangle, a shipping magnate hires a team to go find out what's responsible before it eats the rest of his fleet. **255m/C; DVD.** *UK US* Eric Stoltz; Catherine Bell; Lou Diamond Phillips; Bruce Davison; Michael E. Rodgers; Sam Neill; ***D:*** Craig R. Baxley; ***W:*** Bryan Singer; Rockne S. O'Bannon; Dean Devlin; ***C:*** David Connel; ***M:*** Joseph LoDuca. **TV**

Triangle ½ **2009 (R)** Jess (George) is aboard a sailboat (named the Triangle) with friends when a storm capsizes the boat off the Florida coast. They are rescued by a passing ocean liner, which appears to be deserted, until the killing starts. Then writer/director Smith throws in a time-twisting cycle and the plot falls apart. **98m/C; DVD, Blu-Ray.** Melissa George; Michael Dorman; Rachael Carpani; Emma Lung; Liam Hemsworth; Henry Nixon; Joshua McIvor; ***D:*** Chris Smith; ***W:*** Chris Smith; ***C:*** Robert Humphreys; ***M:*** Christian Henson. **VIDEO**

The Triangle Factory Fire Scandal **1979** Based on the true-life Triangle factory fire at the turn of the century. The fire killed 145 garment workers and drastically changed industrial fire and safety codes. **100m/C; VHS, DVD.** Tom Bosley; David Dukes; Tovah Feldshuh; Janet Margolin; Stephanie Zimbalist; Lauren Front; Stacey Nelkin; Ted Wass; Charlotte Rae; Milton Selzer; Valerie Landsburg; ***D:*** Mel Stuart. **TV**

The Tribe *Plemya* **2015** Set in a Ukrainian school for the deaf, no subtitles or translation of any kind is provided. We're simply thrown into the world of sign language, and left to our own devices. And it works beautifully. Upon enrolling in the boarding school, loner teen Sergey (Fesenko) finds everything in its right place during the day, but all hell breaks loose at night, complete with gang hazings and a secret prostitution ring. A unique and relentlessly intense arthouse experience, challenging the audience with notions of communication and visual art. **132m/C; DVD, Blu-Ray.** *NL UR* Grigoriy Fesenko; Yana Novikova; Rosa Babiy; Alexander Dsiadevich; Alexander Osadchiy; ***D:*** Miroslav Slaboshpitsky; ***W:*** Miroslav Slaboshpitsky; ***C:*** Valentyn Vasyanovych.

Tribulation **2000** Police detective Tom Canboro (Busey) goes up against the evil Messiah (Mancuso) in another entry in the "Left Behind" series of adventures based on the Book of Revelation. **97m/C; DVD.** Gary Busey; Howie Mandel; Margot Kidder; Nick Mancuso; Sherry Miller; Leigh Lewis; ***D:*** Andre Van Heerden; ***W:*** Peter LaLonde; Paul LaLonde; ***C:*** Jiri (George) Tirl.

Tribute **2009** Former child star Cilla McGowan (Murphy) now restores houses and has bought her late grandmother's neglected Virginia farmhouse. Janet Hardy, a famous actress, allegedly died of an overdose in the house 30 years before and there's still a lot of bad blood within the community because Janet was supposedly having an affair with a married man. Neighbor Ford Sawyer (Lewis) is happy to help Cilla out when old family secrets turn into present-day nightmares. Romantic suspense from Lifetime that's based on the book by Nora Roberts. **90m/C; DVD.** Brittany Murphy; Jason Lewis; Tippi Hedren; Diana Scarwid; Christian Oliver; Tiffany Morgan; Wallace Merck; ***D:*** Martha Coolidge; ***W:*** Gary Tieche; ***C:*** Gary Tieche; Johnny E. Jensen. **CABLE**

Tribute to a Bad Man **1956** Hard-nosed rancher Cagney will stop at nothing to retain his worldly possessions in this 1870s Colorado territory western. His ruthless behavior drives girlfriend Papas into the arms of hired hand Dubbins. Spencer Tracy and Grace Kelly were originally cast for the roles of Jeremy Rodock and Jocasta Constantine, but Kelly backed out and Tracy was fired due to differences with director Wise. Based on the short story by Jack Schaefer. **95m/C; VHS, DVD.** James Cagney; Don Dubbins; Stephen McNally; Irene Papas; Vic Morrow; Royal Dano; Lee Van Cleef; James J. Griffith; Onslow Stevens; James Bell; Jeannette Nolan; Bud Osborne; Tom London; Dennis Moore; Buddy Roosevelt; Carl Pitti; ***D:*** Robert Wise; ***W:*** Michael Blankfort; ***M:*** Miklos Rozsa.

Tricheurs *Cheaters* **1984** Scam artists hit largest casino in the world and look forward to golden years of retirement. From the director of "Reversal of Fortune." In French with English subtitles. **95m/C; VHS, DVD.** *FR* Jacques Dutronc; Bulle Ogier; Kurt Raab; Virgilio Teixeira; Steve Baes; ***D:*** Barbet Schroeder.

Trick **1999 (R)** Cheery gay romantic comedy. Quiet Gabriel (Campbell) is a struggling Broadway composer with a horn-dog straight roommate (Beyer) who is constantly taking over their apartment for his one-nighters (and locking Gabe out). Which leaves Gabriel in a dilemma when he meets hunky go-go boy, Mark (Pitok), and the duo can't find a place to be alone. But as the night wears on, they discover that lust may be taking a backseat to some deeper feelings. **90m/C; VHS, DVD.** Christian Campbell; John Paul (J.P.) Pitoc; Tori Spelling; Brad Beyer; Clinton Leupp; Lorri Bagley; Steve Hayes; Missi Pyle; ***D:*** Jim Fall; ***W:*** Jason Schafer; ***C:*** Terry Stacey; ***M:*** David Friedman.

Trick Baby *The Double Con* **1972 (R)** An atypical blaxploitation film based on the novel of the same name by Robert Beck (aka Iceberg Slim). It tells the story of two Philadelphia con men, one black, and one bi-racial but able to pass for white. Making a career out of swindling racists they've decided to retire but past victims are hot on their heels. **89m/C; DVD.** Kiel Martin; Mel Stewart; Dallas Edward Hayes; Vernee Watson-Johnson; ***D:*** Larry Yust; ***W:*** Larry Yust; ***C:*** Isidore Mankofsky.

A Trick of the Mind ½ **2006** Jamie (Holden) spends some time in a mental hospital after her parents' death. Left wealthy and in charge of the family realty business, Jamie soon marries Michael (Johansson). She's contacted by alleged PI Helen (Grant) who claims Michael has a shady past—except there's no apparent evidence. Is Jamie being gaslighted for her inheritance or is she just losing it again? **90m/C; DVD.** Alexandra Holden; Paul Johansson; Stacy Grant; Wanda Cannon; Ben Cole; Mylene Dinh-Robic; Bruce Dawson; ***D:*** Terry Ingram; ***W:*** Jeff Barmash; ***C:*** Michael Balfry; ***M:*** John Sereda. **CABLE**

Trick or Treat ½ **1986 (R)** A high school student is helped to exact violent revenge against his bullying contemporaries. His helper is the spirit of a violent heavy metal rock star who he raises from the dead. Sometimes clever, not terribly scary. **97m/C;**

VHS, DVD. Tony Fields; Marc Price; Ozzy Osbourne; Gene Simmons; Elaine Joyce; Glenn Morgan; Lisa Orgolini; Doug Savant; *D:* Charles Martin Smith; *W:* Joel Soisson; Michael S. Murphy; Rhet Topham; *C:* Robert Elswit.

Trick 'r Treat **2008 (R)** Good old-fashioned fright fest. This Halloween anthology is set in a small Ohio town that celebrates in a big way with various characters recurring over the stories. School principal Steven takes extreme measures to rid himself of trick-or-treaters while a crusty old codger learns tricking rather than treating has dire consequences. A Little Red Riding Hood costume worn by college virgin Laurie attracts some predatory attention; a married couple breaks the Jack o' Lantern holiday rule; and a group of teens use an urban legend to play a trick that backfires on them. **82m/C; DVD, Blu-Ray.** Dylan Baker; Anna Paquin; Lauren Lee Smith; Brian Cox; Leslie Bibb; Tahmoh Penikett; Quinn Lord; *D:* Michael Dougherty; *C:* Glen MacPherson; *M:* Douglas Pipes. **VIDEO**

Tricks of a Woman ½ *Tricks of Love* **2008 (R)** Plain Jane fish-cleaner Dessi is spotted by fashion photographer Rex who makes a bet with rival Albert that he can turn the frump into a successful model. **87m/C; DVD.** Elika Portnoy; Scott Elrod; Carlos Leon; Vincent Pastore; Natasha Lyonne; Ashley Wolfe; Dennis Lemoine; Jordan Carlos; *D:* Todd Norwood; *W:* Todd Norwood; Richard Lasser; *C:* Taylor Gentry; *M:* Cory Gabel. **VIDEO**

Tricks of the Trade **1988 (R)** Goody-two-shoe housewife and hooker accomplice search for husband's murderer. Racy TV fodder. **100m/C; VHS, DVD.** Cindy Williams; Markie Post; Chris Mulkey; James Whitmore, Jr.; Scott Paulin; John Ritter; Apollonia; *D:* Jack Bender. **TV**

Trigger **2010** Childhood friends Vic (Wright) and Kat (Parker) started a Toronto riot grrrl band in the '90s but success, ego, and Vic's drug addiction broke up the duo and their friendship. Ten years later, the women are asked to do a benefit concert, so they reluctantly meet for a tension-filled dinner and try to figure out if they can make their brief reunion work. Director McDonald lathers on the soap, although the leads are certainly worth watching. **83m/C; DVD.** *CA* Molly Parker; Tracy Wright; Don McKellar; Sarah Polley; Callum Keith Rennie; *D:* Bruce McDonald; *W:* Daniel MacIvor; *C:* Jonathan Cliff; *M:* Brendan Canning.

The Trigger Effect ½ **1996 (R)** Nightmare in yuppiedom when a suspicious electromagnetic pulse knocks out all electrical power, telephone, and broadcast signals for hundreds of miles around a tranquil southern California community, which becomes increasingly unsettled. Matt (MacLachlan), wife Annie (Shue), and friend Joe (Mulroney) hang out together during the mystery power outage with lots of mounting tension both within and without. Film, however dread-producing, doesn't really make that much sense. **103m/C; VHS, DVD, Blu-Ray.** Kyle MacLachlan; Elisabeth Shue; Dermot Mulroney; Michael Rooker; Richard T. Jones; Bill Smitrovich; William Lucking; Molly Morgan; Richard Schiff; *D:* David Koepp; *W:* David Koepp; *C:* Newton Thomas (Tom) Sigel; *M:* James Newton Howard.

Trigger Happy ½ *Mad Dog Time* **1996 (R)** Director Bishop (son of Rat-Packer Joey, who's in the film) tells a tale of crime lord Vic (Dreyfuss) and various gangsters in what should be a knowingly cool story but isn't. Vic's about to get out of the loony bin and has informed his enforcer, Ben London (Byrne), to get rid of his rivals and disloyal fellow mobsters in time for his return. Meanwhile, his chief of staff, Mickey (Goldblum), has been romancing both Vic's gal Grace (Lane) and her jealous older sister, Rita (Barkin). This situation does not make Vic happy either. The movie won't make you happy either. **93m/C; VHS, DVD.** Richard Dreyfuss; Gabriel Byrne; Jeff Goldblum; Diane Lane; Ellen Barkin; Gregory Hines; Kyle MacLachlan; Larry Bishop; Burt Reynolds; Henry Silva; ***Cameo(s):*** Joey Bishop; Angie Everhart; Michael J. Pollard; Richard Pryor; Rob Reiner; Billy Idol; *D:* Larry Bishop; *W:* Larry Bishop; *C:* Frank Byers; *M:* Earl Rose.

Trigger, Jr. ½ **1950** Rogers and his Western Show find themselves in the middle of a dispute between intimidated ranchers and an evil local range patrol office. When Trigger is injured by a killer stallion, Roy turns to two unlikely allies—a 10-year-old boy who's scared of horses and frisky Trigger Jr. **67m/B; VHS, DVD, Blu-Ray.** Roy Rogers; Dale Evans; Grant Withers; Pat Brady; Gordon Jones; Peter Miles; George Cleveland; *D:* William Witney; *W:* Gerald Geraghty.

Triggerman ½ *Doc West Returns* **2009 (PG)** Easy-going sequel to "Doc West." Gambling gunslinger Minnesota 'Doc' West (Hill) arrives in town for a poker tournament. He soon figures out that his thieving fellow card players are fixing to cheat their way to victory. **97m/C; DVD.** *IT* Terence Hill; Paul Sorvino; Ornella Muti; Fabrizio Bucci; Micah Alberti; Linus Huffman; *D:* Giulio Base; *W:* Luca Biglione; Marcello Olivieri; *C:* Massimiliano Trevis; *M:* Maurizio de Angelis.

Triggermen **2002 (R)** Two inept con men hit the jackpot after slipping off with a cash-packed suitcase—problem is it's an advance to two hit men to snuff out a mob boss. Naturally they don't split the scene right away and the hit men catch up to them, but the hoopla doesn't end there in this mildly amusing farce. **96m/C; VHS, DVD.** Pete Postlethwaite; Neil Morrissey; Donnie Wahlberg; Adrian Dunbar; Michael Rapaport; Claire Forlani; Amanda Plummer; Saul Rubinek; *D:* John Bradshaw; *W:* Tony Johnston; *C:* Barry Stone; *M:* Terence Gowan; Blair Packham. **VIDEO**

Trilogy of Terror ½ **1975** Black shows her versatility as she plays a tempting seductress, a mousy schoolteacher, and the terrified victim of an African Zuni fetish doll in three horror shorts. **78m/C; VHS, DVD, Blu-Ray.** Karen Black; Robert (Skip) Burton; John Karlen; Gregory Harrison; George Gaynes; James Storm; Kathryn Reynolds; Tracy Curtis; *D:* Dan Curtis; *W:* Richard Matheson; *C:* Paul Lohmann; *M:* Robert Cobert. **TV**

Trilogy of Terror 2 **1996 (R)** Curtis follows up his 1975 TV movie with an okay sequel headed by Anthony. "Graveyard Rats" features flesh-eating, cemetery-dwelling rodents and a greedy wife who bumped off her wealthy husband, a mother strikes a fiendish bargain to bring her drowned son back to life in "Bobby," and the deadly African Zuni fetish doll returns in "He Who Kills." **90m/C; VHS, DVD, Blu-Ray.** Lysette Anthony; Richard Fitzpatrick; Geraint Wyn Davies; Matt Clark; Geoffrey Lewis; Blake Heron; *D:* Dan Curtis; *W:* Dan Curtis; William F. Nolan; Richard Matheson; *C:* Elemer Ragalyi; *M:* Robert Cobert. **CABLE**

Trinity Is Still My Name ½ *Continuavamo A Chiamarlo Trinita* **1975 (G)** Sequel to "They Call Me Trinity." Insouciant bumbling brothers Trinity and Bambino, oblivious to danger and hopeless odds, endure mishaps and adventures as they try to right wrongs. A funny parody of Western cliches that never becomes stale. **117m/C; VHS, DVD, Blu-Ray.** *IT* Bud Spencer; Terence Hill; Harry Carey, Jr.; *D:* E.B. (Enzo Barboni) Clucher.

The Trio **1997** Unconvincing German sex comedy finds gay middle-aged Zobel (George) and his daughter Lizzie (Hain) constantly on the move as they exercise their pickpocketing profession, along with Zobel's lover Karl (Redl). After Karl dies in an auto accident, Lizzie recruits hunky drifter Rudolf (Eitner) to take his place. Which Rudolf does in more ways than one, since he soon becomes the lover of both father and daughter. German with subtitles. **97m/C; VHS, DVD.** *GE* Goetz George; Jeanette Hain; Felix Eitner; Christian Redl; *D:* Hermine Huntgeburth; *W:* Hermine Huntgeburth; Horst Sczerba; Volker Einrauch; *C:* Martin Kukula; *M:* Niki Reiser.

The Trip **1967** A psychedelic journey to the world of inner consciousness, via drugs. A TV director, unsure where his life is going, decides to try a "trip" to expand his understanding. Hopper is the drug salesman, Dern, the tour guide for Fonda's trip through sex, witches, torture chambers, and more. Great period music. **85m/C; VHS, DVD, Blu-Ray.** Peter Fonda; Susan Strasberg; Bruce Dern; Dennis Hopper; Salli Sachse; Barboura Morris; Judith Lang; Luana Anders; Beach Dickerson; Dick Miller; Michael Nader; Michael Blodgett; Caren Bernsen; Katherine Walsh; Peter Bogdanovich; Tom Signorelli; *D:* Roger Corman; *W:* Jack Nicholson; *C:* Arch R. Dalzell; *M:* Barry Goldberg.

The Trip **2002 (R)** In 1973 Los Angeles, young Republican Alan Oakley (Sullivan) is working for an establishment newspaper and denying the fact that he's gay. In fact, Alan's writing a book that's a conservative attack on gay rights. When Alan meets gay rights activist Tommy (Braun), things change personally and professionally. Too bad Alan's manuscript gets published anonymously by envious wannabe lover, Peter (Baker). Film eventually makes its way to 1984 when Alan learns ex-lover Tommy is dying of AIDS in Mexico but would like to see Alan one more time. Not quite as sappy as you may think, since writer/director Swain is certainly sincere, but it's also basic melodrama. **93m/C; VHS, DVD.** Larry Sullivan; Steve Braun; Ray Baker; Art Hindle; Jill St. John; Alexis Arquette; *D:* Miles Swain; *W:* Miles Swain; *C:* Charles L. Barbee; Scott Kevan; *M:* Steven Chesne.

The Trip **2010** Coogan, Brydon, and director Winterbottom reunite (after 2006's "Tristram Shandy: A Cock and Bull Story") to play fictional versions of themselves for this improv Brit comedy. When Steve gets the chance to review high-class restaurants in rural England, he inevitably—and with much ambivalence—takes his agitating best friend, Rob, along for the ride. The pair engages on a wacky adventure characterized by arguments about their lives and impersonations of celebrities like Woody Allen and Michael Caine. Hilarious and insightful, with a unique and honest camaraderie between the leads, it's a trip well worth taking. **107m/C; DVD, Blu-Ray.** *GB* Steve Coogan; Rob Brydon; Claire Keelan; Margo Stilley; Rebecca Johnson; Dolya Gavanski; *D:* Michael Winterbottom; *C:* Ben Smithard.

The Trip to Bountiful **1985 (PG)** An elderly widow, unhappy living in her son's fancy modern home, makes a pilgrimage back to her childhood home in Bountiful, Texas. Based on the Horton Foote play. Fine acting with Oscar-winning performance from Page. **102m/C; VHS, DVD, Blu-Ray.** Geraldine Page; Rebecca De Mornay; John Heard; Carlin Glynn; Richard Bradford; *D:* Peter Masterson; *W:* Horton Foote; *C:* Fred Murphy. Oscars '85: Actress (Page); Ind. Spirit '86: Actress (Page), Screenplay.

The Trip to Bountiful **2014** Lifetime adaptation of the Horton Foote play. Restless widow Carrie Watts (the incomparable Tyson) is a Texas octogenarian who wants to see the place she grew up one last time before she dies. Now living with her son and daughter-in-law, who don't support her adventure, Carrie simply leaves, taking a bus and depending on the kindness of strangers to get her where she's going. Tyson won a Tony award for her role in the 2013 stage revival. **90m/C; DVD.** Cicely Tyson; Blair Underwood; Vanessa Williams; Keke Palmer; Clancy Brown; *D:* Michael Wilson; *W:* Horton Foote; *C:* David (Robert) A. Greene; *M:* John Gromada. **CABLE**

The Trip to Italy ½ **2014** Coogan and Brydon reunite in director Winterbottom's follow-up to the indie comedy hit, and the results are basically more of the same. But that's OK when a film like this is so light-hearted and well-executed. The pair, who are essentially playing themselves, are sent to Italy to have six meals in six different cities. The structure is merely an excuse for the gentlemen to riff on fame, personality, and their bizarre form of friendship. It's essentially a buddy comedy with a dry, British sense of humor, one that produces more laughs than most Hollywood offerings. **108m/C; DVD, Blu-Ray.** *UK IT* Steve Coogan; Rob Brydon; Rosie Fellner; *D:* Michael Winterbottom; *W:* Steve Coogan; Rob Brydon; Michael Winterbottom; *C:* James Clarke.

The Trip to Spain ½ **2017** The solid third entry in The Trip series of faux documentaries starring comedic actors Coogan and Byrdon again playing versions of themselves to great comic effect. The pair travels to various parts of Spain to experience local culinary and cultural scenes and reveal their personal and professional anxieties in the process. Though what they do has some importance, the film primarily runs on their appealing rapport, dueling wits, and celebrity impressions. The fictionalized versions of Coogan and Brydon's families add some filler between the jokes. A delightful film for British comedy fans. **108m/C; DVD, Blu-Ray.** Steve Coogan; Rob Brydon; Marta Barrio; Claire Keelan; Rebecca Johnson; *D:* Michael Winterbottom; *C:* James Clarke.

TripFall ½ **2000 (R)** Tom Williams (Ritter) decides he, wife Gina (Hunter), and their kids need some family time, so they head off on vacation. And run into the nightmare of Eddie (Roberts) and his gang of kidnappers. With his wife and kids in Eddie's slimy hands, Tom has one day to get more than a million bucks together if he wants them back alive. **95m/C; VHS, DVD.** John Ritter; Eric Roberts; Rachel Hunter; *D:* Serge Rodnunsky; *W:* Serge Rodnunsky; *C:* Greg Patterson; *M:* Evan Evans. **VIDEO**

Triple Agent **2004** Rohmer enters murky political territory in his moral spy yarn based on a true crime. In 1936, Tsarist sympathizer Fiodor Voronin (Renko) is living in exile in Paris with his Greek-born wife Arsinoe (Didaskalou). His frequent business trips arouse Arsinoe's suspicions, but Fiodor is not having an affair: he's a spy playing the White Russians against the communists and the fascists in a dangerous and increasingly complicated triple-cross. French, Russian, and German with subtitles. **115m/C; DVD.** *FR IT GR RU SP* Serge Renko; Amanda Langlet; Emmanuel Salinger; Katerina Didaskalou; Cyrielle Clair; Grigori Manoukov; *D:* Eric Rohmer; *W:* Eric Rohmer; *C:* Diane Baratier.

Triple Cross **1967** Plummer is a British safecracker imprisoned on the channel islands at the outbreak of WWII. When the Germans move in, he offers to work for them if they set him free. The Germans buy his story and send him to England, but once there he offers his services to the British as a double agent. Based on the exploits of Eddie Chapman, adapted from his book, "The Eddie Chapman Story." **91m/C; DVD.** *FR UK* Christopher Plummer; Romy Schneider; Trevor Howard; Gert Frobe; Yul Brynner; Claudine Auger; Georges Lycan; Jess Hahn; Howard Vernon; *D:* Terence Young; *W:* Rene Hardy; *C:* Henri Alekan; *M:* Georges Garvarentz.

Triple Dog **2009 (R)** That's as in triple dog dare ya in this teen drama filled with foolish and/or unpleasant characters. Eve's troubled BFF Chapin decides Eve's 16th birthday should be spent with their friends taking on increasingly dangerous and dumb dares. There's also some sort of tie-in to Chapin's hiding what she knows about another student's suicide. **95m/C; DVD, Blu-Ray.** Brittany Robertson; Alexia Fast; Scout Taylor-Compton; Janel Parrish; Emily Tennant; Carly McKillip; Aubrey Mozino; *D:* Pascal Franchot; *W:* Barbara Marshall; *C:* George Campbell; *M:* Ian Honeyman. **VIDEO**

Triple Frontier ½ **2019 (R)** After current private military contractor Santiago "Pope" Garcia (Isaac) raids a drug cartel kingpin's secret lair, he comes up with a plan to steal the $75 million the kingpin has hidden in his home. To pull it off, Garcia needs the help of four of his former special ops cohorts who have struggled in their post-military lives. Tom "Redfly" Davis (Affleck) is a real estate agent in Florida, while William "Ironhead" Miller (Hunnam) gives motivational speeches. The well-planned heist faces some unexpected challenges, including getting away with it. It's a tense, good-looking thriller that's more style than substance. **125m/C; DVD.** Ben Affleck; Oscar Isaac; Charlie Hunnam; Garrett Hedlund; Pedro Pascal; *D:* J.C. Chandor; *W:* J.C. Chandor; Mark Boal; *C:* Roman Vasyanov; *M:* Disasterpeace.

Triple 9 **2015 (R)** Imagine if someone watched a lot of Michael Mann and Sidney Lumet movies and thought he could do the same thing as the masters of macho action examinations of masculinity. You'd have some idea of this dirty, vile disaster that wastes so much talent. Ejiofor leads a group of bank robbers who are working at the behest of a Russian mob wife (Winslet). To accomplish their latest task, they plan to pull a "Triple 9" (the code for "Officer Down") and kill a rookie cop (played by Casey Affleck). The film alternates between not making sense and making you want to take a shower to get rid of its grime. **?m/C; DVD, Blu-Ray.** Chiwetel Ejiofor; Casey Affleck; Anthony Mackie; Woody Harrelson; Aaron Paul; Gal Gadot; Teresa Palmer; Norman Reedus; Kate Winslet; *D:* John Hillcoat; *W:* Matt Cook; *C:* Nicolas Karakatsanis;

M: Claudia Sarne; Bobby Krlic; Atticus Ross; Leopold Ross.

Triple Threat **2019 (R)** When heiress Xiao Xian (Jade) uses her fortune to destroy a dangerous crime syndicate, they threaten her life. Though Xian is heavily guarded, the syndicate puts its best killers on the case. One such killer is Collins (Adkins), who is broken out of his remote Indonesian prison camp by Devereaux (White) and Joey (Bisping) for the job. While they make their way out of the jungle, they create enemies of locals, Long Fei (Chen) and Jaka (Uwais), who have their own enemy in Payu (Jaa). This brutal action-based martial arts film showcases the abilities of its stars but the story is forgettable. **96m/C; DVD.** Tony Jaa; Tiger Hu Chen; Iko Uwais; Scott Adkins; Celina Jade; *D:* Jesse V. Johnson; *W:* Joey O'Bryan; Fangjin Song; Paul Staheli; *C:* Jonathan Hall; *M:* Joel J. Richard.

Triplecross ½ **1995 (R)** Jewel thief Jimmy Ray (Bergin) is after a fortune in diamonds and obsessive FBI agent Oscar (Williams) is looking to bring him down. Oscar decides to use Jimmy Ray's ex-cell mate Teddy (Pare) but Teddy gets involved with J.R.'s girlfriend Julia (Laurence) instead of tending to business. Wooden crime caper. **95m/C; VHS, DVD.** Patrick Bergin; Billy Dee Williams; Michael Paré; Ashley Laurence; *D:* Jeno Hodi. **CABLE**

The Triplets of Belleville *Les Triplettes de Belleville; Belleville Rendez-Vous* **2002 (PG-13)** Surreal French animated tale of a joyless bicycle racer and his eccentric grandmother charms, surprises, and confounds with flights of fancy and wonderfully imaginative scenarios. Champion is a sad little boy who doesn't respond to anything until his grandmother buys him a tricycle. This leads him to become a top-level bike racer who is eventually kidnapped by French mobsters. His stalwart grandma stops at nothing to rescue him. **91m/C; DVD.** *FR BE CA D:* Sylvain Chomet; *W:* Sylvain Chomet; *M:* Benoit Charest. L.A. Film Critics '03: Animated Film, Score.

The Tripper **2006 (R)** Arquette's directorial debut is a lame horror satire that makes you wonder if everyone on set was maybe tripping. Three hippie couples are driving through a North Carolina forest when they're attacked by a psycho wearing a Ronald Reagan mask and fondling sharp and deadly inplements. **93m/C; DVD.** Thomas Jane; Jaime King; Richmond Arquette; Paz de la Huerta; Balthazar Getty; Lukas Haas; Jason Mewes; Paul (Pee-wee Herman) Reubens; David Arquette; *D:* David Arquette; *W:* David Arquette; Joe Harris; *C:* Bobby Bukowski; *M:* Jimmy Haun; Dave Wittman.

Trippin' **1999 (R)** Gregory (Richmond) is a daydreamer who can't keep his mind on his studies until he finds out that the prom queen, Cinny (Campbell), goes for the brainy type. Between fantasies of fame, fortune, and exotic locales, Gregory, with the help of his ne'er-do-well buddies Fish (Torry) and June (Faison), tries to improve his grades and get her to the prom. Likeable cast and a nice message about the importance of getting an education balance out a gratuitous subplot about a local crime boss recruiting June. Lightweight but amusing. **92m/C; VHS, DVD.** Deon Richmond; Maia Campbell; Donald Adeosun Faison; Guy Torry; Harold Sylvester; Stoney Jackson; Michael Warren; Aloma Wright; Bill Henderson; *D:* David Raynr; *W:* Gary Hardwick; *C:* John Aronson.

Trishna **2011 (R)** Director Winterbottom switches genres yet again with this adaptation/update of the Thomas Hardy novel, "Tess of the D'Ubervilles," to contemporary Rajasthan, India. The gorgeous Pinto plays the title character, a woman torn between the tradition of her culture and the beating of her romantic heart. Meanwhile the object of her affection Jay (Ahmed)--the son of a wealthy property developer--faces his own challenges from his family as he pursues her. A piece about not just about romance but how one's situation can destroy hopes and dreams. Unfortunately the end result is cold and Pinto seems disconnected. **113m/C; DVD.** *UK* Freida Pinto; Riz Ahmed; Roshan Seth; *D:* Michael Winterbottom; *W:* Michael Winterbottom; *C:* Marcel Zyskind; *M:* Shigeru Umebayashi.

Tristan & Isolde ½ **2006 (PG-13)** Pretty actors play tragic lovers in a romantic drama based on a Celtic legend. Dark Ages Irish princess Isolde (Myles) is the marriageable bargaining chip for her scheming father (O'Hara), whose aim is to rule the squabbling English tribes. Isolde rescues, and falls in love with, injured warrior Tristan (Franco), who happens to be the champion of powerful Briton Lord Marke (Sewell). Unbeknownst to the lovers, Isolde has been promised to Marke; they try to do the right thing. It's appropriately swoony and teary and noble. **125m/C; DVD, Blu-Ray.** *GB GE US* James Franco; Sophia Myles; Rufus Sewell; David O'Hara; Mark Strong; Henry Cavill; Bronagh Gallagher; Ronan Vibert; Lucy Russell; Thomas Brodie-Sangster; JB Blanc; Graham Mulins; *D:* Kevin Reynolds; *W:* Dean Georgaris; *C:* Arthur Reinhart; *M:* Anne Dudley.

Tristram Shandy: A Cock and Bull Story **2005 (R)** Peculiar film-within-a-film follows Brit comedian Coogan playing an exaggerated version of "Steve Coogan" as he takes the title role in the filming of the eccentric 18th-century novel "The Life and Opinions of Tristram Shandy." Insecure and vain, Coogan annoys the director (Northam) and screenwriter (Hart), while childishly sparring with his primary co-star (Brydon) and ignoring his visiting girlfriend (Macdonald) and their baby. Best for Coogan fans or those interested in movie minutia. **91m/C; DVD.** Steve Coogan; Rob Brydon; Keeley Hawes; Shirley Henderson; Dylan Moran; Jeremy Northam; Naomie Harris; Kelly Macdonald; Elizabeth Berrington; Mark Williams; James Fleet; Ian Hart; Kieran O'Brien; Stephen Fry; Gillian Anderson; David Walliams; Anthony H. Wilson; *D:* Michael Winterbottom; *W:* Martin Hardy; *C:* Marcel Zyskind; *M:* Michael Nyman; Edward Nogria.

The Triumph of Hercules *Il Trionfo di Ercole; Hercules and the Ten Avengers; Hercules vs. the Giant Warriors* **1966** Hercules gets stripped of his powers by a peeved Zeus and must try to battle a sorcercess and 10 giant bronze warriors without them, until Zeus reconsiders. **94m/C; VHS, DVD.** *IT FR* Dan Vadis; Moira Orfei; Pierre Cressoy; Marilu Tolo; Pierro Lulli; *D:* Alberto De Martino; *W:* Roberto Gianviti; Robert Gianviti; *C:* Pier Ludovico Pavoni; *M:* Francesco De Masi.

The Triumph of Love **2001 (PG-13)** Not much of a triumph but not a complete waste of time either. Adapted from Pierre Marivaux's 18th-century play, Sorvino plays Princess Leonide, who knows that her family usurped their throne and she is determined to see its rightful owner, Prince Agis (Rodan), returned to power. Of course, he's a handsome prince and the princess has fallen in love but there are complications that involve her disguising herself as a male philosophy student and insinuating herself into his guardians' (Kingsley, Shaw) austere lives. Deceptions abound. **107m/C; VHS, DVD.** *IT GB* Mira Sorvino; Ben Kingsley; Fiona Shaw; Jay Rodan; Rachael Stirling; Ignazio Oliva; *D:* Clare Peploe; *W:* Clare Peploe; Bernardo Bertolucci; Marilyn Goldin; *C:* Fabio Cianchetti; *M:* Jason Osborn.

The Triumph of Sherlock Holmes ½ **1935** Wontner and Fleming teamed for an early series of Holmesian romps. In one of their best outings, Sherlock Holmes comes out of retirement as a series of bizarre murders of Pennsylvania coal miners lure him back into action. From "The Valley of Fear" by Sir Arthur Conan Doyle. **84m/B; VHS, DVD.** *GB* Arthur Wontner; Ian Fleming; *D:* Leslie Hiscott.

Triumph of the Spirit **1989 (R)** Gritty account of boxer Salamo Arouch's experiences in Auschwitz. The boxer became champion in matches between prisoners conducted for the amusement of Nazi officers. Filmed on location in Auschwitz. **115m/C; VHS, DVD; Open Captioned.** Willem Dafoe; Robert Loggia; Edward James Olmos; Wendy Gazelle; Kelly Wolf; Costas Mandylor; Kario Salem; *D:* Robert M. Young; *W:* Robert M. Young; Andrzej Krakowski; Laurence Heath; Arthur Coburn; Millard Lampell; Shimon Arama; *M:* Cliff Eidelman.

Triumph of the Will ½ *Triumph des Willens* **1934** Director Riefenstahl's formidable, stunning film, documenting Hitler and the Sixth Nazi Party Congress in 1934 in Nuernberg, Germany. The greatest and most artful propaganda piece ever produced. German dialogue. Includes English translation of the speeches. **115m/B; VHS, DVD, Blu-Ray.** *GE D:* Leni Riefenstahl; *W:* Leni Riefenstahl; *C:* Sepp Allgeier; *M:* Herbert Windt.

Trixie **2000 (R)** Performances by a fine ensemble cast are mangled almost as badly as the English language in this wandering comedy-mystery. Trixie (Watson) is a malaprop-spouting security guard at a resort casino who wants to be a detective. She stumbles onto a murder mystery involving bombastic Senator Avery (Nolte) and decides that if she solves the crime, a career as a detective will surely follow. Many false leads are chased, and the theme that not everyone is as they appear is hammered home time and time again. Among the list of usual suspects are a golddigging barfly (Murphy), a washed-up lounge singer (Warren), a two-bit ladies man (Mulroney) and an impressionist/singer with a shady past (Lane). **117m/C; VHS, DVD.** Emily Watson; Nick Nolte; Dermot Mulroney; Nathan Lane; Brittany Murphy; Lesley Ann Warren; Will Patton; Stephen Lang; *D:* Alan Rudolph; *W:* Alan Rudolph; *C:* Jan Kiesser; *M:* Mark Isham; Roger Neill.

Trog **1970** Truly awful no-budget horror flick that was Crawford's final film role. Two students investigate a cave near an English village and disturb the half-man, half-ape that lives there. Local anthropologist Dr. Brockton (Crawford) has the beast/man captured and taken to her lab, discovering he's a prehistoric troglodyte who's soon nicknamed Trog. She wants to study him, but local landowner Sam Murdock (Gough) believes the creature is a threat. Mistreated Trog escapes and proves Murdock right by going on a bloody rampage. **91m/C; DVD.** *GB* Joan Crawford; Michael Gough; Bernard Kay; David Griffin; Kim Braden; Joe Cornelius; *D:* Freddie Francis; *W:* Aben Kandel; *C:* Desmond Dickinson; *M:* John Scott.

Trois Couleurs: Blanc *White; Three Colors: White* **1994 (R)** Bittersweet comedic rags-to-riches tale spiced with revenge and lasting love. "White" focuses on equality and begins when a bewildered Polish hairdresser is divorced by his disdainful French wife, who takes him for everything he has. Returning to his family in Poland, Karol doggedly works his way into wealth. Then he decides to fake his death and leave his fortune to the ex he still loves—or does he? In Polish and French with English subtitles. Part 2 of Kieslowski's trilogy, following "Trois Couleurs: Bleu" and followed by "Trois Couleurs: Rouge." **92m/C; VHS, DVD.** *FR SI PL* Zbigniew Zamachowski; Julie Delpy; Janusz Gajos; Jerzy Stuhr; Aleksander Bardini; Grzegorz Warchol; Cezary Harasimowicz; Jerzy Nowak; Jerzy Trela; Cezary Pazura; Michel Lisowski; Philippe Morier-Genoud; *Cameo(s):* Juliette Binoche; Florence Pernel; *D:* Krzysztof Kieslowski; *W:* Krzysztof Kieslowski; Krzysztof Piesiewicz; *C:* Edward Klosinski; *M:* Zbigniew Preisner. Berlin Intl. Film Fest. '94: Director (Kieslowski).

Trois Couleurs: Bleu *Three Colors: Blue; Blue* **1993 (R)** First installment of director Kieslowski's trilogy inspired by the French tricolor flag. "Blue" stands for liberty—here freedom is based on tragedy as Julie (Binoche) reshapes her life after surviving an accident which killed her famous composer husband and their young daughter. Excellent performance by Binoche, which relies on the internalized grief and brief emotion which flits across her face rather than overwhelming displays for expression. In French with English subtitles. **98m/C; VHS, DVD.** *FR* Juliette Binoche; Benoit Regent; Florence Pernel; Charlotte Very; Helene Vincent; Philippe Volter; Claude Duneton; Hugues Quester; Florence Vignon; Isabelle Sadoyan; Yann Tregouet; Jacek Ostaszewski; *Cameo(s):* Emmanuelle Riva; *D:* Krzysztof Kieslowski; *W:* Krzysztof Kieslowski; Krzysztof Piesiewicz; Slawomir Idziak; Agnieszka Holland; Edward Zebrowski; *C:* Slawomir Idziak; *M:* Zbigniew Preisner. Cesar '94: Actress (Binoche), Film Editing, Sound; L.A. Film Critics '93: Score; Venice Film Fest. '93: Actress (Binoche), Film.

Trois Couleurs: Rouge ½ *Three Colors: Red; Red* **1994 (R)** "Red" is for fraternity in the French tricolor flag and, in director Kieslowski's last film in his trilogy, emotional connections are made between unlikely couples. There's law student Auguste and his girlfriend Karin, young fashion model Valentine, and a nameless retired judge, brought together by circumstance and destined to change each other's lives. Subtle details make for careful viewing but it's a rewarding watch and a visual treat (keep an eye on cinematographer Sobocinski's use of the color red). Binoche and Delpy, who starred in the earlier films, also make an appearance, as Kieslowski uses the finale to tie up loose ends. In French with English subtitles. **99m/C; VHS, DVD.** *FR PL SI* Irene Jacob; Jean-Louis Trintignant; Frederique Feder; Jean-Pierre Lorit; Samuel Le Bihan; Marion Stalens; Teco Celio; Bernard Escalon; Jean Schlegel; Elzbieta Jasinska; *Cameo(s):* Juliette Binoche; Julie Delpy; Benoit Regent; Zbigniew Zamachowski; *D:* Krzysztof Kieslowski; *W:* Krzysztof Kieslowski; Krzysztof Piesiewicz; *C:* Piotr Sobocinski; *M:* Zbigniew Preisner. Cesar '94: Score; Ind. Spirit '95: Foreign Film; L.A. Film Critics '94: Foreign Film; N.Y. Film Critics '94: Foreign Film; Natl. Soc. Film Critics '94: Foreign Film.

Trojan Eddie **1996** Stephen Rea puts his perpetual hangdog mug to good use as the hapless Trojan Eddie, so named for the make of the van in which he transports and sells stolen goods. He is married to the shrewish town tramp, who helps little in raising their two girls and makes fun of his dream of opening his own business. His boss is John Power (Harris), leader of a group of clannish con men. He is teamed with Power's nephew Dermot (Townsend), who's secretly romancing his uncle's much younger wife-to-be. The young lovers take off with the cache of wedding loot on the night of the nuptials, and Power involves Eddie in an all-out search for the couple. After they're caught and pardoned by Power, however, the spiral of betrayal and violence spins faster than ever, with Eddie always eyeing the chance to escape. Excellent rapport between Rea and Harris as their fortunes shift and reverse. **103m/C; VHS, DVD.** Stephen Rea; Richard Harris; Brendan Gleeson; Sean McGinley; Angeline Ball; Brid Brennan; Stuart Townsend; Aislin McGuckin; *D:* Gilles Mackinnon; *W:* Billy Roche; *C:* John de Borman; *M:* John Keane.

The Trojan Horse ½ *The Trojan War; The Mighty Warrior* **1962** Greek warrior Aeneas (Reeves), under the command of Ulysses (Barrymore), gets to hide out in the Trojan horse with his fellow fighters and then get those Trojans when they take the wooden beast into their city. When they're successful, Aeneas takes his guys and decides to go off and found the city of Rome. You were maybe expecting historical or mythological accuracy? **105m/C; VHS, DVD.** *IT FR* Steve Reeves; John Drew (Blythe) Barrymore, Jr.; Juliette Mayniel; Edy Vessel; Lidia Alfonsi; Luciana Angiolillo; Arturo Dominici; Mimmo Palmara; Carlo Tamberlani; Nando Tamberlani; *D:* Giorgio Ferroni; *W:* Ugo Liberatore; *C:* Rino Filippini; *M:* Giovanni Fusco.

The Trojan Horse ½ **2008 (R)** Complicated Canadian thriller that's a sequel to the 2004 miniseries "H2O." Former Prime Minister Tom McLaughlin (Gross) watches in disgust as his countrymen vote for a union with the U.S.A., and Canada is divided into six new states. Tom, secretly backed by a European cartel, runs as an independent candidate for the presidency with his ex-wife, Texas Governor Mary Miller (Burns), as his veep choice. Veteran British journalist Helen Madigan (Scacchi) uncovers a plan to commit voter fraud and her knowledge turns out to be very, very dangerous. **180m/C; DVD.** *CA* Paul Gross; Martha Burns; Greta Scacchi; Tom Skerritt; William Hutt; Clark Johnson; Saul Rubinek; Stephen McHattie; Heino Ferch; Kenneth Welsh; Jean Pearson; *D:* Charles Biname; *C:* Derick Underschultz. **TV**

Trojan War ½ **1997 (PG-13)** Yes, the title does refer to the condom brand. High schooler Brad Kimble (Friedle) has finally convinced dream girl Brooke (Shelton) to get romantic—if he has the proper protection, of course. But as his search is continually thwarted, this gives his best gal pal Lea (Hewitt)?who would like to be something more—the chance to show who really loves him. Harmless, although sexually overt, teen fluff. **90m/C; VHS, DVD.** Jennifer Love Hewitt; Will Friedle; Marley Shelton; Lee Majors; Wendie

Malick; David Patrick Kelly; Anthony Michael Hall; *D:* George Huang; *W:* Andy Burg; Scott Myers; *C:* Dean Semler; *M:* George S. Clinton.

Trojan Women **1971 (G)** Euripides' tragedy on the fate of the women of Troy after the Greeks storm the famous city. The play does not translate well to the screen, in spite of tour-de-force acting. **105m/C; VHS, DVD.** Katharine Hepburn; Vanessa Redgrave; Irene Papas; Genevieve Bujold; Brian Blessed; Patrick Magee; *D:* Michael Cacoyannis. Natl. Bd. of Review '71: Actress (Papas).

Troll **1/2 1986 (PG-13)** A malevolent troll haunts an apartment building and possesses a young girl in hopes of turning all humans into trolls. Sometimes imaginative, sometimes embarrassing. Followed by a sequel. **86m/C; VHS, DVD, Blu-Ray.** Noah Hathaway; Gary Sandy; Anne Lockhart; Sonny Bono; Shelley Hack; June Lockhart; Michael Moriarty; Jennifer Beck; Phil Fondacaro; Brad Hall; Julia Louis-Dreyfus; Albert Band; Charles Band; *D:* John Carl Buechler; *W:* Ed Naha; *C:* Romano Albani; *M:* Richard Band.

Troll 2 **1/2 1992 (PG-13)** A young boy can only rely on his faith in himself when no one believes his warnings about an evil coming to destroy his family. Entering into a nightmare world, Joshua must battle witches' spells and the evil trolls who carry out their bidding. **95m/C; VHS, DVD, Blu-Ray.** Michael Stephenson; Connie McFarland; Gavin Reed; *D:* Drago Floyd; *W:* Claudio Fragasso.

The Troll Hunter *Trollhunter; Trolljegeren* **2011 (PG-13)** Yet another 'found footage' horror story (albeit in Norwegian) covers too much familiar territory to make this monster ride unique, although the fast pace is a blessing. Thomas (Tosterud), Johanna (Morch), and Kalle (Larsen) are three college filmmakers doing a doc on bear poaching. They interview loner Hans (Jespersen) and finally discover he works as a troll hunter for a secret government agency. Seems the various troll species are supposed to stay on a secured reservation but the legendary gigantor creatures would prefer to wreak havoc on the landscape, including livestock and humans. Norwegian with subtitles. **103m/C; DVD, Blu-Ray, Download.** *NO* Glenn Erland Tosterud; Johanna Morch; Tomas Alf Larsen; Otto Jerpersen; Hans Morten Mansen; *D:* André Ovredal; *W:* André Ovredal; *C:* Hallvard Braein.

A Troll in Central Park **1/2 1994 (G)** Animated fantasy about Stanley the troll, who is cast out of his kingdom (because he's a good guy) and winds up in New York's Central Park. There, Stanley brings happiness to a little girl and her skeptical brother, all the while battling the evil troll queen. Strictly average family fare. **76m/C; VHS, DVD.** *V:* Dom DeLuise; Cloris Leachman; Jonathan Pryce; Hayley Mills; Charles Nelson Reilly; Phillip Glasser; Robert Morley; Sy Goraleb; Tawney Sunshine Glover; Jordan Metzner; *D:* Don Bluth; Gary Goldman; *W:* Stu Krieger; *M:* Robert Folk.

Trolls **1/2 2016 (PG)** Way better than it has any right to be given its origins, this animated musical rides by on the charms of its voice stars and an odd sense of humor that keeps it from becoming too saccharine to swallow. Kendrick voices Poppy, sent on a road trip with the only sullen troll in the world, the anxious Branch (Timberlake), to save their kind from a troll-eating group of, well, trolls. There are enough strange jokes and musical choices to keep adults entertained and the kids will be mesmerized by the non-stop bright colors and happy, singing voices. **92m/C; DVD, Blu-Ray.** Anna Kendrick; Justin Timberlake; Zooey Deschanel; Christopher Mintz-Plasse; Christine Baranski; *D:* Mike Mitchell; *W:* Jonathan Aibel; Glenn Berger; *C:* Yong Duk Jhun; *M:* Christophe Beck.

Trolls World Tour **2020 (PG)** Queen Barb (Bloom) is a troll queen with dark ambitions. Once there were six different musical tribes of trolls (pop, country, rock, classical, funk, techno). Though their musical strings were once united, each tribe left their musical string and formed their own society. Barb wants to take control of all six strings, form one guitar, and rule all the trolls. Poppy (Kendrick) tries to stop Barb but becomes entangled in her quest. The hyperactive animated sequel is bright and busy, but in a good way. Also introduces many new characters and impressive voice work by musicians such as George Clinton and Ozzy Osbourne. **90m/C; DVD.** Anna Kendrick; Justin Timberlake; Rachel Bloom; James Corden; Ron Funches; *D:* Walt Dohrn; *W:* Jonathan Aibel; Glenn Berger; Maya Forbes; M. Wallace Wolodarsky; Elizabeth Tippet; *M:* Theodore Shapiro.

Troma's War **WOOF! 1988 (R)** The survivors of an air crash find themselves amid a tropical terrorist-run civil war. Also available in a 105-minute, unrated version. Devotees of trash films shouldn't miss this one. **90m/C; VHS, DVD, Blu-Ray.** Carolyn Beauchamp; Sean Bowen; Michael Ryder; Jessica Dublin; Steven Crossley; Lorayn Lane DeLuca; Charles Kay Hune; Ara Romanoff; Alex Cserhart; Aleida Harris; *D:* Michael Herz; Lloyd Kaufman; *W:* Lloyd Kaufman; Mitchell Dana; Eric Hattler; Thomas Martinek; *C:* James London; *M:* Christopher De Marco.

Tromeo & Juliet **1995 (R)** There've been many versions of Shakespeare, but the Bard may never recover from being "Tromatized." On the outskirts of New York City, teenaged Tromeo Que (Keenan) falls in lust with babe Juliet Capulet (Jensen), but the family feud is still around to cause major disharmony. There's lots of profanity, perversity, and gore to keep your interest. As the movie's tagline says, "Body Piercing. Kinky Sex. Dismemberment. The things that made Shakespeare great." The unrated version is 105 minutes. **95m/C; VHS, DVD.** Will Keenan; Jane Jensen; Debbie Rochon; Lemmy; Valentine Miele; Sean Gunn; *D:* Lloyd Kaufman; *W:* James Gunn; *C:* Brendan Flynt; *M:* Willie Wisely.

Tron **1982 (PG)** A video game designer enters into his computer, where he battles the computer games he created and seeks revenge on other designers who have stolen his creations. Sounds better than it plays. Terrific special effects, with lots of computer-created graphics. **96m/C; VHS, DVD, Blu-Ray, UMD.** Jeff Bridges; Bruce Boxleitner; David Warner; Cindy Morgan; Barnard Hughes; Dan Shor; Peter Jurasik; Tony Stephano; *D:* Steven Lisberger; *W:* Steven Lisberger; *C:* Bruce Logan; *M:* Walter (Wendy) Carlos.

Tron: Legacy **2010 (PG)** In this sequel to 1982's "Tron," Sam Flynn (Hedlund) enters the virtual world his video game designer father, Kevin Flynn (Bridges, reprising the role and then some), disappeared into 20 years earlier. While the CGI, 3-D, breathtaking imagery and soundtrack shine, the story line of the Flynns takes a back seat to the special effects. Sci-fi aficionados and fans of the original won't hesitate to jump into this cyber universe for a state-of-the-art experience by rookie feature film director Kosinski. **125m/C; Blu-Ray.** Garrett Hedlund; Jeff Bridges; Olivia Wilde; Bruce Boxleitner; James Frain; Beau Garrett; Michael Sheen; *D:* Joseph Kosinski; *W:* Edward Kitsis; Adam Horowitz; Richard Jefferies; *C:* Claudio Miranda; *M:* Daft Punk.

Troop Beverly Hills **1989 (PG)** Spoiled housewife Long isn't really spoiled, just misunderstood. She takes over leadership of her daughter's Wilderness Girls troop and finds the opportunity to redeem herself by offering her own unique survival tips to the uncooperative little brats who make up the troop. Everyone learns meaningful life lessons, Long is finally understood, and everyone lives happily ever after in posh Beverly Hills. Sheer silliness makes this one almost painful to watch, a shame since it boasts a good cast whose talent is totally wasted. **105m/C; VHS, DVD, Blu-Ray.** Shelley Long; Craig T. Nelson; Betty Thomas; Mary Gross; Stephanie Beacham; Audra Lindley; Edd Byrnes; Ami Foster; Jenny Lewis; Kellie Martin; *D:* Jeff Kanew; *W:* Pamela Norris; Margaret Grieco Oberman; *M:* Randy Edelman.

Trooper Hook **1/2 1957** Sgt. Hook (McCrea) discovers captive white woman Cora Sutliff (Stanwyck) after capturing a band of Apaches. She'll only return to her homesteader husband Fred (Dehner) alongside her young half-breed son Quito (Lawrence), which brings her a lot of condemnation from the locals, but sympathy from Civil War vet Hook. Fred Sutliff refuses to accept the boy and his Apache father Nanchez (Acosta) is determined to get Quito back, so Hook and Cora have a few problems. **83m/B; DVD.** Joel McCrea; Barbara Stanwyck; John Dehner; Terry Lawrence; Rodolfo Acosta; Earl Holliman; *D:* Charles Marquis Warren; *W:* Martin Berkeley; David Victor; *C:* Ellsworth Fredericks; *M:* Gerald Fried.

Trophy Wife **1/2 2006** Since Kate's (Burns) wealthy husband was going to divorce her, it's no surprise she becomes a suspect when he is murdered. Then an extortionist contacts Kate saying he did the deed so she could collect her substantial inheritance, which he wants a part of or he'll frame her for the crime. With the cops no help, Kate decides she must clear her name herself. **90m/C; DVD.** Brooke Burns; Royston Innes; Peter Benson; Barclay Hope; Kyle Cassie; Jay Brazeau; Gina Holden; *D:* Harvey Kahn; *W:* Pablo F. Fenjves; *C:* Adam Sliwinski. **CABLE**

Tropic of Cancer **1970 (NC-17)** Based on Henry Miller's once-banned, now classic novel, this film portrays the sexual escapades of the expatriate author living in 1920s Paris. Torn stars as the carefree, loose-living writer and Burstyn plays his disgusted wife. **87m/C; VHS, DVD.** Rip Torn; James Callahan; Ellen Burstyn; David Bauer; Phil Brown; *D:* Joseph Strick.

Tropic Thunder **2008 (R)** Dead-on parody of Hollywood self-absorption and egotism has five actors on location in Vietnam filming a war movie with things constantly going wrong. They wind up alone on a remote jungle location where they are mistaken for DEA agents by the local drug lords. Stiller's the vacuous action star, Black's a druggie comedian, and Downey Jr. brilliantly plays an Oscar-winning Method actor who dyes his skin black when he discovers that his grunt character was supposed to be African-American. This and other bits caused some protests from people who didn't get that Stiller was making fun of the film industry's insular cluelessness. Tom Cruise hilariously cameos in a fat suit as a foul-mouthed studio exec. **106m/C; Blu-Ray, On Demand.** Ben Stiller; Robert Downey, Jr.; Jack Black; Jay Baruchel; Danny McBride; Bill Hader; Steve Coogan; Nick Nolte; Brandon T. Jackson; Tom Cruise; Matthew McConaughey; Justin Theroux; Christine Taylor; Amy Stiller; Brandon Soo Hoo; *Cameo(s):* Tobey Maguire; Jon Voight; Tyra Banks; Jennifer Love Hewitt; *D:* Ben Stiller; *W:* Ben Stiller; Justin Theroux; Etan Cohen; *C:* John Toll; *M:* Theodore Shapiro.

Tropical Heat **1993 (R)** When the Maharajah is killed on safari, his grieving widow (D'Abo) files a $5 million insurance claim before returning to India. She's followed by an investigator (Rossovich) who becomes infatuated with the lovely D'Abo. Through palaces, primitive villages, and ancient jungle temples, they are drawn into a mystery involving blackmail and murder. Based on a story by Jag Mundhra, Michael W. Potts, and Simon Levy. **86m/C; VHS, DVD.** Rick Rossovich; Maryam D'Abo; Lee Ann Beaman; Asha Siewkumar; *D:* Jag Mundhra; *W:* Michel W. Potts; *M:* Del Casher.

Tropical Malady **1/2** *Sud pralad* **2004** Maybe it makes more sense to a Thai audience. In present-day Thailand, soldier Keng (Lamnoi) meets country boy Tong (Kaewbuadee) and the two fall in love. Then we go from the natural to the supernatural world and something involving a Thai legend about a shaman who can transform himself into animals. Keng encounters a tiger in the jungle or maybe it's just a spirit tiger and Tong disappears except maybe he's the animal—or maybe not. And there's a talking monkey and the spirit of a dead cow. Thai with subtitles. **120m/C; DVD.** *TH* Banlop Lomnoi; Sakda Kaewbuadee; *D:* Apichatpong Weerasethakul; *W:* Apichatpong Weerasethakul; *C:* Jean-Louis Vialard; Vichet Tanapanitch; Jarin Pengpanitch.

Tropix **1/2 2002** Poor Corrine thinks her hubby whisked her to Costa Rica to salvage their wreck of a marriage only to realize that the no-good cad actually has crooked business dealings on the agenda. When things go haywire she's kidnapped and spends most of her time struggling to cut loose from her captors in the jungle. **98m/C; VHS, DVD.** Keith Brunsmann; Ryan Barton-Grimley; Danielle Bisutti; Michelle Jones; Thomas Scott-Stanton; *D:* Percy Angress; Livia Linden; *W:* Livia Linden; *C:* Luc G. Nicknair. **VIDEO**

The Trotsky **2009** Multicultural comedy finds Montreal teenager Leon Bronstein (Baruchel) convinced that he's the reincarnation of Russian revolutionary Leon Trotsky. Forced to enroll at a public high school for his senior year, Leon tries to politically organize his apathetic peers and battle the fascist regime of principal Berkhoff (Feore) while trying to fulfill his destiny (exile and assassination included). English and French with subtitles. **117m/C; DVD.** *CA* Jay Baruchel; Colm Feore; Emily Hampshire; Michael Murphy; Domini Blythe; Saul Rubinek; Genevieve Bujold; Anne-Marie Cadieux; *D:* Jacob Tierney; *W:* Jacob Tierney; *C:* Guy Dufaux; *M:* Malajube.

Trouble along the Way **1/2 1953** Wayne is a once big-time college football coach who takes a coaching job at a small, financially strapped Catholic college in an effort to retain custody of his young daughter. His underhanded recruiting methods result in his firing—and the probable loss of his daughter. Unusual and sentimental role for Wayne proves he can handle comedy as well as action. **110m/B; VHS, DVD.** John Wayne; Donna Reed; Charles Coburn; Tom Tully; Sherry Jackson; Marie Windsor; Tom Helmore; Dabbs Greer; Leif Erickson; Douglas Spencer; *D:* Michael Curtiz; *W:* Jack Rose; Melville Shavelson; *M:* Max Steiner.

Trouble Bound **1992 (R)** Madsen is Harry, a guy just out of prison, on his way to Nevada with trouble dogging him every step. He's got a dead body in the car trunk, drug dealers after him, and when he offers a lift to a pretty cocktail waitress (Arquette) his luck only gets worse. She plans to kill a Mob boss and it's no secret. Chases and violence. **90m/C; VHS, DVD, Blu-Ray.** Michael Madsen; Patricia Arquette; Florence Stanley; Seymour Cassel; Sal Jenco; *D:* Jeff Reiner; *W:* Darrell Fetty; Francis Delia; *M:* Vinnie Golia.

Trouble in Mind **1986 (R)** Stylized romance is set in the near future in a rundown diner. Kristofferson is an ex-cop who gets involved in the lives of a young couple looking for a better life. Look for Divine in one of her/his rare appearances outside of John Waters' works. **111m/C; VHS, DVD.** Kris Kristofferson; Keith Carradine; Genevieve Bujold; Lori Singer; Divine; Joe Morton; George Kirby; John Considine; Dirk Blocker; Gailard Sartain; Tracy Kristofferson; Allan Nicholls; *D:* Alan Rudolph; *W:* Alan Rudolph; *C:* Toyomichi Kurita; *M:* Mark Isham. Ind. Spirit '86: Cinematog.

Trouble in Paradise **1932** Oh-so-assured sophisticated comedy finds gentleman jewel thief Gaston (Marshall) meeting his match in upscale pickpocket Lily (Hopkins). Even though they team up, their personal relationship doesn't get in the way of their professional ambitions. Gaston cons his way into the graces of wealthy widow Mariette Colet (Francis), who's well-aware she'd being used but is more amused than outraged. The same can't be said of her two devoted and dull suitors (Ruggles, Horton), who don't like the competition. And maybe Gaston is getting a little too interested in Mariette for even Lily's piece of mind. Both leading actresses are flirty and lovely and Marshall is suave and gallant. Because this is a pre-Production Code film, there's lots of sexual innuendo (both visual and verbal) and crime without punishment. **83m/B; VHS, DVD.** Herbert Marshall; Miriam Hopkins; Kay Francis; Charlie Ruggles; Edward Everett Horton; Sir C. Aubrey Smith; Robert Greig; *D:* Ernst Lubitsch; *W:* Grover Jones; Samson Raphaelson; *C:* Victor Milner; *M:* W. Franke Harling.

Trouble in Paradise **1988** Welch stars as a widow stranded in a tropical island paradise with an Australian sailor. The two must struggle as they are stalked by a gang of drug smugglers, hence the title. **92m/C; VHS, DVD.** Raquel Welch; Jack Thompson; Nicholas Hammond; John Gregg; *D:* Di Drew. **TV**

Trouble in Store **1/2 1953** A bumbling department store employee stumbles on a gangster's plot. Fun gags and a good cast. **85m/B; VHS, DVD.** *GB* Margaret Rutherford; Norman Wisdom; Moira Lister; Megs Jenkins; *D:* Jack Paddy Carstairs.

Trouble in the Glen 🦴🦴 1/2 **1954** A Scottish-American soldier returns to his ancestral home and becomes involved in a dispute between the town residents and a lord over a closed road. Uneven script undermines comic idea. **91m/C; VHS, Streaming.** *GB* Orson Welles; Victor McLaglen; Forrest Tucker; Margaret Lockwood; ***D:*** Herbert Wilcox.

Trouble in the Sky 🦴🦴 *Cone of Silence* **1960** Capt. George Gort (Lee) is found guilty of pilot error after a British jet crashes in India. His daughter Charlotte (Seal) asks flight examiner Hugh Dallas (Craig) to investigate and he gets suspicious that there's been a cover-up and that the airliner's design is actually to blame. **90m/B; DVD.** *GB* Michael Craig; Elizabeth Seal; Bernard Lee; Peter Cushing; Noel Willman; George Sanders; Gordon Jackson; ***D:*** Charles Frend; ***W:*** Robert Westerby; ***C:*** Arthur Grant; ***M:*** Gerard Schurmann.

Trouble Man 🦴🦴 **1972 (R)** Mr. T (Hooks), a private eye/problem fixer for hire, is asked by two men running an illegal craps game to find out who keeps robbing them. Things get complicated after the mysterious robbers murder a gang lord, and Mr. T has to prevent a war from breaking out. Marvin Gaye's only music score. **105m/C; DVD, Blu-Ray.** Robert Hooks; Paul Winfield; Ralph Waite; William (Bill) Smithers; Paula Kelly; ***D:*** Ivan Dixon; ***W:*** John D.F. Black; ***C:*** Michel Hugo; ***M:*** Marvin Gaye.

The Trouble with Angels 🦴🦴 1/2 **1966 (PG)** Two young girls turn a convent upside down with their endless practical jokes. Russell is everything a Mother Superior should be: understanding, wise, and beautiful. **112m/C; VHS, DVD, Blu-Ray.** Hayley Mills; June Harding; Rosalind Russell; Gypsy Rose Lee; Binnie Barnes; ***D:*** Ida Lupino; ***C:*** Lionel Lindon; ***M:*** Jerry Goldsmith.

The Trouble With Bliss 🦴 1/2 **2011 (PG-13)** Awkward, irksome quirkiness; Douglas Light co-scripted from his novel "East Fifth Bliss." Morris Bliss (Hall) is 35, has no job, no money, and lives with his widowed father (Fonda). He finds his emotional shell cracking when apartment neighbor Andrea (Liu) makes some bold moves as does aggressive 18-year-old Stephanie (Larson), the daughter of a former high school classmate (Henke). **97m/C; DVD.** Michael C. Hall; Brie Larson; Lucy Liu; Brad William Henke; Peter Fonda; Chris Messina; Sarah Shahi; ***D:*** Michael Knowles; ***W:*** Michael Knowles; Douglas Light; ***C:*** Ben Wolf; ***M:*** Daniel Alcheh.

The Trouble with Girls (and How to Get into It) 🦴🦴🦴 *The Chautauqua* **1969 (G)** A 1920s traveling show manager tries to solve a local murder. Not as much singing as his earlier films, but good attention is paid to details. This is definitely one of the better Elvis vehicles. **99m/C; VHS, DVD.** Elvis Presley; Marlyn Mason; Nicole Jaffe; Sheree North; Edward Andrews; John Carradine; Vincent Price; Joyce Van Patten; Dabney Coleman; John Rubinstein; Anthony Teague; Helene Winston; ***D:*** Peter Tewkesbury.

The Trouble with Harry 🦴🦴🦴 **1955 (PG)** When a little boy finds a dead body in a Vermont town, it causes all kinds of problems for the community. No one is sure who killed Harry and what to do with the body. MacLaine's film debut and Herrmann's first musical score for Hitchcock. **90m/C; VHS, DVD, Blu-Ray.** John Forsythe; Shirley MacLaine; Edmund Gwenn; Jerry Mathers; Mildred Dunnock; Mildred Natwick; Royal Dano; ***D:*** Alfred Hitchcock; ***W:*** John Michael Hayes; ***C:*** Robert Burks; ***M:*** Bernard Herrmann.

The Trouble with Romance 🦴 1/2 **2009** Four romantic vignettes (of varying quality) that take place on the same night in the same hotel. Jack freaks when his hottie one-night stand Jill gets the guilts and starts hallucinating visions of her boyfriend. Karen decides to spice up her marriage to Paul by suggesting a menage a trois but she doesn't know that her chosen third has already slept with her hubby. Stephanie breaks up with immature Jimmy when she decides she'll never come first over his stoner friends. Finally, lonely Charlie hires hooker-with-a-heart-of-gold Nicole for what turns out to be conversation rather than sex. **88m/C; DVD.** Kip Pardue; Jennifer Siebel (Newsom); Josie Davis; David Eigenberg; Roger Fan; Emily Liu; Sheetal Sheth; Portia Dawson; Jordan Belfi; ***D:*** Gene Rhee; ***W:*** Gene Rhee; Sharri Hefner; Mike Su; ***C:*** Nathan Wilson; ***M:*** Daniel Cage.

Trouble with the Curve 🦴🦴 **2012 (PG-13)** Eastwood settles into his well-worn khakis in a role that he can knock out of the park in his sleep--another grizzled old-timer who learns a valuable lesson about life in his twilight years. Widower Gus Lobel is one of baseball's all-time best scouts but his age is starting to betray his skills. His estranged daughter Mickey (Adams) joins him on what could be one final scouting trip and the two bond for the first time. Eastwood, Adams, and Timberlake (as another scout) bring a ton of charisma but the abundance of trivial dialogue strikes them all out. **111m/C; DVD, Blu-Ray.** Clint Eastwood; Amy Adams; Justin Timberlake; John Goodman; Matthew Lillard; Ed Lauter; Robert Patrick; Scott Eastwood; ***D:*** Robert Lorenz; ***W:*** Randy Brown; ***C:*** Tom Stern; ***M:*** Marco Beltrami.

The Trouble with the Truth 🦴🦴🦴 **2011 (R)** When Robert (Shea) and Emily's (Thompson) daughter gets engaged, the divorcees have a reunion dinner that sparks the lingering feelings that remain even after 10 years. The two banter while lightly remembering what drove them apart (infidelity on both sides) although writer/director Hemphill resists the obvious despite the chemistry between his middle-aged leads. **96m/C; DVD.** John Shea; Lea Thompson; Danielle Harris; ***D:*** Jim Hemphill; ***W:*** Jim Hemphill; ***C:*** Roberto Correa; ***M:*** Sean Schafer Hennessy.

Troublemakers 🦴 1/2 **1994 (PG)** Travis (Hill) is the fastest gun in the west—but his brother Moses (Spencer) is the country's meanest bounty hunter. But their mother loves them, and wants both her boys home for Christmas. So she leaves it up to Travis to lure Moses back to the homestead. **98m/C; VHS, DVD.** Terence Hill; Bud Spencer; Anne Kasprik; Ruth Buzzi; Ron Carey; ***D:*** Terence Hill; ***W:*** Jess Hill; ***C:*** Carlo Tafani; ***M:*** Pino Donaggio.

Troublemakers: The Story of Land Art 🦴🦴🦴 **2015** A feature-length documentary examination of the land art movement in the late 1960s and early 1970s. In this period, artists created radical, experimental pieces in desolate desert spaces of the American Southwest. Featuring interviews with many leading twentieth century artists, those who took part in the movement, the art they created, and the impact it had are considered. **72m/C; DVD.** ***D:*** James Crump; ***W:*** James Crump; ***C:*** Robert O'Haire; Alexandre Themistocleous; ***M:*** Peter Alargic; Travis Huff.

Troubles 🦴🦴 1/2 **1988** In 1919, Major Brendan Archer arrives on the coast of Wicklow, Ireland to be reunited with his fiancee, Angela Spencer, at the family hotel, the decaying Majestic. Brendan is puzzled by the changes in both the hotel and Angela and begins to turn his interests to her friend, Sarah Devlin, who is a passionate Irish nationalist. But volatile Irish politics puts the romance in danger. Based on the 1970 novel by J.G. Farrell. **208m/C; VHS, DVD.** *GB* Ian Charleson; Ian Richardson; Sean Bean; Emer Gillespie; Susannah Harker; ***D:*** Christopher Morahan; ***W:*** Charles Sturridge. **TV**

The Troubles We've Seen 🦴🦴 1/2 *Veillees d'armes* **1994** Footage of old and recent war coverage and journalist Marcel Ophuls' own work while in Sarajevo is woven together with interviews of various war correspondents to provide an insider's view of the ethical and philosophical difficulties of covering the insanity of war while clinging to one's own precarious grip on sanity. This in-depth documentary explores topics as diverse as a reporter revealing his own opposition to the war he's covering to the dark truth that, as one subject puts it, "the more horrible the situation, the more successful we become." **224m/C; DVD.** ***D:*** Marcel Ophuls; ***W:*** Marcel Ophuls; ***C:*** Pierre Milon; Pierre Boffety.

Troy 🦴🦴 1/2 **2004 (R)** Petersen's epic telling of the Trojan War finally hit the screen after many delays (including Pitt injuring his Achilles tendon, oh the irony!) and budget-busting incidents. Merely inspired by Homer's "The Iliad," it dispenses with all those pesky Greek gods and makes it all about the warriors. When beautiful Helen (Kruger) flees her Spartan husband Menaleus (Gleeson) with pretty-boy lover Paris (Bloom), her greedy brother-in-law Agamemnon (Cox) decides Troy's wealth is worth a little fighting. Arrogant Achilles (Pitt) is persuaded to join in, and while Paris is no fighter, big brother Hector (Bana) is. Naturally, Achilles and Hector will have to go mano-a-mano (in one of the film's best scenes). Also around to show those youngsters what acting's all about is O'Toole as aging King Priam. It's all handled professionally but it's just not terribly compelling. **162m/C; DVD, Blu-Ray, HD-DVD.** *GB* Brad Pitt; Orlando Bloom; Eric Bana; Peter O'Toole; Diane Kruger; Brendan Gleeson; Brian Cox; Sean Bean; Julian Glover; Julie Christie; Saffron Burrows; John Shrapnel; James Cosmo; Rose Byrne; Garrett Hedlund; Nathan Jones; Vincent Regan; Trevor Eve; Tyler Mane; ***D:*** Wolfgang Petersen; ***W:*** David Benioff; ***C:*** Roger Pratt; ***M:*** James Horner.

The Truce 🦴🦴🦴 *La Tregua* **1996** Adaptation of the novel by Primo Levi, based on his true account of traveling home across Europe after the liberation of Auschwitz at the end of WWII. Tells the story of Levi's arduous journey home to Turin through Eastern Europe, as well as his slow rediscovery of life and hope. Has the trappings of a grand historical epic, but works best as a quiet introspective look at a man trying to reclaim his humanity after experiencing unimaginable horror. Flashback scenes in the camp are appropriately harrowing, but the film loses focus when joining Levi and his ragtag compadres on the road home, sometimes slipping into banal sentimentality or outright melodrama, two things a story this powerful doesn't need. Turturro, who committed to the project several years ago, gives the performance of his career, understated and convincing. Levi committed suicide in 1987, shortly after giving Rosi's adaptation his blessing. **117m/C; VHS, DVD.** *IT FR GE SI* John Turturro; Rade Serbedzija; Massimo Ghini; Stefano Dionisi; Teco Celio; Claudio Bisio; Roberto Citran; Andy Luotto; Agnieszka Wagner; ***D:*** Francesco Rosi; ***W:*** Stefano Rulli; Sandro Petraglia; Tonino Guerra; Francesco Rosi; ***C:*** Pasqualino De Santis; Marco Pontecorvo; ***M:*** Luis Bacalov.

Truck Stop Women 🦴🦴 **1974 (R)** Female truckers become involved in smuggling and prostitution at a truck stop. The mob wants a cut of the business and will do anything to get their way. Better than it sounds. **88m/C; VHS, DVD.** Claudia Jennings; Lieux Dressler; John Martino; Dennis Fimple; Dolores Dorn; Gene Drew; Paul Carr; Jennifer Burton; ***D:*** Mark L. Lester.

Truck Turner 🦴 1/2 **1974 (R)** He's a bounty hunter, he's black and he's up against a threadbare plot. Hayes methodically eliminates everyone involved with his partner's murder while providing groovy soundtrack. Quintessential blaxploitation. **91m/C; VHS, DVD, Blu-Ray.** Isaac Hayes; Yaphet Kotto; Annazette Chase; Nichelle Nichols; Scatman Crothers; Dick Miller; ***D:*** Jonathan Kaplan; ***W:*** Leigh Chapman; ***C:*** Charles F. Wheeler; ***M:*** Isaac Hayes.

Trucker 🦴🦴 **2008 (R)** Diane Ford (Monaghan) is a foul-mouthed, independent loner who works as a long-haul trucker. She unexpectedly (and unwillingly) needs to change her life when her estranged 11-year-old son Peter (Bennett) comes to live with her because his dad Leonard (Bratt) is in the hospital with cancer. Peter is as profane and angry at the situation as his birth mother, who hasn't willingly seen him in years, so the kid has abandonment issues as well. They learn to tolerate each other but don't expect any big bonding, touchy-feely scenes. **90m/C; On Demand.** Michelle Monaghan; Jimmy Bennett; Benjamin Bratt; Nathan Fillion; Joey Lauren Adams; Bryce Johnson; ***D:*** James Mottern; ***W:*** James Mottern; ***C:*** Lawrence Sher; ***M:*** Mychael Danna.

Trucker's Woman 🦴 **1975 (R)** Man takes a job driving an 18-wheel truck in order to find the murderers of his father. **90m/C; VHS, DVD.** Michael Hawkins; Mary Cannon; ***D:*** Will Zens.

Trucks 🦴🦴 **1997 (R)** A group of residents are terrorized by driverless trucks going on a rampage through their small town, which happens to be located in Area 51. Based on the short story by Stephen King and previously filmed as 1986's "Maximum Overdrive." **99m/C; VHS, DVD.** Timothy Busfield; Brenda Bakke; Brendan Fletcher; Jay Brazeau; Amy Stewart; ***D:*** Chris Thomson; ***W:*** Brian Taggert; ***C:*** Rob Draper; Keith Holland; ***M:*** Michael Richard Plowman. **CABLE**

True Believer 🦴🦴 1/2 **1989 (R)** Cynical lawyer, once a '60s radical, now defends rich drug dealers. Spurred on by a young protege, he takes on the hopeless case of imprisoned Asian-American accused of gang-slaying. Tense thriller with good cast. **103m/C; VHS, DVD, Blu-Ray.** James Woods; Robert Downey, Jr.; Yuji Okumoto; Margaret Colin; Kurtwood Smith; Tom Bower; Miguel Fernandes; Charles Hallahan; ***D:*** Joseph Ruben; ***W:*** Wesley Strick; ***C:*** John Lindley; ***M:*** Brad Fiedel.

True Blood 🦴🦴 **1989 (R)** A man returns to his home turf to save his brother from the same ruthless gang who set him up for a cop's murder. **100m/C; VHS, DVD.** Chad Lowe; Jeff Fahey; Sherilyn Fenn; ***D:*** Peter Maris.

True Blue 🦴🦴 **2001 (R)** Rem Macy (Berenger) is supposed to be a seasoned NYPD detective. So why does he behave like a hormonally challenged rookie? He's investigating a severed hand found floating in a Central Park pond that turns out to belong to the roommate of Nikki (Heuring). Nikki begs protection from Macy and he lets her stay in his apartment—which the Hound is sure is standard police procedure. Naturally, this is a really dumb move. **101m/C; VHS, DVD.** Tom Berenger; Lori Heuring; Barry Newman; Pamela Gidley; Soon-Teck Oh; Richard Chevolleau; Leo Lee; ***D:*** J.S. Cardone; ***W:*** J.S. Cardone; ***C:*** Darko Suvak; ***M:*** Timothy S. (Tim) Jones. **VIDEO**

True Colors 🦴🦴 **1991 (R)** Law school buddies take divergent paths in post grad real world. Straight and narrow Spader works for Justice Department while dropout Cusack manipulates friends and acquaintances to further his position as Senator's aid. Typecast, predictable and, moralizing. **111m/C; VHS, DVD.** John Cusack; James Spader; Imogen Stubbs; Mandy Patinkin; Richard Widmark; Paul Guilfoyle; Dina Merrill; Philip Bosco; Brad Sullivan; Don McManus; ***D:*** Herbert Ross.

True Confession 🦴🦴 1/2 **1937** Because he's so honest, lawyer Kenneth Bartlett (MacMurray) isn't financially successful and his aspiring writer wife Helen (Lombard) secretly gets a job. Unfortunately, it's for a rich lech who gets murdered and Helen becomes the prime suspect. Thanks to her overactive imagination (and habitual lying) she allows Ken to believe she's guilty but he decides to prove self-defense at her trial. It's a comedy but Helen's behavior really isn't very funny though Lombard sells it for all she's worth. **85m/B; DVD.** Carole Lombard; Fred MacMurray; John Barrymore; Una Merkel; Edgar Kennedy; Porter Hall; John Murray; Fritz Feld; Hattie McDaniel; ***D:*** Wesley Ruggles; ***W:*** Claude Binyon; ***C:*** Ted Tetzlaff; ***M:*** Frederick "Friedrich" Hollander.

True Confessions 🦴🦴🦴 **1981 (R)** Tale of corruption pits two brothers, one a priest and the other a detective, against each other. Nice 1940s period look, with excellent performances from De Niro and Duvall. Based on a true case from the Gregory Dunne novel. **110m/C; VHS, DVD, Blu-Ray.** Robert De Niro; Robert Duvall; Kenneth McMillan; Charles Durning; Cyril Cusack; Ed Flanders; Burgess Meredith; Louisa Moritz; ***D:*** Ulu Grosbard; ***W:*** John Gregory Dunne; Joan Didion; ***C:*** Owen Roizman; ***M:*** Georges Delerue.

True Confessions of a Hollywood Starlet 🦴🦴 1/2 **2008** Amusing Lifetime showbiz dramedy. Bratty teen Morgan Carter (Levesque) is a singer/actress whose success has led to completely out-of-control behavior. One drink too many lands her in rehab and then her worried mom (Boyd) sends Morgan to her Aunt Trudy (Bertinelli), who lives in Fort Wayne, Indiana. Morgan is supposed to learn how to live like a normal teenager in the boring Midwest, but she's not going to make it easy on anyone, including herself. **87m/C; DVD.** Joanna "JoJo" Levesque; Valerie Bertinelli; Lynda Boyd; Justin Louis; Ian Nelson; Shenae Grimes; ***D:*** Tim Matheson; ***W:*** Elisa Bell; ***C:*** David Herrington; ***M:*** David Schwartz. **CABLE**

True Crime 🦴🦴 1/2 *Dangerous Kiss* **1995 (R)** High school student turns detective when a classmate is killed, hooks up with a police cadet, and finds herself on the trail of a serial killer. **94m/C; VHS, DVD.** Alicia Silverstone; Kevin Dillon; Bill Nunn; Michael Bowen; ***D:*** Pat Verducci; ***W:*** Pat Verducci; ***C:*** Chris Squires; ***M:*** Blake Leyh.

True Crime 🦴🦴 1/2 **1999 (R)** Eastwood, who directs and stars, does a good job developing his character Steve Everett, a flawed reporter who has boozed and womanized his way out of the top of his profession. He is given the assignment to interview death row inmate Frank Beachum (Washington), who is scheduled to die in 24 hours. Everett becomes convinced that Beachum is innocent, and the plot erodes into a trite race against time to save the innocent man. Clint shows his acting chops before the story deflates, however, and his fans will certainly enjoy this one. **127m/C; VHS, DVD, Blu-Ray.** Clint Eastwood; James Woods; Isaiah Washington, IV; Denis Leary; Frances Fisher; Diane Venora; Mary McCormack; Lisa Gay Hamilton; Bernard Hill; Michael McKean; Michael Jeter; Hattie Winston; Laila Robins; Christine Ebersole; Anthony Zerbe; John Finn; Marissa Ribisi; Erik King; Graham Beckel; Sydney Tamiia Poitier; Penny Rae Bridges; Jack Kehler; ***D:*** Clint Eastwood; ***W:*** Larry Gross; Paul Brickman; Stephen Schiff; ***C:*** Jack N. Green; ***M:*** Lennie Niehaus.

True Friends 🦴🦴 **1998 (R)** Amateurish but earnest effort by the three lead actors (who also wrote, directed, and produced in various combinations). In 1980, three 12-year-old Bronx buddies witness local mob boss, Big Tony, kill a man. They've stayed friends and kept the secret for 15 years but now the crime comes back to haunt them. **98m/C; VHS, DVD.** James Quattrochi; Loreto Mauro; Rodrigo Botero; Dan Lauria; MacKenzie Phillips; John Capodice; Peter Onorati; Bertila Damas; Leo Rossi; ***D:*** James Quattrochi; ***W:*** James Quattrochi; Rodrigo Botero; ***C:*** Jeff Baustert; ***M:*** Charles Dayton.

True Grit 🦴🦴🦴 **1969 (G)** Hard-drinking U.S. Marshal Rooster Cogburn (Wayne) is hired by a young girl (Darby) to find her father's killer. Won Wayne his only Oscar. Based on the Charles Portis novel. Prompted sequel, "Rooster Cogburn." **128m/C; VHS, DVD, Blu-Ray.** John Wayne; Glen Campbell; Kim Darby; Robert Duvall; Jeremy Slate; Dennis Hopper; Alfred Ryder; Strother Martin; Jeff Corey; Ron Soble; John Fiedler; James Westerfield; John Doucette; Donald Woods; Edith Atwater; Carlos Rivas; Wilford Brimley; Jay Silverheels; Hank Worden; ***D:*** Henry Hathaway; ***W:*** Marguerite Roberts; ***C:*** Lucien Ballard; ***M:*** Elmer Bernstein. Oscars '69: Actor (Wayne); Golden Globes '70: Actor--Drama (Wayne).

True Grit 🦴🦴🦴 1/2 **2010 (PG-13)** Remake of the 1969 film by the Coen brothers, who stay closer to Charles Portis' elegiac 1968 novel. Fourteen-year-old Mattie Ross (Steinfeld) is determined to bring Tom Chaney (Brolin), her father's killer, to justice. She teams up with fat, aging, one-eyed, drunken Marshal Rooster Cogburn (Bridges) and reward-minded Texas Ranger LaBoeuf (Damon) to track Chaney into hostile Indian territory. If Bridges can't eradicate the memory of Oscar-winning John Wayne as Rooster, he more than holds his own with the trigger-happy character itself, and Steinfeld, in her film debut, is a real find as the feisty, revenge-oriented Mattie. **110m/C; Blu-Ray, On Demand.** Hailee Steinfeld; Jeff Bridges; Matt Damon; Josh Brolin; Barry Pepper; Domhnall Gleeson; Ed Corbin; Elizabeth Marvel; Bruce Green; Paul Rae; Dakin Matthews; Brian Brown; Nicholas Sadler; ***D:*** Joel Coen; Ethan Coen; ***W:*** Joel Coen; Ethan Coen; ***C:*** Roger Deakins; ***M:*** Carter Burwell. British Acad. '10: Cinematog.

True Heart 🦴🦴 1/2 **1997 (PG)** Bonnie (Dunst) and brother Sam (Bryan) are lost in the British Columbian wilderness after surviving a plane crash. They are befriended by a Native American elder (Schellenberg), who guides them through the dangers and back to civilization. Corny dialogue and beautiful scenery. **92m/C; VHS, DVD.** Kirsten Dunst; Zachery Ty Bryan; August Schellenberg; Dey Young; Michael Gross; ***D:*** Catherine Cyran; ***W:*** Catherine Cyran; ***C:*** Christopher Baffa; ***M:*** Eric Allaman.

True Heart Susie 🦴🦴 1/2 **1919** A simple, moving story about a girl who is in love with a man who marries another girl from the city. Silent. **87m/B; Silent; VHS, DVD.** Lillian Gish; Robert "Bobbie" Harron; ***D:*** D.W. Griffith.

True History of the Kelly Gang 🦴🦴 **2020 (R)** After a traumatic, desperate childhood, anti-authoritarian Ned Kelly (MacKay), of Irish lineage, learns how to be an itinerant robber in nineteenth century Australia under the guidance of Harry Power (Crowe). Forming his own gang with members of his sometimes abusive family, Ned and his group have numerous run-ins with the Victorian police and the Kelly family. When Ned declares war on the Australian colonial police, violence ensues. The bloody western stays true to the real life Kelly gang while exploring intense issues related to colonization, poverty, personal brokenness, and societal roles and expectations. **124m/C; DVD.** George MacKay; Ben Corbett; Orlando Schwerdt; Charlie Hunnam; Essie Davis; ***D:*** Justin Kurzel; ***W:*** Shaun Grant; ***C:*** Ari Wegner; ***M:*** Justin Kurzel.

True Lies 🦴🦴 1/2 **1994 (R)** Brain candy with a bang offers eye popping special effects and a large dose of unbelievability. Sort of like a big screen "Scarecrow and Mrs. King" as supposed computer salesman Harry Trasker (Ah-nuld) keeps his spy work secret from mousy, neglected and bored wife Helen (Curtis), who has a few secrets of her own and inadvertantly ends up right in the thick of things. Raunchy and extremely sexist, but not without charm; the stupidity is part of the fun. Perfectly cast sidekick Arnold holds his own as a pig, but Heston is wasted as the head honcho. Tons of special effects culiminate in a smashing finish. Very loosely adapted from the 1991 French comedy "La Total." **114m/C; VHS, DVD.** Arnold Schwarzenegger; Jamie Lee Curtis; Tom Arnold; Bill Paxton; Tia Carrere; Art Malik; Eliza Dushku; Charlton Heston; Grant Heslov; ***D:*** James Cameron; ***W:*** James Cameron; ***C:*** Russell Carpenter; ***M:*** Brad Fiedel. Golden Globes '95: Actress--Mus./Comedy (Curtis); Blockbuster '96: Action Actress, V. (Curtis).

True Love 🦴🦴🦴 **1989 (R)** Low-budget, savagely observed comedy follows the family and community events leading up to a Bronx Italian wedding. Authentic slice-of-life about two young people with very different ideas about what marriage and commitment mean. Acclaimed script and performances. **104m/C; VHS, DVD.** Annabella Sciorra; Ron Eldard; Aida Turturro; Roger Rignack; Michael J. Wolfe; Star Jasper; Kelly Cinnante; Rick Shapiro; Suzanne Costallos; Vincent Pastore; ***D:*** Nancy Savoca; ***W:*** Nancy Savoca; Richard Guay; ***C:*** Lisa Rinzler. Sundance '89: Grand Jury Prize.

True Romance 🦴🦴 1/2 **1993 (R)** Geeky Clarence (Slater) and wide-eyed call girl Alabama (Arquette) meet and fall instantly in love (and marriage). The inept duo inadvertantly steals her pimp's coke and they head to L.A. with the mob in pursuit. Gem performances in small roles include Walken's icily debonair mafioso; Clarence's dad (Hopper), an ex-cop who runs afoul of Walken; Pitt's space-case druggie; Oldman's crazed pimp; and the ghost of Elvis (Kilmer), whom Clarence talks to in times of stress. Horrific violence mixed with very black humor clicks most of the time. Tarantino helped finance "Reservior Dogs" when he sold this script, his first. Unrated version also available. **116m/C; VHS, DVD, Blu-Ray, UMD.** Christian Slater; Patricia Arquette; Gary Oldman; Brad Pitt; Val Kilmer; Dennis Hopper; Christopher Walken; Samuel L. Jackson; Christopher Penn; Bronson Pinchot; Michael Rapaport; Saul Rubinek; Conchata Ferrell; James Gandolfini; Tom Sizemore; Ed Lauter; Maria Pitillo; Gregory Sporleder; Kevin Corrigan; Michael Beach; Frank Adonis; Victor Argo; Paul Ben-Victor; Paul Bates; ***D:*** Tony Scott; ***W:*** Quentin Tarantino; ***C:*** Jeffrey L. Kimball; ***M:*** Hans Zimmer; Mark Mancina.

True Stories 🦴🦴🦴 1/2 **1986 (PG)** Quirky, amusing look at the eccentric denizens of a fictional, off-center Texas town celebrating its 150th anniversary. Notable are Kurtz as the Laziest Woman in America and Goodman as a blushing suitor. Directorial debut of Byrne. Worth a look. **89m/C; VHS, DVD, Blu-Ray.** David Byrne; John Goodman; Swoosie Kurtz; Spalding Gray; Annie McEnroe; Pops Staples; Tito Larriva; Alix Elias; Scott Valentine; Jo Harvey Allen; ***D:*** David Byrne; ***W:*** David Byrne; Beth Henley; Stephen Tobolowsky; ***C:*** Edward Lachman; ***M:*** David Byrne.

True Story 🦴🦴 **2015 (R)** A great performance by Franco can barely be seen in a film that alternates between over- and under-direction on the part of Goold. The filmmaker never gets a grip on why he's telling this odd story of a man named Christian Longo (Franco) who ended up on the FBI's Most Wanted list after killing his family, only to be found hiding under the pseudonym of Michael Finkel, who happened to be a real reporter (Hill) for the New York Times. The real Finkel interviews Longo, trying to figure why he took his identity. Based on Finkel's memoir. **100m/C; DVD, Blu-Ray.** Jonah Hill; James Franco; Felicity Jones; Maria Dizzia; Ethan Suplee; ***D:*** Rupert Goold; ***W:*** Rupert Goold; ***C:*** Masanobu Takayanagi; ***M:*** Marco Beltrami.

The True Story of Jesse James 🦴🦴 1/2 **1957** Ray's brisk-but-bland remake of 1939's "Jesse James" covers the last 18 years of the outlaw's life and is no more true than other film versions. Jesse (Wagner) and brother Frank (Hunter) find post-Civil War life difficult as unrepentent southern sympathizers and take to the outlaw life to survive. Ray does emphasize a theme of youthful rebellion turning to bitterness. **92m/C; DVD, Blu-Ray.** Robert Wagner; Jeffrey Hunter; Hope Lange; Agnes Moorehead; Alan Hale, Jr.; John Carradine; Frank Gorshin; ***D:*** Nicholas Ray; ***W:*** Walter Newman; ***C:*** Joseph Macdonald; ***M:*** Leigh Harline.

True Women 🦴🦴 1/2 **1997 (PG-13)** Sarah McClure (Delany) leaves Georgia with husband Bartlett (Boothe), settles in Texas, and raises her orphaned sister Euphemia (Majorino and Gish), as well as her own family, while Bartlett's off being a Texas Ranger. Euphemia's eventually reunited with her best friend, southern plantation beauty Georgia (Jolie), who's trying to hide the fact that she's part-Cherokee. The ladies suffer through Comanche attacks, the Alamo and the Mexican Army, the Civil War, Reconstruction, and various romantic trials and tribulations, all while being gosh-darn heroic. TV miniseries based on the historical novel by Janice Woods Windle. **170m/C; VHS, DVD.** Dana Delany; Annabeth Gish; Angelina Jolie; Powers Boothe; Tina Majorino; Rachael Leigh Cook; Jeffrey Nordling; Michael Greyeyes; Tony Todd; Terrence Mann; Michael York; Salli Richardson-Whitfield; Irene Bedard; Charles S. Dutton; Julie Carmen; Matthew Glave; John Schneider; ***D:*** Karen Arthur; ***W:*** Christopher Lofton; ***C:*** Thomas Neuwirth; ***M:*** Bruce Broughton. **TV**

Truly, Madly, Deeply 🦴🦴🦴 **1991 (PG)** The recent death of her lover Jamie (Rickman) drives Nina (Stevenson) into despair and anger, until he turns up at her apartment one day. And decides to bring some of his ghostly buddies and hang out. Tender and well written tale of love and the supernatural, with believable characters and plot-line. Playwright Minghella's directorial debut. **107m/C; VHS, DVD.** *GB* Juliet Stevenson; Alan Rickman; Bill Paterson; Michael Maloney; Christopher Rozycki; Keith Bartlett; David Ryall; Stella Maris; ***D:*** Anthony Minghella; ***W:*** Anthony Minghella; ***C:*** Remi Adefarasin; ***M:*** Barrington Pheloung. Australian Film Inst. '92: Foreign Film; British Acad. '91: Orig. Screenplay.

Truman 🦴🦴 1/2 **1995 (PG)** Cable bio follows "Give 'em Hell" Harry (Sinise) from 1917 to 1968. The 33rd U.S. President, derided as a political hack, was determined to prove himself against the odds and by making the tough decisions, including authorizing use of the A-bomb on Japan. Sinise gives the appropriate no-nonsense performance, matched by Scarwid as ever-loyal wife Bess. Based on David McCullough's Pulitzer Prize-winning book. **135m/C; VHS, DVD.** Gary Sinise; Diana Scarwid; Colm Feore; Richard Dysart; James Gammon; Tony Goldwyn; Pat Hingle; Harris Yulin; Leo Burmester; Zeljko Ivanek; David Lansbury; Marian Seldes; Lois Smith; Richard Venture; Daniel von Bargen; ***D:*** Frank Pierson; ***W:*** Thomas (Tom) Rickman; ***C:*** Paul Elliott; ***M:*** David Mansfield. **CABLE**

The Truman Show 🦴🦴🦴🦴 **1998 (PG)** Flawless execution of an eerie, yet fantastical premise, marked by outstanding performances, make this surreal fable a joy to watch from start to finish. Unbeknownst to insurance salesman Truman Burbank, (Carrey) his entire life has been broadcast live on TV in a 24-hour soap opera. When evidence of Truman's fabricated life begins to surface, he plans his escape, upsetting the grand scheme of producer, director and charismatic artist Christof (Harris in a stand-out performance). Carrey's sympathetic, low-key portrayal will make people forget the disappointment of "Cable Guy." Weir handles his satirical theme with craftmen-like precision, never letting his commentary on the power of the tube become too heavy-handed. Carrey reportedly took a pay cut from his $20 million fee in order to star. **102m/C; VHS, DVD, Blu-Ray.** Jim Carrey; Ed Harris; Laura Linney; Noah Emmerich; Natascha (Natasha) McElhone; Holland Taylor; Paul Giamatti; Philip Baker Hall; Brian Delate; Una Damon; ***D:*** Peter Weir; ***W:*** Andrew Niccol; ***C:*** Peter Biziou; ***M:*** Philip Glass; Burkhard Dallwitz. British Acad. '98: Director (Weir), Orig. Screenplay; Golden Globes '99: Actor--Drama (Carrey), Score, Support. Actor (Harris); MTV Movie Awards '99: Male Perf. (Carrey); Natl. Bd. of Review '98: Support. Actor (Harris).

Trumbo 🦴🦴🦴 1/2 **2007 (PG-13)** Dalton Trumbo was one of Hollywood's most fierce, original, and ultimately tarnished screenwriters of the 1950's. Blacklisted by the House Un-American Activities Committee, he was forced to pen scripts under a pseudonym and fake identity, winning an Oscar in the process. Based on his son Christopher's play of the same title, this first-hand account documents his days in the limelight and under the microscope, with Nathan Lane reprising his stage role, but oddly includes eight other actors, reading excerpts from a 1999 volume of Trumbo's collected letters, "Additional Dialogue." Nothing new to Hollywood historians and old-time fans, yet a fascinating examination of a dark period in America. **96m/C; On Demand.** ***D:*** Peter Askin; ***W:*** Christopher Trumbo; ***C:*** Frank Prinzi; Jonathan Furmanski; Fred Murphy; Christopher Norr; ***M:*** Robert Miller.

Trumbo 🦴🦴 1/2 **2015 (R)** Biopic of Dalton Trumbo (Cranston), a mid-twentieth century screenwriter who was blackballed from Hollywood because of his Communist leanings. The dependable Cranston steals the show as he perfectly captures his subject, even if the rest of the film falters somewhat around him. Director Roach's period piece feels hollow despite the strength and determination of the man it's about. **124m/C; DVD, Blu-Ray.** Bryan Cranston; Adewale Akinnuoye-Agbaje; Diane Lane; Elle Fanning; Dame Helen Mirren; ***D:*** Jay Roach; ***W:*** John McNamara; ***C:*** Jim Denault; ***M:*** Theodore Shapiro.

The Trumpet of the Swan 🦴 1/2 **2001 (G)** Disappointing animated adaptation of E.B. White's 1970 children's book has Louis, a mute trumpeter swan, trying to overcome his disability. Louis befriends a human boy who persuades him to learn to read and write, which doesn't help him much in the animal world, but brings him fame in the human one. His father, distraught over his son's "defect," steals a trumpet for him, and Louis learns to play, becoming famous enough to assuage his father's guilt over the theft by paying for the instrument. The animation, story, and (surprisingly) the score, all seem flat, while the script provides nothing in the way of magic. Only the youngest (under 5) of viewers will be distracted, but probably not for very long. **75m/C; VHS, DVD.** ***V:*** Dee Bradley Baker; Jason Alexander; Mary Steenburgen; Reese Witherspoon; Seth Green; Carol Burnett; Joe Mantegna; Sam Gifaldi; ***D:*** Richard Rich; Terry L. Noss; ***W:*** Judy Rothman Rofe; ***M:*** Marcus Miller.

Trust 🦴🦴 **1990 (R)** An obnoxious girl, tossed out by her family after becoming pregnant, forms a loving bond with a strange, possibly deranged guy from an abusive household. Similar in style and theme to Hartley's "The Unbelievable Truth"?a peculiar sardonic comedy/drama not for every taste. **107m/C; DVD, Blu-Ray.** Adrienne Shelly; Martin Donovan; Merritt Nelson; Edie Falco; John MacKay; Marko Hunt; ***D:*** Hal Hartley; ***W:*** Hal Hartley; ***C:*** Michael Spiller; ***M:*** Phil Reed. Sundance '91: Screenplay.

Trust 🦴🦴 1/2 **2010 (R)** Director Schwimmer restrains from exploiting the topic of Internet predators but he tips towards melodrama. Fourteen-year-old Annie Cameron (striking debut for Liberato) falls for the online chat blandishments of alleged teenager Charlie and agrees to a meeting—only to greet a 30-something man. What happens next is predictable and soon becomes a police matter with Annie in denial and her parents (Keener, Owen) devastated. **106m/C; Blu-Ray, On Demand.** Clive Owen; Catherine Keener; Liana Liberato; Viola Davis; Chris Henry Coffey; Jason Clarke; Noah Emmerich; Spencer Curnutt; *D:* David Schwimmer; *W:* Andy Bellin; Rob Festinger; *C:* Andrzej Sekula; *M:* Nathan Larson.

The Trust 1/2 **2016 (R)** Las Vegas cops David Waters (Cage) and Jim Stone (Wood) are broke and disengaged with their jobs. When Waters discovers that a local drug dealer has a large stash of money in his apartment, the pair decides to perform a robbery. Of course, there's no movie if that robbery goes as planned. Cage gives a more subtle performance than usual, but that actually makes the movie less interesting, not more. There's just not enough meat on these bones, even with a Jerry Lewis cameo. **106m/C; DVD, Blu-Ray.** Nicolas Cage; Elijah Wood; Sky Ferreira; Eric Heister; Ethan Suplee; *D:* Alex Brewer; Benjamin Brewer; *W:* Benjamin Brewer; Adam Hirsch; *C:* Sean Porter; *M:* Reza Safinia.

Trust Me **2013 (R)** Inside take on former child actor Howard Holloway (Gregg), now a kids' talent agent, who goes for broke to represent 13-year-old Hollywood newcomer Lydia (Sharbino). Desperately losing his grip on the business, this final plunge with the sharks pits him against a producer (Huffman), a casting director (Janney), and a rival agent (Rockwell). A valiant effort from second-time director-writer-star Gregg, with solid acting and comic timing, but the trust he sets up early on starts to unravel once Lydia's boozing dad staggers onto the scene. What starts out witty and charming, descends into dark family dysfunction without reason. **90m/C; On Demand.** Clark Gregg; Saxon Sharbino; Paul Sparks; Sam Rockwell; Felicity Huffman; Amanda Peet; Allison Janney; *D:* Clark Gregg; *W:* Clark Gregg; *C:* Terry Stacey; *M:* Mark Kilian.

Trust the Man **2006 (R)** Relationship flick finds two Manhattan couples whining and dining in local eateries complaining about each other. Successful actress Rebecca (Moore, real-life wife of director Freundlich) is married to sex-addict stay-at-home dad Tom (Duchovny), and Elaine (Gyllenhaal) is an aspiring writer and live-in girlfriend of Rebecca's brother Tobey (Crudup), a commitment-phobic but cute schlub. Everyone ponders the state of their unions while dabbling in infidelity and self-pity, and despite a few too many moments that are cloying, cliched, or contrived, the leads are good and make things watchable. Tom and Rebecca's two kids are played by Moore and Freundlich's real offspring. **103m/C; DVD.** Julianne Moore; David Duchovny; Billy Crudup; Maggie Gyllenhaal; Garry Shandling; Eva Mendes; Ellen Barkin; James LeGros; Liam Broggy; Dagmara Dominczyk; Justin Bartha; *D:* Bart Freundlich; *W:* Bart Freundlich; *C:* Tim Orr; *M:* Clint Mansell.

The Truth 1/2 **2010** Wealthy Jonathan Davenport and his trophy wife Dana have their home invaded by crazy Gabriel, who ties them up and starts asking questions that have nothing to do with robbing them. Flashbacks show a troubled younger Gabriel who may share a past with both Davenports. Not quite as predictable a thriller as might be imagined but nothing special either. **96m/C; DVD.** John Heard; Erin Cardillo; Brendan Sexton, III; Daniel Baldwin; Erica Shaffer; *D:* Ryan Barton-Grimley; *W:* Ryan Barton-Grimley; *C:* Eric Adkins; *M:* Adrien Capozzi. **VIDEO**

Truth **2015 (R)** James Vanderbilt's well-intentioned drama struggles through too much telling and not enough showing, as the writer/director amplifies its melodrama with fake-sounding speeches and moral proclamations. Cate Blanchett stars as Mary Mapes, the producer of 60 Minutes II, who was embroiled in a controversy when she spearheaded a segment about then-candidate George W. Bush's questionable time in the National Guard. In the end, enough questions about the legitimacy of documents used in the segment cost Mapes and Dan Rather (an effective Robert Redford) their jobs although Vanderbilt argues successfully that politics clouded the heart of the issue—that the story was probably true regardless. **125m/C; DVD, Blu-Ray.** Cate Blanchett; Robert Redford; Topher Grace; Dennis Quaid; Elisabeth Moss; Bruce Greenwood; *D:* James Vanderbilt; *W:* James Vanderbilt; *C:* Mandy Walker; *M:* Brian Tyler.

The Truth about Cats and Dogs **1996 (PG-13)** Funny, intelligent Abby (Garofalo) hosts a popular radio call-in show for pet lovers. When a handsome Brit photographer (Chaplin) phones in with a Great Dane problem, he becomes intrigued by her voice, and asks for a date. Insecure about her looks, Abby asks her beautiful-but-dim girlfriend Noelle (Thurman) to fill in. Naturally, both women fall for the shy Englishman. Charming, updated version of "Cyrano de Bergerac" theme works because of strong lead performances, especially Garofalo, who steals the show with her dry, self-effacing wit. Entertaining romantic comedy features some nice scenes of Santa Monica, too. **97m/C; VHS, DVD, Blu-Ray.** Janeane Garofalo; Uma Thurman; Ben Chaplin; Jamie Foxx; Richard Coca; Stanley DeSantis; Bob Odenkirk; *D:* Michael Lehmann; *W:* Audrey Wells; *C:* Robert Brinkmann; *M:* Howard Shore.

The Truth About Charlie 1/2 **2002 (PG-13)** Jonathan Demme's remake of the Cary Grant-Audrey Hepburn vehicle "Charade" has the same Paris setting and convoluted plot, but not much of the carefree attitude of the original. Regina (Newton) comes home from a vacation and finds that her husband Charlie has been murdered, and that he was more than he seemed, as the police produce several passports that show Charlie with a different name and disguise. She also discovers that she now has a trio of her husband's former colleagues following her, looking for his hidden six million dollars. As an homage to the French New Wave cinema that was blooming when the original was filmed, Demme includes cameos of several luminaries of the genre. **104m/C; VHS, DVD.** Mark Wahlberg; Thandie Newton; Tim Robbins; Joong-Hoon Park; Ted Levine; Lisa Gay Hamilton; Christine Boisson; Stephen (Dillon) Dillane; *Cameo(s):* Charles Aznavour; Anna Karina; *D:* Jonathan Demme; *W:* Jonathan Demme; Stephen Schmidt; Jessica Bendinger; *C:* Tak Fujimoto; *M:* Rachel Portman.

The Truth About Emanuel 1/2 *Eamanuel and the Truth About Fishes* **2013** Sullen teen Emanuel (Scodelario) lashes out at everyone around her until she meets new neighbor Linda (Biel). Emanuel offers to babysit her infant daughter as an excuse to hang out the woman who looks like Emanuel's deceased mom. A ridiculous secret is revealed as Linda turns out to be living a fantasy the self-dramatizing teen vows to protect. It's not terribly convincing. **96m/C; Blu-Ray, On Demand.** Kaya Scodelario; Jessica Biel; Frances O'Connor; Alfred Molina; Aneurin Barnard; Jimmi Simpson; *D:* Francesca Gregorini; *W:* Francesca Gregorini; *C:* Polly Morgan; *M:* Nathan Larson.

The Truth About Jane 1/2 **2000** Fifteen-year-old Jane (Muth) is experiencing her first love. Unfortunately for her family and friends, it's with another girl and they just can't cope. Her mom, Janice (Channing), is especially upset and may lose Jane if she can't find a way to accept her. **91m/C; VHS, DVD.** Stockard Channing; Ellen Muth; James Naughton; RuPaul Charles; Noah Fleiss; Kelly Rowan; Jenny O'Hara; Alicia Lagano; *D:* Lee Rose; *W:* Lee Rose; *C:* Eric Van Haren Noman; *M:* Terence Blanchard. **CABLE**

The Truth About Love **2004** Prudish and plain nurse Alice (Hewitt) gets an anonymous Valentine's Day card and assumes it's meant for her philandering husband. Alice and sister Felicity (Miles) conspire, cooking up their own anonymous love letter to Alice's husband Sam (Mistry) in hopes of proving his infidelity. Twists and turns are plentiful in the Brit love caper along the lines of Bridget Jones or Love Actually. **90m/C; VHS, DVD.** *GB* Jennifer Love Hewitt; Kate Miles; Jimi Mistry; Dougray Scott; Branka Katic; *D:* John Hay; *W:* John Hay; Peter Blore; William Johnston; Rik Carmichael; *C:* Graham Frake; *M:* Debbie Wiseman. **VIDEO**

The Truth About Youth 1/2 **1930** Richard Carewe (Tearle) is pushing for a marriage between his ward, also named Richard (Manners), and his housekeeper's daughter Phyllis (Young). Instead, foolish young Dick is enamored of cabaret singer Kara (Loy), who agrees to marry him because she thinks he's rich. Carewe tries to prevent Phyllis from finding out but he's too blind to see that she doesn't want the younger man anyway. **70m/B; DVD.** Conway Tearle; Loretta Young; Myrna Loy; David Manners; J. Farrell MacDonald; *D:* William A. Seiter; *W:* B. Harrison Orkow; *C:* Arthur C. Miller.

Truth Be Told 1/2 **2011** Appealing cast and an "honesty is the best policy" storyline. Marriage counselor Annie Morgan (Cameron Bure) is single and doesn't always follow her own advice, including the part about truthfulness being essential to relationships. She receives a weekend invitation for her and her family from media mogul Terrance Bishop (Cox) and Annie knows it could lead to her own radio show. She persuades an old friend, widowed dad Mark Crane (Elliott), to pretend to be her hubby but the complications just keep piling up. **95m/C; DVD.** Candace Cameron Bure; David James Elliott; Ronny Cox; Chris Brochu; Emma Gould; Michael Sheets; Antonia DeNardo; Belita Moreno; *D:* Jonathan Frakes; *W:* Wesley Bishop; Alan Marc Levy; *C:* Tim Suhrstedt; *M:* Ernest Troost. **TV**

Truth or Consequences, N.M. **1997 (R)** Yes, the name of the town is real. No, Bob Barker is not the mayor. Dim parolee Raymond (Gallo) and his even dimmer girlfriend Addy (Dickens) are reunited and just want to settle down, to tell the truth. Instead, they fall immediately back into a life of crime. Along with their accomplices Marcus (Williamson) and Curtis (Sutherland), they plan to rip off a drug dealer for big bucks (no whammies!). The heist, of course, goes bad; they steal an RV and kidnap its owners Gordon (Pollack) and Donna (Phillips). An attempt to unload the drugs on a powerful Mafia boss (Steiger) also goes awry, and that starts a real family feud. As the mob hit man (Sheen), the cops, and the crooks all converge on the eponymous New Mexico town, everyone is in jeopardy. Not logical, not original and not good. Directorial debut for Sutherland, who should really quit playing coked-up psychopathic murderers. **106m/C; VHS, DVD, Blu-Ray.** Vincent Gallo; Kim Dickens; Kiefer Sutherland; Mykelti Williamson; Grace Phillips; Kevin Pollak; Martin Sheen; Rod Steiger; Rick Rossovich; John C. McGinley; Max Perlich; *D:* Kiefer Sutherland; *W:* Brad Mirman; *C:* Ric Waite; *M:* Jude Cole.

Truth or Dare 1/2 *In Bed with Madonna; Madonna Truth or Dare* **1991 (R)** A quasi-concert-documentary—here is music superstar Madonna tarted up in fact, fiction, and fantasy—exhibitionism to the nth power. Tacky, self-conscious, and ultimately, if you are a Madonna fan, moving. On camera Madonna stings ex-boyfriend Warren Beatty, disses admirer Kevin Costner, quarrels with her father, reminisces, and does sexy things with a bottle. Oh yes, she occasionally sings and dances. Both those who worship and dislike the Material Girl will find much to pick apart here. **118m/C; VHS, DVD, Blu-Ray.** Madonna; *D:* Alek Keshishian.

Truth or Dare *Blumhouse's Truth or Dare* **2018 (PG-13)** A slasher film centered on a twisted game of truth or dare. During a spring break to the beach, a group of college seniors gather for fun before graduation. Intelligent Olivia (Hale) is convinced to come on the trip by her flirty best friend Markie (Beane), who also convinces other friends like leering Ronnie (Lerner) and openly gay Brad (Szeto). Along with attractive Lucas (Posey) and off-putting law student Tyson (Funk), the group plays truth or dare. To survive the game, the players must remain true to themselves. An unfulfilling genre film full of stock characters and expected plotting. **100m/C; DVD, Blu-Ray.** Lucy Kate Hale; Tyler Posey; Violett Beane; Sophia Ali; Nolan Gerard Funk; *D:* Jeff Wadlow; *W:* Jeff Wadlow; Jillian Jacobs; Michael Reisz; Christopher Roach; *C:* Jacques Jouffret; *M:* Matthew Margeson.

Truth or Die *Doing Life* **1986 (PG-13)** This trite, cliched TV movie chronicles the life of convict Jerry Rosenberg, the first prisoner to earn a law degree from his cell. Still, an uncharacteristic role for sitcom guy Danza. Based on Rosenberg's book "Doing Life." **96m/C; VHS, DVD.** Tony Danza; Jon (John) DeVries; Lisa Langlois; Rocco Sisto; *D:* Gene Reynolds.

Tsotsi 1/2 **2005 (R)** Young Tsotsi and his gang of urban thugs pillage their shantytown-turf outside Johannesburg, South Africa. After stealing a BMW from a wealthy black woman, Tsotsi discovers he's also nabbed her infant son in the backseat. The child's affect on this criminal becomes the centerpiece and eventual redemption behind the story. Unpredictable, violent, and compassionate. Director Gavin Hood constructs a world foreign to most Western audiences, in every sense of the word. **94m/C; DVD.** Kenneth Nkosi; Zenzo Ngqobe; Presley Chweneyagae; Terry Pheto; Mothusi Magano; Israel Makoe; Percy Matsemela; Benny Moshe; Nambitha Mpumlwana; Rapulana Seiphemo; Jerry Mofokeng; *D:* Gavin Hood; *W:* Gavin Hood; *C:* Lance Gewer; *M:* Mark Kilian; Paul Hepker. Oscars '05: Foreign Film.

Tube *Tyubeu* **2003 (R)** After suffering a shocking personal loss, police detective Jay (Kim) finds himself relegated to the ranks of subway cop. He toils away until that fateful day when the good-guy-gone-bad (Park) takes control of the train and terrorizes the community, giving Jay the chance to be a hero again and save the day. While the action in director Woon-hak's Seoul-based debut zips along, the effort lacks that "certain something" (like a well-developed plot) that made its obvious inspirations?"Die Hard" and "Speed"?smash hits. Korean, with English subtitles. **112m/C; VHS, DVD.** Seok-hun Kim; Du-na Bae; Sang-min Park; Byeong-ho Son; Oh-jung Gweon; *D:* Woon-hak Baek; *W:* Woon-hak Baek; Weon-mi Byeon; Jeong-min Kim; Min-ju Kim; *C:* Hong-shik Yun; *M:* Sang-jun Hwang. **VIDEO**

Tuck Everlasting 1/2 **2002 (PG)** Director Jay Russell does an admirable job adapting the beloved 1975 children's novel by Natalie Babbitt into a feature film. Winnie (Bledel) is chafing under the strict discipline of her parents, particularly the rule that forbids her from playing in the nearby woods. One day while sneaking into the forbidden forest, she meets Jesse, a boy from the rough and tumble Tuck clan. He tells her not to drink from a certain spring, but immediately after the warning she is abducted by Jesse's brother Miles (Bairstow). At the Tuck residence, Jesse's parents inform her that the spring is a fountain of youth and that she is not allowed to return home with that knowledge. She begins to fall for young Jesse although she discovers that he is actually 104 years old. **90m/C; DVD.** Alexis Bledel; Jonathan Jackson; Sissy Spacek; William Hurt; Scott Bairstow; Ben Kingsley; Amy Irving; Victor Garber; *Nar:* Elisabeth Shue; *D:* Jay Russell; *W:* James V. Hart; Jeffrey Lieber; *C:* James L. Carter; *M:* William Ross.

Tucker & Dale vs. Evil **2010 (R)** Turning the tables on the horror formulas of killer hillbillies in the woods, Tucker (Tudyk) and Dale (Labine) may wear overalls and wield chainsaws but they're nice, average guys, something ignored by the vacationing college kids who stumble across their cabin and mistake them for serial killers. Of course it doesn't help matters when one of kids turns up missing. A clever, manic genre send-up that smashes gore with humor and makes a fun spoof of both slasher flicks and the stereotypes of city kids and country folks. **89m/C; Blu-Ray, On Demand.** *CA* Tyler Labine; Alan Tudyk; Katrina Bowden; Jesse Moss; Brandon Jay McClaren; Christie Laing; Chelan Simmons; Travis Nelson; Philip Granger; *D:* Eli Craig; *W:* Eli Craig; Morgan Jurgenson; *C:* David Geddes; *M:* Michael Shields.

Tucker: The Man and His Dream **1988 (PG)** Portrait of Preston Tucker, entrepreneur and industrial idealist, who in 1946 tried to build the car of the future and was effectively run out of business by the powers-that-were. Ravishing, ultra-nostalgic lullaby to the American Dream. Watch for Jeff's dad, Lloyd, in a bit role. **111m/C; VHS, DVD, Blu-Ray.** Jeff Bridges; Martin Landau; Dean Stockwell; Frederic Forrest; Mako; Joan Allen; Christian Slater; Lloyd Bridges; Elias Koteas; Nina Siemaszko; Corin "Corky" Nemec; Marshall Bell; Don Novello; Peter Donat; Dean Goodman; Patti Austin; *D:* Francis Ford Coppola; *W:* Arnold Schulman; David Seidler; *M:* Joe Jackson; Carmine Coppola. Golden Globes '89: Support. Actor (Landau); N.Y. Film Critics '88: Support. Actor (Stockwell).

Tuesdays with Morrie 1/2 **1999** Detroit sportswriter Mitch Albom (Azaria) spots his old college prof, 78-year-old Morrie

Schwartz (Lemmon), on ABC's "Nightline" discussing his battle with ALS and his thoughts on death. The workaholic Albom, who has not seen Morrie in 16 years, decides to pay his one-time mentor a visit in Boston. The relationship rekindles and they begin to meet every Tuesday, with Albom coming to question the path his life is taking. Based on Albom's best-selling book. **89m/C; VHS, DVD.** Jack Lemmon; Hank Azaria; John Carroll Lynch; Wendy Moniz; Bonnie Bartlett; Caroline Aaron; Aaron Lustig; Bruce Nozick; ***D:*** Mick Jackson; ***W:*** Thomas (Tom) Rickman; ***C:*** Theo van de Sande; ***M:*** Marco Beltrami. **TV**

Tuff Turf 🦴🦴 **1985 (R)** The new kid in town must adjust to a different social lifestyle and a new set of rules when his family is forced to move to a low-class section of Los Angeles. He makes enemies immediately when he courts the girlfriend of one of the local toughs. Fast-paced with a bright young cast. Music by Jim Carroll, Lene Lovich, and Southside Johnny. **113m/C; VHS, DVD, Blu-Ray.** James Spader; Kim Richards; Paul Mones; Matt Clark; Olivia Barash; Robert Downey, Jr.; Catya (Cat) Sassoon; Claudette Nevins; ***D:*** Fritz Kiersch; ***W:*** Jette Rinck; ***C:*** Willy Kurant; ***M:*** Jonathan Elias.

Tugboat Annie 🦴🦴🦴 **1933** A colossal MGM hit for the very popular Dressler, with Beery as her drunken husband Terry. Son Alec (Young) is the captain of an ocean liner who's in love with Patricia (O'Sullivan), the daughter of liner owner Red Severn (Robertson). Alec wants his mom to leave his dad and come work with him but the loyal Annie refuses, even after Terry crashes the tugboat. Sold at auction and turned into a garbage scow, Annie continues to run the vessel and one stormy night, the ocean liner sends out an SOS and it's the little-scow-that-could to the rescue! Based on a series of Norman Reilly Raine stories published in the "Saturday Evening Post." **88m/B; DVD.** Marie Dressler; Wallace Beery; Robert Young; Maureen O'Sullivan; Willard Robertson; Tammany Young; Frankie Darro; ***D:*** Mervyn LeRoy; ***W:*** Zelda Sears; Eve Greene; ***C:*** Gregg Toland.

Tulip Fever 🦴🦴 **2017 (R)** Despite its all-star cast and prestige feel, this misfired romantic period drama has limited appeal. Amidst the 17th century Amsterdam obsession with tulips, wealthy widower Cornelis Sandvoort (Waltz) hires struggling artist Jan Van Loos (DeHaan) to paint a portrait of himself and his young, unhappy wife Sofia (Vikander). Sofia finds more passion with Jan than her husband, who married her to produce an heir. Scheming with her housekeeper Maria (Grainger), Sofia devises a way to give her husband the baby he wants while allowing her to maintain her relationship with Jan. The cast's decent performances are undermined by the unfocused, twist-heavy narrative. **105m/C; DVD, Blu-Ray.** Alicia Vikander; Dane DeHaan; Jack O'Connell; Holliday Grainger; Tom Hollander; ***D:*** Justin Chadwick; ***W:*** Deborah Moggach; Tom Stoppard; ***C:*** Eigil Bryld; ***M:*** Danny Elfman.

Tully 🦴🦴🦴 *What Happened to Tully; The Truth About Tully* **2000 (R)** Quiet and convincing adaptation of Tom Neal's 1992 short story is set on a Nebraska dairy farm owned by taciturn Tully Coates Sr. (Burrus), who is hiding family secrets from his two sons. Handsome Tully Jr. (Mount) is the local womanizer while younger brother Earl (Fitzgerald) is shy and sensitive. Both have a soft spot for recently-returned neighbor Ella Smalley (Nicholson), who is too smart to fall for Tully's lines even as their friendship veers toward romance. **107m/C; VHS, DVD.** Anson Mount; Julianne Nicholson; Glenn Fitzgerald; Bob Burrus; Catherine Kellner; Natalie Canerday; John Diehl; V. Craig Heidenreich; ***D:*** Hilary Birmingham; ***W:*** Hilary Birmingham; Matt Drake; ***C:*** John Foster; ***M:*** Marcelo Zarvos.

Tully 🦴🦴 **1/2 2018 (R)** A comedy-drama that takes an honest look at the demands of motherhood: Marlo (Theron) is a only few days from giving birth to her unexpected third child. Her son (Fallica) has autism, and her husband (Livingston) travels often for work and lacks understanding about the day-to-day demands of his household. When baby Mia is born, Marlo's brother (Duplass) pays for a night nurse, Tully (Davis), who changes Marlo's life in unexpected ways. Screenwriter Cody and director Reitman unflinchingly and poignantly capture the sometimes surreal feeling of parenting, and Theron's powerful performance and lovely chemistry with Davis give the film its heart. **96m/C; DVD, Blu-Ray, Streaming.** Charlize Theron; Mackenzie Davis; Mark Duplass; Ron Livingston; Emily Haine; ***D:*** Jason Reitman; ***W:*** Diablo Cody; ***C:*** Eric Steelberg; ***M:*** Rob Simonsen.

Tulsa 🦴🦴🦴 **1949** High-spirited rancher's daughter begins crusade to save her father's oil empire when he's killed. Having become ruthless and determined to succeed at any cost, she eventually sees the error of her ways. Classic Hayward. **96m/C; VHS, DVD.** Susan Hayward; Robert Preston; Chill Wills; Ed Begley, Sr.; Pedro Armendariz, Sr.; ***D:*** Stuart Heisler; ***C:*** Winton C. Hoch.

Tumbledown 🦴🦴 **1/2 2016 (R)** A comedy-drama about death, music, and those left behind. After the death of her acclaimed folk singer husband, young widow Hannah (Hall) struggles with daily life in Maine. Andrew (Sudeikis), a New York-based pop culture scholar, crashes into her world when he comes to interview with her. As Hannah and Andrew make a deal to write a biography of her deceased husband together, the pair initially clash but soon find a connection that could be more. Through it all, Andrew must deal with locals, including Hannah's defensive parents (Danner, Masur), as he and Hannah find love in a most unlikely place. **105m/C; DVD, Blu-Ray, Streaming, Download.** Jason Sudeikis; Rebecca Hall; Blythe Danner; Richard Masur; Joe Manganiello; ***D:*** Sean Mewshaw; ***W:*** Desiree Van Til; ***C:*** Seamus Tierney; ***M:*** Daniel Hart; Damien Jurado.

Tumbleweeds 🦴🦴🦴 **1925** William S. Hart's last western. Portrays the last great land rush in America, the opening of the Cherokee Strip in the Oklahoma Territory to homesteaders. Preceded by a sound prologue, made in 1939, in which Hart speaks for the only time on screen, to introduce the story. Silent, with musical score. **114m/B; Silent; VHS, DVD.** William S. Hart; Lucien Littlefield; Barbara Bedford; ***D:*** King Baggot.

Tumbleweeds 🦴🦴 **1/2 1998 (PG-13)** Mary Jo Walker (McTeer) has been married numerous times and been in even more relationships. 12-year-old daughter Ava (Brown) knows that when things go wrong with mom's romantic prospects they pack up and hit the road, which is why they're on their way to San Diego. Of course, Mary Jo meets trucker Jack (O'Connor) along the way and decides to shack up with him when they reach their destination, while the remarkably resilient Ava settles into another new life. But since Mary Jo has such lousy judgment (except about her love for Ava) this mother-daughter duo is headed for rocky times ahead. **104m/C; VHS, DVD.** Janet McTeer; Kimberly J. Brown; Gavin O'Connor; Jay O. Sanders; Lois Smith; Laurel Holloman; Michael J. Pollard; Noah Emmerich; ***D:*** Gavin O'Connor; ***W:*** Gavin O'Connor; Angela Shelton; ***C:*** Dan Stoloff; ***M:*** David Mansfield. Golden Globes '00: Actress--Mus./Comedy (McTeer); Ind. Spirit '00: Debut Perf. (Brown); Natl. Bd. of Review '99: Actress (McTeer); Sundance '99: Filmmakers Trophy.

Tundra 🦴🦴 **1/2** *The Mighty Thunder* **1936** Quasi adventure-drama/documentary set in the Alaskan tundra. A young man, known only as the "Flying Doctor," tends to the sick in small villages throughout the wilderness. But his own survival is at stake when his small plane crashes. Filmed on location. **72m/B; VHS, DVD.** Del Cambre; ***D:*** Norman Dawn.

The Tune 🦴🦴 **1992** 30,000 ink and watercolor drawings make up this animated gem which tells the story of Del (Neiden), a failed songwriter who gets a fresh start when he makes a wrong turn on the freeway and winds up in Flooby Nooby. The strange inhabitants of this town teach Del to throw out his rhyming dictionary and write about his experiences. Plympton's first full-length animated feature. Also includes "The Making of The Tune" and the animated short "Draw." **80m/C; VHS, DVD.** ***V:*** Daniel Neiden; Maureen McElheron; Marty Nelson; Emily Bindiger; Chris Hoffman; ***D:*** Bill Plympton; ***W:*** Maureen McElheron; Bill Plympton; P.C. Vey; ***C:*** John Donnelly; ***M:*** Maureen McElheron.

Tune in Tomorrow 🦴🦴 **1990 (PG-13)** Lovesick young Martin (Reeves) wants to woo divorced older babe aunt-by-marriage Julia (Hershey) and is romantically counseled by wacky soap opera writer Pedro (Falk). Seems even soap operas draw on real life, and Martin's story is immortalized on the airwaves, circa 1951 New Orleans. The story-within-a-story also features Pedro's radio characters coming to hammy life. Sometimes funny, sometimes not (the Albanian jokes are tiresome). Adapted from the novel "Aunt Julia and the Scriptwriter" by Mario Vargas Llosa. **90m/C; VHS, DVD.** Barbara Hershey; Keanu Reeves; Peter Falk; Bill McCutcheon; Patricia Clarkson; Peter Gallagher; Dan Hedaya; Buck Henry; Hope Lange; John Larroquette; Elizabeth McGovern; Robert Sedgwick; Henry Gibson; ***D:*** Jon Amiel; ***W:*** William Boyd; ***C:*** Robert M. Stevens; ***M:*** Wynton Marsalis.

Tunes of Glory 🦴🦴🦴 **1/2 1960** Guinness and Mills are wonderful in this well made film about a brutal, sometimes lazy colonel and a disciplined and educated man moving up through the ranks of the British military. York's film debut. From the novel by James Kennaway, who adapted it for the screen. **107m/C; VHS, DVD, Blu-Ray.** *GB* Alec Guinness; John Mills; Dennis Price; Kay Walsh; Susannah York; ***D:*** Ronald Neame; ***M:*** Malcolm Arnold.

The Tunnel 🦴🦴🦴 **1/2** *Der Tunnel* **2001** Originally produced for German television broadcast. Based on the true story of Harry Melchior (Ferch), an East German swimming champ who fled to West Berlin in 1961 as the wall was going up. Melchior is so committed to getting his sister Lotte (Lara) and her family out of East Berlin that he hatches a plan to dig a tunnel under the wall. Naturally the tunnel becomes a massive undertaking requiring the clandestine enlistment of other West Berliners with loved ones behind the wall. This tense drama is packed with story lines and looming disaster—a rare gem with top notch production values. **157m/C; DVD.** *GE* Heino Ferch; Nicolette Krebitz; Sebastian Koch; Mehmet Kurtulus; Alexandra Maria Lara; Felix Eitner; ***D:*** Roland Suso Richter; ***W:*** Johannes W. Betz; ***C:*** Martin Langer; ***M:*** Harald Kloser; Thomas Wanker. **TV**

The Tunnel of Love 🦴🦴 **1/2 1958** Day and Widmark are a married couple who find themselves over their heads in red tape when they try to adopt a baby. A beautiful, disapproving adoption investigator also causes more problems for the couple when she believes Widmark is less than ideal father material. Widmark is not in his element at comedy but Day and Young (as their next-door neighbor) are fine in this lightweight adaptation of the Joseph Fields-Peter DeVries play. **98m/B; VHS, DVD.** Doris Day; Richard Widmark; Gig Young; Gia Scala; Elisabeth Fraser; Elizabeth Wilson; ***D:*** Gene Kelly; ***W:*** Jerome Chodorov.

Tunnel Rats 🦴🦴 *1968 Tunnel Rats* **2008** A tense and competent actioner from Boll set during the Vietnam War. A special unit of American soldiers, led by Sgt. Hollowborn (Pare), is assigned to infiltrate the maze-like, booby-trapped tunnels used by the Viet Cong. Not for the claustrophobic. **92m/C; DVD.** *GE* Michael Paré; Wilson Bethel; Mitch Eakins; Brandon Fobbs; Erik Eiden; Rocky Marquette; Jane Le; ***D:*** Uwe Boll; ***W:*** Uwe Boll; ***C:*** Mathias Neumann; ***M:*** Jessica de Rooij.

Tunnel Vision 🦴 **1/2 1995 (R)** Detective Kelly Wheatstone (Kensit) and her partner Frank Yanovitch (Reynolds) are after a serial killer whose victims are all beautiful women killed in a ritualistic fashion. But all the clues begin to point to Yanovitch as the one committing the crimes. This one is routine all the way. **100m/C; VHS, DVD.** *AU* Patsy Kensit; Robert Reynolds; Rebecca Rigg; Shane Briant; ***D:*** Clive Fleury; ***W:*** Clive Fleury; ***C:*** Paul Murphy; ***M:*** David Hirschfelder.

Tunnelvision 🦴🦴 **1/2 1976 (R)** A spoof of TV comprised of irreverent sketches. Fun to watch because of the appearances of several now-popular stars. **70m/C; VHS, DVD.** Chevy Chase; John Candy; Laraine Newman; Joe Flaherty; Howard Hesseman; Gerrit Graham; Al Franken; Tom Davis; Ron Silver; ***D:*** Neal Israel.

Turbo 🦴🦴 **1/2 2013 (PG)** Reynolds voices the title character of Turbo, a snail turned superhero when a freak accident gives him the speed to compete in the Indy 500. There's nothing wrong with this little-guy-made-good story other than its over-familiarity making you want to watch the better movies of which it reminds you. This DreamWorks entry has its moments but ultimately registers as more forgettable than entertaining. It's the kind of animated comedy that works well enough while it unfolds but doesn't linger enough to encourage repeat viewing. **96m/C; DVD, Blu-Ray.** ***V:*** Ryan Reynolds; Paul Giamatti; Michael Peña; Samuel L. Jackson; Maya Rudolph; Luis Guzman; Bill Hader; Snoop Dogg; Richard Jenkins; Ken Jeong; Michelle Rodriguez; ***D:*** David Soren; ***W:*** David Soren; Darren Lemke; Robert Siegel; ***C:*** Chris Stover; ***M:*** Henry Jackman.

Turbo: A Power Rangers Movie 🦴 **1996 (PG)** The Power Rangers must battle the evil Divatox (Turner), who's kidnapped the wizard Lerigot so she can use his power to free her even more evil boyfriend Maligore. It's all around cheesy but if you're a five-year-old you may still enjoy the action. **99m/C; VHS, DVD, Blu-Ray.** Jason David Frank; Stephen Antonio Cardenas; John Yong Bosch; Catherine Sutherland; Nakia Burrise; Blake Foster; Paul Schrier; Jason Narvy; Amy Jo Johnson; Austin St. John; Hilary Shepard Turner; Jon Simanton; ***D:*** David Winning; Shuki Levy; ***W:*** Shuki Levy; Shell Danielson; ***C:*** Ilan Rosenberg; ***M:*** Shuki Levy.

Turbo Kid 🦴 **2015** The trend of filmmakers trying to nostalgically pay homage to the '80s midnight madness movies that helped them fall in the love with the form continues. Someone really should stop it. In this Troma-esque horror-comedy, The Kid is a scavenger in a post-apocalyptic world who meets and falls for a girl named Apple. The two will battle the notoriously evil and scenery-chewing Zeus (Ironside), but the plot is just an excuse for gross-out bits that don't quite work. Only the most diehard cult movie fans need apply. Everyone else will either find it disturbing or deadly boring. **90m/C; DVD, Blu-Ray.** Munro Chambers; Laurence Leboeuf; Michael Ironside; Edwin Wright; Aaron Jeffrey; ***D:*** Francois Simard; Anouk Whissell; Yoann-Karl Whissell; ***W:*** Francois Simard; Anouk Whissell; Yoann-Karl Whissell; ***C:*** Jean-Philippe Bernier; ***M:*** Jean-Philippe Bernier; Jean-Nicolas Leupi Le Matos.

Turbulence 🦴 **1/2 1996 (R)** When you fly, it's usually the turbulence that makes you throw up. Well, this movie isn't that bad, but you may experience a touch of nausea. Flight attendant Teri (Holly) is pushing the drink cart on a strangely vacant New York to L.A. Christmas Eve run. Among the passengers are convicted felons Ryan (Liotta) and Stubbs (Gleeson), who are either on their way to a more secure prison or fulfilling the "consumption of airline food" portion of their sentence. The prisoners seize a gun from the marshals and accidentally rub out the cockpit crew. With all the passengers locked away, Teri must battle the serial rapist/killer Ryan as well as learn to fly the plane through a horrible storm. Passengers on the left of the screen may look out and see "Passenger 57," while those on the right can see the ancient monument of "Airport 75." **103m/C; VHS, DVD.** Ray Liotta; Lauren Holly; Hector Elizondo; Brendan Gleeson; Ben Cross; Rachel Ticotin; Jeffrey DeMunn; John Finn; Catherine Hicks; ***D:*** Robert Butler; ***W:*** Jonathan Brett; ***C:*** Lloyd Ahern, II; ***M:*** Shirley Walker.

Turbulence 2: Fear of Flying 🦴🦴 **1999** Group of scared to fly passengers try to overcome their fears aboard a jumbo 747. They will never set foot off the ground again after severe turbulance damages the plane and a nerve gas-carrying terrorist commandeers it. **100m/C; VHS, DVD.** Tom Berenger; Craig Sheffer; Jennifer Beals; Jeffrey Nordling; ***D:*** David Mackay; ***W:*** Kevin Bernhardt; Brendan Broderick; Rob Kerchner. **VIDEO**

Turbulence 3: Heavy Metal **WOOF!** **2000 (R)** Wannable shock rocker Slade Craven (Mann) wants to make his last concert a spectacular affair, so he has a passenger jet modified so he can give his performance, which will be broadcast over the Internet, in mid-air to a select audience. But the plane is hijacked and FBI agent Kate Hayden (Anwar), who just happens to be on board, and hacker Nick Watts (Sheffer) try to prevent a disaster. Stupid plot, stupid characters—all around cheese. **96m/C; VHS, DVD.** Craig Sheffer; Gabrielle Anwar; Monica Schnarre; Rutger Hauer; Joe Mantegna; John Mann; ***D:*** Jorge Montesi; ***W:*** Wade Ferley; ***C:*** Philip Linzey; ***M:*** John McCarthy. **VIDEO**

Turbulent Skies WOOF! 2010 Bad acting, bad CGI, ridiculous plot; even by lowering standards for a cable disaster flick this is a woofer. Faulty software uploaded along with a new supercomputer results in a 747 that goes wonky during its first flight and can't be controlled. The military option is to shoot the plane down (too bad about the passengers) but the computer's inventor thinks he can regain control if he can get onboard. **82m/C; DVD.** Casper Van Dien; Brad Dourif; Nicole Eggert; Patrick Muldoon; Ted Monte; Mark Enticknap; Cal Bartlett; ***D:*** Fred Olen Ray; ***W:*** Fred Olen Ray; ***C:*** Theo Angell; ***M:*** Jason Solowsky. **CABLE**

Turistas 2006 (R) Young, sexy, and often-naked travelers are stuck in Brazil after a bus accident. That doesn't stop them from partying, however, until they wake up the next morning to the not-so-shocking realization that they've been drugged and robbed. The overly-friendly locals aren't what they seem, and soon a crazed surgeon straight out of the book of urban legends is blathering about economic inequality and carving out the visitors' vital organs. Dopey, dull, and not very scary (unless xenophobia counts). **89m/C; DVD.** Josh Duhamel; Melissa George; Olivia Wilde; Desmond Askew; Beau Garrett; Max Brown; Agles Steib; Miguel Lunardi; ***D:*** John Stockwell; ***W:*** Michael Arlen Ross; ***C:*** Enrique Chediak; ***M:*** Paul Haslinger.

Turk 182! 1/2 1985 (PG-13) The angry brother of a disabled fireman takes on City Hall in order to win back the pension that he deserves. He attacks through his graffiti art. Hutton is too heavy for the over-all comic feel of this mostly silly film. **96m/C; VHS, DVD.** Timothy Hutton; Robert Culp; Robert Urich; Kim Cattrall; Peter Boyle; Darren McGavin; Paul Sorvino; ***D:*** Bob (Benjamin) Clark.

Turkish Delight 1/2 1973 Free spirit sculptor falls in love with free spirit gal from bourgeois family and artsy soft porn ensues. That is until a brain tumor puts an end to their fun, and he's left to wallow in flashbacks and more artsy soft porn. Dubbed. Verhoeven later became big boxoffice in the U.S. with "Total Recall." **100m/C; VHS, DVD.** *NL* Monique Van De Ven; Rutger Hauer; Tonny Huurdeman; Wim Van Den Brink; ***D:*** Paul Verhoeven; ***W:*** Gerard Soeteman; ***C:*** Jan De Bont.

Turn Back the Clock 1933 Middle-aged Joe Gimlet (Tracy) is dissatisfied with his life and marriage to high school sweetheart Mary (Clarke), especially after a chance meeting with successful hometown pal Ted Wright (Kruger). A car accident sends Joe into surgery and back to 1910, but with his curret memories intact, and he's determined not to be a sap again. But apparently changing his future doesn't mean Joe's any happier. **79m/B; DVD.** Lee Tracy; Mae Clarke; Otto Kruger; Peggy Shannon; C. Henry Gordon; George Barbier; ***D:*** Edgar Selwyn; ***W:*** Edgar Selwyn; Ben Hecht; ***C:*** Harold Rosson; ***M:*** Herbert Stothart.

Turn It Up 2000 (R) Diamond (Pras) is a talented musician who's involved in the drug trade with childhood friend Gage (Ja Rule). He wants to go legit so he can pursue his music dreams but Gage is a hothead who gets them into more trouble. Then Diamond's girlfriend announces she's pregnant, his mother unexpectedly dies, and his estranged father (Curtis-Hall) turns up. **87m/C; VHS, DVD.** Pras; Vondie Curtis-Hall; Ja Rule; Tamala Jones; Jason Statham; Eugene Clark; ***D:*** Robert Adetuyi; ***W:*** Robert Adetuyi; ***C:*** Hubert Taczanowski; ***M:*** Gary Jones; Happy Walters.

Turn of the Blade 1997 Predictable thriller finds photographer Sam Peyton (Christensen) upset that his wife Kelly (Owens) is more interested in her acting career than in having a baby. It may be safer to have the kid, since Kelly's the lust object for a seedy film director and then a dangerous stalker. Meanwhile, Sam has his own problems with his associate Wendy, who wants their relationship to get personal and wants Kelly out of the way. **91m/C; VHS, DVD.** David Christensen; Crystal Owens; David Keith Miller; Julie Horvath; ***D:*** Bryan Michael Stoller; ***W:*** Mark Bark; ***C:*** Richard A. Jones; ***M:*** Greg Edmonson. **VIDEO**

The Turn of the Screw 1974 Supernatural powers vie with a young governess for control of the souls of the two children in her charge. Redgrave does well in this chilling film adapted from the Henry James story. **120m/C; VHS, DVD.** Lynn Redgrave; Jasper Jacobs; Eva Griffith; ***D:*** Dan Curtis.

The Turn of the Screw 1992 (R) Yet another version of the Henry James classic as a young governess struggles with sexual obsession and the two children in her care who are possessed by evil. **95m/C; VHS, Streaming.** Julian Sands; Patsy Kensit; Stephane Audran; Marianne Faithfull; ***D:*** Rusty Lemorande; ***M:*** Simon Boswell.

The Turn of the Screw 1/2 1999 Solid TV adaptation of the Henry James novel boasts some fine performances in a now familiar story. Miss (May) is the young, too-impressionable governess at Bly manor, whose charges are the overly well-behaved Miles (Sowerbutts) and his younger sister, Flora (Robinson). Soon Miss is seeing ghosts—those of the former governess and another servant, Peter Quint (Salkey), whom she believes are corrupting her innocent children. But maybe the emotional young woman is simply crazy. **80m/C; VHS, DVD.** *GB* Jodhi May; Pam Ferris; Colin Firth; Joe Sowerbutts; Grace Robinson; Jason Salkey; Caroline Pegg; Jenny Howe; ***D:*** Ben Bolt; ***W:*** Nick Dear; ***C:*** David Odd; ***M:*** Adrian Johnston. **TV**

Turn the River 2007 (R) Kailey (a de-glamorized Janssen) is a downtrodden pool hustler who is allowed no contact with her 11-year-old son Gulley (Dornan), so they meet secretly. Kailey's trying to put together the cash so she can just take the kid from his toxic father (Ross) and head for Canada but she makes some majorly dumb mistakes (there's a gun involved). **92m/C; DVD, Blu-Ray.** Famke Janssen; Jamie Dornan; Rip Torn; Matt Ross; Lois Smith; Terry Kinney; Marin Hinkle; John Juback; ***D:*** Christopher Eigeman; ***W:*** Christopher Eigeman; ***C:*** H. Michael Otano; ***M:*** Clogs.

Turner and Hooch 1989 (PG) A dog witnesses a murder, and a fussy cop is partnered with the drooling mutt and a weak script in his search for the culprit. Drool as a joke will only go so far, but Hanks is his usual entertaining self. **99m/C; VHS, DVD; Open Captioned.** Tom Hanks; Mare Winningham; Craig T. Nelson; Scott Paulin; J.C. Quinn; ***D:*** Roger Spottiswoode; ***W:*** Jim Cash; Jack Epps, Jr.; Michael Blodgett; ***C:*** Adam Greenberg; ***M:*** Charles Gross.

The Turning 1/2 ***Home Fires Burning*** **1992** Twenty-two-year-old Cliff Harnish (Dolan) returns home after a four-year absence to shock his family with his strident Neo-Nazi beliefs. May be of curiosity value to Anderson's "X-Files" fans, since she appears (relatively briefly and partially nude) as the guy's girlfriend in a kitchen sex scene. Based on the play by Ceraso. **92m/C; VHS, DVD.** Michael Dolan; Raymond J. Barry; Karen Allen; Tess Harper; Gillian Anderson; ***D:*** L.A. Puopolo; ***W:*** L.A. Puopolo; Chris Ceraso; ***C:*** J. Michael McClary.

Turning Paige 1/2 2001 Teenager Paige is struggling to maintain the status quo in her life while looking after her widowed, recovering alcoholic dad. Her carefully constructed normal life starts to fall apart when her estranged brother Trevor returns home and brings some hard truths that Paige has been hiding into the open. **112m/C; DVD.** *CA* Katharine Isabelle; Nicholas (Nick) Campbell; Torri Higginson; Philip DeWilde; Brendan Fletcher; Nikki Barnett; John Diamond; Chris Kelly; ***D:*** Robert Cuffley; ***W:*** Robert Cuffley; Jason Long; ***C:*** Mark Dobrescu; ***M:*** Michael Shields.

The Turning Point 1/2 1977 (PG) A woman who gave up ballet for motherhood must come to terms as her daughter launches a ballet career and falls for the lead male dancer. The mother finds herself threatened by her daughter's affection toward an old friend who sacrificed a family life for the life of a ballerina. Baryshnikov's film debut. Melodramatic ending and problems due to ballet sequences. **119m/C; VHS, DVD.** Shirley MacLaine; Anne Bancroft; Tom Skerritt; Leslie Browne; Martha Scott; Marshall Thompson; Mikhail Baryshnikov; ***D:*** Herbert Ross; ***W:*** Arthur Laurents; ***C:*** Robert L. Surtees. Golden Globes '78: Director (Ross), Film--Drama; L.A. Film Critics '77: Director (Ross); Natl. Bd. of Review '77: Actress (Bancroft), Support. Actor (Skerritt); Writers Guild '77: Orig. Screenplay.

Turtles Can Fly 1/2 ***Lakposhtha ham parvaz mikonand*** **2004** Director Ghobadi's stark and engrossing tale of the unending daily sufferings of refugee children living on the Iraq-Turkey border as they await the U.S.-led invasion in early 2003. Essentially absent of adults, Ghobadi centers on 13-year-old Satellite (Ebrahim)?who uses his technical savvy to bring TV to the camp so they can watch news channels—along with his rival Hengov, disfigured by landmines, and Hengov's withdrawn sister Agrin who rebuffs Satellite's romantic advances. In Kurdish, with English subtitles. **95m/C; DVD.** *FR IA IQ* Soran Ebrahim; Avaz Latif; Hirsh Feyssal; Saddam Hossein Feysal; Hiresh Feysal Rahman; Abdol Rahman Karim; Ajil Zibari; ***D:*** Bahman Ghobadi; ***W:*** Bahman Ghobadi; ***C:*** Shahriar Assadi; ***M:*** Hossein Alizadeh.

Tusk 1/2 2014 (R) Smith's would-be retirement proved short-lived as this odd horror-comedy proves. Spawned from an admittedly high conversation had during one of Smith's podcast, the writer-director weaves the tale of Wallace Bryton (Long), a podcaster who goes missing deep in the Manitoba wilderness. The investigating team sent to find him discovers that Wallace was taken prisoner by a man who intended to turn him into a walrus. It's neither funny nor scary. It's just weird. One has to admire Smith for trying something this different, but that doesn't mean it works. **102m/C; DVD, Blu-Ray.** *US CA* Michael Parks; Justin Long; Haley Joel Osment; Genesis Rodriguez; Johnny Depp; ***D:*** Kevin Smith; ***W:*** Kevin Smith; ***C:*** James Laxton; ***M:*** Christopher Drake.

The Tuskegee Airmen 1995 (PG-13) Cable drama based on the formation and WWII achievements of the U.S. Army Air Corps' first squadron of black combat fighter pilots, the "Fighting 99th" of the 332nd Fighter Group. They were nicknamed after the segregated military outpost where they trained in Tuskegee, Alabama and distinguished themselves in combat, never losing a single bomber, and receiving more than 800 medals. Cast all do a fine job in what turns out to essentially be a standard action/war movie. Based on a story by former Tuskegee airman, Robert W. Williams. **107m/C; VHS, DVD, Blu-Ray.** Laurence Fishburne; Cuba Gooding, Jr.; Allen Payne; Malcolm Jamal Warner; Courtney B. Vance; Andre Braugher; John Lithgow; Rosemary Murphy; Christopher McDonald; Vivica A. Fox; Daniel Hugh-Kelly; David Harrod; Eddie Braun; Bennet Guillory; ***D:*** Robert Markowitz; ***W:*** Paris Qualles; Ron Hutchinson; Trey Ellis; ***C:*** Ronald Orieux; ***M:*** Lee Holdridge. **CABLE**

Tusks 1/2 ***Fire in Eden*** **1989 (R)** A ruthless hunter tries to kill elephants. **99m/C; VHS, DVD.** Andrew Stevens; John Rhys-Davies; Lucy Gutteridge; Julian Glover; ***D:*** Tara Hawkins Moore.

The Tuxedo 1/2 2002 (PG-13) After an unusual opening non sequiter, movie pits kickmaster Chan against the evil Banning (Coster) out to dehydrate the world via a deadly ingredient in the water supply. Mild mannered taxi driver Jimmy (Chan) takes a job chauffeuring Clark Devlin (Isaacs), a wealthy spy with a secret weapon: the title's near-magical tuxedo that turns the wearer into a martial arts fighting machine. After Devlin's injured, Jimmy dons the supersuit and joins agent Del (Hewitt) in the fight against Banning. Chan is his usual amiable, entertaining self even against this extremely silly backdrop of a movie. Highlight is Chan's stint as a stand-in for soul man James Brown. **98m/C; VHS, DVD.** Jackie Chan; Jennifer Love Hewitt; Jason Isaacs; Debi Mazar; Ritchie Coster; Peter Stormare; Romany Malco; Mia Cottet; ***D:*** Kevin Donovan; ***W:*** Michael J. Wilson; Michael Leeson; ***C:*** Stephen F. Windon; ***M:*** John Debney; Christophe Beck.

The TV Set 1/2 2006 (R) Art vs. commerce in an amusing satire. Writer Mike (Duchovny) is trying to sell a personal project for TV development to a network headed by the predatory Lenny (Weaver). Lenny willfully prefers the mediocre and sleazy as long as it bring in ratings and advertising dollars. She ignores his original vision, but Mike is reassured by new programming head Richard McAllister (Gruffudd) that he'll have his say. Mike is doomed to disappointment. Kasdan worked on "Freaks and Geeks" and "Undeclared" so he knows the territory—maybe too well for those who aren't insiders. **87m/C; DVD.** David Duchovny; Sigourney Weaver; Ioan Gruffudd; Judy Greer; Fran Kranz; Lindsay Sloane; Justine Bateman; Lucy Davis; ***D:*** Jake Kasdan; ***W:*** Jake Kasdan; ***C:*** Uta Briesewitz; ***M:*** Michael Andrews.

Tweek City 1/2 2005 Bumpy indie follows San Francisco drug dealer Bill, who has a crystal meth problem that fuels his insecurities about his half-Latino heritage, his sexuality, and his troubled childhood. Bill can't get past his ex-high school girlfriend getting married and goes on a bender before crashing the wedding. Writer/director Johnson ultimately doesn't know where to take his character or story. **86m/C; DVD.** Giuseppe Andrews; Keith Brunsmann; Elizabeth Bogush; Eva Fisher; ***D:*** Eric Johnson; ***W:*** Eric Johnson; ***C:*** Barry Stone; ***M:*** Jim Latham.

Twelfth Night 1/2 1996 (PG) Director Nunn's take on Shakespeare's gender-bending, romantic-comedy, which is now set in the 1890s. Shipwrecked on an unfriendly Illyrian shore, Viola (Stubbs), believing twin brother Sebastian (Mackintosh) to be dead, disguises herself in male attire and joins the retinue of the lovesick Duke Orsino (Stephens). He's pining for the Countess Olivia (Bonham Carter) and decides to use Viola-turned-Cesario as a surrogate wooer. Too bad Olivia's becoming more interested in her effeminate pseudo-suitor and that Orsino's having a few sexual quandries of his own. **133m/C; VHS, DVD.** *GB* Imogen Stubbs; Helena Bonham Carter; Toby Stephens; Steven Mackintosh; Richard E. Grant; Nigel Hawthorne; Ben Kingsley; Imelda Staunton; Mel Smith; Nicholas Farrell; ***D:*** Trevor Nunn; ***W:*** Trevor Nunn; ***C:*** Clive Tickner; ***M:*** Shaun Davey.

12 2007 (PG-13) Despite the PG-13 rating, it's unlikely any teens will be interested in a Russian courtroom drama inspired by the 1957 film "12 Angry Men." In Mikhalkov's operatic drama, 12 Muscovites (who are nameless) are sent to a decrepit high school gym so they can deliberate a case where an 18-year-old Chechan is accused of murdering his adoptive Russian father. Eleven of the jurors quickly vote guilty while a contrary engineer insists they need to consider the consequences of acquiescing to the government's case without debate. Russian with subtitles. **159m/C; On Demand.** *RU* Sergei Makovetsky; Alexei Petrenko; Nikita Mikhalkov; Sergei Garmash; Valentin Gaft; Yuri Stoyanov; Sergei Gazarov; Mikhail Efremov; Apti Magamaev; ***D:*** Nikita Mikhalkov; ***W:*** Nikita Mikhalkov; Alexander Novototsky; Vladimir Moiseenko; ***C:*** Vladislav Opeliants; ***M:*** Edward Artemiev.

Twelve 2010 (R) Schumacher goes with his self-indulgent, teenage fetishes in this pretentious drug dealer drama adapted from then-17-year-old Nick McDonell's 2002 novel. Mopey White Mike (Crawford) drops out of prep school to deal drugs to his self-indulgent Upper East Side trust-fund acquaintances, but there's trouble with Harlem supplier Lionel (Jackson) that brings in the cops. Title refers to a new street drug that's a combo of cocaine and Ecstasy. **94m/C; Blu-Ray.** Chace Crawford; 50 Cent; Emma Roberts; Rory Culkin; Jeremy White; Billy Magnussen; Emily Meade; Esti Ginzburg; Charlie Saxton; Maxx Bauer; ***Nar:*** Kiefer Sutherland; ***D:*** Joel Schumacher; ***W:*** Jordan Melamed; ***C:*** Steven Fierberg; ***M:*** Harry Gregson-Williams.

12 and Holding 2005 (R) Rudy (Donovan) and his fat buddy Leonard (Camacho) spend the night in their tree house, which is torched by bullies. Leonard is injured (he loses his sense of taste) but Rudy dies. His twin Jacob is barely able to cope (he already has self-esteem issues since a birthmark covers half his face), especially when confronted with his parents' grief and rage. Leonard's survival inspires him to lose weight and get in shape, much to the resentment of his obese parents. Meanwhile, their friend Malee (Weizenbaum) becomes precociously interested in one of her therapist mom's

(Sciorra) patients, a hunky construction worker (Renner). First-rate work by all, with much uncomfortably honest depiction of adolescent bewilderment and fear. **95m/C; DVD.** Zoe Weizenbaum; Jeremy Renner; Conor Donovan; Jesse Camacho; Annabella Sciorra; Linus Roache; Jayne Atkinson; Marcia DeBonis; Michael Fuchs; ***D:*** Michael Cuesta; ***W:*** Anthony Cipriano; ***C:*** Romeo Tirone; ***M:*** Pierre Foldes.

Twelve Angry Men 🦴🦴🦴🦴 **1957** Fonda sounds the voice of reason as a jury inclines toward a quick-and-dirty verdict against a boy on trial. Excellent ensemble work. Lumet's feature film debut, based on a TV play by Reginald Rose. **95m/B; VHS, DVD, Blu-Ray.** Henry Fonda; Martin Balsam; Lee J. Cobb; E.G. Marshall; Jack Klugman; Robert Webber; Ed Begley, Sr.; John Fiedler; Jack Warden; George Voskovec; Edward Binns; Joseph Sweeney; ***D:*** Sidney Lumet; ***W:*** Reginald Rose; ***C:*** Boris Kaufman; ***M:*** Kenyon Hopkins. Berlin Intl. Film Fest. '57: Golden Berlin Bear; British Acad. '57: Actor (Fonda); Natl. Film Reg. '07.

The Twelve Chairs 🦴🦴🦴 **1970 (PG)** Take-off on Russian folktale first filmed in Yugoslavia in 1927. A rich matron admits on her deathbed that she has hidden her jewels in the upholstery of one of 12 chairs that are no longer in her home. A Brooksian treasure hunt ensues. **94m/C; VHS, DVD.** Mel Brooks; Dom DeLuise; Frank Langella; Ron Moody; Bridget Brice; ***D:*** Mel Brooks; ***W:*** Mel Brooks; ***C:*** Djordje Nikolic; ***M:*** Mel Brooks; John Morris.

12 Christmas Wishes For My Dog 🦴 ½ *12 Wishes of Christmas* **2011** Since Laura's living in a 'no pets' apartment, the dog quickly gets stuck in a shelter in this formulaic TV movie. She gets fired and dumped by her boyfriend, becoming fair game when she consults life coach Noel. Laura is told to make 12 wishes for positive changes in her life but she's frivolous and selfish instead. As her wishes come true with unforeseen consequences, she has quite a mess to clean up. **88m/C; DVD.** Elisa Donovan; David O'Donnell; Chonda Pierce; Sarah Thompson; Gabrielle Carteris; Michael Gross; Fred Willard; Michael Bergin; Mo Gaffney; ***D:*** Peter Sullivan; ***W:*** Michael Ciminera; Richard Gnolfo; ***C:*** George Reasner; ***M:*** Matthew Janszen. **TV**

The Twelve Days of Christmas Eve 🦴🦴 ½ **2004 (PG)** Business exec Calvin Carter (Weber) neglects those closest to him in his pursuit of success. When he winds up in the hospital on Christmas Eve, nurse/guardian angel Angie (Shannon) informs Calvin he has 12 chances to make amends and find his true holiday spirit or suffer the consequences. Manages to be more mildly sarcastic than sugary despite its holiday theme. **120m/C; DVD.** Steven Weber; Molly Shannon; Patricia Velasquez; Teryl Rothery; Chad Willett; Vincent Gale; Stefanie von Pfetten; ***D:*** Martha Coolidge; ***W:*** J.B. White; ***C:*** Derick Underschultz; ***M:*** Jennie Muskett. **CABLE**

12 Disasters WOOF! *The 12 Disasters of Christmas* **2012** Lunatic Syfy Channel mayhem in the small town of Calvary, Idaho on Christmas Eve. Eighteen-year-old Jacey, the daughter of Joseph and Mary, must save the world from a cataclysm of not-so-natural disasters that also involve a Mayan prophecy and five gold rings. **90m/C; DVD.** Magda Apanowicz; Ed Quinn; Holly Dignard; Donnelly Rhodes; Roark Critchlow; Kaj-Erik Eriksen; ***D:*** Steven R. Monroe; ***W:*** Sydney Roper; Rudy Thauberger; ***C:*** Anthony C. Metchie; ***M:*** Michael Nielson. **CABLE**

The Twelve Dogs of Christmas 🦴 ½ **2005** Sappy Christmas story set in the Depression. 12-year-old Emma O'Connor (Green) is sent to live with her aunt in a small town and finds out that dogs are newly banned in the community (grrrrr). So it's up to Emma, a large number of pooches, and a school holiday pageant to make everything right. Cute dogs, cute kid—probably tolerable for the younger set. Based on the book by Emma Kragen. **107m/C; DVD, Blu-Ray.** Jordan-Claire Green; John Billingsley; Richard Riehle; Eric Lutes; Bonita Friedericy; Mindy Sterling; John-Kevin Hilbert; ***D:*** Keith Merrill; ***W:*** Keith Merrill; Emma Kragen; ***C:*** Michael Fimognari. **VIDEO**

12 Dogs of Christmas: Great Puppy Rescue 🦴 **2012 (PG)** Dull doggie adventure with too much going on for coherence. Emma O'Connor (Chuchran) returns to her hometown just in time to try and rescue the dog orphanage from greedy tycoon Finneas James (Flanery). Emma puts on a musical to raise the money to save the shelter. **102m/C; DVD; Closed Captioned.** Danielle Chuchran; Sean Patrick Flanery; D.B. Sweeney; ***D:*** Keith Merrill; ***W:*** Keith Merrill; ***C:*** T.C. Christensen; ***M:*** John-Kevin Hilbert. **VIDEO**

Twelve Hours to Kill 🦴 **1960** Dull and routine crime drama. Greek immigrant Martin (Minardos) witnesses a murder and is taken into protective custody. Only the cops are allied with the killers and when Martin is doublecrossed he goes on the lam. **83m/B; DVD.** Nico Minardos; Barbara Eden; Grant Richards; Russ Conway; Gavin MacLeod; ***D:*** Edward L. Cahn; ***W:*** Jerry Sohl; ***C:*** Floyd Crosby; ***M:*** Paul Dunlap.

12 Hours to Live 🦴 ½ **2006** Overwrought crime drama. FBI agent Megan Saunders (Skye) is still devastated about a hesitation that caused her partner's death during a bank robbery. Now the same robber (Durand) has kidnapped teenaged diabetic Amy (Wilson) and is holding her hostage. Amy needs her insulin within 12 hours or she'll go into a diabetic coma but Megan's superior (Coates) doesn't think she's steady enough to do her job. **90m/C; DVD.** Ione Skye; Kevin Durand; Brittney Wilson; Kim Coates; Doug Abraham; Michael Boisvert; Michael Moriarty; ***D:*** George Mendeluk; ***W:*** Patrick Corbett; ***C:*** Mahlon Todd Williams; ***M:*** Clinton Shorter. **CABLE**

12 Men of Christmas 🦴🦴 ½ **2009** Lifetime Christmas romance finds uptight New York publicist E.J. Baxter (Chenoweth) losing both her job and fiance at the office holiday party. She finally finds a tourism job in a small Montana town and decides to boost interest and help fund the volunteer search-and-rescue team by getting the hunks to pose for a spicy calendar, including a potential new beau (Hopkins). The photo montage of the shoot alone is worth the movie's predictability. **87m/C; DVD.** Kristin Chenoweth; Josh Hopkins; Anna Chlumsky; Erin Dilly; Stephen Huszar; Heather Hanson; Craig Eldridge; ***D:*** Arlene Sanford; ***W:*** Jon Maas; ***C:*** Peter Benison; ***M:*** David Lawrence. **CABLE**

12 Monkeys 🦴🦴🦴 **1995 (R)** Forty years after a plague wipes out 99 percent of the human population and sends the survivors underground, scientists send prisoner James Cole (Willis) to the 1990s to investigate the connection between the virus and seriously deranged fanatic Jeffrey Goines (Pitt), whose father happens to be a renowned virologist. Director Gilliam's demented vision is a bit tougher and less capricious than usual, and the convoluted plot and accumulated detail require a keen attention span, but as each piece of the puzzle falls into place the story becomes a fascinating sci-fi spectacle. Pitt drops the pretty-boy image with a nutzoid performance that'll make revelers stop swooning in a heartbeat. Inspired by the 1962 French short "La Jetee." **131m/C; VHS, DVD, Blu-Ray, HD-DVD.** Bruce Willis; Madeleine Stowe; Brad Pitt; Christopher Plummer; David Morse; Frank Gorshin; Jon Seda; ***D:*** Terry Gilliam; ***W:*** David Peoples; Janet Peoples; ***C:*** Roger Pratt; ***M:*** Paul Buckmaster. Golden Globes '96: Support. Actor (Pitt).

12 O'Clock Boys 🦴🦴🦴 **2014** Documentary follows Pug, a 13-year-old coming up in Baltimore's underground dirtbike culture. Director Nathan vividly captures the culture of dirtbike crews as they take over streets and alleyways of urban Baltimore, but the anchor is Pug, who grows up on camera as he struggles with his family life and seeks some replacement in his fellow bikers. Powerful and sympathetic, it misses chances to explore the effect of the bikers' marginally legal activities on their community and falters towards the end, but remains a fascinating exploration of a unique subculture. **72m/C; DVD, Blu-Ray.** ***M:*** Joe Williams.

Twelve o'Clock High 🦴🦴🦴 ½ **1949** Epic drama about the heroic 8th Air Force, with Peck as bomber-group commander sent to shape up a hard-luck group, forced to drive himself and his men to the breaking point. Compelling dramatization of the strain of military command. Includes impressive footage of actual WWII battles. Best-ever flying fortress movie. **132m/B; VHS, DVD, Blu-Ray.** Gregory Peck; Hugh Marlowe; Gary Merrill; Millard Mitchell; Dean Jagger; Paul Stewart; Robert Arthur; John Kellogg; Sam Edwards; Russ Conway; Lawrence (Larry) Dobkin; ***D:*** Henry King; ***W:*** Sy Bartlett; Beirne Lay, Jr.; ***C:*** Leon Shamroy; ***M:*** Alfred Newman. Oscars '49: Sound, Support. Actor (Jagger); Natl. Film Reg. '98.

12:01 🦴🦴 ½ **1993 (PG-13)** It's the "Groundhog Day" premise played for thrills. Barry Thompson (Silverman) is an employee at a scientific research firm who finds himself reliving the same 24-hour period over and over again. And what a day it is—he discovers a secret project is causing the mysterious time warp, falls in love with beauteous scientist Lisa (Slater) and watches as she gets murdered. Can Barry figure out how to stop what's going on and change things enough to save her? Adaptation of the short story "12:01" by Richard Lupoff, which was previously made into a short film. **92m/C; VHS, DVD.** Jonathan Silverman; Helen Slater; Martin Landau; Nicolas Surovy; Jeremy Piven; ***D:*** Jack Sholder. **TV**

12 Rounds 🦴🦴 **2009 (PG-13)** During an FBI sting to capture the notorious Irish terrorist, Miles Jackson (Gillen), things go wrong and detective Danny Fisher (Cena) accidentally kills the terrorist's girlfriend. One year later Jackson busts out of prison and kidnaps Fisher's wife in an act of revenge. The detective then must pass 12 violent challenges in order to save her and take down the deadly con on the streets of New Orleans during Mardi Gras. Veteran action director Harlin loads up on the standard barrage of car chases and fist-pumping action, but a shoddy script leaves much to be explained. WWE wrestler Cena proves capable of handling his new career but he's no Dwayne "The Rock" Johnson, as sad as that may sound. **108m/C; Blu-Ray, On Demand.** John Cena; Aidan Gillen; Steve Harris; Ashley Scott; Brian White; Taylor Cole; Ray Santiago; ***D:*** Renny Harlin; ***W:*** Daniel Kunka; ***C:*** David Boyd; ***M:*** Trevor Rabin.

12 Rounds 3: Lockdown 🦴🦴 **2015 (R)** A cop-centered action crime thriller. After the death of his partner, police detective Shaw (Ambrose) returns to active duty only to discover evidence that ties other officers in his precinct to a murder. Because of his revelation, Shaw is framed for a murder he did not commit. Determined to prove his innocence, he does everything he can to expose the corruption and clear his name. **90m/C; DVD, Blu-Ray, Streaming, Download.** Dean Ambrose; Roger R. Cross; Daniel Cudmore; Lochlyn Munro; Ty Olsson; ***D:*** Stephen Reynolds; ***W:*** Nathan Brookes; Bobby Lee Darby; ***C:*** Mahlon Todd Williams; ***M:*** Nathan Whitehead.

12 Strong 🦴🦴 ½ **2018 (R)** The true, recently declassified, account of the Horse Soldiers, the first Special Forces team deployed to Afghanistan after the 9/11 attacks. Led by Capt. Mitch Nelson (Hemsworth) and fueled by courage and patriotism, the 12-man unit rides on horseback into battle against 50,000 Taliban. The action is intense and realistic, but the film has been Bruckheimered into a superficial war movie that lacks nuance and much resemblance to the real-life soldiers who deserve a better homage. Based on the book "Horse Soldiers" by Doug Stanton. **130m/C; DVD, Blu-Ray.** Chris Hemsworth; Michael Shannon; Michael Peña; Navid Negahban; Trevante Rhodes; ***D:*** Nicolai Fuglsig; ***W:*** Ted Tally; Peter Craig; ***C:*** Rasmus Videbaek; ***M:*** Lorne Balfe.

12 to the Moon 🦴 *Twelve to the Moon* **1960** Astronauts land on the moon and the natives grow restless and forcibly invite the intruders to leave. Upon returning, the crew finds the moonies freezing the earth and decide the easiest way to combat this is to detonate an atom bomb in a volcano. **112m/B; DVD.** Ken Clark; Michi Kobi; Tom Conway; Anthony Dexter; John Wengraf; Anna-Lisa; Phillip Baird; Roger Til; Cary Devlin; Muzaffer Tema; Richard Weber; Robert Montgomery; ***Nar:*** Francis X. Bushman; ***D:*** David Bradley; ***W:*** Fred Gebhardt; DeWitt Bodeen; ***C:*** John Alton; John Alton; ***M:*** Michael Andersen. **VIDEO**

12/12/12 🦴 **2012 (R)** In this latest Asylum mockbuster, Veronica (Sarah Malakul Lane) lies in childbirth as her newborn baby arrives and promptly murders the nurse and doctor. **90m/C; DVD, Blu-Ray, Streaming.** Sara Malakul Lane; Jesus Guevara; Steve Hanks; Carl Donelson; Laura Alexandra Ramos; ***D:*** Jared Cohn; ***W:*** Jared Cohn; ***C:*** Ben Demaree; ***M:*** Graham Denman. **VIDEO**

12 Years a Slave 🦴🦴🦴 **2013 (R)** Director McQueen adapts the true story of Solomon Northup (Ejiofor), a free man kidnapped and forced back into slavery for over a decade. Transferred from owner to owner and ripped from his family, Northup's story becomes a defining one for the horrors of slavery overall. Ejiofor's incredible performance grounds the film but he's ably as sisted by strong supporting work from Fassbender as Northup's most demented abuser and Nyong'o as a slave that Solomon tries to protect. Sometimes a bit too self-conscious of its artistic nature, it still captures the human tragedy of slavery in ways that haven't been documented before. **134m/C; DVD, Blu-Ray.** Chiwetel Ejiofor; Michael Fassbender; Lupita Nyong'o; Sarah Paulson; Paul Dano; Benedict Cumberbatch; Bryan Batt; Paul Giamatti; Scoot McNairy; Michael K(enneth) Williams; Garret Dillahunt; Bill Camp; Alfre Woodard; Brad Pitt; ***D:*** Steve McQueen; ***W:*** John Ridley; ***C:*** Sean Bobbitt; ***M:*** Hans Zimmer. Oscars '13: Actress--Supporting (Nyong'o), Adapt. Screenplay, Film; British Acad. '13: Actor (Ejiofor), Film; Golden Globes '14: Film--Drama; Ind. Spirit '14: Actress--Supporting (Nyong'o), Cinematog., Director (McQueen), Film, Screenplay; Screen Actors Guild '13: Actress--Supporting (Nyong'o).

Twentieth Century 🦴🦴🦴🦴 **1934** Maniacal Broadway director Barrymore transforms shop girl Lombard into a smashing success adored by public and press. Tired of Barrymore's manic-excessive ways, she heads for the Hollywood hills, pursued by the Profile in fine form. **91m/B; DVD.** Carole Lombard; John Barrymore; Walter Connolly; Roscoe Karns; Edgar Kennedy; Ralph Forbes; Charles Lane; Etienne Girardot; Snow Flake; ***D:*** Howard Hawks; ***W:*** Charles MacArthur; Ben Hecht. Natl. Film Reg. '11.

20th Century Women 🦴🦴 ½ **2017 (R)** Mike Mills follows up his Oscar-winning film about his father ("Beginners") with a loosely autobiographical film about his mother. Bening gives a fantastic performance as Dorothea, single mother to Jamie (Zumann) in 1979 Santa Barbara. Helping teach teen Jamie about the ways of the world are room renter Abbie (Gerwig), handyman William (Crudup), and local crush Julie (Fanning). Mills' film is like hazy memories coming back on top of each other, and that makes it hard to grasp and even harder to care about the characters. Still, he draws great performances, especially from Bening and Gerwig. **119m/C; DVD, Blu-Ray.** Annette Bening; Elle Fanning; Greta Gerwig; Billy Crudup; Lucas Jade Zumann; ***D:*** Mike Mills; ***W:*** Mike Mills; ***C:*** Sean Porter; ***M:*** Roger Neill.

Twenty Bucks 🦴🦴🦴 **1993 (R)** Whimsical film follows a $20 bill from its "birth" at a cash machine to its "death" as it is returned to the bank, tattered and torn, for shredding. The bill is passed from owner to owner, sometimes simply and briefly, sometimes altering fate. The original screenplay is nearly 60 years old: Endre Bohem originally drafted it in 1935, and his son revised and updated it. Clever transitions allow the various stories and characters to blend almost seamlessly. The strongest character is Shue's, a young waitress and aspiring writer. Rosenfeld's directorial debut is worth a look. Filmed in Minneapolis. **91m/C; VHS, DVD.** Linda Hunt; David Rasche; George Morfogen; Brendan Fraser; Gladys Knight; Elisabeth Shue; Steve Buscemi; Christopher Lloyd; Sam Jenkins; Kamal Holloway; Melora Walters; William H. Macy; Diane Baker; Spalding Gray; Matt Frewer; Concetta Tomei; Nina Siemaszko; ***D:*** Keva Rosenfeld; ***W:*** Leslie Bohem; Endre Bohem; ***C:*** Emmanuel Lubezki; ***M:*** David Robbins. Ind. Spirit '94: Support. Actor (Lloyd).

Twenty8k 🦴🦴 **2012** Slick Brit crime thriller. Fashion exec Deeva returns to London when her younger brother Vipon is accused of murdering two people. She reconnects with old neighborhood flame Clint, an ex-gang member, as their investigation leads them to Vipon being a scapegoat for crimes involving drugs, prostitution, and police corruption. Title refers to the gang Vipon belongs to. **106m/C; DVD.** *UK* Parminder K. Nagra; Jonas Armstrong; Stephen (Dillon) Dillane; Sebastian Nanena; Kaya Scodelario; Michael Socha; ***D:*** David Kew; Neil Thompson; ***W:*** Paul Abbott; ***C:*** Mike Beresford-Jones; ***M:*** Ruth Barrett.

20 Feet from Stardom **2013 (PG-13)** What must it be like to be so close to fame and yet so far? Neville's documentary captures the lives of backup singers to the stars and how some make the leap to the front of the stage but most do not. With interviews with Merry Clayton, Darlene Love, Patti Austin, Sheryl Crow and many others, Neville takes viewers behind the microphones and into the lives of very talented men and women who simply may not have had the chance to shine like those they support so well. **91m/C; DVD, Blu-Ray.** ***D:*** Morgan Neville; ***C:*** Nicola Marsh; Graham Willoughby. Oscars '13: Feature Doc.; Ind. Spirit '14: Feature Doc.

The 25th Hour **1/2 1967** Despite good performances from Quinn and Lisi, this is a mess of a movie that lurches from comedy to tragedy and back again. Romanian peasant Johann Moritz is forced to leave his beautiful wife Susanna when he's deported to a labor camp during WWII. He escapes, makes it to Hungary, is captured by the Germans (again), but this time a crazy Nazi colonel decides Moritz is perfect for the SS. To save his skin, Johann joins up and is then put on trial by the allies after the war is over. **127m/C; DVD.** Anthony Quinn; Virna Lisi; Gregoire Aslan; Marcel Dalio; Michael Redgrave; Marius Goring; ***D:*** Henri Verneuil; ***W:*** Henri Verneuil; Francois Boyer; Wolf Mankowitz; ***C:*** Andreas Winding; ***M:*** Georges Delerue.

25th Hour **1/2 2002 (R)** Moody, atmospheric character study follows the last 24 hours of freedom for convicted drug dealer Monty Brogan (Norton) before he begins a seven-year sentence. Brogan says his goodbyes to his father, a retired firefighter who now runs a bar paid for with Monty's drug money; his longtime buddies Frank (Pepper), a Wall Street shark, and Jacob (Hoffman), a high school teacher with low self-esteem and a crush on one of his students (Paquin); and girlfriend Naturelle (Dawson), whom he suspects of turning him in. All feel different levels of guilt over letting Monty become involved in "the life." If Lee had stuck to these stories, it would've worked much better, but instead he lays the spectre of 9/11 over the proceedings, creating jarring scenes that sometimes work, but mostly distract from some impressive performances. **132m/C; VHS, DVD, Blu-Ray.** Edward Norton; Philip Seymour Hoffman; Barry Pepper; Rosario Dawson; Anna Paquin; Brian Cox; Isiah Whitlock, Jr.; Michael Genet; Tony Siragusa; Levani Outchanechvili; Misha Kuznetsov; ***D:*** Spike Lee; ***W:*** David Benioff; ***C:*** Rodrigo Prieto; ***M:*** Terence Blanchard. Golden Globes '03: Score.

24 Days *24 jours* **2014** A gripping thriller based on real events from 2006. In January 2006, 23-year-old Ilan Halimi, a Jewish Parisian, is kidnapped by a group who dubbed themselves The Gang of Barbarians. As Halimi's family begs the French police to save their son, the young man is tortured for 24 days before being killed. The film also explores the event in terms of the indifference of those who could have helped him and the anti-Semitism his mother believed played a major role in the response of the police and others who could have helped her son. French with subtitles. **108m/C; DVD, Streaming, Download.** Syrus Shahidi; Zabou Breitman; Pascal Elbe; Jacques Gamblin; Sylvie Testud; ***D:*** Alexandre Arcady; ***W:*** Alexandre Arcady; Emilie Freche; Antoine Lacomblez; ***C:*** Gilles Henry; ***M:*** Armand Amar.

The 24 Hour War **2016** A documentary look at the epic battles between Ford and Ferrari at the 24 Hours of Le Mans races in the 1960s. The feature-length documentary explains the background of this rivalry, which began in 1963. At the time, Ford had its struggles and Ferrari had the most successful racing team in the world. Henry Ford II tried to buy Ferrari from Enzo Ferrari, but months of negotiation led to nothing. Angered that Ferrari would not sell, Henry Ford II vowed to build a race car to rival Ferraris. Ford's GT40 race car was built in response and would ultimately dethrone the dominant Ferraris at Le Mans several times in the 1960s. **98m/C; DVD, Blu-Ray, Streaming, Download.** ***D:*** Nate Adams; Adam Carolla; ***C:*** Derek Bauer. **VIDEO**

24 Hours to Live **2017 (R)** A deeply flawed action film that does not serve the abilities of its leading man. After the death of his wife and son, grief-stricken assassin Travis Conrad (Hawke) takes one last job. During the assignment, he is shot, wakes up on the operating table, and learns that a newly developed technology has been used on him. Though resurrected, Travis only has 24 hours to live and uses that time to seek revenge on those who brought him back to life. Though Hawke tries to sell the lackluster dialogue and skid over the plot holes, the film is not fun enough to suspend disbelief. **93m/C; DVD, Blu-Ray.** Paul Anderson; Ethan Hawke; Rutger Hauer; Nathalie Boltt; Liam Cunningham; ***D:*** Brian Smrz; ***W:*** Zach Dean; Jim McClain; Ron Mita; ***C:*** Ben Nott; ***M:*** Tyler Bates.

The 24th Day **1/2 2004 (R)** Tom learned 24 days ago that he and his wife are infected with HIV and Tom blames Dan—a man whom he had a one-night-stand with five years before. Off he goes to not merely confront Dan—who doesn't even remember Tom—but to take him hostage while his blood is tested with plans for a slow, painful death if it comes back positive. Adapted from writer-director Piccirillo's own stage play—where it should have stayed. **92m/C; VHS, DVD.** Sofia Vergara; James Marsden; Scott Speedman; ***D:*** Tony Piccirillo; ***W:*** Tony Piccirillo; ***C:*** Alan Hostetter; ***M:*** Kevin Manthei. **VIDEO**

20 Million Miles to Earth **1/2 1957** A spaceship returning from an expedition to Venus crashes on Earth, releasing a fast-growing reptilian beast that rampages throughout Rome. Another entertaining example of stop-motion animation master Ray Harryhausen's work, offering a classic battle between the monster and an elephant. **82m/B; DVD, Blu-Ray.** William Hopper; Joan Taylor; Frank Puglia; John Zaremba; Thomas B(rowne). Henry; Jan Arvan; ***D:*** Nathan "Jerry" Juran; ***W:*** Christopher Knopf; Bob Williams; ***C:*** Irving Lippman; ***M:*** Mischa Bakaleinikoff.

29 Palms **1/2 2003 (R)** A law clerk discovers his judge boss thinks he's an undercover FBI agent who knows about some deals with an Indian casino. Fleeing a hitman, he comes to a small desert town, where he not only has to deal with said killer (who had his pay stolen and wants it back), but corrupt local weirdos. Not to be confused with the French film released the same year. **93m/C; DVD, Streaming.** Chris O'Donnell; Jeremy Davies; Michael Lerner; Russell Means; Rachael Leigh Cook; Jon Polito; Michael Rapaport; Bill Pullman; P.J. Byrne; Keith David; Carlos Mencia; ***D:*** Leonardo Ricagni; ***W:*** Tino Lucente; ***C:*** Horacio Maira; ***M:*** Mario Grigorov.

29th & Gay **2005** A year in the life of a 29-year-old gay man, James Sanchez, who longs for love and success. But the average-looking, unemployed actor is trapped by his own idea of what his life should be. Charming if cliched. **87m/C; DVD.** James Vasquez; Mike Doyle; Kali Rocha; Michael Emerson; Nicole Marcks; David McBean; Annie Hinton; ***D:*** Carrie Preston; ***C:*** Mark Holmes; ***M:*** John Avila.

21 Bridges **2019 (R)** After eight NYPD officers are killed during a drug heist, disgraced police detective Andre Davis (Boseman) leads the hunt for the killers. He's made tracking down cop killers his specialty – his cop father was killed on duty when he was young. Over the course of the night, Andre discovers that the killings are part of a wider conspiracy. As the search deepens, he closes all 21 bridges around Manhattan to keep the suspects from leaving the borough. While it covers familiar ground, Boseman and director Kirk have created a thoughtful police drama. **99m/C; DVD, Blu-Ray.** Chadwick Boseman; Sienna Miller; J.K. Simmons; Taylor Kitsch; David Keith; ***D:*** Brian Kirk; ***W:*** Adam Mervis; ***C:*** Paul Cameron; ***M:*** Alex Belcher; Henry Jackman.

21 Jump Street **2012 (R)** Bucking the trend of loathsome remakes of TV series, the creators of 21 Jump Street wisely chose not to translate their '80s cult hit directly but instead to use it as merely a foundation for their wacky comedy. The awkward Schmidt (Hill) and smooth Jenko (Tatum) join the Jump Street police, a group of underperforming cops forced to go undercover at a local high school to investigate a drug ring. With a consistent a string of laughs, it's a more successful product than the show on which it was based—a true rarity. **109m/C; DVD, Blu-Ray.** Jonah Hill; Channing Tatum; Ice Cube; Brie Larson; DeRay David; Dave Franco; Rob Riggle; Holly Robinson Peete; ***Cameo(s):*** Johnny Depp; Peter DeLuise; Richard Grieco; ***D:*** Phil Lord; Christopher Miller; ***W:*** Michael Bacall; ***C:*** Barry Peterson; ***M:*** Mark Mothersbaugh.

Twenty Plus Two **1961** Private eye Tom Adler (Janssen) specializes in missing person cases and links the murder of actor Leroy Dane's (Dexter) secretary to the disappearance of heiress Doris Delaney (Merrill). Except Doris isn't dead but using an alias after thinking she murdered her louse of a lover. Complicating the situation even more is Jacques'(Aubuchon) hiring Tom to search for his missing brother. **102m/B; DVD.** David Janssen; Dina Merrill; Jeanne Crain; Brad Dexter; Agnes Moorehead; Jacques Aubuchon; Robert Strauss; William Demarest; ***D:*** Joseph M. Newman; ***W:*** Frank Grubern; Carl Guthrie; ***C:*** Gerald Fried.

The Twenty Questions Murder Mystery **1/2** *Murder on the Air* **1950** Routine Brit crime programmer. A radio quiz show panel is challenged with an anonymous question that leads to multiple murders since the killer uses the show to name his next victim. **95m/B; DVD.** *GB* Robert Beatty; Rona Anderson; Clifford Evans; Olga Lindo; Edward Lexy; Harold Scott; ***D:*** Paul Stein; ***W:*** Victor Katona; Patrick Kirwan; ***C:*** Ernest Palmer.

22 July **1/2 2018 (R)** The true account of the one-man terrorist attacks that killed 77 people in Norway on July 22, 2011. The crimes themselves occupy the first half-hour, with the bulk of the film devoted to their aftermath from three perspectives: an injured survivor, the national leadership, and the defense attorney. A thriller that ends with messages of hope, resilience, and the triumph of good over evil. Based on the book *One of Us* by Åsne Seierstad. **143m/C; Streaming.** Anders Danielsen Lie; Jonas Strand Gravli; Jon Oigarden; Maria Bock; Thorbjorn Harr; ***D:*** Paul Greengrass; ***W:*** Paul Greengrass; ***C:*** Pål Ulvik Rokseth; ***M:*** Sune Martin.

20,000 Days on Earth **2014** Directors Forsyth and Pollard take a different approach to telling the story of a day-in-the-life of musician Nick Cave, a unique and influential cult superstar. Focusing mostly on the writing and recording of Cave's "Push the Sky Away," the directors allow Cave (also a screenwriter it should be noted) to craft a narrative of his life through voiceover and montage. It's a compelling look into the process of art as much as anything else, perfectly capturing the balance between the persona defined by Cave and how he uses his reality to create it, even if some of it isn't true. **95m/C; DVD, Blu-Ray.** *UK* Nick Cave; ***D:*** Iain Forsyth; Jane Pollard; ***W:*** Nick Cave; Iain Forsyth; Jane Pollard; ***C:*** Erik Alexander Wilson; ***M:*** Nick Cave; Warren Ellis.

20,000 Leagues under the Sea **1916** Outstanding silent adaptation of Jules Verne's "20,000 Leagues Under the Sea" and "The Mysterious Island" filmed with a then revolutionary underwater camera. Much octopus fighting. Look for newly mastered edition. **105m/B; Silent; VHS, DVD.** Matt Moore; Allen Holubar; June Gail; William Welsh; Chris Benton; Dan Hamlon; ***D:*** Stuart Paton; ***W:*** Stuart Paton; ***C:*** Eugene Gaudio. Natl. Film Reg. '16.

20,000 Leagues under the Sea **1/2 1954** From a futuristic submarine, Captain Nemo wages war on the surface world. A shipwrecked scientist and sailor do their best to thwart Nemo's dastardly schemes. Buoyant Disney version of the Jules Verne fantasy. **127m/C; VHS, DVD.** James Mason; Kirk Douglas; Peter Lorre; Paul Lukas; Robert J. Wilke; Carleton Young; ***D:*** Richard Fleischer; ***W:*** Earl Felton; ***C:*** Franz Planer; ***M:*** Paul J. Smith. Oscars '54: Art Dir./Set Dec., Color.

20,000 Leagues Under the Sea **1/2 1997** Silly TV version of the oft-told Verne tale finds marine biologist Aronnax (Crenna) and his assistant/daughter Sophie (Cox) prisoners on Captain Nemo's (Cross) submarine. In the original Verne version, Sophie was a young man—the sex change now means there's lots of boring eye-batting between Sophie, harpoonist Ned Land (Gross), and the jealous Nemo. The underwater photography is nifty but the fish also provide more excitement than the cast. **91m/C; VHS, DVD.** Ben Cross; Richard Crenna; Paul Gross; Julie Cox; Michael Jayston; ***D:*** Michael Anderson, Sr.; ***W:*** Joe Wiesenfeld; ***C:*** Alan Hume; ***M:*** John Scott. **TV**

20,000 Years in Sing Sing **1/2 1933** Based on the book by Sing Sing's reform-minded warden Lewis E. Lawes, who allowed the movie to be shot at the prison with actual prisoners in the crowd scenes. Tough guy Tom Connors (Tracy) soon finds out he's a nobody when he winds up in the joint, so he joins in an escape plan. When things go wrong, Tom decides to work with Warden Long (Byron) and earn a parole instead. Meanwhile, girlfriend Fay (Davis in an ill-fitting ingenue role) turns to sleazy lawyer Finn (Calhern) for help and gets in a serious car crash. And things get worse for Tom. Remade in 1940 as "Castle on the Hudson" with John Garfield in the Tracy role. **81m/B; DVD.** Spencer Tracy; Bette Davis; Bruce Byron; Lyle Talbot; Louis Calhern; Grant Mitchell; Warren Hymer; ***D:*** Michael Curtiz; ***W:*** Brown Holmes; Courtney Terrett; Wilson Mizner; Robert Lord; ***M:*** Bernhard Kaun.

23 Paces to Baker Street **1/2 1956** Blind writer Phillip Hannon (Johnson), who lives on London's Baker Street, overhears a kidnapping plot but can't get the police to believe him. So Phillip asks former fiancee Jean (Miles) and his secretary Matthews (Parker) to help him find the criminals. Some good twists in a tight B-movie crime/mystery. **103m/C; DVD, Blu-Ray.** Maurice Denham; Estelle Winwood; ***D:*** Henry Hathaway; James B. Clark; ***W:*** Nigel Balchin; ***C:*** Milton Krasner; ***M:*** Leigh Harline.

2012 *Twenty Twelve* **2009 (PG-13)** The ending of the Mayan calendar on 12/12/2012 brings about a number of natural disasters and predicts the end of the world. The king of the CGI apocalypse, director Emmerich delivers just that once again and little else. What there is of an actual tale focuses on sci-fi writer Jackson Curtis (Cusack, much too good of an actor for this), his failed marriage to Kate (Peet), and their kids—who Jackson of course has taken on a trip to Yellowstone Park before the world comes unhinged. An hour-too-long, preposterous exercise in computer-generated graphics. **158m/C; Blu-Ray, On Demand.** John Cusack; Amanda Peet; Danny Glover; Chiwetel Ejiofor; Oliver Platt; Thandie Newton; Woody Harrelson; Thomas (Tom) McCarthy; ***D:*** Roland Emmerich; ***W:*** Roland Emmerich; Harald Kloser; ***C:*** Dean Semler; ***M:*** Harald Kloser; Thomas Wanker.

20 Years After **1/2 2008 (R)** A post-apocalyptic saga with bombs and plagues leaving only a few survivors. Sarah (Skye) is pregnant with the first child to be born in 15 years and her only solace is listening to pirate radio DJ Michael (Leonard), whom she turns to for help when her pregnancy is put in danger. Sounds like somebody was reading "Children of Men." **95m/C; DVD.** Azura Skye; Joshua Leonard; Reg E. Cathey; Diane Salinger; Charlie Talbert; Nathan Baesel; ***D:*** Jim Torres; ***W:*** Ron Harris; Jim Torres; ***C:*** William Sweikart; ***M:*** John Heitzenrater; Chris Johnson. **VIDEO**

21 **1/2 2008 (PG-13)** Lacking the $300, 000 needed to attend Harvard, wide-eyed med student Ben Campbell (Sturgess) joins a secret gang of MIT geeks who spend their weekends raking in millions from Vegas casinos. Led by sneaky math prof Mickey Rose (Spacey), who teaches the ways of card counting and hand signals, and under the spell of his new girlfriend Jill (Bosworth), Ben quickly turns to the dark side. Very loosely based on the true exploits in Ben Mezrich's book "Bringing Down the House." Director Luketic should've stayed closer to the original material, but instead focuses solely on Ben and his predictable rise-and-fall drama as high roller who leaves his buddies behind, and the story suffers for it. **122m/C; DVD.** Jim

Sturgess; Kevin Spacey; Kate (Catherine) Bosworth; Aaron Yoo; Jacob Pitts; Laurence Fishburne; Liza Lapira; Sam Golzari; Jack Gilpin; Helen Carey; Josh Gad; Spencer Garrett; Jack McGee; *D:* Robert Luketic; *W:* Peter Steinfeld; Allan Loeb; *C:* Russell Carpenter; *M:* David Sardy.

21 & Over ♪ 1/2 **2013 (R)** The night before his big medical exam, and the night of his 21st birthday, studious college kid Jeff Change (Chon) is surprised by uninvited guests. His old high school pals Casey (Astin) and Miller (Teller) drag Jeff into a wild night of binge drinking, skirt-chasing, and tampon eating (don't ask). Jeff is passed out for much of it, letting the action focus on the party boys' idiotic antics. Standard frat fair, but this raunchy comedy violates rule #1: be funny. Penned by two writers from "The Hangover" who seem to have not much else to offer. **93m/C; DVD, Blu-Ray.** Justin Chon; Skylar Astin; Miles Teller; Sarah Wright; Jonathan Keltz; Francois Chau; *D:* Jon Lucas; Scott Moore; *W:* Jon Lucas; Scott Moore; *C:* Terry Stacey; *M:* Lyle Workman.

21 Days ♪♪ 1/2 *Twenty-One Days Together; The First and the Last* **1940** Dull film somewhat redeemed by its stars. Leigh is a married woman carrying on with Olivier. When her husband confronts them, Olivier accidentally kills him in a fight. They keep quiet but then a mentally deranged man is taken into custody for the crime. Since he will be held 21 days before coming to trial, the lovers decide to spend the time together before Olivier confesses. Based on the play "The First and the Last" by John Galsworthy. **75m/C; VHS, DVD.** *GB* Vivien Leigh; Laurence Olivier; Leslie Banks; Francis L. Sullivan; Hay Petrie; Esme Percy; Robert Newton; *D:* Basil Dean; *W:* Graham Greene; Basil Dean.

21 Grams ♪♪♪ 1/2 **2003 (R)** In his second film (his first in English), Inarritu takes what could have, in the wrong hands, become a trite Lifetime movie, and elevates it in an unusual and compelling fashion. Jack (DelToro), is imprisoned and born-again. Paul (Penn) has a terminal heart disease and needs a transplant. Christina (Watts), a recovering addict, mourns the loss of her family. Of course, the lives of these characters collide. Stellar performances by an excellent cast combine with beautiful cinematography to create a powerful film. Title refers to the amount of weight a body loses upon death. **125m/C; VHS, DVD, Blu-Ray.** Sean Penn; Benicio Del Toro; Naomi Watts; Charlotte Gainsbourg; Melissa Leo; Clea DuVall; Danny Huston; Paul Calderon; *D:* Alejandro Gonzalez Inarritu; *W:* Guillermo Arriaga; *C:* Rodrigo Prieto; *M:* Gustavo Santaolalla. L.A. Film Critics '03: Actress (Watts); Natl. Bd. of Review '03: Actor (Penn).

21 Hours at Munich ♪♪♪ **1976** Made-for-TV treatment of the massacre of Israeli athletes by Arab terrorists at the 1972 Olympics. Well-done. The film was produced using the actual Munich locations. **100m/C; VHS, DVD.** William Holden; Shirley Knight; Franco Nero; Anthony Quayle; Noel Willman; *D:* William A. Graham.

2103: Deadly Wake ♪♪ **1997** A cargo ship is carrying deadly waste, unbeknowst to its crew, which is also unaware that the ship is intended to be sunk (with the crew). **100m/C; VHS, DVD.** *CA GB* Malcolm McDowell; Michael Paré; Heidi von Palleske; Gwynyth Walsh; Hal Eisen; *D:* G. Philip Jackson; *W:* Timothy Lee; Andrew Dowler; Doug Bagot. **VIDEO**

21 Up South Africa: Mandela's Children ♪♪♪ **2008** A South African version of acclaimed series of feature documentaries, UP, that follow a group of children of various races and socio-economic status as they grow up. First filmed in 1992 at the age of 7, this installment visits the 11 South African children who are now 21 years old. In addition to exploring the changes in the personal lives, the effects of the end of apartheid on their opportunities and the challenges they face are considered as well. The AIDS crisis is a particular focus, and has a particular impact on several of the participants. **70m/C; DVD.** *D:* Angus Gibson. **VIDEO**

22 Bullets ♪♪ *L'Immortel* **2010** Efficient French crime thriller. Former Marseilles crime boss Charly Mattei (Reno) is shot 22 times by masked assassins who don't know how to make a head shot. He survives, earning the nickname 'The Immortal', and is generally pissed off someone would bother him in his retirement. Then he learns onetime rival Zacchia (Merad) was behind the attempt and Charly wants his revenge. French with subtitles. **117m/C; DVD, Blu-Ray.** *FR* Jean Reno; Kad Merad; Marina Fois; Jean-Pierre Darroussin; Richard Berry; *D:* Richard Berry; *W:* Richard Berry; Matthieu Delaporte; Alexandre de la Patelliere; *C:* Thomas Hardmeier; *M:* Klaus Badelt.

22 Jump Street ♪♪ 1/2 **2014 (R)** The reboot of the TV series 21 Jump Street as a major comedy franchise continues with remarkable success thanks to the bro-chemistry of affable stars Hill and Tatum. The two leads play Morton Schmidt and Greg Jenko, who are forced back to work undercover at a local college this time to find the supplier of a drug known as "WHYPHY" that's killing students. Of course, the drug dealing plotline is just an excuse for the guys to act like horny, crazed college kids again. Well-cast, funny, and totally carried by Hill and Tatum, this is the surprisingly effective comedy sequel that allows one to look forward to part three. **112m/C; DVD, Blu-Ray.** Amber Stevens; Jonah Hill; Channing Tatum; Ice Cube; Nick Offerman; Jillian Bell; Wyatt Russell; Peter Stormare; *D:* Phil Lord; Christopher Miller; *W:* Michael Bacall; Rodney Rothman; Oren Uziel; *C:* Barry Peterson; *M:* Mark Mothersbaugh.

23 1/2 Hours Leave ♪♪ **1937** Amusing WWI service comedy as a barracks wisecare bets that by the following morning he'll be breakfasting with a general. It's a songfilled remake of a 1919 film, whose star Douglas MacLean later produced this. **73m/B; VHS, DVD.** James Ellison; Terry Walker; Morgan Hill; Arthur Lake; Paul Harvey; *D:* John Blystone.

24 Exposures ♪ 1/2 **2013** Mumblecore's most productive wunderkind, director Swanberg, turns in another micro-budget examination of reality, illusion, and the minutia of relationship struggles. Fetish/erotic gore photographer Billy (fellow mumblecore director, Wingard), comes under investigation by local cop Mike (fellow mumblecore screenwriter, Barrett) after one of his models is murdered. Not only that, but Billy's girlfriend Alex (White), begins to lose her patience for his ever-wandering eye. Unfortunately, this interesting experiment in bare-bones filmmaking is bogged down by stiff performances and illogical character choices. **80m/C; DVD.** Adam Wingard; Simon Barrett; Helen Rogers; Sophia Takal; Mike Brune; Caroline White; *D:* Joe Swanberg; *W:* Joe Swanberg; *C:* Adam Pinney.

Twenty-Four Eyes ♪♪♪ *Nijushi No Hitomi* **1954** Miss Oishi (Takamine), a teacher on a remote Japanese island in the 1920s, attempts to transmit peaceful values to her 12 pupils amidst the clamor of a nation gearing up for war. As she watches them grow up, many of them doomed to an early death, she remains a pillar of quiet strength. In Japanese with English subtitles. **158m/B; VHS, DVD.** *JP* Hideko Takamine; Chishu Ryu; Toshiko Kobayashi; *D:* Keisuke Kinoshita.

24 Hour Party People ♪♪ **2001 (R)** Winterbottom's tribute to the late '70s through early '90s punk rock/rave/acid culture of his native Manchester as seen through the bleary eyes of real-life figure Tony Wilson (Coogan). Wilson is a presenter for Granada TV when he's inspired by a Sex Pistols performance to open a club, the Hacienda, to showcase local bands, including Joy Division (which morphs into New Order) and the Happy Mondays. He also starts Factory Records—both of which eventually fail, thanks to drugs and general craziness. Filmed in a semi-documentary style with Wilson's asides to camera commenting on the scenes. **115m/C; VHS, DVD, Blu-Ray.** *GB* Steve Coogan; Lennie James; Shirley Henderson; Paddy Considine; Andy Serkis; John Simm; Danny Cunningham; Keith Allen; Sean Harris; Chris Coghill; Paul Popplewell; *D:* Michael Winterbottom; *W:* Frank Cottrell-Boyce; *C:* Robby Muller.

The 24 Hour Woman ♪♪ 1/2 **1999 (R)** Perez is Grace, a morning TV talk show producer who has her pregnancy announced on the air, to the surprise of the baby's father (and the show's co-host) Serrano. Heartless executive producer LuPone milks the pregnancy for every ratings point, then callously turns her back on her employee's problems once the baby is delivered. Pressured by the demands of her job and motherhood, Grace has a major mental meltdown in which she confronts her harpy boss on air. Perez shows a more mature side while still retaining her Latina buzzsaw comic gifts. **93m/C; VHS, Streaming.** Rosie Perez; Marianne Jean-Baptiste; Patti LuPone; Karen Duffy; Wendell Pierce; Melissa Leo; Aida Turturro; Diego Serrano; Rosanna Desoto; Alicia Renee Washington; *D:* Nancy Savoca; *W:* Nancy Savoca; Richard Guay; *C:* Teresa Medina; *M:* Louis Vega; Kenny Gonzalez.

24 Hours in London ♪♪ **2000 (R)** In 2009's London, organized crime openly vies with the police for control of the streets. Mob boss Christian (Olsen) has just 24 hours to prevent witness Martha (Smith) from testifying against him for murder or watch his criminal empire vanish. Violent. **91m/C; VHS, DVD.** *GB* Gary Olsen; Tony London; Anjela Lauren Smith; David Sonnethal; Wendy Cooper; Sara Stockbridge; Luke Garrett; *D:* Alexander Finbow; *W:* Alexander Finbow; *C:* Chris Plevin; *M:* Edmund Butt.

24 Hours to Kill ♪ 1/2 **1965** Pilot Jamie (Barker) is forced to land in Beirut because of engine trouble and there's now a 24-hour layover. Purser Norman (Rooney) soon needs his help because he's really a smuggler on the run for stealing gold bullion. The Malouf (Slezak) gang cause problems but Jamie and the flight crew decide to help Norman anyway. Filmed in Lebanon. **94m/C; DVD.** *GB* Lex Barker; Mickey Rooney; Walter Slezak; Helga Sommerfeld; Michael Medwin; Wolfgang Lukschy; *D:* Peter Bezencenet; *W:* Peter Yeldham; *C:* Ernest Steward; *M:* Wilfred Josephs.

24 Nights ♪♪ 1/2 **1999** Twenty-four-year-old Jonathan Parker has never stopped believing in Santa Claus after a magical encounter at the age of four. Now a pot-smoking loser at life and love, he writes a letter to Santa asking for true romance. When Jonathan meets new co-worker Toby, he decides his letter has been answered even though Toby has a longtime boyfriend. But Jonathan will do anything to get what he believes is his Christmas wish. **97m/C; VHS, DVD.** Kevin Isola; Aida Turturro; Steven Mailer; David Burtka; Mary Louise Wilson; *D:* Kieran Turner; *W:* Kieran Turner; *C:* Scott Barnard.

24: Redemption ♪♪ **2008** TV movie is set between the sixth and seventh seasons of the series. Jack Bauer has been contacted by his Special Forces buddy Carl Benton (Carlyle), who now runs an orphanage in the small (fictional) African nation of Sangala. A local warlord is planning a coup and forcing boys to become child soldiers. Jack comes to their rescue (over the mealy-mouthed objections of the bureaucrats at the U.S. embassy) while back home President-Elect Allison Taylor (Jones) should be watching out for unsavory elements in the Capitol. **88m/C; DVD.** Kiefer Sutherland; Robert Carlyle; Cherry Jones; Tony Todd; Powers Boothe; Jon Voight; Gil Bellows; Peter MacNichol; Bob Gunton; Eric Lively; Colm Feore; Sebastien Roche; *D:* Jon Cassar; *W:* Howard Gordon; *M:* Sean Callery. **TV**

25 Fireman's Street ♪♪♪ *Almok a hazrol; Tuzolto utca 25* **1973** An evocative drama about the residents of an old house in Hungary which is about to be torn down, and their evening of remembrances of life before, during and after WWII. In Hungarian with English subtitles. **97m/C; VHS, DVD.** *HU* Rita Bekes; Peter Muller; Lucyna Winnicka; Andras Balint; *D:* Istvan Szabo; *W:* Istvan Szabo; Luca Karall; *C:* Sandor Sara.

27 Dresses ♪ 1/2 **2008 (PG-13)** You know the drill: Hopeless romantic Jane (Heigl) simply adores weddings but is the perennial bridesmaid—literally—with 27 (oft hideous) bridesmaid dresses to prove it. Jane crushes on her boss George (Burns), but he has eyes for her sister Tess (Akerman). In the meantime perennial cynic Kevin (Marsden) has a thing for Jane, but she's too hooked on her boss to pay any attention. What she doesn't realize is that Kevin is actually the writer of a marriage column that Jane has been clipping for years. What ensues is pure romantic-comedy rehash. Heigl's adorable, but alas, this silly chick flick is much less so. **107m/C; DVD, Blu-Ray.** Katherine Heigl; James Marsden; Malin Akerman; Judy Greer; Edward Burns; Melora Hardin; Brian Kerwin; Maulik Pancholy; *D:* Anne Fletcher; *W:* Aline Brosh McKenna; *C:* Peter James; *M:* Randy Edelman.

The 27th Day ♪♪ 1/2 **1957** Temperate cold war allegory has aliens deliver five mysterious capsules to five Earthlings from different countries. Each capsule, if opened, is capable of decimating the population of the entire planet, but is rendered ineffective after 27 days or upon the death of the holder. Wild ending. Based on John Mantley novel. **75m/B; VHS, DVD.** Gene Barry; Valerie French; George Voskovec; Arnold Moss; Stefan Schnabel; Ralph Clanton; Friedrich Ledebur; Mari Tsien; *D:* William Asher; *W:* John Mantley; *C:* Henry Freulich; *M:* Mischa Bakaleinikoff.

28 Days ♪♪ 1/2 **2000 (PG-13)** Hard-partying New York journalist Gwen (Bullock) manages to destroy her sister's wedding reception when she gets drunk and manages to get arrested for DUI. The film's title refers to the amount of time Gwen must spend at a rehab clinic. Naturally, Gwen doesn't really believe she has a problem and that's the first attitude adjustment she has to make. Cliches galore although Bullock is welcomingly spiky rather than sweet. **103m/C; VHS, DVD.** Sandra Bullock; Viggo Mortensen; Dominic West; Diane Ladd; Elizabeth Perkins; Steve Buscemi; Alan Tudyk; Reni Santoni; Marianne Jean-Baptiste; Michael O'Malley; Azura Skye; Margo Martindale; *D:* Betty Thomas; *W:* Susannah Grant; *C:* Declan Quinn; *M:* Richard Gibbs.

28 Days Later ♪♪ 1/2 **2002 (R)** Jim (Murphy) wakes up in a London hospital after an accident and finds the building deserted. London seems deserted as well—until he nearly becomes a victim of blood-drinking zombies. Rescued by Selena (Harris) and Mark (Huntley), Jim learns that animal rights activists released lab chimps who carried a blood-transmitted plague that decimated the population within 28 days. The few uninfected survivors have banded together and decide to head to Manchester, where a military installation is said to be a safe haven. Ick and gore galore. **108m/C; VHS, DVD, Blu-Ray.** *GB US* Cillian Murphy; Megan Burns; Brendan Gleeson; Naomie Harris; Christopher Eccleston; Noah Huntley; *D:* Danny Boyle; *W:* Alex Garland; *C:* Anthony Dod Mantle; *M:* John Murphy.

28 Hotel Rooms ♪ **2012** Long-distance adultery between a nameless cople in a series of hotel rooms over some years. He's a New York writer with a girlfriend (and then wife) and she's a married accountant from Seattle who meet while traveling on business. It's about sex rather than talk and the lack of emotional connection makes for a film as bland as the interchangeable rooms themselves. **82m/C; DVD.** Chris Messina; Marin Ireland; *D:* Matt Ross; *W:* Matt Ross; *C:* Doug Emmett. **VIDEO**

28 Weeks Later ♪♪ 1/2 **2007 (R)** Sequel to "28 Days Later" serves up new flawed protagonists and same old angry zombies ravaging Britain. Don (Carlyle), attacked by a horde infected by the rage virus, leaves his wife Alice (McCormack) behind. Reunited in an American-run safe zone in London, Alice infects Don and all hell breaks loose and American occupiers must fight for their lives, sometimes at the expense of morality. Brutally terrifying and relentlessly paced, director Fresnadillo also injects wit and allegory, although both get buried as the movie progresses into a full-blown bloodfest. **99m/C; DVD, Blu-Ray.** *GB US* Robert Carlyle; Rose Byrne; Jeremy Renner; Harold Perrineau, Jr.; Catherine McCormack; Idris Elba; *D:* Juan Carlos Fresnadillo; *W:* Juan Carlos Fresnadillo; Rowan Joffe; Jesus Olmo; Enrique Lopez Lavigne; *C:* Enrique Chediak.

29th Street ♪♪ 1/2 **1991 (R)** Compelling comedy-drama based on the true story of Frank Pesce, a New York actor who won $6 million in that state's first lottery. Great performance from Aiello, as usual, but the direction falters in the dramatic sequences. Based on the book by Frank Pesce and James Franciscus. **101m/C; VHS, DVD.** Danny Aiello; Anthony LaPaglia; Lainie Kazan; Frank Pesce; Donna Magnani; Rick Aiello; Vic Manni; Ron Karabatsos; Robert Forster; Joe Franklin;

Pete Antico; ***D:*** George Gallo; ***W:*** George Gallo; ***C:*** Steven Fierberg; ***M:*** William Olvis.

2012: Doomsday 2008 (PG-13) Doomsday for anyone watching something this bad. On December 21, 2012—the day the Mayan calendar predicts the world will end—four strangers are drawn to an ancient temple in Mexico. (There's some Christian-oriented Bible/Rapture stuff involved here that never makes much sense.) Meanwhile, scientists discover that a cataclysmic polar shift is causing the Earth's axis to slow. **85m/C; DVD.** Cliff De Young; Dale Midkiff; Ami Dolenz; Joshua Lee; Sara Tomko; Danae Nason; ***D:*** Nick Everhart; ***W:*** Nick Everhart; ***C:*** Mark Atkins; ***M:*** Ralph Rieckermann. **VIDEO**

2046 1/2 **2004 (R)** Wong's quasi-sequel to 2001's "In the Mood for Love" is a swoony, hopeless romance about lovers who meet each other at the wrong time to fall in love. Womanizing Chow (Leung Chui-wai) is a pulp fiction writer who moves into Room 2047 of Hong Kong's Hotel Oriental and gets involved with the beautiful women who briefly occupy Room 2046 ("2046" is also the name of the sci-fi novel Chow is writing). There are two ex-girlfriends named Su Li (Gong Li and Cheung), whom he left behind in Singapore; Lulu/Mimi (Lau), who is murdered; prostitute Bai Ling (Zhang), who becomes Chow's confidante; and Jing (Wong), the daughter of the hotel's owner who's in love with a man her father disapproves of. It certainly looks gorgeous; Japanese and Mandarin with subtitles. **129m/C; DVD.** *CH CH FR GE* Tony Leung Chiu-Wai; Gong Li; Takuya Kimura; Faye Wong; Ziyi Zhang; Carina Lau; Chen "Chang Chen" Chang; Maggie Cheung; Wang Sum; Lam Siu-ping; Thongchai McIntyre; Dong Jie; ***D:*** Wong Kar-Wai; ***W:*** Wong Kar-Wai; ***C:*** Christopher Doyle; Lai Yiu-fai; Kwan Pun-leung; ***M:*** Peer Raben; Shingeru Umebayashi. N.Y. Film Critics '05: Cinematog.; Natl. Soc. Film Critics '05: Cinematog.

Twentynine Palms 1/2 **2003** Director Dumont's first feature made in the U.S. is a grim, moody thriller than grinds on monotonously until a twist near the end triggers an intense situation. L.A. residents David (Wissak) and his French-speaking girlfriend Katia (Golubeva) embark on a trip to the California desert locale of the title. The action mostly consists of motel stops where the eerily laconic couple, who mostly just drive around and bicker, copulate graphically and frequently out of boredom. David accidentally hits a dog, to Katia's horror, but not much else happens until they get hit from behind by a strange vehicle which sets off horrific violence. Seemingly pointless exercise in gratuitous sex and violence. Mostly in English with some French dialogue. **119m/C; VHS, DVD.** *GE FR* Yekaterina (Katia) Golubeva; David Wissak; ***D:*** Bruno Dumont; ***W:*** Bruno Dumont; ***C:*** Georges Lechaptois; ***M:*** Takashi Hirayasu; Bob Brozman.

Twice a Judas *Dos Veces Judas; Due Volte Guida* **1969** An amnesiac is swindled and has his family killed by a ruthless renegade. He wants to get even, even though he can't remember who anyone is. **90m/C; VHS, DVD, Blu-Ray.** *IT SP* Klaus Kinski; Antonio (Tony) Sabato; Emma Baron; Franco Beltramme; Jose Calvo; ***D:*** Nando Cicero; ***W:*** Jaime Jesus Balcazar; ***C:*** Francis Marin; ***M:*** Carol Pes.

Twice Born *Venuto al Mondo* **2012 (R)** Florid, dreary romantic drama complete with ripe dialogue and some questionable casting. Single mom Gemma (Cruz) brings her sullen teenaged son Pietro (Castellitto) to Sarajevo to see an exhibition of photos done by the father he never knew. Plot backtracks to when Italian Gemma and American Diego (Hirsch) met and fell in love at the Sarajevo Olympics. They're desperate to have a child but there are problems and then they get caught up in the Bosnian war, so Pietro's finally going to learn some family secrets. English, Italian, and Bosnian with subtitles. **127m/C; DVD.** *IT* Penelope Cruz; Emile Hirsch; Pietro Castellitto; Adnan Haskovic; Saadet Aksoy; Mira Furlan; Jane Birkin; ***D:*** Sergio Castellitto; ***W:*** Sergio Castellitto; Margaret Mazzantini; ***C:*** Gianfilippo Corticello; ***M:*** Eduardo Cruz.

Twice Dead WOOF! **1988** A family moves into a ramshackle mansion haunted by a stage actor's angry ghost. The ghost helps them battle some attacking delinquent boys. Uninteresting story, poorly done. Never released in theatres. **94m/C; VHS, DVD.** Tom Breznahan; Jill Whitlow; Sam Melville; Brooke Bundy; Todd Bridges; Jonathan Chapin; Christopher Burgard; ***D:*** Bert L. Dragin; ***M:*** David Bergeaud.

Twice in a Lifetime **1985 (R)** Middle-aged man takes stock of his life when he's attracted to Ann-Margret. Realizing he's married in name only, he moves in with his new love while his former wife and children struggle with shock, disbelief, and anger. Well-acted, realistic, and unsentimental. **117m/C; VHS, DVD.** Gene Hackman; Ellen Burstyn; Amy Madigan; Ann-Margret; Brian Dennehy; Ally Sheedy; ***D:*** Bud Yorkin; ***W:*** Colin Welland.

Twice-Told Tales *Nathaniel Hawthorne's "Twice Told Tales"* **1963** Horror trilogy based loosely on three Nathaniel Hawthorne tales, "Dr. Heidegger's Experiment," "Rappaccini's Daughter," and "The House of Seven Gables." Price is great in all three of these well-told tales. **120m/C; VHS, DVD, Blu-Ray.** Vincent Price; Sebastian Cabot; Brett Halsey; Beverly Garland; Richard Denning; ***D:*** Sidney Salkow; ***W:*** Robert E. Kent; ***C:*** Ellis W. Carter; ***M:*** Richard LaSalle.

Twice upon a Yesterday *The Man With Rain in His Shoe; If Only* **1998 (R)** Struggling London actor Victor (Henshall) is a romantic swine. He two-timed girlfriend Sylvia (Headey) and she wisely dumped him and found another guy, Dave (Strong), and they're going to get married. Through some time-travelling magic, Victor is able to relive his fateful moment and prevent Sylvia's going. But she winds up meeting Dave anyway while a confused Victor finds a sympathetic bartender, Louise (Cruz), to listen to his romantic trials. Things are just a little too sappy and meandering but the cast (especially Cruz) are worth watching. **94m/C; VHS, DVD.** *GB* Douglas Henshall; Lena Headey; Mark Strong; Penelope Cruz; Elizabeth McGovern; Eusebio Lazaro; Charlotte Coleman; Gustavo Salmeron; Neil Stuke; ***D:*** Maria Ripoli; ***W:*** Rafa Russo; ***C:*** Javier Salmones.

Twilight *The Magic Hour* **1998 (R)** It's a pleasure to see pros at work, even if the story is a familiar one. In the noir world of L.A., ex-cop, ex-drunk, ex-P.I. Harry Ross (Newman) is living above the garage at the estate of movie star marrieds Jack (Hackman) and Catherine (Sarandon) Ames, for whom Harry has done several jobs. The cancer-stricken Jack asks Harry to handle a blackmail payoff, which seems to resurrect the circumstances of femme fatale Catherine's first husband's alleged suicide. Also involved is Harry's colleague Raymond Hope (Garner)and Harry's ex-flame, Verna (Channing), a cop investigating a murder with ties to the entire ugly situation. **94m/C; VHS, DVD.** Paul Newman; Susan Sarandon; Gene Hackman; James Garner; Stockard Channing; Reese Witherspoon; Giancarlo Esposito; Liev Schreiber; Margo Martindale; John Spencer; M. Emmet Walsh; ***D:*** Robert Benton; ***W:*** Robert Benton; Richard Russo; ***C:*** Piotr Sobocinski; ***M:*** Elmer Bernstein.

Twilight 1/2 **2008 (PG-13)** Misfit Bella Swan (Stewart) moves in with her divorced sheriff father in small-town Forks, Washington, where she struggles to fit into her new high school. However, after being saved from certain death in the school parking lot by mysterious hunk Edward Cullen (Pattinson), she discovers romance and the dark secret behind his family tree: they're all vampires. A pop-culture phenomenon with teen girls, mostly due to Pattinson's instant heartthrob status, but like most book-to-screen translations, some fans of Stephanie Meyer's novel will likely be disappointed. **121m/C; Blu-Ray, On Demand.** Kristen Stewart; Robert Pattinson; Taylor Lautner; Billy Burke; Peter Facinelli; Elizabeth Reaser; Nikki Reed; Jackson Rathbone; Ashley Greene; Kellan Lutz; Cam Gigandet; Rachelle Lefevre; Edi Gathegi; Anna Kendrick; Michael Welch; Gil Birmingham; Justin Chon; Christian Serratos; ***D:*** Catherine Hardwicke; ***W:*** Melissa Rosenberg; ***C:*** Elliot Davis; ***M:*** Carter Burwell.

The Twilight Girls *Les Collegiennes* **1957** Escaping a family scandal, Catherine Royner (Arnaud) enters an exclusive girls boarding school and is immediately introduced to a clique of wealthy girls—one of whom, Monica (Laurent) develops a amourous attraction to the newcomer. Film was originally banned in New York because of the frankness of its lesbian scenes. Deneuve's film debut (under the family name Dorleac) as Adelaide. Her scenes were cut in the version originally released in the U.S. but are restored on the DVD. **83m/B; VHS, DVD.** *FR* Marie-Helene Arnaud; Agnes Laurent; Elga Andersen; Henri Guisol; Estella Blain; Catherine Deneuve; ***D:*** Andre Hunebelle; ***W:*** Jean Lambertie; Jacques Lancien; ***C:*** Paul Cotteret.

Twilight of Honor **1963** Since he was enjoying success as "Dr. Kildare," MGM decided to promote Chamberlain's popularity on the big screen in this average courtroom drama. Young local attorney David Mitchell's given a no-win case of loner Ben Brown (Adams) who's accused of murdering a prominent citizen. He's even confessed, but David becomes suspicious of his story, especially after ambitious state prosecutor Bixby (Gregory) tries to suppress evidence because of a potential scandal. Adams lobbied hard to get an Academy Award nomination and did so. **104m/B; DVD.** Richard Chamberlain; Nick Adams; Joey Heatherton; Claude Rains; Joan Blackman; James Gregory; Pat Buttram; ***D:*** Boris Sagal; ***W:*** Henry Denker; ***C:*** Philip H. Lathrop; ***M:*** Johnny Green.

The Twilight of the Golds 1/2 **1997 (PG-13)** The upper-middle class Jewish Gold family seem conventional if fretful: there's doctor dad Walter (Marshall), concerned mom Phyllis (Dunaway), married daughter Suzanne (Beals), and aspiring theatrical producer son David (Fraser), who's gay. It seems everyone's dealt with David's homosexuality until Suzanne's geneticist husband, Rob Stein (Tenney), informs his pregnant wife that tests on their unborn son show genes statistically link to him being gay. (The theory is unproven.) Suzanne considers abortion and David is understandably upset when no one tries to talk her out of it, beginning a family estrangement. Based on the play by Tolins. **90m/C; VHS, DVD.** Garry Marshall; Faye Dunaway; Jennifer Beals; Brendan Fraser; Jon Tenney; Jack Klugman; Sean O'Bryan; Rosie O'Donnell; ***D:*** Ross Kagen Marks; ***W:*** Jonathan Tolins; Seth Bass; ***C:*** Tom Richmond; ***M:*** Lee Holdridge. **CABLE**

The Twilight of the Ice Nymphs **1997** Welcome once again to filmmaker Maddin's weird world. Peter Glahn (Whitney) is released from prison and travels back to his mythical home in Mandragora, where the sun never sets. At the family ostrich farm, his sister Amelia (Duvall) is smitten with Dr. Solti (Thompson) who has unearthed a mysterious statue of Venus that apparently has strange powers. And Peter gets involved with two women, Zephyr (Krige) and Julianna (Bussieres), who also have ties to the doctor. Deliberately artificial and hallucinatory. **91m/C; VHS, DVD.** *CA* Pascale Bussieres; R.H. Thomson; Alice Krige; Nigel Whitmey; Shelley Duvall; Frank Gorshin; Ross McMillan; ***D:*** Guy Maddin; ***W:*** George Toles; ***C:*** Michael Marshall; ***M:*** John McCulloch.

Twilight People WOOF! *Beasts* **1972 (PG)** When a mad scientist's creations turn on him for revenge, he runs for his life. Boring, gory, with bad make-up and even poorer acting. This one should fade away into the night. **84m/C; VHS, DVD, Blu-Ray.** *PH* John Ashley; Pat(ricia) Woodell; Jan Merlin; Pam Grier; Eddie Garcia; ***D:*** Eddie Romero.

The Twilight Saga: Breaking Dawn, Part 1 **2011 (PG-13)** At this point, the series is strictly for fans. Edward and Bella are married, go on their violent honeymoon, and Bella immediately gets pregnant. This is a dangerous occurrence for Bella's health, since humans aren't meant to have half-vampire babies. The birth scene is intense and causes added trouble for the couple since the Volturi vampires and the Quileute wolf pack take a too-close interest in the baby. And with the marriage, the issue of Bella getting turned into a vampire yet again arises. Adapted from the Stephenie Meyer novel. **117m/C; DVD, Blu-Ray.** Kristen Stewart; Robert Pattinson; Taylor Lautner; Peter Facinelli; Elizabeth Reaser; Ashley Greene; Kellan Lutz; Nikki Reed; Jackson Rathbone; Billy Burke; Anna Kendrick; Dakota Fanning; Michael Sheen; ***D:*** Bill Condon; ***W:*** Melissa Rosenberg; ***C:*** Guillermo Navarro; ***M:*** Carter Burwell.

The Twilight Saga: Breaking Dawn, Part 2 **2012 (PG-13)** The fifth and last film for the Stephenie Meyer's vampire saga. Bella's a vampire and she and husband Edward have to deal with the consequences of their rapidly growing, half-vampire/half-human daughter Renesmee, whose existance has upset the ruling Volturi. Jacob and his werewolf pack get involved since he imprinted on the girl and there's a battle between the Cullen family and friends and those interfering Volturi. It wraps up neatly and Twi-hards should be happy. **115m/C; DVD, Blu-Ray.** Kristen Stewart; Robert Pattinson; Taylor Lautner; Mackenzie Foy; Maggie Grace; Michael Sheen; Peter Facinelli; Elizabeth Reaser; Ashley Greene; ***D:*** Bill Condon; ***W:*** Melissa Rosenberg; ***C:*** Guillermo Navarro; ***M:*** Carter Burwell. Golden Raspberries '12: Worst Actress (Stewart), Worst Director (Condon), Worst Ensemble Cast, Worst Picture, Worst Remake/Sequel, Worst Support. Actor (Lautner).

The Twilight Saga: Eclipse 1/2 **2010 (PG-13)** The third film adapted from Stephenie Meyer's books has Bella (Stewart) reuniting with vampire love Edward Cullen (Pattinson) while maintaining her friendship with werewolf rival Jacob Black (Lautner). Vamp Victoria (Howard) wants revenge on Bella and is behind a series of Seattle kills that are moving closer to her hometown. Also, impatient Bella wants to both lose her humanity and her virginity to Edward but he wants them to marry first (after she graduates). **124m/C; Blu-Ray, On Demand.** Kristen Stewart; Robert Pattinson; Taylor Lautner; Ashley Greene; Peter Facinelli; Elizabeth Reaser; Kellan Lutz; Nikki Reed; Jackson Rathbone; Bryce Dallas Howard; Billy Burke; Anna Kendrick; Dakota Fanning; Jodelle Ferland; Michael Welch; Gil Birmingham; Christian Serratos; Julia Jones; Cameron Bright; Kirsten Prout; Sarah Clarke; Catalina Sandino Moreno; Chaske Spencer; Leah Gibson; Alex Meraz; ***D:*** David Slade; ***W:*** Melissa Rosenberg; ***C:*** Javier Aguirresarobe; ***M:*** Howard Shore. Golden Raspberries '10: Worst Support. Actor (Rathbone).

The Twilight Saga: New Moon *New Moon; Twilight: New Moon* **2009 (PG-13)** When Bella's (Stewart) 18th birthday party at the Cullens' nearly proves fatal for her, vampire beau Edward (Pattinson) abruptly leaves, fearing his attraction might be the death of her. Despondent, Bella and her now-superbuff childhood pal Jacob Black (Lautner) reconnect, leading to a romantic triangle—sort of. Thing is Jacob has his own secret. But her devotion to Edward causes Bella to put herself in harm's way hoping he will return and "save" her. Meanwhile, Edward is in Italy trying to provoke the vampire counsel of the Volturri into killing him. Slow moving and overly mopey, but sure to suck in fanatics by staying true to the second book in Stephenie Meyer's series. **130m/C; Blu-Ray, On Demand.** Kristen Stewart; Robert Pattinson; Taylor Lautner; Ashley Greene; Peter Facinelli; Elizabeth Reaser; Kellan Lutz; Nikki Reed; Jackson Rathbone; Chaske Spencer; Rachelle Lefevre; Edi Gathegi; Billy Burke; Dakota Fanning; Cameron Bright; Michael Sheen; Christopher Heyerdahl; Graham Greene; Anna Kendrick; Michael Welch; Justin Chon; Christian Serratos; ***D:*** Chris Weitz; ***W:*** Melissa Rosenberg; ***C:*** Javier Aguirresarobe; ***M:*** Alexandre Desplat.

The Twilight Samurai 1/2 *Tasogare Seibei* **2002** Director Yamada's long-awaited foray into samurai cinema that was definitely worth the wait. Story takes place in mid-19th century feudal Japan and centers on Seibei (Sanada), a very capable but low-level samurai who must single-handedly take care of his aged, senile mother and two young daughters after the recent death of his wife. The hard-working Seibei makes very little from his clan-appointed jobs and spends the rest of his time doing household chores. Still grieving his wife, the staunchly single Seibei slowly begins to soften to the idea of love until suddenly being dispatched by the clan to take on the rebel Yogo (Tanaka), a master swordsman. Yamada lets the human drama takes center stage over the spectacular swordfighting usually found in this genre. Based on a novel by Shuhei Fujiwara. **129m/C; Blu-Ray.** *JP* Hiroyuki (Henry) Sanada; Ren Osugi; Miki Ito; Rie Miyazawa;

Nenji Kobayashi; Mitsuru Fukikoshi; Hiroshi Kanbe; Min Tanaka; Erina Hashiguchi; ***D:*** Yoji Yamada; ***W:*** Yoji Yamada; Yoshitaka Asama; ***C:*** Mutsuo Naganuma; ***M:*** Isao Tomita.

Twilight Women **1952** Grim Brit drama. Pregnant Vivienne, whose lover has been arrested for murder, finds a room in the grungy London boardinghouse run by Mrs. Alistair. Befriended by roommate Christine, Vivienne learns that Mrs. Alistair runs a black market adoption ring and their eventual confrontation leads to more than one tragedy. **80m/B; DVD.** *GB* Rene Ray; Lois Maxwell; Freda Jackson; Vida Hope; Dora Bryan; Joan Dowling; Laurence Harvey; ***D:*** Gordon Parry; ***W:*** Anatole de Grunwald; ***C:*** Jack Asher; ***M:*** Allan Gray.

Twilight Zone: The Movie ½ **1983 (PG)** Four short horrific tales are anthologized in this film as a tribute to Rod Sterling and his popular TV series. Three of the episodes, "Kick the Can," "It's a Good Life" and "Nightmare at 20,000 Feet," are based on original "Twilight Zone" scripts. Morrow was killed in a helicopter crash during filming. **101m/C; VHS, DVD, Blu-Ray.** Dan Aykroyd; Albert Brooks; Vic Morrow; Kathleen Quinlan; John Lithgow; Billy Mumy; Scatman Crothers; Kevin McCarthy; Bill Quinn; Selma Diamond; Abbe Lane; John Larroquette; Jeremy Licht; Patricia Barry; William Schallert; Burgess Meredith; Cherie Currie; Nancy Cartwright; Dick Miller; Stephen Bishop; Steven Williams; ***D:*** John Landis; Steven Spielberg; George Miller; Joe Dante; ***W:*** John Landis; George Clayton Johnson; Richard Matheson; ***C:*** Allen Daviau; John Hora; Stevan Larner; ***M:*** Jerry Goldsmith.

Twin Dragons *Shuang Long Hui* **1992 (PG-13)** Re-edited and redubbed English version of the Asian all-star film "Seung Lung Wui," a benefit for the Director's Guild of Hong Kong. Stealing the plot from Jean-Claude Van Damme of all people, Chan plays a dual role as twins separated at birth (as if there were any other kinds of twins in movie scripts) who grow up and cross paths. Chan's likable personality saves the trite, allegedly funny comedy jokelets from bouncing too hard, and the action is chop-sockety good. Cameos from Hong Kong big shots like Tsui Hark, Ringo Lam and John Woo. **89m/C; VHS, DVD, Blu-Ray.** *CH* Jackie Chan; Maggie Cheung; Anthony Chan; Philip Chan; Nina Li Chi; Sylvia Chang; James Wong; Kirk Wong; Ringo Lam; John Woo; Tsui Hark; Teddy Robin; ***D:*** Ringo Lam; Tsui Hark; ***W:*** Tsui Hark; Barry Wong; ***C:*** Wing-Hung Wong; Wong Ngor Tai; ***M:*** Michael Wandmacher; Phe Loung.

Twin Falls Idaho **1999 (R)** Eerie romantic drama about a lonely pair of conjoined twins, Francis (Michael Polish) and Blake (Mark Polish) Falls. The handsome 25-year-olds are celebrating their birthday in a shabby hotel room on Idaho Street, which is where hooker Penny (Hicks) shows up. Blake (the strong twin) intends Penny as a present for his fragile brother Francis, whose weakened heart is seemingly kept beating by Blake's sheer will. Initially repulsed, Penny becomes fascinated by their situation and begins to fall for Blake. But just what will happen if Francis does indeed die? The talented Polish brothers are identical but not "Siamese" twins. **110m/C; VHS, DVD.** Michael Polish; Mark Polish; Michele Hicks; Jon(athan) Gries; Patrick Bauchau; Garrett Morris; William Katt; Lesley Ann Warren; Teresa Hill; Holly Woodlawn; ***D:*** Michael Polish; ***W:*** Michael Polish; Mark Polish; ***C:*** M. David Mullen; ***M:*** Stuart Matthewman.

Twin Peaks: Fire Walk with Me **1992 (R)** Prequel to the cult TV series is weird and frustrating, chronicling the week before Laura Palmer's death. Suspense is lacking since we know the outcome, but Lynch manages to intrigue with dreamlike sequences and interestingly offbeat characters. On the other hand, it's exploitative and violent enough to alienate series fans. Includes extremely brief and baffling cameos by Bowie as an FBI agent and Stanton as the manager of a trailer park. Several of the show's regulars are missing, and others appear and disappear very quickly. On the plus side are the strains of Badalamenti's famous theme music and Isaak as an FBI agent with amazingly acute powers of observation. **135m/C; VHS, DVD, Blu-Ray.** *FR* Kyle MacLachlan; Sheryl Lee; Moira Kelly; David Bowie; Chris Isaak; Harry Dean Stanton; Ray Wise; Kiefer Sutherland; Peggy Lipton; Dana Ashbrook; James Marshall; David Lynch; Catherine Coulson; Julee Cruise; Eric (DaRe) Da Re; Miguel Ferrer; Heather Graham; Madchen Amick; Jurgen Prochnow; Grace Zabriskie; ***D:*** David Lynch; ***W:*** David Lynch; ***C:*** Ron Garcia; ***M:*** Angelo Badalamenti.

Twin Sisters ½ **1991** Woman discovers her missing twin sister was a high-priced prostitute and a detective tries to protect her from the lowlifes sis was involved with. **92m/C; VHS, DVD.** Stephanie Kramer; Susan Almgren; Frederic Forrest; James Brolin; ***D:*** Tom Berry; ***M:*** Lou Forestieri.

Twin Warriors ½ *The Tai-Chi Master; Tai ji Zhang San Feng* **1993 (R)** Junbao (Li) and Tianbao (Siu-hou) grow up together in a Shaolin temple where they secretly learn kung fu by observing the monks in training. Eventually, they're kicked out and Junbao joins a group of rebels while Tianbao enlists in the imperial army. He betrays the rebels and Junbao works to become a Tai Chi master in order to defeat his old friend. Dubbed from Cantonese. **91m/C; VHS, DVD, Blu-Ray.** *CH* Jet Li; Chin Siu-hou; Michelle Yeoh; ***D:*** Woo-ping Yuen; ***W:*** Kwong Kim Yip; ***C:*** Tom Lau; ***M:*** Wai Lap Wu.

Twinkletoes **1926** Twink Minasi (Moore) wants to use her dancing skills to escape her life of poverty in London's Limehouse district. Married prizefighter Chuck (Harland) falls for Twink but she resists him until he can free himself from his bitter, drunken wife Cissie (Brockwell). **78m/B; Silent; DVD.** Colleen Moore; Kenneth Harlan; Gladys Brockwell; Tully Marshall; Warner Oland; Lucien Littlefield; ***D:*** Charles Brabin; ***W:*** Winifred Dunn; ***C:*** James Van Trees.

Twins ½ **1988 (PG)** A genetics experiment gone awry produces twins rather than a single child. One is a genetically engineered superman, the other a short, lecherous petty criminal. Schwarzenegger learns he has a brother, and becomes determined to find him, despite their having been raised separately. The two meet and are immediately involved in a contraband scandal. Amusing pairing of Schwarzenegger and DeVito. **107m/C; VHS, DVD.** Arnold Schwarzenegger; Danny DeVito; Kelly Preston; Hugh O'Brian; Chloe Webb; Bonnie Bartlett; Marshall Bell; Trey Wilson; Nehemiah Persoff; ***D:*** Ivan Reitman; ***W:*** William Davies; William Osborne; Timothy Harris; Herschel Weingrod; ***C:*** Andrzej Bartkowiak; ***M:*** Georges Delerue; Randy Edelman.

Twins of Evil *The Gemini Twins; Twins of Dracula; The Virgin Vampires* **1971** Beautiful female twins fall victim to the local vampire, and their God-fearing uncle is out to save/destroy them. Hammer sex and blood-sucking epic starring the Collinsons, who were featured in the October 1970 issue of "Playboy" as the first twin Playmates. **86m/C; VHS, DVD, Blu-Ray, Streaming.** *GB* Madeleine Collinson; Mary Collinson; Peter Cushing; Kathleen Byron; Dennis Price; Damien Thomas; David Warbeck; Katya Wyeth; Maggie Wright; Luan Peters; Kristen Lindholm; Judy Matheson; ***D:*** John Hough; ***W:*** Tudor Gates; ***C:*** Dick Bush.

Twinsitters ½ **1995 (PG-13)** Twins Peter and David Falcone (Peter and David Paul) find themselves unexpectedly saving the life of corrupt businessman Frank Hillhurst (Martin). Hillhurst is turning state's evidence on his crooked operations and his disturbed partners have threatened both his life and the lives of his twin 10-year-old nephews. So Hillhurst hires the Falcones to protect his hellacious pint-sized relatives—who manage to get themselves kidnapped. **93m/C; DVD.** Peter Paul; David Paul; Christian Cousins; Joseph Cousins; Jared Martin; George Lazenby; Rena Sofer; Mother Love; ***D:*** John Paragon; ***W:*** John Paragon.

The Twist ½ *Folies Bourgeoises; Pazzi borghesi; Die Verruckten Reichen* **1976** A tepid French drama chronicling the infidelities of various wealthy aristocrats. The aristocrats are boring, as is the film. In French with English subtitles or dubbed. **105m/C; VHS, Blu-Ray.** *FR* Bruce Dern; Stephane Audran; Ann-Margret; Sydne Rome; Jean-Pierre Cassel; Curt Jurgens; Maria Schell; Charles Aznavour; ***D:*** Claude Chabrol; ***M:*** Manuel De Sica.

Twist **2003** Dark adaption of the Charles Dicken's Oliver Twist novel set amongst the street hustlers and heroin junkies of Toronto's streets. Oliver (Close), a teenage runaway meets up with Dodge (Stahl), a young prostitute. Dodge introduces him to the life of street hustling and the protective wing of Fagin (Farmer), the local pimp. A mindful presence, but not seen on screen is Bill the drug dealer, who controls both Fagin and his lover Nancy (Pelletier), a waitress at the diner where Fagin's boys often hang out. Despite what the title would suggest, the focus of the movie is Dodge as he plies his trade to further his heroin addiction. Works mainly because the young actors are so genuine and compelling. **97m/C; DVD.** *CA* Nick Stahl; Gary Farmer; Michelle-Barbara Pelletier; Joshua Close; Brigid Tierney; Stephen McHattie; Tygh Runyan; ***D:*** Jacob Tierney; ***W:*** Jacob Tierney; ***C:*** Gerald Packer; ***M:*** Ron Proulx.

Twist & Shout *Hab Og Karlighed* **1984 (R)** Sequel to the popular Danish import "Zappa," in which two teenage lovers discover sex and rock and roll. Transcends the teens discovering sex genre. Danish with English subtitles. Profanity, nudity, and sex. **107m/C; VHS, DVD.** *DK* Lars Simonsen; Adam Tonsberg; Ulrikke Juul Bondo; Camilla Soeberg; ***D:*** Bille August; ***W:*** Bille August; ***C:*** Jan Weincke; Aldo (G.R. Aldo) Graziatti.

Twisted **1996 (PG-13)** Four people become trapped in a fantasy world where nothing is as it seems. An airline passenger loses his identity, a housewife finds romance, a con man find a new mark, and a hired killer decides to retire—or at least that's what they believe. From the Australian TV series "Twisted Tales." **86m/C; VHS, DVD.** *AU* Geoffrey Rush; Rachel Ward; Bryan Brown; Kimberly Davies; Shane Briant; ***Nar:*** Bryan Brown; ***D:*** Samantha Lang; Christopher Robbin Collins; Gregor Jordan; Catherine Millar; ***C:*** James Bartle; ***M:*** Nerida Tyson-Chew. **TV**

Twisted **1996** Apt title for a contemporary gay version of "Oliver Twist" set in New York. Homeless 10-year-old orphan Lee (Graves) is brought into the seedy world of brothel owner Andre (Hickey). The youngster is befriended by Angel (Norona) a drug-addicted hustler who's under the sway of abusive pimp Eddie (Crivello). Along with big-hearted drag queen Shiniqua (Porter), Angel tries to rescue Lee from a sordid life. A stylized, operatic melodrama. **100m/C; VHS, DVD.** Keivyn McNeil Graves; William Hickey; David Norona; Anthony Crivello; Billy Porter; ***D:*** Seth Michael Donsky; ***W:*** Seth Michael Donsky; ***C:*** Hernan Toto.

Twisted ½ **2004 (R)** Judd stars as police detective Jessica Shepard in a sleazy, predictable thriller. Jessica likes to drink herself into blackout stupors and have one-night stands, until her hook-ups start turning up dead. Somehow, she ends up in charge of the murder investigation and must hunt down the killer while wondering what she has to do with the crimes. Partner Mike (Garcia) and Police Commissioner Mills (Jackson) are there to keep the pressure on. Oh yeah, and her father went crazy and killed a bunch of people, too. Convoluted backstory, lame plot, and yet another "Ashley Judd in trouble" role adds up to a mediocre turkey and a precipitous step down for director Kaufman. **96m/C; DVD.** Ashley Judd; Samuel L. Jackson; Andy Garcia; Russell Wong; David Strathairn; Camryn Manheim; Mark Pellegrino; Titus Welliver; D.W. Moffett; Richard T. Jones; Leland Orser; ***D:*** Philip Kaufman; ***W:*** Sarah Thorp; ***C:*** Peter Deming; ***M:*** Mark Isham.

Twisted Brain *Horror High* **1974 (R)** An honor student develops a serum that makes him half man and half beast. Now he can exact revenge on all the jocks and cheerleaders who have humiliated him in the past. Cardi is okay, the rest of the cast is awful. Silly, horrific teen monster epic. **89m/C; VHS, DVD.** Pat Cardi; Austin Stoker; Rosie Holotik; John Niland; Joyce Hash; Jeff Alexander; Joe "Mean Joe" Greene; ***D:*** Larry N. Stouffer.

Twisted Justice ½ **1989** Set in 2020, Heavener is a cop determined to stop a ruthless killer. Matters become complicated, however, when his gun is taken away. Now he's forced to rely on his cunning to outwit his sadistic opponent. **90m/C; VHS, DVD.** David Heavener; Erik Estrada; Jim Brown; Shannon Tweed; James Van Patten; Don Stroud; Karen Black; Lori Warren; ***D:*** David Heavener; ***W:*** David Heavener; ***C:*** David Hue.

Twisted Obsession **1990 (R)** A man becomes passionately obsessed with a woman, and it leads to murder. **109m/C; VHS, DVD.** Jeff Goldblum; Miranda Richardson; Anemone; Dexter Fletcher; Daniel Ceccaldi; Liza Walker; Jerome Natali; Arielle Dombasle; ***D:*** Fernando Trueba; ***C:*** Jose Luis Alcaine; ***M:*** Antoine Duhamel.

Twisted Souls ½ *Ecorches* **2005** Marc (Matinez) and Lea (Thierry) are step-siblings who become lovers as adults vacationing in the countryside when a violent storm and an intrusive employer begin driving them towards madness. **70m/C; DVD.** *FR* Vincent Martinez; Mélanie Thierry; Frederic Saurel; ***D:*** Cheyenne Carron; ***W:*** Cheyenne Carron; ***C:*** Antoine Marteau; ***M:*** Olivier Lebe.

Twister **1989 (PG-13)** An intriguing independent feature about a bizarre midwestern family, its feverish eccentricities and eventual collapse. Awaiting a cult following. **93m/C; VHS, DVD.** Dylan McDermott; Crispin Glover; Harry Dean Stanton; Suzy Amis; Jenny Wright; Lindsay Christman; Lois Chiles; William S. Burroughs; Tim Robbins; ***D:*** Michael Almereyda; ***W:*** Michael Almereyda; ***C:*** Renato Berta; ***M:*** Hans Zimmer.

Twister ½ **1996 (PG-13)** Director De Bont's sophomore directorial effort is another non-stop adrenaline drive, but instead of a mad bomber, nature is the bad guy. Hunt leads a team of storm chasing scientists through Oklahoma in hopes of placing robotic sensors inside a tornado. Hunt's soon-to-be ex-husband Paxton rejoins the chase, to spice things up when the skies clear. There's a lot of things flying around, including trucks, houses, cows and the plausibility of the plot. Some nice chemistry between Hunt and Paxton, apparently the only people who can still look attractive in high winds and blowing debris. **105m/C; VHS, DVD, Blu-Ray.** Bill Paxton; Helen Hunt; Cary Elwes; Jami Gertz; Alan Ruck; Lois Smith; Sean M. Whalen; Gregory Sporleder; Abraham Benrubi; Jake Busey; Joey Slotnick; Philip Seymour Hoffman; Jeremy Davies; Zach Grenier; Richard Lineback; Rusty Schwimmer; Alexa Vega; ***D:*** Jan De Bont; ***W:*** Michael Crichton; Anne-Marie Martin; ***C:*** Jack N. Green; ***M:*** Mark Mancina. MTV Movie Awards '97: Action Seq.

Twitch of the Death Nerve *Bay of Blood; Last House on the Left, Part 2; Carnage* **1971 (R)** Four vacationers are relentlessly pursued by a homicidal maniac armed with a sickle, bent on decapitation. Supposedly the inspiration for the "Friday the 13th" series. **87m/C; VHS, DVD, Blu-Ray.** *IT* Claudine Auger; Chris Avram; Isa Miranda; Laura Betti; Luigi Pistilli; Sergio Canvari; Anna M. Rosati; ***D:*** Mario Bava; ***W:*** Mario Bava; Filippo Ottoni; Joseph McLee; Gene Luotto; ***C:*** Mario Bava; ***M:*** Stelvio Cipriani.

Twitches ½ **2005 (PG)** Tweener girls should enjoy the fantasy adventures of twins Camryn and Alex (Tamera & Tia Mowry) who were separated at birth and raised under very different circumstances. Meeting at 21, the twins learn that they were spirited away from their magical kingdom for their own safety and that they are powerful witches. Now they must learn to use their abilities and work together to defeat their evil uncle, Thantos (Fabian). **86m/C; DVD.** Tamera Mowry; Tia Mowry; Kristen Wilson; Jenny Robertson; Patrick Fabian; Patrick Kelly; Arnold Pinnock; Jessica Grieco; Karen Holness; ***D:*** Stuart Gillard; ***W:*** Daniel Berendsen; Melissa Gould; ***C:*** Manfred Guthe; ***M:*** John Van Tongeren. **CABLE**

Twitches Too ½ **2007** Our twin witches return—continuing to learn to control their magical abilities while dealing with living as a family and going to college and having boyfriends and other girl stuff. But the darkness follows Alex and Camryn into the mortal world, so they must return to Coventry to defeat it once and for all. **83m/C; DVD.** Tamera Mowry; Tia Mowry; Kristen Wilson; Patrick Kelly; Kevin Jubinville; Arnold Pinnock; Leslie Seiler; Patrick Fabian; Karen Holness; Chris Gallinger; Nathan Stephenson; ***D:*** Stuart Gillard; ***W:*** Daniel Berendsen; ***C:*** Manfred Guthe; ***M:*** John Van Tongeren. **CABLE**

Twixt 🦴 1/2 **2012 (R)** Horror/thriller that's self-indulgent fluff from Coppola with some surreal B&W dream sequences, including some unnecessary 3D. Boozy, third-rate horror author Hall Baltimore is on a cheap book tour that takes him to an isolated town that was once the site of a mass murder. Staying at the same hotel where Edgar Allan Poe was apparently once a guest, Hall's booze-fueled dreams have him encountering Virginia, a 12-year-old victim, and the ghost of Poe himself. Hall is struggling with his cureent writing when his editor calls, urging a big twist ending (hint, hint). **88m/C; DVD, Blu-Ray.** Val Kilmer; Elle Fanning; Ben Chaplin; Bruce Dern; Joanne Whalley; David Paymer; ***Nar:*** Tom Waits; ***D:*** Francis Ford Coppola; ***W:*** Francis Ford Coppola; ***C:*** Milhai Malaimare, Jr.; ***M:*** Osvaldo Golijov.

Two Bits 🦴🦴 1/2 *A Day to Remember* **1996 (PG-13)** Depression-era drama tells the story of a 12-year-old boy and his emotional coming of age. Title refers to a quarter Gennaro (Barone, in his film debut) seeks in order to attend the grand opening of a glamorous, air-conditioned movie palace. A heavily made-up Pacino (looking suspiciously like Marlon Brando in the garden scene of "The Godfather"), co-stars as the boy's grandfather, who leaves him his last quarter. Gramps promises that he can collect later that day, when, he says, he will die. Fine performances all around and some powerful scenes go a long way toward masking the fact that the material is a bit too thin to stretch over an entire feature film. **85m/C; VHS, DVD.** Al Pacino; Gerlando Barone; Mary Elizabeth Mastrantonio; Joe Grifasi; Joanna Merlin; Andy Romano; Ron McLarty; Donna Mitchell; Patrick Borriello; Mary Lou Rosato; Rosemary DeAngelis; ***V:*** Alec Baldwin; ***D:*** James Foley; ***W:*** Joseph Stefano; ***C:*** Juan Ruiz-Anchia; ***M:*** Jane Musky.

Two Bits & Pepper 🦴🦴 1/2 **1995 (PG)** Bumbling criminals (both played by Piscopo) still manage to kidnap a a young girl and her friend and it's up to the title characters, a pet horse and a pony, to attempt a daring rescue. **90m/C; VHS, DVD.** Joe Piscopo; Lauren Eckstrom; Rachel Crane; Perry Stephens; Kathrin Lautner; Dennis Weaver; ***D:*** Corey Michael Eubanks; ***W:*** Corey Michael Eubanks; ***C:*** Jacques Haitkin; ***M:*** Louis Febre.

Two Brothers 🦴🦴 1/2 **2004 (PG)** Kiddy fare about tiger brothers whose happy cubhood is shattered by the intrusion of Man. Great White Hunter (Pearce) guns down their father, and the cubs are snatched away into captivity. One cub is bought by a cruel circus owner (Scarito); the other becomes a child's (Highmore) pet. Neither can be tamed though, and circumstances reunite them with predictably tender results. Set in Indochina in the 1920s, with gorgeous backdrops of crumbling temples and lush jungles. The tigers are great, but human characters are exaggerated and unbelievable. Director Annaud shows great talent working with animals, as in previous work, "The Bear." Perhaps next time he'll leave out the humans. **109m/C; VHS, DVD.** *FR GB* Guy Pearce; Jean-Claude Dreyfus; Freddie Highmore; Philippine Leroy-Beaulieu; Moussa Maaskri; Vincent Scarito; Mai Anh Le; Oanh Nguyen; Stephanie Lagarde; ***D:*** Jean-Jacques Annaud; ***W:*** Jean-Jacques Annaud; ***C:*** Jean-Marie Dreujou; ***M:*** Stephen Warbeck.

2 Brothers & a Bride 🦴🦴 1/2 *A Foreign Affair* **2003 (PG-13)** Simple-minded siblings Jake (Arquette) and Josh (Nelson) need to find a good (yet equally simple-minded) woman to tend to the chores on the farm since dear old mom passed away. They figure they'll find that lucky girl waiting for them somewhere in Russia. **92m/C; DVD, On Demand.** David Arquette; Tim Blake Nelson; Emily Mortimer; Larry Pine; Lois Smith; Allyce Beasley; Megan Follows; Redmond M. Gleeson; ***D:*** Helmut Schleppi; ***W:*** Geert Heetebrij; ***C:*** M. David Mullen; ***M:*** Todd Holden Capps.

2 by 4 🦴🦴 **1998** Johnnie (Smallhorne) is an Irish construction worker employed by his hard-living Uncle Trump (O'Neill) in New York. Though he's got a steady job, good friends, and a loving girlfriend in Maria (Topper), Johnnie's plagued by nightmares of something that happened in his childhood. And his apparent childhood abuse leads him to drugs, drink, and a certain sexual ambiguity as his repressed memories try to force their way to the surface. **90m/C; VHS, DVD.** Jimmy Smallhorne; Chris O'Neill; Bradley Fitts; Joe Holyoake; Terrence McGoff; Michael Liebman; Ronan Carr; Leo Hamill; Seamus McDonagh; Kimberly Topper; ***D:*** Jimmy Smallhorne; ***W:*** Jimmy Smallhorne; Terrence McGoff; Fergus Tighe; ***C:*** Declan Quinn. Sundance '98: Cinematog.

Two Came Back 🦴 1/2 **1997** Based on a novel, which is based on a true story. A group of young friends decide to sail from California to Vancouver and encounter a storm. They're set adrift at sea, and the rest you can probably guess from the film's title. **90m/C; DVD.** Melissa Joan Hart; Jonathan Brandis; David Gail; Joe Pennell; Susan Walters; Susan Sullivan; Steven Ford; ***D:*** Dick Lowry; ***W:*** Deborah Scaling-Kiley; Meg Noonan; Raymond Hartung; ***M:*** Michael Tavera. **TV**

Two Can Play That Game 🦴 1/2 **2001 (R)** Upwardly mobile Shante (Fox) seems to be the fountain of knowledge for her romantically challenged girlfriends Diedre (Mo'Nique), Karen (Robinson) and Trayce (Jones) on the subject of how to keep a man in line. When she sees her boyfriend Keith (Chestnut) grinding on another woman at a nightclub, however, her credibility takes a blow. She decides on a 10-day plan of action to force Keith back under her thumb. Clued in by his worldly wise buddy Tony (Anderson), however, Keith is well versed in the battle tactics of the opposite sex. Familiar material (director Brown also wrote "How to Be a Player"), spotty performances and the incessant narration by Fox's character make this a game you may want to quit halfway through. **90m/C; VHS, DVD.** Vivica A. Fox; Morris Chestnut; Anthony Anderson; Gabrielle Union; Wendy Raquel Robinson; Tamala Jones; Mo'Nique; Ray Wise; Bobby Brown; Dondre T. Whitfield; ***D:*** Mark Brown; ***W:*** Mark Brown; ***C:*** Alexander Grusynski; ***M:*** Marcus Miller.

Two Days 🦴🦴 **2003** What could be more depressing than being a dejected wanna-be actor? Apparently, not much as Paul Miller (Rudd) decides life isn't much worth living if he can't make it there (or, anywhere). In typical Hollywood fashion, he clings to his last 15 minutes (er, 48 hours) of fame by having his final two days put down on film. Will the filmmakers, his family, or his friends try to stop him? While Rudd tries his best to breathe life into it, this unconventional journey and its requisite destination proves too haphazardly constructed for anyone to truly care. **87m/C; VHS, DVD.** Paul Rudd; Donal Logue; MacKenzie Astin; Adam Scott; Joshua Leonard; Caroline Aaron; Graham Beckel; Marguerite Moreau; Stacey Travis; ***D:*** Sean McGinly; ***W:*** Sean McGinly; ***C:*** Jens Sturup; ***M:*** Alan Ari Lazar. **VIDEO**

2 Days in Paris 🦴🦴🦴 **2007 (R)** Vacationing couple Jack (Goldberg) and Marion (writer/director Julie Delpy) stop off in Paris to see Marion's parents before they go home to New York. Unfortunately for neurotic Jack, the visit isn't exactly how he wanted to wrap up their trip, as he's forced to confront his fear of terrorist attacks, lunch with Marion's French-speaking parents (Delpy's real-life parents Albert Delpy and Pillet), and encounter her ex-boyfriends. The ensuing stresses and culture clash begin to highlight the differences between the two. A funny, if occasionally mean, anti-romantic comedy. **96m/C; DVD.** *FR GE* Julie Delpy; Adam Goldberg; Albert Delpy; Marie Pillet; Adan Jodorowsky; Daniel Bruehl; Alexia Landeau; Alex Nahon; ***D:*** Julie Delpy; ***W:*** Julie Delpy; ***C:*** Lubomir Bakchev.

Two Days in the Valley 🦴🦴🦴 **1996 (R)** Film adds two days with ten characters in one locale and one half dozen separate plots and tries to come up with a dark comedy/thriller and winning debut for Herzfeld. It succeeds, mostly. San Fernando Valley is the backdrop, with a diverse ensemble of disturbed characters thrown together by the murder of a philandering spouse. Disjointed, and some plot threads are left hanging, but there's some fine comic moments and interesting character development, especially Aiello's culinary hitman, Dosmo Pizzo. Theron's Helga adds eye candy. For those too young to remember "Dynasty," you may want to check out the intense cat-fight between Hatcher's Becky Foxx and Helga. **105m/C; VHS, DVD.** Danny Aiello; Jeff Daniels; Marsha Mason; Teri Hatcher; Glenne Headly; James Spader; Eric Stoltz; Greg Cruttwell; Peter Horton; Charlize Theron; Keith Carradine; Louise Fletcher; Austin Pendleton; Paul Mazursky; Kathleen Luong; ***D:*** John Herzfeld; ***W:*** John Herzfeld; ***C:*** Oliver Wood; ***M:*** Anthony Marinelli.

Two Days, One Night 🦴🦴🦴 *Deux Jours, Une Nuit* **2014 (PG-13)** The Dardennes brothers cast a recognizable star in a leading role for the first time in their career, and the result is the best performance of Cotillard's notable filmography. She stars as Sandra, a woman forced out of work by depression and other health issues. When she returns, she's told that her job has been liquidated. She can return to work, but her co-workers would have to forego a sizable bonus to pay her salary. She has two days and one night to get the majority to agree. What would you do? This fascinating drama dissects solidarity in a working world that tries to destroy it. **95m/C; DVD, Blu-Ray.** *BE FR* Marion Cotillard; Fabrizio Rongione; ***D:*** Jean-Pierre Dardenne; Luc Dardenne; ***W:*** Jean-Pierre Dardenne; Luc Dardenne; ***C:*** Alain Marcoen.

Two Deaths 🦴🦴 **1994 (R)** Sex, brutality, power, madness, death, revolution—sounds like a Roeg concoction. In 1989 Romania, the Ceaucescu government is under siege and a civil war rages outside. But inside the opulent apartment of cynical Dr. Daniel Pavenic (Gambon) calmness prevails, as three longtime friends join him for their annual reunion dinner. Dinner is served by Pavenic's housekeeper Ana (Braga), who has a strange, disturbing relationship with the possessive doctor that he relates to his friends. His candor leads to similar revelations by his companions. Based on the novel "The Two Deaths of Senora Puccini" by Stephen Dobyns. **102m/C; VHS, DVD.** *GB* Michael Gambon; Sonia Braga; Patrick Malahide; Nickolas Grace; John Shrapnel; Ion Caramitru; ***D:*** Nicolas Roeg; ***W:*** Allan Scott; ***C:*** Witold Stok; ***M:*** Hans Zimmer.

Two Drifters 🦴 *Odete* **2005** Overwrought tearjerker. Rui is devastated when his lover Pedro is killed in a car accident. This leaves him vulnerable when he meets Odete, whose obsession to have a baby has left her unhinged. She happens to know Pedro's mother Teresa and claims she's carrying Pedro's child and things just go downhill from there. Portuguese with subtitles. **98m/C; DVD.** *PT* Ana Christine de Oliveira; Teresa Madruga; Nuno Gil; Joao Carreira; ***D:*** Joao Pedro Rodrigues; ***W:*** Joao Pedro Rodrigues; Paulo Rebelo; ***C:*** Rui Poças; ***M:*** Frank Beauvais.

Two English Girls 🦴🦴🦴 1/2 *Les Deux Anglaises et le Continent; Anne and Muriel* **1972 (R)** A pre-WWI French lad, with a possessive mother, loves two English sisters, one an impassioned, reckless artist, the other a repressed spinster. Tenderly delineates the triangle's interrelating love and friendship over seven years. Based on the novel "Les Deux Anglaises et le Continent" by Henri-Pierre Roche. In French with English subtitles. **130m/C; VHS, DVD.** *FR* Jean-Pierre Leaud; Kika Markham; Stacey Tendeter; Sylvia Marriott; Marie Mansert; Philippe Leotard; ***D:*** Francois Truffaut; ***W:*** Francois Truffaut; ***C:*** Nestor Almendros; ***M:*** Georges Delerue.

Two Evil Eyes 🦴🦴 *Due Occhi Diabolici* **1990 (R)** Horror kings Romero and Argento each direct an Edgar Allan Poe tale in this release, hence the title. Barbeau, the scheming younger wife of a millionaire, hypnotizes her husband with the help of her lover in "The Facts in the Case of M. Valdemar." When hubby dies too soon to validate changes made in his will, the lovers decide to freeze him for two weeks in order that death can be recorded at the correct time. In "Black Cat" a crime photographer used to photographing gore adopts a feline friend and starts getting sick on the job. **121m/C; VHS, DVD, Blu-Ray.** *IT* Adrienne Barbeau; Ramy Zada; Harvey Keitel; Madeleine Potter; Bingo O'Malley; E.G. Marshall; John Amos; Sally Kirkland; Kim Hunter; Martin Balsam; Tom Atkins; ***D:*** George A. Romero; Dario Argento; ***W:*** George A. Romero; Dario Argento; Franco Ferrini; ***C:*** Giuseppe Maccari; Peter Reniers; ***M:*** Pino Donaggio.

The Two Faces of Dr. Jekyll 🦴🦴 1/2 *House of Fright; Jekyll's Inferno* **1960** Henry Jekyll's (Massie) experiments lead to the release of his suave alter ego Edward Hyde. When Hyde discovers that Jekyll's long-suffering wife has taken up with his best friend, Hyde pits everyone against each other, while Jekyll struggles to retain control over his insidious other half. **87m/C; VHS, DVD, Blu-Ray.** *GB* Paul Massie; Dawn Addams; Christopher Lee; David Kossoff; Francis De Wolff; Oliver Reed; Norma Marla; Terry Quinn; ***D:*** Terence Fisher; ***W:*** Wolf Mankowitz; ***C:*** Jack Asher.

The Two Faces of January 🦴🦴 1/2 **2014 (PG-13)** Amini adapts Patricia Highsmith's novel about a glamorous American couple (Mortensen & Dunst) who arrive in Athens in 1962 and encounter a charismatic young man named Rydal (Isaac). Of course, as with all things Highsmith, no one here is exactly who they seem to be, and a triangle quickly forms with murderous inevitability. The narrative here is not one of the author's best and the film is uneven, but just spending time with these three actors has some value. It's an interesting vacation with beautiful people in beautiful places. **96m/C; DVD, Blu-Ray.** *UK US* Viggo Mortensen; Kirsten Dunst; Oscar Isaac; ***D:*** Hossein Amini; ***W:*** Hossein Amini; ***C:*** Marcel Zyskind; ***M:*** Alberto Iglesias.

Two Family House 🦴🦴 1/2 **1999 (R)** The '50s aren't exactly a time of happiness and prosperity for factory worker Buddy Rispoli. He's a frustrated singer, still haboring dreams of the big time, with a number of failed moneymaking schemes behind him. His latest venture is buying a two-family house where he and his family can live upstairs while he turns the downstairs into a bar. But the current tenants, a pregnant Irish teen and her abusive husband, have other ideas. **109m/C; VHS, DVD.** Michael Rispoli; Kelly Macdonald; Kathrine Narducci; Matt Servitto; Kevin Conway; Michele Santopietro; ***D:*** Raymond De Felitta; ***W:*** Raymond De Felitta; ***C:*** Mike Mayers; ***M:*** Stephen Endelman. Sundance '00: Aud. Award.

2 Fast 2 Furious 🦴🦴 **2003 (PG-13)** 2 dumb 2 believe, but no one seems to care. Walker reprises his role as now-disgraced undercover cop Brian O'Connor, and he's once again upstaged by his co-star. This time it's Tyrese, as childhood pal and new partner-in-undercover-crime Roman. It doesn't really matter, though, because everyone is upstaged by the lovingly photographed cars and the chaos they cause. The continuous action is now in Miami, as the buddies infiltrate the street-racing circuit to bust a Colombian drug ring and some bad cops. **94m/C; VHS, DVD, Blu-Ray, UMD, HD-DVD.** Paul Walker; Tyrese Gibson; Cole Hauser; Eva Mendes; Chris Bridges; Devon Aoki; James Remar; Thom Barry; Michael Ealy; Mark Boone, Jr.; ***D:*** John Singleton; ***W:*** Derek Haas; Michael Brandt; ***C:*** Matthew F. Leonetti; ***M:*** David Arnold.

Two Fathers' Justice 🦴🦴 **1985** Two dads, one tough and one a wimp, seek revenge on the men who killed their kids. **100m/C; VHS, DVD.** Robert Conrad; George Hamilton; Brooke Bundy; Catherine Corkill; Whitney Kershaw; Greg Terrell; ***D:*** Rod Holcomb. **TV**

Two Fathers: Justice for the Innocent 🦴🦴 **1994** Chicago blue-collar widower Stackhouse (Conrad) and wealthy Boston businessman Bradley (Hamilton) are brought together because the same drug dealer murdered their children. The two men team up after learning the killer has escaped from prison and they are determined to get him back behind bars. **94m/C; DVD.** Robert Conrad; George Hamilton; Danny Goldring; Mary Mulligan; Ned Schmidtke; Gary Houston; ***D:*** Paul Krasny; ***W:*** Stephen Zito; ***C:*** Robert Hudececk; ***M:*** Robert Folk. **TV**

Two for Texas 🦴🦴 1/2 **1997** Young buck Holland (Bairstow) and grizzled adventurer Allison (Kristofferson) manage to escape from a Louisiana chain gang and decide to head to Texas so they can join in the Texas Volunteer Army under Sam Houston (Skerritt). Soon, they're part of a group sent to San Jacinto in order to avenge the massacre at the Alamo. Kind of plodding western based on the novel by James Lee Burke. **96m/C; DVD.** Kris Kristofferson; Scott Bairstow; Tom Skerritt; Peter Coyote; Irene Bedard; Victor Rivers; Rodney A. Grant; Marco Rodriguez; Richard Jones; ***D:*** Rod Hardy; ***W:*** Larry Brothers; ***C:*** David Connell; ***M:*** Lee Holdridge. **CABLE**

Two for the Money 🦴🦴 **2005 (R)** Another bigger-than-life role for Al Pacino who plays Walter, the owner of a sports betting advice empire. Walter takes on Brandon Lang (McConaughey) after his incredible football game-picking accuracy gains notice. Brandon, whose NFL hopes were shot down by a career-ending knee injury, moves to Manhattan where under the mentoring of Walter he becomes a game-picking superstar, rocketing into a world of wealth and glamour. Predictably Brandon's hot streak cools, plunging him back to earth. If you can't get enough of Pacino's "Hoo-WAH!" roles, you'll love this one, which borders on self-parody. **124m/C; DVD.** Al Pacino; Matthew McConaughey; Rene Russo; Armand Assante; Jeremy Piven; Jaime King; Kevin Chapman; Gedde Watanabe; Carly Pope; Gerard Plunkett; James Kirk; ***D:*** D.J. Caruso; ***W:*** Dan Gilroy; ***C:*** Conrad W. Hall; ***M:*** Christophe Beck.

Two for the Road 1/2 **1967** On a road trip to the French Riviera, Mark (Finney) and Joanna (Hepburn) look back on more than a decade of marriage and find only fragments of their relationship. Flashbacks to their first meeting and subsequent vacations detail what when wrong and if their love is worth saving. Mancini score adds poignancy to the couple's reflections on their stormy life. Well-acted but the very sixties look has dated badly. **112m/C; VHS, DVD, Blu-Ray.** *GB* Audrey Hepburn; Albert Finney; Eleanor Bron; William Daniels; Claude Dauphin; Nadia Gray; Jacqueline Bisset; Georges Descrieres; Gabrielle Middleton; Judy Cornwell; Irene Hilda; Roger Dann; Libby Morris; Yves Barsac; ***D:*** Stanley Donen; ***W:*** Frederic Raphael; ***C:*** Christopher Challis; ***M:*** Henry Mancini.

Two for the Seesaw **1962** Mitchum stars as a Nebraska attorney who comes to New York and gets involved with MacLaine. Humorous and touching comedy-drama worked better on stage, because the large screen magnified the talkiness of Gibson's play. Unusual casting of Mitchum as a Midwest lawyer and MacLaine as a New York Jewish bohemian. **119m/B; VHS, DVD, Blu-Ray.** Robert Mitchum; Shirley MacLaine; Edmon Ryan; Elisabeth Fraser; Eddie Firestone; Billy Gray; Vic Lundin; ***D:*** Robert Wise; ***W:*** Isobel Lennart; ***M:*** Andre Previn.

Two Friends **1986** Campion's first feature, made for Australian TV, depicts the severing of the friendship between 15-year-olds Kelly (Bidenko) and Louise (Coles). Separated physically and emotionally as they begin growing up and attending different schools, the film flashes back to moments in their once inseparable friendship. **76m/C; VHS, DVD.** *AU* Kris Bidenko; Emma Coles; Peter Hehir; Kris McQuade; ***D:*** Jane Campion; ***W:*** Helen Garner; ***C:*** Julian Penney; ***M:*** Martin Armiger.

Two Girls and a Guy **1998 (R)** Graham and Wagner find out that Downey's been two-timing them and they confront him at his apartment. Only don't expect the usual revenge scenario. Yeah, it's talky, but the dialogue (much of it improvised) is great. Downey is at his best, playing an irresistibly charismatic actor backed into a (real and figurative) corner by his lifestyle while Graham and Wagner avoid the wronged-woman cliches. In one of the all-time male fantasies ever, Downey's character still gets to have sex with one of the women even after his lie has been exposed. The MPAA had a little problem with that, since that scene, like most of the rest of the movie, was shot in real time. The uncut NC-17 version is also available. **92m/C; VHS, DVD.** Robert Downey, Jr.; Heather Graham; Natasha Gregson Wagner; Angel David; Frederique van der Wal; ***D:*** James Toback; ***W:*** James Toback; ***C:*** Barry Markowitz.

Two Girls and a Sailor **1944** Wartime musical revue loosely structured around a love triangle involving a sailor on leave. Vintage hokum with lots of songs. **124m/B; VHS, DVD.** June Allyson; Gloria De Haven; Van Johnson; Xavier Cugat; Jimmy Durante; Tom Drake; Lena Horne; Harry James; Gracie Allen; Virginia O'Brien; Jose Iturbi; Carlos Ramirez; Donald Meek; Ben Blue; ***Cameo(s):*** Buster Keaton; ***D:*** Richard Thorpe; ***C:*** Robert L. Surtees.

Two Girls on Broadway **1940** The Midwest dance team of Eddie Kerns (Murphy) and Molly Mahoney (Blondell) get a rude awakening when Eddie is told that Molly's younger sister Pat (Turner) would make a better Broadway partner. Though Eddie is also involved romantically with Molly, she recognizes that Pat and Eddie are smitten though Pat is denying her feelings by allowing herself to be wooed by wealthy, much-divorced producer Chat Chatsworth (Taylor). Remake of 1929's "Broadway Melody." **71m/B; DVD.** Lana Turner; Joan Blondell; George Murphy; Kent Taylor; Richard Lane; Wallace Ford; ***D:*** S. Sylvan Simon; ***W:*** Jerome Chodorov; Joseph Fields; ***C:*** George J. Folsey.

Two Gladiators 1/2 *I Due Gladiatori* **1964** Loyal Roman senator Tarrunio (Solaro) needs to find the long-lost twin brother (Harrison) of cruel new emperor Commodus (Palmara) and convince him to take his rightful place as ruler. Dubbed. **90m/C; DVD.** *IT* Richard Harrison; Moira Orfei; Mimmo Palmara; Pierro Lulli; Alberto Farnese; Gianni Solaro; Mirko Ellis; ***D:*** Mario Caiano; ***W:*** Mario Caiano; Alfonso Brescia; ***C:*** Pier Ludovico Pavoni; ***M:*** Carlo Franci.

2 Guns 1/2 **2013 (R)** Few films have ever relied more successfully on the incredible screen power of their stars than this effective action-thriller-comedy hybrid. Robert Trench (Washington) is an undercover DEA agent caught up in an investigation with an undercover Naval Intelligence Officer named Michael Stigman (Wahlberg), although the two are unaware that they're actually working on the right side of the law. Surprisingly violent and far too reliant on narrative twists and turns instead of actual character, the two leads can carry a film as well as anyone on the market and in ways that other actors could never imagine. **109m/C; DVD, Blu-Ray.** Denzel Washington; Mark Wahlberg; Paula Patton; Bill Paxton; James Marsden; Edward James Olmos; Fred Ward; Robert John Burke; ***D:*** Baltasar Kormakur; ***W:*** Blake Masters; ***C:*** Oliver Wood; ***M:*** Clinton Shorter.

Two Hands **1998** Black comedy/thriller stars Aussie heartthrob Ledger as teen Jimmy who's got a nothing job in Sydney and would like to improve his prospects. So he agrees to deliver a cash-filled envelope for local gang boss, Pando (Brown), and then promptly loses the money. This sends Jimmy on the run to avoid Pando's retribution. (But the kid still finds some time to romance naive Alex (Byrne).) **104m/C; VHS, DVD.** *AU* Heath Ledger; Bryan Brown; David Field; Rose Byrne; Susie Porter; Tom Long; Steven Vidler; ***D:*** Gregor Jordan; ***W:*** Gregor Jordan; ***C:*** Malcolm McCulloch; ***M:*** Chris Gough. Australian Film Inst. '99: Director (Jordan), Film, Film Editing, Orig. Screenplay, Support. Actor (Brown).

2-Headed Shark Attack WOOF! **2012 (R)** Boobs--and we're not just talking the anatomical kind--rule in this woofer about coeds signed up for a semester at sea where clothing is almost optional. The mutant shark is a tease since it likes to play with its food, which at least offers some amusement. **90m/C; DVD, Blu-Ray.** Brooke Hogan; Carmen Electra; Charlie O'Connell; David Gallegos; ***D:*** Christopher Ray; ***W:*** H. Perry Horton; ***C:*** Stuart Brereton; ***M:*** Chris Ridenour. **VIDEO**

200 Cigarettes **1998 (R)** Directorial debut from former casting director Garcia follows the adventures of various self-absorbed hipsters on New Year's Eve in early '80s New York. The excellent ensemble cast is given spotty material, however. The primary goal of all these rather unlikable characters is to find someone (or anyone) to sleep with before the night is over. They all hook up in this ode to the high life of pre-AIDS promiscuity, but you don't really care about them at all. Chapelle provides the most entertainment as a philosophy-spouting disco cabbie who schleps the shallow partygoers to and fro. **101m/C; VHS, DVD.** Ben Affleck; Casey Affleck; Jay Mohr; Dave Chappelle; Gaby Hoffman; Courtney Love; Christina Ricci; Paul Rudd; Catherine Kellner; Martha Plimpton; Janeane Garofalo; Guillermo Diaz; Angela Featherstone; Brian McCardie; Nicole Ari Parker; Kate Hudson; Elvis Costello; ***D:*** Risa Bramon Garcia; ***W:*** Shana Larsen; ***C:*** Frank Prinzi; ***M:*** Mark Mothersbaugh; Bob Mothersbaugh.

211 1/2 **2018 (R)** An based-on-real-life action-drama about a bank robbery. Meek Kenny (Rainey) is punished for an incident at school with a ride along with cop Mike Chandler (Cage), a bitter widower, and his partner/son-in-law Steve (Cameron), who has just learned his wife is expecting a baby. During the ride along, the trio crosses paths with killer mercenaries who are owed money by a war-profiteer and plan to rob a million dollars from a bank used by their former employer. Though well-paced, the plot is quite predictable and nonsensical. **86m/C; DVD, Blu-Ray, Streaming.** Nicolas Cage; Sophie Skelton; Michael Rainey Jr.; Dwayne Cameron; Amanda Cerny; ***D:*** York Alec Shackleton; ***W:*** York Alec Shackleton; ***C:*** Alexander Krumov; ***M:*** Frederick Wiedmann. **VIDEO**

200 Motels 1/2 **1971 (R)** Rambling, non-narrative self-indulgent video album by and about Frank Zappa and the Mothers of Invention, as they document a long and especially grueling road tour. For fans only. **99m/C; VHS, Streaming.** Ringo Starr; Theodore Bikel; Keith Moon; Janet Ferguson; Lucy Offerall; ***D:*** Frank Zappa; ***W:*** Frank Zappa; ***C:*** Gillian Lynne; ***M:*** Frank Zappa.

200 MPH **2011** A kid starts illegally racing cars made of bad CGI after the death of his brother. Sad attempt at exploiting more famous movies made for car nuts. **90m/C; DVD, Blu-Ray.** Jaz Martin; Darren Anthony Thomas; Paul Logan; Hennely Jimenez; AnnaMaria Demara; ***D:*** Cole S. McKay; ***W:*** Thunder Levin; ***C:*** Alexander Yellen; ***M:*** Chris Ridenhour; Yoshiki Miyamoto. **VIDEO**

Two If by Sea 1/2 *Stolen Hearts* **1995 (R)** Small-time hood Frank (Leary) and his girlfriend Roz (Bullock) hole up in a New England mansion after Frank steals a valuable Matisse painting. Between verbal sparring matches, the two try to mingle with the upper crusty residents with predictable results. Pursuing the pair are the FBI, led by the deluded O'Malley (Kotto), and Frank's bonehead cousin Beano (Robson) and his trio of dim henchmen. Tries to be a caper/romantic comedy but fails to deliver on all fronts. The usually caustic Leary takes some of the edge off of his trademark bitter humor, and the alleged witty repartee is just plain annoying as a result. Nova Scotia turns in a fine performance as New England. **96m/C; VHS, DVD.** Sandra Bullock; Denis Leary; Stephen (Dillon) Dillane; Yaphet Kotto; Wayne Robson; Jonathan Tucker; Mike Starr; Michael Badalucco; Lenny Clarke; John Friesen; ***D:*** Bill Bennett; ***W:*** Denis Leary; Mike Armstrong; ***C:*** Andrew Lesnie.

2 Jacks **2012** Loose adaptation of the Chekhov short story "The Two Hussars" is an empty, low-budget showbiz tale. Legendary director Jack Hussar Sr., now down on his luck, comes to Tinseltown to charm and seduce his way into financing for his new film. Twenty years later, it's the turn of Jack's namesake son, who's working on his first film. He not only lacks his father's chutzpah but the town is now all business and no show. **90m/C; DVD.** Danny Huston; Jack Huston; Sienna Miller; Jacqueline Bisset; Rosie Fellner; Billy Zane; ***D:*** Bernard Rose; ***W:*** Bernard Rose; ***C:*** Bernard Rose; ***M:*** Iryna Orlova; Anatoliy Mamalyga.

The Two Jakes **1990 (R)** Ten years have passed and Jake Gittes is still a private investigator in this sequel to 1974's "Chinatown." When a murder occurs while he's digging up dirt on an affair between the wife of a real estate executive and the executive's partner, Jake must return to Chinatown to uncover the killer and face the painful memories buried there. Despite solid dialogue and effective performances, it's unreasonably difficult to follow if you haven't seen "Chinatown." Outstanding photography by Vilmos Zsigmond. **137m/C; VHS, DVD.** Jack Nicholson; Harvey Keitel; Meg Tilly; Madeleine Stowe; Eli Wallach; Ruben Blades; Frederic Forrest; David Keith; Richard Farnsworth; Tracey Walter; James Hong; Van Dyke Parks; Perry Lopez; Joe Mantell; Rebecca Broussand; ***D:*** Jack Nicholson; ***W:*** Robert Towne; ***C:*** Vilmos Zsigmond; ***M:*** Van Dyke Parks.

Two Lane Blacktop **1971** Counterculture critics darling that failed at the box-office but has since developed a cult following. The Driver (Taylor) and the Mechanic (Wilson) are car freaks in a '55 Chevy, driving the southwestern backroads looking for a race. They meet up with Oates who's at the wheel of a brand-new G.T.O. He proposes they cross-country to D.C. and the winner gets the loser's car. Along the way, everyone's enthusiasm wanes and they part, with Wilson and Taylor driving down a two-lane blacktop as the film literally melts into a bright light. Music includes The Doors, Kris Kristofferson, and Ray Charles. **103m/C; VHS, DVD.** James Taylor; Dennis Wilson; Warren Oates; Laurie Bird; Harry Dean Stanton; ***D:*** Monte Hellman; ***W:*** Rudy Wurlitzer; Will Corry; ***C:*** Jackson Deerson. Natl. Film Reg. '12.

Two Little Bears **1961** Generally harmless kids fantasy. Billy and Timmy Davis dress up as bear cubs for Halloween and then meet a fortuneteller who gives them a spell that can turn them into real live cubs. They try it out and it works, but no one believes them until they show off their new ability to their school principal father. But that just confuses things even more. **83m/B; DVD.** Eddie Albert; Jane Wyatt; Butch Patrick; Donnie Carter; Soupy Sales; Nancy Kulp; ***D:*** Randall Hood; ***W:*** George W. George; ***C:*** Floyd Crosby; ***M:*** Henry Vars.

2 Little Monsters 1/2 *Little Monsters* **2015** A moving drama inspired by a British case in which two young boys murdered a toddler, but were released from prison at 18. At the age of 10, James (Greco) and Carl (Larson) kidnapped and murdered three-year-old David McClendon (Greco). Caught, tried, and convicted, they are placed in separate juvenile facilities until the age of 18. At that time, they are given new names and released into society despite public outcry. Following their lives post-release, the film shows how they try to escape their past, build new lives, and survive the controversy over their release. **107m/C; DVD, Streaming, Download.** Charles Cantrell; Ryan LeBoeuf; Chaz Greco; James Greco; Jackson Larson; ***D:*** David Schmoeller; ***W:*** David Schmoeller; ***C:*** Craig Boydston; ***M:*** Georg Brandl Egloff. **VIDEO**

Two Lovers **2009 (R)** Brooklynite Leonard (Phoenix) is torn between family friend Sandra (Shaw), whom his parents want him to marry, and volatile new neighbor Michelle (Paltrow). Leonard falls in love with Michelle despite the fact that she is being kept by a married man. Gray, known for hard-edged, tough-guy themes, keeps things dark but deeply sensitive in this effectively moody character study of love, loss and the struggle between. Sadly this excellent second collaboration between writer/director Gray and Phoenix (*The Yards*) could be the last if Phoenix follows through on his claim of trading acting for, a-hem, rapping. **110m/C; Blu-Ray, On Demand.** *US FR* Joaquin Rafael (Leaf) Phoenix; Gwyneth Paltrow; Vinessa Shaw; Isabella Rossellini; Elias Koteas; Moni Moshonov; ***D:*** James Gray; ***W:*** James Gray; Richard Menello; ***C:*** Joaquin Baca-Asay.

Two Men Went to War 1/2 **2002** Silly comedy that falls into the "truth is stranger than fiction" category. In 1942, Sgt. King (Cranham) and Pvt. Cuthbertson (Bill), both assigned to the Army Dental Corps, decide to go AWOL in order to see some action. They take a bag of grenades, steal a boat, sneak into France, and go after some Nazi targets. Adapted from Raymond Foxall's book "Amateur Commandos." **108m/C; DVD.** *GB* Kenneth Cranham; Leo Bill; Derek Jacobi; Phyllida Law; James Fleet; Julian Glover; Anthony Valentine; David Ryall; Rosanna Lavelle; ***D:*** John Henderson; ***W:*** Christopher Villiers; Richard Everett; ***C:*** John Ignatius; ***M:*** Richard Harvey.

Two Minute Warning **1976 (R)** A sniper plans to take out the president of the United States at an NFL playoff game in this boring, pointless, disaster film that goes on forever. Features all the ready-made characters inherent in the genre, but, until its too late, precious little of the mayhem. To get caught watching the TV version, which features more characters and an additional subplot, would be truly disastrous. **116m/C; VHS, DVD, Blu-Ray.** Charlton Heston; John Cassavetes; Martin Balsam; Beau Bridges; Marilyn Hassett; David Janssen; Jack Klugman; Walter Pidgeon; Gena Rowlands; ***D:*** Larry Peerce; ***W:*** Ed Hume; ***C:*** Gerald Hirschfeld; ***M:*** Charles Fox.

2 Minutes Later **2007** Graham is sassy and Molina is hunky in this noirish thriller. Mild-mannered insurance agent Michael Dalmar (Molina) goes looking for his missing twin brother Kyle, a Philadelphia photographer who specialized in kink and was notorious for being a jerk. Take-charge private eye Abigail Marks (Graham) teams up with Michael and they decide he should pose as Kyle to see what shakes lose. They get a digital-camera chip from Kyle's last shoot, which points them in a dangerous direction. **70m/C; DVD.** J. Matthew Miller; Michael Molina; Jessica Graham; Peter Sickles; *D:* Robert Gaston; *W:* Robert Gaston; *C:* Jeff Schirmer. **VIDEO**

Two Minutes to Play 🦴 1/2 **1937** College football stars Martin Granville and Jack Gaines are also academic rivals—traditions set by their own fathers. Then they become romantic rivals over cute coed Pat Meredith. As you can tell from the title nothing gets resolved until the final minutes of the big game. **69m/B; DVD.** Bruce Bennett; Edward J. Nugent; Jeanne Martel; Betty Compson; Richard Tucker; Sam Flint; Duncan Renaldo; Grady Sutton; Forrest Taylor; *D:* Robert F. "Bob" Hill; *W:* William Buchanan; *C:* William (Bill) Hyer.

The Two Mrs. Carrolls 🦴🦴 1/2 **1947** Bogart is a psycho-killer/artist who paints portraits of his wives as the Angel of Death—and then kills them. The married Bogart falls for Stanwyck, poisons his current wife, and the two marry. After a few years, Bogart falls for Smith and decides to rid himself of Stanwyck in the same manner as his first killing. Stanwyck, however, becomes increasingly suspicious and calls on an old beau for help. Melodrama cast Bogart against type (not always successfully). Filmed in 1945, but was unreleased until 1947. **99m/B; VHS, Streaming.** Humphrey Bogart; Barbara Stanwyck; Alexis Smith; Nigel Bruce; Pat O'Moore; Ann Carter; *D:* Peter Godfrey.

The Two Mr. Kissels 🦴🦴 **2008** Generously tawdry true-life story (shown on Lifetime) about two brothers whose sibling rivalry, materialism, and marital discord leads to a gruesome conclusion for them both. Wall Streeter Rob (Mount) leaves unstable, adulterous wife Nancy (Tunney) behind while he works in Hong Kong and she decides she wants the money more than the man. Brother Andrew (Stamos) goes the real estate route and marries TV personality Hayley (Egolf) before he turns to shady deals, drugs, and hookers. **86m/C; DVD.** John Stamos; Anson Mount; Robin Tunney; Chuck Shamata; Simon Reynolds; Vincent Walsh; Gretchen Egolf; *D:* Edward Bianchi; *W:* Maria Nation; *C:* Teodoro Maniaci; *M:* Johnny Klimek; Reinhold Heil. **CABLE**

Two Moon Junction 🦴 1/2 **1988 (R)** A soon-to-be-wed Southern debutante enters into a wild love affair with a rough-edged carnival worker. Poorly acted, wildly directed, with many unintentional laughs. **104m/C; VHS, DVD.** Sherilyn Fenn; Richard Tyson; Louise Fletcher; Burl Ives; Kristy McNichol; Millie Perkins; Don Galloway; Herve Villechaize; Dabbs Greer; Milla Jovovich; Screamin' Jay Hawkins; *D:* Zalman King; *W:* Zalman King; *C:* Mark Plummer; *M:* Jonathan Elias. Golden Raspberries '88: Worst Support. Actress (McNichol).

Two Much 🦴 1/2 **1996 (PG-13)** Banderas does double duty as a con man pretending to be twins in order to romance two sisters (Griffith and Hannah). Embarrassingly light comedy suffers from a complicated plot (which still manages to leave holes), weak or non-existent characterization, and a general lack of humor. About the only thing it has going for it is Cusack as a wisecracking secretary. It was on the set of this film that Banderas and Griffith started their real-life romance. While that may have helped the boxoffice and gossip columns in Banderas's homeland, the fireworks didn't find their way to the screen. **118m/C; VHS, DVD, Blu-Ray.** Melanie Griffith; Antonio Banderas; Daryl Hannah; Joan Cusack; Danny Aiello; Eli Wallach; Vincent Schiavelli; *D:* Fernando Trueba; *W:* Fernando Trueba; David Trueba; *C:* Jose Luis Alcaine; *M:* Michel Camilo.

Two Mules for Sister Sara 🦴🦴🦴 **1970 (PG)** American mercenary in 19th century Mexico gets mixed up with a cigar-smoking nun and the two make plans to capture a French garrison. MacLaine and Eastwood are great together. Based on a Boetticher story. **105m/C; VHS, DVD, Blu-Ray.** Clint Eastwood; Shirley MacLaine; *D:* Donald Siegel; *W:* Albert (John B. Sherry) Maltz; *M:* Ennio Morricone.

Two Night Stand 🦴🦴 **2014 (R)** Teller and Tipton star as a genetically blessed couple who have a one-night stand that they still wish could be the end of their relationship. As they plan to slink off into the rest of their lives, a blizzard forces them to stay together. Trapped in a tiny apartment after Manhattan has turned into ice, the pair actually gets to know each other, and, well, you can probably figure it out. The leads are remarkably charming, but the rom-com clichés here stack up, even just in that tiny NYC apartment. **86m/C; DVD, Streaming.** Miles Teller; Analeigh Tipton; Jessica Szohr; *D:* Max Nichols; *W:* Mark Hammer; *C:* Bobby Bukowski; *M:* Neil DeLuca; Matthew DeLuca.

Two Nights with Cleopatra 🦴 1/2 *Due Notti Con Cleopatra* **1954** A piece of Italian pizza involving Cleopatra's double (also played by Loren) falling in love with one of the guards. Notable only for the 19-year-old Sophia's brief nudity. **77m/C; DVD.** *IT* Sophia Loren; Ettore Manni; Alberto Sordi; Paul Muller; Alberto Talegalli; Rolf Tasna; Gianni Cavalieri; Nando (Fernando) Bruno; Riccardo Garrone; Carlo Dale; *D:* Mario Mattoli; *W:* Nino Maccari; Ettore Scola.

Two Ninas 🦴 1/2 **2000 (R)** Dreary romantic comedy finds mopey aspiring writer Marty (Livingston) meeting sarcastic Nina Cohen (Buono) at a party. The two hit it off but then Marty literally runs into Nina 2, i.e. wealthy Nina Harris (Peet), while rollerblading in Central Park. He starts dating her as well. Now Marty has to keep his stories straight and hope the two Ninas never meet, which, of course, they do. **90m/C; VHS, DVD, On Demand.** Ron Livingston; Cara Buono; Amanda Peet; Bray Poor; Jill(ian) Hennessey; *D:* Neil Turitz; *W:* Neil Turitz; *C:* Joaquin Baca-Asay; *M:* Joseph Saba.

Two of a Kind 🦴🦴 **1951** Michael Farrell (O'Brien) is hired by con woman Brandy (Scott) and her shady lawyer lover Vincent (Knox) to impersonate the wealthy McIntyres' long-lost son. He ingratiates himself into the family but things don't go as planned since old man William (Barnett) refuses to change his will. There's some murderous intentions put into play but this minor noir starts out interesting and then turns routine. **75m/B; DVD.** Edmond O'Brien; Lizabeth Scott; Alexander Knox; Terry Moore; Griff Barnett; Virginia Brissac; Robert Anderson; *D:* Henry Levin; *W:* Lawrence Kimble; James Gunn; James Edward Grant; *C:* Burnett Guffey; *M:* George Duning.

Two of a Kind 🦴 **1983 (PG)** Angels make a bet with God—two selfish people will redeem themselves or God can blow up the Earth. Bad acting, awful direction, and the script needs divine intervention. **88m/C; VHS, DVD.** John Travolta; Olivia Newton-John; Charles Durning; Beatrice Straight; Scatman Crothers; Oliver Reed; *D:* John Herzfeld; *C:* Fred W. Koenekamp.

The Two of Us 🦴🦴🦴 1/2 *Le Vieil Homme Et L'Enfant; Claude; The Old Man and the Boy* **1968** Young Jewish boy flees Nazi-occupied Paris to live in the country with an irritable, bigoted guardian. Sensitive, eloquent movie about racial prejudice and anti-Semitism. In French with English subtitles. **86m/B; VHS, DVD.** *FR* Michel Simon; Alain Cohen; Luce Fabiole; Roger Carel; Paul Preboist; Charles Denner; *D:* Claude Berri; *W:* Claude Berri; *C:* Jean Penzer; *M:* Georges Delerue.

Two of Us 🦴🦴 **2000 (PG-13)** A "what-if" look at the friendship between ex-Beatles Paul McCartney and John Lennon. In 1976, Paul (Quinn) is in New York to publicize a concert with his band Wings and he decides to visit estranged mate John (Harris) at the Dakota in a bittersweet effort to make peace with their relationship. **90m/C; VHS, DVD.** Aidan Quinn; Jared Harris; *D:* Michael Lindsay-Hogg; *W:* Mark Stanfield; *C:* Miroslaw Baszak; *M:* David Schwartz. **CABLE**

Two On a Guillotine 🦴🦴 **1965** Horror that's more camp than shock. A botched guillotine trick left the wife/assistant of magician Duke Duquesne without her head and baby daughter Cassie without her mother. When The Great Duquesne dies 20 years later, his will states that his estranged daughter must spend seven nights in his creepy mansion to inherit. Accompanied by reporter (and wannabe beau) Val, Cassie might just die of fright since the crazy magician has left a lot of surprises behind. Final music score for composer Max Steiner. **107m/B; DVD, Blu-Ray.** Connie Stevens; Dean Jones; Cesar Romero; Parley Baer; Virginia Gregg; John Hoyt; *D:* William Conrad; *C:* Sam Leavitt.

Two or Three Things I Know about Her 🦴🦴 *Deux ou Trois Choses Que Je Sais d'Elle* **1966** Inspired by a magazine article about housewife-prostitutes, Godard takes on the bourgeoise. Juliette (Vlady) is a wife and mother who lives in the suburbs of Paris and goes into the city once a week to work as a prostitute in order to buy consumer goods. French with subtitles. **95m/C; VHS, DVD.** *FR* Marina Vlady; Anny (Annie Legras) Duperey; Roger Montsoret; Jean Narboni; Raoul Levy; *D:* Jean-Luc Godard; *W:* Jean-Luc Godard; *C:* Raoul Coutard.

The Two Popes 🦴🦴🦴 **2019 (PG-13)** When Cardinal Jorge Bergoglio (Pryce) tries to retire, Pope Benedict XVI (Hopkins) sidesteps the issue in conversation and talks of their personal differences. Later, Benedict resigns the papacy and becomes pope emeritus. The cardinal is elected to the papacy, becoming Pope Francis. Through it all, the popes take walks and have meaningful conversations, and the theological and personal issues they encounter are analyzed with reflection and humor. Based on the imagined relationship between the two real popes, the drama is both serious and joyful in its exploration of the popes' relationship with memorable performances by both leads. **125m/C; DVD.** Anthony Hopkins; Jonathan Pryce; Juan Minujin; Luis Gnecco; Cristina Banegas; *D:* Fernando Meirelles; *W:* Anthony McCarten; *C:* Cesar Charlone; *M:* Bryce Dessner.

Two Rode Together 🦴🦴 1/2 **1961** A Texas marshal and an army lieutenant negotiate with the Comanches for the return of captives, but complications ensue. **109m/C; DVD, Blu-Ray.** James Stewart; Richard Widmark; Shirley Jones; Linda Cristal; Andy Devine; John McIntire; *D:* John Ford; *W:* Frank Nugent; *C:* Charles Lawton, Jr.; *M:* George Duning.

Two Seconds 🦴🦴 **1932** Hammy crime melodrama. The press arrives at a prison to witness the electric chair execution of convicted murderer John Allen (Robinson). Flashbacks detail the trouble that derails the friendship of ironworker Allen and his pal Bud Clark (Foster) which eventually leads to Allen winding up on Death Row. Title refers to the time it takes the electrical current to reach the chair's occupant. **68m/B; DVD.** Edward G. Robinson; Preston Foster; Vivienne Osborne; J. Carrol Naish; Guy Kibbee; Berton Churchill; *D:* Mervyn LeRoy; *W:* Harvey Thew; *C:* Sol Polito.

Two Shades of Blue 🦴 1/2 **1998 (R)** Surprisingly dull erotic thriller. Writer Hunter is framed for the murder of fiancee Busey, so she assumes the alter ego identity of her novel's sexy heroine in order to hunt for the killer herself. She takes a job as a relay telephone operator for the deaf so she can contact deaf D.A. Matlin. But Matlin has a sexually obsessive relationship with boyfriend Roberts (who's in whacko mode) and Hunter begins to take a voyeuristic delight in their conversations. **103m/C; VHS, DVD.** Rachel Hunter; Marlee Matlin; Eric Roberts; Gary Busey; *D:* James D. Deck; *W:* Ted Williams. **VIDEO**

Two Sisters From Boston 🦴🦴 1/2 **1946** MGM musical comedy. Abigail Chandler (Grayson) writes to her stuffy Boston relatives about her successful opera career but she's really working as a popular singer in a Bowery saloon owned by Spike (Durante). When her aunt, uncle, and prim sister Martha (Allyson) come for a visit, Abigail tries to hide the truth while Spike works to make her opera dreams come true. Much confusion follows. **112m/B; DVD.** Kathryn Grayson; June Allyson; Jimmy Durante; Peter Lawford; Lauritz Melchior; Ben Blue; Thurston Hall; Harry Hayden; Isobel Elsom; Gino Corrado; *D:* Henry Koster; *W:* Myles Connolly; *C:* Robert L. Surtees.

Two Smart People 🦴🦴 1/2 **1946** There's a conniving dame on a New Orleans-bound train who gets a con man, a cop, and a gunsel all involved in her plans. Con man Ace (Hodiak) has some stolen bonds and is caught by cop Simms (Nolan). They are on that train with gunsel Feretti (Cook Jr.), who wants the bonds for himself, and con woman Ricki (Ball), who wants the bonds AND Ace but turns out to have a conscience. Mardi Gras in the Big Easy proves to be a climatic event. **93m/B; DVD.** John Hodiak; Lucille Ball; Lloyd Nolan; Elisha Cook, Jr.; Lloyd Corrigan; Vladimir Sokoloff; *D:* Jules Dassin; *W:* Ethel Hill; Leslie Charteris; *C:* Karl Freund; *M:* George Bassman.

2:13 🦴 1/2 **2009** Police profiler Russell Spivey suffered a breakdown but is called back to duty when the Mask Killer resurfaces. The serial killer tortures his women victims and then leaves an elaborately-made mask at the scene. The reveal of the killer and his reasons (naturally all leading back to Spivey) don't make much sense but until then the hunt is worth watching. **96m/C; DVD, Blu-Ray.** Teri Polo; Mark Pellegrino; Kevin Pollack; Mark Thompson; Dwight Yoakam; Jere Burns; Ken Howard; *D:* Charles Adelman; *W:* Mark Thompson; *C:* David A. Armstrong; *M:* Marc Bonilla. **VIDEO**

2000 Maniacs 🦴🦴 1/2 **1964** One of cult director Lewis' most enjoyably watchable films. A literal Civil War "ghost town" takes its revenge 100 years after being slaughtered by renegade Union soldiers by luring unwitting "yankee" tourists to their centennial festival. The hapless Northerners are then chopped, crushed, ripped apart etc. while the ghostly rebels party. Quite fun in a cartoonishly gruesome sort of way. Filmed in St. Cloud, FL. **75m/C; VHS, DVD, Blu-Ray.** William Kerwin; Connie Mason; Jeffrey Allen; Ben Moore; Gary Bakeman; Jerome Eden; Shelby Livingston; Michael Korb; Yvonne Gilbert; Mark Douglas; Linda Cochran; Vincent Santo; Andy Wilson; *D:* Herschell Gordon Lewis; *W:* Herschell Gordon Lewis; *C:* Herschell Gordon Lewis; *M:* Herschell Gordon Lewis; Larry Wellington.

2001 Maniacs 🦴 1/2 **2005 (R)** Sequel to the 60's film about a southern town of cannibalistic psychopaths who are pretty upset the South lost the Civil War, and who celebrate by inviting Northerners to a festival once a year to torture, kill, and eat them. The overflowing amount of bigotry, gore, and black humor will likely insult many. **87m/C; DVD.** Tim Sullivan; Robert Englund; Giuseppe Andrews; Jay Gillespie; Eli Roth; Lin Shaye; Marla Malcolm; *D:* Tim Sullivan; *W:* Tim Sullivan; Chris Kobin; *C:* Steve Adcock; *M:* Nathan Barr. **VIDEO**

2001 Maniacs: Field of Screams 🦴 *Tim Sullivan's 2001 Maniacs: Field of Screams* **2010 (R)** The annual festival invitees fail to show, and a town of Confederate cannibals take to the road and encounter new victims in the form of a reality TV show. Taking place almost entirely in an empty field full of tents it lacks even the occasional wit of the original. **86m/C; DVD, Streaming.** Bill Moseley; Nivek Ogre; Ahmed Best; Tim Sullivan; Clifford Allen Wagner; Lin Shaye; Christa Campbell; Andrea Leon; *D:* Tim Sullivan; *W:* Tim Sullivan; Chris Kobin; Christopher Tuffin; *C:* Mike Karasick; *M:* Patrick Copeland. **VIDEO**

2010: Moby Dick **WOOF!** **2010** Bizarre science fiction remake of the classic killer whale tale that somehow inexplicably got funding and name actors. **90m/C; DVD, Streaming.** Barry Bostwick; Matt Lagan; Adam Grimes; Michael Teh; Renee O'Connor; *D:* Trey Stokes; *W:* Paul Bales; Herman Melville; *C:* Alexander Yellen; *M:* Chris Ridenhour. **VIDEO**

Two Thousand Women 🦴🦴 1/2 **1944** British female prisoners arrive at a French hotel that's been turned into a German internment camp. RAF airmen land on the grounds after their bomber is hit and Freda and some of the others hide the men until they can plan their escape. Only the women learn there's a German spy amongst them and the situation becomes even more perilous. **97m/B; DVD.** *UK* Phyllis Calvert; Flora Robson; Patricia Roc; Reginald Purdell; James R McKechnie; Renee Houston; Jean Kent; *D:* Frank Launder; *W:* Frank Launder; Sidney Gilliat; *C:* Jack Cox; *M:* Hans May.

2001: A Space Odyssey 🦴🦴🦴🦴 **1968** Space voyage to Jupiter turns chaotic when a computer, HAL 9000, takes over. Seen by some as a mirror of man's historical use of machinery and by others as a grim vision of the future, the special effects and music are still stunning. Critically acclaimed and well accepted by some, simply confusing to others. Martin Balsam originally recorded the voice of HAL, but was replaced by Rain. From Arthur C. Clarke's short story "The Sentinel." Followed by a sequel "2010: The Year We Make Contact." **139m/C; VHS, DVD, Blu-Ray, HD-DVD.** *GB* Keir Dullea; Gary Lockwood; William Sylvester; Dan Richter; Leonard Rossiter; Margaret Tyzack; Robert Beatty; Vivian Kubrick; *V:* Douglas Rain; *D:* Stanley Kubrick; *W:* Stanley Kubrick; Arthur C. Clarke; *C:* Geoffrey Unsworth; John Alcott. Oscars '68: Visual FX; AFI '98: Top 100; Natl. Film Reg. '91.

2001: A Space Travesty 🦴🦴 1/2 **2000 (R)** Nielsen continues his tradition of parodies starring as none-too-bright Marshal "Dick" Dix who must rescue the U.S. president who has been kidnapped by aliens and replaced by a clone. He joins forces with sexy Cassandra (Winter) and heads to planet Vegan on his mission. **99m/C; VHS, DVD.** Leslie Nielsen; Ezio Greggio; Peter Egan; Ophelie Winter; *D:* Allan Goldstein; *W:* Alan Shearman; *C:* Sylvain Brault; *M:* Claude Foisy.

2010: The Year We Make Contact 🦴🦴🦴 **1984 (PG)** Based on Arthur C. Clarke's novel, which is his sequel to "2001: A Space Odyssey." Americans and Russians unite to investigate the abandoned starship Discovery's decaying orbit around Jupiter and try to determine why the HAL 9000 computer sabotaged its mission years before, while signs of cosmic change are detected on and around the giant planet. **116m/C; VHS, DVD.** Roy Scheider; John Lithgow; Dame Helen Mirren; Bob Balaban; Keir Dullea; Madolyn Smith; Mary Jo Deschanel; *V:* Douglas Rain; Candice Bergen; *D:* Peter Hyams; *W:* Peter Hyams; Arthur C. Clarke; *C:* Peter Hyams; *M:* David Shire.

2016: Obama's America 🦴 1/2 **2012 (PG)** Filmed in advance of the 2012 presidential election. Director/producer D'Souza attempts to show Americans the "dark path" the country will take in 2016 if Obama wins his second term--aiming to establish Obama as the harbinger of "Bad Things To Come," i.e. economic collapse, the start of World War III, and more. The film suggests (or, jams down the viewer's throat) that Obama's supposedly radical Kenyan father is responsible for his anti-American politics, among other conspiratorial points. What could actually have been learned about Barack Obama is certainly overshadowed by the sensationalist treatment and downright creepy horror-film music. **87m/C; DVD.** Dinesh D'Souza; Dr. Alice Dewey; Willy Kauai; Dr. Paul Kengor; Barack Obama; *D:* Dinesh D'Souza; John Sullivan; *W:* Dinesh D'Souza; John Sullivan; *M:* Calvin Jones; Greg Kellogg.

2069: A Sex Odyssey 🦴 1/2 **1978 (R)** Team of beautiful, sensuous astronauts are sent to Earth to obtain male sperm which they must bring back to Venus. Tongue-in-cheek soft core sci-fi spoof. **73m/C; VHS, DVD.** Alena Penz; Nina Fredric; Gerti Sneider; Raoul Retzer; Catherine Conti; Heidi Hammer; Michael Mein; Herb Heesel; *D:* George Keil; *W:* Willi Frisch; *C:* Michael Marszalek; Georg Mondi; *M:* Hans Hammerschmid.

Two Tickets to Broadway 🦴🦴 1/2 **1951** A small-town singer and a crooner arrange a hoax to get themselves on Bob Crosby's TV show. Appealing but lightweight. **106m/C; VHS, DVD.** Tony Martin; Janet Leigh; Gloria De Haven; Joi Lansing; *D:* James V. Kern; *M:* Leo Robin; Jule Styne.

Two Tickets to Paradise 🦴🦴 *Dirt Nap* **2006** Three middle-aged buddies finally have to accept the fact that their glory days are behind them—but they're not going down without a fight. Mark's (McGinley) family life is hurt by his serious gambling problem, McGriff (Sweeney) can't give up his rock 'n' roll dreams despite his marital troubles, and nerdy Jason (Hipp) still lives with his parents who run his life. When Jason wins tickets to the College Football Championship Bowl, it makes for an eventful road trip to Florida. Sweeney's directorial debut. **91m/C; DVD.** D.B. Sweeney; John C. McGinley; Paul Hipp; Moira Kelly; Janet Jones; Ed Harris; Ned Bellamy; Pat Hingle; *D:* D.B. Sweeney; *W:* D.B. Sweeney; Brian Currie; *C:* Claudio Rocha; *M:* John E. Nordstrom.

Two Tough Guys 🦴 1/2 *Dos Tipos Duros* **2003** Spanish hitman Paco (Resines) owes money to his boss Don Rodrigo (Alexandre) so he's willing to help out by looking after the Don's dim nephew Alex (Vilches). This includes paying for good-time girl Tatiana (Anaya) although Paco doesn't think this should mean that she can tag along on their next job. Uneasy mix of comedy and violence. Spanish with subtitles. **100m/C; DVD.** *SP* Antonio Resines; Jordi Vilches; Elena Anaya; Rosa Maria Sarda; Manuel Alexandre; *D:* Juan Martinez Moreno; *W:* Juan Martinez Moreno; *C:* Gonzalo F. Berridi; *M:* Alex Martinez.

2:22 🦴 1/2 **2008 (R)** Routine and lackluster crime drama about four criminals who plan a New Year's Eve heist of the safety deposit boxes located in a boutique hotel. Naturally things don't go exactly as expected. The robbers are unpleasant but one of their victims is more so'vengeful drug dealer Curtis. **104m/C; DVD, Blu-Ray.** Mick Rossi; Robert Miano; Aaron Gallagher; Jorge A. Jiminez; Peter Dobson; Val Kilmer; Bruce Kirby; *D:* Phillip Guzman; *W:* Mick Rossi; Phillip Guzman; *C:* Philip Roy; *M:* Danny Saber. **VIDEO**

2: Voodoo Academy 🦴 **2012** A pack of young men stop overnight at a spooky mansion since the road is blocked by fallen trees. Billed as a sequel to the first horror film 'made for girls' though it's set at a house full of gay men slowly being killed off one by one. **76m/C; DVD, Streaming.** Alex Bugaj; Alex Fox; Shane McGlashen; Richie Nuzzolese; Josh Randall; Brandon Schinaman; Michelle Bauer; *D:* David DeCoteau; *W:* Charlie Meadows; *C:* David DeCoteau; *M:* Harry Manfredini. **VIDEO**

Two-Way Stretch 🦴🦴 1/2 **1960** Three prison inmates in a progressive jail plan to break out, pull a diamond heist, and break back in, all in the same night. Fast-paced slapstick farce. **84m/B; VHS, DVD.** *GB* Peter Sellers; Wilfrid Hyde-White; Liz Fraser; David Lodge; *D:* Robert Day.

Two Weeks 🦴 1/2 **2006 (R)** Wan and predictable family drama with a lot of unlikable characters (but not our Sally!). Four squabbling siblings unexpectedly find themselves together for two weeks in order to deal with their mother's upcoming death. Filmmaker Keith (Chaplin) decides to record interviews with mom Anita (Field) while the others cope (or not) in their own ways. **102m/C; DVD.** Sally Field; Ben Chaplin; Julianne Nicholson; Glenn Howerton; Thomas Cavanaugh; Clea DuVall; James Murtaugh; *D:* Steve Stockman; *W:* Steve Stockman; *C:* Stephen Kazmierski; *M:* Hector Pereira.

Two Weeks in Another Town 🦴🦴 **1962** Douglas and Robinson are a couple of Hollywood has-beens who set out to make a comeback picture but meet with adversity at every turn. Extremely sappy melodrama is based on Irwin Shaw's trashy novel and represents one of director Minnelli's poorer efforts. **107m/C; VHS, DVD, Blu-Ray, Streaming.** Kirk Douglas; Edward G. Robinson; Cyd Charisse; George Hamilton; Daliah Lavi; Claire Trevor; James Gregory; Rosanna Schiaffino; George Macready; Stefan Schnabel; Vito Scotti; Leslie Uggams; *D:* Vincente Minnelli; *C:* Milton Krasner.

Two Weeks Notice 🦴🦴 1/2 **2002 (PG-13)** We know that Bullock and Grant are master charmers and they've both done romantic comedies, so perhaps our slight disappointment in this routine pairing can be understood. Irresponsible New York playboy and real estate developer George Wade (Grant) has a history of hiring female attorneys based on looks and not professional ability. Environmental activist Lucy Kelson (Bullock) is somehow roped in as George's latest lawyer/babysitter but she eventually has enough and hands in her, well, the title says it all. Of course, the ditzy duo need to figure out that they're made for each other. **100m/C; VHS, DVD, Blu-Ray.** Sandra Bullock; Hugh Grant; Alicia Witt; Dana Ivey; Robert Klein; Heather Burns; David Haig; Dorian Missick; *D:* Marc Lawrence; *W:* Marc Lawrence; *C:* Laszlo Kovacs; *M:* John Powell.

Two Weeks with Love 🦴🦴 **1950** Reynolds and family wear funny bathing suits in the Catskills in the early 1900s while the Debster sings songs and blushes into young adulthood. **92m/C; VHS, DVD.** Debbie Reynolds; Jane Powell; Ricardo Montalban; Louis Calhern; Ann Harding; Phyllis Kirk; Carleton Carpenter; Clinton Sundberg; Gary Gray; *D:* Roy Rowland.

Two Women 🦴🦴🦴🦴 *La Ciociara* **1961** Widowed Cesira (Loren) and her 13-year-old daughter Rosetta (Brown) travel war-torn Italy during WWII and must survive lack of food, bombings, and brutal soldiers. Tragic, moving, well-directed. Loren received well-deserved Oscar. Based on the novel by Alberto Moravia. In Italian with English subtitles or dubbed. **99m/B; VHS, DVD.** *IT* Sophia Loren; Raf Vallone; Eleonora Brown; Jean-Paul Belmondo; *D:* Vittorio De Sica; *W:* Cesare Zavattini; Vittorio De Sica; *C:* Gabor Pogany; *M:* Armando Trovajoli. Oscars '61: Actress (Loren); British Acad. '61: Actress (Loren); Cannes '61: Actress (Loren); Golden Globes '62: Foreign Film; N.Y. Film Critics '61: Actress (Loren).

The Two Worlds of Jenny Logan 🦴🦴 1/2 **1979** A woman travels back and forth in time whenever she dons a 19th century dress she finds in her old house. She is also able to fall in love twice, in different centuries. Adapted from "Second Sight," a novel by David Williams. Stylish and well made. **97m/C; VHS, DVD.** Lindsay Wagner; Marc Singer; Alan Feinstein; Linda Gray; Constance McCashin; Henry Wilcoxon; Irene Tedrow; Joan Darling; Allen Williams; Pat Corley; Gloria Stuart; *D:* Frank De Felitta. **TV**

Two Years at Sea 🦴🦴 1/2 **2012** An unconventional documentary about an unusual man, shot in 16mm by artist Ben Rivers. The film focuses on Jake, a man who lives very much alone in the middle of the forest. As a young man, Jake spent two years working at sea but longed to live in the forest. After he returned to shore, he moved to a remote forest and lived the isolated life he always wanted to live. The film shows the whole of Jake's life,including surviving in all seasons, working on unusual projects, and enjoying his radical vision to its fullest. **88m/B; DVD.** *D:* Ben Rivers; *W:* Ben Rivers.

2B Perfectly Honest 🦴 1/2 *2BPerfectlyHonest* **2004** Frank and Josh try to strike it rich on the Internet but their agency sinks, making Frank ditch his posh Manhattan digs and—gulp—move back in with ma and pa. Another shot at success appears doomed when they find out their new investors are up to no good. **88m/C; VHS, DVD.** Adam Trese; Andrew McCarthy; John Turturro; Michael Badalucco; Aida Turturro; Robert Vaughn; Hayley Mills; Mark Margolis; Kathleen Chalfant; Bruce MacVittie; *D:* Randel Cole; *W:* Randel Cole; *C:* Christopher La Vasseur; *M:* Jason Frederick. **VIDEO**

Tycoon 🦴🦴 1/2 **1947** Wayne goes to Latin America to build a road for an American industrialist. When the industrialist insists on a shorter but more dangerous route, Wayne must satisfy his own sense of honor. Meanwhile, he's found romance with the industrialist's half-Spanish daughter. Long, but well-acted. **129m/C; VHS, DVD.** John Wayne; Laraine Day; Cedric Hardwicke; Judith Anderson; James Gleason; Anthony Quinn; Jan Sterling; Grant Withers; Paul Fix; Charles Trowbridge; *D:* Richard Wallace; *W:* Borden Chase; John Twist; *C:* William Howard Greene; Harry Wild; *M:* Leigh Harline.

Tycus 🦴🦴 **1998 (R)** Journalist Jake Lowe (Onorati) investigates a suspicious mining company and discovers that visionary Peter Crawford (Hopper) has been building his own vast underground city as a modern-day Noah's Ark. Seems the Tycus comet is on a destruco course with Earth and not much is expected to survive. And when the rest of the world finds out, it'll be a race against time. **94m/C; VHS, DVD.** Dennis Hopper; Peter Onorati; Finola Hughes; Chick Vennera; *D:* John Putch; *W:* Kevin Goetz; *C:* Ross Berryman; *M:* Alexander Baker; Clair Marlo. **VIDEO**

Tyler Perry's A Madea Christmas 🦴 *A Madea Christmas* **2013 (PG-13)** Another entry in Perry's Madea franchise (based on his stage play). It's Christmastime in a small Alabama town where Eileen (Horsford) takes her kooky, cranky aunt Madea to spend the holiday with Eileen's daughter Lacey (Sumpter). But Lacey has a secret--a white husband (Lively) she's hiding from her racist mother--which sets the scene for oh-too-many strained jokes. Though Najimy and Larry the Cable Guy as the husband's parents makes for some fun, it's otherwise the same tired bit--even if it's wrapped in a holiday package. **100m/C; DVD, Blu-Ray.** Tyler Perry; Kathy Najimy; Chad Michael Murray; Anna Maria Horsford; Tika Sumpter; Eric Lively; Larry the Cable Guy; *D:* Tyler Perry; *W:* Tyler Perry; *C:* Alexander Gruszynski; *M:* Christopher Young. Golden Raspberries '13: Worst Actress (Perry).

Tyler Perry's Good Deeds 🦴 1/2 *Good Deeds* **2012 (PG-13)** Successful entrepreneur Wesley Deeds is engaged to an uptown girl when he becomes more interested in a hard-luck single mom. Typical Perry fare. **110m/C; DVD, Blu-Ray.** Tyler Perry; Thandie Newton; Gabrielle Union; Phylicia Rashad; Brian White; Rebecca Romijn; Eddie Cibrian; Jamie Kennedy; Jordenn Thompson; *D:* Tyler Perry; *W:* Tyler Perry; *C:* Alexander Grusynski; *M:* Aaron Zigman.

Tyler Perry's Hell Hath No Fury Like a Woman Scorned: The Play 🦴🦴 **2014** A comedy-drama about a woman's quest to find love gone bad and the aftermath. Successful single woman Anita Lincoln (Riley) has it all—friends, a great job, and a close-knit family. Anita is even paying for her younger sister's wedding. All that Anita lacks is a loving man, and her closest friend seems to have found an ideal man for her online. Ray (Lavender) seems charming, loving, and wealthy, and convinces Anita to marry him in Vegas. But once Randy marries her, he shows his true colors. Anita must adjust to take her life back and ensuring Randy pays for doing her wrong. **117m/C; DVD, Streaming, Download.** Cheryl "Pepsii" Riley; Ray Lavender; Patrice Lovely; Olrick Johnson; Monica Blaire; *D:* Tyler Perry; *W:* Tyler Perry. **VIDEO**

Tyler Perry's Meet the Browns 🦴 1/2 *Meet the Browns* **2008 (PG-13)** Single mother Brenda (Bassett) learns that her father, a man she's never met, has died, so she packs up the family and heads to Georgia for the funeral. There, she and her three children are greeted with varying degrees of Southern hospitality by a batch of half-siblings she never knew existed. Brenda then meets Harry (Fox, in a role not far from home), a handsome retired basketball player who sweeps Brenda off her feet (surprise, surprise). Typical Perry fare, loaded with racial commentary, monologues on family values, and conversations about economic struggle. **101m/C; DVD, Blu-Ray.** Angela Bassett; Rick Fox; Margaret Avery; Frankie Faison; Jenifer Lewis; Sofia Vergara; Lamman Rucker; Irma P. Hall; Tyler Perry; Lance Gross; David Mann; Tamela Mann; Judy Rhee; *D:* Tyler Perry; *W:* Tyler Perry; *C:* Sandi Sissel; *M:* Aaron Zigman.

Tyler Perry's Temptation: Confessions of a Marriage Counselor 🦴 1/2 *Temptation: Confessions of a Marriage Counselor* **2013 (PG-13)** Tyler Perry strikes again, preaching on the dangers of adultery. Judith (Smollett-Bell), an Ivy-League educated therapist for an upscale matchmaking agency, finds herself slowly drifting away from her blue-collar, good-hearted husband Brice (Gross), and gravitating towards social-media mogul stud Harley (Jones). Soon enough, during a business trip, Harley sweeps her off to his New Orleans mansion, revealing a lifestyle filled with drugs and excess. She returns a different woman, much to the confusion and dismay of her husband. An absurdly out-of-touch cliched melodrama, with Perry lacking any understanding of human interaction. Any laughs are unintentional. **111m/C; DVD, Blu-Ray.** Jurnee Smollett; Lance Gross; Vanessa Williams; Brandy Norwood; Ella Joyce; Kim Kardashian; Robbie Jones; *D:* Tyler Perry; *W:* Tyler Perry; *C:* Alexander Grusynski; *M:* Aaron Zigman. Golden Raspberries '13: Worst Support. Actress (Kardashian).

Tyler Perry's The Single Moms' Club 🦴🦴 *The Single Moms' Club* **2014 (PG-13)** Female bonding goes a long way to ingratiate the pic with its target audience. Five women apparently have little in common except that they're single parents with kids at the same prep school. When the kids run a little wild, the moms are called in for a disciplinary hearing and wind up in charge of the school's annual fundraising dance. Thus their club and friendships begin in Tyler's low-key dramedy. **111m/C; DVD, Blu-Ray.** Nia Long; Wendi McLendon-Covey; Amy Smart; Zulay Henao; Cocoa Brown; Eddie Cibrian; Terry Crews; Ryan Eggold; William Levy; Tyler Perry; ***D:*** Tyler Perry; ***W:*** Tyler Perry; ***C:*** Alexander Gruszynski; ***M:*** Christopher Young.

Tyler Perry's Why Did I Get Married? 1/2 *Why Did I Get Married?* **2007 (PG-13)** Four couples—all friends who met as undergrads at a historically black college—navigate the rollercoaster of marriage as they gather for their annual couples retreat. Each is successful (there's a psychologist, lawyer, and pediatrician), but each relationship hides secrets and they begin to unfold over the retreat. One couple argues over having a second child; someone's sleeping with his wife's best friend; another couple fights about everything. Perry, with God's help (a theme throughout most of his work), wraps things up a bit too neatly by the end of the retreat. Despite the drama, though, the characters are both smart and refreshing. **113m/C; DVD.** Tyler Perry; Janet Jackson; Jill Scott; Malik Yoba; Richard T. Jones; Michael Jai White; Lamman Rucker; Sharon Leal; Tasha Smith; Denise Boutte; ***D:*** Tyler Perry; ***W:*** Tyler Perry; ***C:*** Toyomichi Kurita; ***M:*** Aaron Zigman.

Tyler Perry's Why Did I Get Married Too *Why Did I Get Married Too* **2010 (PG-13)** Unnecessary sequel to Tyler Perry's 2007 outing, but comes off more like a series of deleted scenes from the original. The cast returns for an annual retreat to the Bahamas, bunking together in a seaside cabin. Obviously tempers and libidos flair, as these couples re-examine their relationships. Bland, generic visuals add to the drudgery of a watered-down overly-melodramatic script that tries to cram too much filler into a wafer-thin story. **121m/C; Blu-Ray, On Demand.** Tyler Perry; Janet Jackson; Malik Yoba; Sharon Leal; Michael Jai White; Tasha Smith; Amber Stevens; Richard T. Jones; Louis Gossett, Jr.; Cicely Tyson; Jill Scott; ***D:*** Tyler Perry; ***W:*** Tyler Perry; ***C:*** Toyomichi Kurita; ***M:*** Michael Stern.

Typhoon *Taepung* **2006 (R)** Melodramatic action flick, filmed in Korea, Russia, and Thailand, follows North Korean exile Myong-sin (Jang), who's plotting to unleash chemical weapons during a typhoon on both South and North Korea. His family was betrayed and murdered while trying to escape the oppressive regime and he wants payback. Kang (Lee) is the military officer who must stop him. Korean with subtitles. **103m/C; DVD.** *NK* Dong-gun Jang; Lee Mi-yeon; Lee Jung-jae; ***D:*** Kwak Kyung-taek; ***W:*** Kwak Kyung-taek; ***C:*** Hong Kyeng-pyo.

Tyrannosaur **2011** Considine's intense feature film debut is based on his 2008 short "Dog Altogether," which also starred Mullen and Colman. Joseph (Mullen) is a widowed, rage-filled, working-class drunk who's befriended by Christian charity-shop worker Hannah (Colman). Hannah's cheerful manner belies her home life torment since she's married to the insecure, abusive James (Marsan). Joseph was hardly the model husband to his late wife (the title refers to her nickname) and he doesn't believe Hannah's explanations for black eyes and bruises, which unexpectedly gives Hannah the courage to not only confront James but to leave him. **91m/C; DVD.** *GB* Peter Mullan; Olivia Colman; Eddie Marsan; Ned Dennehy; Sally Carman; Samuel Bottomley; Paul Popplewell; Sian Breckin; ***D:*** Paddy Considine; ***W:*** Paddy Considine; ***C:*** Erik Wilson; ***M:*** Chris Baldwin; Dan Baker.

Tyson 1/2 **2008 (R)** Toback uses his longtime friendship with the boxer to draw out the volatile former heavyweight championship in this complex bio. Toback delves into Tyson's troubled childhood, his various boxing triumphs and defeats, his relationships and prison stint, drug addiction and rehabilitation, and what happened after he hung up the gloves for good. **90m/C; Blu-Ray, On Demand.** Mike Tyson; ***D:*** James Toback; ***C:*** Lawrence McConkey; ***M:*** Salaam Remi.

U-571 1/2 **2000 (PG-13)** U.S sub crew is sent to steal an Enigma encryption device from a disabled Nazi U-boat before the Germans can send help. When their own sub is sunk, the Americans, led by Lt. Tyler (McConaughey), take over the German sub and try to make their way back home through enemy destroyers. Long on loud and impressive action sequences, but short on characterization and good dialogue, this one'll work best for adrenalin junkies and those with theatre-quality entertainment systems. **116m/C; VHS, DVD, Blu-Ray, HD-DVD.** Matthew McConaughey; Bill Paxton; Harvey Keitel; Jon Bon Jovi; Jake Weber; David Keith; Terrence "T.C." Carson; Jack Noseworthy; Tom Guiry; Thomas Kretschmann; Erik Palladino; Will Estes; Matthew Settle; Dave Power; Derk Cheetwood; ***D:*** Jonathan Mostow; ***W:*** Jonathan Mostow; David Ayer; Sam Montgomery; ***C:*** Oliver Wood; ***M:*** Richard (Rick) Marvin. Oscars '00: Sound FX Editing.

U-Turn 1/2 *Stray Dogs* **1997 (R)** Bobby (Penn) is a two-bit gambler on his way to pay off the balance of a debt in Las Vegas (the down payment was two of his fingers) when he is stranded in the town of Superior, Arizona. He becomes mixed up with a married couple (Nolte and Lopez), each of whom want Bobby to kill the other. Adding to the fun in this Mayberry on mescaline are the walking grease pit of a mechanic (Thornton) and a local tough guy named TNT (Phoenix), who thinks Bobby is making a play for his nymphet girlfriend (Danes). Also appearing is the stock issue Oliver Stone wise old Indian who dispenses wisdom, or something like it. The characters meet for the predestined showdown in the desert, with predictable results. Stone has a good time taking stereotypical noir characters and putting his unique twist on them, although you may not have as much fun watching them. **125m/C; VHS, DVD, Blu-Ray.** Sean Penn; Jennifer Lopez; Claire Danes; Nick Nolte; Joaquin Rafael (Leaf) Phoenix; Powers Boothe; Billy Bob Thornton; Jon Voight; Abraham Benrubi; Julie Hagerty; Bo Hopkins; Valery (Valeri Nikolayev) Nikolaev; Aida Linares; Laurie Metcalf; Liv Tyler; ***D:*** Oliver Stone; ***W:*** John Ridley; ***C:*** Robert Richardson; ***M:*** Ennio Morricone.

UFO: Target Earth **1974 (G)** Scientist attempts to fish flying saucer out of lake and costs studio $70,000. **80m/C; VHS, DVD.** Nick Plakias; Cynthia Cline; Phil Erickson; ***D:*** Michael de Gaetano.

Ugetsu 1/2 *Ugetsu Monogatari* **1953** The classic film that established Mizoguchi's reputation outside of Japan. Two 16th century Japanese peasants venture from their homes in pursuit of dreams, and encounter little more than their own hapless folly and a bit of the supernatural. A wonderful mix of comedy and action with nifty camera movement. Based on the stories of Akinara Ueda. In Japanese with English subtitles. **96m/B; VHS, DVD, Blu-Ray.** *JP* Machiko Kyo; Masayuki Mori; Kinuyo Tanaka; Eitaro (Sakae, Saka Ozawa) Ozawa; ***D:*** Kenji Mizoguchi; ***W:*** Yoshikata Yoda; ***C:*** Kazuo Miyagawa; ***M:*** Fumio Hayasaka. Venice Film Fest. '53: Silver Prize.

The Ugly 1/2 **1996** Confessed serial killer Simon (Rotondo) has celebrity shrink Karen (Hobbs) evaluate him to determine whether he's cured or has to stand trial for his crimes. Through flashbacks, dream sequences, and fantasies (both Simon's and the doc's), Simon's screwed-up past is revealed: mentally and physically abused by an unstable mother (Ward-Leeland) and picked on by bullies, he commits his first murder at 13. First-time director Reynolds' use of red herrings, alternate points of view, and mixing of perspectives can be hard to follow, but they do ratchet up the suspense. He also doesn't scrimp on the gore, which is highly stylized and effective. **93m/C; VHS, DVD.** *NZ* Paolo Rotondo; Rebecca Hobbs; Jennifer Ward-Lealand; Roy Ward; Vanessa Byrnes; ***D:*** Scott Reynolds; ***W:*** Scott Reynolds; ***C:*** Simon Raby; ***M:*** Victoria Kelly.

The Ugly American 1/2 **1963** A naive American ambassador to a small, civil-war-torn Asian country fights a miniature Cold War against northern communist influence. Too preachy, and the "Red Menace" aspects are now very dated, but Brando's performance is worth watching. Based on the William J. Lederer novel. **120m/C; VHS, DVD, Blu-Ray.** Marlon Brando; Sandra Church; Eiji Okada; Pat Hingle; Arthur Hill; ***D:*** George Englund; ***W:*** Stewart Stern.

The Ugly Dachshund 1/2 **1965** Jones and Pleshette are married dog lovers who raise Dachshunds. When Ruggles convinces them to take a Great Dane puppy, the fun begins! The Great Dane thinks he is a Dachshund because he has been raised with them—just imagine what happens when such a large dog acts as if he is small! Kids will love this wacky Disney film. **93m/C; VHS, DVD.** Dean Jones; Suzanne Pleshette; Charlie Ruggles; Kelly Thordsen; Parley Baer; Mako; ***D:*** Norman Tokar; ***W:*** Albert Aley; ***C:*** Edward Colman; ***M:*** George Bruns.

The Ugly Truth **WOOF!** **2009 (R)** This is NOT what adult women want. Shrewish prude Abby (Heigl) is a morning TV show producer with a long list of requirements for the perfect man, so it's no wonder she's still single. Then loutish ape Mike (Butler), a cable shock jock, is hired to improve ratings with his outrageously chauvinistic rants. He presumes to give Abby advice about man's typical caveman behavior, encouraging her into such ridiculously superficial changes as hair extensions, push-up bras, and vibrating panties. Since apparently Abby has absolutely no pride or dignity, she's easy to dismiss and the flick is all too predictable. A humiliating throwback (or throw-up) in more ways than one and an ugly, desperate example of what is passing for romantic comedy. **95m/C; Blu-Ray, On Demand.** Katherine Heigl; Gerard Butler; Eric Winter; Bonnie Sommerville; Bree Turner; Nick Searcy; Cheryl Hines; John Michael Higgins; Kevin Connolly; Yvette Nicole Brown; Nathan (Nate) Corddry; Noah Mathews; ***D:*** Robert Luketic; ***W:*** Kirsten Smith; Nicole Eastman; Karen McCullah; ***C:*** Russell Carpenter; ***M:*** Aaron Zigman.

UglyDolls 1/2 *Ugly Dolls* **2019 (PG)** An animated musical with a threadbare plot: the plush doll inhabitants of Uglyville venture beyond their town to discover that being different is OK. Make no mistake, this is no "Toy Story." Instead, it took a page from "The Emoji Movie" playbook: quality/originality/message = low; merchandising potential = high. The only redeeming feature is the soundtrack -- most of the characters are voiced by musical artists, not actors (as is painfully apparent). **87m/C; DVD, Blu-Ray, Streaming.** *CA CH US V:* Emma Roberts; Kelly Clarkson; Gabriel "Fluffy" Iglesias; Nick Jonas; Janelle Monáe; ***D:*** Kelly Asbury; ***W:*** Alison Peck; ***M:*** Christopher Lennertz.

UHF **1989 (PG-13)** A loser is appointed manager of a bargain-basement UHF television station. He turns it around via bizarre programming ideas. Some fun parodies of TV enhance this minimal story. Developed solely as a vehicle for Yankovic. **97m/C; VHS, DVD, Blu-Ray.** Weird Al Yankovic; Kevin McCarthy; Victoria Jackson; Michael Richards; David Bowe; Anthony Geary; Stan Brock; Trinidad Silva; Gedde Watanabe; Dr. Demento; Fran Drescher; John Paragon; Emo Philips; Billy Barty; ***D:*** Jay Levey; ***W:*** Weird Al Yankovic; Jay Levey; ***C:*** David Lewis; ***M:*** John Du Prez.

UKM: The Ultimate Killing Machine **2006** Action trash. After turning war hero Dodds (Northwood) into an uncontrollable killing machine, the army decides to experiment on a group of misfits instead, in an effort to turn them into supersoldiers. The side-effects are uncontrollable rage and uncontrollable lust and since this is a co-ed group, the latter wouldn't appear to be a problem. But the human guinea pigs escape, as does the raging Dodds, and the hunt is on! **90m/C; DVD.** *CA* Michael Madsen; John Evans; Simon Northwood; Mak Fyfe; Steve Arbuckle; Victoria Nestorowicz; Erin Mackinnon; Deanna Dezmari; ***D:*** David Mitchell; ***W:*** Tyler Levine; Tim McGregor; ***C:*** Marcus Elliott; ***M:*** Craig McConnell. **VIDEO**

Ulee's Gold **1997 (R)** Slow-paced, deliberate character study, set in the Florida panhandle. Ulysses "Ulee" Jackson (Fonda) is a widowed, middle-aged Vietnam vet who puts most of his energies into his work as a beekeeper, much to the detriment of his family. Son Jimmy (Wood) is in prison and druggie daughter-in-law Helen (Dunford) has disappeared, leaving the taciturn Ulee to care for his troubled granddaughters, teenaged Casey (Biel) and nine-year-old Penny (Zima). But their ordinary lives change when Helen turns up in Orlando with two violent hoods from Jimmy's past and Ulee must not only rescue her but find the emotional release to make them all a home. Splendidly moving performance from Fonda. **111m/C; VHS, DVD, Blu-Ray.** Peter Fonda; Tom Wood; Vanessa Zima; Jessica Biel; Christine Dunford; Patricia Richardson; Steve Flynn; Dewey Weber; J. Kenneth Campbell; ***D:*** Victor Nunez; ***W:*** Victor Nunez; ***C:*** Virgil Marcus Mirano; ***M:*** Charles Engstrom. Golden Globes '98: Actor--Drama (Fonda); N.Y. Film Critics '97: Actor (Fonda).

The Ultimate Gift 1/2 **2007 (PG)** Sentimental, sometimes preachy drama based on Jim Stovall's novel. Trust-fund twentysomething playboy Jason Stevens (Fuller) expects nothing from his estranged grandfather Red's (Garner) will. But Red, via videotaped messages, leaves Jason a fortune—with stipulations that are intended to teach him to be a better person, including bonding with young cancer patient Emily (Breslin). Pic veers off track when Jason goes to Ecuador and gets kidnapped by bandits but manages to right itself. And it's a pleasure to see old pros like Garner, Dennehy, and Cobb at work. **114m/C; DVD.** Drew Fuller; James Garner; Ali Hillis; Abigail Breslin; Lee Meriwether; Brian Dennehy; Bill Cobbs; ***D:*** Michael O. Sajbel; ***W:*** Cheryl McKay; ***C:*** Brian Baugh; ***M:*** Mark McKenzie; Anthony Short.

Ultimate Heist *Le Premier Cercle; Inside Ring* **2009 (R)** Efficient crime actioner. Gangster Milo Malakian (Reno) expects his son Anton (Ulliel) to take over the family business but Anton would prefer to open a legit hotel with girlfriend Elodie (Giocante). The family's latest heist/murder draws the relentless attention of detective Saunier (Bouajila) and he might have his chance to bring the clan down when Malakian plans an airport robbery. French with subtitles. **95m/C; DVD.** *FR IT* Jean Reno; Gaspard Ulliel; Sami Bouajila; Vahina Giocante; Isaac Sharry; ***D:*** Laurent Tuel; ***W:*** Laurent Tuel; Simon Moutairou; Laurent Turner; ***C:*** Laurent Machuel; ***M:*** Alain Kremski.

The Ultimate Life **2013 (PG)** Equally faith-based sequel to 2007's "The Ultimate Gift" offers good family messages delivered in the dullest and most cliched way possible. Having inherited a mega-company from his billionaire grandfather Red, Jason Stevens has turned into a neglectful workaholic. So Jason reads Red's journals to see how he made his fortune and what it did to his life (all shown in flashbacks) in order to learn that money can't buy happiness. **110m/C; DVD, Blu-Ray.** Logan Bartholomew; Ali Hillis; Drew Waters; Elizabeth Ann Bennett; Peter Fonda; Bill Cobbs; Lee Meriwether; Austin James; Abigail Mavity; ***D:*** Michael Landon, Jr.; ***W:*** Brian Bird; Lisa Shillingburg; ***C:*** Christo Bakalov; ***M:*** Mark McKenzie.

The Ultimate Warrior 1/2 **1975 (R)** Yul Brynner must defend the plants and seeds of a pioneer scientist to help replenish the world's food supply in this thriller set in 2012. **92m/C; VHS, DVD.** Yul Brynner; Max von Sydow; Joanna Miles; Richard Kelton; Lane Bradbury; William (Bill) Smith; ***D:*** Robert Clouse; ***W:*** Robert Clouse.

The Ultimate Weapon **1997 (R)** Mercenary Hogan destroys an IRA base camp when he realizes he's been double-crossed. **110m/C; VHS, DVD.** Hulk Hogan; Carl Marotte; Cynthia (Cyndy, Cindy) Preston; Lynne Adams; Daniel Pilon; ***D:*** Jon Cassar; ***C:*** Bert Tougas; ***M:*** Marty Simon. **VIDEO**

Ultrachrist! **2003** It's the 21st century and Jesus is back in town—New York City, to be exact—but soon realizes that the old ways of getting his word out aren't cutting. So he dons a skin-tight superhero suit and assumes the alias Ultrachrist. But Dad isn't thrilled with this newfangled approach and Christ must prove himself, while battling his archenemy the Antichrist. Further proof that one person's blasphemy is another's fun. **92m/C; VHS, DVD.** Jonathan C. Green; Celia A. Montgomery; Dara Shindler; Jordan Hoffman; Danielle Langlois; Samantha Dark; Nathaniel Graves; Bob Cohen; Jurgen Fauth; Marty Grillo; Rob Haussman; Ryan V. McCallum; Steve Montague; Leila Nelson; Michael R. Thomas; ***D:*** Kerry Douglas Dye; ***W:*** Jordan Hoffman; Kerry Douglas Dye; ***C:*** Peter Olsen; ***M:*** Howard Leshaw. **VIDEO**

Ultramarines: A Warhammer 40,000 Movie 1/2 **2010 (R)** Animated film based on the fictional universe of Games

Workshop's Warhammer 40K game. A squad of Space Marines are dispatched to a planet that sent out a distress signal before falling silent. **77m/C; DVD, Blu-Ray, Streaming.** *UK V:* Terence Stamp; John Hurt; Sean Pertwee; Steven Waddington; Donald Sumpter; ***D:*** Martyn Pick; ***W:*** Dan Abnett; ***C:*** Darren Lovell; ***M:*** Adam Harvey. **VIDEO**

Ultraviolet 🦴🦴 ½ **1998** Vampires walk among us. Humans are their food source and now they are threatened by humanity's ability to destroy itself and the vamps want to take control. The CIB, a secret government operation, is determined to prevent that situation. Atmospheric British miniseries in which the term "vampire" is never used—the bloodsuckers are referred to as Code Fives and the title refers to the ultraviolet light that the CIB uses in its work. **360m/C; VHS, DVD.** *GB* Jack Davenport; Susannah Harker; Philip Quast; Idris Elba; Corin Redgrave; Stephen Moyer; Thomas Lockyer; Collette Brown; Fiona Dolman; ***D:*** Joe Ahearne; ***W:*** Joe Ahearne; ***C:*** Peter Greenhalgh; ***M:*** Sue Hewitt. **TV**

Ultraviolet 🦴 **2006 (PG-13)** After being given a virus by the military to create a group of superhumans, sexy vamp Violet (Jovovich) must kick some major butt to save their lives when the powers-that-be decide to terminate them. Their ultimate survival rests within a boy named Six (Bright), whom Violet must protect. Set in a "Matrix"-like future world—a world where no shirt exists that properly fits Violet—writer/director Wimmer seems proud to crudely rip off a mishmash of other such action flicks as "Tomb Raider" and "Kill Bill," not to mention "Resident Evil." **89m/C; DVD, Blu-Ray, UMD.** Milla Jovovich; Cameron Bright; Nick (Nicholas) Chinlund; William Fichtner; Sebastien Andrieu; ***D:*** Kurt Wimmer; ***W:*** Kurt Wimmer; ***C:*** Arthur Wong Ngok Tai; ***M:*** Klaus Badelt.

Ulysses 🦴🦴 ½ *Ulisse* **1955** An Italian made version of the epic poem by Homer, as the warrior returns to his homeland and the ever-faithful Penelope after the Trojan war. Ambitious effort provides for the ultimate mixed review. Douglas is good in the role and his stops along the ten-year way are well visualized. Sometimes sluggish with poor dubbing. Seven writers helped bring Homer to the big screen. **104m/C; VHS, DVD.** *IT* Kirk Douglas; Silvana Mangano; Anthony Quinn; Rossana Podesta; ***D:*** Mario Camerini.

Ulysses 🦴🦴 ½ **1967** James Joyce's probably unfilmable novel was given a noble effort in this flawed film covering a day in the life of Leopold Bloom as he wanders through Dublin. Shot in Ireland with a primarily Irish cast. **140m/B; VHS, DVD.** Milo O'Shea; Maurice Roeves; T.P. McKenna; Martin Dempsey; Sheila O'Sullivan; Barbara Jefford; ***D:*** Joseph Strick; ***W:*** Joseph Strick; Fred Haines; ***C:*** Wolfgang Suschitzky; ***M:*** Stanley Myers.

Ulysses Against the Son of Hercules 🦴 ½ *Ulisse contro Ercole; Ulysses Against Hercules* **1961** Hercules (or his son depending on which version of this film you see) is sent by the Gods to fetch Ulysses who is to be punished for blinding the Cyclops. Captured by curious weird monster people along the way, they bond in their attempts to defeat the world's evils. **99m/C; DVD.** *FR IT* Georges Marchal; Mike Lane; Gabriele Tinti; Alessandra Panaro; ***D:*** Mario Caiano; ***W:*** Mario Caiano; ***C:*** Alvaro Mancori; ***M:*** Angelo Francesco Lavagnino.

Ulysses' Gaze 🦴🦴 *The Look of Ulysses; To Vlemma Tou Odyssea; The Gaze of Ulysses* **1995** Nameless Greek-American filmmaker (Keitel) journeys across the Balkans from Athens to Sarajevo while making a documentary on pioneer filmmakers, the Manakia brothers, who ignored national and ethnic strife in order to record the lives of ordinary people. Keitel has heard that some undeveloped film shot by the brothers has turned up in Sarajevo and he's determined to see it despite the turmoil in Bosnia. Moving and pessimistic depiction of the Balkan conflict seen through a filmmaker's eyes. English and Greek with subtitles. **173m/C; VHS, DVD.** *GR FR IT* Harvey Keitel; Maia Morgenstern; Erland Josephson; Thanassis Vengos; Yorgos Michalokopoulos; Dora Volonaki; ***D:*** Theo Angelopoulos; ***W:*** Theo Angelopoulos; Tonino Guerra; Petros Markaris; ***C:*** Yorgos Arvanitis; ***M:*** Eleni Karaindrou. Cannes '95: Grand Jury Prize.

Ulzana's Raid 🦴🦴🦴 **1972 (R)** An aging scout and an idealistic Cavalry lieutenant lock horns on their way to battling a vicious Apache chieftain. A violent, gritty western that enjoyed critical re-evaluation years after its first release. **103m/C; DVD, Blu-Ray.** Burt Lancaster; Bruce Davison; Richard Jaeckel; Lloyd Bochner; Jorge Luke; ***D:*** Robert Aldrich; ***W:*** Alan Sharp; ***C:*** Joseph Biroc; ***M:*** Frank DeVol.

Umberto D 🦴🦴🦴🦴 **1955** A government pensioner, living alone with his beloved dog, struggles to keep up a semblance of dignity on his inadequate pension. De Sica considered this his masterpiece. A sincere, tender treatment of the struggles involved with the inevitability of aging. In Italian with English subtitles. Laser edition features letterboxed print. **89m/B; VHS, DVD, Blu-Ray.** *IT* Carlo Battista; Maria Pia Casilio; Lina Gennari; ***D:*** Vittorio De Sica; ***W:*** Vittorio De Sica; Cesare Zavattini; ***M:*** Alessandro Cicognini. N.Y. Film Critics '55: Foreign Film.

Umbrellas of Cherbourg 🦴🦴🦴 ½ *Les Parapluies de Cherbourg; Die Regenschirme von Cherbourg* **1964** A bittersweet film operetta with no spoken dialog. Genevieve (Deneuve) is the teenaged daughter of a widow (Vernon) who owns an umbrella shop. She and her equally young boyfriend Guy (Castelnuovo) are separated by his military duty in Algeria. Finding she is pregnant, Genevieve marries the wealthy Roland (Michel), and when her former lover returns, he too marries someone else. But when they meet once again will their love be rekindled? Lovely photography and an evocative score enhance the story. French with subtitles; also available dubbed in English (not with the same effectiveness). **90m/C; VHS, DVD, Blu-Ray.** *FR* Catherine Deneuve; Nino Castelnuovo; Anne Vernon; Ellen Farner; Marc Michel; Mireille Perrey; Jean Champion; Alfred Wolff; Dorothee Blanck; ***D:*** Jacques Demy; ***W:*** Jacques Demy; ***C:*** Jean Rabier; ***M:*** Michel Legrand. Cannes '64: Film.

Un Air de Famille 🦴🦴 *Respectable Families; Family Resemblances* **1996** Comedy, adapted from a play, about a dysfunctional family. They're meeting at the family's rundown bar to celebrate the birthday of son Philippe's (Yordanoff) silly wife, Yolande (Frot). The bar is run by his brother Henri (Bacri), whose wife calls to say she's left him, while their tactless mother (Maurier) frets over their sister, Betty (Jaoui), who's 30 and still single. What no one knows is that Betty has been secretly seeing Denis (Darroussin), the bartender, whom everyone thinks is simple but is actually the only one with any clue to the family's hypocrisy. French with subtitles. **107m/C; VHS, DVD.** *FR* Jean-Pierre Bacri; Agnes Jaoui; Jean-Pierre Darroussin; Catherine Frot; Claire Maurier; Wladimir Yordanoff; ***D:*** Cedric Klapisch; ***W:*** Jean-Pierre Bacri; Agnes Jaoui; Cedric Klapisch; ***C:*** Benoit Delhomme. Cesar '97: Support. Actor (Darroussin), Support. Actress (Frot), Writing.

Un Coeur en Hiver 🦴🦴 ½ *A Heart in Winter* **1993** An anti-romance romantic drama where passion is frozen and real emotion is reserved for the inanimate. Serious Stephane (Auteuil) is a master craftsman at repairing violins; his partner Maxime (Dussollier) runs the business side and deals with the musicians, including beautiful violinist Camille (Beart) with whom he has fallen in love. Camille is single-mindedly fixated on her career and she recognizes a kindred spirit in Stephane but their calculated emotional seduction causes problems for all. Can be frustrating since the smooth surface of the characters is rarely cracked. In French with English titles. **100m/C; VHS, DVD, Blu-Ray.** *FR* Emmanuelle Beart; Daniel Auteuil; Andre Dussollier; Elisabeth Bourgine; Brigitte Catillon; Maurice Garrel; Myriam Boyer; ***D:*** Claude Sautet; ***W:*** Jacques Fieschi; Jerome Tonnerre; ***C:*** Yves Angelo. Cesar '93: Director (Sautet), Support. Actor (Dussollier).

Una 🦴🦴 ½ **2017 (R)** A study of the consequences of pedophilia, based on the 2005 play Blackbird. When Una (Mara) was a young teen, she was seduced by her creepy neighbor Ray (Mendelsohn). He promised to take her to Europe, but abandoned her at a bed and breakfast in a small town. Though Ray served time, the experience left Una unable to experience intimacy and obsessed with Ray. After his release, Ray built a new a life with a new name. Finding his picture in the news, the fixated Una confronts him at his workplace. Mara's exceptional performance as the damaged, crazy Una drives the film's twisted story. **94m/C; DVD.** Rooney Mara; Ben Mendelsohn; Tara Fitzgerald; Ruby Stokes; Riz Ahmed; ***D:*** Benedict Andrews; ***W:*** David Harrower; ***C:*** Thimios Bakatakis; ***M:*** Jed Kurzel.

Una Noche 🦴🦴 **2013** Debut feature from Mulloy features a non-pro cast and a plot that allows some comedy to break the tension, which centers on the efforts of teen friends Raul and Elio to escape Havana for Miami by raft. After hot-headed Raul gets into trouble with the cops, he's desperate to leave his poverty-stricken, black market life behind. Elio is happy to join him even though it means leaving his twin sister, Lila, and keeping his less-than-platonic feelings for Raul a secret. Only an abrupt outcome lets down the story. Spanish with subtitles. **90m/C; DVD.** *US CU UK* Daniel Arrechago; Javier Nunez Florian; Anailin de la Rua de la Torre; ***D:*** Lucy Mulloy; ***W:*** Lucy Mulloy; ***C:*** Trevor Forrest; Shlomo Godder.

Unaccompanied Minors 🦴🦴 ½ **2006 (PG)** Mildly goofy holiday comedy meant for the pre-adolescent crowd finds a disparate group of kids left by various adults at a midwestern airport to begin their solo travels on Christmas Eve. Only there's a blizzard and all flights are cancelled, leaving the little darlings to plot their escape from the control of airport stooge Mr. Porter (Black) and more sympathetic staffer Zach (Valderrama). Mayhem ensues. **87m/C; DVD.** Brett Kelly; Lewis Black; Wilmer Valderrama; Paget Brewster; Tyler James Williams; Dyllan Christopher; Gina Mantegna; Quinn Shephard; Dominique Saldana; Jessica Walter; David Koechner; Rob Corddry; Teri Garr; Michelle Sandler; ***D:*** Paul Feig; ***W:*** Jacob Meszaros; Mya Stark; ***C:*** Christopher Baffa; ***M:*** Michael Andrews.

Unanswered Prayers 🦴🦴 **2010** The 1990 Garth Brooks ballad gets the Lifetime movie treatment. High school football star Ben married cheerleader Lorrie and eventually settled into his family's construction business. Years pass and Ben's (Close) actual high school sweetie Ava (Amick) comes back to town for her mother's funeral. Some drunken reminiscing leads Ben to wonder 'what if', especially when Ava makes it clear she's interested in rekindling that old flame. **88m/C; DVD.** Eric Close; Samantha Mathis; Madchen Amick; Tony Oller; Patty Duke; Jennifer Aspen; Alex Frnka; ***D:*** Steven Schachter; ***W:*** Anne Gerard; Otis Jones; ***C:*** Eric Van Haren Noman; ***M:*** Steve Porcaro. **CABLE**

The Unbearable Lightness of Being 🦴🦴🦴 ½ **1988 (R)** Tomas (Day Lewis), a young Czech doctor in the late 1960s, leads a sexually and emotionally carefree existence with a number of women, including provocative artist Olin. When he meets the fragile Binoche, he may be falling in love for the first time. On the eve of the 1968 Russian invasion of Czechoslovakia the two flee to Switzerland, but Binoche can't reconcile herself to exile and returns, followed by the reluctant Tomas who has lost his position because of his new-found political idealism. They lead an increasingly simple life, drawn ever closer together. The haunting ending caps off superb performances. Based on the novel by Milan Kundera. **172m/C; VHS, DVD.** Daniel Day-Lewis; Juliette Binoche; Lena Olin; Derek de Lint; Erland Josephson; Pavel Landovsky; Donald Moffat; Daniel Olbrychski; Stellan Skarsgard; Tormek Bork; Bruce Myers; Pavel Slaby; Pascale Kalensky; Jacques Ciron; Anne Lonnberg; Laszlo Szabo; Vladimir Valenta; Clovis Cornillac; Leon Lissek; Consuelo de Haviland; ***D:*** Philip Kaufman; ***W:*** Jean-Claude Carriere; Philip Kaufman; ***C:*** Sven Nykvist; ***M:*** Mark Adler; Ernie Fosselius; Leos Janacek. British Acad. '88: Adapt. Screenplay; Ind. Spirit '89: Cinematog.; Natl. Soc. Film Critics '88: Director (Kaufman), Film.

Unbeatable Harold 🦴🦴 **2006 (PG-13)** Harmless quirky comedy with one of those lovable loser leads. Reno, Nevada assistant restaurant manager Harold James (Michaels) tries to help everyone out and do his best, which is why he comes to the aid of Wanda (DeHuff) after she's stranded. Wanda has once again left her cheating boyfriend (McDermott) and Harold gets her a waitress job and then falls in love. **82m/C; DVD.** Gordon Michaels; Nicole DeHuff; Dylan McDermott; Henry Winkler; Robert Peters; Gladys Knight; Taryn Manning; Phyllis Diller; Charles Durning; Lin Shaye; Michelle Phillips; Tim Russ; ***D:*** Ari Palitz; ***W:*** Gordon Michaels; ***C:*** Robert Hayes; ***M:*** Michael A. Reagan. **VIDEO**

The Unbelievable Truth 🦴🦴 ½ **1990 (R)** Ex-con Robocop-to-be Burke meets armageddon-obsessed model and sparks fly until bizarre murder occurs. Quirky black comedy shot in less than two weeks. **100m/C; VHS, DVD, Blu-Ray.** Adrienne Shelly; Robert John Burke; Christopher Cooke; Julia Mueller; Julia McNeal; Mark Bailey; Gary Sauer; Kathrine Mayfield; ***D:*** Hal Hartley; ***W:*** Hal Hartley; ***C:*** Michael Spiller; ***M:*** Jim Coleman.

The Unborn 🦴 ½ **1991 (R)** An infertile wife gets inseminated at unorthodox clinic. But once pregnant she suspects that her unborn baby is a monstrous being. Tasteless B-movie with an A-performance from Adams; if the rest had been up to her standard this could have been another "Stepford Wives." Instead it cops out with cheap gore. **85m/C; VHS, DVD, Blu-Ray.** Brooke Adams; Jeff Hayenga; James Karen; K. Callan; Jane Cameron; ***D:*** Rodman Flender; ***W:*** John Brancato; ***C:*** Wally Pfister; ***M:*** Gary Numan; Michael R. Smith.

The Unborn 🦴 **2009 (PG-13)** Fabulously-gorgeous co-ed Casey Beldon (Yustman) begins seeing disturbing images of a frightening young boy. Fearing she may be losing her sanity as her mother had years before, Casey turns to a Holocaust survivor (Alexander), who explains the events through a family connection to medical experiments performed by the Nazis on Casey's unborn twin brother nicknamed Jumby, who died in utero. Unnerving bugs, a freakish dog, scary mirrors, and the fact that Jumby wants to be born signals the need for Rabbi Sendak (Oldman) to perform an exorcism. The whole Nazi tie-in is a stretch and the final scene stalls, but heck, the Jewish exorcism theme is at least somewhat novel. **86m/C; Blu-Ray, On Demand.** Odette Annable; Gary Oldman; Cam Gigandet; Meagan Good; Jane Alexander; Idris Elba; Carla Gugino; James Remar; ***D:*** David S. Goyer; ***W:*** David S. Goyer; ***C:*** James Hawkinson; ***M:*** Ramin Djawadi; Spring Aspers.

The Unborn 2 🦴 **1994 (R)** Greene's blood-craving baby thinks nothing of feasting off the babysitter until a gun-wielding avenger comes to the rescue. Some notably gross scenes. **84m/C; VHS, DVD.** Michele Greene; Scott Valentine; Robin Curtis; ***D:*** Rick Jacobson.

Unbreakable 🦴🦴 ½ **2000 (PG-13)** Willis reteams with "The Sixth Sense" writer/director Shyamalan for another spooky saga. He's not only the sole survivor of a train crash but he emerged without a scratch, which intrigues Jackson, who suffers from brittle bone disease. Shyamalan still knows how to hold attention, and the look and feel of the movie are mesmerizing, but this time the story doesn't quite hold up. You'll either find this one a keeper or a head-scratcher. **107m/C; VHS, DVD.** Bruce Willis; Samuel L. Jackson; Robin Wright; Spencer Treat Clark; Charlaine Woodard; James Handy; Elizabeth Lawrence; Leslie Stefanson; Eamonn Walker; ***D:*** M. Night Shyamalan; ***W:*** M. Night Shyamalan; ***C:*** Eduardo Serra; ***M:*** James Newton Howard.

Unbroken 🦴🦴 **2014 (PG-13)** Louis Zamperini (O'Connell) should have been an internationally recognized Olympic athlete but his life forever changed when he was shot down over the Pacific in World War II. After barely surviving nearly seven weeks on a life raft, Zamperini was captured by the Japanese, and forced into hard labor in a POW camp. Directed by Jolie, this true story hits all the right notes but does so in such predictable, Hollywood ways as to train them of any sense of danger. It's an oddly flat film, only interesting for O'Connell's remarkable charisma. **137m/C; DVD, Blu-Ray.** Jack O'Connell; Takamasa Ishihara; Domhnall Gleeson; Garrett Hedlund; Finn Wittrock; Jai Courtney; ***D:*** Angelina Jolie; ***W:*** Joel Coen; Ethan Coen; Richard LaGravenese; William Nicholson; ***C:*** Roger Deakins; ***M:*** Alexandre Desplat.

Unbroken: Path to Redemption 🦴🦴 **2018 (PG-13)** A faith-focused sequel to 2014's Unbroken. After competing in the 1939 Olympics, track athlete Louis Zamperini (Hunt) served in the US Army Air Corps. He was shot down during

World War II and tortured in a Japanese prisoner of war camp, before being rescued. Returning home, Louis has post-traumatic stress disorder, including nighly nightmares about his experiences, and feels isolated from his family. Though he tries to move on with his life, he only starts to find peace after attending a religious revival. Too heavy handed in delivering its Christian message than creating a genuine connection with the characters and their stories. **98m/C; DVD, Blu-Ray.** Samuel Hunt; Merritt Patterson; Bobby Campo; David Sakurai; Vincenzo Amato; ***D:*** Harold Cronk; ***W:*** Richard Friedenberg; Ken Hixon; ***C:*** Zoran Popovic; ***M:*** Brandon Roberts.

Uncaged 1/2 **2016** This off-beat horror film explores what happens when a teenager learns the truth about himself and his family. Though Jack (Luskey) was orphaned as a child after a tragedy, he was raised by relatives and grew up with his cousin Brandon (Weiner). At 18, Jack's life takes an unusual turn when he finds himself sleepwalking and waking up naked in the woods with no memory of how he got there. To learn the truth, he straps a camera to his body and learns an unexpected truth about who (and what) he is and his family legacy. Jack's sinister fate might only end with his death. **95m/C; DVD, Streaming, Download.** Gene Jones; Ben Getz; Kyle Kirkpatrick; Garrett Hendricks; Zack Weiner; ***D:*** Daniel Robbins; ***W:*** Daniel Robbins; Mark Rappaport; ***C:*** Rasa Acharya Partin; ***M:*** Brooke Blair; Will Blair. **VIDEO**

Uncaged Heart 1/2 **2007** Single mom Janet Tarr (Warner) works as a prison shrink for potential parolees. She agrees to the parole of bank robber Robert Moss (Spence) and the two begin an affair when he's released. But Robert can't adjust to going straight and commits more crimes that put Janet and her daughter in danger. **90m/C; DVD.** Julie Warner; Sebastian Spence; Jessica Harmon; Emily Hirst; ***D:*** Allan Harmon; ***W:*** Eric Edson; Michele Samit; ***C:*** Randal Platt; ***M:*** Stu Goldberg. **CABLE**

Uncanny 1/2 **2015** A dark-leaning science fiction/fantasy exploration of the nature of artificial intelligence. After a decade of seclusion, inventor David Kressen (Webber) has allowed access to his research facility to a technology reporter, Joy Andrews (Griffiths), for a week. Among Kressen's creations is Adam (Rogers), a humanoid with artificial intelligence and very human-like qualities. Though she experiences a range of reactions to Kressen and Adam, Joy soon discovers there is deception afoot as Adam acts angry and jealous towards her as she begins a relationship with Kressen. **91m/C; DVD, Download.** Mark Webber; Lucy Griffiths; David Clayton Rogers; Rainn Wilson; ***D:*** Matthew Leutwyler; ***W:*** Shanin Chandrasoma; ***C:*** Ross Richardson; ***M:*** Craig Richey.

Uncertain Glory **1944** Errol plays a French thief who's willing to pretend to be a saboteur and die for his country. Based on a story by Joe May and Laszlo Vadnay. **102m/B; VHS, DVD.** Errol Flynn; Paul Lukas; Jean Sullivan; Lucile Watson; Faye Emerson; James Flavin; Douglass Dumbrille; Dennis Hoey; Sheldon Leonard; ***D:*** Raoul Walsh; ***W:*** Laszlo Vadnay; Max Brand.

Uncertainty 1/2 **2008** Bobby (Gordon-Levitt) and a pregnant Kate (Collins) meet on the Brooklyn Bridge to decide their future on a coin toss, with two different, color-coded scenarios that go from dull family drama to silly action-thriller. In the green story, they attend a Fourth of July barbeque at the Brooklyn home of Kate's parents where they discover some disquieting family regrets. In the yellow story, set in Manhattan, the duo finds a cell phone in a taxi and Bobby calls a number, hoping to return the phone to its owner. Instead they are chased around Chinatown by a gunman determined to retrieve the phone, which is apparently part of a blackmail scheme. **101m/C; DVD.** Joseph Gordon-Levitt; Lynn Collins; Assumpta Serna; Olivia Thirlby; ***D:*** Scott McGehee; David Siegel; ***W:*** Scott McGehee; David Siegel; ***C:*** Rain Kathy Li; ***M:*** Peter Nashel.

Uncle Boonmee Who Can Recall His Past Lives *Lung Boonmee Raluek Chat* **2010** Surreal, meandering award-winner from Thailand has dying widower Uncle Boonmee (Saisaymar) being cared for by his sister-in-law Jen as various spirits from his past (including his ghostly wife, dead son in giant monkey form, and a catfish) come to watch over him and he gradually recalls his reincarnations. Will appeal to an arthouse audience who like magic realism but not many others. Thai and French with subtitles. **113m/C; Blu-Ray.** *TH GB FR SP* Thanapat Saisaymar; Jenjira Pongpas; Natthakarn Aphaiwonk; ***D:*** Apichatpong Weerasethakul; ***W:*** Apichatpong Weerasethakul; ***C:*** Sayombhu Mukdeeprom; Yukontorn Mingmonghon.

Uncle Buck **1989 (PG)** When Mom and Dad have to go away suddenly, the only babysitter they can find is good ol' Uncle Buck, a lovable lout who spends much of his time smoking cigars, trying to make up with his girlfriend, and enforcing the teenage daughter's chastity. More intelligent than the average slob/teen comedy with a heart, due in large part to Candy's dandy performance. Memorable pancake scene. **100m/C; VHS, DVD, Blu-Ray; Open Captioned.** John Candy; Amy Madigan; Jean Louisa Kelly; Macaulay Culkin; Jay Underwood; Gaby Hoffman; Laurie Metcalf; Elaine Bromka; Garrett M. Brown; ***D:*** John Hughes; ***W:*** John Hughes; ***C:*** Ralf Bode; ***M:*** Ira Newborn.

Uncle Drew **2018 (PG-13)** After losing his star player to a rival team, Dax (Howery) reluctantly enlists former basketball wizzes to compete in the Rucker Classic street ball tournament. There's joy in watching real-life NBA and WNBA stars (Kyrie Irving, Shaquille O'Neal, Aaron Gordon, Lisa Leslie, Reggie Miller, Nate Robinson, Chris Webber) in prosthetics and grey-haired wigs, dribbling circles around the young punks, and they demonstrate better acting chops than you might expect from non-actors. Light, harmless fun. Based on a series of viral commercials from Pepsi. **103m/C; DVD, Blu-Ray.** Kyrie Irving; Milton Howery; Shaquille O'Neal; Chris Webber; Reginald Miller; ***D:*** Charles Stone, III; ***W:*** Jay Longino; ***C:*** Karsten Gopinath; ***M:*** Christopher Lennertz.

Uncle Joe Shannon **1978** Sentimental twaddle. Trumpet player Joe Shannon's (Young) life is devastated when his wife and child are killed in a fire. He becomes self-destructive until he befriends crippled young Robby (McKeon). Maynard Ferguson does the trumpet playing for Young. **108m/C; DVD.** Burt Young; Doug McKeon; Bobby Cassidy; Madge Sinclair; Jason Bernard; Bert Remsen; ***D:*** Joseph Hanwright; ***W:*** Burt Young; ***C:*** Bill Butler; ***M:*** Bill Conti.

Uncle Nick *10 Cent Christmas; 10 Cent Beer Night: Christmas in Cleveland* **2015** Remember drunken Cousin Eddie from the Vacation movie series? If you've ever kind of wondered what the film would be like from his point of view, there's probably no better example than this. Uncle Nick (Brian Posehn) drunkenly fumbles his way though the holidays, much to the chagrin of his uptight family. He is a walking, talking definition of inappropriate, so you can kind of sympathize with them. At least you could if they weren't somehow more unlikeable than Posehn's character. **81m/C; DVD, Blu-Ray, Streaming.** Brian Posehn; Paget Brewster; Missi Pyle; Scott Adsit; Beau Ballinger; ***D:*** Chris Kasick; ***W:*** Mike Demski; ***C:*** Michael Pescasio; ***M:*** P. Andrew Willis. **VIDEO**

Uncle Nino 1/2 **2003 (PG)** Financially comfortable, but mildly dysfunctional, family headed by clueless dad (Mantegna) gets an unexpected visit from their colorful Italian uncle (Mascarino). He injects a little chaos into their lives, helping them to relax and smell the roses. Saccharin sweet family movie destined to please the masses. **104m/C; Blu-Ray, On Demand.** Joe Mantegna; Anne Archer; Pierrino Mascarino; Trevor Morgan; Gina Mantegna; ***D:*** Robert Shallcross; ***W:*** Robert Shallcross; ***C:*** Hugo Cortina; ***M:*** Larry Pecorella.

Uncle Sam **1996 (R)** The box art is cool but this is basically a video horror. Desert Storm hero Sam Harper (Fralick) returns home—in a coffin. Only he doesn't stay dead and decides to liven up his small town's Fourth of July celebration by dressing up as Uncle Sam and going on a killing spree. **91m/C; VHS, DVD, Blu-Ray.** David "Shark" Fralick; Timothy Bottoms; Robert Forster; Isaac Hayes; Bo Hopkins; ***D:*** William Lustig; ***W:*** Larry Cohen; ***C:*** James Lebovitz; ***M:*** Mark Governor. **VIDEO**

Uncle Tom's Cabin 1/2 **1927** Universal Studios' $2 million production was one of the costliest of the silent era, with more than 2400 actors, and a shooting schedule of 19 months. It follows Harriet Beecher Stowe's abolitionist novel about a black family torn apart by slavery. This version contains heroine Eliza's (Fischer) flight across the ice floes, which was borrowed by D.W. Griffith for his film "Way Down East." **112m/B; Silent; VHS, DVD, Blu-Ray.** James B. Lowe; Margarita Fischer; George Siegmann; Virginia Grey; ***D:*** Harry A. Pollard; ***W:*** Harry A. Pollard; Harvey Thew; ***C:*** Charles Stumar; Jacob Kull; ***M:*** Erno Rapee.

Uncle Was a Vampire *Tempi Duri per i Vampiri; Hard Times for Vampires* **1959** An impoverished Italian count has turned his castle into a hotel. But staying there could be hazardous to a guest's health since the count was bitten by a vampire. **85m/C; VHS, DVD.** *IT* Christopher Lee; Kai (Kay) Fischer; Renato Rascel; Sylva Koscina; Lia Zoppelli; Susanne Loret; ***D:*** Steno; ***W:*** Edoardo Anton; ***C:*** Marco Scarpelli.

Uncommon Valor 1/2 **1983 (R)** After useless appeals to the government for information on his son listed as "missing in action" in Vietnam, Colonel Rhodes takes matters into his own hands. Hackman is solid and believable as always, surrounded with good cast in generally well-paced film. **105m/C; VHS, DVD.** Gene Hackman; Fred Ward; Reb Brown; Randall "Tex" Cobb; Robert Stack; Patrick Swayze; Harold Sylvester; Tim Thomerson; ***D:*** Ted Kotcheff; ***C:*** Stephen Burum; ***M:*** James Horner.

Unconditional **2012 (PG-13)** Based on a true story, this drama centers on finding redemption while dealing with intense emotional pain. Children's book author Samantha Crawford (Collins) suffers deeply when her husband is killed during a mugging gone violent. Two years after the event, the killer has not been found and Sam is ready to end her life. On her way to kill herself, she witnesses a young child being struck by a car and stops to help. Through this event, Sam reconnects with Joe Bradford (Ealy), a childhood friend who now runs an after school program and tries to make life better for the children in the neighborhood without love and family bonds. Subsequent events give Sam closure on her husband's death, find purpose her her life, and much needed unconditional love and forgiveness. **92m/C; DVD, Streaming, Download.** Lynn Collins; Michael Ealy; Bruce McGill; Kwesi Boakye; Diego Klattenhoff; ***D:*** Brent McCorkle; ***W:*** Brent McCorkle; ***C:*** Michael Regalbuto; ***M:*** Brent McCorkle; Mark Petrie.

Unconditional Love **2003 (PG-13)** Watch it for Bates's performance because otherwise there's not much here (or maybe there's too much going on). Chicago housewife Grace Beasley (Bates) is abruptly dumped by hubby Max (Aykroyd) who needs his space. Meanwhile, a Chicago serial killer has just offed closeted lounge singer Victor Fox (Pryce), leaving his in-the-shadows lover Dirk (Everett) to battle with Victor's sister Nola (Redgrave) over his estate. Fan Grace meets Dirk at Victor's funeral, they bond, and decide to hunt for Victor's killer together. Hey, it's one way to deal with unresolved feelings. **122m/C; VHS, DVD.** Kathy Bates; Rupert Everett; Lynn Redgrave; Meredith Eaton; Dan Aykroyd; Jonathan Pryce; Peter Sarsgaard; Stephanie Beacham; Richard Briers; Jack Noseworthy; Daniel Wyllie; ***D:*** P.J. Hogan; ***W:*** P.J. Hogan; Jocelyn Moorhouse; ***C:*** Remi Adefarasin; ***M:*** James Newton Howard.

Unconquered 1/2 **1947** Silly epic about America finds indentured servant Abby (Goddard), meeting Virignia militia man Christopher Holden (Cooper). He nobly buys her contract and frees her but scurvy trader Martin Garth (da Silva) manages to get Abby working in his saloon. Garth also illegally sells guns to the local Seneca Indian tribe and persuades their chief, Guyasuta (Karloff), to attack the colonists. Cooper has to keep rescuing Goddard throughout the movie, as well as battling da Silva and helping the settlers fight Indians. Based on the novel "The Judas Tree" by Neil H. Swanson. **147m/C; VHS, DVD.** Gary Cooper; Paulette Goddard; Howard da Silva; Boris Karloff; Cecil Kellaway; Ward Bond; Katherine DeMille; Henry Wilcoxon; Sir C. Aubrey Smith; Victor Varconi; Virginia Grey; Mike Mazurki; Porter Hall; ***D:*** Cecil B. DeMille; ***W:*** Charles Bennett; Jesse Lasky, Jr.; Frederic M. Frank; ***C:*** Ray Rennahan; ***M:*** Victor Young.

Uncorked 1/2 *At Sachem Farm; Higher Love* **1998 (PG)** British ex-pats gather together in Simi Valley, California to essentially drive each other crazy. Ross (Sewell) is visiting his family in order to close a deal on selling some rare wines so he can get the money to support another get-rich-quick scheme. But he's thwarted by his eccentric Uncle Cullen (Hawthorne) who wants Ross to do something he passionately believes in (which happens to be music). Ross also has a reclusive, nutty brother Paul (Rodgers), and then there's his snooty girlfriend Kendal (Driver) who really wants her ex-boyfriend, Tom (Sporleder) back. It's predictable but pleasant. **95m/C; VHS, DVD.** Rufus Sewell; Nigel Hawthorne; Minnie Driver; Michael E. Rodgers; Gregory Sporleder; Amelia Heinle; Keone Young; ***D:*** John Huddles; ***W:*** John Huddles; ***C:*** Mark Vicente; ***M:*** Jeff Danna.

Uncovered *La Tabla de Flandes* **1994 (R)** Julia (Beckinsale at the beginning of her career) is restoring a 500-year-old painting of a chess game when she discovers an inscription hidden on the painting that says "Who killed the knight?". Some investigation indicates the painter was telling the story of a series of killings that followed the pattern of play in the painting, and that pattern is being duplicated in the present day. Complex and interesting story is undermined by poor acting (Beckinsale's inexperience shows) and inconsistent direction. **112m/C; VHS, DVD.** *GB SP* Kate Beckinsale; John Wood; Sinead Cusack; Peter Wingfield; Helen McCrory; Michael Gough; Art Malik; James Villiers; Paudge Behan; ***D:*** Jim McBride; ***W:*** Jim McBride; Jack Baran; Michael Hirst; ***C:*** Affonso Beato; ***M:*** Philippe Sarde. **VIDEO**

Uncovered: The War on Iraq 1/2 **2004** Documentary presents case against Bush administration's decision to go to war with Iraq through interviews with authorities ranging from weapons inspectors and C.I.A. analysts to ex-military and diplomatic figures. Another in a slew of anti-Bush documentaries released in election year of 2004. Drier and less theatrical than political heavyweight Michael Moore, but the straightforward style make it effective and convincing. **83m/C; DVD.** ***D:*** Robert Greenwald; ***C:*** Richard Perez; Glen Pearcy; Bob Sullivan; Scott Williams; Hamish Campbell; Marc Levy; Bob Seeberger; ***M:*** Jim Ervin; Brad Chiet; Mars Lasar.

Uncut Gems **2019 (R)** When diamond dealer Howard (Sandler) receives a long-awaited black opal, he believes it will resolve his large gambling debts. The day he receives it, his Diamond District store is visited by professional basketball player Kevin Garnett (Garnett) and Howard allows Kevin to borrow it for good luck. Over the next few days, Howard makes a series of similarly bad decisions that increase his debt and further alienate his already scornful family. Sandler gives an extraordinary performance that adds to the the tension-laden film by the Safdie brothers, who have zealously captured a gritty part of New York City. **135m/C; DVD, Blu-Ray.** Adam Sandler; Lakeith Stanfield; Julia Fox; Mike Francesa; Kevin Garnett; ***D:*** Benny Safdie; Josh Safdie; ***W:*** Benny Safdie; Josh Safdie; Ronald Bronstein; ***C:*** Darius Khondji; ***M:*** Oneohtrix Point Never. Ind. Spirit '20: Actor (Sandler), Director (Safdie), Director (Safdie), Film Editing.

The Undead **1957** A prostitute is accidentally sent back to the Middle Ages as the result of a scientific experiment and finds herself condemned to die for witchcraft. Early Corman script filled with convoluted storylines, laughable characters, violence, and heaving bosoms. **75m/B; VHS, DVD.** Pamela Duncan; Richard Garland; Allison Hayes; Mel Welles; Richard Devon; Billy Barty; Dick Miller; Val Dufour; Dorothy Neumann; Aaron Saxon; Bruno VeSota; Paul Blaisdell; ***D:*** Roger Corman; ***W:*** Charles B. Griffith; Mark Hanna; ***C:*** William Sickner; ***M:*** Ronald Stein.

Undead 1/2 **2005 (R)** A freakish meteor shower falls upon the residents of Berkeley, Queensland, tainting the water supply and causing the locals to morph into brain-munching zombies, except, of course, for a few lucky(?) unaffected folks who band together at an outback farmhouse with the area's resident kooky gun nut. As they try to fend off the mutants some aliens arrive. Not much of a point, but then it is a zombie flick. If you like your zombies with an Aussie accent, give this one a try, but don't say you weren't warned. **100m/C; DVD.** Felicity Mason; Mungo McKay; Lisa Cunningham; Dirk Hunter; Emma Randall; Steve Greig; Noel Sheridan; Gaynor Wensley; Eleanor Stillman; Peter Spierig; *D:* Peter Spierig; Michael Spierig; *W:* Peter Spierig; Michael Spierig; *C:* Andrew Strahorn; *M:* Cliff Bradley.

Undead or Alive 2007 (R) Unlikely cowboy Luke (Kattan) and his new partner, army deserter Elmer (Denton), run a con on a corrupt sheriff and escape into the desert. Only they're pursued by angry Sheriff Claypool (Besser) and his posse. The duo meets up with Native American Sue (Rawat) and learn that because of Geronimo's curse all the local white settlers and soldiers are turning into zombies. About as dumb as you can imagine. **91m/C; DVD.** Chris Kattan; James Denton; Navi Rawat; Matt Besser; Christopher Coppola; *D:* Glasgow Phillips; *W:* Glasgow Phillips; *C:* Thomas Callaway; *M:* Ivan Koutikov. **VIDEO**

Undeclared War 1991 (R) Suspenseful espionage thriller that takes you behind the scenes of an international terrorist plot, which has been cleverly disguised as a bloody global revolution. Intense action heightened by conflicts between worldwide intelligence networks, the news media and terrorist organizations. **103m/C; VHS, DVD.** Vernon Wells; David Hedison; Olivia Hussey; Peter Lapis; *D:* Ringo Lam.

Undefeatable ½ 1994 (R) Rothrock is out to avenge the murder of her sister at the hands of a serial killer who, coincidentally, happens to be a martial arts expert. You watch for Cynthia to kick butt not for plot anyway. **88m/C; VHS, DVD.** Cynthia Rothrock; Don Niam; John Miller; Donna Jason; *D:* Godfrey Ho.

The Undefeated 1969 (G) A Confederate and Yankee find they must team up on the Rio Grande. They attempt to build new lives in the Spanish held Mexico territory, but are caught in the battle for Mexican independence. Standard fare made palatable only by Wayne and Hudson. **119m/C; VHS, DVD, Blu-Ray.** John Wayne; Rock Hudson; Lee Meriwether; Merlin Olsen; Bruce Cabot; Ben Johnson; Jan-Michael Vincent; Harry Carey, Jr.; Antonio Aguilar; Roman Gabriel; John Agar; *D:* Andrew V. McLaglen; *C:* William Clothier.

Undefeated 2003 Leguizamo stars and makes his directorial debut in this too-familiar boxing tale. Lex Vargas (Leguizamo) is a tough amateur boxer from Queens who comes under the tutelage of Victor (Serrano). Victor believes in a slow and steady rise but manager Mack (Miller) and promoter Scott Green (Forster) offer up a more enticing proposal. And then Vargas falls for Mack's girlfriend Lizette (Ferlito), who's stringing both men along. As Vargas climbs the boxing ladder, it's suggested that maybe he should take a dive with next opponent, Beveaqua (De Los Reyes), in order to get a bigger payday down the road. Leguizamo broods effectively. **90m/C; VHS, DVD.** John Leguizamo; Nestor Serrano; Omar Benson Miller; Robert Forster; Vanessa Ferlito; Kamar De Los Reyes; Clifton (Gonzalez) Collins, Jr.; Guillermo Diaz; *D:* John Leguizamo; *W:* Frank Pugliese; *C:* Enrique Chediak; *M:* Roy Nathanson; Bill Ware. **CABLE**

Undefeated ½ 2011 Inspiring sports documentary about Bill Courtney and the inner-city high school Manassas Tigers. Courtney is a white businessman in North Memphis, Tennessee who serves as the volunteer football coach for the hard-luck perennial losers, whose players are all African-American. After six years, Courtney has begun to turn the program around and his players are dedicated to winning their first playoff game during their 2009 season though there are still many serious issues off the field. **113m/C; DVD, Blu-Ray.** Bill Courtney; Montrail "Money" Brown; Chavis Daniels; O.C. Brown; *D:* T.J. Martin; Daniel Lindsay; *C:* T.J. Martin; Daniel Lindsay; *M:* Michael Brook; Dan McMahon; Miles Nielsen. Oscars '11: Feature Doc.

The Undefeated 2011 (PG-13) Oddly titled (she has lost, after all), pseudo-documentary of former Alaska governor and 2008 Republican vice-presidential candidate Sarah Palin. Using primarily video clips to recount her political ascension, there is no real life story told. Plays like a nearly two-hour-long advertisement for a presumed run for president in 2012. Loosely based on her 2009 memoir "Going Rogue: An American Life." **113m/C; Blu-Ray.** Andrew Breitbart; Gene Therriault; Judy Patrick; Con Bunde; Jamie Radtke; Sarah Palin; *D:* Stephen K. Bannon; *W:* Stephen K. Bannon; *C:* Dain Valverde; *M:* David Cerbert.

Under California Stars *Under California Skies* **1948** Shady gang making a living rounding up wild horses decides they can make more money by capturing Rogers' horse, Trigger. **71m/C; VHS, DVD.** Roy Rogers; Andy Devine; Jane Frazee; *D:* William Witney.

Under Capricorn ½ 1949 Bergman is an Irish lass who follows her convict husband Cotten out to 1830s Australia where he makes a fortune. She turns to drink, perhaps because of his neglect, and has her position usurped by a housekeeper with designs on her husband. When Bergman's cousin (Wilding) arrives, Cotten may have cause for his violent jealousy. There's a plot twist involving old family skeletons, but this is definitely lesser Hitchcock. Adapted from the Helen Simpson novel. Remade in 1982. **117m/C; VHS, DVD, Blu-Ray.** *GB* Ingrid Bergman; Joseph Cotten; Michael Wilding; Margaret Leighton; Jack Watling; Cecil Parker; Denis O'Dea; *D:* Alfred Hitchcock; *C:* Jack Cardiff.

Under Eighteen 1932 Cautionary pre-Hays Code melodrama. Seamstress Margie Evans (Marsh) is a slum kid during the Depression who wants to help her family out of their money woes by utilizing her natural talents. The beauty meets playboy Howard Raymond (William) and he invites her to his penthouse pool party. He's a lech and her hard-working beau Jimmie (Toomey) tries to get Margie to see the light but she's not such a dumb bunny that Margie doesn't know what Howard wants. Now she has to decide what she's willing to give up. **79m/B; DVD.** Marian Marsh; Warren William; Regis Toomey; Anita Page; Norman Foster; Joyce Compton; Emma Dunn; J. Farrell MacDonald; *D:* Archie Mayo; *W:* Charles Kenyon; *C:* Sidney Hickox.

Under Fire ½ 1983 (R) Three foreign correspondents, old friends from the past working together, find themselves in Managua, witnessing the 1979 Nicaraguan revolution. In a job requiring objectivity, but a situation requiring taking sides, they battle with their ethics to do the job right. Fine performances, including Harris as a mercenary. Interesting view of American media and its political necessities. **128m/C; VHS, DVD, Blu-Ray.** Gene Hackman; Nick Nolte; Joanna Cassidy; Ed Harris; Richard Masur; Hamilton Camp; Jean-Louis Trintignant; *D:* Roger Spottiswoode; *W:* Ron Shelton; Clayton Frohman; *C:* John Alcott; *M:* Jerry Goldsmith.

Under Heavy Fire ½ *Going Back* **2001 (R)** Formulaic "war is hell" story that has lots of flashbacks filled with rather graphic violence. In 1968, the Marines of Echo company came under a friendly fire bombing during a raid on an enemy village in 'Nam. The men blamed their captain, Ramsey (Van Dien), for the incident. Some 30 years later, the survivors (including Ramsey) meet up in Saigon at the request of journalist Kathleen (Otis) to get to the truth. **118m/C; VHS, DVD.** Casper Van Dien; Carre Otis; Jaimz Woolvett; Bobby Hosea; Daniel Kash; Martin Kove; *D:* Sidney J. Furie; *W:* Greg Mellott; *C:* Curtis Petersen; *M:* Amin Bhatia.

Under Hellgate Bridge 1999 (R) Familiar New York crime drama is set in the Astoria neighborhood of Queens. Ryan (Rodrick) is just outa prison (it was a bum rap) and heads home to find slick wiseguy Vincent (LaPaglia) has taken over his territory and his old girlfriend, Carla (Bayne). The situation gets messy. **87m/C; VHS, DVD.** Michael Rodrick; Jonathan LaPaglia; Jordan Bayne; Frank Vincent; Vincent Pastore; Dominic Chianese; Brian Vincent; Careena Melia; *D:* Michael Sergio; *W:* Michael Sergio; *C:* Leland Krane; *M:* Stephan Moccio.

Under Milk Wood ½ 1973 (PG) An adaptation of the Dylan Thomas play about the lives of the residents of a village in Wales. Burton and O'Toole are wonderful in this uneven, but sometimes engrossing film. **90m/C; VHS, DVD.** *GB* Richard Burton; Elizabeth Taylor; Peter O'Toole; Glynis Johns; Vivien Merchant; *D:* Andrew Sinclair.

Under Nevada Skies ½ 1946 Fairly good matinee-era western centers on a missing map to a uranium deposit, climaxing with Rogers heading a posse of Indian allies to the rescue. The Sons of the Pioneers contribute songs. **69m/B; VHS, DVD.** Roy Rogers; George "Gabby" Hayes; Dale Evans; Douglass Dumbrille; Tristram Coffin; Rudolph Anders; Iron Eyes Cody; *D:* Frank McDonald.

Under Oath *Urban Justice; Blood Money* **1997 (R)** Financially strapped cops Scalia and Velez accidentally kill a drug runner in a shakedown and then learn he was an undercover ATF agent. Then they're assigned to investigate their own crime. Cast does good work in slick genre fare. **89m/C; VHS, DVD.** Jack Scalia; James Russo; Eddie Velez; Richard Lynch; Abraham Benrubi; Beth Grant; Clint Howard; Robert LaSardo; *D:* Dave Payne; *W:* Scott Sandin; *C:* Mike Michiewicz; *M:* Roger Neil. **VIDEO**

Under One Roof ½ 2002 Cute Daniel Chang (Wong) is a Chinese-American guy living with his tradition-bound mother (Lee) in San Francisco. She wants grandchildren and keeps introducing her son to suitable Chinese girls. Daniel is keeping secret the fact that he's gay—until mom rents out the basement flat to new-to-the-city Robert (Marks). Daniel's attracted and if Robert reciprocates, Mother Chang is in for a big surprise. Sweet story if unevenly told. **76m/C; VHS, DVD.** Jay Wong; James Marks; Sandra Lee; Vivian Kobayashi; *D:* Todd Wilson; *W:* David Lewis; *C:* Dan Schmeltzer; *M:* Jack Curtis Dubowsky.

Under Pressure 1998 (R) What do you do when your neighbor tries to run your life? It's hot, the kids are cranky, you're cranky, and the guy next door comes over to complain about everything you do. Only he doesn't just complain—he threatens you, but the cops won't do anything to help. **88m/C; VHS, DVD.** Charlie Sheen; Mare Winningham; John Ratzenberger; David Andrews; *D:* Craig R. Baxley; *W:* Betsy Giffen Nowrasteh.

Under Siege 1992 (R) The USS Missouri becomes the battleground for good-guy-with-a-secret-past Seagal. He's up against the deranged Jones, as an ex-Special Forces leader, and Busey, a corrupt naval officer looking to steal the battleship's nuclear arsenal. May be predictable (especially the graphic violence) but the action is fast, the villains swaggering, and Seagal efficient at dispatching the enemy. Work for "Die Hard 3" was reportedly scrapped after Warner announced this film because DH's John McClane was supposed to save the passengers of a boat from terrorists. Sound familiar? **100m/C; VHS, DVD, Blu-Ray, HD-DVD.** Steven Seagal; Tommy Lee Jones; Gary Busey; Patrick O'Neal; Erika Eleniak; Dale Dye; Richard Jones; *D:* Andrew Davis; *W:* J.F. Lawton; *C:* Frank Tidy; *M:* Gary Chang.

Under Siege 2: Dark Territory **1995 (R)** Kicking terrorists' butts and slinging hash have worn out ex-Navy SEAL and gourmet chef Casey Ryback (Seagal), so he takes a little vacation to the Rocky Mountains. By coincidence, the train he boards is command central for psychotic computer expert Dane's (Bogosian) scheme to control the world's deadliest satellite. Pretty familiar territory for Seagal, who's acting technique consists of "look mad and hurt people." Bigger budget means bigger, and more frequent, explosions. Bogosian takes over the Jones/Busey role of evil villain/talented actor. **100m/C; VHS, DVD, Blu-Ray.** Steven Seagal; Eric Bogosian; Katherine Heigl; Morris Chestnut; Everett McGill; Andy Romano; Nick Mancuso; Brenda Bakke; Dale Dye; *D:* Geoff Murphy; *W:* Richard Hatem; *C:* Robbie Greenberg; *M:* Basil Poledouris.

Under Still Waters ½ *Still Waters* **2008** Troubled marrieds Charlie and Andrew decide to spend some time at a lakeside family cabin. Before they even arrive, their journey goes bad when Andrew accidentally hits drifter Jacob. The two take him to the cabin to recuperate but Jacob has a gun and Charlie likes to play mind games, which doesn't bode well. **85m/C; DVD.** Lake Bell; Jason Clarke; Ken Howard; Clifton Collins, Jr.; *D:* Carolyn Miller; *W:* Carolyn Miller; *C:* Matthew Irving; *M:* Tom Heil. **VIDEO**

Under Suspicion ½ 1992 (R) Christmas 1959 in Brighton finds seedy private eye Tony Aaron and his wife faking adultery cases for those desperate to get around England's strict divorce laws. Sordid tale takes a turn when Tony bursts in to snap incriminating photos and finds both his wife and their client, a famous artist, murdered. Dark who-dunnit has some interesting twists that could have made it exceptional rather than the conventional melodrama it turned out to be. Neeson is very good as the charmingly sleazy Tony but nobody else stands out, except the unfortunately miscast San Giacomo. Theatrical feature debut for director Moore. **99m/C; VHS, DVD.** *GB* Liam Neeson; Laura San Giacomo; Alphonsia Emmanuel; Kenneth Cranham; Maggie O'Neill; Martin Grace; Stephen Moore; *D:* Simon Moore; *W:* Simon Moore; *C:* Vernon Layton; *M:* Christopher Gunning. **TV**

Under Suspicion ½ 2000 (R) Not much tension in what aims to be a tension-filled thriller. Hackman is accused of raping and murdering several Puerto Rican women and spends the film being interrogated by detectives Freeman and Jane. Lots of talk but little to connect with in this remake of Claude Miller's very well respected "Garde a Vue." Both Hackman and Freeman co-executive produced. **111m/C; VHS, DVD.** Morgan Freeman; Gene Hackman; Thomas Jane; Monica Bellucci; *D:* Stephen Hopkins; *W:* W. Peter Iliff; Tom Provost; *C:* Peter Levy.

Under the Biltmore Clock **1985** F. Scott Fitzgerald's story, "Myra Meets His Family," is the basis for this American Playhouse installment for PBS. It is outwit or be outwitted in this tale of a fortune-hunting '20s flapper who is outsmarted by the man she has set her sights on when he hires actors to play his eccentric "family." **80m/C; VHS, DVD.** Sean Young; Lenny Von Dohlen; Barnard Hughes; *D:* Neal Miller. **TV**

Under the Boardwalk ½ 1989 (R) A pair of star-crossed teenage lovers struggle through familial and societal differences in 1980s California. This is, like, bogus, ya know. **102m/C; VHS, DVD; Open Captioned.** Keith Coogan; Danielle von Zerneck; Richard Joseph Paul; Hunter von Leer; Tracey Walter; Roxana Zal; Dick Miller; Sonny Bono; Corky Carroll; *D:* Fritz Kiersch; *C:* Don Burgess. **VIDEO**

Under the Cherry Moon ½ 1986 **(PG-13)** Prince portrays a fictional musician of the 1940s who travels to the French Riviera, seeking love and money. Songs include "Under the Cherry Moon," "Kiss," "Anotherloverholeinyohead," "Sometimes It Snows in April," and "Mountains." A vanity flick down to its being filmed in black and white. **100m/B; VHS, DVD, Blu-Ray.** Prince; Jerome Benton; Francesca Annis; Kristin Scott Thomas; *D:* Prince; *C:* Michael Ballhaus. Golden Raspberries '86: Worst Actor (Prince), Worst Director (Prince), Worst Picture, Worst Song ("Love or Money"), Worst Support. Actor (Benton).

Under the Domim Tree ½ *Etz Hadomim Tafus* **1995** Sequel to "The Summer of Aviya," set in 1953, finds 15-year-old Aviya (Cohen) living in an Israeli community with other teenagers who were scarred by the Holocaust. As they get to know one another, each must deal with their own tormented memories. Based on a memoir by Almagor, who plays Aviya's institutionalized mother. Hebrew with subtitles. **102m/C; VHS, DVD.** *IS* Kaipo Cohen; Julino Mer; Ohad Knoller; Orli Perl; Riki Blich; Gila Almagor; *D:* Eli Cohen; *W:* Gila Almagor; Eyal Sher; *C:* David Gurfinkel; *M:* Benny Nagari.

Under the Eiffel Tower ½ 2018 After bourbon salesman Stuart (Walsh) is fired, friends Frank (Wain) and Tillie (Watkins) invite Stuart to tag along on a family trip to France with their young adult daughter Rosalind (Gelula). During the trip, Stuart misunderstands Rosaline's interest and proposes marriage to her in Paris. Repulsed by his actions, the family sends him on his way. Taking a train, he meets a handsome injured soccer player, Liam (Scott), and a French woman, Louise (Godreche). The pair follow her to a French city where they compete for her affections. The romantic comedy suffers from numerous absurd plot twists and cliches. **87m/C; DVD.** Matt Walsh; Judith Godreche; Reid Scott; Michaela Watkins; Gary Cole; ***D:*** Archie Borders; ***W:*** Judith Godreche; Archie Borders; David Henry; ***C:*** Leo Hinstin; ***M:*** Joseph Stephens.

Under the Flag of the Rising Sun 🦴🦴🦴🦴 *Gunki hataweku motoni* **1972** A grieving widow (Hidari) is determined to find the truth behind her husband's court martial and execution on the New Guinea front during the final days of World War II. Interviewing surviving members of her husband's garrison, she encounters conflicting testimonies that form a heart-breaking tapestry of wartime atrocity and desperate measures taken for survival. Subtitled. **96m/C; DVD.** *JP* Sachiko Hidari; Tetsuro Tamba; Kanemon Nakamura; Noboru Mitani; Sanae Nakahara; ***D:*** Kinji Fukasaku; ***W:*** Kinji Fukasaku; Kaneto Shindo; Norio Osada; ***C:*** Hiroshi Segawa; ***M:*** Hikaru Hayashi.

Under the Greenwood Tree 🦴🦴 1/2 **2005** Fancy Day, a local beauty from a wealthy family, is the new schoolteacher in the village of Mellstock. She attracts the romantic interests of wealthy landowner Farmer Shiner, young vicar Reverend Maybold, and laborer Dick Dewey. A loose adaptation of the 1872 novel by Thomas Hardy, much sweeter than his similar quadrangle in "Far from the Madding Crowd." **100m/C; DVD.** *GB* Keeley Hawes; Ben Miles; Tony Haygarth; James Murray; Steve Pemberton; ***D:*** Nicholas Laughland; ***W:*** Ashley Pharoah; ***C:*** John Aspinall; ***M:*** John Lunn; Jim Williams. **TV**

Under the Gun 🦴 1/2 **1995 (R)** Debt-ridden club owner Frank Torrance (Norton) is in trouble with everyone he knows. But he can't clear his debts just by quitting the business, so he decides to fight back. **90m/C; VHS, DVD.** Richard Norton; Kathy Long; Jane Badler; Peter Lindsey; ***D:*** Matthew George; ***W:*** Matthew George; ***C:*** Dan Burstall; ***M:*** Frank Strangio.

Under the Lighthouse Dancing 🦴 1/2 **1997** What began as a vacation for six friends on a picturesque Australian island turns into a mad scramble to fulfill Emma's dying wish to marry Harry. Flat, despite being drawn from actual events. **94m/C; VHS, DVD.** *AU* Jack Thompson; Jacqueline McKenzie; Naomi Watts; Aden (John) Gillett; Philip Holder; Zoe Bertram; ***D:*** Graeme Rattigan; ***W:*** David Giles; Graeme Rattigan; ***C:*** Paul Murphy; ***M:*** Nerida Tyson-Chew. **VIDEO**

Under the Mistletoe 🦴🦴 1/2 **2006** Harmless Christmas fare with an appealing cast. Susan (Newman) and her son Jonathan (Duffield) are still mourning the loss of husband and father Tom (Graham). Except Jonathan insists that Tom's ghost is hanging around to give him advice. Worried, Susan turns to school counselor Kevin (Shanks) for help. Then Jonathan decides to enter his mom in a radio dating contest although he thinks Kevin would really be the right guy to make her happy again. **90m/C; DVD.** Jaime Ray Newman; Michael Shanks; Burkely Duffield; Russell Porter; Conan Graham; Ingrid Torrance; Derek Green; ***D:*** George Mendeluk; ***W:*** Lindsay MacAdam; Jason Riley; ***C:*** Mahlon Todd Williams; ***M:*** Clinton Shorter. **CABLE**

Under the Pavement Lies the Strand 🦴🦴 *Unter dem Pflaster Ist der Strand* **1975** Grischa and Heinrich were fervent radicals during Germany's 1968 student demonstrations. Now stage actors in Berlin, they are feeling older and insignificant until they decide to put their passion into fighting a new abortion bill. But their zeal is tempered by an unexpected pregnancy. First film from Sanders-Brahms; German with subtitles. **106m/B; DVD.** *GE* Grischa Huber; Heinrich Giskes; ***D:*** Helma Sanders-Brahms; ***W:*** Grischa Huber; Heinrich Giskes; Helma Sanders-Brahms; ***C:*** Thomas Mauch.

Under the Piano 🦴🦴 1/2 **1995** Regina Bailio (Stratas) is a failed opera singer-turned-voice teacher whose bitterness leads to her over-protecting her autistic daughter Rosetta (Follows). Meanwhile, Regina's handicapped older daughter Franny (Plummer) tries to help her sister lead the fullest life possible. Set in the 1940s. **92m/C; DVD.** *CA* Teresa Stratas; Amanda Plummer; Megan Follows; James Carroll; Richard Blackburn; Dan Lett; John Juliani; Jackie Richardson; ***D:*** Stefan Scaini; ***W:*** Blair Ferguson; ***C:*** Robert Saad; ***M:*** Christopher Dedrick. **TV**

Under the Rainbow WOOF! **1981 (PG)** Comic situations encountered by a talent scout and a secret service agent in a hotel filled with Munchkins during filming of "The Wizard of Oz." Features midgets, spies, and a prevailing lack of taste. International intrigue adds to the strange attempt at humor. **97m/C; VHS, DVD.** Chevy Chase; Carrie Fisher; Eve Arden; Joseph Maher; Robert Donner; Mako; Pat McCormick; Billy Barty; Zelda Rubinstein; ***D:*** Steve Rash; ***W:*** Pat McCormick; Martin Smith; Harry Hurwitz; Fred Bauer; Pat Bradley.

Under the Red Robe 🦴🦴 1/2 **1936** A French soldier of fortune is trapped into aiding Cardinal Richelieu in his persecution of the Huguenots and winds up falling in love with the sister of his intended victim. Good costume adventure-drama. Sjostrom's last film as a director. **82m/B; VHS, DVD.** *GB* Raymond Massey; Conrad Veidt; Annabella; Romney Brent; ***D:*** Victor Sjostrom; ***C:*** James Wong Howe.

Under the Roofs of Paris 🦴🦴🦴 1/2 *Sous les Toits de Paris* **1929** An early French sound film about the lives of young Parisian lovers. A gentle, highly acclaimed melodrama. In French with English subtitles. **95m/B; VHS, DVD.** *FR* Albert Prejean; Pola Illery; Gaston Modot; Edmond T. Greville; ***D:*** Rene Clair; ***W:*** Rene Clair; ***C:*** Georges Perinal; ***M:*** Armand Bernard.

Under the Same Moon 🦴🦴 1/2 *La Misma Luna* **2007 (PG-13)** A heart-tugger that usually stays just this side of sentimentality. Young Carlitos (Alonso) lives in Mexico with his grandma while his mother Rosario (del Castillo) works illegally as a maid in L.A. Every Sunday she calls him from the same pay phone. When grandma dies, Carlitos decides to cross the border to reunite with his mom. He makes it to Texas but it's a problematic journey from there to California that may be for naught since the fed-up Rosario is deciding whether to return home. English and Spanish with subtitles. **109m/C; DVD.** Adrian Alonso; Maya Zapata; Kate del Castillo; Eugenio Derbez; Gabriel Porras; ***D:*** Patricia Riggen; ***W:*** Ligiah Villalobos; ***C:*** Checco Varese; ***M:*** Carlo Siliotto.

Under the Sand 🦴🦴🦴 *Sous le Sable* **2000** Middleaged Marie (Rampling) has been married for many years to Jean (Cremer). They are vacationing at their summer house and Jean goes for a swim while Marie takes a nap. When she awakens, he has disappeared. A search reveals nothing and Marie must eventually return to Paris and try to go on with her life. But Marie is deep in denial—she speaks as if Jean were still alive and, in fact, she continues to see and interact with—well, whatever spirit of Jean that she has conjured up. Bravura performance from Rampling. French with subtitles. **95m/C; VHS, DVD.** *FR* Charlotte Rampling; Bruno Cremer; Jacques Nolot; Alexandra Stewart; Pierre Vernier; Andree Tainsey; ***D:*** Francois Ozon; ***W:*** Francois Ozon; Marina de Van; Emmanuele Bernheim; Marcia Romano; ***C:*** Jeanne Lapoirie; Antoine Heberle; ***M:*** Philippe Rombi.

Under the Shadow 🦴🦴🦴 **2016 (PG-13)** Nargès Rashidi stars as Shideh, a woman left alone with her young daughter in Tehran in the late '80s. Writer/director Anvari uses the location of a war-torn country for maximum horror. A bomb could fall through the ceiling at any moment. And into this world enters something supernatural, a Djinn, the legendary creature that attaches itself to Shideh and her daughter. This is a harrowing, politically fascinating study of gender, conflict, motherhood, and horror. **84m/C; DVD.** Narges Rashidi; Avin Manshadi; Bobby Naderi; Arash Marandi; Ray Haratian; ***D:*** Babak Anvari; ***W:*** Babak Anvari; ***C:*** Kit Fraser; ***M:*** Gavin Cullen; William McGillivray.

Under the Silver Lake 🦴🦴 **2018 (R)** Scruffy and aimless, 33-year-old Sam (Garfield) makes a connection with Sarah (Keough) at their complex's pool, but when her apartment is cleared out the next morning, he embarks on a code-breaking hunt through LA's underground to unearth the cause of her disappearance. A strange, neo-noir conspiracy flick in which women exist only as playthings for men, and Garfield is an unreliable, perpetually stoned narrator. What you'd get if David Lynch directed *Rear Window*. **139m/C; DVD, Blu-Ray.** Andrew Garfield; Riley Keough; Sydney Sweeney; Jimmi Simpson; Grace Van Patten; ***D:*** David Robert Mitchell; ***W:*** David Robert Mitchell; ***C:*** Mike Gioulakis; ***M:*** Rich Vreeland.

Under the Skin 🦴🦴🦴 **2013 (R)** Possibly the first "thinking man's alien seductress movie," Glazer's eerie, introspective story of an alien (Johansson) disguising herself as human and luring young Scottish men to an ambiguous (i.e. probably bloody) fate doesn't offer any easy answers, but that's part of its charm. Johansson succeeds in making her character feel both human and truly alien, giving a superb performance. Glazer's unsettling commentary on the male gaze is a nice change from the usual outer-space invader story, but might disappoint sci-fi fans looking for explosions and hot-to-trot alien women. **108m/C; DVD, Blu-Ray.** *UK* Scarlett Johansson; Paul Brannigan; ***D:*** Jonathan Glazer; ***W:*** Jonathan Glazer; Walter Campbell; ***C:*** Daniel Landin; ***M:*** Mica Levi.

Under the Sun 🦴🦴 *Under Solen* **1998** In 1956, 40-year-old virgin, Olof (Lassgard), lives on his rather rundown farm in western Sweden—his only friend being the younger Erik (Widerberg), who takes advantage of Olof's generosity. Then Ellen (Bergstrom) turns up in answer to Olof's ad for a housekeeper and the unlikely duo become a romantic couple much to Erik's dismay. So he decides to find out what a beautiful city girl is doing on a remote farm. Based on a short story by H.E. Bates. Swedish with subtitles. **118m/C; VHS, DVD.** *SW* Rolf Lassgard; Helena Bergstrom; Johan Widerberg; Jonas Falk; Linda Ulvaeus; ***D:*** Colin Nutley; ***W:*** Colin Nutley; ***C:*** Jens Fischer; ***M:*** Paddy Moloney.

Under the Tuscan Sun 🦴🦴 1/2 **2003 (PG-13)** Very loose adaptation of the Frances Mayes bestseller has beautiful scenery—both from its leads and Italy. Still in shock from her recent divorce, writer Frances (Lane) is given a change-of-scenery trip by her lesbian best friend Patti (Oh). While traveling in Tuscany, Frances comes across a rundown villa, which she impulsively buys and proceeds to renovate with the aid of some displaced Polish workmen. She begins to make friends with the locals, including handsome Marcello (Bova), with whom she is soon getting romantic. Lane is exuberant as the newly risk-taking Frances but Oh supplies much humor when Patti shows up, pregnant and deserted by her lover, to join Frances's new household. **113m/C; VHS, DVD, Blu-Ray.** Diane Lane; Sandra Oh; Lindsay Duncan; Raoul Bova; Vincent Riotta; Guilia Steigerwalt; Pawel Szajda; Valentine Pelka; Sasa Vulicevic; David Sutcliffe; Kate Walsh; ***D:*** Audrey Wells; ***W:*** Audrey Wells; ***C:*** Geoffrey Simpson; ***M:*** Christophe Beck.

Under the Volcano 🦴🦴🦴 **1984** An alcoholic British ex-consul finds his life further deteriorating during the Mexican Day of the Dead in 1939. His half-brother and ex-wife try to save him from himself, but their affair sends him ever-deeper into his personal hell. Finney's performance is pathetic and haunting. Adapted from the novel by Malcolm Lowry. **112m/C; VHS, DVD.** Albert Finney; Jacqueline Bisset; Anthony Andrews; Katy Jurado; ***D:*** John Huston; ***M:*** John Beal; Alex North. L.A. Film Critics '84: Actor (Finney).

Under the Yum-Yum Tree 🦴🦴 1/2 **1963** When womanizing landlord Hogan's (Lemmon) ex-fiance Irene (Adams) moves out, he doesn't pine. Instead he plots to romance her niece Robin (Lynley) who's just moved into his building. But his romantic shenanigans are thwarted by the presence of fiance David (Jones), who's living platonically with Robin to test their compatibility. Silly sex comedy based on the play by Roman. **110m/C; VHS, DVD.** Jack Lemmon; Carol Lynley; Dean Jones; Edie Adams; Imogene Coca; Paul Lynde; Robert Lansing; Bill Bixby; ***D:*** David Swift; ***W:*** David Swift; Lawrence Roman; ***C:*** Joseph Biroc; ***M:*** Frank DeVol.

Under Western Stars 🦴 **1938** Roy's first starring vehicle. A newly elected congressman goes to Washington and fights battles for his constituents, caught in the middle of the Dust Bowl and drought. **83m/B; VHS, DVD.** Roy Rogers; Smiley Burnette; ***D:*** Jean Yarbrough. Natl. Film Reg. '09.

Underclassman WOOF! **2005 (PG-13)** Venice beach bike cop, Tre (Cannon), gets assigned to prep school to investigate a murder. Sounds like it might have promise, but nope. Even the juxtaposition of Tre—the only African American on the starkly white prep school campus—falls flat amidst cheap jokes and predictably cliched circumstances. Poor Cheech Marin, who plays Tre's boss, adds another thankless role to his resume. Why Tre, a trouble-finding high school dropout, is a cop in the first place, is beyond logic. **95m/C; DVD.** Nick Cannon; Shawn Ashmore; Roselyn Sanchez; Kelly Hu; Ian Gomez; Hugh Bonneville; Richard "Cheech" Marin; Mary Pat Gleason; Angelo Spizzirri; Kaylee DeFer; ***D:*** Marcos Siega; ***W:*** David T. Wagner; Brent Goldberg; ***C:*** David Hennings; ***M:*** BT (Brian Transeau).

Undercover 🦴 1/2 **1994 (R)** Police detective (and hot babe) Cindy Hanen (Massey) gets an undercover assignment to capture a murderer who's targeted an upscale brothel. It's an excuse for interesting undies (or less). **93m/C; VHS, DVD.** Athena Massey; Tom Tayback; Anthony Guidera; Rena Riffel; Jeffrey Dean Morgan; Meg Foster; ***D:*** Alexander Gregory (Gregory Dark) Hippolyte; ***W:*** Lalo Wolf; Oola Bloome; ***C:*** Philip Hurn; ***M:*** Ashley Irwin.

Undercover Angel 🦴🦴 1/2 **1999 (PG-13)** Predictably cheesy but still entertaining movie that features the chubby-cheeked blonde girl from the Welch's Juice TV commercials. Six-year-old Young is left in the care of struggling writer Winters, her mom's old boyfriend. He's attracted to Bleeth and the little moppet charges into the woman's life in order to get the duo together. Oh yeah, and then Young and Winters discover that he's actually her biological father. **93m/C; VHS, DVD.** Yasmine Bleeth; Dean Winters; Emily Mae Young; Lorraine Ansell; Casey Kasem; Richard Eden; James Earl Jones; ***D:*** Bryan Michael Stoller; ***W:*** Bryan Michael Stoller; ***C:*** Bruce Alan Greene; ***M:*** Greg Edmonson. **VIDEO**

Undercover Blues 🦴🦴 1/2 **1993 (PG-13)** Comedy-thriller starring Turner and Quaid as married spies Jane and Jeff Blue, on parental leave from the espionage biz, who are on vacation with their 11-month-old daughter in New Orleans. But the holiday is interrupted when they're recruited by their boss to stop an old adversary from selling stolen weapons. The leads play cute together and the baby is adorable but this is strictly routine escapism. Stick with "The Thin Man" instead. **90m/C; VHS, DVD, Blu-Ray.** Kathleen Turner; Dennis Quaid; Fiona Shaw; Stanley Tucci; Larry Miller; Obba Babatunde; Park Overall; Tom Arnold; Saul Rubinek; Michelle Schuelke; ***D:*** Herbert Ross; ***W:*** Ian Abrams; ***M:*** David Newman.

Undercover Bridesmaid 🦴🦴 1/2 **2012** Amusing Hallmark Channel rom com that is reminiscent of "Miss Congeniality." Tough bodyguard Tanya (Burns) is hired by wealthy Texan Jim Thompson (Harrison) to protect his daughter Daisy (Paggi), who has been receiving death threats before her wedding. Tanya is horrified that this means posing as a girly bridesmaid while investigating likely suspects amongst all the wedding preparations. **86m/C; DVD.** Brooke Burns; Gregory Harrison; Nicole Paggi; Justin Baldoni; Shashawnee Hall; Jay Kenneth Johnson; ***D:*** Matthew Diamond; ***W:*** Gregg Rossen; Brian Sawyer; ***C:*** Maximo Munzi; ***M:*** Lawrence Shragge. **CABLE**

Undercover Brother 🦴🦴 1/2 **2002 (PG-13)** Funny but padded spoof of secret agents and blaxploitation movies. Brother (Griffin) is a secret agent from the B.R.O.T.H.-E.R.H.O.O.D. sent to rescue a black war hero turned presidential candidate (the always-cool Williams) who has been brainwashed in a plot by The Man to destroy African-American culture. More-hit-than-miss comedy finds many targets of all stripes to lampoon, and does so with just the right amount of funk. **85m/C; VHS, DVD, Blu-Ray.** Eddie Griffin; Chris Kattan; Denise Richards; Dave Chappelle; Chi McBride; Aunjanue Ellis;

Neil Patrick Harris; Billy Dee Williams; Jack Noseworthy; Gary Anthony Williams; James Brown; Robert Trumbull; ***Nar:*** J.D. Hall; ***D:*** Malcolm Lee; ***W:*** John Ridley; Michael McCullers; ***C:*** Tom Priestley; ***M:*** Stanley Clarke.

Undercover Maisie 🦴🦴 **1947** The 10th and last film in the tired MGM series has Maisie (Sothern) joining the LAPD to be near her detective boyfriend (Nelson). She's sent undercover to infiltrate a gang of con artists led by a phony swami (Ames), but Maisie's cover is blown and it looks like her police career is going to be a short one. **90m/B; DVD.** Ann Sothern; Barry Nelson; Leon Ames; Mark Daniels; Clinton Sundberg; Dick Simmons; Charles D. Brown; ***D:*** Harry Beaumont; ***W:*** Thelma Robinson; ***C:*** Charles Salerno, Jr.; ***M:*** David Snell.

The Undercover Man 🦴 **1/2 1949** Title is a misnomer since Treasury Agent Frank Warren (Ford) doesn't go undercover in this crime drama filmed in a semi-documentary style. Frank and his partner George Pappas (Whitmore) go after a Chicago mobster for tax evasion but have trouble proving their case since their contacts wind up dead. Story is based on how the feds brought down Al Capone. **85m/B; DVD.** Glenn Ford; James Whitmore; Nina Foch; Barry Kelley; David Wolfe; ***D:*** Joseph H. Lewis; ***W:*** Jack Rubin; Sydney (Sidney) Boehm; ***C:*** Burnett Guffey; ***M:*** George Duning.

Undercover With the KKK 🦴 *My Undercover Years With the KKK* **1978** Don Meredith's acting talents don't extend to playing the real life Gary Thomas Rowe Jr. who's recruited by the FBI in the 1960s to become an informant on the Ku Klux Klan in his Alabama hometown. **97m/C; DVD.** Don Meredith; Slim Pickens; Clifton James; Ed Lauter; Albert Salmi; Margaret Blye; Edward Andrews; ***D:*** Barry Shear; ***W:*** Lane Slater; ***C:*** Robert Moreno; ***M:*** Morton Stevens.

Undercurrent 🦴🦴 **1/2 1946** Minnelli's only foray into film noir is high-gloss melodrama based on the novel "You Were There" by Thelma Strabel. Innocent Ann (Hepburn) marries Alan (Taylor) after a whirlwind romance and then discovers he's not the man she thinks. He may be a murderer and there's some chicanery involving his brother Michael (Mitchum) and the family business. Taylor's in a rare bad guy role while Hepburn seems too sophisticated for her naive wife and Mitchum just seems tired. **116m/B; VHS, DVD.** Katharine Hepburn; Robert Taylor; Robert Mitchum; Edmund Gwenn; Marjorie Main; Clinton Sundberg; Dan Tobin; Jayne Cotter; ***D:*** Vincente Minnelli; ***W:*** Marguerite Roberts; Edward Chodorov; George Oppenheimer; ***C:*** Karl Freund; ***M:*** Herbert Stothart.

Undercurrent 🦴🦴 **1999 (R)** Ex-cop Lamas arrives in Puerto Rico to run a nightclub and is blackmailed into an affair with a mobster's wife. **99m/C; VHS, DVD.** Lorenzo Lamas; Frank Vincent; Brenda Strong; ***D:*** Frank Kerr; ***C:*** Carlos Gaviria; ***M:*** Christopher Lennertz. **VIDEO**

The Underdog 🦴 **1/2 1943** After the bank forecloses, a farm family must move to the city. The family's young son has only his loyal dog to turn to for friendship, but the gallant animal proves his mettle by rounding up a gang of spies plotting some WWII sabotage. Believe it if you dare. **65m/B; VHS, DVD.** Barton MacLane; Bobby Larson; Jan Wiley; ***D:*** William Nigh.

Underdog 🦴 **2007 (PG)** Live-action/CGI combo finds the TV cartoon character making his feature film debut. Beagle Underdog (Lee) goes from ordinary to extraordinary, thanks to an accident in the lab of Dr. Simon Barsinister (Dinklage). He can even talk, which is a big surprise to young owner Jack (Neuberger). Now Underdog's new mission is to protect the citizens of Capitol City, especially lovely spaniel "Sweet" Polly Purebred (Adams), from Barsinister's...well...sinister plans to take over. With a dog as a superhero, there's no way this should have missed. Unfortunately, a handful of inspired moments aren't enough to overcome the generally disjointed and rushed feel of the whole thing. **84m/C; DVD, Blu-Ray.** Peter Dinklage; Patrick Warburton; Alex Neuberger; Taylor Momsen; John Slattery; Brad Garrett; James Belushi; ***V:*** Jason Lee; Amy Adams; ***D:*** Frederick Du Chau; ***W:*** Adam Rifkin; Joe Piscatella; Craig A. Williams; ***C:*** David Eggby; ***M:*** Randy Edelman.

Underdog Kids 🦴🦴 **2015 (PG)** A family action film centered on an underdog karate team. A few weeks before a major karate tournament, the instructor for the Mid-City Community Center's karate team is gone. The situation seems dire until Jimmy "The Lightning Bolt" Lee (Rhee) visits. A former MMA champ and native of the neighborhood, Jimmy reluctantly agrees to coach the misfit kids for the tournament. Facing the undefeated Beverly Hills team, the center kids learn many life lessons about courage, confidence, and honor. **94m/C; DVD, Download.** Phillip Rhee; Mirelly Taylor; Max Gail; Adam Irigoyen; Ryan Potter; ***D:*** Phillip Rhee; ***W:*** Phillip Rhee; ***C:*** Aaron Meister; ***M:*** Arturo Sandoval.

Underground 🦴🦴 **1/2 1941** Eric (Dorn) is a member of the German underground working against the Nazis. But he must conceal his activities from his loyal solider brother Kurt (Lynn). Topical wartime drama still hits home with its story of divided loyalties. **95m/B; VHS, DVD.** Philip Dorn; Jeffrey Lynn; Martin Kosleck; Karen Verne; Mona Maris; Peter Whitney; Ilka Gruning; ***D:*** Vincent Sherman; ***W:*** Charles Grayson; ***C:*** Sidney Hickox; ***M:*** Adolph Deutsch.

Underground 🦴 **1/2 1970** The affable Goulet is miscast as ruthless U.S. agent Joe Dawson, who's out to capture Nazi general Stryker (Duering). Dawson is reluctantly aided by French resistance leader Boulet (Dobkin) and fighter Yvonne (Gaubert), who's put off by Dawson's ruthlessness. Dawson has some private reasons for getting revenge on Stryker. **96m/C; DVD.** *UK* Daniele Gaubert; Lawrence (Larry) Dobkin; Carl Duering; Joachim Hansen; ***D:*** Arthur Nadel; ***W:*** Ron Bishop; ***C:*** Robert Goulet; Ken Talbot; ***M:*** Stanley Myers.

Underground 🦴🦴🦴 *Once Upon a Time There Was a Country; Il Etait une Fois un Pays* **1995** Exhausting black comedy, set in Yugoslavia from 1941 to 1992, follows the adventures of Marko (Manojlovic) and his best friend Blacky (Ristovski). They run a black-market operation and lead Communist Party meetings while trying to avoid the Gestapo in WWII Belgrade. Hiding out in a cellar, where refugees have put together a munitions factory, the treacherous Marko manages to convince everyone that the war is still going on—20 years later in fact—until the truth unexpectedly comes out (thanks to a pet monkey). The final section sees Marko unscrupulously dealing arms and drugs amidst the breakup of Yugoslavia in a civil war and the violence on all sides. **192m/C; VHS, DVD, Blu-Ray.** *FR GE HU* Miki (Predrag) Manojlovic; Lazar Ristovski; Mirjana Jokovic; Slavko Stimac; Ernst Stötzner; Srdan Todorovic; Mirjana Karanovic; Milena Pavlovic; Danilo Stojkovic; Bora Todorovic; Davor Dujmovic; Branislav Lecic; Dragan Nikolic; Hark Bohm; ***Cameo(s):*** Emir Kusturica; ***D:*** Emir Kusturica; ***W:*** Emir Kusturica; Dusan Kovacevic; ***C:*** Vilko Filac; ***M:*** Goran Bregovic. Cannes '95: Film.

The Underground 🦴🦴 **1997 (R)** A rap artist is gunned down by a gang and Sgt. Brian Donnegan (Fahey) and his partner Scully (Tigar) are on the investigation. But when Scully is killed by the same scum, Donnegan is partnered with a rookie (McFall) and the duo must infiltrate L.A.'s music scene to get their suspects. **92m/C; VHS, DVD.** Jeff Fahey; Ken Tigar; Michael McFall; ***D:*** Cole McKay; ***W:*** William Lawlor; ***C:*** Ken Blakey; ***M:*** John Gonzalez.

Underground President 🦴 **2007** Blow (Jones) is a gangster living the good life (or at least as good as it gets for a mid-level thug), when events put the city's drug lords at war and he is called upon to take sides. **87m/C; DVD.** Jermaine Young Jones; Corey McFarlane; Jared Wofford; ***D:*** Tim Warren; ***W:*** Tim Warren; ***C:*** Ricardo Manavello.

Underground: The Julian Assange Story 🦴🦴 **2012** Bland bio, made for Australian TV, primarily covers 1989-91 in the life of WikiLeaks founder Julian Assange. His early years were spent on the run with his left-leaning mother, Christine, and his younger brother, after leaving a cult known as The Family. Settling in Melbourne when Julian is a teenager, he soon becomes part of a hacker group that attacks worldwide computer systems, including U.S. military sites, which gets him trouble with the authorities. **89m/C; DVD.** *AU* Alex Williams; Rachel Griffiths; Anthony LaPaglia; Laura Wheelwright; ***D:*** Robert Connolly; ***W:*** Robert Connolly; ***C:*** Andrew Commis; ***M:*** Francois (Frank) Tetaz. **TV**

Undermind 🦴 **1/2 2003** Dissolute corporate lawyer Derrick (Trammell) wakes up in an altered reality as a low-life criminal named Zane. While Zane's enjoying the perks of Derrick's life, Derrick's finding it hard to manage Zane's bottom-feeder existence. Everything gets tied up neatly. Dwek's debut effort. **113m/C; DVD.** Sam Trammell; Erik Jensen; Susan May Pratt; Tara Subkoff; Celia Weston; Ellen Pompeo; Aasif Mandai; Michael Ryan Segal; ***D:*** Nevil Dwek; ***W:*** Nevil Dwek; ***C:*** Wolfgang Held; ***M:*** Joel Goodman.

The Underneath 🦴🦴🦴 **1995 (R)** Recovering gambling addict Michael Chambers (Gallagher) returns home after skipping out on his debts and his wife Rachel (sultry newcomer Elliott) several years before. Old passions ignite in more ways than one, and Michael's lust for his ex, now married to a hot-tempered hoodlum, leads him to risk it all for a final big score. Moody and tense study of the complexities of emotion is capped by smart lead performances but style wins out over substance and the finale definitely leaves more questions than answers. Remake of the 1949 film noir classic "Criss Cross," based on Don Tracy's novel of the same name. **99m/C; VHS, DVD.** Peter Gallagher; Alison Elliott; William Fichtner; Elisabeth Shue; Adam Trese; Paul Dooley; Joe Don Baker; Anjanette Comer; Harry Goz; Shelley Duvall; Vincent Gaskins; Tony Perenski; Richard Linklater; Dennis Hill; Helen Cates; John Martin; David Jensen; Joseph Chrest; ***D:*** Steven Soderbergh; ***W:*** Steven Soderbergh; Daniel Fuchs; ***C:*** Elliot Davis; ***M:*** Cliff Martinez.

Undersea Kingdom 🦴🦴 **1936** Adventure beneath the ocean floor. In 12 chapters of 13 minutes each; the first chapter runs 20 minutes. Later re-edited into one film, "Sharad of Atlantis." **226m/B; VHS, DVD.** Ray Corrigan; Lon Chaney, Jr.; Lois Wilde; Monte Blue; William Farnum; Smiley Burnette; ***D:*** B. Reeves Eason.

The Undertaker and His Pals 🦴🦴 **1967** Undertaker teams up with diner owners in murder scheme to improve mortician's business and expand restaurateurs' menu. Pretty violent stuff, with some good laughs and a campy flare, but not for every one's palate. **70m/C; VHS, DVD.** Ray Dannis; James Westmoreland; Larrene Ott; Robert Lowery; Sally Frei; ***D:*** David C. Graham; ***C:*** Andrew Janczak.

The Undertaker's Wedding 🦴🦴 **1997 (R)** Undertaker Mario Bellini (Brophy) fakes the death and burial of mob boss Rocco (Wincott) to stem a local mob war but then makes the big mistake of falling in love with the new "widow," Maria (Wuhrer). **90m/C; VHS, DVD.** *CA* Adrien Brody; Jeff Wincott; Kari Wuhrer; Burt Young; Holly Gagnier; Nicholas Pasco; ***D:*** John Bradshaw; ***W:*** John Bradshaw; ***C:*** Edgar Egger.

Undertaking Betty 🦴🦴 **1/2** *Plots with a View* **2002 (PG-13)** In this wacky Brit rom com, shy Boris (Molina) owns a funeral home in a small Welsh town. He's in love with the married Betty (Blethyn), who decides to fake her own death so the two can run away together. Boris has professional and personal competition in crass American Fred (Walken). Betty learns her adulterous husband Hugh (Pugh) and his gold-digging mistress Meredith (Watts) were planning to kill her anyway and she decides to get even first. **94m/C; DVD.** *UK* Brenda Blethyn; Alfred Molina; Christopher Walken; Robert Pugh; Naomi Watts; Lee Evans; ***D:*** Nick Hurran; ***W:*** Frederick Ponzlov; ***C:*** James Welland; ***M:*** Rupert Gregson-Williams.

Undertow 🦴🦴 **1949** Standard B-noir story with some directorial flourishes from Castle. Tony Reagan ran with gangsters before his Army stint and now he plans to stay on the straight-and-narrow and marry Sally. Only her uncle is big in the rackets and Tony gets framed for his murder. On the lam in Chicago, Tony tries to prove he's innocent with the help of new friend Ann. **71m/B; DVD.** Scott Brady; Dorothy Hart; Peggy Dow; John Russell; Bruce Bennett; ***D:*** William Castle; ***W:*** Lee Loeb; Arthur T. Horman; ***C:*** Irving Glassberg.

Undertow 🦴🦴 **2004 (R)** Over-heated southern gothic. Rebellious teen Chris (Bell) lives on a hardscrabble hog farm with widowed dad John (Mulroney) and sickly 10-year-old bro Tim (Alan). Then wicked Uncle Deel (Lucas) shows up, fresh outta prison and with a lot of pent-up resentment and anger toward John (seems John's late wife was Deel's gal first). He demands his share of some rare gold coins bequeathed to him and John, which John believes are cursed. Deel goes all Cain and Abel, which forces the younger duo to grab the gold and take off running. Brit boy Bell manages his Southern twang with aplomb. Filmed on location around Savannah, Georgia. **107m/C; DVD, Blu-Ray.** Jamie Bell; Josh(ua) Lucas; Dermot Mulroney; Shiri Appleby; Patricia Healy; Bill McKinney; Alan Devon; ***D:*** David Gordon Green; ***W:*** David Gordon Green; ***C:*** Tim Orr; ***M:*** Philip Glass.

Underwater 🦴🦴 **2020 (PG-13)** When the hull of an underwater research site cracks and explodes, only six out of hundreds of crew members survive including Norah (Stewart), Le capitaine (Cassel), Henwick (Emily), and Paul (Miller). There is no one to help them on the surface, and all the escape pods have been used or destroyed. To get out alive, they must walk a mile along the ocean floor to another site where they might be working pods. During this perilous journey, they discover that they are not alone. The cinematography and Stewart's performance help the tightly constructed action/monster film overcome a sometimes incoherent story. **95m/C; DVD.** Kristen Stewart; Vincent Cassel; Mamoudou Athie; T.J. Miller; Jessica Henwick; ***D:*** William Eubank; ***W:*** Brian Duffield; Adam Cozad; ***C:*** Bojan Bazelli; ***M:*** Marco Beltrami; Brandon Roberts.

Underworld 🦴🦴 **1996 (R)** Considering the on-screen talent, this crime comedy/thriller is a disappointment. Ex-wiseguy Johnny Crown (Leary) studied psychotherapy in the joint and, when he's released, decides to put his new knowledge to work on bossman Frank Gavilan (Mantegna), who may be behind the hit on Johnny's old man. Contrived dialogue and story but a sleek-looking production. **95m/C; VHS, DVD.** Denis Leary; Joe Mantegna; Annabella Sciorra; Larry Bishop; Abe Vigoda; James Tolkan; Robert Costanzo; ***D:*** Roger Christian; ***W:*** Larry Bishop; ***C:*** Steven Bernstein; ***M:*** Anthony Marinelli.

Underworld 🦴🦴 **2003 (R)** Vampires and Lycans (werewolves) wage a centuries old battle of survival. The aristocratic vampires have been in control, but the lycans have a plan to turn the tide. It involves human med student Michael (Speedman), who has the blood of both in his family. Head vampire warrior Selene (Beckinsale) inexplicably falls in love with him, precipitating a final showdown. Despite the almost constant gunplay and fight scenes, style vs. substance is the overriding battle here, even though it's no contest. Substance gets its butt handed to it, suffering from the absence of allies plot and characterization. On the bright side, Beckinsale can handle the action stuff, and looks great doing it. **121m/C; VHS, DVD, Blu-Ray, UMD.** *US GB GE HU* Kate Beckinsale; Scott Speedman; Michael Sheen; Shane Brolly; Bill Nighy; Erwin Leder; Sophia Myles; Robbie Gee; Wentworth Miller; ***D:*** Len Wiseman; ***W:*** Danny McBride; ***C:*** Tony Pierce-Roberts; ***M:*** Paul Haslinger.

Underworld: Awakening 🦴 *Underworld: New Dawn; Underworld 4: Awakening* **2012 (R)** The franchise that most likely should not have been awakened returns with an uninspired 3D installment that mistakes being loud for being creative. Humans learn that vampires and werewolves are real and a worldwide purge of the creatures ensues. Years later, Selene (Beckinsale) escapes imprisonment into a world where all vamps and Lycans are underground. But they are planning a return and someone close to Selene could be the answer for who will rule the world. Fans will dig seeing Beckinsale back in black leather, and a twist at the end implies she'll be wearing it again. **88m/C; DVD, Blu-Ray.** Kate Beckinsale; Scott Speedman; Stephen Rea; Kris Holden-Ried; Theo James; India Eisley; Charles Dance; Michael Ealy; ***D:***

Mans Marlind; Bjorn Stein; ***W:*** J. Michael Straczynski; Len Wiseman; John Hlavin; Allison Burnett; ***C:*** Scott Kevan; ***M:*** Paul Haslinger.

Underworld: Blood Wars **2016 (R)** Beckinsale can barely disguise how remarkably little she cares about what's happening in the latest and worst entry in the series about vampires and werewolves that has never found a pulse. Selene has been betrayed by her kind, the vampires, and has to fend off attacks by the Lycans at the same time. Only David (James) and his father Thomas (Dance) stand by her side, and the trio soon learns that she may be the only one that can stop all-out war between the two factions. This underwhelming entry shouldn't have seen the light of day. **91m/C; DVD, Blu-Ray, Streaming.** Kate Beckinsale; Theo James; Tobias Menzies; Lara Pulver; Charles Dance; ***D:*** Anna Foerster; ***W:*** Cory Goodman; Kyle Ward; ***C:*** Karl Walter Lindenlaub; ***M:*** Michael Wandmacher.

Underworld: Evolution **1/2 2005 (R)** Selene and Michael are still on the run and still trying to figure out the depths of the various betrayals and who, if anyone, they can trust. This time out they have to deal with the O.G. vampire and werewolf, and there are a few family issues to work out.There's also plenty of backstory, and more of what made the first installment a hit: Beckinsale in black leather, frenetic vampire-on-werewolf battle action, blood, and gunplay. As a bonus, there's a much better villain and script that brings everything home (but don't rule out another sequel). **106m/C; DVD, Blu-Ray, UMD.** Kate Beckinsale; Scott Speedman; Tony Curran; Shane Brolly; Derek Jacobi; Bill Nighy; Steven Mackintosh; Brian Steele; John Mann; Michael Sheen; Sophia Myles; Richard Cetrone; ***D:*** Len Wiseman; ***W:*** Len Wiseman; Danny McBride; ***C:*** Simon Duggan; ***M:*** Marco Beltrami.

Underworld: Rise of the Lycans **1/2 2009 (R)** Third installment in the "Underworld" franchise serves as a prequel for the earlier offeringsand is set a thousand years prior to the original. Explains the origin of the epic conflict between the werewolves and vampires born in the dark ages. Favored Lycan member Lucian (Sheen) falls in love with Sonja (Mitra), the daughter of chief vampire and villain Viktor (Nighy). The affair provokes Viktor's wrath while in turn Lucian instigates an uprising among the Lycans. The two clans do magical battle in mostly inky dark settings with the exception of the blood, which shoots across the screen like fireworks. Nothing surprising or interesting, but hard-core fans will appreciate the history behind the discord. **93m/C; Blu-Ray, UMD, On Demand.** Michael Sheen; Rhona Mitra; Bill Nighy; Shane Brolly; Steven Mackintosh; Kevin Grevioux; Elizabeth Hawthorne; Kate Beckinsale; David Aston; Larry Rew; ***D:*** Patrick Tatopoulos; ***W:*** Danny McBride; Howard McCain; Dirk Blackman; ***C:*** Ross Emery; ***M:*** Paul Haslinger.

The Underworld Story **1/2 1950** Big city journalist at large moves to small-town New England after losing job for unethical reporting and uncovers scheme to frame innocent man for murder. Solid performances. **90m/B; VHS, DVD.** Dan Duryea; Herbert Marshall; Gale Storm; Howard da Silva; Michael O'Shea; Mary Anderson; Gar Moore; Melville Cooper; Frieda Inescort; Art Baker; Harry Shannon; Alan Hale, Jr.; Steve (Stephen) Dunne; Roland Winters; ***D:*** Cy Endfield.

Underworld U.S.A. **1961** A man infiltrates a tough crime syndicate to avenge his father's murder, which winds up with him caught between the mob and the feds. A well-acted and directed look at the criminal underworld. **99m/B; VHS, DVD, Blu-Ray.** Cliff Robertson; Dolores Dorn; Beatrice Kay; Robert Emhardt; Larry Gates; Paul Dubov; Gerald Milton; Richard Rust; Allan Gruener; ***D:*** Samuel Fuller; ***W:*** Samuel Fuller; ***C:*** Hal Mohr; ***M:*** Harry Sukman.

Undiscovered **2005 (PG-13)** Model Brier (James) and songwriter Luke (Strait) meet in New York's subway but Luke is soon off to L.A. to ply his trade. Some time later, Brier heads to the coast to try her luck as an actress and just happens to find Luke again. Brier decides to create some media buzz to help Luke's career, but her plans backfire. Price of fame cliches abound and the music is egregiously bad (although the leads are attractive). **97m/C; DVD.** Pell James; Steven Strait; Kip Pardue; Fisher Stevens; Ashlee Simpson; Shannyn Sossamon; Peter Weller; Carrie Fisher; Stephen Moyer; ***D:*** Meiert Avis; ***W:*** John Galt; ***C:*** Danny Hiele; ***M:*** David Baerwald.

Undisputed **1/2 2002 (R)** Champion boxer James "Ice Man" Chambers is locked up in Sweetwater maximum-security prison for rape, which he claims he didn't commit. Snipes is Monroe Hutchens, a lifer at Sweetwater and fellow boxer, sentenced for beating a man to death. Hutchens is also the prison's undefeated champ of the illegal boxing matches set up by a rough prison guard (Rooker). Smacking of real-life boxer Tyson, Chambers desperately tries to find honor in his unhappy situation and wants to be the first to break Hutchen's winning streak, but Monroe has his reasons for avoiding a smack-down with Chambers. Short on dialogue, pic is a well-cast, lean, mean movie machine. **96m/C; VHS, DVD.** Wesley Snipes; Ving Rhames; Peter Falk; Michael Rooker; Jon Seda; Wes Studi; Fisher Stevens; Dayton Callie; Amy Aquino; Nils Allen Stewart; Denis Arndt; Rose Rollins; ***D:*** Walter Hill; ***W:*** Walter Hill; David Giler; ***C:*** Lloyd Ahern, II; ***M:*** Stanley Clarke.

Undisputed 2: Last Man Standing **2006 (R)** An unnecessary sequel that has few ties to the first pic. Ex-boxing champ George Chambers (White) is making vodka commercials in Russia when he lands in prison on trumped-up charges. Seems the Russian mob wants to pit Chambers against the prison's best fighter, Uri Boyka (Adkins), in a televised match they expect will bring in big gambling bucks. The fights between the leads are impressive but scant as is the rest of the action. **98m/C; DVD.** Michael Jai White; Eli Danker; Ben Cross; Scott Adkins; ***D:*** Isaac Florentine; ***W:*** David White; James Townsend; ***C:*** Ross W. Clarkson; ***M:*** Stephen (Steve) Edwards. **VIDEO**

Undrafted **2016** Based on a true story, this baseball comedy considers the life-changing effects of one game. After being overlooked in the Major League Baseball draft, college star John Mazetti (Tveit) is one of 12 quirky teammates playing what should be a fun summer intramural baseball game. For everyone involved, the game is played as they grapple with the transition from playing baseball to a future that has yet to be defined. It becomes one of the most meaningful of their lives. **90m/C; DVD, Streaming, Download.** Aaron Tveit; Tyler Hoechlin; Joseph Mazzello; Michael Fishman; Chace Crawford; ***D:*** Joseph Mazzello; ***W:*** Joseph Mazzello; ***C:*** Adrian Correia.

The Undying **2009** Dull and dumb supernatural horror/romance. Lonely doctor Barbara Haughton rents a remote house that's built on ground once used as a Civil War field hospital. Maybe that's why the house is haunted by a Confederate soldier named Elijah. Barbara falls in love with her ghost and is determined to make him corporeal by getting Elijah's spirit to inhabit the body of a brain-dead John Doe. Her plan works, but with some serious consequences. **105m/C; DVD.** Robin Weigert; Anthony Carrigan; Jay O. Sanders; Wes Studi; Sybil Temtchine; Paul David Storey; ***D:*** Steven Peros; ***W:*** Steven Peros; ***C:*** Robert F. Smith; ***M:*** Christopher Caliendo.

Une Femme Mariee *A Married Woman* **1964** A series of moments in the life of married Charlotte, a vain, trivial woman who cheats on her pilot husband with an actor. When Charlotte gets pregnant and isn't sure who the father is, she has to decide between the two men. For Godard completists. French with subtitles. **95m/B; DVD.** *FR* Macha Meril; Phillippe LeRoy; Bernard Noel; ***D:*** Jean-Luc Godard; ***W:*** Jean-Luc Godard; ***C:*** Raoul Coutard.

Unearthed **2007** Low budget chase movie involving aliens, a slightly crazed cop, an archaeologist, and an unknown who may also be an alien competing for an artifact dug up at a high-rise project. **93m/C; DVD.** Emmanuelle Vaugier; Luke Goss; Beau Garrett; Charlie (Charles Q.) Murphy; M.C. Gainey; Russell Means; ***D:*** Matthew Leutwyler; ***W:*** Matthew Leutwyler; ***C:*** Ross Richardson; ***M:*** Joseph Bishara.

The Unearthing **1993 (R)** An unwanted pregnancy seems to find a happy solution when a woman decides to marry the heir to a wealthy estate and pass off her child as his. Only the family has some very strange tastes, including a taste for the blood of the unborn. Based on a Filipino vampire legend (!). **83m/C; VHS, DVD.** Norman Moses; Tina Ona Paukstelis; ***D:*** Wyre Martin; Barry Poltermann; ***W:*** Wyre Martin; Barry Poltermann.

The Unearthly **1/2 1957** A mad scientist is trying to achieve immortality through his strange experiments, but all he winds up with is a basement full of mutants. When his two latest about-to-be victims fall in love, the doctor's mutant assistant decides enough is enough and things come to an unpleasant end. Carradine is typecast. Absurd, but fun. **76m/B; VHS, DVD.** John Carradine; Tor Johnson; Allison Hayes; Myron Healey; Karl Johnson; ***D:*** Boris L. Petroff.

Unexpected **1/2 2015 (R)** Writer/director Swanberg draws new dramatic range out of Smulders in the lead role of her drama about a woman dealing with an unplanned pregnancy. Inner-city high school teacher Samantha Abbott (Smulders) ends up pregnant when she least expects it, which brings her closer to Jasmine (Bean), one of her students who happens to be in the same life predicament, although at a younger age and in a different economic situation. The film dodges a few social issues and lacks some depth but Smulders and Bean make it worth a look. **90m/C; DVD, Blu-Ray, Streaming.** Cobie Smulders; Anders Holm; Gail Bean; Elizabeth McGovern; ***D:*** Kris Swanberg; ***W:*** Kris Swanberg; Megan Mercier; ***C:*** Dagmar Weaver-Madsen; ***M:*** Keegan DeWitt.

An Unexpected Love **2003** Kate Meyer (Hope) is frustrated by her life so she separates from her husband (Moffett), leaves her kids behind, and gets a job at a small real estate agency thanks to sympathetic owner Mac Hayes (Crewson). Then Kate finds herself becoming romantically attracted to Mac, which causes problems with her family and friends. Hope's character is on the unpleasant side but Crewson's performance is a gem. **90m/C; DVD.** Leslie Hope; Wendy Crewson; D.W. Moffett; Alison Pill; Margo Martindale; Brent Spiner; Irma P. Hall; Christine Ebersole; ***D:*** Lee Rose; ***W:*** Lee Rose; ***C:*** Jan Kiesser; ***M:*** Velton Ray Bunch. **CABLE**

Unexplained Laughter **1989** A cynical journalist vacations in Wales with her timid vegetarian friend and stumbles across a mystery in this darkly comic British TV-movie. Sold as part of the 'Diana Rigg at the BBC'. **85m/C; VHS, DVD.** *GB* Diana Rigg; Elaine Page; Jon Finch; ***D:*** Gareth Davies; ***W:*** Alun Owen; ***C:*** Ashley Rowe.

Unfaithful **2002 (R)** Director Lyne may be known for such hot-blooded features as "9 1/2 Weeks," "Fatal Attraction," and "Lolita" but he takes a cooler approach to adultery in this melodrama, which was inspired by Claude Chabrol's 1969 film "La Femme Infidele." Connie (a luscious Lane) is a suburban mom, complacently married to regular guy Edward (Gere), who cannot resist having a hot, hot, hot affair with French bookseller Paul (Martinez), whom Connie meets cute while shopping in New York. Edward gets suspicious, Connie tries to break things off, and it turns out there's nothing like a MAN who gets scorned to bring trouble. **123m/C; VHS, DVD, Blu-Ray.** Richard Gere; Diane Lane; Olivier Martinez; Erik Per Sullivan; Dominic Chianese; Zeljko Ivanek; Kate Burton; Chad Lowe; Gary Basaraba; Margaret Colin; ***D:*** Adrian Lyne; ***W:*** Alvin Sargent; William Broyles, Jr.; ***C:*** Peter Biziou; ***M:*** Jan A.P. Kaczmarek. N.Y. Film Critics '02: Actress (Lane), Actress (Lane).

Unfaithfully Yours **1/2 1948** A conductor suspects his wife is cheating on him and considers his course of action. He imagines punishment scenarios while directing three classical works. Well-acted by all, but particularly by Harrison as the egotistical and jealous husband. Another of Sturges' comedic gems. Remade in 1984. **105m/B; DVD.** Rex Harrison; Linda Darnell; Kurt Kreuger; Rudy Vallee; Lionel Stander; Edgar Kennedy; ***D:*** Preston Sturges; ***C:*** Victor Milner.

Unfaithfully Yours **1984 (PG)** A symphony conductor suspects his wife of fooling around with a musician; in retaliation, he plots an elaborate scheme to murder her with comic results. No match for the 1948 Preston Sturges film it's based on. **96m/C; DVD.** Dudley Moore; Nastassja Kinski; Armand Assante; Albert Brooks; Cassie Yates; Richard Libertini; Richard B. Shull; ***D:*** Howard Zieff; ***W:*** Valerie Curtin; Barry Levinson; Robert Klane; ***M:*** Bill Conti.

Unfinished Business **2015 (R)** Vaughn continues to defile film comedy with another disaster. It's hard to figure why he's still getting parts. This time, he stars as a small business owner who takes his two associates (poor Wilkinson and Franco, both too talented for this junk) on a trip to Europe to close the most important deal of their lives. Wacky hijinks ensue. It's all physical, mostly gross-out humor with no opportunity for a bad joke untaken. It's one of those films for which none of the characters are worth rooting for, making their boorish, "Ugly American" behavior harder to stomach. **90m/C; DVD, Blu-Ray.** Vince Vaughn; Tom Wilkinson; Dave Franco; Sienna Miller; June Diane Raphael; ***D:*** Ken Scott; ***W:*** Steve Conrad; ***C:*** Oliver Stapleton; ***M:*** Alex Wurman.

The Unfinished Dance **1/2 1947** Technicolor MGM dance drama. Young ballet student Meg (O'Brian) worships the company's rising star Ariane (Charisse). When visiting prima ballerina La Darina (Booth) takes the lead role in "Swan Lake," Meg is outraged for her idol and does some stage sabotage that goes too far. Thomas makes his film debut as Meg's guardian. Remake of the 1938 French film "Ballerina." **101m/C; DVD.** Margaret O'Brian; Cyd Charisse; Karin (Karen, Katharine) Booth; Danny Thomas; Elinor Donahue; Esther Dale; Thurston Hall; ***D:*** Henry Koster; ***W:*** Myles Connolly; ***C:*** Robert L. Surtees; ***M:*** Herbert Stothart.

An Unfinished Life **1/2 2005 (PG-13)** Crusty Wyoming rancher Einar Gilkyson (Redford) has a rundown property he works a little with his best friend, Mitch Bradley (Freeman), who has been severely mauled by a bear. This furry nemesis was captured and unhappily resides in a local animal park. (That's the symbolism you're smelling, not the bear.) Jean Gilkyson (Lopez), Einar's widowed daughter-in-law has been abused by her lowlife boyfriend Gary (Lewis) for the last time and unwillingly seeks shelter at the ranch with her tough-talking, 11-year-old daughter Griff (Gardner). Einar, who blames Jean for his son's death, grudging allows them to stay temporarily and gradually thaws towards his spunky granddaughter. Much gruff bonding and a family reconciliation finally ensue (with the bear playing its part). Tomboyish Gardner is a delight, though Lopez has little to do and makes an equally slight impression. Best are the interactions between pros Redford and Freeman, whose characters squabble and fuss like a longtime married couple. Co-written by Mark and and Virginia Korus Spragg, and adapted from Spragg's novel. **107m/C; DVD, Blu-Ray.** Robert Redford; Morgan Freeman; Jennifer Lopez; Josh(ua) Lucas; Damian Lewis; Camryn Manheim; Becca Gardner; ***D:*** Lasse Hallstrom; Andrew Mondshein; ***W:*** Mark Spragg; ***C:*** Oliver Stapleton; ***M:*** Christopher Young.

An Unfinished Piece for a Player Piano **1/2 1977** A general's widow invites family and friends to a weekend house party in 1910 Russia. Romantic and familial entanglements begin to intrude in a lyrical adaptation of Chekov's play "Platonov." In Russian with English subtitles. **100m/C; VHS, DVD.** *RU* Alexander Kalyagin; Elena Solovei; Antonina Shuranova; Oleg Tabakov; Yuri Bogatyrev; Nikita Mikhalkov; ***D:*** Nikita Mikhalkov.

Unfinished Song *Song for Marion* **2012 (PG-13)** A gentle dramatic comedy about the healing power of music and community. Arthur (Stamp) is a gruff older gentleman who enjoys his dull and routine life until his beloved wife Marion (Redgrave) convinces him to join her local singing group for seniors. There, Arthur finds new life and adventures while striking up a friendship with the group's leader, Elizabeth (Arterton), while his terminally ill wife enjoys her last days. Through it all, Arthur deals with the death of Marion and re-connects with his estranged son James (Eccleston). **93m/C; DVD, Blu-Ray, Streaming.** *UK* Terence Stamp; Vanessa Redgrave; Gemma Arterton; Christopher Eccleston; Anne Reid; ***D:*** Paul Andrew Williams; ***W:***

Paul Andrew Williams; ***C:*** Carlos Catalan; ***M:*** Laura Rossi.

The Unforeseen 🦴🦴 1/2 **2007** A feature-length documentary how the environment is impacted by human activity, including the American Dream. Focusing on parts of Austin, Texas, the film explores a real estate development that began in the 1980s and created new areas of the city in what had once been wilderness. However, as the development reached Barton Springs, an aquifer and spring-fed swimming spot, the community reacted with disdain. The struggle between growth and preservation is held as an example of similar conflicts in other parts of the United States. **88m/C; DVD.** ***D:*** Laura Dunn; ***C:*** Lee Daniel.

Unforgettable 🦴🦴 **1996 (R)** Unfortunately, the film doesn't live up to its title. On-the-edge medical examiner David Krane (Liotta) has barely escaped conviction for his wife's brutal murder. Living under a cloud of suspicion, he turns to university researcher Martha Briggs (Fiorentino, wasted as a nerdy scientist), whose experiments in memory transference lead David to believe he can uncover the killer. But, like a Chinese puzzle box, one discovery only leads to a further complication. Too many, in fact, for the story to stay focused (and the ending is less than satisfying). **116m/C; VHS, DVD.** Ray Liotta; Linda Fiorentino; Peter Coyote; Christopher McDonald; Kim Cattrall; David Paymer; Kim Coates; Duncan Fraser; Garwin Sanford; ***D:*** John Dahl; ***W:*** Bill Geddie; ***C:*** Jeffrey Jur; ***M:*** Christopher Young.

Unforgettable 🦴🦴 **2017 (R)** Jilted ex-wife Tessa (Heigl) decides to make her ex's fiancee Julia (Dawson), who's trying to escape a turbulent past, pay for usurping her in increasingly psychotic and TV-movie trope ways. Either everyone involved totally bought into the complete campiness of it all, or were completely unaware and were playing it laughably straight. It's hard to tell. And that may be both its biggest strength and most glaring weakness. It's a trainwreck, and is best enjoyed as such. **100m/C; DVD, Blu-Ray.** Katherine Heigl; Rosario Dawson; Geoff Stults; Whitney Cummings; Cheryl Ladd; ***D:*** Denise Di Novi; ***W:*** Christina Hodson; David Leslie Johnson; ***C:*** Caleb Deschanel; ***M:*** Toby Chu.

Unforgivable 🦴🦴 *Impardonnables* **2011** Director/writer Techine's oblique pic starts with the relationship of Francis and Judith and radiates outward in complex patterns tied to family and friends. Writer Francis meets real estate agent Judith when he's looking fior a place to rent in Venice. After a time leap, we see the couple have married. Francis' daughter, Alice, goes missing after a visit and he hires PI Anna Maria--formerly Judith's lover--to find out what's happened, which leads to more drama. French with subtitles. **110m/C; DVD.** *FR* Andre Dussollier; Carole Bouquet; Mélanie Thierry; Adriana Asti; Mauro Conte; Alexis Loret; ***D:*** Andre Techine; ***W:*** Andre Techine; Philippe Djian; ***C:*** Julien Hirsch; ***M:*** Max Richter.

The Unforgiven 🦴🦴🦴 **1960** A western family is torn asunder when it is suspected that the eldest daughter is of Indian birth. Film takes place in 1850s' Texas. One of Huston's weakest ventures, but viewed in terms of 1950s' prejudices it has more resonance. Fine acting from all the cast, especially Gish. Watch for the stunning Indian attack scene. **123m/C; VHS, DVD, Blu-Ray.** Burt Lancaster; Audrey Hepburn; Lillian Gish; Audie Murphy; John Saxon; Charles Bickford; Doug McClure; Joseph Wiseman; Albert Salmi; ***D:*** John Huston.

Unforgiven 🦴🦴🦴 1/2 **1992 (R)** Will Munny (Eastwood) lives a quiet life with his stepchildren on his failing pig farm, but his desperado past catches up with him when the Schofield Kid invites him to a bounty hunt. Munny reluctantly agrees, mistakenly believing that once the killing is through he can take up his peaceful ways again. Enter sadistic sheriff Little Bill Daggett (Hackman), who doesn't want any gunmen messing up his town. Eastwood uses his own status as a screen legend to full advantage as the aging gunman who realizes too late that his past can never be forgotten. Director Eastwood is also in top form with his well-seasoned cast and myth-defying Old West realism. Surprising critical and boxoffice hit. **131m/C; VHS, DVD, Blu-Ray.** Clint Eastwood; Gene Hackman; Morgan Freeman; Richard Harris; Jaimz Woolvett; Saul Rubinek; Frances Fisher; Anna Thomson; David Mucci; Rob Campbell; Anthony James; ***D:*** Clint Eastwood; ***W:*** David Peoples; ***C:*** Jack N. Green; ***M:*** Lennie Niehaus. Oscars '92: Director (Eastwood), Film, Film Editing, Support. Actor (Hackman); AFI '98: Top 100; British Acad. '92: Director (Eastwood), Film, Support. Actor (Hackman); Directors Guild '92: Director (Eastwood); Golden Globes '93: Director (Eastwood), Support. Actor (Hackman); L.A. Film Critics '92: Actor (Eastwood), Director (Eastwood), Film, Screenplay, Support. Actor (Hackman); N.Y. Film Critics '92: Support. Actor (Hackman); Natl. Soc. Film Critics '92: Director (Eastwood), Film, Screenplay, Support. Actor (Hackman).

Unfriended 🦴🦴 1/2 **2015 (R)** Clever concepts in the low-budget horror genre only come along every few years, which is why this very modern riff on "Rear Window" is surprisingly refreshing. The entire piece takes place "on" the screen of a laptop, as high school student Blaire Lily (Hennig) communicates with friends on the one-year anniversary of her childhood friend's suicide (Sossaman). As Blaire and the gang cyber-talk, they notice an unknown user on the account. And then things get weird. A story of a haunting via Skype may not seem effective but it works for what it is. **82m/C; DVD, Blu-Ray.** Heather Sossaman; Matthew Bohrer; Courtney Halverson; Shelley Hennig; Moses Storm; ***D:*** Levan Gabriadze; ***W:*** Nelson Greaves; ***C:*** Adam Sidman.

Unfriended: Dark Web 🦴🦴 **2018 (R)** An unclaimed laptop proves terrifying and deadly to a circle of friends who dare to access its files. Transported into the Dark Web while videochatting with each other, the pals slowly realize that the computer's videos depict real-life violence, but before they can do anything about it, but killer comes after them. Scary in concept and execution, this horror flick won't disappoint casual fans of the genre. **92m/C; DVD.** Colin Woodell; Betty Gabriel; Rebecca Rittenhouse; Andrew Lees; Connor Del Rio; ***D:*** Stephen Susco; ***W:*** Stephen Susco; ***C:*** Kevin Stewart; ***M:*** Andy Ross.

The Unguarded Hour 🦴🦴 **1936** Glossy MGM crime melodrama. Lady Helen Dearden (Young) is in a pickle: she knows Samuel Metford (Digges) didn't murder his wife but if she comes forward as a witness it could ruin her husband Alan's (Tone) career. That's because, at the time, she was paying off a blackmailer (Daniell) about Alan's affair. From there the situation gets more complicated. **87m/B; DVD.** Loretta Young; Franchot Tone; Henry Daniell; Dudley Digges; Roland Young; Aileen Pringle; ***D:*** Sam Wood; ***W:*** Leon Gordon; Howard Emmett Rogers; ***C:*** James Van Trees; ***M:*** William Axt.

The Unguarded Moment 🦴🦴 1/2 **1956** Technicolor trashy suspense. Suburban high school music teacher Lois Conway (Williams) is the object of desire for unbalanced football star Leonard Bennett (Saxon) after she's nice to him. His teen troubles can be blamed on his misogynistic, deranged dad (Andrews in a chilling performance), but only Det. Graham (Nader) believes Lois is being threatened. Williams' first (non-swimming) role after her MGM contract ended. **95m/C; DVD.** Esther Williams; John Saxon; George Nader; Edward Andrews; Les Tremayne; ***D:*** Harry Keller; ***W:*** Herb Meadow; Larry Marcus; ***C:*** William H. Daniels; ***M:*** Herman Stein.

Unhappy Birthday 🦴 1/2 **2010** Atmospheric, but low-on-thrills Brit horror. Newly-pregnant Sadie hasn't told boyfriend Rick her news when he has a surprise of his own. For Sadie's birthday, Rick and their friend Jonny take Sadie to meet Corinne, who claims to be Sadie's long-lost sister. Corinne lives on the remote isle of Amen and they are forced to stay at her cottage when the isle is cut off from the mainland by high tide. This doesn't bode well for the guests. **89m/C; DVD.** *GB* Christina De Vallee; David Paisley; Jonathan Keane; Jill Riddiford; David McGillivray; ***D:*** Mark Harriott; Mike Matthews; ***W:*** Mark Harriott; Mike Matthews; ***C:*** Mark Hammond; ***M:*** Lin Sangster.

The Unholy 🦴 1/2 **1988 (R)** A New Orleans priest battles a demon that's killing innocent parishioners. Confusing and heavy-handed. **100m/C; VHS, Blu-Ray, Streaming; Open Captioned.** Ben Cross; Hal Holbrook; Trevor Howard; Ned Beatty; William Russ; James Dennis (Jim) Carroll; ***D:*** Camilo Vila; ***W:*** Philip Yordan; ***M:*** Roger Bellon.

Unholy 🦴 **2007** After widowed Martha's daughter commits suicide, she and son Lucas decide to investigate, which leads them to brainwashing techniques and government conspiracies. Dull, drab, and confusing. **86m/C; DVD.** Adrienne Barbeau; Nicholas Brendon; Siri Baruc; ***D:*** Daryl Goldberg; ***W:*** Sam Freeman; ***C:*** Jeff Maher. **VIDEO**

Unholy Four 🦴 1/2 *A Stranger Came Home* **1954** An amnesiac returns home after three years to attempt to find out which of his three fishing buddies left him for dead. Confusing at times, but has some suspenseful moments. **80m/B; VHS, DVD, Blu-Ray.** *GB* Paulette Goddard; Paul Carpenter; William Sylvester; Patrick Holt; Russell Napier; ***D:*** Terence Fisher; ***W:*** Michael Carreras; ***C:*** Walter J. (Jimmy W.) Harvey; ***M:*** Ivor Slaney; Leonard Salzedo.

Unholy Rollers 🦴 *Leader of the Pack* **1972 (R)** Jennings stars as a factory worker who makes it big as a tough, violent roller derby star. Typical "Babes-on-Wheels" film that promises nothing and delivers even less. **88m/C; VHS, DVD.** Claudia Jennings; Louis Quinn; Betty Anne Rees; Roberta Collins; Alan Vint; Candice Roman; ***D:*** Vernon Zimmerman.

The Unholy Three 🦴🦴🦴 1/2 **1925** Ventriloquist Chaney, working with other carnival cohorts, uses his talent to gain entrance to homes which he later robs. Things go awry when two of the gang strike out on their own and the victim is killed. When the wrong man is accused, his girl, one of Chaney's gang, begs Chaney to get him free, which he does by using his vocal talents. Chaney decides being a criminal is just too hard and goes back to his ventriloquism. **70m/B; Silent; VHS, DVD.** Lon Chaney, Sr.; Harry Earles; Victor McLaglen; Mae Busch; Matt Moore; Matthew Betz; William Humphreys; ***D:*** Tod Browning.

The Unholy Three 🦴🦴🦴 **1930** Chaney remade his silent hit of 1925 for his first and only talking picture (he died before the film was released). The story is essentially the same. Chaney is a ventriloquist who, with his circus friends, work as scam artists and thieves. When an innocent man is accused of their crimes Chaney tries his ventriloquist tricks to come to his aid, only in this version Chaney is exposed as a fraud and is sent to prison. Rumors that Chaney was a mute had him agreeing to appear in a "talkie" and he actually used five different voices for his various roles. **75m/B; VHS, DVD.** Lon Chaney, Sr.; Lila Lee; Elliott Nugent; Harry Earles; John Miljan; ***D:*** Jack Conway.

Unhook the Stars 🦴🦴 1/2 **1996 (R)** Director Cassavetes does mom Rowlands proud (and she him) with the lead role of widowed Mildred, who discovers there's life after the kids leave the nest. At loose ends, Mildred befriends her wild young neighbor Monica (Tomei), who conveniently needs a babysitter for her solemn six-year-old son, J.J. (Lloyd). Monica also tries to get Mildred to loosen up by taking her to a local joint, where French-Canadian trucker Tommy (Depardieu) knows a good woman when he sees one. Mildred makes some tentative steps towards independence and we get to enjoy the stellar Rowlands once again. **105m/C; VHS, DVD.** Gena Rowlands; Marisa Tomei; Gerard Depardieu; Moira Kelly; Jake Lloyd; David Sherrill; David Thornton; ***D:*** Nick Cassavetes; ***W:*** Nick Cassavetes; Helen Caldwell; ***C:*** Phedon Papamichael; ***M:*** Steven Hufsteter.

Unidentified Flying Oddball 🦴🦴 1/2 **1979 (G)** An astronaut and his robotic buddy find their spaceship turning into a time machine that throws them back into Arthurian times and at the mercy of Merlin the magician. Futuristic version of Twain's "A Connecticut Yankee at King Arthur's Court." **92m/C; VHS, DVD.** Dennis Dugan; Jim Dale; Ron Moody; Kenneth More; Rodney Bewes; ***D:*** Russ Mayberry; ***W:*** Don Tait; ***C:*** Paul Beeson; ***M:*** Ronald Goodwin.

Uniform 🦴🦴 *Zhifu* **2003** A young man goes to work in the family shop in order to help pay his father's medical bills. When a policeman leaves his uniform to be tailored, the young man puts it on and gains instant respect, especially from Zheng, who is also leading another life—as a prostitute. Mandarin with subtitles. **92m/C; DVD.** *CH* Kai Han; Hongli Liang; Hua Qin; ***D:*** Diao Yinan; ***W:*** Diao Yinan; ***C:*** Jingsong Dong; ***M:*** Zi Wan.

The Uninvited 🦴🦴🦴 **1944** Roderick Fitzgerald (Milland) and his sister Pamela (Hussey) buy a house in Cornwall, only to find it is haunted. Doors open and close by themselves, strange scents fill the air, and they hear sobbing during the night. Soon they are visited by a woman (Russell) with an odd link to the house—her mother is the spirit who haunts the house. Chilling and unforgettable, this is one of the first films to deal seriously with ghosts. Based on the novel by Dorothy Macardle. **99m/B; DVD, Blu-Ray.** Ray Milland; Ruth Hussey; Donald Crisp; Cornelia Otis Skinner; Gail Russell; Alan Napier; Dorothy Stickney; ***D:*** Lewis Allen; ***W:*** Dodie Smith; Frank Partos; ***C:*** Charles B(ryant) Lang, Jr.; ***M:*** Victor Young.

The Uninvited WOOF! **1988** A mutant cat goes berserk onboard a luxury yacht, killing the passengers one by one with big, nasty, pointy teeth. **89m/C; VHS, DVD, Blu-Ray.** George Kennedy; Alex Cord; Clu Gulager; Toni Hudson; Eric Larson; Shari Shattuck; Austin Stoker; ***D:*** Greydon Clark.

Uninvited 🦴🦴 1/2 **1993 (R)** Grady is a mysterious old man who leads eight misfits to the top of a sacred mountain with the promise of finding gold. But the fortune hunters have trespassed in a sacred Indian burial ground and find their nightmares becoming a violent reality. **90m/C; VHS, DVD.** Jack Elam; Christopher Boyer; Erin Noble; Bari Buckner; Jerry Rector; Zane Paolo; Dennis Gibbs; Ted Haler; Eno Brutto; ***D:*** Michael Derek Bohusz; ***W:*** Michael Derek Bohusz.

The Uninvited 🦴🦴 1/2 **2009 (PG-13)** Institutionalized for months after a suicide attempt, Anna (Browning) returns home for the first time since the tragic death of her ill mother (Masser) to find that her father (Strathairn) is engaged to Rachel (Banks), mom's nurse during her illness. Suspicious of Rachel's overly saccharin behavior, Anna and sister Alex (Kebbel) soon see Rachel's dark side. By then Anna begins seeing disturbing visions—among them the ghost of her mother delivering a message of doom about the soon-to-be stepmom. Remake of the 2003 Korean horror hit "Changhwa Hongryeon" (A Tale of Two Sisters), its great cinematography and even better locations fall short of delivering the original's uneasy suspense, though the final plot twist is definitely creepy. **87m/C; Blu-Ray, On Demand.** Emily Browning; Elizabeth Banks; Arielle Kebbel; David Strathairn; Maya Massar; Thomas Guard; Jesse Moss; Dean Paul Gibson; ***D:*** Charles Guard; ***W:*** Doug Miro; Carlo Bernard; Craig Rosenberg; ***C:*** Dan Landin; ***M:*** Christopher Young.

Uninvited Guest 🦴🦴 1/2 *An Invited Guest* **1999 (R)** Smooth-talking Silk (Phifer) comes to the suburban home of Howard (Jackson) and Debbie (Morrow) and asks to use their phone. The couple agree and let the stranger in and he promptly takes them and their friends captive. A twist comes unexpected early and takes a little away from the real ending. **103m/C; VHS, DVD.** Mekhi Phifer; Mari Morrow; Mel Jackson; Kim Fields; Malinda Williams; ***D:*** Timothy Wayne Folsome; ***W:*** Timothy Wayne Folsome; ***C:*** Wayne Sells; ***M:*** Gregory Darryl Smith. **VIDEO**

Union City 🦴🦴 **1981 (R)** Deborah "Blondie" Harry's husband gets a little edgy when someone steals the milk. Murder ensues, and they're on the run from the law. Intended as a film noir spoof, and not without some good moments. **82m/C; VHS, DVD.** Deborah Harry; Everett McGill; Dennis Lipscomb; Pat Benatar; Irina Maleeva; Terina Lewis; Sam McMurray; Paul Andor; Tony Azito; CCH Pounder; ***D:*** Mark Reichert; ***W:*** Mark Reichert; ***C:*** Edward Lachman; ***M:*** Chris Stein.

Union Depot 🦴🦴 1/2 **1932** Chic (Fairbanks Jr.) and Scrap Iron (Kibbee) are tramps who find their luck changing when they hang around a train station. First Chic finds some dough and a nice suit in the washroom and gives himself a makeover. Then Scrap Iron finds a checkroom claim ticket—lost by con man The Baron (Hale Sr.)?and redeems it for a violin case full of dough. Meanwhile, stranded chorus girl Ruth (Blondell) is doing a little vamping of Chic so he'll give her the fare to get to her gig in Salt Lake City. But there's trouble when G-men start looking for counterfeit money being passed around the station. **68m/B; DVD.** Douglas Fairbanks, Jr.; Joan Blondell; Guy Kibbee; Alan Hale; George Rosener; David Landau; Earle Foxe; ***D:*** Alfred E. Green; ***W:*** Kubec Glasmon; John Bright; Walter DeLeon; Kenyon Nicholson; ***C:*** Sol Polito.

Union Pacific **1939** Full DeMille treatment highlights this saga about the building of America's first transcontinental railroad. Jeff Butler (McCrea) is the construction overseer who must battle saboteurs and Indians (although the U.S. Cavalry does arrive to save the day). He also gets to fall for self-sufficient postmistress Mollie Monahan (Stanwyck). DeMille borrowed the actual golden spike used to drive in the last rail in 1869 for his reenactment of the completion celebration. Based on the book "Trouble Shooters" by Ernest Haycox. **136m/B; VHS, DVD.** Joel McCrea; Barbara Stanwyck; Robert Preston; Brian Donlevy; Akim Tamiroff; Lynne Overman; Robert Barrat; Anthony Quinn; Stanley Ridges; Henry Kolker; Evelyn Keyes; Regis Toomey; ***D:*** Cecil B. DeMille; ***W:*** Walter DeLeon; Jesse Lasky, Jr.; C. Gardner Sullivan; ***C:*** Victor Milner.

Union Station **1950** Holden plays the chief of the railway police for Chicago's Union Station. He learns the station is to be used as a ransom drop in a kidnapping; but for all his security, the main thug gets away with the money, and the hunt is on. Good acting raises this film above the ordinary. **80m/B; DVD, Blu-Ray.** William Holden; Barry Fitzgerald; Nancy Olson; Jan Sterling; Lee Marvin; Allene Roberts; Lyle Bettger; ***D:*** Rudolph Mate; ***W:*** Sydney (Sidney) Boehm; ***C:*** Daniel F. Fapp; ***M:*** Heinz Roemheld.

United **1/2 2011 (PG-13)** BBC drama based on the true story of the 1958 charter plane crash that killed 23 of the 43 people on board, including eight members of Manchester United's football team. Told from the point-of-view of 19-year-old new player Bobby Carlton (O'Connell) as coach Jimmy Murphy (Tennant) and owner Matt Busby (Scott) try to rebuild the team. **90m/C; DVD.** *UK* Jack O'Connell; David Tennant; Dougray Scott; Sam Claflin; Ben Peel; Dean Andrews; Brogan West; ***D:*** James Strong; ***W:*** Chris Chibnall; ***C:*** Christopher Ross; ***M:*** Clint Mansell. **TV**

A United Kingdom **1/2 2017 (PG-13)** This is the well-meaning but ultimately disappointing true story of King Seretse Khama of Botswana (Oyelowo), who risks political and personal upheaval when he marries a British white woman named Ruth Williams (Pike). Based on Susan Williams' book, director Asante's historical drama set in the 1940s hits all the right notes, but too often plays out like a TV movie, back when the big TV networks made historical dramas like this one. The notable charisma of the two leads keep it somewhat interesting though. **111m/C; Blu-Ray.** David Oyelowo; Rosamund Pike; Tom Felton; Jack Davenport; Laura Carmichael; ***D:*** Amma Asante; ***W:*** Guy Hibbert; ***C:*** Sam McCurdy; ***M:*** Patrick Doyle.

United 93 **2006 (R)** Greengrass' intense, emotional drama covers the hijacking of United Airlines Flight 93 on September 11, 2001. Events alternate between what is happening onboard as the passengers and crew try to disarm the hijackers and what is happening at the FAA, air defense headquarters, and airport control towers as realization dawns about the scope of the disaster and what, if anything, can be done. The Boeing 757 eventually crashed near Shanksville, Pennsylvania, with a total loss of life. Greengrass filmed in the U.K., and a number of the cast are nonprofessionals playing themselves. **111m/C; DVD, Blu-Ray.** David Alan Basche; Richard Bekins; Susan Blommaert; Christian Clemenson; Ray Charleson; Gregg Henry; Polly Adams; Denny Dillon; Khalid Abdalla; Lewis Alsamari; Ben Sliney; Maj. James Fox; Trish Gates; Cheyenne Jackson; ***D:*** Paul Greengrass; ***W:*** Paul Greengrass; ***C:*** Barry Ackroyd; ***M:*** John Powell. British Acad. '06: Director (Greengrass), Film Editing.

U.S. Marshals **1998 (PG-13)** Jones reprises his Oscar-winning role from "The Fugitive" as the hound dog U.S. Marshal Sam Gerard in this lackluster sequel. Gerard tracks down Sheridan (Snipes) who is framed for a double homicide of two federal agents. Gerard's probing reveals that Sheridan really isn't the average Joe he seems, and the presence of shifty agent Downey Jr. further confirms Gerard's suspicions of a government cover-up. Jones remains solid in a popular role, supported well by his sidekick Cosmo (Pantolino). The stunts equal if not better its predecessor, yet a poorly developed Sheridan, compounded by Snipes's lack of intensity drag this chase movie down to a slow crawl. **133m/C; VHS, DVD, Blu-Ray.** Tommy Lee Jones; Robert Downey, Jr.; Wesley Snipes; Joe Pantoliano; Kate Nelligan; Irene Jacob; Daniel Roebuck; Tom Wood; LaTanya Richardson Jackson; Michael Paul Chan; ***D:*** Stuart Baird; ***W:*** John Pogue; ***C:*** Andrzej Bartkowiak; ***M:*** Jerry Goldsmith.

United States of Leland **2003 (R)** Low-key high school student Leland (Gosling) senselessly stabs his ex-girlfriend's autistic brother to death at the beginning of this bleak flick. Director Hoge then spends the rest of his debut film juggling the pieces attempting to define Leland's motivation. Was it his heroin-addicted girlfriend (Malone) who left him for her dealer? Or his emotionally absent novelist father, Albert (Spacey)? Or something else? Meanwhile, Pearl (Cheadle), an aspiring but struggling writer, is Leland's juvenile detention counselor who sees in him an opportunity for his first novel and the hidden agenda has its own consequences. While those encounters provide some lively scenes, and Spacey, Cheadle, and Malone give capable performances, there's no sustaining this disjointed piece. **108m/C; DVD.** Ryan Gosling; Don Cheadle; Chris Klein; Jena Malone; Lena Olin; Kevin Spacey; Michelle Williams; Martin Donovan; Ann Magnuson; Kerry Washington; Sherilyn Fenn; Matt Malloy; Michael Peña; Ron Canada; Troy Winbush; Yolonda Ross; Jim Haynie; Kimberly Scott; Ryan Malgarini; Clyde Kusatsu; Sheeri Rappaport; Angela Paton; Michael Welch; ***D:*** Matthew Ryan Hoge; ***W:*** Matthew Ryan Hoge; ***C:*** James Glennon; ***M:*** Jeremy Enigk.

U.S. Seals **1998 (R)** Absolutely undistinguished action flick pits a team of Navy SEALs against pirates from Kazahkstan. The heroes are jut-jawed guys with crewcuts and cute kids. Lots of stuff blows up. Production values are strictly of the made-for-cable quality. **90m/C; DVD.** Jim (James) Fitzpatrick; Greg Collins; J. Kenneth Campbell; ***D:*** Yossi Wein.

U.S. Seals 2 **1/2 2001 (R)** An ex-SEAL is planning to launch a nuclear strike on the U.S. from a secret Russian missile base unless the good guys can stop him. **95m/C; VHS, DVD.** Damian Chapa; Mike Worth; Marshall Teague; Sophia Crawford; ***D:*** Isaac Florentine; ***W:*** Michael D. Weiss; ***C:*** Peter Belcher; ***M:*** Stephen (Steve) Edwards. **VIDEO**

U.S. SEALs: Dead or Alive *U.S. Navy SEALS: Dead or Alive; Frogmen Operation Stormbringer; U.S. SEALs 3: Frogmen* **2002 (R)** A team of Navy SEALs must locate a cluster bomb before terrorists sell it to the Albania government. The producers no doubt hope the action with be enough cover for the dumb plot and subpar acting, but they're wrong. **93m/C; VHS, DVD.** Tyler Christopher; John Simon Jones; Bentley Mitchum; Gary Murphy; George Stanchev; ***D:*** Franklin A. Vallette; ***W:*** Steve Latshaw; ***C:*** Don E. Fauntleroy; ***M:*** Serge Colbert. **VIDEO**

The U.S. Vs. John Lennon **2006 (PG-13)** A look at peace advocate John Lennon's post-Beatles contributions to music and popular culture that leaves out the man's dark edges (the documentary was made with the cooperation of Yoko Ono, so no surprise there). The focus is on the Nixon's administration paranoid view of Lennon as an enemy to national security and his subjection to wiretapping, surveillance, and a deportation order. Music from Lennon's solo career highlights the visuals and it features an odd group of talking heads, from Geraldo Rivera to Gore Vidal. **99m/C; DVD.** ***D:*** David Leaf; John Scheinfeld; ***W:*** David Leaf; John Scheinfeld; ***C:*** James Mathers.

Universal Soldier **1992 (R)** A reporter discovers a secret government project to design perfect robo-soldiers by using the bodies of dead GIs, including tough guys Lundgren and Van Damme who were killed in Vietnam. But the knowledge is going to get her killed until Van Damme has flashbacks of his past (the soldier's memories have supposedly been erased) and agrees to help her. Lundgren doesn't have the same compassion and goes after them both. Big-budget thriller with some good action sequences and a lot of violence. **98m/C; VHS, DVD, Blu-Ray, UMD.** Jean-Claude Van Damme; Dolph Lundgren; Ally Walker; Ed O'Ross; Jerry Orbach; ***D:*** Roland Emmerich; ***W:*** Dean Devlin; Christopher Leitch; Richard Rothstein; ***C:*** Karl Walter Lindenlaub; ***M:*** Christopher Franke.

Universal Soldier: Day of Reckoning **1/2 2012 (R)** John (Scott Adkins) wakes up from a coma to discover his family has been murdered in a home invasion, and a Universal Soldier wants him dead. His quest to find the man responsible for this leads him to Luc Devereaux (Van Damme), who is building his own religion among the cyborgs. **113m/C; DVD, Blu-Ray, Streaming.** Scott Adkins; Dolph Lundgren; Andrei Arlovski; Jean-Claude Van Damme; Mariah Bonner; ***D:*** John Hyams; ***W:*** John Hyams; Douglas Magnuson; John Greenhalgh; ***C:*** Yaron Levy; ***M:*** Michael Krassner.

Universal Soldier: Regeneration **2009 (R)** Hardcore action in this fifth flick, which reunites Van Damme and Lundgren, as a futuristic terrorist (Arlovski) and his crew take over the Chernobyl nuclear reactor and threaten a meltdown. Dormant universal soldier Luc Deveraux (Van Damme) is reactivated to stop them but the bad guys have UniSol's version (Lundgren) to help them. **98m/C; DVD.** Dolph Lundgren; Jean-Claude Van Damme; Andrei Arlovski; Mike Pyle; Garry Cooper; ***D:*** John Hyam; ***W:*** Victor Ostrovsky; ***C:*** Peter Hyams. **VIDEO**

Universal Soldier: The Return **1999 (R)** The creators of superwarrior Van Damme have double-crossed him and he's out to get even in this sequel (although technically it's the fourth installment after two straight-to-cable releases). After Defense Department cutbacks short circuit the Universal Soldier program, the cyborgs start a rebellion led by an evil computer. Van Damme must battle the renegade warriors while attempting to not muss his hair. The Muscles from Brussels goes back to a proven winner after a series of boxoffice stinkers in hopes that he can kick-start his flagging career. **82m/C; VHS, DVD, Blu-Ray.** Jean-Claude Van Damme; Michael Jai White; Daniel von Bargen; Heidi Schanz; Xander Berkeley; Justin Lazard; ***D:*** Mic Rodgers; ***W:*** John Fasano; William Malone; ***C:*** Michael A. Benson; ***M:*** Don Davis.

Universal Soldiers **2007** Yet another of Asylum's mockbuster films, this time spoofing a Jean-Claude Van Damme film with a suspiciously similar name. Marines are sent to a remote island to save a professor from uppity cyborgs he's been making as military death machines. **85m/C; DVD.** Kristen Quintrall; Dario Deak; Jason S. Gray; Rick Malambri; Angela Vitale; ***D:*** Griff Furst; ***W:*** Geoff Meed; David Michael Latt; ***C:*** Alexander Yellen; ***M:*** David Raiklen. **VIDEO**

Universal Squadrons *Minutemen* **2011** Captain Lance Deakins realizes that the flashbacks he has are about the violent videogame Minutemen that he played while serving in Iraq. It was actually a military experiment to brainwash him and his unit into becoming super-soldiers. Back home in Texas, Lance is being hunted and won't reveal what he was subjected to and any top secret info he's learned. **82m/C; DVD.** Riley Smith; Willa Ford; Barry Corbin; Christian Kane; Marshall Teague; David Born; Bryan Massey; ***D:*** Mark Millhone; ***W:*** Mark Millhone; Daniel Raymond O'Brien; ***C:*** Clay Liford; ***M:*** John David Kent. **VIDEO**

The Unkissed Bride *Mother Goose A Go-Go* **1966 (PG)** A young newlywed couple are driven to distraction by the husband's inexplicable fainting spells and his strange obsession with Mother Goose. **82m/C; VHS, DVD.** Tommy Kirk; Anne Helm; Danica D'Hondt; Henny Youngman; ***D:*** Jack H. Harris.

Unknown **2011 (PG-13)** On business in Berlin, Dr. Martin Harris (Neeson) scrambles to relocate an important briefcase while wife Elizabeth (Jones) waits at the hotel. After a nasty car accident he awakens four days later and discovers another man (Quinn) has assumed his identity and Elizabeth claims not to know him. Conveniently, his ID is back at the hotel and he spends the rest of the movie trying to convince everyone they're wrong. A cool premise that works half the time until things get strange. Mostly half-baked Hitchcockian nonsense, though Neeson does the action genre well. Based on the novel "Out of My Head" by Didier van Cauwelaert. **109m/C; Blu-Ray, On Demand.** Liam Neeson; January Jones; Aidan Quinn; Diane Kruger; Bruno Ganz; Frank Langella; ***D:*** Jaume Collet-Serra; ***W:*** Oliver Butcher; Stephen Cornwell; ***C:*** Flavio Martinez Labiano; ***M:*** John Ottman; Alexander Rudd.

The Unknown Girl *La fille inconnue* **2017** During her last shift at a free clinic, Dr. Jenny Davin (Haenel) refuses to let in a desperate woman after business hours. The woman was a young immigrant prostitute who turns up dead the next day, and guilty Jenny feels that she may have contributed to her demise. Jenny decides to begin her own investigation. As she gets close to the killer's identity, she confronts threats from those who want her to stop looking. Though imperfect, Haenel is strong and sincere. French with subtitles. **113m/C; DVD.** Adèle Haenel; Olivier Bonnaud; Jeremie Renier; Louka Minnella; Christelle Cornil; ***D:*** Jean-Pierre Dardenne; Luc Dardenne; ***W:*** Jean-Pierre Dardenne; Luc Dardenne; ***C:*** Alain Marcoen.

Unknown Island **1/2 1948** Scientists travel to a legendary island where dinosaurs supposedly still exist. Bogus dinosaurs and cliche script. **76m/C; VHS, DVD.** Virginia Grey; Phillip Reed; Richard Denning; Barton MacLane; ***D:*** Jack Bernhard; ***W:*** Jack Harvey; Robert T. Shannon; ***C:*** Fred W. Jackman; ***M:*** Ralph Stanley.

The Unknown Known **2014 (PG-13)** Directed by Academy Award winner Errol Morris, this feature-length documentary look at Donald Rumsfeld, the U.S. Secretary of Defense under President George W. Bush. While the documentary considers Rumsfeld's life, career, and influence, it focuses primarily on his mindset related to the Iraq War. Using arguments and counterarguments, the film looks at the ideas, fears, and certainties of Rumsfeld, how they impacted history, and how they led the United States into war. **103m/C; DVD, Blu-Ray, Streaming, Download.** ***D:*** Errol Morris; ***W:*** Errol Morris; ***C:*** Robert Chappell; ***M:*** Danny Elfman.

Unknown Origin *The Alien Within; Roger Corman Presents: The Alien Within* **1995 (R)** Scientific crew is stuck in an underwater installation with a deadly parasite. It's "Aliens" under the sea but a few twists will tweak your interest. **75m/C; VHS, DVD.** Roddy McDowall; Melanie Shatner; Alex Hyde-White; Don Stroud; ***D:*** Scott Levy; ***W:*** Alex Simon; ***M:*** Christopher Lennertz. **CABLE**

Unknown Powers **WOOF! 1980 (PG)** Science and drama are combined to examine ESP and magic. Are they gifts or curses, and how are peoples' lives affected by them? Members of the cast introduce various sections of this totally inept film. **97m/C; VHS, DVD.** Samantha Eggar; Jack Palance; Will Geer; Roscoe Lee Browne; ***D:*** Don Como.

The Unknown Soldier **1/2 1998** Fine performances in an ultimately depressing drama, with some unexpected twists, focusing on the tragedy of war. When aristocratic Sophia Carey's (Aubrey) ancestral home is turned into a private hospital for WWI soldiers, she seriously takes up her nursing duties. One of her latest patients is an amnesiac, initially mute soldier nicknamed Angel (Mavers) by the men who rescued him in France. Sophia falls hopelessly in love with the traumatized Angel but the working-class Jenny (McGuckin) claims Angel is actually her fiance John and the military police believe he's a deserter wanted for murder. **180m/C; VHS, DVD.** *GB* Juliet Aubrey; Gary Mavers; Aislin McGuckin; ***D:*** Dr. David Drury; ***W:*** Peter Barwood. **TV**

Unknown White Male **1/2 2005 (PG-13)** Spellbinding documentary following the lost life of Doug Bruce, a man with retrograde amnesia. Two years prior Doug took a subway trip to Coney Island; once he arrived he didn't know where he was or why he was there. Since that time, for reasons no one knows, his entire memory has been wiped out. His family, his girlfriend, his home have become pieces in a puzzle he's unable to fit back together. Completely absorbing and provocative. Would make for a wicked psycho-drama. **88m/C; DVD.** ***D:*** Rupert Murray; ***C:*** Orlando Stuart; ***M:*** Mukul.

The Unknown Woman 1/2 *La Sconosciuta* **2006 (R)** Ukrainian Irina was forced into the life of a sex slave but escaped with money stolen from her brutal pimp Muffa. Having made her way to Trieste, Irina gets a job as the nanny to Thea, the fragile adopted daughter of the Adachers, who are gold dealers. Irina has a secret (about a black market baby scam) and Muffa is still determined to find her. Highly disturbing situations and brutal violence involving women and children. Italian with subtitles. **120m/C; DVD.** *IT* Kseniya Rappoport; Michele Placido; Claudia Gerini; Pierfrancesco Favino; Clara Dossena; Piera Degli Esposti; ***D:*** Giuseppe Tornatore; ***W:*** Giuseppe Tornatore; ***C:*** Fabio Zamarion; ***M:*** Ennio Morricone.

Unknown World **1951** A group of scientists tunnel to the center of the Earth to find a refuge from the dangers of the atomic world. Big start winds down fast. Director Terry Morse sometimes credited as Terrell O. Morse. **73m/B; VHS, DVD.** Bruce Kellogg; Marilyn Nash; Victor Kilian; Jim Bannon; ***D:*** Terry Morse; ***M:*** Ernest Gold.

Unlawful Entry **1992 (R)** After a break-in, Karen and Michael Carr naturally call the cops. Handsome, polite policeman Pete Davis responds to the call and agrees to help burglar-proof their home. But Pete has some definite quirks—he falls for the beauteous Karen and begins stalking the couple, deciding to get rid of Michael in order to have his wife. A lurid combination of the worst moments of "Internal Affairs" and "Fatal Attraction" undermines this usually talented cast. **107m/C; VHS, DVD.** Kurt Russell; Ray Liotta; Madeleine Stowe; Roger E. Mosley; Ken Lerner; Deborah Offner; Carmen Argenziano; Andy Romano; Barry W. Blaustein; Dick Miller; ***D:*** Jonathan Kaplan; ***W:*** Lewis Colick; ***C:*** Jamie Anderson; ***M:*** James Horner.

Unleashed *Danny the Dog* **2005 (R)** Fight scenes are taken to seat-jolting heights by renowned martial-arts choreographer Yuen Wo Ping in this live-action cyberpunk cartoon starring Jet Li as Danny the human pit bull. Enslaved from childhood and conditioned to kill without conscience by his ruthless London mobster "owner" Bart (Hoskins), Danny maims and mutilates delinquent debtors when his collar is removed. With the collar he's passive and docile. His accidental liberation sends him to the only person who was ever kind to him, a blind piano tuner (Freeman), who through piano music helps connect him with his humanity. The gangster, alas, returns for Danny resulting in one last showdown of canine love and loyalty. **102m/C; DVD, UMD, HD-DVD.** *US FR GB CH* Jet Li; Morgan Freeman; Bob Hoskins; Michael Jenn; Kerry Gordon; Christian Gazio; Carole Ann Wilson; ***D:*** Louis Leterrier; ***W:*** Luc Besson; ***C:*** Pierre Morel; ***M:*** Massive Attack.

Unlikely Angel 1/2 **1997** Brassy singer Ruby Diamond (Parton) dies suddenly in an accident but is having some trouble entering heaven. St. Peter (McDowall) thinks she's a likely prospect but Ruby needs a few more good deeds before she can get her wings. So she's sent to help a frazzled widower (Kerwin) who's the father of two lonely preteens. **90m/C; VHS, DVD.** Dolly Parton; Roddy McDowall; Brian Kerwin; ***D:*** Michael Switzer.

Unlocked 1/2 **2017 (R)** CIA operative Alice Racine (Rapace) has avoided fieldwork since failing to stop a 2012 terrorist attack in Paris but the agency convinces her to return when an ISIS cell seems posed for an attack there. While questioning a courier with important information, Alice correctly surmises there is more going on. Not knowing who to trust, she's forced on the run, where she is helped only by a local, Amjad (Cole). Rapace's charismatic performance cannot overcome a mundane screenplay. **98m/C; DVD.** Noomi Rapace; Orlando Bloom; Toni Collette; John Malkovich; Michael Douglas; ***D:*** Michael Apted; ***W:*** Peter O'Brien; ***C:*** George Richmond; ***M:*** Stephen Barton.

The Unloved **2009** Morton makes her directorial debut in a harsh look at the overwhelmed British child welfare system. Silent, 11-year-old Lucy has been neglected or abused by her estranged parents and is finally sent to a badly-run group home where she is befriended by older resident Lauren. Lucy prefers to wander the streets, seeking out her ineffectual parents, hoping one of them will be able to take her back. **108m/C; DVD.** *GB* Molly Windsor; Lauren Socha; Robert Carlyle; Susan Lynch; Craig Parkinson; ***D:*** Samantha Morton; ***W:*** Samantha Morton; Tony Grisoni; ***C:*** Tom Townsend.

Unmade Beds **2009** Spanish slacker Axl (Tielve) travels to London with the intention of finding the British man who fathered him during a vacation fling. He stays in a number of squats that are also occupied by fellow squatter Vera (Francois), a romantically-depressed young Frenchwoman. Their confusion over identity, isolation, and their place in the world is similar although their involvement is limited. English and French dialogue. **96m/C; DVD.** *GB* Fernando Tielve; Deborah Francois; Iddo Goldberg; Richard Lintern; Michiel Huisman; ***D:*** Alexis Dos Santos; ***W:*** Alexis Dos Santos; ***C:*** Jakob Ihre.

An Unmarried Woman **1978 (R)** Suddenly divorced by her husband of 17 years, a woman deals with change. She enters the singles scene, copes with her daughter's growing sexuality, and encounters a new self-awareness. Mazursky puts real people on screen from start to finish. **124m/C; VHS, DVD.** Jill Clayburgh; Alan Bates; Cliff Gorman; Michael Murphy; ***D:*** Paul Mazursky; ***W:*** Paul Mazursky; ***M:*** Bill Conti. Cannes '78: Actress (Clayburgh); L.A. Film Critics '78: Screenplay; N.Y. Film Critics '78: Screenplay; Natl. Soc. Film Critics '78: Screenplay.

The Unmistaken Child *Ha-Gilgul* **2008** Israeli documentary chronicles Nepalese monk Tenzin Zopa's years-long search for the reincarnation of a deceased Buddhist master. Senior lamas in India consult Taiwanese astrologers for clues that have disciple Zopa examining a number of young children on his travels to find the new embodiment of Geshe Lama Konchog. Tibetan, Nepali, Hindi, and Taiwanese with subtitles. **104m/C; DVD.** *IS* ***D:*** Nati Baratz; ***W:*** Nati Baratz; Ilil Alexander; ***C:*** Yaron Orbach; ***M:*** Cyril Morin.

The Unnamable **1988** The adaptation of the H.P. Lovecraft story about a particular New England ancestral home haunted by a typically Lovecraftian bloodthirsty demon borne of a woman hundreds of years before. College students, between trysts, investigate the myths about it. Uncut version, unseen in theatres, available only on video good for a few giggles and thrills. **87m/C; VHS, Blu-Ray, Streaming.** Charles Klausmeyer; Mark Kinsey Stephenson; Alexandra Durrell; Laura Albert; Eben Ham; Blane Wheatley; Mark Parra; Katrin Alexandre; ***D:*** Jean-Paul Ouellette; ***W:*** Jean-Paul Ouellette; ***C:*** Tom Fraser.

The Unnamable 2: The Statement of Randolph Carter 1/2 *H.P. Lovecraft's The Unnamable Returns; The Unnamable Returns* **1992 (R)** Randolph Carter is investigating a series of murders at Miskatonic University. Evidence leads Carter back to a 17th-century warlock who had the misfortune to summon an evil creature known as Alyda. The half-demon, half-woman now wants to permanently return to the mortal plane and every new victim just helps her evil purpose along. Based on a story by H.P. Lovecraft. **104m/C; VHS, DVD.** Mark Kinsey Stephenson; John Rhys-Davies; David Warner; Julie Strain; Maria Ford; Charles Klausmeyer; ***D:*** Jean-Paul Ouellette; ***W:*** Jean-Paul Ouellette; ***C:*** Greg Gardiner.

Unnatural 1/2 **1952** A mad scientist creates a souless child from the genes of a murderer and a prostitute. The child grows up to be the beautiful Neff, who makes a habit of seducing and destroying men. Dark, arresting film from a very popular German story. **90m/B; VHS, DVD.** Hildegarde Knef; Erich von Stroheim; Karl-Heinz Boehm; Harry Meyen; Harry Helm; Denise Vernac; Julia Koschka; ***D:*** Arthur Maria Rabenalt.

Unnatural Causes **1986** A dying Vietnam vet believes that his illness is the result of exposure to Agent Orange. With the help of a VA counselor, they lobby for national programs to assist other veterans who have been exposed to the chemical and together bring publicity to the issue. A TV drama that is exceptionally well-acted. **96m/C; VHS, DVD.** John Ritter; Patti LaBelle; Alfre Woodard; John Sayles; Sean McCann; John Vargas; Gwen E. Davis; ***D:*** Lamont Johnson; ***W:*** John Sayles; ***M:*** Charles Fox. **TV**

Unplanned **2019 (R)** While working at a Planned Parenthood clinic, Abby (Bratcher) encounters many young, poor, and/or struggling women who often chose abortion to end their pregnancies. Abby's boss, the ambitious Cheryl (Scott), pressures her to increase the number of abortion procedures to increase profits. Over time, Abby has other experiences that make her question the mission of Planned Parenthood, including when she tries to help a friend's teenage daughter get an abortion but it is botched. Based the best-selling memoir of a former Planned Parenthood staffer turned anti-abortion activist, the drama takes controversial stances through a story that argues why abortion should be considered unsafe. **106m/C; DVD, Blu-Ray.** Ashley Bratcher; Brooks Ryan; Robia Scott; Jared Lotz; Emma Elle Roberts; ***D:*** Chuck Konzelman; Cary Solomon; ***W:*** Chuck Konzelman; Cary Solomon; ***C:*** Drew Maw; ***M:*** Stephen Blake Kanicka.

Unpublished Story **1942** Fast-paced wartime thriller is also a British propaganda flick filmed amidst the London Blitz. War correspondent Bob Randall (Greene) can't understand why his story about a suspicious pacifist organization was killed by government official Lamb (Radford) in favor of a puff piece by reporter Carol Bennett (Hobson). Carol is curious as well and she and Bob team up and discover a group of Nazi sympathizers with too much political power. **91m/B; DVD.** *UK* Richard Greene; Valerie Hobson; Basil Radford; Roland Culver; Miles Malleson; ***D:*** Harold French; ***W:*** Anatole de Grunwald; Patrick Kirwan; ***C:*** Bernard Knowles; ***M:*** Clifton Parker.

The Unquiet 1/2 **2008** Below average ghost story. Paranormal debunker Julie Bishop (Buono) is called to dispel rumors about Blackstone Prison, an abandoned women's facility supposedly haunted by violent spirits. She's not happy to see that her documentary filmmaker ex-husband Tom (Martin) is there to prove the opposite. But something hostile is definitely trapped within the walls. **90m/C; DVD.** Cara Buono; Chris William Martin; Julia Benson; Michael Teigan; Don S. Davis; Zahf Paroo; Tegan Moss; ***D:*** Bill Corcoran; ***W:*** Matt Dorff; ***C:*** Michael Balfry; ***M:*** Misha Segal. **CABLE**

An Unreasonable Man **2006** Straightforward look at the career of crusading consumer advocate Ralph Nader and his presidential aspirations. The self-righteous workaholic frequently exasperated his colleagues and was heavily criticized for siphoning votes away from Al Gore during the contested 2000 election. Documentary is a mix of contemporary interviews and archival footage. **122m/C; DVD.** Ralph Nader; ***D:*** Henriette Mantel; Stephen Skrovan; ***C:*** Mark Raker; ***M:*** Joe Kraemer.

An Unremarkable Life **1989 (PG)** Two aging sisters live symbiotically together, until one views the other's romantic attachment to a charming widower as destructive to her own life. **97m/C; VHS, DVD; Open Captioned.** Shelley Winters; Patricia Neal; Mako; Rochelle Oliver; Charles S. Dutton; Lily Knight; ***D:*** Amin Qamar Chaudhri.

The Unsaid 1/2 *The Ties That Bind* **2001 (R)** After psychologist Michael Hunter's (Garcia) teenaged son commits suicide, he becomes estranged from his wife and daughter and gives up hands-on therapy. But he's persuaded by his former student, Barbara (Polo), to look into one of her social work cases. Now nearly-18, Tommy (Kartheiser) discovered the body of his murdered mother when he was a boy and his father (Bottoms) is in prison for the crime. But Tommy has been keeping a lot of secrets. **110m/C; DVD.** *US CA* Andy Garcia; Vincent Kartheiser; Teri Polo; Linda Cardellini; Sam Bottoms; August Schellenberg; Chelsea Field; Trevor Blumas; Brendan Fletcher; ***D:*** Tom McLoughlin; ***W:*** Miguel Tejada-Flores; Scott Williams; ***C:*** Lloyd Ahern, II; ***M:*** Don Davis.

Unsane 1/2 *Shadow; Sotto gli Occhi dell'Assassino; Tenebrae; Tenebre* **1982** A mystery novelist realizes that a series of bizarre murders strangely resembles the plot of his latest book. Bloody fun from Argento. **91m/C; VHS, DVD, Blu-Ray.** *IT* Anthony (Tony) Franciosa; John Saxon; Daria Nicolodi; Giuliano Gemma; Christian Borromeo; Mirella D'Angelo; Veronica Lario; Ania Pieroni; Carola Stagnaro; John Steiner; Lara Wendel; ***D:*** Dario Argento; ***W:*** Dario Argento; ***C:*** Luciano Tovoli; ***M:*** Claudio Simonetti.

Unsane 1/2 **2018 (R)** An intelligent thriller film about a stalker and the object of his obsession by director Soderbergh. After Valentini (an outstanding Foy) cares for the father of David Strine (Leonard) in the elderly man's final days, David becomes obsessed with her. Because of the effect of his stalking on her, she seeks treatment at a facility that takes her possessions, dehumanizes her, and is perhaps using her insurance money. When it seems that David begins working at the facility, Valentini's concerns are dismissed. **98m/C; DVD, Blu-Ray.** Claire Foy; Joshua Leonard; Sarah Stiles; Marc Kudisch; Amy Irving; ***D:*** Steven Soderbergh; ***W:*** Jonathan Bernstein; James Greer; ***C:*** Steven Soderbergh; ***M:*** Thomas Newman.

The Unseen **2005** College professor Roy Clemens (Harris) returns to his rural Georgia hometown to deal with the death of his father. This also means confronting his estranged childhood friend, volatile redneck Harold Dickerson (Harold). Whatever dark secret they share has also impacted the life of Sammy (Bloch), Harold's blind, simple-minded younger brother who's kept a near-prisoner at home. Southern gothic anchored by some good performances. **99m/C; DVD.** Steve Harris; Catherine Dent; Michelle Clunie; Judah Friedlander; Gale Harrold; Phillip Bloch; ***D:*** Jim Hunter; ***W:*** Jim Hunter; ***M:*** Dean Parker.

Unseen Enemy **2017 97m/C; Streaming.** ***D:*** Janet Tobias; ***W:*** Janet Tobias; ***C:*** Cesar Charlone; Zac Nicholson; ***M:*** John Piscitello.

Unseen Evil **1999 (R)** A group of archeological students accompany their professor to an ancient burial ground for a dig. Unfortunately, the prof wants to uncover a powerful alien force and is prepared to sacrifice anyone necessary. **90m/C; VHS, DVD, Blu-Ray.** Richard Hatch; Tim Thomerson; Robbie (Reist) Rist; Cindi Braun; Frank Ruotolo; Jere Jon; Cindy Pena; ***D:*** Jay Woelfel; ***W:*** Scott Spears; ***C:*** Scott Spears. **VIDEO**

Unshackled 1/2 **2000 (PG-13)** Slightly overdone melodrama tells the true story of Harold Morris, who was sentenced to life at 20 for armed robbery and murder and later helped organize the first interracial basketball team at Georgia State Prison. The team led the way to fully integrating the prison. Eventually paroled, Morris goes on to steer kids away from drugs and crime. Often heavy-handed, but the message is supposed to be inspirational (hence the PG13 rating), and it will be, to some. **106m/C; VHS, DVD.** Burgess Jenkins; James Black; Stacy Keach; Morgan Fairchild; ***D:*** Bart Patton; ***W:*** Harold Morris; ***C:*** Paul Varrieur; ***M:*** Jeffrey Scott Pearson.

The Unsinkable Molly Brown **1964** A spunky backwoods girl is determined to break into the upper crust of Denver's high society and along the way survives the sinking of the Titanic. This energetic version of the Broadway musical contains many Meredith Willson ("Music Man") songs and lots of hokey, good-natured fun. **128m/C; VHS, DVD, Blu-Ray.** Debbie Reynolds; Harve Presnell; Ed Begley, Sr.; Martita Hunt; Hermione Baddeley; ***D:*** Charles Walters; ***C:*** Daniel F. Fapp; ***M:*** Meredith Willson.

Unspeakable 1/2 **2000** James (Cline) and Alice Fhelleps have a nasty, unsatisfying marriage until a car accident turns their life together into a true horror. From that premise, Chad Ferrin spins out a relatively realistic tale of madness and murder. For hard-core horror fans only. **81m/C; DVD.** Robert Cline; Timothy Muskatell; Tina Birchfield; Wolf Dangler; ***D:*** Chad Ferrin; ***W:*** Chad Ferrin; ***C:*** Nicholas Loizides.

Unspeakable 1/2 **2002 (R)** A shrink is sickened when her fancy-pants mind machine shows lots of icky and—could it be—

inhuman stuff going on inside the serial killer's head. Things get funky when he flies the coop after outlasting the electric chair, making the hotheaded warden (Hopper) lose face (really). **109m/C; VHS, DVD.** Michele J. Wolff; Marco Rodriguez; Dina Meyer; Lance Henriksen; Dennis Hopper; Luke McCoubrey; Jim Helton; Jonah Moran; Ron Pantane; Adam Zuckerman; ***D:*** Thomas J. Wright; ***W:*** Luke McCoubrey; ***C:*** Antonio Calvache; ***M:*** Jeff Marsh. **VIDEO**

The Unspeakable Act 🦴🦴 **2013** This drama, the fourth feature by filmmaker Dan Sallitt, explores the incestuous desire of a younger sister for her older brother. At 17, Jackie (Medel) has had sexual feelings for her older brother Matthew (Hirschkron) for years as the pair have been close friends and confidants. Jackie now feels more yearning as he gets ready for college and finds his first girlfriend, Yolanda (Mehner). Longing to retain her childhood fantasies though aware of her brother's sexual disinterest in her, Jackie does all she can to not lose the connection to the world she desires. After Matthew leaves, she learns to face life on her own and meet more available boys. **91m/C; DVD.** Tallie Medel; Sky Hirschkron; Aundrea Fares; Katie Schwartz; Caitlin Mehner; ***D:*** Dan Sallitt; ***W:*** Dan Sallitt; ***C:*** Duraid Munajim.

Unstoppable 🦴🦴🦴 *Imparable* **2010 (PG-13)** The title sums up the pairing of the always-reliable Washington and dynamic Pine, crafted by director Scott, the master of mind-blowing, nonstop (literally) action—splendidly created without relying much on CGI. And it lives up to its name. As an unmanned freight train carrying toxic chemicals gets cut loose in Pennsylvania, it's up to veteran engineer Frank (Washington) and inexperienced conductor Will (Pine) to somehow get the brakes on before disaster strikes. Based in part on actual events, it marks the fifth outing (to date) for the Washington and Scott team. **98m/C; Blu-Ray.** Denzel Washington; Chris Pine; Rosario Dawson; Kevin Chapman; Ethan Suplee; Kevin Dunn; Kevin Corrigan; ***D:*** Tony Scott; ***W:*** Mark Bomback; ***C:*** Ben Seresin; ***M:*** Harry Gregson-Williams.

Unstrung Heroes 🦴🦴 1/2 **1995 (PG)** Semi-autobiographical tale of Steven Lidz (Watt), growing up in 1960s California with a mother who is dying of cancer (MacDowell) and a nutty professor-type father (Turturro) who refuses to accept her illness. A desperate Steven goes to live with his two oddball uncles (Richards and Chaykin) who provide understanding and insight for the youngster, as well as a new name, Franz. Moving and quirky without being sappy, Keaton's feature debut avoids what would've been easy stereotypes. Based on the autobiography by Franz Lidz. **93m/C; VHS, DVD, Blu-Ray.** Andie MacDowell; John Turturro; Michael Richards; Maury Chaykin; Nathan Watt; Kendra Krull; ***D:*** Diane Keaton; ***W:*** Richard LaGravenese; ***C:*** Phedon Papamichael; ***M:*** Thomas Newman.

The Unsuspected 🦴🦴 1/2 **1947** Complicated noir-thriller involving murder, blackmail, amnesia, and an inheritance. Rains is appropriately suave and creepy as Victor Grandison, the host of a successful crime-mystery radio program. Of course it's because Victor is a murderous crazy who is planning to take over the inheritance of allegedly dead niece Matilda (Caulfield). Matilda makes a surprising return to her home, temporarily thwarting Victor, who must also alter his plans when suspicious Steven Howard (North) becomes involved after Steven's friend (and Grandison's secretary) is found dead. **103m/B; DVD.** Claude Rains; Joan Caulfield; Ted North; Audrey Trotter; Hurd Hatfield; Constance Bennett; Fred Clark; Jack Lambert; ***D:*** Michael Curtiz; ***W:*** Ranald MacDougall; ***C:*** Elwood "Woody" Bredell; ***M:*** Franz Waxman.

Untamable Angelique 🦴🦴 1/2 *Indomptable Angelique* **1967** The fourth in the series, following "Angelique and the King." Angelique learns that Joffrey is alive and leaves the court to find him, but her ship is attacked by pirates. Angelique jumps overboard without knowing that the pirate chief is Joffrey in disguise. She's rescued by d'Escrainville (Pigaut) but when she refuses his advances he threatens to sell her at the Candia slave market. Followed by "Angelique and the Sultan." French with subtitles. **95m/C; DVD.** *FR* Michele Mercier; Robert Hossein; Roger Pigaut; Ettore Manni; Bruno Dietrich; ***D:*** Bernard Borderie; ***W:*** Francis Cosne; ***C:*** Henri Persin; ***M:*** Michel Magne.

Untamed 🦴🦴 **1929** Crawford's first starring role in a talkie is as oil heiress Bingo, who was raised in a South American jungle by her recently deceased dad and two guardians, Ben (Torrence) and Howard (Herbert). The men think Bingo needs some city polishing and head to New York. Before long, she's on the prowl in Manhattan, ready to bag penniless Andy McAllister (Montgomery). But a guy's got his pride and he won't marry Bingo until he can support her. **86m/B; DVD.** Joan Crawford; Robert Montgomery; Ernest Torrence; Holmes Herbert; John Miljan; Gwen Lee; ***D:*** Jack Conway; ***W:*** Frank Butler; Sylvia Thalberg; Willard Mack; ***C:*** Oliver Marsh.

Untamed 🦴🦴 1/2 **1955** Hayward undergoes many tribulations as 1850s Irish lass Katie Kildare. When the potatoe famine hits Ireland Katie and husband Shawn emigrate to South Africa as homesteaders. Shawn is quickly killed in a Zulu attack and Katie makes a play for her first love, Paul (Power), who's too busy fighting for a Dutch Free State for romance. Her shifty foreman Kurt (Ehan) likes the missus but he becomes an outlaw. Diamond mines are also involved (as are babies). It's CinemaScope malarkey with some good action sequences. **111m/C; DVD, Blu-Ray.** Susan Hayward; Tyrone Power; Richard Egan; John Justin; Agnes Moorehead; Rita Moreno; ***D:*** Henry King; ***W:*** Talbot Jennings; Frank Fenton; Michael Blankfort; ***C:*** Leo Tover; ***M:*** Franz Waxman.

Untamed Heart 🦴🦴 1/2 **1993 (PG-13)** Adam (Slater), the painfully shy busboy with a heart condition, loves Caroline (Tomei), the bubbly waitress, from afar. She doesn't notice him until he saves her from some would-be rapists and their love blooms in the coffee shop where they both work. Tomei and Slater are both strong in the leads and Perez, as Caroline's best buddy Cindy, hurls comic barbs with ease. Charmingly familiar surroundings help set this formulaic romance apart. Filmed on location in Minneapolis. **102m/C; VHS, DVD, Blu-Ray.** Christian Slater; Marisa Tomei; Rosie Perez; Kyle Secor; Willie Garson; ***D:*** Tony Bill; ***W:*** Tom Sierchio; ***C:*** Jost Vacano; ***M:*** Cliff Eidelman. MTV Movie Awards '93: Kiss (Christian Slater/Marisa Tomei), Most Desirable Male (Slater).

Untamed Love 🦴🦴 **1994** Troubled six-year-old Caitlin's violent behavior (due to abuse) is going to have her institutionalized unless a proper program can be found to help her. Special education teacher Maggie finally seems to be the one that can reach the young girl. Lifetime drama. **92m/C; DVD.** Cathy Lee Crosby; Ashley Laurence; John Getz; Gary Frank; ***D:*** Paul Aaron; ***W:*** Peter W. Nelson; ***C:*** James Glennon; ***M:*** James Di Pasquale. **CABLE**

Untamed Women 🦴 **1952** Cheap lost world pic with fur-clad babes, stock footage dinosaurs, an erupting volcano (more stock footage), cavemen, and four survivors of a military plane crash. They wash up on an uncharted island and Captain Steve Holloway (Conrad) relates their story (in flashbacks) after he's later found on a raft drifting in the ocean. **70m/B; DVD.** Mikel Conrad; Doris Merrick; Richard Monahan; Mark Lowell; Morgan Jones; Judy Brubaker; Midge Ware; Lyle Talbot; ***D:*** W. Merle Connell; ***W:*** George Wallace Sayre; ***C:*** Glen Gano; ***M:*** Raoul Kraushaar.

Untamed Youth 🦴 1/2 **1957** Campy '50s rock 'n' roll youth exploitation flick finds sisters Penny (Van Doren) and Janey (Nelson) arrested in the rural south for hitchhiking and vagrancy. It's all a scam to get them sentenced to a prison farm, which means free labor for head man Tropp's (Russell) cotton-picking operation. Apparently the teens do find the time to bop around to the juke box, with Van Doren's jiggling physical assets on notable display. **80m/B; DVD.** Mamie Van Doren; Lori Nelson; John Russell; Lurene Tuttle; Eddie Cochran; Don Burnett; ***D:*** Howard W. Koch; ***W:*** John C. Higgins; ***C:*** Carl Guthrie; ***M:*** Les Baxter.

Unthinkable 🦴🦴 1/2 **2007** True crime story. Police detective Jamie McDowell (Forbes) still tries to run the life of her 19-year-old son Peter (Grayhm). She opposes his impulsive proposal to Kelly (Levesque), the daughter of her best friend Susan (Hayward), who doesn't approve either. When Kelly dies in an arson fire, her violent ex, Ray (Kosakoski), is first blamed but Jamie realizes the evidence is pointing in Peter's direction instead. **90m/C; DVD.** Michelle Forbes; Steven Grayhm; Elyse Levesque; Rachel Hayward; Graham Kosakoski; Garry Chalk; Philip Granger; Jerry Wasserman; ***D:*** Keoni Waxman; ***W:*** Richard Leder; ***C:*** Eric Goldstein; ***M:*** Jerry Lambert; Harry Manfredini. **CABLE**

Unthinkable 🦴 **2010 (R)** Do the ends justify the means, especially when the means are extreme torture? Nuclear expert turned terrorist Steven Arthur Younger (Sheen) is captured by the FBI after he says he's planted three nuclear bombs in three U.S. cities. Since he refuses to talk, black ops interrogator Henry Humphries (Jackson) is called in to use any means necessary to get the locations. Big ideas but little follows through. **97m/C; DVD.** Samuel L. Jackson; Michael Sheen; Carrie-Anne Moss; Martin Donovan; Brandon Routh; Gil Bellows; Vincent Laresca; Stephen (Steve) Root; ***D:*** Gregor Jordon; ***W:*** Peter Woodward; ***C:*** Oliver Stapleton; ***M:*** Graeme Revell. **VIDEO**

Until September 🦴🦴 **1984 (R)** An American tourist becomes stranded in Paris. She meets and falls in love with a married banker while she is stuck in her hotel. Routine romance. **96m/C; VHS, DVD.** Karen Allen; Thierry Lhermitte; Christopher Cazenove; Johanna Pavlis; ***D:*** Richard Marquand; ***M:*** John Barry.

Until the End of the World 🦴🦴🦴 1/2 *Bis ans Ende der Welt; Jusqu'au Bout du Monde* **1991 (R)** Convoluted road movie set in 1999 follows the travails of Sam Farber (Hurt) through 15 cities in eight countries on four continents as he is chased by Dommartin, her lover (Neill), a bounty hunter, a private detective, and bank robbers, until all wind up in the Australian outback. And this is only the first half of the movie. For true cinematic satisfaction, don't expect logic—just go with the flow. Visually stunning, unexpectedly humorous, with excellent performances from an international cast. Footage created with high definition (HDTV) video technology is a technological first. The soundtrack features Lou Reed, David Byrne, U2, and others. **158m/C; VHS, Blu-Ray, Streaming.** *AU GE FR* William Hurt; Solveig Dommartin; Sam Neill; Max von Sydow; Ruediger Vogler; Ernie Dingo; Jeanne Moreau; David Gulpilil; ***D:*** Wim Wenders; ***W:*** Wim Wenders; Peter Carey; ***C:*** Robby Muller; ***M:*** Graeme Revell.

Until They Sail 🦴🦴 1/2 **1957** Soap opera set in New Zealand during WWII. Plot centers around the lives of four sisters involved in love and murder. Dee's film debut. Based on a story by James Michener. **95m/B; VHS, DVD.** Jean Simmons; Joan Fontaine; Paul Newman; Piper Laurie; Charles Drake; Sandra Dee; Wally Cassell; Alan Napier; ***D:*** Robert Wise; ***W:*** Robert Anderson.

(Untitled) 🦴🦴 **2009 (R)** Parker offers an absurdist look at the contemporary New York art and music scenes and the differences between commerce and personal expression. Humorless Adrian (Goldberg) is a self-important avant-garde composer and his brother Josh (Bailey) is a superficial commercially-successful artist. Adrian begrudges his brother's success, especially since Adrian himself is neither successful nor a particularly good composer. However, ambitious Chelsea art gallery owner Madeleine (Shelton) commissions Adrian for a performance piece to be played during an exhibition by pretentious bad boy Brit Ray (Jones) and his luck may finally change. **96m/C; Blu-Ray, On Demand.** Adam Goldberg; Marley Shelton; Eion Bailey; Vinnie Jones; Lucy Punch; Zak Orth; Michael Panes; Janet Carroll; Ben Hammer; Ptolemy Slocum; ***D:*** Jonathan Parker; ***W:*** Jonathan Parker; Catherine Di Napoli; ***C:*** Svetlana Cvetko; ***M:*** David Lang.

Untogether 🦴 1/2 **2019 (R)** In Los Angeles, one-time successful author Andrea (J. Kirke) is attached to her lover Nick (Dornan), who has published a popular memoir about his experiences as a volunteer in Gaza. Newly sober Andrea also struggles with the potential loss of her creative spark. Elsewhere in L.A., Andrea's sister Tara (L. Kirke) is involved with Martin (Mendelsohn), who wants to revive his creativity by going back to his grunge rock days. Seeking her own meaning, Tara is impressed by an activist rabbi (Crystal). A rambling story that gets lost along the way, it mainly serves as a study of unappealing characters. **98m/C; DVD.** Jamie Dornan; Lola Kirke; Jemima Kirke; Ben Mendelsohn; Billy Crystal; ***D:*** Emma Forest; ***W:*** Emma Forest; ***C:*** Autumn Cheyenne Durald; ***M:*** Robin Foster.

The Untold Story of Emmett Louis Till 🦴🦴🦴 **2005 (PG-13)** Documentary was released to coincide with the 50th anniversary of the 1955 murder of Till, a 14-year-old African American from Chicago who went to visit his grandfather in Money, Mississippi, where he was tortured and killed for allegedly whistling at a white woman. Till's murder became a pivotal moment in the civil rights movement. The Justice Department reopened the case when new evidence came to light, thanks to the years-long investigation of director Beauchamp. Includes TV and newsreel footage and numerous interviews. **70m/C; DVD.** ***D:*** Keith Beauchamp; ***C:*** Rondrick Cowins; Sikay Tang; ***M:*** Jim Papoulis.

The Untouchables 🦴🦴🦴 1/2 **1987 (R)** Big-budget, fast-paced, and exciting re-evaluation of the popular TV series about the real-life battle between Treasury officer Eliot Ness (Costner) and crime boss Al Capone (De Niro) in 1920s Chicago. History sometimes takes a back seat to Hollywood's imagination in the screenplay, but it doesn't really matter since there are splendid performances by De Niro and Connery as Ness' mentor Jimmy Malone to help it look realistic. Costner does a fine job showing the change in Ness from naive idealism to steely conviction. Beautifully filmed with excellent special effects. Note DePalma's long train station/baby carriage scene that's an homage to the 1925 silent Russian classic, "Battleship Potemkin." **119m/C; VHS, DVD, Blu-Ray, HD-DVD.** Kevin Costner; Sean Connery; Robert De Niro; Andy Garcia; Charles Martin Smith; Billy Drago; Richard Bradford; Jack Kehoe; ***D:*** Brian De Palma; ***W:*** David Mamet; ***C:*** Stephen Burum; ***M:*** Ennio Morricone. Oscars '87: Support. Actor (Connery); Golden Globes '88: Support. Actor (Connery); Natl. Bd. of Review '87: Support. Actor (Connery).

Untraceable 🦴 1/2 **2008 (R)** Agent Jennifer Marsh (Lane) is an FBI "cybercrime" expert who must find a killer whose elaborate, torturous murders are broadcast live on the Internet. The twist? The more hits the killer's website gets, the faster he kills his victims. Eventually, Marsh must work to stop the killer and protect her own family as well. Cynical movie that aspires to condemn people's love of exploitative violence while serving up lots of violent exploitation without a shred of irony to redeem it. **100m/C; Blu-Ray.** Diane Lane; Billy Burke; Colin Hanks; Joseph Cross; Mary Beth Hurt; Ty(rone) Giordano; Perla Haney-Jardine; Peter Lewis; Tim De Zarn; ***D:*** Gregory Hoblit; ***W:*** Allison Burnett; Robert Fyvolent; Mark R. Brinker; ***C:*** Anastas Michos; ***M:*** Christopher Young.

Unwed Mother 🦴 **1958** Oh the exploitative teenage drama! Innocent young Betty (Moore) moves to L.A. and is seduced by cad Don (Vaughn). She gets preggers and he promises to marry her but leaves her to fend for herself instead. (The louse!) Betty decides to give the baby up for adoption but isn't sure about her decision. **74m/B; DVD.** Norma Moore; Robert Vaughn; Diana Darrin; Billie Bird; Jeanne Cooper; ***D:*** Walter Doniger; ***W:*** Anson Bond; ***C:*** Lothrop Worth; ***M:*** Emil Newman.

Unzipped 🦴🦴🦴 **1994 (R)** Witty, behind-the-scenes look at whiz-kid fashion designer Isaac Mizrahi as he prepares for the showing of his 1994 collection. Alternately filmed in black-and-white and color in a variety of film stocks, Keeve (Mizrahi's former lover) captures Mizrahi's varying moods, from his creative struggles to his unique sense of humor and gift for mimicry. Highlights include scenes with Mizrahi's doting mother. Fashionphiles will love every minute, and strictly off-the-rack viewers can enjoy the supermodels on parade. **76m/C; VHS, DVD.** ***D:*** Douglas Keeve; ***C:*** Ellen Kuras. Sundance '95: Aud. Award.

Up 🦴🦴🦴 1/2 **2009 (PG)** In Pixar's stunning 10th animated adventure (the first in 3-D), grumpy 78-year-old widower Carl Fredricksen (Asner), a retired balloon salesman, ties thousands of helium balloons to his house so it will be able to float. Carl wants to fulfill the lifelong dream of his late wife by traveling to Paradise Falls in South America in the footsteps of his discredited explorer hero Charles F. Muntz (Plummer). However, he doesn't expect to have a stowaway—enthusiastic eight-year-old Russell (Nagai), who thinks his experience as a Junior Wilderness Explorer will come in handy. Carl and Russell find a gawky bird and some talking dogs, an odd-couple friendship, and a lot of action. **96m/C; Blu-Ray.** ***V:*** Ed Asner; Jordan Nagai; Christopher Plummer; John Ratzenberger; Delroy Lindo; Bob Peterson; Jerome Ranft; ***D:*** Pete Docter; Bob Peterson; ***W:*** Bob Peterson; ***C:*** Patick Lin; ***M:*** Michael Giacchino. Oscars '09: Animated Film, Orig. Score; British Acad. '09: Animated Film, Orig. Score; Golden Globes '10: Animated Film, Orig. Score.

Up Against the Eight Ball 1/2 **2004 (R)** Best friends Monique (Dahl) and Krista (La'Shawn) need money for their last year of college tuition. So they take their pool-hustling skills to a tournament in Vegas with various troubles (romantic and otherwise) accompanying them. Way too predictable in a you-go-girl way. **90m/C; VHS, DVD.** Kym E. Whitley; Iva La'Shawn; Tawny Dahl; Jay Cooper; T. Ashanti Mozelle; ***D:*** Miguel A. Nunez, Jr.; Troy Curvey, Jr.; ***W:*** Keith Sagoes. **VIDEO**

Up and Down *Horem Padem* **2004 (R)** Overstuffed character drama begins with a couple of Czech lowlifes who are transporting a group of illegal immigrants from India. They discover a baby has been left behind in their truck, which they sell to a pawnshop owner who in turn sells the infant to a desperate childless couple who change their lives (breaking off from their hooligan friends) to try starting over as a family. Then there's a second scenario involving a man who's visiting his divorced parents for the first time in 20 years (he'd immigrated to Australia). Martin discovers that his dad lives with Martin's ex-girlfriend and they have an 18-year-old daughter. This makes for a very awkward family lunch, which includes Martin's resentful (and racist) mother. Czech with subtitles. **108m/C; DVD.** Jan Triska; Jaroslav Dusek; Petr Forman; Emilia Vasaryova; Jiri Machacek; Natasa Burger; Ingrid Timkova; Kristyna Liska-Bokova; Pavel Liska; Marek Daniel; Jan Budar; Zdenek Suchy; ***Cameo(s):*** Vaclav Havel; ***D:*** Jan Hrebejk; ***W:*** Jan Hrebejk; ***C:*** Jan Malir; ***M:*** Ales Brezina.

Up at the Villa 1/2 **2000 (PG-13)** The British and American expatriate community in 1938 Florence is the setting for the unlikely romantic travails of respectable British widow Mary Panton (Scott Thomas). She is courted by longtime (and older) friend/diplomat Sir Edgar (Fox) who will offer her a comfortable if dull life in India. But at a party, Mary is paired off with confident American Rowley Flint (Penn), who must unexpectedly help Mary out of a jam involving a dead body. However, politics also plays its part with the rise of fascism. Scott Thomas and Penn may not have any romantic sparks but they do well individually and Bancroft is an amusing scene stealer as a wealthy socialite. Based on a novella by W. Somerset Maugham. **115m/C; VHS, DVD.** *GB* Kristin Scott Thomas; Sean Penn; Anne Bancroft; Derek Jacobi; Jeremy Davies; James Fox; Massimo Ghini; ***D:*** Philip Haas; ***W:*** Belinda Haas; ***C:*** Maurizio Calvesi; ***M:*** Pino Donaggio.

Up Close and Personal **1996 (PG-13)** Ambitious Reno card dealer Tally Atwater (Pfeiffer) wants to get into broadcasting and finds her chance at a Miami TV station where she's mentored by successful veteran-reporter-turned-producer Warren Justice (Redford). They fall in love but find their careers clashing as Tally climbs the media success ladder. Originally inspired by the tragic life of NBC reporter Jessica Savitch, whose problems with drugs and abusive relationships led to a sad ending, film turned into a star-powered romance with media trappings and another variation of "A Star is Born." It's now "suggested" by Alanna Nash's book "Golden Girl." **124m/C; VHS, DVD.** Michelle Pfeiffer; Robert Redford; Kate Nelligan; Stockard Channing; Joe Mantegna; Glenn Plummer; James Rebhorn; Noble Willingham; Scott Bryce; Raymond Cruz; Dedee Pfeiffer; Miguel (Michael) Sandoval; James Karen; ***D:*** Jon Avnet; ***W:*** Joan Didion; John Gregory Dunne; ***C:*** Karl Walter Lindenlaub; ***M:*** Thomas Newman.

Up for Grabs 1/2 **2005** The story of the controversy over ownership of Barry Bonds's record-setting homer is actually more interesting than all the hype leading up to the history-making hit. Following the frenzied scramble for the ball, two men stepped forward into the spotlight—one with the ball and the other claiming he had caught the ball only to have it ripped from his hand in the ensuing struggle. Using news footage of the event as well as eyewitness accounts, documentarian Michael Wranovics shines a light on the absurd clash, which ends up with the two parties in court. **88m/C; DVD.** ***D:*** Michael Wranovics; ***W:*** Michael Wranovics; ***C:*** Zack Richard; Josh Keppel.

Up from the Depths 1/2 **1979 (R)** Something from beneath the ocean is turning the paradise of Hawaii into a nightmare. Prehistoric fish are returning to the surface with one thing on their minds—lunch. "Jaws" rip-off played for humor. **85m/C; VHS, DVD, Blu-Ray.** Sam Bottoms; Suzanne Reed; Virgil Frye; ***D:*** Charles B. Griffith; ***W:*** Alfred Sweeney; ***M:*** James Horner.

Up Goes Maisie **1946** MGM's "Maisie" series (this is the ninth entry) was not only getting tired, it was getting more and more silly. Maisie (Sothern) graduates from business school and takes a secretarial job with inventor Joseph Morton (Murphy), who's working on a revolutionary helicopter design. A rival aircraft manufacturer is out to sabotage or steal Morton's work and it all ends with Maisie taking the controls and flying over L.A. to land the craft in the Pasadena Rose Bowl! **89m/B; DVD.** Ann Sothern; George Murphy; Hillary Brooke; Paul Harvey; Stephen McNally; Ray Collins; Jeff York; ***D:*** Harry Beaumont; ***W:*** Thelma Robinson; ***C:*** Robert Planck; ***M:*** David Snell.

Up in Arms **1944** Danny Kaye's first film presents a typical Kaye scenario: he plays a twitching hypochondriac who is drafted into the Army and sneaks his girlfriend aboard the troopship bound for the Pacific. Features an appearance by the Goldwyn Girls. Remake of the film "The Nervous Wreck." **105m/C; DVD.** Danny Kaye; Dinah Shore; Constance Dowling; Dana Andrews; Margaret Dumont; Lyle Talbot; Louis Calhern; ***D:*** Elliott Nugent; ***W:*** Allen Boretz; Robert Pirosh; Don Hartman; ***C:*** Ray Rennahan; ***M:*** Max Steiner.

Up in Central Park 1/2 **1948** Poor adaptation of the hit Broadway musical (the studio removed much of Romberg's score) about Irish immigrant lass Rosie Moore (Durbin), who teams up with New York reporter John Matthews (Haymes) to expose corrupt politician Boss Tweed (Price). Without the songs, the plot is shown to be wafer-thin. **88m/B; DVD.** Deanna Durbin; Dick Haymes; Vincent Price; Albert Sharpe; Tom Powers; Hobart Cavanaugh; Thurston Hall; ***D:*** William A. Seiter; ***W:*** Dorothy Fields; Herbert Fields; Karl Tunberg; ***C:*** Milton Krasner; ***M:*** Sigmund Romberg.

Up in the Air **2009 (R)** Corporate downsizer Ryan Bingham (Clooney) attributes his commitment phobia to his work, though he seems naturally inclined to distancing himself from too many messy human emotions. Bingham loves his airport life and is deeply offended when his boss (Bateman) pairs him with young go-getter Natalie (Kendrick) whose big idea is to fire people via the Internet. Then Ryan gets distracted by the more mature beauty and wit of fellow traveler Alex (Farmiga), who's equally amenable to no-strings sex. Clooney is made for this role—a debonair, intelligent if somewhat ruthless, man who's become complacent until he finds his own working life threatened, which leads to some midlife questioning. Thankfully, writer/director Reitman refrains from mawkishness and expected changes. Adapted from Walter Kirn's 2002 novel. **109m/C; Blu-Ray, On Demand.** George Clooney; Vera Farmiga; Jason Bateman; Melanie Lynskey; Anna Kendrick; Danny McBride; Chris Lowell; Amy Morton; Sam Elliott; Zach Galifianakis; J.K. Simmons; ***D:*** Jason Reitman; ***W:*** Jason Reitman; Sheldon Turner; ***C:*** Eric Steelberg; ***M:*** Rolfe Kent. British Acad. '09: Adapt. Screenplay; Golden Globes '10: Screenplay; Writers Guild '09: Adapt. Screenplay.

Up Periscope 1/2 **1959** Garner is a demolitions expert unwillingly assigned to a submarine commanded by O'Brien. His mission: to sneak onto a Japanese-held island and steal a top-secret code book. Trouble is, O'Brien may not wait for Garner to complete his mission before taking the sub back underwater. A routine submarine film. **111m/C; VHS, DVD.** James Garner; Edmond O'Brien; Andra Martin; Alan Hale, Jr.; Carleton Carpenter; Frank Gifford; Richard Bakalyan; ***D:*** Gordon Douglas.

Up the Academy *Mad Magazine's Up the Academy; The Brave Young Men of Weinberg* **1980 (R)** Four teenaged delinquents are sent to an academy for wayward boys where they encounter a sadistic headmaster and a gay dance instructor. Sometimes inventive, often tasteless fare from "Mad" magazine. **88m/C; VHS, DVD.** Ron Leibman; Ralph Macchio; Barbara Bach; Tom Poston; Stacey Nelkin; Wendell Brown; Tom Citera; ***D:*** Robert Downey.

Up the Creek 1/2 **1984 (R)** Four college losers enter a whitewater raft race to gain some respect for their school. The soundtrack features songs by Heart, Cheap Trick and The Beach Boys. Routine. **95m/C; VHS, DVD, Blu-Ray.** Tim Matheson; Jennifer Runyon; Stephen Furst; John Hillerman; James B. Sikking; Julia Montgomery; Jeana Tomasina; ***D:*** Robert Butler; ***M:*** William Goldstein.

Up the Down Staircase **1967** A naive, newly trained New York public school teacher is determined to teach the finer points of English literature to a group of poor students. She almost gives up until one student actually begins to learn. Good production and acting. Based on Bel Kaufman's novel. **124m/C; VHS, DVD.** Sandy Dennis; Patrick Bedford; Eileen Heckart; Ruth White; Jean Stapleton; Sorrell Booke; ***D:*** Robert Mulligan.

Up the Junction 1/2 **1968** Dreary, manipulative Brit drama. Bored Polly leaves her comfortable life in Chelsea to go slumming in depressed Battersea. She finds a factory job, a flat, and a boyfriend who wants the good life Polly's left behind. A subplot involved Polly's friendship with sisters Rube and Sylvie and Rube's illegal abortion. **119m/C; DVD, Blu-Ray.** *UK* Suzy Kendall; Dennis Waterman; Adrienne Posta; Maureen Lipman; Michael Gothard; ***D:*** Peter Collinson; ***W:*** Roger Smith; ***C:*** Arthur Lavis; ***M:*** Manfred Mann; Mike Hugg.

Up the Ladder **1925** Presumably that's the ladder of success. Heiress Jane Cornwall (Valli) secretly finances her boyfriend James Van Clinton's (Stanley) latest invention: a telephone that allows both parties to see each other while talking. When it's a success, Jane and James get married. After a few years James gets bored and messes things up. **70m/B; Silent; DVD.** Virginia Valli; Forrest Stanley; Margaret Livingston; Holmes Herbert; Priscilla Moran; George Fawcett; ***D:*** Edward Sloman; ***W:*** Grant Carpenter; Tom McNamara; ***C:*** Jackson Rose.

Up the River 1/2 **1930** Tracy's film debut as convict St. Louis. He breaks out of jail with sidekick Dan (Hymer) and the two go their separate ways but can't keep out of trouble. They wind up back in the joint, this time sharing a cell with rich boy Steve (Bogart). Steve gets blackmailed after his release and his two prison buddies break out again to come to his aid. Ford reworked the original dramatic script into a comedy and shot the film in two weeks. **90m/B; DVD.** Spencer Tracy; Warren Hymer; Humphrey Bogart; Morgan Wallace; Robert Emmett O'Connor; Clare Luce; Joan Lawes; ***D:*** John Ford; ***W:*** Maurine Watkins; William "Buster" Collier, Jr.; ***C:*** Joseph August.

Up the Sandbox **1972 (R)** A bored housewife fantasizes about her life in order to avoid facing her mundane existence. Fine acting from Streisand, with real problems of young mothers accurately shown. **98m/C; VHS, DVD.** Barbra Streisand; David Selby; Jane Hoffman; Barbara Rhoades; ***D:*** Irvin Kershner; ***W:*** Paul Zindel; ***C:*** Gordon Willis; ***M:*** Billy Goldenberg.

Upgrade 1/2 **2018 (R)** Writer-director Leigh Whannell upgrades the entire revenge thriller genre by delivering a flick that's fast, fresh, fun, and flinchingly violent. Grey Trace, crippled in an attack that killed his wife, receives an implant called Stem that enables him to perform superhuman physical feats in his quest for vengeance. Gleefully gory with a surprisingly intelligent subtext. **100m/C; DVD, Blu-Ray.** Logan Marshall-Green; Betty Gabriel; Harrison Gilbertson; Benedict Hardie; Simon Maiden; ***D:*** Leigh Whannell; ***W:*** Leigh Whannell; ***C:*** Stefan Duscio; ***M:*** Jed Palmer.

Upperworld *Upper World* **1934** Wealthy New Yorker Alexander Stream (William) takes up with burlesque dancer Lily (Rogers) since his society wife Hettie (Astor) has no time for him. Lily's sleazy boss Lou (Naish) thinks he can blackmail the married man but there's a couple of shootings and Stream winds up in big trouble after trying to cover up his involvement. This leads to a trial and an ending that feels forced. **72m/B; DVD.** Warren William; Mary Astor; Ginger Rogers; J. Carrol Naish; Sidney Toler; Dickie Moore; Robert Barrat; Andy Devine; ***D:*** Roy Del Ruth; ***W:*** Ben Markson; ***C:*** Gaetano Antonio "Tony" Gaudio.

Uprising **2001** Well-done, realistic miniseries depicts the Warsaw Ghetto uprising of 1943, when Polish Jews, facing deportation to death camps, held off the Nazis for a month using guerilla tactics. Solid script, which avoids melodrama and over-sentimentality, leaves room to show the politics and motivations involved between the people who wanted to negotiate with the Nazis, those who collaborated for self-preservation, and the fighters. Though the whole cast is up to the task, Sobieski's performance stands out, and Schwimmer makes a better showing here than he did in "Band of Brothers." **177m/C; VHS, DVD.** Leelee Sobieski; Hank Azaria; David Schwimmer; Jon Voight; Donald Sutherland; Cary Elwes; Stephen Moyer; Sadie Frost; Radha Mitchell; Mili Avital; Alexandra Holden; John Ales; Eric Lively; Jesper Christensen; ***D:*** Jon Avnet; ***W:*** Jon Avnet; Paul Brickman; ***C:*** Denis Lenoir; ***M:*** Maurice Jarre. **TV**

The Upside **2017 (PG-13)** Dell (Hart) is on parole and needs to prove he is at least looking for a job. Fate intervenes when he finds himself in the same elevator as Phillip (Cranston), a wheelchair-bound multi-millionaire who needs 24-hour care after an accident. Though Dell is not qualified, Phillips likes his attitude and immediately hires him. As the pair spends time together, they are exposed to unexpected life experiences. This American remake of the 2011 hit French film "The Intouchables" falls short of the warmth of the original as well as the true story of the men involved, compounded by the lack of chemistry between Cranston and Hart. **126m/C; DVD.** Kevin Hart; Bryan Cranston; Nicole Kidman; Aja Naomi King; Jahi Di'Allo Winston; ***D:*** Neil Burger; ***W:*** Jon Hartmere; ***C:*** Stuart Dryburgh; ***M:*** Rob Simonsen.

Upside Down 1/2 **2013 (PG-13)** Adam (Sturgess) and Eden (Dunst) live on twinned worlds that pull in opposite directions. In other words, they're literally above and below one another, which makes their Romeo & Juliet love story even harder to pull off. Is love stronger than gravity? Such is the question of this pretty damn silly sci-fi romance, a movie with two engaging leads and a commitment to its out there concept but a story so straight-up stupid (and dialogue to match) that one can't really get invested in it for a second. Echoes of The Adjustment Bureau without the smart script that made that film work. **100m/C; DVD, Blu-Ray.** Jim Sturgess; Kirsten Dunst; Timothy Spall; ***D:*** Juan Diego Solanas; ***W:*** Juan Diego Solanas; ***C:*** Pierre Gill; ***M:*** Benoit Charest.

The Upside of Anger **2005 (R)** Allen gives new meaning to the term ferocious as betrayed suburban Detroit wife Terry Wolfmeyer. Her husband has apparently left Terry and their four beautiful daughters (Witt, Christensen, Russell, Wood) for his secretary. Terry takes to alcohol, anger, and rebellion while the girls run the household. When neighbor Denny (Costner) finds out about her plight, he's eager to make Terry a drinking buddy and possible romantic partner. Genial Denny, who's bored and lonely, is a retired Detroit Tigers pitcher turned radio talk show host. (He's also entranced by the sheer femaleness of the Wolfmeyer home.) There's a certain comfortable, angsty camaraderie to the whole situation that's appealing. Writer/director Binder also takes a small role as Denny's lecherous producer. **118m/C; DVD.** Joan Allen; Kevin Costner; Erika Christensen; Evan Rachel Wood; Keri Russell; Alicia Witt; Mike Binder; Dane Christensen; Holt McCallany; ***D:*** Mike Binder; ***W:*** Mike Binder; ***C:*** Richard Greatrex; ***M:*** Alexandre Desplat; Stephen (Steve) Edwards.

Upstairs and Downstairs **1959** Ambitious young executive Richard works for bride Kate's father and the newlyweds are expected to entertain business clients. Dad suggests they hire some domestic help but they have terrible luck until blonde, Swedish Ingrid comes along. She can do the job but her flirtatious attitude soon proves to be a problem. **90m/C; DVD.** *GB* Michael Craig; Anne Heywood; Mylene Demongeot; James Robertson Justice; Daniel Massey; Sidney James; Claudia Cardinale; Joan Sims; Joan Hickson; ***D:*** Ralph Thomas; ***W:*** Frank Harvey; ***C:*** Ernest Steward; ***M:*** Philip Green.

Upstairs Downstairs **1/2 2011** In this BBC sequel to the 1970s series it's 1936 and 165 Eaton Place has long been unoccupied. The property is bought by diplomat Sir Hallam Holland (Stoppard) and his wife, Lady Agnes (Hawes). They need a staff and Lady Agnes hires Miss Rose Buck (Marsh), who comes back to her former home. The household expands with the arrival of Hallam's imperious mother Lady Maud (Atkins), returning from India with her Sikh secretary (Malik) and pet monkey. Lady Agnes invites her foolish younger sister Lady Persephone (Foy), who flirts with Nazism, causing problems for everyone. Oh yes, the servants have various difficulties as well. **180m/C; DVD.** *GB* Jean Marsh; Keeley Hawes; Ed Stoppard; Eileen Atkins; Claire Foy; Art Malik; Anne Reid; Adrian Scarborough; Ellie Kendrick; Neil Jackson; Helen Bradbury; Alexia James; Blake Ritson; Anthony Calf; Edward Baker-Duly; ***D:*** Euros Lyn; Saul Metstein; ***W:*** Heidi Thomas; ***C:*** Adam Suschitzky; ***M:*** Daniel Pemberton. **TV**

Upstream Color **2013** Daring, inventive, and totally unique, director/writer/actor Carruth's festival hit challenges viewers to not interpret it but allow it to work more as beautiful poetry. Kris (Seimetz) is kidnapped and manipulated (via sci-fi mind control) to turn over her fortune before her essence is removed and transferred into the body of a pig. Yes, you read that right. As her life descends into turmoil, Kris meets Jeff (Carruth) and tries to regain a bit of her individuality and self-control. The plot is secondary to the spell that Carruth weaves with expert editing, perfect sound design, and gorgeous imagery. **96m/C; DVD, Blu-Ray.** Shane Carruth; Amy Seimetz; Andrew Sensenig; Thiago Martins; ***D:*** Shane Carruth; ***W:*** Shane Carruth; ***C:*** Shane Carruth; ***M:*** Shane Carruth.

Uptight **1968** This bleak story of betrayal is a remake of John Ford's "The Informer" (1935). Shortly after the assssination of Martin Luther King, hotheaded unemployed Cleveland steelworker Tank Williams (Mayfield) turns his wanted militant friend, Johnny (Julien), into the cops for a reward. This puts a price on Tank's head for being a snitch. **104m/C; DVD.** Julian Mayfield; Max Julien; Raymond St. Jacques; Roscoe Lee Browne; Juanita Moore; Ruby Dee; ***D:*** Jules Dassin; ***W:*** Julian Mayfield; Ruby Dee; Jules Dassin; ***C:*** Boris Kaufman; ***M:*** Booker T. Jones.

Uptown Girls **1/2 2003 (PG-13)** Cloying female buddy comedy pits a ditsy, down-on-her-luck socialite against an extremely precocious and well-off 8-year-old with annoying results. After her financial manager embezzles her inheritance, spoiled New York trust-fund kid Molly (Murphy) is forced to get a (shudder!) job. She becomes a nanny to young Ray (Fanning), who is largely abandoned by her record exec mum (Locklear in an especially unappealing performance). The two butt heads immediately, but through a series of uninspired events predictably do the role reversal bit—learning from each other how to act more their own ages. Murphy's performance is forced and just plain weird at times. Fanning holds her own against her flaky co-star and dismal script. **93m/C; VHS, DVD, Blu-Ray.** Brittany Murphy; Dakota Fanning; Heather Locklear; Donald Adeosun Faison; Marley Shelton; Austin Pendleton; Jesse Spencer; Polly Adams; ***D:*** Boaz Yakin; ***W:*** Mo Ogrodnik; Julia Dahl; Lisa Davidowitz; ***C:*** Michael Ballhaus; ***M:*** Joel McNeely.

Uptown New York **1932** A young man pressured by his family marries a rich girl instead of the woman he loves, who in turn marries a man she does not love. Routine melodrama. **81m/B; VHS, DVD.** Jack Oakie; Shirley Green; Leon Ames; Shirley Grey; George Cooper; Raymond Hatton; ***D:*** Victor Schertzinger.

Uptown Saturday Night **1/2 1974 (PG)** Two working men attempt to recover a stolen lottery ticket from the black underworld after being ripped off at an illegal gambling place. Good fun, with nice performances from both leads and from Belafonte doing a black "Godfather" parody of Brando. Followed by "Let's Do It Again." **104m/C; VHS, DVD.** Sidney Poitier; Bill Cosby; Harry Belafonte; Flip Wilson; Richard Pryor; Calvin Lockhart; ***D:*** Sidney Poitier; ***W:*** Richard Wesley; ***C:*** Fred W. Koenekamp.

The Upturned Glass **1/2 1947** Brooding crime melodrama told in flashbacks, with an unsatisfying ending and a nonsensical title. London brain surgeon Michael Joyce falls in love with married Emma Wright after saving the life of her young daughter. Unwilling to get caught in a scandal, they break their romance off. When Emma dies in a suspicious fall, Michael is certain she was murdered by jealous sister-in-law Kate and takes his revenge. **90m/B; DVD.** *GB* James Mason; Rosamund John; Pamela Kellino; Brefni O'Rorke; Ann Stephens; Jane Hylton; Morland Graham; ***D:*** Lawrence Huntington; ***W:*** Pamela Kellino; ***C:*** Reg Wyer; ***M:*** Bernard Stevens.

The Uranium Conspiracy **1/2** *Agenten Kennen Keine Tranen* **1978** A secret agent and a mercenary soldier try to stop a shipment of uranium out of Zaire from falling into enemy hands. It won't be easy. German with subtitles. **100m/C; VHS, DVD.** *GE IS IT* Fabio Testi; Janet Agren; Assi Dayan; Siegfried Rauch; Herbert (Fuchs) Fux; ***D:*** Gianfranco Baldanello; Menahem Golan; ***W:*** David Paulsen; August Rieger; ***C:*** Adam Greenberg; ***M:*** Coriolano Gori; Dov Seltzer.

Urban Country **2018** A family friendly drama about a city teen coming into her own in an unexpected environment. Faith (Sharbino) rebels against authority figures including her father (London) and high school principal (Howell). Because of her actions, she ends up in juvenile hall where she questions her life, especially after a visit from her estranged mother Anna (Barley). Upon her release, she visits her dying mother's ranch in Mississippi and they work to mend their relationship. Faith also finds new life with a ranch hand (Marroquin) and the horses that live there. The sincerity of director Smith's film makes for enjoyable viewing. **88m/C; DVD.** Brighton Sharbino; Lou Diamond Phillips; Jason London; Candice Michele Barley; Dean J. West; ***D:*** Teddy Smith; ***W:*** Gianna Montelaro; ***C:*** Teddy Smith; ***M:*** Andrew Morgan Smith.

Urban Cowboy **1/2 1980 (PG)** A young Texas farmer comes to Houston to work in a refinery. After work he hangs out at Gilley's, a roadhouse bar, where he and his friends drink, fight, and prove their manhood by riding a mechanical bull. Film made Winger a star, was an up in Travolta's roller coaster career, and began the craze for country western apparel and dance and them there mechanical bulls. Ride 'em, cowboy! **135m/C; VHS, DVD.** John Travolta; Debra Winger; Scott Glenn; Madolyn Smith; Barry Corbin; ***D:*** James Bridges; ***W:*** James Bridges; Aaron Latham; ***C:*** Reynaldo Villalobos; ***M:*** Ralph Burns.

Urban Crossfire **1/2 1994 (PG-13)** Two veteran white Brooklyn detectives investigating gang violence are aided by a young black patrolman whose partner was killed by a gang leader. Solid cast, fast paced action. **95m/C; VHS, DVD.** Mario Van Peebles; Ray Sharkey; Peter Boyle; Michael Boatman; ***D:*** Dick Lowry.

Urban Ghost Story **1998 (R)** Saddled with guilt after surviving a car wreck that killed her friend, 12-year-old Lizzie suspects that her near-death experience released a nasty ghost that's purposely tormenting her. When no one believes her, her mom enlists the aid of a journalist to prove Lizzie's claims—which only makes life worse as a gaggle of scientists and voyeurs swarm their grungy Glasgow home. **82m/C; VHS, DVD.** Jason Connery; Stephanie Buttle; Heather Ann Foster; Nicola Stapleton; James Cosmo; Elizabeth Berrington; Siri Neal; Andreas Wisniewski; Kenneth Bryans; Carolyn Bonnyman; Alan Owen; Stephen MacDonald; Julie Austin; Nicola Greene; Nick Von Schlippe; David Haddow; Richard Syms; Andy McEwan; Aaron White; Joss Castell-Gydesen; ***D:*** Genevieve Jolliffe; ***W:*** Genevieve Jolliffe; Chris Jones; ***C:*** Jon Walker; ***M:*** Rupert Gregson-Williams. **VIDEO**

Urban Justice **2007 (R)** If you're looking for a brainless, violent flick, then here it is because nothing else is offered. When the police department doesn't pursue the criminals who killed a cop in a drive-by shooting, his dad (Seagal) decides to take on the 'hood and blow the bad guys away himself. **92m/C; DVD.** Steven Seagal; Eddie Griffin; Danny Trejo; Kirk B.R. Woller; Carmen Serano; Cory Hart; ***D:*** Don E. Fauntleroy; ***W:*** Gilmar Fortis, II; ***C:*** Don E. Fauntleroy; ***M:*** Peter Meisner. **VIDEO**

Urban Legend **1998 (R)** Another in the nudge-and-wink genre of horror movies. Screen scream alumni litter the screen in this ode to modern tall tales that may have actually happened to the friend of a cousin of a friend of yours. Natalie (Witt) is the standard good girl who doesn't know why her friends are getting knocked off, even though her folklore prof (Englund) is the guy who played Freddy Krueger, and the voice of Chucky the evil doll is now coming out of her gas station attendant (Dourif). The killer uses urban legends as the theme of his crimes, but he never makes anyone eat Pop Rocks then drink Pepsi. Characters are so irritating you'll cheer when they die. **100m/C; VHS, DVD, Blu-Ray.** Alicia Witt; Jared Leto; Rebecca Gayheart; Loretta Devine; Joshua Jackson; Tara Reid; John Neville; Robert Englund; Brad Dourif; Natasha Gregson Wagner; Danielle Harris; Michael Rosenbaum; ***D:*** Jamie Blanks; ***W:*** Silvio Horta; ***C:*** James Chressanthis; ***M:*** Christopher Young.

Urban Legends 2: Final Cut **1/2 2000 (R)** This entry in the current trend of tongue-in-cheek slasher flicks proves that the genre is like its crazed killer characters. It refuses to die and is getting really ugly. Nearly abandoning the urban legend aspect of the original, the "movie within a movie" schtick is stolen from the "Scream" series as film students compete for the career-starting Hitchcock award at a prestigious film school. Amy (Morrison) decides to base her movie on urban legends after a chat with Reese (Devine), the only returning cast member of the original. Soon, fellow students and their projects get killed in development. Composer and film editor Ottman, making his directorial debut, seems more intent on giving movie cliches a slight twist and making film industry inside jokes than actually delivering a coherent plot. **94m/C; VHS, DVD, Blu-Ray.** Jennifer (Jenny) Morrison; Anthony Anderson; Joseph Lawrence; Matthew Davis; Hart Bochner; Loretta Devine; Marco Hofschneider; Eva Mendes; Michael Bacall; Anson Mount; Jessica Cauffiel; Chas Lawther; ***D:*** John Ottman; ***W:*** Paul Harris Boardman; Scott Derrickson; ***C:*** Brian Pearson; ***M:*** John Ottman.

Urban Legends: Bloody Mary **1/2 2005 (R)** Mary (Fields) dies during prom night because of a jock prank gone wrong. Years later, some slumber party babes giggle and do the "Bloody Mary" chant, only to rouse the restless Mary's spirit, causing her to start playing her own bloody tricks on another group of equally thoughtless jocks. **93m/C; DVD.** Kate Mara; Tina Lifford; Ed Marinaro; Lilith Fields; Robert Vito; Haley McCormick; Olesya Rulin; ***D:*** Mary Lambert; ***W:*** Michael Dougherty; Dan Harris; ***C:*** Ian Fox; ***M:*** Jeff Rona. **VIDEO**

Urban Menace **1999 (R)** Another "the future sucks" urban nightmare. A quarantined wasteland known as "The Downs" is the killing ground for a serial maniac. Two men, Harper and Crow, try to stop the mayhem and discover their murderer isn't even human. Features a hard-core rap and hip-hop soundtrack. **73m/C; VHS, DVD.** Snoop Dogg; Big Pun; Ice-T; Fat Joe; T.J. Storm; Vincent Klyn; Romany Malco; Tahitia; Karen Dyer; Ernie Hudson; ***D:*** Albert Pyun; ***W:*** Tim Story; ***C:*** Philip Alan Waters. **VIDEO**

Urbania **2000 (R)** Urban legends and painful flashbacks are plentifully featured in this disturbing film that finds Charlie (Futterman) restlessly wandering the streets of New York in search of the handsome homophobic stranger (Ball) who turns out to be responsible for the death of Charlie's boyfriend Chris (Keeslar). Directorial debut of Shear; based on Daniel Reitz's play "Urban Folk Tales." **104m/C; VHS, DVD.** Dan Futterman; Matt Keeslar; Josh Hamilton; Samuel Ball; William Sage; Megan Dodds; Alan Cumming; Lothaire Bluteau; Barbara Sukowa; Paige Turco; Gabriel Olds; ***D:*** Jon Shear; ***W:*** Daniel Reitz; ***C:*** Shane Kelly; ***M:*** Marc Anthony Thompson.

Urge **2016 (R)** A thriller centered on the deadly effects of a designer club drug. During a weekend getaway to an island, a group of wealthy friends go to club where its owner (Brosnan) gives them a new designer drug. The drug makes them shed their inhibitions and members of the group begin to act out their every fantasy. The night takes a darker turn when the partying leads to mayhem and violence. **89m/C; DVD, Blu-Ray, Download.** Pierce Brosnan; Justin Chatwin; Danny Masterson; Ashley Greene; Nick Thune; ***D:*** Aaron Kaufman; ***W:*** Jerry Stahl; ***C:*** Lyle Vincent; ***M:*** The Newton Brothers.

Uri: The Surgical Strike **2019** Indian army major Vihaan Singh Shergill (Kaushal) is known for his bravery on the battlefield, while also being an ideal colleague and family man. After he suffers personal loss when militants attack an Indian army outpost in Kashmir, Vihaan volunteers for a revenge mission into Pakistan organized by Indian national security advisor Govind (Rawal) to attack the militants. Based on real events that occurred in 2016, the film brings together characteristics of Bollywood and gritty war movies. Featuring strong action sequences and a memorable performance by Kaushal, it gets dragged out by too many unneeded details. Hindi with subtitles. **138m/C; DVD.** Vicky Kaushal; Paresh Rawal; Yami Gautam; Mohit Raina; Kirti Kulhari; ***D:*** Aditya Dhar; ***W:*** Aditya Dhar; ***C:*** Mitesh Mirchandani; ***M:*** Shashwat Sachdev.

Ursus in the Land of Fire *Ursus nella terra di fuoco; The Son of Hercules in the Land of Fire; The Son of Hercules and Five Giants* **1963** The usual bad guy usurps the throne and begins oppressing the people while his court plots against one another, inspiring the usual invincible local hero to dish out some beefy sixties Italian muscle justice. **87m/C; DVD.** *IT* Ed Fury; Claudia Mori; Luciana Gilli; Adriano Micantoni; ***D:*** Giorgio Simonelli; ***W:*** Marcello Ciorciolini; ***C:*** Luciano Trasatti; ***M:*** Carlo Savina.

Ursus in the Valley of the Lions **1/2** *The Mighty Ursus; Ursus* **1962** Ursus attempts to rescue his love from druids but is dismayed to find that she has taken up homicide in her free time. **92m/C; VHS, DVD.** *IT SP* Ed Fury; Luis Prendes; Moira Orfei; Cristina Gajoni; Maria Luisa Merlo; ***D:*** Carlo Campogalliani.

Us **2019 (R)** During a trip to a Santa Cruz boardwalk in 1986, a young girl wanders into a house of mirrors and comes face to face with her doppelganger. Now an adult, Adelaide (Nyong'o) is tense as she returns to Santa Cruz with her husband Gabe (Duke) and their children. Reluctantly returning to the same area as Adelaide's childhood incident, the family meets old friends at the beach, shakes off a few odd incidents, and spends the evening at home only to encounter the whole family's doppelgangers. Writer/director Peele ("Get Out") has created another complex, multi-layered horror film with impressive performances that begs to be viewed more than once. **120m/C; DVD, Blu-Ray.** *US JP CH* Lupita Nyong'o; Winston Duke; Elisabeth Moss; Tim Heidecker; Shahadi Wright Joseph; ***D:*** Jordan Peele; ***W:*** Jordan Peele; ***C:*** Mike Gioulakis; ***M:*** Michael Abels.

Used Cars **1980 (R)** A car dealer is desperate to put his jalopy shop competitors out of business. The owners go to great lengths to stay afloat. Sometimes too obnoxious, but often funny. **113m/C; VHS, DVD,**

Blu-Ray. Kurt Russell; Jack Warden; Deborah Harmon; Gerrit Graham; Joe Flaherty; Michael McKean; David Lander; Al Lewis; Wendie Jo Sperber; Dick Miller; Rita Taggart; ***D:*** Robert Zemeckis; ***W:*** Robert Zemeckis; Bob Gale; ***C:*** Donald M. Morgan; ***M:*** Patrick Williams.

Used People 1/2 **1992 (PG-13)** A study in ethnicity and characterization, three Oscar-winning actresses lead a talented cast playing a Jewish family living in Queens in 1969. When the father dies, Joe (Mastroianni), an old friend with an old torch for the widow, Pearl (MacLaine), shows up at the funeral and manages to charm her into a date for coffee. Pearl's new relationship with her Italian suitor affects each of the somewhat off-balance family members and washes the whole clan with a sense of hope and renewal. Adpated from screenwriter Graff's play "The Grandma Plays" that was based on memories of his grandmother. Director Kidron's American debut. **116m/C; VHS, DVD.** Shirley MacLaine; Marcello Mastroianni; Kathy Bates; Marcia Gay Harden; Jessica Tandy; Sylvia Sidney; Bob (Robert) Dishy; Joe Pantoliano; Matthew Branton; Louis Guff; Charles Cioffi; Doris Roberts; Helen Hanft; ***D:*** Beeban Kidron; ***W:*** Todd Graff; ***M:*** Rachel Portman.

USS Indianapolis: Men of Courage **2016 (R)** An ineffective look at the harrowing events involving the USS Indianapolis near the end of World War II. In July 1945, the navy ship was sunk by a Japanese sub after delivering the components for the atomic bomb that was dropped on Hiroshima. The 900 sailors who survived spent days floating on lifeboats before two-thirds of them died of injury, disease, and shark attacks. One survivor is Captain McVay (Cage), who is later court-martialed as a scapegoat. **128m/C; DVD.** Nicolas Cage; Tom Sizemore; Thomas Jane; Matt Lanter; James Remar; ***D:*** Mario Van Peebles; ***W:*** Cameron Cannon; Richard Rionda Del Castro; ***C:*** Andrzej Sekula; ***M:*** Laurent Eyquem.

The Usual Suspects 1/2 **1995 (R)** Twisted noir-thriller about some crooks, a $91 million heist, and mysterious crime lord Keyser Soze. Customs agent Kujan (Palminteri) tries to get a straight story out of small-time con man "Verbal" Kint (Spacey) about a burning tanker in the San Pedro harbor, 27 dead bodies, and the other four tempermental criminals involved: ex-cop-turned thief Keaton (Byrne), explosives expert Hockney (Pollak), and hot-headed partners McManus (Baldwin) and Fenster (Del Toro). Nothing is as it seems, and the ending keeps everyone guessing, right up to the final credits. Terrific performances from all complement the intelligent, humorous script. And yes, the title does come from the famous line in "Casablanca." **105m/C; VHS, DVD, Blu-Ray.** Kevin Spacey; Gabriel Byrne; Chazz Palminteri; Kevin Pollak; Stephen Baldwin; Benicio Del Toro; Giancarlo Esposito; Pete Postlethwaite; Dan Hedaya; Suzy Amis; Paul Bartel; Peter Greene; Louis Lombardi; ***D:*** Bryan Singer; ***W:*** Christopher McQuarrie; ***C:*** Newton Thomas (Tom) Sigel; ***M:*** John Ottman. Oscars '95: Orig. Screenplay, Support. Actor (Spacey); British Acad. '95: Orig. Screenplay; Ind. Spirit '96: Screenplay, Support. Actor (Del Toro); Natl. Bd. of Review '95: Support. Actor (Spacey); N.Y. Film Critics '95: Support. Actor (Spacey); Broadcast Film Critics '95: Support. Actor (Spacey).

Utamaro and His Five Women 1/2 *Five Women Around Utamaro; Utamaro O Meguru Gonin No Onna* **1946** Utamaro is a legendary 19th-century Edo artist who gained inspiration from Tokyo's "floating world," of courtesans, brothels, drinking parties, and violent passions. His gorgeous portraits worship women but he dislikes the complications that flesh-and-blood females bring. Heavily stylized look at the artistic impulse. In Japanese with English subtitles. **89m/B; VHS, DVD.** *JP* Minnosuke Bando; Kinuyo Tanaka; Kotaro Bando; Hisato Osawa; Tamezo Mochizuki; Hiroko Kawasaki; ***D:*** Kenji Mizoguchi; ***W:*** Yoshikata Yoda; ***C:*** Shigeto Miki; ***M:*** Hisato Osawa; Tamezo Mochizuki.

Utopia *Atoll K; Robinson Crusoeland; Escapade* **1951** Laurel and Hardy inherit a paradisaical island, but their peace is disturbed when uranium is discovered. Final screen appearance of the team is diminished by poor direction and script. **82m/B; VHS, DVD.** *FR* Stan Laurel; Oliver Hardy; Suzy Delair; Max Elloy; ***D:*** Leo Joannon; ***W:*** Rene Wheeler; Piero Tellini; Monte (Monty) Collins, Jr.; ***C:*** Louis Nee; Armand Thirard; ***M:*** Paul Misraki.

The Utopian Society 1/2 **2003** Low-budget and predictable story about six college students realizing they're not so different after all. The students are supposed to have been working on a group sociology project to describe what they would consider a utopian society. But they blew it off until the night before the paper is due and now seem more interested in bickering and other foolishness than getting down to work, even if it means failing the class. **93m/C; DVD.** Kelvin Yu; Malin Akerman; Austin Nichols; Kristen Ariza; Sam Doumit; Mat Hostetler; ***D:*** John P. Aguirre; ***W:*** Jason Preston; ***C:*** Eric Gustavo Petersen; ***M:*** Eric Hester.

Utu **1983 (R)** A Maori tribesman serving with the colonizing British army in 1870 explodes into ritual revenge when his home village is slaughtered. Filmed in New Zealand. **122m/C; VHS, DVD.** *NZ* Anzac Wallace; Kelly Johnson; Tim Elliot; Bruno Lawrence; ***D:*** Geoff Murphy; ***W:*** Geoff Murphy; Keith Aberdein; ***C:*** Graeme Cowley; ***M:*** John Charles.

U2: Rattle and Hum 1/2 **1988 (PG-13)** Very-well-done concert/documentary, focusing on the Irish band U2 and their 1988 U.S. tour. Filmed in black-and-white and color. **90m/C; VHS, DVD.** ***D:*** Phil Joanou; ***C:*** Robert Brinkmann; Jordan Cronenweth.

Uzumaki 1/2 *Spiral* **2000** In what was originally a manga by famed horror writer Junji Ito, the inhabitants of the small town of Kurozu-cho are obsessed with spirals, which is the symbol of some entity that transforms or destroys anything it encounters. The comic is written in 20 episodes, seven of which make it into the film, which ultimately fails to live up to the spirit of the comic due to its lower budget effects and a lack of closure. **90m/C; DVD.** *JP* Hinako Saeki; Eun-Kyung Shin; Ren Osugi; Denden; Taro Suwa; Eriko Hatsune; Fhi Fan; Keiko Takahashi; Masami Horiuchi; Tooru Teduka; Sadao Abe; Asumi Miwa; Saori Nakane; Yasuki Tanaka; Yuki Murakama; Maki Hamada; Tomoo Fukatsu; Akira Matsuda; Takuto Oyama; Hassei Takano; ***D:*** Higuchinsky; ***W:*** Junji Ito; Kengo Kaji; Takao Nitta; Chika Yasuo; ***C:*** Gen Kobayashi; ***M:*** Keiichi Suzuki; Tetsuro Kashibuchi.

V **1983** Very creepy sci-fi miniseries that spawned a short-lived TV show. Advanced aliens, known as the Visitors, come to Earth on a seemingly friendly quest. But their human-like appearance is a facade—as is their mission. Fake skin masks a repitilian hide and what they want is complete planetary control. Naturally, some earthlings don't fall for their smooth talk and a resistance movement is born. Followed by miniseries conclusion "V: The Final Battle." **190m/C; VHS, DVD.** Marc Singer; Jane Badler; Faye Grant; Robert Englund; Michael Durrell; Peter Gill Nelson; Neva Patterson; Andrew Prine; Richard Herd; Rafael Campos; ***D:*** Kenneth Johnson; ***W:*** Kenneth Johnson. **TV**

V for Vendetta 1/2 **2006 (R)** The Wachowskis and director McTeigue bring Alan Moore's 1980s graphic novel to the big screen (though Moore disowned the film). In the year 2020, disease and chaos have swept America off the top of the global food chain, and dictator Sutler (Hurt) has used the resultant fear to turn Britain into a totalitarian regime. V (Weaving), a masked avenger who uses the legend of Guy Fawkes as both disguise and inspiration, strikes at the government by blowing up Big Ben, promising to return in a year to bring about revolution. On the same night, he also happens to save Evey (Portman) from being raped by the police. She becomes an important ally in his fight. Covers a lot of philosophical ground, but at times glosses over the ideas it presents, costing it much real depth. But it does so with a goodly amount of flash, and not a little artistry. **132m/C; DVD, Blu-Ray, HD-DVD.** Hugo Weaving; Natalie Portman; Stephen Rea; Stephen Fry; John Hurt; Tim Pigott-Smith; Rupert Graves; Roger Allam; Ben Miles; Sinead Cusack; Eddie Marsan; Natasha Wightman; ***D:*** James McTeigue; ***W:*** Lilly Wachowski; Lana Wachowski; ***C:*** Adrian Biddle; ***M:*** Dario Marianelli.

V/H/S 1/2 **2012 (R)** Some men break into a home and stumble upon a series of videotapes that contain footage of a horrific and confusing nature. In one story, a one-night stand goes horribly awry. In another, a woman is tormented via Skype. As with most anthology films, the quality levels fluctuate wildly but there is enough of interest here for fans of the increasingly mocked found-footage genre to find something to like. This anthology comes from a number of the most notable names in the Mumblecore genre like Ti West and Joe Swanberg. **116m/C; DVD, Blu-Ray.** Calvin Reeder; Lane Hughes; Adam Wingard; Joe Swanberg; Sophia Takal; Hanna Fierman; Matt Battinelli-Olpin; ***D:*** Adam Wingard; Joe Swanberg; Matt Battinelli-Olpin; David Bruckner; Tyler Gillett; Justin Martinez; Glenn McQuaid; Chad Villella; Ti West; Simon Barrett; Radio Silence; ***W:*** David Bruckner; Tyler Gillett; Justin Martinez; Glenn McQuaid; Chad Villella; Ti West; Brad Miska; Simon Barrett; Nicholas Tecosky; Radio Silence; ***C:*** Adam Wingard; Tyler Gillett; Justin Martinez; Eric Branco; Andrew Droz Palermo; Victoria K. Warren; Michael J. Wilson.

V/H/S/2 *S-VHS* **2013** Vastly superior to the 2012 anthology film that has apparently sparked a franchise, this follow-up is tighter, scarier, funnier, and smarter that the first movie, even with many of the same contributors. Evans and Tjahjanto's segment ("Safe Haven") is a mini-masterpiece of horror, presenting what could happen if a satanic cult really did find a way to communicate with the other side. It barely beats Hale and Sanchez's brilliant zombie comedy "A Ride in the Park" as best in show. The other segments (by Simon Barrett, Jason Eisener, and Adam Wingard) suffice, but the two middle short films justify a look at the whole thing on their own. **96m/C; DVD, Blu-Ray.** *US CA* Lawrence Michael Levine; Kelsey Abbott; Adam Wingard; Hannah Hughes; Jay Saunders; Epy Kusnandar; Fachry Albar; Hannah Al-Rashid; Samantha Gracie; Rylan Logan; Cohen King; ***D:*** Adam Wingard; Simon Barrett; Eduardo Sanchez; Greg Hale; Timo Tjahjanto; Gareth Evans; Jason Eisener; ***W:*** Simon Barrett; Timo Tjahjanto; Gareth Evans; Jason Eisener; Jamie Nash; John Davies; ***C:*** Tarin Anderson; Abdul Dermawan Habir; Stephen Scott; Seamus Tierney; Jeff Wheaton; ***M:*** James Guymon; Steve Moore; Aria Prayogi; Fajor Yuskemal.

V: The Final Battle 1/2 **1984** It's four-months since the Visitors appeared on earth, proclaiming their false friendship. But a resistance movement knows these reptiles, who hide behind a human appearance, are only interested in harvesting earth's inhabitants as a new food source. Continuation of the TV miniseries "V." **285m/C; VHS, DVD, Blu-Ray.** Marc Singer; Robert Englund; Michael Ironside; ***D:*** Richard T. Heffron.

Va Savoir 1/2 *Who Knows?* **2001 (PG-13)** Romantic farce involving theatre folk. French actress Camille (Balibar) returns to Paris as the star of an Italian theatrical company. She's involved with company director Ugo (Castellitto) but sees her ex, Pierre (Bonaffre), who has a new girlfriend, Sonia (Basler). Meanwhile, Ugo is searching for a lost play by 18th-century writer Goldoni, aided by grad student Do (de Fougerolles) who gets a crush on him, despite her half-brother Arthur's (Todeschini) dislike of the situation. That everyone will interact in each other's lives is a given. French with subtitles. **154m/C; VHS, DVD.** *FR IT GE* Jeanne Balibar; Sergio Castellitto; Jacques Bonnaffe; Marianne Basler; Helene de Fougerolles; Bruno Todeschini; Catherine Rouvel; Claude Berri; ***D:*** Jacques Rivette; ***W:*** Jacques Rivette; Christine Laurent; Pascal Bonitzer; ***C:*** William Lubtchansky.

Vacancy 1/2 **2007 (R)** Standard slasher flick finds bickering estranged couple David (Wilson) and Amy (Beckinsale) stuck in a fleabag motel after having car trouble along a deserted backroad. Their in-room entertainment consists of dusty videotapes of torture snuff flicks they soon realize happened in the very room they're in. Then they figure out they're being watched. Wilson and Beckinsale give their characters a little more depth than the pic probably deserves. **80m/C; DVD, Blu-Ray.** Luke Wilson; Kate Beckinsale; Frank Whaley; Ethan (Randall) Embry; ***D:*** Nimrod Antal; ***W:*** Mark Smith; ***C:*** Andrzej Sekula; ***M:*** Paul Haslinger.

Vacancy 2: The First Cut **2008 (R)** A generally cheap, dreary, and dumb prequel story to the 2007 studio release. Two sleazoids tape the sexual encounters of their no-tell motel guests for fun and profit. A serial killer rents a room and they catch him killing a hooker on video and the killer proposes they team up and turn from sex tapes to snuff films. Then three friends check-in and are about to become the first "stars." **86m/C; DVD.** Agnes Bruckner; David Moscow; Arjay Smith; Trevor Wright; Beau Billingslea; Brian Klugman; ***D:*** Eric Bross; ***W:*** Mark L. Smith; ***C:*** Horacio Marquinez; ***M:*** Jerome Dillon. **VIDEO**

Vacas *Cows* **1991** The political and social climate of the Basque region of Spain is frequently dangerous but the region's cows (the "vacas" of the title) placidly continue as always despite what happens to the humans around them. Covering more than 50 years, from 1875 through the Spanish Civil War, the lives of two families are interwined in emotional conflict through three generations. Spanish with subtitles. **96m/C; VHS, DVD, Blu-Ray.** *SP* Carmelo Gomez; Ana Torrent; Emma Suarez; Pilar Bardem; Kandito Uranga; ***D:*** Julio Medem; ***W:*** Julio Medem; Michel Gaztambide; ***C:*** Carlos Gusi; ***M:*** Alberto Iglesias.

Vacation **2015 (R)** The poisoned genre of the comedy remake gets another dubious entry in this update of the classic Chevy Chase/National Lampoon vehicle for a new generation of mean-spirited, gross-out humor. Helms takes the wheel as Rusty, the eldest Griswold son, determined to make a family vacation memory of his own just like the trip he can never forget from his youth. What follows is a series of adventures and encounters that often end with Rusty or his family being physically assaulted or covered in some form of bodily fluids. A few of the jokes connect but most leave a bad taste. **99m/C; DVD, Blu-Ray, Streaming.** Ed Helms; Christina Applegate; Skyler Gisondo; Steele Stebbins; Beverly D'Angelo; Chevy Chase; ***D:*** John Francis Daley; Jonathan M. Goldstein; ***W:*** John Francis Daley; Jonathan M. Goldstein; ***C:*** Barry Peterson; ***M:*** Mark Mothersbaugh.

Vacation from Marriage 1/2 *Perfect Strangers* **1945** Robert (Donat) and Catherine (Kerr) Wilson are leading dull and unhappy lives, which is why they find their marital separation by the war a blessing in disguise. Robert joins the Navy and becomes a war hero and Cathy regains her self-esteem after joining the WRENs. It's three years before their leaves coincide and both dread their reunion, thinking it might be best to divorce. **92m/B; DVD.** *UK* Robert Donat; Deborah Kerr; Glynis Johns; Ann Todd; Roland Culver; ***D:*** Alexander Korda; ***W:*** Clemence Dane; Anthony Pelissier; ***C:*** Georges Perinal; ***M:*** Clifton Parker. Oscars '46: Story, Story (Dane).

Vacuuming Completely Nude in Paradise 1/2 **2001** Not only is Pete's (Begley) girlfriend tired of stripping to support them but she won't put out until he gets a real job. Off he goes to the local door-to-door vacuum sales office and is placed under the dubious tutelage of polar opposite Tommy (Spall)?a frantic, morally bankrupt, yet very experienced and successful salesman. The jocularity is plentiful in this BBC-TV production as the contest for the "Golden Hoover" pits all the sales folks against Tommy. Spall excels in punching out his frenzied lines while director Boyle's use of the digital video format captures the essence of office life in this grim send-up. **75m/C; VHS, DVD.** Timothy Spall; Michael Begley; Katy Cavanagh; Caroline Ashley; ***D:*** Danny Boyle; ***W:*** Jim Cartwright; ***C:*** Anthony Dod Mantle; ***M:*** John Murphy. **TV**

Vagabond 1/2 *Sans Toit Ni Loi* **1985** Bleak, emotionally shattering, powerful and compelling, this film traces the peripatetic life of an amoral and selfish young French woman who has no regard for social rules and tremendous fear of responsibility in her drifting yet inexorable journey into death. Told via flashbacks from the moment when she is found dead, alone, and unaccounted for by the roadside, this film will not leave you unscathed. Written by New Wave director Varda. In French with English subtitles. **105m/C; VHS, DVD.** *FR* Sandrine Bonnaire; Macha Meril; Stephane Freiss; Elaine Cortadellas; Marthe Jarnias; Yolande Moreau; ***D:*** Agnes Varda; ***W:*** Agnes Varda; ***C:*** Patrick Blossier; ***M:*** Joanne Bruzdowicz. Cesar '86: Actress (Bonnaire); L.A. Film Critics '86: Actress (Bonnaire), Foreign Film.

Vagabond Lady 1935 Department store owner R.D. Spear (Churchill) employs both his wastrel friend Spiggins (Craven) and Spiggins' daughter Josephine (Venable). This is something of a problem since R.D.'s responsible son John (Denny) wants to marry Jo. John's irresponsible brother Tony (Young), who's just returned from sailing around the South Seas, decides he wants the girl as well. **75m/B; DVD.** Robert Young; Evelyn Venable; Reginald Denny; Berton Churchill; Frank Craven; ***D:*** Sam Taylor; ***W:*** Frank Butler; ***C:*** Jack MacKenzie.

Vagabond Lover 1/2 **1929** The amusing tale of the loves, hopes, and dreams of an aspiring saxophone player. Rudy croons through his megaphone in his movie debut. Appealing, with Dressler sparkling in the role of the wealthy aunt. **66m/B; VHS, DVD.** Rudy Vallee; Sally Blane; Marie Dressler; Charles Sellon; Eddie Nugent; ***D:*** Marshall Neilan; ***W:*** James A. Creelman; ***C:*** Leo Tover.

The Vagrant **1992 (R)** Run-of-the-mill creeper with a mind-game playing derelict inhabiting the home of a young exec. A series of murders has this wimp yuppie wondering how to get rid of his unwelcome intruder. **91m/C; VHS, Blu-Ray, Streaming.** Bill Paxton; Michael Ironside; Marshall Bell; Stuart Pankin; ***D:*** Chris Walas.

The Valachi Papers 1/2 **1972 (R)** Joe Valachi (Bronson), serving a life sentence, recouns his life and times as a small-time soldier in the mob. The Feds want him to tell them how the outfit works, and the mob wants him dead. Sometimes violent but overall flatly told story of low-life mob life can be seen as a precursor to the Scorsese mob epics that came later. Bronson turns in a good performance. **125m/C; DVD, Blu-Ray.** Charles Bronson; Lino Ventura; Jill Ireland; Walter Chiari; Joseph Wiseman; Gerald S. O'Loughlin; Amedeo Nazzari; Fausto Tozzi; Angelo Infanti; Pupella Maggio; ***D:*** Terence Young; ***W:*** Stephen Geller; ***C:*** Aldo Tonti; ***M:*** Riz Ortolani; Armando Trovajoli.

Valdez Is Coming 1/2 **1971 (PG-13)** Though not a world-class western, this filmed-in-Spain saga does feature a probing script (based on an Elmore Leonard novel) on the nature of race relations. Fine performance by Lancaster as a Mexican-American who ignites the passions of a town, and ultimately confronts the local land baron. **90m/C; VHS, DVD, Blu-Ray.** Burt Lancaster; Susan Clark; Jon Cypher; Barton Heyman; Richard Jordan; Frank Silvera; Hector Elizondo; ***D:*** Edwin Sherin; ***W:*** David Rayfiel; ***M:*** Charles Gross.

Valentin 1/2 **2002 (PG-13)** Valentin is the overly adorable, 9-year-old, horn-rimmed glasses wearing hero of Agresti's semi-autobiographical drama set in 1960s Buenos Aires. Valentin (Noya) lives with his kooky grandmother (Maura) after being abandoned by his mother and playboy father, (director Agresti) who have long separated. Valentin attempts to rebuild his family by playing Cupid with his dad's current girlfriend, the beautiful and attentive Leticia (Cardinali) while simultaneously charming and inspiring various local, hardened grown-ups. The precocious boy is also an aspiring astronaut, a fact which allows him to dress up in a far-less-than-homemade looking get-up and look cute, which he does for far too much of this sometimes saccharine heart-tugger. Does boast some genuinely touching moments. **86m/C; DVD.** *AR NL* Carmen Maura; Rodrigo Noya; Alejandro Agresti; Jean Pierre Noher; Mex Urtizberea; Julieta Cardinali; ***D:*** Alejandro Agresti; ***W:*** Alejandro Agresti; ***C:*** Jose Luis Cajaraville; ***M:*** Luis Salinas; Paul M. van Brugge.

Valentine **2001 (R)** Slasher film with a former nerd of a killer in a Cupid mask wreaking revenge upon the snooty girls who dissed him in junior high. After one victim's funeral, the remaining four get some threatening Valentines, which they, of course, promptly ignore. Boreanaz is among the doomed babes' boyfriends and a prime suspect. After yet another of the girls falls victim to the demented deity-wannabe, the remaining three grieve by throwing a bash at a swanky mansion with rambling vacant rooms that just scream, well, you get it. Eye-candy cast with mild suspense mix with dubious scripting. The only real victim here is your precious time. **96m/C; VHS, DVD, Blu-Ray.** David Boreanaz; Denise Richards; Marley Shelton; Jessica Capshaw; Katherine Heigl; Johnny Whitworth; Hedy Burress; Jessica Cauffiel; Fulvio Cecere; Daniel Cosgrove; ***D:*** Jamie Blanks; ***W:*** Donna Powers; Wayne Powers; Gretchen J. Berg; Aaron Harberts; ***C:*** Rick Bota; ***M:*** Don Davis.

A Valentine Carol 1/2 **2007** A modern takeoff of "A Christmas Carol." Distinctly unlikeable Seattle radio talk host Ally Simms offers love advice that boils down to being status-conscious and marrying rich. She's getting married herself on Valentine's Day but her deceased mentor Jackie Marley shows up to give cynical Ally a chance to change her ways (via three boyfriend spirits) before it's too late. **90m/C; DVD.** Emma Caulfield; Barbara Niven; John Reardon; Dominic Zamprogna; Tobias Slezak; Doron Bell; Jeremy Jones; Jill Morrison; David Milchard; ***D:*** Mark Jean; ***W:*** Edgar Lyall; ***C:*** Michael Balfry; ***M:*** Peter Allen. **CABLE**

Valentine's Day **2010 (PG-13)** There are only two things missing from this star-studded romantic comedy from schmaltzmeister Marshall. Unfortunately, those things are romance and comedy. Linking the stories of lust, love, and revenge together is the flower store owned by Reed (Kutcher), who is proposing to his conflicted girlfriend Morley (Alba). Stars such as Julia Roberts, Shirley MacLaine, and Anne Hathaway are wasted in this movie that has so many plot lines and characters that nothing is able to emerge as anything other than two-dimensional. The celebrity cameos might have seemed like a good idea, but it's more like "The Love Boat" hit an iceberg and sank. **125m/C; Blu-Ray.** Julia Roberts; Anne Hathaway; Jessica Alba; Jessica Biel; Jennifer Garner; Shirley MacLaine; Queen Latifah; Bradley Cooper; Ashton Kutcher; Jamie Foxx; Topher Grace; Emma Roberts; Taylor Swift; Hector Elizondo; George Lopez; Patrick Dempsey; Eric Dane; Kathy Bates; Taylor Lautner; Larry Miller; Kirsten Schaal; ***D:*** Garry Marshall; ***W:*** Abby Kohn; Marc Silverstein; Katherine Fugate; ***C:*** Charles Minsky; ***M:*** John Debney. Golden Raspberries '10: Worst Actor (Kutcher), Worst Support. Actress (Alba).

Valentino **1977 (R)** Another one of director Russell's flamboyantly excessive screen biographies, this time of silent screen idol Rudolph Valentino (Nureyev). The details hardly matter but the movie is told in flashback from Valentino's funeral to his beginnings as a dance instructor and his eventual success as a screen lover. Nureyev is noticeably stiff in his screen debut but at least he possesses some charisma. **127m/C; VHS, DVD.** *GB* Rudolf Nureyev; Leslie Caron; Michelle Phillips; Carol Kane; Felicity Kendal; Seymour Cassel; Peter Vaughan; William Hootkins; Huntz Hall; David de Keyser; Alfred Marks; Anton Diffring; ***D:*** Ken Russell; ***W:*** Mardik Martin; Ken Russell; John Byrum; ***C:*** Peter Suschitzky; ***M:*** Ferde Grofe, Jr.

Valentino: The Last Emperor 1/2 **2008 (PG-13)** Debuting director Tynauer's documentary examines haute couture and the career of Italian fashion designer Valentino (who retired in 2007 shortly after the two-year shoot was completed). Included are a celebration of the designer's 45-year career and his longtime personal and professional relationship with partner Giancarlo Giammaetti. **96m/C; DVD, Blu-Ray.**

Valerian and the City of a Thousand Planets 1/2 **2017 (PG-13)** An entertaining, if imperfect, science fiction romp by Luc Besson that best succeeds in its striking, memorable visuals. In the 28th century, Valerian (DeHaan) and Laureline (Delevingne) are secret operatives who fight crime throughout the universe. When the important floating city of Alpha is threatened from within, the pair are put on the case. After learning that a horrible mistake there is being covered up by a vast government conspiracy, they go on separate adventures to mitigate the scheme's damage. **137m/C; DVD, Blu-Ray.** Dane DeHaan; Cara Delevingne; Clive Owen; Rihanna; Ethan Hawke; ***D:*** Luc Besson; ***W:*** Luc Besson; ***C:*** Thierry Arbogast; ***M:*** Alexandre Desplat.

Valerie **1957** A surprisingly vicious western with a "Rashomon"-like plot. Civil War vet John Garth (Hayden) is on trial for murdering his in-laws and nearly killing his foreign-born wife Valerie (Ekberg). Three versions of the story follow: John claims Valerie is a slut who seduced his younger brother Herb (Walker) as well as the local minister (among others). Rev. Blake (Steel) denies the affair and claims John was abusive and he took Valerie to her parents' home for safety. Valerie herself says the vicious John was only after her substantial dowry and made up the affair so he could kill Valerie and his own brother. **82m/B; DVD.** Sterling Hayden; Anita Ekberg; Anthony Steel; Peter Walker; John Wengraf; Sydney Smith; ***D:*** Gerd Oswald; ***W:*** Laurence Heath; ***C:*** Ernest Laszlo.

The Valet 1/2 *La Doublure* **2006 (PG-13)** Venal tycoon Pierre Levasseur (Auteuil) is in big trouble when a paparazzo takes a photo of him and supermodel mistress Elena (Taglioni). Seems Pierre's wife Christine (Scott Thomas) owns the majority share of company stock and he can't afford a divorce. Ah, but valet Francois (Elmaleh) was also in the picture, so Pierre pays him (and Elena) to pretend that they are a couple. Francois wants the money to help out true (if oblivious) love Emilie (Ledoyen) but the complications increase in Veber's amusing bedroom farce. French with subtitles. **85m/C; DVD.** *FR* Daniel Auteuil; Kristin Scott Thomas; Virginie Ledoyen; Richard Berry; Gad Elmaleh; Alice Taglioni; Dany Boon; ***D:*** Francis Veber; ***W:*** Francis Veber; ***C:*** Robert Fraisse; ***M:*** Alexandre Desplat.

Valhalla Rising 1/2 **2009** Testosterone-driven gore that's slow-paced thanks to the lack of dialogue and excess of staring to convey thought. Mute Viking warrior One-Eye (Mikkelson), imprisoned in Scotland, slays his captors and sets out for home before falling in with a band of Christian Vikings who plan to sail for Jerusalem (and conquer it). **90m/C; DVD.** *DK* Mads Mikkelsen; Maarten Stevenson; Gordon Brown; Andrew Flanagan; Gary Lewis; Gary McCormack; Alexander Morgan; Jamie Sieves; ***D:*** Nicolas Winding Refn; ***W:*** Nicolas Winding Refn; Roy Jacobsen; ***C:*** Morten Soborg; ***M:*** Peter Kyed.

Valiant 1/2 **2005 (G)** Feature-length film based on the WWII homing pigeons used by the British Armed Forces is cute and short, which should please the kids but the plot development never really gets off the ground. Classic "misfit gets his chance and saves the day" story focuses on Valiant (McGregor), who has not been allowed to join the Royal Homing Pigeon Service until they discover how to turn his short-falling into an asset. Plenty of jokes spoofing war movies of days-gone-by. **80m/C; DVD.** *GB US* ***V:*** Ewan McGregor; Tim Curry; Jim Broadbent; Hugh Laurie; Daniel Roberts; John Cleese; John Hurt; Pip Torrens; Ricky Gervais; Brian Lonsdale; Olivia Williams; Rik Mayall; Sharon Horgan; ***D:*** Gary Chapman; ***W:*** Jordan Katz; George Webster; George Melrod; ***C:*** John Fenner; ***M:*** George Fenton.

Valkyrie 1/2 **2008 (PG-13)** Following the loss of an eye, a hand, and a couple of fingers during an air raid, Claus von Stauffenberg (Cruise), a Colonel in Hitler's Third Reich, realizes he can no longer participate in the destruction and mass murders being carried out by the Fuhrer's SS troops. With several like-minded officers (Branagh, Nighy and Stamp), von Stauffenberg hatches a covert plan to assassinate Hitler (Bamber) and bring back honor to Germany. The historically known failure of the June 1944 plot hangs the story's interest on the thoughts and motivations of those involved and on the plan's details. Much of the action is restrained due to the nature of the career military officers being portrayed, but the suspense of the many near misses and close calls makes for an interesting second half. **120m/C; Blu-Ray, On Demand.** *US GE* Tom Cruise; David Bamber; Matthias Freihof; Carice van Houten; Kenneth Branagh; Eddie Izzard; Thomas Kretschmann; Bill Nighy; Terence Stamp; Kevin McNally; Christian Berkel; Tom Hollander; Kenneth Cranham; ***D:*** Bryan Singer; ***W:*** Christopher McQuarrie; Nathan Alexander; ***C:*** Newton Thomas (Tom) Sigel; ***M:*** John Ottman.

Valley Girl 1/2 *Bad Boyz* **1983 (R)** Slight but surprisingly likeable teen romantic-comedy inspired by Frank Zappa novelty tune. Title stereotype falls for a leather-jacketed rebel. Really. It may look like a music video, but the story is straight from "Romeo and Juliet" via Southern California. Helped launch Cage's career. Music by Men at Work, Culture Club, and others. **95m/C; VHS, DVD, Blu-Ray.** Nicolas Cage; Deborah Foreman; Colleen Camp; Frederic Forrest; Lee Purcell; Elizabeth Daily; Michael Bowen; Cameron Dye; Heidi Holicker; Michelle Meyrink; ***D:*** Martha Coolidge; ***W:*** Wayne Crawford; Andrew Lane; ***C:*** Frederick Elmes; ***M:*** Marc Levinthal; Scott Wilk.

Valley Girl **2020 (PG-13)** Suburban teen queen Julie (Rothe) has a loyal group of friends and is dating the best looking, most vain guy in high school, Mickey (Paul). Though she seems to have it all, she wants something different. When Julie meets Randy (Whitehouse), a punk from the city, at the beach, she finds it. Randy is looking for musical success with his band, but is drawn to Julie as well. After he crashes a party Julie is hosting, they make decisions that alter their life paths forever. This remake of the 1980s teen cult classic will, like, totally disappoint fans of the original. **102m/C; DVD.** Jessica Rothe; Josh Whitehouse; Jessie Ennis; Ashleigh Murray; Chloe Bennet; ***D:*** Rachel Lee Goldenberg; ***W:*** Amy Talkington; ***C:*** Adam Silver; ***M:*** Roger Neill.

Valley Inn 1/2 **2014** A fish-out-of-water comedy-drama about a college student learning about truly finding her path in life. Emily (Scott) attends college in a big city, but moves to rural northwest Arkansas for a summer job selling Christian books. When she arrives in the community, she experiences culture shock as the quirky residents try to make Emily feel welcome in their own way. As she adjusts to her surroundings, she helps locals prepare for the year's major event, the Rodeo of the Ozarks. Though her experience is challenging at times, Emily soon learns much about herself and what she really wants out of life. **120m/C; DVD, Streaming, Download.** Jordan Scott; Joey Lauren Adams; David Lansbury; Natalie Canerday; Mark Landon Smith; ***D:*** Kim Swink; ***W:*** Kim Swink; ***C:*** Blake Elder; ***M:*** Kris Allen; Amos Cochran. **VIDEO**

The Valley Obscured by the Clouds *La Vallee* **1970** A group of dropouts and seekers search for the valley of the gods in the wilds of New Guinea, and experience a sexual and spiritual metamorphosis. In French with English subtitles. **106m/C; VHS, DVD.** *FR* Bulle Ogier; Michael Gothard; Jean-Pierre Kalfon; Jerome Beauvarlet; Monique Giraudy; ***D:*** Barbet Schroeder; ***W:*** Barbet Schroeder; ***C:*** Nestor Almendros; ***M:*** Pink Floyd.

The Valley of Decision **1945** Entertaining poor-girl-meets-rich-boy story with Peck as a wealthy mill owner who falls in love with beautiful housemaid Garson (the Queen of MGM at the time). Set in 1870 Pittsburgh; based on Marcia Davenport's novel. **111m/B; VHS, DVD.** Gregory Peck; Greer Garson; Donald Crisp; Lionel Barrymore; Preston Foster; Gladys Cooper; Marsha Hunt; Reginald Owen; Dan Duryea; Jessica Tandy; Barbara Everest; ***D:*** Tay Garnett; ***W:*** John Meehan; Sonya Levien; ***C:*** Joseph Ruttenberg.

The Valley of Gwangi **1969 (G)** One of the best prehistoric-monster-westerns out there. Cowboys discover a lost valley of dinosaurs and try to capture a vicious, carnivorous allosaurus. Bad move, kemosabe! The creatures move via the stop-motion model animation by f/x maestro Ray Harryhausen, here at his finest. **95m/C; VHS, DVD, Blu-Ray.** James Franciscus; Gila Golan; Richard Carlson; Laurence Naismith; Freda Jackson; Gustavo Rojo; Dennis Kilbane; Mario De Barros; Curtis Arden; Jose Burgos; ***D:*** James O'Connolly; ***W:*** William Bast; Julian More; ***C:*** Erwin Hillier; ***M:*** Jerome Moross.

Valley of Saints 1/2 **2012** An exotic setting adds some interest to this low-key narrative. Living in the economically depressed and politically turbulent Dal Lake region of Kashmir, boatman Gulzar plots with his best friend Afzal to leave and start over elsewhere. A political clash results in a military curfew, and Gulzar passes the time by helping out scientist Asifa, who's researching the lake's pollution problems. Afzal resents the intrusion and fears the budding romance will derail their plans. Kashmiri with subtitles. **82m/C; DVD.** *IN* Gulzar Ahmed Bhat; Mohammed Afzal; Neelofar Hamid; ***D:*** Musa Syeed; ***W:***

Musa Syeed; *C:* Yoni Brook; *M:* Mubashir Mohi-ud-Din.

Valley of the Dolls 🦴🦴 **1967 (PG)** Camp/trash classic was rated as a bomb by many critics but is really of the so-bad-it's-good variety. Three beauties, Jennifer (Tate), Neely (Duke), and Anne (Parkins), dream of Hollywood stardom but fall victim to Hollywood excess, including drug dependency (the "dolls" of the title). There's unhappy love affairs, porno parts, health risks, and hysterics of various kinds—all designed to have you dropping your jaw in disbelief. The bathroom scene between Duke and Hayward involving a wig is not to be missed. Based on the novel by Jacqueline Susann who has a bit part as a reporter. Remade for TV as "Jacqueline Susann's Valley of the Dolls" in 1981. **123m/C; VHS, DVD, Blu-Ray.** Barbara Parkins; Patty Duke; Sharon Tate; Paul Burke; Tony Scotti; Martin Milner; Susan Hayward; Charles Drake; Lee Grant; Alex Davion; Robert H. Harris; Robert Viharo; Joey Bishop; George Jessel; Richard Dreyfuss; ***Cameo(s):*** Jacqueline Susann; *D:* Mark Robson; *W:* Jacqueline Susann; Dorothy Kingsley; Helen Deutsch; *C:* William H. Daniels; *M:* John Williams.

Valley of the Dragons 🦴 **1961** In 1881, two men are caught up and sucked into a passing comet where they discover the inhabitants are rival cave dwellers, living amidst dinosaurs and other prehistoric creatures. Seems the comet has been passing by Earth for millennia, picking up bits of civilization, and the survivors then have to adapt to their new situation. Adaptation of a Jules Verne novel. **82m/B; DVD.** Cesare Danova; Sean McClory; Joan Staley; Danielle De Metz; Gregg Martell; I. Stanford Jolley; *D:* Edward L. Bernds; *W:* Edward L. Bernds; *C:* Brydon Baker; *M:* Ruby Raksin.

Valley of the Heart's Delight 🦴 **1/2 2007** Old-fashioned and somewhat flat retelling of a true crime story from 1933. The title refers to Silicon Valley's previous incarnation as an agricultural area. Ambitious rookie reporter Jack Daumier is assigned to a society story when Blake Walsh, son of local bigwig Horace, gets a job promotion. However, Jack is more interested in dating Blake's sister Helen (Harrison). When Blake is kidnapped, Jack thinks there's a cover-up. **100m/C; DVD.** Gabriel Mann; Pete Postlethwaite; Emily Harrison; Diana Scarwid; Bruce McGill; Tom Bower; Ron Rogge; Joe Mandragona; Michael Sommers; Cully Fredricksen; *D:* Tim Boxell; *W:* Miles Murphy; *C:* Hiro Narita; *M:* Richard Gibbs; Nicholas O'Toole. **VIDEO**

Valley of the Sun 🦴 **1/2 2011** Self-conscious whimsey where a porn star gives relationship advice to senior citizens. Andy (Whitworth) is an adult film star who walks off the set and into a mental hospital. His worried parents, who don't know what Andy does for a living, take him to their Arizona retirement community to regroup. Andy's past doesn't stay in his showbiz closet. **103m/C; DVD.** Johnny Whitworth; Heather Burns; Beth Grant; Barry Corbin; Garrett Morris; Graham Greene; Peter Jason; Bette Ford; *D:* Stokes McIntyre; *W:* Stokes McIntyre; *C:* Jeffrey L. Kimball; *M:* Greg Camp.

Valmont 🦴🦴🦴 **1989 (R)** Another adaptation of the Choderlos de Laclos novel "Les Liaisons Dangereuses." Various members of the French aristocracy in 1782 mercilessly play each other for fools in a complex game of lust and deception. Firth and Bening are at first playfully sensual, then the stakes get too high. They share an interesting bathtub scene. Well-acted, the 1988 Frears version, "Dangerous Liaisons," is edgier. Seeing the two films together makes for interesting comparisons of characters and styles. **137m/C; VHS, DVD.** Colin Firth; Meg Tilly; Annette Bening; Fairuza Balk; Sian Phillips; Jeffrey Jones; Fabia Drake; Henry Thomas; Vincent Schiavelli; T.P. McKenna; Ian McNeice; *D:* Milos Forman; *W:* Jean-Claude Carriere; *M:* Christopher Palmer. Cesar '90: Art Dir./Set Dec., Costume Des.

Value for Money 🦴🦴 **1955** Chayley Broadbent (Gregson) inherited a fortune from his miserly father as well as his skinflint ways. When he and fiancee Ethel (Stephen) squabble, Chayley heads for London and meets gold-digging chorus girl Ruthine (Dors) in a nightclub. She thinks he's poor and rejects Chayley's advances, which hurts his pride. He becomes determined to win her but when will Chayley realize he's after the wrong girl? **90m/C; DVD.** John Gregson; Diana Dors; Susan Stephen; Derek Farr; Frank Pettingell; Joan Hickson; Donald Pleasence; Ernest Thesiger; *D:* Ken Annakin; *W:* William Fairchild; R.F. Delderfield; *C:* Geoffrey Unsworth; *M:* Malcolm Arnold.

Vamp 🦴 **1/2 1986 (R)** Two college freshmen encounter a slew of weird, semi-vampiric people in a seamy red-light district nightclub. Starts cute but goes kinky. Jones is great as the stripping vampire. **93m/C; VHS, DVD, Blu-Ray.** Grace Jones; Chris Makepeace; Robert Rusler; Gedde Watanabe; Sandy Baron; Dedee Pfeiffer; Billy Drago; Lisa Lyons; *D:* Richard Wenk; *W:* Richard Wenk; *C:* Elliot Davis; *M:* Jonathan Elias.

Vampire Academy 🦴🦴 **2014 (PG-13)** Set at a Gothic boarding school, this adaptation of the popular Richelle Mead novels combines the bitchiness and silliness of "Clueless" with the trends of the "Twilight" series. Snarky half-human/half-vampire Rose (Deutch), member of the Dhampir clan, and her BFF Lissa (Fry), a peaceful Moroi vampire, go head to head against a nasty group of evil vampires, known as the Strigoi. A harmless teen vampire flick, with Deutch stealing the show with her relentless spunk and bubblegum fight scenes. **104m/C; DVD, Blu-Ray.** *UK RO* Zoey Deutch; Lucy Fry; Danila Kozlovsky; Cameron Monaghan; Sarah Hyland; Dominic Sherwood; Joely Richardson; Olga Kurylenko; Gabriel Byrne; *D:* Mark S. Waters; *W:* Daniel Waters; *C:* Tony Pierce-Roberts; *M:* Rolfe Kent.

Vampire Assassin 🦴 **2005 (PG-13)** Martial artist Hall is a would-be triple threat in this dull vampire story in which he stars as Derek Washington, an ambitious cop who has a phobia about blood. Which is bad news when Derek realizes bad guy Slovak (Novak) is a blood-sucker. Derek teams up with vampire hunter Master Kao (Okamura) but soon figures out he may have to become what he hates in order to fight this evil. **87m/C; VHS, DVD.** Ron Hall; Mel Novak; Rudy Ray Moore; Gerald Okamura; Anthony Chow; Merry Everest; *D:* Ron Hall; *W:* Ron Hall; *C:* Ed Tillman. **VIDEO**

Vampire at Midnight 🦴 **1/2** *Maria's B Movie Mayhem: Vampire at Midnight* **1988** Fairly stupid homicide detective stalks a rampaging vampire in Los Angeles. Occasional moments of gratuitous sex thrown in for good measure. **93m/C; VHS, DVD.** Jason Williams; Gustav Vintas; Jeanie Moore; Christina Whitaker; Leslie Milne; *D:* Gregory McClatchy.

The Vampire Bat 🦴🦴 **1/2 1932** A mad scientist and a vampire bat and its supernatural demands set the stage for murders in a small town. Sets and actors borrowed from Universal Studios in this low-budget flick that looks and plays better than it should. Weird and very exploitative for 1932, now seems dated. **69m/B; VHS, DVD, Blu-Ray.** Lionel Atwill; Fay Wray; Melvyn Douglas; Dwight Frye; Maude Eburne; George E. Stone; *D:* Frank Strayer; *W:* Edward T. Lowe; *C:* Ira Morgan.

Vampire Bats 🦴 **1/2 2005** Silly sequel to the 2005 TV movie "Locusts." Maddy Rierdon (Lawless) has left her USDA post and moved to Louisiana with husband Dan (Neal) for a position as a college biology professor. When a student is found dead, Maddy figures out he wasn't killed by humans but by mutated vampire bats. So she looks for the bats' lair and a way to eradicate the menace while also exposing that fact that the mutation was caused by corporate pollution of the local river. **90m/C; DVD.** Lucy Lawless; Dylan Neal; Timothy Bottoms; Brett Butler; Tony Plana; Liam Waite; *D:* Eric Bross; *W:* Doug Prochilo; *C:* Horacio Marquinez; *M:* Douglas J. Cuomo. **TV**

Vampire Circus 🦴🦴 **1/2 1971 (R)** A circus appears in an isolated Serbian village in the 19th century but instead of bringing joy and happiness, this circus brings only death, mutilation and misery. It seems all the members are vampires who have the unique ability to transform themselves into animals. They intend to take revenge on the small town, whose inhabitants killed their evil ancestor 100 years previously. Excellent Hammer production. **84m/C; DVD, Blu-Ray.** *GB* Adrienne Corri; Laurence Payne; Thorley Walters; John Moulder-Brown; Lynne Frederick; Elizabeth Seal; Anthony (Corlan) Higgins; Richard Owens; Domini Blythe; David Prowse; *D:* Robert W. Young; *W:* Judson Kinberg; *C:* Moray Grant.

Vampire Clan 🦴 **1/2 2002 (R)** Loosely inspired by real-life events in Florida. A group of teens, hoping to become real vampires, go on the run after murdering one of their members' parents. **86m/C; DVD.** Drew Fuller; Alexandra Breckenridge; Timothy Lee DePriest; Marina Black; Kelly Kruger; Richard Gilliland; *D:* John Webb; *W:* Aaron Pope; *C:* Kristian Bernier.

Vampire Effect 🦴🦴 **1/2** *The Twins Effect; Chin gei bin* **2003 (R)** The evil Duke Dekotes (Hardt) wants to take over the world (and who wouldn't?) but he needs to snuff out Prince Kazaf (Chen)?the last offshoot of European vampire royalty—and round up his blood to do so. When Kazaf attempts to elude the Duke by going to Hong Kong, he unexpectedly falls for Helen (Chen)?who, of course, just happens to the sister of butt-kicking vampire-killer, Reeve (Cheng). There's more! Helen's friend, Gypsy (Chung) wants to get in on the action and so all three band together in an effort to foil the Duke's dastardly plot. Jackie Chan cameos in this supernatural romp. Cantonese, with English subtitles. **88m/C; VHS, DVD.** *CH* Ekin Cheng; Anthony Wong; Jackie Chan; Josie Ho; Charlene (Cheuk-Yin) Choi; Gillian (Yan-Tung) Chung; Edison Chen; Mickey Hardt; Karen Mok; *D:* Dante Lam; *W:* Jack Ng; *C:* Man Po Cheung; *M:* Kwong Wing Chan; Robert Duncan. **VIDEO**

The Vampire Happening 🦴 **1/2 1971 (R)** An actress travels to Translyvania to sell the family castle and discovers to her chagrin that her ancestors were vampires after she unknowingly releases them to party hearty on the local villagers. **101m/C; VHS, DVD.** *GE* Ferdinand "Ferdy" Mayne; Pia Degermark; Thomas Hunter; Yvor Murillo; Ingrid van Bergen; Raoul Retzer; *D:* Freddie Francis; *W:* Karl Heinz Hummel; August Rieger; *C:* Gerard Vandenburg; *M:* Jerry Van Rooyen.

The Vampire Hookers 🦴 *Cemetery Girls; Sensuous Vampires; Night of the Bloodsuckers; Twice Bitten* **1978 (R)** Man in makeup recruits bevy of beautiful bloodsuckers to lure warm blooded victims to his castle. High ham performance by Carradine. **82m/C; VHS, DVD.** *PH* John Carradine; Bruce Fairbairn; Trey Wilson; Karen Stride; Lenka Novak; Katie Dolan; Lex Winter; *D:* Cirio H. Santiago.

Vampire in Brooklyn 🦴 **1995 (R)** Murphy switches gears to play a Carribean vampire traveling to New York in search of his vampiric lady love—who turns out to be half-vamp-half-cop Bassett. As in "Coming to America," Murphy plays multiple characters, but that's three times the disappointment. Stale humor and cheap horror effects do little to break the zombie curse plaguing Murphy's career. Three days into filming, a stunt double for Bassett was killed after doing a routine jump on the set, providing a bad omen Murphy should have heeded. **103m/C; VHS, DVD.** Eddie Murphy; Angela Bassett; Kadeem Hardison; Allen Payne; Zakes Mokae; John Witherspoon; Jsu Garcia; *D:* Wes Craven; *W:* Charles Murphy; Chris Parker; Michael Lucker; *C:* Mark Irwin; *M:* J. Peter Robinson.

Vampire Journals 🦴🦴 **1/2 1996 (R)** Revenge-minded Zachary (Gunn) vows to destroy Ash (Morris), the ancient vampire who created him centuries before, especially when they both become interested in the same mortal woman, Sofia (Cerre). Shot on location in Transylvania. **82m/C; VHS, DVD, Blu-Ray.** David Gunn; Jonathan Morris; Kirsten Cerre; Starr Andreeff; *D:* Ted Nicolaou; *W:* Ted Nicolaou; *C:* Adolfo Bartoli; *M:* Richard Kosinski.

Vampire Killers 🦴 **1/2** *Lesbian Vampire Killers* **2009 (R)** Slapdash, deadpan horror comedy. Lesbian vampire Carmilla (Colloca) has plagued the secluded village of Craigswich for centuries. She turns all the young women at 18 and the men only remain alive if they agree to trick visitors into becoming blood donors. During a hiking trip, milquetoast Jimmy (Horne) and his oversized, lager-swilling best bud Fletch (Corden) meet fellow hiker Lotte (Burning), whose friends have already been converted, and a vampire-killing vicar (McGann) with a plan to stop Carmilla once and for all. Special effects are good (lots of gushing geysers of gore) but it's still surprisingly bland. **86m/C; DVD.** *GB* Matthew Horne; James Corden; MyAnna Buring; Silvia Colloca; Vera Filatova; Ashley Mulheron; Paul McGann; Louise Dylan; Lucy Gaskell; *D:* Phil Claydon; *W:* Paul Hupfield; Stewart Williams; *C:* David Higgs; *M:* Debbie Wiseman.

The Vampire Lovers 🦴🦴 **1/2 1970 (R)** An angry father goes after a lesbian vampire who has ravished his daughter and other young girls in a peaceful European village. Innovative story was soon used in countless other vampire vehicles. Hammer Studio's first horror film with nudity, another addition to the genre which spread rapidly. Based on the story "Carmilla" by Sheridan Le Fanu. Followed by "Lust for a Vampire." **91m/C; VHS, DVD, Blu-Ray.** *GB* Ingrid Pitt; Pippa Steele; Madeleine Smith; Peter Cushing; George Cole; Dawn Addams; Kate O'Mara; Ferdinand "Ferdy" Mayne; Douglas Wilmer; Harvey Hall; Charles Farrell; *D:* Roy Ward Baker; *W:* Tudor Gates; *C:* Moray Grant.

Vampire Night WOOF! **2000** Pretty Peggy (Metcalfe) runs off to Hollywood with stars in her eyes and winds up with an agent, Vezrech (Ryan), whose main talent is supplying fresh blood to his stable of vampire babes. Peggy's brother, Carl (Jerman), gets worried and comes to the big, bad city to find his sis. How can a movie with vampire babes be so dull? **76m/C; VHS, DVD.** Jimmy Jerman; Heather Metcalfe; Robert Michael Ryan; Pat Downey; Eden Rae; *D:* John Robert Stephens; *W:* John Robert Stephens; *C:* Dennis Devine; *M:* Jonathan Price.

Vampire Vixens from Venus 🦴 **1994** Three hideous drug smuggling aliens transform themselves into bodacious babes on earth so they can get what they came for. Seems their drug fix is derived from the life essence of men and they plan to drain every last drop they can. **90m/C; VHS, DVD.** Michelle (McClellan) Bauer; Leon Head; Charlie Callas; Theresa Lynn; J.J. North; Leslie Glass; *D:* Tewd A. Bohus; *W:* Tewd A. Bohus; *C:* Curtis Mattikow; *M:* Ariel Shallit.

Vampirella 🦴 **1/2** *Roger Corman Presents: Vampirella* **1996 (R)** Inhabitants of the planet Drakulon use a synthetic concoction to quench their thirst for blood. When Vampirella's (Soto) stepfather is murdered by rebels, led by Vlad Tepes (Daltrey), she must pursue them to earth to get justice. There she finds two opposing forces—the vampires led by Tepes and a paramilitary group led by Adam Van Helsing (Paul), who's out to cleanse the planet of the interlopers. But it's Vampirella who wants a final confrontation with Tepes (in Las Vegas, no less). **90m/C; VHS, DVD.** Talisa Soto; Roger Daltrey; Richard Joseph Paul; Angus Scrimm; Tom Deters; Cirnna Harney; Brian Bloom; *D:* Jim Wynorski; *W:* Gary Gerani; *C:* Andrea V. Rossotto; *M:* Joel Goldsmith. **CABLE**

Vampire's Kiss 🦴🦴🦴 **1988 (R)** Cage makes this one worthwhile; his twisted transformation from pretentious post-val dude to psychotic yuppie from hell is inspired. If his demented torment of his secretary (Alonso) doesn't give you the creeps, his scene with the cockroach will. Cage fans will enjoy his facial aerobics; Beals fans will appreciate her extensive sucking scenes (she's the vamp of his dreams). More for psych majors than horror buffs. **103m/C; VHS, DVD, Blu-Ray; Open Captioned.** Nicolas Cage; Elizabeth Ashley; Jennifer Beals; Maria Conchita Alonso; Kasi Lemmons; Bob Lujan; David Hyde Pierce; Jessica Lundy; John Michael Higgins; Amy Stiller; Marc Coppola; Debbie Rochon; *D:* Robert Bierman; *W:* Joe Minion; *C:* Stefan Czapsky; *M:* Colin Towns.

Vampires of Sorority Row: Kickboxers From Hell 🦴🦴 **1999** Trailer-trash princess Cindy (Glass) goes to college and pledges a sorority, only to find domineering pledge mistress Denise (Lydon) and a gaggle of vampires causing a commotion. T&A competes with kickboxing action and self-mocking humor (that really works!) for viewers' attention spans. You could do worse on a Saturday night when "Gandhi" is rented and you need a laugh. **80m/C; VHS, DVD.** Christine Lydon; Rich Ward; Kathryn Glass; Rita Fiora; Erika Gardener; Christian Caitlin; Angelica Hayden; *D:* Dennis Devine; Kathryn Glass; *W:* Dennis Devine; *M:* Jonathan Price.

Vampires Suck 🦴 **2010 (PG-13)** Forgettable, lame, and obvious genre spoof of the "Twilight" movies—though thankfully short. Becca (Proske), the angsty teenaged daughter of the local Sporks, Washington sheriff (Bader), falls for broody, pale vampire Edward Sullen (Lanter). Classmate and cat-chasing werewolf Jacob White (Riggi) would rather Becca choose him over the bloodsucker. **82m/C; Blu-Ray.** Matt Lanter; Diedrich Bader; Ken Jeong; Anneliese van der Pol; David DeLuise; Dave Foley; Arielle Kebbel; Jenn Proske; Chris Riggi; Kelsey Ford; Jeff Witzke; ***D:*** Jason Friedberg; Aaron Seltzer; ***W:*** Jason Friedberg; Aaron Seltzer; ***C:*** Shawn Maurer; ***M:*** Christopher Lennertz.

Vamps 🦴 1/2 **2012 (PG-13)** Director Heckerling reunites with "Clueless" star Silverstone for this mildly amusing vampire comedy/romance. Best friends Goody (Silverstone) and Stacy (Ritter) don't drink from humans (but the rat population is in trouble) and are looking for love despite past relationship issues. That's about it. **93m/C; DVD, Blu-Ray.** Alicia Silverstone; Krysten Ritter; Dan Stevens; Justin Kirk; Sigourney Weaver; Richard Lewis; Malcolm McDowell; Wallace Shawn; ***D:*** Amy Heckerling; ***W:*** Amy Heckerling; ***C:*** Tim Suhrstedt; ***M:*** David Kitay.

Vampyr 🦴🦴🦴🦴 *Vampyr, Ou l'Etrange Aventure de David Gray; Vampyr, Der Traum des David Gray; Not against the Flesh; Castle of Doom; The Strange Adventure of David Gray; The Vampire* **1931** Dreyer's classic portrays a hazy, dreamlike world full of chilling visions from the point of view of a young man who believes himself surrounded by vampires and who dreams of his own burial in a most disturbing way. Evil lurks around every corner as camera angles, light and shadow sometimes overwhelm plot. A high point in horror films based on a collection of horror stories by Sheridan Le Fanu. In German with English subtitles. **75m/B; VHS, DVD, Blu-Ray.** *GE FR* Julian West; Sybille Schmitz; Henriette Gerard; Maurice Schutz; Rena Mandel; Jan Hieronimko; Albert Bras; ***D:*** Carl Theodor Dreyer; ***W:*** Carl Theodor Dreyer; Christen Jul; ***C:*** Rudolph Mate; Louis Nee; ***M:*** Wolfgang Zeller.

Vampyres 🦴🦴 1/2 *Vampyres, Daughters of Dracula; Blood Hunger; Satan's Daughters; Daughters of Dracula; Vampire Orgy* **1974 (R)** Alluring female vampires coerce unsuspecting motorists to their castle for a good time, which ends in death. Anulka was the centerfold girl in "Playboy"'s May 1973 issue. **90m/C; VHS, DVD, Blu-Ray.** *GB* Marianne Morris; Anulka; Murray Brown; Brian Deacon; Sally Faulkner; Michael Byrne; Karl Lanchbury; Bessie Love; Elliott Sullivan; ***D:*** Joseph (Jose Ramon) Larraz; ***W:*** Diane Daubeney; ***C:*** Harry Waxman; ***M:*** James Clark.

The Van 🦴 *Chevy Van* **1977 (R)** A recent high school graduate passes on the college scene so he can spend more time picking up girls in his van. A lame sex (and sexist) comedy. **92m/C; VHS, DVD.** Stuart Getz; Deborah White; Danny DeVito; Harry Moses; Maurice Barkin; ***D:*** Sam Grossman; ***W:*** Robert J. Rosenthal; Celia Susan Cotelo; ***C:*** Irv Goodnoff; ***M:*** Steve Eaton.

The Van 🦴🦴🦴 **1995 (R)** The last of writer Roddy Doyle's Barrytown trilogy (following "The Commitments" and "The Snapper") is set in 1989-90, in Dublin, where baker Bimbo (O'Kelly) has just lost his job. Tired of sitting around the pub, he takes his redundancy money and buys a filthy, dilapidated fish 'n' chips van, which he decides to run with best friend Larry (Meany), with their families helping out. The months pass quickly and their venture turns out to be a big success but the close quarters puts a strain on the mens' friendship until Bimbo has another idea. **105m/C; VHS, DVD.** *GB* Donal O'Kelly; Colm Meaney; Ger Ryan; Caroline Rotwell; Neili Conroy; Ruaidhri Conroy; ***D:*** Stephen Frears; ***W:*** Roddy Doyle; ***C:*** Oliver Stapleton; ***M:*** Eric Clapton; Richard Hartley.

Van Gogh 🦴🦴🦴 **1992 (R)** "One doesn't produce 100 masterpieces in a state of depression—Van Gogh died from having had a glimpse of happiness." This is the way director Pialat sums up his approach to the last 67 days in the life of Vincent Van Gogh. Dutronc is skillful in portraying Van Gogh as a man with no excuses, and even a sense of humor. Not a psychological portrait and offers no answers—it's simply one artist's view of another. In French with English subtitles. **155m/C; VHS, DVD, Blu-Ray.** *FR* Jacques Dutronc; Alexandra London; Gerard Sety; Bernard Le Coq; Corinne Bourdon; ***D:*** Maurice Pialat; ***W:*** Maurice Pialat; ***C:*** Gilles Henry; Emmanuel Machuel; ***M:*** Edith Vesperini. Cesar '92: Actor (Dutronc).

Van Helsing 🦴🦴🦴 **2004 (PG-13)** Bram Stoker's title character takes on Frankenstein's monster, the Wolf Man and Count Dracula. Hollywood's macho "Indiana Jones meets James Bond" Van Helsing (Jackman) is a high-tech bow and arrow-slinging, creature-slaying hero who travels with sidekick Carl (Wenham), to Transylvania to kill the head vampire himself (Roxburgh). Sexy gypsy Anna (Beckinsale) turns up seeking to vanquish Dracula and lift a curse her family has suffered for centuries. With chase scenes, a masked ball, nonstop adventure, monsters galore, and a script that doesn't take itself too seriously, this f/x extravaganza will find something to appeal to everyone. **132m/C; DVD, Blu-Ray, UMD, HD-DVD.** *US CZ* Hugh Jackman; Kate Beckinsale; Richard Roxburgh; David Wenham; Shuler Hensley; Elena Anaya; Will(iam) Kemp; Kevin J. O'Connor; Alun Armstrong; Thomas (Tom) Fisher; Samuel West; Robbie Coltrane; Silvia Colloca; Josie Maran; Stephen H. Fisher; ***D:*** Stephen Sommers; ***W:*** Stephen Sommers; ***C:*** Allen Daviau; ***M:*** Alan Silvestri.

Van Nuys Blvd. 🦴 1/2 **1979 (R)** The popular boulevard is the scene where the cool southern California guys converge for cruising and girl watching, so naturally it's where a country hick comes to test his drag racing skills and check out the action. **93m/C; VHS, DVD.** Bill Adler; Cynthia Wood; Dennis Bowen; Melissa Prophet; ***D:*** William Sachs.

Van Wilder: Freshman Year 🦴 1/2 **2008 (R)** The third flick in the franchise is a prequel detailing how Van Wilder (Bennett) became the ultimate college party animal. As he starts his freshman year at Coolidge College, Van Wilder must deal with an uptight Dean and a campus full of girls who have taken a vow of chastity even as he pursues ultimate babe Kaitlin (Cavallari). **100m/C; DVD.** Jonathan Bennett; Steven Talley; Kurt Fuller; Kristin Cavallari; Jerry Shea; ***D:*** Harvey Glazer; ***W:*** Todd McCullough; ***C:*** Shawn Maurer; ***M:*** Nathan Wang. **VIDEO**

Vanessa 🦴 1/2 **2007** Vanessa runs away from home to escape her abusive stepfather and only survives on the streets by turning to prostitution. Just when she decides that suicide is the only way out, she meets a stranger who offers her hope. **88m/C; DVD.** Nick Mancuso; Candice Prentice; ***D:*** Bozidar D. Benedikt; ***W:*** Bozidar D. Benedikt. **VIDEO**

The Vanguard 🦴 1/2 **2008** In the future WWIII has rendered the Earth nearly uninhabitable except for a lush forest occupied by a recluse who may be mankind's last hope against flesh-eating killer mutants who die when you whack them in the head like the zombie--they so totally aren't meant to represent. **89m/C; DVD, Streaming.** *UK* Karen Admiraal; Jack Bailey; Ray Bullock, Jr.; Emma Choy; ***D:*** Matthew Hope; ***W:*** Matthew Hope; ***C:*** David Byrne; ***M:*** Mark Delaney.

Vanilla Sky 🦴🦴 1/2 **2001 (R)** Director Crowe goes existential in this puzzling, surreal thriller, a remake of Alejandro Amenabar's 1997 Spanish film, "Abre los Ojos." Cruise plays David Aames, a publishing magnate and playboy who's got it all except for real love. Just when he thinks he's found it in the form of aspiring dancer Sofia (Cruz, reprising her role from the original), a bitter ex-lover (Diaz) changes the game by inadvertently changing David's pretty face. Fairly straightforward allegory becomes science fiction, where David (and the audience) can't tell dream from reality. Thought-provoking, even deliberately confusing plot may frustrate some. But for those who like to sink their brains into a film, it'll will be rewarding, whether you like the explain-it-all ending or not. Decent acting, dreamy cinematography, and an engaging soundtrack will provide entertainment at the very least. **135m/C; VHS, DVD, Blu-Ray.** Tom Cruise; Penelope Cruz; Cameron Diaz; Jason Lee; Kurt Russell; Noah Taylor; Timothy Spall; Tilda Swinton; Alicia Witt; Johnny Galecki; Michael Shannon; ***D:*** Cameron Crowe; ***W:*** Cameron Crowe; ***C:*** John Toll; ***M:*** Nancy Wilson.

Vanina Vanini 🦴🦴🦴 1/2 **1961** An acclaimed Rossellini historical drama about the daughter of an Italian aristocrat in 1824 who nurses and falls in love with a wounded patriot hiding in her house. Based on a Stendhal short story. In Italian with English subtitles. **113m/B; VHS, DVD.** *IT* Sandra Milo; Laurent Terzieff; ***D:*** Roberto Rossellini.

Vanished 🦴🦴🦴 *Danielle Steel's Vanished* **1995 (PG)** Marielle and Charles are happily married in 1920 Paris until the tragic death of their son breaks them up. Marielle remarries and has another child who gets kidnapped and her estranged husband is arrested for the crime. **120m/C; DVD.** George Hamilton; Lisa Rinna; Robert Hays; Maurice Godin; Alex D. Linz; ***D:*** George Kaczender; ***W:*** Kathleen Rowell; ***C:*** Pierre Mignot; ***M:*** Francois Dompierre. **CABLE**

Vanished 🦴 1/2 **2006** Hope (Cook) and Jake (Rowe) try to rekindle their shaky marriage by vacationing on the island of San Carlos. When Jake suddenly disappears and the cops learn of his chronic infidelities, they dismiss Hope's fears. She starts investigating, is warned off, and discovers Jake was kidnapped by a local voodoo leader because there's a sordid secret in Jake's past. **90m/C; DVD.** A.J. Cook; Brad Rowe; Carlos Ponce; Joemy Blanco; Luis Raul; Oscar H. Guerrero; ***D:*** Michael Switzer; ***W:*** Matt Dorff; ***C:*** Barry Stone. **CABLE**

The Vanished Empire 🦴🦴 **2008** Eighteen-year-old Sergey comes of age in 1973 Moscow, where he's only interested in buying contraband rock albums and imported jeans to impress girlfriend Lyuda. Title refers not only to the changes happening in the U.S.S.R. but also to the site of a vanished civilization that his archeologist grandfather helped to excavate. Russian with subtitles. **105m/C; DVD.** *RU* Aleksandr Lyapin; Lidiya Milyuzina; Armen Dzhigarkhanyan; Ivan Kupreyenko; Yegor Baranovsky; Yanina Kalganova; Olga Tumajkina; ***D:*** Karen Shakhnazarov; ***W:*** Sergei Rokotov; Yevgeni Nikishov; ***C:*** Shandor Berkeshi; ***M:*** Konstantin Shevelyov.

Vanished-Left Behind: Next Generation 🦴 **2016 (PG-13)** Vanished is a boring retread of the Left Behind series containing a teenage romantic triangle meant to appeal to younger viewers. It sabotages itself in this regard by being so heavy handed with it's religious themes it comes across as propaganda implying anyone who disagrees with the central premise is Evil. **88m/C; DVD, Blu-Ray, Streaming.** Mason Dye; Dylan Sprayberry; Brigid Brannagh; Keely Wilson; Rachel Hendrix; ***D:*** Larry A. McLean; ***W:*** Kim Beyer-Johnson; John Considine Johnson; ***C:*** Pete Wages; ***M:*** B.J. Davis; Josh Debney; Andrew Grush. **VIDEO**

The Vanishing 🦴🦴🦴 *Spoorloos* **1988** When his wife suddenly disappears, a young husband finds himself becoming increasingly obsessed with finding her. Three years down the road, his world has become one big, mad nightmare. Then, just as suddenly, the answer confronts him, but the reality of it may be too horrible to face. Well-made dark thriller based on "The Golden Egg" by Tim Krabbe. In French and Dutch with English subtitles. Remade by Sluizer in 1992. **107m/C; VHS, DVD, Blu-Ray.** *NL FR* Barnard Pierre Donnadieu; Johanna Ter Steege; Gene Bervoets; Gwen Eckhaus; Bernadette Le Sache; Tania Latarjet; Lucille Glenn; Roger Souza; ***D:*** George Sluizer; ***W:*** George Sluizer; Tim Krabbe; ***C:*** Toni Kuhn; ***M:*** Henny Vrienten.

The Vanishing 🦴🦴 1/2 **1993 (R)** Director Sluizer remakes his own 1988 Dutch film "Spoorloos" to lesser effect. Tense thriller about the disappearance of a woman (Bullock) at a highway rest stop. Her boyfriend (Sutherland) becomes obsessed with locating her, searching for some three years as he is haunted by her memory. Unlike the Dutch original, the remake resorts to a clumsy ending designed for feel-good appeal. Based on the novel "The Golden Egg" by Tim Krabbe. **110m/C; VHS, DVD, Blu-Ray.** Jeff Bridges; Kiefer Sutherland; Nancy Travis; Sandra Bullock; Park Overall; Lisa Eichhorn; George Hearn; Maggie Linderman; Lynn Hamilton; ***D:*** George Sluizer; ***W:*** Todd Graff; ***M:*** Jerry Goldsmith.

The Vanishing 🦴🦴 1/2 **2019 (R)** On the Scottish Flannan Isle in 1900, three lighthouse keepers—older leader Thomas (Mullan), family man James (Butler), and naive young Donald (Swindells)—are going about their duties when they come across a dead body and a trunk full of gold. As they contemplate what to do, two scowling men appear asking about both questions. Before long, everyone on the island must fight for their survival. Based on a true story known as the Flannan Isle Mystery that remains unsolved, Butler leads an impressive cast but the story loses steam. **106m/C; DVD.** Gerard Butler; Peter Mullan; Connor Swindells; Soren Malling; Olafur Darri Olafsson; ***D:*** Kristoffer Nyholm; ***W:*** Joe Bone; Celyn Jones; ***C:*** Jorgen Johansson; ***M:*** Benjamin Wallfisch.

The Vanishing American 🦴🦴 **1925** The mistreatment of the American Indian is depicted in this sweeping Western epic that stars Dix as Navajo chieftain Nophaie. Nophaie must reconcile the heritage of his people with the 20th century and deal with a crooked government agent. Filmed in Monument Valley and the Betatkin Cliff Dwellings of Arizona. Based on the novel by Zane Grey. **109m/B; Silent; VHS, DVD.** Richard Dix; Noah Beery, Sr.; Lois Wilson; ***D:*** George B. Seitz; ***W:*** Lucien Hubbard; Ethel Doherty; ***C:*** Harry Perry; Charles E. Schoenbaum.

Vanishing Legion 🦴🦴 **1931** Western serial with outdoor action and gunplay. Twelve chapters, 13 minutes each. **156m/B; VHS, DVD.** Frankie Darro; Harry Carey, Sr.; ***D:*** B. Reeves Eason.

The Vanishing of Sidney Hall 🦴🦴 *Sidney Hall* **2017 (R)** A drama about a high school writer and his unexpected success. Titular Sidney (Lerman) aspires to be a great author like Hunter S. Thompson and David Foster Wallace, and believing that his critical teacher Mrs. Hall (Monaghan) does not understand him even though she is a published author. Sidney proves her wrong by writing Suburban Tragedy, a novel which becomes a best-seller. Along the way, he finds love, gains a stalker in the Seeker (Chandler), and realizes that fame comes at a high cost. Despite solid production values, the film is superficial and its power is undercut its attitude towards women. **119m/C; DVD, Blu-Ray, Streaming.** Logan Lerman; Elle Fanning; Michelle Monaghan; Kyle Chandler; Nathan Lane; ***D:*** Shawn Christensen; ***W:*** Shawn Christensen; Jason Dolan; ***C:*** Daniel Katz; ***M:*** Darren Morze.

Vanishing on 7th Street 🦴 **2010 (R)** Remarkably dull and contrived indie horror with chatty characters you won't have any interest in seeing survive. After a citywide power outage, most of Detroit's citizens are sucked up by wraithlike creatures, leaving only piles of clothing behind. Five people make their way to the same bar, which has a generator to keep them alive (at least momentarily). Apparently unable to do anything else, they talk. Baffling that major stars Christensen and Newton headline. **90m/C; DVD, Blu-Ray.** Hayden Christensen; John Leguizamo; Thandie Newton; Jacob Latimore; Taylor Groothius; ***D:*** Brad Anderson; ***W:*** Anthony Jaswinski; ***C:*** Uta Briesewitz; ***M:*** Lucas Vidal.

Vanishing Point 🦴🦴 **1971 (R)** An ex-racer makes a bet to deliver a souped-up car from Denver to San Francisco in 15 hours. Taking pep pills along the way, he eludes police, meets up with a number of characters, and finally crashes into a roadblock. Rock score helps attract this film's cult following. **98m/C; VHS, DVD, Blu-Ray.** Barry Newman; Cleavon Little; Gilda Texter; Dean Jagger; Paul Koslo; Robert Donner; Severn Darden; Victoria Medlin; ***D:*** Richard Sarafian; ***W:*** Guillermo Cain; ***C:*** John A. Alonzo; ***M:*** Jim Bowen; Peter Carpenter.

The Vanishing Virginian 🦴🦴 1/2 **1941** Slice of Americana family comedy/drama. The citizens of Lynchburg, Virginia are struggling with the rapid changes occurring in the early decades of the 20th century. Among those bewildered by all the newfangled ideas are public prosecutor Robert 'Cap'n Bob' Yancey (Morgan) and his wife Rosa (Byington). Their independently-minded children feel differently, including daughter Rebecca (Grayson) who joins the suffragettes. Based on Rebecca Yancey Williams' memoir. **97m/B; DVD.** Frank Morgan; Spring Byington; Kathryn Grayson; Mark Daniels; Johnny Mitchell; Natalie Thompson; Dick(ie) Jones; Juanita Quigley; Scotty Beckett; Elizabeth

Patterson; *D:* Frank Borzage; *W:* Jan Fortune; *C:* Charles Lawton, Jr.; *M:* David Snell.

Vanity Fair **1932** Loy stars in this tale of a wily and manipulative woman looking for the perfect marriage. This was the 58th film for the 27-year-old Loy, but even she couldn't save it. Of course, none of the three films based on the story by Thackeray have done it justice. **67m/B; VHS, DVD.** Myrna Loy; Conway Tearle; Barbara Kent; Walter Byron; Anthony Bushell; Billy Bevan; Montagu Love; Mary Forbes; *D:* Chester M. Franklin.

Vanity Fair ½ **1999** Orphaned Becky Sharp (Little) is beautiful, clever and, despite her poverty, determined to get ahead in society so she can enjoy the same privileges as her posh childhood friend, Amelia Sedley (Grey). And she's not too particular about how she stakes her claim. Based on the novel by William Makepeace Thackeray, this Brit miniseries loses the author's acerbic voice which makes for a bland, though typically lavish, production. **300m/C; VHS, DVD.** Natasha Little; Frances Grey; Nathaniel Parker; Philip Glenister; Jeremy Swift; Roger Ashton-Griffiths; Eleanor Bron; Anton Lesser; Miriam Margolyes; Michele Dotrice; David Bradley; David Ross; *D:* Marc Munden; *W:* Andrew Davies; *C:* Oliver Curtis. **TV**

Vanity Fair ½ **2004 (PG-13)** In William Makepeace Thackeray's novel "Vanity Fair," Becky Sharp is an unrepentant social climber. But with Witherspoon tackling Becky in director Nair's version, such calculation just wouldn't do. Becky still aspires to climb the slippery social ladder in early 19th century Britain, but here she has a heart. Becky first flirts with the wealthy, foppish brother (Maudsley) of her sweet-but-dim friend Amelia (Garai) but cannot bring him to marriage. She then rolls the dice with dashing gambler/soldier Rawdon Crawley (Purefoy). However, things never quite turn out for greedy Becky. Nair's hard-pressed to cover the novel's 30 years and multiple subplots so the film has a rushed feeling. Witherspoon is plucky but the supporting cast of British stalwarts (Hoskins, Atkins, Broadbent, etc.) gives the endeavor its panache. **137m/C; VHS, DVD.** *US GB* Reese Witherspoon; Eileen Atkins; Jim Broadbent; Gabriel Byrne; Romola Garai; Bob Hoskins; Rhys Ifans; Geraldine McEwan; James Purefoy; Jonathan Rhys Meyers; Douglas Hodge; Natasha Little; Tony Maudsley; *D:* Mira Nair; *W:* Matthew Faulk; Mark Skeet; Julian Fellowes; *C:* Declan Quinn; *M:* Mychael Danna.

The Vanquished *I Vinti; Les Vaincus; Youth and Perversion* **1952** Director Michaelangelo Antonioni nearly wasn't able to put forth this controversial trio of nihilistic stories centering on well off youths in Britain, France, and Italy who indulge in crime for their own selfish purposes and end up possibly over their heads. Inspired by headlines of the day, all three stories had to be changed to get the film off the ground. **110m/B; DVD, Blu-Ray.** *FR IT* Franco Interlenghi; Peter Reynolds; Patrick Barr; Fay Compton; Etchika Choureau; Francoise Arnoul; *D:* Michelangelo Antonioni; *W:* Michelangelo Antonioni; *C:* Enzo Serafin; *M:* Giovanni Fusco.

The Vanquisher *Final Target* **2010 (R)** Blindly incoherent action film who's murky plot involves the Bush administration, evil CIA agents, ninja assassins from Japan, terrorists, and an elite unit of the Royal Thai Police composed of sword wielding female models in tight clothing. **90m/C; DVD, Blu-Ray.** *TH* Jacqueline Apitananon; Kessarin Ektawatkul; Sophita Sribanchean; *D:* Manop Udomdej; *W:* Manop Udomdej; *C:* Pipat Piyaka; *M:* Patai Puangchin.

Vantage Point ½ **2008 (PG-13)** Do they celebrate Groundhog day in Spain? U.S. President Ashton (Hurt) has just arrived in Spain to give the opening speech at a global "War on Terror" conference when he's shot. Sheer chaos ensues as eight different versions of the event unfold from eigh points of view. American tourist Howard Lewis (Whitaker) with his videocam; Secret Service agents Thomas Barnes (Quaid) and Kent Taylor (Fox); news producer Rex Brooks (Weaver) and others all saw the event, but in different ways. Is it terrorists or a conspiracy? Sure, each version adds another piece of the puzzle, but by the time it all actually comes together, the audience may be too confused or bored to care. **90m/C; DVD, Blu-Ray.** Dennis Quaid; Matthew Fox; Forest Whitaker; William Hurt; Sigourney Weaver; Bruce McGill; Edgar Ramirez; Said Taghmaoui; Ayelet Zurer; Zoe Saldana; Eduardo Noriega; Richard T. Jones; Holt McCallany; Leonardo Nam; James LeGros; *D:* Stuart Baird; Pete Travis; *W:* Barry L. Levy; *C:* Amir M. Mokri; *M:* Atli Orvarsson.

Vanya on 42nd Street ½ **1994 (PG)** Group of actors in street clothes rehearse a workshop production of Chekhov's play, "Uncle Vanya," in New York's dilapidated New Amsterdam Theater. Theatrical director Gregory first gets his group together in 1989, with Mamet's contemporary adaptation, and they continue to work in private until Malle films their production some four years later before a small, select audience. Shawn, best known for "My Dinner with Andre" portrays Vanya with depth and complexity. The other actors shine as well, often against type, in this complex Russian drama of desperation. **119m/C; VHS, DVD, Blu-Ray.** Wallace Shawn; Julianne Moore; Brooke Smith; Larry Pine; George Gaynes; Lynn Cohen; Madhur Jaffrey; Phoebe Brand; Jerry Mayer; Andre Gregory; *D:* Louis Malle; *W:* Andre Gregory; David Mamet; *C:* Declan Quinn; *M:* Joshua Redman.

Varian's War ½ **2001** Based on the true story of American Varian Fry (Hurt), who is the editor of a foreign affairs publication when he witnesses the Nazi rise in Berlin and decides he must help Europe's Jews despite American neutrality. He heads off to Marseilles where a number of artists and intellectuals wait to escape Vichy France and establishes an underground rescue organization. **120m/C; VHS, DVD.** William Hurt; Julia Ormond; Matt Craven; Maury Chaykin; Alan Arkin; Lynn Redgrave; Remy Girard; Christopher Heyerdahl; Vlasta Vrana; Gloria Carlin; John Dunn-Hill; *D:* Lionel Chetwynd; *W:* Lionel Chetwynd; *C:* Daniel Jobin; *M:* Neil Smolar. **CABLE**

Variety *Vaudeville; Variete* **1925** Simple and tragic tale of a scheming young girl and the two men of whom she takes advantage. The European circus in all its beautiful sadness is the setting. Extraordinary cast and superb cinematography. Silent. **104m/B; Silent; VHS, DVD, Blu-Ray.** *GE* Emil Jannings; Lya de Putti; Warwick Ward; Werner Krauss; *D:* E.A. Dupont; *W:* E.A. Dupont; *C:* Karl Freund.

Variety ½ **1983** Christine (McLeod) gets a job selling tickets at a porno theatre near Times Square and starts getting curious about the milieu. Her relationships begin to change as her interest in pornography becomes all-consuming. **97m/C; VHS, DVD.** Sandy McLeod; Will Patton; Richard Davidson; *D:* Bette Gordon; *W:* Kathy Acker; *C:* Tom DiCillo; *M:* John Lurie.

Variety Lights ½ *Luci del Varieta; Lights of Variety* **1951** Fellini's first (albeit joint) directorial effort, wherein a young girl runs away with a travelling vaudeville troupe and soon becomes its main attraction as a dancer. Filled with Fellini's now-familiar delight in the bizarre and sawdust/tinsel entertainment. In Italian with English subtitles. **93m/B; VHS, DVD.** *IT* Giulietta Masina; Peppino de Filippo; Carla Del Poggio; Folco Lulli; *D:* Federico Fellini; Alberto Lattuada; *W:* Federico Fellini; Alberto Lattuada; Tullio Pinelli; Ennio Flaiano; *C:* Otello Martelli; *M:* Felice Lattuada.

Varsity Blood **2014** A high school horror revenge flick in which a mascot turns the tables on the athletes and cheerleaders. After the Hogeye High School Warriors' Halloween game, the players and cheerleaders head to an out-of-the-way farmhouse for a rowdy party. The group also harbors a dark secret, a fact that comes to light when they are attacked by an unknown guest dressed like the team's Indian warrior mascot. Armed with a battle axe and a bow and arrow, the mascot's thirst for blood and revenge soon makes the party a bloodbath no one will ever forget. **87m/C; DVD, Streaming, Download.** Lexi Giovagnoli; Wesley Scott; Debbie Rochon; Natalie Peyton; Blair Jackson; *D:* Jake Helgren; *W:* Jake Helgren; *C:* Troy Bakewell; *M:* Tom Jemmott. **VIDEO**

Varsity Blues ½ **1998 (R)** After star quarterback Lance (Walker) goes down with an injury, backup Mox (Van Der Beek) learns the perks of stardom in a small Texas town obsessed with high school football. It's not all free six-packs and groupies in whipped cream bikinis, however. He butts heads with blood-and-guts Coach Kilmer (Voight), whose win-at-all-costs philosophy is injuring his players. Mox leads the players in a rebellion against the coach, leaving the usual doubts about the inevitable "big game." The young cast does an admirable job lifting the material above the average jock flick, but it lurches into the gutter a little too often for some tastes. **103m/C; VHS, DVD, Blu-Ray.** James Van Der Beek; Jon Voight; Paul Walker; Ron Lester; Scott Caan; Richard Lineback; Amy Smart; Thomas F. Duffy; Tony Perenski; Tiffany C. Love; Eliel Swinton; Jill Parker Jones; Joe Pichler; Ali Larter; *D:* Brian Robbins; *W:* W. Peter Iliff; *C:* Charles Cohen; *M:* Mark Isham. MTV Movie Awards '99: Breakthrough Perf. (Van Der Beek).

Varsity Show **1937** Broadway producer Chuck Daly (Powell) is an alumnus of Winfield College and offers to produce the annual varsity show to the delight of Betty (Lane) and her fellow students. Only their conservative faculty advisor, Prof. Biddle (Catlett), opposes their choice and Daly bows out to prevent trouble. The students travel to New York on spring break to convince Daly to change his mind and wind up putting on the show there. The big Busby Berkeley dance finale is a tribute to the nation's colleges and got the choreographer an Oscar nomination. Beware the edited version released at 80 minutes. **120m/B; DVD.** Dick Powell; Priscilla Lane; Fred Waring; Walter Catlett; Rosemary Lane; Sterling Holloway; Ted Healy; Mabel Todd; Lee Dixon; *D:* William Keighley; *W:* Warren Duff; Sid Herzig; Richard Macaulay; Jerry Wald; *C:* Sol Polito; George Barnes.

The Vast of Night **2020 (PG-13)** In a small town in 1950s America, the entire community is at a high school basketball game. Everett (Horowitz) and Fay (McCormick) leave the game to go to their jobs: radio show host and town switchboard operator, respectively. When strange things start happening -- weird sounds, static, and interference -- it affects them both. Working together, they use their technology knowledge to make sense of it all. Director Patterson's debut is a low budget indie sci-fi with a relatively common plot, but it's vivid storytelling makes it full of wonder. **89m/C; DVD.** Sierra McCormick; Jake Horowitz; Gail Cronauer; Cheyenne Barton; *V:* Bruce Davis; *D:* Andrew Patterson; *W:* James Montague; Craig W. Sanger; *C:* Miguel Ioann Littin Menz; *M:* Erick Alexander; Jared Bulmer.

Vatel **2000 (PG-13)** Lavish period drama suffers from a dull screenplay and a lack of gusto. In 1671, Sun King Louis XIV (Sands) is ruling with the usual decadence when he and his court are invited to the country chateau of the Prince de Conde (Glover), who's hoping to curry favor. Conde leaves the plans for the royal visit to his steward, Francois Vatel (Depardieu). He must supply food and entertainment to keep the court amused but Vatel provokes envy as well. Depardieu is efficient but the English language cast seems to be primping more than acting. **117m/C; VHS, DVD.** *GB FR* Gerard Depardieu; Uma Thurman; Tim Roth; Julian Glover; Julian Sands; Timothy Spall; Arielle Dombasle; Hywel Bennett; Richard Griffiths; Feodor Atkine; Phillippe LeRoy; Murray Lachlan Young; *D:* Roland Joffé; *W:* Jeanne Labrune; Tom Stoppard; *C:* Robert Fraisse; *M:* Ennio Morricone.

The Vault **2000 (R)** Teacher Mr. Burnett (Lyde) takes four students—Dezaray (Pride), Willy (Priester), Zipper (Walker), and Kyle (Davis) to visit an old high school, which is scheduled to be demolished. (The four kids fit the stereotypes of cheerleader, jock, nerd, and tough guy.) The school was originally a way-station for slaves and the group hopes to rescue some historical items (or something like that). Once they arrive at the school, they meet the eerie security guard Spangler (Papi), who warns them to not venture into the basement. You see, there's a very old locked door in the basement, and behind that door is...ultimate evil. Unfortunately, the film ends just as it's beginning to get interesting. **85m/C; DVD.** Ted Lyde; Shani Pride; Austin Priester; Kyle Walker; Michael Cory Davis; Leopoldo Papi; *D:* James Black.

Vault **2019** In mid-'70s Providence, longtime friends Deuce (Rossi) and Chucky (Standen) have been successfully robbing pawnshops and jewelry stores when they up their game and rob two banks in one day. They are caught and imprisoned when the theft doesn't go right. To get ahead inside, Chucky helps Gerry (Johnson), the right-hand man of local mob boss Raymond (Palminteri). Impressed by the pair, Gerry presents a life and career-changing opportunity for them after their release. Based on true events, the period crime drama works because of the lead characters' friendship and impressive period detail, but ends up overpowered by clichés. **99m/C; DVD.** Theo Rossi; Clive Standen; Samira Wiley; Chazz Palminteri; Don Johnson; *D:* Tom DeNucci; *W:* Tom DeNucci; B. Dolan; *C:* Sam Eilersten; *M:* B. Dolan.

Vault of Horror ½ *Tales from the Crypt II* **1973 (R)** A collection of five terrifying tales based on original stories from the E.C. comic books of the 1950s. Stories include, "Midnight Mess," "Bargain in Death," "This Trick'll Kill You," "The Neat Job," and "Drawn and Quartered." **86m/C; VHS, DVD, Blu-Ray.** *GB* Terry-Thomas; Curt Jurgens; Glynis Johns; Dawn Addams; Daniel Massey; Tom Baker; Michael Craig; Anna Massey; Denholm Elliott; *D:* Roy Ward Baker; *W:* Milton Subotsky.

The Vector File ½ **2003 (R)** Little Mattie got her hands on a wicked DNA code that threatens the world if not kept under wraps forcing dear old dad to fend off the terrorists in pursuit of it. Stars real-life family—Van Dien is Oxenberg's husband and India is her daughter. **92m/C; VHS, DVD.** Casper Van Dien; Catherine Oxenberg; Timothy Balme; William Wallace; Katherine Kennard; India Oxenberg; Roz Turnbull; George Henare; Laurie Foel; Stephen Hall; David Stott; Chic Littlewood; Craig Hall; Paddy Wilson; Paul Norell; Roz Worthington; Chris Easley; *D:* Eliot Christopher; *W:* Iain McFadyen; *C:* Kevin Riley; *M:* Bruce Lynch. **VIDEO**

Vegas **1978** A private detective, with Las Vegas beauties as assistants and pursuers, solves the murder of a teenage runaway girl. Pilot for a TV series. Scriptwriter Mann went on to do "Miami Vice." Currently only available as part of the tv series on dvd. **74m/C; VHS, DVD.** Robert Urich; June Allyson; Tony Curtis; Will Sampson; Greg Morris; *D:* Richard Lang; *W:* Michael Mann. **TV**

Vegas in Space **WOOF!** **1994** Four male astronauts take a secret mission to the planet Clitoris, the all-female pleasure plant where men are forbidden to trod. To capture a heinous villainous, they swallow gender-reversal pills in order to infiltrate the resort as show-girls. Typical Troma trash. Boasts an all-transvestite cast. **85m/C; VHS, DVD.** Doris Fish; Miss X; Ginger Quest; Ramona Fischer; Lori Naslund; Timmy Spence; Silvana Nova; Sandelle Kincaid; Tommy Pace; Arturo Galster; Jennifer Blowdryer; Freida Lay; Tippi; *D:* Phillip R. Ford; *W:* Phillip R. Ford; Doris Fish; Miss X; *C:* Robin Clark; *M:* Ramona Fischer; Timmy Spence.

The Vegas Strip Wars *Las Vegas Strip War* **1984** Rival casino owners battle it out in the land of lady luck. Unmemorable except for Jones's Don King impersonation and the fact that it was Hudson's last TV movie. **100m/C; VHS, DVD.** Rock Hudson; James Earl Jones; Noriyuki "Pat" Morita; Sharon Stone; Robert Costanzo; *D:* George Englund.

Vegas Vacation **1996 (PG)** It may not have come out under the "National Lampoon" banner but you'll recognize both the characters and the situations. The innocent Griswold clan head from their Chicago home to the bright lights and gambling temptations of Las Vegas. Clark (Chase) blows all their money, Ellen (D'Angelo) reveals a hidden passion for Wayne Newton, daughter Audrey (Nichols) decides to become a go-go dancer, and son Rusty (Embry) turns into a high roller who draws the attention of the mob. Oh yeah, dimwit cousin Eddie (Quaid) also tries to supply a few yucks. **98m/C; VHS, DVD, Blu-Ray.** Chevy Chase; Beverly D'Angelo; Randy Quaid; Ethan (Randall) Embry; Miriam Flynn; Marisol Nichols; Shae D'Lyn; Wallace Shawn; Wayne Newton; ***Cameo(s):*** Sid Caesar; Julia Sweeney; Christie Brinkley; *D:* Stephen Kessler; *W:* Elisa Bell; *C:* William A. Fraker; *M:* Joel McNeely.

Vegas Vice 🦴 1/2 *Hard Vice* **1994** Tweed and Jones are Vegas cops after a serial killer, who might be a hooker. Routine. **83m/C; VHS, DVD.** Sam Jones; Shannon Tweed; James Gammon; Tom Fridley; Rebecca Ferratti; Branscombe Richmond; ***D:*** Joey Travolta; ***W:*** Joey Travolta; ***M:*** Jeff Lass.

Vehicle 19 🦴 **2013 (R)** In this action thriller, Michael Woods (Walker) is an American who is breaking parole to travel to South Africa to see his former wife after five years apart. At the airport, he is given the wrong rental car, which was intended for a corrupt cop. Michael soon finds himself deeply involved in a murky situation with a dectective and with a key witness needed at a corruption trial. **85m/C; DVD, Blu-Ray.** *SA US* Paul Walker; Naima McLean; Gys de Villiers; Leyla Haidarian; ***D:*** Mukunda Michael Dewil; ***W:*** Mukunda Michael Dewil; ***C:*** Miles Goodall; ***M:*** James Matthee.

The Velocity of Gary 🦴 1/2 *The Velocity of Gary (Not His Real Name)* **1998 (R)** Melodrama about love, death, and what makes a family is undone by a weak script, strained humor, and a screechy performance by Hayek. Gary's (Jane) a hustler in New York City who's attracted to bisexual porn star Valentino (D'Onofrio). Valentino has a possessive waitress girlfriend, Mary Carmen (Hayek), and she and Gary immediately hate each other and constantly compete for Valentino's affections. But when Valentino falls ill with AIDS, the three move into together and try to put aside their differences. **98m/C; VHS, DVD.** Vincent D'Onofrio; Salma Hayek; Thomas Jane; Olivia D'Abo; ***D:*** Dan Ireland; ***W:*** James Still; ***C:*** Claudio Rocha.

Velocity Trap 🦴🦴 **1999 (R)** In 2150, electronic crime and piracy run rampant throughout the galaxy. Cop Raymond Stokes (Gruner) is assigned to escort a federal banking ship through a section of space, known as the Velocity Run, that's equivalent to the Bermuda Triangle. Along with ship's navigator, Beth Sheffield (Coppola), Stokes must prevent thieves from grabbing the ship's loot and an asteroid from destroying the ship itself. **90m/C; VHS, DVD.** Olivier Gruner; Alicia Coppola; Ken Olandt; Bruce Weitz; Craig Wasson; ***D:*** Phillip J. Roth; ***W:*** Phillip J. Roth. **VIDEO**

Velvet Buzzsaw 🦴🦴 **2019 (R)** Flashy art critic Morf Vandewalt (Gyllenhaal) holds much power in the high-end art world, and can make or break a career with a review. When Josephina (Ashton), the assistant to high-powered agent Rhodora (Russo), finds her upstairs neighbor dead, the art scene, defined by Morf, Rhodora, and others, is changed forever. Josephina's neighbor was a troubled artist who created fantastic paintings and she brings his art into the world, creating a frenzy for the profits. The bloody satire-horror film is ambitious but inconsistent as it makes fun of the high-end art world. **113m/C; DVD.** Jake Gyllenhaal; John Malkovich; Toni Collette; Rene Russo; Daveed Diggs; ***D:*** Dan Gilroy; ***W:*** Dan Gilroy; ***C:*** Robert Elswit; ***M:*** Marco Beltrami; Buck Sanders.

Velvet Goldmine 🦴🦴 **1998 (R)** Director Haynes takes on the excesses of the '70s British glam-rock era. In 1984, journalist Arthur Stuart (Bale) is assigned to write a "Whatever Happened to" article on the 10-year disappearance of vanished superstar Brian Slade (Rhys Meyers as a cross between T-Rex's Marc Bolan and a Ziggy Stardust-era David Bowie). This leads fan Arthur to Slade's viperish ex-wife Mandy (Collette) and his ex-manager Jerry Divine (Izzard). But Arthur discovers the most important relationship in Brian's life was to self-destructive cult idol Curt Wild (MacGregor, channelling Iggy Pop). The flamboyant duo had an equally flamboyant affair that eventual lead to a downward spiral for them both. The story might be average but the visuals are spectacular and MacGregor, especially, is mesmerizing. **120m/C; VHS, DVD, Blu-Ray.** *GB* Ewan McGregor; Jonathan Rhys Meyers; Christian Bale; Toni Collette; Eddie Izzard; Emily Woof; Michael Feast; ***D:*** Todd Haynes; ***W:*** Todd Haynes; ***C:*** Maryse Alberti; ***M:*** Carter Burwell. British Acad. '98: Costume Des.; Ind. Spirit '99: Cinematog.

Velvet Smooth 🦴 **1976 (R)** A protection agency's sultry boss, Velvet Smooth, gets involved solving the problems of a numbers racket. **89m/C; VHS, DVD.** Johnnie Hill; ***D:*** Janace Fink.

The Velvet Vampire 🦴🦴 *Cemetery Girls; Through the Looking Glass; The Waking Hour* **1971 (R)** Yarnall is a sexy, sun-loving, dune buggy-riding vampiress who seduces a young, sexy, swinging, Southern California couple in her desert home. Lots of atmosphere to go along with the blood and nudity. **82m/C; VHS, DVD, Blu-Ray.** Michael Blodgett; Sherry Miles; Celeste Yarnall; Gene Shane; Jerry Daniels; Sandy Ward; Paul Prokop; Chris Woodley; Robert Tessier; ***D:*** Stephanie Rothman; ***W:*** Stephanie Rothman; Maurice Jules; Charles S. Swartz; ***C:*** Daniel Lacambre.

Vendetta 🦴 1/2 **1985** A woman gets herself arrested and sent to the penitentiary in order to exact revenge there for her sister's death. Acting and pacing make this better than the average sexploitation flick. **89m/C; VHS, DVD, Blu-Ray.** Karen Chase; Sandy Martin; Durga McBroom; Kin Shriner; Eugene Robert Glazer; ***D:*** Bruce Logan; ***M:*** David Newman.

Vendetta 🦴🦴 **1999 (R)** Based on a true story. New Orleans politicians and businessman seek to wrest away control of the docks from the Italian family that controls it. An unleashed angry mob leads to the largest lynching in American history. Adapted from the book by Richard Gambino. **117m/C; VHS, DVD.** Christopher Walken; Clancy Brown; Bruce Davison; Joaquim de Almeida; Edward Herrmann; Kenneth Welsh; ***D:*** Nicholas Meyer; ***W:*** Tim Prager; ***C:*** David Franco; ***M:*** John Altman. **CABLE**

Vendetta 🦴🦴 **2015 (R)** An action-packed dramatic thriller about the lengths a man will go to get revenge. Mason (Cain) is a no-nonsense detective who works hard and closes cases. His life is changed forever when his wife is murdered by one of the criminals Mason helped put behind bars. To avenge the murder, Mason deliberately gets himself arrested and sent to prison. Once there, he learns that a new criminal syndicate is emerging and those involved will stop at nothing to protect it. **90m/C; DVD, Blu-Ray, Streaming, Download.** Dean Cain; Paul Wight; Michael Eklund; Ben Hollingsworth; Adrian Holmes; ***D:*** Jen Soska; Sylvia Soska; ***W:*** Justin Shady; ***C:*** Mahlon Todd Williams; ***M:*** The Newton Brothers.

The Venetian Affair 🦴 1/2 **1967** After an American diplomat inexplicably turns suicide bomber at a peace conference in Venice, hard-drinking journalist Bill Fenner is called back into CIA service by his former boss Rosenfeld. Bill is told his ex-wife Sandra's communist sympathies have gotten her involved in the bombing, leading Bill to Venice to try and save her and prevent another explosive situation. Adaptation of the 1963 thriller by Helen MacInnes. **96m/C; DVD.** Robert Vaughn; Elke Sommer; Boris Karloff; Ed Asner; Karl-Heinz Boehm; Felicia Farr; Luciana Paluzzi; Roger C. Carmel; ***D:*** Jerry Thorpe; ***W:*** E. Jack Neuman; ***C:*** Milton Krasner; ***M:*** Lalo Schifrin.

Vengeance Is Mine WOOF! **1974 (R)** A demented farmer captures three criminals and tortures them in horrifyingly sadistic ways. Gratuitously grisly. **90m/C; VHS, DVD.** Ernest Borgnine; Michael J. Pollard; Hollis McLaren; Louis Zorich; Cec Linder; Vladimir Valenta; Al Waxman; Tim Henry; Susan Petrie; ***D:*** John Trent; ***W:*** John Trent; David Main; ***C:*** Marc Champion; ***M:*** Paul Hoffert.

Vengeance Is Mine 🦴🦴🦴 *Fukusho Suruwa Ware Ni Ari* **1979** Told in flashbacks, the film focuses on the life of a habitual criminal whose life of deprivation leads to murder. Contains violence and nudity. Based on a true story. In Japanese with English subtitles. **129m/C; VHS, DVD, Blu-Ray.** *JP* Ken Ogata; Rentaro Mikuni; Mitsuko Baisho; Chocho Miyako; Mayumi Ogawa; Nijiko Kiyokawa; ***D:*** Shohei Imamura; ***W:*** Masuru Baba; ***C:*** Sinsaku Himeda; ***M:*** Shinichiro Ikebe.

The Vengeance of Fu Manchu 🦴 **1967** The third in the Lee series finds Fu Manchu and daughter Lin Tang (Chin) plotting revenge on Scotland Yard commissioner Nayland Smith (Wilmer). He's kidnapped and replaced with a murderous double in order to further the crime syndicate plans of the villains. Based on the characters created by Sax Rohmer. **91m/C; DVD.** *GE* Christopher Lee; Tsai Chin; Douglas Wilmer; Tony Ferrer; Noel Trevarthen; Horst Frank; Wolfgang Kieling; Suzanne Roquette; ***D:*** Jeremy Summers; ***W:*** Harry Alan Towers; ***C:*** John von Kotze; ***M:*** Malcolm Lockyer.

The Vengeance of She 🦴 *The Return of She* **1968** Carol (Berova) is taken for the reincarnation of 2,000-year-old queen, Ayesha, by her immortal lover, King Killikrates (Richardson). The king promises high priest Man Hari (Godfrey) immortality if he can restore Ayesha's soul. But Carol's shrink boyfriend (Judd) isn't crazy about the idea and tries to convince the king otherwise. **101m/C; VHS, DVD, Blu-Ray.** *GB* Olinka (Schoberova) Berova; John Richardson; Derek Godfrey; Edward Judd; Colin Blakely; ***D:*** Cliff Owen; ***W:*** Peter O'Donnell; ***C:*** Peter Suschitzky; ***M:*** Mario Nascimbene.

Vengeance of the Dead 🦴 1/2 **2001** Homegrown horror flick never manages to live up to the big ideas it introduces. Eric (Galvin) journeys to the town of Harvest, to visit his Grandpa (Vollmers). (Although we're never told where he's been or given an idea of how long he's going to stay.) Once he's settled in, Eric has strange nightmares concerning a little girl, an act of violence, and a burning house. These dreams lead him to sleepwalk through the town and commit strange acts of vengeance. The dreams and Eric's behaviors are linked to a crime from many years ago, and a ghostly presence is seeking revenge on those responsible. Despite an interesting premise, the film is slow, boring, and hard to follow at times. Kudos to filmmakers Adams and Picardi for squeezing as much as possible out of their limited budget, but this movie can't overcome its amateur roots. **85m/C; DVD.** Michael Galvin; Mark Vollmers; ***D:*** Don Adams; Harry James Picardi.

Vengeance of the Zombies 🦴 1/2 **1972** A madman seeks revenge by setting an army of walking corpses to stalk the streets of London. **90m/C; VHS, DVD, Blu-Ray.** *SP* Paul Naschy; ***D:*** Leon Klimovsky.

Vengeance Valley 🦴🦴 **1951** Lancaster and Walker are foster brothers with Walker being an envious weasel who always expects Lancaster to get him out of scrapes. Lancaster is even accused of a crime committed by Walker and must work to clear himself. Good cast is let down by uneven direction. **83m/C; VHS, DVD.** Burt Lancaster; Joanne Dru; Robert Walker; Sally Forrest; John Ireland; Hugh O'Brian; ***D:*** Richard Thorpe; ***W:*** Irving Ravetch; ***C:*** George J. Folsey; ***M:*** Rudolph Kopp.

Venice Underground 🦴 **2005 (R)** A group of raw police cadets are selected by the DEA to form a Narcotics unit in Florida. When one of them gets murdered in a turf war, the rest have 48 hours to fix things or be suspended. Apparently the moral of the story is that all Florida agents are young beautiful people driving sports cars, who don't have to worry about being fired after one of their own gets himself killed. **119m/C; DVD.** Randall Batinkoff; Mark Boone, Jr.; Francis Capra; James Duval; Edward Furlong; Ed Lauter; Eric Mabius; ***D:*** Eric Delabarre; ***W:*** Eric Delabarre; ***C:*** Lila Javan; ***M:*** Justin Caine Burnett.

Venice, Venice 🦴🦴 1/2 **1992 (R)** Alternately earnest and satirical, Jaglom pokes fun at himself and movie-making in a movie about, well, himself and movie-making. Consciously straddling the genre fence, he uses real people and events, but adopts a pseudonym, Dean. In Venice, Italy, young filmmaker Alard decides to make a film about Dean/Jaglom, a plot which creates the effect of two mirrors reflecting each other into infinity. Dean/Jaglom and Alard return to Venice, California, where he conducts auditions for a movie in which he will star and direct. Art imitating life or life imitating art? More importantly, does it really matter? **108m/C; VHS, DVD.** Nelly Alard; Henry Jaglom; Suzanne Bertish; Melissa Leo; Daphna Kastner; David Duchovny; Diane Salinger; Zack Norman; Marshall Barer; John Landis; Pierre Cottrell; Edna Fainaru; Klaus Hellwig; ***D:*** Henry Jaglom; ***W:*** Henry Jaglom; ***C:*** Hanania Baer.

Venom WOOF! **1982 (R)** Deadly black mamba is loose in an elegant townhouse, terrorizing big-name cast. The snake continually terrorizes an evil kidnapper, his accomplices and his kidnapped victim. Participants walk through tired cliches with that far-away look in their eyes—like they wish they were anywhere else. Original director Tobe Hooper was replaced. **92m/C; VHS, DVD, Blu-Ray.** *GB* Sterling Hayden; Klaus Kinski; Sarah Miles; Nicol Williamson; Cornelia Sharpe; Susan George; Michael Gough; Oliver Reed; ***D:*** Piers Haggard; ***W:*** Robert B. Carrington; ***M:*** Michael Kamen.

Venom 🦴🦴 **2005 (R)** Swamp-set slasher flick offers redneck Ray (Cramer) getting bitten by a suitcase full of snakes that happened to belong to a voodoo priestess. Ray gets resurrected and goes after all the pretty teens (male and female) who annoyed Ray when he was alive. Hits all the genre highlights, so if voodoo and zombies and gore, oh my, are what you're searching for, look no further. **87m/C; DVD, Blu-Ray.** Agnes Bruckner; Joshua Jackson; Rick Cramer; Meagan Good; Bijou Phillips; Method Man; Laura Ramsey; Pawel Szajda; Stacey Travis; James Pickens, Jr.; Davetta Sherwood; D.J. Cotrona; Marcus Lyle Brown; Deborah Duke; ***D:*** Jim Gillespie; ***W:*** Flint Dille; Brandon Boyce; ***C:*** Steve Mason; ***M:*** James L. Venable.

Venom 🦴🦴 **2018 (PG-13)** When investigative reporter Eddie Brock (Hardy) sneaks around a high-tech laboratory, he accidentally allows a volatile alien specimen to inhabit his body and his consciousness. The alien, known as Venom, controls his body at will and stretches and transforms him into a killing machine. As Eddie tries to manage Venom, he's drawn into a conflict with unhinged billionaire scientist Carlton Drake (Ahmed), who has been trying to tame aliens like Venom to benefit society. Hardy gives an intense, sometimes darkly humorous performance that outshines the uneven, often chaotic origin story of the Marvel comic book antihero. **112m/C; DVD.** Tom (Thomas) Hardy; Michelle Williams; Riz Ahmed; Scott Haze; Reid Scott; ***D:*** Ruben Fleischer; ***W:*** Jeff Pinkner; Scott Rosenberg; Kelly Marcel; ***C:*** Matthew Libatique; ***M:*** Ludwig Göransson.

Venomous 🦴🦴 **2001 (PG-13)** Genetically altered poisonous snakes make their presence felt in a small town by spreading a deadly virus among the human population. To cover up the source of the disease, the military (the snakes are one of their experiments gone wrong) plans to blow up the town. **97m/C; VHS, DVD.** Treat Williams; Mary Page Keller; Brian Poth; J.B. Gaynor; Hannes Jaenicke; Geoffrey Pierson; Catherine Dent; ***D:*** Fred Olen Ray; ***W:*** Dan Golden; Sean McGinley; ***C:*** Andrea V. Rossotto; ***M:*** Neal Acree. **VIDEO**

Venus 🦴🦴🦴 **2006 (R)** The ever-charismatic, though now frail, O'Toole plays a mildly famous charmer of an actor who still takes an interest in a pretty girl, even if the flesh is weak. Maurice's best friend is his grumpy (and equally aged) fellow thespian Ian (Phillips). Ian's grand-niece Jessie (Whittaker) has ostensibly arrived to help him out but the sullen, lower-class teen is more concerned with her own interests. This doesn't prevent Maurice from becoming interested in her, though it might be more a nod to his rogue past than to Jessie herself. Funny and poignant without mawkishness; also notable is the appearance of Redgrave as Maurice's understanding ex-wife. **94m/C; DVD.** *GB* Peter O'Toole; Leslie Phillips; Richard Griffiths; Jodie Whitaker; Vanessa Redgrave; ***D:*** Roger Michell; ***W:*** Hanif Kureishi; ***C:*** Haris Zambarloukos; ***M:*** David Arnold; Corinne Bailey Rae.

Venus and Vegas 🦴 **2010 (R)** Capable cast lost in a borderline caper comedy that's lacking humor and sense. Three bone-headed buddies rob a Vegas warehouse of counterfeit casino chips belonging to old school mobster Frank Santino. The heist goes wrong and Alex ends up in Santino's hands. In retailiation, Stu and Eric kidnap Santino's nephew, Bruno, as their own bargaining chip. The "Venus" part of the title refers to the guys lady friends. **96m/C; DVD, Blu-Ray.** Eddie Guerra; Eddie Kaye Thomas; Donald Adeosun Faison; Jon Polito; Abraham Benrubi; Jaime Pressly; Molly Sims; Roselyn Sanchez; Florence Henderson; Paul Ben-Victor; ***D:*** Demian Lichtenstein; ***W:*** Eddie Guerra; ***C:*** James Chressanthis; ***M:*** Andrew Gross. **VIDEO**

Venus Beauty Institute 🦴🦴 1/2 **1998 (R)** Fortyish Angele (Baye) works at a Paris beauty salon along with proprietor Nadine

(Ogier) and younger colleagues Samantha (Seigner) and Marie (Tantou). Angele refuses to fall in love and picks up men strictly for sex—until she's pursued by Antoine (Le Bihan), a young sculptor who insists he fell in love with her at first sight. (He basically stalks her but Angele is intrigued rather than repulsed by his devotion.) The Institute also has a parade of frequently neurotic customers in romantic dilemmas. French with subtitles. **105m/C; VHS, DVD.** *FR* Nathalie Baye; Bulle Ogier; Samuel Le Bihan; Jacques Bonnaffe; Mathilde Seigner; Robert Hossein; Claire Nebout; Audrey Tautou; ***D:*** Tonie Marshall; ***W:*** Tonie Marshall; ***C:*** Gerard de Battista; ***M:*** Khalil Chahine. Cesar '00: Director (Marshall), Film, Screenplay.

Venus in Fur *La Venus a la fourrure* **2013** Polanski directs this personally reflective drama, his second in a row based on the David Ives play, about a stage director (Amalric) trying to cast the leading role in his latest production. At the end of a busy day of auditions, the captivating Vanda (Seigner, Polanski's wife) enters at the last minute. At first, she's easy to dismiss but the director and the actress begin a sexual game of words, characters, and motivations, blurring the line between person and performer. Polanski is a bit shallow here but he's having more fun than he has in years. French with subtitles. **96m/C; DVD.** *FR PL* Mathieu Amalric; Emmanuelle Seigner; ***D:*** Roman Polanski; ***W:*** Roman Polanski; David Ives; ***C:*** Pawel Edelman; ***M:*** Alexandre Desplat.

Venus in Furs 1/2 *Paroxismus; Puo Una Morta Rivivere Per Amore?; Venus in Peltz* **1970 (R)** Jazz musician working in Rio de Janeiro becomes obsessed with a mysterious woman; she resembles a murder victim whose body he discovered months earlier. Weird mix of horror, sadism, black magic, and soft porn. **70m/C; VHS, DVD.** *GB IT GE* James Darren; Klaus Kinski; Barbara McNair; Dennis Price; Maria Rohm; Margaret Lee; Jess (Jesus) Franco; ***D:*** Jess (Jesus) Franco; ***W:*** Jess (Jesus) Franco; Milo G. Cuccia; Malvin Wald; ***C:*** Angelo Lotti.

Venus Rising **1995 (R)** In the year 2000, Eve and August manage to escape from the island prison on which they were raised. They discover that the mainland world features emotions that are controlled by drugs and love is only a game on the virtual reality network. Hunted, the fugitives try to fit in and figure out what's real and what's fantasy. Be forewarned—Fairchild's role is very small. **91m/C; VHS, DVD.** Audie England; Costas Mandylor; Billy Wirth; Morgan Fairchild; ***D:*** Leora Barish; ***W:*** Leora Barish.

Vera Cruz 1/2 **1953** Two soldiers of fortune become involved in the Mexican Revolution of 1866, a stolen shipment of gold, divided loyalties, and gun battles. Less than innovative plot is made into an exciting action flick. **94m/C; VHS, DVD, Blu-Ray.** Gary Cooper; Burt Lancaster; Denise Darcel; Cesar Romero; George Macready; Ernest Borgnine; Charles Bronson; Jack Elam; ***D:*** Robert Aldrich; ***W:*** Roland Kibbee; James R. Webb; ***C:*** Ernest Laszlo; ***M:*** Hugo Friedhofer.

Vera Drake **2004 (R)** Compassionate, complex drama with a stellar performance by Staunton in the title role. Set in the drab postwar London of 1950, Vera is a cozy, middle-aged married house cleaner who is relentlessly cheery and helpful to all those around her. This includes the poor young women who find themselves "in trouble." Vera, as it happens, is the local abortionist—something her family discovers only when the police descend on them after one of Vera's procedures goes wrong. Her subsequent trial highlights the hypocrisy of the proceedings (matched against Vera's bewildered decency) without becoming overbearing. **125m/C; DVD.** Imelda Staunton; Philip Davis; Peter Wright; Adrian Scarborough; Heather Craney; Alex Kelly; Daniel Mays; Eddie Marsan; Sally Hawkins; Ruth Sheen; Helen Coker; ***D:*** Mike Leigh; ***W:*** Mike Leigh; ***C:*** Dick Pope; ***M:*** Andrew Dickson. British Acad. '04: Actress (Staunton), Costume Des., Director (Leigh).

Verboten! 1/2 **1959** In post-war occupied Berlin, an American G.I. falls in love with a German girl. Good direction maintains a steady pace. **93m/B; VHS, DVD.** James Best; Susan Cummings; Tom Pittman; Paul Dubov; ***D:*** Samuel Fuller; ***W:*** Samuel Fuller; ***C:*** Joseph Biroc.

The Verdict 1/2 **1946** Siegel made his directorial feature film debut in the last film Greenstreet and Lorre would appear in together. In 1890 London, aging Scotland Yard superintendent Grodman (Greenstreet) is forced into retirement after a convicted murderer is found to be innocent—after his execution. He's replaced by pompous Buckley (Coulouris) who soon has a locked room murder on his hands. Naturally he arrests the wrong man (a friend of Grodman's) and then the case turns even more complicated. **86m/B; DVD.** Sydney Greenstreet; Peter Lorre; George Coulouris; Joan Lorring; ***D:*** Terry Morse; ***C:*** Arthur L. Todd; ***M:*** Max Steiner.

The Verdict **1982 (R)** Frank Galvin (Newman) is an alcoholic failed attorney reduced to ambulance chasing. A friend gives him a supposedly easy malpractice case that pits Frank against a powerful establishment Catholic hospital in Boston in what turns out to be a last chance at redeeming himself and his career. Adapted from the novel by Barry Reed. One of Newman's finest performances. **122m/C; VHS, DVD, Blu-Ray.** Paul Newman; James Mason; Charlotte Rampling; Jack Warden; Milo O'Shea; Lindsay Crouse; Edward Binns; Roxanne Hart; James Handy; Wesley Addy; Joe Seneca; Julie Bovasso; ***D:*** Sidney Lumet; ***W:*** David Mamet; ***C:*** Andrzej Bartkowiak; ***M:*** Johnny Mandel. Natl. Bd. of Review '82: Director (Lumet).

Verdict in Blood 1/2 **2002 (R)** When the judge she covered is murdered, reporter Joanne Kilbourne's hunt for the culprit exposes scandalous family secrets. Based on Gail Bowen's serial novel. **90m/C; VHS, DVD.** Wendy Crewson; Shawn Doyle; Zachary Bennett; Neil Crone; Robert Davi; Richard Fitzpatrick; Ken James; Sally Kellerman; Kristen Lehman; Reagan Pasternak; Elizabeth Shepherd; Walter Alza; Alex Campbell; Diego Chambers; Pablo Coffey; Callahan Connor; Angela Gei; Kristen Gutoskie; Natasha La Force; Shawn Laurence; Tony Munch; Paul Robbins; Pamela Wallin; Lila Yee; Jean Yoon; Gail Bowen; Janet Maclean; Andrew Wreggitt; ***D:*** Stephen Williams; ***W:*** Jeremy Hole; ***C:*** David Herrington; ***M:*** Robert Carli. **TV**

Verdict on Auschwitz: The Frankfurt Auschwitz Trial 1963—1965 *Strafsache 4 Ks 2/63: Auschwitz Vor Dem Frankfurter Schwurgericht* **1993** Originally made for German TV, where it was shown as a 3-part documentary. (It was also released in 2005 in a 60-minute version.) This re-release is a loosely structured examination of the 1963-65 trial of 22 Auschwitz SS officers, based on 430 hours of audiotapes. Directors Bickel and Wagner divide this chilling recounting into the investigation, the trial (which included testimony by more than 200 survivors), and the verdict. Testimony is illustrated with footage and photographs as well as archival material. English, German, Polish, and Russian with subtitles. **180m/C; DVD.** *GE* ***Nar:*** Edgar M. Boehke; ***D:*** Rolf Bickel; Dietrick Wagner; ***W:*** Rolf Bickel; Dietrick Wagner; ***C:*** Armin Alker; Dominik Schunk.

Veritas: Prince of Truth **2007 (PG)** A 14-year-old boy decides to fight the cancellation of his favorite comic book and so does the book's main character who comes to life to take offense. Not quite as good as that sounds considering the director seems to have made the common mistake that all comics are written for 5-year-olds when the average age of readership is well into the 30s. **94m/C; DVD.** Sean Patrick Flanery; Bret Loehr; Amy Jo Johnson; Kate Walsh; Tyler Posey; Danny Strong; ***D:*** Arturo Ruiz-Esparza; ***W:*** Arturo Ruiz-Esparza; ***C:*** Arturo de la Rosa; ***M:*** John Massari.

Vernie **2004** Sean and Kristi were once best friends and they reunite when Sean is diagnosed with an inoperable brain tumor. When Sean asks Kristi to have his child, she surprises herself by agreeing. But the ensuing months prove to be more difficult than either of them imagined. A tearjerker with humor, which makes for a generally winning combo. **86m/C; DVD.** Amy Colon; John Riedlinger; Patrick Coyle; Allyson Kearns; Adam Whisner; Heidi Jo Langseth; ***D:*** David Tufford; ***W:*** Kevin Ross; ***C:*** David Doyle; ***M:*** Todd Syring.

The Vernonia Incident 1/2 **1989** Urban guerillas invade a small town, killing the police chief. The townspeople gather up their shotguns and fight back. That's entertainment. **95m/C; VHS, DVD.** David Jackson; Shawn Stevens; Floyd Ragner; Ed Justice; Robert Louis Jackson; ***D:*** Ray Etheridge; ***W:*** Ray Etheridge.

Veronica Guerin 1/2 **2003 (R)** A less than inspired script is nonetheless brought to life by the brilliant acting of Blanchett in the title role of the real-life Irish reporter, who took on a Dublin drug lord in the 1990s. Despite threats and extreme violence, the plucky wife and mother was relentless in her pursuit of the truth. While Guerin pays for her anti-drug crusade with her life, gunned down at a red light in 1996 by a suspected drug-world henchman, pic tones down the martyr factor by presenting a well-rounded character. Hinds effectively plays a sympathetic Guerin informant who tries to warn her of her impending doom. **98m/C; VHS, DVD, Blu-Ray.** Cate Blanchett; Gerard McSorley; Ciaran Hinds; Brenda Fricker; Barry Barnes; David Murray; Joe Hanley; David Herlihy; Gerry O'Brien; Don Wycherley; Colin Farrell; Alan Devine; ***D:*** Joel Schumacher; ***W:*** Carol Doyle; Mary Agnes Donoghue; ***C:*** Brendan Galvin; ***M:*** Harry Gregson-Williams.

Veronica Mars 1/2 **2014 (PG-13)** Fan-worthy adaptation of the cult TV series. A one-time teen PI, Veronica (Bell) has left sleuthing behind in her corrupt coastal hometown of Neptune, California. Now a New York lawyer, Veronica still quickly responds to the pleas of ex-bad boy beau, Logan (Dohring), who's accused of murder. Leaving current boyfriend Piz (Lowell) behind, Veronica uses their 10-year high school reunion as an excuse to come home and start snooping. Familiar faces from the series pop up and Bell is as smart and sassy as ever, but the best relationship onscreen remains that of Veronica and her beloved, bemused dad, Keith (Colantoni). **110m/C; DVD, Blu-Ray, On Demand.** Kristen Bell; Jason Dohring; Enrico Colantoni; Chris Lowell; Percy Daggs, III; Tina Majorino; Ryan Hansen; Francis Capra; Jerry O'Connell; Krysten Ritter; Gaby Hoffman; Ken Marino; Max Greenfield; Andrea Estella; Jamie Lee Curtis; ***Cameo(s):*** James Franco; ***D:*** Rob Thomas; ***W:*** Rob Thomas; Diane Ruggiero; ***C:*** Ben Kutchins; ***M:*** Josh Kramon.

Veronico Cruz 1/2 *La Dueda Interna; The Debt* **1987** Despite its sincerity, Pereira's feature debut offers muddled response to the human waste incurred by the Falklands War. Set in a tiny remote village in the Argentinean mountains, the film's narrative is derived from the growing friendship between a shepherd boy and a teacher from the city. Well-meaning anti-war movie. In Spanish with English subtitles. **96m/C; VHS, DVD.** *AR GB* Juan Jose Camero; Gonzalo Morales; Rene Olaguivel; Guillermo Delgado; ***D:*** Miguel Pereira; ***W:*** Miguel Pereira; Eduardo Leiva Muller; ***C:*** Gerry Feeny; ***M:*** David Eppel; Jaime Torres.

Veronika Decides to Die **2015 (R)** Aimless Veronika (Gellar) feels her life is just meaningless repetition, so she washes down a few handfuls of pills with a bottle of booze. She awakens in a mental institution, told her suicide attempt caused severe heart damage and she doesn't have long to live. Instead of a cathartic bucket list adventure, she oddly opts to stick around the institution and get to know everyone, including handsome mute Edward (Tucker). Filmed in 2009, this well-acted indie plays it small and quiet, but allows its characters to make one too many silly choices. **103m/C; DVD, Blu-Ray.** Sarah Michelle Gellar; Jonathan Tucker; Erika Christensen; David Thewlis; Melissa Leo; ***D:*** Emily Young; ***W:*** Larry Gross; Roberta Hanley; ***C:*** Seamus Tierney; ***M:*** Michael Whalen.

Veronika Voss *Die Sehns Ucht Der Veronika Voss* **1982 (R)** Highlights the real life of fallen film star Sybille Schmitz who finally took her own life out of despair. Played by Zech, Voss is exploited by her physician to turn over all of her personal belongings for morphine. A lover discovers the corruption and reveals it to the authorities. This causes great upheaval resulting in Voss' suicide. Highly metaphoric and experimental in its treatment of its subject. In German with English subtitles. **105m/C; VHS, DVD, Blu-Ray.** *GE* Rosel Zech; Hilmar Thate; Conny Froboess; Anna Marie Duringer; Volker Spengler; ***D:*** Rainer Werner Fassbinder; ***W:*** Pea Frolich; Peter Marthesheimer; ***C:*** Xaver Schwarzenberger; ***M:*** Peer Raben.

Versus 1/2 **2000 (R)** There are 666 portals to the other side, and the 444th (the Forest of Resurrection) is set in Japan, where the local Yakuza have been using it to get rid of dead bodies. Two prisoners have recently taken a girl hostage to escape from a maximum security prison, and the yakuza are supposed to pick them up in the forest and take them to a safe house. Instead a gunfight erupts, after which the dead reanimate and attack the living. One of the prisoners escapes into the forest with the girl, and they desperately search for a way out from their undead pursuers. Over-the-top gore and martial arts fights commence. **119m/C; DVD, Blu-Ray.** *JP* Tak Sakaguchi; Hideo Sakaki; Chieko Masaki; ***D:*** Ryuhei Kitamura; ***W:*** Ryuhei Kitamura; Yudai Yamaguchi; ***C:*** Takumi Furuya; ***M:*** Nobuhiko Morino.

Vertical Limit **2000 (PG-13)** Photographer O'Donnell joins a team of mountain climbers in order to rescue his sister Tunney, who is part of a group trapped on K2. Plot serves mainly as connective tissue for the numerous heart-stopping (and well-done) action sequences. Mountain-fodder cast has few standouts, except maybe Glenn in the crazy-but-wise-old-coot role. **126m/C; VHS, DVD, Blu-Ray.** Chris O'Donnell; Robin Tunney; Bill Paxton; Scott Glenn; Izabela Scorupco; Temuera Morrison; Stuart Wilson; Nicholas Lea; Alexander Siddig; Robert Taylor; Roshan Seth; David Hayman; Ben Mendelsohn; Steve Le Marquand; ***D:*** Martin Campbell; ***W:*** Robert King; Terry Hayes; ***C:*** David Tattersall; ***M:*** James Newton Howard.

The Vertical Ray of the Sun 1/2 **2000 (PG-13)** Slow-moving visual treat set in Hanoi. Three sisters plan a commemorative meal in honor of the anniversary of their mother's death. The two eldest sisters have marital problems and the youngest is so close to their brother that many believe the twosome are sexually involved. Over the course of a month (which ends with the anniversary of their father's death), the women deal with their emotional entanglements. Vietnamese with subtitles. **112m/C; VHS, DVD.** *VT FR* Tran Nu Yen-Khe; Nguyen Nhu Quynh; Le Khanh; Tran Manh Cuong; Chu Ngoc Hung; Ngo Quang Hai; ***D:*** Tran Anh Hung; ***W:*** Tran Anh Hung; ***C:*** Mark Ping Bin Lee; ***M:*** Ton That Tiet.

Vertigo **1958 (PG)** Hitchcock's romantic story of obsession, manipulation and fear. Stewart plays a detective forced to retire after his fear of heights causes the death of a fellow policeman and, perhaps, the death of a woman he'd been hired to follow. The appearance of her double (Novak), whom he compulsively transforms into the dead girl's image, leads to a mesmerizing cycle of madness and lies. Features Herrmann's haunting music. **126m/C; VHS, DVD, Blu-Ray.** James Stewart; Kim Novak; Barbara Bel Geddes; Tom Helmore; Ellen Corby; Henry Jones; Raymond Bailey; Lee Patrick; ***D:*** Alfred Hitchcock; ***W:*** Samuel A. Taylor; ***C:*** Robert Burks; ***M:*** Bernard Herrmann. AFI '98: Top 100; Natl. Film Reg. '89.

Very Annie Mary 1/2 **2000** Sentimental comedy set in a small Welsh village filled with eccentrics. That would include singing baker Jack (Pryce), a tyrannical widower who dominates his gauche, 30-ish daughter Annie-Mary (Griffiths). She's saving up to buy a house of her own when her father is felled by a severe stoke and she must take over running the family bakery (for which she has no talent). What Annie-Mary can do is sing and she decides to enter a talent contest in Cardiff in order to fund a trip to Disneyland for her dying friend Bethan (Page). Very twee. **105m/C; VHS, DVD.** *GB FR* Rachel Griffiths; Jonathan Pryce; Ioan Gruffudd; Matthew Rhys; Kenneth Griffiths; Ruth Madoc; Joanna Page; Radcliffe Grafton; ***D:*** Sara Sugarman; ***W:*** Sara Sugarman; ***C:*** Barry Ackroyd; ***M:*** Stephen Warbeck.

Very Bad Things **1998 (R)** What begins as a not-so-innocent prenuptial bachelor party in Vegas quickly disintegrates into a murderous blood bath. Kyle (Favreau), the groom-to-be, escapes the clutches of his control-freak fiance Laura (Diaz) with some pals, including unscrupulous yuppie Boyd (Slater). When the hired "entertainment" is killed in a freak accident involving a towel hook, Boyd comes up with the idea of burying her body in the desert and going on with the wedding. A pitch-dark comedy of errors ensues. Peter Berg's first stab at writing and directing has some funny moments, mostly the kind you realize afterwards you shouldn't find funny, but relies too heavily on gratuitous gore and shock value. **100m/C; VHS, DVD, Blu-Ray.** Jon Favreau; Christian Slater; Cameron Diaz; Jeremy Piven; Daniel Stern; Leland Orser; Jeanne Tripplehorn; Joey Zimmerman; *D:* Peter Berg; *W:* Peter Berg; *C:* David Hennings; *M:* Stewart Copeland.

A Very Brady Sequel 🦴🦴 1/2 **1996 (PG-13)** They're back! The cast from the surprise hit "The Brady Bunch Movie" returns and Brady mom Carol (Long) is shocked when her presumed dead first husband Roy Martin (Matheson) suddenly appears on their doorstep. The Bradys must travel to Hawaii to attempt to save the family (based on a three-part episode from the original TV series). The stuck-in-the-'70s gang is still too far-out for the '90s, but in Hawaii it's always a sunshine day. Not as good as the first, but still worth a few laughs. **90m/C; VHS, DVD.** Shelley Long; Gary Cole; Tim Matheson; Christopher Daniel Barnes; Christine Taylor; Paul Sutera; Jennifer Elise Cox; Henriette Mantel; Olivia Hack; Jesse Lee; RuPaul Charles; Whip Hubley; John Hillerman; Richard Belzer; David Spade; Barbara Eden; *Cameo(s):* Zsa Zsa Gabor; Rosie O'Donnell; *D:* Arlene Sanford; *W:* Harry Elfont; Deborah Kaplan; Stan Zimmerman; James Berg; *C:* Mac Ahlberg; *M:* Guy Moon.

A Very British Coup 🦴🦴🦴 **1988** McAnally plays Harry Perkins, a former steelworker who gets involved in British politics. Although a left-wing radical, the charismatic Perkins is actually elected Prime Minister. However, his radical policies cause the entrenched government officials to conspire to bring him down. And you thought American politics were dirty! **180m/C; VHS, DVD.** *GB* Ray McAnally; Alan MacNaughton; Keith Allen; Geoffrey Beevers; Jim Carter; Philip Madoc; Tim (McInnerny) McInnerny; *D:* Mick Jackson; *W:* Alan Plater; *C:* Ernest Vincze; *M:* John Keane. **TV**

Very Good Girls 🦴 1/2 **2013 (R)** Another coming-of-age drama filtered through the sexual exploration of young women, this time played by the too-talented-for-this Olsen and Fanning. Gerri (Olsen) and Lilly (Fanning) are teen friends who make a pact to lose their virginity over the same sun-kissed summer before they both end up falling for the same boy (Boyd Holbrook). Naturally, jealousy comes with sexuality, but the material never feels quite right, coming off like a Lifetime TV Movie version of events that thinks it's something deeper. Also features veteran actors Dreyfuss, Moore, and Barkin. **91m/C; DVD, Blu-Ray.** Dakota Fanning; Elizabeth Olsen; Boyd Holbrook; Ellen Barkin; Clark Gregg; Richard Dreyfuss; Demi Moore; Peter Sarsgaard; *D:* Naomi Foner; *W:* Naomi Foner; *C:* Bobby Bukowski; *M:* Jenny Lewis.

A Very Harold & Kumar Christmas 🦴🦴 1/2 **2011 (R)** Harold (Cho) and Kumar (Penn) return for round three of stoner hi-jinks, this time with a Christmas theme, and the result is their liveliest and most consistent adventure to date. With a gleefully manic desire to do whatever it takes to make you laugh, the more-talented lead actors strike the funny bone more often than not as they search for the perfect Christmas tree, dodge gangsters, find themselves "Claymated," have an encounter with Santa himself, and, of course, run into a movie-stealing NPH (aka Neil Patrick Harris) one more time. Far from perfect but funnier than expected. **90m/C; DVD, Blu-Ray.** John Cho; Kal Penn; Paula Garces; Danneel Harris; David Krumholtz; Thomas Lennon; Neil Patrick Harris; Danny Trejo; Elias Koteas; *D:* Todd Strauss-Schulson; *W:* Jon Hurwitz; Hayden Schlossberg; *C:* Michael Barrett; *M:* William Ross.

Very Important Person 🦴🦴 **1961** British satire of wartime POW flicks. Irascible Sir Ernest Pease (Justice) is an eminent scientist on a WWII reconnaissance flight that's testing his new radar invention. When the plane is shot down, Pease winds up in a German POW camp under an alias so the Nazis won't realize his importance. But his fellow Brits think the unpleasant chappie is a snitch or spy. When they realize Pease's value to the war effort, they plan an escape without much cooperation from their VIP. **90m/B; DVD.** *GB* James Robertson Justice; Leslie Phillips; Stanley Baker; Eric Sykes; Richard Wattis; Colin Gordon; Norman Bird; John Forrest; John Le Mesurier; *W:* Jeremy Lloyd; Ken Annakin; Jack Davies; Henry Blyth; *C:* Ernest Steward; *M:* Reg Owen.

A Very Long Engagement 🦴🦴🦴 *Un long dimanche de fiancailles* **2004 (R)** Jeunet reteams with his "Amelie" star Tautou in a bittersweet WWI-era weepie about a young woman who refuses to believe her fiance has died on the battlefield. In 1917, Manech (Ulliel) is the youngest of five soldiers court-martialed and condemned to certain death in a frontline trench. Two years later, Mathilde (Tautou) is equally certain that Manech is still alive, especially when she receives a letter from one of Menach's fellow soldiers. She hires detective Pire (Holgado) to help her investigate; in a parallel story, Tina (Cotillard), the girlfriend of another soldier, is also looking for answers, although for a much-deadlier purpose. French with subtitles; based on the 1991 novel by Sebastien Japrisot. **133m/C; DVD.** *FR* Audrey Tautou; Gaspard Ulliel; Jean Becker; Clovis Cornillac; Marion Cotillard; Jodie Foster; Jean-Claude Dreyfus; Albert Dupontel; Andre Dussollier; Ticky Holgado; Tcheky Karyo; Denis Lavant; Francois Levantal; Chantal Neuwirth; Dominique Pinon; Dominique Bettenfeld; Jean-Pierre Daroussin; Jerome Kircher; Jean-Paul Rouve; Rodolphe Pauly; *D:* Jean-Pierre Jeunet; *C:* Bruno Delbonnel; *M:* Angelo Badalamenti.

A Very Mary Christmas 🦴 1/2 *Expecting Mary* **2010 (PG)** Uneven but rather sweet comedy. Sixteen-year-old pregnant Mary (Rulin) is hitchhiking to L.A. to see her dad when she's given a ride by trucker Horace (Gould). He's stopping in New Mexico to visit his girlfriend Darnella (Gray), who's an aging showgirl at an Indian casino. She offers Mary a place to stay and the eccentric inhabitants of the trailer park help Mary out. **97m/C; DVD.** Olesya Rulin; Elliott Gould; Linda Gray; Della Reese; Lainie Kazan; Cloris Leachman; Fred Willard; *D:* Dan Gordon; *W:* Dan Gordon; *C:* Michael Goi; *M:* Kevin Saunders Hayes.

A Very Merry Daughter of the Bride 🦴🦴 1/2 **2008** Disapproving wedding planner Roxanne (Garcia) isn't merry at all about her mom Rose's (Shaver) whirlwind upcoming nuptials to Jack (Welsh). She offers to handle the wedding details so she can subtly put a kibosh on the whole thing until an unexpected romance with Charlie (Perry) leads Roxanne to reconsider. **90m/C; DVD.** Joanna Garcia; Luke Perry; Helen Shaver; Kenneth Welsh; Jason Priestley; Lucas Bryant; *D:* Leslie Hope; *W:* Leslie Hope; Scott Eastlick; *C:* Adam Kane; *M:* Zack Ryan. **CABLE**

A Very Merry Mix-Up 🦴🦴 1/2 **2013** Alice Chapman is about to meet her future in-laws for the first time without her fiancé. Her trip is a disaster until Matt comes to her rescue, she winds up at the wrong house, and soon realizes she's also romantically involved with the wrong man. Hallmark Channel holiday romance. **90m/C; DVD.** Alicia Witt; Mark Wiebe; Susan Hogan; Richard Fitzpatrick; Lawrence Dane; Scott Gibson; *D:* Jonathan Wright; *W:* Barbara Kymlicka; *C:* Russ Goozee; *M:* Stacey Hersh. **CABLE**

A Very Natural Thing 🦴🦴 **1973** Twenty-six-year-old Jason leaves the priesthood to pursue a gay lifestyle in New York. He becomes a teacher, meets ad exec David, and finds love. Considered to be the first film to explore homosexuality in a realistic manner, made by a gay director, and given national, commercial distribution. **85m/C; VHS, DVD.** Robert Joel; Curt Gareth; Bo White; *D:* Christopher Larkin; *W:* Christopher Larkin; Joseph Coencas; *C:* C.H. Douglass; *M:* Gordon Gottlieb; Bert Lucarelli.

Very Semi-Serious: A Partially Thorough Portrait of New Yorker Cartoonists 🦴🦴 1/2 **2015** An award-winning documentary on the cartoons that appear in The New Yorker and the process behind them. Taking the perspective of cartoon editor Bob Mankoff, the film follows him as he considers the many submissions and pitches he receives each week. The work and personalities of the New Yorker cartoonists as well as the wider cultural impact of the cartoons is considered as well. **83m/C; DVD.** *D:* Leah Wolchok; *C:* Kirsten Johnson; *M:* Max Avery Lichtenstein.

A Very Serious Person 🦴🦴 **2006** Precocious, orphaned 13-year-old Gil (Verhoest) lives with his grandma, Mrs. A (Bergen), and loves their beachside summers. She accepts his budding sexuality (a queen in the making) although he can't accept the fact that she is dying. Mrs. A needs professional nursing that companion Betty (Ivey) can't handle, so she hires prim Danish male nurse Jan (Busch—mostly out of drag). Jan and Gil become friends, but Jan is also overprotective. Knowing that the boy will soon be living with distant relatives, he urges Gil to an unwilling (and unlikely) conformity. **96m/C; DVD.** Charles Busch; Polly Bergen; Dana Ivey; Julie Halston; P.J. Verhoest; Carl Andress; *D:* Charles Busch; *W:* Charles Busch; Carl Andress; *C:* Joseph Parlagreco; *M:* Andrew Sherman.

A Very Special Favor 🦴 1/2 **1965** A typically glossy, smarmy '60s sex farce. Texas oil man Paul Chadwick (Hudson) bests French lawyer Michel Boullard (Boyer) in a court case by seducing the female judge and offers to do him a favor as recompense. Michel asks Paul to romance his uptight shrink daughter Lauren (Caron) who's engaged to a milquetoast (Shawn) but needs a real man to teach her about love. **105m/C; DVD.** Rock Hudson; Leslie Caron; Charles Boyer; Dick Shawn; Norma Varden; Walter Slezak; Larry Storch; Nita Talbot; *D:* Michael Gordon; *W:* Nate Monaster; Stanley Shapiro; *C:* Leo Tover; *M:* Vic Mizzy.

The Very Thought of You 🦴 1/2 *Martha, Meet Frank, Daniel and Laurence* **1998 (PG-13)** Limp romantic comedy finds a trio of longtime London friends clashing over their interest in the same woman. Actor Frank (Sewell), music exec Daniel (Hollander), and painter Laurence (Fiennes) all separately encounter Martha (Potter) and pick her up—without anyone realizing (until late in the movie) how they're all connected. However, Martha's character comes across as a imperious nag, while the men are either petulant, arrogant, or wimpy. You won't care who Martha finally ends up with. **88m/C; VHS, DVD.** *GB* Monica Potter; Rufus Sewell; Joseph Fiennes; Tom Hollander; Ray Winstone; *D:* Nick Hamm; *W:* Peter Morgan; *C:* David C(lark) Johnson; *M:* Ed Shearmur.

The Vessel 🦴🦴 **2016 (PG-13)** A moving and visually stunning parable set in a seaside Latin American village. A decade after 46 children died in a tsunami, the survivors are still reeling. They include Leo (Quintana), who lost his brother in the storm and who was so anguished that his girlfriend Soraya (Mejias) married someone else. Father Douglas (Sheen) tries to convince the village to look to the future with little success. Furthermore, community members are skeptical when Leo survives an accident that kills a friend. When Leo begins to build a boat, the community becomes even more aggressive towards him. **86m/C; DVD.** Lucas Quintana; Martin Sheen; Jacqueline Duprey; Aris Mejias; Hiram Delgado; *D:* Julio Quintana; *W:* Julio Quintana; *C:* Santiago Benet Mari; *M:* Hanan Townshend.

The Veteran 🦴🦴 1/2 **2006** Crazed from his time as a Vietnam War POW, Doc (Ironside) is bent on avenging his abandonment by his comrades and targets Ray (Hosea), who is now a preacher with high political aspirations. Doc lures Ray back to Vietnam and holds him hostage in a hotel while rehashing painful memories (done via vivid flashbacks), not knowing that a government agent (Sheedy) investigating MIAs is trailing the pair. **89m/C; DVD.** Michael Ironside; Bobby Hosea; Ally Sheedy; Kenneth Johnson; Colin Glazer; *D:* Sidney J. Furie; *W:* J. Stephen Maunder. **VIDEO**

V.I. Warshawski 🦴🦴 **1991 (R)** The filmmakers seem to think they can slum with the oldest cliches in detective shows just as long as the tough gumshoe is a woman. They're wrong. Turner is terrific as the leggy shamus of the title (from a popular series of books by Sara Paretsky), but the plot is nothing special, featuring stock characters in the killing of a pro athlete and a real-estate deal. **89m/C; VHS, DVD, Blu-Ray.** Kathleen Turner; Jay O. Sanders; Angela Goethals; Charles Durning; Stephen (Steve) Root; *D:* Jeff Kanew; *W:* Nick Thiel; David Aaron Cohen; *M:* Randy Edelman.

Vibes 🦴 **1988 (PG)** Two screwball psychics are sent on a wild goose chase through the Ecuadorean Andes in search of cosmic power and, of course, fall in love. Flat offering from the usually successful team of writers, Lowell Ganz and Babaloo Mandel ("Splash" and "Night Shift"). Lauper's first starring role (and so far, her last). **99m/C; VHS, DVD, Blu-Ray.** Jeff Goldblum; Cyndi Lauper; Julian Sands; Googy Gress; Peter Falk; Elizabeth Pena; *D:* Ken Kwapis; *W:* Babaloo Mandel; Lowell Ganz; *C:* John Bailey; *M:* James Horner.

Vibrations 🦴🦴 1/2 **1994 (R)** Anamika (Applegate), a dance club manager, befriends TJ (Marshall), a homeless, alcoholic, once-promising musician who lost his hands in a brutal attack. The duo find romance as Anamika encourages TJ to try again. **104m/C; VHS, DVD.** James Marshall; Christina Applegate; Faye Grant; Paige Turco; Bruce Altman; David Burke; Scott Cohen; Shane Butterworth; *D:* Michael Paseornek; *W:* Michael Paseornek; *M:* Bob Christianson.

Vice 🦴 1/2 **2008 (R)** Familiar crime thriller but Madsen makes an effort. Cop Max Walker (Madsen) is on a downhill slide that gains momentum after an undercover drug bust goes bad and the heroin goes missing. As members of his team get offed, Walker turns to fellow cops Sampson (Williamson) and Salt (Hannah) to help him out, especially since the killer may be one of their own. **98m/C; DVD.** Michael Madsen; Daryl Hannah; Mykelti Williamson; Mark Boone, Jr.; Kurupt; Nicholas Lea; John Cassini; *D:* Raul Inglis; *W:* Raul Inglis; *C:* Andrzej Sekula; *M:* Cliff Martinez. **VIDEO**

Vice 🦴 **2015 (R)** What begins as a harmless revision of 1973's "Westworld" guts the premise and nearly destroys the original's legacy. Corrupt tycoon Julian (Willis) has created the ultimate vacation resort for sickos, populated with beautiful cyborgs programmed to play out any twisted fantasy a guest may desire. For the most part, these whims include rape, assault, and general violence again women. When female robot, Kelly (Childers), goes AWOL, the good, the bad, and the ugly set out to nab her first. Director Miller is a master of the bland, pitting one cliche up against another, and apparently bent on dragging down the career of Willis, one boring chase scene at a time. **96m/C; DVD, Blu-Ray.** Bruce Willis; Ambyr Childers; Thomas Jane; Johnathon Schaech; Bryan Greenberg; Charlotte Kirk; *D:* Brian A. Miller; *W:* Andre Fabrizio; Jeremy Passmore; *C:* Yaron Levy.

Vice 🦴🦴 1/2 **2018 (R)** Christian Bale loses himself into the role of Dick Cheney, Vice President to George W. Bush who expands his influence by inserting himself in matters beyond the scope of the mostly symbolic position of VP. How much of the film is true largely depends on your own political leanings, but the talents of the lead actors are undisputed. **132m/C; DVD, Blu-Ray.** Christian Bale; Amy Adams; Sam Rockwell; Steve Carell; Lily Rabe; *D:* Adam McKay; *W:* Adam McKay; *C:* Greig Fraser; *M:* Nicholas Britell. Oscars '18: Makeup; British Acad. '18: Film Editing; Golden Globes '19: Actor--Mus./Comedy (Bale).

Vice Academy 🦴 1/2 **1988 (R)** Two females join the Hollywood vice squad. Allen was a former porn queen. **90m/C; VHS, DVD, Blu-Ray.** Linnea Quigley; Ginger Lynn Allen; Karen Russell; Jayne Hamil; Ken Abraham; Stephen Steward; Jeannie Carol; *D:* Rick Sloane.

Vice Academy 2 🦴 **1990 (R)** Two vice cop babes try to stop a female crime boss from dumping aphrodesiacs in the city's water supply. **90m/C; VHS, DVD, Blu-Ray.** Linnea Quigley; Ginger Lynn Allen; Jayne Hamil; Scott Layne; Jay Richardson; Joe Brewer; Marina Benvenga; Teagan Clive; *D:* Rick Sloane.

Vice Academy 3 **WOOF! 1991 (R)** The worst of the series, and not just because cult actress Linnea Quigley is absent. Wit, pacing and even sets are nonexistent as the girls battle a toxic villainess called Malathion. **88m/C; VHS, DVD, Blu-Ray.** Ginger Lynn Allen; Elizabeth Kaitan; Julia Parton; Jay Richardson; Johanna Grika; Steve Mateo; ***D:*** Rick Sloane; ***W:*** Rick Sloane.

Vice Girls ½ **1996 (R)** Three undercover female cops (all babes naturally) use their brains and bodies to capture a serial killer who gets his jollies by filming his victims before he kills them. Sexy fun. **85m/C; VHS, DVD.** Lana Clarkson; Liat Goodson; Kimberly Roberts; A. Michael Baldwin; Richard Gabai; Caroline Keenan; Hoke Howell; ***D:*** Richard Gabai; ***W:*** A. Michael Baldwin; ***C:*** Gary Graver.

Vice Raid ½ **1960** Carol (Van Doren) is a hooker without a heart of gold who agrees to frame honest cop Whitey Brandon (Coogan) for her boss, Vince Malone (Dexter). One of the louses takes advantage of Carol's kid sister, and she gets even by helping the fired Brandon get evidence on the mobsters. **71m/B; DVD, Blu-Ray.** Mamie Van Doren; Richard Coogan; Brad Dexter; Barry Atwater; Frank Gerstle; Carol Nugent; ***D:*** Edward L. Cahn; ***W:*** Charles Ellis; ***C:*** Stanley Cortez; ***M:*** Paul Sawtell; Bert Shefter.

Vice Squad **1953** B-list crime drama. Over the course of one day, L.A. police captain Barnie Barnaby (Robinson) wants to avenge the death of a colleague and isn't above breaking the law to do so. He's tipped by brothel owner Mona (Goddard) that the killers are planning a bank robbery. **88m/B; DVD.** Edward G. Robinson; Paulette Goddard; Lee Van Cleef; Edward Binns; K.T. Stevens; Porter Hall; Adam Williams; ***D:*** Arnold Laven; ***W:*** Lawrence Roman; ***C:*** Joseph Biroc; ***M:*** Herschel Burke Gilbert.

Vice Squad WOOF! **1982 (R)** Violent and twisted killer-pimp goes on a murderous rampage, and a hooker helps a vice squad plainclothesman trap him. Sleazy and disturbing, with little to recommend it. **97m/C; VHS, DVD, Blu-Ray.** Wings Hauser; Season Hubley; Gary Swanson; Cheryl "Rainbeaux" Smith; ***D:*** Gary Sherman; ***W:*** Robert Vincent O'Neil.

Vice Versa **1988 (PG)** Another 80s comedy about a workaholic father and his 11-year-old son who switch bodies, with predictable slapstick results. Reinhold and Savage carry this, appearing to have a great time in spite of over-done story. **97m/C; VHS, DVD, Blu-Ray.** Judge Reinhold; Fred Savage; Swoosie Kurtz; David Proval; Corinne Bohrer; Jane Kaczmarek; William Prince; Gloria Gifford; ***D:*** Brian Gilbert; ***W:*** Dick Clement; Ian La Frenais; ***M:*** David Shire.

Viceroy's House ½ **2017** An elegant period drama exploring the 1947 independence and partition of India. Britain's last viceroy to India, Lord Mountbatten (Bonneville), and his wife, Lady Edwina (Anderson), employ Hindus, Sikhs, and Muslims in their Delhi household. Overseeing the peaceful transfer of power, Mountbatten considers India's future with political power brokers such as future Indian prime minister Jawaharlal Nehru (Ghani) and Muslim leader Muhammad Ali Jinnah (Smith). Household employees eavesdrop on the proceedings and have their own drama, such as the potential romance between Hindu valet Jeet (Dayal) and his Muslim childhood friend turned translator Aalia (Qureshi). **106m/C; DVD.** Hugh Bonneville; Gillian Anderson; Manish Dayal; Huma Qureshi; Michael Gambon; ***D:*** Gurinder Chadha; ***W:*** Gurinder Chadha; Paul Mayeda Berges; Moira Buffini; ***C:*** Ben Smithard; ***M:*** A.R. Rahman.

The Vicious Kind **2009 (R)** Misogynistic Caleb (Scott) rants to his innocent younger brother Peter (Frost) that his new girlfriend Emma (Snow), who's coming to Thanksgiving dinner, is basically a slut. Caleb is protesting too much since he's got a sexual thing for Emma he won't willingly admit to as well as a corrosive relationship with their brutal father (Simmons). Writer/director Krieger is good at dialogue and characters although the dysfunctional family plot is familiar. **93m/C; DVD.** Adam Scott; Brittany Snow; Alex Frost; J.K. Simmons; ***D:*** Lee Toland Krieger; ***W:*** Lee Toland Krieger; ***C:*** Bradley Stonesifer; ***M:*** Jeff Cardoni.

Vicky Cristina Barcelona ½ **2008 (PG-13)** Two best friends, Vicky (Hall), the stable engaged one, and Cristina (Johansson), the risk-taking impulsive one, decide to spend the summer in Barcelona at the home of Vicky's relatives, Judy and Mark (Clarkson and Dunn). Both are drawn to an eccentric local artist, Juan Antonio (Bardem), and eventually they are charmed into considering a shared romance with the smooth-talker. They're unaware, however, that he is still passionately (and violently) involved with his tempestuous ex-wife (Cruz). Similar in theme and style with most of Woody Allen's later work; as always, Allen's characters speak intelligently and never follow the Hollywood formulas. Cruz infuses the otherwise languid film with needed spark. **96m/C; Blu-Ray, On Demand.** *US SP* Javier Bardem; Rebecca Hall; Scarlett Johansson; Penelope Cruz; Patricia Clarkson; Kevin Dunn; Chris Messina; ***V:*** Christopher Evan Welch; ***D:*** Woody Allen; ***W:*** Woody Allen; ***C:*** Javier Aguirresarobe. Oscars '08: Support. Actress (Cruz); British Acad. '08: Support. Actress (Cruz); Golden Globes '09: Film--Mus./Comedy; Ind. Spirit '09: Screenplay, Support. Actress (Cruz).

Victim ½ **1961** A successful married English barrister (Bogarde) with a hidden history of homosexuality is threatened by blackmail after the death of his ex-lover. When the blackmailers, who are responsible for his lover's suicide, are caught, Bogarde decides to prosecute them himself, even though it means revealing his hidden past. One of the first films to deal straightforwardly with homosexuality. Fine performances. **100m/B; VHS, DVD.** *GB* Dirk Bogarde; Sylvia Syms; Dennis Price; Peter McEnery; Nigel Stock; Donald Churchill; Anthony Nicholls; Hilton Edwards; Norman Bird; Derren Nesbitt; Alan MacNaughton; Noel Howlett; Charles Lloyd-Pack; John Barrie; John Bennett; ***D:*** Basil Dearden; ***W:*** John McCormick; Janet Green; ***C:*** Otto Heller; ***M:*** Philip Green.

Victim of Beauty **1991** A small-town girl comes to the big city and becomes a successful model. However, she then becomes the victim of a fatal attraction killer as all her would-be suitors get killed off one by one. **90m/C; VHS, DVD.** Jennifer Rubin; Sally Kellerman; Stephen Shellen; Peter Outerbridge; ***Cameo(s):*** Michael Ironside; ***D:*** Paul Lynch. **CABLE**

Victim of Love **1991 (PG-13)** A therapist doesn't know whom to believe when she finds out she and one of her more neurotic patients are sharing the same boyfriend. Only the patient claims the man murdered his wife to be with his lover. Who will be the next victim? **92m/C; VHS, DVD.** Pierce Brosnan; JoBeth Williams; Virginia Madsen; Georgia Brown; ***D:*** Jerry London; James Desmarais; ***C:*** Billy Dickson; ***M:*** Richard Stone. **TV**

Victor Frankenstein ½ **2015 (PG-13)** Director McGuigan and writer Landis try to revive the monster story of Dr. Victor Frankenstein. The legendary character is played by McAvoy, but this version is captured through the eyes of a totally re-imagined Igor (Radcliffe), believe it or not. The piece is a loud, obnoxious mess from its very first scene, as Mary Shelley's creation doesn't support being adapted into a hyper-stylized action film. McAvoy and Radcliffe probably needed the money, but both talented actors should have known better. **109m/C; DVD, Blu-Ray.** Daniel Radcliffe; Jessica Brown Findlay; Bronson Webb; James McAvoy; Andrew Scott; Mark Gatiss; ***D:*** Paul McGuigan; ***W:*** Max Landis; ***C:*** Fabian Wagner; ***M:*** Craig Armstrong.

Victor/Victoria **1982 (PG)** Victoria (Andrews), an unsuccessful actress in Depression-era Paris, impersonates a man impersonating a woman and becomes a star. Luscious music and sets. Warren as confused showgirl Norma, and Preston as Andrews' gay mentor Toddy are right on target; Garner is charming as gangster King Marchan, who falls for the woman he thinks she is, with Karras amusing as his bodyguard with a secret, Squash. **133m/C; VHS, DVD, Blu-Ray.** Julie Andrews; James Garner; Robert Preston; Lesley Ann Warren; Alex Karras; John Rhys-Davies; Norman Chancer; Peter Arne; ***D:*** Blake Edwards; ***W:*** Blake Edwards; ***C:*** Dick Bush; ***M:*** Henry Mancini. Oscars '82: Orig. Song Score and/or Adapt.; Cesar '83: Foreign Film; Golden Globes '83: Actress--Mus./Comedy (Andrews); Natl. Bd. of Review '82: Support. Actor (Preston); Writers Guild '82: Adapt. Screenplay.

Victoria ½ **2015** Sebastian Schipper's one-take thriller is a remarkable technical accomplishment, anchored by a breathtaking performance by Laia Costa as the title character, a woman caught up in a very unpredictable night in Berlin. Unlike something like Birdman, in which the cuts are hidden, Schipper's film really was shot in one take, for over two hours. Costa plays Victoria, a woman who meets a cute guy at a club and ends unwittingly becoming the getaway driver for an elaborate heist. The first, talkier half of the film is more interesting as it doesn't suspend belief quiet as much as the second half, but the whole thing is pretty fun. **138m/C; DVD, Blu-Ray.** *GE* Laia Costa; Frederick Lau; Franz Rogowski; Burak Yigit; Max Mauff; Andre Hennicke; ***D:*** Sebastian Schipper; ***W:*** Sebastian Schipper; Olivia Neergaard-Holm; Eike Frederik Schulz; ***C:*** Sturla Brandth Grovlen; ***M:*** Nils Frahm.

Victoria & Abdul **2017 (PG-13)** Queen Victoria, beloved yet isolated in her role as England's monarch, befriends her much-younger Indian footman, forming a loyal alliance that's challenged by nearly everyone over issues of class and race. Based on a true story, but the line between "truth" and the retrospective whitewashing of British colonialism remains unclear. Regardless, this movie is filled with the magnificence of Dame Dench, so any overextension of poetic license may be forgiven. Based on the book by Shrabani Basu. **111m/C; DVD, Blu-Ray.** Dame Judi Dench; Ali Fazal; Tim Pigott-Smith; Eddie Izzard; Adeel Akhtar; ***D:*** Stephen Frears; ***W:*** Lee Hall; ***C:*** Danny Cohen; ***M:*** Thomas Newman.

Victoria & Albert ½ **2001** In this BBC production, fabulous sets and costumes frame the story of Victoria, the girl who would be Queen, and Albert, the husband she weds by arrangement. This is a romantic tale of two people who are put together through politics but come to depend on and love each other through trust and mutual respect. The story is historically accurate, but little things pertaining to the personal relationship and family life are painted a little too rosy. Literary license aside, this is a great, romantic, period drama that makes historical figures from a distant land accessible and friendly while teaching you a little about potentially dry English history. **200m/C; VHS, DVD.** Victoria Hamilton; Jonathan Firth; David Suchet; Diana Rigg; Patrick Malahide; Penelope Wilton; Peter Ustinov; Nigel Hawthorne; ***D:*** John Erman; ***W:*** John Goldsmith; ***C:*** Tony Imi; ***M:*** Alan Parker. **TV**

Victoria the Great ½ **1937** Neagle is appropriately regal in the title role, which covers the reign of Queen Victoria from her coronation in 1837 to her Diamond Jubilee sixty years later (that sequence was filmed in Technicolor). Based on Laurence Housman's 1935 play, "Victoria Regina." Followed by the 1938 sequel "Sixty Glorious Years." **110m/B; DVD.** *GB* Anna Neagle; Anton Walbrook; Walter Rilla; Mary Morris; H.B. Warner; Charles Carson; Felix Aylmer; Arthur Young; James Dale; Grete Wegener; ***D:*** Herbert Wilcox; ***W:*** Charles de Grandcourt; Miles Malleson; ***C:*** Frederick A. (Freddie) Young; William V. Skall; ***M:*** Anthony Collins.

Victory ½ **1981 (PG)** Soccer match between WWII American prisoners of war and a German team is set up so that the players can escape through the sewer tunnels of Paris. Of course they want to finish the game first. Not particularly believable as either a soccer flick (even with Pele and other soccer stars) or a great escape, but watchable. **116m/C; VHS, DVD, Blu-Ray.** Sylvester Stallone; Michael Caine; Max von Sydow; Pele; Carole Laure; Bobby Moore; Daniel Massey; ***D:*** John Huston; ***W:*** Jeff Maguire; Djordje Milicevic; ***C:*** Gerry Fisher; ***M:*** Bill Conti.

The Victory *This Time Forever; Yesterday* **1981 (PG)** In 1967 Montreal, an American college exchange student falls in love with a French-Canadian co-ed. Can love survive their different cultures? **95m/C; VHS, DVD, Streaming.** Vincent Van Patten; Cloris Leachman; Eddie Albert; Claire Pimpare; Nicholas (Nick) Campbell; Jack Wetherall; Jacques Godin; Marthe Mercure; ***D:*** Larry Kent; ***W:*** John Dunning; Bill LaMond; ***C:*** Richard Ciupka; ***M:*** Paule Baillargeon.

Victory ½ **1995 (R)** In 1913, Axel Heyst (Dafoe) is living on a remote island in the Dutch East Indies. He makes a trip to the port town of Surabaya and becomes enamored of Alma (Jacob), a violinist who plays in the hotel's orchestra. Alma is being coerced by hotel owner Schomberg (Yanne) into becoming his mistress and Axel decides to take her with him back to his island. Schomberg then sends a couple of thieves (Neill, Sewell) after them by falsely saying that Axel has amassed a fortune. No happy endings; based on the novel by Joseph Conrad. **99m/C; VHS, DVD.** Willem Dafoe; Irene Jacob; Sam Neill; Rufus Sewell; Jean Yanne; Simon Callow; ***D:*** Mark Peploe; ***W:*** Mark Peploe; ***C:*** Bruno de Keyzer; ***M:*** Richard Hartley.

Victory at Entebbe ½ **1976** An all-star cast in a made-for-TV movie that aired within five months of the actual July 4, 1976, incident in which the PLO hijacked an Air France flight with a number of Israeli and Jewish passengers aboard. Israeli leaders Yitzhak Rabin and Shimon Perez go into action to put a military rescue team together while the plane sits on the tarmac at the Entebbe airport in Uganda, which is under the control of bombastic dictator Idi Amin. **119m/C; DVD.** Helmut Berger; Theodore Bikel; Linda Blair; Kirk Douglas; Richard Dreyfuss; Stefan Gierasch; David Groh; Julius W. Harris; Helen Hayes; Anthony Hopkins; Burt Lancaster; Christian Marquand; Elizabeth Taylor; Jessica Walter; Harris Yulin; ***D:*** Marvin J. Chomsky; ***W:*** Ernest Kinoy; ***C:*** Jim Kilgore; ***M:*** Charles Fox. **TV**

The Video Dead WOOF! **1987 (R)** Gore-farce in which murderous zombies emerge from a possessed TV and wreak havoc. **90m/C; VHS, DVD, Blu-Ray, Streaming.** Roxanna Augesen; Rocky Duvall; Michael St. Michaels; ***D:*** Robert Scott.

Video Violence **1987** A gory spoof about a video store owner who discovers that his customers have grown bored with the usual Hollywood horror movies and decide to shoot some flicks of their own. **90m/C; VHS, DVD.** Art Neill; Jackie Neill; William Toddie; Bart Sumner; ***D:*** Gary P. Cohen.

Video Violence Part 2. . . The Exploitation! **1987** Two sickos named Howard and Eli run a cable TV network where talk show guests are spindled and mutilated. **90m/C; VHS, DVD.** Uke; Bart Sumner; Lee Miller; ***D:*** Gary P. Cohen.

Video Voyeur: The Susan Wilson Story ½ **2002** Based on the true story of Lousiana wife and mother Susan Wilson. Susan (Harmon), husband Gary (Midkiff), and their kids move into her dream house. Next-door neighbor Steve Glover (Sheridan) is an old friend but Susan becomes concerned about his overly helpful nature. Then she discovers that Steve installed video surveillance equipment prior to the Wilson's moving in and has been spying on them every since. This prompts Wilson to lobby for a state law (which passed in 1999) making video voyeurism a felony. **91m/C; VHS, DVD.** Angie Harmon; Jamey Sheridan; Dale Midkiff; Tegan Moss; Garry Chalk; Teryl Rothery; ***D:*** Tim Hunter; ***W:*** Kathleen Rowell; ***C:*** Peter Woeste; ***M:*** Daniel Licht. **VIDEO**

Videodrome **1983** Woods is a cable TV programmer with a secret yen for sex and violence, which he satisfies by watching a pirated TV show. "Videodrome" appears to show actual torture and murder, and also seems to control the thoughts of its viewers—turning them into human VCRs. Cronenberg's usual sick fantasies are definitely love 'em or leave 'em. Special effects by Rick Baker. **87m/C; VHS, DVD, Blu-Ray.** *CA* James Woods; Deborah Harry; Sonja Smits; Peter Dvorsky; ***D:*** David Cronenberg; ***W:*** David Cronenberg; ***C:*** Mark Irwin; ***M:*** Howard Shore. Genie '84: Director (Cronenberg).

Vietnam, Texas **1990 (R)** Vietnam vet leaves his past to become a priest. But he returns to violence when he discovers his Vietnamese daughter is in the hands of Houston's most relentless gangster. **101m/C; VHS, DVD.** Robert Ginty; Haing S. Ngor; Tamlyn Tomita; Tim Thomerson; ***D:*** Robert Ginty; ***W:*** C. Courtney Joyner; Tom Badal.

The Vietnam War **2017 1003m/C; DVD, Blu-Ray, Streaming.** ***D:*** Ken Burns; Lynn Novick; ***W:*** Geoffrey C. Ward; ***C:*** Buddy Squires; ***M:*** David Cieri; Trent Reznor; Atticus Ross. **TV**

View from the Top **2003 (PG-13)** Does for "stewardess-in-training" films what "Feds" did for the buddy-cop genre. Don't remember that one? Exactly. The problem isn't that it's a bad film, it's that it doesn't know what kind of a bad film to be (romance, comedy, or fish-out-of water success story). Paltrow is small-town girl Donna, who aspires to a more worldly life (as a stewardess). After leaving for the big blue, Donna falls in love with Ted (Ruffalo) then loses him. She finds him again only to lose him for a shot at the big time. Other tedious stew school hijinks are involved. "Showgirls" showed more depth and logic. Only Mike Myers's lampooning saves it from being completely dreadful. **87m/C; VHS, DVD.** Gwyneth Paltrow; Christina Applegate; Mark Ruffalo; Candice Bergen; Kelly Preston; Rob Lowe; Joshua Malina; Mike Myers; ***D:*** Bruno Barreto; ***W:*** Eric Wald; ***C:*** Affonso Beato; ***M:*** Theodore Shapiro.

A View to a Kill **1985 (PG)** This James Bond mission takes him to the United States, where he must stop the evil Max Zorin from destroying California's Silicon Valley. Feeble and unexciting plot with unscary villain. Duran Duran performs the catchy title tune. Moore's last appearance as 007. **131m/C; VHS, DVD, Blu-Ray.** *GB* Roger Moore; Christopher Walken; Tanya Roberts; Grace Jones; Patrick Macnee; Lois Maxwell; Dolph Lundgren; Desmond Llewelyn; Robert Brown; ***D:*** John Glen; ***W:*** Michael G. Wilson; ***C:*** Alan Hume; ***M:*** John Barry.

Vigil in the Night ½ **1940** Lombard leaves screwball comedy behind for noble and serious with dull results. English nurse Anne Lee (Lombard) takes the blame for a fatal medical error caused by her younger student sister Lucy (Shirley). Anne eventually gets a job in London at an underfunded, understaffed hospital where tireless Dr. Robert Prescott (Aherne) is working. The hospital is beset by various medical emergencies, including an epidemic, which brings the colleagues closer together. Based on a novel by A.J. Cronin. **96m/B; DVD.** Carole Lombard; Brian Aherne; Anne Shirley; Julien Mitchell; Doris Lloyd; Robert Coote; Brenda Forbes; Peter Cushing; ***D:*** George Stevens; ***W:*** Rowland Leigh; Fred Guiol; P.J. Wolfson; ***C:*** Robert De Grasse; ***M:*** Alfred Newman.

Vigilante WOOF! *Street Gang* **1983 (R)** Frustrated ex-cop, tired of seeing criminals returned to the street, joins a vigilante squad dedicated to law and order. Often ridiculous and heavy handed. **91m/C; VHS, DVD.** Robert Forster; Fred Williamson; Carol Lynley; Rutanya Alda; Richard Bright; Woody Strode; Donald Blakely; Joseph Carberry; Joe Spinell; Frank Pesce; ***D:*** William Lustig; ***W:*** Richard Vetere; ***C:*** James (Momel) Lemmo; ***M:*** Jay Chattaway.

A Vigilante ½ **2019 (R)** Domestic abuse survivor Sadie (Wilde) uses her well-honed boxing skills to save others who are experiencing abuse. When she learns of an abuser, she beats him up and supports those whom he has abused. Though Sadie is committed to helping others, she struggles because of her own abuse experiences, lack of justice, and her violent acts. Sadie is also aware that her abusive husband (Spector) is out in the world, a fact that affects all she does. The first-time filmmaker Daggar-Nickson accurately and thoughtfully captures the pain of abuse in the feminist revenge thriller, and her film showcases Wilde's full commitment to the role. **91m/C; DVD.** Olivia Wilde; Morgan Spector; Kyle Catlett; Betsy Aidem; Cheryse Dyllan; ***D:*** Sarah Daggar-Nickson; ***W:*** Sarah Daggar-Nickson; ***C:*** Alan McIntyre Smith; ***M:*** Danny Bensi; Saunder Jurriaans.

Vigilante Diaries ½ **2016 (R)** A 1990s throwback action adventure centered on a team of anti-hero crime fighters who take part in action-focused missions of rescue and revenge around the world. Led by The Vigilante (Sloan), all members of the team are former black-ops agents who fight for justice with and for opponents as colorful and dangerous as they are. With their escapes chronicled by filmmaker Mike Hanover (Mewes), the team becomes drawn into a bloodbath that involves such bad guys as deadly Armenian mobsters, Mexican cartels and undercover super spies. **107m/C; DVD, Blu-Ray, Streaming, Download.** Paul Sloan; Jason Mewes; Quinton 'Rampage' Jackson; Michael Jai White; Michael Madsen; ***D:*** Christian Sesma; ***W:*** Paul Sloan; Christian Sesma; ***C:*** Anthony J. Rickert-Epstein; ***M:*** Kevin Riepl.

Vigilante Force ½ **1976** Inhabitants of a remote California town turn to troubled Vietnam vet Aaron Arnold and his buddies to stop the lawlessness accompanying an influx of rowdy oil workers. When the vigilantes take advantage of their power, Aaron's younger brother Ben has to put a stop to their taking over the town instead. **89m/C; DVD.** Kris Kristofferson; Jan-Michael Vincent; Victoria Principal; Bernadette Peters; Andrew Stevens; David Doyle; Brad Dexter; Judson Pratt; ***D:*** George Armitage; ***W:*** George Armitage; ***C:*** William Cronjager; ***M:*** Gerald Fried.

The Vigilantes Are Coming
1936 "The Eagle" sets out to avenge his family and upsets a would-be dictator's plot to establish an empire in California. In 12 chapters; the first is 32 minutes, and additional chapters are 18 minutes each. **230m/B; VHS, DVD.** Robert "Bob" Livingston; Kay Hughes; Guinn "Big Boy" Williams; Raymond Hatton; William Farnum; ***D:*** Mack V. Wright; Ray Taylor.

The Viking **1928** Viking Leif Ericsson (Crisp) sails off in search of new lands after disagreeing with his father Eric the Red (Randolf). Leif must also compete with his friend Egil (Woods) and English slave Alwin (Mason) for the affections of Nordic beauty Helga (Starke). Filmed in two-strip Technicolor. **90m/C; Silent; DVD.** Donald Crisp; Anders Randolph; Pauline Starke; Harry Woods; Leroy Mason; ***D:*** Roy William Neill; ***W:*** Jack Cunningham; ***C:*** George Cave.

The Viking Queen **1967** Babe and swordplay saga. After her father dies, Salina (Carita) becomes queen and must protect her British tribe from the Roman occupation. But after tribal rebels attack the Centurions, Roman commander Justinian (Murray) refuses her father a proper burial, even though he and Salina are getting romantic. Then Salina falls into the hands of the evil Octavian (Keir) and he begins a war against the tribes while Justinian is away. When Salina escapes, she joins the fighting. **91m/C; VHS, DVD.** *GB* Carita; Don Murray; Andrew Keir; Donald Houston; Adrienne Corri; Niall MacGinnis; Nicola Pagett; Patrick Troughton; ***D:*** Don Chaffey; ***W:*** Clarke Reynolds; ***C:*** Stephen Dade; ***M:*** Gary Hughes.

The Viking Sagas **1995 (R)** Kjartan (Moeller) is the warrior who must avenge his father's execution, defend his people, and fight for his country's survival against evil oppressors. At least there's a beautiful babe around to offer him some comfort. The Icelandic scenery is the best thing about the movie. **83m/C; VHS, DVD.** Ralph (Ralf) Moeller; Ingibjorg Stefansdottir; Sven-Ole Thorsen; ***D:*** Michael Chapman; ***W:*** Dale Herd; Paul R. Gurian; ***M:*** George S. Clinton.

The Viking Women and the Sea Serpent *The Saga of the Viking Women and Their Voyage to the Waters of the Great Sea Serpent* **1957** When their menfolk go missing the viking women go looking for them and encounter whirlpools, sea monsters, and evil barbarians. Turns out the barbarians are holding their men hostage. It's from Roger Corman so it's a cheap goof. **71m/B; DVD.** Abby Dalton; Susan Cabot; Bradford Jackson; June Kenney; Richard Devon; ***D:*** Roger Corman; ***W:*** Lawrence Louis Goldman; ***C:*** Monroe Askins; ***M:*** Albert Glasser.

Vikingdom **2013** Unpretentious action fantasy. Viking prince Eirick is revived after being killed in battle in order to prevent bad Norse god Thor from gathering relics that will allow him to open the gates of Valhalla so he can conquer and rule over mankind. Naturally, Eirick needs a kick-butt group of warriors to help him. **114m/C; DVD, Blu-Ray.** Dominic Purcell; Craig Fairbrass; Natassia Malthe; Jon Foo; Conan Stevens; Patrick Murray; ***D:*** Yusry Abd Halim; ***W:*** James Coyne; ***C:*** Eric Oh; ***M:*** Edry Abdul Halim. **VIDEO**

The Vikings ½ **1958** A Viking king and his son kidnap a Welsh princess and hold her for ransom. Depicts the Vikings' invasion of England. Great location footage of both Norway and Brittany. Basic costume epic with good action scenes. Narrated by Welles. **116m/C; VHS, DVD, Blu-Ray.** Kirk Douglas; Ernest Borgnine; Janet Leigh; Tony Curtis; James Donald; Alexander Knox; ***Nar:*** Orson Welles; ***D:*** Richard Fleischer; ***W:*** Calder Willingham; ***C:*** Jack Cardiff; ***M:*** Mario Nascimbene; Gerard Schurmann.

Villa Rides **1968** A flying gun-runner aids Francisco "Pancho" Villa's revolutionary Mexican campaign. Considering the talent involved, this one is a disappointment. Check out Brynner's hair. **125m/C; VHS, DVD, Blu-Ray.** Yul Brynner; Robert Mitchum; Charles Bronson; Herbert Lom; Jill Ireland; Robert Towne; Robert Viharo; Frank Wolff; Fernando Rey; Alexander Knox; Diana Lorys; ***D:*** Buzz Kulik; ***W:*** Robert Towne; Sam Peckinpah; ***C:*** Jack Hildyard; ***M:*** Maurice Jarre.

The Village **2004 (PG-13)** So is Shyamalan a one-trick director or are we just anticipating a trick in every film he directs? This solemn supernatural thriller is set in a 19th Century village whose insular, fearful inhabitants have formed an uneasy, unspoken truce with the monsters that live in the woods that surround it. The village elders forbid anyone to go beyond the perimeter but Lucius (Phoenix) becomes determined to defy them. Lucius is in love with blind Ivy (Howard), who is also loved by the village idiot Noah (Brody in an unfortunate role). Except that it's Ivy who finally enters the woods and is soon hearing scary noises coming in her direction. The payoff doesn't measure up to the portentousness. Maybe it's time Shyamalan does a comedy. **120m/C; DVD.** Joaquin Rafael (Leaf) Phoenix; William Hurt; Sigourney Weaver; Adrien Brody; Bryce Dallas Howard; Judy Greer; Jayne Atkinson; Frank Collison; Brendan Gleeson; Cherry Jones; Liz Stauber; Celia Weston; Michael Pitt; John Christopher Jones; Fran Kranz; ***D:*** M. Night Shyamalan; ***W:*** M. Night Shyamalan; ***C:*** Roger Deakins; ***M:*** James Newton Howard.

A Village Affair ½ **1995** Ward is a young wife and mother, living what appears to be a perfect life in a quiet English village, when she meets a neighbor's daughter (Fox) who's just returned from America. Fox makes her interests clear and soon the two women are having an affair that shatters the peacefulness around them. Based on a novel by Joanna Trollope. **108m/C; VHS, DVD.** *GB* Sophie Ward; Kerry Fox; Nathaniel Parker; Claire Bloom; Michael Gough; Barbara Jefford; Jeremy Northam; Rosalie Crutchley; ***D:*** Moira Armstrong; ***W:*** Alma Cullen; ***C:*** John Else. **TV**

The Village Barbershop **2008 (R)** Gruff Reno widower Arthur Leroldi has just buried his longtime barbershop partner. His greedy landlord wants to break the lease and Arthur is having money trouble. He reluctantly hires cosmetologist Gloria, who can also keep the books straight. Gloria seems tough but she's just found out she's pregnant by the guy who just dumped her and the two lost souls find someone they can lean on. **99m/C; DVD.** John Ratzenberger; Shelly Cole; Cindy Pickett; Amos Glick; Josh Hutchinson; ***D:*** Chris Ford; ***W:*** Chris Ford; ***C:*** Cliff Traiman; ***M:*** Michael Tremante.

Village of Dreams **1997** Middle-aged identical twin brothers recall the sweetness of their childhood in a rural Japanese village in 1948. As mischievous eight-year-olds, the duo spend their time playing pranks, spying on their neighbors, and entertaining themselves in the woods and streams. Based on the memoir "The Village of My Paintings" by Seizo Tashima. Japanese with subtitles. **112m/C; VHS, DVD.** *JP* Keigo Matsuyama; Shogo Matsuyama; ***D:*** Yoichi Higashi; ***W:*** Takehiro Nakajima; Yoichi Higashi; ***C:*** Yoshio Shimizu.

Village of the Damned **1960** A group of unusual children are born in a small English village. They avoid their fathers and other men, except for the one who is their teacher. He discovers they are the vanguard of an alien invasion and leads the counter-attack. Exciting and bone-chilling low-budget thriller. From the novel, "The Midwich Cuckoos," by John Wyndham. **78m/B; VHS, DVD, Blu-Ray.** *GB* George Sanders; Barbara Shelley; Martin Stephens; Laurence Naismith; Michael Gwynn; John Phillips; Richard Vernon; Jenny Laird; Richard Warner; Thomas Heathcote; Charlotte Mitchell; John Stuart; Bernard Archard; ***D:*** Wolf Rilla; ***W:*** Wolf Rilla; Stirling Silliphant; George Harley; ***C:*** Geoffrey Faithfull; ***M:*** Ronald Goodwin.

Village of the Damned ½ **1995 (R)** The quiet town of Midwich, California, has been enveloped by a strange force that seems to have impregnated the local women. The albino children born of this incident have disturbing telepathic powers that they display through their bright orange and red eyes—supposedly precipitating a plot to take control. A pale remake of the 1960 British horror classic, which was based on John Wyndham's novel "The Midwich Cuckoos." Fails to capture the eeriness of it's predecessor and is bogged down with awkward casting, absurd dialogue, and a brood of children with glowing eyes that make them less like a threat and more like Nintendo addicts. **98m/C; VHS, DVD, Blu-Ray.** Christopher Reeve; Kirstie Alley; Linda Kozlowski; Mark Hamill; Meredith Salenger; Michael Paré; Peter Jason; Constance Forslund; Karen Kahn; ***D:*** John Carpenter; ***W:*** John Carpenter; David Himmelstein; ***C:*** Gary B. Kibbe; ***M:*** John Carpenter; Dave Davies.

Village of the Giants **1965** A group of beer-guzzling teenagers become giants after eating a mysterious substance invented by a 12-year-old genius. Fun to pick out all the soon-to-be stars. Totally silly premise with bad special effects and minimal plot follow-through. Based on an H.G. Wells story. **82m/C; VHS, DVD.** Ron Howard; Johnny Crawford; Tommy Kirk; Beau Bridges; Freddy Cannon; Toni Basil; Tisha Sterling; Tim Rooney; Charla Doherty; Joe Turkel; ***D:*** Bert I. Gordon; ***W:*** Alan Caillou; ***C:*** Paul Vogel; ***M:*** Jack Nitzsche.

Villain **1971** Grim, seedy, and violent crime drama inspired by real-life gangster Ronnie Kray. Sadistic East End crime boss Vic Dakin (Burton) plans a payroll heist to remain on top of his criminal empire while carrying on with blackmailing pimp Wolfe (McShane). Scotland Yard Inspector Matthews (Davenport) is closing in and is sure he can get the goods from a Dakin associate if Vic doesn't silence the stoolie first. **98m/C; DVD.** *UK* Richard Burton; Nigel Davenport; Ian McShane; Donald Sinden; Joss Ackland; T.P. McKenna; Cathleen Nesbitt; ***D:*** Michael Tuchner; ***W:*** Dick Clement; Ian La Frenais; ***C:*** Christopher Challis; ***M:*** Jonathan Hodge.

The Villain ½ *Cactus Jack* **1979 (PG)** An unfunny spoof of "B" westerns that is almost like a live-action "Roadrunner" cartoon. Douglas plays Cactus Jack, a highwayman who keeps trying to kidnap fair damsel Ann-Margret. Hero Schwarzenegger keeps rescuing her. Lynde is amusing as the uptight Indian chief Nervous Elk. **93m/C; VHS, DVD.** Kirk Douglas; Ann-Margret; Arnold Schwarzenegger; Paul Lynde; Foster Brooks; Ruth Buzzi; Jack Elam; Strother Martin; Robert Tessier; Mel Tillis; ***D:*** Hal Needham; ***W:*** Robert G. Kane; ***C:*** Bobby Byrne; ***M:*** Bill Justis.

The Villain Still Pursued Her
1941 A poor hero and rich villain vie for the sweet heroine in this satire of old-fashioned temperance melodrama. Keaton manages to shine as the hero's sidekick. **67m/B; VHS, DVD.** Anita Louise; Alan Mowbray; Buster Keaton; Hugh Herbert; ***D:*** Edward F. (Eddie) Cline.

Villains ½ **2019 (R)** Frantic couple Mickey (Skarsgard) and Jules (Monroe) are petty criminals who long to move to Florida and a new, better life. Not particularly skilled, the pair robs a gas station then runs out of gas. When they approach a house for help, they find the retro-looking dwelling has a mysterious basement in which a girl (Baumgartner) is chained. The couple's rescue mission is interrupted by the appearance of the home's creepy owners, George (Donovan) and Gloria (Sedgwick), and a cat-and-mouse game of survival. The comedy-thriller genre film is both absurd and unsettling, with a cast that can run with the premise. **89m/C; DVD.** Bill Skarsgård; Maika Monroe; Blake Baumgartner; Jeffrey Donovan; Kyra Sedgwick; ***D:*** Dan Berk; Robert Olsen; ***W:*** Dan Berk; Robert Olsen; ***C:*** Matt Mitchell; ***M:*** Andrew Hewitt.

Vince Vaughn's Wild West Comedy Show *Wild West Comedy Show* **2006 (R)** Part comedy concert film, part backstage documentary follows comedy tour mastermind Vaughn and four up-and-coming comics on a tour across the southern U.S. in 2005. Outside of a visit to a camp of people who had just been displaced by Hurricane Katrina, the film doesn't break out of its basic concept, focusing on the backgrounds of comedians Caparule, Ernst, Maniscalco, and Ahmed and their time on the road, which seems to involve very little partying or getting into trouble. The result is a tour movie that's not particularly wild. For stand-up fans. **100m/C; DVD.** ***Cameo(s):*** Vince Vaughn;

Ahmed Ahmed; John Caparulo; Bret Ernst; Sebastian Mansicalco; ***D:*** Ari Sandel; ***M:*** John O'Brien.

Vincent & Theo 1/2 **1990 (PG-13)** The story of Impressionist painter Vincent van Gogh (Roth), and his brother Theo (Rhys), a gallery owner who loved his brother's work, yet could not get the public to buy it. Increasing despair and mental illness traps both men, as each struggles to create beauty in a world where it has no value. Altman has created a stunning portrait of "the artist" and his needs. The exquisite cinematography will make you feel as if you stepped into van Gogh's work. **138m/C; VHS, DVD, Blu-Ray.** Tim Roth; Paul Rhys; Johanna Ter Steege; Wladimir Yordanoff; ***D:*** Robert Altman; ***W:*** Julian Mitchell; ***C:*** Jean Lepine.

Vincent N Roxxy 1/2 **2017 (R)** A bloody romance that kicks off when small-town Vincent (Hirsch) rescues Roxxy (Kravitz) from big-city attackers. The troubled pair enjoys some lovin' in Vincent's trailer until the gangsters track them down and resume the violence. Hirsch and Kravitz have an easy chemistry and act their hearts out, but neither their performances nor the conclusion justify the film's brutality. **102m/C; DVD.** Emile Hirsch; Zoë Kravitz; Emory Cohen; Zoey Deutch; Scott Mescudi; ***D:*** Gary Michael Schultz; ***W:*** Gary Michael Schultz; ***C:*** Alex Disenhof; ***M:*** Ahmir-Khalib Thompson.

Vincent: The Life and Death of Vincent van Gogh **1987** Van Gogh's work and creativity is examined in a documentary manner through his life and his letters. Thoughtful and intriguing production. Narrated by John Hurt as van Gogh. **99m/C; VHS, DVD.** *AU* ***V:*** John Hurt; ***D:*** Paul Cox; ***W:*** Paul Cox; ***M:*** Norman Kaye.

Vincere *Victory; Win* **2009** Operatically-told, little-known story of Italian dictator Benito Mussolini's ill-fated first wife and son. In 1907, when Benito (Timi) was merely a Socialist union organizer, he meets beautiful Ida Dalser (Mezzogiorno) who's fascinated by his outsized personality and his lust for power (and her). He changes his stance (World War I has him turning fascist) and Ida bears his son in 1915 only to learn he's legally married Rachele (Cescon). The ambitious Benito distances himself from Ida and their child and she becomes obsessed with getting her due, so he has her thrown into an insane asylum. Once he moves on, the only way Ida sees him is through (actual archival) newsreels as he gains governmental control. Italian with subtitles. **128m/C; DVD.** *IT FR* Michela Cescon; Piergiorgio Bellocchio; Paolo Pierobon; Fabrizio Costella; Giovanna Mezzogiorno; Filippo Timi; Fausto Russo Alesi; Bruno Cariello; Francesca Picozza; ***D:*** Marco Bellocchio; ***W:*** Daniela Ceselli; Marco Bellocchio; ***C:*** Daniele Cipri; ***M:*** Carlo Crivelli.

The Vineyard **1989 (R)** Hapless victims are lured to a Japanese madman's island, where he drinks their blood and maintains a questionable immortality. **95m/C; VHS, DVD, Blu-Ray.** James Hong; Karen Witter; Michael Wong; ***D:*** James Hong; Bill Rice.

Vintage Model *Modelo Antiguo* **1992** Carmen hosts a radio program giving romantic advice, though she's lonely and lives on her memories of the past. When she learns she only has a short time to live, Carmen hires a chauffeur to drive her around Mexico City so she can remember. Spanish with subtitles. **97m/C; VHS, DVD.** *MX* Silvia Pinal; Alonso Echanove; ***D:*** Raul Araiza; ***W:*** Consuelo Garrido; Alejandro Pelayo; ***C:*** Rosalio Solano; ***M:*** Osni Cassab.

Violated **1953** Pathetic production about New York police attempting to track down a sex-maniac murderer who slays his victims and then gives them a haircut. Unbelievably bad. **78m/B; VHS, DVD.** Lili Dawn; Mitchell Kowal; Vicki Carlson; William Martel; ***D:*** Walter Strate.

Violence 1/2 **1947** Magazine writer Ann (Coleman) goes undercover to shed light on a scam outfit, the United Defenders—a public service organization that's actually a racket. While hunting down the bad guys, she suffers a bout of amnesia which threatens to blow her cover. **72m/B; DVD.** Nancy Coleman; Michael O'Shea; Sheldon Leonard; ***D:*** Jack Bernhard; ***W:*** Lewis Lantz; Stanley Rubin.

Violence at Noon **1966** Highly disturbing film in which two women protect a brutal sex murderer from the law. Living among a quiet community of intellectuals, this conspiracy ends in a shocking finale in Oshima's stylized masterpiece. In Japanese with English subtitles. **99m/B; VHS, DVD.** *JP* Saeda Kawaguchi; Akiko Koyama; ***D:*** Nagisa Oshima.

Violent Blue 1/2 **2010** A semi-coherent art film about a music composer with writer's block thrown into a cage by her ex-husband, her brother who is being leaned on by criminals, and various weird sex-obsessed whackos of every description. If you like your stories with bondage masks, little in the way of dialogue, and a plot explained in vague metaphor you've got a pretty good one here. **122m/C; DVD.** Silvia Suvadora; Jesse Hlubik; Nick Mancuso; ***D:*** Gregory Hatanaka; ***W:*** Gregory Hatanaka; ***C:*** James Avallone; ***M:*** Toshiyuki Hiraoka.

Violent Cop *Sono Otoko, Kyobo ni Tsuki* **1989** Think "Dirty Harry" to the nth power and you'll have some idea of the kind of cop Detective Azuma (Kitano) is. However, he also gets results, so the boss is willing to overlook the violent way Azuma does his job. His latest case involves a drug-related murder, a sadistic killer, a corrupt friend, and the kidnapping of Azuma's own mentally unstable sister. Not for the squeamish. Japanese with subtitles. **103m/C; VHS, DVD, Blu-Ray.** *JP* Takeshi "Beat" Kitano; Shiro Sano; Maiko Kawakami; Makoto Ashikawa; Shigeru Hiraizumi; Mikiko Otonashi; ***D:*** Takeshi "Beat" Kitano; ***W:*** Hisahi Nozawa; ***C:*** Yasushi Sasakibara; ***M:*** Daisaku Kume.

The Violent Men 1/2 *Rough Company* **1955** Big-time land baron Robinson is trying to push out all other landowners in the valley, including Ford. At first Ford refuses to fight back, but after one of Robinson's henchmen kills one of his hired hands, he starts an all-out war against Robinson to save his land. Stanwyck as Robinson's wife and Keith as his brother are wicked as the two urging him on and having an affair behind his back. Based on the novel "Rough Company" by Donald Hamilton. **95m/C; VHS, DVD.** Glenn Ford; Barbara Stanwyck; Edward G. Robinson; Dianne Foster; Brian Keith; May Wynn; ***D:*** Rudolph Mate; ***C:*** Burnett Guffey.

Violent Ones WOOF! **1968** Three men who are suspected of raping a young girl are threatened with lynching by an angry mob of townspeople. Badly acted, poorly directed, uneven and feeble. **96m/C; VHS, DVD.** Fernando Lamas; David Carradine; ***D:*** Fernando Lamas.

Violent Road 1/2 **1958** Taut B-movie that plays like an Americanized version of the 1953 French pic "Wages of Fear." Six desperate men are transporting volatile chemicals used in rocket fuel over bad mountain roads. Most are in it for the money, but guilt-ridden George (Zimbalist Jr.) developed the fuel and has already seen what the chemicals can do if there's a mishap (think big boom). **86m/B; DVD.** Brian Keith; Efrem Zimbalist, Jr.; Dick Foran; Sean Garrison; Perry Lopez; Arthur Batanides; Merry Anders; Ann Doran; ***D:*** Howard W. Koch; ***W:*** Richard H. Landau; ***C:*** Carl Guthrie; ***M:*** Leith Stevens.

Violent Saturday **1955** Director Fleischer's film noir, set in harsh daylight and filmed in CinemaScope, is less concerned with the crime plot and more with the characters. Three crooks come to an Arizona mining town to case the bank, which they plan to rob on Saturday. They also look at the locals, who turn out to be less-than-upstanding citizens. The bank manager is a peeping tom; the wealthiest man in town is a drunk and his wife cheats on him; some residents are thieves themselves; some are perceived to be cowards; and an Amish farmer must betray his pacifist beliefs to protect his family. **91m/C; DVD, Blu-Ray.** Stephen McNally; Lee Marvin; J. Carrol Naish; Victor Mature; Tommy Noonan; Sylvia Sydney; Margaret (Maggie) Hayes; Richard Egan; Ernest Borgnine; Virginia Leith; Billy Chapin; Dorothy Patrick; Brad Dexter; ***D:*** Richard Fleischer; ***W:*** Sydney (Sidney) Boehm; ***C:*** Charles G. Clarke; ***M:*** Hugo Friedhofer.

Violent Zone **1989** Mercenaries go on a supposed rescue mission in the wilderness. **92m/C; VHS, DVD.** John Douglas; Chard Hayward; Christopher Weeks; ***D:*** John Garwood; ***W:*** David Pritchard; John Bushelman.

Violet & Daisy **2011 (R)** Fast-talking indie flick following two precocious teenage assassins, Violet (Bledel) and Daisy (Ronan), as their daily kill list is interrupted by a target who actually wants to be killed. Out of morbid fascination, the girls hold their fire and listen as the man (Gandolfini) explains the motive behind his death wish. The directorial debut of Fletcher amounts to little more than a cliched homage, as the duo's quirky rapid-fire banter and casual brutality awkwardly borrows from a certain pair of hitmen from a popular '90s indie flick. Luckily, the girls never have to call in The Wolf. **88m/C; DVD, Blu-Ray.** Alexis Bledel; Saoirse Ronan; James Gandolfini; Danny Trejo; Marianne Jean-Baptiste; Tatiana Maslany; ***D:*** Gregory Fletcher; ***W:*** Gregory Fletcher; ***C:*** Vanja Cernjul.

Violet Tendencies **2010** Cohn makes a sweet lead as acerbic, lovable-but-lonely longtime fag hag Violet. Wanting a boyfriend of her own, Violet decides she must—at least temporarily—separate herself from her gay friends in order to find a straight lover. This sends the men into a panic since they don't know what to do without their reliable Violet. **99m/C; DVD.** Mindy Cohn; Marcus Patrick; Jesse Archer; Samuel Whitten; Casper Andreas; Anthony Armand; Adrian Armas; Kim Allen; ***D:*** Casper Andreas; ***W:*** Jesse Archer; ***C:*** Timothy Naylor; ***M:*** Dr. Michael Barry.

Violeta Went to Heaven *Violeta se fue a los cielos* **2013** True story of Chilean artist and musician Violeta Parra (Gavilán). Born into poverty, Parra builds a life as an artist, traveler, and musician, first in her native country and eventually across Europe, often leaving family behind in pursuit of her life as an artist. With an impressionistic style that leaps back and forth in time, the film focuses more on style than biographical details, losing some of the facts of her relationships and revolutionary politics while favoring her internal struggles and contradictions. Gavilán distinguishes herself in the role of Perra, including singing all the songs herself. Based on the memoirs of Perra's son, Angel. **110m/C; DVD.** *CL* Francisca Gavilan; Thomas Durand; ***D:*** Andres Wood; ***W:*** Eliseo Altunaga; ***C:*** Miguel Ioann Littin Menz; ***M:*** Violeta Parra.

Violets Are Blue 1/2 **1986 (PG-13)** Two high-school sweethearts are reunited in their hometown years later and try to rekindle their romance—even though the man is married. **86m/C; VHS, DVD, Streaming.** Kevin Kline; Sissy Spacek; Bonnie Bedelia; John Kellogg; Augusta Dabney; Jim Standford; ***D:*** Jack Fisk; ***W:*** Naomi Foner; ***C:*** Ralf Bode; ***M:*** Patrick Williams.

Violette *Violette Noziere* **1978 (R)** Fascinating true-life account of a 19-year-old French girl in the 1930s who, bored with her life and wanting to be with her lover, decides to poison her parents so she can receive her inheritance. Her mother survives but her father dies, and the girl is sent to prison for murder. Extraordinary performance by Huppert and the film is visually stunning. **122m/C; VHS, DVD.** *FR* Isabelle Huppert; Stephane Audran; Jean Carmet; Jean-Francoise Garreaud; Bernadette LaFont; ***D:*** Claude Chabrol; ***W:*** Odile Barski; Frederic Grendel; ***C:*** Jean Rabier; ***M:*** Pierre Jansen. Cannes '78: Actress (Huppert); Cesar '79: Support. Actress (Audran).

VIP, My Brother Superman 1/2 **1990** The Vips are modern-day descendants of superbeings about to become legends in their own times. SuperVip is broad of chest and pure in spirit while his brother MiniVip possesses only limited powers. From the creator of "Allegro Non Troppo" comes this enticing, amusing piece of animation. **90m/C; VHS, DVD.** *IT* ***D:*** Bruno Bozzetto; ***W:*** Bruno Bozzetto; ***C:*** Luciano Marzetti; ***M:*** Franco Godi.

Viper **1988** A woman battles a cryptic anti-terrorist band to avenge the murder of her husband. **96m/C; VHS, DVD.** Linda Purl; Chris Robinson; James Tolkan; ***D:*** Peter Maris.

Vipers **2008 (R)** Genetically-enhanced snakes escape during a break-in at a research lab. Since they reproduce at an alarming rate, they're soon devouring all the locals, who happen to be stuck on an isolated island. Lots of bad acting and shoddy CGI effects. **89m/C; DVD.** Tara Reid; Jonathan Scarfe; Corbin Bernsen; Don S. Davis; Jessica Steen; Mark Humphrey; Genevieve Buechner; ***D:*** Bill Cocoran; ***W:*** Brian Katkin; ***C:*** Thomas Burstyn; ***M:*** Lawrence Shragge. **VIDEO**

The V.I.P.'s **1963** Slick, sophisticated drama set in the V.I.P. lounge of a British airport. Trapped by fog, several of the passengers get acquainted and are forced to face their problems as they spend the night in the airport lounge. Taylor stars as Frances Andros, a wealthy young woman leaving her husband (Burton) for life in the U.S. with her lover, Jourdan. A movie tycoon, an Australian entrepreneur, his secretary, and a duchess are among the other passengers grounded by the fog. Both Rutherford and Smith give excellent performances and it was a tossup as to which actress would be nominated for the Oscar. **119m/C; VHS, DVD.** *GB* Elizabeth Taylor; Richard Burton; Louis Jourdan; Elsa Martinelli; Margaret Rutherford; Maggie Smith; Rod Taylor; Orson Welles; Linda Christian; Dennis Price; ***D:*** Anthony Asquith; ***W:*** Terence Rattigan; ***C:*** Jack Hildyard; ***M:*** Miklos Rozsa. Oscars '63: Support. Actress (Rutherford); Golden Globes '64: Support. Actress (Rutherford); Natl. Bd. of Review '63: Support. Actress (Rutherford).

Viral 1/2 **2016 (R)** A science fiction/horror drama about the impact of a virus on a community. In a suburban neighborhood, teen sisters Emma (Black-D'Elia) and Stacey (Tipton) lead normal lives until a mysterious parasitic virus hits the community. As the disease spreads quickly throughout the town, the sisters try to barricade themselves in their home to protect themselves. When they realize it may be too late, they are faced with making the choice between surviving and protecting each other. **85m/C; DVD, Blu-Ray, Streaming, Download.** Sofia Black-D'Elia; Analeigh Tipton; Travis Tope; Michael Kelly; Machine Gun Kelly; ***D:*** Henry Joost; ***W:*** Christopher Landon; ***C:*** Magdalena Gorka; ***M:*** Rob Simonsen.

Viral Assassins 1/2 **2000** Surprisingly dark social commentary in a Troma sci fi movie set in a dystopian future. In the new world once your health care bills exceed your perceived worth, the government sends assassins to kill you. They also send out hitmen if you catch any so-called 'super viruses' so you don't spread them. And you thought health care was harsh now. **90m/C; DVD.** Jim Gordon; Ray Kelly; Steve Gatschet; Greg Eisenhuth; Sherri Hewell; ***D:*** Robert Larkin; ***W:*** Robert Larkin; ***C:*** David Deneen; ***M:*** Joe DeMattia. **VIDEO**

Virgil Bliss **2001** Virgil (Jordan) is a mild-mannered career thief from Mississippi who's been paroled to a Brooklyn halfway house after 12 years in the joint. So what's the first thing he does? Well, he listens to his new roomie Manny (Gorman) who maybe wants Virgil to do another job and who introduces him to tough hooker/junkie Ruby (Russell). Naturally, Virgil falls for her and there's more trouble a-coming. **94m/C; VHS, DVD.** Clint Jordan; Kirsten Russell; Anthony Gorman; ***D:*** Joe Maggio; ***W:*** Joe Maggio; ***C:*** Harlan Bosmajian.

Virgin **2003 (R)** Fundamentalist's rebellious daughter becomes pregnant after being drugged and date-raped. Not remembering the assault, she declares herself Virgin Mother to the Second Coming, and is not surprisingly attacked by her family and community. Odd feminist parable seems unsure whether to take itself seriously or not. Intense and unforgettable central performance by Moss does little to rid film of its contrived weirdness. **114m/C; DVD.** Robin Wright; Elisabeth Moss; Daphne Rubin-Vega; Dr. Charles Socarides; Socorro Santiago; Peter Gerety; Stephanie Gatchet; ***D:*** Deborah Kampmeier; ***W:*** Deborah Kampmeier; ***C:*** Ben Wolf.

Virgin among the Living Dead **1971 (R)** Young woman travels to remote castle when she hears of relative's death. Once there, she finds the residents a tad weird and has bad dreams in which zombies chase her. Bizarre even for Franco, who seems to have been going through a "Pasolini" phase while making this one. **90m/C; VHS, DVD, Blu-Ray.** *SP* Christina von Blanc;

Britt Nichols; Howard Vernon; Anne Libert; Rose Kiekens; Paul Muller; ***D:*** Jess (Jesus) Franco.

The Virgin and the Gypsy ½ **1970 (R)** An English girl brought up in a repressive household in 1920s England falls in love with a gypsy. Based on the novel by D.H. Lawrence. Directorial debut of Miles. **92m/C; VHS, DVD.** *GB* Joanna Shimkus; Franco Nero; Honor Blackman; Mark Burns; ***D:*** Christopher Miles; ***W:*** Alan Plater.

Virgin High **1990 (R)** Three young men sneak into an all-girls Catholic boarding school with hilarious consequences. Ward (TV's Robin, from "Batman") makes a special appearance in bondage in this sex farce. **90m/C; VHS, Streaming.** Burt Ward; Linnea Quigley; Tracy Dali; Richard Gabai; Catherine McGuiness; Chris Dempsey; ***D:*** Richard Gabai; ***W:*** Richard Gabai; Jeff Neal.

Virgin Machine *Jungfrauenmaschine* **1988** Lesbian journalist Dorothy Muller (Blum) is unhappy in her native Hamburg and decides to move to California to pursue her idea of romantic love. English and German with English subtitles. **91m/B; VHS, DVD.** *GE* Ina Blum; Susie Bright; Shelley Mars; Dominique Gaspar; ***D:*** Monika Treut; ***W:*** Monika Treut; ***C:*** Elfi Mikesch.

The Virgin of Nuremberg ½ *Horror Castle; Terror Castle; Castle of Terror; La Vergine de Norimberga* **1965** A young woman enters her new husband's ancestral castle and is stalked by the specter of a legendary sadist. **82m/C; VHS, DVD.** *IT* Rossana Podesta; George Riviere; Christopher Lee; Jim Dolen; ***D:*** Anthony M. Dawson.

The Virgin Queen **1955** Davis stars in this historical drama, which focuses on the stormy relationship between the aging Queen and Sir Walter Raleigh. Collins is the lady-in-waiting who is the secret object of Raleigh's true affections. Previously, Davis played Queen Elizabeth I in "Elizabeth and Essex." Davis holds things together. **92m/C; VHS, DVD.** Bette Davis; Richard Todd; Joan Collins; Herbert Marshall; Dan O'Herlihy; Jay Robinson; Romney Brent; ***D:*** Henry Koster.

Virgin Queen of St. Francis High **1988 (PG)** Two high school foes make a bet that one of them can take the "virgin" title away from gorgeous Christensen by summer's end. She has to fight off their advances, but grows to like Straface. **89m/C; VHS, Streaming.** *CA* Joseph R. Straface; Stacy Christensen; J.T. Wotton; ***D:*** Francesco Lucente.

Virgin Sacrifice **1959** A great white hunter looking for zoo-bound jaguars confronts the virgin-sacrificing, Tiger God-revering natives of Guatemala. **67m/C; VHS, DVD.** David DaLie; Antonio Gutierrez; Angelica Morales; Fernando Wagner; ***D:*** Fernando Wagner.

The Virgin Soldiers ½ **1969 (R)** A British comedy about greenhorn military recruits stationed in Singapore, innocent of women as well as battle, and their struggles to overcome both situations. A good cast raises this above the usual low-brow sex farce. Based on the novel by Leslie Thomas. Followed by "Stand Up Virgin Soldiers." **96m/C; VHS, DVD, Blu-Ray.** *GB* Hywel Bennett; Nigel Davenport; Lynn Redgrave; Nigel Patrick; Rachel Kempson; Jack Shepherd; Tsai Chin; ***D:*** John Dexter; ***W:*** John Hopkins.

The Virgin Spring ½ *Jungfrukallan* **1959** Based on a medieval ballad and set in 14th-century Sweden. The rape and murder of young innocent Karin (Pattersson) spurs her father Tore (Van Sydow) to vengeance and he kills her attackers. Over the girl's dead body, the father questions how God could have let any of it happen, but he comes to find solace and forgiveness when a spring bursts forth from the spot. Stunning Bergman compositions. In Swedish with English subtitles; also available in dubbed version. **88m/B; VHS, DVD, Blu-Ray.** *SW* Max von Sydow; Birgitta Valberg; Gunnel Lindblom; Brigitta Pattersson; Axel Duborg; ***D:*** Ingmar Bergman; ***W:*** Ulla Isaakson; ***C:*** Sven Nykvist; ***M:*** Erik Nordgren. Oscars '60: Foreign Film; Golden Globes '61: Foreign Film.

The Virgin Suicides **1999 (R)** The five teenaged Lisbon sisters are all blonde, lovely, and isolated in their 70s suburban life. Mom (Turner) is a rigid, religious harridan while Dad (Woods) is a wimpy math teacher. After 13-year-old Cecilia (Hall) tries to off herself, her parents are encouraged to let the girls socialize and the story becomes the recollections of the narrator (Ribisi), one of the boys fascinated by the quintet. Much of the movie focuses on sexually provocative Lux (Dunst) and her hunky would-be beau, Trip (Hartnett). There's a floaty, listlessly romantic air to the whole production (Coppola's directorial debut), which is based on the novel by Jeffrey Eugenides. **97m/C; VHS, DVD, Blu-Ray.** Kirsten Dunst; Kathleen Turner; James Woods; Josh Hartnett; Hanna Hall; Chelse Swain; A.J. Cook; Leslie Hayman; Danny DeVito; Scott Glenn; Jonathan Tucker; Anthony DeSimone; ***Nar:*** Giovanni Ribisi; ***D:*** Sofia Coppola; ***W:*** Sofia Coppola; ***C:*** Edward Lachman.

Virgin Territory ½ **2007 (R)** If you're expecting a version of "Casanova," this isn't it. Instead, it's a dull rather than swaggering would-be romp with a couple of weak leads. In 14th-century Florence, penniless rogue Lorenzo (Christensen) is known for deflowering the local lovelies. His next likely conquest is Pampinea (Barton), who's also being pursued by a Russian count (Rhys) and an obsessed Italian nobleman (Roth), but of course the two youngsters actually love each other. **97m/C; DVD.** Hayden Christensen; Mischa Barton; Matthew Rhys; Tim Roth; Christopher Ega; ***D:*** David Leland; ***W:*** David Leland; ***C:*** Benjamin Davis; ***M:*** Ilan Eshkeri.

The Virgin Witch ½ *Lesbian Twins* **1970 (R)** Two beautiful sisters are sent to the British countryside, ostensibly for a modeling job. They soon find themselves in the midst of a witches' coven however, and discover one of them is to be sacrificed. The Michelles were "Playboy" magazine's first sister centerfolds. **89m/C; VHS, DVD.** *GB* Anne Michelle; Vicki Michelle; Patricia Haines; Keith Buckley; James Chase; Neil Hallett; ***D:*** Ray Austin.

Virginia *What's Wrong With Virginia* **2010 (R)** Off-balance Southern comedy-drama. Virginia (Connelly) is an unstable single mom living with her illegitimate son Emmett (Gilbertson) in a Virginia beach town. Emmett falls in love with Jessie (Roberts), the daughter of local sheriff Richard Tipton (Harris). This is trouble in so many ways, including the fact that the married Morman with some sexual kinks is his mom's longtime lover. **110m/C; DVD.** Jennifer Connelly; Ed Harris; Harrison Gilbertson; Emma Roberts; Amy Madigan; Toby Jones; ***D:*** Dustin Lance Black; ***W:*** Dustin Lance Black; ***C:*** Eric Alan Edwards; ***M:*** Nick Urata.

Virginia City **1940** Action-packed western drama set during the Civil War. Flynn is a Union soldier who escapes from a Confederate prison run by Scott, after learning of a gold shipment being sent by Southern sympathizers to aid the Confederacy. He ends up in Virginia City (where the gold-laden wagon train is to leave from) and falls for a dance-hall girl (Hopkins) who turns out to be a Southern spy working for Scott but who falls for Flynn anyway. Bogart is miscast as a half-breed outlaw who aids Scott but wants the gold for himself. Considered a follow-up to "Dodge City." **121m/C; VHS, DVD.** Errol Flynn; Miriam Hopkins; Randolph Scott; Humphrey Bogart; Frank McHugh; Alan Hale; Guinn "Big Boy" Williams; Douglass Dumbrille; Charles Halton; ***D:*** Michael Curtiz; ***M:*** Max Steiner.

The Virginia Hill Story **1976** Fictionalized biography of mobster Bugsy Siegel's girlfriend who, in the mid-'50s, was subpoenaed to appear before the Kefauver investigation on crime in the U.S. As the examining lawyer presents questions regarding her background and connections with the underworld, we see the story of her life. **90m/C; VHS, DVD.** Dyan Cannon; Harvey Keitel; Robby Benson; Allen Garfield; John Vernon; ***D:*** Joel Schumacher. **TV**

The Virginian ½ **1946** Cowboy good guy, known as the Virginian (McCrea), and his best pal Steve (Tufts) both fall for Molly (Britton), the Eastern-bred schoolmarm who's come to their Wyoming town. Steve wants to make some quick money and joins up with leader Trampas' (Donlevy) cattle rustling gang. So the Virginian is forced to chose between friendship and the code of the west and Molly wonders if she can accepts the country's harsh ways. Based on Owen Wister's 1902 novel. **87m/C; DVD.** Joel McCrea; Sonny Tufts; Barbara Britton; Brian Donlevy; Fay Bainter; Tom Tully; Henry O'Neill; William Frawley; ***D:*** Stuart Gilmore; ***W:*** Frances Goodrich; Albert Hackett; ***C:*** Harry Hallenberger; ***M:*** Daniele Amfitheatrof.

The Virginian ½ **1999** Yet another remake (this one unremarkable but watchable) of Owen Wister's 1902 novel. Pullman (who also directed) is the cowboy of the title, who is out for a brutal brand of justice against an unscupulous rancher. But his methods upset his schoolmarm sweetie (Lane). **95m/C; DVD.** Bill Pullman; Diane Lane; John Savage; Dennis Weaver; Harris Yulin; Colm Feore; Gary Farmer; James Drury; ***D:*** Bill Pullman; ***W:*** Larry Gross; ***C:*** Peter Wunstorf; ***M:*** Nathan Barr. **CABLE**

The Virginity Hit **WOOF! 2010 (R)** Dumb, crude, and predictable teen sex comedy shot on handheld digital cameras and edited to represent a series of YouTube clips. Four insufferable New Orleans teenage boys decide to commemorate their first time but only nerdy Matt can't succeed with his dream girl Nicole. Alleged hijinks and much humiliation follow—all captured on camera. **90m/C; DVD.** Matt Bennett; Zack Pearlman; Jacob Davich; Justin Kline; Nicole Weaver; ***D:*** Andrew Gurland; Huck Botko; ***W:*** Andrew Gurland; Huck Botko; ***C:*** Luke Geissbuhler.

Viridiana **1961** Innocent Viridiana (Pinal), with strong ideas about goodness, visits her worldly uncle, Don Jaime's (Rey), home before she takes her vows as a nun. He has developed a sick obsession for her, but after drugging Viridiana, Don Jaimefinds he cannot violate her purity. He tells her, however, she is no longer chaste so she will not join the church. After her uncle's suicide, Viridiana learns she and his illegitimate son Jorge (Rabal) have inherited her uncle's rundown estate. Viridiana opens the house to all sorts of beggars, who take shameless advantage, while Jorge works slowly to restore the estate and improve the lives of those around him. Considered to be one of Bunuel's masterpieces and a bitter allegory of Spanish idealism versus pragmatism and the state of the world. Spanish with subtitles. **90m/B; VHS, DVD.** *SP MX* Silvia Pinal; Francisco Rabal; Fernando Rey; Margarita Lozano; Victoria Zinny; ***D:*** Luis Bunuel; ***W:*** Luis Bunuel; Julio Alajandro; ***C:*** Jose F. Aguayo. Cannes '61: Film.

Virtual Assassin *Cyberjack* **1995 (R)** 21st century sci-fi actioner finds the crooked Zef (James) leading his band of thugs into a research lab to steal a powerful computer virus. Naturally, the janitor (Dudikoff) just happens to be an ex-cop with a score to settle with Zef. Predictable but with decent special effects. **99m/C; VHS, DVD.** *CA JP* Michael Dudikoff; Brion James; Jon Cuthbert; Suki Kaiser; James Thom; ***D:*** Robert Lee; ***W:*** Eric Poppen.

Virtual Combat **1995 (R)** Ex-cop Quarry (Wilson) teams up with some cybergirls to stop a madman who's able to manipulate virtual reality programs into living beings and releases a killer who wants to lead a destructive virtual army. **97m/C; VHS, DVD.** Don "The Dragon" Wilson; Athena Massey; Loren Avedon; Kenneth McLeod; Turhan Bey; Stella Stevens; Michael Bernardo; ***D:*** Andrew Stevens; ***W:*** William C. Martell; ***C:*** David J. Miller; ***M:*** Claude Gaudette.

Virtual Desire ½ **1995 (R)** Brad Collins is bored with his marriage and finds some excitement via sexual games on the Internet. But someone is taking a very close interest in Brad's virtual amours and when his wife is murdered, Brad becomes the prime suspect. **92m/C; VHS, DVD.** Michael Meyer; Julie Strain; Gail Harris; ***D:*** Noble Henri; ***W:*** Pete Slate; ***C:*** Gary Graver; ***M:*** Leo Nichols.

Virtual Encounters ½ **1996 (R)** Top-drawer soft-core fluff follows busy executive Amy (Elizabeth Kaitan), whose birthday present is a session of virtual wish fulfillment at a high-tech fantasyland. The fantasies involve masks, leather, desks, broccoli. . .well, O.K., the broccoli is an exaggeration. This is sexy and kinky, not sick. The action is slickly staged and well photographed by director Richards. Also available in an unrated version at 84 minutes. **80m/C; VHS, DVD.** Elizabeth Kaitan; Taylore St. Claire; Rob Lee; ***D:*** Cybil (Sybil) Richards; ***C:*** Cybil (Sybil) Richards.

Virtual Girl **2000 (R)** Computer programmer John Lewis (Dixon) is working on an erotic virutal reality program that features a cyber-slut (Curtis). When said vixen gets rejected by her creator, she gets very, very angry. Erotica that makes the best use of its low-budget and Curtis' assets. **84m/C; VHS, DVD.** Richard Gabai; Charlie Curtis; Max Dixon; ***D:*** Richard Gabai. **VIDEO**

Virtual Obsession ½ *Host* **1998** ABC TV movie. Terminally ill Juliet Spring becomes obsessed with her boss Dr. Joe Messenger, who's designed a super-computer that's currently running Salt Lake City. But Joe knows 'Albert" can do more and Juliet shows him he's right when she uploads her consciousness to Albert and then has her body cryogenically frozen. However Juliet's obsession with Joe only grows and she wants him to join in her virtual reality. **133m/C; DVD.** Peter Gallagher; Bridgette Wilson-Sampras; Mimi Rogers; Jake Lloyd; Andy Comeau; Robert Vaughn; ***D:*** Mick Garris; ***W:*** Mick Garris; Preston Sturges, Jr.; ***C:*** Shelly Johnson; ***M:*** Nicholas Pike. **TV**

Virtual Sexuality **1999 (R)** Teen comedy, set in London, that has an amusing virtual reality plot. Cute 17-year-old Justine (Fraser) decides school stud Alex (O'Brien) is the perfect guy to lose her virginity to. But he's only interested in school vamp, "Hoover" (Bell). So Justine enters a virtual reality makeover machine at a technology fair in order to create an electronic facsimile of her perfect man. But a malfunction causes Justine to split in two'herself (with amnesia) and her perfect man, the bewildered male creation Jake (Penry-Jones). Based on the novel by Chloe Rayban. **92m/C; VHS, DVD.** *GB* Laura Fraser; Rupert Penry-Jones; Kieran O'Brien; Luke De Lacey; Natasha Bell; Steve John Shepherd; Laura Macaulay; Marcelle Duprey; ***D:*** Nick Hurran; ***W:*** Nick Fisher; ***C:*** Brian Tufano; ***M:*** Rupert Gregson-Williams.

Virtuality **2009** This failed TV pilot movie is a stylish bit of sci fi set aboard the starship Phaeton, which has begun a 10-year journey to explore a distant planetary system. The crew is filming a reality TV series to explain things to the folks back home and their only chance for privacy is a series of virtual reality modules. Tensions rise and naturally things begin to go wrong. **88m/C; DVD.** Nikolaj Coster-Waldau; Sienna Guillory; James D'Arcy; Clea DuVall; Ritchie Coster; Erik Jensen; Omar Metwally; Kerry Bishe; Joy Bryant; Nelson Lee; Jose Pablo Cantillo; Gene Farber; ***D:*** Peter Berg; ***W:*** Ronald D. Moore; Michael Taylor; ***C:*** Stephen McNutt; ***M:*** Lisa Coleman; Wendy Melvoin. **TV**

Virtue **1932** Low-budget programmer from Columbia Pictures. New York hooker Mae (Lombard) stiffs genial cab driver Jimmy (O'Brien) of his fare but wants to make good when she wants to reform. They marry after a whirlwind romance but Mae falls for a scam involving Gert (Grey), another ex-hooker who gets murdered. Mae gets blamed and Jimmy turns to the bottle until his friend Frank (Bond) convinces him to stick with his innocent wife. **87m/B; DVD.** Carole Lombard; Pat O'Brien; Mayo Methot; Ward Bond; Jack LaRue; Shirley Grey; Willard Robertson; ***D:*** Edward Buzzell; ***W:*** Robert Riskin; ***C:*** Joseph Walker.

Virtuosity ½ **1995 (R)** Ex-cop-with-a-tragic-past Parker Barnes (Washington) is sprung from prison to help capture computer-generated killer Sid 6.7 (Crowe), who escapes from cyberspace and goes on a rampage in 1997 Los Angeles. Seems this virtual reality bad guy has a personality composed of some 200 serial killers and criminal minds so Parker's got his work cut out for him. But criminal-behavior psychologist Madison Carter (Lynch) is around to lend her expert advice. Both the charismatically evil Crowe and the sufferingly noble Washington are wasted in this effects-laden thriller that sacrifices character for flash. **105m/C; VHS, DVD, Blu-Ray.** Denzel Washington; Russell Crowe; Kelly Lynch; Stephen Spinella; William Forsythe; Louise Fletcher; William Fichtner; Costas Mandylor; Kevin J. O'Connor; ***D:*** Brett Leonard; **W:** Eric Bernt; **C:** Gale Tattersall; **M:** Christopher Young.

Virunga 🦴🦴🦴 **2014** An enraging documentary calling out a large corporation that's threatening to steamroll the Congo's landscape in search for oil. What begins as an expose piece eventually picks up the momentum of an action thriller. Director Orlando von Einsiedel allows the viewer to slowly side with him, never pushing his politics too early. He simply allows four central figures to speak for him, from a mountain gorilla caretaker to park wardens, finally settling on French journalist Melanie Gouby to push the message home. **90m/C; Streaming.** *UK* **D:** Orlando Von Einsiedel; **W:** Orlando Von Einsiedel; **C:** Orlando Von Einsiedel; Franklin Dow; **M:** Patrick Jonsson.

Virus 🦴🦴 *Fukkatsu no Hi* **1982 (PG)** After nuclear war and plague destroy civilization, a small group of people gather in Antarctica and struggle with determination to carry on life. A look at man's genius for self-destruction and his endless hope. **102m/C; VHS, DVD.** *JP* George Kennedy; Sonny Chiba; Glenn Ford; Robert Vaughn; Stuart Gillard; Stephanie Faulkner; Ken Ogata; Bo Svenson; Olivia Hussey; Chuck Connors; Edward James Olmos; **D:** Kinji Fukasaku.

Virus 🦴 ½ **1996 (PG-13)** Secret Service agent Ken Fairchild (Bosworth) finds out that biological-warfare chemicals have been spilt in a national park that's the site for an ecological summit between the president and world leaders. It's up to Fairchild and a park ranger (Pinsent) to battle the minions of the chemical's manufacturer who wants to keep the whole thing quiet. **90m/C; VHS, DVD.** Brian Bosworth; Leah K. Pinsent; **D:** Allan Goldstein.

Virus 🦴 ½ **1998 (R)** Curtis, Sutherland, and Baldwin are members of a tugboat crew whose boat has been wrecked by a typhoon. They take refuge aboard a Russian research ship only to discover the Russian crew has been eliminated by a strange life form. The electricity-based alien considers humanity a virus and begins making bizarre killing machines out of body parts and machinery. The plot also seems pieced together from other sci-fi horror movies that did it better. **100m/C; VHS, DVD, Blu-Ray.** Jamie Lee Curtis; William Baldwin; Donald Sutherland; Joanna Pacula; Sherman Augustus; Clifford Curtis; Marshall Bell; Julio Oscar Mechoso; Yuri Chervotkin; Keith Flippen; **D:** John Bruno; **W:** Chuck Pfarrer; Dennis Feldman; **C:** David Eggby; **M:** Joel McNeely.

Virus X 🦴 *H1N1: Virus X* **2010 (R)** Doctors in a secret lab believe they are helping the world by creating a mutant flu strain, when in actuality they're helping a rich old woman who hopes to get richer selling the vaccine for the new virus. Predictably the disease gets loose and she sends her pet robot to smite them before the infected doctors get free. **85m/C; DVD, Streaming.** Jai Day; Domiziano Arcangeli; Joe Zaso; Dylan Vox; Sybil Danning; **D:** Ryan Stevens Harris; **W:** Ryan Stevens Harris; Jeremiah Campbell; **C:** Ryan Stevens Harris; **M:** Shawn K. Clement. **VIDEO**

Vision 🦴🦴 **2009** German biopic covers the long life of 12th-century Benedictine nun Hildegard von Bingen, a mystic who claims to receive visions directly from God. The nuns share the Disibodenberg cloister and Hildegard's behavior frequently usurps and angers the brothers' authority. Eventually forced to plead her case before the pope, Hildegard is also allowed to establish her own cloister away from male influence. German with subtitles. **110m/C; DVD.** *GE* Barbara Sukowa; Hannah Herzprung; Lena Stolze; Heino Ferch; Alexander Held; Sunnyi Melles; David Striesow; **D:** Margarethe von Trotta; **W:** Margarethe von Trotta; **C:** Axel Block; **M:** Chris Heynne.

Vision Quest 🦴🦴 ½ *Crazy for You* **1985 (R)** A high school student wants to win the Washington State wrestling championship and the affections of a beautiful older artist. He gives it his all as he trains for the meet and goes after his "visionquest." A winning performance by Modine raises this above the usual teen coming-of-age movie. Madonna sings "Crazy for You" in a nightclub. Based on novel by Terry Davis. **107m/C; VHS, DVD, Blu-Ray.** Matthew Modine; Linda Fiorentino; Ronny Cox; Roberts Blossom; Daphne Zuniga; Charles Hallahan; Michael Schoeffling; Forest Whitaker; Gary Kasper; James Gammon; Harold Sylvester; Raphael Sbarge; **D:** Harold Becker; **W:** Darryl Ponicsan; **C:** Owen Roizman; **M:** Tangerine Dream.

Visions 🦴🦴 **2016 (R)** A haunted vineyard drives a pregnant woman to the brink of insanity. When Eveleigh (Fisher) moves with her husband David (Mount) to their new vineyard home, she is looking forward to less hectic lifestyle and the birth of her first child. As soon as she moves there, however, she keeps seeing visions of a hooded figure and hears horrible noises. Because no one by Eveleigh sees or hears them, her well-being is brought into question. To prove her sanity, Eveleigh consults a local medium who tells her the bloody history of the vineyard. As the dark conspiracy emerges, Eveleigh must act to save herself and that of her unborn child. **82m/C; DVD, Streaming, Download.** Isla Fisher; Anson Mount; Gillian Jacobs; Joanna Cassidy; Eva Longoria; **D:** Kevin Greutert; **W:** L.D. Goffigan; Lucas Sussman; **C:** Michael Fimognari; **M:** Anton Sanko. **VIDEO**

Visions of Evil 🦴 *So Sad About Gloria* **1975** A young woman, recently released from a mental institution, is plagued by a series of terrifying visions when she moves into a house where a brutal axe murder took place. **85m/C; VHS, DVD, Blu-Ray.** Lori Sanders; Dean Jagger; Robert Ginnaven; Lou Hoffman; Seymour Trietman; Linda Wyse; **D:** Harry Z. Thomason; **W:** Marshall Riggan; **C:** James Roberson; **M:** Jerald Reed.

Visions of Light: The Art of Cinematography 🦴🦴🦴 **1993** Excellent documentary on the way films look and how the art of photographing movies can contribute as much, if not more, than cast, director, and script. Scenes from 125 films, from "Birth of a Nation" to "GoodFellas" are shown, with commentary from a number of cinematographers, including Gordon Willis, William A. Fraker, Conrad Hall, Ernest Dickerson, Vilmos Zsigmond, and Michael Chapman, on how they achieved certain effects and their collaborations with the director of the film. **95m/C; VHS, DVD.** **D:** Arnold Glassman; Stuart Samuels; Todd McCarthy; **W:** Todd McCarthy; **C:** Nancy Schreiber. N.Y. Film Critics '93: Feature Doc.; Natl. Soc. Film Critics '93: Feature Doc.

Visions of Murder 🦴🦴 **1993** Psychologist Jesse Newman (Eden) is told by patient Gloria Hager (Finlay) that her husband is abusive. Jesse starts having visions that Gloria's husband Truman (O'Quinn) murders her and dumps the body in the San Francisco Bay. The cops don't believe Jesse until the body is found and then she becomes a suspect, especially after they find out that Jesse had a previous mental breakdown. **90m/C; DVD.** Barbara Eden; Anita Finlay; Terry O'Quinn; Erika Flores; James Brolin; Joan Pringle; Scott Bryce; **D:** Michael Ray Rhodes; **W:** Julie Moskowitz; Gary Stephens; **C:** Steve (Steven) Shaw; **M:** Michael Hoenig. **TV**

Visions of Sugarplums 🦴 **1999** Amateurish and filled with stereotypes that makes for more bah-humbug than a jolly holiday. Happy gay New Yorkers Joey and Bruce are thrown into a panic by the sudden visit of Joey's conservative parents, who don't know about their son's alternative lifestyle. Bruce is temporarily kicked out of the apartment but the truth comes out anyway. **78m/C; DVD.** Edward Fasulo; Mark Hardin; Mary Jean Feton; Vincent Wares; **D:** Edward Fasulo; **W:** Anthony Bruce; **C:** Chun Lee; **M:** Marty Dunayer. **VIDEO**

The Visit 🦴🦴 **1964** Teenage orphan Karla is seduced by Serge, but when she gets pregnant, he rejects her and small-minded townsfolk drive her out. Years later, Karla (Bergman) returns to the poor community an extremely wealthy widow and makes the residents a devil's bargain to get her revenge on her former lover (Quinn). Bergman gives a powerful performance as the cold, calculating lead. The movie ending is different from that of Friedrich Durrenmatti's play. **100m/B; DVD.** *GE IT FR* Ingrid Bergman; Anthony Quinn; Valentina Cortese; Irina Demick; Hans-Christian Blech; **D:** Bernhard Wicki; **W:** Ben Barzman; **C:** Armando Nannuzzi; **M:** Richard Arnell.

The Visit 🦴🦴🦴 **2000 (R)** Harper leads an excellent cast in this story of Alex, a man imprisoned for a rape he may not have committed who only seeks the acceptance and love of his family. Through visits with his estranged, successful brother (Obatunde), his loving mother (Gibbs), and his disapproving father (Williams), as well as a prison psychiatrist (Rashad) and a childhood friend (Chong), Alex finds the peace he seeks. Yes, it sounds hokey, but the excellent performances and steady, subtle direction make it all work. The parole board scene is a highlight. **107m/C; VHS, DVD.** Hill Harper; Obba Babatunde; Billy Dee Williams; Marla Gibbs; Rae Dawn Chong; Phylicia Rashad; Talia Shire; David Clennon; Glynn Turman; Efrain Figueroa; Amy Stiller; **D:** Jordan Walker-Pearlman; **W:** Jordan Walker-Pearlman; **C:** John L. (Ndiaga) Demps, Jr.; **M:** Michael Bearden.

The Visit 🦴🦴 **2015 (PG-13)** Shyamalan returns to the world of horror after a few total disasters, and the result is a step-up from the total garbage he's been making, but still pretty flawed. Young filmmaking student Becca (DeJonge) and her brother Tyler (Oxenbould) head out to visit the grandparents (Dunagan, McRobbie) that they've never met after an estrangement from Mom (Hahn). From the beginning, Nana & Pop Pop are acting funny, and things get stranger from there. Shyamalan's film, as it typically is, is built on a twist most people will see coming. It's funny, but forgettable. **94m/C; DVD, Blu-Ray.** Olivia DeJonge; Ed Oxenbould; Kathryn Hahn; Deanna Dunagan; Peter McRobbie; **D:** M. Night Shyamalan; **W:** M. Night Shyamalan; **C:** Maryse Alberti.

Visiting Hours 🦴 *The Fright; Get Well Soon* **1982 (R)** Psycho-killer slashes his female victims and photographs his handiwork. Grant is one of his victims who doesn't die, so the killer decides to visit the hospital and finish the job. Fairly graphic and generally unpleasant. **101m/C; VHS, DVD, Blu-Ray.** *CA* Lee Grant; William Shatner; Linda Purl; Michael Ironside; **D:** Jean-Claude Lord; **W:** Brian Taggert; **M:** Jonathan Goldsmith.

The Visitor 🦴 ½ **1980 (R)** Affluent handsome doctor and mate conspire with grisly devil worshippers to conceive devil child. **90m/C; VHS, DVD, Blu-Ray.** Mel Ferrer; Glenn Ford; Lance Henriksen; John Huston; Shelley Winters; Joanne Nail; Sam Peckinpah; **D:** Giullo Paradisi.

The Visitor 🦴🦴🦴 ½ **2007 (PG-13)** Ubiquitous character actor Jenkins runs away with his lead role in McCarthy's humanistic drama. Widowed professor Walter Vale reeks of being stuck in his lonely, boring rut of a life. On a rare visit to New York, Walter finds immigrants Tarek (Sleiman) and his girlfriend Zainab (Gurira) living in his infrequently-used city apartment, the victims of a renter's scam. Walter allows them to stay until something can be figured out and is befriended by the gregarious Tarek, a musician. Unfortunately, Tarek runs into a bureaucratic nightmare (he's outstayed his visa) when he's arrested and incarcerated in a detention center. This brings Tarek's mother Mouna (Abbass) into the picture, which furthers Walter's re-emergence as a participant rather than a mere observer of life. **108m/C; DVD, Blu-Ray.** Richard Jenkins; Hiam Abbass; Haaz Sleiman; Danai Gurira; **D:** Thomas (Tom) McCarthy; **W:** Thomas (Tom) McCarthy; **C:** Oliver Bokelberg; **M:** Jan A.P. Kaczmarek. Ind. Spirit '09: Director (McCarthy).

Visitor Q 🦴🦴 *Bijita Q* **2001 (R)** Director Takashi Miike is known for surreal, disturbing films, and this is him at his most over the top. In a very unusual family, the father is a reality television host/reporter shunned by his fellow workers (in a documentary on young women becoming prostitutes he tries to convince his own daughter to sleep with him). The mother is a heroin addict so far gone she can barely communicate. Her son, bullied brutally at school, has taken to torturing her for relief. To say they have 'issues' is seriously downplaying it. Then one day a young man hits the father over the head with a rock, moves in, and begins terrorizing the family in one of the most hallucinatory films ever made. **90m/C; DVD.** *JP* Kenichi Endo; Shaun Hood; Joel Hookey; Virginia Carraway; Charlie Fitzgerald; Iain Kelso; Mia Blake; **D:** Takashi Miike; **W:** David Fane; **C:** Hideo Yamamoto; **M:** Koji Endo.

The Visitors 🦴🦴 *Les Visiteurs* **1995 (R)** Time travel comedy features 12th-century knight Godefroy (Reno) and his vassal Jacquasse (Clavier) crossing paths with a powerful witch (and evidently pissing her off) since she casts a spell causing Godefroy to accidentally kill his father-in-law. So Godefroy contacts a wizard to give him a time travel potion so he can go back and stop the shooting. Too bad the potion hurls knight and vassal forward into present-day France. French with subtitles. **106m/C; VHS, DVD.** *FR* Jean Reno; Christian Clavier; Mariann (Marie-Anne) Chazel; Valerie Lemercier; Christian Bujeau; **D:** Jean-Marie Poire; **W:** Christian Clavier; Jean-Marie Poire; **C:** Jean-Yves Le Mener; **M:** Eric Levi.

Visitors 🦴 ½ **2003 (R)** Supernatural thriller that turns a bit silly. After six months on a solo sailing trip aournd the world, Georgia's (Mitchell) sloop is becalmed for several days. Not very stable to begin with (she has the requisite dark past), Georgia begins to hallucinate, only these ghostly encounters leave behind physical reminders of their presence. **88m/C; VHS, DVD.** *AU* Radha Mitchell; Susannah York; Ray Barrett; Tottie Goldsmith; **D:** Richard Franklin; **W:** Everett De Roche; **C:** Ellery Ryan; **M:** Nerida Tyson-Chew.

Visitors 🦴🦴 ½ **2013** A black-and-white experiment in cinematic poetry from U.S. director Reggio, pasting together 74 shots that each last roughly one minute. Ancient trees with leathered bark, a contemplative gorilla, and humans gazing into the camera's lens like they're confused aliens, all playing out overtop a rhythmic score from legendary composer Philip Glass. And as beautiful as the imagery may be, the overall effect is likely more compelling in a museum rather than a living room. **87m/B; DVD, Blu-Ray.** **D:** Godfrey Reggio; **W:** Godfrey Reggio; **C:** Graham Berry; Trish Govoni; Tom Lowe; **M:** Philip Glass.

Vita & Virginia 🦴🦴 **2019** Already well-known writer Virginia Woolf (Debicki) is experiencing mental illness and intense emotions as her novel Mrs. Dalloway is published. In this tumultuous period, she meets socialite/writer Vita Sackville-West (Arterton). As Virginia becomes infatuated with vibrant Vita, her career begins to take off. Though their relationship brings Virginia a muse, Vita must deal with a disapproving mother (Rossellini). The biographical romance flounders as it tries to be too many different kinds of movies. And the spark between Vita and Virginia is talked about rather than shown, making it seem like the talented actresses that play them lack chemistry. **110m/C; DVD.** Gemma Arterton; Elizabeth Debicki; Isabella Rossellini; Rupert Penry-Jones; Peter Ferdinando; **D:** Chanya Button; **W:** Chanya Button; Eileen Atkins; **C:** Carlos De Carvalho; **M:** Isobel Waller-Bridge.

Vital Signs 🦴 **1990 (R)** Hackneyed drama about six medical students enduring the tribulations of their profession. **102m/C; VHS, DVD, Blu-Ray.** Adrian Pasdar; Diane Lane; Jack Gwaltney; Laura San Giacomo; Jane Adams; Tim Ransom; Bradley Whitford; Lisa Jane Persky; William Devane; Norma Aleandro; Jimmy Smits; James Karen; Telma Hopkins; **D:** Marisa Silver; **W:** Jeb Stuart; **M:** Miles Goodman.

Viva Knievel **WOOF!** *Seconds to Live* **1977 (PG)** Crooks plan to sabotage Knievel's daredevil jump in Mexico and then smuggle cocaine back into the States in his coffin. Unintentionally campy. **106m/C; VHS, DVD.** Evel Knievel; Gene Kelly; Lauren Hutton; Red Buttons; Leslie Nielsen; Cameron Mitchell; Marjoe Gortner; Albert Salmi; Dabney Coleman; ***Cameo(s):*** Frank Gifford; **D:** Gordon Douglas; **C:** Fred H. Jackman, Jr.; **M:** Charles Bernstein.

Viva Las Vegas 🦴🦴 ½ *Love in Las Vegas* **1963** Race car driver Elvis needs money to compete against rival Danova in the upcoming Las Vegas Grand Prix. He takes a job in a casino and romances fellow employee Ann-Margret, who turns out to be his rival for the grand prize in the local talent competition. Good pairing between the two leads, and the King does particularly well with the title song. **85m/C; VHS, DVD, Blu-Ray, HD-DVD.** Elvis Presley; Ann-Margret; William Demarest; Jack Carter; Cesare Danova; Nicky Blair; Larry Kent; **D:** George Sidney; **C:** Joseph Biroc.

Viva Maria! 🦴🦴 ½ **1965 (R)** Tongue-in-cheek comedy with Bardot and Moreau as two dancers (both named Maria) in a show traveling through Mexico. The two become incensed by the poverty of the peasants and decide to turn revolutionary (especially after Moreau has an affair with revolutionary leader Hamilton, who promptly gets killed). The two French sex symbols are a fine match. **119m/C; DVD, Blu-Ray.** *FR IT* Jeanne Moreau; Brigitte Bardot; George Hamilton; Paulette Dubost; Claudio Brook; ***D:*** Louis Malle; ***W:*** Louis Malle; Jean-Claude Carriere; ***C:*** Henri Decae; ***M:*** Georges Delerue.

Viva Max 1/2 **1969** A blundering modern-day Mexican general and his men recapture the Alamo, and an equally inept American force, headed by Winters, is sent to rout them out. Mostly works, with some very funny scenes. Ustinov is great. **93m/C; VHS, DVD.** Peter Ustinov; Jonathan Winters; John Astin; Pamela Tiffin; Keenan Wynn; ***D:*** Jerry Paris.

Viva Zapata! **1952** Chronicles the life of Mexican revolutionary Emiliano Zapata. Brando is powerful as he leads the peasant revolt in the early 1900s, only to be corrupted by power and greed. Quinn well deserved his Best Supporting Actor Oscar for his performance as Zapata's brother. Based on the novel "Zapata the Unconquered" by Edgcumb Pinchon. **112m/B; VHS, DVD, Blu-Ray.** Marlon Brando; Anthony Quinn; Jean Peters; Margo; Arnold Moss; Joseph Wiseman; Mildred Dunnock; ***D:*** Elia Kazan; ***W:*** John Steinbeck; ***M:*** Alex North. Oscars '52: Support. Actor (Quinn); British Acad. '52: Actor (Brando); Cannes '52: Actor (Brando).

Vivacious Lady **1938** Appealing romantic comedy about a mild-mannered college professor who marries a chorus girl. Problems arise when he must let his conservative family and his former fiance in on the marriage news. Good performances. **90m/B; DVD.** Ginger Rogers; James Stewart; James Ellison; Beulah Bondi; Charles Coburn; Jack Carson; Franklin Pangborn; Dorothy Moore; ***D:*** George Stevens.

Vlad 1/2 **2003** Four grad students travel to Romania to study the vile legend of Vlad Drakul (aka Dracula) per a Bucharest professor's request. While inside his tomb (what could possibly go wrong?) they end up taking a harrowing trip back in time thanks to a mysterious necklace. **98m/C; VHS, DVD.** Billy Zane; Brad Dourif; Francesco Quinn; John Rhys-Davies; Claudiu Bleont; Paul Popowich; Kam Heskin; Nicholas Irons; Monica Davidescu; Iva Hasperger; Emil Hostina; Guy Siner; Mircea Stoian; Andreea Macelaru; Alin Panc; Alexandera Velniciuc; Zoltan Butuc; Anca-Ioana Androne; Adrian Pintea; Ian Ionescu; Catalin Rotaru; Cristian Popa; ***D:*** Michael D. Sellers; ***W:*** Michael D. Sellers; Tony Shawkat; ***C:*** Viorel Sergovici, Jr.; ***M:*** Christopher Field. **VIDEO**

Voice from the Stone 1/2 **2017 (R)** A dramatic thriller set in Tuscany, based on Silvio Raffo's book. A skilled nurse specializing in children, Verena (Clarke) is hired for young Jakob (Dring). The boy has been mute since his beloved mother Malvina (Murino) died. As Verena tries to reach Jakob, she learns that he believes his mother speaks to him through the walls. After Verena is convinced to wear a dress of Malvina's, she experiences a sexual awakening that involves Jakob's father Klaus (Csokas). As Verena's place in the household grows, she believes she hears Malvina speaking to her as well. Atmospheric but lacking true suspense. **94m/C; DVD.** Emilia Clarke; Marton Csokas; Caterina Murino; Remo Girone; Lisa Gastoni; ***D:*** Eric D. Howell; ***W:*** Andrew Shaw; ***C:*** Peter Simonite; ***M:*** Michael Wandmacher.

The Voice of Merrill 1/2 *Murder Will Out* **1952** Has a blackmailing secretary been killed by unhappy publisher Ronald Parker (Kendall)? Or ailing, unpleasant, but successful writer Jonathan Roach (Justice)? Or Roach's unhappy wife Alycia (Hobson) who is having an affair with struggling author Hugh Allen (Underdown)? Scotland Yard investigates. Title refers to the radio serial, penned but disowned by Roach, which leads to a final twist. **83m/B; DVD.** *GB* Valerie Hobson; Edward Underdown; James Robertson Justice; Henry Kendall; Garry Marsh; ***D:*** John Gilling; ***W:*** John Gilling; ***C:*** Monty Berman; ***M:*** Frank Cordell.

The Voice of the City 1/2 **1929** Actor, writer, and director Willard Mack made his talkie debut in his own film, starring as police detective Biff Myers. Biff realizes gangsters have set-up escaped con Bobby Doyle and he's fallen for their tricks. Biff doesn't like being taken for a mug and wants to capture the real bad guys. **85m/B; DVD.** Willard Mack; Robert Ames; Sylvia Field; Jim Farley; Clark Marshall; John Miljan; ***D:*** Willard Mack; ***W:*** Willard Mack; ***C:*** Maximilian Fabian.

The Voice of the Turtle 1/2 **1947** In this charming WWII-set romance, New York actress Sally Middleton (Parker) feels sorry for Army Sgt. Bill Page (Reagan) after her pal Olive (Arden) stands him up for a date with an officer. Since Bill's on a weekend pass, Sally lets him sleep on her couch and the duo are soon smitten. John Van Druten adapted from his Broadway play. **103m/B; DVD.** Eleanor Parker; Ronald Reagan; Eve Arden; Wayne Morris; Kent Smith; ***D:*** Irving Rapper; ***W:*** John Van Druten; ***C:*** Sol Polito; ***M:*** Max Steiner.

The Voices 1/2 **2015 (R)** Off-kilter horror-comedy is the first English-language pic for French-Iranian director Satrapi, but something's lost in translation. Jerry (Reynolds) seems like a shy, normal guy, except for the meds he has to take according to his court-appointed shrink (Weaver), and his evil-talking cat Mr. Whiskers and doofus talking dog Bosco (Reynolds does the voices for both). He's encouraged to pursue office crush Fiona (Atherton) but it unexpectedly results in a bloody knife, a dead deer, and human heads in the fridge after Jerry turns to his pets for advice. **103m/C; DVD, Blu-Ray.** Ryan Reynolds; Gemma Arterton; Jacki Weaver; Anna Kendrick; Ella Smith; ***D:*** Marjane Satrapi; ***W:*** Michael R. Perry; ***C:*** Maxime Alexandre; ***M:*** Olivier Bernet.

Voices from Beyond 1/2 *Voci dal Profondo* **1990** After wealthy Giorgio Mainardi hemorrhages to death, his daughter Rosy (Huff) returns home from college to attend the funeral. She soon begins to have strange dreams in which her father claims that he was murdered, and begs Rosy to discover the identity of the killer. In flashbacks, we learn that Giorgio did something to enrage everyone in the household before he died, so there are many suspects. While the revelation of the murderer is actually surprising, the rest of the film is a boring mess. While director Fulci is well-known for his liberal use of gore and his occasionally creepy visuals, this film has neither. The acting isn't very good, and the atrocious dubbing only makes matters worse. **91m/C; DVD, Blu-Ray.** *IT* Dulio Del Prete; Karina Huff; Pascal Persiano; Lorenzo Flaherty; Bettina Giovannini; Damiano Azzos; ***D:*** Lucio Fulci; ***W:*** Piero Regnoli; ***M:*** Stelvio Cipriani.

Voices of Iraq **2004** In April of 2004 a crew of American filmmakers distributed 150 video cameras to citizens of Iraq. Given full artistic and legal license to speak at will, the citizens participate in an unbiased experiment showing the true sentiment of the war-torn country. Surprisingly, there is little complaint of the U.S. and coalition's occupying troops and rampant hatred against their former dictator, Saddam Hussein; which leads us to believe that perhaps the cameras were given to select sects, rather that random citizens, or likely a dictatorship in the editing room. Still, it makes for an empowering tool in the struggle of a wounded country. **79m/C; DVD.** ***M:*** Narcicyst; Euphrates.

The Void 1/2 **2001 (R)** Physicist Eva Soderstrom (Tapping) discovers that industrialist Thomas Abernathy (McDowell) is experimenting with creating an artificial black hole on Earth. This isn't a good thing so Eva hooks up with Dr. Steven Price (Paul) to stop Abernathy. So-so thriller. **90m/C; VHS, DVD.** Amanda Tapping; Adrian Paul; Malcolm McDowell; Andrew McIlroy; ***D:*** Gilbert M. Shilton; ***W:*** Gilbert M. Shilton; Geri Cudia Barger; ***C:*** Attila Szalay; ***M:*** Ross Vannelli.

The Void **2017** A violent, gory indie horror siege narrative. In a foggy small town, rookie cop Daniel (Poole) must protect residents from a murderous cult by hiding out in the subterranean levels of a local hospital. The cult members are allied with grossly deformed humanoid monsters with tentacles, and they transform or kill anyone who opposes them. People who have experience a loss related to childbirth are especially targeted. Human survivors must kill the cult members, who hide their faces with white sheets, or face their own extinction. A paper-thin plot and lack of imagination make for an underwhelming film. **90m/C; DVD.** Aaron Poole; Kenneth Welsh; Daniel Fathers; Kathleen Munroe; Ellen Wong; ***D:*** Jeremy Gillespie; Steven Kostanski; ***W:*** Jeremy Gillespie; Steven Kostanski; ***C:*** Samy Inayeh; ***M:*** Blitz/Berlin; Joseph Murray; Menalon Music; Lodewijk Vos.

Volcano **1997 (PG-13)** L.A. has already had to deal with earthquakes, mudslides, raging fires, riots and the acting career of Anna Nicole Smith. Now it's completely roasted by millions of gallons of molten lava. This overblown Rescue 911 has Mike Roark (Jones), the standard take-charge guy, trying to avert total destruction while being assisted by the brainy-but-beautiful seismologist Dr. Amy Barnes (Heche). Many tongue-in-cheek jokes about the general state of chaos in L.A. even on the best of days; but aside from these, the dialogue is cheesy beyond belief. The special effects are very impressive, however. Wilshire Blvd. was actually recreated on a 17-acre set (believed to be the biggest ever) in order to meet its fiery doom. **120m/C; VHS, DVD, Blu-Ray.** Tommy Lee Jones; Anne Heche; Gaby Hoffman; Don Cheadle; Keith David; John Corbett; Michael Rispoli; John Carroll Lynch; Jacqueline Kim; ***D:*** Mick Jackson; ***W:*** Billy Ray; Jerome Armstrong; ***C:*** Theo van de Sande; ***M:*** Alan Silvestri.

Volunteers **1985 (R)** Ivy League playboy joins the newly formed Peace Corps to escape gambling debts and finds himself on a bridge-building mission in Thailand. Has its comedic moments, especially with Candy. **107m/C; VHS, DVD.** Tom Hanks; John Candy; Rita Wilson; Tim Thomerson; Gedde Watanabe; George Plimpton; Ernest Harada; ***D:*** Nicholas Meyer; ***W:*** David Isaacs; Ken Levine; ***C:*** Ric Waite; ***M:*** James Horner.

Volver *To Return* **2006 (R)** Almodovar and the women. The writer/director tackles domestic melodrama when frustrated cleaner Raimunda (Cruz) is forced into drastic action to protect her daughter Paula (Cobo). In addition, Raimunda's hairdresser sister Sole (Duenas) is suddenly confronted by their mother Irene's (Maura) ghost, who takes up residence with Sole and helps out in her salon in order to rectify some mistakes she made with her daughters. Much sly humor and female bonding and yes, Cruz is wearing a prosthetic backside to give her that sexy sway. Spanish with subtitles. **111m/C; DVD, Blu-Ray.** *SP* Penelope Cruz; Lola Duenas; Carmen Maura; Chus (Maria Jesus) Lampreave; Blanca Portillo; Yohana Cobo; Maria Isabel Diaz; Antonio de la Torre; Carlos Blanco; Leonardo Rivera; ***D:*** Pedro Almodóvar; ***W:*** Pedro Almodóvar; ***C:*** Jose Luis Alcaine; ***M:*** Alberto Iglesias.

Von Ryan's Express **1965** An American Air Force colonel leads a group of prisoners-of-war in taking control of a freight train in order to make their exciting escape from a WWII P.O.W. camp in Italy. Strong cast. **117m/C; VHS, DVD, Blu-Ray.** Frank Sinatra; Trevor Howard; Brad Dexter; Raffaella Carra; Sergio Fantoni; John Leyton; Vito Scotti; Edward Mulhare; Adolfo Celi; James Brolin; James B. Sikking; Wolfgang Preiss; John van Dreelen; Richard Bakalyan; Michael Goodliffe; Michael St. Clair; Ivan Triesault; ***D:*** Mark Robson; ***W:*** Wendell Mayes; Joseph Landon; ***C:*** William H. Daniels; ***M:*** Jerry Goldsmith.

The Von Trapp Family: A Life of Music **2015** Based on the autobiography "Memories Before and After 'The Sound of Music'," the story of the von Trapp family from the eldest daughter's perspective. Agathe von Trapp (Bennett) escapes Austria and the tense political situation there as World War II begins with her family. Despite many challenges faced by her and her family, she seeks her own path in music, moves to the United States, and builds a successful life. **98m/C; DVD, Streaming, Download.** Eliza Bennett; Lauryn Canny; Yvonne Catterfeld; Annette Dasch; Marco Dott; ***D:*** Ben Verbong; ***W:*** Christoph Silber; Tim Sullivan; ***C:*** Jan Fehse; ***M:*** Enis Rotthoff. **VIDEO**

Voodoo **1995 (R)** College student Andy (Feldman) must battle a fraternity, lead by an evil voodoo priest, when they decide to make his girlfriend their next human sacrifice. **91m/C; VHS, DVD.** Corey Feldman; Sarah Douglas; Jack Nance; Joel J. Edwards; ***D:*** Rene Eram; ***W:*** Brian DiMuccio; Dino Vindeni; ***C:*** Dan Gillham; ***M:*** Keith Bilderbeck.

Voodoo Academy **2000** Imagine an episode of "Scooby Doo" crossed with a Calvin Klein ad and you'll get the idea of what video veteran Dave DeCoteau is doing in what he calls "the first horror film made for girls." A Bible college is a front for voodoo activity. The all-male students run around in their underwear trying to figure out what's going on. **100m/C; DVD.** Riley Smith; Chad Burns; Debra Meyer; ***D:*** David DeCoteau.

Voodoo Dawn **1989 (R)** Two New Yorkers travel to the Deep South to visit a friend who, it turns out, is the latest victim in a series of really gross voodoo murders. A beautiful girl is written into the plot, and the New York guys have an excuse to stay in voodooville, even though bimbolina's southern accent comes and goes for no discernable reason. Filmed near Charleston, South Carolina, and co-written by Russo of "Night of the Living Dead" fame. **83m/C; VHS, DVD.** Raymond St. Jacques; Theresa Merritt; Gina Gershon; Kirk Baily; Billy "Sly" Williams; J. Grant Albrecht; Tony Todd; ***D:*** Steven Fierberg; ***W:*** John A. Russo; Jeffrey Delman.

Voodoo Dawn 1/2 **1999** Crazy con Frank Barlow (Madsen) has learned voodoo rites in prison and is using his power to get revenge on his brother's killer. Predictable crime drama despite the occult trappings. **93m/C; VHS, DVD.** Michael Madsen; Rosanna Arquette; Balthazar Getty; Phillip Glasser; James Russo; ***D:*** Andrzej Sekula. **VIDEO**

Voodoo Moon 1/2 **2005** More silly than scary. Cole (Mabius) and Heather (Carpenter) were the only survivors when a demonic presence destroyed their town. For many years, Cole has been learning how to destroy the demon and now returns with his psychic sis to put his knowledge to the test. **89m/C; DVD.** Eric Mabius; Charisma Carpenter; Alison Grace; Jeffrey Combs; Jayne Heitmeyer; John Amos; Dee Wallace; ***D:*** Kevin VanHook; ***W:*** Kevin VanHook; ***C:*** Matt Steinauer; ***M:*** Ludek Drizhal. **CABLE**

Voodoo Possession 1/2 **2014 (R)** A horror film that explores demon possession and the depths of brotherly love. Since he was a small child, Aiden Chase (Caltagirone) has felt a deep sense of guilt related to his brother. As an adult, Aiden goes on a search for his missing sibling. Traveling to an insane asylum in Haiti, he finds that the hospital administrator Billy Kross (Trejo) and all the residents are possessed by a voodoo spirit. This demonic spirit longs for blood and plain, tormenting the living and the dead. To save his brother and their souls, Aiden travels to a spirit world to confront the force causing so much pain. **94m/C; DVD, Streaming, Download.** Danny Trejo; Ryan Caltagirone; Kerry Knuppe; David Thomas Jenkins; Treva Etienne; ***D:*** Walter Boholst; ***W:*** Walter Boholst; ***C:*** Matthias Schubert; ***M:*** Pez Wilson. **VIDEO**

Voulez-Vous Danser avec Moi? 1/2 *Come Dance with Me; Do You Want to Dance with Me?* **1959** Lighthearted comedy-mystery with a sexy Bardot starring as the newly married Virginie. After a quarrel with her husband Herve (Vidal), she follows him to a dance studio and finds him incriminated in the murder of the studio's owner. So Virginie decides to go undercover as an instructor to clear her husband's name. Based on the novel "The Blonde Died Dancing" by Kelley Roos. French with subtitles. **91m/C; VHS, DVD.** *FR IT* Brigitte Bardot; Henri Vidal; Dawn Addams; Philippe Nicaud; Serge Gainsbourg; Dario Moreno; ***D:*** Michel Boisrond; ***W:*** Annette Wademant; ***C:*** Robert Lefebvre; ***M:*** Henri Crolla.

The Vow **2012 (PG-13)** Inspired by true events, yes, it's sappy and cliched but this romance is saved by the tenacity of Tatum's performance and MacAdams pretty appeal. A car accident put newlywed Paige (McAdams) into a coma and when she regains consciousness she's suffering from severe memory loss. Her husband Leo (Tatum) vows to win her love all over again while Paige struggles to rebuild her life when the recen years have been wiped out. Leo also has to go up against Paige's controlling parents (Lange, Neill), who would be happy to see him gone as would her ex-fiance Jeremy (Speedman), who now has a second chance.

104m/C; DVD, Blu-Ray. Rachel McAdams; Channing Tatum; Scott Speedman; Sam Neill; Jessica Lange; ***D:*** Michael Sucsy; ***W:*** Michael Sucsy; Abby Kohn; Marc Silverstein; ***C:*** Rogier Stoffers; ***M:*** Michael Brook; Rachel Portman.

Vox Lux **2018 (R)** At a memorial service after a mass shooting at her middle school, young Celeste sings a ballad that propels her to pop stardom. Cut to 18 years later, when Natalie Portman's Celeste tours in promotion of her latest album, *Vox Lux*, while grappling with her fame, her past, and a terrorist attack loosely related to her celebrity. Writer/director Brady Corbet raises a multitude of questions about modern society, but fails to answer any of them in a meaningful way. **110m/C; DVD, Blu-Ray.** Natalie Portman; Jude Law; Raffey Cassidy; Stacy Martin; Jennifer Ehle; ***D:*** Brady Corbet; ***W:*** Brady Corbet; ***C:*** Lol Crawley; ***M:*** Scott Walker.

Voyage in Italy 1/2 *Journey to Italy; Voyage to Italy; The Lonely Woman; Strangers* **1953** Narrative of a marriage finds unhappy English couple Bergman and Sanders travelling by car to Naples. However, various crises manage to reunite them. Critically mauled upon its release, this third collaboration between Bergman and Rossellini, following "Stromboli" and "Europa '51," later became a big hit with New Wave directors. **83m/B; VHS, DVD, Blu-Ray.** *IT* Ingrid Bergman; George Sanders; ***D:*** Roberto Rossellini; ***W:*** Roberto Rossellini; Vitaliano Brancatti; ***C:*** Enzo Serafin; ***M:*** Renzo Rossellini.

Voyage of the Damned **1976 (G)** The story of one of the most tragic incidents of WWII. In 1939, 1,937 German-Jewish refugees fleeing Nazi Germany are bound for Cuba aboard the Hamburg-America liner S.S. St. Louis. They are refused permission to land in Cuba (and everywhere else) and must sail back to Germany and certain death. Based on the novel by Gordon Thomas and Max Morgan-Witts. **155m/C; VHS, DVD, Blu-Ray.** *GB* Faye Dunaway; Max von Sydow; Oskar Werner; Malcolm McDowell; Orson Welles; James Mason; Lee Grant; Katharine Ross; Ben Gazzara; Lynne Frederick; Wendy Hiller; Jose Ferrer; Luther Adler; Sam Wanamaker; Denholm Elliott; Nehemiah Persoff; Julie Harris; Maria Schell; Jonathan Pryce; Janet Suzman; Helmut Griem; Michael Constantine; Victor Spinetti; ***D:*** Stuart Rosenberg; ***W:*** Steve Shagan; David Butler; ***C:*** Billy Williams; ***M:*** Lalo Schifrin. Golden Globes '77: Support. Actress (Ross).

Voyage of the Rock Aliens **1987** A quasi-satiric space farce about competing alien rock stars. **97m/C; VHS, DVD.** Pia Zadora; Tom Nolan; Craig Sheffer; Rhema; Ruth Gordon; Michael Berryman; Jermaine Jackson; Alison La Placa; ***D:*** James Fargo; ***W:*** Edward Gold; S. James Guidotti; ***C:*** Gilbert Taylor; ***M:*** Jack White.

Voyage of the Unicorn 1/2 **2000 (G)** Based vaguely on the novel "Voyage of the Bassett," a professor and his two daughters are whisked off to a fantasy realm to prevent trolls from destroying it. Made forn the Hallmark Channel. **132m/C; DVD.** Beau Bridges; Chantal Conlin; Heather McEwen; MacKenzie Gray; ***D:*** Philip Spink; ***W:*** Dan Levine; ***C:*** John Spooner; ***M:*** Daryl Bennett. **CABLE**

The Voyage of the Yes **1972 (PG)** Two teenagers, one white and one black, in a small sailboat hit rough weather and battle the elements while learning about themselves. Average TV movie. **100m/C; VHS, DVD.** Desi Arnaz, Jr.; Mike Evans; Beverly Garland; Skip Homeier; Della Reese; Scoey Mitchell; ***D:*** Lee H. Katzin. **TV**

A Voyage 'Round My Father **1989** John Mortimer's adaptation of his semi-autobiographical stage play. Olivier is the eccentric, opinionated blind barrister-father and Bates the exasperated son as both try to come to terms with their stormy family relationship. Well-acted and directed. **85m/C; VHS, DVD.** *GB* Laurence Olivier; Alan Bates; Jane Asher; Elizabeth Sellars; ***D:*** Alvin Rakoff. **TV**

Voyage to the Beginning of the World *Journey to the Beginning of the World; Viagem ao Principio do Mundo* **1996** Autobiographical piece by 88-year-old director de Oliveira, who has been making movies since the silent film era. Mastroianni, in his last role, plays the somewhat fictionalized director named Manoel who travels to Portugal to shoot a film. Along the way he points out crumbling landmarks that he remembers from his childhood, an apt metaphor for the memories where the majority of his life now resides. Along with him is French actor Afonso (Gautier), who makes a visit to an elderly aunt (de Castro) who poignantly tells Afonso about his father and the way things used to be. Slow moving but lyrical ode to aging and the changing perspective it gives. French and Portuguese with subtitles. **93m/C; VHS, DVD.** *PT* Marcello Mastroianni; Jean-Yves Gautier; Leonor Silveira; Diogo Doria; Isabel de Castro; ***D:*** Manoel de Oliveira; ***W:*** Manoel de Oliveira; ***C:*** Renato Berta; ***M:*** Emmanuel Nunes.

Voyage to the Bottom of the Sea **1961** The crew of an atomic submarine must destroy a deadly radiation belt which has set the polar ice cap ablaze. Fun stuff, with good special effects and photography. Later became a TV series. **106m/C; VHS, DVD, Blu-Ray.** Walter Pidgeon; Joan Fontaine; Barbara Eden; Peter Lorre; Robert Sterling; Michael Ansara; Frankie Avalon; ***D:*** Irwin Allen; ***W:*** Irwin Allen; Charles Bennett; ***C:*** Winton C. Hoch; ***M:*** Paul Sawtell; Bert Shefter.

Voyage to the Planet of Prehistoric Women **WOOF!** *Gill Woman; Gill Women of Venus* **1968** Astronauts journey to Venus, where they discover a race of gorgeous, sea-shell clad women led by Van Doren, as well as a few monsters. Incomprehensible but fun. The third film incorporating the Russian "Planeta Burg" footage. Directed (and narrated) by Bogdanovich under the pseudonym Derek Thomas. **78m/C; VHS, DVD.** Mamie Van Doren; Mary Mark; Paige Lee; Aldo Roman; Margot Hartman; ***Nar:*** Peter Bogdanovich; ***D:*** Peter Bogdanovich; ***W:*** Henry Ney.

Voyage to the Prehistoric Planet 1/2 *Voyage to a Prehistoric Planet* **1965** In the year 2020, an expedition to Venus is forced to deal with dinosaurs and other perils. In the making of this movie, Roger Corman edited in special effects and additional footage from a recently acquired Russian film, "Planeta Burg," and his own "Queen of Blood." **80m/C; VHS, DVD.** Basil Rathbone; Faith Domergue; Marc Shannon; Christopher Brand; ***D:*** Curtis Harrington.

The Voyeur **1994** After ten years of marriage, a couple tries to ignite those sexual fires by spending a weekend in Napa Valley and indulging in erotic sexual games. Based on Lonnie Barbach's book "Erotic Edge." **80m/C; VHS, DVD, Blu-Ray.** Al Sapienza; Kim (Kimberly Dawn) Dawson; ***D:*** Deborah Shames; ***W:*** Udana Power.

Vulture's Eye **2004** Why is it that a bunch of sexy ladies can't roam the pleasant Virginia countryside without having some creepy evil-doer Count lurking about? Thank goodness there's a stereotypical coot of a Southern doctor around to try to save the poor women's souls. That and the special strength they get from just being friends. Who knew that just having pals keeps ya from joining the undead! **100m/C; DVD.** Brooke Paller; Anne Flosnik; Jason King; Fred Iacovo; James Nalitz; Eve Young; ***D:*** Frank Sciurba; ***W:*** Frank Sciurba. **VIDEO**

W 1/2 *I Want Her Dead* **1974 (PG)** A woman and her husband are terrorized and must find out why. A single letter "W" is found at the scene of the crimes. Notable only as model Twiggy's first film. **95m/C; VHS, DVD.** Twiggy; Dirk Benedict; John Vernon; Eugene Roche; ***D:*** Richard Quine.

W. **2008 (PG-13)** Stone's take on the life and times of President George W. Bush is surprisingly conventional and restrained. Bush (played convincingly by Brolin) spends his early years as a troubled alcoholic, rebelling against his privileged upbringing, fighting his father (Cromwell), and watching as his brother Jeb became the chosen one. Still, somehow, he climbs the political ladder high enough to become the leader of the free world. All the key players are here—vice-presidential strategist Dick Cheney (Dreyfuss), master political consultant Karl Rove (Jones), Defense Secretary Donald Rumsfeld (Glenn), and first lady Laura Bush (Banks). Told in non-linear fashion, flashing back to key moments in W.'s upbringing and to the major decisions he was forced to make as president, it's a solid drama, but nothing out of the ordinary from most celebrity biopics. Ultimately, it highlights both his incompetence, and his humanity. **131m/C; DVD, Blu-Ray.** Josh Brolin; Elizabeth Banks; Thandie Newton; Richard Dreyfuss; Scott Glenn; Ioan Gruffudd; James Cromwell; Ellen Burstyn; Noah Wyle; Jason Ritter; Jeffrey Wright; Jesse Bradford; Rob Corddry; Toby Jones; Sayed Badreya; Michael Gaston; ***D:*** Oliver Stone; ***W:*** Stanley Weiser; ***C:*** Phedon Papamichael; ***M:*** Paul Cantelon.

Wabash Avenue 1/2 **1950** Enjoyable musical, set during Chicago's 1893 Colombian Exposition, is a basic rehash of 1943's "Coney Island." Singer/dancer Ruby Summers (Grable) works for Mike Stanley (Harris) at his Wabash Avenue club but wants something classier. Broadway producer Andy Clark (Mature), Mike's rival, falls for Ruby and wants to take her to New York but Mike is determined to keep her. **92m/C; DVD.** Betty Grable; Victor Mature; Phil Harris; Reginald Gardiner; Margaret Hamilton; ***D:*** Henry Koster; ***W:*** Charles Lederer; Harry Tugend; ***C:*** Arthur E. Arling.

The WAC From Walla Walla 1/2 **1952** Smalltown farm girl Judy (Canova) accidentally joins the Army and decides to make the best of her new life as a soldier. Although the Army might not survive. Judy even defeats a couple of spies trying to steal missile plans through her constant klutziness. **83m/B; DVD.** Judy Canova; Steve (Stephen) Dunne; George Cleveland; June Vincent; Irene Ryan; Thurston Hall; Roy Barcroft; Allen Jenkins; ***D:*** William Witney; ***W:*** Arthur T. Horman; ***C:*** Jack Marta; ***M:*** R. Dale Butts.

Wackiest Ship in the Army 1/2 **1961** A completely undisciplined warship crew must smuggle an Australian spy through Japanese waters during WWII. Odd, enjoyable mixture of action and laughs. Became a TV series. In the middle of the war effort, Nelson straps on a guitar and sings "Do You Know What It Means to Miss New Orleans." **99m/C; VHS, DVD.** Jack Lemmon; Ricky Nelson; Chips Rafferty; John Lund; Mike Kellin; Patricia Driscoll; ***D:*** Richard Murphy.

Wackiest Wagon Train in the West **1977 (G)** Hapless wagon master is saddled with a dummy assistant as they guide a party of five characters across the West. Based on the minor TV sitcom "Dusty's Trail." Produced by the same folks who delivered the similarly premised TV series "Gilligan's Island" and "The Brady Bunch." **86m/C; VHS, DVD.** Bob Denver; Forrest Tucker; Jeannine Riley; William Cort; Ivor Francis; Lori Saunders; ***D:*** Elroy Schwartz; ***W:*** Sherwood Schwartz; Elroy Schwartz. **TV**

The Wackness 1/2 **2008 (R)** Loner Luke Shapiro (Peck) peddles pot and navel-gazes as he contemplates graduation, the long summer prior to college, parental issues, and a serious lack of confidence with girls. He strikes up an unlikely yet drug-based friendship with his therapist, Dr. Squires (Kingsley, who although a jack-of-all-trades actor is kinda creepy as a pot-head), who has issues of his own, namely a failing marriage and a general lack of maturity. The good doctor seems to have an undue interest in getting Luke laid, although he's not hip to Luke's interest in his own stepdaughter Stephanie (Thirlby). The coming-of-age storyline meanders in a stoner haze around 1994 New York, which doesn't seem long ago enough to be treated in a period movie. **95m/C; Blu-Ray, On Demand.** Josh Peck; Ben Kingsley; Famke Janssen; Olivia Thirlby; Mary-Kate Olsen; Jane Adams; Method Man; Talia Balsam; David Wohl; Bob (Robert) Dishy; ***D:*** Jonathan Levine; ***W:*** Jonathan Levine; ***C:*** Petra Korner; ***M:*** David Torn.

Wadjda **2013 (PG)** A deceptively simple film given its subject matter--a young girl who wants to buy and ride a bicycle—that is far more complex given its setting: Saudi Arabia. Not only are girls like 10-year-old Wadjda not allowed to ride bikes but they have numerous other restrictions for the sake of modesty. Wadjda wants to race a local boy and so she works to save up enough money to buy a green bike, discovering that a school religious competition on the Koran may be her best opportunity to do so. Arabic with subtitles. **98m/C; DVD, Blu-Ray.** *SD GE* Waad Mohammed; Reem Abdullah; Abdullrahman Al Gohani; Ahd; Sultan Al Assaf; ***D:*** Haifaa Al-Mansour; ***W:*** Haifaa Al-Mansour; ***C:*** Lutz Reitemeier; ***M:*** Max Richter.

Wag the Dog 1/2 **1997 (R)** Based on the book "American Hero" by Larry Beinhart and adapted by Hilary Henkin and David Mamet. Over-the-top Hollywood producer (Hoffman) is hired by White House officials to stage a military attack against the U.S. to divert media attention from accusations that the President fondled a Girl Scout. Show biz insiders say Hoffman's Motss resembles one-time studio head Robert Evans; Washington insiders wonder if it's a documentary. In fact, the entire film is one big insider's joke. Luckily, it's smart enough, and short enough, to avoid becoming tiresome. Look for cameos by Woody Harrelson and Willie Nelson. Filmed in a speedy 29 days on a $15 million budget. **96m/C; VHS, DVD.** Dustin Hoffman; Robert De Niro; Anne Heche; Woody Harrelson; Denis Leary; Willie Nelson; Andrea Martin; Suzanne Cryer; Suzy Plakson; John Michael Higgins; Kirsten Dunst; William H. Macy; Michael Belson; ***D:*** Barry Levinson; ***W:*** Hilary Henkin; David Mamet; ***C:*** Robert Richardson; ***M:*** Mark Knopfler. Natl. Bd. of Review '97: Support. Actress (Heche).

Wages of Fear *Le Salaire de la Peur* **1955** American oil company controls a desolate Central American town whose citizens desperately want out—so desperately that four are willing to try a suicide mission to deliver nitroglycerine to put out a well-fire raging 300 miles away. The company's cynical head has offered $2000 to each man, enough to finance escape from the hell-hole they live in. Complex, multi-dimensional drama concentrates on character development for the first half—crucial to the film's greatness. This is the restored version. Remade by William Friedkin as "Sorcerer" in 1977. Based on a novel by Georges Arnaud. In French with English subtitles. **138m/B; VHS, DVD, Blu-Ray.** *FR* Yves Montand; Charles Vanel; Peter Van Eyck; Vera Clouzot; Folco Lulli; William Tubbs; ***D:*** Henri-Georges Clouzot; ***W:*** Henri-Georges Clouzot; ***C:*** Armand Thirard; ***M:*** Georges Auric. British Acad. '54: Film; Cannes '53: Actor (Vanel), Film.

Wagner: The Complete Epic **1985** The unedited version of the epic miniseries dramatizing the life of German composer Richard Wagner. The excellent photography does justice to the elaborate production, shot on some 200 different locations. The actors cringe in the presence of the subject's grandeur; Burton, a shell of his former cinematic self, is painful to watch in his last released film. Frankly, this is way too long. Also available in a edited 300-minute version, which is still too long. **540m/C; VHS, DVD.** *GB HU* Richard Burton; Vanessa Redgrave; Ralph Richardson; John Gielgud; Laurence Olivier; Franco Nero; ***D:*** Tony Palmer. **TV**

Wagon Master **1950** Two cowboys are persuaded to guide a group of Mormons, led by Bond, in their trek across the western frontier. They run into a variety of troubles, including a band of killers who joins the wagon train to escape a posse. Sensitively directed, realistic and worthwhile. Inspired the TV series "Wagon Train." Also available colorized. **85m/B; VHS, DVD, Blu-Ray.** Ben Johnson; Joanne Dru; Harry Carey, Jr.; Ward Bond; Jane Darwell; James Arness; ***D:*** John Ford.

Wagons East **1994 (PG-13)** Fed up with prairie hardships, pioneers decide to hitch up to a wagon train and head east. Candy (who died during filming) plays the drunken former wagonmaster hired to get them back home, with Lewis (out of his depth) as a neurotic ex-doctor, and McGinley stuck in the role of a gay bookseller that reeks of stereotypical mannerisms. Script is desperate for humor, which it never finds, and it's hard to watch Candy's performance knowing this mess was his last role. **100m/C; VHS, DVD.** John Candy; Richard Lewis; Ellen Greene; John C. McGinley; Robert Picardo; William Sanderson; Thomas F. Duffy; Russell Means; Rodney A. Grant; Michael Horse; Gailard Sartain; Lochlyn Munro; Stuart Proud Eagle Grant; Melinda Culea; ***D:*** Peter Markle; ***W:*** Matthew Carlson; Jerry Abrahamson.

The Wagons Roll at Night 1/2 **1941** The circus wagons that is. Remake of 1937's "Kid Galahad" transfers the action from the boxing arena to the circus arena. Nick Coster (Bogart) is the owner of the failing enterprise, romancing fortune teller Flo (Sidney) while trying to protect his innocent sister, Mary (Leslie) from the seedy side of life. This would have been easier if sis hadn't fallen for the new lion tamer, Matt Varney (Albert). Nick tries to break up the lovebirds with predictable results. Based on the novel by Francis Wallace. **84m/B; VHS, DVD, Streaming.** Humphrey Bogart; Sylvia Sidney; Eddie Albert; Joan Leslie; Sig Rumann; Cliff Clark; Charles Foy; Frank Wilcox; ***D:*** Ray Enright; ***W:*** Barry Trivers; Fred Niblo, Jr.; ***C:*** Sidney Hickox; ***M:*** Heinz Roemheld.

Wagons West 1/2 **1952** Jeff Curtis (Cameron) is leading a wagon train from Missouri to California but gunrunners have been supplying the Cheyenne who are now on the warpath. While fending off Indian attacks, Jeff discovers the gunrunners are part of the wagon train. **70m/C; DVD.** Rod Cameron; Henry (Kleinbach) Brandon; Frank Ferguson; Riley Hill; Noah Beery, Jr.; I. Stanford Jolley; ***D:*** Ford Beebe; ***W:*** Daniel Ullman; ***C:*** Harry Neumann; ***M:*** Marlin Skiles.

Wagons Westward 1/2 **1940** Twin brothers David (Warren Hull) and Tom (Wayne Hull) Cook can't be more different, and when their father dies they take very different paths. Tom moves in with Uncle Hardtack (Hayes) in New Mexico and David stays home to care for their mother (Brissac). As adults, Tom (Morris) becomes an outlaw gunman and David (Morris) becomes a Marshall, eventually charged with apprehending his brother. While classically western, the story adds the twists of mistaken identity and double-crossing as it creeps to a final confrontation. **70m/B; DVD.** Wayne Hull; Warren Hull; Chester Morris; Anita Louise; Buck Jones; Ona Munson; George "Gabby" Hayes; ***D:*** Lew Landers; ***W:*** Harrison Jacobs; Joseph Moncure March; ***C:*** Ernest Miller.

Wah-Wah **2005 (R)** Grant debuts as a writer/director in an autobiographical family story set in Swaziland in the late 1960s on the eve of the African nation's independence from Britain. Young Ralph (Fox) catches his mother Lauren (Richardson) committing adultery. Lauren walks out on the family, and husband/father Harry (Byrne) takes to drink, sending Ralph to boarding school. When the boy returns (now played by Hoult), he discovers his father has suddenly married a brash American, Ruby (Watson). Ruby becomes the teenager's ally, which is a good thing since the ex-pat colony is breaking apart, Harry's drinking makes him violent, and Ralph's mother suddenly decides to return. **97m/C; DVD.** *GB FR* Gabriel Byrne; Miranda Richardson; Emily Watson; Julie Walters; Nicholas Hoult; Celia Imrie; Julian Wadham; Fenella Woolgar; Sid Mitchell; Zachary Fox; Ian Roberts; ***D:*** Richard E. Grant; ***W:*** Richard E. Grant; ***C:*** Pierre Aim; ***M:*** Patrick Doyle.

Waikiki Wedding **1937** Enjoyable musical about a scheming pineapple promoter (Crosby) who meets the woman of his dreams in a contest he concocted. Contest winner Ross dislikes Hawaii and wants to go home and Crosby must keep her from going. . .first for business reasons and later, for love. Supporting cast includes Hawaiian Prince Leilani and a pig. Lots of song and dance and Hawaiian sunsets, along with Burns and Raye, the other couple destined for love on the islands, keep the story moving. **89m/B; DVD.** Bing Crosby; Bob Burns; Martha Raye; Shirley Ross; George Barbier; Leif Erickson; Grady Sutton; Granville Bates; Anthony Quinn; ***D:*** Frank Tuttle; ***W:*** Frank Butler; Don Hartman; Walter DeLeon; Francis Martin; ***C:*** Karl Struss; ***M:*** Leo Robin; Ralph Rainger. Oscars '37: Song ("Sweet Leilani").

The Wailer 1/2 *La Llorona* **2006** Low-budget and cliched horror story based on a Mexican legend. Six vacationing Americans are offered a mountain cabin by a local. Only the place is haunted by the ghost of a crying woman who murdered her children to be with her lover. For some reason, the ghost decides to dispense with her visitors. **85m/C; DVD.** Vanessa Rice; John Patrick Jordan; Hugo Medina; Brenda Lynn Mejia; Monique Barajas; Nicole Daniels; Rocael Leiva; ***D:*** Andres Navia; ***W:*** Rafy Rivera; ***C:*** Curtis Petersen; ***M:*** Richard John Baker. **VIDEO**

The Wailing 1/2 *Goksung* **2016** Rural Korean police struggle to deal with a rash of killings seemingly inspired by a sickness that coincidentally appears with a Japanese stranger. Political and social subtext may be lost on those unfamiliar with Korean culture, and like many supernatural K-horror tales this is ambiguous enough for you to decide on what the events really mean. **156m/C; DVD, Blu-Ray, Streaming.** *SK US* Do Won Kwak; Jung-min Hwang; Jun Kunimura; Woo-hee Chun; Kim Hwan-hee; ***D:*** Hong-jin Na; ***W:*** Hong-jin Na; ***C:*** Kyung-Pyo Hong.

Waist Deep **2006 (R)** Violent urban gangsta pic more or less delivers as expected. Parolee O2 (Gibson) is trying to live the straight and narrow when he gets carjacked with his son sleeping in the back seat. Was it a deliberate snatch and did his snarling mad dog rival Meat (The Game) have something to do with it? No matter—O2 is gonna get his little boy back at any cost—with some help from street-smart honey Coco (Good). **97m/C; DVD, Blu-Ray, HD-DVD.** Tyrese Gibson; Meagan Good; Larenz Tate; Kimora Lee Simmons; H. Hunter Hall; The Game; ***D:*** Vondie Curtis-Hall; ***W:*** Vondie Curtis-Hall; Darin Scott; ***C:*** Shane Hurlbut; ***M:*** Terence Blanchard.

The Wait **2013 (R)** Moments after the death of their mother, Angela (Malone) and Emma (Sevigny) receive a mysterious phone call vaguely implying that she will return to life shortly. The two sisters, stuck in the limbo of grief and wanting to believe, seek ways to occupy themselves. Believer Emma chases away the funeral home and prepares for Mom's post-resurrection party, while not-so-sure Angela finds herself attracted to the neighbor (Grimes). Nothing much happens in this aimless indie movie. **96m/C; On Demand.** Chloë Sevigny; Jena Malone; Devon Gearhart; Luke Grimes; Michael O'Keefe; ***D:*** M. Blash; ***W:*** M. Blash; ***C:*** Kasper Tuxen; ***M:*** Owen Pallett.

Wait until Dark **1967** A photographer unwittingly smuggles a drug-filled doll into New York, and his blind wife, alone in their apartment, is terrorized by murderous crooks in search of it. A compelling thriller based on the Broadway hit by Frederick Knott, who also wrote "Dial M for Murder." The individual actors' performances were universally acclaimed in this spinetingler. **105m/C; VHS, DVD, Blu-Ray.** Audrey Hepburn; Alan Arkin; Richard Crenna; Efrem Zimbalist, Jr.; Jack Weston; ***D:*** Terence Young; ***W:*** Robert B. Carrington; ***C:*** Charles B(ryant) Lang, Jr.; ***M:*** Henry Mancini.

Waiting **2000** Actor wannabe/slacker/waiter Sean (Keenan) is told by his dad that he has 30 days to find a job, an apartment, and something to do with his life. And dad doesn't mean that Sean should continue to wait tables at a South Philly mob-run Italian eatery—and maybe he could find a nice girl as well. **80m/C; VHS, DVD, UMD.** Will Keenan; Hannah Dalton; Kerri Kenney; Harry Philabosian; Lloyd Kaufman; Ron Jeremy; ***D:*** Patrick Hasson; ***W:*** Patrick Hasson; ***C:*** Michael Pearlman.

Waiting WOOF! **2005 (R)** Any laughs that might have been squeezed from this comedy set at ShenaniganZ—an eatery more mall-generic than a blend of Bennigan's and Applebee's—have been derailed by the genuinely pathetic lives of the staff and their patrons. Solid cast, led by Reynolds, is given table scraps in the form of predictable food pranks and self-loathing gags. **93m/C; DVD, Blu-Ray.** Ryan Reynolds; Anna Faris; Justin Long; David Koechner; Luis Guzman; Chi McBride; Alanna Ubach; Vanessa Lengies; Max Kasch; Dane Cook; Jordan Ladd; Emmanuelle Chriqui; Wendie Malick; John Francis Daley; Kaitlin Doubleday; Robert Patrick Benedict; Andy Milonakis; ***D:*** Rob McKittrick; ***W:*** Rob McKittrick; ***C:*** Matthew Irving; ***M:*** Adam Gorgoni.

The Waiting City 1/2 **2009 (R)** After Australians Ben and Fiona travel to Calcutta to pick up their adopted daughter, lawyer Fiona finds herself dealing with the red tape while musician Ben wanders around the city. He meets Scarlett, who shares his laid-back attitude, which not only heightens the differences between husband and wife but adds to the strains in their marriage. **107m/C; DVD.** *AU* Radha Mitchell; Joel Edgerton; Isabel Lucas; Samrat Chakrabarti; ***D:*** Claire McCarthy; ***W:*** Claire McCarthy; ***C:*** Densen Baker; ***M:*** Michael Yezerski.

Waiting for Dublin 1/2 **2007** A snorer of a WWII comedy set in neutral Ireland with a silly premise and a sillier resolution (but very pretty County Galway scenery). In 1944, American pilot Mike is in a Chicago nightclub and makes a very large bet with a mobster (about how many enemy planes he can shoot down) that Mike seems destined to lose after being forced to land his damaged plane in rural Ireland. **84m/C; DVD.** Andrew Keegan; Jade Yourell; Hugh O'Conor; Guido de Craene; Jenne Decleir; Frank Kelly; Des Braiden; ***D:*** Roger Tucker; ***W:*** Chuck Conaway; ***C:*** Marc Felperlaan; ***M:*** Alfred Van Acker.

Waiting for Forever 1/2 **2011 (PG-13)** Despite some solid performances, the plot makes for an unsuccessful, queasy rom com. Will Donner (Sturridge) has obvious mental problems that are ignored. He's become fixated on childhood best friend Emma (Bilson) to the point of stalking her when she becomes an L.A. actress although she's apparently unaware of his presence. Emma returns home to visit her parents (Danner, Jenkins) and Will follows and decides he will finally make a romantic overture. **95m/C; DVD.** Thomas Sturridge; Rachel Bilson; Blythe Danner; Richard Jenkins; Scott Mechlowicz; Matthew Davis; Jaime King; Nicole Blonsky; ***D:*** James Keach; ***W:*** Steve Adams; ***C:*** Matthew Irving; ***M:*** Damian Katkhuda; Nick Urata. **VIDEO**

Waiting for Guffman **1996 (R)** The eccentric citizens of Blaine, Missouri, plan an original musical ("Red, White, and Blaine") to celebrate the town's 150th anniversary with the aid of former New Yorker and semi-hysteric Corky St. Claire (Guest) as their director. Everyone's very game—and almost completely talentless. The Guffman of the title is the Broadway producer Corky knows and whom he's invited to see their disaster-in-the-making. A little too deliberately quirky for its own good. **84m/C; VHS, DVD, Blu-Ray.** Christopher Guest; Eugene Levy; Catherine O'Hara; Parker Posey; Fred Willard; Lewis Arquette; Matt Keeslar; Paul Dooley; Paul Benedict; Bob Balaban; Larry Miller; Brian Doyle-Murray; Bob Odenkirk; ***D:*** Christopher Guest; ***W:*** Christopher Guest; Eugene Levy; ***C:*** Roberto Schaefer; ***M:*** Christopher Guest; Michael McKean; Harry Shearer.

Waiting for Superman 1/2 **2010 (PG)** Guggenheim's dynamic expose of the failing U.S. public school system with its monetary waste, unfulfilled potential, and social and generational failure. It's shown from the view of five children (and their families) who are dependent on a lottery system to get into charter schools that offer a better education. There's also a focus on the intractability of the American Federation of Teachers for real educational change. Title comes from a comment made by educational reformer Geoffrey Canada who, as a boy, thought Superman might come to save him from life in the South Bronx. **102m/C; Blu-Ray, On Demand.** ***D:*** Davis Guggenheim; ***W:*** Davis Guggenheim; Billy Kimball; ***C:*** Erich Roland; ***M:*** Christophe Beck.

Waiting for the Light 1/2 **1990 (PG)** When a woman takes over a small-town diner, she gets the surprise of her life. Seems an angel has made his home there and now the townsfolk are flocking to see him. MacLaine is wonderful and Garr is fetching and likeable. Set during the Cuban missile crisis. Enjoyable, tame comedy. **94m/C; VHS, DVD.** Shirley MacLaine; Teri Garr; Vincent Schiavelli; John Bedford Lloyd; ***D:*** Christopher Monger; ***W:*** Christopher Monger.

Waiting for the Moon 1/2 **1987 (PG)** Hunt as Alice B. Toklas is a relative treat in this ponderous, frustrating biopic about Toklas and Gertrude Stein, her lover. Made for "American Playhouse" on PBS. **88m/C; VHS, DVD.** Linda Hunt; Linda Bassett; Andrew McCarthy; Bruce McGill; Jacques Boudet; Bernadette LaFont; ***D:*** Jill Godmilow; ***W:*** Mark Magill; ***C:*** Andre Neau. Sundance '87: Grand Jury Prize. **TV**

The Waiting Game 1/2 **1998** College friends Sarah (West) and Amy (Abdul) work at the same art gallery but things start to get dicey when Sarah gets dragged into a mystery involving her Uncle Lowell (Hinkle), undercover CIA agent Adrian (Potter), and some smuggled artifacts. From the Harlequin Romance Series; adapted from the Jayne Ann Krentz novel. **95m/C; DVD.** *CA* Chandra West; Chris Potter; Paula Abdul; Jonathan Crombie; John Pyper-Ferguson; Art Hinkle; ***D:*** Vic Sarin; ***W:*** Barbara O'Kelly; Peter Lauterman; Jennifer Black; ***C:*** Vic Sarin; ***M:*** John McCarthy. **TV**

The Waiting Game **1999** Group of actor wannabes are working in a New York restaurant while waiting for the proverbial big break. They fall in and out of lust and love and suffer audition humiliation and other trials. **81m/C; VHS, DVD.** Michael Raynor; Will Arnett; Terumi Matthews; Dan Riordan; Debbon Ayer; ***D:*** Ken Liotti; ***W:*** Ken Liotti; ***C:*** Rich Eliano; ***M:*** Jim Farmer.

The Waiting Room **2007** Sentimental South London-set romantic drama. Single mom Anna is separated from Toby and has started a casual affair with neighbor George, the husband of her best friend Jem. Nurse Stephen, who lives with Fiona, works in a retirement home and meets cute with Anna at a train station when he follows absent-minded patient Roger. They are smitten but neglect to get each other's names or phone numbers and must rely on another chance meeting if anything is to occur. **106m/C; DVD.** Anne-Marie Duff; Ralf Little; Rupert Graves; Frank Finlay; Zoe Telford; Christine Bottomley; Adrian Bower; Phyllida Law; ***D:*** Roger Goldby; ***W:*** Roger Goldby; ***C:*** James Aspinall; ***M:*** Edmund Butt.

The Waiting Room **2012** Peter Nicks spent five months in the crowded emergency room at the public Highland Hospital in Oakland, California, where the patients are mostly uninsured, black, poor, and with no other options. Nicks' offers an apolitical composite day of waiting and the bureaucracy of a stretched to the breaking point health care system. **81m/C; DVD.** ***D:*** Peter Nicks; ***C:*** Peter Nicks; ***M:*** William Ryan Fritch.

The Waiting Time 1/2 **1999** Post-Cold War thriller based on the novel by Gerald Seymour. Tracy Barnes (Turner) is a corporal in the British Intelligence Corps who makes a seemingly unprovoked attack on German politician Dieter Krause (Becker). Befriended by solicitor's clerk Joshua Mantle (Thaw), the duo travel to Berlin to make sense of things but Joshua finds himself involved in the decade-old murder of Tracy's German lover and with the dreaded East German secret police. **150m/C; VHS, DVD.** *GB* John Thaw; Zara Turner; Hartmut Becker; Mark Pegg; Struan Rodger; Colin Baker; Christien Anholt; ***D:*** Stuart Orme; ***W:*** Patrick Harbinson; ***C:*** Peter Middleton; ***M:*** Colin Towns. **TV**

Waiting to Exhale **1995 (R)** Adaptation of Terry McMillan's novel about four African-American women hoping to reach the point in their love lives when they can relax and stop waiting for the right man. After the string of dogs and users they choose, you want to tell them not to hold their breath. The women are supposed to be close friends, but all of their stories are broken up into vignettes. This erodes the ensemble feeling of the movie, but performances are strong all around. Retaining the book's feel of just-between-friends girl talk, it may be a little harsh for those who are, shall we say, estrogen-challenged. A lush R&B soundtrack is the perfect backdrop for the ladies' soulful yearning for real love. **120m/C; VHS, DVD.** Whitney Houston; Angela Bassett; Loretta Devine; Lela Rochon; Gregory Hines; Dennis Haysbert; Mykelti Williamson; Michael Beach; Leon; Wendell Pierce; Donald Adeosun Faison; Jeffrey D. Sams; Lamont Johnson; ***Cameo(s):*** Wesley Snipes; ***D:*** Forest Whitaker; ***W:*** Ronald Bass; ***C:*** Toyomichi Kurita; ***M:*** Kenneth "Babyface" Edmonds. MTV Movie Awards '96: Song ("Sittin' Up in My Room").

Waitress WOOF! *Soup to Nuts* **1981 (R)** Three beautiful girls are waitresses in a crazy restaurant where the chef gets drunk, the kitchen explodes, and the customers riot. Awful premise, worse production. **85m/C; VHS, DVD.** Jim Harris; Carol Drake; Carol Bever; ***D:*** Lloyd Kaufman; ***W:*** Charles Kaufman; Michael Stone; ***C:*** Lloyd Kaufman.

Waitress **2007 (PG-13)** Sweet as, well, pie. Waitress Jenna (the radiantly appealing Russell) is a pie-baking phenom in her southern community. She's also fixing to leave her abusive jerk husband Earl (Sisto) when she discovers she's pregnant. Jenna looks for support from her diner co-workers while baking up outrageous concoctions ("I Hate My Husband Pie") that reflect her changing moods. She also decides to have a fling with her sweetly flustered OB-GYN (Fillion), and from there, the tale is uneven but cute nonetheless. Writer/director/actress Shelly (who plays Dawn) was murdered in November 2006 just after completing the film. **107m/C; DVD.** Keri Russell; Nathan Fillion; Cheryl Hines; Lew Temple; Jeremy Sisto; Edward Jemison; Andy Griffith; Darby Stanchfield; Adrienne Shelly; ***D:*** Adrienne Shelly; ***W:*** Adrienne Shelly; ***C:*** Matthew Irving; ***M:*** Andrew Hollander.

Wake 🦴 1/2 **2009 (R)** Carys Reitman (Phillips) has been morbidly obsessed with death since her younger sister died years before. She goes to strangers' memorial services and funerals and is best friends with undertaker Shane (Masterson). While paying her respects to Anna, Carys manages to accidentally misappropriate the dead woman's engagement ring and then pretends to be a friend in order to return the ring to Anna's fiance Tyler (Somerhalder), which causes more problems. The contrivances become increasingly annoying as the film stumbles along. **97m/C; DVD.** Bijou Phillips; Danny Masterson; Marguerite Moreau; Jane Seymour; Ian Somerhalder; Kevin Alejandro; David Zayas; Ian Gomez; ***D:*** Ellie Kanner; ***W:*** Lennox Wiseley; ***C:*** Gavin Kelly; ***M:*** Brad Segal.

Wake Island 🦴🦴🦴 **1942** After Pearl Harbor, a small group of Marines face the onslaught of the Japanese fleet on a small Pacific Island. Although doomed, they hold their ground for 16 days. Exciting, realistic, and moving. The first film to capitalize on early "last stands" of WWII; also among the most popular war movies. Shown to soldiers in training camps with great morale-raising success. **88m/B; VHS, DVD.** Robert Preston; Brian Donlevy; William Bendix; MacDonald Carey; Albert Dekker; Walter Abel; Rod Cameron; Barbara Britton; Mikhail Rasumny; Bill Goodwin; Damian O'Flynn; Frank Albertson; Hugh Beaumont; Hillary Brooke; James Brown; Don Castle; Frank Faylen; Mary Field; William Forrest; Alan Hale, Jr.; Charles Trowbridge; Philip Van Zandt; Phillip Terry; ***D:*** John Farrow; ***W:*** W.R. Burnett; Frank Butler; ***C:*** William Mellor; Theodor Sparkuhl; ***M:*** David Buttolph. N.Y. Film Critics '42: Director (Farrow).

Wake Me When It's Over 🦴 1/2 **1960** A complicated bureaucratic screwup causes WWII vet Gus Brubaker (Shawn) to be drafted again and he's sent to the remote Japanese island of Shima. The assignment is so boring that Capt. Stark (Kovacs) is constantly thinking of ways to keep his men occupied and Gus comes up with a plan to use up surplus G.I. supplies. They'll build a hotel on the island to bring tourists and dollars to the locals but things get dicey in this silly, overlong military comedy. **126m/C; DVD.** Dick Shawn; Ernie Kovacs; Jack Warden; Margo Moore; Nobu McCarthy; Don Knotts; Parley Baer; ***D:*** Mervyn LeRoy; ***W:*** Richard L. Breen; ***C:*** Leon Shamroy; ***M:*** Cyril Mockridge.

Wake of the Red Witch 🦴🦴 1/2 **1949** Wayne captains the ship of the title and battles shipping tycoon Adler for a fortune in pearls and the love of a beautiful woman (Russell). Wayne shows impressive range in a non-gun-totin' role. **106m/B; DVD, Blu-Ray.** John Wayne; Gail Russell; Gig Young; Luther Adler; Henry Daniell; ***D:*** Edward Ludwig; ***W:*** Harry Brown; Kenneth Gamet; ***C:*** Reggie Lanning; ***M:*** Nathan Scott.

Wake Up and Dream 🦴🦴 1/2 **1946** After her brother Jeff (Payne) enlists in the Navy, young Nella (Marshall) is looked after by the other boardinghouse residents, includng elderly Henry (Bevans), who's built a boat on wheels that he goes 'sailing' in. When Jeff is declared MIA, Nella is convinced that he's on the special island he told Nella about and she's determined to use Henry's boat to find him. Payne may have star billing but he's MIA for most of the movie. Based on the Robert Ntahn novel "The Enchanted Voyage." **92m/C; DVD.** John Payne; June Haver; Connie Marshall; Clem Bevans; Charlotte Greenwood; John Ireland; ***D:*** Lloyd Bacon; ***W:*** Elick Moll; ***C:*** Harry Jackson; ***M:*** Cyril Mockridge.

Wake Up and Live 🦴🦴 1/2 **1937** Columnist Walter Winchell and bandleader Ben Bernie play themselves in this musical comedy that has the two manufacture a radio fued for publicity and ratings. Singer Eddie Kane (Haley) gets a job as a studio tour guide because he freezes up every time he gets in front of a microphone. Singing host Alice (Faye) encourages Eddie to practice in the studio but his vocals go out live and soon everyone wants to know who 'The Phantom Troubadour' is. **91m/B; DVD.** Alice Faye; Jack Haley; Walter Winchell; Ben Bernie; Patsy Kelly; Ned Sparks; Grace Bradley; Walter Catlett; ***D:*** Sidney Lanfield; ***W:*** Jack Yellen; Harry Tugend; ***C:*** Edward Cronjager.

Wake Wood 🦴🦴 **2010** Modern Hammer horror. Patrick and Louise Daly move to the isolated Irish community of Wake Wood after the death of their young daughter Alice. They soon hear of a pagan ritual that allows the village inhabitants to bring back the recently dead for three days—with strict conditions and consequences. A not-quite-right Alice returns but the Dalys don't want to let her go again and she doesn't want to leave. **90m/C; DVD, Blu-Ray.** *GB IR* Eva Birthistle; Aidan Gillen; Timothy Spall; Ella Connolly; Amelia Crowley; Brian Gleeson; Ruth McCabe; ***D:*** David Keating; ***W:*** David Keating; Brendan McCarthy; ***C:*** Chris Maris.

Wakefield 🦴🦴 1/2 **2017 (R)** An introspective and voyeuristic examination of identity and marriage. Dissatisfied with his life as attorney, husband, and father, Howard Wakefield rashly decides to hide in the attic of his suburban garage. Hours turn into months as he spies on his family by day and scavenges by night. Garner delivers a top-notch performance, and you'll be mesmerized by Cranston despite disliking his character. The ending is abrupt, but it remains true to the short story by E.L. Doctorow. **106m/C; DVD.** Bryan Cranston; Jennifer Garner; Beverly D'Angelo; Ian Anthony Dale; Jason O'Mara; ***D:*** Robin Swicord; ***W:*** Robin Swicord; ***C:*** Andrei Bowden Schwartz; ***M:*** Aaron Zigman.

Waking Life 🦴🦴 1/2 **2001 (R)** Linklater's innovative and visually groundbreaking look at dreams, life, and philosophy doesn't really seem to have a plot. What it does have is several vignettes of people mostly just talking about the above subjects. What makes it stunning is the look of the project. Linklater "filmed" the scenes on digital video, then had a group of artists digitally "paint" over the footage, assigning different artists different scenes or actors so as to have a variety of styles. The result is a trippy experiment that might not appeal to many people except philosophy majors, computer geeks, or chemically altered college students. Film buffs looking for something new would do well to check it out. **99m/C; VHS, DVD.** Richard Linklater; Glover Gill; Julie Delpy; Wiley Wiggins; Ethan Hawke; Adam Goldberg; Nicky Katt; Steven Soderbergh; ***D:*** Richard Linklater; ***W:*** Richard Linklater; ***C:*** Richard Linklater; Tommy Pallotta; ***M:*** Glover Gill. N.Y. Film Critics '01: Animated Film.

Waking Madison 🦴 1/2 **2010 (R)** Suicidal Madison Walker suffers from multiple personality disorder. She finds her illness too much to cope with and decides to confine herself to her New Orleans apartment for 30 days, keeping a video diary for her shrink. Madison hopes to learn what past traumas triggered her problems while the doctor tries to figure out if what Madison reveals is truth or fantasy. **89m/C; DVD.** Sarah Roemer; Elisabeth Shue; Imogen Poots; Will Patton; Taryn Manning; Frances Conroy; ***D:*** Katherine Brooks; ***W:*** Katherine Brooks; ***C:*** Rob Sweeney; ***M:*** Klaus Badelt.

Waking Ned Devine 🦴🦴🦴 1/2 **1998 (PG)** Old Ned Devine has the winning ticket for the Irish National Lottery—unfortunately, the shock has killed him. Jackie O'Shea (Bannen) and the other 50 still-living residents of Tulaigh Morh conspire to fool a bored lottery official (Dempsey) into thinking that Michael O'Sullivan (Kelly) is Devine, so that they can share the wealth. As each obstacle to the payoff is overcome, a larger hurdle appears, and the comedy becomes more and more screwball until it reaches its darkly comic conclusion. Warm and full of blarney, but never becomes too sappy, or contrived. Filmed on the beautiful Isle of Man and accented with a fine score full of Celtic melodies. Veteran cast carries off even the most improbable gags (including Kelly's buck-naked motorcycle ride). **91m/C; VHS, DVD.** Ian Bannen; David Kelly; Fionnula Flanagan; Susan Lynch; James Nesbitt; Maura O'Malley; Robert Hickey; Paddy Ward; James Ryland; Fintan McKeown; Matthew Devitt; Eileen Dromey; Dermot Kerrigan; Brendan F. Dempsey; ***D:*** Kirk Jones; ***W:*** Kirk Jones; ***C:*** Henry Braham; ***M:*** Shaun Davey.

Waking the Dead 🦴🦴 1/2 **2000 (R)** Director Gordon's uneven but earnest adaptation of the Scott Spencer novel features Crudup as Fielding Pierce, an aspiring politician haunted by the death ten years earlier of his activist girlfriend Sarah (Connelly) in a car bombing. As Fielding begins a run at the Senate, he starts to see Sarah in crowds, wondering if the reports of her death were exaggerated, and doubting his sanity. The love story angle gets a lot of play, yet manages to be unconvincing, and the frequent jumps back and forth in time are jarring. Crudup and Connelly seem in over their heads at times. **105m/C; VHS, DVD, Blu-Ray.** Billy Crudup; Jennifer Connelly; Molly Parker; Janet McTeer; Paul Hipp; Sandra Oh; Hal Holbrook; Lawrence Dane; ***D:*** Keith Gordon; ***W:*** Robert Dillon; ***C:*** Tom Richmond; ***M:*** tomandandy.

Waking Up in Reno 🦴 1/2 **2002 (R)** Redneck road pic where romance goes awry for two couples on the way to a monster truck show in Nevada. Ringleader is Little Rock car dealer Lonnie Earl (Thornton), who fools around on his wife Darlene (Richardson) with the aptly named Candy (Theron) under the nose of his best friend and Candy's husband Roy (Swayze). Candy, who desperately wants to get pregnant, is always fooling around in the back seat with Roy while Lonnie enters a steak eating contest. Cruz appears as a hooker Roy meets in a sleazy hotel bar. Flimsy setup gives way to the disappointing payoff, and you soon realize its all over but the shouting. **100m/C; VHS, DVD.** Billy Bob Thornton; Charlize Theron; Patrick Swayze; Natasha Richardson; Holmes Osborne; Chelcie Ross; Brent Briscoe; Wayne Federman; Penelope Cruz; Mark Fauser; ***Cameo(s):*** Tony Orlando; ***D:*** Jordan Brady; ***W:*** Brent Briscoe; Mark Fauser; ***C:*** William A. Fraker; ***M:*** Marty Stuart.

Waking Up Wally **2005** Innocuously-told true story based on hockey dad Walter Gretzky (McCamus), whose debilitating brain aneurysm made him forget, among other things, his famous son Wayne's (Holden-Reid) sports achievements. The family struggles through rehabilitation as Walter's lack of short-term memory leads to frustration before he (and they) can accept his limitations. Based on the memoir "Walter Gretzky: On Family, Hockey and Healing." **?m/CDVD.** *CA* Tom McCamus; Kris Holden-Ried; Victoria Snow; Tara Spencer-Nairn; Carey Feeham; ***D:*** Dean Bennett; ***W:*** Carol Hay; ***C:*** Roger Vernon; ***M:*** Christopher Dedrick. **TV**

Wal-Mart: The High Cost of Low Price 🦴🦴🦴 1/2 **2005** Greenwald's latest documentary investigates the economic impact of the retail giant on everyday people, from its own workers to competing business owners in rural areas to the consumer in general. Gives voice to the views of those opposed to the practices of the company. **98m/C; DVD.** ***D:*** Robert Greenwald; ***C:*** Kristy Tully; ***M:*** John (Gianni) Frizzell.

The Walk 🦴🦴 **2015 (PG)** Zemeckis pulls every technically marvelous trick out of his bag to recreate something we haven't really seen in film before—a 3D high-wire act between the Twin Towers, the one notoriously performed by Philippe Petit in 1974 and chronicled in the Oscar-winning "Man on Wire." The result is a film that looks great but feels hollow, especially in its first, interminable hour before the actual feat. Gordon-Levitt plays Petit, who is captured as a force of nature, always scheming and dreaming his way to the impossible. The actual walk is amazing but the narration that tells us exactly what Petit was thinking and feeling was a tragic mistake. **100m/C; DVD, Blu-Ray.** Joseph Gordon-Levitt; Charlotte Le Bon; Ben Kingsley; James Badge Dale; Ben Schwartz; ***D:*** Robert Zemeckis; ***W:*** Robert Zemeckis; Christopher Browne; ***C:*** Dariusz Wolski; ***M:*** Alan Silvestri.

Walk a Crooked Mile 🦴 1/2 **1948** Red Scare pic. After a security leak is discovered at a California atomic plant, FBI agent Dan O'Hara is partnered with Scotland Yard detective Philip Grayson. The case takes them to San Francisco and a communist spy ring. Documentary-style filming is enhanced by location shooting. **91m/B; DVD.** Dennis O'Keefe; Louis Hayward; Onslow Stevens; Louise Allbritton; Carl Esmond; Raymond Burr; Philip Van Zandt; ***D:*** Gordon Douglas; ***W:*** George Bruce; ***C:*** George Robinson; ***M:*** Paul Sawtell.

A Walk Among the Tombstones 🦴🦴 1/2 **2014 (R)** Neeson goes a little darker, turning to noir from the action genre that has made him a surprisingly robust star in his later career. He stars in writer/director Frank's surprisingly brutal film as Matt Scudder, a former cop turned private eye. A drug dealer's wife has been kidnapped and killed, and the dealer (Stevens) needs Scudder's help to find the people responsible. A bit misanthropic and violent, viewers should be warned that this is more depressing than escapism. Adapted from the Lawrence Block novel. **114m/C; DVD, Blu-Ray.** Liam Neeson; Dan Stevens; Brian "Astro" Bradley; David Harbour; Adam David Thompson; ***D:*** Scott Frank; ***W:*** Scott Frank; ***C:*** Mihai Malaimare, Jr.; ***M:*** Carlos Rafael Rivera.

Walk, Don't Run 🦴🦴 1/2 **1966** Romantic comedy involving a British businessman (Grant) unable to find a hotel room in Tokyo due to the crowds staying for the 1964 summer Olympic Games. He winds up renting a room from an Embassy secretary (Eggar) and then meets and invites Hutton, a member of the U.S. Olympic walking team, also without a place to stay, to share it with him. Grant then proceeds to play matchmaker, despite the fact that Eggar has a fiance. Grant's last film. Innocuous, unnecessary remake of "The More the Merrier." **114m/C; VHS, DVD.** Cary Grant; Samantha Eggar; Jim Hutton; John Standing; Miiko Taka; ***D:*** Charles Walters; ***M:*** Quincy Jones.

Walk East on Beacon 🦴 1/2 **1952** Red scare propaganda based on a "Reader's Digest" story credited to J. Edgar Hoover. Boston FBI agent Belden is assigned to find the commies behind a security leak. Top Soviet spy Alex is blackmailing refugee scientist Kafer, who notifies the feds. But that spy's no dummy and he kidnaps Kafer, intending to spirit him back to the U.S.S.R. by sub. **98m/B; DVD.** George Murphy; Karel Stepanek; Finlay Currie; Virginia Gilmore; Peter Capell; ***D:*** Alfred Werker; ***W:*** Leo Rosten; ***C:*** Joseph Brun; ***M:*** Louis Applebaum.

Walk Hard: The Dewey Cox Story 🦴 1/2 **2007 (R)** Yet another double entendre smut-fest from screenwriter Apatow (and director/writer Kasdan), who mock every music bio cliche they can twang a guitar at. Reilly goes silly for his title role as a white boy singer (with a family tragedy that haunts him) who gets that devil rock 'n' roll in his soul and finds it leads to drugs and debauchery, if not the love of a woman (Fisher) too good for him. Much like a novelty record it's clever for a moment but repeated exposure may cause brain damage. **96m/C; DVD, Blu-Ray.** John C. Reilly; Jenna Fischer; Raymond J. Barry; Kristen Wiig; Tim Meadows; Harold Ramis; Margo Martindale; Chris Parnell; Matt Besser; David Krumholtz; Frankie Muniz; Jack White; Justin Long; Paul Rudd; Jason Schwartzman; Rance Howard; Martin Starr; Jack McBrayer; Jane Lynch; Simon Helberg; Jack Black; John Michael Higgins; Jonah Hill; Craig Robinson; ***D:*** Jake Kasdan; ***W:*** Jake Kasdan; Judd Apatow; ***C:*** Uta Briesewitz; ***M:*** Michael Andrews.

A Walk in My Shoes 🦴🦴 1/2 **2010** In this NBC TV movie, overbearing high school teacher Trish Fahey is frustrated by underachieving students and blames bad parenting. When popular basketball star Justin Kremer consistently underperforms in her class, Trish has him suspended from the team. After meeting mysterious Molly, Trish has a car accident and wakes up as Cindy Kremer, Justin's hard-pressed single mom and learns what the Kremer family's life is really like. **84m/C; DVD.** Nancy Travis; Jackson Pace; Cameron Deane Stewart; Jana Lee Hamblin; Yara Martinez; Philip Winchester; ***D:*** John Kent Harrison; ***W:*** Wesley Bishop; ***M:*** Lawrence Shragge. **TV**

A Walk in the Clouds 🦴🦴 1/2 **1995 (PG-13)** Gorgeously photographed, if sappy, romantic fantasy finds WWII vet Paul Sutton

(Reeves), returning to his unhappy marriage and salesman job. So when the good-hearted Paul meets beautiful Victoria (Sanchez-Gijon), the pregnant and unmarried daughter of a possessive Napa vineyard owner (Giannini), he's more than happy to help by posing as her husband. Naturally, dad is livid at their "marriage" and Paul falls in love with his sham bride. Quinn gets to do his part as wise family patriarch and yes, there's even a grape harvest (and some grape stomping) to put everyone in the proper romantic mood. Based on the 1942 Italian film "Four Steps in the Clouds." **103m/C; VHS, DVD.** Keanu Reeves; Aitana Sanchez-Gijon; Giancarlo Giannini; Anthony Quinn; Angelica Aragon; Evangelina Elizondo; Freddy Rodriguez; Debra Messing; ***D:*** Alfonso Arau; ***W:*** Robert Mark Kamen; ***C:*** Emmanuel Lubezki; ***M:*** Leo Brouwer. Golden Globes '96: Score.

Walk in the Spring Rain 1/2 **1970 (PG)** The bored wife of a college professor follows him to rural Tennessee when he goes on sabbatical, where she meets the married Quinn and the two begin an affair. When Quinn's disturbed son learns of the affair, he attacks the woman, with tragic results. Fine cast should have had better effect on low-key script. **98m/C; VHS, DVD, Streaming.** Ingrid Bergman; Anthony Quinn; Fritz Weaver; Katherine Crawford; Tom Fielding; Virginia Gregg; ***D:*** Guy Green; ***W:*** Stirling Silliphant; ***C:*** Charles B(ryant) Lang, Jr.; ***M:*** Elmer Bernstein.

A Walk in the Sun 1/2 *Salerno Beachhead* **1946** The trials of a group of infantrymen in WWII from the time they land in Italy to the time they capture their objective, a farmhouse occupied by the Germans. Excellent ensemble acting shows well the variety of civilians who make up any fighting force and explores their fears, motivations, and weaknesses. Producer and director Milestone also made "All Quiet on the Western Front" and the Korean War masterpiece "Pork Chop Hill." Released in the final days of the war, almost concurrently with two other WWII films of the first echelon, "The Story of G.I. Joe" and "They Were Expendable." **117m/B; VHS, DVD.** Dana Andrews; Richard Conte; John Ireland; Lloyd Bridges; Sterling Holloway; George Tyne; Norman Lloyd; Herbert Rudley; Richard Benedict; Huntz Hall; James B. Cardwell; George Offerman, Jr.; Steve Brodie; Matt Willis; Alvin Hammer; Chris Drake; Victor Cutler; Jay Norris; ***D:*** Lewis Milestone; ***W:*** Robert Rossen; Harry Brown; ***C:*** Russell Harlan; ***M:*** Freddie Rich; Earl Robinson. Natl. Film Reg. '16.

A Walk in the Woods **2015 (R)** A well-meaning but inert film, Kwapis' dramedy proved that there's no audience out there not tapped by Hollywood to make a profit off of. Bill Bryson (Redford) has spent two decades in England and seeks to reconnect with his beloved United States by hiking the Appalachian Trail with his buddy Stephen Katz (Nolte). The two bicker and reconnect as they wander through the woods and audiences doze off. It's a well-meaning but flat movie that's not bad if you just want to spend a couple hours with two legends. **105m/C; DVD, Blu-Ray.** Robert Redford; Nick Nolte; Emma Thompson; Mary Steenburgen; Kristen Schaal; Nick Offerman; ***D:*** Ken Kwapis; ***W:*** Michael Arndt; Bill Holderman; ***C:*** John Bailey; ***M:*** Nathan Larson.

Walk Like a Man 1/2 **1987 (PG)** In a take-off of Tarzan movies, Mandel plays a man raised by wolves. Comic problems arise when he is found by his mother and the family attempts to civilize him. Juvenile script wastes fine cast. **86m/C; VHS, DVD.** Howie Mandel; Christopher Lloyd; Cloris Leachman; Colleen Camp; Amy Steel; George DiCenzo; ***D:*** Melvin Frank.

Walk of Shame **2014 (R)** Contrived, unfunny farce that wastes the comedic talents of Banks. After L.A. newscaster Meghan is dumped by her fiancée and passed over for a promotion, she gets drunk and has a one-night stand with bartender Gordon (Marsden). She learns the promotion is possible after all, but she must get across town for an interview, though she's now minus her car, phone, and purse, under trying circumstances (including being repeatedly mistaken for a hooker). **95m/C; DVD, Blu-Ray.** Elizabeth Banks; James Marsden; Gillian Jacobs; Sarah Wright; Ethan Suplee; Bill Burr; Larry (Lawrence) Gilliard, Jr.; ***D:*** Steven Brill; ***W:*** Steven Brill; ***C:*** Jonathan Brown; ***M:*** John Debney.

A Walk on the Moon 1/2 **1999 (R)** Goldwyn's promising directorial debut has 30-ish, vaguely restless Jewish housewife Pearl (Lane) vacationing in the Catskills in the summer of 1969 with her family: teenage daughter Alison (Paquin), son Daniel (Boriello), and intrusive mother-in-law Lillian (Feldshuh). Hubby Marty (Schreiber) is working in the city and visits on the weekends. When sensitive hippie blouse peddler Walker (Mortensen) catches her eye, she decides it's time to catch up on the '60s and her lost teenage years. When she takes off for Woodstock and happens upon her daughter, the family drama is intensified. Pearl's turmoil and motivations are handled well by Lane and the screenwriter Gray, and neither of the men vying for her are cardboard stereotypes, but the abruptly feel-good ending may not work for some. **107m/C; VHS, DVD.** Diane Lane; Liev Schreiber; Viggo Mortensen; Anna Paquin; Tovah Feldshuh; Bobby Boriello; Lisa Bronwyn Moore; ***D:*** Tony Goldwyn; ***W:*** Pamela Gray; ***C:*** Anthony B. Richmond; ***M:*** Mason Daring.

Walk on the Wild Side **1962** In 1930s New Orleans, a man searches for his long-lost love, finds her working in a whorehouse and fights to save her from the lesbian madame Stanwyck. Melodrama, based only loosely on the Nelson Algren novel and adapted by cult novelist John Fante, with Edmund Morris. Much-troubled on the set, and it shows. **114m/B; DVD.** Jane Fonda; Laurence Harvey; Barbara Stanwyck; Capucine; Anne Baxter; ***D:*** Edward Dmytryk; ***W:*** John Fante; Edmund Morris; ***C:*** Joe MacDonald; ***M:*** Elmer Bernstein.

Walk the Dark Street 1/2 **1956** Big game hunter Frank Garrick is angry over his brother's death in Korea and blames his commanding officer, Dan Lawton, who has come to offer his condolences. He proposes a big bucks hunting 'game' on the L.A. streets and Dan agrees, not knowing the psycho has a deadly agenda. **72m/B; DVD.** Chuck Connors; Don Ross; Regina Gleason; ***D:*** Wyott Ordung; ***W:*** Wyott Ordung; ***C:*** Brydon Baker; ***M:*** Paul Dunlap.

Walk the Line 1/2 **2005 (PG-13)** Phoenix embodies The Man in Black, warts and all in this excellent biopic showing Johnny Cash's family strife, rise as an early 50s rock star, through his battle with drugs, and his long courtship of June Carter (an equally brilliant Witherspoon). Script and actors never shy away from the more disturbing aspects of Cash's personality and life, which makes for a powerful, if not always comfortable, film. Phoenix and Witherspoon did all their own singing, and they do it well enough to make you wonder if it's the real thing. **135m/C; DVD, Blu-Ray.** Joaquin Rafael (Leaf) Phoenix; Reese Witherspoon; Ginnifer Goodwin; Robert Patrick; Dallas Roberts; Larry Bagby; Dan John Miller; Shelby Lynne; Tyler Hilton; Waylon Malloy Payne; Shooter Jennings; ***D:*** James Mangold; ***W:*** James Mangold; Gill Dennis; ***C:*** Phedon Papamichael; ***M:*** T-Bone Burnett. Oscars '05: Actress (Witherspoon); British Acad. '05: Actress (Witherspoon), Sound; Golden Globes '06: Actor--Mus./Comedy (Phoenix), Actress--Mus./Comedy (Witherspoon), Film--Mus./Comedy; N.Y. Film Critics '05: Actress (Witherspoon); Natl. Soc. Film Critics '05: Actress (Witherspoon); Screen Actors Guild '05: Actress (Witherspoon).

A Walk to Remember 1/2 **2002 (PG)** Sweet and swoony teen romance with attractive leads, based on the Nicholas Sparks novel, and set in Beaufort, North Carolina. Popular student Landon Carter (West) gets into trouble for a school prank and must perform some afterschool community activities. This brings him into contact with Reverend Sullivan's (Coyote) serious daughter, Jamie (Moore), who thinks Landon's a doof. They both get over their misconceptions to start a romance but their new relationship is tested when Jamie reveals a heartbreaking secret. **101m/C; DVD.** Mandy Moore; Shane West; Peter Coyote; Daryl Hannah; Lauren German; Clayne Crawford; ***D:*** Adam Shankman; ***W:*** Karen Janszen; ***C:*** Julio Macat; ***M:*** Mervyn Warren.

Walkabout 1/2 **1971 (PG)** Beautifully told and filmed story (by Roeg in his debut) about a nameless young brother (John, Roeg's six-year-old son) and sister (Agutter), who are abandoned in the Australian outback when their father kills himself. The children wander, with little chance of survival, until a young aborigine (Gumpilil) finds them. He interrupts his own "walkabout," a rite of passage, to teach them to survive, leading to betrayal and tragedy. Based on a novel by James Vance Marshall. **100m/C; VHS, DVD.** *AU* Jenny Agutter; Lucien John; David Gulpilil; John Meillon; ***D:*** Nicolas Roeg; ***W:*** Edward Bond; ***C:*** Nicolas Roeg; ***M:*** John Barry.

Walker **1987 (R)** Slapdash, tongue-in-cheek historical pastiche about the real-life American William Walker (played previously in "Burn!" by Marlon Brando), and how he led a revolution in Nicaragua in 1855 and became its self-declared president. A bitter, revisionist farce never for a moment attempting to be accurate. Matlin's unfortunate, though fortunately brief, follow-up to her Oscar-winning performance. **95m/C; VHS, DVD.** Ed Harris; Richard Masur; Peter Boyle; Rene Auberjonois; Marlee Matlin; Miguel (Michael) Sandoval; ***D:*** Alex Cox; ***W:*** Rudy Wurlitzer; ***M:*** Joe Strummer.

The Walker 1/2 **2007 (R)** Carter (Harrelson), an extravagantly gay DC insider who spends most of his time escorting rich married women to public events, ends up in the middle of the investigation of the murder of a powerful Beltway lobbyist who was having an affair with Carter's married friend Lynn (Scott Thomas). In order to protect her and clear his own name, Carter must find the real killer himself while his carefully cultivated status in DC society collapses. Harrelson's performance stands out, but otherwise this is a run-of-the mill crime drama that flirts awkwardly with political commentary. **107m/C; On Demand.** *GB US* Woody Harrelson; Kristin Scott Thomas; Lauren Bacall; Lily Tomlin; Moritz Bleibtreu; Ned Beatty; Willem Dafoe; Geff Francis; Steven Hartley; Mary Beth Hurt; ***D:*** Paul Schrader; ***W:*** Paul Schrader; ***C:*** Chris Seager; ***M:*** Anne Dudley.

Walker Payne 1/2 **2006 (R)** Self-conscious drama with some strongly suggestive scenes of cruelty to animals. Walker Payne (Patric) is a divorced ex-con who's laid off from his mining job in rural Illinois in the late 1950s. Walker's hateful ex-wife Luanne (de Matteo) won't let him near his daughters until he hands over $5K so she can go to nursing school. His one potential asset is entering his faithful pit bull Brute in a backwoods dogfighting match. **117m/C; DVD.** Jason Patric; Drea De Matteo; KaDee Strickland; Sam Shepard; Bruce Dern; ***D:*** Matt Williams; ***W:*** Alex Paraskevas; ***C:*** James L. Carter; ***M:*** Mason Daring.

Walker: Texas Ranger: One Riot, One Ranger 1/2 **1993 (PG-13)** Norris sticks with the action-adventure mode with this tv pilot movie about Cordell Walker, a good guy with a code and some martial arts skills, who teams up with an ex-gridiron star and a female district attorney to go after lawbreakers. This time its bank robbers and three hoods after a teenaged girl. **96m/C; VHS, DVD.** Chuck Norris; Sheree J. Wilson; Clarence Gilyard, Jr.; Gailard Sartain; Floyd "Red Crow" Westerman; James Drury; ***D:*** Virgil W. Vogel; ***W:*** Louise McCarn. **TV**

Walking and Talking 1/2 **1996 (R)** Low-budget, lighthearted estrogen romp through the lives of two best friends in New York, Amelia (Keener) and Laura (Heche), going through commitment crises. Freshman writer/director Holofcener scores by making a lackluster story imminently watchable. Likable cast of mostly unknowns (Heche was deemed a rising star at a recent Cannes Festival) deliver Holofcener's clever and humorous exchanges. Corrigan's video store clerk and all-around "ugly guy" is a highlight. Brit Bragg brings in a worthy score. **86m/C; VHS, DVD.** Anne Heche; Catherine Keener; Liev Schreiber; Todd Field; Kevin Corrigan; Randall Batinkoff; Joseph Siravo; Vincent Pastore; Lynn Cohen; Andrew Holofcener; ***D:*** Nicole Holofcener; ***W:*** Nicole Holofcener; ***C:*** Michael Spiller; ***M:*** Billy Bragg.

Walking Deceased *Walking with the Dead* **2015 (R)** A satiric/comic take on the zombie apocalypse. After being hospitalized and in a coma for six weeks, Sheriff Lincoln (Sheridan) wakes up to find the world is a month into a zombie takeover. He connects with a group of survivors which include four who guy by the names of their favorite cities for safety reasons and the sheriff's entreprenuerial-minded 10-year-old son Chris (Galyon). Also part of the group is Romeo (Ogletree), a zombie with a penchant for voiceovers who has convinced the group he is really not a zombie but just slow. The ragtag group is forced from their safe minicamp to find a rumored safe haven, leading to unexpected dangers. **88m/C; DVD, Download.** Dave Sheridan; Mason Dakota Galyon; Troy Ogletree; Tim Ogletree; Joey Oglesby; ***D:*** Scott Dow; ***W:*** Tim Ogletree; ***C:*** Shaun Hart.

Walking on Water **2002** Gavin (Bonney) has been suffering from leukemia for a long time and has asked his friends and housemates—Charlie (Colosimo), Anna (Theodorakis), and Frank (Bishop)?to help him die with dignity at home. In the end, this means Charlie must quietly assist Gavin's suicide, which leaves him haunted by grief and guilt. He's not the only one unable to cope as Gavin's friends and family all struggle in their separate ways. **90m/C; VHS, DVD.** *AU* Vince Colosimo; Maria Theodorakis; Nicholas Bishop; Nathaniel Dean; Judi Farr; David Bonney; Anne Lise Phillips; Daniel Roberts; ***D:*** Tony Ayres; ***W:*** Roger Monk; ***C:*** Robert Humphreys; ***M:*** Antony Partos. Australian Film Inst. '02: Actor (Dean), Actress (Theodorakis), Screenplay, Support. Actress (Farr).

Walking Out 1/2 **2017 (PG-13)** Based on a 1988 short story by David Quammen, this wilderness adventure by filmmaker siblings Alex and Andrew Smith offers a respectable exploration of how one teen connects with his estranged father and learns the depth of his inner strength. A 14-year-old suburban dweller, David (Wiggins) visits his father Cal (Bomer), an outdoorsman and survivalist, in Montana. When Cal takes David on a moose hunting trip deep in the mountains, things go wrong from the first and David is forced to take action to ensure their survival. **95m/C; DVD, Blu-Ray.** Matt Bomer; Josh Wiggins; Bill Pullman; Alex Neustaedter; Lily Gladstone; ***D:*** Alex Smith; Andrew J. Smith; ***W:*** Alex Smith; Andrew J. Smith; ***C:*** Todd McMullen; ***M:*** Ernst Reijseger.

The Walking Stick **1970** Having a leg withered by polio gives Deborah (Eggar) low self-esteem, leaving her romantically vulnerable to the charms of artist Leigh Hartley (Hemmings). She works at an upscale London auction house and Leigh persuades Deborah to help him with a jewel heist he says is to set up their future together. Adapted from a Winston Graham novel. **101m/C; DVD.** *UK* Samantha Eggar; David Hemmings; Emlyn Williams; Phyllis Calvert; Ferdinand "Ferdy" Mayne; Francesca Annis; ***D:*** Eric Till; ***W:*** George Bluestone; ***C:*** Arthur Ibbetson; ***M:*** Stanley Myers.

Walking Tall 1/2 **1973 (R)** A Tennessee sheriff takes a stand against syndicate-run gambling and his wife is murdered in response. Ultra-violent crime saga wowed the movie going public and spawned several sequels and a TV series. Based on the true story of folk-hero Buford Pusser, admirably rendered by Baker. **126m/C; VHS, DVD, Blu-Ray.** Joe Don Baker; Elizabeth Hartman; Noah Beery, Jr.; Gene Evans; Rosemary Murphy; Felton Perry; ***D:*** Phil Karlson; ***W:*** Mort Briskin; ***C:*** Jack Marta; ***M:*** Walter Scharf.

Walking Tall 1/2 **2004 (PG-13)** Changes abound in this ho hum retelling of the 1973 version as the good guy now goes by Chris Vaughn (The Rock) who's single and lives in Washington. Luckily, he's still carrying the big stick and taking care of business (although, oddly enough, director Bray contemplated swapping it out for an aluminum bat—c'mon, is nothing sacred?) And he does just that with the authority one would expect from The Rock, whose presence is commanding yet surprisingly subtle (something he could not have learned from his wrestling days) allowing him to rise above the mediocre script and sub-par character development. Johnny Knoxville effectively serves as the comic-relief/sidekick guy while Neal McDonough sleepwalks through what could have been a fun villain role. **86m/C; VHS, DVD, Blu-Ray.** Dwayne "The Rock" Johnson; Johnny Knoxville; Neal McDonough; Kristen Wilson; Khleo Thomas; John Beasley; Barbara Tarbuck; Michael Bowen; Ashley Scott; ***D:*** Kevin Bray; ***W:*** David Klass; Channing Gibson; David Levien; Brian Koppelman; *C:* Glen MacPherson; *M:* Graeme Revell.

Walking Tall: Lone Justice 🦴 **2007 (R)** Low-grade actioner that has nothing to do with the original franchise. Sheriff Nick Prescott (Sorbo) has retired but it doesn't last long when he's caught up in a federal case against a drug lord and his gang who are determined to wipe out all witnesses. **94m/C; DVD.** Kevin Sorbo; Haley Ramm; Laurent Martin; Rodrigo De La Rosa; Jennifer Sipes; *D:* Tripp Reed; *W:* Joe Halpin; Ben Strassmann; *C:* Jas Shelton; *M:* Eric Wurst; David Wurst. **VIDEO**

Walking Tall: Part 2 🦴🦴 **1975 (PG)** Club-wielding Tennessee sheriff Buford Pusser, this time played less memorably by Svenson, attempts to find the man who killed his wife. Even more violent than the original. **109m/C; VHS, DVD, Blu-Ray.** Bo Svenson; Noah Beery, Jr.; Angel Tompkins; Richard Jaeckel; *D:* Earl Bellamy.

Walking Tall: The Final Chapter 🦴 1/2 **1977 (PG)** The final months in the life of Tennessee sheriff Buford Pusser and the mystery surrounding his death. It wasn't the final chapter. Still to come: a TV flick and series. **112m/C; VHS, DVD, Blu-Ray.** Bo Svenson; Forrest Tucker; Leif Garrett; Morgan Woodward; *D:* Jack Starrett; *C:* Robert B. Hauser.

Walking Tall: The Payback 🦴 1/2 **2007 (R)** Nick Prescott (Sorbo) returns to his hometown in time to see the redneck mafia murder his father. Since no one else seems interested in pursuing it, he initiates a traditional bar brawl to let the bad guys know he's a comin' for them. **88m/C; DVD.** Kevin Sorbo; Richard Dillard; A.J. Buckley; Bentley Mitchum; Gail Cronauer; Eric Wurst; *D:* Tripp Reed; *W:* Brian Strasmann; *C:* Jas Shelton; *M:* David Wurst.

Walking the Edge 🦴 1/2 **1983 (R)** A widow hires a taxi driver to help her seek vengeance against the men who killed her husband and her son. Forster does what he can with the lousy story and script. **94m/C; VHS, DVD.** Robert Forster; Nancy Kwan; Joe Spinell; Aarika Wells; *D:* Norbert Meisel; *W:* Curt Allen; *C:* Ernie Poulos; *M:* Jay Chattaway.

Walking the Halls 🦴 1/2 **2012** Lurid Lifetime drama is cluttered with too many issues. L.A. high school senior Casey Benson is having problems at home with her parents' marriage disintegrating so she's flattered when Amber, leader of the popular girls, invites her to join them in some fun. That 'fun' turns out to be a prostitution ring organized by school security guard, Jack, who gives Casey trouble when she wants out. **90m/C; DVD.** Caitlin Thompson; Marie Avgeropoulos; Jamie Luner; Matthew Alan; Al Sapienza; Lindsay Taylor; Arden Cho; *D:* Doug Campbell; *W:* Doug Campbell; *C:* Eric Anderson; *M:* Steve Gurevitch. **CABLE**

Walking Thunder 🦴🦴 1/2 **1994 (PG)** The McKay family are stranded in the Rocky Mountains in 1850 when their wagon is destroyed by a grizzly bear. But they're rescued by a mountain man (Read) and a Sioux medicine man (Thin Elk), who introduce young Jacob to a number of adventures. It's wholesome, old-fashioned kid entertainment. **95m/C; VHS, DVD.** John Denver; James Read; David Tom; Chief Ted Thin Elk; *Nar:* Brian Keith; *D:* Craig Clyde; *W:* Craig Clyde; *M:* John Scott.

Walking with Dinosaurs 3D 🦴 1/2 **2013 (PG)** CGI dinosaurs against real backgrounds might have been interesting if the creators of this awful film had any respect for either their audience or their subject matter. Alex (Leguizamo) is a prehistoric bird who narrates the tale of three dinosaurs (Long, Sircar, Stone) on their journey from youth to adulthood. The paper-thin script makes "Ice Age" sequels look dense, and the inept plot is just an excuse for CGI effects and juvenile humor to get little ones through the brief running time. The voice work is awful--and with no educational or entertainment value whatsoever, this flick needs to be extinct. **87m/C; DVD, Blu-Ray.** *V:* Karl Urban; John Leguizamo; Justin Long; *D:* Barry Cook; Neil Nightingale; *W:* John Collee; *C:* John Brooks; *M:* Paul Leonard-Morgan.

Walking with the Enemy 🦴 1/2 **2013 (PG-13)** Clumsy WWII thriller very loosely based on real events, desperate to inspire and uplift. In a courageous move, fictitious Hungarian peasant Elek Cohen (Armstrong) slips into the disguise of a Nazi officer to track down his dislocated family. Once in awhile, the story distracts itself with scenes that seem to be from a different, and much better, movie altogether, focusing on strong-willed Hungarian leader Horthy (Kingsley) and his battles with Nazi questioning. In the end, this cliched military drama tries to cram too many big ideas into a small movie, and too much gloss into a low-budget indie. **124m/C; DVD.** Jonas Armstrong; Hannah Tointon; Ben Kingsley; Burn Gorman; *D:* Mark Schmidt; *W:* Kenny Golde; *C:* Dean Cundey; *M:* Tim Williams.

The Wall 🦴🦴🦴 1/2 *Guney's The Wall; Le Mur; Duvar* **1983** The last film by Guney, author of "Yol," about orphaned boys in prison in the Turkish capitol of Ankara trying to escape and/or rebel after ceaseless rapings, beatings and injustice. An acclaimed, disturbing film made from Guney's own experience. He died in 1984, three years after escaping from prison. Brutal and horrifying. In Turkish with English subtitles. **117m/C; VHS, DVD.** *TU* Ayse Emel Mesci; Saban; Sisko; *D:* Yilmaz Guney; *W:* Yilmaz Guney.

The Wall 🦴🦴🦴 **1999** Three stories that focus on the Vietnam Veterans Memorial and some of the objects left there. "The Pencil Holder" finds young Ben Holst (Blumas) living with his stiff-necked Army colonel father (Olmos) in Saigon in 1969 where he's mistaken by a dying soldier (Chevolleau) for his own son. "The Badge" is the good-luck toy sheriff's badge that black soldier Bracey Mitchell (Glover) clings to as he hides from the Vietcong and dreams of home. "The Player" is conniving wheeler-dealer Bishop (Whaley), who runs a base nightclub and gets his comeuppance from self-sacrificing soldier Luis (DeLorenzo), who's a guitar-playing whiz. **94m/C; DVD.** Edward James Olmos; Richard Chevolleau; Trevor Blumas; Dean McDermott; Savion Glover; Ruby Dee; Martin Roach; Linette Robinson; Frank Whaley; Michael Delorenzo; Ron White; Matthew Ferguson; *D:* Joseph Sargent; *W:* Scott Abbott; Charles Fuller; Patrick Sheane Duncan; *C:* Donald M. Morgan; *M:* Larry Brown. **CABLE**

Wall 🦴🦴🦴 1/2 *Mur* **2004** Documentary from veteran filmmaker Simone Bitton. This time she takes on the security fence being erected to divide Israel from the West Bank. Use of the term "wall" gives a hint of the filmmaker's opinion of the security fence. Israeli officials resist the use of any term apart from "fence." The strength of this documentary is in its balanced view. While showing the wall from many locations it is never clear what side of the wall is being viewed. Ultimately the wall reveals itself as a divider of people and land that neither Israelis nor Palestinians embrace. **98m/C; DVD.** *D:* Simone Bitton; *W:* Simone Bitton; *C:* Jacques Bouquin.

The Wall 🦴 1/2 **2013** Pretension overwhelms character, logic, and entertainment in this adaptation of Marlen Haushofer's hit novel. Gedeck plays the unnamed lead (and virtually only) character, a woman who goes to a remote hunting cottage only to find herself surrounding by an invisible wall. With only a dog and a cow as companions, she is forced to live off the land for an undefined number of years, keeping a detailed diary, which makes up the bulk of the film's storytelling. Beautiful vistas can't hide the lack of relatable behavior. **108m/C; DVD.** *GE AT* Martina Gedeck; *D:* Julian Polsler; *W:* Julian Polsler; *C:* Markus Fraunholz; Martin Gschlacht; Bernhard Keller.

The Wall 🦴🦴 1/2 **2017 (R)** After victory has been declared in Iraq, an American sniper (Cena) and his spotter (Taylor-Johnson) are pinned down by an unseen enemy sniper. Liman's taut, claustrophobic thriller shows what he can do given excellent material to work with. Not all of the plot works, but Liman is able to limit the damage with driving intensity and ferocity. **90m/C; DVD, Blu-Ray.** Aaron Taylor-Johnson; John Cena; Laith Nakli; *D:* Doug Liman; *W:* Dwain Worrell; *C:* Roman Vasyanov.

WALL-E 🦴🦴🦴 1/2 **2008 (G)** Another winner from Pixar that's both sweet and edgy (that whole global disaster thing is a bummer). Lonely robot WALL-E (Waste Allocation Load Lifter Earth-Class) has been cleaning up Earth for 700 years after it was abandoned by those destructive, messy humans. Sleek droid EVE (Extra-terrestrial Vegetation Evaluator) comes calling to see if it's okay for humans to return and WALL-E is instantly smitten. So when EVE completes her assignment, WALL-E latches on and returns with her to Axiom, the giant spaceship housing the couch potato consumers that barely pass for human to let them know the big news. Oscar-winning sound designer Ben Burtt provides WALL-E's beeps, boops, and other noises. **97m/C; Blu-Ray.** *V:* Fred Willard; Jeff Garlin; Ben Burtt; Sigourney Weaver; Kathy Najimy; John Ratzenberger; Elissa Knight; *D:* Andrew Stanton; *W:* Andrew Stanton; Jim Reardon; *C:* Jeremy Lasky; *M:* Thomas Newman. Oscars '08: Animated Film; British Acad. '08: Animated Film; Golden Globes '09: Animated Film.

Wall of Noise 🦴 1/2 **1963** After fighting with his girlfriend (Provine), horse trainer Joel Tarrant (Hardin) takes a job with contractor Matt Rubio (Meeker) whose younger wife, Laura (Pleshette), is more interested in man flesh than horse flesh. When the husband gets wise, Joel is fired, so he borrows money to buy a promising horse to enter in a race. Pic doesn't end as you may expect. **112m/B; DVD.** Ty Hardin; Suzanne Pleshette; Ralph Meeker; Dorothy Provine; Simon Oakland; Murray Matheson; *D:* Richard Wilson; *W:* Joseph Landon; *C:* Lucien Ballard; *M:* William Lava.

Wall Street 🦴🦴🦴 **1987 (R)** Stone's energetic, high-minded big business treatise in which naive, neophyte stockbroker Bud Fox (Charlie Sheen) is seduced into insider trading by sleek entrepreneur Gordon Gekko (Douglas), much to his blue-collar father's (Martin Sheen) chagrin. A fast-moving drama of '80s-style materialism with a mesmerizing, award-winning performance by Douglas as greed personified. Expert direction by Stone, who co-wrote the not-very-subtle script. His father, to whom this film is dedicated, was a broker. Look for Stone in a cameo. **126m/C; VHS, DVD, Blu-Ray.** Michael Douglas; Charlie Sheen; Martin Sheen; Daryl Hannah; Sean Young; James Spader; Hal Holbrook; Terence Stamp; Richard Dysart; John C. McGinley; Saul Rubinek; James Karen; Josh Mostel; Millie Perkins; Cecilia Peck; Grant Shaud; Franklin Cover; Oliver Stone; Paul Guilfoyle; *D:* Oliver Stone; *W:* Oliver Stone; Stanley Weiser; *C:* Robert Richardson; *M:* Stewart Copeland. Oscars '87: Actor (Douglas); Golden Globes '88: Actor--Drama (Douglas); Natl. Bd. of Review '87: Actor (Douglas); Golden Raspberries '87: Worst Support. Actress (Hannah).

Wall Street 2: Money Never Sleeps 🦴🦴 **2010 (PG-13)** Gordon Gekko's (Douglas) "greed is good" mantra from Stone's 1987 pic is updated when he tries for a second chance after being released from prison. Wall Street broker Jake Moore (LaBeouf), who's involved with Gordon's estranged daughter Winnie (Mulligan), needs him as a mentor in a personal vendetta against slick financial raider Bretton James (Brolin) just as the global financial markets begin their collapse. A treat to see Douglas as Gekko again but the movie itself doesn't hold up to the high standards of the original. **133m/C; DVD, Blu-Ray.** Michael Douglas; Shia LaBeouf; Carey Mulligan; Frank Langella; Josh Brolin; Susan Sarandon; Vanessa Ferlito; Eli Wallach; Austin Pendleton; *D:* Oliver Stone; *W:* Allan Loeb; Stephen Schiff; *C:* Rodrigo Prieto; *M:* Craig Armstrong.

Wallace & Gromit in The Curse of the Were-Rabbit 🦴🦴🦴 1/2 **2005 (G)** Will appeal to adult audiences more than a stop-action animation film would at first seem to warrant. But don't worry, there's still plenty for the kiddies. The dynamic duo is faced with the responsibility of guarding the gardens for miles around in preparation for the annual Giant Vegetable Fete. But rabbits are eating all of the vegetables! Inventor Wallace comes up with a humane way to solve the pesky bunny issue, but it's more complicated than that. The painstakingly millimeter by millimeter claymation is impressive enough. That the characters manage to be expressive, and hilarious, is sheer brilliance. **85m/C; DVD, Blu-Ray.** *GB V:* Peter Sallis; Ralph Fiennes; Helena Bonham Carter; Nicholas C. Smith; Liz Smith; Peter Kay; *D:* Nick Park; Steve Box; *W:* Nick Park; Steve Box; Bob Baker; Mark Burton; *C:* Tristan Oliver; Dave Alex-Riddett; *M:* Julian Nott; Hans Zimmer. Oscars '05: Animated Film; L.A. Film Critics '05: Animated Film; Broadcast Film Critics '05: Animated Film.

Wallenberg: A Hero's Story 🦴🦴🦴 **1985** Excellent TV biopic based on the true story of Swedish diplomat Raoul Wallenberg (Chamberlain), who came from a wealthy Christian banking family, and who worked at the Swedish embassy in WWII Budapest. Disgusted by the Nazis, he arranges for the escape of more than 100,000 Hungarian Jews by claiming they are Swedish citizens. He earns the enmity of a radical Adolf Eichmann (Colley) but Wallenberg's still unknown fate came at the hands of the Soviets and his probable disappearance into a gulag prison. **188m/C; DVD.** Richard Chamberlain; Alice Krige; Kenneth Colley; Melanie Mayron; Stuart Wilson; Bibi Andersson; David Robb; Mark Rylance; *D:* Lamont Johnson; *W:* Gerald Green; *C:* Charles Correll; *M:* Ernest Gold. **TV**

Walls of Glass 🦴🦴 1/2 *Flanagan* **1985 (R)** An aging New York cabby tries to make it as an actor. Effective performances by all override the thin plot. Slow and uneven, but involving. **85m/C; VHS, DVD.** Geraldine Page; Philip Bosco; William Hickey; Olympia Dukakis; Brian Bloom; Linda Thorson; *D:* Scott Goldstein.

The Walls of Hell 🦴🦴 *Intramuros* **1964** Lt. Jim Sorenson (Mahoney) leads guerilla fighters into the city of Manila, aided by freedom fighter Nardo (Poe), to defeat desperate Japanese troops hold up in the city. **88m/B; VHS, DVD.** *PH* Jock Mahoney; Fernando Poe, Jr.; Mike Parsons; *D:* Gerardo (Gerry) De Leon; Eddie Romero; *W:* Eddie Romero; Cesar Amigo; Ferde Grofe, Jr.; *C:* Felipe Sacdalan; *M:* Tito Arevalo.

Walter and Henry 🦴🦴🦴 **2001** Walter (Larroquette) and his 12-year-old son Henry (Braun) live in a trailer in Brooklyn and (barely) make ends meet as street musicians in the city. However, after Walter has a psychotic breakdown and is institutionalized, Henry is forced to live with his rigid grandfather (Coburn) from whom Walter has been estranged for years. And slowly, Henry begins to adapt, and even enjoy, his new life. **90m/C; VHS, DVD.** John Larroquette; James Coburn; Kate Nelligan; Nicholas Braun; *D:* Daniel Petrie; *W:* Geoffrey Sharp; *C:* Michael Storey; *M:* Christopher Dedrick. **CABLE**

Waltz across Texas 🦴🦴 1/2 **1983** Young oil man Jastrow and good-lookin' rock scientist Archer at first don't take to each other, but there's something in the air, and romance blossoms. Jastrow and Archer cowrote and coproduced, and cohabitated as spouses in real-life. **100m/C; VHS, DVD.** Terry Jastrow; Anne Archer; Mary Kay Place; Richard Farnsworth; *D:* Ernest Day; *C:* Robert Elswit.

Waltz King 🦴🦴 **1963** Typically hokey Disney biography of the young composer Johann Strauss during his Old Viennese heyday. Fine music, pretty German locations. Well-made family fare. **94m/C; VHS, DVD.** Kerwin Mathews; Senta Berger; Brian Aherne; *D:* Steve Previn.

Waltz of the Toreadors 🦴🦴🦴 *The Amorous General* **1962** Retired general Sellers doesn't care for his wealthy, shrewish wife and tries to re-kindle a 17-year-old romance with a French woman. It doesn't work out (seems his illegitimate son also has a soft spot for the lady), but the general decides to keep his eyes open for other possibilities. Interestingly cast adaptation of Jean Anouilh's play. Sellers is hilarious, as usual. **105m/C; VHS, DVD.** *GB* Peter Sellers; Dany Robin; Margaret Leighton; Cyril Cusack; *D:* John Guillermin; *W:* Wolf Mankowitz; *C:* John Wilcox; *M:* Richard Addinsell.

A Waltz Through the Hills 🦴🦴 **1988** Two orphans head into the Australian outback and experience many adventures en route to the coast where they can set sail for England and their grandparents. Aired on PBS as part of the "Wonderworks" series. **116m/C; VHS, DVD.** Tina Kemp; Andre Jansen; Ernie Dingo; Dan O'Herlihy; *D:* Frank Arnold.

Waltz with Bashir 🦴🦴🦴 1/2 *Vals in Bashir* **2008 (R)** Animated autobiographical account of director Folman's experiences as a former member of the Israeli army and participant in the 1982 Israeli-Lebanese war—the brutal massacre of civilians in response to the assassination of Lebanese president Bashir Gemayel—and the role his military unit played. Folman's repressed memories first play out as frightening images in the recurring dream of a friend who is also a combat survivor, then proceed to scenes of war, conversations in a cafe, and a final realistic glimpse of war's aftermath. The visions are psychedelic while the realism is stark and uncomfortable. In Hebrew with subtitles. **87m/C; Blu-Ray, On Demand.** *FR IS GE* ***D:*** Ari Folman; ***W:*** Ari Folman; ***M:*** Max Richter. Directors Guild '08: Documentary Director (Folman); Golden Globes '09: Foreign Film.

Waltzing Anna 🦴 1/2 **2006 (PG-13)** Greedy Dr. Charlie Keegan gets nailed for insurance fraud and must work six months in an upstate New York nursing home to keep his license. The place is run by an equally shady operator and Keegan just passes the time until his conscience is pricked by beautiful nurse Jill. Well-meaning but predictable and maudlin. **108m/C; DVD.** Emmanuelle Chriqui; Pat Hingle; Betsy Palmer; Artie Lange; Robert Capelli, Jr.; Mackenzie Milone; Paige Turco; Grant Shaud; Marilyn Chris; Casey Siemaszko; ***D:*** Doug Bollinger; ***W:*** Robert Capelli, Jr.; Doug Bollinger; ***C:*** Yaron Orbach; ***M:*** Tony McAnany. **VIDEO**

Wanda *Barbara Loden's Wanda* **1970 102m/C; DVD, Blu-Ray.** Barbara Loden; Michael Higgins; Jerome Thier; Dorothy Shupenes; ***W:*** Barbara Loden; ***C:*** Nicholas T. Proferes. Natl. Film Reg. '17.

Wanda Nevada 🦴 1/2 **1979 (PG)** Gambler Fonda wins nubile young Shields in a poker game, so he drags her with him to the Grand Canyon to look for gold. Director/star Fonda sure picked a lemon for his only screen appearance with dad Henry (a grizzled old varmint appearing briefly). Shields is in her usual form—stellar for a shampoo commercial. **105m/C; VHS, DVD, Blu-Ray.** Peter Fonda; Brooke Shields; Henry Fonda; Fiona Lewis; Luke Askew; Ted Markland; Severn Darden; Paul Fix; ***D:*** Peter Fonda.

Wanda, the Sadistic Hypnotist 🦴 **1967** A comely vixen hypnotizes an innocent pedestrian, ties him up and whips him to indulge her whims. Despite the "victim's" protests, she unleashes a gang of sexually playful women on him, and he is subjected to a multitude of "tortures." **70m/C; VHS, DVD.** Katharine Shubeck; Janice Sweet; Dick Dangerfield; Daryl Cobinot; ***D:*** Gregory Corarito.

Wanderers 🦴🦴🦴 1/2 **1979 (R)** Richard Price's acclaimed novel about youth gangs coming of age in the Bronx in 1963. The "Wanderers," named after the Dion song, are a gang of Italian-American teenagers about to graduate high school, who prowl the Bronx with the feeling that something is slipping away from them. Fascinating, funny and touching. Manz is unforgettable as a scrappy gal. A wonderful 60s soundtrack (Dion, the Four Seasons) colors this "coming of age the hard way" film. **113m/C; VHS, DVD, Blu-Ray.** Ken Wahl; John Friedrich; Karen Allen; Linda Manz; Richard Price; Toni Kalem; Tony Ganios; Alan Rosenberg; Jim Youngs; Val Avery; Dolph Sweet; Olympia Dukakis; Erland van Lidth; ***D:*** Philip Kaufman; ***W:*** Philip Kaufman; Rose Kaufman; ***C:*** Michael Chapman.

The Wandering Earth 🦴🦴 1/2 *Liu lang di qiu* **2019** Years after the Sun became overactive and Earth was transformed into a planet-sized spaceship as an act of survival, new challenges emerge as this Earth is on course to crash into Jupiter. Two teams of astronauts take action to save it: a two-man skeleton crew, Peiqiang Liu (Wu) and Makarov (Sharogradsky), and an exploratory crew led by Peiqiang's son Qi (Qu) and his partner Duoduo Han (Zhao). Visually stunning, director Gwo uniquely brings together familiar elements from other sci-fi movies and successfully emphasizes the value of teamwork. Mandarin with subtitles. **125m/C; DVD.** Jing Wu; Chuxiao Qu; Guangjie Li; Man-Tat Ng; Jin Mai Jaho; ***D:*** Frant Gwo; ***W:*** Frant Gwo; Gong Geer; Junce Ye; Yan Dongxu; Yang Zhixue; Ruchang Ye; ***C:*** Michael Liu; ***M:*** Roc Chen.

Wandering Jew 🦴🦴 1/2 **1920** An excellent print of the rare Austrian film version of the classic legend, one of at least three silent versions. A Jew is condemned to wander the earth for eternity. **65m/B; VHS, DVD.** *AT* Rudolf Schildkraut; Joseph Schildkraut; Ernst Bath; Else Osterheim; Josef Schreiter; ***D:*** Otto Kreisler; ***W:*** Heinrich Glucksmann.

Wanderlust 🦴🦴 1/2 **2012 (R)** Happily married couple George (Rudd) and Linda (Aniston) are fleeing from career failures and a steep mortgage in New York City when they stumble upon Elysium, a commune that seems the exact karmic opposite of the urbanite lifestyle they're leaving behind. Director Wain's comedy is a bit inconsistent and particularly weak in the final act but the film serves as an amazing spotlight for Rudd, who's arguably never been funnier. Theroux, Alda, Marino, Peele, and many more round out one of the best comedy ensembles of the last several years (even if Aniston's character is sadly underdeveloped). **98m/C; DVD, Blu-Ray.** Paul Rudd; Jennifer Aniston; Justin Theroux; Kathryn Hahn; Malin Akerman; Lauren Ambrose; Joe Lo Truglio; Alan Alda; Ken Marino; ***D:*** David Wain; ***W:*** David Wain; Ken Marino; ***C:*** Michael Bonvillain; ***M:*** Craig Wedren.

Wannabes 🦴🦴 **2001** Angelo (DeMeo) and his younger brother Paulie (Dubin) are waiters in a New York neighborhood joint where the local mob boss is Santo (Vitrelli). Tired of being abused, particularly by Santo's spoiled son Vinny (D'Onofrio), Angelo, Paulie and a couple of their buds become successful bookies and go into loansharking and other criminal activities. Santo likes Angelo's gumption and makes him his protege, much to Vinny's anger. Familiar stereotypes abound. **110m/C; VHS, DVD.** Joe (Johnny) Viterelli; Joseph (Joe) D'Onofrio; William DeMeo; Conor Dubin; Raymond Serra; ***D:*** William DeMeo; Charles A. Addessi; ***W:*** William DeMeo.

The Wannsee Conference 🦴🦴🦴 1/2 *Wannseekonferenz* **1984** A startling, important film depicting, in real time, the conference held at the Wannsee on January 20, 1942, during which 14 members of the Nazi hierarchy decided in 85 minutes the means and logistics of effecting the Final Solution. Recreated from the original secretary's notes. Horrifying and chilling. Along with "Shoah," a must-see for understanding the Holocaust and the psychology of genocide. In German with English subtitles. **87m/C; VHS, DVD.** *GE* Dietrich Mattausch; Gerd Brockmann; Friedrich Beckhaus; Robert Atzorn; Jochen Busse; Hans-Werner Bussinger; Harald Dietl; Peter Fitz; Reinhard Glemnitz; Dieter Groest; Martin Luttge; Anita Mally; Gerd Riegauer; ***D:*** Heinz Schirk; ***W:*** Paul Mommertz; ***C:*** Horst Schier.

Wanted 🦴 1/2 **1998 (R)** Jimmy Scrico (Sutton) has accidentally shot a mob boss. Naturally, this means he's on the run from the vengeful wiseguys and he finds sanctuary in a Catholic school where Jimmy's befriended by Father Donnelly (Busfield). Then the bad guys catch up with him. **90m/C; VHS, DVD.** Michael Sutton; Timothy Busfield; Robert Culp; Tracey Gold; James Quattrochi; ***D:*** Terence M. O'Keefe; ***W:*** Terence M. O'Keefe; Mark Evan Schwartz; ***C:*** Richard A. Jones.

Wanted 🦴🦴🦴 **2008 (R)** Russian-born director Bekmambetov keeps the pace smoking and makes Michael Bay (and others of his ilk) look like hacks and wimps. Or like Wesley Gibson (McAvoy) when we first meet him—a humiliated office drone. Picked up by Fox (Jolie), Wesley's informed that the dad he never knew was just killed and also happened to be an assassin who belonged to a secret society called the Fraternity. Wesley is taken to meet boss Sloan (Freeman) and told to man up so he can get revenge on rogue Cross (Kretschmann), who offed his pops. After some brutal training, Wes heads for his confrontation. The violence is as excessive as it is ridiculous. So what? It's also well-done. Adapted from Mark Millar and J.G. Jones's cult comic. **110m/C; Blu-Ray, On Demand.** James McAvoy; Angelina Jolie; Morgan Freeman; Terence Stamp; Thomas Kretschmann; Common; Marc Warren; David O'Hara; Kristi Hager; Konstantin Khabensky; Dato Bakhtadze; ***D:*** Timur Bekmambetov; ***W:*** Michael Brandt; Derek Haas; Chris Morgan; ***C:*** Mitchell Amundsen; ***M:*** Danny Elfman.

Wanted: Babysitter **WOOF! 1975** A young student accidentally becomes involved by her roommate in a plot to kidnap the child she is babysitting. Schneider is truly awful; Italian comic Pazzetto is at sea in a bad role as her boyfriend. Also released as "The Babysitter." **90m/C; VHS, DVD.** Robert Vaughn; Vic Morrow; Maria Schneider; Renato Pozzetto; Nadja Tiller; Carl Mohner; Sydne Rome; ***D:*** Rene Clement.

Wanted Dead or Alive 🦴 1/2 **1986 (R)** Ex-CIA agent Hauer is now a high-tech bounty hunter assigned to bring in an international terrorist. When the terrorist kills Hauer's friend and girlfriend, he forgets the $50, 000 bonus for bringing him in alive. Official "sequel" to the Steve McQueen TV series with Hauer as the McQueen character's great-grandson. The link is meaningless, and the plot is a thin excuse for much violence and anti-terrorist flag-waving. **104m/C; VHS, DVD, Blu-Ray.** Rutger Hauer; Gene Simmons; Robert Guillaume; William Russ; Jerry Hardin; Mel Harris; ***D:*** Gary Sherman; ***W:*** Brian Taggert; ***C:*** Alex Nepomniaschy; ***M:*** Joe Renzetti.

The War 🦴🦴 1/2 **1994 (PG-13)** Post-Vietnam war drama, set in 1970 Mississippi, centers on a children's battle over a treehouse but becomes a sermon on love, death, family values, pacifism, and the physical and spiritual wounds of war. After helping son Stu (Wood) and daughter Lidia (Randall) build their treehouse, troubled Vietnam vet Stephen Simmons (Costner) tries to coax Stu to make peace with the bullies trying to take it over. However cliched, director Avnet allows a talented cast of kids to thoughtfully express a child's view of the world but gosh-darn-it the preachy tone can get down-right annoying. **126m/C; VHS, DVD, HD-DVD.** Elijah Wood; Kevin Costner; Lexi (Faith) Randall; Mare Winningham; Christine Baranski; Bruce A. Young; Gary Basaraba; Raynor Scheine; Nick Searcy; Lucas Black; ***D:*** Jon Avnet; ***W:*** Kathy McWorter; ***C:*** Geoffrey Simpson; ***M:*** Thomas Newman.

War 🦴 **2007 (R)** Yet another of Jet Li's urban action/martial arts flicks, this time featuring British action import Statham. Rogue (Li) is an assassin manipulating two crime families into a bloody gang war. Crawford (Statham) is the FBI agent chasing him. Did Rogue kill Crawford's partner? Why is Rogue starting a gang war? Does it matter? The movie is mostly about explosions and gunfire, at the expense of the charisma and action skills of Statham and Li. What plot exists owes much to "Yojimbo" and "A Fistful of Dollars," minus the depth and the appeal of the Asian martial-arts movies that gave Li his start, leaving a noisy, forgettable mess. **103m/C; DVD, Blu-Ray.** Jet Li; Jason Statham; John Lone; Devon Aoki; Luis Guzman; Saul Rubinek; Ryo Ishibashi; Sung Kang; Mathew St. Patrick; Nadine Velazquez; ***D:*** Philip G. Atwell; ***W:*** Lee Anthony Smith; Gregory J. Bradley; ***C:*** Pierre Morel; ***M:*** Brian Tyler.

A War 🦴🦴🦴 *Krigen* **2015 (R)** The conflict in Afghanistan and the impact of war on the family of soldiers is explored through the story of a Danish company commander and the difficult decision he must make in the heat of battle. **115m/C; DVD, Blu-Ray.** Pilou Asbaek; Dar Salim; Tuva Novotny; Alex Hogh Andersen; Soren Malling; ***D:*** Tobias Lindholm; ***W:*** Tobias Lindholm; ***C:*** Magnus Nordenhof Jønck; ***M:*** Sune Wagner.

War 🦴🦴 **2019** Indian anti-terrorist agents Kabir (Roshan) and Khalid (Shroff) work together to nab an evil international arms dealer/terrorist, Rizwan Ilyasi (Vasta). However, each man has issues with the other and worries about being betrayed; Kabir does not particularly like Khalid because his father betrayed his country. To help in the quest to find Rizwan, Kabir brings in a reluctant civilian, Naina (Kapoor), with whom he becomes romantically involved. A Bollywood action-adventure, The plot is a bit odd, but it serves primarily as a star vehicle for Roshan and Shroff with decent musical numbers. Hindi, Tamil, and Telugu with subtitles. **155m/C; DVD.** Hrithik Roshan; Tiger Shroff; Vaani Kapoor; Ashutosh Rana; Anupriya Goenka; ***D:*** Siddharth Anand; ***W:*** Siddharth Anand; Shridhar Raghavan; ***C:*** Ben Jasper; ***M:*** Vishal Dadlani; Shekhar Ravjiani.

War and Peace 🦴🦴 1/2 **1956** Lengthy adaptation of Tolstoy's great (and likewise lengthy) novel about three families caught up in Russia's Napoleonic Wars from 1805 to 1812; filmed in Rome. Bad casting and confused script (by six writers) are somewhat overcome by awesome battle scenes and Hepburn. Remade in 1968. **208m/C; VHS, DVD, Blu-Ray.** Audrey Hepburn; Mel Ferrer; Henry Fonda; Anita Ekberg; Vittorio Gassman; John Mills; Oscar Homolka; Herbert Lom; Helmut Dantine; Tullio Carminati; Barry Jones; Milly Vitale; Maria Ferrero; Wilfred Lawson; May Britt; Jeremy Brett; Lea Seidl; Patrick Crean; Sean Barrett; Richard Dawson; ***D:*** King Vidor; ***W:*** King Vidor; Bridget Boland; Mario Camerini; Ennio de Concini; Ivo Perilli; Irwin Shaw; Robert Westerby; ***C:*** Jack Cardiff; Aldo Tonti; ***M:*** Nino Rota. Golden Globes '57: Foreign Film.

War and Peace 🦴🦴🦴 **1968** The massive Russian production of Leo Tolstoy's masterpiece, adapting the classic tome practically scene by scene. All of the production took place in the Soviet Union. So painstaking that it took more than five years to finish, no other adaptation can touch it. Hugely expensive ($100 million, claimed the Russians), wildly uneven production. Great scenes of battle and aristocratic life. Though this version is far from perfect, one asks: Is it humanly possible to do screen justice to such a novel? In Russian with English subtitles. On four tapes. (Beware the two-part, poorly dubbed version that was also released.) **373m/C; VHS, DVD, Blu-Ray.** *RU* Lyudmila Savelyeva; Sergei Bondarchuk; Vyacheslav Tihonor; Hira Ivanov-Golarko; Irina Gubanova; Antonina Shuranova; ***D:*** Sergei Bondarchuk; ***C:*** Jack Cardiff. Oscars '68: Foreign Film; Golden Globes '69: Foreign Film; N.Y. Film Critics '68: Foreign Film.

War and Peace 🦴🦴 1/2 **1973** Lengthy BBC production of the lengthy Tolstoy masterpiece that follows the trials and triumphs of two Russian families whose lives intersect against a backdrop of the Napoleonic Wars. On 6 cassettes. **750m/C; VHS, DVD.** *GB* Anthony Hopkins; Alan Dobie; Faith Brook; Morag Hood; Colin Baker; Neil Stacey; ***D:*** John Howard Davies; ***W:*** Jack Pulman.

War & Remembrance 🦴 1/2 **1988** Tedious sequel to the epic TV miniseries "The Winds of War," based on the novel by Herman Wouk. Historical fiction is created around the events of WWII, including Nazi persecution and naval battles in the Pacific. Followed by "War and Remembrance: The Final Chapter." On seven cassettes. **840m/C; VHS, DVD.** Robert Mitchum; Jane Seymour; Hart Bochner; Victoria Tennant; Barry Bostwick; Polly Bergen; David Dukes; Michael Woods; Sharon Stone; Robert Morley; Sami Frey; Topol; John Rhys-Davies; Ian McShane; William Schallert; Jeremy Kemp; Steven Berkoff; Robert Hardy; Ralph Bellamy; John Gielgud; Charles Lane; ***D:*** Dan Curtis. **TV**

War & Remembrance: The Final Chapter 🦴 1/2 **1989** The final episodes of Herman Wouk's sweeping saga, following "The Winds of War" and "War and Remembrance," deal with the struggle of a Jewish family in war-torn Europe. Natalie and her son, Louis, are trapped in a ghetto under the reign of a vicious Nazi, who considers a bribe for the sake of the mother and son. On five cassettes. **600m/C; VHS, DVD.** Robert Mitchum; Jane Seymour; Hart Bochner; Victoria Tennant; Polly Bergen; David Dukes; Michael Woods; Sharon Stone; Robert Morley; Sami Frey; Topol; John Rhys-Davies; Ian McShane; William Schallert; Jeremy Kemp; Steven Berkoff; Robert Hardy; Ralph Bellamy; John Gielgud; ***D:*** Dan Curtis. **TV**

War Arrow 🦴🦴 **1953** Army Major Howell Brady (Chandler) is sent by Washington to end the Kiowa uprisings in Texas in this cavalry vs. Indians western. Along the way, he tries to win the heart of O'Hara. **79m/C; VHS, DVD.** Maureen O'Hara; Jeff Chandler; Suzan Ball; John McIntire; Noah Beery, Jr.; Henry (Kleinbach) Brandon; Dennis Weaver; Jay Silverheels; ***D:*** George Sherman; ***W:*** John Michael Hayes.

The War at Home 🦴 1/2 **1996 (R)** In 1972 Vietnam vet Jeremy Collier (Estevez) has been home in the Dallas suburbs for a year but the war and its effects still linger. Mom Maureen (Bates) is a conservative control freak and dad Bob (Sheen) just can't connect, while teenaged sis Karen (Williams) is going through her own rebellion. The tense situation comes to a bitter head over a Thanksgiving weekend. Based on the 1984 play "Home Front" by James Duff. **124m/C; VHS, DVD, Blu-Ray.** Kathy Bates; Martin

Sheen; Emilio Estevez; Kimberly Williams; Carla Gugino; Geoffrey Blake; Corin "Corky" Nemec; Ann Hearn; *D:* Emilio Estevez; *W:* James Duff; *C:* Peter Levy; *M:* Basil Poledouris.

The War Bride **2001** Slow and sometimes tedious homefront drama but Friel's a firecracker. Cockney Lily (Friel) makes a whirlwind wartime marriage to Canadian soldier Charlie (Young) and is eventually granted citizenship and shipped off to her husband's home country. Lily's in for a rude shock when she sees that she'll be living on a small hardscrabble ranch in rural Alberta with her unwelcoming in-laws—Charlie's mother Betty (Fricker) and polio-stricken sister Sylvia (Parker). But this city sparrow is determined to make the best of things, although it's not going to be easy. **96m/C; DVD.** *GB CA* Anna Friel; Brenda Fricker; Molly Parker; Aden Young; Loren Dean; Julie Cox; *D:* Lyndon Chubbuck; *C:* Ronald Orieux; *M:* John Sereda.

War Dogs 1/2 **2016 (R)** David Packouz (Teller) and Efraim Diveroli (Hill) are buddies with little focus or potential in Miami Beach during the Iraq War. Using a little-known government initiative to their advantage, the pair bids on a U.S. military contract and eventually land a $300 million deal to provide weapons to the Afghani Military. Of course, the rich life they think they're going to live quickly gets really, really dangerous. This "based on a true story" is a bad fit for director Phillips ("Hangover"), who's great at the men behaving badly aspect but fumbles the rest. It leaves a bad taste in your mouth. **114m/C; DVD, Blu-Ray.** Jonah Hill; Miles Teller; Kevin Pollak; Bradley Cooper; Shaun Toub; Ana de Armas; *D:* Todd Phillips; *W:* Todd Phillips; Stephen Chin; Jason Smilovic; *C:* Lawrence Sher; *M:* Cliff Martinez.

War Drums **1957** Well-intentioned but heavy-handed western from United Artists. Apache chief Mangas Coloradas (Barker) is told to keep his warriors from breaking a peace treaty. White gold miners violate its terms by prospecting on tribal land causing the Apaches attack. Mangas' friend, settler Luke Fargo (Johnson), tries to find a solution. **75m/C; DVD.** Les Barker; Ben Johnson; Joan Taylor; Larry Chance; Richard Cutting; John Colicos; John Pickard; *D:* Reginald LeBorg; *W:* Gerald Drayson Adams; *C:* William Margulies; *M:* Les Baxter.

War Eagle, Arkansas 1/2 **2007 (PG-13)** Promising high school baseball player Enoch (Grimes) has a crushing stutter and a demanding grandfather (Dennehy) pushing his own frustrated athletic dreams onto his grandson. Enoch's best friend is motormouth 'Wheels' (McCabe), who is confined to a wheelchair because of cerebral palsy. When Enoch gets a girlfriend (Traya) and an out-of-state college sports scholarship, Wheels gets resentful that Enoch is leaving him behind. **93m/C; DVD.** Luke Grimes; Dan McCabe; Brian Dennehy; Misti Traya; Mare Winningham; Mary Kay Place; James McDaniel; Lynsee Provence; *D:* Robert Milazzo; *W:* Graham Gordy; *C:* Masanobu Takayanagi. **VIDEO**

War Flowers 1/2 **2012** Mediocre and fairly predictable Civil War melodrama. Southerner Sarabeth Ellis (Ricci) is left alone with her daughter, Melody, when her husband John goes off to fight for the Confederates. She finds badly wounded Union soldier Louis McIntire (Gedrick), who was left for dead at the site of a nearby battle. Sarabeth secretly takes Louis in and cares for him while awaiting word of her husband's fate, which may not matter to her so much when the two fall in love. **100m/C; DVD, Blu-Ray.** Christina Ricci; Jason Gedrick; Gabrielle Popa; Tom Berenger; Bren Foster; *D:* Serge Rodnunsky; *W:* Serge Rodnunsky; *C:* Andrew Mclean; *M:* Evan Evans. **VIDEO**

War for the Planet of the Apes 1/2 **2017 (PG-13)** A breathtaking conclusion to an impressive, intelligent trilogy. With the human race all but decimated by a pandemic, the ruthless Colonel (Harrelson) mobilizes a group of insurgent humans, along with traitorous apes, to annihilate the simian species once and for all. Caesar (a typically stellar Serkis), the peaceful leader of apes, must choose between doing what's "right" and what's right for his species. There's much to sink your teeth into: biblical allegories, civil rights comparisons, and computer graphics so magical you'll believe you're watching actual apes riding horses. **140m/C; DVD, Blu-Ray.** Andy Serkis; Woody Harrelson; Steve Zahn; Karin Konoval; Amiah Miller; *D:* Matt Reeves; *W:* Matt Reeves; Mark Bomback; *C:* Michael Seresin; *M:* Michael Giacchino.

War Goddess 1/2 *Le Guerriere dal seno nudo; Les Amazones* **1974** Once a year, the Amazons fight to decide who will be queen before hiring Greek soldiers to conceive children with so they can keep their tribe going. This year ends in ambush by another tribe and the Amazons assume the Greeks are at fault and gear up for war. **84m/C; DVD.** *FR IT SP* Angelo Infanti; Sabine Sun; Luciana Paluzzi; *D:* Terence Young; *W:* Terence Young; Richard Aubrey; Luciano Vincenzoni; Charles Spaak; Antonio Recoder; Arduino (Dino) Maiuri; Robert Graves; Massimo De Rita; Serge de la Roche; *C:* Aldo Tonti; Alejandro Ulloa; *M:* Riz Ortolani.

War Horse 1/2 **2011 (PG-13)** Also a 1982 children's novel by Michael Morpurgo and a Broadway play, Spielberg's adaptation is intentionally sentimental, delivering a gorgeously timeless film that could have been made 70 years ago, for better or worse. Farm boy Albert Narracott (Irvine) trains a beloved horse named Joey to save his drunken father's (Mullan) farm in England only to watch it get sold to the British cavalry. The horse goes through a series of owners during WWI, always trying to work his way back home. But the story never really comes together and is surprisingly lifeless. **146m/C; DVD, Blu-Ray.** Jeremy Irvine; Emily Watson; Peter Mullan; David Thewlis; Benedict Cumberbatch; Tom Hiddleston; Toby Kebbell; Niels Arestrup; *D:* Steven Spielberg; *W:* Lee Hall; Richard Curtis; *C:* Janusz Kaminski; *M:* John Williams.

War Hunt **1962** Psychological war drama is the film debut of Redford. Roy Loomis (Redford) is a new recruit for a frontline platoon in Korea where the vets soon strip him of all heroic illusions. In order to gain valuable intel, the platoon's captain (Aidman) allows crazy Pvt. Endore (Saxon) to go on solitary night patrols where he stalks and kills North Koreans. But Endore isn't about to respect a ceasefire and goes too far. **81m/B; DVD.** John Saxon; Robert Redford; Charles Aidman; Sydney Pollack; Gavin MacLeod; Tom Skerritt; Tommy Matsuda; *D:* Denis Sanders; *W:* Stanford Whitmore; *C:* Ted D. McCord; *M:* Bud Shank.

War in Space *Battle of the Stars; Anno Zero - Guerra Nello Spazio; Year Zero - War in Sace* **1977** Powerful U.N. Space Bureau Starships and UFOs band together to battle alien invaders among the volcanoes and deserts of Venus. **91m/C; VHS, DVD.** *IT* John Richardson; Gaetano Balestrieri; Yanti Sommer; *D:* Alfonso Brescia; *W:* Alfonso Brescia; *C:* Silvio Fraschetti; *M:* Marcello Giombini.

War, Inc. 1/2 **2008 (R)** Over-the-top black comedy lampoons American wartime operations in Iraq. Hauser (Cusack) is a hitman sent to Turaquistan, a fictional country occupied by U.S. troops and run by an American corporation called Tamerlane, to assassinate a Middle Eastern oil barren named Omar Sharif (not actually played by Omar Sharif, of course). While there he falls for a reporter (Tomei), who mistakes him for another money-hungry executive. Several prominent political figures are roasted, including Dan Akroyd's obvious take on Dick Cheney as an ex-veep and current head of Tamerlane, running the corporation while sitting on the toilet (literally). Still, it's a little too angry and smug to work, as it awkwardly pushes its self-important sermon amid the silly jokes. **107m/C; DVD, Blu-Ray.** John Cusack; Hilary Duff; Marisa Tomei; Joan Cusack; Ben Kingsley; Dan Aykroyd; Lyubomir Neikov; Ben Cross; Ned Bellamy; Shirly Brener; *D:* Joshua Seftel; *W:* John Cusack; Jeremy Pikser; Mark Leyner; *C:* Zoran Popovic; *M:* David Robbins.

The War Lord **1965** Set in the 11th century, Heston stars as Chrysagon, a Norman knight and war lord who commands a peasant village. While battling his enemies, he becomes enamored of a peasant girl named Bronwyn (Forsyth), who is unfortunately engaged to someone else. Pulling rank, Chrysagon uses an ancient law that allows noblemen the first night with a bride and the two fall in love. The two vow to never part, but that sets the stage for even more bloody battles. Fine acting and great production values make this a well-adapted version of the play "The Lovers" by Leslie Stevens. **121m/C; VHS, DVD, Blu-Ray.** Charlton Heston; Richard Boone; Rosemary Forsyth; Guy Stockwell; Niall MacGinnis; Henry Wilcoxon; James Farentino; Maurice Evans; Michael Conrad; *D:* Franklin J. Schaffner; *W:* John Collier; Millard Kaufman; *C:* Russell Metty.

War Lover 1/2 **1962** An American daredevil flying captain and his co-pilot find themselves vying for the affections of a woman during WWII in England. Seeks human frailty beneath surface heroism. McQueen is impressive, no thanks to mediocre script. Excellent aerial photography, and featuring one of only a very few serviceable WWII B-17s then remaining. Based on John Hersey's novel. **105m/B; VHS, DVD.** *GB* Steve McQueen; Robert Wagner; Shirley Anne Field; Bill Edwards; Gary Cockrell; *D:* Philip Leacock; *W:* Howard Koch.

War Machine 1/2 **2017** A war satire about a real-life U.S. general who, instead of cleaning up the U.S. military's efforts in Afghanistan, disobeys orders by trying to win the war. Pitt's over-the-top performance, awkward mannerisms, and raspy, holding-his-breath voice are acting choices that may be quirks of the general himself but are a bit hard to get used to. Based on Michael Hastings book, "The Operators: The Wild and Terrifying Inside Story of America's War in Afghanistan." **122m/C; Streaming.** Brad Pitt; Topher Grace; Emory Cohen; Anthony Michael Hall; John Magaro; *D:* David Michod; *W:* David Michod; *C:* Dariusz Wolski; *M:* Nick Cave; Warren Ellis. **VIDEO**

War of the Buttons 1/2 **1995 (PG)** Two sleepy Irish fishing villages provide childish battle grounds for two groups of local lads. The Ballys (Ballydowse village), lead by Fergus (Fitzgerald), and the Carricks (Carrickdowse), with leader Geronimo (Coffey), have an intense rivalry and capture by the other gang leads to the removal of every clothing button for the unfortunate captive. When Fergus becomes a Carrick victim, he organizes a retaliatory strike, and emotions threaten to overwhelm all concerned. Based on the French novel "La Guerre des Boutons" by Louis Pergaud. Filmed on location in West Cork, Ireland. **94m/C; VHS, DVD.** Gregg Fitzgerald; John Coffey; Liam Cunningham; Paul Batt; Eveanna Ryan; Colm Meaney; Johnny Murphy; *D:* John Roberts; *W:* Colin Welland; *C:* Bruno de Keyzer; *M:* Rachel Portman.

War of the Buttons 1/2 *La Nouvelle Guerre des Boutons* **2012 (PG-13)** In his hometown, rebellious pre-teen Lebrac (Texier) pours fuel on the fire started by two gangs of boys from nearby villages. The childish behavior must be set aside when Lebrac falls in love with Violette (Bachelier), a young Jewish girl who could be found by the Nazis. A manipulative and old-fashioned piece of dreck that tells a story set in WWII France that tries to teach audiences a lesson about humanity but does so with such heavy fists that viewers are more likely to feel abused than moved. Adapted from the 1912 novel by Louis Pergaud. French with subtitles. **100m/C; DVD.** *FR* Jean Texier; Ilona Bachelier; Laetitia Casta; Clement Godefroy; Theophile Baquet; *D:* Christophe Barratier; *W:* Christophe Barratier; Stephane Keller; Thomas Langmann; Philippe Lopes-Curval; *C:* Jean Poisson; *M:* Philippe Rombi.

War of the Colossal Beast 1/2 *The Terror Strikes; Revenge of the Colossal Man* **1958** This sequel to "The Amazing Colossal Man" finds the 70-foot Colonel Manning even angrier at the attempts to kill him than he was in the first film. So he wreaks more havoc until scolded by his sister into committing suicide for being such a troublemaker. Cheesy special effects but good for a laugh. **68m/B; VHS, DVD.** Dean Parkin; Sally Fraser; Russ Bender; Rico Alaniz; Roger Pace; Charles Stewart; *D:* Bert I. Gordon; *W:* Bert I. Gordon; George Worthing Yates; *C:* Jack Marta; *M:* Albert Glasser. **VIDEO**

War of the Gargantuas *Duel of the Gargantuas; Frankenstein Monsters: Sanda vs. Gairath; Furankenshutain No Kaiju: Sanda tai Gailah; Sanda tai Gailah* **1970 (G)** Tokyo is once again the boxing ring for giant monsters. This time it's a good gargantua (half human, half monster) against a bad gargantua. This is a strange one. **92m/C; VHS, DVD.** *JP* Russ Tamblyn; Kumi Mizuno; Kenji Sahara; Jun Tazaki; Kipp Hamilton; Haruo Nakajima; Nobuo Nakamura; Ikio Sawamura; Yoshifumi Tajima; *D:* Inoshiro Honda; *W:* Inoshiro Honda; Takeshi Kimura; Kaoru Mabuchi; *C:* Hajime Koizumi; *M:* Akira Ifukube.

The War of the Planets *I Diafonidi Portano la Morte* **1965** The second film in the camp Italian sci fi series (preceded by "The Wild, Wild Planet"). In the 21st century, light cloud aliens use Mars as their base to steal all Earth's space stations. They either kill or brainwash the crews until they can invade and carry out some evil plan. Dubbed. **97m/C; DVD.** *IT* Tony Russel; Lisa Gastoni; Franco Nero; Carlo Giustini; Enzo Fiermonte; Linda Sini; *D:* Anthony M. Dawson; *W:* Renato Moretti; Ivan Reiner; *C:* Riccardo (Pallton) Pallottini; *M:* Angelo Francesco Lavagnino.

The War of the Roses **1989 (R)** Acidic black comedy about a well-to-do suburban couple who can't agree on a property settlement in their divorce so they wage unreserved and ever-escalating combat on each other, using their palatial home as a battleground. Expertly and lovingly (if that's the word) directed by DeVito, who plays the lawyer. Turner and Douglas are splendid. Adapted from the novel by Warren Adler. **116m/C; VHS, DVD, Blu-Ray.** Michael Douglas; Kathleen Turner; Danny DeVito; Marianne Saegebrecht; Sean Astin; G.D. Spradlin; Peter Donat; Heather Fairfield; Dan Castellaneta; Danitra Vance; Tony Crane; *D:* Danny DeVito; *W:* Michael Leeson; *C:* Stephen Burum; *M:* David Newman.

War of the Satellites 1/2 **1958** Advanced alien race gets snippy when earthlings prepare for their first manned spaceflight. There's also a zombie scientist resurrected to sabotage the mission in this fast and cheap Corman production made to capitalize on the USSR's Sputnik launch. **66m/B; DVD.** Dick Miller; Richard Devon; Susan Cabot; Eric Sinclair; Michael Fox; Robert Shayne; *D:* Roger Corman; *W:* Lawrence Louis Goldman; *C:* Floyd Crosby; *M:* Walter Greene.

War of the Wildcats 1/2 *In Old Oklahoma* **1943** Fast-moving western with Wayne as a tough cowboy battling a powerful land baron. They fight over land, oil and a woman. Unusual because Wayne's character acts on behalf of the Indians to drill and transport oil. **102m/B; DVD, Blu-Ray.** John Wayne; Martha Scott; Albert Dekker; George "Gabby" Hayes; Sidney Blackmer; *D:* Albert Rogell; *W:* Ethel Hill; Eleanore Griffin; *C:* Jack Marta; *M:* Walter Scharf.

The War of the Worlds 1/2 **1953** H.G. Wells's classic novel of the invasion of Earth by Martians, updated to 1950s California, with spectacular special effects of destruction caused by the Martian war machines. Pretty scary and tense; based more on Orson Welles's radio broadcast than on the book. Still very popular; hit the top 20 in sales when released on video. Classic thriller later made into a TV series. Produced by George Pal, who brought the world much sci-fi, including "The Time Machine," "Destination Moon," and "When Worlds Collide," and who appears here as a street person. **85m/C; VHS, DVD.** Gene Barry; Ann (Robin) Robinson; Les Tremayne; Lewis Martin; Robert Cornthwaite; Sandro Giglio; George Pal; Jack Kruschen; Carolyn Jones; Alvy Moore; William Phipps; Paul Frees; *V:* Cedric Hardwicke; *D:* Byron Haskin; *W:* Barre Lyndon; *C:* George Barnes; *M:* Leith Stevens. Natl. Film Reg. '11.

War of the Worlds **2005 (PG-13)** Spielberg and Cruise re-team in this modern sci-fi remake of the H.G. Wells classic 1898 novel (George Pal produced the 1953 film version) though the M-word (Martians, that is) is never actually uttered here. Dockworker Ray Ferrier (Cruise) is a distant dad forced together with his teenage son Robbie (Chatwin) and 10-year-old daughter Rachel (Fanning) for the weekend. That dysfunctional scene is cut short by powerful lightning strikes that activate massive underground three-legged alien machines bent on destroying every human in sight, which puts Ray and his brood on the run. Typical breathtaking Spielberg special effects abound;

Cruise shows why he's an A-lister. **118m/C; DVD, Blu-Ray.** Tom Cruise; Dakota Fanning; Miranda Otto; Tim Robbins; Justin Chatwin; Rick Gonzalez; David Alan Basche; Yul Vazquez; Lenny Venito; Lisa Ann Walter; Ann (Robin) Robinson; Gene Barry; ***Nar:*** Morgan Freeman; ***D:*** Steven Spielberg; ***W:*** David Koepp; Josh Friedman; ***C:*** Janusz Kaminski; ***M:*** John Williams.

War of the Worlds 2: The Next Wave **2008 (R)** The sequel to 2005's "H.G. Wells' War of the Worlds" just dissipates whatever good will the first flick engendered by being ridiculous and dull. Two years after the first Martian invasion, astronomer George Herbert is hiding out in the woods with his son when he makes some nasty discovery about what the Martians are doing with human bodies, finds his son has been taken, and then the humans decide to take their battle to Mars before another invasion starts. **85m/C; DVD.** C. Thomas Howell; Christopher Reid; Kim Little; Danna Brady; Jonathan Levit; Darren Dalton; Jonathan Nation; Dashiell Howell; Fred Griffith; ***D:*** C. Thomas Howell; ***W:*** Eric Forsberg; ***C:*** Mark Atkins; ***M:*** Ralph Rieckermann. **VIDEO**

War on Everyone **2017 (R)** John Michael McDonagh's black comedy too often plays like a comedian who advertises himself as edgy but hasn't exactly honed his material beyond offensive. Skarsgard and Pena play a pair of corrupt cops who get entangled with a criminal sociopath (James) who may be even more dangerous than they are. This is the kind of movie that opens with one character asking another if a mime makes a sound if hit by a car, and then they hit a mime with a car. At least every other joke falls flat but the two leads do their best to pick them up. **98m/C; DVD, Blu-Ray.** Alexander Skarsgård; Michael Peña; Theo James; Tessa Thompson; Paul Reiser; ***D:*** John Michael McDonagh; ***W:*** John Michael McDonagh; ***C:*** Bobby Bukowski; ***M:*** Lorne Balfe.

War Paint **1/2 1953** Decent western adventure from United Artists. Lt. Billings is leading an Army troop through Death Valley to deliver a peace treaty before a deadline elapses. Chief Grey Cloud's son Taslik offers to be their guide, but the troop's water runs low and renegade attacks increase before Billings' finally figures out that Taslik and his sister Wanima are trying to sabotage his mission. **89m/C; DVD.** Robert Stack; Joan Taylor; Keith Larsen; Charles McGraw; Peter Graves; Robert J. Wilke; Douglas Kennedy; ***D:*** Lesley Selander; ***W:*** Richard Alan Simmons; Martin Berkeley; ***C:*** Gordon Avil; ***M:*** Emil Newman; Arthur Lange.

The War Room **1993 (PG)** Eye opening, sometimes disturbing documentary presents a behind the scenes peek at what really goes on during a Presidential campaign. When filming began in June '92 Bill Clinton was an unknown political quantity and advisors George Stephanopoulous and James Carville were masterminding his campaign. The "War Room" refers to the building in Little Rock where they struggled to organize a small army of volunteers into a winning team. Highlights include the Democratic National Convention, the North Carolina leg of Clinton's campaign bus tour, three Presidential debates, and the week leading up to election night. **93m/C; VHS, DVD, Blu-Ray.** ***D:*** Chris Hegedus; D.A. Pennebaker; ***C:*** D.A. Pennebaker; Kevin Rafferty. Natl. Bd. of Review '93: Feature Doc.

War Room **2015 (PG)** Bland faith-based indie drama that focuses on Christian wish fulfillment via heavy handed dialogue. Struggling in her marriage to Tony (Stallings), Elizabeth Jordan (Shirer) crosses paths with Miss Clara (Abercrombie). The elderly prayer warrior introduces Elizabeth to the concept of a spiritual "war room" as a means of healing her life. Tony does not become a better husband, father, and believer until he is fired from his job, but sees the light by film's end. The lead actors give emotional, sincere performances but it is not enough to overcome its issues. **120m/C; DVD.** Karen Abercrombie; Priscilla Shirer; T.C. Stallings; Tenae Downing; Alena Pitts; ***D:*** Alex Kendrick; ***W:*** Alex Kendrick; Stephen Kendrick; ***C:*** Bob Scott; ***M:*** Paul Mills.

War Story **2014** Tediously depressing and narratively thin, Jackson's drama features a strong central performance from Keener but is nonetheless forgettable. The actress stars as Lee, a war photographer at a low point in her life, holed up in a hotel room as she deals with deep emotional trauma. Jackson makes the crucial mistake of turning Lee's backstory into a mystery, making for a film lacking enough emotional answers to care. Keener is good and Ben Kingsley pops up in a great scene, but by the time Lee's history is revealed, you'll have checked out. **90m/C; DVD.** Catherine Keener; Hafsia Herzi; Ben Kingsley; Vincenzo Amato; ***D:*** Mark Jackson; ***W:*** Mark Jackson; Kristin Gore; ***C:*** Reed Morano; ***M:*** Dave Eggar.

War Tapes **2006** Director Scranton gave digital video cameras to members of a New Hampshire National Guard unit deployed to Iraq. They filmed what they saw, did, and experienced, and sent the footage back. She gave them tips on improving technique and edited it down to a 97-minute movie. The experiment works best when showing the day-to-day dangers of the war. **97m/C; DVD.** ***D:*** Dan Wallin; ***C:*** P.H. O'Brien; Peter Ciardelli; ***M:*** Norman Arnold.

The War Wagon **1967** The Duke plans revenge on Cabot, the greedy mine owner who stole his gold claim and framed him for murder for which he spent years in prison. He assembles a gang to aid him, including a wise-cracking Indian (Keel) and the man sent by Cabot to kill him (Douglas). Wayne's plan is to steal the gold being shipped in Cabot's armor-plated stagecoach, the "war wagon." Well-written, good performances, lots of action. Based on the book "Badman" by Clair Huffaker. **101m/C; VHS, DVD, Blu-Ray.** John Wayne; Kirk Douglas; Howard Keel; Robert Walker, Jr.; Keenan Wynn; Bruce Dern; Bruce Cabot; Joanna Barnes; ***D:*** Burt Kennedy; ***W:*** Clair Huffaker; ***C:*** William Clothier; ***M:*** Dimitri Tiomkin.

War Witch *Rebelle* **2012** Tells the harrowing story of 12-year-old Komona, kidnapped by rebel soldiers who destroy her village and force her to kill to survive. Two years later, she's pregnant and, thanks to a hallucinatory tree sap, has ghostly visions that help save the group, leading their leader to dub her a 'war witch.' Her experiences of carnage don't stop even after she and her friend Magician manage to desert. The film doesn't say specifically in which central African country the civil war is taking place, it was filmed in the Democratic Republic of Congo. French and Lingala with subtitles. **90m/C; DVD.** *CA* Rachel Mwanza; Serge Kanyinda; Mizinga Mwinga; ***D:*** Kim Nguyen; ***W:*** Kim Nguyen; ***C:*** Nicolas Bolduc.

The War Within **2005 (R)** Pakistani student Hassan (Akhtar) is kidnapped from his Paris home and tortured for three years in a detention center during which time he becomes a radicalized Jihadist. After being released he is smuggled into New York where he is to play a key role in a plot to bomb targets in the city. Hassan's friend Sayeed (Bamji) allows him to stay in his home in New Jersey while Hassan is working within a sleeper cell. This sets up a sharp contrast between the western lifestyle of Sayeed's family and the extremist activities of Hassan and his cell. The chilling plausibility of the storyline makes up for any weakness in execution. **90m/C; DVD.** Ayad Akhtar; Nandana Sen; Firdous Bamji; Sarita Choudhury; John Ventimiglia; Mike McGlone; Charles Daniel Sandoval; Varun Sriram; Anjeli Chapman; Ajay Naidu; Aasif Mandvi; ***D:*** Joseph Castelo; ***W:*** Joseph Castelo; Ayad Akhtar; Tom Glynn; ***C:*** Lisa Rinzler; ***M:*** David Holmes.

The War Zone **1998 (R)** Harrowing and uncompromising look at a working class British family torn apart by incest and abuse. Dad (Winstone) has just moved the family to a small Devon town—a move resented by his children, 18-year-old Jessie (Belmont) and 15-year-old Tom (Cunliffe). Mum (Swinton) is too busy with a new baby to see what's going on but lonely Tom gradually (and later graphically) becomes aware that something not right is happening between Jessie and their father. Roth's disquieting directing debut; based on Stuart's novel. **98m/C; VHS, DVD.** *GB* Ray Winstone; Tilda Swinton; Lara Belmont; Freddie Cunliffe; Aisling O'Sullivan; Colin Farrell; Annabelle Apsion; Kate Ashfield; ***D:*** Tim Roth; ***W:*** Alexander Stuart; ***C:*** Seamus McGarvey; ***M:*** Simon Boswell.

Warbirds **WOOF! 2008** This WWII-set creature feature woofer has slightly better CGI than your typical Sci Fi Channel original but it doesn't make up for the bad acting and beyond dumb plot. Officer Jack Toller (Krause) is involved in a secret mission that has a crew of female pilots transporting a weapon to a Pacific island. A storm forces the plane down on the wrong island, which is the land that time forgot since it's populated by flying dinosaurs (and Japanese soldiers). **86m/C; DVD.** David Jensen; Brian Kruase; Jamie Elle Mann; Tohoru Masamune; Lucy Faust; ***D:*** Kevin Gendreau; ***W:*** Kevin Gendreau; ***C:*** Adolfo Bartoli; ***M:*** Margaret Guinee. **CABLE**

Warcraft **2016 (PG-13)** A horde of Orcs invades the planet Azeroth and a group of humans and dissenting Orcs have to stop them in director/co-writer Jones' adaptation of the hit video game. Heavy on CGI, bad make-up, and forced mythology, no one seems to have made an effort to deliver a film that would appeal to anyone outside of the game's loyal fan base. This is fan fiction at its worst—loud and foolish. **123m/C; DVD, Blu-Ray.** Daniel Wu; Ben Schnetzer; Travis Fimmel; Paula Patton; Ben Foster; Dominic Cooper; Toby Kebbell; ***D:*** Duncan Jones; ***W:*** Duncan Jones; Charles Leavitt; ***C:*** Simon Duggan; ***M:*** Ramin Djawadi.

The Ward **1/2** *John Carpenter's The Ward* **2010 (R)** Briskly-paced, old-fashioned horror (it's set in the 1960s) from Carpenter has troubled firebug Kristen one of a quartet of young women confined to a psych ward under the care of sinister Dr. Stringer. Kristen claims to see the ghost of a dead patient who's out for revenge. But she is in a nuthouse, so who's going to believe her? **88m/C; DVD, Blu-Ray.** Amber Heard; Danielle Panabaker; Lyndsy Fonseca; Laura-Leigh; Mamie Gummer; Jared Harris; Mika Boorem; ***D:*** John Carpenter; ***W:*** Michael Rasmussen; Shawn Rasmussen; ***C:*** Yaron Orbach; ***M:*** Mark Kilian.

Ward No. 6 **1/2** *Palata No. 6* **2009** Contemporary update of Anton Chekov's 1892 short story. Dr. Khobotov is showing a documentary film crew around a provincial mental asylum when they encounter former director-turned-patient Ragin. Flashbacks show how the lonely alcoholic's one pleasure was his philosophical discussions with his patient Gromov and how they ultimately just increased Ragin's depression and isolation. Russian with subtitles. **83m/C; DVD.** *RU* Vladimir Ilin; Aleksey Vertkov; Evgeniy Stychkin; Viktor Solovyov; Aleksandr Pankratov Chyornyy; ***D:*** Karen Shakhnazarov; Aleksandr Gornovsky; ***W:*** Karen Shakhnazarov; Aleksandr Borodyyanskiy; ***C:*** Aleksndr Kuznetsov; ***M:*** Evgeny Kadimsky.

WarGames **1/2 1983 (PG)** A young computer whiz, thinking that he's sneaking an advance look at a new line of video games, breaks into the country's NORAD missile-defense system and challenges it to a game of Global Thermonuclear Warfare. The game might just turn out to be the real thing. Slick look at the possibilities of an accidental start to WWIII. Entertaining and engrossing, but with a B-grade ending. **110m/C; VHS, DVD, Blu-Ray.** Matthew Broderick; Dabney Coleman; John Wood; Ally Sheedy; ***D:*** John Badham; ***W:*** Walter F. Parkes; Lawrence Lasker; ***C:*** William A. Fraker; ***M:*** Arthur B. Rubinstein.

WarGames: The Dead Code *WarGames 2* **2008 (PG-13)** The U.S. government has created a supercomputer authorized to assassinate terrorists, which it does by running an online terrorist attack simulation and sending a drone armed with nukes to kill anyone who's good at it. Seems pretty short-sighted even for government officials. **100m/C; DVD.** Matt Lanter; Amanda Walsh; Colm Feore; Chuck Shamata; Maxim Roy; ***D:*** Stuart Gillard; ***W:*** Randall Badat; ***C:*** Bruce Chun; ***M:*** John Van Tongeren.

Warhead **1/2 1996 (R)** Special Forces Ranger Tannen (Zagarino) has to stop a renegade military group, led by his former compatriot Craft (Lara), that have stolen a nuclear warhead and are threatening Washington. **97m/C; VHS, DVD.** Frank Zagarino; Joe Lara; Elizabeth Giordano; ***D:*** Mark Roper; ***W:*** Jeff Albert; ***C:*** Rod Stewart; ***M:*** Robert O. Ragland.

Warlock **1959** Claustrophic, resonant town-bound tale of a marshal (Fonda) and his adoring sidekick (Quinn) who clean up a town which then turns against him. Unusual story, fine performances carry this well beyond the run-of-the-mill cow flick. Fonda re-established himself at the box office as a western star, after "Stage Struck" and "Twelve Angry Men." From the novel by Oakley Hall. Look for "Bones" McCoy from "Star Trek" in a bit part. **122m/C; VHS, DVD, Blu-Ray.** Henry Fonda; Anthony Quinn; Richard Widmark; Dorothy Malone; Wallace Ford; Richard Arlen; Regis Toomey; DeForest Kelley; ***D:*** Edward Dmytryk; ***W:*** Robert Alan Aurthur.

Warlock **1/2 1991 (R)** It's 1691 and the most powerful warlock (Sands) in the New World is only hours away from execution. Luckily, his pal, Satan, whisks him (and witchhunter Grant, by mistake) three hundred years in the future to present-day Los Angeles, where he crash-lands in Singer's house. Surprisingly witty dialogue and neat plot twists outshine occasionally cheesy special effects. **103m/C; VHS, DVD.** Richard E. Grant; Julian Sands; Lori Singer; Mary Woronov; Richard Kuss; Kevin O'Brien; Anna Levine; Allan Miller; David Carpenter; ***D:*** Steve Miner; ***W:*** David N. Twohy; ***C:*** David Eggby; ***M:*** Jerry Goldsmith.

Warlock 3: The End of Innocence **1998 (R)** Kris (Laurence) decides to spend a weekend in the abandoned 16th-century family manor that she has inherited. Disturbed by visions, she comes to realize that her family has a legacy of witchcraft and now she is the sacrifical target of a warlock (Payne). Predictable, although Payne is sufficiently chilling. **94m/C; VHS, DVD.** Bruce Payne; Ashley Laurence; Angel Boris; Boti Ann Bliss; Paul Francis; Rick Hearst; Jan Schweiterman; ***D:*** Eric Freiser; ***W:*** Eric Freiser; Bruce David Eisen. **VIDEO**

Warlock Moon **1/2 1973** Young woman is lured to a secluded spa and falls prey to a coven of witches. **75m/C; VHS, DVD, Blu-Ray.** *MX* Laurie Walters; Joe Spano; Edna Macafee; Ray Goman; Steve Solinsky; Charles Raino; ***D:*** Bill Herbert.

Warlock: The Armageddon **1/2 1993 (R)** Sequel finds Sands back again as the sinister Warlock. This time he's out to gather six Druidic rune stones which have the power to summon Satan's emissary (in the wrong hands) or to stop his nefarious activities (in the right ones). A sect in a small California town serves as the keeper of the stones, only their designated champions are two unprepared teenagers. Sands has all the fun, gleefully dispatching his would-be opponents with some good special effects. **93m/C; VHS, DVD.** Julian Sands; Chris Young; Paula Marshall; Steve Kahan; Charles Hallahan; R.G. Armstrong; Bruce Glover; Zach Galligan; Dawn Ann Billings; Joanna Pacula; ***D:*** Anthony Hickox; ***W:*** Kevin Rock; Sam Bernard; ***C:*** Gerry Lively; ***M:*** Mark McKenzie.

Warlords **1/2 1988 (R)** Lone soldier Carradine battles mutant hordes in a post-apocalyptic desert. Amateurish futuristic drivel. **87m/C; VHS, DVD.** David Carradine; Sid Haig; Ross Hagen; Fox Harris; Robert Quarry; Victoria Sellers; Brinke Stevens; Dawn Wildsmith; ***D:*** Fred Olen Ray.

Warlords *Tou Ming Zhuang* **2008 (R)** Historical war melodrama following the emotional brotherhood and brutal split of a trio of bandits, turned warlords, during the Taiping Rebellion of the 1860s in China. General Pang Qingyun (Li), surviving a massacre of his soldiers, joins with wandering thieves Er-Hu (Lau) and Wen-Xiang (Kaneshiro) with a renewed sense of rebellion. Their loyalty is eventually tested by a romantic triangle that develops between Pang, Er-Hu, and courtesan Lian (Xu). Includes an epic battle scene that gives "Braveheart" a run for its blood. Powerful Chinese import from veteran director Peter Chan. Mandarin with subtitles. **110m/C; Blu-Ray, On Demand.** *CH CH* Jet Li; Andy Lau; Takeshi Kaneshiro; Jinglei Xu; ***D:*** Peter Chan; ***W:*** Tin Chun; Jojo Hui; Oi Wah Lam; Huang Jianxin; Lan Xu; ***C:*** Arthur Wong; ***M:*** Kwong Wing Chan; Peter Kam; Leon Ko.

Warlords of the 21st Century **1/2** *Battletruck* **1982** Bandit gang speed around the galaxy in an indestructible battle cruiser. Then the boys are challenged by a space lawman. Gratuitously violent action pic lacking real action. Filmed on planet New Zealand. **91m/C; VHS, DVD.** Michael Beck; Annie McEnroe; James Wainwright; ***D:*** Harley Cokliss; ***W:*** Harley Cokliss; Irving Austin; John Beech; ***C:*** Chris Menges.

Warm Blooded Killers 🦴🦴 **2001 (R)** Quirky, likeable comedy has brother/sister hitmen (hitpersons?) John and Vicky doing well for themselves until Vicky's boyfriend angers John. Being what he is, John ices the guy, then finds out he was the boss's godson. Disorganized crime hi-jinks ensue. **84m/C; DVD.** Mick Murray; Constance Zimmer; F. William Parker; Carmen Argenziano; ***D:*** Nicholas Siapkaris; Stephen Langford; ***W:*** Stephen Langford; ***C:*** Charles L. Barbee; ***M:*** Matthew Olivo. **VIDEO**

Warm Bodies 🦴🦴 **½ 2013 (PG-13)** Director Levine's horror-comedy proves that there's still life in the overdone zombie genre when it's approached in a fresh way. R (Hoult) is one of the undead after the zombie apocalypse but he's starting to evolve. When R sees Julie (Palmer), he falls instantly in love with her but this Romeo & Juliet seem supernaturally doomed from the start. Levine's twist is clever and surprisingly heartfelt with two incredibly likeable young lead stars. A zombie movie that's not brain-dead! **97m/C; DVD, Blu-Ray.** Nicholas Hoult; Teresa Palmer; Rob Corddry; John Malkovich; Dave Franco; Cory Hardrict; Analeigh Tipton; ***D:*** Jonathan Levine; ***W:*** Jonathan Levine; ***C:*** Javier Aguirresarobe; ***M:*** Marco Beltrami.

Warm Summer Rain 🦴 **½ 1989 (R)** A young couple meet under unusual circumstances and develop a relationship in a desert cabin as they reflect on their unfulfilled pasts. Lust, self-doubt and longing for something to hold onto draw them together as the days pass. Thoroughly self-indulgent romantic comedy that's oddly self-pitying and poorly directed. **85m/C; VHS, DVD.** Kelly Lynch; Barry Tubb; ***D:*** Joe Gayton.

A Warm Wind 🦴🦴 **2011** David learns his cousin Buck, a U.S. Marine, has been severely wounded in Iraq and is coming home and decides to help out, although his family disapproves. Buck accepts David moving in with him as Buck tries to adjust to being home with a physical handicap, a traumatic brain injury, and PTSD. **92m/C; DVD.** Brent King; Tyler Haines; Zac Titus; Landon Ashworth; Robert Sisko; ***D:*** Jeff London; ***W:*** Jeff London; ***C:*** Ben Demaree; ***M:*** Mark Krench.

Warning Shadows 🦴🦴🦴 **1923** Classic example of interior German Expressionism. Brilliantly portrays a jealous husband's emotions and obsessions through shadows. Innocent events seem to reek of sin. A seldom-seen study of the oft-precarious distinction between love and obsession; directly influenced by the classic "The Cabinet of Dr. Caligari." Silent with German and English titles. **93m/B; Silent; VHS, DVD.** *GE* Fritz Kortner; Ruth Weyher; Alexander Granach; Rudolf Klein-Rogge; Max Gulstorff; ***D:*** Arthur Robison; ***W:*** Arthur Robison; ***C:*** Fritz Arno Wagner.

Warning Shot 🦴🦴 **½ 1967** Lots of familiar faces make an appearance in this fast-paced crime drama. L.A. police Sgt. Tom Valens (Janssen) is accused of being trigger-happy after killing a man he swears was armed. No gun is found and the dead man was a well-respected doctor. Suspended and charged with manslaughter, Valens is given a week to investigate and clear his name and he discovers a conspiracy. **100m/C; DVD.** David Janssen; Ed Begley, Sr.; Keenan Wynn; Sam Wanamaker; Lillian Gish; Stefanie Powers; Eleanor Parker; George Grizzard; George Sanders; ***D:*** Buzz Kulik; ***W:*** Mann Rubin; ***C:*** Joseph Biroc; ***M:*** Jerry Goldsmith.

Warning Sign 🦴 **½ 1985 (R)** A high-tech thriller in which a small town is terrorized by the accidental release of an experimental virus at a research facility. Shades of "The Andromeda Strain" and "The China Syndrome," though less originality and quality. **99m/C; VHS, DVD, Blu-Ray.** Sam Waterston; Kathleen Quinlan; Yaphet Kotto; Richard Dysart; Rick Rossovich; ***D:*** Hal Barwood; ***W:*** Hal Barwood; Matthew Robbins; ***C:*** Dean Cundey.

Warp Speed 🦴 **½ 1981** An empty spaceship is found adrift and a psychic is brought in to see if her power to cause the film to go into flashback mode can reveal what happened to the crew who were on their way to Saturn. Cheesy TV fare. **88m/C; DVD.** Barry Gordon; Adam West; Camille Mitchell; David Chandler; ***D:*** Allan Sandler; ***W:*** Peter Dawson; ***C:*** Jose Luis Mignone; ***M:*** Robert Emenegger. **TV**

The Warrior 🦴🦴 **2001 (R)** If you've ever watched a samurai movie, this effort will seem familiar (although less violent). Warrior Lafcadia (Khan) is an indentured enforcer in the northwest Indian state of Rajasthan. During his latest pillage with his men, Lafcadia has a mystical vision and decides to lay down his sword, which enrages his master who sends other warriors after him. Seeking redemption, Lafcadia follows his vision into the Himalayas accompanied by a young thief (Mani) and a blind woman (Marfatia) on a pilgrimage. Hindi with subtitles; there is also an English-language version. **86m/C; DVD.** Irfan Khan; Puru Chhibber; Mandakini Goswami; Sunita Sharma; Noor Mani; Damayanti Marfatia; Firoz Khan; Anupam Shyam; ***D:*** Asif Kapadia; ***W:*** Tim Miller; Asif Kapadia; ***C:*** Roman Osin; ***M:*** Dario Marianelli.

Warrior 🦴🦴🦴🦴 **2011 (PG-13)** On a collision course are two men—Tommy Conlon (Hardy), a traumatized soldier who has returned home with wounds too deep to see, and his estranged brother Brendan (Edgerton), a man who fights to save his home and family from economic crisis. Both men struggle to deal with their recovering-alcoholic, formerly-abusive father (a commanding Nolte). Director O'Connor's piece pounds gloriously past standard sports movie stereotypes and creates a complex story in which the final act, though anticipated, has two fully-developed protagonists without a clear favorite. **140m/C; DVD, Blu-Ray.** Tom (Thomas) Hardy; Joel Edgerton; Nick Nolte; Jennifer (Jenny) Morrison; Frank Grillo; Kevin Dunn; Noah Emmerich; ***D:*** Gavin O'Connor; ***W:*** Gavin O'Connor; Anthony Tambakis; Cliff Dorfman; ***C:*** Masanobu Takayanagi; ***M:*** Mark Isham.

The Warrior & the Sorceress 🦴 **½ 1984 (R)** Mercenary Carradine offers his services to rival factions fighting for control of a water well in an impoverished desert village located on a planet with two suns. He attempts to aggravate the conflicts between the factions, playing the shifty go-between. The sorceress is topless throughout. "A Fistful of Dollars" goes to outer space. Inoffensive, except that better judgment is expected of Carradine. **81m/C; VHS, DVD.** David Carradine; Luke Askew; Maria Socas; Harry Townes; ***D:*** John Broderick; ***W:*** John Broderick.

Warrior of Justice 🦴 **1996** Karate instructor has one of his students disappear after competing in a secret tournament. He then uncovers a black market ring specializing in selling human organs that's run by a former opponent. **90m/C; VHS, DVD.** Richard Lynch; Jorge (George) Rivero; Nick (Nicholas, Niko) Hill; Ian Jacklin; Jorgo Ognenovski; ***D:*** Jorgo Ognenovski; Mike Tristano.

Warrior of the Lost World WOOF! **1984** A warrior must destroy the evil Omega Force who tyrannically rules the world in the distant future, etcetera, etcetera. One-size-fits-all premise; horrible special effects; miserably directed. Only for really hard-core Pleasence fans. **90m/C; VHS, DVD.** Robert Ginty; Persis Khambatta; Donald Pleasence; ***D:*** David Worth.

Warrior Queen 🦴🦴 **½ 2003** Boudica (Kingston) is the leader of her tribe in first-century Briton, which is under Roman rule. Sickened by the increasing demands of the Emperor Nero and his occupying troops, Boudica unites the fractious Celt tribes to lead an onslaught on the Roman camps. But the Romans did not conquer the world by giving in. **90m/C; VHS, DVD.** *GB* Alex Kingston; Steven Waddington; Hugo Speer; Gary Lewis; Emily Blunt; Leanne Rowe; Ben Faulks; ***D:*** Bill Anderson; ***W:*** Andrew Davies; ***C:*** Tudor Lucaciu; ***M:*** Nina Humphreys. **TV**

The Warriors 🦴🦴 **½** *The Dark Avenger* **1955** Swashbuckling adventure about Prince Edward's valiant rescue of Lady Joan and her children from the clutches of the evil Count De Ville. Flynn looks old and pudgy, but buckles his way gallantly through intrepid adventure. Also the last Flynn to see: fun, but more or less completely derivative and familiar. Filmed in England. **85m/C; DVD.** *UK* Errol Flynn; Peter Finch; Joanne Dru; Yvonne Furneaux; Noel Willman; Michael Hordern; ***D:*** Henry Levin; ***W:*** Daniel Ullman; ***C:*** Guy Green.

The Warriors 🦴🦴 **½ 1979 (R)** Action story about a turf battle between NYC street gangs that rages from Coney Island to the Bronx. Silly plot works because of fine performances and direction, excellent use of action and color, and nonstop pace. Fight scenes are very carefully, even obviously, choreographed. **94m/C; VHS, DVD, Blu-Ray, HD-DVD.** Michael Beck; James Remar; Deborah Van Valkenburgh; Thomas G. Waites; David Patrick Kelly; Mercedes Ruehl; Dorsey Wright; David Harris; Brian Tyler; Tom McKitterick; Steve James; Robert Townsend; Lynne Thigpen; Terry Michos; ***D:*** Walter Hill; ***W:*** Walter Hill; David Shaber; ***C:*** Andrew Laszlo; ***M:*** Barry DeVorzon.

A Warrior's Heart 🦴 **½ 2011 (PG)** Brisk, cliched, but not unappealing, sports drama. Showboating high school lacrosse player Conor Sullivan turns his anger over his Marine dad's death into viciousness on the field and gets kicked off the team. Duke Wayne, a comrade of his dad's, drags Conor off to a work camp for some tough-love discipline. The teen is focused so he can prove himself to his coach and get reinstated for the big game. And yes, there's even time for a romance with the coach's daughter. **95m/C; DVD.** Kellan Lutz; Ashley Greene; Adam Beach; Gabrielle Anwar; Aaron Hill; William Mapother; ***D:*** Michael F. Sears; ***W:*** Martin Dugard; ***C:*** Thomas Callaway; ***M:*** Alec Puro.

Warriors of the Wasteland WOOF! *The New Barbarians; I Nuovi Barbari* **1983 (R)** It's the year 2019, and the world has been devastated by a nuclear war. The few survivors try to reach a distant land which emits radio signals indicating the presence of human life. They are hindered by attacks from the fierce homosexual Templars, led by a self-proclaimed priest called One. Mindless rip-off of "Road Warrior" and obviously made on the proverbial shoestring budget. Dubbed. **92m/C; VHS, DVD, Blu-Ray.** *IT* Fred Williamson; Giancarlo Prete; Anna Kanakis; ***D:*** Enzo G. Castellari.

Warriors of Virtue 🦴🦴 **½ 1997 (PG)** Teenaged Ryan Jefers (Yedidia) is transported to the land of Tao where he learns the five virtues (righteousness, benevolence, integrity, wisdom, and loyalty) from the kangaroo-like Warmblood warriors, who live in harmony with humans. Then he must use his knowledge to fight the evil Komodo (MacFadyen), who wishes to steal the energy from Tao to make himself immortal. Nice message for the kids, with enough action to keep them interested, but the Warmbloods are dorky-looking. **101m/C; VHS, DVD.** Mario Yedidia; Angus MacFadyen; Marley Shelton; Chao-Li Chi; ***D:*** Ronny Yu; ***W:*** Michael Vickerman; Hugh Kelley; ***C:*** Peter Pau; ***M:*** Don Davis.

Wasabi 🦴 **½ 2001 (R)** This is one Japanese dip you probably won't care to sample. Hubert (Reno) is a hard-assed, violence-prone French cop, who is forced to take a vacation. He winds up in Tokyo at the funeral of a woman he loved years before. He also discovers he's been left a screechy punk daughter, Yumi (Hirosue), he didn't know about, a mysterious key, and 200 million (in dollars) in the bank. And then the yakuza get involved. High-concept and fast-paced but not particularly entertaining. French and Japanese with subtitles. **94m/C; VHS, DVD.** *FR JP* Jean Reno; Michel Muller; Carole Bouquet; Ryoko Hirosue; ***D:*** Gerard Krawczyk; ***W:*** Luc Besson; ***C:*** Gerard Sterin; ***M:*** Éric Serra.

The Wash 🦴🦴 **2001 (R)** Sean (Dre) loses his job and has his car booted, so pal Dee Loc (Snoop Dogg) helps him out with some news about an opening at the car wash where he works. Soon Sean is assistant manager under crusty owner Mr. Washington (Wallace). Between dealing with the resentment of Loc, and the kidnapping of the boss, along with the usual supply of quirky characters and subplots, Sean has his hands full in this very laid-back, low-key tribute to 1977's "Car Wash." Appealing performances, moments of inspired comedy, and plenty of cameos to watch for make this a pleasant way to kill some time. **96m/C; VHS, DVD.** Snoop Dogg; Dr. Dre; DJ Pooh; George Wallace; Tommy (Tiny) Lister; Alex Thomas; Arif S. Kinchen; Demetrius Navarro; Thomas Chong; Pauly Shore; Lamont Bentley; Bruce Bruce; Shari Watson; Shawn Fonteno; Angell Conwell; ***D:*** DJ Pooh; ***W:*** DJ Pooh; ***C:*** Keith L. Smith.

Washington: Behind Closed Doors 🦴🦴 **1977** ABC miniseries based on co-conspirator John Erlichman's 1976 novel "The Company" about the CIA, Nixon, the presidency, and Watergate. CIA director Bill Martin (Robertson) is afraid info about dirty dealings will get out when Republican president Richard Monckton (Robards) takes office. Monckton's interest in settling old political scores leads to a lot of unsavory business that threatens the entire administration. **540m/C; DVD.** Cliff Robertson; Jason Robards, Jr.; Robert Vaughn; Harold Gould; Barry Nelson; Tony Bill; David Selby; Andy Griffith; John Houseman; Stefanie Powers; Lois Nettleton; ***D:*** Gary Nelson; ***W:*** Eric Bercovici; David W. Rintels; ***C:*** Joseph Biroc; ***M:*** Dominic Frontiere. **TV**

Washington Heights 🦴🦴 **2002 (R)** Washington Heights is an upper west side Manhattan neighborhood largely populated by immigrants from the Dominican Republic. Widower Eddie Ramirez (Milian) provides for his family by running a bodega and would like his twenty-something son Carlos (Perez) to take over the business. But Carlos is a cartoonist with dreams of his own, who wants to move out of the 'hood, although his girlfriend Maggie (Navedo) is reluctant. Then Eddie is shot and Carlos is forced to mind the store, which makes the son feel even more trapped by circumstance. An effective portrayal (warts-and-all) that has something of a pat ending. **85m/C; VHS, DVD.** Manny Perez; Tomas Milian; Danny Hoch; Andrea Navedo; Jude Ciccolella; Bobby Cannavale; Judy Reyes; Callie (Calliope) Thorne; David Zayas; ***D:*** Alfredo de Villa; ***W:*** Alfredo de Villa; Nat Moss; ***C:*** Claudio Chea; ***M:*** Leigh Roberts.

Washington Square 🦴🦴🦴 **1997 (PG)** Adaptation of Henry James' novel, which was previously filmed as "The Heiress." Set in 19th-century New York City (filmed in Baltimore), wealthy spinster Catherine Sloper (Leigh), against the will of her overbearing father (Finney), is pursued by a handsome fortune hunter (Chaplin). Director Holland tends to bluntly simplify James' complex undertones, and Leigh's facial ticks can't equal "The Heiress'" Olivia de Havilland's painful plainness; nonetheless, definitely worth seeing. **115m/C; VHS, DVD, Blu-Ray.** Jennifer Jason Leigh; Ben Chaplin; Albert Finney; Maggie Smith; Judith Ivey; Betsy Brantley; Jennifer Garner; Peter Maloney; Robert Stanton; Scott Jaeck; ***D:*** Agnieszka Holland; ***W:*** Carol Doyle; ***C:*** Jerzy Zielinski; ***M:*** Jan A.P. Kaczmarek.

The Wasp Woman 🦴 **½ 1959** In her quest for eternal beauty, a woman uses a potion made from wasp enzymes. Naturally, she turns into a wasp monster at night. Good fun, courtesy of Corman. **84m/B; VHS, DVD, Blu-Ray.** Susan Cabot; Anthony Eisley; Barboura Morris; Michael Marks; William Roerick; Frank Gerstle; Bruno VeSota; Frank Wolff; Lynn Cartwright; Roy Gordon; ***D:*** Roger Corman; ***W:*** Leo Gordon; ***C:*** Harry Neumann; ***M:*** Fred Katz.

The Wasp Woman 🦴🦴 **1996 (R)** Equally campy cable remake of the 1959 flick finds ex-supermodel-turned-cosmetics company exec Janice Starlin (Rubin) discovering that her fading beauty is causing problems both with her company and her love life. So she turns to a mysterious doctor for help and injects herself with his untested serum, an experimental wasp hormone. She's hoping to discover a fountain of youth and is instead transformed into a nasty-tempered giant insect. Cool, disgusting makeup/costuming. **81m/C; VHS, DVD.** Jennifer Rubin; Daniel J. Travanti; Maria Ford; Doug Wert; ***D:*** Jim Wynorski; ***W:*** Daniella Purcell; ***M:*** Terry Plumeri. **CABLE**

Wassup Rockers 🦴🦴 **2006 (R)** A group of South Central Salvadoran teens hang out, skateboarding, working their punk-rock band, chasing girls—two of whom happen to be rich, so the boys travel to Beverly Hills and get into trouble and then scamper back to their 'hood. The teens are first-time actors basically playing themselves and, for Clark, the film is almost surprisingly sweet. **99m/C; DVD, On Demand.** Carlos Ramirez; Jonathan Velasquez; Francisco Pedrasa; Milton Valesquez; Usvaldo Panameno; Eddie Velasquez; Luis Rojas Salgado; Iris Zelaya; Rosalia; Laura Cellner; Jessica Steinbaum; *D:* Larry Clark; *W:* Larry Clark; *C:* Steve Gainer; *M:* Harry Cody.

Waste Land 1/2 **2010** Brazilian artist Vik Muniz's past work includes recreating famous paintings out of unconventional and/or discarded materials. Returning to Brazil, he begins photographing the garbage pickers ('catadore') who live and work by scavenging and recycling trash from Jardim Gramacho, the world's largest landfill. He concentrates on six workers, including Tiao, who organizes the workers to protect their rights; Irma, who finds unspoiled food to feed them; and Zumbi, who makes a lending library from discarded books. Muniz then uses his photographs as the basis for an art series called "Pictures of Garbage." English and Portuguese with subtitles. **99m/C; On Demand.** *GB D:* Lucy Walker; *C:* Aaron Phillips; Dudu Miranda; Heloisa Passos; *M:* Moby.

A Waste of Shame 1/2 **2005** Shakespeare wrote 154 sonnets—most of them about a 'fair youth' and some about a 'dark lady.' In this speculation, the youth is William Herbert (Sturridge), the son of the Earl of Pembroke, and the lady is half-Moor prostitute Lucie (Varma). The middle-aged Shakespeare (Graves) goes back and forth between the two while neglecting his family back in Stratford. Unfortunately, Sturridge plays William as such a pretty blank that you'll wonder if the poet/playwright just sees the young man as a tabula rosa for his work while his petty jealousy over Lucie's profession gets wearying. **85m/C; DVD.** *GB* Rupert Graves; Thomas Sturridge; Indira Varma; Zoe Wanamaker; Anna Chancellor; Andrew Tiernan; Nicholas (Nick) Rowe; *D:* John McKay; *W:* William Boyd; *C:* Tim Palmer; *M:* Kevin Sargent. **TV**

Wasted *Farewell Bender* **2006 (R)** Impressive debut for Oates despite the seemingly familiar plot. In 1996, three high school buddies reunite several years after graduation for the funeral of their friend Bender. Mitch (Pardue) is a golden college boy, nice guy Stan (Thomas) is a municipal worker, and Dixon (Cooke) is perpetually wasted and blaming himself for being unable to rescue Bender from drowning. The trio takes to reliving their hell-raising teen exploits before realizing it's time to face reality, grow up, and move on. **92m/C; DVD.** Kip Pardue; Eddie Kaye Thomas; Josh Cooke; Kaley Cuoco; Marisa Coughlan; Alexandra Holden; *D:* Mat Oates; *W:* Mat Oates; Jeremiah Lowder; *C:* Paul Marshall; *M:* Tree Adams.

Wasted on the Young **2010 (R)** Australian teen drama with a plot that may seem familiar. Stepbrothers Zack and Darren occupy opposite ends of the high school hierarchy. Zack's the bullying jock and Darren the sullen nerd. Then, at Zack's blowout party, Xandrie, whom Darren has a crush on, is drugged and raped. When she's afraid to pursue the matter, Darren is determined to get justice for her, no matter the consequences. **97m/C; DVD.** *AU* Oliver Ackland; Alex Russell; Adelaide Clemens; *D:* Ben C. Lewis; *W:* Ben C. Lewis; *C:* Dan Freene.

Wasteland *The Rise* **2013** Harvey (Treadaway) was framed and put away by a local crime lord (Maskell). Out now and seeking revenge, he sets in motion a complicated plan with the help of his mates and despite the warnings of his girl (Kirby). The lackluster Brit crime drama fails by never presenting protagonists worth giving a damn about in any way. Director/writer Athale's misfire has some notable style but nowhere near enough substance, and ends up feeling like a limp imitation of similar genre flicks. **108m/C; Streaming.** *UK* Luke Treadaway; Iwan Rheon; Matthew Lewis; Vanessa Kirby; Timothy Spall; Neil Maskell; Gerard Kearns; *D:* Rowan Athale; *W:* Rowan Athale; *C:* Stuart Bentley; *M:* Neil Athale.

The Watch 1/2 **2008** Efficient thriller. College psych student Cassie (DuVall) is still trying to overcome the trauma of a childhood kidnapping. In order to finish her thesis on PTSD in children, she agrees to participate in an isolation experiment by becoming a fire lookout for a month. However, when strange things start happening in the woods, Cassie realizes that her past has something to do with her present danger. **90m/C; DVD.** Clea DuVall; Elizabeth Whitmere; James A. Woods; Victoria Sanchez; Morgan Kelly; Robert Reynolds; *D:* Jim Donovan; *W:* Ben Ripley; *C:* Manfred Guthe; *M:* Luc St. Pierre. **CABLE**

The Watch *Neighborhood Watch* **2012 (R)** Stiller and Vaughn continue to prove that they reside on the latter half of their popularity cycles with this sci-fi comedy that plays up both of their worst habits as comedians. Vaughn screams and Stiller mugs as the two most prominent members of a neighborhood watch (which also includes much-funnier Hill and Ayoade) who stumble across an alien invasion in suburbia. With a bizarre blend of obscene jokes and clichéd, sitcom-ish humor, it comes off as a work that was mangled in rewrites or the editing room more than anything else. **102m/C; DVD, Blu-Ray, Streaming.** Ben Stiller; Vince Vaughn; Jonah Hill; Richard Ayoade; Rosemarie DeWitt; Will Forte; *D:* Akiva Schafer; *W:* Evan Goldberg; Seth Rogen; Jared Stern; *C:* Barry Peterson; *M:* Christophe Beck.

Watch Me **1996 (R)** Photog Paul (Medford) is inspired by new neighbor babe Elise (Burns) and secretly snaps her through the window. Meanwhile, Elise is peeking in on Paul's would-be gal Samantha (Burton) who's having sex with his best bud Alex (Sherwin). Paul of course wants to get more personally involved with Elise (especially after he finds out about Samantha). Lots of nudity—no heat. **90m/C; VHS, DVD.** Robert Medford; Kelly Burns; Jennifer Burton; Steven Sherwin; *D:* Lipo Ching; *W:* Beth Salmon; *C:* Andreas Kossak; *M:* Yoav Goren.

Watch on the Rhine 1/2 **1943** Couple involved with the anti-Nazi underground has escaped the country, but is pursued and harassed by Nazi agents. Adapted by Hammett and Hellman from her play. Performed on stage before the U.S. entered the war, it was the first American play and movie to portray the ugliness of fascism as an ideology, as opposed to the more devious evil of its practical side. The Production Code at the time required that a killer always be punished; the murderer (whose screen motives had been noble) refused to film the offending scene, which explains the tacked-on ending. Superb drama from a pair of highly gifted writers and a great cast. Shumlin also directed the play. **114m/B; VHS, DVD.** Bette Davis; Paul Lukas; Donald Woods; Beulah Bondi; Geraldine Fitzgerald; George Coulouris; Henry Daniell; Helmut Dantine; Donald Buka; Anthony Caruso; Clyde Fillmore; Howard Hickman; Creighton Hale; Kurt Katch; Clarence Muse; Alan Hale, Jr.; Frank Reicher; Mary (Marsden) Young; Lucile Watson; *D:* Herman Shumlin; *W:* Lillian Hellman; Dashiell Hammett; *C:* Hal Mohr; Merritt B. Gerstad; *M:* Max Steiner. Oscars '43: Actor (Lukas); Golden Globes '44: Actor--Drama (Lukas); N.Y. Film Critics '43: Actor (Lukas), Film.

Watch the Birdie 1/2 **1950** It's Skelton three times over as cameraman, father, and grandfather! First, he accidentally films a scam that would send the lovely Miss Dahl filing for bankruptcy. Later a crazy chase scene unfolds, that will have viewers rolling, as Skelton the cameraman nabs the bad guys and turns them over to the cops. Light fun that will charm Skelton fans. **70m/B; VHS, DVD.** Red Skelton; Arlene Dahl; Ann Miller; Leon Ames; *D:* Jack Donohue.

The Watcher **2000 (R)** Serial killer Reeves leaves clues for burned-out FBI agent Spader as to who his next victim will be so Spader will get back in the game. Start with a direct-to-video feel, add a plot cribbed from better serial killer thrillers, throw in a bunch of showy visual effects and Reeves' hysterical line readings, and you've got a night of talking back to the TV, MST3K-style. It's ridiculous, but that's half the fun. **97m/C; VHS, DVD, Blu-Ray.** Keanu Reeves; James Spader; Marisa Tomei; Ernie Hudson; Chris Ellis; Robert Cicchini; Jenny (Jennifer) McShane; Yvonne Niami; Gina Alexander; Joe Sikora; Rebekah Louise Smith; *D:* Joe Charbanic; *W:* Joe Charbanic; David Elliott; Clay Ayers; *C:* Michael Chapman; *M:* Marco Beltrami.

The Watcher in the Woods **1981 (PG)** When an American family rents an English country house, the children are haunted by the spirit of a long-missing young girl. A very bland attempt at a ghost story. **83m/C; VHS, DVD.** Bette Davis; Carroll Baker; David McCallum; Ian Bannen; Lynn-Holly Johnson; Kyle Richards; Frances Cuka; Richard Pasco; *D:* John Hough; *W:* Brian Clemens; *C:* Alan Hume; *M:* Stanley Myers.

Watchers **1988 (R)** From the suspense novel by Dean R. Koontz, a secret experiment goes wrong, creating half-human monsters. A boy and his extremely intelligent dog are soon pursued. Low-budget, Corman-influenced production is tacky but effective. **99m/C; VHS, DVD.** Barbara Williams; Michael Ironside; Corey Haim; Duncan Fraser; Blu Mankuma; Dale Wilson; Colleen Winton; *D:* Jon Hess; *W:* Bill Freed; *C:* Richard Leiterman; *M:* Joel Goldsmith.

Watchers 2 **1990 (R)** Sequel to "Watchers" follows the further adventures of a super-intelligent golden retriever who leads a Marine to an animal psychologist and then attempts to warn them both of a mutant killer. The dog says woof, but this movie doesn't quite. Fun for lovers of hounds or horror flicks. **101m/C; VHS, DVD.** Marc Singer; Tracy Scoggins; *D:* Thierry Notz; *M:* Rick Conrad.

Watchers 3 1/2 **1994 (R)** A secret military outpost in the South American jungles is attacked by a carnivorous predator. Ex-military convicts are sent to rescue the remaining survivors and to make certain the government experiment that started the terror never comes to light. **95m/C; VHS, DVD.** Wings Hauser; Gregory Scott Cummins; Daryl Roach; John K. Linton; Lolita Ronalds; Frank Novak; *D:* Jeremy Stanford.

Watchers Reborn **1998 (R)** Genetically engineered mutants stalk the innocent with only a hyper-intelligent golden retriever (of course!) able to stop them. Based on the novel "Watchers" by Dean R. Koontz. **83m/C; VHS, DVD.** Mark Hamill; Lisa Wilcox; Stephen Macht; Lou Rawls; Floyd Levine; Gary Collins; Kane Hodder; *D:* John Carl Buechler; *W:* Sean Dash; *M:* Terry Plumeri.

Watching the Detectives 1/2 **2007** Oddball romantic comedy that fails to deliver on the appeal of its leads. Movie geek/video store owner Neil (Murphy) is obsessed with film noir and he can spot a femme fatale when she walks into his joint. Violet (Liu) is big on spontaneity, but when they start dating, her penchant for increasingly dangerous practical jokes has Neil questioning her sanity. Bogie never had this kind of trouble with Bacall. **91m/C; DVD.** Cillian Murphy; Lucy Liu; Michael Panes; Jason Sudeikis; Callie (Calliope) Thorne; *D:* Paul Soter; *W:* Paul Soter; *C:* Christopher Lanzenberg; *M:* Nathan Barr. **VIDEO**

Watchmen **2009 (R)** In an alternate reality of 1985, superheroes have been outlawed or taken under government control. Vigilante Rorschach (Haley) investigates the murder of a former superhero, which reunites him with some old, albeit flawed, colleagues: Dr. Manhattan (Crudup), a giant glowing blue nudist; Silk Spectre II (Akerman), the sexy daughter of a former superhero; and Nite Owl (Wilson), a Batman-knock off. After investigation, the Watchmen uncover a conspiracy to discredit and kill the retired crimefighters. The unconventional structure and focus on backstories often make it difficult to follow. Director Snyder's highly-anticipated and ambitious attempt to bring Alan Moore's post-modern cult graphic novel to the big screen will inevitably upset some fanboys, and send others to orgasmic heights, but overall, it's an uneven disappointment. **161m/C; Blu-Ray, On Demand.** Jackie Earle Haley; Billy Crudup; Jeffrey Dean Morgan; Matthew Goode; Carla Gugino; Malin Akerman; Stephen McHattie; Patrick Wilson; Matt Frewer; *D:* Zack Snyder; *W:* David Hayter; Alex Tse; *C:* Larry Fong; *M:* Tyler Bates.

Water **1985 (PG-13)** The resident governor of a Caribbean British colony juggles various predatory interests when a valuable mineral water resource is found. The good cast is wasted in this all-too-silly effort. **89m/C; VHS, DVD.** *GB* Michael Caine; Brenda Vaccaro; Leonard Rossiter; Valerie Perrine; Jimmie Walker; *Cameo(s):* Eric Clapton; George Harrison; Fred Gwynne; Ringo Starr; *D:* Dick Clement; *W:* Dick Clement; Ian La Frenais; Bill Persky.

Water **2005 (PG-13)** Following Hindu custom in 1938 India, when child bride Chuyia's (Sarala) aged husband dies, her family sends her to live in exile in an ashram for widows. Chuyia can't understand and rebels against the restrictions until she is befriended by religious, middle-aged Shakuntala (Biswas) and beautiful, young Kalyani (Ray). Kalyani is forced to work as a prostitute to help support the ashram but falls in love with Narayan (Abraham), whose progressive views are inspired by Gandhi. However, their involvement leads to both tragedy and freedom. The last of Mehta's trilogy following "Fire" and "Earth." Hindi with subtitles. **117m/C; DVD.** *CA* Seema Biswas; Lisa Ray; Raghuvir Yadav; Kulbashan Kharbanda; John Abraham; Sarala; Manorama; Vidula Javalgekar; Vinay Pathak; Gerson Da Cunha; Mohan Jhangiani; *D:* Deepa Mehta; *C:* Giles Nuttgens; *M:* Mychael Danna; A.R. Rahman.

Water Babies *Slip Slide Adventures* **1979 (G)** When a chimney sweep's 12-year-old apprentice is wrongly accused of stealing silver, the boy and his dog fall into a pond and eventually rescue some of the characters they find there. Combination of live-action and animated fairy-tale story set in 19th-century London. Boring, unless you're a young child with equivalent standards. Based on the book by Charles Kingsley. **93m/C; VHS, DVD.** *GB* James Mason; Billie Whitelaw; David Tomlinson; Paul Luty; Sammantha Coates; *D:* Lionel Jeffries.

The Water Diviner 1/2 **2015 (R)** Russell Crowe makes his directorial debut with this well-meaning but flat drama that veers between melodrama, history lesson, and action film. Set after the Battle of Gallipoli in 1915, Crowe plays an Australian farmer named Connor who learns that his three sons sent to war will not be returning home again. He decides to travel to Turkey to find the young men, or at least find their bodies in order to give them a proper burial. He ends up staying at a hotel in Istanbul, where he meets Ayshe (Kurylenko), a supportive manager. Crowe is a workmanlike director, not giving this film the personality or scope it needed. **111m/C; Blu-Ray.** Russell Crowe; Olga Kurylenko; Yilmaz Erdogan; Cem Yilmaz; Jai Courtney; *D:* Russell Crowe; *W:* Andrew Knight; Andrew Anastasios; *C:* Andrew Lesnie; *M:* David Hirschfelder.

Water Drops on Burning Rocks *Gouttes d'Eau sur Pierres Brulantes* **1999** Director Ozon pays tribute to late German director Rainer Werner Fassbinder by resurrecting his unproduced play. In the '70s, 50-year-old businessman Leopold (Giraudeau) picks up 19-year-old Franz (Zidi), who winds up moving in, though the mismatched duo fight constantly. When Franz's former girlfriend, Anna (Sagnier), shows up, Leopold even begins seducing her. Then transexual Vera (Thomson), Leopold's ex-girlfriend, also comes back. And it's a very messy foursome, indeed. French with subtitles. **82m/C; VHS, DVD.** *FR* Bernard Giraudeau; Anna Thomson; Malik Zidi; Ludivine Sagnier; *D:* Francois Ozon; *W:* Francois Ozon; *C:* Jeanne Lapoirie.

Water for Elephants 1/2 **2011 (PG-13)** In this Depression-era drama, veterinary student Jacob (Pattinson) can't complete his exams after a family tragedy leaves him penniless. He joins the second-rate Benzini Brothers traveling circus and makes the mistake of falling in love with star performer Marlena (Witherspoon) who's married to abusive animal trainer August (Waltz). The most poignant moments occur when Jacob and Marlena tend to the main attraction, an elephant named Rosie, with whom Jacob develops a means of nonverbal communication. Try as they might, the leads don't quite click but it's still worth watching. Adapted from Sara Gruen's novel. **120m/C; DVD, Blu-Ray, On Demand.** Reese Witherspoon; Robert Pattinson; Christoph Waltz; Hal Holbrook; Paul Schneider; Tim Guinee; Mark Povinelli; *D:* Francis Lawrence; *W:* Richard LaGravenese; *C:* Rodrigo Prieto; *M:* James Newton Howard.

The Water Horse: Legend of the Deep 1/2 **2007 (PG)** The water horse turns out to be the Loch Ness Monster and this charming family film explains how it got into that Scottish loch. Lonely young Angus (Etel) is living with his stern housekeeper mum (Watson) and sister Kirstie (Xi) on a Scottish estate while dad is off fighting in WWII. Angus finds an egg on the beach that hatches into a cute, mischievous critter Angus names Crusoe that soon grows to mammoth size. So he must secretly be transported to the loch under the noses of snooty British soldiers stationed on the property. Visual effects are good. Based on the novel by Dick King-Smith. **111m/C; Blu-Ray, On Demand.** *GB US* Alex(ander Nathan) Etel; Emily Watson; Ben Chaplin; David Morrissey; Priyanka Xi; Brian Cox; ***D:*** Jay Russell; ***W:*** Robert Nelson Jacobs; ***C:*** Oliver Stapleton; ***M:*** James Newton Howard.

The Waterboy **1998 (PG-13)** Another in a continuing line of deliberately stupid comedies finds Sandler a not-too-bright, constantly picked-on waterboy for a lousy Louisiana college football team. After a player taunts him once too often, he tackles the big guy, and is suddenly promoted to player—much to the dismay of his overprotective mother, Bates. Loser player turns loser team into winners after some contrived obstacles: you've seen it before, but Sandler cultists (and less discerning football fans) will love it anyway. **90m/C; VHS, DVD.** Adam Sandler; Kathy Bates; Henry Winkler; Fairuza Balk; Jerry Reed; Larry (Lawrence) Gilliard, Jr.; Blake Clark; Rob Schneider; Clint Howard; Allen Whiting; Robert Kokol; ***D:*** Frank Coraci; ***W:*** Adam Sandler; Tim Herlihy; ***C:*** Steven Bernstein; ***M:*** Alan Pasqua.

The Waterdance **1991 (R)** Autobiographical film based on the experiences of writer/co-director Jimenez. When writer Joel Garcia (Stoltz) is paralyzed in a hiking accident he finds himself dealing with not only the rehab process itself but his feelings, the feelings of his married lover, and those of his fellow patients. Deals unsentimentally with all the physical adjustments, including the sexual ones. Resolutions may be predictable but the performances rise above any script weaknesses. The title refers to Hill's dream of dancing on water—and the fear of drowning if he stops. **106m/C; VHS, DVD.** Eric Stoltz; Wesley Snipes; William Forsythe; Helen Hunt; Elizabeth Pena; Grace Zabriskie; ***D:*** Neal Jimenez; Michael Steinberg; ***W:*** Neal Jimenez; ***C:*** Mark Plummer; ***M:*** Michael Convertino. Ind. Spirit '93: First Feature, Screenplay; Sundance '92: Aud. Award, Screenplay.

Waterfront **1944** Nazis coerce German-Americans into helping them in WWII-era San Francisco. Credulity defying spy doings, but that's okay. Fairly entertaining wartime drama about paranoia on the home front. **68m/B; VHS, DVD.** John Carradine; J. Carrol Naish; Terry Frost; Maris Wrixon; Edwin Maxwell; ***D:*** Steve Sekely.

Waterhole Number 3 **1/2 1967 (PG)** Three Confederate army buddies steal a fortune in gold bullion from the Union Army and hide it in a waterhole in the desert. One of the funnier entries in the Western comedy genre. **95m/C; DVD.** James Coburn; Carroll O'Connor; Margaret Blye; Claude Akins; Bruce Dern; Joan Blondell; James Whitmore; ***D:*** William A. Graham; ***W:*** Robert R. Young; ***C:*** Robert Burks; ***M:*** Dave Grusin.

Waterland **1992 (R)** Meandering drama about a history teacher who tries to solve a personal crisis by using his class as a sounding board to describe his troubled past in England. Dark secrets abound, including incest, madness, murder, and the terrifying love between the teacher and his childhood bride. Melancholy, overwrought but partially redeemed by the lead performances of Irons and his (real-life and cinematic) wife, Cusack. The film's setting has been unfortunately moved from London to Pittsburgh, destroying story links. Based on the novel by Graham Swift. **95m/C; VHS, DVD.** Jeremy Irons; Ethan Hawke; Sinead Cusack; John Heard; Grant Warnock; Lena Headey; Pete Postlethwaite; Cara Buono; ***D:*** Stephen Gyllenhaal; ***W:*** Peter Prince; ***C:*** Robert Elswit; ***M:*** Carter Burwell.

Waterloo Bridge **1940** In London during WWI, Capt. Roy Cronin (Taylor), a soldier from an aristocratic family, begins a tragic romance with ballet dancer Myra Lester (Leigh) when they meet by chance on the foggy Waterloo Bridge. She loses her job and when Roy is listed as dead, Myra's despair turns her to prostitution. But when Roy returns from POW camp, they once again meet by accident on Waterloo Bridge, and their romance resumes, with Myra struggling to conceal her shameful secret. Four-hanky drama with fine performances by Leigh (her first after "Gone with the Wind") and Taylor. Based on the play by Robert E. Sherwood. **109m/B; VHS, DVD.** Vivien Leigh; Robert Taylor; Lucile Watson; Sir C. Aubrey Smith; Maria Ouspenskaya; Virginia Field; ***D:*** Mervyn LeRoy; ***W:*** S.N. Behrman; George Froeschel; Hans Rameau; ***C:*** Joseph Ruttenberg; ***M:*** Herbert Stothart.

Waterloo Road **1/2 1945** Wartime romantic melodrama. Jim is separated from wife Tillie due to his active service in the war. She takes up with smoothie Ted, who's a lying shirker, and when Jim finds out, he goes AWOL. He hunts down Ted and wins back Tillie by beating the blighter silly during an air raid. **73m/B; DVD.** *UK GB* John Mills; Joy Shelton; Stewart Granger; Alastair Sim; Alison Leggatt; Beatrice Varley; George Carney; ***D:*** Sidney Gilliat; ***W:*** Sidney Gilliat; ***C:*** Arthur Crabtree.

Watermelon Man **1970 (R)** The tables are turned for a bigoted white guy when he wakes up one morning to discover he has become a black man. Broad comedy with not much place to go is still engaging. Cambridge takes on both roles, appearing in unconvincing white makeup. **97m/C; VHS, DVD.** Godfrey Cambridge; Erin Moran; Estelle Parsons; Howard Caine; D'Urville Martin; Kay Kimberly; Paul Williams; ***D:*** Melvin Van Peebles; ***W:*** Herman Raucher; ***C:*** Herman Raucher; ***M:*** Melvin Van Peebles.

The Watermelon Woman **1997** Cheryl (Dunye) is a young, black, lesbian video store clerk who wants to be a documentary filmmaker. She becomes obsessed with a black actress seen in some 1930s black films, who was known only as the "Watermelon Woman." Doing research, Cheryl discovers the woman's name was Fae Richards (Bronson) and that she was a lesbian who had an affair with her white director. While deciding to film a documentary about Fae, Cheryl's personal life begins to parallel Fae's when she briefly falls for white customer, Diana (Turner). **85m/C; VHS, DVD.** Cheryl Dunye; Valerie Walker; Guinevere Turner; Lisa Marie Bronson; ***D:*** Cheryl Dunye; ***W:*** Cheryl Dunye; ***C:*** Michelle Crenshaw; ***M:*** Paul Shapiro.

Waterproof **1999 (PG-13)** Reynolds is oddly cast but very effective as Eli, a Jewish shopkeeper who is shot by a young would-be robber, Thaniel (Dye). To protect him from prosecution, Thaniel's mother, Tyree (Grace), whisks her son and Eli to her childhood home in Waterproof, Louisiana. She's been away for 15 years and finds a great deal of tension with her family, but they are willing to take Tyree and Thaniel in to assist them. The film examines the struggles that exist between family members and individuals from differing ethnic backgrounds. Without becoming overwrought, the film delivers positive message while being entertaining. Special kudos to Jones, who overcomes his comic reputation by portraying a man with severe brain damage. **94m/C; DVD.** Burt Reynolds; April Grace; Cordereau Dye; Whitman Mayo; Anthony Lee; Orlando Jones; Ja'net DuBois; ***D:*** Barry Berman.

Water's Edge **2003** Tense little thriller finds New Yorkers Robert (Fillion) and Molly (West) relocating to a small town and the rustic lakeside cabin that Robert inherited from his father. But this friendly town hides some dirty secrets, including blackmail and murder. **?m/CVHS, DVD.** Nathan Fillion; Chandra West; Emmanuelle Vaugier; Daniel Baldwin; Andrew Moxham; ***D:*** Harvey Kahn; ***W:*** Craig Brewer. **VIDEO**

Watership Down **1/2 1978 (PG)** Wonderfully animated story based on Richard Adams's allegorical novel about how a group of rabbits escape fear and overcome oppression while searching for a new and better home. It's really an adult theme with sufficient violence to the poor wittle wabbits to scare the kiddies. **92m/C; VHS, DVD, Blu-Ray.** *GB V:* Ralph Richardson; Zero Mostel; John Hurt; Denholm Elliott; Harry Andrews; Michael Hordern; Joss Ackland; Richard Briers; ***D:*** Martin Rosen; ***W:*** Martin Rosen.

Waterworld **1/2 1995 (PG-13)** "The Man From Atlantis" meets "Mad Max." Industry knives sharpened with glee before release, with some insiders calling this luck-impaired project "Fishtar" and "Kevin's Gate." Most of the estimated $150 million budget seems to have ended up on screen, which makes for a visually striking, and at times daunting, film. Costner, who did just about everything but cater the meals, stars as Mariner, a mutant man-fish who reluctantly helps human survivors search for the mythical Dryland since the polar ice caps melted, flooding the earth. The bad guys are the Smokers, led by the evil Hopper, who can play these roles in his sleep. Entertaining, but not riveting, as the budget and PR hype leads one to expect. The floating set was anchored (not very well, apparently) off the Hawaiian coast and was lost once during a tropical storm. Costner bet the boat on this one and lost more than just money. **135m/C; VHS, DVD, Blu-Ray, HD-DVD.** Kevin Costner; Dennis Hopper; Jeanne Tripplehorn; Tina Majorino; Michael Jeter; R.D. Call; Robert Joy; Jack Kehler; Zakes Mokae; Sab Shimono; Jack Black; Kim Coates; John Toles-Bey; Ari Barak; Sean M. Whalen; Robert LaSardo; Lee Arenberg; ***D:*** Kevin Reynolds; ***W:*** Peter Rader; Marc Norman; David N. Twohy; ***C:*** Dean Semler; ***M:*** James Newton Howard. Golden Raspberries '95: Worst Support. Actor (Hopper).

The Watsons Go to Birmingham **2013 (PG)** A period drama based on the best-selling book, The Watsons Go to Birmingham. In the summer of 1963, the African-American Watson family faces internal tensions. Living in Flint, Michigan, father Daniel (Harris) and mother Wilona (Rose) have three children. When their teenage delinquent eldest son Byron (Knight) continues to act inappropriately, Daniel and Wilona decide the family needs the perspective and influence of no nonsense Grandma Sands (Richardson). Making a road trip to Birmingham, Alabama, to see her, the family learns that life in the South is very different than in Michigan and unexpectedly experiences history. **87m/C; DVD, Streaming, Download.** Bryce Clyde Jenkins; Harrison Knight; Skai Jackson; Anika Noni Rose; Wood Harris; LaTanya Richardson Jackson; ***D:*** Kenny Leon; ***W:*** Caliope Brattlestreet; Stephen Glantz; Tonya Lewis Lee; ***C:*** James Chressanthis; ***M:*** Mervyn Warren. **VIDEO**

The Wave *Die Welle* **2008** In 1967, history teacher Ron Jones found himself having trouble explaining to his students how Germany willingy allowed the Nazis to rise to power, and decided to do an experiment to show them instead by slowly turning the class into fascists. He ended it in less than a week because he began to lose control of the experiment. Eventually the experimnt was novelized and made into this film which transports the setting from California to Germany. Teacher Wenger (Jurgen Vogel) is unable to convince his class that the Nazis could ever again come to power, and makes the mistake of creating the movement himself to prove it to them. **107m/C; DVD.** *GE* Jurgen Vogel; Frederick Lau; Max Riemelt; Jennifer Ulrich; Christiane Paul; ***D:*** Dennis Gansel; ***W:*** Dennis Gansel; Johnny Dawkins; Ron Birnbach; Peter Thorwarth; ***C:*** Torsten Breuer; ***M:*** Heiko Maile. **VIDEO**

The Wave *Bolgen* **2015 (R)** A clever Norwegian take on the American disaster movie. A real fjord, called Geiranger, suffers a rock slide causing a lot of land to make its way into the water. The resulting tsunami threatens to bury an entire town in water. Luckily, the residents are prepared with an alarm system and bunkers in which to hide. Now, if scientist Kristian (Joner) can only convince them that it's time to run for cover. It's a simple action movie, done well, especially the centerpiece sequence that gives it a name. **104m/C; Blu-Ray, Streaming.** *NO* Kristoffer Joner; Ane Dahl Torp; Jonas Hoff Oftebro; Eili Harboe; Fridtjov Saheim; ***D:*** Roar Uthaug; ***W:*** John Kare Raake; Harald Rosenlow-Eeg; ***C:*** John Christian Rosenlund; ***M:*** Magnus Beite.

Waves **2019 (R)** Handsome Florida teen Tyler (Harrison) seems to have it all. He's a successful high school wrestler with beautiful girlfriend Alexis (Demie) and a loving sister Emily (Russell) and caring stepmother Catherine (Goldsberry). Though Tyler's father is stern, Ronald (Brown) believes he is helping to make his son successful. A shoulder injury kicks off a series of events that cause Tyler's life to unravel. Despite tragic events, the family tries to endure and move forward. Beautifully acted, it's an empathetic exploration of extreme pain and the long-term effects of bad decisions. **135m/C; DVD, Blu-Ray.** Taylor Russell; Kelvin Harrison, Jr.; Alexa Demie; Renee Goldsberry; Sterling K. Brown; ***D:*** Trey Edward Shults; ***W:*** Trey Edward Shults; ***C:*** Drew Daniels; ***M:*** Trent Reznor; Atticus Ross.

Wax Mask **1/2** *M.D.C. Maschera di Cera* **1997** Liner notes state that this loose remake of "House of Wax" was to have been directed by Lucio Fulci ("Zombie," "The Black Cat") who died before he could begin work. It was produced in part by Dario Argento, but the important thing for horror fans to know is that this one owes just as much to Stuart Gordon's "Re-Animator." It takes the same gleeful approach to outrageous medical horror and sex, though overall, it is a much more polished looking film with expensive production values, an attractive (if unknown in America) young cast, and a sharply focused image. The setting is Paris and Rome in the early 20th century. Sonia (Mondello) witnessed the brutal murder of her parents as a child. Years later, she goes to work for Boris Volkoff (Hossein), whose macabre wax museum hides terrible secrets. Director Sergio Stivaletti came to the job through special effects expertise and his work here (in both capacities) is very good. This is a man to watch. The plot goes much too far for the film ever to find a large mainstream audience, and that's the point of Grand Guignol horror. **98m/C; DVD, Blu-Ray.** *IT FR* Robert Hossein; Romina Mondello; Ricardo Serventi Longhi; ***D:*** Sergio Stivaletti; ***W:*** Lucio Fulci; ***C:*** Sergio Salvati. **VIDEO**

Waxwork **1/2 1988 (R)** A wax museum opens up, and it is soon evident that the dummies are not what they seem. Garbled nonthriller. Available in a 100-minute unrated version. **97m/C; VHS, DVD, Blu-Ray.** Zach Galligan; Deborah Foreman; Michelle Johnson; Dana Ashbrook; Miles O'Keeffe; Patrick Macnee; David Warner; John Rhys-Davies; ***D:*** Anthony Hickox; ***W:*** Anthony Hickox; ***C:*** Gerry Lively; ***M:*** Roger Bellon.

Waxwork 2: Lost in Time **1/2** *Lost in Time* **1991 (R)** A young couple (Galligan and Schnarre) barely escape with their lives when the infamous waxworks museum burns down. A severed hand also gets loose and follows Schnarre home and murders her stepfather, leaving her to take the blame. In order to prove her innocence, the couple must travel through a bizarre time machine. Extraordinary special effects, strange plot twists, and recreations of scenes from past horror movies make this a highly entertaining sequel. **104m/C; VHS, DVD, Blu-Ray.** Zach Galligan; Alexander Godunov; Bruce Campbell; Michael Des Barres; Monica Schnarre; Martin Kemp; Sophie Ward; Marina Sirtis; Juliet Mills; John Ireland; Patrick Macnee; David Carradine; Drew Barrymore; ***D:*** Anthony Hickox; ***W:*** Anthony Hickox; ***C:*** Gerry Lively.

The Way **1/2 2010 (PG-13)** Father/son inspirational pic as writer/director Estevez bases some of his story on personal experiences as well as Jack Hitt's book "Off the Road: A Modern-Day Walk Down the Pilgrim's Route in Spain" and gives the lead role to his dad Martin Sheen. When his son David (Estevez) is killed while starting his pilgrim's trek in France, widower Tom Avery (Sheen) decides to fulfill David's last wish by scattering his ashes along the 400-kilometer route of Spain's Camino de Santiago. Naturally, it becomes a sort of emotional and spiritual re-awakening as Tom picks up some travelling companions along the way. **123m/C; DVD, Blu-Ray.** Martin Sheen; Yorick Van Wageningen; Deborah Kara Unger; James Nesbitt; Antonio Gil; Emilio Estevez; ***D:*** Emilio Estevez; ***W:*** Emilio Estevez; ***C:*** Juanmi (Juan Miguel) Azpiroz; ***M:*** Tyler Bates.

The Way Ahead *The Immortal Battalion* **1944** Reed filmed in a semi-documentary style to tell a gritty story of civilian conscripts who must be molded into a fighting unit. That's the thankless job of Sgt. Fletcher (Hartnell) and Lt. Perry (Niven). However, when the new platoon is sent to North Africa to fight Rommel's Afrika Korps, they realize the value of their hated training. **115m/B; DVD.** *GB* David Niven; William Hartnell; Leslie Dwyer; Stanley Holloway; James Donald; Jimmy Hanley; Raymond Huntley; Hugh Burden; ***D:*** Carol Reed; ***W:*** Peter Ustinov; Eric Ambler; ***C:*** Derick Williams; Guy Green; ***M:*** William Alwyn.

The Way Back 1/2 **2010 (PG-13)** Inspired by the incredible true story of a group of men who escaped a 1940s Red Army prison in Siberia, surviving a 4,000 mile trek to freedom. An American, going by "Mr. Smith" (Harris), a Russian named Valka (Farrell), and their fellow escapees cross the Siberian arctic, the Gobi desert, and the Himalayas to reach safety. The dangerous terrain, along with gritty performances, lends itself to a sense of realism. Ultimately writer and director Weir takes too many liberties, resulting in a near fictionalization of the events. Too many questions remain and actual survival skills are glossed over. Those looking for the truth should stick to the book by Slavomir Rawicz. **132m/C; Blu-Ray, On Demand.** Jim Sturgess; Colin Farrell; Ed Harris; Saoirse Ronan; Mark Strong; Gustaf Skarsgard; Alex Potocean; Sebastian Urzendowsky; Dragos Bucur; ***D:*** Peter Weir; ***W:*** Peter Weir; ***C:*** Russell Boyd; ***M:*** Burkhard von Dallwitz.

The Way Back 1/2 **2020 (R)** Affleck delivers a career-high performance as Jack Cunningham, a former high school basketball star who abandoned the game until he's asked to return as coach of his alma mater's struggling team. Like any good underdog/redemption sports flick, this one packs an emotional punch, and the final seconds before the buzzer will have you on the edge of your seat. **108m/C; DVD, Blu-Ray.** Ben Affleck; Al Madrigal; Janina Gavankar; Michaela Watkins; Brandon Wilson; ***D:*** Gavin O'Connor; ***W:*** Brad Ingelsby; ***C:*** Eduard Grau; ***M:*** Rob Simonsen.

Way Down East **1920** Melodramatic silent drama of a country girl who is tricked into a fake marriage by a scheming playboy. The famous final scene of Gish adrift on the ice floes is in color. One of Griffith's last critical and popular successes. Includes the original Griffith-approved musical score. Remade in 1935 with Henry Fonda. **107m/B; Silent; VHS, DVD, Blu-Ray.** Lillian Gish; Richard Barthelmess; Lowell Sherman; Creighton Hale; Burr McIntosh; Kate Bruce; Florence Short; ***D:*** D.W. Griffith; ***W:*** D.W. Griffith; Joseph R. Grismer; ***C:*** Billy (G.W.) Bitzer; Hendrik Sartov.

The Way Home 1/2 **2001 (PG)** Because his mother has lost her job, a seven-year-old boy (Yoo) is forced to leave the city of Seoul to stay with his wizened mute grandmother (Kim) in her ranshackle rural hut. The spoiled kid can't believe he has to do without fast food, let alone indoor plumbing and other modern conveniences. But what the boy eventually comes to realize is that his grandmother loves him unconditionally. Korean with subtitles. **85m/C; VHS, DVD.** *NK* Seung-Ho Yoo; Eul-Boon Kim; Hyo-Hee Dong; ***D:*** Jeong-Hyang Lee; ***W:*** Jeong-Hyang Lee; ***C:*** Hong-Shik Yoon; ***M:*** Dae-Hong Kim; Yan-Hee Kim.

Way of a Gaucho **1952** Martin (Calhoun), a gaucho in Argentina in the 1870s, avoids a prison sentence by joining the army. He deserts and forms an outlaw band that's hunted by his former commander Salinas (Boone). Martin realizes he doesn't have much of a future and he really just wants to marry his pregnant girlfriend Teresa (Tierney) and settle down. **91m/C; DVD.** Rory Calhoun; Gene Tierney; Richard Boone; Hugh Marlowe; Everett Sloane; ***D:*** Jacques Tourneur; ***W:*** Philip Dunne; ***C:*** Harry Jackson; ***M:*** Sol Kaplan.

A Way of Life 1/2 **2004** One of those unrelentingly bleak British kitchen-sink dramas with a completely unsympathetic lead. Leigh-Anne is a young, trouble-prone, unemployed single mum who hangs out with a bunch of racist losers to the concern of her granny, who wants custody of Leigh-Ann's baby daughter. When she takes the baby to the hospital after a minor accident, suspicious doctors insist on keeping the child and paranoid Leigh-Anne blames her immigrant neighbor for her problems, resulting in more tragedy. **91m/C; DVD.** Brenda Blethyn; Nathan Jones; Stephanie James; Gary Sheppeard; Dean Wong; Sara Gregory; Oliver Haden; ***D:*** Amma Asante; ***W:*** Amma Asante; ***C:*** Ian Wilson; ***M:*** David Gray.

Way of the Gun 1/2 **2000 (R)** Two unsuccessful career criminals (Phillippe and Del Toro) take up kidnapping and hold a surrogate mother (Lewis) for ransom. Only the parents-to-be are mobbed up and send two thugs (Diggs and Katt) and a philosophical enforcer (Caan) to get her back unharmed. McQuarrie shows that he still has the knack for twisty plots, surprise revelations, and cool dialogue, but he lets the proceedings drag on a little longer than they need to. He's also not shy about heaping on the violence and crude language (which isn't necessarily bad, just consider yourself forewarned). **118m/C; VHS, DVD.** Ryan Phillippe; Benicio Del Toro; Juliette Lewis; James Caan; Taye Diggs; Nicky Katt; Scott Wilson; Kristen Lehman; Geoffrey Lewis; Dylan Kussman; ***D:*** Christopher McQuarrie; ***W:*** Christopher McQuarrie; ***C:*** Dick Pope; ***M:*** Joe Kraemer.

The Way of the West *The Moutie; Lawman* **2011 (R)** In this inept and confusing Canadian actioner, west means the Yukon Territory in the late 1800s. Disgraced Mountie Wade Grayling is sent to scout the location for a new outpost. He stumbles across a tent city occupied by immigrants where everyone is forced to grow opium for a Russian gang. Pare is the nominal love interest. **83m/C; DVD.** *CA* Andrew W. Walker; Jessica Pare; Earl Pastko; George Buza; ***D:*** Wyeth Clarkson; ***W:*** Wyeth Clarkson; Charles Johnston; ***C:*** Rene Smith; ***M:*** Ivan Barbotin. **VIDEO**

Way of the Wicked **2014** Superficial, derivative horror tale about a priest who still questions how a young boy died five years after his suspicious death. It's basically don't make teenager Robbie angry and don't come between him and his dream girl, Heather. **92m/C; DVD, Blu-Ray.** Christian Slater; Vinnie Jones; Emily Tennant; Jake Croker; Jedidiah Goodacre; Matthew Robert Kelly; ***D:*** Kevin Carraway; ***W:*** Matthew Robert Kelly; ***C:*** Curtis Petersen; ***M:*** Christopher Nickel.

The Way of War 1/2 **2008 (R)** Paramilitary operative David Wolfe (Gooding Jr.) is assigned to kill a Middle Eastern terrorist. While on the job (which goes bad), David learns about a U.S. government conspiracy and tries to expose the truth before getting silenced himself. Plot feels like a tired retread of other military and conspiracy flicks. **87m/C; DVD, Blu-Ray.** Cuba Gooding, Jr.; J.K. Simmons; John Terry; Lance Reddick; ***D:*** John Carter; ***W:*** John Carter; Scott Schafer; ***M:*** James Melvin. **VIDEO**

The Way Out *Dial 999* **1956** Average crime drama starring Nelson as a fugitive accused of killing a bookie. **90m/C; VHS, Streaming.** *GB* Gene Nelson; Mona Freeman; John Bentley; Michael Goodliffe; Sydney Tafler; ***D:*** Montgomery Tully.

Way Out West **1937** The classic twosome journey way out west to deliver the deed to a gold mine to the daughter of their late prospector pal. The obligatory romance is missing, but you'll be laughing so hard you won't notice. One of Stan and Ollie's best. Score includes the song "Trail of the Lonesome Pine." Also included on this tape is a 1932 Todd and Pitts short, "Red Noses." Available colorized. **86m/B; VHS, DVD.** Stan Laurel; Oliver Hardy; Rosina Lawrence; James Finlayson; Sharon Lynne; Zasu Pitts; William Haines; ***D:*** James W. Horne.

Way Past Cool **2000 (R)** Two gangs, both made up of pre-teens, are pitted against each other by a 16-year-old drug dealer, with all the gang staples, including turf battles, shootouts, drinking (and we're not talking juice boxes), and swearing. Sorry, can't think of a single redeeming thing about it. **96m/C; VHS, DVD.** Wayne Collins; Adam Davidson; Terence Williams; Kareem Woods; Wes Charles, Jr.; Jonathan Roger Neal; Luchisha Evans; D'andre Jenkins; D'esmond Jenkins; Partap Khalsa; ***D:*** Adam Davidson; ***W:*** Yule Caise; Jess Mowry; ***C:*** Amy Vincent; ***M:*** Zen Amen. **VIDEO**

The Way To Fight *Kenka no hanamichi: Oosaka saikyo densetsu* **1996** Kazuyoshi Tamai is a serious street brawler and the toughest guy in his school. Similarly Takeshi Hamada is the toughest boy of his school, and they have challenged one another to see who is the best. Due to a series of missteps they miss one another, and years later Kazuyoshi is a Bantamweight boxing champion while Takeshi has become a famous pro wrestler. Meeting once again, they decide to continue their rivalry. Unusually normal fare for director Takashi Miike. **114m/C; DVD.** *JP* Takeshi Caesar; Ryoko Imamura; Kazuki Kitamura; ***D:*** Takashi Miike; ***W:*** Masa Nakamura; Seijun Ninomiya; ***C:*** Hideo Yamamoto.

The Way to the Stars 1/2 *Johnny in the Clouds* **1945** In 1942, young RAF pilot Peter Penrose (Mills) is mentored by his squadron leader David Archdale (Redgrave), who is married to Toddy (John), the manager of the squadron's local inn. Peter falls for London evacuee Iris (Asherson) but breaks things off when David is killed, believing fighting men shouldn't get involved in romance. It takes Toddy to show Peter that life must go on. **87m/B; DVD.** *GB* John Mills; Michael Redgrave; Rosamund John; Renee Asherson; Trevor Howard; Stanley Holloway; Basil Radford; Felix Aylmer; Douglass Montgomery; Bonar Colleano; Anatole de Grunwald; ***D:*** Anthony Asquith; ***W:*** Terence Rattigan; ***C:*** Derick Williams; ***M:*** Nicholas Brodszky.

The Way Way Back **2013 (PG-13)** Rockwell delivers the charming comedic performance that fans of his have been hoping to see for years in this remarkably likable directorial debut by the Oscar-winning writers of "The Descendants." Duncan (James) is the center of this familiar tale of "the summer that changed a teen's life". On a summer vacation, he meets a cute girl (Robb), deals with his mom's (Collette) obnoxious new boyfriend (Carell), and finds himself on a seasonal job at a water park run by Rockwell charmer. The ensemble cast is strong from top to bottom and writer/directors Faxon and Rash know how to deliver the laughs. **103m/C; DVD.** Liam James; Toni Collette; Steve Carell; Sam Rockwell; Allison Janney; AnnaSophia Robb; Maya Rudolph; Rob Corddry; Amanda Peet; Nat Faxon; Jim Rash; ***D:*** Nat Faxon; Jim Rash; ***W:*** Nat Faxon; Jim Rash; ***C:*** John Bailey; ***M:*** Rob Simonsen.

The Way We Live Now 1/2 **2002** Based on the 1875 novel by Anthony Trollope, this adaptation centers around shady financier Augustus Melmotte (Suchet). An economic boom is sweeping through Europe in the 1870s and Melmotte arrives in London with a scheme to buy himself a place in Victorian society. Melmotte is even willing to sacrifice his daughter Marie (Henderson) who has developed an infatuation for debt-ridden but aristocratic Sir Felix Carbury (Macfadyen). The question for all this greedy bunch is who will get the better of whom? **300m/C; VHS, DVD.** *GB* David Suchet; Shirley Henderson; Matthew Macfadyen; Cheryl Campbell; Paloma Baeza; Douglas Hodge; Miranda Otto; Cillian Murphy; Michael Riley; Allan Corduner; David Bradley; Jim Carter; Oliver Ford Davies; Joanna David; ***D:*** David Yates; ***W:*** Andrew Davies; ***C:*** Chris Seager; ***M:*** Nicholas Hooper. **TV**

The Way We Were **1973 (PG)** Big boxoffice hit follows a love story between opposites from the 1930s to the 1950s. Streisand is a Jewish political radical who meets the handsome WASP Redford at college. They're immediately attracted to one another, but it takes years before they act on it and eventually marry. They move to Hollywood where Redford is a screenwriter and left-wing Streisand becomes involved in the Red scare and the blacklist, much to Redford's dismay. Though always in love, their differences are too great to keep them together. An old-fashioned and sweet romance, with much gloss. Hit title song sung by Streisand. Adapted by Arthur Laurents from his novel. **118m/C; VHS, DVD, Blu-Ray.** Barbra Streisand; Robert Redford; Bradford Dillman; Viveca Lindfors; Herb Edelman; Murray Hamilton; Patrick O'Neal; James Woods; Sally Kirkland; Lois Chiles; Susan Blakely; Allyn Ann McLerie; Marcia Mae Jones; Diana Ewing; George Gaynes; ***D:*** Sydney Pollack; ***W:*** Arthur Laurents; ***C:*** Harry Stradling, Jr.; ***M:*** Marvin Hamlisch. Oscars '73: Orig. Dramatic Score, Song ("The Way We Were"); Golden Globes '74: Song ("The Way We Were").

The Way West 1/2 **1967** A wagon train heads to Oregon. A poor and muddled attempt at recreating the style of a John Ford western. What really galls is that it's based on the Pulitzer-winning novel by A.B. Guthrie Jr. Boy, is the book better than the movie. Field's first film. **122m/C; VHS, DVD, Blu-Ray.** Kirk Douglas; Robert Mitchum; Richard Widmark; Lola Albright; Michael Witney; Stubby Kaye; Sally Field; Jack Elam; ***D:*** Andrew V. McLaglen; ***C:*** William Clothier.

Wayne's World **1992 (PG-13)** Destined to become one of the top movies of all time—Not! This "Saturday Night Live" skit proved to be so popular that it got its own movie, not unlike the plot, which has slimy producer Benjamin Oliver (Lowe) take the public access "Wayne's World" into the world of commercial television. The zany duo of Wayne (Myers) and Garth (Carvey) are as much fun on the big screen as they were on SNL and there are many funny moments, several of which are destined to become comedy classics. A huge boxoffice hit that spawned a sequel. It also spawned Lorne Michaels's desperate attempts to match its success with other non-bigscreen worthy skits from the show. **93m/C; VHS, DVD, Blu-Ray.** Mike Myers; Dana Carvey; Rob Lowe; Tia Carrere; Brian Doyle-Murray; Lara Flynn Boyle; Kurt Fuller; Colleen Camp; Donna Dixon; Ed O'Neill; Alice Cooper; Meat Loaf Aday; ***D:*** Penelope Spheeris; ***W:*** Mike Myers; Bonnie Turner; Terry Turner; ***C:*** Theo van de Sande; ***M:*** J. Peter Robinson. MTV Movie Awards '92: On-Screen Duo (Mike Myers/Dana Carvey).

Wayne's World 2 **1993 (PG-13)** Good-natured rerun of the original has plenty of sophomoric gags, but feels tired. Wayne and Garth are on their own, planning a major concert, Waynestock. "If you book them they will come," Jim Morrison says in a dream. Meanwhile, Wayne's girlfriend (Carrere) is falling for slimeball record promoter Walken. Offers a few brilliantly funny segments. If you liked the "Bohemian Rhapsody" spot in the original, get ready for the Village People here. Heston has a funny cameo, and Walken and Basinger push the limits without going over the top. Feature film debut for director Surjik. **94m/C; VHS, DVD, Blu-Ray.** Mike Myers; Dana Carvey; Tia Carrere; Christopher Walken; Ralph Brown; Kim Basinger; James Hong; Chris Farley; Ed O'Neill; Olivia D'Abo; Kevin Pollak; Drew Barrymore; Charlton Heston; Rip Taylor; Bob Odenkirk; Michael A. (M.A.) Nickles; ***D:*** Stephen Surjik; ***W:*** Mike Myers; Bonnie Turner; Terry Turner; ***C:*** Francis Kenny; ***M:*** Carter Burwell.

The Wayward Bus 1/2 **1957** Watered-down version of the John Steinbeck novel. A small charter bus lumbers along a 50-mile stretch of California mountain road. Pouring rain makes driving treacherous but that's nothing compared to the drama amongst the passengers, who include a stripper, traveling salesman, and the bus driver's alcoholic wife. **89m/B; DVD, Blu-Ray.** Rick Jason; Joan Collins; Jayne Mansfield; Dan Dailey; Dolores Michaels; Larry Keating; Kathryn Givney; Will Wright; ***D:*** Victor Vicas; ***W:*** Ivan Moffat; ***C:*** Charles G. Clarke; ***M:*** Leigh Harline.

W.E. 1/2 **2011 (R)** Although Madonna-as-director is not in the Uwe Boll category, she should stick to her music career. Underwhelming, awkward, and dull romantic drama features the dual story of the scandalous 1930s romance between Wallis Simpson (Riseborough) and the man who would briefly become King Edward VIII (D'Arcy) and 1990s New Yorker Wally Winthrop (Cornish), who becomes obsessed with the story. But as romantically-minded, mopey Wally researches the strong-minded American divorcee and the weak-willed British royal, she discovers that their marriage didn't turn out the way she thought. At least the flick looks glamorous. **119m/C; DVD, Blu-Ray.** Abbie Cornish; Andrea Riseborough; James D'Arcy; Oscar Isaac; Natalie Dormer; Laurence Fox; James Fox; Richard Coyle; Judy Parfitt; Geoffrey Palmer; Katie McGrath; David Harbour; ***D:*** Madonna; ***W:*** Madonna; Alek Keshishian; ***C:*** Hagen Bogdanski; ***M:*** Abel Korzeniowski. Golden Globes '12: Song ("Masterpiece").

We All Fall Down **2000** Disturbing urban drama about addiction and friendship. The death of his mother propels struggling Vancouver actor Michael (Belsher) deeper into his drug habit, which suits his best friend, junkie/artist Kris (Cummins), just fine. Following a friend's drug-related death, Michael struggles to get clean, pushing away from Kris and his temptations. Ryan (Robertson), Kris' girlfriend, is also fed up and looks to Michael for solace, adding an extra complication. **92m/C; DVD.** *CA* Martin Cummins; Francoise Robertson; Helen Shaver; Nicholas

(Nick) Campbell; Darcy Belsher; Rene Auberjonois; Barry Pepper; Ryan Reynolds; *D:* Martin Cummins; *W:* Martin Cummins; Richard C. Burton; *C:* Andreas Poulsson; *M:* Jim Byrnes.

We All Loved Each Other So Much ♪♪♪ 1/2 **1977** Sensitive comedy follows three friends over 30 years, beginning at the end of WWII. All three have loved the same woman, an actress. Homage to friendship and to postwar Italian cinema. Includes a full-scale re-creation of the fountain scene in "La Dolce Vita." In Italian with English subtitles. **124m/C; VHS, DVD.** *IT* Vittorio Gassman; Nino Manfredi; Stefano Satta Flores; Stefania Sandrelli; Marcello Mastroianni; Federico Fellini; Anita Ekberg; Vittorio De Sica; *D:* Ettore Scola.

We Are Legion: The Story of the Hacktivists ♪♪ **2012** Director/writer Knappenberger's documentary follows the underground movement of 'hacker-activists' including the loose online collective known as Anonymous. Going back to the roots of hacking, he introduces the 4Chan site that hosts various message boards, and interviews hackers, scholars, and journalists about the social phenomenon. **93m/C; DVD.** *D:* Brian Knappenberger; *W:* Brian Knappenberger; *C:* Dan Krauss; Lincoln Else; Scott Sinkler; *M:* John Dragonnetti.

We Are Marshall ♪♪ 1/2 **2006 (PG)** The tight-knit community of Huntington, West Virginia, grieves after the real-life tragedy of a plane crash that killed 75 Marshall University football players, coaches, staff, and boosters in 1970. The school's president decides to end the program until the student body gathers together with its "We are Marshall!" peprally chant (repeated often throughout). Enter coach Jack Lengyel (a spirited McConaughey) to lead the piecing together of the team and win over the doubters. Occasional goosebumpy moments give way to a dull script and, oddly enough, entirely too much on-field action. **131m/C; DVD, Blu-Ray, HD-DVD.** Matthew McConaughey; Matthew Fox; Anthony Mackie; David Strathairn; Ian McShane; Kate Mara; January Jones; Kimberly Williams; *D:* McG; *W:* Jamie Linden; *C:* Shane Hurlbut; *M:* Christophe Beck.

We are Still Here ♪♪ 1/2 **2015** The timeless B-movie queen Barbara Crampton enlivens an otherwise-stale genre entry. She stars as Anne, a woman whose teenage son recently died in a car crash. She moves to New England to try to start a new life with her husband, only to learn that the house into which they have moved is also home to a family of vengeful spirits. As in a number of superior horror films, depression manifests itself in the supernatural. The strangely violent, bloody final act nearly resurrects the dull first hour, but this is for hardcore fans of the genre of star alone. **83m/C; DVD, Blu-Ray, Streaming.** Barbara Crampton; Andrew Sensenig; Lisa Marie; Larry Fessenden; Monte Markham; *D:* Ted Geoghegan; *W:* Ted Geoghegan; *C:* Karim Hussain; *M:* Wojciech Golczewski. **VIDEO**

We Are the Best! ♪♪♪ **2013** Swedish director Moodysson has long been interested in atypical communities and so it makes sense that he would be drawn to the union that forms around musical movements such as punk. It is 1980s Stockholm, long after the end of the punk rock movement, but don't say that to Bobo (Barkhammar), Klara (Grosin), or Hedvig (LeMoyne), three misfit pre-teen girls who embrace the style, tunes, and worldview of their punk forefathers. Moodysson showcases how music and fashion can create community for people, especially kids, who need it desperately. Adapted from his wife Coco's graphic novel. Swedish with subtitles. **102m/C; DVD, Blu-Ray.** *SW DK* Mira Barkhammar; Mira Grosin; Liv LeMoyne; *D:* Lukas Moodysson; *W:* Lukas Moodysson; *C:* Ulf Brantas.

We Are the Hartmans ♪ 1/2 **2011** Sitcom humor with some added in indie sweetness. The owner (Chamberlain) of Hartman's Rock Club falls ill and can't manage the business, his estranged family immediately want to sell the place. Only they are unprepared for how the club's eccentric longtime regulars react to the unwelcome news. **84m/C; DVD.** Richard Chamberlain; Ben Curtis; Jennifer Restivo; Jonah Spear; *D:* Laura Newman; *W:* Laura Newman; Peter Brash; *C:* Paul Rondeau; *M:* Alec Puro. **VIDEO**

We Are What We Are ♪ 1/2 *Somos Lo Que Hay* **2011** Cannibals—that's what this poor Mexico City family are—in writer-director Grau's disturbing, bloody debut combo of horror and family drama. They all have trouble coping when the patriarch of the clan drops dead, and bitter, angry mom and her three sheltered, squabbling kids must now bring home the human chow themselves. Meanwhile, inept cops indifferently investigate a series of street murders. Spanish with subtitles. **89m/C; Blu-Ray.** *MX* Paulina Gaitan; Francisco Barreiro; Alan Chavez; Carmen Beato; Jorge Zarate; Esteban Soberanes; Humberto Yanez; *D:* Jorge Grau; *W:* Jorge Grau; *C:* Santiago Sanchez; *M:* Enrico Chapela.

We Are What We Are ♪♪♪ **2013 (R)** Horror director Mickle remakes the Mexican flick about a family who adheres to an ancient tradition that dictates they must commit acts of cannibalism to stay together. When the matriarch of said family passes away, the task of finding sustenance for the Parkers transfers to the two daughters. As the authorities get closer and closer to the Parker family secret, the girls crack under the pressure of a tradition that they don't really want to continue. Mickle strikes a mesmerizing tone reminiscent of old-fashioned Gothic horror, aided by great performances all around, especially from the young Garner and vet Parks. **105m/C; DVD, Blu-Ray.** Ambyr Childers; Julia Garner; Bill Sage; Kelly McGillis; Michael Parks; *D:* Jim Mickle; *W:* Jim Mickle; Nick Damici; *C:* Ryan Samul; *M:* Jeff Grace.

We Are Your Friends ♪ **2015 (R)** There's so little story behind this drama that it's almost impossible to recap the plot. It's about a DJ (Efron) and some people he knows. That's about it. By the time a love triangle sprouts up between Efron, Bentley, and Ratajkoswki, most viewers will have checked out. The lack of any hook to sell actually made this one of the biggest bombs of 2015, although it's nowhere near awful enough to really warrant that hatred. It's just forgettable. **96m/C; DVD.** Zac Efron; Wes Bentley; Emily Ratajkowski; Jonny Weston; Shiloh Fernandez; *D:* Max Joseph; *W:* Max Joseph; Meaghan Oppenheimer; *C:* Brett Pawlak; *M:* Matt Simpson.

We Bought a Zoo ♪♪ 1/2 **2011 (PG)** Based on a 2007 memoir, director Crowe tells the story of Benjamin Mee (Damon), a man who needed a change after the death of his wife, so he picked up his family and moved into a rundown private zoo in California. Tasked with trying to get the zoo back up and running while also helping his teenage son and little girl get over losing their mother, the Mees learn Hollywood-ized lessons about grief and moving on. Sentimental to be sure, but in such an expertly-done way by Crowe and Damon that it feels real instead of succumbing to typical melodrama. **124m/C; DVD, Blu-Ray.** Matt Damon; Scarlett Johansson; Patrick Fugit; Thomas Haden Church; Stephanie Szostak; Elle Fanning; John Michael Higgins; Angus MacFadyen; Colin Ford; Maggie Elizabeth Jones; Peter Riegert; J.B. Smoove; *D:* Cameron Crowe; *W:* Aline Brosh McKenna; *C:* Rodrigo Prieto; *M:* Jonsi.

We Can't Go Home Again ♪♪ **1973** Filmmaker Nicholas Ray turned to teaching his art towards the end of his life, and this film is the result of that. A semi-documentary/arthouse project it is the result of him filming his students and them filming him, presented in a montage. **170m/B; DVD, Blu-Ray.** Richie Bock; Tom Farrell; Danny Fisher; Jill Gannon; Jane Heymann; *D:* Nicholas Ray; *W:* Tom Farrell; Nicholas Ray; Susan Ray; *C:* Richie Bock; Danny Fisher; Peer Bode; Mark Goldstein; Stanley Liu; Steve Maurer. **VIDEO**

We Come As Friends ♪♪ 1/2 **2014** In this feature-length documentary, filmmaker Hubert Sauper explores the stories, people, and places in Sudan shortly before the country was divided into two separate countries in 2011. In his discussions with the Sudanese, those making important decisions, and people of various nationalities working in Sudan, Sauper touches on such issues as colonialism, wars, and resources, and the tensions between all these issues and the people shaping Sudan's future in big and small ways. **110m/C; DVD, Download.** *D:* Hubert Sauper; *W:* Hubert Sauper; *C:* Hubert Sauper; Barney Broomfield; *M:* Slim Twig. **VIDEO**

We Die Young ♪♪ **2019 (R)** Fourteen-year-old Lucas (Rodriguez) lives in Washington, D.C., and is a reluctant member of the notorious gang Mara Salvatrucha, headed locally by brutal Rincon (Castaneda) and his hot-headed second in command Jester (MacGechan). As part of his duties, Lucas delivers pain killers to drug-addicted veteran David (Van Damme) at his auto shop and is charged with helping Rincon make a deal with a dangerous drug cartel. At the same time, Lucas tries to prevent his younger brother from joining the gang. Though the film relies on racial stereotypes and gangster movie cliches, it has features notable performances by Van Damme and Castaneda. **92m/C; DVD, Blu-Ray.** Jean-Claude Van Damme; David Castaneda; Elijah Rodriguez; Nicholas Sean Johnny; Charlie MacGechan; Ivan Vatsov; *D:* Lior Geller; *W:* Lior Geller.

We Dive at Dawn ♪♪♪ **1943** Interesting, tense British submarine drama. The "Sea Tiger" attempts to sink the German battleship "Brandenburg" off Denmark. Good cast. Mills prepared for the role by riding an actual submarine, turning "a pale shade of pea-green" when it crash-dived. **98m/B; VHS, DVD.** *GB* Eric Portman; John Mills; *D:* Anthony Asquith; *W:* Val Valentine; *C:* Jack Cox.

We Don't Belong Here ♪ 1/2 **2017 (R)** Widow Nancy (Keener) struggles to cope with her young adult children. Each has a major problem: Max (Yelchin) is gay and suicidal; pop singer Elisa (Keough) is in a destructive relationship and estranged from her mother; Lily (Dever), the youngest, is bipolar and exploring her sexuality. Though Nancy's best friend Joanne (Rudolph) keeps her grounded, she becomes concerned when Max goes missing. The story is told through revealing flashbacks and a nonlinear format which gets confusing, despite strong performances. **92m/C; DVD.** Catherine Keener; Anton Yelchin; Kaitlyn Dever; Riley Keough; Annie Starke; *D:* Peer Pedersen; *W:* Peer Pedersen; *C:* Doug Emmett; *M:* Michael Yezerski. **VIDEO**

We Don't Live Here Anymore ♪♪ **2004 (R)** A quartet of 30-somethings discover adultery and betrayal have repercussions in this adaptation of two novellas by Andre Dubus. Best friends Jack (Ruffalo) and Hank (Krause) teach at a small college; Jack's married to Terry (Dern), Hank to Edith (Watts). Both couples have children; neither marriage is happy. Jack and Edith are in lust and enjoy woodland trysts while waiting to get caught. Serial womanizer Hank is seemingly unconcerned when he finds out but Terry is driven by fury to punish Jack by screwing Hank and then telling her husband—who doesn't react as expected. They're whiny, indecisive, self-involved, angry, weak, occasionally passionate, but not a group you'd want to spend a lot of time with (despite the capable performances from all four actors). **101m/C; DVD.** Mark Ruffalo; Laura Dern; Peter Krause; Naomi Watts; Jennifer Bishop; Sam Charles; Haili Page; *D:* John Curran; *W:* Larry Gross; *C:* Maryse Alberti; *M:* Lesley Barber; Laurie Parker.

We Have Your Husband ♪♪ **2011** In 2007, American-born Jayne, her husband Eduardo, and their children are living on their ranch outside a peaceful Mexican town. At least until Eduardo, the son of a newspaper publisher, is kidnapped. Jayne doesn't have access to the millions of dollars demanded by the kidnappers but she's determined to get her husband released safely. Lifetime movie based on a true story. **90m/C; DVD.** Teri Polo; Esai Morales; Olivia D'Abo; Nicholas Gonzalez; William R. Moses; Danny Mora; *D:* Eric Bross; *W:* J.B. White; *C:* Horacio Marquinez; *M:* Joseph Julian Gonzalez. **CABLE**

We Live Again ♪♪ 1/2 **1934** Costume melodrama adapted from the Tolstoy novel "Resurrection." Prince Dmitri (March) seduces and betrays childhood sweetheart, peasant Katusha (Sten). Years later, she's a prostitute charged with murder while he's one of the jurors. He vows to change his hedonistic ways and help her. **82m/B; DVD.** Fredric March; Anna Sten; Jane Baxter; Sir C. Aubrey Smith; Sam Jaffe; *D:* Rouben Mamoulian; *W:* Preston Sturges; *C:* Gregg Toland; *M:* Alfred Newman.

We Monsters ♪♪ *Wir Monster* **2015** A neo-noir thriller about a family's misguided web of lies. When Paul (Nebbou) and Christine (Tscharre) decide to separate, their teenage daughter Sarah (Fautz) does not take the news well. Knowing Sarah could do just about anything, they are not shocked when she murders her best friend. Believing that Sarah needs to be protected, they hide the crime. Though their guilt brings the family back together, there is no way out of the deceit and deadly intentions the situation brings. German with subtitles. **95m/C; DVD.** Mehdi Nebbou; Ulrike C. Tscharre; Janina Fautz; Britta Hammelstein; Daniel Drewes; *D:* Sebástian Ko; *W:* Sebastian Ko; Marcus Seibert; *C:* Andreas Kohler; *M:* Durbeck & Dohmen. **VIDEO**

We Need to Talk About Kevin ♪♪♪ **2011 (R)** A memory piece that unfolds after the title character (Miller) commits a high school killing spree and his mother Eva (Swinton) tries to piece together how her child became an internationally-known monster, or if he was born that way. Eva is forced to examine her own life—as a single woman, her marriage to the happy-go-lucky Franklin (Reilly, solid as usual), and as mother to a child whose erratic behavior has caused turmoil. No simple conclusions exist in director Ramsay's intensely complex film, the greatest strength of which is the heart-rending turn by Swinton. Based on the lauded 2003 novel by Lionel Shriver. **111m/C; DVD, Blu-Ray.** *US GB* Tilda Swinton; John C. Reilly; Ezra Miller; Jasper Newell; Ashley Gerasimovich; Siobhan Fallon; *D:* Lynne Ramsey; *W:* Lynne Ramsey; Rory Kinnear; *C:* Seamus McGarvey; *M:* Johnny Greenwood.

We of the Never Never ♪♪♪ **1982 (G)** In turn-of-the-century Australia a city-bred woman marries a cattle rancher and moves from civilized Melbourne to the barren outback of the Northern Territory. Based on the autobiographical story written by Jeannie Gunn, the first white woman to travel in the aboriginal wilderness. She finds herself fighting for her own rights as well as for those of the aborigines in this sincere, well-done film. **136m/C; VHS, DVD.** *AU* Angela Punch McGregor; Arthur Dignam; Tony Barry; *D:* Igor Auzins.

We Own the Night ♪♪ **2007 (R)** Nightclub manager Bobby (Phoenix) has distanced himself from his cop father Bert (Duvall) and brother Joseph (Wahlberg) to work for Russian mobster Marat (Moshonov) and his drug-dealing nephew Vadim (Veadov). After a raid, Vadim attacks Joseph, and Bobby nervously agrees to become an informant. The performances are okay (everyone's done better work) but Mendes is inarguably hot as Bobby's personal party girl. Set in late 1980s Brooklyn, this stark crime story superficially harkens back to the police dramas of the 70s. **117m/C; DVD, Blu-Ray.** Joaquin Rafael (Leaf) Phoenix; Mark Wahlberg; Robert Duvall; Eva Mendes; Moni Moshonov; Alex Veadov; Danny Hoch; Tony Musante; Antoni Corone; *D:* James Gray; *W:* James Gray; *C:* Joaquin Baca-Asay; *M:* Wojciech Kilar.

We Steal Secrets: The Story of WikiLeaks ♪♪ **2013 (R)** Documentarian Gibney delves into the world of information hacker Julian Assange and exposes a new angle on a man many consider a martyr and hero. On a crusade against government cover-ups, the controversial snooper tags troubled U.S. Army private Bradley Manning for some major dirt. Gibney's version of the story takes no prisoners, showing how Obama's wolves went to town on a defenseless Manning after Assange squeezed the truth from him. Thoroughly researched and meticulously mapped out, the events unfold like a taut thriller. **130m/C; DVD.** *D:* Alex Gibney; *W:* Alex Gibney; *C:* Maryse Alberti; *M:* Will Bates.

We the Animals ♪♪♪ **2018 (R)** Based on a semi-autobiographical novel by Justin Torres, this coming-of-age drama relates the story of three Puerto Rican-American brothers living hand-to-mouth with their dysfunctional parents in upstate New York. Writer-director Zagar is known for documentaries and shorts, and this film feels a bit of both, with grainy vignettes chronicling the growth of the boys and the dissolution of the family unit. It's not a happy story, but it feels real. **94m/C; DVD, Blu-Ray.** Sheila Vand; Raúl Castillo; Evan Rosado; Josiah Gabriel; Isaiah Kristian; ***D:*** Jeremiah Zagar; ***W:*** Jeremiah Zagar; Daniel Kitrosser; ***C:*** Zak Mulligan; ***M:*** Nick Zammuto.

We the Living 1/2 **1942** The torpid long-lost and restored Italian version of Ayn Rand's unique political tome. Deals with a young Soviet woman in revolutionary Petrograd who is slowly ruined by the system and her affair with a romantic counter-revolutionary. Made under the Fascists' nose during WWII. A fascinating dialectic between utopian melodrama and Rand dogma. In Italian with subtitles. **174m/B; VHS, DVD.** *IT* Alida Valli; Rossano Brazzi; Fosco Giachetti; ***D:*** Goffredo Alessandrini.

We Were Dancing 1/2 **1942** Shearer made only one more film after this frothy effort before retiring from acting and it's a loose adaptation of Noel Coward's play "Tonight at 8:30." Penniless Vicki (Shearer) is engaged to wealthy Hubert Tyler (Bowman) but abandons him for dashing Nicki (Douglas) under the impression he has dough. He thinks the same about her and they get married before realizing they're a couple of cons. Trying another scam, the duo are exposed by Nicki's ex-lover Linda (Patrick) but it doesn't stop them for long. **94m/B; DVD.** Norma Shearer; Melvyn Douglas; Gail Patrick; Lee Bowman; Marjorie Main; Reginald Owen; Alan Mowbray; Florence Bates; ***D:*** Robert Z. Leonard; ***W:*** George Froeschel; Claudine West; Hans Rameau; ***C:*** Robert Planck; ***M:*** Bronislau Kaper.

We Were Here **2011** Frank documentary from Weissman details the AIDS crisis in San Francisco's Castro neighborhood and how the community united to care for its often disenfranchised inhabitants. It begins in the late 1970s and goes through the present day with interviews from activists and survivors as well as archival photographs and news footage. **90m/C; DVD.** ***D:*** David Weissman; Bill Weber; ***C:*** Marsha Kahm; ***M:*** Holcolmbe Waller.

We Were One Man *Nous Etions Un Seul Homme* **1980** In 1943, simple French peasant Guy finds wounded German soldier Rolf hiding in the woods and brings him to his cottage to recover. Eventually, Guy and Rolf's growing friendship turns sexual but when Rolf realizes he needs to leave for fear of capture, Guy makes a shocking decision. French with subtitles. **105m/C; DVD.** *FR* Serge Avedikian; Piotr Stanislas; Catherine Albin; ***D:*** Philippe Vallois; ***W:*** Philippe Vallois; ***C:*** Francois About; ***M:*** Jean-Jacques Ruhlmann.

We Were Soldiers 1/2 **2002 (R)** Writer-director Wallace once again tackles the fact-based miltary epic, with outstanding results. Recounting the battle of the la Drang Valley in 1965, the first major land battle for U.S. troops in Vietnam, the story focuses on Lt. Col. Hal Moore (Gibson) and his leadership of the 7th Air Cavalry at LZ X-Ray. Moore's combination of experience, leadership, instinct, knowledge, and genuine concern for his men make him seem too good to be true, but Gibson's portrayal, and the fact that Moore is real, help to erase disbelief. Inevitable comparisons with "Black Hawk Down" are justified, as both pics deal with chaotic battlefields and the heroism of the soldiers who must fight their way out of situations they were trained, but not quite prepared, for. But this movie goes beyond the battle to show the impact to families back home, as well as giving a nod of respect to the enemy. Elliot stands out as Moore's right-hand man, as does Pepper as reporter Galloway, while Stein, Russell, and Kinnear do well playing against type. Based on the book "We Were Soldiers Once...and Young" by Lt. Gen. Harold G. Moore (Ret.) and Joseph L. Galloway. **137m/C; VHS, DVD, Blu-Ray, HD-DVD.** Mel Gibson; Madeleine Stowe; Greg Kinnear; Sam Elliott; Chris Klein; Keri Russell; Barry Pepper; Don Duong; Ryan Hurst; Marc Blucas; Jsu Garcia; Clark Gregg; Desmond Harrington; Blake Heron; Dylan Walsh; Robert Bagnell; Josh Daugherty; Jon Hamm; Erik MacArthur; Simbi Khali; Mark McCracken; Taylor Momsen; Daniel Roebuck; Keith Szarabajka; Sloane Momsen; Matthew Lang; Edwin Morrow; Billinger C. Tran; ***D:*** Randall Wallace; ***W:*** Randall Wallace; ***C:*** Dean Semler; ***M:*** Nick Glennie-Smith.

Weakness **2010** High school teacher Joshua Polansky's life falls apart just before summer vacation and exposes all the flaws in his character as he tries to cope. His mother dies, his angry autistic brother gets thrown out of his assisted living home, and his wife Elizabeth has an affair and leaves him. A bewildered and hurt Josh begins dating former student Danielle without realizing that colleague Katharine is interested and his best friend Bart is jealous. **98m/C; DVD.** Bobby Cannavale; June Diane Raphael; Keith Nobbs; Lily Rabe; Danielle Panabaker; Josh Charles; Phyllis Somerville; Daniel Sunjata; ***D:*** Michael Melamedoff; ***W:*** Michael Melamedoff; ***C:*** Harlan Bosmajian; ***M:*** Neil Halstead.

The Weapon **1956** Young Erik finds a gun in a bombed-out building in postwar London and runs away after accidentally shooting a playmate. Ballistics ties the gun to the unsolved murder of a U.S. Army officer, which gets American Capt. Mark Andrews involved. His snooping upsets some unsavory types, including the killer who's hunting Erik to get the gun back first. **78m/B; DVD, Blu-Ray.** *UK* Steve Cochran; Lizabeth Scott; Herbert Marshall; Jon Whiteley; George Cole; Nicole Maurey; ***D:*** Val Guest; ***W:*** Fred Freiberger; ***C:*** Reginald Wyer; ***M:*** James Stevens.

Weaponized *Swap* **2016** A sci-fi action thriller centered on a futuristic war on terror, a robotic virus, and the fate of the country. When the Pentagon is the target of a terrorist attack, a new war on terror is launched. One new form of combat is being developed with the support of private military contractor Kyle Norris (Sizemore), who ensures that Professor Clarence Peterson (Rourke) can move forward with his biomechanical weapons program. The professor's weapon is the robotic virus, which allows soldiers to switch consciousness with machines. Though the program is promising, it is also being abused and could be deadly if it falls into the wrong hands. Detective Walker (Messner) unintentionally learns about the program and does all he could while protecting his family from those who will take any action to keep the program alive. **91m/C; DVD, Blu-Ray, Streaming, Download.** Tom Sizemore; Johnny Messner; Mickey Rourke; Taylor Cole; Jon Foo; ***D:*** Timothy Woodward, Jr.; ***W:*** Sean Ryan; ***C:*** Pablo Diez; ***M:*** Sid De La Cruz. **VIDEO**

Weapons of Mass Distraction **1997 (R)** Two megalomanical multimedia tycoons set out to destroy each other in this black comedy. Lionel Powers (Byrne) wants to buy pro football's Tucson Titans and so does his arch-rival Julian Messenger (Kingsley). So there's bribery and blackmail and airing of dirty family laundry all over the place. No heroes here but occassionally some sharp satire. **105m/C; VHS, DVD.** Gabriel Byrne; Ben Kingsley; Mimi Rogers; Jeffrey Tambor; Illeana Douglas; Paul Mazursky; Kathy Baker; Chris Mulkey; R. Lee Ermey; Caroline Aaron; Jason Lee; Christina Pickles; ***D:*** Stephen Surjik; ***W:*** Larry Gelbart; ***C:*** Alar Kivilo; ***M:*** Don Davis. **CABLE**

Weary River **1929** When he winds up in the big house, gangster Jerry Larrabee (Barthelmess) finds he has a talent for singing that's encouraged by the Warden (Holden). Jerry's success gets him a pardon from the governor but he discovers going straight isn't so easy. Released with title cards and limited dialogue as well as music and sound effects. Title refers to the most popular of the songs that Jerry sings. **89m/B; DVD.** Richard Barthelmess; Louis Natheaux; Betty Compson; William Holden; George E. Stone; ***D:*** Frank Lloyd; ***W:*** Bradley King; ***C:*** Ernest Haller.

Weather Girl **2009 (R)** Seattle TV weather girl Sylvia Miller (O'Kelley) trashes her career in a spectacular on-air rant when she publicly reviles her boyfriend, clueless host Dale Waters (Harmon), after discovering that he is cheating on her. Unable to land another broadcast job, Sylvia moves in with her slacker younger brother Walt (Devlin), finds a job as a waitress, and takes up the offer of Walt's friend Byron (Adams) to be her rebound guy. It's all about the sex since neither are looking for any commitments or romance and you can see where this is going, can't you. **92m/C; On Demand.** Tricia O'Kelley; Patrick J. Adams; Ryan Devlin; Mark Harmon; Kaitlin Olson; Jane Lynch; Marin Hinkle; Jon Cryer; Blayne Weaver; Alex Kapp Horner; ***D:*** Blayne Weaver; ***W:*** Blayne Weaver; ***C:*** Brandon Trost; ***M:*** Andrew Hollander.

Weather in the Streets 1/2 **1984 (PG)** A young woman enters into an ill-fated love affair after spending a few moments with an aristocratic married man. Cliched drama set in England between the two world wars. **108m/C; VHS, DVD.** Michael York; Joanna Lumley; Lisa Eichhorn; Isabel Dean; Norman Pitt; ***M:*** Carl Davis.

The Weather Man 1/2 **2005 (R)** David Spitz (Cage) is a weatherman in Chicago. Not really much of a movie in that fact alone. What makes this story move is that, as his Pulitzer Prize-winning father Robert (Caine) points out, he isn't a particularly good one. David's life seems to consistently point out to him the fact that he's not actually good at much at all. To illustrate the point, strangers on the street thank him for his rotten forecast with fast food showers. Just as Dave's life sinks to a new low, he is offered a prestigious position on a morning show in New York. Cage and Caine are excellent. **102m/C; DVD.** Nicolas Cage; Michael Caine; Hope Davis; Gemmenne de la Pena; Nicholas Hoult; Michael Rispoli; Gil Bellows; Judith McConnell; Anne Marie Howard; ***D:*** Gore Verbinski; ***W:*** Steve Conrad; ***C:*** Phedon Papamichael; ***M:*** Hans Zimmer.

The Weather Underground **2002** Documentary insightfully studies the Weather Underground, the radical group that called for and practiced violence and unrest as an alternative to the peaceful, and in their view, ineffectual protests that were going on at the time. Also explores the issues and atmosphere of the times that bhrough about the division in society that made the Weather Underground a semi-viable movement for a time, before disillusionment set in. **92m/C; DVD.** ***D:*** Sam Green; Bill Siegel; ***C:*** Andrew Black; Federico Salsano; ***M:*** Dave Cerf; Amy Domingues.

Weather Wars *Storm War* **2011** The sons of a formerly famous climate scientist, who has fallen into disrepute, suspect their father is behind unusual weather when they find out that all his enemies are dead. **91m/C; Blu-Ray.** Wes Brown; Erin Cahill; Stacy Keach; Jason London; Gary Grubbs; ***D:*** Todor Chapkanov; ***W:*** Paul A. Birkett; ***C:*** Thomas Callaway; ***M:*** Andrew Morgan Smith. **VIDEO**

Web of the Spider *Nella Stretta M Orsa Del Ragno; In the Grip of the Spider; Dracula in the Castle of Blood; And Comes the Dawn...But Colored Red* **1970** Kinski as Poe is really the only good thing about this run-of-the-mill horror outing. A man stays the night in a spooky house to prove it's not haunted. Remake of "Castle of Blood." **94m/C; VHS, DVD, Blu-Ray.** *GE FR IT* Anthony (Tony) Franciosa; Klaus Kinski; Michele Mercier; Peter Carsten; Karin (Karen) Field; ***D:*** Anthony M. Dawson.

Webs **2003** Electrical workers investigating a power source coming from an abandoned building discover a deserted lab. They accidentally activate a device that transports them to a savage parallel universe occupied by cannibalistic spider-people with a very hungry queen. But does she mate first before biting your head off? A Sci-Fi Channel original. **87m/C; DVD.** Richard Grieco; Kate Greenhouse; Colin Fox; Richard Yearwood; Jeff Douglas; Dylan Bierk; ***D:*** David Wu; ***W:*** Greenville Case; Robinson Young; ***C:*** Richard Wincenty; ***M:*** Lawrence Shragge. **CABLE**

A Wedding 1/2 **1978 (PG)** The occasion of a wedding leads to complications galore for the relatives and guests on the happy day. Silent film legend Gish's 100th screen role. Miserable, self-indulgent outing for Altman, who went through quite a dry spell after "Nashville." **125m/C; VHS, DVD.** Mia Farrow; Carol Burnett; Lillian Gish; Lauren Hutton; Viveca Lindfors; Geraldine Chaplin; Paul Dooley; Howard Duff; Dennis Christopher; Peggy Ann Garner; John Considine; Nina Van Pallandt; Dina Merrill; Pat McCormick; Vittorio Gassman; Desi Arnaz, Jr.; Tim Thomerson; Allan Nicholls; Pam Dawber; Dennis Franz; Bert Remsen; Gavan O'Herlihy; ***D:*** Robert Altman; ***W:*** John Considine; Robert Altman; Allan Nicholls; Patricia Resnick.

The Wedding Banquet *Xiyan; Hsi Yen* **1993 (R)** Charming story about a clash of customs and secrets. Naturalized American Wai Tung (Chao, in his film debut) lives comfortably with his lover Simon (Lichtenstein) while hiding the fact that he's gay from his Chinese parents. To appease his parents and get his "wife" (Chin) a green card, he marries for convenience and watches as the deception snowballs. Comedy of errors was shot on a small budget ($750,000) and examines small details with as much care as the larger ones. A fine effort from director Lee that's solidly humorous, but also poignant. In English and Chinese with subtitles. **111m/C; VHS, DVD, Blu-Ray.** *TW* Winston Chao; May Chin; Mitchell Lichtenstein; Sihung Lung; Ah-Leh Gua; Michael Gaston; Jeffrey Howard; ***D:*** Ang Lee; ***W:*** Ang Lee; Neil Peng; James Schamus; ***C:*** Jong Lin.

Wedding Bell Blues **1996 (R)** Three 30ish single friends/roommates cope with a variety of crises. Pregnant Tanya (Porikova) learns that her boyfriend Tom (Edson) has no intention of marrying her, Micki's (Warner) fiance has just called off their wedding, and Jasmine's (Douglas) conservative parents are upset by their promiscuous daughter's approach to life. Stressed, the women decide to seek their fortunes in Vegas—preferably through some quickie marriages and even quickier divorces. Looks like it was shot on a shoestring budget and the lighting could be better, but the dialogue rings true and the actors do a decent job. Look for Seinfeld's TV mom as Micki's overbearing mother and Jackson as a disgruntled shopper. Reynolds plays herself. **100m/C; VHS, DVD.** Illeana Douglas; Paulina Porizkova; Julie Warner; John Corbett; Jonathan Penner; Richard Edson; Charles Martin Smith; Stephanie Beacham; Carla Gugino; Leo Rossi; John Capodice; Victoria Jackson; Jeff Seymour; ***Cameo(s):*** Debbie Reynolds; ***D:*** Dana Lustig; ***W:*** Annette Goliti Gutierrez; ***C:*** Kent Wakeford; ***M:*** Paul Christian Gordon; Tal Bergman.

The Wedding Bros. *The Marconi Bros.* **2008 (R)** Anthony and Carmine Marconi dutifully work in the family carpet business while Anthony takes classes at the community college and Carmine gambles in Atlantic City in an effort to change their lives. An unexpected meeting with Long Island wedding video producer Mo Brown has the brothers impulsively deciding to become crazy Mo's new assistants, which doesn't go so well. **83m/C; DVD.** Dan Fogler; Brendan Sexton, III; Jon Polito; Patti D'Arbanville; Zoe Lister-Jones; Steven Randazzo; Yul Vasquez; ***D:*** Michael Canzoniero; Marco Ricci; ***W:*** Michael Canzoniero; Marco Ricci; ***C:*** Brian Hubbard; ***M:*** Carlo Giacco.

The Wedding Chapel 1/2 **2013** Newly single and down on her luck, artist Sara visits her mom, Rita, and joins the crusade to save an historic church. Rita gets the chance to rekindle a long ago romance while Sara gets a second chance as well--and not just romantically. **92m/C; DVD.** *CA* Emmanuelle Vaugier; Shelley Long; Barclay Hope; Mark Deklin; ***D:*** Vanessa Parise; ***W:*** Kele McGlohon; Bruce Spiegelman; ***C:*** Danny Nowak. **VIDEO**

Wedding Crashers **2005 (R)** Womanizing buds John (Wilson) and Jeremy (Vaughn) are divorce mediators who crash weddings in order to pick up Ms. Right Now. Only John really falls for engaged Claire (McAdams), who's the daughter of eccentric politician William Cleary (Walken), and the duo find themselves spending the weekend at the family's waterfront estate. Harkens back to the "Animal House/Blues Brothers/Caddyshack" glory days of R-rated comedy, earning the rating and plenty of laughs. Vaughn and Wilson do what they do best, and have great chemistry. Walken, though underused, is effective. Stumbles a little toward the end, but not enough to spoil the festivities. **119m/C; DVD, Blu-Ray, UMD.** Owen Wilson; Vince Vaughn; Rachel McAdams; Christopher Walken; Jane Seymour; Will Ferrell; Ellen A. Dow; Isla Fisher; Bradley Cooper; Ron Canada; Henry Gibson; Keir O'Donnell; Dwight Yoakam; Rebecca De Mornay; David Conrad; Larry Joe Campbell; Jennifer (Jenny) Alden; Geoff Stults; Diora Baird; ***D:*** David Dobkin; ***W:*** Bob Fisher; Steve Faber; ***C:*** Julio Macat; ***M:*** Rolfe Kent.

The Wedding Date 1/2 **2005 (PG-13)** Complete waste of two attractive, amusing leads. High-strung New Yorker Kat (Messing) must fly to London for her self-absorbed half-sister Amy's (Adams) wedding. To her horror, the best man is her ex-fiance Jeff (Sheffield), who dumped her. Refusing to appear alone and needy, especially to her critical mother Bunny (Taylor), Kat decides to hire handsome escort Nick (Mulroney) to accompany her as her new beau. Nick is intelligent and somewhat mysterious; Kat is confused. There are various pre-wedding complications as sub-plots. Predictability rules. **90m/C; DVD, Blu-Ray, HD-DVD.** Debra Messing; Dermot Mulroney; Amy Adams; Jack Davenport; Jeremy Sheffield; Peter Egan; Holland Taylor; Sarah Parish; Jolyon James; C. Gerod Harris; Martin Barrett; Jay Simon; Stephen Lobo; ***D:*** Clare Kilner; ***W:*** Dana Fox; ***C:*** Oliver Curtis.

Wedding Daze ☆ 1/2 *The Pleasure of Your Company* **2006 (R)** Muddled and somewhat vulgar rom com that tries too hard for yuks. Anderson's (Biggs) been in a funk since his fiancee died after an embarrassing incident. Best pal Ted (Weston) thinks Anderson should get back in the dating game but, instead, he proposes to the next woman he meets, who happens to be quirky coffee shop waitress Katie (Fisher). And she accepts. **90m/C; DVD.** Jason Biggs; Isla Fisher; Joe Pantoliano; Joanna Gleason; Edward Herrmann; Mark Consuelos; Rob Corddry; Margo Martindale; Chris Diamantopoulos; Matt Malloy; Jay O. Sanders; Heather Goldenhersch; ***D:*** Michael Ian Black; ***W:*** Michael Ian Black; ***C:*** Dan Stoloff; ***M:*** Peter Nashel.

The Wedding Director ☆ 1/2 *Il Regina di Matrimoni* **2006** Troubled film director Franco Elica unexpectedly winds up in a small Sicilian town where he becomes the guest of fan Enzo Baiocco, the local wedding videographer. Franco is asked if he will shoot some footage of an upcoming wedding but he falls in love with bride-to-be Bona the instant he meets her. Italian with subtitles. **100m/C; DVD.** *FR IT* Sergio Castellitto; Sami Frey; Maurizio Donadoni; Donatella Finocchiaro; Bruno Cariello; Simona Nobili; Gianni Carina; ***D:*** Marco Bellocchio; ***W:*** Marco Bellocchio; ***C:*** Pasquale Mari; ***M:*** Riccardo Giagni.

The Wedding Gift ☆☆☆ *Wide-Eyed and Legless* **1993 (PG-13)** Offbeat charm and humor go a long way to overcome the inherent tragedy in this true story made for British TV. Longtime happily marrieds Diana (Walters) and Deric (Broadbent) Longden are struggling to cope with Diana's mysterious and increasingly debilitating illness, which causes blackouts, pain, and the inability to use her limbs. Diana comes to accept the fact that she's going to die and decides to find her hubby a new wife, aided by Deric's friendship with a blind novelist (Thomas). Terrific performances keep the mawkishness at bay. Based on Deric Longden's books "Diana's Story" and "Lost for Words." **87m/C; VHS, DVD.** *GB* Julie Walters; Jim Broadbent; Sian Thomas; Thora Hird; Andrew Lancel; Anastasia Mulrooney; ***D:*** Richard Loncraine; ***W:*** Jack Rosenthal; ***C:*** Remi Adefarasin. **TV**

The Wedding Guest ☆☆ **2018 (R)** Though Jay (Patel) tells people he has traveled from London to Pakistan to attend an old friend's wedding, in reality he's going to kidnap a bride, Samira (Apte), and take her across the border to his employer and her secret boyfriend Deepesh (Sarbh). The situation grows complicated during the kidnapping, when a guard is killed, and the manipulative Samira and the brooding Jay are on the run in India. As Jay becomes more protective of Samira, he learns the situation is not what it seems. A neo-film noir full of crimes and double crosses, the stylistic film features beautiful scenery and charismatic actors. **97m/C; DVD, Blu-Ray.** *UK* Dev Patel; Radhika Apte; Jim Sarbh; Nish Nathwani; Harish Khanna; ***D:*** Michael Winterbottom; ***W:*** Michael Winterbottom; ***C:*** Giles Nuttgens; ***M:*** Harry Escott.

Wedding in Blood ☆☆☆ *Les Noces Rouges* **1974 (PG)** Two French lovers plot to kill their respective spouses, and proceed to do so amid calamity and much table-turning. Sharp social satire and suspenseful mystery. Based on a true story. In French with English subtitles. **98m/C; VHS, DVD.** *FR IT* Claude Pieplu; Stephane Audran; Michel Piccoli; ***D:*** Claude Chabrol; ***W:*** Claude Chabrol; ***C:*** Jean Rabier.

A Wedding in Galilee ☆☆☆ *Noce In Galilee* **1987** The elder of a Palestinian village is given permission to have a traditional wedding ceremony for his son if Israeli military officers can attend as the guests of honor. As the event approaches, conflicts arise among the villagers, the family, and the Israelis. Long but fascinating treatment of traditional culture in the modern world amidst political tension. In Arabic and Hebrew, with English subtitles. **113m/C; VHS, DVD.** *BE FR* Ali M. El Aleili; Nazih Akleh; Anna Achdian; ***D:*** Michel Khleifi.

Wedding in White ☆☆ **1972 (R)** A rape and out-of-wedlock pregnancy trouble a poor British clan living in Canada during WWII. Sad, glum way to spend an evening. Kane is good in a non-comic role. Her screen father cares more for her honor than he does for her. **103m/C; VHS, DVD.** *CA* Donald Pleasence; Carol Kane; Leo Phillips; ***D:*** William Fruet.

The Wedding Night ☆ 1/2 **1935** Weepie melodrama with both leads miscast. Washed-up writer Tony Barrett (Cooper) heads to his Connecticut farmhouse with wife Dora (Vinson), hoping to become inspired. He takes an interest in Polish farm girl Manya (Sten), who's engaged to dull Fredrik (Bellamy), and decides to use her life as the basis for his new book. Bored Dora heads back to the city and Tony and Manya get closer than they should, with her old-world upbringing clashing with his more modern ways. **82m/B; DVD.** Gary Cooper; Anna Sten; Helen Vinson; Ralph Bellamy; Sig Rumann; Esther Dale; Walter Brennan; ***D:*** King Vidor; ***W:*** Edith Fitzgerald; ***C:*** Gregg Toland; ***M:*** Alfred Newman.

The Wedding Party ☆ 1/2 **1969** Apprehensive groom is overwhelmed by his too-eager bride and her inquisitive relatives at a prenuptial celebration. Hokey, dull, would-be comedy. First screen appearances of both Clayburgh and De Niro (spelled DeNero in the credits). **90m/C; VHS, DVD, Blu-Ray.** Jill Clayburgh; Robert De Niro; William Finley; ***D:*** Brian De Palma; Cynthia Munroe; Wilford Leach; ***W:*** Brian De Palma.

The Wedding Party ☆☆ 1/2 *Thank God He Met Lizzie* **1997 (R)** Predictable wedding comedy has thirtysomething Guy (Roxburgh) searching for the perfect woman. Finally he meets Lizzie (Blanchett) and the twosome are soon involved in lavish wedding preparations before they really have a chance to get to know each other. In fact, Guy begins dreaming of former love, Jenny (O'Connor), in the middle of the ceremony! **91m/C; DVD.** *AU* Richard Roxburgh; Cate Blanchett; Frances O'Connor; Linden Wilkinson; Michael K. Ross; John Gaden; Genevieve Mooy; Rhett Walton; Deborah Kennedy; ***D:*** Cherie Nowlan; ***W:*** Alexandra Long; ***C:*** Kathryn Milliss; ***M:*** Martin Armiger. Australian Film Inst. '97: Support. Actress (Blanchett).

The Wedding Plan ☆☆ 1/2 *Laavor et hakir* **2017 (PG)** An appealing romantic comedy with heart and hope. Weeks before her wedding, Ultra-Orthodox Jew Michal (Kooler) finds herself jilted by her fiance. Michal refuses to cancel anything because she is certain God will provide her with a replacement in time. In the ensuing days, the indomitable Michal goes on a series of unsuccessful dates and takes a pilgrimage to the Ukraine to visit the shrine of a rabbi. Though she connects with pop star Yos (Zehavi) there, the self-aware Michal realizes he is not what she seeks. Supported by loved ones, formidable Michal's faithful journey illustrates the power of belief. Hebrew with subtitles. **110m/C; DVD.** Noa Koler; Amos Tamam; Oz Zehavi; Irit Sheleg; Ronny Merhavi; ***D:*** Rama Burshtein; ***W:*** Rama Burshtein; ***C:*** Amit Yasur; ***M:*** Roy Edri.

The Wedding Planner ☆☆ 1/2 **2001 (PG-13)** A film that's a bridesmaid instead of a bride. Mary Fiore (Lopez) is a workaholic wedding planner in San Francisco who has no love life of her own. The driven Mary meets cute with aw-shucks doctor Steve Edison (McConaughey) who, naturally, turns out to be the fiance of Mary latest client, heiress Fran (Wilson). Not that the attractive duo can stay away from each other despite their good intentions. The leads nearly carry the film on charm alone before the script finally lets them down. **105m/C; VHS, DVD.** Jennifer Lopez; Matthew McConaughey; Bridgette Wilson-Sampras; Justin Chambers; Alex Rocco; Judy Greer; Kevin Pollak; Joanna Gleason; Charles Kimbrough; Fred Willard; Kathy Najimy; ***D:*** Adam Shankman; ***W:*** Michael Ellis; Pamela Falk; ***C:*** Julio Macat; ***M:*** Mervyn Warren.

Wedding Present ☆☆ **1936** After "Big Brown Eyes," Grant and Bennett were reteamed for this screwy—but not very funny—screwball comedy. Rusty (Bennett) and Charlie (Grant) are newspaper reporters. When Charlie gets a promotion to editor, he becomes insufferable and Rusty quits. She decides to marry boring writer Dodacker (Nagel) and Charlie goes out of his way to find her the perfect wedding present, which turns out to be himself. Grant's last contract film for Paramount. **81m/B; DVD.** Cary Grant; Joan Bennett; Conrad Nagel; Gene Lockhart; William Demarest; Inez Courtney; ***D:*** Richard Wallace; ***W:*** Joseph Anthony; ***C:*** Leon Shamroy.

The Wedding Ringer ☆☆ **2015 (R)** Hart continues his domination of the comedy market with this semi-funny tale. Jimmy Callahan (Hart) runs a unique service as a "Best Man for Hire" for those without enough friends to find their own. Enter the sweet but awkward Doug (Gad), someone who needs Jimmy's services. Cue wacky slapstick and silly humor. Hart and Gad make a decent comedy duo but their schtick gets old before the movie ends. It's another case of a mediocre script that everyone forgot to punch up after the leads were cast, figuring they could handle the rest. **101m/C; DVD, Blu-Ray.** Josh Gad; Kevin Hart; Kaley Cuoco; Ken Howard; Mimi Rogers; Colin Kane; Alan Ritchson; Aaron Takahashi; Cloris Leachman; Olivia Thirlby; Ignacio Serricchio; ***D:*** Jeremy Garelick; ***W:*** Jeremy Garelick; Jay Lavender; ***C:*** Bradford Lipson; ***M:*** Christopher Lennertz.

The Wedding Singer ☆☆ 1/2 **1997 (PG-13)** Despite almost nonexistent pacing and a script full of holes, "Singer" is an enjoyably goofy look at the mid '80s. Surprisingly toned-down and appealing Sandler is Robbie Hart, wedding singer, ultimate nice guy, and rock-star wanna-be, who's jilted at the altar. Waitress Barrymore is engaged to a skirt-chasing stock broker. It's immediately clear that they belong together, and the rest of the movie is spent on them chasing each other through various contrived obstacles, to the obvious ending. Features great cameos by punk-rocker Billy Idol, Jon Lovitz (as a rival wedding singer), and Steve Buscemi (excellent as the groom's jealous "dad always liked you best" brother). Musical highlight is Sandler's heartfelt rendition of the J. Geils Band's "Love Stinks." Isn't it a little scary that we're already spoofing the '80s? **96m/C; VHS, DVD, Blu-Ray.** Adam Sandler; Drew Barrymore; Christine Taylor; Allen Covert; Matthew Glave; Ellen A. Dow; Angela Featherstone; Alexis Arquette; Christina Pickles; Jon Lovitz; Steve Buscemi; Kevin Nealon; ***Cameo(s):*** Billy Idol; ***D:*** Frank Coraci; ***W:*** Tim Herlihy; ***C:*** Tim Suhrstedt; ***M:*** Teddy Castellucci. MTV Movie Awards '98: Kiss (Adam Sandler/Drew Barrymore).

The Wedding Song ☆☆ *Le Chant des Mariees* **2009** In 1942 Nazi-occupied Tunis, 16-year-old Muslim Nour (Borval) is engaged to her cousin Khaled (Oudghiri). Generally confined to the women's quarters, Nour shares the same courtyard with equally young French Jew Myriam (Brochere) and the girls have maintained an emotional friendship. When Myriam's mother (Albou) is forced to pay a huge fine for being a Jewish resident, it means her daughter is unwillingly betrothed to a much-older doctor (Abkarian). Their differences continue to heighten as the Nazis spread propaganda and Nour becomes resentful that Myriam is seemingly getting the life that she wants. Arabic, French and German with subtitles. **100m/C; DVD.** *FR* Simon Abkarian; Karin Albou; Lizzie Brochere; Olympe Borval; Najib Oudghiri; ***D:*** Karin Albou; ***W:*** Karin Albou; ***C:*** Laurent Brunet; ***M:*** Francoise-Eudes Chanfrault.

Wedding Wars ☆☆ 1/2 **2006** Fluff comedy with a serious message. Shel (Stamos) is a gay wedding planner who's in charge of brother Ben's (Dane) nuptials to Maggie (Somerville), the daughter of the governor of Maine. When Shel learns that Ben's boss, Governor Welling (Brolin), opposes gay marriage, he picks up a picket sign and goes on strike. Soon, gays across the country are leaving their jobs to join in Shel's protest, and the wedding, which has been turned over to the tacky Mrs. Fairfield (Kash), is a disaster waiting to happen. **87m/C; DVD.** John Stamos; Eric Dane; Bonnie Somerville; James Brolin; Sean Maher; Linda Kash; Rosemary Dunsmore; Jayne (Jane) Eastwood; Sean McCann; ***D:*** Jim Fall; ***W:*** Stephen Mazur; ***C:*** Ron Stannett. **CABLE**

The Wedding Year ☆☆ **2019 (R)** Self-centered Mara (Hyland) wants to be a photographer but works in a boutique and parties her way through life. Though she is unsure about wanting to be married, she becomes involved with aspiring chef Jake (Williams). Though the couple is financially challenged, they are invited to seven weddings over the course of a year and spend thousands of dollars on presents, flights, outfits, and hotels. The wedding circuit experience challenges their own relationship, as Mara's commitment issues come back. The generic romantic comedy also has rather unappealing characters, though Hyland makes the most of Mara. **90m/C; DVD.** Sarah Hyland; Tyler James Williams; Keith David; Kristen Johnston; Anna Camp; ***D:*** Robert Luketic; ***W:*** Donald Diego; ***C:*** Tom Banks; ***M:*** Raney Shockne.

Wee Willie Winkie ☆☆☆ **1937 (PG)** A precocious little girl is taken in by a British regiment in India. Sugar-coated. If you're a cinematic diabetic, be warned. If you're a Temple fan, you've probably already seen it. If not, you're in for a treat. Inspired by the Rudyard Kipling story. **99m/B; VHS, DVD.** Shirley Temple; Victor McLaglen; Sir C. Aubrey Smith; June Lang; Michael Whalen; Cesar Romero; Constance Collier; ***D:*** John Ford; ***C:*** Arthur C. Miller.

Week-End in Havana ☆☆ 1/2 **1941** Set in pre-revolution Cuba, this frothy musical finds salesgirl Faye on a long-awaited cruise when her ship gets stranded in Havana. She's escorted around town by shipping-official Payne and catches the eye of gambler-lothario Romero, who has a jealous girlfriend in Miranda. Fun fluff. **80m/C; VHS, DVD.** Alice Faye; John Payne; Cesar Romero; Carmen Miranda; Cobina Wright, Jr.; George Barbier; Sheldon Leonard; Billy Gilbert; ***D:*** Walter Lang; ***W:*** Karl Tunberg; ***M:*** Alfred Newman.

Weekend ☆☆☆ **1967** A Parisian couple embark on a drive to the country. On the way they witness and are involved in horrifying highway wrecks. Leaving the road they find a different, equally grotesque kind of carnage. Godard's brilliant, surreal, hyper-paranoiac view of modern life was greatly influenced by the fact that his mother was killed in an auto accident in 1954 (he himself suffered a serious motorcycle mishap in 1975). In French with English subtitles. **105m/C; VHS, DVD, Blu-Ray.** *FR IT* Mireille Darc; Jean Yanne; Jean-Pierre Kalfon; Valerie Lagrange; Jean-Pierre Leaud; Yves Beneyton; ***D:*** Jean-Luc Godard; ***W:*** Jean-Luc Godard; ***M:*** Antoine Duhamel.

The Weekend ☆☆ 1/2 **2000** Marian (Unger) and John (Harris) Kerr are hosting a weekend for family and friends at their upstate New York home to remember John's half-brother Tony (Sweeney) who died of AIDS a year before. Gathered are Tony's lover Lyle (Conrad) and his new boyfriend Robert (Duval) as well as neighbors Laura (Rowlands) and her daughter Nina (Shields). Turns out that mostly everybody was enamored of Tony and some unpleasant truths come out after too much wine. Good cast in a very gabby drama. Based on the novel by Peter Cameron. **97m/C; VHS, DVD.** *GB US* Deborah Kara Unger; Jared Harris; Gena Rowlands; D.B. Sweeney; Brooke Shields; David Conrad; James Duval; Gary Dourdan; ***D:*** Brian Skeet; ***W:*** Brian Skeet; ***C:*** Ron Fortunato; ***M:*** Dan (Daniel) Jones; Sarah Class.

Weekend ☆☆ **2011** Understated Brit drama. Introverted Russell (Cullen) concludes his Friday nightclubbing by picking up uninhibited Glen (New). Their morning-after chat includes Glen with a tape recorder asking Russell some very intimate questions, claiming he's working on an art project about gay sexuality. Noncommittal Glen also tells Russell that he's moving to America but in the intervening time there's a lot of conversation and sex. **96m/C; DVD, Blu-Ray.** *UK* Tom Cullen; Chris New; ***D:*** Andrew Haigh; ***W:*** Andrew Haigh; ***C:*** Ula Pontikos; ***M:*** James Edward Barker.

Weekend at Bernie's ☆☆ 1/2 *Hot and Cold* **1989 (PG-13)** Two computer nerds discover embezzlement at their workplace after being invited to their boss's beach house for a weekend party. They find their host murdered. They endeavor to keep up appearances by (you guessed it) dressing and strategically posing the corpse during the party. Kiser as the dead man is memorable, and the two losers gamely keep the silliness flowing. Lots of fun. **101m/C; VHS, DVD, Blu-Ray; Open Captioned.** Andrew McCarthy; Jonathan Silverman; Catherine Mary Stewart; Terry Kiser; Don Calfa; Louis Giambalvo; ***D:*** Ted Kotcheff; ***W:*** Robert Klane; ***C:*** Francois Protat; ***M:*** Andy Summers.

Weekend at Bernie's 2 1/2 **1993 (PG)** Unlikely but routine sequel to the original's cavorting cadaver slapstick, except now McCarthy and Silverman are frantically hunting for Bernie's (Kiser) cash stash, a quest that takes them and poor dead Bernie to the Caribbean. See Bernie get stuffed in a suitcase, see Bernie hang glide, see Bernie tango, see Bernie attract the opposite sex. Thin script with one-joke premise done to death but fun for those in the mood for the postmortem antics of a comedic stiff. Plenty of well-executed gags involving the well-preserved corpse (particularly one that's been dead for two films now) should lure back fans of the 1989 original. **89m/C; VHS, DVD.** Andrew McCarthy; Jonathan Silverman; Terry Kiser; Steve James; Troy Beyer; Barry Bostwick; ***D:*** Robert Klane; ***W:*** Robert Klane; ***M:*** Peter Wolf.

Weekend at the Waldorf
1945 Glossy, americanized remake of "Grand Hotel" set at the famous Park Avenue hotel, the Waldorf-Astoria, in New York City. Turner and Rogers star in the roles originated by Joan Crawford and Greta Garbo. Johnson and Pidgeon play their love interests. Combining drawing room comedy with slapstick and a touch of romance proved to be a hit, as this film was one of the top grossers of 1945 and was just what war-weary moviegoers wanted to see. Based on the play "Grand Hotel" by Vicki Baum. **130m/B; VHS, DVD.** Ginger Rogers; Walter Pidgeon; Van Johnson; Lana Turner; Robert Benchley; Edward Arnold; Leon Ames; Warner Anderson; Phyllis Thaxter; Keenan Wynn; Porter Hall; Samuel S. Hinds; ***D:*** Robert Z. Leonard; ***W:*** Samuel Spewack; Bella Spewack; Guy Bolton.

Weekend Pass **1984 (R)** Moronic rookie sailors who have just completed basic training are out on a weekend pass, determined to forget everything they have learned. They find this surprisingly easy to do. **92m/C; VHS, DVD.** D.W. Brown; Peter Ellenstein; Phil Hartman; Patrick Hauser; Chip McAllister; ***D:*** Lawrence Bassoff; ***W:*** Lawrence Bassoff; ***C:*** Bryan England.

Weekend with the Babysitter
WOOF! *Weekend Babysitter* **1970 (R)** Sordid teen drama about a weekend babysitter who goes to a film director's house and babysits everyone but the kids, running into a heroin-smuggling ring along the way. Casting-couch story with a twist. **93m/C; VHS, DVD.** Susan (Suzan) Roman; George E. Carey; James Almanzar; Luanne Roberts; ***D:*** Don Henderson.

Weepah Way for Now **2015** Sisters Elle and Joey (Aly and AJ Michalka) plan one last party to bring their friends and loved ones together before they head out on a musical tour. Plans for unity are soon squashed when their divorced parents and ex-boyfriends show up, because what's a fun gathering for if not the soul crushing despair easily induced by relatives? Reportedly a semi-autobiographical film about their lives and career, it makes no distinction between what really happened and what didn't (not that most people will care). **89m/C; DVD, Blu-Ray, Streaming.** AJ Michalka; Alyson Michalka; Mimi Rogers; Amanda Crew; ***V:*** Saoirse Ronan; ***D:*** Stephen Ringer; ***W:*** Stephen Ringer; ***C:*** Stephen Ringer; ***M:*** Michael Einziger; Ann Marie Simpson. **VIDEO**

The Weight of Water **2000 (R)** Photographer Jean (McCormack) arrives at Smuttynose Island, off the coast of New Hampshire, to research an infamous 1873 ax-murder case involving two Norwegian immigrant women (Cartlidge, Shaw) a local man (Hinds), and an unreliable witness (Polley). You see their story in flashback as Jean struggles with her own domestic dilemmas—her drunken poet husband Thomas (Penn), his brother Rich (Lucas), and Rich's sexy girlfriend Adaline (Hurley). Jealousy, lies, and betrayal abound in both stories. Based on the novel by Anita Shreve. **105m/C; VHS, DVD.** Catherine McCormack; Sarah Polley; Sean Penn; Josh(ua) Lucas; Elizabeth Hurley; Ciaran Hinds; Ulrich Thomsen; Anders W. Berthelsen; Katrin Cartlidge; Vinessa Shaw; ***D:*** Kathryn Bigelow; ***W:*** Alice Arlen; Christopher Kyle; ***C:*** Adrian Biddle; ***M:*** David Hirschfelder.

Weird Science **1985 (PG-13)** Hall is appealing, and Hughes can write dialogue for teens with the best of them. However, many of the jokes are in poor taste, and the movie seems to go on forever. Hall and his nerdy cohort Mitchell-Smith use a very special kind of software to create the ideal woman who wreaks zany havoc in their lives from the outset. **94m/C; VHS, DVD, Blu-Ray.** Kelly Le Brock; Anthony Michael Hall; Ilan Mitchell-Smith; Robert Downey, Jr.; Bill Paxton; ***D:*** John Hughes; ***W:*** John Hughes; ***C:*** Matthew F. Leonetti; ***M:*** Ira Newborn.

Weirdsville 1/2 **2007 (R)** Heroin addict pals Dexter (Speedman) and Royce (Bentley) live in tiny Weedsville in Northern Ontario. They owe their dealer Omar (Bhaneja) and agree to deal drugs for him to settle their account. Royce's girlfriend and sometimes-hooker Matilda (Manning) seemingly overdoses on Omar's goods, and the brilliant pair decide to get rid of her by burying her in the boiler room of a drive-in theatre where Dexter briefly worked. But they run into complications. 1) She's still alive, and 2) they figure this out only after they've accidentally stumbled upon some Satanists in the middle of a human sacrifice. Pursued by the Satanists, they've still got to figure out how to pay Omar. Some would doubt the humor in heroin addiction, and this pic will definitely reinforce that doubt. **90m/C; DVD.** ***CA*** Scott Speedman; Wes Bentley; Taryn Manning; Matt Frewer; Greg Bryk; Maggie Castle; Raoul Bhaneja; Joe Dinicol; Jordan Prentice; Dax Ravina; ***D:*** Allan Moyle; ***W:*** Willem Wennekers; ***C:*** Adam Swica; ***M:*** Michael Doherty; John Rowley.

Welcome Home **1989 (R)** A missing-in-action Vietnam vet (Kristofferson) leaves his wife and children in Cambodia to return to America more than 15 years after he was reported dead. He finds his first wife remarried and discovers a teenaged son he unknowingly fathered. This plotless, sporadically moving film was Schaffner's last. **92m/C; VHS, Streaming.** Kris Kristofferson; JoBeth Williams; Sam Waterston; Brian Keith; Trey Wilson; Thomas Wilson Brown; ***D:*** Franklin J. Schaffner; ***C:*** Fred W. Koenekamp; ***M:*** Henry Mancini. **CABLE**

Welcome Home **2018 (R)** After the relationship between Cassie (Ratajkowski) and Bryan (Paul) suffers because of Cassie's infidelity, the couple takes a trip to Italy to repair it. They rent a large village in the countryside hoping to work through her betrayal and his feelings of anguish. The tensions between them are heightened by a mysterious, menacing neighbor who watches all they do through electronic surveillance devices. Federico (Scamarcio) is a charming yet sinister man who encourages tortured Bryan's feelings of resentment while acting as Cassie's shoulder to cry on. The thriller plays on fears of voyeurism and technology but is quite predictable aside from an interesting ending. **97m/C; DVD.** Emily Ratajkowski; Aaron Paul; Riccardo Scamarcio; Katy Saunders; Alice Bellagamba; ***D:*** George Ratliff; ***W:*** David Levinson; ***C:*** Shelly Johnson; ***M:*** Bear McCreary.

Welcome Home Roscoe Jenkins 1/2 **2008 (PG-13)** Cultures clash and cliches abound when hotshot Hollywood talk-show host Roscoe Jenkins (Lawrence) returns home to small-town Georgia with his dim fiancee (Bryant) and young son for his parents' 50th wedding anniversary. His unimpressed family-including horndog sister Betty (Mo'Nique), studly brother Otis (Duncan), slick cousin Reggie (Epps), and nemesis Clyde (Cedric the Entertainer)?doesn't exactly roll out the red carpet. In no time, old rivalries make for put-downs, pot-shots, and sight gags that alternate between amusing and embarrassing, until a not-unexpected but somewhat ironic dose of schmaltz finally ends the tedium. **113m/C; DVD.** Martin Lawrence; Margaret Avery; James Earl Jones; Joy Bryant; Michael Clarke Duncan; Cedric the Entertainer; Mike Epps; Mo'Nique; Louis C.K.; Nicole Ari Parker; Damani Roberts; ***D:*** Malcolm Lee; ***W:*** Malcolm Lee; ***C:*** Greg Gardiner; ***M:*** David Newman.

Welcome Home, Roxy Carmichael **1990 (PG-13)** Ryder, as a young misfit, is the bright spot in this deadpan, would-be satire. Hollywood star Roxy Charmichael returns to her small Ohio hometown and begins fantasizing that she is really her mother. It is obvious why this deadpan, hard-to-follow movie was a boxoffice flop. **98m/C; VHS, DVD.** Winona Ryder; Jeff Daniels; Laila Robins; Dinah Manoff; Ava Fabian; Robbie Kiger; Sachi (MacLaine) Parker; ***D:*** Jim Abrahams; ***C:*** Paul Elliott.

Welcome Home, Soldier Boys
WOOF! **1972** Bleak, brutal, and banal pic that's supposed to reflect on how badly Vietnam vets were treated when they returned home. Four vets pool their dough to drive to California, but are disillusioned by their reception along the way. Broke by the time they reach New Mexico, they rob a gas station and then go on a rampage, before putting on their uniforms again and waiting for a final showdown with the authorities. **91m/C; DVD.** Joe Don Baker; Paul Koslo; Elliot Street; Alan Vint; Geoffrey Lewis; Billy Green Bush; ***D:*** Richard Compton; ***W:*** Guerdon (Gordon) Trueblood; ***C:*** Donald Birnkrant; ***M:*** Ronee Blakley.

Welcome Says the Angel
2001 Drifter Joshua (Jacobs) winds up at a seedy bar in Hollywood where he's picked up by Ana (Hauer) and the two go off to her loft. In the morning, Josh finds himself handcuffed, his wallet and Ana gone. She returns after getting her heroin fix but refuses to let Josh go. They begin to bond (must be Stockholm Syndrome) and Josh vows to get her off drugs when he finally gets free. Maybe he wants to handcuff her instead. No-budgeter but the leads work well together. **90m/C; VHS, DVD.** Jon Jacobs; Aysha Hauer; ***D:*** Philippe Dib; ***W:*** Jon Jacobs; Philippe Dib; ***C:*** Gabor Satanyl; ***M:*** Nels Cline; George Lockwood.

Welcome Stranger 1/2 **1947** New doctor's ideas clash with the old doctor's ways in a small town until the younger saves the live of the elder. Crosby and Fitzgerald star as the two clashing medics in this reunion of the cast of "Going My Way." He wins the heart of the town and the heart of local teacher Caulfield in the meantime. Sheekman's script calls for Marx Brothers'-like comedy and director Nugent appears in a cameo as another doctor. **107m/B; VHS, DVD.** Bing Crosby; Barry Fitzgerald; Joan Caulfield; Wanda Hendrix; Frank Faylen; Elizabeth Patterson; Robert Shayne; Don Beddoe; Percy Kilbride; Larry Young; ***Cameo(s):*** Elliott Nugent; ***D:*** Elliott Nugent; ***W:*** Arthur Sheekman; ***C:*** Lionel Lindon; ***M:*** Johnny Burke; James Van Heusen.

Welcome to Acapulco 1/2 **2019** Video game designer Mathew (Kingsbaker) plans on debuting his new game at an event in New Mexico. His situation becomes complicated when he wakes up drunk along the way in Acapulco, Mexico, and the CIA demands that he produce a mysterious package. Stranger yet, he is rescued by Adriana (Serradilla), who claims to be his wife. As Mathew tries to understand the conspiracy he has stumbled into, he encounters evil bounty hunter Hyde (Madsen), a corrupt U.S. senator (Sorvino), and a wealthy businessman Jake (Baldwin). Though the film has energy, it has a convoluted plot. **88m/C; DVD.** William Baldwin; Michael Madsen; Bradley Gregg; Ana Serradilla; Michael Kingsbaker; ***D:*** Guillermo Ivan; ***W:*** Garry Charles; ***C:*** Saro Varjabedian; ***M:*** Javier Bayon; Luc Suarez. **VIDEO**

Welcome to Collinwood **2002 (R)** Ensemble comedy by the brothers Russo is a remake of the 1958 Italian classic, "Big Deal on Madonna Street." Collinwood is home to a group of hopelessly inept, dim wanna-be criminals. The dubious crew consists of single father Riley (Macy), Leon (Washington), Toto (Jeter), Pero (Rockwell) and Basil (Davoli). Broad character bits are highlighted by the always brilliant Macy and an amusing Rockwell. Producer Clooney provides a highlight as a wheelchair-bound safe cracker. A little too over-the-top, but accurately cops original's hilarious comic climax as the boys break down a wall to get at the safe. **86m/C; VHS, DVD.** Luis Guzman; Michael Jeter; Patricia Clarkson; Andrew Davoli; Isaiah Washington, IV; William H. Macy; Sam Rockwell; Gabrielle Union; Jennifer Esposito; George Clooney; ***D:*** Anthony Russo; Joe Russo; ***W:*** Anthony Russo; Joe Russo; ***C:*** Lisa Rinzler; Charles Minsky; ***M:*** Mark Mothersbaugh.

Welcome to Hard Times 1/2 **1967** Haphazard western based on the E.L. Doctorow novel. Aging lawyer Will Blue (Fonda) is the mayor of the small town of Hard Times, which lives up to its name when a nameless drifter (Ray) torments its citizens and burns the town to the ground. Will vows to help the few remaining residents rebuild, and newcomer Zar (Wynn) opens a successful brothel/saloon. The drifter returns and this time Will has to take a stand. **103m/C; DVD.** Henry Fonda; Aldo Ray; Janice Rule; Keenan Wynn; Royal Dano; Warren Oates; Paul Fix; Michel Shea; Arlene Golonka; Fay Spain; Janis Page; Kalen Liu; Lon Chaney, Jr.; Elisha Cook, Jr.; ***D:*** Burt Kennedy; ***W:*** Burt Kennedy; ***C:*** Harry Stradling, Jr.; ***M:*** Harry Sukman.

Welcome to Hollywood **2000** Filmmaker Rifkin plays himself in this mockumentary that follows the career of actor Nick Decker (Markes) from wannabe to superstar, which includes his romance with married actress Everhart (playing herself). **89m/C; VHS, DVD.** Adam Rifkin; Tony Markes; Angie Everhart; ***D:*** Adam Rifkin; Tony Markes.

Welcome to Marwen 1/2 **2018 (PG-13)** Based on a true story, this inspirational film profiles Mark Hogancamp (Carell), who was beaten nearly to death outside a N.Y. bar in 2000. As part of his emotional and physical recovery, he created the miniature town of Marwen, where his doll-avatar is a WWII soldier who suffers obstacles but ultimately overcomes them, often with the help of female dolls representing women he knows in real life. A touching tale of resilience, imagination, and artistry, inspired by the 2010 documentary *Marwencol*. **116m/C; DVD, Blu-Ray.** Steve Carell; Leslie Mann; Diane Kruger; Merritt Wever; Janelle Monáe; ***D:*** Robert Zemeckis; ***W:*** Robert Zemeckis; Caroline Thompson; ***C:*** C. Kim Miles; ***M:*** Alan Silvestri.

Welcome to Me **2015 (R)** Walking that fine line between exploiting mental illness and capturing it, Piven's dramedy only works because of Wiig's fearless performance. Everything else around her doesn't quite connect. Alice Klieg is a mentally unstable shut-in who has no friends and spends her days rewatching old VHS tapes of Oprah Winfrey for inspirational messages. She wins the lottery and spends her money on an Oprah-esque show of her own. Of course, the producers are willing to take the cash, even though Klieg clearly needs more than a camera in her face. **87m/C; DVD, Blu-Ray.** Kristen Wiig; Wes Bentley; Linda Cardellini; Joan Cusack; Loretta Devine; ***D:*** Shira Piven; ***W:*** Eliot Laurence; ***C:*** Eric Alan Edwards; ***M:*** David Robbins.

Welcome to Mooseport 1/2 **2004 (PG-13)** Romano's big-screen debut is a weak-scripted mess that has him running for mayor of his stock-character quirky small town against former president Hackman. Romano plays average schlub (Everybody Loves) Handy Harrison, who gets into politics when ex-President Monroe "Eagle" Cole (Hackman) hits on his long-time, waiting-for-commitment girlfriend (Tierney). A golf match for the town and her heart ensues. Hackman turns in a dependable performance but Romano shuffles through, depending too much on the audience's familiarity with his TV character while Tierney taps her foot impatiently. Riddled with stereotypical characters, the movie never moves past utterly predictable, and the laughs are few and far between. Director Petrie obviously wants to conjure the charm of old Frank Capra movies, but only manages to reach the level of a bad sitcom pilot that drags on for far too long. **110m/C; DVD.** Ray Romano; Gene Hackman; Marcia Gay Harden; Maura Tierney; Christine Baranski; Fred Savage; Rip Torn; June Squibb; Wayne Robson; John Rothman; Karl Pruner; ***D:*** Donald Petrie; ***W:*** Tom Schulman; Doug Richardson; ***C:*** Victor Hammer; ***M:*** John Debney.

Welcome to New York 1/2 **2015 (R)** The somewhat true-life misadventures of former IMF chief and French presidential candidate, Dominique Strauss-Kahn, through the twisted eyes of former exploitation director Abel Ferrara. Ripped from the headlines, and Strauss-Kahn now dubbed Mr. Devereaux (Depardieu), begins nearly as a soft-core porn take on a very public sex scandal, slowly transforming into a biting character study of a powerful politician stripped of all his freedoms (and clothes) and eventually taken to Riker's Island. A complicated and challenging portrait of a feared man, who's living in a constant state of fear. **125m/C; DVD, Blu-Ray.** Jacqueline Bisset; Gerard Depardieu; Amy Ferguson; Drena De Niro; Paul Calderon; ***D:*** Abel Ferrara; ***W:*** Abel Ferrara; Christ Zois; ***C:*** Ken Kelsch.

Welcome to Paradise 🦴🦴 1/2 **2007 (PG)** Uplifting family drama has single mom and controversial preacher Debbie Laramie (Bernard) transferred from her large urban ministry to the small, depressed town of Paradise, Texas. She meets a lot of resistance from her parishioners and the church's charter is in danger of being revoked. But when the church burns down, everyone finds a reason to work together. **105m/C; DVD.** Crystal Bernard; Brian Dennehy; Bobby Edner; Nick Searcy; Brad Stine; Beth Grant; Ken Jenkins; William Shockley; ***D:*** Brent Huff; ***W:*** William Shockley; Brent Huff; ***C:*** Robert Hayes; ***M:*** Steve Pierson.

Welcome to Sarajevo 🦴🦴🦴 1/2 **1997 (R)** Fresh, unusual take on the siege of Sarajevo in 1992. A group of news correspondents, including British reporter Michael Henderson (Dillane), find themselves in the middle of the siege, and become disillusioned when the conflict is largely ignored by the rest of the world. Film sheds perspective when a particularly bloody massacre takes a backseat to the marital troubles of the royal family. Henderson becomes personally involved when his daily coverage of an orphanage sparks him to become a hero to the orphaned Emily (Sarajevan actress Nusevic). Intermingling actual news footage, Winterbottom shows the violence on a personal level. Solid supporting characters include Harrelson as the wonderfully egotistic American celeb journalist. Strong emotional content is tempered by the smart and savvy gallows humor, which keeps melodrama miles away. Loosely based on a true story by ITN reporter, Michael Nicholson. **102m/C; VHS, DVD.** Stephen (Dillon) Dillane; Woody Harrelson; Marisa Tomei; Kerry Fox; Emily Lloyd; Goran Visnjic; Juliet Aubrey; Emira Nusevic; James Nesbitt; Igor Dzambazov; Gordana Gadzic; Drazen Sivak; Vesna Orel; ***D:*** Michael Winterbottom; ***W:*** Frank Cottrell-Boyce; ***C:*** Daf Hobson; ***M:*** Adrian Johnston.

Welcome to Spring Break 🦴 1/2 *Nightmare Beach* **1988 (R)** College co-eds are stalked by a killer on the beaches of Florida. **92m/C; VHS, DVD, Blu-Ray.** John Saxon; Michael Parks; Nicolas De Toth; Sarah Buxton; Lance LeGault; Rawley Valverde; ***D:*** Umberto Lenzi; ***W:*** Umberto Lenzi; ***M:*** Claudio Simonetti.

Welcome to the Dollhouse 🦴🦴 1/2 **1995 (R)** Eleven-year-old, glasses-wearing Dawn Wiener (Matarazzo) is the middle child of a middle-class family in an average New Jersey town. It's her first year in junior high and Dawn's bewildered—by school, by family, by life in general, and where she fits in. Puberty sucks. **87m/C; VHS, DVD, Blu-Ray.** Heather Matarazzo; Brendan Sexton, III; Daria Kalinina; Matthew Faber; Angela Pietropinto; Eric Mabius; ***D:*** Todd Solondz; ***W:*** Todd Solondz; ***C:*** Randy Drummond; ***M:*** Jill Wisoff. Ind. Spirit '97: Debut Perf. (Matarazzo); Sundance '96: Grand Jury Prize.

Welcome to the Jungle 🦴 1/2 **2013** No, it's not that Guns 'n' Roses biopic that we're all waiting for. This ridiculous comedy centers on an office outing gone horribly awry when a corporate retreat ends up in the hands of an unhinged former Marine brilliantly named Storm Rothchild (a game Van Damme). Putting spoiled yuppies in harm's way makes for the kind of broad comedy that works better in sitcom form, a feeling that's enhanced by the cast of TV veterans that makes up the ensemble (including Adam Brody, Rob Huebel, and Megan Boone). Some funny moments but nowhere near memorable or consistent enough. **95m/C; DVD, Blu-Ray.** Jean-Claude Van Damme; Adam Brody; Rob Huebel; Megan Boone; Eric Edelstein; Kristen Schaal; ***D:*** Rob Meltzer; ***W:*** Jeff Kauffman; ***C:*** Eric Haase; ***M:*** Karl Preusser.

Welcome to the Punch 🦴🦴 **2013 (R)** Flashy, undemanding good cop vs. everyone else story. London detective Max Lewinsky (an uinlikely McAvoy) is after master criminal Jacob (Strong) when he's seriously injured. Three years later, Max gets the chance to take Jacob down again when the bad guy's teenaged son gets caught during a heist. Jacob, who's retired to Iceland, is lured back home and it should be straightforward enough except Max's corrupt boss Geiger (Morrissey) is in cahoots with a crooked politician although that plotline remains ill-defined. **99m/C; DVD, Blu-Ray.** *UK* James McAvoy; Mark Strong; David Morrissey; Andrea Riseborough; Robert Portal; Peter Mullan; Jason Flemyng; Elyes Gabel; ***D:*** Eran Creevy; ***W:*** Eran Creevy; ***C:*** Ed Wild; ***M:*** Harry Escott.

Welcome to the Rileys 🦴🦴 **2010 (R)** After the traumatic death of their daughter, salesman Doug (Gandolfini) and his wife Lois (Leo) are merely going through the motions of their marriage. When Doug goes to a convention in Katrina-ravaged New Orleans he encounters stripper/hooker Mallory (Stewart), who reminds him of his lost child. His paternal instincts overwhelm him, and he moves into her run-down shack to try to protect her. Agoraphobic Lois then heads south to try to bring her husband back. Unlikely healing begins to flourish like the mildew on the intentionally grubby set design. Directed by Jake Scott, son of renowned director Ridley Scott. **110m/C; Blu-Ray, On Demand.** James Gandolfini; Melissa Leo; Kristen Stewart; Eisa Davis; Joseph Chrest; Ally Sheedy; ***D:*** Jake Scott; ***W:*** Ken Hixon; ***C:*** Christopher Soos; ***M:*** Marc Streitenfeld.

Welcome II the Terrordome 🦴 1/2 **1995 (R)** Yet another future apocalypse. Terrordome is a city collapsing under pollution, filled with corrupt police, where blacks are confined to ghettos with rampant gang violence and drugs. Spike's young nephew is killed in a police raid and his sister goes on a shooting spree, which draws more rage and has Spike being forced to choose between his homies and his preggers white girlfriend. **98m/C; VHS, DVD.** *GB* Saffron Burrows; Valentine Nonyela; Suzette Llewellyn; Felix Joseph; ***D:*** Ngozi Onwurah; ***W:*** Ngozi Onwurah.

Welcome to Woop Woop 🦴 1/2 **1997 (R)** Hit-or-miss (mostly miss) comedy about a con man meeting his match in a small Australian town of redneck eccentrics. On the lam, Teddy (Schaech) nevertheless offers a ride to buxom blonde Angie (Porter), whom he meets at a gas station. The next thing he knows (having been drugged), Teddy wakes up in the nightmarish community of Woop Woop, where Angie announces they've gotten married. And Angie's violent father, Daddy-O (Taylor), makes it clear his new son-in-law has no chance of making it out alive. Based on the book "The Dead Heart" by Douglas Kennedy. **97m/C; VHS, DVD.** *AU* Johnathon Schaech; Rod Taylor; Susie Porter; Dee Smart; Richard Moir; Rachel Griffiths; Barry Humphries; ***D:*** Stephan Elliott; ***W:*** Michael Thomas; ***C:*** Mike Molloy; ***M:*** Stewart Copeland.

The Well 🦴🦴🦴 **1951** A young black girl disappears and a white man (Morgan) is accused of kidnapping her. When it is discovered that the girl is trapped in a deep well, Morgan's expertise is needed to help free her. **85m/B; VHS, DVD.** Richard Rober; Harry (Henry) Morgan; Barry Kelley; Christine Larson; ***D:*** Leo Popkin; Russell Rouse; ***C:*** Ernest Laszlo.

The Well 🦴🦴 **1997** Repression, isolation, and tragedy set in barren rural Australia. Drab, middleaged Hester (Rabe) hires spirited teenager Katherine (Otto) to help out on her bleak farm. Hester soon becomes emotional dependent on Katherine, who eventually convinces her to sell the property so they can travel to Europe. (Yes, "The Servant" will come to mind.) But a car accident (caused by Katherine) claims the life of a mystery man and Hester decides to hide the body in an unused well. Then they discover all their money has been stolen, probably by their dead friend, and just who's going down the well to retrieve it? Based on a novel by Elizabeth Jolley. **101m/C; VHS, DVD.** *AU* Pamela Rabe; Miranda Otto; Paul Chubb; ***D:*** Samantha Lang; ***W:*** Laura Jones; ***C:*** Mandy Walker; ***M:*** Stephen Rae. Australian Film Inst. '97: Actress (Rabe), Adapt. Screenplay, Art Dir./Set Dec.

Well-Digger's Daughter 🦴🦴🦴 *La Fille Du Puisatier* **1946** As her lover goes off to war, a well-digger's daughter discovers that she is pregnant causing both sets of parents to feud over who's to blame. This is the first film made in France after the end of WWII and marks the return of the French film industry. In French with English subtitles. **142m/B; VHS, DVD.** *FR* Raimu; Josette Day; Fernandel; Charpin; ***D:*** Marcel Pagnol.

The Well-Digger's Daughter 🦴🦴 *La Fille du Puisatier* **2011** Old-fashioned family melodrama that's a remake of Marcel Pagnol's 1940 pic. Poor widower Pascal Amoretti asks his teenage daughter Patricia to come back from Paris to help him look after her sisters. Dashing pilot Jacques, the son of bourgeois townsfolk, makes his move on the beauty before returning to the war and she, of course, winds up pregnant. Papa does not take the news well at all. French with subtitles. **107m/C; DVD, Blu-Ray.** *FR* Daniel Auteuil; Astrid Berges-Frisbey; Nicolas Duvauchelle; Kad Merad; Jean-Pierre Darroussin; Sabine Azema; ***D:*** Daniel Auteuil; ***W:*** Daniel Auteuil; ***C:*** Jean-Francois Robin; ***M:*** Alexandre Desplat.

We'll Meet Again 🦴🦴 1/2 **1982** Cliched but touching miniseries set in a quiet English town in 1943. At least the town was quiet until the arrival of a bomber group from the U.S. Army Eighth Air Force. Soon the Yanks are chasing the local girls and getting into trouble while their commander (Shannon) finds himself falling for a married doctor (York). **690m/C; VHS, DVD.** *GB* Michael J. Shannon; Susannah York; Ronald Hines; Ed Devereaux; Christopher Malcolm; Patrick O'Connell; Joris Stuyck; ***D:*** Christopher Hodson. **TV**

We'll Meet Again 🦴 1/2 **2002 (PG-13)** Having been unjustly thrown in the slammer for six years for her husband's slaying makes the strong-willed Molly intent on hunting down the real killer with the aide of reporter pal Fran. But, as often is the case in these Mary Higgins Clark adaptations, the truth could have deadly results for the women. **100m/C; VHS, DVD.** Laura Leighton; Brandy Ledford; Andrew Jackson; Anne Openshaw; Bryan Genesse; Beverley Elliott; Paul Campbell; Gedeon Burkhard; Paula Shaw; Steve Archer; Karin Konoval; Michael Eklund; Eva DeViveiros; Patti Allan; Sam MacMillan; Taayla Markell; ***D:*** Michael Storey; ***W:*** Michael Thoma; John Benjamin Martin; ***C:*** Henry Lebo; ***M:*** Claude Foisy. **TV**

The Wendell Baker Story 🦴 1/2 **2005 (PG-13)** Con man Wendell (Luke Wilson) bumbles from a fake-ID con to prison to working at a seedy retirement hotel where the nurses (Griffin and Owen Wilson) are scamming Medicare, stealing medicine, and forcing the residents to work for food. Wendell takes the side of the residents (Cassel, Stanton, and Kristofferson) and lazy hijinks ensue. Or something. All three Wilsons (including director Andrew) try hard to make a lazy 70s stoner comedy but mostly coast on their proven talent while rehashing themes done better elsewhere. **95m/C; DVD.** Luke Wilson; Owen Wilson; Seymour Cassel; Eddie Griffin; Kris Kristofferson; Eva Mendes; Harry Dean Stanton; Jacob Vargas; Spencer Scott; Buck Taylor; Jo Harvey Allen; Azura Skye; Paul M. Wright; Mathew Greer; Will Ferrell; ***D:*** Luke Wilson; Andrew Wilson; ***W:*** Luke Wilson; ***C:*** Steve Mason; ***M:*** Aaron Zigman.

Wendigo 🦴🦴 1/2 **2001 (R)** Manhattanites George (Weber), Kim (Clarkson), and their eight-year-old son Miles (Sullivan) are heading out of the city for a weekend at a friend's farmhouse in upstate New York. Distracted George hits a deer, which enrages backwoods hunter Otis (Speredakos) who was trailing the buck. Quiet Miles notices the tension between his parents but weird things really begin to happen when a mysterious man gives Miles a Wendigo figure, a creature in Native American mythology that has destructive powers, which Miles now seems to command. **91m/C; VHS, DVD, Blu-Ray.** Patricia Clarkson; Jake Weber; Erik Per Sullivan; John Speredakos; Christopher Winkoop; ***D:*** Larry Fessenden; ***W:*** Larry Fessenden; ***C:*** Terry Stacey; ***M:*** Michelle DiBucci.

Wendy and Lucy 🦴🦴🦴 **2008 (R)** Director Reichhardt crafts a stripped-down and poignant gem of Wendy's (Williams) never-quite-finished and financially challenged journey from Indiana to Alaska, where she attempts to free herself from an unemployed, dead-end existence. With her lovable mutt, Lucy, as her sole traveling companion, Wendy just can't seem to catch a break along the way. In Oregon her beat-up Honda breaks down and she finds herself locked up, hit with a fine, and dogless after trying to lift some jerky and dog food from the local market. An honest but not sentimental portrait of the realities of life in America normally hidden away. **80m/C; Blu-Ray, On Demand.** Michelle Williams; William Oldham; John Robinson; Will Patton; Larry Fessenden; Wally Dalton; ***D:*** Kelly Reichardt; ***W:*** Kelly Reichardt; Jonathan Raymond; ***C:*** Sam Levy.

Went to Coney Island on a Mission from God. . . Be Back by Five 🦴🦴 **1998 (R)** Daniel (Cryer), Stan (Stear), and Richie (Baez) were all best neighborhood friends while growing up in Brooklyn. Now it's years later and Stan and Daniel have lost touch with Richie, whom they hear is a mentally ill vagrant living under the boardwalk at Coney Island. So they decide to ditch their boring lives and track him down. Flashbacks to earlier incidents get confusing if not tedious. **94m/C; VHS, DVD, Blu-Ray.** Jon Cryer; Rick Stear; Rafael Baez; Ione Skye; Frank Whaley; Peter Gerety; Akili Prince; Aesha Waks; Dominic Chianese; ***D:*** Richard Schenkman; ***W:*** Richard Schenkman; Jon Cryer; ***C:*** Adam Beekman; ***M:*** Midge Ure.

We're Back! A Dinosaur's Story 🦴🦴 1/2 **1993 (G)** Animated adventures of a pack of revived dinosaurs who return to their old stomping grounds—which are now modern-day New York City. Smart-mouth human boy Louie and his girlfriend Cecilia take the dinos under their wing (so to speak), wise them up to modern life, and try to prevent their capture by the evil Professor Screweyes. Slow-moving with some violence. Adapted from the book by Hudson Talbott. **78m/C; VHS, DVD, Blu-Ray.** ***V:*** John Goodman; Felicity Kendal; Walter Cronkite; Joey Shea; Jay Leno; Julia Child; Kenneth Mars; Martin Short; Rhea Perlman; Rene LeVant; Blaze Berdahl; Charles Fleischer; Yeardley Smith; ***D:*** Dick Zondag; Ralph Zondag; Phil Nibbelink; Simon Wells; ***W:*** John Patrick Shanley.

We're No Angels 🦴🦴🦴 **1955** Three escapees from Devil's Island hide out with the family of a kindly French storekeeper on Christmas Eve. Planning to rob the family, they end up helping them with various financial, romantic, and familial problems. Somewhat stagey, but great dialogue and excellent cast make for enjoyable holiday fare. One of Bogart's few comedies. From the French stage play of the same name, later remade with De Niro and Penn. **103m/C; VHS, DVD.** Humphrey Bogart; Aldo Ray; Joan Bennett; Peter Ustinov; Basil Rathbone; Leo G. Carroll; Lea Penman; John Smith; Gloria Talbott; John Baer; ***D:*** Michael Curtiz; ***W:*** Ranald MacDougall; ***C:*** Loyal Griggs; ***M:*** Frederick "Friedrich" Hollander.

We're No Angels 🦴🦴 1/2 **1989 (R)** Two escaped cons disguise themselves as priests and get in the appropriate series of jams. De Niro and Penn play off each other well, turning in fine comic performances. Distantly related to the 1955 film of the same name and the David Mamet play. **110m/C; VHS, DVD.** Robert De Niro; Sean Penn; Demi Moore; Hoyt Axton; Bruno Kirby; James Russo; John C. Reilly; Ray McAnally; Wallace Shawn; ***D:*** Neil Jordan; ***W:*** David Mamet; ***C:*** Philippe Rousselot; ***M:*** George Fenton.

We're Not Dressing 🦴🦴🦴 **1934** Loose musical adaptation of J.M. Barrie's "The Admirable Crichton" with the butler transformed into singing sailor Crosby. Fabulously wealthy heiress Lombard invites her pals for a South Seas yachting adventure. Only the ship gets wrecked and everyone winds up on a small island where the practical Crosby whips everyone into shape (and romances Lombard). Burns and Allen supply additional comedy as a pair of botanists who just happen to be studying the local fauna. **74m/B; VHS, DVD.** Bing Crosby; Carole Lombard; George Burns; Gracie Allen; Ethel Merman; Leon Errol; Ray Milland; ***D:*** Norman Taurog; ***W:*** Horace Jackson; Francis Martin; ***M:*** Harry Revel; ***M:*** Mack Gordon.

We're Not Married 🦴🦴🦴 **1952** Five couples learn that they are not legally married when a judge realizes his license expired before he performed the ceremonies. The story revolves around this quintet of couples who now must cope with whether or not they really do want to be married. Although the episodes vary in quality, the Allen-Rogers sequence is excellent. Overall, the cast performs well in this lightweight comedy. **85m/B; VHS, DVD.** Ginger Rogers; Fred Allen; Victor Moore; Marilyn Monroe; Paul Douglas; David Wayne; Eve Arden; Louis Calhern; Zsa Zsa Gabor; James Gleason; Jane Darwell; Eddie Bracken; Mitzi Gaynor; Selmer Jackson; Lee Marvin; ***D:*** Edmund Goulding; ***W:*** Nunnally Johnson; Dwight Taylor; ***C:*** Leo Tover; ***M:*** Cyril Mockridge.

We're the Millers **2013 (R)** A likable pot dealer named David (Sudeikis) is forced to create a fake family in order to more easily sneak past the border on a massive drug run. He convinces a local stripper named Rose (Aniston) to pretend to be his wife and mother to Casey (Roberts) and Kenny (Poulter). Wacky hi-jinks ensue. Director Thurber's comedy has a great cast and clever premise but it's incredibly slow-paced and feels like a movie that was written by four people--which it was. Still, there are enough funny moments for a rainy-night rental but it's a missed opportunity at comedy greatness. **110m/C; DVD, Blu-Ray.** Jason Sudeikis; Jennifer Aniston; Emma Roberts; Will Poulter; Ed Helms; Nick Offerman; Kathryn Hahn; Molly C. Quinn; ***D:*** Rawson Marshall Thurber; ***W:*** Bob Fisher; Steve Faber; Sean Anders; John Morris; ***C:*** Barry Peterson; ***M:*** Theodore Shapiro; Ludwig Göransson.

Were the World Mine 1/2 **2008** Timothy is out and proud, which makes him a target at his private boys' high school. He also has a crush on jock Jonathan and gets a chance when he's cast as Puck in the school production of 'A Midsummer Night's Dream.' Tim discovers a magic love potion that makes the target of the potion fall hopelessly in love with the first person they see, which Tim makes sure are of the same sex, thus turning a bunch of homophobes into lovesick fools. A musical teen fantasy with risk-taking pizzazz. **95m/C; DVD.** Wendy Robie; Zelda Williams; David Darlow; Tanner Cohen; Nathaniel David Becker; Judy McLane; Ricky Goldman; Jill Larson; ***D:*** Tom Gustafson; ***W:*** Tom Gustafson; Cory James Krueckeberg; ***C:*** Kira Kelly; ***M:*** Jessica Fogle.

The Werewolf 1/2 **1956** Low-budget horror offers a sympathetic portrayal of the title character. Duncan March (Ritch) is found in a car wreck by a couple of scientists who use him as a guinea pig, injecting him with a radiated serum (50s = nuclear fears). It turns the amnesiac into a werewolf when he's under stress, which is pretty much all the time, and soon he's a hunted man-beast. **83m/B; DVD.** Steven Ritch; Don Megowan; Harry Lauter; George Lynn; S. John Launer; Joyce Holden; ***D:*** Fred F. Sears; ***W:*** Robert E. Kent; ***C:*** Edward Linden; ***M:*** Mischa Bakaleinikoff.

Werewolf **1995 (R)** A remote desert town is stricken by an ancient curse that turns its occupants into werewolves at the full moon. This doesn't help the tourism industry. **99m/C; DVD.** Jorge (George) Rivero; Fred Cavalli; Adrianna Miles; Richard Lynch; Joe Estevez; R(ichard) C(arlos) Bates; Heidi Bjorn; Randall Oliver; Nena Belini; Tony Zarindast; ***D:*** Tony Zarindast; ***W:*** Tony Zarindast; ***C:*** Robert Hayes; Dan Gilman.

Werewolf of London 1/2 **1935** A scientist searching for a rare Tibetan flower is attacked by a werewolf. He scoffs at the legend, but once he's back in London, he goes on a murderous rampage every time the moon is full. Dated but worth watching as the first werewolf movie made. **75m/B; DVD, Blu-Ray.** Henry Hull; Warner Oland; Valerie Hobson; Lester Matthews; Spring Byington; Lawrence Grant; Zeffie Tilbury; ***D:*** Stuart Walker; ***W:*** Robert H. Harris; John Colton; ***C:*** Charles Stumar.

Werewolf of Washington **1973 (PG)** Stockwell is a White House press secretary with a problem—he turns into a werewolf. And bites the President, among others. Sub-plot involves a short mad scientist who operates a secret monster-making lab in a White House bathroom. Occasionally engaging horror spoof and political satire made during Watergate era. **90m/C; VHS, DVD.** Dean Stockwell; Biff McGuire; Clifton James; Jane House; Beeson Carroll; Michael Dunn; Nancy Andrews; Stephen Cheng; Barbara Siegel; ***D:*** Milton Moses Ginsberg; ***W:*** Milton Moses Ginsberg; ***C:*** Robert M. "Bob" Baldwin, Jr.; ***M:*** Arnold Freed.

Werewolf: The Beast Among Us **2012 (R)** Hokey, simple horror. A group of 19th-century bounty hunters come to a remote Transylvanian village in search of a werewolf. The townsfolk have dealt with the creatures before, but something about the beast is different this time. **93m/C; DVD, Blu-Ray.** Ed Quinn; Stephen Rea; Steven Bauer; Nia Peeples; Adam Croasdell; Ana Ularu; ***D:*** Louis Morneau; ***W:*** Louis Morneau; Catherine Cyran; ***C:*** Philip Robertson; ***M:*** Michael Wandmacher. **VIDEO**

The Werewolf vs. the Vampire Woman 1/2 *Shadow of the Werewolf; Blood Moon; Night of Walpurgis; La Noche de Walpurgis* **1970 (R)** Hirsute Spanish wolfman teams with two female students in search of witch's tomb. One is possessed by the witch, and eponymous title results. **82m/C; VHS, DVD.** *SP GE* Paul Naschy; Gaby Fuchs; Barbara Capell; Patty (Patti) Shepard; Valerie Samarine; Julio Pena; Andres Resino; ***D:*** Leon Klimovsky; ***W:*** Paul Naschy; ***C:*** Leopoldo Villasenor; ***M:*** Anton Abril.

Werewolves on Wheels WOOF! **1971 (R)** A group of bikers are turned into werewolves due to a Satanic spell. A serious attempt at a biker/werewolf movie, however, too violent and grim, not at all funny, and painful to sit through. McGuire had a hit with "Eve of Destruction." **85m/C; VHS, DVD.** Stephen Oliver; Severn Darden; D.J. Anderson; Duece Barry; Billy Gray; Barry McGuire; ***D:*** Michel Levesque.

Wes Craven Presents Mind Ripper *Mind Ripper* **1995 (R)** A top secret government experiment, intended to produce a superhuman, goes wrong and traps the scientists in a remote desert outpost with their deadly, pissed-off creation. **90m/C; VHS, DVD.** Lance Henriksen; John Diehl; Natasha Gregson Wagner; Dan Blom; Claire Stansfield; ***D:*** Joe Gayton; ***W:*** Jonathan Craven; Phil Mittleman; ***C:*** Fernando Arguelles; ***M:*** J. Peter Robinson.

Wes Craven Presents: They 1/2 *They* **2002 (PG-13)** Maybe Wes should stop presenting this stuff and start writing and directing it again. It might turn out better. Derivative horror flick has psych grad student Julia (Regan) visited by childhood friend and fellow nightmare sufferer Billy, who tells her that something's after them. She doesn't believe him until her old nightmares return and spooky things start happening. Starts off genuinely creepy and appropriately scary, but loses itself in cliches and other plot devices you've seen done better elsewhere. Regan gives a good debut performance, though. **100m/C; VHS, DVD, Blu-Ray.** Laura Regan; Marc Blucas; Ethan (Randall) Embry; Dagmara Dominczyk; Jon Abrahams; Jay Brazeau; Alexander Gould; ***D:*** Robert Harmon; ***W:*** Brendan William Hood; ***C:*** Rene Ohashi; ***M:*** Elia Cmiral.

Wes Craven's New Nightmare *Nightmare on Elm Street 7* **1994 (R)** Seems the six previous conjurings of Freddy's tortured but fictional soul have inadvertently created a real supernatural force bent on tormenting the lives of retired scream queen Langenkamp, her son (Hughes), writer-director Craven, and surprisingly mild alter-ego Englund. Craven's solution is to write a script that reunites series principals for a final showdown with the slashmaster in Hell. Clever and original in a genre known for neither trait, this movie-in-a-movie-about-a-movie is equal parts playful gimmick and inspired terror that will give even the most seasoned Kruegerphile the heebie-jeebies. **112m/C; DVD, Blu-Ray.** Robert Englund; Heather Langenkamp; Miko Hughes; David Newsom; Tracy Middendorf; Fran Bennett; John Saxon; Wes Craven; Robert Shaye; Sara Risher; Marianne Maddalena; ***D:*** Wes Craven; ***W:*** Wes Craven; ***C:*** Mark Irwin; ***M:*** J. Peter Robinson.

West Beirut *West Beyrouth* **1998** Muslim teenagers Tarek (Doueiri, the director's younger brother) and Omar (Chamas) and their new friend, the Christian May (Al Amin), live in an apartment complex in Muslim-controlled West Beirut in 1975. The date is significant since Muslim and Christian militias are battling for control of the Lebanese city and, since their school is closed, the teens have little better to do than to explore the forbidden. Arabic with subtitles. **105m/C; VHS, DVD.** *FR* Rami Doueiri; Mohamad Chamas; Rola Al Amin; Leila Karam; ***D:*** Ziad Doueiri; ***W:*** Ziad Doueiri; ***C:*** Ricardo Jacques Gale; ***M:*** Stewart Copeland.

West-Bound Limited 1/2 **1923** A Romantic adventurer rescues a girl from certain death as a train is about to hit her, and the two fall in love. Lucky for him, she happens to be the boss' daughter. This film is a good example of classic silent melodrama with music score. **70m/B; Silent; VHS, DVD.** John Harron; Ella Hall; Claire McDowell; ***D:*** Emory Johnson.

West Is West **1987** Vikram arrives in San Francisco from Bombay to attend university and discovers that his sponser has returned to India. With little money, he gets a room in a seedy hotel run by an Indian immigrant, who also gives Vikram a menial job. As he begins to explore the city Vikram meets arty punk Sue, but with his visa running out and the INS ready to deport him, Vikram needs to convince Sue to a green card marriage. **80m/C; VHS, DVD.** Ashutosh Gowariker; Heidi Carpenter; Pearl Padamsee; ***D:*** David Rathod; ***W:*** David Rathod; ***C:*** Christopher Tufty.

West New York **1996 (R)** Ex-cop Tom Coletti (Vincent) has a job in Jersey, disposing of old bank bonds. He comes up with a scheme to skim some of the bonds but the news leaks to the local mob boss, Carmine (Pastore). He's unhappy he's not being cut in and decides to put out a hit to show his displeasure, so Coletti has to get to him first. **90m/C; VHS, DVD.** Frank Vincent; Vincent Pastore; Victor Colicchio; Brian Burke; Gian DiDonna; Gloria Darpino; Brian McCormick; ***D:*** Phil Gallo.

West of Broadway 1/2 **1931** WWI vet Jerry Seevers (Gilbert) returns to New York and his hard-drinking socialite life. Since his fiance Anne (Evans) dumped him, Jerry drunkenly marries party girl Dot (Moran). He sobers up and heads to his Arizona ranch, planning a divorce but Dot has other ideas. The ethnic comic relief is questionable for modern audiences but there's nothing wrong with Gilbert's acting--or voice. **73m/B; DVD.** John Gilbert; Lois Moran; Madge Evans; Ralph Bellamy; El Brendel; Hedda Hopper; Willie Fung; ***D:*** Harry Beaumont; ***W:*** Ralph Graves; Bess Meredyth; ***C:*** Merritt B. Gerstad.

West of Here 1/2 **2002 (R)** Predictable and dull road story that's the directorial debut of Masterson, whose sister does him the favor of co-starring. When Josiah (Butz) is killed in a car crash, his cousin and songwriting partner Gil (Hamilton) decides to leave his boring life in Boston and hit the road to San Francisco to settle Josiah's affairs. Along the way, Gil just happens to reconnect with his old college flame (Masterson), and she comes along for the ride. **80m/C; DVD.** Josh Hamilton; Norbert Lee Butz; Mary Stuart Masterson; Guillermo Diaz; Tate Donovan; ***D:*** Peter Masterson; ***W:*** Jay Sweet; ***C:*** Peter Masterson; ***M:*** Timothy Cutler; Todd Park Mohr.

West of Memphis **2012 (R)** Another investigative documentary (following the "Paradise Lost" trilogy from Joe Berlinger and Bruce Sinofsky) about the notorious miscarriage of justice case and the defendents known as the West Memphis Three. Convicted in 1993 of murdering three 8-year-old boys in West Memphis, Arkansas, Jason Baldwin and Jesse Misskelly Jr. were sentenced to life in prison while Damien Echols was given the death penalty. Berg's documentary details a protracted legal battle to free the men as well as offering evidence pointing to other more likely suspects. **147m/C; DVD, Blu-Ray.** ***D:*** Amy Berg; ***W:*** Amy Berg; Billy McMillin; ***C:*** Maryse Alberti; Ronan Killeen; ***M:*** Nick Cave; Warren Ellis.

West of the Pecos 1/2 **1945** Rill (Hale) is a society gal on her way to the family ranch in Texas. She's disguised as a boy for safety, which turns out to be a smart idea when outlaws attack the stagecoach. Fortunately, Pecos Smith (Mitchum) is also around to lend a hand. Based on the novel by Zane Grey; first filmed in 1935. **66m/B; VHS, DVD.** Robert Mitchum; Barbara Hale; Richard Martin; Thurston Hall; Rita (Paula) Corday; Russell Hopton; Harry Woods; ***D:*** Edward Killy; ***C:*** Russell Metty.

West Point **1927** Typical role for Haines as he plays wealthy practical joker Brice Wayne who angers his fellow West Point cadets with his arrogance despite his stardom on the gridiron. Brice falls for local girl Betty (Crawford), who's more than his match although even she tires of his juvenile ways. Brice sulkily resigns after clashing with his coach until he finally realizes he has to man up when the big Army-Navy game is at stake. **95m/B; Silent; DVD.** William Haines; Joan Crawford; William "Billy" Bakewell; Neil Neely; Ralph Emerson; Leon Kellar; ***D:*** Edward Sedwick; ***W:*** Joe Farnham; ***C:*** Ira Morgan.

The West Point Story 1/2 *Fine and Dandy* **1950** Cagney stars as an on-the-skids Broadway director offered a job staging a show at West Point. Seems cadet MacRae has written a musical and his uncle happens to be a producer. Cagney, with girlfriend Mayo, finds all the rules and regulations getting the better of his temper, so much so that he's told unless he can conform to academy standards the show won't go on! Day is the showgirl MacRae falls for. Cagney's energy and charm carry the too-long film but it's not one of his better musical efforts. **107m/B; VHS, DVD.** James Cagney; Virginia Mayo; Gordon MacRae; Doris Day; Roland Winters; Gene Nelson; Alan Hale, Jr.; Wilton Graff; Jerome Cowan; ***D:*** Roy Del Ruth; ***W:*** John Monks, Jr.; Charles Hoffman; Irving Wallace; ***M:*** Sammy Cahn; Jule Styne.

West Side Story 1/2 **1961** Gang rivalry and ethnic tension on New York's West Side erupts in a ground-breaking musical. Loosely based on Shakespeare's "Romeo and Juliet," the story follows the Jets and the Sharks as they fight for their turf while Tony and Maria fight for love. Features frenetic and brilliant choreography by co-director Robbins, who also directed the original Broadway show, and a high-caliber score by Bernstein and Sondheim. Wood's voice was dubbed by Marni Nixon and Jimmy Bryant dubbed Beymer's. **151m/C; VHS, DVD, Blu-Ray.** Natalie Wood; Richard Beymer; Russ Tamblyn; Rita Moreno; George Chakiris; Simon Oakland; Ned Glass; Yvonne Wilder; ***D:*** Robert Wise; Jerome Robbins; ***W:*** Ernest Lehman; ***C:*** Daniel F. Fapp; ***M:*** Leonard Bernstein; Stephen Sondheim. **Oscars '61: Art Dir./Set Dec., Color, Color Cinematog., Costume Des. (C), Director (Wise), Film, Film Editing, Scoring/Musical, Sound, Support. Actor (Chakiris), Support. Actress (Moreno); AFI '98: Top 100; Directors Guild '61: Director (Robbins), Director (Wise); Golden Globes '62: Film--Mus./Comedy, Support. Actor (Chakiris), Support. Actress (Moreno); Natl. Film Reg. '97; N.Y. Film Critics '61: Film.**

The West Wittering Affair **2005** Kathy (Sutcliffe) borrows a weekend retreat and invites her friends Jaime (Scheinmann) and Natasha (Cardinale), whose boyfriend Greg (Anneh) is also supposed to come. But Natasha suspects him of cheating and shows up alone, leading to an evening of too much booze and confessions and Jaime having sex with both women (separately). And this misbegotten experience still resounds with problems three years later. Ensemble comedy/drama that was frequently improvised. **90m/C; DVD.** *GB* Danny Scheinmann; Sarah Sutcliffe; Rebecca Cardinale; David Annen; ***D:*** David Scheinmann; ***W:*** Danny Scheinmann; Sarah Sutcliffe; ***C:*** David Scheinmann; ***M:*** Marc Tschantz.

Westbound **1958** One of the lesser western collaborations between Boetticher and Scott. Union officer John Hayes (Scott) is charged with starting up a stagecoach line that will deliver gold shipments from California. Setting up in the small Colorado town of Julesberg, Hayes runs into serious opposition from Confederate supporter (and town leader) Clay Putnam (Duggan) and his henchmen. **72m/C; DVD.** Randolph Scott; Virginia Mayo; Andrew Duggan; Karen Steele; Michael Dante; Michael Pate; Wally Brown; ***D:*** Budd Boetticher; ***W:*** Berne Giler; ***C:*** J. Peverell Marley; ***M:*** David Buttolph.

Western 1996 Spaniard Paco (Lopez), a traveling rep for a shoe manufacturer in France, picks up hitchhiking Russian emigre Nino (Bourdo) and soon finds himself minus car, shoe samples, and luggage. He's rescued by local beauty Marinette (Vitali) and, since he's been fired, decides to hang around the town where she lives. But when Paco spots Nino again, he promptly beats him up, sending the Russian to the hospital. Oddly, this serves as a bond for the two men and they decide to do a little traveling through Brittany together, with Paco trying to teach the naive Nino how to pick up pretty girls. Funny, if extended, French road trip. French with subtitles. **136m/C; VHS, DVD.** *FR* Sergi Lopez; Sacha Bourdo; Elisabeth Vitali; Marie Matheron; Basile Siekoua; ***D:*** Manuel Poirier; ***W:*** Jean-Francois Goyet; Manuel Poirier; ***C:*** Nara Keo Kosal; ***M:*** Bernardo Sandoval. Cannes '97: Special Jury Prize.

Western Stars 2019 (PG) A documentary on the life, music, and 35-year career of singer/songwriter Bruce Springsteen. Co-directed by the Boss himself, this inviting biopic offers archival footage, personal narration, and a live performance in a 100-year-old barn of all 13 songs from his "Western Stars" album. **83m/C; DVD.** Bruce Springsteen; Patti Scialfa; ***D:*** Bruce Springsteen; Thom Zimny; ***C:*** Joe DeSalvo; ***M:*** Bruce Springsteen.

Western Union 1/2 1941 A lavish, vintage epic romantically detailing the political machinations, Indian warfare, and frontier adventure that accompanied the construction of the Western Union telegraph line from Omaha, Nebraska, to Salt Lake City, Utah, during the Civil War. A thoroughly entertaining film in rich Technicolor. This was Lang's second western, following his personal favorite, "The Return of Frank James." Writer Carson utilized the title, but not the storyline, of a Zane Grey book. The German Lang showed himself a master of the most American of genres, yet made only one more western, "Rancho Notorious" (1952), another masterpiece. **94m/C; DVD, Blu-Ray, Streaming.** Randolph Scott; Robert Young; Dean Jagger; Slim Summerville; Virginia Gilmore; John Carradine; Chill Wills; Barton MacLane; Minor Watson; Charles Middleton; Irving Bacon; ***D:*** Fritz Lang; ***W:*** Robert Carson; ***C:*** Edward Cronjager; ***M:*** David Buttolph.

The Westerner 1/2 1940 Cooper stars as Cole Hardin, a sly, soft-spoken drifter who champions Texas border homesteaders in a land war with the legendary Judge Roy Bean (Brennan). Known as "The Law West of the Pecos," Bean sentences Hardin hang as a horse thief, but he breaks out of jail. Hardin then falls for damsel Jane-Ellen (Davenport) and stays in the area, advocating the rights of homesteaders, and has to have a final confrontation with the judge. Brennan's Bean is unforgettable and steals the show from Cooper. Film debuts of actors Tucker and Andrews. Amazing cinematography; Brennan's Oscar was his third, making him the first performer to pull a hat trick. **100m/B; VHS, DVD.** Gary Cooper; Walter Brennan; Doris Davenport; Fred Stone; Chill Wills; Dana Andrews; Forrest Tucker; Charles Halton; Lupita Tovar; Tom Tyler; Lillian Bond; ***D:*** William Wyler; ***W:*** Jo Swerling; Niven Busch; W.R. Burnett; ***C:*** Gregg Toland; ***M:*** Dimitri Tiomkin. Oscars '40: Support. Actor (Brennan).

Westward Bound 1/2 1930 Rich boy Bob Lansing (Wilsey) gets mixed up in a publicity incident at a nightclub where he meets Montana rancher Marge Holt (Ray). Having embarrassed his senator father, Bob and his chauffeur Ben (Corbett) are sent out west where they are mistaken for a couple of rustlers. Bob also meets Marge again but she's reluctant to clear up their identity problems. **65m/B; DVD.** Buffalo Bill, Jr.; Allene Ray; Ben (Benny) Corbett; Buddy Roosevelt; Yakima Canutt; Tom London; Fern Emmett; ***D:*** Harry S. Webb; ***W:*** Carl Krusada; ***C:*** William Nobles.

Westward Ho, the Wagons! 1/2 1956 The promised land lies in the west, but to get there these pioneers must pass unfriendly savages, thieves, villains, and scoundrels galore. Suitable for family viewing, but why bother? Well, the cast does include four Mouseketeers. **94m/B; VHS, DVD, Streaming.** Fess Parker; Kathleen Crowley; Jeff York; Sebastian Cabot; George Reeves; ***D:*** William Beaudine; ***M:*** George Bruns.

Westward the Women 1951 Buck Wyatt (Taylor) is a scout hired to wagon-train 150 mail-order brides from Chicago to California. When his lustful hired hands turn out to be all hands, Buck and the ladies must fight off attacking Indians on their own. Notable film allowing women to be as tough as men is not your typical western. Based on the Frank Capra story. **116m/C; VHS, DVD.** Robert Taylor; Denise Darcel; Hope Emerson; John McIntire; Beverly Dennis; Lenore Lonergan; Marilyn Erskine; Julie Bishop; Renata Vanni; Frankie Darro; George Chandler; ***D:*** William A. Wellman; ***W:*** Charles Schnee; ***C:*** William Mellor; ***M:*** Jeff Alexander.

Westworld 1973 (PG) Crichton wrote and directed this story of an adult vacation resort of the future which offers the opportunity to live in various fantasy worlds serviced by lifelike robots. Brolin and Benjamin are businessmen who choose a western fantasy world. When an electrical malfunction occurs, the robots begin to go berserk. Brynner is perfect as a western gunslinging robot whose skills are all too real. **90m/C; VHS, DVD.** Yul Brynner; Richard Benjamin; James Brolin; Dick Van Patten; Majel Barrett; ***D:*** Michael Crichton; ***W:*** Michael Crichton; ***C:*** Gene Polito; ***M:*** Fred Karlin.

Wet Gold 1984 A beautiful young woman and three men journey to retrieve a sunken treasure. Nice scenery. Proves that it is possible to make "The Treasure of the Sierra Madre" without making a classic. John Huston, where are you? **90m/C; VHS, DVD.** Brooke Shields; Brian Kerwin; Burgess Meredith; Tom Byrd; ***D:*** Dick Lowry. **TV**

Wet Hot American Summer 2001 (R) Send-up of late 70s/early 80s camp flicks like "Meatballs" and "Little Darlings" focuses on the counselors trying to get laid and/or stoned on the last weekend of a Maine summer camp in 1981 while the youngsters in their charge are thrown around like chew toys. Beth (Garofalo) is the camp director with the hots for an astrophysicist (Pierce) who finds that the camp is in danger of being crushed by Skylab. The plot also involves many other cast members trying to sleep with many other cast members, but to detail more of the story would take crucial print space away from the genius that is the Vietnam vet camp cook (Meloni), whose spiritual advisor is a can of mixed vegetables. Take that whatever way you want, but trust us, you really have to see it to believe it. **97m/C; VHS, DVD, Blu-Ray.** Janeane Garofalo; David Hyde Pierce; Michael Showalter; Marguerite Moreau; Paul Rudd; Zak Orth; Christopher Meloni; A.D. Miles; Molly Shannon; Bradley Cooper; Michael Ian Black; Amy Poehler; Marisa Ryan; Elizabeth Banks; Kevin Sussman; Gideon Jacobs; ***D:*** David Wain; ***W:*** Michael Showalter; David Wain; ***C:*** Ben Weinstein; ***M:*** Theodore Shapiro; Craig Wedren.

The Wet Parade 1/2 1932 Heavy-handed adaptation of the Upton Sincalir novel about the evils of alcohol and the problems with Prohibition. The southern Chilcote family, headed by Roger, run a bootlegging business. The New York Tarletons have Pow spending most of his time in speakeasys. Both men come to bad ends, leaving their families to suffer. **120m/B; DVD.** Dorothy Jordan; Robert Young; Walter Huston; Lewis Stone; Neil Hamilton; Myrna Loy; Jimmy Durante; ***D:*** Victor Fleming; ***W:*** John Lee Mahin; ***C:*** George Barnes; ***M:*** William Axt.

Wetbacks 1956 Fishing boat skipper Jim Benson (Bridges) agrees to help the U.S. Immigration Department nab smugglers who want to use Benson's vessel to carry illegal immigrants from Mexico into the U.S. **89m/C; VHS, DVD.** Lloyd Bridges; Nancy Gates; Barton MacLane; John Hoyt; Harold (Hal) Peary; Nacho Galindo; ***D:*** Hank McCune; ***W:*** Pete LaRoche; ***C:*** Brydon Baker; ***M:*** Les Baxter.

Wetherby 1985 (R) Playwright David Hare's first directorial effort, which he also wrote, about a Yorkshire schoolteacher whose life is shattered when a young, brooding stranger comes uninvited to a dinner party, and then shoots himself in her living room. Compelling but oh, so dark. Richardson, who plays a young Redgrave, is actually Redgrave's daughter. **97m/C; VHS, DVD.** *GB* Vanessa Redgrave; Ian Holm; Dame Judi Dench; Joely Richardson; Tim (McInnerny) McInnery; Suzanna Hamilton; ***D:*** David Hare; ***W:*** David Hare; ***M:*** Nick Bicat. Berlin Intl. Film Fest. '85: Golden Berlin Bear; Natl. Soc. Film Critics '85: Actress (Redgrave).

Wetlands *Feuchtgebiete* 2013 Purposefully grotesque, this coming-of-age story is unlike any other. It's the story of Helen (Juri), an 18-year-old German girl who learns that her sexual proclivities tend to the truly strange. While in the hospital, Helen narrates the story of her sexual awakening in dirty bathrooms and other unhygienic places. At what point is director Wnendt just pushing buttons to provoke the audience? The answer will be different for everyone, but this is an undeniably unique sexual adventure. A little bit more story would have helped. German with subtitles. **109m/C; DVD, Blu-Ray.** *GE* Carla Juri; Marlen Kruse; Meret Becker; Axel Milberg; Christoph Letkowski; ***D:*** David Wnendt; ***W:*** David Wnendt; Claus Falkenberg; ***C:*** Jakub Bejnarowicz; ***M:*** Enis Rotthoff.

Whacked! 2002 (R) Adopted brothers Mark and Tony go from the rough streets of Brooklyn to jobs as professional killers: one for the Mob, the other for the CIA. The discovery of a plot to steal millions from the government reunites them to protect a witness and bring down the scheme. Standard actioner has some good stunt work going for it. **91m/C; DVD.** Paul Sampson; Patrick Muldoon; Carmen Electra; Judge Reinhold; Michael (Mike) Papajohn; ***D:*** James Bruce; ***W:*** Paul Sampson; Matthew Goodman; ***C:*** Dan Heigh.

The Whale 1/2 2013 Innocuous BBC TV movie that's based on the true story that inspired Herman Melville's "Moby Dick." In 1820, the Nantucket whaling ship Essex is struck by a sperm whale and sinks. Eight surviving crew members then struggle to survive, trying to make a grueling sea voyage to Peru in their long-boats. **90m/C; DVD.** *UK* Charles Furness; Martin Sheen; Jonas Armstrong; Adam Rayner; Jassa Ahluwalia; ***D:*** Alrick Riley; ***W:*** Terry Cafolla; ***C:*** David Raedeker; ***M:*** Debbie Wiseman. **TV**

Whale Rider 1/2 2002 (PG-13) Pai (Castle-Hughes, wonderful in her film debut) is a very determined 12-year-old Maori girl whose very traditional grandfather Koro (Paratene) is the tribal chief. Pai's father (Curtis) should be the next in line but after the death of his wife and Pai's infant twin brother, he's left the family. Although the stubborn Koro loves Pai, he refuses to see his granddaughter as a possible successor and won't train her in the customs that he teaches to the Maori boys. So Pai observes and learns on her own—ready to show everyone that she has what it takes. Title refers to the legend that their ancestor arrived in their land on the back of a whale. Adapted from the 1986 novel by Witi Ihimaera. **105m/C; VHS, DVD, Blu-Ray.** *NZ GE* Keisha Castle-Hughes; Rawiri Paratene; Vicky Haughton; Clifford Curtis; ***D:*** Niki Caro; ***W:*** Niki Caro; ***C:*** Leon Narbey; ***M:*** Lisa Gerrard. Ind. Spirit '04: Foreign Film.

The Whales of August 1/2 1987 Based on the David Berry play, the story of two elderly sisters—one caring, the other cantankerous, blind, and possibly senile—who decide during a summer in Maine whether or not they should give up their ancestral house and enter a nursing home. Gish and Davis are exquisite to watch, and the all-star supporting cast is superb—especially Price as a suave Russian. Lovingly directed by Anderson in his first US outing. **91m/C; VHS, DVD, Blu-Ray.** Lillian Gish; Bette Davis; Vincent Price; Ann Sothern; Mary Steenburgen; Harry Carey, Jr.; Tisha Sterling; Margaret Ladd; ***D:*** Lindsay Anderson; ***W:*** David Berry; ***C:*** Mike Fash. Natl. Bd. of Review '87: Actress (Gish).

Wham-Bam, Thank You Spaceman 1/2 1975 (R) Very silly stuff about aliens with fiberglass heads and balloon ears that inflate when they become excited. They transport themselves to Earth in a tiny set decorated with tinfoil where most of the action takes place. Their mission: to impregnate Earth women to save their race. Though the female nudity is abundant, the sexual action is pretty tame by today's standards. **79m/C; DVD.** Jay Rasumny; Samuel Mann; Dyanne Thorne; Maria Arnold; Valda Hansen; Sandy Carey; John Ireland, Jr.; ***D:*** William A. Levey; ***W:*** Shlomo D. Weinstein; ***C:*** David Platnik; ***M:*** Miles Goodman; David White.

What a Carve-Up! *No Place Like Homicide* 1962 A group of relatives gather in an old, spooky mansion to hear the reading of a will. Tries too hard. Remake of "The Ghoul." **87m/B; VHS, DVD.** *GB* Kenneth Connor; Sidney James; Shirley Eaton; Donald Pleasence; Dennis Price; Michael Gough; ***D:*** Pat Jackson.

What a Girl Wants 1/2 2003 (PG) Another movie intended for the tweenie girl set ala "The Princess Diaries." Spunky Daphne Reynolds (Bynes) lives in Manhattan with her single bohemian mom Libby (Preston). Daphne has never met her Dad, a once-adventurous English lord, Sir Henry Dashwood (Firth), who has gone all staid and stuffy. So Daph takes off for London to introduce herself. Henry's got a political career to think about so the arrival of this brash American teen is a less than happy occasion, especially to Henry's fiancee, manipulative Glynnis (Chacellor) and her snobby daughter Clarissa (Cole). But you just know that Daphne will get everything she wants (including this really cute English boy). Adapted from a play and previously filmed as 1958's "The Reluctant Debutante" with Sandra Dee. **104m/C; VHS, DVD.** Amanda Bynes; Colin Firth; Kelly Preston; Eileen Atkins; Anna Chancellor; Jonathan Pryce; Oliver James; Christina Cole; Sylvia Syms; Ben Scholfield; ***D:*** Dennie Gordon; ***W:*** Elizabeth Chandler; Jenny Bicks; ***C:*** Andrew Dunn; ***M:*** Rupert Gregson-Williams.

What a Life 1/2 1939 High school student Henry Aldrich (Cooper) needs to quit the pranks and clean up his image of being the worst kid in school, made harder by his dad's former status as big man on campus at Princeton. Fortunately Henry pulls it all together. This character was so popular that subsequent films were spawned. **75m/B; DVD.** Jackie Cooper; Betty Field; John Howard; Janice Logan; Vaughan Glaser; ***D:*** Theodore Reed; ***W:*** Charles Brackett; Clifford Goldsmith; ***C:*** Victor Milner.

What about Bob? 1991 (PG) Bob, a ridiculously neurotic patient, follows his psychiatrist on vacation, turning his life upside down. The psychiatrist's family find Bob entertaining and endearing. Murray is at his comedic best; Dreyfuss's overly excitable characterization occasionally wears thin. **99m/C; VHS, DVD.** Richard Dreyfuss; Bill Murray; Julie Hagerty; Charlie Korsmo; Tom Aldredge; Roger Bowen; Fran Brill; Kathryn Erbe; Doris Belack; Susan Willis; ***D:*** Frank Oz; ***W:*** Tom Schulman; Alvin Sargent; ***C:*** Michael Ballhaus; ***M:*** Miles Goodman.

What About Your Friends: Weekend Getaway 1/2 2002 Heartfelt adventures of three bright African-American high school friends as they seek out college scholarships at a weekend retreat and begin to realize the powerful life changes that await them—including the possibility that they'll be heading in different directions. **89m/C; VHS, DVD.** Keisha Knight Pulliam; Angell Conwell; Monica McSwain; Kym E. Whitley; Edwin Morrow; Salim Grant; Alexis Fields; Louis Gossett, Jr.; Denise Dowse; Ella Joyce; Troy Winbush; ***D:*** Niva Dorell; ***W:*** Kim Watson; ***C:*** Jurgen Baum; ***M:*** Andre Mayon. **TV**

What Color Is Love? 2008 Lifetime drama based on a true story. White sports fan Nicole Alpern (Finnigan) falls for married black basketball player Ty Rivers (Cross). She gives birth to their mixed-race son but when the affair ends, Rivers sues for sole custody because Nicole can't relate to the baby's black heritage and he will encounter prejudice. Nicole fights back and finds a lawyer (Savant) who's willing to take the case to Canada's highest court. **90m/C; DVD.** Jennifer Finnigan; Roger R. Cross; Doug Savant; Chilton Crane; Glynis Davies; John Treleaven; Enuka Okuma; ***D:*** Gary Harvey; ***W:*** Shelley Eriksen; ***C:*** Kamal Derkaoui; ***M:*** Shaun Tozer. **CABLE**

What Comes Around 1985 (PG) A good-ole-boy drama about a doped-up country singer who is kidnapped by his brother for his own good. The singer's evil manager sends his stooges out to find him. Might have been funny, but isn't. But is it meant to be? Good Reed songs; mildly interesting plot. **92m/C; VHS, DVD.** Jerry Reed; Bo Hopkins; Arte Johnson; Barry Corbin; ***D:*** Jerry Reed.

What Comes Around *Veiled Truth* **2006** Carolyn Logan (Vaugier) has kept her teenage prostitute past from her aspiring politician husband Andy (Newbern). She put her pimp Jake (Ramsay) in jail but now he's out and wants revenge. Jake owes Russian mobster Victor (Mancuso) and wants Carolyn to make nice with the crime boss. **90m/C; DVD.** Emmanuelle Vaugier; Bruce Ramsay; George Newbern; Nick Mancuso; Josh Hayden; ***D:*** Monika Mitchell; ***W:*** Lauren Dale; ***C:*** Anthony C. Metchie; ***M:*** John Sereda; Michael Thomas. **CABLE**

What Did You Do in the War, Daddy? ½ **1966** Unfunny comedy set in WWII about a group of weary American soldiers trying to get a small town in Sicily to surrender. Things don't go smoothly thanks to a combination soccer game/wine festival, not to mention the Germans deciding to attack. Director Edwards comedic verve deserted him. **119m/C; VHS, Blu-Ray, Streaming.** Dick Shawn; James Coburn; Sergio Fantoni; Giovanna Ralli; Aldo Ray; Harry (Henry) Morgan; Carroll O'Connor; Jay Novello; Vito Scotti; ***D:*** Blake Edwards; ***W:*** William Peter Blatty; Blake Edwards; ***M:*** Henry Mancini.

What Doesn't Kill You **2008 (R)** Brian (Ruffalo) and his childhood pal Paulie (Hawke) have been doing low-end work for local South Boston hood Pat (Goodman) for years. Paulie is impatient to break away for more lucrative work, but the married Brian has become a drug addict and Pat knows how to keep him in line. A prison stint has Brian trying to go straight but he's terrified at the changes surrounding him. Especially good performances from leads Ruffalo and Hawke though the story may seem familiar. **100m/C; Blu-Ray, On Demand.** Mark Ruffalo; Ethan Hawke; Amanda Peet; Will Lyman; Lenny Clarke; Angela Featherstone; Donnie Wahlberg; Brian Goodman; ***D:*** Brian Goodman; ***W:*** Donnie Wahlberg; Brian Goodman; Paul T. Murray; ***C:*** Christopher Norr; ***M:*** Alex Wurman.

What Dreams May Come **1998 (PG-13)** Romantic idea and lushly colorful computer imagery combine with sappy dialogue to turn surreal fantasy into very average digital hocus-pocus. Dr. Chris Neilsen (Williams) and his artist-wife Annie (Sciorra) lose their two children to a traffic accident. Four years later the doctor himself is killed in a freak accident. He finds that his heaven is much like a painting done by his wife (or Monet or Van Gogh) of their dream cottage. Chris is just getting used to the "rules" when he learns that his wife has committed suicide, damning her to hell. Unable to accept eternal separation, he begins an odyssey to find her. For the first half hour, Williams alternates between a "Patch Adams" rehearsal and over-emoting into the tear-filled eyes of Sciorra. Very loosely adapted from a 20-year-old Richard Matheson novel. **113m/C; VHS, DVD, Blu-Ray, HD-DVD.** Robin Williams; Annabella Sciorra; Cuba Gooding, Jr.; Max von Sydow; Rosalind Chao; Jessica Brooks Grant; Josh Paddock; ***D:*** Vincent Ward; ***W:*** Ronald Bass; ***C:*** Eduardo Serra; ***M:*** Michael Kamen. Oscars '98: Visual FX.

What Ever Happened To. . . ½ *What Ever Happened to Baby Jane* **1993** Sisters play sisters as the Redgraves (in their first film together) tackle this remake of "What Ever Happened to Baby Jane?" in all its demented glory. Former actress Blanche (Vanessa) and former child star "Baby Jane" (Lynn) are living in a decaying mansion, which Blanche, confined to a wheelchair, is talking about selling. "Baby" snaps (not that she was ever very stable) and proceeds to torment her sis (more than usual). **94m/C; VHS, DVD.** Vanessa Redgrave; Lynn Redgrave; Bruce A. Young; Amy Steel; John Scott Clough; John Glover; ***D:*** David Greene; ***W:*** Brian Taggert.

What Ever Happened to Baby Jane? ½ **1962** Davis and Crawford portray aging sisters and former child stars living together in a decaying mansion. When the demented Jane (Davis) learns of her now-crippled sister's (Crawford) plan to institutionalize her, she tortures the wheelchair-bound sis. Davis plays her part to the hilt, unafraid of Aldrich's unsympathetic camera, and the viciousness of her character. She received her 10th Oscar nomination for the role. **132m/B; VHS, DVD, Blu-Ray.** Bette Davis; Joan Crawford; Victor Buono; Anna Lee; B.D. Merrill; Maidie Norman; ***D:*** Robert Aldrich; ***W:*** Lukas Heller; ***C:*** Ernest Haller; ***M:*** Frank DeVol.

What Goes Up **2009 (R)** Depressed New York reporter Babbitt comes to the Concord, New Hampshire hometown of teacher Christa McAuliffe to interview high school students about her space shuttle mission. But everyone's lives are affected when the Challenger mission proves fatal. Too much teen angst (and bad acting) and odd plot threats (suicide, pregnancy, bogus stories) to make this pic watchable. **115m/C; DVD.** Steve Coogan; Hilary Duff; Olivia Thirlby; Josh Peck; Molly Shannon; Molly Price; Max Hoffman; Andrea Brooks; ***D:*** Jonathan Glatzer; ***W:*** Jonathan Glatzer; Robert Lawson; ***C:*** Antonio Calvache; ***M:*** Roddy Bottum. **VIDEO**

What Happened, Miss Simone? **2015** This rich, insightful biographical documentary explores the life, career, and influence of singer Nina Simone. Her performances were musically enthralling, and she was considered a musical genius by a legion of devoted critics and fans. Though the African-American vocalist had carved her own distinctive identity, she came to fame amidst the turmoil of the Civil Rights movement in the mid-twentieth century. Includes Simone's own autobiographical tapes, archival films, and revealing interviews, the film explores her commitment to the cause, race issues in the United States, and the challenges she faced in this tumultuous period. Filmmaker Liz Garbus's balanced yet complex approach presents Simone the singer and the person to new generations while illuminating racial tensions still in play in the United States. **101m/C; DVD, Blu-Ray.** ***D:*** Liz Garbus; ***C:*** Igor Martinovic.

What Happened Was. . . **1994 (R)** Two-character study about a weirdly nightmarish first date. Law secretary Jackie (Sillas) has been eyeing bookish paralegal Michael (Noonan) and finally invites him for dinner at her loft. The two struggle to relax and make small talk that turns into some unexpected soul baring. Emotionally distant Michael is unexpectedly hostile about his job and claims to be writing an expose of their law firm while overly friendly Jackie is writing a children's book, which turns out to be jarringly violent and apparently autobiographical. Provides an idiosyncratic, if limited, appeal thanks to a compelling performance by Sillas. **92m/C; VHS, Streaming.** Tom Noonan; Karen Sillas; ***D:*** Tom Noonan; ***W:*** Tom Noonan; ***C:*** Joe DeSalvo; ***M:*** Tom Noonan. Sundance '94: Grand Jury Prize, Screenplay.

What Happens in Vegas ½ **2008 (PG-13)** Wanna bet how this one's gonna go? Strangers Jack (Kutcher) and Joy (Diaz) are in Vegas escaping their respective personal bad luck when when a hotel snafu sticks them in the same room. Several cocktails and one wild night later, they wake up married. Too bad they hate each other, because thanks to a twist in the already ridiculous and deteriorating plot, a quarter gets tossed in a slot and the newlyweds are rich. So who makes off with the $3 million? And might these impossibly good-looking losers be made for each other after all? Queen Latifah's appearance as a marriage counselor is lackluster, while pretty much everyone else overacts and over gesiculates in an attempt to make the gags funny, with little success. Note to Hollywood: Don't base movies on catchy marketing slogans if you can't make them at least half as clever as a 30-second commercial. **99m/C; Blu-Ray, On Demand.** Cameron Diaz; Ashton Kutcher; Lake Bell; Rob Corddry; Queen Latifah; Treat Williams; Dennis Miller; Dennis Farina; Zach Galifianakis; Jason Sudeikis; Michelle Krusiec; Krysten Ritter; Deirdre O'Connell; ***D:*** Tom Vaughan; ***W:*** Dana Fox; ***C:*** Matthew F. Leonetti; ***M:*** Christophe Beck.

What Happens Next **2011** After wealthy New York socialite Paul Greco (Lindstrom) sells his business, he doesn't know what to do with his extra time. His overbearing sister Elise (Malick) gets Paul a dog and during a daily walk to the park, Paul and his pooch meet fellow dog-owner Andy (Murrah), a young, gay ad exec, and their casual meetings start heading somewhere that confuses them both. Complicating their undefined situation are Elise and Andy's sister Roz (Cigliuti), who are both uncomfortable with Andy's interest in the older, seemingly straight man. **100m/C; DVD.** Jon Lindstrom; Chris Murrah; Wendie Malick; Natalie Cigliuti; Ariel Shafir; ***D:*** Jay Arnold; ***W:*** Jay Arnold; ***C:*** Joe Meccariello; ***M:*** Kerry Muzzey. **VIDEO**

What Have I Done to Deserve This? *Que He Hecho Yo Para Merecer Esto!?* **1985** A savage parody on Spanish mores, about a speed-addicted housewife who ends up selling her son and killing her husband with a ham bone. Black, black comedy, perverse and funny as only Almodovar can be. In Spanish with subtitles. Nudity and profanity. **100m/C; VHS, DVD.** Carmen Maura; Chus (Maria Jesus) Lampreave; ***D:*** Pedro Almodóvar; ***W:*** Pedro Almodóvar.

What If ½ **2013 (PG-13)** An inept variation on the millennial rom-com that somehow finds a way to take popular actors Radcliffe and Kazan and make you dislike them. Radcliffe plays the heartbroken Wallace to Kazan's doe-eyed pixie girl Chantry, who is portrayed with such misogynist undertones that feminists should have protested the film. Chantry has a boyfriend, so she enters the "Friend Zone" with Wallace, despite obvious chemistry. Everyone knows exactly where this tale is headed so it becomes about the journey, and this trip is filled with poop jokes and deeply unlikable characters. **98m/C; DVD, Blu-Ray.** *CA IR* Daniel Radcliffe; Zoe Kazan; Rafe Spall; Adam Driver; Mackenzie Davis; Megan Park; ***D:*** Michael Dowse; ***W:*** Elan Mastai; ***C:*** Rogier Stoffers; ***M:*** A.C. Newman.

What If God Were the Sun? **2007** ER nurse Jamie (Chabert) suffers a bad case of grief and guilt when her hospitalized estranged father dies while she is with another patient. Her out-of-control emotions get her transferred to long-term care where elderly cancer patient Mrs. Esienbloom (Rowlands) hires Jamie as a home nurse. Though terminally ill, Mrs. Eisenbloom has unwavering faith, which leads Jamie to examine her own lack of belief. Based in part on the novel by TV psychic John Edwards. **90m/C; DVD.** Lacey Chabert; Gena Rowlands; Sarah Rafferty; Sam Trammell; Klea Scott; Diana Reis; Amanda Brugel; ***D:*** Stephen Tolkin; ***W:*** Janet Dulin Jones; Jamie Pachino; ***C:*** Robin Loewen; ***M:*** Laura Karpman. **CABLE**

What It's All About ½ *El Perque de Tot Plegat* **1995** Fifteen brief comic stories, set in Barcelona, that explore faith, desire, love, doubt, and other emotions. Based on the book by Quim Monzo. Spanish with subtitles. **96m/C; DVD.** *SP* Lluis Homar; Alex Casanovas; Camilo Rodriguez; Rosa Gamiz; Pepa Lopez; Rosa Novell; ***D:*** Ventura Pons; ***W:*** Ventura Pons; ***C:*** Carles Gusi; ***M:*** Carles Cases.

What Just Happened ½ **2008 (R)** Fictionalized version of producer Art Linson's memoirs follows two weeks in the course of A-list Hollywood producer Ben (DeNiro), who is suddenly caught up in a massive career snag. His Sean Penn movie is tanking at test screening, and now, Bruce Willis refuses to lose a few pounds or shave his beard for a new part. It's funny at times, but unlike the exaggerated, flashy television series "Entourage" or Altman's satire "The Player," this realistic behind-the-scenes look at Hollywood unconsciously appeals mostly to those involved in the industry. However, DeNiro's sharp, subtle performance is a welcome return to more grounded material, after a long stretch of goofy or over-hyped roles. *CNT Language, some violent images, sexual content and some drug material. **113m/C; Blu-Ray, On Demand.** Robert De Niro; Bruce Willis; Sean Penn; Stanley Tucci; John Turturro; Robin Wright; Michael Wincott; Catherine Keener; Kristen Stewart; Lily Rabe; ***D:*** Barry Levinson; ***W:*** Art Linson; ***C:*** Stephane Fontaine; ***M:*** Marcelo Zarvos.

What Katy Did ½ **1999** Canadian telefilm based on Susan Coolidge's 1872 children's book. Rebellious, 13-year-old Katy Carr is a challenge to her widowed physician father and Aunt Izzie, who is helping to raise her siblings. But when Katy suffers a serious accident that confines her to her room, it changes her attitude. **88m/C; DVD.** *CA* Alison Pill; Kevin Whately; Martha Burns; Megan Follows; Michael Cera; Dean Stockwell; ***D:*** Stacey Stewart Curtis; ***W:*** Olivia Hetreed; ***C:*** Derek Rogers; ***M:*** Tony Flynn. **TV**

What Lies Beneath **2000 (PG-13)** Empty-nester Pfeiffer wanders around a seemingly haunted house suspecting neighbors of murder and finding out more about her scientist husband's past than she'd like. Zemeckis shoots for Hitchcockian suspense but manages mostly intermittent jolts and occasional wit. The "surprise" ending, telegraphed by the film's marketing campaign, has nothing to do with the film's first hour, which has everything to do with atmosphere and setting up distractions. **130m/C; VHS, DVD.** Harrison Ford; Michelle Pfeiffer; Diana Scarwid; Joe Morton; James Remar; Miranda Otto; Amber Valletta; Katharine Towne; Victoria Birdwell; ***D:*** Robert Zemeckis; ***W:*** Clark Gregg; ***C:*** Don Burgess; ***M:*** Alan Silvestri.

What Lola Wants **2015 (R)** In this romantic action drama, a teenager on the run falls in love with someone who may betray her. Lola Franklin (Lowe) is 16 and part of a well-known family in Hollywood when she fakes her own kidnapping and runs off on a mysterious journey across the United States. In a roadside diner in the desert of New Mexico, she meets Marlo (Knapp), a teenager with a complicated life. The pair fall in love, but when Marlo learns of a reward being given for Lola's return, he must make a difficult choice of Lola and her trip or the funds to ensure his past stays in the past. **81m/C; DVD, Blu-Ray, Streaming, Download.** Sophie Lowe; Beau Knapp; Dale Dickey; Robert Taylor; Charles S. Dutton; ***D:*** Rupert Glasson; ***W:*** Rupert Glasson; ***C:*** Eric Leach; ***M:*** John Gray. **VIDEO**

What Love Is ½ **2007 (R)** Trouble, that's what it is, especially in this talky production. Nice guy Tom (Gooding) has his live-in girlfriend (Pratt) leave him on Valentine's Day just as he was about to propose. His buds come over (followed by their gals) to offer relationship advice despite being equally clueless. **93m/C; DVD.** Cuba Gooding, Jr.; Matthew Lillard; Anne Heche; Gina Gershon; Sean Astin; Tamala Jones; Judy Tylor; Shiri Appleby; Mars Callahan; Victoria Pratt; Andrew Daily; ***D:*** Mars Callahan; ***W:*** Mars Callahan; ***C:*** David G. Stump; ***M:*** Erik Godal.

What Maisie Knew **2012 (R)** Maisie (Aprile) knows that the adults in her life act more like children. After her parents (Moore and Coogan) split up and begin relationships with other people (Skarsgard and Vanderham), Maisie becomes, like so many other children that are products of divorce, little more than a pawn in an emotional game. Great performances all around highlight a heartbreaking story, based loosely on the Henry James novel, that avoids melodrama on its way to provoking true emotion. Incredibly smart and remarkably perceptive about the way families not only break apart but how children are forced to move on through those broken pieces. **99m/C; DVD, Blu-Ray.** Julianne Moore; Steve Coogan; Alexander Skarsgård; Joanna Vanderham; Onata Aprile; ***D:*** Scott McGehee; David Siegel; ***W:*** Nancy Doyne; Carroll Cartwright; ***C:*** Giles Nuttgens; ***M:*** Nick Urata.

What Matters Most ½ **2001** High school basketball star Lucas Warner (Allen) is the son of a prominent family in their small Texas community. His father (Teague) doesn't approve of Lucas falling in love with wrong-side-of-the-tracks Heather (Cole). When Heather becomes pregnant, the teens plan to run away and get married but an accident leaves Lucas in a coma. **105m/C; DVD.** Chad Allen; Marshall Teague; Polly Cole; Shonda Farr; Tamara Clatterbuck; Gary Driver; ***D:*** Jane Cusumano; ***W:*** Jane Cusumano; ***C:*** Michael Goi; ***M:*** Sean Morris.

What Men Want **2019 (R)** Raised by a single father (Roundtree), adult Ali (Henson) works as sports agent in a mostly white, mostly male firm. Though she acts like and is accepted as one of the guys, she does not become a partner because her clients are not in the NFL, NBA, or MLB. After unexpectedly getting the power to hear men's thoughts, Ali uses this new ability to gain an NBA draft pick as a client, but realizes the effects of her actions on herself and her life. This gender-reverse remake of "What Women Want" (2000) draws strength from Henson's multi-faceted performance. **117m/C; DVD, Blu-Ray.** Taraji P. Henson; Josh Brener; Kellan Lutz; Tracy Morgan; Max Greenfield; ***D:*** Adam Shankman; ***W:*** Tina Gordon Chism; Peter Huyck; Alex Gregory; ***C:*** Jim Denault; ***M:*** Brian Tyler.

What Planet Are You From? **2000 (R)** Two jokes, no waiting! Shandling's feature film debut tries to be a comment on how differently men and women view sex and relationships, but it spends most of its time with a humming penis. Shandling is an alien sent from a planet of test tube people to impregnate an earth woman, once he's given the proper equipment (which has the previously mentioned unfortunate feature). He disguises himself as Harold, a bank executive, and gets dating tips from a philandering co-worker (Kinnear) who recommends AA meetings as a great pickup place. His direct approach ("You smell nice") somehow attracts a recovering alcoholic (Bening) who's on the biological clock. The other joke (and better of the two) involves a hen-pecked FAA inspector who's suspicious of Harold's origins. Shandling's limited range is exposed, and the juvenile script doesn't do him any favors. **107m/C; VHS, DVD, Blu-Ray.** Garry Shandling; Annette Bening; Greg Kinnear; Ben Kingsley; Linda Fiorentino; John Goodman; Richard Jenkins; Caroline Aaron; Judy Greer; Nora Dunn; Ann Cusack; Camryn Manheim; Janeane Garofalo; Stacey Travis; Willie Garson; Sarah Silverman; ***D:*** Mike Nichols; ***W:*** Garry Shandling; Michael Leeson; Edward Solomon; Peter Tolan; ***C:*** Michael Ballhaus; ***M:*** Carter Burwell.

What Price Glory? **1952** Remake of the 1926 silent classic about a pair of comradely rivals for the affections of women in WWI France. Strange to have Ford directing an offbeat comedy, but it works: masterful direction, good acting. Demarest broke both legs in a motorcycle accident during shooting. **111m/C; VHS, DVD.** James Cagney; Dan Dailey; Corinne Calvet; William Demarest; James Gleason; Robert Wagner; Max (Casey Adams) Showalter; Craig Hill; Marisa Pavan; ***D:*** John Ford.

What Price Hollywood? **1932** Aspiring young starlet decides to crash film world by using an alcoholic director as her stepping stone. Bennett is lovely; Sherman is superb as an aging, dissolute man who watches his potential slip away. From a story by Adela Rogers St. Johns. Remade three times as "A Star is Born." **88m/B; DVD.** Constance Bennett; Lowell Sherman; Neil Hamilton; ***D:*** George Cukor; ***W:*** Robert Presnell, Sr.; Gene Fowler, Sr.; Jane Murfin; Ben Markson; Allen Rivkin; Rowland Brown; ***C:*** Charles Rosher; ***M:*** Max Steiner.

What the #$*! Do We Know? ½ **2004** Excruciatingly upbeat New Agers' guide to the perplexed. Follows a confused woman (Maitlin) through the troubles of daily life with annoying animation and talking heads helping her search for meaning. Supposed exploration of quantum theory and its impact is a queasy mishmash of pop- and pseudo-science, with some mysticism made to please the starry-eyed and vacant. **108m/C; VHS, DVD.** Marlee Matlin; Elaine Hendrix; John Ross Bowie; Robert Bailey, Jr.; Barry Newman; Larry Brandenburg; ***D:*** Mark Vicente; William Arntz; Betsy Chasse; ***W:*** William Arntz; Betsy Chasse; Matthew Hoffman; ***C:*** David Bridges; ***M:*** Christopher Franke.

What the Deaf Man Heard **1998** Sly comedy starts off in the '40s with 10-year-old Sammy (Muniz) winding up alone in the small town of Barrington, Georgia after his single mother (Peters) vanishes. Since she told him to keep silent, Sammy continues to obey her—even when he's taken in by kindly bus station manager Norm (Skerritt). Soon everyone believes Sammy is deaf and mute and this doesn't change as Sammy grows to adulthood (Modine) as the local handyman. In fact, everyone is happy to confide in Sammy so he knows everyone's secrets—not always a happy situation. Based on the novel "What the Deaf-Mute Heard" by G.D. Gearino. **107m/C; VHS, DVD.** Matthew Modine; Tom Skerritt; Judith Ivey; Claire Bloom; James Earl Jones; Jerry O'Connell; Anne Bobby; Stephen Spinella; Jake Weber; Bernadette Peters; Frankie Muniz; ***D:*** John Kent Harrison; ***W:*** Robert W. Lenski; ***C:*** Eric Van Haren Noman; ***M:*** J.A.C. Redford. **TV**

What the Peeper Saw *Night Hair Child; Child of the Night; Diabolica Malicia* **1972** The wife of a wealthy author finds her comfortable life turning into a terrifying nightmare when her young stepson starts acting funny. Juicy and terrifying. **97m/C; VHS, DVD, Blu-Ray.** Britt Ekland; Mark Lester; Hardy Kruger; Lilli Palmer; Harry Andrews; ***D:*** Andrea Bianchi; ***W:*** Andrea Bianchi; ***C:*** Luis Cuadrado; Harry Waxman; ***M:*** Stelvio Cipriani.

What They Had ½ **2018 (R)** A woman must fly back to her hometown when her Alzheimer's-stricken mother wanders into a blizzard. The return home forces her to confront her past. **101m/C; DVD, Streaming.** Hilary Swank; Michael Shannon; Robert Forster; Blythe Danner; Taissa Farmiga; ***D:*** Elizabeth Chomko; ***W:*** Elizabeth Chomko; ***C:*** Roberto Schaefer; ***M:*** Danny Mulhern.

What Time Is It There? **2001** Hsiao Kang (Lee) earns a living on the streets of Taipei by selling cheap wristwatches. Shiang-Chyi (Chen) wants to buy the watch Hsiao is wearing because it displays two time zones and she is flying to Paris. After she leaves, Hsiao suddenly decides to change all the watches on display to Paris time—and then all the watches and clocks he can find all around the city, even a gigantic clock on a building—in order to keep a connection with her. French and Chinese with subtitles. **116m/C; VHS, DVD.** *TW* Kangsheng Lee; Shiang-chyi Chen; Tien Miao; Yiching Lu; ***Cameo(s):*** Cecilia Yip; Jean-Pierre Leaud; ***D:*** Ming-liang Tsai; ***W:*** Ming-liang Tsai; Pi-ying Yang; ***C:*** Benoit Delhomme.

What to Do in Case of Fire ½ *Was Tun, Wenn's Brennt?* **2002 (R)** In 1987, six friends, part of an anarchist group in Berlin, make a bomb and place it in an empty building. It sits there until it's inadvertently detonated 15 years later. Although no one is injured, there is no statute of limitations on their crime. Veteran police detective Manowsky (Lowitsch) knows just who to look for and goes after the group's two remaining holdouts Tim (Schweiger) and Hotte (Feifel). The cops find incriminating materials and the buddies must now seek out their four former members in order to get them all off the hook. German with subtitles. **101m/C; VHS, DVD.** *GE* Til Schweiger; Sebastian Blomberg; Nadja Uhl; Martin Feifel; Matthias Matschke; Doris Schretzmayer; ***D:*** Gregor Schnitzler; ***W:*** Stefan Dahnert; Anne Wild; ***C:*** Andreas Berger; ***M:*** Stephan Zacharias; Stephan Gade.

What to Expect When You're Expecting ½ **2012 (PG-13)** This false adaptation of a nonfiction book presents nothing that even resembles the real world. The ensemble comedy filled with clichés of how Hollywood views pregnancy and parenthood, is an insult to women, families, fathers, doctors, and even the unborn. As various couples--with an odd abundance of various personal situations--prepare for parenthood they each face their own challenges. Some of the cast members come out more unscathed than others (Quaid, Decker, Banks) but others should be ashamed (Rock, Lopez, Diaz). Ask any real parent about their life and find a more entertaining story. **110m/C; DVD, Blu-Ray; Closed Captioned.** Cameron Diaz; Jennifer Lopez; Elizabeth Banks; Chace Crawford; Brooklyn Decker; Ben Falcone; Anna Kendrick; Matthew Morrison; Dennis Quaid; Chris Rock; Rodrigo Santoro; Joe Manganiello; Thomas Lennon; Wendi McLendon-Covey; ***D:*** Kirk Jones; ***W:*** Shauna Cross; Heather Hach; ***C:*** Xavier Perez Grobet; ***M:*** Mark Mothersbaugh.

What Up? *The Sweep* **2008 (R)** Nothing much, that's for sure in this dumb comedy with an overly-familiar plot. Janitors Tyrone (Hardison) and Jerome (Godfrey) find a briefcase full of cash and blow it all. Then they discover it was mob money and they have a week to pay it back—or else. **82m/C; DVD.** Kadeem Hardison; Godfrey; Sonny Bermudez; ***D:*** Dale Stelly; ***W:*** Dale Stelly; Marvin Hayes; ***C:*** Keith L. Smith; ***M:*** Jason Solowsky.

What We Become ½ *Sorgenfri* **2016** This foreign film hit could be described as "Fear the Danish Dead." Another end of the world riff, this one taking the micro approach of focusing on a family trying to survive as the undead apocalypse unfolds. Bo Mikkelson's film effectively centers on a traditional clan (father, mother, sister, brother) as the small town around them becomes quarantined after a suspicious virus erupts. As the family hears screams and gunshots around their neighborhood, the tension rises, and Mikkelson deftly plays the final act, even if his film ends a bit too abruptly, just as it's getting most interesting. Danish with subtitles. **85m/C; DVD, Blu-Ray.** Mille Dinesen; Ole Dupont; Marie Hammer Boda; Troels Lyby; Mikael Birkkjaer; ***D:*** Bo Mikkelsen; ***W:*** Bo Mikkelsen; ***C:*** Adam Philp; ***M:*** Martin Pedersen.

What We Did on Our Holiday ½ **2015 (PG-13)** A comedy-drama about family secrets and the limitations in keeping them. As part of a gathering with their extended family, Doug (Tennant) and Abi (Pike) travel to Scotland with their kids—Lottie (Jones), Mickey (Smalldridge), and Jess (Turnbull)—in tow. Over the course of their time together, the kids begin to innocently reveal many aspects of their family life including intimate details about their parents. Doug and Abi fear their children will tell the biggest secret of all—about their marriage and their future together. **95m/C; DVD, Blu-Ray, Streaming, Download.** Rosamund Pike; David Tennant; Emilia Jones; Bobby Smalldridge; Harriet Turnbull; ***D:*** Andy Hamilton; Guy Jenkin; ***W:*** Andy Hamilton; Guy Jenkin; ***C:*** Martin Hawkins; ***M:*** Alex Heffes.

What We Do in the Shadows ½ **2014** Waititi and Clement direct, write, and star in this hysterical spoof of the international obsession with vampires through the lens of reality TV. Vlago, Vladislav, Deacon, and Petyr are four bloodsuckers who share a flat in Wellington in this hybrid of "The Real World" and "Twilight." The result is one of the best mockumentaries in years, a really smart, clever satire of not just our obsession with vampire culture but human relationships. These four guys are just trying to get by in a world in which they don't really belong. It's smart, and remarkably funny, destined to become a cult classic. **87m/C; DVD, Blu-Ray.** *NZ* Taika Waititi; Jemaine Clement; Jonathan Brugh; Ben Fransham; Jackie Van Beek; Cori Gonzalez-Macuer; ***D:*** Taika Waititi; Jemaine Clement; ***W:*** Taika Waititi; Jemaine Clement; ***C:*** Richard Bluck; DJ Stipsen.

What We Do Is Secret ½ **2007 (R)** Clear, engagingly personal take on the California punk scene and a self-destructive icon. Jan Paul Beahm recreates himself as Darby Crash (West), songwriter and leader of 1970s SoCal punk band the Germs?-and a junkie. A man with a five-year plan, Crash is a rule-breaker determined to find success his way and then kill himself (which he did in 1980). The look seems remarkably accurate, and surviving bandmate Pat Smear also taught the actors to recreate the Germs' performances. **92m/C; DVD.** Shane West; Bijou Phillips; Rick Gonzalez; Noah Segan; Ashton Holmes; Tina Majorino; Azura Skye; Ray Park; Sebastien Roche; ***D:*** Rodger Grossman; ***W:*** Rodger Grossman; ***C:*** Andrew Huesbscher; ***M:*** Anna Waronker.

What Women Want ½ **2000 (PG-13)** Male-chauvinist Gibson gets electrocuted in his bathroom and suddenly has the power to hear women's thoughts, which aren't very complimentary towards him. Gibson, obviously enjoying himself, shines in this intermittently funny, lightweight but enjoyable romantic comedy. Sublety and restraint are in short supply, but Gibson's performance, especially when he's doing his neo-Rat Pack act, makes up for the overindulgences. **123m/C; VHS, DVD.** Mel Gibson; Helen Hunt; Marisa Tomei; Lauren Holly; Bette Midler; Mark Feuerstein; Ashley Johnson; Judy Greer; Alan Alda; Delta Burke; Valerie Perrine; Lisa Edelstein; Sarah Paulson; Ana Gasteyer; Loretta Devine; Eric Balfour; Logan Lerman; ***D:*** Nancy Meyers; ***W:*** Josh Goldsmith; Cathy Yuspa; ***C:*** Dean Cundey; ***M:*** Alan Silvestri.

What Women Want *Wo Zhi Nu Ren Zin; I Know a Woman's Heart* **2010** Chinese adaptation of the 2000 Paramount Mel Gibson release has a bland script that lets down its stars. Chauvinist ad exec Zigang Sun expects to be promoted but is passed over for Yilong Li, who's better attuned to modern women. An electrical storm leaves Sun with the freakish ability to hear women's thoughts and, once he gets over the shock, he uses his new talent to his personal and professional advantage. English and Mandarin with subtitles. **100m/C; DVD.** *CH* Andy Lau; Gong Li; Chengru Li; Yuan Li; ***D:*** Daming Chen; ***W:*** Daming Chen; ***C:*** Max Wang; ***M:*** Christopher O'Young.

What Your Eyes Don't See *Ojos Que No Ven* **1999** Abelardo Sachs is the owner/editor of a political magazine. He's murdered in his home by a masked gunman. As the police start investigating, everyone in Sachs's life has their own theory on whether the killing was political or personal. Spanish with subtitles. **90m/C; VHS, DVD.** *AR* Mauricio Dayub; Luis Luque; Malena Solda; Gaston Pauls; Alejandra Flechner; ***D:*** Beda Docampo Feijoo; ***W:*** Beda Docampo Feijoo; Enrique Cortes; ***C:*** Ricardo Rodriguez; ***M:*** Ivan Wyszogrod.

Whatever Happened to Aunt Alice? **1969 (PG)** After murdering her husband to inherit his estate, a poor, eccentric widow develops an awful habit: she hires maids, only to murder them and steal their savings. The only evidence is a growing number of trees by the drive. Sleuth Ruth Gordon (of "Harold and Maude" fame, acting here just as odd) takes the job in hopes of solving the mystery. Thoroughly amusing. **101m/C; VHS, DVD, Blu-Ray.** Geraldine Page; Ruth Gordon; Rosemary Forsyth; Robert Fuller; Mildred Dunnock; ***D:*** Lee H. Katzin; ***W:*** Theodore Apstein; ***C:*** Joseph Biroc; ***M:*** Gerald Fried.

Whatever It Takes ½ **2000 (PG-13)** Dopey teen romancer, with the usual attractive cast, that tries to be a modern version of "Cyrano de Bergerac." Ya got cutie boy-next-door-type Ryan (West) and his sensitive best pal Maggie (Sokoloff), who is, of course, his unknown soulmate. But Ryan pines for snobby hottie Ashley (O'Keefe). Meanwhile, Maggie has won the eye of jock Chris (Franco). So Chris and Ryan team up so that each can get their dream girl before the prom. You know how everything turns out. **94m/C; VHS, DVD.** Marla Sokoloff; Jodi Lyn O'Keefe; Shane West; James Franco; Julia Sweeney; Richard Schiff; Aaron Paul; Colin Hanks; ***D:*** David Raynr; ***W:*** Mark Schwahn; ***C:*** Tim Suhrstedt; ***M:*** Ed Shearmur.

Whatever Works ½ **2009 (PG-13)** You'd think Allen (in his 42nd film) would get tired of trotting out the same old obsessions and characters, although the script is allegedly recycled from the 1970s. Allen's protagonist is even more mopey, misanthropic, and ridiculous than usual: aging New Yorker Boris (David), a self-proclaimed scientific genius, who upends his uptown life and moves into a dingy apartment near Chinatown. A chance meeting with beautiful young southern runaway Melody (Wood) leads to an odd relationship (and then marriage) until her repressed, conservative parents (Clarkson, Begley Jr.) show up and there are further extreme character transformations. **92m/C; Blu-Ray, On Demand.** *US FR* Larry David; Evan Rachel Wood; Patricia Clarkson; Ed Begley, Jr.; Henry Cavill; Michael McKean; ***D:*** Woody Allen; ***W:*** Woody Allen; ***C:*** Harris Savides.

Whatever You Say *Mon Idole; My Idol* **2002** Bastien (Canet) works as the abused assistant to Philippe (Lefebvre), the egotistical host of a popular TV reality show. He puts up with the humiliations for a chance to pitch his own ideas to producer Broustal (Berleand), who suddenly invites Bastien to his country home for the weekend. Bastien soon figures out that his TV opportunity is tied to pleasing Broustal's younger wife Clara (Kruger) but there's something so unsettling about the situation that all Bastien wants is a way out. Directorial debut for Canet; French with subtitles. **110m/C; DVD.** *FR* Guillaume Canet; Francois Berleand; Diane Kruger; Philippe Lefebvre; Daniel Prevost; Clotilde Courau; ***D:*** Guillaume Canet; ***W:*** Guillaume Canet; Philippe Lefebvre; ***C:*** Christophe Offenstein; ***M:*** Alexandra Sinclair.

What's Cooking? **2000 (PG-13)** Follows the Thanksgiving tradition of feasting amid household tension through the stories of four American families: one Jewish, one Latino, one Vietnamese, and one African American. Culture clashes, generation gaps, sexual identities, divorce, and other family flash points get addressed with sincere writing and delicate acting by all involved. Written by India-born English director Chadha and her Japanese-American husband Berges—you can't more all-American than that. **109m/C; VHS, DVD.** Alfre Woodard; Joan Chen; Julianna Margulies; Mercedes Ruehl; Kyra Sedgwick; Lainie Kazan; Dennis Haysbert; Victor Rivers; Douglas Spain; A. Martinez; Maury Chaykin; Estelle Harris; Will Yun Lee; Kristy Wu; ***D:*** Gurinder Chadha; ***W:*** Gurinder Chadha; Paul Mayeda Berges; ***C:*** Jong Lin; ***M:*** Craig Pruess.

What's Eating Gilbert Grape *Gilbert Grape* **1993 (PG-13)** Offbeat is mildly descriptive. Depp stars as Gilbert Grape, the titular head of a very dysfunctional family living in a big house in a small Iowa town. His Momma (Cates) weighs more than 500 pounds and hasn't left the house in seven years, he has two squabbling teenage sisters, and 17-year-old brother Arnie (DiCaprio) is mentally retarded and requires constant supervision. What's a good-hearted grocery clerk to do? Well, when free-spirited Becky (Lewis) is momentarily marooned in town, Gilbert may have found a true soulmate. Performances, especially DiCaprio's, save this from the oddball/cute factor although flick would have benefitted from streamlining, particularly the scenes involving Depp and bad-haircut Lewis. Based on the novel by Hedges. **118m/C; VHS, DVD.** Johnny Depp; Leonardo DiCaprio; Juliette Lewis; Mary Steenburgen; Darlene Cates; Laura Harrington; Mary Kate Schellhardt; Kevin Tighe; John C. Reilly; Crispin Glover; Penelope Branning; ***D:*** Lasse Hallstrom; ***W:*** Peter Hedges; ***C:*** Sven Nykvist; ***M:*** Alan Parker; Bjorn Isfalt. Natl. Bd. of Review '93: Support. Actor (DiCaprio).

What's Good for the Goose 1/2 **1969** Stuffy, married financial institution executive's lifestyle receives a major overhaul when he attends a banking conference and meets a beautiful and free-spirited young woman whom he takes as a lover. Unfortunately, he perpetually finds her in bed with other men, and then his wife gets in on the act, too. Classic British humor. **104m/C; VHS, DVD.** *GB* Norman Wisdom; Sarah Atkinson; Sally Bazely; Sally Geeson; Derek Francis; Terence Alexander; David Lodge; ***D:*** Menahem Golan; ***W:*** Norman Wisdom; Menahem Golan; ***C:*** William Brayne; ***M:*** Reg Tilsley.

What's Love Got to Do with It? 1/2 **1993 (R)** Energetic biopic of powerhouse songstress Tina Turner. Short sequences cover her early life before moving into her abusive relationship with Ike and solo comeback success. Bassett may not look like Tina, but her exceptionally strong performance leaves no question as to who she's supposed to be, even during on-stage Tina sequences. Some credibility is lost when Turner is shown in the final concert sequence—Gibson would have been wise to let Bassett finish what she started. Fishburne is a sympathetic but still chilling Ike, rising to the challenge of showing both Ike's initial charm and longtime cruelty. Based on "I, Tina" by Turner and Kurt Loder. **118m/C; VHS, DVD.** Angela Bassett; Laurence Fishburne; Vanessa Bell Calloway; Jenifer Lewis; Phyllis Stickney; Khandi Alexander; Pamela Tyson; Penny Johnson; Rae'ven (Alyia Larrymore) Kelly; Robert Miranda; Chi McBride; Damon Hines; ***D:*** Brian Gibson; ***W:*** Kate Lanier; ***C:*** Jamie Anderson; ***M:*** Stanley Clarke. Golden Globes '94: Actress--Mus./Comedy (Bassett); Blockbuster '95: Female Newcomer, V. (Bassett).

What's New Pussycat? *Quoi De Neuf, Pussycat?* **1965** A young engaged man, reluctant to give up the girls who love him, seeks the aid of a married psychiatrist who turns out to have problems of his own. Allen's first feature as both actor and screenwriter. Oscar-nominated title song sung by Tom Jones. **108m/C; VHS, DVD, Blu-Ray.** Peter Sellers; Peter O'Toole; Romy Schneider; Paula Prentiss; Woody Allen; Ursula Andress; Capucine; ***D:*** Clive Donner; ***W:*** Woody Allen; ***M:*** Burt Bacharach; Hal David.

What's the Matter with Helen? 1/2 **1971 (PG)** Two women, the mothers of murderous sons, move to Hollywood to escape their past and start a new life. They open a school for talented children, and seem to be adjusting to their new lives until strange things start happening. It is soon revealed that one of the mothers is a psychotic killer, and the other mother becomes part of an eerie finale. A fine starring vehicle for two aging actresses. Great score. **101m/C; VHS, DVD, Blu-Ray.** Debbie Reynolds; Shelley Winters; Dennis Weaver; Agnes Moorehead; Micheal MacLiammoir; ***D:*** Curtis Harrington.

What's the Worst That Could Happen? **2001 (PG-13)** Billionaire DeVito catches thief Lawrence robbing his mansion and, in retaliation, takes the man's lucky charm ring. Since Lawrence just received the ring from new girlfriend Ejogo, he'll do anything to get it back. It becomes an escalating, and ultimately tiresome, war of revenge and humiliation. The large and talented cast are given neither the script or the room to really shine, but some of the supporters fare well. Leguizamo, Fichtner, and Headly stand out, but Lawrence and DeVito should've been reined in a bit. **95m/C; VHS, DVD.** Martin Lawrence; Danny DeVito; Nora Dunn; William Fichtner; Glenne Headly; John Leguizamo; Bernie Mac; Carmen Ejogo; Larry Miller; Richard Schiff; Ana Gasteyer; Sascha Knopf; Siobhan Fallon Hogan; GQ; Lenny Clarke; ***D:*** Sam Weisman; ***W:*** Matthew Chapman; ***C:*** Anastas Michos; ***M:*** Tyler Bates.

What's Up, Doc? **1972 (G)** A shy musicologist from Iowa (Ryan) travels to San Francisco with his fiance (Kahn) for a convention. He meets the eccentric Streisand at his hotel and becomes involved in a chase to recover four identical flight bags containing top secret documents, a wealthy woman's jewels, the professor's musical rocks, and Streisand's clothing. Bogdanovich's homage to the screwball comedies of the '30s. Kahn's feature film debut. **94m/C; VHS, DVD.** Barbra Streisand; Ryan O'Neal; Kenneth Mars; Austin Pendleton; Randy Quaid; Madeline Kahn; ***D:*** Peter Bogdanovich; ***W:*** David Newman; Buck Henry; Robert Benton; ***M:*** Artie Butler. Writers Guild '72: Orig. Screenplay.

What's Up, Hideous Sun Demon? *Revenge of the Sun Demon* **1983** Bad 50s monster movie redubbed and re-edited into a story about suntan lotion gone awry. **71m/B; DVD, Streaming.** Bill Capizzi; Barbara Goodson; Jay Leno; ***V:*** Bernard Behrens; Zachary Berger; ***D:*** Craig Mitchell; ***W:*** Craig Mitchell; ***C:*** Steve Dubin; John Lambert; ***M:*** Fredric Myrow. **VIDEO**

What's Up, Scarlet? **2005** Successful L.A. matchmaker Scarlet Zabrinski is constantly at odds with her overbearing mother Ruth and her pothead brother Benjamin. Scarlet has no interest in a relationship of her own until a fender-bender introduces her to scatter-brained but sultry actress Sabrina. Learning Sabrina's homeless, Scarlet impulsively invites her to stay at her home, but is clueless about her burgeoning feelings for Sabrina until Ben makes a play for her. **84m/C; DVD.** Musetta Vander; Sally Kirkland; Jere Burns; Susan Priver; ***D:*** Anthony Caldarella; ***W:*** Anthony Caldarella; ***C:*** Geza Sinkovics; ***M:*** Stephen Graziano.

What's Up, Tiger Lily? **1966** This legitimate Japanese spy movie?"Kagi No Kag" (Key of Keys), a 1964 Bond imitation—was re-edited by Woody Allen, who added a new dialogue track, with hysterical results. Characters Terri and Suki Yaki are involved in an international plot to secure egg salad recipe; Allen's brand of Hollywood parody and clever wit sustain the joke. Music by the Lovin' Spoonful, who make a brief appearance. **90m/C; VHS, DVD.** *JP* Tatsuya Mihashi; Mie Hama; Akiko Wakabayashi; China Lee; Eisei Amamoto; Kumi Mizuno; Tadao Nakamura; ***Nar:*** Woody Allen; ***D:*** Woody Allen; Senkichi Taniguchi; ***W:*** Woody Allen; Julie Bennett; Frank Buxton; Louise Lasser; Mickey Rose; Bryan Wilson; Kazuo Yamada; ***C:*** Kazuo Yamada; ***M:*** Jack Lewis.

What's Your Number? 1/2 **2011 (R)** An awful excuse for a "chick flick" that finds Faris once again starring in material beneath her skills as a comedic actress. Based on Karyn Bosnak's novel, Faris plays a woman in a mid-life dating crisis who goes back through the 20 men she's slept with in the hope of finding Mr. Right even as he (Evans) so obviously lives across the hall. Dialogue that never rings true serves as the foundation for a script awash in misogyny that, most importantly, just isn't ever funny. A talented supporting cast looks lost in a romantic comedy that doesn't really qualify as either. **106m/C; DVD, Blu-Ray.** Anna Faris; Chris Evans; Dave (David) Annable; Mike Vogel; Joel McHale; Thomas Lennon; Ari Gaynor; Andy Samberg; Zachary Quinto; Ed Begley, Jr.; Blythe Danner; Oliver Jackson-Cohen; Heather Burns; ***D:*** Mark Mylod; ***W:*** Jennifer Crittenden; Gabrielle Allan; ***C:*** J.(James) Michael Muro; ***M:*** Aaron Zigman.

The Wheeler Dealers *Separate Beds* **1963** Garner plays a supposedly penniless investor (actually a Texas millionaire) who comes to New York stock analyst Remick for investment advice. Her shyster boss (Backus) tells her to sell the aw-shucks cowboy worthless stock which turns out to be worth a fortune. Zany spoof of Wall Street ethics. **100m/C; VHS, DVD, Blu-Ray.** James Garner; Lee Remick; Jim Backus; Phil Harris; Shelley Berman; Chill Wills; John Astin; Louis Nye; ***D:*** Arthur Hiller.

Wheelman 1/2 **2017** Though just out of prison, the wheelman (Grillo) reluctantly takes a bank robbery job because of financial, family, and mob debt pressures. Ordered by an anonymous caller to leave the two robbers behind after they put the loot in his trunk, the wheelman must learn who has set him up. Through numerous phone calls and a discussion with his sketchy contractor Clay (Dillahunt), the wheelman tries to learn the truth while also taking calls from his beloved teen daughter Katie (Carmichael). Shot in his car, the film has cliched moments but is an effective character study. **82m/C; DVD.** Frank Grillo; Caitlin Carmichael; Garret Dillahunt; Wendy Moniz; John Cenatiempo; ***D:*** Jeremy Rush; ***W:*** Jeremy Rush; ***C:*** Juanmi (Juan Miguel) Azpiroz; ***M:*** Brooke Blair; Will Blair.

When a Man Falls in the Forest *Desires of a Housewife* **2007 (R)** Three former high school classmates meet middle age. Architect Gary (Hutton) is disillusioned by his job and estranged from his equally depressed wife (Stone); Travis (Vince) still suffers the effects from a long-ago accident; and Bill (Baker), a janitor at Gary's office, listens to an instructional tape on lucid dreaming, imaging a life he will never have the nerve to live. It's all low-key and bleak. **86m/C; DVD.** Timothy Hutton; Dylan Baker; Pruitt Taylor Vince; Sharon Stone; Nicholas Elia; ***D:*** Ryan Eslinger; ***W:*** Ryan Eslinger; ***C:*** Lawrence Sher; ***M:*** Billy Corgan; John Sereda.

When a Man Loves **1927** Adaptation of the novel "Manon Lescault" by Abbe Prevost. Chevalier Fabien des Grieux (Barrymore) rescues Manon (Costello) after her brother offers her to the Comte de Morfontaine (de Grasse) but she eventually returns to him because Manon likes what Morfontaine's wealth brings. When des Grieux reenters her life, he tries cheating at cards as a way to support them but that only gets Manon imprisoned on a convict ship. **112m/B; Silent; DVD.** John Barrymore; Dolores Costello; Sam De Grasse; Warner Oland; Holmes Herbert; Stuart Holmes; Bertram Grassby; ***D:*** Alan Crosland; ***W:*** Bess Meredyth; ***C:*** Byron Haskin.

When a Man Loves a Woman 1/2 *To Have and to Hold; Significant Other* **1994 (R)** Time to get suspicious when song titles become film titles. Alice Green (Ryan) is the mother in a perfect little family, with a loving husband (Garcia), two little girls, and a satisfying career. She's also a closet alcoholic. Less about her alcoholism than the effect on her family and her hubby in particular, shown as a '90s sort of guy who allows Alice to keep her secret. Ryan's detox treatments and struggle back to sobriety are fertile ground for psycho-babble and 12-step cliches, but solid performances save this picture from drying out. **126m/C; VHS, DVD.** Meg Ryan; Andy Garcia; Lauren Tom; Philip Seymour Hoffman; Tina Majorino; Mae Whitman; Ellen Burstyn; Eugene Roche; LaTanya Richardson Jackson; ***D:*** Luis Mandoki; ***W:*** Ronald Bass; Al Franken; ***C:*** Lajos Koltai; ***M:*** Zbigniew Preisner. Blockbuster '95: Drama Actress, V. (Ryan).

When a Stranger Calls 1/2 **1979 (R)** Babysitter is terrorized by threatening phone calls and soon realizes that the calls are coming from within the house. Story was expanded from director Walton's short film "The Sitter." Distasteful and unlikely, though the first half or so is tight and terrifying. **97m/C; VHS, DVD, Blu-Ray.** Carol Kane; Charles Durning; Colleen Dewhurst; Rachel Roberts; Rutanya Alda; Carmen Argenziano; Kirsten Larkin; Ron O'Neal; Tony Beckley; ***D:*** Fred Walton; ***W:*** Fred Walton; Steve Feke; ***C:*** Don Peterman.

When a Stranger Calls **2006 (PG-13)** The call is still coming from (gasp!) inside the house in this remake of the 1979 nail-biter, except the house is now a modern high-tech glass palace (strangely without caller ID though)?in the middle of nowhere, of course (because that's where most palaces are). The violence that marked the original is toned down to make it more teen-friendly. Unfortunately, so is the suspense. **100m/C; DVD, Blu-Ray, UMD.** Camilla Belle; Tommy Flanagan; Tessa Thompson; Brian Geraghty; Clark Gregg; Derek de Lint; David Denman; Madeline Carroll; Kate Jennings Grant; Arthur Young; Steve Eastin; Katie Cassidy; ***V:*** Lance Henriksen; ***D:*** Simon West; ***W:*** Jake Wade Wall; ***C:*** Peter Menzies, Jr.; ***M:*** James Dooley.

When a Stranger Calls Back 1/2 **1993 (R)** Sequel to "When a Stranger Calls" finds college student Julia Jenz (Schoelen) still trying to put her life together five years after a terrifying ordeal with a stalker. She turns to her advisor Jill (Kane), who went through a similar fate, but once Jill becomes involved she again becomes the pawn of a psychopath. It's up to retired detective John Clifford (Durning), who saved Jill before, to do his heroics once again. Scary opening sequence but suspense peters out toward the end. **94m/C; VHS, DVD, Blu-Ray.** Carol Kane; Charles Durning; Jill Schoelen; Gene Lythgow; Karen Austin; ***D:*** Fred Walton; ***W:*** Fred Walton; ***C:*** David Geddes; ***M:*** Dana Kaproff. **CABLE**

When a Woman Ascends the Stairs *Onna Ga Kaidan O Agaru Toki* **1960** A young widow with an elderly mother and a useless brother supports them all by working as a Ginza bar hostess. As she approaches the perilous professional age of 30, Keiko must decide whether to open her own bar or marry once again. In Japanese with English subtitles. **110m/B; VHS, DVD.** *JP* Hideko Takamine; Tatsuya Nakadai; Masayuki Mori; ***D:*** Mikio Naruse.

When Brendan Met Trudy **2000** Irish romantic comedy by the writer of such standout novels as "The Commitments" and "The Snapper." Brendan (McDonald) is somewhat of a pansy-boy who attracts his polar opposite Trudy (Montgomery), a street-smart sort of girl and falls in love. Brendan, a straitlaced schoolteacher, soon learns that Trudy moonlights as a thief, and after the initial shock wears off, joins his outlaw honey in some good old-fashioned felonious fun. The true fun of the film, though, is its constant classic film references, such as when a misadventure lands Brendan in the gutter, he is reminded of William Holden in "Sunset Boulevard." Even if you're not a film buff, thought, you'll still enjoy this offbeat comic romp. **95m/C; VHS, DVD.** *IR GB* Peter McDonald; Flora Montgomery; Marie Mullen; Pauline McLynn; Don Wycherley; ***D:*** Kieron J. Walsh; ***W:*** Roddy Doyle; ***C:*** Ashley Rowe; ***M:*** Richard Hartley.

When Calls the Heart 1/2 **2013** Hallmark Channel drama based on the first book in Janette Oke's Canadian West series. In 1910, young Elizabeth Stanton (Drayton) is nervous about leaving her New England home to accept her first teaching job until she finds her namesake aunt's diary and learns she did the same thing. Elizabeth Thatcher (Grace) leaves her high society life for the struggles of a 19th-century frontier town in the foothills of the Canadian Rockies. There, she finds a new purpose and love with handsome Mountie, Wynn Delaney (Amell). **90m/C; DVD.** Maggie Grace; Stephen Amell; Jean Smart; Lori Loughlin; Tygh Runyan; Poppy Drayton; ***D:*** Michael Landon, Jr.; ***W:*** Michael Landon, Jr.; ***C:*** Christo Bakalov; ***M:*** Lee Holdridge. **CABLE**

When Did You Last See Your Father? 1/2 **2007 (PG-13)** Blake (Firth) returns to the town where he was born to reconnect with his dying father (Broadbent), realizing it's too late to say the things he's wanted to say for so long. Told in episodes, with flashbacks to a past when the two would go camping together and dad was teaching son to drive. Director Tucker tells this sad story with lush landscape photography and a melodramatic score, often framing the characters in mirrors, as if they're only reflecting, and not truly there. It all works; it's just not very pleasant. **92m/C; DVD, Streaming.** Jim Broadbent; Colin Firth; Juliet Stevenson; Gina McKee; Matthew "Stymie" Beard; Sarah Lancashire; Elaine Cassidy; Claire Skinner; ***D:*** Anand Tucker; ***W:*** David Nicholls; ***C:*** Howard Atherton; ***M:*** Barrington Pheloung.

When Do We Eat? 🦴 1/2 **2005 (R)** Stereotypical dysfunctional family comedy. The Stuckman family's Passover Seder doesn't go smoothly since no one seems to get along. Although patriarch Ira (Lerner) is feeling no pain after stoner son Zeke (Feldman) doses him with ecstasy. **86m/C; DVD.** Michael Lerner; Lesley Ann Warren; Ben Feldman; Jack Klugman; Shiri Appleby; Mili Avital; Meredith Scott Lynn; Adam Lamberg; Max Greenfield; Cynda Williams; ***D:*** Salvador Litvak; ***W:*** Salvador Litvak; Nina Davidovich; ***C:*** M. David Mullen; ***M:*** Mark Adler.

When Eight Bells Toll 🦴🦴 **1971** MacLean adapted his own adventure novel in which naval secret service agent Philip Calvert (Hopkins) discovers that millions in gold bullion is being stolen. He and agent Hunslett (Redgrave) travel to Scotland, posing as marine biologists; there they encounter hostile Scottish locals and a suspicious Greek tycoon, Skouras (Hawkins), who has a very attractive companion (Delon). Hawkins had lost his voice to throat cancer so his lines were dubbed by actor Charles Gray. **94m/C; VHS, DVD, Blu-Ray.** *GB* Anthony Hopkins; Corin Redgrave; Jack Hawkins; Nathalie Delon; Robert Morley; Derek Bond; Ferdinand "Ferdy" Mayne; Maurice Roeves; ***D:*** Etienne Perier; ***W:*** Alistair MacLean; ***C:*** Arthur Ibbetson; ***M:*** Angela Morley.

When Every Day Was the Fourth of July 🦴🦴 1/2 **1978** A nine-year-old girl asks her father, a lawyer, to defend a mute handyman accused of murder, knowing this will bring on him the contempt of the community. Well handled, but see "To Kill a Mockingbird" first. Based on producer/director Curtis's childhood. Sequel: "The Long Days of Summer." **100m/C; VHS, DVD.** Katy Kurtzman; Dean Jones; Louise Sorel; Harris Yulin; Chris Petersen; Geoffrey Lewis; Scott Brady; Henry Wilcoxon; Michael Pataki; ***D:*** Dan Curtis. **TV**

When Evil Calls 🦴 1/2 **2006 (R)** Well, don't answer! In this horror parody, a sleazy narrator (Pertwee) informs the audience of the consequences of a deadly text message circulating among high school students. The message grants the recipient's wish—to be popular, thin, beautiful, etc.?as long as the text gets passed on to two more students. Of course the wish is "granted" in the most gory (and often naked) way possible. Originally a 20-episode series made to be downloaded to a cell phone and then re-edited. **76m/C; DVD.** *GB* Jennifer Lim; Dominique Pinon; Sean Pertwee; Sean Brosnan; Chris (Christopher) Barrie; Rick Warden; Chris Barrie; ***D:*** Johannes Roberts; ***W:*** Johannes Roberts; ***C:*** John Raggett; ***M:*** Alex Taylor. **VIDEO**

When Father Was Away on Business 🦴🦴🦴 1/2 *Otac na Sluzbenom Putu* **1985 (R)** Set in 1950s Yugoslavia. A family must take care of itself when the father is sent to jail for philandering with a woman desired by a Communist Party offical. The moving story of the family's day-to-day survival is seen largely through the eyes of the father's six-year-old son, who believes dad is "away on business." In Yugoslavian with English subtitles. **144m/C; VHS, DVD.** *YU* Moreno D'E Bartolli; Miki (Predrag) Manojlovic; Mirjana Karanovic; ***D:*** Emir Kusturica; ***W:*** Abdullah Sidran; ***C:*** Vilko Filac; ***M:*** Zoran Simjanovic. Cannes '85: Film.

When Good Ghouls Go Bad 🦴🦴 1/2 **2001 (PG)** Twelve-year-old Danny has just moved to a new town where he discovers that because of a town curse no one is allowed to celebrate Halloween. So Danny teams up with his recently departed Uncle Fred (Lloyd) to drive away the prankster ghouls who have been causing all the mischief. Based on a story by R.L. Stine. **93m/C; VHS, DVD.** Christopher Lloyd; Tom Amandes; Joe Pichler; ***D:*** Patrick Read Johnson; ***W:*** Patrick Read Johnson; ***C:*** Brian J. Breheny; ***M:*** Christopher Gordon. **TV**

When Harry Met Sally... 🦴🦴🦴 **1989 (R)** Romantic comedy follows the long relationship between two adults who try throughout the changes in their lives (and their mates) to remain platonic friends—and what happens when they don't. Wry and enjoyable script is enhanced by wonderful performances. Another directorial direct hit for "Meathead" Reiner, and a tour de force of comic screenwriting for Ephron, with improvisational help from Crystal. Great songs by Sinatra sound-alike Connick. **96m/C; VHS, DVD, Blu-Ray.** Billy Crystal; Meg Ryan; Carrie Fisher; Bruno Kirby; Steven Ford; Lisa Jane Persky; Michelle Nicastro; Harley Jane Kozak; Tracy Reiner; ***D:*** Rob Reiner; ***W:*** Nora Ephron; ***C:*** Barry Sonnenfeld; ***M:*** Harry Connick, Jr; Marc Shaiman. British Acad. '89: Orig. Screenplay.

When Hell Broke Loose 🦴 1/2 **1958** Routine WWII actioner about a small-time crook (Bronson) who joins the Army, changes his ways because of the love of a good woman, and gets a chance to be a hero when he stumbles upon a Nazi assassination plot against General Eisenhower. **78m/B; VHS, Streaming.** Charles Bronson; Violet Rensing; Richard Jaeckel; Arvid Nelson; Robert Easton; ***D:*** Kenneth Crane; ***W:*** Oscar Brodney.

When He's Not a Stranger 🦴🦴🦴 **1989** Lyn is a college freshman who goes to a campus party hosted by the football team. When Ron, the star quarterback, invites Lyn to his dorm room, the situation gets out of hand. Only Lyn calls it rape and Ron calls her a liar. Intense performances are a highlight of this well-done story. **100m/C; VHS, DVD.** Annabeth Gish; John Terlesky; Kevin Dillon; Paul Dooley; Kim Meyers; ***D:*** John Gray. **TV**

When I Find the Ocean 🦴🦴 **2006 (PG)** It's 1965. Lily (Holly) is 12 and lives in Alabama with her mother Jenny (Redford) and her grandparents (Ladd, Majors). She's still heartbroken over her sailor father's disappearance at sea and is keeping secret the fact that her mother's new boyfriend Dean (Tyson) has been abusing her. Lily finally decides to escape to the ocean—in a rowboat—to feel closer to her father's memory. **104m/C; DVD.** Amy Redford; Diane Ladd; Lee Majors; Richard Tyson; Graham Greene; Bernie Casey; David "Shark" Fralick; Lily Matland Holly; ***D:*** Tonya S. Holly; ***W:*** Tonya S. Holly; ***C:*** Mario DiLeo; ***M:*** Flavio Motalla.

When in Rome 🦴 **2009 (PG-13)** Unlucky in love, Beth Harper (Bell) travels to Rome to see her newlywed sister. She impulsively steals some coins from the city's magical fountain of love and must deal with the men who suddenly fall hopelessly in love with her in this chemistry-free romantic comedy. What little potential the flimsy premise contains is trampled by the terrible script, one-note characters, and utterly inept direction. The cast is left trying too hard for laughs that were never there to begin with. **91m/C; Blu-Ray.** Kristen Bell; Josh Duhamel; Will Arnett; Jon Heder; Anjelica Huston; Alexis Dziena; Peggy Lipton; Keir O'Donnell; Kate Micucci; Bobby Moynihan; Dax Shepard; ***D:*** Mark Steven Johnson; ***W:*** David Diamond; David Weissman; ***C:*** John Bailey; ***M:*** Christopher Young.

When Justice Fails 🦴🦴 **1998 (R)** Vigilante goes after rapists. **90m/C; VHS, DVD.** Jeff Fahey; Marlee Matlin; Monique Mercure; Carl Marotte; ***D:*** Allan Goldstein; ***W:*** Tony Kayden; ***C:*** Barry Gravelle.

When Ladies Meet 🦴🦴 1/2 *Strange Skirts* **1941** Entertaining story of a love quadrangle that features several of MGM's top stars of the '40s. In this remake of the 1933 film, Crawford plays a novelist and an early proponent of the women's liberation movement. She falls in love with her publisher (Marshall), who just happens to be married to Garson. Meanwhile, Taylor, who is in love with Crawford, attempts to show her that he isa more suitable match for her than Marshall, but Crawford has yet to catch on.The lengthy dialogue on women's rights is badly dated, but the real-life rivalry between Crawford and Garson adds a certain bite to their witty exchanges. **105m/B; VHS, DVD.** Joan Crawford; Robert Taylor; Greer Garson; Herbert Marshall; Spring Byington; ***D:*** Robert Z. Leonard; ***W:*** Anita Loos; S.K. Lauren.

When Love Comes 🦴🦴 **1998** Katie Keen (Owen) is a 40ish one-hit pop singer who decides to return home to New Zealand to rethink her fading career and life with her manager/lover Eddie (Westaway). Her best pal is still Stephen (Prast) who is involved with the younger Mark (O'Gorman), a songwriter. Mark's friends Fig (Brunning) and Sally (Hawthorne) have a band and ask Katie to sing on a recording. Everyone eventually winds up at Katie's seaside home trying to make potentially life-altering decisions. **94m/C; DVD.** *NZ* Rena Owen; Dean O'Gorman; Simon Prast; Nancy Brunning; Simon Westaway; Sally Hawthorne; ***D:*** Garth Maxwell; ***W:*** Garth Maxwell; Peter Wells; Rex Pilgrim; ***C:*** Darryl Ward; ***M:*** Chris Anderton.

When Love Is Not Enough: The Lois Wilson Story 🦴🦴 **2010** A Hallmark Hall of Fame production based on the true story of the founder of Al-Anon. Lois (Ryder) marries Bill Wilson (Pepper) in 1917 but it turns out he's a self-destructive alcoholic. Lois loyally stands by him (for many, many years) through his constant pledges to quit and all their other problems until he finds a support group, which leads to Bill's cofounding of Alcoholics Anonymous. Lois' experiences then lead her to create a corresponding group for families. It's admirable, meant to be inspirational, storytelling but frustrating as well (Lois' suffering can get wearying). **90m/C; DVD.** Winona Ryder; Barry Pepper; John Bourgeois; Rosemary Dunsmore; Ellen Dubin; ***D:*** John Kent Harrison; ***W:*** William G. Borchert; Camille Thomasson; ***C:*** Miroslaw Baszak; ***M:*** Lawrence Shragge. **TV**

When Nature Calls **WOOF!** **1985 (R)** A city family "gets back to nature" in this collection of mostly ineffective gags and poor satirical ideas. Probably your first and last chance to see Liddy and Mays on screen together. **76m/C; VHS, DVD.** Davie Orange; Barbara Marineau; Nicky Beim; Tina Marie Staiano; Willie Mays; G. Gordon Liddy; ***D:*** Charles Kaufman.

When Night Is Falling 🦴🦴🦴 **1995 (R)** Camille (Bussieres) is a professor of mythology at a Calvinist college in Toronto and engaged to theologian Martin (Czerny). Vaguely unsatisfied, Camille meets Petra (Crawford), a trapeze artist in a traveling circus, gets drawn into her world, falls in love, and must decide what she wants from her life. Lots of yearning, romance, and fantasy. Lesbian lovemaking scenes caused a ratings problem (the MPAA originally deemed them worthy of NC-17). **96m/C; VHS, DVD.** *CA* Pascale Bussieres; Rachael Crawford; Henry Czerny; David Fox; Don McKellar; Tracy Wright; ***D:*** Patricia Rozema; ***W:*** Patricia Rozema; ***C:*** Douglas Koch; ***M:*** Lesley Barber.

When the Bough Breaks 🦴🦴 **1986** A psychologist helps the police with the case of a murder-suicide witnessed by a child. He finds one sick secret society at work in this unkinder, ungentler TV thriller, based on the novel by Jonathan Kellerman. Danson coproduced. **100m/C; VHS, DVD.** Ted Danson; Richard Masur; Rachel Ticotin; David Huddleston; James Noble; Kim Miyori; Merritt Butrick; ***D:*** Waris Hussein.

When the Bough Breaks 🦴🦴 **1993 (R)** A Texas police chief (Sheen) discovers seven severed hands and turns to a forensic expert (Walker) for help. But then the specialist discovers a psychic link between a mentally disturbed child and the serial killer. **103m/C; VHS, DVD.** Ally Walker; Martin Sheen; Ron Perlman; ***D:*** Michael Cohn; ***W:*** Michael Cohn; ***C:*** Michael Bonvillain.

When the Bough Breaks 🦴 **2016 (PG-13)** John and Laura Taylor (Chestnut and Hall) are a happy couple, hoping to have a baby soon. They struggle to conceive, and so they hire a surrogate to serve as their baby mama. At first, everything seems to be going well with Anna (Sinclair), but as her pregnancy advances, so does her obsession with John. With echoes of thrillers like "Fatal Attraction" and "Hand That Rocks the Cradle," this modern spin should only insult viewers, especially women, as it treats pregnancy as something that drives you crazy. The cast is better than the material, but this isn't even B-movie fun. **107m/C; DVD, Blu-Ray.** Morris Chestnut; Regina Hall; Jaz Sinclair; Romany Malco; Theo Rossi; ***D:*** Jon Cassar; ***W:*** Jack Olsen; ***C:*** David Moxness; ***M:*** John (Gianni) Frizzell.

When the Boys Meet the Girls 🦴 1/2 **1965** Silly '60s musical romance that's an update of George Gershwin's "Girl Crazy." Ginger Gray (Francis) and her father Phin (Faylen) are going to lose their Nevada ranch thanks to his gambling debts. Wealthy Danny Churchill (Presnell) convinces them to turn the property into a dude ranch for those waiting for their divorce decrees to come through. **97m/C; DVD.** Connie Francis; Harve Presnell; Sue Ane Langdon; Frank Faylen; ***D:*** Alvin Ganzer; ***W:*** Robert E. Kent; ***C:*** Paul Vogel; ***M:*** Fred Karger.

When the Clouds Roll By 🦴🦴🦴 1/2 **1919** Psycho-satire pits demented doctor against Fairbanks in experiment to make him suicidal basket case. Fairbanks seems to contract ferocious nightmares, passionate superstitions, a spurning lover, and a warrant for his arrest, none of which suppresses his penchant for acrobatics. **77m/B; Silent; VHS, DVD.** Douglas Fairbanks, Sr.; Herbert Grimwood; Kathleen Clifford; Frank Campeau; Ralph Lewis; Daisy Robinson; Albert MacQuarrie; ***D:*** Victor Fleming.

When the Game Stands Tall 🦴 1/2 **2014 (PG)** Based on the story of Concord, California's Spartans high school football team, who stomped their way to an astounding 151-game winning streak by 2004. Off the gridiron, though, tensions mount, and despite the best efforts of Coach Ladoucer (Caviezel) and his assistant (Chiklis), the team is more about trophies than comradery. Clipping along at breakneck speed through rousing locker room pep talks and workout montages, the victories come to a screeching halt when the team is confronted with adversity. A typical heart-warming sports gusher--gooey, pseudo-religious, and predictable, this melodrama fumbles its own Hail Mary. **115m/C; DVD, Blu-Ray.** Jim Caviezel; Michael Chiklis; Laura Dern; Clancy Brown; Alexander Ludwig; Matthew Daddario; Ser'darius Blain; Stephan James; ***D:*** Thomas Carter; ***W:*** Scott Marshall Smith; ***C:*** Michael Lohmann; ***M:*** John Paesano.

When the Last Sword is Drawn 🦴🦴🦴 *Mibu gishi den* **2002** In the last days of the Tokugawa Shogunate a group of samurai known as the Shinsegumi remain loyal to the Shogun after the Emperor decides to modernize Japan by eliminating the Shogun and his samurai because he feels they are unnecessary, touching off a civil war. Told mostly in flashback it is the story of one misunderstood samurai and his friend caught in the middle between the countries current and former governments, and his tragic story. **143m/C; DVD.** *JP* Kiichi Nakai; Koichi Sato; Yui Natsukawa; Takehiro Murata; Miki Nakatani; Yuji Miyake; ***D:*** Yojiro Takita; ***W:*** Takehiro Nakajima; Jiro Asada; ***C:*** Takashi Hamada; ***M:*** Joe Hisaishi.

When the Party's Over 🦴🦴 1/2 **1991 (R)** Twenty-somethings share a southern California house and a hip—but ultimately empty—lifestyle. **114m/C; VHS, DVD.** Rae Dawn Chong; Fisher Stevens; Elizabeth Berridge; Sandra Bullock; Brian McNamara; Kris Kamm; ***D:*** Matthew Irmas.

When the Screaming Stops 🦴 **1973 (R)** A hunter is hired to find out who has been cutting the hearts out of young women who reside in a small village near the Rhine River. Turns out it's a she-monster who rules a kingdom beneath the river. Bad effects; gory gore; outlandish plot. All the ingredients, in other words, of a classic dog. **86m/C; VHS, DVD.** *SP* Tony Kendall; Helga Line; Silvia Tortosa; ***D:*** Armando de Ossorio.

When the Sky Falls 🦴🦴 **1999** Gritty bio loosely focuses on the last years of crusading Dublin journalist Veronica Gerin, who was murdered in 1996. Sinead Hamilton (Allen) has angered Dublin politicians, the IRA, police, and crime bosses with her investigation into the city's drug scene. She ticks off bad guy Dave Hackett (Flynn) and even tough detective Mackey (Bergin) tries to warn her but threats only make Hamilton more determined to do her expose. **107m/C; VHS, DVD.** *IR* Joan Allen; Patrick Bergin; Liam Cunningham; Gerard Flynn; Kevin McNally; Jimmy Smallhorne; Jason Barry; Pete Postlethwaite; Des McAleer; Ruaidhri Conroy; ***D:*** John MacKenzie; ***W:*** Michael J. Sheridan; Ronan Gallagher; Colum McCann; ***C:*** Seamus Deasy; ***M:*** Pol Brennan.

When the Wind Blows 🦴🦴🦴 **1986** An animated feature about a retired British couple when their peaceful—and naive—life in the country is destroyed by nuclear war. Poignant, sad, and thought-provoking, and just a little scary. Features the voices of Ashcroft and Mills; Roger Waters, David Bowie, Squeeze, Genesis, Hugh Cornell, and Paul Hardcastle all contribute to the soundtrack. Based on the novel by Raymond Briggs. **80m/C; VHS, DVD, Blu-Ray.** *GB V:* Peggy Ashcroft; John Mills; *D:* Jimmy T. Murakami.

When Time Expires 🦴🦴 **1997 (PG-13)** Extraterrestrial scientist Travis Beck (Grieco) time travels from the future to present-day earth to stop the planet's destruction by evil forces. **93m/C; VHS, DVD.** Richard Grieco; Cynthia Geary; Mark Hamill; Tim Thomerson; Chad Everett; *D:* David Bourla; *W:* David Bourla; *C:* Dean Lent; *M:* Todd Hayen. **CABLE**

When Time Ran Out 🦴 **1980 (PG)** A volcano erupts on a remote Polynesian island covered with expensive hotels and tourists with no way to escape. Contains scenes not seen in the theatrically released print of the film. A very good cast is wasted in this compilation of disaster film cliches. **144m/C; VHS, DVD.** Paul Newman; Jacqueline Bisset; William Holden; Ernest Borgnine; Edward Albert; Barbara Carrera; Valentina Cortese; Burgess Meredith; Noriyuki "Pat" Morita; Red Buttons; *D:* James Goldstone; *W:* Stirling Silliphant; *C:* Fred W. Koenekamp; *M:* Lalo Schifrin.

When Trumpets Fade 🦴🦴 **1/2 1998 (R)** Private Manning (Eldard) is the only survivor of his platoon, which is caught in the Battle of the Hurtgen Forest along the Belgian-German border in 1944. Manning is interested in nothing more than his own survival but his skills attract the attention of an officer (Donovan) who promptly promotes him to sgt. (and soon, lieutenant) and gives him his own platoon of raw recruits to whip into shape. **93m/C; VHS, DVD.** Ron Eldard; Zak Orth; Frank Whaley; Dylan Bruno; Martin Donovan; Timothy Olyphant; Dan Futterman; Dwight Yoakam; Devon Gummersall; Jeffrey Donovan; *D:* John Irvin; *W:* William W. Vought; *C:* Thomas Burstyn; *M:* Geoffrey Burgon. **CABLE**

When Two Worlds Collide 🦴🦴🦴 **1/2 2016** A documentary look at the conflict between capitalism and government-backed business interests versus indigenous populations and their desire to protect the land in Peru. In that country, President Alan Garcia begins to extract oil, minerals, and gas from previously untouched lands around the Amazon. He is opposed most forcefully by indigenous leader Alberto Pizango, who wants to keep indigenous lands untouched. The documentary shows how the conflict escalates from a war of words to a violent conflict. **103m/C; DVD.** *D:* Heidi Brandenburg; Mathew Orzel; *M:* H. Scott Salinas.

When We Were Kings 🦴🦴🦴 **1/2 1996 (PG)** Chronicles the 1974 heavyweight championship fight, held in Zaire, between underdog Muhammad Ali and George Foreman. Gast uses original footage of the pre-fight hype as well as current interviews from George Plimpton and Norman Mailer (who covered the fight at the time) and Spike Lee. **94m/C; VHS, DVD, Blu-Ray.** *D:* Leon Gast. Oscars '96: Feature Doc.; Broadcast Film Critics '96: Feature Doc.

When Will I Be Loved 🦴 **1/2 2004 (R)** Cynical, chilly wannabe thriller stars Campbell as wealthy dilettante Vera Barrie who's involved with a shady, sometimes violent street hustler named Ford (Weller). Needing money, Ford sells Vera's favors to a visiting Italian media mogul (Chianese), but manipulative Vera turns the tables by working out her own devious deal. Despite its brief length, film's rambling and semi-improvised dialogue and structure does the story no favors, although the city of New York is richly displayed. **81m/C; DVD.** Neve Campbell; Dominic Chianese; Frederick Weller; Karen Allen; Barry Primus; Abdullah Ibrahim; James Toback; Joelle Carter; *D:* James Toback; *W:* James Toback; *C:* Lawrence McConkey; *M:* Oli "Power" Grant.

When Willie Comes Marching Home 🦴🦴🦴 **1950** Insightful (and funny) satire from Ford with equally well-done dramatic moments. William Kluggs (Dailey) wants to become a hero when he enlists, but instead he's assigned to be the gunnery instructor in his own hometown. A town joke, Bill finally gets his chance as a B-17 gunner but winds up being rescued by members of the French Resistance. After aiding them, he does become a hero but is sworn to secrecy by his superiors. Bill then has to endure more abuse from the folks at home until everything is revealed. **90m/C; DVD.** Dan Dailey; William Demerest; Bill Calvert; Lloyd Corrigan; Colleen Townsend; James Lydon; Evelyn Varden; *D:* John Ford; *W:* Mary Loos; Richard Sale; *C:* Leo Tover; *M:* Alfred Newman.

When Women Had Tails 🦴 **1/2** *Quando De Donne Avevando La Coda* **1970 (R)** A primitive comedy about prehistoric man's discovery of sex. And boy, did they ever discover it. Harmless (more or less), though not exactly cerebral. Followed by "When Women Lost Their Tails." **99m/C; VHS, DVD.** *IT* Senta Berger; Frank Wolff; *D:* Pasquale Festa Campanile; *M:* Ennio Morricone.

When Women Lost Their Tails 🦴 **1975 (R)** Ostensible sequel to "When Women Had Tails" about prehistoric cavemen and their sexual habits. **94m/C; VHS, DVD.** *IT* Senta Berger; *D:* Pasquale Festa Campanile; *M:* Ennio Morricone.

When Worlds Collide 🦴🦴 **1/2 1951 (G)** Another planet is found to be rushing inevitably towards earth, but a select group of people attempt to escape in a spaceship; others try to maneuver their way on board. Oscar-quality special effects and plot make up for cheesy acting and bad writing. **81m/C; VHS, DVD.** Richard Derr; Barbara Rush; Larry Keating; Peter Hansen; *D:* Rudolph Mate; *W:* Sydney (Sidney) Boehm; *C:* William Howard Greene; *M:* Leith Stevens.

When's Your Birthday? 🦴🦴 **1/2 1937** Brown stars in this comedy about a prize-fighter who is working his way through astrology school with his fighting skills. The stars, in turn, tell him when to fight. Lame zaniness (what other kind is there?) meant as a vehicle for Brown, though Kennedy is funnier. The opening sequence, an animated cartoon showing the influence of the moon over the planets, was filmed in Technicolor. **77m/B; VHS, DVD.** Joe E. Brown; Marian Marsh; Edgar Kennedy; *D:* Harry Beaumont.

Where Angels Fear to Tread 🦴🦴🦴 **1991 (PG)** Another turn-of-the-century tale of the English in Italy from the pen of E.M. Forster. Widowed, 40ish Lilia (Mirren) is urged by her stuffy in-laws to spend some time in Italy. Much to everyone's dismay she impulsively marries a 21-year-old Italian—with disastrous consequences. Based on Forster's first novel, the characters are more stereotypical and the story less defined than his later works and the movies made from them. Impressive performances and beautiful settings make up for a somewhat lackluster direction that isn't up to the standards set by the team of Merchant Ivory, responsible for the Forster films "A Room with a View" and "Howard's End." **112m/C; VHS, DVD.** *GB* Rupert Graves; Helena Bonham Carter; Judy Davis; Dame Helen Mirren; Giovanni Guidelli; Barbara Jefford; Thomas Wheatley; Sophie Kullman; *D:* Charles Sturridge; *W:* Charles Sturridge; Tim Sullivan; Derek Granger; *C:* Michael Coulter; *M:* Rachel Portman.

Where Angels Go, Trouble Follows 🦴🦴 **1/2 1968** Follow-up to "The Trouble with Angels," with Russell reprising her role as the wise Mother Superior challenged by her mischief loving students. Younger, modern nun Stevens tries to convince Russell to update her old-fashioned ways and persuades her to take the convent students on a bus trip to a California peace rally. A very young Saint James is one of the convent's irrepressible troublemakers. Very dated but still mildly amusing. **94m/C; VHS, DVD.** Rosalind Russell; Stella Stevens; Binnie Barnes; Mary Wickes; Susan St. James; Dolores Sutton; Alice Rawlings; *Cameo(s):* Milton Berle; Arthur Godfrey; Van Johnson; Robert Taylor; *D:* James Neilson; *W:* Blanche Hanalis.

Where Are My Children? 🦴🦴 **1994** ABC TV movie based on a true story. Single mom Vanessa Meyer is mysteriously arrested by the FBI for a petty crime and does a brief prison stint. Upon her release, she discovers her three children have been put up for illegal adoption and she spends the next 25 years trying to reunite her family. **89m/C; DVD.** Marg Helgenberger; Corbin Bernsen; Chris Noth; *D:* George Kaczender; *W:* Michael Zagor; *C:* Laszlo George; *M:* Craig Safan. **TV**

Where Are the Children? 🦴 **1/2 1985 (R)** Based on Mary Higgins Clark's best-seller. A woman who was cleared of murdering the children from her first marriage remarries. Then the children from her second marriage are kidnapped. Sustains suspense completely, until it falls apart. **92m/C; VHS, Streaming.** Jill Clayburgh; Max Gail; Barnard Hughes; Clifton James; Harley Cross; Elisabeth Harnois; Elizabeth Wilson; Frederic Forrest; *D:* Bruce Malmuth.

Where Are Your Children? 🦴🦴 **1944** Cautionary juvie drama. Lonely 16-year-old Judy (Storm) falls for Danny Cheston (Cooper), who has some questionable friends. First they spike her drink and she winds up in policy custody, then, after Danny joins the Navy, they persuade Judy to ride with them to his base in San Diego. Only Judy doesn't know the car is stolen and she's soon an accessory to murder! After Judy lands in the slammer, Danny comes to her rescue. **73m/B; DVD.** Gale Storm; Jackie Cooper; Patricia Morison; John Litel; Gertrude Michael; Anthony Warde; Neyle Morrow; *D:* William Nigh; *W:* George Wallace Sayre; *C:* Mack Stengler.

Where Children Play 🦴🦴 **2015** Complex drama about the power of making peace with the past and live a better life. Because of a difficult, abusive childhood, Bellissima (Parris) left home but never found the happy future she sought because of the past. When her mother dies, however, she returns home and must face the father who abused her and provide care to him. In confronting her family's history, she finds forgiveness, gains healing, and opens her heart to love. **105m/C; DVD, Streaming, Download.** Teyonah Parris; Edwina Findley Dickerson; Brian White; Macy Gray; Kylee Russell; *D:* Leila Djansi; *W:* Leila Djansi; *C:* Pete Villani; *M:* Igor Vrabac; Ken Worth. **VIDEO**

Where Danger Lives 🦴🦴 **1950** Tough guy Mitchum plays a patsy. Young Dr. Jeff Cameron is intrigued when he treats beautiful Margo (Domergue), who attempted suicide. After Jeff gets all hot and bothered, he learns that the older man (a sneering Rains) he thought was her father, is actually her husband. During a boozy confrontation, the cuckold husband winds up dead, the doc gets a concussion, and Margo insists they have to make a run for the border. The French Domergue was a sultry, but not particularly talented, protege of Howard Hughes. **82m/B; DVD.** Robert Mitchum; Faith Domergue; Claude Rains; Maureen O'Sullivan; Charles Kemper; Billy House; Philip Van Zandt; Ralph Duke; *D:* John Farrow; *W:* Charles Bennett; *C:* Nicholas Musuraca; *M:* Roy Webb.

Where Eagles Dare 🦴🦴🦴 **1968 (PG)** During WWII, a small group of Allied commandos must rescue an American general held by the Nazis in a castle in the Bavarian Alps. Relentless plot twists and action keep you breathless. Well-made suspense/adventure. Alistair MacLean adapted his original screenplay into a successful novel. **158m/C; VHS, DVD, Blu-Ray.** *GB* Clint Eastwood; Richard Burton; Mary Ure; Michael Hordern; Anton Diffring; Ingrid Pitt; Patrick Wymark; Robert Beatty; Donald Houston; Derren Nesbitt; Ferdinand "Ferdy" Mayne; Peter Barkworth; William Squire; Neil McCarthy; Brook Williams; Vincent Ball; *D:* Brian G. Hutton; *W:* Alistair MacLean; *C:* Arthur Ibbetson; *M:* Ronald Goodwin.

Where God Left His Shoes 🦴🦴 **2007** Stabile's drama stacks the deck against his homeless boxer but, thanks to a strictly unsentimental performance by lead Leguizamo, refrains from schmaltz. Frank is a washed-up fighter who is forced into a New York homeless shelter with his family right before Christmas. He has a chance at low-income housing if Frank can quickly find a job but he's illiterate and has a criminal record that's further limiting his prospects. It's so real and awkward it can be hard to watch but worth the effort. **110m/C; DVD.** Leonor Varela; David Castro; Samantha Rose; John Leguizamo; *D:* Salvatore Stabile; *W:* Salvatore Stabile; *C:* Vanja Cernjul; *M:* Jeff Beal.

Where Have All the People Gone? 🦴 **1974** Solar explosion turns most of Earth's inhabitants to dust while the Anders family vacations in a cave. The family tries to return home amid the devastation. Bad timing, bad acting, bad script. **74m/C; VHS, DVD.** Peter Graves; Kathleen Quinlan; Michael-James Wixted; George O'Hanlon, Jr.; Verna Bloom; *D:* John Llewellyn Moxey. **TV**

Where Hearts Lie 🦴🦴 **2016** A dramatic thriller about the wide impact of poor choices. In Brooklyn, Brave Williams (Mulzac) is a real estate mogul in the making and generous to his family and community. His world is turned upside down when he meets Nikki (Sanderson), a woman who wants to latch on to his happiness and his success. Because of his relationship and marriage to Nikki, Brave stands to lose his business, his sanity, and ultimately, the safety of his child. **116m/C; DVD, Streaming, Download.** Alexander Mulzac; Erin Sanderson; Clifton Powell; Mizan Kirby; Luis Morales; *D:* Tony Lindsay; *W:* Tony Lindsay; *C:* Ambrose Eng. **VIDEO**

Where Hope Grows 🦴🦴 **1/2 2015 (PG-13)** A drama about self-discovery. Calvin (Polaha) had a promising professional baseball career that ended abruptly because he began suffering panic attacks at the plate. Now he spends much of his time drinking with friends. It is not until he meets Produce (DeSanctis), a young man with Down syndrome who is employed at a grocery store, and forms an unexpected friendship with him that Calvin truly begins to find peace within himself, put his life back in order, and bond with his own estranged teenaged daughter. **95m/C; DVD, Blu-Ray, Streaming, Download.** Kristoffer Polaha; David DeSanctis; McKaley Miller; Michael Grant; William Zabka; *D:* Chris Dowling; *W:* Chris Dowling; *C:* Alexandre Lehmann; *M:* Kyle Newmaster.

Where in the World Is Osama Bin Laden? 🦴🦴 **2006 (PG-13)** Daddy-to-be Spurlock decides he needs to make the world safer for his first child by hunting down Osama bin Laden. Not quite serious documentary, not quite comedy, although it would benefit from picking a side and sticking with it. Surprisingly he's only assaulted once, in an Orthodox Jewish neighborhood in Israel. Apparently they didn't find him amusing. **90m/C; DVD.** Morgan Spurlock; Alexandra Jamieson; *D:* Morgan Spurlock; *W:* Morgan Spurlock; Jeremy Chilnick; *C:* Daniel Marracino. **VIDEO**

Where Is Kyra? 🦴🦴 **1/2** *Deceit* **2017 (R)** A bleak drama set in working class Brooklyn. Economically challenged Kyra's (Pfeiffer) world is small. Recently divorced and unemployed, she moves back in with her elderly, ailing mother (Shepherd) to care for her while looking for a part-time job. After her mother's death, Kyra's situation grows more dire and she concocts a plan to stay afloat. Isolated from human contact, Kyra finds comfort with Doug (Sutherland), a man she meets in a dive bar. The situation grows more desperate when she involves him in her scheme for survival. Outstanding cinematography and a brava performance by Pfeiffer. **98m/C; DVD, Blu-Ray.** Michelle Pfeiffer; Kiefer Sutherland; Suzanne Shepherd; Sam Robards; Elizabeth Evans; *D:* Andrew Dosunmu; *W:* Darci Picoult; *C:* Bradford Young; *M:* Philip Miller.

Where Is My Friend's House? 🦴🦴 *Where is the Friend's Home?; Khaneh-Je Doost Kojast?* **1987** At the village school, Mohamed is told by his teacher that he'll be expelled if he doesn't do his homework in the required exercise book. But that evening schoolmate Ahmed realizes he's taken Mohamed's book by mistake so he sets off to find his friend's house in a neighboring village. However, Ahmed gets lost and none of the adults he meets will help him. Farsi with subtitles. Followed by "Life and Nothing More..." and "Through the Olive Trees." **90m/C; VHS, DVD.** *IA* Babek Ahmed Poor; Ahmed Ahmed Poor; Kheda Barech Defai; *D:* Abbas Kiarostami; *W:* Abbas Kiarostami; *C:* Farhad Saba.

Where It's At 🦴 **1/2 1969** Where it's at? Well it's not with this disjointed, generational father/son drama. A.C. Smith (Janssen) owns Caesar's Palace in Vegas and expects his Princeton-educated son Andy (Drivas) to be as shady and hard as he is. The kid's a sensitive disappointment until he uses his business acumen to wrest control of the casino away from his dad. Writer/director

Kanin is apparently well out of his comfort zone since the situations and dialogue are dull and familiar. **104m/C; Streaming.** David Janssen; Robert Drivas; Rosemary Forsyth; Brenda Vaccaro; Don Rickles; Edy Williams; *D:* Garson Kanin; *W:* Garson Kanin; *C:* Burnett Guffey; *M:* Benny Golson.

Where Love Has Gone ♪♪ 1/2 **1964** A soaper about a teenage daughter who kills her nympho mother's current boyfriend. Her divorced parents end up dragging the ordeal out in a murder trial/custody battle and a lot of family skeletons come out of their closets. Davis is the manipulative grand dame grandmother. Based on the novel by Harold Robbins. **114m/C; VHS, DVD, Blu-Ray.** Bette Davis; Susan Hayward; Joey Heatherton; Jane Greer; George Macready; *D:* Edward Dmytryk; *W:* John Michael Hayes.

Where Sleeping Dogs Lie ♪♪ **1991 (R)** A struggling writer moves into an abandoned California home five years after a wealthy family was murdered there. While doing research for his novel on their brutal killings, he revives their ghosts as well as the very real presence of their killer. **92m/C; VHS, DVD.** Dylan McDermott; Tom Sizemore; Sharon Stone; *D:* Charles Finch.

Where the Boys Are ♪♪ 1/2 **1960** Four college girls go to Fort Lauderdale to have fun and meet boys during their Easter vacation. Features the film debuts of Francis, who had a hit single with the film's title song, and Prentiss. Head and shoulders above the ludicrous '84 remake. **99m/C; VHS, DVD, Blu-Ray.** George Hamilton; Jim Hutton; Yvette Mimieux; Connie Francis; Paula Prentiss; Dolores Hart; Frank Gorshin; Barbara Nichols; Rory Harrity; Chill Wills; Jack Kruschen; *D:* Henry Levin; *W:* George Wells; *C:* Robert J. Bronner; *M:* Pete Rugolo; Georgie Stoll.

Where the Boys Are '84 WOOF! 1984 (R) Horrible remake of the 1960 comedy still features girls searching for boys during spring break in Fort Lauderdale. Telling about its era: charm gives way to prurience. **95m/C; VHS, DVD.** Lisa Hartman Black; Wendy Schaal; Lorna Luft; Lynn-Holly Johnson; Christopher McDonald; *D:* Hy Averback; *W:* Jeff Burkhart; *C:* James A. Contner; *M:* Sylvester Levay. Golden Raspberries '84: Worst Support. Actress (Johnson).

Where the Buffalo Roam ♪ 1/2 **1980 (R)** Early starring role for Murray as the legendary "gonzo" journalist Hunter S. Thompson. Meandering satire based on Thompson's books "Fear and Loathing in Las Vegas" and "Fear and Loathing on the Campaign Trail '72." Either confusing or offensively sloppy, depending on whether you've read Thompson. Music by Neil Young, thank goodness, or this might be a woof. **98m/C; VHS, DVD, Blu-Ray.** Bill Murray; Peter Boyle; Susan Kellerman; Bruno Kirby; Rene Auberjonois; R.G. Armstrong; Rafael Campos; Craig T. Nelson; Danny Goldman; Leonard Frey; *D:* Art Linson; *W:* John Kaye; *C:* Tak Fujimoto; *M:* Neil Young.

Where the Day Takes You ♪♪ 1/2 **1992 (R)** Runaways on Hollywood Boulevard are depicted in an unfortunately heavy-handed drama. King (Mulroney) is the slightly older leader of a group of street kids who tries to discourage his friends from getting involved in the violence and drugs they see all around them. He falls in love with new runaway Heather (Boyle) but their love is blighted by the relentless bleakness of their lives. Among the other members of King's "family" are Astin, as a young druggie in thrall to his older dealer (MacLachlan) and Getty, as a young hustler drawn to violence. The story's predictability undercuts some convincing acting. **105m/C; VHS, DVD, Blu-Ray.** Dermot Mulroney; Lara Flynn Boyle; Balthazar Getty; Sean Astin; James LeGros; Ricki Lake; Kyle MacLachlan; Robert Knepper; Peter Dobson; Stephen Tobolowsky; Will Smith; Adam Baldwin; Christian Slater; Nancy McKeon; Alyssa Milano; David Arquette; Leo Rossi; Rachel Ticotin; *V:* Laura San Giacomo; *D:* Marc Rocco; *W:* Michael Hitchcock; Kurt Voss; Marc Rocco; *M:* Mark Morgan.

Where the Green Ants Dream ♪♪ 1/2 *Wo Die Grunen Ameisen Traumen* **1984** A mining excavation in the Outback is halted by Aborigines who declare ownership of the sacred place where the mythical green ants are buried. A minor entry in the Herzog vision of modern-versus-primal civilization. Too obvious and somehow unsure of itself artistically. **99m/C; VHS, DVD, Blu-Ray.** *GE* Bruce Spence; Wandjuk Marika; Roy Marika; Ray Barrett; Norman Kaye; Colleen Clifford; *D:* Werner Herzog.

Where the Heart Is ♪♪ **1990 (R)** Wealthy dad Coleman kicks his spoiled kids out on the streets to teach them the value of money. Meant as farce with a message. Flops in a big way; one senses it should have been much better. **111m/C; VHS, DVD.** Dabney Coleman; Uma Thurman; Joanna Cassidy; Suzy Amis; Crispin Glover; Christopher Plummer; David Hewlett; Maury Chaykin; Dylan Walsh; Ken Pogue; Sheila Kelley; Robbie Coltrane; *D:* John Boorman; *W:* John Boorman; Telsche Boorman; *C:* Peter Suschitzky; *M:* Peter Martin. Natl. Soc. Film Critics '90: Cinematog.

Where the Heart Is ♪♪ *Home Is Where the Heart Is* **2000 (PG-13)** Pregnant 17-year-old Novalee Nation (Portman) is on her way to California with her no-good boyfriend Willy Jack (Bruno), who abandons her at an Oklahoma WalMart. Without friends or funds, Novalee hides out in the store until she gives birth there. Suddenly a local celeb, Novalee finds shelter with eccentric Sister Husband (Channing) and becomes best pals with fecund single mom, Lexi (Judd). Novalee also gets a potential romance with shy librarian Forney (Frain). Superficially one-note sap and Portman seems miscast. Based on the novel by Billie Letts. **115m/C; VHS, DVD.** Natalie Portman; Ashley Judd; Stockard Channing; James Frain; Dylan Bruno; Joan Cusack; Keith David; Richard Jones; Sally Field; *D:* Matt Williams; *W:* Lowell Ganz; Babaloo Mandel; *C:* Richard Greatrex; *M:* Mason Daring.

Where the Hot Wind Blows ♪♪ *La Legge; La Loi; The Law* **1959** Marietta (Lollobrigida) is a poor girl in a Sicilian fishing village who's in love with Enrico (Mastroianni), an equally impoverished engineer. But she comes up with a unique way to get money for her dowry even as she's pursued by every male in town. Meanwhile, local mobster Brigante (Montand) wants to make sure than his son Francisco (Mattioli) doesn't get too involved with the unsuitable Lucrezia (Mercouri). Italian with subtitles. **120m/B; VHS, DVD.** *FR IT* Gina Lollobrigida; Marcello Mastroianni; Yves Montand; Melina Mercouri; Raf Mattioli; Pierre Brasseur; Paolo Stoppa; *D:* Jules Dassin; *W:* Jules Dassin; Francoise Giroud; *C:* Otello Martelli; *M:* Roman Vlad.

Where the Money Is ♪♪ 1/2 **2000 (PG-13)** Famed bank robber Henry (Newman) fakes a stroke so he can get transferred from prison to a nursing home. Carol (Fiorentino) is the bored former prom queen nurse who knows he's faking and enlists his help in pulling one more job. She also brings along dull but devoted hubby Wayne (Mulroney). The characters, and the superb actors playing them, are the main reasons to see this one. Newman is still more charismatic than 90% of the leading men around, while Fiorentino and Mulroney seem inspired just by being on the same set with him. The lightweight script depends heavily on the audience's knowledge of Newman's filmography and the standard caper comedy conventions, but still manages to entertain. **90m/C; VHS, DVD.** Paul Newman; Linda Fiorentino; Dermot Mulroney; Susan Barnes; Bruce MacVittie; Dorothy Gordon; Anne Pitoniak; Irma St. Paule; *D:* Marek Kanievska; *W:* E. Max Frye; Topper Lilien; Carroll Cartwright; *C:* Thomas Burstyn; *M:* Mark Isham.

Where the North Begins ♪ 1/2 **1923** Rin Tin Tin and his French fur trapper master Gabriel Dupre (McGrail) come to the aid of Dupre's sweetheart Felice (Adams), who is coveted by dastardly trading post manager Shad Galloway (Hartigan). **75m/B; Silent; DVD.** Walter McGrail; Claire Adams; Pat Hartigan; Fred Huntley; *D:* Chester M. Franklin; *W:* Raymond L. Schrock.

Where the Red Fern Grows ♪♪ 1/2 **1974 (G)** A young boy in Dust Bowl-era Oklahoma learns maturity from his love and responsibility for two Redbone hounds. Well produced, but tends to be hokey; good family fare. Followed by a sequel nearly 20 years later. **97m/C; VHS, DVD.** James Whitmore; Beverly Garland; Jack Ging; Lonny (Lonnie) Chapman; Stewart Petersen; *D:* Norman Tokar; *W:* Douglas Day Stewart; Eleanor Lamb; *C:* Dean Cundey; *M:* Lex de Azevedo.

Where the Red Fern Grows: Part 2 ♪♪ 1/2 **1992 (G)** Sequel to one of the most popular family movies of all time starring Brimley as Grandpa Coleman. Set deep in the Louisiana woods, this magical coming of age tale will touch the hearts of young and old viewers alike. **105m/C; VHS, DVD.** Wilford Brimley; Doug McKeon; Lisa Whelchel; Chad McQueen; *D:* Jim McCullough, Sr.; *W:* Samuel Bradford; *C:* Joseph M. Wilcots; *M:* Robert Sprayberry.

Where the River Runs Black ♪♪ **1986 (PG)** An orphaned Indian child is raised in the Brazilian jungles by river dolphins. He is eventually befriended by a kindly priest who brings him into the modern world of violence and corruption. Slow pace is okay until the boy arrives at the orphanage, at which point the dolphin premise sadly falls by the wayside. **96m/C; VHS, DVD.** Charles Durning; Peter Horton; Ajay Naidu; Conchata Ferrell; Alessandro Rabelo; Castulo Guerra; *D:* Christopher Cain; *C:* Juan Ruiz-Anchia; *M:* James Horner.

Where the Rivers Flow North ♪♪ 1/2 **1994 (PG-13)** Vermont logger Noel Lord (Torn) has lived on the land all his life and doesn't want to sell out to the power company. His blunt-talking Indian housekeeper/lover Bangor (Cardinal) knows it's best to take the money and move on. Set in 1927 and adapted from the novella by Howard Frank Mosher. Flat storytelling with a good performance by Cardinal. **104m/C; VHS, DVD.** Rip Torn; Tantoo Cardinal; Bill Raymond; Mark Margolis; John Griesemer; Amy Wright; Dennis Mientka; Jusef Bulos; Michael J. Fox; Treat Williams; *D:* Jay Craven; *W:* Jay Craven; Don Bredes; *C:* Dr. Paul Ryan.

Where the Road Meets the Sun ♪ 1/2 **2011** Two parallel male friendships, which also deal with L.A.'s diverse immigrant culture, are tracked in Yong's drama. Having fled Japan after recovering from a coma, hitman Takashi struggles with flashbacks while depressed hotel clerk Blake (who has divorce issues) lends some sympathy. Brit Guy has an expired visa and is getting by on his charm as is illegal Mexican busboy Julio who is trying to get more money to help his family. **93m/C; DVD.** Will Yun Lee; Eric Mabius; Fernando Noriega; Luke Brandon Field; Elsa Pataky; Emmanuelle Vaugier; *D:* Mun Chee Yong; *W:* Mun Chee Yong; *C:* Gavin Kelly; *M:* Patrick Kirst.

Where the Sidewalk Ends ♪♪ 1/2 **1950** Preminger and Hecht are credited with developing the character of the rogue cop/detective who uses violence to get justice. The son of a career criminal, detective Mark Dixon (Andrews) is over-zealous in his pursuit of bad guys. He accidentally beats to death gambler/murder suspect Ken Paine (Stevens) while trying to put away mob boss Tommy Scalise (Merrill). Dixon attempts to make the death look like a mob hit but innocent cabbie Taylor (Tully) becomes the prime suspect because his daughter Morgan (Tierney) was married to the louse. Dixon falls for the widow and tries to clear her pop while still wanting to nail Scalise. **94m/B; DVD, Blu-Ray.** Dana Andrews; Gene Tierney; Gary Merrill; Bert Freed; Tom Tully; Karl Malden; Craig Stevens; Ruth Donnelly; Robert F. Simon; *D:* Otto Preminger; *W:* Ben Hecht; *C:* Joseph LaShelle; *M:* Cyril Mockridge.

Where the Spies Are ♪♪ 1/2 **1965** Generally amusing spy spoof stars suave Niven as country physician Jason Love, who gets recruited by a former WWII intelligence colleague for an assignment where the cover is a medical convention in Beirut. Love learns the spy game as he goes along when he must prevent the assassination of a Middle Eastern prince by the Russians. Pretty Dorleac is decorative as Love's French contact. Based on the James Leasor novel "Passport to Oblivion." **112m/C; DVD.** *UK* David Niven; Francoise Dorleac; Cyril Cusack; John Le Mesurier; Noel Harrison; Nigel Davenport; Eric Pohlmann; *D:* Val Guest; *W:* Val Guest; Wolf Mankowitz; *C:* Arthur Grant; *M:* Mario Nascimbene.

Where the Truth Lies ♪♪ 1/2 **1999** Dana Sue Lacey (Matlin) is the deaf campaign manager for a candidate who has just been murdered. When she becomes the prime suspect and goes to trial, attorney Lillian Rose Martin (King) has her work cut out for her since Dana refuses to cooperate. But the past and its secrets cannot stay hidden any longer. **92m/C; VHS, DVD.** Marlee Matlin; Regina King; Philip Lester; Robert Blanche; Linden Ashby; Brian McNamara; Susan Walters; *D:* Nelson McCormick; *W:* Marshall Goldberg; *C:* Bill Roe; *M:* Peter Manning Robinson. **CABLE**

Where the Truth Lies ♪♪ **2005** Lanny (Bacon) and Vince (Firth) were a successful '50s showbiz duo (think Martin & Lewis) whose act broke up in 1957 over a sensational scandal involving a dead blonde (Blanchard) in a bathtub. Fifteen years later, ambitious and nubile blonde journalist Karen (a miscast Lohman) is trying to write Vince's bio and wants to know what really happened. Except truth is a subjective idea at best and the men still prefer their secrets to remain that way. A menage a trois scene upset the MPAA so director Egoyan released his voyeuristic noir drama unrated. Adapted from the novel by Rupert Holmes. **107m/C; DVD, Blu-Ray.** *US CA GB* Kevin Bacon; Colin Firth; Alison Lohman; Rachel Blanchard; David Hayman; Maury Chaykin; Kristin Adams; Sonja Bennett; Deborah Grover; Beau Starr; *D:* Atom Egoyan; *W:* Atom Egoyan; *C:* Paul Sarossy; *M:* Mychael Danna.

Where the Wild Things Are ♪♪ **2009 (PG)** You have to wonder who writer/director Jonze's audience is truly meant to be since the pic's anarchic sophistication seems geared to adults who grew up with Maurice Sendak's 1963 picture book, although children will see the appeal of Max's own wild behavior and facing their fears. Having tested his frazzled single mom's (Keener) patience once too often, tantrum-throwing Max (newcomer Records) is sent to his room. Instead, wearing his white wolf costume, Max runs outside, boards a boat, and makes his way to the island where the Wild Things (who now have names and distinctive personalities) live. They crown Max their ruler but there are lots of parallels to the world—and troubles—Max left behind. The Wild Things, as created by Jim Henson's Creature Shop, are particularly amazing. **101m/C; DVD, Blu-Ray.** Catherine Keener; Max Records; Mark Ruffalo; Pepita Emmerichs; *V:* Forest Whitaker; James Gandolfini; Paul Dano; Catherine O'Hara; Lauren Ambrose; Chris Cooper; *D:* Spike Jonze; *W:* Spike Jonze; Dave Eggers; *C:* Lance Acord; *M:* Carter Burwell; Karen O (Orzolek).

Where There's a Will ♪ 1/2 **1955** Mild comedy about a Cockney family that inherits a rundown Devon farm. Alfie (Dwyer), aided by housekeeper Annie (Harrison), is determined to rebuild and make a go of the property despite the reluctance of the rest of his family who want to return to London. **79m/B; DVD.** *GB* Leslie Dwyer; Kathleen Harrison; George Cole; Thelma Ruby; Ann Hanslip; Dandy Nichols; *D:* Vernon Sewell; *W:* Vernon Sewell; R.F. Delderfield; *C:* Basil Emmott; *M:* Robert Sharples.

Where There's Life ♪♪ 1/2 **1947** Wisecracking Hope is a New York DJ about to be married to Marshe when he discovers he's the heir to the kingdom of Borovia (whose last king was assassinated). Hasso works her feminine wiles as the general who's guarding Hope when the assassins come after him. Oh, and Marshe and her cop brother Bendix are tracking him down to go through with the wedding ceremony. Frantic antics. **75m/B; VHS, DVD.** Bob Hope; Signe Hasso; William Bendix; Vera Marshe; George Coulouris; George Zucco; Dennis Hoey; John Alexander; *D:* Sidney Lanfield; *W:* Melville Shavelson; Allen Boretz.

Where Time Began ♪♪ **1977 (G)** The discovery of a strange manuscript of a scientist's journey to the center of the earth leads to the decision to re-create the dangerous mission. Based on Jules Verne's classic novel "Journey to the Center of the Earth," but not anywhere near as fun or stirring. **87m/C; VHS, DVD.** Kenneth More; Pep Munne; Jack Taylor; *D:* J(uan) Piquer Simon.

Where to Invade Next ♪ 1/2 **2015 (R)** Michael Moore reaches his most smug apex with a travelogue documentary, in which he goes to various countries with the express purpose of "invading" them to take something they do better than the United States and bring it home with him. So, for example, in Italy, he learns how important better vacation time and maternity leaves helps society. In France, he talks to kids about their school lunches, which never include fried food. Race, gender imbalance, history denial and more are included, but Moore can't keep himself out of the conversation, and most of the insights feel superficial at best. **110m/C; DVD, Blu-Ray.** Michael Moore; *D:* Michael Moore; *C:* Rick Rowley; Jayme Roy.

Where Truth Lies 🦴🦴 **1996 (R)** After a severe breakdown, troubled psychiatrist Ian Lazarre (Savage) is sent to a clinic run by the sinister Dr. Renquist (McDowell). Lazarre's given an experimental drug that causes him to have visions of executed serial killer Jonas Keller (Forrest) and also to develop ESP. The plot doesn't make much sense in any case. **92m/C; VHS, DVD.** John Savage; Kim Cattrall; Malcolm McDowell; Sam Jones; Eric Pierpoint; Candice Daly; Dennis Forrest; *D:* William H. Molina; *W:* Ted Perkins; *C:* William H. Molina; *M:* David Wurst; Eric Wurst.

Where'd You Go, Bernadette 🦴🦴 **2019 (PG-13)** Early in her career, Bernadette Fox (Blanchett) was an ambitious architect with a bright future. After suffering a major professional setback and becoming a mother, she ends up a recluse in the Seattle mansion she shares with husband Elgie (Crudup) and their now-teen daughter Bee (Nelson). When Bee wants to take a family trip to Antarctica, Bernadette panics and must face personal problems that compel her to take a journey of self-discovery without telling her family where she has gone. Blanchett is the only saving grace for Linklater's weak adaptation of the 2012 Maria Semple novel. **104m/C; DVD.** Cate Blanchett; Kristen Wiig; Judy Greer; Billy Crudup; Emma Nelson; *D:* Richard Linklater; *W:* Richard Linklater; Holly Gent; Vincent Palmo; *C:* Shane F. Kelly; *M:* Samuel Lipman; Graham Reynolds.

Where's Marlowe? 🦴🦴 **1998 (R)** Sendup of both indie filming and the private eye genre in a b&w and color combo. NYU film school grads Crawley (Def) and Edison (Livingston) decide to make a documentary about private investigators and choose nearly bankrupt L.A. detectives Boone (Ferrer) and Murphy (Slattery) as their subjects. The dicks latest case seems to involve a wife, a mistress, and, soon, Murphy's demise and the two film students decide to lend a more active hand in solving the case. **99m/C; VHS, DVD.** Miguel Ferrer; John Slattery; John Livingston; Mos Def; Allison Dean; Clayton Rohner; Barbara Howard; Elizabeth Schofield; *D:* Daniel Pyne; *W:* Daniel Pyne; John Mankiewicz; *C:* Greg Gardiner; *M:* Michael Convertino.

Where's Poppa? 🦴🦴🦴 *Going Ape* **1970** A Jewish lawyer's senile mother constantly ruins his love life, and he considers various means of getting rid of her, including dressing up as an ape to scare her to death. Filled with outlandish and often tasteless humor, befitting its reign as a black comedy cult classic. Adapted by Robert Klane from his novel. **84m/C; VHS, DVD, Blu-Ray.** George Segal; Ruth Gordon; Trish Van Devere; Ron Leibman; Rae Allen; Vincent Gardenia; Barnard Hughes; Paul Sorvino; Rob Reiner; Garrett Morris; *D:* Carl Reiner; *W:* Robert Klane; *C:* Jack Priestley; *M:* Jack Elliott.

Where's Willie? 🦴🦴 **1977 (G)** Willie is a very bright boy; perhaps a little too bright. When he reveals his latest invention to the folks in his small town, everyone is out to get him. **91m/C; VHS, DVD.** Guy Madison; Henry Darrow; Kate Woodville; Marc Gilpin; *D:* John Florea.

Which Way Home 🦴🦴 **2009** Director Cammisa follows several children and teens who travel from their homes (in Honduras, Guatemala, and Mexico) aboard a freight train used by migrant workers to make their way close to the U.S./Mexico border in an effort to make an illegal crossing into the United States. No violence is shown on camera but the children, some of whom are interviewed at shelters and detention centers after being apprehended by authorities, talk of being robbed, beaten, and witnessing crimes. Spanish with subtitles. **90m/C; DVD.** *D:* Rebecca Cammisa; *C:* Rebecca Cammisa; Lorenzo Hagerman; Eric Goethals; *M:* James Lavino.

Which Way Is Up? 🦴🦴 **1/2 1977 (R)** Pryor plays three roles in this story of an orange picker who accidentally becomes a union hero. He leaves his wife and family at home while he seeks work in Los Angeles. There he finds himself a new woman, starts a new family, and sells out to the capitalists. American version of the Italian comedy "The Seduction of Mimi" tries with mixed success for laughs. Pryor as a dirty old man is the high point. **94m/C; VHS, DVD.** Richard Pryor; Lonette McKee; Margaret Avery; Morgan Woodward; Marilyn Coleman; *D:* Michael A. Schultz; *W:* Carl Gottlieb; *C:* John A. Alonzo.

Which Way to the Front? 🦴 **1/2 1970 (G)** Assorted Army rejects form a guerilla band and wage their own small-scale war during WWII. **96m/C; VHS, DVD.** Jerry Lewis; Jan Murray; George L. Baxt; Steve Franken; *D:* Jerry Lewis; *W:* Dee Caruso.

Whiffs 🦴 **1975 (PG)** A gullible man plays guinea pig in an Army experiment on germ warfare which leaves him with the intellect of a chimpanzee. Naturally, he then devises a plan to use the volatile gas in a chain of bank robberies. The title is appropriate—this movie is a stinker. **91m/C; DVD.** Elliott Gould; Eddie Albert; Harry Guardino; Godfrey Cambridge; Jennifer O'Neill; Alan Manson; *D:* Ted Post; *W:* Malcolm Marmorstein; *C:* David M. Walsh; *M:* John Cameron.

While She Was Out 🦴 **2008 (R)** Dopey woman-in-jeopardy flick. Abused wife Della (Basinger) heads to the mall on Christmas Eve and attracts the unwanted attention of four teen sociopaths. She finds herself running to a deserted construction site with a toolbox and a desire to kick some male tail. **88m/C; DVD.** Kim Basinger; Lukas Haas; Craig Sheffer; Jamie Starr; Leonard Wu; Luis Chavez; *D:* Susan Montford; *W:* Susan Montford; *C:* Steve Gainer; *M:* Paul Haslinger.

While the City Sleeps 🦴🦴🦴 **1956** Three newspaper reporters vie to crack the case of a sex murderer known as "The Lipstick Killer" with the editorship of their paper the prize. Good thriller with the emphasis on the reporters' ruthless methods of gaining information rather than on the killer's motivations. Lang's last big success. Based on "The Bloody Spur" by Charles Einstein. **100m/B; VHS, DVD, Blu-Ray.** Dana Andrews; Rhonda Fleming; George Sanders; Howard Duff; Thomas Mitchell; Ida Lupino; Vincent Price; Mae Marsh; *D:* Fritz Lang; *C:* Ernest Laszlo.

While We're Young 🦴🦴 **1/2 2014 (R)** Filmmaker Josh (Stiller) and his wife Cornelia (Watts) are feeling the burn of middle age when they become creatively inspired by young couple Jamie (Driver) and Darby (Seyfried). Jamie is a filmmaker who looks up to Josh, while Josh needs a bit of youthful energy in his life. Of course, the story eventually shows the differences between the two men. While writer/director Baumbach takes a few easy shots at hipsters, one of his best casts assembled (Stiller in particular) makes for an enjoyable comedy nonetheless. **94m/C; DVD, Blu-Ray.** Naomi Watts; Ben Stiller; Adam Driver; Amanda Seyfried; Maria Dizzia; Adam Horovitz; *D:* Noah Baumbach; *W:* Noah Baumbach; *C:* Sam Levy; *M:* James Murphy.

While You Were Sleeping 🦴🦴🦴 **1995 (PG)** Feel-good romantic comedy finds lonely Lucy Moderatz (Bullock) collecting tokens for the Chicago train system and admiring Yuppie lawyer Peter Callaghan (Gallagher) as he commutes to and fro. Fate conspires to throw them together when Lucy rescues Peter after a mugging. Trouble is, he's not conscious so Lucy goes to the hospital with him, where she's mistaken for his fiancee. She continues the charade and is warmly welcomed by the Callaghan family, with the exception of Peter's brother, Jack (Pullman), who smells a rat even as he falls under the token collector's spell. Meanwhile, Peter remains in a coma, allowing Jack and Lucy to supply romantic comedy. Gallagher brings a serenity to his role as the unconscious Peter, while Bullock and Pullman take the predictable plot and deliver performances that earn them another notch on the climb to stardom. **103m/C; VHS, DVD.** Sandra Bullock; Bill Pullman; Peter Gallagher; Jack Warden; Peter Boyle; Glynis Johns; Micole Mercurio; Jason Bernard; Michael Rispoli; Ally Walker; Monica Keena; *D:* Jon Turteltaub; *W:* Fred Lebow; Daniel G. Sullivan; *C:* Phedon Papamichael; *M:* Randy Edelman. Blockbuster '96: Comedy Actress, T. (Bullock), Comedy Actress, V. (Bullock).

The Whip and the Body 🦴🦴 **1/2** *Night Is the Phantom; What* **1963** Mario Bava's 19th-century ghost/love/revenge story makes a belated arrival on home video. Nevena (Lavi) is about to be married when her ex-lover Kurt (Lee), soon to be her brother-in-law, shows up. The rest of the action is almost pure Gothic with a moody castle for setting, secret passages, ladies wandering the hallways late at night in their diaphanous gowns. Though the story doesn't quite live up to the title, it is very sexually charged for its time and Lee turns in an aggressive performance. **88m/C; DVD, Blu-Ray.** *IT* Christopher Lee; Daliah Lavi; Tony Kendall; Harriet Medin; Isli Oberon; *D:* Mario Bava; *W:* Ernesto Gastaldi; Ugo Guerra; Luciano Martino; *C:* Ubaldo Terzano; *M:* Carlo Rustichelli.

Whip It 🦴🦴🦴 **2009 (PG-13)** Desperate to break from the clutches of her controlling mom (Harden) and her small-town Texas beauty pageant life, misfit teen Bliss (Page) is drawn to all-girls roller derby. After secretly joining the Hurl Scouts team in nearby Austin, she quickly becomes a crowd favorite as Babe Ruthless. Adapted by Cross from her 2007 novel "Derby Girl," this coming-of-age story is dipped in the delicious roller derby culture where girls rule. And not only did Barrymore craft an engaging female-power action comedy for her directorial debut, but she also dons some skates as tough chick Smashley Simpson—a particular treat is seeing her and Page do much of their own skating. **111m/C; DVD, Blu-Ray.** Ellen Page; Kristen Wiig; Juliette Lewis; Eve; Zoe Bell; Alia Shawkat; Ari Graynor; Sydney Bennett; Marcia Gay Harden; Daniel Stern; Jimmy Fallon; Drew Barrymore; *D:* Drew Barrymore; *W:* Shauna Cross; *C:* Robert Yeoman; *M:* The Section Quartet.

Whiplash 🦴🦴 **1948** Routine boxing/romance. California artist/boxer Michael (Clark) falls for vacationing Laurie (Smith) and follows her back to New York where he learns she's married and sings in the nightclub run by her husband Rex (Scott). Rex had to retire from the ring after a crippling accident left him in a wheelchair and he decides to train Michael to fulfill his own lost dreams. That is, until he learns about Michael and Laurie's affair and his jealousy turns vicious. **91m/B; DVD.** Dane Clark; Alexis Smith; Zachary Scott; Eve Arden; Jeffrey Lynn; S.Z. Sakall; Alan Hale; Douglas Kennedy; *D:* Lewis Seiler; *W:* Gordon Kahn; Maurice Geraghty; Harriet Frank, Jr.; *C:* J. Peverell Marley; *M:* Franz Waxman.

Whiplash 🦴🦴🦴 **2014 (R)** One of the best films of 2014, and the winner of both the Grand Jury and Audience Awards at Sundance. Teller stars as Andrew Neyman, a drum student at the most prestigious music school in New York City. After the school's most notorious jazz band instructor, Mr. Fletcher (a frighteningly compelling Simmons), takes an interest in Andrew, a battle of wills unfolds. Andrew knows he has talent but Fletcher believes there are no more dangerous words in the English language than "good job," and that only pressure turns coal into a diamond. It's a thrilling drama from first frame to last. **106m/C; DVD, Blu-Ray.** Miles Teller; J.K. Simmons; Paul Reiser; Melissa Benoist; Austin Stowell; *D:* Damien Chazelle; *W:* Damien Chazelle; *C:* Sharone Meir; *M:* Justin Hurwitz. Oscars '14: Actor--Supporting (Simmons), Film Editing, Sound; British Acad. '14: Actor--Supporting (Simmons), Film Editing, Sound; Golden Globes '15: Actor--Supporting (Simmons); Ind. Spirit '15: Actor--Supporting (Simmons); Screen Actors Guild '14: Actor--Supporting (Simmons).

Whipped 🦴 **2000 (R)** It's probably aiming for sophisticated, adult romantic comedy but all it achieves is smut. Sexpot Mia (Peet) is forced to deal with the arrested development of three Manhattan yuppies (Van Holt, Domke, Abrahams) who have prehistoric attitudes towards women. They all discover they are dating her but none wants to give Mia up and they become rivals for her questionable affections. Very unlikeable characters; very unpleasant. **82m/C; VHS, DVD.** Amanda Peet; Brian Van Holt; Judah Domke; Zorie Barber; Jonathan Abrahams; Callie (Calliope) Thorne; *D:* Peter M. Cohen; *W:* Peter M. Cohen; *C:* Peter B. Kowalsk; *M:* Michael Montes.

Whipsaw 🦴🦴 **1/2 1935** Vivian (Loy), Ed (Stephens), and Harry (Clement) are jewel thieves who make their way from Paris to New York with stolen pearls. Vivian meets Ross (Tracy), who's trying to pass himself off as a crook but Vivian soon figures out he's a G-man. Still, he comes in handy when Vivian skips out on her partners—only to be followed cross-country by a rival gang after the goods. Loy is lovely and Tracy does right by her as the hero who falls for the shady dame. **88m/B; DVD.** Myrna Loy; Spencer Tracy; Harvey Stephens; Clay Clement; William Harrigan; Robert Gleckler; Robert Warwick; *D:* Sam Wood; *W:* Howard Emmett Rogers; *C:* James Wong Howe; *M:* William Axt.

Whirlpool 🦴🦴 **1/2 1934** Thinking her husband has died in prison, Helen Rankin (Lee) remarries and their daughter Sandra (Arthur) grows up to be a reporter. Actually Buck (Holt) didn't want Helen waiting around and, after he gets out of the joint, he changes his name and opens a hot nightclub that Sandra frequents. She recognizes Buck from an old photo but the father/daughter reunion is complicated by his underworld connections, Helen's (unwitting) bigamy, and the fact that Sandra's stepdad is a judge. **73m/B; DVD.** Jack Holt; Jean Arthur; Donald Cook; Lila Lee; Willard Robertson; John Miljan; Ward Bond; Allen Jenkins; *D:* Roy William Neill; *W:* Dorothy Howell; Ethel Hill; *C:* Benjamin (Ben H.) Kline.

Whirlpool 🦴🦴 **1949** Ann Sutton (Tierney) has managed to keep her kleptomania from her L.A. shrink husband William (Conte). When she gets caught shoplifting, sinister hypnotist David Korvo (Ferrer) comes to her rescue and takes her on as a patient. However, he's setting Ann up to take the fall for the murder of his mistress (O'Neill), whom William happened to be treating. With Ann a suspect, William teams up with detective Colton (Bickford) and uses hypnosis to turn the tables on Korvo. Screenwriter Hecht was on the blacklist so he used the pseudonym Lester Barstow for Preminger's paint-by-numbers noir. **97m/B; DVD, Blu-Ray.** Gene Tierney; Richard Conte; Jose Ferrer; Charles Bickford; Barbara O'Neil; Eduard Franz; Constance Collier; *D:* Otto Preminger; *W:* Ben Hecht; Andrew Solt; *C:* Arthur C. Miller; *M:* David Raskin.

Whirlygirl 🦴🦴 **2004 (R)** Naive prep school student James (Morris) follows an exotic dancer known as Whirlygirl (Mazur) to New York, ditching school to learn about life. Based on a true story. **95m/C; DVD.** Monet Mazur; Julian Morris; Fran Kranz; Daniel Franzee; *D:* Jim Wilson; *W:* Pete McCormack; *C:* Christo Bakalov; *M:* Deborah Lurie. **VIDEO**

Whiskey Galore 🦴🦴🦴 **1/2** *Tight Little Island* **1948** During WWII, a whiskey-less Scottish island gets a lift when a ship, carrying 50,000 cases of spirits, wrecks off the coast. A full-scale rescue operation and the evasion of both local and British government authorities ensue. The classic Ealing studio comedy is based on the actual wreck of a cargo ship off the Isle of Eriskay in 1941. **81m/B; VHS, DVD.** *GB* Basil Radford; Joan Greenwood; Gordon Jackson; James Robertson Justice; *D:* Alexander MacKendrick.

Whiskey Tango Foxtrot 🦴🦴 **2016 (R)** Fey tries to stretch her range with this dramedy based on the memoir by Kim Barker, "The Taliban Shuffle: Strange Days in Afghanistan and Pakistan." One of the first female journalists to report on the Middle East, Barker probably has an interesting story to tell. This isn't it. Fey's delivery is bland and, more importantly, Carlock's screenplay can't figure out its intention. Not funny enough to be a comedy but not dramatic enough for a drama. It's got a so-that-happened approach to a unique chapter in journalistic history. Fey and Barker deserved better. **112m/C; DVD, Blu-Ray, Streaming.** Tina Fey; Margot Robbie; Martin Freeman; Alfred Molina; Billy Bob Thornton; Christopher Abbott; *D:* Glenn Ficarra; John Requa; *W:* Robert Carlock; *C:* Xavier Perez Grobet; *M:* Nick Urata.

Whisper 🦴 **1/2 2007 (R)** Kidnappers (Holloway, Callies, Edgerton, Rooker) abduct the 10-year-old adoptive son (Woodruff) of a wealthy socialite only to find out that the boy is one of those demon spawn kiddies with his own agenda. Woodruff is a lot scarier than the kid they got for "The Omen" remake so this routine horror show has something going for it. **95m/C; DVD.** Josh Holloway; Sarah Wayne Callies; Blake Woodruff; Joel Edgerton; Michael Rooker; Dulé Hill; Teryl Rothery; *D:* Stewart Hendler; *W:* Christopher Borrelli; *C:* Dean Cundey; *M:* Jeff Rona. **VIDEO**

Whisper 2: L'Aventure Continue ♂♂ *Ostwind 2* **2016** The follow-up to Ostwind finds Mika (Binke) returning to her grandmother's for summer vacation. Happy to see her horse Ostwind again, she is concerned about wounds she finds on him. Mika is also distressed by her grandmother's facility, Kaltenbach, going bankrupt. She decides to enter a tournament to win prize money and help her grandmother. However, Ostwind does not perform well during training. When the stallion runs into the forest on day, she finds that he connects with a gray mare. Its owner appears and offers his help to Mika in winning the tournament. German with subtitles. **103m/C; DVD.** Hanna Binke; Jannis Niewohner; Marvin Linke; Amber Bongard; Cornelia Froboess; *D:* Katja von Garnier; *W:* Lea Schmidbauer; *C:* Torsten Breuer; *M:* Annette Focks. **VIDEO**

The Whisperers ♂♂ **1966** Dank British drama set in a dank, dreary Manchester flat. Addled old-age pensioner Maggie Ross is certain that voices are whispering to her. Her son Charlie is a thief and hides money from his latest heist in Maggie's closet but when she finds it, Maggie is certain that it's some kind of long-lost inheritance. She makes the mistake of telling her greedy neighbor Mrs. Noonan and suffers the consequences. **105m/B; DVD, Blu-Ray.** *GB* Edith Evans; Eric Portman; Ronald Fraser; Avis Bunnage; Gerald Sim; *D:* Bryan Forbes; *W:* Bryan Forbes; *C:* Gerry Turpin; *M:* John Barry.

Whispering City ♂♂♂ **1947** A female reporter receives an inside tip incriminating a prominent attorney in a murder committed several years earlier. She tries to get the evidence she needs before she becomes his latest victim. Highly suspenseful, thanks to competent scripting and directing. **89m/B; VHS, DVD.** *CA* Helmut Dantine; Mary Anderson; Paul Lukas; *D:* Fedor Ozep.

Whispering Ghosts ♂ ½ **1942** H. H. Van Buren (Milton Berle) plays a detective on a radio show and for whatever unguessable reason decides he can do it for real too, attempting to solve a murder that's several years old. **75m/B; DVD.** Milton Berle; Brenda Joyce; John Shelton; John Carradine; Willie Best; *D:* Alfred Werker; *W:* Lou Breslow; Philip MacDonald; *C:* Lucien Ballard; *M:* Leigh Harline; Emil Newman; David Buttolph; Cyril Mockridge. **VIDEO**

Whispering Shadow ♂♂ **1933** Serial starring the master criminal known as the "faceless whisperer." Twelve chapters, 13 minutes each. **156m/B; VHS, DVD, Blu-Ray.** Bela Lugosi; Robert Warwick; *D:* Al(bert) Herman; Colbert Clark.

Whispering Smith ♂♂♂ **1948** Ladd's first film in color and his first starring role in a western. Smith (Ladd) is a soft-spoken but tough railroad detective after a gang of train robbers. This puts him in contact with childhood friend Murray Sinclair (Preston), a railroad employee suspiciously involved with crooked rancher Barney Rebstock (Crisp). After another series of train derailments and thefts, Smith is reluctantly forced to confront Sinclair about his part in the crimes. Based on the Frank Spearman novel and previously filmed as a William S. Hart silent western. **88m/C; DVD.** Alan Ladd; Robert Preston; Brenda Marshall; Donald Crisp; Frank Faylen; William Demarest; John Eldredge; Will Wright; J. Farrell MacDonald; Fay Holden; *D:* Leslie Fenton; *W:* Frank Butler; Karl Kamb; *C:* Ray Rennahan; *M:* Adolph Deutsch.

Whispers ♂♂ **1989 (R)** Psycho Le Clerc repeatedly bothers writer Tennant even though she seems to have killed him. This dismays police guy Sarandon. Based on the novel by Dean R. Koontz. **96m/C; VHS, DVD.** Victoria Tennant; Chris Sarandon; Jean LeClerc; *D:* Douglas Jackson; *W:* Anita Doohan; Don Carmody.

Whispers: An Elephant's Tale ♂♂ ½ **2000 (G)** Odd anthropomorphic film made up entirely of nature footage is similar in some respects to "The Adventures of Milo & Otis." As with that film, here we have animals photographed in the wilds of Africa, with various actors supplying voices for the animals. The film opens with the birth of Whispers (Derryberry), an elephant. While his herd is roaming, he gets lost and can't find his mother Gentle Heart (Archer). Wandering through the bush, he meets another elephant named Groove (Bassett). Groove isn't very fond of Whispers at first, but she ultimately decides to help him find his mom. Along the way, they meet a variety of interesting animals and encounter some evil poachers. An entertaining film, but it also feels very artificial. The end result is a film with some amazing photography, but a story which comes across as hollow. **72m/C; DVD.** *V:* Debi Derryberry; Anne Archer; Angela Bassett; Joanna Lumley; Kevin M. Richardson; Alice Ghostley; Betty White; Kathryn Cressida; Joan Rivers; *D:* Dereck Joubert; *W:* Dereck Joubert; Jordan Moffet; Holly Goldberg Sloan; *C:* Dereck Joubert; *M:* Trevor Rabin.

Whispers and Lies ♂ ½ **2008** Jill (Hart) accompanies her cousin Patti (Milligan) on a vacation to an island off the Oregon coast so Patti can meet a man she only knows through an online dating service. Patti soon disappears and when Jill starts searching she uncovers the island's strange secret—no one has died there in centuries. **90m/C; DVD.** Melissa Joan Hart; Deanna Milligan; Susan Hogan; G. Patrick Currie; Damon Runyan; Stefan Arngrim; *D:* Penelope Buitenhuis; *W:* John Murlowski; *C:* Adam Sliwinski; *M:* Michael Neilsen. **CABLE**

Whispers in the Dark ♂♂ **1992 (R)** A psychiatrist counsels two odd patients—one is an ex-con turned painter with a violent streak, the other is a woman who reveals her kinky sexual experiences with a mystery man. Things get interesting when the doctor finds out her new lover is her patient's mystery man, and the patient turns up murdered. Confusing thriller seems forced but the experienced cast is worth watching. **103m/C; VHS, DVD.** Annabella Sciorra; Jamey Sheridan; Anthony LaPaglia; Jill Clayburgh; John Leguizamo; Deborah Kara Unger; Alan Alda; Anthony Heald; *D:* Christopher Crowe; *W:* Christopher Crowe; *C:* Michael Chapman; *M:* Thomas Newman.

The Whistle Blower ♂♂♂ **1987** A young government worker in England with a high-security position mysteriously dies. His father, a former intelligence agent, begins investigating his son's death and discovers sinister Soviet-related conspiracies. A lucid, complex British espionage thriller. Adapted from the John Hale novel by Julian Bond. **98m/C; VHS, DVD.** *GB* Michael Caine; Nigel Havers; John Gielgud; James Fox; Felicity Dean; Gordon Jackson; Barry Foster; David Langton; *D:* Simon Langton; *W:* Julian Bond; *C:* Fred Tammes; *M:* John Scott.

Whistle Stop ♂♂ **1946** A small-town girl divides her attentions between low-life gambler Raft, and villainous nightclub owner McLaglen, who plans a robbery-murder to get rid of any rivals. A forgettable gangster drama. **85m/B; VHS, DVD.** George Raft; Ava Gardner; Victor McLaglen; *D:* Leonide Moguy; *W:* Philip Yordan.

The Whistleblower ♂♂♂ **2011 (R)** Weisz stars as former heartland police officer, Kathryn Bolkovac, who uncovers an underage sex-trafficking scandal in postwar Bosnia in this harrowing true story while serving on an U.N. peacekeeping force. When she brings the story to light, though, the powers-that-be initiate a massive cover-up that puts not only her job but her life in jeopardy. Despite a melodramatic and cliched screenplay, Weisz gives a stellar performance along with solid support from Strathairn and Redgrave. **112m/C; DVD, Blu-Ray.** *CA GE* Rachel Weisz; Vanessa Redgrave; David Strathairn; Monica Bellucci; Benedict Cumberbatch; David Hewlett; Liam Cunningham; *D:* Larysa Kondracki; *W:* Larysa Kondracki; Ellis Kirwan; *C:* Kieran McGuigan; *M:* Mychael Danna.

Whistling in Brooklyn ♂♂ ½ **1943** Skelton again plays radio crime-solver Wally Benton in this third and last entry following "Whistling in the Dark" and "Whistling in Dixie." A cop-killer and the Brooklyn Dodgers baseball team figure in the mystery, which finds Skelton a suspect in the crimes. **87m/B; VHS, DVD.** Red Skelton; Ann Rutherford; Jean Rogers; Rags Ragland; Ray Collins; Henry O'Neill; William Frawley; Sam Levene; *D:* S. Sylvan Simon; *W:* Wilkie Mahoney; Nat Perrin; *C:* Lester White; *M:* George Bassman.

Whistling in Dixie ♂♂ ½ **1942** The second appearance of Skelton as radio sleuth Wally "The Fox" Benton (following "Whistling in the Dark") finds him traveling to Georgia with girlfriend Carol (Rutherford). She's worried about an ex-sorority sister who knows the secret of a hidden Civil War treasure. When Wally gets involved, humorous trouble follows. Followed by "Whistling in Brooklyn." **73m/B; VHS, DVD.** Red Skelton; Ann Rutherford; George Bancroft; Guy Kibbee; Diana Lewis; Peter Whitney; Rags Ragland; *D:* S. Sylvan Simon; *W:* Nat Perrin; Wilkie Mahoney; *C:* Clyde De Vinna.

Whistling in the Dark ♂♂♂ **1941** Skelton plays Wally Benton, a radio sleuth nicknamed "The Fox," in the first of a three-film series. Veidt (an always excellent villain) is the leader of a phony religious cult, after the money of one of his followers. He decides to kidnap Skelton and have him come up with a plan for the perfect murder but of course there are all sorts of comic complications. Skelton's first starring role is a clever comic mystery and a remake of the 1933 film. Followed by "Whistling in Dixie" and "Whistling in Brooklyn." **78m/B; VHS, DVD.** Red Skelton; Ann Rutherford; Conrad Veidt; Virginia Grey; Rags Ragland; Eve Arden; Donald "Don" Douglas; Don Costello; Paul Stanton; William Tannen; Reed Hadley; *D:* S. Sylvan Simon; *W:* Harry Clork; Albert Mannheimer; Robert MacGunigle; *C:* Sidney Wagner.

The White Angel ♂♂ *L'Angelo Bianco* **1955** Sequel to 1952's "Nobody's Children." Luisa became a nun after her separation from her lover Guido and the alleged death of their son. Guido marries but suffers another family tragedy and finds his only solace when he meets Luisa's double—gold-digging nightclub floozy Lina. Italian with subtitles. **100m/B; DVD.** *IT* Amedeo Nazzari; Yvonee Sanson; Alberto Farnese; Phillipe Hersent; Flora Lillo; *D:* Raffaello Matarazzo; *W:* Raffaello Matarazzo; Aldo De Benedetti; *C:* Tonino Delli Colli; *M:* Ottavio Scotti.

The White Balloon ♂♂♂ ½ *Badkonake Sefid* **1995** Beautifully told story from the viewpoint of determined seven-year-old Teheranian Razieh (Mohammadkhani), who wants to properly celebrate the Islamic New Year by buying a particularly plump goldfish (a symbol of harmony) from the pet shop. She manages to beg the money from her mother and sets off but, distracted by the street sights, Reziah loses the banknote, which falls into a street grate. Various characters seek to help her out but it's Reziah's resourceful brother Ali (Kafili) who gets a balloon seller to finally retrieve the money. Farsi with subtitles. **85m/C; VHS, DVD.** *IA* Aida Mohammadkhani; Mohsen Kafili; Fereshteh Sadr Orfani; Anna Bourkowska; Mohammad Shahani; Mohammad Bahktiari; *D:* Jafar Panahi; *W:* Abbas Kiarostami; *C:* Farzad Jowdat. N.Y. Film Critics '96: Foreign Film.

White Bird in a Blizzard ♂♂ **2014 (R)** Teenager Kat Connor (Woodley) has always known that her mother Eve (Green) was a bit left of center, but even she's surprised when mommy dearest up and disappears one average suburban day. In director/writer Araki's '80s drama, nothing is quite what it seems. Did Dad Brock (Meloni) have something to with Mom's disappearance? Kat's boyfriend Phil (Fernandez)? Araki is more concerned with another apathetic teen coming-of-age story as the mystery fades into the background. Woodley grounds the piece and Green is her typical over-the-top greatness but eventually the movie fails them both. **91m/C; DVD, Blu-Ray, Streaming.** Shailene Woodley; Eva Green; Shiloh Fernandez; Thomas Jane; Christopher Meloni; Gabourey Sidibe; Angela Bassett; *D:* Gregg Araki; *W:* Gregg Araki; *C:* Sandra Valde-Hansen; *M:* Robin Guthrie; Harold Budd.

White Boy Rick ♂♂ **2018 (R)** In 1980s Detroit, Richard Wershe Jr. (Merritt), dubbed White Boy Rick, lives with his gun dealer father, Richard Sr. (an impressive McConaughey) and drug addict sister Dawn (Powley). Though Rick Sr. dreams of opening video stores, he can barely support his family and Rick steps up by infiltrating local gangs for money as an informant for the FBI. When the gig ends and Rick is left unsupported, he turns to dealing drugs, a trade he learned while an informant, and suffers unintended consequences. Based on actual events, it's the classic case of a good story not told well. **111m/C; DVD, Blu-Ray.** Matthew McConaughey; Richie Merritt; Bel Powley; Jennifer Jason Leigh; Brian Tyree Henry; *D:* Yann Demange; *W:* Andy Weiss; Logan Miller; Noah Miller; *C:* Tat Radcliffe; *M:* Max Richter.

White Boyz ♂♂ *Whiteboys* **1999 (R)** Flip (Hoch) and his friends long to be gangsta rappers, despite being white and from Iowa. He fantasizes about duets with his idol Snoop Doggy Dogg while dealing baking soda passed off as cocaine to dimwit yuppie disco patrons. He befriends recent Chicago transplant Khalid (Bird) and persuades him to take Flip and his poseur posse to the Cabrini Green projects, where Flip discovers his gangsta fantasy pales in comparison to the real thing. Uneven performances and a rather phat-free script water down an undeniably good premise. **92m/C; VHS, DVD.** Danny Hoch; Dash Mihok; Eugene Bird; Mark Webber; Piper Perabo; Bonz Malone; *D:* Marc Levin; *W:* Danny Hoch; Marc Levin; Richard Stratton; Garth Belcon; *C:* Mark Benjamin.

The White Buffalo ♂♂ *Hunt to Kill* **1977 (PG)** A strange, semi-surreal western parable about the last days of Wild Bill Hickok (Bronson) and his obsession with a mythical white buffalo that represents his fear of mortality. Something of a "Moby Dick" theme set in the Wild West. Clumsy but intriguing. **97m/C; VHS, DVD, Blu-Ray; Open Captioned.** Charles Bronson; Jack Warden; Will Sampson; Kim Novak; Clint Walker; Stuart Whitman; John Carradine; Slim Pickens; Cara Williams; Douglas Fowley; *D:* J. Lee Thompson; *M:* John Barry.

White Chicks ♂ ½ **2004 (PG-13)** Two African-American FBI agents (Shawn and Marlon Wayans) are assigned to protect two wealthy white heiresses from a kidnapping plot. When the sisters are bruised and refuse to be seen in public, the guys disguise themselves as the heiresses to uncover the kidnappers. Hilarity allegedly ensues. Crazy premise could've been mined for class, culture and gender clash material, but instead lunges down the easy path of junior high humor. Too bad, since the Wayans brothers can be very funny when they play it smart. Disconcerting layers of latex and makeup make them look more like bizarre androgynous aliens than debutantes. **108m/C; DVD, UMD.** Marlon Wayans; Shawn Wayans; Brittany Daniel; Jaime King; Jessica Cauffiel; Busy Philipps; Frankie Faison; John Heard; Lochlyn Munro; Maitland Ward; Anne Dudek; Terry Crews; Eddie Velez; Faune A. Chambers; Rochelle Aytes; Jennifer Carpenter; Drew Sidora; Casey Lee; Suzy Joachim; *D:* Keenen Ivory Wayans; *W:* Marlon Wayans; Shawn Wayans; Keenen Ivory Wayans; Michael Anthony Snowden; Andrew McElfresh; Xavier Cook; *C:* Steven Bernstein; *M:* Teddy Castellucci.

White Christmas ♂♂♂ **1954** Two ex-army buddies become a popular comedy team and play at a financially unstable Vermont inn at Christmas for charity's sake. Many swell Irving Berlin songs rendered with zest. Paramount's first Vista Vision film. **120m/C; VHS, DVD, Blu-Ray.** Bing Crosby; Danny Kaye; Rosemary Clooney; Vera-Ellen; Dean Jagger; *D:* Michael Curtiz; *W:* Norman Panama; *C:* Loyal Griggs.

The White Cliffs of Dover ♂♂♂ **1944** Prime example of a successful 40s "women's weepie." American Dunne goes to England in 1914, falls in love, and marries the British Marshal. He joins the WWI troops and is killed, without knowing he had a son. Dunne raises the boy in England as a new threat looms with the rise of Hitler. Now grown, he goes off to do his duty and she joins the Red Cross, where she sees him again among the wounded, another victim of the ravages of war. Dunne is fine in her noble, sacrificing role. McDowall is the young son with Taylor (with whom he'd already worked in "Lassie Come Home") as a childhood friend. Based on the poem by Alice Duer Miller. Bring the hankies. **126m/B; VHS, DVD.** Irene Dunne; Alan Marshal; Frank Morgan; Peter Lawford; Gladys Cooper; May

Whitty; Sir C. Aubrey Smith; Roddy McDowall; Van Johnson; Elizabeth Taylor; June Lockhart; John Warburton; Jill Esmond; Norma Varden; Tom Drake; Arthur Shields; Brenda Forbes; Edmund Breon; Clyde Cook; Isobel Elsom; Lumsden Hare; Miles Mander; Ian Wolfe; *D:* Clarence Brown; *W:* George Froeschel; Jan Lustig; Claudine West; *C:* George J. Folsey; *M:* Herbert Stothart.

White Coats 1/2 *Intern Academy* **2004** Low-brow comedy about the misadventures (medical and personal) of the interns at chaotic St. Albert's Hospital. Many gross-out jokes and familiar comedy names, but not much else to recommend it. **98m/C; DVD.** *CA* Dave Thomas; Patrick Kelly; Viv Leacock; Dave Foley; Peter Oldring; Ingrid Kavelaars; Dan Aykroyd; Maury Chaykin; Carly Pope; Matt Frewer; Saul Rubinek; *C:* John Spooner.

The White Cockatoo 1/2 **1935** Sue Talley (Muir) is having a reunion with her brother Jim (Cortez), whom she hasn't seen in 20 years. They're meeting at an isolated hotel in France to work out the clues to obtaining their inheritance but they aren't the only ones who want the money. Based on the mystery by Mignon G. Eberhart. **73m/B; DVD.** Jean Muir; Ricardo Cortez; Ruth Donnelly; Minna Gombell; Walter Kingsford; John Eldredge; *D:* Alan Crosland; *W:* Ben Markson; Lillie Hayward; *C:* Tony Gaudio.

White Comanche 1/2 **1968** Campy, violent spaghetti western with Shatner playing mixed-race twin brothers. Notah is a renegade Comanche who takes peyote and Johnny Moon is a drifter cowboy. Johnny is always being blamed for crimes committed by his brother and must have a final showdown with him. **94m/C; DVD.** *SP* William Shatner; Joseph Cotten; Perla Cristal; Rossana Yanni; Mariano Vidal Molina; Luis Prendes; *D:* Jose Briz Mendez; *W:* Frank Gruber; Robert I. Holt; *C:* Francisco Fraile; *M:* Jean Ledrut.

The White Countess 1/2 **2005 (PG-13)** As you might expect from a Merchant Ivory production, the period styling is gorgeous even if the story is a little finicky. Set on the eve of Japan's WWII invasion of China in 1936, the film follows Sofia (Richardson) who lives in Shanghai, where she supports her family of exiled Russian aristocrats by scratching out a living as an exotic dancer and prostitute. She meets expatriate American Todd Jackson (Fiennes), who recognizes Sofia as the ideal hostess for his new nightclub, The White Countess. Richardson and Fiennes truly make the viewer care about their wounded characters, even as their business and personal relationships spirals downwards thanks to the chaos of war. **138m/C; DVD.** *US CH GB GE* Ralph Fiennes; Natasha Richardson; Vanessa Redgrave; Hiroyuki (Henry) Sanada; Lynn Redgrave; Allan Corduner; Da(nniel) Ying; Jean-Pierre Lorit; Lee Pace; Madeleine Potter; John Wood; Madeleine Daly; Dan Herzberg; Pierre Seznec; Luoyong Wang; *D:* James Ivory; *W:* Kazuo Ishiguro; *C:* Christopher Doyle; *M:* Richard Robbins.

The White Crow 1/2 **2018 (R)** A biopic about Rudolf Nureyev, the legendary Russian ballet dancer who, during the height of the 1960s Cold War, was part of a touring company to Paris. Experiencing the Western freedom that didn't exist in his homeland, he dared to elude the KGB and risk treason in order to defect. The dance scenes are elegant and captivating, but the movie's political themes take center stage, removing much of the passion from his story. Inspired by Julie Kavanagh's book, "Rudolf Nureyev: The Life." **127m/C; DVD.** *FR UK* Oleg Ivenko; Ralph Fiennes; Adele Exarchopoulos; Sergei Polunin; Chulpan Khamatova; *D:* Ralph Fiennes; *W:* David Hare; *C:* Mike Eley; *M:* Ilan Eshkeri.

The White Dawn 1/2 **1975 (PG)** Three whalers are stranded in the Arctic in the 1890s and are taken in by an Eskimo village. They teach the villagers about booze, gambling, and other modern amenities. Resentment grows until a clash ensues. All three leads are excellent, especally Oates. Much of the dialogue is in an Eskimo language, subtitled in English, as in "Dances with Wolves." **110m/C; DVD.** Warren Oates; Timothy Bottoms; Louis Gossett, Jr.; Simonie Kopapik; Joanasie Salomonie; *D:* Philip Kaufman; *W:* James A. Houston; Thomas Rickman; *C:* Michael Chapman; *M:* Henry Mancini.

The White Diamond **2004** Herzog's documentary (which he also narrates) begins with a brief history of flight and then moves on to the eccentricities of British aeronautical engineer Graham Dorrington, who designs a two-person airship meant to be used for scientific research in the Amazon rain forest. Herzog records their expedition to Guyana as they try to get Dorrington's aircraft to fly. Dorrington's crew is supported by local Guyanese diamond miners, including Mark Anthony Yhap, whose christening of the airship gives the film its title. **90m/C; DVD.** *GE GB JP* *D:* Werner Herzog; *C:* Henning Brummer; Klaus Scheurich; *M:* Ernst Reijseger; Eric Spitzer-Marlyn.

White Dog **1982** Young actress Julie Sawyer (McNichol) finds a white stray dog that she adopts, but she soon learns that the dog has been conditioned to kill blacks. She takes the dog to black animal trainer Keys (Winfield), who believes that the dog can be re-trained. Fuller's controversial drama about racism scared off the studio (Paramount) who dumped the picture without more than a token release. **90m/C; DVD.** Kristy McNichol; Paul Winfield; Burl Ives; Jameson Parker; Lynne Moody; Samuel Fuller; *D:* Samuel Fuller; *W:* Samuel Fuller; Curtis Hanson; *C:* Bruce Surtees; *M:* Ennio Morricone.

White Fang 1/2 **1936** In this loose adaptation of the Jack London novel, Sylvia Burgess (Muir) and her brother, Hal (Beck), inherit a gold mine in the frozen north. They hire guide Scott (Whalen) who protects Sylvia after Hal commits suicide, but dastardly saloon owner Smith (Carradine) tries to get the mine for himself by claiming Scott murdered Hal. Oh yeah, half-dog/half-wolf White Fang comes to the good guys' rescue. **70m/B; DVD.** Michael Whalen; Jean Muir; Slim Summerville; John Carradine; Jane Darwell; Thomas Beck; *D:* David Butler; *W:* Gene Fowler, Sr.; *C:* Arthur C. Miller.

White Fang **1991 (PG)** Boy befriends canine with big teeth and both struggle to survive in third celluloid rendition of Alaska during the Gold Rush. Beautiful cinematography. Fun for the entire family based on Jack London's book. Followed by "White Fang 2: The Myth of the White Wolf." **109m/C; VHS, DVD.** Klaus Maria Brandauer; Ethan Hawke; Seymour Cassel; James Remar; Susan Hogan; *D:* Randal Kleiser; *W:* Jeanne Rosenberg; Nick Thiel; David Fallon; *C:* Tony Pierce-Roberts; *M:* Basil Poledouris.

White Fang 2: The Myth of the White Wolf **1994 (PG)** White boy and his wolf-dog lead starving Native American tribe to caribou during the Alaskan Gold Rush. Simplistic story with obvious heroes and villains, yes, but this is also wholesome (and politically correct) family fare compliments of Disney. Focuses less on the wolf, a flaw, and more on Bairstow and his love interest Craig, a Haida Indian princess, while exploring Native American mythology and dreams in sequences that tend to stop the action cold. Still, kids will love it, and there are plenty of puppies to achieve required awwww factor. Beautiful scenery filmed on location in Colorado and British Columbia. **106m/C; VHS, DVD.** Scott Bairstow; Alfred Molina; Geoffrey Lewis; Charmaine Craig; Victoria Racimo; Paul Coeur; Anthony Michael Ruivivar; Al Harrington; ***Cameo(s):*** Ethan Hawke; *D:* Ken Olin; *W:* David Fallon; *M:* John Debney.

White Fang and the Hunter **1985 (G)** The adventures of a boy and his dog who survive an attack from wild wolves and then help to solve a murder mystery. Loosely based on the novel by Jack London. **87m/C; VHS, DVD.** Pedro Sanchez; Robert Woods; *D:* Al (Alfonso Brescia) Bradley.

White Fire *Three Steps to the Gallows* **1953** Brady, in search of his lost brother, gets involved in a smuggling ring. Seems the brother is falsely accused of murder and about to hang. Brady and bar singer Castle solve the case. Good photography; bad script. **82m/C; VHS, DVD.** *GB* Scott Brady; Mary Castle; Ferdinand "Ferdy" Mayne; *D:* John Gilling.

White Fire **1984** Two jewel thieves will stop at nothing to own White Fire, a two hundred-carat diamond. **90m/C; VHS, DVD, Blu-Ray.** Robert Ginty; Fred Williamson; Belinda Mayne; Jess Hahn; *D:* Jean Marie Pallardy; *W:* Edward John Francis; *C:* Roger Fellous; *M:* Vicky Brown.

White Frog **2012** Nick, who's 15 and has Asperger's Syndrome, is at a loss when his protective, popular older brother Chazz dies in an accident. His traditional Chinese-American parents are separately grieving, but in their loss are ignoring Nick, so Chazz's best friends Doug and Randy look after him. As Nick gets to know his brother's friends, he also learns that Chazz had a life his family knew nothing about. **93m/C; DVD.** Booboo Stewart; Gregg Sulkin; Tyler Posey; Harry Shum, Jr.; B.D. Wong; Joan Chen; Kelly Hu; *D:* Quentin Lee; *W:* Fabienne Wen; Ellie Wen; *C:* Yasu Tanida; *M:* Steven Pranoto.

White Girl 1/2 **2016** The title of Elizabeth Wood's controversial Sundance drama refers to both the cocaine that flows plentifully throughout it and its lead character, a wild child named Leah (Saylor). Leah moves to New York City at a young age and falls in love with partying, sex, and doing drugs. She also falls for a local tough guy with a heart of gold named Blue (movie-stealing Brian Marc). After a night goes awry, Blue ends up in jail, and Leah does whatever she can to get him out. Wood's shallow drama feels too often like it's just trying to shock people. **88m/C; DVD, Blu-Ray.** Morgan Saylor; Brian Marc; Justin Bartha; Chris Noth; Adrian Martinez; *D:* Elizabeth Wood; *W:* Elizabeth Wood; *C:* Michael Simmonds.

White Gold **1928** Shepherd's son weds Mexican woman and his disgruntled father contrives apparent rendezvous between the wife and a ranch-hand, who's found dead in her bedroom. Seems no one believes the wife's story. Unprecedented, dark, silent drama. **73m/B; Silent; VHS, DVD.** Jetta Goudal; Kenneth Thomson; George Bancroft; George Nicholls, Jr.; Clyde Cook; *D:* William K. Howard.

White Heat 1/2 **1949** A classic gangster film with one of Cagney's best roles as a psychopathic robber/killer with a mother complex. The famous finale—perhaps Cagney's best-known scene—has Cagney trapped on top of a burning oil tank shouting "Made it, Ma! Top of the world!" before the tank explodes. Cagney's character is allegedly based on Arthur "Doc" Barker and his "Ma," and his portrayal is breathtaking. Also available colorized. **114m/B; VHS, DVD, Blu-Ray.** James Cagney; Virginia Mayo; Edmond O'Brien; Margaret Wycherly; Steve Cochran; John Archer; Wally Cassell; *D:* Raoul Walsh; *W:* Ivan Goff; Ben Roberts; *C:* Sidney Hickox; *M:* Max Steiner. Natl. Film Reg. '03.

White Hot: The Mysterious Murder of Thelma Todd **1991** Thelma Todd was a Hollywood starlet found dead under strange circumstances in 1935. Buffs have sought a solution to the maybe-murder ever since; this treatment (based on the book "Hot Toddy" by Andy Edmunds) leaves too many loose ends for purists and isn't sufficiently gripping for the uninitiated. **95m/C; DVD.** Loni Anderson; Robert Davi; Paul Dooley; Lawrence Pressman; *D:* Paul Wendkos; *W:* Robert E. Thompson. **TV**

White House Down 1/2 **2013 (PG-13)** Emmerich blows up the White House again in this bit of nonsense that follows quickly on the heels of the similarly-themed "Olympus Has Fallen" and falls short. Tatum stars as a wannabe Secret Service Agent who just happens to be at the most recognizable home in the world on the day that one man (Woods) tries to start World War III. Working with the charismatic President (a movie-stealing Foxx, the only one who knows to play this silliness with a wink and a smile), Tatum's agent fights the terrorists and tries to save his little girl. **131m/C; DVD, Blu-Ray.** Channing Tatum; Jamie Foxx; Joey King; Jason Clarke; James Woods; Maggie Gyllenhaal; Richard Jenkins; Lance Reddick; Michael Murphy; *D:* Roland Emmerich; *W:* James Vanderbilt; *C:* Anna Foerster; *M:* Harald Kloser.

White Hunter, Black Heart **1990 (PG)** Eastwood casts himself against type as Hustonesque director who is more interested in hunting large tusked creatures than shooting the film he came to Africa to produce. Based on Peter Viertel's 1953 account of his experiences working on James Agee's script for Huston's "African Queen." Eastwood's Huston impression is a highlight, though the story occasionally wanders off with the elephants. **112m/C; VHS, DVD.** Clint Eastwood; Marisa Berenson; George Dzundza; Jeff Fahey; Timothy Spall; Charlotte Cornwell; Mel Martin; Alun Armstrong; Richard Vanstone; *D:* Clint Eastwood; *W:* Peter Viertel; James Bridges; Burt Kennedy; *C:* Jack N. Green; *M:* Lennie Niehaus.

White Huntress 1/2 *Golden Ivory* **1957** Two brothers venturing into the jungle encounter a beautiful young woman, the daughter of a settlement leader. Meanwhile, a killer is on the loose. **86m/C; VHS, DVD.** *GB* Robert Urquhart; John Bentley; Susan Stephen; *D:* George Breakston.

White Irish Drinkers 1/2 **2010 (R)** In 1975, teenager Brian Leary and his older brother Danny are living with their abusive alcoholic dad and ineffectual mom in an Irish-American Brooklyn neighborhood. Sensitive Brian works at the local movie theater where his boss Whitey has a crazy plan to book the Rolling Stones for a brief concert. Thug Danny tries to bully Brian into helping him rob the theater of the concert proceeds so they can finance an escape from the 'hood. **109m/C; DVD.** Nick Thurston; Geoff Wigdor; Peter Riegert; Stephen Lang; Karen Allen; Zachary Booth; Leslie Murphy; Ken Jennings; *D:* John Gray; *W:* John Gray; *C:* Seamus Tierney; *M:* Mark Snow.

The White Legion 1/2 **1936** Workers and engineers push their way through steaming jungles and reeking swamps while building the Panama Canal. Many fall victim to yellow fever. Physician Keith does some medical sleuthing and saves the day. Plodding, predictable drama. **81m/B; VHS, DVD.** Ian Keith; Tala Birell; Snub Pollard; *D:* Karl Brown.

White Lies **1998 (R)** Catherine (Polley), a freshman college student at a liberal university, feels alienated from her peers and finds solace in an online chat room. She becomes increasingly involved with the shadowy National Identity Movement and becomes their spokesperson before understanding what they really represent and that they're a group of neo-Nazis. **92m/C; VHS, DVD.** *CA* Sarah Polley; Tanya Allen; Jonathan Scarfe; Lynn Redgrave; Joseph Kell; Albert Schultz; *D:* Keri Skogland; *W:* Dennis Foon. **TV**

White Lightning 1/2 *McKlusky* **1973 (PG)** Good ol' boy Reynolds plays a moonshiner going after the crooked sheriff who murdered his brother. Good stunt-driving chases enliven the formula. The inferior sequel is "Gator." **101m/C; VHS, DVD, Blu-Ray.** Burt Reynolds; Ned Beatty; Bo Hopkins; Jennifer Billingsley; Louise Latham; *D:* Joseph Sargent; *W:* William W. Norton, Sr.; *M:* Charles Bernstein.

White Line Fever 1/2 **1975 (PG)** A young trucker's search for a happy life with his childhood sweetheart is complicated by a corrupt group in control of the long-haul trucking business. Well-done action film of good triumphing over evil. **89m/C; VHS, DVD, Blu-Ray.** Jan-Michael Vincent; Kay Lenz; Slim Pickens; L.Q. Jones; John David Garfield; *D:* Jonathan Kaplan; *W:* Jonathan Kaplan; Ken Friedman; *C:* Fred W. Koenekamp.

The White Lioness *Den Vita Lejoninnan* **1996** A young woman is found murdered in the Swedish countryside and the small town cop investigating realizes it's a more complicated case than he can handle. Especially when the crime leads him to Russia and South Africa and an international terrorist organization. Based on the novel by Henning Mankell. Swedish with subtitles. **104m/C; VHS, DVD.** *SW* Rolf Lassgard; Basil Appollis; Jesper Christensen; Nelson Mandela; *D:* Per (Pelle) Berglund; *W:* Lars Bjorkman; *C:* Tony Forsberg; *M:* Thomas Lindahl.

White Man's Burden **1995 (R)** In a world where blacks have all the wealth and power, and whites comprise the struggling underclasses, Caucasian factory worker Louis Pinnock (John Travolta) is fired by his bigoted black CEO (Belafonte) due to a misunderstanding. Driven by poverty-level financial strain, Louis kidnaps his wealthy boss to show him how the other half lives. Gimmicky premise is full of reversed stereotypes, such as black cops beating a white guy, and skinheads taking over as inner-city gangsters. Treads too lightly, and rehashes too many familiar stories, to make any real impact. Travolta had to be talked into this role by "Pulp Fiction" producer Lawrence Bender. **89m/C; VHS, DVD.** John Travolta; Harry Belafonte; Kelly Lynch; Margaret Avery; Tom Bower; Carrie Snodgress; Sheryl Lee Ralph; ***D:*** Desmond Nakano; ***W:*** Desmond Nakano; ***C:*** Willy Kurant; ***M:*** Howard Shore.

White Material 🦴🦴 **2010** Disturbing, brooding, chaotic drama from writer/director Denis. French-born Maria Vial (Huppert) has long-lived on a coffee plantation in some unnamed African country that is now in the midst of a brutal civil war. Stubborn and willfully blind to the danger, she refuses to leave her property as the rebels and child soldiers, who want to get rid of all the white European colonists, as well as the regime's army come closer. French with subtitles. **106m/C; Blu-Ray.** *FR* Isabelle Huppert; Christopher Lambert; Nicolas Duvauchelle; Michel Subor; Isaach de Bankole; Adele Ado; Ali Barkai; Daniel Tchangang; Marie N'Diaye; ***D:*** Claire Denis; ***W:*** Claire Denis; ***C:*** Yves Cape; ***M:*** Stuart S. Staples.

White Men Can't Jump 🦴🦴 **1992 (R)** Sometimes they can't act either. Small-time con man Harrelson stands around looking like a big nerd until someone dares him to play basketball and he proves to be more adept than he looks. After he beats Snipes, they become friends and start hustling together. Harrelson lays to rest the rumor that he can't act; here, he proves it. Fast-paced, obscenity-laced dialogue does not cover up for the fact that the story hovers between dull and dismal, redeemed only by the surreal "Jeopardy" game show sequence and the convincing b-ball action. Snipes manages to rise above the material as well as the rim, while Perez, as wooden Woody's spitfire Hispanic girlfriend, is appropriately energetic. **115m/C; VHS, DVD, Blu-Ray.** Wesley Snipes; Woody Harrelson; Rosie Perez; Tyra Ferrell; Cylk Cozart; Kadeem Hardison; Ernest Harden, Jr.; John Jones; ***D:*** Ron Shelton; ***W:*** Ron Shelton; ***C:*** Russell Boyd; ***M:*** Bennie Wallace.

White Mile 🦴🦴 **1/2 1994 (R)** Abusive L.A. advertising exec Dan Cutler (Alda) invites his top execs and important clients on a white-water rafting expedition along the Chilko River in the Canadian Rockies (filmed at Northern California's Russian River). But competition and arrogance causes the deaths of several participants and the widow of one sues the agency for damages. Alda excels in arrogant, self-serving nastiness. Fact-based TV movie based on court transcripts. **97m/C; VHS, DVD.** Alan Alda; Peter Gallagher; Robert Loggia; Fionnula Flanagan; Dakin Matthews; Bruce Altman; Robert Picardo; Max Wright; Jack Gilpin; Ken Jenkins; ***D:*** Robert Butler; ***W:*** Michael Butler.

White Mischief 🦴🦴🦴 **1988 (R)** An alternately ghastly and hilarious indictment of the English upper class between the World Wars, and the decadence the British colonists perpetrated in Kenya, which came to world attention with the murder of the philandering Earl of Errol in 1941. Exquisitely directed and photographed. Acclaimed and grandly acted, especially by Scacchi; Howard's last appearance. **108m/C; VHS.** Greta Scacchi; Charles Dance; Joss Ackland; Sarah Miles; John Hurt; Hugh Grant; Geraldine Chaplin; Trevor Howard; Murray Head; Susan Fleetwood; Alan Dobie; Jacqueline Pearce; ***D:*** Michael Radford; ***W:*** Michael Radford; ***C:*** Roger Deakins; ***M:*** George Fenton.

White Night Wedding 🦴 **1/2** *Brluogumin* **2008** Maybe Icelandic humor doesn't travel well or maybe this sour would-be comedy just isn't funny. Middle-aged widower Jon (Gudnason) and his much younger fiancee and former student Thora (Eliasdottir) are getting married in 24 hours. However, everyone, even the engaged couple, believe the marriage is probably a bad idea. Icelandic with subtitles. **96m/C; DVD.** *IC* Hilmir Snaer Gudnason; Margaret Vilhjalmsdottir; Olfia Hronn Jonsdottir; Throstur Leo Gunnarsson; ***D:*** Baltasar Kormakur; ***W:*** Baltasar Kormakur; Olafur Egill Egilsson; ***C:*** Bergsteinn Bjorgulfsson; ***M:*** Sigurdur Gardarsson.

White Nights 🦴🦴🦴 *Le Notti Bianche* **1957** Based on a love story by Dostoyevski. A young woman pines for the return of her sailor while a mild-mannered clerk is smitten by her. Both of their romantic fantasies are explored the dance-hall cadence is mixed with dreamy, fantastic flashbacks. In Italian with English subtitles. Equally good Soviet version made in 1959. **107m/C; VHS, DVD.** *IT FR* Maria Schell; Jean Marais; Marcello Mastroianni; Clara Calamai; Giorgio Listuzzi; ***D:*** Luchino Visconti; ***W:*** Luchino Visconti; Suso Cecchi D'Amico; ***C:*** Giuseppe Rotunno; ***M:*** Nino Rota.

White Nights 🦴🦴 **1/2 1985 (PG-13)** A Russian ballet dancer who defected to the U.S. (Baryshnikov) is a passenger on a jet that crashes in the Soviet Union. With the aid of a disillusioned expatriate tap dancer (Hines), he plots to escape again. The excellent dance sequences elevate the rather lame story. **135m/C; VHS, DVD, Blu-Ray.** Mikhail Baryshnikov; Gregory Hines; Isabella Rossellini; Dame Helen Mirren; Jerzy Skolimowski; Geraldine Page; ***D:*** Taylor Hackford; ***C:*** David Watkin; ***M:*** Michel Colombier. Oscars '85: Song ("Say You, Say Me"); Golden Globes '86: Song ("Say You, Say Me").

White Noise 🦴 **2005 (PG-13)** Despite an eerily effective marketing campaign—touting the science behind Electronic Voice Phenomenon (EVP), in which ghosts use electric static to contact the living—this cheap Michael Keaton vehicle should have gone straight to video. After architect Jonathan Rivers (Keaton) loses his wife Anna (West) in a suspicious accident, he retreats into despair. That is, until a stranger (McNeice) convinces Rivers that Anna is sending him messages from beyond the grave via EVP. Rivers becomes obsessed with the transmissions, which awakens a malevolent force unamused with his meddling. The last hour plays like a low budget "Final Destination" retread. **101m/C; VHS, DVD, Blu-Ray, HD-DVD.** Michael Keaton; Chandra West; Deborah Kara Unger; Ian McNeice; Sarah Strange; Nicholas Elia; Mike Dopud; ***D:*** Geoffrey Sax; ***W:*** Niall Johnson; ***C:*** Chris Seager; ***M:*** Claude Foisy.

White Noise 2: The Light 🦴 **1/2 2007 (PG-13)** After Abe Dale's (Fillion, playing it straight and dull) family is killed and he is saved from an attempted suicide, Abe comes back from his near-death experience seeing white auras around people who are about to die. But in preventing their deaths, Abe learns there's an unexpected price to pay, since those he saves turn into demons after 72 hours—unless they die again. **99m/C; DVD, Blu-Ray, HD-DVD.** Nathan Fillion; Katee Sackhoff; Craig Fairbrass; Teryl Rothery; Adrian Homes; William Macdonald; ***D:*** Patrick Lussier; ***W:*** Matt Venne; ***C:*** Brian Pearson; ***M:*** Normand Corbeil. **VIDEO**

White Oleander 🦴🦴 **1/2 2002 (PG-13)** Pfieffer plays against type as an ice cold mother who controls her daughter Astrid's (Lohman) life from the prison where she's serving a life sentence for murder. Astrid is forced into an odyssey through the foster care system, where she is taken in by a string of damaged foster moms, including a born-again ex-stripper (Wright Penn), a needy ex-actress (Zellweger) and a greedy Russian ragpicker (Efremova). Astrid changes her looks as well as her psyche for each of these faux-mothers, but finally learns to break away and become her own person with some help from fellow foster child Paul (Fugit). The performances are good across the board, but director Kosminsky seems more interested in making the all-star cast of actresses look good then giving them an interesting story to tell. **110m/C; DVD.** Alison Lohman; Michelle Pfeiffer; Robin Wright; Renée Zellweger; Patrick Fugit; Billy Connolly; Cole Hauser; Noah Wyle; Amy Aquino; Svetlana Efremova; ***D:*** Peter Kosminsky; ***W:*** Mary Agnes Donoghue; ***C:*** Elliot Davis; ***M:*** Thomas Newman.

The White Orchid 🦴🦴 **1954** Romantic triangle ventures into the wilds of Mexico in search of Toltec ruins. Exceptional sets. **81m/C; VHS, DVD.** William Lundigan; Peggy Castle; Armando Silvestre; Rosenda Monteros; ***D:*** Reginald LeBorg.

White Palace 🦴🦴 **1/2 1990 (R)** Successful widowed Jewish lawyer Spader is attracted to older, less educated hamburger waitress Sarandon, and ethnic/cultural strife ensues, as does hot sex. Adapted from the Glenn Savan novel, it starts out with promise but fizzles toward the end. **103m/C; VHS, DVD.** Susan Sarandon; James Spader; Jason Alexander; Eileen Brennan; Griffin Dunne; Kathy Bates; Steven Hill; Rachel Levin; Corey Parker; Spiros Focas; Renee Taylor; Kim Myers; ***D:*** Luis Mandoki; ***W:*** Alvin Sargent; Ted Tally; ***C:*** Lajos Koltai; ***M:*** George Fenton.

White Pongo WOOF! **1945** A policeman goes undercover with a group of British biologists to capture a mythic white gorilla believed to be the missing link. A camp jungle classic with silly, cheap special effects. **73m/B; VHS, DVD.** Richard Fraser; Maris Wrixon; Lionel Royce; Al Eben; Gordon Richards; Michael Dyne; George Lloyd; ***D:*** Sam Newfield; ***W:*** Raymond L. Schrock; ***C:*** Jack Greenhalgh.

The White Raven 🦴🦴 **1998 (R)** Nazi war criminal Markus Straud (Rubes) agrees to be interviewed only by Chicago journalist Tully Windsor (Silvers). During the war, Straud hid a priceless diamond and various factions think he's finally going to reveal where the stone is. But Straud only offers a series of cryptic clues that lead Windsor back home, with the bad guys in pursuit. **92m/C; VHS, DVD.** Ron Silver; Jan Rubes; Joanna Pacula; Roy Scheider; ***D:*** Andrew Stevens; ***W:*** Michael Blodgett; ***C:*** Michael Slovis; ***M:*** David Wurst; Eric Wurst.

White Reindeer 🦴🦴 **1/2 2013** Suzanne (Hollyman) is a polite, relatively average realtor in the Washington DC 'burbs who learns that her husband Jeff (Williams) has been having an affair with a stripper named Fantasia (Lemar-Goldsborough). After her world is shattered, she tracks down the stripper and actually forms a relationship. A bit sitcomish, this quiet, simple indie has modest charms and goals but it works--largely because the charming Hollyman gives a genuine, believable performance. **82m/C; DVD.** Anna Margaret Hollyman; Joe Swanberg; Nathan Williams; Laura Lemar-Goldsborough; ***D:*** Zachary Clark; ***W:*** Zachary Clark; ***C:*** Daryl Pittman; ***M:*** Fritz Myers.

The White Ribbon 🦴🦴 *Das Weisse Band* **2009 (R)** Gorgeously filmed in black-and-white, Haneke's disturbing drama is best-suited to film aficionados. Misfortunes befall the small German Protestant agricultural town of Eichwald shortly before World War I, changing from minor disturbances to outright atrocities as longtime neighbors turn suspicious and vengeful. Narrated by the town's schoolteacher (Friedel)?years after the events have taken place—the town has a strict and brutal moral code and hierarchy with the children (and women) being punished for the slightest suspected infraction while the adult males carry on as they please. It comes as neither a surprise that the abused children are behind the havoc nor that the horrors depicted are only a prelude to the horrors of the upcoming war. German with subtitles. **150m/B; Blu-Ray, On Demand.** *GE AT FR IT* Ulrich Tukur; Burghart Klaussner; Josef Bierbichler; Christian Friedel; Leonie Benesch; Ursina Lardi; Steffi Kuhnert; Rainer Bock; Gariela Maria Shcmeide; ***Nar:*** Ernst Jacobi; ***D:*** Michael Haneke; ***W:*** Michael Haneke; ***C:*** Christian Berger. Golden Globes '10: Foreign Film.

White River 🦴 *The White River Kid* **1999 (R)** Embarassingly bad would-be comedy based on the book "The Little Brothers of St. Mortimer" by John Fergus Ryan. Broth Edgar (Hoskins) is a fake monk, teamed up with illegal immigrant Morales Pittman (Banderas), in a scam involving selling cheap "socks for God." Traveling through Arkansas they meet up with serial killer "The White River Kid" (Bentley), his girlfriend Apple Lisa Weed (Dickens) and her eccentric family, a blind prostitute (Barkin), and a singing, corrupt sheriff (Travis). Not that you'll be interested in any of them. **99m/C; VHS, DVD.** Bob Hoskins; Antonio Banderas; Wes Bentley; Kim Dickens; Ellen Barkin; Randy Travis; Beau Bridges; Swoosie Kurtz; ***D:*** Arne Glimcher; ***W:*** David Leland; ***C:*** Michael Chapman; ***M:*** John (Gianni) Frizzell.

White Sands 🦴🦴 **1/2 1992 (R)** When a dead man's body is found at a remote Indian reservation clutching a gun and a briefcase filled with $500,000, the local sheriff (Dafoe) takes his identity to see where the money leads. Using a phone number found on a piece of paper in the dead man's stomach, the sheriff follows clues until he finds himself mixed up with a rich woman (Mastrantonio) who sells black market weapons and uses the money to support "worthy" causes, and an FBI man (Jackson) who uses him as bait to lure a CIA turncoat/arms dealer (Rourke). Sound confusing? It is, and despite the strong cast and vivid scenery of the southwest United States, this film just doesn't cut it. **101m/C; VHS, DVD, Blu-Ray.** Willem Dafoe; Mary Elizabeth Mastrantonio; Mickey Rourke; Mimi Rogers; Samuel L. Jackson; M. Emmet Walsh; James Rebhorn; Maura Tierney; Beth Grant; Miguel (Michael) Sandoval; John Lafayette; Jack Kehler; ***Cameo(s):*** Fred Dalton Thompson; John P. Ryan; ***D:*** Roger Donaldson; ***W:*** Daniel Pyne; ***C:*** Peter Menzies, Jr.; ***M:*** Patrick O'Hearn.

White Shadows in the South Seas 🦴🦴 **1/2 1929** Alcohol, drugs, and prostitution take their toll on the native population of Tahiti in this early talkie. Blue plays a western doctor who marries the daughter of a native chief. However, he finds greed for the island's pearl treasures drawing other unscrupulous westerners to destroy the unspoiled paradise. **88m/B; VHS, DVD.** Monte Blue; Robert Anderson; Raquel Torres; ***D:*** W.S. Van Dyke; ***C:*** Clyde De Vinna. Oscars '29: Cinematog.

The White Sheik 🦴🦴🦴 *Lo Sceicco Bianco* **1952** Fellini's first solo effort. A newly wed bride meets her idol from the comic pages (made with photos, not cartoons; called fumetti) and runs off with him. She soon finds he's as ordinary as her husband. Brilliant satire in charming garb. Remade as "The World's Greatest Lover." Woody Allen's "The Purple Rose of Cairo" is in a similar spirit. In Italian with subtitles. **86m/B; VHS, DVD.** *IT* Alberto Sordi; Giulietta Masina; Brunella Bovo; Leopoldo Trieste; ***D:*** Federico Fellini; ***W:*** Federico Fellini; Tullio Pinelli; Ennio Flaiano; ***C:*** Arturo Galea; ***M:*** Nino Rota.

The White Sin 🦴🦴 **1924** An innocent country girl hires on as maid of a rich woman and is seduced and abandoned by the woman's profligate son, but everything turns out all right by the end of the third handkerchief. Silent with original organ music. **93m/B; Silent; VHS, DVD.** Madge Bellamy; John Bowers; Billy Bevan; ***D:*** William A. Seiter.

The White Sister 🦴🦴🦴 **1/2 1923** Gish is an Italian aristocrat driven from her home by a conniving sister. When her true love (Colman) is reported killed she decides to become a nun and enters a convent. When her lover does return he tricks her into leaving the convent but before he can persuade her to renounce her vows Vesuvius erupts and he goes off to warn the villagers, dying for his efforts. Gish then re-dedicates herself to her faith. Colman's first leading role, which made him a romantic star. Filmed on location in Italy. **108m/B; Silent; VHS, DVD.** Lillian Gish; Ronald Colman; Gail Kane; J. Barney Sherry; Charles Lane; ***D:*** Henry King.

The White Sister 🦴🦴 **1933** There's little chemistry between Hayes and Gable in this wartime romance, based on the 1909 novel by Francis Marion Crawford, but Fleming keeps the worst of the melodrama down. Italian princess Angela runs away with army officer Giovanni but he must leave her when WWI begins. When he's presumed dead, she enters a convent. But a twist of fate forces Angela to make a life-altering decision. **110m/B; DVD.** Helen Hayes; Clark Gable; Lewis Stone; Louise Closser Hale; Edward Arnold; Alan Edwards; Mary Robson; ***D:*** Victor Fleming; ***W:*** Donald Stewart; ***C:*** William H. Daniels; ***M:*** Herbert Stothart.

White Slave 🦴 *Amazonia: The Catherine Miles Story* **1986 (R)** An Englishwoman is captured by bloodthirsty cannibals and, rather than being eaten, is tormented and made a slave. **90m/C; VHS, DVD.** Elvive Avoray; Will Gonzales; Andrew Louis Coppola; ***D:*** Mario Gariazzo.

White Squall 🦴🦴 **1/2 1996 (PG-13)** Based on the 1960 true story of 13 young men who become students at Ocean Academy, a year-long adventure spent aboard the brigantine Albatross. Bridges plays the ship's captain and surrogate dad. The boys agonize over their various crises, making the first half of the movie into a veritable "Dead Poets

Yachting Society." However, a sudden storm overtakes the ship in the Caribbean and several crew members are killed. There's a shift to a "Caine Mutiny" type trial in which Bridges must prove the tragedy was not his fault while the survivors rally to his defense. Director Scott excels at showing the fury of nature in the prolonged storm scene, but takes his time getting there. **128m/C; VHS, DVD, Blu-Ray.** Jeff Bridges; Scott Wolf; Caroline Goodall; Balthazar Getty; John Savage; Jeremy Sisto; Jason Marsden; David Selby; Zeljko Ivanek; Ryan Phillippe; David Lascher; Eric Michael Cole; Julio Oscar Mechoso; Ethan (Randall) Embry; ***D:*** Ridley Scott; ***W:*** Todd Robinson; ***C:*** Hugh Johnson; ***M:*** Jeff Rona.

The White Squaw **1956** Minor western plagued by stereotypes. Mixed-race Ectay-O-Wahnee has grown up with the Sioux. Swedish immigrant Swanson wants to drive the tribe off their land so he can start a ranch but cattleman Garth comes to their aid after Swanson is responsible for the death of the young woman's white father. **75m/B; DVD.** May Wynn; David Brian; William Bishop; Paul Birch; Frank De Kova; ***D:*** Ray Nazarro; ***W:*** Les Savage; ***C:*** Henry Freulich; ***M:*** Mischa Bakaleinikoff.

The White Storm *Sao du* **2013 (R)** An action crime thriller centered on the wide effects of an undercover police operation going very bad. Three police officers—who are also lifelong friends—work for the Narcotics Bureau of the Hong Kong Police Department and involved in a case to bring a well-known Thai drug lord to justice. Their lives are changed forever during the sting operation when things do not go as planned, and they must chose which one of them must die. Five years later, the two surviving friends want to gain revenge for their friend but eventually competing against each other for their very lives. Cantonese and Thai with subtitles. **140m/C; DVD, Blu-Ray, Streaming, Download.** Ching-Wan Lau; Louis Koo; Nick Cheung; Hoi-Pang Lo; Quan Yuan; ***D:*** Benny Chan; ***W:*** Benny Chan; Manfred Wong; ***C:*** Anthony Pun; ***M:*** Nicolas Errera.

White Tiger **½ 1923** Three crooks pull off a major heist and hide out in a mountain cabin where their mistrust of each other grows. **81m/C; VHS, DVD.** Priscilla Dean; Matt Moore; Raymond Griffith; Wallace Beery; ***D:*** Tod Browning.

White Tiger **½ 1995 (R)** DEA agent Mike Ryan (Daniels) decides to take the law into his own fists when his partner Grogan (Craven) is murdered by Chinese gang/drug leader Victor Chow (Tagawa). **93m/C; VHS, DVD.** Gary Daniels; Matt Craven; Cary-Hiroyuki Tagawa; Julia Nickson-Soul; ***D:*** Richard Martin; ***W:*** Gordon Melbourne; ***C:*** Gregory Middleton; ***M:*** Graeme Coleman.

The White Tower **1950** Five men and a woman set out to scale the infamous White Tower in the Alps. Each person's true nature is revealed as he or she scales the peak, which has defied all previous attempts. Slightly overwrought, but exciting. Filmed in Technicolor on location in the Swiss Alps. **98m/C; DVD.** Glenn Ford; Claude Rains; Cedric Hardwicke; Oscar Homolka; Lloyd Bridges; ***D:*** Ted Tetzlaff; ***W:*** Paul Jarrico; ***C:*** Ray Rennahan; ***M:*** Roy Webb.

White Water Summer **½** *Rites of Summer* **1987 (PG)** A group of young adventurers trek into the Sierras, and find themselves struggling against nature and each other to survive. Bacon is the rugged outdoorsman (yeah, sure) who shows them what's what. Chances are it was never at a theatre near you, and with good reason. **90m/C; VHS, DVD.** Kevin Bacon; Sean Astin; Jonathan Ward; Matt Adler; K.C. Martel; ***D:*** Jeff Bleckner; ***M:*** Michael Boddicker.

White Wedding **½ 2010** In this genial South African comedy, would-be bridegroom Elvis (Nkosi) suffers a series of road misadventures as he and best man Tumi (Seiphemo) travel from Johannesburg to Cape Town for what he expects will be a traditional white wedding. However, bride-to-be Ayanda (Msutwana) is caught between European and African traditions, last-minute interference, and the sudden reappearance of a flashy ex-boyfriend that brings out Elvis' jealousy. **93m/C; Blu-Ray, On Demand.** *SA* Kenneth Nkosi; Zandie Msutwana; Rapulana Seiphemo; Jodie Whitaker; Sylvia Mngzekeza; Mbulelo Grootboom; ***D:*** Jann Turner; ***W:*** Kenneth Nkosi; Rapulana Seiphemo; Jann Turner; ***C:*** Willie Nel; ***M:*** Joel Assiazky.

White Witch Doctor **1953** Jungle melodrama. Nurse Ellen Burton (Hayward) comes to the Belgian Congo in 1907 to minister to the Bakuba tribe. She hires Lonni Douglas (Mitchum) and his partner Huysman (Slezak) as her guides, but they're more interested in the rumors of tribal gold. Ellen proves her medical worth while Lonni, who's fallen for her, turns good guy against his greedy parter. **95m/C; DVD.** Susan Hayward; Robert Mitchum; Walter Slezak; Timothy Carey; ***D:*** Henry Hathaway; ***W:*** Ivan Goff; Ben Roberts; ***C:*** Leon Shamroy; ***M:*** Bernard Herrmann.

White Wolves 2: Legend of the Wild **½ 1994 (PG)** Troubled teens are on a school assignment involving a conservation foundation's rescue of a pair of young wolves. They must overcome lots of obstacles, including the fact that they can't stand each other. Average teens-in-the-woods adventure. **95m/C; VHS, DVD.** Corin "Corky" Nemec; Justin Whalin; Jeremy London; Elizabeth Berkley; Ernie Reyes, Jr.; Ele Keats; ***D:*** Terence H. Winkless; ***C:*** John Aronson.

White Wolves 3: Cry of the White Wolf **½ 1998 (PG)** A plane crash strands three teens in the wilderness where they must depend on themselves, and the mystical white wolf, for survival. **82m/C; VHS, DVD.** Rodney A. Grant; Mercedes McNab; Robin Clarke; Tracy Brooks Swope; Mick Cain; Margaret Howell; ***D:*** Victoria Muspratt.

White Woman **½ 1933** Laughton chews scenery (and a disgusting moustache) in this jungle melodrama. Widow Judith (Lombard) is trying to make a living as a singer and is desperate enough to marry wealthy rubber plantation owner Horace Prin. When she's living on his remote Malaysian estate, she discovers hubby is cruel and jealous, leaving Judith to fall for handsome-but-troubled overseer David (Taylor). David is sent away and replaced by chain gang fugitive Ballister (Bickford), who challenges Horace, and much over-acting ensues. **70m/B; DVD.** Charles Laughton; Carole Lombard; Kent Taylor; Charles Bickford; Percy Kilbride; ***D:*** Stuart Walker; ***W:*** Gladys Lehman; Samuel Hoffenstein; ***C:*** Harry Fischbeck.

The White Zombie **1932** Lugosi followed his success in "Dracula" with the title role in this low-budget horror classic about the leader of a band of zombies who wants to steal a beautiful young woman from her new husband. Set in Haiti; the first zombie movie. Rich and dark, though ludicrous. Based on the novel "The Magic Island" by William Seabrook. **73m/B; VHS, DVD, Blu-Ray.** Bela Lugosi; Madge Bellamy; John Harron; Joseph Cawthorn; Robert Frazer; Brandon Hurst; George Burr Macannan; Frederick Peters; Dan Crimmins; Clarence Muse; ***D:*** Victor Halperin; ***W:*** Garnett Weston; ***C:*** Arthur Martinelli; ***M:*** Xavier Cugat.

WhiteForce **1988 (R)** A secret agent tracks an enemy. His government tracks him. He runs around with a big machine gun and a couple of hand grenades. He fires the gun and throws the grenades. **90m/C; DVD.** Sam Jones; Kimberly Pistone; ***D:*** Eddie Romero.

Whiteout **½ 2009 (R)** Disturbingly violent thriller is set in Antarctica's Amundsen-Scott Station days before the winter closes down travel. Carrie Stetko (Beckinsale), the only U.S. Marshal assigned to the post, hopes to wrap up an uneventful two-year stint, but the station's first homicide victim shows up just as a brutal storm approaches. Stetko's not going anywhere, right? Yeah, and neither is this movie. As dead scientists pile up, Stetko gets assistance from mentoring father figure/pilot Doc (Skerritt) and special UN investigator, Robert (Macht). Flashbacks to a Russian plane crash in 1957 hint at the back-story but the storm, big parkas, and frenetically filmed action make it difficult to follow the unfolding mystery. On a good note, the gorgeous Beckinsale delivers her obligatory disrobing and shower scene very early in the film so, guys, if you doze off in the final third...you're good. **101m/C; Blu-Ray.** Kate Beckinsale; Gabriel Macht; Tom Skerritt; Columbus Short; Alex O'Loughlin; Shawn Doyle; ***D:*** Dominic Sena; ***W:*** Chad Hayes; Carey Hayes; Jon Hoeber; Erich Hoeber; ***C:*** Christopher Soos; ***M:*** John (Gianni) Frizzell.

Whitey: United States of America v. James J. Bulger **2014** Was James "Whitey" Bulger a notorious criminal mastermind or an FBI mole? Or both? Director Berlinger was granted the most access to this legendary Boston gangster's story in history, and what he found detailed a startling relationship between Bulger and the Department of Justice. Did our government allow Bulger to rule his criminal empire, even encouraging it at times? The film spins its wheels a bit too often (it could be at least 20 minutes shorter), but Bulger's story is never boring and captures something unique about how crime and the enterprise designed to stop it can become intertwined. **130m/C; DVD, Blu-Ray.** ***D:*** Joe Berlinger; ***C:*** Robert Richman; Etienne Sauret; ***M:*** Wendy Blackstone.

Whitney **2015** Bassett's directorial debut is this sympathetic Lifetime biopic that focuses on a brief period (1989-1995) in the life of tragic singer Whitney Houston when she meets fellow singer Bobby Brown and the two fall in love and marry. The lovely DaCosta shows Whitney's vulnerability although it's fairly standard showbiz fare. (Houston's vocals are supplied by Deborah Cox.) **92m/C; DVD.** Yaya DaCosta; Arlen Escarpeta; Yolonda Ross; Suzzanne Douglass; Mark Rolston; ***D:*** Angela Bassett; ***W:*** Shem Bitterman; ***C:*** Anastas Michos. **CABLE**

Whitney **½ 2018 (R)** An intimate look at the rise and tragically premature demise of one of the greatest singers of all time, Whitney Houston. Director Kevin Macdonald celebrates the beauty of her voice and her accomplishments, but he also probes his interviewees for answers to the hard questions. At once a moving tribute and a cautionary tale about true identity. **120m/C; DVD, Blu-Ray.** *US UK* Whitney Houston; Bobby Brown; Bobbi Kristina Brown; Cissy Houston; Clive Davis; ***D:*** Kevin MacDonald; ***W:*** Kevin MacDonald; ***C:*** Nelson Hume; ***M:*** Adam Wiltzie.

Whity **1970** Whity (Kaufman) is the illegitimate mulatto son of the wealthy white man for whom he works. An equally exploited barmaid (Schygulla) convinces Whity his one chance for freedom is to murder his masters. Kaufman was one of Fassbinder's boyfriends and the personal tensions and obsessions of their relationship spilled onto the screen. German with subtitles. **102m/C; DVD.** *GE* Gunther Kaufman; Hanna Schygulla; Ulli Lommel; Harry Baer; Rainer Werner Fassbinder; ***D:*** Rainer Werner Fassbinder; ***W:*** Rainer Werner Fassbinder; ***C:*** Michael Ballhaus; ***M:*** Peer Raben.

Who Do You Love **½ 2008** Engaging biography of Leonard Chess (Nivola), the founder of Chicago's blues/rock label Chess Records. Leonard is running the family junkyard with brother Phil (Abrahams) but wants a more glamorous life so he persuades his bro to sell the business and open a nightclub with him, putting the profits into a record label. The mercurial, ambitious Leonard deals either dubiously or generously with his various acts, including Muddy Waters (Oyelowo) and Willie Dixon (McBride). Of course the best part about the flick is the music. **90m/C; DVD.** Miko Defoor; Keb' Mo'; Robert Randolph; Alessandro Nivola; David Oyelowo; Chi McBride; Jon Abrahams; Megalyn Echikunwoke; Marika Dominczyk; ***D:*** Jerry Zaks; ***W:*** Bob Conte; Peter Martin Wortmann; ***C:*** David Franco; ***M:*** Jeff Beal.

Who Done It? **1942** Average Abbott and Costello comedy about two would-be radio mystery writers, working as soda-jerks, who play detective after the radio station's president is murdered. **77m/B; VHS, DVD.** Bud Abbott; Lou Costello; William Gargan; Patric Knowles; Louise Allbritton; Don Porter; Jerome Cowan; William Bendix; Mary Wickes; ***D:*** Erle C. Kenton.

Who Done It? **½ 1956** Film debut of the rakish Hill as ice-rink sweeper, Hugo Dill. When Dill comes into some money and a dog, he launches a private investigating firm. A woman enters the picture and Hugo discovers his sleuthing has gotten him in over his head. Lots of typical gags and car chases. **85m/B; VHS, DVD.** *GB* Benny Hill; Belinda Lee; David Kossoff; Ernest Thesiger; Garry Marsh; George Margo; Denis Shaw; Fred Schiller; Jeremy Hawk; Thorley Walters; Philip Stainton; Stratford Johns; ***D:*** Basil Dearden; ***W:*** T.E.B. Clarke; ***C:*** Otto Heller; ***M:*** Philip Green.

Who Framed Roger Rabbit **½ 1988 (PG)** Technically marvelous, cinematically hilarious, eye-popping combination of cartoon and live action create a Hollywood of the 1940s where cartoon characters are real and a repressed minority working in films. A 'toon-hating detective is hired to uncover the unfaithful wife of 2-D star Roger, and instead uncovers a conspiracy to wipe out all 'toons. Special appearances by many cartoon characters from the past. Coproduced by Touchstone (Disney) and Amblin (Spielberg). Adapted from "Who Censored Roger Rabbit?" by Gary K. Wolf. **104m/C; VHS, DVD, Blu-Ray; Open Captioned.** Bob Hoskins; Christopher Lloyd; Joanna Cassidy; Alan Tilvern; Stubby Kaye; ***V:*** Charles Fleischer; Mae Questel; Kathleen Turner; Amy Irving; Mel Blanc; June Foray; Frank Sinatra; ***D:*** Robert Zemeckis; ***W:*** Jeffrey Price; Peter S. Seaman; ***C:*** Dean Cundey; ***M:*** Alan Silvestri. Oscars '88: Film Editing, Visual FX; Natl. Film Reg. '16.

Who Gets to Call It Art? **½ 2005** Jumbled documentary about the unlikely career of Metropolitan Museum of Art curator Henry Geldzahler, who died in 1994, and his 1969 landmark 408-piece exhibition entitled "New York Painting and Sculpture: 1940-1970" that showcased works from 43 artists, including Jackson Pollock, Jasper Johns, Willem de Kooning, Andy Warhol, and David Hockney. **80m/C; DVD.**

Who Is Clark Rockefeller? **2010** Somewhat campy true crime Lifetime drama finds wealthy Bostonian Sandra (Stringfield) marrying suave Clark (McCormack), who claims to be related to the Rockefeller family. After 12 years of marriage, Sandra heads to divorce court and gets custody of their daughter Reigh (Lind). This leads to parental kidnapping and the exposure of Clark's long-running con. **90m/C; DVD.** Eric McCormack; Sherry Stringfield; Emily Alyn Lind; Regina Taylor; Stephen McHattie; ***D:*** Mikael Salomon; ***W:*** Edithe Swensen; ***C:*** John Dyer; ***M:*** Jeff Toyne. **CABLE**

Who is Cletis Tout? **½ 2002 (R)** This nostalgic spoof of/homage to classic movies revolves around the efforts of cornered man Trevor (Slater) to convince a film-loving hitman that he is not Cletis Tout, a reporter that the mob wants dead. Critical Jim (Allen) is a button man with time on his hands, so he has Trevor tell him the story like he was pitching a movie idea to a studio executive. The tale contains many obvious Hollywood plot machinations and references including a prison break, a pretty girl, elaborate con jobs and true love. Trevor is also not above taking cues from Jim, changing the story when his captor is displeased by part of it. Good premise tends to get too cute with the material, but all in all a fun ride. **92m/C; VHS, DVD.** Tim Allen; Christian Slater; Portia de Rossi; Richard Dreyfuss; Billy Connolly; Peter MacNeill; Richard Chevolleau; RuPaul Charles; ***D:*** Christopher Ver Wiel; ***W:*** Christopher Ver Wiel; ***C:*** Jerzy Zielinski; ***M:*** Randy Edelman.

Who Is Julia? **1986** CBS TV movie. Beautiful Julia North's body is crushed in a terrible accident but her brain is functioning. Plain Mary Frances (Winningham) is brain dead but her body is intact. So the doctors transplant Julia's brain into Mary Frances' body but the memories are only those of Julia who can't relate to her alien body or Mary Frances' family. But Julia's own husband rejects her because she's not gorgeous anymore. So just who is Julia now? Ridiculous premise but Winningham sells it with her sincerity. **93m/C; DVD.** Mare Winningham; Jameson Parker; Jonathan Banks; Jeffrey DeMunn; Mason Adams; Bert Remsen; ***D:*** Walter Grauman; ***W:*** James Sadwith; ***C:*** Thomas Del Ruth; ***M:*** Robert Drasnin. **TV**

Who Is Killing the Great Chefs of Europe? *Too Many Chefs; Someone is Killing the Great Chefs of Europe* **1978 (PG)** A fast-paced, lightly handled black comedy. When a gourmand, well-played by Morley, learns he must lose weight to live, a number of Europe's best chefs are murdered according to their cooking specialty. A witty, crisp, international mystery based on Ivan and Nan Lyon's novel. **112m/C; VHS, DVD.** George Segal; Jacqueline Bisset; Robert Morley; Jean-Pierre Cassel; Philippe Noiret; Jean Rochefort; Joss Ackland; Nigel Havers; ***D:*** Ted Kotcheff; ***M:*** Henry Mancini. L.A. Film Critics '78: Support. Actor (Morley).

Who Is Simon Miller? **2011** Made-for-television family adventure. Simon Miller is always away on business trips, but then he calls to warn his wife of danger and goes missing. Meredith and his two kids search Simon's office and discover a number of passports with different names and realize Simon has been keeping potentially deadly secrets. **90m/C; DVD.** Loren Dean; Robin (Robyn) Lively; Skyler Day; Drew Koles; Christine Baranski; Anthony Lemke; ***D:*** Paolo Barzman; ***W:*** Sheryl J. Anderson; ***C:*** Pierre Jodoin; ***M:*** Ned Bouhalassa. **TV**

Who Killed Bambi? 1/2 *Qui a tu Bambi?* **2003** Proving that hospitals are creepy in any language, this French thriller uses the hygienic facade of the medical profession as its backdrop for terror. Isabelle (Quinton) is a nursing student, beginning her first residency at a large, isolated hospital. After she faints on the job, her cousin Veronique (Jacob) nicknames her "Bambi," due to her inability to stay on her feet. When the stoic, handsome Dr. Philipp (Lucas) believes that Isabelle's fainting spells might be cured by an operation, she goes under his care, only to discover that Philipp has a penchant for molesting female patients while they're unconscious. Thus begins a protracted cat-and-mouse struggle between doctor and nurse, which reaches increasingly improbable heights. **121m/C; DVD.** Laurent Lucas; Catherine Jacob; Sophie Quinton; Doc Mateo; ***D:*** Gilles Marchand; ***C:*** Pierre Milon; ***M:*** Alexandre Beaupain; Lily Margot; Francois Eudes.

Who Killed the Electric Car? 1/2 **2006 (PG)** Advocate Paine looks at the history of the EV1, the first mass-produced electric automobile, introduced by General Motors in California in 1996 after the state passed legislation requiring automakers to make a portion of their vehicles with zero-emission engines. Despite protests, GM pulled the cars (which were only available by lease) in 2000, citing lack of consumer interest among other reasons. Paine uncovers the EV1's ultimate fate—crushed at GM's Nevada desert proving ground. **92m/C; DVD.** ***D:*** Charles Paine; ***W:*** Charles Paine; ***C:*** Thaddeus Wadleigh; ***M:*** Michael Brook.

Who Loves the Sun **2006** Arthur and Mary Bloom are surprised when their son Daniel's childhood friend Will suddenly shows up at their lakeside cabin. The guys had a falling out when Will found Daniel cheating with Will's wife Maggie and Will disappeared for five years. Blooms summon Daniel (and Maggie) for a weekend confab with Will to confront their problems. **94m/C; DVD.** *CA* Lukas Haas; Adam Scott; Molly Parker; R.H. Thomson; Wendy Crewson; ***D:*** Matthew Bissonnette; ***W:*** Matthew Bissonnette; ***C:*** Arthur E. Cooper; ***M:*** Mac McCaughan.

Who Made the Potatoe Salad? **2005 (R)** Vulgar comedy that wastes a lot of potential. Bumbling San Diego cop Michael (White) proposes to his girlfriend Ashley (Frederique) and insists that they travel to L.A. for Thanksgiving to inform her family. Ashley has been keeping everyone in the dark—Michael knows nothing about them and they know nothing about him, so let the trouble begin. It seems Ashley's dad (Powell) is a former Black Panther who doesn't want a pig for a son-in-law, her brother June Bug (Davis) is a hip-hop slinging thug, and her ex (Griffin) is a con. **90m/C; DVD.** Jaleel White; Clifton Powell; DeRay Davis; Eddie Griffin; Jenna Frederique; Ella Joyce; Tommy (Tiny) Lister; ***D:*** Damon "Coke" Daniels; ***W:*** Damon "Coke" Daniels; ***C:*** Geary McLeod; ***M:*** Geoff Levin. **VIDEO**

Who Saw Her Die? *Chi l'Ha Vista Morire* **1972** Sculptor Franco (Lazenby) is visited by his preteen daughter Roberta (Elmi) at his Venice home. Roberta goes missing and is found dead in a canal. When Franco and his estranged wife Elizabeth (Strindberg) investigate, they learn that there has been a cover-up concerning the murders of several other children. Italian with subtitles. **94m/C; DVD, Blu-Ray.** *IT* George Lazenby; Anita Strindberg; Nicoletta Elmi; Adolfo Celi; Peter Chatel; ***D:*** Aldo Lado; ***W:*** Aldo Lado; Francesco Barilli; ***M:*** Ennio Morricone.

Who Shot Pat? 1/2 *Who Shot Patakango?; Brooklyn Love Story* **1992 (R)** Funny, nostalgic, coming of age story set in '50s Brooklyn. Knight stars as Bic Bickham, the leader of a clean-living "gang" of seniors at a Brooklyn vocational school. Memorable vintage soundtrack features hits by legendary artists Chuck Berry and Bo Diddly. **102m/C; VHS, DVD.** David Edwin Knight; Sandra Bullock; Kevin Otto; Aaron Ingram; Brad Randall; ***D:*** Robert Brooks; ***W:*** Robert Brooks; Halle Brooks; ***C:*** Robert Brooks.

Who Slew Auntie Roo? 1/2 *Whoever Slew Auntie Roo?; Gingerbread House* **1971 (PG)** An updated twist on the Hansel and Gretel fairy tale. Features Winters as an odd, reclusive widow mistaken for the fairy tale's children-eating witch by one of the orphans at her annual Christmas party—with dire consequences. **90m/C; VHS, DVD, Blu-Ray.** Shelley Winters; Ralph Richardson; Mark Lester; Lionel Jeffries; Hugh Griffith; ***D:*** Curtis Harrington; ***W:*** Robert Blees.

Who the Hell is Juliette? 1/2 *¿Quien diablos es Juliette?* **1998** This insightful, humorous feature-length documentary considers the commonalities of two women from very different circumstances while also providing a reflection on the filmmaking process. The documentarian, cinematographer Carlos Macovich, was shooting a video in Cuba starring Mexican model Fabiola Quiroz, when he met Yuliet Ortega, a teenage prostitute. He soon learned they had not seen their fathers in many years and began filming this documentary. Macovich focused on the lives of the two women and the process of making the documentary itself. **91m/C; DVD.** ***D:*** Carlos Marcovich; ***W:*** Carlos Marcovich; Carlos Cuaron; ***C:*** Carlos Marcovich; ***M:*** Alejandro Marcovich.

Who Was That Lady? 1/2 **1960** In this outlandish comedy, Ann (Leigh) is quick to accuse her chemistry prof husband David (Curtis) of hanky-panky when she misreads a situation with a student. Panicked, David calls his swinging single pal Michael (Martin) for advice. Michael's a TV writer and tells David to pass himself off as an undercover FBI agent looking for spies. Only the lies come to the attention of a real FBI agent--and some Soviet agents. Curtis and Leigh were married at the time of filming. **114m/B; DVD.** Tony Curtis; Janet Leigh; Dean Martin; James Whitmore; Barbara Nichols; John McIntire; Larry Storch; Simon Oakland; ***D:*** George Sidney; ***W:*** Norman Krasna; ***C:*** Harry Stradling, Sr.; ***M:*** Andre Previn.

Whole New Thing **2005** Precocious 13-year-old Emerson (Webber in his feature debut) has been home-schooled by his hippie parents Kaya (Jenkins) and Rog (Joy). Worried about his social skills, Kaya decides androgynous Emerson should now attend public school, where he's promptly beaten up, which Emerson takes with remarkable poise. He's not so self-possessed about his gay middle-aged English teacher, Don (McIvor), on whom Emerson develops a major crush. Don fends off Emerson's inappropriate advances while suffering through a midlife crisis—one shared by Emerson's parents, who are having marital problems. **92m/C; DVD.** *CA* Rebecca Jenkins; Robert Joy; Callum Keith Rennie; Daniel MacIvor; Aaron Webber; ***D:*** Amnon Buchbinder; ***W:*** Daniel MacIvor; Amnon Buchbinder; ***C:*** Christopher Ball; ***M:*** David Buchbinder.

The Whole Nine Yards 1/2 **2000 (PG-13)** Wimpy dentist Oz (Perry) has his life turned to chaos when former hit man Jimmy (Willis) moves in next door, inspiring his wife Sophie (Arquette), who's bored and wants Oz dead for the insurance money, and Jill, Oz's receptionist, who aspires to be a hit woman herself. Sophie nags Oz into a plot to alert Jimmy's former employers of his whereabouts, which brings in a whole bunch of new over-the-top characters, all of whom want somebody dead. While it's true that most of the plot elements are not only ridiculous, but cribbed from other hit man movies, this one works because the actors all do fine jobs (except maybe Arquette), and seem to be having a good time. One of those movies that plays much better on video than on the big screen. **101m/C; VHS, DVD, Blu-Ray.** Bruce Willis; Matthew Perry; Michael Clarke Duncan; Natasha Henstridge; Amanda Peet; Rosanna Arquette; Kevin Pollak; Harland Williams; ***D:*** Jonathan Lynn; ***W:*** Mitchell Kapner; ***C:*** David Franco; ***M:*** Randy Edelman.

The Whole Shebang **2001** Low-key, sentimental romantic comedy. After the heir to the Barzini fireworks company blows himself up during a little extra-marital nookie, Pop (Giannini) sends for Neapolitan cousin Giovanni (Tucci, heavy on the shtick) to come to New Jersey as a replacement. Giovanni has been suicidally lovesick over a heartless beauty (Champa) but his luck may change when he meets his cousin's not-so-brokenhearted widow, Val (Fonda). Val is being wooed by Joey Zito (DeSando), whose family is eager to learn Pop's pyrotechnical secrets. A big fireworks competition (which was filmed in Naples) adds some pow. **97m/C; DVD.** *US CA* Stanley Tucci; Bridget Fonda; Giancarlo Giannini; Talia Shire; Anthony DeSando; Anna Maria Alberghetti; Jo Champa; Alexander Milani; ***D:*** George Zaloom; ***W:*** Jeff Rothberg; George Zaloom; ***C:*** Jacek Laskus; ***M:*** Evan Lurie.

The Whole Ten Yards 1/2 **2004 (PG-13)** Apparently, this is one yard too many. Stretching the premise of the original into a better-left-undone mess, sequel reunites dorky dentist Oz (Perry) with ex-hitman Jimmy the Tulip (Willis) and his still-aspiring hit woman wife Jill (Peet), who are trying to live on the down-low in Mexico. Jill is still trying (and failing) to become an assassin while Jimmy's attempts at blending in consist of pretending to be a house-husband to terrifically bad comic effect. Oz, meanwhile is living in L.A. with wife Cynthia (Henstridge). Shred of a plot centers around the revenge scheme of Lazlo Gogolak (Pollack), whose son Janni (also Pollack) was whacked by Oz and the Tulip in the not great but infinitely better original. Joyless performances by all underscored by a spectacularly bad Pollack. **99m/C; DVD.** Bruce Willis; Matthew Perry; Amanda Peet; Kevin Pollak; Natasha Henstridge; Frank Collison; Johnny Messner; Silas Weir Mitchell; Tasha Smith; ***D:*** Howard Deutch; ***W:*** Mitchell Kapner; George Gallo; ***C:*** Neil Roach; ***M:*** John Debney.

The Whole Town's Talking **1935** Meek clerk Arthur Jones (Robinson) usually leads an uneventful life, until the police arrest him, thinking he's escaped mobster Killer Mannion (Robinson again). Arthur manages to prove his identity and is issued an ID card to settle the confusion, but the mix-up has hit the papers and when Mannion finds out about his double, he steals the card and kidnaps Arthur's Aunt Agatha (Ellsler) and coworker Wilhelmina (Arhtur) to ensure his cooperation. Mannion goes on a crime spree and Arthur must figure a way out of his double trouble. Based on a novel by William R. Burnett. **95m/B; DVD, Blu-Ray.** Edward G. Robinson; Jean Arthur; Arthur Hohl; Wallace Ford; Arthur Byron; Donald Meek; Paul Harvey; Effie Ellsler; ***D:*** John Ford; ***W:*** Jo Swerling; Robert Riskin; ***C:*** Joseph August.

The Whole Truth 1/2 **2016 (R)** Richard Ramsay (Reeves) has a difficult new client, the son (Basso) of a good friend (Zellweger). The young man murdered his father. On this, there is no disagreement. But did he do so in self-defense or is he perhaps protecting another killer? He's not talking. This is the kind of John Grisham Lite courtroom drama they made every other week in the late '90s, and they stopped making for a reason. It's all harmless enough, but a few ridiculous final act twists that defy all logic make it feel somehow more insulting. **93m/C; DVD, Blu-Ray.** Keanu Reeves; Renée Zellweger; Gugu Mbatha-Raw; Gabriel Basso; James Belushi; ***D:*** Courtney Hunt; ***C:*** Jules O'Loughlin; ***M:*** Evgueni Galperine; Sacha Galperine.

The Whole Wide World **1996 (PG)** Adaptation of Novalyne Price Ellis' memoirs about her friendship with "Conan the Barbarian" pulp writer Robert E. Howard. In 1933, proper young Cross Plains, Texas schoolteacher (and aspiring writer) Price (Zellweger) arranges an introduction to local eccentric Howard (D'Onofrio), who lives with his overprotective, dying mother (Wedgeworth) and respected doctor father (Presnell) while churning out his bloody tales. Howard has few, if any, social skills but his unpredictability appeals to the sensible Price and the two have a turbulent emotional relationship that never blooms into a full romance. Howard committed suicide in 1936 at the age of 30. **111m/C; VHS, DVD, Blu-Ray.** Renée Zellweger; Vincent D'Onofrio; Ann Wedgeworth; Harve Presnell; Helen Cates; Benjamin Mouton; Michael Corbett; Marion Eaten; Leslie Berger; Chris Shearer; Sandy Walper; Dell Aldrich; Libby Villari; Antonia Bogdanovich; Elizabeth D'Onofrio; Stephen Marshall; ***D:*** Dan Ireland; ***W:*** Michael Scott Myers; Novalyne Price Ellis; ***C:*** Claudio Rocha; ***M:*** Hans Zimmer; Harry Gregson-Williams.

Who'll Stop the Rain? 1/2 *Dog Soldiers* **1978 (R)** A temperamental Vietnam vet (Nolte) is enlisted in a smuggling scheme to transport a large amount of heroin into California. An excellent blend of drama, comedy, action, suspense, and tragedy. Based on Robert Stone's novel "Dog Soldiers." Outstanding period soundtrack by Creedence Clearwater Revival, including title song. Violent and compelling tale of late-'60s disillusionment. **126m/C; VHS, DVD, Blu-Ray.** Nick Nolte; Tuesday Weld; Michael Moriarty; Anthony Zerbe; Richard Masur; Ray Sharkey; David Opatoshu; Charles Haid; Gail Strickland; ***D:*** Karel Reisz; ***W:*** Judith Rascoe; ***C:*** Richard H. Kline; ***M:*** Laurence Rosenthal.

Wholly Moses! **WOOF!** **1980 (PG)** Set in biblical times, this alleged comedy concerns a phony religious prophet who begins to believe that his mission is to lead the chosen. Horrible ripoff of "Life of Brian," released the previous year. What a cast—what a waste! **125m/C; VHS, DVD.** Dudley Moore; Laraine Newman; James Coco; Paul Sand; Dom DeLuise; Jack Gilford; John Houseman; Madeline Kahn; Richard Pryor; John Ritter; ***D:*** Gary Weis.

Whoopee! **1930** Cantor stars in his first sound picture as a rich hypochondriac sent out west for his health, where he encounters rugged cowboys and Indians. Filmed in two-color Technicolor and based on Ziegfeld's 1928 Broadway production with the same cast. Dances supervised by Busby Berkeley. **93m/C; DVD.** Eddie Cantor; Ethel Shutta; Paul Gregory; Eleanor Hunt; Betty Grable; ***D:*** Thornton Freeland; ***W:*** William Conselman; ***C:*** Ray Rennahan; Gregg Toland; Lee Garmes.

The Whoopee Boys **1986 (R)** A New York lowlife in Palm Beach tries to reform himself by saving a school for needy children so his rich girlfriend will marry him. Full of unfunny jokes and very bad taste, with no redeeming qualities whatever. **89m/C; VHS, DVD, Blu-Ray.** Michael O'Keefe; Paul Rodriguez; Denholm Elliott; Carol(e) Shelley; Eddie Deezen; Marsha Warfield; Elizabeth Arlen; Joe Spinell; Robert Gwaltney; Stephen Davies; Taylor Negron; Greg Germann; David Keith; Noelle Parker; Dan O'Herlihy; Lucinda Jenney; ***D:*** John Byrum; ***W:*** Jeff Buhai; ***C:*** Ralf Bode; ***M:*** Jack Nitzsche.

Who's Afraid of Virginia Woolf? **1966 (R)** Nichols debuts as a director in this biting Edward Albee play. A teacher and his wife (Segal and Dennis) are invited to the home of a burned-out professor and his foul-mouthed, bitter, yet seductive wife (Burton and Taylor). The guests get more than dinner, as the evening deteriorates into brutal verbal battles between the hosts. Taylor and Dennis won Oscars; Burton's Oscar-nominated portrait of the tortured husband is magnificent. Richard and Liz's best film together. **127m/B; VHS, DVD, Blu-Ray.** Richard Burton; Elizabeth Taylor; George Segal; Sandy Dennis; ***D:*** Mike Nichols; ***W:*** Ernest Lehman; ***C:*** Haskell Wexler; ***M:*** Alex North. Oscars '66: Actress (Taylor), Art Dir./Set Dec., B&W, B&W Cinematog., Costume Des. (B&W), Support. Actress (Dennis); British Acad. '66: Actor (Burton), Actress (Taylor), Film; Natl. Bd. of Review '66: Actress (Taylor); Natl. Film Reg. '13; N.Y. Film Critics '66: Actress (Taylor).

Who's Got the Action? 1/2 **1963** Martin and Turner are a husband and wife divided by his love of playing the ponies. In order to keep his gambling under control Turner schemes to become his new bookie. But when Martin suddenly goes on a winning streak, the new bookie is in trouble with her former competition, who just happen to be the Mob. Strained, flat comedy with Turner especially miscast. **93m/C; VHS, DVD, Blu-Ray.** Lana Turner; Dean Martin; Walter Matthau; Eddie Albert; Nita Talbot; Margo; Paul Ford; John McGiver; Jack Albertson; *D:* Daniel Mann; *W:* Jack Rose.

Who's Got the Black Box? *La Route de Corinthe* **1967** Spy spoof has NATO security agent Robert Ford (Marquand) investigating the whereabouts of 15 black boxes jamming American radar installations in Greece. Robert is killed and his wife Shanny (Seberg) is framed for the crime, but she convinces Robert's former partner Dex (Ronet) to help her find the real criminals. French with subtitles. **90m/C; DVD.** *FR IT* Jean Seberg; Maurice Ronet; Christian Marquand; Michel Bouquet; Saro Urzi; Claude Chabrol; *D:* Claude Chabrol; *W:* Claude Brule; Daniel Boulanger; *C:* Andre Genoves; *M:* Pierre Jansen.

Who's Harry Crumb? 1/2 **1989 (PG-13)** Bumbling detective Candy can't even investigate a routine kidnapping! His incompetence is catching: the viewer can't detect a single genuinely funny moment. Candy is the only likeable thing in this all-around bad, mindless farce. **95m/C; VHS, DVD, Blu-Ray.** John Candy; Jeffrey Jones; Annie Potts; Tim Thomerson; Barry Corbin; Shawnee Smith; Valri Bromfield; Renee Coleman; Joe Flaherty; Lyle Alzado; James Belushi; Stephen Young; *D:* Paul Flaherty; *W:* Robert Conte; *M:* Michel Colombier.

Who's Minding the Mint? **1967** A money checker at the U.S. Mint must replace $50,000 he accidentally destroyed. He enlists a retired money printer and an inept gang to infiltrate the mint and replace the lost cash, with predictable chaos resulting. Non-stop zaniness in this wonderful comedy that never got its due when released. Thieves who befriend Hutton include Denver of "Gilligan's Island" and Farr, later of "M*A*S*H." **97m/C; VHS, Streaming.** Jim Hutton; Dorothy Provine; Milton Berle; Joey Bishop; Bob Denver; Walter Brennan; Jamie Farr; *D:* Howard Morris; *C:* Joseph Biroc.

Who's Minding the Store? 1/2 **1963** Well, it's certainly not Lewis, who plays poodle sitter Raymond Phiffier who's in love with rich girl Barbara (St. John). Barbara's imperious mother (Moorehead) is determined to break up the duo and hires Raymond to work at the family department store (hoping he'll be a disaster), instead he becomes a success in his own slapstick way. **90m/C; VHS, DVD, Blu-Ray, Streaming.** Jerry Lewis; Jill St. John; Agnes Moorehead; John McGiver; Ray Walston; Nancy Kulp; *D:* Frank Tashlin; *W:* Frank Tashlin; Harry Tugend; *C:* W. Wallace Kelley; *M:* Joseph J. Lilley.

Who's That Girl? **1987 (PG)** A flighty, wrongly convicted parolee kidnaps her uptight lawyer and they have wacky adventures as she goes in search of the crumb that landed her in the pokey. Plenty of Madonna tunes, if that's what you like; they briefly keep you from wondering why you're not laughing. Kind of a remake (a bad one) of "Bringing Up Baby" (1938). **94m/C; VHS, DVD.** Madonna; Griffin Dunne; John Mills; Haviland (Haylie) Morris; Albert "Poppy" Popwell; *D:* James Foley; *C:* Jan De Bont. Golden Raspberries '87: Worst Actress (Madonna).

Who's That Knocking at My Door? *J.R.; I Call First* **1968** Interesting debut for Scorsese, in which he exercises many of the themes and techniques that he polished for later films. An autobiographical drama about an Italian-American youth growing up in NYC, focusing on street life, Catholicism and adolescent bonding. Begun as a student film called "I Call First"; later developed into a feature. Keitel's film debut. **90m/B; VHS, DVD.** Harvey Keitel; Zena Bethune; *D:* Martin Scorsese.

Who's the Man? **1993 (R)** Two clowning companions who work in a barbershop in Harlem get recruited onto the police force to investigate a murder. Doctor Dre and Ed Lover (themselves) make use of their hip-hop music connections and full-throttle slapstick humor to enliven the search. Salt of "Salt 'n' Pepa," is the female lead and Ice-T plays a gangster. First-time director Demme works his star duo for both foolish and vulgar humor. Filming done mostly on location in Harlem. Includes a lengthy list of cameo appearances by several hip-hop performers. For fans; based on a story by Dre, Lover, and Seth Greenland. **124m/C; VHS, DVD.** Ed Lover; Cheryl "Salt" James; Ice-T; Jim Moody; Colin Quinn; Kim Chan; Rozwill Young; Badja (Medu) Djola; Richard Bright; Denis Leary; Andre B. Blake; Bill Bellamy; Louis Freese; *D:* Ted (Edward) Demme; *W:* Seth Greenland; *M:* Michael Wolff.

Who's Who **1978** In a satire on climbing the British social ladder, workers in a London brokerage firm struggle with class issues and find the higher you climb, the more you find greed, pettiness, and stupidity. **75m/C; VHS, DVD.** *GB* Bridget Kane; Simon Chandler; Adam Norton; Philip Davis; Joolia Cappleman; *D:* Mike Leigh; *W:* Mike Leigh. **TV**

Who's Your Caddy? 1/2 **2007 (PG-13)** Rap mogul C-Note (Patton) tries to become a member at the conservative Carolina Pines country club, where he's opposed by snobby club president Cummings (Jones). But C-Note blackmails his way in, causing predictable havoc. Vulgarity and stereotypes abound. **93m/C; DVD.** Antwan Andre Patton; Jeffrey Jones; Sherri Shepherd; Faizon Love; Jenifer Lewis; Tamala Jones; Andy Milonakis; Chase Tatum; *D:* Don Michael Paul; *W:* Don Michael Paul; Bradley Allenstein; Robert Henny; *C:* Thomas Callaway; *M:* Jon Lee.

Who's Your Monkey 1/2 *Throwing Stars* **2007 (R)** Four longtime buddies are in a crisis after doctor Mark (Grimes) kills a threatening local drug dealer and they need to get rid of the body. And, uh, animal porn is a main plot point, which would explain the monkey. **86m/C; DVD.** Scott Grimes; Jason London; Scott Michael Campbell; David DeLuise; Kevin Durand; Wayne Knight; Ali Hillis; Susan May Pratt; *D:* Todd Breau; *W:* Ryan Steckloff; *C:* Michael Jacob Kerber; *M:* Ron Alan Cohen. **VIDEO**

Whose Life Is It Anyway? 1/2 **1981 (R)** Black humor abounds. Sculptor Dreyfuss is paralyzed from the neck down in an auto accident. What follows is his struggle to persuade the hospital authorities to let him die. Excellent cast headed impressively by Dreyfuss; Lahti as his doctor and hospital head Cassavetes also are superb. From Brian Clark's successful Broadway play. **118m/C; VHS, DVD.** Richard Dreyfuss; John Cassavetes; Christine Lahti; Bob Balaban; Kenneth McMillan; Kaki Hunter; Thomas Carter; *D:* John Badham; *W:* Reginald Rose; Brian Clark.

Whose Streets? 1/2 **2017 (R)** This revealing documentary explores the aftermath of the 2014 shooting of 18-year-old Michael Brown, a young black man, by a white police officer, Darren Wilson, in Ferguson, Missouri. Told solely from the point of view of activists and citizens who protested in the wake of the shooting, the film offers a subjective, in-the-moment account of the incidents that followed, such as the use of tear gas against these civilians. Showing how these residents responded to such events--and how they felt white authorities responded to them--tells an important story. **90m/C; DVD.** *D:* Sabaah Folayan; Damon Davis; *C:* Lucas Alvarado-Farrar; *M:* Samora Pinderhughes.

Why Am I Doing This? **2009** Ensemble Hollywood comedy. Struggling actor Tony (Chang) is only hired for Asian stereotype roles when he finds work at all. He makes ends meet with catering and children's birthday gigs. His black roommate Lester (Montgomery) is a cerebral stand-up comedian who's constantly told he's not edgy enough. Both have some romantic complications but most of the humor comes out of the L.A. showbiz scene. **118m/C; DVD.** Tom Huang; Anthony Montgomery; Sheetal Sheth; Lynn Chen; Joe Torry; Emma Caulfield; Valarie Pettiford; Obba Babatunde; Teddy Chen Culver; Dion Basco; Tamlyn Tomita; Gerry Bednob; *D:* Tom Huang; *W:* Tom Huang; *C:* Jeff Bollman; *M:* Timo Chen.

Why Be Good? **1929** Saucy silent stars the delightful Moore as flapper shopgirl Pert Kelly, who isn't thought to be good enough for the love-struck son of the boss. Dad suggests Jr. take Pert to a hot club to see how she behaves. And since Pert's no dummy, she shows everyone how much fun it is to be bad. **81m/B; Silent; DVD.** Colleen Moore; Neil Hamilton; Edward Martindel; Bodil Rosing; John St. Polis; *D:* William A. Seiter; *W:* Carey Wilson; *C:* Sidney Hickox.

Why Change Your Wife? 1/2 **1920** A rare, recently re-discovered silent comedy. Swanson and Meighan play married couple Beth and Robert who find themselves drifting apart after ten years of marriage. Robert becomes involved with someone else and Beth demands a divorce. After Robert remarries, Beth decides she wants him back and the real fun begins as she tries every trick in the book to regain her ex-husband. Piano scored. **100m/B; Silent; VHS, DVD.** Gloria Swanson; Thomas Meighan; Bebe Daniels; *D:* Cecil B. DeMille.

Why Do Fools Fall in Love? **1998 (R)** Frankie Lymon was a teen do-wop singing sensation in the mid-'50s but a career slide led to heroin addiction and an OD death at the age of 25 in 1968. The other thing Frankie liked to do was marry—without bothering to get divorced. So there are three would-be widows battling for what's left of Lymon's estate: R&B singer Zola Taylor (Berry), goodtime girl and single mom Elizabeth Waters (Fox), and churchgoing schoolteacher Emira Eagle (Rochon). The ladies pull out of the stops but Lymon remains a mystery. **115m/C; VHS, DVD.** Larenz Tate; Halle Berry; Lela Rochon; Vivica A. Fox; Paul Mazursky; Pamela Reed; Little Richard; Ben Vereen; Lane Smith; Alexis Cruz; *D:* Gregory Nava; *W:* Tina Andrews; *C:* Edward Lachman; *M:* Stephen James Taylor.

Why Do They Call It Love When They Mean Sex? *Por Que Lo Llaman Amor Cuando Quieren Decir Sexo?* **1992** Gloria (Forque) works in a live-sex act but is forced to change partners and work with inexperienced Manu (Sanz), who needs some quick cash because of gambling debts. But everything goes well until Manu's respectable parents meet Gloria and think the duo are just a nice conventional couple. **115m/C; VHS, DVD.** *SP* Jorge Sanz; Veronica Forque; Fernando Colomo; Fernando Guillen; Rosa Maria Sarda; Alejandra Grepi; Elisa Matilla; Isabel Ordaz; *D:* Manuel Gomez Pereira; *W:* Manuel Gomez Pereira; *C:* Hans Burman; *M:* Manuel Tena.

Why Does Herr R. Run Amok? *Warum Lauft Herr R Amok?* **1969** Notorious Fassbinder black comedy about a middle-class man, unable to cope with the increasing problems of modern life, who suddenly murders his family. The characters are called by the actors' names to heighten the sense of reality. Film is based on a case history. In German with English subtitles. **88m/C; VHS, DVD.** *GE* Kurt Raab; Lilith Ungerer; Amadeus Fengler; Hanna Schygulla; Franz Maron; *D:* Rainer Werner Fassbinder; Michael Fengler; *W:* Rainer Werner Fassbinder; Michael Fengler.

Why Has Bodhi-Darma Left for the East **1989** Set in a remote monastery in the Korean mountains, film follows an old master, close to death, who must lead his disciples in their search for spiritual freedom. The film's title is a Zen koan—an unanswerable riddle that serves as an aid on the path to enlightenment. Korean with subtitles. **135m/C; VHS, DVD.** *NK* Hae-Jin Huang; Su-Myong Ko; Yi Pan-Yong; Sin Won-Sop; *D:* Bae Young-kyun; *W:* Bae Young-kyun; *C:* Bae Young-kyun.

Why Him? **2016 (R)** The super-talented cast here offers a few jokes and the premise is fun, but it doesn't really go anywhere and isn't nearly as funny as it should be. John Hamburg, who wrote "Meet the Parents" and its sequel returns to that well again with the twist being that the potential son-in-law is the problem child in the dynamic. When Ned Fleming (a game Cranston) meets the Silicon Valley billionaire boyfriend (Franco, in full annoyance mode) of his daughter, he immediately hates him. Can the two men come together over the mutual love for the same woman? Probably. But silly stuff happens first. **111m/C; DVD, Blu-Ray.** James Franco; Bryan Cranston; Zoey Deutch; Megan Mullally; Cedric the Entertainer; Keegan Michael Key; Griffin Gluck; *D:* John Hamburg; *W:* John Hamburg; Ian Helfer; *C:* Kris Kachikis; *M:* Theodore Shapiro.

Why I Wore Lipstick to My Mastectomy 1/2 **2006** True story based on the memoir by TV exec Geralyn Lucas. Happily married and excited by her new job, 27-year-old Geralyn (Chalke) is thrown when she's diagnosed with breast cancer. She decides to go public and (with a strong support system) uses humor to help her cope with surgery, chemo, and her fears. **90m/C; DVD.** Jay Harrington; Lally Cadeau; Harvey Atkin; Robin Brule; Patti LaBelle; Sarah Chalke; *D:* Peter Werner; *W:* Nancey Silvers. **CABLE**

Why Must I Die? 1/2 *Thirteen Steps to Death* **1960** Low-budget sensationalism from AIP and director Del Ruth's last pic. Singer Lois King (Moore) walks out on her crook boyfriend Eddie (Ames) to make a new life. She falls for club owner Kenny Randall (Harvey) before Eddie and his hard-boiled new squeeze Dottie (Paget) show up, wanting Lois to help them rob the joint. Trigger-happy Dottie kills Kenny but it's Lois who's tried, convicted, and sentenced to death row. When unrepentant Dottie is imprisoned on another crime, can Lois convince her to tell the truth or will she soon be getting the shock of her life? **86m/B; DVD.** Terry Moore; Debra Paget; Bert Freed; Juli Reding; Phil Harvey; Lionel Ames; Fred Sherman; *D:* Roy Del Ruth; *W:* Richard Bernstein; George Waters; *C:* Ernest Haller; *M:* Richard LaSalle.

Why Shoot the Teacher **1979** A young teacher sent to a one-room schoolhouse in a small prairie town in Saskatchewan during the Depression gets a cold reception on the cold prairie. One of the more popular films at the Canadian box office. Cort was Harold in "Harold and Maude." Based on the novel by Max Braithwaite. **101m/C; VHS, DVD.** *CA* Bud Cort; Samantha Eggar; Chris Wiggins; *D:* Silvio Narizzano; *W:* James DeFelice.

Why Stop Now 1/2 *Predisposed* **2012 (R)** In this absurd dramedy, piano prodigy Eli (Eisenberg) tries to get his coke-addict mom Penny (Leo) into rehab on the day of his big music conservatory audition. She can't be admitted since she's momentarily off drugs, and they head to Penny's dealer Sprinkles (Morgan) to score. As luck would hav it, Sprinkles is out of product and needs Spanish-speaking Eli to negogiate with his Latino supplier. Pic wanders from annoying to kooky to distracting and back again. **88m/C; DVD, Blu-Ray.** Jesse Eisenberg; Melissa Leo; Tracy Morgan; Isiah Whitlock, Jr.; Paul Calderon; Sarah Ramos; Emma Rayne Lyle; *D:* Philip Dorling; Ron Nyswaner; *W:* Philip Dorling; Ron Nyswaner; *C:* Ben Kutchins; *M:* Spencer David Hutchings.

The Wicked *Outback Vampires* **1989** Though packaged as serious horror, this is a cheap, tacky spoof with folks stranded at the country residence of a vampire family. Sole point of interest: these Transylvanian cliches take place in the Australian outback. Kids might actually like this (gore isn't severe), if they can surmount the thick Down Under accents. **87m/C; VHS, DVD.** Brett Cumo; Richard Morgan; Angela Kennedy; Maggie Blinco; John (Roy Slaven) Doyle; *D:* Colin Eggleston.

Wicked **1998 (R)** Fourteen-year-old Ellie (Stiles) has a big Electra complex—she's desperate to get Daddy Ben's (Moses) attention (he's too busy boffing their au pair) and get rid of Mom Karen (Field). Then Karen is murdered and Detective Boland (Parks) first suspects their sleazy neighbor, Lawson (Muldoon), with whom Karen had been carrying on. But Inger, Ellie's younger sister, notices that things aren't, well, normal between her sibling and their pop. But the twists aren't done yet. **87m/C; VHS, DVD.** Julia Stiles; William R. Moses; Chelsea Field; Patrick Muldoon; Michael Parks; Vanessa Zima; *D:* Michael Steinberg; *W:* Eric Weiss; *C:* Bernd Heinl; *M:* Eric Martinez.

Wicked Blood **2013** Southern-fried family gothic with overdone narration and metaphors. Chess prodigy Hannah (Breslin) copes with her father's sudden death, her sibling rivalry with older sister Amber (Vega), and her Uncle Donny's (Temple) drug addiction by going to work for local Louisiana drug/crime kingpin, Frank Stinson (Bean). There, Hannah discovers Amber's biker boyfriend, Wild Bill (Purefoy), has some drug connections of his own. **92m/C; DVD, Blu-Ray.** Abigail Breslin; Alexa Vega; Sean Bean; Lew Temple; James Purefoy; Jake Busey; *D:* Mark Young; *W:* Mark Young; *C:* Gregg Easterbrook; *M:* Elia Cmiral. **VIDEO**

Wicked City 🦴🦴🦴 **1989** Wild and woolly anime is similar in tone to a James Bond movie. In fact, the whole production has a mid-'60s look. A young man named Taki is picked up by a sexy woman in a bar and regrets his decision when she does one of those really icky transformations. Seems she's a visitor from the parallel Black World of monsters. He's an agent of the Black Guard, a secret intelligence organization that protects the Earth from these supernatural bad guys. The story revolves around Guiseppi Mayart, a strange little character who looks (and acts!) like an oversexed E.T., and is the key to a treaty between the two worlds. Taki and his reluctant female partner Makea are assigned to guard the debauched diplomat. **82m/C; DVD.** *JP V:* Greg Snegoff; Michael J. Reynolds; Alexandra Kenworthy; *D:* Yoshiaki Kawajiri; *W:* Kisei Choo; *C:* Kinichi Ishikawa.

Wicked City 🦴🦴 **1992** Humans are uneasily coexisting with Reptoids (creatures that can assume human shape) in this sci-fi tale based on a Japanese comic strip. Then Hong Kong police discover a plot by the Reptoids to destroy mankind and rule the world (what else is new). Nifty special effects. Available dubbed or in Cantonese with subtitles. **88m/C; VHS, DVD.** *CH* Jacky Cheung; Leon Lai; Michelle Li; Tatsuya Nakadai; Yuen Woo Ping; Roy Cheung; *D:* Peter Mak; *W:* Tsui Hark; Roy Szeto; *C:* Wai Keung (Andrew) Lau; Joe Chan; *M:* Richard Yuen.

The Wicked Lady 🦴🦴 **1945** Posh but lame costume drama about a bored 17th century noblewoman who takes to highway robbery to spice up her life. Credulity-stretcher extraordinaire. Based on "The Life and Death of Wicked Lady Skelton" by Magdalen King-Hall. Mason is cheeky as a fellow highwayman. Remade in 1983 with Faye Dunaway. **103m/B; DVD.** *UK* James Mason; Margaret Lockwood; Patricia Roc; Michael Rennie; Felix Aylmer; Enid Stamp-Taylor; Griffith Jones; *D:* Leslie Arliss; *W:* Leslie Arliss; Aimee Stuart; *C:* Jack Cox; *M:* Hans May.

Wicked Lake 🦴 **1/2 2008** Four lesbian witches go to a remote mountain cabin to perform a ritual, get insulted and assaulted by the local rednecks, and take bloody revenge at midnight when their powers spontaneously pop into being. There's no one to root for in this film—not the doltish cowardly men, not the smart slutty psychopaths who like to get naked and make out when they're not getting even in the bloodiest of ways. Wait, maybe there is someone to root for. **95m/C; DVD.** Will Keenan; Robin Sydney; Tim Thomerson; Carlee Baker; Frank Birney; Michael Esparza; Eryn Joslyn; Eve Mauro; Marc Senter; *D:* Zach Passero; *W:* Chris Sivertson; Adam Rockoff; *C:* Stephen Osborn; *M:* Al Jourgensen. **VIDEO**

Wicked Little Things 🦴 **1/2 2007 (R)** Karen (Lori Heuring) moves her family to a remote house in the mountains after losing her husband (and all the family's money.) Her bad luck continues to hold, as it turns out her new place is infested with dead people. **94m/C; DVD, Blu-Ray, Streaming.** Lori Heuring; Scout Taylor-Compton; Chloë Grace Moretz; Geoffrey Lewis; Ben Cross; *D:* J.S. Cardone; *W:* Boaz Davidson; Ben Nedivi; *C:* Emil Topuzov; *M:* Tim Wynne-Jones.

Wicked Stepmother 🦴 **1989 (PG-13)** A family discovers that an aged stepmother is actually a witch. Davis walked off the film shortly before she died, and was replaced by Carrera. Davis's move was wise; the result is dismal, and would have been had she stayed. As it is the viewer wonders: How come the stepmother isn't Davis anymore? Davis's unfortunate last role. **90m/C; VHS, DVD.** Bette Davis; Barbara Carrera; Colleen Camp; Lionel Stander; David Rasche; Tom Bosley; Seymour Cassel; Evelyn Keyes; Richard Moll; Laurene Landon; James Dixon; *D:* Larry Cohen; *W:* Larry Cohen; *C:* Bryan England; *M:* Robert Folk.

Wicked Ways 🦴🦴 *A Table for One* **1999 (R)** Matt Draper (Rooker) is a bigamist. And when wife Ruth (De Mornay) discovers his other life, she becomes determined to make the vow "till death do us part" a reality. Watchable cast in a familiar storyline. **110m/C; VHS, DVD.** Rebecca De Mornay; Michael Rooker; Lisa Zane; Mark Rolston; Peter Dobson; *D:* Ron Senkowski; *W:* Ron Senkowski; *C:* Chris Walling; *M:* Evan Evans. **VIDEO**

Wicked, Wicked **WOOF! 1973** Crummy slasher pic filmed in 'Duo-Vision,' which is just a split-screen process doing nothing to enhance this dull story. A psycho handyman who works at a California resort likes to dismember the guests. Music is the original score from the 1925 silent classic "The Phantom of the Opera." **95m/C; DVD.** Randolph (Randy) Roberts; Scott Brady; David Bailey; Tiffany Bolling; Edd Byrnes; Diane McBain; *D:* Richard L. Bare; *W:* Richard L. Bare; *C:* Frederick Gately; *M:* Philip Springer.

The Wicked, Wicked West 🦴🦴 *Painted Angels* **1997 (R)** Follows the desolate lives of several prostitutes and their pragmatic madam Annie Ryan (Fricker) in a prairie town bordello in the 1870s. **108m/C; VHS, DVD.** Brenda Fricker; Kelly McGillis; Bronagh Gallagher; Meret Becker; Lisa Jakub; *D:* Jon Sanders; *W:* Jon Sanders; *C:* Gerald Packer.

The Wicker Man 🦴🦴🦴 **1/2 1975** The disappearance of a young girl leads a devoutly religious Scottish policeman to an island whose denizens practice bizarre pagan sexual rituals. An example of occult horror that achieves its mounting terror without gratuitous gore. The first original screenplay by playwright Shaffer. Beware shortened versions that may still lurk out there; the 103-minute restored director's cut is definitive. **103m/C; VHS, DVD, Blu-Ray.** *GB* Edward Woodward; Christopher Lee; Britt Ekland; Diane Cilento; Ingrid Pitt; Lindsay Kemp; Irene Sunters; Walter Carr; Geraldine Cowper; Lesley Mackie; *D:* Robin Hardy; *W:* Anthony Shaffer; *C:* Harry Waxman; *M:* Paul Giovanni.

The Wicker Man **WOOF! 2006 (PG-13)** What was originally creepily foreboding (with a shocker ending) has turned into a laughable muddle in this remake of the 1973 Brit horror pic. An overwrought Cage stars as troubled cop Edward Malus, who looks into the disappearance of ex-fiance Willow's (Beahan) young daughter. This involves traveling to an isolated island community off the Washington coast, where Malus discovers a matriarchal community of beekeepers led by Sister Summerisle (Burstyn) practicing pagan goddess rites. Why LaBute wanted to do this story in the first place is a bigger mystery than why it turned out so badly. **97m/C; DVD.** Nicolas Cage; Ellen Burstyn; Kate Beahan; Frances Conroy; Molly Parker; Leelee Sobieski; Diane Delano; Erika-Shaye Gair; Michael Wiseman; Aaron Eckhart; James Franco; Jason Ritter; *D:* Neil LaBute; *W:* Neil LaBute; *C:* Paul Sarossy; *M:* Angelo Badalamenti.

Wicker Park 🦴🦴 **2004 (PG-13)** A sluggish homage to the 1996 French thriller "L'Appartement." Chicago advertising exec Matthew (Hartnett) is engaged to Rebecca (Pare), his boss' sister, when he thinks he sees his one true love, Lisa (Kruger), who disappeared from his life two years before. Matt cancels a business trip and tells no one except best bud Luke (Lillard) as he hunts for the dame. This leads him to an apartment rented by the mysterious Alex (Byrne), who was Lisa's neighbor. Romantic obsession, stalking, and many confusing flashbacks ensue and everyone, except for the goofy Lillard, seems quite glum. **115m/C; DVD.** Josh Hartnett; Rose Byrne; Matthew Lillard; Diane Kruger; Christopher Cousins; Jessica Pare; *D:* Paul McGuigan; *W:* Brandon Boyce; *C:* Peter Sova; *M:* Cliff Martinez; Liza Richardson.

The Wicker Tree 🦴 **2010 (R)** Hardy directed the infinitely scary "The Wicker Man" in 1973 but this late companion pic is much tamer fare. A couple of clueless missionaries from Texas decide to bring the good word to a quaint Scottish village at the invite of Sir Lachlan, who owns the local nuclear power plant. They're so patronizing and dumb you can't wait for them to become the usual sacrifices. **96m/C; DVD, Blu-Ray.** *UK* Brittania Nicol; Henry Garrett; Graham McTavish; Honeysuckle Weeks; Jacqueline Leonard; Clive Russell; *D:* Robin Hardy; *W:* Robin Hardy; *C:* Jan Pester; *M:* John Scott.

Wide Awake 🦴🦴 **1/2 1997 (PG)** After the death of his beloved grandfather (Loggia), a young Catholic school boy (Cross) begins a mission to find God in order to find out if his grandpa is O.K. He asks difficult questions of his parents (Leary and Delaney) and teachers, including O'Donnell as a sports obsessed nun who compares Jesus and his disciples to a baseball team. He explores Judaism, Islam and Buddhism as well as Christianity. Finally he has an encounter with an angel that restores his faith. While Cross comes across well, the fellow youngsters in the movie have a stagy stiffness to their lines and expressions that lend the movie a hokey feel. **88m/C; VHS, DVD.** Joseph Cross; Dana Delany; Rosie O'Donnell; Denis Leary; Robert Loggia; Dan Lauria; Timothy Reifsnyder; Camryn Manheim; *D:* M. Night Shyamalan; *W:* M. Night Shyamalan; *C:* Adam Holender; *M:* Edmund Choi.

Wide Awake 🦴 **1/2 2007** Medical researcher Cassie Wade (Peregrym) suffers from narcolepsy and is working on a potential drug cure. After discovering that the drug trials have been sabotaged, Cassie turns to reporter Robert Turner (Lemke) for help. A conspiracy is involved but Cassie has to stay awake to stay alive. **90m/C; DVD.** Missy Peregrym; Anthony Lemke; Scott Wickware; Joseph Di Mambro; Michael McMurtry; Derek McGrath; Jim Codrington; *D:* Penelope Buitenhuis; *W:* Brian McCarthy; *C:* Alwyn Kumst; *M:* Stacey Hersh. **CABLE**

The Wide Blue Road 🦴🦴🦴 *La Grande Strada Azzurra* **1957** Neo-realist melodrama stars Montand as stubborn fisherman Squarcio, who lives with his family in a small village off the Adriatic Sea. Determined to support his family by any means, he scorns the nets used by his fellow fisherman and instead goes illegal dynamite fishing. Successful at first, this practice leads to tragedy for Squarcio and his family. Pontecorvo's debut film; Italian with subtitles. **99m/C; VHS, DVD.** *IT* Yves Montand; Alida Valli; Francisco Rabal; Frederica Ranchi; Ronaldo Bonacchi; *D:* Gillo Pontecorvo; *W:* Gillo Pontecorvo; Franco Solinas; *C:* Mario Montuori; *M:* Carlo Franci.

Wide Open Faces 🦴🦴 **1938** Every crook in town is looking for some missing stolen loot. Soda jerk Brown outwits them all in his own inimitable way. The story may be predictable, but Brown's physical humor keeps things interesting. **67m/B; VHS, DVD.** Joe E. Brown; Jane Wyman; Alison Skipworth; Alan Baxter; Lucien Littlefield; Sidney Toler; Berton Churchill; Barbara Pepper; Stanley Fields; Horace Murphy; *D:* Kurt Neumann; *C:* Paul Vogel.

Wide Sargasso Sea 🦴🦴 **1992 (NC-17)** Jamaica in the 1840s is a seething, mysterious paradise—a former British slave colony with a mix of powerful voodoo culture, beauty, and eroticism providing a very potent brew, a perfect setting for this soaper. Based on the novel by Jean Rhys, which is something of a prequel to Charlotte Bronte's "Jane Eyre." Properly English Edward Rochester meets and marries the tragic Antoinette—the same mad wife locked in the attic in the Bronte novel. Explicit nudity and sex earn the NC-17, but the film is tragic without being sensationalized. Also available in an edited R-rated and unrated versions. **98m/C; VHS, DVD.** *AU* Karina Lombard; Nathaniel Parker; Rachel Ward; Michael York; Martine Beswick; Claudia Robinson; Rowena King; Huw Christie Williams; *D:* John Duigan; *W:* Jan Sharp; Carole Angier; John Duigan; *C:* Geoff Burton; *M:* Stewart Copeland.

Wide Sargasso Sea 🦴🦴 **1/2 2006** TV adaptation made for the BBC that's based on the 1966 novel by Jean Rhys, which she wrote as a prequel to Charlotte Bronte's "Jane Eyre." Young Edward Rochester (Spall) goes to Jamaica to make his fortune and meets Creole beauty Antoinette Cosway-Mason (Hall). Her family offers a substantial dowry and they swiftly marry—before Edward learns about Antoinette's tragic past or the madness that runs in her family. Lust, betrayal, and revenge follow. Previously (and explicitly) filmed in 1993. **84m/C; DVD.** *GB* Rafe Spall; Rebecca Hall; Nina Sosanya; Victoria Hamilton; Fraser Ayres; Karen Meagher; Lorraine Burroughs; Alex Robertson; *D:* Brendan Maher; *W:* Stephen Greenhorn; *C:* David Luther; *M:* Nina Humphreys. **TV**

Widow Couderc 🦴🦴🦴 **1974** A provincial widow unknowingly includes an escaped murderer among her liaisons. Based on a novel by Georges Simenon. In French with English subtitles. **92m/C; VHS, DVD.** *FR* Simone Signoret; Alain Delon; *D:* Pierre Granier-Deferre.

The Widow of Saint-Pierre 🦴🦴🦴 *La Veuve de Saint-Pierre* **2000 (R)** Saint-Pierre is a remote French-run island off the coast of Newfoundland. In 1849, drunken sailor Neel Auguste (Kusturica) is involved in a murder and condemned to death via guillotine—known as the "widow." But the island doesn't have one and it must be sent from another French colony. In the meantime, Auguste is in the custody of the local military officer, Le Capitaine (Auteuil), whose compassionate wife (Binoche) has a repentent Auguste released to do chores for the islanders. But the more Auguste becomes part of the community, the more the townspeople become uneasy about the rightness of his fate. French with subtitles. **112m/C; VHS, DVD.** *FR* Juliette Binoche; Daniel Auteuil; Emir Kusturica; Michel Duchaussoy; Sylvie Moreau; Sarah McKenna; Reynald Bouchard; Philippe Magnan; *D:* Patrice Leconte; *W:* Claude Faraldo; *C:* Eduardo Serra; *M:* Pascal Esteve.

Widow on the Hill 🦴🦴 **2005** Oh-so-trashy true crime story. Blonde bombshell nurse Linda Dupree (Henstridge) is hired by wealthy Virginia rancher Hank Cavanaugh (Brolin) to look after his dying wife Felicia (Duquet). Too soon after their mother's death for his disgusted daughters, Jenny (Staite) and Monica (Deines), the besotted widower marries Linda, changes his will, and dies himself. Jenny is suspicious and certain that Linda helped both deaths along and she's going to prove it. **90m/C; DVD.** Natasha Henstridge; James Brolin; Jewel Staite; Melinda Deines; Michelle Duquet; Jeff Roop; Gabriel Hogan; *D:* Peter Svatek; *W:* Stephen Harrigan; *C:* David (Robert) A. Greene; *M:* Danny Lux. **CABLE**

The Widowing of Mrs. Holroyd 🦴🦴 **1995** Adapted from an early play by D.H. Lawrence and based on memories of his parents' tempestuous marriage. Mrs. Holroyd (Wanamaker) wishes her blustering coal miner husband (Firth) dead after she falls in love with another man (Dillane). When he suddenly does die, she finds her life changing in unexpected ways. **90m/C; DVD.** *GB* Zoe Wanamaker; Colin Firth; Stephen (Dillon) Dillane; Brenda Bruce; *D:* Katie Mitchell. **TV**

Widows 🦴🦴 **1/2 2002 (PG-13)** A gang of professional thieves are double-crossed and killed during the attempted theft of a Vermeer from an art gallery. When the police bring in their widows for questioning, Dolly (Ruehl) gets suspicious about the circumstances. So she recruits the other women to avenge their men's deaths and to carry out the original heist. **168m/C; VHS, DVD.** Mercedes Ruehl; Brooke Shields; Rosie Perez; N'Bushe Wright; Jay O. Sanders; Nigel Bennett; Colm Feore; Rod Wilson; Jacob Davis; Lark Voorhies; *D:* Geoffrey Sax; *W:* Lynda La Plante; *C:* Alan Caso; *M:* Simon Boswell. **TV**

Widows 🦴🦴🦴 **2018 (R)** After her beloved husband Harry Rawlins (Neeson) dies in a robbery gone bad, Veronica (Davis) has little time to mourn. She and the three widows of his co-conspirators face a multimillion dollar debt and threats from crime lord Jatemme (Kaluuya). Veronica decides to attempt the heist by partnering with Linda (Rodriguez), Alice (Debicki), and Belle (Erivo), using the plans her late husband left behind. Director/co-screenwriter McQueen has crafted an intense yet entertaining Chicago-set thriller based on the Lynda La Plante novel. Featuring an all-star cast, Davis is at the top of her game as the widow who leads this unlikely group of thieves. **128m/C; DVD, Blu-Ray.** Viola Davis; Liam Neeson; Jon Bernthal; Manuel Garcia-Rulfo; Michelle Rodriguez; *D:* Steve McQueen; *W:* Steve McQueen; Gillian Flynn; *C:* Sean Bobbitt; *M:* Hans Zimmer.

Widow's Peak 🦴🦴 **1/2 1994 (PG)** 1920s Irish community is run by a dictatorship of well-to-do widows with Mrs. Doyle-Counihan (Plowright) at the helm. Troubles begin for the town non-widow (Farrow) upon the arrival of recently widowed Broome (Richardson), who attracts Dunbar, the nitwit son of Plowright. Entertaining performances (Farrow shows that success is possible after the Wood-man) and beautiful scenery help boost a script that seems torn between whimsical comedy and dark drama. **102m/C; VHS, DVD.** *GB* Mia Farrow; Joan Plowright; Natasha Richardson; Adrian Dunbar; Jim Broadbent; John Kavanagh; Gerard McSorley; Anne Kent; Rynagh O'Grady; Michael James Ford; Garrett Keogh; ***D:*** John Irvin; ***W:*** Hugh Leonard; ***C:*** Ashley Rowe; ***M:*** Carl Davis.

Wiener-Dog 🦴🦴 1/2 **2016 (R)** Solondz turns his cynical worldview to the vantage point of a dachshund, who travels from foster family to foster family, allowing the writer/director to continue his chronicles of suburban malaise and dysfunction. If you don't like one story, another will come along, but the feeling that Solondz doesn't really like his characters is still a hard one to shake. While the film feels looser and more enjoyable than most of his works, most nonfans will want to avoid. **88m/C; DVD, Blu-Ray.** Keaton Nigel Cooke; Tracy Letts; Julie Delpy; Greta Gerwig; Kieran Culkin; Danny DeVito; Zoe Mamet; Michael James Shaw; Ellen Burstyn; ***D:*** Todd Solondz; ***W:*** Todd Solondz; ***C:*** Edward Lachman; ***M:*** James Lavino.

Wieners 🦴 **2008 (R)** Typically infantile gross-out comedy. Buddies Joel (Kranz), Ben (Levi), and Wyatt (Thompson) travel cross-country in a custom weiner van in order to confront smarmy daytime talk show therapist Dr. Dwayne (Hammond). The doc encouraged Joel's girlfriend to break up with him, humiliating Joel live and nationwide. Along the route the boys pass out free hot dogs and encounter a number of disgusting situations and weird people. And beware—McCarthy (as the trio's hot-for-teacher fantasy) has only one scene despite her promo prominence. **93m/C; DVD.** Fran Kranz; Zachary Levi; Darrell Hammond; Jenny McCarthy; Keenan Thompson; Andy Milonakis; ***D:*** Mark Steilen; ***W:*** Suzanne Francis; Gabe Grifoni; ***C:*** Walt Lloyd; ***M:*** David Kitay. **VIDEO**

The Wife 🦴🦴 **1995 (R)** The routine of married psychotherapists Jack (Noonan) and Rita (Hagerty), who live in an isolated Vermont farmhouse, is disrupted by the unexpected (and unwelcome) appearance of Jack's patient Cosmo (Shawn), who's in crisis, and his wife Arlie (Young). Everyone's got secrets and marital dilemmas that come spilling out over too much wine. A variation on "Who's Afraid of Virginia Woolf?" **101m/C; VHS, DVD.** Tom Noonan; Julie Hagerty; Karen Young; Wallace Shawn; ***D:*** Tom Noonan; ***W:*** Tom Noonan; ***C:*** Joe DeSalvo; ***M:*** Tom Noonan.

The Wife 🦴🦴 1/2 **2017 (R)** A fascinating drama that explores cracks in an unhealthy marriage. For decades, Joan Castleman (Close) has supported her author husband Joe (Pryce) by anticipating and meeting his every need. When Joe receives the long-awaited call that he has won the Nobel Prize for literature, he looks to Joan for support. At a small celebration the couple holds at their home, Joe receives adoration while Joan serves champagne and dismisses suggestions that she deserves thanks. As truths about their past and present are revealed, Joan gains the strength to come into her own. Strong performances by Pryce and, especially, Close. **100m/C; DVD, Blu-Ray.** *US SW UK* Glenn Close; Jonathan Pryce; Christian Slater; Max Irons; Elizabeth McGovern; ***D:*** Bjorn Runge; ***W:*** Jane Anderson; ***C:*** Ulf Brantas; ***M:*** Jocelyn Pook. Golden Globes '19: Actress--Drama (Close); Ind. Spirit '19: Actress (Close); Screen Actors Guild '17: Actress (Close).

Wife, Husband and Friend 🦴🦴 **1939** New York singing teacher Hugo (Romero) persuades housewife Doris (Young) that she can become a professional. Businessman hubby Leonard (Baxter) goes along with the farce while secretly taking lessons from opera diva Cecil (Barnes). Neither of their debuts go as planned. Based on the James M. Cain story "Two Can Sing" and remade as 1949's "Everybody Does It." **80m/B; DVD.** Loretta Young; Warner Baxter; Binnie Barnes; Cesar Romero; Eugene Pallette; ***D:*** Gregory Ratoff; ***W:*** Nunnally Johnson; ***C:*** Ernest Palmer.

Wife Versus Secretary 🦴🦴🦴 1/2 **1936** Excellent acting against type creates a near-perfect picture of romantic relationships. Harlow and Gable play a secretary and her boss who have a wonderful professional relationship, but Loy worries something else is afoot. Could have been a heavy-handed soap opera, but the witty dialogue and Brown's fine pacing make it much more. Stewart later claimed that he purposely messed up his romantic scenes with Harlow in order to spend more time in her arms. **89m/B; VHS, DVD.** Clark Gable; Jean Harlow; Myrna Loy; May Robson; Hobart Cavanaugh; James Stewart; George Barbier; Gilbert Emery; Gloria Holden; ***D:*** Clarence Brown; ***W:*** John Lee Mahin; Norman Krasna; Alice Duer Miller; ***C:*** Ray June; ***M:*** Herbert Stothart; Edward Ward.

Wife Wanted 🦴 1/2 **1946** Fading film star Carole Raymond Francis) unknowingly gets mixed-up in a real estate scam and a lonely hearts racket that's actually a crime front for blackmail and murder. Set-up to take the fall, Carole doesn't know whether to trust newshound William Tyler (Shayne) or try to bring the criminals to justice herself. Mongram pic was Francis's last before her retirement. **70m/B; DVD.** Kay Francis; Robert Shayne; Veda Ann Borg; Paul Cavanagh; Teala Loring; John Gallaudet; ***D:*** Phil Karlson; ***W:*** Sidney Sutherland; ***C:*** Harry Neumann.

Wigstock: The Movie 🦴🦴 1/2 **1995 (R)** Documentary of the eponymous annual Labor Day event in Manhattan, billed as the Super Bowl of drag. Shils intercuts stage numbers with interviews from a variety of the talented, witty festival performers, such as Lypsinka, Mistress Formika, and RuPaul. One of the best numbers is performed by the Dueling Bankheads (as in Tallulah) singing "Born to Be Wild." Like the event itself, documentary is more a celebration than a probing, psychological look at drag. Won't appeal to everyone, but a lot of fun for those who can appreciate high hair and high fashion. **92m/C; VHS, DVD.** RuPaul Charles; John (Lypsinka) Epperson; Alexis Arquette; ***D:*** Barry Shils; ***C:*** Wolfgang Held; Michael Barrow; ***M:*** Peter Fish; Robert Reale.

Wilbur Wants to Kill Himself 🦴🦴🦴 **2002 (R)** Indeed, Wilbur (Sives) does want to die as the opening sequence shows him eager to swallow some pills in one of his many, varied attempts to join his deceased parents. When he becomes homeless his responsible, easy-going brother, Harbour (Rawlins), who lives above their father's old dingy bookstore, provides refuge even after Harbour's new wife and her nine-year-old daughter move in. With this unconventional family unit, Danish director Scherfig's first English offering exquisitely spans the spectrum of human emotion as it shuffles between humor as dark and dreary as its backdrop (Glasgow) and the morbidity inherent in such a tale. **106m/C; DVD.** *SW GB DK FR* Adrian Rawlins; Shirley Henderson; Jamie Sives; Lisa McKinlay; Mads Mikkelsen; Susan Vidler; Julia Davis; ***D:*** Lone Scherfig; ***W:*** Lone Scherfig; Anders Thomas Jensen; ***C:*** Jorgen Johansson; ***M:*** Joachim Holbek.

The Wilby Conspiracy 🦴🦴🦴 **1975 (PG)** A political activist and an Englishman on the wrong side of the law team up to escape the clutches of a prejudiced cop in apartheid Africa. The focus of the film is on the chase, not the political uprising taking place around it. Well-done chase film with fine performances throughout. **101m/C; VHS, DVD, Blu-Ray.** Sidney Poitier; Michael Caine; Nicol Williamson; Prunella Gee; Persis Khambatta; Saeed Jaffrey; Rutger Hauer; Helmut Dantine; ***D:*** Ralph Nelson; ***W:*** Rod Amateau.

The Wild 🦴🦴 1/2 **2006 (G)** No, it's not "Madagascar 2" although you'd be forgiven for thinking so. Here young lion cub Ryan (Cipes) decides he needs to get out from under his dad Samson's (Sutherland) roar, so he escapes from a New York zoo and stows away on an Africa-bound ship. Dad follows along with opinionated giraffe Bridget (Garofalo) and her bossy squirrel admirer, Benny (Belushi); dopey anaconda Larry (Kind); and snooty, campy koala, Nigel (a very enjoyable Izzard). When they get to Africa, Nigel gets mistaken for a god by a herd of wildebeests, led by the sinister Kazar (Shatner), who challenges Samson for supremacy. **85m/C; DVD, Blu-Ray.** ***V:*** Kiefer Sutherland; James Belushi; Eddie Izzard; Janeane Garofalo; Greg Cipes; Richard Kind; William Shatner; Colin Hay; Don Cherry; Lenny Venito; Patrick Warburton; Kevin M. Richardson; ***D:*** Steve "Spaz" Williams; ***W:*** Edward Decter; John J. Strauss; Mark Gibson; Philip Halprin; ***M:*** Alan Silvestri.

Wild 🦴🦴🦴 **2014 (R)** Witherspoon stars in this adaptation of Cheryl Strayed's memoir about walking a California hiking trail for hundreds of miles to find herself again. Through flashbacks, we see how Cheryl fell off the human radar after the death of her mother (the phenomenal Dern), and became addicted to drugs and anonymous sex in the process. The idea that someone needs to physically challenge herself to get back to center has rarely been so well-drawn in a feature film, thanks mostly to Witherspoon's excellent performance, but also thanks to Nick Hornby's script, which expertly takes what is mostly an internal journey and makes it external. **115m/C; DVD, Blu-Ray.** Reese Witherspoon; Laura Dern; Thomas Sadoski; Gaby Hoffman; W. Earl Brown; ***D:*** Jean-Marc Vallee; ***W:*** Nick Hornby; ***C:*** Yves Bélanger.

A Wild Affair 🦴🦴 **1963** A tease of a title for this trendy '60s Brit comedy that's more silly than sexy. Engaged secretary Marjorie (Kwan in her Mary Quant fashions and Vidal Sassoon haircut) wants to have a little fun before settling down to married life so she attends her company Christmas party where everyone is known to get drunk and let their inhibitions go. But when Marjorie's lecherous boss (Terry-Thomas) is the one making the indecent proposal, what will she decide to do? **88m/C; DVD.** *UK* Nancy Kwan; Terry-Thomas; Betty Marsden; Victor Spinetti; Bessie Love; ***D:*** John Krish; ***W:*** John Krish; ***C:*** Arthur Ibbetson; ***M:*** Martin Slavin.

Wild America 🦴🦴🦴 **1997 (G)** Warner Bros. invades Disney's well-marked territory of family-friendly real-life adventure with this bio of famed nature documentarians Mark, Marty, and Marshall Stouffer. Pic focuses on the origins of the boys' fascination with animals, which started when their parents gave them a used 16mm camera to mess around with. After getting some footage of backyard wildlife, they're hooked, and hit the road to find more dangerous (and endangered) beasts to shoot (in the good way). As you would expect, the scenery and camera work are splendid, and any expected wild animal gore and violence has been toned way down. There's plenty to hold the interest of adults as well as children, with a big assist going to the clever script. Title is taken from Marty Stouffer's long-running PBS nature series. **105m/C; VHS, DVD, Blu-Ray.** Jonathan Taylor Thomas; Devon Sawa; Scott Bairstow; Jamey Sheridan; Frances Fisher; Tracey Walter; Don Stroud; Sonny Shroyer; ***D:*** William Dear; ***W:*** David Michael Wieger; ***C:*** David Burr; ***M:*** Joel McNeely.

The Wild Angels 🦴🦴 1/2 **1966 (PG)** Excessively violent film but B-movie classic about an outlaw biker gang and the local townspeople. Typical Corman fodder was one of AIP's most successful productions. **124m/C; VHS, DVD, Blu-Ray.** Peter Fonda; Nancy Sinatra; Bruce Dern; Diane Ladd; Michael J. Pollard; Gayle Hunnicutt; Peter Bogdanovich; Dick Miller; ***D:*** Roger Corman; ***W:*** Peter Bogdanovich; Charles B. Griffith; ***C:*** Richard Moore; ***M:*** Michael Curb.

Wild at Heart 🦴🦴🦴 1/2 **1990 (R)** Dern and Cage are on the lam, going across country to escape her mother, his parole officer, and life. Humorous and frightening, sensual and evocative as only Lynch can be. Sweet love story of Sailor and Lula is juxtaposed with the violent and bizarre, obsessive brand of love of the people they encounter. Unmistakable Wizard of Oz imagery sprinkled throughout, as are some scenes of graphic violence. Ladd is unnerving as Dern's on-screen mother (she also has the role off-screen). **125m/C; VHS, DVD, Blu-Ray.** Nicolas Cage; Laura Dern; Diane Ladd; Willem Dafoe; Isabella Rossellini; Harry Dean Stanton; Crispin Glover; Grace Zabriskie; J.E. Freeman; Freddie Jones; Sherilyn Fenn; Sheryl Lee; Albert "Poppy" Popwell; Jack Nance; Charlie Spradling; William Morgan Sheppard; ***D:*** David Lynch; ***W:*** David Lynch; ***C:*** Frederick Elmes; ***M:*** Angelo Badalamenti. Cannes '90: Film; Ind. Spirit '91: Cinematog.

Wild Beauty 🦴 1/2 **1927** Former soldier Bill Moran (Allan) returns home from WWI with Rex the Wonder Horse, whom he rescued on the battlefield. Bill enters Rex in a race to help save his girlfriend Helen's (Marlowe) family ranch but crooks have other ideas (there's a mare involved). **65m/B; Silent; DVD.** Hugh Allan; June Marlowe; William Bailey; Jack Pratt; Scott Seaton; Hayes Robinson; ***D:*** Henry MacRae; ***W:*** Edward Meagher; ***C:*** John Stumar.

Wild Bill 🦴🦴 1/2 **1995 (R)** Realistic, unheroic portrait of Wild Bill Hickok (Bridges), seen mostly in flashback. From trapper and lawman to his last days in Deadwood, South Dakota, focus is on the events haunting the glaucoma-stricken, opium-addicted legend in his later years, such as twice deserting his true love (Lane). Action packed first 20 minutes mellows along with the aging Hickok and the rest gets a bit talky for a Western, albeit an arty one. Bridges's Hickok is brilliant, but Barkin is given a somewhat tedious Calamity Jane. Based on the novel "Deadwood" by Pete Dexter and the play "Fathers and Sons" by Thomas Babe. **97m/C; VHS, DVD, Blu-Ray.** Jeff Bridges; Ellen Barkin; John Hurt; Diane Lane; Keith Carradine; Christina Applegate; Bruce Dern; James Gammon; David Arquette; Marjoe Gortner; ***D:*** Walter Hill; ***W:*** Walter Hill; ***C:*** Lloyd Ahern, II; ***M:*** Van Dyke Parks.

Wild Boys of the Road 🦴🦴 **1933** During the depths of the Great Depression, two high school sophomores decide to strike out on the road in order to find work and help out their families. Meeting other teens in similar straits along the way, they encounter hardhip, police harassmant, exploitation, and run-ins with both criminals and the law. Considered lurid and sensational in its day. **77m/B; DVD.** Frankie Darro; Rochelle Hudson; Sterling Holloway; Minna Gombell; Robert Barrat; Edwin Phillips; Dorothy Coonan; Ward Bond; Alan Hale, Jr.; Grant Mitchell; Claire McDowell; ***D:*** William A. Wellman; ***W:*** Earl Baldwin; ***C:*** Arthur L. Todd. Natl. Film Reg. '13.

The Wild Bunch 🦴🦴🦴🦴 **1969 (R)** Acclaimed western about a group of aging outlaws on their final rampage, realizing time is passing them by. Highly influential in dialogue, editing style, and lyrical slow-motion photography of violence; Peckinpah's main claim to posterity. Holden and Ryan create especially memorable characters. Arguably the greatest western and one of the greatest American films of all times. Beware of shortened versions; after a pre-release showing to the East Coast critics, producer Feldman cut key scenes without Peckinpah's knowledge or consent. **145m/C; VHS, DVD, Blu-Ray, HD-DVD.** William Holden; Ernest Borgnine; Robert Ryan; Warren Oates; Strother Martin; L.Q. Jones; Albert Dekker; Bo Hopkins; Edmond O'Brien; Ben Johnson; Jaime Sanchez; Emilio Fernandez; Dub Taylor; ***D:*** Sam Peckinpah; ***W:*** Walon Green; Sam Peckinpah; ***C:*** Lucien Ballard; ***M:*** Jerry Fielding. AFI '98: Top 100; Natl. Film Reg. '99; Natl. Soc. Film Critics '69: Cinematog.

The Wild Card 🦴 1/2 **2003** Four crooks take on a new task by kidnapping a trophy wife—who's been fooling around with a gangster—but their Vegas luck runs out once the typical backstabbing seeps in. **90m/C; VHS, DVD.** Ron Dean; Mik Scriba; Jim Petersmith; Timothy Patrick Klein; Marty Maguire; Hilary Tuck; Barbara Alyn Woods; John J. Dalesandro; Zelda Rubinstein; ***D:*** Tom Whitus; ***W:*** Tom Whitus; ***C:*** Richard Siegel; ***M:*** Trebor Murray; Terry Quiet; Sugar Free Allstars; Deon Vozov. **VIDEO**

Wild Card 🦴 1/2 **2015 (R)** Down-on-his-luck Las Vegas bodyguard Nick (Statham) wants cash to leave town, so he rents himself out to nefarious clientele in need of muscle. Episodic to a fault, femme fatales and an endless stream of thugs come and go, spouting one cliche after another. Luckily, most of these silly walk-on roles go to familiar faces. An unfortunate misuse of talent from Oscar-winning screenwriter William Goldman, who adapted the script from his own 1985 trash novel, "Heat," which first flopped onto the screen in 1986. **92m/C; DVD, Blu-Ray.** Jason Statham; Michael Angarano; Milo Ventimiglia; Dominik Garcia-Lorido; Sofia Vergara; Max Casella; Stanley Tucci; Hope Davis; Jason Alexander; Anne Heche; ***D:*** Simon West; ***W:*** William Goldman; ***C:*** Shelly Johnson; ***M:*** Dario Marianelli.

Wild Cherry 🦴 1/2 **2009 (R)** Stupid teen sex comedy. High school seniors/best friends (and virgins) Katlyn, Helen, and Trish are outraged to learn that they are in the football team's book of sexual conquests to be. They decide to humiliate the three football players who have been trying to date them (frozen sperm is involved in one prank) but the guys aren't quite the raunchy doofs they seem. **85m/C; DVD, Blu-Ray.** Rumer Willis; Tania Raymonde; Kristin Cavallari; Ryan Merriman; Jesse Moss; John White; Tia Carrere; Rob Schneider; Bryan Clarke; ***D:*** Dana Lustig; ***W:*** Chris Charney; ***C:*** Michael Marshall; ***M:*** Chris Ainscough.

The Wild Child 1/2 *L'Enfant Sauvage* **1970 (G)** The brilliant film based on the journal of a 19th century physician who attempts to educate and civilize a young boy who has been found living in the wilderness, without any comprehension of human life. Tenderly told coming of age tale, with surprising sensitivity for its subject. In French with English subtitles. **85m/B; VHS, DVD.** *FR* Jean-Pierre Cargol; Francois Truffaut; Jean Daste; Francoise Seigner; Paul Ville; ***D:*** Francois Truffaut; ***W:*** Francois Truffaut; Jean Gruault; ***C:*** Nestor Almendros; ***M:*** Antoine Duhamel. Natl. Bd. of Review '70: Director (Truffaut); Natl. Soc. Film Critics '70: Cinematog.

Wild Child 1/2 **2008 (PG-13)** When pampered Malibu teen Poppy (Roberts) finally crosses the line, her fed-up dad (Quinn) packs her off to an all-girls British boarding school where the brash American is instantly disliked by the reigning clique, headed by Harriet (King). Poppy eventually learns from headmistress Mrs. Kingsley (Richardson) that her mysterious mother attended the school and she finds some teen romance with Mrs. Kingsley's son, Freddie (Pettyfer). A bit choppy but sweet for tweens as girl power rules. **98m/C; DVD, Blu-Ray.** *GB* Emma Roberts; Natasha Richardson; Alex Pettyfer; Shirley Henderson; Aidan Quinn; Kimberly Nixon; Georgia King; Juno Temple; Sophie Wu; Daisy Donovan; Shelby Young; Nick Frost; ***D:*** Nick Moore; ***W:*** Lucy Dahl; ***C:*** Chris Seager; ***M:*** Michael Price. **VIDEO**

The Wild Country 1/2 *The Newcomers* **1971 (G)** Children's fare detailing the trials and tribulations of a Pittsburgh family moving into an inhospitable Wyoming ranch in the 1880s. Based on the novel "Little Britches" by Ralph Moody. **92m/C; VHS, DVD, Streaming.** Steve Forrest; Ron Howard; Clint Howard; Rance Howard; ***D:*** Robert Totten; ***M:*** Robert F. Brunner.

Wild Country 1/2 **2005 (R)** The low budget is something of a problem since the beastie in this teen horror flick isn't very scary. Kelly Ann (Shields) is on a hike in the Scottish Highlands with some friends when they find an abandoned baby. As they try to get the tyke to safety, a wolf-life creature starts stalking and killing them. **72m/C; DVD.** *GB* Martin Compston; Peter Capaldi; Kevin Quinn; Samantha Shields; Nicola Muldoon; Jamie Quinn; ***D:*** Craig Strachan; ***W:*** Craig Strachan; ***C:*** Jan Pester.

The Wild Duck 1/2 **1984 (PG)** A father discovers that his beloved daughter is illegitimate and turns against her. To regain his love, she plans to sacrifice her most prized possession. Irons overacts; Ullmann almost disappears into the woodwork. Child star Jones is insufferable, and the whole family squeaks with "literary" pomposity. A horrid adaptation of the classic Ibsen play. **96m/C; VHS, DVD.** *AU* Jeremy Irons; Liv Ullmann; Lucinda Jones; Arthur Dignam; ***D:*** Henri Safran.

Wild Geese **1978 (R)** The adventure begins when a veteran band of mercenaries land deep inside Africa to rescue the imprisoned leader of an emerging African nation, in the interest of protecting British commercial interest. Their mission meets an unexpected turn when they are betrayed by their financial backers. Too much training in the early part; too long; too much dialogue. Where's the action? **132m/C; VHS, DVD, Blu-Ray.** *GB* Richard Burton; Roger Moore; Richard Harris; Hardy Kruger; Stewart Granger; Frank Finlay; Jeff Corey; ***D:*** Andrew V. McLaglen; ***W:*** Reginald Rose.

The Wild Goose Lake 1/2 *Nan Fang Che Zhan De Ju Hui* **2020** After he accidentally kills a police officer that he'd mistaken for a rival gangster, Zenong Zhou flees to Wild Goose Lake, a resort area known for criminal activity. There, he's approached by Aiai Liu, a prostitute acting as emissary for her pimp, who threatens to turn Zhou in for the reward. A highly atmospheric spin on the classic noir crime thriller. **113m/C; DVD.** Ge Hu; Lun-Mei Kwei; Fan Liao; Wan Qian; Dao Qi; ***D:*** Yi'nan Diao; ***W:*** Yi'nan Diao; ***C:*** Jingsong Dong.

Wild Grass *Les Herbes Folles* **2009 (PG)** Despite its MPAA rating, it's unlikely that anyone but adult fans of director Resnais will be interested in his surreal arthouse melodrama. Married 60-something Georges (Dussollier) finds single red-haired dentist Marguerite's (Azema) stolen wallet and becomes intrigued by her life to the point of obsession, until she begins to find his harassment interesting. Adaptation of the Christian Gailly novel, "The Incident." French with subtitles. **113m/C; On Demand.** *FR IT* Sabine Azema; Andre Dussollier; Anne Consigny; Emmanuelle Devos; Mathieu Amalric; Michel Vuillermoz; Sara Forestier; Nicolas Duvauchelle; Vladimir Consigny; ***Nar:*** Edouard Baer; ***D:*** Alain Resnais; ***W:*** Alex Reval; Laurent Herbiert; ***C:*** Eric Gautier; ***M:*** Mark Snow.

Wild Grizzly 1/2 **1999 (PG)** A grizzly escapes from a mountain community and rampages through the small town of Pine Lake. Teenaged newcomer John Harding, Ranger Frank Bradford, wildlife tracker Jack Buck, and land developer Harlan Adams are all on a bear hunt for their own reasons. **100m/C; VHS, DVD.** Daniel Baldwin; Fred (John F.) Dryer; Michele Greene; Steve Reevis; Brendan O'Brien; John Hurley; Courtney Peldon; Riley Smith; ***D:*** Sean McNamara. **VIDEO**

Wild Guitar **WOOF!** **1962** A swinging youth cycles into Hollywood and, improbably, becomes an instant teenidol. Considered a top contender for "Worst Picture of All Time" honors. **92m/B; VHS, DVD.** Arch Hall, Jr.; Ray Dennis Steckler; Carolyn Brandt; Bob Crumb; Nancy Czar; Marie Denn; Arch (Archie) Hall, Sr.; ***D:*** Ray Dennis Steckler; ***W:*** Arch (Archie) Hall, Sr.; Joe Thomas; Bob Wehling; ***C:*** Joseph Mascelli; ***M:*** Alan O'Day.

Wild Hearts Can't Be Broken **1991 (G)** Depicts the true-life story of Sonora Webster, a small town Georgia girl who runs away from a foster home to join a carnival in the early 1930s, hoping to become a stunt rider. She becomes a horse-diver (a Depression-era sideshow phenomena) and is blinded in a diving accident, but returns to find romance and ride again. Storyline has little screen tension, but it doesn't detract from this fresh family film with a feisty heroine, a sweet romance, and horses. Nice U.S. screen debut for British actress Anwar. **89m/C; VHS, DVD.** Gabrielle Anwar; Cliff Robertson; Dylan Kussman; Michael Schoeffling; Kathleen York; Frank Renzulli; ***D:*** Steve Miner; ***W:*** Oley Sassone; ***M:*** Mason Daring.

Wild Hogs **2007 (PG-13)** Four middle-aged buddies in Cincinnati get together on the weekends to indulge their mild sides by putting on their leather jackets and riding their hogs around town. Then Woody (Travolta) gets the bright idea to go on a road trip. Their first blunder is enraging a true outlaw biker gang, led by Jack (Liotta). Their second is to get stuck in a desert nowheres-ville, which at least allows shy Dudley (Macy) to go gaga over waitress Maggie (Tomei). And yes, there's a showdown between the biker boys. You'll laugh, but you'll probably wonder why in the morning. **99m/C; DVD, Blu-Ray.** John Travolta; Tim Allen; Martin Lawrence; William H. Macy; Ray Liotta; Marisa Tomei; Kevin Durand; M.C. Gainey; Jill(ian) Hennessey; Tichina Arnold; Stephen Tobolowsky; John C. McGinley; ***D:*** Walt Becker; ***W:*** Brad Copeland; ***C:*** Robbie Greenberg; ***M:*** Teddy Castellucci.

Wild Horse Canyon **1925** Yakima Canutt, the man credited with creating the profession of stunt man, stars in this tale about a lady rancher who requires saving from her evil foreman. The climactic stampede scene gives Yakima a chance to demonstrate a high dive off a cliff and a somersault onto his horse. Silent, with musical score. **68m/B; Silent; VHS, DVD.** Yakima Canutt; Edward Cecil; Helene Rosson; Jay Talbet; ***D:*** Ben F. Wilson.

Wild Horse Hank **1979** A young woman risks everything to save a herd of wild mustangs from being slaughtered for use as dog food. Creena is good; otherwise, it's sentimental family fare. Based on the novel "The Wild Horse Killers" by Mel Ellis. **94m/C; VHS, DVD.** *CA* Linda Blair; Richard Crenna; Michael Wincott; Al Waxman; ***D:*** Eric Till.

Wild Horses **1982** A man attempts to make a living by capturing and selling wild horses. Adventure fans will love this film which deals with the common theme of man against nature. **88m/C; VHS, DVD.** *NZ* Keith Aberdein; John Bach; Robyn Gibbes; ***D:*** Derek Morton.

Wild Horses **1984** Ex-rodeo champ Rogers is hankering to escape his dull life. He joins a roundup of wild horses and with Dawber's help exposes a bureaucrat's scheme for them. Rogers is likable and sings, but the supporting cast carries this one. Made for TV. **90m/C; VHS, DVD.** Kenny Rogers; Pam Dawber; Ben Johnson; Richard Masur; David Andrews; Karen Carlson; ***D:*** Dick Lowry. **TV**

Wild Horses **2015 (R)** The once-great Duvall continues to frustrate with this barely released drama which he wrote, directed, and stars in. Duvall plays a Southern rancher who catches his youngest son in the arms of another man and throws him out of the house, banishing him for life. Fifteen years later, the rancher is changing and growing, especially when the black sheep (Franco) returns to confront him. The rancher's other son KC (Hartnett) is even less welcoming of his brother's return, having adopted some of dear old dad's prejudices. The setting and performers are well-used here but the script is flat and uninspired. **100m/C; DVD, Blu-Ray, Streaming.** Robert Duvall; James Franco; Josh Hartnett; Luciana Pedraza; Angie Cepeda; ***D:*** Robert Duvall; ***W:*** Robert Duvall; Michael Shell; ***C:*** Barry Markowitz; ***M:*** Tim Williams.

Wild in the Country 1/2 **1961** Backwoods delinquent Presley is aided in his literary aspirations by woman psychiatrist Lange. Okay, so that's fairly novel. Strange plot lines but in general Elvis is going to college and reading and writing and singing and playing his guitar. Meanwhile Weld wanders around seductively to provide that hint of Tennessee Williams ambience as interpreted by Odet but hey, who cares? Interesting if convoluted Elvis dramatic turn. **114m/C; VHS, DVD, Blu-Ray.** Elvis Presley; Hope Lange; Tuesday Weld; Millie Perkins; John Ireland; Gary Lockwood; Alan Napier; ***D:*** Philip Dunne; ***W:*** Clifford Odets; ***C:*** William Mellor.

Wild in the Streets 1/2 **1968** Satire set in the future, where a malcontent rock star becomes president after the voting age is lowered to 14. Adults over 30 are imprisoned and fed a daily dose of LSD. The president gets his comeuppance when challenged by even younger youths. Very groovy, very political in its own way, very funny. **97m/C; VHS, DVD, Blu-Ray.** Christopher Jones; Shelley Winters; Hal Holbrook; Richard Pryor; Diane Varsi; Millie Perkins; Ed Begley, Sr.; Barry Williams; Dick Clark; ***D:*** Barry Shear; ***W:*** Robert Thom; ***C:*** Richard Moore; ***M:*** Les Baxter.

Wild Is the Wind **1957** Larger-than-life romantic melodrama. Italian-born Nevada rancher Gino (Quinn) sends for his late wife's sister Gioia (Magnani) in an arranged marriage. She's soon neglected and miserable because Gino can't let go of his first wife's memory, so Gioia turns to his adopted son, ranch hand Bene (Franciosa), for comfort. The symbolism is heavy-handed but the performances compensate. Johnny Mathis sings the Oscar-nominated title tune. **114m/B; Streaming.** Anthony Quinn; Anna Magnani; Anthony (Tony) Franciosa; Dolores Hart; Joseph Calleia; Lili Valenty; ***D:*** George Cukor; ***W:*** Arnold Schulman; ***C:*** Charles B(ryant) Lang, Jr.; ***M:*** Dimitri Tiomkin.

The Wild Life *Robinson Crusoe* **2016 (PG)** A kid-friendly animated feature loosely based on the titular character and the story in Daniel Defoe's classic novel. On a small tropical island, chatty parrot Tuesday (Thornton) and his quirky animal friends live in paradise. Unlike most of the other residents, Tuesday wants to learn more about the world. After a violent storm, sailor Robinson Crusoe (Schweighofer) is washed ashore. While Tuesday sees Robinson as a way off the island, Robinson needs the animals to survive on the island. The harmonious island life that emerges becomes threatened when two savage cats try to take control, leading Crusoe and the animals to truly understand the importance of friendship. **91m/C; DVD, Blu-Ray, Streaming, Download.** Yuri Lowenthal; David Howard Thornton; Kaya Yanar; Cindy aus Marzahn; Dieter Hallervorden; ***D:*** Vincent Kesteloot; Ben Stassen; ***W:*** Domonic Paris; ***M:*** Ramin Djawadi.

The Wild Man of the Navidad 1/2 **2008** A flick made to be seen at a drive-in, where its cheesy low-budget aesthetic can be properly appreciated. A legendary bloodthirsty creature has been terrorizing the town of Sublime, Texas along the Navidad River for over 200 years. Wimpy Dale S. Rogers (Meek) nightly leaves a dead rabbit to appease the beast but when Rogers finally allows hunting on his land and the Wild Man gets winged, he also gets mighty perturbed. **85m/C; DVD.** Justin Meeks; Tony Wolford; Charlie Hurtin; Alex Garcia; Stacy Meeks; Edmond Geyer; Bob Wood; ***D:*** Justin Meeks; Duane Graves; ***W:*** Justin Meeks; Duane Graves; ***C:*** Duane Graves; ***M:*** Charlie Hurtin.

The Wild North **1952** Wilderness adventure finds French trapper Jules Vincent (Granger) on the lam for a self-defense killing. He's being tracked by inexperienced Mountie Pedley (Corey) who manages to get himself in lots of trouble thanks to a blizzard and an attack by wolves. When Pedley is injured, Jules decides to do the right thing and save his life. Filmed around Sun Valley, Idaho in the Boulder Mountains. **97m/C; DVD.** Stewart Granger; Wendell Corey; Cyd Charisse; Morgan Farley; J.M. Kerrigan; ***D:*** Andrew Marton; ***W:*** Frank Fenton; ***C:*** Robert L. Surtees; ***M:*** Bronislau Kaper.

Wild Oats **2016 (PG-13)** An unexpected windfall leads to an adventure for a widow in this comedy. After the death of her husband, retired widow Eva (MacLaine) receives a life insurance check. Though it should be for $50,000, it is accidentally made out for $5 million. Evie uses the money to go on the trip of a lifetime with her newly single best friend Maddie (Lange). During their trip, they become both media sensations and fugitives from justice over the check. **86m/C; DVD, Streaming, Download.** Shirley MacLaine; Jessica Lange; Demi Moore; Ptolemy Slocum; Colin Walker; ***D:*** Andy Tennant; ***W:*** Claudia Myers; Gary Kanew; ***C:*** Jose Luis Alcaine; ***M:*** George Fenton.

Wild On the Beach **WOOF!** **1965** Low, low-budget indie that has very little beach to be seen and certainly isn't wild. Two groups of college kids--one male and one female--are given use of the same beach house on the same spring weekend. Sonny & Cher make their first screen appearance in this Beach Party rip-off. **76m/B; DVD.** Frankie Randall; Sherry Jackson; Booth Colman; Russ Bender; ***D:*** Maury Dexter; ***W:*** Harry Spalding; ***C:*** Jacques Marquette; ***M:*** Jimmie Haskell.

The Wild One 1/2 **1954** The original biker flick: two motorcycle gangs descend upon a quiet midwestern town and each other. Brando is the leader of one (Marvin leads the other), struggling against social prejudices and his own gang's lawlessness to find love and a normal life. The classic tribute to 1950s rebelliousness. Based vaguely on a real incident in California. Quaint after nearly 40 years, but still the touchstone for much that has come since, and still a central role in Brando's now-long career. Brando himself believes it failed to explore motivations for youth gangs and violence, only depicting them. Banned in Britain until 1967. **79m/B; VHS, DVD, Blu-Ray.** Marlon Brando; Lee Marvin; Mary Murphy; Robert Keith; Jerry Paris; Alvy Moore; Jay C. Flippen; Peggy Maley; Bruno VeSota; ***D:*** Laszlo Benedek; ***W:*** John Paxton; ***C:*** Hal Mohr; ***M:*** Leith Stevens.

Wild Ones on Wheels **WOOF!** *Drivers to Hell* **1962** A gang of teenage hot-rod punks meet an ex-con in the Mojave desert who is searching for the half-a-million bucks he buried there years earlier. Before they find out where the money is, they kill him. In an attempt to find the stash, they kidnap the dead con's wife, hoping she'll sing like a bird. Plenty of unintended laughter. **92m/B; VHS, DVD.** Francine York; Edmund Tontini; Robert Blair; Ray Dennis Steckler; ***D:*** Rudolph

Cusumano; *W:* Eugene Pollack; *C:* Ray Dennis Steckler.

Wild Oranges 🦴🦴 **1924** Widower John Woolfolk (Mayo) is sailing his yacht along the Georgia coast with his friend Paul Halvard (Sterling) when they make anchor in an inlet to get fresh water. John discovers a dilapidated mansion where homicidal brute Iscah (Post) is holding southern beauty Millie (Valli) and her grandfather (de Brulier) as virtual hostages and he tries to rescue them (with mixed success). Vidor shot on Florida locations. **85m/B; Silent; DVD.** Frank Mayo; Virginia Valli; Charles A. Post; Nigel de Brulier; Ford Sterling; *D:* King Vidor; *W:* King Vidor; *C:* John Boyle.

Wild Orchid 🦴 **1990 (R)** One of the most controversial theatrical releases of 1990. Rourke is a mystery millionaire involved with two beautiful women in lovely Rio de Janeiro. Bisset is strange as an international real estate developer with unusual sexual mores. Very explicit sex scenes, but otherwise mostly boring and unbelievable. Rourke allegedly took his method-acting technique to the limit in the last love scene with Otis. Available in an unrated version as well. From the producers of "9 1/2 Weeks." Followed by an unrelated sequel. **107m/C; VHS, DVD, Blu-Ray.** Mickey Rourke; Jacqueline Bisset; Carre Otis; Assumpta Serna; Bruce Greenwood; *D:* Zalman King; *W:* Zalman King; *C:* Gale Tattersall; *M:* Simon Goldenberg; Geoff MacCormack.

Wild Orchid 2: Two Shades of Blue **WOOF!** **1992 (R)** Blue's jazz-musician, heroin-addict dad dies after a bad fix and she's sold into prostitution, until she runs away to find her true love and live a "normal" life. Effort from soft-core expert King has nothing to do with the first "Wild Orchid" and is almost laughably bad. Siemaszko is whiny, the plot is unbelievable, and the dialogue is unintentionally funny. Yes, you get sex, lots of it, but rather than passionate, it merely looks staged. Also available in an unrated version at 111 minutes. **105m/C; VHS, DVD.** Nina Siemaszko; Wendy Hughes; Brent Fraser; Robert Davi; Tom Skerritt; Joe Dallesandro; Christopher McDonald; Liane (Alexandra) Curtis; *D:* Zalman King; *W:* Zalman King.

Wild Orchids 🦴🦴 ½ **1928** A husband suspects his wife of infidelity while they take a business cruise to Java. One of Garbo's earliest silent films. Garbo is lushly surrounded with great scenery, costumes and sets, making the best of her as she makes the best of a cheery tale. **119m/B; Silent; VHS, DVD.** Greta Garbo; Lewis Stone; Nils Asther; *D:* Sidney Franklin; *C:* William H. Daniels.

Wild Palms 🦴🦴 **1993** In 2007 Los Angeles, Harry (Belushi) takes a job at a TV station that offers virtual reality programming to viewers, only this isn't benign technology. Delany is stuck in a thankless role as his wife, Cattrall is his former lover, but Dickinson has the most fun as Harry's power-mad mother-in-law who's also a sadistic co-conspirator of a nasty senator (Loggia). Lesson in weird style over substance really doesn't make much sense, but unlike "Twin Peaks" (to which this TV miniseries was heavily compared) it at least has an ending. Executive producer Stone has a cameo which concerns the JFK conspiracy. Based on the comic strip by Wagner. In two parts. **300m/C; VHS, DVD.** James Belushi; Robert Loggia; Dana Delany; Kim Cattrall; Angie Dickinson; Ernie Hudson; Bebe Neuwirth; Nick Mancuso; Charles Hallahan; Robert Morse; David Warner; Ben Savage; Bob Gunton; Brad Dourif; Charles Rocket; ***Cameo(s):*** Oliver Stone; *D:* Phil Joanou; Kathryn Bigelow; Keith Gordon; Peter Hewitt; *W:* Bruce Wagner; *C:* Phedon Papamichael; *M:* Ryuichi Sakamoto.

The Wild Parrots of Telegraph Hill 🦴🦴🦴 **2003 (G)** This cute little documentary is for the birds. But the birds are cool, man. Free-spirit Mark Bittner moved to San Francisco during the dawn of the hippie age with dreams of becoming a professional musician. Instead of flocking fans, he acquired a flock of parrots. Over the next 25 years these escaped tropical pets often roosted on his front porch, finding the climate nice and the owner quite hospitable. Soon enough they began following him everywhere, even when he was forced to move. Bittner grows to be a local icon and tourist attraction, kind of like the Birdman of San Francisco. A tender little character study about the bohemian nature of life. **83m/C; DVD.** *D:* Judy Irving; *C:* Judy Irving.

Wild Party 🦴🦴 ½ **1974 (R)** It's 1929, a year of much frivolity in Hollywood. Drinking, dancing, maneuvering and almost every sort of romance are the rule of the night at silent film comic Jolly Grimm's sumptuous, star-studded party that climaxes with, among other things, a murder. Well performed but somehow hollow; ambitious Ivory effort unfortunately falls short. Based on Joseph Moncure March's poem, and loosely on the Fatty Arbuckle scandal. **90m/C; VHS, DVD.** Raquel Welch; James Coco; Perry King; David Dukes; Royal Dano; Tiffany Bolling; *D:* James Ivory; *C:* Walter Lassally.

The Wild Pear Tree 🦴🦴🦴 *Ahlat Agaci* **2018** Recent college graduate and high-minded author Sinan (Demirkol) travels regularly between the city of Canakkale and the small town where he grew up to visit his family. Unaware that he insults everyone he meets, Sinan looks down on everyone, including a former romantic interest, Hatice (Erguclu), and his gambler father Idris (Cemcir). After an encounter with a famous author, Suleyman (Keskin), Sinan's perspective on his life and future is shifted with unexpected results. The film balances an exploration of social and political concerns with a character study of young, idealistic writer using humor, relatable characters, and a sense of young romanticism. Turkish with subtitles. **188m/C; DVD, Blu-Ray.** Dogu Demirkol; Murat Cemcir; Bennu Yildirimlar; Hazar Ergüçlü; Serkan Keskin; *D:* Nuri Bilge Ceylan; *W:* Nuri Bilge Ceylan; Akin Aksu; Ebru Ceylan; *C:* Gokhan Tiryaki; *M:* Mirza Tahirovic.

Wild Pony 🦴 **1983** A young boy spurns his new stepfather, preferring to live with his pony instead. Reversal of the evil-stepmother-and-girl-loves-horse theme. **87m/C; VHS, DVD.** Marilyn Lightstone; Art Hindle; Josh Byrne; *D:* Kevin Sullivan; *M:* Hagood Hardy.

Wild Rebels 🦴 **1971 (R)** A two-faced member of a ruthless motorcycle gang informs the police of the gang's plans to rob a bank. Lots of bullet-flying action. Dumb, ordinary biker flick; star Pastrano was a former boxing champ in real life. **90m/C; VHS, DVD.** Steve Alaimo; Willie Pastrano; John Vella; Bobbie Byers; *D:* William Grefe.

Wild Reeds 🦴🦴🦴 *Les Roseaux Sauvages* **1994** Emotional coming of age tale set in 1962 (at the end of the French war in Algeria) and focusing on three classmates at a French boarding school. Sensitive Francois (Morel) is just coming to the realization that he likes boys, particularly working-class Serge (Rideau) who's attracted to Francois's confidante Maite (Bouchez). The provocateur is Algerian-born Henri (Gorny), a bitter political militant who enjoys his battles with classmates and teachers alike. Politics and youthful passions are forced into crises. French historical/political context may prove a barrier. French with subtitles. **110m/C; VHS, DVD.** *FR* Gael Morel; Stephane Rideau; Elodie Bouchez; Frederic Gorny; Michele Moretti; *D:* Andre Techine; *W:* Gilles Taurand; Olivier Massart; Andre Techine; *C:* Jeanne Lapoirie; *M:* Chubby Checker. Cesar '95: Director (Techine), Film, Writing; L.A. Film Critics '95: Foreign Film; Natl. Soc. Film Critics '95: Foreign Film.

Wild Riders **WOOF!** *Angels for Kicks* **1971 (R)** Two ruthless, amoral bikers molest, kidnap, rape, and beat two beautiful, naive young society ladies. Despicable story, with deplorable acting, but the ending, in which a husband slays a biker with a cello, surely is unique. **91m/C; VHS, DVD.** Alex Rocco; Elizabeth Knowles; Sherry Bain; Arell Blanton; *D:* Richard Kanter.

Wild River 🦴🦴 **1960** Social drama from Kazan. In 1933, Tennessee Valley Authority administrator Chuck Glover (Clift) is sent to a rural community to make certain the locals are relocated before a new dam along the Tennessee River floods their property. Eighty-year-old Ella Garth (Van Fleet) refuses to leave the family land and Chuck isn't making any friends among the locals, except for Ella's lonely widowed granddaughter Carol (Remick). **115m/C; DVD, Blu-Ray.** Montgomery Clift; Lee Remick; Jo Van Fleet; Albert Salmi; Jay C. Flippen; Bruce Dern; James Westerfield; Barbara Loden; Robert Earl Jones; *D:* Elia Kazan; *W:* Paul Osborn; *C:* Ellsworth Fredricks; *M:* Kenyon Hopkins.

Wild Rose 🦴🦴🦴 **2018 (R)** Young Scottish woman Rose (Buckley) wants to be a country singer. Though raised in a working class section of Glasgow by her bakery attendant mother (Walters), Rose believes that she belongs in Nashville. After spending a year in prison on drug charges, Rose not only pursues her dream of country stardom but also must connect with her young children, Wynonna (Littlefield) and Lyle (Mitchell), who barely know her. With a premise as familiar as a country song, the drama succeeds because it meets those expectations in unexpected ways led by the charismatic Buckley. **101m/C; DVD.** Jessie Buckley; Julie Walters; Craig Parkinson; Sophie Okonedo; Jamie Sives; *D:* Tom Harper; *W:* Nicole Taylor; *C:* George Steel; *M:* Jack Arnold.

Wild Rovers 🦴🦴 **1971 (PG)** An aging cowboy and his younger colleague turn to bank robbing and are pursued by a posse in a wacky comedy-adventure from director Edwards. Uneven script and too much referential baggage (faint shades of "Butch Cassidy") doom this valiant effort, with the two stars hanging right in there all the way. **138m/C; VHS, DVD, Blu-Ray.** William Holden; Ryan O'Neal; Karl Malden; Lynn Carlin; Tom Skerritt; Joe Don Baker; Rachel Roberts; Moses Gunn; *D:* Blake Edwards; *W:* Blake Edwards; *M:* Jerry Goldsmith.

Wild Side 🦴🦴 **1995 (R)** Bank employee Alex (Heche) moonlights as a hooker and gets caught in a federal sting operation. Forced to inform on one of her clients, Bruno (Walken), who's involved in a money-laundering scheme, Alex complicates matters by falling in love with Bruno's mistress, Victoria (Chen). The unrated version is 96 minutes. Original director Cammell (who retained his screenwriter's credit) removed his name from the film after disagreeing with cuts made by the production company. **90m/C; VHS, DVD.** Anne Heche; Christopher Walken; Joan Chen; Steven Bauer; *D:* Franklyn Brauner; *W:* Donald Cammell; China Cammell.

Wild Stallion 🦴 ½ **1952** Top Kick, Dan Light's colt, escapes during an Indian raid and grows up into a wild white stallion. Dan's determined to capture and retrain the horse, who returns his loyalty after an Indian attack and a pack of wolves leave an injured Dan in trouble. **70m/C; DVD.** Ben Johnson; Edgar Buchanan; Martha Hyer; Hugh Beaumont; Hayden Rorke; *D:* Lewis D. Collins; *W:* Daniel Ullman; *C:* Harry Neumann; *M:* Marlin Skiles.

The Wild Stallion 🦴 ½ **2009 (G)** Family flick with a preservation message. City girl Hannah wants to photograph wild mustangs for a school project so her dad arranges a stay at his friend Matty's ranch. Matty's daughter CJ and Hannah team up and find a legendary black stallion but learn his herd is threatened by corporate greed. **86m/C; DVD.** Miranda Cosgrove; Danielle Chuchran; Connie Sellecca; Fred Ward; Robert Wagner; Paul Sorvino; *D:* Craig Clyde; *W:* Craig Clyde; *C:* Jason Brunner; *M:* Sam Cardon. **VIDEO**

Wild Strawberries 🦴🦴🦴🦴 *Smultron-Stallet* **1957** Bergman's landmark film of fantasy, dreams and nightmares. An aging professor, on the road to accept an award, must come to terms with his anxieties and guilt. Brilliant performance by Sjostrom, Sweden's first film director and star. Excellent use of flashbacks and film editing. An intellectual and emotional masterpiece. In Swedish with English subtitles. **90m/B; VHS, DVD, Blu-Ray.** *SW* Victor Sjostrom; Bibi Andersson; Max von Sydow; Ingrid Thulin; Gunnar Bjornstrand; Folke Sundquist; Bjorn Bjelvenstam; *D:* Ingmar Bergman; *W:* Ingmar Bergman; *C:* Gunnar Fischer; *M:* Erik Nordgren. Golden Globes '60: Foreign Film.

Wild Style 🦴🦴 **1983** Zoro, a mild-mannered Bronx teenager, spends his evenings spray-painting subway cars. Intended as a depiction of urban street life, including graffiti, breakdancing and rap music. Mildly interesting social comment, but unconvincing as cinema. Too "realistic," with too little vision. **82m/C; VHS, DVD.** Lee George Quinones; Fredrick Braithwaite; Dondi White; *D:* Charlie Ahearn; *M:* Fred Brathwaite.

Wild Tales 🦴🦴🦴 ½ *Relatos Salvajes* **2014** This Argentinian Oscar nominee for Best Foreign Language Film is a delightfully twisted collection of six short films featuring people in unique situations. Writer/director Szifron has a keen, clever voice when it comes to the way people behave when pushed to make rash decisions and a strong visual eye that keeps his anthology film humming even as it jumps protagonists every twenty minutes or so. Szifron has a remarkable ability to keep his stories intriguing even though we don't spend much time in them. They could really all be adapted into feature length films. **122m/C; DVD, Blu-Ray.** *AR SP* Maria Marull; Dario Grandinetti; Julieta Zylberberg; Cesar Bordon; Leonardo Sbaraglia; Walter Donado; Ricardo Darin; Oscar Martinez; Erica Rivas; Diego Gentile; *D:* Damian Szifron; *W:* Damian Szifron; *C:* Javier Julia; *M:* Gustavo Santaolalla. British Acad. '15: Foreign Film.

Wild Target 🦴🦴 **2010 (PG-13)** Lurching between brutality and slapstick, this attempt at a zany heist comedy fails to satisfy either sense or sense of humor. Proper British hit man Victor (Nighy) is hired to kill art thief Rose (Blunt), who stole a Rembrandt from his client (Everett). He finds that he can't bring himself to pull the trigger after developing a soft spot for Rose. Instead, he begins to act as her bodyguard and starts falling for the pretty con artist. Then again, he alludes that he may be gay. The excellent cast of British actors keeps a stiff upper lip, but they can't save the confusing mess of a plot (which also can't decide what it is). **96m/C; Blu-Ray.** *GB* Bill Nighy; Emily Blunt; Rupert Grint; Martin Freeman; Rupert Everett; Eileen Atkins; Gregor Fisher; *D:* Jonathan Lynn; *W:* Lucinda Coxon; *C:* David Johnson; *M:* Michael Price.

Wild Things 🦴🦴 **1998 (R)** Titillating pulp friction can't decide between modern noir and swampy spoof. Miami guidance counselor and high school heartthrob fodder Sam Lombardo (Dillon) lectures on sex crimes and gets accused of rape by two school girls: snotty rich Kelly (Richards) and trailer trash Suzie (Campbell). The seemingly upright investigator (Bacon) tries to figure out who's telling the truth. Murray pops up doing his best Bill Murray, but his hilarious presence doesn't play next to the oh-so-serious Dillon and gang. Even more out of place is Wagner's wooden cameo as Kelly's lawyer. Speaking of wooden, the normally fine Russell is reduced to similar stereotype as Kelly's vampy, conniving mother. Endless exercise in audience manipulation has plot twists and turns relentlessly continue through the credits for no apparent reason. **108m/C; VHS, DVD, Blu-Ray.** Matt Dillon; Neve Campbell; Kevin Bacon; Denise Richards; Theresa Russell; Daphne Rubin-Vega; Bill Murray; Robert Wagner; Carrie Snodgress; Jeff(rey) Perry; Marc Macaulay; *D:* John McNaughton; *W:* Stephen Peters; *C:* Jeffrey L. Kimball; *M:* George S. Clinton. L.A. Film Critics '98: Support. Actor (Murray).

Wild Things 2 🦴🦴 **2004 (R)** Bad-girl classmates Brittney (Ward) and Maya (Arcieri) try to get their hands on an inheritance and insurance money by using their looks and other talents to doublecross each other or anyone else who might be after the same thing. Basically the same scenario as the original, only not as well plotted or acted. Seems like the only reason it got made was to get a new pair of girls to make out in a pool. Not that there's anything wrong with that. **95m/C; DVD.** Susan Ward; Leila Arcieri; Katie Stuart; Anthony John (Tony) Denison; Linden Ashby; Joe Michael Burke; Isaiah Washington, IV; Dylan Kussman; Ron Dean; Kathy Neff; *D:* Jack Perez; *W:* Ross Helford; Andy Hurst; *M:* Andrew Feltenstein; John Nau. **VIDEO**

Wild Things 3: Diamonds in the Rough 🦴 **2005 (R)** It's the same basic plot (and the same sorts of sexual shenanigans) with different actresses in revealing swimwear or less. Pampered Marie is furious when stepdad Jay won't turn over the diamonds she inherited in her mother's will. How convenient that Jay is suddenly arrested for the roofie rape of bad girl Elena. Think the two teens know each other? Think it's all a scam? Even the cops smell something and it's not sun tan lotion. **87m/C; DVD.** Serah D'Laine; Brad Johnson; Sandra McCoy; Ron

Melendez; Linden Ashby; Dina Meyer; ***D:*** Jay Lowi; ***W:*** Andy Hurst; Ross Helford; ***C:*** Hubert Taczanowski; ***M:*** Steven Stern. **VIDEO**

Wild Things: Foursome WOOF!
2010 Could this franchise sink any lower into self-indulgent stupidity and recycled plots? Florida playboy Carson (Angel) is accused of rape but it's all a scam. Then his wealthy dad (Daddo) is killed in an accident that might not be so accidental. Lots of bikini-clad chicks but the simulated sex is dull and the blank-faced actors can barely move and talk at the same time. **91m/C; DVD.** Ashley Parker Angel; Jillian Murray; Marne(tte) Patterson; Jessie Nickson; John Schneider; Cameron Daddo; Ethan Smith; Josh Randall; ***D:*** Andy Hurst; ***W:*** Howard Zemski; Monty Featherstone; ***C:*** Jeffrey D. Smith; ***M:*** Steven Stern. **VIDEO**

The Wild Thornberrys Movie 🦴🦴🦴 ½ **2002 (PG)** Big-screen adaptation of the popular Nickelodeon toon provides all the action, sly wit, and fully-realized characters that fans would expect. Newcomers will be entertained as well, no matter what age. The Thornberrys are nature documentary filmmakers, led by dad Nigel (Curry) and mom Marianne (Carlisle). Their intrepid brood includes angsty teen Debbie and half-feral Donnie, but the real star is daughter Eliza (Chabert), who can communicate with the animals and has a sarcastic monkey pal, Darwin (Kane). When Eliza's new playmate, a cheetah cub, is taken by poachers (Everett and Tomei), she has to escape a stuffy boarding school, where she was sent by her proper English grandmum, to save him and her family. African setting and rollicking action translate well to the big screen, but shouldn't lose anything when it returns to your TV for the numerous video viewings. Some scenes involving the poachers may be a little scary for younger kids. **88m/C; VHS, DVD.** ***V:*** Lacey Chabert; Tom Kane; Tim Curry; Lynn Redgrave; Danielle Harris; Flea; Jodi Carlisle; Rupert Everett; Marisa Tomei; Kevin M. Richardson; Obba Babatunde; Alfre Woodard; Melissa Greenspan; Brock Peters; Brenda Blethyn; ***D:*** Jeff McGrath; Cathy Malkasian; ***W:*** Kate Boutilier; ***M:*** Drew Neumann.

Wild Tigers I Have Known 🦴 ½ **2006** Experimental and abstract debut feature by Archer. 13-year-old Logan (Stumpf) and his best friend, science nerd Joey (Paradise), seem to be physically developing slower than their classmates, much to Joey's dismay. Logan, however, is emotionally maturing and discovering that he likes boys, especially rugged ninth-grader Rodeo (White), whose own feelings towards his precocious worshipper are ambiguous. Originally released at 98 minutes. **88m/C; DVD.** Malcolm Stumpf; Fairuza Balk; Kim Dickens; Tom Gilroy; Patrick White; Max Paradise; ***D:*** Cam Archer; ***W:*** Cam Archer; ***C:*** Aaron Platt; ***M:*** Nate Archer.

Wild Wheels WOOF! 1969 (PG) A group of dune-buggy enthusiasts seek revenge against a gang of motorcyclists who have ravaged a small California beach town. **81m/C; VHS, DVD.** Casey Kasem; Dovie Beams; Terry Stafford; Robert Dix; Bobby Clark; ***D:*** Ken Osborne; ***W:*** Ken Osborne; ***C:*** Ralph Waldo; ***M:*** Harley Hatcher.

Wild, Wild Planet 🦴 ½ **1965** Alien beings from a distant planet are miniaturizing Earth's leaders in a bid to destroy our planet, and a dubbed, wooden hero comes to the rescue. A rarely seen Italian SF entry, great fun for genre fans. A must for "robot girls in skin tight leather outfits" completists. **93m/C; VHS, DVD.** *IT* Tony Russell; Lisa Gastoni; Massimo Serato; Franco Nero; ***D:*** Anthony M. Dawson.

Wild Wild West 🦴 **1999 (PG-13)** A wild, wild waste of time, money, and star power that saw director Sonnenfeld and star Smith re-team (after "Men In Black") for this western spy spoof based on the 60s TV series. Government agents James T. West (Smith) and master-of-disguise Artemus Gordon (Kline) are sent to stop diabolical wheelchair-bound scientist, Dr. Arliss Loveless (Branagh), from assassinating President Ulysses S. Grant in 1867. The budget was $100 million but the elaborate sets and effects are more hokey than cool and some money should have been spent on the script. And a black James West just doesn't work, no matter Smith's charm. **105m/C; VHS, DVD.** Will Smith; Kevin Kline; Kenneth Branagh; Salma Hayek; M. Emmet Walsh; Ted Levine; Musetta Vander; Bai Ling; Rodney A. Grant; Frederique van der Wal; Garcelle Beauvais; Sofia Eng; ***D:*** Barry Sonnenfeld; ***W:*** Brent Maddock; S.S. Wilson; Jeffrey Price; Peter S. Seaman; ***C:*** Michael Ballhaus; ***M:*** Elmer Bernstein. Golden Raspberries '99: Worst Director (Sonnenfeld), Worst Picture, Worst Screenplay, Worst Song ("Wild Wild West").

Wild, Wild West Revisited 🦴🦴 ½ **1979** A feature-length reprise of the tongue-in-cheek western TV series. Irreverent and fun, in the spirit of its admirable predecessor—though it's probably just as well the proposed new series didn't see fruition. **95m/C; VHS, DVD.** Robert Conrad; Ross Martin; Harry (Henry) Morgan; Rene Auberjonois; ***D:*** Burt Kennedy. **TV**

Wild Women of Wongo 🦴 ½ **1959** The denizens of a primitive isle, essentially beautiful women and ugly men, meet the natives of a neighboring island, handsome men and ugly women. Not quite bad enough to be true camp fun, but stupidly silly in a low-budget way. **73m/C; VHS, DVD.** Pat Crowley; Ed Fury; Adrienne Bourbeau; Jean Hawkshaw; Johnny Walsh; ***D:*** James L. Wolcott; ***W:*** Cedric Rutherford; ***C:*** Harry Walsh.

Wild Zero 🦴🦴 **2000** KISS had "Phantom of the Park," and the Japanese punk band Guitar Wolf has this film. Young fan Ace goes to see his favorite band Guitar Wolf in concert, and they have a gunfight with their soon-to-be-former manager—then aliens invade and turn people into flesh-eating zombies. Ace finds a girlfriend who wasn't always a girl and summons the band to whoop some behind. Meant to be campy with cheesy effects, it has a trippy charm. **98m/C; DVD.** *JP* Shiro Namiki; Yoshiyuki Morishita; Guitar Wolf; Bass Wolf; Drum Wolf; Masasahi Endo; Kwancharu Endo; Makoto Inamiya; Haruka Nakajo; Taneko; Masao; Tawaki Fusamori; Akihiko Murata; Kae Egawa; Hideaki Skiguchi; ***D:*** Tetsuro Takeuchi; ***W:*** Tetsuro Takeuchi; Satoshi Takagi; ***C:*** Motoki Kobayashi; ***M:*** Guitar Wolf.

Wildcat 🦴🦴 **1942** Crabbe, famous as the serials' Flash Gordon, is a villain in this petrochemical adventure. The hero overextends his credit when he buys an oil well and must produce a gusher or else. **73m/B; VHS, DVD.** Richard Arlen; Arline Judge; Buster Crabbe; William Frawley; Arthur Hunnicutt; Elisha Cook, Jr.; William Benedict; ***D:*** Frank McDonald; ***W:*** Maxwell Shane; ***C:*** Fred H. Jackman, Jr.

Wildcats 🦴🦴 **1986 (R)** A naive female phys-ed teacher (Hawn) is saddled with the job of coach for a completely undisciplined, inner city, high school football team. Formulaic, connect-the-dots comedy; moderately funny, and of course Hawn triumphs in adversity, but at nearly two hours a very long sitcom episode. **106m/C; VHS, DVD.** Goldie Hawn; James Keach; Swoosie Kurtz; Bruce McGill; M. Emmet Walsh; Woody Harrelson; Wesley Snipes; Tab Thacker; Jsu Garcia; ***D:*** Michael Ritchie; ***M:*** James Newton Howard.

Wilde 🦴🦴 **1997 (R)** The witty Wilde is making something of a resurgence in film, plays, and books. The Irish author/playwright (portrayed by look-alike Fry) is enjoying the London limelight and his family life with wife Constance (Ehle) and their two sons, while privately acknowledging his attraction to men. Unfortunately, this leads Oscar into a mad passion for sulky, neurotic pretty boy Bosie Douglas (Law), whose aristocratic father, the Marquess of Queensbury (Wilkinson), wants moral revenge on Wilde. His affair with Bosie leads to a celebrated trial for Oscar and a tragic outcome. Adapted from the biography by Richard Ellman. **115m/C; VHS, DVD.** *GB* Stephen Fry; Jude Law; Vanessa Redgrave; Jennifer Ehle; Michael Sheen; Zoe Wanamaker; Tom Wilkinson; Gemma Jones; Judy Parfitt; ***D:*** Brian Gilbert; ***W:*** Julian Mitchell; ***C:*** Martin Fuhrer; ***M:*** Debbie Wiseman.

The Wilde Wedding 🦴🦴 **2017 (R)** A romantic comedy about the complicated relationships involved with a wedding. Retired movie star Eve Wilde (Close) is hosting her wedding to celebrated novelist Harold Alcott (Stewart) at her upscale, upstate New York home. Guests include family members such as her first husband Laurence Darling (Malkovich), their three sons, and Harold's three daughters. As the wedding draws closer, Eve wonders if she can really accommodate a fourth husband, Harold wonders if he can change from his libertine ways, and Laurence wonders about his lingering feelings for Eve. The film suffers from too many stereotypical characters, but the great leading trio makes it worth the ride. **95m/C; DVD.** Glenn Close; John Malkovich; Patrick Stewart; Minnie Driver; Grace Van Patten; ***D:*** Damian Harris; ***W:*** Damian Harris; ***C:*** Paula Huidobro; ***M:*** P.T. Walkley.

Wilder 🦴🦴 *Slow Burn* **2000 (R)** Maverick cop Della Wilder (Grier) and her partner Harlan Lee (Orzari) are assigned to investigate the murder of the ex-lover of Dr. Sam Charney (Hauer). He seems the most likely suspect but the detectives find out that this is one in a series of deaths and it's not the usual sort of serial killer. In fact, the crimes are tied into a giant pharmaceutical company and Della decides to use Charney's medical expertise to prove it—if they can survive the investigation. **92m/C; VHS, DVD.** *CA* Pam Grier; Rutger Hauer; Romano Orzari; John Dunn-Hill; Eugene Clark; Serge Houde; ***D:*** Rodney Gibbons; ***W:*** Terry Abrahamson; ***C:*** Bert Tougas; ***M:*** Michael Corriveau; Robert Marchaud. **VIDEO**

Wilder Napalm 🦴 ½ **1993 (PG-13)** Lame comedy about two at-odds brothers, the woman they both love, and their dangerous pyrokinetic abilities. Wilder (Howard) and Wallace (Quaid) Foudroyant have been feuding for years—and not just over the fact that Wallace is in love with Wilder's wife Vida (Winger). Wallace wants to use their family "gift" to become rich and famous but Wilder doesn't want them to exploit their fiery powers. They finally decide on an incendiary showdown to settle the score once and for all. Good actors lost in witless characters and a incoherent plot. **109m/C; VHS, DVD.** Dennis Quaid; Arliss Howard; Debra Winger; M. Emmet Walsh; Jim Varney; Mimi Lieber; Marvin J. McIntyre; ***D:*** Glenn Gordon Caron; ***W:*** Vince Gilligan; ***M:*** Michael Kamen.

Wilderness 🦴🦴 ½ **1996 (R)** Quiet British librarian Alice White (Ooms) is keeping quite a secret. It seems when there's a full moon, she gets a little furry. She tries to cope with her affliction by seeing a shrink (Kitchen) but the weasel just wants to exploit her. And just try explaining you're a werewolf to the new guy (Teale) in your life. Think gothic romance more than straight horror. Made for British TV. **90m/C; VHS, DVD.** *GB* Amanda Ooms; Michael Kitchen; Owen Teale; Gemma Jones; ***D:*** Ben Bolt; ***W:*** Andrew Davies; Bernadette Davis. **TV**

Wilderness Love 🦴🦴 ½ *Personally Yours* **2002** Handsome Alaskan rancher Jesse (Nordling) is a divorced dad and since his kids worry he'll never find someone to love again, they decide to submit his photo to a lonely-hearts magazine. His profile draws attention from lots of eligible women but Jesse's perfect romance may still be his ex-wife Susannah (Bertinelli). **90m/C; DVD.** Jeffrey Nordling; Valerie Bertinelli; Brittney Irvin; Michael Welch; Donnelly Rhodes; Andrea Roth; Emily Tennant; ***D:*** Jeff Reiner; ***W:*** Jill Blotevogel; ***C:*** Feliks Parnell; ***M:*** Don Davis. **TV**

The Wildest Dream: The Conquest of Everest 🦴🦴 ½ **2010 (PG)** In 1999, American mountaineer Conrad Anker was part of a team that recovered the body of George Mallory—75 years after the British mountaineer vanished in 1924, along with climbing partner Andrew Irvine, while attempting to make the first ascent to the summit of Mount Everest. Includes archival footage and recreations of the climb and recovery efforts along with readings from Mallory's letters and other narration. Mallory offered his now-famous rationale for climbing Everest as "because it's there." **94m/C; Blu-Ray.** Conrad Anker; Leo Houlding; ***V:*** Hugh Dancy; Ralph Fiennes; Natasha Richardson; Alan Rickman; ***Nar:*** Liam Neeson; ***D:*** Anthony Geffen; ***W:*** Mark Halliley; ***C:*** Chris Openshaw; Ken Sauls; ***M:*** Joel Douek.

Wildfire 🦴🦴 **1988 (PG)** As teenagers, Frank and Kay run away to get married but Frank is sent to prison for robbing a bank and Kay winds up making a new life for herself. Released from prison after eight years, Frank discovers Kay is married with two children and doesn't want anything further to do with him. But when Frank violates his parole, Kay discovers she can't leave him again and the two go on the run together. **98m/C; VHS, Streaming.** Steven Bauer; Linda Fiorentino; Will Patton; Marshall Bell; ***D:*** Zalman King; ***W:*** Zalman King; Matthew Bright; ***C:*** Bill Butler; ***M:*** Maurice Jarre.

Wildfire 7: The Inferno 🦴🦴 **2002** Nell was wrongly imprisoned for killing her abusive husband and her in-laws have cut all contact between Nell and her daughter Sophie. To secure a parole, Nell enters an inmate forest firefighting program, and a heroic deed eventually leads her to the Wildfire 7 unit. Naturally, Nell's big test comes with an out-of-control national park fire where her estranged daughter happens to be camping. **94m/C; DVD.** Tracey Gold; Alexander Walters; Jennifer Geiger; Woody Jeffreys; Tahmoh Penikett; Nathaniel Arcand; Joanna Cassidy; ***D:*** Jason Bourque; ***W:*** Dana Stone; ***C:*** Mahlon Todd Williams; ***M:*** John Sereda; Michael Thomas. **CABLE**

Wildflower 🦴🦴🦴 **1991** Set in the Depression-era South, Alice is a 17 year-old partially deaf girl who also suffers from epilepsy. Her stepfather believes she's possessed and confines her to a shed. Growing up ignorant and abused Alice is befriended by a neighboring brother and sister who decide to rescue her. A three-hankie family picture with moving performances and inspirational themes. Based on the novel "Alice" by Sara Flanigan. **94m/C; VHS, DVD.** Patricia Arquette; Beau Bridges; Susan Blakely; William McNamara; Reese Witherspoon; Collin Wilcox-Paxton; Norman (Max) Maxwell; Heather Lynch; Allison Smith; Richard Olsen; Mary Page; ***D:*** Diane Keaton; ***W:*** Sara Flanigan; ***C:*** Janusz Kaminski; ***M:*** Jon Gilutin; Ken Edwards. **CABLE**

Wildflowers 🦴🦴 ½ *Wild Flowers* **1999 (R)** Cathy (DuVall) is a 17-year-old tomboy who lives on a houseboat with her single dad (Arana). Longing for a female role model, Cally stumbles across hippie artist Sabine (Hannah) and gets involved in her life and a past that has some secrets Cally may not want to uncover. Especially fine performance by DuVall. **98m/C; VHS, DVD.** Clea DuVall; Daryl Hannah; Tomas Arana; Eric Roberts; Irene Bedard; James Gandolfini; John Doe; ***D:*** Melissa Painter; ***W:*** Melissa Painter; ***C:*** Dr. Paul Ryan.

Wildlife 🦴🦴🦴 **2018 (PG-13)** In 1960 Montana, Jerry (Gyllenhaal) and Jeanne (Mulligan) are married with teenage son Joe (Oxenbould). When Jerry loses his job, Jeanne takes one at the local YMCA. As Jerry drifts away from his family again, the break grows when he takes a position fighting wildfires. As Joe longs for his father's return, his mother starts a relationship with Warren (Camp) who seems to offer more stability. The directorial debut of actor Dano is moving and emotional with memorable performances by Gyllenhaal and Mulligan. **104m/C; DVD, Blu-Ray.** Jake Gyllenhaal; Carey Mulligan; Bill Camp; Ed Oxenbould; Zoe Margaret Colletti; ***D:*** Paul Dano; ***W:*** Paul Dano; Zoe Kazan; ***C:*** Diego Garcia; ***M:*** David Lang.

Wildling 🦴🦴 **2018 (R)** Anna (Powley) grows up alone in a locked attic, and only has knowledge of the world through a man she calls Daddy (Douif). He claims that he has been protecting her from a child-eating beast, the Wildling. When Anna hits puberty, Daddy tells her that she is ill. She ends up in the hospital and learns the world is much more complex than Daddy told her. Living with local sheriff Ellen (Tyler), Anna is drawn to the nearby forest. An intelligent, well-constructed horror film that shows the influence of the Brothers Grimm and Roald Dahl while offering a strong female perspective. **92m/C; DVD.** Liv Tyler; Brad Dourif; Bel Powley; James LeGros; Mike Faist; ***D:*** Fritz Bohm; ***W:*** Fritz Bohm; Florian Eder; ***C:*** Toby Oliver; ***M:*** Paul Haslinger.

Will Penny 🦴🦴🦴 ½ **1967** Just back from a cattle drive, a range-wandering loner looks for work in the wrong place and offends a family of outlaws who come after him. His escape from them leads to another kind of trap—one set by a love-hungry woman (Hackett, in a strong performance). Heston considers this film his personal best, and he's probably right. Superbly directed western, with excellent cinematography and professional, realistic portrayals, flopped in theatres, moviegoers preferring simultaneous Heston outing "Planet of the Apes." **109m/C; VHS, DVD.** Charlton Heston; Joan Hackett; Donald Pleasence; Lee Majors; Bruce Dern; Anthony Zerbe; Ben Johnson; Clifton James; Jon(athan) Gries; ***D:*** Tom Gries; ***W:*** Tom Gries; ***C:*** Lucien Ballard; ***M:*** Elmer Bernstein.

Will Success Spoil Rock Hunter? 1/2 **1957** Dated advertising satire finds ad man Hunter (Randall) hoping to get the key to the executive washroom but he may instead find himself on the unemployment line unless he can convince the profitable Stay-Put lipstick account not to change agencies. One day Rock sees movie star Rita Marlowe (Mansfield), and her kissable lips, on TV and tries to convince her to endorse the product. But she'll only agree if he'll pose as her new boyfriend to make ex-beau Bobo (Mansfield's real-life hubby Hargitay) jealous. Naturally, the lipstick ads take off bigtime but success does indeed spoil Rock (at least temporarily). Very slightly based on the play by George Axelrod. **94m/C; VHS, DVD, Blu-Ray.** Tony Randall; Jayne Mansfield; Betsy Drake; Mickey Hargitay; John Williams; Henry Jones; Joan Blondell; ***Cameo(s):*** Groucho Marx; ***D:*** Frank Tashlin; ***W:*** Frank Tashlin; ***C:*** Joe MacDonald; ***M:*** Cyril Mockridge. Natl. Film Reg. '00.

Will You Merry Me? **2008** In this Lifetime holiday comedy, Rebecca Fine is from an upper-crusty Jewish L.A. family while Henry Kringle's (really?!) parents are tradition-bound Christians from Wisconsin. The immature couple gets engaged and decides to introduce the potential in-laws by having the Kringles invite the Fines to Madison the week of Hanukah. Let's just say Henry and Rebecca have good intentions. **90m/C; DVD.** Vikki Krinsky; Tommy Lioutas; Wendie Malick; Cynthia Stevenson; David Eisner; Patrick McKenna; ***D:*** Nisha Ganatra; ***W:*** Karen McClellan; ***C:*** Yuri Yakubiw; ***M:*** David Buchbinder. **CABLE**

Willard **2003 (PG-13)** Willard is back (in the form of Glover) and he brought the rats with him. He's the beaten-down son to a hateful, domineering mom, and the punching bag for his brutish boss (Ermey). The twist in this one is that he communicates with fuzzy, white Socrates, instead of the apparently steroid-fueled giant rat Ben, which causes a vermin power struggle. Sometimes clever (the original Willard, Bruce Davison, is seen in a painting as this Willard's deceased father), but mostly soulless remake does have the advantage of Glover's presence in a role that seems made for him. He goes all-out and over-the-top to portray Willard's swirling psychosis and ever-escalating delusions of grandeur. **95m/C; VHS, DVD, Blu-Ray.** Crispin Glover; R. Lee Ermey; Laura Elena Harring; Jackie Burroughs; David Parker; ***D:*** Glen Morgan; ***W:*** Glen Morgan; ***C:*** Robert McLachlan; ***M:*** Shirley Walker.

William & Catherine: A Royal Romance 1/2 **2011** Ticky-tacky and dull Hallmark Channel version of the romance of Prince William (Amboyer) and Catherine Middleton (St. Clair) who both come across as attractive but boring. They're university friends first and a courtship and engagement eventually follows. There's no wedding re-enactment here. **90m/C; DVD; Closed Captioned.** Dan Amboyer; Alice St. Clair; Jane Alexander; Victor Garber; Jean Smart; Stanley Eldridge; ***D:*** Linda Yellen; ***W:*** Linda Yellen; ***C:*** Gabriel Kosuth; ***M:*** Patrick Seymour. **CABLE**

William & Kate **2011** Rushed into production Lifetime cheesefest cashed in on the fascination of the British royal romance of Prince William and Kate Middleton. The leads don't look like the people they're portraying and the dialogue is laughable even if the situations are (possibly) true as it goes from their university meeting in 2001 to their engagement in 2010. **83m/C; DVD.** Ben Cross; Nico Evers-Swindell; Camilla Luddington; Justin Hanlon; Serena Scott Thomas; Christopher Cousins; Mary Elise Hayden; Samantha Whittaker; Jonathan Patrick Moore; Richard Reid; ***D:*** Mark Rosman; ***W:*** Nancy Silvers; ***C:*** Anthony B. Richmond. **CABLE**

William Shakespeare's A Midsummer Night's Dream 1/2 *A Midsummer Night's Dream* **1999 (PG-13)** Shakespeare's fantasy/romance/comedy is transported to turn-of-the-century Tuscany where Oberon (Everett), King of the Fairies, is fighting with his queen, Titania (Pfeiffer). Their spats lead to trouble for a variety of humans, including the hapless Bottom (Kline), who winds up with a donkey's head replacing his own. Kline is the most at ease with his role (Everett and Pfeiffer, primarily, have to look beautiful, which they do), while the younger foursome of would-be lovers (Flockhart, Bale, Friel, and West) prove to be less than memorable, as does the entire production. **115m/C; VHS, DVD.** Rupert Everett; Michelle Pfeiffer; Kevin Kline; Stanley Tucci; Calista Flockhart; Dominic West; Christian Bale; David Strathairn; Sophie Marceau; John Sessions; Anna Friel; Roger Rees; Max Wright; Gregory Jbara; Bill Irwin; Sam Rockwell; Bernard Hill; ***D:*** Michael Hoffman; ***W:*** Michael Hoffman; ***C:*** Oliver Stapleton; ***M:*** Simon Boswell.

William Shakespeare's Romeo and Juliet *Romeo and Juliet* **1996 (PG-13)** Bright, loud update of Shakespeare's tragedy of feuding families and first love. Contemporary fantasy setting, Verona Beach, and attitude (the Montagues and the Capulets are business rivals), with the 16th-century Elizabethan language intact, although Luhrmann's said to have cut half the text. Hot-blooded Romeo (DiCaprio) takes one look at angelic Juliet (Danes) and falls immediately in love/lust. This doesn't please Juliet's family, including quick-tempered cousin Tybalt (Leguizamo) who goes after Romeo with far-reaching consequences. DiCaprio's remarkable and the young duo look wonderful together. A big hit with the teens. Filmed in Mexico City. **120m/C; VHS, DVD, Blu-Ray.** Leonardo DiCaprio; Claire Danes; John Leguizamo; Paul Sorvino; Brian Dennehy; Diane Venora; Pete Postlethwaite; Paul Rudd; Harold Perrineau, Jr.; Jesse Bradford; Miriam Margolyes; Vondie Curtis-Hall; Christina Pickles; M. Emmet Walsh; ***D:*** Baz Luhrmann; ***W:*** Baz Luhrmann; Craig Pearce; ***C:*** Donald McAlpine; ***M:*** Nellee Hooper. British Acad. '97: Adapt. Screenplay, Art Dir./Set Dec., Director (Luhrmann), Score; MTV Movie Awards '97: Female Perf. (Danes).

The Willies **1990 (PG-13)** Three youngsters gross each other out with juvenile tales of horror and scariness while camping out in the backyard. Pointless but not without a few yuks (in both senses of the term). **120m/C; VHS, DVD.** James Karen; Sean Astin; Kathleen Freeman; Jeremy Miller; ***D:*** Brian Peck.

The Willoughbys 1/2 **2020 (PG)** Though Father (Short) and Mother (Krakowski) love each other very much, they do not feel the same way about their four children, Tim (Forte), Jane (Cara), and twins both named Barnaby (Cullen), and neglect them. After years of this treatment, the children send their parents on a dangerous trip hoping to become orphans. At the same time, the siblings have support in the form of sweet nanny Linda (Rudolph) and kind candy maker Commander Melanoff (Crews). Though more than a little dark, the animated feature is bright, full of memorable details and visual jokes, and fully embraces fantasy. **90m/C; DVD.** Will Forte; Maya Rudolph; Alessia Cara; Terry Crews; Martin Short; ***D:*** Kris Pearn; Rob Lodermeier; ***W:*** Kris Pearn; Mark Stanleigh; ***C:*** Sebastian Brodin; ***M:*** Mark Mothersbaugh. **VIDEO**

Willow 1/2 **1988 (PG)** Blockbuster fantasy epic combines the story of Moses with "Snow White," dwarves and all. Willow is the little Nelwyn who finds the lost baby Daikini and is assigned the task of returning her safely to her people. Willow discovers that the girl is actually a sacred infant who is destined to overthrow the evil queen Bavmorda and rule the land. As you might expect from executive producer George Lucas, there is much action and plenty of clever, high-quality special effects. But the "Star Wars"-esque story (by Lucas) is strangely predictable, and a bit too action-packed. Not really for children. **118m/C; VHS, DVD, Blu-Ray.** Warwick Davis; Val Kilmer; Jean Marsh; Joanne Whalley; Billy Barty; Pat Roach; Ruth Greenfield; Patricia Hayes; Gavan O'Herlihy; Kevin Pollak; ***D:*** Ron Howard; ***W:*** Bob Dolman; ***C:*** Adrian Biddle; ***M:*** James Horner.

Willow Creek **2013** Writer/director Goldthwait shifts makes a found-footage movie about a wannabe celebrity and his girlfriend trying to find Bigfoot. It's a successful slow-burn of a film as the director spends most of the time exploring how communities build up around urban legends. It's not until the last 10-15 minutes that the "horror" of the piece kicks in but the wait is worth it as Goldthwait proves to have a sense of how to use sound design and forced perspective, putting viewers right in the tent as something makes a very loud bump in the night. **80m/C; DVD, Blu-Ray.** Bryce Johnson; Alexie Gilmore; ***D:*** Bobcat Goldthwait; ***W:*** Bobcat Goldthwait; ***C:*** Evan Phelan.

Willy Wonka & the Chocolate Factory 1/2 **1971 (G)** When the last of five coveted "golden tickets" falls into the hands of sweet but very poor Charlie, he and his Grandpa Joe get a tour of the most wonderfully strange chocolate factory in the world. The owner is the most curious hermit ever to hit the big screen. He leads the five young "winners" on a thrilling and often dangerous tour of his fabulous factory. Adapted from Roald Dahl's "Charlie and the Chocolate Factory." Without a doubt one of the best "kid's" movies ever made; a family classic worth watching again and again. **100m/C; VHS, DVD, Blu-Ray, HD-DVD.** Gene Wilder; Jack Albertson; Denise Nickerson; Peter Ostrum; Roy Kinnear; Aubrey Woods; Michael Bollner; Ursula Reit; Leonard Stone; Dodo Denney; Julie Dawn Cole; Gunter Meisner; ***D:*** Mel Stuart; ***W:*** Roald Dahl; ***C:*** Arthur Ibbetson; ***M:*** Leslie Bricusse; Anthony Newley; Walter Scharf. Natl. Film Reg. '14.

Wilma **1977** Based on the true story of Wilma Rudolph, a young black woman who overcame childhood illness to win three gold medals at the 1960 Olympics. Plodding made-for-TV biography suffers from sub-par script and acting. **100m/C; VHS, DVD.** Shirley Jo Finney; Joe Seneca; Cicely Tyson; Jason Bernard; Denzel Washington; Larry B. Scott; Norman Matlock; ***D:*** Bud Greenspan; ***C:*** Arthur Ornitz; ***M:*** Irwin Bazelon. **TV**

Wilson **1944** Biography of Woodrow Wilson from his days as the head of Princeton University, to the governorship of New Jersey, and as U.S. President during WWI. After the war, Wilson conceives of the League of Nations but is unable to sell it to a U.S. still bent on isolationism. This lavish film won critical plaudits but was a major money-loser. **154m/C; DVD.** Alexander Knox; Charles Coburn; Geraldine Fitzgerald; Thomas Mitchell; Ruth Nelson; Ruth Ford; Cedric Hardwicke; Vincent Price; William Eythe; Mary Anderson; Sidney Blackmer; Stanley Ridges; Eddie Foy, Jr.; Charles Halton; ***D:*** Henry King; ***W:*** Lamar Trotti; ***C:*** Leon Shamroy; ***M:*** Alfred Newman. Oscars '44: Color Cinematog., Film Editing, Orig. Screenplay, Sound; Golden Globes '45: Actor--Drama (Knox).

Wilson **2017 (R)** Craig Johnson directs this adaptation of the Daniel Clowes graphic novel with mixed results. Stars Harrelson and Dern do their best in this acerbic comedy, and they're typically great, but overall the film is inconsistent and frustrating. Harrelson plays the title character, a man who reunites with his estranged wife (Dern), only to discover he has a teenage daughter. Wilson is perhaps a bit too sour, to the point that it's difficult to relate to his cynicism, which takes away from what he's forced to go through with his new-found daughter. **94m/C; DVD, Blu-Ray.** Woody Harrelson; Laura Dern; Cheryl Hines; David Warshofsky; Isabella Amara; ***D:*** Craig Johnson; ***W:*** Daniel Clowes; ***C:*** Frederick Elmes; ***M:*** Jon Brion.

Wimbledon 1/2 **2004 (PG-13)** Harmlessly predictable romantic comedy set in the tennis world, where weary 30-something Brit Peter Colt (Bettany) is coming to the end of his career with his final Wimbledon tournament. He meets cute with aggressive American super-player Lizzie Bradbury (Dunst), who's managed by her control-freak dad, Dennis (Neill). Lizzie's up for a little serve-and-volley and Peter suddenly finds his game (not to mention his love life) reinvigorated. Suddenly, he's a contender! But Lizzie is having second thoughts when love interferes with her concentration. After all, love in tennis is a big zero. Bettany is all self-deprecating charm while Dunst manages to be both smug and vulnerable. **98m/C; DVD, Blu-Ray.** Kirsten Dunst; Paul Bettany; Sam Neill; Jon Favreau; Bernard Hill; Eleanor Bron; Nikolaj Coster-Waldau; Austin Nichols; Robert Lindsay; James McAvoy; ***D:*** Richard Loncraine; ***W:*** Adam Brooks; Jennifer Flackett; Marc Levin; ***C:*** Darius Khondji; ***M:*** Ed Shearmur.

Win a Date with Tad Hamilton! **2004 (PG-13)** Typical young-love romance has small-town girl Rosalee (Bosworth) fall for actor-outsider Tad (Duhamel) while boy-next-door Pete (Grace) pines away in silence for her. Tad's agent (Lane) and manager (Hayes)--both oh so cleverly sharing the same name, Richard Levy—concoct the "win a date" contest to fix the bad boy image that's made him tabloid fodder. Rosalee is chosen and, to no one's surprise, Tad becomes intrigued. He pursues her much to Pete's dismay, and the usual dance ensues. Bosworth's down-to-earth appeal saves the formulaic concept but one wonders what prompted Broadway success Lane to take the bit role. **96m/C; VHS, DVD.** Kate (Catherine) Bosworth; Topher Grace; Ginnifer Goodwin; Josh Duhamel; Nathan Lane; Sean P. Hayes; Gary Cole; Kathryn Hahn; Stephen Tobolowsky; Amy Smart; Octavia L. Spencer; ***D:*** Robert Luketic; ***W:*** Victor Levin; ***C:*** Peter Lyons Collister; ***M:*** Ed Shearmur.

Win Win 1/2 **2011 (R)** Easygoing, modest dramedy. Struggling lawyer Mike Flaherty(Giamatti) moonlights as the high school coach of the very unsuccessful wrestling team. With some shady legal moves and for financial gain, Mike becomes the legal guardian of confused, elderly Leo Poplar (Young) and sticks him in an assisted-living facility when Leo's runaway teenage grandson Kyle (Shaffer) reappears. A star wrestler, the Flahertys take him in to help out the team. However, Kyle is then followed by his broke, fresh-out-of-rehab mom Cindy (Lynskey). Shaffer, an actual wrestler, isn't quite up to the complexities of his acting debut but he's surrounded by seasoned talent. **106m/C; Blu-Ray, On Demand.** Paul Giamatti; Alex Shaffer; Melanie Lynskey; Amy Ryan; Bobby Cannavale; Jeffrey Tambor; Burt Young; Margo Martindale; David Thompson; ***D:*** Thomas (Tom) McCarthy; ***W:*** Thomas (Tom) McCarthy; ***C:*** Oliver Brokelberg; ***M:*** Lyle Workman.

Winchell 1/2 **1998 (R)** Flamboyant biopic of powerful journalist/radio personality Walter Winchell (Tucci), whose career stretched from the 1930s into the '50s. Winchell blurred the line between hard news and tabloid gossip and used his influence politically to re-elect President Roosevelt and get the U.S. involved in WWII. But he was also arrogant and mean-spirited and his grandiosity eventually proved to be his downfall. Based on the 1976 book "Walter Winchell: His Life and Times" by Winchell's longtime ghostwriter Herman Klurfeld. **105m/C; VHS, DVD.** Stanley Tucci; Paul Giamatti; Glenne Headly; Christopher Plummer; Xander Berkeley; Kevin Tighe; Frank Medrano; Vic Polizos; Megan Mullally; Victoria Platt; ***D:*** Paul Mazursky; ***W:*** Scott Abbott; ***C:*** Robbie Greenberg; ***M:*** Bill Conti. **CABLE**

Winchester 1/2 **2018 (PG-13)** A horror flop that's far less interesting than the true story that inspired it. Widowed Sarah Winchester, heiress to the Winchester rifle fortune, is convinced that she's being haunted by the souls of people killed in the Civil War by her family's guns. A psychic tells her that she'll be safe as long as her mansion is never fully constructed, so in 1886, contractors start working around the clock for nearly four decades, building room upon room, doors that open into walls, a staircase that leads to nowhere, and other architectural oddities. Instead of showcasing more of this fascinating structure, the Spierigs opted for cheap scares featuring bloodied spirits. Even the fabulous Mirren couldn't do justice to the terror and madness that haunted Sarah more than any ghost did. **99m/C; DVD, Blu-Ray.** Dame Helen Mirren; Jason Clarke; Sarah Snook; Finn Scicluna-O'Prey; Emm Wiseman; ***D:*** Michael Spierig; Peter Spierig; ***W:*** Michael Spierig; Peter Spierig; Tom Vaughan; ***C:*** Ben Nott; ***M:*** Peter Spierig.

Winchester '73 1/2 **1950** Superb acting and photography characterize this classic, landmark western. Simple plot—cowboy Stewart pursues his stolen state-of-the-art rifle as it changes hands—speeds along and carries the viewer with it, ending with an engrossing and unforgettable shoot-out. Almost singlehandedly breathed new life into the whole genre. Laser videodisc version contains a special narration track provided by Stewart. Mann's and Stewart's first teaming. **82m/C; VHS, DVD.** James Stewart; Shelley Winters; Stephen McNally; Dan Duryea; Millard Mitchell; John McIntire; Will Geer; Jay C. Flippen; Rock Hudson; Tony Curtis; Charles Drake; ***D:*** Anthony Mann; ***C:*** William H. Daniels. Natl. Film Reg. '15.

The Wind 🦴 **1987** Foster is terrorized by Hauser while attempting to write her next thriller in Greece. Let's hope her book is more exciting than this movie. Shot on location in Greece. **92m/C; VHS, DVD, Blu-Ray.** Meg Foster; Wings Hauser; Steve Railsback; David McCallum; Robert Morley; ***D:*** Nico Mastorakis; ***W:*** Nico Mastorakis; Fred C. Perry; ***C:*** Andreas Bellis; ***M:*** Stanley Myers; Hans Zimmer.

Wind 🦴🦴 **1/2 1992 (PG-13)** Sailor Will Parker (Modine) chooses the opportunity to be on the America's Cup team over girlfriend Grey and then has the dubious honor of making a technical error that causes their loss. Undaunted, he locates Grey and her new engineer boyfriend (Skarsgard) and convinces them to design the ultimate boat for the next set of races. ESPN carried extensive coverage of the America's Cup races for the first time in the summer of '92 and viewers discovered that a little goes a long way. The same holds true for "Wind" which has stunning race footage, but little else. The script lacks substance and was written as filming progressed, and it shows. **123m/C; VHS, DVD, Blu-Ray.** Matthew Modine; Jennifer Grey; Cliff Robertson; Jack Thompson; Stellan Skarsgard; Rebecca Miller; Ned Vaughn; ***D:*** Carroll Ballard; ***W:*** Rudy Wurlitzer; Mac Gudgeon; ***C:*** John Toll; ***M:*** Basil Poledouris.

The Wind 🦴🦴 **1/2 2019 (R)** In 19th-century frontier America, Lizzy (Gerard) lives in a relatively isolated cabin with husband Isaac (Zukerman). Her husband is gone for long periods of time, so Lizzy spends much of her time alone, except for visits from her superstitious, flighty neighbor Emma (Tilles). Emma's belief in demons haunting the American plains deeply affects the mind of religious Lizzy, who has long believed she is surrounded by supernatural forces. A unique combination of western and horror, it's an intriguing character study of Lizzie as she slowly loses her grip on reality. **86m/C; DVD.** Caitlin Gerard; Ashley Zukerman; Miles Anderson; Julia Goldani Telles; Dylan McTee; ***D:*** Emma Tammi; ***W:*** Teresa Sutherland; ***C:*** Lyn Moncrief; ***M:*** Ben Lovett.

Wind and Cloud: The Storm Riders 🦴 *Tian xia; Storm Riders* **2004** Marketed as a sequel to the original "Storm Riders" film, but it is instead a film cobbled together from a TV series that's a sequel to a similar film. Since the series is 30 hours long, and this film is less than three hours, the plot suffers. It has been 12 years since Wind and Cloud fought their duel, and a new Evil has arisen to plague the land. It's assumed Wind and Cloud will come together, but an evil pill has turned Wind to the dark side. **109m/C; DVD.** *CH* Sonny Chiba; Aaron Kwok; Yiu-Cheung Lai; Kristy Yang; Ekin Chang; ***D:*** Raymond Lee; Shui Chung Yuet; ***W:*** Wing-Shing Ma; ***M:*** Akira Inoue.

The Wind and the Lion 🦴🦴🦴 **1975 (PG)** In turn-of-the-century Morocco, a sheik (Connery) kidnaps a feisty American woman (Bergen) and her children and holds her as a political hostage. President Teddy Roosevelt (Keith) sends in the Marines to free the captives, who are eventually released by their captor. Directed with venue and style by Milius. Highly entertaining, if heavily fictionalized. Based very loosely on a historical incident. **120m/C; DVD, Blu-Ray.** Sean Connery; Candice Bergen; Brian Keith; John Huston; Geoffrey Lewis; Steve Kanaly; Vladek Sheybal; Nadim Sawalha; Roy Jenson; Larry Cross; Simon Harrison; Polly Gottesmann; Marc Zuber; ***D:*** John Milius; ***W:*** John Milius; ***C:*** Billy Williams; ***M:*** Jerry Goldsmith.

The Wind Cannot Read 🦴🦴 **1958** Sentimental wartime romance. RAF officer Michael Quinn (Bogarde) is transferred to India to learn Japanese so he can interrogate POWs. He falls in love with his teacher Sabbi (Tani) and they secretly marry. Michael is captured after being sent to the front and becomes a prisoner of the Japanese. In the camp, the prisoners hear British radio propaganda and Michael recognizes Sabbi's voice. But one day her broadcasts stop and he becomes desperate to escape. **115m/C; DVD.** *UK* Dirk Bogarde; Yoko Tani; Ronald Lewis; John Fraser; Henry Okawa; ***D:*** Ralph Thomas; ***W:*** Richard Mason; ***C:*** Ernest Steward; ***M:*** Angelo Francesco Lavagnino.

Wind Chill 🦴🦴 **2007 (R)** Two college students are heading home for Christmas break. Driving in whiteout conditions, they get stuck in a snowbank on a deserted road without heat or a phone signal. But staying alive through the night may not be just a matter of the weather as it seems the ghosts of those who died on that road would like some more company. **91m/C; DVD, Blu-Ray.** Emily Blunt; Ashton Holmes; Martin Donovan; Ned Bellamy; ***D:*** Gregory Jacobs; ***W:*** Steven Katz; Joesph Gangemi; ***C:*** Dan Laustsen; ***M:*** Clint Mansell.

A Wind from Wyoming 🦴 **1/2 1994 (R)** Lea's boyfriend leaves her for her mother. Her father is determined to win back his wife by means of a hypnotist. Her chubby sister is obsessed with a celebrated author who somehow falls for Lea. When the hypnotist decides he wants Lea he turns the author into a woman-hater. Humorous look at dysfunctional families and the mysteries of love through a plot that is a bit hard to follow. Subtitled. **99m/C; VHS, DVD.** *CA FR* Francois Cluzet; France Castel; Michel Cote; Marc Messier; Sarah-Jeanne Salvy; Celine Bonnier; Donald Pilon; ***D:*** Andre Forcier; ***W:*** Andre Forcier; Patrice Arbour; Jacques Marcotte; ***C:*** Georges Dufaux; ***M:*** Christian Gaubert.

The Wind Rises 🦴🦴🦴 **1/2** *Kaze tachinu* **2013 (PG-13)** Visually splendid, elegiac animated drama from Japanese master Miyazaki was inspired by the life of innovative aviation engineer Jiro Horikoshi and tubercular novelist Tatsuo Hori (the film is dedicated to both). Jiro's too nearsighted to be a pilot but takes his love of flying to Mitsubishi where he becomes a rising star in the aviation industry. Since it's the 1930s, Jiro's troubled by the increasing likelihood of war as he works on what will become the 'Zero' fighter plane. Also part of the pic is the tender love story of Jiro and his TB-stricken wife, Naoko. Japanese, French, German, and Italian with subtitles. **126m/C; DVD, Blu-Ray.** *JP V:* Hideaki Anno; Miori Takimodo; Hidetoshi Nishijima; Masahiko Nishimura; Stephen Alpert; Mansai Nomura; ***D:*** Hayao Miyazaki; ***W:*** Hayao Miyazaki; ***M:*** Joe Hisaishi.

Wind River 🦴🦴 **1/2 1998 (PG-13)** In 1855 Utah, there's trouble between the settlers and the Shoshone tribe. The wife of Chief Washakie (Means) dreams that a wolf threatens the tribe and a young blond warrior saves them. So the chief sends Moragoni (Martinez) to find the boy. Moragoni meets 15-year-old settler Nicolas Wilson (Heron) and believes him to be the dream warrior and Nicolas agrees to live with the Shoshone and learn their ways. But eventually, Nicolas must choose between his real and adopted families. Based on "The White Indian Boy" by Elijah Nicolas, which was inspired by actual events. **97m/C; VHS, DVD.** Blake Heron; A. Martinez; Russell Means; Wes Studi; Karen Allen; Patricia Van Ingen; Joe Wandell; ***D:*** Tom Shell; ***W:*** Tom Shell; Elizabeth Hansen; ***C:*** Lawrence Schweich; ***M:*** Jeff Marsh. **VIDEO**

Wind River 🦴🦴🦴 **2017 (R)** When a young woman is found murdered on an Indian reservation in Wyoming, an FBI Agent (Olsen) enlists a local game tracker to help solve the case. Renner's restrained performance channels the quiet intensity of a hunter, and Olsen excels as a person admitted, but not embraced, in a foreign land. Wintry cinematography and understated dialogue mirror the residents' isolation in this superb, character-driven, psychological thriller. **107m/C; DVD, Blu-Ray.** Jeremy Renner; Elizabeth Olsen; Jon Bernthal; Martin Sensmeier; Julia Jones; ***W:*** Taylor Sheridan; ***C:*** Ben Richardson; ***M:*** Nick Cave; Warren Ellis.

The Wind That Shakes the Barley 🦴🦴🦴 **2006** Loach's take on the Irish fight for independence from Great Britain, which resulted in the partitioning of the country. In 1920, Damien O'Donovan (Murphy) is expecting to study medicine in London, but repeated run-ins with British soldiers find him joining his activist brother, Teddy (Delaney), in the IRA. However, following the Anglo-Irish Peace Agreement, the brothers find themselves on opposite sides—Teddy is willing to support an Irish Free State while the zealous Damien continues pursuing the dream of a totally independent country. Loach is unafraid to show the ruthlessness on both sides and the bitterness and tragedy that still lingers. **127m/C; DVD.** *SP IT GE IR GB* Cillian Murphy; Liam Cunningham; Mary Riordan; Padraic Delaney; Orla Fitzgerald; Laurence Barry; ***D:*** Ken Loach; ***W:*** Paul Laverty; ***C:*** Barry Ackroyd; ***M:*** George Fenton.

Windbag the Sailor 🦴 **1/2 1936** Ben Cutlet (Hay) only captains a small canal barge but likes to brag about his fictitious sea-going adventures. He's hired to take command of a ship that, unbeknownst to him, is supposed to be scuttled in an insurance scam. The crew mutinies and Cutlet and two stowaways find themselves on an island inhabited by cannibals, but Ben manages to use his tall tales to his advantage. **85m/B; DVD.** *GB* Will Hay; Moore Marriott; Graham Moffatt; Norma Varden; Kenneth Warrington; Dennis Wyndham; Amy Veness; ***D:*** William Beaudine; ***W:*** Will Hay; Marriott Edgar; George Edgar; Stafford Dickens; ***C:*** Jack Cox; ***M:*** Louis Levy.

Windjammer 🦴🦴 **1937** Western star O'Brien took a break from the lone prairie to make this seafaring rescue drama. He is a deputy state's attorney who signs up for a yacht race in order to serve a subpoena. Bad guys arrive on the scene, and the initially moody yacht denizens rely on our trusty hero to save them. Decent adventure. **75m/B; VHS, DVD.** George O'Brien; Constance Worth; ***D:*** Sam Newfield.

The Window 🦴🦴🦴 **1/2 1949** A little boy (Disney star Driscoll, intriguingly cast by director, Tetzlaff) has a reputation for telling lies, so no one believes him when he says he witnessed a murder...except the killers. Almost unbearably tense, claustrophobic thriller about the helplessness of childhood. Tetzlaff clearly learned more than a thing or two from the master, Hitchcock, for whom he photographed "Notorious." Based on the novella "The Boy Who Cried Murder" by Cornell Woolrich. Driscoll was awarded a special miniature Oscar as Outstanding Juvenile for his performance. **73m/B; VHS, DVD.** Bobby Driscoll; Barbara Hale; Arthur Kennedy; Ruth Roman; ***D:*** Ted Tetzlaff.

Window Theory 2004 Aimless Ethan (Large) returns to his hometown to stop the wedding of his high school honey Stephanie (O'Dell) to his ex-best friend Jeff (Flynn). Ethan wants her back but he's such an immature jerk—especially to women—that Steph is well rid of him. Since the lead is so unpleasant you really want him to get pummeled but that's about all. **?m/CDVD.** *CA* Luke Kirby; Alexandra Holden; Carly Pope; James Duval; Corey Large; Jennifer O'Dell; Luke Flynn; Paul Johannson; Tom Lenk; John Cassini; ***D:*** Andrew Putschoegl; ***W:*** Kyle Kramer; ***C:*** Andrew Huebscher; ***M:*** Miles Ito.

Window to Paris 🦴🦴 **1995 (PG-13)** East and West meet unexpectedly when a young music teacher (Dontsov) rents a room in St. Petersburg with a secret window that opens onto a Paris rooftop. Loony adventures ensue as Dontsov and his friends escape their dreary existence to exploit the bounties of Western capitalism in this sharp satire of Russian social ills. Relentless humor based on cross-cultural stereotypes wears thin (the Russians are cantankerous drunks; the Parisians, self-important snobs), but it keeps a sunny cast upon what could have been a scathing commentary. Russian and French with subtitles. **92m/C; VHS, DVD.** *RU FR* Serguej Dontsov; Agnes Soral; Viktor Michailov; Nina Oussatova; ***D:*** Yuri Mamin; ***W:*** Arkadi Tigai; Yuri Mamin; ***M:*** Aleksei Zalivalov; Yuri Mamin.

Windows 🦴 **1980 (R)** A lonely lesbian (Ashley) becomes obsessed with her quiet neighbor (Shire) and concocts a plot to get close to her. Director Willis is known for his unbeatable cinematography, most notably for Woody Allen in "Manhattan." His debut in the chair is a miserable, offensive flop. **93m/C; VHS, DVD, Blu-Ray.** Talia Shire; Joe Cortese; Elizabeth Ashley; Kay Medford; Linda Gillin; ***D:*** Gordon Willis; ***C:*** Gordon Willis; ***M:*** Ennio Morricone.

Windrunner 🦴🦴 **1/2 1994 (PG)** Angry at his football-star dad and rejected by the local high school team, Greg Cima (Wiles) finds an unlikely ally in the spirit of Native American Olympic hero Jim Thorpe (Means). Seems Thorpe needs some aid to return to the spirit world and, by coaching Cima, he'll also get the help he needs. Believable performances and an exploration of the power of Native American mysticism help the unlikely premise along. **110m/C; VHS, DVD.** Russell Means; Jason Wiles; Amanda Peterson; Margot Kidder; Jake Busey; Max Casella; Bruce Weitz; ***D:*** William Clark; ***W:*** Mitch Davis; ***M:*** Arthur Kempel.

The Winds of Kitty Hawk 🦴🦴 **1978** Visually interesting but talky account of the Wright brothers attempt to beat their rival Glenn Curtiss and his backer, phone man Alexander Graham Bell. Rule of thumb: Fast-forward through the parts when they are on the ground, or see Stacy Keach's public-TV version instead. **96m/C; VHS, DVD.** Michael Moriarty; David Huffman; Kathryn Walker; Eugene Roche; John Randolph; Scott Hylands; ***D:*** E.W. Swackhamer; ***M:*** Charles Bernstein.

Winds of Terror 🦴 **1/2** *WW3* **2001** FBI special agent Larry Sullivan (Hutton) is called in to investigate the sudden and mysterious deaths of a number of passengers aboard a cruise ship. It turns out to be biological terrorism and Sullivan must find out who's behind the act before they strike again. **100m/C; VHS, DVD.** Timothy Hutton; Terry O'Quinn; Lane Smith; Marin Hinkle; Michael Constantine; Vanessa L(ynne) Williams; ***D:*** Robert Mandel; ***W:*** Daniel Taplitz; ***C:*** Claudio Chea. **TV**

The Winds of War 🦴🦴 **1983** Excruciatingly long and dull miniseries based on Herman Wouk's bestseller about WWII. The book was much better; Mitchum appears to be fighting sleep unsuccessfully for much of the show. Two follow-ups were produced: "War and Remembrance" and "War and Remembrance: The Final Chapter." **900m/C; VHS, DVD.** Robert Mitchum; Ali MacGraw; Ralph Bellamy; Polly Bergen; Jan-Michael Vincent; David Dukes; John Houseman; Victoria Tennant; Peter Graves; Topol; Ben Murphy; Jeremy Kemp; Anton Diffring; Lawrence Pressman; Andrew Duggan; Barbara Steele; Charles Lane; ***D:*** Dan Curtis. **TV**

The Windsplitter 🦴 **1971** Obvious and amateurish 70s generation gap flick. Small-town Texan Bobby Joe (McMullan) goes to Hollywood and becomes a successful actor. When he returns home for a visit, the right-wing townsfolk are shocked to see a long-haired, motorcycle-riding hippie. And they turn vigilante to run him out of town. Filmed in Houston. **100m/C; DVD.** Jim McMullan; Paul Lambert; Joyce Taylor; ***D:*** Julius Feigelson; ***W:*** Julius Feigelson; ***C:*** Fred Kaplan; ***M:*** Al Capps.

Windtalkers 🦴🦴 **2002 (R)** Woo's WW II drama squanders a promising premise and turns it into a by-the-book war flick. The plot is inspired by the true story of Navaho Native Americans recruited by the Marines in order to use their language as an unbreakable code. Sgt. Enders (Cage) is a Marine assigned to protect one of these men, Pvt. Yahzee (Beach), but he also has orders to kill him if capture is imminent to protect the secrets of the code. The stage is then set for some of Woo's favorite themes: betrayal, duty and explosive bloody violence. Unfortunately, the characters are trite and the violence a bit overwhelming. **134m/C; VHS, DVD, Blu-Ray.** Nicolas Cage; Adam Beach; Christian Slater; Noah Emmerich; Mark Ruffalo; Peter Stormare; Brian Van Holt; Frances O'Connor; Jason Isaacs; Martin Henderson; Roger Willie; ***D:*** John Woo; ***W:*** John Rice; Joe Batteer; ***C:*** Jeffrey L. Kimball; ***M:*** James Horner.

Windwalker 🦴🦴🦴 **1981** Howard, the only cast member who is not a Native American, is an aged chief who shares the memories of his life with his grandchildren. Filmed in the Crow and Cheyenne Indian languages and subtitled in English throughout. A beautifully photographed, intelligent independent project. **108m/C; VHS, DVD.** Trevor Howard; James Remar; Dusty Iron Wing McCrea; ***D:*** Keith Merrill.

A Wing and a Prayer 🦴🦴🦴 **1944** Better-than-average WWII Air Force action flick. Battles rage throughout the Pacific theater and the men aboard the aircraft carrier struggle to do their part to save the world for freedom. Fine cast receives Hathaway's excellent unsentimental direction. **97m/B; VHS, DVD.** Don Ameche; Dana Andrews; William Eythe; Charles Bickford; Cedric Hardwicke; Kevin O'Shea; Richard Jaeckel; Harry (Henry) Morgan; ***D:*** Henry Hathaway; ***W:*** Jerome Cady; ***C:*** Glen MacWilliams; ***M:*** Hugo Friedhofer.

Wing Chun **1994** Wing Chun (Yeoh) battles horse stealing bandits and the male chauvinists around her that don't think a woman can be strong and independent (as well as a fighting expert). Chinese with subtitles or dubbed. **93m/C; VHS, DVD.** *CH* Michelle Yeoh; Donnie Yen; Waise Lee; ***D:*** Yuen Woo Ping.

Wing Commander WOOF! 1999 (PG-13) Unintentionally amusing sci-fi action flick combines elements from old WWII pilot movies, "Top Gun," and "Star Trek." Hot-shot space pilots (Prinz Jr. and Lillard) battle an evil race of aliens that resembles a heavily armed version of the cast of "Cats." Their real battle is with the heinous dialogue and techno-babble they are forced to regurgitate. Adapted from a video game. **105m/C; VHS, DVD, Blu-Ray.** Freddie Prinze, Jr.; Matthew Lillard; Saffron Burrows; Tcheky Karyo; Jurgen Prochnow; David Suchet; David Warner; ***D:*** Chris Roberts; ***W:*** Kevin Droney; ***C:*** Thierry Arbogast; ***M:*** Kevin Kiner.

Winged Migration ½ *Le Peuple Migrateur; Traveling Birds* **2001 (G)** Exhilarating documentary that follows the migratory patterns of birds. Shot from 1998 to 2001 by some 15 cinematographers throughout 40 countries, using a variety of gliders, balloons, and long-lensed cameras to get close enough to record the working muscles on a crane's back, among other sights. Terns float on arctic ice, rockhopper penguins waddle, gannets feed, sand grouse perform their mating dance, and flocks fly. The minimal narration identifies the birds and their journeys. English and French with subtitles. **89m/C; VHS, DVD, Blu-Ray.** *FR GE SP IT SI* ***Nar:*** Jacques Perrin; ***D:*** Jacques Perrin; ***W:*** Jacques Perrin; Stephane Durand; ***C:*** Bernard Lutic; Thierry Machado; Olli Barbe; Michel Benjamin; Sylvie Carcedo; Laurent Charbonnier; Luc Drion; Laurent Fleutot; Philippe Garguil; Dominique Gentil; Stephane Martin; Fabrice Moindrot; Ernst Sasse; Michel Terasse; Thierry Thomas; ***M:*** Bruno Coulais.

Wings ½ **1927** The silent classic about friends, Rogers and Arlen, their adventures in the Air Corps during WWI, and their rivalry for the hand of a woman. Contains actual footage of combat flying from the Great War. Won the very first Best Picture Oscar. Too-thin plot hangs on (barely) to the stirring, intrepid dogfight scenes. **139m/B; Silent; VHS, DVD, Blu-Ray.** Clara Bow; Charles "Buddy" Rogers; Richard Arlen; Gary Cooper; Jobyna Ralston; El Brendel; Richard Tucker; Henry B. Walthall; Roscoe Karns; Gunboat Smith; Julia Swayne Gordon; Arlette Marchal; Carl von Haartman; William A. Wellman; ***D:*** William A. Wellman; ***W:*** Hope Loring; John Monk Saunders; Louis D. Lighton; ***C:*** Harry Perry; ***M:*** J.S. Zamecnik. Oscars '28: Film; Natl. Film Reg. '97.

Wings in the Dark ½ **1935** The first (of three) pairings for Grant and Loy. Pilot Ken Gordon (Grant) is working on expanding airplane safety equipment when he meets stunt aviatrix Sheila Mason (Loy). Ken is blinded in an explosion and, unbeknownst to him, Sheila begins helping him financially. When she gets into trouble while flying in heavy fog, Ken is able to come to her rescue using his new safety instruments. Good flying sequences. **75m/B; DVD.** Cary Grant; Myrna Loy; Roscoe Karns; Hobart Cavanaugh; Dean Jagger; Bert Hanlon; ***D:*** James Flood; ***W:*** Dale Van Every; Jack Kirkland; Frank Partos; E. H. Robinson; ***C:*** Dewey Wrigley; William Mellor.

Wings of Danger *Dead on Course* **1952** A pilot tries to save his friend from blackmailing gold smugglers. **72m/B; VHS, DVD.** *GB* Zachary Scott; Kay Kendall; Robert Beatty; Naomi Chance; ***M:*** Malcolm Arnold.

Wings of Desire ½ *Der Himmel Uber Berlin* **1988 (PG-13)** An ethereal, haunting modern fable about angels Damiel (Ganz) and Cassiel (Sander), who observe human life in and above the broken existence of Berlin. Their attention is particularly focused on Homer (Bois), an elderly poet, American actor Peter Falk (playing himself), and a lovely French trapeze performer named marion (Dommartin). But the more Damiel observes, the more he longs to experience desire—emotional and physical—as humans do. A moving, unequivocable masterpiece, with as many beautiful things to say about spiritual need as about the schizophrenic emptiness of contemporary Germany; Wenders' magnum opus. German with subtitles, and with black-and-white sequences. **130m/C; VHS, DVD.** *GE* Bruno Ganz; Peter Falk; Solveig Dommartin; Otto Sander; Curt Bois; ***D:*** Wim Wenders; ***W:*** Wim Wenders; Peter Handke; ***C:*** Henri Alekan; ***M:*** Jurgen Knieper. Ind. Spirit '89: Foreign Film; L.A. Film Critics '88: Cinematog., Foreign Film; N.Y. Film Critics '88: Cinematog.; Natl. Soc. Film Critics '88: Cinematog.

Wings of Eagles ½ **1957** Hollywood biography of Frank 'Spig' Wead, a famous WWI aviation pioneer turned screenwriter. Veers wildly from comedy to stolid drama, though Bond's lampoon of Ford as "John Dodge" is justly famous. **110m/C; VHS, DVD.** John Wayne; Ward Bond; Maureen O'Hara; Dan Dailey; Edmund Lowe; Ken Curtis; Kenneth Tobey; Sig Rumann; Veda Ann Borg; ***D:*** John Ford; ***C:*** Paul Vogel.

The Wings of the Dove ½ **1997 (R)** Beautifully acted and filmed romance "inspired by" Henry James's 1902 novel. Updated to 1910, this triangular tale focuses on well-bred- but-penniless Kate Croy (Bonham Carter), who's been taken in by her imperious Aunt Maude (Rampling) with the expectation that she marry well. And this doesn't mean Kate's present beau, poor journalist Milton Densher (Roache). But when Kate meets gentle American heiress Millie Theale (Elliott), learns she's dying, and that she's also intrigued by Merton, the wheels begin to turn. A trip to Venice sets Kate's plan in motion but leads to unexpected developments for all concerned. **101m/C; VHS, DVD.** *GB* Helena Bonham Carter; Linus Roache; Alison Elliott; Elizabeth McGovern; Charlotte Rampling; Alex Jennings; Michael Gambon; ***D:*** Iain Softley; ***W:*** Hossein Amini; ***C:*** Eduardo Serra; ***M:*** Gabriel Yared. British Acad. '97: Cinematog., Makeup; L.A. Film Critics '97: Actress (Bonham Carter); Natl. Bd. of Review '97: Actress (Bonham Carter); Broadcast Film Critics '97: Actress (Bonham Carter).

Wings of the Morning ½ **1937** Maria (Annabella), a descendant of Spanish gypsies, comes to Ireland with her grandmother (Vanbrugh) who's entering a horse in the Epsom Downs Derby. Maria disguises herself as a boy so she can ride in the race but is discovered by Canadian horse-trainer Kerry (Fonda), who promptly falls in love with her. Legendary tenor John McCormack sings several songs. The first British movie to be filmed in Technicolor. **89m/C; VHS, DVD.** *GB* Annabella; Henry Fonda; Edward Underdown; Irene Vanbrugh; Leslie Banks; Stewart Rome; ***D:*** Harold Schuster; ***W:*** Tom Geraghty; ***C:*** Jack Cardiff; Henry Imus; Ray Rennahan; ***M:*** Arthur Benjamin.

Wings of the Navy ½ **1939** A romantic triangle turns out to be a minor matter in what looks more like a naval recruitment film set at the Pensacola Naval Air Training Station. Veteran flyer Cass is wooing Irene when rookie pilot, brother Jerry, turns up. After being crippled in a crash, Cass designs an experimental fighter that Jerry is determined to test despite the danger. **88m/B; DVD.** George Brent; Olivia de Havilland; John Payne; Frank McHugh; John Litel; Victor Jory; ***D:*** Lloyd Bacon; ***W:*** Michael Fessier; ***C:*** Arthur Edeson.

The Winner **1996 (R)** Philip (D'Onofrio) is on a winning streak at the Vegas Pair-A-Dice casino and the target of estranged brother Wolf (Madsen), temperamental lounge singer Louise (DeMornay), and various other con artists and thugs, all of whom want to separate him from his winnings. Lots of good actors but this Vegas story is nothing new. Based on the play "A Darker Purpose" by Riss. **90m/C; VHS, Streaming.** Vincent D'Onofrio; Michael Madsen; Rebecca De Mornay; Delroy Lindo; Frank Whaley; Billy Bob Thornton; Richard Edson; ***D:*** Alex Cox; ***W:*** Wendy Riss; ***C:*** Denis Maloney; ***M:*** Daniel Licht.

Winner Take All **1932** Cagney stars as egocentric palooka Jimmy Kane, who's currently taking a rest cure in New Mexico paid for by his New York fans. He meets widowed Peggy (Nixon), whose son Dickie (Moore) is ill. Jimmy heads back to the city for a title bout and promises to send for them, but flirty society dame Joan (Bruce) nearly causes Jimmy to ruin both his personal and professional lives. **70m/B; DVD.** James Cagney; Marion (Marian) Nixon; Dickie Moore; Virginia Bruce; Guy Kibbee; ***D:*** Roy Del Ruth; ***W:*** Wilson Mizner; Robert Lord; ***C:*** Robert B. Kurrle; ***M:*** W. Franke Harling.

Winner Takes All *The Boy Who Had Everything* **1984 (R)** A young college student during the Vietnam War comes to grips with maturity and growing pains. **94m/C; VHS, DVD.** *AU* Jason Connery; Diane Cilento; Lewis Fitz-Gerald; Laura Williams; ***D:*** Stephen Wallace; ***W:*** Stephen Wallace; ***C:*** Geoff Burton; ***M:*** Ralph Schneider.

Winners of the West **1940** A landowner schemes to prevent a railroad from running through his property. The railroad's chief engineer leads the good guys in an attempt to prevent sabotage. A fun serial in 13 chapters, full of shooting, blown-up bridges, locomotives afire, etc., and, of course, the requisite damsel in distress. **250m/B; VHS, DVD.** Anne Nagel; Dick Foran; James Craig; Harry Woods; ***D:*** Ray Taylor; Ford Beebe.

Winners Take All **1987 (PG-13)** A handful of friends compete in Supercross races. Spirited but thoroughly cliche sports flick. **103m/C; VHS, DVD.** Don Michael Paul; Kathleen York; Robert Krantz; Gerardo Mejia; ***D:*** Fritz Kiersch.

Winnie Mandela ½ **2013 (R)** Heavy-handed, paint-by-numbers biopic of Winnie Mandela (Hudson) and her marriage to the imprisoned Nelson Mandela (Howard) as she struggles with South Africa's apartheid system. Roodt's drama seems more about Winnie's wardrobe than her own imprisonment and social crusade and it can't quite deal with her later descent into notoriety. English and Xhosa with subtitles. Hudson gets to sing an unfortunately treacly song over the end credits. **107m/C; DVD, Blu-Ray.** *SA CA* Jennifer Hudson; Terrence Howard; Elias Koteas; Wendy Crewson; ***D:*** Darrell Roodt; ***W:*** Darrell Roodt; Andre Pieterse; ***C:*** Mario Janelle; ***M:*** Laurent Eyquem.

Winnie the Pooh **2011 (G)** Walt Disney Pictures went short, sweet, and old-fashioned (a hand-drawn look rather than CGI) in its return to a big-screen animated adventure for Pooh and his friends in the Hundred Acre Woods. Inspired by five A.A. Milne stories, including Pooh's constant search for honey, Eeyore's missing tail, and the mistaken notion that Christopher Robin is in danger. The title tune is sung by Zooey Deschanel. **69m/C; DVD, Blu-Ray, On Demand.** ***V:*** Jim (Jonah) Cummings; Craig Ferguson; Tom Kenny; Travis Oates; Bud Luckey; Kristen Anderson-Lopez; Jack Boulter; Wyatt Dean Hall; Huell Howser; ***Nar:*** John Cleese; ***D:*** Stephen John Anderson; Don Hall; ***C:*** Julio Macat; ***M:*** Henry Jackman.

Winning **1969 (PG)** A race car driver (Newman) will let nothing, including his new wife (Woodward), keep him from winning the Indianapolis 500. Newman does his own driving. Thomas' film debut. **123m/C; VHS, DVD, Blu-Ray.** Paul Newman; Joanne Woodward; Robert Wagner; Richard Thomas; Clu Gulager; ***D:*** James Goldstone; ***W:*** Howard Rodman; ***C:*** Richard Moore; ***M:*** Dave Grusin.

The Winning of Barbara Worth ½ **1926** Orphaned Barbara (Banky) has been raised by rancher Jefferson Worth (Lane), whose dream is to irrigate the desert. She's in love with foreman Abe Lee (young and gorgeous Cooper) until Willard Holmes (Colman) comes to town. Holmes is an engineer who has been hired by a land speculator to dam the local river but the speculator cheats the ranchers and uses cheap materials on the dam, setting up a spectacular disaster that has Holmes and Lee joining forces. King filmed on location in Nevada. Based on the novel by Harold Bell Wright. **89m/B; Silent; DVD.** Vilma Banky; Ronald Colman; Gary Cooper; Charles Lane; E.J. Ratcliffe; ***D:*** Henry King; ***W:*** Frances Marion; ***C:*** Gregg Toland; Georges Barens; ***M:*** Ted Henkel.

The Winning Season ½ **2009 (PG-13)** Divorced, hard-drinking loser Bill (Rockwell) is estranged from his teen daughter Molly (Dowdeswell). Then he's asked by his friend Terry (Corddry), who's the new principal at Molly's high school, to coach the pathetic girls' varsity basketball team. The mouthy players are a match for their disdainful coach but they learn from each other in a refreshingly non-sappy manner. **104m/C; DVD, Streaming.** Sam Rockwell; Shana Dowdeswell; Emma Roberts; Shareeka Epps; Emily Rios; Rooney Mara; Meaghan Witri; Melanie Hinkle; Rob Corddry; Margo Martindale; ***D:*** James C. Strouse; ***W:*** James C. Strouse; ***C:*** Frank DeMarco.

The Winning Team ½ **1952** Reagan stars in this biography of baseball legend Grover Cleveland Alexander and Day plays his dedicated wife. Some controversial issues were glossed over in the film, such as Alexander's real-life drinking problem and the fact that he had epilepsy. Although this was one of Reagan's favorite roles, he was upset by the studio's avoidance of all-too-human problems. Nonetheless, it's an entertaining enough movie about a very talented ballplayer. **98m/B; VHS, DVD.** Doris Day; Ronald Reagan; Frank Lovejoy; Eve Miller; James Millican; Russ Tamblyn; ***D:*** Lewis Seiler.

Winning: The Racing Life of Paul Newman ½ **2015** A feature-length documentary look at actor Paul Newman's obsession with car racing. An Academy Award winning actor and philanthropist, Newman began racing at the age of 47 and immediately became passionate about the sport. The documentary explores the depths of his passion, which was so intense that Newman nearly gave up acting. Racing for 35 years, Newman won four national championships as a driver and eight as an owner. Interviews with Mario Andretti, Robert Redford, and Patrick Dempsey are included. **83m/C; DVD, Streaming, Download.** ***D:*** Adam Carolla; ***W:*** Adam Carolla; Nate Adams; ***C:*** Marten Tedin; ***M:*** Extreme Music.

The Winslow Boy ½ **1948** A cadet at the Royal Naval College is wrongly accused of theft and expelled. Donat as the boy's lawyer leads a splendid cast. Despite consequences for his family, the boy's father (Hardwicke) sues the government and fights his son's battle, as the case makes the papers and he approaches bankruptcy. Plot would seem far-fetched if it weren't based on fact. Absorbing. Based on a play by Rattigan, who co-wrote the script. **112m/B; VHS, Streaming.** *GB* Robert Donat; Cedric Hardwicke; Margaret Leighton; Frank Lawton; Kathleen Harrison; Basil Radford; ***D:*** Anthony Asquith; ***W:*** Terence Rattigan; ***C:*** Frederick A. (Freddie) Young.

The Winslow Boy **1998 (G)** Mamet successfully treads on unfamiliar ground with this English period piece in which young Ronnie Winslow (Edwards) is accused of stealing and expelled from military school. His father (Hawthorne) becomes determined to clear his name at whatever cost. And the cost is to be high, for his family, his health, and his moderate fortune. He hires renowned lawyer Sir Robert Morton (Northam), also with consequences for family and bank balance. Although based on a real case, the story largely ignores the main events of the scandal, focusing on its effects on the various family members. Strong performances are led by Northam and Hawthorne. Based on Terence Rattigan's play. **104m/C; VHS, DVD.** Nigel Hawthorne; Jeremy Northam; Rebecca Pidgeon; Gemma Jones; Guy Edwards; Matthew Pidgeon; Colin Stinton; Aden (John) Gillett; Perry Fenwick; Sarah Flind; Sara Stewart; Alan Polanski; Neil North; ***D:*** David Mamet; ***W:*** David Mamet; ***C:*** Benoit Delhomme; ***M:*** Alaric Jans.

Winter a Go-Go **1965** It's a beach party flick moved to the slopes with all the silly cliches intact. Jeff (Wellman Jr.) inherits a rundown ski lodge and persuades some friends to help him turn it into the hot spot for the hip crowd of snow bunnies and cool guys. **87m/C; DVD.** William A. Wellman; James Stacy; Beverly Adams; Tom Nardini; Anthony Hayes; Jill Donahue; Walter Mascow; ***D:*** Richard

Benedict; *W:* Bob Kanter; Reno Carell; *C:* Jacques "Jack" Marquette; *M:* Harry Betts.

Winter Break 1/2 *Sheer Bliss* **2002 (R)** Cheesy-but-amusing comedy for those who liked "American Pie." College grad Matt (Ventimigila) is wondering what to do about getting a job when his best bud, Peter (Thomas), persuades him to join their friends in Aspen for the winter. They're basically out to enjoy themselves—until Matt finds romance with Michelle (Lawson). **98m/C; VHS, DVD, On Demand.** Milo Ventimiglia; Eddie Kaye Thomas; Maggie Lawson; Justin Urich; Eddie Mills; George Lazenby; Rachel Wilson; *D:* Marni Banack; *W:* Mark Botvinick; *C:* George Mooradian; *M:* Hope Botvinick. **VIDEO**

The Winter Guest **1997 (R)** Rickman's directorial debut looks at the lives of eight people living in a remote and icy Scottish village, focusing on the fictional relationship between real-life mother and daughter Law and Thompson. Introspective and somewhat stagey, but fine performances and excellent use of the desolate landscape make this a worthwhile debut effort. Based on the play by Sharman Macdonald, which he and Rickman adapted for the screen. **106m/C; VHS, DVD.** *GB* Emma Thompson; Phyllida Law; Sheila Reid; Sandra Voe; Gary Hollywood; Arlene Cockburn; Douglas Murphy; Sean Biggerstaff; Tom Watson; *D:* Alan Rickman; *W:* Alan Rickman; Sharman MacDonald; *C:* Seamus McGarvey; *M:* Michael Kamen.

Winter in Wartime *Oorlogswinter* **2010 (R)** Loss of innocence wartime melodrama. In January 1945, the Nazis occupy Holland and bored 14-year-old Michiel (Lakemeier) is disgusted that his realistic father, the town's mayor, placates their leaders. Instead, the naive teenager hopes to help out the Resistance and gets his chance when he witnesses an RAF plane get shot down and pilot Jamie (Campbell Bower) bail out. So Michiel vows to help him escape capture. Adapted from Jan Turlouw's 1972 semiautobiographical novel. English, Dutch, and German with subtitles. **103m/C; Blu-Ray, On Demand.** *NL* Yorick Van Wageningen; Jamie Campbell Bower; Martijn Lakemeier; Raymond Thir; Melody Klaver; Anneke Blok; Jesse Van Driel; Mees Peiknenburg; Dan van Husen; *D:* Martin Koolhoven; *W:* Paul Jan Nelissen; Martin Koolhoven; Mieke de Jong; *C:* Guido van Gennep; *M:* Pino Donaggio.

Winter Kill **1974** A failed TV pilot finds Griffith starring as the sheriff of a ski resort town troubled by a serial killer who spray-paints messages near his victims. The town council wants the crimes solved before tourist season begins or sheriff Sam will be out of a job. **97m/C; DVD.** Andy Griffith; John Calvin; Sheree North; Lawrence Pressman; Eugene Roche; John Larch; Nick Nolte; Joyce Van Patten; Tim O'Connor; *D:* Jud Taylor; *W:* John Michael Hayes; David Karp; *C:* Frank Stanley; *M:* Jerry Goldsmith. **TV**

Winter Kills **1979 (R)** Distinctive political black comedy suffers a hilariously paranoid version of American public life. Nick Kegan (Bridges) has been drifting through life ever since his older brother, a U.S. president, was assassinated 15 years earlier. His eccentric father (Huston) wants to draw Nick back into the family by claiming a conspiracy, but as Nick begins to dig into the past, he does uncover political machinations. Uneven, but well worth seeing; flopped at the boxoffice, but was re-edited (with the original ending restored) and re-released in 1983. Elizabeth Taylor (as Lola Comante) went unbilled. Based on the novel by Richard Condon. **97m/C; VHS, DVD, Blu-Ray.** Jeff Bridges; John Huston; Anthony Perkins; Richard Boone; Sterling Hayden; Eli Wallach; Ralph Meeker; Belinda Bauer; Dorothy Malone; Toshiro Mifune; Elizabeth Taylor; Donald Moffat; Tisa Farrow; Brad Dexter; Joe Spinell; *D:* William Richert; *W:* William Richert; *C:* Vilmos Zsigmond; *M:* Maurice Jarre.

The Winter Light 1/2 *Nattvardsgaesterna* **1962** The second film in Bergman's famous trilogy on the silence of God, preceded by "Through a Glass Darkly" and followed by "The Silence." Bleak and disturbing view of a tortured priest who searches for the faith and guidance he is unable to give his congregation. Hard to swallow for neophyte Bergmanites, but challenging, deeply serious and rewarding for those accustomed to the Swede's angst. Polished and personal. In Swedish with English subtitles. **80m/B; VHS, DVD, Blu-Ray.** *SW* Gunnar Bjornstrand; Ingrid Thulin; Max von Sydow; *D:* Ingmar Bergman; *W:* Ingmar Bergman; *C:* Sven Nykvist.

Winter Lily **1998** Disturbing shocker. Photographer Peter (Gilmore) checks into a remote B&B where the only inhabitants are owner Agatha (Berryman) and her 14-year-old daughter Lily (Laferriere) who is confined to her bedroom by illness. When Peter finds Lily's diary, he discovers that she is dying because her parents are refusing her medical aid. Is this as a punishment for her affair with a much-older man? And just where is Lily's violent absent father (Bergeron) anyway? **90m/C; VHS, DVD.** *CA* Dorothee Berryman; Danny Gilmore; Jean-Pierre Bergeron; Kimberley Laferriere; *D:* Roshel Bissett; *W:* Roshel Bissett.

Winter Meeting **1948** Overwrought drama with Bette Davis starring as a spinster poetess who falls in love with a war hero who wants to be a priest. Very talky script, of interest only as the sole romantic lead for James Davis, whose claim to fame was westerns and the TV series "Dallas" as 'Jim' Davis. **104m/B; DVD.** Bette Davis; Janis Paige; James Davis; John Hoyt; Florence Bates; Walter Baldwin; Ransom Sherman; *D:* Bretaigne Windust; *W:* Catherine Turney; *C:* Ernest Haller; *M:* Max Steiner.

Winter of Frozen Dreams **2008** Based on the 1970s true crime murder case of Barbara Hoffman, a Madison, Wisconsin college student who worked as a massage parlor hooker. When her jittery fiance Jerry Davies reports finding a body frozen in the snow, it's not long until Detective Lulling makes them the prime suspects. Turns out Barb seduces her clients into leaving her money and then kills them. The first televised murder trial in the United States. **92m/C; DVD.** Thora Birch; Brendan Sexton, III; Leo Fitzpatrick; Dean Winters; Keith Carradine; Scott Cohen; Dan Moran; *D:* Eric Mandelbaum; *W:* Eric Mandelbaum; *C:* Brian O'Carroll; *M:* Kenneth Lampl.

The Winter of Our Dreams 1/2 **1982** Down Under slice of seamy life as a heroin-addicted prostitute becomes involved with an unhappy bookshop owner. Davis shines in otherwise slow and confusing drama. **89m/C; VHS, DVD.** *AU* Judy Davis; Bryan Brown; Cathy Downes; Baz Luhrmann; Peter Mochrie; Mervyn Drake; Margie McCrae; Marcie Deane-Johns; *D:* John Duigan. Australian Film Inst. '81: Actress (Davis).

Winter on Fire: Ukraine's Fight for Freedom **2015** An unflinching look at the Ukrainian Revolution of 2013-14 from an on-the-ground perspective. The 93-day-long protest against the Ukrainian government is chronicled with footage shot by both documentarian Evgeny Afineevsky and activists taking part. Though the protest begins peacefully, violent government action against protestors only raises the stakes and leads to more people joining their cause. The documentary captures the bravery of the protestors in the face of brutality and serves a testament to the human spirit. **102m/C; DVD.** *D:* Evgeny Afineevsky; *W:* Den Tolmor; *C:* Evgeny Afineevsky; Oleg Balaban; Maxim Bernakevich; Ruslan Ganushchak; Eduard Georgadze; Inna Goncharova; Kostyantyn Ignatchuk; Alex Kashpur; Lizogub Khrystyna; Lina Klebanova; Kirill Kniazev; Damian Kolodiy; Maria Komar; Viktor Kozhevnikov; Yuriy Krivenko; Vladimir Makarevich; Arturas Morozovas; Dmytro Patyutko; Pavlo Peleshok; Viacheslav Poliantsev; Galyna Sadomtseva-Nabaranchuk; Constantin Shandybin; Zhenya Shynkar; Ielizaveta Smith; Oleg Tandalov; Tsvetkov Vyacheslav; Igor Zakharenko; *M:* Jasha Klebe.

Winter Passing 1/2 **2005 (R)** Reese (Deschanel) is a disillusioned actress living an empty life in New York, trying not to acknowledge the fact that her mother has recently died and she hasn't seen her father, a reclusive, alcoholic, once-famous novelist, in years. Motivated by an editor's (Madigan) offer of big money for potential love letters written by her parents long ago, Reese reluctantly returns to Michigan to reconnect with her mislaid father. Upon her arrival she's greeted by Corbit (Ferrell), her father's spaced-out caretaker, and Shelly (Warner), who handles her father's business matters. Dancing between humor and affection, the characters all carefully paint a portrait of loneliness and awakening. However, that dance is often a little too slow. Inspired performances, especially in Ferrell's wise restraint. **98m/C; DVD, Blu-Ray.** Zooey Deschanel; Ed Harris; Will Ferrell; Amelia Warner; Amy Madigan; Dallas Roberts; Deirdre O'Connell; Robert Beitzel; *D:* Adam Rapp; *W:* Adam Rapp; *C:* Terry Stacey; *M:* John Kimbrough.

Winter People 1/2 **1989 (PG-13)** A clock-making widower and a woman living alone with her illegitimate son experience tough times together with feuding families in a Depression-era Appalachian community. Silly, rehashed premise doesn't deter McGillis, who gamely gives a fine performance. Based on the novel by John Ehle. **109m/C; VHS, DVD.** Kurt Russell; Kelly McGillis; Lloyd Bridges; Mitchell Ryan; Jeffrey Meek; Eileen Ryan; Amelia Burnette; *D:* Ted Kotcheff; *W:* Carol Sobieski; *M:* John Scott.

Winter Sleep 1/2 **2014** Turkish director Ceylan challenges viewers with this three-hour-plus drama that features his typical lack of traditional action but allows for dense, deep characters. Aydin is a former actor who is now running a small hotel in central Anatolia (shot again with Ceylan's typically gorgeous eye, bringing beauty to even the most mundane landscapes). Aydin is married to Nihal, with whom he often fights, and runs the hotel with his sister Necla, who is dealing with the ripple effect of divorce. Ceylan has an amazing ability to draw as much character out of silence and bitter stares as most directors do with pages of dialogue. **196m/C; DVD.** *TU* Haluk Bilginer; Melisa Sozen; Demet Akbag; *D:* Nuri Bilge Ceylan; *W:* Nuri Bilge Ceylan; Ebru Ceylan; *C:* Gokhan Tiryaki.

Winter Sleepers 1/2 *Winterschlafer* **1997** Angsty and slow (completely unlike the director's breakthrough "Run Lola Run"). Rebecca (Daniel) is waiting at a mountain chalet for her boyfriend Marco (Ferch) to show up. When Marco leaves his keys in his car, Rene (Matthes) takes it for a joy ride and gets into an accident, eventually meeting Laura (Sellem) the nurse, who owns the chalet. The foursome wind-up together but nothing much matters. Based on the novel "Expense of the Spirit" by Pyszora, who co-wrote the screenplay. German with subtitles. **124m/C; VHS, DVD.** *GE* Heino Ferch; Floriane Daniel; Ulrich Matthes; Marie-Lou Sellem; Josef Bierbichler; *D:* Tom Tykwer; *W:* Tom Tykwer; Anne-Francois Pyszora; *C:* Frank Griebe; *M:* Tom Tykwer; Johnny Klimek; Reinhold Heil.

Winter Solstice **2004 (R)** Such a sad, sad gut-wrencher. But it's so good at being sad. Jim Winters (LaPaglia) is the struggling father of a motherless family still trying to get by without her, five years after a tragic car accident. Jim's two sons, Gabe and Peter, don't want to grab hold when he reaches out to them. They're mad at the life they live. Thankfully, writer/director Josh Sternfeld doesn't bother with much plot, something that normally distracts from emotion and character examination in these types of films. These people live and suffer, and let us watch—we wonder what'll happen to them when the movie ends. Its effect lingers long after the credits. **90m/C; DVD.** Anthony LaPaglia; Aaron Stanford; Mark Webber; Allison Janney; Michelle Monaghan; Ron Livingston; Brandon Sexton, III; Ebon Moss-Bachrach; *D:* Josh Sternfeld; *W:* Josh Sternfeld; *C:* Harlan Bosmajian; *M:* John Leventhal.

The Winter War *Talvisota* **1989** One of the best Finnish films ever tells the story of the Russian war on Finland and the Finnish defense in 1939-41. **195m/C; VHS, DVD.** Esko Nikkari; Tomi Salmela; Vesa Vierikko; Samuli Edelmann; Teemu Koskinen; Esko Kovero; Eero Maenpaa; Konsta Makela; Taneli Makela; Heikki Paavilainen; Antti Raivio; Miitta Sorvali; Martti Suosalo; Timo Torikka; *D:* Pekka Parikka; *W:* Pekka Parikka; *C:* Kari Sohlberg; *M:* Jukka Haavisto; Juha Tikko.

Winterbeast **1992** Winter resort community dwellers begin mysteriously disappearing until somebody remembers that the resort was built over a sacred Indian burial ground. Sgt. Bill Whitman, the valiant park ranger and his Barney Fife-like assistant Stillman, question the town's wise old sage, Sheldon, who's sitting on a secret that could threaten the entire community. **77m/C; VHS, Streaming.** Tim R. Morgan; Mike Magri; Bob Harlow; Charles Majka; Dori May Kelly; *D:* Christopher Thies; *W:* Christopher Thies; *M:* Michael Perilstein.

Winter's Bone **2010 (R)** Tense backwoods indie drama with an outstanding performance by Lawrence as proud, overwhelmed teenager Ree. She lives in a bleak, poor Missouri Ozarks community, looking after two younger siblings and her mentally ill mother. Her meth-cooking dad has disappeared, skipping bail on a drug bust, and they'll be evicted since he put the house up as bond. Ree is determined to find her dad though she's warned off by increasingly hostile locals who believe in keeping their business private. Adaptation of the Daniel Woodrell novel. **99m/C; DVD.** Jennifer Lawrence; John Hawkes; Kevin Breznahan; Dale Dickey; Garret Dillahunt; Sheryl Lee; Lauren Sweetser; Tate Taylor; *D:* Debra Granik; *W:* Debra Granik; Anne Rosellini; *C:* Michael McDonough; *M:* Dickon Hinchliffe. Ind. Spirit '11: Support. Actor (Hawkes), Support. Actress (Dickey).

Winter's Tale **2014 (PG-13)** Carelessly pieced together from Mark Helprin's popular fantasy novel, this driveling cornball fluff has no idea what direction it's going. Like most storybook set-ups, sparks fly when orphaned badboy thief Peter (Farrell) falls in love with privileged Beverly (Brown Findlay). Tragedy befalls their star-crossed love, prompting Peter to turn to magical gems and guardian angels in order to defy mortality and pull off gooey miracles. Crowe's in there as a demon named Pearly. A total head scratcher, guaranteed to confuse anyone not familiar with the novel. **118m/C; DVD, Blu-Ray.** Colin Farrell; Jessica Brown Findlay; Russell Crowe; William Hurt; Jennifer Connelly; Eva Marie Saint; Graham Greene; Will Smith; *D:* Akiva Goldsman; *W:* Akiva Goldsman; *C:* Caleb Deschanel; *M:* Hans Zimmer; Rupert Gregson-Williams.

Winterset 1/2 **1936** A son seeks to clear his father's name of a falsely accused crime 15 years after his electrocution. Powerful at the time, though time has lessened its impact. Loosely based on the trial of Sacco and Vanzetti and adapted from Maxwell Anderson's Broadway play, with stars in the same roles. Meredith's film debut. **85m/B; VHS, DVD.** Burgess Meredith; Margo; John Carradine; *D:* Alfred Santell.

Wintertime 1/2 **1943** Forgettable and mindless Henie musical. Plot revolves around Henie travelling in Canada with her wealthy uncle, and saving an old, run-down hotel. An appearance by Woody Herman and his Orchestra give the film a much-needed boost. Based on a story by Arthur Kober. **82m/B; DVD.** Sonja Henie; Jack Oakie; Cesar Romero; Carole Landis; S.Z. Sakall; Cornel Wilde; Woody Herman; *D:* John Brahm; *W:* E. Edwin Moran; Jack Jevne; Lynn Starling.

Wired **2008** Bank employee Louise Evans (Whittaker) gets a promotion and is then targeted by thugs Phillip (Fox) and Manesh (Ahmed). They work for a money-laundering crime family and want her to intercept a money transfer. The men know Louise defrauded the bank and use blackmail to keep her in line while undercover cop Crawford Hill (Stephens) tries to protect Louise and do his job—though Louise also knows how to protect herself. **134m/C; DVD.** *GB* Jodie Whittaker; Toby Stephens; Laurence Fox; Riz Ahmed; Ramon Tikaram; *D:* Kenny Glenaan; *W:* Kate Brooke; *C:* Tony Slater-Ling; *M:* Stephen McKeon. **TV**

Wiretapper 1/2 **1955** Shallow crime drama based on the autobiography of Jim Vaus. Petty criminal Jim Vaus is doing electrical repair work at the home of mobster Charles Rumson when he discovers the place is bugged by the feds. The grateful crook gets Jim work wiretapping the cops and electronically fixing horse races, but his criminal success puts a strain on his marriage. Wife Alice insists they go to hear evangelist Billy Graham preach to help Jim find the right path. **85m/B; DVD.** Bill Williams; Georgia Lee; Douglas Kennedy; Stanley Clements; Paul Picerni; *D:* Dick Ross; *W:* John O'Dea; *C:* Ralph Woolsey; *M:* Ralph Carmichael.

Wirey Spindell **1999** Self-indulgent clap-trap about a self-satisfied creep. The title character (Schaeffer) is engaged to beautiful Tabatha (Thorne) but has become suddenly impotent due to extreme premarital jitters. This little dilemma leads Wirey to explore his childhood and druggie high school/college years (when the character is played by Mabius), his first love, and his falling for Tabatha. Problem is Wirey isn't a very interesting character. **101m/C; VHS, DVD.** Eric Schaeffer; Callie (Calliope) Thorne; Eric Mabius; Samantha Buck; ***D:*** Eric Schaeffer; ***W:*** Eric Schaeffer; ***C:*** Kramer Morgenthau; ***M:*** Amanda Kravat.

Wisdom 1/2 **1987 (R)** Unemployed young guy (Estevez) becomes a bank robber with Robin Hood aspirations, coming to the aid of American farmers by destroying mortgage records. Estevez became the youngest person to star in, write, and direct a major motion picture. And, my goodness, it shows. **109m/C; VHS, DVD.** Emilio Estevez; Demi Moore; Tom Skerritt; Veronica Cartwright; ***D:*** Emilio Estevez; ***M:*** Danny Elfman.

Wise Blood 1/2 **1979 (PG)** Gothic drama about a drifter who searches for sin and becomes a preacher for a new religion, The Church Without Christ. Excellent cast in achingly realistic portrayal of ersatz religion, southern style. Many laughs are more painful than funny. Superb, very dark comedy from Huston. Adapted from the Flannery O'Connor novel. **106m/C; VHS, DVD.** Brad Dourif; John Huston; Ned Beatty; Amy Wright; Harry Dean Stanton; ***D:*** John Huston; ***M:*** Alex North.

Wise Guys 1/2 **1986 (R)** Two small-time hoods decide to rip off the mob. When their boss figures out their plan he decides to set them up instead. Lame black comedy that has too few moments. **100m/C; DVD.** Joe Piscopo; Danny DeVito; Ray Sharkey; Capt. Lou Albano; Dan Hedaya; Julie Bovasso; Patti LuPone; ***D:*** Brian De Palma; ***M:*** Ira Newborn.

Wisecracks **1993** Women comics perform and talk about their work in this documentary directed by Gail Singer. The comics featured have, in some cases, little more in common than their work, but all share interesting perspectives on what they do. Interesting mix of performance clips and interviews sometimes includes banal comments about the nature of comedy, but is more often insightful, especially remarks by seasoned vet Phyllis Diller. Although there exists here the potential for an angry feminist diatribe on gender-based humor, the focus is more towards talented women who are just plain funny. **93m/C; VHS, DVD. *D:*** Gail Singer.

Wisegal 1/2 **2008** Tough Brooklyn widow Patty Montanari (Milano) has two young sons to support. While selling contraband smokes for some local wiseguys, Patty catches the eye of married crime boss Frank Russo (Gedrick), who gives Patty a nightclub to manage. Then mob honcho Salvatore Palmeri (Caan) insists Patty transport cash from New York across the border to his Canadian operations. Patty eventually wants out, especially when the feds start closing in. Inspired by a true story; an original Lifetime movie. **89m/C; DVD.** Alyssa Milano; Jason Gedrick; James Caan; Janet Wright; Alessandro Costantini; Kyle Harrington; ***D:*** Jerry Ciccoritti; ***W:*** Shelley Evans; ***C:*** Gerald Packer; ***M:*** John (Gianni) Frizzell. **CABLE**

Wisegirls *Wise Girls* **2002** Estrogen-injected mob flick follows Meg (Sorvino), a med school grad who moves back to New York and takes a job waitressing in a mob-infested restaurant. Trying to divorce herself from a disastrous past, Meg gets wise to just which family owns this family-owned establishment. She's less than thrilled but the worst she has to deal with is reluctantly accepting money from their boss (Nascarelli), who admires her medical skills, and fending off advances from his odious son (Maelen), until she witnesses a murder and finds herself on the wrong side of the law. Plot contains interesting twists right down to the satisfying end. Sorvino performs ably while Walters is a standout and Carey proves she has stuff to make it on the big screen. Tired premise, however, takes some of the fun out this gangster chick flick. **96m/C; VHS, DVD.** Mira Sorvino; Mariah Carey; Melora Walters; Arthur J. Nascarella; Christian Maelen; Joseph Siravo; ***D:*** David Anspaugh; ***W:*** John Meadows; ***C:*** Johnny E. Jensen; ***M:*** Keith Forsey.

Wish I Was Here **2014 (R)** Aidan Bloom (Braff) is a struggling actor with a wife and two kids, who is forced to a crossroads by the fact that his father (Patinkin) is dying. Notoriously known as the film that Braff funded through his fans by using Kickstarter, the result is a work that proves that perhaps producers are necessary for the creative process. Given complete creative freedom, Braff succumbs to all of his filmmaking weaknesses, making a dramedy that underlines every emotional beat while making none of them feel real. **106m/C; DVD, Blu-Ray.** Zach Braff; Kate Hudson; Mandy Patinkin; Joey King; Pierce Gagnon; Josh Gad; Jim Parsons; ***D:*** Zach Braff; ***W:*** Zach Braff; Adam J. Braff; ***C:*** Lawrence Sher; ***M:*** Rob Simonsen.

Wish Upon **2017 (PG-13)** Miserable high schooler Clare finds an old music box that grants her seven wishes, so she wishes for world peace and an end to global hunger. Of course she doesn't! She wants revenge on enemies and sweet stuff for herself. Gruesome deaths ensue, thanks to the demon living in the box. Move along--nothing original or scary here. **90m/C; DVD, Blu-Ray.** Joey King; Ryan Phillippe; Ki Hong Lee; Shannon Purser; Sydney Park; ***D:*** John R. Leonetti; ***W:*** Barbara Marshall; ***C:*** Michael Galbraith; ***M:*** tomandandy.

Wish upon a Star 1/2 **1996 (PG)** Battling teenage sisters Alexia (Heigl) and Haley (Harris) wind up switching identities when bookish Haley wishes on a falling star to be like popular Alexia. Naturally, this confuses everyone but the sisters get to see how their other sibling feels. **90m/C; VHS, DVD.** Katherine Heigl; Danielle Harris; Scott Wilkinson; Mary Parker Williams; Don Jeffcoat; Lois Chiles; ***D:*** Blair Treu; ***W:*** Jessica Barondes; ***C:*** Brian Sullivan; ***M:*** Ray Colcord.

Wish You Were Dead 1/2 **2000 (R)** Schnook insurance adjuster MacBeth (Elwes) naively signs over his million dollar life insurance policy to slutty "girlfriend" Sally (Steenburgen), who promptly hires hit woman Jupiter (Hendrix) to get rid of the excess baggage. Only Jupiter can't get over what a nice guy MacBeth is and falls in love with him instead—which doesn't mean Sally is giving up. **89m/C; VHS, DVD.** Cary Elwes; Mary Steenburgen; Elaine Hendrix; Christopher Lloyd; Billy Ray Cyrus; Robert Englund; Sally Kirkland; Gene Simmons; Shannon Tweed; ***D:*** Valerie McCaffrey; ***W:*** Scott Firestone; ***C:*** David Klein. **VIDEO**

Wish You Were Here *Too Much* **1987** Poignant yet funny slice of British post-war life roughly based on the childhood memoirs of famous madame, Cynthia Payne. A troubled and freedom-loving teenager expresses her rebellion in sexual experimentation. Mum is dead and Dad just doesn't understand, so what's a girl to do, but get the boys excited? Lloyd, in her first film, plays the main character with exceptional strength and feistiness. Payne's later life was dramatized in the Leland-scripted "Personal Services." **92m/C; VHS, DVD.** *GB* Emily Lloyd; Tom Bell; Clare Clifford; Barbara Durkin; Geoffrey Hutchings; Charlotte Barker; Chloe Leland; Trudy Cavanagh; Jesse Birdsall; Geoffrey Durham; Pat Heywood; ***D:*** David Leland; ***W:*** David Leland; ***C:*** Ian Wilson; ***M:*** Stanley Myers. British Acad. '87: Orig. Screenplay; Natl. Soc. Film Critics '87: Actress (Lloyd).

Wish You Were Here **2012 (R)** When Dave Flannery (Edgerton), springs an impromptu vacation at a Cambodian beach resort on his wife Alice (Price), her sister Steph (Palmer) and Steph's new boyfriend Jeremy (Palmer), the group learns the dangers of excess. They live it up, drinking, dancing, and drugging, leading to a delirious night of adultery. Finally regain consciousness, they're back home in Australia but without Jeremy. Fearful of revealing too much to the authorities, they manipulate their stories to conceal the truth. The events unfold slowly, with the entire cast twisting their characters into surprisingly self-destructive messes. An unpredictable vacation hallucination, loaded with risks and suspense. **89m/C; DVD.** *AU* Felicity Price; Joel Edgerton; Teresa Palmer; Antony Starr; ***D:*** Kieran Darcy-Smith; ***W:*** Felicity Price; Kieran Darcy-Smith; ***C:*** Jules O'Loughlin; ***M:*** Rosie Chase.

Wishful Thinking **1992** A lovelorn screenwriter rescues a peculiar man from mysterious assassins and receives a magical writing pad for his efforts. It seems that whatever Michael writes on the paper will come true, so he decides to write himself into the life of the luscious Diane. **94m/C; VHS, DVD.** Murray Langston; Michelle Johnson; Ruth Buzzi; Billy Barty; Johnny Dark; Ray "Boom Boom" Mancini; Vic Dunlop; Kip Addotta; ***D:*** Murray Langston.

Wishful Thinking 1/2 **1996 (R)** Elizabeth (Beals) and Max (Le Gros) have been living together for four years. When Max doesn't want to get married, Elizabeth becomes withdrawn but Max decides she's having an affair. As he becomes more and more jealous, a third party enters the picture. Lena (Barrymore) decides she wants Max herself and devises a plan to get him at any cost. **89m/C; VHS, DVD.** Drew Barrymore; Jennifer Beals; James LeGros; Mel Gorham; Eric Thal; Jon Stewart; ***D:*** Adam Park; ***W:*** Adam Park.

Wishmaster *Wes Craven Presents Wishmaster* **1997 (R)** An evil genie grants wishes to those who stumble upon him, but he also gets his kicks by destroying the lives of those naive enough to play along. Anemic horror tale that's as thin on plot as it is on scares. Standard-issue exploding chest cavities and flying heads can't easily erase the boredom. Make-up artist turned director Kurtzman should have wished for some directorial skills, because he hasn't got a clue. Don't be misled by Wes Craven's name, his association with this dud is meant to lure the least discriminating of horror fans. **90m/C; VHS, DVD, Blu-Ray.** Tammy Lauren; Andrew Divoff; Robert Englund; Chris Lemmon; Tony Crane; Wendy Benson; Jenny O'Hara; Tony Todd; Kane Hodder; ***D:*** Robert Kurtzman; ***W:*** Peter Atkins; ***C:*** Jacques Haitkin; ***M:*** Harry Manfredini.

Wishmaster 2: Evil Never Dies **1998 (R)** The Djinn is awakened by thief Morgana during a botched robbery and, in order to gain the souls he needs, the Djinn allows himself to be put in prison where he can offer wishes to the prisoners. But Morgana, aided by a priest, tries to stop him before the Djinn can destroy humanity. **96m/C; VHS, DVD, Blu-Ray.** Andrew Divoff; Paul Johansson; Holly Fields; Bokeem Woodbine; Tommy (Tiny) Lister; ***D:*** Jack Sholder; ***W:*** Jack Sholder; ***C:*** Carlos Gonzalez; ***M:*** David Williams. **VIDEO**

Wishmaster 3: Beyond the Gates of Hell 1/2 **2001 (R)** Baxter College history prof Joel Barash (Connery) has a crush on student Diana (Cook) who has been helping him out. Unfortunately, her help includes releasing the demonic Djinn from its puzzle box. The Djinn then possesses Barash and goes after Diana to grant her three wishes. Diana knows there's a trick but her fellow students aren't so smart and their wishes have nasty results. Diana can wish to spare her friends but the only thing that will really destroy the evil is the magical Sword of Justice. **92m/C; VHS, DVD, Blu-Ray.** A.J. Cook; Jason Connery; Tobias Mehler; Aaron Smolinksi; Louisette Geiss; John Novak; ***D:*** Chris Angel; ***W:*** Alexander Wright. **VIDEO**

Wishmaster 4: The Prophecy Fulfilled **2002 (R)** Same old, same old. The Djinn (Novak) gets released by Lisa (Spencer-Nairn) whose boyfriend Steven (Trucco) has been paralyzed in an accident. She gets the usual three wishes that don't come out the way she intended. This time if Lisa does her third wish, the Djinn brotherhood are released from hell—or something like that. Usual gore and Spencer-Nairn takes her clothes off and has a gratuitous sex scene. **92m/C; VHS, DVD, Blu-Ray.** John Novak; Tara Spencer-Nairn; Michael Trucco; Victor Webster; John Benjamin Martin; ***D:*** Chris Angel; ***W:*** John Benjamin Martin; ***M:*** Daryl Bennett; Jim Guttridge. **VIDEO**

The Wistful Widow of Wagon Gap *The Wistful Widow* **1947** Lou, a traveling salesman, accidentally kills a man, and according to the law of the west he has to take care of the dead man's widow and children—all seven of them. Because the family is so unsavory, Lou knows that no other man will kill him, so he allows himself to be appointed sheriff and clears the town of lowlifes. Usual Abbott & Costello fare is highlighted with their zany antics. **78m/B; VHS, DVD.** Bud Abbott; Lou Costello; Marjorie Main; George Cleveland; Gordon Jones; William Ching; Peter Thompson; Glenn Strange; Olin Howlin; ***D:*** Charles T. Barton.

Wit **2001** A tough topic buoyed by Thompson's fierce performance and Nichols expert direction. Middleaged scholar Vivian Bearing (Thompson) has dedicated her work to studying the holy sonnets of John Donne. The poet's life-and-death issues take on new meaning when Vivian learns she has stage-four ovarian cancer and she agrees to undergo the most aggressive treatment available. She puts herself in the care of veteran researcher Dr. Kelekian (Lloyd) and his internist Dr. Posner (Woodward), a former student of Vivian's. Their insensitivity sparks her bitter wit as Vivian realizes the inevitable truth. Based on the 1997 Pulitzer Prize-winning play by Margaret Edson. **98m/C; VHS, DVD.** Emma Thompson; Christopher Lloyd; Audra McDonald; Jonathan M. Woodward; Eileen Atkins; Harold Pinter; ***D:*** Mike Nichols; ***W:*** Emma Thompson; Mike Nichols; ***C:*** Seamus McGarvey. **CABLE**

The Witch *The VVitch: A New-England Folktale* **2016 (R)** Robert Eggers breakthrough Sundance horror hit is an elaborate, historically detailed nightmare based on actual testimony from the Salem Witch Trials that supposes what if the reports of witchcraft were true? It is 1630 New England and a family of five has been kicked out of their religious community, forced to the edge of civilization. When the youngest disappears, the true evil in the woods come forward and slow, terrifying chunks built more around mood than narrative. Eggers transports us back in time and drops us in the middle of a horrifying vision. **92m/C; DVD, Blu-Ray.** Anya Taylor-Joy; Ralph Ineson; Kate Dickie; Harvey Scrimshaw; Ellie Grainger; Lucas Dawson; ***D:*** Robert Eggers; ***W:*** Robert Eggers; ***C:*** Jarin Blaschke; ***M:*** Mark Korven. Ind. Spirit '17: First Feature, First Screenplay.

Witch Who Came from the Sea 1/2 **1976 (R)** Witch terrorizes all the ships at sea, but doesn't exactly haunt the viewer. **98m/C; VHS, DVD, Blu-Ray.** Millie Perkins; Lonny (Lonnie) Chapman; Vanessa Brown; Peggy (Margaret) Feury; Rick Jason; ***D:*** Matt Cimber.

Witchboard 1/2 **1987 (R)** During a college party, a group of friends bring out the Ouija board and play with it for laughs. One of the girls discovers she can use the board to communicate with a small boy who died years before. In her effort to talk with him she unwittingly releases the evil spirit of an ax murderer who haunts and murders members of the group. An entertaining, relatively inoffensive member of its genre that displays some attention to characterization and plot. **98m/C; VHS, DVD, Blu-Ray.** Todd Allen; Tawny Kitaen; Stephen Nichols; Kathleen Wilhoite; Burke Byrnes; Rose Marie; James W. Quinn; Judy Tatum; Gloria Hayes; J.P. Luebsen; Susan Nickerson; ***D:*** Kevin S. Tenney; ***W:*** Kevin S. Tenney; ***C:*** Roy Wagner; ***M:*** Dennis Michael Tenney.

Witchboard 3: The Possession 1/2 **1995 (R)** A Ouija board opens the gates to hell (yet again or we wouldn't have a movie) and the board's spirit steals Brian's soul and takes control of his body—much to the bewilderment of his girlfriend Julie. **93m/C; VHS, DVD.** David Nerman; Locky Lambert; Cedric Smith; Donna Sarrasin; ***D:*** Peter Svatek; ***W:*** Kevin S. Tenney; Jon Ezrine; ***C:*** Barry Gravelle.

Witchcraft WOOF! **1988 (R)** A young mother meets a couple killed three centuries ago for performing witchcraft. They want her baby, of course, to be the son of the devil. "Rosemary's Baby" rip-off, that is thoroughly predictable. **90m/C; VHS, DVD.** Anat "Topol" Barzilai; Gary Sloan; Mary Shelley; Deborah Scott; Alexander Kirkwood; Lee Kisman; Edward Ross Newton; ***D:*** Robert Spera; ***W:*** Jody Savin; ***C:*** Jens Sturup; ***M:*** Randy Miller.

Witchcraft 2: The Temptress **1990 (R)** A sensuous woman seduces an innocent young man into the rituals of witchcraft and the occult. Sequel to "Witchcraft" does not succeed where original failed, but does have a fair share of sex and violence. **88m/C; VHS, DVD.** Charles Solomon, Jr.; Mia Ruiz; Delia Sheppard; ***D:*** Mark Woods; ***W:*** Jim

Henson; Sal Manna; *C:* Jens Sturup; *M:* Miriam Cutler.

Witchcraft 4: Virgin Heart 🦴 **1992 (R)** Supernatural horror continues as attorney Will Spanner sinks even deeper into his enemy's satanic trap in this shocking sequel to the popular series. His only hope is to use his own black magic powers and to enlist the help of a seductive stripper (Penthouse Pet Strain). **92m/C; VHS, DVD.** Charles Solomon, Jr.; Julie Strain; Clive Pearson; Jason O'Gulihar; Lisa Jay Harrington; Barbara Dow; *D:* James Merendino.

Witchcraft 6: The Devil's Mistress 🦴 **1994 (R)** Police detectives Lutz and Garner's new case involves young women turning up naked and dead. Turns out satanic disciple Savanti is expected to impress the boss with a virgin sacrifice before an impending eclipse. But since virgins are scarce, he's having a real tough time. Practically no gore but lots of skin, along with hit-or-miss humor. **86m/C; VHS, DVD.** Kurt Alan; John E. Holiday; Bryan Nutter; Jerry Spicer; Shannon Lead; *D:* Julie Davis; *W:* Julie Davis.

Witchcraft 7: Judgement Hour 🦴 **1995 (R)** Modern-day warlock must sacrifice his earthly existence to kill an evil vampire. **91m/C; VHS, DVD.** David Byrnes; April Breneman; Alisa Christensen; John Cragen; Loren Schmalle; *D:* Michael Paul Girard; *W:* Peter Fleming; *C:* Denis Maloney; *M:* Miriam Cutler.

Witchcraft 9: Bitter Flesh 🦴 **1996 (R)** Yet another sequel to the endless erotic horror series finds the LAPD investigating a series of murders. They get a tip from a strange call girl who claims to be chanelling the spirit of a warlock, who's about to open the gates to hell. **90m/C; VHS, DVD.** Landon Hall; David Byrnes; Stephanie Beaton; Mikul Robins; *D:* Michael Paul Girard; *W:* Stephen J. Downing; *C:* Jeff Gateman; *M:* Michael Paul Girard.

Witchcraft 10: Mistress of the Craft 🦴 **1998** Witch Celeste Sheridan has been hunting Raven and her band of vampires outside London. Meanwhile, LAPD detective Lucy Lutz arrives in London with an extradition order for Satanic serial killer, Hyde. But Raven and her vamps free Hyde in order to have him help in a ritual power-enhancing ceremony. After Celeste finds out, she teams up with Lucy and Interpol agent Chris Dixon to hunt down Raven and Hyde before they can finish their demonic work. **90m/C; VHS, DVD.** Wendy Cooper; Eileen Daly; Stephanie Beaton; Kerry Knowlton; Sean Harry; Frank Scantori; Emily Bouffante; Lynn Michelle; *D:* Elisar Cabrera; *W:* Elisar Cabrera; *C:* Alvin Leong. **VIDEO**

Witchcraft 11: Sisters in Blood 🦴 ½ **2000 (R)** A college production of "Macbeth" resurrects three long-dead witches. Full of fuzzy occult logic and semi-undressed girls in peril. **90m/C; VHS, DVD.** Stephanie Beaton; Mikul Robins; James Servais; Miranda Odell; Laura Ian Richards; Kathleen St. Lawrence; *D:* Ron Ford; *W:* Ron Ford; *C:* Scott Spears. **VIDEO**

Witchery 🦴 *La Casa 4; Ghosthouse 2; Witchcraft* **1988** A photographer and his girlfriend vacation at a New England hotel where they discover a horrifying, satanic secret. One by one (as always, in this kind of bad flick, in the interest of "suspense"), people are killed off. Seems it's a witch, bent on revenge. Forget room service and bar the door. Laurenti used the pseudonym Martin Newlin. **96m/C; VHS, DVD, Blu-Ray.** David Hasselhoff; Linda Blair; Catherine Hickland; Hildegarde Knef; Leslie Cumming; Bob Champagne; Richard Farnsworth; Michael Manches; *D:* Fabrizio Laurenti.

The Witches 🦴🦴 ½ *The Devil's Own* **1966** Gwen Mayfield (Fontaine) accepts a teaching position at Haddaby School. She wants to put terrifying memories of work in Africa behind her, but finds that the bucolic English country town is just as dangerous. The sense of menace isn't as strong as it is in the similar "Wicker Man," and the film isn't one of the strongest entries from the Hammer Studio, but it is up to their high standards in terms of production values and acting. **90m/C; DVD, Blu-Ray.** Joan Fontaine; Kay Walsh; Alec McCowen; Ann Bell; John Collin; Michele Dotrice; Gwen Ffrangcon Davies; Ingrid Brett; *D:* Cyril Frankel; *W:* Nigel Kneale; *C:* Arthur Grant; *M:* Richard Rodney Bennett.

The Witches 🦴🦴🦴 ½ **1990 (PG)** Nine-year-old boy on vacation finds himself in the midst of a witch convention, and grand high witch Huston plans to turn all children into furry little creatures. The boy, with the help of his good witch grandmother, attempts to prevent the mass transmutation of children into mice. Top-notch fantasy probably too spooky for the training wheel set. Wonderful special effects; the final project of executive producer Jim Henson. Based on Roald Dahl's story. **92m/C; VHS, DVD, Blu-Ray.** Anjelica Huston; Mai Zetterling; Jasen Fisher; Rowan Atkinson; Charlie Potter; Bill Paterson; Brenda Blethyn; Jane Horrocks; *D:* Nicolas Roeg; *W:* Allan Scott; *C:* Harvey Harrison; *M:* Stanley Myers. L.A. Film Critics '90: Actress (Huston); Natl. Soc. Film Critics '90: Actress (Huston).

The Witches Hammer WOOF! **2006 (R)** An action-horror woofer with a stupid plot, bad acting, and lame action and CGI effects. Rebecca is turned into a vampire and then recruited by a secret organization to battle a power-hungry vamp who wants to rule over humans. Title refers to a book of magic that falls into the bad vamp's hands. **91m/C; DVD.** Claudia Coulter; Stephanie Beacham; Tom Dover; Harold Gasnier; Sally Reeve; Jonathan Sidgwick; Jason Tompkins; Maga Rodriguez; *D:* James Eaves; *W:* James Eaves; *C:* John Raggett; *M:* Mark Conrad Chambers. **VIDEO**

The Witches of Eastwick 🦴🦴 ½ **1987 (R)** "Mad Max" director Miller meets Hollywood in this unrestrained, vomit-filled treatment of John Updike's novel about three lonely small-town New England women and their sexual liberation. A strange, rich, overweight and balding, but nonetheless charming man knows their deepest desires and makes them come true with decadent excess. Raunchy fun, with Nicholson over-acting wildly as the Mephisto. Miller lends a bombastic violent edge to the effort, sometimes at the expense of the story. Filmed on location in Cohasset, Massachusetts. **118m/C; VHS, DVD.** Jack Nicholson; Cher; Susan Sarandon; Michelle Pfeiffer; Veronica Cartwright; Richard Jenkins; Keith Joakum; Carel Struycken; *D:* George Miller; *W:* Michael Cristofer; *C:* Vilmos Zsigmond; *M:* John Williams. L.A. Film Critics '87: Actor (Nicholson); N.Y. Film Critics '87: Actor (Nicholson).

The Witches of Oz 🦴 ½ *Dorothy and the Witches of Oz* **2011** In this silly SyFy Channel miniseries, a modern-day Dorothy Gale (Rojas) writes bestselling children's books based on her grandfather's stories of Oz. Dorothy leaves Kansas to complete her latest book for a New York publisher and discovers Oz is real and based on her own repressed childhood memories. The Wicked Witch of the West (Swenson) figures it's time to cause chaos in the real world unless Dorothy can stop her. A shorter (101 minutes) version has also been released under the title "Dorothy and the Witches of Oz." **164m/C; DVD, Blu-Ray.** Paulie Rojas; Eliza Swenson; Ethan (Randall) Embry; Sean Astin; Mia Sara; Billy Boyd; Christopher Lloyd; Lance Henriksen; *D:* Leigh Scott; *W:* Eliza Swenson; Leigh Scott; Chris Campbell; *C:* Leigh Scott; *M:* Eliza Swenson. **CABLE**

Witches of the Caribbean 🦴 **2005 (R)** Troubled teen Angela (Cavazos) is plagued by nightmares of a witch being burned at the stake. She heads to a Caribbean retreat to participate in a program organized by psychotherapist Professor Avebury (Cassidy) but evil things happen when her fellow patients start to disappear. The scenery is pretty but there's little else to recommend in this standard witch tale. **82m/C; DVD.** Joanna Cassidy; Nicole Cavazos; Nicole Marie Monica; Kelly Giddish; Michael King; Nina Tapanin; Kyle Jordan; *D:* David DeCoteau; *W:* Jana K. Arnold; *C:* Robert Hayes. **VIDEO**

The Witching WOOF! *Necromancy* **1972** Poorly made story of man's continuing quest for supernatural power. Welles slums as the high priest out to get victim Franklin. **90m/C; VHS, DVD, Blu-Ray.** Orson Welles; Pamela Franklin; Michael Ontkean; Lee Purcell; Lisa James; Harvey Jason; Terry Quinn; *D:* Bert I. Gordon; *W:* Bert I. Gordon; Gail March; *C:* Winton C. Hoch.

The Witchmaker 🦴 *Legend of Witch Hollow; Witchkill* **1969** Remote, crocodile-infested bayou in Louisiana is the scene of witchcraft and the occult as young girls are murdered in order for a group of witches to become youthful again. **101m/C; VHS, DVD, Blu-Ray.** John Lodge; Alvy Moore; Thordis Brandt; Anthony Eisley; Shelby Grant; Robyn Millan; Helene Winston; *D:* William O. Brown; *W:* William O. Brown.

Witchouse 🦴🦴 **1999 (R)** Elizabeth (McKinney), a modern-day witch, invites some fellow college students to an off-campus party at her creepy mansion. But it turns out they are all descendants of witch-hunters who burned Elizabeth's ancestor at the stake. And now it's time for revenge. **90m/C; VHS, DVD.** David Oren Ward; Ashley Mckinney; Matt Raftery; Monica Serene Garnich; Brooke Muller; Ariauna Albright; Marissa Tait; Dane Northcutt; Kimberly Pullis; *D:* Jack Reed; *W:* Matthew Jason Walsh; *C:* Viorel Sergovici, Jr. **VIDEO**

Witchouse 2: Blood Coven 🦴🦴 ½ **2000 (R)** Four unmarked graves are discovered by a strange house that is about to be torn down. The graves may be related to Lilith, a witch burned to death in the area. When a professor and her students come to investigate they find the locals aren't very friendly—especially after people start dying. Has Lilith return to take revenge? **82m/C; VHS, DVD.** Ariauna Albright; Andrew Prine; Nicholas Lanier; Elizabeth Hopgood; *D:* J.R. Bookwalter. **VIDEO**

Witchouse 3: Demon Fire 🦴🦴 **2001 (R)** Stevie (Rochon) and Rose (Krause) are filming a documentary on witchcraft, when their old friend Annie (Dempsey) comes to visit. Annie is seeking refuge from her abusive boyfriend and her buddies are glad to oblige. As part of the documentary, the three women conduct a mock seance, and inadvertently raise the spirit of the evil witch Lilith (Stevens). Soon, strange things happen and the corpses start piling up. Is Lilith real, or has one of the girls gone insane? As with the other films in this series, director Bookwalter is able to put every nickel up on-screen and create an interesting movie. This one isn't great art, nor does it want to be. It's simply a horror film that offers cheap thrills, attractive ladies, and a brief escape from reality. **77m/C; DVD.** Debbie Rochon; Tanya Dempsey; Tina Krause; Brinke Stevens; *D:* J.R. Bookwalter.

The Witch's Mirror 🦴🦴 **1960** A sorceress plots to destroy the murderer of her god-daughter. The murderer, a surgeon, begins a project to restore the disfigured face and hands of his burned second wife, and he doesn't care how he gets the materials. For true fans of good bad horror flicks. Badly dubbed (which adds to the charm); dark (of course); and offbeat (naturally). **75m/B; VHS, DVD.** *MX* Rosita (Rosa) Arenas; Armando Calvo; Isabela Corona; Dina De Marco; *D:* Chano Urueto.

Witchslayer Gretl 🦴 *Gretl: Witch Hunter* **2012** Numbing SyFy Channel cheapie with even worse special effects than usual. Twenty years after his encounter with a witch, Hansel (McGillian) has become a witch slayer. He returns to the forest to avenge the death of his sister Gretl (Doherty) only to discover that she's not dead but possessed by a witch and is their queen. **87m/C; DVD.** Paul McGillion; Shannen Doherty; Sarain Boylan; Emilie Ullerup; Jefferson Brown; *D:* Mario Azzopardi; *W:* Brook Durham; *C:* Russ Goozee; *M:* Stacey Hersh. **CABLE**

Witchville 🦴 ½ **2010** Douglas knows how to be witchy and that helps along this low-budget Syfy sword-and-sorcery original that has a few too many silly plot meanderings. After the death of his father, Prince Malachy (Goss) returns to his famine-ravaged kingdom. Witch-hunter Kramer (Thorp) blames all their troubles on the Red Queen (Douglas), who wants to conquer Malachy's kingdom and Malachy and his knights try to stop her. **89m/C; DVD.** Luke Goss; Simon Thorp; Sarah Douglas; Ed Speleers; Andrew Pleavin; MyAnna Buring; Ian Virgo; *D:* Pearry Reginald Teo; *W:* John Werner; Amy Krell; *C:* Ginnin Cheung; *M:* Neal Acree. **CABLE**

With a Friend Like Harry 🦴🦴🦴 *Harry, He's Here to Help; Harry, un Ami Qui Vous Veut du Bien; Harry, A Friend Who Wishes You Well* **2000 (R)** Twisted, surprisingly funny black comedy about a sociopath. Michel (Lucas), wife Claire (Seigner), and their three young daughters have embarked on the vacation from hell as they head to their summer home. At a rest stop, Michel happens to meet Harry (Lopez), a high school acquaintance who remembers Michel very well. Before they know it, Claire and Michel are sharing their farmhouse with Harry and his sexy girlfriend, the aptly named Plum (Guillemin). Harry's a very, very generous (if off-kilter) guy—in fact, he'll do anything to make Michel's life better, even kill. French with subtitles. **117m/C; VHS, DVD.** *FR* Sergi Lopez; Laurent Lucas; Mathilde Seigner; Sophie Guillemin; *D:* Dominik Moll; *W:* Dominik Moll; Gilles Marchand; *C:* Mathieu Poirot-Delpech; *M:* David Whitaker. Cesar '01: Actor (Lopez), Director (Moll), Film Editing, Sound.

With a Song in My Heart 🦴🦴🦴 **1952** Showbiz drama based on the life of singer Jane Froman, with a stellar performance by Hayward. Told in flashback; Jane (Hayward) gets her first big break in radio and decides to marry mentor Don (Wayne), who becomes increasingly jealous of her success. During a WWII troop tour, Jane's plane crashes near Lisbon and she's rescued by pilot John Burn (Calhoun), who falls in love as Jane slowly recuperates. Aided by faithful nurse Clancy (Ritter), Jane is eventually strong enough to try for a comeback and Don finally realizes that their marriage is over. Froman herself dubbed the singing for Hayward. **117m/C; DVD.** Susan Hayward; Thelma Ritter; Rory Calhoun; David Wayne; Robert Wagner; Helen Westcott; Una Merkel; Leif Erickson; *D:* Walter Lang; *W:* Lamar Trotti; *C:* Leon Shamroy; *M:* Alfred Newman. Oscars '52: Orig. Score.

With Honors 🦴🦴 ½ **1994 (PG-13)** Pesci is a bum who finds desperate Harvard student Fraser's Honors thesis, and, like any quick-witted bum with a yen for literature, holds it for ransom. Desperate to salvage his future gold card, Fraser and his roommates agree to fix Joe's homeless state. Self-involved students learn something about love and life while Madonna drones in the background. Fraser is believable as the ambitious student about to endure Pesci's enlightenment. Pesci is Pesci, doing his best to overcome numerous script difficulties. **100m/C; VHS, DVD.** Joe Pesci; Brendan Fraser; Moira Kelly; Patrick Dempsey; Josh Hamilton; Gore Vidal; *D:* Alek Keshishian; *W:* William Mastrosimone; *C:* Sven Nykvist; *M:* Patrick Leonard.

With Six You Get Eggroll 🦴🦴 *A Man in Mommy's Bed* **1968 (G)** A widow with three sons and a widower with a daughter elope and then must deal with the antagonism of their children and even their dogs. Brady Bunch-esque family comedy means well, but doesn't cut it. Hershey's debut. Jamie Farr, William Christopher, and Vic Tayback have small parts. To date, Day's last big-screen appearance. **95m/C; VHS, DVD.** Doris Day; Brian Keith; Pat Carroll; Alice Ghostley; Vic Tayback; Jamie Farr; William (Bill) Christopher; Barbara Hershey; *D:* Howard Morris; *C:* Harry Stradling, Jr.

Within Our Gates 🦴🦴 **1920** Boston teacher Sylvia Landry has her engagement broken thanks to rival Alma Pritchard so she moves back to her southern hometown of Piney Woods to work in an all-black school. When the school has financial problems, Sylvia returns to Boston to raise money and white doctor Vivian falls in love with her. Sylvia leaves again and the smitten Vivian turns to Alma to find her. Pioneering African-American director Micheaux didn't shy away from controversy and his powerful depictions of beatings, attempted rape, and lynchings are still shocking. **78m/B; Silent; DVD, Blu-Ray.** Mattie Peters; Evelyn Preer; Flo Clements; Jack Chenault; Charles D. Lucas; Ralph Johnson; Grant Gorman; William Stark; William S. Smith; Bernice Ladd; James D. Ruffin; *D:* Oscar Micheaux; *W:* Oscar Micheaux.

Within the Law 🦴🦴 **1923** After being falsely convicted of theft, shopgirl Mary Turner (Talmadge) spends three years in prison and can't find a job after her release. Then, New York con man Joe Garson (Cody) comes to Mary's aid and becomes her mentor. Mary's revenge mark is Richard Gilder (Mulhall), the son of department store owner Edward (Kilgour) who sent her to the joint, and she gets Richard to fall in love with her. **96m/B; Silent; DVD.** Norma Talmadge; Lew Cody; Eileen Percy; Jack Mulhall; Joseph Kilgour; Ward Crane; Arthur Stuart Hull; Helen Ferguson; ***D:*** Frank Lloyd; ***W:*** Frances Marion; ***C:*** Norbert Brodine; Tony Gaudio.

Within the Rock 🦴🦴 **1996 (R)** Space crew must shift a wandering moon before it collides with earth but beyond that problem they've got an alien predator that's escaped. **91m/C; VHS, DVD.** Xander Berkeley; Bradford Tatum; Brian Krause; Caroline Barclay; Calvin Levels; Earl Boen; Dale Dye; ***D:*** Gary J. Tunnicliffe; ***W:*** Gary J. Tunnicliffe; ***C:*** Adam Kane; ***M:*** Tony Fennell; Rod Gammons.

Withnail and I 🦴🦴🦴 **1/2 1987 (R)** A biting and original black comedy about a pair of unemployed, nearly starving English actors during the late 1960s. They decide to retreat to a country house owned by Withnail's uncle, for a vacation and are beset by comic misadventures, particularly when the uncle, who is gay, starts to hit on his nephew's friend. Robinson, who scripted "The Killing Fields," makes his successful directorial debut, in addition to drafting the screenplay from his own novel. Co-produced by George Harrison and Richard Starkey (Ringo Starr). **108m/C; VHS, DVD.** *GB* Richard E. Grant; Paul McGann; Richard Griffiths; Ralph Brown; Michael Elphick; ***D:*** Bruce Robinson; ***W:*** Bruce Robinson; ***C:*** Peter Hannan; ***M:*** David Dundas.

Without a Clue 🦴🦴 **1/2 1988 (PG)** Spoof of the Sherlock Holmes legend, in which Holmes is actually portrayed by a bumbling, skirt-chasing actor, and Watson is the sole crime-solving mastermind, hiring the actor to impersonate the character made famous by the doctor's published exploits. The leads have some fun and so do we; but laughs are widely spaced. **107m/C; VHS, DVD, Blu-Ray.** *GB* Michael Caine; Ben Kingsley; Jeffrey Jones; Lysette Anthony; Paul Freeman; Nigel Davenport; Peter Cook; Pat Keen; ***D:*** Thom Eberhardt; ***W:*** Gary Murphy; Larry Strawther; ***M:*** Henry Mancini.

Without a Paddle 🦴🦴 **1/2 2004 (PG-13)** A harmlessly stupid buddy flick finds three lifelong friends—phobic Dan (Green), surfer dude Jerry (Lillard), and loudmouth Tom (Shepard)?mourning the unexpected death of pal Billy. Uneasily pushing 30, these faux grown-ups decide to pursue a childhood fantasy by heading into the Oregon woods to search for the lost treasure of '70s crime legend, D.B. Cooper. Now the real fun begins as they deal with growling bears, canoeing the rapids, redneck pot farmers, tree-huggers, and, briefly, a charismatically grizzled Burt Reynolds. There's a lot of standard scatological and slapstick humor as well as many nostalgic '70s and '80s references that may be lost on a younger crowd. **99m/C; VHS, DVD, Blu-Ray, UMD.** Seth Green; Matthew Lillard; Dax Shepard; Ethan Suplee; Abraham Benrubi; Rachel Blanchard; Burt Reynolds; Christina Moore; Bonnie Somerville; Ray Baker; ***D:*** Steven Brill; ***W:*** Jay Leggett; Mitch Rouse; Fred Wolf; Harris Goldberg; Tom Nursall; ***C:*** Jonathan Brown; ***M:*** Christophe Beck.

Without a Paddle: Nature's Calling 🦴 **1/2 2009 (PG-13)** Doofus buddy comedy. Workaholic Ben (James) and easy-going Zach (Turner) were childhood buds who drifted apart. Ben's one outside interest is his longtime crush on would-be sweetheart Heather (Riley), now a tree hugger living in the wilderness. Zach decides he and Ben can reconnect, accompanied by Brit nature enthusiast Nigel (Young), by heading into the woods and tracking Heather down so Ben can finally tell her how he feels. **90m/C; DVD, Blu-Ray.** Kristopher Turner; Oliver James; Amber McDonald; Rik Young; Madison Riley; Jerry Rice; ***D:*** Ellory Elkayem; ***W:*** Stephen Mazur; ***C:*** Thomas Callaway. **VIDEO**

Without a Trace 🦴🦴 **1983 (PG)** One morning, a six-year-old boy is sent off to school by his loving mother, never to return. The story of the mother's relentless search for her son. Cardboard characters, wildly unrealistic ending that is different from the real-life incident on which it's based. Scripted by Gutcheon from her book "Still Missing." Jaffe's directorial debut. **119m/C; VHS, DVD.** Kate Nelligan; Judd Hirsch; Stockard Channing; David Dukes; ***D:*** Stanley R. Jaffe; ***C:*** John Bailey; ***M:*** Jack Nitzsche.

Without Evidence 🦴🦴 **1996** When Oregon correctional director Michael Francke (Garrett) is visiting younger brother Kevin (Plank) in Florida, he mentions his suspicions about an operation within his department involving drugs in prison. Then the next phone call Kevin gets is that Michael's been murdered. When he heads to Oregon, Kevin seems to be getting the official runaround and becomes increasingly suspicious about a coverup. A tension-building true story that remains unsolved. **90m/C; VHS, DVD.** Scott Plank; Anna Gunn; Andrew Prine; Angelina Jolie; Paul Perri; Allen Nause; Ernie Garrett; ***D:*** Gill Dennis; ***W:*** Gill Dennis; Phil Stanford; ***C:*** Victor Nunez; ***M:*** Franco Piersanti.

Without Limits 🦴🦴🦴 *Pre* **1997 (PG-13)** Second biopic about '70s long-distance runner Steve Prefontaine (after 1996's "Prefontaine") focuses mainly on Prefontaine's (Crudup) relationship with his University of Oregon coach Bill Bowerman (Sutherland), who later was a co-founder of Nike. Also explores the heartbreak of the 1972 Olympics. Crudup does a fine job exploring the runner's playful arrogance, fearlessness, and iconoclasm (especially when dealing with the corrupt AAU). Sutherland, playing a three-dimensional character for the first time in a while, gives a fine performance. Kenny Moore, a close friend and fellow '72 Olympian, wrote the script with director Towne, with the full cooperation of Bowerman and Prefontaine's girlfriend. **117m/C; DVD.** Billy Crudup; Donald Sutherland; Monica Potter; Jeremy Sisto; Matthew Lillard; Billy Burke; Dean Norris; Gabriel Olds; Judith Ivey; ***D:*** Robert Towne; ***W:*** Robert Towne; Kenny Moore; ***C:*** Conrad L. Hall; ***M:*** Randy Miller.

Without Love 🦴🦴 **1/2 1945** Tracy is a scientist, Hepburn, a woman with an empty basement for his laboratory. Since the neighbors would be scandalized by the idea of unmarried people living together, however platonically, they decide to get married, although each has sworn off romance. Snappy dialogue, expertly rendered by the Tracy/Hepburn team. Terrific supporting cast keeps this minimally plotted outing afloat. Adapted from the play of the same name by Philip Barry. **113m/B; VHS, DVD.** Spencer Tracy; Katharine Hepburn; Lucille Ball; Keenan Wynn; Carl Esmond; Patricia Morison; Felix Bressart; ***D:*** Harold Bucquet; ***W:*** Donald Ogden Stewart; ***C:*** Karl Freund.

Without Men 🦴 **1/2 2011 (R)** Battle of the sexes comedy. The women of a remote Latin American mountain village are left to fend for themselves when all the men are recruited to fight in the country's civil war. The women grow to enjoy their freedom and aren't about to go back to their old ways when American reporter Gordon shows up with their menfolk in tow. **83m/C; DVD, Blu-Ray.** Eva Longoria; Christian Slater; Kate del Castillo; Oscar Nunez; Maria Conchita Alonso; Guillermo Diaz; Paul Rodriguez; Judy Reyes; ***D:*** Gabriela Tagliavini; ***W:*** Gabriela Tagliavini; ***C:*** Andrew Strahorn; ***M:*** Carlo Siliotto. **VIDEO**

Without Reservations 🦴🦴 **1/2 1946** Hollywood-bound novelist Colbert encounters Marine flyer Wayne and his pal (DeFore) aboard a train. She decides he would be perfect for her newest movie. They both dislike her famous book and don't realize they're traveling with the renowned author. Misadventures and misunderstandings abound as this trio make their way to Tinseltown. Of course, Colbert and Wayne fall in love. Boxoffice success with a tired script and too few real laughs. The Duke is interesting but miscast. Based on the novel "Thanks, God, I'll Take It From Here" by Jane Allen. **101m/B; VHS, DVD.** Claudette Colbert; John Wayne; Don DeFore; Phil Brown; Frank Puglia; ***Cameo(s):*** Louella Parsons; Cary Grant; Jack Benny; ***D:*** Mervyn LeRoy; ***C:*** Milton Krasner.

Without Warning 🦴 **1980** Low-budget sci-fi/horror has some teens going camping when they're attacked by flying, flesh-sucking disks. A crazy old coot and a hunter come to the survivors' rescue, then learn they are being hunted by an alien who's come to Earth after new prey. **89m/C; DVD, Blu-Ray.** Martin Landau; Jack Palance; Cameron Mitchell; Tarah Nutter; Christopher S. Nelson; Neville Brand; Larry Storch; Sue Ane Langdon; Ralph Meeker; David Caruso; ***D:*** Greydon Clark; ***W:*** Daniel Grodnik; ***C:*** Dean Cundey.

Witless Protection WOOF! **2008 (PG-13)** Another unsuccessful, unnecessary, and unfunny vehicle for Larry the Cable Guy. This time around Larry plays a dimwitted cop who kidnaps a woman in witness protection because he thinks the FBI agents at her side are ruthless drug dealers. Genius screenplay! It take about 90 minutes for him to realize his mistake, allowing plenty of time to insert lame fart jokes and zingers about Arabs along the way. Larry needs to start making like a real cable guy and keep us waiting a long time before we see the likes of him on screen again. **97m/C; DVD, Blu-Ray.** Larry the Cable Guy; Ivana Milicevic; Yaphet Kotto; Peter Stormare; Jenny McCarthy; Eric Roberts; Joe Mantegna; ***D:*** Charles Robert Carner; ***W:*** Charles Robert Carner; ***C:*** Michael Goi; ***M:*** Eric Allaman.

Witness 🦴🦴🦴 **1/2 1985 (R)** A young Amish boy, Samuel Lapp (Haas), traveling from his father's funeral witnesses a murder in a Philadelphia bus station. Investigating detective John Book (Ford, in one of his best roles) soon discovers the killing is part of a conspiracy involving corruption in his department. He follows the child and his young widowed mother, Rachel (McGillis) to their home in the country. A thriller with a difference, about the encounter of alien worlds, with a poignant love story. McGillis, in her first major role, is luminous as the Amish mother, while Ford is believable as both a cop and a sensitive man. An artfully crafted drama, richly focusing on the often misunderstood Amish lifestyle. **112m/C; VHS, DVD, Blu-Ray.** Harrison Ford; Kelly McGillis; Alexander Godunov; Lukas Haas; Josef Sommer; Danny Glover; Patti LuPone; Viggo Mortensen; Robert Earl Jones; ***D:*** Peter Weir; ***W:*** William Kelley; Earl W. Wallace; ***C:*** John Seale; ***M:*** Maurice Jarre. Oscars '85: Film Editing, Orig. Screenplay; Writers Guild '85: Orig. Screenplay.

The Witness 🦴 **1/2** *Fish Out of Water* **1999 (PG)** Teen discovers an arsonist's plot to burn down a historic museum. Cheesy Canadian 'action' flick fails to deliver any thrillls, spills, or, well, action. **95m/C; VHS, DVD.** John Heard; Susan Almgren; Patrick Thomas; Christopher Heyerdahl; ***D:*** Geoffrey Edwards; ***W:*** Richard Gourdreau; ***C:*** Georges Archambault; ***M:*** Jerry Devilliers. **VIDEO**

The Witness Files 🦴 **1/2 2000 (R)** Sandy (Butler) has been imprisoned for the murder of her abusive husband. Corrupt politician Frank Sutton (Flatman) arranges for her release so he can use her special talents (she does makeup special effects) for his own nefarious ends. But Sandy hooks up with a detective (Nerman) to doublecross Sutton. Watch "F/X" instead unless you're a particular fan of Butler. **97m/C; VHS, DVD.** Yancy Butler; David Nerman; Barry Flatman; Matthew Harbour; ***D:*** Douglas Jackson. **VIDEO**

Witness for the Prosecution 🦴🦴🦴 **1/2 1957** An unemployed man is accused of murdering a wealthy widow whom he befriended. Ailing defense attorney Laughton can't resist taking an intriguing murder case, and a straightforward court case becomes increasingly complicated in this energetic adaptation of an Agatha Christie story and stage play. Outstanding performances by Laughton, with excellent support by real life wife, Lanchester, as his patient nurse. Power, as the alleged killer, and Dietrich, as his enigmatic wife, are top-notch. **116m/B; VHS, DVD, Blu-Ray.** Charles Laughton; Tyrone Power; Marlene Dietrich; Elsa Lanchester; John Williams; Henry Daniell; Una O'Connor; Ian Wolfe; Torin Thatcher; Norma Varden; Francis Compton; Philip Tonge; Ruta Lee; Ottola Nesmith; J. Pat O'Malley; ***D:*** Billy Wilder; ***W:*** Harry Kurnitz; Billy Wilder; ***C:*** Russell Harlan; ***M:*** Matty Malneck. Golden Globes '58: Support. Actress (Lanchester).

Witness Protection 🦴🦴🦴 **1999** Highly watchable performances raise this cable movie about mobsters above the average. Boston goodfella Bobby Batton (Sizemore) turns state's evidence after he's betrayed by his cronies. He and his family are placed in the witness protection program under the eye of a U.S. marshal (Whitaker) but living as a regular mook proves difficult. Bobby's wife (Mastrantonio) is bitter, his kids are angry and confused, and there are no easy endings. Based on a 1996 New York Times Magazine article by Robert Sabbag. **105m/C; VHS, DVD.** Tom Sizemore; Forest Whitaker; Mary Elizabeth Mastrantonio; Shawn Hatosy; Richard Portnow; ***D:*** Richard Pearce; ***W:*** Daniel Therriault; ***C:*** Fred Murphy; ***M:*** Cliff Eidelman. **CABLE**

Witness to Murder 🦴🦴 **1954** Atmospheric L.A.-set noir. Cheryl Draper sees a woman being strangled to death from her window, but the killer covers his tracks and the cops don't find any evidence of a crime. However, the killer decides to tidy up loose ends by setting Cheryl up to seem crazy, which will explain her 'suicide'. Fortunately, one police detective does believe her. **83m/B; DVD, Blu-Ray.** Barbara Stanwyck; George Sanders; Gary Merrill; Jesse White; Harry Shannon; ***D:*** Roy Rowland; ***W:*** Chester Erskine; ***C:*** John Alton; ***M:*** Herschel Burke Gilbert.

Witness to the Mob 🦴 **1/2 1998 (R)** Originally an NBC miniseries, this mob saga tells the true story of Sammy "The Bull" Gravano (Turturro), who turned state's evidence against his boss, John Gotti. Manages to hit every cliche and stereotype along the way. **172m/C; VHS, DVD.** Nicholas Turturro; Tom Sizemore; Debi Mazar; Frankie Valli; Abe Vigoda; Philip Baker Hall; Frank Vincent; Michael Imperioli; Lenny Venito; Vincent Pastore; Kirk Acevedo; Richard Bright; ***D:*** Thaddeus O'Sullivan; ***W:*** Stanley Weiser; ***C:*** Frank Prinzi; ***M:*** Stephen Endelman. **TV**

The Witness Vanishes 🦴 **1/2 1939** The fifth and final installment of Universal's "Crime Club" series follows the murders of several British newspaper executives who had their rival committed to an insane asylum so they could take over his newspaper, the London Sun. When he escapes, he plants their premature obits in the newspaper and then goes on with their executions as published. **66m/B; DVD.** Barlowe Borland; Edmund Lowe; Wendy Barrie; Bruce Lester; Walter Kingsford; Forrester Harvey; Vernon Steele; ***D:*** Otis Garrett; ***W:*** Robertson White; ***C:*** Arthur Martinelli.

The Witnesses 🦴🦴 *Les Temoins* **2007** Set in 1984, friends are forced to consider their fears when confronted by the early days of the AIDS epidemic. Writer Sarah (Beart) and her cop husband Mehdi (Bouajila) have an arrangement allowing liaisons. Sarah's close friend Adrien (Blanc), a middle-aged gay doctor, is enamored of provincial young Manu (Libereau) who agrees to be his platonic companion. When Adrien and Manu visit Sarah and Mehdi during a summer holiday, Manu and Mehdi begin a secret affair. Then Manu gets sick, Adrien becomes an early fighter against the new disease, and Sarah learns what's been going on and reacts unexpectedly. French with subtitles. **115m/C; DVD.** *FR* Emmanuelle Beart; Michel Blanc; Johan Libereau; Julie Depardieu; Sami Bouajila; ***D:*** Andre Techine; ***W:*** Andre Techine; Laurent Guyot; Viviane Zingg; ***C:*** Julien Hirsch; ***M:*** Philippe Sarde.

Wittgenstein 🦴🦴 **1993** Complicated, experimental portrait of Viennese-born philosopher Ludwig Wittgenstein (Johnson), executed as a series of blackout sketches (that feature a green Martian dwarf and such friends as Bertrand Russell and Ottoline Morrell). Assumes a familiarity with the eccentric Wittgenstein's ideas but does manage to convey some emotion and wit. **75m/C; VHS, DVD.** *GB* Karl Johnson; Michael Gough; Tilda Swinton; John Quentin; Nabil Shaban; ***D:*** Derek Jarman; ***W:*** Derek Jarman; Terry Eagleton; Ken Butler.

Wives and Daughters 🦴🦴 **1/2 2001** Charming adaptation of Elizabeth Gaskell's 1864 chronicle of family ties, romance, and scandal set in an 1820s English country town. Our heroine is modest Molly Gibson (Waddell), whose widower doctor father (Paterson) marries ambitious Hyacinth (Annis), who has a beautiful daughter, Cynthia (Hawes), who's Molly's age. Then there's the local gentry, Squire Hamley (Gambon), and his two sons, the poetic Osborne (Hollander) and the scientific Roger (Howell). Molly becomes everyone's confidante, but also has her own secrets. **300m/C; VHS, DVD.** *GB*

Justine Waddell; Keeley Hawes; Francesca Annis; Bill Paterson; Michael Gambon; Penelope Wilton; Tom Hollander; Anthony Howell; Ian Carmichael; Iain Glen; Barbara Leigh-Hunt; Tonia Chauvet; Shaughan Seymour; Barbara Flynn; Deborah Findlay; ***D:*** Nicholas Renton; ***W:*** Andrew Davies. **TV**

The Wives He Forgot **2006** Generally a comic mystery with some dramatic moments. A man injured in a car accident stumbles into the law office of Charlotte St. John (Ringwald). After a hospital visit, she learns he has amnesia so Charlotte befriends the newly-named Gabriel (Humphrey) and then falls in love. Too bad his past is suddenly revealed and Charlotte must defend her beau. But he may not be quite the sleaze he seems. **90m/C; DVD.** Molly Ringwald; Mark Humphrey; Shannon Sturges; Maxim Roy; Linda Thorson; Karl Pruner; ***D:*** Mario Azzopardi; ***W:*** J. J. Jamieson; ***C:*** Michael Storey; ***M:*** Eric Cadesky. **CABLE**

Wives under Suspicion ½ **1938** While prosecuting a man who murdered his wife out of jealousy, a district attorney finds his own home life filled with similar tension. Director Whale's unnecessary remake of his own earlier film, "The Kiss Before the Mirror." He is best known for "Frankenstein." **75m/B; VHS, DVD.** Warren William; Gail Patrick; Constance Moore; William Lundigan; ***D:*** James Whale.

The Wiz **1978 (G)** Black version of the long-time favorite "The Wizard of Oz," based on the Broadway musical. Ross plays a Harlem schoolteacher who is whisked away to a fantasy version of NYC in a search for her identity. Some good character performances and musical numbers, but generally an overblown and garish effort with Ross too old for her role. Pryor is poorly cast, but Jackson is memorable as the Scarecrow. High-budget ($24 million) production with a ton of name stars, lost $11 million, and cooled studios on black films. Horne's number as the good witch is the best reason to sit through this one. **133m/C; VHS, DVD.** Diana Ross; Michael Jackson; Nipsey Russell; Ted Ross; Mabel King; Thelma Carpenter; Richard Pryor; Lena Horne; ***D:*** Sidney Lumet; ***W:*** Joel Schumacher; ***C:*** Oswald Morris; ***M:*** Quincy Jones.

The Wizard ½ **1989 (PG)** Facing the dissolution of his dysfunctional family, a youngster decides to take his autistic, video game-playing little brother across the country to a national video competition. Way too much plot in pretentious, blatantly commercial feature-length Nintendo ad, featuring the kid from "The Wonder Years." For teen video addicts only. **99m/C; VHS, DVD, Blu-Ray.** Fred Savage; Beau Bridges; Christian Slater; Luke Edwards; Jenny Lewis; ***D:*** Todd Holland; ***W:*** David Chisholm.

The Wizard of Gore **1970 (R)** The prototypical Lewis splatter party, about a magician whose on-stage mutilations turn out to be messily real. High camp and barrels of bright movie blood. **96m/C; VHS, DVD, Blu-Ray.** Ray Sager; Judy Cler; Wayne Ratay; Phil Laurenson; Jim Rau; Don Alexander; Monika Blackwell; Corinne Kirkin; John Elliott; ***D:*** Herschell Gordon Lewis; ***W:*** Allen Kahn; ***C:*** Alex Ameri; Daniel Krogh; ***M:*** Larry Wellington.

The Wizard of Gore **2007 (R)** Remake of the 1970 flick lives up to its title. Underground magician Montag the Magnificent (a perfect fit for Glover) has an extremely graphic act where he dismembers chosen females from the audience, although they reappear healthy. Too bad they don't stay that way. Amateur detective Edmund Bigelow (Pardue) learns the women are later found in pieces in the exact same way as in the magic show. As Bigelow keeps digging, his sanity becomes suspect, especially since Montag is ever only seen onstage. Maybe he doesn't exist at all? **97m/C; DVD.** Crispin Glover; Kip Pardue; Bijou Phillips; Jeffrey Combs; Brad Dourif; Joshua John Miller; ***D:*** Jeremy Kasten; ***W:*** Zach Chassler; ***C:*** Christopher Duddy; ***M:*** Steve Porcaro.

The Wizard of Oz ½ **1925** An early silent version of the L. Frank Baum fantasy, with notable plot departures from the book and later 1939 adaptation, starring long-forgotten comedian Semon as the Scarecrow, supported by a pre-Laurel Hardy as the Tin Woodman. With music score. **96m/B; Silent; VHS, DVD.** Larry Semon; Dorothy Dwan; Bryant Washburn; Charles Murray; Oliver Hardy; Josef Swickard; Virginia Pearson; ***D:*** Larry Semon; ***W:*** Larry Semon; L. Frank Baum, Jr.; ***C:*** Leonard Smith; Frank B. Good; Hans Koenekamp.

The Wizard of Oz **1939** From the book by L. Frank Baum. Fantasy about a Kansas farm girl (Garland, in her immortal role) who rides a tornado to a brightly colored world over the rainbow, full of talking scarecrows, munchkins and a wizard who bears a strange resemblance to a Kansas fortuneteller. She must outwit the Wicked Witch if she is ever to go home. Delightful performances from Lahr, Bolger, and Hamilton; King Vidor is uncredited as co-director. Director Fleming originally wanted Deanna Durbin or Shirley Temple for the role of Dorothy, but settled for Garland who made the song "Over the Rainbow" her own. She received a special Academy Award for her performance. **101m/C; VHS, DVD, Blu-Ray.** Judy Garland; Margaret Hamilton; Ray Bolger; Jack Haley; Bert Lahr; Frank Morgan; Charley Grapewin; Clara Blandick; Mitchell Lewis; Billie Burke; ***D:*** Victor Fleming; ***W:*** Noel Langley; ***C:*** Harold Rosson; ***M:*** Herbert Stothart. Oscars '39: Orig. Score, Song ("Over the Rainbow"); AFI '98: Top 100; Natl. Film Reg. '89.

Wizards ½ **1977 (PG)** A good, bumbling sorcerer battles for the sake of a magic kingdom and its princess against his evil brother who uses Nazi propaganda films to inspire his army of mutants. Profane, crude, & typically Bakshian fantasy with great graphics. Animated. **81m/C; VHS, DVD.** ***V:*** Bob Holt; Jesse Wells; Richard Romanus; David Proval; ***D:*** Ralph Bakshi; ***W:*** Ralph Bakshi; ***M:*** Andrew Belling.

Wizards of the Demon Sword **1994 (R)** Group of warriors battle over a sword with the power to control the world. **90m/C; VHS, DVD.** Lawrence Tierney; Michael Berryman; Russ Tamblyn; Lyle Waggoner; Blake Bahner; Heidi Paine; Dan Speaker; Jay Richardson; Dawn Wildsmith; ***D:*** Fred Olen Ray; ***W:*** Dan Golden; Ernest Farino.

The Wizards of Waverly Place: The Movie ½ **2009 (G)** In this Disney Channel original (derived from the TV series), Alex (Gomez), Max (Austin), Justin (Henrie), and their parents go on a Caribbean vacation but 16-year-old Alex gets pouty over being told what to do. She inadvertently wishes her parents had never met and makes them forget all about their family. Max tries to prevent his parents from endangering their future while Alex and Justin try to find the Stone of Dreams to reverse the spell. **98m/C; DVD.** Selena Gomez; David Henrie; Jake T. Austin; Maria Canals-Barrera; David DeLuise; Jennifer Stone; Steve Valentine; ***D:*** Lev L. Spiro; ***W:*** Daniel Berendsen; ***C:*** David Makin; ***M:*** Kenneth Burgomaster. **CABLE**

Woke Up Dead **2009** Dull, repetitive zombie comedy originally shown as a webisode TV series. Drex Greene wakes up in a bathtub, apparently dead from drowning, after taking a mystery pill. He goes to wannabe filmmaker roommate Matt and med student Cassie for help since he's turned into some kind of zombie who's developing superpowers (and a craving for cows' brains). **84m/C; DVD.** Jon Heder; Josh Gad; Krysten Ritter; Wayne Knight; Daniel Roebuck; Meital Dohan; ***D:*** Tim O'Donnell; ***W:*** John Fasano; ***C:*** Theo Angell. **VIDEO**

Wolf ½ **1994 (R)** Harrison's original script is massaged by Nichols into an upscale new age men's movement horror spectacle lacking a suitable climax. Stressed out Manhattan book editor Will Randall's (Nicholson) car hits a wolf on a country road and he's bitten when he tries to help the animal. Normally a wishy-washy guy, he notices some distinctly hairy changes to both his body and personality, leading him to make some drastic changes at work by knocking off his firm's greedy honchos and taking over. Talk about being ruthless in business. Boss' daughter Pfeiffer takes a shine to Randall's new animal magnetism, but is just visual candy. Walks a fine line between black comedy, camp, romance, and horror, though Jack baying at the moon seems sort of campy. **125m/C; VHS, DVD.** Jack Nicholson; Michelle Pfeiffer; James Spader; Kate Nelligan; Christopher Plummer; Richard Jenkins; Om Puri; Eileen Atkins; David Hyde Pierce; Ron Rifkin; Prunella Scales; Oz (Osgood) Perkins, II; Jennifer Nicholson; ***D:*** Mike Nichols; ***W:*** Wesley Strick; Jim Harrison; ***C:*** Giuseppe Rotunno; ***M:*** Ennio Morricone.

Wolf Blood ½ **1925** When Dick (Chesebro) is hurt in an accident, Dr. Horton uses wolf's blood for a transfusion. Soon there are unexplained deaths and Dick fears he's becoming a man-beast. Early precursor to the wolfman films. **68m/B; Silent; VHS, DVD.** George Chesebro; Marguerite Clayton; Ray Hanford; Roy Watson; Milburn (Milt) Morante; ***D:*** George Chesebro; George Mitchell.

Wolf Creek **2005 (R)** In the Australian Outback, three young adults, Ben (Phillips), Liz (Magrath) and Kristy (Morassi) are on a cross-country car trip. Having purchased a cheap junker for the trek, the threesome find they've been stranded in the bush when the car fails to start. In an unlikely stroke of luck, a tow truck-driving bushman named Mick (Jarratt) appears and assures them he can repair the car but must tow them back to his compound. So begins the unrelenting stream of torturous (to them and the audience) horrors. More than a wee bit over the top. **95m/C; DVD, HD-DVD.** John Jarratt; Kestie Morassi; Nathan Phillips; Cassandra Magrath; ***D:*** Greg Mclean; ***W:*** Greg Mclean; ***C:*** William Gibson; ***M:*** Francois (Frank) Tetaz.

Wolf Creek 2 **2013** Add another film to the list of sequels that no one asked for. Director McLean tries his damnedest to take the murderer from the first film, Mick Taylor (Jaratt), and turn him into a Jason Voorhees or Michael Myers icon of the genre with embarrassing results. Mick goes after a German couple who happen into his gore-filled part of the Australian outback. And he kills them, bringing in another fly for his over-fed spider. It's just a waste of time on nearly every level—never scary, never thrilling, never interesting, never justifying its existence. **106m/C; DVD, Blu-Ray.** *AU* John Jarratt; Ryan Corr; Phillipe Klaus; Shannon Ashlyn; ***D:*** Greg Mclean; ***W:*** Greg Mclean; Aaron Sterns; ***C:*** Toby Oliver; ***M:*** Johnny Klimek.

The Wolf Hour **2019 (R)** In 1977 New York City, writer June Leigh (Watts) is a recluse in her well-worn South Bronx apartment. Though June was once an admired counterculture figure, she has isolated herself because one of her books destroyed her family. As she lives in squalor, she is visited by people including her supportive sister (Ehle), a delivery guy/hustler (Harrison), and a creepy cop (Cohen). When that summer's blackout begins, June's fears that someone is trying to harm her are amplified. Watts is outstanding and director Griffin captures the city's grittiness but it's otherwise forgettable. **99m/C; DVD.** Naomi Watts; Jennifer Ehle; Jeremy Bobb; Brennan Brown; Emory Cohen; ***D:*** Alistair Banks Griffin; ***W:*** Alistair Banks Griffin; ***C:*** Khalid Mohtaseb; ***M:*** Danny Bensi; Saunder Jurriaans.

The Wolf Man ½ **1941** Fun, absorbing classic horror with Chaney as a man bitten by werewolf Lugosi. His dad thinks he's gone nuts, his screaming gal pal just doesn't understand, and plants on the Universal lot have no roots. Ouspenskaya's finest hour as the prophetic gypsy woman. Ow-ooo! Chilling and thrilling. **70m/B; VHS, DVD, Blu-Ray.** Lon Chaney, Jr.; Claude Rains; Maria Ouspenskaya; Ralph Bellamy; Bela Lugosi; Warren William; Patric Knowles; Evelyn Ankers; Forrester Harvey; Fay Helm; ***D:*** George Waggner; ***W:*** Curt Siodmak; ***C:*** Joseph Valentine; ***M:*** Charles Previn; Hans J. Salter; Frank Skinner.

Wolf Moon ½ *Dark Moon Rising* **2009 (R)** Decent special efforts in a horror story that turns increasingly silly. Small town teen Amy falls for newcomer Dan who reveals that he's inherited a werewolf curse from his vicious father Bender. Local sheriff Sam is investigating a series of killings when ex-cop Thibodeaux shows up and informs her that he and Bender have an old score to settle, with the young lovers getting caught in the middle. **124m/C; DVD.** Max Ryan; Billy Drago; Maria Conchita Alonso; Chris Mulkey; Sid Haig; Lin Shaye; Ginny Weirick; Chris Divecchio; ***D:*** Dana Mennie; ***W:*** Dana Mennie; ***C:*** Mark Ream; ***M:*** Geoff Gibbons. **VIDEO**

The Wolf of Wall Street **2013 (R)** Jordan Belfort (DiCaprio) started his life on Wall Street on the day that the market collapsed, forcing him back to the beginning and teaching him to live completely and fully in the moment because there may be no tomorrow. And so Belfort cheated his clients, slept around on his wife, and did whatever drug he could get his hands on. He also made a fortune. Martin Scorsese, writer Winter, DiCaprio, and Hill work together to deliver an adrenalin shot of cinema, pushing their incredible story forward for three hours and pulling no punches along the way. It's a masterpiece of bad behavior. **180m/C; DVD, Blu-Ray.** Leonardo DiCaprio; Jonah Hill; Margot Robbie; Matthew McConaughey; Kyle Chandler; Rob Reiner; Jon Bernthal; Jon Favreau; Jean Dujardin; Joanna Lumley; Cristin Milioti; Christine Ebersole; Shea Whigham; Katarina Cas; P.J. Byrne; Ethan Suplee; ***D:*** Martin Scorsese; ***W:*** Terence Winter; ***C:*** Rodrigo Prieto. Golden Globes '14: Actor--Mus./Comedy (DiCaprio).

Wolf Totem *Le dernier loup* **2015 (PG-13)** Based on the novel by Jiang Rong, a dramatic exploration of one man's experience during the Cultural Revolution in China. In 1967, Mao is imposing severe changes on China and its culture. That year, Chen Zhen (Feng), a young student in Beijing is forced to leave the city to live with nomadic herdsmen in Inner Mongolia. There, he adopts a wolf and witness how civilization, wolf packs, and local residents are impacted by the changes taking place. Mandarin and Mongolian with subtitles. **121m/C; DVD, Blu-Ray, Streaming, Download.** Shaofeng Feng; Shawn Dou; Ankhnyam Ragchaa; Zhusheng Yin; Baasanjav Mijid; ***D:*** Jean-Jacques Annaud; ***W:*** Jean-Jacques Annaud; Alain Godard; Lu Wei; John Collee; ***C:*** Jean-Marie Dreujou; ***M:*** James Horner.

Wolfcop ½ **2015** A horror comedy centered on a drunken cop who becomes an drunken WolfCop! Working in the small community of Woodhaven, Lou Garou (Fafard) is an unmotivated law enforcement officer. He avoids investigating anything that would take time from his drinking. That is, until he looks into an incident just outside of town one night. When he wakes up, he sees that a pentagram has been cut into his chest and he is being transformed into a wolfman. Lou's new focus becomes finding out what happened to him and why, drawing on all the cop skills he avoided using to date. **79m/C; DVD, Blu-Ray, Streaming, Download.** Leo Fafard; Amy Matysio; Sarah Lind; Corinne Conley; Jesse Moss; ***D:*** Lowell Dean; ***W:*** Lowell Dean; ***C:*** Peter Larocque; ***M:*** Toby Bond; Shooting Guns. **VIDEO**

Wolfen **1981 (R)** Surrealistic menace darkens this original and underrated tale of super-intelligent wolf creatures terrorizing NYC. Police detective Finney tries to track down the beasts before they kill again. Notable special effects in this thriller, which covers environmental and Native American concerns while maintaining the tension. Feature film debuts of Hines and Venora. Based on the novel by Whitley Strieber. **115m/C; VHS, DVD, Blu-Ray.** Albert Finney; Gregory Hines; Tom Noonan; Diane Venora; Edward James Olmos; Dick O'Neill; Dehl Berti; Peter Michael Goetz; Sam Gray; Ralph Bell; ***D:*** Michael Wadleigh; ***W:*** Michael Wadleigh; David Eyre; ***C:*** Gerry Fisher; ***M:*** James Horner.

The Wolfman **1982** Colin Glasgow is summoned back to his family manor to attend the funeral of his father. Unbeknownst to Colin, his father was actually murdered by his children who are in thrall to a Satanist priest. The family stalls Colin, hoping their father's "curse" will be passed on to him at the next full moon. It does, and Colin turns into a werewolf and begins a small rural rampage. Extremely amateurish gothic horror attempt in the Universal/"Dark Shadows" vein. The sets and models look flimsy and the acting is like that of a bad stage-play. **102m/C; VHS, DVD.** Earl Owensby; Kristina Reynolds; Sid Rancer; Julian Morton; ***D:*** Worth Keeter; ***W:*** Worth Keeter; ***C:*** Darrell Cathcart; ***M:*** David Floyd; Arthur Smith.

The Wolfman **2009 (R)** Inspired by the 1941 horror classic starring Lon Chaney, this foggy homage shows what happens when family dysfunction gets hairy. Lawrence Talbot (Del Toro) returns to his family's estate to help his brother's fiance Gwen (Blunt) after said brother ends up gnawed and gnarly. Reunited with his estranged father (Hopkins), Lawrence learns that a bloodthirsty creature is feasting on the villagers. While strolling on the moors, Lawrence is also attacked but survives. Now a werewolf, Lawrence must deal with his bestial nature, a family secret, and Scotland Yard detective Aberline (Weaving). Fairly true to the spirit of the original, you will be rooting for the reluctant Wolfman by the end. **102m/C; Blu-Ray.** Benicio Del Toro; Emily Blunt; Anthony Hopkins; Hugo Weaving; Geraldine Chaplin; Art Malik; Asa Butterfield; Simon Merrells; Mario Marin-Borquez; Cristina Contes; ***D:*** Joe Johnston; ***W:*** Andrew Kevin Walker; David Self; ***C:*** Shelly Johnson; ***M:*** Danny Elfman. Oscars '10: Makeup.

Wolverine *Code Name: Wolverine* **1996 (R)** Former Navy SEAL Harry Gordini (Sabato Jr.) and his family are vacationing in Italy where he becomes an unwitting drug smuggler. After the drug cartel kidnaps his wife and son, Harry uses his training to attempt a rescue before the authorities intervene. Based on the book by Frederick Forsyth. Supplies the required action quotient. **91m/C; VHS, DVD.** Antonio Sabato, Jr.; Richard Brooks; Traci Lind; Daniel Quinn; ***D:*** David S. Jackson; ***W:*** Robert T. Megginson; ***C:*** Denis Maloney; ***M:*** Christopher Franke. **TV**

The Wolverine **2013 (PG-13)** A surprisingly adult and robust superhero movie that replaces the cartoonish approach of "X-Men Origins: Wolverine." Originally developed by Darren Aronofsky, this one-off-adventure based on a legendary 1982 comic sees Logan/Wolverine (Jackman) heading to Japan, where he's stripped of his immortal powers and forced to deal with the human side of his superhero persona. But the strong story gets weighed down by CGI clichés in the final act though Mangold's film still works. **126m/C; DVD, Blu-Ray.** Hugh Jackman; Tao Okamoto; Rila Fukushima; Will Yun Lee; Svetlana Khodchenkova; Famke Janssen; Hiroyuki (Henry) Sanada; Brian Tee; ***D:*** James Mangold; ***W:*** Mark Bomback; Scott Frank; ***C:*** Ross Emery; ***M:*** Marco Beltrami.

The Wolves *Shussho Iwai* **1982** Gosha shows the world of the yakuza (gangster) during the 1920s. Reminiscent of the samurai, the movie combines ancient Japanese culture with the rapidly changing world of 20th century Japan. In Japanese with English subtitles. **131m/C; VHS, DVD.** *JP* Tatsuya Nakadai; Noboru Ando; Komake Kurihara; Kyoko Enami; Isao Natsuyagi; ***D:*** Hideo Gosha; ***W:*** Hideo Gosha; ***C:*** Kozo Okazaki; ***M:*** Masaru Sato.

Wolves in the Snow *Des Chiens dans la Neige* **2002** When Lucie finds out her husband Antoine has been cheating on her for years, she accidentally kills him in a rage. Unwilling to go to jail, she tries to figure out how to dispose of the body. But cheating wasn't all Antoine was hiding—he was also involved in money laundering for the mob. When a couple of hoods show up to question Lucie about Antoine's whereabouts, she lies. Now they think he's skipped out of town with a bag of missing cash and that Lucie knows more than she's telling. French with subtitles. **95m/C; DVD.** *CA* Marie Josee Croze; Jean-Philippe Ecoffey; Romano Orzari; Anne Roussel; Frederic Gilles; Antoine Lacomblez; ***D:*** Michael Welterlin; ***W:*** Antoine Lacomblez; Michael Welterlin; ***C:*** Yves Bélanger; ***M:*** Alain Mouysset.

The Wolves of Kromer **1998** A modern-day fairytale set in the rural English town of Kromer. The hypocritical townspeople are mean-spirited gossips who look down upon the local wolf population (in this case very attractive young human/beasts in fur coats and long tails). Seth (Williams) has just "come out" as a wolf and fallen for promiscuous Gabriel (Layton). Meanwhile, two servants are poisoning their cruel mistress and plan to point accusing fingers at the wolves, giving the human populace the excuse they need for violence. Based on the play by Lambert, who wrote the screenplay. **77m/C; VHS, DVD.** *GB* Lee Williams; James Layton; Rita Davies; Margaret Towner; Rosemary Dunham; Angharad Rees; Kevin Moore; Leila Lloyd-Evelyn; Matthew Dean; David Prescott; ***Nar:*** Boy George; ***D:*** Will Gould; ***W:*** Charles Lambert; Matthew Read; ***C:*** Laura Remacha; ***M:*** Basil Moore-Asfouri.

Wolvesbayne **1/2 2009** Syfy Channel horror mayhem. Russell Bayne is attacked by a werewolf and gets turned. Minions of vampire Von Griem try to kidnap him because he's apparently in possession of one of four amulets necessary to fully restore first vampire queen Lilith. When they fail, Bayne teams up with Jacob Van Helsing and his crew in a vampire/lycan/hunter smackdown. **92m/C; DVD, Blu-Ray.** Jeremy London; Mark Dacascos; Yancy Butler; Rhett Giles; Christy Carlson Romano; Stephanie Honore; ***D:*** Griff Furst; ***W:*** Leigh Scott; ***C:*** Bill Posley; ***M:*** Miles Hankins. **CABLE**

The Woman **1/2 2011 (R)** A film so brutally violent that it caused a public outcry at Sundance, director/writer McKee's horror/drama is not for the squeamish but offers a unique, riveting take on the misogyny often hidden behind the picket fence. Chris Cleek (Bridgers) is arguably the most disturbing cinematic creation of 2011, a controlling family man who finds a feral woman (McIntosh) in the woods and chains her up in his backyard shed—something of a family "pet." The ensuing torture and abhorrent treatment she receives is disturbing, but the final act reveals a darker secret that truly sends audiences reeling. **101m/C; DVD, Blu-Ray.** Sean Bridges; Angela Bettis; Pollyanna McIntosh; Zach Rand; Carlee Baker; Lauren Ashley Carter; Shylla Molhusen; ***D:*** Lucky McKee; ***W:*** Lucky McKee; Jack Ketchum; ***C:*** Alex Vendler; ***M:*** Sean Spillane.

A Woman, a Gun and a Noodle Shop *A Simple Noodle Story; San Qiang Pai'an Jingqi* **2010 (R)** Zhang's remake of the Coen brothers 1984 film "Blood Simple," is transferred to a dusty desert town sometime during China's feudal past. Cheapskate Wang owns a roadside inn, doesn't pay his help, and neglects his wife who's having an affair with their young cook. She decides to bump off the old grouch but Wang is suspicious and hires a cop to kill off the adulterous lovers but there's a certain farcical quality to the entire deadly situation. Mandarin with subtitles. **95m/C; Blu-Ray.** *CH* Honglei Sun; Xiao Shen-Yang; Dahong Ni; Yan Ni; Ye Cheng; Mao Mao; ***D:*** Yimou Zhang; ***W:*** Zhengchao Xu; Jianquan Shi; ***C:*** Xiaoding Zhao; ***M:*** Lin Zhao.

A Woman, A Part **1/2 2017** Anna Baskin (Siff) is a 44-year-old actress stuck in something of a mid-life crisis. She's a workaholic who has achieved a reasonable degree of fame on a TV show but she hates the work. She abruptly quits the gig, returning to New York to find the roots of why she became an actress in the first place. The quest leads her to a personally revealing role, but she realizes she must confront several of the demons of her past if she wants to move on. Siff is fantastic in a story that's not often told. **97m/C; DVD.** Maggie Siff; Cara Seymour; John Ortiz; Dagmara Dominczyk; Khandi Alexander; ***D:*** Elisabeth Subrin; ***W:*** Elisabeth Subrin; ***C:*** Chris Dapkins.

The Woman Between **1931** Beautiful Julie does love her wealthy older husband John but their marriage caused trouble with John's children and she never met his son, Victor. While returning to New York from France, Julie has a shipboard romance with a man named Paul Niles. She breaks off the affair after she learns something horrifying about him. **73m/B; DVD, Blu-Ray.** Lili Damita; Lester Vail; O.P. Heggie; Miriam Seegar; Anita Louise; William Morris; ***D:*** Victor Schertzinger; ***W:*** Howard Estabrook; ***C:*** J. Roy Hunt.

A Woman Called Golda **1982** Political drama following the life and career of Golda Meir, the Israeli Prime Minister and one of the most powerful political figures of the 20th century. Davis portrays the young Golda, Bergman taking over as she ages. Superior TV bio-epic. **192m/C; VHS, DVD.** Ingrid Bergman; Leonard Nimoy; Anne Jackson; Ned Beatty; Robert Loggia; Judy Davis; ***D:*** Alan Gibson; ***W:*** Steven Gethers; Harold Gast. **TV**

A Woman Called Moses **1/2 1978** The story of Harriet Ross Tubman, who bought her freedom from slavery, founded the underground railroad, and helped lead hundreds of slaves to freedom before the Civil War. Wonderful performance by Tyson but the telefilm is bogged down by a so-so script. Based on the novel by Marcy Heldish. **200m/C; VHS, DVD.** Cicely Tyson; Dick Anthony Williams; Will Geer; Robert Hooks; Hari Rhodes; James Wainwright; ***D:*** Paul Wendkos; ***W:*** Lonnie Elder, III; ***M:*** Coleridge-Taylor Perkinson. **TV**

The Woman From Monte Carlo **1/2 1931** When the French cruiser Lafayette is sunk by German submarines, Captain Corlaix (Huston) is accused of negligence and put on trial. His much-younger wife Lottie (Dagover), one of the rescued survivors, was dallying with Lt. D'Orlelles (William) onboard and must reveal her adultery to save her husband from a court-martial. Remake of the 1928 silent "The Night Watch." **65m/B; DVD.** Walter Huston; Lil Dagover; Warren William; John Wray; George E. Stone; Robert Warwick; ***D:*** Michael Curtiz; ***W:*** Harvey Thew; ***C:*** Ernest Haller.

Woman Hater **1949** Delightful farce about the belief in the single life. Confirmed bachelor plays games with a single woman. They eventually disregard their solitary ways in favor of romance. **101m/B; VHS, DVD.** Stewart Granger; Edwige Feuillere; Ronald Squire; Mary Jerrold; ***D:*** Terence Young.

A Woman, Her Men and Her Futon **1992 (R)** A beautiful woman tries to find her identity by having a number of lovers but none can satisfy her every need. **90m/C; VHS, DVD.** Jennifer Rubin; Lance Edwards; Grant Show; Michael Ceveris; Delaune Michel; Robert Lipton; ***D:*** Mussef Sibay; ***W:*** Mussef Sibay; ***C:*** Michael J. Davis; ***M:*** Joel Goldsmith.

A Woman Hunted **1/2 2003 (PG-13)** Lainie Wheeler's (Paul) car breaks down in the middle of nowhere and she's happy when good samaritan Harry (Higgins) stops and offers her a ride. She shouldn't be. **94m/C; DVD.** *CA* Alexandra Paul; Linden Ashby; Michele Greene; Jonathan Higgins; Maxim Roy; ***D:*** Morrie Ruvinsky; ***W:*** Morrie Ruvinsky; ***C:*** Bruno Philip; ***M:*** Richard Bowers. **VIDEO**

The Woman Hunter **1/2 1972** A wealthy woman recovering from a traffic accident in Mexico believes someone is after her for her jewels and possibly her life. Eden dressed well, if nothing else; suspense builds ploddingly to a "Yeah, sure" climax. **73m/C; VHS, DVD.** Barbara Eden; Robert Vaughn; Stuart Whitman; Syd Chaplin; Larry Storch; Enrique Lucero; ***D:*** Bernard L. Kowalski. **TV**

Woman in Black **1/2 1989** Chilling ghost story set in 1925 and adapted from the novel by Susan Hill. Soliciter Arthur Kidd is sent to a remote house to settle the estate of a client. He's haunted by the mysterious figure of a woman in black, who according to the locals, has put a curse on the village. Arthur's driven close to the edge of sanity by the ghostly figure and the tragedy that haunts the past. **100m/C; VHS, DVD.** *GB* Adrian Rawlins; Bernard Hepton; David Daker; Pauline Moran; ***D:*** Herbert Wise; ***W:*** Nigel Kneale. **TV**

The Woman in Black **1/2 2012 (PG-13)** A pulpy Hammer Films adaptation of Susan Hill's 1983 novel. Young lawyer Arthur Kipps (Radcliffe) travels to a clearly-haunted estate so his employer can take ownership. Going through the paperwork he discovers the legend of the title character, a ghost who portends the death of children in the small town nearby. Filled with jump scares and loud sound cues, there are some definite chill moments and is far more haunting than its advertising let on, even if Radcliffe's slightly passive as a protagonist. Coincidentally, actor Adrian Rawlins, who played the role of Harry Potter's father, also starred as Arthur in a 1989 British TV adaptation. **95m/C; DVD, Blu-Ray.** *GB* Daniel Radcliffe; Ciaran Hinds; Janet McTeer; Shaun Dooley; Sophie Stuckey; Roger Allam; Alisa Khazanova; Liz White; Ashley Foster; ***D:*** James H. Watkins; ***W:*** Jane Goldman; ***C:*** Tim Maurice-Jones; ***M:*** Marco Beltrami.

The Woman in Black 2: Angel of Death **1/2 2015 (PG-13)** The Hammer Films banner returns for a follow-up to the surprisingly successful 2012 hit but they lose most of the mood and atmosphere that made that film work. Back at Eel Marsh House, director Harper's horror film is a lot more of the same—shadowy figures in black prowling the grounds of a haunted house. An old-fashioned ghost story is welcome in an era of overcooked horror movies but a strong first act is sabotaged by the inevitable jump cuts and loud noises that have dominated the modern-day genre. Just because it's loud doesn't mean it's scary. **98m/C; DVD, Blu-Ray.** *UK CA* Phoebe Fox; Helen McCrory; Oaklee Pendergast; Jeremy Irvine; Adrian Rawlins; Leanne Best; ***D:*** Tom Harper; ***W:*** Jon Croker; ***C:*** George Steel; ***M:*** Marco Beltrami; Marcus Trump; Brandon Roberts.

Woman in Brown **1/2** *The Vicious Circle; The Circle* **1948** It's Hungary, 1882, and five Jewish men are on trial for the murder of a man who actually committed suicide. Despite the prejudice and hatred from the locals, their lawyer believes in and fights for their innocence. **77m/B; VHS, DVD.** Conrad Nagel; Fritz Kortner; Reinhold Schunzel; Philip Van Zandt; Eddie LeRoy; Edwin Maxwell; ***D:*** W. Lee Wilder.

Woman in Gold **2015 (PG-13)** Noted as Austria's "Mona Lisa", Gustav Klimt's painting "Woman in Gold" had originally been confiscated from its original owner by the Nazis, then placed in a Vienna museum after the war. Fast-forward to the late 90s, Maria Altmann (Mirren), niece of the actual woman in gold, must hire junior lawyer Randol Schoenberg (Reynolds) to uphold a new law that allows looted treasures to be returned to their rightful owner. The silly back-and-forth between the two characters takes center stage, like some mismatched buddy cop flick or off-kilter romantic comedy. Milking this twice-told tale, director Simon Curtis oversimplifies this somewhat complicated true-life story for easy digestion and maximum emotional schmaltz. **109m/C; DVD, Blu-Ray.** Dame Helen Mirren; Ryan Reynolds; Daniel Brühl; Katie Holmes; Tatiana Maslany; ***D:*** Simon Curtis; ***W:*** Alexi Kaye Campbell; ***C:*** Ross Emery; ***M:*** Martin Phipps; Hans Zimmer.

The Woman in Green *Sherlock Holmes and the Woman in Green* **1949** Murder victims are found with missing index fingers, and it's up to Holmes and Watson to try to solve this apparently motiveless crime. Available colorized. **68m/B; VHS, DVD.** Basil Rathbone; Nigel Bruce; Hillary Brooke; Henry Daniell; Paul Cavanagh; Frederick Worlock; Mary Gordon; Billy Bevan; ***D:*** Roy William Neill; ***W:*** Bertram Millhauser; ***C:*** Virgil Miller.

Woman in Hiding **1/2 1949** Killer spouse alert in this effective '50s noir. Seldon Clark (McNally) expects his marriage to Deborah Chandler (Lupino) to restore his family's fortunes in their southern mill town. He tries to bump her off in a car accident on their honeymoon, so she plays dead. Ex-soldier Keith Ramsey (Duff) unwittingly gives her away to her psycho hubby until he realizes she's actually in danger. **92m/B; DVD, Blu-Ray.** Ida Lupino; Stephen McNally; Howard Duff; Peggy Dow; John Litel; ***D:*** Michael Gordon; ***W:*** Roy Huggins; Oscar Saul; ***C:*** William H. Daniels; ***M:*** Frank Skinner.

The Woman in Red **1935** Shelby Barrett and Johnny Wyatt are both employed in the stables of wealthy Mrs. Nicholas. The widow is interested in a personal relationship with Johnny while rich Eugene Fairchild feels the same about Shelby but the duo elopes instead. Still, Shelby feels obligated to help out Fairchild with a party aboard his yacht that leads to a guest's drowning. Only a mysterious "woman in red" can come to his aid. **68m/B; DVD.** Barbara Stanwyck; Gene Raymond; John Eldredge; Genevieve Tobin; Dorothy Tree; Phillip Reed; Russell Hicks; Edward Van Sloan; Arthur Treacher; ***D:*** Robert Florey; ***W:*** Peter Milne; Mary C. McCall; ***C:*** Sol Polito.

The Woman in Red **1/2 1984 (PG-13)** Executive Wilder's life unravels when he falls hard for stunning Le Brock. Inferior Hollywood-ized remake of the ebulliant "Pardon Mon Affaire." Somehow the French seem to do the sexual force thing with more verve, but this one has its moments, and Wilder is likeable. Music by Stevie Wonder. **87m/C; VHS, DVD.** Gene Wilder; Charles Grodin; Kelly Le Brock; Gilda Radner; Judith Ivey; Joseph Bologna; ***D:*** Gene Wilder; ***W:*** Gene Wilder; ***M:*** John Morris. Oscars '84: Song ("I Just Called to Say I Love You"); Golden Globes '85: Song ("I Just Called to Say I Love You").

Woman in the Dunes *Suna No Onna; Woman of the Dunes* **1964** Splendid, resonant allegorical drama. A scientist studying insects in the Japanese sand dunes finds himself trapped with a woman in a hut at the bottom of a pit. Superbly directed and photographed (by Hiroshi Segawa). Scripted by Kobo Abe from his acclaimed novel. In Japanese with English subtitles. **123m/B; VHS, DVD, Blu-Ray.** *JP* Eiji Okada; Kyoko Kishida; Koji Mitsui; Hiroko Ito; Sen Yano; ***D:*** Hiroshi Teshigahara; ***W:*** Kobe Abe; ***C:*** Hiroshi Segawa; ***M:*** Toru Takemitsu. Cannes '64: Grand Jury Prize.

The Woman in the Fifth 🦴 *Le Femme du 5e* **2011 (R)** Dreary, silly French psycho-thriller finds failed American writer Tom (Hawke) in Paris trying to reconnect with his family. When he fails, the desperate man takes a job working for his thug landlord Sezer (Guesmi) as a night watchman and is all too susceptible to the charms of the elegant, mysterious widow Margit (Scott Thomas), who encourages him to start writing again. However, since Tom's grip on his sanity seems fragile at best, what's actually going on is suspect. English and French with subtitles. **85m/C; DVD.** *FR PL UK* Ethan Hawke; Kristin Scott Thomas; Joanna Kulig; Samir Guesmi; Delphine Chuillot; Julie Papillon; ***D:*** Pawel Pawlikowski; ***W:*** Pawel Pawlikowski; ***C:*** Ryszard Lenczewski; ***M:*** Max de Wardener.

Woman in the Moon 🦴🦴 1/2 *By Rocket to the Moon; Girl in the Moon* **1929** Assorted people embark on a trip to the moon and discover water, and an atmosphere, as well as gold. Lang's last silent outing is nothing next to "Metropolis," with a rather lame plot (greedy trip bashers seek gold), but interesting as a vision of the future. Lang's predictions about space travel often hit the mark. Silent with music. **115m/B; Silent; VHS, DVD, Blu-Ray.** *GE* Klaus Pohl; Willy Fritsch; Gustav von Wagenheim; Gerda Maurus; ***D:*** Fritz Lang.

Woman in the Shadows 🦴🦴 *Woman in the Dark* **1934** A ex-con retreats to the woods for serenity and peace, but is assaulted by mysterious women, jealous lovers, and gun-slinging drunks, until he explodes. A man can only take so much. From a Dashiell Hammett story. **70m/B; DVD.** Fay Wray; Ralph Bellamy; Melvyn Douglas; Roscoe Ates; Joe King; ***D:*** Phil Rosen; ***C:*** Joseph Ruttenberg.

Woman in the Window 🦴🦴🦴 **1944** Psycho-melodrama finds staid college professor Richard Wanley straying off the straight and narrow into a world of trouble—thanks to beautiful model Alice (Bennett). She invites him over but when her jealous boyfriend Claude (Loft) arrives unexpectedly, he attacks them both and Richard kills Claude in self-defense. Thinking no one will believe them, and afraid of scandal, the inept duo bury the body in the woods. Too bad Richard's best friend Frank (Massey) is the D.A. and there's a blackmailer around. Or is there? Surprise ending. Based on the novel "Once Off Guard" by J.H. Wallis. **99m/B; VHS, DVD, Blu-Ray.** Edward G. Robinson; Joan Bennett; Raymond Massey; Arthur Loft; Dan Duryea; Edmund Breon; Dorothy Peterson; Robert (Bobby) Blake; ***D:*** Fritz Lang; ***W:*** Nunnally Johnson; ***C:*** Milton Krasner; ***M:*** Arthur Lange.

The Woman in White 🦴🦴 1/2 **1997** The happy hours half-sisters, outgoing Marian (Fitzgerald) and shy Laura (Waddell), spend with their eccentric Uncle Fairlie (Richardson) soon turn sinister when Laura is married off to the seemingly charming Sir Percival Glyde (Wilby). Sir Percival quickly appears to be conspiring with the suspicious Count Fosco (Callow) to take control of Laura's money. When Marian visits her sister, she's alarmed by Laura's decline and equally unnerved by the mysterious woman in white, Anne (Vidler), who seems to know Glyde and tries to warn the sisters of impending danger. Based on the novel by Wilkie Collins, who also wrote "The Moonstone." **120m/C; DVD.** *UK* Tara Fitzgerald; Justine Waddell; James Wilby; Simon Callow; Ian Richardson; Andrew Lincoln; Susan Vidler; John Standing; Corin Redgrave; ***D:*** Tim Fywell; ***W:*** David Pirie; ***M:*** David Ferguson. **TV**

The Woman Inside 🦴 1/2 **1983 (R)** Low-budget gender-bender depicts the troubled life of a Vietnam veteran who decides on a sex-change operation to satisfy his inner yearnings. Blondell's unfortunate last role as his/her aunt. Cheesy like Limburger; almost too weird and boring even for camp buffs. **94m/C; VHS, DVD.** *CA* Gloria Manon; Dr. Dave Clark; Joan Blondell; ***D:*** Joseph Van Winkle; ***W:*** Steve(n) Fisher.

A Woman Is a Woman 🦴🦴🦴 *Une Femme Est une Femme; La Donna E Donna* **1960** Godard's affectionate sendup of Hollywood musicals is a hilarious comedy about a nightclub dancer (Karina) who desperately wants a baby. When boyfriend Belmondo balks, she asks his best friend Brialy. Much ado is had, with the three leads all splendid. Godard's first film shot in color and cinemascope, with great music. In French with English subtitles. **88m/C; VHS, DVD.** *FR* Jean-Claude Brialy; Jean-Paul Belmondo; Anna Karina; Marie DuBois; ***D:*** Jean-Luc Godard; ***W:*** Jean-Luc Godard; ***C:*** Raoul Coutard; ***M:*** Michel Legrand.

Woman Is the Future of Man 🦴🦴🦴 *Yeojaneun namjaui miraeda* **2004** While meeting for lunch, two old Korean friends Mun-ho (Ji-tae) and Hyeon-gon (Tae-woo) reminisce over too much rice wine about a girl they both dated years before, Seon-hwa (Hyeon-a), and how each regrets mistreating her. Even though the men have moved on with their lives—Mun-ho is a married college art lecturer while Hyeon-gon is a hopeful filmmaker—they decide to visit Seon-hwa but find that life has not gone quite as well for her. In Korean, with English subtitles. **88m/C; DVD, Blu-Ray.** Yoo Jitae; Kim Taewoo; Sung Hyunah; ***D:*** Hong Sang-soo; ***W:*** Hong Sang-soo; ***C:*** Kim Hyungkoo; ***M:*** Chong Yongjin.

The Woman Next Door 🦴🦴🦴 *La Femme d'a Cote* **1981 (R)** One of Truffaut's last films before his sudden death in 1984. The domestic drama involves a suburban husband who resumes an affair with a tempestuous now-married woman after she moves next door, with domestic complications all around. An insightful, humanistic paean to passion and fidelity by the great artist, though one of his lesser works. Supported by strong outings from the two leads. In French with English subtitles. **106m/C; VHS, DVD.** *FR* Gerard Depardieu; Fanny Ardant; Michele Baumgartner; Veronique Silver; Roger Van Hool; ***D:*** Francois Truffaut; ***W:*** Suzanne Schiffman; ***C:*** William Lubtchansky; ***M:*** Georges Delerue.

Woman Obsessed 🦴🦴 **1959** Hayward suffers well and Boyd is a hunk in this melodrama. Recent widow Mary (Hayward) is afraid of losing her Saskatchewan farm until she hires strong-but-silent logger Fred (Boyd) to help out. Her young son Robbie (Holmes) is okay with the new guy until Mary and Fred marry (too quickly) and Fred's child raising ideas turn out to be somewhat primitive. He also has a temper and Mary is ready to give Fred the heave-ho until disaster strikes. **102m/C; DVD.** Susan Hayward; Stephen Boyd; Dennis Holmes; Barbara Nichols; Ken Scott; Theodore Bikel; Arthur Franz; ***D:*** Henry Hathaway; ***W:*** Sydney (Sidney) Boehm; ***C:*** William Mellor; ***M:*** Hugo Friedhofer.

Woman of Desire 🦴 **1993 (R)** Christina Ford (Derek) is a femme fatale who is yachting with rich boyfriend Ted when there is a terrible storm. Christina, Ted, and yacht captain Jack are washed overboard and Jack is found washed ashore with no memory. When Christina turns up she claims Jack killed Ted. So Jack gets a lawyer, Walter J. Hill (played by the redoubtable Mitchum) but is he wily enough to discredit the deceitful Christina? Bo's body is once again on display. Also available in an unrated version. **97m/C; VHS, DVD.** Bo Derek; Jeff Fahey; Steven Bauer; Robert Mitchum; ***D:*** Robert Ginty; ***W:*** Robert Ginty; ***C:*** Hanro Mohr; ***M:*** Rene Veldsman.

A Woman of Independent Means 🦴🦴🦴 **1994 (PG)** Leisurely family miniseries, based on the 1979 novel by Elizabeth Forsythe Hailey. Fields stars as the title character, Bess Steed Garner (based on the author's maternal grandmother), a well-off Texas belle who marries childhood sweetheart Robert Steed (Goldwyn) in 1907 and settles down to family life. Of course, nothing is settled as Beth bears children, Robert tries to make a go of his insurance business, their families interfere, and tragedy strikes. **316m/C; VHS, DVD.** Sally Field; Tony Goldwyn; Brenda Fricker; Charles Durning; Ron Silver; Sheila McCarthy; Ann Hearn; ***D:*** Robert Greenwald.

A Woman of Substance 🦴🦴 1/2 **1984** The woman of the title, Emma Harte, rises from poverty to wealth and power through self-discipline, enduring various romantic disappointments and tragedies along the way. Based on the novel by Barbara Taylor Bradford. Followed by "Hold the Dream." **300m/C; VHS, DVD.** Jenny Seagrove; Barry Bostwick; Deborah Kerr; Liam Neeson; Diane Baker; George Baker; Peter Chelsom; Peter Egan; Christopher Gable; Christopher Guard; Gayle Hunnicutt; John Mills; Nicola Pagett; Saskia Reeves; Miranda Richardson; ***D:*** Don Sharp; ***W:*** Lee Langley; ***C:*** Ernest Vincze; ***M:*** Nigel Hess. **TV**

The Woman of the Town 🦴🦴 1/2 **1944** Frontier marshal and newspaperman Bat Masterson is portrayed convincingly by Dekker as a very human hero who seeks justice when the woman he loves, a dance hall girl who works in the town for social causes, is killed by an unscrupulous rancher. Fictionalized but realistic western shows "heroes" as good, ordinary people. **90m/B; VHS, DVD.** Claire Trevor; Albert Dekker; Barry Sullivan; Henry Hull; Porter Hall; Percy Kilbride; ***D:*** George Archainbaud; ***M:*** Miklos Rozsa.

A Woman of the World 🦴🦴 **1925** After being betrayed in love, sophisticated Italian Countess Elnora (Negri) decides to visit distant cousins in their conservative Iowa town. She causes a scandal with her liberated behavior that both disturbs and intrigues stuffy DA Granger (Herbert) and he tries to run her out of town. Outraged, Elnora uses a handy horsewhip to teach him some manners, which apparently—uh—excites the guy since he changes his mind. Definitely offers a melodramatic shock. **70m/B; Silent; DVD.** Pola Negri; Holmes Herbert; Chester Conklin; Lucille Ward; Charles Emmet Mack; Blanche Mehaffey; Guy Oliver; ***D:*** Malcolm St. Clair; ***W:*** Lucille Ward; Pierre Collings; ***C:*** Bert Glennon.

Woman of the Year 🦴🦴🦴🦴 **1942** First classic Tracy/Hepburn pairing concerns the rocky marriage of a renowned political columnist and a lowly sportswriter. Baseball scene with Hepburn at her first game is delightful. Hilarious, rich entertainment that tries to answer the question "What really matters in life?" Tracy and Hepburn began a close friendship that paralleled their quarter-century celluloid partnership. Hepburn shepherded Kamin and Lardner's Oscar-winning script past studio chief Louis B. Mayer, wearing four-inch heels to press her demands. Mayer caved in, Tracy was freed from making "The Yearling," and the rest is history. **114m/B; VHS, DVD, Blu-Ray.** Spencer Tracy; Katharine Hepburn; Fay Bainter; Dan Tobin; Reginald Owen; Roscoe Karns; William Bendix; Minor Watson; ***D:*** George Stevens; ***W:*** Ring Lardner, Jr.; Michael Kanin; ***C:*** Joseph Ruttenberg; ***M:*** Franz Waxman. Oscars '42: Orig. Screenplay; Natl. Film Reg. '99.

The Woman on Pier 13 🦴 1/2 **1950** Brad Collins (Ryan) is now the VP of a San Francisco shipping company but in his wayward youth (and under another name), he was a dockworker who joined the Communist Party. Now he's being blackmailed by Commie Vanning (Gomez), who wants Brad to call a strike or else. Wife Nan (Day) is confused by Brad's strange behavior, which leads to all sorts of complications in this Red Scare melodrama. The title makes no sense but audiences disliked the preview title "I Married a Communist." **73m/B; DVD.** Robert Ryan; Laraine Day; John Agar; Thomas Gomez; Janis Carter; Richard Rober; William Talman; ***D:*** Robert Stevenson; ***W:*** Charles Grayson; Robert D. (Robert Hardy) Andrews; ***C:*** Nicholas Musuraca; ***M:*** Leigh Harline.

The Woman on the Beach 🦴🦴 **1947** Director Jean Renoir's last Hollywood film ventured into atypical film noir territory. A violent quarrel with his unhappy wife Peggy (Bennett) had aging artist Tod Butler (Bickford) losing both his eyesight and career. Peggy wanders along the beach near the Coast Guard base where she meets traumatized Lt. Scott Burnett (Ryan), who soon becomes obsessed with her. He's also convinced that Tod is faking his blindness and wants to prove it by some dangerous means. After an unsuccessful preview, Renoir and RKO heavily re-cut the film before its release but it didn't help the boxoffice. **71m/B; DVD.** Joan Bennett; Robert Ryan; Nan Leslie; Charles Bickford; Walter Sande; Irene Ryan; ***D:*** Jean Renoir; ***W:*** Jean Renoir; Frank Davis; ***C:*** Harry Wild; Leo Tover; ***M:*** Hanns Eisler.

Woman On the Run 🦴🦴 **1950** Modest crime melodrama shot on location in San Francisco. Frank Johnson (Elliott) witnesses a mob hit, tells the cops, and decides to go into hiding on his own. Indifferent wife Eleanor (Sheridan) thinks he's finally left their foundering marriage until informed otherwise. She agrees to help out but decides to trust overly-friendly reporter Danny Leggett (O'Keefe) as she searches for her husband. **77m/B; DVD, Blu-Ray.** Ann Sheridan; Ross Elliott; Dennis O'Keefe; Robert Keith; Frank Jenks; John Qualen; ***D:*** Norman Foster; ***W:*** Norman Foster; Alan Campbell; ***C:*** Hal Mohr; ***M:*** Emil Newman; Arthur Lange.

Woman on Top 🦴🦴 1/2 **2000 (R)** Mildly amusing romantic comedy that's held together by the charm of its lead. Beautiful Brazilian Isabella (Cruz) suffers from extreme motion sickness, which means she must always be in control. She's a whiz in the kitchen and her talents make her husband's (Benicio) restaurant a big success. But Izzie takes off for San Francisco when she discovers Toninho with another gal. Thanks to her culinary skills (and some magical realism), Isabella soon has her own cable cooking show and men (literally) falling at her feet. First there's "Like Water for Chocolate," then there's "Simply Irresistible," and now "Woman" completes the trifecta of food overwhelming the emotions. **93m/C; VHS, DVD.** Penelope Cruz; Harold Perrineau, Jr.; Mark Feuerstein; Murilo Benicio; John de Lancie; ***D:*** Fina Torres; ***W:*** Vera Blasi; ***C:*** Thierry Arbogast; ***M:*** Luis Bacalov.

The Woman Racket 🦴 1/2 **1930** Smitten cop Tom Hayes prevents employee Julia from being arrested during a speakeasy raid and they soon marry. Julia's quickly bored with being a poor cop's wife and wants to go back to work. Tom disapproves, she leaves him, and gangster Chris Miller eventually gets Julia involved in murder. Silent screen star Sweet's first feature-length sound picture. **70m/B; DVD.** Blanche Sweet; Tom Moore; John Miljan; Robert Agnew; ***D:*** Albert Kelley; Robert Ober; ***W:*** Albert S. Le Vino; ***C:*** J. Peverell Marley.

A Woman Rebels 🦴🦴 1/2 **1936** A young Victorian woman challenges Victorian society by fighting for women's rights. Excellent performance from Hepburn lifts what might have been a forgettable drama. Screen debut of Van Heflin. Based on Netta Syrett's "Portrait of a Rebel." **88m/B; VHS, DVD.** Katharine Hepburn; Herbert Marshall; Elizabeth Allan; Donald Crisp; Van Heflin; ***D:*** Mark Sandrich.

Woman They Almost Lynched 🦴 1/2 **1953** Low-budget oater with women running the show. At the end of the Civil War, a quiet Ozark town becomes a refuge for renegades such as Charles Quantrill, the James brothers, and Cole Younger. Sally's brother is killed, and she takes over running the saloon until Union soldiers circling the area accused her of being a Confederate spy. **90m/B; DVD, Blu-Ray.** Joan Leslie; Audrey Totter; Brian Donlevy; Nina Varela; Ben Cooper; James Brown; Jim Davis; John Lund; ***D:*** Allan Dwan; ***W:*** Steve Fisher; ***C:*** Reggie Lanning; ***M:*** Stanley Wilson.

Woman, Thou Art Loosed 🦴🦴 1/2 **2004 (R)** Critics may have been divided on this pic's merits but female audiences gave it strong word-of-mouth support. Based on the self-help novel by charismatic Bishop T.D. Jakes (who plays himself), "Woman" follows the lifelong misfortunes of Michelle (a ferocious Elise), a young black victim of poverty, rape, drug addiction, and eventual imprisonment for murder. The flashback structure of the story (Jakes offers a compassionate ear as Michelle tells her story) is somewhat distracting, but Foster's script offers multi-dimensional characters even if it's a little self-conscious. **99m/C; DVD.** Kimberly Elise; Loretta Devine; Debbi (Deborah) Morgan; Michael Boatman; Clifton Powell; Sean Blakemore; Ricky Harris; ***D:*** Michael A. Schultz; ***C:*** Reinhart Pesche.

Woman Times Seven 🦴🦴 1/2 *Sept Fois Femme; Sette Volte Donna* **1967 (PG)** Italian sexual comedy: seven sketches, each starring MacLaine with a different leading man. Stellar cast and good director should have delivered more, but what they have provided has its comedic moments. **99m/C; VHS, DVD, Blu-Ray.** *IT FR* Shirley MacLaine; Peter Sellers; Rossano Brazzi; Vittorio Gassman; Lex Barker; Elsa Martinelli; Robert Morley; Alan Arkin; Michael Caine; Patrick Wymark; Anita Ekberg; Philippe Noiret; Elspeth March; ***D:*** Vittorio De Sica.

A Woman under the Influence 🦴🦴🦴 **1974 (R)** Strong performances highlight this overlong drama about a family's disintegration. Rowlands is the lonely, middle-aged housewife who's having a breakdown and Falk is her blue-collar husband who can't handle what's going on. **147m/C; VHS, DVD, Blu-Ray.** Gena Rowlands; Peter Falk; Matthew Cassel; Matthew Laborteaux; Christina Grisanti; ***D:*** John Cassavetes; ***W:*** John Cassavetes; ***C:*** Caleb Deschanel; Mitch Breit. Golden Globes '75: Actress--Drama (Rowlands); Natl. Bd. of Review '74: Actress (Rowlands); Natl. Film Reg. '90.

Woman Walks Ahead 🦴🦴 ½ **2017 (R)** Historical drama about a meeting between portrait painter Catherine Weldon (Chastain) and Lakota chief Sitting Bull (Greyeyes), based on true events. Widowed Catherine travels from her New York City home to the Standing Rock reservation with the goal of painting the portrait of Sitting Bull. Though the commanding officer (Hinds) in the region tries to dissuade her, Catherine insists on meeting Sitting Bull. The destitute leader agrees to sit for her for $1,000 and the pair find unexpectedly common ground. Though the film is well-meaning and features beautiful scenery, it unsuccessfully brings together the marginalization of women with the genocide of Native Americans. **101m/C; DVD, Blu-Ray, Streaming.** Jessica Chastain; Michael Greyeyes; Chaske Spencer; Sam Rockwell; Bill Camp; ***D:*** Susanna White; ***W:*** Steven Knight; ***C:*** Mike Eley; ***M:*** George Fenton.

Woman Wanted 🦴🦴 **1998 (R)** Vivacious Emma Riley (Hunter) is hired by as a live-in housekeeper by widowed professor Richard Goddard (Moriarty) and his troubled son Wendell (Sutherland). Both men fall in love with her and Emma, who loves Richard, nevertheless has a one-nighter with Wendell. Then she winds up pregnant. Rather yakky but these are actors who are worth watching. Based on the novel by Glass, who also wrote the screenplay. **110m/C; VHS, DVD.** Holly Hunter; Michael Moriarty; Kiefer Sutherland; ***D:*** Kiefer Sutherland; ***W:*** Joanna McClelland Glass. **CABLE**

The Woman Who Came Back 🦴🦴 **1945** A young woman who believes she suffers from a witch's curse returns to her small hometown with unhappy results. Good cast; bad script. Indifference inducing. **69m/B; VHS, DVD.** Nancy Kelly; Otto Kruger; John Loder; Ruth Ford; Jeanne Gail; ***D:*** Walter Colmes; ***W:*** Dennis J. Cooper; Lee Willis; ***C:*** Henry Sharp; ***M:*** Edward Plumb.

The Woman Who Loved Elvis 1993 TV movie about an obsessive fan who converts her home into an Elvis shrine. **?m/CVHS, DVD.** Roseanne; Tom Arnold; Cynthia Gibb; Sally Kirkland; Danielle Harris; Joe Guzaldo; ***D:*** Bill Bixby. **TV**

A Woman Without Love 🦴🦴🦴 **1951** A rarely seen film from Bunuel's Mexican period based on a classic Guy de Maupassant tale about a forbidden romance. Family tragedy results later when the husband "misbequeaths" his fortune. Minor but fascinating bug-the-bourgeoisie Bunuel. In Spanish with English subtitles. **91m/C; VHS, Streaming.** *MX* Rosario Granados; Julio Villareal; Tito Junco; ***D:*** Luis Bunuel.

The Womaneater 🦴🦴 **1959** This '50s oddity makes a belated appearance on home video. Dr. James Moran (Coulouris) returns from the depths of the Amazon jungle (obviously a set filled with plastic plants) with a miraculous tree that's a close cousin of "Audrey" in the original "Little Shop of Horrors." To maintain its healing powers, the doctor must feed it a steady diet of young women. Not a good sign for his sexy housekeeper Sally (Day). It's every bit as silly as it sounds, swiftly paced and short. **71m/B; VHS, DVD.** *GB* George Coulouris; Robert MacKenzie; Norman Claridge; Marpessa Dawn; Jimmy Vaughan; Vera Day; ***D:*** Charles Saunders; ***W:*** Brandon Fleming; ***C:*** Ernest Palmer; ***M:*** Edwin Astley.

A Woman's a Helluva Thing 🦴🦴 **2001 (R)** Lewd men's magazine publisher Houston loses his macho swagger when he heads home for his mother's funeral and learns that not only did she have a lesbian lover but that it's his ex-girlfriend, and that she stands to inherit the entire estate. **94m/C; VHS, DVD.** Angus MacFadyen; Penelope Ann Miller; Ann-Margret; Kathryn Harrold; Mary Kay Place; Barry Del Sherman; Paul Dooley; Jonas Chernick; ***D:*** Karen Leigh Hopkins; ***W:*** Karen Leigh Hopkins; ***C:*** Barry Parrell; ***M:*** Louis Febre; Thomas Kilzer. **VIDEO**

A Woman's Face 🦴🦴🦴 *En Kvinnas Ansikte* **1938** An unpleasant, bitter woman with a hideous scar on her face blackmails illicit lovers as a form of revenge for a happiness she doesn't know. She even plots to murder a child for his inheritance. But after plastic surgery, she becomes a nicer person and doubts her plan. Lean, tight suspense with a bang-up finale. In Swedish with English subtitles. Remade in Hollywood in 1941. **100m/B; VHS, DVD.** *SW* Ingrid Bergman; Anders Henrikson; Karin Carlsson; Georg Rydeberg; Goran Bernhard; Tore Svennberg; ***D:*** Gustaf Molander.

A Woman's Face 🦴🦴🦴 **1941** A physically and emotionally scarred woman becomes part of a blackmail ring. Plastic surgery restores her looks and her attitude. Begins with a murder trial and told in flashbacks; tight, suspenseful remake of the 1938 Swedish Ingrid Bergman vehicle. Climax will knock you out of your chair. **107m/B; VHS, DVD.** Joan Crawford; Conrad Veidt; Melvyn Douglas; Osa Massen; Reginald Owen; Albert Bassermann; Marjorie Main; Donald Meek; Charles Quigley; Henry Daniell; George Zucco; Robert Warwick; ***D:*** George Cukor; ***W:*** Donald Ogden Stewart; Elliot Paul; ***C:*** Robert Planck; ***M:*** Bronislau Kaper.

A Woman's Guide to Adultery 🦴🦴 ½ **1993** Four female friends, living and working in London, find their lives turned upside down by their passions for unavailable men. Political advisor Jo (Donohoe) is involved with married politician Martin (McElhinney) while art tutor Jennifer (Gillies) wants her student David (Morrissey), despite his having a live-in girlfriend. Ad execs Helen (Lacey) and Michael (Dunbar) find their marriage in tatters when Helen admits to an affair with their boss and photographer Rose (Russell) breaks her own rule about adultery by getting involved with married university instructor Paul (Bean). Based on the novel by Carol Clewlow. Made for TV. **145m/C; VHS, DVD.** *GB* Theresa Russell; Amanda Donohoe; Sean Bean; Adrian Dunbar; Ingrid Lacey; Fiona Gillies; Neil Morrissey; Danny (Daniel) Webb; Ian McElhinney; Julie Peasgood; Caroline Lee-Johnson; ***D:*** David Hayman; ***W:*** Frank Cottrell-Boyce; ***C:*** Graham Frake; ***M:*** Daemion Barry. **TV**

Womb 🦴🦴 *Clone* **2010** Rebecca (Eva Green) and Thomas (Matt Smith) are childhood friends who become lovers when they are reunited as adults. When Thomas is taken from her again in a car accident, Rebecca decides to be impregnated with his clone. **111m/C; DVD, Blu-Ray, Streaming.** *FR GE HU* Eva Green; Matt Smith; Lesley Manville; Peter Wright; Hannah Murray; ***D:*** Benedek Fliegauf; ***W:*** Benedek Fliegauf; ***C:*** Peter Szatmari; ***M:*** Max Richter. **VIDEO**

The Women 🦴🦴🦴 ½ **1939** A brilliant adaptation of the Clare Boothe Luce stage comedy about a group of women who destroy their best friends' reputations at various social gatherings. Crawford's portrayal of the nasty husband-stealer is classic, and the fashion-show scene in Technicolor is one not to miss. Hilarious bitchiness all around. Remade semi-musically as "The Opposite Sex." Another in that long list of stellar 1939 pics. **133m/B; VHS, DVD, Blu-Ray.** Norma Shearer; Joan Crawford; Rosalind Russell; Joan Fontaine; Mary Boland; Lucile Watson; Margaret Dumont; Paulette Goddard; Ruth Hussey; Marjorie Main; ***D:*** George Cukor; ***W:*** Anita Loos; ***C:*** Joseph Ruttenberg. Natl. Film Reg. '07.

The Women 🦴 ½ *Les Femmes; The Vixen* **1968** Plodding romantic comedy about a blocked writer and his muse. Dizzy Clara (Bardot) is secretary to middle-aged womanizer Jerome (Ronet), who is attempting to work on his memoirs. Inspired by her beauty, Jerome sets out to seduce Clara, which also reinvigorates his writing. But he's thinking fling and she's thinking something more permanent. French with subtitles. **86m/C; VHS, DVD.** *FR IT* Brigitte Bardot; Maurice Ronet; Anny (Annie Legras) Duperey; Jean-Pierre Marielle; Christina Holme; ***D:*** Jean Aurel; ***W:*** Jean Aurel; Cecil Saint-Laurent; ***C:*** Claude Lecomte; ***M:*** Luis Fuentes, Jr.

Women 🦴🦴 ½ *Elles* **1997** Linda (Maura) is a journalist who asks her equally middleaged female friends what they would do with three wishes. Wishes may not help as the ladies suffer through career and family crises, infidelity, affairs, and aging. French with subtitles. **94m/C; VHS, DVD.** *FR* Carmen Maura; Miou-Miou; Marthe Keller; Marisa Berenson; Guesch Patti; Joaquim de Almeida; Didier Flamand; Morgan Perez; ***D:*** Luis Galvao Teles; ***W:*** Don Bohlinger; Luis Galvao Teles; ***C:*** Alfredo Mayo; ***M:*** Alejandro Masso.

The Women 🦴🦴 ½ **2008 (PG-13)** Only borrowing the title and a few ideas from the 1939 film, and mostly just taking inspiration for the original play by Clare Booth Luce—this all-female comedy is very much its own. Wiser and funnier than the women in "Sex and the City," four close friends help each other get through the ups and downs of life—one married with four kids (Messing), one married to a Wall Street millionaire who's cheating on her (Ryan), one a successful fashion magazine editor (Bening), and one who's simply a lesbian (Smith), nothing more. However, even with sharp, honest dialogue and an amazing cast, the introduction of too many characters and too much melodrama ruins what could have been truly great. By the way, take the title literally: not a single man is ever on screen. **114m/C; Blu-Ray, On Demand.** Meg Ryan; Annette Bening; Eva Mendes; Debra Messing; Jada Pinkett Smith; Bette Midler; Candice Bergen; Carrie Fisher; Cloris Leachman; Debi Mazar; Joanna Gleason; Ana Gasteyer; India Ennenga; Lynn Whitfield; ***D:*** Diane English; ***W:*** Diane English; ***C:*** Anastas Michos; ***M:*** Mark Isham.

Women & Men: In Love There Are No Rules 🦴🦴 ½ **1991 (R)** Extravaganza chronicling the relationships of three couples, each adapted from the short story of a renowned author. Irwin Shaw's "Return to Kansas City" tells of a young boxer who is prematurely pushed into a match by his ambitious wife. In Carson McCullers' "A Domestic Dilemma," a marriage begins to crumble thanks to an alcoholic wife. Finally, Henry Miller's "Mara" has an aging man and a young Parisian prostitute spending a revealing evening together. **90m/C; VHS, DVD.** Matt Dillon; Kyra Sedgwick; Ray Liotta; Andie MacDowell; Scott Glenn; Juliette Binoche; Jerry Stiller; ***D:*** Kristi Zea; Walter Bernstein; Mike Figgis. **CABLE**

Women & Men: Stories of Seduction 🦴🦴 ½ **1990** Three famous short stories are brought to the screen in this made-for-TV collection. Mary McCarthy's "The Man in the Brooks Brothers Shirt," Dorothy Parker's "Dusk Before Fireworks," and Hemingway's "Hills Like White Elephants" between them cover every aspect of male-female relationships. Since there are three casts and three directors, there is little to join the stories in style, calling attention to some flaws in pacing and acting ability; still, worth watching. **90m/C; VHS, DVD.** James Woods; Melanie Griffith; Peter Weller; Elizabeth McGovern; Beau Bridges; Molly Ringwald; ***D:*** Ken Russell; Tony Richardson; Frederic Raphael.

Women from the Lake of Scented Souls 🦴🦴 **1994** Mournful film, set in a rural Chinese village, focuses on matriarchal businesswoman Xiang (Gaowa), who runs the local sesame oil making factory that has just attracted the attention of Japanese investors. Seems the water of the nearby lotus-covered lake, scene of local tragedies, is Xiang's special ingredient. With her newfound wealth, Xiang is able to purchase a very reluctant bride, Huanhuan (Yujuan), for her mentally retarded son—a disaster in the making. Rich detail and nuanced performances; Chinese with subtitles. **105m/C; VHS, DVD.** *CH* Siqin Gaowa; Wu Yujuan; Lei Luosheng; Chen Baoguo; ***D:*** Xie Fei; ***W:*** Xie Fei; ***C:*** Bao Xianran; ***M:*** Wang Liping.

Women in Bondage 🦴 ½ **1943** Lurid wartime propaganda from Monogram. Margot Bracken (Patrick) returns to the fatherland when war is declared and her husband is sent to the Russian front. She's appointed section leader of the local Hitler Youth movement but finds it hard to indoctrinate the teenaged girls into Nazi doctrine when she sees some of the horrors for herself. **71m/B; DVD.** Gail Patrick; Nancy Kelly; H.B. Warner; William Henry; ***D:*** Steve Sekely; ***W:*** Houston Branch; ***C:*** Mack Stengler.

Women in Love 🦴🦴🦴 **1970 (R)** Atmospheric drama of two steamy affairs, based on D.H. Lawrence's classic novel. Forward-thinking artist Gudrun (Jackson) and her teacher sister Ursula (Linden) are introduced to Gerald (Reed) and Rupert (Bates). The more conventional Ursual and Rupert marry while Gudrun and Gerald have an affair that ends violently when Gudrun takes up with another man. Deservedly Oscar-winning performance by Jackson; controversial nude wrestling scene with Bates and Reed is hard to forget. Followed nearly two decades later (1989) by a "prequel": "The Rainbow," also from Lawrence, also directed by Russell and featuring Jackson. **129m/C; VHS, DVD, Blu-Ray.** *GB* Glenda Jackson; Jennie Linden; Alan Bates; Oliver Reed; Michael Gough; Eleanor Bron; Vladek Sheybal; ***D:*** Ken Russell; ***W:*** Larry Kramer; ***C:*** Billy Williams; ***M:*** Georges Delerue. Oscars '70: Actress (Jackson); Golden Globes '71: Foreign Film; Natl. Bd. of Review '70: Actress (Jackson); N.Y. Film Critics '70: Actress (Jackson); Natl. Soc. Film Critics '70: Actress (Jackson).

Women in Love 🦴🦴 **2011** BBC drama combines D.H. Lawrence's novels "Women in Love" and its prequel "The Rainbow" to follow the pre-WWI lives of sisters Ursula and Gudrun Brangwen and their passionate involvement with friends Rupert Birkin and Gerald Crich. The men's nude wrestling scene--memorable in Ken Russell's 1970 film--remains, albeit shown under different circumstances. **179m/C; DVD.** *UK* Rachael Stirling; Rosamund Pike; Rory Kinnear; Joseph Mawle; Olivia Grant; James Alexander; ***D:*** Miranda Bowen; ***W:*** William Ivory; ***C:*** George Steel; ***M:*** Chris Letcher. **TV**

Women in Trouble 🦴🦴 **2009 (R)** Director Gutierrez unleashes an uninhibited soap opera about the intersecting lives of a number of women dealing with life-altering crises. Newly pregnant porn star Elektra (Gugino) gets stuck in an elevator with nervous neurotic Doris (Britton). Meanwhile her X-rated co-star Holly Rocket (Palicki) takes on a private client with her pal Bambi (Chriqui). As the plotlines intertwine, the characters are linked by a series of coincidences and their effects. Raunchy behavior and dialogue may offend those with delicate sensibilities. Shot in twelve days on a low budget, this is the first installment in a planned trilogy. The soundtrack is by esteemed alt-rocker Robyn Hitchcock. **95m/C; Blu-Ray, On Demand.** Adrianne Palicki; Isabella Gutierrez; Carla Gugino; Connie Britton; Emmanuelle Chriqui; Sarah Clarke; Marley Shelton; Rya Kihlstedt; Caitlin Keats; Cameron Richardson; Josh Brolin; Simon Baker; Joseph Gordon-Levitt; ***D:*** Sebastian Gutierrez; ***W:*** Sebastian Gutierrez; ***C:*** Cale Finot; ***M:*** Robyn Hitchcock.

The Women of Brewster Place 🦴🦴🦴 **1989** Seven black women living in a tenement fight to gain control of their lives. (Men in general don't come out too well.) Excellent, complex script gives each actress in a fine ensemble headed by Winfrey (in her TV dramatic debut) time in the limelight. Pilot for the series "Brewster Place." Based on the novel by Gloria Naylor. Winfrey was executive producer. **180m/C; VHS, DVD.** Oprah Winfrey; Mary Alice; Olivia Cole; Robin Givens; Moses Gunn; Jackee; Paula Kelly; Lonette McKee; Paul Winfield; Cicely Tyson; ***D:*** Donna Deitch; ***W:*** Karen Hall; ***C:*** Alexander Grusynski; ***M:*** David Shire. **TV**

Women of Valor 🦴 ½ **1986** During WWII, a band of American nurses stationed in the Philippines are captured by the Japanese and struggle to survive in a brutal POW camp. TV feature was made 40 years too late, adding up to a surreal experience.

95m/C; VHS, DVD. Susan Sarandon; Kristy McNichol; Alberta Watson; Valerie Mahaffey; Suzanne Lederer; Pat Bishop; Terry O'Quinn; Neva Patterson; ***D:*** Buzz Kulik; ***C:*** Mike Fash; ***M:*** Georges Delerue. **TV**

The Women on the Sixth Floor 1/2 *Les Femmes du 6e Etage* **2010** Breezy French comedy set in Paris in 1962. Bourgeois stockbroker Jean-Louis and his neurotic, socialite wife Suzanne can't cope when their longtime maid quits. They hire newcomer Maria, who is one of several Spanish maids living in tiny rooms on the 6th floor of the building and working for various tenants. Jean-Louis is soon taken by their joie de vivre--as well as Maria's other charms--and expands his outlook on life. French and Spanish with subtitles. **104m/C; DVD.** *FR* Fabrice Luchini; Sandrine Kiberlain; Natalia Verbeke; Carmen Maura; Lola Duenas; Berta Ojea; ***D:*** Philippe Le Guay; ***W:*** Philippe Le Guay; Jerome Tonnerre; ***C:*** Jean-Claude Larrieu; ***M:*** Jorge Arriagada.

Women on the Verge of a Nervous Breakdown 1/2 *Mujeres al Borde de un Ataque de Nervios* **1988 (R)** Surreal and hilarious romp through the lives of film dubber Maura, her ex-lover, his crazed wife, his new lover, his son, and his son's girlfriend. There's also Maura's friend Barranco, who inadvertantly lent her apartment to Shiite terrorists and now believes the police are after her as an accomplice in an airline hijacking. They meet in a comedy of errors, missed phone calls, and rental notices, while discovering the truth and necessity of love. Fast-paced and full of black humor, with loaded gazpacho serving as a key element. Introduced Almodovar to American audiences. In Spanish with English subtitles. **88m/C; VHS, DVD, Blu-Ray.** *SP* Carmen Maura; Fernando Guillen; Julieta Serrano; Maria Barranco; Rossy de Palma; Antonio Banderas; ***D:*** Pedro Almodóvar; ***W:*** Pedro Almodóvar; ***C:*** Jose Luis Alcaine; ***M:*** Bernardo Bonezzi. N.Y. Film Critics '88: Foreign Film.

Women vs. Men **2002 (R)** Michael (Mantegna) is a typical married guy bewildered when Dana (Lahti), his wife of 20 years, begins behaving out of character. (She's basically fed up with her hubby and their boring marriage.) His best bud Bruce (Reiser) decides they should go to a strip club and commiserate but doesn't know that Dana is following them. Furious, Dana reports the guys' sleazy night out to Bruce's wife, Brita (Headley). Equally peeved, they kick their husbands out, leading Michael and Bruce to get advice from their swinger divorced buddy Nick (Pastorelli). Basic battle-of-the-sexes flick. **88m/C; VHS, DVD.** Joe Mantegna; Christine Lahti; Paul Reiser; Glenne Headly; Jennifer Coolidge; Robert Pastorelli; Marshall Herskovitz; Jon Polito; ***D:*** Chazz Palminteri; ***W:*** David J. Burke. **CABLE**

Women Who Kill **2017 91m/C; DVD, Blu-Ray, Streaming.** Annette O'Toole; Sheila Vand; Deborah Rush; Tami Sagher; Grace Rex; ***D:*** Ingrid Jungermann; ***W:*** Ingrid Jungermann; ***C:*** Robert Leitzell.

Women Without Men *Zanan Bedoone Mardan* **2009** Intertwined narrative about four Iranian women in August, 1953 when a CIA-backed coup topples the government and installs the Shah. There's would-be political activist Munis who kills herself (which doesn't prevent her reappearance in the plot); her religiously observant friend Faezeh; unhappily married Fakhri who leaves her overbearing army general husband to buy an orchard; and runaway prostitute Zarin who takes refuge there. Adapted from Shahrnush Parsipur's magical realist novel; Farsi with subtitles. **95m/C; Blu-Ray.** *AT FR GE* Pegah Ferydoni; Artia Shahrzad; Shabnam Toloui; Orsi Toth; Bijan Daneshmand; ***D:*** Shirin Neshat; Shoja Azari; ***W:*** Shirin Neshat; Shoja Azari; Steven Henry Madoff; ***C:*** Martin Gschlacht; ***M:*** Ryuichi Sakamoto; Abbas Bakhtiari.

The Women's Balcony 1/2 *Ismach Hatani* **2016** A profound comedy about a devout Orthodox community that includes sharp commentary about fanaticism, sexism, and tolerance. In a Jerusalem neighborhood, the women's balcony in a gender-segregated synagogue collapses during a bar mitzvah and leaves the building unsafe. The incident renders the elderly rabbi unable to lead. He is replaced by the charismatic Rabbi David (Aviv Alush), who tells the flock that the collapse is God's judgement, oversees the reconstruction project, and wants to ban women from the new synagogue's main room all together. Rabbi David's anti-woman pronouncements affect marriages, friendships, and alliances. The character-driven humor offers sharp insights while entertaining. Hebrew with subtitles. **96m/C; DVD.** Evelin Hagoel; Igal Naor; Orna Banai; Einat Saruf; Avraham Aviv Alush; ***D:*** Emil Ben-Shimon; ***W:*** Shlomit Nehama; ***C:*** Ziv Berkovich.

Women's Prison **1955** Babes-behind-bars with an uninhibited performance by Lupino as sadistic prison warden Amelia Van Zandt. Amelia takes out her frustrations on her inmates despite doc Crane (Duff) trying to make improvements in their care. Fed-up cons Brenda (Sterling) and Mae (Moore) decide it's simpler to start a riot after Amelia's evil ways led to the death of prisoner Joan (Totter). **80m/B; DVD.** Ida Lupino; Jan Sterling; Cleo Moore; Howard Duff; Audrey Totter; Phyllis Thaxter; Warren Stevens; Mae Clarke; ***D:*** Lewis Seiler; ***W:*** Crane Wilbur; Jack DeWitt; ***C:*** Lester White; ***M:*** Mischa Bakaleinikoff.

Women's Prison Escape 1/2 *Cell Block Girls; Thunder County* **1974** Four tough broads blow the pen and are forced to high-tail it through the Everglades. They can't decide which is worse, the snakes and 'gators, or the corrupt and sleazy life they left behind. Only cinematic pairing of Rooney and Lurch. **90m/C; VHS, DVD.** Ted Cassidy; Chris Robinson; Mickey Rooney; ***D:*** Chris Robinson.

Wonder 1/2 **2017 (PG)** A warm, moving look at a pivotal year in the life of a young boy born with genetic abnormalities. After years of medical treatment and being homeschooled by his mother Isabel (Roberts), 10-year-old August "Auggie" Pullman (Tremblay) is an imaginative, funny boy who is obsessed with science. Attending Beecher Prep for the first time, Auggie is tormented by some students but finds a true friend in Jack Will (Jupe), a scholarship student. Full of empathy and emotion. **113m/C; DVD, Blu-Ray.** Jacob Tremblay; Owen Wilson; Izabela Vidovic; Julia Roberts; Mandy Patinkin; ***D:*** Stephen Chbosky; ***W:*** Stephen Chbosky; Steve Conrad; Jack Thorne; ***C:*** Don Burgess; ***M:*** Marcelo Zarvos.

Wonder Bar **1934** This Pre-Hays Code Jolson pic pushes the limits for suggestiveness with Busby Berkeley doing his usual extravagant choreography. Al Wonder (Jolson) is the owner of a Paris nightspot who's in love with dancer Inez (Del Rio). So's band singer Tommy (Powell) but Inez only has eyes for her gigolo partner Harry (Cortez). Harry's cheating with married socialite Liane (Francis) and there's a bunch more subplots about the customers and such. Jolson (in blackface) does the now-very dated (not to mention strange) song 'I'm Going to Heaven on a Mule' accompanied by a number of black children with all the angels black as well. **84m/B; DVD.** Al Jolson; Dick Powell; Dolores Del Rio; Ricardo Cortez; Kay Francis; Guy Kibbee; Ruth Donnelly; Louise Fazenda; ***D:*** Lloyd Bacon; ***W:*** Earl Baldwin; ***C:*** Sol Polito.

Wonder Boys **2000 (R)** Curis Hanson's excellent follow up to "L.A. Confidential" pits professor and former literary star Grady (Douglas in his finest performance in years) against a strange case of writer's block, his flamboyant New York editor (Downey), an approaching literary festival, and several converging mid-life crises. His wife's just left, he's having an affair with the school chancellor (McDormand), who's the wife of his boss and has just informed him that she's pregnant, and his prize pupil is a death-obsessed compulsive liar (Maguire) who shoots his boss's dog and steals a valuable piece of memorabilia. On paper it seems chaotic, but the screwball comedy manages to be subtle and understated. Based on Michael Chambon's novel. **112m/C; VHS, DVD.** Michael Douglas; Tobey Maguire; Frances McDormand; Katie Holmes; Robert Downey, Jr.; Richard Thomas; Rip Torn; Philip Bosco; Jane Adams; ***D:*** Curtis Hanson; ***W:*** Steve Kloves; ***C:*** Dante Spinotti; ***M:*** Christopher Young. Oscars '00: Song ("Things Have Changed"); Golden Globes '01: Song ("Things Have Changed").

Wonder Man 1/2 **1945** When a brash nightclub entertainer (Kaye) is killed by gangsters, his mild-mannered twin brother (Kaye) takes his place to smoke out the killers. One of Kaye's better early films. The film debuts of Vera-Ellen and Cochran. Look for Mrs. Howell of "Gilligan's Island." **98m/C; DVD.** Danny Kaye; Virginia Mayo; Vera-Ellen; Steve Cochran; S.Z. Sakall; Otto Kruger; Natalie Schafer; ***D:*** H. Bruce Humberstone; ***W:*** Don Hartman; Jack Jevne; Eddie Moran; Philip Rapp; Melville Shavelson; ***C:*** Victor Milner; ***M:*** Ray Heindorf.

Wonder Park **2019 (PG)** Smart June (Denski) is close with her mother (Garner), and they spend hours creating an imaginary world centered on a fabulous theme park called Wonder Park. When June's mom is diagnosed with a life-threatening illness, she must go away for treatment and June's father (Broderick) sends reluctant June to a math camp. On her way there, June gets off the bus, wanders in the forest, and finds a complete yet rundown version of Wonder Park. June must take action to save the park and the depressed talking animals who live there. A rather bland animated film that awkwardly waffles between sorrow and fun and games. **85m/C; DVD, Blu-Ray.** *SP US* Sofia Mali; Jennifer Garner; Ken Hudson Campbell; Kenan Thompson; Mila Kunis; ***D:*** Dylan Brown; ***W:*** Josh Appelbaum; André Nemec; ***C:*** Juan Garcia Gonzalez; ***M:*** Steven Price.

Wonder Wheel 1/2 **2017 (PG-13)** A problematic Woody Allen film that explores a love triangle in early 1950s Coney Island. Living in the middle of the amusement park, Ginny (Winslet) struggles with her disappointing life. She is married to the crude Humpty (Belushi) and has a pyromaniac for a young son. Her world is turned upside down by the appearance of Mickey (Timberlake), a lifeguard and wannabe playwright. Their affair is cut short when Humpty's daughter Carolina (Temple) shows up as she hides from her mobster husband and takes up with Mickey. Though the film is bright at times, it suffers from improbable plot turns and overwrought performances. **101m/C; DVD, Blu-Ray.** Jim Belushi; Juno Temple; Justin Timberlake; Kate Winslet; Max Casella; ***D:*** Woody Allen; ***W:*** Woody Allen; ***C:*** Vittorio Storaro.

Wonder Woman 1/2 **1974** Before Lynda Carter gave the spandex a try, Cathy Lee Crosby starred in this ABC TV movie adaptation of the DC Comics heroine. Less of a superhero and more of a superspy, this one has Wonder Woman as a 70s espionage agent instead of her traditional role of fighting the Nazis in WWII. **73m/C; DVD.** Cathy Lee Crosby; Kaz Garas; Andrew Prine; Ricardo Montalban; Charlene Holt; ***D:*** Vincent McEveety; ***W:*** John D.F. Black; William M. Marston; ***C:*** Joseph Biroc; ***M:*** Artie Butler. **TV**

Wonder Woman **2017 (PG-13)** Glorious and long-overdue tribute to the Amazon princess. After Diana (Gadot) rescues Trevor (Pine) from his wrecked biplane off the shores of Themyscira, she abandons her idyllic island of female warriors with the singular determination to kill Ares, thereby exorcising evil from mankind and halting the war to end all wars. Gadot's Diana wears her heart on her gold cuffs, sporting a charming naïveté that belies powers still largely unexplored but already understood enough to lead men into battle. Finally, a female superhero movie worthy of--and welcomed into--the DC pantheon. **141m/C; DVD, Blu-Ray.** Gal Gadot; Chris Pine; Connie Nielsen; Robin Wright; Danny Huston; ***D:*** Patty Jenkins; ***W:*** Allan Heinberg; ***C:*** Matthew Jensen; ***M:*** Rupert Gregson-Williams.

The Wonderful Country **1959** American gunslinger/gunrunner Martin Brody is living in Mexico but heads to Texas to do a deal for his boss, Castro. Brody breaks a leg and is looked after by Ellen, the wife of Army Major Colton. A gun shipment is stolen and Brody's boss is an unhappy man. A Texas Ranger is also involved and the various plot threads tangle up Brody more and more. Baseball great Satchel Paige has a role as a Buffalo Soldier. **98m/C; DVD.** Robert Mitchum; Julie London; Gary Merrill; Pedro Armendariz, Sr.; Victor Manuel Mendoza; Jack Oakie; Albert Dekker; Charles McGraw; Leroy Robert Paige; ***D:*** Robert Parrish; ***W:*** Robert Ardrey; ***C:*** Floyd Crosby; Alex Phillips; ***M:*** Alex North.

The Wonderful Ice Cream Suit 1/2 **1998 (PG)** Slapstick hokum based on Bradbury's 1957 story "The Magic White Suit." Cash-poor barrio sharpster Gomez (Mantegna) would like to buy a flashy white suit he sees in a shop window and manages to convince four more men of roughly the same size to pony up some money and have shares in the suit. Each take a turn wearing the garment and find their various dreams coming true. **77m/C; VHS, DVD, Streaming.** Joe Mantegna; Esai Morales; Edward James Olmos; Clifton (Gonzalez) Collins, Jr.; Gregory Sierra; Liz Torres; Sid Caesar; Howard Morris; Lisa Vidal; Mike Moroff; ***D:*** Stuart Gordon; ***W:*** Ray Bradbury; ***C:*** Mac Ahlberg.

Wonderful Town 1/2 **2007** When a seaside community is almost destroyed by a Tsunami, a young architect volunteers to spend two months there to help rebuild the community. When he falls in love with a hotel owner, they have to be careful as the small town doesn't like outsiders, and she doesn't feel it would be safe for her family to know she is seeing one. Which of course means it's obviously not safe for them to date. **92m/C; DVD.** *TH* Anchalee Saisoontorn; Supphasit Kansen; Dul Yaambunying; ***D:*** Aditya Assarat; ***W:*** Aditya Assarat; ***C:*** Ampornpol Yukol; ***M:*** Koichi Shimizu.

Wonderful World 1/2 **2009 (R)** Once a semi-successful children's music performer, discontented, pot-smoking misanthrope Ben Singer (Broderick playing the ultimate mope) is now floundering in his proofreading job and as a weekend dad. He's such a hopeless downer that even his tween daughter Sandra (Ferland) is refusing his custodial visits. Ben's only friendship is with his Sengalese roommate Ibou (Williams), who falls into a diabetic coma and then becomes part of a managed medical care nightmare. Ben decides a lawsuit against the city is the way to go but that has unexpected consequences, including the arrival of Ibou's hopeful sister Khadi (Lathan) who moves in with Ben (and starts him rethinking his depressing ways) while her brother's fate is being decided. **95m/C; DVD.** Matthew Broderick; Michael K(enneth) Williams; Sanaa Lathan; Jodelle Ferland; Ally Walker; Philip Baker Hall; Jesse Tyler Ferguson; ***D:*** Joshua Goldin; ***W:*** Joshua Goldin; ***C:*** Daniel Shulman; ***M:*** Craig Richey.

Wonderland **1999** Slice of London pic covers four November days in the lives of sisters Debbie (Henderson), Nadia (McKee), and Molly (Parker) and their daily struggles—single parenthood, bad dates, pregnancy, separation, unemployment, and their equally frustrated parents. Yet the film is about the ability to survive rather than about succumbing to despair. **108m/C; VHS, DVD.** *GB* Shirley Henderson; Gina McKee; Molly Parker; Ian Hart; John Simm; Stuart Townsend; Kika Markham; Jack Shepherd; ***D:*** Michael Winterbottom; ***W:*** Laurence Coriat; ***C:*** Sean Bobbitt; ***M:*** Michael Nyman.

Wonderland **2003 (R)** Inferior true-crime drama about down-on-his-luck, druggie porn star John C. Holmes (Kilmer) who got mixed up in a 1981 quadruple homicide at 8763 Wonderland Avenue, where Holmes partied and bought his drugs. Kudrow, in a standout performance, plays his long-suffering wife Sharon and Bosworth his much-younger girlfriend Dawn. While emphasis is on the crime and what role Holmes played in it, pic may have benefited from further exploring the relationship between Sharon and Dawn, who became life-long friends. The anatomically gifted Holmes, is adequately portrayed by Kilmer. Told in confused, back and forward chronology, events and motivations muddle an interesting story much better articulated in director Anderson's fictitious but far superior ode to the porno industry, "Boogie Nights." **99m/C; VHS, DVD.** Val Kilmer; Kate (Catherine) Bosworth; Lisa Kudrow; Dylan McDermott; Eric Bogosian; Josh(ua) Lucas; Christina Applegate; Tim Blake Nelson; Ted Levine; Natasha Gregson Wagner; Janeane Garofalo; Franky G.; M.C. Gainey; Carrie Fisher; Faizon Love; ***D:*** James Cox; ***W:*** James Cox; Captain Mauzner; Todd Samovitz; D. Loriston Scott; ***C:*** Michael Grady; ***M:*** Michael A. Levine.

The Wonders 1/2 *Le Meraviglie; Land der Wunder* **2015** A delicate family story told in the way only writer/director Alice Rohrwacher can tell it. Gelsomina (Alexandra Lungu) has three younger sisters, and lives a peaceful, almost lyrical life. She is a part of a family of beekeepers in the Tuscan countryside, a group who watches their idyllic world change forever when they're asked to be a part of a TV show. At the same time, a troubled young man enters this estrogen-heavy world. Rohrwacher's film is unique in its manner and style, almost replicating those final days of summer when we still enjoy the sun but know things are about to change. **100m/C; DVD.** *GE IT SI* Alba Rohrwacher; Maria Alexandra Lungu; Sam Louwyck; Sabine Timoteo; Agnese Graziani; Monica Bellucci; *D:* Alice Rohrwacher; *W:* Alice Rohrwacher; *C:* Helene Louvart; *M:* Piero Crucitti.

Wonderstruck 1/2 **2017 (PG)** Based on a novel by Brian Selznick (who also wrote the screenplay), this warm drama blends the quests of two deaf children, separated by 50 years, to locate someone: Ben tries to track down his absent father, and Rose seeks out a mother-figure in a famous actress. Unlike most movies for -- and starring -- children, this film is quiet and intelligent, with gorgeous cinematography and artfully woven time jumps (Rose's scenes are black and white). The intersection between the two stories can be seen from far off, but its predictability doesn't diminish the journey. The first film for Simmonds, deaf in real life, who utterly lights up the screen. **117m/C; DVD, Blu-Ray.** Oakes Fegley; Julianne Moore; Michelle Williams; Millicent Simmonds; Tom Noonan; *D:* Todd Haynes; *W:* Brian Selznick; *C:* Edward Lachman; *M:* Carter Burwell.

Wonderwall: The Movie **1969** Weird psychedelic curio. Middle-aged professor Oscar Collins accidentally knocks a hole in his apartment wall, letting him peek at his young and beautiful model neighbor, Penny Lane. So he's an obsessed voyeur. Score is by George Harrison. **82m/C; DVD, Blu-Ray.** *UK* Jack MacGowran; Jane Birkin; Irene Handl; *D:* Joe Massot; *W:* G. Cabrera Infante; *C:* Harry Waxman; *M:* George Harrison.

Wondrous Oblivion **2006 (PG)** Though 11-year-old David (Smith) loves the sport of cricket, he lacks the skills, so when a cricket-loving Jamaican family moves in next door he's overjoyed. The family's patriarch, Dennis Samuels (Lindo) offers to teach him. While the young Jewish boy at first has no qualms about befriending the Samuels, the rest of their South London neighbors aren't so accepting, it being the racially-charged 1960s and all, and eventually David finds himself in an awkward situation. Avoids being sappy, and Lindo really rules as the father. **106m/C; DVD.** Sam Smith; Jo Stone-Fewings; Emily Woof; Leagh Conwell; Dominic Barklem; Delroy Lindo; Carol MacReady; Yasmin Paige; Stanley Townsend; *D:* Paul Morrison; *W:* Paul Morrison; *C:* Nina Kellgren; *M:* Ilona Sekacz. **VIDEO**

Won't Back Down 1/2 **2012 (PG)** Two very talented actresses, Davis and Gyllenhaal, prove that all of the acting ability in the world can't overcome the kind of muck that this screenplay delivers. The two play mothers trying to reform their children's failing inner city school and dealing with all of the Hollywood clichés that come with it. Education reform is an important issue in the new millennium as big-city schools continue to fail the next generation and so director Barnz's melodramatic handling of such a serious concern feels altogether exploitative. Only the sincerity of Davis and Gyllenhaal keep it from Lifetime TV movie territory. **121m/C; DVD, Blu-Ray.** Maggie Gyllenhaal; Viola Davis; Oscar Isaac; Rosie Perez; Ving Rhames; Lance Reddick; Marianne Jean-Baptiste; Bill Nunn; Emily Ann Lind; Dante Brown; Holly Hunter; *D:* Daniel Barnz; *W:* Daniel Barnz; *C:* Roman Osin; *M:* Marcelo Zarvos.

Won't You Be My Neighbor? 1/2 **2018 (PG-13)** An honest and moving portrayal of Fred Rogers, the host of the children's television show "Mr. Rogers' Neighborhood." The man was far more than a mild-mannered cardigan wearer. His genuine kindness, compassion, and patience were boundless, uplifting children and adults alike. He embraced the Civil Rights movement, and even testified before Congress to save PBS from being gutted to fund the Vietnam War. This doc features archive footage of Rogers along with interviews of some of the people he inspired over the decades. **94m/C; DVD, Blu-Ray.** Fred Rogers; Joanne Rogers; Betty Aberlin; Jim Rogers; Yo-Yo Ma; *D:* Morgan Neville; *C:* Graham Willoughby; *M:* Jonathan Kirkscey. Ind. Spirit '19: Feature Doc.

Woo **1997 (R)** Knock-out party girl Darlene "Woo" Bates (Pinkett Smith) agrees to a blind date with nice-guy law student Tim (Davidson) on the advice of her cross-dressing psychic. Tim wants to do the right thing and be honorable, but Woo seduces, endangers, and humiliates him at every turn. When Tim finally stands up for himself, she has a change of heart and appreciates his better qualities. Somewhat mean-spirited comedy trods familiar urban cliches and blind-date disaster territory, but Pinkett Smith's turn could be a star-maker. **80m/C; VHS, DVD.** Jada Pinkett Smith; Tommy Davidson; Duane Martin; Dave Chappelle; LL Cool J; Paula Jai Parker; Darrell Heath; Pam Grier; Jsu Garcia; Isaac Hayes; *D:* Daisy von Scherler Mayer; *W:* David C(lark) Johnson; *C:* Jean Lepine; *M:* Michel Colombier.

The Wood 1/2 **1999 (R)** Follows the friendship of three young black men growing up together during the 80s in Inglewood, California. Through the use of flashbacks, their lives are traced from junior high to the imminent wedding day of one of the trio. Mike (Epps) and Slim (Jones) are also forced to track down reluctant groom Roland (Diggs), sober him up, and get him to the church on time. Newcomer Famuyiwa based the script on his own life. Good cast is left with little interesting to do in this likable, but bland, nostalgia-fest. **107m/C; VHS, DVD.** Omar Epps; Sean Nelson; Richard T. Jones; Taye Diggs; Trent Cameron; Malinda Williams; Duane Finley; Sanaa Lathan; De'Aundre Bonds; LisaRaye; Cynthia Martells; Tamala Jones; Elayne J. Taylor; *D:* Rick Famuyiwa; *W:* Rick Famuyiwa; *C:* Steven Bernstein; *M:* Robert Hurst.

Woodchipper Massacre WOOF! **1989** Aunt Tess is frozen in the freezer, waiting to be turned into whatever the fleshy equivalent of woodchips is by her three unloving relations, and her totally evil son has just broken out of prison looking to retrieve his inheritance. You think you have problems? You'll have one less if you leave this one on the shelf. **90m/C; VHS, DVD.** Jon McBride; Patricia McBride; *D:* Jon McBride.

The Wooden Man's Bride **1994** The inhabitants of this austere 1920s, northwest Chinese community live in stone fortresses, fearful of being attacked by roving armed bandits. Which is what happens to the bridal party of Young Mistress (Lan), who's kidnapped by bandit leader Tang (Mingjun). She's released unharmed when her servant Kui (Shih) impresses Tang with his bravery but her bridegroom has been killed in a freak accident and formidable Madame Liu (Yumei), who runs the fortress, forces her to marry a wooden likeness of the deceased. Despairing Young Mistress begins an affair with Kui, which can only end badly. Mandarin with subtitles. **114m/C; VHS, DVD.** *CH* Wang Lan; Chang Shih; Wang Yu-mei; Kao Mingjun; *D:* Huang Jianxin; *W:* Yang Zhengguang; *C:* Zhang Xiaoguang; *M:* Zhang Dalong.

The Woods **2003 (R)** In 1965, isolated Falburn Academy is an all-girls New England boarding school. Troublesome new student Heather (Bruckner) is determined to get thrown out so she can return home, but she's got other problems. It seems the surrounding woods are giving Heather nightmares, her classmates start disappearing, and sinister headmistress Mrs. Traverse (Clarkson) wants to recruit Heather as a witch. Campbell is briefly seen as Heather's clueless pop. **91m/C; DVD.** Agnes Bruckner; Patricia Clarkson; Rachel Nichols; Bruce Campbell; *D:* Lucky McKee; *W:* David Ross; *C:* John R. Leonetti; *M:* John (Gianni) Frizzell. **VIDEO**

The Woods Have Eyes **2007** Cheap backwoods horror about summer campers in upstate New York. Joe and Carmine scare the kids with the campfire legend of killer Cappy's Cabin. They then persuade the youngsters to go into the woods and look for the cabin so they can frighten them some more, but the cabin turns out to be a real place and occupied by Cappy and his homicidal twin sons. **87m/C; DVD, Blu-Ray.** Joseph Anthony; Garrett Harrison; Michael Bolten; Taylor Jeffers; A.J. Diafero; Cody Greer; John Kyle; Michael Christeas; Adam Dunnells; *D:* Anthony Indelicato; *W:* Anthony Indelicato; Jason Noto; *C:* Valentina Caniglia. **VIDEO**

Woodshock 1/2 **2017 (R)** In a foggy northern California town, Theresa (Dunst) helps her terminally ill mother (Traylor) commit suicide. As Theresa processes this traumatic event, she continues to work in a medical marijuana dispensary, lacks helpful relationships with her boyfriend Nick (Cole) and boss Keith (Asbaek), and repeatedly wanders in a forest. Though the debut feature by designer sisters Kate and Laura Mulleavy--the creative force behind Rodarte--successfully emphasizes its 1970s-inspired visual elements at times, this hazy, dull drama lacks a coherent plot and compelling characters. **100m/C; DVD, Blu-Ray.** Kirsten Dunst; Joe Cole; Pilou Asbaek; Steph Duvall; Jack Kilmer; *D:* Kate Mulleavy; Laura Mulleavy; *W:* Kate Mulleavy; Laura Mulleavy; *C:* Peter Flinckenberg; *M:* Peter Raeburn.

The Woodsman **2004 (R)** Kassell's feature debut is not for the faint-hearted. How do you not depict a convicted pedophile of young girls as a monster? It's a measure of Bacon's talents as Walter that if you can't sympathize with his character (and you're not asked to), you do come to some understanding of his torment. Recently paroled after a 12-year prison term, Walter finds a job in a lumberyard and an apartment opposite a grade school. As Walter struggles to keep his sexual impulses in check, he starts his first adult relationship with equally scarred co-worker Vickie (Bacon's wife Sedgwick), even as receptionist Mary-Kay (Eve) and cop Lucas (Mos Def) become suspicious of withdrawn Walter's behavior. Disturbing without becoming explicit and with a sliver of hopefulness in its resolution. Co-writer Fechter adapted from his play. **87m/C; DVD.** Kevin Bacon; Kyra Sedgwick; Eve; Mos Def; David Alan Grier; Benjamin Bratt; Michael Shannon; Hannah Pilkes; Carlos Leon; *D:* Nicole Kassell; *W:* Nicole Kassell; Steven Fechter; *C:* Xavier Perez Grobet; *M:* Nathan Larson.

Woodstock **1970 (R)** Step into the way-back machine and return to the times of luv, peace, and understanding. Powerful chronicle of the great 1969 Woodstock rock concert celebrates the music and lifestyle of the late '60s. More than 400,000 spectators withstood lack of privacy, bathrooms, parking, and food while wallowing in the mud for four days to catch classic performances by a number of popular performers and groups. Martin Scorcese helped edit the documentary, trail-blazing in its use of split-screen montage. A director's cut is available at 225 minutes. **180m/C; VHS, DVD, Blu-Ray.** *D:* Michael Wadleigh. Oscars '70: Feature Doc.; Natl. Film Reg. '96.

Word Wars: Tiles and Tribulations on the Scrabble Circuit **2004** Four unconventional competitors make their way to the 2002 National Scrabble Tournament in San Diego pursing the $25, 000 grand prize. The characters are authentic oddballs, their world becomes more arcane and peculiar the longer you're in it, and the suspense approaches desperation at the end, all of which makes the film watchable in this age of reality TV. **80m/C; DVD.** *D:* Eric Chaikin; Julian Petrillo; *C:* Laela Kilbourn; *M:* Thor Madsen.

Wordplay **2006** Creadon looks at the passion of crossword puzzle fans and champions by following "New York Times" crossword puzzle editor Will Shortz as he prepares for the 28th annual American Crossword Puzzle Tournament in 2005. He interviews puzzle designers, competitors, and such crossword puzzlers as John Stewart, Bill Clinton, and Ken Burns. **90m/C; DVD.** *D:* Patrick Creadon; *W:* Patrick Creadon; Christine O'Malley; *C:* Patrick Creadon; *M:* Peter Golub.

The Words **2012 (PG-13)** Struggling novelist Rory (Cooper) stumbles across the lost pages of a novel in a leather case bought by his wife (Saldana, serving as eye candy) and publishes it as his own. Problem is, the actual writer is an old man (Irons) who confronts Rory. This leads to a barrage of unnecessary characters appearing and disappearing too quickly, all with a confounding timeline that shifts between eras. The basis of the story, as most Ernest Hemingway fans would know, is his unpublished works (through 1922) that were packed in a briefcase then lost by his wife on a train. If only this story was as compelling. **96m/C; DVD, Blu-Ray.** Dennis Quaid; Bradley Cooper; Jeremy Irons; Zoe Saldana; Olivia Wilde; J.K. Simmons; *D:* Brian Klugman; Lee Sternthal; *W:* Brian Klugman; Lee Sternthal; *C:* Antonio Calvache; *M:* Marcelo Zarvos.

Words and Music 1/2 **1948** Plot based on the careers of Rodgers and Hart is little more than a peg on which to hang lots of classic songs, sung by a parade of MGM stars. Also includes Kelly's dance recreation of "Slaughter on Tenth Avenue." Good advice: if no one's singing or dancing, fast forward. **122m/C; VHS, DVD.** Mickey Rooney; Tom Drake; Judy Garland; Gene Kelly; Lena Horne; Mel Torme; Cyd Charisse; Marshall Thompson; Janet Leigh; Betty Garrett; June Allyson; Perry Como; Vera-Ellen; Ann Sothern; *D:* Norman Taurog; *M:* Richard Rodgers.

Words and Pictures 1/2 **2013 (PG-13)** It's hard to believe that a romantic movie starring the wildly charismatic Owen and Binoche could be this dull but Schepisi's latest stinker accomplished the near-impossible. Believe it or not, the title is not merely generic. Owen plays an English teacher; Binoche plays an art teacher. They collide at an upscale prep school as the students there try to prove which is more valuable, words or pictures. Of course, they fall in love and deal with their own troubled pasts at the same time. And everyone smiles and skips off into the sunset. **111m/C; DVD, Blu-Ray.** Clive Owen; Juliette Binoche; Bruce Davison; Amy Brenneman; *D:* Fred Schepisi; *W:* Gerard Di-Pego; *C:* Ian Baker; *M:* Paul Grabowsky.

Words by Heart 1/2 **1984** An African American family in turn of the century Missouri faces issues of discrimination and prejudice. Twelve-year-old Lena wins a speech contest and begins to question their place in the community and their aspirations for a better life. Based on a book by Ouida Sebestyen. Aired by PBS as part of the "Wonderworks" family movie series. **116m/C; VHS, DVD.** Charlotte Rae; Robert Hooks; Alfre Woodard; *D:* Robert Thompson. **TV**

The Work **2017** A deeply powerful documentary about men, prison rehabilitation, and intensive group therapy. Shot in Folsom State Prison, the film explores the complex emotions and dynamics during a four-day session in which convicts and members of the public come together for group therapy. The free men share and initially experience catharsis merely by being there, but soon reveal some of their own emotional release. Some of the incarcerated also share their stories and feelings, and achieve honest understanding of their pain. **89m/C; DVD.** *D:* Jairus McLeary; Gethin Aldous; *C:* Arturo Santamaria.

Working Girl **1988 (R)** Romantic comedy set in the Big Apple has secretary Tess McGill (Griffith) working her way to the top in spite of her manipulative boss Katherine Parker (Weaver in a powerful parody). Tess gets her chance to shine when Katherine breaks a leg and she strikes a business deal with Jack Trainer (Ford)that turns to romance. A 1980s Cinderella story that's sexy, funny, and sharply written and directed. Nice work by Ford, but this is definitely Griffith's movie. And keep an eye on Tess's gal pal Cynthia (Cusack). **115m/C; VHS, DVD, Blu-Ray.** Melanie Griffith; Harrison Ford; Sigourney Weaver; Joan Cusack; Alec Baldwin; Philip Bosco; Ricki Lake; Nora Dunn; Olympia Dukakis; Oliver Platt; James Lally; Kevin Spacey; Robert Easton; *D:* Mike Nichols; *W:* Kevin Wade; *C:* Michael Ballhaus; *M:* Carly Simon; Rob Mounsey. Oscars '88: Song ("Let the River Run"); Golden Globes '89: Actress--Mus./Comedy (Griffith), Film--Mus./Comedy, Song ("Let the River Run"), Support. Actress (Weaver).

Working Girls **1975 (R)** Three girls who share an apartment in Los Angeles are willing to do anything for money. And they do. For lack of anything else to recommend, watch for the striptease by Peterson, better known as Elvira on TV. **80m/C; VHS, DVD.** Sarah Kennedy; Laurie Rose; Mark Thomas; Cassandra Peterson; *D:* Stephanie Rothman.

Working Girls **1987** An acclaimed, controversial look by independent filmmaker Borden into lives of modern brothel prostitutes over the period of one day. The sex is realistically candid and perfunctory; the docudrama centers on a prostitute who is a Yale graduate and aspiring photographer living with a female lover. Compelling, touching, and lasting, with sexually candid language and scenery. **93m/C; VHS, DVD.** Amanda Goodwin; Louise Smith; Ellen McElduff; Maurisia Zach; Janne Peters; Helen Nicholas; ***D:*** Lizzie Borden; ***W:*** Lizzie Borden; Sandra Kay; ***C:*** Judy Irola; ***M:*** David Van Tiegham.

The Working Man 🦴🦴 ½ **1933** Rich shoe manufacturer John Reeves (Arliss) is upset when his rival dies because he misses the competition. Leaving his own business in the hands of his know-it-all nephew Benjamin (Albright), Reeves meets Tommy (Newton) and Jenny (Davis) Hartland, the offspring of his late competitor, and realizes they're squandering their inheritance. He manipulates his way into their company, revamps it, and then goes after his own business (to teach Ben a lesson) before revealing who he actually is to the Hartlands. **77m/B; DVD.** George Arliss; Bette Davis; Theodore Newton; Hardie Albright; Gordon Westcott; J. Farrell MacDonald; ***D:*** John G. Adolfi; ***W:*** Maude Howell; Charles Kenyon; ***C:*** Sol Polito.

Working Miracles 🦴🦴 ½ *Healing Hands* **2010** Hallmark Channel original. School janitor Buddy Hoyt (Cibrian) is just an average guy until an accident puts him in a coma. When he awakens, Buddy discovers he has the power to heal but his new gift is problematic since it takes an enormous toll on him physically and starts affecting his relationship with fiancee Alice (Sheridan). **100m/C; DVD.** Eddie Cibrian; Lisa Sheridan; Alexandra Holden; Patrick Duffy; Meagen Fay; ***D:*** Bradford May; ***W:*** Steven H. Berman; ***C:*** Maximo Munzi; ***M:*** Lawrence Shragge.

The World According to Garp 🦴🦴🦴 **1982 (R)** Comedy turns to tragedy in this relatively faithful version of John Irving's popular (and highly symbolic) novel, adapted by Steve Tesich. Chronicles the life of T.S. Garp, a struggling everyman beset by the destructive forces of modern society. Nevertheless, Garp maintains his optimism even as his life unravels around him. At the core of the film is a subplot involving a group of extreme feminists inspired in part by Garp's mother, the author of "A Sexual Suspect." Close and Lithgow (as a giant transsexual) are spectacular, while Williams is low-key and tender as the beleagured Garp. Ultimately pointless, perhaps, but effectively and intelligently so. **136m/C; VHS, DVD, Blu-Ray.** Robin Williams; Mary Beth Hurt; John Lithgow; Glenn Close; Hume Cronyn; Jessica Tandy; Swoosie Kurtz; Amanda Plummer; Warren Berlinger; Brandon Maggart; George Roy Hill; ***D:*** George Roy Hill; ***W:*** Steve Tesich; ***C:*** Miroslav Ondricek; ***M:*** David Shire. L.A. Film Critics '82: Support. Actor (Lithgow), Support. Actress (Close); Natl. Bd. of Review '82: Support. Actress (Close); N.Y. Film Critics '82: Support. Actor (Lithgow).

World and Time Enough 🦴 ½ **1995** Sculptor Mark's (Guidry) father compulsively designed Gothic cathedrals and after his death Mark decides to build his own version in a field belonging to a sympathetic cleric. Meanwhile, his equally eccentric lover, garbage-collector Joey (Giles), goes on a search for his birth parents. Lots of symbols, not much sense. **90m/C; VHS, DVD.** Matt Guidry; Gregory G. Giles; Kraig Swartz; Peter Macon; ***D:*** Eric Mueller; ***W:*** Eric Mueller; ***C:*** Kyle Bergersen; ***M:*** Eugene Huddleston.

A World Apart 🦴🦴🦴 ½ **1988 (PG)** Cinematographer Menges' first directoral effort is a blistering, insightful drama told from the point of view of a 13-year-old white girl living in South Africa, oblivious to apartheid until her crusading journalist mother is arrested under the 90-Day Detention Act, under which she might remain in prison permanently. Political morality tale is also a look at the family-vs-cause choices activists must make. Heavily lauded, with good reason; the autobiographical script is based on Slovo's parents, persecuted South African journalists Joe Slovo and Ruth First. **114m/C; VHS, DVD.** *GB* Barbara Hershey; Jodhi May; Linda Mvusi; David Suchet; Jeroen Krabbe; Paul Freeman; Tim Roth; Jude Akuwidike; Albee Lesotho; ***D:*** Chris Menges; ***W:*** Shawn Slovo; ***C:*** Peter Biziou; ***M:*** Hans Zimmer. British Acad. '88: Orig. Screenplay; Cannes '88: Actress (Hershey), Actress (May), Actress (Mvusi), Grand Jury Prize; N.Y. Film Critics '88: Director (Menges).

World for Ransom 🦴 ½ **1954** Low-budget noir from Monogram. In shady post-war Singapore, vet-turned-PI Mike Callahan gets involved in a conspiracy when a black marketer kidnaps a nuclear scientist. The husband of Mike's wartime lover Frennessey is involved and there's an unexpected twist when Mike solves the case. **82m/B; DVD, Blu-Ray.** Dan Duryea; Gene Lockhart; Patric Knowles; Marian Carr; Arthur Shields; Reginald Denny; Douglass Dumbrille; Nigel Bruce; ***D:*** Robert Aldrich; ***W:*** Lindsay Hardy; ***C:*** Joseph Biroc; ***M:*** Frank DeVol.

The World Gone Mad 🦴🦴 ½ *The Public Be Hanged; Public Be Damned* **1933** During Prohibition, a tough reporter discovers the district attorney is the intended victim of a murder plot involving crooked Wall Street types. Full circle: this interesting drama of white-collar crime is again topical, though dialogue heavy and desultory. **70m/B; DVD.** Pat O'Brien; Louis Calhern; J. Carrol Naish; Evelyn Brent; Neil Hamilton; Mary Brian; ***D:*** Christy Cabanne; ***W:*** Edward T. Lowe; ***C:*** Ira Morgan.

The World in His Arms 🦴🦴 ½ **1952** Action and romance, circa 1850. Seal hunter Jonathan Clark (Peck) and his crew are in San Francisco when he meets beautiful Countess Marina Selanova (Blyth), who's fleeing an arranged marriage and is anxious to join her Uncle (Rumann), who happens to be the Governor General of Alaska (which is under Russian control). The twosome fall quickly in love but Marina's kidnapped by her would-be fiance, Prince Semyon (Esmond), who takes off for Alaska and Clark must go to rescue his love. Based on the book by Rex Beach. **104m/C; VHS, DVD.** Gregory Peck; Ann Blyth; Anthony Quinn; Carl Esmond; Sig Rumann; John McIntire; Hans Conried; Andrea King; ***D:*** Raoul Walsh; ***W:*** Borden Chase; ***C:*** Russell Metty; ***M:*** Frank Skinner.

The World Is Not Enough 🦴🦴 ½ **1999 (PG-13)** Brosnan returns in the 19th James Bond adventure in which 007 is sent to protect Elektra King (Marceau), the daughter of a murdered oil tycoon who was also an old friend of M's (Dench). The threat appears to come from terrorist Renard (Carlyle), who has a bullet in the brain courtesy of MI6 that has made him impervious to pain. Renard's playing the nuclear explosion card, which leads to this episode's Bond girl, nuclear weapons expert (!) Dr. Christmas Jones (Richards), who has minimal impact but looks fetching and (of course) falls for the dashing spy's charms. The numerous action sequences overwhelm the characters and Bond has little to pit himself against since the villains are so low-key. There is a welcome darker edge to both Bond's character and the plot that the franchise should build on, rather than trying to top its death-defying stunts each time. **125m/C; VHS, DVD, Blu-Ray.** Pierce Brosnan; Sophie Marceau; Denise Richards; Robert Carlyle; Dame Judi Dench; John Cleese; Desmond Llewelyn; Robbie Coltrane; Samantha Bond; Michael Kitchen; Colin Salmon; Maria Grazia Cucinotta; David Calder; Serena Scott Thomas; Ulrich Thomsen; Goldie; ***D:*** Michael Apted; ***W:*** Neal Purvis; Robert Wade; Bruce Feirstein; ***C:*** Adrian Biddle; ***M:*** David Arnold. Golden Raspberries '99: Worst Support. Actress (Richards).

The World Made Straight 🦴🦴 **2015 (R)** Meandering drama set in 1971. It's hard times in a North Carolina Appalachian community. Teenager Travis loses his job and home, and he's taken in by teacher-turned-pot dealer Leonard, who's haunted by the area's Civil War past, including a massacre that Travis learns involved his own kin. Travis makes the mistake of stealing some pot from the violent hillbilly Toomeys, leading to even more problems. Adapted from Ron Rash's 2006 novel. **119m/C; DVD, Blu-Ray.** Jeremy Irvine; Noah Wyle; Minka Kelly; Steve Earle; Haley Joel Osment; Adelaide Clemens; Marcus Hester; ***D:*** David Burris; ***W:*** Shane Danielsen; ***C:*** Tim Orr.

The World Moves On 🦴🦴 **1934** In 1825, the Girards and the Warburtons are the most prominent families in the New Orleans cotton industry. A will unites them in business, which expands overseas to England, France, and Germany. But after some four generations, their business empire is destroyed by WWI and the stock market crash. Tone plays a Girard and Carroll a Warburton who find love over several incarnations. **104m/B; DVD.** Madeleine Carroll; Franchot Tone; Lumsden Hare; Reginald Denny; Raul Roulien; Sig Rumann; Louise Dresser; Stepin Fetchit; Dudley Digges; ***D:*** John Ford; ***W:*** Reginald Berkeley; ***C:*** George Schneiderman; ***M:*** Hugo Freidhofer.

The World of Apu 🦴🦴🦴🦴 *Apu Sansat; Apur Sansar* **1959** Finale of director Ray's acclaimed Apu trilogy (following "Pather Panchali" and "Aparajito"). Aspiring writer Apu drops out of the university for want of money and takes up with an old chum. An odd circumstance leads him to marry his friend's cousin, whom he comes to love. She dies in childbirth (though her baby boy lives); Apu is deeply distraught, destroys the novel he was working on, and becomes a wanderer. His friend finds him five years later and helps him begin again with his young son. Wonderfully human, hopeful story told by a world-class director. From the novel "Aparajito" by B. Bandopadhaya. In Bengali with English subtitles. **103m/B; VHS, DVD, Blu-Ray.** *IN* Soumitra Chatterjee; Sharmila Tagore; Alok Charkravarty; Swapan Makerji; ***D:*** Satyajit Ray; ***W:*** Satyajit Ray; ***M:*** Ravi Shankar.

The World of Henry Orient 🦴🦴🦴 ½ **1964** Charming, eccentric comedy about two 15-year-old girls who, madly in love with an egotistical concert pianist, pursue him all around New York City. Sellers is hilarious, Walker and Spaeth are adorable as his teen groupies; Bosley and Lansbury are great as Walker's indulgent parents. For anyone who has ever been uncontrollably infatuated. Screenplay by the father/daughter team, Nora and Nunnally Johnson, based on Nora Johnson's novel. **106m/C; VHS, DVD, Blu-Ray.** Peter Sellers; Tippy Walker; Merrie Spaeth; Tom Bosley; Angela Lansbury; Paula Prentiss; Phyllis Thaxter; Bibi Osterwald; ***D:*** George Roy Hill; ***W:*** Nunnally Johnson; Nora Johnson; ***C:*** Boris Kaufman; ***M:*** Elmer Bernstein.

The World of Kanako 🦴🦴 *Kawaki* **2015** This adaptation of a hit novel is the kind of gore-driven insanity that Takashi Miike used to make more often. Akikazu (Yakusho) is a retired cop who is drawn back into a violent world when his daughter Kanako goes missing. He investigates her disappearance and gets drawn into an underground society of drugs, sex, and extreme violence. The result is a film that unabashedly displays its desire to provoke (complete with "Batman"-esque sound words on the screen like "Kill!"). The insanity gets a bit numbing long before it's even half-over, but you have to admire the commitment. Japanese with subtitles. **118m/C; DVD, Blu-Ray.** Koji Yakusho; Nana Komatsu; Satoshi Tsumabuki; Hiroya Shimizu; Fumi Nikaido; ***D:*** Tetsuya Nakashima; ***W:*** Tetsuya Nakashima; Miako Tadano; Nobuhiro Monma; ***C:*** Shoichi Ato.

The World of Suzie Wong 🦴🦴 **1960** Asian prostitute Kwan plays cat-and-mouse with American painter Holden. She lies to him about her profession, her family, and herself. His association with her ruins relationships in his life. Why, then, does he not get a clue? Good question, not answered by this soap opera that would be a serious drama. Offensively sanitized picture of the world of prostitution in an Asian metropolis. On the other hand, it's all nicely shot, much of it on location in Hong Kong. Based on Paul Osborn's play which was taken from Richard Mason's novel. **129m/C; DVD.** *UK* William Holden; Nancy Kwan; Sylvia Syms; Michael Wilding; Laurence Naismith; Jacqueline "Jackie" Chan; ***D:*** Richard Quine; ***W:*** John Patrick; ***C:*** Geoffrey Unsworth; ***M:*** George Duning.

World of the Depraved 🦴 *Mundo Depravados* **1967** Tango (Storm) runs an exercise club for young lovelies that are systematically being stalked by the mysterious full moon sex killer. Enter police detectives Riley and Hamilton (Decker, Reed), joking types who peep on their charges through keyholes, etc. When the plot finally gets around to the issue of the killer, the point of the movie has already been made clear. Silly, trivial, sophomoric humor lacking a trace of sincerity. Volume 6 of Frank Henenlotter's Sexy Shockers series. **73m/C; VHS, DVD.** Tempest Storm; Johnnie Decker; Larry Reed; ***D:*** Herbert Jeffries; ***W:*** Herbert Jeffries.

World on a Wire 🦴🦴 *Welt am Draht* **1973** Fassbinder's slow-moving sci fi story, originally made for German TV. Cybernetics engineer Fred Stiller worked on the Simulacron computer project that created a virtual reality world with computer-generated people who think they're human. The project leader dies suddenly leading Fred to a corporate and government conspiracy. Adapted from Daniel F. Galouye's 1964 novel "Simulacron-3." German with subtitles. **212m/C; DVD, Blu-Ray.** *GE* Klaus Lowitsch; Barbara Valentin; Ulli Lommel; Gunter Lamprecht; Wolfgang Schenck; Ivan Desny; ***D:*** Rainer Werner Fassbinder; ***W:*** Rainer Werner Fassbinder; Fritz Muller-Scherz; ***C:*** Michael Ballhaus; ***M:*** Gottfried Hungsberg.

World Trade Center 🦴🦴🦴 **2006 (PG-13)** Stone directs a 9/11 drama about John McLoughlin (Cage) and Will Jimeno (Pena), two Port Authority policemen trapped in the World Trade Center after they went in as part of the rescue team. Film follows their efforts at survival and escape with the efforts of others to save them, and the fears of their families. Stone shot in chronological order to heighten the reality and tension and had the survivors and their families on the set as well. He puts aside the cynicism and paranoia for an elegantly told tale of extraordinary heroism by ordinary people. **129m/C; DVD, Blu-Ray, HD-DVD.** Nicolas Cage; Michael Peña; Maria Bello; Maggie Gyllenhaal; Jay Hernandez; Stephen Dorff; Michael Shannon; ***D:*** Oliver Stone; ***W:*** Andrea Berloff; ***C:*** Seamus McGarvey; ***M:*** Craig Armstrong.

World Traveler 🦴🦴 ½ **2001 (R)** One day, thirtysomething NYC architect Cal (Crudup) leaves his wife and son, gets into the family station wagon, and hits the road to drive cross country in this frustrating film. Although Crudup is a fine actor, the viewer never learns Cal's motives for leaving his life behind except that he's not the nicest guy around, considering the way he treats some of the people he meets on his trip, including construction worker Carl (Derricks) whose marriage Cal damages, and various female hitchhikers. Not a lot really happens as Cal searches for himself (apparently) and the film ultimately falls flat. **104m/C; VHS, DVD.** *US CA* Billy Crudup; Julianne Moore; Cleavant Derricks; David Keith; Mary McCormack; James LeGros; Karen Allen; Liane Balaban; ***D:*** Bart Freundlich; ***W:*** Bart Freundlich; ***C:*** Terry Stacey; ***M:*** Clint Mansell.

The World Unseen 🦴🦴 **2007 (PG-13)** In 1952 Cape Town, rebellious young South Asian Amina co-owns a cafe where social outcasts can meet even if it means defying apartheid laws. Amina is immediately attracted to a new customer, browbeaten wife and mother Miriam, who owns a small country store with her traditional and controlling husband Omar. Amina pursues Miriam when Omar is conveniently away but there's bound to be trouble. **94m/C; DVD.** *GB SA* Lisa Ray; Sheetal Sheth; Parvin Dabas; Natalie Becker; David Dennis; Grethe Fox; Colin Moss; ***D:*** Shamin Sarif; ***W:*** Shamin Sarif; ***C:*** Mike Downie; ***M:*** Shigeru Umebayashi.

World War II: When Lions Roared 🦴🦴 ½ **1994** The "Lions" are Franklin Delano Roosevelt, Winston Churchill, and Joseph Stalin. The three Allied leaders formed an uneasy alliance to crush Hitler and Mussolini, all against much internal treachery. Uses lots of WWII newsreel footage. **186m/C; VHS, DVD.** John Lithgow; Bob Hoskins; Michael Caine; Ed Begley, Jr.; Jan Triska; ***D:*** Joseph Sargent; ***W:*** David W. Rintels; ***C:*** John A. Alonzo. **TV**

World War III 🦴🦴 ½ **1986** How's that for a title? A Russian plot is afoot to seize and destroy the Alaskan pipeline. When the plot is discovered, negotiation is needed to prevent world war. Executive branch showdown ensues between U.S. prez Hudson and Soviet chief Keith. Director Boris Sagal was killed on location, whereupon Greene took over, and shooting was moved indoors with dramatic tension lost in the transition. **186m/C; DVD.** Brian Keith; David Soul; Rock Hudson; Cathy Lee Crosby; Katherine Helmond; Robert Prosky; James Hampton; Richard Yniguez; Herbert Jefferson, Jr.; ***D:*** David Greene; ***W:*** Robert L. Joseph. **TV**

World War Z **2013 (PG-13)** Pitt plays the only man who stands between us and the undead apocalypse as the convoluted script takes him away from his family and around the world in search of a way to stop the brain-eating maniacs. Director Forster's action sequences are bumpy at best and the opening act is as clunky as a zombie trying to open a door. The movie ends strong but it's an undead chore getting there. The troubled production of this adaptation of Max Brooks's hit book led to problems that remain on the screen--it almost works but it isn't enough to feast on. **116m/C; DVD, Blu-Ray.** Brad Pitt; Mireille Enos; James Badge Dale; Daniella Kertesz; Ludi Boeken; ***D:*** Marc Forster; ***W:*** Matthew Michael Carnahan; Drew Goddard; Damon Lindelof; ***C:*** Robert Richardson; ***M:*** Marco Beltrami.

The World Was His Jury **1/2 1958** Low-budget courtroom drama. Ship's captain Jerry Barrett (McQueeney) is on trial for criminal negligence after an ocean liner disaster claimed many lives. His defense atorney, David Carson (O'Brien), stakes his reputation on geting to the truth. **82m/B; DVD.** Edmond O'Brien; Robert McQueeney; Mona Freeman; Karin (Karen, Katharine) Booth; John Beradino; Richard Cutting; ***D:*** Fred F. Sears; ***W:*** Herbert Abbott Spiro; ***C:*** Benjamin (Ben H.) Kline.

World Without End **1/2 1956** Silly CinemaScope sci fi with beautiful babes and hunky heroes. During their return trip from Mars, four astronauts black out, enter a time warp, and crash-land on a future Earth after an atomic war has nearly wiped out humanity. The remaining 'normal' humans live underground while mutants and giant spiders rule the surface. Naturally, the spacemen decide to make the planet safe for civilization again. **80m/C; DVD, Blu-Ray.** Hugh Marlowe; Nancy Gates; Rod Taylor; Nelson Leigh; Christopher Dark; Booth Colman; Shirley Patterson; Lisa Montell; Everett Glass; ***D:*** Edward L. Bernds; ***W:*** Edward L. Bernds; ***C:*** Ellsworth Fredericks; ***M:*** Leith Stevens.

Worlds Apart *Enas allos kosmos* **2017** A drama featuring three interwoven stories set in Athens during Greece's crisis involving immigration issues, a financial meltdown, and a potential civil war. In one segment, Daphne (Vakali), a young Greek woman, falls in love with Farris (Barhom), a Syrian refugee but must manage her father, Antonis (Chatzisavvas), who blames the loss of his business on refugees. In another, corporate manager Giorgos (Papakaliatis) has a failing marriage and a stressful work life. A third features Sebastian (Simmons), a lonely German, who meets broke housewife Maria (Kavoyianni) weekly to buy her perishables. it seems sincere but overly calculated. Greek and Arabic with subtitles. **113m/C; DVD.** J.K. Simmons; Maria Kavoyianni; Andrea Osvart; Christopher Papakaliatis; Tawfeek Barhom; ***D:*** Christopher Papakaliatis; ***W:*** Christopher Papakaliatis; ***C:*** Yannis Drakoularakos; ***M:*** Kostas Christides.

The World's End **2013 (R)** Twenty years after attempting an epic pub crawl designed to close the night at a pub called The World's End, five childhood friends (Pegg, Frost, Freeman, Considine, and Marsan) reunite to finish what they couldn't when they were younger. They also happen to attempt this legendary event on the night that the world looks like it's about to end for real in director Wright's third riff on classic genre films (zombie hit "Shaun of the Dead" and buddy-cop comedy "Hot Fuzz"), he and his favorite collaborators hit gold again, balancing heartfelt humor with cleverly-designed genre plotting. It's a blast. **109m/C; DVD, Blu-Ray.** *UK* Simon Pegg; Nick Frost; Martin Freeman; Paddy Considine; Eddie Marsan; Rosamund Pike; David Bradley; Pierce Brosnan; ***D:*** Edgar Wright; ***W:*** Simon Pegg; Edgar Wright; ***C:*** Bill Pope; ***M:*** Steven Price.

The World's Fastest Indian **2005 (PG-13)** Burt Munro (a refreshingly un-scary Hopkins) is the town "crazy old guy," a kooky New Zealander with a dream of setting a land-speed motorcycle record at Bonneville Flats, Utah. The Indian in the title is the bike, a 1920 Indian Scout, which, with Munro's constant tinkering, flies at a blistering 201 mph across the desert with Munro at its helm. A true story, told here by the same director of the 1971 documentary about Munro, "Offerings to the God of Speed." Mildly schmaltzy, but well-told and all heart. **127m/C; DVD.** *US NZ* Anthony Hopkins; Diane Ladd; Aaron Murphy; Paul Rodriguez; Chris(topher) Williams; Christopher Lawford; Annie Whittle; ***D:*** Roger Donaldson; ***W:*** Roger Donaldson; ***C:*** David Gribble; ***M:*** J. Peter Robinson.

The World's Greatest Athlete **1973 (G)** Lame Disney comedy about a Tarzan-like jungle-man (Vincent) recruited by an unsuccessful American college coach (Amos) and his bumbling assistant (Conway). Fun special effects, weak script add up to mediocre family fare. Cameo by Howard Cosell as—who else??himself. **89m/C; VHS, DVD.** Jan-Michael Vincent; Tim Conway; John Amos; Roscoe Lee Browne; Dayle Haddon; ***Cameo(s):*** Howard Cosell; ***D:*** Robert Scheerer; ***W:*** Dee Caruso; ***M:*** Marvin Hamlisch.

World's Greatest Dad **2009** Sweet-yet-twisted story of failed writer/high school teacher/single dad Lance Clayton (Williams) whose life unexpectedly takes a turn for the better after his jackass, porn-obsessed, teenage son Kyle (Sabara), accidentally kills himself by auto-erotic asphyxiation. Lance rearranges the scene to appear as though Kyle hung himself, even composing a suicide letter. The note becomes public and Kyle is remembered with great affection by those who hours before hated him, or never even knew him, and Lance is suddenly a much sought-after instructor. This unintended attention leads Lance to compose an entire diary of Kyle's, which also gets out-of-control recognition. Williams remarkably laces this heavy-handed material with just the right dollop of comedy while writer/director Goldthwait continues to emerge as a dark comedy genius. **99m/C; Blu-Ray, On Demand.** Robin Williams; Daryl Sabara; Alexie Gilmore; Henry Simmons; Evan Martin; Tom Kenny; Mitzi McCall; Jermaine Williams; Toby Huss; Michael Thomas Moore; Lorraine Nicholson; ***D:*** Bobcat Goldthwait; ***W:*** Bobcat Goldthwait; ***C:*** Horacio Marquinez; ***M:*** Gerald Brunskill.

World's Greatest Lover **1/2 1977 (PG)** Milwaukee baker Rudi Valentine, played oft-hilariously by Wilder, tries to make it big in 1920s Hollywood. He has a screen test as a Hollywood movie sheik, but his wife (Kane) leaves him for the real McCoy. Episodic and uneven, it's alternately uproarious, touching and downright raunchy. **89m/C; VHS, DVD.** Gene Wilder; Carol Kane; Dom DeLuise; Fritz Feld; Carl Ballantine; Michael Huddleston; Matt Collins; Ronny Graham; ***D:*** Gene Wilder; ***W:*** Gene Wilder.

The Worm Eaters **WOOF! 1977 (PG)** Mean developers want to take over a reclusive worm farmer's land. He unleashes his livestock on them. The bad guys turn into'eeck!?"worm people." A truck runs over our hero nearly 75 minutes too late to save the viewer. **75m/C; VHS, DVD.** Herb Robins; Barry Hostetler; Lindsay Armstrong Black; Joseph Sacket; Robert Garrison; Mike Garrison; ***D:*** Herb Robins; ***W:*** Herb Robins; ***C:*** Willis Hawkins; ***M:*** Theodore Stern.

The Worst Witch **1/2 1986 (G)** Fantasy about a school for young witches where the educational lessons never go quite as planned. Adapted from the children's book "The Worst Witch" by Jill Murphy. **70m/C; VHS, DVD.** Diana Rigg; Charlotte Rae; Tim Curry; Fairuza Balk; ***D:*** Robert M. Young.

Worth: The Testimony of Johnny St. James **2012** A dramatic look at one man's attempt to turn his life around. Johnny St. James (Johnson) was a seminary student when his wife was killed by a drunk driver. Losing all hope and his faith, he becomes an alcoholic. After a decade, he decides to start going to Alcoholic Anonymous meetings but finds his first meeting is run by the driver, who has tried to change his life. Though Johnny makes plans to avenge his wife's death, he finds his own redemption in the process. **90m/C; DVD.** Jeffrey Johnson; Vincent Irizarry; Veronica Rodriguez; Ashley Noel; Eric Roberts; ***D:*** Jenn Page; ***W:*** Jason Horton; ***C:*** Steve Snyder. **VIDEO**

Worth Winning **1/2 1989 (PG-13)** A notoriously eligible Philadelphia bachelor takes a bet to become engaged to three women within three months, and finds himself in hot water. A critically dead-in-the-water chucklefest. **103m/C; VHS, DVD.** Mark Harmon; Lesley Ann Warren; Madeleine Stowe; Maria Holvoe; Mark Blum; Andrea Martin; Alan Blumenfeld; Brad Hall; Tony Longo; ***D:*** Will MacKenzie; ***W:*** Sara Parriott; Josann McGibbon.

Would Be Kings **2008 (R)** Cousins and best friends, as well as drug-squad cops, Patrick (Currie) and Jamie (Bass) find their own lives and the lives of their families threatened by dirty money and department corruption. Originally made for Canadian TV. **90m/C; DVD.** *CA* Currie Graham; Ben Bass; Maxim Roy; Stana Katic; Michelle Nolden; Natasha Henstridge; Robert Forster; Stephen McHattie; ***D:*** David Wellington; ***W:*** Tassie Cameron; Esta Spalding; ***C:*** David Perrault; ***M:*** Ron Sures. **TV**

Woyzeck **1978** Chilling portrayal of a man plunging into insanity. Mired in the ranks of the German Army, Woyzeck is harassed by his superiors and tortured in scientific experiments, gradually devolving into homicidal maniac. Based on Georg Buchner play. In German with English subtitles. **82m/C; VHS, DVD, Blu-Ray.** *GE* Klaus Kinski; Eva Mattes; Wolfgang Reichmann; Josef Bierbichler; ***D:*** Werner Herzog; ***W:*** Werner Herzog; ***C:*** Jorge Schmidt-Reitwein.

Woyzeck **1994** Woyzeck (Kovacs) is a flagman in a decaying trainyard—caught between his cruel employer, poverty, and his distant wife. In order to make a little extra money, he agrees to take part in a bizarre medical experiment. Increasingly pushed to the edge, Woyzeck snaps when he learns his wife is having an affair. Based on the play by Georg Buchner. Hungarian with subtitles. **93m/B; VHS, DVD.** *HU* Lajos Kovacs; Diana Vacaru; Aleksandr Porokhovshchikov; Sandor Gaspar; ***D:*** Janos Szasz; ***W:*** Janos Szasz; ***C:*** Tibor Mathe.

Wozzeck **1947** The corpse of murderer Franz Wozzeck (Meisel) is being used in an anatomy lecture, while medical student Buchner (Eckard) tells Wozzeck's tragic story in flashbacks. A soldier, Wozzeck endures humiliation in order to barely support his wife Marie (Zulch) and their child. The beautiful Marie allows herself to be seduced by another soldier (Haussler), as Wozzeck's physical and mental health declines. And then Franz learns of her infidelity. Based on the drama by Georg Buchner. German with subtitles. **94m/B; VHS, DVD.** Kurt Meisel; Helga Zulch; Richard Haussler; Max Eckard; ***D:*** Georg C. Klaren; ***W:*** Georg C. Klaren; ***C:*** Bruno Mondi; ***M:*** Herbert Trantow.

WR: Mysteries of the Organism **1971** Makavejev's breakthrough film, a surreal, essayist exploration of the conflict/union between sexuality and politics—namely, Wilheim Reich and Stalin. A raunchy, bitterly satiric non-narrative that established the rule-breaking Yugoslav internationally. In Serbian with English subtitles. **84m/C; VHS, DVD.** Milena Dravic; Jagoda Kaloper; Tuli Kupferberg; Jackie Curtis; ***D:*** Dusan Makavejev; ***W:*** Dusan Makavejev.

The Wraith **1/2 1987 (PG-13)** Drag-racing Arizona teens find themselves challenged by a mysterious, otherworldly stranger. Hot cars; cool music; little else to recommend it. Lousy script; ludicrous excuse for a premise. Most of the stars herein are related to somebody famous. **92m/C; VHS, DVD.** Charlie Sheen; Nick Cassavetes; Sherilyn Fenn; Randy Quaid; Matthew Barry; Clint Howard; Griffin O'Neal; ***D:*** Mike Marvin; ***W:*** Mike Marvin.

Wrangler **1/2 1988** When an Australian rancher dies his daughter tries to hang on to the family ranch from a ruthless creditor. She also has to deal with the attentions of two men—one a businessman and the other a cattleman, both equally dashing and handsome. Beautiful scenery of the Australian Outback as well as romance and adventure. **93m/C; VHS, DVD.** Jeff Fahey; Tushka Bergen; Steven Vidler; Richard Moir; Shane Briant; Drew Forsythe; Cornelia Frances; Sandy Gore; Frederick Parslow; ***D:*** Ian Barry; ***W:*** John Sexton; ***M:*** Mario Millo.

The Wrath of God **1/2 1972** Escapist actioner that may or may not be a western satire depending on the viewer. In any case, Oliver Van Horne (Mitchum) is a con man posing as a priest with a gun in his bible and a switchblade crucifix. He, Irish rebel Emmet Keogh (Hutchinson), and bootlegger Jennings (Buono) are captured by Col. Santilla (Colicos) in a nowhere south of the border community. They're offered safe passage out if they get rid of crazed despot Tomas de la Plata (Langella). Hayworth's last film role as Tomas' unhappy mama. Based on a Jack Higgins novel. **111m/C; DVD.** Robert Mitchum; Ken Hutchison; Victor Buono; Frank Langella; John Colicos; Rita Hayworth; Paula Pritchett; Gregory Sierra; ***D:*** Ralph Nelson; ***W:*** Ralph Nelson; ***C:*** Alex Phillips, Jr.; ***M:*** Lalo Schifrin.

The Wrath of the Gods **1914** Boyish American sailor Tom Wilson (Borzage) is shipwrecked near a Japanese village. He soon falls in love with local beauty, Toya San (Aoki). But their forbidden romance leads to divine retribution (she's under a curse) in the form of a volcanic eruption. **?m/B; Silent; DVD.** Frank Borzage; Sessue Hayakawa; Tsuru Aoki; Kisaburo Kurihara; ***D:*** Reginald Barker; ***W:*** Thomas Ince.

Wrath of the Titans **1/2** *Clash of the Titans 2* **2012 (PG-13)** In this sequel to "Clash of the Titans," demigod Perseus (Worthington) must leave his quiet life when the Olympian gods start losing control of the Titans and their leader Kronos. When Zeus is betrayed and imprisoned in the underworld, Perseus sets out with some remaining allies to rescue his father and save the world. **99m/C; DVD, Blu-Ray.** Sam Worthington; Rosamund Pike; Toby Kebbell; Bill Nighy; Liam Neeson; Edgar Ramirez; Ralph Fiennes; Danny Huston; ***D:*** Jonathan Liebesman; ***W:*** Dan Mazeau; David Leslie Johnson; Steven Knight; ***C:*** Ben Davis; ***M:*** Javier Navarrete.

Wreck-It Ralph **1/2 2012 (PG)** Continuing the trend of bad guys who want to be good ("Megamind," "Despicable Me," etc.), Disney's 3D-animated adventure is a modestly successful comedy with lots of visual candy for the kiddies. Ralph (Reilly) is an '80s video arcade bad guy forced to leave his own game to finally change his fate. He encounters sassy Vanellope von Schweetz (Silverman), a young girl also ostracized in her game and the two form an uneasy partnership. Like the video games that its characters inhabit, the film is a little too 2D. A bit sluggish and repetitive despite a few solid laughs (and knowing references for video game geeks). **101m/C; DVD, Blu-Ray.** ***V:*** John C. Reilly; Sarah Silverman; Jack McBrayer; Jane Lynch; Alan Tudyk; ***D:*** Rich Moore; ***W:*** Jennifer Lee; Phil Johnston; ***M:*** Henry Jackman.

The Wreck of the Mary Deare **1/2 1959** Slow-moving adventure drama focusing on the wreck of the freighter called the Mary Deare. Heston plays a ship salvager who comes upon a seemingly empty ship one night and Cooper is the only crew member on board. Special effects are the main attraction in this interesting sea drama. Film originally was to be directed by Hitchcock, but he turned down the offer to do "North by Northwest." **105m/C; VHS, DVD.** *GB* Gary Cooper; Charlton Heston; Michael Redgrave; Emlyn Williams; Cecil Parker; Alexander Knox; Virginia McKenna; Richard Harris; ***D:*** Michael Anderson, Sr.; ***W:*** Eric Ambler.

Wrecked **2010 (R)** A nameless man (Brody) wakes up in a car wreck in the middle of nowhere. He's injured, has amnesia, two dead passengers, lots of moolah, and a gun. None of this turns out to be very interesting, especially when the man starts wandering in the woods, trying to find some help and having hallucinations. **90m/C; DVD, Blu-Ray.** Adrien Brody; Caroline Dhavernas; Jacob Blair; Ryan Robbins; ***D:*** Michael Greenspan; ***W:*** Christopher Dodd; ***C:*** James Liston; ***M:*** Michael Brook.

Wrecker **1/2** *Juggernaut* **2015** An action-thriller about a road trip gone very, very bad. Best friends Emily (Hutchison) and Leslie (Whitburn) decide to take a road trip into the desert. Their travel plans take a bad turn when Emily decides to leave the highway to take a short cut. On this back road, the friends must fight for their lives when a mysterious yet psychotic trucker starts to follow them forces them to play an endless game of cat and mouse that puts their survival at stake. **83m/C; DVD.** Anna Hutchison; Andrea Whitburn; Jennifer Koenig; Michael Dickson; Ashley Evans; ***D:*** Michael Bafaro; ***W:*** Michael Bafaro; Evan Tylor; *C:* Jon Thomas; Ian MacDougall; *M:* Vincent Mai.

Wrecking Crew ☆ 1/2 **1942** Competitive coworkers Matt (Arlen) and Duke (Morris) reduce skyscrapers to rubble but they must work together when they are trapped atop a collapsing building. **73m/B; DVD.** Richard Arlen; Chester Morris; Jean Parker; Esther Dale; Joseph (Joe) Sawyer; Evelyn Brent; Alexander Granach; *D:* Frank McDonald; *W:* Maxwell Shane; Richard Murphy; *C:* Fred H. Jackman, Jr.; *M:* Freddie Rich.

The Wrecking Crew ☆☆ **1968** The fourth and final of Martin's Matt Helm spy spoof series. Matt and bumbling babe Freya (Tate) must save the world from economic doom when evildoer Massimo (Green) steals $1 billion in gold. Tate was murdered several months after the film's release. **105m/C; VHS, DVD.** Dean Martin; Sharon Tate; Nigel Green; Elke Sommer; Nancy Kwan; Tina Louise; John Larch; Wilhelm von Homburg; Tony Giorgio; *D:* Phil Karlson; *W:* William McGivern; *C:* Sam Leavitt; *M:* Hugo Montenegro.

The Wrecking Crew ☆ 1/2 **1999 (R)** Ice-T heads the title "crew," a government-sponsored (secret) hit squad that's sent to the Motor City to clean up the mess made by gangmaster Snoop Dogg. **81m/C; VHS, DVD.** Ice-T; Snoop Dogg; David Askew; Ernie Hudson, Jr.; *D:* Albert Pyun; *W:* Hannah Blue. **VIDEO**

The Wrestler ☆ **1973** All-star wrestling, which is fictional anyway, gets said treatment in the appropriate way. Honest promoter (yeah, sure) bumps heads with bad-guy crooks who want in on the action. Made-for-TV opportunity for Asner to slum. **103m/C; VHS, DVD.** Ed Asner; Elaine Giftos; Verne Gagne; Harold Sakata; *D:* James Westman; *W:* Eugene Gump; *C:* Gil Hubbs; *M:* William Allen Castleman.

The Wrestler ☆☆☆☆ **2008 (R)** In the 1980's, Randy "The Ram" Robinson was a huge star in a small wrestling circuit. Over the years, his health has deteriorated, his daughter (Wood) has turned her back on him, and his trailer in New Jersey can't keep out winter. However, a proposed 20th anniversary rematch with his legendary nemesis lures him back into the ring for one more shot at glory. This prayer for redemption is financed by his part-time supermarket job, but, unfortunately, the affection from his stripper girlfriend (Tomei) runs cold once the money's tucked away. Heart-wrenching, funny, and never succumbs to cheap sports-movie melodrama. A triumphant comeback for Rourke with his infamously abused face and body, guided by cult director Darren Aronofsky. **109m/C; Blu-Ray, On Demand.** Mickey Rourke; Marisa Tomei; Evan Rachel Wood; *D:* Darren Aronofsky; *W:* Robert Siegel; *C:* Maryse Alberti; *M:* Clint Mansell. British Acad. '08: Actor (Rourke); Golden Globes '09: Actor--Drama (Rourke), Song ("The Wrestler"); Ind. Spirit '09: Actor (Rourke), Cinematog., Film.

Wrestling Ernest Hemingway ☆☆ **1993 (PG-13)** A shy barber and a rollicking sea captain, both 75 and retired, form an unlikely companionship in a Florida retirement mecca. Duvall is the persnickety introvert who quietly follows routine and Harris is the would-be ladies' man whose endless tall tales include having tangled with Papa Hemingway in his youth. They share walks in the park, little league baseball from the bleachers, and coffee klatches that reveal the emptiness of their lives. Director Haines' focus on the principals' emotional baggage considerably dampens the proceedings. Depression in the elderly may be a topic that is not quite ready to come out of Hollywood's closet. **123m/C; VHS, DVD.** Robert Duvall; Richard Harris; Piper Laurie; Shirley MacLaine; Sandra Bullock; *D:* Randa Haines; *W:* Steve Conrad; *C:* Lajos Koltai; *M:* Michael Convertino.

Wrestling with Alligators ☆☆ 1/2 **1998** Quiet, coming-of-ager stars Palladino as Maddy, a teenager escaping a tragic past in Florida and finding comfort in her new-found friends at an all-female boarding house on the New Jersey shore in 1959. Lulu's Look Out offers the tough teenager a place to find herself, with the help of proprietor Lulu (Bloom), an eccentric silent-screen star, and residents Mary (Shelly), an artist, and the beautiful Claire (Richardson), a French war widow. Tomboy Maddy finds herself attracted to a man for the first time when she meets carnival worker Will (Trammell). Then, when Claire becomes pregnant by the local garage owner (Sanders), Maddy finds herself growing up even more as she comes to the aid of her newfound family, which is beginning to show signs of serious strain. Unassuming portrait of four very different women is a worthy effort, with the leads displaying convincing chemistry. **95m/C; VHS, DVD.** Aleksa Palladino; Joely Richardson; Claire Bloom; Adrienne Shelly; Sam Trammell; Jay O. Sanders; Tom Guiry; Sloane Shelton; Angelica Torn; Schuyler Grant; *D:* Laurie Weltz; *W:* Laurie Weltz; *C:* Richard Dallett; *M:* Andrew Hollander.

The Wretched ☆☆ **2008** Seven college students are conducting soil research at a farm when they discover the diary of the wife or a former owner and accidentally stumble into a curse Then, they have to deal with ghosts and possessions. Definitely not your average college experience. **92m/C; On Demand, Download.** Lara Adkins; Mark Booker; Mike Delange; Melanie Gillis; Chelsie Hartness; Matt Harwell; Jessica Hotovy; Eliot Irvin; Daniel B. Iske; Wendy Iske; Nick Sanchez; Michelle Schrage; Matt Tatroe; Sarah Wald; William Wassem; *D:* Daniel B. Iske; *W:* Scott Coleman; *C:* Daniel B. Iske; *M:* James Iske.

A Wrinkle in Time ☆☆ 1/2 **2018 (PG)** This adaptation of Madeleine L'Engle's classic novel makes a valiant effort at capturing the story's imagination, but the heavy use of special effects and glittery eye shadow is more distracting than magical. Meg (Reid), a middle schooler struggling with low self-esteem and the disappearance of her physicist father (Pine), uncovers a 5th dimension that, with the help of three celestial guides, will lead her to her dad and enable her to free him from evil forces. The first live-action film by writer Jennifer Lee, better known for such animated hits as *Frozen* and *Zootopia.* **109m/C; DVD, Blu-Ray.** Storm Reid; Oprah Winfrey; Reese Witherspoon; Mindy Kaling; Levi Miller; *D:* Ava DuVernay; *W:* Jennifer Lee; Jeff Stockwell; *C:* Tobias A. Schliessler; *M:* Ramin Djawadi.

Wristcutters: A Love Story ☆☆ **2006 (R)** What could be worse than a miserable life? A miserable afterlife, that's what. Croatian director Goran Dukic takes a stark and quirky peek at the limbo that exists between the two. Zia (Fugit) is dumped by girlfriend Desiree (Bibb) and decides to end it all, hoping for relief from his misery. But he finds himself stuck in an afterlife that is marginally like the one he just left, only duller, and with worse jobs. A cast of kooky characters who have also offed themselves shares the limbo world, two of which are wild Russian rocker Eugene (Whigham) and derelict clown Kneller (an aptly-cast Waits). Zia cheers up just a bit when he finds out that Desiree followed his lead and he goes on a roadtrip to find her, but ends up falling for Mikal (Sossamon), who swears she's there by mistake and is trying to get home. **88m/C; DVD, On Demand.** Patrick Fugit; Shannyn Sossamon; Shea Whigham; Leslie Bibb; Tom Waits; Mark Boone, Jr.; Mary Pat Gleason; Abraham Benrubi; Will Arnett; Clayne Crawford; John Hawkes; Jake Busey; Sarah Roemer; Azura Skye; Eddie Steeples; Nick Offerman; *D:* Goran Dukic; *W:* Goran Dukic; *C:* Vanja Cernjul; *M:* Bobby Johnston.

Written on the Wind ☆☆☆ 1/2 **1956** Sirk's frenzied, melodrama-as-high-art dissection of both the American Dream and American movies follows a Texas oil family's self-destruction through wealth, greed and unbridled lust. Exaggerated depiction of and comment on American ambition and pretension, adapted from Robert Wilder's novel. **99m/C; VHS, DVD.** Lauren Bacall; Rock Hudson; Dorothy Malone; Robert Stack; Robert Keith; Grant Williams; Edward Platt; Harry Shannon; *D:* Douglas Sirk; *W:* George Zuckerman; *C:* Russell Metty. Oscars '56: Support. Actress (Malone).

The Wrong Arm of the Law ☆☆☆ **1963** Loopy gangster yarn about a trio of Aussie gangsters who arrive in London and upset the local crime balance when they dress up as cops and confiscate loot from apprehended robbers. General confusion erupts among the police, the local crooks, and the imposters. Riotous and hilarious, with Sellers leading a host of familiar faces. **94m/B; VHS, DVD.** *GB* Peter Sellers; Lionel Jeffries; Nanette Newman; Bernard Cribbins; Dennis Price; *D:* Cliff Owen; *M:* Richard Rodney Bennett.

The Wrong Box ☆☆☆ **1966** Two elderly Victorian brothers try to kill each other so that one of them may collect the large inheritance left to them. Based on a Robert Louis Stevenson novel. Well-cast black comedy replete with sight gags, many of which flop. **105m/C; VHS, DVD.** *GB* Peter Sellers; Dudley Moore; Peter Cook; Michael Caine; Ralph Richardson; John Mills; *D:* Bryan Forbes; *W:* Larry Gelbart; *M:* John Barry.

Wrong Cops ☆☆ **2013** The third film directed by Quentin Dupieux is an absurdist cop comedy. Living and working in Los Angeles, Officer Duke (Burnham) knows he is not an ideal police officer. Corrupt, a drug dealer, and a bully, Duke is obsessed with electronic music. Duke does not stick out in his department because his fellow depraved cops include a sexual abuser, an extortionist, and an extremis—none of whom is particularly concerned with solving crimes. Duke threatens their ability to get away with it all when accidentally shoots a manwhile holding a teenager captive. Believing the man is dead, Duke stuffs the body in the trunk, soon learns that his colleagues are not going to be much help in disposing of the body, and that there may not be a body after all. **82m/C; DVD, Blu-Ray, Streaming, Download.** Mark Burnham; Eric Judor; Steve Little; Brian Warner; Grace Zabriskie; *D:* Quentin Dupieux; *W:* Quentin Dupieux; *C:* Quentin Dupieux; *M:* Quentin Dupieux.

The Wrong Guy ☆☆ **1996 (PG-13)** Hit-and-miss spoof of "man on the run" movies. Nerdy exec Nelson Hibbert (Foley) threatens his boss in front of a bunch of people and is later seen running from the man's office, screaming, covered in blood, and holding a knife. Although the police quickly figure out Nelson is not the killer, Nelson doesn't know this and he keeps ending up in the wrong place at the wrong time. **87m/C; VHS, DVD, Blu-Ray.** *CA* Dave Foley; David Anthony Higgens; Jennifer Tilly; Joe Flaherty; Alan Scarfe; Kenneth Welsh; Enrico Colantoni; Colm Feore; *D:* David Steinberg; *W:* Dave Foley; David Anthony Higgens; Jay Kogen; *C:* David Makin; *M:* Lawrence Shragge.

The Wrong Guys ☆ **1988 (PG)** Five giants of stand-up comedy star as a group of men who reunite their old boy scout pack and go camping. A crazed convict mistakes them for FBI agents. It's supposed to get zany after that, but succeeds only in being clumsy and embarassing. **86m/C; VHS, DVD.** Richard Lewis; Richard Belzer; Louie Anderson; Tim Thomerson; Franklin Ajaye; John Goodman; Ernie Hudson; Timothy Van Patten; *D:* Danny Bilson; *W:* Danny Bilson; Paul DeMeo.

Wrong Is Right ☆☆ *The Man With The Deadly Lens* **1982 (R)** A black action comedy about international terrorism, news reporting and the CIA. Connery is terrific, as usual, as a TV reporter in a head-scratching attempt at satire of our TV-influenced society. **117m/C; VHS, DVD.** Sean Connery; Katharine Ross; Robert Conrad; George Grizzard; Henry Silva; G.D. Spradlin; John Saxon; Leslie Nielsen; Robert Webber; Rosalind Cash; Hardy Kruger; Dean Stockwell; Ron Moody; Jennifer Jason Leigh; *D:* Richard Brooks; *W:* Richard Brooks; *C:* Fred W. Koenekamp.

The Wrong Man ☆☆☆ 1/2 **1956** Night-club musician Fonda is falsely accused of a robbery and his life is destroyed. Taken almost entirely from the real-life case of mild-mannered bass player "Manny" Balestrero; probes his anguish at being wrongly accused; and showcases Miles (later to appear in "Psycho") and her character's agony. Harrowing, especially following more light-hearted Hitchcock fare such as "The Trouble with Harry." Part of the "A Night at the Movies" series, this tape simulates a 1956 movie evening with a color Bugs Bunny cartoon, "A Star Is Bored," a newsreel and coming attractions for "Toward the Unknown." **126m/B; VHS, DVD, Blu-Ray.** Henry Fonda; Vera Miles; Anthony Quayle; Nehemiah Persoff; *D:* Alfred Hitchcock; *C:* Robert Burks.

The Wrong Move ☆☆ 1/2 **1978** A loose adaptation of Goethe's "Sorrows of Young Werther" by screenwriter Peter Handke. Justly acclaimed and engrossing, though slow. Kinski's first film. A young poet, searching for life's meaning, wanders aimlessly through Germany. In German with English subtitles. **103m/C; VHS, DVD, Blu-Ray.** *GE* Nastassja Kinski; Hanna Schygulla; Ruediger Vogler; Hans-Christian Blech; *D:* Wim Wenders.

Wrong Side of Town ☆ **2010 (R)** Ex-SEAL Bobby now makes his living doing landscaping, with one client being mobster Seth Bordas. Seth's coked-up brother Ethan nearly rapes Bobby's wife Dawn and gets accidentally dead. Seth puts a bounty out on Bobby and kidnaps his teenage daughter Brianna too, so Bobby turns to fellow vet Big Ronnie for help. Acting varies between wooden and over-the-top, the plot's a cliche, but the low-budget action scenes are fairly decent. **104m/C; DVD, Blu-Ray.** Rob van Dam; Ja Rule; Edrick Browne; Dave Batista; Jerry Katz; Brooke Frost; Lara Grice; Ross Britz; Ava Santana; *D:* David DeFalco; *W:* David DeFalco; *C:* Thomas Lembcke; *M:* Jim Kaufman. **VIDEO**

Wrong Turn ☆ 1/2 **2003 (R)** Six friends are involved in a car crash that strands them in the West Virginia mountains where they are hunted by disfigured, inbred, cannibalistic mountain men. Typical victim-by-number horror flick offers no twists on the genre and only slight wit by its doomed cast. Don't expect to see this one on the West Virginia Tourist Board's recommended list. **85m/C; DVD, Blu-Ray.** Eliza Dushku; Jeremy Sisto; Emmanuelle Chriqui; Desmond Harrington; Lindy Booth; Kevin Zegers; Julian Richings; Garry Robbins; Ted Clark; Yvonne Gaudry; David Huband; Joel Harris; Wayne Robson; James Downing; *D:* Rob Schmidt; *W:* Alan B. McElroy; *C:* John Bartley; *M:* Elia Cmiral.

Wrong Turn 2: Dead End ☆ **2007 (R)** Retired special forces officer Dale Murphy (Rollins) is the host of a reality TV show where contestants must survive in a remote West Virginia wilderness. But they don't expect to find themselves being hunted by an inbred family of cannibals. Just as sleazy and gross as it sounds. **93m/C; DVD, Blu-Ray.** Henry Rollins; Erica Leerhsen; Daniella Alonso; Texas Battle; Crystal Lowe; Aleksa Palladino; Steve Braun; Kimberly Caldwell; *D:* Joe Lynch; *W:* Turi Meyer; Al Septien; *C:* Robin Loewen; *M:* Bear McCreary. **VIDEO**

Wrong Turn 3: Left for Dead ☆ **2009** This franchise, featuring lots of gore and violence, should be left as well but continues to carry on with its typical plot. Three Finger and his inbred cannibal clan get a two-fer when a group of innocent campers take a wrong turn and then a bunch of escaped cons also become prey for the stabbings, decapitations, vivisections, and various other graphically-depicted deaths. **92m/C; DVD, Blu-Ray.** Janet Montgomery; Tamer Hassan; Chucky Venice; Gil Kolirin; Borislav Iliev; Tom Frederic; *D:* Declan O'Brien; *W:* Connor James Delaney; *C:* Lorenzo Senatore; *M:* Claude Foisy. **VIDEO**

Wrong Turn 4: Bloody Beginnings **WOOF! 2011** Gore and nudity and cannibal hillbilly brothers. One Eye, Three Finger, and Saw Tooth have fresh meat when college kids out for a weekend break get stranded by a blizzard and take shelter in an abandoned mental hospital. **94m/C; DVD, Blu-Ray.** Daniel Skene; Sean Skene; Scott Johnson; *D:* Declan O'Brien; *W:* Declan O'Brien; *C:* Michael Marshall; *M:* Claude Foisy. **VIDEO**

Wrong Turn at Tahoe ☆ 1/2 **2009 (R)** If you can buy Gooding Jr. as a tough mob cohort you might buy the flick (at least as a passable time-waster). Mob debt collector Joshua finds himself in trouble when his boss (Ferrer) is doublecrossed by a powerful drug dealer (Keitel). **90m/C; DVD.** Cuba Gooding, Jr.; Miguel Ferrer; Harvey Keitel; Louis Mandylor; Noel Guglielmi; Johnny Messner; Mike Starr; Alex Meneses; Leonor Varela; *D:* Franck Khalfoun; *W:* Eddie Nickerson; *C:* Christopher LaVasseur; *M:* Nicholas Pike. **VIDEO**

The Wronged Man ☆☆ 1/2 **2010** Lifetime drama based on a true story. Calvin Willis (Ali) is serving a life sentence without parole after being convicted of raping an 11-year-old special needs girl. Louisiana paralegal Janet Gregory (Ormond) stumbles across the case file after her defense attorney boss dies and, after reading about shaky testimony and withheld evidence, she starts a 20-year battle to overturn his conviction. **90m/C; DVD.** Julia Ormond; Mahershala Ali; Lisa Arrindell Anderson; Tonea Stewart; Bruce McKinnon; Omar J. Dorsey; *D:* Tom McLoughlin; *W:* Teena Booth; *C:* Shelly Johnson; *M:* Stephen Endelman. **CABLE**

Wrongfully Accused 1/2 **1998 (PG-13)** Yet another Nielsen spoof, with "The Fugitive" (along with several other movies) the target this time around. He's violinist Ryan Harrison who has a tryst with socialite Lauren Goodhue (Le Brock) and then gets convicted of her husband Hibbing's (York) murder. Harrison escapes, determined to find the actual killer—the one-armed, one-legged, and one-eyed man—while being hunted by Marshal Fergus Falls (Crenna). This is one genre that's definitely had its day, with more clunkers than chuckles. **85m/C; VHS, DVD.** Leslie Nielsen; Richard Crenna; Kelly Le Brock; Melinda McGraw; Michael York; Sandra Bernhard; *D:* Pat Proft; *W:* Pat Proft; *C:* Glen MacPherson; *M:* Bill Conti.

WUSA 1/2 **1970** Heavy-handed social drama. Cynical down-and-out Rheinhardt (Newman) comes to New Orleans and prevails on con man buddy Farley (Harvey) to get him a job at the local, right-wing radio station owned by Bingamon (Hingle). He gets involved with part-time hooker Geraldine (Woodward) and befriends naive social worker Rainey (Perkins) and it all leads to tragedy. **115m/C; DVD, Blu-Ray.** Paul Newman; Joanne Woodward; Anthony Perkins; Laurence Harvey; Pat Hingle; Cloris Leachman; Michael Anderson, Jr.; Robert Quarry; B.J. Mason; Wayne Rogers; Moses Gunn; *D:* Stuart Rosenberg; *W:* Robert Stone; *C:* Richard Moore; *M:* Lalo Schifrin.

Wuthering Heights **1939** The first screen adaptation of Emily Bronte's romantic novel about the doomed love between Heathcliff and Cathy on the Yorkshire moors. Dynamically captures the madness and ferocity of the classic novel, remaining possibly the greatest romance ever filmed. Excellent performances from Wyler's sure direction, particularly Olivier's, which made him a star, and Oberon in her finest hour as the exquisite but selfish Cathy. Remade twice, in 1953 (by Luis Bunuel) and in 1970. **104m/B; VHS, DVD.** Laurence Olivier; Merle Oberon; David Niven; Geraldine Fitzgerald; Flora Robson; Donald Crisp; Cecil Kellaway; Leo G. Carroll; Miles Mander; Hugh Williams; *D:* William Wyler; *W:* Ben Hecht; Charles MacArthur; *C:* Gregg Toland; *M:* Alfred Newman. Oscars '39: B&W Cinematog.; AFI '98: Top 100; Natl. Film Reg. '07; N.Y. Film Critics '39: Film.

Wuthering Heights 1/2 **1970 (G)** The third screening of the classic Emily Bronte romance about two doomed lovers. Fuest's version features excellent photography, and Calder-Marshall's and Dalton's performances are effective, but fail even to approach the intensity and pathos of the 1939 film original (or of the book). Filmed on location in Yorkshire, England. **105m/C; VHS, DVD, Blu-Ray.** *GB* Anna Calder-Marshall; Timothy Dalton; Harry Andrews; Pamela Brown; Judy Cornwell; James Cossins; Rosalie Crutchley; Hilary Dwyer; Hugh Griffith; Ian Ogilvy; *D:* Robert Fuest; *W:* Patrick Tilley; *C:* John Coquillon; *M:* Michel Legrand.

Wuthering Heights 1/2 **1998** Yet another adaptation of Emily Bronte's 1847 gothic romance. Cavanah plays the embittered Heathcliff while Brady is the wilfull Cathy, whose desire for a life of ease places them both on a tragic path that haunts them even after death. **120m/C; VHS, DVD.** *GB* Robert Cavanah; Orla Brady; Crispin Bonham Carter; Peter Davison; *W:* David Skynner; *M:* Warren Bennett; Neil McKay. **TV**

Wuthering Heights **2009** Umpteenth version of the Emily Bronte tragedy is well-staged but an intense Hardy isn't well-matched by petulant newcomer Riley. Heathcliff (Hardy) is a poor Gypsy boy adopted into the Earnshaw family where he and Cathy (Riley) find they are soulmates. Unfortunately, Cathy chooses to marry proper aristocrat Edgar Linton (Lincoln) and a furious Heathcliff, who has made his own fortune, decides on a spiteful revenge. **150m/C; DVD.** *GB* Tom (Thomas) Hardy; Burn Gorman; Andrew Lincoln; Rebecca Night; Tom Payne; Sarah Lancashire; Charlotte Riley; Rosalind Halstead; *D:* Coky Giedroyc; *W:* Peter Bowken; *C:* Ulf Brantas; *M:* Ruth Barrett. **TV**

Wuthering Heights 1/2 **2012** Emily Bronte's sweeping tale of painful, passionate love is given a fresh take in this adaptation that uses shaky camera footage, minimal dialogue, no score to speak of and a gritty reality befitting the bleak English moors on which the story takes place. Cathy (Beer) and Heathcliff (Glave) bond as children when Cathy's father comes home with the West Indian Heathcliff. Cathy's duties and Heathcliff's dark, brooding tendencies drive them apart; her older brother (Shaw) plots to destroy Heathcliff. This Heights features a black Heathcliff, a departure from previous film adaptations. **129m/C; DVD, Blu-Ray.** *UK* Kaya Scodelario; James Howson; Lee Shaw; Shannon Beer; Solomon Glave; Paul Hilton; Simone Jackson; Nichola Burley; James Northcote; Amy Wren; Steve Evets; *D:* Andrea Arnold; *W:* Andrea Arnold; Olivia Hetread; *C:* Robbie Ryan.

W.W. and the Dixie Dancekings 1/2 **1975** Set in Nashville in the 1950s, this easygoing comedy stars the irrepressible Reynolds as W.W. Bright, a gas station robber who carjacks the Dixie Dancekings, a country music band. W.W. becomes their manager and sets about getting them noticed in the country music capitol and onstage at the Grand Ole Opry. **91m/C; DVD.** Burt Reynolds; Conny Van Dyke; Jerry Reed; Ned Beatty; James Hampton; Art Carney; *D:* John G. Avildsen; *W:* Thomas Rickman; *C:* James A. Crabe; *M:* Dave Grusin.

WWJD: What Would Jesus Do? *What Would Jesus Do?* **2010 (PG)** When small town pastor Henry Maxwell (Gleason) rejects helping a drifter (Schneider) who comes to his church for aid, he realizes he needs to renew his faith. So he and some other townsfolk decide to ask 'what would Jesus do?' before they make a decision. **88m/C; DVD.** John Schneider; Jim Gleason; Maxine Bahns; Adam Gregory; Mark Arnold; *D:* Thomas Makowski; *W:* Joseph Nasser; *C:* Robert Kraetsch; *M:* Stu Goldberg. **VIDEO**

Wyatt Earp 1/2 **1994 (PG-13)** Revisionist epic suffers from bad timing as it follows "Tombstone" in telling the story of tarnished badge Earp (Costner), his brothers, and tubercular friend Doc Holliday (Quaid). Costner is barely believable as a 20-something lad, but fares better as he ages. Forty pounds lighter and likely delusional from lack of food, Quaid is unrecognizable but terrific, hacking his way to supporting Oscar territory. 'Course, Val Kilmer got there first. Huge cast finds screen time precious, even though film is some 40 minutes too long, due to prolonged intro to early Wyatt life. Originally envisioned as a TV miniseries till sheriff Costner took a hankering to bring tall tale to the big screen. Filmed on location in Sante Fe, New Mexico. For the full Earp effect, see it with "Tombstone" and relive the legend. **191m/C; VHS, DVD, Blu-Ray, HD-DVD.** Kevin Costner; Dennis Quaid; Gene Hackman; Jeff Fahey; Mark Harmon; Michael Madsen; Catherine O'Hara; Bill Pullman; Isabella Rossellini; Tom Sizemore; JoBeth Williams; Mare Winningham; Betty Buckley; Adam Baldwin; Rex Linn; Todd Allen; David Andrews; Linden Ashby; Annabeth Gish; Joanna Going; Martin Kove; Tea Leoni; James (Jim) Caviezel; Karen Grassle; Owen Roizman; James Gammon; Randle Mell; Lewis Smith; Ian Bohen; Alison Elliott; MacKenzie Astin; John Dennis Johnston; Jack Kehler; Kris Kamm; Michael Huddleston; John Doe; *D:* Lawrence Kasdan; *W:* Dan Gordon; Lawrence Kasdan; *C:* Owen Roizman; *M:* James Newton Howard. Golden Raspberries '94: Worst Actor (Costner), Worst Remake/Sequel.

Wyatt Earp's Revenge 1/2 **2012 (PG-13)** Low-budget western. Kilmer has a small role as an aged Earp who's giving an interview, resulting in flashbacks to the action. After Earp's gal Dora is murdered by the Kenedy brothers, not even their powerful rancher father can save them. Earp gets his posse--Bat Masterson, Doc Holliday, Charlie Bassett, and Bill Tighman--together and they start riding. **93m/C; DVD.** Shawn Roberts; Matt Dallas; Scott Whyte; Levi Fiehler; Wilson Bethel; Val Kilmer; Trace Adkins; Daniel Booko; Steven Grayhm; *D:* Michael Feifer; *W:* Darren B. Shepherd; *C:* Roberto Schein; *M:* Andres Boulton. **VIDEO**

Wyoming Renegades **1955** Routine western from Columbia Pictures. After doing time for riding with Butch Cassidy, outlaw Brady Sutton (Carey) wants to go straight. However, Sutyon's neighbors start looking like a lynch mob when Butch and his gang rob the town's bank and they're sure Brady was involved. **73m/C; DVD.** Phil Carey; Gene Evans; Martha Hyer; William Bishop; Douglas Kennedy; Roy Roberts; *D:* Fred F. Sears; *W:* David Lang; *C:* Lester White.

Wyvern **2009** Sci Fi Channel movie has global warming thawing out the non-fire breathing dragon that's been stuck in the ice in Alaska. Naturally hungry, the wyvern chows down on the residents of isolated Beaver Mills who are celebrating the summer solstice. This time the CGI of the flying beastie is actually acceptable. Last role for Don S. Davis who plays the town's retired military kook. **89m/C; DVD.** Nick (Nicholas) Chinlund; Erin Karpluk; Barry Corbin; Elaine Miles; Don S. Davis; John Shaw; *D:* Stephen R. Monroe; *W:* Jason Bourque; *C:* C. Kim Miles; *M:* Pinar Toprak. **CABLE**

The Wyvern Mystery **2000** Confusing and stodgy Gothic mystery based on an 1869 novel by Sheridan Le Fanu. As a child, Alice is taken in by Squire Fairfield (Jacobi) when her tenant father dies. Alice grows up into a beautiful young woman (Watts) and the Squire has lustful designs on her but is bested when Alice runs off and marries Fairfield's son Charles (Glen). The newlyweds wind up at an isolated Fairfield property that apparently has a curse on it and a now-pregnant Alice begins to have nightmares of tragedy. Watts is demure and Jacobi chews the scenery; everything else is a follow-the-numbers folly. **118m/C; DVD.** *UK* Naomi Watts; Derek Jacobi; Iain Glen; Jack Davenport; Aisling O'Sullivan; Ellie Haddington; *D:* Alex Pillai; *W:* David Pirie; *C:* Simon Maggs; *M:* Philip Appleby. **TV**

The X-Files 1/2 *The X-Files: Fight the Future* **1998 (PG-13)** The TV series' fifth-season cliffhanger continues in the big screen adaptation, which supposedly has a plot clear enough so viewers unfamiliar with the series can still figure out what's going on. Creator Chris Carter uses the show's "mythology" episodes to have FBI agents Mulder (Duchovny) and Scully (Anderson) battling a global conspiracy involving the Cigarette-Smoking Man (Davis) and an international syndicate, colonizing aliens, and related paranormal perplexities. The big budget allows for some big action sequences and special effects and the two leads have a comfortable partnership. **120m/C; VHS, DVD.** David Duchovny; Gillian Anderson; Martin Landau; William B. Davis; John Neville; Armin Mueller-Stahl; Blythe Danner; Mitch Pileggi; Terry O'Quinn; Jeffrey DeMunn; Lucas Black; Glenne Headly; *D:* Rob Bowman; *W:* Chris Carter; Frank Spotnitz; *C:* Ward Russell; *M:* Mark Snow.

The X Files: I Want to Believe **2008 (PG-13)** A decade after the first movie and six years since the TV series ended its run, the dynamic paranormal-investigating duo of Mulder (Duchovny) and Scully (Anderson) are drawn back to their FBI roots. While investigating a string of bizarre, though not particularly supernatural murders, they are prodded along by a disgraced priest (played by an unexpectedly low-key Connolly) and his seemingly psychic visions. The X-philes audience will enjoy having them back in action, but will likely miss those wacky aliens. **104m/C; Blu-Ray, On Demand.** David Duchovny; Gillian Anderson; Billy Connolly; Xzibit; Amanda Peet; Callum Keith Rennie; Adam Godley; Mitch Pileggi; *D:* Chris Carter; *W:* Chris Carter; Frank Spotnitz; *C:* Bill Roe; *M:* Mark Snow.

X-Men 1/2 **2000 (PG-13)** The Marvel Comics characters, who were born with genetic mutations that give them superpowers, get their shot at the big screen. Wheelchair-bound telepath Charles Xavier (Stewart), AKA Professor X, runs a school to help others learn to use their mutant powers. The good guys, who seeks to work with humans, fight against the Magneto (McKellen)-led Brotherhood, who feel mankind is expendable. The story is simple enough for newbies to follow and takes itself seriously (no camp allowed) but doesn't have a lot of surprises and, except for Wolverine (Jackman), the characters aren't very involving. The setup calls for a sequel, which may flesh things out. **104m/C; VHS, DVD, Blu-Ray, UMD.** Patrick Stewart; Ian McKellen; Famke Janssen; Hugh Jackman; James Marsden; Halle Berry; Rebecca Romijn; Ray Park; Tyler Mane; Anna Paquin; Bruce Davison; Shawn Ashmore; *D:* Bryan Singer; *W:* David Hayter; *C:* Newton Thomas (Tom) Sigel; *M:* Michael Kamen.

X-Men: Apocalypse **2016 (PG-13)** Rarely have so many talented people been involved in such a loud, CGI-heavy blockbuster disaster. Much like Bryan Singer's original series ended with an overcooked three-quel ("The Last Stand"), the new series with quality entries "First Class" and "Days of Future Past" ends in disaster. This time, the X-Men have to fight the villainous Apocalypse (Isaac) before he destroys the world. Overcrowded with characters and smothered with destructive special effects that become numbing, this is a textbook example of how not to do a superhero sequel. Bigger is not better. **144m/C; DVD.** James McAvoy; Michael Fassbender; Jennifer Lawrence; Nicholas Hoult; Oscar Isaac; Tye Sheridan; Bryan Singer; Sophie Turner; Olivia Munn; Ben Hardy; Alexandra Shipp; *D:* Bryan Singer; *W:* Simon Kinberg; *C:* Newton Thomas (Tom) Sigel; *M:* John Ottman.

X-Men: Days of Future Past **2014 (PG-13)** Let's get all the X-Men together! The latest entry in the hit Marvel franchise merges the worlds of the original Bryan Singer franchise with the attempted reboot/prequel directed by Matthew Vaughn. Why settle for one Magneto when you can have two? Recapping the plot with so many characters would be near impossible but let's just say the present-day mutant superheroes need the help of the X-Men from the past. Time travel, dozens of characters, expertly-staged action—it may not make a ton of sense and it gets cluttered under the weight of its own ensemble-merging but it's also often explosive fun. **131m/C; DVD, Blu-Ray.** Hugh Jackman; James McAvoy; Patrick Stewart; Ian McKellen; Michael Fassbender; Jennifer Lawrence; Peter Dinklage; Nicholas Hoult; Halle Berry; Evan Peters; *D:* Bryan Singer; *W:* Simon Kinberg; *C:* Newton Thomas (Tom) Sigel; *M:* John Ottman.

X-Men: First Class **2011 (PG-13)** Good casting and a decent story keep this prequel to the Marvel Comic X-Men saga moving along with energy and flair. Set in 1962 (with scenes going back to WWII), it follows the friendship of Charles Xavier (McAvoy) and Erik Lensherr (Fassbender) as they decide how best to utilize their mutant powers. When a rift develops over stopping evil Sebastian Shaw (Bacon) and his own mutant forces, the break between Professor X's X-Men and Magneto's Brotherhood begins. **132m/C; DVD, Blu-Ray, On Demand.** James McAvoy; Michael Fassbender; Rose Byrne; January Jones; Kevin Bacon; Nicholas Hoult; Lucas Till; Jason Flemyng; Oliver Platt; Jennifer Lawrence; Edi Gathegi; Caleb Landry Jones; Alex Gonzales; Zoë Kravitz; *D:* Matthew Vaughn; *W:* Matthew Vaughn; Ashley Edward Miller; Jane Goldman; Zack Stentz; *C:* John Mathieson; *M:* Henry Jackman.

X-Men Origins: Wolverine **2009 (PG-13)** Jackman stars as the angry, adamantium-clawed mutant for the fourth time in this conventional, though briskly moving, popcorn flick from the Marvel Comics universe as we learn how James became Logan/Wolverine. James and his half-brother Victor (Schreiber) join in various wars throughout the decades. Eventually this draws the attention of nefarious General William Stryker (Huston) and his Team X mutant Army unit. Wolverine comes to regret his participation but will never be allowed to lead a peaceful life. Other mutants make appearances, with Reynolds (as Deadpool) and Kitsch (as Gambit) making the most of their screen time. **107m/C; Blu-Ray, On Demand.** Hugh Jackman; Liev Schreiber; Ryan Reynolds; Dominic Monaghan; Taylor Kitsch; Kevin Durand; Danny Huston; will.i.am; Daniel Henney; Lynn Collins; *D:* Gavin Hood; *W:* David Benioff; Skip Woods; *C:* Donald McAlpine; *M:* Harry Gregson-Williams.

X-Men: The Last Stand 1/2 *X-Men 3* **2006 (PG-13)** Last stand? More like "can't stand." Hack-a-licious director Brett Ratner tarnishes the legacy of Bryan Singer's above-average superhero series with this lazy, unimaginative bore. Forget all the subtlety and coolness from the first two X-Men movies, because Ratner's replaced them with cheap-looking FX, incoherent storytelling, and barely disguised misogyny. Professor X's merry mutants have to contend with a resurrected Jean Grey (reborn as the all powerful Phoenix) and a new "cure" that threatens to wipe out mutantkind forever. Sounds intriguing, but you won't believe how often your eyes will involuntarily roll as major characters die stupidly, plot holes run rampant, and Wolverine cries like a wuss every ten minutes. **104m/C; DVD, Blu-Ray.** Patrick Stewart; Ian McKellen; Hugh Jackman; Famke Janssen; Halle Berry; Anna Paquin; Rebecca Romijn; Kelsey Grammer; Ben Foster; James Marsden; Shawn Ashmore; Daniel Cudmore; Ellen Page; Aaron Stanford; Vinnie Jones; Dania Ramirez; Olivia Williams; Shohreh Aghdashloo; Cameron Bright; Michael Murphy; Bill Duke; Eric Dane; Haley Ramm; Josef Sommer; Connor Widdows; Shauna Kain; Ken Leung; Kea Wong; Anthony Heald; Makenzie Vega; ***D:*** Brett Ratner; ***W:*** Zak Penn; Simon Kinberg; ***C:*** Dante Spinotti; ***M:*** John Powell.

X: The Man with X-Ray Eyes 🦴🦴🦴 *The Man with the X-Ray Eyes; X* **1963** First-rate Corman has Milland gain power to see through solid materials. Predates Little Caesars campaign. **79m/C; VHS, DVD, Blu-Ray.** Ray Milland; Diana Van Der Vlis; Harold J. Stone; John Hoyt; Don Rickles; Dick Miller; Jonathan Haze; Morris Ankrum; Barboura Morris; ***D:*** Roger Corman; ***W:*** Ray Russell; Robert Dillon; ***C:*** Floyd Crosby; ***M:*** Les Baxter.

X The Unknown 🦴 1/2 **1956** Geologist Adam Royston (Jagger) is sent to investigate a radioactive spot where a mysterious and deadly fissure has appeared. Seems a mud something that feeds on radiation bursts out of the Earth's surface every 50 years or so and kills. Now, it's expanding its territory. **78m/B; VHS, DVD, Blu-Ray.** Dean Jagger; Leo McKern; Edward Chapman; John Harvey; William Lucas; Anthony Newley; ***D:*** Leslie Norman; ***W:*** Jimmy Sangster; ***C:*** Gerald Gibbs; ***M:*** James Bernard.

X2: X-Men United 🦴🦴🦴 *X-Men 2* **2003 (PG-13)** The regulars are back as Prof. Xavier's X-Men must join forces with Magneto's mutants to battle a greater evil: a power-mad, mutant-hating general (Cox) out to find and eliminate all mutants. Cox is great as the general, full of self-righteousness and silky menace, properly denying his character the small moments of sympathy allowed to McKellan's Magneto. The story is better than in the original, even though it jams as much, if not more exposition into the plot and lingers too long on the teen romance between Rogue and Iceman. Script provides a well-executed and exciting central plot, while leaving plenty of threads and new characters that audiences will be anxious to follow in "X-Men 3." Special effects are fantastic, but they don't overshadow the story. **134m/C; VHS, DVD, Blu-Ray, UMD.** Patrick Stewart; Ian McKellen; Famke Janssen; Hugh Jackman; James Marsden; Halle Berry; Rebecca Romijn; Anna Paquin; Shawn Ashmore; Brian Cox; Alan Cumming; Kelly Hu; Bruce Davison; Aaron Stanford; Katie Stuart; Cotter Smith; Daniel Cudmore; Peter Wingfield; Michael Reid MacKay; Keely Purvis; Jill Teed; Alf Humphreys; James Kirk; ***D:*** Bryan Singer; ***W:*** Michael Dougherty; Daniel P. "Dan" Harris; ***C:*** Newton Thomas (Tom) Sigel; ***M:*** John Ottman.

X, Y & Zee 🦴 1/2 *Zee & Co.* **1972 (R)** A brassy, harsh version of the menage a trois theme, wherein the vicious wife (Taylor) of a philanderer (Caine) decides to avenge herself by seducing his mistress. An embarrassment for everyone involved. **110m/C; VHS, DVD, Blu-Ray.** Michael Caine; Elizabeth Taylor; Susannah York; Margaret Leighton; ***D:*** Brian G. Hutton; ***W:*** Edna O'Brien; ***C:*** Billy Williams.

Xala 🦴🦴🦴🦴 *The Curse; Impotence* **1975** Sembene is at the height of his powers in this bitter and brilliantly witty tale of a self-satisfied, "Europeanized" black businessman (he washes his Mercedes with Evian) who is suddenly struck down by the dreaded 'xala' curse, which causes impotence. As he searches desperately?-and in all the wrong places?-for a cure, his refusal to recognize the genesis of his condition explodes into both a tragic portrait of cultural enslavement and a sharp satire of man's endless capacity for self-delusion. Despite being heavily censored in Senegal, it is nevertheless one of Sembene's most widely seen and thoroughly entertaining films. Be prepared: the last sequence is sobering and unsparing. **123m/C; DVD.** Douta Seck; Makhouredia Gueye; Thierno Leye; Dieynaba Niang; Miriam Niang; Iliamane Sagna; Seune Samb; Abdoulaye Seck; Younouss Seye; ***D:*** Ousmane Sembene; ***W:*** Ousmane Sembene; ***C:*** Georges Caristan; Orlando L. Lopez; Seydina D. Saye; Farba Seck; ***M:*** Samba Diabara Samb.

Xanadu WOOF! **1980 (PG)** Dorky star-vehicle remake (of 1947's "Down to Earth") eminently of its era, which is now better forgotten. Newton-John is a muse who descends to Earth to help two friends open a roller disco. In the process she proves that as an actor, she's a singer. Kelly attempts to soft shoe some grace into the proceedings, though he seems mystified as anyone as to why he's in the movie. Don Bluth adds an animated sequence. **96m/C; VHS, DVD, Blu-Ray.** Olivia Newton-John; Michael Beck; Gene Kelly; Sandahl Bergman; ***D:*** Robert Greenwald; ***W:*** Richard Danus; ***C:*** Victor Kemper; ***M:*** Barry DeVorzon. Golden Raspberries '80: Worst Director (Greenwald).

Xchange 🦴🦴🦴 *X Change* **2000 (R)** In the near future, bio-technology advances allow people to transfer their minds into the bodies of others. The process called "floating" lets anyone "travel" by having his or her consciousness transmitted anywhere in the world. When anti-corporate terrorists assassinate a powerful CEO, Baldwin is called in to investigate the murder. He is transported to San Francisco, where he ends up occupying the body of the lead terrorist (MacLachlan). Then he must fight to reclaim his body. The concept is more than compelling, and the action sequences generally overcome the relative low budget of the production. **110m/C; VHS, DVD.** *CA* Stephen Baldwin; Kyle MacLachlan; Kim Coates; Pascale Bussieres; ***D:*** Allan Moyle. **VIDEO**

Xiu Xiu: The Sent Down Girl 🦴🦴🦴 *Tian Yu* **1997 (R)** To foil Chinese censors, first-time director Chen was forced into guerilla filmmaking (accounting for the film's somewhat rough look) in this moving effort set during the Cultural Revolution. In 1975, teenaged city girl Xiu-Xiu (Lu Lu) is sent down to a remote corner of Tibet to learn horse training from peasant Lao Jin (Lopsang). She expects only to be gone six-months but is instead stuck, forgotten, on the plains. In desperation, Xiu-Xiu begins to trade sexual favors in exchange for the chance to return home. Based on the novel "Tian Yu" (Heavenly Bath) by co-writer Geling. Mandarin with subtitles. **99m/C; VHS, DVD.** Lu Lu; Lopsang; ***D:*** Joan Chen; ***W:*** Joan Chen; Yan Geling; ***C:*** Lu Yue; ***M:*** Johnny Chen.

Xtro WOOF! **1983 (R)** An Englishman, abducted by aliens three years before, returns to his family with a deadly, transforming disease. Slime-bucket splatter flick notable for the scene where a woman gives birth to a full-grown man, and various sex slashings. **80m/C; VHS, DVD.** *GB* Philip Sayer; Bernice Stegers; Danny Brainin; Simon Nash; Maryam D'Abo; David Cardy; Anna Wing; Peter Mandell; Robert Fyfe; ***D:*** Harry Bromley-Davenport; ***W:*** Robert Smith; Iain Cassie; ***C:*** John Metcalfe; ***M:*** Harry Bromley-Davenport.

Xtro 2: The Second Encounter 🦴🦴 **1991 (R)** Research facility conducts an experiment to transfer people to a parallel dimension. Out of the three researchers sent to the other side, only one returns, unconscious. Turns out that he is playing host to a biohazardous creature brought over from the other dimension who escapes into the air shafts and threatens to kill everyone in the building. One more problem: if the creature isn't killed, the computer system will fill the building with radiation. Sound familiar? It should, because this is a low-budget remake of "Alien." Good photography, adequate acting, but Vincent just isn't credible as a brilliant scientist. A sequel to "Xtro" in name only. **92m/C; VHS, DVD.** *CA* Jan-Michael Vincent; Paul Koslo; Tara Buckman; Jano Frandsen; Nicholas Lea; W.F. Wadden; Rolf Reynolds; Nic Amoroso; Tracy Westerholm; ***D:*** Harry Bromley-Davenport.

Xtro 3: Watch the Skies 🦴🦴 **1995 (R)** Military unit arrives at a remote island where the government has covered up a UFO landing. However, the island is now inhabited by a pissed-off alien whose mate has been killed. **90m/C; VHS, DVD, Blu-Ray.** Sal Landi; Jim Hanks; Robert Culp; Andrew Divoff; Karen Moncrieff; ***D:*** Harry Bromley-Davenport; ***W:*** Daryl Haney.

XX 🦴 1/2 **2017 (R)** A horror anthology in the vein of the V/H/S movies but with only female directors is a fantastic idea but the result is sadly flat and frustrating. The four directors—Vuckovic ("The Box"), St. Vincent, as Clark ("The Birthday Party"), Benjamin ("Don't Fall"), and Kusama ("Her Only Living Son")—bring a unique perspective to this typically male genre. But that doesn't stop at least half from just not working. Kusama's, which could be viewed as a sequel to a '70s classic, is the only one worth seeking out. Hopefully they will try this again with better scripts and better results. **80m/C; DVD, Blu-Ray.** Natalie Brown; Melanie Lynskey; Breeda Wool; Christina Kirk; Peter DaCunha; ***D:*** Roxanne Benjamin; Karyn Kusama; St. Vincent; Jovanka Vuckovic; ***W:*** Roxanne Benjamin; Karyn Kusama; St. Vincent; Jovanka Vuckovic; ***C:*** Ian Anderson; Tarin Anderson; Patrick Cady; ***M:*** St. Vincent; Jefferson Friedman; Carly Paradis; The Gifted; Craig Wedren.

XX/XY 🦴🦴 1/2 **2002 (R)** In 1993, Coles Burroughs (Ruffalo) is studying film at Sarah Lawrence, meets fellow students Sam (Stange) and Thea (Robertson), and tries a menage a trois until pairing up with Sam for awhile. Ten years later, Coles is an ad exec living with longtime girlfriend Claire (Wright), Thea runs a restaurant with husband Miles (Thornton), and Sam has just returned from London after breaking her engagement. Sam and Coles meet accidentally and they're soon rekindling their long-ago flame. The sexual intrigue comes to a head during a weekend in the Hamptons. **91m/C; VHS, DVD.** Mark Ruffalo; Maya Stange; Kathleen Robertson; Petra Wright; David Thornton; Kel O'Neill; Joshua Spafford; Zach Shaffer; ***D:*** Austin Chick; ***W:*** Austin Chick; ***C:*** Uta Briesewitz.

XXX 🦴🦴 1/2 **2002 (PG-13)** Director Rob Cohen attempts to update the secret agent flick for the X Games crowd with this stunt-riddled explosion fest. Xander "XXX" Cage (Diesel) is a former extreme athlete recruited by NSA agent Gibbons (Jackson) after he's busted stealing a senator's car. Xander is given a choice between jail time or becoming a special ops agent. He then spends the rest of the movie jumping off, sliding down and blowing up plot devices. If you're looking for an introspective drama about feelings, move along. If you're looking to watch things go "Boom!" while a thick-necked mumbling guy acts like a jackass, then put it in and get some popcorn. Cohen and Diesel previously teamed up on the unexpected hit "The Fast and the Furious," so the bets on the duo remaking "Steel Magnolias" as their next project have officially been taken off the board. **111m/C; VHS, DVD, Blu-Ray, UMD.** Vin Diesel; Samuel L. Jackson; Asia Argento; Marton Csokas; Danny Trejo; Michael Roof; Tom Everett; Richy Muller; Werner Daehn; ***D:*** Rob Cohen; ***W:*** Rich Wilkes; ***C:*** Dean Semler; ***M:*** Randy Edelman.

xXx: Return of Xander Cage 🦴 1/2 **2017 (PG-13)** Vin Diesel returns to one of the characters who made him a star in this long-delayed sequel that delivers some action goods but too much nonsensical dialogue in between the fun moments. Diesel plays Xander Cage, thought dead but secretly in hiding, brought back to work by handler Augustus Gibbons (Jackson). Bad guy Xiang (Donnie Yen) is trying to obtain an unstoppable weapon known as the Pandora's Box, and Cage recruits a team of fellow mercenaries to stop him. It's occasionally B-movie fun in a way that justifies a rental. **96m/C; DVD, Blu-Ray, Streaming.** Vin Diesel; Donnie Yen; Deepika Padukone; Tony Jaa; Nina Dobrev; ***D:*** D.J. Caruso; ***W:*** F. Scott Frazier; ***C:*** Russell Carpenter; ***M:*** Robert Lydecker; Brian Tyler.

XXX: State of the Union **2005 (PG-13)** Ice Cube replaces Vin Diesel (whose character, Xander Cage, is pointedly and dismissively pronounced dead about 20 minutes in) as Darius Stone, a former Navy SEAL in Gibbons' (Jackson) old unit jailed nine years ago for leading a mutiny against a general. When members of that old SEAL unit begin disappearing and Gibbons' XXX HQ is attacked, the two team up to find out why. What they find is an attempted military coup by the Secretary of Defense (Dafoe). To no one's surprise, there's plenty of explosions, gunplay, car chases, and mayhem, and none of it makes a damn bit of sense. But for those who enjoy that sort of thing, it is a wild ride. Don't expect anything resembling believability, though. **94m/C; DVD, Blu-Ray, UMD.** Ice Cube; Samuel L. Jackson; Willem Dafoe; Scott Speedman; Peter Strauss; Nona Gaye; Michael Roof; Sunny Mabrey; Xzibit; John G. Connolly; ***D:*** Lee Tamahori; ***W:*** Simon Kinberg; ***C:*** David Tattersall; ***M:*** Marco Beltrami.

Y Tu Mama Tambien 🦴🦴 1/2 *And Your Mother Too* **2001** Mexican teenagers Julio (Bernal) and Tenoch (Luna) envision a guilt-free, sex-filled summer when their girlfriends go to Europe on vacation. At a wedding, they meet Luisa (Verdu), the wife of Tenoch's cousin, and begin a flirtation, telling her of their planned trip to a secluded (and non-existent) beach. When Luisa discovers her husband's infidelity, she decides to join the boys on their trip, and their adolescent sexual fantasies turn to emotional upheaval when she seduces them separately. Believe it or not, this is a comedy (and a funny one), with "American Pie" type jokes and shenanigans sprinkled throughout. But since this movie has a brain, and something of a soul, the consequences aren't always slapstick-funny. Spanish with subtitles. **105m/C; VHS, DVD, Blu-Ray.** *MX* Gael Garcia Bernal; Diego Luna; Maribel Verdu; ***D:*** Alfonso Cuarón; ***W:*** Alfonso Cuarón; Carlos Cuaron; ***C:*** Emmanuel Lubezki. Ind. Spirit '03: Foreign Film; L.A. Film Critics '02: Foreign Film; N.Y. Film Critics '02: Foreign Film; Natl. Soc. Film Critics '02: Foreign Film.

The Yakuza 🦴🦴 1/2 *Brotherhood of the Yakuza* **1975 (R)** An ex G.I. (Mitchum) returns to Japan to help an old army buddy find his kidnapped daughter. He learns the daughter has been kidnapped by the Japanese version of the Mafia (the Yakuza) and he must call on old acquaintances to help free her. A westernized oriental gangster drama with a nice blend of buddy moments, action, ancient ritual, and modern Japanese locations. **112m/C; DVD, Blu-Ray.** Robert Mitchum; Richard Jordan; Ken Takakura; Brian Keith; Herb Edelman; ***D:*** Sydney Pollack; ***W:*** Paul Schrader; Leonard Schrader; Robert Towne; ***M:*** Dave Grusin.

Yakuza Apocalypse 🦴🦴 1/2 *Gokudou daisensou* **2015 (R)** Takashi Miike may have slowed his ridiculously prodigious output in recent years but he proves with this gangster epic that he hasn't lost his twisted sense of humor and abundance of style. Like the films that made Milike a cult star, this one is nearly impossible to describe. It involves vampires, yakuza members, and a guy in a frog suit. There are assassins, martial arts masters, extreme gore, and more of the insanity we've come to expect from the director of Ichi the Killer. It may have been decades since Miike's gonzo style redefined Japanese cinema but he shows no signs of slowing down. **115m/C; DVD, Blu-Ray, Streaming.** *JP* Hayato Ichihara; Lily Frankie; Yayan Ruhian; ***D:*** Takashi Miike; ***W:*** Yoshitaka Yamaguchi; ***C:*** Hajime Kanda; ***M:*** Koji Endo.

Yalom's Cure 🦴🦴 1/2 **2014** A feature-length biographical documentary on influential psychotherapist Irvin D. Yalom. In addition to offering background information on the best-selling author and respected scholar, the documentary offers an existential exploration of the human mind and psyche. Though these discussions, Yalom's groundbreaking work in psychotherapy is explored and his wisdom is shared. **77m/C; DVD, Blu-Ray.** ***D:*** Sabine Gisiger; ***W:*** Sabine Gisiger; ***C:*** Helena Vagnieres; ***M:*** Balz Bachmann.

A Yank at Eton 🦴🦴 1/2 **1942** Thematic sequel to 1938's "A Yank at Oxford" finds football-loving American teen Timothy Dennis (Rooney) trading Notre Dame for traditional boys school Eton when his mother marries an Englishman and settles them in across the pond. Naturally, free-spirited Tim has some adjusting to do as does his staid new stepbrother--and fellow student--Peter (Bartholomew). **88m/B; DVD.** Mickey Rooney; Freddie Bartholomew; Edmund Gwenn; Peter

Lawford; Ian Hunter; Marta Linden; Juanita Quigley; Alan Mowbray; ***D:*** Norman Taurog; ***W:*** George Oppenheimer; Lionel Houser; Thomas Phipps; ***C:*** Karl Freund; Charles Lawton, Jr.; ***M:*** Bronislau Kaper.

Yank in Libya 🦴 ½ **1942** No, not the American bombing raid of Khadafy, rather a low-budget WWII adventure pitting an American man and an English girl against Libyan Arabs and Nazis. **65m/B; VHS, DVD.** Walter Woolf King; Joan Woodbury; H.B. Warner; Parkyakarkus (Harry Einstein); ***D:*** Al(bert) Herman; ***W:*** Arthur St. Claire; Sherman Lowe; ***C:*** Edward Linden.

A Yank in the R.A.F. 🦴🦴 ½ **1941** Power's enthusiastic performance as a brash American pilot boosts this dated WWII adventure. He and his British allies seem more concerned over who gets showgirl Betty Grable than in the Nazis, but climactic air attacks retain excitement. Produced by Darryl F. Zanuck to drum up American support for embattled Britain and France. **98m/B; VHS, DVD.** Tyrone Power; Betty Grable; John Sutton; Reginald Gardiner; ***D:*** Henry King.

Yankee Buccaneer 🦴🦴 ½ **1952** With the arrival of impulsive Lt. David Farragut (Brady), Naval Captain David Porter's (Chandler) frigate is given a new assignment. The crew and ship are to sail to the Caribbean, disguised as pirates, and stop the criminals who have been preying on America's merchant fleet. Portuguese countess Donna (Ball) comes aboard since the pirates are threatening to overthrow her government, but when she and Farragut are captured, it's the noble Porter to their rescue. **86m/C; DVD.** Jeff Chandler; Scott Brady; Suzan Ball; Joseph Calleia; George Mathews; Rodolfo Acosta; David Janssen; ***D:*** Fred de Cordova; ***W:*** Charles K. Peck, Jr.; ***C:*** Russell Metty; ***M:*** Milton Rosen.

Yankee Clipper 🦴🦴 ½ **1927** Deceit, treachery, and romance are combined in this depiction of a fierce race from China to New England between the American ship Yankee Clipper, and the English ship Lord of the Isles. Silent. **68m/B; Silent; VHS, DVD.** William Boyd; Elinor Fair; Frank "Junior" Coghlan; John Miljan; Walter Long; ***D:*** Rupert Julian.

Yankee Doodle Dandy 🦴🦴🦴🦴 **1942** Nostalgic view of the Golden Era of show business and the man who made it glitter—George M. Cohan. His early days, triumphs, songs, musicals and romances are brought to life by the inexhaustible Cagney in a rare and wonderful song-and-dance performance. Told in flashback, covering the Irishman's struggling days as a young song writer and performer to his salad days as the toast of Broadway. Cagney, never more charismatic, dances up a storm, reportedly inventing most of the steps on the spot. **126m/B; DVD, Blu-Ray.** James Cagney; Joan Leslie; Walter Huston; Richard Whorf; Irene Manning; Rosemary DeCamp; Jeanne Cagney; S.Z. Sakall; Walter Catlett; Frances Langford; Eddie Foy, Jr.; George Tobias; Michael Curtiz; ***D:*** Michael Curtiz; ***W:*** Robert Buckner; ***C:*** James Wong Howe. Oscars '42: Actor (Cagney), Scoring/Musical, Sound; AFI '98: Top 100; Natl. Film Reg. '93; N.Y. Film Critics '42: Actor (Cagney).

Yankee Zulu 🦴🦴 **1995 (PG)** A young black boy, Zulu, and a young white boy, Rhino, begin a friendship in their South African homeland that is torn apart by apartheid. Twenty-five years later, they are reunited by chance and forced into race-reversal roles that lead to a number of comedic disasters and a renewal of their boyhood friendship. **89m/C; VHS, Streaming.** *SA* Leon Schuster; John Matshikiza; Wilson Dunster; Terri Treas; ***D:*** Gray Hofmeyr; ***W:*** Leon Schuster; Gray Hofmeyr.

The Yankles 🦴 ½ **2009 (PG-13)** Religious sports drama that's sometimes preachy and sometimes amusing, all done (noticeably) on a shoestring budget. A prison sentence for numerous DUIs ruined the career of baseball player Charlie Jones (Wimmer). A paroled Charlie reluctantly agrees to serve as a baseball coach to fulfill his community service requirements even though his wannabe players are all orthodox yeshiva students with little experience (or apparent ability). **115m/C; DVD, Blu-Ray.** Brian Wimmer; Donny Most; Bart Johnson; Michael Buster; Susanne Sutchy; Kenneth F. Brown; ***D:*** David R. Brooks; ***W:*** David R. Brooks; Zev Brooks; ***C:*** Boris Price; ***M:*** Eddie Hernandez. **VIDEO**

Yanks 🦴🦴 **1979** An epic-scale but uneventful drama depicts the legions of American soldiers billeted in England during WWII, and their impact—mostly sexual—on the staid Britons. No big story, no big deal, despite a meticulous recreation of the era. **139m/C; VHS, DVD, Blu-Ray.** Richard Gere; Vanessa Redgrave; William Devane; Lisa Eichhorn; Rachel Roberts; Chick Vennera; Arlen Dean Snyder; Annie Ross; ***D:*** John Schlesinger; ***W:*** Colin Welland; Walter Bernstein; ***C:*** Dick Bush; ***M:*** Richard Rodney Bennett. British Acad. '79: Support. Actress (Roberts); Natl. Bd. of Review '79: Director (Schlesinger).

The Yards 🦴🦴 ½ **2000 (R)** Director James Gray presents a gloomy, tragic New York story once again in his follow-up to "Little Odessa." Just out of the joint, Leo (Wahlberg) returns home to find that his mother Val (Burstyn) is suffering from a heart condition and his girl Erica (Theron) has taken up with his best friend Willie (Phoenix). Deciding to do right by mom, Leo decides to get a job with his Uncle Frank (Caan), whose company makes and repairs New York City trains. He discovers that his uncle isn't as squeaky clean as he thought when he joins Willie's crew, running highly illegal errands for Frank. On a sabotage mission to a competing company, Willie murders a security guard and tries to pin the crime on Leo. Leo is now chased by the cops and Uncle Frank's "family." Gray's writing is superb and the cast turns in good performances as well, although Theron's Noo Yawk accent tends to grate. **115m/C; VHS, DVD, Blu-Ray.** Mark Wahlberg; James Caan; Charlize Theron; Joaquin Rafael (Leaf) Phoenix; Ellen Burstyn; Faye Dunaway; Tony Musante; Steve Lawrence; Victor Argo; Tomas Milian; Victor Arnold; Chad Aaron; Andrew Davoli; Robert Montano; ***D:*** James Gray; ***W:*** James Gray; Matt Reeves; ***C:*** Harris Savides; ***M:*** Howard Shore. Natl. Bd. of Review '00: Support. Actor (Phoenix).

The Yarn Princess 🦴🦴 ½ **1994** With her family threatened by separation, mentally retarded Marjorie Thomas (Smart) must prove to state authorities that she has the ability to take care of her six sons when husband Jake (Pastorelli) falls victim to severe schizophrenia. Boutsikaris plays Smart's defense lawyer. Average made for TV movie about a handicapped woman beating the odds. **92m/C; VHS, DVD.** Jean Smart; Robert Pastorelli; Dennis Boutsikaris; Peter Crook; ***D:*** Tom McLoughlin; ***W:*** Dalene Young. **TV**

The Year Dolly Parton Was My Mom 🦴🦴 ½ **2011** It's 1976 and 11-year-old Elizabeth finds her parents boring and conservative--not at all like her best friend Annabelle's mother, Stella, who's a big fan of Dolly Parton's music. Elizabeth accidentally finds out she's adopted and suddenly decides that Dolly is her birth mother. Elizabeth runs away to meet Dolly at her concert in Minneapolis, even though she lives in Manitoba. **95m/C; DVD.** *CA* Julia Stone; Rebecca Croll; Rebecca Windheim; Macha Grenon; Gil Bellows; ***D:*** Tara Johns; ***W:*** Tara Johns; ***C:*** Claudine Sauve.

A Year in Provence 🦴🦴🦴 **1989** Retired London executive Peter Mayle and his wife Annie decide to leave England to live in the south of France. They buy a 200-year-old farmhouse and experience all the trials and amusements of forging a new life in a different country, complete with different language and customs. They hoped for tranquility and what they got were eccentric neighbors, endless renovations, lots of company, and a taste for good food and drink. Based on Mayle's autobiographical novels "A Year in Provence" and "Tonjours Provence" and filmed on location. **360m/C; VHS, DVD.** *GB* John Thaw; Lindsay Duncan; Bernard Spiegel; Jean-Pierre Delage; Maryse Kuster; Louis Lyonnet; ***D:*** David Tucker; ***W:*** Michael Sadler. **TV**

The Year My Parents Went on Vacation 🦴🦴 *O Ano em que Mus Pais Sairam de Ferais* **2007 (PG)** In 1970, Brazil is ruled by a military dictatorship, which forces the activist parents of 12-year-old Mauro (Joelsas) to go underground to escape arrest. So Mauro finds himself being cared for by his grandfather's grumpy neighbor Shlomo (Haiut), a member of the Orthodox Jewish community in San Paulo. Mauro's naturally confused and lonely as he tries to adjust to his new circumstances in this fairly familiar and sentimental tale. Portuguese, Hebrew, and Yiddish with subtitles. **103m/C; DVD.** *BR* Caio Blat; Michel Joelsas; Germano Haiut; Daniela Piepszyk; Liliana Castro; Simone Spoladore; Eduardo Moreira; Paulo Autran; ***D:*** Cao Hamburger; ***W:*** Braulio Mantovani; Cao Hamburger; Claudio Galperin; Anna Muylaert; ***C:*** Adriano Goldman; ***M:*** Beto Villares.

The Year My Voice Broke 🦴🦴🦴 **1987 (PG-13)** Above-average adolescent drama: a girl breaks a boy's heart by getting pregnant by a tougher, older boy, then leaves town. Blues-inducing, explicit, and not pleasant, but good acting from newcomers carries the day. Followed by "Flirting." **103m/C; VHS, DVD.** *AU* Noah Taylor; Leone Carmen; Ben Mendelsohn; Graeme Blundell; Lynette Curran; Malcolm Robertson; Judi Farr; Bruce Spence; ***D:*** John Duigan; ***W:*** John Duigan; ***C:*** Geoff Burton; ***M:*** Christine Woodruff. Australian Film Inst. '87: Film.

The Year of Getting to Know Us 🦴 ½ **2008 (R)** Cliched dysfunctional family comedy. New York-based writer Chris Rocket reluctantly returns home to Florida after dad Ron suffers a debilitating stroke. Flashbacks show Chris' childhood as he is pulled between his crazy parents, leaving him a commitment-phobe who has never grown up. **90m/C; DVD.** Jimmy Fallon; Sharon Stone; Tom Arnold; Lucy Liu; Tony Hale; Illeana Douglas; Chase Ellison; ***D:*** Patrick Sisam; ***W:*** Patrick Sisam; Rick Velleu; ***C:*** Lisa Rinzler; ***M:*** John Swihart.

The Year of Living Dangerously 🦴🦴🦴 ½ **1982 (PG)** Political thriller features Gibson as immature, impulsive Australian journalist Guy Hamilton, who's covering a political story in Indonesia, circa 1965. During the coup against President Sukarno, he becomes involved with British attache Jill Bryant (Weaver) at the height of the bloody fighting and rioting in Jakarta. Hunt is excellent as male photographer Billy Swan, central to the action as the moral center. Rumored to be based on the activities of CNN's Peter Arnett, although the original source is a novel by C.J. Koch, who reportedly collaborated/battled with Weir on the screenplay. Fascinating, suspenseful film, set up brilliantly by Weir, with great romantic chemistry between Gibson and Weaver. Shot on location in the Philippines (then moved to Sydney after cast and crew were threatened). First Australian movie financed by a U.S. studio. **114m/C; VHS, DVD.** *AU* Mel Gibson; Sigourney Weaver; Linda Hunt; Michael Murphy; Noel Ferrier; Bill Kerr; ***D:*** Peter Weir; ***W:*** Peter Weir; David Williamson; Christopher (C.J.) Koch; ***C:*** Russell Boyd; ***M:*** Maurice Jarre. Oscars '83: Support. Actress (Hunt); L.A. Film Critics '83: Support. Actress (Hunt); Natl. Bd. of Review '83: Support. Actress (Hunt); N.Y. Film Critics '83: Support. Actress (Hunt).

Year of the Comet 🦴🦴 **1992 (PG-13)** Amusing adventure/romantic comedy throws straightlaced Maggie (Miller) with carefree Oliver (Daly) in a quest for a rare bottle of wine. Fine wine is Maggie's passion, and snagging this particular bottle will boost her status in the family business. Oliver is a pretzels and beer kind of guy, but his boss wants this bottle and will pay a lot to get it. Wants to be another "Romancing the Stone," but plot and characters are too thin. Nice chemistry between Miller and Daly sort of saves this one despite a disappointing script. Beautiful location shots of Scotland. **135m/C; VHS, Blu-Ray, Streaming.** Penelope Ann Miller; Timothy Daly; Louis Jourdan; Art Malik; Ian Richardson; Ian McNeice; Timothy Bentinck; Julia McCarthy; Jacques Mathou; ***D:*** Peter Yates; ***W:*** William Goldman; ***M:*** Hummie Mann.

Year of the Dog 🦴🦴 **2007 (PG-13)** Peggy (Shannon) is your basic single, middle-aged office drone whose one true love is her beagle, Pencil. When Pencil suddenly dies, Peggy goes off the deep end in her grief. Looking for a sense of purpose, Peggy takes up the cause of animal rights, with the encouragement of fellow activist Newt (Sarsgaard), and also adopts every stray she sees. Shannon plays her character absolutely straight: Peggy might be nuts, she might be unsympathetic sometimes, but she's completely sincere and those animals are lucky to have her. Screenwriter (and actor) White makes his directorial debut. **98m/C; DVD.** Molly Shannon; Peter Sarsgaard; Laura Dern; Thomas (Tom) McCarthy; Regina King; John C. Reilly; Josh Pais; ***D:*** Mike White; ***W:*** Mike White; ***C:*** Tim Orr; ***M:*** Christophe Beck.

Year of the Dragon 🦴🦴 ½ **1985 (R)** Polish police Captain Stanley White of the NYPD vows to neutralize the crime lords running New York's Chinatown. Brilliant cinematography, well-done action scenes with maximum violence, a racist hero you don't want to root for, murky script, and semi-effective direction are the highlights of this tour through the black market's underbelly and hierarchy. Based on Robert Daley's novel. **136m/C; VHS, DVD.** Mickey Rourke; John Lone; Ariane; Leonard Termo; Raymond J. Barry; Jack Kehler; ***D:*** Michael Cimino; ***W:*** Oliver Stone; Michael Cimino.

Year of the Gun 🦴🦴 ½ **1991 (R)** McCarthy is an American journalist in Rome who begins a novel based on the political instability around him, using the names of real people in his first draft. Soon, ambitious photojournalist Stone wants to collaborate with him, and the Red Brigade terrorist group wants to "remove" anyone associated with the book. Although failing on occasion to balance the thin line it establishes between reality and perception, "Gun" aspires to powerful drama, offering a realistic look at the lives and priorities of political terrorists. Love scenes between Stone and McCarthy are torrid. **111m/C; VHS, DVD.** Andrew McCarthy; Sharon Stone; Valeria Golino; John Pankow; Mattia Sbragia; George Murcell; ***D:*** John Frankenheimer; ***W:*** David Ambrose; Jay Presson Allen; ***M:*** Bill Conti.

Year of the Horse 🦴🦴 **1997 (R)** Jarmusch's documentary on the nearly 30-year rock phenomenon of Neil Young & Crazy Horse. Looking as gritty as some of Horse's riffs sound, pic intercuts footage of the band's performances in '76, '86, and the latest '96 European and U.S. tours shot on Super-8, High Fi-8 video, and 16 mm. Jarmusch wisely lets songs run full-length with complete performances intact, though lesser fans of the band may not be as thrilled about that. Falls short in capturing the spirit and essence of the band and their drive to stay together after all these years, but does show some cool behind-the-scenes moments that make it worthwhile to rock fans. **107m/C; VHS, DVD.** ***D:*** Jim Jarmusch.

Year of the Quiet Sun 🦴🦴🦴 ½ **1984 (PG)** A poignant, acclaimed love story about a Polish widow and an American soldier who find each other in the war-torn landscape of 1946 Europe. Beautifully rendered, with a confident sense of time and place, making this much more than a simple love story. In Polish with English subtitles. **106m/C; VHS, DVD.** *PL GE* Scott Wilson; Maja Komorowska; ***D:*** Krzysztof Zanussi. Venice Film Fest. '84: Film.

Year One 🦴 ½ **2009 (PG-13)** Comic shtick filled with jokes that were old when the Old Testament wasn't. Jack Black naturally looks like a caveman and Michael Cera naturally looks like a dweeb, which happen to fit their characters, who are dumb hunter-gatherers who get kicked out of their tribe for not pulling their weight. Somehow these Neanderthals stumble into various biblical situations, such as witnessing Cain kill Abel, and wind up in Sodom where Zed decides it would be fun to proclaim himself a religious deity (good for getting chicks). **97m/C; Blu-Ray, UMD, On Demand.** Jack Black; Michael Cera; Olivia Wilde; June Raphael; David Cross; Oliver Platt; Hank Azaria; Christopher Mintz-Plasse; Paul Rudd; Harold Ramis; Vinnie Jones; ***D:*** Harold Ramis; ***W:*** Harold Ramis; Gene Stupnitsky; Lee Eisenberg; ***C:*** Alar Kivilo; ***M:*** David Kitay; Theodore Shapiro.

The Yearling 🦴🦴🦴 ½ **1946** This family classic is a tear-jerking adaptation of the Marjorie Kinnan Rawlings novel about a young boy's love for a yearling fawn during the post Civil-War era. His father's encouragement and his mother's bitterness play against the story of unqualified love amid poverty and the boy's coming of age. Wonderful footage of Florida. Jarman was awarded a special Oscar as outstanding child actor. **128m/C; VHS, DVD.** Gregory Peck; Jane Wyman; Claude Jarman, Jr.; Chill

Wills; Henry Travers; Jeff York; Forrest Tucker; June Lockhart; Margaret Wycherly; *D:* Clarence Brown; *C:* Charles Rosher. Oscars '46: Color Cinematog.; Golden Globes '47: Actor--Drama (Peck).

The Yearling ☙☙ 1/2 **1994** TV remake of the classic Marjorie Kinnan Rawlings novel about a boy and his orphaned fawn. The Baxters are struggling in '30s Florida: Pa Penny (Strauss) is a hardscrabble farmer and severe Ma Ora (Smart) has lost three of her four children. Surviving son, 12-year-old Jody (Horneff), gets more than his share of life's hard lessons—with even his adored pet causing problems. On the cloying side, the 1946 big-screen version is still the one to watch. Filmed in South Carolina. **98m/C; VHS, DVD.** Peter Strauss; Jean Smart; Wil Horneff; Brad Greenquist; Jarred Blanchard; Philip Seymour Hoffman; Nancy Moore Atchison; *D:* Rod Hardy; *W:* Joe Wiesenfeld; *M:* Lee Holdridge.

Yella ☙☙☙ **2007** Yella, a woman from the former East Germany, lands a job in the western city of Hanover, where she plans to break free of her violent, estranged husband Ben. Despite the abuse, Yella continues to give in to her husband's demands and finds that her past will not stop haunting her. She bounces from one strange encounter to another as writer-director Petzold slices a tightly wound psychological thriller out of a timeline that weaves from present to past. **89m/C; DVD.** *GE* Hinnerk Schoenemann; David Striesow; Christian Redl; Michael Wittenborn; *D:* Christian Petzold; *W:* Christian Petzold; *C:* Hans Fromm.

Yelling to the Sky ☙ 1/2 **2011** Fighting between her parents forces Sweetness (Zoe Kravitz) to move into a neighborhood and school much rougher than she is used to, and she finds herself turning to crime to find a way back out. **95m/C; DVD, Blu-Ray, Streaming.** Zoë Kravitz; Jason Clarke; Gabourey Sidibe; Tim Blake Nelson; Sonequa Martin; *D:* Victoria Mahoney; *W:* Victoria Mahoney; *C:* Reed Morano; *M:* David Wittman.

Yellow ☙☙ **1998** Eight Korean-American teens have big plans for their graduation night in L.A. but they didn't originally include trying to help Sin Lee (Chung) recover the large sum of his dad's dough that he lost. They get into more trouble trying to round up the cash and Sin reacts to their friendly efforts by running away and making things worse for himself. **90m/C; VHS, DVD.** Soon-Teck Oh; Amy Hill; Michael Chung; Burt Bulos; Angie Suh; Mia Suh; Jason J. Tobin; Lela Lee; Mary Chen; John Cho; *D:* Chris Chan Lee; *W:* Chris Chan Lee; *C:* Ted Cohen; *M:* John Oh.

Yellow ☙☙ **2006 (R)** Cliched though energetic follow-your-dreams pic. Classically trained dancer Amaryllis (very sultry Sanchez) moves from San Juan to New York hoping to dance on Broadway. Needing a job while she auditions, Amaryllis works as a stripper (whose nom de pole is "Yellow") and soon has a favorite client, depressed doctor Christian (Sweeney), who wants to sweep Amaryllis away from all the sleaze. **90m/C; DVD.** Roselyn Sanchez; D.B. Sweeney; Bill Duke; Manny Perez; Jamie Tirelli; Erika Michaels; *D:* Alfredo de Villa; *W:* Roselyn Sanchez; Nacoma Whobery; *C:* Claudio Chea; *M:* Andre Abujamra.

The Yellow Birds ☙☙ **2017 (R)** An Iraq War drama focusing on two American soldiers, adapted from a novel by veteran Kevin Powers. At Army basic training, 18-year-old Daniel "Murph" Murphy (Sheridan) meets 20-year-old Brandon Bartle (Ehrenreich). Though the pair are from different social classes, both are from Virginia and Bartle feels protective of the more innocent Murph. When they are shipped out to Iraq, the terrorizing experience of urban warfare deeply affects them both. Once back home, Bartle's processing of his experience negatively impacts himself and those around him. Though the acting is strong, the premise is overused. **94m/C; DVD, Blu-Ray, Streaming.** Alden Ehrenreich; Tye Sheridan; Toni Collette; Jason Patric; Jack Huston; *D:* Alexandre Moors; *W:* David Lowery; R.F.I. (Ronnie) Porto; *C:* Daniel Landin; *M:* Adam Wiltzie.

Yellow Cargo ☙☙ **1936** Ingenious "B" movie about a pair of undercover agents who blow the lid off a smuggling scam. It seems that the smugglers have been masquerading as a movie crew, and use disguised Chinese "extras" to transport their goods. The agents pose as actors to infiltrate the gang. **70m/B; VHS, DVD.** Conrad Nagel; Eleanor Hunt; Vince Barnett; Jack La Rue; Claudia Dell; *D:* Crane Wilbur; *W:* Crane Wilbur.

The Yellow Handkerchief ☙☙☙ **2008 (PG-13)** Just out of prison, Brett (Hurt) is hoping his ex-wife May (Bello) will take him back, so he hitches a ride with teenage misfits Martine (Stewart) and Gordy (Redmayne) back to Louisiana. As they travel the three strangers come to trust, understand, and help one another. Hurt leads with an excellent performance in this movie that's unafraid to sit back and let the character dynamics unfold slowly and gracefully, avoiding excessive sentimentality. Title refers to Brett's request that May should hang a yellow handkerchief outside the house if she says yes. Adapted from a 1971 short story by Pete Hamill. **102m/C; DVD, Blu-Ray.** William Hurt; Maria Bello; Kristen Stewart; Eddie Redmayne; Veronica Russell; *D:* Udayan Prasad; *W:* Erin Dignam; *C:* Chris Menges; *M:* Eef Barzelay; Jack Livesey.

The Yellow Rolls Royce ☙ 1/2 **1964** Uneven anthology veers from comedy to drama within the same plot. In the 1920s, Charles, the Marquis of Frinton, buys wife Eloise the exotic Phantom II Rolls as an anniversary gift though later he discovers her in it with another man. American gangster Paolo Maltese buys the car in the 1930s when he takes moll/fiancee Mae on an Italian tour. He's called away and Mae flirts with photographer Stefano, which is dangerous if Paolo finds out. By 1941 the Rolls is a shabby shadow of its former self for wealthy American Gerda Millet who's driving to Yugoslavia and finds herself in the resistance against the Nazis. **122m/C; DVD.** *GB* Rex Harrison; Jeanne Moreau; Edmund Purdom; Moira Lister; George C. Scott; Shirley MacLaine; Alain Delon; Art Carney; Ingrid Bergman; Omar Sharif; Joyce Grenfell; Michael Hordern; *D:* Anthony Asquith; *W:* Terence Rattigan; *C:* Jack Hildyard; *M:* Riz Ortolani.

Yellow Sky ☙☙☙ **1948** Emerging from the nearby wilderness, a gang of outlaws, led by the amoral Stretch Dawson (Peck), sneak into a nearby town and rob the local bank. Though the gang is pursued by local garrison soldiers, the soldiers stop the chase once they realize the criminals are heading straight into the desert. The men struggle to survive in the unforgiving terrain, only finding what seems to be a respite in a ghost town inhabited only by a feisty woman named Mike (Baxter) and her prospector grandfather (Barton).The classic Western by filmmaker Wellman is a forceful study of the primal struggles of humanity. **98m/B; DVD.** Gregory Peck; Anne Baxter; Richard Widmark; John Russell; Robert Arthur; *D:* William A. Wellman; *W:* Lamar Trotti; W.R. Burnett; *C:* Joseph Macdonald; *M:* Alfred Newman.

Yellow Submarine ☙☙☙ 1/2 **1968 (G)** The acclaimed animated fantasy based on a plethora of mid-career Beatles songs, sees the Fab Four battle the Blue Meanies for the sake of Sgt. Pepper, the Nowhere Man, Strawberry Fields, and Pepperland. The first full-length British animated feature in 14 years features a host of talented cartoonists. Fascinating LSD-esque animation and imagery. Speaking voices provided by John Clive (John), Geoff Hughes (Paul), Peter Batten (George), and Paul Angelis (Ringo). The Beatles themselves do appear in a short scene at the end of the film. Martin fills in as music director, and Segal of "Love Story" fame co-scripts. **87m/C; VHS, DVD, Blu-Ray.** *GB V:* John Clive; Geoff Hughes; Peter Batten; Paul Angelis; Dick Emery; Lance Percival; George Harrison; John Lennon; Paul McCartney; Ringo Starr; *D:* George Duning; Dick Emery; *W:* Erich Segal; Al Brodax; Jack Mendelsohn; Lee Minoff; *M:* George Harrison; John Lennon; Paul McCartney; Ringo Starr.

Yellowbeard ☙☙ **1983 (PG)** An alleged comedy with a great cast who wander about with little direction. Follows the efforts of an infamous pirate (Chapman) to locate a buried treasure using the map tattooed on the back of his son's head. Final role for Feldman, who died during production. **97m/C; VHS, DVD, Blu-Ray.** Graham Chapman; Peter Boyle; Richard "Cheech" Marin; Thomas Chong; Peter Cook; Marty Feldman; Martin Hewitt; Michael Hordern; Eric Idle; Madeline Kahn; James Mason; John Cleese; Susannah York; David Bowie; Monte Landis; Kenneth Mars; Ferdinand "Ferdy" Mayne; Beryl Reid; *D:* Mel Damski; *W:* Graham Chapman; Peter Cook; Bernard McKenna; *C:* Gerry Fisher; *M:* John Morris.

Yellowneck ☙☙ **1955** A handful of Confederate Army soldiers desert, hoping to cross the Florida Everglades and eventually reach Cuba. The swamp takes its toll, however, and one by one the men fall by the wayside. A sole survivor reaches the coast. Will the escape boat be waiting for him? **83m/C; VHS, DVD.** Lin McCarthy; Stephen Courtleigh; Berry Kroeger; Harold Gordon; Bill Mason; *D:* R. John Hugh.

Yentl ☙☙ 1/2 **1983 (PG)** The famous Barbra adaptation of Isaac Bashevis Singer's story set in 1900s Eastern Europe about a Jewish girl who masquerades as a boy in order to study the Talmud, and who becomes enmeshed in romantic miscues. Lushly photographed, with a repetitive score that nevertheless won an Oscar. Singer was reportedly appalled by the results of Streisand's hyper-controlled project. **134m/C; VHS, DVD, Blu-Ray.** Barbra Streisand; Mandy Patinkin; Amy Irving; Nehemiah Persoff; Steven Hill; Allan Corduner; Ruth Goring; David de Keyser; Bernard Spear; *D:* Barbra Streisand; *C:* David Watkin; *M:* Michel Legrand; Alan Bergman; Marilyn Bergman. Oscars '83: Orig. Song Score and/or Adapt.; Golden Globes '84: Director (Streisand), Film--Mus./Comedy.

Yerma ☙☙ **1999** Yerma (Sanchez-Gijon) desperately wants a child but is unable to conceive. The village wise woman (Papas) puts the blame on Yerma's husband Juan (Diego). As her obsession grows so does Yerma's hatred of her husband and she is tempted to seduce shepherd Victor (Cabrero) to fulfill her longings, which are now driving her to the edge of insanity. Based on a drama by Federico Garcia Lorca. Spanish with subtitles. **118m/C; VHS, DVD.** *SP* Aitana Sanchez-Gijon; Irene Papas; Juan Diego; Jesus Cabrero; *D:* Pilar Tavora; *W:* Pilar Tavora; *C:* Acacio De Almeida; *M:* Vincente Sanchez.

Yes ☙☙ 1/2 **2004 (R)** When She (Allen) and He (Abkarian) cross paths in London some serious sexual fireworks go off and, at first, they ignore their cultural differences—She's an Irish-American scientist trapped in a dead-end marriage to a rich politician and He's a Lebanese refugee and surgeon-turned-chef. All good things must come to an end, though, as he despises Western culture while she questions Islamic values. Tries too hard to push its post-9/11 political message, as it awkwardly uses poetic meter for dialogue. **99m/C; DVD.** Joan Allen; Simon Abkarian; Sam Neill; Shirley Henderson; Sheila Hancock; Samantha Bond; Gary Lewis; Raymond Waring; Stephanie Leonidas; Wil (Wilbert) Johnson; *D:* Sally Potter; *C:* Alexei Rodionov; *M:* Sally Potter.

Yes, Giorgio ☙☙ **1982 (PG)** Opera singer Pavarotti in his big-screen debut. He has an advantage over other non-actors trapped in similar situations (e.g., Hulk Hogan): He can sing (but of course, not wrestle). Lame plot (famous opera star falls for lady doctor) is the merest excuse for the maestro to belt out "If We Were in Love," "I Left My Heart in San Francisco," and arias by Verdi, Donizetti, and Puccini. **111m/C; VHS, DVD.** Luciano Pavarotti; Kathryn Harrold; Eddie Albert; James Hong; *D:* Franklin J. Schaffner; *W:* Norman Steinberg; *M:* John Williams.

Yes Man ☙☙ **2008 (PG-13)** After a heartbreaking divorce, glum bank employee Carl (Carrey) attends a self-help seminar, where the eccentric speaker convinces him to stop saying "no" and start saying "yes"?to everything. Soon he finds himself bungee jumping off a bridge, learning Korean, and somehow becoming an overall better person through his new positive mantra, even meeting a girl (Deschanel—who's much too young for Carrey). A simple premise comes across as tame and shallow while goofball Carrey stretches it to the limit with very few glimpses of his true talents. Based on the memoir by Danny Wallace, an actual participator in the "yes" self-help program. **104m/C; Blu-Ray, On Demand.** Jim Carrey; Zooey Deschanel; Terence Stamp; Sasha Alexander; Bradley Cooper; Danny Masterson; Molly Sims; Rhys Darby; Fionnula Flanagan; John Michael Higgins; *D:* Peyton Reed; *W:* Nicholas Stoller; Jarrad Paul; Andrew Mogel; *C:* Robert Yeoman; *M:* Lyle Workman; Mark Oliver Everett.

The Yes Men ☙☙ **2003 (R)** Documentary follows a couple of anti-government pranksters, Andy Bichlbaum and Mike Bonanno, who travel around impersonating representatives of the World Trade Organization. They disrupt various economic conferences, give fake interviews and speeches, and generally behave like nitwits. They also seem to be the only ones getting the supposed joke. Fighting the man has never been so bland. **80m/C; DVD.** *D:* Chris Smith; Dan Ollman; Sarah Price; *C:* Chris Smith; Dan Ollman; Sarah Price.

Yesterday ☙☙ 1/2 **2019 (PG-13)** Jack (Patel) is a struggling musician who lives with his parents in Suffolk and is managed by his friend Ellie (James). He is ready to give up on his dream of musical success when a 12-second blackout across the world results in small changes, including most everyone forgetting the Beatles and their songs. However, Jack remembers, plays the songs publicly, and claims them as his own This results in a meteoric rise in his musical career, though one that comes a cost for him personally and romantically. It has many feel-good moments and an interesting concept, but its troubles aren't so...far away... **116m/C; DVD, Blu-Ray.** Himesh Patel; Lily James; Sophia Di Martino; Ellise Chappell; Meera Syal; *D:* Danny Boyle; *W:* Richard Curtis; *C:* Christopher Ross; *M:* Daniel Pemberton.

The Yesterday Machine **WOOF!** **1963** Camp sci-fi: A mad doctor tries to bring back Hitler. Don't worry, though: the good guys win. Predictable, dumb drivel. **85m/B; VHS, DVD.** Tim Holt; James Britton; Jack Herman; *D:* Russ Marker.

Yesterday, Today and Tomorrow ☙☙☙ 1/2 *Ieri, Oggi E Domani; She Got What She Asked For* **1964** Trilogy of comic sexual vignettes featuring Loren and her many charms. She plays a black marketeer, a wealthy matron, and a prostitute. Funny, and still rather racy. Loren at her best, in all senses; includes her famous striptease for Mastroianni. **119m/C; VHS, DVD, Blu-Ray.** *IT FR* Sophia Loren; Marcello Mastroianni; Tony Pica; Giovanni Ridolfi; Tecla Scarano; Armando Trovajoli; *D:* Vittorio De Sica; *W:* Eduardo de Filippo; *C:* Giuseppe Rotunno; *M:* Armando Trovajoli. Oscars '64: Foreign Film; British Acad. '64: Actor (Mastroianni).

Yesterday's Enemy ☙☙ **1959** In 1942, British Captain Langford (Baker) and his men, cut off by the Japanese advance into Burma, take refuge in a jungle village. Langford discovers coded plans for an attack and is determined to get info from an uncooperative prisoner. He resorts to brutal means and his methods are later turned against him. **94m/B; DVD.** *UK* Stanley Baker; Leo McKern; Guy Rolfe; Gordon Jackson; Philip Ahn; Bryan Forbes; *D:* Val Guest; *W:* Peter R. Newman; *C:* Arthur Grant.

Yeti **WOOF!** **2008** Part of the Syfy Channel's "Maneater" series. A college football team's plane crashes in the Himalayas and they not only have to survive the environment but the attacks of a hungry Yeti. A guy in a furry suit isn't scary, although seeing a bunch of whiny college kids get munched is always fun. **87m/C; DVD.** Carly Pope; Marc Menard; Peter DeLuise; Crystal Lowe; Brandon Jay McClaren; Elfina Luk; Adam O'Byrne; Ed Marinaro; *D:* Paul Ziller; *W:* Rafael Jordan; *C:* Curtis Peterson; *M:* Michael Richard Plowman. **CABLE**

Yeti: A Love Story **WOOF!** **2008** Along with importing cheap products to Walmart, China apparently now also imports homosexual rapist Yetis from Tibet for the use of homicidal American cultists. Or so you'd believe after watching this film, which also implies that pillow fights are life-altering events that convince women to turn lesbian, and that by sharing chocolate and talking afterwards, victims of rape and their attackers can fall in love. Just beyond bad. **90m/C; DVD.** Adam Balivet; Brie Bouslaugh; Laura Glascott; Eric Gosselin; Adam Malamut; Joe Mande; Jim Martin; Loren Mash; David Paige;

Noah Wolfe; *D:* Eric Gosselin; Adam Deyoe; *W:* Eric Gosselin; Jim Martin; Adam Deyoe; Moses Roth; *C:* Eric Gosselin; Adam Deyoe. **VIDEO**

Yi Yi *A One and a Two...* **2000** N.J. Jian is a middle-aged partner in a Taipei computer firm that needs to innovate if the business is to stay profitable. NJ thinks about teaming up with Japanese games designer, Ota, but a number of family difficulties begin to distract him and things unravel even more while NJ is on a business trip to Japan. Japanese and Mandarin with subtitles. **173m/C; VHS, DVD, Blu-Ray.** *JP TW* Elaine Jin; Nianzhen Wu; Kelly Lee; Jonathan Chang; Issey Ogata; Suyun Ke; *D:* Edward Yang; *W:* Edward Yang; *C:* Weihan Yang; *M:* Kai-li Peng. Cannes '00: Director (Yang); L.A. Film Critics '00: Foreign Film; N.Y. Film Critics '00: Foreign Film; Natl. Soc. Film Critics '00: Film.

Yog, Monster from Space *Kessen Nankai No Daikaiju; Nankai No Daikaiju; The Space Amoeba* **1971 (G)** When a spaceship crashes somewhere near Japan, the aliens in it create monsters out of ordinary critters in order to destroy all the cities. A promoter gets a gleam in his eye and sees the potential for a vacation spot featuring the viscious creatures. Standard Japanese monster flick utilizing the usual out-of-synch dub machine. Dubbed. **105m/C; VHS, DVD.** *JP* Akira Kubo; Yoshio Tsuchiya; Kenji Sahara; Atsuko Takahashi; Yukiko Kobayashi; Yu Fujiki; Noritake Saito; *D:* Inoshiro Honda; *W:* Ei Ogawa; *C:* Taiichi Kankura; *M:* Akira Ifukube.

Yoga Hosers **2016 (PG-13)** Since he left the studio system, writer/director Kevin Smith has absolutely no one left to tell him when he has a horrible idea. Two of the supporting characters from the awful Tusk—yoga-loving, cellphone-addicted, 15-year-old Winnipeg girls Colleen Collette and Colleen McKenzie (Lily-Rose Depp and Harley Quinn Smith, the director's daughter)—have to save the world from Nazi sausages. Yes, Nazi sausages. There was a time when Smith doing a teenage apocalypse story might have been fun, but he's lost so much of his filmmaking edge. **88m/C; DVD, Blu-Ray.** Lily-Rose Depp; Harley Quinn Smith; Johnny Depp; Adam Brody; Tony Hale; Ralph Garman; *D:* Kevin Smith; *W:* Kevin Smith; *C:* James Laxton; *M:* Christopher Drake.

Yogi Bear 1/2 **2010 (PG)** When a greedy, conniving mayor (Daly) plans to sell off Jellystone Park, it's up to Yogi Bear and Boo-Boo (voiced perfectly by Ackroyd and Timberlake) to find a way to save their home, with the help of former nemesis Ranger Smith (Cavanagh). Based on the animated Hanna-Barbera classic TV show but filmed in 3D CG/live-action, it seamlessly puts talking bears into the real world. But with neither the wit nor charm of the original cartoon, the tired, contrived plot is what's not to be believed. **82m/C; Blu-Ray.** T.J. Miller; *V:* Dan Aykroyd; Justin Timberlake; Tom Cavanagh; Andy Daly; Anna Faris; *D:* Eric Brevig; *W:* Brad Copeland; Jeffrey Ventimilia; Joshua Sternin; *C:* Peter James; *M:* John Debney.

Yojimbo **1961** Two clans vying for political power bid on the services of a laconic masterless samurai Sanjuro (Mifune), who comes to their small town in 1860. The samurai sells his services to both parties, with devastating results for all. Japanese with subtitles or dubbed. Re-made by Sergio Leone as the 1964 western "A Fist Full of Dollars." **110m/B; VHS, DVD, Blu-Ray.** *JP* Toshiro Mifune; Eijiro Tono; Isuzu Yamada; Seizaburo Kawazu; Kamatari (Keita) Fujiwara; Takashi Shimura; Tatsuya Nakadai; Daisuke Kato; Yoshio Tsuchiya; Susumu Fujita; Hiroshi Tachikawa; Kyu Sazanka; Ko Nishimura; Ikio Sawamura; Yoko Tsukasa; *D:* Akira Kurosawa; *W:* Akira Kurosawa; Hideo Oguni; Ryuzo Kikushima; *C:* Kazuo Miyagawa; *M:* Masaru Sato.

Yolanda and the Thief 1/2 **1945** A charming, forgotten effort from the Arthur Freed unit about a con man who convinces a virginal South American heiress that he is her guardian angel. Songs include a lengthy Dali-esque ballet built around "Will You Marry Me?" **109m/C; VHS, DVD.** Fred Astaire; Lucille Bremer; Leon Ames; Mildred Natwick; *D:* Vincente Minnelli; *C:* Charles Rosher; *M:* Arthur Freed; Harry Warren.

Yonkers Joe 1/2 **2008 (R)** Palminteri is in familiar territory as a crooked gambler and bad dad. Joe heads up a group of con artists who scam unsuspecting marks at various gambling venues from Atlantic City to Vegas. One thing not going his way is the sudden reappearance of his mentally-handicapped 20-year-old son, Joe Jr. (Guiry), whose aggression has gotten him kicked out of his group home. The kid resents dad's parental neglect and dad resents the kid upsetting his plans. Think they can find some common ground and come to an understanding? **102m/C; On Demand.** Chazz Palminteri; Christine Lahti; Tom Guiry; Michael Lerner; Linus Roache; Michael Rispoli; Roma Maffia; *D:* Robert Celestino; *W:* Robert Celestino; *C:* Michael Fimognari; *M:* Chris Hajian.

Yor, the Hunter from the Future *Il Mondo Di Yor; The World of Yor* **1983 (PG)** Lost in a time warp where the past and the future mysteriously collide, Yor sets out on a search for his real identity, with his only clue a golden medallion around his neck. **88m/C; VHS, DVD, Blu-Ray, Streaming.** *IT* Reb Brown; Corinne Clery; John Steiner; *D:* Anthony M. Dawson; *W:* Anthony M. Dawson; Robert Bailey.

Yossi 1/2 **2012** Director Fox catches up with one of the title characters from his highly-acclaimed 2003 offering "Yossi and Jagger" in this light but accomplished affair. Shaken from depression, Dr. Yossi Hoffman (Knoller) has yet to come out and lives a lonesome life in Tel Aviv. He takes a trip to Eilat, where he meets a young--and unabashedly gay--Israeli IDF officer named Tom (Zehavi) and begins to live again. Perhaps a little overly sentimental, this heartwarmer is a crowd-pleaser with an engaging cast. **84m/C; DVD.** *IS* Ohad Knoller; Oz Zehavi; Lior Ashkenazi; Orly Silbersatz Banai; *D:* Eytan Fox; *W:* Itay Segal; *C:* Guy Raz; *M:* Keren Ann.

Yossi & Jagger **2002** Lior (Levi) and Yossi (Knoller) are soldiers stationed at a remote and snowy Army base on the Israeli-Lebanese border. They also happen to be lovers. They're discreet—Yossi is a career military officer—but Lior, who's nicknamed "Jagger" because of his charisma, is ready to leave the service and come out of the closet so they can live together. Tensions are heightened when two female soldiers, Goldie (Furstenberg) and Yaeli (Koren), arrive and Yaeli immediately makes a play for Jagger. Just as the truth about Yossi and Jagger seems certain to come out, the unit is sent on a dangerous night mission. Restraint is the word for director Fox, which only makes the situation more intense. Hebrew with subtitles. **71m/C; DVD.** *IS* Ohad Knoller; Yehuda Levi; Hani Furstenberg; Aya Koren; Assi Cohen; Sharon Reginiano; Erez Kahana; *D:* Eytan Fox; *W:* Avner Bernheimer; *C:* Yaron Sharf; *M:* Ivri Lider.

You Again 1/2 **2010 (PG)** One-time brace-faced high school nerd Marni (Bell), now grown-up and good-looking, discovers years later that her brother is about to marry Joanna (Yustman), the bully who made her adolescence a living hell. Coincidentally, her mother (Curtis) went through the same ugly duckling years in high school, tormented by the bride's Aunt Ramona (Weaver). Cue the uncomfortable reunion between the warring families for the wedding ceremony. Sounds like a decent idea for a screwball farce, but incorrectly shoots for a warm-hearted romantic comedy. Total waste of big-time female talent and star power, including White's typecast turn as the dopey grandma. **105m/C; Blu-Ray.** Kristen Bell; Odette Annable; Jamie Lee Curtis; Sigourney Weaver; James Wolk; Betty White; Victor Garber; Kristin Chenoweth; Cloris Leachman; Patrick Duffy; Meagan Holder; Christine Lakin; Billy Unger; Kyle Bornheimer; Daryl Hall; Catherine Bach; Staci Keanan; Dwayne "The Rock" Johnson; *D:* Andy Fickman; *W:* Moe Jelline; *C:* David Hennings; *M:* Nathan Wang.

You Ain't Seen Nothin' Yet 1/2 *Vous N'avez Encore Rien Vu* **2012** A postmodern take on the world of theatre brings a group of actors together to the home of recently deceased playwright Antoine d'Anthac (Podalydès). Turns out, these actors all worked on d'Anthac's adaptation of "Eurypides," which is now being performed by a younger theatre company. A video recording by the late director makes a plea for the group to resurrect their performances in a new retelling, but doesn't give clear direction, leaving the troupe to fend for themselves. Ninety-year-old Resnais' movie is artfully edited and carefully paced, but often tries to cram too many ideas into a short span of time. French with subtitles. **115m/C; DVD.** *FR* Sabine Azema; Pierre Arditti; Anne Consigny; Lambert Wilson; Michel Piccoli; Mathieu Amalric; Denis Podalydes; *D:* Alain Resnais; *W:* Laurent Herbiert; Alex Reval; *C:* Eric Gauthier; *M:* Mark Snow.

You and I **2011 (R)** Poor acting and a stupid plot. Janie is an American party girl living in Moscow. She meets Russian aspiring model Lana at a concert where they bond over their mutual obsession with the pop duo t.A.T.u. The girls fall in love, but the situation is complicated by Lana finding out how sordid the fashion world can be and Janie's increasing drug use. **101m/C; DVD.** Mischa Barton; Shantel VanSanten; Charlie Creed-Miles; Anton Yelchin; Bronson Pinchot; *D:* Roland Joffé; *W:* Shawn Schepps; Andrew Cullen; *C:* Philip Robertson; *M:* Jeff Cardoni. **VIDEO**

You and Me 1/2 **1938** Joe Dennis (Raft) is an ex-con now employed at the same department store as Helen (Sidney). They fall in love and marry without Helen admitting she's on parole herself and the rules forbid her to wed. When Joe realizes his marriage is illegal (and his wife's a liar), he picks up with his old gang and plans a robbery. Schizophrenic film is an uneasy mixture of comedy, pathos, romance, crime, and even some songs by Lang's associate Kurt Weill. **90m/B; DVD.** George Raft; Sylvia Sidney; Harry Carey, Sr.; Robert Cummings; Barton MacLane; Warren Hymer; Roscoe Karns; George E. Stone; *D:* Fritz Lang; *W:* Virginia Van Upp; *C:* Charles B(ryant) Lang, Jr.; *M:* Boris Morros.

You and Me *Toi et Moi* **2006** Ariane (Depardieu) writes for illustrated romance magazines but her own life is lovelorn since her boyfriend Farid (Sisley) isn't about to commit to her. Meanwhile, Ariane is oblivious to the interest of mason Pablo (Mencheta), who's working in her apartment building. Ariane's serious sister Lena (Cotillard), a classical cellist, has a dull boyfriend and is ready to succumb to the cocky charms of rakish violinist Mark (Zaccai) but it's a brief interlude that disrupts Lena's life more than she could have imagined. French with subtitles. **95m/C; DVD.** *FR* Julie Depardieu; Marion Cotillard; Jonathan Zaccai; Tomer Sisley; Sergio Peris-Mencheta; Eric Berger; Chantal Lauby; *D:* Julie Curval; *W:* Julie Curval; *C:* Philippe Guilert; *M:* Sebastien Schuller.

You Are Here * **2000 (R)** You are a big loser. (Well, maybe not you personally but you get the idea.) Your job sucks, your love life sucks, life sucks in general. So you decide to quit your job and do what you've always wanted to do. And then your boss comes along and offers you a promotion. Now what? This indie feature gives you some possibilities. **86m/C; VHS, DVD.** Todd Peters; Randall Jaynes; Ajay Naidu; Caroline Hall; Larry Fessenden; Heather Burns; *D:* Jeff Winner; *W:* Jeff Winner; *C:* Bryan Pryzpek; *M:* Byron Estep.

You Are Not Alone *Due Er Ikke Alene* **1978** Two boarding school boys find their friendship turning into first love. But the film doesn't completely dwell on this—when a fellow student is about to be expelled for a prank, the classmates organize a strike against the stern headmaster. Danish with subtitles. **90m/C; DVD.** *CZ* Ove Sprogoe; Anders Agenso; Peter Bjerg; *D:* Ernst Johansen; Lasse Nielsen; *W:* Lasse Nielsen; Bent Petersen; *C:* Henrik Herbert.

You Belong to Me **2007** Whether you want to or not. Jeffrey (Sauli) thinks Rene (Lucas) is the man of his dreams and impulsively decides to move into the same New York apartment building. Overly-attentive landlady Gladys (D'Arbanville, properly horrific) doesn't have a good explanation as to why the previous tenant left all his stuff behind and it's too late to leave when Jeffrey discovers Rene has a live-in lover. Jeffrey starts getting creeped out by the strange goings-on and suspicious when he hears a faint voice calling for help. **82m/C; DVD.** Daniel Serafini Sauli; Patti D'Arbanville; Heather Alicia Simms; Duane Boutte; Julien Lucas; *D:* Sam Zalutsky; *W:* Sam Zalutsky; *C:* Jonathan Furmanski; *M:* John Turner. **VIDEO**

You Can Count On Me **1999 (R)** Sammy (Linney) is a single mom who works at the local bank in her small hometown. Orphaned at an early age, she has grown apart from her younger brother Terry (Ruffalo), who's become a self-destructive wanderer. When Terry comes for a visit, the love they still share as siblings conflicts with their unease over their adult selves and what they now expect from each other. Great performances and no pat resolutions. **109m/C; VHS, DVD.** Laura Linney; Mark Ruffalo; Matthew Broderick; Jon Tenney; Rory Culkin; ***Cameo(s):*** Kenneth Lonergan; *D:* Kenneth Lonergan; *W:* Kenneth Lonergan; *C:* Stephen Kazmierski; *M:* Lesley Barber. Ind. Spirit '01: First Feature, Screenplay; L.A. Film Critics '00: Screenplay; N.Y. Film Critics '00: Actress (Linney), Screenplay; Natl. Soc. Film Critics '00: Actress (Linney), Screenplay; Sundance '00: Grand Jury Prize, Screenplay; Writers Guild '00: Orig. Screenplay.

You Can't Cheat an Honest Man **1939** The owner of a misfit circus suffers a variety of headaches including the wisecracks of Charlie McCarthy. Contains Field's classic ping-pong battle and some of his other best work. **79m/B; VHS, DVD.** W.C. Fields; Edgar Bergen; Constance Moore; Eddie Anderson; Mary Forbes; Thurston Hall; *D:* George Marshall; *C:* Milton Krasner.

You Can't Escape Forever **1942** Newspaper editor Steve Mitchell (Brent) gets into trouble when journalist (and gal pal) Laurie Abbott (Marshall) gets a big story wrong. Steve gets demoted to a lovelorn column and turns out to be a success but he still pursues his interest in crime boss Greer (Ciannelli), working with Laurie to get the goods on the bad guy. **77m/B; DVD.** Brenda Marshall; George Brent; Gene Lockhart; Eduardo Ciannelli; Roscoe Karns; Paul Harvey; Edith Barrett; *W:* Jo Graham; Hector Chevigny; Fred Niblo, Jr.; *C:* James Van Trees; Gaetano Antonio "Tony" Gaudio.

You Can't Get Away With Murder **1939** Crime thriller. Teenager Johnny Stone (Halop) has stolen the gun of his sister Madge's (Page) cop fiance Fred (Stephens). He gives it to his mentor, hardened criminal Frank Wilson (Bogart), who uses it to set Fred up for a murder rap in a botched robbery. Fred is convicted and winds up in Sing Sing on Death Row. Frank and Johnny are also sent to the joint and Johnny's conscience starts bothering him but Fred is afraid he's going turn rat and engineers a breakout to take care of the problem. **79m/B; DVD.** Humphrey Bogart; Billy Halop; Gale Page; Harvey Stephens; Henry Travers; John Litel; Joe Sawyer; Joe Downing; Harold Huber; Joseph Crehan; *D:* Lewis Seiler; *W:* Robert Buckner; Kenneth Gamet; Don Ryan; *C:* Sol Polito; *M:* Heinz Roemheld.

You Can't Have Everything 1/2 **1937** Wannabe serious playwright Judith (Faye) meets cute with Broadway musical director George (Ameche), who talks producer Sam (Wininger) into buying Judith's latest opus even though it's terrible. After turning the work into a musical, George dumps hard-boiled girlfriend Lulu (Lee) and gets Judith a part in the now-successful work, but Lulu isn't going quietly. The Ritz Brothers offer some comic relief. **100m/B; DVD.** Alice Faye; Don Ameche; Charles Winninger; Gypsy Rose Lee; Tony Martin; *D:* Norman Taurog; *W:* Karl Tunberg; Harry Tugend; Jack Yellen; *C:* Lucien N. Andriot.

You Can't Hurry Love **1988 (R)** A jilted-at-the-altar Ohio bachelor moves to Los Angeles and flounders in the city's fast-moving fast lane. A dull film with Fonda, daughter of "Easy Rider" Peter, playing a minor role. **92m/C; VHS, DVD.** David Leisure; Scott McGinnis; Sally Kellerman; Kristy McNichol; Charles Grodin; Anthony Geary; Bridget Fonda; David Packer; Frank Bonner; *D:* Richard Martini; *C:* Peter Lyons Collister.

You Can't Take It with You 1/2 **1938** The Capra version of the Kaufman-Hart play about an eccentric New York family and their non-conformist houseguests. Alice Sycamore (Arthur), the stable family member of an offbeat clan of free spirits, falls for Tony Kirby (Stewart), the down-to-earth son of a snooty, wealthy and not always quite honest family. Amidst the confusion over this love affair, the two families rediscover the simple joys of life. **127m/B; VHS, DVD, Blu-Ray.** James Stewart; Jean Arthur; Lionel Barrymore; Spring Byington; Edward Arnold; Mischa Auer; Donald Meek; Samuel S. Hinds; Ann Miller; H.B. Warner; Halliwell Hobbes; Dub Taylor; Mary Forbes; Eddie Anderson; Harry Davenport; Lillian Yarbo; ***D:*** Frank Capra; ***W:*** Robert Riskin. Oscars '38: Director (Capra), Film.

You Can't Take It With You **1979** Amusing CBS TV adaptation of Moss Hart and George Kaufman's play. Most of the Sycamore family is eccentric, if not crazy, but they want to make a good impression for granddaughter Alice's sake. She's invited her fiancee and his strait-laced parents for dinner but they turn up on the wrong day. **97m/C; DVD.** Art Carney; Jean Stapleton; Blythe Danner; Barry Bostwick; Eugene Roche; Beth Howland; Paul Sand; Polly Holliday; Robert Mandan; Mildred Natwick; ***D:*** Paul Bogart; ***W:*** Paul Bogart; ***C:*** Roy Barnett; ***M:*** Arthur B. Rubinstein. **TV**

You Don't Know Jack **2010** Pacino restrains himself in a thought-provoking portrait of scrappy, stubborn pathologist Dr. Jack Kevorkian and his medically assisted suicide crusade that ultimately landed him in prison. The HBO drama covers Michigan's 'Dr. Death' from the age of 61 to his release (after a conviction for second-degree murder) at the age of 79. **134m/C; DVD.** Al Pacino; Susan Sarandon; Danny Huston; Brenda Vaccaro; John Goodman; ***D:*** Barry Levinson; ***W:*** Adam Mazer; ***C:*** Eigil Bryld; ***M:*** Marcelo Zarvos. **CABLE**

You Don't Mess with the Zohan **2008 (PG-13)** Over-the-top comedy featuring Adam Sandler's latest incarnation, the Zohan—an Israeli commando who fakes his death in order to move to New York and fulfill his dream of becoming a hairdresser. Armed with a superhero-sized crotch and a desire to please the babes, the Zohan becomes a minor celebrity in the Big Apple, but runs into trouble once his homeland finds out. Vulgar and unapologetic, as Sandler will say or do just about anything to anyone (even a cat) for a laugh?-but not very funny. Still, it's nice to see Sandler as something other than a dull dad or soft-hearted boyfriend. **113m/C; Blu-Ray, UMD.** Adam Sandler; John Turturro; Emmanuelle Chriqui; Nick Swardson; Rob Schneider; Barry Livingston; Shelley Berman; Omid Abtahi; Lainie Kazan; Dave Matthews; Ido Mosseri; Michael Buffer; ***Cameo(s):*** Mariah Carey; ***D:*** Dennis Dugan; ***W:*** Adam Sandler; Robert Smigel; Judd Apatow; ***C:*** Michael Barrett; ***M:*** Rupert Gregson-Williams.

You Got Served **2004 (PG-13)** Friends David (Grandberry) and Elgin (Houston)?both from real-life hip hop groups, B2K and IMx, respectively—have a falling out before the big street-dance contest that could earn them $50,000. David is a bit of a tomcat and wants to date Elgin's cute sister, Liyah (Freeman). There's also the issue of the busted drug run. This is about as complex as the story gets. Rookie writer-director Stokes—also of B2K with music-video directing credits—puts all the dancers' energy and talent out there but chops up the segments, thus diminishing the overall effect. Oh and, just to be clear, "you got served" means "I beat you...and BAD." So there. **94m/C; DVD, Blu-Ray, UMD.** Marques Houston; Michael "Bear" Taliferro; Omari (Omarion) Grandberry; Jarell (J-Boog) Houston; DeMario (Raz B) Thornton; Dreux (Lil' Fizz) Frederic; Jennifer Freeman; Christopher Jones; Meagan Good; Steve Harvey; Jackee; Malcolm David Kelly; ***Cameo(s):*** Kimberly (Lil' Kim) Jones; ***D:*** Christopher B. Stokes; ***W:*** Christopher B. Stokes; ***C:*** David Hennings; ***M:*** Tyler Bates.

You Gotta Stay Happy **1/2 1948** Heiress Dee Dee Dillwood (Fontaine) marries the man (Parker) her family approves of and realizes her mistake on their wedding night honeymoon in New York. Distraught, she manages to hide out in the room of failing airplane cargo company owner Marvin Payne (Stewart). He takes her with him on a California-bound cargo flight that winds up crashlanding in a field. By this time Dee Dee and Marvin are in love but then he finds out the truth about his would-be fiancee. **101m/B; DVD.** James Stewart; Joan Fontaine; Eddie Albert; Willard Parker; Roland Young; Halliwell Hobbes; Stanley Prager; Mary Forbes; Percy Kilbride; William "Billy" Bakewell; Arthur Walsh; ***D:*** H.C. Potter; ***W:*** Karl Tunberg; ***C:*** Russell Metty; ***M:*** Daniele Amfitheatrof.

You Kill Me **2007 (R)** Hit man in love. Frank (Kingsley) is a killer for his Polish mob family in Buffalo. Only his drinking problem wrecks havoc and he screws up eliminating rival Irish mob boss O'Leary (Farina). So Frank's Uncle Roman (Hall) sends him to San Francisco to sober up. Frank begins attending AA meetings (which are hilarious given Frank's profession) and gets a job at a funeral home. He also finds a grown-up romance with tough sales exec Laurel (a breezy Leoni), who doesn't faze easily. Still, Frank's family back home is being squeezed. Kingsley, who's done a lot of crap lately, proves again why the Brits bothered to knight him. **92m/C; DVD.** Ben Kingsley; Tea Leoni; Dennis Farina; Philip Baker Hall; Bill Pullman; Luke Wilson; Jayne (Jane) Eastwood; John Dahl; Marcus Thomas; Alison Sealy-Smith; ***W:*** Christopher Markus; Stephen McFeely; ***C:*** Jeffrey Jur; ***M:*** Marcelo Zarvos.

You Know My Name **1999** Elliott is perfectly cast in this true story of legendary lawman-turned-moviemaker Bill Tilghman. Tilghman was connected to the Earp Brothers and then segued into early filmmaking, trying to produce authentic silent westerns in what turned out to be an ill-fated venture. In 1924, toward the end of his life, Tilghman is called upon by the law-abiding citizens of oil-rich boomtown Cromwell, Oklahoma to clean up its dens of iniquity. But Tilghman finds himself unexpectedly opposed by corrupt federal agent Wiley (Howard). **94m/C; VHS, DVD.** Sam Elliott; Arliss Howard; Carolyn McCormick; James Gammon; R. Lee Ermey; Sheila McCarthy; Jonathan Young; Nataalia Rey; James Parks; ***D:*** John Kent Harrison; ***W:*** John Kent Harrison; ***C:*** Kees Van Oostrum; ***M:*** Lawrence Shragge. **CABLE**

You Know What Sailors Are **1959** In this enjoyably silly military comedy, drunken naval officer Sylvester Green and his pals come up with a prank, attaching some painted junk to a foreign ship. His captain questions its purpose causing Green to lie that it's new radar equipment. He sinks himself deeper into chaos as the lies expand. **90m/C; DVD.** *UK* Donald Sinden; Bill Kerr; Sarah Lawson; Akim Tamiroff; Michael Hordern; Naunton Wayne; ***D:*** Ken Annakin; ***W:*** Peter Rogers; ***C:*** Reginald Wyer; ***M:*** Malcolm Arnold.

You Light Up My Life WOOF! **1977 (PG)** Sappy sentimental story of a young singer trying to break into the music business. Debbie Boone's version of the title song was a radio smash, the constant playing of which drove many people over the edge. **91m/C; VHS, DVD.** Didi Conn; Michael Zaslow; Melanie Mayron; Joe Silver; Stephen Nathan; ***D:*** Joseph Brooks; ***W:*** Joseph Brooks; ***C:*** Eric Saarinen; ***M:*** Joseph Brooks. Oscars '77: Song ("You Light Up My Life"); Golden Globes '78: Song ("You Light Up My Life").

You Lucky Dog **2010** This Hallmark Channel melodrama leaves no cliche behind. Lisa comes home for her mother's funeral to learn the family farm is in trouble and her brother Jim has decided to raise sheep to pay the bills though their dad doesn't approve. When Lisa brings in border collie Lucky to herd the woolies more problems ensue. Of course Lucky is smarter than any of the humans and also proves to be heroic. **89m/C; DVD.** Natasha Henstridge; Harry Hamlin; Lawrence Dane; Anthony Lemke; Geri Hall; ***D:*** John Bradshaw; ***W:*** Kevin Commins; ***C:*** Russ Goozee; ***M:*** Stacey Hersh. **CABLE**

You May Not Kiss the Bride **2012 (PG-13)** Poor schlub photographer Bryan (Annable) marries beauty Masha (McPhee) at the 'request' of her Croatian mobster father, who wants to get her a green card. A Tahitian honeymoon doesn't go as planned when the bride gets kidnapped. Suvari, as Bryan's lustful assistant, actually steals a number of scenes from everyone involved, but the whole production has a cheap look. Shelved for a few years, this inert rom-com saw a brief theatrical life with the TV success of its two stars before returning to the dust bin of movie history. **100m/C; DVD.** Dave (David) Annable; Katharine McPhee; Rob Schneider; Mena Suvari; Ken Davitian; Tia Carrere; Kevin Dunn; Vinnie Jones; Kathy Bates; ***D:*** Rob Hedden; ***W:*** Rob Hedden; ***C:*** Russ T. Alsobrook; ***M:*** Geoff Zanelli.

You, Me and Dupree **2006 (PG-13)** Call it "The Marriage Crasher." Having recently lost his job, home, and car, down-and-out Dupree (Wilson) becomes the houseguest from hell of his best friend Carl (Dillon) and Carl's reluctant new bride, Molly (Hudson). Dupree strings together rude and crude antics while his hosts react with predictable dismay and lack of confrontation skills; a mugging Douglas adds further strain as a menacing father-in-law who stirs the pot. But Dupree's sleazy charm contrasts with Carl's uptight angst, giving Molly plenty of opportunities to offer cute and soulful looks. Too bad they couldn't be funnier in the process. **108m/C; DVD, Blu-Ray, HD-DVD.** Owen Wilson; Matt Dillon; Kate Hudson; Michael Douglas; Amanda Detmer; Seth Rogen; Todd Stashwick; Harry Dean Stanton; ***D:*** Anthony Russo; Joe Russo; Peter Ellis; ***W:*** Michael LeSieur; ***C:*** Charles Minsky; ***M:*** Rolfe Kent.

You Move You Die **1/2 2007** Micro-budget Kiwi crime comedy, filmed in real time, that actually improves as it rolls along. Despite being a professional criminal, Mike (Sterling) gets mugged and robbed of the engagement ring he's just bought. He and psycho pal Rob (Harrison) have no problem resorting to violence as they careen through various Auckland neighborhoods in an effort to retrieve his property. **92m/C; DVD.** *NZ* Bruce Hopkins; Ketzal Sterliing; Julian Harisson; Patrick Clarke; ***D:*** Ketzal Sterliing; ***W:*** Ketzal Sterliing; ***C:*** Ketzal Sterliing.

You Must Be Joking! **1/2 1965** Wacky "mod" slapstick comedy. Crazy Army psychologist Foskett wants to see if he can transform five soldiers through a series of odd tests over a 48-hour period. Their goal is to gather symbols of the British way of life to preserve for posterity in case of a nuclear war. Why this involves a French singer's hair is for the Brits to understand. **99m/C; DVD.** *UK* Michael Callan; Lionel Jeffries; Denholm Elliott; Bernard Cribbins; Lee Montague; Terry-Thomas; Patricia Viterbo; Wilfrid Hyde-White; ***D:*** Michael Winner; ***W:*** Alan Hackney; ***C:*** Geoffrey Unsworth; ***M:*** Laurie Johnson.

You Must Remember This **1992** When Uncle Buddy (Guillaume) receives a mysterious trunk, Ella's curiosity gets the best of her. She opens the trunk to discover a number of old movies made by W.B. Jackson—Uncle Buddy. Ella takes the films to a movie archive to find out about her uncle's past as an independent black filmmaker. After researching the history of black cinema, Ella convinces her uncle to be proud of his contribution to the film world. Includes a viewers' guide. Part of the "Wonderworks" series. **110m/C; VHS, DVD.** Robert Guillaume; Tim Reid; Daphne Maxwell Reid; Vonetta McGee.

You Never Can Tell **1/2 1951** Fantasy-comedy has an eccentric millionaire willing his fortune to his German Shepherd, King, with secretary Ellen as the trustee. When King is poisoned, he winds up in the animal equivalent of Purgatory while Ellen is accused of killing the dog so she can inherit. King is reincarnated in human form as PI Rex Shepherd and must convince Ellen that her smooth-talking fiancé is the bad guy. **78m/B; DVD.** Dick Powell; Peggy Dow; Charles Drake; Joyce Holden; ***D:*** Lou Breslow; ***W:*** Lou Breslow; ***C:*** Maury Gertsman; ***M:*** Hans J. Salter.

You Only Live Once **1/2 1937** Ex-con Fonda wants to mend his ways and tries to cross into Canada with his girlfriend in tow. Impressively scripted, but a glum and dated Depression-era tale. **86m/B; VHS, DVD, Blu-Ray.** Henry Fonda; Sylvia Sidney; Ward Bond; William Gargan; Barton MacLane; Margaret Hamilton; Jean Dixon; Warren Hymer; Charles "Chic" Sale; Guinn "Big Boy" Williams; Jerome Cowan; John Wray; Jonathan Hale; Ben Hall; Jean Stoddard; Wade Boteler; Henry Taylor; Walter DePalma; ***D:*** Fritz Lang; ***W:*** C. Graham Baker; Gene Towne; ***C:*** Leon Shamroy.

You Only Live Twice **1/2 1967 (PG)** 007 travels to Japan to take on archnemesis Blofeld, who has been capturing Russian and American spacecraft in an attempt to start WWIII. Great location photography; theme sung by Nancy Sinatra. Implausible plot, however, is a handicap, even though this is Bond. **125m/C; VHS, DVD, Blu-Ray.** *GB* Sean Connery; Mie Hama; Akiko Wakabayashi; Tetsuro Tamba; Karin Dor; Charles Gray; Donald Pleasence; Tsai Chin; Bernard Lee; Lois Maxwell; Desmond Llewelyn; ***D:*** Lewis Gilbert; ***W:*** Roald Dahl; ***C:*** Frederick A. (Freddie) Young; ***M:*** John Barry.

You Said a Mouthful **1/2 1932** Joe Holt (Brown) moves to California after inventing an unsinkable swimsuit. On Catalina Island, socialite Alice Brandon (Rogers) mistakes Joe for a marathon swimmer and assumes he's going to compete in a 21-mile race to the mainland that has a significant cash prize. She's anxious for Joe to show up her pompous ex-beau Ed (Foster), but since Joe can't actually swim, will his unsinkable suit save the day? Water hijinks ensue. **70m/B; DVD.** Joe E. Brown; Ginger Rogers; Preston Foster; Sheila Terry; Allen 'Farina' Hoskins; Harry Gribbon; ***D:*** Lloyd Bacon; ***W:*** Robert Lord; ***C:*** Richard Towers.

You Should Have Left **2020 (R)** Middle-aged screenwriter Theo Conroy (Bacon) was accused of contributing to the death of his first wife, who took pills and drowned in a bathtub, but he has maintained his innocence. The incident still colors his life years later, even though he is married to younger actress Susanna (Seyfried). To get away from it all, the couple takes their young daughter Ella (Essex) to a secluded rental home in Wales. Once they are inside, the building plays with their sense of reality. The low budget horror flick tries but can't be rescued despite the talented cast. **93m/C; DVD.** Kevin Bacon; Amanda Seyfried; Avery Tiiu Essex; Colin Blumenau; Lowri-Ann Richards; ***D:*** David Koepp; ***W:*** David Koepp; ***C:*** Angus Hudson; ***M:*** Geoff Zanelli. **VIDEO**

You So Crazy **1/2** *Martin Lawrence You So Crazy* **1994** Scandalous star of TV show "Martin" and host of HBO's "Def Comedy Jam" follows in the footsteps of raunchy humorists Richard Pryor and Eddie Murphy. Threatened with an NC-17 rating, Lawrence refused to edit and Miramax, the original distributor, dropped it. It was picked up by Samuel Goldwyn, who released the original version, uncut and unrated. Filmed live at the Brooklyn Academy of Music, Lawrence displays too little of his considerable talent, and too much vulgarity and poor taste. **85m/C; VHS, DVD.** Martin Lawrence; ***D:*** Thomas Schlamme; ***W:*** Martin Lawrence; ***C:*** Arthur Albert.

You Stupid Man **1/2 2002** Actually, "you stupid movie" would be more appropriate. First-timer Burns (brother of Ed) does his own NY romantic-comedy to mixed effect. Geeky writer Owen (Krumholtz) loses hot blonde girlfriend Chloe (Richards) to L.A.'s bright lights and TV fame. So he goes on a blind date and meets brunette babe Nadine (Jovovich) and they eventually get cozy. Then Chloe's TV show gets cancelled and she comes home to the Big Apple and wants Owen back. Is this a Woody Allen fantasy or what? **95m/C; DVD.** David Krumholtz; Denise Richards; Milla Jovovich; William Baldwin; Dan Montgomery, Jr.; Jessica Cauffiel; ***D:*** Brian Burns; ***W:*** Brian Burns; ***C:*** David Herrington; ***M:*** David Schwartz.

You Talkin' to Me? **1987 (R)** Fledgling actor who idolizes De Niro moves to the West Coast for his big break. He fails, so he dyes his hair blond and digs the California lifestyle. Embarrassingly bad. **97m/C; VHS, Streaming.** Chris Winkler; Jim Youngs; Faith Ford; ***D:*** Charles Winkler; ***W:*** Charles Winkler.

You Tell Me **2006** Three twenty-something slacker buddies on New York's Lower East Side continue to screw up their romantic lives by listening to each other's bad advice. Flint (Fenkart) has been dumped and is crashing at Jeff's (Ledoux) apartment; Jeff has just discovered that both his girlfriend and his mother (who's left his dad) have been cheating; and floundering Gray's (Cary) talented girlfriend is about to break big in the art world, leaving him even more insecure. **88m/C; DVD.** Jack Davidson; Joshua Cary; David Ledoux; Bryan Fenkart; Amber McDonald; Maren Levin; Ciara Pressler; ***D:*** Joshua Cary; ***W:*** Joshua Cary; David Ledoux; Bryan Fenkart; ***C:*** Colin Bressler; ***M:*** Charles Newman. **VIDEO**

You Were Never Lovelier 1/2 **1942** Charming tale of a father who creates a phony Romeo to try to interest his daughter in marriage. Astaire appears and woos Hayworth in the flesh. The dancing, of course, is superb, and Hayworth is stunning. **98m/B; VHS, DVD.** Fred Astaire; Rita Hayworth; Leslie Brooks; Xavier Cugat; Adolphe Menjou; Larry Parks; *D:* William A. Seiter; *M:* Jerome Kern; Johnny Mercer.

You Were Never Really Here **2017 (R)** Phoenix simmers as a disturbed veteran who brutally rescues young girls who've been kidnapped and trafficked as sex slaves. Based on the novel by Jonathan Ames, it's an arty rendition of a vengeance quest, with poetic touches that balance the horrific violence. Winner of Cannes Film Festival awards for best actor and best screenplay. **89m/C; DVD, Blu-Ray.** Joaquin Rafael (Leaf) Phoenix; Judith Roberts; Ekaterina Samsonov; John Doman; Alex Manette; *D:* Lynne Ramsay; *W:* Lynne Ramsay; *C:* Thomas Townend; *M:* Jonny Greenwood. Ind. Spirit '19: Film Editing.

You Will Meet a Tall Dark Stranger **2010 (R)** Tiring ensemble comedy-drama from Allen is somewhat redeemed by a stellar cast. A group of not-terribly interesting characters always think their romantic and working relationships can be changed by looking outside rather than fixing what's wrong within themselves. Marital troubles abound for several couples, there's foolishness by young and old, and flirtations with spirituality via a psychic. **98m/C; Blu-Ray, On Demand.** *GB SP* Naomi Watts; Josh Brolin; Gemma Jones; Anthony Hopkins; Pauline Collins; Freida Pinto; Antonio Banderas; Lucy Punch; Roger Ashton-Griffiths; *D:* Woody Allen; *W:* Woody Allen; *C:* Vilmos Zsigmond.

You Wont Miss Me 1/2 **2009** Freshly discharged from a mental hospital, Shelly (Schnabel) is a troubled 23-year-old Brooklyn hipster wandering the streets for trouble. Whether it be sex with strangers, absurd acting auditions, or just yelling in public, Shelly can't seem to find much of anything. A snapshot portrait of a person disconnected with both society and possibly herself. Director and co-writer Russo-Young captures the grunge of this NY world and gets a realistic performance from Schnabel, but to little avail. So aimless in scope that the line between irritating art imitating irritating life becomes very much blurred. (And, yes, it's too cool for an apostrophe.) **81m/C; DVD.** Stella Schnabel; Simon O'Connor; Zachary Tucker; Borden Capalino; Carlen Altman; Rene Ricard; Josephine Wheelwright; Aaron Katz; *D:* Ry Russo-Young; *W:* Stella Schnabel; Ry Russo-Young; *C:* Kitao Sakurai; Ku-Ling Siegel; *M:* Will Bates.

You'll Find Out **1940** A comic mix of music and mystery as Kay Kyser and his Band, along with a debutante in distress, are terrorized by Lugosi, Karloff, and Lorre. **97m/B; VHS, DVD.** Peter Lorre; Kay Kyser; Boris Karloff; Bela Lugosi; Dennis O'Keefe; Helen Parrish; *D:* David Butler.

You'll Get Over It *A Cause d'un Garcon* **2002** Seventeen-year-old high schooler Vincent (Baumgartner) is the star of the swim team; has a pretty girlfriend, Noemie (Maraval); and a best pal, Stephane (Comar). But Vincent is also seeing the older Bruno (Ohlund) and struggling with maintaining his secret. Then, new student Benjamin (Elkaim) obviously pursues Vincent and he's outted before the whole school—resulting in feelings of betrayal on all fronts. Soon, Vincent is discovering who his friends really are. French with subtitles. **90m/C; DVD.** *FR* Julien Baumgartner; Francois Comar; Julie Marawal; Nils Ohlund; Jeremie Elkaim; *D:* Fabrice Cazeneuve; *W:* Vincent Molina; *C:* Stephan Massis; *M:* Michel Portal. **TV**

You'll Never Get Rich **1941** A Broadway dance director is drafted into the Army, where his romantic troubles cause him to wind up in the guardhouse more than once. He of course gets the girl. Exquisitely funny. **88m/B; DVD, Blu-Ray.** Fred Astaire; Rita Hayworth; Robert Benchley; *D:* Sidney Lanfield; *W:* Michael Fessier; Ernest Pagano; *C:* Philip Tannura.

Young Adam 1/2 **2003 (NC-17)** Writer/director Mackenzie uses the grim backdrop of 1950s Scotland for the richly dark character drama of his second feature. McGregor is Joe, a sexually charged but emotionally and morally devoid transient who finds work, room, and board on a barge owned by Les (Mullan) and his wife Ella (Swinton) who share a loveless marriage. When the body of a young woman washes up and is fished out by the barge-dwellers it sets off various reactions in all three. Joe seduces Ella under the nose of the emotionally repressed Les and a series of flashbacks reveal more about Joe's past and his relationship with Cathie (Mortimer), a young woman who reminds him of the deceased. Moody, noirish and visually engaging with stellar portrayals by all. Based on a novel by Alexander Trocchi. **98m/C; DVD.** *FR GB* Ewan McGregor; Tilda Swinton; Peter Mullan; Emily Mortimer; Jack McElhone; *D:* David Mackenzie; *W:* David Mackenzie; *C:* Giles Nuttgens; *M:* David Byrne.

Young Adult 1/2 **2011 (R)** Teen lit writer Mavis Gary (Theron) has never found as much popularity, stability, or happiness as when she was Prom Queen in a small Minnesota town. Trying to rekindle the time at which she was on her highest life pedestal, she returns home to steal her high school sweetheart Buddy (Wilson) from his wife and new baby. Theron is brassy, never asking the viewer to like her or expect a typical Hollywood morality tale. Oswalt, as a disabled former classmate she dubbed "the hate crime kid," grounds the piece in a supporting role. **94m/C; DVD, Blu-Ray.** Charlize Theron; Patrick Wilson; Patton Oswalt; Elizabeth Reaser; J.K. Simmons; Collette Wolfe; Jill Eikenberry; Richard Bekins; Mary Beth Hurt; *D:* Jason Reitman; *W:* Diablo Cody; *C:* Eric Steelberg; *M:* Rolfe Kent.

Young America **1932** Juvenile delinquent Arthur (Conlon) is paroled by Judge Blake (Bellamy) into the care of his strict aunt (Graham) but he runs away to stay with his best friend Nutty (Borzge) and Nutty's grandma (Mercer). When grandma gets sick, the boys steal medicine from druggist Jack Doray (Tracy) and get caught. Soft-hearted Mrs. Doray (Kenyon) takes Arthur in over hubby's objections but the kid becomes a hero after witnessing a robbery at the drugstore and outwitting the crooks. **70m/B; DVD.** Spencer Tracy; Doris Kenyon; Ralph Bellamy; Beryl Mercer; Anne Shirley; Robert E. Homans; Tommy Conlon; Raymond Borzage; Betty Jane Graham; *D:* Frank Borzage; *W:* William Counselman; *C:* George Schneiderman; *M:* George Lipschultz.

The Young Americans **1993 (R)** Tough New York cop John Harris (Keitel) is sent to London to aid the police with their investigations into a series of killings related to a drug smuggling operation working out of the club scene. Harris wants to tie everything to the sleazeball gangster Carl Frazer (Mortensen) that he's been trailing. Slick formula with hard-working cast. Debut for 25-year-old director Cannon. **108m/C; VHS, DVD.** *GB* Harvey Keitel; Viggo Mortensen; Iain Glen; John Wood; Keith Allen; Craig Kelly; Thandie Newton; Terence Rigby; *D:* Danny Cannon; *W:* Danny Cannon; David Hilton; *M:* David Arnold.

Young & Beautiful 1/2 *Jeune et Jolie* **2013** Teenaged Isabelle (Vach) goes from virgin to call girl quickly, hooking up in seedy hotel rooms with older men. The great modern French filmmaker Ozon portrays her not as a nymphomaniac or traditional prostitute, but almost as an object to be purchased—oblivious to the human connection of it all. Even the money doesn't seem to drive her. What does? In this story of a young woman's sexual awakening, there is much left up in the air, but Ozon does so with his typical dose of style, sexuality, and top-notch filmmaking. French with subtitles. **95m/C; DVD.** *FR* Marine Vacth; Lucas Prisor; Johan Leysen; Geraldine Pailhas; *D:* Francois Ozon; *W:* Francois Ozon; *C:* Pascal Marti; *M:* Philippe Rombi.

Young and Innocent *The Girl Was Young* **1937** Somewhat uneven thriller about a police constable's daughter who helps a fugitive prove he didn't strangle a film star. **80m/B; VHS, DVD.** *GB* Derrick DeMarney; Nova Pilbeam; Percy Marmont; Edward Rigby; Mary Clare; John Longden; George Curzon; Basil Radford; Pamela Carme; George Merritt; J.H. Roberts; Jerry Verno; H.F. Maltby; Beatrice Varley; Syd Crossley; Frank Atkinson; Torin Thatcher; *D:* Alfred Hitchcock; *W:* Charles Bennett; Alma Reville; Gerald Savory; Antony Armstrong; Edwin Greenwood; *C:* Bernard Knowles; *M:* Louis Levy.

The Young and Prodigious T.S. Spivet 1/2 **2015 (PG)** This action-adventure drama focuses on a gifted child with a dark secret and the journey he takes. Ten-year-old T.S. Spivet (Catlett) lives on a ranch in Montana with his unusual family, which includes a mother obsessed with the morphology of beetles and a cowboy father. Deeply interested in cartography, T.S. also is the inventor of a perpetual motion machine. When he receives a call from the Smithsonian that he is the winner of the Baird prize for his machine, he leaves a note for his family and jumps on a freight train to attend the reception in his honor in Washington, D.C. The Smithsonian does not know his age, nor does T.S. really understand that his his twin brother Layton died during one of his experiments. **105m/C; DVD, Blu-Ray, Streaming, Download.** Kyle Catlett; Helena Bonham Carter; Judy Davis; Callum Keith Rennie; Niamh Wilson; *D:* Jean-Pierre Jeunet; *W:* Jean-Pierre Jeunet; Guillaume Laurant; *C:* Thomas Hardmeier; *M:* Denis Sanacore.

Young at Heart 1/2 **1954** Fanny Hurst's lighthearted tale of a cynical hard-luck musician who finds happiness when he falls for a small town girl. A remake of the 1938 "Four Daughters." **117m/C; DVD, Blu-Ray.** Frank Sinatra; Doris Day; Gig Young; Ethel Barrymore; Dorothy Malone; Robert Keith; Elisabeth Fraser; Alan Hale, Jr.; *D:* Gordon Douglas; *W:* Julius J. Epstein; Liam O'Brien; *C:* Ted D. McCord; *M:* Ray Heindorf.

Young@Heart **2007 (PG)** The other side of the spectrum from Don Argott's documentary "Rock School." This time around director Walker spotlights the Young at Heart Chorus, an eclectic nursing home choir that specializes in classic and indie rock. They run through staples by the Clash, the Bee Gees, and David Bowie, while struggling to learn Sonic Youth's "Schizophrenia" and James Brown's "I Feel Good." Lead by pseudo-radical teacher Bob Cilman, who probably spends too much time gushing over his pupils but never backs down from the challenge. Begins light and peppy, with corny jokes from the singers, but gradually darkens as their stories turn to age, depression, and death. Don't worry; it's wrapped up nice and pretty. **107m/C; On Demand.** *Nar:* Stephen Walker; *D:* Stephen Walker; *C:* Edward Marritz.

Young Bess 1/2 **1953** Simmons and real-life husband Granger star in this splashy costume drama about 16th century England's young Queen. Features outstanding performances by Simmons as Elizabeth I and Laughton (repeating his most famous role) as Henry VIII. Based on the novel by Margaret Irwin. **112m/C; VHS, DVD.** Jean Simmons; Stewart Granger; Deborah Kerr; Charles Laughton; Kay Walsh; Guy Rolfe; Kathleen Byron; Cecil Kellaway; Rex Thompson; Elaine Stewart; *D:* George Sidney; *W:* Jan Lustig; Arthur Wimperis; *C:* Charles Rosher; *M:* Miklos Rozsa.

Young Caruso *Enrico Caruso: Leggenda di Una Voce* **1951** Dramatic biography of legendary tenor Enrico Caruso, following his life from childhood poverty in Naples to the beginning of his rise to fame. Dubbed in English. **78m/B; VHS, DVD.** *IT* Gina Lollobrigida; Ermanno Randi; Gino Saltamerenda; Maria V. Tasnady; *D:* Giacomo Gentilomo; *W:* Giacomo Gentilomo; *C:* Tino Santoni; *M:* Carlo Franci.

Young Cassidy **1965** Colorful biopic based on the autobiography of Irish playwright Sean O'Casey. Poor Dubliner John Cassidy (Taylor) does manual labor, secretly trains with the revolutionaries, and writes about working-class life. Eventually his plays get noticed and produced by the Abbey Theatre, but Cassidy is worried about losing his voice when he's taken up by the literary establishment. John Ford started the picture but fell ill and was replaced by Jack Cardiff. **110m/C; DVD.** Rod Taylor; Julie Christie; Edith Evans; Michael Redgrave; Flora Robson; Maggie Smith; Sian Phillips; *D:* Jack Cardiff; *W:* John Whiting; *C:* Edward (Ted) Scaife; *M:* Sean O'Riada.

Young Catherine **1991** Made-for-TNT account of Russia's strongest female ruler, the girl who would be Catherine the Great. Star-studded cast and excellent production values. Script and strong cast make Ormond look like a lightweight. Filmed in Leningrad. **150m/C; DVD.** Vanessa Redgrave; Christopher Plummer; Marthe Keller; Franco Nero; Julia Ormond; Maximilian Schell; Reece Dinsdale; Mark Frankel; *D:* Michael Anderson, Sr.; *W:* Chris Bryant; *C:* Ernest Day; *M:* Isaak Shvarts. **CABLE**

Young Dr. Kildare 1/2 **1938** The first of nine films in the MGM series starring Lew Ayres in the title role. Rather than practicing medicine back home with his father, James Kildare takes an internship at Blair General in New York where irascible Dr. Gillespie (Barrymore) becomes his mentor. Kildare gets into various scrapes over medical decisions that nearly get him fired but, naturally, he's right. **81m/B; DVD.** Lew Ayres; Lionel Barrymore; Lynne Carver; Nat Pendleton; Jo Ann Sayers; Samuel S. Hinds; *D:* Harold Bucquet; *W:* Willis Goldbeck; Harry Ruskin; *C:* John Seitz; *M:* David Snell.

Young Doctors in Love **1982 (R)** Spoof of medical soap operas features a chaotic scenario at City Hospital, where the young men and women on the staff have better things to do than attend to their patients. Good cast keeps this one alive, though many laughs are forced. Includes cameos by real soap star, including then-General Hospital star Moore. **95m/C; VHS, DVD, Blu-Ray.** Dabney Coleman; Sean Young; Michael McKean; Harry Dean Stanton; Hector Elizondo; Patrick Macnee; Pamela Reed; Saul Rubinek; ***Cameo(s):*** Demi Moore; Janine Turner; *D:* Garry Marshall; *W:* Michael Elias; Rich Eustis; *M:* Maurice Jarre.

Young Einstein **1989 (PG)** A goofy, irreverent Australian farce starring, directed, co-scripted and co-produced by Serious, depicting Einstein as a young Outback clod who splits beer atoms and invents rock and roll. Winner of several Aussie awards. Fun for the kids. **91m/C; VHS, DVD.** *AU* Yahoo Serious; Odile Le Clezio; John Howard; Pee Wee Wilson; Su Cruickshank; Lulu Pinkus; Kaarin Fairfax; Jonathan Coleman; *D:* Yahoo Serious; *W:* Yahoo Serious; David Roach; *C:* Jeff Darling; *M:* Martin Armiger; William Motzing; Tommy Tycho.

Young Frankenstein **1974 (PG)** Young Dr. Frankenstein (Wilder), a brain surgeon, inherits the family castle back in Transylvania. He's skittish about the family business, but when he learns his grandfather's secrets, he becomes obsessed with making his own monster. Wilder and monster Boyle make a memorable song-and-dance team to Irving Berlin's "Puttin' on the Ritz," and Hackman's cameo as a blind man is inspired. Garr ("What knockers!" "Oh, sank you!") is adorable as a fraulein, and Leachman ("He's vass my—boyfriend!") is wonderfully scary. Wilder saves the creature with a switcheroo, in which the doctor ends up with a certain monster-sized body part. Hilarious parody. **108m/B; VHS, DVD, Blu-Ray.** Peter Boyle; Gene Wilder; Marty Feldman; Madeline Kahn; Cloris Leachman; Teri Garr; Kenneth Mars; Richard Haydn; Gene Hackman; Liam Dunn; Monte Landis; *D:* Mel Brooks; *W:* Gene Wilder; Mel Brooks; *C:* Gerald Hirschfeld; *M:* John Morris. Natl. Film Reg. '03.

The Young Girl and the Monsoon 1/2 **1999** Successful photojournalist and divorced dad Hank (Kinney) agrees to take care of 13-year-old daughter Constance (Muth) while her mother, with whom she usually lives, is out of town. Constance is a mass of teenage contradictions—constantly testing her boundaries (and Hank's sanity and patience). Hank has kept his work and life, including the fact that his girlfriend is a twentysomething model named Erin (Avital), from Constance but there's an explosion in every conversation. **93m/C; VHS, DVD.** Terry Kinney; Ellen Muth; Mili Avital; Diane Venora; Tim Guinee; Domenick Lombardozzi; *D:* James Ryan; *W:* James Ryan; *C:* Ben Wolf; *M:* David Carbonara.

The Young Girls of Rochefort 1/2 *Les Demoiselles de Rochefort* **1968** Twins sisters Delphine and Solange (played by sisters Deneuve and

Dorleac) dream of romance, which first appears in the forms of salesmen Etienne (Chakiris) and Bill (Dale), who are minor distractions for the real thing—artistic sailor Maxence (Perrin) and concert pianist Andy (Kelly). Demy's followup to the more compelling "The Umbrellas of Cherbourg" is still an equally candy-colored musical fantasy. Rochefort (like Cherbourg) is an actual town that Demy took over for filming. **125m/C; VHS, DVD, Blu-Ray.** *FR* Catherine Deneuve; Francoise Dorleac; George Chakiris; Grover Dale; Gene Kelly; Jacques Perrin; Danielle Darrieux; Michel Piccoli; Pamela Hart; Jacques Riberolles; Leslie North; ***D:*** Jacques Demy; ***W:*** Jacques Demy; ***C:*** Ghislan Cloquet; ***M:*** Michel Legrand.

Young Goethe in Love 1/2 *Goethe!* **2011** Cliched fictional biopic of the German writer. Goethe fails his bar exams in 1772, and his dad sends him to a dull country town to work as a court clerk. Attending a dance, he meets lively Lotte and they have a secret romance since he's poor and she must marry his wealthy boss to help out her penniless family. Oh, the romantic angst! German with subtitles. **100m/C; DVD.** *GE* Alexander Fehling; Miriam Stein; Moritz Bleibtreu; Volker Bruch; ***D:*** Philipp Stolzl; ***W:*** Philipp Stolzl; Christoph Muller; ***C:*** Kolja Brandt; ***M:*** Ingo Frenzel.

The Young Graduates **1971 (PG)** Hormonally imbalanced teens come of age in spite of meandering plot. Features "Breaking Away" star Christopher in big screen debut. **99m/C; VHS, DVD.** Patricia Wymer; Steven Stewart; Gary Rist; Bruce Kirby; Jennifer Ritt; Dennis Christopher; ***D:*** Robert Anderson.

Young Guns 1/2 **1988 (R)** A sophomoric Wild Bunch look-alike that ends up resembling a western version of the Bowery Boys. Provides a portrait of Billy the Kid and his gang as they move from prairie trash to demi-legends. Features several fine performances by a popular group of today's young stars. **107m/C; VHS, DVD, Blu-Ray, UMD.** Emilio Estevez; Kiefer Sutherland; Lou Diamond Phillips; Charlie Sheen; Casey Siemaszko; Dermot Mulroney; Terence Stamp; Terry O'Quinn; Jack Palance; Brian Keith; Patrick Wayne; Sharon Thomas; ***D:*** Christopher Cain; ***W:*** John Fusco; ***C:*** Dean Semler; ***M:*** Anthony Marinelli; Brian Backus; Brian Banks.

Young Guns 2 **1990 (PG-13)** Brat Pack vehicle neo-Western sequel about Billy the Kid (Estevez) and his gang. Told as an account by Brushy Bill Roberts who, in 1950, claims to be the real Billy the Kid and recounts his continuing adventures with Doc (Sutherland), Chavez (Phillips) and Pat Garrett (Petersen). Not bad for a sequel, thanks mostly to Petersen. **105m/C; VHS, DVD, Blu-Ray.** Emilio Estevez; Kiefer Sutherland; Lou Diamond Phillips; Christian Slater; William L. Petersen; Alan Ruck; R.D. Call; James Coburn; Balthazar Getty; Jack Kehoe; Robert Knepper; Jenny Wright; Tracey Walter; Ginger Lynn Allen; Jon Bon Jovi; Viggo Mortensen; Leon Rippy; Bradley Whitford; Scott Wilson; John Hammil; ***D:*** Geoff Murphy; ***W:*** John Fusco; ***C:*** Dean Semler; ***M:*** Alan Silvestri. Golden Globes '91: Song ("Blaze of Glory").

Young Guns of Texas **1962** Minor western with inadequate performances by the kids of various stars. While searching for his brother, Tyler (Conway) befriends Jeff (McCrea) and Lily (Ladd), daughter of landowner Jesse (Lowery), who thinks the young men have kidnapped her. Instead, the two have taken Lily to her Comanche-raised love, Morgan (Mitchum), so they can marry. Dad rustles up a posse to go after the young 'uns but you won't much care. **78m/C; DVD.** Gary Conway; Jody McCrea; Alana Ladd; James Mitchum; Robert Lowery; Chill Wills; ***D:*** Maury Dexter; ***W:*** Harry Spalding; ***C:*** John M. Nickolaus, Jr.; ***M:*** Paul Sawtell; Bert Shefter.

Young Hercules 1/2 **1997 (PG-13)** Seventeen-year-old Herc (Bohen) is a confused teen, torn between his mortal and immortal sides. So concerned mom Alcmene sends the kid to Cherion's academy where Herc can learn to be a warrior and where he'll meet friends and rivals Iolus (O'Gorman), Prince Jason (Conrad), and the beautiful Yvenna (Stewart). Oh yes, war god Ares (Smith) also shows up, trying to prevent half-brother Herc and his friends from obtaining the golden fleece for Jason's dying father. **93m/C; VHS, DVD.** Ian Bohen; Dean O'Gorman; Johna Stewart; Chris Conrad; Kevin Smith; ***D:*** T.J. Scott; ***W:*** Robert Tapert; Andrew Dettmann; Daniel Truly; ***C:*** John Mahaffie; ***M:*** Joseph LoDuca. **VIDEO**

Young Ideas **1943** Widow Jo Evans (Astor) is a bestselling romance author whose college-age children, Jeff (Reid) and Susan (Peters), are thrown into a tizzy when mom suddenly marries Professor Michael Kingsley (Marshall). They sabotage their newlyweded bliss but their plans fall apart when Susan becomes romantically interested in her drama teacher (Carlson). **77m/B; DVD.** Mary Astor; Herbert Marshall; Susan Peters; Elliott Reid; Richard Carlson; ***D:*** Jules Dassin; ***W:*** Ian McLellan Hunter; ***C:*** Charles Lawton, Jr.; ***M:*** George Bassman.

The Young in Heart **1938** A lonely, old woman allows a family of conartists into her life for companionship. Impressed by her sweet nature, the parasitic brood reforms. The cute comedy was a real crowd-pleaser in its day, especially after the bittersweet ending was replaced with a happier variety. Based on the novel "The Gay Banditti" by I.A.R. Wylie. **90m/C; VHS, DVD, Blu-Ray.** Janet Gaynor; Douglas Fairbanks, Jr.; Paulette Goddard; Roland Young; Billie Burke; Minnie Dupree; Richard Carlson; Charles Halton; ***D:*** Richard Wallace; ***W:*** Charles Bennett; Paul Osborn.

Young Ivanhoe 1/2 **1995** Ivanhoe learns how to be a warrior, with some help from Robin Hood and the Black Knight, inspiring others to follow him into battle to save their land from seizure by the Norman invaders. **96m/C; VHS, DVD.** Stacy Keach; Nick Mancuso; Margot Kidder; Kris Holden-Ried; Rachel Blanchard; Matthew Daniels; ***D:*** Ralph L. (R.L.) Thomas; ***W:*** Ralph L. (R.L.) Thomas; Frank Encarnacao; ***C:*** John Berrie; ***M:*** Alan Reeves.

The Young Kieslowski 1/2 **2015 (R)** A broad comedy from the creator of "Harold & Kumar Go to White Castle." Brian Kielowski (Malgarini) and Leslie Mallard (Richardson) are students at Caltech and virgins. They have a drunken one-night stand and become pregnant with twins. As they deal with their feelings for each other and take a trip through California, they also must face their own neuroses and their families as they decide what path to take. **104m/C; DVD, Streaming, Download.** Ryan Malgarini; Haley Lu Richardson; Joshua Malina; Melora Walters; James LeGros; ***D:*** Kerem Sanga; ***W:*** Kerem Sanga; ***C:*** Ricardo Diaz; ***M:*** John Swihart.

Young Lady Chatterly 2 1/2 **1985** A poor sequel to the popular MacBride film, with only the name of the Lawrence classic. Chatterly inherits the family mansion and fools around with the servants and any one else who comes along. Unrated version with 13 minutes of deleted footage is also available. **87m/C; VHS, DVD.** Sybil Danning; Adam West; Harlee MacBride; ***D:*** Alan Roberts.

The Young Land 1/2 **1959** Less-than-inspiring western does feature a good performance by Hopper as malcontent bully Hatfield Carnes. Carnes kills a respected Mexican in a barroom gunfight in 1848 California and sheriff Jim Ellison (Wayne) is quick to call territorial judge Isham (O'Herlihy) to ensure a fair trial—with the rest of the Spanish-speaking town looking on in skepticism. Based on the story "Frontier Frenzy" by John Reese. **88m/C; VHS, DVD.** Dennis Hopper; Patrick Wayne; Dan O'Herlihy; Yvonne Craig; Ken Curtis; Pedro Gonzalez-Gonzalez; ***D:*** Ted Tetzlaff; ***W:*** Norman S. Hall; ***C:*** Winton C. Hoch; Henry Sharp; ***M:*** Dimitri Tiomkin.

The Young Lions **1958** A cynical WWII epic following the experiences of a young American officer and a disillusioned Nazi in the war's last days. Martin does fine in his first dramatic role. As the Nazi, Brando sensitively considers the belief that Hitler would save Germany. A realistic anti-war film. **167m/B; VHS, DVD, Blu-Ray.** Marlon Brando; Montgomery Clift; Dean Martin; Hope Lange; Barbara Rush; Lee Van Cleef; Maximilian Schell; May Britt; Dora Doll; Liliane Montevecchi; Parley Baer; Arthur Franz; Hal Baylor; Richard Gardner; Herbert Rudley; L.Q. Jones; ***D:*** Edward Dmytryk; ***W:*** Edward Anhalt; ***C:*** Joe MacDonald; ***M:*** Hugo Friedhofer.

Young Man with a Horn **1950** Dorothy Baker's novel, which was loosely based on the life of jazz immortal Bix Beiderbecke, was even more loosely adapted for this film, featuring Kirk as an angst-ridden trumpeter who can't seem to hit that mystical "high note." **112m/B; VHS, DVD.** Kirk Douglas; Doris Day; Lauren Bacall; Hoagy Carmichael; ***D:*** Michael Curtiz.

Young Man With Ideas **1952** Mild domestic comedy. Shy Montana attorney Maxwell Webster (Ford) moves his wife Julie (Roman) and their kids to L.A. to start over. Their home phone number used to belong to a bookie and when Julie jokingly accepts a bet, gangster Brick Davis (Leonard) expects the winning wager to be honored. Instead, Maxwell's first case as a California attorney is to defend himself! **84m/B; DVD.** Glenn Ford; Ruth Roman; Sheldon Leonard; Nina Foch; Denise Darcel; Donna Corcoran; Mary Wickes; ***D:*** Mitchell Leisen; ***W:*** Arthur Sheekman; ***C:*** Joseph Ruttenberg; ***M:*** David Rose.

Young Master **1980** Chan, searching for his missing brother, is mistaken for a fugitive and has to save himself from bounty hunters and police. Oh, and get the real bad guys so he can clear his name. Chinese with subtitles or dubbed. **90m/C; VHS, DVD.** *CH* Jackie Chan; Pai Wei; Ing-Sik Whang; Kien Shih; ***D:*** Jackie Chan; ***W:*** Jackie Chan; ***M:*** Akira Inoue.

The Young Messiah 1/2 **2016 (PG-13)** A manipulative and melodramatic retelling of the story of Jesus Christ as a child. We see Jesus at age seven, his family departing Egypt to return to Nazareth. It's a kid's movie about Jesus! It's not the concept here that's flawed but the execution. Everyone looks like they're going through the motions. At least the biblical epics of the '50s and '60s had some cheese value. This is just boring. Based on the 2011 book by Anne Rice, originally titled "Christ the Lord: Out of Egypt: A Novel." **111m/C; DVD, Blu-Ray.** Adam Greaves-Neal; Sara Lazzaro; Vincent Walsh; Jonathan Bailey; Sean Bean; ***D:*** Cyrus Nowrasteh; ***W:*** Cyrus Nowrasteh; Betsy Giffen Nowrasteh; ***C:*** Joel Ransom; ***M:*** John Debney.

Young Mr. Lincoln 1/2 **1939** A classy Hollywood biography of Lincoln in his younger years from log-cabin country boy to idealistic Springfield lawyer. A splendid drama, and one endlessly explicated as an American masterpiece by the French auteur critics in "Cahiers du Cinema." **100m/B; VHS, DVD, Blu-Ray.** Henry Fonda; Alice Brady; Marjorie Weaver; Arleen Whelan; Eddie Collins; Ward Bond; Donald Meek; Richard Cromwell; Eddie Quillan; Charles Halton; ***D:*** John Ford; ***W:*** Lamar Trotti. Natl. Film Reg. '03.

The Young Nurses *Nightingale; Young L.A. Nurses 3* **1973 (R)** The fourth entry in the Roger Corman produced "nurses" series. Three sexy nurses uncover a drug ring run from their hospital, headed by none other than director Fuller. Also present is Moreland, in his last role. Preceded by "The Student Nurses," "Private Duty Nurses," "Night Call Nurses," followed by "Candy Stripe Nurses." Also on video as "Young L.A. Nurses 3." **77m/C; VHS, DVD.** Jean Manson; Ashley Porter; Angela Gibbs; Zack Taylor; Dick Miller; Jack La Rue; William Joyce; Sally Kirkland; Allan Arbus; Mary Doyle; Don Keefer; Nan Martin; Mantan Moreland; Samuel Fuller; ***D:*** Clinton Kimbrough; ***W:*** Howard R. Cohen; ***M:*** Greg Prestopino.

The Young One 1/2 *La Joven; Island of Shame* **1961** Traver (Hamilton) is a black jazz musician who escapes from his southern town when he's wrongly accused of raping a white woman. He hides out on a small island which is used as a private hunting ground for rich sportsmen, overseen by Miller (Scott), the game keeper. Hamilton gets work as the new handyman and becomes close to the young Evalyn (Meersman). When Miller rapes Evalyn, it's Traver who's once again accused until things can be put right. Racist elements are heavy-handed; one of Bunuel's lesser efforts. Based on the story "Travelin' Man" by Peter Matthiessen. **94m/B; VHS, DVD.** *MX* Bernie Hamilton; Zachary Scott; Kay Meersman; Claudio Brook; Graham Denton; ***D:*** Luis Bunuel; ***W:*** Luis Bunuel; Hugo Butler.

Young Ones 1/2 **2014 (R)** Paltrow divides his oppressive sci fi western into three chapters told by each of his male protagonists. In the near future, water is a dwindling resource and much of the land is a desert. Grim Ernest Holm has a farm, but makes his living hauling supplies and protecting his property. His rebellious daughter marries arrogant Flem Lever, who has his own plans for the land, while Ernest's son Jerome discovers a betrayal and takes his revenge in the final chapter. **100m/C; Blu-Ray, Streaming.** Michael Shannon; Nicholas Hoult; Kodi Smit-McPhee; Elle Fanning; Aimee Mullins; ***D:*** Jake Paltrow; ***W:*** Jake Paltrow; ***C:*** Giles Nuttgens; ***M:*** Nathan Johnson.

Young People 1/2 **1940 (G)** Temple's 12 in this lesser vehicle and almost-adolesence doesn't serve her well with this tired plot. She's an orphan adopted by showbiz team Oakie and Greenwood who've decided to retire to rural life. They even get to put on a show to prove to the small-minded small-towners what a swell trio they are. Temple's last film for 20th-Century Fox does include nostalgic clips from earlier Shirley hits, including "Stand Up and Cheer" and "Curly Top," to explain her character's background. **78m/C; VHS, DVD.** Shirley Temple; Jack Oakie; Charlotte Greenwood; Arleen Whelan; George Montgomery; Kathleen Howard; ***D:*** Allan Dwan; ***W:*** Edwin Blum; Don Ettlinger.

The Young Philadelphians *The City Jungle* **1959** Ambitious young lawyer Newman works hard at making an impression on the snobbish Philadelphia upper crust. As he schemes and scrambles, he woos debutante Rush and defends buddy Vaughn on a murder charge. Long, but worth it. Part of the "A Night at the Movies" series, this package simulates a 1959 movie evening with a Bugs Bunny cartoon, "People Are Bunny," a newsreel and coming attractions for "The Nun's Story" and "The Hanging Tree." **136m/B; DVD.** Paul Newman; Barbara Rush; Alexis Smith; Billie Burke; Brian Keith; John Williams; Otto Kruger; Robert Vaughn; ***D:*** Vincent Sherman; ***C:*** Harry Stradling, Sr.; ***M:*** Ernest Gold.

The Young Poisoner's Handbook **1994 (R)** Based on the true story of London teenager Graham (O'Conor), who's obsessed with chemistry and at odds with his stepmother. So, he poisons her chocolates and she dies. Sent to Broadmoor prison for the criminally insane, Graham comes under the care of Dr. Ziegler (Sher), who, eight years later, recommends Graham for parole. Now working in a photographic lab, Graham decides to experiment with doctoring his co-workers tea—which results in eight more deaths before Graham is caught. Locked up again, Graham spends his time writing a poisoner's handbook for Dr. Ziegler. Be warned that the sufferings of the poisoned victims are gruesome. **99m/C; VHS, DVD.** *GB* Hugh O'Conor; Anthony Sher; Ruth Sheen; Charlotte Coleman; Roger Lloyd-Pack; Paul Stacey; Samantha Edmonds; Charlie Creed-Miles; ***D:*** Benjamin Ross; ***W:*** Benjamin Ross; Jeff Rawle; ***C:*** Hubert Taczanowski; ***M:*** Robert (Rob) Lane; Frank Strobel.

The Young Savages **1961** Gang warfare in New York's East Harlem. Three Italian teenagers are accused of murdering another teen—a blind Puerto Rican boy. Assistant DA Hank Bell (Lancaster), who grew up on the same mean streets, doesn't think the case is as cut-and-dry as presented and determines that the deceased was not the innocent victim he's portrayed to be. Routine juvenile delinquent drama based on the novel "A Matter of Conviction" by Evan Hunter. **103m/B; VHS, DVD, Blu-Ray.** Burt Lancaster; Dina Merrill; Edward Andrews; Shelley Winters; Vivian Nathan; Larry Gates; Telly Savalas; John Davis Chandler; Neil Nephew; Stanley Kristien; ***D:*** John Frankenheimer; ***W:*** Edward Anhalt; J.P. Miller; ***C:*** Lionel Lindon; ***M:*** David Amram.

Young Sherlock Holmes **1985 (PG-13)** Holmes and Watson meet as schoolboys. They work together on their first case, solving a series of bizarre murders gripping London. Watch through the credits for an interesting plot twist. Promising "what if" sleuth tale crashes and burns, becoming a typical high-tech Spielberg film. Second half bears too strong a resemblance to "Indiana Jones and the Temple of Doom." **109m/C; VHS, DVD.** Nicholas (Nick) Rowe; Alan Cox; Sophie Ward; Freddie Jones; Michael Hordern;

D: Barry Levinson; *W:* Chris Columbus; *M:* Bruce Broughton.

The Young Stranger **1957** Hal, the neglected teenaged son of movie producer Thomas Ditmar, is only defending himself when he gets into a fight with older theater manager Grubbs. The cops think that Hal is just another juvie delinquent as dad finally realizes he needs to pay some attention to his parental duties. Frankenheimer's feature film debut is an adaptation of the 1955 TV play "Deal a Blow," which he also directed. **84m/B; DVD.** James MacArthur; James Daly; Kim Hunter; Whit Bissell; James Gregory; *D:* John Frankenheimer; *W:* Robert Dozier; *C:* Robert Planck; *M:* Leonard Rosenman.

Young Tiger WOOF! *Police Woman; Rumble in Hong Kong* **1974 (R)** A really cheesy Chan movie where he plays a bad guy, followed by a 12-minute documentary featuring Jackie Chan, kung-fu sensation, demonstrating his skills. **102m/C; VHS, DVD.** *CH* Jackie Chan; Qui Yuen; Ken Jeong; Gam Woo; *D:* Hdeng Tsu.

Young Tom Edison **½ 1940** Two teenaged years in the life of Thomas Alva Edison, as he drives his family crazy with his endless experiments on his way to becoming the famed inventor. Rooney manages to be enthusiastic without being overwhelming. Followed by "Edison the Man," with Spencer Tracy in the adult role. **82m/B; VHS, DVD.** Mickey Rooney; Fay Bainter; George Bancroft; Virginia Weidler; Eugene Pallette; Victor Kilian; Bobby Jordan; Lloyd Corrigan; *D:* Norman Taurog; *W:* Dore Schary; Bradbury Foote; Hugo Butler.

The Young Victoria **2009 (PG)** Depicting the early years of the reign of Queen Victoria (Blunt), period piece artfully blends the court intrigues and eventual emotion that led to her marriage to Prince Albert (Friend). Victoria must learn to rule as well as navigate the manipulations of her mother (Richardson) and uncle (Kretschmann), who both wish to be the power behind the throne. Victoria and Albert begin to warm to each other in their mutual dislike of their meddling elders, and love blossoms. Producers include Martin Scorsese and Sarah Ferguson, Duchess of York, whose daughter Beatrice appears as a lady-in-waiting. Sadly, inquiries concerning Prince Albert in a can remain unanswered as this edition went to print. **104m/C; Blu-Ray, On Demand.** Emily Blunt; Rupert Friend; Paul Bettany; Miranda Richardson; Jim Broadbent; Thomas Kretschmann; Mark Strong; Jesper Christensen; Harriet Walter; Julian Glover; Michael Maloney; Michaela Brooks; *D:* Jean-Marc Vallee; *W:* Julian Fellowes; *C:* Hagen Bogdanski; *M:* Ilan Eshkeri. Oscars '09: Costume Des.; British Acad. '09: Costume Des., Makeup.

Young Warlord *King Arthur, the Young Warlord* **1975** Arthur roams western England in 500 AD, leading a band of guerrilla cavalrymen. When the Saxons invade, Arthur unites the tribe, holds off the attack and becomes king. **97m/C; VHS, DVD.** Oliver Tobias; Michael Gothard; Jack Watson; Brian Blessed; *D:* Peter Sasdy.

Young Winston **1972 (PG)** Based on Sir Winston Churchill's autobiography "My Early Life: A Roving Commission." Follows him through his school days, journalistic career in Africa, early military career, and his election to Parliament at the age of 26. Ward is tremendous as the prime minister-to-be. **145m/C; VHS, DVD, Streaming.** *GB* Simon Ward; Robert Shaw; Anne Bancroft; John Mills; Jack Hawkins; Ian Holm; Anthony Hopkins; Patrick Magee; Edward Woodward; Jane Seymour; *D:* Richard Attenborough. Golden Globes '73: Foreign Film.

Youngblood **1986 (R)** An underdog beats the seemingly insurmountable odds and becomes a hockey champion. Some enjoyable hockey scenes although the success storyline is predictable. **111m/C; VHS, DVD, Blu-Ray.** Rob Lowe; Patrick Swayze; Cynthia Gibb; Ed Lauter; George Finn; Fionnula Flanagan; Keanu Reeves; *D:* Peter Markle.

Youngblood Hawke **½ 1964** Glossy potboiler adapted from the Herman Wouk novel. Ambitious Kentucky truck driver Youngblood Hawke (Franciscus) is determined to become a famous writer in New York. Editor Jeanne Green (Pleshette) helps him achieve success but he breaks her heart when he succumbs to the lure of shallow society. Hawke eventually finds his career on the rocks and must head back south to find himself. **137m/C; DVD.** James Franciscus; Suzanne Pleshette; Genevieve Page; Edward Andrews; Mildred Dunnock; Mary Astor; Eva Gabor; Lee Bowman; John Dehner; *D:* Delmer Daves; *W:* Delmer Daves; *C:* Charles Lawton, Jr.; *M:* Max Steiner.

The Youngest Profession **½ 1943** Starstruck teens Joan (Wielder) and Patricia (Porter) are serious autograph hounds and are determined to get the signatures of their favorite MGM stars into their books when they find out they're in New York. They're like squealy, polite stalkers. Cameos include Greer Gawson, Lana Turner, Walter Pidgeon, William Powell, and Robert Taylor. **82m/B; DVD.** Virginia Weidler; Jean Porter; Edward Arnold; Marta Linden; Marjorie Gateson; Thurston Hall; John Carroll; Agnes Moorehead; *D:* Edward Buzzell; *W:* George Oppenheimer; Charles Lederer; *C:* Charles Lawton, Jr.; *M:* David Snell.

Your Cheatin' Heart **1964** Glossy MGM bio of country music legend Hank Williams (an oddly-cast Hamilton) and the price of fame. Hank grows up poor in Alabama, learns to play the guitar, and marries Audrey who will help him with his career path on the radio and at the Grand Ole Opry. But Williams falls prey to the dangers of alcohol and road life. Features the vocals of a teenage Hank Williams Jr. on the soundtrack. **99m/B; DVD.** George Hamilton; Susan Oliver; Red Buttons; Rex Ingram; Donald Losby; Shary Marshall; Arthur O'Connell; *D:* Gene Nelson; *W:* Stanford Whitmore; *C:* Ellis W. Carter; *M:* Fred Karger.

Your Friends & Neighbors **1998 (R)** If these are your friends and neighbors, you should reconsider your decisions and address. Six yuppies lie, cheat and deceive their way around the block in La Bute's tale of modern suburban immorality. Weasel Jerry (Stiller) sleeps with Mary (Brenneman), the supposedly happy wife of his old friend Barry (Eckhart). Meanwhile, his live-in girlfriend (Keener) is having a lesbian affair with art gallery employee Cheri (Kinski), and chilly misogynist Cary (Patric) seduces and discards a string of women. Excellent performances by the entire cast bring this nasty group to life and La Bute provides riveting if unsettling material for them. **99m/C; VHS, DVD.** Jason Patric; Nastassja Kinski; Ben Stiller; Catherine Keener; Aaron Eckhart; Amy Brenneman; *D:* Neil LaBute; *W:* Neil LaBute; *C:* Nancy Schreiber.

Your Highness **2011 (R)** Embarrassing, raunchy stoner comedy set in a Dungeons and Dragons fantasy world. The valiant Prince Fabious (Franco) must trek through dangerous land to save his bride (Deschanel), who's been kidnapped by the evil wizard Leezar (Theroux). But according to his father's wishes, Fabious must drag along his slovenly brother Thadeous (McBride). Joining them along the way is Xena-esque Isabel (Portman), who's under constant pressure by Thadeous to get either high or naked. Shameless waste of royal talent, including the normally sharp director Green, on fart jokes and prepubescent boob obsession. **102m/C; Blu-Ray, On Demand.** Danny McBride; James Franco; Natalie Portman; Zooey Deschanel; Justin Theroux; Toby Jones; Damian Lewis; Charles Dance; *D:* David Gordon Green; *W:* Danny McBride; Ben Best; *C:* Tim Orr; *M:* Steve Jablonsky.

Your Love Never Fails **2011** Hallmark Channel family drama. Working mom Laura would love to spend more time with her daughter, Kelsey. When Kelsey's dad, Dylan, files for joint custody, Laura returns to Texas to confront the life she left behind. **96m/C; DVD.** Elisa Donovan; Brad Rowe; Tom Skerritt; Kirstin Dorn; Fred Willard; Catherine Hicks; John Schneider; *D:* Michael Feifer; *W:* Michael Feifer; Peter Sullivan; *C:* Kobi Zaig-Mendez; *M:* Andres Boulton. **CABLE**

Your Name *Kimi no na wa.* **2017 (PG)** A visually striking anime film by writer/director Makoto Shinkai about the human condition with a Freaky Friday-esque twist. High school student Mitsuha (Kamishiraishi) lives in the village of Itomori and has no connection to Taki (Kamiki), who lives in Tokyo. One day, Taki wakes up and realizes that he is in Mitsuha's body, and vice versa. The next day, they are switched back. They soon learn that they randomly switch places while sleeping, and begin to help each other with their lives. When they stop switching, Taki tries to find Mitusha, who has disappeared. A moving blend of beautiful images and story. **106m/C; DVD.** Ryunosuke Kamiki; Mone Kamishiraishi; Ryo Narita; Aoi Yuki; Nobunaga Shimazaki; *D:* Makoto Shinkai; *W:* Makoto Shinkai; Clark Cheng; *C:* Makoto Shinkai; *M:* Radwimps.

Your Sister's Sister **2011 (R)** Jack (Duplass) can't get over his brother's death, so his best friend, Iris (Blunt), tells him to use her family's island cabin and figure out what to do next. Only problem is the cabin is already occupied by Iris's older sister, Hannah (DeWitt), who's just broken up with her longtime girlfriend. Too much tequila and an unwise decision later means when Iris unexpectedly shows up, Hannah and Jack decide to keep quiet about the night before. But everyone seems to have a secret that will be revealed. Talky dramedy but with winning performances. **90m/C; DVD, Blu-Ray, Streaming.** Mike Birbiglia; Rosemarie DeWitt; Emily Blunt; Mark Duplass; *D:* Lynn Shelton; *W:* Lynn Shelton; *C:* Benjamin Kasulke; *M:* Vinny Smith.

Your Turn Darling *A Toi de Faire, Mignonne; L'Agente Federale Lemmy Caution; Ladies Man* **1963** French espionage thriller with Constantine once again playing Lemmy Caution, a U.S. secret agent involved with a gang of spies. **93m/B; VHS, DVD.** *FR* Eddie Constantine; Gaia Germani; Elga Andersen; *D:* Bernard Borderie; *W:* Bernard Borderie; *C:* Henri Persin; *M:* Paul Misraki.

Your Vice is a Closed Room and Only I Have the Key **½** *Il tuo vizio e una stanza chiusa e solo io ne ho la chiave; Excite Me; Eye of the Black Cat; Gently Before She Dies* **1972** Italian writer Oliviero (Pistilli) enjoys tormenting and belittling women, especially his wife. When one of his mistresses is brutally murdered, followed by similar crimes, he becomes a suspect. His behavior toward his wife worsens and is witnessed by his scheming niece and the family's cat. Satisfying giallo heavily influenced by Poe. **96m/C; DVD, Blu-Ray.** *IT* Luigi Pistilli; Anita Strindberg; Edwige Fenech; Ivan Rassimov; *D:* Sergio Martino; *W:* Adriano Bolzoni; Ernesto Gastaldi; Luciano Martino; Sauro Scavolini; *C:* Giancarlo Ferrando; *M:* Bruno Nicolai.

You're a Big Boy Now **1966** Kastner, a virginal young man working in the New York Public Library, is told by his father to move out of his house and grow up. On his own, he soon becomes involved with manhating actress Hartman and a discotheque dancer. A wild and weird comedy. Coppola's commercial directorial debut. **96m/C; VHS, DVD.** Elizabeth Hartman; Geraldine Page; Peter Kastner; Julie Harris; Rip Torn; Michael Dunn; Tony Bill; Karen Black; *D:* Francis Ford Coppola; *W:* Francis Ford Coppola.

You're In the Navy Now **½ 1951** Mild naval comedy. The green new skipper (Cooper) of a submarine chaser has a crew as inexperienced as he is. They must all cope with an experimental steam engine installed for testing—the ship is nicknamed the USS Teakettle—which results in a lot of problems. The sixth collaboration between star Cooper and director Hathaway. **93m/B; DVD.** Gary Cooper; Eddie Albert; John McIntire; Ray Collins; Harry von Zell; Jack Webb; Jane Greer; *D:* Henry Hathaway; *W:* Richard Murphy; *C:* Joseph Macdonald; *M:* Cyril Mockridge.

You're Never Too Young **1955** Slapstick remake of 1942's "The Major and the Minor." Wilbur Hoolick comes into possession of a stolen diamond that thief Noonan wants back. Disguising himself as an 11-year-old boy to get half price train fare, Wilbur involves teachers Bob and Nancy in his scheme when he tries hiding out at the all-girls school where they teach. **102m/C; DVD.** Jerry Lewis; Dean Martin; Raymond Burr; Diana Lynn; Mitzi McCall; Nina Foch; *D:* Norman Taurog; *W:* Sidney Sheldon; *C:* Daniel F. Fapp; *M:* Walter Scharf.

You're Next **½ 2013 (R)** Erin (the great Vinson) ends up at the family reunion from Hell when her new boyfriend's (Bowen) clan is attacked in their remote home. As the body count rises, Erin is forced to fight back against three home invaders with a secret plan. Director Wingard's 2011 festival hit earned a theatrical release two years later and proved it had lost none of its blunt power. Wingard and writer Barrett deliver a lean machine of an old-fashioned horror flick more focused on the crunch of bone and spray of blood than narrative tricks in an era when so many are bloated messes. **94m/C; DVD, Blu-Ray.** Sharni Vinson; AJ Bowen; Joe Swanberg; Nicholas Tucci; Wendy Glenn; Margaret Laney; Amy Seimetz; Ti West; Rob Moran; Barbara Crampton; *D:* Adam Wingard; *W:* Simon Barrett; *C:* Andrew Droz Palermo; *M:* Kyle McKinnon.

You're Only Young Once **½ 1937** The second Andy Hardy comedy is one of the series' best as each of the characters gets a chance to shine and Rooney's tendency to mug is yet to become overwhelming. Judge and Mrs. Hardy take the family to Catalina Island for a vacation. While his father is determined to go deep-sea fishing, Andy is more interested in romancing local girl Jerry Lane (Lynn). **78m/B; DVD.** Mickey Rooney; Lewis Stone; Fay Holden; Cecilia Parker; Sara Haden; Eleanor Lynn; Ann Rutherford; Frank Craven; Ted Pearson; *D:* George B. Seitz; *W:* Kay Van Riper; *C:* Lester White; *M:* David Snell.

You're So Cupid **½ 2010 (G)** Sweet family comedy about romance. High school seniors and fraternal twins, tomboy Emma and shy Lily both fall for Connor and become rivals for his interest. That is until they learn that their parents' marriage has lost its spark and is in trouble. This is strange due to dad Daniel's secret life of bringing couples together. Now it's up to the girls to remind mom and dad about true love. **93m/C; DVD.** Brian Krause; Lauren Holly; Caitlin Meyer; Danielle Chuchran; Jeremy Sumpter; Chad Hively; Malese Jow; *D:* John Lyde; *W:* Sally Meyer; *M:* Jimmy Schafer. **VIDEO**

Yours, Mine & Ours **½ 1968** Bigger, better, big screen version of "The Brady Bunch." It's the story of a lovely lady (Ball) with eight kids who marries a a widower (Fonda) who has ten. Imagine the zany shenanigans! Family comedy manages to be both wholesome and funny. Based on a true story. **114m/C; VHS, DVD.** Lucille Ball; Henry Fonda; Van Johnson; Tim Matheson; Tom Bosley; Tracy Nelson; Morgan Brittany; *D:* Melville Shavelson; *W:* Melville Shavelson; *C:* Charles F. Wheeler; *M:* Fred Karlin.

Yours, Mine & Ours **2005 (PG)** Over-the-top slapstick, remake of the 1968 Lucille Ball/Henry Fonda farce about blending a large family. Helen (Russo) and Frank (Quaid) shared a brief high school romance. Now it's 30 years (and 18 kids) later, they're both single, and the romance rekindles at a reunion. Conflict between the kids, their jobs, and their differing child-raising philosophies ensues, as do sporadic fits of humor. Fun and safe enough family viewing. **90m/C; VHS, DVD.** Dennis Quaid; Rene Russo; Rip Torn; Linda Hunt; Jerry O'Connell; David Koechner; Sean Faris; Katija Pevec; Tyler Patrick Jones; Danielle Panabaker; Drake Bell; Miranda Cosgrove; Dean Collins; Haley Ramm; Brecken Palmer; Bridger Palmer; Ty Panitz; Miki Ishikawa; Slade Pearce; Little JJ; Andrew Vo; Jennifer Habib; Jessica Habib; Nicholas Roget-King; *D:* Raja Gosnell; *W:* Ron Burch; David Kidd; *C:* Theo van de Sande; *M:* Christophe Beck.

Youth **2015 (R)** Sorrentino loses his grip on character in his follow-up to his multi-award winning The Great Beauty. As is often the case with successful foreign film, Sorrentino moves to English with this drama and one can sense that the language not being his first led to the film's odd rhythm and pretentious dialogue. Caine stars as Fred Ballinger, a retired conductor who is on vacation in the Alps with his best friend (Keitel) and daughter (Weisz). The result is a bizarrely episodic film, filled with interesting exchanges with great actors that don't connect or amount to much of anything at all. **124m/C; DVD, Blu-Ray.** Harvey Keitel; Michael Caine; Paul Dano; Rachel Weisz; Alex MacQueen; Jane Fonda; *D:* Paolo Sorrentino; *W:* Paolo Sorrentino; *C:* Luca Bigazzi; *M:* David Lang.

Youth in Revolt **2010 (R)** In this dark comedy about love and surviving puberty, over-bright, under-sexed teenage intellectual Nick Twisp (Cera) meets dream girl Sheeni (Doubleday) in a trailer park and is determined to be with her at any cost, no matter how absurd. Along the path to her heart, he lies, cheats, steals, invents a French bad-boy persona, destroys a city block, and becomes a fugitive from the police, all while dealing with his divorced parents (Smart, Buscemi), sleazy authority figures, and oddball peers. Cera puts a funny twist on the "awkward teenager" cliche as Nick and his remorseless alter ego, Francois, whose bad judgment, faux-Frenchman accent, and raging hormones turn dysfunction into chaos wherever he goes. Based on the cult novel by C.D. Payne, the zany moments abound but the manic pace sometimes misses the biting satire and insight of the source. **90m/C; Blu-Ray, On Demand.** Michael Cera; Steve Buscemi; Jean Smart; Justin Long; Portia Doubleday; Ray Liotta; Ari Graynor; Fred Willard; Zach Galifianakis; Erik Knudsen; M. Emmet Walsh; Mary Kay Place; *D:* Miguel Arteta; *W:* Gustin Nash; *C:* Chuy Chavez; *M:* John Swihart.

Youth Without Youth **2007 (R)** A disappointing return to directing for Francis Ford Coppola after a ten-year hiatus. Dominic (Roth) is a 70-year-old Romanian linguist who fears he'll die alone a failure and, on the eve of World War II, decides to kill himself. But his suicide plans are interrupted when he's struck by lightning and somehow begins to grow younger. Scientists of the Third Reich snatch him up for observation and soon he meets Veronica (Lara), a sexy German spy who is coincidentally also struck by lightning, but begins to age rapidly. A muddled and tiring story that would've been better suited as a "Twilight Zone" episode. **124m/C; Blu-Ray.** Tim Roth; Alexandra Maria Lara; Bruno Ganz; Andre Hennicke; Alexandra Pirici; *D:* Francis Ford Coppola; *W:* Francis Ford Coppola; *C:* Mihai Malaimare, Jr.; *M:* Osvaldo Golijov.

You've Got a Friend **2007** A Hallmark Channel movie set in 1976. Twelve-year-old Bobby's (McLaughlin) parents die in a car accident, and he's sent to live with his Uncle Jeff (Brooks) and Aunt Gayle (Connor). Struggling to adjust, Bobby befriends town recluse and Vietnam vet Jim (Schneider), who helps Bobby with his dream of building a racer to enter the American Soapbox Derby despite his uncle's objections. **90m/C; DVD.** John Schneider; Dylan McLaughlin; Jason Brooks; Kate Connor; Chase Ellison; Bitty Schram; Mark Rolston; *D:* James A. Contner; *W:* Oliver Robins; *C:* James Warren; *M:* Kevin Kiner. **CABLE**

You've Got Mail **1/2 1998 (PG)** Third remake of "The Shop Around the Corner" ("In the Good Old Summertime" was number 2) finds independent bookstore owner Ryan battling Hank's bookstore conglomerate to stay in business. How does this qualify as a romantic comedy? Because they're flirting with each other anonymously by e-mail. Third teaming of Ryan and Hanks relies, almost too much, on their considerable chemistry. Soundtrack music was chosen for maximum on-screen and record store effect. Must-see for hopeless romantics and fans of Hanks and/or Ryan. Others must decide based on tolerance for meet-cute situations and lightweight romantic comedy. **119m/C; VHS, DVD.** Meg Ryan; Tom Hanks; Parker Posey; Greg Kinnear; Jean Stapleton; Steve Zahn; Dave Chappelle; Dabney Coleman; John Randolph; Michael Badalucco; Heather Burns; Hallee Hirsh; *D:* Nora Ephron; *W:* Nora Ephron; *C:* John Lindley; *M:* George Fenton.

You've Ruined Me, Eddie *The Touch of Flesh* **1958** A spoiled rich girl gets knocked up and her boyfriend will never know peace again. Meanwhile, their once quiet town is outraged. **76m/B; VHS, DVD.** Charles Martin; Robert Cannon; Ted Marshall; Jeanne Rainer; Sue Ellis; Josie Hascall; *D:* R. John Hugh; *C:* Charles T. O'Rork.

Yu-Gi-Oh! The Movie: Pyramid of Light **2004 (PG)** Yu-Gi-Oh hits the big screen with the television cartoon's storyline (picking up at the end of the series' third season) and gameplay in tow, meaning only fans (and their suffering parents) need to see it. Yu-GI-Oh, whose body hosts an Egyptian spirit, plays a combat monster game, apparently for the future of humanity and occasionally for the players' souls. The Pyramid of Light in question is the most powerful card, and controls the destiny of the players. If your kids aren't fans, count yourself lucky. If they are, keep in mind that game cards were given out as inticement to get people into the theater. **89m/C; VHS, DVD.** *JP V:* Eric Stuart; Dan Green; Maddie (Maddeleine) Blaustein; Wayne Grayson; Scottie Ray; Tara Jayne; Frank Frankson; *D:* Hatuki Tsuji; *W:* Norman Grossfeld; Matthew Drdek; Lloyd Goldfine; *C:* Hiroaki Edamitsu; *M:* Elik Alvarez.

The Yum-Yum Girls **1/2 1978 (R)** Pair of innocent girls arrive in NYC to pursue their dreams. Gives an inside looks at the fashion industry. Not as funny or as cute as it wants to be. **89m/C; VHS, DVD.** Judy Landers; Tanya Roberts; Barbara Tully; Michelle Daw; *D:* Barry Rosen.

Yuma **1970** An old-style Western about a sheriff (Walker) who rides into town, cleans it up, and saves his own reputation from a plot to discredit him. Dull in places, but action-packed ending saves the day. **73m/C; VHS, DVD.** Clint Walker; Barry Sullivan; Edgar Buchanan; *D:* Ted Post; *M:* George Duning. **TV**

Yuri Nosenko, KGB **1/2 1986** Fact-based account of a KGB defector and the CIA agent who must determine if he's on the up-and-up. **85m/C; VHS, DVD.** *GB* Tommy Lee Jones; Oleg Rudnik; Josef Sommer; Ed Lauter; George Morfogen; Stephen D. Newman; *D:* Mick Jackson. **TV**

Z **1969** The assassination of a Greek nationalist in the 1960s and its aftermath are portrayed by the notorious political director as a gripping detective thriller. Excellent performances, adequate cinematic techniques, and important politics in this highly acclaimed film. **128m/C; VHS, DVD.** *FR* Yves Montand; Jean-Louis Trintignant; Irene Papas; Charles Denner; Georges Geret; Jacques Perrin; Francois Perier; Marcel Bozzuffi; *D:* Constantin Costa-Gavras; *W:* Constantin Costa-Gavras; *M:* Mikis Theodorakis. Oscars '69: Film Editing, Foreign Film; Cannes '69: Actor (Trintignant), Special Jury Prize; Golden Globes '70: Foreign Film; N.Y. Film Critics '69: Director (Costa-Gavras), Film; Natl. Soc. Film Critics '69: Film.

Z for Zachariah **1/2 2015 (PG-13)** A futuristic sci-fi dramatic thriller about the last survivors on Earth, based on the novel by Robert C. O'Brien. After a nuclear war, Ann Burden (Robbie) is a young woman believes she might be the only human being still alive. That is, until she connects with a man, John Loomis (Ejiofor) who has been desperately searching for others. The frantic man is a scientist who has been ill with radiation exposure. Over time, the pair bond and form an understanding which is challenged when they meet a third person—Caleb (Pine) another man looking for fellow survivors. **98m/C; DVD, Blu-Ray, Streaming, Download.** Margot Robbie; Chiwetel Ejiofor; Chris Pine; *D:* Craig Zobel; *W:* Nissar Modi; *C:* Tim Orr; *M:* Heather McIntosh.

Zabriskie Point **1970 (R)** Antonioni's first U.S. feature. A desultory, surreal examination of the American way of life. Worthy but difficult. Climaxes with a stylized orgy in Death Valley. **112m/C; VHS, DVD.** Mark Frechette; Daria Halprin; Paul Fix; Rod Taylor; Harrison Ford; G.D. Spradlin; *D:* Michelangelo Antonioni; *W:* Michelangelo Antonioni; Sam Shepard; Fred Gardner; Tonino Guerra; Clare Peploe.

Zachariah **1/2 1970 (PG)** A semi-spoof '60s rock western, wherein two gunfighters given to pursuing wealth-laden bands of outlaws separate and experience quixotic journeys through the cliched landscape. Scripted by members of The Firesign Theater and featuring appearances by Country Joe and The Fish, The New York Rock Ensemble, and The James Gang. **93m/C; VHS, DVD, Blu-Ray.** Don Johnson; John Rubinstein; Pat Quinn; Dick Van Patten; William Challee; Country Joe McDonald; Elvin Jones; Doug Kershaw; Lawrence Kubik; Hank Worden; *D:* George Englund; *W:* Peter Bergman; Joe Massot; Phil(ip) Proctor; Philip Austin; David Ossman; *C:* Jorge Stahl, Jr.; *M:* Jimmie Haskell.

Zack and Miri Make a Porno **2008 (R)** Longtime platonic friends Zack (Rogan) and Miri (Banks), in desperate need of quick cash, decide to, as the title warns, make their own skin flick. Rather than sexy or smutty, they aim for goofy and ridiculous, particularly when converting "Star Wars" to "Star Whores." And, since this is actually a well-disguised romantic comedy, Zack and Miri eventually find they may be more than friends. Luckily, their on-screen chemistry keeps the perfect balance of nasty and nice. Rogan's signature crude charm is still fresh despite often-inconsistent Kevin Smith writing and directing in place of usual suspect Judd Apatow. **101m/C; Blu-Ray, On Demand.** Seth Rogen; Elizabeth Banks; Craig Robinson; Jason Mewes; Jeff Anderson; Traci Lords; Ricky Mabe; Brandon Routh; Katie Morgan; Justin Long; Gerry Bednob; *D:* Kevin Smith; *W:* Kevin Smith; *C:* David Klein; *M:* James L. Venable.

Zack & Reba **1998 (R)** When Reba (Murphy) calls off her wedding a week before the ceremony, her fiance commits suicide. Guilt-ridden, Reba returns to her hometown of Spooner and its eccentric residents, which include shotgun-toting grandma, Beulah (Reynolds), and her grief-stricken grandson Zack (Flanery), who can't seem to get over the death of his wife. Naturally, Beulah thinks Zack and Reba are just made for each other. **91m/C; VHS, DVD.** Sean Patrick Flanery; Brittany Murphy; Debbie Reynolds; Kathy Najimy; Martin Mull; Michael Jeter; *D:* Nicole Bettauer; *W:* Jay Stapleton; *C:* Mark Irwin; *M:* Joel McNeely.

Zalmen or the Madness of God **1/2 1975** Elie Wiesel's mystical story about a rabbi's struggle against religious persecution in post-Stalin Russia. **120m/C; VHS, DVD.** Joseph Wiseman; Dianne Wiest; *D:* Peter Levin; *W:* Elie Wiesel. **TV**

Zama **1/2 2017** Based on the acclaimed Argentine novel by Antonio Di Benedetto. Don Diego de Zama is an officer in the Spanish empire assigned to a remote town in Paraguay in the 18th century. There, he awaits reassignment to a position closer to his wife and children in Buenos Aires, but as governor after governor ignore him, he turns his attention to capturing the bandit Vicuña Porto as a way of relieving his existential gloom. Hauntingly beautiful, with comedic flashes that mock European colonialism. **115m/C; DVD, Blu-Ray.** Daniel Gimenez Cacho; Lola Duenas; Matheus Nachtergaele; Juan Minujin; Nahuel Cano; *D:* Lucrecia Martel; *W:* Lucrecia Martel; *C:* Rui Poças.

Zandalee WOOF! **1991 (R)** The sexual adventures of a bored sexy young woman who has a fling with her husband's friend. Bad script, graphic sex. Also available in an unrated version. **100m/C; VHS, DVD.** Nicolas Cage; Judge Reinhold; Erika Anderson; Viveca Lindfors; Aaron Neville; Joe Pantoliano; Ian Abercrombie; Marisa Tomei; Zach Galligan; *D:* Sam Pillsbury; *W:* Mari Kornhauser.

Zandy's Bride **1/2 1974 (PG)** Basic story about a rancher who sents for a mail-order bride. She's shocked by his ill-treatment of her and stands up to his bullying, thus winning his respect and love. Beautiful scenery, courtesy of Big Sur, California, but predictable all-around and essentially a waste of an experienced cast. Based on the novel "The Stranger" by Lillian Bos Ross. **97m/C; DVD.** Gene Hackman; Liv Ullmann; Eileen Heckart; Harry Dean Stanton; Joe Santos; Sam Bottoms; Susan Tyrrell; Frank Cady; *D:* Jan Troell; *W:* Marc Norman; *C:* Jordan Cronenweth; *M:* Michael Franks.

Zapped! **1982 (R)** Teen genius discovers he possesses telekinetic powers. He does the natural thing, using his talent to remove clothing from nearby females. A teen boy's dream come true. **98m/C; VHS, DVD, Blu-Ray.** Scott Baio; Willie Aames; Robert Mandan; Felice Schachter; Scatman Crothers; Roger Bowen; Marya Small; Greg Bradford; Hilary Beane; Sue Ane Langdon; Heather Thomas; Merritt Butrick; LaWanda Page; Rosanne Katon; *D:* Robert J. Rosenthal; *M:* Charles Fox.

Zapped Again **1989 (R)** The lame-brained sequel to 1982's "Zapped" about a high schooler who has telekinetic powers and lust on his mind. **93m/C; VHS, DVD.** Todd Eric Andrews; Kelli Williams; Reed Rudy; Linda Blair; Karen Black; Lyle Alzado; Rossie (Ross) Harris; *D:* Doug Campbell.

Zarak **1/2 1956** Zarak Khan becomes an outlaw after being banished by his father. British Major Michael Ingram is sent to stop the bandits and he and Zarak develop a grudging respect for each other. Ingram is captured by the sadistic Ahmad and Zarak risks his life to free his enemy. The CinemaScope/Technicolor cinematography and the Moroccan desert locations make up for the routine adventure story. **96m/C; DVD.** *GB* Victor Mature; Michael Wilding; Peter Illing; Anita Ekberg; Frederick Valk; Patrick McGoohan; *D:* Terence Young; *W:* Richard Maibaum; *C:* Cyril Knowles; *M:* Auyar Hosseini.

Zardoz **1973** A surreal parable of the far future (2293), when Earth society is broken into strict classes: a society of intellectuals known as the Eternals, a society of savages called the Brutals, and an elite unit of killers, naturally named the Exterminators, who keep the order. The Exterminators worship a stone god named Zardoz, but killer Zed (Connery) discovers that it's merely a futuristic version of "The Wizard of Oz" and that the Eternals have been manipulating the social order. His presence causes chaos and destruction (but he does get all the babes). Visually interesting but pretentious. **105m/C; VHS, DVD, Blu-Ray.** *GB* Sean Connery; Charlotte Rampling; John Alderton; Sara Kestelman; Sally Anne Newton; Niall Buggy; Christopher Casson; Bosco Hogan; Jessica Swift; *D:* John Boorman; *W:* John Boorman; *C:* Geoffrey Unsworth; *M:* David Munrow.

Zarkorr! The Invader **1996 (PG)** Aliens studying earth decide humans need a challenge (like we don't have enough problems of our own) so they send a 185-foot tall, laser-eyed monster to crush (American) cities and cause general terror in the population. And who's our hero? A postal worker—aided by a five-inch tall alien girl. Low-budget spoof has its moments, but eventually wears thin. **80m/C; VHS, DVD.** Rhys Pugh; Deprise Grossman; Mark Hamilton; Charles Schneider; Eileen Wesson; *D:* Aaron Osborne; *W:* Benjamin Carr; *C:* Joe C. Maxwell; *M:* Richard Band.

Zathura **2005 (PG)** Ten year old Walter (Hutcherson) and six year old Danny (Bobo) both fight for overstressed dad's (Robbins) attention, but he's too busy. Older sister Lisa (Stewart) is charged with babysitting the two, but she could care less. Until they all find themselves trapped in the bizarre space-world of Zathura, a game which comes to life as they play. Sort-of sequel to "Jumanji," also done by Chris Van Allsburg. Fabulous special effects and a fantastical plot is exciting stuff for both children and adults. **113m/C; DVD, UMD.** Jonah Bobo; Josh Hutcherson; Dax Shepard; Kristen Stewart; Tim Robbins; *V:* Frank Oz; *D:* Jon Favreau; *W:* David Koepp; John Kamps; *C:* Guillermo Navarro; *M:* John Debney.

Zatoichi **1/2** *The Blind Swordsman: Zatoichi* **2003 (R)** Versatile and popular filmmaker Kitano (who also takes on the lead role under his actor's pseudonym) kicks butt as a legendary 19th-century samurai (an iconic figure in Japanese film and TV). The blind masseur/gambler hides his sword in his walking stick and the plot, such as it is, involves loner Zatoichi helping out geisha Okino (Daike) and her cross-dressing brother Osei (Tachibana) in their quest for revenge on the Ginzo gang, who slaughtered their family and who are now threatening the local peasants. Which makes a good excuse for Zatoichi to challenge the gang and their own formidable samurai Hattori (Asano). Lots of stylized violence and some slapstick gags; Japanese with subtitles. **115m/C; DVD.** *JP* Tadanobu Asano; Takeshi "Beat" Kitano; Michiyo Ogusu; Guadalcanal Taka; Daigoro Tachibana; Yuko Daike; Ittoku Kishibe; Saburo Ishikura; *D:* Takeshi "Beat" Kitano; *W:* Takeshi "Beat" Kitano; *C:* Katsumi Yanagijima; *M:* Keiichi Suzuki.

Zatoichi: Master Ichi and a Chest of Gold **1964** A violent thriller about a blind gambler and former samurai who tries to clear his name after being framed for a gold robbery. Adapted from a novel by Kazuo Miyagawa. In Japanese with English subtitles. **83m/C; VHS, DVD, Blu-Ray.** *JP* Shintaro Katsu; Tomisaburo Wakayama;

D: Kazuo Ikehiro; *W:* Shozaburo Asai; *C:* Kazuo Miyagawa; *M:* Ichiro Saito.

Zatoichi: The Blind Swordsman and the Chess Expert **1965** Zatoichi, the blind gambler and former samurai, befriends a master chess player and gets involved with Japanese gangsters. In Japanese with English subtitles. **87m/C; VHS, DVD, Blu-Ray.** *JP* Shintaro Katsu; Mikio Narita; Chizu Hayashi; Kaneko Iwasaki; Gaku Yamamoto; *D:* Kenji Misumi; *W:* Daisuke Ito; *C:* Chishi Makiura; *M:* Akira Ifukube.

Zatoichi: The Blind Swordsman and the Fugitives *Zatoichi and the Fugitives* **1968** This time Zatoichi, the blind masseur and master swordsman, is pitted against a band of outlaws. When the local bandits brutalize the countryside Zatoichi steps in to defend the weak and faces a showdown with outlaw leader Genpachiro. In Japanese with English subtitles. **82m/C; VHS, DVD, Blu-Ray.** *JP* Shintaro Katsu; Yumiko Nogawa; Kayo Mikimoto; Kyosuke Machida; *D:* Kimiyoshi Yasuda.

Zatoichi: The Blind Swordsman's Vengeance *Zatoichi's Vengeance* **1966** Zatoichi defends a dying man against a group of gangsters who have taken over an isolated village. In Japanese with English subtitles. **83m/C; VHS, DVD, Blu-Ray.** *JP* Shintaro Katsu; Shigeru Amachi; Kei Sato; Mayumi Ogawa; *D:* Tokuzo Tanaka.

Zatoichi: The Life and Opinion of Masseur Ichi *The Tale of Zatoichi* **1962** The first film in the action series about the Zen-like blind masseur, gambler, and swordsman. Zatoichi is drawn into a revenge match between two ruthless gangs. When one gang tries to hire him the other hires a savage killer. This sets in motion a war between the yakuza gangs and mercenary samurai. In Japanese with English subtitles. **96m/C; VHS, DVD, Blu-Ray.** *JP* Shintaro Katsu; Masayo Mari; Ryuzo Shimada; Gen Mitamura; Shigeru Amachi; *D:* Kenji Misumi.

Zatoichi vs. Yojimbo ½ *Zatoichi Meets Yojimbo; Zato Ichi To Yojimbo* **1970** The legendary blind warrior-samurai, Zatoichi, wants to retire, but his village is being held captive by outlaws. He is forced to fight Yojimbo, the crude wandering samurai without a master, and the sparks really fly! This was a comic send-up of Akiro Kurosawa's "Yojimbo" with Mifune recreating his role here and playing it for laughs. Subtitled. **90m/C; VHS, DVD.** *JP* Toshiro Mifune; Shintaro Katsu; Osamu Takizawa; *D:* Kihachi Okamoto; *W:* Tetsuro Yoshida.

Zatoichi: Zatoichi's Flashing Sword **1964** Blind swordsman Zatoichi gets caught up in a feud between two competing yakuza bosses. When Zatoichi declares his alliegence to Tsumugi, the unhappy Yasu tries to get his revenge. In Japanese with English subtitles. **82m/C; VHS, DVD, Blu-Ray.** *JP* Shintaro Katsu; Mayumi Nagisa; Naoko Kubo; Ryutaro Gami; Yutaka Nakamura; *D:* Kazuo Ikehiro.

Zazie dans le Metro ½ *Zazie in the Underground; Zazie in the Subway* **1961** One of Malle's early movies, this is one of the best of the French New Wave comedies. A young girl, wise beyond her years, visits her drag queen uncle in Paris. She wants to ride the subway, but the ensuing hilarious adventures keep her from her goal. In French with English subtitles. **92m/C; VHS, DVD, Blu-Ray.** *FR* Catherine Demonget; Philippe Noiret; Carla Marlier; *W:* Louis Malle.

Zebra Force **1976 (R)** Group of army veterans embark on a personal battle against organized crime, using their military training with deadly precision. Non-distinguished substandard action-adventure. **81m/C; VHS, DVD.** Mike Lane; Richard X. Slattery; Rockne Tarkington; Glenn Wilder; Anthony Caruso; *D:* Joe Tornatore.

Zebra in the Kitchen ½ **1965** A 12-year-old boy living in a small town is upset when he sees the run-down condition of the local zoo. So he decides to set all the animals free, which causes pandemonium in the town. Pleasant family fare. **92m/C; VHS, DVD.** Jay North; Martin Milner; Andy Devine; Joyce Meadows; Jim Davis; *D:* Ivan Tors.

Zebra Lounge **2001** Wendy (Swanson) and Alan (Baldwin) Barnet feel their marriage has gotten dull, so they place an ad in a swingers' magazine that leads them to the Zebra Lounge. There they meet the more experienced Jack (Daddo) and Louise (Ledford) Bauer who take them on a new sexual trip. But the Barnets soon discover that their new partners are not the emotionally stable people to get involved with. **92m/C; VHS, DVD.** *CA* Stephen Baldwin; Kristy Swanson; Cameron Daddo; Brandy Ledford; *D:* Keri Skogland; *W:* Claire Montgomery; Monte Montgomery; *C:* Barry Parrell. **VIDEO**

Zebrahead **1992 (R)** Zack and Nikki are two high schoolers in love—which would be okay except Zack's white and Nikki's black. Writer/director Drazan's expressive debut features one of last appearances by Sharkey as Zack's dad. Outstanding performances by the young and largely unknown cast, particularly Rapaport and Wright, and a great musical score enrich the action. Filmed on location in Detroit, with plenty of authentic Motown scenery to chew on, including Cody High School and a shootout at the eastside Skateland. Developed with assistance by the Sundance Institute. **102m/C; VHS, DVD.** Michael Rapaport; N'Bushe Wright; Ray Sharkey; DeShonn Castle; Ron Johnson; Marsha Florence; Paul Butler; Abdul Hassan Sharif; Dan Ziskie; Candy Ann Brown; Helen Shaver; Luke Reilly; Martin Priest; Kevin Corrigan; *D:* Tony Drazan; *W:* Tony Drazan; *C:* Maryse Alberti; *M:* Taj Mahal. Sundance '92: Filmmakers Trophy.

Zebraman ½ *Zeburaman* **2004** Junior high teacher Shinichi is a failure at life. His wife hates him, his daughter is slutty, and his son spends his days being bullied. Shinichi spends most of his time daydreaming about his favorite TV show from his childhood, "Zebraman" (think "Power Rangers" on drugs). Eventually he begins dressing up as Zebraman and going out into the city streets at night. At some point he meets a villain named Crabhead and kicks him unconscious. Then the aliens invade and begin possessing people and killing young girls, turning Shinichi into a superhero, whether he wants the job or not. Oddly lighthearted for a Takashi Miike flick. **115m/C; DVD.** *JP* Sho Aikawa; Atsuro Watabe; Akira (Tsukamoto) Emoto; Ren Osugi; Kyoka Suzuki; Yui Ichikawa; Koen Kondo; Ryo Iwamatsu; Teruyoshi Uchimura; *D:* Takashi Miike; *W:* Kankuro Kudo; *C:* Kazunari Tanaka; *M:* Koji Endo.

A Zed & Two Noughts **1988** A serio-comic essay by the acclaimed British filmmaker. Twin zoologists, after their wives are killed in an accident, explore their notions of death by, among other things, filming the decay of animal bodies absconded from the zoo. Heavily textured and experimental; Greenaway's second feature film. **115m/C; VHS, DVD.** *GB* Eric Deacon; Brian Deacon; Joss Ackland; Andrea Ferreol; Frances Barber; *D:* Peter Greenaway; *W:* Peter Greenaway; *C:* Sacha Vierny; *M:* Michael Nyman.

Zeder ½ *Revenge of the Dead; Zeder: Voices from Beyond* **1983** A young novelist (Lavia) discovers fragments of curious documents on the ribbon of a used typewriter bought by his wife (Canovas). He comes to think that they suggest research into immortality. The rest of the film combines elements of suspense with horror in a fairly slow-moving, serious plot with references to Val Lewton's "Cat People." **98m/C; VHS, DVD, Blu-Ray.** *IT* Gabriele Lavia; Anne Canovos; *D:* Pupi Avati; *W:* Pupi Avati; Antonio Avati; Maurizio Costanzo.

Zelary ½ **2003 (R)** Eliska (Geislerova) is a confident young medical student in 1943 Prague whose life is interrupted by the Nazi invasion. She joins the resistance, but her cell is soon discovered, forcing her to flee with a sympathetic patient (Cserhalmi) to a rural village. In order to avert suspicion, she must marry the man and try to fit in. Slowly and gracefully follows Eliska's initial hesitation with her new benefactor and environment until she is won over by their kindness and strength of character. Lovingly shot and acted, if a bit overlong. **150m/C; DVD.** *CZ AT* Anna Geislerova; Ivan Trojan; Jan Hrusinsky; Iva Bittova; Tomas Zatecka; Jaroslava Adamova; *D:* Ondrej Trojan; *W:* Petr Jarchovsky; *C:* Asen Sopov; *M:* Petr Ostouchov.

Zelig ½ **1983 (PG)** Documentary spoof stars Allen as Leonard Zelig, the famous "Chameleon Man" of the 1920s, whose personality was so vague he would assume the characteristics of those with whom he came into contact, and who had a habit of showing up among celebrities and at historic events. Filmed in black-and-white; intersperses bits of newsreel and photographs with live action. Allen-style clever filmmaking at its best. **79m/B; VHS, DVD, Blu-Ray.** Woody Allen; Mia Farrow; Susan Sontag; Saul Bellow; Irving Howe; *D:* Woody Allen; *W:* Woody Allen; *C:* Gordon Willis. N.Y. Film Critics '83: Cinematog.

Zemsta *The Revenge* **2002** In the 17th century, two feuding noblemen occupy different parts of the same crumbling castle because of their declining fortunes. They live to make each other miserable and marry money. Papkin (Polanski), a boastful popinjay, is enlisted by Czesnik to help him woo a supposedly wealthy widow in return for the chance at romancing Czesnik's pretty niece, who has her own romantic plans. Adapted from the play by Aleksander Fredro. Polish with subtitles. **100m/C; VHS, DVD.** *PL* Roman Polanski; Janusz Gajos; Andrzej Seweryn; Kasia (Katarzyna) Figura; Agata Buzek; Rafal Krolikowski; *D:* Andrzej Wajda; *W:* Andrzej Wajda; *C:* Pawel Edelman; *M:* Wojciech Kilar.

Zentropa *Europa* **1992 (R)** Clever cinematic allusions and visuals aside, this is essentially a conventional thriller. German-American pacifist Leopold travels to Germany in 1945 to help in the postwar rebuilding. He finds work as a sleeping-car conductor for a giant railway system called Zentropa and finds himself romancing the mysterious Katharina, who draws the hapless Leopold into an intrigue involving Nazi sympathizers. Director von Trier uses the voice of Von Sydow as an omniscient narrator to address the audience and move the story along. Filmed primarily in black-and-white with bursts of color denoting dramatic moments. In English and German with English subtitles. **112m/C; VHS, DVD.** *GE* Jean-Marc Barr; Barbara Sukowa; Udo Kier; Eddie Constantine; *Nar:* Max von Sydow; *D:* Lars von Trier; *W:* Niels Vorsel; Lars von Trier.

Zeppelin ½ **1971 (G)** During WWI, the British enlist the aid of York as a double agent. His mission is to steal Germany's plans for a super-dirigible. Accompanying the Germans on the craft's maiden voyage, York discovers they are actually on a mission to steal British treasures. Although the script is poor, the battle scenes and the airship itself are very impressive. **102m/C; VHS, DVD.** *GB* Michael York; Elke Sommer; Peter Carsten; Marius Goring; Anton Diffring; Andrew Keir; Rupert Davies; Alexandra Stewart; *D:* Etienne Perier.

Zeram *Zeiram; Zeiramu* **1991** Zeram is a giant renegade space alien lured to earth by a female bounty hunter. How does she expect to capture it? Why with a warp machine, space bazooka, electric shield, and a computer named Bob, of course. Dubbed. **92m/C; VHS, DVD.** *JP* Yuko Moriyama; Yukihiro Hotaru; Kunihiko Ida; *D:* Keita Amemiya; *W:* Hajime Matsumoto; *C:* Hiroshi Kidokoro; *M:* Hirokazu Ohta.

Zeram 2 *Zeiram 2; Zeiramu* **1994** Moriyama returns to play Investigator Iria, an intergalactic bounty hunter, who is assisted by her computer, Bob. Iria has been given a new android as a trainee, but it malfunctions during a battle and turns on her. The android is infected with a Zeram, an evil alien force. To make matters worse, Iria's partner Fujikuro (Sabu) has betrayed her and is trying to steal an ancient artifact which Iria possesses. Trapped and in need of assistance, Iria calls on her old friends Teppei (Iida) and Kamiya (Hotaru), two bumbling electricians to help her. The film is non-stop fun, as it mixes amazing action scenes, gross monsters, and slapstick comedy seamlessly to create an entertaining sci-fi treat. **100m/C; DVD.** *JP* Yukihiro Hotaru; Kunihiko Iida; Yuko Moriyama; *D:* Keito Amamiya.

Zero ½ **1997** The first feature by avant-garde filmmaker James Fotopoulos is a 16mm film, shot in black and white and hand tinted. The experimental horror film centers a man (Buckley) who descends into an isolated dark place. Obsessed with pornography and violence, he becomes increasingly mentally unstable and has visions which further his mental breakdown. The state of his mind is physically manifested by a cyst growing on his arm. **142m/B; DVD.** Matthew Buckley; *D:* James Fotopoulos; *C:* John Wagner; *M:* Tom Nicholl. **VIDEO**

Zero **2018** A pint-sized, 30-something bachelor with quart-sized arrogance pursues two women, a wheelchair-bound intellectual and a Bollywood icon, before taking his life in an entirely new direction: outer space. Taking a page from the Austin Powers handbook, director Aanand Rai delivers a strange comedy that defies expectations (and logic), but is, perhaps, bound by culture. **164m/C; DVD.** *IN* Shahrukh Khan; Anushka Sharma; Katrina Kaif; Salman Khan; Bill Billions; *D:* Aanand L. Rai; *W:* Himanshu Sharma; *C:* Manu Anand.

Zero Boys WOOF! **1986 (R)** Teenage survivalists in the Californian wilderness are stalked by a murderous lunatic. Exploitative and mean-spirited. **89m/C; VHS, DVD, Blu-Ray.** Daniel Hirsch; Kelli Maroney; Nicole Rio; Joe Estevez; *D:* Nico Mastorakis; *W:* Nico Mastorakis; Fred C. Perry; *C:* Steve (Steven) Shaw; *M:* Stanley Myers; Hans Zimmer.

Zero Charisma ½ **2013** Adult nerd king Scott (Eidson) lives a contented life in his grandmother's house, hosting a weekly fantasy role playing meet-up with the local geeks and discussing the differences in horsepower between the Millennium Falcon and the Starship Enterprise. However, hipster nerd newcomer Miles (Graham) challenges his very existence--he not only has a hot girlfriend, but can definitively answer that timeless spaceship question. An indie underdog tale that follows an unlikable guy through his journey of bitterness and self-pity with enough humor to coast most of the way. **86m/C; Streaming.** Sam Eidson; Garrett Graham; Katie Folger; Anne Gee Byrd; Brock England; Cyndi Williams; *D:* Katie Graham; Andrew Matthews; *W:* Andrew Matthews; *C:* Ellie Ann Fenton; *M:* Bobby Tahouri.

Zero Dark Thirty **2012 (R)** Kathryn Bigelow delivers yet again with this riveting, exhaustively detailed retelling of the hunt for Osama Bin Laden. Chastain gives the best performance of 2012 as Maya, the woman who was on the front line of the CIA investigation after 9/11 and led the most famous manhunt of the modern age. With pitch-perfect levels of tension, Bigelow and her writer on The Hurt Locker, Mark Boal, hit every major beat from 2001 to 2011 and capture not only a decade of the fight against terrorism but ask the question of where it led us and where we go from here. A true accomplishment on every level. **157m/C; DVD, Blu-Ray.** Jason Clarke; Jessica Chastain; Kyle Chandler; Mark Strong; Joel Edgerton; Chris Pratt; *D:* Kathryn Bigelow; *W:* Mark Boal; *C:* Greig Fraser; *M:* Alexandre Desplat. Oscars '12: Sound FX Editing; Golden Globes '13: Actress--Drama (Chastain); Writers Guild '12: Orig. Screenplay.

Zero Days ½ **2016 (PG-13)** Masterful documentarian Alex Gibney turns to the dangerous world of malware for his latest non-fiction film about the ever-changing face of technology and how we live with it. His focus here is Stuxnet, a malware that was actually used by the United States and Israel in 2010 on an Iranian nuclear facility. The problem is that Stuxnet didn't behave like our government wanted it to, and spread beyond Iran. What does this mean for the future of technological warfare? Should private citizens be afraid of what our governments can do with a computer as much as what they can do with a bomb? **116m/C; DVD.** David Sanger; Emad Kiyaei; Eric Chien; Liam O'Murchu; Gary D. Brown; *D:* Alex Gibney; *W:* Alex Gibney; *C:* Antonio Rossi; Avner Shahaf; Brett Wiley; *M:* Will Bates.

Zero Degrees Kelvin ½ *Zero Kelvin; Kjaerlighetens Kjotere* **1995** Brrrr! Get the ice scraper ready, because you may have to clear off your TV screen in this chilly tale of trappers in 1920s Greenland. Henrik Larsen (Eidsvold), a poet living in Oslo, decides to join the band of trappers after his girlfriend Gertrude (Martens) spurns his marriage proposal. On his arrival in the stark and frozen landscape, he is forced to share a cabin with the stoic, silent Holm (Sundquist) and the lewd, violent Randbaek (Skarsgard). Randbaek holds the newcomer and his city-boy ways in disdain, creating an air of tension and menace that inevitably results in a clash between the two. Instead of dwelling on the action aspect, director Moland uses the minimalist landscape to echo the psychological battles the men must face with the frigid terrain and between themselves. Norwegian with subtitles. **113m/C; VHS, DVD.** *NO* Gard B. Eidsvold; Stellan Skarsgard; Bjorn Sundquist; Camilla Martens; ***D:*** Hans Petter Moland; ***W:*** Hans Petter Moland; Lars Bill Lundholm; ***C:*** Philip Ogaard; ***M:*** Terje Rypdal.

Zero Effect ½ **1997 (R)** A cross between Howard Hughes and Sherlock Holmes, brilliant, eccentric detective Daryl Zero (Pullman), who, along with his harried helper Steve Arlo (Stiller), takes on the case of a blackmailed timber tycoon (O'Neal) in this comedic whodunit. The normally reclusive sleuth bites the bullet and agrees to trek to Oregon to personally investigate the particularly intriguing case, which also involves an attractive paramedic (Dickens). Pullman pulls off another quirky leading man performance with flair. Stiller is stellar as the exasperated assistant. Fresh idea and hip humor mark this debut for 22-year-old writer/director Kasdan, son of director Lawrence Kasdan. **150m/C; DVD.** Bill Pullman; Ben Stiller; Ryan O'Neal; Kim Dickens; Angela Featherstone; ***D:*** Jake Kasdan; ***W:*** Jake Kasdan; ***C:*** Bill Pope.

Zero Hour! ½ **1957** Passengers and crew aboard an airliner become sick from food poisoning and the only way to avoid disaster is to find someone on board who can fly the plane—and hasn't had fish for dinner! Yep, it's the film that inspired the classic spoof "Airplane!" And for that, it deserves an extra half bone. **81m/B; DVD.** Dana Andrews; Linda Darnell; Sterling Hayden; Geoffrey Toone; Jerry Paris; Peggy King; Charles Quinlivan; Patricia Tiernan; Elroy "Crazylegs" Hirsch; Willis Bouchey; Robert Stevenson; Mary Newton; ***Nar:*** William Conrad; ***D:*** Hall Bartlett; ***W:*** Hall Bartlett; John C. Champion; Arthur Hailey; ***C:*** John F. Warren.

Zero Patience **1994** Yes, it's an audacious film musical about AIDS myths and ghosts and Victorian explorers—among other things. Infamous Patient Zero (Fauteux) is the Canadian flight attendant reputed to have carried the virus to North America. Ghostly Zero pleads for someone to tell his story and his cause is taken up by Victorian explorer Sir Richard Francis Burton (Robinson), who happens to have achieved eternal life after an encounter with the Fountain of Youth, and who is also preparing an exhibit on contagious diseases. Sharp mix of politics, humor, and fantasy. **100m/C; DVD.** *CA* John Robinson; Normand Fauteux; Dianne Heatherington; Ricardo Keens-Douglas; ***D:*** John Greyson; ***W:*** John Greyson; ***M:*** Glenn Schellenberg.

Zero Population Growth ½ *Z.P.G.* **1972** In the 21st century the government has decreed that no babies may be born for a 30-year span in order to control the population. But Chaplin and Reed secretly have a child and when they are discovered are sent to be executed. Maudlin and simplistic. **95m/C; VHS, DVD, Blu-Ray.** Oliver Reed; Geraldine Chaplin; Diane Cilento; Don Gordon; Bill Nagy; Sheila Reid; David Markham; ***D:*** Michael Campus; ***W:*** Frank De Felitta; Max Ehrlich; ***C:*** Mikael Salomon; Michael Reed; ***M:*** Jonathan Hodge.

The Zero Theorem ½ **2013 (R)** More ambitious than exceptional, Gilliam returns to another vision of the future that the filmmaker has said is the final chapter of The Dystopian Trilogy with "Brazil" and "12 Monkeys." Qohen Leth's (Waltz) a man who has become little more than a cog in the machine. He's a hacker who plugs into technology all day until he stumbles on the reason for human existence. At that point, management steps in and tries to distract him from breaking free of his societal bonds. The cast is talented enough, Gilliam still has a striking visual style, and Tilda Swinton raps! **107m/C; DVD, Blu-Ray, Streaming.** *UK* Christoph Waltz; Matt Damon; Mélanie Thierry; Lucas Hedges; David Thewlis; ***D:*** Terry Gilliam; ***W:*** Pat Rushin; ***C:*** Nicola Pecorini; ***M:*** George Fenton.

Zero Tolerance ½ **1993 (R)** FBI agent Jeff Douglas (Patrick) is assigned to travel to Mexico and pick up a drug-runner who works for the White Hand cartel, whose latest product is liquid heroin. When they are ambushed Douglas is forced to carry a shipment of drugs across the border—the lives of his wife and child hang in the balance. But after the dirty deed is done, Douglas finds his family has been murdered anyway. So he sets out to execute the cartel druglords. **92m/C; VHS, DVD.** Robert Patrick; Miles O'Keeffe; Mick Fleetwood; Titus Welliver; Jeffrey Anderson-Gunter; Gustav Vintas; Michael Gregory; Maurice Lamont; ***D:*** Joseph Merhi; ***W:*** Jacobsen Hart.

Zero Tolerance *2 Guns: Zero Tolerance* **2015 (R)** A Thailand-set action crime thriller centering on a quest for revenge over a family member's murder. Former CIA operatives Johnny (Nguyen) and Peter (Boonthanakit) seek the killer of Johnny's daughter Angel (Paosut). After Angel's death, they learn that Angel was working as a high-end escort. To avenge her demise and find out the truth about her life and her death, the pair violently search through the city of Bangkok, shooting a number of pimps, drug cartel members, and others in the process. **89m/C; DVD, Streaming, Download.** Dustin Nguyen; Sahajak Boonthanakit; Nina Paosut; Scott Adkins; Gary Daniels; ***D:*** Kaos; ***W:*** Kaos; ***C:*** Kaos; ***M:*** Dan Bewick. **VIDEO**

Zeroville ½ **2019 (R)** Arriving in Los Angeles in 1969 to begin a film career, Vikar (Franco, who also directs) loves old Hollywood but feels that change is on the horizon. While learning about film editing from Dotty (Weaver), he begins a romance with beautiful actress Soledad (Fox) and grows attached to her daughter Zazi (King). Franco also has a tumultuous relationship with outrageous producer Rondell (Ferrell). An adaptation of the popular Steve Erickson novel, Franco blends fact and fiction in his satiric exploration of Vikar's time in Hollywood. But, somewhere along the way, the director gets lost and the ridiculousness takes over. **96m/C; DVD.** James Franco; Megan Fox; Seth Rogen; Joey King; Danny McBride; ***D:*** James Franco; ***W:*** Paul Felten; Ian Olds; ***C:*** Bruce Thierry Cheung; ***M:*** Johnny Jewel.

Zeta One *Alien Women; The Love Factor* **1969** A soft-core British science fiction yarn about scantily clad alien babes and the special agent who's trying to uncover their secret. It's all very sketchy, silly and campy, though pleasantly cast with plenty of lovely British actresses. **86m/C; VHS, DVD, Blu-Ray.** *GB* James Robertson Justice; Charles Hawtrey; Robin Hawdon; Anna Gael; Brigitte Skay; Dawn Addams; Valerie Leon; Yutte Stensgaard; Wendy Lingham; Rita Webb; Caroline Hawkins; ***D:*** Michael Cort; ***W:*** Michael Cort; Christopher Neame; Alistair McKenzie; ***C:*** Jack Atcheler; ***M:*** John Hawksworth.

Zeus and Roxanne **1996 (PG)** Hey, I know! Let's combine "Flipper" and "Benji" with "The Parent Trap!" You know, for the kids! Marine biologist and single mom Mary Beth (Quinlan) meets her unconventional (and conveniently widowed) new neighbor Terry (Guttenberg) and his dog Zeus. Cuteness ensues. Mary Beth's daughters and Terry's young son go about getting the two adults together. Meanwhile, Zeus and Roxanne, Mary Beth's dolphin, strike up a unique friendship of their own. Showing up to provide drama is evil guy Claude (Vosloo), who is vying for the same grant as Mary Beth. Unlikely animal couple steals the show, and the story would have benefitted from focusing on the entertaining bond between those two and less on the human romance. Not much appeal for anyone over the age of nine. **98m/C; VHS, DVD.** Kathleen Quinlan; Steve Guttenberg; Arnold Vosloo; Miko Hughes; Dawn McMillan; Majandra Delfino; ***D:*** George Miller; ***W:*** Tom Benedek; ***C:*** David Connell; ***M:*** Bruce Rowland.

Zhou Yu's Train ½ *Zhou Yu de Huoche* **2002 (PG-13)** Gong Li stars in this slick romantic drama as porcelain painter, Zhou Yu, who's in love with teacher/poet Chen Ching (Leung Kar-fai). Because he lives in a distant village, Zhou takes the train twice a week so they can be together. Chen begins to feel overwhelmed and transfers to an even farther away town; meanwhile, Zhou becomes friendly with another train passenger, Zhang (Honglei). Gong also plays another character, Xiu, who's involved with Chen and wants to know about his time with Zhou. Except maybe nothing is what it first seems since director's Sun's theme is that love is how you want it to appear (or something like that). Based on the novella "Zhou Yu's Cry" by Bei Cun. Mandarian with subtitles. **97m/C; DVD.** Honglei Sun; Gong Li; Tony Leung Kar-fai; Li Zhixiong; Shi Chunling; Liu Wei; Gao Jingwen; Dai Ke; Pan Weiyan; Huang Mo; ***D:*** Sun Zhou; ***W:*** Sun Zhou; Bei Cun; Zhang Mei; ***C:*** Wang Yu.

Ziegfeld Follies ½ **1946** A lavish revue of musical numbers and comedy sketches featuring many MGM stars of the WWII era. Highlights include Astaire and Kelly's only duet and a Astaire-Bremer ballet number. **115m/C; VHS, DVD.** Fred Astaire; Judy Garland; Gene Kelly; Red Skelton; Fanny Brice; William Powell; Jimmy Durante; Edward Arnold; Lucille Bremer; Hume Cronyn; Victor Moore; Lena Horne; Lucille Ball; Esther Williams; ***D:*** Vincente Minnelli; ***C:*** Charles Rosher.

Ziegfeld Girl **1941** Three star-struck girls are chosen for the Ziegfeld follies and move on to success and heartbreak. Lavish costumes and production numbers in the MGM style. **131m/B; VHS, DVD.** James Stewart; Judy Garland; Hedy Lamarr; Lana Turner; Tony Martin; Jackie Cooper; Ian Hunter; Charles Winninger; Al Shean; Edward Everett Horton; Philip Dorn; Paul Kelly; Eve Arden; Dan Dailey; Fay Holden; Felix Bressart; Mae Busch; Reed Hadley; ***D:*** Robert Z. Leonard.

ZigZag ½ *Zig Zag* **1970** Terminally ill Paul Cameron (Kennedy) looks to provide for his family by framing himself for an unsolved murder to collect the reward money. He collapses at his trial, has surgery, and is cured, which really puts Paul in the hot seat. **105m/C; DVD.** George Kennedy; Eli Wallach; Anne Jackson; Steve Ihnat; Walter Brooke; William Marshall; Pamela Murphy; Dana Elcar; ***D:*** Richard A. Colla; ***W:*** John T. Kelley; ***C:*** James A. Crabe; ***M:*** Oliver Nelson.

ZigZag **2002 (R)** Louis "ZigZag" Fletcher (Jones) is an autistic 15-year-old who lives in fear of his dad Fletcher (Snipes), an abusive drug addict. ZigZag works as a dishwasher for the foul-mouthed Toad (Platt), and his one caring friend is his volunteer Big Brother, Dean (Leguizamo), who has cancer. ZigZag steals $9,000 from Toad to give to his dad and Dean goes to a loan shark (Goss) to get the money to return to Toad's safe before he realizes it's missing. Based on the novel by Landon J. Napoleon; Goyer's directorial debut. The sort of story that can easily descend into sap but doesn't, thanks to some fearless performances and Goyer's tight control. **101m/C; VHS, DVD.** Sam Jones, III; John Leguizamo; Wesley Snipes; Oliver Platt; Natasha Lyonne; Sherman Augustus; Luke Goss; Michael Greyeyes; Elizabeth Pena; ***D:*** David S. Goyer; ***W:*** David S. Goyer; ***C:*** James L. Carter; ***M:*** Grant Lee Phillips.

Zipper **2015 (R)** Patrick Wilson continues to make questionable career decisions in this tawdry, trivial drama. Sam Ellis (Wilson) is a federal prosecutor with a great career and supportive wife (Headey). Of course, he has to throw it all away on a night with a high-end escort. It turns out that Sam is a sex addict. He can't stop with the prostitutes, even as it tears his life apart. This is almost a defiantly dumb movie in which people do and say things that no one does or says in real life. Everyone in it is above it. So are you. **103m/C; DVD.** Patrick Wilson; Lena Headey; Ray Winstone; Richard Dreyfuss; John Cho; ***D:*** Mora Stephens; ***W:*** Mora Stephens; Joel Viertel; ***C:*** Antonio Calvache; ***M:*** H. Scott Salinas.

Zipperface **1992** A Palm Beach serial killer is making mincemeat of the local prostitutes. In order to capture the scum, the prerequisite beautiful police detective goes undercover only to find herself the killer's biggest thrill. **90m/C; VHS, DVD.** Dona Adams; Jonathan Mandell; David Clover; Trisha Melynkov; Richard Vidan; Harold Cannon; Bruce Brown; Rikki Brando; Timothy D. Lechner; John Dagnen; ***D:*** Mansour Pourmand; ***W:*** Barbara Bishop; ***C:*** F. Smith Martin; ***M:*** Jim Halfpenny.

Zita ½ **1968** Young, shy Ann (Shimkus) learns that her adored Aunt Zita (Paxinou) is dying, but she's unable to accept the idea of parting from her great friend and confidant. She also finds it too heartbreaking to remain in the house with the deathly ill Zita, so she runs off into the Parisian night, looking to lose herself in the clubs and cafes, and meeting a young man in the process. When Ann returns home, she's able to face the situation through newly opened eyes. Shimkus turns in a sweet, sympathetic performance, and the cinematography is both otherworldly and intoxicating. Rarely seen, quietly contemplative film is a knockout. **92m/C; DVD.** Suzanne Flon; Katina Paxinou; Joanna Shimkus; ***D:*** Robert Enrico; ***C:*** Jean Boffety; ***M:*** Francois de Roubaix.

The Zodiac **2005 (R)** Under-realized account of the notorious Zodiac Killer, who infamously terrorized the San Francisco area in the late '60s and has eluded the police to this day. Depressingly bland and straightforward, unintentionally looking like an episode of "Columbo." The killer is seen in shadow and cops are bogged down in exposition and melodrama. Do not confuse this clunker with the masterful David Fincher-helmed "Zodiac" (although they probably hope you will). **92m/C; DVD.** Justin Chambers; Robin Tunney; Rory Culkin; William Mapother; Brad William Henke; Rex Linn; Philip Baker Hall; Ian Scott Mcgregor; Marty Lindsey; Shelby Alexis Irey; Natassia Costa; Kris Palm; Nate Dushku; Katelin Chesna; Jodi Feder; Kathryn Howell; George Maguire; Carolyne Smith; Munda Razooki; ***D:*** Alexander Bulkley; ***W:*** Kelly Bulkley; ***C:*** Denis Maloney; ***M:*** Michael Suby.

Zodiac ½ **2007 (R)** Drawn-out and detailed examination (with strong performances) of the still-unsolved Bay Area serial killings from the 1970s. The self-named Zodiac sends cryptic messages to the San Francisco Chronicle, where dissolute reporter Paul Avery (Downey Jr.) is on the crime beat. The paper's editorial cartoonist, Robert Graysmith (Gyllenhaal), figures out the killer's cipher and becomes obsessed with helping out. Then, SFPD detectives Dave Toschi (Ruffalo) and William Armstrong (Edwards) are assigned to the case, which eventually goes cold. Graysmith later wrote about the killings and drew his own conclusions as to the Zodiac's identity. **156m/C; DVD, Blu-Ray, HD-DVD.** Mark Ruffalo; Jake Gyllenhaal; Robert Downey, Jr.; Brian Cox; Chloë Sevigny; John Carroll Lynch; Charles Fleischer; Zach Grenier; Philip Baker Hall; Elias Koteas; Donal Logue; Dermot Mulroney; John Terry; John Getz; Adam Goldberg; Candy Clark; John Lacy; James Le Gros; ***D:*** David Fincher; ***W:*** James Vanderbilt; ***C:*** Harris Savides; ***M:*** David Shire.

The Zodiac Killer ½ **1971 (R)** Based on a true story, this tells the violent tale of the San Francisco murders that occurred in the late 1960s. Doesn't have the suspense it should. **87m/C; VHS, DVD, Blu-Ray.** Tom Pittman; Hal Reed; Bob Jones; Ray Lynch; ***D:*** Tom Hanson.

Zodiac: Signs of the Apocalypse **2014** Usual nonsensical--and forgettable--Syfy Channel disaster pic. An archeological dig reveals an ancient stone apparatus carved with signs of the zodiac. Professor Neil Martin is brought in to figure out the device, but every time it's messed with another not-so-natural disaster occurs. It's up to a couple of crazies to tie the stone and disasters together and do something about both. **90m/C; DVD.** Joel Gretsch; Reilly Dolman; Christopher Lloyd; Andrea Brooks; Emily Holmes; Ben Cotton; Aaron Douglas; ***D:*** W.D. Hogan; ***W:*** David Sanderson; ***C:*** Anthony C. Metchie. **CABLE**

Zoe ½ **2001** Teenager Zoe (Zima) longs to escape her abusive homelife and explore her Native American heritage through a Cherokee spirit guide. So she and two girlfriends (who want to go to Hollywood) run away from home and start their journey, eventually crossing paths with middle-aged Englishwoman Cecilia (Seagrove) whose mother's last request was to have her ashes scattered in the mountains of New Mexico. Recognizing a kindred spirit, Zoe leaves her friends to follow Cecilia and find her spirit guide. **92m/C; VHS, DVD.** Vanessa Zima; Jenny Seagrove; Stephi Lineburg; Victoria Davis; Gordon Tootoosis; Kim Greist; ***D:*** Deborah Attoinese; ***W:*** Deborah Attoinese; Amy Dawes; ***C:*** Samuel Ameen; ***M:*** Dan Pinnella.

Zoltan. . . Hound of Dracula ½ *Dracula's Dog* **1978** The vampire and his bloodthirsty dog go to Los Angeles to find the last of Count Dracula's living descendants. Campy and just original enough to make it almost worth watching. **85m/C; VHS, DVD, Blu-Ray.** Michael Pataki; Reggie Nalder; Jose Ferrer; Jan Shutan; Libbie Chase; John Levin; Cleo Harrington; Simmy Bow; JoJo D'Amore; ***D:*** Albert Band; ***W:*** Frank Ray Perilli; ***C:*** Bruce Logan; ***M:*** Andrew Belling.

Zombi Child 1/2 **2020** In early 1960s Haiti, Clairvuius (Bijou) enters a zombified state and spends years being exploited as a laborer. The story of his fate is intercut with that of teenagers at an elite all-girls school in present day France. At this school, Fanny (Labeque) misses her boyfriend Pablo (El Alami). Fanny befriends new student Melissa (Louimat), a Haitian who moved to Paris after her parents died, and wants her to use voodoo to get closer to Pablo. The political horror-drama is a little daring, a little fascinating, and a little awkward exploration of colonialism and voodoo. French with subtitles. **103m/C; DVD.** Louise Labeque; Wislanda Louimat; Katiana Milfort; Mackenson Bijou; Adile David; ***D:*** Bertrand Bonello; ***W:*** Bertrand Bonello; ***C:*** Yves Cape; ***M:*** Bertrand Bonello.

Zombie *Zombie Flesh-Eaters; Island of the Living Dead; Zombi 2* **1980** Italian-made white-men-in-the-Caribbean-with-flesh-eating-zombies cheapie. **91m/C; VHS, DVD, Blu-Ray.** *IT* Tisa Farrow; Ian McCulloch; Richard Johnson; Al Cliver; Auretta Gay; Olga Karlatos; Stefania D'Amario; Lucio Fulci; Ugo Bologna; Monica Zanchi; ***D:*** Lucio Fulci; ***W:*** Elisa Briganti; Dardano Sacchetti; ***C:*** Sergio Salvati; ***M:*** Fabio Frizzi; Giorgio Tucci.

Zombie High *The School That Ate My Brain* **1987 (R)** Students at a secluded academy are being lobotomized by the school president. Mindless, in two senses of the word. **91m/C; VHS, Blu-Ray, Streaming.** Virginia Madsen; Richard Cox; Kay E. Kuter; James Wilder; Sherilyn Fenn; Paul Williams; Scott Coffey; Clare Carey; Walter Addison; ***D:*** Ron Link; ***W:*** Aziz Ghazal; Tim Doyle; Elizabeth Passerelli; ***C:*** Brian Coyne; David Lux; ***M:*** Daniel May.

Zombie Honeymoon **2004** Generally successful mix of pathos, comedy, and horror. Denise (Coogan) and Danny (Sibley) are on their honeymoon when Danny is attacked by a zombie. Denise is inconsolable until Danny returns—a changed man. Neither his increasing bloodlust or physical disintegration can drive Denise away. Is that true love or what? **83m/C; DVD.** Neal Jones; Tracy Coogan; Graham Sibley; Tonya Cornelisse; David M. Wallace; Phil Catalano; ***D:*** Dave Gebroe; ***W:*** Dave Gebroe; ***C:*** Ken Seng; ***M:*** Michael Tremante.

Zombie Island Massacre **1984 (R)** In this trying film, tourists travel to see a voodoo ritual, and then are systematically butchered by the rite-inspired zombies. Featuring former congressional wife and "Playboy" magazine model Jenrette. **89m/C; VHS, DVD, Blu-Ray.** Rita Jenrette; David Broadnax; ***D:*** John N. Carter.

Zombie Lake *El Lago de los Muertos Vivientes; The Lake of the Living Dead* **1980** Killed in an ambush by villagers during WWII, a group of Nazi soldiers turned zombies reside in the town's lake, preying on unsuspecting swimmers, especially dog paddling nude young women. Laughable FX, almost bad enough to be good. From the team that produced "Oasis of the Zombies." **90m/C; VHS, DVD, Blu-Ray.** *FR SP* Howard Vernon; Pierre Escourrou; Anouchka; Anthony (Jose, J. Antonio, J.A.) Mayans; Nadine Pascale; Jean Rollin; ***D:*** Jean Rollin; J.A. Laser; ***W:*** Jess (Jesus) Franco; Julian Esteban.

Zombie Nightmare **WOOF! 1986 (R)** A murdered teenager is revived by a voodoo queen and slaughters his punk-teen assailants. Cheap and stupid just about sums this one up. Music by Motorhead, Death Mask, Girlschool, and Thor. **89m/C; VHS, DVD, Blu-Ray.** Adam West; Jon Mikl Thor; Tia Carrere; Frank Dietz; Linda Singer; Mandn E. Turbride; Hamibh McEwen; ***D:*** John Bravman.

Zombie Strippers **2008** The Bush administration, elected to a fourth term, creates a virus to reanimate dead tissue in order to ensure a supply of eternal soldiers to fight the never-ending Iraq war. Unfortunately the virus is only stable in women, and it eventually spreads from the lab to a nearby illegal strip club run by Ian (Englund). His best stripper Kat (Jameson) becomes infected, and suddenly the local rednecks can't spend enough money to watch her take her clothes off, causing jealousy in the other dancers, who promptly infect themselves to make more money. A subtle little film with perhaps some political commentary. **94m/C; DVD, Blu-Ray.** Robert Englund; Joey Medina; John Hawkes; Whitney Anderson; Jenna Jameson; Roxy Saint; Shamron Moore; Penny Drake; Jennifer Holland; Jeanette Sousa; Calvin Green; Catero Colbert; Carmit Levite; Zak Kilberg; Billy Beck; Adam J. Smith; Jen Alex Gonzalez; Laura Bach; Jessica Custodio; Travis Wood; Brad Milne; Shannon Malone; Gary Kraus; Jim Roof; Asante Jones; David O'Kelley; ***D:*** Jay Lee; ***W:*** Jay Lee; ***C:*** Jay Lee; ***M:*** Billy White Acre. **VIDEO**

Zombieland 1/2 **2009 (R)** The world is overrun by the undead and a rag-tag group of survivors must cling together to outwit and outgun the relentless zombie scourge. Teaming up are two unlikely survivors—a pathetically frightened kid from Ohio, Columbus (Eisenberg), and the fearsome Twinkie-loving zombie slayer, Tallahassee (Harrelson)--who face down the rotting menace with dark wit and shotgun blasts to the head. They connect with Wichita (Stone) and Little Rock (Breslin) and the four unleash a ghoulish road movie that somehow remains light-hearted and charming. **88m/C; Blu-Ray, On Demand.** Woody Harrelson; Jesse Eisenberg; Emma Stone; Abigail Breslin; Amber Heard; Bill Murray; Derek Graf; ***D:*** Ruben Fleischer; ***W:*** Rhett Reese; Paul Wernick; ***C:*** Michael Bonvillain; ***M:*** David Sardy.

Zombieland: Double Tap **2019 (R)** A sequel that takes the action and farce of the first installment and adds fresh characters and faster, more evolved zombies. Ten years after we left them, the makeshift family of survivors, led by patriarch Tallahassee (Harrelson), obliterates the undead from the plains states to the White House with deadly force and rapid-fire comedy. More than worth the wait! **99m/C; DVD, Blu-Ray.** Woody Harrelson; Jesse Eisenberg; Emma Stone; Abigail Breslin; Zoey Deutch; ***D:*** Ruben Fleischer; ***W:*** Dave Callaham; Rhett Reese; Paul Wernick; ***C:*** Chung-hoon Chung; ***M:*** David Sardy.

Zombies of Mass Destruction *ZMD: Zombies of Mass Destruction* **2010 (R)** Violent horror comedy with a political/social agenda that takes a little too long to get to the first zombie attack. Port Gamble, Washington is being overrun by zombies. Iranian-born film student Frida, who's suspected of being a terrorist by the conservative locals, teams up with gay Tom and his partner Lance to stop the invasion before the entire town is infected. **92m/C; DVD, Blu-Ray.** Janette Armand; Doug Fahl; Cooper Hawkins; Bill Johns; Russell Hodgkinson; ***D:*** Kevin Hamedani; ***W:*** Kevin Hamedani; Ramon Isao; ***C:*** John Guleserian; ***M:*** Andrew Rohrmann. **VIDEO**

Zombies of Moratau **WOOF! 1957** A diver and his girlfriend seek to retrieve an undersea treasure of diamonds protected by zombies. So boring you'll want to die. CUrrently only sold as part of a collection. **70m/B; VHS, DVD.** Gregg (Hunter) Palmer; Allison Hayes; Autumn Russel; Joel Ashley; ***D:*** Edward L. Cahn.

Zombies of the Stratosphere *Satan's Satellites* **1952** A serial in 12 chapters in which a cosmic policeman fights Zombies attempting to blow the Earth out of orbit. Also available in a 93-minute, colorized version. **152m/B; VHS, DVD.** Judd Holdren; Aline Towne; Leonard Nimoy; John Crawford; Ray Boyle; Craig G. Kelly; ***D:*** Fred Brannon.

Zombies on Broadway 1/2 *Loonies on Broadway* **1944** Two press agents travel to the Caribbean in search of new talent, but find Lugosi performing experiments on people and turning them into sequel material. RKO hoped this would be equally successful follow-up to "I Walked with a Zombie." **68m/B; VHS, DVD.** Wally Brown; Alan Carney; Bela Lugosi; Anne Jeffreys; Sheldon Leonard; Frank Jenks; Russell Hopton; Joseph (Joe) Vitale; Ian Wolfe; Louis Jean Heydt; Darby Jones; Sir Lancelot; ***D:*** Gordon Douglas; ***W:*** Robert E. Kent; Lawrence Kimble; ***C:*** Jack MacKenzie; ***M:*** Roy Webb.

Zombieworld 1/2 **2015** Using a newscast as an means of organizing an anthology-type zombie film, short segments of how zombies are taking over the world explore how this event is unfolding. Reports come from various locations in North America, Ireland, Australia, and Europe, each with a different twist. Despite the rising tide of the undead, there are human survivors trying to make it in this crazy, nearly end of the world tale. **100m/C; DVD, Streaming, Download.** Bill Oberst, Jr.; Steven Barton; Mike Hardy; Therese Lentz; Jennifer Oakley; ***D:*** Jesse Baget; Adrian Cardona; Rafa Dengra; Luke Guidici; Phil Haine; Peter Horn; Jared Marshall; Cameron McCulloch; David Munoz; Adam O'Brien; Zachary Ramelan; Paul Shrimpton; Vedran Marjonovic Wekster; Tommy Woodard; ***W:*** Adrian Cardona; Rafa Dengra; Luke Guidici; Jared Marshall; Cameron McCulloch; David Munoz; Adam O'Brien; Zachary Ramelan; Paul Shrimpton; Vedran Marjonovic Wekster; Tommy Woodard; Stefania Moscato; Jonathan Brown; Raven Cousens; Graham Taylor; ***M:*** Jeff McDonough.

Zone of the Dead **1978** A mortician is using his morgue for other than embalming—and it isn't pretty! **81m/C; VHS, DVD.** John Ericson; Ivor Francis; Charles Aidman; Bernard Fox.

Zone 39 **1996** Sci-fi thriller vibrates with impending doom. A 40-year war results in an uneasy peace between two rival factions. Guard Leo (Phelps) has gone a little loopy after the death of his wife and is assigned to patrol the remote outpost of Zone 39, where a severe contamination is spreading. Thanks to the illegal drug Novan that Leo keeps taking, he's also experiencing flashbacks of his wife and other ghostly figures. The spectacularly desolate setting is a dry salt lake located in Woomera, Australia. **93m/C; VHS, DVD.** *AU* Peter Phelps; William Zappa; Caroline Beck; Brad Byquar; Alex Menglet; Jeff Kovski; ***D:*** John Tatoulis; ***W:*** Deborah Parsons; ***C:*** Peter Zakhavor; ***M:*** Burkhard Dallwitz.

Zone Troopers 1/2 **1984 (PG)** Five American G.I.'s in WWII-ravaged Europe stumble upon a wrecked alien spacecraft and enlist the extraterrestrial's help in fending off the Nazis. **86m/C; VHS, DVD, Blu-Ray, Streaming.** Timothy Van Patten; Tim Thomerson; Art LaFleur; Biff Manard; ***D:*** Danny Bilson; ***W:*** Danny Bilson; Paul DeMeo; ***C:*** Mac Ahlberg; ***M:*** Richard Band.

Zontar, the Thing from Venus **1966** Scientist is taken over by alien batlike thing from Venus, and attempts to take over the Earth. A parody of itself. **68m/C; VHS, DVD.** John Agar; Anthony Huston; Susan Bjorman; Pat Delaney; Warren Hammack; Neil Fletcher; ***D:*** Larry Buchanan; ***W:*** Larry Buchanan; Hillman Taylor; ***C:*** Robert Alcott. **TV**

Zookeeper 1/2 **2011 (PG)** Slapstick family-oriented comedy with James as fun-loving but lonely zookeeper Griffin Keyes. The animals at the Franklin Park Zoo are fond of lovelorn Griffin and want to help him out when he decides to make a second attempt at wooing the completely wrong gal, icy snob Stephanie (Bibb). They confess that they can talk—and begin offering romantic advice that doesn't exactly work for humans. **102m/C; DVD, Blu-Ray, On Demand.** Kevin James; Leslie Bibb; Rosario Dawson; Ken Jeong; Donnie Wahlberg; Joe Rogan; Nat Faxon; ***V:*** Cher; Nick Nolte; Sylvester Stallone; Jon Favreau; Judd Apatow; Adam Sandler; Faizon Love; Maya Rudolph; ***D:*** Frank Coraci; ***W:*** David Ronn; Jay Sherick; Nicky Bakay; Rock Reuben; ***C:*** Michael J. Bennett; ***M:*** Rupert Gregson-Williams.

The Zookeeper's Wife **2017 (PG-13)** Chastain does everything in her acting power to elevate this saccharine adaptation of Diane Ackerman's non-fiction book, but the result is still a manipulative mess. She plays Antonina Zabinski, one of the keepers of the Warsaw Zoo in the 1930s. At the end of the decade, she's given a chance to not only help save the animals being destroyed by the constant bombing of the beginning of World War II but a chance to help protect Jews on the run from the Third Reich. By lessening the true atrocity of the situation to appeal to a wide audience, Zabinski's true bravery feels lessened as well. **127m/C; DVD, Blu-Ray.** Jessica Chastain; Daniel Brühl; Johan Heldenbergh; Michael McElhatton; Iddo Goldberg; ***D:*** Niki Caro; ***W:*** Angela Workman; ***C:*** Andrij Parekh; ***M:*** Harry Gregson-Williams.

Zoolander 1/2 **2001 (PG-13)** Stiller plays Derek Zoolander, an absurdly vacuous and successful male model who's brainwashed into becoming an assassin by over-the-top designer Mugatu (Ferrell). It seems that a foreign prime minister is committed to cutting off the supply of cheap third world labor for the fashion industry, and Zoolander is the only model stupid enough to have his noggin scrubbed clean. He develops a friendship with arch-rival model Hansel (Wilson), and the dim duo try to stop the nefarious plot. Packed to the gills with celebrity cameos, including Heidi Klum, Donald Trump and, yes, Fabio. Ran into unexpected controversy because the intended target is the prime minister of Malaysia (and the Malaysians naturally objected). **89m/C; VHS, DVD, Blu-Ray.** Ben Stiller; Owen Wilson; Christine Taylor; Will Ferrell; Milla Jovovich; Jerry Stiller; Jon Voight; David Duchovny; ***D:*** Ben Stiller; ***W:*** Ben Stiller; John Hamburg; Drake Sather; ***C:*** Barry Peterson; ***M:*** David Arnold.

Zoolander 2 1/2 **2016 (PG-13)** Most jokes can't be funny twice. It's why so few comedy sequels have worked. Comedy plays off the unexpected, and there's nothing unpredictable or fresh about this long-delayed sequel to the Stiller hit about Derek Zoolander, a movie that playfully skewered an industry in need of parody. In the sequel, Derek and Hansel (Wilson) are called in when the world's most beautiful people are being executed, sending a signal with Zoolander's trademark look before they die. It's all an excuse for wacky hijinks and a never-ending string of cameos. When Kiefer Sutherland and Benedict Cumberbatch give the funniest performances, you're in trouble. **102m/C; DVD, Blu-Ray.** Ben Stiller; Owen Wilson; Christine Taylor; Penelope Cruz; Will Ferrell; Kristen Wiig; Benedict Cumberbatch; Cyrus Arnold; ***D:*** Ben Stiller; ***W:*** Ben Stiller; Justin Theroux; Nicholas Stoller; John Hamburg; ***C:*** Dan(iel) Mindel; ***M:*** Theodore Shapiro. Golden Raspberries '16: Actress--Supporting (Wiig), Worst Actress.

Zoom **2006 (PG)** Superhero Captain Zoom (Allen) has retired and gotten soft. But he's called back into action when he's needed to turn a group of misfit kids into the next generation of superheroes so that the world can be saved once again. Based on the graphic novel by Jason Lethcote. Definitely the weak link in the "kids dealing with superpowers" genre. **88m/C; DVD.** Tim Allen; Courteney Cox; Chevy Chase; Spencer Breslin; Kevin Zegers; Kate Mara; Michael Cassidy; Ryan Newman; Rip Torn; Thomas F. Wilson; ***D:*** Peter Hewitt; ***W:*** Adam Rifkin; David Berenbaum; ***C:*** David Tattersall; ***M:*** Christophe Beck.

Zoot Suit **1981 (R)** Based on Luis Valdez' play, this murder mystery/musical is rooted in the historical Sleepy Lagoon murder in the 1940s. Valdez plays a Mexican-American accused of the crime. His friends (and defense lawyers) rally around him to fight this travesty of justice. Lots o'music and dancing. **104m/C; VHS, DVD, Blu-Ray.** Edward James Olmos; Daniel Valdez; Tyne Daly; Charles Aidman; John Anderson; ***D:*** Luis Valdez; ***W:*** Luis Valdez. Natl. Film Reg. '19.

Zootopia *Zootropolis* **2016 (PG)** Disney's effort is a clever, if slightly overlong and undercooked, adventure film about how we shouldn't really be defined by what society says we can and cannot be (aren't they all about that a little bit?). In a world in which various species interact and the predator/prey dynamic has been eliminated, Judy Hopps (Goodwin), a plucky rabbit, wants to be a cop. When the case of a lifetime lands in her lap, she learns she'll need the assistance of petty thief Nick Wilde (Bateman). It's fun, and totally diverting, just not quite as deep as it thinks it is. **108m/C; DVD, Blu-Ray, Streaming.** ***V:*** J.K. Simmons; Maurice LaMarche; Alan Tudyk; Bonnie Hunt; Ginnifer Goodwin; Jason Bateman; Idris Elba; Octavia Spencer; Jenny Slate; Nate Torrence; ***D:*** Byron Howard; Rich Moore; ***W:*** Don Lake; Byron Howard; Rich Moore; Jared Bush; Josie Trinidad; Jim

Reardon; Phil Johnston; Jennifer Lee; Dan Fogelman; ***M:*** Michael Giacchino. Oscars '16: Animated Film; Golden Globes '17: Animated Film.

Zora Is My Name! 1/2 *My Name Is Zora* **1990** The funny, moving story of Zora Neal Hurston, a Black writer known for her stories and folklore of the rural South of the '30s and '40s. From PBS's American Playhouse. **90m/C; VHS, DVD.** Ruby Dee; Louis Gossett, Jr.; Roger E. Mosley; Flip Wilson; ***D:*** Neema Barnette; ***W:*** Ann Wallace; ***M:*** Olu Dara.

Zorba the Greek 1/2 *Zormba* **1964** A young British writer (Bates) comes to Crete to find himself by working his father's mine. He meets Zorba, an itinerant Greek laborer (Quinn), and they take lodgings together with an aging courtesan, who Zorba soon romances. The writer, on the other hand, is attracted to a lovely young widow. When she responds to him, the townsmen jealously attack her. Zorba teaches the young man the necessary response to life and its tragedies. Based on a novel by Nikos Kazantzakis. Masterpiece performance from Quinn. Beautifully photographed, somewhat overlong. Film later written for stage production. **142m/B; VHS, DVD, Blu-Ray.** Anthony Quinn; Alan Bates; Irene Papas; Lila Kedrova; ***D:*** Michael Cacoyannis; ***C:*** Walter Lassally. Oscars '64: Art Dir./Set Dec., B&W, B&W Cinematog., Support. Actress (Kedrova); Natl. Bd. of Review '64: Actor (Quinn).

Zorro 1/2 *El Zorro la belva del Colorado; El Zorro* **1974 (G)** Italian take on the Zorro legend is a light romp, with Delon as the masked one careful not to take the proceedings too seriously. Recently arrived California governor Diego runs afoul of corrupt officials and dons the famous cape and mask to help the peasants. Mostly aims to please the kids but should keep adults interested, too. **120m/C; DVD, Blu-Ray.** *IT FR* Alain Delon; Stanley Baker; Adriana Asti; Marino (Martin) Mase; Giacomo "Jack" Rossi-Stuart; Moustache; Ottavia Piccolo; Giampiero Albertini; Enzo Cerusico; ***D:*** Duccio Tessari; ***W:*** Giorgio Arlorio; ***C:*** Giulio Albonico; ***M:*** Guido de Angelis; Maurizio de Angelis.

Zorro Rides Again **1937** Zorro risks his life to outwit gangsters endeavoring to secure ancestor's property. In 12 chapters; the first runs 30 minutes, the rest 17. **217m/B; VHS, DVD.** John Carroll; Helen Christian; Noah Beery, Sr.; Duncan Renaldo; ***D:*** William Witney; John English.

Zorro, the Gay Blade 1/2 **1981 (PG)** Tongue-in-cheek sword play with Hamilton portraying the swashbuckling crusader and his long-lost brother, Bunny Wigglesworth, in this spoof of the Zorro legend. The fashion-conscious hero looks his best in plum. Leibman is fun to watch. **96m/C; VHS, DVD.** George Hamilton; Lauren Hutton; Brenda Vaccaro; Ron Leibman; Donovan Scott; James Booth; Helen Burns; Clive Revill; Eduardo Noriega; ***D:*** Peter Medak; ***W:*** Greg Alt; ***C:*** John A. Alonzo; ***M:*** Ian Fraser.

Zorro's Black Whip **1944** A young girl dons the mask of her murdered brother (Zorro) to fight outlaws in the old West. Serial in 12 episodes. **182m/B; VHS, DVD.** George Lewis; Linda Stirling; Lucien Littlefield; Francis McDonald; Tom London; ***D:*** Spencer Gordon Bennet; ***W:*** Wallace Grissell.

Zorro's Fighting Legion **1939** Zorro forms a legion to help the president of Mexico fight a band of outlaws endeavoring to steal gold shipments. A serial in 12 chapters. **215m/B; VHS, DVD.** Reed Hadley; Sheila Darcy; Edmund Cobb; John Merton; C. Montague Shaw; Budd Buster; Carleton Young; ***D:*** William Witney; John English; ***W:*** Barney A. Sarecky; Frank (Franklyn) Adreon; Morgan Cox; ***C:*** Reggie Lanning; ***M:*** William Lava.

Zotz! **1962** The holder of a magic coin can will people dead by uttering "zotz"; spies pursue the mild-mannered professor who possesses the talisman. Adapted from a Walter Karig novel. Typical William Castle fare; his gimic in the theatrical release of the movie was to distribute plastic "zotz" coins to the theatre patrons. **87m/B; VHS, DVD.** Tom Poston; Julia Meade; Jim Backus; Fred Clark; Cecil Kellaway; Margaret Dumont; Jimmy Hawkins; ***D:*** Ray Russell; William Castle; ***W:*** Ray Russell; ***C:*** Gordon Avil; ***M:*** Bernard Green.

Zou Zou 1/2 **1934** Lavish backstage musical/drama of a laundress who fills in for the leading lady on opening night and becomes a hit. Baker's talking picture debut. In French with English subtitles. **92m/B; VHS, DVD.** *FR* Josephine Baker; Jean Gabin; ***D:*** Marc Allegret.

The Zoya Factor **2019** Ad agency Zoya (Kapoor) employee is assigned to work a photo shoot with an Indian cricket team. She meets and falls in love with player Nikhil (Salmaan). She tells him and his team that her family has been considered a lucky charm for cricket matches by her family since birth. When the underperforming team starts to win matches, its members start to believe Zoya really is a lucky charm, a situation which makes Nikhil uncomfortable as his relationship with her becomes more serious. The light romantic comedy is predictable but feelgood and features a strong performance by Kapoor. Hindi with subtitles. **134m/C; DVD.** Sonam Kapoor; Dulquer Salmaan; Sanjay Kapoor; Angad Bedi; Diksha Juneja; ***D:*** Abhishek Sharma; ***M:*** Shankar-Ehsaan-Loy.

Zu Warriors *Shu shan zheng zhuan; The Legend of Zu* **2001 (PG-13)** Back in the 1980s, director Tsui Hark made a neat little fantasy film called "Zu: Warriors of the Magic Mountain." In the 1990s he decided to update it, and did a cgi remake called "Legend of Zu." Eventually Miramax got the U.S. release rights to it and decided to rename it as "Zu Warriors" (which the original film is also called, causing some confusion), cutting 20 minutes of time from the length and dubbing and re-editing the chopped-up remainder. The result is an incomprehensible mess that was universally panned, which is why it didn't get a theatrical release like the other properties Miramax acquired. **80m/C; DVD.** *CH* Ziyi Zhang; Cecilia Cheung; Louis Koo; Sammo Hung; Patrick Tam; Kelly Lin; Jacky Wu; Ekin Cheng; ***D:*** Tsui Hark; ***W:*** Tsui Hark; ***C:*** Hang-Seng Poon; Herman Yau; William Yim; ***M:*** Ricky Ho.

Zu: Warriors from the Magic Mountain *Shu Shan* **1983** The forces of evil are plotting to take over the world and a warrior endures the perils of the Zu Mountains in order to find the Twin Swords, the only weapons capable of defeating the demons. Cantonese with subtitles or dubbed. **98m/C; VHS, DVD.** *CH* Adam Cheng; Yuen Biao; Brigitte Lin; Sammo Hung; Moon Lee; ***D:*** Tsui Hark; ***C:*** Bill Wong.

Zulu 1/2 **1964** In 1879, a small group of British soldiers try to defend their African outpost from attack by thousands of Zulu warriors. Amazingly, the British win. Dated colonial epic based on an actual incident; battle scenes are magnificent. Prequel "Zulu Dawn" (1979) depicts British mishandling of the situation that led to the battle. **139m/C; VHS, DVD, Blu-Ray.** Michael Caine; Jack Hawkins; Stanley Baker; Nigel Green; Ulla Jacobsson; James Booth; Paul Daneman; Neil McCarthy; Gary Bond; Patrick Magee; Dickie Owen; Larry Taylor; Dennis Folbigge; Ivor Emmanuel; Glynn Edwards; David Kernan; ***Nar:*** Richard Burton; ***D:*** Cy Endfield; ***W:*** Cy Endfield; John Prebble; ***C:*** Stephen Dade; ***M:*** John Barry.

Zulu Dawn **1979 (PG)** An historical epic about British troops fighting the Zulus at Ulandi in 1878. Shows the increasing tensions between the British colonial government and the Zulus. Stunning landscapes unfortunately don't translate to the small screen. Good but unoriginal colonial-style battle drama. **117m/C; VHS, DVD, Blu-Ray.** Burt Lancaster; Peter O'Toole; Denholm Elliott; Nigel Davenport; John Mills; Simon Ward; Bob Hoskins; Freddie Jones; ***D:*** Douglas Hickox; ***M:*** Elmer Bernstein.

Zuma Beach 1/2 **1978** With her career in trouble, depressed singer Bonnie Katt (Somers) decides to head to the beach for a day of relaxing in the sun. A bunch of high school boys recognize her and start drooling while Bonnie decides to offer some friendly advice to the guys and their bikini-clad girlfriends. Harmless fluff with Somers doing justice to her swimwear. **98m/C; DVD.** Suzanne Somers; Steven Keats; Michael Biehn; Kimberly Beck; Perry Lang; Rosanna Arquette; Timothy Hutton; P.J. Soles; Tanya Roberts; Mark Wheeler; Biff Warren; ***D:*** Lee H. Katzin; ***W:*** John Carpenter; John Herman Shaner; William A. Schwartz; ***C:*** Hector Figueroa; ***M:*** Dick Halligan. **TV**

Zus & Zo *This and That; Hotel Paraiso* **2001** Sisters Michelle (Poorta), Wanda (Blok), and Sonja (Hendrickx) are dismayed to learn that their gay younger brother Nino (Derwig) is going to marry Bo (Reijn) in order to collect on an inheritance. Thanks to a clause in their parents' will, he will become the sole owner of the family's waterfront hotel in Portugal, which each sister thinks should come to her, and which each believes that Nino will soon sell. So they scheme to break up the couple while avoiding their own domestic crises. Dutch with subtitles. **100m/C; VHS, DVD.** *NL* Sylvia Poorta; Anneke Blok; Monic Hendrickx; Jacob Derwig; Halina Reijn; Theu Boermans; Jaap Spijkers; Pieter Embrechts; Annet Nieuwenhuyzen; ***D:*** Paula van der Oest; ***W:*** Paula van der Oest; ***C:*** Bert Pot; ***M:*** Fons Merkies.

Zvenigora **1928** Dovzhenko's first major film, and a lyrical revelation in the face of Soviet formality: a passionate, funny fantasy tableaux of 1,000 years of Ukrainian history, encompassing wild folk myths, poetic drama, propaganda and social satire. Silent. **73m/B; Silent; VHS, DVD.** *RU* Nikolai Nademsky; Alexander Podorozhny; Semyon Svashenko; ***D:*** Alexander Dovzhenko.

Category List

The Category Index contains genre, sub-genre, thematic, or significant scene classifications, ranging from the very general terms (Western, Sports Comedies) to the fairly particular (Heists: Casinos, Ninjas, Grandparents). The terms are defined (more or less) below. We've done our best to provide serious subject references while also including fun categories and lists to make your video viewing experience a little more enjoyable. No one list is all-inclusive. We are continuously reclassifying, adding, and subtracting movies. Many of the categories in this list are new, and therefore represent only a beginning. We're also trying to pare down or eliminate some of the bigger categories. *VideoHound* invites readers to participate in this pastime by sending in suggestions for new categories and adding movies to existing ones. **An asterisk (*) denotes a new category for this edition.**

ABBA-ca-dabra: The Swedish '70s group inspired some cinematic flair

Abortion: Contoversial issue supposedly settled with Roe v. Wade

Adoption & Orphans: Cute kids lacking permanent authority figures, ranging from *Annie* to *Wild Hearts Can't Be Broken*

Adultery: Gettin' a little on the side; usually ends badly

Adventure Drama: Action with more attention to dramatic content—*Apocalypse Now* to *Robin Hood, Prince of Thieves*

Advertising: Corporate shenanigans at the agency—*How to Get Ahead in Advertising* to *The Horse in the Gray Flannel Suit*

Africa: *Out of Africa* to *Zulu Dawn*

African America: Dominant African American themes

AIDS: Someone usually dies; *An Early Frost* to *Longtime Companion*

Airborne: Contraptions up in the sky

Alaska: The 49th state, home of the Iditarod and site of many manly Jack London adventures

Alcatraz: Prison island off San Francisco, aka *The Rock*

Alien Babes: Women who possess otherworldly beauty (and appetites)

Alien Beings—Benign: Friendly space visitors, including *Howard the Duck* and little buddy *E.T.*

Alien Beings—Vicious: Not-so-friendly space visitors, notably the multi-jawed *Alien* continually harassing Sigourney Weaver

Alien Cops: The long arm (tentacle?) of the outer space law

Aliens Are People, Too: Space visitors pretend to be human, or just take over the bodies—*Invasion of the Body Snatchers* kinda stuff

Alzheimer's/Dementia: Loved ones gradually forget everything as they age. Not a very funny subject

Amateur Sleuths: . . .and I woulda gotten away with it, too, if it weren't for those meddling kids!

American South: Theatrics amid much brow mopping and drawling; *A Streetcar Named Desire* rattling down *Flamingo Road*

America's Heartland: Flyover country, includes the Midwest, Bible Belt, Great Plains, and all the other places that aren't a Coast

Amnesia: Phone call for *Anastasia*

Amsterdam: City in the Netherlands where many vices are legal—just ask Vincent Vega

Amusement Parks: Cotton candy, ferris wheels, Coney Island, *Godzilla on Monster Island, Rollercoaster*

Angels: Benevolent winged visitors from above: *Wings of Desire*

Animated Musicals: Boys, girls, dogs, ducks, birds, mice, and monkeys croon; many of Disney vintage, including *Aladdin* and *Sleeping Beauty*

Animated Sci-Fi: To boldly go where no cartoon has gone before!

Animation & Cartoons: Antics of Daffy, Donald, Bugs, Mickey, Chip, Dale, Tom, Jerry, Fred, Wilma, Charlie, and the rest of the gang

Anime: Animated cartoons from Japan with cult following

Anthology: More than one story to a package

Anti-Heroes: From *Billy Jack* to *Dirty Harry* to *Thelma & Louise*

Anti-War War Movies: Recognizes that war really is hell—from *All Quiet on the Western Front* to *Paths of Glory*

Apartheid: Afrikaans term for racial segregation in South Africa

Apartments & Apartment Buildings: Why do they call 'em apartments when they're all together? The building or an apartment becomes important to the plot.

Arab Culture: Dominant Arab-American themes.

Archery: Shooting an arrow, sometimes for sport, sometimes for war, sometimes for food, sometimes to defend Sherwood Forest from the Sheriff of Notingham.

Architects & Architecture: People designing buildings for other people to build

Army Training, Sir Tales of basic training, or boot camp, if you prefer. Are those *Stripes* on your *Full Metal Jacket*?

Art & Artists: They paint, pause, and propagate with equal passion

Asia: *China White, Red Dust, Sand Pebbles*

Asian America: Asian experience in the US—*The Joy Luck Club, Come See the Paradise*

Assassinations: Lincoln, *JFK, La Femme Nikita, Times of Harvey Milk*, and more

Astronauts: Houston, we have a problem.

At the Drive-In: Scenes in which people watch movies. . .at the drive-in.

At the Movies: The movie within a movie or movies about watching the movies, from *The Purple Rose of Cairo* to *Last Action Hero* to *Matinee*

At the Video Store: Scenes from a video store, *Clerks, Remote Control*

Atlanta: Home of the Braves, Ted Turner, CNN, and that annoying Tomahawk Chop. Sherman dropped in a while back with some rowdy friends.

Atlantic City: Gambling mecca of the East Coast, aka Trumptown

Atlantis: The mythical undersea kingdom that's home to Aquaman and mermaids, supposedly

Auditions: Trying to get that part that'll be the Big Break

Aunts & Uncles, Nieces & Nephews: Extended family members you usually spend Thanksgiving with. In the movies, they're usually causing trouble

Autism: Tales of families dealing with the mysterious condition

Babysitting: Supervision of small-fry pranksters not your own; *Uncle Buck* to *The Hand that Rocks the Cradle*

Bachelor Party: The groom's last foray into debauchery before the big day; all hell generally breaks loose

Bad Bosses: When he says he wants that report by 5:00 or heads will roll. . .it may not be a figure of speech

Bad Dads: Daddy-Os with unpredictable mean streak: *The Shining, Kiss Daddy Goodbye*

Ballet: On your toes—*The Turning Point*

Ballooning: Up, up and away, or *Around the World in 80 Days*

Baltimore: Take a look at the Maryland city, hometown of director Barry Levinson and favorite digs of John Waters

Bar & Grill: Most, if not all, of the action takes place in a drinking establishment.

Barcelona: Second largest city in Spain is the capital of Catalonia; setting for recent Olympics, and some cool movies.

Baseball: Action on the diamond, ranging from *Bull Durham* to *A League of Their Own* to *Rookie of the Year*

Basketball: Roundball thrillers, including the memorable *The Fish that Saved Pittsburgh* and *White Men Can't Jump*

Bathroom Scenes: Plot points in the potty; sometimes sexy, sometimes scary, sometimes mundane, but always plenty of TP on hand

Bats: Flying rodents that fly into your hair and sometimes turn into centuries-old Eastern European aristocrats with strange eating habits

Bears: Most of 'em are looking for more than just pic-i-nic baskets

The Beat Generation: They set the stage for the Hippies of the '60s by hitting the

* = new to this edition

road and questioning the Establishment's version of the world

Beatniks: Jazz beards, bongos, poetry that doesn't rhyme, berets

Beauty Pageants: From the heartless to the hilarious, beauty is a big business—*Smile* girls!

Beer: Mmmmm, beer. The cause and solution to all of Homer's problems. The cities of St. Louis and Milwaukee are fueled by it. . .so is your brother-in-law

Bees: Flying insects that whore around with every flower they can get their hairy little legs on, and then make delicious honey. Sometimes they get mad and go on mass stinging sprees

Belfast: Northern Ireland city, Van Morrison's hometown (but that's not what it's famous for)

Berlin: City in Germany divided after WWII, now it's one big happy city again

Bermuda Triangle: That place in the Pacific where ships, planes, and plot continuity tend to disappear

Beverly Hills: Fancy-pants area of L.A.; home of Cops, Troops, Vamps, and 30-year-old teenagers

Bicycling: Two wheels, no motor, much leg action and sweating

Big Cats: Lions and Tigers and Panthers and Jaguars and other large felines that sports teams get named after.

Big Digs: Anthropology and archaeology, from Indiana Jones to various mummy on-the-loose stories

Big Rigs: *Smokey and the Bandit* speed down *Thieves' Highway* in a *Convoy*

Bigfoot/Yeti: Large, hairy, seldom-seen beast with really big feet

Bikers: Usually with a mean streak and traveling in leather-clad packs

Biopics—Artists: True stories of artists' lives. Find out if they were really starving or not

Biopics—Cops & Robbers: True stories of real life criminals and the real-life cops who arrested 'em

Biopics—Military: True stories of the men and women who fought this (and other) country's wars

Biopics—Musicians: From European composers to punk rock icons, they usually end up being tales of over-indulgence and others ripping them off

Biopics—Politics: True stories of the politicians who lead countries, states, and municipalities

Biopics—Religious: Life stories of church leaders, reformers, saints, and the occasional deity

Biopics—Royalty: Life stories of kings, queens, czars. They ran things before politicians were invented

Biopics—Science/Medical: Life stories of the people who invented the medicine and products that make modern life. . .modern

Biopics—Showbiz: Life stories of those who entertain us. It ain't always all glamour and happy endings

Biopics—Sports: Life stories of those we admire for their athletic prowess

Biopics—Writers: Life stories of those who put thoughts, stories, or manifestos to paper and became famous for it

Birds: Beaks, feathers, talons, bird #%!; *The Birds, Beaks: The Movie, Howard the Duck*

Birthdays: Congratulations on making it through another year!

Bisexuality: Going both ways—*Basic Instinct, Three of Hearts*

Black Comedy: Funny in a biting or despairing sort of way, from *The Addams Family* to *The Hospital*

Black Gold: Oil, that is; aka *Oklahoma Crude*

Black Market: Shady characters can get that hard-to-find item, for a hefty price. Usually it's hard to find because of a war or oppressive regime, or just an aversion to sales tax

Blackmail: I'm gonna tell, unless. . . *The Last Seduction, Letter to My Killer*

Blackout: Boom Boom, Out go the lights! In the whole city, usually

Blaxploitation: '70s remakes of horror classics, as well as B-movies made with the black audience in mind

Blind Date: Usually set up by friends or family members with the best of intentions, they rarely result in the best of relationships

Blindness: Can't see or sight impaired; *Afraid of the Dark*

Blizzards: Big snow storms, usually overblown by over-excited local weather people.

Bodyguards: Costner looks after Whitney's personal business

Bookies: Place your bets!. . .illegally with these guys

Books and Bookstores: Literary works (such as this) and the places where they can be found, as a major plot device: *La Lectrice* to *Crossing Delancey*

Boom!: Really big explosions, bombs, and other noisy or fiery messes popular in big budget action flicks

Boomer Reunions: thirty-somethings gather and reminisce: *The Big Chill*

Bootleggers: Transporters of illegal booze, usually back in the 1920s. . .or in the backwoods of the South

Bosnia: Has played host to Olympics and ethnic strife

Boston: Beantown, where everybody knows your name.

Bounty Hunters: Bring 'em back dead or alive—for a price

Bowling: Heavy round ball is thrown down waxed alley toward club-like pins; all fall down

Boxing: Yo, Adrian!

Brains!: Disturbing scenes of brains being extracted, forcibly, from the brainpan

Brainwashed: Minds get scrubbed clean of what they used to know so someone can put in whatever they want; generally orders to do bad things

Break-Ups: They usually happen in the second act of romantic comedies, before the happy ending. Although sometimes they are the plot

Bridges: For crossing, or if you're in a war movie, defending and/or blowing up

Bringing Up Baby: *Look Who's Talking* to *Raising Arizona*, plus infants with that little something different—*Alien 3, Enemy Mine, Basket Case 3: The Progeny*

Brush with Fame: Ordinary characters interact with famous people, either as plot poits or coincidence. Think Tyson in *The Hangover* or De Niro and Snipes in *The Fan*

Buddhism: Eastern religion with bald guys

Buddy Cops: Couple of police hanging together, usually practicing limited repartee at a donut shop; *Lethal Weapon, Tango and Cash*

Buffalo, NY: Upstate New York city that's home to lots of snow and a famously perennial runner-up football team

Bullfighters & Bullfighting: 0dquo;Sport0dquo; pitting Spaniards with red capes and swords vs. future Big Macs with horns

Burglars: Thievery by stealth, usually at night, and using cool equipment, like in *Entrapment*

Buried Alive: I'm not quite dead, yet! Hello, Mr. grave digger person, hello!

Buses: Large truck-like passenger vehicles—*Speed, The Big Bus, The Trip to Bountiful*

Cabbies: Where to, Mac?

Calcutta: Big, overpopulated city in India

Cambodia: Small country in Southeast Asia bordering Vietnam. Haven't had much luck with politics in the last few decades

Camelot (New): The exploits of JFK, Jackie, and various relatives and hangers-on

Camelot (Old): The exploits of King Arthur and his *Knights of the Round Table*

Campers/RVs: Portable homes on wheels. 0dquo;What do we have? We have one heavily-armed recreational vehicle!0dquo;

Campus Capers: What really goes on at college—*Assault of the Party Nerds*

Canada: Renfrew of the Mounties plus lots of wilderness and the occasional hockey puck

Canadian Mounties: The Great White North version of cops. They always get their man

Canine Cops: Four-legged police who really take a bite out of crime

Cannibalism: People who eat people are the luckiest people; *Alive, Rabid Grannies, Cannibal Women in the Avocado Jungle of Death, The Cook, the Thief, His Wife & Her Lover*

Capitol Capers: Hollywood versions of hijinks in Washington, D.C.—*Dave, Mr. Smith Goes to Washington, All the President's Men*

Caribbean: Tropical vacation destination, home to sandy beaches, cool breezes, palm trees, excellent baseball players, hurricanes, and reggae

Carnivals & Circuses: Big top, little top, domes: *Shakes the Clown* to *Rollercoaster*, plus *Big Top Pee Wee, State Fair,* and metaphoric circuses: *Brewster McCloud, La Strada*

Casbah: Come with me. . .we will make beautiful musics togezher

Catholic School: Educational arm of the church of Rome, usually run by ruler-wielding nuns

Cats: Lesser vertebrate nonetheless much beloved by Hollywood

Cattle Drive: Git along little doggies!

Cattle Rustlers/Horse Thieves: Someone stole our little doggies (or horsies)

Cave People: From the most primitive (*The Clan of the Cave Bear*) to the fairly modernized (*The Flintstones*)

Caves: Holes in the ground where monsters, bats, and Flintstones live

Central America: That chunk of land stuck between North America and South America

Chain Gangs: Shakin'it over here, Boss! Prisoners working on the side of the road, or making little ones out of big ones

Checkered Flag: *Eat My Dust;* racing in the street or on the track; *The Last American Hero*

Cheerleaders: Give me an A! *The Positively True Adventures of the Alleged Texas Cheerleader-Murdering Mom* meets *Revenge of the Cheerleaders*

Chefs: The fancy-schmancy preparers of fancy-schmancy foods at fancy-schmancy eateries. They have cool hats that make them seem a lot taller

Chess: Game that involves much strategy and forward thinking. . .as well as a lot of staring, sitting, and generally looking unconscious. Not a really good spectator sport

Chicago: City in Illinois, right at the bottom of Lake Michigan

Child Abuse: Not very funny at all—*Mommie Dearest, Fallen Angel*

Childhood Buddies: The pals we hang around with before puberty hits

China: *The Last Emperor* to *Red Sorghum* to *The World of Suzie Wong*

Christmas: Reindeer, Santa, children make appearance amid much sentimentality

Church Choirs: Big groups of singers in robes who sing in. . .church (Duh!). Can I get an Amen?

CIA/NSA: Men and women of the Agency. You know, the good spies. . .uh, usually

Cincinnati: Southern Ohio city, home to German immigrants, Jerry Springer, and the Big Red Machine (and we're not talking about Ivan Drago)

Cinderella Stories: Gal down on her luck meets fairy godmother (or father) and finds true love—*Pretty Woman, Flashdance, Cinderella*

City-Squishing Behemoths: 0dquo;Don't you hate it when you keep stepping on those little cars?0dquo; 0dquo;Yeah! The little critters inside are always so noisy!0dquo;

Civil Rights: Fighting for equality—*The Autobiography of Miss Jane Pittman, Mississippi Burning*

Civil War: The Yankees against the Confederates; aka *The Blue and the Gray*

Civil War (non-U.S.): People in the same (foreign) country fighting and killing over religion, politics, tribal affiliation, or anything else that makes people kill their own countrymen

Clergymen: Non-Catholic (they're covered elsewhere) men and women of the cloth

Cleveland: 0dquo;The Mistake by the Lake,0dquo; home to the Rock 'n' Roll Hall of Fame, a very cinematic baseball team, and some of the most 'rabid' football fans in the country

Cloning Around: Makin' copies—of people or animals. *Multiplicity* to *Jurassic Park*

Clowns: Big red noses, huge feet, painted smiles frighten many

Coaches/Managers: They design the plays, pick the players, and make the speeches for the teams that win all those improbably 'underdog defies the odds' movies

Coast Guard: They, well, guard the coast, and help boaters, and bust smugglers, as well as other cool maritime duties

Cockroaches: Creepy crawlies signifying the work of the supernatural, or a lack of housekeeping skills

Cold Spots: Set in a frostbitten locale with lots of shivering; *Ice Station Zebra, Never Cry Wolf, Quest for Fire*

Cold War Spies: Spy vs. Spy pitting various U.S. and British alphabet soup agencies against the Commies

Coma: Some sort of head trauma usually leads to extended nap time

Comedy Anthologies: More than one yuk fest on a cassette

Comedy Mystery: Wacky whodunits like *Murder by Death, Clue*

Comedy Sci-Fi: Laughs in space! *Spaceballs*

Comic Adventure: Adventurous romps liberally laced with humor: *Romancing the Stone* to *Bird on a Wire* to *Crocodile Dundee*

Comic Books: Colorful tales of superheroes and adventure play a big part in the plot, unless your mom threw 'em out

Comic Cops: Police officers that catch laughs as they catch the bad guys. Think Axel Foley or those cut-ups from the *Police Academy* series

Coming of Age: Hard-fought adolescent battle for adulthood, led by *American Graffiti, The Apprenticeship of Duddy Kravitz, The Karate Kid*

Communists & Communism: Way left-wingers politically. They used to run Eastern Europe, but now they just rant in coffeehouses. The ones in Asia are still around, though

Computers: Bits and bytes play major role

Concentration/Internment Camps: Nazis used them for their 0dquo;final solution0dquo; while the U.S. used them to imprison Japanese-Americans

Contemporary Noir: Dark and moody or tributes to dark and moody that pay homage to the original Film Noir genre—*Blue Velvet, 9½ Weeks, sex, lies, and videotape, Wild Orchid*

Corporate Shenanigans: Big Business runs amuck—*Barbarians at the Gate, Wall Street*

Cousins: Progeny of your parents' sibs.

Cover-Ups: It's not the crime that trips you up, it's

* = new to this edition

trying to keep people from finding out about it. . .

Creepy Houses: Scary dwellings—*Amityville Horror* 1 through 33

Crime Doesn't Pay: When the perfect crime. . .isn't.

Crime Drama: Gangster family dysfunction, heists gone awry, packin' pathos with your piece. *The Godfather, Goodfellas, Reservoir Dogs.*

Crime Sprees: Bad guy, gal or couple goes on a crime binge and other tales of obsessive criminal activity, including *Bonnie & Clyde, The Boys Next Door*

Crimedy: formerly *So I Amuse You?* Wisenheimer Guys—funny felons, amusing miscreants, if you will

Crimes of Passion: Love, sex, and death

Criminally Insane: They don't really care if crime pays, they're just following orders from the voices.

The Crusades: 0dquo;Holy0dquo; wars between Christians and Muslims in the middle ages.

Cuba: Fidel's Island, where the survivors vote themselves off and the winners make it 90 miles north to become high-priced baseball players.

Cuban Missile Crisis: Two weeks in 1962 when the U.S. and the Soviet Union came close to blowing up the world over some missiles in Cuba

Cubicle Hell: Toiling thanklessly in the land of Dilbert

Cults: Something like a gang but more intense and usually governed by a state of mind similar to irrationality—*Helter Skelter*

Culture Clash: Hilarity ensues (or sometimes not) as people from vastly different backgrounds try to interact. *Deliverance, Witness, George of the Jungle*

Custer's Last Stand: is what whites called it. Native Americans probably had a different name for it. Either way, it didn't end well for Custer

Custody Battles: People, mostly divorced couples, fight over who keeps the kids. *Kramer vs. Kramer, Losing Isaiah*

Cuttin' Heads: Barber shops and Beauty salons are the scenes of all or most of the 0dquo;action0dquo;

Cyberpunk: Dark, moody, futuristic flicks—*Blade Runner, Freejack, Tank Girl*

Dallas: Big city in Texas. Home of the Cowboys, J.R., and scandal among the rich

Dance Fever: Whole lotta foot-tapping going on, including *An American in Paris, Daddy Long Legs,* and *Dirty Dancing*

Dates from Hell: Fun evening for two singles turns into a nightmare for one of them—*Bye Bye Love, Singles, Something Wild*

Day Care/Nursery School: Babysitting warehouse where parents drop off their kids while they make money to pay for daycare

A Day In The Life: All the action takes place within a 24-hour period

DEA: G-men on the front lines of America's War on Drugs

Deadly Implants: Where is that ticking coming from?

Deafness: Can't hear or hearing impaired; *Bridge to Silence, The Miracle Worker*

Death & The Afterlife: Could be ghosts, could be voices from the beyond, could be any number of post-dead things—*Beetlejuice, Carnival of Souls, Flatliners, Poltergeist, Weekend at Bernie's*

Death Row: Waitin' for a call from the Governor; *Dead Man Walking, Angels with Dirty Faces*

Dedicated Teachers: From *The Dead Poet's Society* to *The Blackboard Jungle* to *The Miracle Worker*

Deep Blue: The sea around us, including *ffolkes* and *Splash*

Deep Woods Offed: People go into the woods, but they don't come out. Gonna make 'em squeal like a. . .well, you know. . .

Demons & Wizards: Swords, sorcery and wrinkled old men with wands—*The Alchemist, The Hobbit, The Sword & the Sorcerer*

Dental Mayhem: Toothpickin' uproars; *Marathon Man, The Dentist*

Deserts: Endless beach minus the water—*Ishtar, Lawrence of Arabia*

Detective Spoofs: Putting together clues in humorous fashion—*The Adventures of Sherlock Holmes' Smarter Brother, The Naked Gun*

Detroit: The Motor City, home of Motown, lots of cars, and. . .VideoHound

Devils: Some may meet on *Judgment Day*

Devil's Island: French Island prison in the South Atlantic

Diner: Most of the story, or at least important parts of it, occur in the smallish, very informal eating establishment

Dinosaurs: *Jurassic Park* and other less animated thundering lizards

Disaster Flicks: Natural and man-made, including 47 *Airport* sequels

Disco Musicals: '70s tackiness reigns supreme, from *Saturday Night Fever* to *Xanadu*

Disease of the Week: Bulimia, anorexia, polio, cancer, and so on

Disorganized Crime: Stupid crime, including *Amos and Andrew, Dog Day Afternoon, Home Alone, Quick Change*

Divorce: Breaking up is hard to do; *Accidental Tourist, Heartburn, Kramer vs. Kramer*

Doctors & Nurses: Men and women in scrubs concerned about health of complete strangers for profit, often to the dismay of the patient—*Autopsy, Candy Stripe Nurses, Dead Ringers*

Documentary: Real life manipulated on film—*A Brief History of Time, The Last Waltz, Paris Is Burning, Roger and Me*

Domestic Abuse: *This Boy's Life, The Burning Bed, What's Love Got to Do With It?*

Doublecross!: Usually happens when there's no more honor among thieves, like in *Payback*

Down Under: Australian, New Zealand settings—*The Rescuers Down Under, Gallipoli, The Man from Snowy River, The Thorn Birds*

Downsized: Getting the pink slip, precipitating new opportunities, or maybe some unlawful activity

Dragons: Legendary medieval lizards, usually with fiery dispositions; *Dragonheart, Pete's Dragon*

Dropouts People who just couldn't finish what they started. . .it all seemed so promising back in kindergarten

Drug Abuse: Life with a drugstore cowboy; consumption of drugs, mostly illegal or in extra-large dosages

Dublin: Irish capitol city, home to *The Commitments*

Dying for a Promotion: . . .or killing for one. Guess those business ethics seminars were a waste of money

Ears!: Bloody detachment and general maiming of. . .

Earthquakes: The Earth moved! Common occurrence in California

Easter: Holiday in the early spring celebrated with giant rabbits, eggs, chocolate, bonnets. . .and gruesome movies depicting the crucifixion

Eastern Europe: Basically everything east of Germany and west of Asia

Eco-Vengeance!: Nature wreaks havoc on man—watch out for *Alligators, Frogs* and *Piranhas*

Edinburgh: Scottish capital city. They pronounce it 0dquo;Goff0dquo; instead of 0dquo;Golf0dquo; according to Judge Smails.

Egypt-Ancient: Mummies, Pharaohs, Pyramids, when they were brand new

Elementary School/Junior High: tough transitional time, where recess and playgrounds give way to locker partners and puberty

Elephants: Pachyderms play a BIG part in the plot—*Dumbo, Larger Than Life*

Elevators: Sometimes the oddest things happen in them. . .

Emerging Viruses: Deadly virus spreads like wildfire as frantic medical personnel search for a cure; think ebola

The Empire State Building: *King Kong* liked to hang there.

Errant Educators: Teachers, coaches, or principals who may not have the kids' best interests in mind, maybe because they're aliens (*The Faculty*), or they're just mean (*Teaching Mrs. Tingle*)

Escaped Cons: They busted outta the joint, now they're makin' a run for it. *Con Air, We're No Angels, Papillon, Fled*

Eskimos: Native North Americans who reside in particularly frosty climates

Evil Doctors: Don't go to these guys for a checkup—*Malice, Dead Ringers,* and *Doctor X*

Ex-Cons: Former guests of state or federal penal institutions

Ex-Cops: Former members of the law enforcement community

Exchange Students: Kids come over here to sample our educational wares, and maybe some host family's nubile offspring. . .or we go over there and do the Ugly American thing

Executing Revenge: Bad guys come back from being executed to cause more trouble. *Fallen, Shocker*

Exorcism & Exorcists: Priests try to evict evil spirits from pea-soup-spewing, head-twirling victims of possession.

Explorers: Going boldly where no man or woman has regularly gone before

Extraordinary Pairings: Jesse James meets Frankenstein's Daughter

Eyeballs!: Unnerving scenes involving pupils, irises, lids, and occasionally, lashes

Fairs & Expositions: Short term amusement parks: *State Fair*

Family Adventure: Families find themselves in perilous or thrilling predicaments; ingenuity and derring-do usually ensues

Family Comedy: Families find themselves in amusing situations; hilarity may or may not ensue

Family Drama: Families struggling through tragedy, daily life, difficult circumstances, or too few bathrooms; teardrops and recriminations are usually involved

Family Horror: The whole clan gets scared and/or chased by the knife-wielding maniac or spooky ghosts rather than just the nubile teenagers. The family that screams together. . .

Family Reunions: Vacations or picnics where extended family members get together to reintroduce themselves to each other, eat a lot of food, and pretend they have something in common besides surnames.

Fantasy: Tales of the imagination, including *Alice* and her looking glass, *E.T., Ladyhawke, My Stepmother Is an Alien*

Farm Livin': Down on the farm; *Bitter Harvest, Pelle the Conqueror, Jean de Florette, The River*

Fashion: The world of crazy clothing

Fast Zombies: The undead who can do more than just shamble

Fatsuit Acting: Actors get big parts, and lots of padding to go with 'em

FBI: The Bureau. Federal cops with an internal focus and a dress code

Female Bonding: Women get together, usually to the men's dismay; *Waiting to Exhale*

Female Spies: The fairer sex uses its feminine assets and wiles to get the other side's secrets

Femme Fatale: She done him and him and him wrong

Fencing: En garde, dude

Film Noir: Dark and moody or tributes to dark and moody—*Farewell, My Lovely, The Postman Always Ring Twice, The Third Man, Who Framed Roger Rabbit?*

Filmmaking: The making of a film within a film: *The Player*

Firemen: *Backdraft, Frequency,* and other tales of brave people with hoses

Fires: *Frankenstein, Quest for Fire, Pyrates*

The First Time: Y'know, the first time you had. . .when you broke your. . .when you made. . .when you first. . .uh, did it. . .with another person

Flashback: Why, I remember like it was yesterday. It all started when. . .*The Usual Suspects, Casablanca*

Flatulence: Embarrassing gaseous emissions

Floods: Water, water everywhere

Florence: Not Alice's grits-kissing pal, but the city in Italy

Florida: Beaches, retirement communities, swamps, Spring Training, Disney World.

Folklore & Legend: Age-old adult tales covering Atlantis, little people, faeries, Paul Bunyan, and the like

Football: Everything from terrorist attacks on the Superbowl (*Black Sunday*) to prison competition (*The Longest Yard*) plus *Diner*

Foreign Cops: The long arm of the law in other countries, or visiting law enforcement representatives helping catch international baddies here in the good ole U.S. of A.

Foreign Intrigue: Overseas mystery, with emphasis on accent and location

Frame-ups: Someone's set up to take the rap: *My Cousin Vinny* to *Consenting Adults*

France: From *Dirty Rotten Scoundrels* to *The Moderns* to *Gigi* to *The Last Metro* to *Killer Tomatoes Eat France*

Fraternities & Sororities: Those fun-lovin' campus cut-ups who're always pulling pranks or getting offed in bad slasher flicks

French Revolution: Starving peasants have had enough, and a few royals lose their heads

Front Page: *Citizen Kane, All the President's Men, The Philadelphia Story,* and other journalistic stories

Fugitives: Running from the law; *Breathless, Nowhere to Hide, Posse*

Funerals: The final good-bye—*Four Weddings and a Funeral, Gardens of Stone, The Big Chill*

Funeral Homes: A place to say your final good-bye. Not the funnest place in the world, especially if you're the one in the box

Funny Money: Counterfeiting, and all the action movie stuff that goes with it

Future Cop: The future of law enforcement

Future Shock: Someone from our past comes to our present, or someone from our present goes to our future; *Sleeper, Just Visiting*

Gambling: Aces and Eights, *The Color of Money, Eight Men Out, Honeymoon in Vegas*

Game Shows: *The Running Man* and *Queen for a Day*

Gangs: Criminally enterprising teens and adults running in packs: *State of Grace, Miller's Crossing, Public Enemy, The Wanderers*

Gay Best Friend: The Greek Chorus of most romantic comedies, commenting on (and sometimes prompting) the mistakes of the main protagonists

Gays: Gay themes—*Kiss of the Spider Woman, The Hunger*

Gender Bending: *The Crying Game, La Cage aux Folles, Her Life as a Man* and other instances of boys becoming girls and vice versa

Generation X: Slacking in the '90s—*Reality Bites, Singles*

Genetics: Fooling with the double helix—*The Fly*

Genies: *Aladdin* finds magic lamp filled with compressed Robin Williams

Genocide/Ethnic Cleansing: One ethnic group thinks it is so superior to another that the other group must be completely destroyed. Words cannot describe the stupidity of this view

Genre Spoofs: Wacky takes on serious films, starting with the granddaddy of them all: *Airplane!*

Germany: *The Blue Angel, Wings of Desire*

Ghosts, Ghouls, & Goblins: *Ghostbusters, Topper, Poltergeist*

Giants: *The Amazing Colossal Man* visits *Village of the Giants*

Gifted Children: Kids show amazing talents that astound adults, from *Rookie of the Year* to *Little Man Tate*

Glasgow: Scottish city, not the capital of Scotland.

Go Fish: Casting a line in the river that runs through it; *Man of Aran, A Fish Called Wanda, Captains Courageous*

Going Native: Outsiders try to blend in; *Dances with Wolves, The Swiss Family Robinson*

Going Postal: Neither rain, snow, sleet, nor dead of night. . . .Hello, Newman

Going Straight: Trying to stay on the right side of the law so you can stay on the right side of prison bars, after you've already sampled the wrong side of both

Golf: Slow boring game best experienced on screen (0dquo;Be the ball, Danny0dquo;)

Gospel Music: Inspirational music usually sung by people in church or who really like church

Grand Hotel: Checkout time is noon; *Blame It on the Bellboy*

Grand Theft Auto: Boosting cars for fun and/or profit. Just like on *Cops*, chases usually ensue

Grandparents: Your parents' parents, the ones who spoil you and drive your folks crazy

Great Britain: Thwarted royals (*Charles & Diana: A Palace Divided, Edward and Mrs. Simpson*), kings (*King Ralph*), queens (*The Naked Civil Servant*), class distinctions (*The Ruling Class*), vanished empires (*Cromwell, A Man for All Seasons*), criminals (*The Krays, The Long Good Friday*) plus multiple stiff upper lips, the Brontes, and Dickens

Great Depression: The era, not the state of mind—*Bound for Glory, Of Mice and Men, The Grapes of Wrath, Rambling Rose*

Great Escapes: Seizing the day for freedom—*The Big Doll House, Escape from Alcatraz, Papillon*

Greece—Ancient: In the immortal words of Socrates, 0dquo;I drank what?0dquo;

Greece—Modern: They don't walk around in sheets and philosophize anymore, at least not in public

Grim Reaper: Time's up when the pale bald guy wearing a hood and carrying garden implements comes looking for you.

Growing Older: *On Golden Pond, *batteries not included, Cocoon, Driving Miss Daisy, The Shootist, The Wild Bunch*

Gunslingers: Old West killers for hire. Sometimes they killed the bad guys, sometimes they were the bad guys

Gym Class: The bane of un-athletic schoolkids throughout the country

Gymnastics: Human pretzels like *Nadia*

Gypsies: Fortune tellers with scarves around their heads and vaguely-European accents, or modern day con men are the two basic movie types

Hackers: Computer whiz kids cause havoc—or just change their grades

Halloween: *Trick or Treat!*

Hallucinations/Illusions: Stuff looks real, but it's all in yer head, man!

Handyman Specials: Houses that need a little work to be livable. . .unless you're a ghost, serial killer, or otherwise disinclined to hire an inspector

Hard Knock Life: Poverty and bad luck; *City of Joy, The Match Factory Girl*

Harlem: Part of New York City you don't see in the tourism brochures

Hawaii: The 50th state, fun in the sun, if the volcanoes are behaving.

Heads! Disturbing (or fun) scenes of heads being forcibly removed from the bodies they formerly controlled

Hearts!: Unnerving scenes involving human hearts, generally seen by the audience and almost always still pumping

Heaven Sent: Visits or returns from the place where good souls and all dogs go—*Field of Dreams* to *Made in Heaven* to *Oh God!*

Heists: Crooks plan and carry out elaborate jobs

Heists—Armored Car: Crooks plan and carry out jobs on armored cars

Heists—Art: Crooks plan and carry out jobs to steal works of art, *The Thomas Crown Affair*

Heists—Bank: Crooks plan and carry out early withdrawals, sometimes incurring substantial penalties

Hests—Cars/trucks: Crooks plan and carry out jobs on cars or trucks, or for cars and trucks, hopefully after they've come to a complete stop

Heists—Casinos: Crooks plan to steal from the one-armed bandits; *Ocean's Eleven are 3000 Miles From Graceland*

Heists—Gold/Precious Metals: Elaborate plans to go for the gold, or silver, or platinum. Bronze isn't that valuable in this game

Heists—Jewels: Ya gotta be cool to get the ice, just ask the *Reservoir Dogs*

Heists—Stagecoach: Old West crooks plan and carry out jobs on stagecoaches, the buses of their day

Heists—Trains: Not the whole train, just the good stuff inside it. *Butch Cassidy and the Sundance Kid* liked the choo-choos

Hell: Not a place you wanna end up. The forecast calls for continued hot, with a 0% chance of freezing over.

Hell High School: Place where adolescents gather against their will; also known as *Rock 'n' Roll High School*

The Help—Female: Maids, nannies, governesses, cooks, housekeepers

The Help—Male: Butlers, chauffeurs, manservants, valets

Hide the Dead Guy: What to do with those pesky bodies after the killing's done?

High School: This is for those few movies where high school isn't treated like the hellish experience we all seem to remember it being

High School Reunions: Adults gather to impress other adults they didn't like as adolescents

Hijacked!: Terrorists take over various modes of transportation, causing much action-movie heroics

Hinduism: Movies relating to the main religion of the sub-continent

Hispanic America: Dominant Hispanic American themes (*Salsa, Mi Vida Loca*)

Historical Comedy: Famous and not-so-famous events of the past, played for laughs

Historical Detectives: It's elementary! Sherlock, meet Elliot Ness.

Historical Drama: Usually at least loosely based on a real incident or personality

Historical Romance: Smooches, longing looks, and other activities exchanged between historical personages

Hit Men/Women: Boys and girls armed with silencers; *Prizzi's Honor, Romeo is Bleeding*

Hockey: *Slap Shot* and other icy tales of passing the puck

Holidays: Easter, Thanksgiving, New Year's, Halloween, but generally not Christmas

Holocaust: *Playing for Time, Schindler's List*

Home Alone: Kids find themselves without adult supervision—*Adventures in Babysitting* to *Young Sherlock Holmes*

Home Invasion: Uninvited guests drop by. . .usually intent on larceny, mayhem, or a place to hide out

The Homefront—England: Air raids, stiff upper lips, they were a lot closer to the action, and were just as worried about their sons and husbands.

The Homefront—U.S./Canada: The war at home during WWII—looking for spies, rationing, waiting for word about 0dquo;the boys.0dquo;

Homeless: Street people with no homes

Homicide: Murder most foul! It's what usually gets those wacky buddy-cop movies started

Honeymoon: Where the bride and groom go after the wedding's over to. . .get acquainted

Hong Kong: Land of the really cool action flick; Chow Yun-Fat and Jackie Chan became stars there. Great Britain gave it back to the Chinese

Horrible Holidays: Holidays with a ghoulish twist—*Bloody New Year, Halloween, My Bloody Valentine, Silent Night, Bloody Night*

Horror Anthologies: More than one scarefest per package

Horror Comedy: Tongue-in-bloody cheek—*The Fearless Vampire Killers, Piranha, Sorority Babes in the Slimeball Bowl-A-Rama*

Horses: Can you say *Black Beauty?*

Hospitals & Medicine: Dysfunctional institutional health care—*Article 99, The Hospital, One Flew Over the Cuckoo's Nest, Young Doctors in Love*

Hostage!: People held against their will for bargaining purposes

Houston: That big city in Texas where J.R. didn't live, but Roger Clemens does.

Human Sacrifice: You do NOT want to get volunteered for this. People croak other people hoping to appease or please some perceived higher power

Hunted!: Humans tracking humans for trophy purposes

Hunting: Where's dat wascally wabbit? *Caddyshack, The Bear, White Hunter, Black Heart*

Hurricanes: Natural disasters that involve much wind, water, boarded windows, and debris

I Was a Teenage Criminal: When teenagers steal, kill, or generally have a total lack of respect for the law . It's that damn rock 'n' roll music, I tell ya!

Illegal Immigration: Give us your tired, your poor, your huddled masses. . .unless they try to sneak in

I'm Not Dead, Yet! Reports of their demise have been greatly exaggerated

Immigration: Melting pot stories—*Avalon, Far and Away, Living on Tokyo Time*

Immortality: I wanna live forever

Impending Retirement: Gold watch, a party, some tearful goodbyes. . .but there's always those darn loose ends to tie up first

Inheritance: The stuff your folks give you after they die. Could lead to the worst sort of sibling rivalry

In-Laws: The family you marry into; usually a source of conflict and punchlines

Incest: Implied or actual relationships among family members—*The Grifters, Spanking the Monkey*

India: On the road to *Bombay*

The Inquisition, What a Show!: The Spanish Inquisition, that is. No one expects it. Spanish Catholic Church officials got a little, um, enthusiastic, in their recruiting efforts in the late 1400s

Insomnia: Can't sleep at night

Insurance: Usually the cure for the above category, unless someone's killing, scamming, or frauding for the money it pays

Internet Borne: It's not just for naughty pics or fantasy sports anymore. You can find either love or death on the World Wide Web.

Interpol: International police force that fights crime and terrorism when it crosses many borders

Interracial Affairs: Couple from different racial backgrounds cause trauma for family and friends—*Mississippi Masala, Jungle Fever*

Inventors & Inventions: Those wacky folks and their newfangled machines; *Chitty Chitty Bang Bang*

Invisibility: Now you see 'em, now you don't

Iraq: Maybe you've heard of it. . .oil-rich country in the Middle East? We've been poking around there for a while now?

Ireland: Aye, make that a pint for take away; *The Field, Cal, The Playboys*

Islam: Religious themes, concentrating on Muslims

Island Fare: Thin, isolated stretch of land surrounded by water; notorious for encouraging natural appetites in men and women

Israel: *Cast a Giant Shadow, Exodus*

Istanbul, not Constantinople: Former seat of the Eastern Roman Empire, now the Turks run things.

Italy: Passion, vino, lust, vino, Sophia Loren

It's a Conspiracy, Man!: Just because you're paranoid doesn't mean they're not out to get you

It's the End of the World! Skynet, zombies, giant space rocks, pandemics, nuclear war. . .they're all coming for ya

Jamaica: Caribbean Island country to head to when you need to hear some reggae, inhale, or get your groove back

Japan: *Land of the Rising Sun, Godzilla, Hiroshima, Mon Amour*

Jazz & Blues: Uniquely American music form performed mostly by tragic figures. . .in the movies, anyway.

Jealousy: The green-eyed monster that causes a lot of crimes. I know you didn't just look at MY man!

Jerusalem: Much-fought-over Holy City, it's ground zero for much of the world's religious population.

Jockeying for Position: Horse racing flicks like *Seabiscuit*

Joke and Dagger: *Spies Like Us* can be funny, even when the mission is *Top Secret!*

Judaism: *Fiddler on the Roof* meets *Funny Girl*

Jungle Stories: Tarzan, tribes, trees, treasure, temperature, temptresses, tigers

Junior Jocks: Kids got out onto the field, court, pitch, or rink to emulate their sports heroes, or just for fun, or to please their vicariously-thrilled parents.

Juvenile Delinquents: Teenaged troublemakers, Kiddie crime sprees, When Children Attack. The dirty-faced kids who always spoke with Brooklyn accents in the old movies.

Karaoke: This Japanese import usually runs best on alcohol

KGB: Not the crazy Russian poker player from *Rounders* but the former Soviet Union's spy organization

Kidnapped!: Held for ransom or just for the heck of it—*A Perfect World, Raising Arizona*

Killer Apes and Monkeys: *King Kong* lives on *The Planet of the Apes*

Killer Appliances: Defrosted refrigerator goes on killing binge

Killer Beasts: Cloned dinosaurs run amuck in backyard, destroying patio

Killer Brains: Literally has a mind of its own, i.e., *The Brain That Wouldn't Die*

Killer Bugs: Giant and/or miserably mean spiders,

* = new to this edition

ants, bees, worms, flies, slugs, tarantulas, wasps, and other creepy things

Killer Cars: You should have changed *Christine*'s oil

Killer Clowns: Confirming what everybody knows: clowns are evil

Killer Dogs: Fido takes a walk on the wild side—*Cujo*, baby

Killer Dreams: More like nightmares on elm street

Killer Kats: Kitties with a killer instinct

Killer Kiddies: *Children of the Corn* hang out on the outskirts of the *Village of the Damned*. . .isn't that near the 7-Eleven of Doom?

Killer Pigs: Bacon gets its revenge

Killer Plants: Too much fertilizer produces killer tomatoes (stewed)

Killer Reptiles: *Godzilla* and pals, not rampaging lawyers

Killer Rodents: Nasty mice, rats, bats, and shrews

Killer Sea Critters: Just when you thought it was safe to go back in the water; formerly *Sea Critter Attack*

Killer Spouses: Watch their eyes very closely when you get to the 0dquo;. . .until death do you part0dquo; portion of the vows

Killer Teens: Teenagers act on the worst of their hormone and angst-fueled impulses

Killer Toys: Demented play things develop homicidal urges; why hello, Chucky

Killing Sprees: A person, or sometimes a couple, decides that a bunch of people need killin' in a short amount of time

King of Beasts (Dogs): Need we say more?

Korean War: *M*A*S*H* and friends

L.A.: Smoggy city in California also known as Los Angeles or the City of Angels; includes Hollywood & Beverly Hills

Labor & Unions: *Hoffa* and other working stiffs

Lacrosse: It's like hockey, on grass

Late Bloomin' Love: Better late than not blooming at all

Law & Lawyers: Tom Cruise joins *The Firm* and other realistic legal adventures

Leprechauns: The wee mischievous people of Irish lore who carry around pots o' gold

Lesbians: Lesbian themes—*Lianna, Bar Girls*

Libraries & Librarians: Important things happen where you can't talk—sometimes people even read!

Lifeguards: Rescuers of the swimming-challenged

Little People: Dwarves, munchkins, leprechauns, oompa-loompas and the like

London: City in merry old England, home to many generations of the most famous royals

Loner Cops: *Dirty Harry* Syndrome

Long Distance Love: Couples try to do the long-distance relationship thing, usually unsuccessfully

Look Ma! I'm on TV!: TV becomes real life—*The Truman Show*, live from *Pleasantville*

Lost Worlds: From *Brigadoon* to *The People That Time Forgot*

Lottery Winners: Ordinary schmoes get rich quick. Be careful what you wish for. . .

Louisiana: Southern state on the bayou; where the Mississippi ends and the party begins (at Mardi Gras time)

Lovable Loonies: Crazy, but not Norman Bates crazy; *Crazy People, Benny & Joon*

Lovers on the Lam: Couples commit crimes and find themselves on the run—*Badlands, Natural Born Killers, True Romance*

Mad Scientists: *The Brain That Wouldn't Die* spends an evening with *Frankenhooker*

Madrid: Capital of Spain, it has museums, great nightlife, and a pretty famous soccer team

Magic: Hocus pocus, often with evil intent

Magic Carpet Rides: *Aladdin* joins *Sinbad the Sailor* for *The Golden Voyage of Sinbad*

Mail-Order Brides: Shipping is okay, but I've got a problem with this handling charge!

Makeovers: When 'ugly' people become pretty by taking off glasses and putting on makeup, or letting their hair out of a bun

Making Friends: Using spare parts to create semi-articulate, reasonable facsimiles of people. *Young Frankenstein* meets *Frankenhooker*

Marriage Hell: Divorce is the preferred exit strategy, but an uncooperative spouse usually has other ideas

Marriages of Convenience: Will you marry me so I can inherit boatloads of cash or not get deported? Oh, how romantic!

Mars: The Red Planet, which gave us (supposedly) little green men and the Illudium-Q Explosive Space Modulator.

Martial Arts: Fists of Aluminum Foil; much head-kicking, rib-crunching, chopsocky action

Masseurs: People who knead people. . .

Matchmakers & Matchmaking: The people you gave money to to find the love of your life for you before the internet came along

Mathemagicians: Smarties with a good head for figures, but sometimes balancing the fine edge of sanity

May-December Romance: Older people meet younger people and the romantic sparks fly; *Harold and Maude* visit *Atlantic City*.

The Meaning of Life: The search for the elusive answer—*My Life, The Remains of the Day, Shadowlands*

Medieval Romps: Dirty peasants, deodorized and glorified kings and queens, splendid knights in shining armor, and one for all and all for one

Meltdown: Or how I learned to stop worrying and love the bomb; also bad wiring at local nuclear plants

Memphis: The other city in Tennessee; Elvis' home

Men in Prison: Working on a chain gang; what we have here is a failure to communicate

Mental Hospitals: Storage area for those not on speaking terms with Mr. Reality

Mental Retardation: *Bill, Charly*, Dominick, Lenny, Raymond (definitely)

Mercenaries: *Dogs of War* who like the killin' if they get paid enough

Mermaids: Half woman, half fish, alright! *The Little Mermaid* makes a big *Splash*

Metamorphosis: Ch-ch-ch-changes—From *The Fly* to *Wolf*

Meteors, Asteroids & Comets: Chunks of stuff wizzing through space, sometimes they land and cause problems

Mexico: *South of Santa Fe* and *Against All Odds*

Miami: Extremely warm coastal city in southern Florida

Michigan: The Great Lakes State, home to Jeff Daniels, Motown, the U.P., breakfast cereal, and *VideoHound!*

Middle East: Desert fare and camel close-ups ranging from *Ishtar* to *Lawrence of Arabia* to *The Jewel of the Nile*

Midlife Crisis: The point in a man's life when he trades in his car and wife for a newer, faster model. Neither decision ends well, usually

Military—Air Force: Flyboys fight America's aerial battles

Military—Army: GIs, Grunts, Dogfaces

Military Comedy: Marching to a different drummer, including *Stripes, M*A*S*H* and *No Time for Sergeants*

Military Crimes & Trials: Courtroom drama in the Armed Forces; *A Few Good Men* didn't follow the *Rules of Engagement* on their *Paths to Glory*

Military—Foreign: Armed forces of other nations are the focus

Military—Marines: Jarheads. The first ones in and the last ones out.

Military—Navy: Fighting on the high seas and in the air

Military Romance: One or both of the lovebirds are in the military

Military School: Kids get sent there to learn discipline, the art of war, and how to march in a straight line. Sometimes they learn too well and take over (*Taps*)

Military Westerns: Here comes the cavalry! Occasionally, *They Died with Their Boots On*

Milwaukee: Wisconsin home of beer, brats, the Brewers, Bucks, and lots and lots of snow

Miners & Mining: Helmets with the little flashlights are nifty; *Matewan* and *McCabe & Mrs. Miller*

Minnesota: Northern state that makes Michigan seem like the tropics. Home of the Twin cities and Prince, eh?

Missing Persons: People who disappear for a variety of reasons, sometimes because other people have taken them away

Missionaries: On a mission from God to save native populations

Mistaken Identity: You mean to say you're not the King of France?

Mockumentary: Movies in which actors pretend to be real people being followed around by fake documentary crews that are actually real filmmaking crews; *This is Spinal Tap*'s genre, and they're still *Best in Show* at it.

Model Citizens: Fashion and models are the center of attention—but isn't that the point? *Looker, Gia, Unzipped, Ready to Wear*

Modern Cowboys: Fun-lovin' rascals adept at riding horses through busy city streets or with a yen to experience mid-life crisis by doing a rodeo

Modern Shakespeare: The Bard's stories are brought into modern times, sometimes with his dialogue intact, sometimes re-written for contemporary ears.

Monkeyshines: Critters from the jungle, sometimes cute and fluffy, often wreaking havoc—*Congo, Monkey Trouble, Outbreak*

Monks: Of the Catholic-Friar-Tuck, Tibetan-Buddhist and *Bulletproof* varieties

Monster Moms: Loving on the outside, evil on the inside—*Mommie Dearest, Serial Mom*

Monster Yuks: Monster movies where the creatures are more funny, or cuddly, than scary

Montana: Northern plains state, home to wide-open spaces and the occasional wide-eyed loon living on a 0dquo;compound0dquo;

Monte Carlo/Monaco: European playgrounds of the rich, famous, and occasional suave secret agent

Montreal: Cosmopolitan city of francophones currently in Canada

Moonshiners: Distillers of illegal whiskey, in all its redneck forms. Mmmmm, corn squeezins!

Mormons: Religious sect headquartered in Utah; they're big on knocking on strangers' doors, polygamy, and *Reservoir Dogs* wardrobes

Morticians/Undertakers: The people who staff funeral homes. Generally creepier in the movies than they are in real life

Moscow: City in Russia (the country formerly known as USSR) that has the Kremlin and Lenin's corpse

Moscow Mafia: The Russian Mob

Motor Vehicle Dept.: *Chitty Chitty Bang Bang* at the *Car Wash*, plus *Tucker, Herbie*, and the *Repo Man*

Motorcycles: Two-wheeled transportation with a powerful motor strapped to it. Made Steve McQueen, Marlon Brando, and Peter Fonda even cooler than they already were.

Mountaineering: *Cliffhangers*

Mummies: Dead guys with leather-like skin, often wrapped in sheets

Museums: Big buildings that contain old paintings, sculptures, treasures. . .and the occasional ancient man-eating beastie

Musical Comedy: Laughter, singing, and dancing

Musical Drama: Singing and dancing, less laughter, more tension

Musical Fantasy: Singing and dancing in a figment of someone's imagination

Mutiny: Gang of disgruntled sailors takes over the ship

Mythology: Tales of the ancient gods and goddesses, and how they liked messing with us mewre mortals

Nannies & Governesses: Musically-inclined women raise kids for rich people too busy to do it themselves

Nashville: Tennessee city that country music and Robert Altman made famous

Nashville Narratives: *Honkytonk Man* elopes with the *Coal Miner's Daughter*

National Guard: Branch of the military that goes where they're needed most. Sometimes it's natural disasters in their own back yard, sometimes it's a tense social situation where order is needed, sometimes it's a patch of desert thousands of miles away

Native America: Dancing with the wolves on *Pow Wow Highway*

Nazis & Other Paramilitary Slugs: *The Boys from Brazil* and *The Dirty Dozen* plus SS she-wolf *Ilsa* and modern David Duke adaptations

Near-Death Experiences: Brushes with the Reaper, usually resulting in some extra powers upon the victim's return

Negative Utopia: Things seemed so perfect until. . .

Netherlands: Not to be confused with the nether regions, which are often prominently displayed in some areas of Amsterdam.

New Jersey Butt of too many New Yorkers' jokes; home of The Chairman, The Boss, The Trump, and Jay & Silent Bob

New Orleans: City in Louisiana that boasts the Mardi Gras and cajun cookin'

New Year's Eve: Stay up late, count down with Dick Clark, drink too much, greet the New Year feeling like. . .

New York, New York: It's a hell of a town. . .

Newlyweds: Ah, the first year of marriage; the honeymoon, settling into your new life together, hanging out with Bob Eubanks. . .

News at 11: Broadcast 0dquo;journalism0dquo;; in which some local hairdo spends most of a half-hour telling you what he's gonna tell you, and the rest of the time scaring the bejeezus outta ya

Niagara Falls: Little upstate New York border town where honeymooners and barrel riders gather. Oh yeah, they have some water thing there, too. . .

Nice Mice: Cute anthropomorphic or cartoon rodents, rather than the disease-carrying vermin variety

Nightclubs: *Casablanca*, of course

9/11: Films dealing with the events and aftermath of that day

Ninjas: Stealthy martial arts assassins in pajamas

No-Exit Motel: Sleazy motels with extremely lenient late-checkout policies

Not-So-True Identity: People pass themselves off as something else; *Soul Man, Gentleman's Agreement*

Nuns & Priests: Collars and habits; *Agnes of God, The Cardinal, Going My Way, Nuns on the Run, Sister Act*

Nuclear Energy: Keeping the lights on by splitting some atoms. Doesn't always have a happy outcome

Nuns With Guns: Sister

* = new to this edition

Mary Margaret has traded up from the ol' yardstick. Better practice that penmanship.

Nursploitation!: *Night Call Nurses* offer *Tender Loving Care* in *The Hospital of Terror*

Obsessive Love: You like me. You really, really, *really* like me.

Occult: Witches, warlocks, devil worshippers, spell makers, spell breakers, haunted houses, and so on

Office Surprise: Office supplies used as weapons

Ohio: Midwestern Rust Belt state most famous for being really flat.

Oldest Profession: It's not accounting

The Olympics: *Chariots of Fire* and other tales of athletic discipline

On the Rocks: Alcoholism, alcohol, barflies, moonshining, Prohibition—*Arthur, Days of Wine and Roses, Papa's Delicate Condition, My Favorite Year*

One Last Job: Crooks just wanna retire to a warm climate and enjoy their ill-gotten booty, but someone is always pullin' 'em back in!

Only the Lonely: 50 ways to play solitaire—*The Cemetery Club, The Heart Is a Lonely Hunter, Sleepless in Seattle*

Opera: Shouting in a melodic way while in costume

Orchestra Conductors: Those guys who stand in front of the musicians and wave thir little sticks around. Probably not a lot of action movies here

Order in the Court: Courtroom tales, including *The Accused, And Justice for All, A Few Good Men, Witness for the Prosecution*

Organ Transplants: Taking parts from one body that doesn't need 'em anymore and putting 'em into a body that does.

Organized Crime: Gangsters with Franklin Planners

Otherwise Engaged: Couple buys ring, sets date, and gets ready to march down the aisle, sometimes with a new fiancee—*Moonstruck, Only You, Sleepless in Seattle*

Out of Order: Movies in which the director's vision was not chronologically 20/20. Think *Memento* or any Quentin Tarantino movie

Out of This World Sex: Doin' the intergalactic nasty, usually with unfortunate results for earthlings

Pacific Islands: Hawaii, Tahiti, Philippines, etc.

Paperboys: Kids who toss papers everywhere but your front porch

Parades & Festivals: *Animal House* and *Ferris Bueller's Day Off*

Paradise Gone Awry: You'd think it'd be perfect, but you'd be mistaken

Parallel Universes: There's a whole other world out there—*Cool World, Who Framed Roger Rabbit?*

Paramedics: Part doctor, part fireman, part delivery driver. Cool!

Pardners: Buddies in the Old West; Butch & Sundance, Wyatt Earp & Doc Holliday, the guys from *Silverado*

Parenthood: Moms, dads, substitutes—*Dutch, Ma Barker's Killer Brood, Father of the Bride, Three Men and a Baby, Yours, Mine, and Ours, Raising Arizona*

Paris: Ze city in France with rude occupants and ze Eiffel Tower

Party Hell: *Psycho Girls* have fun at a sleepover until *Monsters Crash the Pajama Party* and it becomes *The Slumber Party Massacre*

Patriotism & Paranoia: Run the flag up the pole and salute it—Rambo, Patton, Norris, etc.

Peace: *Friendly Persuasion, Gandhi*

Peculiar Partners: Odd pairings, usually in buddy cop movies. *Stop, Or My Mom Will Shoot!* and any dog-as-a-cop movie.

Pen Pals: Strangers correspond through the mail (or cyberspace) and become friends. . .or sometimes more

Penguins: Cute waddling flightless birds from Antarctica in tuxedos

Period Piece: Costume epics or evocative of a certain time and place; now divided into eras for your time traveling pleasure

- **15th Century**—*Braveheart* and other tales of the end of the Middle Ages
- **16th Century**—The Renaissance; rebirth of culture, art, science
- **17th Century**—The Enlightenment, or Age of Reason
- **18th Century**—Revolutions all over the place
- **19th Century**—more war, plus the Industrial Revolution
- **20th Century**—Epics that span more than one decade
- **1900s**—the decade that began the now-completed 20th century
- **1910s**—stories not involving World War I
- **1920s**—Roaring '20s, Age of Jazz, Prohibition, Babe Ruth
- **1930s**—stories not involving the Depression
- **1940s**—stories not involving World War II
- **1950s**—Rock 'n' Roll, Elvis, Eisenhower, McCarthyism, Civil Rights movement begins
- **1960s**—assassinations, hippies, Vietnam, along with more mundane concerns
- **1970s**—bad clothes, Watergate, disco, Elvis dies. . .let's just forget this decade happened
- **1980s**—Reagan, Iran-Contra, John Hughes angst-fests, big hair, and greed

Persian Gulf War: Smart bombs away

Philadelphia: Famous Pennsylvania city that's home to *Rocky*, the Liberty Bell, cheesesteaks, and M. Night Shyamalan films

Phobias!: Ee-eeeeeeeeeeeeeek!

Phone Sex: Is it really the next best thing to being there?

Phone Terror: *Don't Answer the Phone*

Physical Problems: *My Left Foot, Coming Home, The Elephant Man, The Other Side of the Mountain, Untamed Heart, The Waterdance*

Pigs: Loveable swine—*Gordy, Babe the Gallant Pig*

Pirates: Avast, ye scurvy dogs! *Captain Blood* drops in on *Treasure Island*

Pittsburgh: City in western Pennsylvania, home of sports teams fond of the colors black and yellow.

Plastic Surgery: Using surgery to give you what nature didn't, or to take away some of the unwanted stuff with which nature was overly generous

Poetry: Not exactly a booming category, but think of *Poetic Justice*

Poisons: *Arsenic and Old Lace* and *D.O.A.*

Poker: Card game where fortunes, property, wives, etc can be won or lost in a myriad of ways: Texas Hold 'em; Stud, Draw (particularly in the Old West)

Police Detectives: They get paid to bust open the big cases amid wild car chases and gunplay.

Politics: *Bob Roberts, Mandela, Whoops Apocalypse*

Polygamy: I now pronounce you man and wife, and wife. . .and wife. You may kiss the brides

Pool: *The Hustler*

Pornography: *Hardcore, Body Double*

Portland (Oregon, not Maine): Northwestern city, home to lots of trees and rain, beautiful scenery, and the Trailblazers

Possession: Supposedly it's 9/10ths of the law, but in these movies it's 9/10ths of the plot when spirits or demons try to move into a body that's already occupied

Post Apocalypse: No more convenience stores

Postwar: After effects of war, generally WWI or WWII but sometimes the Civil War, the War of 1812, the Revolutionary War, and the Ohio Automobile Dealers War

POW/MIA: Captured by the enemy

Pregnant Men: Ahh-nuld fails the *Rabbit Test*

Pregnant Pauses: Humorous takes on pregnancy and birth—*Nine Months, She's Having a Baby*

Prep School: Where the children of the elite meet to learn how to be upper-crusty

Presidency: Mr. Lincoln, *JFK*, LBJ, FDR, and, of course, *Dave*

Price of Fame: What goes up. . .

Prison Breaks: Getting out of the big house before your sentence is up without the aid of the parole board

Private Eyes: There's no such thing as a simple little case. . .

Prohibition Gangs: The bootleggers and criminals who ran the booze, gambling, prostitution, and corruption of the Roaring 20s.

Prom: A night you'll always remember. . .which isn't necessarily a good thing. Right, *Carrie*?

Protests: Hell no, we won't go (to bad movies)! Make popcorn, not war!

Psychic Abilities: I see dead people! Or the future, or read minds, or have telekenesis. . .

Psychotics/Sociopaths: *Killer Inside Me, Reservoir Dogs, The Stepfather*

Publicists: People who suck up to the press so celebrities don't have to

Puerto Rico: Caribbean island that could become the 51st state

Punk Rock: Anarchic semi-musical revolution of the late 70s, where the message (if you could decipher it) was more important that the melody. Way, way more important.

Puppets: Usually with strings, but also muppets

Rabbis: Jewish clergy

Rabbits: *Harvey* has a *Fatal Attraction* for the *Nasty Rabbit*

Raccoons: Furry little scavengers who remembered to wear their masks when they went to pull a heist on your garbage.

Race Against Time: Tick, tock, tick, tock—*China Syndrome, Lorenzo's Oil*

Radio: Over the airwaves—*Choose Me, The Fisher King, Radio Days, Sleepless in Seattle*

Rags to Riches: Grit, determination, and hustling (or just pure dumb luck) lead to fortune—*Trading Places, Working Girls*

Rape: Victims and often their revenge

Rats!: Rodent critters who obviously went with a different PR firm than their mouse cousins

Real Estate: Everyone's gotta live somewhere, and most want to live on land they own. That's where agents, scams, and deals come in

REALLY Bad TV: When TV sucks. . .you into another dimension. How can there be anything good on when your TV is possessed?

Rebel With a Cause: Bucking the establishment for a reason

Rebel Without a Cause: Bucking the establishment just because it's the establishment

The Red Cross: Organization that helps those in need of blood, disaster relief, and war relief; also monitors treatment of POWs

Red Scare: Cold War and Communism—*The Commies Are Coming, The Commies Are Coming, Reds*

Reefer Madness: Tales of the demon weed.

Reggae: Jamaican musical style that fits well with the island's laid-back vibe and is also strangely apropos for the preceding category

Rehab: Drying out, sobering up. . .walking around in bathrobes.

Reincarnation: Why is everyone somebody famous in a past life?

Religion: *Witness, The Last Temptation of Christ*

Religious Epics: Charlton Heston parts the Red Sea—religion on a really big scale

Renegade Body Parts: Hands, fingers, eyes, brains with a life of their own

Rent-a-Cop: Security guys who sit or stand at the entrance to your favorite bank, grocery store, warehouse, clothing store, etc. Sometimes they are collateral damage in heists flicks, sometimes they are (usually imbalanced) proagonaists in action-comedies.

Repressed Men: Often British (*see* Anthony Hopkins or Hugh Grant), always with plenty of stiffness in upper lip and little elsewhere

Rescue Missions: I'll save you—*The Searcher, Free Willy*

Rescue Missions Involving Time Travel: I'll save you in another dimension—*Back to the Future*

The Resistance: WWII rebels with an anti-Nazi cause

Reunited: Usually after a long absence caused by extreme circumstances

Revolutionary War: Fought over tea

Rio: As in de Janeiro—that swingin' South American party town.

A River Runs Through the Plot: Long, sometimes winding and narrow body of water the main characters may have to get over, around, through or travel down, or fish in to get to the end of the story

Road Trip: Escapism courtesy of two- and four-wheel vehicles—*Easy Rider, Coupe de Ville, Pee Wee's Big Adventure, Wild at Heart*

Robots/Androids: Mechanical but fascinating, like the one Tom replaced Katie with; *Blade Runner* and *The Terminator*

Rock Flicks: Movies about real or made up rockers, starring rock stars, or featuring bands in concert; *Eddie & the Cruisers, The Last Waltz, Almost Famous*

Rodeos: Rope tricks with steers

Rogue Cops: Corruption in the PD, cops on the take, etc. Usually, *Internal Affairs* gets involved

Role Reversal: Vice versa; empathy test—*Freaky Friday, My Fair Lady, Switch, Soul Man*

Roller Skating: Strap some wheels to your feet and away you go, either disco dancing, exercising, racing, or chasing roadrunners

Romantic Adventures: Love among the chases and explosions—*The African Queen, Romancing the Stone*

Romantic Mystery: Like there's a bigger mystery than the opposite sex??

Romantic Triangles: Three where there's only room for two—*The Age of Innocence, Casablanca, Three of Hearts*

Rome—Ancient Emperors ran the show, feeding Christians to the lions, using V for U, having orgies, and throwing up on purpose. . .those were the days!

Rome—Modern: Capital city of Italy. The Pope has a little place there

Roommates from Hell: Sometimes they won't do the dishes, sometimes they're homicidal—*Single White Female*

Royalty: Emperors, kings, queens, princes, princesses, crowns, scepters

Royalty, British: Emperors, kings, queens, etc in Merry Olde England

Royalty, French: Kings and queens who ran France when they didn't surrender to any foreigner who happened by

Royalty, Russian: Emperors, czars, and czarinas who ran things in Moscow till those mean old Bolsheviks showed up

Runaways: Kids leave home without permission, bad things usually ensue

Running: Jogging, panting, collapsing

Russia/USSR: Back in what used to be the USSR

Russian Revolution: 1917, when the Bolsheviks kicked out the Czar, set up the Soviet Union, and got Russia out of WWI

Rwanda: Troubled country in Africa being torn apart by war, poverty, and disease

Sail Away: Vessels on the water—*Mutiny on the Bounty, Erik the Viking, Mister Roberts*

St. Petersburg: The one in Russia, seat of the old monarchy. You wouldn't wanna have spring break here

Saints: *Bernadette, Saint Joan, A Time for Miracles*

Salespeople: Have I got a deal for you. . .

Samurai: Bodyguards to royalty and nobility in ancient Japan, sometimes they had to freelance

San Diego: Sunny (is there any other kind?) Southern California city close to Mexico

San Francisco: Set in the Northern California city known for hills and sourdough bread

Satanism: *Speak of the Devil*

Satire & Parody: Biting social commentary or genre spoofs, including *Being There, Airplane!, Down and Out in Beverly Hills, I'm Gonna Git You Sucka, Monty Python's The Meaning of Life, The Player*

Savannah: the city in Georgia, with the southern belles and the big social events

Savants: Half-minded geniuses; *Rain Man, Forrest Gump*

Scams, Stings & Cons: The hustle—*The Billionaire Boys Club, The Color of Money, A Fish Called Wanda, The Grifters, The Sting*

Scared 'Chuteless: Jumping out of airplanes without the proper equipment. Good candidates for a bad case of cement poisoning

School Daze: Education, school, and teachers, generally grammar school days—*Lean on Me, Dead Poet's Society, To Sir, with Love, Teachers*

Sci Fi Romance: Lookin' for love in space. And we're not just talkin' about Capt. Kirk makin' it with green chicks

Sci Fi Westerns: You ain't from around heah, is ya?

Science & Scientists: *Altered States, Darkman, Them, They, Son of Flubber, The Story of Louis Pasteur*

Scotland: Lush hills, thick brogues, kilts, bagpipes, and *Whiskey Galore*

Scotland Yard: British coppers oddly not located anywhere near Scotland.

Screwball Comedy: Snappy repartee between a man and a woman dealing with an impossibly silly situation

Scuba: Wet suits, including *The Abyss, Navy SEALS*

Sculptors: Artists who like to work with clay, rock, hammers, and chisels

Sea Disasters: We've sprung a leak—*The Poseidon Adventure*

Seattle: Showcases the city in Washington state where it rains a lot; the home of grunge rock

Second Chance: Another opportunity to set things right, fix mistakes, redeem yourself, or all of the above

Secret Service: Bodyguards to the First Family, they also investigate counterfeiting

Serial Killers: They just won't stop—*Henry: Portrait of a Serial Killer, The Rosary Murders*

Sex & Sexuality: Focus is on lust, for better or worse—*Alfie, Barbarella, Emmanuelle, Looking for Mr. Goodbar, Rambling Rose, She's Gotta Have It*

Sex on the Beach: Flashing the fish and getting sand in the darnedest places; the most famous couple was in *From Here to Eternity* and *Airplane!* lost no time making fun of them

Sexual Abuse: Victims and their stories—*Twin Peaks, Fire Walk with Me*

Sexual Harassment: When I say no, I mean it

Shipwrecked: Stranded on an island when your boat sinks

Shops & Shopping: When commerce at the mall is a major plot point.

Shore Leave: Sailors on vacation, usually with money in their pockets and women on their minds

Showbiz Comedies: Laughter behind the scenes in Hollywood or on Broadway

Showbiz Dramas: Tension behind the scenes in Hollywood or on Broadway

Showbiz Horror: Bloody mayhem or creepy goings-on behind the scenes in Hollywood or on Broadway

Showbiz Musicals: Singing and dancing behind the scenes in Hollywood or on Broadway

Showbiz Thrillers: Screaming behind the scenes in Hollywood or on Broadway

Shrinkage: People become very, very small. Honey, I Shrunk Rick Moranis's Career

Shrinks: Psychiatry or equivalent, with *The Prince of Tides, One Flew Over the Cuckoo's Nest*

Shutterbugs: Photographers and their pictures—*The Public Eye, The Eyes of Laura Mars, Peeping Tom*

Sibling Rivalry: Brothers and sisters fighting over. . .well, anything, but usually romance or parental affection or wealth.

Sieges/Standoffs: If you don't come out, we'll sit here and make sure you want to come out eventually, usually by cutting off all food, power, and contact with the outside world

Silent Films: No small talk/no big talk/no talk talk

Single Parents: Divorced or widowed, they're doing the work of two—and they're back in the dating scene, usually assisted by matchmaking kids

Singles: Not always swinging but still solidly unmarried—*About Last Night, Singles, When Harry Met Sally*

Skateboarding: Teens on wheels—*Gleaming the Cube*

Skating: Roller and ice, including *The Cutting Edge, Xanadu*

Skiing: Slap on a couple of waxed boards and off you go—*Downhill Racer, Swing-ing Ski Girls*

Skinheads: Nazi wannabes wreak havoc and cause trouble

Skydiving: Jumping from a plane with a polyester slip

Slapstick Comedy: Humor of the physical sort, including Abbott and Costello, the Marx Brothers, sports comedies, Ernest, Pink Panther, Home Alone, the Three Stooges

Slasher Flicks: Horror movies in which unsuspecting and promiscuous teens get sliced, diced, and julienned by knife, machete, drill, chainsaw, and/or farm implement-wielding maniacs

Slavery: *Roots, Spartacus*

Slice of Life: Moveis that highlights the everyday or quieter dramas of life, usually having to do with friendships, long-term romances, or family relationships.

Slob Comedy: Happily dumb comedies that provide plenty of laughs and quotes for adolescent boys of all ages. *Animal House, Stripes, Caddyshack* are the Holy Trinity

Small-Town Sheriffs: Think Sly in *Cop Land*, or Buford Pusser of *Walking Tall* fame

Smuggler's Blues: Making, transporting, and selling the drugs. Don't *Blow* your cool in the *Traffic*.

Snakes: Slithering creatures who frighten many—*Raiders of the Lost Ark*

Sniper: Military (and sometimes not) sharpshooters who can kill from a distance

Snowboarding: Kinda like skiing, except it's one big board attached to your feet, instead of two skinny ones. Oh, and no poles

Soccer: Known as football outside of the USA—*Victory, Ladybugs*

Softball: Baseball-like sport played with a larger ball, aluminum bats, beer, and much enthusiasm by guys with bad knees.

South America: Right below North America—*Aguirre, the Wrath of God, The Mission*

Southern Belles: Southern gals ooze charm—*Blaze, Driving Miss Daisy, Steel Magnolias*

Space Operas: Going where no spam has gone before—*Alien, Star Trek, 2001: A Space Odyssey, Apollo 13*

Spaghetti Western: Clint with a squint, *A Fistful of Dollars, My Name is Nobody, Once Upon a Time in the West*

Spain: Southern European country that's been home to conquerors, explorers, Moors, and Antonio Banderas

Spanish Civil War: Franco and the Fascists vs. the defenders of the newly-elected Socialist government. A preview of how WWII would be fought

Spiders: Eight-legged creepy crawlies spinning their webs, sometimes in the service of cartoon pigs

Spies & Espionage: Trench coats, dark glasses, Bond, *North by Northwest*

Sports Comedies: Humorous athletic tales, generally not based on a true story

Sports Documentaries: Non-fiction examinations of athletes and the games they play

Sports Dramas: Intense athletic tales, often based on a true story

Sports Romance: One or both of the lovebirds is a jock

Spring Break: Colleges and high schools empty their kids into the streets of Florida, Mexico and other exotic locales, where they search for beer and sex. . .if we remember correctly

Spy Kids: Agents with a safe house on Sesame Street

Stagestruck: Stories of the theatre; *Broadway Melody* sung at the *Stage Door* by *The Dolly Sisters*

Stalked: No, I do not want to switch to MCI

Star Gazing: Not Hollywood stars, astrology/astronomy type stars

Stay-at-Home Dads: *Mr. Mom* takes care of the kids while Mom goes to the office. . .or just goes

Stepparents: New spouse hiding either alien origins or sociopathic tendencies greets existing clan

Stewardesses: *Three Guys Named Mike* go to *Stewardess School* and meet *Blazing Stewardesses*

Storytelling: *Amazing Stories, Grim Prairie Tales*

Strained Suburbia: Neighborhood is not what it seems—*Dennis the Menace, Neighbors, Edward Scissorhands*

Strippers: Take it off, take it all off

Struggling Artists: It's hard not to struggle when your work only becomes valuable after you're dead

Struggling Musicians: Talented, but still reaching for the top

Stuntmen: Guys (and gals) paid to take the fall (and punch, and crash) for the stars

Stupid Is. . .: Stupidity on purpose—*Billy Madison, Dumb and Dumber*, or dumbness as a plot device—*Being There, Forrest Gump*

Submarines: Deep sea diving; *Das Boot, Up Periscope, Run Silent, Run Deep, Hunt for Red October*

Subways: A train for shorter trips—*Speed, The Taking of Pelham One Two Three*

Suicide: Self-inflicted premature ends—*The Big Chill, Scent of a Woman, Romeo and Juliet*

Summer Camp: Where children go to misbehave, including *Meatballs* and *Sleepaway Camp*

Super Heroes: Men and women of extraordinary strength and abilities wearing silly- looking costumes

Supernatural Comedies: *Beetlejuice* marries *She-Devil* and they take *The Ghost Train* to their *Haunted Honeymoon*

Supernatural Horror: Forces from beyond terrorize those who are here

Supernatural Martial Arts: Kung fu *From Beyond the Grave*

Supernatural Westerns: Forces from beyond terrorize cowboys in the Old West

Surfing: Awesome wave, dude! *Mad Wax, The Surf Movie, Surf Nazis Must Die, Endless Summer*

Survival: *Alive, The Bridge over the River Kwai, Testament*

Suspended Animation: Frozen in time—*Coma, Late for Dinner*

Swashbucklers: Crossed swords and rope swinging, including *Robin Hood*, Zorro, various Musketeers, *Captain Blood, The Three Amigos*

Swimming: Ranging from *Gremlins* to *Jaws* to *The Swimmer* to *Cocoon*

Swingers: *Bob & Carol & Ted & Alice* try *Group Marriage* and Carol and Alice become *Swinging Wives*

Sword & Sandal: *See* Arnold Schwarzenegger's early career

Sydney: Big Aussie city; recent site of Olympic glory

Tale of the Tape: Videocassettes or audiocassettes are important plot devices. . .so remember to rewind

Talking Animals: *Dr. Doolittle* treats *Babe*

Tanks: Armored, heavily armed difference-makers that roll over anything and symbolized the mechanization of war.

Tattoos: *The Illustrated Man* visits *Cape Fear* to do battle with *Cyber Bandits*

Taxing Situations: The IRS comes looking for the gummint's cut of the action. Gol' dang revenooers!

Technicolor Yawn: What goes down sometimes comes back up—*The Exorcist, Parenthood, Monty Python's Meaning of Life*

Technology—Rampant: Machines that wreak havoc—*Metropolis, Death Ray 2000, Blade Runner*

Teen Adventure: Teenagers move into the action-adventure genre and create their own brand of havoc

Teen Comedy: Teenagers yuk it up in school or out. Usually has a lot to do with sex, bodily functions, and defying authority (preferably all three at once)

Teen Drama: Kinda redundant. Teenagers deal with VERY IMPORTANT issues, or stuff that seems that way at the time, anyway.

Teen Horror: Horror flicks where the body count is skewered toward the 15-19 demographic (isn't that pretty much all of 'em?)

Teen Musicals: Teens sing and dance, probably while texting their BFF. OMG!

Teen Romance: Teenagers falling in love, or lust

Teen Sci fi/fantasy: Teenagers encounter unexplainable phenomena or weird happenings that don't involve their own hormones

Televangelists: Salesmen on late-night or Sunday morning TV with plastic hair and shiny suits who want to help you get to heaven. . .if you have the cash

Tennis: Anyone?

Terminal Confusion: Luggage gets mixed up at the airport, bus station, etc. Trouble usually follows

Terminal Illness: Someone's gonna die a tragic death from a horrible disease, but probably not before falling in love or doing something inspirational. Usually not considered comedy premise

Terror in Tall Buildings: From *Die Hard* to *Speed* to *The Towering Inferno*

Terrorism: Love affairs with hidden bombs

** = new to this edition*

Texas: Southern state that once was a country. . .and they never let anyone forget it. Apparently everything is bigger there.

Thanksgiving: Huge dinner, football, familial angst, turkey coma, Christmas shopping may now commence

There Goes the Neighborhood: Those nice new neighbors turn out out to be psychos, terrorists, aliens, or worse. . .tool borrowers!

The Third Degree: Where were you on the night of. . .

This Is My Life: Autobiographies starring the subject—Muhammed Ali in *The Greatest*, Audie Murphy goes *To Hell and Back*

This Is Your Life: Biography and autobiography, including *The Babe Ruth Story, Amazing Howard Hughes, Amadeus, Catherine the Great, Great Balls of Fire, Raging Bull, What's Love Got to Do With It?*

3-D Flicks: Bring your special glasses

Thumbs Up: Hitchin' a ride—*Even Cowgirls Get the Blues, The Hitcher*

Tibet: So I says 0dquo;Hey, Lama, how's about a little somethin' for the effort. . .0dquo;

Tijuana: City in Mexico that holds a special allure for Americans looking for various flavors of debauchery

Time Travel: Fast forward or reverse with Bill and Ted, *Dr. Who, Back to the Future,* and *Peggy Sue Got Married*

Time Warped: You wake up in an era not your own; *Austin Powers*, the Bradys and the Cleavers coping with the '90s

Titanic: The unsinkable ship that hit an iceberg its first time out. . .and sunk. It was in all the papers

To the Moon!: *Apollo 13, From the Earth to the Moon*

Tokyo: Crowded city in Japan terrorized by Godzilla

Torn in Two (or More): *Sybil* and *Dr. Jekyll and Mr. Hyde* are *Raising Cain* leading *Separate Lives* on the *Edge of Sanity*

Toronto: Big city in Canada where they don't make you speak French. Home of Skydome and the Hockey Hall of Fame

Toys: *Babes in Toyland, The Toy, Toys*

Trailer Parks: Tornado magnets in which portable homes not on wheels congregate

Trains: Rhythm of the clackity clack—*Romance on the Orient Express, Throw Momma from the Train, Running Scared, The Silver Streak*

Trapped with a Killer!: And there's no escape—*Dead Calm, Misery, The Shining*

Treasure Hunt: Looking for hidden riches—*Klondike Fever, Treasure of Sierra Madre, Romancing the Stone*

Trees & Forests: Can't see one for the other, that wilderness paradox—includes *Mr. Sycamore* and *The Wizard of Oz*

Triads: Chinese organized crime outfit. Chow-Yun Fat is always shooting it out with 'em in John Woo flicks

True Crime: Based on fact, including *The Boston Strangler, The Executioner's Song, Helter Skelter*

True Stories: Approximations of real-life events often significantly fictionalized for the screen, including *All The President's Men, Chariots of Fire, Cry Freedom, Heart Like a Wheel, The Killing Fields, Silkwood*

Twins: *Double Trouble, Double Vision, Mirror Images*

Twister!: The big wind not caused by Mexican food that picks up heavy things (houses, cows, trucks) and deposits them elsewhere

Under My Skin: People (or cartoon characters) get inside a guy's pelt, and crawl around for a little while

Undercover Cops: Cops pretend they're bad guys to catch more bad guys, but sometimes they get *In Too Deep*

Unexplained Phenomena: No apparent reason for an event

Unhappy Meals Dining experience is marred by familial angst, unfortunate incidents, or people keeling over dead

Unhealthy Romance: People fall in love with each other before (or after) one of them gets very sick.

U.S. Marshals: Law enforcement branch that transports prisoners, hunts down fugitives, and in the Old West, handled the showdown duties

Up All Night: Movie takes place mostly after the sun goes down and *Before Sunrise*

Urban Comedy: Taking the *Soul Plane* to the *Car Wash*, and then to the *Barbershop*. Then maybe head to *The Cookout. Are We There Yet?*

Urban Drama: *American Me* to *Boyz N the Hood* to *Grand Canyon* to *Zebrahead*

Urban Gangstas: Gangs fight it out for their piece of the mean streets of the inner city; *Colors, New Jack City*

Urban Legends: No, really! It totally happened to my cousin's neighbor's sister's hairdresser!

The USO: Entertained the troops through two world wars and a variety of police actions—with Bob Hope usually leading the way

Vacation Hell: When the annual two-week respite from work goes horribly wrong. Usually starts with someone asking the skeevy gas station attendant for directions

Vacations: Getting away from it all, yet bringing the family.

Vampire Babes: Blood sucking dames—*The Brides of Dracula*

Vampire Spoof: Comedic blood suckers, including *Buffy, Andy Warhol's Dracula, Dracula Sucks*

Vampires: More serious vein of blood sucking varmint, including *Dracula* in his many manifestations

Vaudeville: Low-tech form of popular entertainment that employed comedians before radio, TV, comedy clubs, and the internets came along.

Venice: Italian city of gondolas

Veterans: Retired fighting men (and women)—*Alamo Bay* to *Who'll Stop the Rain*

Veterinarians: Animal doctors. Plasma! Dog Plasma!

Videogames Interactive digital games that long ago replaced human interacton and eye contact as the preferred method of home entertainment for kids and geeks all over the world

Vietnam War: *Platoon, Hamburger Hill, Apocalypse Now, Good Morning, Vietnam*

Vigilantes: Individuals take the law into their own hands—*Death Wish, The Outlaw Josey Wales*

Vikings: Rowdy guys with horns on their hats who like boat trips. . .Not those guys, the ones from Scandinavia!

Virtual Reality: High-tech video game that seems real. . .to computer geeks

Viva Las Vegas!: Celebrating America's tackiest city—*Honeymoon in Vegas, Sister Act*

Volcanoes: Mountain blowing off steam, including *Joe Versus the Volcano*

Volleyball: *Side Out* used to be the only one till we remembered the bare-chested boys from *Top Gun*

Voodoo: From *Angel Heart* to *How to Stuff a Wild Bikini* to *Weekend at Bernie's 2*

Vote for Me!: Political campaigns for various offices, from student council (*Election*) to U.S. President (*The Candidate*)

Wagon Train: Westward, Ho! Prairie Schooners play a big part in Westerns. . .such as getting people to the West

Waitresses: *Alice Doesn't Live Here Anymore*, she went to *Atlantic City* to get some *Mystic Pizza*

Wall Street: The financial capital of the U.S., makers of vast sums of money and occasional global financial crises

War Between the Sexes: Men and women battle for supremacy—*It Happened One Night, The King and I, He Said, She Said, Romancing the Stone, When Harry Met Sally, The War of the Roses, Thelma & Louise*

War Brides: Soldier meets girl and they get hitched, then he bring her home to his mother country

War, General: Generally any conflict that defies other classification—*The Alamo, Gunga Din, The Last of the Mohicans*

Weathermen: Guys on the news who stand in front of a map and 0dquo;predict0dquo; whether or not it will rain. Isn't there always a 50% chance of rain? Either it'll rain or it won't

Wedding Bells: Memorable weddings; *Father of the Bride, Four Weddings and a Funeral, Sixteen Candles, The Wedding*

Wedding Hell: Horror-filled or anxiety-ridden weddings; *The Blood Spattered Bride, The Brides Wore Blood, The Graduate, Wedding Banquet*

Werewolves: Full moon wonders, like *Wolf*

West Virginia: Mountainous state that's home to two horror movie franchises, a few country music stars, coal mining, Hatfields, and McCoys.

Western Comedy: Gags and horses—*Ballad of Cable Hogue, Blazing Saddles, Rancho Deluxe, Support Your Local Sheriff*

Westerns: Cowboys, cowgirls, horses and jingle jangling spurs on the frontier

Westrogens: The Old West through women's eyes

Whales: Really big seafaring mammals. It's best to just stay out of their way. . .Just ask *Pinocchio*

White Slavery: People get kidnapped or tricked into lives of involuntary servitude (usually sexual).

Whitewater Rafting: Wild ride down a raging river, often in the company of a psycho

Widows & Widowers: The one who's left when a spouse dies; *Dragonfly, Sleepless in Seattle*

Wild Kingdom: Animals on their own and interacting with confused humans, including *The Bear, Dumbo, Born Free, Free Willy, Never Cry Wolf*

Wilderness: More trees than a forest, plus wild critters—*The Life and Times of Grizzly Adams*

Wine & Vinyards: Spirits from the grape, and the places the grapes came from

Wisconsin: Chilly northern state, makers of beer and dairy products, land of Cheeseheads.

Witchcraft: From *Hocus Pocus* to *Three Sovereigns for Sarah* to *The Wizard of Oz*

Witness Protection Program: Rat out your 0dquo;associates,0dquo; get a new identity

Wolves: Your dog's out-of-control cousin. Usually the heavy in fairy tales

Women Cops: Female officers of the law

Women in Prison: The things that go on in the big doll house

Women in War: Nurses, WACs, WAVES, USO performers, sometimes prisoners—they also served. . .

Wonder Women: *Attack of the 50-Foot Woman, Ripley, La Femme Nikita, Supergirl*

Words Come to Life: Characters literally jump off the page

Workin' for a Livin': Focuses on working stiffs and their jobs

World War I: The First Big One, including *African Queen, Gallipoli, Grand Illusion*

World War I Spies: Espionage in the Great War. Think *Mata Hari*

World War II: The Last Big One, including *A Bridge Too Far, Guadalcanal Diary, The Guns of Navarone, Hope and Glory, Memphis Belle, Tora! Tora! Tora!*

World War II Spies: British and American agents who used stealth and deception to fight the Nazis

Wrestling: Choreographed sport involving men and women—*No Holds Barred, All the Marbles, Wrestling Women vs. the Aztec Ape*

Writers: Tortured souls who put pen to paper when they're not putting bottle to lips. Does not include the ink-stained wretches of the journalistic trade

Wrong Side of the Tracks: Often involves relationship with someone on the right side—*Cannery Row, The Flamingo Kid, Pretty in Pink, White Palace*

Yakuza: Japanese version of the Mafia, very organized crime

Yoga: Exercise you do sitting in one place that makes you all bendy

You Are Getting Sleepy!: Hypnosis, its practitioners, and effects, including glazed looks and strange behavior. . .Right, Katie, er, Kate?

You Big Dummy!: Ventriloquists have wooden dolls do their talking (or killing) for them

You Lose, You Die: Sports goes nuts—only the winner survives; *Arena, Rollerball, Tron*

Yuppie Nightmares: Young adults find best-laid plans for attaining wealth and privilege going astray—*Baby Boom, Desperately Seeking Susan, The Mighty Ducks, Pacific Heights, Something Wild, Wall Street*

Ziegfeld Follies: The big thing in entertainment before there was the interwebs. . .or TV. . .or movies. . .or radio

Zombie Soldiers: Recently undead in the army—*They Saved Hitler's Brain*

Zombies: Recently undead everywhere—*I Walked with a Zombie, Night of the Living Dead*

Category Index

The Category Index includes subject terms ranging from straight genre descriptions (Crime Drama, Romantic Comedy, etc.) to more off-the-wall themes (Nuns with Guns, Eyeballs!). These terms can help you identify unifying themes (Baseball, Heists), settings (Miami, Period Piece: 1950s), events (The Great Depression, World War II), occupations (Clowns, Police Detectives, Doctors & Nurses), or suddenly animate objects (Killer Appliances, Killer Cars). Category definitions and cross-references precede the index; category terms are listed alphabetically. Release year is now included in this index. **A tipped triangle indicates a video rated three bones or higher.**

ABBA-ca-da-bra

The Adventures of Priscilla, Queen of the Desert '94 ▸
Mamma Mia! '08
Muriel's Wedding '94 ▸

Abortion

After Tiller '13 ▸
Balzac and the Little Chinese Seamstress '02
The Carey Treatment '72
Chance at Heaven '33
Choices '86
The Cider House Rules '99 ▸
Citizen Ruth '96
The Crime of Father Amaro '02 ▸
Daddy's Gone A-Hunting '69 ▸
The Doctor and the Girl '49
Dogma '99
Eye of God '97 ▸
Fast Times at Ridgemont High '82 ▸
Flanders '06
4 Months, 3 Weeks and 2 Days '07 ▸
Goldstein '64
Grandma '15 ▸
Happy Endings '05
If These Walls Could Talk '96
Knight of Cups '15
Meant to Be '12
Men in White '34
Never Rarely Sometimes Always '20 ▸
Obvious Child '14 ▸
October Baby '12
Palindromes '04 ▸
Panic in Needle Park '71 ▸
A Private Matter '92 ▸
Rain Without Thunder '93
Rude '96
Signs & Wonders '00
Silent Victim '92
The Story of Women '88 ▸
Swing Vote '99
Things You Can Tell Just by Looking at Her '00
Too Soon to Love '60
Unplanned '19
Up the Junction '68
Vera Drake '04 ▸

Action-Adventure

See *Action-Comedy; Adventure Drama; Comic Adventure; Disaster Flicks; Martial Arts; Romantic Adventure; Swashbucklers*

Action-Comedy

Abominable '19
The Accidental Spy '01
Action Force: The Movie '87
Adventures in Zambezia '12
After the Sunset '04
Agent Cody Banks 2: Destination London '04
All at Sea '57
American Ultra '15
The Angry Birds Movie '16
Ant-Man '15 ▸
Ant-Man and the Wasp '18 ▸
Antboy '14
Around the World in 80 Days '04
Assault of the Sasquatch '09
Attack the Block '11
Avengers: Age of Ultron '15
Bachelor Games '16
Bad Boys for Life '20
Bait '00
Barely Lethal '15
Battle Creek Brawl '80
The Baytown Outlaws '12
Bending the Rules '12
Beverly Hills Chihuahua '08
Blue Iguana '18
The Bodyguard 2 '07
The Bodyguard '04
Bon Cop Bad Cop '06
Bounty Hunters 2: Hardball '97
The Brothers Grimsby '16
Camouflage '00
Casa de mi Padre '12
Cat Run '11
Central Intelligence '16
Charlie's Angels '00
Charlie's Angels '19
Charlie's Angels: Full Throttle '03
Chill Factor '99
Colossal '17
Compadres '16
Concrete Cowboys '79
Coronado '03
Deadpool 2 '18
Deadpool '16
D.E.B.S. '04
Detective Bureau 2-3: Go to Hell Bastards! '63
Don't Kill It '17
Double Agent 73 '80
Double Take '01
Drive Hard '14
The Emoji Movie '17
Enter the Warriors Gate '17
Evil Behind You '06
The Family '13
Finding Steve McQueen '19
Free Fire '17
G-Force '09
The Gentlemen '20
Get Smart '08
Ghostbusters '16
Gorgeous '99
Greed In the Sun '64
Guardians of the Galaxy '14 ▸
Guardians of the Galaxy Vol. 2 '17 ▸
Gun Shy '17
Guns, Girls and Gambling '11
Hancock '08
The Happytime Murders '18
The Heat '13
Here Comes the Boom '12
Hit and Run '12
The Hitman's Bodyguard '17
Holmes & Watson '18
Holy Flame of the Martial World '83
Hot Fuzz '07 ▸
Hot Pursuit '15
Hot Rod '07
Hot Tamale '06
House of Fury '05
I Spy '02
I'm for the Hippopotamus '79
The Incredible Burt Wonderstone '13
The Incredibles '04 ▸
Incredibles 2 '18 ▸
Intermission '03 ▸
Jackie Chan's The Myth '05
Johnny English Reborn '11
Johnny English Strikes Again '18
Jumanji: The Next Level '19
Jumanji: Welcome to the Jungle '17
Just Getting Started '17
Keeping Up with the Joneses '16
Kelly's Heroes '70
Kick-Ass '10 ▸
Kick-Ass 2 '13
Killers '10
Killing Gunther '17
Kim Possible '19
Kingsman: The Golden Circle '17
Kiss Kiss Bang Bang '05 ▸
Knight and Day '10
Knights of Badassdom '13
Kung Fu Hustle '04
Kung Fu Panda 3 '16 ▸
Ladrones '15
Laughing to the Bank '13
Legend of the Liquid Sword '93
The LEGO Batman Movie '17 ▸
The LEGO Movie 2: The Second Part '19
The Lego Movie '14 ▸
The LEGO Ninjago Movie '17
Let's Be Cops '14
The Librarian: Curse of the Judas Chalice '08
The Librarian: Quest for the Spear '04
The Librarian: Return to King Solomon's Mines '06
The Liquidator '65
The Lovebirds '20
Low Heights '02
MacGruber '10
Machete Kills '13
The Machine Girl '07
The Man '05
Man of the House '05
Manborg '11
Masterminds '16
Maximum Impact '18
The Medallion '03
Meltdown '95
Men in Black: International '19
Mickey, Donald, Goofy: The Three Musketeers '04
Middle School: The Worst Years of My Life '16
Mike and Dave Need Wedding Dates '16
Miracles '89
Miss Congeniality 2: Armed and Fabulous '05
Mr. Right '16
Moana '16 ▸
Monster Trucks '16
My Spy '19
My Super Ex-Girlfriend '06
New York Minute '04
Next Day Air '09
The Nice Guys '16 ▸
Night at the Museum: Battle of the Smithsonian '09
Nim's Island '08
Ocean's 8 '18
Ocean's Twelve '04
One for the Money '12
The 100-Year-Old Man Who Climbed Out the Window and Disappeared '15
Onward '20 ▸
OSS 117: Lost in Rio '09
The Other Guys '10
Outside Bet '12
The Pacifier '05
Paper Soldiers '02
Partners '99
Pineapple Express '08 ▸
Pirates of the Caribbean: At World's End '07
Pirates of the Caribbean: On Stranger Tides '11
Pixels '15
Pokémon Detective Pikachu '19
Project A '83
Project A: Part 2 '87
Railroad Tigers '17
Ralph Breaks the Internet '18
Ratchet & Clank '16
RED 2 '13
RED '10
Red Shadow '01
Ride Along 2 '16
Ride Along '14
Robinson Crusoe: The Great Blitzkrieg '08
RoboGeisha '06
The Rundown '03
Running on Karma '03
Rush Hour '98
Rush Hour 3 '07
Sahara '05
Sausage Party '16
Scooby-Doo 2: Monsters Unleashed '04
Scott Pilgrim *vs.* the World '10
Season of the Witch '10
The Secret Life of Pets 2 '19
Seoul Raiders '05
Shaft '19
Shanghai Express '86
Shaolin Soccer '01
Shazam! '19
Silver Case '11
Snatched '17
South Sea Woman '53
The Southern Star '69
Spark: A Space Tail '17

Spenser Confidential '20
Spider-Man 2 '04 ►
Spider-Man: Far from Home '19 ►
Spies in Disguise '19
Spy '15 ►
The Spy Next Door '10
The Spy Who Dumped Me '18
Starsky & Hutch '04
Storks '16
Stuber '19
The Taint '10
Taxi '04
Teen Titans Go! To the Movies '18
Teenage Mutant Ninja Turtles: Out of the Shadows '16
This Means War '12
Thor: Ragnarok '17 ►
Thunderbirds '04
Timmy Failure: Mistakes Were Made '20
Total Dhamaal '19
Tremors 4: The Legend Begins '04
Tropix '02
The Tuxedo '02
21 Jump Street '12 ►
21 & Over '13
22 Jump Street '14
Underclassman '05
Underdog '07
Unfinished Business '15
Violet & Daisy '11
War Dogs '16
War on Everyone '17
Warm Blooded Killers '01
The Wedding Ringer '15
Welcome to Acapulco '19
Welcome to the Jungle '13
White Chicks '04
The Whole Ten Yards '04
Yakuza Apocalypse '15
Yoga Hosers '16
You Don't Mess with the Zohan '08
Your Highness '11
Zebraman '04
Zombieland: Double Tap '19 ►
Zootopia '16 ►

Adolescence

***See** Coming of Age; Hell High School; Summer Camp; Teen Comedy; Teen Drama; Teen Horror; Teen Musicals; Teen Romance*

Adoption & Orphans

***See also** Custody Battles; Hard Knock Life; Only the Lonely*

Across the Great Divide '76
Admission '13
Adopt a Highway '19
Adopted '09
Adoption '75 ►
Adoration '08
The Affair of the Necklace '01
After the Wedding '06 ►
Aladdin '92 ►
Alex Rider: Operation Stormbreaker '06
Aliens '86 ►
All Mine to Give '56
Alone in the Dark '05
Altered Minds '13
Always Goodbye '38
The Amazing Mrs. Holiday '43
Anastasia '97
Andre '94
Anne of Green Gables '34 ►
Anne of Green Gables '85 ►
Annie '82
Annie '99 ►
Annie '14
August Rush '07
Azumi '03 ►
Babes on Broadway '41
Bachelor Mother '39 ►
Back to the Secret Garden '01
Ballet Shoes '07
Bambi '42 ►
Batman Begins '05 ►
Batman Forever '95 ►
Battle Hymn '57
Before I Wake '15
The Beniker Gang '83
Beverly Lewis' The Shunning '11
Beyond the Blue Horizon '42
Big Daddy '99
Big Red '62
The Big Wedding '13
Black Dynamite '09
The Blind Side '09
Blossoms in the Dust '41
Blues Brothers 2000 '98
Bobbie's Girl '02
Bogus '96
The Book Thief '13
Born Free '66 ►
Born to Win '16
The Boy with the Green Hair '48 ►
Brand Upon the Brain! '06 ►
Breakfast on Pluto '05
The Breaks '99
The Bride Goes Wild '48
Bright Eyes '34
The Brothers Grimsby '16
Brute '97
Casa de los Babys '03 ►
Catfish in Black Bean Sauce '00
The Chateau '01
The Children Nobody Wanted '81 ►
The Children of Huang Shi '08
Children of the Corn 3: Urban Harvest '95
Chronicle of a Boy Alone '64
The Cider House Rules '99 ►
City Boy '93 ►
City Streets '38
Close to My Heart '51
The Country Bears '02
A Cry from the Streets '57
Crystalstone '88
Daddy Long Legs '19
Daddy Long Legs '55 ►
Dangerous Orphans '86
D.A.R.Y.L. '85
David Copperfield '35 ►
David Copperfield '70
David Copperfield '99
Days of Being Wild '91 ►
Deadly Sanctuary '68
Dear Wendy '05
December Boys '07
Deep Waters '48
Despicable Me '10
The Devil's Backbone '01
Dick Tracy '90 ►
Dondi '61
Eagle's Shadow '84
The Education of Little Tree '97 ►
Emile '03
Escape to Witch Mountain '75 ►
The Family Holiday '07
The Family Jewels '65
Family of Strangers '93
Far from the Madding Crowd '15
The Father Clements Story '87
Father Is a Bachelor '50
The Fireball '50
First Love '39
Flirting with Disaster '95 ►
Forbidden '32
Foster '18
Four Brothers '05
Free Willy '93
The Geisha Boy '58
Gigantic '08
Glass House: The Good Mother '06
Gloria '98
Glorious 39 '09
The Goldfinch '19
The Great Diamond Robbery '53
Great Expectations '34
Great Expectations '46 ►
Great Expectations '81
Great Expectations '99
Great Expectations '11
Great Expectations '12
The Great Water '04
The Green Years '46
Happy Endings '05
Hell's House '32
A Home at the End of the World '04
A Home of Our Own '75
Hotel for Dogs '09
Hugo '11 ►
Hurt '09
I Am David '04
Ida '13 ►
The Identical '14
Il Futuro '13
I'm Glad My Mother Is Alive '09
Immediate Family '89
The Infidel '10
The Inheritance '97
Instant Family '18
Invisible Mom 2 '99
The Italian '05
James and the Giant Peach '96 ►
Jane Eyre '34
Jane Eyre '44 ►
Jane Eyre '83 ►
Jane Eyre '96 ►
Jane Eyre '97
June '15
The Jungle Book '16 ►
Juno '07 ►
Kidnapped '05 ►
Kings and Queen '04 ►
The Land Before Time '88 ►
Laugh, Clown, Laugh '28 ►
Lemony Snicket's A Series of Unfortunate Events '04
The Light Between Oceans '16
Like Dandelion Dust '09
Like Mike '02
Lilo & Stitch '02 ►
Lion '16 ►
The Little Kidnappers '90
Little Men '98
Little Miss Nobody '36
The Little Princess '87
Little Secrets '02
Loggerheads '05 ►
Losing Isaiah '94 ►
Lost Angel '43
The Lost Child '00
Love Come Down '00
Love Finds a Home '09
Love Takes Wing '09
Lovely & Amazing '02 ►
Love's Unending Legacy '07
Luce '19 ►
Machine Gun Preacher '11
Mad Max: Beyond Thunderdome '85
Madeline '98
The Magic Christian '69 ►
Major Payne '95
Man, Woman & Child '83
Manchester by the Sea '16 ►
Marion Bridge '02
Martian Child '07
Meet the Robinsons '07
The Memory Keeper's Daughter '08
Men & Chicken '15
Men On Her Mind '44
Mercury Rising '98
The Mexican Spitfire's Baby '41
Mighty Aphrodite '95
Mighty Joe Young '49
Mighty Joe Young '98
Milwaukee, Minnesota '03
Min & Bill '30
Miral '10
Miss Peregrine's Home for Peculiar Children '16
The Missing Person '09
Mr. Peabody & Sherman '14
The Mistress of Spices '05
Moll Flanders '96
Monsieur Ibrahim '03 ►
Mostly Martha '01 ►
Mother and Child '09
The Mudlark '50
My Blue Heaven '50
My Dog Shep '46
My Life as a Zucchini '16 ►
My Lucky Elephant '13
My Name is Modesty: A Modesty Blaise Adventure '04
Mysteries of Lisbon '10
Nacho Libre '06
Napoleon and Samantha '72 ►
No Reservations '07
Nob Hill '45
Norbit '07
Nothing But the Night '72
October Baby '12
The Odyssey of the Pacific '82
Off Season '01
The Official Story '85 ►
Oliver! '68 ►
Oliver & Company '88
Oliver Twist '22 ►
Oliver Twist '33
Oliver Twist '48 ►
Oliver Twist '82 ►
Oliver Twist '85 ►
Oliver Twist '97
Oliver Twist '00 ►
Oliver Twist '05 ►
Oliver Twist '07
One Desire '55
One Good Cop '91
The Orphan '79
Orphan '09
The Orphanage '07 ►
Orphans '87 ►
Orphans of the Storm '21 ►
Our Children '12
Our Little Sister '16
The Outsiders '83
The Overbrook Brothers '09
Owd Bob '97
The Owl and the Sparrow '07
Paddy O'Day '35
Pan '15
Paper Moon '73 ►
Peck's Bad Boy '34
Pennies from Heaven '36
Penny Serenade '41 ►
Perfume: The Story of a Murderer '06
Pete's Dragon '16
Phantasm '79
Philomena '13
Pictures of Hollis Woods '07
Pixote '81 ►
Play for Me '01
Pollyanna '60 ►
Possessing Piper Rose '11
The Prince of Central Park '77 ►
Problem Child '90
Queen Kelly '29 ►
The Quest '96
The Quiet '05
Rags to Riches '87
Raising Heroes '97
Rebecca of Sunnybrook Farm '17
Relative Strangers '06
The Rescuers '77 ►
Rikisha-Man '58 ►
Rodeo Rhythm '42
Romance of the Limberlost '38
Room for One More '51
Rose Hill '97
The Royal Tenenbaums '01 ►
Saddle Tramp '47
Sally '29
Sally of the Sawdust '25
Samantha '92
Scandal at Scourie '53
Scaramouche '23
The Search for Santa Paws '10
Second Best '94 ►
The Secret Garden '49 ►
The Secret Garden '84
The Secret Garden '87 ►
The Secret Garden '93
The Secret of Moonacre '08
Secrets and Lies '95
Shannon's Rainbow '09
A Shine of Rainbows '09
Shooting Fish '98
Shoplifters '18 ►
Sidewalks of London '38 ►
Simon and the Oaks '12
A Simple Twist of Fate '94
Sioux City '94
666: The Child '06
The Sleepy Time Gal '01
Snow Dogs '02
Snow White and the Seven Dwarfs '37 ►
A Soldier's Daughter Never Cries '98
Spark: A Space Tail '17
Spin '04
Station Jim '01
The Story of an African Farm '04
Strange Relations '02
A Stranger's Heart '07
Stuart Little '99
Sugar Cane Alley '83 ►
The Sugarland Express '74 ►
Sunday Dinner for a Soldier '44
Superman: The Movie '78 ►
Susannah of the Mounties '39
Tarzan Finds a Son '39 ►
Ted 2 '15
Ten Inch Hero '07
That Hagen Girl '47
Then She Found Me '07
These Wilder Years '56
The Thief Lord '06
33 Postcards '11
Three Identical Strangers '18 ►
Three Secrets '50
The Three Stooges '12
Three Stripes in the Sun '55
Ticking Clock '10
The Tie That Binds '95
Tish '42
Tom & Thomas '02
Tom Jones '98 ►
Torch Singer '33
The Tunnel of Love '58
24: Redemption '08
Twisted '96
The Unknown Woman '06
Unwed Mother '58
Vanity Fair '04
A Very Serious Person '06
The Waiting City '09
Welcome to Sarajevo '97 ►
Whacked! '02
Where Are My Children? '94
Where the River Runs Black '86
Wild Hearts Can't Be Broken '91 ►
Wilson '17
Winter's Tale '14
Wuthering Heights '09
Young People '40
Yours, Mine & Ours '05

Adultery

Addicted '14
Albatross '11
All the Good Ones Are Married '07
An American Affair '09
And Never Let Her Go '01
And While We Were Here '13
Angela '02
Anglo-Saxon Attitudes '92
Anna Karenina '12
Another Life '01
Answers to Nothing '11
Arbitrage '12 ►
Asylum '05
The Babysitters '07
Back Street '41
Bad Blonde '53
Bed and Board '70 ►
Before the Devil Knows You're Dead '07 ►
Before the Rains '07
Before We Go '14
Bel Ami '12
Betrayed: A Story of Three Women '95
The Big Picture '10
A Bigger Splash '15
Birdsong '12
Blind Corner '63
Bloom '03
Blue Blood '07
Bread and Tulips '01 ►
The Bridges of Madison County '95 ►
Bright Days Ahead '14
Brothers '04 ►
Burn After Reading '08
The Burning Plain '08
Café Society '16
The Canyons '13
Car Trouble '86
Carnival of Crime '62
Cat City '08
Caught in the Act '04
Change of Plans '09
Cheaters' Club '06
Chicago '02 ►
Cinema Verite '11
Closer '04 ►
Coastlines '02
Coco Chanel & Igor Stravinsky '09
A Coeur Joie '67
Coffin '11
Colombiana '11
Come Live With Me '40
Cool and the Crazy '94
Counsellor-at-Law '33 ►
Cover '08
Curse of the Golden Flower '06
Daisy Kenyon '47
Dangerous Liaisons '03
Darkness Falls '98
The Daughter '15
Day of Reckoning '33
Day-Time Wife '39
Dead Gorgeous '02
The Decalogue '88 ►
Derailed '05
The Descendants '11 ►
The Details '11
The Devil and the Deep '32
The Devil Wears Prada '06
Diary of a Mad Black Woman '05
Die Mommie Die! '03
The Divine Lady '29
Doctor Zhivago '65 ►
Doctor Zhivago '03
Don't Make Waves '67
The Door in the Floor '04 ►
Dot the I '03
The Duchess '08 ►
The Dying Gaul '05 ►
Elena Undone '10
Extract '09
Faithless '00 ►
Familia '05
The Family That Preys '08
The Family Tree '10
Fatal Attraction '87 ►
Fatal Desire '05
The File on Thelma Jordon '50 ►
Flashbacks of a Fool '08
The Foot Fist Way '08
44 Inch Chest '09
Fracture '07
The Freebie '10
From the Terrace '60
The Front Runner '18
Gilles' Wife '04
The Golden Bowl '00
Golden Exits '17
The Good Girl '02 ►
Goodbye to Language '14 ►
The Goose and the Gander '35
Gospel of Deceit '06
Hall Pass '11
Happily Ever After '04
Happy, Happy '10
The Hatchet Man '32
Haunted Highway '05
He Loves Me '11
Head On '04
The Healer '02
Heart '99
The Heart of Me '02
Heart of Stone '01
Heights '04
Hitched '01
Hollywoodland '06
Hope Gap '20
The Housemaid '10
Housewife '34
I Smile Back '15
I Take This Woman '40
I Think I Love My Wife '07
The Ice Storm '97 ►
If I Were Free '33
In My Country '04
In Secret '13

► = rated three bones or higher

In the Mood for Love '00
Incendiary '08
The Innocent '76
Interlude '68
Intermission '03 ►
The Invisible Woman '13 ►
Jarhead '05
Jeff, Who Lives at Home '12
Jewel Robbery '32
Just Another Love Story '08
Just Before Nightfall '71
The Kate Logan Affair '10
The Kids Are All Right '10 ►
The Killer Must Kill Again '75
Knight of Cups '15
La Femme Infidele '69 ►
Lady Chatterley '10 ►
Land Girls '09
Landline '17
Lansdown '01
Lantana '01 ►
Last Night '10
The Last Sentence '12
Le Divorce '03
The Ledge '11
Leo '02
The Letter '29
Lies & Alibis '06
Life of Crime '13
Little Chenier: A Cajun Story '06
Little Children '06 ►
Liz & Dick '12
The Loft '14
Lord of War '05 ►
Love and Money '80
Love Ranch '10
Lovely & Amazing '02 ►
The Lovers '17 ►
Lovers of Hate '10
Loving '70
Lulu Belle '48
Lymelife '08
The Man in the Net '59
The Man Who Wasn't There '01 ►
Match Point '05 ►
Meet Bill '07
Melinda and Melinda '05
Melo '86
The Monkey's Mask '00
Motives '03
Murder in the Hamptons '05
My Golden Days '15 ►
My Life Without Me '03
My Wife's Best Friend '52
Nathalie '03
Never Forever '07
Night Editor '46
Nina Takes a Lover '94
No Brother of Mine '07
No Money Down '97
No More Ladies '35
Non-Fiction '18
Nora Prentiss '47
Nurse 3D '13
Obsession '49
One Hour Photo '02 ►
100 Mile Rule '02
The Oranges '12
The Other Man '08
The Other Woman '08
The Other Woman '14
Our Idiot Brother '11
Our Little Sister '16
Out of Time '03
The Painted Veil '06
Parnell '37
A Perfect Man '13
Petulia '68 ►
Possession '02
The Prowler '51
Psyche 59 '64
Queen of Hearts '19
A Rage to Live '65
Rain '01
The Reckoning '03 ►
Reconstruction '03
Resistance '03
Revenge '17
Revolutionary Road '08
Romance & Cigarettes '05
Romulus, My Father '07 ►
Say Nothing '01
The Scarlet Letter '34
The Scarlet Letter '73 ►
The Scarlet Letter '79 ►
The Scarlet Letter '95
The Sea of Grass '47
Second Skin '99
Secrets of Eden '12
The Sentinel '06
Separate Lies '05
A Serious Man '09 ►
A Severed Head '70
Shed No Tears '48
The Shooting Party '85 ►
Sidewalks of New York '01
Signs & Wonders '00
Sitting Target '72
Six Days, Six Nights '94
Sleep Easy, Hutch Rimes '00
Sleuth '07
Snow Angels '07 ►
Someone Behind the Door '71
Sordid Lives '00
Spring 1941 '08
The Square '08
Steam: A Turkish Bath '96 ►
Street of Women '32
Stronger Than Desire '39
Such Good Friends '71
Suckerfish '99
Summer of '04 '06
A Summer Place '59
Summer Storm '44
Suspense '46
Sylvia '03
Tangerine '15
The Taste of Others '00 ►
Tempted '01
10 Rules for Sleeping Around '13
Their Own Desire '29
Therese Raquin '80
Things to Come '16 ►
Thirst '09 ►
Those We Love '32
Three Blondes in His Life '61
3-Way '04
Three Wise Girls '32
Thrill of the Kill '06
Thunder in Dixie '65
Tick Tock '00 ►
Time Regained '99
To Have and to Hold '06
Tornado '43
Town and Country '01
The Toy Wife '38
Tre '06
Tristan & Isolde '06
28 Hotel Rooms '12
The Two Jakes '90
Tyler Perry's Temptation: Confessions of a Marriage Counselor '13
Undertaking Betty '02
Une Femme Mariee '64
Unfaithful '02 ►
Unfaithfully Yours '48 ►
Unfaithfully Yours '84
The Unguarded Hour '36
Up the Ladder '25
The Valet '06
The Voice of Merrill '52
Wah-Wah '05
Waitress '07 ►
Waking Up in Reno '02
The Walker '07
Wall of Noise '63
Waterloo Road '45
We Don't Live Here Anymore '04
When the Bough Breaks '16
Who Loves the Sun '06
The Witnesses '07
A Woman, a Gun and a Noodle Shop '10
The Woman From Monte Carlo '31
The Women '08
Y Tu Mama Tambien '01
Yes '04
You Will Meet a Tall Dark Stranger '10
Young Adam '03 ►

Adventure Drama

Ace of Aces '33
Action in the North Atlantic '43
Ad Astra '19 ►
The Admirable Crichton '57
The Adventures of Huck Finn '93 ►
The Adventures of Huckleberry Finn '39 ►
The Adventures of Milo & Otis '89 ►
The Adventures of the Wilderness Family '76
The Adventures of Tom Sawyer '38 ►
Afghan Luke '11
Against the Sun '15
Against the Wild II: Survive the Seregenti '16
Age of the Hobbits '12
Air Force '43 ►
Air Force One '97 ►
Aladdin '19
Alaska '96
Alexander Nevsky '38 ►
Ali Baba and the Forty Thieves '43
Allan Quatermain and the Lost City of Gold '86
Alligator Alley '72
Aloha, Bobby and Rose '74
The Amazing Panda Adventure '95
America '24
American Empire '42
Angels of the City '89
Apocalypse Now '79 ►
Apocalypto '06 ►
Apollo 13 '95 ►
Appointment with Crime '45
The Arab Conspiracy '76
Archer's Adventure '85
Arctic '18
Arctic Blue '93
Around the World in 80 Days '56 ►
Around the World in 80 Days '89
Ashura '05
Assassination '87
Attila '01
The Aviator '85
A-X-L '18
Azumi '03 ►
Back to God's Country '53
Backdraft '91
Bang Rajan '00 ►
Barbary Coast '35 ►
The Baron '88
Bataan '43
The Battle of El Alamein '68
Battle of the Eagles '79
Battleforce '78
Beau Geste '39 ►
The Beautiful Country '04
The Bells of Death '68
Beneath the 12-Mile Reef '53
Benji: Off the Leash! '04
Benji the Hunted '87
Beowulf '07 ►
Beowulf & Grendel '06
Between Heaven and Hell '56 ►
Beyond Rangoon '95
Big Bad Mama '74
Big Miracle '12
The Big Push '75
The Big Scam '79
The Big Turnaround '88
Bigfoot: The Unforgettable Encounter '94
Billy Budd '62 ►
Black Arrow '48 ►
Black Dawn '05
Black Jack '79
Black Moon Rising '86
Blackbeard '06
Blackout '78
Blood and Sand '41 ►
Blood Diamond '06
Bloom '03
Blown Away '94
The Blue and the Gray '82
Blue Fin '78
The Blue Lamp '49 ►
Blue Thunder '83
The Bodyguard from Beijing '94
Bombardier '43
Border Blues '03
The Bounty '84
The Bourne Supremacy '04 ►
Breakdown '96 ►
The Breed '01
Brighty of the Grand Canyon '67
Brotherhood of Death '76
A Bullet Is Waiting '54
Bumblebee '18 ►
By Way of the Stars '92
Cadence '89
California '63
The Call of the Wild '35 ►
Call of the Wild '72
The Call of the Wild '20
Call of the Wilderness '32
Call of the Yukon '38
Campbell's Kingdom '57
Casablanca Express '89
Casshern '04
The Castilian '63
Casualties of War '89 ►
Catwoman '04
Cellular '04
Chain Reaction '80
Chain Reaction '96
Chains of Gold '92
The Challenge '38 ►
The Charge of the Light Brigade '36 ►
The Children of Huang Shi '08
Children of the Wild '37
China Gate '57 ►
Clarence, the Cross-eyed Lion '65 ►
Clash of the Titans '10
Clear and Present Danger '94
The Climbers '19
Code Name: Emerald '85
Code Name: Wild Geese '84
Code of Honor '16
Cold Skin '18
Command Decision '48
Commando Attack '67
Con Air '97 ►
Conspiracy Theory '97 ►
Coogan's Bluff '68 ►
The Corruptor '99 ►
Corsair '31
The Count of Monte Cristo '12
The Count of Monte Cristo '34 ►
The Count of Monte Cristo '99
The Count of Monte Cristo '02
Courage Mountain '89
Crimebusters '79
Crimson Romance '34
Crimson Tide '95 ►
Crouching Tiger, Hidden Dragon: Sword of Destiny '16
The Curse of King Tut's Tomb '06
Da 5 Bloods '20
The Da Vinci Treasure '06
Dam Busters '55 ►
Danger Beneath the Sea '02
Dangerous Ground '96
Dark Kingdom: The Dragon King '04
Dark Tide '12
The Darkside '87
Day of the Falcon '11
Days of Thunder '90
Deadlock '91
Deadly Sanctuary '68
Dear Eleanor '16
Death in the Garden '56
The Death Merchant '91
The Deceivers '88
The Decks Ran Red '58
Deliverance '72 ►
Destination Tokyo '43
Dick Tracy '90 ►
Die Hard '88 ►
Die Hard 2: Die Harder '90 ►
Die Hard: With a Vengeance '95
A Different Loyalty '04 ►
Dive Bomber '41 ►
A Dog's Way Home '19
Don Verdean '15
Doomsdayer '00
Down to the Sea in Ships '22
Dragon Storm '04
Dragonfly Squadron '54
Duma '05 ►
Each Dawn I Die '39
The Eagle '11
The Eagle Has Landed '77 ►
The Eagle Huntress '16 ►
East of Borneo '31
Edge of Honor '91
Eight Below '06
Embrace of the Serpent '15
The Emerald Forest '85 ►
Enchanted Island '58
Enemy Below '57 ►
Enemy of the State '98
The Enforcer '51
Eraser '96
Escape Room '19
Escape to Witch Mountain '75 ►
Evel Knievel '72
Everest '15
Executive Decision '96
Fallen '17
Fangs of the Wild '54
Fantasy Island '20
Far from Home: The Adventures of Yellow Dog '94
A Far Off Place '93
Farewell to the King '89
Ferry to Hong Kong '59
55 Days at Peking '63 ►
The Fighting Prince of Donegal '66
Fireball 500 '66
Firepower '79
Five Deadly Venoms '78 ►
Flame Over India '59 ►
The Flash '90
Flight of the Grey Wolf '76
Flipper '63 ►
Flowing Gold '40
Flying Leathernecks '51 ►
Flying Tigers '42
Follow Me '69
For Whom the Bell Tolls '43 ►
Fort Saganne '84
Fortunes of War '94
Forty Thousand Horsemen '41
The Four Feathers '39 ►
The Four Feathers '78
Four Warriors '15
F.P. 1 '33
F.P. 1 Doesn't Answer '33
Free Willy '93
Free Willy 2: The Adventure Home '95
Free Willy 3: The Rescue '97
The Fugitive '93 ►
Fugitive Champion '99
Full Eclipse '93
Fury to Freedom: The Life Story of Raul Ries '85
Future Zone '90
The Gaucho '27 ►
The Ghost and the Darkness '96
Gods of Egypt '16
Gold '16
The Golden Compass '07
Goldrush: A Real Life Alaskan Adventure '98
Gone in 60 Seconds '74
Goyokin '69 ►
Great Adventure '75
The Great Escape '63 ►
The Great Locomotive Chase '56
The Great Train Robbery '79 ►
The Green Glove '52
The Grey '12
Greystoke: The Legend of Tarzan, Lord of the Apes '84
Grizzly Mountain '97
Guadalcanal Diary '43
The Guardian '01
Guerillas in Pink Lace '64
Gunga Din '39 ►
Hackers '95
The Halls of Montezuma '50
Hamlet '90 ►
Hangfire '91
Harry Potter and the Goblet of Fire '05 ►
Harry Potter and the Prisoner of Azkaban '04
Have Sword, Will Travel '69
The Heartbreak Kid '07
Heaven & Hell '78
Hell Commandos '69
Hell Divers '31
Hell in the Pacific '69 ►
Hell Squad '85
Hell to Eternity '60
Hellcats of the Navy '57
Hellfighters '68
Hell's Angels '30 ►
Hero's Island '62
Hidalgo '04
Himalaya '99 ►
Hired to Kill '73
Hit! '73
Homeward Bound: The Incredible Journey '93 ►
Horatio Hornblower '99 ►
Horatio Hornblower: The Adventure Continues '01 ►
Hostile Waters '97
Hostiles '17
The Houdini Serial '20
House of Traps '81
Huck and the King of Hearts '93
Hudson's Bay '40
Hugo '11 ►
The Hunger Games: Mockingjay-Part 2 '15
The Hunt for Red October '90 ►
The Hunter '12
The Huntsman: Winter's War '16
Hurricane Smith '92
Hustler Squad '76
Ill Met By Moonlight '57
Immortal Sergeant '43
Immortals '11
In Enemy Hands '04
In Harm's Way '65
In Love and War '91
In Search of a Golden Sky '84
In Search of Fellini '17
In the Name of the King: A Dungeon Siege Tale '08
In Which We Serve '43 ►
Indiana Jones and the Kingdom of the Crystal Skull '08
Indiana Jones and the Last Crusade '89 ►
Indiana Jones and the Temple of Doom '84 ►
Initiation '87
Into Thin Air: Death on Everest '97
The Intruder '04 ►
IO '19
The Iron Mask '29
Iron Will '93
Island in the Sky '53 ►
Isle of Forgotten Sins '43
Jack London's The Call of the Wild '97
JAG '95
Jamaica Inn '39
Jamaica Inn '82
Jason and the Argonauts '00
Jem and the Holograms '15
Jet Pilot '57
Joey '98
Johnny Mnemonic '95
The Journey of Natty Gann '85 ►
Journey to the Center of the Earth '88
Juggernaut '74 ►
Jungle '52
The Jungle Book '16 ►
Junglee '19
Jurassic Park 3 '01
Jurassic Park '93 ►
Jurassic World '15
Jurassic World: Fallen Kingdom '18
The Karate Kid '84 ►
The Karate Kid: Part 2 '86
The Karate Kid: Part 3 '89
Kavik the Wolf Dog '80
The Keeper: The Legend of Omar Khayyam '05
Keeping Track '86
Kicks '16
Kid Colter '85
Kidnapped '38
Kidnapped '48

► = rated three bones or higher

Kidnapped '60
Kidnapped '05 ▶
The Killer '90 ▶
The Killer Elite '75
King Arthur '04
King of New York '90 ▶
King Solomon's Mines '50 ▶
King Solomon's Mines '85
King Solomon's Treasure '76
Kings of the Sun '63
Kiss and Kill '68
Klondike Fever '79
Knives of the Avenger '65
Kon-Tiki '12
K2: The Ultimate High '92
La Guerre Est Finie '66 ▶
Lady Cocoa '75
Lassie, Come Home '43
Lassiter '84
The Last Hunter '80
Last Knights '15
The Last of the Finest '90
The Last of the Mohicans '32
The Last of the Mohicans '36
The Last of the Mohicans '92 ▶
The Last Place on Earth '85
The Last Riders '90
Lean on Pete '17 ▶
Legend of Billie Jean '85
The Legend of Cryin' Ryan '98
The Legend of Johnny Lingo '03
The Legend of Sea Wolf '75
Legend of the Northwest '78
The Legend of Wolf Mountain '92
Lethal Weapon 2 '89 ▶
Liane, Jungle Goddess '56
Life of Pi '12 ▶
Lightning Hutch '26
The Lion King '19
Lion of the Desert '81 ▶
Loaded Guns '75
Lockdown '90
The Losers '10
The Lost City of Z '17 ▶
The Lost World: Jurassic Park 2 '97
The Lost Zeppelin '29
Macao '52 ▶
The Mad Bomber '72
The Man from U.N.C.L.E. '15
The Man in the Iron Mask '39 ▶
The Man in the Iron Mask '97
The Man in the Iron Mask '98 ▶
Man of Legend '71
The Man Who Killed Hitler and Then the Bigfoot '19
The Martian '15 ▶
The Mask of Zorro '98 ▶
Massacre in Dinosaur Valley '85
The Master of Ballantrae '53
Master of the Flying Guillotine '75
Max '15
The McConnell Story '55
Memphis Belle '90 ▶
Men in War '57
Miami Vice '84
Midnight Crossing '87
Midway '76
Milo & Otis '89
MirrorMask '05
Ms. 45 '81 ▶
Moby Dick '56 ▶
Moby Dick '98 ▶
Money Train '95
Monos '19 ▶
The Moon-Spinners '64
Moran of the Lady Letty '22
Mountain Family Robinson '79
Mountain of the Cannibal God '79
Moving Target '89
Murder Without Motive '92
The Mutiny of the Elsinore '39
My Dog Shep '46
Mysterious Island '05
Naked Jungle '54 ▶
Ned Kelly '03
The Negotiator '98
Night Crossing '81
Noah '14
The Non-Stop Flight '26
Noon Sunday '75
The North Star '43 ▶
North West Frontier '59
Northern Pursuit '43
Northwest Passage '40 ▶
Number One with a Bullet '87
Objective, Burma! '45 ▶
Oceans of Fire '86
Odongo '56
The Odyssey '97
One Armed Executioner '80
127 Hours '10 ▶
One Man Force '89
One Minute to Zero '52
One of Our Aircraft Is Missing '41 ▶
One That Got Away '57 ▶
Ong Bak 2 '08
Operation Cross Eagles '69
Operation Haylift '50
Operation Thunderbolt '77
Opposing Force '87
Outbreak '94 ▶
Outlaw Blues '77
The Package '89
Paco '75
Palindromes '04 ▶
Pan '15
Papillon '73 ▶
Party Line '88
The Passage '79
Passenger 57 '92
The Patriot '86
Patriot Games '92 ▶
The Peacemaker '97
The Peanut Butter Falcon '19
Penitentiary 2 '82
Penitentiary '79
The Perils of Gwendoline '84
The Phantom '96
Pirates of Treasure Island '06
Platoon '86 ▶
Plunder Road '57
Policewomen '73
Pork Chop Hill '59 ▶
Portrait of a Hitman '77
The Predator '18
The Presidio '88
Prey '19
Prime Target '91
Prince Brat and the Whipping Boy '95 ▶
Prince of Persia: The Sands of Time '10
Prisoner in the Middle '74
The Prisoner of Zenda '22
Promare '19
PT 109 '63
Pursuit of the Graf Spee '57
Queen's Messenger II '01
Radio Patrol '37
Raid on Entebbe '77 ▶
Raid on Rommel '71
Raiders of the Lost Ark '81 ▶
The Rains of Ranchipur '55
Rampage '18
Rambo '08
Ran '85 ▶
The Real Glory '39 ▶
Reap the Wild Wind '42
Remedy '05
Renegades '89
The Replacement Killers '98
Report to the Commissioner '75 ▶
The Rescue '88
The Return of the Scarlet Pimpernel '37
Revelation '00
The Revenant '15 ▶
Revenge '90
Riot in Cell Block 11 '54 ▶
Risen '16
The River Wild '94
Robin Hood: Prince of Thieves '91
RoboCop '87 ▶
Rogue One: A Star Wars Story '16 ▶
Ronin '98
Rudyard Kipling's The Jungle Book '94
Run for the Sun '56
Runaway Train '85 ▶
Running Free '00
Running out of Time '99 ▶
The Saint '97
The St. Valentine's Day Massacre '67
The Sand Pebbles '66 ▶
Sands of Iwo Jima '49 ▶
Savage Justice '88
Savage Sam '63
Savage Streets '83
Scaramouche '52 ▶
The Scarlet Coat '55
The Scorpion King 4: Quest for Power '15
Scott of the Antarctic '48
Sea Chase '55
Sea Devils '53
Sea Gypsies '78
The Sea Hawk '40 ▶
Sea Wolves '81
Seal Team '08
Search and Destroy '81
Secret of Stamboul '36
See You Yesterday '19
Sell Out '76
Sergeant York '41 ▶
Seven Alone '75
Sex Crimes '92
The Shadow '94
Shadow Force '92
Shark! '68
Sharpe's Peril '08
She '35
She '65
She Came to the Valley '77
Shogun Assassin '80
The Siege '98
The Siege of Firebase Gloria '89
The Silent Enemy '58
The Silver Stallion: King of the Wild Brumbies '93
The Sinister Urge '60
Sink the Bismarck '60 ▶
Sins of Rome '54
6 Below: Miracle on the Mountain '17
Six Pack '82
The Sky Crawlers '08
Sky Riders '76
S.M.A.R.T. Chase '18
Smugglers '75
Sniper '92
Sniper 2 '02
Sniper 3 '04
The Snow Walker '03
Sodom and Gomorrah '62
Soldier of Fortune '55
Sorcerer '77
S.O.S. Iceberg '33
Soul Vengeance '75
Souls at Sea '37
Spawn of the North '38
Special Forces '68
The Specialist '94
Speed '94 ▶
Spider-Man 2 '04 ▶
The Spider Returns '41
The Spider's Web '38
Spin '04
Spirit of the Eagle '90
Spree '79
Squanto: A Warrior's Tale '94 ▶
Standing Up '13
Star Trek: Insurrection '98
Steamboy '05
The Steel Claw '61
The Steel Helmet '51 ▶
The Steel Lady '53
Steele Justice '87
Steele's Law '91
The Sting '73 ▶
Stolen '12
The Stone Killer '73
Storm Boy
Storm Over the Nile '55
Strange Days '95 ▶
Street Crimes '92
Street War '76
Streets of Fire '84
Strike Force '75
Sub Down '97
Sudden Death '95
Sundown '41
Sunset Grill '92
The Swiss Family Robinson '60 ▶
Switchback '97
Sword Masters: Brothers Five '70
Sword Masters: The Battle Wizard '77
The Taking of Pelham One Two Three '74 ▶
Tank '83
Taps '81
Target of Opportunity '04
The Tartars '61
10,000 A.D.: The Legend of the Black Pearl '08
10,000 B.C. '08
Terminal Error '02
Terminator Genisys '15
Theeb '15 ▶
Thelma & Louise '91 ▶
They Were Expendable '45 ▶
This Must Be the Place '12
Those Calloways '65
The Three Musketeers '21 ▶
The Three Musketeers '11
Three the Hard Way '74
Throw Down '00
Thunder Alley '67
Thunderbirds '04
A Tiger Walks '64
Tim Tyler's Luck '37
Timbuktu '59
Tom Sawyer '73
Tomb Raider '18
Top Gun '86 ▶
Tour of Duty '87
Toy Soldiers '91
Tracks '14
The Transporter '02
Treasure Guards '11
Tribulation '00
Triple Cross '67 ▶
Triple Frontier '19
Trouble in Paradise '88
True Blood '89
True Heart '97
Truth or Die '86
Turbo Kid '15
2012 '09
The Twilight Saga: Breaking Dawn, Part 2 '12
Twisted Justice '89
Two Brothers '04
Two Came Back '97
Unconquered '47
U.S. Marshals '98
U.S. Seals '98
Up Periscope '59
Vanished-Left Behind: Next Generation '16
The Vector File '03
Vigilante Diaries '16
Von Ryan's Express '65 ▶
Wake Island '42 ▶
Wake Up and Dream '46
The Walk '15
A Walk in the Sun '46 ▶
A Walk in the Woods '15
Walking Out '17
A Waltz Through the Hills '88
The Warrior '01
We Dive at Dawn '43 ▶
When the Last Sword is Drawn '02 ▶
Whisper 2: L'Aventure Continue '16
White Fang '36
White Fire '53
White Squall '96
The White Tower '50 ▶
White Witch Doctor '53
White Wolves 2: Legend of the Wild '94
Wild Riders '71
Wind and Cloud: The Storm Riders '04
A Wing and a Prayer '44 ▶
Winning '69 ▶
The World in His Arms '52
World War III '86
A Wrinkle in Time '18
The Year of Living Dangerously '82 ▶
Yellowneck '55
Young Warlord '75
Zarak '56
Zeppelin '71
Zulu '64
Zulu Dawn '79 ▶

Advertising

***See also* Front Page**

The Agency '81
And Now a Word From Our Sponsor '13
Artists and Models '37
Beer '85
Bounce '00
Branded '12
Capital Games '13
Carpool Guy '05
Confessions of an American Bride '05
Crazy People '90
Creep '15
Dear Me: A Blogger's Tale '08
Derailed '05
DROP Squad '94
Eros '04
A Fool and His Money '88
The Girl Can't Help It '56
The Girl From Mexico '39
Giving It Up '99
Group Sex '10
Having a Wild Weekend '65
Her Husband's Affairs '47
The Horse in the Gray Flannel Suit '68
Housewife '34
How to Get Ahead in Advertising '89 ▶
How to Lose a Guy in 10 Days '03
The Hucksters '47 ▶
I Want to Get Married '11
In Good Company '04 ▶
A Job to Kill For '06
The Joneses '09
Kids in the Hall: Brain Candy '96
Knife Fight '13
Kramer vs. Kramer '79 ▶
Lost in America '85 ▶
Lover Come Back '61
Loving '70
The Man in the Gray Flannel Suit '56
The Mexican Spitfire Out West '40
Mr. Blandings Builds His Dream House '48 ▶
Mr. Mom '83 ▶
Mr. Write '92
My Girlfriend's Boyfriend '10
A Nanny for Christmas '10
No '12
Nothing in Common '86
Nothing to Lose '96
One Night Stand '97 ▶
Passion '13
Perfect Stranger '07
Picture Perfect '96
POM Wonderful Presents: The Greatest Movie Ever Sold '11
Pretty Baby '50
Pursuit of Happiness '01
Putney Swope '69 ▶
Renaissance Man '94
Revolution #9 '01
Santa Claus: The Movie '85
The Smurfs '11
Son of the Mask '05
Surviving Christmas '04
Sweet November '01
Syrup '13
The Thrill of It All! '63
Thunder in the City '37 ▶
Transformers: The Movie '86
Waikiki Wedding '37 ▶
What Women Want '00
What Women Want '10
White Mile '94
Will Success Spoil Rock Hunter? '57
The Zoya Factor '19

Africa

***See also* Apartheid**

Abdulla the Great '56
Ace Ventura: When Nature Calls '95
Adopted '09
Adventures in Zambezia '12
Africa Screams '49
An African Election '11
The African Queen '51 ▶
African Rage '78
African Treasure '52
Against the Wild II: Survive the Seregenti '16
The Air Up There '94
Algiers '38 ▶
Allan Quartermain and the Temple of Skulls '08
Allan Quatermain and the Lost City of Gold '86
The Ambassador '11
Amistad '97 ▶
And Now Ladies and Gentlemen '02
Atlantics '19 ▶
Attack on Darfur '09
Babel '06 ▶
Babies '10 ▶
The Bang Bang Club '10
Bang! Bang! You're Dead! '66
Beasts of No Nation '15
Beyond Borders '03
The Big Alligator River '79
Black Hawk Down '01 ▶
Black Jesus '68
Black Panther '18 ▶
Blended '14
Blood Diamond '06
Blood Monkey '07
Blue Crush 2 '11
Boesman & Lena '00
Bomba and the Hidden City '50
Bomba and the Jungle Girl '52
Bomba on Panther Island '49
Bomba, the Jungle Boy '49
Bopha! '93 ▶
The Boy Who Harnessed the Wind '19
The Boys of Baraka '05
The Bride & the Beast '58
Call Me Bwana '63
Cape of Good Hope '04
Captain Phillips '13 ▶
Changing Times '04
Cheetah '89
Chocolat '88 ▶
Cobra Verde '88
Cold Case Hammarskjöld '19 ▶
The Color of Freedom '07
Coming to America '88 ▶
Concerning Violence '14
Congo '95
Congo Maisie '40
The Constant Gardener '05 ▶
Curious George '06
Dangerous Ground '96
Darfur Now '07
Dark of the Sun '68
Darwin's Nightmare '04 ▶
The Desert Fox '51 ▶
Deserter '02
The Devil Came on Horseback '07 ▶
Disgrace '08
District 9 '09 ▶
The Dogs of War '81
Dominion: Prequel to the Exorcist '05
Drums of Africa '63
A Dry White Season '89 ▶
Duma '05 ▶
East of Kilimanjaro '57
The Egyptian '54
An Elephant Called Slowly '69
Elephant Stampede '51
Endgame '09
Ernest Goes to Africa '97
Escape from Pretoria '20
A Far Off Place '93
15 Minutes of War '19
The Fighting Rats of Tobruk '44
Firefall '94
Fishing Without Nets '14
Five Weeks in a Balloon '62
The Flame Trees of Thika '81 ▶
The Forgiven '18
Fort Saganne '84
The Four Feathers '02

▶ = *rated three bones or higher*

Free Willy: Escape from Pirate's Cove '10
Ganja and Hess '73
The Garden of Allah '36 ▶
George of the Jungle '97 ▶
The Ghost and the Darkness '96
God Grew Tired of Us '06 ▶
The Gods Must Be Crazy 2 '89
The Gods Must Be Crazy '84 ▶
Golden Dawn '30
The Golden Idol '54
The Golden Salamander '51
A Good Man in Africa '94
Gorillas in the Mist '88 ▶
Greystoke: The Legend of Tarzan, Lord of the Apes '84
Guns at Batasi '64
Half-Caste '04
Hard to Forget '98
The Harvesters '19
Hatari! '62 ▶
Heat of the Sun '99 ▶
Hideous Kinky '99
A Hijacking '13 ▶
Holiday in the Wild '19
Honey 3: Dare to Dance '16
Hotel Rwanda '04
I Am Not a Witch '18
I Dreamed of Africa '00
I'm for the Hippopotamus '79
In a Better World '10
In Desert and Wilderness '01
In My Country '04
In the Army Now '94
Inside '96 ▶
The Intouchables '12
Invictus '09 ▶
Jane '17 ▶
Jericho '38
The Jewel of the Nile '85
Jungle Drums of Africa '53
Jungle Man-Eaters '54
Killer Leopard '54
Killers '88
The King Is Alive '00
King Kong '33 ▶
King Solomon's Mines '37 ▶
King Solomon's Mines '50 ▶
King Solomon's Mines '85
The Kitchen Toto '87 ▶
Kongo '32
The Last Adventure '67
The Last Face '17
The Last King of Scotland '06 ▶
The Last Outpost '35
The Last Tree '19
The League of Extraordinary Gentlemen '03
The Legend of Tarzan '16
The Librarian: Return to King Solomon's Mines '06
Life, Above All '10
The Lion Hunters '51
The Lion King 1 1/2 '04 ▶
The Lion King: Simba's Pride '98
Lord of the Jungle '55
The Lost Patrol '34 ▶
The Lost Volcano '50
The Lost World '92
Lullaby '08
Lumumba '01 ▶
Machine Gun Preacher '11
Madagascar: Escape 2 Africa '08
Mama Africa '02
Mandabi '68 ▶
Mandela '87 ▶
Mandela and de Klerk '97
Mandela: Long Walk to Freedom '13
Manhattan Baby '82
March or Die '77
Mark of the Gorilla '58
The Mark of the Hawk '57 ▶
Mary and Martha '13
Mediterranea '15 ▶
Mighty Joe Young '49
Mighty Joe Young '98
Miraculous Journey '48
Mister Johnson '91 ▶
Mogambo '53 ▶
Monster from Green Hell '58
Moolaade '04
Mother of George '13 ▶
Mountains of the Moon '90 ▶
The Naked Prey '66 ▶
Night of the Sorcerers '70
Nowhere in Africa '02
Odongo '56
Out of Africa '85 ▶
The Passenger '75 ▶
Pepe Le Moko '37 ▶
Pride of Africa '97
Primeval '07
Queen of Katwe '16 ▶
Red Scorpion '89
The Redemption of General Butt Naked '11
Return to Africa '89
Revolt '17
Rope of Sand '49
Running Wild '99
Safari Drums '53
Sahara '05
Sanders of the River '35 ▶
Sands of the Kalahari '65
Sarafina! '92 ▶
Seal Team 8: Behind Enemy Lines '14
Secret Obsession '88
7 Days in Entebbe '18
Shaft in Africa '73
Shaka Zulu '83 ▶
Shaka Zulu: The Last Great Warrior '01
Shake Hands With the Devil: The Journey of Romeo Dallaire '04 ▶
The Sheltering Sky '90 ▶
Shooting Dogs '05
Simba '55 ▶
The Sins of Rachel Cade '61
Skeleton Coast '89
The Snows of Kilimanjaro '52 ▶
Something of Value '57 ▶
Song of Freedom '36
Soul Power '08
The Southern Star '69
Stander '03
Storm Over the Nile '55
The Story of an African Farm '04
Submergence '18
Sundown '41
Tarzan '99 ▶
Tarzan and the Lost City '98
Tears of the Sun '03
They Will Have to Kill Us First: Malian Music in Exile '15
13 Hours: The Secret Soldiers of Benghazi '16
Timbuktu '15 ▶
Time to Kill '89
To Walk with Lions '99
Tobruk '66
Tremors 5: Bloodlines '15
Tsotsi '05 ▶
21 Up South Africa: Mandela's Children '08 ▶
24: Redemption '08
A United Kingdom '17
Untamed '55
Vehicle 19 '13
Virunga '14 ▶
Wah-Wah '05
War Witch '12
We Come As Friends '14
When We Were Kings '96 ▶
White Hunter, Black Heart '90 ▶
White Material '10
White Mischief '88 ▶
White Wedding '10
The Wild '06
Wild Geese '78
The Wild Thornberrys Movie '02 ▶
Winnie Mandela '13
A World Apart '88 ▶
The World Unseen '07
Xala '75 ▶
Yankee Zulu '95
Zulu '64
Zulu Dawn '79 ▶

African America

Aaliyah: The Princess of R&B '14
Aaron Loves Angela '75
About Last Night '14
Above the Rim '94
Acrimony '18
Addicted '14
The Affair '95
Akeelah and the Bee '06
Ali '01
All About the Benjamins '02
All About You '01
Always Outnumbered Always Outgunned '98 ▶
Amazing Grace '19 ▶
American Gangster '07 ▶
American Son '19
American Violet '09
America's Dream '95 ▶
And Then Came Love '07
And Then There Was You '13
The Angel Levine '70
Anne Rice's The Feast of All Saints '01
Annie '14
Antwone Fisher '02 ▶
Ashes and Embers '82
The Autobiography of Miss Jane Pittman '74 ▶
Baadasssss! '03 ▶
Baby Boy '01
Baggage Claim '13
Ballast '08
Bamboozled '00
The Banker '20
B.A.P.'s '97
Barbershop 2: Back in Business '04 ▶
Barbershop '02 ▶
Barbershop: The Next Cut '16
Beasts of the Southern Wild '12 ▶
Beauty Shop '05 ▶
Bebe's Kids '92
Being Elmo: A Puppeteer's Journey '11
Beloved '98
The Best Man '99 ▶
The Best Man Holiday '13
The Best of Enemies '19
Better Dayz '02
Betty & Coretta '13
The Big Dis '89
Big Mommas: Like Father, Like Son '11
Biggie & Tupac: The Story Behind the Murder of Rap's Biggest Superstars '02
Biker Boyz '03
Bingo Long Traveling All-Stars & Motor Kings '76 ▶
Bird '88 ▶
The Birth of a Nation '16
Black and Blue '19
Black and White '99 ▶
Black Brigade '69
Black Coffee '14
Black Dynamite '09
Black Eye '74
Black Girl '66 ▶
Black Godfather '74
Black Gunn '72
The Black King '32
Black Knight '01
Black Like Me '64
Black Listed '03
Black Nativity '13
The Black Panthers: Vanguard of the Revolution '15 ▶
Black Sister's Revenge '76
Blackbird '14
BlacKkKlansman '18 ▶
Blade '98
Blind Faith '98
The Blind Side '09
Blood Brothers '93
Blood Done Sign My Name '10
Blue Collar '78 ▶
Blues '08
Boardinghouse Blues '48
Bodied '17 ▶
Body and Soul '24
Boesman & Lena '00
The Bounce Back '16
A Boy. A Girl. A Dream. '18
Boycott '02 ▶
The Boys of Baraka '05
Boyz N the Hood '91 ▶
Breaking a Monster '16 ▶
The Breaks '99
Brian Banks '18
Bright Road '53
Bringing Down the House '03
The Brother from Another Planet '84 ▶
Brother John '70 ▶
Brother to Brother '04
The Brothers '01 ▶
Brown Sugar '02
Bucktown '75
Buffalo Soldiers '97 ▶
Bulworth '98 ▶
Cabin in the Sky '43 ▶
Carmen: A Hip Hopera '01
Carmen Jones '54 ▶
Carter High '15
Catfish in Black Bean Sauce '00
Caught Up '98
CB4: The Movie '93
Champs '15 ▶
The Chateau '01
The Cherokee Kid '96
Chi-raq '15 ▶
Christmas at Water's Edge '04
Christmas in Canaan '09
Christmas in Compton '12
Chuck Berry: Hail! Hail! Rock 'n' Roll '87 ▶
Civil Brand '02
Class Act '91
Clemency '19
Clockers '95 ▶
Code Name: The Cleaner '07
College Road Trip '08
The Color Purple '85 ▶
Coming to America '88 ▶
The Confidant '10
Consinsual '10
Conviction '02
Cool Breeze '72
Cooley High '75 ▶
Cora Unashamed '00
The Corner '00
Corrupt '99
Cotton Comes to Harlem '70 ▶
The Courage to Love '00
Cover '08
Cranford '08
Crooklyn '94 ▶
Crossover '06
Crown Heights '02
Da 5 Bloods '20
Da Sweet Blood of Jesus '14
Daddy's Little Girls '07
Dancing in September '00
Dangerous Evidence: The Lori Jackson Story '99
Daughters of the Dust '91 ▶
Dave Chappelle's Block Party '06 ▶
A Day in the Life '09
A Day Late and a Dollar Short '14
The Day Shall Come '19
Dead Heist '07
Dead Presidents '95
Dear White People '14 ▶
The Defiant Ones '58 ▶
Deliver Us from Eva '03
Detroit '17 ▶
Devil in a Blue Dress '95 ▶
Diary of a Mad Black Woman '05
Dirty Laundry '07
Disappearing Acts '00
Disorderlies '87
Divided We Stand '00
Divine Intervention '07
Django Unchained '12 ▶
Do the Right Thing '89 ▶
Dolemite Is My Name '19 ▶
Don't Be a Menace to South Central While Drinking Your Juice in the Hood '95
Don't Let Go '19
Double Take '01
Double Wedding '10
Down to Earth '01
Dreamgirls '06 ▶
DROP Squad '94
Drumline '02 ▶
Drums O'Voodoo '34
Dynamite Chicken '70
Edge of the City '57
An Encounter with the Messiah '15
Everyday Black Man '10
Eve's Bayou '97 ▶
The Express '08
The Family That Preys '08
A Family Thing '96 ▶
Far from Heaven '02 ▶
Farming '19
Fat Albert '04
Father of Lies '07
Fear of a Black Hat '94
Fences '16 ▶
Fifty Shades of Black '16
Final Comedown '72
Finding Buck McHenry '00
Firehouse '87
First Sunday '08
The Fits '16
The Five Heartbeats '91 ▶
Five Nights in Maine '16
Fly by Night '93
Foolish '99
For Colored Girls '10
For One Night '06
For Real '02
Forgiveness '15
42 '13 ▶
48 Hrs. '82 ▶
Four '12
Four of Hearts '13
Foxy Brown '74
Frankie and Alice '10
Free of Eden '98
Freedom Song '00 ▶
Fresh '94
Fresh Dressed '15
Friday '95
Friday After Next '02
From Above '13
Fruitvale Station '13
G '02
The Gabby Douglas Story '14
Gang in Blue '96
Get On the Bus '96 ▶
Get On Up '14
Get Rich or Die Tryin' '05
Ghetto Dawg 2: Out of the Pits '05
Ghetto Dawg '02
Ghosts of Mississippi '96
Gifted Hands: The Ben Carson Story '09
Gimme the Loot '12
Girl from Chicago '32
The Glass Shield '95
Glory '89 ▶
Glory Road '06
Go Tell It on the Mountain '84
The Golden Child '86
A Good Day to Die '95
Good Fences '03
Good Hair '09
Gordon Glass '07
The Gospel '05 ▶
Gospel Hill '08
The Grace Card '11
Graffiti Bridge '90
Greased Lightning '77
The Great Debaters '07 ▶
The Great White Hope '70
The Greatest '77
The Green Mile '99
The Green Pastures '36 ▶
Grindin' '07
Guess Who's Coming to Dinner '67 ▶
Guilty by Association '03
The Guy from Harlem '77
Hale County This Morning, This Evening '18 ▶
Half Nelson '06 ▶
Half Slave, Half Free '85
Hallelujah! '29 ▶
Halls of Anger '70
Hangin' with the Homeboys '91 ▶
Hard Lessons '86
Harlem Nights '89
Harriet '19
Hav Plenty '97 ▶
Having Our Say: The Delany Sisters' First 100 Years '99
He Got Game '98
Head of State '03
The Heart Specialist '06
Heaven Ain't Hard to Find '10
Heavens Fall '06
The Help '11 ▶
Hendrix '00
A Hero Ain't Nothin' but a Sandwich '78
Hidden Figures '17 ▶
High Flying Bird '19
Higher Learning '94
The Hit '06
Holiday Rush '19
Hollywood Shuffle '87
Homecoming '13
Honeydripper '07
Hoodlum '96
Hoop Dreams '94 ▶
Hopelessly in June '11
House Party 2: The Pajama Jam '91
House Party 3 '94
House Party '90 ▶
How High '01
How I Spent My Summer Vacation '97
How Stella Got Her Groove Back '98
How to Eat Your Watermelon in White Company (and Enjoy It) '05 ▶
How U Like Me Now? '92 ▶
The Hurricane '99 ▶
Hurry Sundown '67
The Hustle '08
Hustle & Flow '05 ▶
I Accidentally Domed Your Son '04
I Am Not Your Negro '17 ▶
I Can Do Bad All By Myself '09
I Got the Hook-Up '98
I Think I Love My Wife '07
Identity Crisis '90
Idlewild '06
If Beale Street Could Talk '18 ▶
I'm Gonna Git You Sucka '88 ▶
Imitation of Life '34
Imitation of Life '59 ▶
In His Father's Shoes '97
In My Father's House '15 ▶
In the Heat of the Night '67 ▶
Incognito '99
The Inheritance '10
The Inkwell '94
Internet Dating '08
Introducing Dorothy Dandridge '99 ▶
Intruder in the Dust '49 ▶
The Jackie Robinson Story '50 ▶
Jada '08
The Janky Promoters '09
Jason's Lyric '94
Jasper, Texas '03
Jazz on a Summer's Day '59
J.D.'s Revenge '76
The Jesse Owens Story '84
Jimi: All Is by My Side '14
Jo Jo Dancer, Your Life Is Calling '86
Joe and Max '02 ▶
The Joe Louis Story '53
Johnny B. '00
Johnson Family Vacation '04
The Josephine Baker Story '90 ▶
Juanita '19
Juice '92
Jump In! '07
Jumping the Broom '11
Junior's Groove '97
Just Another Girl on the I.R.T. '93
Just Mercy '19 ▶
Just Wright '10
Kansas City '95 ▶
Keanu '16

▶ = rated three bones or higher

- Keep the Faith, Baby '02
- The Keeper '96
- Killer Diller '48
- Killer of Sheep '77 ▸
- King '78 ▸
- Kingdom Come '01
- Kings '17
- Kings of the Evening '08
- Kiss the Bride '10
- The Klansman '74
- Krush Groove '85
- Lady Sings the Blues '72
- The Land '16
- The Landlord '70
- The Last Black Man in San Francisco '19 ▸
- The Last Dragon '85
- Last Holiday '06
- The Last Letter '13
- The Last of the Mobile Hotshots '69
- Laughing to the Bank '13
- Lean on Me '89 ▸
- The Learning Tree '69
- The Least Among You '09
- The Least of These '08
- Lee Daniels' The Butler '13
- The Lena Baker Story '08
- A Lesson Before Dying '99 ▸
- Let It Shine '12
- Let's Do It Again '75
- Liberty Heights '99
- Life & Nothing More '17
- Life of a King '13
- Life Support '07 ▸
- Lift '01
- Lilies of the Field '63 ▸
- Little '19
- Little John '02
- Little Richard '00
- Livin' Large '91
- The Long Walk Home '89 ▸
- Losing Isaiah '94 ▸
- Lost Boundaries '49
- The Lottery Ticket '10
- Lotto Land '95
- Love and Other Four Letter Words '07
- Love Beat the Hell Outta Me '00
- Love Don't Cost a Thing '03
- Love Goggles '99
- Love Jones '96 ▸
- Love Songs '99
- A Low Down Dirty Shame '94
- Luce '19 ▸
- LUV '13
- Madea Goes to Jail '09
- Madea's Big Happy Family '11
- Madea's Family Reunion '06
- Madea's Witness Protection '12
- Mahogany '75
- Malcolm X '92 ▸
- Mama Flora's Family '98
- A Man Called Adam '66
- Man in the Mirror: The Michael Jackson Story '04
- The Man with the Iron Fists '12
- Mandela and de Klerk '97
- Manderlay '05
- Medicine for Melancholy '08
- Meet the Blacks '16
- Menace II Society '93 ▸
- Middle of Nowhere '12 ▸
- Miles Ahead '16 ▸
- Miracle at St. Anna '08
- Miracle in Harlem '48
- Miss Evers' Boys '97
- Miss Juneteenth '20
- Mississippi Burning '88 ▸
- Mississippi Masala '92 ▸
- Mr. & Mrs. Loving '96 ▸
- Mister Johnson '91 ▸
- Mr. Ricco '75
- Mixing Nia '98
- Mo' Better Blues '90
- Mo' Money '92
- Monsters and Men '18
- Monster's Ball '01 ▸
- Moon over Harlem '39
- Moonlight '16 ▸
- Mooz-Lum '10
- More Money More Family '15
- Morris from America '16 ▸
- Mudbound '17 ▸
- Murda Muzik '03
- My Brother '06
- My Girlfriend's Back '10
- My Side Piece '16
- Mysterious Ways '15
- Native Son '19
- New Jack City '91
- New Jersey Drive '95
- Next Friday '00
- Night Catches Us '10
- Night Comes On '18 ▸
- Night School '18
- Nightjohn '96
- Nina '16
- 1982 '16
- 96 Minutes '11
- No Way Back '74
- No Way Out '50
- Noah's Arc: Jumping the Broom '08
- Nora's Hair Salon 2: A Cut Above '08
- Nora's Hair Salon '04
- Norbit '07
- The North Star '16
- Not Easily Broken '09
- Nothing but a Man '64
- Notorious '09
- Of Boys and Men '08
- The Old Settler '01
- On the Edge '02
- Once Upon a Time . . . When We Were Colored '95 ▸
- One False Move '91 ▸
- Original Gangstas '96
- Othello '01 ▸
- The Other Brother '02
- Our America '02
- Our Family Wedding '10
- Our Song '01 ▸
- Out of Sync '95
- Paid in Full '02
- Panther '95
- Paper Soldiers '02
- Parallel Sons '95
- Pariah '11 ▸
- Paris Is Burning '91 ▸
- Passing Glory '99 ▸
- Pastime '91 ▸
- A Patch of Blue '65
- Paul Robeson '77
- Peeples '13
- Penitentiary '79
- Percentage '13
- The Perfect Holiday '07
- The Perfect Man '11
- Personals '00
- Phantom Punch '09
- Phat Beach '96
- Phat Girlz '06
- The Photograph '20
- The Piano Lesson '94 ▸
- Pimp '18
- Pinky '49 ▸
- Playin' For Love '15 ▸
- Poetic Justice '93
- Pootie Tang '01
- Preacher's Kid '10
- The Preacher's Wife '96
- Preaching to the Choir '05
- Precious: Based on the Novel 'Push' by Sapphire '09 ▸
- Premature '20
- Presenting Princess Shaw '16
- Pride '07
- The Princess and the Frog '09 ▸
- The Proud Family Movie '05
- Proud Mary '18
- Purlie Victorious '63
- Purple Rain '84
- The Pursuit of Happyness '06
- Putney Swope '69 ▸
- Queen & Slim '19 ▸
- Quest '17
- Quiet Fire '91
- Race '99
- Race '16
- Race to Freedom: The Story of the Underground Railroad '94
- Radio '03
- A Rage in Harlem '91 ▸
- A Raisin in the Sun '61 ▸
- A Raisin in the Sun '08
- Raising the Heights '97
- Rappin' '85
- The Reading Room '05
- Rebound: The Legend of Earl 'The Goat' Manigault '96
- The Red Sneakers '01
- Red Tails '12
- Relative Stranger '09
- Repentance '14
- Rhapsody '01
- Ricochet '91 ▸
- Ride '98
- Ride Along 2 '16
- The River Niger '76
- Rock the Paint '05
- Rockwell: A Legend of the Wild West '93
- Roll Bounce '05 ▸
- Roman J. Israel, Esq. '17
- Romeo Must Die '00
- Roots '77 ▸
- Roots: The Gift '88
- Roots: The Next Generation '79 ▸
- The Rosa Parks Story '02
- Rosewood '96 ▸
- Ruby Bridges '98
- Rude '96
- The Salon '05
- Santa and Pete '99
- Saving God '08
- The Scar of Shame '27
- School Daze '88 ▸
- Scott Joplin '77
- The Secret Life of Bees '08 ▸
- Selma '14 ▸
- Selma, Lord, Selma '99
- Separate but Equal '91 ▸
- Sepia Cinderella '47
- Sergeant Rutledge '60 ▸
- Set It Off '96 ▸
- Seventeen Again '00
- The '70s '00
- Shadows '60 ▸
- Shaft '71 ▸
- Shaft '00 ▸
- Shaft '19
- Shaft's Big Score '72
- Shanty Tramp '67
- She Hate Me '04
- Sheba, Baby '75
- She's Gotta Have It '86 ▸
- She's Not Our Sister '11
- The Show '95
- Silent Cry Aloud '16
- The Simple Life of Noah Dearborn '99
- A Simple Promise '07
- The Sin Seer '15
- Six Degrees of Separation '93
- The '60s '99
- Slam '98
- Snow Dogs '02
- A Soldier's Story '84 ▸
- Something New '06
- Something the Lord Made '04
- Song of Freedom '36
- Soul Food '97
- Soul Men '08
- Soul of the Game '96 ▸
- Soul Plane '04
- Soul Survivor '95
- Soul Vengeance '75
- Sounder '72 ▸
- South Central '92
- Spark '98
- Sparkle '76
- Speed-Dating '10
- Sprung '96
- Steel Magnolias '12 ▸
- Step '17
- Stomp the Yard '07
- Stomp the Yard 2: Homecoming '10
- Straight out of Brooklyn '91
- Strange Fruit '04
- A Stranger in the Kingdom '98
- Strapped '93
- Strong Island '17 ▸
- Sudie & Simpson '90 ▸
- Sugar Hill '74
- Sugar Hill '94
- Summer's End '99
- The Sun Is Also a Star '19
- Superfly '72
- SuperFly '18
- The Suspect '14
- Sweet Sweetback's Baadasssss Song '71 ▸
- Take a Giant Step '59
- Tales from the Hood '95
- Talk to Me '07
- Tap '89
- Tar '97
- The Temptations '98
- 10,000 Black Men Named George '02
- The Tenants '06
- They Call Me Sirr '00
- Thicker than Water '99
- A Thin Line Between Love and Hate '96
- Think Like a Man '12
- Think Like a Man Too '14
- 35 and Ticking '10
- 30 Years to Life '01
- This Christmas '07
- Three Can Play That Game '07
- Three Strikes '00
- Three the Hard Way '74
- Thurgood '11 ▸
- Tick... Tick... Tick '70
- The Tiger Woods Story '98
- A Time to Kill '96 ▸
- To Sir, with Love '67
- To Sleep with Anger '90 ▸
- Toe to Toe '09
- Toni Morrison: The Pieces I Am '19 ▸
- Top Five '14 ▸
- The Trip to Bountiful '14 ▸
- Trippin' '99
- Truck Turner '74
- Turn It Up '00
- The Tuskegee Airmen '95 ▸
- 12 Years a Slave '13 ▸
- Two Can Play That Game '01
- Tyler Perry's A Madea Christmas '13
- Tyler Perry's Good Deeds '12
- Tyler Perry's Hell Hath No Fury Like a Woman Scorned: The Play '14
- Tyler Perry's Meet the Browns '08
- Tyler Perry's Temptation: Confessions of a Marriage Counselor '13
- Tyler Perry's Why Did I Get Married? '07
- Tyler Perry's Why Did I Get Married Too '10
- Undercover Brother '02
- Undisputed '02
- The Untold Story of Emmett Louis Till '05 ▸
- Up Against the Eight Ball '04
- Uptight '68
- Vicky Cristina Barcelona '08
- Waist Deep '06
- Waiting to Exhale '95 ▸
- The Wash '01
- Watermelon Man '70
- The Watermelon Woman '97
- The Watsons Go to Birmingham '13
- Waves '19 ▸
- Welcome Home Roscoe Jenkins '08
- What About Your Friends: Weekend Getaway '02
- What Happened, Miss Simone? '15 ▸
- What Men Want '19
- What Up? '08
- What's Love Got to Do with It? '93
- When We Were Kings '96 ▸
- Where Children Play '15
- Where Hearts Lie '16
- White Chicks '04
- White Dog '82
- White Man's Burden '95
- White Men Can't Jump '92
- Whitney '15
- Who Do You Love '08
- Who Made the Potatoe Salad? '05
- Who's Your Caddy? '07
- Whose Streets? '17
- Why Am I Doing This? '09
- Within Our Gates '20
- The Wiz '78
- Woman, Thou Art Loosed '04
- The Women of Brewster Place '89 ▸
- The Wood '99
- Words by Heart '84
- You Got Served '04
- You Must Remember This '92
- You So Crazy '94
- Zebrahead '92 ▸
- Zora Is My Name! '90

AIDS

***See also** Disease of the Week*

- Alive and Kicking '96
- All About My Mother '99 ▸
- And the Band Played On '93 ▸
- Angels in America '03 ▸
- Because of You '95
- Before Night Falls '00 ▸
- Behind the Red Door '02
- Blue '93
- Boys on the Side '94
- BPM (Beats Per Minute) '17
- Close My Eyes '91
- Close to Leo '02
- Common Threads: Stories from the Quilt '89 ▸
- Conspiracy of Silence '03
- The Constant Gardener '05 ▸
- The Cure '95
- Dallas Buyers Club '13 ▸
- Darwin's Nightmare '04 ▸
- Desert Migration '16 ▸
- An Early Frost '85 ▸
- The Event '03
- Forrest Gump '94 ▸
- Gia '98
- Girl, Positive '07
- Green Plaid Shirt '96
- Heaven's a Drag '94
- A Home at the End of the World '04
- Homeless to Harvard: The Liz Murray Story '03
- The Hours '02 ▸
- How to Survive a Plague '12 ▸
- It's My Party '95
- Jeanne and the Perfect Guy '98
- Jeffrey '95
- Kids '95
- Life, Above All '10
- Life Support '07 ▸
- Loggerheads '05 ▸
- Longtime Companion '90 ▸
- Love Thy Neighbor '02
- Love! Valour! Compassion! '96
- The Man I Love '97
- My Own Country '98
- No One Sleeps '01
- The Normal Heart '14 ▸
- One Night Stand '97 ▸
- Our Sons '91
- Parting Glances '86 ▸
- The Perfect Son '00
- Peter's Friends '92
- Philadelphia '93 ▸
- Playing by Heart '98
- Postcards from America '95
- Rent '05
- A River Made to Drown In '97
- Sex Positive '09
- Summer 1993 '17 ▸
- Sweet Jane '98
- This Girl's Life '03
- The Trip '02
- The 24th Day '04
- 21 Up South Africa: Mandela's Children '08 ▸
- The Velocity of Gary '98
- The Visit '00 ▸
- We Were Here '11
- The Witnesses '07
- Zero Patience '94

Air Disasters

***See** Airborne; Disaster Flicks; Sea Disasters*

Airborne

***See also** Air Disasters; Stewardesses*

- Above and Beyond '53 ▸
- Above and Beyond '06
- Ace Drummond '36
- Ace of Aces '33
- Aces: Iron Eagle 3 '92
- Active Stealth '99
- Adventures of Smilin' Jack '43
- Afterburn '92 ▸
- Air America '90
- Air Eagles '31
- Air Force '43 ▸
- Air Force One '97 ▸
- Air Hawks '35
- Air Rage '01
- Airborne '98
- Airboss '97
- Airplane 2: The Sequel '82
- Airplane! '80 ▸
- Airplane vs. Volcano '14
- Airport '75 '75
- Airport '77 '77
- Airport '70 ▸
- Altitude '10
- Altitude '17
- Always '89
- Amelia '09
- Amelia Earhart: The Final Flight '94
- Angels One Five '54
- Appointment in London '53
- The Aviator '85
- Baggage Claim '13
- The Bamboo Blonde '46
- Battle of Britain '69
- Battle of the Eagles '79
- Beyond the Time Barrier '60
- Biggles '85
- Birds of Prey '72
- Black Thunder '98
- The Blue Max '66
- Blue Thunder '83
- Boeing Boeing '65
- Bombardier '43
- Bombers B-52 '57
- Brewster McCloud '70 ▸
- Bulletproof '96
- By Dawn's Early Light '89
- Calcutta '47
- Can You Keep a Secret? '19
- Canal Zone '42
- Captains of the Clouds '42
- Central Airport '33
- Chain Lightning '50
- China Clipper '36
- Christopher Strong '33
- Con Air '97 ▸
- The Concorde: Airport '79 '79
- Crash Landing '58
- Crimson Romance '34
- The Crowded Sky '60
- Cry Terror! '58
- Dark Blue World '01
- The Dawn Patrol '30 ▸
- Dawn Patrol '38 ▸
- Deadly Encounter '72 ▸
- Delta Force '86
- Desert Thunder '99
- Desperate Search '52
- Die Hard 2: Die Harder '90 ▸
- Disney's The Kid '00
- Dive Bomber '41 ▸
- Dr. Strangelove, or: How I Learned to Stop Worrying and Love the Bomb '64 ▸
- Dragonfly Squadron '54
- Drop Zone '94
- The Eagle and the Hawk '33 ▸
- Executive Decision '96
- The Family Jewels '65
- Fate Is the Hunter '64
- Fighter Squadron '48
- Final Approach '08
- Final Destination '00
- Final Mission '93
- Fire Birds '90
- Firefox '82
- First Light '10
- Five Weeks in a Balloon '62
- Flat Top '52
- Flight '12 ▸
- Flight Angels '40
- Flight Command '40

▸ = rated three bones or higher

Flight from Glory '37
Flight of Black Angel '91
Flight of the Intruder '90
The Flight of the Phoenix '65 ►
Flight 7500 '16
Flightplan '05
Fly Away Home '96 ►
Flyboys '06
Flying Blind '41
The Flying Deuces '39 ►
Flying Down to Rio '33
The Flying Fleet '29
Flying High '31
Flying Leathernecks '51 ►
Flying Tigers '42
For the Moment '94
Forget Paris '95
Freedom Strike '98
French Kiss '95
The Geisha Boy '58
God is My Co-Pilot '45
Going Wild '30
The Great Waldo Pepper '75 ►
Hell Divers '31
Hell's Angels '30 ►
High Flyers '37
High Road to China '83
Higher Ground '88
Hijacked '12
The Horror at 37,000 Feet '73
Hostage Flight '85
Hot Shots! '91 ►
The Hunters '58
Hypersonic '02
I'm So Excited '13
Independence Day '96 ►
Interceptor '92
Into the Sun '92
Iron Eagle '86
Iron Eagle 2 '88
Iron Eagle 4 '95
The Island at the Top of the World '74
It Happened at the World's Fair '63
Jack Brown, Genius '94
Jet Pilot '57
Julie '56
Keep 'Em Flying '41
La Bamba '87 ►
La Grande Vadrouille '66 ►
Lafayette Escadrille '58
L'Annee Sainte '76
Left Behind '14
The Left Hand of God '55 ►
Living on Velvet '35
Look Who's Talking Now '93
Love Affair '32
Love Affair '94
Love is in the Air '13
Low Heights '02
Mach 2 '00
Malta Story '53
The Man with the Golden Gun '74
The Mark '12
The McConnell Story '55
Memphis Belle '90 ►
Men Against the Sky '40
Men of the Fighting Lady '54 ►
Men with Wings '38
Mercy Mission '93
Millennium '89
Mirror Wars: Reflection One '05
Moon Pilot '62
Murder on Flight 502 '75
Mystery Squadron '33
Night Flight '33
1941 '79
No Highway in the Sky '51 ►
Non-Stop '14
The Non-Stop Flight '26
October Sky '99 ►
One of Our Aircraft Is Missing '41 ►
1,000 Plane Raid '69
Only Angels Have Wings '39 ►
Operation Dumbo Drop '95
Pandora's Clock '96
Parachute Jumper '32
Paradise, Hawaiian Style '66
Passenger 57 '92
Pearl Harbor '01
The Phantom '96
Phone Call from a Stranger '52
Piece of Cake '88
Pilot X '37
Planes '13
Planes: Fire & Rescue '14
Power Dive '41
Pushing Tin '99 ►
Reach for the Sky '56
The Red Baron '08
Red Eye '05 ►
Red Sky '14
Red Tails '12
Revenge of the Red Baron '93
The Right Stuff '83 ►
Robot Pilot '41
Saigon '47
7 Days in Entebbe '18
7500 '12
Shadow of the Eagle '32
Six Days, Seven Nights '98
633 Squadron '64
Sky Riders '76
Skyway '33
Slattery's Hurricane '49
Snakes on a Plane '06
The Sound Barrier '52
The Space Between '10
Special Delivery '08
Spirit of St. Louis '57 ►
Spitfire '42 ►
Steal the Sky '88
Stealth '05
Stealth Fighter '99
Stephen King's The Langoliers '95
Stephen King's The Night Flier '96
Strategic Air Command '55
Stuart Little 2 '02 ►
Survivor '80
Swing Shift Maisie '43
Tactical Assault '99
Tail Spin '39
Tarnished Angels '57 ►
Task Force '49
Terminal Velocity '94
Test Pilot '38 ►
Those Magnificent Men in Their Flying Machines '65 ►
Three Came to Kill '61
Thunder Birds '42
Tip On a Dead Jockey '57
Today We Live '33
Top Gun '86
Toward the Unknown '56
Trouble in the Sky '60
Turbulence '96
Turbulent Skies '10
The Tuskegee Airmen '95 ►
Twelve o'Clock High '49 ►
24 Hours to Kill '65
Up Goes Maisie '46
Up in the Air '09 ►
View from the Top '03
Waiting for Dublin '07
War Lover '62
The Way to the Stars '45
The Wedding Singer '97
We'll Meet Again '82
The White Diamond '04 ►
The Wind Rises '13 ►
The Winds of Kitty Hawk '78
A Wing and a Prayer '44 ►
Wings '27
Wings in the Dark '35
Wings of Danger '52
Wings of Eagles '57
Wings of the Navy '39
You Gotta Stay Happy '48
Zeppelin '71

Airplanes

***See** Air Disasters; Airborne*

Alaska

***See also** Cold Spots*

Against the Wild '14
Alaska '96
Avalanche '99
Back to God's Country '53
Balto '95 ►
Bears '14
Beyond '11
Big Miracle '12
The Big White '05
The Call of the Wild '35 ►
Call of the Wild '72
Call of the Wild '93
The Call of the Wild '20
Dear Lemon Lima '09
Deep Winter '08
The Edge '97
Extreme Limits '01
Eye of the Beholder '99
First Descent '05
The Fourth Kind '09
The Gold Rush '25 ►
Goldrush: A Real Life Alaskan Adventure '98
The Great Alone '15
The Grey '12
Grizzly Man '05 ►
Higher Ground '88
Hold the Dark '18
Insomnia '02 ►
Into the Wild '07 ►
Jack London's The Call of the Wild '97
Klondike Annie '36
Klondike Fever '79
Klondike Fury '42
The Last Winter '06
Limbo '99
Long Shot '19
Mystery, Alaska '99
Never Cry Wolf '83 ►
North to Alaska '60 ►
Northern Lights '09
On Deadly Ground '94
The Proposal '09
The Road to Utopia '46 ►
Runaway Train '85 ►
The Simpsons Movie '07 ►
Snow Buddies '08
Spawn of the North '38
The Spoilers '42 ►
Spoilers of the North '47
Sweet Virginia '17
30 Days of Night '07
Togo '19 ►
The Trail of '98 '28
The Undefeated '11
Wilderness Love '02
Wyvern '09

Alcatraz

***See also** Great Escapes; Men in Prison*

Birdman of Alcatraz '62 ►
Dark Passage '47
The Enforcer '76
Escape from Alcatraz '79 ►
Half Past Dead '02
The Last Gangster '37
Murder in the First '95
Point Blank '67
The Rock '96 ►
Skidoo '68
X-Men: The Last Stand '06

Alcoholism

***See** On the Rocks*

Alien Babes

***See also** Alien Beings--Benign; Alien Beings--Vicious; Aliens Are People, Too*

Alien Visitor '95
Beach Babes 2: Cave Girl Island '95
Cat Women of the Moon '53
Cocoon '85 ►
The Day the Earth Stopped '08
Decoys '04
Decoys: The Second Seduction '07
Dude, Where's My Car? '00
Guardians of the Galaxy '14 ►
Guardians of the Galaxy Vol. 2 '17 ►
How To Talk To Girls At Parties '17
Interceptor Force 2 '02
Invasion of the Star Creatures '63
Leprechaun 4: In Space '96
Mars Attacks! '96
Men in Black 2 '02
My Stepmother Is an Alien '88
Planet of Blood '66
Queen of Outer Space '58
The Sender '98
Species '95
Species 2 '98
Species 3 '04
Species 4: The Awakening '07
Star Trek: First Contact '96 ►
Under the Skin '13 ►
Vampire Vixens from Venus '94
Vampirella '96

Alien Beings--Benign

***See also** Alien Babes; Alien Beings--Vicious; Alien Cops; Aliens Are People, Too; Out of This World Sex; Space Operas*

Absolutely Anything '17
The Abyss '89 ►
Aftershock '88
Alien from L.A. '87
Alien Nation '88
Alien Nation: Body and Soul '95
Alien Nation: Dark Horizon '94
Alien Nation: Millennium '96
Alien Nation: The Enemy Within '96
Aqua Teen Hunger Force Colon Movie Film for Theaters '07
Arrival '16 ►
The Aurora Encounter '85
Avatar '09 ►
Avengers: Endgame '19 ►
*batteries not included '87
Battle for Terra '09 ►
The Big Empty '04
Big Meat Eater '85
The Brother from Another Planet '84 ►
The Cat from Outer Space '78
Chicken Little '05
Close Encounters of the Third Kind '77 ►
Cocoon '85 ►
Cocoon: The Return '88
Communion '89
Coneheads '93
The Cosmic Eye '71 ►
The Cosmic Man '59
Dark City '97
The Day the Earth Stood Still '51 ►
The Day the Earth Stood Still '08
District 9 '09 ►
Doctor Who '96
Earth Girls Are Easy '89
Earth to Echo '14
Earth *vs.* the Flying Saucers '56
The Empire Strikes Back '80 ►
Enemy Mine '85
Escape to Witch Mountain '75 ►
E.T.: The Extra-Terrestrial '82 ►
The Ewok Adventure '84
The Ewoks: Battle for Endor '85
Explorers '85
Femalien 2 '98
Femalien '96
Fire in the Sky '93
Flight of the Navigator '86
Galaxy Quest '99
The Ghastly Love of Johnny X '12
Gremlins 2: The New Batch '90 ►
Gremlins '84 ►
Groom Lake '02
Guardians of the Galaxy '14 ►
Guardians of the Galaxy Vol. 2 '17 ►
The Hidden '87 ►
The Hitchhiker's Guide to the Galaxy '05 ►
Honeymoon '14
Howard the Duck '86
I Am Number Four '11
I'll Believe You '07
It Came from Outer Space '53 ►
Josh Kirby. . . Time Warrior: Chapter 5, Journey to the Magic Cavern '96
Jupiter Ascending '15
Labyrinth '86 ►
The Last Mimzy '07
The Last Starfighter '84
Leroy and Stitch '06
Lilo & Stitch 2: Stitch Has a Glitch '05 ►
Lilo & Stitch '02 ►
The Lost Skeleton of Cadavra '01
Mac and Me '88
Man of Steel '13
The Man Who Fell to Earth '76 ►
Mars Needs Moms '11
The Mating Habits of the Earthbound Human '99
Max Steel '16
Men in Black '97 ►
Men in Black: International '19
Midnight Special '16 ►
Missile to the Moon '59
Monsters '10
Moon Pilot '62
Morons from Outer Space '85
Munchie '92
Muppets from Space '99
My Favorite Martian '98
My Stepmother Is an Alien '88
My Uncle: The Alien '96
Mysterious Two '82
Outlaw Prophet '01
Pajama Party '64
Paul '11
The Phantom Planet '61
Planet 51 '09
Real Men '87
Repo Man '83 ►
Return of the Jedi '83 ►
Riddler's Moon '98
Riverworld '10
Rock Jocks '12
The Rocket Man '54
Search for the Gods '75
A Shaun the Sheep Movie: Farmageddon '19 ►
Simon '80
Sonic the Hedgehog '20
Spaced Invaders '90
Star Knight '85
Star Trek 3: The Search for Spock '84
Star Trek 4: The Voyage Home '86 ►
Star Trek '09 ►
Star Trek: Beyond '16 ►
Star Trek: First Contact '96 ►
Star Trek: Into Darkness '13 ►
Star Wars '77 ►
Star Wars: Episode 1-The Phantom Menace '99 ►
Stardust Memories '80
Starman '84 ►
Suburban Commando '91
Super 8 '11
Super Mario Bros. '93
Supergirl '84
Superman: The Movie '78 ►
Superman 2 '80 ►
Superman 3 '83
Superman 4: The Quest for Peace '87
Teenage Mutant Ninja Turtles 2: The Secret of the Ooze '91
The Toe Tactic '08
Transformers: Age of Extinction '14
Transformers: The Last Knight '17
The 27th Day '57
UFO: Target Earth '74
Vegas in Space '94
Voyage of the Rock Aliens '87
What Planet Are You From? '00
When Time Expires '97
Zarkorr! The Invader '96
Zeta One '69

Alien Beings--Vicious

***See also** Alien Babes; Alien Beings--Benign; Alien Cops; Aliens Are People, Too; Out of This World Sex; Space Operas*

Absolutely Anything '17
Actium Maximus: War of the Alien Dinosaurs '05
The Adventures of Buckaroo Banzai Across the Eighth Dimension '84 ►
AE: Apocalypse Earth '13
Alien 3 '92
Alien '79 ►
Alien Abduction '14
Alien Agent '07
Alien Apocalypse '05
Alien Contamination '81
Alien: Covenant '17
Alien Dead '79
Alien Factor 2: The Alien Rampage '01
The Alien Factor '78
Alien 51 '04
Alien Hunter '03
Alien Invasion Arizona '07
Alien Lockdown '04
Alien Massacre '67
Alien Nation: Dark Horizon '94
Alien Outlaw '85
Alien Prey '78
Alien Raiders '08
Alien: Resurrection '97 ►
Alien Seed '89
Alien Siege '05
Alien Storm '12
Alien Terminator '95
Alien 3000 '04
Alien Trespass '09
Alien 2 on Earth '80
Alien Uprising '12
Alien *vs.* Predator '04
Alienator '89
Aliens '86 ►
Aliens in the Attic '09
Aliens *vs.* Predator: Requiem '07
Alive '02
The Alpha Incident '76
Altered '06
The Ambushers '67
American Warship '12
American Warships '01
The Angry Red Planet '59
Area 51 '11
Area 51 '15
The Arrival 2 '98
The Arrival '96
Arrival '16 ►
The Astro-Zombies '67
Atomic Rulers of the World '65
Atomic Submarine '59
Attack from Mars '88
Avengers: Infinity War '18 ►
AVH: Alien *vs.* Hunter '07
Baberellas '03
Backlash: Oblivion 2 '95
Bad Channels '92
Bad Taste '88 ►
Battle Beyond the Stars '80
Battle for Skyark '15
Battle: Los Angeles '11
Battle of the Worlds '61
Battle Planet '08
Battlefield Earth '00
Battleship '12
Battlestar Galactica '78
The Beast With a Million Eyes '56
Beware! The Blob '72
Bio Hazard '85
The Blob '58
The Blob '88 ►
Bloodsuckers from Outer Space '83
Blue Flame '93
Body Snatchers '93
The Brain from Planet Arous '57
Breeders '86
Breeders '97
Brightburn '19
Captain Marvel '19 ►
Captive State '19
Cat Women of the Moon '53

► = rated three bones or higher

Class of Nuke 'Em High 3: The Good, the Bad and the Subhumanoid '94
Cold and Dark '05
The Colony '98
Color Out of Space '19
Cowboys & Aliens '11
Creature '85
Creature of Darkness '09
Creeping Terror '64
The Cremators '72
Crimson Force '05
Critters '86
Critters 2: The Main Course '88
Critters 3 '91
Critters 4 '91
Crossworlds '96
The Curse '87
The Dark '79
Dark Breed '96
Dark Skies '13
Dark Star '74 ►
Dark Universe '93
The Darkest Hour '11
Day the World Ended '55
The Day the World Ended '01
Day Time Ended '80
Dead Space '90
Deep Evil '04
Deep Red '94
Destination Inner Space '66
Destination: Outer Space '10
Destroy All Planets '68
Devil Girl from Mars '54
Dr. Alien '88
Doctor Who '96
Dollman '90
Dracula *vs.* Frankenstein '69
Dragon Storm '04
Dreamcatcher '03
Earth *vs.* the Flying Saucers '56
Edge of Tomorrow '14 ►
The Empire Strikes Back '80 ►
Encounter at Raven's Gate '88
End of the World '76
Endangered Species '02
Epoch: Evolution '03
Evil Alien Conquerors '02
Evil Brain from Outer Space '65
Evils of the Night '85
Evolution '01
Extraterrestrial '14
The Eye Creatures '65
Eyes Behind the Stars '72
The Faculty '98
Fantastic Four: Rise of the Silver Surfer '07
The Fear Chamber '68
Feeders '96
The Fifth Element '97
The 5th Wave '16
Final Days of Planet Earth '06
Final Fantasy: The Spirits Within '01
First Man into Space '59
Flesh Eaters from Outer Space '05
Flight to Mars '52
Forbidden World '82
Forbidden Zone: Alien Abduction '96
Frankenstein Meets the Space Monster '65
Freaks of Nature '15
Freezer Burn: The Invasion of Laxdale '08
From Beyond '86 ►
From Other Worlds '04
Galaxy Invader '85
Galaxy of Terror '81
Galaxy Quest '99
Gamera *vs.* Guiron '69
Gamera *vs.* Zigra '71
Genesis II '73
Ghidrah the Three Headed Monster '65
The Giant Claw '57
The Giant Spider Invasion '75
God Told Me To '76
Godzilla: Final Wars '04
Godzilla *vs.* King Ghidora '91
Godzilla *vs.* the Cosmic Monster '74
Goobers! '97
Grand Tour: Disaster in Time '92
The Green Slime '68
Gremlins 2: The New Batch '90 ►
Gremlins '84 ►
Guardians of the Galaxy '14 ►
Guardians of the Galaxy Vol. 2 '17 ►
The Guyver '91
Guyver 2: Dark Hero '94
Hands of Steel '86
Hell Swarm '00
H.G. Wells' War of the Worlds '05
The Hidden 2 '94
The Hidden '87 ►
The High Crusade '92
High Plains Invaders '09
The Hitchhiker's Guide to the Galaxy '05 ►
Horror of the Blood Monsters '70
The Host '13
H.P. Lovecraft's The Color Out of Space '10
The Human Duplicators '64
Hybrid '97
I Am Number Four '11
I Come in Peace '90
I Married a Monster from Outer Space '58
Impostor '02
Independence Day '96 ►
Independence Day: Resurgence '16
Independence Daysaster '13
Inseminoid '80
Interceptor Force '99
Invader '91
Invaders from Mars '53
Invaders from Mars '86
Invasion! '99
Invasion '07
The Invasion '07
Invasion: Earth '98
Invasion Earth: The Aliens Are Here! '87
Invasion for Flesh and Blood '94
Invasion of the Animal People '62
Invasion of the Bee Girls '73 ►
Invasion of the Body Snatchers '56 ►
Invasion of the Body Snatchers '78 ►
Invasion of the Girl Snatchers '73
Invasion of the Neptune Men '61
Invasion of the Pod People '07
Invasion of the Space Preachers '90
Invisible Adversaries '77
Invisible Invaders '59
Island of the Burning Doomed '67
It Came from Outer Space '53 ►
It! The Terror from Beyond Space '58
J-Men Forever! '79 ►
Jimmy Neutron: Boy Genius '01
John Carpenter's Ghosts of Mars '01
Journey to the Seventh Planet '62
Jupiter Ascending '15
Killer Klowns from Outer Space '88
Killer Tongue '96
Killers from Space '54
Kraa! the Sea Monster '98
Kronos '57
Laserhawk '99
Lazer Team '16
The LEGO Movie 2: The Second Part '19
Leroy and Stitch '06
Lethal Target '99
Leviathan '89
Life '17
Liquid Sky '83 ►
Lost in Space '98
Man of Steel '13
Mark of the Astro-Zombies '02
Mars Attacks! '96
Mars Needs Women '66
The Martian Chronicles: Part 3 '79
Mass Effect: Paragon Lost '12
Men in Black 2 '02
Men in Black '97 ►
Men in Black: International '19
Message from Space '78
Mindwarp '91
Mom and Dad Save the World '92
The Monolith Monsters '57
Monster '78
Monster a Go-Go! '65
Monster High '89
Monsters: Dark Continent '15
Monsters *vs.* Aliens '09
Munchies '87
Murdercycle '99
The Mysterians '58
Negadon: The Monster from Mars '05
Night Beast '83
Night Caller from Outer Space '66
Night of the Creeps '86
Night Skies '07
Not of This Earth '88
Not of This Earth '96
Oblivion '94
Outlander '08
Overtime '11
Pacific Rim '13
Pacific Rim: Uprising '18
Peacemaker '90
Phantom from Space '53
The Phantom Planet '61
The Pink Chiquitas '86
Pitch Black '00 ►
Pixels '15
Plan 9 from Outer Space '56
The Planet '06
Planet of Blood '66
Predator '87
Predator 2 '90
The Predator '18
Predators '10
Princess of Mars '09
Progeny '98
Prometheus '12
The Puppet Masters '94
Quatermass 2 '57 ►
The Quatermass Experiment '56 ►
Queen of Blood '66
Radar Men from the Moon '52
Ratchet & Clank '16
Reactor '78
The Recall '17
Recon 2023: The Gauda Prime Conspiracy '08
Reptilian '99
Return of the Aliens: The Deadly Spawn '83
Return of the Jedi '83 ►
Revenge of the Teenage Vixens from Outer Space '86
Revolt '17
Riddick '13
The Rig '10
Riverworld '10
Robin Cook's Invasion '97
Robinson Crusoe: The Great Blitzkrieg '08
Robot Monster '53
Robot World '15
Rock 'n' Roll Nightmare '85
Roswell: The Aliens Attack '99
Scared to Death '80
Sci-Fighters '96
Showdown at Area 51 '07
Signs '02 ►
The Silencers '96
Skyline '10
Slaughterhouse Five '72
The Snow Devils '67
The Space Children '58
Space Chimps '08
Space Jam '96
Space Master X-7 '58
Species '95
Species 2 '98
Specimen '97
Spider-Man 3 '07
Spiders '13
Split Second '92
Star Crystal '85
Star Hunter '95
Star Trek: The Motion Picture '79
Star Trek 3: The Search for Spock '84
Star Trek '09 ►
Star Trek: Beyond '16 ►
Star Trek: First Contact '96 ►
Star Wars '77 ►
Star Wars: Episode 1-The Phantom Menace '99 ►
Stargate '94
Stargate: Continuum '08
Stephen King's The Langoliers '95
Stephen King's The Tommyknockers '93
Storage 24 '12
Stranded '13
Strange Invaders '83 ►
Stranger from Venus '54
Super Buddies '13
Super 8 '11
Super Mario Bros. '93
Superman 2 '80 ►
Supernova '99
Taken '02
Teenage Space Vampires '99
Teenagers from Outer Space '59
10 Cloverfield Lane '16 ►
Terminal Invasion '02
Terror of Mechagodzilla '78
They '77
They Are Among Us '04
They Came from Beyond Space '67
They Live '88
The Thing '51 ►
The Thing '82
The Thing '11
This Island Earth '55
Threshold '03
Thrill Seekers '99
Time Runner '92
Time Walker '82
Transformers '07
Transformers: Age of Extinction '14
Transformers: Dark of the Moon '11
Transformers: Revenge of the Fallen '09
Transformers: The Last Knight '17
12 to the Moon '60
20 Million Miles to Earth '57
2001: A Space Travesty '00
Undead '05
Unearthed '07
Unknown Origin '95
Unseen Evil '99
V '83 ►
V: The Final Battle '84
Vampire Vixens from Venus '94
Venom '18
Village of the Damned '60 ►
Village of the Damned '95
Virus '98
War in Space '77
The War of the Planets '65
War of the Satellites '58
War of the Worlds 2: The Next Wave '08
The War of the Worlds '53 ►
War of the Worlds '05 ►
The Watch '12
When Time Expires '97
Wicked City '92
Wild, Wild Planet '65
Wild Zero '00
Within the Rock '96
Without Warning '80
The World's End '13 ►
The X-Files '98
Xtro '83
Xtro 2: The Second Encounter '91
Xtro 3: Watch the Skies '95
Zarkorr! The Invader '96
Zathura '05 ►
Zebraman '04
Zeram 2 '94 ►
Zeram '91
Zombies of the Stratosphere '52
Zontar, the Thing from Venus '66

Alien Cops

***See also** Alien Babes; Alien Beings--Benign; Alien Beings--Vicious; Aliens Are People, Too; Extraordinary Pairings; Space Operas*

Alien Trespass '09
The Hidden 2 '94
The Hidden '87 ►
Peacemaker '90
The Silencers '96

Aliens Are People, Too

***See also** Alien Babes; Alien Beings--Benign; Alien Beings--Vicious*

The Adventures of Buckaroo Banzai Across the Eighth Dimension '84 ►
Alien 3 '92
Alien '79 ►
Alien Avengers '96
Alien: Resurrection '97 ►
Alien Trespass '09
Aliens '86 ►
Annihilation '18
The Arrival '96
Artifacts '08
The Astronaut's Wife '99
Body Snatchers '93
The Chronicles of Riddick '04
Earth Girls Are Easy '89
The Faculty '98
The Hidden 2 '94
The Hidden '87 ►
The Hitchhiker's Guide to the Galaxy '05 ►
The Host '13
I Married a Monster from Outer Space '58
Impostor '02
InAlienable '08
Infected '08
The Invader '96
Invaders from Mars '53
Invaders from Mars '86
Invasion of the Body Snatchers '56 ►
Invasion of the Body Snatchers '78 ►
Invasion of the Pod People '07
K-PAX '01
Mars Attacks! '96
Meet Dave '08
Men in Black 2 '02
Men in Black '97 ►
My Favorite Martian '98
My Stepmother Is an Alien '88
Not of This Earth '57
Outlander '08
Planet of the Vampires '65
Predator Island '05
The Puppet Masters '94
Species 2 '98
Species 3 '04
Specimen '97
Starman '84 ►
Starship Troopers 2: Hero of the Federation '04
Stranger from Venus '54
Superman Returns '06
Taken '02
Terminal Invasion '02
The Thing '51 ►
The Thing '82
The Thing '11
Thrill Seekers '99
Under the Skin '13 ►
V '83 ►
V: The Final Battle '84
Venom '18

Alzheimer's/Dementia

Alive Inside '14 ►
Away From Her '06 ►
Capone '20
Deep Blue Sea '99
Diminished Capacity '08
Hamlet & Hutch '14
Happy End '17
Iris '01 ►
The Leisure Seeker '17
The Looking Glass '16
Poetry '10
The Reagans '04
Remember '15
Rise of the Planet of the Apes '11 ►
Safe House '99
A Separation '11
A Short History of Decay '13
A Song for Martin '01
Speed of Life '99
Starlet '12 ►
Still Alice '14 ►
Still Mine '13 ►
What They Had '18

Amateur Sleuths

Ace Ventura Jr.: Pet Detective '08
After the Thin Man '36 ►
Agatha Christie's A Caribbean Mystery '83
Agatha Christie's Murder is Easy '82
Agatha Christie's Murder with Mirrors '85
Awakening the Zodiac '17
Beautiful '09
The Bishop Murder Case '30
Blair Witch '16
The Body in the Library '84
The Casino Murder Case '35
Clubhouse Detectives '96
A Date With the Falcon '42
Emil and the Detectives '64
Ex-Mrs. Bradford '36 ►
The Falcon and the Co-Eds '43
The Falcon in Danger '43
The Falcon Strikes Back '43
Fast and Furious '39
Fast and Loose '39
Fast Company '38
Fletch '85
Fletch Lives '89
Footsteps in the Dark '41
Forty Naughty Girls '37
Gallant Sons '40
Gambling Daughters '41
The Gay Falcon '41
Get a Clue '02
Girl Missing '33
The Girl on the Train '16
The Glass Key '42 ►
Gumshoe '72
In Your Dreams '07
Killer Hair '09
Kit Kittredge: An American Girl '08
Man from Cairo '54
The Mandarin Mystery '37
Manhattan Murder Mystery '93 ►
Mary Higgins Clark: Lucky Day '02
Matinee Idol '33
Messenger of Death '88
Miss Pinkerton '32
Mr. Arkadin '55 ►
Mr. Holmes '15
Murder Ahoy '64
Murder at the Gallop '63 ►
Murder in a Small Town '99
Murder Most Foul '65 ►
Murder On a Bridle Path '36
Murder On a Honeymoon '35
Murder On the Blackboard '34
Murder She Said '61
Mystery Kids '99
Nancy Drew '07
Nancy Drew, Reporter '39
Nobody Else But You '11
The Oxford Murders '08
Penguin Pool Murder '32
The Plot Thickens '36

► = rated three bones or higher

A Plumm Summer '08
The Raven '12
Ruby in the Smoke '06
The Shadow in the North '07
Shadow of the Thin Man '41 ▸
A Shot in the Dark '35
The Silent Passenger '35
Song of the Thin Man '47
Speedy Death '99 ▸
Star of Midnight '35
Strange Affair '44
Summer of 84 '18
They Might Be Giants '71 ▸
The Thin Man '34 ▸
The Thin Man Goes Home '44
13th Guest '32
Unconditional Love '03
Veronica Mars '14
Voulez-Vous Danser avec Moi? '59
Whistling in Brooklyn '43
Whistling in Dixie '42
Whistling in the Dark '41 ▸
The Wizard of Gore '07

American Indians

See *Native America*

American South

See also *Atlanta; Memphis; Miami; Nashville; Nashville Narratives; New Orleans; Savannah; Southern Belles*

Ada '61
Ain't No Way Back '89
Albino Farm '09
All the King's Men '06
All the Real Girls '03 ▸
Alleged '10
Alligator Alley '72
An American Haunting '05
Among Brothers '05
Andersonville '95 ▸
Angel Baby '61
Angel Heart '87
The Apostle '97 ▸
April Love '57
The Autobiography of Miss Jane Pittman '74 ▸
The Baby Dance '98 ▸
Baby Doll '56 ▸
Bad Country '14
The Ballad of the Sad Cafe '91
Ballast '08
Bandwagon '95
Barbara Frietchie '24
Bastard out of Carolina '96
Beasts of the Southern Wild '12 ▸
Beautiful Creatures '13
Beer for My Horses '08
The Beguiled '70 ▸
The Beguiled '17
Belizaire the Cajun '86
Beneath the Mississippi '08
Between Heaven and Hell '56 ▸
Beulah Land '80
Big Bad Love '02
Big Boy '30
The Big Easy '87 ▸
Big Fish '03 ▸
Big Momma's House '00
The Birth of a Nation '16
Black Like Me '64
Black Snake Moan '07
Black Widow Murders: The Blanche Taylor Moore Story '93
Blood Done Sign My Name '10
Bloodworth '10
Blue Ridge Fall '99
Boxcar Bertha '72
Boycott '02 ▸
Bright Leaf '50
Bright Road '53
Broken Bridges '06
Bucktown '75
Camilla '94
The Campaign '12
Cape Fear '61 ▸
Carnal Innocence '11
Carolina Blues '44
The Cat and the Canary '39
Cat on a Hot Tin Roof '58 ▸
Cat on a Hot Tin Roof '84
Catch.44 '11
Caught in the Act '04
The Chamber '96
Charms for the Easy Life '02
Child of God '14
Children On Their Birthdays '02
Christmas In Conway '13
Christy '94
Claudelle Inglish '61
Cold Mountain '03 ▸
Colonel Effingham's Raid '45
The Color Purple '85 ▸
Come Early Morning '06
Cookie's Fortune '99 ▸
Cool Hand Luke '67 ▸
Crazy in Alabama '99
Crazy Like a Fox '04
Creature '11
Crossroads '86
CSA: The Confederate States of America '04
Cypress Edge '99
Daddy & Them '99
Daltry Calhoun '05
Dancer, Texas-Pop. 81 '98 ▸
Dead Birds '04
Deadline '12
The Death of Dick Long '19
The Delta '97
Delta Heat '92
The Descent 2 '09
Dirty Laundry '07
Divine Secrets of the Ya-Ya Sisterhood '02
Dixiana '30
Django Unchained '12 ▸
Down in the Delta '98 ▸
Driving Miss Daisy '89 ▸
The Drowning Pool '75
Drum '76
Due East '02
The Dukes of Hazzard '05
The Dynamiter '11
Elizabethtown '05
Enemies Among Us '10
Eve's Bayou '97 ▸
A Family Thing '96 ▸
The Fighting Temptations '03
Final Cut '88
Fireball 500 '66
The First Saturday in May '08
Flamingo Road '49 ▸
Fled '96
Fletch Lives '89
Follow That Car '80
Footloose '11
For Real '02
For Sale by Owner '09
Forrest Gump '94 ▸
Foxfire '87 ▸
Frailty '02 ▸
Freedom Song '00 ▸
Freedom Summer '14
Fried Green Tomatoes '91 ▸
The Fugitive Kind '60
The Gambler from Natchez '54
Game Time: Tackling the Past '11
The General's Daughter '99
George Wallace '97
Get Low '09 ▸
Gettysburg '93 ▸
Ghosts of Mississippi '96
Gideon's Army '13
The Gift '00
The Gingerbread Man '97
The Glass Menagerie '87 ▸
Gods and Generals '03
God's Little Acre '58 ▸
Gone with the Wind '39 ▸
A Good Baby '99
Good Intentions '10
Goodbye Solo '08
Goodbye to All That '14
The Grass Harp '95
Great Balls of Fire '89
The Great Santini '80 ▸
Great World of Sound '07
Green Book '18 ▸
The Green Mile '99
Hannah Montana: The Movie '09
Hard Drivin' '60
Harlan County War '00
The Heart Is Deceitful Above All Things '04
Heart o' the Hills '19
The Heart of Dixie '89
Heavens Fall '06
Hell and Back Again '11
The Help '11 ▸
Heroes of the Heart '94
Hero's Island '62
Highway 301 '50
Home from the Hill '60 ▸
The Home Front '02
Hometown Legend '02
Honeydripper '07
Hootch Country Boys '75
Hounddog '08
The Hunley '99
Hunter's Moon '97
Hurricane Season '09
Hush, Hush, Sweet Charlotte '65 ▸
I Walk the Line '70
I'd Climb the Highest Mountain '51 ▸
In Old Kentucky '35
In the Electric Mist '08
In the Family '11
In the Flesh '97
In the Heat of the Night '67 ▸
Inherit the Wind '99
The Inheritance '10
Intruder in the Dust '49 ▸
Invitation to a Gunfighter '64
Jayne Mansfield's Car '13
Jesse James' Women '54
Jezebel '38 ▸
John Grisham's The Rainmaker '97
The Journey of August King '95
Joyful Noise '12
Judge Priest '34 ▸
Kalamity '10
Kentucky '38
Kentucky Kernels '34
Kentucky Moonshine '38
Killing Season '13
Kings of the Evening '08
Kiss of Fire '98
The Klansman '74
Lady for a Night '42
The Ladykillers '04
Lake City '08
The Last Confederate: The Story of Robert Adams '05
Last Dance '96
Last Kind Words '12
The Last of the Mobile Hotshots '69
The Last Song '10
Lawless '12
The Ledge '11
The Legend of Gator Face '96
The Lena Baker Story '08
A Lesson Before Dying '99 ▸
Life '99
Lifted '10
A Lion Is in the Streets '53 ▸
The List '07
Little Accidents '14
Little Chenier: A Cajun Story '06
The Little Colonel '35 ▸
Little Richard '00
Lolly-Madonna XXX '73
Lone Star State of Mind '02
The Lords of Discipline '83
The Loss of a Teardrop Diamond '08
The Lost & Found Family '09
Louisiana Story '48 ▸
The Lucky One '12
Lure of the Wilderness '52
Macon County Line '74
Madea's Family Reunion '06
Madea's Witness Protection '12
Main Street '10
Manderlay '05
Mandingo '75
Manglehorn '15
Many Rivers to Cross '55
Masterminds '16
Meeting Daddy '98
The Mermaid Chair '06
Midnight in the Garden of Good and Evil '97
Misconceptions '08
Miss Evers' Boys '97
Miss Firecracker '89 ▸
Mississippi '35
Mississippi Burning '88 ▸
Mississippi Masala '92 ▸
Mr. & Mrs. Loving '96 ▸
Misty '61
Monster's Ball '01 ▸
Moonshine Mountain '64
The Moonshine War '70
Morgan's Ferry '99
Morning Glory '93
Mothman '10
The Mothman Prophecies '02
Mud '12 ▸
Murder in Coweta County '83
The Murder of Mary Phagan '87 ▸
Murder on the Bayou '91 ▸
Muscle Shoals '13 ▸
My Cousin Vinny '92 ▸
My Dog Skip '99 ▸
My Louisiana Sky '02 ▸
My Mom's New Boyfriend '08
My Own Country '98
My Own Love Song '10
The Neon Bible '95
Netherworld '90
The New Daughter '10
No Mercy '86
Norma Rae '79 ▸
Norman Rockwell's Shuffleton's Barbershop '13
North and South Book 1 '85 ▸
North and South Book 2 '86 ▸
Not Since You '09
The Notebook '04
Nothing but a Man '64
O Brother Where Art Thou? '00
An Occasional Hell '96
Ode to Billy Joe '76
On the Run '73
On Valentine's Day '86
Once Upon a Time . . . When We Were Colored '95 ▸
One False Move '91 ▸
The Only Thrill '97
Other Voices, Other Rooms '95
Paradise '91 ▸
Paradise Lost 3: Purgatory '11
Passion Fish '92 ▸
The Patriot '00
Perfect Harmony '91
The Phenix City Story '55
Plain Dirty '04
Poor Pretty Eddie '73
Preacher's Kid '10
Primary Colors '98
The Prince of Tides '91 ▸
Princess Protection Program '09
Purlie Victorious '63
Queen Bee '55
Radio '03
Rambling Rose '91 ▸
A Real American Hero '78
The Reaping '07
Red Dirt '99
Redemption Road '10
Reel Love '11
Reflections in a Golden Eye '67
The Relic '96
Return to Mayberry '85
Rich in Love '93
Ride the Wild Fields '00
Ride with the Devil '99
Ripe '97
The Rising Place '02
Road to Nashville '67
Romance of the Limberlost '38
Roots '77 ▸
Roots: The Next Generation '79 ▸
The Rosa Parks Story '02
The Rose Tattoo '55 ▸
Rosewood '96 ▸
Ruby Gentry '52
Ruby's Bucket of Blood '01
The Runaway '00
Rustin '01
Safe Haven '13
The St. Francisville Experiment '00
Saratoga Trunk '45
Scarlett '94
Scorchers '92
The Secret Life of Bees '08 ▸
Secretariat '10
Selma '14 ▸
Selma, Lord, Selma '99
Serena '14
Seven Angry Men '55
Shadrach '98
Shag: The Movie '89 ▸
Shanty Tramp '67
Sherman's March '86 ▸
The Simple Life of Noah Dearborn '99
A Single Shot '13
Sins of the Father '01 ▸
Sister, Sister '87
Six-Pack Annie '75
Sixteen '72
Sling Blade '96 ▸
A Slipping Down Life '99
Smokey Bites the Dust '81
Snuffy Smith, Yard Bird '42
Soldier's Girl '03 ▸
Something for the Boys '44
Something the Lord Made '04
Something to Talk About '95
Sonny '02
Sounder '72 ▸
Southern Comfort '81 ▸
The Southerner '45 ▸
Sparrows '26 ▸
Stand Up and Fight '39
Steel Magnolias '12 ▸
Storm Warning '51
Stormswept '95
Storyville '92
Strange Fruit '04
The Strangers '08
Straw Dogs '11
A Streetcar Named Desire '51 ▸
A Streetcar Named Desire '95
Summer and Smoke '61
Summer's End '99
Swamp Fire '46
Swanee River '39
Sweet Bird of Youth '62 ▸
Sweet Bird of Youth '89
Sweet Country Road '83
Sweet Home Alabama '02
Swimming '00
Swing Your Lady '38
Tammy and the Bachelor '57
Tammy and the Doctor '63
Tammy Tell Me True '61
Tank '83
Texasville '90
That Evening Sun '09 ▸
They Won't Forget '37 ▸
This Stuff'll Kill Ya! '71
Tick... Tick... Tick '70
Tigerland '00 ▸
A Time to Kill '96 ▸
To Kill a Mockingbird '62 ▸
Tobacco Road '41
Tornado Valley '09
The Trail of the Lonesome Pine '36 ▸
The Traveling Executioner '70
The Trial '10
Tribute '09
The Trip to Bountiful '85 ▸
Tune in Tomorrow '90
Two Moon Junction '88
2000 Maniacs '64
2001 Maniacs '05
2001 Maniacs: Field of Screams '10
Tyler Perry's Meet the Browns '08
Undercover With the KKK '78
Undertow '04
The Unseen '05
Untamed Youth '57
The Untold Story of Emmett Louis Till '05 ▸
The Vanishing Virginian '41
Video Voyeur: The Susan Wilson Story '02
Virginia '10
Voodoo Dawn '89
Vulture's Eye '04
Waitress '07 ▸
Walk in the Spring Rain '70
A Walk to Remember '02
Walking Tall '73
Walking Tall: Part 2 '75
Walking Tall: The Final Chapter '77
The War '94
The Waterboy '98
We Are Marshall '06
Welcome Home Roscoe Jenkins '08
The Wet Parade '32
What Comes Around '85
When I Find the Ocean '06
Widow on the Hill '05
Wild Oranges '24
Wild River '60
Wild Things '98
Wildflower '91 ▸
Wise Blood '79 ▸
Within Our Gates '20
A Woman Called Moses '78
Woman in Hiding '49
The World Made Straight '15
Wrong Turn '03
The Yellow Handkerchief '08 ▸
Youngblood Hawke '64
Your Cheatin' Heart '64

America's Heartland

See also *Slice of Life*

About Schmidt '02 ▸
An American Crime '07
American Teen '08
America's Heart and Soul '04
Arachnophobia '90
The Awakening Land '78
The Basket '99
Bloomington '10
Boys Don't Cry '99 ▸
Butter '12
Carried Away '95
Cedar Rapids '11 ▸
The Children Nobody Wanted '81 ▸
Children of the Corn '84
Children of the Corn 4: The Gathering '96
Doc Hollywood '91
Eye of God '97 ▸
Eye of the Storm '98
Fargo '96 ▸
Feed the Fish '09
Field of Dreams '89 ▸
Fire in the Sky '93
Fried Green Tomatoes '91 ▸
Grandview U.S.A. '84
Grumpier Old Men '95
Hard Promises '92
Hard Rain '97
Height of the Sky '99
A History of Violence '05 ▸
Home In Indiana '44
Home of the Giants '07
Homecoming '09
Horton Foote's Alone '97
Hush '98
In Cold Blood '96
Iowa '05
Joshua '02
Late Bloomers '95
Leave It to Beaver '97
Leaves of Grass '09
The Locusts '97
Lonesome Jim '06 ▸
Lovely, Still '08
Macon County Line '74
The Major and the Minor '42 ▸
Meet Monica Velour '10
The Milagro Beanfield War '88 ▸
Mumford '99 ▸
Murphy's Romance '85 ▸
The Music Man '62 ▸
My Cousin Vinny '92 ▸
Nebraska '13 ▸
NoNames '10
Normal Life '96
Northfork '03

▸ = rated three bones or higher

Now and Then '95
Oklahoma! '55 ►
Our Town '40 ►
Our Town '77 ►
Our Town '89
Pearl Diver '04
Phenomenon '96
Powder '95
Promised Land '12
Return to Mayberry '85
The Rider '17
Ring the Bell '13
Saving Grace B. Jones '09
Shotgun Stories '07
Signs '02 ►
The Slaughter Rule '01
Steel Magnolias '89 ►
Straight from the Heart '03
The Straight Story '99 ►
Sugar '09 ►
A Thousand Acres '97
To the Wonder '12
To Wong Foo, Thanks for Everything, Julie Newmar '95
The Toilers and the Wayfarers '97
Tom and Huck '95 ►
The Tree of Life '11 ►
True Confessions of a Hollywood Starlet '08
Tully '00 ►
Twister '96
Waiting for Guffman '96
Where the Heart Is '00
Win a Date with Tad Hamilton! '04
The Winning Season '09

Amnesia

The Addams Family '91
Amateur '94 ►
Amnesia '96
Anastasia '56 ►
Anastasia: The Mystery of Anna '86
The Anomaly '15
Another Woman '94
Armistead Maupin's More Tales of the City '97
Awake '19
The Back Trail '24
Before I Go to Sleep '14
Blind Horizon '04
The Blonde '92
The Blue Gardenia '53 ►
Bomba and the Hidden City '50
The Bourne Identity '88 ►
The Bourne Identity '02 ►
The Bourne Supremacy '04 ►
The Bourne Ultimatum '07 ►
The Bumblebee Flies Anyway '98
Caravan '46
Clean Slate '94
Code Name: The Cleaner '07
Coming Home '14
Crack-Up '46
Crossroads '42
Cure '97 ►
Dangerously We Live '41
Dead Again '91 ►
The Descent 2 '09
Desperately Seeking Susan '85
Diabolically Yours '67
Dr. Gillespie's New Assistant '42
Driftwood '97
88 '15
Empire of the Wolves '05
Eternal Sunshine of the Spotless Mind '04 ►
Experiment '05
Facing Windows '03
The Family Tree '10
50 First Dates '04
The Forgotten '04
The Ghost '04
The Girl on the Train '16
Gone, But Not Forgotten '03
The Great Dictator '40 ►
Hana & Alice '04 ►
Hancock '08
Hardwired '09
Headshot '17
High Stakes '93
Hysteria '64
I Feel Pretty '18
The I Inside '04
I Love You Again '40 ►
Identity Unknown '45
Inferno '99
Into the Arms of Strangers '07
The Jacket '05
Jackie Chan's Who Am I '98
Jane Doe '83
Jericho '01
Killerman '19
The Killing Jar '96
Kiss Me Deadly '08
Libel '59
The Long Kiss Goodnight '96
Lost Honeymoon '47
Love Letters '45
The Majestic '01
Malice in Wonderland '09
The Man Without a Past '02 ►
The Matrimonial Bed '30
The Memory of a Killer '03
Men in Black 2 '02
Men in Black '97 ►
Mirage '66 ►
Mission of Death '97
Mister Buddwing '66
Mulholland Drive '01 ►
The Muppets Take Manhattan '84 ►
Never Forget '08
The Night Before the Night Before Christmas '10
Night of the Hunted '80
Not My Life '06
Overboard '87
Overboard '18
Paycheck '03
Pit of Darkness '61
Project X '68
A Pure Formality '94
Random Harvest '42 ►
Rascals '38
Regarding Henry '91 ►
Return of the Soldier '82 ►
The Right of Way '31
A River Called Titas '73 ►
The Road to Hong Kong '62
The Saddest Music in the World '03
San Saba '08
The Search for Santa Paws '10
The Second Woman '51
The Sender '82
Shattered '91
Shock '79
Smooch '11
Snow 2: Brain Freeze '08
Someone Behind the Door '71
Somewhere in the Night '46
Southland Tales '06
Speed Dating '07
Spellbound '45 ►
Strange Awakening '58
The Stranger '87 ►
The Stranger '10
Swelter '14
10 Minutes Gone '19
The Third Day '65
XIII '08
36 Hours '64 ►
Till Human Voices Wake Us '02
Time Lapse '01
Total Recall '90 ►
Trap for Cinderella '13
Twice a Judas '69
Unholy Four '54
The Unknown Soldier '98
Unknown White Male '05 ►
The Unsuspected '47
Upstream Color '13 ►
Virtual Sexuality '99
The Vow '12
Welcome to Marwen '18
The Werewolf '56
The Wives He Forgot '06
Wrecked '10

Amsterdam

The Amsterdam Connection '78
Anne Frank: The Whole Story '01 ►
The Attic: The Hiding of Anne Frank '88
The Bourne Supremacy '04 ►
Business is Business '71
Deuce Bigalow: European Gigolo '05
The Diary of Anne Frank '59 ►
The Diary of Anne Frank '08
Holy Rollers '10
Hostel '06
Katie Tippel '75
Nightwatching '07
Ocean's Twelve '04
Operation Amsterdam '60
Paid '06
Puppet on a Chain '72
Snapshots '02
Stoner Express '16

Amusement Parks

***See also** Carnivals & Fairs & Expositions*

Action Point '18
Adventureland '09 ►
The Beast from 20,000 Fathoms '53
Bebe's Kids '92
Beverly Hills Cop 3 '94
Big '88 ►
Carnival of Blood '71
Carnival of Souls '62 ►
The Crying Game '92 ►
Curse of the Headless Horseman '72
Dr. Giggles '92
Fatal Attraction '87 ►
Final Destination 3 '06
Free Willy: Escape from Pirate's Cove '10
Funland '89
Gangster World '98
Getting Even with Dad '94
Godzilla on Monster Island '72
Hell Fest '18
Hot Cars '56
Jimmy Neutron: Boy Genius '01
KISS Meets the Phantom of the Park '78
The Lady from Shanghai '48 ►
Liliom '30
Little Fugitive '06
Lucky Days '08
Luv '67
Mighty Joe Young '98
My Life '93
National Lampoon's Vacation '83 ►
1941 '79
Omega Doom '96
Piranha 3DD '11
Postal '07
Rollercoaster '77
Rugrats in Paris: The Movie '00 ►
Scooby-Doo '02
The Slams '73
A Slipping Down Life '99
Strangers on a Train '51 ►
The Third Man '49 ►
3 Ninjas: High Noon at Mega Mountain '97
Tremors 3: Back to Perfection '01
The Way Way Back '13 ►
Wonder Park '19
Wonder Wheel '17
Zombieland '09 ►

Angels

***See also** Heaven Sent*

Absolution '03
Almost an Angel '90
Always '89
Angel-A '05
The Angel Levine '70
Angels in America '03 ►
Angels in the Endzone '98
Angels in the Infield '00
Angels in the Outfield '51 ►
Angels in the Outfield '94
The Bishop's Wife '47 ►
Cabin in the Sky '43 ►
Christmas Angel '11
Christmas at Water's Edge '04
The Christmas Box '95
Christmas Magic '11
City of Angels '98
Click '06
The Contractor '07
Cowboys and Angels '00
Date with an Angel '87
Defending Your Life '91 ►
Dogma '99
Down to Earth '01
Fallen '97
Fallen '17
Faraway, So Close! '93
Fear No Evil '80
Field of Dreams '89 ►
For Heaven's Sake '50
Forever Darling '56
Gabriel & Me '01
Gabriel Over the White House '33 ►
Get Smart '08
The Green Pastures '36 ►
Heart and Souls '93
Heaven Can Wait '78 ►
The Heavenly Kid '85
Here Comes Mr. Jordan '41 ►
The Horn Blows at Midnight '45 ►
I Married an Angel '42
It Came Upon a Midnight Clear '84
It's a Wonderful Life '46 ►
Kindergarten Ninja '94
The Last Will and Testament of Rosalind Leigh '12
Legion '10
Levitation '97
A Life Less Ordinary '97
The Littlest Angel '69
Made in Heaven '87
Michael '96
Miracle in Milan '51 ►
The Mortal Instruments: City of Bones '13
Neil Gaiman's NeverWhere '96
$9.99 '08
No News from God '01
Northfork '03
One Magic Christmas '85
A Perfect Day '06
The Perfect Holiday '07
The Preacher's Wife '96
The Prophecy '95
The Prophecy 2: Ashtown '97
The Prophecy 3: The Ascent '99
Pure Country 2: The Gift '10
A Season for Miracles '99
Signed, Sealed, Delivered for Christmas '14
Slam Dunk Ernest '95
Soultaker '90
Stairway to Heaven '46 ►
Story of Mankind '57
Sundays at Tiffany's '10
Teen Spirit '11
The Twelve Days of Christmas Eve '04
Two of a Kind '83
Unlikely Angel '97
Waiting for the Light '90
Wide Awake '97
Wings of Desire '88 ►
Winter's Tale '14

Animals

***See** Bears; Birds; Cats; Horses; King of Beasts (Dogs); Penguins; Wild Kingdom*

Animated Musicals

***See also** Animation & Cartoons*

Adam Sandler's 8 Crazy Nights '02
Aladdin '92 ►
All Dogs Go to Heaven '89
All Dogs Go to Heaven 2 '95
American Pop '81
An American Tail '86
An American Tail: Fievel Goes West '91
Anastasia '97
Beauty and the Beast '91 ►
Cats Don't Dance '97
Charlotte's Web '73
Chico & Rita '10
Cinderella '50 ►
Fantasia/2000 '00
Frozen '13 ►
Gay Purr-ee '62
The Grinch '18
Happy Feet '06 ►
Hercules '97 ►
Home on the Range '04
Hoodwinked '05 ►
The Hunchback of Notre Dame '96 ►
The Jungle Book '67 ►
The King and I '99
Lady and the Tramp '55 ►
Legends of Oz: Dorothy's Return '14
The Lion King '94 ►
The Little Mermaid '89 ►
The Magic Voyage '93
Melody Time '48 ►
Mulan '98
The Nightmare Before Christmas '93 ►
The Pebble and the Penguin '94
Pink Floyd: The Wall '82
Pinocchio '40 ►
Pocahontas '95 ►
Prince of Egypt '98 ►
The Princess and the Frog '09 ►
Quest for Camelot '98
The Return of Jafar '94
The Road to El Dorado '00
Robin Hood '73 ►
Rock-a-Doodle '92
Shinbone Alley '70
Sing '16
Sleeping Beauty '59 ►
Snow White and the Seven Dwarfs '37 ►
South Park: Bigger, Longer and Uncut '99
The Swan Princess '94
The Swan Princess 2: Escape from Castle Mountain '97
Tangled '10 ►
The Thief and the Cobbler '96 ►
Thumbelina '94
Tim Burton's Corpse Bride '05 ►
Trolls '16
The Trumpet of the Swan '01
The Tune '92
Water Babies '79
Yellow Submarine '68 ►

Animated Sci-Fi

Battle for Terra '09 ►
Big Hero 6 '14
Bionicle 3: Web of Shadows '05
The Congress '13
The Dalmarian Chronicles '03
Despicable Me 2 '13
Despicable Me 3 '17
Despicable Me '10
Escape From Planet Earth '13
Final Fantasy: The Spirits Within '01
Fly Me to the Moon '08
Heavy Metal '81 ►
Home '15
Howl's Moving Castle '04
The Incredibles '04 ►
Inspector Gadget's Biggest Caper Ever '05
The Iron Giant '99 ►
Jimmy Neutron: Boy Genius '01
Leroy and Stitch '06
Mars Needs Moms '11
Mass Effect: Paragon Lost '12
Meet the Robinsons '07
Monsters *vs.* Aliens '09
9 '09 ►
Phantom Boy '16
Planet 51 '09
Pokemon 3: The Movie '01
Renaissance '06
Space Chimps '08
Star Wars: The Clone Wars '08
Steamboy '05
Titan A.E. '00
Transformers: The Movie '86
WALL-E '08 ►
Yu-Gi-Oh! The Movie: Pyramid of Light '04

Animation & Cartoons

***See also** Animated Musicals*

Abominable '19
Action Force: The Movie '87
The Addams Family '19
Adventures in Zambezia '12
The Adventures of Ichabod and Mr. Toad '49 ►
The Adventures of Mark Twain '85 ►
The Adventures of Tintin '11
Aladdin and the King of Thieves '96
Alice in Wonderland '50
Alice in Wonderland '51 ►
Allegro Non Troppo '76 ►
Alpha and Omega '10
Alvin and the Chipmunks: Road Chip '15
The Angry Birds Movie '16
The Angry Birds Movie 2 '19
Animal Crackers '17
Animal Farm '55 ►
Anomalisa '16 ►
The Ant Bully '06
Antz '98 ►
Aqua Teen Hunger Force Colon Movie Film for Theaters '07
Arctic Dogs '19
The Aristocats '70 ►
Arthur Christmas '11
Astro Boy '09
Atlantis: The Lost Empire '01
Ava & Lala '14
Babar: The Movie '88
Balto '95
Bambi '42 ►
Barnyard '06
Batman: Mask of the Phantasm '93
Beavis and Butt-Head Do America '96
Bebe's Kids '92
Bee Movie '07
Beneath the Flesh '09
Beowulf '07 ►
The Black Cauldron '85
Bolt '08 ►
The Book of Life '14
The Boss Baby '17
The Boxtrolls '14
Boy & the World '15 ►
Brave '12
The Breadwinner '17 ►
A Bug's Life '98 ►
Butterfly Ball '76
Captain Underpants: The First Epic Movie '17
Cars 2 '11
Cars 3 '17
Cars '06 ►
A Cat in Paris '11
Cheech & Chong's Animated Movie! '13
Chicago 10 '07 ►
Chicken Little '05
Chicken Run '00 ►
Chico & Rita '10
A Christmas Carol '09
Christopher Robin '18
Cinderella '12
Cinderella III: A Twist in Time '07
Clifford's Really Big Movie '04
Cloudy with a Chance of Meatballs 2 '13
Cloudy with a Chance of Meatballs '09
Coco '17 ►
Cool World '92
Coraline '09 ►
The Cosmic Eye '71 ►
The Croods '13
Curious George '06
The Dagger of Kamui '85 ►

► = rated three bones or higher

Delgo '08
Delhi Safari '12
Dilili in Paris '18
Dinosaur '00
Disney's Teacher's Pet '04 ▶
Dr. Seuss' Horton Hears a Who! '08 ▶
Dr. Seuss' The Lorax '12
Doogal '05
Doug's 1st Movie '99 ▶
DuckTales the Movie: Treasure of the Lost Lamp '90
Early Man '18
The Emoji Movie '17
Epic '13
Ernest & Celestine '13
Everyone's Hero '06
Evil Toons '90
Fantasia '40 ▶
Fantastic Mr. Fox '09 ▶
Fantastic Planet '73 ▶
Far Out Isn't Enough: The Tomi Ungerer '13
Ferdinand '17
Ferngully: The Last Rain Forest '92
Finding Dory '16 ▶
Finding Nemo '03 ▶
Fire and Ice '83
Flight of Dragons '82
Flushed Away '06 ▶
The Fox and the Hound '81 ▶
Frankenweenie '12 ▶
Free Birds '13
Fritz the Cat '72 ▶
Frozen II '19 ▶
Garfield: A Tail of Two Kitties '06
Garfield: The Movie '04
Gargoyles, The Movie: The Heroes Awaken '94
Ghost in the Shell '95 ▶
Gnomeo & Juliet '11
The Good Dinosaur '15
A Goofy Movie '94
The Great Mouse Detective '86 ▶
Guardians of the Lost Code '10
Gulliver's Travels '39
Gulliver's Travels '77
Gumby: The Movie '95
Happily Ever After '93
Happily N'Ever After '07
Happy Feet Two '11
The Haunted World of El Superbeasto '09
Heavy Metal 2000 '00
Heavy Traffic '73 ▶
Hey Arnold! The Movie '02
Hey Good Lookin' '82
Hey There, It's Yogi Bear '64
The Hobbit '78 ▶
Home on the Range '04
Hoodwinked '05 ▶
Hoodwinked Too! Hood *vs.* Evil '11
Hoppity Goes to Town '41
Hotel Transylvania 2 '15
Hotel Transylvania '12
Hotel Transylvania 3: Summer Vacation '18
How to Train Your Dragon 2 '14
How to Train Your Dragon '10
How to Train Your Dragon: The Hidden World '19 ▶
I Lost My Body '19 ▶
Ice Age '02 ▶
Ice Age: Collision Course '16
Ice Age: Continental Drift '12
Ice Age: Dawn of the Dinosaurs '09
Ice Age: The Meltdown '06
Igor '08
The Illusionist '10 ▶
The Incredibles '04 ▶
Incredibles 2 '18 ▶
Inside Out '15 ▶
The Invincible Iron Man '07
Isle of Dogs '18 ▶
Jetsons: The Movie '90
Journey Back to Oz '71
Kaena: The Prophecy '03
Kahlil Gibran's The Prophet '15 ▶
Klaus '19 ▶
Kubo and the Two Strings '16 ▶
Kung Fu Panda 2 '11 ▶
Kung Fu Panda 3 '16 ▶
The Land Before Time '88 ▶
The Land Before Time 2: The Great Valley Adventure '94
The Land Before Time 3: The Time of the Great Giving '95
The Land Before Time 4: Journey Through the Mists '96
The Land Before Time 5: The Mysterious Island '97
The Land Before Time 6: The Secret of Saurus Rock '98
Land Before Time 7: The Stone of Cold Fire '00
The Last Unicorn '82
Leap! '16
Legend of the Guardians: The Owls of Ga'Hoole '10 ▶
The LEGO Batman Movie '17 ▶
The LEGO Movie 2: The Second Part '19
The Lego Movie '14 ▶
The LEGO Ninjago Movie '17
A Letter to Momo '11
Life, Animated '16 ▶
Lilo & Stitch 2: Stitch Has a Glitch '05
The Lion King '19
The Lion King 1 1/2 '04 ▶
The Little Mermaid '75
Little Nemo: Adventures in Slumberland '92
The Little Prince '16 ▶
Looney Looney Looney Bugs Bunny Movie '81 ▶
The Lord of the Rings '78
Loving Vincent '17
Mad Monster Party '68
Madagascar: Escape 2 Africa '08
Madagascar 3: Europe's Most Wanted '12
Madagascar '05
Man from Button Willow '65
The Many Adventures of Winnie the Pooh '77
Marco Polo, Jr. '72
Mary and Max '09
Megamind '10 ▶
Mickey, Donald, Goofy: The Three Musketeers '04
Minions '15
The Miracle Maker: The Story of Jesus '00
Miss Hokusai '16
Missing Link '19
Mr. Peabody & Sherman '14
Moana '16 ▶
Monster House '06 ▶
A Monster in Paris '11
Monsters, Inc. '01 ▶
Monsters University '13
Mulan 2 '04
My Dog Tulip '09 ▶
My Entire High School Sinking Into the Sea '17
My Life as a Zucchini '16 ▶
My Little Pony: The Movie '17
Ne Zha '19
Nine Lives of Fritz the Cat '74
$9.99 '08
Norm of the North '16
The Nut Job 2: Nutty by Nature '17
The Nut Job '14
The Nutcracker Prince '91
Oliver & Company '88
Once Upon a Forest '93
101 Dalmatians '61 ▶
1001 Arabian Nights '59
Only Yesterday '16 ▶
Onward '20 ▶
Open Season 2 '08
Open Season 3 '10
Open Season '06
Over the Hedge '06 ▶
An Oversimplification of Her Beauty '13
Paddington 2 '17 ▶
The Painting '11 ▶
ParaNorman '12 ▶
The Peanuts Movie '15
Penguins of Madagascar '14
Persepolis '07 ▶
Peter Pan '53 ▶
Peter Rabbit '18
Phantom Boy '16
Phantom Tollbooth '69 ▶
Phantom 2040 Movie: The Ghost Who Walks '95
Piglet's Big Movie '03
The Pirates! Band of Misfits '12
The Pirates Who Don't Do Anything: A VeggieTales Movie '08
The Plague Dogs '82
Planes '13
Planes: Fire & Rescue '14
Playmobil: The Movie '19
The Point '71
Pokémon Detective Pikachu '19
Pokemon the Movie: The Power of Us '18
The Polar Express '04
Ponyo '08 ▶
Postman Pat: The Movie '14
The Powerpuff Girls Movie '02 ▶
The Princess and the Goblin '94
Promare '19
The Proud Family Movie '05
Puss in Boots '11 ▶
Queer Duck: The Movie '06
The Rabbi's Cat '11
Ralph Breaks the Internet '18
Rango '11 ▶
Ratatouille '07 ▶
Ratchet & Clank '16
The Red Turtle '17 ▶
Reef 2: High Tide '12
The Rescuers '77 ▶
The Rescuers Down Under '90
Resident Evil: Vendetta '17
The Return of the King '80
Return to Never Land '02
Rio 2 '14
Rio '11
Rise of the Guardians '12
Robots '05
Rock & Rule '83
Rock Dog '17
Rover Dangerfield '91
Ruben Brandt, Collector '18
Rugrats Go Wild! '03
Rugrats in Paris: The Movie '00 ▶
The Rugrats Movie '98 ▶
Sausage Party '16
Scoob! '20
The Secret Life of Pets 2 '19
The Secret of Kells '09
The Secret of NIMH 2 '98
The Secret of NIMH '82 ▶
The Secret World of Arrietty '10 ▶
Sgt. Stubby: An American Hero '18
Shark Tale '04
Shaun the Sheep Movie '15 ▶
A Shaun the Sheep Movie: Farmageddon '19 ▶
Sherlock Gnomes '18
Shrek 2 '04 ▶
Shrek '01 ▶
Shrek Forever After '10
Shrek the Third '07
The Simpsons Movie '07 ▶
Sinbad and the Eye of the Tiger '77
Sinbad: Legend of the Seven Seas '03
Sing '16
The Singing Princess '49
Smallfoot '18
Smurfs: The Lost Village '17
Sonic the Hedgehog '20
Spark: A Space Tail '17
Spider-Man: Into the Spider-Verse '18 ▶
Spies in Disguise '19
Spirit: Stallion of the Cimarron '02
Spirited Away '01
The SpongeBob SquarePants Movie '04
The Star '17
Starchaser: The Legend of Orin '85
Steamboy '05
Storks '16
Strange Magic '15
Streetfight '75
Stuart Little 3: Call of the Wild '06
Superman: Unbound '13
Surf's Up '07
The Sword in the Stone '63 ▶
The Tale of Despereaux '08
The Tale of the Princess Kaguya '13 ▶
Tarzan '99 ▶
Teen Titans Go! To the Movies '18
The Three Caballeros '45
TMNT: Teenage Mutant Ninja Turtles '07
Todd McFarlane's Spawn '97 ▶
Tom and Jerry: The Movie '93
Tom Thumb '58 ▶
Tower '16 ▶
Toy Story '95 ▶
Toy Story 2 '99 ▶
Toy Story 3 '10 ▶
Toy Story 4 '19 ▶
The Triplets of Belleville '02 ▶
A Troll in Central Park '94
Trolls '16
Trolls World Tour '20
Turbo '13
UglyDolls '19
Up '09 ▶
Valiant '05
Very Semi-Serious: A Partially Thorough Portrait of New Yorker Cartoonists '15
VIP, My Brother Superman '90
Waking Life '01
Walking with Dinosaurs 3D '13
Wallace & Gromit in The Curse of the Were-Rabbit '05 ▶
Watership Down '78
We're Back! A Dinosaur's Story '93
When the Wind Blows '86 ▶
The Wild Life '16
The Wild Thornberrys Movie '02 ▶
The Willoughbys '20
The Wind Rises '13 ▶
Winnie the Pooh '11 ▶
Wizards '77
Wonder Park '19
Wreck-It Ralph '12
Yogi Bear '10
Your Name '17 ▶
Yu-Gi-Oh! The Movie: Pyramid of Light '04
Zootopia '16 ▶

Anime

***See also** Animation & Cartoons*

Bleach the Movie 4: Hell Verse '10
The Castle of Cagliostro '80
Colorful: The Motion Picture '10 ▶
The Dagger of Kamui '85 ▶
The Dark Myth '90
Dragonball: Evolution '09
Grave of the Fireflies '88 ▶
Howl's Moving Castle '04
Mirai '18 ▶
Miss Hokusai '16
My Neighbor Totoro '88
Only Yesterday '16 ▶
Otaku No Video '91 ▶
Paprika '06
Pokemon: The First Movie '99
Pokemon the Movie 2000: The Power of One '00
Pom Poko '94
Princess Mononoke '98 ▶
The Sky Crawlers '08
Spriggan '98
Steamboy '05
Summer Wars '09 ▶
Toward the Terra '80
Wicked City '89 ▶

Anthology

***See also** Comedy Anthology; Horror Anthology*

The ABCs of Death '12
The Acid House '98
Actors and Sin '52
The Air I Breathe '07
America's Dream '95 ▶
The Ballad of Buster Scruggs '18 ▶
Bambole '65
Beyond the Clouds '95
Black Sabbath '64 ▶
Boys Life '94
Burning Daylight '10
Call Me Crazy '13
Cat's Eye '85
The Chaplin Revue '58
Charade '53
Coffee and Cigarettes '03 ▶
Crash '05 ▶
Creepshow III '06
Deadtime Stories '86
The Decameron '70 ▶
Decameron Nights '53
Dogville Shorts '30
Dolls '02 ▶
Eros '04
Erotique '94
Fantasia/2000 '00
Film Socialisme '10
Four Rooms '95
From Beyond the Grave '73
A Girl Thing '01
The Great New Wonderful '06
Halfmoon '95
The Heyday of the Insensitive Bastards '17
If I Had a Million '32
If These Walls Could Talk 2 '00
If These Walls Could Talk '96
It's a Big Country '51
Kaos '85 ▶
Kisses in the Dark '97
Kwaidan '64 ▶
Le Plaisir '52
Loggerheads '05 ▶
Love Songs '99
Mama Africa '02
Melody Time '48 ▶
Mickey the Great '39
More American Graffiti '79
Mystery Train '89 ▶
New York, I Love You '09
Night Gallery '69 ▶
Night on Earth '91 ▶
Nightmares '83
Nine Lives '05 ▶
Noel '04
Paisan '46 ▶
Paris, je t'aime '06
Personal Velocity: Three Portraits '02 ▶
Picture Windows '95
Pulp Fiction '94 ▶
The Queens '66
Red Shoe Diaries '92
Red Shoe Diaries 2: Double Dare '92
Red Shoe Diaries 3: Another Woman's Lipstick '93
Red Shoe Diaries 4: Auto Erotica '93
Red Shoe Diaries 5: Weekend Pass '95
Red Shoe Diaries 6: How I Met My Husband '95
Red Shoe Diaries 7: Burning Up '96
Red Shoe Diaries 8: Night of Abandon '97
Red Shoe Diaries: Four on the Floor '96
Red Shoe Diaries: Luscious Lola '00
Red Shoe Diaries: Strip Poker '96
Red Shoe Diaries: Swimming Naked '00
Rio, I Love You '14
The Rising of the Moon '57
The Robert Benchley Miniatures Collection '35
Robot Stories '03
Route 30 '08
Short Cuts '93 ▶
Sin City '05
Sin City: A Dame to Kill For '14
Six in Paris '68
Slacker '91 ▶
Subway Stories '97
Tale of Tales '15
Tales of Erotica '93
Tales of Manhattan '42 ▶
Tales of the Unexpected '91
Tales That Witness Madness '73
The Ten '07
That's Dancing! '85 ▶
That's Entertainment '74 ▶
That's Entertainment, Part 2 '76
That's Entertainment, Part 3 '93
3 Backyards '10
Three Days of Rain '02
To Die, Or Not '99
Tokyo! '09
Trick 'r Treat '08 ▶
The Trouble with Romance '09
Twice-Told Tales '63 ▶
Twilight Zone: The Movie '83
Twisted '96
Two Days in the Valley '96 ▶
Vanishing Legion '31
The Wall '99 ▶
What It's All About '95
Wild Tales '14 ▶
Women & Men: In Love There Are No Rules '91
Women & Men: Stories of Seduction '90
The Yellow Rolls Royce '64

Anti-Heroes

***See also** Loner Cops; Rebel With a Cause*

Aeon Flux '05
Bad Santa 2 '16
Belly '98
Big Bad Love '02
Billy Jack '71
Blade '98
Bonnie & Clyde '67 ▶
Born Losers '67
Butch Cassidy and the Sundance Kid '69 ▶
Casino '95 ▶
A Civil Action '98
The Dead Pool '88
Dirty Harry '71 ▶
Easy Rider '69 ▶
The Enforcer '76
Gang Related '96
Hell or High Water '16 ▶
Hero '92 ▶
Hulk '03
Hustle '04
In a Lonely Place '50 ▶
Last Man Standing '96
Lock, Stock and 2 Smoking Barrels '98 ▶
Magnum Force '73
Niagara, Niagara '97
Palookaville '95 ▶
Playing God '96
The Punisher '04
Rebel without a Cause '55 ▶
Robin Hood: Prince of Thieves '91
The Secret Agent '96
Set It Off '96
Shaun of the Dead '04 ▶
16 Blocks '06 ▶
Steal This Movie! '00
Street Kings '08
Sudden Impact '83
Suicide Squad '16
Surviving Picasso '96
Ten Benny '98
Thelma & Louise '91 ▶
Things to Do in Denver When You're Dead '95 ▶

To Wong Foo, Thanks for Everything, Julie Newmar '95
Traveller '96 ▸
The Trial of Billy Jack '74
Trojan Eddie '96 ▸
True Crime '99
12 Monkeys '95 ▸
U-Turn '97
Ultraviolet '06
V for Vendetta '06
The Weather Man '05
Wisdom '87
Yojimbo '61 ▸

Anti-War War Movies

***See also** Satire & Parody*
All Quiet on the Western Front '30 ▸
All Quiet on the Western Front '79
Amazing Grace & Chuck '87
American Pastoral '16
Anthropoid '16
Apocalypse Now '79 ▸
Beach Red '67 ▸
Beasts of No Nation '15
Beaufort '07 ▸
The Big Parade '25 ▸
Born on the Fourth of July '89 ▸
The Bridge '59
The Bridges at Toko-Ri '55 ▸
The Burmese Harp '56 ▸
Bushido: The Cruel Code of the Samurai '63 ▸
Castle Keep '69 ▸
Catch-22 '70 ▸
The Charge of the Light Brigade '68
Civilization '16 ▸
Come and See '85 ▸
Coming Home '78 ▸
The Cuckoo '02
Cup Final '92
The Dawn Patrol '30 ▸
Dr. Strangelove, or: How I Learned to Stop Worrying and Love the Bomb '64 ▸
The Eagle and the Hawk '33 ▸
Fahrenheit 9/11 '04 ▸
Fires on the Plain '59 ▸
Forbidden Games '52 ▸
The Four Horsemen of the Apocalypse '21 ▸
The Four Horsemen of the Apocalypse '62
Gallipoli '81 ▸
Glory '89 ▸
Grand Illusion '37 ▸
Hamburger Hill '87
Hell in the Pacific '69 ▸
Henry V '89 ▸
Hombres Armados '97 ▸
J'accuse! '19 ▸
Jarhead '05
Joyeux Noel '05 ▸
JSA: Joint Security Area '00 ▸
King and Country '64 ▸
The King of Hearts '66 ▸
La Guerre Est Finie '66 ▸
Land of Mine '15
Latino '85
Les Carabiniers '63 ▸
M*A*S*H '70 ▸
M*A*S*H: Goodbye, Farewell & Amen '83 ▸
Master of the World '61
A Midnight Clear '92 ▸
Mission to Death '66
No Greater Glory '34
No Man's Land '01
Nurse Edith Cavell '39 ▸
Oh! What a Lovely War '69
Our Music '04
Paths of Glory '57 ▸
Platoon '86 ▸
Pretty Village, Pretty Flame '96 ▸
Prisoner of the Mountains '96 ▸
The Red Badge of Courage '51 ▸
Revolution '85
The Road to Glory '36
The Sky Crawlers '08
The Steel Helmet '51 ▸
Straight into Darkness '04
The Tiger and the Snow '05
The Tin Drum '79 ▸
Too Late the Hero '70 ▸
Veronico Cruz '87
Wackiest Ship in the Army '61
War Horse '11
War Hunt '62
What Price Glory? '52 ▸
The Young Lions '58 ▸

Apartheid

***See also** Africa; Civil Rights*
After the Rain '99
The Bang Bang Club '10
Boesman & Lena '00
Bopha! '93 ▸
Catch a Fire '06
The Color of Freedom '07
Cry Freedom '87
Cry, the Beloved Country '95 ▸
Dangerous Ground '96
Disgrace '08
District 9 '09 ▸
A Dry White Season '89 ▸
Endgame '09
Escape from Pretoria '20
The Forgiven '18
Funeral for an Assassin '77
In My Country '04
Inside '96 ▸
Invictus '09 ▸
Mandela '87 ▸
Mandela and de Klerk '97
Mandela: Long Walk to Freedom '13
The Power of One '92
The Quarry '98
Sarafina! '92 ▸
21 Up South Africa: Mandela's Children '08 ▸
The Wilby Conspiracy '75 ▸
Winnie Mandela '13
A World Apart '88 ▸
The World Unseen '07
Yankee Zulu '95

Apartments & Apartment Buildings

Adam '09
Among Brothers '05
Amour '12 ▸
The Apartment '60 ▸
Apartment for Peggy '48
Apartment 12 '06
Apartment Zero '88 ▸
Aquarius '16 ▸
As Good As Dead '10
As Good As It Gets '97 ▸
Baby Mama '08
BachelorMan '03
Barefoot in the Park '67 ▸
Berlin Syndrome '17
Boystown '07
Breakfast at Tiffany's '61 ▸
Brightest Star '14
The Bubble '06
Bunny and the Bull '09
The Caller '11
Carnage '11
Chef's Special '08
Christina '10
Columbus Circle '10
Compulsion '13
A Couch in New York '95
Crashing '07
Dark Water '02
The Debt '10
Designing Woman '57 ▸
The Disappearance of Alice Creed '09
The Disaster Artist '17 ▸
Down Terrace '10
Down With Love '03
The Dreamers '03
The Echo '08
Elsa & Fred '14
Everly '14
The Exploding Girl '09
The Extra Man '10
Falling Up '08
The Fifth Horseman Is Fear '64
Filth and Wisdom '08
Final Draft '07
Fine Dead Girls '02
Fish Tank '09 ▸
Flight of the Red Balloon '08
For Colored Girls '10
44 Inch Chest '09
Four and a Half Women '05
4:44 Last Day on Earth '11
Getting High '06
Ghostbusters '84 ▸
Good Dick '08
A Good Man '14
Good Neighbors '10
The Grudge 3 '09
The Haunting of Helena '12
The Hedgehog '09
Hidden in Silence '96
High-Rise '16
Homeless to Harvard: The Liz Murray Story '03
The Idle Rich '29
Inside Paris '06
Joe's Apartment '96
Johnny Doesn't Live Here Any More '44
Julie & Julia '09 ▸
Kettle of Fish '06
Kill the Poor '03
The Killing Floor '06
A Kiss in the Dark '49
La Chinoise '67
La Cucina '07
Lady in the Water '06
The Landlord '70
The Last International Playboy '08
Last Tango in Paris '73 ▸
L'Auberge Espagnole '02 ▸
Laura '44 ▸
The Ledge '11
Left Bank '08
Les Cousins '59
Let Me In '10
Let the Right One In '08
The Lifeguard '13
The Loft '14
Love '71 ▸
The Man in 3B '16
The Man Who Played God '32
Mary, Mary '63
Mister 880 '50
Mr. Popper's Penguins '11
Mood Indigo '13
Moscow, Belgium '08
The Motive '18
Moving Malcolm '03
Mulberry Street '06
Multiple Sarcasms '10
My Old Lady '14
My Piece of the Pie '11
My Sister Eileen '42
My Worst Nightmare '11
A Near-Death Experience '08
The Neighbor '07
Next Day Air '09
$9.99 '08
No Escape '53
No Home Movie '15
Nymphomaniac, Volume 1 '13
The Odd Couple '68 ▸
The Ones Below '16
Paris '08
The Penthouse '10
A Perfect Murder '98
Pieces of April '03
Please Give '10
Pornography: A Thriller '10
Precious: Based on the Novel 'Push' by Sapphire '09 ▸
Pushover '54
Quarantine '08
Rafter Romance '33
Rear Window '54 ▸
The Rebound '09
[Rec] '07
[Rec] 2 '09
Redemption '13
Repulsion '65 ▸
The Resident '10
Rope '48 ▸
Rosemary's Baby '68 ▸
A Safe Place '71
The Salesman '16 ▸
Sarah's Key '10
The Secret Life of Pets '16
Seven Stages to Achieve Eternal Bliss '20
Shame '11 ▸
Single White Female '92
Sister '12
Sliver '93
Small Apartments '12
Snowglobe '07
Someone Like You '01
Something Wild '61
The Sunset Limited '11
The Tenant '76 ▸
35 Shots of Rum '08
A Thousand Kisses Deep '11
Timekeeper '98
Tiny Furniture '10 ▸
The Trouble With Bliss '11
12 Christmas Wishes For My Dog '11
Two Girls and a Guy '98 ▸
Two Lovers '09 ▸
Two Night Stand '14
Under the Shadow '16 ▸
Under the Silver Lake '18
Unfaithful '02 ▸
The Visitor '07 ▸
Wait until Dark '67 ▸
Waking Madison '10
Warning Shot '67
What Love Is '07
What We Do in the Shadows '14
Whatever Works '09
The Whisperers '66
The Wolf Hour '19
The Women on the Sixth Floor '10
Wonderwall: The Movie '69
You and Me '06
You Belong to Me '07

Arab Culture

***See also** Islam; Middle East*
American East '07
Amreeka '09 ▸
The Big Sick '17 ▸
David & Layla '07
The Insult '17 ▸
Sufat Chol '16 ▸
Towelhead '07
Vita & Virginia '19
Wadjda '13 ▸

Archaeology

***See** Big Digs*

Archery

The Adventures of Robin Hood '38 ▸
The Avengers '12 ▸
Brave '12
Deliverance '72 ▸
The Hunger Games '12 ▸
The Hunger Games: Catching Fire '13 ▸
The Hunger Games: Mockingjay--Part 1 '14
Killing Season '13
Lord of the Rings: The Fellowship of the Ring '01 ▸
Lord of the Rings: The Two Towers '02 ▸
Lord of the Rings: The Return of the King '03 ▸
Rambo: First Blood, Part 2 '85
Robin Hood '22 ▸
Robin Hood '73 ▸
Robin Hood '91 ▸
Robin Hood '10
Robin Hood: Men in Tights '93
Robin Hood: Prince of Thieves '91
Robin Hood. . . The Legend: Robin Hood and the Sorcerer '83
The Story of Robin Hood & His Merrie Men '52 ▸
Sword of Sherwood Forest '60

Architects & Architecture

Amateur Night '16
The Architect '06
At First Sight '98
Beat Girl '60
The Belly of an Architect '91 ▸
The Book of Love '16
The Brady Bunch Movie '95 ▸
The Cocoanuts '29
Columbus '17 ▸
Dead End '37 ▸
Dead of Night '45 ▸
Death Wish '74
Fear '96
For Sale by Owner '09
The Fountainhead '49 ▸
Hard to Get '38
Heaven '99
High-Rise '16
The House Next Door '06
Housesitter '92
Indecent Proposal '93
Isn't It Romantic '19
It's Complicated '09
Journey to the Lost City '58
Just Around the Corner '38
Just Looking '99
A Kind of Murder '16
Land of the Pharaohs '55
Les Biches '68 ▸
Life as a House '01
Living in Peril '97
Lost Honeymoon '47
Me, Myself and Her '16
My Architect: A Son's Journey '03 ▸
Mystic Pizza '88 ▸
A Name for Evil '70
One Fine Day '96
The Palm Beach Story '42 ▸
Pillars of the Earth '10
Reaching for the Moon '13
Retour Chez Ma Mere '16
The Serpent's Kiss '97
Shattered '91
A Smile Like Yours '96
Strangers When We Meet '60
The Tempest '82 ▸
Three Men and a Baby '87 ▸
Three to Tango '99
Til There Was You '96
The Towering Inferno '74
Town and Country '01
A Very Brady Sequel '96
Where'd You Go, Bernadette '19
White Noise '05
Wonderful Town '07

Army Training, Sir!

Band of Brothers '01 ▸
Billy Lynn's Long Halftime Walk '16
Biloxi Blues '88
The Boys in Company C '77
Buck Privates '41
D.I. '57
Full Metal Jacket '87 ▸
In the Army Now '94
Private Valentine: Blonde & Dangerous '08
Queen and Country '14
Stripes '81
Tell It to the Marines '26
There's Something About a Soldier '43
Thunder Birds '42
Tigerland '00 ▸

Art & Artists

***See also** Biopics: Artists; Biopics: Musicians; Sculptors; Struggling Artists; Struggling Musicians; This Is Your Life; Writers*
Age of Consent '69
The Agony and the Ecstasy '65
Ai Weiwei: Never Sorry '12 ▸
All the Vermeers in New York '91 ▸
An American in Paris '51 ▸
Anamorph '07
Andrei Rublev '66 ▸
Angel '07
Art House '16
Art Machine '12
Art School Confidential '06
Artemisia '97
Artists and Models '55
As Good As It Gets '97 ▸
At Eternity's Gate '18
The B-Side: Elsa Dorfman's Portrait Photography '17
Back Against the Wall '00
Backbeat '94 ▸
Basquiat '96 ▸
Bean '97 ▸
Beautiful Losers '08
The Belly of an Architect '91 ▸
The Best Offer '13
Between Something & Nothing '08
Big Eden '00
Big Eyes '14
Blue is the Warmest Color '13 ▸
The Blue Light '32 ▸
Bluebeard '44
Body Strokes '95
Boogie Woogie '09
A Bread Factory, Part One '18 ▸
A Bread Factory, Part Two '18 ▸
Bride of the Wind '01
Brideshead Revisited '08
Brush with Fate '03
A Bucket of Blood '59 ▸
The Burnt Orange Heresy '20
Camille Claudel '89 ▸
Caravaggio '86 ▸
Caravaggio '07
Carrington '95
Cashback '06
Castle Keep '69 ▸
Cave of Forgotten Dreams '11 ▸
Changing Habits '96
Chasing Amy '97
Chihwaseon: Painted Fire '02
The Christmas Cottage '08
Circle of Two '80
Clara '19
Color Me Blood Red '64
Color of Night '94
The Competition '80 ▸
The Con Artist '10
Crucible of Terror '72
Crumb '94 ▸
Cutie and the Boxer '13 ▸
The Da Vinci Code '06 ▸
Dead Man's Eyes '44
Death in Venice '71 ▸
Dedication '07
The Designated Mourner '97
Detonator 2: Night Watch '95
The Devil's Candy '17
Dirty Pictures '00
Dishonored Lady '47
A Dog of Flanders '99
Don't Leave Home '18
Don't Think Twice '16
Don't Worry, He Won't Get Far on Foot '18
Drew: The Man Behind the Poster '13
Driller Killer '79
Ebony Tower '86
Echoes '83
Eddie the Sleepwalking Cannibal '12
Edie in Ciao! Manhattan '72
Edvard Munch '74
Entre-Nous '83 ▸
The Escape '18
Euphoria '19
Everything You Want '05
Exit Through the Gift Shop '10
The Face of Love '13
Faces Places '17
Fake '10
Fakers '04
The Family Fang '16
Far Out Isn't Enough: The Tomi Ungerer '13
Fear and Loathing in Las Vegas '98
Final Portrait '17
Finding Altamira '16
Florence Foster Jenkins '16
For No Good Reason '13
The Forger '15
Four Corners of Suburbia '05
Framed '90
Framed '10
Frida '84
Frida '02

From the Mixed-Up Files of Mrs. Basil E. Frankweiler '95
Frozen in Fear '00
Gambit '12
Georgia O'Keefe '09
Getting High '06
Ghosted '09
The Girl from Jones Beach '49
Girl with a Pearl Earring '03 ▸
The Glass Castle '17
The Goldfinch '19
Golem: The Petrified Garden '93
Gothic '87 ▸
Goya in Bordeaux '99
Goya's Ghosts '06
Gradiva '06
Great Expectations '97
Green Dragon '01
A Harlot's Progress '06
The Hideaways '73
The Hollars '16
Holy Matrimony '43 ▸
Horse Girl '20
The Horse's Mouth '58 ▸
Horsey '99
Hour of the Wolf '68 ▸
House of D '04
House of Horrors '46
House of Wax '53 ▸
How to Steal a Million '66 ▸
Hullabaloo over Georgie & Bonnie's Pictures '78
Hunger '66
I Shot Andy Warhol '96 ▸
If Lucy Fell '95
In America '02 ▸
In the City of Sylvia '07
Incognito '97
Inferno '16
The Iris Effect '04
It Seemed Like a Good Idea at the Time '75
I've Heard the Mermaids Singing '87 ▸
Jean-Michel Basquiat: The Radiant Child '10 ▸
Jimmy Zip '00
Junebug '05 ▸
Kate Plays Christine '16 ▸
The Keeper of the Bees '35
La Belle Noiseuse '90 ▸
An L.A. Minute '18
Ladies of Leisure '30
The Lady From Lisbon '42
Leaving Metropolis '02
Lennon Naked '10
Les Biches '68 ▸
Let the Sunshine In '17
The Life of Emile Zola '37 ▸
Lily & Kat '15
Little Ashes '09
Live, Love and Learn '37
Local Color '06
Look Both Ways '05
Love & Sex '00
Love Is the Devil '98 ▸
Loving Vincent '17
Lowriders '17
Lucky Partners '40
Luscious '97
Lust for Life '56 ▸
The Man in the Net '59
The Man Who Lived at the Ritz '91
Marina Abramovic the Artist Is Present '12
Marwencol '10
Max '02
The Mermaid Chair '06
The Meyerowitz Stories (New and Selected) '17 ▸
Migrating Forms '00
The Mill and the Cross '11
Mirror, Mirror 3: The Voyeur '96
Miss Hokusai '16
Mr. Art Critic '07
Mr. Jones '14
Mr. Turner '14 ▸
Mistral's Daughter '84
The Moderns '88 ▸
Mojave '15
Moll Flanders '96
The Monuments Men '13
The Moon and Sixpence '43 ▸
Morgan: A Suitable Case for Treatment '66
Mortdecai '15
Moulin Rouge '52 ▸
Mrs. Lowry & Son '19
Museum Hours '13 ▸
My Best Friend '06
My Left Foot '89 ▸
My Lucky Elephant '13
My Mother's Smile '02
Mystery of Picasso '56 ▸
Never Look Away '18 ▸
Never Met Picasso '96
New York Stories '89 ▸
The Next Big Thing '02
Nightwatching '07
The Object of Beauty '91 ▸
The Orgasm Diaries '10
An Oversimplification of Her Beauty '13
The Painted Lady '97 ▸
The Painting '11 ▸
Panzer '13
A Perfect Murder '98
The Picasso Summer '69
Picture Windows '95
Pictures of Hollis Woods '07
Pollock '00 ▸
Portrait in Terror '66
Portrait of a Lady on Fire '19 ▸
Portrait of Jennie '48 ▸
Postcards from America '95
Presenting Princess Shaw '16
Prick Up Your Ears '87 ▸
Primal Secrets '94
A Question of Attribution '91
A Quiet Place in the Country '69
The Reckless Hour '31
Rembrandt '36 ▸
The Rendering '02
Renoir '12
Retribution '88
A River Made to Drown In '97
Ruben Brandt, Collector '18
The Sandpiper '65
Savage Messiah '72 ▸
The Science of Sleep '06
Scream, Baby, Scream '69
Screaming Mimi '58
Seraphine '08 ▸
Sheer Madness '84 ▸
The Shell Seekers '06
The Silver Chalice '54
Sirens '94
Six Days, Six Nights '94
Slaves of New York '89
Speak '04 ▸
Spiral '07
The Square '17
Starry Night '99
Stay '05
Stealing Beauty '96
Still Breathing '97
The Still Life '07
Strange Affair '44
Street Angel '28
Summer Hours '08
Summer in February '13
A Sunday in the Country '84 ▸
Sunday in the Park with George '86 ▸
Superstar: The Life and Times of Andy Warhol '90 ▸
Surviving Picasso '96
Sweet Thing '00 ▸
Synecdoche, New York '08 ▸
Take Her, She's Mine '63
The Tenant of Wildfell Hall '96
The Testament of Orpheus '59 ▸
The Thomas Crown Affair '99 ▸
The Time Being '12
The Time Traveler's Wife '09
Tim's Vermeer '13 ▸
Titanic '97 ▸
Track of the Vampire '66
Troublemakers: The Story of Land Art '15 ▸
Tulip Fever '17
200 Cigarettes '98
Two If by Sea '95
The Two Mrs. Carrolls '47
Two Much '96
Uncovered '94
(Untitled) '09
Utamaro and His Five Women '46
Van Gogh '92 ▸
Velvet Buzzsaw '19
Very Semi-Serious: A Partially Thorough Portrait of New Yorker Cartoonists '15
Vicky Cristina Barcelona '08
Vincent & Theo '90 ▸
Vincent: The Life and Death of Vincent van Gogh '87 ▸
Washington Heights '02
Waste Land '10
What Dreams May Come '98
White Oleander '02
Who Gets to Call It Art? '05
Woman in Gold '15
The Woman on the Beach '47
Words and Pictures '13
World and Time Enough '95
The World of Suzie Wong '60
Wrestling with Alligators '98
The Yes Men '03

Asia

See also China; Japan

The Act of Killing '13 ▸
The Age of Shadows '16
All I See Is You '17
Almayer's Folly '12
Anna and the King '99
Asian Connection '16
Babies '10 ▸
Bang Rajan '00 ▸
Bangkok Dangerous '08
The Beautiful Country '04
Beyond Borders '03
Beyond Rangoon '95
Bitter/Sweet '09
The Breadwinner '17 ▸
Brokedown Palace '99
A Bullet in the Head '90 ▸
Catfish in Black Bean Sauce '00
Chaos Factor '00
Chasing Freedom '04
Chihwaseon: Painted Fire '02
City of Ghosts '03
Crazy Rich Asians '18 ▸
Croc '07
Dheepan '16
Diamond Dogs '07
The Eagle Huntress '16 ▸
Eat Drink Man Woman '94 ▸
Eat, Pray, Love '10
The Elephant King '06
Elephant White '11
Emmanuelle '74
Emmanuelle, the Joys of a Woman '76
Entrapment '99
Escape to Burma '55
Flower Drum Song '61
Fortunes of War '94
The Great Challenge '04
The Hangover, Part 2 '11
Hard Target 2 '16
Headshot '17
Holly '07
Indochine '92 ▸
The Intended '02
The Intruder '04 ▸
Jackie Chan's First Strike '96 ▸
The Killing Fields '84 ▸
The King '18
Knockdown '11
K2: The Ultimate High '92
Kubo and the Two Strings '16 ▸
The Lady '11
Lara Croft: Tomb Raider '01
The Lark Farm '07
Little Buddha '93
Lost Horizon '37 ▸
Madeo '09
Malaya '49
The Man with the Golden Gun '74
Memories of Murder '03
The Missing Picture '13
Mission Mangal '19
Moebius '13
Mongol '07 ▸
The Mongols '60
Monkey Kingdom '15 ▸
My Lucky Elephant '13
Never Back Down: No Surrender '16
No Escape '15
Oldboy '03 ▸
Ong-Bak '03 ▸
Only God Forgives '13
Pieta '13 ▸
A Prayer Before Dawn '18 ▸
Purple Butterfly '03 ▸
The Quest '96
The Quiet American '02 ▸
The Railway Man '13
Rambo '08
Red Dust '32 ▸
A River Called Titas '73 ▸
Rogue Trader '98
S21: The Khmer Rouge Killing Machine '03 ▸
The Sand Pebbles '66 ▸
The Scent of Green Papaya '93 ▸
Shanghai Surprise '86
Sherpa '15 ▸
The Story of the Weeping Camel '03 ▸
Street Fighter: The Legend of Chun-Li '09
Tarzan's Three Challenges '63
The Taste of Money '12
That's the Way I Like It '99
Three . . . Extremes '04
A Town Like Alice '56
Trade of Innocents '12
Two Brothers '04
Typhoon '06
The Ugly American '63
The Vertical Ray of the Sun '00
Wake Island '42 ▸
Wolf Totem '15
Woman Is the Future of Man '04 ▸
World for Ransom '54

Asian America

Almost Perfect '11
American Fusion '05
The Beautiful Country '04
Better Luck Tomorrow '02 ▸
Chan Is Missing '82 ▸
Charlotte Sometimes '02
Color of a Brisk and Leaping Day '95
Combination Platter '93
Come See the Paradise '90 ▸
Dim Sum: A Little Bit of Heart '85 ▸
Dim Sum Funeral '08
Double Happiness '94 ▸
Eat a Bowl of Tea '89 ▸
Golden Gate '93
Green Dragon '01
The Joy Luck Club '93 ▸
Linsanity '13
Living on Tokyo Time '87
The Lucky One '12
MDMA '18
Old San Francisco '27
Only the Brave '06
The People I've Slept With '09
Red Doors '05
Romeo Must Die '00
Shanghai Kiss '07
Son of the Gods '30
Strawberry Fields '97
A Thousand Years of Good Prayers '07
The Wedding Banquet '93 ▸
White Frog '12
Why Am I Doing This? '09
Yellow '98

Assassination

See also Camelot (New); Foreign Intrigue; Hit Men/Women; Spies & Espionage

Abraham Lincoln '30
The Ace of Hearts '21
African Rage '78
All the King's Men '49 ▸
The American Friend '77 ▸
The American Soldier '70
Anna '19
The Anomaly '15
Anthropoid '16
The Arab Conspiracy '76
Ashes and Diamonds '58 ▸
Assassin X '16
Assassination '87
The Assassination Bureau '69 ▸
The Assassination of Jesse James by the Coward Robert Ford '07 ▸
The Assassination of Richard Nixon '05
Assassin's Bullet '12
Assassin's Creed '16
The Assignment '17
Avengers: Endgame '19 ▸
Avengers: Infinity War '18 ▸
Azumi 2 '05
Azumi '03 ▸
Beautiful Beast '95
Beyond Valkyrie: Dawn of the Fourth Reich '16
Black Box '12
Black Sunday '77
Blind Horizon '04
Blow Out '81 ▸
Bobby '06
The Bourne Identity '02 ▸
The Bourne Ultimatum '07 ▸
Brass Target '78
Brother Orchid '40 ▸
The Brotherhood of the Rose '89
Caracara '00
Center of the Web '92
Chain of Command '15
Clear All Wires! '33
Cleopatra '99
The Clockmaker '73 ▸
Counterstrike '03
Crooked '05
The Dallas Connection '94
Dangerous Pursuit '89
The Day of the Dolphin '73
The Day of the Jackal '73 ▸
Dead Zone '83 ▸
Death Force '78
Death to Smoochy '02
Decommissioned '16
The Destructors '74
Diamond Run '90
The Dirty Dozen: The Next Mission '85
The Domino Principle '77
Eagle Eye '08
The Eagle Has Landed '77 ▸
ECCO '19
The Eleventh Hour '08
Eliminators '16
Elizabeth '98 ▸
Emmanuelle, the Queen '79
The Emperor and the Assassin '99
End Game '06
Enigma '82
The Evil That Men Do '84
Excellent Cadavers '99
Excessive Force 2: Force on Force '95
Executive Action '73
Expert Weapon '93
F/X '86 ▸
Fatal Deception: Mrs. Lee Harvey Oswald '93
Fatal Justice '93
Flashpoint '84
Foul Play '78 ▸
Free Fall '14
Friday Foster '75
From Russia with Love '63 ▸
Funeral for an Assassin '77
Gandhi '82 ▸
Ghosts of Mississippi '96
The Guardsman '15
Guns for Hire '15
Hangmen Also Die '42
Harum Scarum '65
Hero '02 ▸
Hidden Assassin '94
Hit Lady '74
The Hunted '94
The Hunted '03
I Spit on Your Corpse '74
In the Line of Fire '93 ▸
Intent to Kill '58
The Interpreter '05 ▸
The Interview '14
Interview with the Assassin '02
Invitation to a Gunfighter '64
The Jackal '97
Jackie '16 ▸
Jason Bourne '16
JFK '91 ▸
John Wick: Chapter 2 '17 ▸
John Wick: Chapter 3-Parabellum '19 ▸
Judgment Night '93
The Kennedys '11
Kill Castro '80
The Killer Elite '75
Killer Likes Candy '78
Killers Anonymous '19
The Killing Device '92
Killing Gunther '17
Killing Kennedy '13
Killing Lincoln '13
King Richard and the Crusaders '54
La Femme Nikita '91 ▸
La Scorta '94 ▸
Lady Snowblood: Love Song of Vengeance '74
The Last Boy Scout '91
London Has Fallen '16
The Long Kiss Goodnight '96
Love and Anarchy '73 ▸
Loves & Times of Scaramouche '76
Lumumba '01 ▸
Malcolm X '92 ▸
The Man Who Killed Hitler and Then the Bigfoot '19
The Man Who Knew Too Much '34 ▸
The Man Who Knew Too Much '56
The Man with the Golden Gun '74
The Manchurian Candidate '62 ▸
Maniac '77
Mechanic: Resurrection '16
The Mercenaries '80
Mercenary: Absolution '15
Mercury Rising '98
The Mermaid '16 ▸
Michael Collins '96 ▸
Mr. Right '16
Momentum '15
Most Wanted '97
Munich '05 ▸
My Little Assassin '99
Nashville '75 ▸
Navy Blues '37
Nick of Time '95
Night of the Assassin '70
Ninja Assassin '09
Nowhere to Hide '83
Omar Khayyam '57
Operation C.I.A. '65
Operation Daybreak '75
The Ordeal of Dr. Mudd '80 ▸
The Parallax View '74 ▸
Parkland '13
The Plot to Kill Hitler '90
Point of No Return '93
Polar '19
PT 109 '63
Puerto Vallarta Squeeze '04
Queen's Messenger II '01
Rampage: President Down '16
Red Eye '05 ▸
Red Scorpion '89
Reign of Assassins '10
Revenge of the Pink Panther '78
RFK '02
RoboGeisha '06
Rogue Male '76
Ruby '92
Russian Roulette '75
Sabotage '96
Scorpio '73
Seven Days in May '64 ▸
Shinobi no Mono '62 ▸
Shinobi no Mono 2: Vengeance '63 ▸
Shooter '07
The Silencers '96
Silent Trigger '97
The Sisters Brothers '18
6 Underground '19
Snake Eyes '98

▸ = rated three bones or higher

Soul Assassin '01
Spenser: The Judas Goat '94
Stalking Danger '86
Steele's Law '91
Stopover Tokyo '57
Suddenly '54 ►
Supreme Sanction '99
The Tall Target '51
The Target '15
Taxi Driver '76 ►
The Terminator '84 ►
The Terrorist '98
XIII '08
13 Minutes '17
This Gun for Hire '90
Three Came to Kill '61
Times of Harvey Milk '83 ►
Triple Threat '19
24 Hours to Live '17
Two Minute Warning '76
The Vanquisher '10
Vantage Point '08
Veronica Guerin '03
When Hell Broke Loose '58
Where There's Life '47
Winter Kills '79►
Xchange '00►
XXX: State of the Union '05
Yojimbo '61►
Z '69►
Zoolander '01

Astronauts

***See also** Space Operas*
Ad Astra '19►
Alien Apocalypse '05
Alien: Covenant '17
Apollo 13 '95►
Apollo 18 '11
Apollo 11 '19►
Approaching the Unknown '16
Armageddon '98
Armstrong '19
The Astronaut Farmer '07
The Astronaut's Wife '99
Beneath the Planet of the Apes '70
Capricorn One '78►
Collision Earth '11
Countdown '68
Crimson Force '05
Deep Impact '98
Earth II '71
Escape From Planet Earth '13
Fantastic Four '05
First Man '18
Fly Me to the Moon '08
From the Earth to the Moon '98►
Gattaca '97►
Gravity '13►
In the Shadow of the Moon '07►
Interstellar '14
Journey to the Seventh Planet '62
Life '17
Love '11
Marooned '69
Mission to Mars '00
Moon '09
Moonwalkers '16
Pandorum '09
Planet 51 '09
Planet of the Apes '68►
Planet of the Apes '01►
Queen of Blood '66
Red Planet '00
The Reluctant Astronaut '67
The Right Stuff '83►
RocketMan '97
Sergeant Deadhead '65
The Sky's No Limit '84
Solaris '02
The Space Between Us '17
Space Buddies '08
Space Chimps '08
Space Cowboys '00►
Space Warriors '13
Species 2 '98
Stranded '13
Strange New World '75
3022 '19
Time Warp '81
12 to the Moon '60
2001: A Space Odyssey '68►
2010: The Year We Make Contact '84 ►
World Without End '56
Zero '18

Astronomy & Astrology

***See** Star Gazing*

At the Drive-In

***See also** At the Movies*
Dead End Drive-In '86
Drive-In '76
Drive-In Massacre '74
Grease '78 ►
Lone Star '95 ►
The Outsiders '83
Pee-wee's Big Adventure '85 ►
Targets '68 ►
Twister '96

At the Movies

Alien Trespass '09
Anguish '88
Apartment Zero '88►
The Artist '11►
Attack from Mars '88
The Aviator '04►
Bonnie & Clyde '67►
Boogie Nights '97►
Brutal Massacre: A Comedy '07
The Cheetah Girls: One World '08
Cinema Paradiso '88►
Come See the Paradise '90►
CQ '01
The Creeps '97
Cyxork 7 '06
Dark Night '17
Day for Night '73►
The Deal '08
Demons '86
Desperately Seeking Susan '85
The Dying Gaul '05►
Finding Bliss '09
For Ever Mozart '96
Foul Play '78►
Full Frontal '02
Get Shorty '95►
Goodbye, Dragon Inn '03
Gremlins 2: The New Batch '90►
Gremlins '84►
The Hard Way '91►
Hitchcock '12
Hollywood Hotel '37
I Love Your Work '03
In and Out '97►
In the Electric Mist '08
Inglourious Basterds '09►
The Inner Circle '91►
Into the West '92►
Invasion Earth: The Aliens Are Here! '87
Johnny Dangerously '84
The Kid and I '05
L.A. Twister '04
Last Action Hero '93
The Last Picture Show '71►
The Last Shot '04
The Long Day Closes '92►
Love and Death on Long Island '97
Marigold '07
Matinee '92
Merton of the Movies '47
Military Intelligence and You! '06
Mr. Bean's Holiday '07
The Movie House Massacre '78
My Faraway Bride '06
A Nightmare on Elm Street 4: Dream Master '88
Otto: Or, Up with Dead People '08
Passion '82
Polyester '81
Popcorn '89
The Projectionist '71►
The Purple Rose of Cairo '85►
The Real Blonde '97
Reel Paradise '05►
The Replacement Killers '98
Sabotage '36 ►
Scenes from a Mall '91
Scream '96 ►
Scream 2 '97 ►
Scream 3 '00
Shadow of the Vampire '00 ►
Simone '02
Slippery Slope '06
Slipstream '07
Something Short of Paradise '79
South Park: Bigger, Longer and Uncut '99
Tampopo '86 ►
Tartuffe '25
Teen Beach Movie '13
Things to Do in Denver When You're Dead '95 ►
Trailer, the Movie '99
Tristram Shandy: A Cock and Bull Story '05
Trojan Eddie '96►
Tropic Thunder '08►
Two Bits '96
Variety '83
Venice, Venice '92
Wes Craven's New Nightmare '94►
What Just Happened '08
White Heat '49►
Who Framed Roger Rabbit '88►
Zack and Miri Make a Porno '08►

At the Video Store

***See also** At the Drive-In; At the Movies*
Be Kind Rewind '08
Beyond the Gates '16
Clerks '94►
EDtv '99
End of the World '13
Film Geek '06
The Fisher King '91►
Good Dick '08
Heart of the Beholder '05►
How to be a Serial Killer '08
Jersey Girl '04
Little Fish '05►
Love and Death on Long Island '97
Scream '96►
The Sisterhood of the Traveling Pants 2 '08
Tainted '98
Take Me Home Tonight '11
Video Violence '87
Watching the Detectives '07
The Watermelon Woman '97

Atlanta

***See also** American South*
Beauty Shop '05►
Coma '12
Cyborg '89
Daddy's Little Girls '07
Diary of a Mad Black Woman '05
Driving Miss Daisy '89►
The Dukes of Hazzard '05
Echo of Murder '00
The Eleventh Victim '12
Gone with the Wind '39►
The Gospel '05►
In the Flesh '97
Let It Shine '12
Let's Do It Again '75
Like a Boss '20
The Lottery Ticket '10
The Murder of Mary Phagan '87►
96 Minutes '11
No Good Deed '14
Richard Jewell '19►
Ride Along '14
Sabotage '14
Scarlett '94
Sharky's Machine '81
Sherman's March '86►
Stomp the Yard '07
Stomp the Yard 2: Homecoming '10
SuperFly '18
Three Can Play That Game '07

Atlantic City

Atlantic City '44
Atlantic City '81►
Beaches '88 ►
The Burglar '57
Convention Girl '35
Duane Hopwood '05 ►
Fatal Desire '05
$5 a Day '08
5 Star Day '10
Gunshy '98 ►
The King of Marvin Gardens '72
The Lemon Sisters '90
Owning Mahowny '03
Snake Eyes '98
Sour Grapes '98
Three Little Girls In Blue '46
Where the Truth Lies '05
Yonkers Joe '08

Atlantis

The Amazing Captain Nemo '78
Atlantis, the Lost Continent '61
Atlantis: The Lost Empire '01
Hercules and the Captive Women '63
Journey to the Center of the Earth '59►
Journey to the Center of the Earth '99
Journey to the Center of the Earth '08
20,000 Leagues under the Sea '16►
20,000 Leagues under the Sea '54►
20,000 Leagues Under the Sea '97

Auditions

All About Nina '18
Audition '99
Billy Elliot '00►
Center Stage: Turn It Up '08
Chain of Souls '00
A Chorus Line '85
Dancing Co-Ed '39
The Daughter of Rosie O'Grady '50
Dickie Roberts: Former Child Star '03
The Dolly Sisters '46
Don't Think Twice '16
Every Little Step '08
Fame '80►
Flashdance '83
Girls Just Want to Have Fun '85
Go For It! '10
Great World of Sound '07
The Guru '02
Hairspray '88►
Hollywood Homicide '03
Hollywood, Je T'Aime '09
Honkytonk Man '82
I Want Someone to Eat Cheese With '06
Inside Daisy Clover '65
Kiss Kiss Bang Bang '05►
Love Songs '84
Make It Happen '08
National Lampoon Presents Cattle Call '06
Never Say Macbeth '07
Pipe Dream '02
Preacher's Kid '10
Shakespeare in Love '98►
Sharpay's Fabulous Adventure '11
Showgirls '95
Smiley Face '07
Stage Fright '14
Swing Hostess '44
The Thing Called Love '93
Three Sailors and a Girl '53
Too Young to Kiss '51
True Romance '93
Undiscovered '05
Venus in Fur '13►
Why Stop Now '12
Yellow '06
You Light Up My Life '77

Aunts & Uncles, Nieces & Nephews

The Addams Family '91
Addams Family Values '93
Airborne '93
Alex Rider: Operation Stormbreaker '06
All in a Night's Work '61
The Amazing Spider-Man '12 ►
American Movie '99 ►
Apartment Troubles '15
April Love '57
Around June '08
Arsenic and Old Lace '44 ►
ATL '06
Audrey's Rain '03
August '95
Auntie Mame '58 ►
Aussie and Ted's Great Adventure '09
The Bad Man '41
The Ballad of the Sad Cafe '91
Ballast '08
Banjo Hackett '76
Bedtime Stories '08
Beethoven's 5th '03
Bereavement '10
Betsy's Wedding '90
The Beverly Hillbillies '93
Beverly Hills Chihuahua '08
Blind Faith '98
Blood Ties '92
Bottoms Up '06
Brewster's Millions '45
Brewster's Millions '85
Bright Eyes '34
Brighton Beach Memoirs '86
Broken Lullaby '94
Broken Trail '06►
Bye-Bye '96
Café Society '16
Camille '07
The Camomile Lawn '92
Campus Rhythm '43
Caryl of the Mountains '36
Casino Royale '67
Casper '95►
Charley's Aunt '41►
Chase a Crooked Shadow '58
Child in the House '56
Choose Connor '07
Christie's Revenge '07
The Christine Jorgensen Story '70
Christmas Caper '07
Christmas Mail '10
Christmas with Holly '12
City on Fire '87
Clifford '92
Colleen '36
Come Undone '00
Cookie's Fortune '99►
Country Life '95
Cousin Bette '97
Cracked Nuts '31
Crazy in Alabama '99
Cutthroat Island '95
Damien: Omen 2 '78
Dark Blue '03►
Daughter of Keltoum '01
David & Layla '07
The Dead '87►
Deadfall '93
Deadtime Stories '86
Desert Bloom '86►
Devotion '46
Diminished Capacity '08
Dogma '99
The Dolly Sisters '46
Domain '09
Don't Bother to Knock '52
Double Trouble '67
Down in the Delta '98►
The Dream Catcher '99
The Dukes of Hazzard '05
The Dukes of Hazzard: The Beginning '06
East Side Story '07
Emile '03
The Escape Artist '82►
The Family Jewels '65
Family Reunion '81
Fast Girl '07
A Father's Choice '00
Fielder's Choice '05
The Fighting Temptations '03
Finding Amanda '08
Fine Manners '26
First Love '39
Flipper '96►
For Real '02
Fragment of Fear '70
Frankenstein Reborn '98
From Prada to Nada '11
Gallipoli '81►
Ghost Cat '03
The Ghost of Greville Lodge '00
Gifted '17
Gigi '58►
Ginger and Cinnamon '03
The Girl From Mexico '39
The Glass House '01
The Godfather, Part 3 '90►
The Golden Compass '07
The Good Son '93
A Good Year '06
The Grass Harp '95
Great Expectations '34
Great Expectations '46►
Great Expectations '81
Great Expectations '97
Great Expectations '99
The Great Outdoors '88
Greedy '94
Green Dragon '01
The Gypsy Moths '69
Hamlet '48►
Hamlet '90►
Hamlet '96►
Hamlet '00►
Hamlet '01
Hannibal Rising '07
Hard Rain '97
Harry Potter and the Sorcerer's Stone '01►
Harry's War '84
Hatchet 2 '10
Hatfields & McCoys '12►
Haunting Sarah '05
The Hearse '80
Hellraiser '87►
Hidalgo '04
High School '40
High School Confidential '58
Hit Man '72
Home In Indiana '44
The Homecoming '73►
Honkytonk Man '82
House Party 3 '94
Housekeeping '87►
How to Be a Latin Lover '17
I Can Do Bad All By Myself '09
I Remember Mama '48►
Ida '13►
I'll Be Seeing You '44
In Country '89
In the Family '11
The Inheritance '10
The Intended '02
International Velvet '78
I.Q. '94
It's Only Money '62
Jack and Diane '12
Jake's Corner '08
Jamaica Inn '39
James and the Giant Peach '96►
Jason and the Argonauts '00
Journey to the Center of the Earth '08
Judy Moody and the Not Bummer Summer '11
Junior Miss '45
The Keeper of the Bees '35
Kentucky '38
Kidnapped '38
Kidnapped '05►
King Arthur: Legend of the Sword '17
Kingdom Come '01
Kiss the Girls '97
Land of Plenty '04
The Last New Yorker '07
Le Divorce '03
Lebanon, PA '10
The Legend of Fritton's Gold '09
Lemony Snicket's A Series of Unfortunate Events '04
Les Destinees '00
The Life and Adventures of Nicholas Nickleby '81►
A Light in the Darkness '02
The Lion King '94►
The Lion King 1 1/2 '04►
The Longshots '08
Loose Ankles '30

► = rated three bones or higher

Thumbsucker '05 ▶
Touching Home '08
Transfixed '01
Turn It Up '00
U-Turn '97
Ultimate Heist '09
Underworld: Evolution '05
The Unguarded Moment '56
Virgin '03
Wannabes '01
The War Zone '98
Washington Square '97 ▶
We the Animals '18 ▶
When Did You Last See Your Father? '07
Where the Hot Wind Blows '59
The Whole Truth '16
Wilson '17
The Winning Season '09
Wolf Moon '09
Yonkers Joe '08
ZigZag '02 ▶

Ballet

See also Dance Fever
The Accompanist '20
Afternoon of a Faun '13 ▶
Alive and Kicking '96
An American in Paris '51 ▶
Ballets Russes '05 ▶
Black Swan '10 ▶
Black Tights '60
Brain Donors '92
Center Stage '00
Center Stage: Turn It Up '08
Centerstage: On Pointe '16
The Children of Theatre Street '77 ▶
The Company '03 ▶
Dance, Girl, Dance '40
The Dancer Upstairs '02
Dancers '87
First Position '11
George Balanchine's The Nutcracker '93
Girl '18 ▶
Gold Diggers in Paris '38
Grand Hotel '32 ▶
Invitation to the Dance '56
Leap! '16
Limelight '52 ▶
Mao's Last Dancer '09
Margot '09
Never Let Me Go '53
Nijinsky '80
Nine Months '95
The Obsession '06
Passion '13
Petals on the Wind '14
The Red Danube '50
The Red Shoes '48 ▶
Save the Last Dance 2 '06
Secundaria '14
Shall We Dance '37 ▶
The Story of Three Loves '53
Summer Interlude '50 ▶
Suspiria '77 ▶
The Tales of Hoffmann '51
Talk to Her '02 ▶
The Turning Point '77
The Unfinished Dance '47
Waterloo Bridge '40 ▶
The White Crow '18

Ballooning

The Adventures of Baron Munchausen '89 ▶
The Aeronauts '19
Around the World in 80 Days '56 ▶
Around the World in 80 Days '89
Around the World in 80 Days '04
Danny Deckchair '03
Enduring Love '04
Five Weeks in a Balloon '62
Frankenstein Island '81
The Great Race '65
Jules Verne's Mysterious Island '10
The Lost Zeppelin '29
Men Don't Leave '89
Mysterious Island '61 ▶
Night Crossing '81
Octopussy '83
Olly Olly Oxen Free '78
Police Academy 4: Citizens on Patrol '87
Queen of the Jungle '35
Those Magnificent Men in Their Flying Machines '65 ▶
The Wizard of Oz '39 ▶

Baltimore

Adventure in Baltimore '49
The Alien Factor '78
And Justice for All '79
Avalon '90 ▶
The Boys of Baraka '05
Cause of Death '00
The Climb '97
Crash and Burn '07
Diner '82 ▶
A Dirty Shame '04
Duck '05
First Sunday '08
Hairspray '88 ▶
Hairspray '07 ▶
He Said, She Said '91
He's Just Not That Into You '09
The Hit '01
Homicide: The Movie '00
Ladder 49 '04
Liberty Heights '99
Management '09
My Brother Talks to Horses '47
Pecker '98
Polyester '81
The Raven '12
The Salon '05
Seven Days of Grace '06
Sleepless in Seattle '93 ▶
Step Up 2 the Streets '08
Steve Martini's The Judge '01
The Sum of All Fears '02
Tin Men '87
12 O'Clock Boys '14 ▶

Bar & Grill

See also Nightclubs
Albino Alligator '96
Americano '05
Ash Wednesday '02
Avengement '19
Bar Girls '95
Bar Hopping '00
Barb Wire '96
Barfly '87 ▶
Barstool Cowboy '08
Bedazzled '68 ▶
Before Sunrise '94
Bottoms Up '06
The Broken Hearts Club '00 ▶
Bucktown '75
Burnzy's Last Call '95
Cocktail '88
Coyote Ugly '00
Crazy Eyes '12
Crocodile Dundee '86 ▶
Death Proof '07
Dial 1119 '50
Dinner Rush '00 ▶
Dose of Reality '12
The Driftless Area '16
The Drop '14 ▶
The Exiles '61
Feast 2: Sloppy Seconds '08
Feast '06
Flickering Lights '01
The Florentine '98
From Dusk Till Dawn '95
From Dusk Till Dawn 2: Texas Blood Money '98
From Dusk Till Dawn 3: The Hangman's Daughter '99
Headless Body in Topless Bar '96
Hedwig and the Angry Inch '00 ▶
Hi-Life '98
Hysterical Blindness '02
The Iceman Cometh '60 ▶
The Iceman Cometh '73
Intimacy '00
Jake's Corner '08
John Carpenter's Vampires '97
Kings '07
Knock Down the House '19
The Last Time I Committed Suicide '96
Lemonade Joe '64
Little Boy Blue '97
Luminarias '99
Margarita Happy Hour '01
Mistresses '19
Mondays in the Sun '02
Money Kings '98
Nobody '99
One Night at McCool's '01
Overnight '03 ▶
Pee-wee's Big Adventure '85 ▶
Phenomenon '96
Portland Expose '57
Rare Birds '01
Restaurant '98
The Riot Club '15
Road House 2: Last Call '06
Road House '89
Roadie '11
Roxanne '87 ▶
Ruby's Bucket of Blood '01
Satin '10
Secret Agent of Japan '42
Sexy Evil Genius '13
Stand-Ins '97
Stickmen '01
Still Waiting '08
Super Size Me 2: Holy Chicken! '19
Support the Girls '18
Table One '00
The Taste of Others '00 ▶
The Tavern '00
Tod@s Caen '19
Tree's Lounge '96
Twice upon a Yesterday '98
Two Family House '99
Un Air de Famille '96
Urban Cowboy '80
Urbania '00
Vanishing on 7th Street '10
The White Countess '05 ▶

Barcelona

See also Madrid; Spain
Biutiful '10
The Bobo '67
Body Armour '07
Chase a Crooked Shadow '58
The Cheetah Girls 2 '06
Dark Habits '84
Face of Terror '04
Food of Love '02
Gaudi Afternoon '01
L'Auberge Espagnole '02 ▶
Nico and Dani '00
[Rec] 2 '09
Reflections '08
The Sea Change '98
Vicky Cristina Barcelona '08
What It's All About '95

Baseball

Air Bud 4: Seventh Inning Fetch '02
Alibi Ike '35
Amazing Grace & Chuck '87
Angels in the Infield '00
Angels in the Outfield '51 ▶
Angels in the Outfield '94
The Babe '92
Babe Ruth Story '48
The Bad News Bears '76 ▶
The Bad News Bears '05
The Bad News Bears Go to Japan '78
The Bad News Bears in Breaking Training '77
Ball of Wax '03
Bang the Drum Slowly '73 ▶
Benched '18
The Benchwarmers '06
Big Leaguer '53
Bingo Long Traveling All-Stars & Motor Kings '76 ▶
The Break-Up '06
Brewster's Millions '85
The Bronx Is Burning '07
Bull Durham '88 ▶
Calvin Marshall '09
The Catcher '98
The Catcher Was a Spy '18
Chasing 3000 '07
Chicken Little '05
Cobb '94 ▶
Curveball '15
Damn Yankees '58 ▶
Diminished Capacity '08
Ed '96
Eight Men Out '88 ▶
Elmer the Great '33
Everybody Wants Some!! '16
Everyone's Hero '06
The Fan '96
Fear Strikes Out '57 ▶
Fences '16 ▶
Fever Pitch '05
Field of Dreams '89 ▶
The Final Season '07
Finding Buck McHenry '00
For Love of the Game '99
42 '13 ▶
Frequency '00
Game 6 '05
The Geisha Boy '58
The Great American Pastime '56
Hardball '01
Home Run '13
Home Run Showdown '10
How Do You Know '10
Hustle '04
Ironweed '87 ▶
It's Good to Be Alive '74
It's My Turn '80
The Jackie Robinson Story '50 ▶
Jim Thorpe: All American '51
The Kid From Cleveland '49
Kill the Umpire '50
The King '05
A League of Their Own '92 ▶
Life '99
The Life and Times of Hank Greenberg '99 ▶
Little Big League '94
A Little Inside '01
Love Affair: The Eleanor & Lou Gehrig Story '77 ▶
Major League '89
Major League 2 '94
Major League 3: Back to the Minors '98
The Man from Left Field '93
Million Dollar Arm '14
Mr. Baseball '92
Mr. Destiny '90
Mr. 3000 '04
Moneyball '11 ▶
The Natural '84 ▶
The Open Road '09
Pastime '91 ▶
Perfect Game '00
The Perfect Game '09
The Phenom '16
Pride of St. Louis '52
The Pride of the Yankees '42 ▶
Rhubarb '51
Ring the Bell '13
The Rookie '02 ▶
Rookie of the Year '93
The Sandlot '93 ▶
The Sandlot 2 '05
The Sandlot 3: Heading Home '07
The Scout '94
61* '01 ▶
The Slugger's Wife '85
Soul of the Game '96 ▶
Squeeze Play '79
Stealing Home '88
The Stratton Story '49 ▶
Sugar '09 ▶
Summer Catch '01
Take Me Out to the Ball Game '49
Taking Care of Business '90
Talent for the Game '91
Three Wishes '95
Tiger Town '83
Trouble with the Curve '12
Undrafted '16
Up for Grabs '05
The Upside of Anger '05 ▶
War Eagle, Arkansas '07
Where Hope Grows '15
Whistling in Brooklyn '43
Wide Awake '97
The Winning Team '52
Woman of the Year '42 ▶
The Yankles '09

Basketball

Above the Rim '94
The Absent-Minded Professor '61 ▶
Adam Sandler's 8 Crazy Nights '02
Air Bud '97
The Air Up There '94
Alien: Resurrection '97 ▶
The Basket '99
The Basketball Diaries '95
Believe in Me '06
Big and Hairy '98
Big Shot: Confessions of a Campus Bookie '02
Black and White '99 ▶
Blue Chips '94
The Cable Guy '96
Celtic Pride '96
Coach '78
Coach Carter '05 ▶
The Cookout '04
Cornbread, Earl & Me '75
Crossover '06
Eddie '96
Fast Break '79
Final Shot: The Hank Gathers Story '92
Finding Forrester '00
The Fish that Saved Pittsburgh '79
Flubber '97
Forget Paris '95
Glory Road '06
Grown Ups '10
Guarding Eddy '04
Halls of Anger '70
Harvard Man '01
He Got Game '98
The Heart of the Game '05
Heaven Is a Playground '91
High Flying Bird '19
High School Musical 3: Senior Year '08
Home of the Giants '07
Hoop Dreams '94 ▶
Hoosiers '86 ▶
The Hot Flashes '13
Hurricane Season '09
Inside Moves '80
John Tucker Must Die '06
Just Wright '10
Juwanna Mann '02
King of the Jungle '01
Like Mike '02
Linsanity '13
Love and Basketball '00 ▶
The Mighty Macs '09
More Than a Game '08
O '01 ▶
One on One '77
Passing Glory '99 ▶
Pistol: The Birth of a Legend '90
The Playaz Court '07
Playin' For Love '15 ▶
Pleasantville '98 ▶
Porky's Revenge '85
Rebound '05
Rebound: The Legend of Earl 'The Goat' Manigault '96
The Red Sneakers '01
Rock the Paint '05
The St. Tammany Miracle '94
A Season on the Brink '02
Semi-Pro '08
The Sixth Man '97
Slam Dunk Ernest '95
Space Jam '96
Sunset Park '96
Tall Story '60
Teen Wolf '85
That Championship Season '82
That Championship Season '99
Through the Fire '05 ▶
Thunderstruck '12
Tyler Perry's Meet the Browns '08
Uncle Drew '18
Uncut Gems '19 ▶
Unshackled '00
The Way Back '20
White Men Can't Jump '92
The Winning Season '09

Bathroom Scenes

About Last Night. . . '86 ▶
American Gigolo '79
An American Werewolf in London '81 ▶
Angel Blue '97
Arachnophobia '90
Austin Powers: International Man of Mystery '97 ▶
Body Double '84 ▶
Brain Damage '88
Breathless '83
Bull Durham '88 ▶
Bulletproof '96
Club Paradise '86
Color of Night '94
The Cook, the Thief, His Wife & Her Lover '90 ▶
Copycat '95
Diabolique '55 ▶
Diabolique '96
Dressed to Kill '80
Dumb & Dumber '94
An Eye for an Eye '95
Fatal Attraction '87 ▶
Full Metal Jacket '87 ▶
Ghostbusters 2 '89
He Knows You're Alone '80
High Anxiety '77
Jerry Maguire '96 ▶
Jinxed '82
Jurassic Park '93 ▶
The Legacy '79
Lethal Weapon 2 '89 ▶
Liar Liar '97
The Light of the Moon '17 ▶
Married to the Mob '88 ▶
Midnight Express '78 ▶
Mister Roberts '55 ▶
Mixed Nuts '94
National Lampoon's Vacation '83 ▶
9 to 5 '80
An Officer and a Gentleman '82 ▶
Poltergeist '82 ▶
Poltergeist 2: The Other Side '86
Porky's '82
Posers '02
The Postman Always Rings Twice '81
Psycho '60 ▶
Psycho 2 '83
Psycho '98
Pulp Fiction '94 ▶
Red Lights '12
St. Elmo's Fire '85
Satan's Sadists '69
Scarface '83 ▶
Schizo '77
Serious Moonlight '09
Shakes the Clown '92
Shattered Image '98
The Shining '80
Silkwood '83 ▶
Stripes '81
Tequila Sunrise '88
They Came from Within '75
Tie Me Up! Tie Me Down! '90
True Romance '93
Valley Girl '83
Valmont '89 ▶
Very Bad Things '98
Working Girl '88 ▶

Bats

See also Eco-Vengeance!; Up All Night; Wild Kingdom
The Bat People '74
Batman Begins '05 ▶
Batman Forever '95 ▶
Batman Returns '92
Bats '99
Bats: Human Harvest '07
The Devil Bat '41
Nightwing '79
The Vampire Bat '32
Vampire Bats '05

BBC TV Productions

An Adventure in Space and Time '13
The Affair '95
All Passion Spent '86
And Now for Something Completely Different '72 ▶

▶ = rated three bones or higher

Aristocrats '99
The Bad Mother's Handbook '07
Berkeley Square '98
The Best of Men '12
Birdsong '12
Broken '13
The Buccaneers '95 ▶
The Buddha of Suburbia '92 ▶
Burton and Taylor '13
Christabel '89
The Chronicles of Narnia '89 ▶
Cold Comfort Farm '94 ▶
Count Dracula '77
Cranford '08
The Crimson Petal and the White '12
Dangerous Corner '83
The Diary of Anne Frank '08
Doctor Who '96
The Duchess of Duke Street '78 ▶
Edge of Darkness '86
Elizabeth R '72 ▶
Emma '72
Emma '09
The Escape Artist '13 ▶
The Final Cut '95 ▶
First Light '10
The Flame Trees of Thika '81 ▶
Florence Nightingale '08
Fortunes of War '87 ▶
The Girl '12
Going for Gold: The '48 Games '12
The Golden Bowl '72 ▶
Great Expectations '99
Great Expectations '11
The Haunted Airman '06
He Knew He Was Right '04
Hidden '11
The Hitchhiker's Guide to the Galaxy '81 ▶
House of Cards '90 ▶
How Many Miles to Babylon? '82
The Ice House '97 ▶
The Insurance Man '86
Invasion: Earth '98
Ivanhoe '97 ▶
Jude the Obscure '71
King Lear '98 ▶
Lady Chatterley '92
The Lady Vanishes '13
Lennon Naked '10
Little Dorrit '08
Little Lord Fauntleroy '95
Lorna Doone '01 ▶
The Lost Language of Cranes '92 ▶
Mansfield Park '85
Martin Chuzzlewit '94
Middlemarch '93 ▶
Mrs. Brown '97 ▶
Much Ado About Nothing '05
My Brother Jonathan '85
The Mystery of Edwin Drood '12
Neil Gaiman's NeverWhere '96
Northanger Abbey '87
The Old Curiosity Shop '07
Oranges Are Not the Only Fruit '89
Our Mutual Friend '98
Page Eight '11
A Perfect Spy '88
Persuasion '71
Persuasion '95 ▶
Poldark 2 '75 ▶
Poldark '75 ▶
Portrait of a Lady '67
Pride and Prejudice '95 ▶
Priest '94
A Question of Attribution '91
A Respectable Trade '98
Return to Cranford '09
Robin Hood. . . The Legend: Robin Hood and the Sorcerer '83
Rogue Male '76
A Room With a View '08
The Scarlet Pimpernel '99
The Scarlet Pimpernel 2: Mademoiselle Guillotine '99
The Scarlet Pimpernel 3: The Kidnapped King '99
The Sculptress '97
The Secret Garden '84
Sense & Sensibility '85
Shades of Fear '93
Sharpe's Peril '08
She Fell Among Thieves '78
The Singing Detective '86 ▶
The Sinking of the Laconia '10
Six Wives of Henry VIII '71 ▶
South Riding '11
Speedy Death '99 ▶
A Tale of Two Cities '89 ▶
The Tenant of Wildfell Hall '96
Testament of Youth '79
Therese Raquin '80
Thicker Than Water '93
To Play the King '93 ▶
Toast '10
Tom Jones '98 ▶
The Triangle '05
Unexplained Laughter '89
United '11
Upstairs Downstairs '11
Vanity Fair '99
Victoria & Albert '01
The Wedding Gift '93 ▶
Women in Love '11
A Year in Provence '89 ▶

Beach Blanket Bingo

See Lifeguards; Sex on the Beach; Surfing; Swimming

Bears

See also Wild Kingdom

Almost Heroes '97
Alpha and Omega '10
The Bear '89 ▶
Bears '14
The Bears & I '74
Body at Brighton Rock '19
Born in China '17
Brave '12
Brigsby Bear '17
Brother Bear 2 '06
Brother Bear '03
The Country Bears '02
Deadtime Stories '86
Dr. Dolittle 2 '01
Earth '07
The Edge '97
Ernest & Celestine '13
Gentle Giant '67
The Golden Compass '07
The Great Outdoors '88
Grizzly '76
Grizzly Falls '99
Grizzly Man '05 ▶
Grizzly Rage '07
The Hotel New Hampshire '84
The Journey Home '14
The Jungle Book 2 '03
The Jungle Book '67 ▶
King of the Grizzlies '69
Kung Fu Panda '08 ▶
Kung Fu Panda 2 '11 ▶
Legends of the Fall '94
The Many Adventures of Winnie the Pooh '77
Norm of the North '16
Open Season 3 '10
Paddington 2 '17 ▶
Paddington '14 ▶
Pandas '18 ▶
The Parent Trap '61
The Polar Bear King '94
Rudyard Kipling's The Jungle Book '94
Rudyard Kipling's the Second Jungle Book: Mowgli and Baloo '97
Spirit Bear: The Simon Jackson Story '05
Ted '12 ▶
True Heart '97
Two Little Bears '61
An Unfinished Life '05
Wild Grizzly '99
Winnie the Pooh '11 ▶
Without a Paddle '04
Yogi Bear '10

The Beat Generation

Beat '00
Big Sur '13
Heart Beat '80
Howl '10
Kill Your Darlings '06
Kill Your Darlings '13
The Last Time I Committed Suicide '96
On the Road '12

Beatniks

Beat Girl '60
A Bucket of Blood '59 ▶
Expresso Bongo '59
Funny Face '57 ▶
Hairspray '88 ▶
The Last Time I Committed Suicide '96
The Prime Time '60
So I Married an Axe Murderer '93

Beauty Pageants

Ass Backwards '13
Beautiful '00
Beauty Queen Butcher! '91
The Case of the Lucky Legs '35
Drop Dead Gorgeous '99
The Duchess of Idaho '50
Elvis and Annabelle '07
Fast and Furious '39
Happy, Texas '99 ▶
I Know What You Did Last Summer '97 ▶
Little Miss Sunshine '06 ▶
Miss All-American Beauty '82
Miss Bala '12
Miss Bala '19
Miss Cast Away '04
Miss Congeniality '00
Miss Congeniality 2: Armed and Fabulous '05
Miss Firecracker '89 ▶
Miss Juneteenth '20
No Contest '94
On My Way '14
Shag: The Movie '89 ▶
Slap Her, She's French '02
Smile '75 ▶
Waikiki Wedding '37 ▶

Beer

See also On the Rocks

Beer '85
Beer League '06
Beerfest '06
Drinking Buddies '13
Happy Hour '87
The Jolly Boys' Last Stand '00
Kicked in the Head '97
The Lady Eve '41 ▶
The Nugget '02
The Saddest Music in the World '03
Smokey and the Bandit '77
Strange Brew '83
Swing Vote '08
Take This Job & Shove It '81
Uncle Nick '15
Young Einstein '89

Bees

See also Killer Bugs and Slugs

Bee Movie '07
Bright Road '53
Candyman 2: Farewell to the Flesh '94
Candyman 3: Day of the Dead '98
Candyman '92
Colony: The Endangered World of Bees '11
Honeyland '19 ▶
Microcosmos '96 ▶
The Secret Life of Bees '08 ▶
The Swarm '78
Tell It to the Bees '19
The Wonders '15

Behind Bars

See Great Escapes; Men in Prison; Women in Prison

Behind the Scenes

See At the Movies

Belfast

See also Dublin; Ireland

Circle of Deceit '94
The Devil's Own '96 ▶
An Everlasting Piece '00
Fifty Dead Men Walking '08
Four Days in July '85
Hennessy '75
Hunger '08
In the Name of the Father '93 ▶
The Merry Gentleman '08
The Mighty Celt '05
'71 '14 ▶
Shadow Dancer '12 ▶

Berlin

See also Germany

Adam Resurrected '08
Aimee & Jaguar '98
The Apple '80
The Assignment '97
Atomic Blonde '17
Before the Fall '04
Bent '97
Berlin Correspondent '42
Berlin Job '12
Berlin Syndrome '17
Berlin Tunnel 21 '81
The Blue Hour '91
The Bourne Supremacy '04 ▶
Cabaret '72 ▶
Charlie Chan at the Olympics '37
Cherry Blossoms '08
Christina '10
Christopher and His Kind '11 ▶
Cold Room '84
The Company '07
The Crooked Web '55
Dead Pigeon on Beethoven Street '72
The Debt '10
Demons '86
Dr. Ehrlich's Magic Bullet '40
Downfall '04 ▶
The Edukators '04
Eurotrip '04
Faraway, So Close! '93
Flightplan '05
Fraulein '58
Funeral in Berlin '66 ▶
Generation War '13
Germany Year Zero '48 ▶
Go for Zucker '05
Good Bye, Lenin! '03 ▶
The Good German '06
Gotcha! '85
Hidden Agenda '99
Hitler: Beast of Berlin '39
Indiana Jones and the Last Crusade '89 ▶
The Innocent '93
Invincible '01
The Iron Petticoat '56
Judgment in Berlin '88
King of Thieves '04
Kuhle Wampe, Or Who Owns the World? '32
The Legend of Rita '99
The Lives of Others '06 ▶
Lola and Billy the Kid '98
The Looking Glass War '69
Man On a String '60
The Mistake '91
Mother Night '96 ▶
The Murderers Are Among Us '46
Night People '54
Obsession '97
Otto: Or, Up with Dead People '08
Run Lola Run '98 ▶
Salmonberries '91
The Search '48 ▶
The Serpent's Egg '78
Shining Through '92
The Song of Songs '33
Stop Me Before I Kill! '60
Summer Palace '06 ▶
Suspiria '18
Taking Sides '01 ▶
They Came to Blow Up America '43
3 '10
The Tigress '93
Timecop 2: The Berlin Decision '03
The Truce '96 ▶
The Tunnel '01 ▶
Under the Pavement Lies the Strand '75
Unknown '11
Verboten! '59
The Waiting Time '99
What to Do in Case of Fire '02
Wings of Desire '88 ▶

Bermuda Triangle

Airport '77 '77
The Bermuda Depths '78
Bermuda Tentacles '14
Gulliver's Travels '10
The Land That Time Forgot '09
Lost Voyage '01
The Triangle '01
The Triangle '05

Beverly Hills

Allie & Me '97
Anywhere But Here '99
B.A.P.'s '97
Beverly Hills Chihuahua 2 '10
Beverly Hills Chihuahua '08
Beverly Hills Cop '84
Beverly Hills Cop 2 '87
Beverly Hills Cop 3 '94
Clueless '95 ▶
A Death in California '85
Down and Out in Beverly Hills '86
The Hollywood Knights '80
Housewife '72
Just Married '03
The Kreutzer Sonata '08
Legally Blonde '01
Legally Blondes '09
The Lincoln Lawyer '11
Meet the Blacks '16
A Nanny for Christmas '10
The Pool Boys '10
Pretty Woman '90 ▶
The Return of the Beverly Hillbillies '81
Slums of Beverly Hills '98 ▶
Troop Beverly Hills '89
Wassup Rockers '06

Bicycling

American Flyers '85
And Soon the Darkness '70
The Armstrong Lie '13 ▶
Beijing Bicycle '01
The Bicycle Thief '48 ▶
Bicycling With Moliere '13
Blood Trails '06
BMX Bandits '83
Breaking Away '79 ▶
Butch Cassidy and the Sundance Kid '69 ▶
E.T.: The Extra-Terrestrial '82 ▶
The Flying Scotsman '06
Go Further '03
Ithaca '16
The Lovebirds '20
Morgan '12
Pee-wee's Big Adventure '85 ▶
Phantom Pain '09
Premium Rush '12 ▶
The Program '15
Quicksilver '86
Tracers '15
The Triplets of Belleville '02 ▶

Big Battles

See Civil War; Korean War; Persian Gulf/Iraq War; Revolutionary War; Vietnam War; World War One; World War Two

Big Cats

See also Jungle Stories; Wild Kingdom

Across the Moon '94
The Adventures of Tarzan '21
Androcles and the Lion '52
The Big Cat '49
Bringing Up Baby '38 ▶
Cat People '42 ▶
Charlie the Lonesome Cougar '67
Cheetah '89
Doctor Dolittle '67
The Ghost and the Darkness '96
I Dreamed of Africa '00
Ice Age '02 ▶
Island of Lost Souls '32 ▶
Jungle Hell '55
The Leopard Man '43
Les Misérables '19
Life of Pi '12 ▶
The Lion King '94 ▶
The Lost Jungle '34
Maneater '07
Passion in the Desert '97
Primal '19
Rampage '63
Rugrats Go Wild! '03
Talladega Nights: The Ballad of Ricky Bobby '06
Terror Is a Man '59
A Tiger Walks '64
The Wild '06

Big Digs

Ancient Evil: Scream of the Mummy '00
Ancient Relic '02
Appointment With Death '10
Around the Bend '04
Belphegor: Phantom of the Louvre '01
Blood from the Mummy's Tomb '71
The Body '01
Charlie Chan in Egypt '35
Curse of the Faceless Man '58
Dead Are Alive '72
Deadly Intent '88
Exorcist: The Beginning '04
The Golden Salamander '51
Indiana Jones and the Last Crusade '89 ▶
Indiana Jones and the Temple of Doom '84 ▶
Labyrinth '12
The Last Templar '09
Legend of the Lost Tomb '97
The Librarian: Return to King Solomon's Mines '06
The Lost Treasure of the Grand Canyon '08
March or Die '77
The Mask '61
Merry Andrew '58
The Mole People '56
The Mummy '32 ▶
The Mummy '99
Mummy's Boys '36
The Mummy's Hand '40
The Mummy's Shroud '67
National Treasure: Book of Secrets '07
Opa! '05
The Pharaoh's Curse '57
The Pyramid '14
Raiders of the Lost Ark '81 ▶
Return to Treasure Island '54
The Ruins '08
Russell Mulcahy's Tale of the Mummy '99
Search for the Gods '75
Secre of the Andes '98
Sound of Horror '64
Stargate '94
Suez '38
Tower of the Firstborn '98
Treasure Guards '11
Unseen Evil '99
The Vanished Empire '08
Zodiac: Signs of the Apocalypse '14

Big Rigs

See also Motor Vehicle Dept.; Road Trip

The Art of War 3: Retribution '08
Big Trouble in Little China '86
Black Dog '98
Breakdown '96 ▶
Breaker! Breaker! '77
California Straight Ahead '25

▶ = rated three bones or higher

Citizens Band '77 ▸
Code Two '53
Convoy '78
Death in Small Doses '57
Desperate '47
Duel '71 ▸
Every Which Way But Loose '78
F.I.S.T. '78
Great Smokey Roadblock '76
Hi-Jacked '50
Hijack Highway '55
Joy Ride 2: Dead Ahead '08
Joy Ride '01 ▸
Larger Than Life '96
The Long Haul '57
Maximum Overdrive '86
The National Tree '09
The Off Hours '11
The Other Side of the Mountain, Part 2 '78
Pee-wee's Big Adventure '85 ▸
Road Games '81
Road Rage '01
Smokey and the Bandit '77
Smokey and the Bandit 2 '80
Smokey and the Bandit, Part 3 '83
Sorcerer '77
The Sure Thing '85 ▸
They Drive by Night '40 ▸
Trucker '08
Trucks '97
Violent Road '58
Wages of Fear '55 ▸
White Line Fever '75

Bigfoot/Yeti

Abominable '06
The Abominable Snowman '57
Assault of the Sasquatch '09
Big and Hairy '98
Bigfoot '70
Bigfoot: The Lost Coast Tapes '12
Bigfoot: The Unforgettable Encounter '94
The Capture of Bigfoot '79
Clawed: The Legend of Sasquatch '05
Frostbiter: Wrath of the Wendigo '94
Harry and the Hendersons '87
Legend of Boggy Creek '75
Little Bigfoot 2: The Journey Home '97
Little Bigfoot '96
The Man Who Killed Hitler and Then the Bigfoot '19
Night of the Demon '80
Return to Boggy Creek '77
Route 30 '08
Sasquatch '76
Sasquatch '02
The Sasquatch Gang '06
Shriek of the Mutilated '74
The Snow Creature '54
Snowbeast '77
Strange Wilderness '08
Willow Creek '13
Yeti '08
Yeti: A Love Story '08

Bikers

***See also** Motorcycles; Road Trip*

Angels from Hell '68
Angels Hard As They Come '71
Angels' Wild Women '72
Any Which Way You Can '80
Beach Party '63
Beyond the Law '92
Bigfoot '70
Born to Ride '11
Bury Me an Angel '71
C.C. & Company '70
Charms '73
Cleopatra Jones '73
Cyborg Conquest '09
Cyclone '87
Cymbeline '15
Death Valley '04
Easy Rider '69 ▸
Easy Wheels '89
Eaters '15
Exit Speed '08
Ghost Rider: Spirit of Vengeance '12
The Girl on a Motorcycle '68
The Glory Stompers '67
Hell Ride '08
Hellblock 13 '97
Hellcats '68
Hell's Angels on Wheels '67
Hell's Angels '69 '69
Hell's Bloody Devils '70
In Your Face '77
Lone Hero '02
The Losers '70
Mammuth '10
Mask '85 ▸
Me & Will '99
The Naked Angels '69
One Week '08
Peacekillers '71
Pee-wee's Big Adventure '85 ▸
Psychomania '73
Recoil '11
The Road '00
Roadside Prophets '92
Run, Angel, Run! '69
Satan's Sadists '69
Savages from Hell '68
She-Devils on Wheels '68
The Sweet Life '03
The Sweet Ride '68
These Are the Damned '63
Traffik '18
12 O'Clock Boys '14 ▸
Werewolves on Wheels '71
Wicked Blood '13
The Wild Angels '66
The Wild One '54 ▸
Wild Rebels '71
Wild Riders '71
Wild Zero '00
The World's Fastest Indian '05 ▸

Biography

***See** Biopics: Artists; Biopics: Cops & Biopics: Military; Biopics: Musicians; Biopics: Politics; Biopics: Religious; Biopics: Science/Medical; Biopics: Showbiz; Biopics: Sports; Biopics: Writers; This Is My Life; This Is Your Life*

Biopics: Artists

***See also** Art & Artists*

At Eternity's Gate '18
The B-Side: Elsa Dorfman's Portrait Photography '17
Ballets Russes '05 ▸
Basquiat '96 ▸
Camille Claudel '89 ▸
Caravaggio '86 ▸
Caravaggio '07
Carrington '95
Chihwaseon: Painted Fire '02
Chris & Don: A Love Story '07 ▸
Crumb '94 ▸
The Danish Girl '15
Drew: The Man Behind the Poster '13
Edvard Munch '74
Far Out Isn't Enough: The Tomi Ungerer '13
Final Portrait '17
Frida '84
Frida '02
Fur: An Imaginary Portrait of Diane Arbus '06
Georgia O'Keefe '09
Girl with a Pearl Earring '03 ▸
Goya in Bordeaux '99
Henri Langlois: The Phantom of the Cinematheque '04 ▸
Herblock: The Black & the White '13
In the Realms of the Unreal '04 ▸
Klimt '06
Little Ashes '09
Love Is the Devil '98 ▸
Loving Vincent '17
Lust for Life '56 ▸
Maudie '17 ▸
Miss Hokusai '16
Mr. Turner '14 ▸
Modigliani '04
Moulin Rouge '52 ▸
Mrs. Lowry & Son '19
Never Look Away '18 ▸
Pollock '00 ▸
Postcards from America '95
Professor Marston and the Wonder Women '17
Rembrandt '36 ▸
The Salt of the Earth '14 ▸
Savage Messiah '72 ▸
Searching For Sugar Man '12 ▸
Seraphine '08 ▸
Surviving Picasso '96
Tell Them Who You Are '05
Van Gogh '92 ▸
Vincent & Theo '90 ▸
Vincent: The Life and Death of Vincent van Gogh '87 ▸
Welcome to Marwen '18
The White Crow '18
Woman Walks Ahead '17
Yalom's Cure '14

Biopics: Cops & Robbers

***See also** Crime Drama; True Crime*

Aileen: Life and Death of a Serial Killer '03 ▸
Al Capone '59 ▸
Bandit Queen '94
Black Mass '15
BlacKkKlansman '18 ▸
Bonanno: A Godfather's Story '99
Bonnie & Clyde '67 ▸
Bonnie & Clyde '13
Bronson '09
The Buccaneer '58
Bugsy '91 ▸
Bundy: A Legacy of Evil '08
Butch Cassidy and the Sundance Kid '69 ▸
Capone '20
Chopper '00
Crown Heights '17
Dillinger '45 ▸
Dillinger '73
The Dog '14 ▸
Domino '05
Duffy of San Quentin '54
Extremely Wicked, Shockingly Evil and Vile '19
The Fear of 13 '15 ▸
Freeheld '15
The General '98 ▸
Goodfellas '90 ▸
Gotti '96
Gotti '18
The Hillside Stranglings '04
I Am a Fugitive from a Chain Gang '32 ▸
I Shot Jesse James '49 ▸
The Infiltrator '16
J. Edgar '11
The King of the Roaring '20s: The Story of Arnold Rothstein '61
Lansky '99
Last Days of Frank & Jesse James '86
The Left-Handed Gun '58 ▸
Legend '15
Lepke '75
Lizzie '18
Lucky Luciano '74
Mad Dog Coll '61
Madame Sata '02
Melvin Purvis: G-Man '74
Mesrine: Part 1-Killer Instinct '08
Mesrine: Part 2-Public Enemy Number 1 '08
Mr. Nice '10
Monster '03 ▸
Ned Kelly '70
Ned Kelly '03
The Outlaw '43
The Private Files of J. Edgar Hoover '77
A Real American Hero '78
The Rise and Fall of Legs Diamond '60
The Rise of the Krays '16
Stander '03
Sugartime '95
True History of the Kelly Gang '20
Walking Tall '73
Walking Tall: Part 2 '75
Walking Tall: The Final Chapter '77
Whitey: United States of America v. James J. Bulger '14
Wild Bill '95
The Wolf of Wall Street '13 ▸
Wyatt Earp '94
You Know My Name '99 ▸

Biopics: Military

***See also** Civil War; Korean War; Military: Air Force; Military: Army; Military: Foreign; Military: Marines; Military: Navy; True Stories; Vietnam War; World War One; World War Two*

Alexander '04
Alexander the Great '55
And Starring Pancho Villa as Himself '03 ▸
Antwone Fisher '02 ▸
Attila '01
Battle Hymn '57
Benedict Arnold: A Question of Honor '03
The Big Red One '80 ▸
A Bright Shining Lie '98
Carve Her Name with Pride '58
Cast a Giant Shadow '66
Chapayev '34 ▸
Clive of India '35
Cromwell '70
The Desert Fox '51 ▸
The First Texan '56
The Gallant Hours '60 ▸
Genghis Khan: To the Ends of the Earth and Sea '07
Geronimo '93 ▸
God is My Co-Pilot '45
Hacksaw Ridge '16
I Remember Nelson '82
Ike: Countdown to D-Day '04
The Last Days of Patton '86
Lawrence of Arabia '62 ▸
The Long Gray Line '55 ▸
The Lost Bladesman '16
MacArthur '77
Max Manus: Man of War '08
Megan Leavey '17
Men of Honor '00
Mongol '07 ▸
Monsieur N. '03 ▸
Napoleon '55
Orde Wingate '76
Outlaw King '18
Patton '70 ▸
PT 109 '63
The Red Baron '08
Spitfire '42 ▸
To Hell and Back '55
War Dogs '16
We Were Soldiers '02 ▸

Biopics: Musicians

***See also** Biopics: Showbiz; Nashville Narratives; Showbiz Dramas*

Aaliyah: The Princess of R&B '14
Ain't In It For My Health: A Film About Levon Helm '10 ▸
AKA Doc Pomus '12 ▸
All Eyez on Me '17
Amadeus '84 ▸
Amy '15 ▸
Backbeat '94 ▸
Bandwagon '95
Beats, Rhymes and Life: The Travels of a Tribe Called Quest '11 ▸
Beethoven '36
The Benny Goodman Story '55
Beyond the Sea '04
Biggie & Tupac: The Story Behind the Murder of Rap's Biggest Superstars '02
Bird '88 ▸
Blaze '18 ▸
Bohemian Rhapsody '18
Born to Be Blue '15 ▸
Bound for Glory '76 ▸
Bride of the Wind '01
The Buddy Holly Story '78 ▸
Callas Forever '02
Coal Miner's Daughter '80 ▸
Cobain: Montage of Heck '15 ▸
Control '07
Crazy '08
David Crosby: Remember My Name '19
De-Lovely '04
Deep in My Heart '54
The Devil and Daniel Johnston '05 ▸
DIG! '04 ▸
Don't Look Back '67
The Doors '91
Eat That Question: Frank Zappa in His Own Words '16 ▸
The Eddy Duchin Story '56
8 Mile '02 ▸
El Cantante '06
Elvis: The Movie '79
End of the Century: The Story of the Ramones '03 ▸
The Fabulous Dorseys '47
Fade to Black '04 ▸
Farinelli '94
The Five Pennies '59
Florence Foster Jenkins '16
For Love or Country: The Arturo Sandoval Story '00
The Gene Krupa Story '59
George Harrison: Living in the Material World '11
Get On Up '14
The Glenn Miller Story '54 ▸
Great Balls of Fire '89
The Great Caruso '51
The Great Waltz '38 ▸
Green Book '18 ▸
Greetings from Tim Buckley '12
The Harmonists '99
Harmony Lane '35
Hendrix '00
Hilary and Jackie '98 ▸
I Dream of Jeannie '52
The Idol '15 ▸
I'll See You in My Dreams '51
I'm Not There '07 ▸
Immortal Beloved '94
Impromptu '90 ▸
In His Life: The John Lennon Story '00
Interrupted Melody '55 ▸
The Invisibles '99
Irish Eyes Are Smiling '44
The Jacksons: An American Dream '92
Jersey Boys '14
Jimi: All Is by My Side '14
Johnny Winter: Down & Dirty '14
Justin Bieber: Never Say Never '11
Katy Perry: Part of Me '12
Killa Season '06
La Bamba '87 ▸
Lady Sings the Blues '72
Leto '19
Let's Get Lost '88 ▸
The Life and Loves of Mozart '59
Linda Ronstadt: The Sound of My Voice '19 ▸
Lisztomania '75
Little Richard '00
Loretta Lynn: Still a Mountain Girl '16
Love & Mercy '15 ▸
Love Me or Leave Me '55 ▸
The Magic Bow '47
Mahler '74 ▸
Man in the Mirror: The Michael Jackson Story '04
Marguerite '16 ▸
Marianne & Leonard: Words of Love '19
Mayor of the Sunset Strip '03 ▸
Melody Master '41
Metallica: Some Kind of Monster '04 ▸
Miles Ahead '16 ▸
Mo' Better Blues '90
Mozart's Sister '10
New York Doll '05 ▸
Nico Icon '95 ▸
Night and Day '46
The Night We Called It a Day '03
Nina '16
Notorious '09
Over the Waves '49
Passion '99
Pavarotti '19
Pearl Jam Twenty '11
The Pianist '02 ▸
The Polka King '18
Protecting the King '07
The Rat Pack '98
Ray '04 ▸
Rhapsody in Blue '45 ▸
Rhapsody of Spring '98
Ring of Fire '13
Rolling Thunder Revue: A Bob Dylan Story by Martin Scorsese '19 ▸
The Runaways '10
Selena '96
Sex & Drugs & Rock & Roll '10
Seymour: An Introduction '15 ▸
Shine '95 ▸
Sid & Nancy '86 ▸
Song of Love '47 ▸
A Song to Remember '45 ▸
Song Without End '60
Spring Symphony '86
Springsteen & I '13 ▸
Stoned '05
Straight Outta Compton '15 ▸
The Strauss Family '73
Swanee River '39
Sweet and Lowdown '99
Sweet Dreams '85
Take Me Home: The John Denver Story '00
Taking Sides '01 ▸
The Temptations '98
32 Short Films about Glenn Gould '93 ▸
This Is Elvis '81
Three Little Words '50
Till the Clouds Roll By '46
Tous les Matins du Monde '92 ▸
20,000 Days on Earth '14 ▸
Two of Us '00
The U.S. Vs. John Lennon '06
Violeta Went to Heaven '13 ▸
The Von Trapp Family: A Life of Music '15
Wagner: The Complete Epic '85
Walk Hard: The Dewey Cox Story '07
Walk the Line '05 ▸
Waltz King '63
Western Stars '19 ▸
What Happened, Miss Simone? '15 ▸
What We Do Is Secret '07
What's Love Got to Do with It? '93
Whitney '18
Why Do Fools Fall in Love? '98
Words and Music '48
Young Caruso '51
Your Cheatin' Heart '64

Biopics: Politics

***See also** Capitol Capers; Politics; True Stories; Vote for Me!*

Abe Lincoln in Illinois '40 ▸
Abraham Lincoln '30
Amazing Grace '06 ▸
American Dharma '18
Balzac and the Little Chinese Seamstress '02
The Betty Ford Story '87 ▸
Blaze '89
Bobby '06

▸ = rated three bones or higher

Casino Jack '10
Cesar Chavez '14
Chappaquiddick '17
Che '08
Churchill '17
Citizen Cohn '92
Citizen K '19
A Dangerous Man: Lawrence after Arabia '91 ▸
Darkest Hour '17 ▸
The Death of Adolf Hitler '84
The Devil's Double '11
Disraeli '79 ▸
Downfall '04 ▸
Dream West '86
Eleanor & Franklin '76 ▸
Eleanor: First Lady of the World '82
Enemy of Women '44
Fatal Deception: Mrs. Lee Harvey Oswald '93
The Fifth Estate '13
The First Texan '56
The Front Runner '18
Gandhi '82 ▸
The Gathering Storm '02 ▸
George Wallace '97
Giuliani Time '05
Give 'Em Hell, Harry! '75 ▸
Going Upriver: The Long War of John Kerry '04
Gore Vidal's Lincoln '88
Hamilton '20 ▸
Hitler '62
Hitler: The Last Ten Days '73
Hitler: The Rise of Evil '03
House of Saddam '08
Hyde Park on Hudson '12
Il Divo '08
Imperial Venus '63
Into the Storm '09
The Iron Lady '11
Jackie '16 ▸
Jackie, Ethel, Joan: The Kennedy Women '01
Jefferson in Paris '94
The Jesse Ventura Story '99
JFK: Reckless Youth '93
John Adams '08
Juarez '39
Keep the Faith, Baby '02
Killing Lincoln '13
Koch '13 ▸
Kundun '97 ▸
The Lady '11
The Last Emperor '87 ▸
Last Four Days '77
The Last King of Scotland '06 ▸
LBJ '17
The Liberator '13
Lincoln '12 ▸
Loro '19
Lumumba '01 ▸
Magnificent Doll '46
The Magnificent Yankee '50 ▸
Mandela '87 ▸
Mandela: Long Walk to Freedom '13
Mark Felt: The Man Who Brought Down the White House '17
Marshall '17
Michael Collins '96 ▸
Mitt '14
Monsieur N. '03 ▸
The Motorcycle Diaries '04 ▸
Mussolini & I '85
Napoleon '03
Neruda '16
Nixon '95 ▸
Operation Finale '18
Parnell '37
Path to War '02
Pinochet's Last Stand '06
RBG '18 ▸
The Reagans '04
Red Joan '19
The Report '19
RFK '02
Robert Kennedy and His Times '90
Rudy: The Rudy Giulani Story '03
Saint Judy '19
Secret Honor '85 ▸
Selma '14 ▸
The Sicilian '87
Snowden '16
Southside with You '16 ▸
The Special Relationship '10
Sunrise at Campobello '60 ▸
Thurgood '11 ▸
Truman '95
The Undefeated '11
The Unknown Known '14 ▸
Vice '18
Viceroy's House '17
Viva Zapata! '52 ▸
W. '08 ▸
Wilson '44 ▸
Winnie Mandela '13
A Woman Called Golda '82 ▸
Young Mr. Lincoln '39 ▸

Biopics: Religious

***See also** Islam; Judaism; Religion*

Ben-Hur '16
Bernadette '90
Brother Sun, Sister Moon '73
Cardinal Richelieu '35
The Case for Christ '17
Crazy Wisdom: The Life & Times of Chogyam Trungpa Rinpoche '11
The Eyes of Tammy Faye '00
The Flowers of St. Francis '50 ▸
From a Far Country: Pope John Paul II '81
The Gospel of John '15
Have No Fear: The Life of Pope John Paul II '05
The Hoodlum Priest '61 ▸
I Am Michael '17
I'm Not Ashamed '16
Jesus of Nazareth '77 ▸
Joan of Arc '48
Joan of Arc '99
Kundun '97 ▸
The Letters '15
Luther '03
Machine Gun Preacher '11
The Messenger: The Story of Joan of Arc '99
Passion of Joan of Arc '28 ▸
The Passion of the Christ '04 ▸
Paul, Apostle of Christ '18
The Real Joan of Arc '08
Saint Joan '57
St. Patrick: The Irish Legend '00
The Scarlet & the Black '83
Sebastiane '79 ▸
Sister Aimee: The Aimee Semple McPherson Story '06
The Song of Bernadette '43 ▸
Therese '86 ▸
Therese: The Story of Saint Therese of Lisieux '04
A Time for Miracles '80
The Two Popes '19 ▸
Vision '09

Biopics: Royalty

***See also** Politics; Royalty; Royalty, British; Royalty, Russian; True Stories*

The Abdication '74
Caesar the Conqueror '63
Catherine the Great '34
Catherine the Great '95
The Countess '09
Diana '13
Diana: Her True Story '93
The Duchess '08 ▸
Edward and Mrs. Simpson '80
Elizabeth '98 ▸
Elizabeth R '72 ▸
Elizabeth I '05 ▸
Elizabeth: The Golden Age '07
The Favourite '18 ▸
Genghis Khan: To the Ends of the Earth and Sea '07
Grace of Monaco '14
The King '19 ▸
Lady Jane '85 ▸
Ludwig '72
Mad Love '01
Marie Antoinette '38
Mary of Scotland '36 ▸
Mary Queen of Scots '18
Nicholas and Alexandra '71
Princess Kaiulani '09
The Queen's Sister '05
The Rise of Louis XIV '66 ▸
Six Wives of Henry VIII '71 ▸
Sixty Glorious Years '38
A United Kingdom '17
Victoria & Abdul '17
Victoria the Great '37
The Virgin Queen '55 ▸
Warrior Queen '03
William & Catherine: A Royal Romance '11

Biopics: Science/Medical

***See also** This Is My Life; This Is Your Life*

The Aeronauts '19
Armstrong '19
A Beautiful Mind '01 ▸
Breathe '17
A Dangerous Method '11
Dark Waters '19 ▸
Darwin's Darkest Hour '09
The Doctor '91
Dr. Ehrlich's Magic Bullet '40
The Elephant Man '80 ▸
Experimenter '15
First Man '18
Flash of Genius '08
Florence Nightingale '85
Florence Nightingale '08
The Girl in White '52
The Great Moment '44
Hidden Figures '17 ▸
The Imitation Game '14 ▸
Infinity '96
The Inventor: Out For Blood In Silicon Valley '19
Jane '17 ▸
Jobs '13
Kinsey '04 ▸
Kon-Tiki '12
The Lady With the Lamp '51
Madame Curie '43 ▸
The Miracle Worker '62 ▸
The Miracle Worker '79 ▸
The Miracle Worker '00
Nurse Edith Cavell '39 ▸
The Prisoner of Shark Island '36
Steve Jobs: The Man in the Machine '15
The Story of Alexander Graham Bell '39 ▸
Temple Grandin '10 ▸
The Theory of Everything '14
Theremin: An Electronic Odyssey '95 ▸
Unplanned '19
You Don't Know Jack '10
Young Tom Edison '40

Biopics: Showbiz

***See also** Price of Fame*

Alex in Wonderland '70
All That Jazz '79 ▸
The Amazing Howard Hughes '77
And Everything Is Going Fine '10
The Ann Jillian Story '88
Anna Nicole '13
The Audrey Hepburn Story '00
Auto Focus '02 ▸
The Aviator '04 ▸
Baadasssss! '03 ▸
Becoming Mike Nichols '16
Behind the Candelabra '13
Beyond the Sea '04
Blonde '01
The Bodyguard '92
Bojangles '01
Bombshell '19
The Brittany Murphy Story '14
Broadway '42
Burton and Taylor '13
The Cat's Meow '01
Cecil B. Demented '00
Celine '08
Chaplin '92 ▸
Charlotte Rampling: The Look '11
Christine '16
Coco Before Chanel '09
Confessions of a Dangerous Mind '02
De Palma '16 ▸
Dear Brigitte '65
Deceptive Practice: The Mysteries and Mentors of Ricky Jay '13 ▸
The Disaster Artist '17 ▸
Dolemite Is My Name '19 ▸
The Dolly Sisters '46
Dragon: The Bruce Lee Story '93 ▸
Ed Wood '94 ▸
The Eddie Cantor Story '53
Eight Miles High '07
Eisenstein in Guanajuato '15
Elaine Stritch: Shoot Me '14 ▸
Factory Girl '06
Falco '08
Film Stars Don't Die in Liverpool '17
Flynn '96
Frances '82 ▸
From the Journals of Jean Seberg '95
Funny Girl '68 ▸
Funny Lady '75
Gainsbourg: A Heroic Life '10
The George Raft Story '61
Go West, Young Man '36
The Goddess '58 ▸
Gods and Monsters '98 ▸
Golden Girl '51
Goodbye, Norma Jean '75
Grace Kelly '83
Grace of Monaco '14
The Great Ziegfeld '36 ▸
The Greatest Showman '17
Gypsy '62 ▸
Gypsy '93
Hal '18 ▸
Harlow '65
Haywire '80
The Helen Morgan Story '57
Henri Langlois: The Phantom of the Cinematheque '04 ▸
Hitchcock '12
Houdini '53
Houdini '14
How to Eat Your Watermelon in White Company (and Enjoy It) '05 ▸
The I Don't Care Girl '53
I'm Still Here '10
Introducing Dorothy Dandridge '99 ▸
James Dean '76
James Dean '01
James Dean: Live Fast, Die Young '97
The Jayne Mansfield Story '80
Jeanne Eagels '57
Jersey Boys '14
Joan Rivers: A Piece of Work '10
Jolson Sings Again '49
The Jolson Story '46 ▸
The Josephine Baker Story '90 ▸
Judy '19 ▸
Just About Famous: A Film About Celebrity Impersonators '15
Kate Plays Christine '16 ▸
La Vie en Rose '07
The Last Ride '12
The Legend of Lylah Clare '68
Legend of Valentino '75
Lennon Naked '10
Lenny '74 ▸
Life '15 ▸
Life Itself '14 ▸
Life with Judy Garland-Me and My Shadows '01 ▸
Lillian Russell '40
Lillie '79 ▸
Liz & Dick '12
Look for the Silver Lining '49
The Look of Love '13
Love, Antosha '19 ▸
The Love Goddesses '65 ▸
Madame Sata '02
Man in the Mirror: The Michael Jackson Story '04
Man of a Thousand Faces '57 ▸
Man on the Moon '99
Margot '09
Mayor of the Sunset Strip '03 ▸
Merton of the Movies '47
Mr. X: Leos Carax '14 ▸
Mommie Dearest '81
My Favorite Year '82 ▸
My Gal Sal '42
My Wild Irish Rose '47
Nijinsky '80
Norma Jean and Marilyn '95
The Notorious Bettie Page '06
Nowhere Boy '09
One Chance '13
Paul Robeson '77
Pavarotti '19
The Perils of Pauline '47
Permanent Midnight '98
A Portrait of James Dean: Joshua Tree, 1951 '12
Prisoner of Paradise '02 ▸
Queenie '87
Quiet Days in Hollywood '97
The Reagans '04
Resistance '20
Ricky Nelson: Original Teen Idol '99
RKO 281 '99 ▸
Rocketman '19 ▸
Roman Polanski: Wanted and Desired '08 ▸
Roseanne for President! '16
Sal '11
Scott Joplin '77
Seberg '19
The Seven Little Foys '55 ▸
Shattered Innocence '87
Sinatra '92
So This Is Love '53
Stan & Ollie '18 ▸
Star! '68
The Story of Vernon and Irene Castle '39 ▸
The Story of Will Rogers '52
Superstar: The Life and Times of Andy Warhol '90 ▸
Talk to Me '07
Taxi zum Klo '81 ▸
Tell Them Who You Are '05
Telstar: The Joe Meek Story '08
That's Entertainment '74 ▸
That's Entertainment, Part 2 '76
That's Entertainment, Part 3 '93
This Is Elvis '81
Thursday's Child '43
To Be Takei '14
Too Much, Too Soon '58
Topsy Turvy '99 ▸
Trumbo '15
Up Close and Personal '96 ▸
Valentino '77
Veronika Voss '82 ▸
What Ever Happened to Baby Jane? '62 ▸
White Hot: The Mysterious Murder of Thelma Todd '91
White Hunter, Black Heart '90 ▸
Whitney '15
Who Do You Love '08
Winning: The Racing Life of Paul Newman '15
Won't You Be My Neighbor? '18 ▸
Yankee Doodle Dandy '42 ▸

Biopics: Sports

***See also** Baseball; Basketball; Football; Hockey; The Olympics; Running; Soccer; Sports Drama*

Ali '01
The Armstrong Lie '13 ▸
Babe! '75 ▸
The Babe '92
Babe Ruth Story '48
Battle of the Sexes '17
Big Leaguer '53
Bleed for This '16
The Blind Side '09
Bobby Jones: Stroke of Genius '04
Borg vs. McEnroe '17 ▸
Boy in Blue '86
Breaking the Surface: The Greg Louganis Story '96
Breakthrough '19
Brian Banks '18
Brian's Song '71 ▸
Brian's Song '01
Carnera: The Walking Mountain '08
Champions '84
Chariots of Fire '81 ▸
Chasing Mavericks '12
Chuck '17
Cinderella Man '05 ▸
Coach Carter '05 ▸
Cobb '94 ▸
Dempsey '83
Diego Maradona '19 ▸
Don King: Only in America '97
The Eagle Huntress '16 ▸
Eddie the Eagle '16
The Express '08
Fast Company '78
The Fencer '15 ▸
Fighting with My Family '19
Final Shot: The Hank Gathers Story '92
The Flying Scotsman '06
Ford v Ferrari '19 ▸
42 '13 ▸
Full Out '15
The Gabby Douglas Story '14
Gentleman Jim '42 ▸
Gleason '16 ▸
Grambling's White Tiger '81
Greased Lightning '77
The Great White Hope '70
The Greatest '77
The Hammer '11
Hands of Stone '16
Heart Like a Wheel '83
Hustle '04
I, Tonya '17 ▸
Ip Man 2 '10
Ip Man 4: The Finale '19
Ip Man '08
It's Good to Be Alive '74
The Jackie Robinson Story '50 ▸
The Jesse Owens Story '84
Jim Thorpe: All American '51
Joe and Max '02 ▸
The Joe Louis Story '53
The Junction Boys '02
The Keeper '18
Knute Rockne: All American '40 ▸
The Last American Hero '73 ▸
Linsanity '13
A Matador's Mistress '08
The Mercy '19
Miracle '04 ▸
Mr. Hockey: The Gordie Howe Story '13
Pawn Sacrifice '15
Phantom Punch '09
Pistol: The Birth of a Legend '90
A Prayer Before Dawn '18 ▸
Prefontaine '96
Pride '07
Pride of St. Louis '52
The Pride of the Yankees '42 ▸
The Program '15
Queen of Katwe '16 ▸
Race '16
Raging Bull '80 ▸
Rebound: The Legend of Earl 'The Goat' Manigault '96
Richard Jewell '19 ▸
Richard Petty Story '72
The Rocket '05 ▸
Rocky Marciano '99
The Rookie '02 ▸
Running Brave '83
Rush '13 ▸
Seabiscuit '03 ▸
A Season on the Brink '02

▸ = rated three bones or higher

Secretariat '10
Senna '11
6 Below: Miracle on the Mountain '17
61* '01 ▸
Snake & Mongoose '13
Somebody Up There Likes Me '56 ▸
Soul Surfer '11
Through the Fire '05 ▸
The Tiger Woods Story '98
Tommy's Honour '17
Tyson '08
Unbroken: Path to Redemption '18
Wilma '77
The Winning Team '52
Without Limits '97 ▸

Biopics: Writers

The Adventures of Mark Twain '44 ▸
Agatha '79
Agatha Christie: A Life in Pictures '04
All Is True '18
Almost Famous '00 ▸
An Angel at My Table '89 ▸
Author: The JT LeRoy Story '16
Balzac: A Life of Passion '99 ▸
The Barretts of Wimpole Street '34 ▸
A Beautiful Day in the Neighborhood '19 ▸
Before Night Falls '00 ▸
Big Sur '13
Borstal Boy '00
Bright Star '09
The Broken Tower '11
Byron '03
Can You Ever Forgive Me? '18 ▸
Capote '05 ▸
Children of the Century '99
Chris & Don: A Love Story '07 ▸
Christopher and His Kind '11 ▸
Coming Through '85
Cross Creek '83
Daphne '07
Derrida '02
Devotion '46
The Disappearance of Garcia Lorca '96
Dreams With Sharp Teeth '07 ▸
The Edge of Love '08
Finding Neverland '04 ▸
Genius '16
Gonzo: The Life and Work of Dr. Hunter S. Thompson '08 ▸
Goodbye Christopher Robin '17
Gothic '87 ▸
Hammett '82
Hannah Arendt '12
Hans Christian Andersen '52
Haunted Summer '88
Heart Beat '80
Hemingway & Gelhorn '12
Henry & June '90 ▸
How to Lose Friends & Alienate People '08
Howl '10
I Shot Andy Warhol '96 ▸
In the Realms of the Unreal '04 ▸
Infamous '06
The Invisible Woman '13 ▸
Iris '01 ▸
Isn't She Great '00
Jack London '44
James Joyce: A Portrait of the Artist as a Young Man '77 ▸
Joseph Pulitzer: Voice of the People '18
Jungle '17
The Keeper: The Legend of Omar Khayyam '05
The Lady in the Van '15
Last Call: The Final Chapter of F. Scott Fitzgerald '02
The Last Sentence '12
The Last Station '09
The Lost Boys '78 ▸
Magic Beyond Words: The JK Rowling Story '11
The Man Who Invented Christmas '17
Mary Shelley '17
Mike Wallace Is Here '19 ▸
Mishima: A Life in Four Chapters '85 ▸
Miss Austen Regrets '07
Miss Potter '06
Mrs. Parker and the Vicious Circle '94
My Childhood '38 ▸
My Left Foot '89 ▸
Nelson Algren: The End Is Nothing, the Road Is All '15
Nerolio '96
Neruda '16
Nora '00
Papa: Hemingway in Cuba '16
The Passion of Ayn Rand '99
Pinero '01
The Post '17 ▸
Postcards from America '95
The Professor and the Madman '19
Quiet Days in Clichy '90
A Quiet Passion '17
Reaching for the Moon '13
Rebel in the Rye '17
The Road from Coorain '02
Roughly Speaking '45
Salinger '13
The Secret Diaries of Miss Anne Lister '10
The Secret Life of Mrs. Beeton '06
The Sessions '12 ▸
Shadowlands '93 ▸
Sylvia '03
Take My Advice: The Ann & Abby Story '99
A Tale of Love and Darkness '16
Tolkien '19
Tom & Viv '94 ▸
Total Eclipse '95
The Trials of Oscar Wilde '60 ▸
Trumbo '07 ▸
Veronica Guerin '03
Vita & Virginia '19
A Waste of Shame '05
Wilde '97
Young Cassidy '65
Young Goethe in Love '11
Zora Is My Name! '90

Birds

All Hands on Deck '61
The Angry Birds Movie '16
The Angry Birds Movie 2 '19
Babe '95 ▸
Batman Returns '92
Beaks: The Movie '87
The Big Year '11
The Bird Men '13
Bird People '14
A Birder's Guide to Everything '14
Birdman of Alcatraz '62 ▸
The Birds '63 ▸
Blood Freak '72
The Blue Bird '40 ▸
Brewster McCloud '70 ▸
Chicken People '16 ▸
Chicken Run '00 ▸
Chronicle of the Raven '04
Clash of the Titans '81
Cockfighter '74 ▸
Continental Divide '81
The Crow '93
The Crow 2: City of Angels '96
Cry of the Penguins '71
Days and Nights '14
Duck '05
The Eagle Huntress '16 ▸
Earth: One Amazing Day '17 ▸
Everything's Ducky '61
Flu Birds '08
Fly Away Home '96 ▸
Free Birds '13
The Giant Claw '57
The Golden Child '86
The Hawk Is Dying '06
Healing '15
The Hide '08
High Anxiety '77
Hoot '06
Howard the Duck '86
Kes '69 ▸
Ladyhawke '85
Legend of the Guardians: The Owls of Ga'Hoole '10 ▸
Love Happens '09
The Man With a Cloak '51
Million Dollar Duck '71
My Son, My Son, What Have Ye Done '09
Paulie '98
The Pebble and the Penguin '94
Queer Duck: The Movie '06
The Rage '07
Rare Birds '01
The Rescuers Down Under '90
Rio 2 '14
Rio '11
Roadkill '11
Ruby Blue '07
Sesame Street Presents: Follow That Bird '85
Something for the Birds '52
The Song of Sparrows '08
Spies in Disguise '19
Spirit of the Eagle '90
Storks '16
Storm Boy
Stuart Little 2 '02 ▸
Super Size Me 2: Holy Chicken! '19
The Trumpet of the Swan '01
Up '09 ▸
Valiant '05
The Wild Parrots of Telegraph Hill '03 ▸
Winged Migration '01 ▸

Birthdays

Abner the Invisible Dog '13
Alexander and the Terrible, Horrible, No Good, Very Bad Day '14
Alpha Male '06
Angus, Thongs and Perfect Snogging '08
Because I Said So '07
Bending the Rules '12
Bloody Birthday '80
The Boys in the Band '70
Cat on a Hot Tin Roof '58 ▸
Cat on a Hot Tin Roof '84
The Celebration '98
Child's Play '88
City Slickers '91 ▸
Clown '16
Creatures from the Pink Lagoon '07
Criminal Ways '03
Damien: Omen 2 '78
David's Birthday '09
Dirty 30 '16
Duck Season '04 ▸
Emma's Wish '98
5 Star Day '10
4 Months, 3 Weeks and 2 Days '07 ▸
Friends and Family '01
The Game '97 ▸
Giant Little Ones '19
The Great Beauty '13
Happy Birthday to Me '81
Happy Death Day 2U '19
Happy Death Day '17
Ice Men '04
The Jerk '79
Kawa '11
The Kitchen '12
Little Fockers '10
Little Fugitive '06
Meet Joe Black '98
Mrs. Doubtfire '93
Motherhood '09
Never Goin' Back '18
On Golden Pond '81 ▸
The Oogieloves in the Big Balloon Adventure '12
Ordinary World '16
Passenger Side '09
Peep World '10
Phoenix '06
Pizza '05
Please Give '10
Project X '11
The Proposal '09
Quinceanera '06 ▸
Rabid Grannies '89
7 Things to Do Before I'm 30 '08
The Sisters '05
Sitcom '97
Sixteen Candles '84 ▸
16 Wishes '10
Skinwalkers '07
Something Borrowed '11
Spooner '08
Summer Hours '08
10 '79
That's Life! '86
13 Going on 30 '04
30 Years to Life '01
This Is 40 '12
The Time of His Life '55
To Gillian on Her 37th Birthday '96
Traffik '18
Triple Dog '09
21 & Over '13
The Twilight Saga: New Moon '09
Un Air de Famille '96
Unhappy Birthday '10
What's Eating Gilbert Grape '93 ▸
Working Girl '88 ▸

Bisexuality

***See also** Gays; Lesbians*

Appropriate Behavior '14
April's Shower '03
Basic Instinct '92
Bedrooms and Hallways '98
California Suite '78 ▸
Caravaggio '07
A Change of Heart '98
Confusion of Genders '00
Criminal Lovers '99
The Crying Game '92 ▸
Daphne '07
Dog Day Afternoon '75 ▸
Dona Herlinda & Her Son '86
Dry Cleaning '97
Eros '04
Extreme Private Eros: Love Song 1974 '74
Female Perversions '96
Harry and Max '04
Hellbent '04
Hotel America '81
Kaboom '11
Kiss Me Again '06
Laurel Canyon '02
Les Biches '68 ▸
Liquid Sky '83 ▸
Mary, Mary, Bloody Mary '76
The Mysteries of Pittsburgh '08
One to Another '06
A Portrait of James Dean: Joshua Tree, 1951 '12
Puccini for Beginners '06
The Rules of Attraction '02
Showgirls '95
Sunday, Bloody Sunday '71 ▸
Those Who Love Me Can Take the Train '98
3 '10
Three of Hearts '93
Threesome '94
The Trio '97
The 24th Day '04
The Velocity of Gary '98
Velvet Goldmine '98

Black Comedy

***See also** Comedy; Satire & Parody*

Abigail's Party '77
The Acid House '98
Adam's Apples '05
The Addams Family '91
Addams Family Values '93
Adult World '13
The Advocate '93 ▸
After Hours '85 ▸
The Alarmist '98
Alice '88 ▸
American Strays '96
The Americanization of Emily '64 ▸
Amputee with an Axe '73
Angels Over Broadway '40 ▸
The Anniversary '68
The Ape '05
Ariel '89 ▸
Arsenic and Old Lace '44 ▸
The Art of Self-Defense '19 ▸
Art School Confidential '06
The Assassination Bureau '69 ▸
Assault of the Killer Bimbos '88
The Atomic Kid '54
Bad Boy Bubby '93
The Ballad of Buster Scruggs '18 ▸
Barking Dogs Never Bite '00 ▸
Barton Fink '91 ▸
Beat the Devil '53 ▸
Beatriz at Dinner '17
Beautiful People '99
The Bed Sitting Room '69
Beg! '94
A Beginner's Guide to Endings '10
Being John Malkovich '99 ▸
Berlinguer I Love You '77
Beyond the Gates '16
Bizarre Bizarre '39 ▸
The Black House '00
Black Pond '11
Boogie Woogie '09
Brazil '85 ▸
Bread and Chocolate '73 ▸
Break a Leg '03
Breaking & Exiting '18
Brewster McCloud '70 ▸
The Bride of Frank '96
Bringing Out the Dead '99
Buffalo 66 '97 ▸
Buffet Froid '79 ▸
Burke & Hare '10
Burying the Ex '15
Cabaret Balkan '98
The Cable Guy '96
Canadian Bacon '94
Careful '92
The Cars That Ate Paris '74 ▸
Catch-22 '70 ▸
Catfight '17
Chalk '06
Cheap Thrills '14
Checking Out '89
Choice of Weapons '76
The Choirboys '77
Choke '08
City Unplugged '95
Clay Pigeons '98
Clerks '94 ▸
Cold Souls '09
Coldblooded '94
The Color Wheel '11
Come Drink with Me '65 ▸
The Comic '69 ▸
Consuming Passions '88
The Cook, the Thief, His Wife & Her Lover '90 ▸
Counter Clockwise '16
Coup de Torchon '81 ▸
Crimes of the Heart '86
The Criminal Life of Archibaldo de la Cruz '55 ▸
Critical Care '97
Crocodile Tears '98
Cruel Restaurant '08
Curdled '95
The Curve '97
The Dark Backward '91
Day at the Beach '98
A Day in the Death of Joe Egg '71 ▸
Dead or Alive: Final '02
Dead Silence '98
Deadly Advice '93
Death at a Funeral '10
Death Becomes Her '92 ▸
The Death of Stalin '17 ▸
Death Racers '08
Death to Smoochy '02
Deathgasm '15
Delicatessen '92 ▸
Delivered '98
Demon '16 ▸
The Details '11
Dinner for Schmucks '10
Dr. Strangelove, or: How I Learned to Stop Worrying and Love the Bomb '64 ▸
A Dog's Breakfast '07
Dogtooth '09
Don McKay '09
Don's Party '76 ▸
Don't Worry, He Won't Get Far on Foot '18
The Doom Generation '95 ▸
Down Terrace '10
The Dress '96
Drop Dead Gorgeous '99
Drop Dead Gorgeous '10
Duplex '03
Eat the Rich '87
Eating Raoul '82 ▸
8 Heads in a Duffel Bag '96
El Crimen Perfecto '04
Ellie '84
Elvis Has Left the Building '04
The End '78 ▸
Enid Is Sleeping '90
Envy '04
Eternal Sunshine of the Spotless Mind '04 ▸
Eulogy '04
The Ex '07
eXistenZ '99
The Exterminating Angel '62 ▸
Familiar Strangers '08
The Family Tree '10
Fargo '96 ▸
The Favourite '18 ▸
Female Trouble '74
A Fine Madness '66 ▸
The Firemen's Ball '68 ▸
A Fish Called Wanda '88 ▸
Four Bags Full '56
Four Rooms '95
Freaked '93
Frogs for Snakes '98
Fun With Dick and Jane '05
The Funeral '84 ▸
Funny Bones '94 ▸
Funny, Dirty Little War '83
Gas-s-s-s! '70
The Gazebo '59 ▸
Get Out '17 ▸
Getting Away With Murder '96
Ghost Chase '88
Ghost Writer '07
The Girl From Monaco '08
Go for Zucker '05
God Bless America '11
Goldstein '64
Goodbye, Dragon Inn '03
Grand Theft Parsons '03
Gravesend '97
The Greasy Strangler '16
The Green Butchers '03
Greetings '68 ▸
Gridlock'd '96 ▸
Grosse Pointe Blank '97 ▸
Guilty as Charged '92
Happiness '98 ▸
The Happiness of the Katakuris '01
Happy Death Day '17
Harold and Maude '71 ▸
Hawks '89
He Died With a Falafel in His Hand '01
Head Above Water '96
Headless Body in Topless Bar '96
Heart Condition '90
Heathers '89 ▸
Henry Fool '98 ▸
Hexed '93
Hi, Mom! '70 ▸
High Heels '91 ▸
Highway 61 '91
A Hole in One '04
Home Sweet Home '82
The Honey Pot '67
The Hospital '71 ▸
The Hot Rock '70 ▸
The House of Yes '97
The House That Jack Built '18
How Harry Became a Tree '01
How Tasty Was My Little Frenchman '71
How to be a Serial Killer '08

▸ = rated three bones or higher

► = rated three bones or higher

Ashes of Time '94 ▶
At First Sight '98
Ballad in Blue '66
Balls of Fury '07
Blackout '50
Blind '14 ▶
Blind Corner '63
Blind Date '84
Blind Dating '06
Blind Fear '89
Blind Fury '90
Blind Justice '94
Blind Revenge '10
Blind Witness '89
Blindness '08
Blindsight '06 ▶
Blink '93
Broken Embraces '09 ▶
Butterflies Are Free '72 ▶
Cactus '86
City for Conquest '40 ▶
City Lights '31 ▶
Cold Comes the Night '14
The Color of Paradise '99
Connor's War '06
Crazy Love '07 ▶
Crimes & Misdemeanors '89 ▶
The Cyclone Ranger '35
Dancer in the Dark '99
Daredevil '03
Dead Man's Eyes '44
Don't Breathe '16 ▶
Don't Look Now '73 ▶
Eight Witnesses '54
An Encounter with the Messiah '15
The Eye '02
The Eye '08
Eyes in the Night '42
A Family Thing '96 ▶
Fort Defiance '51
The Goddess of 1967 '00
Good Luck '96
Happy Times '00
The Haunting of Marsten Manor '07
Hollywood Ending '02
The Human Monster '39
I Am Potential '15
Ice Castles '79
Ice Castles '10
Ichi '08
Il Futuro '13
Incantato '03
Jennifer 8 '92
Julia's Eyes '10
The Killer '90 ▶
La Roue '23 ▶
Language of the Enemy '07
Last Game '80
Life on a String '90
The Lookout '07 ▶
Lost in the Dark '07
Love Is Blind '19
Love Story '44
Magnificent Obsession '35
The Man Who Had Everything '20
Mask '85 ▶
The Mighty Ursus '61
Minnesota Clay '65
The Miracle Worker '62 ▶
The Miracle Worker '79 ▶
The Miracle Worker '00
Mischief Night '13
Mr. Magoo '97
My Blind Brother '16
The Night Digger '71
Night Gallery '69 ▶
Night Is My Future '47
Night on Earth '91 ▶
Night Song '47
Nowhere in Sight '01
Octavia '82
On Dangerous Ground '51 ▶
Once Upon a Time in Mexico '03 ▶
Other Men's Women '31
A Patch of Blue '65 ▶
A Place Called Home '04
Places in the Heart '84 ▶
Possessed '05
Pride of the Marines '45 ▶
Proof '91 ▶
Psyche 59 '64
Ray '04 ▶
Red Dragon '02
Red Lights '12
Return of the Evil Dead '75
Ringside Maisie '41
The Scent of a Woman '75
Scent of a Woman '92 ▶
Schlock '73
Second Sight '99 ▶
See No Evil '71 ▶
See No Evil, Hear No Evil '89
Seven Pounds '08
7th Heaven '27
Sneakers '92
A Song From the Heart '99
Things You Can Tell Just by Looking at Her '00
This Woman Is Dangerous '52
The Ticket '17
Touch the Top of the World '06
The Toxic Avenger '86
23 Paces to Baker Street '56
Unleashed '05
The Unseen '05
Until the End of the World '91 ▶
The Village '04
A Voyage 'Round My Father '89 ▶
Wait until Dark '67 ▶
The Whales of August '87 ▶
The White Countess '05 ▶
Wild Hearts Can't Be Broken '91 ▶
Wings in the Dark '35
The Woman on the Beach '47
Young Frankenstein '74 ▶
Zatoichi '03 ▶
Zatoichi: The Blind Swordsman and the Chess Expert '65
Zatoichi: The Blind Swordsman's Vengeance '66

Blizzards

See also Cold Spots

Barricade '12
The Day of the Outlaw '59
Deadfall '12
Deliver Us From Evil '73
Edge of Winter '16
8 Women '02 ▶
The Finest Hours '16
The Last Stop '99
Lost Holiday: The Jim & Suzanne Shemwell Story '07
Lost in the Dark '07
Murder on the Orient Express '10 ▶
One Special Night '99
Operation Haylift '50
Osso Bucco '08
Ravenous '99
The Shining '80
Shut In '16
Slim '37
Snow Day '00
Snowbound: The Jim and Jennifer Stolpa Story '94
Stephen King's The Storm of the Century '99
Terminal Invasion '02
Track of the Cat '54
Trapped in Paradise '94
The Wild North '52
Wrong Turn 4: Bloody Beginnings '11

Boating

See Sail Away

Bodyguards

Absolute Power '97
Assassination '87
Avenging Angelo '02
Be Cool '05
Black Belt '92
Blackjack '97
Blade of the Immortal '17
Body Armour '07
The Bodyguard 2 '07
The Bodyguard '92
The Bodyguard '04
The Bodyguard from Beijing '94
The Chase '46
Close '19
Disorder '16
Drillbit Taylor '08
Eastern Promises '07 ▶
Fatal Beauty '87
Final Voyage '99
Finish Line '08
First Kid '96
Get Shorty '95 ▶
The Girl From Monaco '08
Guarding Tess '94
Half a Loaf of Kung Fu '78
Heat '87
The Hitman's Bodyguard '17
In the Line of Fire '93 ▶
In the Mix '05
Incognito '99
The Keeper '09
La Scorta '94 ▶
The Librarian: Quest for the Spear '04
London Boulevard '10
A Lovely Way to Die '68
Man on Fire '04
Mr. Nanny '93
My Bodyguard '80 ▶
On Guard! '03 ▶
An Ordinary Man '18
The Princess Diaries 2: Royal Engagement '04
Protecting the King '07
Pushed to the Limit '92
Sabotage '96
Secret Window '04
The Taste of Others '00 ▶
Time and Tide '00
Transporter 2 '05
Undercover Bridesmaid '12
Wild Card '15

Bookies

See also Gambling; Organized Crime

Bad Lieutenant '92 ▶
Big Shot: Confessions of a Campus Bookie '02
Bloodhounds of Broadway '52
Bookies '03
Buffalo 66 '97 ▶
Dinner Rush '00 ▶
Esther Waters '48
Even Money '06
40 Pounds of Trouble '62
Guys and Dolls '55 ▶
Hollywood or Bust '56
Little Miss Marker '34 ▶
Little Miss Marker '80
Lucky Number Slevin '06
Player 5150 '08
Race Street '48
The Runner '99
Salty O'Rourke '45
Saratoga '37
Scene of the Crime '49
711 Ocean Drive '50
Shadow of the Thin Man '41 ▶
She's Got Everything '37
Snatch '00 ▶
Sorrowful Jones '49
Starsky & Hutch '04
The System '53
U-Turn '97
Young Man With Ideas '52

Books & Bookstores

American Animals '18 ▶
The Answer Man '09
Army of Darkness '92 ▶
The Art of the Steal '13
Austenland '13
The Babadook '14 ▶
Better Than Chocolate '99
Bickford Shmeckler's Cool Ideas '06
Book Club '18
The Book of Eli '10
The Book Thief '13
The Bookshop '18
The Boy Who Harnessed the Wind '19
Breakin' All The Rules '04
The Bride Goes Wild '48
Burglar '87
Capote '05 ▶
Careless '07
Cross Creek '83
Crossing Delancey '88 ▶
Desperado '95 ▶
Don't Worry, We'll Think of a Title '66
The Edge of Heaven '07 ▶
84 Charing Cross Road '86 ▶
Everything You Want '05
Evil Dead '83
Fahrenheit 451 '66 ▶
Fairfield Road '10
Falling in Love '84
Fast and Loose '39
Fast Company '38
Funny Face '57 ▶
A Girl Cut in Two '07
Halloween II '09
Hit Parade '10
The Hitchhiker's Guide to the Galaxy '05 ▶
The Hoax '06
The Hobbit: The Desolation of Smaug '13 ▶
Hocus Pocus '93
I, Madman '89
In the Mouth of Madness '95
Inkheart '09
The Jane Austen Book Club '07 ▶
Love Between the Covers '15
The Love Letter '99
The Mysteries of Pittsburgh '08
The NeverEnding Story '84 ▶
A Night to Remember '42 ▶
The Ninth Gate '99
Not So Dusty '56
Notting Hill '99 ▶
The Pagemaster '94
The Paper Chase '73 ▶
Phenomenon '96
Priest of Love '81
The Professor and the Madman '19
QB VII '74 ▶
The Reader '08
Remarkable Power '08
The Russia House '90
Saving Mr. Banks '13
Scary Stories to Tell in the Dark '19
The Seven Year Itch '55 ▶
Simon and the Oaks '12
Snapshots '02
The Spiderwick Chronicles '08 ▶
Stone Reader '02 ▶
Suburban Girl '07
Tristram Shandy: A Cock and Bull Story '05
Warlock '91
Wilbur Wants to Kill Himself '02 ▶
You've Got Mail '98

Boom!

See Adventure Drama; Fires

Boomer Reunions

See also Period Piece: 1960s

The Big Chill '83 ▶
The Brutal Truth '99
Come as You Are '05
Everything Relative '96
The Foursome '06
I Melt With You '11
I Think I Do '97
Indian Summer '93
Infested: Invasion of the Killer Bugs '02
It Was One of Us '07
Lifeguard '76
A Mighty Wind '03 ▶
Not Since You '09
Old Joy '06 ▶
Peter's Friends '92
Pretty Ugly People '08
Return of the Secaucus 7 '80 ▶
Spin the Bottle '97
Standing Still '05
That Championship Season '99

Boot camp

The Girl He Left Behind '56

Bootleggers

See also Beer; On the Rocks; Organized Crime; Prohibition Gangs

Bugsy Malone '76
Carbine Williams '52
Caught Plastered '31
The Crusader '32
Dixie Jamboree '44
Fireball 500 '66
The Guilty Generation '31
The Helen Morgan Story '57
Hell's House '32
I Walk Alone '48
The Infiltrator '16
Izzy & Moe '85
Lady for a Day '33 ▶
Last Man Standing '96
Lawless '12
The Little Giant '33
The Moonshine War '70
Once Upon a Time in America '84 ▶
Parachute Jumper '32
Pocketful of Miracles '61 ▶
Public Enemy '31 ▶
The Roaring Twenties '39 ▶
Scarface '31 ▶
The Secret Six '31 ▶
A Slight Case of Murder '38
Smokey and the Bandit '77
The Untouchables '87 ▶
War Dogs '16
The Wet Parade '32

Bosnia

Beautiful People '99
Behind Enemy Lines '01
For Ever Mozart '96
Go West '05
Grbavica: The Land of My Dreams '06
Harrison's Flowers '02
The Hunting Party '07
In the Land of Blood and Honey '11
Killing Season '13
No Man's Land '01
Pretty Village, Pretty Flame '96 ▶
Savior '98 ▶
Shot Through the Heart '98 ▶
Sniper 2 '02
Twice Born '12
Ulysses' Gaze '95
Underground '95 ▶
Welcome to Sarajevo '97 ▶
The Whistleblower '11 ▶

Boston

The Actress '53
Acts of Contrition '95
Adrenalin: Fear the Rush '96
Alex & Emma '03
Athena '54
Bad Manners '98
A Beautiful Mind '01 ▶
Before and After '95
Behind the Red Door '02
Black Irish '07
Blown Away '94
Body Count '97
Boondock Saints '99
The Boondock Saints II: All Saints Day '09
The Boston Strangler '68
The Boston Strangler: The Untold Story '08
Breeders '97
By the Gun '14
The Carey Treatment '72
Celtic Pride '96
Children of Invention '09
Christmas in Boston '05
Coma '78 ▶
The Company Men '10
Criminal Law '89
Dealing: Or the Berkeley-to-Boston Forty-Brick Lost-Bag Blues '72
Debbie Macomber's Trading Christmas '11
The Departed '06 ▶
Dr. Jekyll and Mr. Hyde '08
Edge of Darkness '10
The Equalizer '14
Everybody Wants to Be Italian '08
Fake '10
Fear Strikes Out '57 ▶
Fever Pitch '05
The Forbidden Kingdom '08
Free Fire '17
Fuzz '72
Game 6 '05
Gone Baby Gone '07 ▶
Good Will Hunting '97
Goon '12
The Great Moment '44
Guy and Madeline on a Park Bench '09 ▶
The Heat '13
H.M. Pulham Esquire '41
I Don't Know How She Does It '11
Infected '08
Jesse Stone: Innocents Lost '11
Jesse Stone: No Remorse '10
Jill the Ripper '00
Legally Blonde '01
Lemony Snicket's A Series of Unfortunate Events '04
Little Men '98
Little Shots of Happiness '97
Love Story '70 ▶
The Makeover '13
The Matchmaker '97
Misconceptions '08
Money Kings '98
Monument Ave. '98
My Best Friend's Girl '08
Mystic River '03 ▶
Never Met Picasso '96
Next Stop, Wonderland '98
The Parent Trap '61
The Parent Trap '98
Patricia Cornwell's At Risk '10
Patricia Cornwell's The Front '10
Patriots Day '17
The Proposition '97
Proud Mary '18
The Rendering '02
Sail a Crooked Ship '61
The Scarlet Letter '34
The Scarlet Letter '73 ▶
The Scarlet Letter '95
Sci-Fighters '96
The Shocking Miss Pilgrim '47
Shuttle '09
Southie '98
Spenser: Ceremony '93
Spenser Confidential '20
Spenser: Pale Kings & Princes '94
Spenser: The Judas Goat '94
Squeeze '97
Stiffs '06
Stonados '13
Stronger '17 ▶
Thin Air '00
The Town '10 ▶
Tuesdays with Morrie '99
21 '08
The Verdict '82 ▶
Walk East on Beacon '52
What Doesn't Kill You '08
What's the Worst That Could Happen? '01
Who Is Clark Rockefeller? '10
Within Our Gates '20
Witness Protection '99 ▶

Bounty Hunters

All About the Benjamins '02
American Streetfighter 2: The Full Impact '97
Avenging Angel '07
The Awakening '95
Awakening the Zodiac '17
Banjo Hackett '76
The Big Gundown '66
Bounty '09
The Bounty Hunter '10
Bounty Hunters 2: Hardball '97
Bounty Hunters '96
Bounty Killer '13
California '77
Call of the Wilderness '32
Cold Harvest '98
The Condemned 2 '16
Constantine '05
Critters '86
Critters 2: The Main Course '88
Dead or Alive '02
Django Unchained '12 ▶

▶ = rated three bones or higher

Domino *'05*
The Empire Strikes Back *'80* ▶
Execution *'68*
A Fistful of Dollars *'64* ▶
For a Few Dollars More *'65*
Ghost Rider *'07*
Ghost Rider: Spirit of Vengeance *'12*
The Glove *'78*
The Good, the Bad and the Ugly *'67* ▶
The Good, the Bad, the Weird *'08*
Guardians of the Galaxy *'14* ▶
Hannah's Law *'12*
Hansel & Gretel: Witch Hunters *'12*
Home for Christmas *'93*
The Hunter *'80*
Jonah Hex *'10*
Kidnapped *'05* ▶
Kill Zone *'08*
The Last of the Dogmen *'95*
Lethal *'04*
Mannaja: A Man Called Blade *'77*
Midnight Run *'88* ▶
Most Wanted *'97*
Moving Target *'96*
Mud *'12* ▶
Mythica 2: The Darkspore *'15*
No Country for Old Men *'07* ▶
One Fine Day, When Django Met Sartana *'70*
One for the Money *'12*
Only *'20*
Outlaws and Angels *'16*
Return of the Jedi *'83* ▶
The Rundown *'03*
Shadow on the Mesa *'13*
Showdown at Boot Hill *'58*
6 Guns *'10*
Slipstream *'89*
Smokin' Aces 2: Assassins' Ball *'10*
The Spikes Gang *'74*
Star Wars *'77* ▶
Star Wars: Episode 2-Attack of the Clones *'02* ▶
Subhuman *'04*
Terminal Impact *'95*
The Tracker *'88*
29 Palms *'03*
Wanted Dead or Alive *'86*
Werewolf: The Beast Among Us *'12*
The Wild Goose Lake *'20*

Bowling

Alien 2 on Earth *'80*
The Big Lebowski *'97* ▶
Blood and Bone *'09*
Dream with the Fishes *'97*
Family Man *'00*
The Flintstones *'94*
Fright Night 2 *'88*
Grease 2 *'82*
Greedy *'94*
Kingpin *'96*
League of Ordinary Gentlemen *'04* ▶
Mr. Wonderful *'93*
Pleasantville *'98* ▶
Strike *'07*
Uncle Buck *'89* ▶

Boxing

Abbott and Costello Meet the Invisible Man *'51* ▶
Against the Ropes *'04*
Ali *'01*
The All-American Boy *'73*
Animal 2 *'07*
Annapolis *'06*
Any Day *'15*
Any Which Way You Can *'80*
Back Roads *'81*
Bad Blonde *'53*
The Bad Man of Brimstone *'38*
Bare Knuckles *'10*
Battling Butler *'26*
Be Yourself *'30*
Before the Fall *'04*
A Beginner's Guide to Endings *'10*
Belle of the Nineties *'34*
Best of the Best *'89*
The Big Man: Crossing the Line *'91* ▶
Black Cloud *'04*
Blade Boxer *'97*
Bleed for This *'16*
Body and Soul *'47* ▶
Body & Soul *'81*
Body and Soul *'98*
The Boxer *'97*
The Boxer and the Bombshell *'08*
Breakdown *'53*
The Cage *'89*
Cain and Mabel *'36*
Cardboard Boxer *'16*
Carnera: The Walking Mountain *'08*
The Champ *'32* ▶
The Champ *'79*
Champion *'49* ▶
Champs *'15* ▶
Chuck *'17*
Cinderella Man *'05* ▶
City for Conquest *'40* ▶
Cock & Bull Story *'03*
Confessions of a Pit Fighter *'05*
Counter Punch *'71*
Creed *'15* ▶
Creed II *'18*
The Crowd Roars *'38*
Dempsey *'83*
Diggstown *'92*
Don King: Only in America *'97*
Donnybrook *'18*
Far and Away *'92*
Fat City *'72* ▶
Fight Club *'99* ▶
Fight to the Finish *'16*
The Fighter *'52* ▶
The Fighter *'10* ▶
Fighting *'09*
A Fighting Man *'14*
Firepower *'93*
From Mexico With Love *'09*
Gentleman Jim *'42* ▶
Girlfight *'99* ▶
Gladiator *'92*
Glass Chin *'14*
Golden Boy *'39* ▶
Golden Gloves *'40*
The Great White Hope *'70*
The Great White Hype *'96*
The Greatest *'77*
Grudge Match *'13*
The Hammer *'07*
Hands of Stone *'16*
Hard Times *'75* ▶
The Harder They Fall *'56* ▶
Heart *'87*
Hell's Kitchen NYC *'97*
Here Comes Mr. Jordan *'41* ▶
Homeboy *'75*
Homeboy *'88*
The Hurricane *'99* ▶
I Spy *'02*
The Irish in Us *'35*
Joe and Max *'02* ▶
The Joe Louis Story *'53*
Jump In! *'07*
The Kid *'97*
Kid Dynamite *'43*
The Kid from Brooklyn *'46*
Kid Galahad *'37* ▶
Kid Galahad *'62*
Kid Monk Baroni *'52*
Killer McCoy *'47*
Killer's Kiss *'55*
Knockdown *'11*
Knockout *'11*
Knuckle *'11* ▶
Knucklehead *'10*
Like It Is *'98* ▶
Little Old New York *'23*
Locked Down *'10*
Love Come Down *'00*
Love Ranch *'10*
Love Songs *'99*
Made *'01*
The Main Event *'79*
Mandingo *'75*
Meatballs 2 *'84*
Milky Way *'36*
Million Dollar Baby *'04* ▶
Mr. Moto's Gamble *'38*
Movie, Movie *'78*
Navy Way *'44*
Never Back Down: No Surrender *'16*
Night and the City *'92* ▶
No News from God *'01*
Ocean's Eleven *'01* ▶
Off Limits *'53*
On the Waterfront *'54* ▶
Only God Forgives *'13*
The Opponent *'89*
The Opponent *'01*
Out of the Furnace *'13*
Palooka *'34*
Penitentiary 2 *'82*
Penitentiary *'79*
Pepe El Toro *'53*
Phantom Punch *'09*
The Philly Kid *'12*
Play It to the Bone *'99*
Poor Man's Game *'06* ▶
The Power of One *'92*
A Prayer Before Dawn *'18* ▶
Price of Glory *'00*
Prison Shadows *'36*
Prize Fighter *'79*
The Prizefighter and the Lady *'33* ▶
Pulp Fiction *'94* ▶
The Quest *'96*
The Quiet Man *'52* ▶
Raging Bull *'80* ▶
Real Steel *'11*
Requiem for a Heavyweight *'56* ▶
Requiem for a Heavyweight *'62* ▶
Resurrecting the Champ *'07*
Ricky 1 *'88*
Right Cross *'50*
The Ring *'27*
The Ring *'52*
Ring of Death *'08*
Ringside Maisie *'41*
Rocky *'76* ▶
Rocky 2 *'79*
Rocky 3 *'82*
Rocky 4 *'85*
Rocky 5 *'90*
Rocky Balboa *'06*
Rocky Marciano *'99*
Rude *'96*
Rust and Bone *'12* ▶
Schizo *'04*
The Set-Up *'49* ▶
Shiner *'00*
Snake Eyes *'98*
Snatch *'00* ▶
Somebody Up There Likes Me *'56* ▶
Southpaw *'15*
Spenser Confidential *'20*
Spin a Dark Web *'56*
The Spirit of Youth *'37*
Split Decisions *'88*
The Sting 2 *'83*
Street Crimes *'92*
Swing Fever *'43*
Teen Wolf Too *'87*
They Made Me a Criminal *'39*
Tough Enough *'83*
The Trials of Muhammad Ali *'13* ▶
Triumph of the Spirit *'89* ▶
Tyson *'08*
Undefeated *'03*
Undisputed 2: Last Man Standing *'06*
Undisputed *'02*
When We Were Kings *'96* ▶
When's Your Birthday? *'37*
Whiplash *'48*
A Wind from Wyoming *'94*
Winner Take All *'32*

Brains!

***See also** Eyeballs!; Heads!; Renegade Body Parts*
The Black Sleep *'56*
Bride of Re-Animator *'89*
Colossus of New York *'58*
Dawn of the Dead *'78* ▶
Gamebox 1.0 *'04*
George A. Romero's Land of the Dead *'05* ▶
Hannibal *'01*
Hardwired *'09*
Igor *'08*
Indiana Jones and the Temple of Doom *'84* ▶
The Man with Two Brains *'83* ▶
Messiah of Evil *'74*
Night of the Living Dead *'68* ▶
Return of the Living Dead: Rave to the Grave *'05*
The Space Children *'58*
Who Is Julia? *'86*
Woke Up Dead *'09*

Brainwashed

Becky Sharp *'35*
Brainjacked *'09*
A Clockwork Orange *'71* ▶
Cypher *'02* ▶
Disturbing Behavior *'98*
DROP Squad *'94*
The Fearmakers *'58*
In Like Flint *'67*
The Ipcress File *'65* ▶
The Manchurian Candidate *'62* ▶
The Manchurian Candidate *'04* ▶
The Mind Benders *'63*
Mind Snatchers *'72*
1984 *'56* ▶
No Dead Heroes *'87*
On Her Majesty's Secret Service *'69* ▶
Operation Delta Force 5: Random Fire *'00*
Our Children *'12*
Patty Hearst *'88*
Rock Slyde: Private Eye *'09*
Simon *'80*
Timebomb *'91*
Unholy *'07*
Universal Squadrons *'11*
Zoolander *'01*
Zoolander 2 *'16*

Break-Ups

***See also** Divorce*
All Nighter *'17*
And So They Were Married *'36*
Annie Hall *'77* ▶
Appropriate Behavior *'14*
Better Off Single *'16*
The Break-Up *'06*
The Breakup Artist *'04*
The Broken Hearts Club *'00* ▶
Casablanca *'42* ▶
Cashback *'06*
Casual Encounters *'16*
Comet *'14*
The Devil Wears Prada *'06*
Faithless *'32*
Fight to the Finish *'16*
(500) Days of Summer *'09*
Flannel Pajamas *'06*
Forgetting Sarah Marshall *'08*
A Glimpse Inside the Mind of Charles Swan III *'12*
Gone with the Wind *'39* ▶
Heartbreaker *'10*
Hold Your Peace *'11*
Holiday Breakup *'16*
Homecoming *'09*
The Hottest State *'06*
How to Make Love to a Woman *'09*
Inside Paris *'06*
It's Love I'm After *'37*
The Jane Austen Book Club *'07* ▶
Joshy *'16*
Just Before I Go *'15*
Kalamity *'10*
Kilimanjaro *'13*
The Last Five Years *'14* ▶
Le Divorce *'03*
Midsommar *'19*
Mr. Right *'16*
My Blueberry Nights *'07*
Nick & Norah's Infinite Playlist *'08* ▶
Nights and Weekends *'08*
The Old Homestead *'35*
Postcards from the Edge *'90* ▶
Prime *'05*
Puccini for Beginners *'06*
Room at the Top *'59* ▶
St. Elmo's Fire *'85*
Save the Date *'12*
The Spy Who Dumped Me *'18*
Sweet November *'68*
Table 19 *'17*
Time Freak *'18*
2 Days in Paris *'07* ▶
Under the Tuscan Sun *'03*
Valentine's Day *'10*
The Waiting Room *'07*
The Way We Were *'73* ▶
What Love Is *'07*
What's Your Number? *'11*

Bridges

The Amazing Spider-Man *'12* ▶
Bataan *'43*
The Bridge *'59*
The Bridge at Remagen *'69*
The Bridge of San Luis Rey *'44* ▶
The Bridge of San Luis Rey *'05*
The Bridge on the River Kwai *'57* ▶
Bridge to Hell *'87*
A Bridge Too Far *'77*
The Bridges at Toko-Ri *'55* ▶
The Bridges of Madison County *'95* ▶
Carnival of Souls *'62* ▶
Chappaquiddick *'17*
Crossing the Bridge *'92*
Dream with the Fishes *'97*
The Edge *'10*
Final Destination 5 *'11*
5 Flights Up *'15*
For Whom the Bell Tolls *'43* ▶
George of the Jungle *'97* ▶
The Ghost and the Darkness *'96*
The Girl on the Bridge *'98* ▶
Graffiti Bridge *'90*
It's a Wonderful Life *'46* ▶
The Longest Day *'62* ▶
The Lovers on the Bridge *'91*
Meteor Storm *'10*
The Night the Bridge Fell Down *'83*
Ode to Billy Joe *'76*
Saturday Night Fever *'77*
Saving Private Ryan *'98* ▶
Stranded *'35*
Tarzan's New York Adventure *'42*
The Truman Show *'98* ▶
21 Bridges *'19*
Uncertainty *'08*
Volunteers *'85*
Waterloo Bridge *'40* ▶

Bringing Up Baby

***See also** Parenthood; Pregnant Men; Pregnant Pauses*
Addams Family Values *'93*
And Baby Makes Six *'79*
Angie *'94*
Babies *'10* ▶
Baby *'00*
Baby Boom *'87*
Baby Boy *'01*
Baby Broker *'81*
Baby Geniuses *'98*
Babyfever *'94*
Baby's Day Out *'94*
Bachelor Mother *'39* ▶
Basket Case 3: The Progeny *'92*
Black Market Babies *'45*
Blondie Brings Up Baby *'39*
Bobbikins *'59*
The Boy *'16*
Brink of Life *'57*
The Brood *'79*
Brother Rat and a Baby *'40*
Bundle of Joy *'56*
The Child *'05*
Claudia and David *'46*
Close to My Heart *'51*
Cotton Mary *'99*
The Court Jester *'56* ▶
The Cradle *'06*
Cries in the Dark *'06*
A Dad for Christmas *'06*
Dad On the Run *'00*
Declaration of War *'11*
East Side of Heaven *'39*
Eastern Promises *'07* ▶
The Ex *'07*
Family Man *'00*
Fanny *'61* ▶
Fear of Fear *'75*
Fill the Void *'12*
The First Time *'52*
For Keeps *'88*
Four and a Half Women *'05*
Four Days in July *'85*
Friends with Kids *'12*
Ghost Son *'06*
A Good Baby *'99*
Grave of the Vampire *'72*
The Great Lie *'41* ▶
Happy Christmas *'14*
Hell's Heroes *'30*
Her Sister's Secret *'46*
A Hole in the Head *'59*
Hours *'13*
House of Women *'62*
Hush Little Baby *'07*
I Don't Want to Be Born *'75*
In Search of a Golden Sky *'84*
It's Alive *'74* ▶
It's Alive 2: It Lives Again *'78*
It's Alive 3: Island of the Alive *'87*
Jack and Sarah *'95*
The Last Trimester *'06*
Lazybones *'25*
Life As We Know It *'10*
Life Happens *'11*
The Light Between Oceans *'16*
Lion's Den *'08*
Little Man *'06*
Little Man Tate *'91* ▶
Look Who's Talking *'89* ▶
Look Who's Talking, Too *'90*
Malay Nights *'32*
Meet the Fockers *'04*
Monika *'52*
My Baby Is Missing *'07*
Nanny Insanity *'06*
Neighbors *'14*
Nobody's Baby *'37*
Nobody's Baby *'01*
Not of This World *'99*
The Note 3: Notes from the Heart Healer *'12*
Novel Romance *'06*
The Omen *'06*
Penny Serenade *'41* ▶
Problem Child 2 *'91*
Psycho 4: The Beginning *'90*
Raising Arizona *'87* ▶
Ricky *'09*
Robin-B-Hood *'06*
Robot Stories *'03*
Rock-A-Bye Baby *'57*
Rosemary's Baby *'68* ▶
The Rugrats Movie *'98* ▶
Rumpelstiltskin *'86*
Sacred Ground *'83*
Sarah's Child *'96*
Scarred *'84*
Scary Movie 5 *'13*
Sex and Lucia *'01*
She's So Lovely *'97*
Shoot 'Em Up *'07*
The Snapper *'93* ▶
Son of Godzilla *'66*
Song o' My Heart *'30*
A Song of Innocence *'05*
Spy Kids 4: All the Time in the World *'11*
A Stranger in Town *'95*
The Sugarland Express *'74* ▶
Superbabies: Baby Geniuses 2 *'04*
Susan Slade *'61*
The Switch *'10*
Table for Five *'83*
The Terminator *'84* ▶
Test Tube Babies *'48*
The 13th Floor *'88*
Three Godfathers *'36*
Three Men and a Baby *'87* ▶
Three Men and a Cradle *'85* ▶
Three Men and a Little Lady *'90*
Tish *'42*
Tsotsi *'05* ▶
The 24 Hour Woman *'99*
The Unborn 2 *'94*
Unnatural *'52*

▶ = rated three bones or higher

Untamed '55
Up and Down '04
Voice from the Stone '17
The War Zone '98
A Way of Life '04
Willow '88
A Woman Is a Woman '60 ▶

Brothers & Sisters

See *Family Adventure; Family Comedy; Family Drama; Sibling Rivalry; Twins*

Brush with Fame

Always Woodstock '15
Atlantic City '81 ▶
Being John Malkovich '99 ▶
Big Fan '09
Celtic Pride '96
Charley Varrick '73 ▶
Commandos Strike at Dawn '43
Courage Under Fire '96 ▶
Derby Day '52
Don't Think Twice '16
Escape from L.A. '96
The Fan '81
The Fan '96
Fanboys '09
Feel the Beat '20
Florence Foster Jenkins '16
Galaxina '80
Hairspray '07 ▶
Hands of Stone '16
The Hangover '09
Hidalgo '04
King of Comedy '82 ▶
Misery '90 ▶
Moscow, Belgium '08
Notting Hill '99 ▶
Play Misty for Me '71 ▶
Win a Date with Tad Hamilton! '04
Zombies on Broadway '44

Buddhism

The Calamari Wrestler '04
The Covenant '06
Crazy Wisdom: The Life & Times of Chogyam Trungpa Rinpoche '11
The Cup '99
The Departure '17
Green Snake '93
Kundun '97 ▶
Little Buddha '93
Raw Force '81
Seven Years in Tibet '97
Siddhartha '72
Spring, Summer, Fall, Winter. . . and Spring '03 ▶
Temptation of a Monk '94
The Unmistaken Child '08
Why Has Bodhi-Darma Left for the East '89

Buddies

See *Buddy Cops*

Buddy Cops

See also *Buddies; Canine Cops; Women Cops*

Another 48 Hrs. '90
Another Stakeout '93
Bad Boys '95
Bad Boys 2 '03
Bad Boys for Life '20
The Black Dahlia '06
Blue Streak '99
Bon Cop Bad Cop '06
Bright '17
Car 54, Where Are You? '94
City Heat '84
Code Two '53
Collision Course '89
Cop Land '97 ▶
Cop Out '10
The Corruptor '99 ▶
Courageous '11
Dirty '05
End of Watch '12 ▶
Exit to Eden '94
48 Hrs. '82 ▶
Freebie & the Bean '74
The Glimmer Man '96
The Hard Way '91 ▶
The Heat '13
Hollywood Homicide '03
Hot Fuzz '07 ▶
Internal Affairs '90
Java Heat '13
La Chevre '81 ▶
Lethal Weapon '87 ▶
Lethal Weapon 2 '89 ▶
Lethal Weapon 3 '92
Lethal Weapon 4 '98
The Man '05
A Man Apart '03
Men in Black '97 ▶
Metro '96
Miami Vice '06
Money Train '95
Mulholland Falls '95
National Lampoon's Loaded Weapon 1 '93
Nighthawks '81
The Other Guys '10
The Presidio '88
Red Heat '88
Renegades '89
The Rookie '90
Rush Hour 2 '01
Rush Hour 3 '07
Samurai Cop '89
Shakedown '88
Shoot to Kill '88 ▶
Show Dogs '18
Simon Sez '99
Speed '94 ▶
Stakeout '87
Starsky & Hutch '04
The Super Cops '74
Tango and Cash '89
Taxi '04
The Trust '16
22 Jump Street '14
White Chicks '04

Buffalo, NY

Best Friends '82
Bruce Almighty '03
Buffalo 66 '97 ▶
Buffaloed '20
Dames '34 ▶
Evan Almighty '07
Frozen River '08 ▶
Gypsy '62 ▶
The Last Seduction '94 ▶
Manna from Heaven '02
The Savages '07 ▶
You Kill Me '07 ▶

Bullfighters & Bullfighting

See also *Spain*

Around the World in 80 Days '56 ▶
Around the World in 80 Days '89
Blood and Sand '22
Blood and Sand '41 ▶
Blood and Sand '89
The Bobo '67
Bolero '84
Bullfighter & the Lady '50
Carnage '02
El Matador '03
Ferdinand '17
The Happy Thieves '61
Matador '86
The Matador '06 ▶
A Matador's Mistress '08
Pandora and the Flying Dutchman '51
The Sun Also Rises '57
Talk to Her '02 ▶

Burglars

See also *Crime Doesn't Pay; Crime Drama; Disorganized Crime; Heists*

Absolute Power '97
After Hours '85 ▶
Allie & Me '97
Armed Response '13
Bad Samaritan '18
Breaking and Entering '06
Bullet '94
Burglar '87
Criss Cross '48 ▶
Deadfall '12
Don't Breathe '16 ▶
The Edukators '04
Entrapment '99
Family Business '89
Federal Hill '94
Floating '97
Following '99
Gambit '66
The General '98 ▶
Home Alone '90 ▶
The Hot Rock '70 ▶
Hudson Hawk '91
I Don't Feel at Home in This World Anymore '17 ▶
Let Him Have It '91 ▶
Little Sweetheart '90
Millions '05 ▶
Murph the Surf '75
Paper Soldiers '02
Picture Windows '95
Ping! '99
The Pink Panther '64 ▶
Poor White Trash '00
P.S. Your Cat is Dead! '02
Raffles '30 ▶
Raffles '39
Row Your Boat '98
The Set Up '95
Sworn to Justice '97
The Thief of Paris '67 ▶
Villains '19

Buried Alive

Beneath '13
Beneath the Darkness '12
Buried '10
Buried Alive '90
Coffin '11
The Fall of the House of Usher '49
The Fall of the House of Usher '60 ▶
The Fall of the House of Usher '80
Kill Bill Vol. 2 '04 ▶
Macabre '58
The Oblong Box '69
Oxygen '99
Premature Burial '62
Project Solitude: Buried Alive '09
Seed '08
3 Days Gone '08
Three . . . Extremes '04
Trapped: Buried Alive '02

Buses

The Adventures of Priscilla, Queen of the Desert '94 ▶
Almost Famous '00 ▶
Beavis and Butt-Head Do America '96
The Big Bus '76
Bluebird '13
Boycott '02 ▶
Bull Durham '88 ▶
Bus Driver '16
Bus Stop '56 ▶
Bustin' Loose '81 ▶
Detour to Terror '80
Dirty Harry '71 ▶
Exit Speed '08
Ferris Bueller's Day Off '86 ▶
Forrest Gump '94 ▶
Friday the Thirteenth '33
The Fugitive '93 ▶
The Gauntlet '77
Get On the Bus '96 ▶
Heart and Souls '93
The Interpreter '05 ▶
Jeepers Creepers 2 '03
The Journey '59
Juanita '19
Keane '04 ▶
The King Is Alive '00
La Mission '09
The Laughing Policeman '74
A League of Their Own '92 ▶
Love Field '91
Magic Trip: Ken Kesey's Search for a Kool Place '11
Margaret '11
Mexican Bus Ride '51
My Life in Ruins '09
National Lampoon's Senior Trip '95
Pardon My Sarong '42
Paterson '16 ▶
Planes, Trains & Automobiles '87
Ride '98
The Runaway Bus '54
Selena '96
Shuttle '09
Siam Sunset '99
The Siege '98
Sixteen Candles '84 ▶
Somewhere Slow '14
The Space Between '10
Speed '94 ▶
Spice World: The Movie '97
Still Crazy '98 ▶
Sunday in New York '63
The Sweet Hereafter '96 ▶
Swordfish '01
Three Days to Vegas '07
Track the Man Down '55
The Trip to Bountiful '85 ▶
The Trip to Bountiful '14 ▶
Vince Vaughn's Wild West Comedy Show '06
Wassup Rockers '06
The Wayward Bus '57
Where Angels Go, Trouble Follows '68

Business and industry news--Pacific Islands

Fast & Furious Presents: Hobbs & Shaw '19

Cabbies

All or Nothing '02
Better Than Sex '00
Big City '37
The Bishop's Wife '47 ▶
Blood & Donuts '95
Born Romantic '00
Carry On Cabby '63
Chicago Cab '98
Claire Dolan '97
Cold Dog Soup '89
Collateral '04 ▶
Conspiracy Theory '97 ▶
A Crime '06
Crocodile Dundee '86 ▶
Crossing Delancey '88 ▶
Cyclo '95
Daylight '96
D.C. Cab '84
Die Laughing '80
Doc Hollywood '91
Drowning on Dry Land '00
Escape from New York '81
Extremely Dangerous '99
Fall '97
The Family Jewels '65
The Fifth Element '97
For Hire '98
For Pete's Sake '74
Giallo '09
Girl Crazy '32
Goodbye Solo '08
Last Cab to Darwin '16 ▶
Look Who's Talking '89 ▶
The Love Trap '29
Malice in Wonderland '09
Mexico City '00
Midsummer Madness '07
My Best Friend '06
My Son the Fanatic '97 ▶
Night on Earth '91 ▶
99 River Street '53
Old Stone '16
Pulp Fiction '94 ▶
Race to Witch Mountain '09
Radio Cab Murder '54
Scrooged '88
Seeding of a Ghost '86
She's the One '96
Sorry, Haters '05
Stir Crazy '80
Stolen '12
Stuber '19
Take Me Home '11
Taxi! '32
Taxi '04
Taxi Blues '90 ▶
Taxi Driver '76 ▶
3 A.M. '01 ▶
Three Days of Rain '02
Too Bad She's Bad '54
Total Recall '90 ▶
The Town Is Quiet '00
200 Cigarettes '98
Vintage Model '92
Virtue '32

Calcutta

See also *India*

Baraka '93 ▶
Born Into Brothels: Calcutta's Red Light Kids '04
Calcutta '47
City of Joy '92
Lion '16 ▶
The Quest '96
The Waiting City '09

Cambodia

See also *Asia; Vietnam War*

Apocalypse Now '79 ▶
City of Ghosts '03
First They Killed My Father '17
Fortunes of War '94
The Killing Fields '84 ▶
S21: The Khmer Rouge Killing Machine '03 ▶
Swimming to Cambodia '87 ▶

Camelot (New)

See also *Assassination; Presidency*

Bobby '06
Fatal Deception: Mrs. Lee Harvey Oswald '93
Jackie '16 ▶
Jackie Bouvier Kennedy Onassis '00
Jackie, Ethel, Joan: The Kennedy Women '01
JFK '91 ▶
JFK: Reckless Youth '93
Kennedy '83
The Kennedys '11
Killing Kennedy '13
Missiles of October '74 ▶
Parkland '13
PT 109 '63
RFK '02
Robert Kennedy and His Times '90
Ruby '92
Thirteen Days '00 ▶

Camelot (Old)

See also *Medieval Romps; Swashbucklers*

Arthur's Quest '99
Camelot '67
A Connecticut Yankee in King Arthur's Court '49
Excalibur '81 ▶
First Knight '95
A Kid in King Arthur's Court '95
Kids of the Round Table '96
King Arthur '04
King Arthur, the Young Warlord '75
A Knight in Camelot '98
Knights of the Round Table '53
Merlin '98 ▶
Merlin and the Book of Beasts '09
Merlin and the War of the Dragons '08
Merlin's Apprentice '06
Mists of Avalon '01 ▶
Monty Python and the Holy Grail '75 ▶
Prince Valiant '54
Quest for Camelot '98
The Sword in the Stone '63 ▶
Sword of Lancelot '63
Sword of the Valiant '83
Transformers: The Last Knight '17

Campers/RVs

About Schmidt '02 ▶
Barefoot '14
Breathless '12
Brokeback Mountain '05 ▶
Jackie '12
The Long, Long Trailer '54
Lost in America '85 ▶
Meet the Fockers '04
Roadkill '11
RV '06
Sightseers '12
Stripes '81
We're the Millers '13

Campus Capers

See also *Fraternities & Hell High School; School Daze*

Abandon '02
The Absent-Minded Professor '61 ▶
Acceptance '09
Accepted '06
Accident '67
The Affairs of Dobie Gillis '53
All-American Murder '91
American Animals '18 ▶
American Chai '01
American Pie Presents: Beta House '07
American Pie Presents: The Naked Mile '06
American Psycho 2: All American Girl '02
American Virgin '09
Andy Hardy's Blonde Trouble '44
Answer This '10
Assault of the Party Nerds '89
At Middleton '13
Auto Recovery '08
Back to School '86
A Beautiful Mind '01 ▶
Berkeley '05
Beyond Dream's Door '88
B.F.'s Daughter '48
Bickford Shmeckler's Cool Ideas '06
Big Shot: Confessions of a Campus Bookie '02
Black Christmas '75
Blondie Goes to College '42
Blood Cult '85
Blood Sisters '86
Bloomington '10
Blue Chips '94
Blue Like Jazz '12
Boogeyman 3 '08
Boys and Girls '00
Breeders '97
Bride of Killer Nerd '91
Bring It On Again '03
Burn, Witch, Burn! '62
Burning Sands '17
The Campus Corpse '77
Campus Man '87
Campus Rhythm '43
Carnal Knowledge '71 ▶
Casino Jack '10
Charley's Aunt '41 ▶
The Cheerleaders '72
Cheers for Miss Bishop '41
Circle of Friends '94
College '08
College Humor '33
College Swing '38
The Computer Wore Tennis Shoes '69
Confessions of Sorority Girls '94
Confidentially Connie '53
The Cousins '59 ▶
The Crimson Rivers '01
Cruel Intentions 3 '04
Cult '07
The Curve '97
Damsels in Distress '11
Dancing Co-Ed '39
Dark Matter '07
Dead Man on Campus '97
Dealing: Or the Berkeley-to-Boston Forty-Brick Lost-Bag Blues '72
Dear White People '14 ▶
Decoys '04
Decoys: The Second Seduction '07
Defying Gravity '99
Devil in the Flesh 2 '00
Divided We Stand '00
Do You Love Me? '46
Doctor in the House '53 ▶
Dorm That Dripped Blood '82
Down to You '00
Dread '09
Drumline '02 ▶
Elegy '08
Eleven Men and a Girl '30
The Express '08
The 5th Quarter '10

▶ = rated three bones or higher

Final Exam '81
First Daughter '04
Fist Fight '17
Flubber '97
Footnote '11
Foreign Student '94
Francis Goes to West Point '52
Frat Party '09
Fraternity Vacation '85
The Freshman '25 ▶
The Freshman '90
Freshman Orientation '04
Fright Night 2 '88
Game of Your Life '11
Get Yourself a College Girl '64
Getting Away With Murder '96
Ghoulies 3: Ghoulies Go to College '91
Girl Crazy '43 ▶
The Girl Most Likely to. . . '73
Girls Night Out '83
Glory Daze '96
Goat '16
God's Not Dead '14
Going Greek '01
Good '08
Good News '47
Good Will Hunting '97
Goodbye My Fancy '51
Gossip '99
Gotcha! '85
The Great Debaters '07 ▶
Gross Anatomy '89
Happy Death Day '17
Happy Hell Night '92
Harold and Kumar Go to White Castle '04
Harrad Experiment '73
Harrad Summer '74
Harvard Man '01
The Heart of Dixie '89
Heart of Stone '01
Hell Night '81
High Time '60
Higher Learning '94
A Holiday Heist '11
Home Before Dark '58
Horse Feathers '32 ▶
H.O.T.S. '79
The House Bunny '08
House of the Dead 2: Dead Aim '05
The House on Sorority Row '83
House Party 2: The Pajama Jam '91
How High '01
How I Got into College '89
How I Spent My Summer Vacation '97
Huddle '32
The Human Stain '03
I Don't Buy Kisses Anymore '92
I'll Be Home for Christmas '98
In the Blood '06
Indignation '16
The Initiation '84
Initiation of Sarah '78
The Initiation of Sarah '06
I.Q. '94
Iris '01 ▶
Is There Life Out There? '94
Judas Kiss '11
The Junction Boys '02
Kaboom '11
Keep the Faith, Baby '02
Kicking and Screaming '95 ▶
Kill Katie Malone '10
Kill Your Darlings '13
Killer Me '01
Killer Party '86
A Killing Spring '02
Kilroy Was Here '47
Knock Outs '92
Lady Killer '97
Larry Crowne '11
Legacy '08
Legally Blonde '01
Liberal Arts '12
Little Ashes '09
Loser '00
Love and Basketball '00 ▶
Love and Debate '06
Lucky Jim '58
The Male Animal '42
Malice '93
Man of the House '05
Mazes and Monsters '82
Me Without You '01
Midnight Madness '80
The Mirror Has Two Faces '96
The Misadventures of Merlin Jones '63
Mrs. Washington Goes to Smith '09
Mona Lisa Smile '03
The Monkey's Mask '00
Monkey's Uncle '65
Monster on the Campus '59
Monsters University '13
Mooz-Lum '10
Mortuary Academy '91
Mother Is a Freshman '49
My Lucky Star '38
My Sex Life. . . Or How I Got into an Argument '96
National Lampoon's Adam & Eve '05
National Lampoon's Animal House '78 ▶
National Lampoon's Ratko: The Dictator's Son '09
National Lampoon's Van Wilder 2: The Rise of Taj '06
National Lampoon's Van Wilder '02
Navy Blue and Gold '37
Necessary Roughness '91
Needle '10
New Best Friend '02
A Night in the Life of Jimmy Reardon '88
Night of the Creeps '86
Nightwish '89
Nobel Son '08
Now You See Him, Now You Don't '72
Nutty Professor 2: The Klumps '00
The Nutty Professor '63 ▶
The Nutty Professor '96 ▶
An Occasional Hell '96
Odd Jobs '85
Old Man Rhythm '35
Old School '03
Oleanna '94
100 Girls '00
Ordinary Sinner '02
The Oxford Murders '08
The Paper Chase '73 ▶
Party Animal '83
The Party Never Stops '07
P.C.U. '94
The Perfect Student '11
Pieces '83
Pigskin Parade '36
Pitch Perfect '12
The Plastic Age '25
Poison Ivy 4: The Secret Society '08
Poster Boy '04
Pound of Flesh '10
Preppies '82
The Prince & Me '04
The Prodigy '98
The Program '93
Prozac Nation '01
Pumpkin '02
Raw '17
Real Genius '85 ▶
A Reason to Believe '95
Red Letters '00
Return to Halloweentown '06
Revenge of the Nerds '84
Revenge of the Nerds 2: Nerds in Paradise '87
Revenge of the Nerds 3: The Next Generation '92
Ring of Terror '62
Ripper: Letter from Hell '01
Road Trip '00
Road Trip: Beer Pong '09
Roommate '84
The Roommate '11
Roommates '95
Rosalie '38
R.P.M.* (*Revolutions Per Minute) '70
Rudy '93
The Rules of Attraction '02
Rush Week '88
Scent of a Woman '92 ▶
School Daze '88 ▶
School Spirit '85
Scream 2 '97 ▶
The Secret Life of Girls '99
The Seniors '78
Sensation '94
Senseless '98
A Serious Man '09 ▶
Sex Kittens Go to College '60
She's Working Her Way Through College '52
Silent Scream '80
The Sixth Man '97
The Skulls '00
The Skulls 2 '02
Sky High '84
Slackers '02
A Small Circle of Friends '80
Smart People '08
Sniper '75 ▶
So This Is College '29
So Undercover '13
The Social Network '10 ▶
Sorority Babes in the Slimeball Bowl-A-Rama '87
Sorority Boys '02
Sorority House Massacre '86
Sorority House Massacre 2: Nighty Nightmare '92
Sorority House Vampires '95
Sorority Row '09
Sorority Wars '09
Soul Man '86
Soul Survivors '01
South Beach Academy '96
Spellbound '41
Splatter University '84
Splitz '84
Spring Break '83
Starter for 10 '06
The Sterile Cuckoo '69 ▶
Still Alice '14 ▶
Stomp the Yard '07
Stomp the Yard 2: Homecoming '10
Stonebrook '98
Storytelling '01 ▶
Stricken '98
The Strongest Man in the World '75
The Substitute 3: Winner Takes All '99
Summer Palace '06 ▶
The Sure Thing '85 ▶
Surviving Desire '91 ▶
Sydney White '07
Sylvia '03
Tall Lie '53
Tall Story '60
Tammy Tell Me True '61
Teen Wolf Too '87
Tenure '09
That's My Boy '51
Those Glamour Girls '39
Threesome '94
Toga Party '77
Too Young to Marry '07
Tower '16 ▶
Transylmania '09
21 '08
21 & Over '13
22 Jump Street '14
Two Minutes to Play '37
Underclassman '05
Unforgettable '96
The Unnamable 2: The Statement of Randolph Carter '92
The Unnamable '88
Up the Creek '84
Urban Legend '98
Urban Legends 2: Final Cut '00
The Utopian Society '03
Vampires of Sorority Row: Kickboxers From Hell '99
Van Wilder: Freshman Year '08
Varsity Show '37
The Victory '81
Voodoo '95
Voodoo Academy '00
Waking the Dead '00
The Waterboy '98
We Are Marshall '06
What Lies Beneath '00
When He's Not a Stranger '89 ▶
Wishmaster 3: Beyond the Gates of Hell '01
Witchboard '87
With Honors '94
Wonder Boys '00 ▶
Young Ideas '43

Canada

See also Cold Spots; Hockey

Above and Beyond '06
The Adjuster '91
The Agency '81
All Hat '07
Alpha and Omega '10
Anne of Avonlea '87 ▶
Anne of Green Gables '34 ▶
Anne of Green Gables '85 ▶
The Apprenticeship of Duddy Kravitz '74 ▶
Ararat '02 ▶
Atlantic City '81 ▶
Autumn Hearts: A New Beginning '07
Beautiful Dreamers '92
Being Canadian '15 ▶
Big Bear '98
Big Meat Eater '85
Big Red '62
Black Christmas '75
Black Mountain Side '16
Black Robe '91 ▶
Blood Relations '87
The Bloody Brood '59
Blue State '07
Boy in Blue '86
The Boys '97
The Boys Club '96
The Boys of St. Vincent '93 ▶
Brand Upon the Brain! '06 ▶
The Brood '79
Buffalo Jump '90 ▶
Bullies '86
By Way of the Stars '92
The Calling '14
Camilla '94
Campbell's Kingdom '57
The Canadian '26
Canadian Bacon '94
The Captive '14
Cathy's Curse '77
The Changeling '80
Circle of Two '80
Class of 1984 '82
Clean '04
Clean, Shaven '93
Closet Monster '16
Cloudburst '11 ▶
A Cry in the Wild '90 ▶
Curtains '83
Dan Candy's Law '73
Dance Me Outside '95
Dancing in the Dark '86
Daughter of Death '82
Dead Ringers '88 ▶
Deadfall '12
Dear Zachary: A Letter to a Son About His Father '08 ▶
Deathdream '72
The Decline of the American Empire '86 ▶
The Demons '19
Deranged '74 ▶
The Deserters '83
Desperate Search '52
Disappearances '06
Distant Thunder '88
Dog Pound Shuffle '75 ▶
The Dog Who Stopped the War '84
A Doll's House '73 ▶
Dudley Do-Right '99
Eddie and the Cruisers 2: Eddie Lives! '89
Eddie the Sleepwalking Cannibal '12
Edge of Madness '02
Emile '03
The Enemy '01
Everything's Gone Green '06
Far Side of the Moon '03
The Fast Runner '01 ▶
Festival Express '03 ▶
Fly Away Home '96 ▶
For the Moment '94
Freezer Burn: The Invasion of Laxdale '08
Frozen River '08 ▶
Ginger Snaps '01
Ginger Snaps: Unleashed '04
Goon '12
Goon: Last of the Enforcers '17
The Grand Seduction '13
Grey Owl '99
Grizzly Falls '99
Grown Up Movie Star '10
Hard Core Logo '96
Heck's Way Home '95
Henry & Verlin '94
Hey, Happy! '01
Hoax for the Holidays '10
Holy Matrimony '94
Home Again '13
The Horses of McBride '12
House of the Living Dead '73
Hudson's Bay '40
Ice Men '04
The Incredible Journey '63
Intersection '93
Into the Forest '16
Invasion! '99
Iron Road '08
The Journey Home '14
Karla '06
The Killing Machine '09
Lassie's Great Adventure '62
Last Wedding '01
Leaving Metropolis '02
The Little Kidnappers '90
Love and Human Remains '93 ▶
Love on the Side '04
Maelstrom '00
Magic in the Water '95
Margaret's Museum '95 ▶
Marianne & Leonard: Words of Love '19
Maudie '17 ▶
Men with Brooms '02
Mesrine: Part 1-Killer Instinct '08
Mommy '14 ▶
Murderball '05 ▶
My American Cousin '85 ▶
My Life Without Me '03
A Name for Evil '70
Narrow Margin '90
New Waterford Girl '99
The Newton Boys '97
Nomads of the North '20
Northern Extremes '93
Nothing Too Good for a Cowboy '98
Now & Forever '02
One Week '08
The Other Half '17
Perfect Sisters '14
The Perfect Son '00
Playing House '06
Poor Man's Game '06 ▶
Re-Generation '04
Restless Spirits '99
The Right of Way '31
The Rocket '05 ▶
Rose Marie '36 ▶
Rust '09
The Saddest Music in the World '03
Saint Ralph '04
Scandal at Scourie '53
Shattered City: The Halifax Explosion '03
The Shipping News '01
Small Town Murder Songs '10
The Snow Walker '03
Some Girls '88
South Park: Bigger, Longer and Uncut '99
Spenser: A Savage Place '94
Spirit Bear: The Simon Jackson Story '05
Spirit Rider '93 ▶
The Stone Angel '07
Strange Brew '83
Strangers in Good Company '91 ▶
Stryker '04
Super Troopers 2 '18
The Sweet Hereafter '96 ▶
Tail Lights Fade '99
Taking Lives '04
That Beautiful Somewhere '06
Time Lock '57
Tokyo Cowboy '94
Torso '02
The Trojan Horse '08
Turning Paige '01
Tusk '14
The Way of the West '11
Wedding in White '72
Weirdsville '07
When Calls the Heart '13
Who Loves the Sun '06
The Widow of Saint-Pierre '00 ▶
Woman Obsessed '59
The Year Dolly Parton Was My Mom '11
Yoga Hosers '16

Canadian Mounties

See also Canada

Canadian Bacon '94
Caryl of the Mountains '36
Dan Candy's Law '73
Death Hunt '81
Dudley Do-Right '99
Fort Vengeance '53
Northern Pursuit '43
Rose Marie '36 ▶
Rose Marie '54 ▶
Saskatchewan '54
Susannah of the Mounties '39
The Way of the West '11
When Calls the Heart '13
The Wild North '52

Canine Cops

See also Extraordinary Pairings; King of Beasts (Dogs)

The Dog Who Saved Summer '15
K-9 3: P.I. '01
K-9 '89
K-911 '99
See Spot Run '01
Sherlock: Undercover Dog '94
Top Dog '95
Turner and Hooch '89

Cannibalism

Adrenalin: Fear the Rush '96
Alien Prey '78
Alive '93
Alive or Dead '08
Anthropophagus: The Grim Reaper '80
Appetites '15
The Bad Batch '17
Bad Meat '11
Bad Taste '88 ▶
The Beast Must Die '75
Beast of the Yellow Night '70
Beware! Children at Play '95
Bio-dead '09
Bleeders '97
Blood Diner '87
Blood Feast '63
Blood Hook '86
Blood Sisters '86
Bloodsucking Freaks '75
Bloodsucking Pharoahs of Pittsburgh '90
Body Count '87
Bone Tomahawk '15
A Boy and His Dog '75
Brainjacked '09
The 'Burbs '89
Buried Alive '81
Cannibal Apocalypse '80
Cannibal Campout '88
Cannibal Holocaust '80
Cannibal! The Musical '96
Cannibal Women in the Avocado Jungle of Death '89
The Chilling '89
C.H.U.D. '84
Consuming Passions '88
The Cook, the Thief, His Wife & Her Lover '90 ▶
Corporate Animals '19
The Corpse Grinders '71
Crazy Fat Ethel II '85
Dawn of the Dead '78 ▶

Dawn of the Dead '04 ▶
Dawn of the Mummy '82
The Day '11
Delicatessen '92 ▶
Demon Barber of Fleet Street '36
Deranged '74 ▶
The Descent '05
Devil Hunter '08
Doctor X '32
The Donner Party '09
Doomsday '08
Eat the Rich '87
Eaters '15
Eating Raoul '82 ▶
Ed Gein '01
Eddie the Sleepwalking Cannibal '12
Emerald Jungle '80
Enchanted Island '58
Feeders '96
Fiend '83
Flesh Eating Mothers '89
Freakshow '95
Frightmare '74
The Further Adventures of Tennessee Buck '88
The Green Butchers '03
The Green Inferno '14
Grim Reaper '81
Gruesome Twosome '67
Hannibal '01
Hannibal Rising '07
Hansel & Gretel '13
Hansel & Gretel Get Baked '13
He Never Died '15
Hell of the Living Dead '83
The Hills Have Eyes '77
The Hills Have Eyes 2 '07
The Hills Have Eyes '06
How Tasty Was My Little Frenchman '71
Human Beasts '80
I Am Omega '07
I Drink Your Blood '71
I Eat Your Skin '64
Igor & the Lunatics '85
Incredible Melting Man '77
Insanitarium '08
Jeepers Creepers 2 '03
Jeepers Creepers 3 '17
Jeepers Creepers '01
Land of Death '03
Leatherface: The Texas Chainsaw Massacre 3 '89
The Mad Butcher '72
Mom '89
The Monster Club '85
Motel Hell '80
Mountain of the Cannibal God '79
Murderer's Keep '70
Night of the Living Dead '68 ▶
Night of the Living Dead '90
Night of the Zombies '81
Nightstalker '81
The Offspring '87
Parents '89 ▶
The Perverse Countess '73
Porcile '69
Rabid Grannies '89
Ravenous '99
Raw '17
Raw Force '81
Raw Meat '72
Redneck Zombies '88
The Road '09
Robinson Crusoe '54
Serenity '05 ▶
The Severed Arm '73
The Silence of the Lambs '91 ▶
Skinned Alive '08
Slaughterhouse '87
Slave Girls from Beyond Infinity '87
Society '92
Soylent Green '73
Stag Night '08
Suspended Animation '02
Tales from the Darkside: The Movie '90
Tenderness of the Wolves '73
Terror at Red Wolf Inn '72
Texas Chainsaw 3D '13
The Texas Chainsaw Massacre 2 '86
The Texas Chainsaw Massacre '74
The Texas Chainsaw Massacre '03
The Texas Chainsaw Massacre: The Beginning '06
The 13th Warrior '99
Three on a Meathook '72
The Time Machine '02
Tooth and Nail '07
2001 Maniacs '05
2001 Maniacs: Field of Screams '10
The Undertaker and His Pals '67
Warlock Moon '73
We Are What We Are '11
We Are What We Are '13 ▶
Windbag the Sailor '36
The Woman '11
The Womaneater '59
Wrong Turn '03
Wrong Turn 2: Dead End '07
Wrong Turn 3: Left for Dead '09
Wrong Turn 4: Bloody Beginnings '11
Zombie '80
Zombie Island Massacre '84
Zombie Lake '80

Capitol Capers

Abraham Lincoln '30
Absolute Power '97
Adventure in Washington '41
All the President's Men '76 ▶
Alpha Alert '13
The Amazing Captain Nemo '78
An American Affair '99
The American President '95 ▶
Atlas Shrugged: Part 1 '11
The Aviator '04 ▶
Beavis and Butt-Head Do America '96
Born Yesterday '50 ▶
Born Yesterday '93
Breach '07
Bulworth '98 ▶
Burn After Reading '08
The Capitol Conspiracy '99
The Captive City '52
Charlie Wilson's War '07
The Company '07
The Contender '00
Cupid & Cate '00
Dave '93 ▶
The Day Reagan Was Shot '01
DC 9/11: Time of Crisis '04
The Devil's Teardrop '10
Dick '99 ▶
The Distinguished Gentleman '92
The Double '11
End Game '06
Enemy of the State '98
Eraser '96
Fahrenheit 9/11 '04 ▶
Fair Game '10 ▶
Fatwa '06
The Fearmakers '58
First Kid '96
Get On the Bus '96 ▶
Get Smart '08
Government Girl '43
The Growing Pains Movie '00
Guilty by Association '03
Head of State '03
Heavenly Days '44
Hostile Makeover '09
The Hunting of the President '04
In the Line of Fire '93 ▶
In the Loop '09
The Invasion '07
JFK '91 ▶
Johnny Doesn't Live Here Any More '44
Judge Hardy's Children '38
Judicial Indiscretion '07
Killer Hair '09
Killing Lincoln '13
Lee Daniels' The Butler '13
Legally Blonde 2: Red White & Blonde '03
Life of a King '13
Lincoln '12 ▶
Lions for Lambs '07
Man of the Year '06
The Manchurian Candidate '62 ▶
The Manchurian Candidate '04 ▶
Mars Attacks! '96
Massacre '34
Master Spy: The Robert Hanssen Story '02
Minority Report '02 ▶
Miss Sloane '16
Mister 880 '50
Mr. Smith Goes to Washington '39 ▶
Most Wanted '97
Murder at 1600 '97
My Fellow Americans '96
My Son John '52
National Lampoon's Senior Trip '95
Night at the Museum: Battle of the Smithsonian '09
Nixon '95 ▶
Nothing But the Truth '08 ▶
Olympus Has Fallen '13
Open Cam '05
Operation Avalanche '16
Path to War '02
Power and Beauty '02
The President's Analyst '67 ▶
Primary Colors '98
Protocol '84
Rampage: Capital Punishment '14
Random Hearts '99
The Recruit '03
Rendezvous '35
Return of the Living Dead: Rave to the Grave '05
Seance '06
The Seduction of Joe Tynan '79
1776 '72 ▶
The Shadow Conspiracy '96
Sherlock Holmes in Washington '43
Snowden '16
Something for the Birds '52
State of Play '09 ▶
The State Within '06
Suicide Squad '16
Talk to Me '07
Thank You for Smoking '06
Three Days of the Condor '75 ▶
Traffic '00 ▶
Trial by Media '00
24: Redemption '08
Vice '18
W. '08 ▶
Wag the Dog '97
The Walker '07
Washington: Behind Closed Doors '77
White House Down '13
Without Love '45
XXX: State of the Union '05

Caribbean

See also Island Fare

Agatha Christie's A Caribbean Mystery '83
Arrowsmith '31
Caribe '87
The Comedians '67
Countryman '83
Dr. No '62 ▶
Dragonard '88
Emperor Jones '33
Heartbreak Ridge '86 ▶
How Stella Got Her Groove Back '98
I Walked with a Zombie '43 ▶
Live and Let Die '73
Maximum Thrust '88
The Mighty Quinn '89
The Pirate '48 ▶
Pirates of the Caribbean: Dead Men Tell No Tales '17
The Serpent and the Rainbow '87
The Spanish Prisoner '97 ▶
To Have & Have Not '44 ▶
Voodoo Possession '14

Carnivals & Circuses

See also Amusement Parks; Clowns; Fairs & Expositions

Air Eagles '31
Alien 51 '04
Around a Small Mountain '09
At the Circus '39
Ava's Magical Adventure '94
Barney's Great Adventure '98
Barnum '86
Batman Forever '95 ▶
Behind the Sun '01
Berserk! '67
Beyond the Blue Horizon '42
The Big Circus '59
Big Fish '03 ▶
Big Top Pee-wee '88
Billy Rose's Jumbo '62 ▶
Black Jack '79
Black Orpheus '58 ▶
Brewster McCloud '70 ▶
The Cabinet of Dr. Caligari '19 ▶
Candyman 2: Farewell to the Flesh '94
Carnival of Souls '62 ▶
Carnival of Souls '98
Carnival Story '54
Carny '80 ▶
Carny '09
Carousel '56 ▶
Castle of the Living Dead '64
Central Airport '33
Chad Hanna '40
The Circus '28 ▶
Circus of Fear '67
Circus of Horrors '60
Circus World '64
Cirque du Freak: The Vampire's Assistant '09
Clifford's Really Big Movie '04
The Clowns '71 ▶
The Court Jester '56 ▶
Dante's Inferno '35
Death Mask '98
Dixiana '30
Down the Shore '11
Elvira Madigan '67 ▶
Encore '52 ▶
Execution '68
The Fantasticks '95
Fear '90
Final Destination 3 '06
Flamingo Road '49 ▶
Fox and His Friends '75 ▶
Freaked '93
Freaks '32 ▶
Freakshow '95
Freakshow '07
The Funhouse '81
Girl On the Run '53
Grease '78 ▶
The Greatest Show on Earth '52 ▶
He Who Gets Slapped '24 ▶
High, Wide and Handsome '37
Incredibly Strange Creatures Who Stopped Living and Became Mixed-Up Zombies '63
It's a Small World '50
Jeanne Eagels '57
The Jerk '79
Julia Misbehaves '48 ▶
Killer Klowns from Outer Space '88
La Strada '54 ▶
Larger Than Life '96
The Last Circus '10
The Last Days of Summer '07
Laugh, Clown, Laugh '28 ▶
Lili '53 ▶
The Little Mermaid '18
Lola Montes '55 ▶
Looking for Trouble '96
Love in Bloom '35
Luther the Geek '90
Madagascar 3: Europe's Most Wanted '12
Man on a Tightrope '53
The Man Who Laughs '27 ▶
Merry Andrew '58
MirrorMask '05
Moscow on the Hudson '84 ▶
Nightmare Alley '47
One Arabian Night '20 ▶
Open Season 3 '10
Outrage '93
Painted Faces '29
Passion Play '10
Peck's Bad Boy with the Circus '38
Pennies from Heaven '36
Polly of the Circus '32
Portrait of an Assassin '49
P.T. Barnum '99
Rain or Shine '30
The Red Dwarf '99
Revenge of the Nerds '84
The Road to Zanzibar '41 ▶
Roustabout '64
The Rousters '90
Sally of the Sawdust '25
Santa Sangre '90 ▶
Sawdust & Tinsel '53 ▶
The Serpent's Egg '78
7 Faces of Dr. Lao '63 ▶
Shakes the Clown '92
She Creature '01
She-Freak '67
The Show '27
So Dear to My Heart '49 ▶
Something Wicked This Way Comes '83
Splinterheads '09
State Fair '62
The Story of Three Loves '53
Strong Man '26 ▶
Texas Carnival '51
They Gave Him a Gun '37
31 '16
Toby Tyler '59 ▶
Trapeze '56 ▶
Two Moon Junction '88
The Unholy Three '25 ▶
The Unholy Three '30 ▶
Vampire Circus '71
Variety '25 ▶
Variety Lights '51 ▶
The Wagons Roll at Night '41
Water for Elephants '11
When Night Is Falling '95 ▶
Wild Hearts Can't Be Broken '91 ▶
Wilder Napalm '93
You Can't Cheat an Honest Man '39 ▶

Casbah

Aladdin '92 ▶
Algiers '38 ▶
The Battle of Algiers '66 ▶
Carry On Spying '64
The Desert Song '43
Kismet '55
Pepe Le Moko '37 ▶

Catholic School

Absolution '81
The Blackcoat's Daughter '17
Boys Town '38 ▶
The Craft '96
The Dangerous Lives of Altar Boys '02 ▶
Doubt '08 ▶
Going My Way '44 ▶
Heaven Help Us '85
House of D '04
Kentucky Fried Movie '77 ▶
Loving Annabelle '06
Perfect Parents '06
Prom Queen '04
Ready? OK! '08
Sister Act 2: Back in the Habit '93
Stolen Summer '02
True Crime '95

Cats

See also Big Cats; Killer Kats

The Adventures of Milo & Otis '89 ▶
Alice in Wonderland '50
Alice in Wonderland '51 ▶
Alice in Wonderland '85
Alice in Wonderland '99
Alien '79 ▶
An American Tail '86
Angus, Thongs and Perfect Snogging '08
The Aristocats '70 ▶
Austin Powers: International Man of Mystery '97 ▶
Babe '95 ▶
Babe: Pig in the City '98
Batman Returns '92
The Big Cat '49
The Black Cat '34 ▶
The Black Cat '41
The Black Cat '81
Bolt '08 ▶
The Cat from Outer Space '78
A Cat in Paris '11
Cat People '82
Cats '19
Cats & Dogs '01
Cats & Dogs: The Revenge of Kitty Galore '10
Cats Don't Dance '97
Cat's Eye '85
Catwoman '04
The Corpse Grinders '71
Disney's Teacher's Pet '04 ▶
Dr. Seuss' The Cat in the Hat '03
Fritz the Cat '72 ▶
The Future '11
Garfield: A Tail of Two Kitties '06
Garfield: The Movie '04
Gay Purr-ee '62
Ghost Cat '03
Good Neighbors '10
Harry and Tonto '74 ▶
Hocus Pocus '93
Homeward Bound: The Incredible Journey '93 ▶
Homeward Bound 2: Lost in San Francisco '96
The Incredible Journey '63
Inside Llewyn Davis '13 ▶
Ju-On: The Grudge '03
Keanu '16
Kedi '17 ▶
Kiki's Delivery Service '98
Kuroneko '68 ▶
The Late Show '77 ▶
The LEGO Ninjago Movie '17
Marmaduke '10
Meet the Fockers '04
Men in Black '97 ▶
Migrating Forms '00
Milo & Otis '89
Miss Minoes '01
Mr. Roosevelt '17
Mouse Hunt '97 ▶
Murder of a Cat '14
Night of a Thousand Cats '72
Nine Lives '16
Oliver & Company '88
Pet Sematary '89
Pet Sematary '19
Puss in Boots '11 ▶
Return of Chandu '34
Rhubarb '51
Sabrina the Teenage Witch '96
The Secret Life of Pets 2 '19
Seven Deaths in the Cat's Eye '72
Shrek 2 '04 ▶
SMART: Specialized Mobile Animal Rescue Team '16
The Smurfs '11
The Stars Fell on Henrietta '94
A Street Cat Named Bob '16
Stuart Little '99
Stuart Little 2 '02 ▶
That Darn Cat '65
That Darn Cat '96
The Three Lives of Thomasina '63 ▶
Tom and Jerry: The Movie '93
Treasure Buddies '12
Two Evil Eyes '90
The Uninvited '88
Your Vice is a Closed Room and Only I Have the Key '72

▶ = rated three bones or higher

Cattle Drive

***See also** Pardners; Westerns; Westrogens*

Alvarez Kelly '66
Australia '08
The Australian Story '52
Born Free '66 ►
Canyon River '56
Cast a Long Shadow '59
The Cowboys '72 ►
Far Country '55 ►
Go West '25 ►
Gun for a Coward '57
The Last Sunset '61
Lonesome Dove '89 ►
Overlanders '46 ►
The Proposition '97
Robbers' Roost '55
Saddle Tramp '47
The Tall Men '55

Cattle Rustlers/Horse Thieves

Cattle Town '52
Chisum '70
Gun for a Coward '57
Home on the Range '04
The Last Ride of the Dalton Gang '79
Lonesome Dove '89►
Missouri Breaks '76
The Moonlighter '53
The Showdown '40

Cave People

Alpha '18
Beach Babes 2: Cave Girl Island '95
Being Human '94
The Cave '05
Cave Girl '85
Cave Women on Mars '08
Caveman '81
The Clan of the Cave Bear '86
Creatures the World Forgot '70
The Croods '13
Early Man '18
Encino Man '92
The Flintstones '94
The Flintstones in Viva Rock Vegas '00
History of the World: Part 1 '81
Iceman '84►
The Last Dinosaur '77
National Lampoon's The Stoned Aged '07
One Million B.C. '40
1,000 Years From Now '52
Prehistoric Women '50
Quest for Fire '82►
Teenage Caveman '58
10,000 B.C. '08
Trog '70
Untamed Women '52
Valley of the Dragons '61
When Women Had Tails '70
When Women Lost Their Tails '75
Year One '09

Caves

Ace in the Hole '51►
Afghan Knights '07
Alien 2 on Earth '80
As Above, So Below '14
The Bat People '74
Cave-In! '79
Cave of Forgotten Dreams '11►
The Cavern '05
Corporate Animals '19
The Descent 2 '09
The Descent '05
Finding Altamira '16
Fixed Bayonets! '51►
47 Meters Down: Uncaged '19
George and the Dragon '04
The Hills Have Eyes 2 '07
How to Train Your Dragon 2 '14
Invasion of the Star Creatures '63
The Last Descent '16
The Lost Skeleton of Cadavra '01
The Monuments Men '13
No Place on Earth '12
Sanctum '11
Time Trap '17
Trog '70
Turistas '06

Central America

***See also** Mexico; South America*

Apocalypto '06 ►
Appointment in Honduras '53
The Art of Travel '08
Carla's Song '97
Carnival in Costa Rica '47
Che '08
Crude: The Real Price of Oil '09
Delta Force Commando '87
Devil Wears White '86
El Norte '83►
The Evil That Men Do '84
The Firing Line '91
Hombres Armados '97►
Latino '85
The Laundromat '19
Marie Galante '34►
The Mosquito Coast '86
No Turning Back '01
Romero '89
Salvador '86►
Solo '96
Sugar '09►
The Tailor of Panama '00►
Torrid Zone '40
Toy Soldiers '84
Under Fire '83►
Virgin Sacrifice '59
Wages of Fear '55►

Chain Gangs

Chain Gang '50
Chain Gang Girls '08
Chain Gang Women '72
Cool Hand Luke '67►
The Defiant Ones '58►
Fled '96
I Am a Fugitive from a Chain Gang '32►
O Brother Where Art Thou? '00
Sullivan's Travels '41►

Checkered Flag

***See also** Motor Vehicle Dept.*

American Graffiti '73►
Baffled '72
Banzai Runner '86
The Big Wheel '49
Bobby Deerfield '77
Born 2 Race '11
Brewster McCloud '70►
Bullitt '68►
Cannonball '76
Cannonball Run 2 '84
Cannonball Run '81
Cannonball Run Europe: The Great Escape '05
Cars 2 '11
Cars 3 '17
Cars '06►
The Checkered Flag '63
The Circuit '08
Corky '72
The Crowd Roars '32
Days of Thunder '90
Death Race '08
Death Race 2000 '75
Death Race 3: Inferno '12
Death Racers '08
The Devil on Wheels '47
Diamonds Are Forever '71►
Dirty Mary Crazy Larry '74►
Down and Derby '05
Dragstrip Girl '57
Dragstrip Girl '94
Driven '01
The Dukes of Hazzard '05
Dust to Glory '05►
Eat My Dust '76
The Fast and the Furious '54
The Fast and the Furious: Tokyo Drift '06
Fast Company '78
Fast Girl '07
Faster, Pussycat! Kill! Kill! '65
Finish Line '08
Fireball 500 '66
The First Auto '27
Genevieve '53 ►
Goldfinger '64 ►
Grand Prix '66
Grandview U.S.A. '84
Grease '78 ►
Greased Lightning '77
The Great Race '65
Gumball Rally '76
Hard Drivin' '60
Heart Like a Wheel '83
The Heavenly Kid '85
Hell on Wheels '67
Herbie: Fully Loaded '05
Herbie Goes Bananas '80
Herbie Goes to Monte Carlo '77
Hot Rod Girl '56
Landspeed '01
The Last American Hero '73►
Last Chase '81
The Last Ride '04
Le Mans '71►
The Lively Set '64
A Man and a Woman: 20 Years Later '86
Need for Speed '14
Phantom Racer '09
Pit Stop '67►
The Race '09
Race for Life '55
Race the Sun '96
Rebel without a Cause '55►
Red Line '96
Red Line 7000 '65
Redline '07
Richard Petty Story '72
Road Racers '59
Rush '13►
Senna '11
Shaker Run '85
Six Pack '82
Smash Palace '82
Smokey and the Bandit '77
Snake & Mongoose '13
Speed '36
Speed Racer '08
Speedway '29
Speedway '68
Spinout '66
Stroker Ace '83
Talladega Nights: The Ballad of Ricky Bobby '06
Ten Laps to Go '36
Those Daring Young Men in Their Jaunty Jalopies '69
3 Weeks to Daytona '11
Thunder Alley '67
Thunder in Carolina '60
Thunder in Dixie '65
To Please a Lady '50
Treasure Raiders '07
Turbo '13
2 Fast 2 Furious '03
200 MPH '11
Van Nuys Blvd. '79
Vanishing Point '71
Viva Las Vegas '63
Winning '69►
Winning: The Racing Life of Paul Newman '15
The Wraith '87
You've Got a Friend '07

Cheerleaders

***See also** Campus Capers; Hell High School*

American Beauty '99►
Attack of the 50 Foot Cheerleader '12
BASEketball '98
Bring It On '00
Bring It On Again '03
Bring It On: All or Nothing '06
Bring It On: Fight to the Finish '09
Bring It On: In It to Win It '07
Buffy the Vampire Slayer '92►
But I'm a Cheerleader '99
Cheerleader Camp '88
The Cheerleaders '72
Cheerleaders' Wild Weekend '85
Death Proof '07
Fired Up! '09
Flesh Gordon 2: Flesh Gordon Meets the Cosmic Cheerleaders '90
Grease '78 ►
I Love You, Beth Cooper '09
Jeepers Creepers 2 '03
John Tucker Must Die '06
Kids in America '05
Lucas '86 ►
The Majorettes '87
Man of the House '05
National Lampoon's Animal House '78 ►
The New Guy '02
#1 Cheerleader Camp '10
Pep Squad '98
Pom Pom Girls '76
Poms '19
The Positively True Adventures of the Alleged Texas Cheerleader-Murdering Mom '93►
The Prankster '10
Raising Genius '04
Ready? OK! '08
The Replacements '00
Revenge of the Cheerleaders '76
Satan's Cheerleaders '77
Slap Her, She's French '02
Starsky & Hutch '04
Sugar & Spice '01►
The Swinging Cheerleaders '74
Tragedy Girls '17►
Varsity Blues '98

Chefs

Abe '20
Always Be My Maybe '19
Angels Fall '07
April's Shower '03
Autumn in New York '00
Big Night '95
Bitter Feast '10
Burnt '15
Chef '14
Chef's Special '08
East Side Sushi '15►
El Bulli: Cooking in Progress '11
Felicia's Journey '99►
A Fine Mess '86
Frank & Lola '16
Funny About Love '90
Hotel Mumbai '18
The Hundred-Foot Journey '14
Julie & Julia '09►
Kitchen Privileges '00
Last Holiday '50►
Love and Mary '07
Love's Kitchen '11
Making the Rules '14
Mr. Church '16
Mr. Nice Guy '98
Mostly Martha '01►
No Reservations '07
Oldboy '03►
The Ramen Girl '08
Ratatouille '07►
South Park: Bigger, Longer and Uncut '99
Tampopo '86►
A Taste of Romance '12
Today's Special '09►
Tortilla Soup '01
Who Is Killing the Great Chefs of Europe? '78►

Chess

Alice Through the Looking Glass '66
Brooklyn Castle '12►
The Chess Player '27
The Chinese Cat '44
Computer Chess '13
Dangerous Moves '84►
The Dark Horse '14►
Fresh '94
Knight Moves '93
Knights of the South Bronx '05
Life of a King '13
The Luzhin Defence '00
The Other Man '08
Pawn Sacrifice '15
Queen of Katwe '16 ►
Queen to Play '09
Searching for Bobby Fischer '93 ►
The Seventh Seal '56 ►
Stalag 17 '53 ►
Swept from the Sea '97
The Thomas Crown Affair '68 ►
Treasure of Fear '45
Wicked Blood '13
Zatoichi: The Blind Swordsman and the Chess Expert '65

Chicago

Above the Law '88
Adventures in Babysitting '87
Amreeka '09 ►
And Now a Word From Our Sponsor '13
Angel Eyes '01
The Architect '06
Baby on Board '08
Bad City '06
Barbershop '02►
The Beast of the City '32
Beauty Shop '05►
Beginning of the End '57
Big Town '87
The Blues Brothers '80►
Blues Brothers 2000 '98
Bomb Squad '97
Bordertown '06
The Break-Up '06
The Bride Comes Home '35
Cadillac Records '08►
Call Northside 777 '48►
Candyman '92
Captive State '19
Category 6: Day of Destruction '04
Chain Reaction '96
Chasing Papi '03
Chi-raq '15►
Chicago '02►
Chicago Cab '98
Chicago Confidential '57
Chicago Overcoat '09
Chicago 10 '07►
Christmas With the Kranks '04
Code of Silence '85
The Company '03►
Crime Spree '03
The Current War: Director's Cut '19
Deadline '00
Death Wish '18
Derailed '05
Diminished Capacity '08
Divergent '14
Doorway to Hell '30
Down in the Delta '98►
Dragonfly '02
The Earl of Chicago '40
Elmer the Great '33
Everyone's Hero '06
A Family Thing '96►
Ferris Bueller's Day Off '86►
Finding Vivian Maier '14
First Time Felon '97
5 Star Day '10
The Fixer '97
For Hire '98
The Front Page '74
The Fugitive '93►
Go For It! '10
Go Into Your Dance '35
Goldstein '64
Grand Piano '13
The Grudge 3 '09
Happy Christmas '14
Hardball '01
Heaven Is a Playground '91
Her Fatal Flaw '06
Hey! Hey! USA! '38
High Fidelity '00►
Holiday Heart '00
Home Alone '90►
Home Alone 3 '97
I, Robot '04
I Want Someone to Eat Cheese With '06
In Bloom '13►
In My Father's House '15►
The Interrupters '11►
Jerry and Tom '98
John Q '02
Just Visiting '01
Killer Instinct: From the Files of Agent Candice DeLong '03
Kissing a Fool '98
The Lake House '06
Lamb '16
The Last Rites of Joe May '11
LOL '12
Lords of Soaptown: The True Story of Freestyle Walking '16
Louder Than a Bomb '10
Love and Action in Chicago '99
Love Jones '96 ►
Love That Brute '50
Mad Dog and Glory '93 ►
Make It Happen '08
Mercury Rising '98
The Merry Gentleman '08
Mickey One '65
The Million Dollar Rip-Off '76
Miss March '09
My Best Friend's Wedding '97
My Big Fat Greek Wedding '02
My Reputation '46
Native Son '19
The Negotiator '98
Never Been Kissed '99
The Newton Boys '97
Next of Kin '89
Nights and Weekends '08
No Brother of Mine '07
Nothing Like the Holidays '08
Obsessed '02
Of Boys and Men '08
On the Line '01
Osso Bucco '08
Our America '02
Outing Riley '04
Primal Fear '96
The Promotion '08
Proof '05►
Public Enemies '09
A Raisin in the Sun '08
Rampage '18
The Relic '96
Resurrection '99
The Return of Joe Rich '11
Return to Me '00
Risky Business '83►
Robin and the 7 Hoods '64
Roll Bounce '05►
Running Scared '86
Save the Last Dance '01
Shall We Dance? '04
Shattered '07
Shut-Eye '03
The Song of the Lark '01
Source Code '11►
Southside with You '16►
Stir of Echoes '99
Stir of Echoes 2: The Homecoming '07
Stolen Summer '02
Stony Island '77
Straight Talk '92
Stranger Than Fiction '06
Studs Lonigan '60
Super Hybrid '10
Surviving Christmas '04
Sweepings '33
Syncopation '42
Taking Care of Business '90
Tall, Dark and Handsome '41
The Third Miracle '99
Three to Tango '99
The Tiger Hunter '17
The Time Traveler's Wife '09
To Sir, With Love 2 '96
Transformers: Dark of the Moon '11
Trust '10
Uncle Buck '89►
Uncle Nino '03
Unconditional Love '03
The Undercover Man '49
Undertow '49
U.S. Marshals '98
The Untouchables '87►
Wabash Avenue '50
Wanted '08►

► = rated three bones or higher

The Watcher '00
The Weather Man '05
While You Were Sleeping '95 ▸
The White Raven '98
Who Do You Love '08
The Whole Nine Yards '00
Wicker Park '04
Widows '18 ▸
Wild Boys of the Road '33
Witless Protection '08

Child Abuse

Alias Betty '01
America '09
An American Crime '07
Antwone Fisher '02 ▸
Appointment With Death '10
The Awakening '11
Bad Education '04 ▸
Bastard out of Carolina '96
Bereavement '10
Bloodline '19
The Book of Henry '17
Born Into Brothels: Calcutta's Red Light Kids '04
Boy Wonder '10
The Boys of St. Vincent '93 ▸
A Brother's Kiss '97
Brute '97
Bully '11 ▸
The Butterfly Effect '04
Capernaum '18 ▸
The Captive '14
Capturing the Friedmans '03 ▸
Cronicas '04
Darkness '02
Dear Frankie '04
The Demons '19
Dolores Claiborne '94 ▸
Dominick & Eugene '88 ▸
Don't Tell '05
Dust of Life '95
El Bola '00
Ellen Foster '97
Evil '03 ▸
Father Hood '93
The Final Cut '04
Fireflies in the Garden '08
Foster '18
Gardens of the Night '08
Girl Rising '13 ▸
The Great Water '04
The Hanging Garden '97
The Heart Is Deceitful Above All Things '04
Hidden '09
Holly '07
The Hunt '13 ▸
I Know My First Name Is Steven '89
Impulse '74
Indictment: The McMartin Trial '95 ▸
Joe the King '99
Judgment '90 ▸
Just Ask My Children '01
Killer Me '01
King of Devil's Island '10
Lamb '85
Lime Salted Love '06
A Long Way Home '01
The Lost Son '98
Love's Unending Legacy '07
Martyrs '16
Mea Maxima Culpa: Silence in the House of God '12
Michael '11
Minding the Gap '18 ▸
Mockingbird Don't Sing '01
Mommie Dearest '81
Monsoon Wedding '01 ▸
Monster's Ball '01 ▸
The Mudge Boy '03
My Guardian Angel '16
Mysterious Skin '04 ▸
Never Take Candy From a Stranger '60
A Nightmare on Elm Street '10
The Offence '73 ▸
Older Than America '08
Oliver Twist '05 ▸
Osama '03 ▸
The Poker House '09
Polisse '11 ▸
Postcards from America '95
Precious: Based on the Novel 'Push' by Sapphire '09 ▸
Radio Flyer '92
Raising Cain '92
Ray & Liz '19
Ripe '97
River Red '98
Runaway '05
Running Scared '06
Sanitarium '13
The Scamp '57
The Shed '19
Short Eyes '79 ▸
Short Term 12 '13 ▸
Shot in the Heart '01 ▸
The Silence '10 ▸
Sleepers '96
Sleepwalking '08
South Bronx Heroes '85
The Stepdaughter '00
The Stolen Children '92 ▸
Taming Andrew '00
This Boy's Life '93 ▸
Threat of Exposure '02
Towelhead '07
Trade of Innocents '12
Transamerica '05 ▸
Turn the River '07
2 by 4 '98
The Unloved '09
Untamed Love '94
When I Find the Ocean '06
Where Children Play '15
The White Ribbon '09
Wildflower '91 ▸
Wildling '18
The Woodsman '04
You Were Never Really Here '17 ▸
ZigZag '02 ▸

Childhood Buddies

Ace Ventura Jr.: Pet Detective '08
Aliens in the Attic '09
Always Be My Maybe '19
Antboy '14
Babysitters Beware '08
Because of Winn-Dixie '05
The BFG '16
Black Jack '79
Bloodhounds of Broadway '52
Booky's Crush '09
Bridge to Terabithia '07
Captain Underpants: The First Epic Movie '17
Children On Their Birthdays '02
Christmas in Canaan '09
Cop Car '15
Crown Heights '17
Diary of a Wimpy Kid 2: Rodrick Rules '11
Disobedience '17
Dreamcatcher '03
El Bola '00
Extraterrestrial '14
The Fits '16
The Florida Project '17 ▸
The Gold Retrievers '10
The Happy Road '57
How to Train Your Dragon '10
I Declare War '12
I'm Not Scared '03
In a Better World '10
The Inevitable Defeat of Mister & Pete '13
Jack Goes Home '16
Julia '77 ▸
The Jungle Book 2 '03
Keeping the Faith '00
The Kid with a Bike '11
Kisses '08 ▸
Kit Kittredge: An American Girl '08
The Kite Runner '07 ▸
Knuckle Sandwich '04
The Last Time I Saw Macao '13
Let Me In '10
Let the Right One In '08
Lilo & Stitch '02 ▸
Little Men '34
Little Men '16 ▸
The Little Rascals Save the Day '14
Mid90s '18
Mountains May Depart '16 ▸
Mysterious Skin '04 ▸
The Night Before '15
No Strings Attached '11
Now and Then '95
Once Upon a Time in America '84 ▸
Paradise Now '05 ▸
Penrod and Sam '31
Pete's Dragon '16
Popstar: Never Stop Never Stopping '16 ▸
Raiders!: The Story of the Greatest Fan Film Ever Made '16 ▸
The Rainbow Tribe '11
Ramona and Beezus '10
The Robin Hood Gang '98
Scout's Guide to the Zombie Apocalypse '15
Shorts: The Adventures of the Wishing Rock '09
Snowmen '10
The Song of Names '19
Stand by Me '86 ▸
Summer Eleven '10
Ted '12 ▸
Thoroughbreds '17
A Time for Dancing '00
Unconditional '12
Wadjda '13 ▸
War Dogs '16
What About Your Friends: Weekend Getaway '02
Without a Paddle '04

Childhood Visions

***See** Home Alone*

Children

***See** Animated Musicals; Animation & Childhood Visions; Storytelling*

China

***See also** Asia*

Abominable '19
Adventures of Smilin' Jack '43
Ai Weiwei: Never Sorry '12 ▸
The Amazing Panda Adventure '95
American Factory '19 ▸
Ash Is Purest White '18 ▸
Ashes of Time Redux '08
Back to 1942 '12
Balzac and the Little Chinese Seamstress '02
Beijing Bicycle '01
Beyond the Next Mountain '87
The Bitter Tea of General Yen '33 ▸
Black Mask '96
Blood Brothers '07
The Blue Kite '93 ▸
Born in China '17
Call of Heroes '16
Charlie Chan in Shanghai '35
The Children of Huang Shi '08
China '43
China Cry '91
China Girl '42
Chinese Box '97
Chinese Odyssey 2002 '02
City of Life and Death '09
The Climbers '19
Coming Home '14
Crouching Tiger, Hidden Dragon: Sword of Destiny '16
Crows and Sparrows '49 ▸
Curse of the Golden Flower '06
Dangerous Liaisons '12
Deadly Target '94
Dragon Blade '15
Dragon Seed '44
East Palace, West Palace '96
The Emperor and the Assassin '99
The Emperor's Shadow '96
Empire of Assassins '11
Empire of the Sun '87 ▸
Enter the Warriors Gate '17
The Farewell '19 ▸
Farewell My Concubine '93
The Final Master '16
Flowers of Shanghai '98
The Flowers of War '11
The Forbidden Kingdom '08
Formula 17 '04
14 Blades '14
The General Died at Dawn '36 ▸
The Good Earth '37 ▸
The Good, the Bad, the Weird '08
Goodbye, Dragon Inn '03
The Grandmaster '13
The Great Magician '11
A Great Wall '86 ▸
The Great Wall '17
The Guardsman '15
Happy Times '00
The Hatchet Man '32
Hero '02 ▸
House of Flying Daggers '04 ▸
The Inn of the Sixth Happiness '58 ▸
International Settlement '38
Ip Man 3 '16
Ip Man '08
Iron & Silk '91
Jade Warrior '06
Jet Li's Fearless '06
John Rabe '09
Journey to the West '14
The Joy Luck Club '93 ▸
Ju Dou '90 ▸
The Karate Kid '10
The Keys of the Kingdom '44 ▸
Kill Bill Vol. 2 '04 ▸
The Killer '90 ▸
The King of Masks '99 ▸
Kingdom of Blood: The Final Battle '16
Kung Fu Hustle '04
Kung Fu Panda '08 ▸
Kung Fu Panda 2 '11 ▸
Kung Fu Panda 3 '16 ▸
Lan Yu '01
The Last Emperor '87 ▸
The Last Time I Saw Macao '13
The Lost Bladesman '16
The Lost Empire '01
Lust, Caution '07
M. Butterfly '93
The Man with the Iron Fists '12
Mao's Last Dancer '09
Marco Polo '07
Mission: Impossible 3 '06 ▸
Mr. Wu '27
Mountains May Depart '16 ▸
Mulan 2 '04
Mulan '98
The Mummy: Tomb of the Dragon Emperor '08
Ne Zha '19
1911 '11
Not One Less '99
Oil for the Lamps of China '35
Old Stone '16
Once Upon a Time in China '91 ▸
Once Upon a Time in China III '93 ▸
One Child Nation '19 ▸
The Painted Veil '06
Pandas '18 ▸
Pavilion of Women '01
The Promise '05
Purple Butterfly '03 ▸
Railroad Tigers '17
Raise the Red Lantern '91 ▸
Red Cliff '08 ▸
Red Corner '97
Red Firecracker, Green Firecracker '93
The Red Violin '98
Reign of Assassins '10
Rhapsody of Spring '98
Riding Alone for Thousands of Miles '05
The Road Home '01 ▸
The Sand Pebbles '66 ▸
Secret Agent of Japan '42
Seventh Moon '08
Shadow Magic '00
Shanghai '09 ▸
Shanghai Express '32 ▸
Shanghai Triad '95 ▸
Skyscraper '18
S.M.A.R.T. Chase '18
Smile '05
Snow Flower and the Secret Fan '11
Soldier of Fortune '55
The Sorcerer and the White Snake '13
Spy Game '01
The Story of Qiu Ju '91 ▸
Summer Palace '06 ▸
Tai-Pan '86
Tell It to the Marines '26
Temptation of a Monk '94
Temptress Moon '96
Thank you, Mr. Moto '37
Think Fast, Mr. Moto '37
Three Kingdoms: Resurrection of the Dragon '08
To Live '94 ▸
Together '02
A Touch of Sin '13 ▸
2046 '04
Typhoon '06
The Wandering Earth '19
Warlords '08 ▸
What Women Want '10
The White Countess '05 ▸
The Wild Goose Lake '20
Wolf Totem '15
Women from the Lake of Scented Souls '94
The Wooden Man's Bride '94
The World of Suzie Wong '60
Xiu Xiu: The Sent Down Girl '97 ▸
Zhou Yu's Train '02

Christianity

***See** Religion; Religious Epics*

Christmas

***See also** Holidays; Horrible Holidays*

All I Want for Christmas '91
All I Want for Christmas '07
All Through the House '15
Almost Christmas '16
Alvin and the Chipmunks '07
An American Christmas Carol '79
American Gun '02 ▸
And So They Were Married '36
Angels Sing '13
Annie Claus is Coming to Town '11
Arthur Christmas '11
ATM '12
Babes in Toyland '61
A Bad Moms Christmas '17
Bad Santa 2 '16
Bad Santa '03
Batman Returns '92
Battle of the Bulbs '10
Beethoven's Christmas Adventure '11
Believe '16
A Belle for Christmas '14
Ben Is Back '18
Bernard and the Genie '91
The Best Man Holiday '13
Better Watch Out '17
Bikini Bloodbath Christmas '09
The Bishop's Wife '47 ▸
Black Christmas '75
Black Christmas '06
Black Christmas '19
Black Nativity '13
Blast of Silence '61
A Boyfriend for Christmas '04
Breakaway '02
Call Me Claus '01
Call Me Mrs. Miracle '10
Cancel Christmas '11
The Case for Christmas '11
Cast Away '00 ▸
Chasing Christmas '05
The Children '08
Christmas, Again '15
Christmas Angel '09
Christmas Angel '11
Christmas at Water's Edge '04
The Christmas Blessing '05
The Christmas Box '95
Christmas Caper '07
The Christmas Card '06
A Christmas Carol '38 ▸
A Christmas Carol '51 ▸
A Christmas Carol '84 ▸
A Christmas Carol '99
A Christmas Carol '09
Christmas Child '03
The Christmas Choir '08
The Christmas Clause '08
Christmas Comes Home to Canaan '11
Christmas Comes to Willow Creek '87
The Christmas Consultant '12
The Christmas Cottage '08
Christmas Cupid '10
Christmas Do-Over '06
Christmas Eve '15
Christmas Evil '80
The Christmas Hope '09
A Christmas Horror Story '15
Christmas in Boston '05
Christmas in Canaan '09
Christmas in Compton '12
Christmas in Connecticut '45 ▸
Christmas in Connecticut '92
Christmas In Conway '13
Christmas in July '40 ▸
Christmas in Paradise '07
Christmas in the Clouds '01
Christmas in Wonderland '07
Christmas Lodge '11
Christmas Magic '11
Christmas Mail '10
The Christmas Miracle of Jonathan Toomey '07
Christmas on Mars '08
The Christmas Ornament '13
The Christmas Pageant '11
A Christmas Proposal '08
The Christmas Shoes '02
A Christmas Story 2 '12
A Christmas Story '83 ▸
A Christmas Tale '08 ▸
The Christmas That Almost Wasn't '66
Christmas Town '08
A Christmas Tree Miracle '13
A Christmas Wedding '06
A Christmas Wedding Tail '11
The Christmas Wife '88
A Christmas Wish '11
Christmas with Holly '12
Christmas With the Kranks '04
A Christmas Without Snow '80
Come Dance With Me '12
Comfort and Joy '03
Cover Up '49
Crazy for Christmas '05
The Crossing '00
A Dad for Christmas '06
Daddy's Home 2 '17
The Dead '87 ▸
Dear Santa '98
Dear Santa '11
Debbie Macomber's Trading Christmas '11
Deck the Halls '06
A Dennis the Menace Christmas '07
Die Hard '88 ▸
Diner '82 ▸
Dr. Seuss' How the Grinch Stole Christmas '00
A Dog Named Christmas '09
The Dog Who Saved Christmas '09
The Dog Who Saved Christmas Vacation '10
The Dog Who Saved the Holidays '12
Dondi '61
Don't Open Till Christmas '84
Dorm That Dripped Blood '82
Elf '03 ▸
Ernest Saves Christmas '88

Exit Speed '08
Expired '07
F6 Twister '12
Fall Down Dead '07
The Family Holiday '07
Family Man '00
The Family Stone '05
Felicidades '00
Filth '13
The Fitzgerald Family Christmas '12
Fitzwilly '67
Four Christmases '08
Fred Claus '07
Friday After Next '02
Friends & Lovers '99
Frozen River '08 ▶
Funny Farm '88
Gangster Squad '13
The Gathering '77
The Gathering: Part 2 '79
George Balanchine's The Nutcracker '93
The Gift of Love '90
Gift of the Magi '10
Go '99 ▶
A Golden Christmas 2: The Second Tail '11
A Golden Christmas '09
The Good Witch's Gift '10
A Grandpa for Christmas '07
Gremlins '84 ▶
Happy Christmas '14
Heidi '37
Heidi '67
Heidi '93 ▶
Hell's Heroes '30
Here Comes Santa Claus '84
Hi-Life '98
His and Her Christmas '05
Hitched for the Holidays '12
Hoax for the Holidays '10
Hobo's Christmas '87
Hogfather '06
The Holiday '06
Holiday Affair '49
Holiday Baggage '08
A Holiday Heist '11
Holiday in Handcuffs '07
Holiday in the Wild '19
Holiday Inn '42 ▶
Holiday Rush '19
Holiday Spin '12
Holiday Switch '07
Holiday Wishes '06
Holly's Holiday '12
Home Alone '90 ▶
Home Alone 2: Lost in New York '92
Home Alone 3 '97
Home Alone: The Holiday Heist '12
Home By Christmas '06
Home for Christmas '90
Homecoming '09
Homecoming: A Christmas Story '71
The Horses of McBride '12
A House Without a Christmas Tree '72
The Ice Harvest '05
I'll Be Home for Christmas '98
I'll Be Seeing You '44
It Came Upon a Midnight Clear '84
It Happened on 5th Avenue '47
It's a Wonderful Life '46 ▶
Jack Frost '98
Jingle All the Way 2 '14
Jingle All the Way '96
Joyeux Noel '05 ▶
Junior Miss '45
Just Friends '05
Klaus '19 ▶
The Knight Before Christmas '19
Kramer *vs.* Kramer '79 ▶
Krampus '15
La Buche '00
Lady on a Train '45 ▶
Last Christmas '19
Last Ounce of Courage '12
The Lemon Drop Kid '51
Let It Snow '19
Lethal Weapon '87 ▶
The Lion in Winter '68 ▶
The Lion in Winter '03 ▶
The Little Drummer Girl '84 ▶
Little Women '94 ▶
The Long Kiss Goodnight '96
Look Who's Talking Now '93
Lost Holiday: The Jim & Suzanne Shemwell Story '07
Love Actually '03
Love at the Christmas Table '12
Lovely, Still '08
Love's Christmas Journey '11
Lucky Christmas '11
Ma Saison Preferee '93 ▶
Make the Yuletide Gay '09
The Man Who Invented Christmas '17
March of the Wooden Soldiers '34 ▶
The March Sisters at Christmas '12
Merry Christmas, Mr. Lawrence '83 ▶
The Merry Gentleman '08
Merry In-Laws '12
A Midnight Clear '92 ▶
Midnight Clear '06
A Midwinter's Tale '95
Miracle at Sage Creek '05
Miracle in the Wilderness '91
Miracle on 34th Street '47 ▶
Miracle on 34th Street '94
Mrs. Miracle '09
Mrs. Santa Claus '96
Mr. St. Nick '02
Mr. Soft Touch '49
Mistletoe Over Manhattan '11
Mixed Nuts '94
Moonlight & Mistletoe '08
The Most Wonderful Time of the Year '08
The Muppet Christmas Carol '92
My Uncle: The Alien '96
A Nanny for Christmas '10
National Lampoon's Christmas Vacation 2: Cousin Eddie's Big Island Adventure '03
National Lampoon's Christmas Vacation '89
The National Tree '09
The Night Before '15
The Night Before the Night Before Christmas '10
The Night of the Hunter '55 ▶
Night Train '09
The Nightmare Before Christmas '93 ▶
Noel '04
Noelle '19
Northpole '14
Nothing Like the Holidays '08
November Christmas '10
The Nutcracker and the Four Realms '18
The Nutcracker Prince '91
Off Season '01
Office Christmas Party '16
Oh Christmas Tree! '13
On Strike for Christmas '10
One Christmas '95
One Magic Christmas '85
P2 '07
Parental Guidance '98
A Perfect Day '06
The Perfect Holiday '07
The Polar Express '04
Powder Blue '09
Prancer '89
Prancer Returns '01
The Preacher's Wife '96
Pride and Glory '08
A Princess for Christmas '11
'R Xmas '01
The Railway Children '70 ▶
Rare Exports: A Christmas Tale '10
Recipe for a Perfect Christmas '05
The Ref '93 ▶
Reindeer Games '00
Remember the Night '40 ▶
The Resurrection of Gavin Stone '17
Riot '96
The Robe '53
Roots: The Gift '88
A Royal Christmas '14
Santa & Me '13
Santa and Pete '99
Santa Baby '06
Santa Baby 2: Santa Maybe '09
Santa Buddies '09
Santa Claus Conquers the Martians '64
Santa Claus: The Movie '85
The Santa Clause '94
The Santa Clause 2 '02
The Santa Clause 3: The Escape Clause '06
The Santa Incident '10
Santa Paws 2: The Santa Pups '12
The Santa Suit '10
The Santa Trap '02
Saving Christmas '14
Scrooge '70
Scrooged '88
The Search for Santa Paws '10
A Season for Miracles '99
Sheitan '06
Signed, Sealed, Delivered for Christmas '14
Silent Night '02
Silent Night '12
Silent Night, Deadly Night '84
Silent Night, Deadly Night 2 '87
Silent Night, Deadly Night 3: Better Watch Out! '89
Silent Night, Deadly Night 5: The Toymaker '91
Christmas All Over Again '16
Sleepless in Seattle '93 ▶
Small Town Santa '14
Snow '04
Snow 2: Brain Freeze '08
A Snow Globe Christmas '13
Snowglobe '07
Snowmen '10
Stalag 17 '53 ▶
The Star '17
A Star for Christmas '12
The Sum of Us '94 ▶
Surviving Christmas '04
Susan Slept Here '54
Tenth Avenue Angel '47
This Christmas '07
Three Godfathers '36
Three Godfathers '48 ▶
Three Wise Women '11
To Grandmother's House We Go '94
Together Again for the First Time '08
Too Cool for Christmas '04
The Town That Banned Christmas '06
Trading Places '83
Trail of Robin Hood '50
Trapped in Paradise '94
The Traveler '10
Turbulence '96
12 Christmas Wishes For My Dog '11
The Twelve Days of Christmas Eve '04
12 Disasters '12
The Twelve Dogs of Christmas '05
12 Dogs of Christmas: Great Puppy Rescue '12
12 Men of Christmas '09
24 Nights '99
Tyler Perry's A Madea Christmas '13
Unaccompanied Minors '06
Uncle Nick '15
Under the Mistletoe '06
Untamed Heart '93
A Very Harold & Kumar Christmas '11
A Very Mary Christmas '10
A Very Merry Mix-Up '13
Visions of Sugarplums '99
Where God Left His Shoes '07
While She Was Out '08
While You Were Sleeping '95 ▶
White Christmas '54 ▶
White Reindeer '13
Who Slew Auntie Roo? '71
Why Him? '16
Will You Merry Me? '08

Church Choirs

***See also** Gospel Music; Nuns & Priests*

Amazing Grace '19 ▶
As It Is In Heaven '04
Bite '16
The Chorus '04
The Christmas Choir '08
A Christmas Without Snow '80
The Fighting Temptations '03
First Sunday '08
Gabrielle '13 ▶
The Gospel '05 ▶
I Can Only Imagine '18
Let It Shine '12
The Preacher's Wife '96
Preaching to the Choir '05
Sister Act '92
Sister Act 2: Back in the Habit '93
Sunday School Musical '08

CIA/NSA

***See also** Foreign Intrigue; Spies & Espionage*

The A-Team '10 ▶
Act of Valor '12
Agent Cody Banks '03
Altered Minds '13
The Amateur '82
American Assassin '17
American Made '17
American Ultra '15
Anna '19
Argo '12 ▶
Army of One '16
The Assignment '97
Avalanche Express '79
Bad Company '02
Ballistic: Ecks *vs.* Sever '02
Ballistica '10
Bang! Bang! You're Dead! '66
A Beautiful Mind '01 ▶
Beirut '18
Black Dawn '05
Black Water '18
Bloodfist 8: Hard Way Out '96
Body of Lies '08
Bomb Squad '97
The Bourne Legacy '12 ▶
The Bourne Supremacy '04 ▶
The Bourne Ultimatum '07 ▶
Burn After Reading '08
Call Me Bwana '63
The Capitol Conspiracy '99
Central Intelligence '16
Chain Reaction '96
Charlie Wilson's War '07
C.I.A.: Code Name Alexa '92
C.I.A. 2: Target Alexa '94
Class of 1999 2: The Substitute '93
Clear and Present Danger '94
The Cold Light of Day '12
The Company '07
Company Business '91
Confessions of a Dangerous Mind '02
Connor's War '06
Conspiracy of Fear '96
Conspiracy Theory '97 ▶
Contract Killers '08
Contract to Kill '16
Countdown: Jerusalem '09
Crackerjack 3 '00
Crash & Byrnes '99
Crimes of the Past '09
Criminal '16
The Crocodile Hunter: Collision Course '02
Decommissioned '16
The Defector '66
The Detonator '06
Diplomatic Siege '99
Domino '19
The Double '11
The Double Man '67
Double Team '97
D.R.E.A.M. Team '99
Drone '17
Dying of the Light '14
The Eiger Sanction '75
Enemies Among Us '10
The Expendables 2 '12
The Expendables 3 '14
Exterminator '80
Extraction '15
Extreme Limits '01
Eye See You '01
Eyeborgs '09
Fair Game '10 ▶
Farewell '09 ▶
Fay Grim '06
Felony '95
A Few Days in September '06
The Fourth Angel '01
Game of Death '10
The Girl Who Knew Too Much '69
The Glimmer Man '96
A Good Day to Die Hard '13
Good Kill '15
The Good Shepherd '06
Harold & Kumar Escape from Guantanamo Bay '08
Hudson Hawk '91
The Hunt for Red October '90 ▶
The In-Laws '03
Innocent Bystanders '72
The Interview '14
Jack Ryan: Shadow Recruit '14
Jason Bourne '16
Just Another Secret '89
Kill Castro '80
Kill the Messenger '14 ▶
Killer Likes Candy '78
Knock Off '98
The Kremlin Letter '70
The Listening '06
The Long Kiss Goodnight '96
Lumumba '01 ▶
Man On a String '60
Man on Fire '04
Mark Felt: The Man Who Brought Down the White House '17
Maximum Conviction '12
Maximum Impact '18
Memoirs of an Invisible Man '92
MI-5 '15
Mile 22 '18
Militia '99
Mission: Impossible 2 '00 ▶
Mission: Impossible '96 ▶
Mission: Impossible-Fallout '18 ▶
Most Wanted '97
My Brother's War '97
My Little Assassin '99
My Spy '19
Nixon '95 ▶
No Safe Haven '87
Nothing But the Truth '08 ▶
The November Man '14
The Numbers Station '13
The Objective '08
Once Upon a Time in Mexico '03 ▶
Operation Avalanche '16
Operation C.I.A. '65
Pandora's Clock '96
Patriot Games '92 ▶
The Peacemaker '97
The Price of the Bride '90
Puerto Vallarta Squeeze '04
The Quiet American '02 ▶
Rain Fall '09
The Recruit '03
RED '10
Red Serpent '02
Rendition '07
The Report '19
Safe House '12
Sahara '05
The Sellout '76
The Shadow Conspiracy '96
Shadow Man '06
The Siege '98
Silent Partner '05
The Situation '06
Sky High '84
Sniper 3 '04
Snowden '16
The Spanish Prisoner '97 ▶
Spartan '04 ▶
The Speed of Thought '11
Spies Like Us '85
The Spook Who Sat by the Door '73
Spy '15 ▶
Spy Games '99
Sticks '98
Subterfuge '98
The Sum of All Fears '02
Sunstorm '01
Swordfish '01
Syriana '05 ▶
The Take '16
Target '85
Target of Opportunity '04
This Means War '12
3 Days to Kill '14
Time Lapse '01
To the Limit '95
Traitor '08
Unlocked '17
The Venetian Affair '67
The Waiting Game '98
Washington: Behind Closed Doors '77
White Sands '92
X-Men: First Class '11 ▶
XXX '02
XXX: State of the Union '05
Yuri Nosenko, KGB '86
Zero Dark Thirty '12 ▶
Zero Days '16
Zero Tolerance '15

Cincinnati

***See also** America's Heartland*

Airborne '93
Beloved '98
Dirty Pictures '00
Eight Men Out '88 ▶
Fresh Horses '88
The Great Buck Howard '09 ▶
Hustle '04
Jimmy & Judy '06
Kit Kittredge: An American Girl '08
Pride of Jesse Hallum '81
Scream 2 '97 ▶
Wild Hogs '07
With a Song in My Heart '52 ▶

Cinderella Stories

Angus '95
Another Cinderella Story '08
Arthur '81 ▶
Au Pair 2: The Fairy Tale Continues '01
Au Pair '99
B.A.P.'s '97
Beauty and the Boss '33
Boogie Nights '97 ▶
Born Yesterday '50 ▶
Born Yesterday '93
Camp Rock '08
Celestial Clockwork '94
The Church Mouse '34
Cinderella '50 ▶
Cinderella Man '05 ▶
A Cinderella Story '04
A Cinderella Story: Once Upon a Song '11
Cinderfella '60
Dreamer: Inspired by a True Story '05
Ella Enchanted '04 ▶
Ever After: A Cinderella Story '98 ▶
Evita '96
First Love '39
Flashdance '83
For Real '02
Geek Charming '11
The Glass Slipper '55
Hands of Stone '16
Hero '92 ▶
Just Friends '05
The Little Mermaid '89 ▶
The Love Trap '29
Maid in Manhattan '02
Maid to Order '87
Milk Money '94
The Mirror Has Two Faces '96
Mrs. Winterbourne '96

▶ = rated three bones or higher

Mister Cinderella '36
Monte Carlo '11
More Than a Miracle '67
My Fair Lady '64 ▶
Once Around '91
Picture This! '08
Pretty Woman '90 ▶
The Prince & Me '04
The Princess Diaries 2: Royal Engagement '04
The Princess Diaries '01
A Princess for Christmas '11
Pygmalion '38 ▶
Rags '12
The Red Mill '27
Saint Ralph '04
Sally '29
She's All That '99
The Slipper and the Rose '76
Splash '84
A Star Is Born '37 ▶
This Is the Night '32
Up Close and Personal '96 ▶
Working Girl '88 ▶
The World of Suzie Wong '60

Circuses

***See** Carnivals & Clowns*

City-Squishing Behemoths

***See also** Alien Beings--Vicious; Monster Yuks*

Atragon '63
Cloverfield '08
Colossal '17
Death Kappa '10
Dragon Wars '07
Frankenstein Conquers the World '64
Gamera the Brave '06
The Giant Behemoth '59
Godzilla '98
Godzilla '14 ▶
Godzilla Against Mechagodzilla '02
Godzilla: Final Wars '04
Godzilla, King of the Monsters '56
Godzilla: King of the Monsters '19
Godzilla, Mothra, and King Ghidorah: Giant Monsters All-Out Attack '01
Godzilla-Tokyo S.O.S. '03
Godzilla vs. Destroyah '95
Godzilla vs. Megaguirus '00
Godzilla vs. Mothra '92
Godzilla vs. SpaceGodzilla '94
Hellboy II: The Golden Army '08 ▶
Jack the Giant Killer '13
King Kong Escapes '67
Kraa! the Sea Monster '98
Legend of the Dinosaurs and Monster Birds '77
Mega Shark vs. Crocosaurus '10
Negadon: The Monster from Mars '05
Pacific Rim '13
Pacific Rim: Uprising '18
Shin Godzilla '16
Transformers: The Last Knight '17
War of the Colossal Beast '58

Civil Rights

***See also** Apartheid; Slavery*

Ali '01
The Autobiography of Miss Jane Pittman '74 ▶
The Best of Enemies '19
Betty & Coretta '13
Blood Done Sign My Name '10
Bloody Sunday '01 ▶
Boycott '02 ▶
Bucktown '75
Cesar Chavez '14
The Color Purple '85 ▶
The Conversation '74 ▶
Crazy in Alabama '99
Dangerous Evidence: The Lori Jackson Story '99
Detroit '17 ▶
Driving Miss Daisy '89 ▶
A Dry White Season '89 ▶
The Express '08
Final Comedown '72
For One Night '06
Free, White, and 21 '62
Freedom Road '79
Freedom Song '00 ▶
Freedom Summer '14
Gang in Blue '96
George Wallace '97
Get On the Bus '96 ▶
Ghosts of Mississippi '96
Gospel Hill '08
The Great Debaters '07 ▶
Hairspray '07 ▶
Half Slave, Half Free '85
Hawmps! '76
The Heart of Dixie '89
Hidden Agenda '90
I Am Not Your Negro '17 ▶
Just Mercy '19 ▶
King '78 ▶
The Kitchen Toto '87 ▶
The Lawless '50
Long Shadows '86
The Long Walk Home '89 ▶
Loving '16 ▶
Marshall '17
The McMasters '70
Mississippi Burning '88 ▶
Mr. & Mrs. Loving '96 ▶
Not Like Everyone Else '06
On the Basis of Sex '18
Panther '95
RBG '18 ▶
The Red Fury '84
The Ring '52
The Rising Place '02
The Rosa Parks Story '02
Rosewood '96 ▶
Ruby Bridges '98
Seberg '19
The Secret Life of Bees '08 ▶
Selma '14 ▶
Selma, Lord, Selma '99
A Soldier's Story '84 ▶
The Trials of Muhammad Ali '13 ▶
The Two of Us '68 ▶
The Untold Story of Emmett Louis Till '05 ▶
We of the Never Never '82 ▶
What Happened, Miss Simone? '15 ▶
WUSA '70

Civil War

***See also** American South; Period Piece: 19th Century; Southern Belles*

Abraham Lincoln '30
Abraham Lincoln: Vampire Hunter '12
Advance to the Rear '64
Alvarez Kelly '66
Andersonville '95 ▶
The Andersonville Trial '70 ▶
Bad Company '72 ▶
Band of Angels '57
Barbara Frietchie '24
The Beguiled '70 ▶
The Beguiled '17
The Birth of a Nation '15 ▶
The Black Dakotas '54
The Blue and the Gray '82
The Bushwackers '52
Bushwick '17
California '77
Cavalry Charge '51
Cold Brook '18
Cold Mountain '03 ▶
The Conspirator '10
Copper Canyon '50
Copperhead '13
CSA: The Confederate States of America '04
Dark Command '40 ▶
Dead Birds '04
Death of a Nation '18
Drums in the Deep South '51
Escape from Fort Bravo '53
Field of Lost Shoes '14
Fort Defiance '51
Fort Yuma Gold '66
Friendly Persuasion '56 ▶
The General '26 ▶
Gettysburg '93 ▶
The Ghost Brigade '93
Glory '89 ▶
Gods and Generals '03
Golden Girl '51
Gone with the Wind '39 ▶
The Good, the Bad and the Ugly '67 ▶
Gore Vidal's Lincoln '88
The Great Locomotive Chase '56
Gun for 100 Graves '68
Hangman's Knot '52
Hatfields & McCoys '12 ▶
Hellbenders '67
Hellgate '52
The Horse Soldiers '59
How the West Was Won '63 ▶
The Hunley '99
Innocent Voices '04
It Happened in New Orleans '36
Johnny Shiloh '63
Kansas Pacific '53
Kansas Raiders '50
The Keeping Room '15
Killing Lincoln '13
The Last Confederate: The Story of Robert Adams '05
The Last Face '17
Last Stand at Saber River '96
Lincoln '12 ▶
Little Women '33 ▶
Little Women '49 ▶
Little Women '78
Little Women '94 ▶
The Littlest Rebel '35
The Love Letter '98
Love Me Tender '56
The McMasters '70
Menace on the Mountain '70
Mysterious Island '61 ▶
North and South Book 1 '85 ▶
North and South Book 2 '86 ▶
Of Human Hearts '38
The Old Maid '39 ▶
Oldest Confederate Widow Tells All '95 ▶
Operator 13 '34
The Ordeal of Dr. Mudd '80 ▶
The Outlaw Josey Wales '76 ▶
The Outriders '50
Pharoah's Army '95
Queen '93 ▶
Raiders of Ghost City '44
Raintree County '57
Rebel in Town '56
Rebel Vixens '69
The Red Badge of Courage '51 ▶
Ride with the Devil '99
Rocky Mountain '50
The Romance of Rosy Ridge '47
The Rose and the Jackal '90
The Sacketts '79
Sahara '05
Shadow of Chikara '77
The Shadow Riders '82
Shenandoah '65 ▶
Siege at Red River '54
Sommersby '93
South of St. Louis '48
A Southern Yankee '48
Swanee River '39
True Women '97
The Undefeated '69
Virginia City '40 ▶
War Flowers '12
Westbound '58
Woman They Almost Lynched '53
Yellowneck '55

Civil War (non U.S.)

***See also** Genocide/Ethnic Cleansing; Spanish Civil War; War, General*

Beirut '18
Black Ops '20
Darfur Now '07
Dheepan '16
A Field in England '14 ▶
For Greater Glory '12
The Good Lie '14
Guernica '16
Incendies '10 ▶
John Carter '12
Last Men In Aleppo '17 ▶
Of Gods and Men '10 ▶
Pillars of the Earth '10
Rambo '08
To Kill a King '03
24: Redemption '08
White Material '10

Classic Horror

***See** Horror Anthology*

Clergymen

***See also** Nuns & Religion; Religious Epics*

Adventure in Baltimore '49
All Saints '17
Angel Baby '61
Angels and Insects '95 ▶
The Apostle '97 ▶
As It Is In Heaven '04
Avenging Angel '07
Because of Winn-Dixie '05
The Birth of a Nation '16
The Bishop's Wife '47 ▶
Black Nativity '13
Blood Done Sign My Name '10
The Bridge of San Luis Rey '05
Brimstone '17
Captain Salvation '27
Changeling '08 ▶
The Club '16 ▶
Cold Turkey '71 ▶
A Congregation of Ghosts '09
Corpus Christi '19 ▶
Creation '09
Darklight '04
Devotion '46
Dragnet '87
Elmer Gantry '60 ▶
The Europeans '79 ▶
First Reformed '17
First Sunday '08
Footloose '84
Footloose '11
Get Low '09 ▶
God's Not Dead '14
The Good Catholic '17
The Gospel '05 ▶
The Grace Card '11
Hallelujah! '29 ▶
Heaven With a Gun '69
Home Movie '08
The Hustle '08
The Identical '14
The King '05
Ladies of the House '08
Let It Shine '12
Little Church Around the Corner '23
Little Minister '34 ▶
A Man Called Peter '55 ▶
Mercy Streets '00
Middletown '06
Miss Sadie Thompson '53 ▶
Mr. Belvedere Rings the Bell '51
Mitch Albom's Have a Little Faith '11
My Wife's Best Friend '52
The Night of the Hunter '55 ▶
Night on Earth '91 ▶
Noah's Ark '28
One Foot in Heaven '41
Outlaws and Angels '16
The Pastor's Wife '11
Pillars of the Earth '10
Polly of the Circus '32
Preacher's Kid '10
The Preacher's Wife '96
Purlie Victorious '63
The Quick and the Dead '95
Rain '32
The Rector's Wife '94
Red Riding, Part 1: 1974 '09
Red Riding, Part 2: 1980 '09
Red Riding, Part 3: 1983 '09
Red State '11
Rust '09
Salvation Boulevard '11
Saving God '08
The Scarlet Letter '34
The Scarlet Letter '73 ▶
The Scarlet Letter '79 ▶
The Scarlet Letter '95
The Second Chance '06
Secrets of Eden '12
Serious Charge '59
Signs '02 ▶
Silence '16 ▶
Sirens '94
Snow White: A Deadly Summer '12
Something Beneath '07
Sunday School Musical '08
Valerie '57
A Walk to Remember '02
The Windsplitter '71
Wise Blood '79 ▶
Woman, Thou Art Loosed '04
WWJD: What Would Jesus Do? '10

Cleveland

***See also** America's Heartland; Cincinnati; Ohio*

Against the Ropes '04
American Splendor '03 ▶
Antwone Fisher '02 ▶
Draft Day '14
The Fortune Cookie '66 ▶
Howard the Duck '86
The Kid From Cleveland '49
Kill the Irishman '11
The Land '16
Major League '89
Major League 2 '94
The Oh in Ohio '06
The Rocker '08
The Soloist '09
Stranger than Paradise '84 ▶
Uptight '68
Welcome to Collinwood '02
Wild Boys of the Road '33

Cloning Around

Alien: Resurrection '97 ▶
Astro-Zombies M3: Cloned '10
Attack of the Sabretooth '05
The Boys from Brazil '78
Clone '05
Clone Hunter '09
The Clonus Horror '79
D'Agostino '12
Godsend '04
Hitman: Agent 47 '15
The Island '05
Jurassic Park '93 ▶
The Last Sentinel '07
Leroy and Stitch '06
The Lost World: Jurassic Park 2 '97
Moon '09
Multiplicity '96
Never Let Me Go '10
Repli-Kate '01
Replicant '01
Resident Evil: Extinction '07
Resurrection of Zachary Wheeler '71
The 6th Day '00
Species '95
Species 2 '98
Species 4: The Awakening '07
Spy Kids '01 ▶
Star Trek: Nemesis '02
Star Wars: Episode 2-Attack of the Clones '02 ▶
Strange New World '75
2001: A Space Travesty '00
Womb '10

Clowns

***See also** Carnivals & Killer Clowns*

All Hallow's Eve '13
Carnival of Souls '98
Clown '16
Clown Murders '83
Clownhouse '88
The Clowns '71 ▶
The Court Jester '56 ▶
The Family Jewels '65
The Funhouse '81
Funland '89
He Who Gets Slapped '24 ▶
House of 1000 Corpses '03
It '17 ▶
It Chapter Two '19
Joker '19 ▶
Killer Klowns from Outer Space '88
The Man Who Laughs '27 ▶
Mr. Jingles '06
Painted Hero '95
Pee-wee's Big Adventure '85 ▶
Poltergeist '82 ▶
Quick Change '90
Rize '05 ▶
Shakes the Clown '92
S.I.C.K. Serial Insane Clown Killer '03
Spawn '97 ▶
Stephen King's It '90
Stitches '12
13 Moons '02
31 '16
To Catch a Killer '92 ▶

Coaches & Managers

Backwards '12
Bad Parents '12
Benched '18
Bleed for This '16
Calvin Marshall '09
Cowgirls 'n Angels '12
Crooked Arrows '12
Cyber Seduction: His Secret Life '05
D2: The Mighty Ducks '94
Dear Lemon Lima '09
The 5th Quarter '10
Game Time: Tackling the Past '11
The Great American Pastime '56
Grown Ups '10
Hands of Stone '16
Home Run Showdown '10
The Hot Flashes '13
Huddle '32
Hurricane Season '09
In Search of Greatness '18 ▶
McFarland USA '15
Men with Brooms '02
The Mighty Ducks '92
Miles from Nowhere '09
Miracle '04 ▶
The Oklahoma City Dolls '81
Overcomer '19
The Perfect Game '09
Personal Best '82 ▶
Playing for Keeps '12
Pretty Maids All In a Row '71
Racing for Time '08
Touchback '11
The Way Back '20
When the Game Stands Tall '14
Win Win '11
The Winning Season '09
The Yankles '09

Coast Guard

***See also** Military: Navy; Sail Away*

Don Winslow of the Coast Guard '43
The Finest Hours '16
The Guardian '06
Waking the Dead '00
Wetbacks '56
The Woman on the Beach '47
Yours, Mine & Ours '05

Cockroaches

***See also** Killer Bugs and Slugs*

Addicted to Love '96
Bird on a Wire '90
The Craft '96
Creepshow '82
Honey, We Shrunk Ourselves '97
Joe's Apartment '96
Just Married '03
Men in Black '97 ▶
Mimic '97
The Nest '88
Pacific Heights '90 ▶
Shinbone Alley '70
Team America: World Police '04 ▶
Vampire's Kiss '88 ▶
WALL-E '08 ▶

▶ = rated three bones or higher

Cold Spots

The Abominable Snowman '57
Absolute Zero '05
Absolution '97
Adam Sandler's 8 Crazy Nights '02
Adult World '13
Alaska '96
Alien *vs.* Predator '04
And So They Were Married '36
Arctic Blue '93
Arctic Dogs '19
Arctic Tale '07
Atomic Submarine '59
Avalanche '99
Balto '95
The Big Push '75
Black Cadillac '03
Bluebird '13
Boa '02
Bog '84
Call of the Wild '93
The Call of the Wild '20
Chalet Girls '11
Challenge To Be Free '76
Chasing Ice '12►
Chilly Dogs '01
Christmas Comes to Willow Creek '87
Climbing High '38
Cold Prey II '08
Cool Runnings '93
Courage Mountain '89
The Crimson Rivers '01
Cry of the Penguins '71
The Day the Earth Froze '59
Dead of Winter '87►
Dead Snow '09
Dead Snow: Red *vs.* Dead '14►
Devil's Island '96
Devil's Pass '13
Die Another Day '02
Doctor Zhivago '65►
The Donner Party '09
The Double Man '67
Downhill Willie '96
Edge of Winter '16
The Eiger Sanction '75
The Empire Strikes Back '80►
Encounters at the End of the World '07►
Everyman's War '09
Extreme Ops '02
Fallen Angel '03
Far North '07
The Fast Runner '01►
The Fate of the Furious '17
Feed the Fish '09
Firefox '82
Fixed Bayonets! '51►
The Forbidden Quest '93
Force Majeure '14►
The Frankenstein Theory '13
Fred Claus '07
Freezer '14
Friends & Lovers '99
Frozen '10
Frozen '13►
Frozen River '08►
Get Yourself a College Girl '64
The Golden Compass '07
Good Neighbors '10
Happy Feet '06►
Happy Feet Two '11
Heart of Light '97
The Heroes of Telemark '65
How I Ended This Summer '10
I Met Him in Paris '37
Ice Age '02►
Ice Age: Collision Course '16
Ice Age: Continental Drift '12
Ice Age: Dawn of the Dinosaurs '09
Ice Men '04
Ice Palace '60
Ice Quake '10
The Ice Runner '93
Ice Soldiers '13
Ice Spiders '07
Ice Station Zebra '68
Ice Twisters '09
Iceman '19
Into the White '12
Into Thin Air: Death on Everest '97
Iron Will '93
Island in the Sky '53►
Jack Frost 2: Revenge of the Mutant Killer Snowman '00
Jack Frost '98
Jack London's The Call of the Wild '97
Jade Warrior '06
The Juniper Tree '87
Kavik the Wolf Dog '80
Klondike Annie '36
Laila '29
Land Ho! '14
The Last Place on Earth '85
The Last Stop '99
L'Iceberg '05
Lost in Alaska '52
The Lost Zeppelin '29
Lovers of Hate '10
Lovers of the Arctic Circle '98
Map of the Human Heart '93
Meltdown '06
The Mountain Between Us '17
MXP: Most Xtreme Primate '03
Mystery, Alaska '99
Nanook of the North '22►
Never Cry Wolf '83►
Nobody Else But You '11
North Face '08►
North Star '96
North to Alaska '60►
Operation Haylift '50
Ordeal in the Arctic '93
Out Cold '01
The Pebble and the Penguin '94
Post Impact '04
Quest for Fire '82►
Rare Exports: A Christmas Tale '10
Reindeer Games '00
Salmonberries '91
The Santa Clause 2 '02
The Santa Clause 3: The Escape Clause '06
Shackleton '02►
She '35
The Shining '80
Silent Hunter '94
A Simple Plan '98►
Sister '12
Smilla's Sense of Snow '96
Snow Angels '07►
Snow Day '00
The Snow Devils '67
Snow Dogs '02
The Snow Queen '02
Snow Shark '11
The Snow Walker '03
Snowboard Academy '96
Snowbound: The Jim and Jennifer Stolpa Story '94
Snowmen '10
Snowpiercer '14►
Sometimes They Come Back. . . For More '99
Spawn of the North '38
The Spoilers '42►
Spy Games '99
Stargate: Continuum '08
Sub Down '97
Suspended Animation '02
The Thaw '09
The Thing '51►
The Thing '82
The Thing '11
30 Days of Night '07
Titanic 2 '10
Transsiberian '08►
The Troll Hunter '11
Two Night Stand '14
Unaccompanied Minors '06
Vertical Limit '00
The Viking Sagas '95
Virus '82
The White Dawn '75
White Fang 2: The Myth of the White Wolf '94
White Fang '36
White Wolves 3: Cry of the White Wolf '98
Whiteout '09
The Wild Pear Tree '18►
The Wildest Dream: The Conquest of Everest '10
Wind Chill '07
Wind River '17►
Winter a Go-Go '65
Winter Break '02
Winter of Frozen Dreams '08
Winter Passing '05
Winter People '89
Winter Sleepers '97
The Winter War '89►
The X Files: I Want to Believe '08
X2: X-Men United '03►
Yeti '08
Yossi & Jagger '02
Zero Degrees Kelvin '95

Cold War

***See also** Cold War Spies; Communists & Red Scare*

Cold War Spies

***See also** Communists & Red Scare*

Act of War '96
Alamut Ambush '86
Atomic Blonde '17
Avalanche Express '79
Big Jim McLain '52
Billion Dollar Brain '67
Bridge of Spies '15►
Call Me Bwana '63
The Chairman '69
Code Name: Dancer '87
Cold War Killers '86
The Company '07
Company Business '91
Company Man '00
Conspirator '49
Deadly Recruits '86
The Defector '66
A Different Loyalty '04►
Diplomatic Courier '52►
The Eiger Sanction '75
Embassy '72
The English Patient '96►
Enigma '82
The Falcon and the Snowman '85►
Farewell '09
Final Assignment '80
Firefox '82
Firehead '90
For Your Eyes Only '81►
The Fourth Protocol '87►
From Russia with Love '63►
Funeral in Berlin '66►
The Girl Hunters '63
The Good Shepherd '06
Gotcha! '85
The House on Carroll Street '88
The Human Factor '79
The Hunt for Red October '90►
The Ice Runner '93
Ice Station Zebra '68
The In-Laws '79►
The Innocent '93
The Inside Man '84
The Ipcress File '65►
Jet Pilot '57
Jumpin' Jack Flash '86
Kill Castro '80
Laser Mission '90
The Living Daylights '87►
The Looking Glass War '69
M. Butterfly '93
Mackintosh Man '73
Man On a String '60
The Man Who Knew Too Little '97
The Manchurian Candidate '62►
The Mercenaries '80
Nasty Rabbit '64
Night Flight from Moscow '73
Night People '54
No Dead Heroes '87
No Way Out '87►
Octopussy '83
Operation Avalanche '16
Operation C.I.A. '65
The Osterman Weekend '83
Our Man in Havana '59►
The Package '89
The Peking Blond '68
A Perfect Spy '88
Philby, Burgess and MacLean: Spy Scandal of the Century '84
Pickup on South Street '53►
The Prize '63►
Provocateur '96
A Question of Attribution '91
Ravishing Idiot '64
Red Sparrow '18
The Russia House '90
Russian Roulette '75
Scorpio '73
Secret Weapons '85
Sell Out '76
Shack Out on 101 '55►
Sky High '84
Spies Like Us '85
Spy Games '99
The Spy Who Came in from the Cold '65►
S*P*Y*S '74
Steal the Sky '88
Stopover Tokyo '57
The Tamarind Seed '74
Telefon '77
The Thief '52
Tinker Tailor Soldier Spy '11►
Topaz '69►
Torn Curtain '66
Where the Spies Are '65
The Whistle Blower '87►
White Nights '85
Yuri Nosenko, KGB '86

Coma

***See also** Disease of the Week; Doctors & Hospitals & Medicine*

Absolution '05
Anaconda '96
Awakenings '90►
Bad Dreams '88
Between the Darkness and the Dawn '85
The Big Sick '17►
Brainwaves '82
The Brothers Solomon '07
Catfight '17
The Cell '00
Children of the Corn 666: Isaac's Return '99
Columbus '17►
Coma '78►
Coma '12
Critical Care '97
The Dead Zone '02
Devil Doll '64
Eden '98
18 Again! '88
Face/Off '97►
Forever Young '92
Forget Me Not '09
Ghost Dad '90
Good Bye, Lenin! '03►
A Grandpa for Christmas '07
Grindstone Road '07
Halloween 4: The Return of Michael Myers '88
Halloween 5: The Revenge of Michael Myers '89
Hannah Free '09
Hard to Kill '89
Hoax for the Holidays '10
If I Stay '14
Insidious '10
The Invisible '07
Just Another Love Story '08
Just like Heaven '05
Kickin' It Old Skool '07
Kids in the Hall: Brain Candy '96
Kill Bill Vol. 1 '03►
Miss March '09
Monkeybone '01
New Best Friend '02
The 9th Life of Louis Drax '16
The Patience Stone '13►
Patrick '78
Patrick '13
Peppermint '18
Possession '08
Rocky 2 '79
Run & Jump '13
The Safety of Objects '01
Saint Ralph '04
Salvation Boulevard '11
Seven Hours to Judgment '88
Shock! '46
Snow Flower and the Secret Fan '11
Such Good Friends '71
3 Women '77►
28 Days Later '02
Unleashed '05
The Vow '12
Walking Deceased '15
What Matters Most '01
While You Were Sleeping '95►
Working Miracles '10

Comedy

***See also** Black Comedy; Comedy Anthology; Comedy Mystery; Comedy Sci-Fi; Comic Adventure; Crimedy; Detective Spoofs; Genre Spoofs; Horror Comedy; Military Comedy; Musical Comedy; Satire & Screwball Comedy; Showbiz Comedies; Slapstick Comedy; Sports Comedy; Stupid Is...; Western Comedy*

Comedy Anthology

Amazon Women on the Moon '87
And Now for Something Completely Different '72►
Boccaccio '70 '62
Everything You Always Wanted to Know about Sex (But Were Afraid to Ask) '72►
Foreplay '75
The Groove Tube '72
Hollywood Boulevard '76
Kentucky Fried Movie '77►
Looney Looney Looney Bugs Bunny Movie '81►
Monty Python's The Meaning of Life '83►
Movie 43 '13
National Lampoon Goes to the Movies '81
New York Stories '89►
No Sleep 'Til Madison '02
Nora's Hair Salon '04
Plaza Suite '71►
Queen for a Day '51
SuperGuy: Behind the Cape '02
Tunnelvision '76
Woman Times Seven '67
Yours, Mine & Ours '68

Comedy Drama

***See** Black Comedy; Comedy*

Comedy Mystery

***See also** Black Comedy; Comedy; Comedy Drama; Genre Spoofs; Horror Comedy; Satire & Parody*

Adventure in Manhattan '36
Arsene Lupin Returns '38
The Captain Hates the Sea '34
The Cat and the Canary '39
Charade '63►
Clubhouse Detectives '96
Clue '85
Curse of the Pink Panther '83
Dark and Stormy Night '09
Deathtrap '82
Fast and Furious '39
Fast and Loose '39
Fast Company '38
Forty Naughty Girls '37
Get a Clue! '98
Goodbye, Lover '99
The Gracie Allen Murder Case '39
Hail, Caesar! '16►
High Anxiety '77
Hoodwinked '05►
Hostile Makeover '09
It's a Wonderful World '39
Jim Hanvey, Detective '37
Kill or Cure '62
Killer Hair '09
Kiss Kiss Bang Bang '05►
Lady on a Train '45►
Maisie '39
Maisie Goes to Reno '44
The Man with Two Faces '34
Mortal Transfer '01
Murder by Death '76
Murder by Invitation '41
Murder On a Bridle Path '36
Murder On a Honeymoon '35
Murder On the Blackboard '34
Mystery Kids '99
The Notorious Landlady '62
Penguin Pool Murder '32
The Pink Panther '64►
The Pink Panther '06
The Pink Panther Strikes Again '76►
The Plot Thickens '36
The Princess Comes Across '36►
Return of the Pink Panther '74
Revenge of the Pink Panther '78
Safe House '99
The Scenesters '09
Scoop '06
The Sex Thief '74
A Shot in the Dark '64►
Sinister Hands '32
The Smiling Ghost '41
Strange Affair '44
Towards Zero '07
Trail of the Pink Panther '82
Trixie '00
Voulez-Vous Danser avec Moi? '59
Whistling in Brooklyn '43
Whistling in Dixie '42
Whistling in the Dark '41►
The Wives He Forgot '06
Zero Effect '97

Comedy Sci-Fi

***See also** Comedy; Comic Adventure; Genre Spoofs; Satire & Parody*

The Absent-Minded Professor '61►
Absolutely Anything '17
Alien Avengers '96
Aliens in the Attic '09
Attack the Block '11
Baberellas '03
Beach Babes 2: Cave Girl Island '95
Birds Do It '66
Bug Buster '99
Class of Nuke 'Em High 2: Subhumanoid Meltdown '91
Class of Nuke 'Em High 3: The Good, the Bad and the Subhumanoid '94
Class of Nuke 'Em High '86
Clockstoppers '02
Coneheads '93
Destination Mars '06
Dinosaur Valley Girls '96
Earth Girls Are Easy '89
Evolution '01
Freezer Burn: The Invasion of Laxdale '08
From Other Worlds '04
Galaxy Quest '99
Ghost Team '16
Hell Comes to Frogtown '88
Hellboy '04
The Hitchhiker's Guide to the Galaxy '05►
Honey, I Blew Up the Kid '92
Honey, I Shrunk the Kids '89
Honey, We Shrunk Ourselves '97
Horror in the Wind '08
Howard the Duck '86
Ice Pirates '84
The Incredibles '04►
Invasion! '99
Invasion of the Star Creatures '63
Men in Black 2 '02
Men in Black 3 '12
Men in Black '97►
Monarch of the Moon '05

My Favorite Martian '98
My Uncle: The Alien '96
No Men Beyond This Point '15
Paul '11
Petticoat Planet '96
Robot & Frank '12 ▶
Robots '05
Rock Jocks '12
The Rocket Man '54
Sergeant Deadhead '65
Sleeper '73 ▶
Son of Flubber '63
Space Station 76 '14
Spaceballs '87
Spaceship '81
Star Kid '97 ▶
Super Buddies '13
Surge of Power: The Stuff of Heroes '04
Theodore Rex '95
The Watch '12
Wham-Bam, Thank You Spaceman '75
What's Up, Hideous Sun Demon? '83
Zoom '06

Comic Adventure

Adventures in Babysitting '87
The Adventures of Bullwhip Griffin '66
Agent Cody Banks '03
Air America '90
Alien from L.A. '87
All the Way, Boys '73
Alvin and the Chipmunks: Chipwrecked '11
The Ambushers '67
Andy and the Airwave Rangers '89
Angel of H.E.A.T. '82
Angels Hard As They Come '71
Another 48 Hrs. '90
Another Stakeout '93
The Ant Bully '06
Avenging Disco Godfather '76
The Babymakers '12
Back Roads '81
Back to the Future '85 ▶
Back to the Future, Part 2 '89
Back to the Future, Part 3 '90 ▶
Bad Santa 2 '16
Bagdad Cafe '88 ▶
Baywatch '17
Beverly Hills Cop '84
Beverly Hills Cop 2 '87
Beverly Hills Cop 3 '94
The Big Lebowski '97 ▶
The Big Slice '90
The Big White '05
Bingo '91
Bird on a Wire '90
Black Tight Killers '66 ▶
Bloodstone '88
Blue Iguana '88
Body Trouble '92
Bon Voyage '03 ▶
Bridget Jones: The Edge of Reason '04
Brink's Job '78 ▶
Brothers O'Toole '73
Burglar '87
California Straight Ahead '25
Cannibal Women in the Avocado Jungle of Death '89
Cannonball Run 2 '84
Cannonball Run '81
Cartouche '62 ▶
Chan Is Missing '82 ▶
Charlie's Angels '19
Chasers '94
Cheaper by the Dozen 2 '05
CHIPS '17
City Heat '84
Clear All Wires! '33
Collision Course '89
Congo Maisie '40
Crocodile Dundee 2 '88
Crocodile Dundee '86 ▶
Danny Deckchair '03
Dirt Bike Kid '86
Doctor Detroit '83
Dog Pound Shuffle '75 ▶
Dolemite 2: Human Tornado '76
Don Verdean '15
Doogal '05
Double Crossbones '51
Drop Dead Sexy '05
Early Man '18
Every Girl Should Have One '78
Feds '88
The Fifth Musketeer '79
Flipper '96 ▶
Forever Young '92
48 Hrs. '82 ▶
Foul Play '78 ▶
The Further Adventures of Tennessee Buck '88
Garfield: The Movie '04
Ghostbusters 2 '89
Ghostbusters '84 ▶
Girls Trip '17 ▶
Gold Rush Maisie '40
The Golden Child '86
Gozu '03
The Grand Budapest Hotel '14 ▶
Gringo '18
Gulliver's Travels '10
Gunmen '93
Harriet the Spy '96
Hellboy '04
Here We Go Again! '42
High Road to China '83
The House '17
How to Be a Latin Lover '17
How to Eat Fried Worms '06
Hudson Hawk '91
In Like Flint '67
It's in the Bag! '45
Jackass Presents: Bad Grandpa '13
Jackie Chan's Who Am I '98
Jake Speed '86
Jane & the Lost City '87
The Jewel of the Nile '85
Jumanji: The Next Level '19
Kamikaze Girls '04
Kazaam '96
Kindergarten Cop '90
King Kung Fu '87
The Kings of Summer '13
Klaus '19 ▶
Kuffs '92
Last Action Hero '93
Last Holiday '06
Last Vegas '13
Lemony Snicket's A Series of Unfortunate Events '04
Leonard Part 6 '87
The Life Aquatic with Steve Zissou '04
Looking for Trouble '96
A Low Down Dirty Shame '94
Lust in the Dust '85 ▶
Mad About Money '37
Madigan's Millions '67
Magic Kid '92
Maisie Gets Her Man '42
A Man Called Sarge '90
The Man Who Wasn't There '83
The Man with One Red Shoe '85
Masterminds '16
Memoirs of an Invisible Man '92
Midnight Madness '80
Midnight Run '88 ▶
Mr. Billion '77
Mr. Nanny '93
Mr. Nice Guy '98
Mr. Robinson Crusoe '32
Mr. Superinvisible '73
Mitchell '75
Mo' Money '92
Mob Story '90
Mom and Dad Save the World '92
Moms' Night Out '14
The Money '75
Money Talks '97
Monkey Hustle '77
Monkey's Uncle '65
Moonwalkers '16
Mulan 2 '04
Muppet Treasure Island '96
Muppets Most Wanted '14
My Dog, the Thief '69
My Science Project '85
No Deposit, No Return '76
Nobody's Fool '18
The Nut Job '14
O Brother Where Art Thou? '00
Off the Lip '04
Office Christmas Party '16
Old Goats '13
Operation Condor 2: The Armour of the Gods '86
Operation Dumbo Drop '95
Our Man Flint '66
Over the Hill '93
Palookaville '95 ▶
Pippi Goes on Board '69
Pippi in the South Seas '70
Pippi Longstocking '69
Pippi on the Run '70
Pirates of the Caribbean: Dead Man's Chest '06
Pizza '05
Pootie Tang '01
The Prince of Thieves '48
Puss in Boots '11 ▶
Red Lion '69
The Reivers '69 ▶
Rendezvous '35
Return of the Rebels '81
Romancing the Stone '84 ▶
Rough Night '17
Royal Flash '75 ▶
Rumble in the Bronx '96
Running Scared '86
Rush Hour '98
Russkies '87
Sausage Party '16
The Savage '75
Scoob! '20
The Secret Life of Pets '16
Sherlock: Undercover Dog '94
Shrek 2 '04 ▶
Silver Streak '76 ▶
Ski Patrol '89
Sky High '84
Sleepwalk with Me '12
Slither '73 ▶
Smokey and the Bandit '77
Smokey and the Bandit 2 '80
Smokey and the Bandit, Part 3 '83
Smokey & the Judge '80
Smokey Bites the Dust '81
Speedy '28 ▶
Spies, Lies and Naked Thighs '91
S*P*Y*S '74
The Squeeze '87
Stakeout '87
Stand-In '85
The Starving Games '13
Steelyard Blues '73
Stepmonster '92
The Sting 2 '83
Stingray '78
Stop! or My Mom Will Shoot '92
Stuntwoman '81
Suburban Commando '91
The Suitors '88
Summer Night with Greek Profile, Almond Eyes & Scent of Basil '87
Super Fuzz '81
Surf Nazis Must Die '87
Surf Ninjas '93
Survivors '83
Swashbuckler '76
Tag '18
The Tall Blond Man with One Black Shoe '72 ▶
Teenage Mutant Ninja Turtles: The Movie '90
Teenage Mutant Ninja Turtles 2: The Secret of the Ooze '91
Teenage Mutant Ninja Turtles 3 '93
Teenage Mutant Ninja Turtles '14
That Sinking Feeling '79 ▶
They Met in Bombay '41
30 Minutes or Less '11
Those Daring Young Men in Their Jaunty Jalopies '69
Those Fantastic Flying Fools '67
Those Magnificent Men in Their Flying Machines '65 ▶
Three Amigos '86
Three Fugitives '89
The Three Musketeers '74 ▶
3 Ninjas '92
3 Ninjas Kick Back '94
3 Ninjas Knuckle Up '95
3, 2, 1...Frankie Go Boom '12
Thunder and Lightning '77
Toga Party '77
Tom and Huck '95 ▶
Too Hot to Handle '38 ▶
Top Dog '95
Topkapi '64 ▶
Tough Guys '86
Trenchcoat '83
Trolls World Tour '20
Trouble in Store '53
True Lies '94
Twin Dragons '92
Twins '88
Ultrachrist! '03
Under the Rainbow '81
Up the Creek '84
Uptown Saturday Night '74
Vampire Effect '03
Van Nuys Blvd. '79
Vice Academy 2 '90
Vice Academy 3 '91
Vice Academy '88
Viva Maria! '65
Wackiest Ship in the Army '61
Walk of Shame '14
Wallace & Gromit in The Curse of the Were-Rabbit '05 ▶
We're No Angels '89
When the Clouds Roll By '19 ▶
Why Him? '16
The Wild Life '16
The Willoughbys '20
Without a Paddle '04
Wrong Is Right '82
Year of the Comet '92
You May Not Kiss the Bride '12
The Yum-Yum Girls '78
Zoolander 2 '16

Comic Books

American Splendor '03 ▶
American Ultra '15
Antboy '14
Aquaman '18
Artists and Models '55
Captain America: Civil War '16 ▶
Captain Marvel '19 ▶
Chasing Amy '97
Comic Book: The Movie '04 ▶
Comic-Con Episode IV: A Fan's Hope '11
The Dangerous Lives of Altar Boys '02 ▶
Dark Justice '00
The Death of Stalin '17 ▶
Guardians of the Galaxy '14 ▶
Hellboy '19
I, Frankenstein '13
I Want to Go Home '89
Jay and Silent Bob Strike Back '01
Joker '19 ▶
Justice League '17
Mallrats '95
People Places Things '15
Professor Marston and the Wonder Women '17
Son of the Mask '05
Spider-Man: Into the Spider-Verse '18 ▶
Thor: Ragnarok '17 ▶
Venom '18
Veritas: Prince of Truth '07
X-Men: Apocalypse '16

Comic Cops

See also Disorganized Crime

The Animal '01
Big Trouble '02
Cop Out '10
Dragnet '87
Feds '88
Freebie & the Bean '74
Inspector Clouseau '68
It Seemed Like a Good Idea at the Time '75
K-9 '89
Mambo Italiano '03
Me, Myself, and Irene '00 ▶
The Naked Gun: From the Files of Police Squad '88 ▶
Naked Gun 33 1/3: The Final Insult '94
Naked Gun 2 1/2: The Smell of Fear '91
National Lampoon's Loaded Weapon 1 '93
The Other Guys '10
Police Academy '84
Police Academy 2: Their First Assignment '85
Police Academy 3: Back in Training '86
Police Academy 4: Citizens on Patrol '87
Police Academy 5: Assignment Miami Beach '88
Police Academy 6: City under Siege '89
Police Academy 7: Mission to Moscow '94
Reno 911! Miami '07
Rush Hour '98
Rush Hour 2 '01
Super Troopers '01
Superbad '07 ▶
Taxi '04
Turner and Hooch '89

Coming of Age

A Nos Amours '84 ▶
About Scout '15 ▶
Across the Great Divide '76
Adult World '13
Adventures in Zambezia '12
Ah, Wilderness! '35 ▶
Alexandria. . . Why? '78
All Fall Down '62
All I Wanna Do '98
All I Want '02
All Over Me '96 ▶
All the Right Moves '83
All the Wilderness '14
All Things Fair '95
Amarcord '74 ▶
American Graffiti '73 ▶
An American Rhapsody '01 ▶
An American Summer '90
Americano '05
. . .And the Earth Did Not Swallow Him '94
And Then We Danced '20 ▶
Angels in Stardust '14
Anne Frank: The Whole Story '01 ▶
Anne of Green Gables '85 ▶
Anthony Adverse '36
Anywhere But Here '99
Aparajito '58 ▶
The Apprenticeship of Duddy Kravitz '74 ▶
The Art of Getting By '11
As Cool As I Am '13
Au Revoir les Enfants '87 ▶
An Awfully Big Adventure '94
Babe '95 ▶
Baby It's You '82 ▶
Babyteeth '20 ▶
Back Door to Heaven '39 ▶
Barnyard '06
Batman Begins '05 ▶
The Battle of Shaker Heights '03
Battle Royale '00
Beach Rats '17
Beautiful Ohio '06
Beautiful Thing '95 ▶
Beneath the Harvest Sky '14
Big '88 ▶
The Big Bet '85
The Big Night '51
The Big Red One '80 ▶
Big Time Adolescence '20
Billy Bathgate '91
A Birder's Guide to Everything '14
Black Cloud '04
Black Nativity '13
Black Peter '63
Blackbird '14
Blinded by the Light '19 ▶
Blue Car '03 ▶
Blue Fin '78
The Blue Kite '93 ▶
The Blue Lagoon '80
Blue River '95
Blue Velvet '86 ▶
Boarding School '18
Bonjour Monsieur Shlomi '03 ▶
Borstal Boy '00
Boy Erased '18
The Boys in Company C '77
Boys Life '94
The Boys of 2nd Street Park '03 ▶
Brave New Girl '04
Breaking Away '79 ▶
Bridge to Terabithia '07
Brighton Beach Memoirs '86
Brigsby Bear '17
A Brilliant Young Mind '14
Broken '13
A Bronx Tale '93 ▶
Brother to Brother '04
The Buddha of Suburbia '92 ▶
Butterfly '98 ▶
By Way of the Stars '92
Call Me by Your Name '17 ▶
Calvin Marshall '09
Can't Buy Me Love '87
Carnal Knowledge '71 ▶
Carrie Pilby '17
Carry Me Home '04
Catherine Cookson's The Cinder Path '94
Catherine Cookson's The Dwelling Place '94
Catherine Cookson's The Glass Virgin '95
Cemetery Junction '10
The Childhood of a Leader '16
The Chorus '04
Christy '94
A Ciambra '17
The Cider House Rules '99 ▶
Circle of Friends '94
Circumstance '11
City Boy '93 ▶
Class '83
Class of '44 '73
Clip '13
Closely Watched Trains '66 ▶
Closet Monster '16
Cocktail '88
The Cold Lands '13
The Color of Money '86 ▶
Come and See '85 ▶
Come Undone '00
Coming Home '98
Coming Soon '99
Courage Mountain '89
Courtship '87 ▶
Cowboys & Angels '04 ▶
Crossing the Bridge '92
Crutch '04
A Cry in the Wild '90 ▶
Cry of Battle '63
Culpepper Cattle Co. '72
Cyclo '95
D3: The Mighty Ducks '96
Dakota '88
Dallas 362 '03
Damien: Omen 2 '78
Dancer, Texas-Pop. 81 '98 ▶
The Dangerous Lives of Altar Boys '02 ▶
The Dark Side of the Sun '88
The Darkest Corner of Paradise '10
David Copperfield '70
David Copperfield '99
David Holzman's Diary '67 ▶
Dead Beat '94
Dead Poets Society '89 ▶
December '91
December Boys '07
The Deer Hunter '78 ▶
The Demons '19
Desert Bloom '86 ▶
The Devil's Playground '76 ▶
The Diary of a Teenage Girl '15 ▶
Diner '82 ▶
Dirty Dancing '87 ▶
The Doe Boy '01
Dogfight '91 ▶
Dope '15 ▶
Dragstrip Girl '57

▶ = rated three bones or higher

Dreamland '06 ▸
Driving Lessons '06
Dutch Girls '87
Eat Drink Man Woman '94 ▸
Edge of Seventeen '99
The Edge of Seventeen '16 ▸
The Education of Little Tree '97 ▸
Edward Scissorhands '90 ▸
Eighth Grade '18 ▸
Ellen Foster '97
Eragon '06
The Eyes of Youth '19
Fandango '85
Fast Times at Ridgemont High '82 ▸
Father '67 ▸
Fellini Satyricon '69 ▸
Fierce People '05
First Love '70
The First Time '69
5 Time Champion '11
The Flamingo Kid '84 ▸
Flipped '10
For a Lost Soldier '93
Forever Young '85
Fort Tilden '14
Four and a Half Women '05
The 400 Blows '59 ▸
Foxes '80
Friends Forever '86 ▸
Gas Food Lodging '92 ▸
A Generation '54 ▸
A Gentleman's Game '01
Get Real '99
The Getting of Wisdom '77
Gidget '59
Gimme Shelter '14
Ginger & Rosa '13
Ginger Snaps '01
Girl '98
Girl in Progress '12
The Girl in the Sneakers '99
A Girl of the Limberlost '90 ▸
Girlfight '99 ▸
Girls Can't Swim '99
The Giver '14
The Glass Castle '17
Go For It! '10
Go Tell It on the Mountain '84
Goats '12
Going All the Way '97
The Good Humor Man '05
Good Kids '16
Goodbye, Columbus '69 ▸
Goodbye, My Lady '56
The Graduate '67 ▸
The Grass Harp '95
The Great Outdoors '88
The Great Santini '80 ▸
The Great Water '04
Gregory's Girl '80 ▸
Grown Ups '80
A Guide to Recognizing Your Saints '06
Hairspray '88 ▸
Hala '19
Hammers over the Anvil '91
Hangin' with the Homeboys '91 ▸
Hard Choices '84 ▸
Harry Potter and the Order of the Phoenix '07 ▸
Hearts in Atlantis '01
Heathers '89 ▸
Heaven Help Us '85
A Hero Ain't Nothin' but a Sandwich '78
Hey Hey It's Esther Blueberger '08
Hole in the Sky '95
Holy Girl '04 ▸
Holy Matrimony '94
Homeboy '88
Homework '82
The Horse '82 ▸
Horse Camp '14
The Horsemen '70
Hot Moves '84
Hounddog '08
The Hour of the Star '85 ▸
House of D '04
The House of Tomorrow '18
How to Build a Girl '20
Huck and the King of Hearts '93
The Human Comedy '43 ▸
Hurricane Streets '96
I Capture the Castle '02
I Don't Want to Talk About It '94
I Killed My Mother '09
I Love You, I Love You Not '97
I Vitelloni '53 ▸
If Looks Could Kill '91
Il Sorpasso '63
I'm Not Scared '03
In Her Shoes '05 ▸
In Praise of Older Women '78
In Search of Fellini '17
In the Custody of Strangers '82 ▸
The Incredible Mrs. Ritchie '03
Indian Paint '64
The Inevitable Defeat of Mister & Pete '13
The Inheritors '82
Introducing the Dwights '07
Inventing the Abbotts '97
Invisible Circus '00
The Islander '88
It Felt Like Love '14
Ithaca '16
Jerry Maguire '96 ▸
JFK: Reckless Youth '93
Jinn '18
Jitters '10
Joe the King '99
Joey '85
Johnny Be Good '88
Jory '72
The Journey of Jared Price '00
The Journey of Natty Gann '85 ▸
Just Henry '11
Just Looking '99
Kamikaze Girls '04
The Karate Kid '84 ▸
The Karate Kid: Part 2 '86
The Karate Kid: Part 3 '89
Keeping Up with the Steins '06
Kicking and Screaming '95 ▸
Kicks '16
King Jack '16 ▸
King of the Gypsies '78
The Kings of Summer '13
Kings Row '41 ▸
The Kitchen Toto '87 ▸
La Boum '81
Labyrinth '86 ▸
Lady Bird '17 ▸
The Last Tree '19
Late Bloomers '11
The Learning Tree '69
The Legend of Johnny Lingo '03
Let's Make a Movie '11
L'Homme Blesse '83 ▸
Liam '00
L.I.E. '01
Life & Nothing More '17
Like A Bride '94 ▸
The Lion King '94 ▸
The Lion King '19
Little Men '16 ▸
The Little Prince '16 ▸
A Little Romance '79 ▸
Little Women '49 ▸
Little Women '78
Little Women '18
Lola Versus '12
The Long Day Closes '92 ▸
The Lords of Flatbush '74
Love Film '70
Lucas '86 ▸
Maid to Order '87
Malena '00
The Man from Snowy River '82
The Man in the Moon '91 ▸
A Man of Passion '88
The Man Without a Face '93
Marker '05
Marking Time '03
Matinee '92
Me and Orson Welles '09
Mean Creek '04 ▸
Mean Streets '73 ▸
Meet Monica Velour '10
The Member of the Wedding '52 ▸
Memoirs of a Geisha '05
Metropolitan '90 ▸
Mickey '48
A Midnight Clear '92 ▸
Mid90s '18
Milk Money '94
Mischief '85
Monika '52
Monsieur Ibrahim '03 ▸
Moonlight '16 ▸
More American Graffiti '79
Morris from America '16 ▸
The Mudge Boy '03
Murmur of the Heart '71 ▸
My American Cousin '85 ▸
My Bodyguard '80 ▸
My Brilliant Career '79 ▸
My Brothers '10
My Friend Dahmer '17
My Girl 2 '94
My Girl '91
My Life As a Dog '85 ▸
My Life on Ice '02
My One and Only '09
My Summer of Love '05
My Tutor '82
Mystic Pizza '88 ▸
Negative Happy Chainsaw Edge '08
Neon Signs '96
New Waterford Girl '99
Next Stop, Greenwich Village '76 ▸
Nicholas Nickleby '46 ▸
Nicholas Nickleby '02 ▸
Nico and Dani '00
Night Has Settled '14
A Night in the Life of Jimmy Reardon '88
1969 '89 ▸
No Regrets for Our Youth '46 ▸
No Time for Sergeants '58 ▸
The Nostradamus Kid '92
November Criminals '17
Now and Then '95
Nowhere in Africa '02
October Baby '12
Odd Birds '85
Oddballs '84
Ode to Billy Joe '76
Of Time and the City '08
Old Enough '84
One on One '77
Open Road '13
Oranges Are Not the Only Fruit '89
The Other Side of Sunday '96
Other Voices, Other Rooms '95
Our Little Sister '16
Out of the Blue '80 ▸
Outside Providence '99
The Outsiders '83
Over the Edge '79 ▸
A Painted House '03
The Pallbearer '95
Palookaville '95 ▸
The Paper Chase '73 ▸
Paper Towns '15
Paradise '82
Pariah '11 ▸
The Passing of Evil '70
Pather Panchali '54 ▸
Pauline at the Beach '83 ▸
P.C.U. '94
Peck's Bad Boy '34
Penguins '19 ▸
The Perks of Being a Wallflower '12 ▸
Persepolis '07 ▸
Peter Lundy and the Medicine Hat Stallion '77
Pitch Perfect '12
A Place in the World '92 ▸
Platoon '86 ▸
Portrait of a Lady '67
Portrait of a Lady '96 ▸
The Power of One '92
Promised Land '88 ▸
A Prophet '09 ▸
Prozac Nation '01
Purgatory House '04
Quadrophenia '79 ▸
Quinceanera '06 ▸
The Rabbit Is Me '65
Racing with the Moon '84 ▸
The Rage In Placid Lake '03
Rain '01
Raise Your Voice '04
Rambling Rose '91 ▸
The Razor's Edge '46 ▸
The Razor's Edge '84
Real Women Have Curves '02 ▸
A Real Young Girl '75
Red Dirt '99
The Red Fury '84
The Reivers '69 ▸
Restless Spirits '99
Ricochet River '98
Ride with the Devil '99
Risky Business '83 ▸
The River '51 ▸
A River Runs Through It '92 ▸
River's End '05
The Road from Coorain '02
Roger Dodger '02 ▸
A Room with a View '86 ▸
Rudyard Kipling's The Jungle Book '94
Rumble Fish '83 ▸
A Rumor of Angels '00
The Run of the Country '95 ▸
The Runaways '10
Running with Scissors '06
Rushmore '98 ▸
St. Elmo's Fire '85
Samurai 1: Musashi Miyamoto '55 ▸
The Sandlot '93 ▸
Sands of Iwo Jima '49 ▸
Sarafina! '92 ▸
Savage Is Loose '74
Say Anything '89 ▸
Scent of a Woman '92 ▸
The Scent of Green Papaya '93 ▸
Schizo '04
Season of Change '94
Secondhand Lions '03
Secrets '82
A Separate Peace '04
Seven Minutes in Heaven '86
Shaking the Tree '92
She's Out of Control '89
Shipwrecked '90
Shout '91
Showgirls '95
Simon Birch '98
The Sisterhood of the Traveling Pants '05
Sixteen '72
Skateland '10
Skipped Parts '00
Slash '16
The Slingshot '93 ▸
Slums of Beverly Hills '98 ▸
Small Time '14
Smile '05
Smooth Talk '85 ▸
So B. It '17
Soldier of Orange '78 ▸
A Soldier's Daughter Never Cries '98
Soldiers of Change '06
Some Kind of Wonderful '87
Somersault '04
Something in the Air '13
Songs My Brother Taught Me '15 ▸
Sounder '72 ▸
SpaceCamp '86
Spanking the Monkey '94 ▸
The Spectacular Now '13 ▸
Spring, Summer, Fall, Winter. . . and Spring '03 ▸
Square Dance '87
The Squid and the Whale '05 ▸
Star Wars '77 ▸
Star Wars: Episode 1-The Phantom Menace '99 ▸
Still Green '07
Studs Lonigan '60
Submarine '10 ▸
Sugar Kisses '13
Summer '03 '18
Summer Holiday '48
Summer Interlude '50 ▸
Summer of '42 '71 ▸
Summer's End '99
Sunset Rock '16
Sunset Song '16
Surfacing '14
Sweet 15 '90
Swimming '00
Swing Kids '93
The Sword in the Stone '63 ▸
Taste of Death '68
Teen Spirit '18
Teenage Mutant Ninja Turtles 2: The Secret of the Ooze '91
Telling Lies in America '96
Terri '11
Tex '82
That Brennan Girl '46
That Naughty Girl '58
That Night '93
That Was Then. . . This Is Now '85
Theeb '15 ▸
There Goes My Baby '92
36 Fillete '88 ▸
This Boy's Life '93 ▸
This Is England '06
Those Glory, Glory Days '83
Thumbsucker '05 ▸
Tiger Eyes '13
Time of the Gypsies '90 ▸
Toby Tyler '59 ▸
Toe to Toe '09
The Tollbooth '04
Tonio Kroger '65
Top Gun '86
Totally F***ed Up '94
A Tree Grows in Brooklyn '45 ▸
The Tree of Life '11 ▸
Tumbleweeds '98
20th Century Women '17
Twist & Shout '84 ▸
Two Bits '96
Undertow '04
Unexpected '15
Unstrung Heroes '95
The Vanished Empire '08
Vision Quest '85
The Wackness '08
Wah-Wah '05
Walking and Talking '96
Wanderers '79 ▸
The Way To Fight '96
We the Animals '18 ▸
West Beirut '98
Whale Rider '02 ▸
What About Your Friends: Weekend Getaway '02
What's Eating Gilbert Grape '93 ▸
Where the Red Fern Grows: Part 2 '92
White Oleander '02
Who Shot Pat? '92
Whole New Thing '05
Who's That Knocking at My Door? '68 ▸
Why Shoot the Teacher '79 ▸
Wide Awake '97
Wild America '97 ▸
The Wild Child '70 ▸
Wild Reeds '94 ▸
Wild Tigers I Have Known '06
Wildlife '18 ▸
Winner Takes All '84
Winter in Wartime '10
With Honors '94
The Women's Balcony '16
Wonder Boys '00 ▸
Wrestling with Alligators '98
Wuthering Heights '12
Y Tu Mama Tambien '01
The Year My Voice Broke '87 ▸
The Yearling '46 ▸
The Yearling '94
Yelling to the Sky '11
The Young Graduates '71
Young Guns 2 '90
Young Sherlock Holmes '85
Young Tom Edison '40
Youngblood '86
You're a Big Boy Now '66 ▸
Youth in Revolt '10
Zapped! '82
Zoe '01

Communists & Communism

***See also** Cold War Spies; Red Scare; Russia/USSR*

Ai Weiwei: Never Sorry '12 ▸
The Army of Crime '10
Assignment: Paris '52
Baaria '09
Balzac and the Little Chinese Seamstress '02
Bitter Harvest '17
Black Peter '63
British Agent '34
Cambridge Spies '03
The Chairman '69
Cold War '18 ▸
Dark Blue World '01
The Death of Stalin '17 ▸
Disco and Atomic War '14
Divided Heaven '64
Dust of Life '95
Electra, My Love '74
The Fearmakers '58
Frida '02
The Girl Who Knew Too Much '69
Good Bye, Lenin! '03 ▸
The Great Water '04
I Served the King of England '07 ▸
Indiana Jones and the Kingdom of the Crystal Skull '08
Innocent Voices '04
The Iron Petticoat '56
Katyn '07
Kimjongilia '09
La Chinoise '67
The Lost City '05
Man On a String '60
Man on a Tightrope '53
Mao's Last Dancer '09
My Son John '52
Neruda '16
Night People '54
Oil for the Lamps of China '35
The Phynx '70
Red Joan '19
Reds '81 ▸
S21: The Khmer Rouge Killing Machine '03 ▸
The Seventh Dawn '64
Spy in the Sky '58
To Commit a Murder '67
Trial '55
Trumbo '15
The Tunnel '01 ▸
The Vanished Empire '08
The Venetian Affair '67
Walk a Crooked Mile '48
The Woman on Pier 13 '50

Computers

***See also** Robots, Cyborgs & Androids*

Agatha Christie's Murder is Easy '82
Alchemy '05
Alien '79 ▸
Antitrust '00
Big Momma's House 2 '06
Blackhat '15
Blast '04
Computer Chess '13
The Computer Wore Tennis Shoes '69
Conceiving Ada '97
Control Alt Delete '08
Copycat '95
Cyberstalker '96
Dangerous Game '90
Dean Koontz's Black River '01
Dee Snider's Strangeland '98
Demon Seed '77 ▸
Desk Set '57 ▸
Dopamine '03
The Dying Gaul '05 ▸
Entrapment '99
Evilspeak '82
Eyeborgs '09
Fair Game '95
The Fifth Estate '13
The First $20 Million is Always the Hardest '02
Friend Request '16

▸ = rated three bones or higher

The Gallows Act II '19
The Great Hack '19 ▶
Hackers '95
Hard Drive '94
The Honeymoon Machine '61
Hostile Intent '97
How to Make a Monster '01
The Human Factor '75
The Hummingbird Project '18
The Internet's Own Boy: The Story of Aaron Swartz '14 ▶
Johnny Mnemonic '95
Jumpin' Jack Flash '86
Jurassic Park '93 ▶
Lawnmower Man 2: Beyond Cyberspace '95
The Lawnmower Man '92
Live Free or Die Hard '07
Lo and Behold: Reveries of the Connected World '16 ▶
The Matrix '99 ▶
The Matrix Reloaded '03
Menno's Mind '96
Mission: Impossible 2 '00 ▶
Mission: Impossible '96 ▶
Mother '13
Nerve '16
The Net 2.0 '06
The Net '95
Net Games '03
New World Disorder '99
Nirvana '97
Office Space '98
Once Upon a Spy '80
Open Windows '14
Pi '98
The Pirates of Silicon Valley '99
Pulse '01
Ratter '16
Resident Evil '02
Revenge of the Nerds '84
The Scorpio Factor '90
Searching '18 ▶
Sex Kittens Go to College '60
Shredderman Rules '07
Silicon Cowboys '16
Silicon Towers '99
Sneakers '92
The Social Network '10 ▶
Stealing Candy '04
Steve Jobs '15 ▶
Sunset Rock '16
Superman 3 '83
Terminal Error '02
This Thing of Ours '03
Tin Man '83
Tom Clancy's Netforce '98
Trapped '06
Unfriended: Dark Web '18
Virtual Assassin '95
Virtual Desire '95
The Wandering Earth '19
WarGames '83
WarGames: The Dead Code '08
We Are Legion: The Story of the Hacktivists '12
Weird Science '85
You've Got Mail '98
Zero Days '16
The Zero Theorem '13

Concentration/Internment Camps

See also Nazis & POW/MIA

Adam Resurrected '08
Anne Frank: The Whole Story '01 ▶
Army of Shadows '69 ▶
Autumn Hearts: A New Beginning '07
Bent '97
Blindness '08
The Boy in the Striped Pajamas '08 ▶
Come See the Paradise '90 ▶
The Counterfeiters '07 ▶
Death in Love '08
Denial '16
The Devil's Arithmetic '99
The Edge '10
Escape '40
Fateless '05 ▶
The Girl of Your Dreams '99
God on Trial '08
The Great Raid '05
The Great Water '04
Green Dragon '01
The Grey Zone '01
The Hiding Place '75
Hitler: Beast of Berlin '39
Holocaust '78 ▶
I Am David '04
I Love You, I Love You Not '97
In the Land of Blood and Honey '11
Landscape After Battle '70
The Last Butterfly '92
Life Is Beautiful '98 ▶
Merry Christmas, Mr. Lawrence '83 ▶
The Ninth Day '04 ▶
Only the Brave '06
Out of the Ashes '03
Paradise Road '97
Playing for Time '80 ▶
Red Dawn '84
The Road to Guantanamo '06
S21: The Khmer Rouge Killing Machine '03 ▶
Schindler's List '93 ▶
Seven Beauties '76 ▶
Shoah '85 ▶
The Siege '98
Snow Falling on Cedars '99
Son of Saul '15 ▶
Sophie's Choice '82 ▶
Triumph of the Spirit '89 ▶
The Truce '96 ▶
Verdict on Auschwitz: The Frankfurt Auschwitz Trial 1963-1965 '93 ▶

Contemporary Noir

See also Crime Drama; Film Noir; Private Eyes

Across the Hall '09
After Dark, My Sweet '90 ▶
After Hours '85 ▶
After the Storm '01
Against All Odds '84
Albino Alligator '96
The American Friend '77 ▶
Angel Heart '87
Animal Kingdom '09 ▶
Bad Education '04 ▶
Barocco '76
Best Laid Plans '99
Betty Blue '86 ▶
Beyond a Reasonable Doubt '09
The Big Easy '87 ▶
The Big Empty '98 ▶
The Black Dahlia '06
Blade Runner '82 ▶
Blood & Concrete: A Love Story '91
Blood Simple '85 ▶
Blue Velvet '86 ▶
Bodies, Rest & Motion '93
Body Double '84 ▶
Body Heat '81 ▶
Brick '06 ▶
Bring Me the Head of Alfredo Garcia '74
Bringing Out the Dead '99
Broken Embraces '09 ▶
Bulletproof Heart '95 ▶
Cafe Society '97
Cape Fear '91 ▶
Chandler '71
Cherry Crush '07
Chinatown '74 ▶
Choose Me '84 ▶
City of Industry '96
Croupier '97 ▶
Cutter's Way '81
Dance with a Stranger '85 ▶
Dark City '97
Dark Diamond '16
Dark Hearts '12
Deceiver '97
Deepwater '05
Devil in a Blue Dress '95 ▶
The Devil You Know '05
D.O.A. '88
Dogwatch '97
Don McKay '09
Dressed to Kill '80
The Driver '78
Dylan Dog: Dead of Night '11
The Embalmer '03 ▶
Experiment in Terror '62 ▶
Eyes of Laura Mars '78
Fatal Attraction '87 ▶
52 Pick-Up '86
First Degree '95
Flypaper '97
Following '99
Forever Mine '99
The Girl in a Swing '89
The Girl On the Train '13
Goodbye, Lover '99
The Grifters '90 ▶
Guncrazy '92
Hammett '82
Hard Eight '96 ▶
The Hi-Lo Country '98
Hit Me '96
Hollywoodland '06
The Hot Spot '90
The Hustle '75
Jigsaw '99
Kill Me Again '89
The Kill-Off '89
Killing Zoe '94
Kiss of Death '94
Kiss Tomorrow Goodbye '00
L.A. Confidential '97 ▶
The Last Seduction '94 ▶
Le Cercle Rouge '70 ▶
Le Samourai '67 ▶
Let the Devil Wear Black '99
Lights in the Dusk '06
The Limey '99 ▶
A Little Trip to Heaven '05
Live Flesh '97 ▶
The Locusts '97
The Long Goodbye '73 ▶
The Lookout '07 ▶
Love Walked In '97
The Manchurian Candidate '62 ▶
Manhunter '86 ▶
Marlowe '69
Mercy Streets '00
The Million Dollar Hotel '99
The Missing Person '09
Mulholland Falls '95
The Music of Chance '93
Narrow Margin '90
The Nickel Ride '74
Night Moves '75 ▶
9 1/2 Weeks '86
No Good Deed '02
No Way Out '87 ▶
Nobody '07
Novocaine '01
One False Move '91 ▶
Palmetto '98
Payback '98 ▶
The Perfect Sleep '08
Performance '70 ▶
Place Vendome '98 ▶
Promised Land '88 ▶
The Public Eye '92 ▶
Pulp Fiction '94 ▶
Purple Noon '60 ▶
Red Riding, Part 1: 1974 '09
Red Riding, Part 2: 1980 '09
Red Riding, Part 3: 1983 '09
Red Rock West '93 ▶
Redbelt '08 ▶
Reservoir Dogs '92 ▶
The Rich Man's Wife '96
River of Grass '94
Rock Slyde: Private Eye '09
Romeo Is Bleeding '93
Rushlights '13
The Salton Sea '02
sex, lies and videotape '89 ▶
Shattered '91
The Silence of the Lambs '91 ▶
Simpatico '99
Sin City '05
Sin City: A Dame to Kill For '14
A Slight Case of Murder '99
Something Wild '86
The Spanish Prisoner '97 ▶
The Square '08
Sticks '98
Stormy Monday '88
Taxi Driver '76 ▶
Tequila Sunrise '88
Things to Do in Denver When You're Dead '95 ▶
To Live & Die in L.A. '85
The Tourist '10
Track 29 '88
Trouble in Mind '86 ▶
True Believer '89
True Confessions '81 ▶
Twilight '98 ▶
Two Days in the Valley '96 ▶
The Two Jakes '90
2 Minutes Later '07
U-Turn '97
The Underneath '95 ▶
Union City '81
The Usual Suspects '95 ▶
The Walker '07
Watching the Detectives '07
We Monsters '15
When Will I Be Loved '04
Where the Truth Lies '05
Who'll Stop the Rain? '78 ▶
Wild at Heart '90 ▶
Wild Orchid 2: Two Shades of Blue '92
Wild Orchid '90
Wild Things '98
You Kill Me '07 ▶

Cooking

See Chefs

Cops

See Alien Cops; Biopics: Cops & Buddy Cops; Canine Cops; Comic Cops; DEA; FBI; Future Cop; Historical Detectives; Loner Cops; Police Detectives; Private Eyes; Rogue Cops; Small-Town Sheriffs; Undercover Cops; Women Cops

Corporate Shenanigans

See also Advertising; Dying for a Promotion; Salespeople; Workin' for a Livin'

Ablaze '00
The Accountant '16
The Alarmist '98
The Alchemists '99
All in a Night's Work '61
Anacondas: Trail of Blood '09
Andy Hardy Comes Home '58
Antitrust '00
Any Wednesday '66
The Apartment '60 ▶
April Fools '69
Arbitrage '12 ▶
Arthur Hailey's The Moneychangers '76
As Young As You Feel '51 ▶
The Associate '79
The Associate '96
Atlas Shrugged: Part 1 '11
Atlas Shrugged 2: The Strike '12
Atlas Shrugged 3: Who Is John Galt? '14
Au Pair 2: The Fairy Tale Continues '01
August '08
Avalanche '99
Avatar '09 ▶
Baby Geniuses '98
Bad Company '94
The Bad Man '41
The Bad Sleep Well '60 ▶
The Bank '01
Barbarians at the Gate '93 ▶
Barbershop 2: Back in Business '04 ▶
BASEketball '98
Beggars in Ermine '34
Behind Office Doors '31
Believe '07
The Best of Everything '59 ▶
Betting on Zero '16
Big Business '88
The Big One '98
Big Trees '52 ▶
The Bikini Car Wash Company 2 '92
The Bikini Car Wash Company '90
Blonde Ambition '07
Blood Red '88
Bloodsucking Bastards '15
Body & Soul '93 ▶
Boiler Room '00 ▶
Bombshell '97
Bone Eater '07
Boom Town '40 ▶
Boomerang '92
The Boss of It All '06
Boys Will Be Boys '97
Bright Leaf '50
Burning Daylight '28
The Business of Strangers '01
The Caller '08
Campbell's Kingdom '57
Capital '12
Capitalism: A Love Story '09
The Capture of Bigfoot '79
The Carpetbaggers '64
Cash McCall '60
Catwoman '04
Chairman of the Board '97
Changing Lanes '02 ▶
Chasing the Green '09
The Chateau Meroux '11
The China Syndrome '79 ▶
C.H.O.M.P.S. '79
Christmas in Compton '12
The Circle '17
A Civil Action '98
Class of Nuke 'Em High 2: Subhumanoid Meltdown '91
The Clearstream Affair '15
Clockwatchers '97
The Closet '00
The Coca-Cola Kid '84 ▶
Cold Turkey '71 ▶
Collision '09
The Colony '95
Comedy of Power '06
Comic Book: The Movie '04 ▶
Conductor 1492 '24
Consuming Passions '88
Corporate Affairs '90
Corporate Affairs '07
Corporate Animals '19
Cosmopolis '12 ▶
Cow Belles '06
The Crime of Monsieur Lange '36 ▶
Cyborg 2 '93
Cypher '02 ▶
Dark Streets '08
A Dark Truth '12
Dark Waters '19 ▶
Daybreakers '09
The Daydreamer '70
Deadlier Than the Male '67
Dealers '89
Death Collector '89
Death Machine '95
Demonlover '02
The Devil & Miss Jones '41 ▶
The Devil's Advocate '97
Dinocroc Vs. Supergator '10
Disclosure '94
Do or Die '03
Dr. Dolittle '98
Dodsworth '36 ▶
Double Play '96
Duplicity '09
The Early Bird '25
Edge of Darkness '10
The Efficiency Expert '92
8.5 Hours '08
Empire '02
Empire Records '95
Employees' Entrance '33 ▶
End of the Line '88
Enron: The Smartest Guys in the Room '05 ▶
Equity '16
Erin Brockovich '00 ▶
Escape: Human Cargo '98 ▶
Escape Room '19
Executive Koala '06 ▶
Executive Suite '54 ▶
The Family That Preys '08
Fast Food Nation '06 ▶
Fierce Creatures '96
Fire Down Below '97
Firetrap '01
First Degree '98
The First $20 Million is Always the Hardest '02
Flash of Genius '08
The Flintstones '94
FM '78
Food, Inc. '08
For Love or Money '93
Ford: The Man & the Machine '87
Forest Warrior '95
The Founder '17 ▶
Freaked '93
Gas Pump Girls '79
GasLand '10
Get to Know Your Rabbit '72
Glengarry Glen Ross '92 ▶
Good Burger '97
Good Neighbor Sam '64 ▶
Goodfellas '90 ▶
Gorgeous '99
Government Girl '43
Green Sails '00
Gremlins 2: The New Batch '90 ▶
Gringo '18
Gung Ho '86
Hackers '95
Haiku Tunnel '00
Halloween 3: Season of the Witch '82
Hamlet '00 ▶
Happy Hour '87
The Harder They Come '72
Hardwired '09
Head Office '86
Headhunters '11
Heart o' the Hills '19
Heartbeat Detector '07
Her Husband's Affairs '47
Herbie Rides Again '74
Hey Arnold! The Movie '02
His Girl Friday '40 ▶
Hold the Dream '86
Honky Tonk Freeway '81
Hoot '06
How Do You Know '10
How the West Was Fun '95
How to Get Ahead in Advertising '89 ▶
How to Succeed in Business without Really Trying '67 ▶
The Hucksters '47 ▶
The Hudsucker Proxy '93 ▶
I Can Get It For You Wholesale '51
I Heart Huckabees '04
I Love Trouble '94
I Witness '03
In Good Company '04 ▶
In the Company of Men '96
Infected '08
The Informant! '09
The Inheritance '76
Inside Job '10 ▶
The Insider '99 ▶
The International '09
The Inventor: Out For Blood In Silicon Valley '19
Iron Man '08 ▶
Iron Man 2 '10 ▶
It Happened to Jane '59
Ivory Tower '97
Jack and the Beanstalk: The Real Story '01
Janice Beard '99
Jobs '13
Joe Somebody '01
John Grisham's The Rainmaker '97
Johnny Mnemonic '95
Just My Luck '35
The Kansan '43
Kids in the Hall: Brain Candy '96
Killer Wave '07
A Kiss Before Dying '91
La Truite '83 ▶
Ladies Who Do '63
Land of Promise '74
The Last Time '06
The Late Shift '96
The Lavender Hill Mob '51 ▶
Lawnmower Man 2: Beyond Cyberspace '95
Les Destinees '00
Let the Devil Wear Black '99
Life Stinks '91
Limit Up '89
The List '07
The Listening '06
Little Bigfoot '96
Little Giant '46

▶ = rated three bones or higher

Lloyds of London '36 ▶
Local Hero '83 ▶
Lola '81
Looney Tunes: Back in Action '03
Love and Money '80
Love Crime '10
The Loved One '65
Ma and Pa Kettle at Waikiki '55
Main Street '10
Major League '89
The Man in the Gray Flannel Suit '56
The Man in the White Suit '51 ▶
The Manchurian Candidate '04 ▶
Margin Call '11 ▶
Married to It '93
Master '16
Material Girls '06
A Matter of WHO '62
Maxed Out: Hard Times, Easy Credit and the Era of Predatory Lenders '06
Meet Joe Black '98
Memron '04
Metal Tornado '11
Michael Clayton '07 ▶
Micmacs '09
Millions '90
Miss Grant Takes Richmond '49
Miss Minoes '01
Missionary Man '07
Mr. Accident '99
Mr. Average '06
Mr. Destiny '90
Mo' Money '92
Mobius '13
A Model Employee '02
Monkey Hustle '77
Monsters, Inc. '01 ▶
Monsterwolf '10
Moola '07
Moon 44 '90
Moon Zero Two '70
A Most Violent Year '14 ▶
Mutants '08
Naked Gun 2 1/2: The Smell of Fear '91
Network '76 ▶
Never 2 Big '98
New Rose Hotel '98
9 to 5 '80
No Smoking '55
Noble House '88
Nowhere to Run '93
Office Christmas Party '16
Office Killer '97
Office Space '98
Oil for the Lamps of China '35
Okja '17 ▶
Oktober '98
Old English '30
On Again-Off Again '37
One, Two, Three '61 ▶
Open Season '95
Orchids to You '35
The Other Guys '10
Other People's Money '91
The Other Side of Midnight '77
Out Cold '01
Outfoxed: Rupert Murdoch's War on Journalism '04 ▶
Outland '81
The Pajama Game '57 ▶
The Paper '94 ▶
Paranoia '13
Parrish '61
Patterns '56 ▶
Paycheck '03
Perfume '01
The Pirates of Silicon Valley '99
The Player '92 ▶
Pootie Tang '01
Power '86
The Power and the Glory '33
The Power and the Prize '56
Primal Scream '87
The Prime Gig '00
Private Parts '96
Private Wars '93
The Promotion '08
P.U.N.K.S. '98
Purpose '02
Putney Swope '69 ▶
The Queen of Mean '90
Quicksand '01
Quicksand: No Escape '91
Race the Sun '96
The Rainmakers '35
Rancid Aluminium '00
Red Ensign '34
The Reluctant Agent '89
Resident Evil: Retribution '12
Richie Rich '94
Rick '03
Rising Sun '93 ▶
RoboCop '87 ▶
RoboCop 2 '90
RoboCop 3 '91
Robots '05
Roger & Me '89 ▶
Rogue Trader '98
Rollover '81
The Runner '15
Ruthless '48
Sabrina '95
Sahara '05
Scrooged '88
The Search for John Gissing '01
Second Act '18
The Secret of Hidden Lake '06
The Secret of My Success '87
Secretary '02 ▶
Sensations of 1945 '44
Shark Swarm '08
The Shawshank Redemption '94 ▶
She Hate Me '04
Shining Star '75
A Shock to the System '90 ▶
Side Effects '05
Silicon Cowboys '16
Silicon Towers '99
The Silver Horde '30
The Simple Life of Noah Dearborn '99
Sins '85
The 6th Day '00
Skyscraper Souls '32 ▶
The Smell of Success '09
Smilla's Sense of Snow '96
Solid Gold Cadillac '56 ▶
Solitary Man '10 ▶
Soul Assassin '01
The Spanish Prisoner '97 ▶
Special Delivery '08
Spirit Bear: The Simon Jackson Story '05
Stand-In '37 ▶
The State Within '06
Step Up Revolution '12
The Storm '09
Stormy Monday '88
The Story of O, Part 2 '87
Strange Bedfellows '65
Strange Brew '83
The Strongest Man in the World '75
The Summit '08
Sunshine State '02 ▶
Swimming with Sharks '94 ▶
Switching Channels '88
Synapse '95
Syrup '13
Taffin '88
Take This Job & Shove It '81
The Taste of Others '00 ▶
A Taxing Woman '87 ▶
The Temp '93
There Will Be Blood '07 ▶
They Came Together '14
They Drive by Night '40 ▶
3 Ninjas Knuckle Up '95
Tiger Heart '96
Tin Men '87
Tommy Boy '95
Toni Erdmann '16 ▶
Too Big to Fail '11
The Toxic Avenger, Part 3: The Last Temptation of Toxie '89
Toxic Skies '08
Toys '92
The Trade '03
Trading Places '83
Tucker: The Man and His Dream '88 ▶
The TV Set '06
Two Weeks Notice '02
Undercurrent '46
Unfinished Business '15
The Unforeseen '07
Vampire Bats '05
Vendetta '99
Virus '96
The Void '01
Wal-Mart: The High Cost of Low Price '05 ▶
Wall Street '87 ▶
War, Inc. '08
The Way We Live Now '02
Weapons of Mass Distraction '97
Weekend at Bernie's 2 '93
Weekend at Bernie's '89
Welcome to the Jungle '13
What Women Want '10
The Wheeler Dealers '63 ▶
Which Way Is Up? '77
White Mile '94
Who Killed the Electric Car? '06
Who's Who '78
A Wild Affair '63
The Wild Stallion '09
Wilder '00
Wolf '94
Working Girl '88 ▶
The Working Man '33
The World Gone Mad '33
The World Moves On '34
World on a Wire '73
Yella '07 ▶
You've Got Mail '98

Courtroom Drama

See Law & Order in the Court

Cousins

See also Aunts & Brothers & Sisters

The Addams Family '91
The Age of Innocence '34
The Age of Innocence '93 ▶
Airborne '93
Almost Strangers '01 ▶
American Cousins '02
American Pie Presents: Beta House '07
Arsenic and Old Lace '44 ▶
Barbershop 2: Back in Business '04 ▶
Barcelona '94 ▶
Berlin Job '12
Black Coffee '14
Blanche Fury '48
Blood & Chocolate '07
Body Count '97
Brighton Beach Memoirs '86
The Buttercup Chain '70
Bye-Bye '96
The Camomile Lawn '92
Catherine Cookson's The Black Candle '92
Cheech and Chong's Next Movie '80
The Chronicles of Narnia: The Voyage of the Dawn Treader '10
Coffee and Cigarettes '03 ▶
Corky of Gasoline Alley '51
Cousin, Cousine '76 ▶
The Cousins '59 ▶
Cousins '89 ▶
Dangerous Liaisons '12
The Dinner '17
Doctor Zhivago '03
Dolphin Tale '11
Dragonwyck '46
Dreaming About You '92
The Drop '14 ▶
The Dukes '07
The Dukes of Hazzard '05
The Dukes of Hazzard: The Beginning '06
First Love '39
The Four Horsemen of the Apocalypse '21 ▶
The Four Horsemen of the Apocalypse '62
Friday After Next '02
Go for Zucker '05
The Godfather, Part 3 '90 ▶
Going Greek '01
The Good Son '93
The Good Witch's Family '11
Gothic '87 ▶
The Great Gatsby '13
The Great Outdoors '88
The Groomsmen '06
The Guru '02
A Guy Thing '03
The Heartbreak Kid '07
The Hillside Stranglings '04
How I Live Now '13
iCrime '11
I'll Be Seeing You '44
The Immigrant '13 ▶
The Importance of Being Earnest '52 ▶
The Importance of Being Earnest '02
In Secret '13
The Inheritance '97
The Inheritance '10
The Intended '02
Invisible Mom 2 '99
Jude '96 ▶
Jude the Obscure '71
Kiss of Death '94
Kissin' Cousins '64
Kissing Cousins '08
Les Cousins '59
Little Girl Lost: The Delimar Vera Story '08
Little Old New York '23
Living Will '10
Magic Magic '13
Mansfield Park '99
Mansfield Park '07
Maryam '00
The Merry Widow '25 ▶
Miss Firecracker '89 ▶
Money from Home '53
More Money More Family '15
My American Cousin '85 ▶
My Baby's Daddy '04
My Cousin Rachel '52
My Cousin Rachel '17
My Cousin Vinny '92 ▶
Nanny McPhee Returns '10
National Lampoon's Christmas Vacation '89
National Lampoon's Vacation '83 ▶
Next Friday '00
Night Catches Us '10
No Boundaries '09
Nora's Hair Salon 2: A Cut Above '08
On Guard! '03 ▶
One Night at McCool's '01
Osso Bucco '08
Percentage '13
Phat Girlz '06
The Players Club '98 ▶
The Pool Boys '10
The Pope of Greenwich Village '84
Portrait of a Lady '67
Portrait of a Lady '96 ▶
Prisoner of Zenda '37 ▶
Rabbit-Proof Fence '02 ▶
Reducing '31
Reviving Ophelia '10
The Rugrats Movie '98 ▶
St. Urbain's Horseman '07
The Secret Garden '49 ▶
The Secret Garden '84
The Secret Garden '87 ▶
The Secret Garden '93
Slums of Beverly Hills '98 ▶
Smother '08
Sour Grapes '98
Stranger than Paradise '84 ▶
Striking Distance '93
Summer of Fear '78
The Take '09
Traveller '96 ▶
Twelfth Night '96
Uncaged '16
Vegas Vacation '96
A Warm Wind '11
We're No Angels '55 ▶
West of Here '02
What Katy Did '99
Whispers and Lies '08
The Yards '00

Cover-Ups

See also Blackmail; Corporate Shenanigans; Frame-Ups; Politics

Absolute Power '97
All the President's Men '76 ▶
An American Affair '09
Assassination of a High School President '08
Barb Wire '96
The Bay '12
Black and Blue '19
Blow The Man Down '19
Born of Earth '08
Capricorn One '78 ▶
CAT. 8 '13
Chain of Command '15
The China Syndrome '79 ▶
City Hall '95 ▶
Clear and Present Danger '94
Client 9: The Rise and Fall of Eliot Spitzer '10
Cold Case Hammarskjöld '19 ▶
Coma '78 ▶
The Constant Gardener '05 ▶
Cop Land '97 ▶
Courage Under Fire '96 ▶
Cover Up '49
Cover-Up '91
The Da Vinci Code '06 ▶
A Dark Truth '12
Dave '93 ▶
Dead Rising: End Game '16
The Debt '07
Defense of the Realm '85 ▶
Enemy of the State '98
Erased '12
Erin Brockovich '00 ▶
Executive Action '73
Felony '13
A Few Good Men '92 ▶
The Fourth Kind '09
Gang Related '96
Gone Baby Gone '07 ▶
Good Night, and Good Luck '05 ▶
The Good Shepherd '06
Green Zone '10 ▶
Hidden Agenda '90
Holiday Breakup '16
I Am Vengeance '18
In the Valley of Elah '07 ▶
The Insider '99 ▶
Insomnia '97 ▶
Insomnia '02 ▶
The Inventor: Out For Blood In Silicon Valley '19
Jason Bourne '16
JFK '91 ▶
L.A. Confidential '97 ▶
The Last Full Measure '19
The Man Who Cheated Himself '50
Michael Clayton '07 ▶
Misconduct '16
Mothman '10
Murder at 1600 '97
The Negotiator '98
Nixon '95 ▶
No Way Out '87 ▶
The Odessa File '74
Operation Avalanche '16
Page Eight '11
The Parallax View '74 ▶
Poetry '10
The Post '17 ▶
Pride and Glory '08
Primary Colors '98
Puncture '11
The Report '19
Report to the Commissioner '75 ▶
The Scent of Rain & Lightening '17
Serpico '73 ▶
Silkwood '83 ▶
Smoke Screen '10
State of Play '03 ▶
State of Play '09 ▶
Street Kings '08
Super Dark Times '17
Syriana '05 ▶
Thunderheart '92 ▶
Transpecos '16
True Confessions '81 ▶
21 Bridges '19
Wag the Dog '97
The Whistle Blower '87 ▶
Winter Kills '79 ▶
Wrong Cops '13
The X-Files '98
The X Files: I Want to Believe '08
Z '69 ▶

Credits Chaos!

See Genre Spoofs; Satire & Parody

Creepy Houses

See also Supernatural Horror

Abattoir '17
The Accursed '57
Alarm '08
An American Werewolf in Paris '97
The Amityville Horror '79
Amityville 2: The Possession '82
Amityville 3: The Demon '83
Amityville 4: The Evil Escapes '89
The Amityville Horror '05
Amityville 1992: It's About Time '92
Angel of the Night '98
The Attic '06
Bag of Bones '11
The Bat Whispers '30
Believe '99
Beneath '07
Beneath Us '20
Beyond Evil '80
The Black Castle '52
The Black Cat '41
The Black Widow '05
The Blancheville Monster '63
Blondie Has Trouble '40
Blood Island '68
Blood Legacy '73
Bones '01
Bonnie and Clyde vs. Dracula '08
Brahms: The Boy II '19
Break-In '06
Burnt Offerings '76
Candles at Nine '44
Carnage '84
Casper '95 ▶
Castle Freak '95
Castle of Blood '64
Castle of the Living Dead '64
The Cat and the Canary '39
The Cat and the Canary '79
The Changeling '80
Chasing Sleep '00
Chronicle of the Raven '04
Circle '10
Clive Barker's Book of Blood '08
Cold Creek Manor '03
The Collection '12
The Collector '09
The Colony '95
The Cradle '06
The Craft '96
Crescendo '69
Dark and Stormy Night '09
Dark House '09
Dark Mirror '07
Dark Water '02
Darkness '02
Dead Birds '04
A Dead Calling '06
Dead Collections '12
Deadline '09
Demon Seed '77 ▶
The Devil's Mercy '07
The Diary of Ellen Rimbauer '03
Die Sister, Die! '74
The Disappointments Room '16
Dolls '87
Don't Be Afraid of the Dark '73
Don't Be Afraid of the Dark '11
The Doorway '00
Down a Dark Hall '18
Dragonwyck '46
Dream House '11

8213: Gacy House '10
Endless Night '71
The Evil '78
Evil Laugh '86
Evil Remains '04
Evil Toons '90
The Fall of the House of Usher '49
The Fall of the House of Usher '60 ▶
Fear in the Night '47 ▶
Fertile Ground '10
Flowers in the Attic '87
For Sale by Owner '09
Francis in the Haunted House '56
Fright Night '85
Funnyman '94
Get Out '17 ▶
The Ghastly Ones '68
The Ghost and Mr. Chicken '66
The Ghost Breakers '40 ▶
Ghost in the Invisible Bikini '66
The Ghost of Dragstrip Hollow '59
The Ghost of Greville Lodge '00
Ghost Team '16
Girls School Screamers '86
The Glass House '01
Goblin '93
The Good Witch '08
Great Expectations '97
Grindstone Road '07
The Grudge '04
The Grudge 2 '06
Halloween: Resurrection '02
Haunted '95
Haunted Echoes '08
A Haunted House 2 '14
A Haunted House '13
The Haunted Mansion '03
Haunter '13
The Haunting '63 ▶
The Haunting '99
The Haunting in Connecticut 2: Ghosts of Georgia '13
The Haunting in Connecticut '09
The Haunting of Hell House '99
The Haunting of Marsten Manor '07
The Haunting of Winchester House '09
The Heirloom '05
Hereditary '18 ▶
Home Movie '08
House 2: The Second Story '87
House '86 ▶
The House Next Door '06
House of Bodies '13
House of Bones '09
House of Darkness '48
House of 9 '05
The House of Secrets '37
House of the Dead '78
The House of the Devil '09 ▶
House of the Living Dead '73
The House of the Seven Gables '40
The House of Usher '06
House on Haunted Hill '58
House on Haunted Hill '99
The House on Tombstone Hill '92
The House that Dripped Blood '71
The House That Jack Built '18
House Where Evil Dwells '82
Il Futuro '13
In Her Mother's Footsteps '06
The Innocents '61 ▶
Insidious '10
Insidious: The Last Key '18
It Comes at Night '17
Jane Eyre '11
Ju-On 2 '00
Keyhole '11
Killer Pad '06
Knocking on Death's Door '99
Last Hour '08
The Last Will and Testament of Rosalind Leigh '12
The Legend of Hell House '73 ▶
Light from Light '19 ▶
The Little Stranger '18
The Making of a Lady '12
Malice '93
Marked '07
The Mephisto Waltz '71 ▶
The Messengers '07
Midnight Bayou '09
Miss Pinkerton '32
Monster House '06 ▶
Mother's Day '80
Mouse Hunt '97 ▶
Munster, Go Home! '66
Murder by Death '76
Murder by Invitation '41
Murder Mansion '70
The Nesting '80
Nevermore '07
The New Daughter '10
Night Nurse '77
Night of the Demons 2 '94
Night of the Demons '09
Office Killer '97
The Old Dark House '32 ▶
The Orphanage '07 ▶
The Others '01 ▶
Our Mother's House '67
Panic Room '02
Paranoiac '62
The People under the Stairs '91
Personal Shopper '17 ▶
The Perverse Countess '73
The Pit and the Pendulum '09
Psycho '60 ▶
Psycho 2 '83
Psycho 3 '86
Psycho 4: The Beginning '90
Psycho '98
Psychosis '10
The Quiet Ones '14
A Quiet Place in the Country '69
The Raven '07
A Reflection of Fear '73
Restraint '08
Return to House on Haunted Hill '07
Revenge in the House of Usher '82
The Rocky Horror Picture Show '75 ▶
Rooms for Tourists '04
The St. Francisville Experiment '00
Salem's Lot '79
Scary Movie 2 '01
Secret Window '04
Secrets in the Walls '10
7 Below '11
7 Days to Live '00
The Shining '80
Shock '79
Shut In '16
Silent Scream '80
Sister, Sister '87
6 Degrees of Hell '12
The Skeleton Key '05
The Skeptic '09
The Skin I Live In '11
Smart House '00
The Smiling Ghost '41
Spectre '96
Spirit Lost '96
Stephen King's Rose Red '02
Stormswept '95
Superstition '82
Teenage Exorcist '93
Terror House '97
Terror in the Haunted House '58
Terror Tract '00
The Third Clue '34
13 Gantry Row '98
13 Ghosts '60
13 Ghosts '01
13 Seconds '03
Treasure of Fear '45
Two On a Guillotine '65
2: Voodoo Academy '12
The Uninvited '44 ▶
Visions '16
Visions of Evil '75
Warlock 3: The End of Innocence '98
Web of the Spider '70
What a Carve-Up! '62
Wild Oranges '24
Winchester '18
Witchouse 2: Blood Coven '00
Witchouse '99
The Woman in Black 2: Angel of Death '15
The Woman in Black '12
The Wyvern Mystery '00

Crime & Criminals

See *Biopics: Cops & Crime Drama; Crime Sprees; Crimes of Passion; Disorganized Crime; Frame-Ups; Fugitives; Gangs; Grand Theft Auto; Heists; Hit Men/Women; Juvenile Delinquents; Killer Spouses; Organized Crime; Scams, Stings & Serial Killers; Smuggler's Blues; True Crime; Urban Drama; Vigilantes*

Crime Doesn't Pay

See also *Crime Drama; Crimedy; Disorganized Crime; Heists*

All Things to All Men '13
Alpha Dog '06
American Heist '15
Animal Kingdom '09 ▶
Appointment With Danger '51
The Ardennes '17
Armored '09
The Australian Story '52
Bad Guys '08
Bad Men of Tombstone '49
Bad Samaritan '18
The Bag Man '14
The Bank Job '07
The Bank Job '08 ▶
Berlin Job '12
Big Bag of $ '09
Billionaire Boys Club '18
Blondie Johnson '33
Blue Blood '07
Bookies '03
The Boss '16
The Breaking Point '50 ▶
Brotherhood '10
Buffaloed '20
The Burglar '57
Burnt Money '00
Caliber 9 '72
Carjacked '11
Carnival of Wolves '96
Cellmates '12
The Chaperone '11
City on Fire '87
Cocaine Cowboys 2: Hustlin' with the Godmother '08
Crime Wave '54
Cry of the City '48
Decisions '10
Deliver Us From Evil '73
The Demolisher '15
Detour '17
Detour to Terror '80
The Devil Is a Sissy '36
Dog Eat Dog '16
Don't Breathe '16 ▶
Double Indemnity '44 ▶
Dragged Across Concrete '18
The Driftless Area '16
Drive '11 ▶
Easy Money '10 ▶
Easy Money: Hard to Kill '12
The Elder Son '06
The Entitled '11
Eyewitness '56
Federal Hill '94
Flypaper '11
Fog Over Frisco '34
Fool's Gold: The Story of the Brink's-Mat Robbery '92
44 Minutes: The North Hollywood Shootout '03
Freakshow '07
The Front Line '06
Get Lucky '13
Good Intentions '10
The Good Neighbor '16
Good People '14
The Good Samaritan '12
Graduation '07
Grand Slam '67
The Happy Thieves '61
Hard Times '09
The Hateful Eight '15 ▶
Henry's Crime '10
Hero Wanted '08
High Life '09
High School Big Shot '59
Highway 301 '50
The Hitman Diaries '09
Home of the Giants '07
Horrible Bosses 2 '14
How to Rob a Bank '07
The Human Centipede 3: The Final Sequence '15
Inside Men '12
Invisible Stripes '39
Julia '08
K-11 '11
Kidnapped '74
The Killing '56 ▶
Killing Them Softly '12
A Kind of Murder '16
King Cobra '16
Klepto '03
Krews '10
The Ladykillers '04
Lansdown '01
Layer Cake '05 ▶
Le Deuxieme Souffle '66
Leaves of Grass '09
Life of Crime '13
Lift '01
Liliom '30
Living & Dying '07
The Lookout '07 ▶
Lords of the Barrio '02
Love Is Colder Than Death '69
Macbeth '06
Machine Gun McCain '69
Man-Trap '61
Manos sucias '15 ▶
Mob Rules '10
Mother's Day '10
1922 '17
No Orchids for Miss Blandish '48
No Time to Be Young '57
Nobel Son '08
The Nut Job '14
Ocean's 11 '60
Plastic '14
The Poker Club '08
The Postman Always Rings Twice '46 ▶
The Postman Always Rings Twice '81
A Prayer Before Dawn '18 ▶
Pressed '11
Priceless '16
Pushover '54
The Red Lily '24
Redemption '13
Reykjavik-Rotterdam '08
Road to Paradise '30
Rob the Mob '14
RocknRolla '08
Roman J. Israel, Esq. '17
7 Minutes '15
Shut-Eye '03
Sinful Davey '69
Sleepless '17
A Slight Case of Murder '38
The Square '08
Stand Off '11
The Steel Trap '52
A Step Out of Line '71
Stranger by the Lake '13 ▶
Suburbicon '17
The Suspect '14
Sympathy for Mr. Vengeance '02 ▶
They Came to Rob Las Vegas '68
Three Strangers '46
Tomorrow You're Gone '12
A Touch of Sin '13 ▶
Tread Softly Stranger '58
Trespass '11
The Trust '16
Two Tough Guys '03
2:22 '08
A Vigilante '19
Villains '19
Wasteland '13
Wheelman '17
The Wolf of Wall Street '13 ▶
You Can't Get Away With Murder '39
Young America '32

Crime Drama

See also *Adventure Drama; Biopics: Cops & Crime Sprees; Crimes of Passion*

Abandoned '47
The Accountant '16
Acolytes '08
Across the Line: The Exodus of Charlie Wright '10
Acts of Contrition '95
Again, the Ringer '64
Against the Law '98
Age Out '19
Ain't Them Bodies Saints '13 ▶
The Air I Breathe '07
Ajami '09 ▶
Al Capone '59 ▶
Albino Alligator '96
Alex Cross '12
Alias French Gertie '30
Alibi '29
All Things to All Men '13
Ambushed '13
American Animals '18 ▶
An American Dream '66
American Gangster '07 ▶
American Heist '15
American Hustle '13 ▶
American Me '92 ▶
American Pastoral '16
And Never Let Her Go '01
Angel-A '05
Angels Wash Their Faces '39
Angels with Dirty Faces '38 ▶
Animal Kingdom '09 ▶
Another Day in Paradise '98
Another Man's Poison '52
Arbitrage '12 ▶
Arc '06
The Ardennes '17
Armored '09
Asian Connection '16
The Asphalt Jungle '50 ▶
Assault on Precinct 13 '76 ▶
Assault on Precinct 13 '05
The Assignment '17
At Close Range '86 ▶
Aurora '10
Awake '19
Baby Broker '81
Backfire '50
Backlash '99
Bad Blonde '53
Bad Boys '83 ▶
Bad City '06
Bad Country '14
Bad Guys '08
Bad Lieutenant '92 ▶
Bad Lieutenant: Port of Call New Orleans '09
Bad Times at the El Royale '18
Bad Turn Worse '14
The Bag Man '14
Bait '02
Bangkok Dangerous '00
Bangkok Dangerous '08
The Bank Job '08 ▶
Barefoot Boy '38
Baseline Killer '08
Basic Instinct 2 '06
Beach Patrol '79
Beast Cops '98 ▶
The Beast of the City '32
Beatdown '10
Beautiful '09
Bedevilled '55
Before the Devil Knows You're Dead '07 ▶
Behind the Green Lights '35
Belly '98
Ben Is Back '18
Berlin Job '12
Bernie '12 ▶
Best Laid Plans '99
Betrayed '44
The Betrayed '08
A Better Way to Die '00
Between Midnight and Dawn '50
Beyond the Trophy '12
The Big Boodle '57
The Big Caper '57
Big House, U.S.A. '55
The Big I Am '10
The Big Picture '10
The Big Shot '42
The Big Turnaround '88
Billionaire Boys Club '87
Billionaire Boys Club '18
Billy Bathgate '91
Birds of Passage '18 ▶
Bitter Sweet '98
Biutiful '10
Black and Blue '19
The Black Bird '26
Black Heat '76
The Black Legion '37 ▶
Black Market Babies '45
Black Out '12
Black Rain '89
Black Samson '74
Blackrock '97
Blackwell's Island '39
Blast of Silence '61
The Bletchley Circle '13
Blind Corner '63
Blind Trust '06
Blind Woman's Curse '70
Blink '93
Blondie Johnson '33
Blood and Bones '04
Blood & Wine '96
Blood Brother '18
Blood Brothers '07
Blood, Guts, Bullets and Octane '99
Blood In . . . Blood Out: Bound by Honor '93
Blood Money '98
Blood Money '17
Blood Ties '13
Blood Vows: The Story of a Mafia Wife '87
Blue-Eyed Butcher '12
Blue Hill Avenue '01
Blue Ridge Fall '99
Blues '08
Body Count '97
Bodywork '99
Boiling Point '93
Bonanno: A Godfather's Story '99
Bond of Fear '56
Bonnie's Kids '73
The Boondock Saints II: All Saints Day '09
Border Incident '49
Bordertown '06
Borough of Kings '98 ▶
The Boss '56
The Boss '73
Bought and Sold '03
The Box '03
Boy Who Caught a Crook '61
Boy Wonder '10
The Brave One '07
Brawl in Cell Block 99 '17
Breaking In '18
Breaking News '04
Breaking Point '09
Brighton Rock '10
Broken City '13
A Bronx Tale '93 ▶
A Brooklyn State of Mind '97
Brooklyn's Finest '09
Brother '97
Brother '00 ▶
The Brothers Rico '57
The Bubble '06
Bugsy '91 ▶
Bullet Head '17
Bullet to the Head '12
Bullhead '11
Bunco Squad '50
B.U.S.T.E.D. '99
The Burnt Orange Heresy '20
The Business '05
Butterfly Collectors '99
Buzzard '15 ▶
By the Gun '14
Bye-Bye '96
Cage of Evil '60
Caged Animal '10
Caliber 9 '72

▶ = rated three bones or higher

The Call '13
The Calling '14
Capone '89
Capone '20
The Captive City '52
Carbon Copy '69
Career Woman '36
Carnival of Crime '62
Cash on Demand '61
Casino '95 ▶
Castle on the Hudson '40 ▶
Catacombs '64
Catch.44 '11
Catherine Cookson's The Black Candle '92
The Cats '68
Caught in the Crossfire '10
Cement '99
The Ceremony '63
Certain Prey '11
Chain Gang '50
Chain Link '08
Changeling '08 ▶
Charlie '04
Chasing Ghosts '05
The Cheat '31
Chicago Confidential '57
Chicago Overcoat '09
Child 44 '15
China Heat '90
Citizen Gangster '11
City of Fear '59
City of Men '07 ▶
The City of Violence '06
Classe Tous Risque '60 ▶
Cleaverville '07
Close Range '15
Close Your Eyes '02
Coastlines '02
Code Two '53
Cold Comes the Night '14
Collateral '04 ▶
Collide '17
The Color of Lies '99
Compulsion '08
Confidence '03
The Connection '15
Contraband '12
The Contract '07
Convict Women '74
Convicted '50
Cool Breeze '72
Cop Au Vin '85
Cop Hater '58
Cop Land '97 ▶
The Counterfeit Plan '57
Counterplot '59
The Courier '19
Cover Up '49
The Cradle of Courage '20
Crash '05 ▶
Creepy '16 ▶
Crime and Punishment in Suburbia '00
Crime Boss '72
Crime Wave '54
Crimebroker '93
Criminal '04
Criminal '16
Criminal Activities '15
Criminal Desire '98
Criminal Intent '05
Crimson Gold '03
Cronicas '04
The Crooked Web '55
Crown Heights '17
The Crusader '32
Cry of the City '48
Cry Terror! '58
Crypto '19
Cuck '19
Cure '97 ▶
The Cutter '05
Cybergeddon '12
Cyclo '95
Dad Savage '97
The Damned Don't Cry '50
A Dangerous Profession '49
Dark Crimes '16
The Dark Knight Rises '12 ▶
Dark Night '17
The Darkest Corner of Paradise '10
A Daughter's Conviction '06
The Day They Robbed the Bank of England '60
Dead Bodies '03
Dead by Sunset '95
Dead End Kids: Little Tough Guy '38
Dead Man Down '13
Dead or Alive 2 '00
Dead Presidents '95
Deadfall '12
Deadly Honeymoon '10
Deadly Relations '93
Dean Koontz's Intensity '97
Death in Small Doses '57
Death Note 2: The Last Name '07
Death Note 3: L Change the World '08
Death Note '06 ▶
Death Sentence '07
The Debt '03
Deceit '04
Decisions '10
Decoy '46
The Deliberate Stranger '86 ▶
Den of Thieves '18
The Departed '06 ▶
Derailed '05
Destroyer '18
Detour '17
Detroit '17 ▶
The Devil's in the Details '13
Devil's Knot '14
Dial 1119 '50
Dilemma '97
Dillinger '45 ▶
Dillinger '73
Dillinger and Capone '95
The Dinner '17
Dirty '05
Dirty Harry '71 ▶
Dirty Lies '16
The Disappearance of Alice Creed '09
Distorted '18
District 13: Ultimatum '09
Doctor Chance '97
Dogville '03
Domino '19
Donnie Brasco '96 ▶
Don't Cry Now '07
Doorway to Hell '30
Down Three Dark Streets '54
Dragged Across Concrete '18
The Driftless Area '16
The Drop '14 ▶
Drug War '13 ▶
Dust Be My Destiny '39
Eastern Promises '07 ▶
Easy Money '10 ▶
Easy Money: Hard to Kill '12
ECCO '19
Ed McBain's 87th Precinct: Heatwave '97
Edge of Darkness '10
The Edukators '04
88 '15
88 Minutes '08
El Padrino '04
Element of Doubt '96
Elle '16 ▶
Elsewhere '09
Empire of the Wolves '05
End of Watch '12 ▶
Endgame '01
Endure '10
The Entitled '11
Entrapment '99
The Equalizer 2 '18
The Equalizer '14
Equity '16
The Escape Artist '13 ▶
Escobar: Paradise Lost '15
Essex Boys '99
Everybody Knows '18
Exclusive Story '36
Exposed '16
Extasis '96
Extremely Wicked, Shockingly Evil and Vile '19
Eyewitness '56
The Face of an Angel '14
The Face of Fu Manchu '65
The Factory '10
Fallen Angels '95
Family in Hiding '06
Family of Cops 2: Breach of Faith '97
Family of Cops 3 '98
The Fanatic '19
Fast Five '11
FBI Code 98 '63
Felony '13
Few Options '11
15 Minutes '01
The 15:17 to Paris '18
The Fifth Estate '13
A Fig Leaf for Eve '44
The File of the Golden Goose '69
Filth '13
Final Engagement '07
Fingers '78 ▶
Firewall '06
First Kill '17
Five Days '07
Flawless '07
Flower & Snake '04
Flypaper '97
For You I Die '47
Force of Evil '49 ▶
Foreign Land '95
The Forgiven '18
.45 '06
Four Boys and a Gun '57
4.3.2.1 '10
Framed '47
Freedomland '06
Freelancers '12
Friendship, Secrets and Lies '79
The Frightened Man '52
Frisco Jenny '32
Frisco Kid '35
The Front Line '06
The Frontier '16
The Frozen Ground '13
Full Time Killer '01
'G' Men '35 ▶
Gang Busters '55
Gang Related '96
Gangster Squad '13
Genealogies of a Crime '97
The General '98 ▶
Get Carter '71 ▶
Get Carter '00
Get Lucky '13
Get Rich or Die Tryin' '05
Ghost Dog: The Way of the Samurai '99
The Girl in the Spider's Web '18
Girl On the Run '53
The Girl Who Kicked the Hornet's Nest '10
The Girl Who Knew Too Much '69
The Girl Who Played With Fire '10
The Girl With the Dragon Tattoo '09 ▶
The Girl With the Dragon Tattoo '11 ▶
Glass Chin '14
Gloria '80
Gloria '98
Go for Sisters '13
The Godfather '72 ▶
The Godfather, Part 2 '74 ▶
The Godfather, Part 3 '90 ▶
Golden Gloves '40
Goldstone '18
Gomorrah '08 ▶
Gone Baby Gone '07 ▶
Gone Dark '03
Gone in 60 Seconds '00
Gonin 2 '96
Good Day for It '11
The Good Liar '19
A Good Man '14
Good People '14
Good People, Bad Things '08
The Good Samaritan '12
Good Time '17 ▶
Goodfellas '90 ▶
Gotti '18
Gozu '03
Graceland '12
Graduation '17
Grand Central Murder '42
Grand National Night '53
The Guilty '92
The Guilty '18 ▶
The Guilty Generation '31
Guns '08
Gunshy '98 ▶
Gutshot Straight '14
Harry Brown '09
The Hatchet Man '32
Hate Crime '05
Haven '04
Heat '95 ▶
The Heavy '09
The Heineken Kidnapping '11
Hell Bound '57
Hell's Bloody Devils '70
Hell's Half Acre '54
Hell's House '32
Her Forgotten Past '33
Hero Wanted '08
Hickey & Boggs '72
Hidden '05 ▶
High & Low '62 ▶
High Wall '47
The Highway Man '99
A History of Violence '05 ▶
The Hollow Point '16
Holy Rollers '10
Homicide '49
Honor Thy Father '73
Hood Vengeance '09
Hoodlum '96
Hoodrats 2 '08
Hostage '05
Hot Cars '56
Hotel Artemis '18
House of Bamboo '55
House of the Rising Sun '11
How It All Went Down '03
How to Kill a Judge '75
The Hunt for the I-5 Killer '11
The Hunted '48
The Hurricane Heist '18
Hustlers '19 ▶
Hyena '15
I Am Wrath '16
I Don't Feel at Home in This World Anymore '17 ▶
I Escaped from the Gestapo '43
I Saw the Devil '10
I Walk Alone '48
I Wouldn't Be in Your Shoes '48
The Iceman '12
I'll Get You '53
I'll Sleep When I'm Dead '03 ▶
Illegal Business '06
In Cold Blood '67 ▶
In Cold Blood '96
In Order of Disappearance '14
In the Line of Duty: Ambush in Waco '93
In the Line of Duty: The FBI Murders '88 ▶
In the Valley of Elah '07 ▶
In Too Deep '99
Incognito '97
Infamous '20
Infernal Affairs '02 ▶
Infernal Affairs 2 '03
Infernal Affairs 3 '03
Inferno '99
The Innocent Sleep '95
Inside Man '06 ▶
Inside Men '12
Inside Out '11
Internal Affairs '90
Interview With a Hitman '12
Into the Blue '05
The Intruder '04 ▶
Iowa '05
Iris Johansen's The Killing Game '11
The Irishman '19 ▶
I.T. '16
The Italian Connection '73
Jacked Up '01
Jackie Brown '97 ▶
Jesse Stone: Benefit of the Doubt '12
Jesse Stone: Death in Paradise '06
Jesse Stone: Night Passage '06
Jesse Stone: No Remorse '10
Jesse Stone: Stone Cold '05
Jindabyne '06
John Wick: Chapter 3-Parabellum '19 ▶
Johnny Cool '63
Joint Body '11
Journey to the End of the Night '06
Judicial Indiscretion '07
Juice '92
Julia '08
Julie '56
Just Before Nightfall '71
Kalifornia '93
Kansas City '95 ▶
Key Largo '48 ▶
Key Witness '47
Kidnap Syndicate '76
Kill a Dragon '67
Kill for Me '12
Kill Me Tomorrow '57
Killa Season '06
A Killer Among Friends '92
Killer Cop '02
The Killer Inside Me '10
The Killer Is Loose '56
Killer Joe '11
Killerman '19
The Killers '46 ▶
Killers Anonymous '19
The Killing Jar '10
The Killing of a Chinese Bookie '76
Killing Them Softly '12
Killing Zoe '94
Killshot '09
The King '18
King of the Ants '03
The King of the Roaring '20s: The Story of Arnold Rothstein '61
King of the Underworld '39
Kiss Me...Kill Me '76
Kiss the Girls '97
The Kitchen '19
Klepto '03
Knives Out '19 ▶
Kontroll '03 ▶
The Korean '08
Labyrinth of Lies '14
Lady Snowblood '73 ▶
Lansky '99
Larceny in her Heart '46
The Last Diamond '14
The Last Don 2 '98
The Last Don '97
The Last Gangster '37
Last Hour '08
The Last Lullaby '08 ▶
Last Man Standing '96
The Last Mile '59
Last Rampage '17
The Last Ride '04
The Last Run '71
The Last Stand '13
The Last Time I Saw Macao '13
Law Abiding Citizen '09
The Lawless '07
Lawless '12
Layer Cake '05 ▶
Le Deuxieme Souffle '66
Le Samourai '67 ▶
Legend '15
Les Misérables '19
Let Us Live '39
Lethal Victims '87
The Liability '12
Liar's Poker '99
Lies and Illusions '09
Lies My Mother Told Me '05
The Life Before This '99
Life Tastes Good '99
Lightning Strikes Twice '51
Lights in the Dusk '06
Lila & Eve '15
The Limey '99 ▶
The Lincoln Lawyer '11
The Line '08
The Lineup '58
Little Caesar '30 ▶
Little Odessa '94
Live by Night '16
Live Like a Cop, Die Like a Man '76
Lizzie '18
The Locator 2: Braxton Returns '09
Logan's War: Bound by Honor '98
London Boulevard '10
London Fields '18
The Lone Wolf Meets a Lady '40
Lonely Hearts '06
The Long Good Friday '80 ▶
The Long Memory '53
The Lookalike '14
The Lookout '07 ▶
Loophole '54
Loosies '11
Lord of War '05 ▶
Lords of the Barrio '02
The Lost Angel '04
The Lost Capone '90 ▶
The Lost Samaritan '08
Love Among Thieves '86
Love Is Colder Than Death '69
Love to Kill '97
A Lovely Way to Die '68
Lowriders '17
Lucky Luciano '74
Lucky Number Slevin '06
Lulu '02
M '31 ▶
Macbeth '06
Madeo '09
Mafia '11
Magic Man '10
The Maltese Falcon '31 ▶
The Maltese Falcon '41 ▶
The Man in the Net '59
Man in the Vault '56
A Man Named Rocca '61
Man on a Ledge '12
Man on a Swing '74
Man on Fire '04
Man-Trap '61
The Man Who Cheated Himself '50
Manhunt '01
The Marked One '63
Master '16
Match Point '05 ▶
McCanick '14
MDMA '18
Mean Streets '73 ▶
Meet Mr. Callaghan '54
Melissa '97 ▶
Memento '00 ▶
Memories of Murder '03
Men of Respect '91
Menace II Society '93 ▶
Mercy Streets '00
Meskada '10
Mesrine: Part 2-Public Enemy Number 1 '08
Metro Manila '13
The Miami Story '54
Miami Vice '06
Michael Clayton '07 ▶
Middle Men '10
Midnight Episode '50
Midnight Mary '33
Miller's Crossing '90 ▶
The Millerson Case '47
The Million Dollar Rip-Off '76
Millions '05 ▶
The Ministers '09
Misfire '14
Miss Bala '12
Miss Bala '19
Missing Girls '36
Mr. Brooks '07
Mr. Ricco '75
Mr. Soft Touch '49
Mob Rules '10
Mobius '13
Mobsters '91
Momentum '15
Money Kings '98
Money Monster '16
Mongo's Back In Town '71
Monument Ave. '98
The Morrison Murders '96
Motherless Brooklyn '19
Mother's Day '10
Motives 2-Retribution '07
The Mugger '58
The Mule '18 ▶
Munich '05 ▶
Murder by Contract '58
Murder By Two '60
Murder in New Hampshire: The Pamela Smart Story '91
Murder, Inc. '60
Murder Is My Beat '55
The Murder Man '35
Murder on the Orient Express '17 ▶
Murder With Pictures '36
Murderland '09

▶ = rated three bones or higher

Crime

My Baby Is Missing '07
My Son, My Son, What Have Ye Done '09
Mysteria '11
Mysterious Mr. Nicholson '47
Narc '02 ▸
The Narrows '08
Natural Born Killers '94
Necessity '88
Ned Kelly '03
Need for Speed '14
Neighboring Sounds '12 ▸
Neon Signs '96
Neruda '16
Never Die Alone '04
New Blood '99
New Jack City '91
New Orleans Uncensored '55
The Next Hit '08
The Nickel Ride '74
Night Editor '46
Night Falls on Manhattan '96 ▸
The Night Heaven Fell '57
Night Hunter '19
Nightcrawler '14 ▸
Nightwaves '03
9 Souls '03
99 Homes '14 ▸
No Alibi '00
No Country for Old Men '07 ▸
No Escape '53
No Good Deed '14
No Tomorrow '99
Normal Life '96
Notorious But Nice '33
November Criminals '17
Now You See Me '13
No. 3 '97
Officer Down '13
Once Upon a Time in America '84 ▸
Once Upon a Time in Anatolia '12 ▸
Once Upon a Time in Brooklyn '13
One False Move '91 ▸
One Girl's Confession '53
One Tough Cop '98
Only God Forgives '13
An Ordinary Man '18
Our Paradise '11
Out of Line '00
Out of Sight '98 ▸
Out of the Fog '41
The Outfit '73
Outrage '10
The Outsider '14
A Packing Suburbia '99
Pain & Gain '13
Painted Faces '29
The Painted Lady '97 ▸
Pale Saints '97
Palmetto '98
Paper Bullets '41
Paper Bullets '99
The Paperboy '12
Papillon '17
Parachute Jumper '32
Parker '13
Partners '09
Party Girl '58 ▸
Past Tense '06
Pawn '13
Payback '98 ▸
The Perfect Sleep '08
The Perfect Student '11
Persons Unknown '96
Petty Crimes '02
Phantom Lady '44 ▸
The Phantom of Crestwood '32
The Phantom of Paris '31
Phantom Raiders '40
The Phenix City Story '55
Phoenix '98
The Phenix City Story '55 ▸
Pickup Alley '57
Piercing '18
Pigalle '95
Pimp '18
Piranhas '19
Pit of Darkness '61
The Place Beyond the Pines '13 ▸
Plain Truth '04
The Playaz Court '07
Played '06
Playing God '96
Point Blank '10
The Poison Rose '19
Polar '19
Police, Adjective '09
Polisse '11 ▸
The Pope of Greenwich Village '84
Pound of Flesh '10
The Power of Few '13
Precious Cargo '16
Pressed '11
Presumed Dead '06
The Prey '11
Pride of Africa '97
Prince of Poisoners: The Life and Crimes of William Palmer '98
Prisoners '13 ▸
A Prophet '09 ▸
The Proposition '05
Prosecuting Casey Anthony '13
Proud Mary '18
The Public Defender '31
Public Enemies '09
Public Enemy '31 ▸
Public Enemy '02
Puerto Vallarta Squeeze '04
Pulp Fiction '94 ▸
The Purple Gang '59
Purple Noon '60 ▸
Pusher '96
Pushover '54
Q & A '90
Race Street '48
Radio Cab Murder '54
Rage '14
Raiders from Beneath the Sea '64
Railroaded '47
Rampart '11
Rancid '04
Ransom! '56
The Raven '12
Raven's Ridge '97
Read My Lips '01
Real Time: Siege at Lucas Street Market '00
Reaper '15
Reasonable Doubt '14
The Reckoning '14
Recoil '53
The Red-Haired Alibi '32
Red Light '49
Red Riding, Part 1: 1974 '09
Red Riding, Part 2: 1980 '09
Red Riding, Part 3: 1983 '09
Redacted '07
Redemption '13
Reindeer Games '00
Reprisal '18
Reservoir Dogs '92 ▸
Restraint '08
Revenge of the Green Dragons '14
Revolver '75
Revolver '05
Reykjavik-Rotterdam '08
Riot on 42nd Street '87
Rise of the Footsoldier '07
The Rise of the Krays '16
The River King '05
Road Ends '98
The Roaring Twenties '39 ▸
Rob the Mob '14
Romeo Must Die '00
The Rook '99
Row Your Boat '98
Rude Boy: The Jamaican Don '03
Rumble on the Docks '56
Run All Night '15
Runner Runner '13
Running Out of Time 2 '06
Running Scared '06
Running with the Devil '19
Sacrifice '11
Safe House '12
The Saint Meets the Tiger '43
Savage Island '03
Savages '12
A Scandal in Paris '46
Scarface '31 ▸
Scarface '83 ▸
Scene of the Crime '49
Scenes of the Crime '01
Schoolgirl Hitchhikers '73
Score '95
The Score '01
The Second Track '62
The Secret in Their Eyes '09 ▸
Secret in Their Eyes '15
The Secret Six '31 ▸
Secret Witness '88
See You Yesterday '19
The Sellout '51
Senorita Justice '03
Setup '11
Seven '95 ▸
7 Boxes '14 ▸
7 Days in Entebbe '18
711 Ocean Drive '50
7 Minutes '15
Sexy Beast '00 ▸
Shade '03
Shadow of Doubt '35
Shadowboxer '06
Shakedown on the Sunset Strip '88
Shanghai '09 ▸
She Played With Fire '57
Shifty '08
Shoot First, Die Later '74
Shoot to Kill '88 ▸
Shoplifters '18 ▸
Showdown '94
Shut-Eye '03
Shutter Island '09 ▸
Siberia '18
Side Street '50
The Silence '10 ▸
A Simple Favor '18 ▸
A Simple Plan '98 ▸
Sin City: A Dame to Kill For '14
Singham '11
A Single Shot '13
Sirens '02
The Sisters Brothers '18
Sitting Target '72
Six Ways to Sunday '99
16 Blocks '06 ▸
Skyscraper '18
Sleepless '17
Slow Burn '05
Small Town Murder Songs '10
Smalltime '96
S.M.A.R.T. Chase '18
The Sniper '52
The Snorkel '58
Snowden '16
The Snowman '17
Society Lawyer '39
Solo '06
The Son of No One '11
Sonatine '96 ▸
Spanish Judges '99
Speed Kills '18
The Spider Returns '41
Spin a Dark Web '56
The Square '08
Stage Struck '48
Stakeout '62
Stander '03
The Standoff at Sparrow Creek '19
Stash House '12
State of Grace '90 ▸
State Property 2 '05
The Steel Trap '52
A Step Out of Line '71
Steve Martini's The Judge '01
Steve Martini's Undue Influence '96
Stiletto '08
Straight out of Compton '99
The Strange Case of Dr. Rx '42
Strange Fruit '04
Street Gun '96
Street Kings '08
Street Kings 2: Motor City '11
Sugarhouse '07
Sun Don't Shine '12
SuperFly '18
The Suspect '05
Suspect Zero '04
Suspense '46
Suspicion '03
The Sweeney '12
Sweet Sixteen '02 ▸
Swelter '14
Sworn Enemies '96
The System '53
The Take '09
The Take '16
Take Me '01
Takers '10
Taking Lives '04
The Taking of Pelham 123 '09
Tapped Out '03
10 Minutes Gone '19
Tension '50
10th & Wolf '06
Term Life '16
Terminal '18
The Tesseract '03
Texas Killing Fields '11
That Naughty Girl '58
They Call It Murder '71
They Gave Him a Gun '37
They Made Me a Fugitive '47
Thick as Thieves '99
Things to Do in Denver When You're Dead '95 ▸
Third World Cop '99
13 West Street '62
The 36th Precinct '04 ▸
33 Postcards '11
This Day and Age '33
This Is Not a Love Song '02
This Side of the Law '50
This Thing of Ours '03
This Woman Is Dangerous '52
The Thomas Crown Affair '68 ▸
The 3 Marias '03
Thrill of the Kill '06
Thugs '96
Thugz '04
Thumbsucker '05 ▸
Tiger Bay '33
Today You Die '05
Tom Clancy's Netforce '98
Tomorrow Is Another Day '51
Tomorrow We Live '42
Tortured '08
A Touch of Sin '13 ▸
Tower '16 ▸
The Town '10 ▸
Toxic '07
Tracers '15
Track the Man Down '55
Trance '13
Transformed '05
Transsiberian '08 ▸
Tread Softly Stranger '58
Trespass '11
Trespass Against Us '16
Trick Baby '72
Triple Frontier '19
Triple 9 '15
Trojan Eddie '96 ▸
Trophy Wife '06
True Friends '98
True History of the Kelly Gang '20
Tsotsi '05 ▸
Turn It Up '00
Twelve '10
Twelve Hours to Kill '60
12 Hours to Live '06
12 Rounds 3: Lockdown '15
12 Rounds '09
Twenty8k '12
29 Palms '03
21 Bridges '19
The Twenty Questions Murder Mystery '50
22 July '18
23 Paces to Baker Street '56
22 Bullets '10
24 Exposures '13
Two Fathers: Justice for the Innocent '94
2 Guns '13
200 MPH '11
2 Little Monsters '15
Two Seconds '32
Two Smart People '46
2:22 '08
Ultimate Heist '09
Uncut Gems '19 ▸
Under Hellgate Bridge '99
The Undercover Man '49
Underground President '07
Undermind '03
The Underneath '95 ▸
The Unguarded Hour '36
United States of Leland '03
The Untouchables '87 ▸
The Upturned Glass '47
The Valachi Papers '72
Vampire Clan '02
The Vanquished '52
Vault '19
Venice Underground '05
The Verdict '46
Vice '08
Vice Raid '60
Vice Squad '53
Victoria '15
Villain '71
Vincent N Roxxy '17
Violent Blue '10
Violent Saturday '55
The Voice of the City '29
Waist Deep '06
A Walk Among the Tombstones '14
The Walker '07
The Walking Stick '70
Wanda '70
Warning Shot '67
Way of the Gun '00
We Own the Night '07
The Weapon '56
Welcome to the Punch '13
West New York '96
Wetbacks '56
Whacked! '02
What Comes Around '06
What Doesn't Kill You '08
Wheelman '17
When the Sky Falls '99
Where the Sidewalk Ends '50
Whipsaw '35
Whirlpool '49
White Boy Rick '18
The White Storm '13 ▸
Whiteout '09
The Whole Truth '16
Wicked Blood '13
Widows '18 ▸
Wife Wanted '46
Wild Card '15
The Wild Goose Lake '20
Wind River '17 ▸
Wired '08
Wiretapper '55
Without Evidence '96
Witness to the Mob '98
The Woman '11
The Woman in Red '35
Woman On the Run '50
The Woman Racket '30
The World of Kanako '15
Wozzeck '47
The Yards '00
Yellow Sky '48 ▸
You Can't Get Away With Murder '39
You Will Meet a Tall Dark Stranger '10
Young Adam '03 ▸
The Young Americans '93
Zero Tolerance '15
ZigZag '70
Zodiac '07

Crime Sprees

See also Fugitives; Lovers on the Lam

American Violence '17
Arizona '18
The Art of Self-Defense '19 ▸
Attack the Gas Station '99
Avengement '19
Awakening the Zodiac '17
Baby Driver '17 ▸
Baise Moi '00
The Big Bounce '69
Bloodline '19
Bonnie & Clyde '67 ▸
Bonnie & Clyde '13
Border Radio '88
Born Killers '05
The Boys Next Door '85
Burning Life '94
Butterfly Kiss '94
Cannonball Run Europe: The Great Escape '05
The Chant of Jimmie Blacksmith '78 ▸
Cop Killers '73
Corrupted Minds '06
Crackers '84
Cut Off '06
The Day of the Wolves '71
Dead End Kids: Little Tough Guy '38
Den of Thieves '18
Enemy Gold '93
15 Minutes '01
The First Purge '18
Forsaken '15
Fudoh: The New Generation '96
Fun With Dick and Jane '05
Girls Against Boys '12
Hangman '17
Heat '95 ▸
Hell or High Water '16 ▸
High Rolling in a Hot Corvette '77
Highway 301 '50
The House That Jack Built '18
Idiot Box '97
Imperium '16
In Cold Blood '96
Infamous '20
Jesse Stone: No Remorse '10
Jigsaw '17
John Doe: Vigilante '14 ▸
Joker '19 ▸
Keanu '16
Kichiku: Banquet of the Beasts '04
A Killer in the Family '83
The Lawless '07
Lawless '12
Lewis and Clark and George '97
A Little Thing Called Murder '06
Love and a .45 '94
Love Is Colder Than Death '69
Mad Dog Killer '77
Marauders '16
The Meanest Man in Texas '19
Mechanic: Resurrection '16
Meeting Evil '12
Mercury Plains '16
Murder One '88
Naked Youth '59
Natural Born Killers '94
Newtown '16 ▸
Normal Life '96
On the Run '73
The One '01
One Way Out '95
Piano Man '96
Point Break '15
Public Enemies '09
The Purple Gang '59
Rampage '87
Rampage: President Down '16
Reprisal '18
The Rise of the Krays '16
Ruben Brandt, Collector '18
Saw '04
Saw 2 '05
Set It Off '96
Shopping '93
The Snowtown Murders '12 ▸
Solace '16
Son of a Gun '14
The Sorcerers '67
Stander '03
Steelyard Blues '73
Stuff Stephanie in the Incinerator '89
Sworn Enemies '96
Takers '10
That Sinking Feeling '79 ▸
Thieves Like Us '74 ▸
The Tie That Binds '95
Tracers '15
True History of the Kelly Gang '20
The Vanishing '19
Virtuosity '95
Waist Deep '06
Wanda '70
When Brendan Met Trudy '00 ▸
The Whole Town's Talking '35 ▸

▸ = rated three bones or higher

Why Does Herr R. Run Amok? '69

Crimedy

See also Comic Cops; Disorganized Crime

Absolutely Fabulous: The Movie '16
Adventure in Manhattan '36
Analyze That '02
Analyze This '98 ▶
Armed Response '13
The Art of the Steal '13
Ask a Policeman '38
Avenging Angelo '02
Bad Actress '11
Bad Santa 2 '16
Baywatch '17
Beethoven's Big Break '08
Beg! '94
Bending the Rules '12
Betsy's Wedding '90
Big Nothing '06
Big Trouble '02
The Biggest Bundle of Them All '68
Blonde and Blonder '07
Blood & Concrete: A Love Story '91
Boys Will Be Boys '35
Break '09
Breaking & Exiting '18
The Brooklyn Heist '08
The Brothers Bloom '09
Burn After Reading '08
The Busy Body '67
Carry On Matron '72
Cash '08
Chaos & Cadavers '03
The Chaperone '11
Christmas in Wonderland '07
Compadres '16
The Con Artist '10
Cop Out '10
Corky Romano '01
Crazy on the Outside '10
The Crew '00
Crimes of Fashion '04
Criminal Ways '03
The Day Shall Come '19
Dead Fish '04
Dead Lenny '06
Dead Man Running '09
Defendor '09
Dog Gone '08
The Dog Who Saved Christmas Vacation '10
The Dog Who Saved Summer '15
The Dogfather '10
Dom Hemingway '13
Down Terrace '10
Drive Hard '14
Duffy '68
The Dukes '07
8 Heads in a Duffel Bag '96
ExTerminators '09
Fakers '04
The Fall of the American Empire '19
The Family '13
Finding Steve McQueen '19
First Sunday '08
Fitzwilly '67
Flypaper '11
Forget About It '06
Freaky Deaky '12
Friends and Family '01
Gambit '12
Game Night '18
The Gentlemen '20
Get Hard '15
Get Shorty '95 ▶
Gigli '03
The Girl Most Likely to. . . '73
Going in Style '17
Good Intentions '10
Good Morning, Boys '37
The Great Diamond Robbery '53
The Guard '11 ▶
The Happy Thieves '61
Hard Times '09
Harry in Your Pocket '73
Henry's Crime '10
Hi, Nellie! '34
High Life '09
Hit and Run '12
Hit By Lightning '14
Hit Parade '10
A Holiday Heist '11
Hoodlum & Son '03
Horrible Bosses '11
The House '17
The Hustle '19
Identity Thief '13
The Inveterate Bachelor '58
It All Came True '40
It Shouldn't Happen to a Dog '46
I've Got Your Number '34
The Jerky Boys '95
Jewel Robbery '32
Jimmy the Gent '34
The Job '09
Judy & Punch '20
Kaleidoscope '66
Kangaroo Jack '02
Kick-Ass 2 '13
Kill Me Quick, I'm Cold '67
Kill Your Friends '16
Knockaround Guys '01
Ladrones '15
Larceny, Inc. '42
Last Day of Summer '10
The Last Godfather '10
The Laundromat '19
Leaves of Grass '09
Legacy '08
Let Go '11
Lies & Alibis '06
Life of Crime '13
Logan Lucky '17 ▶
The Love Punch '13
Love That Brute '50
The Lovebirds '20
Lowlife '18
Mad Dog and Glory '93 ▶
Mad Money '08
Madness in the Method '19
Mafia! '98
The Maiden Heist '08
Maisie Goes to Reno '44
Malice in Wonderland '09
Margin for Error '43
Married to the Mob '88 ▶
Masterminds '16
The Mexican '01
Micmacs '09
Miss Nobody '10
Miss Pinkerton '32
Mister 880 '50
Mr. Nice '10
Monsieur Gangster '63
The Murderer Lives at Number 21 '42
My Mom's New Boyfriend '08
National Lampoon Presents: Endless Bummer '09
A New Wave '07
Next Day Air '09
The Nitwits '35
The Nuisance '33
Ocean's 8 '18
Ocean's Thirteen '07 ▶
One for the Money '12
One More Time '70
Oscar '91
Osso Bucco '08
Paddington 2 '17 ▶
Paul Blart: Mall Cop 2 '15
Paul Blart: Mall Cop '09
Perrier's Bounty '09
Pineapple Express '08 ▶
Plastic '14
Play Dead '09
Postman's Knock '62
Prizzi's Honor '85 ▶
Pros and Ex-cons '05
Public Menace '35
The Return of Joe Rich '11
R.I.P.D. '13
Robin-B-Hood '06
RocknRolla '08
Sail a Crooked Ship '61
Saintly Sinners '62
The Scenesters '09
Seven Psychopaths '12 ▶
Sexy Evil Genius '13
Shaft '19
Silver Case '11
Skidoo '68
A Slight Case of Larceny '53
A Somewhat Gentle Man '10
The Southern Star '69
The Spirit '87
Spring Breakers '13 ▶
Stand Off '11
Stand Up Guys '12
Staten Island '09
Strictly Sinatra '01
The Strike '16
Sweet Revenge '76
Table One '00
Tall, Dark and Handsome '41
30 Minutes or Less '11
Thoroughbreds '17
Three Billboards Outside Ebbing, Missouri '17 ▶
Tower Heist '11
Tragedy Girls '17 ▶
True Confession '37
29 Palms '03
Undercover Maisie '47
Up Goes Maisie '46
Venus and Vegas '10
War on Everyone '17
Welcome to Acapulco '19
The Wendell Baker Story '05
We're the Millers '13
The Whole Nine Yards '00
Wild Target '10
Women Who Kill '17
You Move You Die '07

Crimes of Passion

The Amy Fisher Story '93
Are You Listening? '32
Backfire '88
Bad Boy Bubby '93
The Big Clock '48 ▶
Bizarre '87
Blood Vows: The Story of a Mafia Wife '87
The Blue Dahlia '46 ▶
Born to Kill '47 ▶
The Canal '14
Casque d'Or '52 ▶
China Moon '91
Concealed Weapon '94
Crime of Passion '57
The Crucible '96 ▶
Deadbolt '92
Deception '46 ▶
Fatal Attraction '87 ▶
The Gingerbread Man '97
I Love You to Death '90
Jade '95
Knots '05
Lethal Lolita-Amy Fisher: My Story '92
The Love Flower '20
The Lovers and the Despot '16
The Mask of Diijon '46
Murder in New Hampshire: The Pamela Smart Story '91
Murder Rap '87
Niagara '52
The People *vs.* Jean Harris '81 ▶
Rancid '04
Secret Beyond the Door '48
Sex Crimes '92
The Shooting Party '77
Single White Female '92
Snowden '16
To Die For '95 ▶
Tomorrow Never Comes '77
Victim of Beauty '91
Woman in the Window '44 ▶
Wozzeck '47

Criminally Insane

See also Crime Sprees; Torn in Two (or More)

Amputee with an Axe '73
Basement Jack '09
Birds of Prey: And the Fantabulous Emancipation of One Harley Quinn '20
The Blancheville Monster '63
Blood Night: The Legend of Mary Hatchet '09
Carnage Park '16
Christmas on Mars '08
Circle '10
The Dark Knight '08 ▶
The Demolisher '15
The Devil Inside '12
Dial 1119 '50
The 11th Hour '14
The Fanatic '19
The Haunting of Sharon Tate '19
High Tension '03
I Am Not A Serial Killer '16
Interrogation '16
The Intruder '19
Knock Knock '15
Last Resort '09
Love Sick Love '12
Mansion of the Doomed '76
Meadowland '15
Medium Raw: Night of the Wolf '10
Parasomnia '08
Ricochet '91 ▶
Shutter Island '09 ▶
Sleep Tight '11
Son of Sam '08
Split '16
31 '16
Toxic '07
Unbreakable '00

The Crusades

The Adventures of Robin Hood '38 ▶
Arn: The Knight Templar '07
Four Warriors '15
King Richard and the Crusaders '54
Kingdom of Heaven '05 ▶
Labyrinth '12
Lionheart '90
Robin and Marian '76
Robin Hood: Prince of Thieves '91

Cuba

See also Red Scare

Assault of the Rebel Girls '59
Before Night Falls '00 ▶
The Big Boodle '57
Camp X-Ray '14
Cassanova Was a Woman '15
Central Airport '33
Che '08
Chico & Rita '10
The Company '07
Company Man '00
Cuba '79 ▶
Cuban Blood '03
Dance with Me '98
Dirty Dancing: Havana Nights '04
A Few Good Men '92 ▶
Fidel '02 ▶
For Love or Country: The Arturo Sandoval Story '00
The Godfather, Part 2 '74 ▶
Guantanamera '95 ▶
Guantanamero '07
The Gun Runners '58
Havana '90
Hello, Hemingway '90
Key Largo '48 ▶
A Lady Without Passport '50
Lansky '99
The Last Supper '76 ▶
The Lost City '05
A Message to Garcia '36
Missiles of October '74 ▶
The Motorcycle Diaries '04 ▶
The Old Man and the Sea '58 ▶
The Old Man and the Sea '90
Original Sin '01
Our Man in Havana '59 ▶
Papa: Hemingway in Cuba '16
The Perez Family '94
Plato's Run '96
Rough Riders '97
Ruby '92
Santiago '56
Scarface '83 ▶
Secundaria '14
Sicko '07
South of the Border '09
Strawberry and Chocolate '93 ▶
Things I Left in Havana '97
Thirteen Days '00 ▶
Una Noche '13
Who the Hell is Juliette? '98

Cuban Missile Crisis

An American Affair '09
Blast from the Past '98
The Good Shepherd '06
Jackie, Ethel, Joan: The Kennedy Women '01
Kennedy '83
Matinee '92
Missiles of October '74 ▶
A Single Man '09 ▶
Taken '02
Thirteen Days '00 ▶
Topaz '69 ▶
X-Men: First Class '11 ▶

Cubicle Hell

See also Bad Bosses; Workin' for a Livin'

Bloodsucking Bastards '15
Clockwatchers '97
He Was a Quiet Man '07
A Job to Kill For '06
Office Space '98
Operation: Endgame '10
Tokyo Sonata '09 ▶

Cults

See also Occult; Satanism

Alien Nation: Millennium '96
Apostle '18
As Good As Dead '10
Bad Dreams '88
Bad Times at the El Royale '18
Batman Begins '05 ▶
The Believers '87
Believers '07
Beware! Children at Play '95
Black Zoo '63
Bloodbath '76
Borderland '07
Burial of the Rats '95
Chain of Souls '00
Children of the Corn 2: The Final Sacrifice '92
Children of the Corn '09
Cobra Woman '44
Cthulhu '08
Cult of the Cobra '55
The Day Shall Come '19
Deadly Blessing '81
The Deceivers '88
The Devil's Prey '01
Drive Angry '11
The Endless '17
Eye of the Devil '67
Fatal Passion '94
Faults '15
Force: Five '81
Forever Evil '87
The French Atlantic Affair '79
The Guyana Tragedy: The Story of Jim Jones '80
Hellraiser: Deader '05
Helter Skelter '76
Helter Skelter Murders '71
Holy Hell '16
Holy Smoke '99
In God's Country '07
In the Line of Duty: Ambush in Waco '93
Isaac Asimov's Nightfall '00
Jug Face '13
June '15
Kaboom '11
The Last Lovecraft: Relic of Cthulhu '09
The Lodge '19
Lord of Illusions '95
The Love-Ins '67
The Loved One '65
Mandy '18
The Manson Family '04
Martha Marcy May Marlene '11 ▶
The Mephisto Waltz '71 ▶
Midnight Special '16 ▶
Midsommar '19
The Mighty Ursus '61
Mind, Body & Soul '92
Mindstorm '01
The Nameless '99
Next One '84
Night of the Death Cult '75
Not Forgotten '09
Postal '07
Purana Mandir '84 ▶
Putney Swope '69 ▶
The Pyx '73 ▶
The Reincarnate '71
Revenge '86
Rock Slyde: Private Eye '09
Sabaka '55
The Sacrament '13
Safe '95 ▶
Savage Messiah '02
Servants of Twilight '91
Seven Stages to Achieve Eternal Bliss '20
Shock 'Em Dead '90
The Snake People '68
Soul's Midnight '06
Sound of My Voice '11
The Source Family '13
Spellbinder '88
The Stranglers of Bombay '60
They Crawl '01
Thou Shalt Not Kill. . .Except '87
Ticket to Heaven '81 ▶
Ultrachrist! '03
Vampire Clan '02
Withnail and I '87 ▶
Wolfcop '15
Yeti: A Love Story '08

Culture Clash

ABCD '99
American Adobo '02
American Chai '01
American Factory '19 ▶
American Fusion '05
An American Rhapsody '01 ▶
American Venus '07
Amreeka '09 ▶
Appropriate Behavior '14
Babe: Pig in the City '98
Babel '06 ▶
The Baby Dance '98 ▶
Bandidas '06
Battles of Chief Pontiac '52
Beatriz at Dinner '17
The Beautiful Country '04
Before the Rains '07
The Bengali Night '88
The Beverly Hillbillies '93
Beverly Hills Chihuahua '08
Beyond Honor '05
Black Robe '91 ▶
Blindspotting '18
The Bookshop '18
Borat: Cultural Learnings of America for Make Benefit Glorious Nation of Kazakhstan '06 ▶
Brand New Day '10
Breaking and Entering '06
Bride & Prejudice '04
Bringing Down the House '03
The Brother from Another Planet '84 ▶
Cabaret '72 ▶
Carla's Song '97
Caterina in the Big City '03
Catfish in Black Bean Sauce '00
Chalet Girls '11
The Chateau '01
Chicken Tikka Masala '05
Chutney Popcorn '99
City of Ghosts '03
City of Joy '92
The Class '08
The Comfort of Strangers '91 ▶
Compulsion '08
Concrete Cowboys '79
Coneheads '93
The Cookout '04
Crash '05 ▶
crazy/beautiful '01
Crocodile Dundee '86 ▶
Crocodile Dundee in Los Angeles '01
Dark Matter '07
David & Layla '07
Dead Heart '96 ▶
Deliverance '72 ▶
Devdas '55 ▶
Devdas '02 ▶
Did You Hear About the Morgans? '09
Disengagement '07
Down in the Delta '98 ▶
The Dreamers '03

▶ = rated three bones or higher

East Is East '99 ▶
The Emerald Forest '85 ▶
Encino Man '92
The Europeans '79 ▶
Everything is Illuminated '05 ▶
Falling for Grace '06
The Family Stone '05
The Fast and the Furious: Tokyo Drift '06
A Few Best Men '11
For Richer or Poorer '97
The Foul King '00
From Above '13
From Prada to Nada '11
G '02
George of the Jungle '97 ▶
Georgia Rule '07
Get Him to the Greek '10
The Glory Brigade '53
God's Not Dead 2 '16
Gonzo: The Life and Work of Dr. Hunter S. Thompson '08 ▶
Gorillas in the Mist '88 ▶
The Great New Wonderful '06
Green Dragon '01
Greystoke: The Legend of Tarzan, Lord of the Apes '84
The Guard '11 ▶
The Guru '02
Heart of Light '97
Heat and Dust '82 ▶
Hello Goodbye '08
A Hologram for the King '16
Holy Man '98
The Hoodlum '19
The Hundred-Foot Journey '14
I Want to Go Home '89
The Idle Rich '29
The Infidel '10
Japanese War Bride '52
Jimmy Vestvood: Amerikan Hero '16
Jumping the Broom '11
Just Like a Woman '13
Just Visiting '01
Kumiko the Treasure Hunter '14 ▶
The Landlord '70
Language of the Enemy '07
The Last Samurai '03 ▶
Late Marriage '01
L'Auberge Espagnole '02 ▶
Lawrence of Arabia '62 ▶
Le Divorce '03
Like A Bride '94 ▶
Lila Says '04
Lilting '14 ▶
The Lost Child '00
Lullaby '14
Malibu's Most Wanted '03
A Man Called Ove '15 ▶
The Man Who Knew Infinity '16
Marigold '07
Marking Time '03
Maryam '00
Meet the Fockers '04
Meet the Parents '00 ▶
Midsummer Madness '07
Mighty Fine '12
The Mission '86 ▶
Mississippi Masala '92 ▶
Mister Johnson '91 ▶
Mixing Nia '98
Monsieur Lazhar '11
Moonlighting '82 ▶
Mooz-Lum '10
Moscow on the Hudson '84 ▶
The Namesake '06 ▶
The Nephew '97
Oh Lucy! '17
On Chesil Beach '17
One Long Night '07
OSS 117: Lost in Rio '09
The Other End of the Line '08
The Other Son '12 ▶
Our Family Wedding '10
Outsourced '06
A Passage to India '84 ▶
Pathfinder '07
Piccadilly '29
Quigley Down Under '90
Red Doors '05
Rescue from Gilligan's Island '78
River Queen '05
Rock My World '02
Rodgers & Hammerstein's South Pacific '01
Rush Hour '98
Saving Face '04
The Science of Sleep '06
Shadow Magic '00
Shanghai Knights '03
Shanghai Noon '00
The Sheltering Sky '90 ▶
Shogun '80 ▶
Snow Dogs '02
The Snow Walker '03
Songcatcher '99 ▶
South Pacific '58 ▶
Spanglish '04
Splash '84
Starman '84 ▶
Stonewall '15
Strangers with Candy '06
Super Troopers 2 '18
Swept from the Sea '97
Tamara Drewe '10
Tammy Tell Me True '61
They Will Have to Kill Us First: Malian Music in Exile '15
Thunderheart '92 ▶
Tokyo Cowboy '94
2 Brothers & a Bride '03
Uncle Nino '03
Wanderlust '12
Wasabi '01
Wassup Rockers '06
The Wedding Night '35
West Is West '87
White Material '10
Witness '85 ▶
A Woman of the World '25
The Women on the Sixth Floor '10
Wondrous Oblivion '06 ▶
Yelling to the Sky '11
Yes '04
Zorba the Greek '64 ▶

Custer's Last Stand

Little Big Man '70 ▶
Seventh Cavalry '56

Custody Battles

See also Divorce; Order in the Court; Single Parents

Bag of Bones '11
Big Daddy '99
Black or White '14
Captain Fantastic '16
Careful, He Might Hear You '84 ▶
Changing Lanes '02 ▶
The Child Stealer '79
The Courtship of Andy Hardy '42
A Dad for Christmas '06
Daddy's Little Girls '07
Dark Water '02
Dream House '11
Edge of Winter '16
Evelyn '02 ▶
Faithless '00 ▶
A Father's Choice '00
Gaudi Afternoon '01
Gifted '17
The Good Mother '88
I Am Sam '01
In the Family '11
Irreconcilable Differences '84
Kramer *vs.* Kramer '79 ▶
Like Dandelion Dust '09
Losing Isaiah '94 ▶
The Man I Married '40
Menashe '17
Mrs. Doubtfire '93
My Silent Partner '06
Rain Man '88 ▶
Special Delivery '08
Steve Martini's Undue Influence '96
Taken From Me: The Tiffany Rubin Story '10
Third Person '13
Who Is Clark Rockefeller? '10
Your Love Never Fails '11

Cuttin' Heads

Abbott and Costello in Hollywood '45
Allie & Me '97
Barbershop 2: Back in Business '04 ▶
Barbershop '02 ▶
The Beautician and the Beast '97
The Big Tease '99
Black Shampoo '76
Blow Dry '00
Born to Win '71
Caramel '07 ▶
Chain of Fools '00
Claire Dolan '97
Coming to America '88 ▶
The Crying Game '92 ▶
Demon Barber of Fleet Street '36
Earth Girls Are Easy '89
Educating Rita '83 ▶
An Everlasting Piece '00
The French Touch '54
Frolics on Ice '39
Good Hair '09
The Hairdresser's Husband '92
Hairspray '88 ▶
Hellbent '04
Honey '03
House of Traps '81
Killer Hair '09
The Man Who Wasn't There '01 ▶
The Matrimonial Bed '30
Mississippi Burning '88 ▶
Nora's Hair Salon 2: A Cut Above '08
Norman Rockwell's Shuffleton's Barbershop '13
Nutty Professor 2: The Klumps '00
Poetic Justice '93
Reducing '31
Runaway Bride '99 ▶
The Salon '05
Shampoo '75
Spotlight Scandals '43
Steel Magnolias '89 ▶
Steel Magnolias '12 ▶
Stigmata '99
Sweeney Todd: The Demon Barber of Fleet Street '84
Sweeney Todd: The Demon Barber of Fleet Street '07
Venus Beauty Institute '98
The Village Barbershop '08
You Don't Mess with the Zohan '08

Cyberpunk

Arcade '93
Blade Runner '82 ▶
Code Hunter '02
The Crow 2: City of Angels '96
Cyborg '89
Cyborg 2 '93
Cyborg Soldier '94
Death Games '02
Demolition Man '93
Escape from L.A. '96
Escape from New York '81
The Fifth Element '97
Freejack '92
The Gene Generation '07
Hackers '95
Johnny Mnemonic '95
Lawnmower Man 2: Beyond Cyberspace '95
The Lawnmower Man '92
Mad Max '80 ▶
Mad Max: Beyond Thunderdome '85
Natural City '03
Nemesis '93
Project X '68
The Road Warrior '82 ▶
RoboCop '87 ▶
RoboCop 2 '90
RoboCop 3 '91
Rubber's Lover '97
Stealing Candy '04
Tank Girl '94
TekWar '94
Terminator 2: Judgment Day '91 ▶
The Terminator '84 ▶
Tetsuo: The Iron Man '92
Tetsuo 2: Body Hammer '97
Total Recall '90 ▶
Tron '82
Tron: Legacy '10
Universal Soldier '92
Universal Soldier: The Return '99
Virtual Combat '95
Virtuosity '95

Dads

See Bad Dads; Monster Moms; Parenthood; Stepparents

Dallas

See also Black Gold; Houston; Texas

Asteroid '97
A Cool, Dry Place '98
Dallas Buyers Club '13 ▶
Dr. T & the Women '00 ▶
Free, White, and 21 '62
JFK '91 ▶
Love Field '91
The Night of the White Pants '06
North Dallas Forty '79 ▶
Ruby '92
Steele's Law '91
Suspect Zero '04
Talk Radio '88 ▶
The Thin Blue Line '88 ▶
A Woman of Independent Means '94 ▶
The X-Files '98

Dance Fever

See also Ballet; Disco Musicals

The Accompanist '20
Alive and Kicking '96
All That Jazz '79 ▶
An American in Paris '51 ▶
Anchors Aweigh '45 ▶
And Then We Danced '20 ▶
April in Paris '52
Assassination Tango '03 ▶
Babes in Arms '39
The Band Wagon '53 ▶
The Barefoot Contessa '54 ▶
The Barkleys of Broadway '49 ▶
Battle of the Year '13
Battlefield America '12
Beat Street '84
Because of You '95
The Belle of New York '52
Bert Rigby, You're a Fool '89
Billy Elliot '00 ▶
Billy Rose's Jumbo '62 ▶
Black Orpheus '58 ▶
Blood Wedding '81 ▶
Bloody Homecoming '12
Body Rock '84
Bojangles '01
Boogie Nights '97 ▶
Bootmen '00
Born to Dance '36
Breakin' 2: Electric Boogaloo '84
Breakin' '84
Broadway '42
Broadway Melody of 1940 '40
Cabin in the Sky '43 ▶
Can-Can '60
Captain January '36
Carefree '38 ▶
Carmen '83 ▶
Center Stage '00
Center Stage: Turn It Up '08
Centerstage: On Pointe '16
A Chorus Line '85
Climax '18
Come Dance at My Wedding '09
Come Dance With Me '12
Cover Girl '44 ▶
Cuban Fury '14
Cunningham '19
Curdled '95
Daddy Long Legs '55 ▶
Dames '34 ▶
Dance Flick '09
Dance with Me '98
Dancehall Queen '97
Dancing Lady '33
Delightfully Dangerous '45
Dirty Dancing '87 ▶
Dirty Dancing: Havana Nights '04
Doll Face '46
Downton Abbey '19 ▶
El Amor Brujo '86 ▶
Everybody's Dancin' '50
Everyone Says I Love You '96 ▶
Everything I Have is Yours '52
Fame '80 ▶
Fame '09
Fast Forward '84
Faster, Pussycat! Kill! Kill! '65
Feel the Beat '20
The Fits '16
Flashdance '83
Flower Drum Song '61
Flying Down to Rio '33
Follies Girl '43
Follow the Fleet '36 ▶
Footlight Parade '33 ▶
Footloose '84
Footloose '11
The Forbidden Dance '90
42nd Street '33 ▶
The FP '12
French Can-Can '55 ▶
From Dusk Till Dawn '95
The Full Monty '96 ▶
Full Out '15
The Gay Divorcee '34 ▶
Ginger & Fred '86 ▶
Girl '18 ▶
Girl in Gold Boots '69
Girls Just Want to Have Fun '85
Give a Girl a Break '53
The Glass Slipper '55
Gloria Bell '18
Go For It! '10
Gold Diggers of 1933 '33 ▶
Gold Diggers of 1935 '35 ▶
Grease 2 '82
Grease '78 ▶
Groove '00 ▶
Hair '79 ▶
Hairspray '88 ▶
Hairspray '07 ▶
Happy Feet '06 ▶
The Harvey Girls '46 ▶
High Strung '16
Hit the Deck '55
Hocus Pocus '93
Holiday Spin '12
Honey 2 '14
Honey 3: Dare to Dance '16
Honey '03
How She Move '08
Human Traffic '99
Idiot's Delight '39 ▶
The In Crowd '88
It Started in Naples '60 ▶
Just Like a Woman '13
Kickin' It Old Skool '07
Kiss Me Kate '53 ▶
Lambada '89
Last Dance '91
The Last Days of Disco '98 ▶
Leading Ladies '10
Les Girls '57
Let's Dance '50
Lilo & Stitch 2: Stitch Has a Glitch '05
Liquid Dreams '92
Lives of Performers '72
Look Who's Talking '89 ▶
Love N' Dancing '09
Mad Hot Ballroom '05 ▶
Make It Happen '08
Make Your Move '13
Mamma Mia! '08
Manhattan Merenque! '95
Mantis in Lace '68
Margot '09
Marigold '07
Marilyn Hotchkiss' Ballroom Dancing & Charm School '06
Michael '96
Michael Jackson's This Is It '09
Music in My Heart '40
The Next Step '95
One Perfect Day '04
Orgy of the Dead '65
Out to Sea '97
Paris Is Burning '91 ▶
Party Girl '58 ▶
Pennies from Heaven '81 ▶
Pina '11
The Pirate '48 ▶
Portrait of a Showgirl '82
Pulp Fiction '94 ▶
Queen of the Stardust Ballroom '75 ▶
Risky Business '83 ▶
Rize '05 ▶
Roberta '35 ▶
Romance in Manhattan '34
Romy and Michele's High School Reunion '97
Rooftops '89
Roseland '77 ▶
Salsa '88
Satin Rouge '02
Saturday Night Fever '77
Save the Last Dance 2 '06
Save the Last Dance '01
Scent of a Woman '92 ▶
Seamless '00
Second Chorus '40
Secundaria '14
Seven Brides for Seven Brothers '54 ▶
Shag: The Movie '89 ▶
Shall We Dance '37 ▶
Shall We Dance? '96 ▶
Shall We Dance? '04
Showgirls '95
Silk Stockings '57 ▶
Singin' in the Rain '52 ▶
Siren of the Tropics '27
Slashdance '89
Spirit of '76 '91
Spork '10
Staying Alive '83
Step '17
Step Up 3D '10
Step Up '06
Step Up: All In '14
Step Up Revolution '12
Step Up 2 the Streets '08
Stomp the Yard '07
Stomp the Yard 2: Homecoming '10
The Story of Vernon and Irene Castle '39 ▶
Strictly Ballroom '92 ▶
Stripped to Kill 2: Live Girls '89
Summer Stock '50 ▶
Sunset Strip '91
Suspiria '18
Sweet Charity '69 ▶
Swing Kids '93
Swing Time '36 ▶
Take Me Out to the Ball Game '49
Take the Lead '06
Tango '98
The Tango Lesson '97
Tap '89
Teen Wolf '85
Thank God It's Friday '78
That's Dancing! '85 ▶
That's Entertainment, Part 2 '76
That's Entertainment, Part 3 '93
That's the Way I Like It '99
They Shoot Horses, Don't They? '69 ▶
Those Lips, Those Eyes '80
A Time for Dancing '00
Top Hat '35 ▶
The Turning Point '77
Twinkletoes '26
The Unfinished Dance '47
Urban Cowboy '80
Voulez-Vous Danser avec Moi? '59
We Are Your Friends '15
West Side Story '61 ▶
What's the Matter with Helen? '71
Words and Music '48
Yankee Doodle Dandy '42 ▶
Yellow '06
You Got Served '04
You Were Never Lovelier '42 ▶
You'll Never Get Rich '41 ▶
Zatoichi '03 ▶
Ziegfeld Follies '46

Ziegfeld Girl '41 ▸
Zou Zou '34

Dates from Hell

***See also** Singles*
After Hours '85 ▸
Better Off Single '16
Blind Date '87
Body Shots '99
Bride of Chucky '98
The Brothers Solomon '07
Bye Bye, Love '94
Casual Encounters '16
Fatal Secrets '09
The 40 Year Old Virgin '05 ▸
Get Out '17 ▸
Harold and Maude '71 ▸
Let the Sunshine In '17
Love by the 10th Date '17
The Lovebirds '20
Mike and Dave Need Wedding Dates '16
Mr. Woodcock '07
My Best Friend's Girl '08
Night of the Creeps '86
Perfect Strangers '03
The Personals '98
Reality Bites '94
Singles '92 ▸
Something Wild '86
The Third Wheel '02
Tod@s Caen '19
Walking and Talking '96
The Wedding Plan '17
What Happened Was. . . '94
Woo '97

Day Care/Nursery School

***See also** Babysitting*
Daddy Day Camp '07
Daddy Day Care '03
The Hunt '13 ▸
Indictment: The McMartin Trial '95 ▸
Superbabies: Baby Geniuses 2 '04
Toy Story 3 '10 ▸

A Day in the Life. . .

***See also** Up All Night*
Allegiance '12
American Graffiti '73 ▸
At Middleton '13
Barbershop '02 ▸
Before I Fall '17
Before Sunrise '94
Before Sunset '04 ▸
Bella '06
Ben Is Back '18
The Best Man '97
Bobby '06
Bomb Squad '97
The Breakfast Club '85 ▸
Caffeine '06
Call It a Day '37
Ca$h '06
Certified Copy '10
Conversations with Other Women '05
Crank '06
Dark Night '17
The Day He Arrives '11
A Day in the Life '09
The Daytrippers '96
Deadlocked '00
Derby Day '52
Falling '06
Ferris Bueller's Day Off '86 ▸
Flypaper '97
For One More Day '07
Four Christmases '08
Free Samples '12
Friday the Thirteenth '33
Fruitvale Station '13
Full Frontal '02
Gideon's Day '58
Groundhog Day '93 ▸
Happy Death Day '17
Haunter '13
Head On '98 ▸
Heights '04
In a Day '06
Interceptor Force '99
Judy Berlin '99
The Liability '12
The Life Before This '99
Little Athens '05
The Living Wake '07
Magnolia '99 ▸
Mandabi '68 ▸
Marie and Bruce '04
McCanick '14
Midaq Alley '95 ▸
Miss Pettigrew Lives for a Day '08 ▸
Mrs. Dalloway '97
Most Beautiful Island '17
Motherhood '09
My Mother's Courage '95
96 Minutes '11
One Fine Day '96
Orphans '97
Oslo, August 31st '11
Passenger Side '09
People I Know '02
Ride Along '14
Sal '11
Say Hello to Yesterday '71
The Secret Life of Pets '16
'71 '14 ▸
Shrek Forever After '10
A Single Man '09 ▸
Sleepless Night '11 ▸
Small Town Saturday Night '10
Spy Game '01
Stand Up Guys '12
Sunday '96
Sunset Strip '99
Support the Girls '18
Time Code '00
Top Five '14 ▸
Training Day '01
Transpecos '16
Trapped '02
Trojan War '97
True Crime '99
12:01 '93
25th Hour '02
20,000 Days on Earth '14 ▸
24 Hours in London '00
Ulysses '67
Vice Squad '53
Walk of Shame '14
White Night Wedding '08
Why Stop Now '12
Working Girls '87 ▸
Zuma Beach '78

DEA

***See also** Buddy Cops; FBI; Smuggler's Blues; Undercover Cops*
Ambushed '13
Basic '03
Cash Crop '99
Cocaine Cowboys 2: Hustlin' with the Godmother '08
Codename: Wildgeese '84
Crash & Byrnes '99
Drug Wars: The Camarena Story '90 ▸
El Gringo '12
End of a Gun '16
Gang Related '96
Gringo '18
Hollow Point '95
Homefront '13
The Infiltrator '16
Love Lies Bleeding '07
A Low Down Dirty Shame '94
A Man Apart '03
Marked for Death '90
Martial Outlaw '93
Misfire '14
Miss Bala '19
The Mule '18 ▸
Road House 2: Last Call '06
Running with the Devil '19
Sabotage '14
Savages '12
Snitch '13
Speed Kills '18
Traffic '00 ▸
2 Guns '13
White Tiger '95

Deadly Implants

Alien: Resurrection '97 ▸
Blind Date '84
Bombshell '97
Drive '96
Escape from L.A. '96
Escape from New York '81
Fortress '93
King of Kong Island '78
Live Wire: Human Timebomb '95
Star Trek: First Contact '96 ▸
Synapse '95
Terminal Impact '95
The Terminal Man '74
Total Recall '90 ▸

Deafness

***See also** Physical Problems*
Amy '81
Babel '06 ▸
Bangkok Dangerous '00
Beyond Silence '96
Bridge to Silence '89
Children of a Lesser God '86 ▸
Cop Land '97 ▸
Dead Silence '96
Dear Frankie '04
Dummy '79
The Family Stone '05
Four Weddings and a Funeral '94 ▸
Goya in Bordeaux '99
The Hammer '11
Hear No Evil '93
The Heart Is a Lonely Hunter '68 ▸
Immortal Beloved '94
In the Company of Men '96
It's All Gone, Pete Tong '04
Johnny Belinda '48 ▸
Listen to Your Heart '10
Love N' Dancing '09
The Man Who Played God '32
Mea Maxima Culpa: Silence in the House of God '12
The Miracle Worker '62 ▸
The Miracle Worker '79 ▸
The Miracle Worker '00
Mr. Holland's Opus '95 ▸
Murderer's Keep '70
Music Within '07
Orphan '09
The Parts You Lose '19
Personal Effects '09
Psych-Out '68
The Quiet '05
Read My Lips '01
A Scene at Sea '92
See No Evil, Hear No Evil '89
Sincerely Yours '55
The Song of Sparrows '08
Staten Island '09
The Story of Alexander Graham Bell '39 ▸
A Summer to Remember '84
Suspect '87
Sweet Nothing in My Ear '08
Tin Man '83
The Tribe '15 ▸
Two Shades of Blue '98
Where the Truth Lies '99
Wonderstruck '17

Death & the Afterlife

***See also** Angels; Funerals; Ghosts, Ghouls, & Heaven Sent; Hell; Immortality; Occult; Reincarnation; Suicide; Terminal Illness*
Abattoir '17
The ABCs of Death '12
The Adderall Diaries '16
After Life '98
After.life '10
Aftermath '17
Afterwards '08
The Alchemist '81
Alive and Kicking '96
All About My Mother '99 ▸
All Hallow's Eve 2 '15
All Hallow's Eve '13
All of Me '84
All That Jazz '79 ▸
All the Wilderness '14
Always '89
The Ambassador '11
Amexico '16
The Amityville Horror '79
Amityville 2: The Possession '82
Amityville 3: The Demon '83
Amityville 4: The Evil Escapes '89
Amityville 1992: It's About Time '92
Angel Eyes '01
Angel Heart '87
Angel on My Shoulder '46 ▸
Angels Crest '11
Annabelle: Creation '17
The Anomaly '15
Appetites '15
The Asphyx '72 ▸
At the Death House Door '08 ▸
Audrey Rose '77
August: Osage County '13
The Autopsy of Jane Doe '16
Autumn Blood '14
Avanti! '72
Awaken '15
Baby Girl Scott '87
Backtrack '16
Backwoods '87
Bad Day for the Cut '17
Barricade '12
Beetlejuice '88 ▸
Before I Fall '17
Being Flynn '12
Between Two Worlds '44
Beyond Tomorrow '40
Biggie & Tupac: The Story Behind the Murder of Rap's Biggest Superstars '02
Bill & Ted's Bogus Journey '91
Black Butterfly '17
Black Death '10
The Black Water Vampire '13
Blithe Spirit '45 ▸
Blood of the Vampire '58
Bloody Homecoming '12
Bloody New Year '87
Body '15
The Bone Yard '90
The Book of Henry '17
The Book of Life '14
The Boy '16
Boys on the Side '94
BPM (Beats Per Minute) '17
Bulletproof Heart '95 ▸
Burnt Offerings '76
Camp Dread '14
The Canterville Ghost '44
Carnival of Souls '62 ▸
Carousel '56 ▸
Cas & Dylan '15
Castle of the Creeping Flesh '68
The Cat and the Canary '27 ▸
Catching Faith '15
Cathy's Curse '77
Cemetery Man '95
Chances Are '89 ▸
The Changeling '80
Charlie St. Cloud '10
Chasing Ghosts '14
Chicken With Plums '11
The Child '76
Chosen '16
Christine '16
A Christmas Carol '38 ▸
A Christmas Carol '51 ▸
A Christmas Carol '84 ▸
A Christmas Carol '99
A Christmas Horror Story '15
Chronic '16
City of Angels '98
Cocaine Cowboys 2: Hustlin' with the Godmother '08
Coco '17 ▸
Cold Heaven '92
Collateral Beauty '16
Colony: The Endangered World of Bees '11
The Condemned 2 '16
Countdown '19
Courage Under Fire '96 ▸
A Crooked Somebody '18
A Cross to Bear '12
The Crow '93
The Crow 2: City of Angels '96
The Crow: Wicked Prayer '05
Curse of Chucky '13
The Curse of Downers Grove '15
Curse of the Cat People '44 ▸
Curse of the Living Corpse '64
Curse of the Witching Tree '15
Daddy's Dyin'. . . Who's Got the Will? '90
Dark Victory '39 ▸
The Day It Came to Earth '77
Day of the Mummy '14
Dead Heat '88
Dead Leaves '98
Dead Mate '88
Dead Rising: End Game '16
Dean '17
Dear Zachary: A Letter to a Son About His Father '08 ▸
The Death and Life of John F. Donovan '19
Death Becomes Her '92 ▸
The Death Curse of Tartu '66
Death Takes a Holiday '34 ▸
The Deaths of Ian Stone '07
Decommissioned '16
Defending Your Life '91 ▸
Deja Vu '84
Demolition '15
Departures '08
Despiser '03
The Devil & Max Devlin '81
Diablo '16
The Diabolical Dr. Z '65
The Discovery '17
Do You Believe? '15
D.O.A. '49 ▸
D.O.A. '88
Dr. Death, Seeker of Souls '73
Dr. Hackenstein '88
Doctor Phibes Rises Again '72
Dominique '79
Dona Flor and Her Two Husbands '78 ▸
Donkey Skin '70 ▸
Donovan's Brain '53 ▸
Don't Go in the House '80
Don't Let Go '19
Don't Let Me Die on a Sunday '98
Down to Earth '01
Dragonfly '02
The Driftless Area '16
The Duel '16
The Duellists '77 ▸
Eaters '15
11-11-11 '11
Encounter with the Unknown '75
The End '78 ▸
The English Patient '96 ▸
Enter the Void '09
The Entertainer '60 ▸
Estate of Insanity '64
Eternity and a Day '97
Everest '15
An Evergreen Christmas '14
Every Thing Will Be Fine '15
Evil Spirits '91
Executive Suite '54 ▸
Exit Plan '20
Expired '07
Exposed '16
The Eye '08
The Eyes of My Mother '16
A Fantastic Woman '18
The Farewell '19 ▸
Fathers and Daughters '16
Fearless '93 ▸
51 Birch Street '05 ▸
The Final Destination '09
Final Destination 5 '11
First They Killed My Father '17
Five Nights in Maine '16
Flatliners '90
Flatliners '17
Flight 7500 '16
Fluke '95
For Roseanna '96
45 Years '15 ▸
Free Fall '14
Frida '02
Friendly Fire '79 ▸
The Frighteners '96
Frightmare '81
Frisk '95
From the Dead of Night '89 ▸
The Funeral '84 ▸
Funeral Home '82
Garbo Talks '84
Gates of Heaven '78 ▸
Gates of Hell '80
The Ghost '63
Ghost '90 ▸
The Ghost and Mrs. Muir '47 ▸
A Ghost Story '17 ▸
Ghosts of Berkeley Square '47
Girl Rising '13 ▸
The Goldfinch '19
Gotham '88 ▸
The Green Room '78
Griffin and Phoenix: A Love Story '76
Guernica '16
Hachiko: A Dog's Tale '09
Happy Death Day '17
Hardcore Henry '15
The Hatching '16
Haunter '13
Hawks '89
He Never Died '15
Heart and Souls '93
Heart Condition '90
Heaven '87
Heaven Can Wait '43 ▸
Heaven Can Wait '78 ▸
The Heavenly Kid '85
Heaven's a Drag '94
Hello Again '87
Hercules the Legendary Journeys, Vol. 4: In the Underworld '94
Here Comes Mr. Jordan '41 ▸
Hereafter '10
Hereditary '18 ▸
Hideaway '94
High Plains Drifter '73
High Spirits '88
Highlander: Endgame '00
Highway 61 '91
The Hoarder '15
Hocus Pocus '93
Hold That Ghost '41 ▸
Home Invasion '16
Homecoming '13
The Hours '02 ▸
Human Nature '02
I Bury the Living '58 ▸
I Spit on Your Grave: Vengeance Is Mine '15
I Walked with a Zombie '43 ▸
If There's a Hell Below '16
I'm Losing You '98
In Order of Disappearance '14
In the Fade '17
The Indestructible Man '56
Infected '13
Infinity '96
Into the Abyss '11 ▸
Into the West '92 ▸
Intruso '93
The Invisible '07
Irreplaceable You '18
It Came Upon a Midnight Clear '84
It's a Wonderful Life '46 ▸
It's All So Quiet '13
It's My Party '95
Jack Goes Home '16
Jackie '16 ▸
Jacob's Ladder '90
Jamie Marks Is Dead '13
Jesse '11
Jigsaw '17
Johnny Winter: Down & Dirty '14
Judge & Jury '96
Just like Heaven '05
Kate Plays Christine '16 ▸
Kickboxer: Vengeance '16
Kingdom of Blood: The Final Battle '16
Kiss Me Goodbye '82
Kiss of Death '77
Kissed '96
The Lady in the Car with Glasses and a Gun '16
The Lady in White '88 ▸
Lady Macbeth '17 ▸
Lamb '16
The Last Best Year '90
Last Cab to Darwin '16 ▸

Last Flag Flying '17
The Last Heist '16
The Last Letter '13
Last Light '93
The Last Word '17
Left in Darkness '06
The Legend of Hell House '73 ▶
The Letters '15
Lies I Told My Little Sister '14
Liliom '35 ▶
Living Doll '90
Lone Survivor '13
Look Both Ways '05
The Looking Glass '16
Louder Than Bombs '16
Louder Than Words '14
Love Letters '99 ▶
Love Unto Death '84
The Loved One '65
Lullaby '14
Macbeth '48 ▶
Macbeth '71 ▶
Made in Heaven '87
Magical Girl '14 ▶
Magnolia '99 ▶
The Man from Elysian Fields '01 ▶
The Man in 3B '16
The Man with Two Lives '42
Mannequin '87
Marvin's Room '96
Mausoleum '83
Maxie '85
Maya Dardel '17
Meet Joe Black '98
Mermaid '00
The Midnight Hour '86
The Miracle of the Bells '48
Mischief Night '13
Misconduct '16
Mr. Right '16
Money Monster '16
Monkeybone '01
A Monster Calls '17
Monty Python's The Meaning of Life '83 ▶
Moonlight and Valentino '95
Moonlight Mile '02 ▶
More Money More Family '15
Mortuary Academy '91
Mother and Son '97
Murder of a Cat '14
Must Read After My Death '09
My Bloody Banjo '15
My Cousin Rachel '17
My Guardian Angel '16
My Life '93
Mysterious Ways '15
Mythica: The Iron Crown '16
Natural Selection '12
Necropolis '87
Neo Ned '05
The Newlydeads '87
Night of the Death Cult '75
Night of the Demons 2 '94
Night of the Demons '88
Night of the Living Dead '68 ▶
Night of the Living Dead '90
The Nightcomers '72
Nightmare Castle '65
Nostalgia '18
November Criminals '17
The Nun '18
Oh, Heavenly Dog! '80
On Borrowed Time '39 ▶
The Oracle '85
Other People '16
The Other Side of the Door '16
Our Children '12
Our Sons '91
Over Her Dead Body '08
Passed Away '92
Passion '13
A Perfect Day '16
Personal Shopper '17 ▶
Pet Sematary '89
Pet Sematary '19
Phantasm '79
Phantasm 2 '88
Phantasm 3: Lord of the Dead '94
The Phantom Chariot '20
A Pigeon Sat on a Branch Reflecting on Existence '14 ▶
Poltergeist '82 ▶
Poltergeist 2: The Other Side '86
Poltergeist 3 '88
The Poltergeist of Borley Forest '13
Ponette '95
Portrait of Jennie '48 ▶
The Possessed '77
The Premonition '75
Promises in the Dark '79
The Prophecy '95
P.S. I Love You '07
Psychomania '73
Purgatory House '04
Queen of Earth '15 ▶
Ready or Not '19 ▶
Reaper '15
The Reckoning '14
Rememory '17
Resident Evil: Vendetta '17
Resurrection of Zachary Wheeler '71
Retribution '88
Revenge of the Dead '84
Riding the Bullet '04
Rimfire '49
A River Made to Drown In '97
Riverworld '10
Robo-Dog '15
Robot Stories '03
Rough Night '17
The Rue Morgue Massacres '73
Run Hide Die '15
Saturn in Opposition '07
Scared Stiff '53 ▶
School Spirit '85
Scrooge '70
Scrooged '88
7 Days to Live '00
The Seventh Seal '56 ▶
The Shack '17
Shannon's Rainbow '09
Sherpa '15 ▶
Shock Waves '77
Sibling Rivalry '90
The Sin Seer '15
Sins of Our Youth '16
6 Plots '12
The Sixth Man '97
The Sixth Sense '99 ▶
Sole Survivor '84
Solid State '12
Some Kind of Hate '15
Sometimes They Come Back '91
Somewhere Tomorrow '85
Son of Saul '15 ▶
Songs My Brother Taught Me '15 ▶
Soultaker '90
South Park: Bigger, Longer and Uncut '99
Southbound '16
Sparks '13
Spawn '97 ▶
Stagecoach: The Texas Jack Story '16
Stand by Me '86 ▶
Standoff '16 ▶
Star Trek 3: The Search for Spock '84
Storm '05
Strange But True '19
The Strange Case of Angelica '10
Strangers of the Evening '32
Struck by Lightning '12
The Substitute Wife '94
Suburbicon '17
The Summit '13
Supernatural '33
Sweet Virginia '17
Teeth and Blood '15
Tell Me a Riddle '80
Tequila Body Shots '99
They Came Back '04
Things to Do in Denver When You're Dead '95 ▶
13 Ghosts '60
13 Hours: The Secret Soldiers of Benghazi '16
13 Moons '02
Tigers Are Not Afraid '19 ▶
Tim Burton's Corpse Bride '05 ▶
To Dance with the White Dog '93 ▶
To Die, Or Not '99
To Dust '19
To Gillian on Her 37th Birthday '96
Topper '37 ▶
Topper Returns '41 ▶
Traded '16
Trash Fire '16
Trick or Treat '86
Truly, Madly, Deeply '91 ▶
12 and Holding '05 ▶
12 Rounds 3: Lockdown '15
24 Days '14
24 Hours to Live '17
Twice Dead '88
Two Days '03
2 Little Monsters '15
Two of a Kind '83
Unconditional '12
Under the Lighthouse Dancing '97
Under the Sand '00 ▶
The Undertaker's Wedding '97
The Unknown Girl '17
The Unnamable '88
Unnatural '52
Unstrung Heroes '95
Vendetta '15
The Vessel '16
Voice from the Stone '17
Vulture's Eye '04
The Wait '13
Weekend at Bernie's 2 '93
Weekend at Bernie's '89
What Dreams May Come '98
When Two Worlds Collide '16 ▶
Where Children Play '15
Whispers '89
White Noise 2: The Light '07
Worth: The Testimony of Johnny St. James '12
Wristcutters: A Love Story '06
Yossi '12
The Young and Prodigious T.S. Spivet '15
Young@Heart '07 ▶
A Zed & Two Noughts '88 ▶
Zero Tolerance '15
Zombieworld '15
Zone of the Dead '78

Death Row

See also Executing Revenge; Men in Prison; Women in Prison

An American Tragedy '31
American Violence '17
Angels with Dirty Faces '38 ▶
At the Death House Door '08 ▶
Beyond the Call '96
Black Angel '46
Bundy: A Legacy of Evil '08
Castle on the Hudson '40 ▶
Cell 2455, Death Row '55
The Chamber '96
Clemency '19
The Condemned '07
Convicted '04
Daniel '83
Dead Man Walking '95 ▶
Decoy '46
Desperate Measures '98
The Detective '68 ▶
88 Minutes '08
The Executioner's Song '82
The Fear of 13 '15 ▶
Gamer '09
The Green Mile '99
Hellblock 13 '97
I Want to Live! '58 ▶
Identity '03
In Cold Blood '67 ▶
In Cold Blood '96
Just Mercy '19 ▶
Killer: A Journal of Murder '95
Killer by Nature '10
Last Dance '96
The Last Mile '59
The Lena Baker Story '08
A Lesson Before Dying '99 ▶
Let Him Have It '91 ▶
Let Us Live '39
Letters from a Killer '98
The Life of David Gale '03
Lost Behind Bars '06
Lost Highway '96
Mommy 2: Mommy's Day '96
Monster's Ball '01 ▶
Multiple Sarcasms '10
The Murder Man '35
Nora Prentiss '47
The Paperboy '12
Paradise Lost 3: Purgatory '11
Pennies from Heaven '36
A Place in the Sun '51 ▶
Prisoner '07
The Riverman '04
Safe in Hell '31
The Seventh Sign '88
Shot in the Heart '01 ▶
The State Within '06
The Sun Sets at Dawn '50
The Thin Blue Line '88 ▶
The Traveling Executioner '70
Trial by Fire '18
True Crime '99
20,000 Years in Sing Sing '33
Two Seconds '32
Under Suspicion '92
Why Must I Die? '60
The Widow of Saint-Pierre '00 ▶
You Can't Get Away With Murder '39

Dedicated Teachers

See also Elementary School/Junior High; Errant Educators; Hell High School; School Daze

Akeelah and the Bee '06
Amy '81
Anna and the King '99
Around the Block '13
Bad Teacher '11
Because They're Young '60
Beyond the Blackboard '11
Blackboard Jungle '55 ▶
Born Yesterday '50 ▶
Born Yesterday '93
Bossa Nova '99
Boys Will Be Boys '35
Bright Road '53
The Browning Version '94
Burn, Witch, Burn! '62
Butterfly '98 ▶
Carried Away '95
Chalk '06
Cheaters '00
Cheers for Miss Bishop '41
Children of a Lesser God '86 ▶
Child's Play '72
The Chorus '04
Christy '94
Ciao, Professore! '94
The Class '08
Coach Carter '05 ▶
Comic Book: The Movie '04 ▶
Coming Out '89
The Corn Is Green '45 ▶
The Corn Is Green '79 ▶
The Country Teacher '08
Cracks '09
Dangerous Minds '95
Dead Poets Society '89 ▶
Detachment '12
Detention '03
Disney's Teacher's Pet '04 ▶
Eden '98
Educating Rita '83 ▶
Election '99 ▶
The Emperor's Club '02
The English Teacher '13
The Explosive Generation '61
Fever Pitch '05
Fighting the Odds: The Marilyn Gambrell Story '05
Freedom Writers '07
Friday Night Lights '04 ▶
G.B.H. '91
Girl, Positive '07
Girl's Dormitory '36
Go For It! '10
Good Morning, Boys '37
Good Morning, Miss Dove '55
Goodbye, Mr. Chips '39 ▶
Goodbye, Mr. Chips '69
Goodbye, Mr. Chips '02
The Great Debaters '07 ▶
The Great O'Malley '36
The Green '11
Half Nelson '06 ▶
Halls of Anger '70
Hamlet 2 '08 ▶
Happy-Go-Lucky '08 ▶
Heart of America '03
Here Comes the Boom '12
High School High '96
Highland Park '13
The History Boys '06
Homework '82
How You Look to Me '05
The Hunt '13 ▶
If Lucy Fell '95
The Incredible Mrs. Ritchie '03
Inherit the Wind '60 ▶
Inherit the Wind '99
Institue Benjamenta or This Dream People Call Human Life '95
An Invisible Sign '11
It All Starts Today '99
Kindergarten Cop '90
Knights of the South Bronx '05
Larry Crowne '11
Lean on Me '89 ▶
Leaves of Grass '09
A Lesson Before Dying '99 ▶
Life Is a Bed of Roses '83
Like Father Like Son '05
Little Men '34
Mad Hot Ballroom '05 ▶
Madame Sousatzka '88 ▶
The Male Animal '42
Matilda '96 ▶
The Miracle Worker '62 ▶
The Miracle Worker '79 ▶
The Miracle Worker '00
Mr. Holland's Opus '95 ▶
Mona Lisa Smile '03
Monsieur Lazhar '11
Murder On the Blackboard '34
Music of the Heart '99
Necessary Roughness '91
Newtown '16 ▶
The Next Karate Kid '94
Night Visitor '89
Not One Less '99
October Sky '99 ▶
Oktober '98
187 '97
The Paper Chase '73 ▶
The Piano Teacher '01
Powder '95
Precious: Based on the Novel 'Push' by Sapphire '09 ▶
The Prime of Miss Jean Brodie '69 ▶
The Prime of Miss Jean Brodie '78
The Principal '87
Race the Sun '96
Rachel, Rachel '68 ▶
Rachida '05 ▶
Rebound '05
Remember the Day '41
Renaissance Man '94
The Road Home '01 ▶
The Rookie '02 ▶
School of Life '06
School of Rock '03 ▶
Shooting Dogs '05
A Smile as Big as the Moon '12
A Song From the Heart '99
South Riding '11
Stand and Deliver '88 ▶
Student Seduction '03
The Substitute '96
Summer School '87
Sunset Park '96
Take a Girl Like You '70
Take the Lead '06
Tammy Tell Me True '61
Teachers '84
Tenure '09
Term of Trial '63
That's What I Am '11
Thunder Soul '10
To Sir, With Love 2 '96
To Sir, with Love '67
Twenty-Four Eyes '54 ▶
Untamed Love '94
Up the Down Staircase '67 ▶
Weakness '10
When Calls the Heart '13
Whiplash '14 ▶
Wildcats '86
Within Our Gates '20
The Woman in Black 2: Angel of Death '15
Won't Back Down '12
Words and Pictures '13
You're Never Too Young '55

Deep Blue

See also Go Fish; Sail Away; Shipwrecked; Submarines

The Abyss '89 ▶
Adrift '18
Andre '94
Assault on a Queen '66
The Beast '96
Beneath the Blue '10
The Big Blue '88
Crimson Tide '95 ▶
Danger Beneath the Sea '02
Dark Descent '02
Dark Tide '12
Deep Blue '03 ▶
Deep Blue Sea '99
Deepwater Horizon '16
Destination Inner Space '66
ffolkes '80
Finding Nemo '03 ▶
Flipper '96 ▶
47 Meters Down '17
1492: Conquest of Paradise '92
Free Willy '93
Free Willy 2: The Adventure Home '95
Free Willy 3: The Rescue '97
Happy Feet '06 ▶
Hello Down There '69
Men of Honor '00
Mission of the Shark '91 ▶
Moby Dick '98
Namu, the Killer Whale '66
Oceans '09 ▶
The Rig '10
Sanctum '11
Shipwrecked '90
The Silent Enemy '58
Splash '84
The Spy Who Loved Me '77
Submergence '18
Tarzan and the Mermaids '48
30,000 Leagues Under the Sea '07
Underwater '20
Waterworld '95
Wind '92

Deep Woods Offed

Abominable '06
Albino Farm '09
Altered '06
Are You Scared 2 '09
Backwoods '08
Bad Meat '11
The Barrens '12
Barricade '12
Big Bad Wolf '06
Bigfoot '70
Bigfoot: The Lost Coast Tapes '12
Black Mountain Side '16
Blackwoods '02
Blair Witch '16
Bloodmyth '09
The Cabin in the Woods '12 ▶
Convict Women '74
Cottage Country '13
Creature '11
Dawning '09
The Day '11
Dead Snow '09
Deliverance '72 ▶
Don't Go in the Woods '81
Don't Go in the Woods '10
Edge of Winter '16

▶ = rated three bones or higher

Evil Dead '13
Hidden '09
The Hills Have Eyes '77
The Hills Have Eyes 2 '07
The Hills Have Eyes '06
The Hills Have Eyes, Part 2 '84
Hold Your Breath '12
Honeymoon '14
I Spit on Your Grave '10
It Comes at Night '17
Jug Face '13
Last Kind Words '12
The Legend of Bloody Jack '07
Mimesis '11
Mr. Jones '14
The Monster '16
Night Fright '67
Preservation '14
Prey '10
Project Solitude: Buried Alive '09
Psychotica '10
Pumpkinhead '88
A Quiet Place '18▸
Snow Shark '11
Summer's Moon '09
13th Child: Legend of the Jersey Devil '02
Tucker & Dale *vs.* Evil '10▸
Tusk '14
Undertow '04
Willow Creek '13
Without Warning '80
Wolf Creek '05
The Woman '11
The Woods Have Eyes '07
The Wretched '08
Wrong Turn '03
Wrong Turn 2: Dead End '07
Wrong Turn 3: Left for Dead '09

Demons & Wizards

***See also** Occult*
Abe's Tomb '07
The Alchemist '81
Along Came the Devil 2 '19
Along Came the Devil '18
Arabian Adventure '79
Army of Darkness '92▸
Arthur's Quest '99
Ashura '05
The Barrens '12
The Basement '89
Belphegor: Phantom of the Louvre '01
Beneath Still Waters '05
Beyond the Dunwich Horror '08
Black Magic '06
The Black Waters of Echo's Pond '10
Bleach the Movie 4: Hell Verse '10
Blood Creek '09
Blood: The Last Vampire '09
Bloodlust: Subspecies 3 '93
Bloodstone: Subspecies 2 '92
Born of Fire '87
Bram Stoker's Shadowbuilder '98
Brotherhood of Blood '08
Byleth: The Demon of Incest '72
The Church '98▸
The Color of Magic '08
Conan the Barbarian '82▸
Conan the Destroyer '84
The Conjuring 2 '16
The Conjuring '13▸
Constantine '05
The Convent '00
Cthulhu '08
Dark Kingdom: The Dragon King '04
The Dark Myth '90
Darklight '04
Dead Waters '94
Death Note 2: The Last Name '07
Death Note 3: L Change the World '08
Death Note '06▸
Deathgasm '15
The Deaths of Ian Stone '07
Deathstalker 4: Match of Titans '92
Deathstalker '83
Demon Rage '82
Demonoid, Messenger of Death '81
Demons '86
Demons of Ludlow '75
Demonstone '89
Despiser '03
The Devil Inside '12
Doctor Strange '16▸
Don't Kill It '17
Don't Knock Twice '17
Dororo '07
Eragon '06
Ernest Scared Stupid '91
Evil Behind You '06
Evil Dead '83
Evil Dead 2: Dead by Dawn '87
Evil Dead '13
Evil Toons '90
Excalibur '81▸
Fading of the Cries '10
Fantasia '40▸
Fantastic Beasts and Where to Find Them '16
Fantastic Beasts: The Crimes of Grindelwald '18
Fire and Ice '83
Funnyman '94
Gate 2 '92
The Gate '87
Ghost Son '06
Ghost Team '16
The Giants of Thessaly '60
Goosebumps '15▸
Gor '88
The Graves '10
The Guardian '01
Harry Potter and the Deathly Hallows, Part 2 '11▸
Harry Potter and the Goblet of Fire '05▸
Harry Potter and the Order of the Phoenix '07
Harry Potter and the Prisoner of Azkaban '04
The Hazing '04
Heartless '10
Hellboy '04
Hellboy '19
Hellions '15
Hellraiser '87
Hellraiser 4: Bloodline '95
Hellraiser: Deader '05
Hellraiser: Revelations '11
The Heroic Trio '93
The Hobbit '78▸
The Hobbit: An Unexpected Journey '12
The Hobbit: The Battle of the Five Armies '14
The Horror at 37,000 Feet '73
Howl's Moving Castle '04
I Am Zozo '12
I, Frankenstein '13
In the Name of the King: A Dungeon Siege Tale '08
Insidious: The Last Key '18
The Invincible Iron Man '07
The Invoking 2 '15
The Invoking '13
Jack-O '95
Jade Warrior '06
Jennifer's Body '09
Jezebeth '11
Jinn '14
June '15
Just Visiting '01
The King and I '99
Krull '83
Ladyhawke '85
The Legacy '79
Lights Out '16
Lord of the Rings: The Fellowship of the Ring '01▸
Lord of the Rings: The Two Towers '02▸
Lord of the Rings: The Return of the King '03▸
The Magic Blade '08
Manborg '11
Max Payne '08
The Mephisto Waltz '71▸
Merlin and the Book of Beasts '09
Merlin and the War of the Dragons '08
Merlin's Apprentice '06
The Minion '98
Mirror, Mirror '90
The Mortal Instruments: City of Bones '13
Mother of Tears '08
My Name Is Bruce '08
Mysterious Museum '99
Ne Zha '19
Necromentia '09
Night of the Demons 3 '97
Night of the Demons '09
Nightmare Man '06
The Nun '18
Ouija: Origin of Evil '16
Painted Skin: The Resurrection '12
Paranormal Activity 3 '11
Paranormal Movie '13
Possessed '00
Princess Raccoon '05
Pumpkinhead 2: Blood Wings '94
Pumpkinhead 3: Ashes to Ashes '06
Pumpkinhead 4: Blood Feud '07
Pumpkinhead '88
Purana Mandir '84▸
The Raven '63▸
Rawhead Rex '87
Red Sonja '85
The Return of the King '80
Rock & Rule '83
Satanic '15
Savage Harvest 2: October Blood '06
Seizure '74
Silent Hill: Revelation 3D '12
Silent Night, Deadly Night 4: Initiation '90
Sinthia: The Devil's Doll '70
The Smurfs '11
The Soul Guardians '98
Stay Awake '87
Stoned Bros. '09
Supergirl '84
Survival Island '02
Sword & the Sorcerer '82
The Sword in the Stone '63▸
Tales from the Crypt Presents Demon Knight '94
Tales from the Crypt Presents Ritual '02
Tales of Halloween '15
Talisman '98
13th Child: Legend of the Jersey Devil '02
Thor the Conqueror '83
Time Barbarians '90
Trancers 4: Jack of Swords '93
Transformers: The Last Knight '17
Troll 2 '92
Troll '86
Ultramarines: A Warhammer 40,000 Movie '10
The Unholy '88
The Unnamable 2: The Statement of Randolph Carter '92
Voodoo Moon '05
Voodoo Possession '14
The Wailing '16
Warlock '91
Warlock: The Armageddon '93
Willow '88
Winter's Tale '14
Wish Upon '17
The Witchmaker '69
The Wizards of Waverly Place: The Movie '09
Your Highness '11
Zu Warriors '01
Zu: Warriors from the Magic Mountain '83

Dental Mayhem

***See also** Doctors & Evil Doctors*
Almost Heroes '97
Brazil '85▸
Captives '94
Charlie and the Chocolate Factory '05▸
The Dentist 2: Brace Yourself '98
The Dentist '96
Dentist In the Chair '60
Diabolique '55▸
Don't Raise the Bridge, Lower the River '68
Ernest & Celestine '13
Finding Nemo '03▸
Ghost Town '08▸
Horrible Bosses '11
Horsemen '09
Houseguest '94
The In-Laws '79▸
Little Shop of Horrors '60▸
Little Shop of Horrors '86▸
Marathon Man '76▸
Novocaine '01
One Sunday Afternoon '33
The Paleface '48▸
Poltergeist 2: The Other Side '86
Reign Over Me '07
The Secret Lives of Dentists '02▸
Serial Mom '94▸
The Shakiest Gun in the West '68
Snow Dogs '02
Strawberry Blonde '41▸
Toothless '97
12 Monkeys '95▸
The Whole Nine Yards '00
The Whole Ten Yards '04
Wild Grass '09

Desert War/Foreign Legion

***See** Deserts; Persian Gulf/Iraq War*

Deserts

***See also** Desert War/Foreign Legion*
The Adventures of Priscilla, Queen of the Desert '94▸
Alien Outlaw '85
Alien Trespass '09
Alive or Dead '08
American Strays '96
Another Dawn '37
Appetites '15
Ashes of Time Redux '08
Back of Beyond '95
The Bad Batch '17
Baja '95
The Barbarian '33
The Beast With a Million Eyes '56
Beavis and Butt-Head Do America '96
The Big Bang '11
The Big Empty '04
Bitter Victory '58
Bone Dry '07
Broken Arrow '95
Camel Spiders '11
Carnage Park '16
Children of Dune '03
Dark Country '09
Death Race 3: Inferno '12
Death Valley '04
Desert Blue '98
The Desert Fox '51▸
Desert Hearts '86▸
Desert Heat '99
Desert Migration '16▸
The Desert Rats '53▸
The Desert Song '53
Desert Winds '95
Desierto '16
Destination Gobi '53
Detour to Terror '80
The Devil's Tomb '09
Dolan's Cadillac '09
Drowning on Dry Land '00
Duma '05▸
Dune '84
Dune '00
Dust to Glory '05▸
Eaters '15
Echoes '15
The English Patient '96▸
Entertainment '15
Escape From Zahrain '62
Evolution '01
A Far Off Place '93
Faster, Pussycat! Kill! Kill! '65
Feast '06
Five Graves to Cairo '43▸
Flight of the Phoenix '04
The Forsaken '01
The Four Feathers '02
The Frontier '16
Grand Theft Parsons '03
Greed In the Sun '64
Harem Girl '52
Hell's Heroes '30
Hidalgo '04
The Hill '65
The Hills Have Eyes '06
Holes '03▸
House of Sand '05▸
In the Army Now '94
Indiana Jones and the Last Crusade '89▸
Ishtar '87
Japanese Story '03▸
The Jewel of the Nile '85
Jumanji: The Next Level '19
Kill Your Darlings '06
The Lark Farm '07
Larry McMurtry's Dead Man's Walk '96
Last Days in the Desert '16▸
The Last Templar '09
Lawrence of Arabia '62▸
Legend of the Lost Tomb '97
Legionnaire '98
Lost '05
Mad Max '80▸
Mad Max: Beyond Thunderdome '85
Mad Max: Fury Road '15▸
The Men Who Stare at Goats '09
Miss Cast Away '04
Mojave '15
Mojave Moon '96
Mongolian Death Worm '10
Monsters: Dark Continent '15
Morocco '30▸
The Mummy '99
The Mummy '17
Natural Born Killers '94
Off the Map '03▸
Operation Condor '91
The Passenger '75▸
Passion in the Desert '97
Patriot Games '92▸
Phoenix Forgotten '17
Picking Up the Pieces '99
The Prisoner '09
The Road to Morocco '42▸
Road to Paloma '14
The Road Warrior '82▸
Rubber '10
Sahara '43▸
Sahara '95
Sahara '05
Samson and Delilah '96
Sands of the Kalahari '65
Scorpion Spring '96
Sea of Sand '58
The Sheik '21▸
The Sheltering Sky '90▸
Shoot or Be Shot '02
Slow Burn '00
Southbound '16
Southwest Passage '54
Star Wars '77▸
Stargate '94
The Steel Lady '53
The Story of the Weeping Camel '03▸
Strawberry Fields '97
Sufat Chol '16▸
Tarzan's Desert Mystery '43
Taxi for Tobruk '60▸
Theeb '15▸
They Came to Rob Las Vegas '68
The Three Burials of Melquiades Estrada '05▸
Three Godfathers '36
Timbuktu '59
Tower of the Firstborn '98
The ToyBox '18
Tracks '14
Transpecos '16
Treasure Guards '11
Tremors 2: Aftershocks '96
Tremors '89
Troublemakers: The Story of Land Art '15▸
Twentynine Palms '03
The Way Back '10
White Sands '92
The Wind and the Lion '75▸
Zarak '56

Detective Spoofs

***See also** Comic Cops; Disorganized Crime; Genre Spoofs; Private Eyes*
Ace Ventura Jr.: Pet Detective '08
Ace Ventura: Pet Detective '93
Ace Ventura: When Nature Calls '95
The Adventures of Sherlock Holmes' Smarter Brother '78▸
Assault of the Party Nerds 2: Heavy Petting Detective '95
Blondes Have More Guns '95
Camouflage '00
Carry On Dick '75
Carry On Screaming '66
The Cheap Detective '78▸
Clean Slate '94
Clue '85
The Crooked Circle '32
Cry Uncle '71
The Curse of the Jade Scorpion '01
Curse of the Pink Panther '83
Dead Men Don't Wear Plaid '82
Detective School Dropouts '85
Dragnet '87
Fatal Instinct '93
Gumshoe '72
Hoodwinked '05▸
The Hound of the Baskervilles '77
Inspector Gadget 2 '02
Inspector Gadget '99
Inspector Hornleigh '39
Love Happy '50
The Man with Bogart's Face '80
Murder by Death '76
My Favorite Brunette '47
The Naked Gun: From the Files of Police Squad '88▸
Naked Gun 33 1/3: The Final Insult '94
Naked Gun 2 1/2: The Smell of Fear '91
Night Patrol '85
Oh, Heavenly Dog! '80
One Body Too Many '44
The Pink Chiquitas '86
The Pink Panther '64▸
The Pink Panther Strikes Again '76▸
The Private Eyes '80
Pure Luck '91
Rentadick '72
Return of the Pink Panther '74
Revenge of the Pink Panther '78
Ryder P.I. '86
Second Sight '89
A Shot in the Dark '64▸
Trail of the Pink Panther '82
Who Done It? '42
Who Done It? '56
Who's Harry Crumb? '89
Without a Clue '88
Zero Effect '97

Detectives

***See** Amateur Sleuths; CIA/NSA; Cops; Detective Spoofs; FBI; Historical Detectives; Police Detectives; Private Eyes*

Detroit

***See also** Checkered Flag; Motor Vehicle Dept.*
Aspen Extreme '93
Assault on Precinct 13 '05
Beverly Hills Cop '84

Beverly Hills Cop 2 '87
Beverly Hills Cop 3 '94
Bird on a Wire '90
Brick Mansions '14
Burn '12 ▸
The Butterfly Effect 3: Revelation '09
Buzzard '15 ▸
Chameleon Street '89 ▸
Collision Course '89
Coupe de Ville '90
Crossing the Bridge '92
Crossover '06
Detroit '17 ▸
Detroit 9000 '73
Detroit Rock City '99
Dreamgirls '06 ▸
8 Mile '02 ▸
Exit Wounds '01
Flash of Genius '08
Four Brothers '05
Freaky Deaky '12
Game of Death '10
Gifted Hands: The Ben Carson Story '09
Gridlock'd '96▸
Grosse Pointe Blank '97▸
Gun '10
The Hardys Ride High '39
Hoffa '92▸
Indian Summer '93
It Follows '15▸
Kin '18
The Last Word '95
The Life and Times of Hank Greenberg '99▸
Life of Crime '13
Lost River '15
The Man '05
Mr. Mom '83▸
Mitch Albom's Have a Little Faith '11
Narc '02▸
Only Lovers Left Alive '13
Out of Sight '98▸
Paper Lion '68
Presumed Innocent '90▸
Private Parts '96
The Purple Gang '59
Renaissance Man '94
R.I.C.C.O. '02
Ringmaster '98
RoboCop '87▸
RoboCop 2 '90
RoboCop 3 '91
RoboCop '14
Roger & Me '89▸
Scarecrow '73
Sparkle '12
Standing in the Shadows of Motown '02▸
Street Boss '09
Street Kings 2: Motor City '11
S.W.A.T.: Firefight '11
Tainted '98
Tiger Town '83
True Romance '93
Tucker: The Man and His Dream '88▸
The Upside of Anger '05▸
Vanishing on 7th Street '10
White Boy Rick '18
The Wrecking Crew '99
Zebrahead '92▸

Devils

Bedazzled '68▸
Bedazzled '00
Blackwater Valley Exorcism '06
Cell 213 '11
Constantine '05
The Craft '96
Crazy as Hell '02
Crocodile Tears '98
Damn Yankees '58▸
Dark Angel: The Ascent '94
Deal of a Lifetime '99
Devil '10
The Devil & Max Devlin '81
The Devil Incarnate '13
The Devils '71▸
The Devil's Advocate '97
The Devil's Candy '17
Doktor Faustus '82
End of Days '99
The Exorcism of Emily Rose '05▸
Exorcist: The Beginning '04
Faust '26 ▸
Gates of Hell 2: Dead Awakening '96
Ghost Rider '07
Ghost Rider: Spirit of Vengeance '12
The Haunted World of El Superbeasto '09
Hocus Pocus '93
The Imaginarium of Doctor Parnassus '09
Last Days in the Desert '16 ▸
The Last Exorcism '10
The Last Exorcism Part II '13
Legend '86
Little Nicky '00
Lost Souls '00
The Mangler '94
Mother Joan of the Angels '60▸
Needful Things '93
The Ninth Gate '99
No News from God '01
The Omen '06
The Prophecy '95
Rattlesnake '19
Second Time Lucky '84
666: The Beast '07
South Park: Bigger, Longer and Uncut '99
Stephen King's The Stand '94
Story of Mankind '57
Tales from the Hood '95
12/12/12 '12
The Witches of Eastwick '87

Devil's Island

***See also** Great Escapes; Men in Prison*

Crescendo '69
The Life of Emile Zola '37▸
Papillon '73▸
Passage to Marseilles '44▸
Strange Cargo '40
We're No Angels '55▸

Diner

***See also** Bar & Waiters & Waitresses*

Alice Doesn't Live Here Anymore '74
Alien Trespass '09
American East '07
American Strays '96
Blood Diner '87
Blue Iguana '18
The Box '03
Cafe '10
Catch.44 '11
A Christmas Wish '11
Coffee and Cigarettes '03▸
Deterrence '00
Diner '82▸
Empire Falls '05
Eye of the Storm '91
Fallen Angel '45
Five Easy Pieces '70▸
Flakes '07
Force of Execution '13
Frankie and Johnny '91▸
Gasoline Alley '51
Gloomy Sunday '02▸
God Bless the Broken Road '18
Heavy '94▸
Her Secret '33
Here on Earth '00
Into the Fire '88
It Could Happen to You '94
The Killing Jar '10
Kisses in the Dark '97
Last Chance Cafe '06
Legion '10
Leo '02
Loveless '83
The Maldonado Miracle '03
Monster's Ball '01▸
My Blueberry Nights '07
The Off Hours '11
One Girl's Confession '53
Parallel Sons '95
Pawn '13
Pennies from Heaven '36
Petrified Forest '36▸
Pulp Fiction '94▸
Queen of Hearts '89▸
Recipe for Disaster '03
A Season for Miracles '99
Six-Pack Annie '75
Sliding Doors '97
Swamp Shark '11
Swimming '00
Trouble in Mind '86 ▸
The Undertaker and His Pals '67
Waiting for the Light '90
Waitress '07 ▸
When Harry Met Sally. . . '89 ▸

Dinosaurs

***See also** Killer Beasts*

Actium Maximus: War of the Alien Dinosaurs '05
Age of Dinosaurs '13
Anonymous Rex '04
At the Earth's Core '76
Baby. . . Secret of the Lost Legend '85
Barney's Great Adventure '98
Carnosaur 2 '94
Carnosaur 3: Primal Species '96
Carnosaur '93
Caveman '81
Clifford '92
Cowboys vs Dinosaurs '15
The Crater Lake Monster '77
Dinosaur '00
Dinosaur Valley Girls '96
Dinosaurus! '60
Dinotopia '02
The Eden Formula '06
The Giant Behemoth '59
The Good Dinosaur '15
Ice Age: Collision Course '16
Ice Age: Dawn of the Dinosaurs '09
Inspector Gadget's Biggest Caper Ever '05
Josh Kirby. . .Time Warrior: Chapter 1, Planet of the Dino-Knights '95
Journey to the Center of the Earth '08
Jurassic Park 3 '01
Jurassic Park '93▸
Jurassic World '15
Jurassic World: Fallen Kingdom '18
King Kong '05▸
The Land Before Time '88▸
The Land Before Time 2: The Great Valley Adventure '94
The Land Before Time 3: The Time of the Great Giving '95
The Land Before Time 4: Journey Through the Mists '96
The Land Before Time 5: The Mysterious Island '97
The Land Before Time 6: The Secret of Saurus Rock '98
Land Before Time 7: The Stone of Cold Fire '00
Land of the Lost '09
The Land That Time Forgot '75
The Land That Time Forgot '09
The Land Unknown '57
The Last Dinosaur '77
The Lost Continent '51
The Lost World '25
The Lost World '60
The Lost World '92
The Lost World '02
The Lost World: Jurassic Park 2 '97
Massacre in Dinosaur Valley '85
Meet the Robinsons '07
My Science Project '85
A Nymphoid Barbarian in Dinosaur Hell '94
100 Million BC '08
One Million B.C. '40
One Million Years B.C. '66
One of Our Dinosaurs Is Missing '75
Pee-wee's Big Adventure '85 ▸
The People That Time Forgot '77
Planet of the Dinosaurs '80
Pterodactyl Woman from Beverly Hills '97
Raptor Island '04
Return to the Lost World '93
Rise of the Dinosaurs '13
Sherlock Holmes '10
Sound of Horror '64
Super Mario Bros. '93
Tarzan's Desert Mystery '43
Teenage Caveman '58
Theodore Rex '95
Toy Story '95 ▸
Toy Story 2 '99 ▸
Unknown Island '48
Untamed Women '52
The Valley of Gwangi '69 ▸
Valley of the Dragons '61
Walking with Dinosaurs 3D '13
Warbirds '08
We're Back! A Dinosaur's Story '93

Disaster Flicks

***See also** Air Disasters; Meltdown; Sea Disasters*

Absolute Zero '05
Adrift '18
Aftermath '17
Aftershock: Earthquake in New York '99
Airplane vs. Volcano '14
Airport '75 '75
Airport '77 '77
Airport '70▸
Alive '93
The Andromeda Strain '08
Anna's Storm '07
The Apocalypse '07
Armageddon '98
Assignment Outer Space '61
Asteroid '97
Asteroid vs. Earth '14
Atomic Train '99
Avalanche '78
Avalanche '99
Avalanche Express '79
The Beasts Are On the Streets '78
Beyond the Poseidon Adventure '79
The Big Bus '76
Britannic '00
The Cassandra Crossing '76
CAT. 8 '13
Category 7: The End of the World '05
Category 6: Day of Destruction '04
Cave-In! '79
The China Syndrome '79▸
City Beneath the Sea '71
The Concorde: Airport '79 '79
Countdown: Jerusalem '09
Crack in the World '65
Crash Landing '58
The Crowded Sky '60
Dante's Peak '97
The Day After Tomorrow '04
The Day the Sky Exploded '57
Daybreak '01
Daylight '96
Deadly Shift '08
Deep Core '00
Deep Impact '98
Deepwater Horizon '16
Descent '05
Disaster Movie '08
Disaster Zone: Volcano in New York '06
Doomsday Prophecy '11
Earthquake '74
Earth's Final Hours '12
Earthstorm '06
Eve of Destruction '13
Exploding Sun '13
F6 Twister '12
Falling Fire '97
Fallout '01
Fatal Contact: Bird Flu in America '06
Fire '77
Fire From Below '09
Firestorm '97
Firetrap '01
500 MPH Storm '13
Flood! '76
Flood '07
Flood: A River's Rampage '97
40 Days and Nights '12
4:44 Last Day on Earth '11
Gale Force '01
Geostorm '17
Gray Lady Down '77
Hanging By a Thread '79
Hard Rain '97
The High and the Mighty '54 ▸
The Hindenburg '75
The Hole '98
The Hurricane '37 ▸
Hurricane '74
Hurricane '79
The Hurricane Heist '18
Ice Quake '10
Ice Twisters '09
Impact '09
The Impossible '12▸
In Old Chicago '37▸
An Inconvenient Sequel: Truth to Power '17
Independence Day '96▸
Into the Storm '14
Judgment Day '99
Krakatoa East of Java '69
LA Apocalypse '14
Last Days of Pompeii '35
The Last Voyage '60
The Last Warrior '99
The Last Woman on Earth '61
Lightning: Fire from the Sky '00
The Lost Missile '58
Magma: Volcanic Disaster '06
Malibu Shark Attack '09
Mayday at 40,000 Feet '76
Megafault '09
Meltdown '06
Metal Tornado '11
Meteor '79
Meteor Apocalypse '10
Meteor Storm '10
Miami Magma '11
Monster '08
Morning Departure '50
The Night the Bridge Fell Down '83
A Night to Remember '58▸
NYC: Tornado Terror '08
Only the Brave '17▸
Out of the Inferno '13
Pandemic '07
Pandora's Clock '96
Panic in the Skies '96
The Perfect Storm '00
Planet on the Prowl '65
Polar Storm '09
Pompeii '14
Poseidon '06
The Poseidon Adventure '72
The Poseidon Adventure '05
Power Play '02
The Rains Came '39
The Rains of Ranchipur '55
Raise the Titanic '80
Red Planet '00
Right at Your Door '06
St. Helen's, Killer Volcano '82
Scorcher '02
Seattle Superstorm '12
Sharknado 2: The Second One '14
Sharknado 3: Oh Hell No! '15
Sharknado: The 4th Awakens '16
Snowblind '78
Snowbound: The Jim and Jennifer Stolpa Story '94
Solar Attack '06
S.O.S. Titanic '79
Spiders '13
Stonados '13
Stonehenge Apocalypse '10
The Storm '09
Storm Cell '08
Storm Seekers '08
Super Eruption '11
Super Storm '12
Supernova '05
Terror in the Mall '98
Terror on the 40th Floor '74
Terror Peak '03
The 33 '15
Titanic 2 '10
Titanic '97 ▸
Titanic '12
Tornado Valley '09
The Towering Inferno '74
Toxic Skies '08
Trapped: Buried Alive '02
Turbulent Skies '10
12 Disasters '12
2012 '09
2012: Doomsday '08
Twister '96
Two Minute Warning '76
Tycus '98
Unstoppable '10▸
Velocity Trap '99
Volcano '97
The Wave '15▸
Weather Wars '11
When Time Ran Out '80
White Squall '96
Wildfire 7: The Inferno '02
Zero Hour! '57
Zodiac: Signs of the Apocalypse '14

Disco Musicals

Can't Stop the Music '80
Car Wash '76
Funkytown '11
KISS Meets the Phantom of the Park '78
Pirate Movie '82
The Rocky Horror Picture Show '75▸
Roll Bounce '05▸
Saturday Night Fever '77
Thank God It's Friday '78
The Wiz '78
Xanadu '80

Disease of the Week

***See also** AIDS; Emerging Viruses*

The Affair '73▸
And Now Ladies and Gentlemen '02
The Ann Jillian Story '88
As Good As It Gets '97▸
Away From Her '06▸
Batman and Robin '97
Beaches '88▸
The Blue Butterfly '04
Bobby Deerfield '77
The Book of Stars '99
The Boy in the Plastic Bubble '76
Breathe '17
Brian's Song '71▸
Brian's Song '01
Bubble Boy '01
Camille '36▸
The Cassandra Crossing '76
Champions '84
Checking Out '89
Children of the Corn 4: The Gathering '96
Chimera Strain '19
Chinese Box '97
A Christmas Tale '08▸
C.H.U.D. '84
Cleo from 5 to 7 '61▸
Cold Harvest '98
Contaminated Man '00
Contracted '13
Crash Course '00
Cries and Whispers '72▸
Crystal Heart '87
A Cure for Wellness '17
The Curse '87
A Dark Truth '12
Daybreak '93
Dead Space '90
Decoding Annie Parker '13
Dick Barton, Special Agent '48
The Doctor '91
Dr. Akagi '98
Doctor Bull '33
Down in the Delta '98▸
A Dream of Kings '69▸
Dying Young '91

▸ = rated three bones or higher

An Early Frost '85 ▸
East of Kilimanjaro '57
The End '78 ▸
Equals '16
Erin Brockovich '00 ▸
Escape '12
Euphoria '19
Extraordinary Measures '10
50/50 '11 ▸
The Fireball '50
The First Deadly Sin '80
First Do No Harm '97
Five Feet Apart '19
Griffin and Phoenix: A Love Story '76
Hangman's Curse '03
Here on Earth '00
Hilary and Jackie '98 ▸
Incredible Melting Man '77
Interrupted Melody '55 ▸
Invasion '07
Iris '01 ▸
Isle of the Dead '45
Isn't She Great '00
Jack '96
John Grisham's The Rainmaker '97
Killer by Night '72
The Last Best Year '90
Last Breath '96
The Last Man on Earth '64
A Little Bit of Heaven '11
Look Both Ways '05
Lorenzo's Oil '92 ▸
Love Affair: The Eleanor & Lou Gehrig Story '77 ▸
Love and Other Drugs '10
Love Story '70 ▸
The Man Who Killed Hitler and Then the Bigfoot '19
Marvin's Room '96
Mary and Martha '13
A Matter of WHO '62
Midnight Sun '18
Miles to Go '86
Miss Evers' Boys '97
Molokai: The Story of Father Damien '99
My Life '93
Nasty Rabbit '64
Niagara, Niagara '97
Night Unto Night '49
On Her Majesty's Secret Service '69 ▸
One True Thing '98 ▸
Osmosis Jones '01
The Painted Veil '06
Panic in Echo Park '77
The Paradise Virus '03
Parting Glances '86 ▸
Philadelphia '93 ▸
Pictures of Hollis Woods '07
The Plague Dogs '82
Poetry '10
The Pride of the Yankees '42 ▸
Promises in the Dark '79
A Quiet Duel '49
Rabid '77
Reborn '81
The Returned '14
The Road to Wellville '94
Run & Jump '13
Safe House '99
The Satan Bug '65
Scott Joplin '77
Shadowlands '93 ▸
The Silver Streak '34
Simon Birch '98
Six Weeks '82
A Song for Martin '01
Steel Magnolias '89 ▸
Stepmom '98 ▸
Stigma '73
Strange Relations '02
Sunchaser '96
Terms of Endearment '83 ▸
Terror Creatures from the Grave '66
That Russell Girl '08
The Tic Code '99
A Time to Remember '03
Unseen Enemy '17
Venomous '01
Waking Up Wally '05
The Wedding Gift '93 ▸
What We Become '16
The White Legion '36
Xtro '83
ZigZag '02 ▸

Disorganized Crime

***See also** Comic Cops; Crime Doesn't Pay; Crimedy; Organized Crime*

The Adventures of Pluto Nash '02
The Adventures of Rocky & Bullwinkle '00
Airheads '94
Albino Alligator '96
All About the Benjamins '02
All Saint's Day '98
Allie & Me '97
Amos and Andrew '93
The Apple Dumpling Gang '75
The Apple Dumpling Gang Rides Again '79
Armed and Dangerous '86
Baby's Day Out '94
Bait '00
Bandits '01
Beautiful Creatures '00
Before the Devil Knows You're Dead '07 ▸
Big Nothing '06
Big Trouble '02
Born Bad '97
Bottle Rocket '95
Buffalo 66 '97 ▸
Children of Hannibal '98
Cop and a Half '93
Crackers '84
Crime Spree '03
Disorganized Crime '89
Dr. Otto & the Riddle of the Gloom Beam '86
Dog Eat Dog '16
Drowning Mona '00
Dying to Get Rich '98
8 Heads in a Duffel Bag '96
Ernest Goes to Jail '90
Everybody's Famous! '00
Face '97
Fargo '96 ▸
Find Me Guilty '06 ▸
A Fine Mess '86
Fish in a Barrel '01
Get Shorty '95 ▸
Glitch! '88
Goodbye South, Goodbye '96
Gravesend '97
Gridlock'd '96 ▸
Gringo '18
The Gun in Betty Lou's Handbag '92
Gun Shy '00
Happy New Year '87
Headless Body in Topless Bar '96
Held Up '00
Henry's Crime '10
Her Alibi '88
Herbie Goes Bananas '80
High Heels and Low Lifes '01
Hit Me '96
Home Alone '90 ▸
Home Alone 2: Lost in New York '92
Hoods '98
I Wonder Who's Killing Her Now? '76
Idiot Box '97
In Bruges '08
The Italian Job '69
The Jerky Boys '95
Keys to Tulsa '96
Kicked in the Head '97
Kill Me Later '01
Killing Zoe '94
Knockaround Guys '01
The League of Gentlemen '60 ▸
Leather Jackets '90
L.I.E. '01
Lock, Stock and 2 Smoking Barrels '98 ▸
Love, Honour & Obey '00
Lucky Numbers '00
A Man, a Woman, and a Bank '79
Man of the House '95
Masterminds '16
Menage '86 ▸
Mexican Hayride '48
Miss Grant Takes Richmond '49
Mixed Nuts '94
More Dogs Than Bones '00
A New Wave '07
Ocean's 11 '60
Once in the Life '00
Once Upon a Crime '92
101 Dalmatians '96
102 Dalmatians '00
Palookaville '95 ▸
Partners '99
The Perfect Score '04
Perpetrators of the Crime '98
Picking Up the Pieces '99
Ping! '99
Poor White Trash '00
Quick Change '90
Reservoir Dogs '92 ▸
River Red '98
Ruthless People '86 ▸
Safe Men '98
St. Benny the Dip '51
Scorched '02
See No Evil, Hear No Evil '89
See Spot Run '01
Shark Tale '04
Sister Act '92
Sitting Ducks '80 ▸
A Slight Case of Murder '99
Small Time Crooks '00
Snatch '00 ▸
Stealing Harvard '02
Stop! or My Mom Will Shoot '92
Suicide Kings '97
The Super '91
Survivors '83
Things to Do in Denver When You're Dead '95 ▸
Thrilled to Death '88
Too Many Crooks '59
Trapped in Paradise '94
Triggermen '02
Truth or Consequences, N.M. '97
Two If by Sea '95
Two Tough Guys '03
Warm Blooded Killers '01
Welcome to Collinwood '02
What's the Worst That Could Happen? '01
The Wrong Arm of the Law '63 ▸
The Young in Heart '38 ▸
Zoolander '01

Divorce

***See also** Marriage; Single Parents; Singles; Stepparents*

Abandoned and Deceived '95
The Accidental Tourist '88 ▸
A.C.O.D. '13
Alimony Madness '33
All I Want for Christmas '91
All the Good Ones Are Married '07
Angels in America '03 ▸
The Assassination of Richard Nixon '05
The Awful Truth '37 ▸
Back Against the Wall '00
Barney's Version '10
Bart Got a Room '08
Behaving Badly '89
The Big Wedding '13
Black Coffee '14
Blue Car '03 ▸
Blue Valentine '10
Breaking Up Is Hard to Do '79
Bringing Down the House '03
Bye Bye, Love '94
California Suite '78 ▸
Can She Bake a Cherry Pie? '83
Catch Me If You Can '02
Celebrity '98 ▸
Chicken Every Sunday '48
City by the Sea '02
Clara's Heart '88
Crazy, Stupid, Love. '11 ▸
Criminal Intent '05
Cross My Heart '88
The Cry of the Owl '09
Cyrus '10
Daisy Kenyon '47
Dead Cool '04
Definitely, Maybe '08 ▸
Desert Hearts '86 ▸
Diary of a Mad Black Woman '05
Divorce American Style '67
Divorce His, Divorce Hers '72
Divorce Wars: A Love Story '82
The Divorcee '30
Divorce-Italian Style '62 ▸
Dr. T & the Women '00 ▸
Dodson's Journey '01
Duane Hopwood '05 ▸
Duck Season '04 ▸
Dying to Get Rich '98
Early Frost '84
Eat, Pray, Love '10
Edie & Pen '95
Empire Falls '05
Enough Said '13 ▸
E.T.: The Extra-Terrestrial '82 ▸
Extraterrestrial '14
Faces '68 ▸
Faithless '00 ▸
Falling Down '93
Family Pictures '93 ▸
The First Wives Club '96
The Five '10
5x2 '04
Flirting with Forty '09
Fool's Gold '08
For Richer or Poorer '97
The Full Monty '96 ▸
Gloria '13 ▸
The Good Father '87 ▸
The Good Mother '88
Goodbye Love '34
Goodbye to All That '14
The Goose and the Gander '35
Gossip '08
Hard Promises '92
Haywire '80
The Healer '02
Heartbreakers '01
Heartburn '86 ▸
Heaven's Door '12
Hello I Must Be Going '12
High Society '56 ▸
History Is Made at Night '37 ▸
Home By Christmas '06
Hope Floats '98
Hope Gap '20
House Arrest '96
How to Be a Latin Lover '17
How to Commit Marriage '69
How to Deal '03
Hullabaloo '40
Humor Me '17
The Hungry Ghosts '09
Husbands and Wives '92 ▸
I Wish '11 ▸
In Love We Trust '07
Interiors '78 ▸
Intolerable Cruelty '03
Irreconcilable Differences '84
It's Complicated '09
Just Before I Go '15
Just Go With It '11
Kramer vs. Kramer '79 ▸
Labor Day '13
The Land of Steady Habits '18
The Last Gangster '37
The Last Song '10
Late Marriage '01
Laws of Attraction '04
Le Divorce '03
Les Destinees '00
Let Us Be Gay '30
Let's Do It Again '53
Let's Make It Legal '51
Liar Liar '97
The Liberation of L.B. Jones '70
Life of the Party '18
Living Out Loud '98
Love '05
The Love Punch '13
Love, Wedding, Marriage '11
Loveless '18 ▸
Maisie Goes to Reno '44
Making Plans for Lena '09
Marie '85 ▸
Marriage on the Rocks '65
Marriage Story '19 ▸
The Marrying Kind '52
May in Summer '13
Me & Mrs. Jones '02
Me and You and Everyone We Know '05 ▸
The Misfits '61 ▸
Mrs. Doubtfire '93
Mr. Skeffington '44 ▸
Mr. Wonderful '93
Mother '96
The Motive '18
Must Love Dogs '05
My One and Only '09
Nadine '87
Necessary Parties '88
Never Say Goodbye '46
The Night of the White Pants '06
Nocturnal Animals '16
Nothing in Common '86
Now and Then '95
Ocean's Eleven '01 ▸
The Odd Couple '68 ▸
Old Acquaintance '43
Old School '03
The Parent Trap '61
The Parent Trap '98
Parnell '37
Payment on Demand '51
Peace, Love & Misunderstanding '11
Peggy Sue Got Married '86
The Personals '83
Petulia '68 ▸
Play It Again, Sam '72 ▸
The Prize Pulitzer '89
The Rebound '09
Reckless '97 ▸
Reno '39
Results '15
The Rich Are Always With Us '32
Rich in Love '93
Riptide '34 ▸
Road Hard '15
The Santa Clause '94
Saraband '03 ▸
Scenes from a Marriage '73 ▸
Second Best '05
Second Honeymoon '37
Secret Lives of Second Wives '08
The Secret of Zoey '02
See You in the Morning '89
Serving Sara '02
Shattered Silence '71
Signs & Wonders '00
So Well Remembered '47
Something's Gotta Give '03 ▸
The Squid and the Whale '05 ▸
The Starter Wife '07
Starting Over '79 ▸
Stepmom '98 ▸
Strange Bedfellows '65
Stuck in Love '12
Sweet Revenge '90
Table for Five '83
Tell It to the Judge '49
Thank You for Smoking '06
That Old Feeling '96
Then She Found Me '07
Things to Come '16 ▸
Three Wise Girls '32
Till Murder Do Us Part '92
Town and Country '01
The Trouble with the Truth '11 ▸
Twister '96
Under the Tuscan Sun '03
Unforgettable '17
An Unmarried Woman '78 ▸
The Upside of Anger '05 ▸
Wah-Wah '05
The War of the Roses '89 ▸
We Monsters '15
The Weather Man '05
Welcome to Mooseport '04
What Maisie Knew '12 ▸
What We Did on Our Holiday '15
When the Boys Meet the Girls '65
Who Is Clark Rockefeller? '10
Wilderness Love '02
Yella '07 ▸

Doctors & Nurses

***See also** AIDS; Dental Mayhem; Disease of the Week; Emerging Viruses; Evil Doctors; Hospitals & Nursploitation!; Shrinks*

Adam Resurrected '08
After Tiller '13 ▸
Afterwards '08
Alias the Doctor '32
All Creatures Great and Small '74 ▸
Alone in the Dark '82
Anatomy 2 '03
And the Band Played On '93 ▸
The Android Affair '95
The Angriest Man in Brooklyn '14
Anne of Green Gables: The Continuing Story '99
Any Given Sunday '99 ▸
Arachnophobia '90
Armistead Maupin's More Tales of the City '97
Arrowsmith '31
Article 99 '92
Ashanti, Land of No Mercy '79
The Asphyx '72 ▸
At First Sight '98
Atonement '07 ▸
Attack the Block '11
Augustine '12
Awake '07
Awakenings '90 ▸
Baby Girl Scott '87
Back to You and Me '05
Bad for Each Other '53
Bad Medicine '85
Badge of Faith '15
Bank Holiday '38
Battle Circus '53
Battle Zone '52
Beautiful People '99
Behind the Mask '99
Between Two Women '45
Beyond Borders '03
Beyond Re-Animator '03
Bikini House Calls '96
Bikini Med School '98
Black Friday '40
Blade '98
Bless the Child '00
Blind Justice '94
Bliss '96
Blood Mania '70
Blood Work '02
Body Parts '91
Bone Daddy '97
Brain Dead '89 ▸
Breast Men '97
Brute Force '47 ▸
The Bumblebee Flies Anyway '98
Burke & Hare '10
Calling Dr. Gillespie '42
Calling Dr. Kildare '39
Candy Stripe Nurses '74
Carancho '10
The Caretakers '63
The Carey Treatment '72
Carry On Again Doctor '69
Carry On Doctor '68 ▸
Carry On Matron '72
Castle of the Creeping Flesh '68
Caught '49 ▸
Children of the Century '99
Children of the Corn 4: The Gathering '96
Choices of the Heart: The Margaret Sanger Story '95
Christie's Revenge '07
Christmas In Conway '13
Chronic '16
The Cider House Rules '99 ▸
Circus of Horrors '60
The Citadel '38 ▸
City of Angels '98
City of Joy '92
The Clonus Horror '79
Coastlines '02
Coma '78 ▸
Coma '12
Concussion '15

Congo Maisie '40
Contagion '11 ▶
Corregidor '43
Corridors of Blood '58
Courageous Dr. Christian '40
Crimes & Misdemeanors '89 ▶
Crisis '50
Critical Care '97
Cry Havoc '43
A Cure for Wellness '17
Dallas Buyers Club '13 ▶
Dangerously We Live '41
Dante 01 '08
Dark City '97
Dark Delusion '47
Darling Companion '12
Dead in a Heartbeat '02
Dead Ringers '88 ▶
Dead Sleep '91
Death Becomes Her '92 ▶
The Death of Mr. Lazarescu '05
Decoding Annie Parker '13
Decoy '46
Deep Crimson '96
Depth Charge '08
The Details '11
Diagnosis: Death '09
Dirty Pretty Things '03 ▶
Doc Hollywood '91
The Doctor '91
Dr. Akagi '98
Dr. Alien '88
The Doctor and the Devils '85
The Doctor and the Girl '49
Doctor at Large '57
Doctor at Sea '56
Dr. Bell and Mr. Doyle: The Dark Beginnings of Sherlock Holmes '00
Dr. Black, Mr. Hyde '76
Doctor Blood's Coffin '62
Doctor Bull '33
Doctor Butcher M.D. '80
Dr. Cyclops '40
Dr. Death, Seeker of Souls '73
Doctor Detroit '83
Dr. Dolittle '98
Dr. Dolittle 2 '01
Doctor Dolittle '67
Dr. Ehrlich's Magic Bullet '40
Doctor Faustus '68
Dr. Frankenstein's Castle of Freaks '74
Dr. Gillespie's Criminal Case '43
Dr. Gillespie's New Assistant '42
Doctor in Clover '66
Doctor in Distress '63
Doctor in Love '60
Doctor in the House '53 ▶
Dr. Jekyll and Mr. Hyde '73
Dr. Jekyll & Mr. Hyde '99
Dr. Jekyll and Mr. Hyde '08
Dr. Kildare Goes Home '40
Dr. Kildare's Crisis '40
Dr. Kildare's Strange Case '40
Dr. Kildare's Victory '42
Dr. Kildare's Wedding Day '41
Dr. Mabuse, The Gambler '22 ▶
Dr. Mabuse *vs.* Scotland Yard '64
Doctor Strange '16 ▶
Dr. T & the Women '00 ▶
Doctor Takes a Wife '40 ▶
Dr. Tarr's Torture Dungeon '75
Doctor Who '96
Doctor X '32
Doctor Zhivago '65 ▶
Doctor Zhivago '03
The Doctor's Dilemma '58
Doctors' Wives '70
Dolittle '20
Dominick & Eugene '88 ▶
Don McKay '09
Don't Look in the Basement '73
Dragonfly '02
The Dreaming '88
Drunken Angel '48 ▶
East of Borneo '31
The Egyptian '54
The Elephant Man '80 ▶
Emmanuelle in the Country '78
An Enemy of the People '77
The English Patient '96 ▶
Evolution '16
Excuse Me for Living '12
Extraordinary Measures '10
Extreme Measures '96
Eyes Wide Shut '99
False Faces '32
Fantastic Voyage '66 ▶
A Farewell to Arms '57
Fatal Error '99
Fatal Trust '06
The Fifth Horseman Is Fear '64
Finding Normal '13
First Do No Harm '97
Five '11 ▶
Flame of the West '45
Flatliners '90
Flatliners '17
The Flesh and the Fiends '60
Flesh Feast '69
Florence Nightingale '85
Florence Nightingale '08
Flowers for Algernon '00
Foreign Body '86
The Fortune Cookie '66 ▶
Fragile '05
Fragments '08
The Fugitive '93 ▶
Generation War '13
Gifted Hands: The Ben Carson Story '09
The Girl in White '52
Girl, Interrupted '99
The Girl Who Kicked the Hornet's Nest '10
The Good Doctor '11
Good Morning, Miss Dove '55
The Grand Seduction '13
The Great Moment '44
The Green Light '37
The Green Years '46
Gross Anatomy '89
Guest in the House '44
Gun Shy '00
Halloween 2: The Nightmare Isn't Over! '81
Hard to Kill '89
Harold and Kumar Go to White Castle '04
He Loves Me . . . He Loves Me Not '02
Healer '36
The Heart Specialist '06
Hellgate '52
A Hole in One '04
Holy Girl '04 ▶
Hombres Armados '97 ▶
The Home Front '02
Honor Among Thieves '68
The Horrible Dr. Hichcock '62
The Horror Chamber of Dr. Faustus '59 ▶
Horror Hospital '73
The Hospital '71 ▶
Hospital of Terror '78
House Calls '78 ▶
How I Killed My Father '03 ▶
Hybrid '07
Hysteria '11
I Never Promised You a Rose Garden '77 ▶
I Take This Woman '40
I Thank a Fool '62
In a Better World '10
In Dreams '98
The In-Laws '79 ▶
In Love and War '96
Inch'Allah '12
The Incredible Journey of Dr. Meg Laurel '79 ▶
Inhale '10
InSight '11
Intent to Kill '58
Internes Can't Take Money '37
The Interns '62
Jekyll & Hyde. . . Together Again '82
Johnny Belinda '48 ▶
Junior '94
Just like Heaven '05
Killer by Night '72
Killing Moon '00
The Killing of a Sacred Deer '17
King of the Underworld '39
The King's Speech '10 ▶
Kiss and Make Up '34
Klondike Fury '42
Knucklehead '15 ▶
Kongo '32
La Sentinelle '92
The Lady With the Lamp '51
Language of the Enemy '07
The Last Enemy '08
The Last Face '17
The Last King of Scotland '06 ▶
The Late Bloomer '16
Laurel Canyon '02
The Lazarus Syndrome '79
Like Father, Like Son '87
A Little Bit of Heaven '11
The Little Stranger '18
Living Proof '08
Looking for an Echo '99
Love '05
Love Finds a Home '09
Love for Rent '05
Love Hurts '09
Love Is a Many-Splendored Thing '55
Love Takes Wing '09
Love's Unfolding Dream '07
Macabre '58
Mad Love '35 ▶
The Mad Monster '42
The Madness of King George '94 ▶
Magnificent Obsession '35
Making Babies '19
Making Love '82
Malice '93
The Man From Yesterday '32
A Man to Remember '38
The Man Who Turned to Stone '57
Maniac Nurses Find Ecstasy '94
Marvin's Room '96
M*A*S*H '70 ▶
M*A*S*H: Goodbye, Farewell & Amen '83 ▶
The Mask of Fu Manchu '32
Master and Commander: The Far Side of the World '03 ▶
Matter of Trust '98
Maze '01
The Medicine Show '01
Meet Dr. Christian '39
Memories of Me '88
The Memory Keeper's Daughter '08
Men in White '34
Mesmer '94
Metamorphosis: The Alien Factor '93
The Millerson Case '47
The Millionairess '60
The Mind of Mr. Soames '70
Miranda '48
Misconceptions '08
Miss Evers' Boys '97
Miss Pinkerton '32
Mr. North '88
Mockingbird Don't Sing '01
Molly '99
The Money Trap '65
A Monster with a Thousand Heads '15 ▶
Monty Python's The Meaning of Life '83 ▶
Mother Didn't Tell Me '50
The Mountain '19
Murder On the Home Front '13
Murder Once Removed '71
The Music Never Stopped '11
My Baby Is Missing '07
My Brother Jonathan '85
My Own Country '98
The National Health '73
National Lampoon Presents RoboDoc '08
Nell '94
Night Call Nurses '72
Night Monster '42
Night Nurse '31 ▶
Night Nurse '77
Nine Months '95
The 9th Life of Louis Drax '16
No Sad Songs For Me '50
No Way Out '50
Nobody's Baby '37
Noel '04
Nomads '86
Nora Prentiss '47
The Normal Heart '14 ▶
Not as a Stranger '55
Not of This Earth '57
Not of This Earth '96
Nurse 3D '13
Nurse '80
The Nurse '97
Nurse Betty '00 ▶
Nurse Edith Cavell '39 ▶
Nuts! '16 ▶
Obsessed '02
Old Swimmin' Hole '40
One Flew Over the Cuckoo's Nest '75 ▶
One Man's Journey '33
Only Love '98
Operation Heartbeat '69
Operation Mad Ball '57
Opium: Diary of a Madwoman '07
The Ordeal of Dr. Mudd '80 ▶
The Other Love '47
Out of the Ashes '03
Outbreak '94 ▶
The Painted Veil '06
Pandemic '07
Panic in Echo Park '77
Panic in the Streets '50 ▶
Paper Mask '91
Paradise: Hope '13
Paris After Dark '43
Parkland '13
Passchendaele '10
Patch Adams '98
Pathology '08
The Patriot '99
Pearl Harbor '01
The People *vs.* Dr. Kildare '41
People Will Talk '51 ▶
Persona '66 ▶
Petulia '68 ▶
Phenomenon '96
Planet Terror '07
Playing God '96
The Pregnancy Pact '10
Prescription Thugs '16
The Princess and the Warrior '00 ▶
The Prisoner of Shark Island '36
Private Duty Nurses '71
Promises in the Dark '79
Psych: 9 '10
Purple Hearts '84
A Quiet Duel '49
Race Against Time '00
Rage '72
Rasen '98
Re-Generation '04
The Real Glory '39 ▶
Reckless '97 ▶
Reckless: The Sequel '98 ▶
The Red Baron '08
Red Beard '65 ▶
Respire '09
Restoration '94 ▶
Return to Sender '15
The Road to Wellville '94
Robin Cook's Terminal '96
Rodgers & Hammerstein's South Pacific '01
Roommates '95
A Royal Affair '12 ▶
Run & Jump '13
Saadia '53
Salem's Lot '04
Saw '04
Saw 3 '06
Say It With Songs '29
The Scribbler '14
The Secret of Dr. Kildare '39
Seducing Doctor Lewis '03
Series 7: The Contenders '01
Serving in Silence: The Margarethe Cammermeyer Story '95 ▶
The She-Creature '56
She Devil '57
A Short Stay in Switzerland '09
The Singing Detective '03
The Sins of Rachel Cade '61
Sisters of War '10
The Skeleton Key '05
Slaughter Hotel '71
Smart People '08
So Proudly We Hail '43 ▶
So Well Remembered '47
Solace '16
Someone Behind the Door '71
Something the Lord Made '04
Something's Gotta Give '03 ▶
Sour Grapes '98
South Pacific '58 ▶
Speed Dating '07
The Spring '00
State of Emergency '94
Stigma '73
A Stolen Face '52
Strange Lady in Town '55
The Student Nurses '70
Sublime '07
Sun Choke '16
The Sun Is Also a Star '19
Sunchaser '96
The Surgeon '94
Symphony of Six Million '32
Talk to Her '02 ▶
The Tall Man '12
The Target '15
Tarzan and the Great River '67
Tarzan's Fight for Life '58
Tarzan's Hidden Jungle '55
Tears of the Sun '03
Tell It to the Bees '19
Tell It to the Marines '26
Tell No One '06 ▶
Tender Loving Care '73
Testament of Youth '79
Testimony of Two Men '77
Things You Can Tell Just by Looking at Her '00
30 Years to Life '01
This Woman Is Dangerous '52
Three Men in White '44
Three Wise Women '11
Thunder on the Hill '51
Torn Apart '04
Touched '05
Trial by Media '00
Tundra '36
The Twelve Days of Christmas Eve '04
The Twilight of the Ice Nymphs '97
The Unbearable Lightness of Being '88 ▶
The Undying '09
The Uninvited '09
Unknown '11
The Unknown Soldier '98
Untogether '19
The Upturned Glass '47
A Very Serious Person '06
Vigil in the Night '40
Virus X '10
Vital Signs '90
Vulture's Eye '04
Waitress '07 ▶
Waltzing Anna '06
Ward No. 6 '09
Welcome Stranger '47
What Dreams May Come '98
What If God Were the Sun? '07
What Katy Did '99
When Did You Last See Your Father? '07
Where Danger Lives '50
Where the Money Is '00
White Coats '04
White Witch Doctor '53
Who Killed Bambi? '03
Widow on the Hill '05
Wit '01 ▶
Witness for the Prosecution '57 ▶
The Witnesses '07
Women of Valor '86
Women's Prison '55
The X Files: I Want to Believe '08
Yes '04
You Don't Know Jack '10
Young Dr. Kildare '38
Young Doctors in Love '82
The Young Nurses '73
Zelary '03 ▶
Zero Hour! '57

Documentary

See also Docudrama

The Act of Killing '13 ▶
An African Election '11
After Innocence '05 ▶
After Tiller '13 ▶
Afternoon of a Faun '13 ▶
Ai Weiwei: Never Sorry '12 ▶
Aileen: Life and Death of a Serial Killer '03 ▶
Ain't In It For My Health: A Film About Levon Helm '10 ▶
Air Guitar Nation '06 ▶
AKA Doc Pomus '12 ▶
Alive Inside '14 ▶
Almost Holy '16 ▶
Amazing Grace '19 ▶
The Ambassador '11
America: Imagine the World Without Her '14
American Dharma '18
American Dream '90 ▶
American Factory '19 ▶
American Grindhouse '10
American Movie '99 ▶
American Mystic '10
American Swing '08
American Teen '08
America's Heart and Soul '04
Among the Believers '15 ▶
Amy '15 ▶
And Everything Is Going Fine '10
Anvil! The Story of Anvil '09
Apollo 11 '19 ▶
Araya '59
Arctic Tale '07
The Aristocrats '05 ▶
Armadillo '11
Armstrong '19
Art House '16
As Goes Janesville '12
Assassination of Trotsky '72
At the Death House Door '08 ▶
The Atomic Cafe '82 ▶
Author: The JT LeRoy Story '16
Awesome! I F***in' Shot That! '06 ▶
The B-Side: Elsa Dorfman's Portrait Photography '17
Babies '10 ▶
Bad Reputation '18
Ballets Russes '05 ▶
A Band Called Death '13 ▶
Baraka '93 ▶
Bathtubs Over Broadway '18 ▶
Batkid Begins '15
The Beaches of Agnes '08
Bears '14
Beats, Rhymes and Life: The Travels of a Tribe Called Quest '11 ▶
Beautiful Losers '08
Becoming Mike Nichols '16
Before the Flood '16
Being Canadian '15 ▶
Being Elmo: A Puppeteer's Journey '11
Best Kept Secret '13
Best of Enemies '15 ▶
Best Worst Movie '09 ▶
Betting on Zero '16
Beyond Clueless '14
The Big One '98
Big Star: Nothing Can Hurt Me '13 ▶
Bigger Stronger Faster '08
The Biggest Little Farm '18 ▶

▶ = rated three bones or higher

S21: The Khmer Rouge Killing Machine '03 ▶
Salinger '13
The Salt of the Earth '14 ▶
Samsara '12
Sasquatch '76
Searching For Sugar Man '12 ▶
Secundaria '14
Senna '11
The September Issue '09
78/52: Hitchcock's Shower Scene '17 ▶
Sex Positive '09
Seymour: An Introduction '15 ▶
Shake Hands With the Devil: The Journey of Romeo Dallaire '04 ▶
Sherman's March '86 ▶
Sherpa '15 ▶
Shine a Light '08
Shoah '85 ▶
The Show '95
Shut Up Little Man! An Audio Misadventure '11
Sicko '07
Side by Side '12 ▶
Silicon Cowboys '16
SMART: Specialized Mobile Animal Rescue Team '16
Sneakerheadz '15
Somm '13
The Sorrow and the Pity '71 ▶
Sound City '13 ▶
The Source Family '13
South of the Border '09
Spellbound '02 ▶
Springsteen & I '13 ▶
The Square '13
Standard Operating Procedure '08 ▶
Standing in the Shadows of Motown '02 ▶
Step '17
Step Into Liquid '03 ▶
Steve Jobs: The Man in the Machine '15
Stone Reader '02 ▶
Stop Making Sense '84 ▶
The Story of the Weeping Camel '03 ▶
Strong Island '17 ▶
The Summit '13
Super Size Me 2: Holy Chicken! '19
Super Size Me '04 ▶
Superstar: The Life and Times of Andy Warhol '90 ▶
Surfwise '07 ▶
Sweetgrass '09
Swimming to Cambodia '87 ▶
Tabloid '10
The T.A.M.I. Show '64 ▶
Tarnation '03
Tea with the Dames '18
Tell Them Who You Are '05
Theremin: An Electronic Odyssey '95 ▶
They Shall Not Grow Old '19 ▶
They Will Have to Kill Us First: Malian Music in Exile '15
The Thin Blue Line '88 ▶
This Film Is Not Yet Rated '06
This is Not a Film '10 ▶
This May Be the Last Time '14
Three Identical Strangers '18 ▶
Through the Fire '05 ▶
Thunder Soul '10
Tickled '16 ▶
The Tillman Story '10 ▶
Time to Choose '16 ▶
Times of Harvey Milk '83 ▶
Tim's Vermeer '13 ▶
To Be Takei '14
Tokyo-Ga '85 ▶
Tokyo Olympiad '66 ▶
Tomorrow We Disappear '14
Toni Morrison: The Pieces I Am '19 ▶
Touching the Void '03
Tower '16 ▶
The Trials of Muhammad Ali '13 ▶
Triumph of the Will '34 ▶
Troublemakers: The Story of Land Art '15 ▶
The Troubles We've Seen '94 ▶
Trumbo '07 ▶
Truth or Dare '91
12 O'Clock Boys '14 ▶
20 Feet from Stardom '13 ▶
The 24 Hour War '16
21 Up South Africa: Mandela's Children '08 ▶
2016: Obama's America '12
Two Years at Sea '12
Tyson '08
Uncovered: The War on Iraq '04
The Undefeated '11
The Unforeseen '07
The U.S. Vs. John Lennon '06
The Unknown Known '14 ▶
Unknown White Male '05 ▶
The Unmistaken Child '08
An Unreasonable Man '06 ▶
Unseen Enemy '17
The Untold Story of Emmett Louis Till '05 ▶
Unzipped '94 ▶
Up for Grabs '05
Valentino: The Last Emperor '08
Verdict on Auschwitz: The Frankfurt Auschwitz Trial 1963-1965 '93 ▶
Very Semi-Serious: A Partially Thorough Portrait of New Yorker Cartoonists '15
The Vietnam War '17
Vince Vaughn's Wild West Comedy Show '06
Virunga '14 ▶
Visions of Light: The Art of Cinematography '93 ▶
Visitors '13
Voices of Iraq '04 ▶
Waiting for Superman '10
The Waiting Room '12
Wal-Mart: The High Cost of Low Price '05 ▶
Wall '04 ▶
Waltz with Bashir '08 ▶
The War Room '93 ▶
War Tapes '06 ▶
Waste Land '10
We Are Legion: The Story of the Hacktivists '12
We Can't Go Home Again '73
We Come As Friends '14
We Steal Secrets: The Story of WikiLeaks '13
We Were Here '11
The Weather Underground '02 ▶
West of Memphis '12
Western Stars '19 ▶
What Happened, Miss Simone? '15 ▶
When Two Worlds Collide '16 ▶
When We Were Kings '96 ▶
Where in the World Is Osama Bin Laden? '06
Where to Invade Next '15
Which Way Home '09
The White Diamond '04 ▶
Whitey: United States of America v. James J. Bulger '14
Whitney '18
Who Gets to Call It Art? '05
Who Killed the Electric Car? '06
Who the Hell is Juliette? '98
Whose Streets? '17
Wigstock: The Movie '95
The Wild Parrots of Telegraph Hill '03 ▶
The Wildest Dream: The Conquest of Everest '10
Winged Migration '01 ▶
Winning: The Racing Life of Paul Newman '15
Winter on Fire: Ukraine's Fight for Freedom '15 ▶
Wisecracks '93 ▶
Won't You Be My Neighbor? '18 ▶
Woodstock '70 ▶
Word Wars: Tiles and Tribulations on the Scrabble Circuit '04 ▶
Wordplay '06 ▶
The Work '17 ▶
Yalom's Cure '14
Year of the Horse '97
The Yes Men '03
Young@Heart '07 ▶

Dolls That Kill

See Killer Toys

Domestic Abuse

See also Sexual Abuse

The Abduction '96
Angel Eyes '01
Au Hasard Balthazar '66
Beyond Betrayal '94
The Break Up '98
The Burning Bed '85 ▶
The Caller '11
Casualties '97
Columbus Circle '10
Dangerous Child '01
Dangerous Game '93
Dear Frankie '04
Edge of Madness '02
Enough '02
Evil '03 ▶
Expired '07
Fallen Angel '99
Falling Down '93
.45 '06
Garrison '07
The Gift '00
Harm's Way '07
Hidden Away '13
The House Next Door '01
The Human Stain '03
The Ice House '97 ▶
In the Bedroom '01 ▶
Instinct to Kill '01
The Invisible Man '20 ▶
John John in the Sky '00
Kill for Me '12
Lea '96
Lift '01
Like Dandelion Dust '09
Love Come Down '00
Love Letters '45
Lovelace '13
A Memory In My Heart '99
The Merry Gentleman '08
Mesmerized '84
Mortal Thoughts '91
Nil by Mouth '96
Olivia '83
100 Feet '08
The Opponent '01
The Pastor's Wife '11
Personal Velocity: Three Portraits '02 ▶
Personal Vendetta '96
Plain Dirty '04
Prairie Fever '08
Preacher's Kid '10
Private Violence '14 ▶
Reviving Ophelia '10
Ryna '05
The Secrets of Comfort House '06
Secrets of Eden '12
Shattered Dreams '90
Sleep Easy, Hutch Rimes '00
Sleeping with the Enemy '91
Sparkle '12
Stranger in My Bed '05
Take My Eyes '03
The Tenant of Wildfell Hall '96
This Boy's Life '93 ▶
A Thousand Kisses Deep '11
Tyrannosaur '11
An Unfinished Life '05
Valerie '57
Vanessa '07
A Vigilante '19
Visions of Murder '93
Visitor Q '01
Waitress '07 ▶
We the Animals '18 ▶
What's Love Got to Do with It? '93
While She Was Out '08
Your Vice is a Closed Room and Only I Have the Key '72

Doofus Dads

See Bad Dads; Dads; Single Parents; Slapstick Comedy; Stepparents

Doublecross!

See also Crime Drama; Heists; Scams, Stings & Cons

The Asphalt Jungle '50 ▶
Assassin X '16
Broken City '13
Caliber 9 '72
Ca$h '06
Casino Royale '06 ▶
Catch.44 '11
Circus '00
The Code '09
Colorado Territory '49
The Contractor '07
Criss Cross '48 ▶
Cypher '02 ▶
Decoy '46
Diamond Run '96
The Diplomat '08
Direct Contact '09
Dot the I '03
Double Cross '06
The Family '70
The File of the Golden Goose '69
Framed '47
Game of Chance '10
Grand Slam '67
The Gun Runners '58
The Hades Factor '06
The Handmaiden '16 ▶
Heist '01 ▶
High School Big Shot '59
Hunt to Kill '10
I Walk Alone '48
The Italian Job '03 ▶
Journey to the End of the Night '06
Just Another Secret '89
The Kane Files '10
The Kremlin Letter '70
A Lady of Chance '28
The Last Run '71
The Legend of Tarzan '16
Lucky Number Slevin '06
Machete '10
Mara Maru '52
The Moonshine War '70
National Lampoon's Gold Diggers '04
Niagara '52
No Good Deed '02
Our America '02
Our Kind of Traitor '16
Out of the Past '47 ▶
Parker '13
Partners '99
Payback '98 ▶
Point Blank '10
Pulse 2: Afterlife '08
Road of No Return '09
Score '95
The Sentinel '06
Seoul Raiders '05
The Set Up '95
Shutter '05
Sniper 3 '04
The Split '68
The Stranger '10
Swindled '04
Thicker than Water '99
Tick Tock '00 ▶
Total Dhamaal '19
Trance '13
Twelve Hours to Kill '60
The Ultimate Weapon '97
Wild Things 2 '04
Wild Things '98
A Woman, a Gun and a Noodle Shop '10
Wrong Turn at Tahoe '09

Down Under

Absolute Deception '13
Adam's Woman '70
Adore '13
The Adventures of Priscilla, Queen of the Desert '94 ▶
Age of Consent '69
The Alice '04
Alien Visitor '95
Animal Kingdom '09 ▶
Animals '15 ▶
Australia '08
The Australian Story '52
Back of Beyond '95
Barry McKenzie Holds His Own '74
Battle Cry '55 ▶
Beautiful '09
Beautiful Kate '09 ▶
Black Water '07
Blackrock '97
Blood Surf '00
Bootmen '00
Brand New Day '10
Bride Flight '08
Brides of Christ '91
Broken Hill '09
Candy '06
The Cars That Ate Paris '74 ▶
The Castle '97
The Chant of Jimmie Blacksmith '78 ▶
Children of the Revolution '95
Chopper '00
The Clinic '10
Cloudstreet '11
Country Life '95
Crocodile Dundee 2 '88
Crocodile Dundee '86 ▶
Crocodile Dundee in Los Angeles '01
The Crocodile Hunter: Collision Course '02
Crush '09
A Cry in the Dark '88 ▶
The Cup '11
Danny Deckchair '03
Dead Alive '93
Dead Heart '96 ▶
December Boys '07
The Desert Rats '53 ▶
Dingo '90
Disgrace '08
The Dish '00 ▶
Do or Die '01
Down Under '86
The Dreaming '88
The Dressmaker '16
Drive Hard '14
Fair Game '86
Fat, Sick & Nearly Dead '11
Fatal Honeymoon '12
A Few Best Men '11
Fierce Creatures '96
15 Amore '98
Finding Nemo '03 ▶
Forty Thousand Horsemen '41
Gallipoli '81 ▶
Garage Days '03
Geordie '55
The Getting of Wisdom '77
The Goddess of 1967 '00
Goldstone '18
The Good Wife '86
Hammers over the Anvil '91
The Hard Word '02
Head On '98 ▶
Heavenly Creatures '94 ▶
Heaven's Burning '97
Holy Smoke '99
Howling 3: The Marsupials '87
The Hunter '12
Hurricane Smith '92
In Her Skin '09
The Incredible Journey of Mary Bryant '05
The Irishman '78
Jackie Chan's First Strike '96 ▶
Japanese Story '03 ▶
Jindabyne '06
Kangaroo Jack '02
Kings in Grass Castles '97
Lake Mungo '08
Lantana '01 ▶
Last Cab to Darwin '16 ▶
Last Ride '09
The Light Between Oceans '16
A Little Bit of Soul '97
Little Boy Lost '78
Love Serenade '96
Mad Dog Morgan '76
The Man from Snowy River '82
Marking Time '03
Maslin Beach '97
Mission: Impossible 2 '00 ▶
Modern Love '07
Moving Out '83
Muriel's Wedding '94 ▶
My Brilliant Career '79 ▶
My Year Without Sex '09
The Mystery of a Hansom Cab '12
Nature's Grave '08
Ned Kelly '70
Ned Kelly '03
Nevil Shute's The Far Country '85
Newcastle '08
The Night We Called It a Day '03
The Nugget '02
On the Beach '59 ▶
On the Beach '00
Once Were Warriors '94 ▶
Oranges and Sunshine '10 ▶
Oscar and Lucinda '97
Outback '71 ▶
Overlanders '46 ▶
Passion '99
Perfect Strangers '03
Plum Role '07
Praise '98 ▶
Prisoners of the Sun '91 ▶
Quigley Down Under '90
Rabbit-Proof Fence '02 ▶
Race the Sun '96
Rebel '85
Reckless Kelly '93
Red Hill '10
The Reef '10
The Rescuers Down Under '90
Return to Snowy River '88 ▶
Ride a Wild Pony '75 ▶
The Right Hand Man '87
River Queen '05
The Road from Coorain '02
Robbery under Arms '57
Rogue '07
Romulus, My Father '07 ▶
The Rover '14
Sanctum '11
Shine '95 ▶
The Shrimp on the Barbie '90
Siam Sunset '99
The Silver Stallion: King of the Wild Brumbies '93
Sirens '94
The Snowtown Murders '12 ▶
Son of a Gun '14
Stingaree '34
Stoned Bros. '09
Strange Bedfellows '04
Strange Fits of Passion '99
Strictly Ballroom '92 ▶
Summer City '77
The Sundowners '60 ▶
Sweet Talker '91
The Tattooist '07
Terror Peak '03
33 Postcards '11
The Thorn Birds '83 ▶
Tim '79
Top of the Lake '13 ▶
A Town Like Alice '56
Tracker '10
Tracks '14
Two Hands '98 ▶
Undead '05
Under Capricorn '49
Under the Lighthouse Dancing '97
Underground: The Julian Assange Story '12
Walkabout '71 ▶
A Waltz Through the Hills '88
We of the Never Never '82 ▶
Welcome to Woop Woop '97
Where the Green Ants Dream '84
The Winter of Our Dreams '82
Wish You Were Here '12
Wolf Creek 2 '13
Wolf Creek '05
Wrangler '88

▶ = *rated three bones or higher*

Downsized
Alan Partridge '13 ▶
Believe '07
Capitalism: A Love Story '09
The Company Men '10
Days and Clouds '07
Downsizing '17
Drunk Parents '19
Everything Must Go '10
Falling Down '93
The Full Monty '96 ▶
Fun with Dick and Jane '77
Fun With Dick and Jane '05
The Greening of Whitney Brown '11
Hank and Mike '08
The Internship '13
Larry Crowne '11
The Long Summer of George Adams '82
Love on the Dole '41 ▶
The M Word '14
Mad Money '08
Margin Call '11 ▶
Mondays in the Sun '02
My Piece of the Pie '11
New in Town '09
Office Space '98
Oh Christmas Tree! '13
Ramona and Beezus '10
Roger & Me '89 ▶
Two Days, One Night '14 ▶
Up in the Air '09 ▶
Wanderlust '12

Dragons
***See also** Medieval Romps*
Adventures of a Teenage Dragonslayer '10
Age of the Dragons '11
Beowulf '07 ▶
Beyond Sherwood Forest '09
Captain Sinbad '63
Come and Find Me '16
Dragon Storm '04
Dragon Wars '07
Dragonheart 3: The Sorcerer's Curse '15
Dragonheart '96
Dragonheart: A New Beginning '00
Dragonquest '09
Dragonslayer '81 ▶
Dungeons and Dragons '00
Eragon '06
Erik the Viking '89
Fire & Ice: The Dragon Chronicles '08
George and the Dragon '04
Ghidrah the Three Headed Monster '65
Goliath and the Dragon '61
Grimm's Snow White '12
Harry Potter and the Goblet of Fire '05 ▶
The Hobbit: An Unexpected Journey '12
The Hobbit: The Battle of the Five Armies '14
How to Train Your Dragon 2 '14
How to Train Your Dragon '10
How to Train Your Dragon: The Hidden World '19 ▶
In the Name of the King 2: Two Worlds '11
In the Name of the King 3: The Last Mission '14
Jabberwocky '77
Jack the Giant Killer '62 ▶
Jason and the Argonauts '63 ▶
Knights of Bloodsteel '09
The Magic Sword '62
Merlin and the War of the Dragons '08
Mulan 2 '04
Mulan '98
The Mummy: Tomb of the Dragon Emperor '08
The NeverEnding Story '84 ▶
1945 '17 ▶
Pete's Dragon '77
Pete's Dragon '16
Pufnstuf '70
Quest for Camelot '98
Reign of Fire '02
Seventh Son '15
The Seventh Voyage of Sinbad '58 ▶
Sherlock Holmes '10
Shrek '01 ▶
Sleeping Beauty '59 ▶
Wyvern '09

Drama
***See** Adventure Drama; Comedy Drama; Coming of Age; Crime Drama; Docudrama; Historical Drama; Musical Drama; Showbiz Dramas; Sports Drama; Urban Drama*

Dream Girls
***See** Beauty Pageants*

Dropouts
Boiler Room '00 ▶
Choke '08
Frankenhooker '90
Free Samples '12
Gold Star '17
The Great Buck Howard '09 ▶
The Scar '48
Street Girls '75
Trust '90
Young Man with a Horn '50 ▶
Zabriskie Point '70 ▶

Drug Use & Abuse
***See also** On the Rocks; Reefer Madness; Rehab*
About Cherry '12
Above the Law '88
Aces: Iron Eagle 3 '92
Across the Tracks '89
Acts of Worship '01
The Adderall Diaries '16
Afghan Luke '11
Afterschool '08
Air America '90
Alien Nation '88
All That Jazz '79 ▶
Almost Holy '16 ▶
Alphabet City '84
Altered States '80 ▶
American Cowslip '09
Amongst Friends '93
The Amsterdam Connection '78
Angel Dusted '81
Animals '15 ▶
Anna Nicole '13
The Anniversary Party '01 ▶
Another Day in Paradise '98
Another Happy Day '11
Another Lonely Hitman '95
Arc '06
Armistead Maupin's Tales of the City '93
Around the Fire '98
Assassin of Youth '35
Autopsy: A Love Story '02
Avenging Disco Godfather '76
Awakenings of the Beast '68
B. Monkey '97
Bachelorette '12
Back in Action '94
Bad Boys '95
Bad Bush '09
Bad Lieutenant '92 ▶
Bad Lieutenant: Port of Call New Orleans '09
Bad Medicine '85
Baja '95
Baked in Brooklyn '16
The Barbarian Invasions '03 ▶
The Basketball Diaries '95
Basquiat '96 ▶
The Beach '00
The Beach Bum '19
Beat '00
Beautiful Boy '18
Behind the Candelabra '13
Being Charlie '16
Belly '98
Ben Is Back '18
Better Living Through Chemistry '14
The Betty Ford Story '87 ▶
The Big Lebowski '97 ▶
Bigger Stronger Faster '08
Bird '88 ▶
Black Circle Boys '97
The Blackout '97
Blast-Off Girls '67
Blood & Concrete: A Love Story '91
Blood Father '16 ▶
Blood Freak '72
Blood In . . . Blood Out: Bound by Honor '93
Bloodbath '76
The Bloody Brood '59
Blow '01
Blowin' Smoke '99
Blue Sunshine '78
Bongwater '98
Boogie Boy '98
Boogie Nights '97 ▶
Booksmart '19
The Boost '88
Borderline '50
Born to Lose '99
Born to Win '71
Bottled Up '13
Boundaries '18
The Boys of 2nd Street Park '03 ▶
Brave New World '98
Breaking Point '09
Bright Lights, Big City '88
Bringing Out the Dead '99
Brittany Runs a Marathon '19
Broken Vessels '98 ▶
Brotherhood of Justice '86
A Brother's Kiss '97
Bully '01
Burnt '15
Burnt Money '00
Busting '74
Bye-Bye '96
Cake '14
Candy '06
The Canyons '13
Capital Punishment '96
Carlito's Way '93 ▶
Carlito's Way: Rise to Power '05
Cartel '90
Casa de mi Padre '12
Casino '95 ▶
Catch the Heat '87
Caught '96
Cause of Death '90
Cement '99
Chained Heat 2 '92
Chains of Gold '92
Cheech and Chong: Still Smokin' '83
Cheech and Chong: Things Are Tough All Over '82
Cheech & Chong's Animated Movie! '13
Chelsea Walls '01
The Children of Times Square '86
Christiane F. '82 ▶
The Chumscrubber '05
Chungking Express '95 ▶
The Cider House Rules '99 ▶
Circuit '02
City by the Sea '02
City of Ghosts '03
Class of 1984 '82
Clean '04
Clean and Sober '88 ▶
Climax '18
Clip '13
Clockers '95 ▶
Cocaine Angel '06
Cocaine Cowboys 2: Hustlin' with the Godmother '08
Cocaine Cowboys '79
Cocaine Fiends '36
Cocaine: One Man's Seduction '83
Coffy '73
Coldfire '90
Condemned '15
Confessions of a Vice Baron '42
Confessions of an Opium Eater '62
The Connection '61 ▶
Contraband '80
The Corner '00
Corridors of Blood '58
The Counselor '13
Countryman '83
Courage '86 ▶
Crack House '89
crazy/beautiful '01
Crescendo '69
A Cross to Bear '12
Crossing the Bridge '92
The Crow 2: City of Angels '96
Cruel Intentions '98
Crutch '04
Crystal Fairy & the Magical Cactus '13
The Curfew Breakers '57
Cut and Run '85
Dangerous Game '93
Dark Days '00
The Dark Side of Love '12
Darkman 3: Die Darkman Die '95
Day of the Cobra '84
Day of the Maniac '77
Dazed and Confused '93 ▶
Dead Presidents '95
Dead Ringers '88 ▶
Death in Small Doses '57
The Death of Richie '76
Death Wish 4: The Crackdown '87
Deep Cover '92
Delta Heat '92
Desperado '95 ▶
Desperate Lives '82
The Destructors '74
The Devil's Sleep '51
Diane '18
Dick '99 ▶
Dr. Jekyll and Mr. Hyde '20 ▶
Dr. Jekyll and Mr. Hyde '32 ▶
Dr. Jekyll and Mr. Hyde '41 ▶
Dr. Jekyll and Mr. Hyde '68
Dr. Jekyll and Mr. Hyde '73
Dogs in Space '87
Don Peyote '14
Donnybrook '18
Don't Look Back '96 ▶
The Doom Generation '95 ▶
Dot.Kill '05
Down in the Delta '98 ▶
Down to the Bone '04
Dream with the Fishes '97
Drug War '13 ▶
Drugstore Cowboy '89 ▶
Drunks '96
Dusty and Sweets Mcgee '71
Easy Kill '89
Easy Money '10 ▶
Easy Rider '69 ▶
Ed Wood '94 ▶
Edge of Sanity '89
Edie in Ciao! Manhattan '72
El Cantante '06
End of a Gun '16
The End of Innocence '90
End of Watch '12 ▶
Enter the Dragon '73 ▶
Equilibrium '02
The Escapist '08
Excuse Me for Living '12
Exit Speed '08
Extreme Prejudice '87
Factory Girl '06
Falco '08
Fat Kid Rules the World '12
Fatal Beauty '87
Fear and Loathing in Las Vegas '98
Federal Hill '94
Fierce People '05
54 '98
Filth '13
The Final Patient '05
Fiona '98
Fire Birds '90
The Five Heartbeats '91 ▶
Fix '08
The Flaming Teen-Age '56
Flashback '89 ▶
Flesh '68 ▶
Fletch '85
Flight '12 ▶
Four Friends '81 ▶
Foxes '80
Frances '82 ▶
French Connection 2 '75 ▶
The French Connection '71 ▶
Fresh '94
Funkytown '11
The Fury of the Wolfman '70
Garage Days '03
The Gene Krupa Story '59
Georgia '95 ▶
Get Him to the Greek '10
Getting High '06
Gia '98
Gimme Shelter '14
Ginger Snaps: Unleashed '04
Go '99 ▶
Godmoney '97
Gone Dark '03
Good Boys '19
Good Kids '16
The Good Samaritan '12
The Good Thief '03 ▶
Goodfellas '90 ▶
Gordon's War '73
Gothic '87 ▶
Gracie's Choice '04
Gridlock'd '96 ▶
Gunmen '93
Hair '79 ▶
Half-Baked '97
Half Nelson '06 ▶
Hangman's Curse '03
Happiness Runs '10
Happy Tears '09
Harry in Your Pocket '73
Harsh Times '05
Harvard Man '01
Hateship Loveship '13
A Hatful of Rain '59
Haunted Summer '88
The Heart Is Deceitful Above All Things '04
Heart of America '03
Heat '72 ▶
Heaven Knows What '15 ▶
Heaven's Prisoners '95
Hell's Kitchen NYC '97
Help Wanted Female '68
Hendrix '00
Her Smell '19
The Hero '17
A Hero Ain't Nothin' but a Sandwich '78
Heroes for Sale '33 ▶
Hidden in the Woods '16
Hideaway '09
High Art '98
High Life '09
High Risk '81
Hit! '73
Holding Trevor '07
Holiday Heart '00
A Home at the End of the World '04
Home Run '13
Homefront '13
Homegrown '97
Homeless to Harvard: The Liz Murray Story '03
Honey Boy '19 ▶
The Hooked Generation '69
Horrible Bosses '11
Horse Girl '20
Horsey '99
The House I Live In '12
House of Versace '13
Hugo Pool '97
Human Traffic '99
The Hungry Ghosts '09
Hussy '80
Hyena '15
I Come in Peace '90
I Drink Your Blood '71
I Got Five on It '05
I Melt With You '11
I Smile Back '15
Icarus '17
Idle Hands '99
Igby Goes Down '02 ▶
I'm Dancing as Fast as I Can '82
I'm So Excited '13
In Bloom '13 ▶
In Hot Pursuit '77
In My Pocket '11
In the Fade '17
In the Flesh '97
The Inevitable Defeat of Mister & Pete '13
The Intouchables '12
The Invisibles '99
Iowa '05
Island Monster '53
Jaguar Lives '79
Jane Doe '96
Jay and Silent Bob Reboot '19
Jeanne Eagels '57
Jekyll and Hyde '90
Jekyll & Hyde. . . Together Again '82
Jennifer On My Mind '71
Jesus' Son '99
Jo Jo Dancer, Your Life Is Calling '86
John Dies at the End '12
Johnny Winter: Down & Dirty '14
Judy '19 ▶
Jumpin' at the Boneyard '92
K-11 '11
Kaboom '11
Keanu '16
Keep the Lights On '12 ▶
Keys to Tulsa '96
Kicked in the Head '97
Kids '95
Kids in the Hall: Brain Candy '96
Kill or Be Killed '93
Kill Your Friends '16
Killing Zoe '94
The Killing Zone '90
The King of Staten Island '20
Kongo '32
La Bamba '87 ▶
La Vie en Rose '07
Lady Sings the Blues '72
The Land of Steady Habits '18
The Last Black Man in San Francisco '19 ▶
The Last of the Finest '90
The Last Stand '13
Lenny '74 ▶
Less Than Zero '87
Lethal Obsession '87
Lethal Weapon '87 ▶
Let's Get Harry '87
Let's Get Lost '88 ▶
License to Kill '89 ▶
Life is Hot in Cracktown '08
Life Support '07 ▶
Lifted '10
Light Sleeper '92
Limitless '11
Little Fish '05 ▶
Live and Let Die '73
Loaded '94
Loaded '08
Loaded Guns '75
London '05
Long Day's Journey into Night '62 ▶
Long Day's Journey into Night '88
The Look of Love '13
The Lookalike '14
Loser '97
Lost Angels '89
Love Come Down '00
The Love-Ins '67
Love Liza '02
Lovelace '13
Low Tide '19
Lucy '14
Lullaby '08
LUV '13
MacArthur Park '01
Madea Goes to Jail '09
Magic Trip: Ken Kesey's Search for a Kool Place '11
Magnolia '99 ▶
Mainline Run '98
The Man with the Golden Arm '55 ▶
A Marine Story '10
Marked for Death '90
Max Payne '08
Maybe I'll Come Home in the Spring '71
McQ '74
MDMA '18
Me and You '12
Midnight Cop '88
Midnight Express '78 ▶
Midsommar '19
Mike's Murder '84
Misconduct '16
Mission Manila '87
Mrs. Parker and the Vicious Circle '94
Mister America '19
Mixed Blood '84

Mob War '88
The Mod Squad '99
More '69
The Mustang '19 ▸
My Life and Times with Antonin Artaud '93 ▸
The Mystery of Edwin Drood '35
The Mystery of Edwin Drood '12
Naked Lunch '91 ▸
Narc '02 ▸
Narco Cultura '13 ▸
The Narcotics Story '58
The Narrows '08
National Lampoon's Senior Trip '95
Never Die Alone '04
New Best Friend '02
New Jack City '91
New York Doll '05 ▸
Nico Icon '95 ▸
The Night of the Iguana '64 ▸
The Night of the White Pants '06
Nil by Mouth '96
1982 '16
Ninja in the U.S.A. '88
No Escape, No Return '93
No Vacancy '99
The Odd Way Home '13
Office Christmas Party '16
Olga's Girls '64
On the Outs '05
On Thin Ice '03
One False Move '91 ▸
100 Streets '17
One Man's Justice '95
One Perfect Day '04
Opium and Kung-Fu Master '84 ▸
Opium: Diary of a Madwoman '07
The Organization '71 ▸
Oslo, August 31st '11
Out of Sync '95
Over the Edge '79 ▸
Pace That Kills '28
Pandaemonium '00
Panic in Needle Park '71 ▸
Parked '10
Party Monster '03
People I Know '02
The People *vs.* Larry Flynt '96 ▸
Perception '06
Perfect Victims '08
Performance '70 ▸
Permanent Midnight '98
Pete's Meteor '98
Pigalle '95
Pinero '01
Point of No Return '93
The Poker House '09
Police '85
The Poppy Is Also a Flower '66
Postcards from the Edge '90 ▸
Praise '98 ▸
Prescription Thugs '16
Prey for Rock and Roll '03 ▸
Prime Cut '72
The Private Lives of Pippa Lee '09
Protector '85
Prozac Nation '01
Psych-Out '68
Psychotica '10
Pulp Fiction '94 ▸
Puncture '11
Punk Love '06
Puppet on a Chain '72
Pure '02 ▸
Purgatory House '04
Pusher '96
Quiet Cool '86
Quitters '16
Rage and Honor '92
Rapid Fire '92
Rated X '00
Raw Target '95
Ray '04 ▸
Rebound: The Legend of Earl 'The Goat' Manigault '96
Red Blooded American Girl '90
Red Heat '88
Red Surf '90
Remedy '05
Rent '05
Requiem for a Dream '00 ▸
Retribution '98
Return to Paradise '98 ▸
Revenge of the Ninja '83
The Rhythm Section '19
Ricochet '91 ▸
Riding in Cars with Boys '01
Ring of Fire '13
Riot on Sunset Strip '67
Rites of Passage '12
River's Edge '87 ▸
The Rose '79 ▸
The Royal Tenenbaums '01 ▸
Rude '96
Run This Town '20
Running Out of Time '94
Running Scared '86
Running with Scissors '06
Running with the Devil '19
Rush '91 ▸
Rushlights '13
Saints and Sinners '95
The Salton Sea '02
A Scanner Darkly '06
Scarface '83 ▸
Scorpion Spring '96
Secret Agent Super Dragon '66
The Secret of Zoey '02
The Seven-Per-Cent Solution '76 ▸
The '70s '00
Shameless '94
Shattered Innocence '87
She Shoulda Said No '49
Shelter '15
Sherlock Holmes '09
Short Term 12 '13 ▸
The Show '95
Showdown in Little Tokyo '91
Shrooms '07
Sicario: Day of the Soldado '18
Sid & Nancy '86 ▸
Side Effects '13 ▸
6 Below: Miracle on the Mountain '17
The '60s '99
Skidoo '68
Slattery's Hurricane '49
Slave '09
SLC Punk! '99
The Slender Thread '65 ▸
The Smell of Success '09
The Snake People '68
Sorted '04
The Souvenir '19 ▸
Sparkle '12
Special '06
Speed of Life '99
Spenser: Pale Kings & Princes '94
Spun '02
Stella Does Tricks '96
Still Crazy '98 ▸
Stoned '05
The Stoned Age '94
Stoned Bros. '09
Stoner Express '16
Straight A's '13
Strange Days '95 ▸
A Street Cat Named Bob '16
Street Girls '75
Street Wars '91
Streetwalkin' '85
Strike Force '75
Submarino '10
The Substitute 3: Winner Takes All '99
The Substitute '96
Sugarhouse '07
Suicide Kings '97
Super Bitch '73
Super Troopers 2 '18
Superfly '72
SuperFly '18
Surrender Dorothy '98
The Sweet Hereafter '96 ▸
Sweet Jane '98
Synanon '65
T2 Trainspotting '17
Taken for Ransom '13
Talons of the Eagle '92
Teenage Devil Dolls '53
TekWar '94
The Temptations '98
Temptress Moon '96
The Tesseract '03
Things We Lost in the Fire '07
The Third Man '49 ▸
Tideland '05
The Tingler '59 ▸
To Write Love On Her Arms '14
Tombstone '93 ▸
Too Young to Die '90
Torchlight '85
The Town Is Quiet '00
Traffic '00 ▸
Traffik '90 ▸
Trainspotting '95 ▸
Trash '70
Trespass '92
Trigger '10
The Trip '67
Tropic Thunder '08 ▸
Trouble in Paradise '88
The Trust '16
Tweek City '05
21 Grams '03 ▸
24 Hour Party People '01
Twin Peaks: Fire Walk with Me '92
Twisted '96
Ulee's Gold '97 ▸
Under Hellgate Bridge '99
Urge '16
Valley of the Dolls '67
Vanishing Point '71
Vault '19
Velvet Goldmine '98
Virgil Bliss '01
Wait until Dark '67 ▸
Walk Hard: The Dewey Cox Story '07
Walk the Line '05 ▸
Wanda, the Sadistic Hypnotist '67
Wasteland '13
We All Fall Down '00
Weekend with the Babysitter '70
Weirdsville '07
Welcome Says the Angel '01
What Doesn't Kill You '08
What Have I Done to Deserve This? '85 ▸
What We Do Is Secret '07
White Girl '16
Whitney '18
Who'll Stop the Rain? '78 ▸
Why Do Fools Fall in Love? '98
Why Stop Now '12
Wicked Blood '13
Wild Bill '95
Wild in the Streets '68
The Winter of Our Dreams '82
Withnail and I '87 ▸
Woman, Thou Art Loosed '04
Women on the Verge of a Nervous Breakdown '88 ▸
Wonder Boys '00 ▸
Wonderland '03
Woodshock '17
Woodstock '70 ▸
The World Made Straight '15
Wrong Cops '13
You and I '11
The Young Americans '93
Zero Tolerance '93
ZigZag '02 ▸
Zone 39 '96

Drugs

See ***Drug Use & Abuse***

Dublin

See also ***Ireland***
About Adam '00
Agnes Browne '99
Circle of Friends '94
The Commitments '91 ▸
The Dead '87 ▸
Disco Pigs '01
Echoes '88
8.5 Hours '08
Evelyn '02 ▸
The Front Line '06
The General '98 ▸
Girl with Green Eyes '64
In Bruges '08
The Informer '35 ▸
Intermission '03 ▸
Into the West '92 ▸
Killing Bono '11
Kisses '08 ▸
Leap Year '10
The Lonely Passion of Judith Hearne '87 ▸
Michael Collins '96 ▸
My Left Foot '89 ▸
Nora '00
Once '06
Ordinary Decent Criminal '99
Perrier's Bounty '09
Pete's Meteor '98
The Quare Fellow '62
Red Roses and Petrol '03
Rory O'Shea Was Here '04
A Secret Affair '99
The Snapper '93 ▸
The Tiger's Tale '06
Triage '09
Ulysses '67
The Van '95 ▸
Veronica Guerin '03
When Brendan Met Trudy '00 ▸
When the Sky Falls '99
Young Cassidy '65

Dying for a Promotion

See also ***Bad Bosses; Corporate Shenanigans; Office Surprise***
El Crimen Perfecto '04
He Was a Quiet Man '07
A Job to Kill For '06
Office Killer '97
The Promotion '08
Severance '06
A Shock to the System '90 ▸
The Temp '93

Ears!

See also ***Eyeballs!; Renegade Body Parts***
At Eternity's Gate '18
Baby Driver '17 ▸
Blue Velvet '86 ▸
Django '68
Feeling Minnesota '96
High Plains Drifter '73
I, Madman '89
Lust for Life '56 ▸
Reservoir Dogs '92 ▸
Say It Isn't So '01
The Sound of Silence '19
Van Gogh '92 ▸
Vincent & Theo '90 ▸
White Mischief '88 ▸

Earthquakes

See also ***Disaster Flicks; L.A.; San Francisco***
Aftershock '12
Aftershock: Earthquake in New York '99
Black Scorpion 2: Ground Zero '96
The Colossus of Rhodes '61
Cyxork 7 '06
Daybreak '01
Deadly Shift '08
Disaster Movie '08
Earthquake '74
Earthquake in Chile '74
Escape from L.A. '96
The Great Los Angeles Earthquake '91
The Last Warrior '99
Life and Nothing More . . . '92
Megafault '09
Old San Francisco '27
Phenomenon '96
Power Play '02
The Rains Came '39
San Andreas '15
San Francisco '36 ▸
The Seventh Sign '88
Shakedown '02
Underwater '20

Easter

See also ***Holidays; Religion; Religious Epics***
Angel of Death '02
Dead Snow '09
Easter Parade '48 ▸
Fourth Wise Man '85
Hank and Mike '08
Jesus '00
Jesus Christ, Superstar '73 ▸
Jesus of Montreal '89 ▸
Jesus of Nazareth '77 ▸
The Long Good Friday '80 ▸
Mary, Mother of Jesus '99
The Passion of the Christ '04 ▸
Resurrection '99
The Robe '53

Eastern Europe

All My Loved Ones '00
Anthropoid '16
Assassin's Bullet '12
Assignment: Paris '52
The Baroness and the Butler '38
Black Peter '63
Blood & Chocolate '07
Born to Raise Hell '10
Brute '97
California Dreamin' '07
Cat Run '11
Charlie Countryman '13
Cold War '18 ▸
The Crooked Road '65
Crystal Swan '20 ▸
Dark Blue World '01
The Death of Mr. Lazarescu '05
Divided We Fall '00
Don't Look Up '08
Double Identity '10
Dracula: The Dark Prince '01
Dust '01
8mm 2 '05
The Emperor's Candlesticks '37
Eva '09
Everything is Illuminated '05 ▸
A Film Unfinished '10
5 Days of War '11
4 Months, 3 Weeks and 2 Days '07 ▸
Four Sons '40
Fright Night 2: New Blood '13
Ghost Rider: Spirit of Vengeance '12
Ghouls '07
Gloomy Sunday '02 ▸
The Good Fairy '35 ▸
Graduation '17
The Grand Budapest Hotel '14 ▸
The Great Water '04
Highly Dangerous '50
Hostel '06
Hot Enough for June '64
I Am David '04
I Served the King of England '07 ▸
Ida '13 ▸
In Darkness '11
Invincible '01
The Ister '04 ▸
Katyn '07 ▸
Kontroll '03 ▸
The Lady Vanishes '13
Last Holiday '06
Love '05
Made in Romania '10
Man on a Tightrope '53
Mercenaries '11
Metamorphosis '07
Midsummer Madness '07
An Ordinary Man '18
Outpost: Black Sun '12
The Pianist '02 ▸
Police, Adjective '09
The Polka King '18
Second in Command '05
The Secret Invasion '64
Severance '06
The Shrine '10
Special Forces '03
Spies of Warsaw '13
Spring 1941 '08
Sunset '18
They're Watching '16
Train '08
Transylmania '09
The Troubles We've Seen '94
Up and Down '04
Walking with the Enemy '13
Wallenberg: A Hero's Story '85 ▸
Winter on Fire: Ukraine's Fight for Freedom '15 ▸
XXX '02
The Yellow Rolls Royce '64
Youth Without Youth '07
Zelary '03 ▸

Eat Me

See ***Cannibalism; Eco-Vengeance!; Killer Beasts; Killer Bugs and Slugs; Killer Plants***

Eating

See ***Cannibalism; Chefs***

Eco-Vengeance!

See also ***Killer Beasts; Killer Bugs and Slugs; Killer Plants; Killer Reptiles; Killer Rodents; Killer Sea Critters***
Aberration '97
Alligator '80 ▸
Anaconda '96
Ants '77
Arachnophobia '90
Before the Flood '16
Body Snatchers '93
The Core '03
Dark Waters '19 ▸
Day of the Animals '77
The Day the Earth Stood Still '08
Deadly Harvest '72
Falling Fire '97
Ferngully: The Last Rain Forest '92
The Fire Next Time '93
Food of the Gods '76
Frogs '72
Grizzly '76
Habitat '97
The Happening '08
Honeyland '19 ▸
The Host '06 ▸
Idaho Transfer '73
An Inconvenient Sequel: Truth to Power '17
Jaws '75 ▸
Jaws 2 '78
Jaws 3 '83
Jaws: The Revenge '87
Jurassic Park '93 ▸
Just Eat It '14
Killer Bees '02
Kingdom of the Spiders '77
The Last Winter '06
Magic in the Water '95
Mega Python Vs. Gatoroid '11
The Mermaid '16 ▸
Nature's Grave '08
Night Moves '13
No Blade of Grass '70
On Deadly Ground '94
Phantom 2040 Movie: The Ghost Who Walks '95
Piranha '78
Piranha 2: The Spawning '82
Pom Poko '94
Ponyo '08 ▸
Prey '10
Prophecy '79
The Ruins '08
Seeds of Destruction '11
Shark Swarm '08
The Simpsons Movie '07 ▸
Snakehead Terror '04
Something Beneath '07
Squirm '76
The Swarm '78
The Thaw '09
Thunder Bay '53 ▸
Ticks '93
The Toxic Avenger '86
Virus '96

Edibles

See ***Cannibalism***

▸ = rated three bones or higher

Edinburgh
***See also** Scotland*
The Body Snatcher '45 ▸
Burke & Hare '10
Clive Barker's Book of Blood '08
Death Defying Acts '07
Filth '13
Greyfriars Bobby '61
The Illusionist '10 ▸
Mister Foe '07
The Prime of Miss Jean Brodie '69 ▸
The Prime of Miss Jean Brodie '78
T2 Trainspotting '17
Trainspotting '95 ▸

Egypt--Ancient
Agora '09
Cleopatra '34
Cleopatra '63
Cleopatra '99
Day of the Mummy '14
The Egyptian '54
Exodus: Gods and Kings '14
Gods of Egypt '16
Land of the Pharaohs '55
The Mummy '32 ▸
The Mummy '59 ▸
The Mummy '99
The Mummy '17
The Mummy Returns '01
The Pharaoh's Curse '57
Prince of Egypt '98 ▸
Princess of the Nile '54
The Scorpion King '02
The Slave '62
Two Nights with Cleopatra '54
Yu-Gi-Oh! The Movie: Pyramid of Light '04

Elementary School/ Junior High
***See also** School Daze*
Adventures of a Teenage Dragonslayer '10
Akeelah and the Bee '06
Alice Upside Down '07
American Girl: Chrissa Stands Strong '09
Anna and the King of Siam '46 ▸
Arlo the Burping Pig '16
Bad Teacher '11
Bee Season '05 ▸
Big Bully '95
Billy Madison '94
Booky's Crush '09
The Boys of Baraka '05
Bright Road '53
Brooklyn Castle '12 ▸
Captain Underpants: The First Epic Movie '17
Caterina in the Big City '03
Chicken Little '05
Children of a Lesser God '86 ▸
The Children's Hour '61
The Chorus '04
The Clique '08
Cooties '14
Dear Dumb Diary '13
Dear Lemon Lima '09
Diary of a Wimpy Kid 2: Rodrick Rules '11
Diary of a Wimpy Kid '10
Eden '98
Eighth Grade '18 ▸
Finn on the Fly '09
Flipped '10
Gifted '17
Gooby '09
Good Boys '19
Goodbye, Mr. Chips '39 ▸
Goodbye, Mr. Chips '69
Gym Teacher: The Movie '08
Half Nelson '06 ▸
Happy-Go-Lucky '08 ▸
Harold '08
Hoot '06
How to Eat Fried Worms '06
I Wish '11 ▸
In a Better World '10
An Invisible Sign '11
It All Starts Today '99
Jack '96
Kindergarten Cop 2 '16
Kindergarten Cop '90
Knights of the South Bronx '05
Lifted '10
Little '19
Little Men '98
Little Monsters '19
The Little Princess '39 ▸
A Little Princess '95 ▸
Lloyd '00
Lovesick '14
Lower Learning '08
Mad Hot Ballroom '05 ▸
The Magnet '50
Mail to the Chief '00
Matilda '96 ▸
Max Keeble's Big Move '01
Mean Creek '04 ▸
Middle School: The Worst Years of My Life '16
Milton's Secret '16
Mr. Peabody & Sherman '14
Monsieur Lazhar '11
Music of the Heart '99
My Guardian Angel '16
Newtown '16 ▸
Notebook '19
Phoebe in Wonderland '08
Ramona and Beezus '10
Rebound '05
Saint Ralph '04
School of Rock '03 ▸
Shooting Dogs '05
Shorts: The Adventures of the Wishing Rock '09
Shredderman Rules '07
The Sixth Sense '99 ▸
Sleepover '04
Son of Rambow '07
Spy School '08
Star Kid '97 ▸
That's What I Am '11
Timmy Failure: Mistakes Were Made '20
Treehouse Hostage '99
12 and Holding '05 ▸
Unconditional '12
The Vessel '16
Whole New Thing '05
Wild Tigers I Have Known '06
Wonder '17
Won't Back Down '12

Elephants
***See also** Carnivals & Wild Kingdom*
Babar: The Movie '88
Beyond the Blue Horizon '42
Billy Rose's Jumbo '62 ▸
Chad Hanna '40
Dr. Seuss' Horton Hears a Who! '08 ▸
Dumbo '19
Earth '07
Ele, My Friend '93
Elephant Boy '37 ▸
An Elephant Called Slowly '69
The Elephant King '06
Elephant Stampede '51
Elephant Walk '54
Fantasia '40 ▸
Freddy Got Fingered '01
George of the Jungle '97 ▸
Hannibal Brooks '69
Holiday in the Wild '19
The Impossible Elephant '02
Junglee '19
Jupiter's Darling '55
Larger Than Life '96
Looking for Trouble '96
Lord of the Jungle '55
The Love Guru '08
My Lucky Elephant '13
Operation Dumbo Drop '95
The Owl and the Sparrow '07
The Prince & Me 4: The Elephant Adventure '10
Smokey and the Bandit 2 '80
Tarzan and the Huntress '47
Tarzan and the She-Devil '53
Tarzan Goes to India '62
Tarzan Triumphs '43
Tarzan's Hidden Jungle '55
Tarzan's Three Challenges '63
Water for Elephants '11
Whispers: An Elephant's Tale '00
White Hunter, Black Heart '90 ▸

Elevators
***See also** Terror in Tall Buildings*
Alpha Alert '13
Basic Instinct '92
Blackout '07
Blast from the Past '98
Christmas Eve '15
The Client '94
Cursed '04
Deceived '91
Deep Rising '98
Devil '10
Die Hard '88 ▸
El Crimen Perfecto '04
Fatal Attraction '87 ▸
Free Fall '14
In the Line of Fire '93 ▸
Just My Luck '06
Mallrats '95
The Man with Two Brains '83 ▸
Mission: Impossible '96 ▸
Mixed Nuts '94
Nick of Time '95
9/11 '17
The Omen '76
Poltergeist 3 '88
Pretty Woman '90 ▸
The Secret of My Success '87
The Shaft '01
The Shaggy Dog '06
The Silence of the Lambs '91 ▸
Sleepless in Seattle '93 ▸
Speed '94 ▸
Terminator 2: Judgment Day '91 ▸
Thoroughly Modern Millie '67
The Towering Inferno '74
Toy Story 2 '99 ▸
True Lies '94
The Untouchables '87 ▸
What about Bob? '91 ▸
Willy Wonka & the Chocolate Factory '71 ▸

Emerging Viruses
***See also** Disease of the Week*
Adrenalin: Fear the Rush '96
And the Band Played On '93 ▸
The Andromeda Strain '71
The Andromeda Strain '08
Antiviral '12
Battle of the Damned '14
The Bay '12
Beast Within '08
Blindness '08
Body Armor '96
Cabin Fever '03
Carriers '09
Condemned '15
Contagion '11 ▸
Contaminated Man '00
Cooties '14
Daybreakers '09
Derailed '02
Doomsday '08
Escape from L.A. '96
Fatal Contact: Bird Flu in America '06
Fatal Error '99
Feardotcom '02
Future Fear '97
Gangland '00
The Girl with All the Gifts '17
The Hades Factor '06
I Am Legend '07 ▸
Inferno '16
The Invasion '07
It Comes at Night '17
The Killer That Stalked New York '47
Killing Moon '00
The Last Enemy '08
The Millerson Case '47
Mimic '97
Mission: Impossible 2 '00 ▸
Only '20
Outbreak '94 ▸
Pandemic '07
Pandemic '09
Pandora's Clock '96
Panic in the Streets '50 ▸
The Patriot '99
The Rage '07
[Rec] 2 '09
[REC] 4: Apocalyse '14
Resident Evil '02
Resident Evil: Apocalypse '04
Resident Evil: Extinction '07
Resident Evil: Retribution '12
Retreat '11
The Returned '14
Robin Cook's Invasion '97
Sahara '05
The Satan Bug '65
Sci-Fighters '96
Shakedown '02
Stephen King's The Stand '94
The Summit '08
Terror Inside '08
Thirst '09 ▸
Time Bomb '08
Toxic Skies '08
12 Monkeys '95 ▸
28 Days Later '02
28 Weeks Later '07
Ultraviolet '06
Viral Assassins '00
Virus X '10
World War Z '13
Xala '75 ▸
Zero Patience '94

Empire State Building
***See also** New York, New York*
An Affair to Remember '57
Enchanted '07
King Kong '33 ▸
King Kong '76
Love Affair '39 ▸
Love Affair '94
On the Town '49 ▸
Percy Jackson & The Olympians: The Lightning Thief '10
The Shadow '94
Sleepless in Seattle '93 ▸

Erotic Thrillers
***See** Sex & Sexuality*

Errant Educators
***See also** Dedicated Teachers; Hell High School*
The Beguiled '17
Blue Car '03 ▸
Disturbing Behavior '98
Dumb and Dumberer: When Harry Met Lloyd '03
The Faculty '98
Fist Fight '17
Loving Annabelle '06
Lower Learning '08
Notes on a Scandal '06 ▸
The Obsession '06
Outback '71 ▸
Teaching Mrs. Tingle '99
When Brendan Met Trudy '00 ▸
Wild Things '98

Escaped Cons
***See also** Fugitives; Great Escapes; Men in Prison*
Aftershock '12
Ain't Them Bodies Saints '13 ▸
Another Man's Poison '52
Axe '06
Bandits '01
Between Midnight and Dawn '50
Big House, U.S.A. '55
Big Momma's House '00
Black Cat Run '98
Bond of Fear '56
Chasers '94
Circle '10
Colorado Territory '49
Con Air '97 ▸
Convict Women '74
Cool Hand Luke '67 ▸
Crime Wave '54
Dark Passage '47
Dead of Night '99
Deadlock '91
Deadly Isolation '05
Deep Valley '47
The Defiant Ones '58 ▸
Do or Die '01
Double Jeopardy '99
Duets '00
Easy Money: Hard to Kill '12
Escape from Alcatraz '79 ▸
Face/Off '97 ▸
The Falcon Takes Over '42
Firestorm '97
Fled '96
48 Hrs. '82 ▸
From Dusk Till Dawn '95
The Fugitive '93 ▸
Gang Busters '55
Go With God Gringo '66
The Goonies '85
Great Expectations '34
Great Expectations '46 ▸
Great Expectations '97
Great Expectations '99
Gunfight at Comanche Creek '64
Happy, Texas '99 ▸
Harold & Kumar Escape from Guantanamo Bay '08
Heart of the Storm '04
Hell's Half Acre '54
His Greatest Gamble '34
I Am a Fugitive from a Chain Gang '32 ▸
Identity '03
The Incredible Journey of Mary Bryant '05
Instinct to Kill '01
Jailbreakers '94
Jailbreakin' '72
Jeopardy '53
Johnny Was '05
A Killer in the Family '83
Labor Day '13
Larceny, Inc. '42
The Last Hard Men '76
The Last House on the Left '09
The Last Marshal '99
The Last Run '71
Le Cercle Rouge '70 ▸
Le Deuxieme Souffle '66
Lewis and Clark and George '97
Lonely Are the Brave '62 ▸
A Long Ride From Hell '68
Lost in the Dark '07
Mad Dog Killer '77
The Mighty '98 ▸
Morgan's Ferry '99
Mud '12 ▸
Next Friday '00
The Night Holds Terror '55
Night Screams '87
9 Souls '03
No Good Deed '14
Nobody's Baby '01
Nothing to Lose '08
O Brother Where Art Thou? '00
One Way Passage '32
Out of Sight '98 ▸
Papillon '73 ▸
Parallel Sons '95
Passage to Marseilles '44 ▸
Passenger 57 '92
A Perfect World '93
The Pledge '08
Point Blank '98
The Prey '11
Prison on Fire 2 '91
Proximity '00
Raising Arizona '87 ▸
Rapture '65
Red Letters '00
Rites of Passage '99
Runaway Train '85 ▸
San Quentin '37
A Scandal in Paris '46
7 Mummies '06
Shutter Island '09 ▸
Slow Burn '00
Spider-Man 3 '07
Spoiler '98
Stakeout '87
The Stunt Man '80 ▸
Thunder County '74
Tomorrow We Live '42
Two for Texas '97
Up the River '30
The Voice of the City '29
We're No Angels '55 ▸
We're No Angels '89
Where the Money Is '00
The Wrong Guys '88
Wrong Turn 3: Left for Dead '09
Wrongfully Accused '98

Eskimos/Inuit
Chloe & Theo '15
Map of the Human Heart '93
Nanook of the North '22 ▸
On Deadly Ground '94
Smilla's Sense of Snow '96
S.O.S. Iceberg '33
The White Dawn '75

Europe
***See** Amsterdam; Barcelona; Eastern Europe; France; Germany; Great Britain; Greece--Ancient; Greece--Modern; Italy; Russia/USSR; Spain*

Evil Doctors
***See also** Doctors & Mad Scientists*
The Abominable Dr. Phibes '71 ▸
Anatomy '00 ▸
The Awful Dr. Orloff '62
Baby Geniuses '98
Batman Begins '05 ▸
Bats: Human Harvest '07
The Beasts of Marseilles '57
Blackmale '99
Bloodrayne: The Third Reich '11
Body Melt '93
Captive '98
A Cure for Wellness '17
The Curious Dr. Humpp '70
Curse of the Puppet Master: The Human Experiment '98
Dead Ringers '88 ▸
Death and the Maiden '94 ▸
The Debt '10
The Dentist '96
Dr. Alien '88
The Doctor and the Devils '85
Dr. Black, Mr. Hyde '76
Doctor Blood's Coffin '62
Doctor Butcher M.D. '80
Dr. Cyclops '40
Dr. Death, Seeker of Souls '73
Dr. Frankenstein's Castle of Freaks '74
Dr. Giggles '92
Dr. Goldfoot and the Bikini Machine '66
Dr. Hackenstein '88
Dr. Jekyll and Mr. Hyde '20 ▸
Dr. Jekyll and Mr. Hyde '41 ▸
Dr. Jekyll and Mr. Hyde '68
Dr. Jekyll and Mr. Hyde '73
Dr. Jekyll and Sister Hyde '71
Dr. Jekyll and the Wolfman '71
Dr. Jekyll's Dungeon of Death '82
Dr. Mabuse, The Gambler '22 ▸
Dr. Mabuse *vs.* Scotland Yard '64
Dr. No '62 ▸
Dr. Orloff and the Invisible Man '72
Dr. Otto & the Riddle of the Gloom Beam '86
Doctor Phibes Rises Again '72
Dr. Tarr's Torture Dungeon '75
Doctor X '32
Eli '19
Extreme Measures '96
Four Skulls of Jonathan Drake '59
The Frozen Dead '66
Gallery of Horrors '67
The Haunted Airman '06

The Human Centipede: First Sequence '10
I Sell the Dead '09
Insanitarium '08
Jekyll and Hyde '90
Mad Doctor of Blood Island '68
The Magician '26
Malice '93
The Man Who Could Cheat Death '59
Night of the Bloody Apes '68
Not My Life '06
Obsession '49
Prince of Poisoners: The Life and Crimes of William Palmer '98
Psychic Experiment '10
The Return of the Swamp Thing '89
The Skin I Live In '11
Slaughter Hotel '71
Subject Two '06
Turistas '06
The Two Faces of Dr. Jekyll '60
Victor Frankenstein '15
The Ward '10
Who Killed Bambi? '03

Exchange Students

See also Elementary School/ Junior High; High School; Teen Comedy; Teen Drama

Amanda Knox: Murder on Trail in Italy '11
American Pie '99▶
Better Off Dead '85
Breathe In '13
Cashback '06
The Comebacks '07
Grease 2 '82
Grease '78▶
Hey Hey It's Esther Blueberger '08
Kiss Me Again '06
L'Auberge Espagnole '02▶
Monster High '89
National Lampoon's Van Wilder '02
Porky's Revenge '85
Sixteen Candles '84▶
Slap Her, She's French '02
Son of Rambow '07
Sydney White '07

Ex-Cons

See also Crime Drama; Escaped Cons; Men in Prison; Women in Prison

A Nous la Liberte '31▶
Adopt a Highway '19
Alias the Doctor '32
All Hat '07
Always Outnumbered Always Outgunned '98▶
American Heart '92▶
American Madness '32
And Now My Love '74
The Anderson Tapes '71▶
Animal '05
Another Earth '11
Any Day '15
Any Number Can Win '63
Appointment with Crime '45
The Ardennes '17
Army of One '16
The Art of the Steal '13
Baby Boy '01
The Badlanders '58
The Bank Job '07
Barbershop 2: Back in Business '04▶
Barbershop '02▶
Benefit of the Doubt '93
Beyond Desire '94
Beyond Suspicion '00
The Big Scam '79
Billy Jack Goes to Washington '77
Black Dog '98
Blindspotting '18
Blood and Bone '09
Blood Brother '18
Blood Father '16▶
Blood Ties '13
Bloody Mama '70
Blue Eyes '09
Blue Iguana '18
Bonded by Blood '09
Bound '96
The Box '03
Boy A '07
Bringing Up Bobby '11
Bug '06
Bustin' Loose '81▶
Caliber 9 '72
Carlito's Way '93▶
Ca$h '06
Caught Up '98
Chain Link '08
The Chaperone '11
The Chase '91
City Island '09
Coastlines '02
Cold Creek Manor '03
The Collector '09
The Con Artist '10
Confessions of a Pit Fighter '05
The Confidant '10
Cool Breeze '72
Corpus Christi '19▶
Crazy on the Outside '10
Crime Wave '54
Dead Heat '01
Dead Heat on a Merry-Go-Round '66▶
Dead Man Running '09
The Disappearance of Alice Creed '09
Disorganized Crime '89
Dog Eat Dog '16
Dolemite '75
Dom Hemingway '13
Dragon Eyes '12
The Dream Catcher '99
Drop Zone '94
East of the River '40
The Echo '08
Eye of God '97▶
Eye of the Tiger '86
Fallen Angels '95
Family Business '89
Farewell, My Lovely '75▶
Fast Five '11
Faster '10
Father of Invention '11
Feeling Minnesota '96
Fever '91
Few Options '11
Fight to the Finish '16
A Fighting Man '14
Flesh '32
Framed for Murder '07
Frankie and Johnny '91▶
Getting Out '94
The Glove '78
Go for Sisters '13
Going Home '71
Going Places '74▶
The Good Samaritan '12
Graveyard of Honor '02
The Guilty '92
Gun Hill Road '11
Guncrazy '92
The Hard Word '02
Headless Body in Topless Bar '96
The Heavy '09
The Heist '89
Hell's Kitchen NYC '97
Henry: Portrait of a Serial Killer '90▶
Henry's Crime '10
Hi-Jacked '50
High Life '09
High Tide '80
Home of the Giants '07
Home Team '98
The Hoodlum Priest '61▶
Horrible Bosses '11
House of the Rising Sun '11
The Hunted '48
I Love You Phillip Morris '10
I Thank a Fool '62
I Walk Alone '48
If Tomorrow Comes '86
In Cold Blood '67▶
In Cold Blood '96
In Your Eyes '14
The Interrupters '11▶
The Intouchables '12
Invisible Stripes '39
Islander '06
I've Loved You So Long '08▶
Jada '08
Jail Party '04
Joe '13▶
Joint Body '11
Judge Dredd '95
Judicial Indiscretion '07
Kansas City Confidential '52▶
Keeping Mum '05
The Killing '56▶
Kin '18
Kings of the Evening '08
Kiss of Death '47▶
Kiss of Death '94
Klepto '03
La Mission '09
Larceny, Inc. '42
The Last Gangster '37
Last Ride '09
The Lazarus Project '08
Le Cercle Rouge '70▶
Le Doulos '61▶
Leo '02
Let Go '11
Levity '03
Life During Wartime '09
Life of a King '13
Like Dandelion Dust '09
The Limey '99▶
Little Children '06▶
Live Flesh '97▶
Loan Shark '52
London Boulevard '10
The Long Memory '53
Luck of the Draw '00
Lulu Belle '48
Machine Gun McCain '69
Machine Gun Preacher '11
Mad Bad '07
Manito '03▶
The Marked One '63
Masked and Anonymous '03
Max Dugan Returns '83
McCanick '14
Mercy Streets '00
The Mighty '98▶
The Million Dollar Rip-Off '76
The Moonshine War '70
Morning Glory '93
Murder at Devil's Glen '99
Murder, My Sweet '44▶
My Baby's Daddy '04
My Summer of Love '05
Mystic River '03▶
Nancy Steele Is Missing '37
Natural Selection '11
Need for Speed '14
Never Back Down 2: The Beatdown '11
Never Down '06
Nobody's Fool '18
Ocean's Eleven '01▶
Oceans of Fire '86
Odds Against Tomorrow '59▶
On the Run '73
Once Upon a Time in Brooklyn '13
One Girl's Confession '53
The Onion Field '79▶
The Outfit '73
Outlaw Blues '77
Outside In '17
Paid '30
Paint and Powder '25
Pale Flower '64
Palmetto '98
Paper Bullets '41
The Passion of Anna '70▶
Pawn '13
Pennies from Heaven '36
Phantom Punch '09
The Philly Kid '12
Pinero '01
Played '06
Poor Man's Game '06▶
Possession '08
Powder Blue '09
Pros and Ex-cons '05
Q (The Winged Serpent) '82▶
Raising Arizona '87▶
The Rambler '13
Rappin' '85
The Ravagers '65
Read My Lips '01
Recoil '11
Red Light '49
Red Road '06
Red Water '01
Reform Girl '33
The Revengers '72
Revolver '05
Reykjavik-Rotterdam '08
Riff Raff '92▶
Row Your Boat '98
Rude '96
Ruslan '09
Saintly Sinners '62
Saving God '08
Say It With Songs '29
Scarecrow '73
A Score to Settle '19
The Set Up '95
Sexy Evil Genius '13
Sherrybaby '06
Shooters '00
Small Time Crooks '00
A Small Town in Texas '76
Soda Springs '11
Spring Forward '99
Stakeout '62
Stealing Candy '04
Stick '85
Stolen '12
Stolen Face '52
Straight Time '78▶
Strangers with Candy '06
Street Angel '28
Street Law '95
Suicide Squad '16
Sushi Girl '12
The Swap '71
Swordfish '01
Synanon '65
The Take '09
Tenth Avenue Angel '47
Terror Among Us '81
This is Martin Bonner '13
This Is Not a Love Song '02
Three Fugitives '89
3000 Miles to Graceland '01
The Time of His Life '55
Tomorrow Is Another Day '51
Tomorrow You're Gone '12
Tough Guys '86
The Trail to Hope Rose '04
Transit '12
2 Fast 2 Furious '03
The Unbelievable Truth '90
Uncaged Heart '07
Under Capricorn '49
The Upside '17
Vehicle 19 '13
Waist Deep '06
Wall Street 2: Money Never Sleeps '10
The Wendell Baker Story '05
What Comes Around '06
Whirlpool '34
Whispers in the Dark '92
Wild Ones on Wheels '62
Within the Law '23
Woman in the Shadows '34
Wonderland '03
The Yankles '09
The Yellow Handkerchief '08▶
You and Me '38
You Only Live Once '37

Ex-Cops

See also Private Eyes; Rent-a-Cop

American Streetfighter 2: The Full Impact '97
Back to Back '96
A Better Way to Die '00
Black Eye '74
Black Scorpion '95
Blackway '16
Body Chemistry 2: Voice of a Stranger '91
Broken City '13
Brown's Requiem '98
Choice of Weapons '76
The Commuter '18
Dark World '08
Day of the Cobra '84
Dead Evidence '00
Dead Heat '01
End of Days '99
Fast Five '11
Fatal Desire '05
Final Payback '99
Gang Boys '97
Girls Night Out '83
The Glove '78
Go for Sisters '13
The Heist '96
Hope Ranch '02
Hostage Hotel '00
House of the Rising Sun '11
Identity '03
The Invader '96
The Isle '01
It Had to Be You '00
Jesse Stone: Innocents Lost '11
Jill the Ripper '00
Kansas City Confidential '52▶
Kick-Ass '10▶
Le Cercle Rouge '70▶
Little Children '06▶
A Lovely Way to Die '68
Mad Max '80▶
Midnight Run '88▶
Mirrors '08
The Morning After '86
An Occasional Hell '96
Odds Against Tomorrow '59▶
Once a Thief '96▶
One Shoe Makes It Murder '82
The Onion Field '79▶
Persons Unknown '96
Physical Evidence '89
Piece of the Action '77
Prime Time Murder '92
Q & A '90
Raising Arizona '87▶
Raw Justice '93
Raw Nerve '99
Romeo Must Die '00
Saw '04
Separate Lives '94
Sin '02
Spenser Confidential '20
Street Corner Justice '96
Trouble in Mind '86▶
True Romance '93
Twilight '98▶
Undercurrent '99
Underdog '07
The Usual Suspects '95▶
Vigilante '83
Virtual Assassin '95
Virtual Combat '95
Virtuosity '95
A Walk Among the Tombstones '14
West New York '96

Executing Revenge

See also Death & Death Row; Men in Prison

Acts of Vengeance '17
American Assassin '17
Ben-Hur '16
Blowback '99
Death Wish '18
Exorcist 3: Legion '90
Fallen '97
The First Power '89
Gallery of Horrors '67
The Horror Show '89
I Know What You Did Last Summer '97▶
The Indestructible Man '56
Jason Bourne '16
Judge & Jury '96
The Killing of a Sacred Deer '17
The Lazarus Project '08
Lethal Dose '03
The Man They Could Not Hang '39
Mechanic: Resurrection '16
Munich '05▶
My Cousin Rachel '17
The Salesman '16▶
Septembers of Shiraz '16
Sherlock Holmes '09
Shocker '89
Soldier '98
Tamara '05
The 3 Marias '03
Upgrade '18

Existentialism

See The Meaning of Life

Exorcism & Exorcists

See also Nuns & Supernatural Horror

The Amityville Horror '05
Beyond the Hills '13
Blackwater Valley Exorcism '06
Dead Waves '06
Deliver Us From Evil '14
The Devil Inside '12
Dominion: Prequel to the Exorcist '05
Drag Me to Hell '09
The Exorcism of Emily Rose '05▶
The Exorcist '73▶
Extra Ordinary '20
Insidious '10
The Last Exorcism '10
The Last Exorcism Part II '13
London Voodoo '04
Lost Souls '00
Naked Evil '66
Ouija: Origin of Evil '16
The Possessed '77
Possessed '00
The Possession of Michael King '14
Repossessed '90
The Rite '11
Scary Movie 2 '01
Teenage Exorcist '93
30 Nights of Paranormal Activity with the Devil Inside the Girl with the Dragon Tattoo '12
The Unborn '09

Explorers

The Adventures of Marco Polo '38
Almost Heroes '97
Apollo 13 '95▶
Atlantis: The Lost Empire '01
Cabeza de Vaca '90▶
Call Me Bwana '63
Carry On Columbus '92
The Cavern '05
Christopher Columbus '49
Congo '95
Dora and the Lost City of Gold '19
The Far Horizons '55
The Forbidden Quest '93
Forgotten City '98
1492: Conquest of Paradise '92
How Tasty Was My Little Frenchman '71
King Solomon's Mines '50▶
King Solomon's Mines '85
Kong: Skull Island '17
The Last Descent '16
The Last Dinosaur '77
The Last Place on Earth '85
The Lost City of Z '17▶
The Lost World '92
The Lost World '02
The Lost Zeppelin '29
The Magic Voyage '93
Marco Polo '07
Missing Link '19
Mountains of the Moon '90▶
The New World '05▶
Shackleton '02▶
She '35
Smurfs: The Lost Village '17
3022 '19
Up '09▶
The Valley Obscured by the Clouds '70
Wake of the Red Witch '49

Extraordinary Pairings

Abbott and Costello Meet Frankenstein '48▶
Alien *vs.* Predator '04
All About the Benjamins '02
Almost Heroes '97
Alpha '18
Bela Lugosi Meets a Brooklyn Gorilla '52
Billy the Kid Versus Dracula '66
The Breed '01
Bulletproof Monk '03
Dr. Jekyll and the Wolfman '71
Doctor Sleep '19▶
Dracula *vs.* Frankenstein '71
Frankenstein Meets the Space Monster '65
Frankenstein Meets the Wolfman '42▶
Freddy *vs.* Jason '03

▶ = rated three bones or higher

The Hollywood Strangler Meets the Skid Row Slasher '79
Jesse James Meets Frankenstein's Daughter '65
King Kong *vs.* Godzilla '63
Living Out Loud '98
My Giant '98
Phantom Boy '16
Rush Hour '98
Santa Claus Conquers the Martians '64
Shirin '09
The Tomorrow Man '19

Eyeballs!

See also Hearts!; Renegade Body Parts

Anguish '88
Austin Powers: International Man of Mystery '97 ▸
The Birds '63 ▸
A Clockwork Orange '71 ▸
The Crawling Eye '58
Damien: Omen 2 '78
Demolition Man '93
Die Hard 2: Die Harder '90 ▸
Evil Dead 2: Dead by Dawn '87
The Eye '08
The Eye Creatures '65
Eyes of Laura Mars '78
Friday the 13th, Part 3 '82
The Fury '78
The Godfather '72 ▸
Halloween 2: The Nightmare Isn't Over! '81
I Origins '14
Idle Hands '99
In the Eyes of a Killer '09
Lazy Eye '16
Julia's Eyes '10
Mansion of the Doomed '76
Minority Report '02 ▸
Nightwatch '96
Peeping Tom '60 ▸
The Phantom '96
Pitch Black '00 ▸
Rocky '76 ▸
Scanners '81
See No Evil '06
Silver Bullet '85
Sleepy Hollow '99 ▸
Strange Behavior '81
Summer School '87
The Terminator '84 ▸
The Ticket '17
True Lies '94
Wild Palms '93
X: The Man with X-Ray Eyes '63 ▸
Zombie '80

Fairs & Expositions

See also Amusement Parks; Carnivals & Circuses

Babe '95 ▸
Charlotte's Web '73
Howling 6: The Freaks '90
It Happened at the World's Fair '63
Ma and Pa Kettle at the Fair '52
Megasnake '07
My Girl '91
Shag: The Movie '89 ▸
State Fair '45 ▸

Family Adventure

The Adventures of the Wilderness Family '76
Against the Wild '14
Against the Wild II: Survive the Seregenti '16
Alaska '96
Alice Through the Looking Glass '16
All Mine to Give '56
The BFG '16
Brave '12
Call of the Forest '49
Chang: A Drama of the Wilderness '27 ▸
Cop Dog '08
Crusade: A March through Time '06
Disappearances '06
A Dog's Way Home '19
Dolphin Tale 2 '14
Dolphin Tale '11
Dora and the Lost City of Gold '19
Dumbo '19
Escape from Wildcat Canyon '99
Far from Home: The Adventures of Yellow Dog '94
The Five '10
Frozen '13 ▸
Further Adventures of the Wilderness Family, Part 2 '77
The Happening '08
The Hunters '13
The Impossible '12 ▸
Inkheart '09
Isle of Dogs '18 ▸
The Jensen Project '10
The Journey Home '14
The Jungle Book '16 ▸
The Kid Who Would Be King '19 ▸
Kubo and the Two Strings '16 ▸
The Lego Movie '14 ▸
Lightning: Fire from the Sky '00
Little Bigfoot 2: The Journey Home '97
Little House on the Prairie '74 ▸
The Lost Medallion: The Adventures of Billy Stone '13
The Lost Treasure of Sawtooth Island '99
The Mummy: Tomb of the Dragon Emperor '08
Mysterious Museum '99
Nancy Drew '07
Nico the Unicorn '98
Nim's Island '08
Pete's Dragon '16
Planes '13
Planes: Fire & Rescue '14
Return to Nim's Island '13
The River Wild '94
R.L. Stine's The Haunting Hour: Don't Even Think About It '07
Rolling Family '04
The Secret Life of Walter Mitty '13
Secret of the Cave '06
Secrets of the Mountain '10
Sgt. Stubby: An American Hero '18
Show Dogs '18
Speed Racer '08
The Spiderwick Chronicles '08 ▸
Spy Kids 4: All the Time in the World '11
Storm Boy
The Swiss Family Robinson '60 ▸
Those Calloways '65
Tom & Thomas '02
Vacation '15
Veritas: Prince of Truth '07
Voyage of the Unicorn '00
Whisper 2: L'Aventure Continue '16
Who Is Simon Miller? '11
Wild America '97 ▸
The Wild Thornberrys Movie '02 ▸
The Willoughbys '20
The Wizards of Waverly Place: The Movie '09
Zeus and Roxanne '96

Family Comedy

See also Aunts & Bad Dads; Brothers & Cousins; Dads; Family Drama; Family Reunions; Monster Moms

Abner the Invisible Dog '13
About Adam '00
Acceptance '09
Ace Ventura Jr.: Pet Detective '08
A.C.O.D. '13
The Addams Family '91
The Addams Family '19
Addams Family Values '93
Adventure in Baltimore '49
Air Bud 5: Buddy Spikes Back '03
Alexander and the Terrible, Horrible, No Good, Very Bad Day '14
Alvin and the Chipmunks '07
American Fusion '05
And Baby Makes Six '79
And You Thought Your Parents Were Weird! '91
Andy Hardy Comes Home '58
Are We Done Yet? '07
Are We There Yet? '05
Au Pair 2: The Fairy Tale Continues '01
Au Pair 3: Adventure in Paradise '09
Au Pair '99
Aussie and Ted's Great Adventure '09
Baby of the Bride '91
Babysitters Beware '08
Battle of the Bulbs '10
Bedtime Stories '08
Beethoven's 4th '01
Belles on Their Toes '52
Bend It Like Beckham '02 ▸
Betsy's Wedding '90
The Beverly Hillbillies '93
Big and Hairy '98
Big Bully '95
The Big Day '99
The Big Wedding '13
Blended '14
Bobbikins '59
Bon Voyage! '62
The Boss Baby '17
The Brady Bunch Movie '95 ▸
California Dreaming '07
Call It a Day '37
The Canterville Ghost '86
Car Babes '06
Cars '06 ▸
The Chaperone '11
Cheaper by the Dozen 2 '05
Cheaper by the Dozen '50 ▸
Cheaper by the Dozen '03
Chef '14
Chicken Every Sunday '48
Christmas Caper '07
The Christmas Clause '08
The Christmas Consultant '12
Christmas Do-Over '06
Christmas in Compton '12
Christmas in Wonderland '07
A Christmas Story 2 '12
A Christmas Story '83 ▸
Christmas Town '08
A Christmas Wedding Tail '11
Christmas With the Kranks '04
Chutney Popcorn '99
City Island '09
Click '06
Coffee Date '06
Cold Comfort Farm '94 ▸
College Road Trip '08
Collier & Co.: Hot Pursuit '06
Colombiana '11
Comfort and Joy '03
Coneheads '93
Cote d'Azur '05
The Courtship of Andy Hardy '42
Crazy on the Outside '10
Daddy & Them '99
Daddy Day Camp '07
Daddy's Dyin'. . . Who's Got the Will? '90
Daddy's Home '15
Dan in Real Life '07
The Daytrippers '96
Dear Mr. Prohack '49
Death at a Funeral '07
Dennis the Menace '93
A Dennis the Menace Christmas '07
Diary of a Wimpy Kid 2: Rodrick Rules '11
Diary of a Wimpy Kid '10
Diary of a Wimpy Kid: Dog Days '12
Diary of a Wimpy Kid: The Long Haul '17
Dirty Laundry '07
The Do-Deca-Pentathlon '12
Dr. Dolittle '98
Dr. Dolittle 2 '01
Dog Gone '08
The Dog Who Saved Christmas '09
The Dog Who Saved Christmas Vacation '10
The Dog Who Saved Summer '15
The Dog Who Saved the Holidays '12
The Dogfather '10
Doogal '05
Down and Derby '05
East Is East '99 ▸
East Side of Heaven '39
Eat a Bowl of Tea '89 ▸
El Carro '04
Elopement '51
Everybody's Fine '09
A Family Affair '37
The Family Holiday '07
Family Honeymoon '49
The Family Plan '05
The Family Stone '05
The Family Tree '10
Family Weekend '13
Father Is a Bachelor '50
Father of the Bride '50 ▸
Father of the Bride '91
Father of the Bride Part 2 '95
Father's Little Dividend '51 ▸
Firehouse Dog '07
First Kid '96
Fishtales '07
Folks! '92
Four Christmases '08
Frank '07
Freaky Friday '76
Freaky Friday '03 ▸
Fred Claus '07
Fun Size '12
The Game Plan '07
Garfield: A Tail of Two Kitties '06
Getting Even with Dad '94
The Girl Next Door '53
Girl *vs.* Monster '12
Go for Zucker '05
Good Morning '59 ▸
Goosebumps 2: Haunted Halloween '18
The Great Outdoors '88
Grown Ups 2 '13
Grown Ups '10
Guess Who '05
The Guilt Trip '12
Hannah Montana: The Movie '09
Happy Tears '09
The Happy Years '50
The Hardys Ride High '39
Harry and the Hendersons '87
Has Anybody Seen My Gal? '52
Hello Down There '69
Holiday for Lovers '59
Holiday in Handcuffs '07
Holiday Rush '19
Honey, I Blew Up the Kid '92
Honey, I Shrunk the Kids '89
Honey, We Shrunk Ourselves '97
Hoot '06
Hotel for Dogs '09
House of Fury '05
Houseboat '58
How Sweet It Is! '68
Humble Pie '07
The Hybrids Family '16
I Do '06
I Don't Know How She Does It '11
I Downloaded a Ghost '04
I-See-You.Com '06
Ice Age: The Meltdown '06
The Idle Rich '29
Imagine That '09
The Incredibles '04 ▸
Incredibles 2 '18 ▸
Inside Out '15 ▸
Introducing the Dwights '07
Invisible Mom 2 '99
The Irish in Us '35
Jack and Jill '11
Jesus Henry Christ '12
Johnson Family Vacation '04
Judge Hardy and Son '39
Judge Hardy's Children '38
Judy Moody and the Not Bummer Summer '11
Jumping the Broom '11
Jungle 2 Jungle '96
Junior Miss '45
Juno '07 ▸
Just Peck '09
Kathleen '41
Keeping Up with the Steins '06
The Kids Are All Right '10 ▸
Krippendorf's Tribe '98
The Last Request '06
Leave It to Beaver '97
Little Fockers '10
A Little Romance '79 ▸
The Little Vampire '00
The Longshots '08
Look Who's Talking '89 ▸
Look Who's Talking Now '93
Look Who's Talking, Too '90
Loose Cannons '10
The Lost Princess '05
Love the Coopers '15
Love, Wedding, Marriage '11
Madea's Big Happy Family '11
Madea's Family Reunion '06
Madea's Witness Protection '12
Maisie Was a Lady '41
Make the Yuletide Gay '09
The Man On the Flying Trapeze '35
Manna from Heaven '02
Marley & Me '08
Marley & Me: The Puppy Years '11
Marmaduke '10
Mayor Cupcake '11
Meddling Mom '13
Meet the Fockers '04
Meet the Robinsons '07
The Merry Frinks '34
Merry In-Laws '12
Middle School: The Worst Years of My Life '16
Minions '15
Mr. Blandings Builds His Dream House '48 ▸
Mr. Mom '83 ▸
Mr. Popper's Penguins '11
Mr. Scoutmaster '53
Mr. Troop Mom '09
Monster-in-Law '05
More of Me '07
Mother Is a Freshman '49
My Brother Talks to Horses '47
My Mother Likes Women '02
My One and Only '09
My Summer Story '94
A Nanny for Christmas '10
Nanny McPhee '06
Nanny McPhee Returns '10
National Lampoon's Christmas Vacation '89
National Lampoon's European Vacation '85
National Lampoon's Vacation '83 ▸
Natural Selection '11
Nature Calls '12
Never Too Late '65
The Night of the White Pants '06
Nine Lives '16
No Dessert Dad, 'Til You Mow the Lawn '94
No Room for the Groom '52
Noelle '19
Nothing Like the Holidays '08
The Oath '18
The Odd Life of Timothy Green '12
Opposite Day '09
Our Family Wedding '10
Our Idiot Brother '11
Our Italian Husband '04
Out West With the Hardys '38
Oy Vey! My Son is Gay! '09
The Pacifier '05
The Parent Trap '61
The Parent Trap '98
The Parent Trap II '86
Parental Guidance '12
Parenthood '89 ▸
Peace, Love & Misunderstanding '11
Peeples '13
Permanent '17
Ping Pong Summer '14
Please Don't Eat the Daisies '60
Post Grad '09
The Prince and the Pauper '07
The Proud Family Movie '05
Racing Stripes '05
The Rainbow Tribe '11
Raising Flagg '06
Ramona and Beezus '10
Ratatouille '07 ▸
Recipe for a Perfect Christmas '05
Recipe for Disaster '03
Red Doors '05
The Remarkable Mr. Pennypacker '59
Robots '05
The Rocker '08
The Rocket Man '54
Rudo y Cursi '09
Rumor Has It. . . '05
RV '06
Santa Baby '06
The Santa Trap '02
Saving Christmas '14
Saving Face '04
Secondhand Lions '03
Serial Mom '94 ▸
7 Things to Do Before I'm 30 '08
The Shaggy Dog '06
Shorts: The Adventures of the Wishing Rock '09
Show Dogs '18
The Simpsons Movie '07 ▸
Sing '16
Sing You Sinners '38
Christmas All Over Again '16
Skidoo '68
Smallfoot '18
Smother '08
Snowglobe '07
Soccer Mom '08
Sordid Lives '00
Spanglish '04
Step Brothers '08
Step Dogs '13
Stuart Saves His Family '94
The Stupids '95
A Successful Calamity '32
Surviving Christmas '04
The Sweeter Side of Life '13
Swing Vote '08
Take Her, She's Mine '63
A Tale of Two Pizzas '03
That's My Boy '12
They Had to See Paris '29
The Thing About My Folks '05
This Christmas '07
This Is 40 '12
A Thousand Words '12
Thunderstruck '12
Today's Special '09 ▸
Together Again for the First Time '08
The Tollbooth '04
Tommy and the Cool Mule '09
Too Busy to Work '32
Trading Mom '94
Two Little Bears '61
Tyler Perry's A Madea Christmas '13
Tyler Perry's Meet the Browns '08
Tyler Perry's Why Did I Get Married? '07
Uncle Buck '89 ▸
Uncle Nick '15
Uncle Nino '03
Up and Down '04
Valiant '05
Vegas Vacation '96
A Very Brady Sequel '96
A Very Merry Daughter of the Bride '08
Wallace & Gromit in The Curse of the Were-Rabbit '05 ▸
We Are the Hartmans '11

▸ = rated three bones or higher

Welcome Home Roscoe Jenkins '08
What about Bob? '91 ▸
When Do We Eat? '05
Where There's a Will '55
Who Made the Potatoe Salad? '05
Wilderness Love '02
Will You Merry Me? '08
The Willoughbys '20
Wilson '17
A Yank at Eton '42
The Year of Getting to Know Us '08
You Again '10
You Can't Take It With You '79
You're Only Young Once '37
You're So Cupid '10
Yours, Mine & Ours '68
Yours, Mine & Ours '05

Family Drama

***See also** Aunts & Bad Dads; Brothers & Cousins; Dads; Family Comedy; Family Reunions; Monster Moms*

Aardvark '18
Abandoned and Deceived '95
Abe '20
About Sunny '12 ▸
Absolution '05
The Accidental Tourist '88 ▸
Accidents Happen '09
Across to Singapore '28
The Actress '53
Adam Had Four Sons '41
Adore '13
The Adventures of Sebastian Cole '99
Affliction '97 ▸
After the Storm '17 ▸
Agnes Browne '99
Albatross '11
Alice in Wonderland '66 ▸
Alice Upside Down '07
All Fall Down '62
All I Desire '53
All Mine to Give '56
All or Nothing '02
All Passion Spent '86
All the Light in the Sky '13 ▸
Alpha Male '06
Altered Minds '13
Always Goodbye '38
American Beauty '99 ▸
American East '07
An American Haunting '05
American Heart '92 ▸
American History X '98
American Pastoral '16
American Son '19
Amongst Women '98
Amreeka '09 ▸
. . .And the Earth Did Not Swallow Him '94
Angel Dusted '81
Angela '94
Angela's Ashes '99
Angels Crest '11
Animal '05
Anne Frank: The Whole Story '01 ▸
Annie's Point '05
The Anniversary '68
Another Happy Day '11
Antonia's Line '95
Anywhere But Here '99
Apres Lui '07
April Morning '88
Around June '08
Around the Bend '04
Astoria '00
The Astronaut Farmer '07
At Close Range '86 ▸
Atonement '07 ▸
August '95
August: Osage County '13
August Rush '07
Aurora Borealis '06
Avalon '90 ▸
The Awakening Land '78
Baaria '09
Back to You and Me '05
The Bad Mother's Handbook '07
Badge of Faith '15
Badland '07
The Ballad of Jack and Rose '05 ▸
The Ballad of Narayama '58 ▸
Ballast '08
The Barbarian Invasions '03 ▸
The Battle of Shaker Heights '03
Beautiful Boy '10
Beautiful Boy '18
Beautiful Kate '09 ▸
Beautiful Ohio '06
Because of Winn-Dixie '05
Becoming Jane '07
Bee Season '05 ▸
Beginners '10 ▸
Behind the Sun '01
Being Flynn '12
Ben-Hur '16
Best of Youth '03 ▸
Betrayed at 17 '11
The Betsy '78
The Better Angels '14 ▸
A Better Life '11 ▸
The Betty Ford Story '87 ▸
Between the Darkness and the Dawn '85
Beverly Lewis' The Confession '13
Beverly Lewis' The Shunning '11
Beyond Honor '05
Billy Elliot '00 ▸
The Bird Can't Fly '07
Birds of America '08
Biutiful '10
The Black Balloon '09
Black Irish '07
Black or White '14
Blame It on Fidel '06
Blood and Bones '04
Blood Ties '13
Bloodworth '10
Bluebird '13
Bomber '09
Bombers B-52 '57
Born 2 Race '11
Bound by a Secret '09
Boy Erased '18
Boy Who Caught a Crook '61
Boyhood '14 ▸
The Boys Are Back '09
Brideshead Revisited '08
Bridge to Terabithia '07
Bridge to the Sun '61
Bringing Ashley Home '11
Bringing Up Bobby '11
Broken Bridges '06
Broken Wings '02 ▸
The Bronte Sisters '79
The Brontes of Haworth '73
Brooklyn Lobster '05
Brothers '04 ▸
Brothers '09
The Brothers Karamazov '58 ▸
Burning Cane '19
Burning Man '11
The Burning Plain '08
The Butcher Boy '97 ▸
The Cake Eaters '07
Call of the Wild 3D '09
Canvas '06
Capernaum '18 ▸
Carnage '11
Catching Faith '15
Caterina in the Big City '03
Catherine Cookson's Colour Blind '98
Catherine Cookson's The Black Velvet Gown '92
Catherine Cookson's The Cinder Path '94
Catherine Cookson's The Fifteen Streets '90
Catherine Cookson's The Man Who Cried '93
Catherine Cookson's The Wingless Bird '97
The Cats '68
The Celebration '98
Chain Link '08
Charlie & Me '08
Charlie St. Cloud '10
Charms for the Easy Life '02
Chasing 3000 '07
The Children Are Watching Us '44 ▸
Chloe '09
Chlorine '13
Christmas Angel '11
The Christmas Blessing '05
The Christmas Box '95
Christmas Comes Home to Canaan '11
The Christmas Cottage '08
The Christmas Hope '09
Christmas in Canaan '09
Christmas in Paradise '07
Christmas Lodge '11
The Christmas Shoes '02
A Christmas Tale '08 ▸
A Christmas Tree Miracle '13
A Christmas Wish '11
Christmas with Holly '12
The Chronicles of Narnia: The Lion, the Witch and the Wardrobe '05
Cider with Rosie '99
Cinderella Man '05 ▸
Cinema Verite '11
The Circuit '08
Cleaverville '07
Close to Leo '02
Cloudstreet '11
The Clown '53
The Cold Light of Day '12
Cold Turkey '13
Come Dance at My Wedding '09
The Conquerors '32
Conviction '10
Cookie's Fortune '99 ▸
Copperhead '13
Courage '09
Cowgirls 'n Angels '12
Crimes of the Past '09
The Crow Road '96
The Crowd Roars '32
The Cup '11
Cyber Seduction: His Secret Life '05
Cymbeline '15
Daddy's Little Girls '07
Damage '92 ▸
Dancing at Lughnasa '98
Daniel's Daughter '08
Dark Blue Almost Black '06
Dark Horse '11
The Dark Side of Love '12
The Daughter '15
Daughters Courageous '39
Daughters of the Dust '91 ▸
David's Birthday '09
A Day Late and a Dollar Short '14
Days and Nights '14
Days of Being Wild '91 ▸
Dear Frankie '04
Dear Santa '11
The Death of the Heart '87
A Decent Proposal '06
The Derby Stallion '05
The Descendants '11 ▸
Desire Under the Elms '58
Disengagement '07
Distant Voices, Still Lives '88 ▸
Divorce Wars: A Love Story '82
The Doctor and the Girl '49
The Doctor's Dilemma '58
A Dog Named Christmas '09
Dogtooth '09
Doing Time on Maple Drive '92
Dolly Parton's Coat of Many Colors '15
Domain '09
Don't Come Knocking '05
Don't Cry Now '07
Don't Tell '05
Douchebag '10
Down in the Delta '98 ▸
Down to the Bone '04
Downton Abbey '19 ▸
Dreamer: Inspired by a True Story '05
Dreams and Shadows '10
Driveways '19 ▸
Duma '05 ▸
The Dynamiter '11
East of the River '40
Eat Drink Man Woman '94 ▸
The Edge of Heaven '07 ▸
Eight Days to Live '06
Eighteen '04
Elena '11
Elizabethtown '05
Emile '03
Emma's Wish '98
Empire Falls '05
The Etruscan Smile '19
Evelyn '02 ▸
The Evening Star '96
An Evergreen Christmas '14
Every Day '10
Every Second Counts '08
Everyday '12
Everything Strange and New '09
Eve's Bayou '97 ▸
Extraordinary Measures '10
Extremely Loud and Incredibly Close '11
Eye of the Dolphin '06
Falling Angels '03
Family Pictures '93 ▸
Family Reunion '81
The Family Secret '24
The Family Secret '51
The Family That Preys '08
Fanny and Alexander '83 ▸
The Fate of the Furious '17
Father of My Children '09
Fathers and Daughters '16
A Father's Choice '00
Feast of July '95
Fences '16 ▸
Feu Mathias Pascal '26
Field of Vision '11
Fielder's Choice '05
The Fields '11
Fierce People '05
The 5th Quarter '10
The Fighter '10 ▸
Fill the Void '12
Film Socialisme '10
Finding Home '03
Fiorile '93 ▸
Fireflies in the Garden '08
Fireproof '08
A Fish in the Bathtub '99
Fish Tank '09 ▸
The Fitzgerald Family Christmas '12
Five and Ten '31
Five Finger Exercise '62
Five Nights in Maine '16
5 Time Champion '11
Flambards '78
Flame in the Streets '61
The Flame Trees of Thika '81 ▸
Flash of Genius '08
Flicka '06
Flicka: Country Pride '12
Flight of the Red Balloon '08
Flipped '10
Flowers in the Attic '14
Follow the Stars Home '01
A Fond Kiss '04
Footnote '11
For One More Day '07
Fort McCoy '11
40 Love '15
Four Men and a Prayer '38
Four Mothers '41
Four Sheets to the Wind '07
Four Wives '39
Frailty '02 ▸
Frankie '19
Free Style '09
Fudoh: The New Generation '96
Full Out '15
Gabriel & Me '01
Gallant Lady '33
Game Time: Tackling the Past '11
Gas Food Lodging '92 ▸
Georgia Rule '07
Germany Year Zero '48 ▸
Ghost Cat '03
Giant '56 ▸
Gideon's Daughter '05
Girl in Progress '12
Girl Most Likely '12
The Glass Castle '17
Glorious 39 '09
Going Home '71
Gold Star '17
Goodbye Christopher Robin '17
Gotti '18
The Grace Card '11
Grace Is Gone '07 ▸
Gracie '07
Gracie's Choice '04
The Greatest '09
The Greening of Whitney Brown '11
Grey Gardens '09 ▸
Grown Up Movie Star '10
Gun Hill Road '11
Hamlet '96 ▸
Hamlet & Hutch '14
Happiness '98 ▸
Hara-Kiri: Death of a Samurai '11
Harvest '10
The Harvesters '19
Hateship Loveship '13
A Hatful of Rain '59
The Haunting in Connecticut '09
Heaven Is for Real '14
Heaven's Door '12
Helen '09
Hellion '13 ▸
Henry & Verlin '94
Her Sister's Secret '46
Hesher '10
Hidden Places '06
Higher Ground '11 ▸
A History of Violence '05 ▸
Hoax for the Holidays '10
Holiday Baggage '08
The Hollars '16
Home '08
Home '09
Home for the Holidays '95
Home In Indiana '44
A Home of Our Own '93
Homecoming '96
Honey 3: Dare to Dance '16
Horse Camp '14
A Horse Tale '15
The Horses of McBride '12
Hounddog '08
House of D '04
The House of the Spirits '93
The House of Yes '97
How the Garcia Girls Spent Their Summer '05
Humboldt County '08
Hunger Point '03
Hush Little Baby '93
I Am Love '09 ▸
I Am Potential '15
I Can Only Imagine '18
I Killed My Mother '09
I Remember Mama '48 ▸
I Smile Back '15
I Wish '11 ▸
The Ice Storm '97 ▸
The Identical '14
Illegal Tender '07
I'm Glad My Mother Is Alive '09
Imaginary Heroes '05
In a Better World '10
In America '02 ▸
In Her Shoes '05 ▸
In the Family '11
In the Land of Women '06
Incendies '10 ▸
Infinitely Polar Bear '14
The Inheritance '76
The Inheritance '97
Inside Paris '06
The Intended '02
The Interrogation of Michael Crowe '02
Into the West '92 ▸
Inventing the Abbotts '97
I've Loved You So Long '08 ▸
Jack of the Red Hearts '15 ▸
Jada '08
Jake's Corner '08
James White '15 ▸
Janie Jones '10
Japanese War Bride '52
Jayne Mansfield's Car '13
JFK: Reckless Youth '93
Joshua '07 ▸
Julien Donkey-boy '99
Julieta '16
Junebug '05 ▸
Just Ask My Children '01
Just Business '08
Just Henry '11
Kabei: Our Mother '08
The Karate Kid '10
Kate's Secret '86
The Kennedys '11
Kes '69 ▸
A Kid Like Jake '18
Kill the Poor '03
Killer of Sheep '77 ▸
King Jack '16 ▸
King of the Corner '04 ▸
King of the Gypsies '78
Kingdom Come '01
Kings and Queen '04 ▸
Kit Kittredge: An American Girl '08
Knucklehead '15 ▸
Labor Day '13
Laila '29
Lake City '08
Lake Effects '12
The Last Cowboy '03
The Last Hard Men '76
The Last Mimzy '07
The Last Movie Star '17
Last Ounce of Courage '12
Last Ride '09
The Last Song '10
Last Summer In the Hamptons '96 ▸
Last Weekend '14
Leaves of Grass '09
Leaving Barstow '08
Legendary '10
Legends of the Fall '94
Leolo '92 ▸
Liam '00
Lies My Mother Told Me '05
Life, Above All '10
Life & Nothing More '17
Life as a House '01
Life Begins at Eight-Thirty '42
Life Is Sweet '90 ▸
Life Support '07 ▸
Lifted '10
The Light Between Oceans '16
Lightning Bug '04
Like Dandelion Dust '09
Like Father Like Son '05
Like Father, Like Son '13
Limbo '99
Little Boy Blue '97
Little Dorrit '08
The Little Foxes '41 ▸
Little Girl Lost: The Delimar Vera Story '08
A Little Help '11
Little Men '16
The Little Mermaid '18
Little Miss Nobody '36
Little Miss Sunshine '06 ▸
Little Women '18
Little Women '19 ▸
Lonesome Jim '06 ▸
The Long Day Closes '92 ▸
Long Lost Son '06
The Long Shot '04
A Long Way Home '01
Look at Me '04 ▸
Look in Any Window '61
The Looking Glass '16
Lorenzo's Oil '92 ▸
The Lost & Found Family '09
The Lost City '05
Lost Embrace '04
The Lost Language of Cranes '92 ▸
Louder Than Bombs '16
Louder Than Words '14
Love Comes Softly '03
Loveless '18 ▸
The Lovely Bones '09
Loverboy '05
Love's Abiding Joy '06
Love's Christmas Journey '11
Love's Enduring Promise '04
Love's Everlasting Courage '11
Love's Long Journey '05
Love's Unending Legacy '07
Lymelife '08
Ma Saison Preferee '93 ▸
Madeo '09
Magical Girl '14 ▸
The Magnificent Ambersons '42 ▸
The Magnificent Ambersons '02
Make Way for Tomorrow '37

▸ = rated three bones or higher

Making Plans for Lena '09
A Man to Remember '38
Manchester by the Sea '16 ▸
Manito '03 ▸
The March Sisters at Christmas '12
Margot at the Wedding '07
Martha Marcy May Marlene '11 ▸
Martian Child '07
Martin (Hache) '97
May in Summer '13
Meadowland '15
Meant to Be '12
Melancholia '11 ▸
Memorial Day '12
A Memory In My Heart '99
The Memory Keeper's Daughter '08
Metro Manila '13
Middletown '06
Mighty Fine '12
Mildred Pierce '11
Miles from Nowhere '09
Milton's Secret '16
Miracle Run '04
Miracles From Heaven '16
Mirai '18 ▸
Miss Austen Regrets '07
Miss Juneteenth '20
Mr. Church '16
Mr. Wu '27
Mobile Homes '19
Moebius '13
Mokey '42
Molly Moon and The Incredible Book of Hypnotism '15
A Monster Calls '17
Moondance Alexander '07
Morning '10
The Morrison Murders '96
The Motel Life '12
Mother and Child '09
Mothers Cry '30
A Mother's Gift '95
Motives 2-Retribution '07
Mozart's Sister '10
Ms. Purple '19
Mulligans '08
The Music Never Stopped '11
Must Read After My Death '09
My Boy Jack '07
My Brother '06
My Brother Jonathan '85
My Brother the Devil '12
My Brothers '10
My Dog the Champion '14
My Family '94 ▸
My Life So Far '98
My Mother's Smile '02
My Sister's Keeper '09
My Son John '52
My Year Without Sex '09
The Myth of Fingerprints '97
Nancy '18
Nancy Steele Is Missing '37
The Nanny Express '08
The National Tree '09
Nearing Grace '05
Nebraska '13 ▸
New Blood '99
New Morals for Old '32
A Night for Dying Tigers '10
Night Has Settled '14
Night Moves '75 ▸
A Nightmare Come True '97
Nil by Mouth '96
99 Homes '14 ▸
No Brother of Mine '07
No More Orchids '32
No Pay, Nudity '16
No Reservations '07
No Sad Songs For Me '50
Noah '14
Noble Things '08
Nobody Knows '04
Nobody Walks '12
Normal '07
Norman Rockwell's Shuffleton's Barbershop '13
November Christmas '10
O Pioneers! '91
October Baby '12
Of Boys and Men '08
Of Human Hearts '38
Of Two Minds '12
Off the Map '03 ▸
An Old-Fashioned Thanksgiving '08
On Thin Ice '03
Once Were Warriors '94 ▸
One Day You'll Understand '08
One Foot in Heaven '41
The One I Wrote For You '14
One Man's Journey '33
One Night at Susie's '30
The Open Road '09
Ordinary People '80 ▸
Other People '16
The Other Son '12 ▸
Other Voices, Other Rooms '95
Our Children '12
Our Little Sister '16
Our Mother's House '67
Our Wild Hearts '13
Out of the Furnace '13
Out of the Woods '05
Owd Bob '97
A Painted House '03
Pampered Youth '25
Paradise, Texas '05
The Paradise Virus '03
Pariah '11 ▸
The Past '13 ▸
Pearl Diver '04
People Like Us '12
Perception '06
Petals on the Wind '14
Philomena '13
Phoebe in Wonderland '08
The Piano Lesson '94 ▸
Pieces of April '03
A Place Called Home '04
Plain Truth '04
Please Give '10
Poor Man's Game '06 ▸
Pope Dreams '06
Prayers for Bobby '09 ▸
Preacher's Kid '10
Pride and Glory '08
The Private Lives of Pippa Lee '09
Private Property '06
The Prize Winner of Defiance, Ohio '05 ▸
Promise '86 ▸
Promises to Keep '85
Proof '05 ▸
Protecting the King '07
The Pursuit of Happyness '06
The Quiet Family '98 ▸
The Quiet Room '96
The Quitter '34
Quitters '16
Rabbit Hole '10 ▸
The Race '09
Rachel Getting Married '08 ▸
Rails & Ties '07
The Railway Children '70 ▸
The Railway Children '00 ▸
Rain '06
A Raisin in the Sun '08
Ratcatcher '99
Real Steel '11
Real Women Have Curves '02 ▸
Rebel in Town '56
Red Roses and Petrol '03
The Red Tent '14
Relative Stranger '09
Relative Strangers '99
Remember Me '10
Reno '39
Reservation Road '07
Return '11
Return to Zero '14
Revolutionary Road '08
Riding in Cars with Boys '01
A River Runs Through It '92 ▸
The River Why '10
River's End '05
Rocket Gibraltar '88 ▸
Romulus, My Father '07 ▸
Room '15
Roughly Speaking '45
The Royal Tenenbaums '01 ▸
Run & Jump '13
Running on Empty '88 ▸
Running with Scissors '06
Rust '09
Ryna '05
Safe Passage '94
The Safety of Objects '01
Saraband '03 ▸
Sarah, Plain and Tall '91 ▸
Sarah, Plain and Tall: Skylark '93
Sarah, Plain and Tall: Winter's End '99 ▸
Sasha '10
The Savages '07 ▸
Saving Grace B. Jones '09
Saving Shiloh '06
The Scamp '57
Scandal at Scourie '53
The Sea of Grass '47
A Secret '07 ▸
The Secret Heart '46
The Secret Life of Bees '08 ▸
The Secret of Roan Inish '94 ▸
A Separation '11
A Serious Man '09 ▸
Seven Angry Men '55
Seventeen Years '99 ▸
Sex and the Single Mom '03
Shannon's Rainbow '09
Sheeba '05
The Shell Seekers '06
She's Not Our Sister '11
She's Too Young '04
A Shine of Rainbows '09
The Shipping News '01
Shoplifters '18 ▸
A Sierra Nevada Gunfight '13
Silence of the Heart '84 ▸
Silent Cry Aloud '16
A Simple Life '11 ▸
Sin Nombre '09 ▸
Since Otar Left. . . '03
Sister '12
The Sisters '05
Sleepwalking '08
Small Town Saturday Night '10
Smart People '08
So B. It '17
Socrates '18 ▸
Solitary Man '10 ▸
Someday This Pain Will Be Useful to You '11
Somewhere '10
The Song of Sparrows '08
Songs My Brother Taught Me '15 ▸
Sons and Lovers '60 ▸
The Son's Room '00 ▸
Sorry We Missed You '20 ▸
Soul Surfer '11
Sparkle '12
Spencer's Mountain '63
Stand Clear of the Closing Doors '13 ▸
Starred Up '13 ▸
Staying Vertical '16
Steamboy '05 ▸
Steel City '06
Still Alice '14 ▸
Stolen Summer '02
The Stone Angel '07
Storm Cell '08
The Stray '17
Stuck in Love '12
Success Is the Best Revenge '84
Sufat Chol '16 ▸
Summer Hours '08
A Summer in Genoa '08
The Sundowners '60 ▸
Surprise, Surprise '09
Sway '06
Sweepings '33
Sweet Nothing in My Ear '08
Swimming Upstream '03
Take Shelter '11 ▸
The Talent Given Us '04 ▸
Talhotblond '12
Taming Andrew '00
Teenage Rebel '56
Tennessee '08
10th & Wolf '06
Tenth Avenue Angel '47
The Tenth Circle '08
Testimony of Two Men '77
Tetro '09
Texas Rein '16
That Evening Sun '09 ▸
That Russell Girl '08
That's My Man '47
Then She Found Me '07
Things We Lost in the Fire '07
Think of Me '11
35 Shots of Rum '08
Those People Next Door '52
Those We Love '32
Though None Go With Me '06
Three Bad Sisters '56
3 Generations '17
Three Priests '08
Through a Glass Darkly '61 ▸
Thunder In the Valley '47
Tiger Eyes '13
Time of the Wolf '03 ▸
Time Out of Mind '14
Time to Leave '05 ▸
Tiny Furniture '10 ▸
To Be Fat Like Me '07
To Live '94 ▸
Toast '10
Tobacco Road '41
Tokyo Sonata '09 ▸
Too Much, Too Soon '58
Too Young to Be a Dad '02
Tortilla Soup '01
Touching Home '08
Towelhead '07
Track of the Cat '54
Transamerica '05 ▸
The Tree '10
Trouble with the Curve '12
Trust '10
Tugboat Annie '33 ▸
Turning Paige '01
12 and Holding '05 ▸
21 Grams '03 ▸
The Twilight of the Golds '97
Two Weeks '06
Typhoon '06
Un Air de Famille '96
Uncertainty '08
Uncle Nino '03
Under the Piano '95
Under the Same Moon '07
Underdog Kids '15
Undertow '04
An Unexpected Love '03
Up and Down '04
The Upside of Anger '05 ▸
Upstairs Downstairs '11
Urban Country '18
The Vanishing Virginian '41
The Vicious Kind '09
Volver '06 ▸
Wakefield '17
Waking Up Wally '05
A Walk in My Shoes '10
Walking with Dinosaurs 3D '13
The War '94
The War Bride '01
War of the Buttons '12
The War Zone '98
Washington Heights '02
The Water Horse: Legend of the Deep '07
Waves '19 ▸
The Way '10
We Are What We Are '11
We Bought a Zoo '11
We Monsters '15
We Need to Talk About Kevin '11 ▸
We Own the Night '07
We the Animals '18 ▸
Weepah Way for Now '15
Welcome to Paradise '07
Welcome to the Dollhouse '95
Welcome to the Rileys '10
The Well-Digger's Daughter '11
The Wet Parade '32
What Katy Did '99
What They Had '18
What's Cooking? '00 ▸
What's Eating Gilbert Grape '93 ▸
When Did You Last See Your Father? '07
When Father Was Away on Business '85 ▸
When I Find the Ocean '06
Where Are My Children? '94
Where Children Play '15
Where God Left His Shoes '07
Where It's At '69
Whirlpool '34
The Whisperers '66
White Irish Drinkers '10
White Material '10
White Reindeer '13
Who Is Simon Miller? '11
Widow on the Hill '05
Wildlife '18 ▸
Winter Passing '05
Winter Solstice '04 ▸
Winter's Bone '10 ▸
Wish I Was Here '14
A Woman of Independent Means '94 ▸
The Wonders '15
Wonderstruck '17
Wondrous Oblivion '06 ▸
The World Moves On '34
Wuthering Heights '12
The Year Dolly Parton Was My Mom '11
Yelling to the Sky '11
Yonkers Joe '08
You Lucky Dog '10
Young Ideas '43
Your Love Never Fails '11

Family Horror

Alien Abduction '14
Along Came the Devil 2 '19
Along Came the Devil '18
An American Haunting '05
The Amityville Horror '79
Amityville 4: The Evil Escapes '89
Amityville Dollhouse '96
The Amityville Horror '05
Amityville 1992: It's About Time '92
The Attic '06
Audrey Rose '77
Barricade '12
The Boy '16
Brahms: The Boy II '19
Burnt Offerings '76
The Caretaker '16
Color Out of Space '19
The Conjuring '13 ▸
The Cradle '06
Damien: Omen 2 '78
Dark House '14
The Diary of Ellen Rimbauer '03
The Dinner Party '20
Don't Be Afraid of the Dark '73
Don't Be Afraid of the Dark '11
The Exorcist '73 ▸
Feu Mathias Pascal '26
Goosebumps 2: Haunted Halloween '18
The Guest '14
A Haunted House '13
The Haunting in Connecticut '09
Hereditary '18 ▸
Insidious '10
Jinn '14
Last House on the Left '72
The Last House on the Left '09
The Little Stranger '18
The Lodge '19
The Lodgers '17
Mama '13 ▸
Mary '19
Mother's Day '10
Oculus '14
The Omen '76
The Others '01 ▸
Paranormal Activity '09 ▸
Paranormal Activity 2 '10
Paranormal Activity 4 '12
Paranormal Activity 5: The Ghost Dimension '15
Paranormal Activity: The Marked Ones '14
Pet Sematary '19
Poltergeist '82 ▸
Poltergeist 2: The Other Side '86
Poltergeist 3 '88
Poltergeist '15
The Prodigy '19
A Quiet Place '18 ▸
The Shining '80
Sinister 2 '15
The Stepfather '87 ▸
Stepfather 2: Make Room for Daddy '89
Stepfather 3: Father's Day '92
The Stepfather '09
Summer 1993 '17 ▸
3 from Hell '19
Trash Fire '16
The Uninvited '44 ▸
The Uninvited '09
Us '19 ▸
The Visit '15
We Are What We Are '13 ▸
The Witch '16 ▸
You Should Have Left '20
You're Next '13

Family Reunions

***See also** Aunts & Brothers & Cousins; Dads; Family Comedy; Family Drama; Grandparents; Vacations*

Abducted: The Carlina White Story '12
Aberdeen '00
Alias Betty '01
Almost Christmas '16
Almost Strangers '01 ▸
Altered Minds '13
American Heart '92 ▸
Around a Small Mountain '09
Around the Bend '04
August Rush '07
Autumn Sonata '78 ▸
Back Home '90
Banner 4th of July '13
Behind the Red Door '02
A Better Life '11 ▸
Blood Father '16 ▸
Blue River '95
Broken Bridges '06
Brothers '04 ▸
The Cake Eaters '07
Carnegie Hall '47
Catfish in Black Bean Sauce '00
A Christmas Tale '08 ▸
The Claim '00
Come Dance at My Wedding '09
Come to Daddy '20
Crimes of the Past '09
Daddy Nostalgia '90 ▸
Dan in Real Life '07
Dangerous Relations '93
The Darjeeling Limited '07 ▸
Dark Shadows '12
The Daughter '15
Daughters Courageous '39
Dawning '09
Days and Nights '14
Death at a Funeral '07
Death at a Funeral '10
The Deep End of the Ocean '98
Despicable Me 3 '17
Disengagement '07
Don't Tell '05
Edge of Winter '16
Elf '03 ▸
The Emerald Forest '85 ▸
Euphoria '19
Familiar Strangers '08
Family Reunion '81
A Family Thing '96 ▸
Finding Dory '16 ▸
The Fitzgerald Family Christmas '12
Frankie '19
Fred Claus '07
The Gathering '77
The Gathering: Part 2 '79
Good Day for It '11
The Growing Pains Movie '00
Growing Pains: Return of the Seavers '04
A Guide to Recognizing Your Saints '06
Halloween '07
The Heartbreak Kid '07
The Hollars '16
Housekeeping '87 ▸
How I Killed My Father '03 ▸

I Know My First Name Is Steven '89
I'm Glad My Mother Is Alive '09
In My Father's House '15 ►
The Inheritance '10
Jeremy's Family Reunion '04
Jumpin' at the Boneyard '92
Junebug '05 ►
Lake Effects '12
Language of the Enemy '07
Leaves of Grass '09
Legendary '10
Leon the Pig Farmer '93
Lion '16 ►
Little Fockers '10
Little Sister '16 ►
The Lost Child '00
A Loving Father '02
Lullaby '14
Machete '10
A Madea Family Funeral '19
Madea's Family Reunion '06
Magnolia '99►
Margot at the Wedding '07
Marion Bridge '02
The Mayor of Casterbridge '03
Montana Sky '07
Mother and Child '09
The Nephew '97
Nobody's Fool '94►
Nothing Like the Holidays '08
Nowhere Boy '09
On Golden Pond '81►
One More Time '15
Oranges and Sunshine '10►
Paris, Texas '83►
Passed Away '92
Peace, Love & Misunderstanding '11
Peeples '13
Prey '10
The Princess Diaries '01
Promises to Keep '85
Pure Country 2: The Gift '10
Pushing Hands '92
The Reception '05
Red Roses and Petrol '03
Relative Stranger '09
The Reunion '11
River Red '98
The Searchers '56►
Secrets and Lies '95
75 Degrees '00
Shannon's Rainbow '09
The Skeleton Twins '14►
A Somewhat Gentle Man '10
Starred Up '13►
Summer Hours '08
The Talent Given Us '04►
Taming Andrew '00
That Russell Girl '08
This Christmas '07
This Modern Age '31
Those Who Love Me Can Take the Train '98
Three Identical Strangers '18►
A Time to Remember '03
Together Again for the First Time '08
Towards Zero '07
Tron: Legacy '10
28 Weeks Later '07
Two Weeks '06
Tyler Perry's Meet the Browns '08
Under the Same Moon '07
Welcome Home Roscoe Jenkins '08
What a Girl Wants '03
What They Had '18
Where Are My Children? '94
Whirlpool '34
The White Cockatoo '35
Wilson '17
Winter Passing '05
A Woman of the World '25
You Can Count On Me '99►

Family Ties

See Aunts & Brothers & Cousins; Dads; Grandparents; In-Laws; Parenthood; Stepparents; Twins

Family Viewing

See Animation & Fantasy; Musical Fantasy; Storytelling

Fantasy

See also Animation & Musical Fantasy

A Nous la Liberte '31 ►
About Time '13
The Adventurer: The Curse of the Midas Box '13
Adventures of a Teenage Dragonslayer '10
The Adventures of Baron Munchausen '89 ►
The Adventures of Mark Twain '85 ►
The Adventures of Pinocchio '96
The Adventures of Sharkboy and Lavagirl in 3-D '05
Age of the Dragons '11
Age of the Hobbits '12
Aladdin '19
Alice '88►
Alice in Wonderland '33
Alice in Wonderland '66►
Alice in Wonderland '85
Alice in Wonderland '99
Alice in Wonderland '10
Alice Through the Looking Glass '66
Alice Through the Looking Glass '16
Alien from L.A. '87
Almighty Thor '11
. . .Almost '90
Amazing Mr. Blunden '72
Amazons '86
American Fable '17
The Amphibian Man '61
Angel-A '05
Angel on My Shoulder '46►
Annihilation '18
Aquaman '18
Aquamarine '06
Arabian Adventure '79
Arthur and the Invisibles '06
Ashik Kerib '88►
Ashura '05
Assassin's Creed '16
Atlantics '19►
Atlantis, the Lost Continent '61
Atlantis: The Lost Empire '01
Atlas '60
Ator the Fighting Eagle '83
Attack of the Gryphon '07
Avengers: Endgame '19►
Avengers: Infinity War '18►
Babe '95►
Babe: Pig in the City '98
Baby. . . Secret of the Lost Legend '85
Barbarella '68
Barbarian Queen '85
Baron Munchausen '43►
Batman '89►
Batman and Robin '97
Batman Forever '95►
Batman Returns '92
*batteries not included '87
Beastly '11
Beastmaster '82
Beauties of the Night '52
Beautiful Creatures '13
This Beautiful Fantastic '17
Beauty and the Beast '14
Beauty and the Beast '17
Beowulf & Grendel '06
Bernard and the Genie '91
Between Two Worlds '44
Beyond Atlantis '73
Beyond Tomorrow '40
The BFG '16
Big '88►
Big Top Pee-wee '88
Biggles '85
Bill & Ted's Excellent Adventure '89
The Bishop's Wife '47►
The Black Cauldron '85
Blade: Trinity '04
Bleach the Movie 4: Hell Verse '10
Blithe Spirit '45►
BloodRayne '06
The Blue Bird '40 ►
The Boy Who Could Fly '86 ►
Branded '12
Bridge to Terabithia '07
Bright '17
The Brothers Grimm '05
Bunraku '10
Butterfly Sword '93
Cabin Boy '94
The Canterville Ghost '44
The Canterville Ghost '96
Cars '06 ►
The Cat from Outer Space '78
Cats '19
The Cave of the Silken Web '67
Cemetery of Splendor '15 ►
Cerberus '05
Charley and the Angel '73
Charlie and the Chocolate Factory '05►
The Christmas That Almost Wasn't '66
The Chronicles of Narnia '89►
The Chronicles of Narnia: Prince Caspian '08
The Chronicles of Narnia: The Lion, the Witch and the Wardrobe '05
The Chronicles of Narnia: The Voyage of the Dawn Treader '10
Cinderella '12
Cinderella 2000 '78
Cirque du Soleil: Worlds Away '12
City of Ember '08
The City of Lost Children '95►
The Clan of the Cave Bear '86
Clash of the Titans '81
Clash of the Titans '10
Click '06
The Cobbler '14
Cocoon '85►
Cocoon: The Return '88
The Color of Magic '08
Colorful: The Motion Picture '10►
Come Drink with Me '65►
The Company of Wolves '85►
Conan the Barbarian '82►
Conan the Barbarian '11
Conan the Destroyer '84
The Congress '13
Conquest '83
Conquest of Mycene '63
Constantine '05
Coraline '09►
Cross '11
Crossworlds '96
Crouching Tiger, Hidden Dragon: Sword of Destiny '16
The Crow '93
The Crow 2: City of Angels '96
The Curious Case of Benjamin Button '08►
The Curse of King Tut's Tomb '06
Curse of the Cat People '44►
Darby O'Gill & the Little People '59►
The Dark Crystal '82►
Dark Kingdom: The Dragon King '04
The Day the Earth Froze '59
The Dead Don't Die '19
Death Takes a Holiday '34►
Death Trance '05
Deathstalker 2: Duel of the Titans '87
Deathstalker 4: Match of Titans '92
Deathstalker '83
Delgo '08
Desperate Living '77
Despiser '03
The Devil & Max Devlin '81
Devil of the Desert Against the Son of Hercules '62
Digging Up the Marrow '14
Dinotopia '02
Doctor Sleep '19►
Doctor Strange '16►
Dolittle '20
Donkey Skin '70 ►
Donovan's Echo '11
Don't Kill It '17
Dororo '07
Dragon Wars '07
Dragonball: Evolution '09
Dragonheart 3: The Sorcerer's Curse '15
Dragonheart '96
Dragonheart: A New Beginning '00
Dragonquest '09
Dragonslayer '81 ►
Dream a Little Dream 2 '94
Dream a Little Dream '89
Dreamchild '85 ►
Dreamscape '84
Drop Dead Fred '91
Dumbo '19
Dungeonmaster '83
Dungeons and Dragons '00
Edward Scissorhands '90►
Elektra '05
Ella Enchanted '04►
Elysium '13
Emmanuelle 4 '84
Enchanted '07
The Enchanted Cottage '45
The Endless '17
Epic '13
Epoch: Evolution '03
Eragon '06
Eraserhead '78►
E.T.: The Extra-Terrestrial '82►
Every Day '18
Everybody Says I'm Fine! '06
The Ewok Adventure '84
The Ewoks: Battle for Endor '85
Excalibur '81►
Explorers '85
Extra Ordinary '20
Fading of the Cries '10
Fallen '17
Fantastic Beasts and Where to Find Them '16
Fantastic Beasts: The Crimes of Grindelwald '18
The Fantastic Night '42►
Fantasy Island '76
Fantasy Island '20
Faraway, So Close! '93
Field of Dreams '89►
The Final Programme '73
Fire and Ice '83
Fire & Ice: The Dragon Chronicles '08
The Five '10
Five Element Ninjas '82
Flight of Dragons '82
Flight of the Navigator '86
Fluke '95
The Forbidden Kingdom '08
The Four '12
Four Warriors '15
Francis Goes to the Races '51
Francis the Talking Mule '49►
French Quarter '78
Frozen II '19►
Gamera the Brave '06
George and the Dragon '04
The Ghost and Mrs. Muir '47►
Ghost Chase '88
A Ghost Story '17►
Ghostwarrior '86
The Giants of Thessaly '60
Gladiators 7 '62
The Glass Slipper '55
The Gnome-Mobile '67
Gods of Egypt '16
Godzilla: Final Wars '04
Godzilla: King of the Monsters '19
Godzilla, Mothra, and King Ghidorah: Giant Monsters All-Out Attack '01
Godzilla-Tokyo S.O.S. '03
Godzilla *vs.* Mothra '92
Godzilla *vs.* SpaceGodzilla '94
Going Postal '10
The Golden Compass '07
Golden Voyage of Sinbad '73
The Golem '20►
Goliath Against the Giants '63
Goliath and the Barbarians '60
Goliath and the Dragon '61
Goliath and the Sins of Babylon '64
Goobers! '97
The Good Night '07
Gor '88
The Great Wall '17
The Great Yokai War '05
Grimm's Snow White '12
The Grinch '18
Guardians of the Lost Code '10
Guinevere '94
Gulliver's Travels '39
Gulliver's Travels '77
Gulliver's Travels '95
A Gun, a Car, a Blonde '97
Happy as Lazzaro '18 ►
Harry Potter and the Chamber of Secrets '02►
Harry Potter and the Deathly Hallows, Part 1 '10►
Harry Potter and the Deathly Hallows, Part 2 '11►
Harry Potter and the Goblet of Fire '05►
Harry Potter and the Order of the Phoenix '07
Harry Potter and the Prisoner of Azkaban '04
Harry Potter and the Sorcerer's Stone '01►
Harvey '50►
Hawk the Slayer '81
Heartbreak Hotel '88
Heaven & Hell '78
Heaven Can Wait '43►
Heaven Can Wait '78►
A Heavenly Vintage '09
Heavy Metal '81►
Helen of Troy '56
Hellboy '19
Hellboy II: The Golden Army '08►
Herbie Rides Again '74
Hercules '58
Hercules '14
Hercules and the Captive Women '63
Hercules in the Haunted World '64
Hercules, Prisoner of Evil '64
Hercules Unchained '59
Here Comes Mr. Jordan '41►
Hey There, It's Yogi Bear '64
Highlander 2: The Quickening '91
Highlander: Endgame '00
Highlander: The Final Dimension '94
The Hobbit '78►
The Hobbit: An Unexpected Journey '12
The Hobbit: The Battle of the Five Armies '14
The Hobbit: The Desolation of Smaug '13►
Hobgoblins '87
Hogfather '06
The Holes '72
Holy Flame of the Martial World '83
Holy Motors '12►
Hook '91
Hoppity Goes to Town '41
Horrors of the Red Planet '64
The House with a Clock in Its Walls '18
How to Train Your Dragon: The Hidden World '19►
Howl's Moving Castle '04
The Hunger Games '12►
The Hunger Games: Catching Fire '13►
The Hunger Games: Mockingjay--Part 1 '14
The Huntsman: Winter's War '16
The I Inside '04
I Lost My Body '19►
Immortals '11
The Impossible Elephant '02
In My Dreams '14
In the Name of the King: A Dungeon Siege Tale '08
In the Name of the King 2: Two Worlds '11
In the Name of the King 3: The Last Mission '14
In Time '11
The Incredible Hulk '08
The Incredible Mr. Limpet '64
Incubus '65
The Indian in the Cupboard '95
Indiana Jones and the Last Crusade '89 ►
Inkheart '09
The Invasion of Carol Enders '74
The Invincible Gladiator '62
Invisible Agent '42
Invisible: The Chronicles of Benjamin Knight '93
Isn't It Romantic '19
It Happened Tomorrow '44
It's a Wonderful Life '46►
Jack Frost '98
Jack the Giant Killer '62►
Jack the Giant Killer '13
Jack the Giant Slayer '13
Jackie Chan's The Myth '05
Jacob Two Two Meets the Hooded Fang '99
James and the Giant Peach '96►
Jason and the Argonauts '63►
Jason and the Argonauts '00
Jem and the Holograms '15
Jimmy, the Boy Wonder '66
Jonathan Livingston Seagull '73
Josh Kirby. . .Time Warrior: Chapter 1, Planet of the Dino-Knights '95
Josh Kirby. . . Time Warrior: Chapter 2, The Human Pets '95
Josh Kirby. . . Time Warrior: Chapter 3, Trapped on Toyworld '95
Josh Kirby. . . Time Warrior: Chapter 4, Eggs from 70 Million B.C. '95
Josh Kirby. . . Time Warrior: Chapter 5, Journey to the Magic Cavern '96
Journey Beneath the Desert '61
Journey to Promethea '10
Journey to the Center of the Earth '59►
Journey to the Center of the Earth '99
Journey to the Lost City '58
Journey to the West '14
Jumanji '95
Jumanji: The Next Level '19
The Jungle Book '42
Jungle Boy '96
Jungle Hell '55
Jurassic World: Fallen Kingdom '18
Just like Heaven '05
Just My Luck '06
Justice League '17
Kaena: The Prophecy '03
Kazaam '96
A Kid in Aladdin's Palace '97
The Kid Who Would Be King '19►
Kids of the Round Table '96
King Kong '33►
King Kong '76
King Kong '05►
Kismet '44
Kiss Me Goodbye '82
Knights of Badassdom '13
Knights of Bloodsteel '09
Kriemhilde's Revenge '24►
Krull '83
Kull the Conqueror '97
L.A. Story '91►
Labou '07
Labyrinth '86►
Lady in the Water '06
Ladyhawke '85
The Lake House '06
Land of Doom '84
The Land of Faraway '87
The Last Airbender '10

► = rated three bones or higher

The Last Days of Pompeii '60
The Last Mimzy '07
The Last Unicorn '82
The Last Warrior '18
The Last Witch Hunter '15
Le Magnifique '76
Legend '86
The Legend of Cryin' Ryan '98
The Legend of Hercules '14
Legend of the Guardians: The Owls of Ga'Hoole '10 ▶
Legend of the Liquid Sword '93
Legion of Iron '90
Lemony Snicket's A Series of Unfortunate Events '04
Leprechaun 2 '94
A Letter to Momo '11
The Lickerish Quartet '70
Like Father, Like Son '87
The Lion of Thebes '64 ▶
Little '19
The Little Mermaid '75
The Little Mermaid '18
Little Monsters '89
Little Nemo: Adventures in Slumberland '92
Logan's Run '76
Lord of the Rings: The Fellowship of the Ring '01 ▶
Lord of the Rings: The Two Towers '02 ▶
The Lord of the Rings '78
Lord of the Rings: The Return of the King '03 ▶
The Lost Continent '51
The Lost Empire '01
The Lost Medallion: The Adventures of Billy Stone '13
The Lost Princess '05
Lost River '15
The Lost Treasure of Sawtooth Island '99
The Loves of Hercules '60
The Luck of the Irish '48
The Machine '13
Maciste in Hell '60
Mad About Men '54
Made in Heaven '87
The Magic Blade '08
The Magic Carpet '51
Magic in the Water '95
The Magic Voyage of Sinbad '52
The Magical Legend of the Leprechauns '99
The Magician '58 ▶
Making Contact '86
Maleficent '14
Maleficent: Mistress of Evil '19
The Man Who Could Work Miracles '37 ▶
The Man Who Killed Don Quixote '18
Mannequin 2: On the Move '91
Marco Polo, Jr. '72
The Mark 2: Redemption '13
Marker '05
The Martian Chronicles: Part 1 '79
The Martian Chronicles: Part 2 '79
The Martian Chronicles: Part 3 '79
Mary Poppins Returns '18
Master of the World '61
Masters of the Universe '87
Maxie '85
Mazes and Monsters '82
Medusa Against the Son of Hercules '62
Meet Joe Black '98
Merlin '98 ▶
Merlin and the Book of Beasts '09
Merlin and the War of the Dragons '08
Merlin's Apprentice '06
The Mermaid '16 ▶
Michael '96
A Midsummer Night's Dream '35 ▶
Mighty Joe Young '49
Mighty Joe Young '98
Mighty Morphin Power Rangers: The Movie '95
Million Dollar Duck '71
Miracle Beach '92
Miracle in Milan '51 ▶
Mirai '18 ▶
Miranda '48
MirrorMask '05
Miss Peregrine's Home for Peculiar Children '16
Mr. Destiny '90
Mr. Magorium's Wonder Emporium '07
Mr. Nobody '13
Mr. Rice's Secret '00
The Mistress of Atlantis '32
The Mistress of Spices '05
Mists of Avalon '01 ▶
Mole Men Against the Son of Hercules '61
Momentum '03
Monkeybone '01
A Monster Calls '17
Mood Indigo '13
Moon over Tao '97 ▶
More Than a Miracle '67
Mortal Engines '18
Mortal Kombat 1: The Movie '95
Mortal Kombat 2: Annihilation '97
Mowgli: Legend of the Jungle '18
The Mummy '17
Munchie '92
The Muppets' Wizard of Oz '05
My Bloody Banjo '15
My Neighbor Totoro '88
My Science Project '85
My Stepmother Is an Alien '88
Mysterious Island '05
Mysterious Museum '99
Mythica 2: The Darkspore '15
Mythica: A Quest for Heroes '15
Mythica: The Iron Crown '16
Mythica: The Necromancer '15
Nanny McPhee '06
The Navigator '88 ▶
Ne Zha '19
Neil Gaiman's NeverWhere '96
Neither Heaven Nor Earth '16
The NeverEnding Story '84 ▶
NeverEnding Story 2: The Next Chapter '91
The NeverEnding Story 3: Escape from Fantasia '94
Neverland '11
Nico the Unicorn '98
Night Across the Street '12
The Night Before the Night Before Christmas '10
Night Tide '61
Night Watch '04
The Nightmare Before Christmas '93 ▶
Nine Lives '16
Nine Lives of Fritz the Cat '74
Noelle '19
November '05 ▶
The Nutcracker and the Four Realms '18
The Ogre '96
100 Monsters '68
One Magic Christmas '85
1001 Arabian Nights '59
Onmyoji 2 '03
Onmyoji '01
Orpheus '49 ▶
Outlander '08
Oz the Great and Powerful '13
The Pagan Queen '09
The Pagemaster '94
Painted Skin '93
Painted Skin: The Resurrection '12
Pan '15
Pandora and the Flying Dutchman '51
Pan's Labyrinth '06 ▶
Parasite '03
Patchwork Girl of Oz '14
Peau D'Ane '71 ▶
Penelope '06
Percy Jackson & The Olympians: The Lightning Thief '10
Percy Jackson: Sea of Monsters '13
Peter Ibbetson '35
Peter Pan '24
Peter Pan '53 ▶
Peter Pan '03 ▶
Pete's Dragon '77
Pete's Dragon '16
The Phantom Chariot '20
Phantom Tollbooth '69 ▶
Piano Tuner of Earthquakes '05
The Plague Dogs '82
Pleasantville '98 ▶
The Point '71
Pokemon the Movie: The Power of Us '18
The Polar Bear King '94
Pom Poko '94
Powder '95
Prancer '89
Prehistoric Bimbos in Armageddon City '93
Prehistoric Women '50
Prelude to a Kiss '92
The Price of Milk '00
Prince of Persia: The Sands of Time '10
Princess: A Modern Fairytale '08
Private Passions '85
The Promise '05
Pufnstuf '70
Radio Flyer '92
Ralph Breaks the Internet '18
Ratboy '86
Re-Cycle '06
Real Men '87
Red Riding Hood '11
Red Sonja '85
The Rescuers Down Under '90
Restless Spirits '99
Return from Witch Mountain '78
The Return of Jafar '94
Return of the Fly '59
The Return of the King '80
Return to Fantasy Island '77
Return to Never Land '02
Return to Oz '85
Return to the Lost World '93
Riverworld '10
R.L. Stine's The Haunting Hour: Don't Even Think About It '07
Robots '05
Rock & Rule '83
The Rook '99
Rookie of the Year '93
Ruby Sparks '12
Salome's Last Dance '88
Samson '61
Samson and His Mighty Challenge '64
Samson and the 7 Miracles of the World '62
Santa Claus Conquers the Martians '64
Santa Claus: The Movie '85
The Saragossa Manuscript '65
The Science of Sleep '06
The Scorpion King 3: Battle for Redemption '11
Scott Pilgrim *vs.* the World '10
Sea People '00
Search for the Gods '75
The Secret Life of Walter Mitty '13
The Secret of Loch Ness '08
The Secret of Moonacre '08
The Secret of NIMH '82 ▶
The Secret of Roan Inish '94 ▶
The Seeker: The Dark Is Rising '07
7 Faces of Dr. Lao '63 ▶
Seventh Son '15
The Seventh Voyage of Sinbad '58 ▶
The Shack '17
The Shaggy Dog '59
The Shaggy Dog '06
Shanks '74
The Shape of Water '17 ▶
Shazam! '19
She '25
She '83
Shrek 2 '04 ▶
Shrek '01 ▶
Shrek Forever After '10
Sidekick '05
Siegfried '24 ▶
A Simple Wish '97
Simply Irresistible '99
Sinbad and the Eye of the Tiger '77
Sinbad of the Seven Seas '89
Christmas All Over Again '16
Skellig: The Owl Man '09
Slave Girls from Beyond Infinity '87
Smallfoot '18
Snow White: A Tale of Terror '97
Snow White and the Huntsman '12
Snow White: The Fairest of Them All '02
Solarbabies '86
Solo: A Star Wars Story '18
Something Wicked This Way Comes '83
Son of Hercules in the Land of Darkness '63
Son of Kong '33
Son of Samson '62
The Sorcerer and the White Snake '13
Sorry to Bother You '18
A Sound of Thunder '05
Southland Tales '06
Spark: A Space Tail '17
The Spiderwick Chronicles '08 ▶
Splash '84
Spring '15 ▶
Stairway to Heaven '46 ▶
Stalker '79 ▶
Stand Up and Cheer '34
Star Wars: The Rise of Skywalker '19
Stardust '07 ▶
Starry Night '99
Steel Dawn '87
Story of Mankind '57
Storybook '95
Strange Magic '15
Stray '19
Sucker Punch '11
Super Mario Bros. '93
Supergirl '84
Superman: The Movie '78 ▶
Superman 2 '80 ▶
Superman 3 '83
Superman 4: The Quest for Peace '87
Superman Returns '06
Sword & the Sorcerer '82
The Sword in the Stone '63 ▶
Sword Masters: The Battle Wizard '77
Sword Masters: Web of Death '76
Sword of the Valiant '83
Tale of Tales '15
Tales of an Ancient Empire '11
Tall Tale: The Unbelievable Adventures of Pecos Bill '95
Tamara '05
Tank Girl '94
Tanya's Island '81
Teenage Mutant Ninja Turtles: The Movie '90
Teenage Mutant Ninja Turtles '14
The 10th Kingdom '00
Test Tube Teens from the Year 2000 '93
The Testament of Dr. Cordelier '59 ▶
The Testament of Orpheus '59 ▶
They Came Back '04
The Thief and the Cobbler '96 ▶
The Thief Lord '06
The Thief of Bagdad '40 ▶
The Thief of Bagdad '24 ▶
The Thief of Bagdad '78
Thor '11 ▶
Thor and the Amazon Women '60
Thor the Conqueror '83
Thor: The Dark World '13
Three Wishes '95
The Three Worlds of Gulliver '59
The 3 Worlds of Gulliver '60
Thunderbirds '04
Thunderstruck '12
Tideland '05
Tigers Are Not Afraid '19 ▶
Tim Burton's Corpse Bride '05 ▶
Time Bandits '81
Time Barbarians '90
The Time of Their Lives '46
The Time Traveler's Wife '09
Timestalkers '87
Tin Man '07
Tobor the Great '54
The Toe Tactic '08
Tom Thumb '58 ▶
Toy Story '95 ▶
Toy Story 2 '99 ▶
Toy Story 4 '19 ▶
Trading Mom '94
Transformers: The Movie '86
The Trip '67
A Troll in Central Park '94
Tropical Malady '04
Trouble in Mind '86 ▶
The Tune '92
Turbo: A Power Rangers Movie '96
12 Christmas Wishes For My Dog '11
20,000 Leagues under the Sea '54 ▶
20,000 Leagues Under the Sea '97
The Twilight of the Ice Nymphs '97
Twisted '96
Twitches '05
Twitches Too '07
Two Little Bears '61
The Two Worlds of Jenny Logan '79
UglyDolls '19
Ulysses Against the Son of Hercules '61
Uncle Boonmee Who Can Recall His Past Lives '10
Undersea Kingdom '36
Unidentified Flying Oddball '79
Ursus in the Land of Fire '63
Ursus in the Valley of the Lions '62
Uzumaki '00
Valerian and the City of a Thousand Planets '17
The Valley of Gwangi '69 ▶
The Vast of Night '20 ▶
Veritas: Prince of Truth '07
Vibes '88
Vice Versa '88 ▶
The Viking Women and the Sea Serpent '57
Vikingdom '13
Voyage of the Unicorn '00
Warcraft '16
The Warrior & the Sorceress '84
Warriors of Virtue '97
The Water Horse: Legend of the Deep '07
Watership Down '78
Welcome to Marwen '18
What Dreams May Come '98
What Men Want '19
Where the Wild Things Are '09
The White Sheik '52 ▶
Wild Women of Wongo '59
Wildling '18
William Shakespeare's A Midsummer Night's Dream '99
Willow '88
Wind and Cloud: The Storm Riders '04
Window to Paris '95
Wings of Desire '88 ▶
Winter's Tale '14
The Witches of Oz '11
Witchslayer Gretl '12
The Wizard of Oz '25
Wizards '77
Wizards of the Demon Sword '94
The Wolves of Kromer '98
Wonder Woman '74
The Worst Witch '86
Wrath of the Titans '12
A Wrinkle in Time '18
Yesterday '19
Yoga Hosers '16
Yor, the Hunter from the Future '83
You Never Can Tell '51
Your Name '17 ▶
Youth Without Youth '07
Yu-Gi-Oh! The Movie: Pyramid of Light '04
Zapped! '82
Zardoz '73
Zathura '05 ▶
Zombi Child '20
Zone Troopers '84
Zu Warriors '01
Zu: Warriors from the Magic Mountain '83

Farm Livin'

See also America's Heartland

Adam's Woman '70
Alambrista! '77
Alien Storm '12
All Roads Lead Home '08
All Saints '17
American Fable '17
. . .And the Earth Did Not Swallow Him '94
Animal Farm '99
Autumn Blood '14
The Back-Up Plan '10
Bad Day for the Cut '17
Balloon Farm '97
Barnyard '06
Beautiful Kate '09 ▶
Bennett's War '19
The Biggest Little Farm '18 ▶
Bitter Harvest '81 ▶
Bloodsuckers from Outer Space '83
Born in 68 '08
The Bridges of Madison County '95 ▶
Broken Harvest '94
Buffalo Jump '90 ▶
Bullhead '11
California Solo '12
The Canadian '26
Captain Boycott '47
Captain Fantastic '16
Cash Crop '98
The Castaway Cowboy '74
Cesar Chavez '14
Charlotte's Web '73
Charlotte's Web '06 ▶
Chicken Run '00 ▶
Christmas in Canaan '09
The Cider House Rules '99 ▶
City Girl '30
Claudia '43
Cold Comfort Farm '94 ▶
Cold Mountain '03 ▶
Color Out of Space '19
Country '84 ▶
Country Life '95
Crypto '19
The Curse '87
Curse of the Starving Class '94
Dark Fields '09
Dark River '18
Dark Waters '19 ▶
Days of Heaven '78 ▶
Deadly Stranger '88
December Bride '91
Deep Valley '47
Desire Under the Elms '58
The Devil & Daniel Webster '41 ▶
Disgrace '08
Django: Last Killer '67
Doc Hollywood '91
Dog Day '83
A Dog Named Christmas '09
A Dog's Journey '19

Dream Boy '08
The Dukes of Hazzard '05
Earth '30 ▶
Edges of the Lord '01
Egg and I '47 ▶
Fantastic Mr. Fox '09 ▶
Far from the Madding Crowd '97 ▶
Far from the Madding Crowd '15
The Farmer Takes a Wife '35
The Farmer's Other Daughter '65
The Field '90 ▶
The Fields '11
15 Amore '98
The Final Storm '09
Freezer Burn: The Invasion of Laxdale '08
Giant '56 ▶
The Girl from Paris '02 ▶
God's Little Acre '58 ▶
God's Own Country '17 ▶
Gold Is Where You Find It '38
The Good Old Boys '95
The Grapes of Wrath '40 ▶
The Green Promise '49
The Greening of Whitney Brown '11
Growing the Big One '09
Happy as Lazzaro '18 ▶
Harvest '11
Harvest of Fire '95
The Harvesters '19
Healing '15
A Hidden Life '19
Home on the Range '04
Horton Foote's Alone '97
Hostile Border '16
Hurry Sundown '67
I'll Wait for You '41
In the Winter Dark '98
The Inheritors '98
Irresistible '20
It's All So Quiet '13
Japanese War Bride '52
Jean de Florette '87 ▶
Kampai! For the Love of Sake '16
The Kettles in the Ozarks '56
Kings in Grass Castles '97
Land Girls '09
Last Kind Words '12
Little John '02
Love Begins '11
Love's Everlasting Courage '11
Ma and Pa Kettle at Home '54
The Mating Game '59 ▶
Mean Dreams '17
Messengers 2: The Scarecrow '09
Mifune '99
The Milagro Beanfield War '88 ▶
Missouri Traveler '58 ▶
Morning Glory '93
Mudbound '17 ▶
My Man and I '52
Nanny McPhee Returns '10
1922 '17
November Christmas '10
Nowhere in Africa '02
Nowhere to Run '93
The Old Homestead '35
Our Daily Bread '34 ▶
The Outsider '02
The Outskirts '98 ▶
Owd Bob '97
A Painted House '03
Pearl Diver '04
Pelle the Conqueror '88 ▶
Peter Rabbit '18
Places in the Heart '84 ▶
The Price of Milk '00
The Proposition '96
The Purchase Price '32
The Race '09
Rapture '65
Riddler's Moon '98
Ride the Wild Fields '00
The River '84
The Road from Coorain '02
Rock-a-Doodle '92
The Romance of Rosy Ridge '47
Romulus, My Father '07 ▶
Ruggles of Red Gap '35 ▶
Sarah, Plain and Tall: Skylark '93
Sarah, Plain and Tall: Winter's End '99 ▶
Secondhand Lions '03
A Shaun the Sheep Movie: Farmageddon '19 ▶
Signs '02 ▶
Sommersby '93
Son-in-Law '93
Sounder '72 ▶
South Riding '11
The Southerner '45 ▶
Spring 1941 '08
The Stars Fell on Henrietta '94
Steal Big, Steal Little '95
Still Mine '13 ▶
The Stone Boy '84 ▶
Summer of the Monkeys '98
Summertime '16
The Sundowners '60 ▶
Sunrise '27 ▶
Temple Grandin '10 ▶
That Evening Sun '09 ▶
This Is My Father '99
A Thousand Acres '97
To the Stars '20
Tobacco Road '41
Tommy and the Cool Mule '09
Tonight We Raid Calais '43
Total Western '00
The Tree of Wooden Clogs '78 ▶
Tully '00 ▶
2 Brothers & a Bride '03
Under the Sun '98
Vacas '91
War Horse '11
The Wedding Night '35
The Well '97
Where There's a Will '55
White Material '10
Wisdom '87
Woman Obsessed '59
The Yearling '94
You Lucky Dog '10
Young Ones '14

Farming

See Farm Livin'

Fashion

Absolutely Fabulous: The Movie '16
Artists and Models Abroad '38
Beau Brummell: This Charming Man '06
Bill Cunningham New York '10
The Bitter Tears of Petra von Kant '72
Bratz '07
Coco Before Chanel '09
Coco Chanel '08
Coco Chanel & Igor Stravinsky '09
Crimes of Fashion '04
The Devil Wears Prada '06
Don't Tell Mom the Babysitter's Dead '91
The Dress '96
The Dressmaker '16
Fashions of 1934 '34
Fresh Dressed '15
The Garment Jungle '57
Hourglass '95
House of Versace '13
I Can Get It For You Wholesale '51
In Fabric '18
Intern '00
The Intern '15
Irene '40
Kill by Inches '99
Kinky Boots '06
A Life of Her Own '50
Lovely to Look At '52 ▶
Made in Paris '65
Mademoiselle C '13
McQueen '18 ▶
My Lucky Star '38
102 Dalmatians '00
Perfume '01
Phantom Thread '17 ▶
Phat Girlz '06
Portraits Chinois '96
Princess Daisy '83
Puerto Ricans in Paris '16
Ready to Wear '94
Ripple Effect '07
Romy and Michele's High School Reunion '97
Scruples '80
Selena '96
The September Issue '09
Sins '85
Tales of Manhattan '42 ▶
27 Dresses '08
Unzipped '94 ▶
Valentino: The Last Emperor '08
Yours, Mine & Ours '05
Zoolander 2 '16

Fast Zombies

Cell '16
Dawn of the Dead '04 ▶
Dead Mine '12
The Girl with All the Gifts '17
Outpost: Rise of the Spetsnaz '13
Rise of the Zombies '12
Super Size Me 2: Holy Chicken! '19
28 Days Later '02
28 Weeks Later '07
Wicked Little Things '07
World War Z '13
Zombieland: Double Tap '19 ▶

Fatsuit Acting

America's Sweethearts '01
Austin Powers 2: The Spy Who Shagged Me '99 ▶
Austin Powers In Goldmember '02
Big Momma's House 2 '06
Big Momma's House '00
Big Mommas: Like Father, Like Son '11
Dance Flick '09
Date Movie '06
Death Becomes Her '92 ▶
Hairspray '07 ▶
Just Friends '05
Madea's Big Happy Family '11
Madea's Witness Protection '12
Monty Python's The Meaning of Life '83 ▶
My Mom's New Boyfriend '08
Norbit '07
Nutty Professor 2: The Klumps '00
The Nutty Professor '96 ▶
The Santa Clause '94
The Santa Clause 2 '02
The Santa Clause 3: The Escape Clause '06
Shallow Hal '01
Stephen King's Thinner '96
To Be Fat Like Me '07
Tropic Thunder '08 ▶
Tyler Perry's A Madea Christmas '13

FBI

See also CIA/NSA; Crime Drama; Detectives

Absolute Deception '13
Across the Line: The Exodus of Charlie Wright '10
After the Sunset '04
Airboss '97
Along Came a Spider '01
Altitude '17
American East '07
American Meltdown '04
American Yakuza '94
Analyze That '02
Analyze This '98 ▶
Angel Has Fallen '19
The Art of War '00
Assassin's Bullet '12
The Astronaut Farmer '07
Back in Business '96
Bait '00
Ballistic: Ecks vs. Sever '02
Balls of Fury '07
Beavis and Butt-Head Do America '96
Best Men '98
Betrayed '88
A Better Way to Die '00
Big House, U.S.A. '55
Big Momma's House 2 '06
Big Momma's House '00
Big Mommas: Like Father, Like Son '11
Big Trouble '02
Bird on a Wire '90
Black Dog '98
Black Mass '15
Black Moon Rising '86
Black Sunday '77
Black Widow '87 ▶
Blade: Trinity '04
Blast '04
Bless the Child '00
Blood, Guts, Bullets and Octane '99
Blood Work '02
Bloodfist 5: Human Target '93
Boondock Saints '99
Boss of Bosses '99
Breach '07
The Breed '01
Broken Trust '95
Bugs '03
Capone '89
Caracara '00
Catch Me If You Can '02
The Cell 2 '09
The Cell '00
Certain Prey '11
Chain Reaction '96
Chasing Papi '03
CHIPS '17
Circle '10
City of Ghosts '03
Civic Duty '06
Clay Pigeons '98
The Clearing '04 ▶
The Client '94
Cloak & Dagger '84
Club Fed '90
The Company You Keep '12
Confessions of a Nazi Spy '39
Corky Romano '01
Crash and Burn '07
Crime Spree '03
Crimes of Fashion '04
The Crimson Code '99
Cry Terror! '58
Cybergeddon '12
Dead Bang '89
Dead Silence '96
Deadly Honeymoon '10
Deadly Impact '09
Death is Nimble, Death is Quick '67
Deja Vu '06
Desperate Hours '90
The Devil's Teardrop '10
Die Hard '88 ▶
Dillinger '73
Dillinger and Capone '95
Domino '05
Donnie Brasco '96 ▶
The Double '11
Double Take '01
Double Vision '02
Down Three Dark Streets '54
Eagle Eye '08
Echelon Conspiracy '09
88 Minutes '08
Eliminators '16
F/X '86 ▶
Face/Off '97 ▶
Fake '10
A Family of Spies '90
Fast Five '11
FBI Code 98 '63
FBI Girl '52
FBI: Negotiator '05
The FBI Story '59 ▶
Feds '88
Felony '95
Final Approach '08
Final Destination '00
Finish Line '08
The Firm '93 ▶
Flashback '89 ▶
Flight to Nowhere '46
The Flock '07
Follow That Car '80
Formosa Betrayed '09
Frailty '02 ▶
Full Disclosure '00
G-Force '09
'G' Men '35 ▶
Ginostra '02
The Gold Racket '37
Golden Gate '93
Government Agents vs. Phantom Legion '51
Grosse Pointe Blank '97 ▶
The Guard '11 ▶
Gun '10
Half Past Dead '02
Hannibal '01
Hard Cash '01
Harvard Man '01
The Heat '13
Hellboy '04
Hell's Bloody Devils '70
Higher Ground '88
Hollow Point '95
The House on Carroll Street '88
House on 92nd Street '45 ▶
The Hunted '03
I Was a Communist for the FBI '51
I Was a Zombie for the FBI '82
I'll Get You '53
Imperium '16
iMurders '08
In the Line of Duty: The FBI Murders '88 ▶
The Informant! '09
The Interpreter '05 ▶
Interrogation '16
J. Edgar '11
The Jackal '97
Java Heat '13
Johnnie Gibson F.B.I. '87
Justice for Natalee '11
The Kane Files '10
Kill Me Later '01
Kill Switch '08
Killer Instinct: From the Files of Agent Candice DeLong '03
Kindergarten Cop 2 '16
The Kingdom '07
The Last Shot '04
The Last Stand '13
The Last Templar '09
Lesser Evil '06
Let 'Em Have It '35
Lethal '04
Little Nikita '88
Live Wire '92
Live Wire: Human Timebomb '95
Man of the House '05
Manhunter '86 ▶
Marauders '16
Married to the Mob '88 ▶
Master Spy: The Robert Hanssen Story '02
Maximum Risk '96
Me and the Mob '94
Medium Cool '69 ▶
Melvin Purvis: G-Man '74
Mercury Rising '98
Mickey Blue Eyes '99
Midnight Run '88 ▶
Mindhunters '05
Mindstorm '01
Minutemen '08
Miss Congeniality '00
Miss Congeniality 2: Armed and Fabulous '05
Mississippi Burning '88 ▶
Molly's Game '17
Momentum '03
Most Wanted '97
My Blue Heaven '90
My Mom's New Boyfriend '08
My Son John '52
Naked Lies '98
Next '07
The Night Holds Terror '55
Night Hunter '19
No Way Back '96
Not Forgotten '09
Now You See Me '13
Nowhere Land '98
Pandemic '07
Panther '95
Parkland '13
Partners in Crime '99
Path to Paradise '97
Pickup Alley '57
Plughead Rewired: Circuitry Man 2 '94
Point Break '15
The Private Files of J. Edgar Hoover '77
Public Enemies '09
The Punisher '04
Pups '99
The Rage '96
Ransom '96 ▶
Raw Deal '86
Red Dragon '02
Red: Werewolf Hunter '10
The Reluctant Agent '89
The Return of Eliot Ness '91
Returned '15
Richard Jewell '19 ▶
Ride the Pink Horse '47 ▶
The River Murders '11
Road Ends '98
Rob the Mob '14
Robin of Locksley '95
The Rock '96 ▶
Rollercoaster '77
Runner Runner '13
Rush Hour '98
Sabotage '96
Safehouse '08
Saw 4 '07
Saw 5 '08
Saw 6 '09
Seberg '19
Secret in Their Eyes '15
Secrets of an Undercover Wife '07
See Spot Run '01
Serial Bomber '96
Shattered Image '93
Shoot to Kill '88 ▶
Shooter '07
Sicario '15 ▶
Sicario: Day of the Soldado '18
The Siege '98
The Silence of the Lambs '91 ▶
The Silencer '99
Skin '18 ▶
Slaughter of the Innocents '93
Sleeper Cell '05
Smashing the Rackets '38
Smokin' Aces '07
Smokin' Aces 2: Assassins' Ball '10
Snakes on a Plane '06
So Undercover '13
Solace '16
Spartan '04 ▶
The Stickup '01
Stolen '12
Stone Cold '91
The Stranger '10
Street Boss '09
Sugartime '95
Sunstorm '01
Surveillance '08
Suspect Zero '04
Switchback '97
Taking Lives '04
10th & Wolf '06
That Darn Cat '65
That Darn Cat '96
They Came to Blow Up America '43
This Woman Is Dangerous '52
3 Ninjas '92
Thunderheart '92 ▶
Tom Clancy's Netforce '98
Torque '04
Tortured '08
The Town '10 ▶
Trail of a Serial Killer '98
Traitor '08
Triplecross '95
Turbulence 3: Heavy Metal '00
12 Hours to Live '06
Twin Peaks: Fire Walk with Me '92
Undercover Blues '93
Undercover With the KKK '78
Union Depot '32

▶ = rated three bones or higher

U.S. Marshals '98
Unthinkable '10
The Untouchables '87 ▶
The Usual Suspects '95 ▶
Valley of the Heart's Delight '07
Walk a Crooked Mile '48
Walk East on Beacon '52
War '07
The Watcher '00
The Weather Underground '02 ▶
Whipsaw '35
White Boy Rick '18
White Chicks '04
White Sands '92
Who Is Clark Rockefeller? '10
Who Was That Lady? '60
Wild Side '95
Wind River '17 ▶
Winds of Terror '01
Wisegal '08
Witless Protection '08
The X-Files '98
The X Files: I Want to Believe '08
Zero Tolerance '93

Female Bonding

***See also** Women; Wonder Women*

Across the Moon '94
Adua and Her Friends '60
All I Wanna Do '98
Allie & Me '97
Always Shine '16 ▶
Amusement '08
Antonia's Line '95
Aquamarine '06
Ass Backwards '13
Attack on Leningrad '09
Baby Mama '08
Bachelorette '12
Bad Moms '16
Bandits '99
The Banger Sisters '02
B.A.P.'s '97
Beaches '88 ▶
Beautiful Creatures '00
Bend It Like Beckham '02 ▶
Berkeley Square '98
Best Friends '05
The Best Man Holiday '13
Best Night Ever '14
Betrayed: A Story of Three Women '95
Between Strangers '02
The Big Bad Swim '06
Black Rock '12
The Bletchley Circle '13
Blonde and Blonder '07
Blue Crush '02 ▶
Bonneville '06
Book Club '18
Boys on the Side '94
Bride Flight '08
Bride Wars '09
Bridesmaids '11 ▶
The Buccaneers '95 ▶
Burning Life '94
The Business of Strangers '01
Cadillac Ranch '96
Calendar Girls '03
Camilla '94
Caramel '07 ▶
Casa de los Babys '03 ▶
The Cemetery Club '93
Chaos '01
Charms for the Easy Life '02
Chasing Papi '03
The Cheetah Girls 2 '06
The Cheetah Girls '03
Clockwatchers '97
Cold Mountain '03 ▶
Coming Soon '99
Confessions of a Teenage Drama Queen '04
Connie and Carla '04
Cracks '09
The Craft '96
Crossroads '02
Crush '02
Damsels in Distress '11
Dancing at the Blue Iguana '00
Daughters of the Dust '91 ▶
Dead Gorgeous '02
Desert Hearts '86 ▶
Divine Secrets of the Ya-Ya Sisterhood '02
Don't Tell '05
The Double Life of Eleanor Kendall '08
Dreamgirls '06 ▶
Dreamland '06 ▶
The Dreamlife of Angels '98 ▶
8 Women '02 ▶
Emma '96 ▶
Emma '97 ▶
Evening '07
Everything Relative '96
ExTerminators '09
Falling '06
Fatal Secrets '09
The First Wives Club '96
4 Months, 3 Weeks and 2 Days '07 ▶
4.3.2.1 '10
Foxfire '96
Frances Ha '13 ▶
Freeway 2: Confessions of a Trickbaby '99
Fried Green Tomatoes '91 ▶
Friend Request '16
Friends with Money '06
G.B.F. '13
Georgia Rule '07
Getting Played '05
Girl, Interrupted '99
A Girl Thing '01
Girlhood '14 ▶
Girls Can't Swim '99
Girls Town '95
Girls Trip '17 ▶
Go For It! '10
The Heidi Chronicles '95
High Heels and Low Lifes '01
Hilary and Jackie '98 ▶
Hollywood Wives: The New Generation '03
Home Room '02 ▶
The Hot Flashes '13
The House Bunny '08
How to Make an American Quilt '95
Hustlers '19 ▶
Hysterical Blindness '02
The Ice House '97 ▶
Inconceivable '17
Irene in Time '09
Jackie, Ethel, Joan: The Kennedy Women '01
The Jane Austen Book Club '07 ▶
John Tucker Must Die '06
The Joy Luck Club '93 ▶
Joyful Noise '12
Just a Little Harmless Sex '99
Just Like a Woman '13
Keep Your Powder Dry '45
The Killing Club '01
Lace 2 '85
Lace '84
Laggies '13
Land Girls '09
The Last of the Blonde Bombshells '00
The Last Word '17
The Lemon Sisters '90
The Life Before Her Eyes '07
Life Happens '11
Life Partners '14
Lisa, Bright and Dark '73
Little Witches '96
Live-In Maid '04
Live Nude Girls '95
Living Out Loud '98
Losing Chase '96
Lovesong '17
Luminarias '99
Mad Money '08
The Magdalene Sisters '02 ▶
Mamma Mia! '08
Manny & Lo '96 ▶
Margarita Happy Hour '01
Me & Will '99
Me Without You '01
The Mermaid Chair '06
Miss Congeniality 2: Armed and Fabulous '05
Miss Pettigrew Lives for a Day '08 ▶
Miss You Already '15
Mists of Avalon '01 ▶
Mona Lisa Smile '03
Moonlight and Valentino '95
Morvern Callar '02
The Moth Diaries '11
My Little Pony: The Movie '17
9 to 5 '80
Nobody's Baby '37
Nora's Hair Salon '04
Notes on a Scandal '06 ▶
Now and Then '95
One True Thing '98 ▶
The Other Woman '14
Our Blushing Brides '30
Our Song '01 ▶
Passion Fish '92 ▶
A Perfect Ending '12
Phat Girlz '06
The Pink Conspiracy '07
Pitch Perfect 2 '15
Pitch Perfect 3 '17
Prey for Rock and Roll '03 ▶
Private Benjamin '80
Proxy '13
P.S. I Love You '07
The Red Tent '14
Redemption Trail '13
Return to Cranford '09
Revenge of the Bridesmaids '10
Rip It Off '02
Romy and Michele's High School Reunion '97
Rough Night '17
The Runaways '10
Secret Society '00
Set It Off '96
Seven Days of Grace '06
Sex and the City: The Movie '08
Sex and the City 2 '10
The Sisterhood of the Traveling Pants '05
The Sisterhood of the Traveling Pants 2 '08
The Smokers '00
Snatched '17
Snow Flower and the Secret Fan '11
Some Mother's Son '96 ▶
Some Prefer Cake '97
Spring Breakdown '08
Stand-Ins '97
Starlet '12 ▶
The Starter Wife '07
Steel Magnolias '89 ▶
Steel Magnolias '12 ▶
Stepmom '98 ▶
Stranded '06
Sucker Punch '11
Sugar & Spice '01 ▶
The Sweetest Thing '02
Tanner Hall '09
Tea with Mussolini '99
Tea with the Dames '18
Terranova '91
That's What She Said '12
Thelma & Louise '91 ▶
These Girls '05
These Old Broads '01
Things You Can Tell Just by Looking at Her '00
Thirteen '03 ▶
This Matter of Marriage '98
Thoroughbreds '17
Three Wise Girls '32
Three Wise Women '11
Toe to Toe '09
Tragedy Girls '17 ▶
Trigger '10
Two Can Play That Game '01
Two Friends '86
Tyler Perry's The Single Moms' Club '14
Under the Tuscan Sun '03
Unhook the Stars '96
Up Against the Eight Ball '04
Up the Junction '68
Uptown Girls '03
Very Good Girls '13
Vulture's Eye '04
Waiting to Exhale '95 ▶
Waitress '07 ▶
Walking and Talking '96
The Ward '10
Water '05
Wedding Bell Blues '96
The Wedding Song '09
The Well '97
Where the Heart Is '00
Whip It '09 ▶
Widows '02
Wild Child '08
Wildflowers '99
Wisegirls '02
A Woman's Guide to Adultery '93
Women '97
The Women '08
Women in Trouble '09
You and I '11
Zoe '01

Female Spies

***See also** Spy Kids; World War One Spies; World War Two Spies*

The Abductors '72
Allied '16
Atomic Blonde '17
Call Me Bwana '63
Caprice '67
C.I.A.: Code Name Alexa '92
The Court Jester '56 ▶
D.E.B.S. '04
The Exception '17
Harriet the Spy '96
Head in the Clouds '04
Inglourious Basterds '09 ▶
Mata Hari '32 ▶
Mr. & Mrs. Smith '05 ▶
Monte Carlo '86
My Favorite Blonde '42 ▶
Notorious '46 ▶
Operator 13 '34
Red Joan '19
Red Sparrow '18
Salt '10 ▶
Secret of Stamboul '36
Shining Through '92
Spy Kids 2: The Island of Lost Dreams '02 ▶
Spy Kids 3-D: Game Over '03
Spy Kids '01 ▶
The World Is Not Enough '99

Feminism

***See** Women; Wonder Women*

Femme Fatale

***See also** Wonder Women*

Addams Family Values '93
Algiers '38 ▶
All About Eve '50 ▶
The Amy Fisher Story '93
Atomic Blonde '17
Austin Powers: International Man of Mystery '97 ▶
Austin Powers 2: The Spy Who Shagged Me '99 ▶
Azumi 2 '05
Azumi '03 ▶
Bad Blonde '53
Basic Instinct 2 '06
Basic Instinct '92
Batman and Robin '97
Beautiful Beast '95
The Beguiled '17
Beverly Hills Ninja '96
Beverly Hills Vamp '88
The Big Bounce '69
Big Town '87
The Black Dahlia '06
Black Heaven '10
Black Widow '87 ▶
Blind Woman's Curse '70
Blonde Ice '48
Blood of Dracula '57
The Blood Spattered Bride '72
Blown Away '93
The Blue Angel '30 ▶
Blue Seduction '09
Blues in the Night '41
Body Heat '81 ▶
Body of Evidence '92
Body Trouble '92
Bound '96
The Bridesmaid '04
Broken Embraces '09 ▶
The Brothers Grimm '05
Brute Force '47 ▶
Buddy Boy '99
Bulletproof Heart '95 ▶
Caesar and Cleopatra '46
Cage of Evil '60
Carmen: A Hip Hopera '01
Carried Away '95
Casque d'Or '52 ▶
Champagne for Caesar '50 ▶
Chicago '27
Clash by Night '52 ▶
Clean Slate '94
Cleopatra '34
Cleopatra '63
Cleopatra '99
A Crime '06
Crime of Passion '57
Criss Cross '48 ▶
Cruel Intentions '98
Crush '93
The Crush '93
The Dallas Connection '94
The Damned Don't Cry '50
Dance Hall '41
Dangerous Ground '96
Dangerous Liaisons '88 ▶
Dangerous Liaisons '03
Dead Reckoning '47 ▶
Death Game '77
Deception '08
Decoy '46
Detour '46 ▶
The Devil's Daughter '91
Diamond Run '96
Disclosure '94
Dishonored Lady '47
Dr. Jekyll and Sister Hyde '71
Don McKay '09
Double Indemnity '44 ▶
Dream Lover '93
The Dressmaker '16
Drive a Crooked Road '54
Drowning by Numbers '87 ▶
Emmanuelle, the Queen '79
Eve of Destruction '90
Eye of the Beholder '99
The Fall '98
Fallen Angel '99
Fangs of the Living Dead '68
Far from the Madding Crowd '67 ▶
Faster, Pussycat! Kill! Kill! '65
Femme Fatale '02
The File on Thelma Jordon '50 ▶
Final Analysis '92
First Name: Carmen '83 ▶
Flame of the Islands '55
The Flesh and the Devil '27 ▶
Focus '15
A Fool There Was '14
Framed '47
Frankenhooker '90
The Gingerbread Man '97
The Girl Hunters '63
Girl in His Pocket '57
The Girl On the Train '13
Give 'Em Hell Malone '09
Great Flamarion '45
The Grifters '90 ▶
The Hard Word '02
Hellgate '89
Hit Me '96
Hostel '06
Human Desire '54
Hustlers '19 ▶
I Spit on Your Corpse '74
Impact '49 ▶
Inner Sanctum '91
Intersection '93
Into the Fire '88
Invasion of the Bee Girls '73 ▶
The Iron Mistress '52
Jay and Silent Bob Strike Back '01
The Jayne Mansfield Story '80
Jezebel '38 ▶
Kill Bill Vol. 1 '03 ▶
Kill Bill Vol. 2 '04 ▶
Kill Cruise '90
The Killers '46 ▶
Lady and the Tramp '55 ▶
Lady for a Night '42
Lady Frankenstein '72
The Lady from Shanghai '48 ▶
Lady Snowblood '73 ▶
The Lair of the White Worm '88 ▶
The Last Seduction 2 '98
The Last Seduction '94 ▶
Le Samourai '67 ▶
Leave Her to Heaven '45 ▶
The Legend of the Shadowless Sword '08
The Legend of the Wolf Woman '77
Lemora, Lady Dracula '73
Les Vampires '15 ▶
Lethal Lolita-Amy Fisher: My Story '92
Lethal Seduction '97
Lights in the Dusk '06
Like a Fish Out of Water '99
The Little Foxes '41 ▶
Lonely Hearts '06
Love Is a Gun '94
Love Sick Love '12
Love Walked In '97
The Machine '13
Mado '76 ▶
The Malibu Beach Vampires '91
Malice '93
The Maltese Falcon '41 ▶
Man, Pride and Vengeance '67
Mantis in Lace '68
Married to the Mob '88 ▶
Massacre '56
Mata Hari '32 ▶
Mata Hari '85
Medusa Against the Son of Hercules '62
Mesa of Lost Women '52
Ms. 45 '81 ▶
A Model Employee '02
Mountaintop Motel Massacre '86
Nana '55 ▶
The Natural '84 ▶
Net Games '03
Night Editor '46
The Night Evelyn Came Out of the Grave '71
Night Tide '61
The Ninth Gate '99
No Good Deed '02
No Way Out '87 ▶
Novocaine '01
An Occasional Hell '96
Of Human Bondage '34 ▶
Of Human Bondage '64
On Her Majesty's Secret Service '69 ▶
One Night at McCool's '01
The Opposite of Sex '98
Out Cold '89
Out of the Past '47 ▶
Palmetto '98
Party Girl '30
Pepe Le Moko '37 ▶
Planet of Blood '66
Playing God '96
Point of No Return '93
Poison Ivy '92
Poison Ivy 2: Lily '95
Poison Ivy 4: The Secret Society '08
The Postman Always Rings Twice '46 ▶
Pretty Poison '68 ▶
Prey of the Chameleon '91
Pushover '54
Queen Bee '55
The Quick and the Dead '95
Race Street '48
The Rage: Carrie 2 '99
A Rage in Harlem '91 ▶
Ran '85 ▶
Reckless '35
Red Sparrow '18
Roadblock '51
Rock Slyde: Private Eye '09
Salome '53
Samson and Delilah '49 ▶
Samson and Delilah '84
Samson and Delilah '96
Scandal '89 ▶
Scarlet Street '45 ▶
Schemes '95
Sea of Love '89 ▶
Second Skin '00
Secret Weapons '85
Seven Sinners '40 ▶
Sex and Death 101 '07

▶ = rated three bones or higher

The Showgirl Murders '95
Sin City: A Dame to Kill For '14
Sins of Jezebel '54
Snow White and the Seven Dwarfs '37 ▶
Some Came Running '58 ▶
Something Wild '86
Southside 1-1000 '50
The Specialist '75
Species '95
Spin a Dark Web '56
The Spirit '08
The Strange Woman '46
Sunrise '27 ▶
Sunset Boulevard '50 ▶
Suspicious Minds '96
The Temp '93
The Temptress '26
A Thin Line Between Love and Hate '96
Tomie '99
Too Late for Tears '49 ▶
The Tourist '10
Truth or Dare '91
U-Turn '97
Under Suspicion '92
Valmont '89 ▶
Vanity Fair '32
The Velvet Vampire '71
Venus in Furs '70
The Wasp Woman '59
When the Bough Breaks '16
When Will I Be Loved '04
Who Framed Roger Rabbit '88 ▶
Wicked Ways '99
Winter of Frozen Dreams '08
Woman of Desire '93
Wrongfully Accused '98
XXX: State of the Union '05

Fencing

See also Swashbucklers
The Court Jester '56 ▶
Dangerous Beauty '98 ▶
The Fencer '15 ▶
The Last Musketeer '00
Rob Roy '95 ▶
Sunshine '99

Fifties

See Period Piece: 1950s

Film Noir

See also Contemporary Noir
Act of Violence '48
Al Capone '59 ▶
Amateur '94 ▶
The American Side '16
Angel Face '52 ▶
Appointment With Danger '51
The Asphalt Jungle '50 ▶
Beyond a Reasonable Doubt '56
The Big Clock '48 ▶
Big Combo '55 ▶
The Big Heat '53 ▶
The Big Sleep '46 ▶
Black Angel '46 ▶
Black Widow '54
Blast of Silence '61
Blonde Ice '48
The Blue Dahlia '46 ▶
The Blue Gardenia '53 ▶
A Blueprint for Murder '53
Bob le Flambeur '55 ▶
Boomerang '47 ▶
Born to Kill '47 ▶
The Bribe '48
Brute Force '47 ▶
The Burglar '57
Caged '50 ▶
Calcutta '47
The Conspirators '44
Cornered '45 ▶
Crack-Up '46
Crime Wave '54
Criss Cross '48 ▶
Crossfire '47 ▶
Cry of the City '48
Dangerous Crossing '53
A Dangerous Profession '49
Dark City '50
Dark Corner '46 ▶
Dark Mirror '46 ▶
Dark Passage '47
Dark Streets '08
The Darkest Corner of Paradise '10
David Harding, Counterspy '50
Dead Again '91 ▶
Dead Awake '01
Deadline at Dawn '46
Decoy '46
Desperate '47
Destination Murder '50
Detour '46 ▶
D.O.A. '49 ▶
Don't Bother to Knock '52
Double Indemnity '44 ▶
Drive a Crooked Road '54
The Element of Crime '84
The Enforcer '51
Fallen Angel '45
Farewell, My Lovely '75 ▶
Fear in the Night '47 ▶
Female On the Beach '55
The File on Thelma Jordon '50 ▶
Force of Evil '49 ▶
Framed '47
Frantic '58 ▶
The Frontier '16
Gilda '46 ▶
The Glass Key '42 ▶
Gotham '88 ▶
Grand Central Murder '42
Gun Crazy '49 ▶
He Walked by Night '48 ▶
Hell's Half Acre '54
High & Low '62 ▶
High Sierra '41 ▶
Highway 301 '50
The Hitch-Hiker '53 ▶
House of Bamboo '55
Human Desire '54
The Hunted '48
I Wouldn't Be in Your Shoes '48
In a Lonely Place '50 ▶
Jericho '15 ▶
Jigsaw '49 ▶
Johnny O'Clock '47
Key Largo '48 ▶
The Killer Is Loose '56
The Killer That Stalked New York '47
The Killers '46 ▶
Killer's Kiss '55
The Killing '56 ▶
King Creole '58
Kiss Me Deadly '55 ▶
Kiss of Death '47 ▶
The Lady from Shanghai '48 ▶
Lady in the Lake '46
Laura '44 ▶
Le Doulos '61 ▶
Leave Her to Heaven '45 ▶
Lightning Strikes Twice '51
The Long Night '47
Loophole '54
Macao '52 ▶
The Maltese Falcon '41 ▶
Man in the Vault '56
The Man Who Cheated Himself '50
The Mask of Dimitrios '44 ▶
Mikey & Nicky '76
Mildred Pierce '45 ▶
Ministry of Fear '44 ▶
Mr. District Attorney '41
The Mob '51
Motherless Brooklyn '19
Murder, My Sweet '44 ▶
Mystery Street '50
The Naked City '48 ▶
Naked Kiss '64
The Narrow Margin '52 ▶
Niagara '52
Night and the City '50 ▶
Night Editor '46
Nightfall '56 ▶
Nightmare Alley '47
99 River Street '53
No Orchids for Miss Blandish '48
Nobody Lives Forever '46 ▶
Nocturne '46
Nora Prentiss '47
Obsession '49
Odds Against Tomorrow '59 ▶
On Dangerous Ground '51 ▶
Our Man in Havana '59 ▶
Out of the Past '47 ▶
Over-Exposed '56
Panic in the Streets '50 ▶
Phantom Lady '44 ▶
Phoenix '14 ▶
The Phenix City Story '55 ▶
Pickup on South Street '53 ▶
Plunder Road '57
The Poison Rose '19
Portland Expose '57
Portrait of an Assassin '49
The Postman Always Rings Twice '46 ▶
The Postman Always Rings Twice '81
The Pretender '47
The Prowler '51
Railroaded '47
Raw Deal '48 ▶
The Red House '47 ▶
Rendez-vous '85 ▶
Ride the Pink Horse '47 ▶
Road House '48
Roadblock '51
Rope '48 ▶
Scandal Sheet '52
The Scar '48
Scarlet Street '45 ▶
Serenity '19
The Set-Up '49 ▶
Shockproof '49
Side Street '50
Signal 7 '83
Sleep, My Love '48
So Dark the Night '46
Somewhere in the Night '46
Sorry, Wrong Number '48 ▶
Southside 1-1000 '50
Stage Struck '48
Stolen Face '52
Story of a Love Affair '50
Strange Illusion '45
Strange Impersonation '46
The Strange Love of Martha Ivers '46 ▶
Sudden Fear '52 ▶
Sunset Boulevard '50 ▶
Sweet Smell of Success '57 ▶
T-Men '47 ▶
Tension '50
They Live by Night '49 ▶
The Third Man '49 ▶
This Gun for Hire '42 ▶
Three Strangers '46
3-Way '04
Too Late for Tears '49 ▶
Touch of Evil '58 ▶
Two of a Kind '51
Under the Silver Lake '18
Undercurrent '46
Undertow '49
Underworld U.S.A. '61 ▶
The Unsuspected '47
Violence '47
Violent Saturday '55
Where Danger Lives '50
Where the Sidewalk Ends '50
While the City Sleeps '56 ▶
Whirlpool '49
White Heat '49 ▶
The Window '49 ▶
Witness to Murder '54
Woman in Hiding '49
The Woman on the Beach '47
World for Ransom '54
The Wrong Man '56 ▶

Filmmaking

See also At the Movies; Behind the Scenes
Abbott and Costello Meet the Keystone Kops '54
The Adjuster '91
An Alan Smithee Film: Burn, Hollywood, Burn '97
Alexandria Again and Forever '90
All the Wrong Places '00
An Almost Perfect Affair '79
An American Carol '08
American Grindhouse '10
American Movie '99 ▶
And Everything Is Going Fine '10
. . .And God Spoke '94
And Starring Pancho Villa as Himself '03 ▶
Ararat '02 ▶
Art House '98
Baadasssss! '03 ▶
Backslash '05
Barton Fink '91 ▶
Be Kind Rewind '08
The Beaches of Agnes '08
Beautiful Losers '08
Becoming Mike Nichols '16
Berberian Sound Studio '12
Best Worst Movie '09 ▶
Beyond the Clouds '95
The Black Water Vampire '13
The Blair Witch Project '99
Bloodbath in Psycho Town '89
Body Chemistry 3: Point of Seduction '93
Bombay Talkie '70
Boogie Vision '77
Bowfinger '99 ▶
Brigsby Bear '17
Café Society '16
Cameraperson '16 ▶
Camp Dread '14
Cannes Man '96
Charlotte Rampling: The Look '11
Chasing Ghosts '14
Children Shouldn't Play with Dead Things '72
Cinema Verite '11
Contempt '64 ▶
The Cool Surface '92
CQ '01
Creep '15
Dangerous Game '93
Danny Roane: First Time Director '06
David Holzman's Diary '67 ▶
The Day He Arrives '11
De Palma '16 ▶
The Dead Hate the Living '99
A Decade Under the Influence '02 ▶
Deep in the Heart (of Texas) '98
The Disaster Artist '17 ▶
Dolemite Is My Name '19 ▶
Don Quixote '92
Ed Wood '94 ▶
Eisenstein in Guanajuato '15
Elvis in Hollywood '93 ▶
Entourage '15
Exit Through the Gift Shop '10
F/X 2: The Deadly Art of Illusion '91
Father of My Children '09
Fellini: I'm a Born Liar '03
Festival at Cannes '02
Film Geek '06
Film Socialisme '10
A Film Unfinished '10
Final Cut '88
The Final Project '16
Five Came Back '17 ▶
Flickers '80
Full Tilt Boogie '97
Geek Charming '11
Get Shorty '95 ▶
Gosford Park '01 ▶
Gossip '00
Hail, Caesar! '16 ▶
Hal '18 ▶
Hearts of Darkness: A Filmmaker's Apocalypse '91 ▶
Hi, Mom! '70 ▶
Hit and Runway '01
Hitchcock '12
Hitchcock/Truffaut '15
Hotel '01
The House of Seven Corpses '73
How It All Went Down '03
How to Eat Your Watermelon in White Company (and Enjoy It) '05 ▶
How to Make a Monster '58
I Want Candy '07
Identification of a Woman '82
I'll Do Anything '93
Intervista '87 ▶
Iron Cowboy '68
It's All True '93
Jay and Silent Bob Reboot '19
The Kid Stays in the Picture '02 ▶
King Cobra '16
Kisses in the Dark '97
La Petite Lili '03
The Last Broadcast '98 ▶
The Last Porno Flick '74
Let's Make a Movie '11
The Life of Lucky Cucumber '08
Living in Oblivion '94 ▶
Loaded '94
Lost Behind Bars '06
Lost in La Mancha '03 ▶
The Lovers and the Despot '16
The M Word '14
The Man Who Killed Don Quixote '18
Me and Earl and the Dying Girl '15 ▶
Mia Madre '16
The Mirror Crack'd '80
Mr. X: Leos Carax '14 ▶
Mistress '91
The Moon & the Stars '07
Movie 43 '13
Mute Witness '95
My Dream Is Yours '49
My Life's in Turnaround '94
Nightmare in Blood '75
Nightmare in Wax '69
Of Time and the City '08
On an Island with You '48
One Hundred and One Nights '95
Operation Avalanche '16
The Other Side of the Wind '18
Overnight '03 ▶
Pain and Glory '19 ▶
Passion '82
The People *vs.* George Lucas '10
The Pickle '93
Pipe Dream '02
The Player '92 ▶
The Pornographer '00
Raiders!: The Story of the Greatest Fan Film Ever Made '16 ▶
RKO 281 '99 ▶
Rules Don't Apply '16
Safari Drums '53
Safe Conduct '01 ▶
The Search for One-Eye Jimmy '94
Secret File of Hollywood '62
Seed of Chucky '04
78/52: Hitchcock's Shower Scene '17 ▶
Sex is Comedy '02
Shoot or Be Shot '02
A Slave of Love '78 ▶
Slaves of Hollywood '99
Souls for Sale '23
Sound of My Voice '11
The Souvenir '19 ▶
Special Effects '85
Spenser: A Savage Place '94
Stand-In '85
Storytelling '01 ▶
The Stunt Man '80 ▶
Sullivan's Travels '41 ▶
The Swap '71
Sweet Liberty '86
Swimming with Sharks '94 ▶
The Tale '18 ▶
The Tango Lesson '97
Teeth and Blood '15
Their Finest '17 ▶
To Be Fat Like Me '07
Tristram Shandy: A Cock and Bull Story '05
Two Weeks in Another Town '62
Ulysses' Gaze '95
Venice, Venice '92
Vigilante Diaries '16
Visions of Light: The Art of Cinematography '93 ▶
Voyage to the Beginning of the World '96 ▶
We Can't Go Home Again '73
Wes Craven's New Nightmare '94 ▶
Where's Marlowe? '98
White Hunter, Black Heart '90 ▶
Who the Hell is Juliette? '98
You Know My Name '99 ▶
You Must Remember This '92

Firemen

See also Fires
Ablaze '00
The Accidental Husband '08
Always '89
Backdraft '91
Be My Valentine '13
Blast '04
Burn '12 ▶
Club Paradise '86
Collateral Damage '02
Evolution '01
Fahrenheit 451 '66 ▶
15 Minutes '01
Fire Serpent '07
Fire With Fire '12
Firefight '03
Firefighter '86
Firehouse '72
Firehouse '87
Firehouse Dog '07
Firelight '12
The Firemen's Ball '68 ▶
Fireproof '08
Firestorm '97
For the Love of Grace '08
Frequency '00
The Guys '02 ▶
Hellfighters '68
I Do (But I Don't) '04
I Heart Huckabees '04
I Now Pronounce You Chuck and Larry '07
Just One Time '00
The King of Staten Island '20
Ladder 49 '04
Mercury Man '06
Miss March '09
Only the Brave '17 ▶
Out of the Inferno '13
Playing with Fire '19
Point of Origin '02
Red Skies of Montana '52
Reign of Fire '02
Roxanne '87 ▶
Sheeba '05
Smoke Jumpers '08
Trespass '92
Turk 182! '85
World Trade Center '06 ▶

Fires

See also Boom!; Disaster Flicks; Firemen
Ablaze '00
Always '89
Backdraft '91
Bellflower '11
Blue Smoke '07
The Burning Bed '85 ▶
The Burning Plain '08
Burning Rage '84
Carrie '76 ▶
The Claim '00
The Cremators '72
Dinosaurus! '60
Don't Go in the House '80
Endless Love '81
Face of Fire '59
Fire '77
Fire From Below '09
Fire Serpent '07
Fire With Fire '12
Fireball '09
Firefight '03
Firehead '90
Firestarter 2: Rekindled '02
Firestarter '84
Firestorm '97
Firetrap '01
Flashfire '94
For the Love of Grace '08
Frankenstein '31 ▶
Ghost Rider '07
Ghost Rider: Spirit of Vengeance '12
God's Not Dead: A Light in Darkness '18
Hellboy II: The Golden Army '08 ▶
In Old Chicago '37 ▶

▶ = rated three bones or higher

Inferno '01
Interview with the Vampire '94
Island of the Burning Doomed '67
Ladder 49 '04
The Lion King '94 ▸
Little Girl Lost: The Delimar Vera Story '08
Little Men '98
Look Who's Talking, Too '90
Meet the Parents '00 ▸
Mighty Joe Young '49
Night Alarm '34
Oil '78
Only the Brave '17 ▸
Out of the Inferno '13
The Outsiders '83
Planes: Fire & Rescue '14
Point of Origin '02
Pretty Poison '68 ▸
Promare '19
A Pyromaniac's Love Story '95
Quest for Fire '82 ▸
Rain or Shine '30
Red Skies of Montana '52
Rosewood '96 ▸
Save the Tiger '73 ▸
Skyscraper '18
Smoke Jumpers '08
Specimen '97
Spontaneous Combustion '89
Subversion '79
SuperFire '02
Terror on the 40th Floor '74
Ticks '93
The Towering Inferno '74
Trash Fire '16
Trial by Fire '18
The Triangle Factory Fire Scandal '79
12 and Holding '05 ▸
Unthinkable '07
Volcano '97
Wilder Napalm '93
Wildfire 7: The Inferno '02
Wildlife '18 ▸
The Witness '99
The Woman on the Beach '47

The First Time

***See also** Sex & Sexuality*

American Pie '99 ▸
American Pie Presents: Book of Love '09
Bart Got a Room '08
Biloxi Blues '88
Blue Lagoon: The Awakening '12
Carrie Pilby '17 ▸
The Crime of Father Amaro '02 ▸
Date and Switch '13
December Boys '07
Dreaming About You '92
Driving Lessons '06
Easy A '10 ▸
An Education '09 ▸
Equals '16
Everything, Everything '17
Fast Times at Ridgemont High '82 ▸
The First Time '12
Food of Love '02
Getting It '06
Ginger and Cinnamon '03
The House of Tomorrow '18
Juno '07 ▸
The Last Request '06
Losin' It '82
Lymelife '08
Marie Antoinette '06
Meet Monica Velour '10
Miss March '09
My Tutor '82
National Lampoon's Adam & Eve '05
Nico and Dani '00
Now Is Good '12
Porky's '82
Pretty Baby '78 ▸
The Reader '08
Risky Business '83 ▸
The Rules of Attraction '02
Running with Scissors '06
Sade '00
The Sessions '12 ▸
Sex Drive '08
Sex Ed '14
Skipped Parts '00
Submarine '10 ▸
Tadpole '02
Take a Girl Like You '70
The Ten '07
The To Do List '13
Very Good Girls '13
The Virginity Hit '10
The Wackness '08
White Bird in a Blizzard '14
Wild Cherry '09
Young & Beautiful '13
The Young Kieslowski '15

Flashback

Absolution '05
Adam Resurrected '08
Adoration '08
Against the Current '09
Albert's Memorial '09
All In '06
All Over the Guy '01
All the King's Men '06
Alpha Male '06
Amazing Grace '06 ▸
America '09
American Beauty '99 ▸
Americano '11
Amores Perros '00 ▸
Amour '12 ▸
Anglo-Saxon Attitudes '92
Anne Rice's The Feast of All Saints '01
Antonia's Line '95
Antwone Fisher '02 ▸
Appointment With Death '10
Appropriate Behavior '14
Ararat '02 ▸
The Army of Crime '10
Autumn Hearts: A New Beginning '07
Back of Beyond '95
Backfire '50
Bad Timing: A Sensual Obsession '80
Badla '19
The Bamboo Blonde '46
Bandits '01
Barney's Version '10
Batman Forever '95 ▸
Beau Geste '39 ▸
Beau Travail '98
Beautiful Kate '09 ▸
Behind Enemy Lines 2: Axis of Evil '06
Behind the Red Door '02
Being Flynn '12
Bella '06
Belles on Their Toes '52
Beloved '98
Best Laid Plans '99
Best Man Down '12
The Best of Me '14
Beverly Lewis' The Shunning '11
Beyond Borders '03
Beyond Victory '31
Big Fish '03 ▸
The Big Shot '42
Billy Lynn's Long Halftime Walk '16
Birdsong '12
Black Book '06 ▸
Black Christmas '06
The Blackcoat's Daughter '17
Blackout '07
Blackthorn '11
Blind Faith '98
Blood Brothers '07
Blood Creek '09
Blue Valentine '10
Bonanno: A Godfather's Story '99
Bonded by Blood '09
Boondock Saints '99
Born Killers '05
Boss of Bosses '99
Boy A '07
Boy Wonder '10
Boys '95
Brand Upon the Brain! '06 ▸
Breaking Up '97
Bright Lights '30
The Broken '08
Broken Embraces '09 ▸
Broken Harvest '94
Brothers Three '07
Brush with Fate '03
The Brutal Truth '99
Bullhead '11
Bunny and the Bull '09
Burning Man '11
The Business of Fancydancing '02
Buster's Mal Heart '17
The Caller '08
The Camomile Lawn '92
Camp Dread '14
Can't Hardly Wait '98
The Captive City '52
Carbine Williams '52
Carmen '03
Carrie '02
Carried Away '95
Casablanca '42 ▸
Casanova '05 ▸
Catch Me If You Can '02
Catch.44 '11
Catfish in Black Bean Sauce '00
Cell 2455, Death Row '55
Cell 211 '09
Cello '05
Cement '99
Chaos Theory '08
Character '97
Charming Billy '98
Chasing 3000 '07
Chicken With Plums '11
The Chorus '04
Citizen Kane '41 ▸
Cleanskin '12
Closing the Ring '07
Coco Chanel '08
Coldwater '14
Come and Find Me '16
Come Undone '00
Company Man '00
The Concert '09
The Constant Gardener '05 ▸
Courage Under Fire '96 ▸
Cover '08
Crash Landing '58
Creation '09
Criminal Lovers '99
The Crowded Sky '60
Dad Savage '97
Danny Roane: First Time Director '06
Dark Blue World '01
Dawn at Socorro '54
The Debt '07
The Debt '10
Deceit '06
December Boys '07
Decoy '46
Deeply '99
Definitely, Maybe '08 ▸
Desire Me '47
The Devil Is a Woman '35 ▸
The Devil You Know '05
Diary of a Suicide '73
The Diplomat '08
Dirty Tricks '00
The Disappearance of Garcia Lorca '96
Divine Secrets of the Ya-Ya Sisterhood '02
The Diving Bell and the Butterfly '07 ▸
A Dog Named Christmas '09
Dogfight '91 ▸
Dolores Claiborne '94 ▸
Don Juan (Or If Don Juan Were a Woman) '73
Don't Look Up '08
Don't Tell '05
Drew Peterson: Untouchable '12
Drifter '09
Drowning Mona '00
Dust '01
Eat, Pray, Love '10
Eddie and the Cruisers '83
Edward Scissorhands '90 ▸
Eichmann '07
Eighteen '04
El Cantante '06
Emile '03
The Emperor's Club '02
Eternity and a Day '97
Evening '07
Event Horizon '97
Eve's Bayou '97 ▸
Exotica '94 ▸
Extraordinary Rendition '07
Eye of God '97 ▸
Facing Windows '03 ▸
Faithless '00 ▸
Fallen Angel '03
A Family Thing '96 ▸
Far North '07
Far Side of the Moon '03
Fatal Deception: Mrs. Lee Harvey Oswald '93
Fate Is the Hunter '64
Fear and Loathing in Las Vegas '98
Fedora '78
Fever Pitch '96
Fight Club '99 ▸
Final '01
Finding Home '03
Fireflies in the Garden '08
Flags of Our Fathers '06 ▸
Flashbacks of a Fool '08
Flick '07
Flight From Ashiya '64
The Forbidden Quest '93
Forget Me Not '09
The Forgotten '04
Four Boys and a Gun '57
Four Corners of Suburbia '05
The 4th Dimension '06
Frailty '02 ▸
Frankie and Alice '10
Friday the Thirteenth '33
From Above '13
Fur: An Imaginary Portrait of Diane Arbus '06
Gangster No. 1 '00
Genealogies of a Crime '97
The General '98 ▸
The General's Daughter '99
Ghosted '09
G.I. Joe: The Rise of Cobra '09
Gifted Hands: The Ben Carson Story '09
Girl of the Night '60
The Girl On the Train '13
The Girl on the Train '16
Gloomy Sunday '02 ▸
God is My Co-Pilot '45
The Goddess of 1967 '00
The Godfather, Part 2 '74 ▸
Godmoney '97
Gods and Monsters '98 ▸
Good '08
The Good Guy '10
Good Morning, Miss Dove '55
The Good Shepherd '06
A Good Year '06
Graduation '07
The Grand Budapest Hotel '14 ▸
The Great Water '04
Green Lantern '11
Greetings from Tim Buckley '12
Grey Owl '99
Grimm Love '06
Grizzly Falls '99
Guantanamero '07
A Guide to Recognizing Your Saints '06
The Halliday Brand '57
Halloween II '09
Handsome Harry '09
Hanging By a Thread '79
The Hanging Garden '97
Haywire '80
Headspace '02
Heart '99
The Heart of Me '02
Heartless '10
Hearts in Atlantis '01
Hedwig and the Angry Inch '00 ▸
Helas pour Moi '94
Hellraiser 4: Bloodline '95
Hemingway & Gelhorn '12
Henry Poole Is Here '08 ▸
Hero '02 ▸
Hero Wanted '08
The Hi-Lo Country '98
Hidden '05 ▸
Hidden '09
High Fidelity '00 ▸
Highlander: Endgame '00
Hiroshima, Mon Amour '59 ▸
Hitman '07
H.M. Pulham Esquire '41
The Hole '01
Holes '03 ▸
Hollywoodland '06
A Home at the End of the World '04
Horatio Hornblower: The Adventure Continues '01 ▸
Horns '13
A Horrible Way to Die '10
Houdini '98
Hours '13
How I Killed My Father '03 ▸
The Human Stain '03
The Hunted '03
I Dream of Murder '06
I Give It a Year '13
I Served the King of England '07 ▸
I Was Happy Here '66
I'm Glad My Mother Is Alive '09
In His Life: The John Lennon Story '00
In Praise of Love '01
In the Family '11
Incendies '10 ▸
Inferno '99
The Inheritance '10
Inside Men '12
Instinct '99
The Insurance Man '86
Into the Wild '07 ▸
An Invisible Sign '11
Invitation '51
Jackie's Back '99
Jacob's Ladder '90
Jane Eyre '11
Jennifer On My Mind '71
Jerry and Tom '98
Jesse Stone: Innocents Lost '11
Jet Li's Fearless '06
John Dies at the End '12
John John in the Sky '00
Johnny Dangerously '84
Julie & Julia '09 ▸
Julieta '16
Just Another Love Story '08
Just Married '03
Kalamity '10
Karla '06
Keep the Faith, Baby '02
Keillers Park '05
The Kennedys '11
Kicking and Screaming '95 ▸
Killing Bono '11
Killing Season '13
Lace 2 '85
Lace '84
Ladder 49 '04
The Lady Gambles '49
Lansky '99
The Last Circus '10
The Last Letter '04
Last Orders '01 ▸
The Last Posse '53
Last Ride '09
The Last Templar '09
The Lawless Breed '52 ▸
Leave Her to Heaven '45 ▸
The Ledge '11
Legacy '10
The Legend of Bagger Vance '00
The Legend of Lizzie Borden '75 ▸
The Legend of Lylah Clare '68
The Legend of 1900 '98
Lennon Naked '10
Les Voleurs '96 ▸
Letter from an Unknown Woman '48 ▸
Liebestraum '91
Life '99
The Life Before Her Eyes '07
The Life Before This '99
The Life of David Gale '03
Life Tastes Good '99
Lilting '14 ▸
Lime Salted Love '06
The Little Prince '16 ▸
Lizzie '18
The Locket '46
The Lone Ranger '13
Lone Star '95 ▸
The Long Night '47
The Lords of Salem '13
The Loss of Sexual Innocence '98
The Lost Valentine '11
Love Come Down '00
Love Letters '99 ▸
Lumumba '01 ▸
Mad Love '01
Man Down '16
A Man to Remember '38
Maniac '12
Mao's Last Dancer '09
Marilyn Hotchkiss' Ballroom Dancing & Charm School '06
A Marine Story '10
The Marrying Kind '52
Martha Marcy May Marlene '11 ▸
A Matador's Mistress '08
Matango '63
Maybe I'll Come Home in the Spring '71
McCanick '14
Memento '00 ▸
Memorial Day '12
Men On Her Mind '44
Mercy '09
Mesrine: Part 2-Public Enemy Number 1 '08
Middle Men '10
Midnight Mary '33
Miracle at St. Anna '08
Mrs. Dalloway '97
Mrs. Harris '05
Mr. Peabody & Sherman '14
Mr. Woodcock '07
Mitch Albom's Have a Little Faith '11
The Moment '13
Mongol '07 ▸
Monsieur N. '03 ▸
The Mortician '11
The Motel Life '12
Mother Night '96 ▸
Mother of Mine '05 ▸
Murder at Devil's Glen '99
Murder in Greenwich '02
Murder in the Hamptons '05
Murderous Intent '06 ▸
My Brother '06
My Name is Modesty: A Modesty Blaise Adventure '04
My Son, My Son, What Have Ye Done '09
The Mystery of a Hansom Cab '12
The Neon Bible '95
Never Been Kissed '99
New Blood '99
Night Editor '46
Night Train to Lisbon '13
Nightmare '07
Nina Takes a Lover '94
The 19th Wife '10
The Ninth Configuration '79 ▸
Nobody Else But You '11
Nora's Will '09
Norman Rockwell's Shuffleton's Barbershop '13
The Note '07
Notes on a Scandal '06 ▸
Now and Then '95
Nymphomaniac, Volume 1 '13
Obsessed '09
Oculus '14
Once Upon a Time in America '84 ▸
Once Upon a Time in Mexico '03 ▸
One Day You'll Understand '08
One Sunday Afternoon '33
Only Love '98
Only Yesterday '16 ▸
Operation Secret '52
Oriana '85
Oscar and Lucinda '97
Outlander '08
The Outrage '64
The Owls '09
Paid in Full '02
Pain and Glory '19 ▸
Passage to Marseilles '44 ▸
The Pastor's Wife '11
Payment on Demand '51

▸ = *rated three bones or higher*

Perestroika '09
The Perfume of Yvonne '94
Perfume: The Story of a Murderer '06
Permanent Midnight '98
Peter Ibbetson '35
The Phantom Carriage '21 ▸
The Phantom of Crestwood '32
The Phantom of Hollywood '74
Pilot No. 5 '43
Place of Execution '09
Potiche '10 ▸
The Power and the Glory '33
Premonition '07
Pretty Village, Pretty Flame '96 ▸
The Private Lives of Pippa Lee '09
Private Peaceful '12
The Proposition '97
P.S. I Love You '07
Psych: 9 '10
Racing Daylight '07
A Rather English Marriage '98
The Razor's Edge '46 ▸
The Razor's Edge '84
The Reader '08
Red Meat '98
Red Riding, Part 3: 1983 '09
Red Roses and Petrol '03
The Red Violin '98
Remarkable Power '08
Remember the Day '41
Reservoir Dogs '92 ▸
Respire '09
The Return '06
Ricky Nelson: Original Teen Idol '99
The Riddle '07
The Rising Place '02
The Road '09
The Road Home '01 ▸
Road Trip: Beer Pong '09
Romy and Michele's High School Reunion '97
The Rules of Attraction '02
Runaway '05
Ruthless '48
The Safety of Objects '01
Salem's Lot '04
The Salton Sea '02
Sarah's Key '10
Saw 3 '06
Saw 3D: The Final Chapter '10
Saw 4 '07
Saw 5 '08
Sea Wife '57
Secondhand Lions '03
A Secret '07 ▸
The Secrets of the Summer House '08
The Sensation of Sight '06
Sergeant Rutledge '60 ▸
Seven Pounds '08
Sex & Drugs & Rock & Roll '10
Sex & Lies in Sin City: The Ted Binion Scandal '08
Sex and Lucia '01
Shake Hands With the Devil '07
Shattered '91
The Shell Seekers '06
Sherlock Holmes '10
Shining Through '92
Short Night of Glass Dolls '71
Shot in the Heart '01 ▸
Simon Birch '98
Simpatico '99
Sister Aimee: The Aimee Semple McPherson Story '06
The Skin I Live In '11
Slattery's Hurricane '49
SLC Punk! '99
Slow Burn '05
Slumdog Millionaire '08 ▸
Smoke Signals '98
Snapshots '02
Snow Angels '07 ▸
Snow Falling on Cedars '99
Snow Flower and the Secret Fan '11
So Well Remembered '47
Solaris '02
The Son of No One '11
Son of Sam '08
South Sea Woman '53
Spider '02 ▸
Spy Game '01
Steal This Movie! '00
Stealing Home '88
Stella Does Tricks '96
Stephanie Daley '06
Stephen King's It '90
Stolen '09
The Stone Angel '07
Stoned '05
The Stoning of Soraya M. '08
Storm Seekers '08
Straight into Darkness '04
The Stranger '10
Stricken '98
The String '09
Submergence '18
A Summer in Genoa '08
Sun Choke '16
Sweet and Lowdown '99
Sweet Nothing in My Ear '08
Swept from the Sea '97
Swindled '04
T-Men '47 ▸
Tamara Drewe '10
Tangled '01
Tell No One '06 ▸
Temple Grandin '10 ▸
The Tenant of Wildfell Hall '96
Tetro '09
A Texas Funeral '99
That Evening Sun '09 ▸
There Be Dragons '11
There's Something about Mary '98 ▸
Things We Lost in the Fire '07
13 '10
This Is My Father '99
Though None Go With Me '06
Till Human Voices Wake Us '02
Total Eclipse '95
Trap for Cinderella '13
Trespass '11
The Truth '10
Tuck Everlasting '02
28 Days '00
Twice Born '12
Two for the Road '67 ▸
Two Friends '86
Two Seconds '32
The Ugly '96
The Ultimate Life '13
Unbreakable '00
Under Heavy Fire '01
The Underneath '95 ▸
Universal Squadrons '11
The Unknown Woman '06
Untamed Women '52
The Upturned Glass '47
Urbania '00
The Usual Suspects '95 ▸
The Valachi Papers '72
Valentino '77
Valerie '57
Velvet Goldmine '98
Waiting for Forever '11
Walkabout '71 ▸
Ward No. 6 '09
The Watch '08
The Way '10
W.E. '11
The Wedding Party '97
The Weekend '00
The Weight of Water '00
Weirdsville '07
Welcome to Collinwood '02
Went to Coney Island on a Mission from God. . . Be Back by Five '98
What Dreams May Come '98
When Did You Last See Your Father? '07
White Night Wedding '08
Who is Cletis Tout? '02
Why Do Fools Fall in Love? '98
The Wicker Man '06
Wicker Park '04
Wild '14 ▸
Wild Bill '95
The Wild Bunch '69 ▸
With a Song in My Heart '52 ▸
Within Our Gates '20
Witness for the Prosecution '57 ▸
The Wood '99
The Words '12
Wozzeck '47
Wyatt Earp's Revenge '12
X-Men: First Class '11 ▸
The Year of Getting to Know Us '08
Zone 39 '96

Flatulence

Austin Powers: International Man of Mystery '97 ▸
Austin Powers In Goldmember '02
Beavis and Butt-Head Do America '96
Bio-Dome '96
Blazing Saddles '74 ▸
Dr. Dolittle '98
Dr. Dolittle 2 '01
Dumb & Dumber '94
Ed '96
Friday After Next '02
Grumpier Old Men '95
Jay and Silent Bob Strike Back '01
A Knight's Tale '01
Larry the Cable Guy: Health Inspector '06
The Lion King '94 ▸
Lost and Found '99
The Love Guru '08
Major Payne '95
Mystery Men '99
National Lampoon's Senior Trip '95
Nutty Professor 2: The Klumps '00
The Nutty Professor '96 ▸
Osmosis Jones '01
Rain Man '88 ▸
The Road to Wellville '94
RocketMan '97
The Santa Clause '94
Spy Kids 4: All the Time in the World '11
Sugar & Spice '01 ▸

Flight

See Airborne

Flood

See also Disaster Flicks

The Day After Tomorrow '04
Flood! '76
Flood '07
Flood: A River's Rampage '97
Hard Rain '97
Heroes of the Heart '94
An Inconvenient Sequel: Truth to Power '17
The Last of the Mobile Hot-shots '69
The Last Wave '77 ▸
Lost City Raiders '08
Noah '14
Noah's Ark '99
Other Men's Women '31
The Rains Came '39
The River '84
Saving Grace B. Jones '09
Terror in the Mall '98
Thunder on the Hill '51
Torrent '26
Waterworld '95
The Winning of Barbara Worth '26

Florence

See also Italy

Light in the Piazza '61
Madonna of the Seven Moons '45
Obsession '76
Romola '25
A Room with a View '86 ▸
A Room With a View '08
Tea with Mussolini '99
Up at the Villa '00
Virgin Territory '07

Florida

See also American South; Miami

Adaptation '02 ▸
American Son '19
Aquamarine '06
Automaton Transfusion '06
Bart Got a Room '08
The Beach Bum '19
Because of Winn-Dixie '05
Bending All the Rules '02
Big Leaguer '53
Birds Do It '66
Blue Car '03 ▸
Blue City '86
Body Heat '81 ▸
The Boynton Beach Club '05
Bully '01
Canvas '06
The Chaos Experiment '09
Christine '16
Coastlines '02
Crawl '19
The Devil's Advocate '97
Dolphin Tale 2 '14
Dolphin Tale '11
Doorway to Hell '30
Elmore Leonard's Gold Coast '97
Endure '10
Escape From Tomorrow '13
Fascination '04
A Flash of Green '85
The Florida Project '17 ▸
Follow That Dream '61
Free Ride '13
Gidget Gets Married '72
Girl Missing '33
A Golden Christmas 2: The Second Tail '11
Grace Is Gone '07 ▸
Great Expectations '97
The Gun Runners '58
The Hawk Is Dying '06
The Heart Specialist '06
Heartbreakers '01
Hello Down There '69
Honky Tonk Freeway '81
House of Wax '05
I'll Believe You '07
In Her Shoes '05 ▸
Infamous '20
Juke Girl '42
Just Cause '94
Kate Plays Christine '16 ▸
Larry the Cable Guy: Health Inspector '06
Like Dandelion Dust '09
Live by Night '16
Marley & Me '08
Meet the Fockers '04
Mega Python Vs. Gatoroid '11
Miami Blues '90
Monster '03 ▸
Murder.com '08
Never Back Down '08
Night Unto Night '49
Off Season '01
Out of Time '03
Over 21 '45
Pain & Gain '13
Palmetto '98
The Paperboy '12
The Parent Trap II '86
The Perfect Wedding '12
Porky's 2: The Next Day '83
Porky's '82
Porky's Revenge '85
Prosecuting Casey Anthony '13
The Queen of Versailles '12 ▸
Race to Space '01
Raging Hormones '99
Recount '08
The Return of the Swamp Thing '89
River of Grass '94
The Riverman '04
Rosewood '96 ▸
Seminole '53
A Short History of Decay '13
The Sleepy Time Gal '01
Still Green '07
Storm Seekers '08
Sun Don't Shine '12
Sunday Dinner for a Soldier '44
Sunlight Jr. '13
Sunshine State '02 ▸
Terror Inside '08
Things Behind the Sun '01
Two Tickets to Paradise '06
Ulee's Gold '97 ▸
Waves '19 ▸
Wild Things 2 '04
Wild Things 3: Diamonds in the Rough '05
Wild Things '98
Wild Things: Foursome '10
Wrestling with Alligators '98
The Year of Getting to Know Us '08
The Yearling '46 ▸
The Yearling '94

Flying Saucers

See Alien Babes; Alien Beings--Benign; Alien Beings--Vicious; Alien Cops; Aliens Are People, Too; Out of This World Sex; Space Operas

Folklore & Legends

See also Storytelling

Abominable '06
Abominable '19
Aladdin '19
Almighty Thor '11
Assassin's Creed '16
Ben-Hur '16
Beowulf & Grendel '06
Black Orpheus '58 ▸
Blair Witch '16
The Blair Witch Project '99
Bluebeard '09
Bone Eater '07
The Book of Life '14
Brotherhood of the Wolf '01
The Brothers Grimm '05
Candyman 2: Farewell to the Flesh '94
Candyman '92
Chunhyang '00
Coyote Waits '03
Cropsey '10
Crossroads '86
The Cry: La Llorona '07
Darby O'Gill & the Little People '59 ▸
Demon '16 ▸
Donkey Skin '70 ▸
Down to Earth '47
Erik the Viking '89
The Fast Runner '01 ▸
Faust '26 ▸
Gabbeh '96 ▸
The Giant of Marathon '60
The Giant of Metropolis '61
The Giants of Thessaly '60
Golden Voyage of Sinbad '73
Goliath Against the Giants '63
Goliath and the Barbarians '60
Goliath and the Dragon '61
Goliath and the Sins of Babylon '64
Guinevere '94
Heart of Glass '74 ▸
Helen of Troy '56
Hercules 2 '85
Hercules the Legendary Journeys, Vol. 1: And the Amazon Women '94
Hercules the Legendary Journeys, Vol. 2: The Lost Kingdom '94
Hercules the Legendary Journeys, Vol. 3: The Circle of Fire '94
Hercules the Legendary Journeys, Vol. 4: In the Underworld '94
Holidays '16
If They Tell You I Fell '89
Into the West '92 ▸
Inugami '01 ▸
Invitation to the Dance '56
Iphigenia '77 ▸
Jade Warrior '06
Jason and the Argonauts '63 ▸
Journey to the West '14
Kibakichi 2 '04
Kibakichi '04
King Arthur '04
Kismet '20 ▸
Krampus '15
Kriemhilde's Revenge '24 ▸
Kubo and the Two Strings '16 ▸
The Legend of Bloody Mary '08
The Legend of Gator Face '96
Legend of the Guardians: The Owls of Ga'Hoole '10 ▸
Leprechaun 2 '94
Life on a String '90
The Lost Empire '01
Magic in the Water '95
A Midsummer Night's Dream '68
A Midsummer Night's Dream '96
Moana '16 ▸
Monty Python and the Holy Grail '75 ▸
Mulan '98
Ne Zha '19
Ned Kelly '03
Nightmare '07
The Odyssey '97
Ondine '09
Out of Time '00
The Pagan Queen '09
Pandora and the Flying Dutchman '51
Pay the Ghost '15
Phedre '68
Phoenix '78
Pied Piper '72
Red Riding Hood '11
The Relic '96
Rise of the Guardians '12
Santa and Pete '99
Scream of the Banshee '11
The Secret of Navajo Cave '76
The Secret of Roan Inish '94 ▸
The Seventh Stream '01
Siegfried '24 ▸
Skinwalker '02
Son of Samson '62
The Song of Hiawatha '97
The Tale of the Princess Kaguya '13 ▸
Tall Tale: The Unbelievable Adventures of Pecos Bill '95
13th Child: Legend of the Jersey Devil '02
Thor '11 ▸
Thor and the Amazon Women '60
Transformers: The Last Knight '17
Tristan & Isolde '06
The Troll Hunter '11
Tropical Malady '04
Ulysses '55
Urban Legend '98
Urban Legends: Bloody Mary '05
Ursus in the Valley of the Lions '62
Walking Tall '04
Wendigo '01
Whale Rider '02 ▸
The Wild Man of the Navidad '08
Zvenigora '28 ▸

Food

See also Edibles

Food industry

Jiro Dreams of Sushi '12 ▸

Football

Ace Ventura: Pet Detective '93
Air Bud 2: Golden Receiver '98
All the Right Moves '83
Angels in the Endzone '98
Any Given Sunday '99 ▸
Backfield in Motion '91
The Best of Times '86
Big Fan '09
Black Sunday '77
The Blind Side '09
Blue Ridge Fall '99

Brian Banks '18
Brian's Song '71 ▶
Brian's Song '01
Buffalo 66 '97 ▶
Carter High '15
Catching Faith '15
Cheaper by the Dozen '03
Cheerleaders' Wild Weekend '85
College Humor '33
The Comebacks '07
Concussion '15
Diner '82 ▶
Draft Day '14
Easy Living '49
Eleven Men and a Girl '30
Everybody's All American '88
The Express '08
Field of Vision '11
The 5th Quarter '10
The Fortune Cookie '66 ▶
The Freshman '25 ▶
Friday Night Lights '04 ▶
Full Ride '02
The Galloping Ghost '31
The Game Plan '07
Game Time: Tackling the Past '11
Gleason '16 ▶
Good Luck '96
Good News '47
Grambling's White Tiger '81
Gridiron Gang '06
Gus '76
Heaven Can Wait '78 ▶
Hold 'Em Jail '32
Hometown Legend '02
Horse Feathers '32 ▶
Huddle '32
Invincible '06 ▶
Jerry Maguire '96 ▶
Jim Thorpe: All American '51
Johnny Be Good '88
The Junction Boys '02
Knute Rockne: All American '40 ▶
The Last Boy Scout '91
Last Game '80
Leatherheads '08
Little Giants '94
The Longest Yard '74 ▶
The Longest Yard '05
The Longshots '08
Lucas '86 ▶
Man of the House '05
Mean Girls 2 '11
Midnight Heat '95
Miles from Nowhere '09
Monday Night Mayhem '02
My All American '15
Navy Blue and Gold '37
Necessary Roughness '91
North Dallas Forty '79 ▶
The Oklahoma City Dolls '81
Paper Lion '68
Pigskin Parade '36
Players '03
Possums '99
The Program '93
Radio '03
Remember the Titans '00 ▶
The Replacements '00
Roberta '35 ▶
Romeo Must Die '00
Rudy '93
Run the Race '19
Rustin '01
A Saintly Switch '99
School Ties '92 ▶
Semi-Tough '77
Silver Linings Playbook '12 ▶
The Slaughter Rule '01
So This Is College '29
That's My Boy '51
They Call Me Sirr '00
Touchback '11
Trouble along the Way '53
Two Minute Warning '76
Two Minutes to Play '37
Undefeated '11
Varsity Blood '14
Varsity Blues '98
The Waterboy '98
We Are Marshall '06
West Point '27
When the Game Stands Tall '14
Wild Cherry '09
Wildcats '86
Windrunner '94

Foreign Cops

***See also** Foreign Intrigue; Interpol; Police Detectives*

The Bourne Supremacy '04 ▶
Carry On Constable '60
Collision Course '89
Cop Au Vin '85
Coup de Torchon '81 ▶
Cradle 2 the Grave '03
Dudley Do-Right '99
Framed '93 ▶
Hard-Boiled '92
Hot Fuzz '07 ▶
Infernal Affairs '02 ▶
Insomnia '97 ▶
Inspector Clouseau '68
Jet Li's The Enforcer '95
The Killer '90 ▶
La Balance '82 ▶
La Scorta '94 ▶
Le Deuxieme Souffle '66
Mad Dog Killer '77
The Medallion '03
The Pink Panther '64 ▶
The Pink Panther '06
Police Story '85
Prime Suspect '92 ▶
Red Heat '88
The Return of Dr. Mabuse '61
Return of the Pink Panther '74
Revenge of the Pink Panther '78
Rush Hour '98
Rush Hour 2 '01
Rush Hour 3 '07
A Shot in the Dark '64 ▶
The Siege of Sidney Street '60
Slumdog Millionaire '08 ▶
Touch of Evil '58 ▶
Traffic '00 ▶
Transporter 3 '08
Transsiberian '08 ▶

Foreign Intrigue

***See also** Spies & Espionage*

Above Suspicion '43 ▶
Ambassador Bill '31
Anne of Green Gables: The Continuing Story '99
Austin Powers: International Man of Mystery '97 ▶
Battle Beneath the Earth '68
Call Him Mr. Shatter '74
Catch Me a Spy '71
Cover-Up '91
Crimson Tide '95 ▶
The Day of the Jackal '73 ▶
The Destructors '74
Devil Wears White '86
Diamonds Are Forever '71 ▶
Diplomatic Courier '52 ▶
Dr. No '62 ▶
The Dogs of War '81
Don't Drink the Water '69
The Eiger Sanction '75
The Emperor's Candlesticks '37
Enigma '82
The Executioner '70
Foreign Correspondent '40 ▶
The Fourth Protocol '87 ▶
Frederick Forsyth's Icon '05
The Glimmer Man '96
Half Moon Street '86
Hamlet '96 ▶
Haywire '12 ▶
The Human Factor '75
The Hunt for Red October '90 ▶
The Interpreter '05 ▶
Jack Ryan: Shadow Recruit '14
Jaguar Lives '79
Jumpin' Jack Flash '86
Lady L '65
License to Kill '89 ▶
The Little Drummer Girl '84 ▶
The Magnificent Two '67
The Man Who Knew Too Little '97
The Man Who Knew Too Much '34 ▶
The Man Who Knew Too Much '56
Marathon Man '76 ▶
The Mask of Dimitrios '44 ▶
The Odessa File '74
Panama Hattie '42
Postmark for Danger '56
Reilly: Ace of Spies '87 ▶
Return of the Man from U.N.C.L.E. '83
Return to Paradise '98 ▶
Rollover '81
The Russia House '90
Saigon: Year of the Cat '87
The Secret Agent '96
6 Underground '19
Sniper: Ghost Shooter '16
The Spy Who Came in from the Cold '65 ▶
They Met in Bombay '41
The Third Man '49 ▶
360 '12
Tokyo Joe '49
Too Bad She's Bad '54
Topaz '69 ▶
Torn Curtain '66
Undeclared War '91
The White Countess '05 ▶
The Wind and the Lion '75 ▶

Foreign Legion

***See** Desert War/Foreign Legion*

Frame-Ups

The A-Team '10 ▶
Abbott and Costello Meet the Invisible Man '51 ▶
Accused at 17 '09
Agatha Christie's The Pale Horse '96
Along the Rio Grande '41
Angel Has Fallen '19
Angels Wash Their Faces '39
Animal 2 '07
Another Pair of Aces: Three of a Kind '91 ▶
The Art of War 3: Retribution '08
The Art of War '00
Backfire '50
The Badlanders '58
Bedroom Eyes '86
Beyond a Reasonable Doubt '09
Big City '37
The Big Clock '48 ▶
Big Score '83
The Big Shot '42
The Black Sleep '56
Blackout '54
Blade: Trinity '04
Blind Trust '06
Bombay Mail '34
The Bourne Supremacy '04 ▶
Breakdown '53
Broken City '13
Buried Alive '39
Candyman 3: Day of the Dead '98
Capital Punishment '96
The Ceremony '63
Chain Reaction '96
Chicago Confidential '57
City Hall '95 ▶
Consenting Adults '92
Corruption '33
Crackerjack '38
Crime and Punishment in Suburbia '00
The Crooked Road '65
Dark Corner '46 ▶
Deadline at Dawn '46
Death Race '08
Death Sentence '74
Delta Force One-The Lost Patrol '99
Demons from Her Past '07
The Desperadoes '43
Deuce Bigalow: European Gigolo '05
Devil Doll '36 ▶
Double Take '01
Dredd '12 ▶
Each Dawn I Die '39
Eagle Eye '08
Executive Koala '06 ▶
Extremely Dangerous '99
F/X '86 ▶
Family of Cops '95
Fatal Call '12
Final Payback '99
Five Guns to Tombstone '60
Forbidden Trail '32
Forfeit '07
Framed '47
Framed '75
Framed '93 ▶
Framed for Murder '07
The Fugitive '93 ▶
Game of Death '10
Gang Related '96
The Gay Buckaroo '32
Get Rita '75
The Girl in the News '41
The Girl Who Played With Fire '10
The Glimmer Man '96
Gun Duel In Durango '57
Her Fatal Flaw '06
Hi-Jacked '50
Hot Cars '56
How to Frame a Figg '71
The Hunted '48
In Time '11
An Innocent Man '89
Judge Dredd '95
Junglee '19
Kill Switch '08
Kiss of the Dragon '01
The Lady Confesses '45
Legacy of Rage '86
Legally Blondes '09
Let's Go to Prison '06
Letters from a Killer '98
Life Begins at Forty '35
The Life of Emile Zola '37 ▶
A Lizard in a Woman's Skin '71
Louisiana Purchase '41
Macon County Line '74
A Man Named Rocca '61
Man Outside '88
The Man Who Came Back '08
The Manhunt '86
The Mighty Quinn '89
Misfire '14
Mission: Impossible-Ghost Protocol '11 ▶
Mr. Wise Guy '42
Most Wanted '97
Motel Blue '98
Moving Target '96
Moving Target '00
Murder '30 ▶
Murphy's Law '86
My Cousin Vinny '92 ▶
My Fellow Americans '96
My Man and I '52
Natural Born Pranksters '16
The Net 2.0 '06
Never 2 Big '98
Nightwatch '96
No Escape '53
No Escape, No Return '93
North by Northwest '59 ▶
Now and Forever '82
Old Mother Riley's New Venture '49
Out of the Past '47 ▶
Out of Time '03
Outlaw's Son '57
Palmetto '98
Papillon '17
Past Sins '06
Phantom Lady '44 ▶
Plato's Run '96
Presumed Innocent '90 ▶
The Price of Fear '56
Prime Suspect '88
Prison Break '38
Prison on Fire '87
The Public Defender '31
RED '10
Red Corner '97
Return of the Frontiersman '50
The Rich Man's Wife '96
Ricochet '91 ▶
Road House '48
Sabotage '96
Saboteur '42 ▶
Sabu '04
The Secret Bride '35
The Sentinel '06
The Shadow Conspiracy '96
Shakes the Clown '92
Shelter '98
Shooter '07
Slow as Lightning '23
Smoke Screen '10
Spenser Confidential '20
Stir Crazy '80
Storm Catcher '99
Street Kings '08
The Take '16
Tank '83
TekWar '94
Thick as Thieves '99
Torque '04
Tracker '10
Trophy Wife '06
12 Rounds 3: Lockdown '15
Undertow '49
Undisputed 2: Last Man Standing '06
U.S. Marshals '98
Vice Raid '60
White Fire '53
Who's Got the Black Box? '67
Wife Wanted '46
Wild Things '98
The Yards '00
You Can't Get Away With Murder '39

France

***See also** Paris*

The Advocate '93 ▶
The Affair of the Necklace '01
Albert's Memorial '09
The Ambassador's Daughter '56
An American in Paris '51 ▶
An American Werewolf in Paris '97
Anatomy of Hell '04
And Soon the Darkness '70
Angelique '64
Angelique and the King '66
Angelique and the Sultan '68
Angelique: The Road to Versailles '65
Any Human Heart '11
Apres-Vous '03
Arch of Triumph '48 ▶
Arch of Triumph '85
Army of Shadows '69 ▶
Around a Small Mountain '09
At Eternity's Gate '18
Au Hasard Balthazar '66
Augustine '12
Ballets Russes '05 ▶
Battle of the Rails '46 ▶
The Beaches of Agnes '08
The Beasts of Marseilles '57
Bedtime Story '63
Before Sunset '04 ▶
Beneath Hill 60 '10
The Better 'Ole '26
Beyond Victory '31
Big Fella '37
Birdsong '12
Black Girl '66 ▶
Black Heaven '10
The Black Tulip '64
Blue is the Warmest Color '13 ▶
Bluebeard's Eighth Wife '38
Bon Voyage '03 ▶
Borsalino '70 ▶
BPM (Beats Per Minute) '17
Breakthrough '50
Breathless '59 ▶
Brotherhood of the Wolf '01
Buffet Froid '79 ▶
By the Sea '15
Can-Can '60
Cannes Man '96
Captain Scarlett '53
Cardinal Richelieu '35
Carnage '02
Carve Her Name with Pride '58
Catch Me If You Can '02
Cave of Forgotten Dreams '11 ▶
Cesar '36 ▶
Charade '63 ▶
Charlotte Gray '01
The Chateau '01
The Childhood of a Leader '16
Chocolat '00 ▶
The Chorus '04
Classe Tous Risque '60 ▶
The Clearstream Affair '15
Climax '18
Coco Chanel '08
The Color of Lies '99
Come Undone '00
The Connection '15
Cosmos '16
The Count of Monte Cristo '02
Criminal Lovers '99
The Cross of Lorraine '43
Daguerreotypes '75 ▶
Danton '82 ▶
Days of Glory '06
Derrida '02
Desire Me '47
Desiree '54
Diane '55
Diary of a Chambermaid '16
Dirty Rotten Scoundrels '88 ▶
Disorder '16
The Dreamlife of Angels '98 ▶
The Duellists '77 ▶
Dunkirk '17 ▶
8 Women '02 ▶
The Elusive Corporal '62 ▶
Ever After: A Cinderella Story '98 ▶
The Family '13
Fanfan la Tulipe '51 ▶
Farewell, My Queen '12 ▶
The Fatal Image '90
Festival at Cannes '02
Fidelio: Alice's Odyssey '14
The Fighting Eagle '27
5x2 '04
Flyboys '06
Forget Paris '95
40 Love '15
The 4 Musketeers '05
Frantic '88 ▶
Frantz '17 ▶
French Connection 2 '75 ▶
French Kiss '95
French Postcards '79
The French Woman '79
Full Speed '96
Games of Love and Chance '03
Gentlemen Prefer Blondes '53 ▶
Gigi '58 ▶
Gilles' Wife '04
Girls Can't Swim '99
The Good Thief '03 ▶
A Good Year '06
Goodbye to Language '14 ▶
Goya in Bordeaux '99
The Grapes of Death '78
Hail Mafia '65
Happily Ever After '04
Happy End '17
Hate '95 ▶
He Loves Me . . . He Loves Me Not '02
Heart of a Nation '43 ▶
A Heavenly Vintage '09
Hellraiser 4: Bloodline '95
Hemingway's Garden of Eden '08
Henri Langlois: The Phantom of the Cinematheque '04 ▶
Hidden '05 ▶
Hijack Highway '55
Holy Motors '12 ▶
Hors Satan '11
The Horseman on the Roof '95
How to Steal a Million '66 ▶
The Hundred-Foot Journey '14
The Hustle '19
I Stand Alone '98
Imitation General '58
Impromptu '90 ▶
The Intouchables '12
The Intruder '04 ▶
Invasion Quartet '61
Is Paris Burning? '66 ▶
It All Starts Today '99
I've Loved You So Long '08 ▶
Jealousy '13 ▶
Jeanne la Pucelle '94

▶ = rated three bones or higher

Jefferson in Paris '94
Joan of Arc '48
Joan of Arc '99
Joan of Paris '42 ▶
The Josephine Baker Story '90 ▶
Journey's End '18
Just Visiting '01
Killer Tomatoes Eat France '91
Killing Zoe '94
Kings and Queen '04 ▶
Kings Go Forth '58
A Knight's Tale '01
La Ceremonie '95 ▶
La Collectionneuse '67
La France '07
La Marseillaise '37 ▶
La Petite Jerusalem '05
La Petite Lili '03
La Vie Promise '02
Labyrinth '12
Ladies' Man '62
The Lady in the Car with Glasses and a Gun '16
Lafayette Escadrille '58
The Last Diamond '14
The Last Metro '80 ▶
Last Tango in Paris '73 ▶
The Last Time I Saw Paris '54
The Last Train '74
Le Corbeau '43 ▶
Le Million '31 ▶
Leap! '16
Lemming '05
Les Destinees '00
Les Miserables '35 ▶
Les Miserables '57 ▶
Les Miserables '78 ▶
Les Miserables '97 ▶
Let the Sunshine In '17
The Life of Emile Zola '37 ▶
Lila Says '04
Lolo '15
The Longest Day '62 ▶
Love Is a Ball '63
Love Me if You Dare '03
Lovely to Look At '52 ▶
Loves & Times of Scaramouche '76
Lulu '02
Ma and Pa Kettle on Vacation '53
Madame Bovary '91 ▶
Madame Claude '77
Magic in the Moonlight '14
The Man in the Iron Mask '39 ▶
The Man in the Iron Mask '77 ▶
The Man in the Iron Mask '97
The Man in the Iron Mask '98 ▶
The Man of My Life '06
Man on the Eiffel Tower '48 ▶
The Man Who Lies '68
Maniac '63
Marie Antoinette '38
Marie Antoinette '06
Marius '31 ▶
Maximum Risk '96
Meet the Guilbys '15
The Midwife '17 ▶
Mr. Bean's Holiday '07
Mr. Klein '76 ▶
The Moderns '88 ▶
Modigliani '04
Moliere '07
Mondovino '04
Monkeys, Go Home! '66
Monsieur Beaucaire '24
Monsieur Beaucaire '46 ▶
Monsieur N. '03 ▶
Monsieur Verdoux '47 ▶
The Moon and Sixpence '43 ▶
Moulin Rouge '52 ▶
The Mountain '56
Murderous Maids '00
My Father's Glory '91 ▶
My Life on Ice '02
Napoleon '55
Napoleon and Josephine: A Love Story '87
Neither Heaven Nor Earth '16
A New Kind of Love '63
New World '95
The Night and the Moment '94
Nobody Else But You '11
On My Way '14
On Tour '10
Operation Mad Ball '57
Overdrive '17
Papillon '17
Paris Can Wait '17
Passion '19
Passion '82
Passion of Joan of Arc '28 ▶
Passion of Mind '00
The Past '13 ▶
Paths of Glory '57 ▶
The Picasso Summer '69
Portrait of a Lady on Fire '19 ▶
The Princess of Montpensier '10 ▶
Prisoner of Honor '91 ▶
Quality Street '37
Queen Margot '94 ▶
Queens of the Ring '13
Quiet Days in Clichy '90
Raw '17
Read My Lips '01
Ready to Wear '94
The Real Joan of Arc '08
The Red Inn '51
Reign of Terror '49
Renoir '12
Resistance '20
Retour Chez Ma Mere '16
Reunion in France '42
Revenge of the Musketeers '63
Revenge of the Musketeers '94
Ridicule '96 ▶
The Road to Glory '36
Roman de Gare '07
Romantics Anonymous '10
Round Midnight '86 ▶
The Rules of the Game '39 ▶
Rust and Bone '12 ▶
Sade '00
Saint Joan '57
The Scapegoat '59
The Scarlet Pimpernel '99
The Scarlet Pimpernel 2: Mademoiselle Guillotine '99
The Scarlet Pimpernel 3: The Kidnapped King '99
The Scarlet Pimpernel '34 ▶
The Scarlet Pimpernel '82 ▶
The Sergeant '68
Sex is Comedy '02
Sgt. Stubby: An American Hero '18
The Shadow Within '07
Silk Stockings '57 ▶
Sister My Sister '94
A Soldier's Daughter Never Cries '98
Something in the Air '13
The Square Peg '58
The Statement '03
Staying Vertical '16
Stolen Holiday '37
Straight into Darkness '04
Strayed '03 ▶
Suite 16 '94
A Summer's Tale '96
Summertime '16
Surviving Picasso '96
Sweet Ecstasy '62
Swimming Pool '03 ▶
The Take '16
A Tale of Two Cities '36 ▶
A Tale of Two Cities '58 ▶
A Tale of Two Cities '80
The Tanks Are Coming '51
The Taste of Others '00 ▶
Tender Is the Night '62
Theatre of Death '67
Therese '12
Therese Raquin '80
Therese: The Story of Saint Therese of Lisieux '04
Things to Come '16 ▶
This Land Is Mine '43 ▶
Those Magnificent Men in Their Flying Machines '65 ▶
Timeline '03
To Catch a Thief '55 ▶
Tonight We Raid Calais '43
Tous les Matins du Monde '92 ▶
The Town Is Quiet '00
Transit '18
The Transporter '02
The Transporter Refueled '15
The Trench '99
Tropic of Cancer '70 ▶
The 24 Hour War '16
22 Bullets '10
Two Thousand Women '44
Uncertain Glory '44
Underground '70
The Unknown Girl '17
Untamable Angelique '67
Until September '84
Valmont '89 ▶
Varian's War '01
Vatel '00
A Very Long Engagement '04 ▶
The Walk '15
War Horse '11
War of the Buttons '12
We Were One Man '80
Welcome to New York '15
Western '96
What Price Glory? '52 ▶
When a Man Loves '27
The White Cockatoo '35
Who Killed Bambi? '03
Window to Paris '95
With a Friend Like Harry '00 ▶
A Year in Provence '89 ▶
Zombi Child '20

Fraternities & Sororities

See also Campus Capers

American Pie Presents: Beta House '07
Among Brothers '05
Black Christmas '75
Black Christmas '06
Brotherhood '10
Burning Sands '17
The Campus Corpse '77
College '08
Confessions of Sorority Girls '94
Damsels in Distress '11
Dead Man on Campus '97
Defying Gravity '99
Fraternity Massacre at Hell Island '07
Freshman Orientation '04
Friendship, Secrets and Lies '79
Funny About Love '90
Goat '16
Going Greek '01
Happy Hell Night '92
Hell Night '81
H.O.T.S. '79
The House Bunny '08
The Initiation '84
Initiation of Sarah '78
The Initiation of Sarah '06
Insecticidal '05
Kilroy Was Here '47
Legacy '08
Midnight Madness '80
National Lampoon's Adam & Eve '05
National Lampoon's Animal House '78 ▶
National Lampoon's Van Wilder 2: The Rise of Taj '06
National Lampoon's Van Wilder '02
Neighbors '14
Old School '03
Pumpkin '02
Revenge of the Nerds '84
Ring of Terror '62
Scream 2 '97 ▶
Senseless '98
The Skulls 2 '02
So This Is College '29
So Undercover '13
Sorority Babes in the Slimeball Bowl-A-Rama '87
Sorority Boys '02
Sorority House Massacre '86
Sorority House Massacre 2: Nighty Nightmare '92
Sorority House Vampires '95
Sorority Row '09
Sorority Wars '09
Stomp the Yard '07
Stomp the Yard 2: Homecoming '10
Sydney White '07
Tall Lie '53
22 Jump Street '14
Urban Legend '98

French Revolution

The Black Tulip '64
Brotherhood of the Wolf '01
Danton '82 ▶
Farewell, My Queen '12 ▶
The Lady and the Duke '01
Marie Antoinette '38
Marie Antoinette '06
Pandaemonium '00
Reign of Terror '49
The Return of the Scarlet Pimpernel '37
Ridicule '96 ▶
The Scarlet Pimpernel '99
The Scarlet Pimpernel '34 ▶
The Scarlet Pimpernel '82 ▶
A Tale of Two Cities '36 ▶
A Tale of Two Cities '58 ▶
A Tale of Two Cities '80
A Tale of Two Cities '89 ▶

Friendship

See Buddies; Buddy Cops; Childhood Buddies; Female Bonding; Pardners

Front Page

See also Paperboys; Shutterbugs

Abandoned '47
Absence of Malice '81
Absolution '05
Ace in the Hole '51 ▶
Action in Arabia '44
Adventure in Manhattan '36
The Adventures of Tintin '11
Afghan Luke '11
After Office Hours '35
Against the Ropes '04
All Hands on Deck '61
All the President's Men '76 ▶
Alleged '10
America's Sweethearts '01
AngKor: Cambodia Express '81
Anima '98
Another Time, Another Place '58
Anzio '68
Area 51 '11
Assassination of a High School President '08
Assignment: Paris '52
Attack on Darfur '09
Attack on Leningrad '09
Beauty & the Briefcase '10
The Beniker Gang '83
Berlin Correspondent '42
Between the Lines '77 ▶
Beyond a Reasonable Doubt '09
Beyond Re-Animator '03
Big Brown Eyes '36
Big Miracle '12
Big News '29
Blackwell's Island '39
Blessed Event '32 ▶
Blonde for a Day '46
Bloody Proof '99 ▶
The Blue Gardenia '53 ▶
Boeing Boeing '65
Bordertown '06
The Bounty Hunter '10
The Boys Are Back '09
Brenda Starr '86
Bright Lights, Big City '88
Broadway Melody of 1936 '35 ▶
Brown Sugar '02
Bruce Almighty '03
Brutal Massacre: A Comedy '07
The Business of Fancydancing '02
Call Northside 777 '48 ▶
The Captive City '52
The Case of the Scorpion's Tail '71
Chain Gang '50
Chicago '27
The Children of Huang Shi '08
Chinese Box '97
Circumstantial Evidence '35
Citizen Kane '41 ▶
Clear All Wires! '33
Close to My Heart '51
Cobb '94 ▶
Cold Blooded '00
The Company You Keep '12
Confirm or Deny '41
Continental Divide '81
Control Room '04 ▶
Corruption '33
Crazy for Christmas '05
Crazy Heart '09
Criminal Act '88
Crocodile Dundee '86 ▶
Crocodile Dundee in Los Angeles '01
The Crooked Road '65
Cry Freedom '87
Cut and Run '85
Dancing Co-Ed '39
The Daring Young Man '35
Dark and Stormy Night '09
Dark Secrets '95
A Daughter's Conviction '06
Deadline '87
Deadline '00
Deadline '12
Dear Viola '14
Death Has a Bad Reputation '90
Deep Impact '98
Defense of the Realm '85 ▶
Design for Scandal '41
Diary of a Serial Killer '97
The Disappearance of Garcia Lorca '96
Don't Look Down '98
Don't Torture a Duckling '72
Double Exposure '82
Each Dawn I Die '39
Easy to Wed '46
Echo of Murder '00
Eight Men Out '88 ▶
Elles '11
Exclusive Story '36
Extramarital '98
Eyes Behind the Stars '72
Eyes of a Stranger '81
A Face in the Fog '36
Fair Game '10 ▶
Far Cry '08
Father Hood '93
Final Assignment '80
Fit for a King '37
5 Days of War '11
Five Star Final '31
A Flash of Green '85
Fletch '85
Fletch Lives '89
Fog Over Frisco '34
Footsteps '98
For One Night '06
Forbidden '32
The Forbidden Quest '93
Forbidden Trail '32
Foreign Correspondent '40 ▶
Four's a Crowd '38
Francis Covers the Big Town '53
French Film '08
Frisco Kid '35
The Front Page '31 ▶
The Front Page '74
Front Page Woman '35
The Front Runner '18
Full Disclosure '00
Full Frontal '02
Fun '94
Generation Kill '08 ▶
Gentleman's Agreement '47 ▶
Get a Clue '02
The Ghost and Mr. Chicken '66
Ghosted '09
The Gilded Lily '35
Girl On the Run '53
The Girl Who Kicked the Hornet's Nest '10
The Girl Who Played With Fire '10
The Girl With the Dragon Tattoo '09 ▶
The Girl With the Dragon Tattoo '11 ▶
Golden Gloves '40
Good Advice '01
The Great Muppet Caper '81 ▶
Gunshy '98 ▶
The Guys '02 ▶
Harrison's Flowers '02
Headline Woman '35
Heat Wave '90 ▶
Hellraiser: Deader '05
Herblock: The Black & the White '13
Hero '92 ▶
Hi, Nellie! '34
His and Her Christmas '05
His Girl Friday '40 ▶
Hit the Ice '43
Honeymoon with Mom '06
Hostile Makeover '09
How to Lose a Guy in 10 Days '03
How to Lose Friends & Alienate People '08
The Hudsucker Proxy '93 ▶
Hue and Cry '47 ▶
Hustling '75 ▶
I Cover the Waterfront '33
I Love Trouble '94
The Image '89
Imagining Argentina '04
Impact Point '08
Impolite '92
In and Out '97 ▶
In My Country '04
Infected '08
The Infiltrator '95
The Innocent Sleep '95
The Insider '99 ▶
It Happened Tomorrow '44
It Shouldn't Happen to a Dog '46
It's Love Again '36
Joe Gould's Secret '00
John Dies at the End '12
Johnny Come Lately '43
Journey for Margaret '42 ▶
Just Off Broadway '42
Just One of the Guys '85
Keeper of the Flame '42
Kill the Messenger '14 ▶
Killer Hair '09
The Killing Device '92
The Killing Fields '84 ▶
A Killing Spring '02
King of the Newsboys '38
Kit Kittredge: An American Girl '08
L.A. Confidential '97 ▶
La Dolce Vita '60 ▶
Ladies Crave Excitement '35
The Last Debate '00
The Last Gangster '37
The Last Sentence '12
The Last Word '95
The Last Word '17
The Lawless '50
Leatherheads '08
Legacy '10
Legalese '98
Let It Rain '08
Libeled Lady '36 ▶
Life Begins at Forty '35
The Life of David Gale '03
Living It Up '54
Lost Angel '43
The Lost Valentine '11
Love Is a Many-Splendored Thing '55
Love Is News '37 ▶
The Love Machine '71
The Luck of the Irish '48
Making Mr. Right '08
Malarek '89
Man of Iron '81 ▶
Man of Steel '13
Marley & Me '08
The Mask '94 ▶
Me & Mrs. Jones '02
Mean Season '85
Meet John Doe '41 ▶
The Men Who Stare at Goats '09
Message in a Bottle '98
Michael '96

▶ = rated three bones or higher

► = rated three bones or higher

RoboCop 2 '90
RoboCop '14
Rush Hour 2 '01
Split Second '92
Timecop '94
Wolfen '81 ►

Future Shock

See also Post-Apocalypse; Time Travel; Time Warped

A. I.: Artificial Intelligence '01
Aeon Flux '05
Alita: Battle Angel '19
Allegiant '16
Amerigeddon '16
Andron: The Black Labyrinth '16
Austin Powers: International Man of Mystery '97 ►
Back to the Future, Part 2 '89
Battle for Skyark '15
Bicentennial Man '99
Bill & Ted's Excellent Adventure '89
Blade Runner 2049 '17
Branded '12
Brave New World '98
Captive State '19
Casshern '04
Children of Men '06►
Chrysalis '07
City of Ember '08
Dead or Alive: Final '02
The Deal '05
Death Games '02
Death Racers '08
Divergent '14
Division 19 '19
Doomsday '08
Equals '16
Forever Young '92
The Fountain '06
Franklyn '08
Future World '18
Ghost in the Shell '17
Ghostwarrior '86
Homo Sapiens '16
Idiocracy '06
Immortal '04
Just Visiting '01
The Last Man '19
Late for Dinner '91
Lost City Raiders '08
Manborg '11
Minority Report '02►
Natural City '03
No Men Beyond This Point '15
The Philadelphia Experiment '84
Planet of the Apes '68►
The Postman '97
Privilege '67
Renaissance '06
Repo Men '10
RoboCop '14
Roger Corman's Death Race 2050 '17
The Rover '14
Six: The Mark Unleashed '04
Sleeper '73►
A Sound of Thunder '05
10,000 A.D.: The Legend of the Black Pearl '08
The Terminators '09
Ultramarines: A Warhammer 40,000 Movie '10
Ultraviolet '06
Universal Soldier: Regeneration '09
Viral Assassins '00
The Visitors '95
WALL-E '08►
The Wandering Earth '19
World Without End '56

Gambling

See also Viva Las Vegas!

Alex & Emma '03
Alibi Ike '35
All In '06
All or Nothing at All '93
Any Number Can Play '49
Any Number Can Win '63
Atlantic City '81►
Back to the Future, Part 2 '89
Bad Lieutenant: Port of Call New Orleans '09
Barry Lyndon '75 ►
A Beginner's Guide to Endings '10
Beverly Lewis' The Confession '13
The Big Boodle '57
Big Shot: Confessions of a Campus Bookie '02
Big Town '87
A Billion for Boris '90
Birds & the Bees '56
Bitter Sweet '33
Bitter Sweet '40
Bob le Flambeur '55 ►
Bookies '03
The Boys '97
Buffalo 66 '97 ►
Bugsy '91 ►
But the Flesh Is Weak '32
Caddyshack '80►
Canyon Passage '46►
Casino '95►
Casino Royale '06►
Catherine Cookson's The Gambling Man '98
Charlie Chan at Monte Carlo '37
Charlie Chan at the Race Track '36
The Cheat '31
The Cheaters '76
Circus '00
Cockfighter '74►
The Color of Money '86►
The Condemned 2 '16
The Confidant '10
The Cooler '03►
Croupier '97►
The Dalton Girls '57
Dark Hazard '34
Dead Heat '01
Deadly Impact '84
The Debt '98
The Deli '97
Diamonds Are Forever '71►
Diggstown '92►
Dinner Rush '00►
Doc West '09
Dona Flor and Her Two Husbands '78►
Double Down '01
Double Dynamite '51
Doughboys '08
The Duchess and the Dirtwater Fox '76
Duke of the Derby '62
Easy Money '83
Eight Men Out '88►
Elmer the Great '33
Even Money '06
Eyes of an Angel '91
Familia '05
Feu Mathias Pascal '26
Finding Amanda '08
A Fine Mess '86
Firepower '93
Five Card Stud '68
Flame of the Barbary Coast '45
Flame of the Islands '55
The Flamingo Kid '84►
Force of Evil '49►
Four Rooms '95
The Foxes of Harrow '47
Frankie and Johnny '65
The Gamble '88
The Gambler '74►
The Gambler '97
The Gambler '14
The Gambler & the Lady '52
The Gambler, the Girl and the Gunslinger '09
Get Shorty '95►
Gilda '46►
Girl Most Likely '12
Glory Years '87
God's Pocket '14
The Good Thief '03►
The Great Mike '44
The Great Sinner '49
Guns, Girls and Gambling '11
Gutshot Straight '14
Guys and Dolls '55►
Hard Eight '96►
Hardball '01
The Harder They Fall '56►
Headin' for Trouble '31
Heat '95 ►
Heaven '99
Hell's Angels '69 '69
Hi-Life '98
Homicide '49
The Honeymoon Machine '61
Hoodlum '96
The House '17
The House on 56th Street '33
Huck and the King of Hearts '93
Hustle '04
The Hustler '61 ►
In Like Flint '67
Indecent Proposal '93
Intacto '01
Jinxed '82
Kaleidoscope '66
Killer McCoy '47
Lady for a Night '42
The Lady Gambles '49
Las Vegas Hillbillys '66
Las Vegas Lady '76
Last Vegas '13
Lay the Favorite '12
Le Million '31►
The Lemon Drop Kid '51
Let It Ride '89
Let's Do It Again '75
Let's Make It Legal '51
Liberty Heights '99
Little Miss Marker '34►
Little Miss Marker '80
Living to Die '91
Lock, Stock and 2 Smoking Barrels '98►
Lookin' to Get Out '82
Lost in America '85►
Lucky Grandma '20
Lucky You '07
Luckytown '00
Manhattan Melodrama '34►
The Marrying Man '91
Maverick '94
McCabe & Mrs. Miller '71►
McHale's Navy '64
Mean Machine '01
Michael Clayton '07►
Michael Shayne: Private Detective '40
Mickey One '65
The Mississippi Gambler '53
Mississippi Grind '15►
Mr. Lucky '43►
Money from Home '53
Money Kings '98
Money Train '95
Monte Carlo '30
Murderers' Row '66
My Blueberry Nights '07
My Brother Talks to Horses '47
My Darling Clementine '46►
My Little Chickadee '40►
No Man of Her Own '32
Ocean's Eleven '01►
Ocean's Thirteen '07►
Oklahoma Kid '39►
The Old Curiosity Shop '07
One Last Ride '03
One Tough Cop '98
Order to Kill '73
Oscar and Lucinda '97
Our Man Flint '66
Out to Sea '97
Owning Mahowny '03
Paradise Island '30
Passionada '02
Phoenix '98
Pink Cadillac '89
Player 5150 '08
Players '03
Poker Alice '87
Poolhall Junkies '02
The Queen of Spades '49►
Quintet '79
Rain Man '88►
Rat Race '01
Reno '39
Rimfire '49
The Ringer '05
The Roaring Twenties '39►
Robin-B-Hood '06
The Rocking Horse Winner '49
Ruggles of Red Gap '35►
The Runner '99
Runner Runner '13
Saint John of Las Vegas '09
Salty O'Rourke '45
Sgt. Bilko '95
Shade '03
The Shadow Man '53
The Shanghai Gesture '42
Showgirls '95
Silver Queen '42
Sky Full of Moon '52
Song of the Thin Man '47
Sorrowful Jones '49
Sour Grapes '98
Spent '00
Sporting Blood '31
The Squeeze '87
The Squeeze '15
Stacy's Knights '83
Stickmen '01
The Sting '73 ►
Strike It Rich '90
Support Your Local Sheriff '69►
Swing Time '36►
The Tailor of Panama '00►
Taking Chances '09
Tall Story '60
Talons of the Eagle '92
Ten Benny '98
Tennessee's Partner '55
That's My Man '47
Things Change '88►
Thoroughbreds Don't Cry '37
3000 Miles to Graceland '01
A Throw of Dice '29►
Tomcats '01
Trading Places '83
21 '08
29th Street '91
Two for the Money '05
Uncle Buck '89►
Uncut Gems '19►
The Underneath '95►
Uptown Saturday Night '74
The Vegas Strip Wars '84
Vegas Vacation '96
Violence '47
Walking Tall '73
The Westerner '40►
Who's Got the Action? '63
The Wild Pear Tree '18►
The Winner '96
Wise Guys '86
Yonkers Joe '08

Game Shows

Champagne for Caesar '50►
The Computer Wore Tennis Shoes '69
Confessions of a Dangerous Mind '02
Deathrow Gameshow '88
Everything You Always Wanted to Know about Sex (But Were Afraid to Ask) '72►
Groundhog Day '93►
Mallrats '95
Mr. Average '06
National Lampoon's European Vacation '85
Nerve '16
Queen for a Day '51
Quiz Show '94►
The Running Man '87
Shock Treatment '81
Starter for 10 '06
10th Victim '65►
13 Sins '13
White Men Can't Jump '92

Gangs

See also Juvenile Delinquents; Moscow Mafia; Organized Crime; Urban Gangstas

All Dogs Go to Heaven '89
Alley Cat '84
American Me '92►
Angel Town '89
Angels Die Hard '70
Antisocial Behavior '07
Ash Is Purest White '18►
Assault on Precinct 13 '76►
Bad Bunch '76
Behave Yourself! '52
Belly '98
A Better Tomorrow, Part 1 '86
A Better Tomorrow, Part 2 '88
Beyond the Law '92
Beyond the Trophy '12
Big Bad Mama 2 '87
Big Bad Mama '74
The Big Brawl '80
Biggie & Tupac: The Story Behind the Murder of Rap's Biggest Superstars '02
Black Caesar '73
The Black Cobra '87
Black Gestapo '75
Blood Brothers '93
Blood Father '16 ►
Blood In . . . Blood Out: Bound by Honor '93
The Bloody Brood '59
Bloody Mama '70
Blue '68
Blue Spring '01
Blue Story '20
Boardwalk '79
Bonnie & Clyde '67►
Borderline '50
Borsalino '70►
Boss of Big Town '43
Boulevard Nights '79
Boyz N the Hood '91►
Bra Boys '07
Bring Me the Head of Alfredo Garcia '74
Broadway Danny Rose '84►
The Bronx War '90
Brother Orchid '40►
Bulldog Drummond's Bride '39
Bullet '94
Bullets or Ballots '38►
Cartouche '62►
C.C. & Company '70
Chains of Gold '92
The Chase '46
El Chicano '19
China O'Brien '88
Chrome and Hot Leather '71
City of God '02
City of Men '07►
Class of 1984 '82
Class of 1999 2: The Substitute '93
Class of 1999 '90
Coach Carter '05►
Code of Silence '85
Contraband '80
Cookie '89
Cop in Blue Jeans '78
Corrupted Minds '06
Cosh Boy '52
Crime in the Streets '56
The Cross & the Switchblade '72
The Crow: Wicked Prayer '05
Cry-Baby '90►
Cry of a Prostitute: Love Kills '72
Dangerous Ground '96
The Dark Horse '14►
The Day It Came to Earth '77
Deadly Encounter '72►
Dear Wendy '05
Death Sentence '07
Defiance '79
Designing Woman '57►
Destroyer '18
Deuces Wild '02
Devil's Angels '67
Dillinger '45►
Dillinger '73
Dirty '05
Disorganized Crime '89
Diva '82►
Dixie Jamboree '44
The Doberman Gang '72
The Dog Who Stopped the War '84
The Don Is Dead '73
Dragon Eyes '12
Drive By '01
Each Dawn I Die '39
East L.A. Warriors '89
The Education of Sonny Carson '74
Emil and the Detectives '64
The Enforcer '51
The Enforcer '76
Escape from L.A. '96
Every Which Way But Loose '78
Exterminator '80
Eye of the Tiger '86
Farming '19
Fight Club '99 ►
Foolish '99
Forced Vengeance '82
Forever, Lulu '87
Four Deuces '75
Foxy Brown '74
Full Eclipse '93
'G' Men '35 ►
The Gambler & the Lady '52
Gambler's Choice '44
Game of Death '79
Gang Boys '97
Gang Busters '42
Gang Justice '94
Gangland '00
Gangs of New York '02►
The Gangster '47
Gangway '37
Gimme Shelter '70
The Glory Stompers '67
Gone Are the Days '84
A Good Man '14
Goodfellas '90►
Gran Torino '08►
The Great Mike '44
Green Street Hooligans '05►
The Grissom Gang '71►
Guns Don't Argue '57
Hard As Nails '01
Hard Lessons '86
Hawk's Vengeance '96
Heartbreaker '83
Hellcats '68
High Sierra '41►
Homeboy '75
Hoodlum Empire '52
I Died a Thousand Times '55
I, Mobster '58
I'd Give My Life '36
Imperium '16
The Irishman '19►
Jinxed '82
Johnny Apollo '40
Johnny Dangerously '84
Jungleground '95
Key Largo '48►
Kill or Be Killed '15
Killer Dill '47
Kung Fu Hustle '04
La Balance '82►
Lady in a Cage '64►
Lady in Red '79
The Last Diamond '14
Last Man Standing '96
The Last Ride of the Dalton Gang '79
The Last Riders '90
Latin Dragon '03
Leather Jackets '90
Lepke '75
Lethal Obsession '87
Like a Puppet Out of Strings '05
Linewatch '08
Little Dragons '80
Little Laura & Big John '73
The Longshot '86
Love Me or Leave Me '55►
Lucky Grandma '20
Lucky Luciano '74
Ma Barker's Killer Brood '60
Manhattan Merry-Go-Round '37
Marked Woman '37►
Men of Respect '91
Menace II Society '93►
The Meteor Man '93
Mexican Gangster '08
Mi Vida Loca '94
Midnight '34
Miracle in Harlem '48
Miss Bala '12
Mr. Majestyk '74
Mob Story '90
Mob War '88
Murda Muzik '03
My Brother the Devil '12
Mystery Date '91
The Naked Angels '69
Ned Kelly '03
Never a Dull Moment '68

► = rated three bones or higher

Never Let Go '60
Never Love a Stranger '58
The New Kids '85
96 Minutes '11
99 & 44/100 Dead '74
No Trace '50
The Noose Hangs High '48 ▶
Omega Doom '96
One Man's Justice '95
Original Gangstas '96
The Outsiders '83
A Packing Suburbia '99
Paco '75
Paradise in Harlem '40
Pariah '98
Parole, Inc. '49
The Payoff '43
Peacekillers '71
Performance '70 ▶
Petrified Forest '36 ▶
Pickup on South Street '53 ▶
Pierrot le Fou '65 ▶
Prayer of the Rollerboys '91
Prime Cut '72
The Prime Time '60
The Principal '87
Prize Fighter '79
Pulp '72
The Purifiers '04
The Racket '51 ▶
The Racketeer '29
Raging Phoenix '09
Rapid Fire '92
The Reading Room '05
Renegades '89
Return of the Dragon '73
Return of the Rebels '81
Revenge '90
Revenge of Sartana '65
Revenge of the Green Dragons '14
Revenge of the Ninja '83
Ricochet '91 ▶
The Rise and Fall of Legs Diamond '60
The Rise of the Krays '16
The Ritz '76 ▶
Rooftops '89
Rumble Fish '83 ▶
Rumble in the Bronx '96
Running Woman '98
Satan's Sadists '69
Scared Stiff '53 ▶
Scarface '83 ▶
The Second Chance '06
The Secret Life of Pets '16
Senorita Justice '03
The Set-Up '49 ▶
Sexton Blake and the Hooded Terror '38
Shaft '71 ▶
Shank '09
Shining Star '75
Shoot the Piano Player '62 ▶
Sidewalks of New York '31
16 Years of Alcohol '03
Skin '18 ▶
Slam '98
Sleight '17
Smart Alecks '42
Some Like It Hot '59 ▶
South Central '92
Speedy '28 ▶
Splinter '06
Stavisky '74 ▶
Steel '97
Sticky Fingers '88
Stingray '78
Stone Cold '91
Street Corner Justice '96
Street Crimes '92
The Street King '02
The Street with No Name '48 ▶
Stryker '04
The Substitute '96
Sucker Free City '05 ▶
T-Bird Gang '59
Tactical Force '11
Teenage Doll '57
Teenage Gang Debs '66
Thicker than Water '99
Three Strikes '00
Tigers Are Not Afraid '19 ▶
Tokyo Tribe '15
Too Late for Tears '49 ▶
Torque '04
Treed Murray '01
Trouble in Store '53
Truck Stop Women '74
True Believer '89
True Blood '89
Tuff Turf '85
Twenty8k '12
The Underground '97
Underground President '07
The Underworld Story '50
Urban Crossfire '94
Vietnam, Texas '90
Vincent N Roxxy '17
The Virginia Hill Story '76
Waist Deep '06
Wanderers '79 ▶
The Warriors '79
We Die Young '19
West Side Story '61 ▶
The Wild Goose Lake '20
The Wild One '54 ▶
Wonder Man '45
Wonderful Town '07
The Wrecking Crew '99
The Wrong Arm of the Law '63 ▶
Year of the Dragon '85
The Young Savages '61

Gay Best Friend

As Good As It Gets '97 ▶
Baggage Claim '13
Dare '09
Date and Switch '13
For a Good Time, Call... '12
G.B.F. '13
A Home at the End of the World '04
Mannequin 2: On the Move '91
Mannequin '87
My Best Friend's Wedding '97
The Next Best Thing '00
The Object of My Affection '98
The Perks of Being a Wallflower '12 ▶

Gays

***See also** Bisexuality; Gender Bending; Lesbians*

The Accompanist '20
Adam & Steve '05
AKA '02
Aleksandr's Price '13
Alive and Kicking '96
All Over the Guy '01
American Beauty '99 ▶
Anatomy of Hell '04
And the Band Played On '93 ▶
And Then We Danced '20 ▶
Angels in America '03 ▶
Another Country '84
Antarctica '08
Any Day Now '12 ▶
Apart from Hugh '94
Arabian Nights '74 ▶
Arizona Sky '08
Armistead Maupin's More Tales of the City '97
Armistead Maupin's Tales of the City '93
As Good As It Gets '97 ▶
August '11
B. Monkey '97
The Bachelor Weekend '13
Bad Education '04 ▶
Bam Bam & Celeste '05 ▶
Be Cool '05
Beach Rats '17
BearCity '10
Beastly Boyz '06
Beat '00
Beautiful Something '16
Beautiful Thing '95 ▶
Bedrooms and Hallways '98
Before I Forget '07
Before Night Falls '00 ▶
Beginners '10 ▶
Behind the Candelabra '13
Behind the Red Door '02
Beloved '11
Beloved/Friend '99
Bent '97
The Best Exotic Marigold Hotel '12 ▶
The Best Way '76
Between Love & Goodbye '08
Between Something & Nothing '08
Beyond the Walls '12
The Big Brass Ring '99
Big Eden '00
The Big Tease '99
Billy's Hollywood Screen Kiss '98
The Birdcage '95 ▶
Blackbird '14
Blast from the Past '98
Blitz '11
Blue '93
Boat Trip '03
Bohemian Rhapsody '18
Boondock Saints '99
Born in 68 '08
Borstal Boy '00
Boulevard '15
Boy Culture '06
Boy Erased '18
The Boy With the Sun in His Eyes '09
The Boys in the Band '70
Boys Life '94
Boystown '07
BPM (Beats Per Minute) '17
Breakfast on Pluto '05
Breakfast With Scot '07
Breaking the Surface: The Greg Louganis Story '96
Brideshead Revisited '08
Broadway Damage '98
Brokeback Mountain '05 ▶
The Broken Hearts Club '00 ▶
The Broken Tower '11
Brother to Brother '04
Bruno '09
The Bubble '06
B.U.S.T.E.D. '99
Burning Blue '14
Burnt Money '00
The Business of Fancydancing '02
Cabaret '72 ▶
Call Me by Your Name '17 ▶
Cambridge Spies '03
Camp '03
Capital Games '13
Carandiru '03
Caresses '97
Carrington '95
The Celluloid Closet '95 ▶
Chef's Special '08
Chicken Tikka Masala '05
Children of Hannibal '98
Chris & Don: A Love Story '07 ▶
Christopher and His Kind '11 ▶
Chuck & Buck '00
Cinema Verite '11
Circuit '02
City in Panic '86
The City of Your Final Destination '09
Clapham Junction '07
Close to Leo '02
The Closet '00
Coffee Date '06
C.O.G. '13
Colonel Redl '84 ▶
Color Me Kubrick '05
Come Undone '00
Coming Out '89
The Conformist '71 ▶
Connie and Carla '04
The Conrad Boys '06
The Cost of Love '11
Cote d'Azur '05
The Country Teacher '08
Cowboys and Angels '00
Cowboys & Angels '04 ▶
Creatures from the Pink Lagoon '07
Crocodile Tears '98
Cruel Intentions '98
Cruising '80
The Crying Game '92 ▶
Cthulhu '08
The Curiosity of Chance '06
Curse of the Queerwolf '87
The Dark Side of Love '12
David Searching '97
David's Birthday '09
Days '02
De-Lovely '04
The Death and Life of John F. Donovan '19
Death in Venice '71 ▶
D.E.B.S. '04
The Deep End '01 ▶
Defying Gravity '99
The Delta '97
Demolition '15
Desert Migration '16 ▶
The Detective '68 ▶
Die Mommie Die! '03
Different Story '78
Dirty Girl '10
Dirty Laundry '07
A Dirty Shame '04
The Dog '14 ▶
Dog Gone Love '03
Doing Time on Maple Drive '92
Domain '09
Dream Boy '08
Dress Gray '86 ▶
Drift '00
The Dying Gaul '05 ▶
An Early Frost '85 ▶
East Palace, West Palace '96
East Side Story '07
Eating Out 2: Sloppy Seconds '06
Eating Out 3: All You Can Eat '09
Eating Out 4: Drama Camp '11
Eating Out: The Open Weekend '11
Eban and Charley '01
Edge of Seventeen '99
Edward II '92
The Embalmer '03 ▶
Enduring Love '04
An Englishman in New York '09
The Event '03
The Everlasting Secret Family '88
Eyes Wide Open '09
Facing Windows '03
The Falls: Covenant of Grace '16
The Falls: Testament of Love '13
Far from Heaven '02 ▶
Father's Day '12
Finding Mr. Wright '11
Finding North '97
First Love and Other Pains / One of Them '99
Floating '97
The Fluffer '01
Food of Love '02
For a Good Time, Call... '12
For a Lost Soldier '93
Forgive and Forget '99
Formula 17 '04
Four '12
A Four Letter Word '07
Four More Years '10
Four Weddings and a Funeral '94 ▶
Fox and His Friends '75 ▶
Frank McKlusky, C.I. '02
Fraternity Massacre at Hell Island '07
Freak Show '18
Freshman Orientation '04
Friends and Family '01
Friends & Lovers '99
Frisk '95
From Beginning to End '09
Full Speed '96
Fun Down There '88
Funkytown '11
The Gay Bed and Breakfast of Terror '07
The Gay Deceivers '69
Gayby '12
Get Real '99
Ghost Writer '07
Go Fish '94 ▶
Go West '05
Gods and Monsters '98 ▶
God's Own Country '17 ▶
Gone, But Not Forgotten '03
Goodbye, Dragon Inn '03
Gorgeous '99
The Graffiti Artist '04
The Green '11
Green Plaid Shirt '96
Grief '94
Grown Up Movie Star '10
Guys and Balls '04
Handsome Harry '09
The Hanging Garden '97
Happy Endings '05
Happy, Texas '99 ▶
Happy Together '96
Hard Pill '05
Harry and Max '04
Harvest '11
The Harvesters '19
Hate Crime '05
Head On '98 ▶
Heartbeats '11
Heaven's a Drag '94
Heights '04
Hellbent '04
Hey, Happy! '01
Hideaway '09
His Secret Life '01 ▶
The History Boys '06
Hit and Runway '01
Hold Your Peace '11
Holding Trevor '07
Hollywood, Je T'Aime '09
A Home at the End of the World '04
Home for the Holidays '95
Hopelessly in June '11
Horror in the Wind '08
The Hours '02 ▶
How to Survive a Plague '12 ▶
Howl '10
Hustler White '96
I Am Michael '17
I Can't Sleep '93
I Do '13 ▶
I Killed My Mother '09
I Love You Baby '01
I Love You Phillip Morris '10
I Now Pronounce You Chuck and Larry '07
I Think I Do '97
I Want to Get Married '11
Ice Blues: A Donald Strachey Mystery '08
Ice Men '04
If You Only Knew '00
Illuminata '98
I'm So Excited '13
The Imitation Game '14 ▶
In and Out '97 ▶
In Bloom '13 ▶
In the Blood '06
In the Family '11
In the Flesh '97
Lazy Eye '16
Infamous '06
The Iron Ladies 2 '03
The Iron Ladies '00
It's In the Water '96
It's My Party '95
It's the Rage '99
Jeffrey '95
Jitters '10
The Journey of Jared Price '00
Judas Kiss '11
Just One Time '00
Kawa '11
Keep the Lights On '12 ▶
Keillers Park '05
King Cobra '16
Kiss Kiss Bang Bang '05 ▶
Kiss Me Deadly '08
Kiss Me, Guido '97
Kiss Me...Kill Me '76
Kiss of the Spider Woman '85 ▶
Kiss the Bride '07
Km. 0 '00
La Cage aux Folles '78 ▶
La Cage aux Folles 2 '81
La Cage aux Folles 3: The Wedding '86
La Leon '07
La Mission '09
Lan Yu '01
The Laramie Project '02 ▶
Last Days '05
Latter Days '04
Lawless Heart '01
The Leather Boys '63
Leather Jacket Love Story '98
Leaving Metropolis '02
Let My People Go! '11
L'Homme Blesse '83 ▶
L.I.E. '01
Lie Down with Dogs '95
Like It Is '98 ▶
Like It Never Was Before '95
Lilies '96
Lilting '14 ▶
The Line of Beauty '06
Lisa Picard Is Famous '01
Little Ashes '09
Little Miss Sunshine '06 ▶
The Living End '92
Loggerheads '05 ▶
Lola and Billy the Kid '98
Long-Term Relationship '06
Longtime Companion '90 ▶
Loose Cannons '10
The Lost Language of Cranes '92 ▶
Love and Death on Long Island '97
Love and Human Remains '93 ▶
Love and Other Disasters '06
Love Is Strange '14 ▶
Love Is the Devil '98 ▶
Love Kills '98
Love, Simon '18 ▶
Love! Valour! Compassion! '96
Ludwig '72
Luminarias '99
Luster '02
Madagascar Skin '95
Madame Sata '02
Make the Yuletide Gay '09
Making Love '82
Mambo Italiano '03
The Man I Love '97
The Man of My Life '06
Marathon '09
Matrimonium '05
Matthew Shepard Is a Friend of Mine '14
Maurice '87 ▶
Men Men Men '95
The Men Next Door '12
Menage '86 ▶
Merci Docteur Rey '04 ▶
The Mexican '01
Midnight Cowboy '69 ▶
Midnight Dancers '94
Midnight in the Garden of Good and Evil '97
Miles '17
Milk '08 ▶
Misconceptions '08
Mr. Right '06
The Moon & the Stars '07
Moonlight '16 ▶
Morgan '12
Mouth to Mouth '95
The Mudge Boy '03
Mulligans '08
My Beautiful Laundrette '85 ▶
My Best Friend's Wedding '97
My Own Private Idaho '91 ▶
Mysterious Skin '04 ▶
The Naked Civil Servant '75 ▶
Naked Lunch '91 ▶
Nasty Baby '15
Nerolio '96
Never Met Picasso '96
Newcastle '08
The Next Best Thing '00
Next Year in Jerusalem '98
Nico and Dani '00
The Night Listener '06
Nighthawks '78
Nijinsky '80
Free Fall '13
No One Sleeps '01
Noah's Arc: Jumping the Broom '08
The Normal Heart '14 ▶
Norman, Is That You? '76
O Fantasma '00
The Object of My Affection '98
Okoge '93
On the Other Hand, Death '08
The One '11
One Kiss '16
Open Cam '05
The Opposite of Sex '98
Ordinary Sinner '02
Other Voices, Other Rooms '95
Otto: Or, Up with Dead People '08

▶ = rated three bones or higher

Our Lady of the Assassins '01
Our Paradise '11
Our Sons '91
Out at the Wedding '07
Out in the Dark '12 ▶
Outing Riley '04
Outrage '09
Oy Vey! My Son is Gay! '09
Pain and Glory '19 ▶
The Painted Lady '97 ▶
Parallel Sons '95
Paris Is Burning '91 ▶
Parting Glances '86 ▶
Partners '82
The Party '17
The Perfect Son '00
The Perfect Wedding '12
Perfume '01
The Perfume of Yvonne '94
Petunia '13
Philadelphia '93 ▶
Phoenix '06
The Pillow Book '95
Plan B '09
Pornography: A Thriller '10
Possible Loves '00 ▶
Postcards from America '95
Poster Boy '04
Prayers for Bobby '09 ▶
Prick Up Your Ears '87 ▶
Pride '14 ▶
Priest '94 ▶
Private Romeo '11
Prom Queen '04
P.S. Your Cat is Dead! '02
Queer Duck: The Movie '06
Querelle '83
Quiet Days in Hollywood '97
Quinceanera '06 ▶
Raising Heroes '97
The Raven '07
Ready to Wear '94
The Reception '05
Red Dirt '99
Redwoods '09
Reflections in a Golden Eye '67
Regular Guys '96
Relax. . . It's Just Sex! '98
Rent '05
Rites of Passage '99
The Ritz '76 ▶
A River Made to Drown In '97
Rock Haven '07
Rocketman '19 ▶
The Rocky Horror Picture Show '75 ▶
Role/Play '10
Rope '48 ▶
Rude '96
Sasha '10
Satan's Brew '76
Saturday Night at the Baths '75
Savage Grace '07
Save Me '07
Saved! '04
Say Uncle '05
The Sculptress '97
Second Best '05
Second Skin '99
Seducing Maarya '99
The Sergeant '68
Sex Positive '09
The Shadows '07
Shakespeare's Merchant '05
Shank '09
Shelter '07
Shock to the System '06
Shut Up Little Man! An Audio Misadventure '11
A Single Man '09 ▶
Sitcom '97
Smoke '93
Socrates '18 ▶
Sordid Lives '00
Speedway Junky '99
Spent '00
Spring Forward '99
The State Within '06
Steam: A Turkish Bath '96 ▶
Stonewall '95 ▶
Stonewall '15
Strange Bedfellows '04
Strange Fits of Passion '99
Strange Fruit '04
Stranger by the Lake '13 ▶
Strawberry and Chocolate '93 ▶
The String '09
The Sum of Us '94 ▶
Sunday, Bloody Sunday '71 ▶
Surge of Power: The Stuff of Heroes '04
Surprise, Surprise '09
Surveillance 24/7 '07
Sweet November '01
Swoon '91 ▶
Taboo '99
The Talented Mr. Ripley '99
Tarnation '03
Taxi zum Klo '81 ▶
Testosterone '03
That's Not Us '15
These Foolish Things '06
Third Man Out: A Donald Strachey Mystery '05
Those Who Love Me Can Take the Train '98
Three to Tango '99
Threesome '94
Time to Leave '05 ▶
Times Have Been Better '06
Times of Harvey Milk '83 ▶
To Be Takei '14
To Play or to Die '91
The Toilers and the Wayfarers '97
Tomcats '01
Too Cool for Christmas '04
Too Much Sun '90
Torch Song Trilogy '88
Total Eclipse '95
Totally F***ed Up '94
Touch of Pink '04
Transamerica '05 ▶
Trick '99 ▶
The Trio '97
The Trip '02
Tropical Malady '04
The 24th Day '04
29th & Gay '05
24 Nights '99
The Twilight of the Golds '97
Twist '03 ▶
Twisted '96
2: Voodoo Academy '12
Unconditional Love '03
Under One Roof '02
Urbania '00
Valentino: The Last Emperor '08
Velvet Buzzsaw '19
Very Annie Mary '00
A Very Natural Thing '73
A Very Serious Person '06
Victim '61 ▶
Victor/Victoria '82 ▶
Villain '71
Violet Tendencies '10
Visions of Sugarplums '99
The Walker '07
Walking on Water '02
Water Drops on Burning Rocks '99
We Were Here '11
We Were One Man '80
The Wedding Banquet '93 ▶
Wedding Wars '06
The Weekend '00
Weekend '11
Were the World Mine '08
What Happens Next '11
When Love Comes '98
Whole New Thing '05
Wild Horses '15
Wild Reeds '94 ▶
Wild Tigers I Have Known '06
Wilde '97
Withnail and I '87 ▶
The Witnesses '07
Wittgenstein '93
The Wolves of Kromer '98
World and Time Enough '95
Yeti: A Love Story '08
Yossi '12
Yossi & Jagger '02
You Belong to Me '07
You'll Get Over It '02
Zero Patience '94
Zombies of Mass Destruction '10
Zus & Zo '01

Gender Bending

***See also** Gays; Lesbians; Role Reversal*

The Adventures of Priscilla, Queen of the Desert '94 ▶
The Adventures of Sebastian Cole '99
All About My Mother '99 ▶
All the Queen's Men '02
Anything for Love '93
The Assignment '17
At War with the Army '50
The Badge '02
The Ballad of Little Jo '93
Better Than Chocolate '99
Big Mommas: Like Father, Like Son '11
Blue Murder at St. Trinian's '56 ▶
The Breadwinner '17 ▶
Chinese Odyssey 2002 '02
The Christine Jorgensen Story '70
Come Drink with Me '65 ▶
Connie and Carla '04
The Cost of Love '11
The Crying Game '92 ▶
Dallas Buyers Club '13 ▶
The Damned '69
The Danish Girl '15
Desperate Living '77
Different for Girls '96 ▶
Dr. Jekyll and Ms. Hyde '95
Dress to Kill '07
Dressed to Kill '80
Eating Out 4: Drama Camp '11
Ed Wood '94 ▶
The Extra Man '10
A Fantastic Woman '18
First a Girl '35
Flawless '99
Gaudi Afternoon '01
Girl '18 ▶
A Girl Like Me: The Gwen Araujo Story '06
Glen or Glenda? '53
Go West '05
Gun Hill Road '11
Hairspray '88 ▶
Hedwig and the Angry Inch '00 ▶
He's My Girl '87
Holiday Heart '00
I Like It Like That '94 ▶
I Shot Andy Warhol '96 ▶
I Want What I Want '72
I Was a Male War Bride '49 ▶
In a Year of 13 Moons '78
The Iron Ladies 2 '03
The Iron Ladies '00
It's Pat: The Movie '94
Just One of the Girls '93
Just One of the Guys '85
K-11 '11
A Kid Like Jake '18
Kill Your Darlings '06
Kinky Boots '06
La Cage aux Folles '78 ▶
La Cage aux Folles 2 '81
La Cage aux Folles 3: The Wedding '86
Laurence Anyways '12
Law of Desire '86 ▶
Lilies '96
Little Old New York '23
Lola and Billy the Kid '98
Lulu '02
Lust in the Dust '85 ▶
M. Butterfly '93
Ma Vie en Rose '97 ▶
Madame Sata '02
The Merchant of Venice '04 ▶
Mrs. Doubtfire '93
Mixed Nuts '94
My Son, the Vampire '52
Myra Breckinridge '70
The New Girlfriend '14
The Newlydeads '87
Nobody's Perfect '90
Normal '03
Nuns on the Run '90
Old Mother Riley in Paris '38
Old Mother Riley, MP '39
Old Mother Riley's Ghosts '41
On Each Side '07
On the Basis of Sex '18
Outrageous! '77 ▶
Paris Is Burning '91 ▶
Peacock '09
Pink Flamingos '72
Polyester '81
Psycho '60 ▶
The Rocky Horror Picture Show '75 ▶
The Romance of Astrea and Celadon '07
She's the Man '06
The Silence of the Lambs '91 ▶
Soldier's Girl '03 ▶
Some Like It Hot '59 ▶
Sorority Boys '02
Spork '10
Stonewall '95 ▶
Surrender Dorothy '98
Switch '91 ▶
Tangerine '15
Those Who Love Me Can Take the Train '98
3 Generations '17
Tipping the Velvet '02
To Wong Foo, Thanks for Everything, Julie Newmar '95
Tootsie '82 ▶
Torch Song Trilogy '88
Transamerica '05 ▶
Transfixed '01
Trash '70
Twelfth Night '96
Twisted '96
Vegas in Space '94
Velvet Goldmine '98
Victor/Victoria '82 ▶
Water Drops on Burning Rocks '99
The Wedding Singer '97
White Chicks '04
Wigstock: The Movie '95
Wild Zero '00
The Woman Inside '83
Woman on Top '00
The World According to Garp '82 ▶
The Year of Living Dangerously '82 ▶
Yentl '83
Zatoichi '03 ▶
Zazie dans le Metro '61 ▶

Generation X

All the Wrong Places '00
Bandwagon '95
The Beach '00
Beautiful Girls '96 ▶
Before Sunrise '94
Blade '98
Bodies, Rest & Motion '93
Bottle Rocket '95
Charlie White '04
Chasing Amy '97
Clerks '94 ▶
Don't Do It '94
Dream for an Insomniac '96
Empire Records '95
Flakes '07
Floundering '94
Gen-X Cops '99
Glory Daze '96
Half-Baked '97
Home '05
Into the Wild '07 ▶
Keys to Tulsa '96
Kicked in the Head '97
Kicking and Screaming '95 ▶
Knocked Up '07
Little Athens '05
Loaded '94
The Low Life '95
Mallrats '95
Mama's Boy '07
Meet the Deedles '98
101 Ways (The Things a Girl Will Do to Keep Her Volvo) '00
Party Girl '94
Reality Bites '94
S.F.W. '94
Singles '92 ▶
Slacker '91 ▶
Sleep with Me '94
Something More '99
Strange Fits of Passion '99
20th Century Women '17
When the Party's Over '91

Genetics

***See also** Mad Scientists; Metamorphosis*

Alien Nation: Body and Soul '95
Biohazard: The Alien Force '95
The Boys from Brazil '78
Corn '04
Dark Metropolis '10
Dinocroc Vs. Supergator '10
District 9 '09 ▶
Eli '19
Extraordinary Measures '10
The Fly '86 ▶
The Fly 2 '89
The Fly '58 ▶
Forbidden World '82
Gattaca '97 ▶
The Gene Generation '07
Godsend '04
Ice Soldiers '13
The Island of Dr. Moreau '96
Little Joe '19
Mega Piranha '10
Metamorphosis: The Alien Factor '93
Mimic '97
Re-Generation '04
The Return of the Swamp Thing '89
Rise of the Planet of the Apes '11 ▶
Sabretooth '01
The Sender '98
Species 2 '98
Splice '10
The Twilight of the Golds '97
Wes Craven Presents Mind Ripper '95
X-Men: Days of Future Past '14 ▶
X-Men: First Class '11 ▶
X-Men: The Last Stand '06

Genies

***See also** Magic Carpet Rides*

Aladdin '92 ▶
Aladdin '19
Aladdin and the King of Thieves '96
Arabian Nights '00
Bernard and the Genie '91
The Brass Bottle '63
Jinn '14
Kazaam '96
A Kid in Aladdin's Palace '97
Miracle Beach '92
The Return of Jafar '94
The Thief of Bagdad '40 ▶
The Thief of Baghdad '24 ▶
The Thief of Baghdad '78
Three Wishes '95
Wishmaster 4: The Prophecy Fulfilled '02
Wishmaster '97

Genocide/Ethnic Cleansing

***See also** Civil War (non U.S.); The Holocaust*

Ararat '02 ▶
Attack on Darfur '09
Beyond Borders '03
Blood Diamond '06
Darfur Now '07
The Devil Came on Horseback '07 ▶
First They Killed My Father '17
Hotel Rwanda '04
John Rabe '09
The Killing Fields '84 ▶
The Lark Farm '07
The Last King of Scotland '06 ▶
The Promise '17
S21: The Khmer Rouge Killing Machine '03 ▶
Shooting Dogs '05
Sometimes in April '05 ▶
Swimming to Cambodia '87 ▶
Tears of the Sun '03

Genre Spoofs

***See also** Comedy Sci-Fi; Credits Chaos!; Detective Spoofs; Satire & Vampire Spoof; Western Comedy*

Airplane 2: The Sequel '82
Airplane! '80 ▶
All Through the Night '42 ▶
April Fool's Day '86
Austin Powers: International Man of Mystery '97 ▶
Austin Powers 2: The Spy Who Shagged Me '99 ▶
Beverly Hills Ninja '96
The Big Bus '76
Black Dynamite '09
Blazing Saddles '74 ▶
Blondes Have More Guns '95
Blood & Concrete: A Love Story '91
Blubberella '11
Bollywood Hero '09
Boogie Woogie '09
Bugsy Malone '76
Cairo '42
Cannibal! The Musical '96
Casino Royale '67
Chinese Odyssey 2002 '02
Code Name: The Cleaner '07
The Comebacks '07
The Cool Ones '67
Corky Romano '01
Creature from the Haunted Sea '60
Creatures from the Pink Lagoon '07
Dance Flick '09
Dark and Stormy Night '09
Date Movie '06
Disaster Movie '08
Dogville Shorts '30
Don't Be a Menace to South Central While Drinking Your Juice in the Hood '95
Don't Worry, We'll Think of a Title '66
Drive-In '76
18 Fingers of Death '05
Epic Movie '07
Fatal Instinct '93
Fathom '67
Fay Grim '06
Ferocious Female Freedom Fighters '88
Flesh Gordon '72
Frankenstein's Great Aunt Tillie '83
Fright Flick '10
Further Up the Creek '58
Galactic Gigolo '87
Galaxina '80
Get Crazy '83
Get Smart '08
Ghoul School '90
The Godson '98
Happily N'Ever After '07
Hatchet 2 '10
Hatchet '07
Hell Comes to Frogtown '88
Hercules '97 ▶
High Anxiety '77
Hot Fuzz '07 ▶
Hot Shots! '91 ▶
Hot Shots! Part Deux '93
The Hound of the Baskervilles '77
Hysterical '83
I'm Gonna Git You Sucka '88 ▶
Invasion! '99
J-Men Forever! '79 ▶
Jake Speed '86
Johnny English '03
Johnny English Reborn '11
Kentucky Fried Movie '77 ▶
Kung Fu Hustle '04
Kung Pow! Enter the Fist '02
Last Action Hero '93
Lemonade Joe '64
The Little Giant '33
The Lost Skeleton of Cadavra '01
Lust in the Dust '85 ▶
Mafia! '98
The Man Who Knew Too Little '97

▶ = rated three bones or higher

Revenge of the Red Baron '93
Riding the Bullet '04
The Ring 2 '05
The Ring Virus '99
Rings '17
Ringu 0 '01
Ringu 2 '99
Ringu '98 ▸
River: The Legend of La Llorona '06
The St. Francisville Experiment '00
Sanitarium '13
Scary Movie 2 '01
Scary Stories to Tell in the Dark '19
Scoob! '20
Scoop '06
Screaming Dead '03
Seance '06
Secrets in the Walls '10
The Secrets of the Summer House '08
Seeding of a Ghost '86
7 Angels in Eden '07
Seventh Moon '08
Shadow People '13
Shut In '16
Shutter '05
Shutter '08
Silent Hill '06
Silent Tongue '92
The Simian Line '99
6 Degrees of Hell '12
The Sixth Man '97
The Sixth Sense '99▸
Sleepy Hollow '99▸
Soft for Digging '01
Some Kind of Hate '15
Sometimes They Come Back. . . Again '96
Somewhere Tomorrow '85
Soultaker '90
Spectre '96
The Spiderwick Chronicles '08▸
Spirit Lost '96
Spirited Away '01
Spooky Buddies '11
Spooky Stakeout '16
Still Small Voices '07
Stir of Echoes '99
Stir of Echoes 2: The Homecoming '07
Stitches '12
Stormswept '95
Straight A's '13
Tales of Halloween '15
Things '93
13 Gantry Row '98
13 Ghosts '60
13 Ghosts '01
13 Seconds '03
30 Nights of Paranormal Activity with the Devil Inside the Girl with the Dragon Tattoo '12
Tigers Are Not Afraid '19▸
The Time of Their Lives '46
To Gillian on Her 37th Birthday '96
Tomie '99
Topper '37▸
Topper Returns '41▸
The Turn of the Screw '74
The Turn of the Screw '92
The Turn of the Screw '99
Twice Dead '88
Twixt '12
Ugetsu '53▸
The Unborn '09
Uncle Boonmee Who Can Recall His Past Lives '10
Under the Mistletoe '06
Under the Sand '00▸
Under the Shadow '16▸
The Undying '09
Unfriended '15
The Uninvited '44▸
The Uninvited '09
The Unquiet '08
Urban Ghost Story '98
Uzumaki '00
A Valentine Carol '07
Versus '00
Visitors '03
Volver '06▸
The Wailer '06
The Ward '10
The Watcher in the Woods '81
We are Still Here '15
What Lies Beneath '00
When Good Ghouls Go Bad '01
When I Find the Ocean '06
White Noise '05
Winchester '18
Wind Chill '07
Windrunner '94
The Woman in Black 2: Angel of Death '15
Woman in Black '89
The Woman in Black '12
The Wretched '08
Wuthering Heights '98
Zero Patience '94

Giants

Attack of the 50 Foot Cheerleader '12
Attack of the 50 Foot Woman '58
Attack of the 50 Ft. Woman '93
Attack of the 60-Foot Centerfold '95
Beavis and Butt-Head Do America '96
The BFG '16
Big Fish '03▸
Boggy Creek II '83
Bride of the Monster '55
Cyclops '56
The Deadly Mantis '57
Dr. Cyclops '40
Ella Enchanted '04▸
Evil Alien Conquerors '02
The Fallen Ones '05
Giant from the Unknown '58
Godzilla *vs.* Megalon '76
Honey, I Blew Up the Kid '92
Humongous '82
Igor '08
The Iron Giant '99▸
Jack and the Beanstalk '09
Jack the Giant Slayer '13
Josh Kirby. . . Time Warrior: Chapter 2, The Human Pets '95
Kronos '57
Mighty Joe Young '49
Mighty Joe Young '98
My Giant '98
The Mysterians '58
The Nutty Professor '96▸
The Phantom Planet '61
The Princess Bride '87▸
The Spy Who Loved Me '77
Starship Troopers '97▸
Tarantula '55▸
Teenage Mutant Ninja Turtles: The Movie '90
Teenage Mutant Ninja Turtles 2: The Secret of the Ooze '91
Them! '54▸
The 3 Worlds of Gulliver '60
Tremors 2: Aftershocks '96
Tremors '89
Village of the Giants '65
War of the Colossal Beast '58
Zarkorr! The Invader '96

Gifted Children

***See also** Childhood Visions*
And You Thought Your Parents Were Weird! '91
Bee Season '05▸
The Book of Henry '17
Brad's Status '17
Dear Brigitte '65
Doctor Sleep '19▸
Escape to Witch Mountain '75▸
Gifted '17
The Girl with All the Gifts '17
Joshua '07▸
Kim Possible '19
Lemony Snicket's A Series of Unfortunate Events '04
Little Man Tate '91▸
Loverboy '05
Matilda '96▸
Midnight Special '16▸
Miss Peregrine's Home for Peculiar Children '16
Powder '95
Push '09
Real Genius '85 ▸
Ricky '09
Rookie of the Year '93
Searching for Bobby Fischer '93 ▸
Valentin '02
The Young and Prodigious T.S. Spivet '15

Gigolos

***See** Oldest Profession*

Glasgow

***See also** Scotland*
American Cousins '02
Beautiful Creatures '00
The Big Tease '99
Carla's Song '97
Dear Frankie '04
Doomsday '08
A Fond Kiss '04
My Name Is Joe '98
Nina's Heavenly Delights '06
Not Another Happy Ending '13
On a Clear Day '05
Orphans '97
Perfect Sense '11
The Purifiers '04
Red Road '06
Wilbur Wants to Kill Himself '02▸

Go Fish

***See also** Deep Blue; Killer Sea Critters*
Alamo Bay '85
Almost Heaven '06
Around the World Under the Sea '65
Bait Shop '08
Beyond All Limits '59
Big Fish '03▸
Bright Future '03▸
Captains Courageous '37▸
Captains Courageous '95
Chubasco '67
Darwin's Nightmare '04▸
The Day of the Dolphin '73
Dodson's Journey '01
Doomwatch '72
Finding Nemo '03▸
A Fish Called Wanda '88▸
Flipper '96▸
Forrest Gump '94▸
Frankenfish '04
Free Willy '93
Gone Fishin' '97
Grumpier Old Men '95
Grumpy Old Men '93▸
The Incredible Mr. Limpet '64
The Islander '88
Islander '06
The Isle '01
It Came from Beneath the Sea '55▸
Jaws '75▸
Jaws 2 '78
Jaws 3 '83
Jaws: The Revenge '87
La Terra Trema '48▸
Leviathan '13
The Life Aquatic with Steve Zissou '04
Like a Fish Out of Water '99
Limbo '99
Love Serenade '96
Maelstrom '00
Man of Aran '34▸
Man's Favorite Sport? '63
Mega Piranha '10
Megalodon '03
Milwaukee, Minnesota '03
Moby Dick '56▸
Moby Dick '98
My Summer Story '94
92 in the Shade '76▸
Northern Extremes '93
The Old Man and the Sea '58▸
The Old Man and the Sea '90
On Golden Pond '81▸
Ondine '09
Orca '77
Out of the Fog '41
Ponyo '08 ▸
Red Water '01
Reel Love '11
Respiro '02
Riff Raff '35
A River Runs Through It '92 ▸
The River Why '10
Salmon Fishing in the Yemen '11
Scorpion with Two Tails '82
The Sea '02
Seducing Doctor Lewis '03
The Seventh Stream '01
Shark Hunter '79
Shark Tale '04
Spawn of the North '38
Spoilers of the North '47
The SpongeBob SquarePants Movie '04
Tabu: A Story of the South Seas '31▸
Thunder Bay '53▸
Tiger Shark '32
The Treasure of Jamaica Reef '74
Up from the Depths '79
Where the Hot Wind Blows '59
The Wide Blue Road '57▸
You're Only Young Once '37
Zeus and Roxanne '96

Going Native

Apocalypse Now '79▸
The Blue Lagoon '80
The Bounty '84
Captain Fantastic '16
Congo '95
Dances with Wolves '90▸
The Emerald Forest '85▸
Farewell to the King '89
Four Frightened People '34
George of the Jungle '97▸
Growing Up Smith '17
Jeremiah Johnson '72▸
Jungle 2 Jungle '96
Krippendorf's Tribe '98
The Legend of Tarzan '16
Lord of the Flies '63▸
Lord of the Flies '90
The Lost City of Z '17▸
A Man Called Horse '70▸
The Mosquito Coast '86
Mutiny on the Bounty '35▸
Mutiny on the Bounty '62
Outback '71▸
Pagan Island '60
Paradise '82
The Return of a Man Called Horse '76
A Stranger Among Us '92
The Swiss Family Robinson '60▸

Going Postal

Alan Partridge '13▸
Appointment With Danger '51
Cop Au Vin '85
Dead Letter Office '98
Dear God '96
The Devil Inside '12
84 Charing Cross Road '86▸
Going Postal '98
Going Postal '10
He Was a Quiet Man '07
The Inspectors 2: A Shred of Evidence '00
The Inspectors '98
A Letter to Three Wives '49▸
Letters from a Killer '98
The Minus Man '99
Overnight Delivery '96
The Postman '94▸
The Postman '97
Postman's Knock '62
See Spot Run '01
The Shop Around the Corner '40▸
Side Street '50
You've Got Mail '98

Going Straight

***See also** Ex-Cons*
Action Man '67
Alias French Gertie '30
Almost an Angel '90
Angels with Dirty Faces '38 ▸
Baby, Take a Bow '34
The Badlanders '58
Barbershop '02 ▸
The Big Caper '57
Blood Ties '13
Bloodhounds of Broadway '52
Bloodhounds of Broadway '89
Boogie Boy '98
Boy A '07
Boys in Brown '49
Carlito's Way '93 ▸
Chain Link '08
The Chaperone '11
City of Bad Men '53
Colorado Territory '49
The Con Artist '10
Confessions of a Pit Fighter '05
Crazy on the Outside '10
Dead Man Running '09
Family Business '89
Few Options '11
The Good Samaritan '12
Gun Brothers '56
Gun Duel In Durango '57
The Hangman '59
Hard Luck '01
I'll Wait for You '41
Invisible Stripes '39
Jacked Up '01
Johnny Handsome '89▸
Joint Body '11
The Kane Files '10
Kiss of Death '47▸
Kiss of Death '94
La Mission '09
Lady Killer '33▸
Larceny, Inc. '42
The Lena Baker Story '08
London Boulevard '10
Love That Brute '50
A Man Named Rocca '61
The Mayor of 44th Street '42
Mercy Streets '00
Midnight Mary '33
The Mind Reader '33
No Man of Her Own '32
Once Upon a Time in Brooklyn '13
One Way Out '95
Paper Bullets '41
Piece of the Action '77
Radio Cab Murder '54
Reykjavik-Rotterdam '08
Saving God '08
Silverado '85▸
Straight Time '78▸
Strapped '93
Tall, Dark and Handsome '41
Tenth Avenue Angel '47
Tequila Sunrise '88
Uncaged Heart '07
The Usual Suspects '95▸
Weary River '29
We're No Angels '55▸
What a Life '39
What Doesn't Kill You '08
Wyoming Renegades '55
You Only Live Once '37

Golf

About Fifty '11
Alpha and Omega '10
Babe! '75▸
Blades '89
Bobby Jones: Stroke of Genius '04
The Caddy '53
Caddyshack 2 '88
Caddyshack '80▸
Carefree '38▸
Chasing the Green '09
Enter the Dragon '73▸
The Foursome '06
A Gentleman's Game '01
Goldfinger '64▸
Golf in the Kingdom '10
The Greatest Game Ever Played '05
Happy Gilmore '96
Houseguest '94
In Like Flint '67
Just Getting Started '17
The Legend of Bagger Vance '00
Love in the Rough '30
Mulligan '00
Mulligans '08
My Favorite Brunette '47
National Lampoon's Golf Punks '99
Once You Kiss a Stranger '69
Pat and Mike '52 ▸
The Price of Milk '00
Second Best '05
Seven Days in Utopia '11
Shelter Island '03
Space Jam '96
Spring Fever '27
The Squeeze '15
The Sweetest Thing '02
There's Something about Mary '98 ▸
The Tiger Woods Story '98
Tin Cup '96▸
Tommy's Honour '17
Who's Your Caddy? '07

Good Earth

***See** Trees & Wilderness*

Gospel Music

Amazing Grace '19▸
America's Heart and Soul '04
Black Nativity '13
The Fighting Temptations '03
The Gospel '05▸
Joyful Noise '12
Preacher's Kid '10
The Preacher's Wife '96
Preaching to the Choir '05
Ray '04▸
Sister Act '92
Sister Act 2: Back in the Habit '93

Governesses

***See** The Help: Female; Nannies & Governesses*

Grand Hotel

***See also** No-Exit Motel*
Across the Hall '09
The Adventurer: The Curse of the Midas Box '13
An Affair of Love '99
Agent of Death '99
Albatross '11
Albert Nobbs '11
Almost Strangers '01▸
America's Sweethearts '01
And Now Ladies and Gentlemen '02
Ants '77
Appetite '98
Bart Got a Room '08
The Best Exotic Marigold Hotel '12▸
Beverly Hills Chihuahua 3: Viva La Fiesta! '12
The Big Kahuna '00
Billy Madison '94
Bird People '14
Blame It on the Bellboy '92
Blondie Takes a Vacation '39
Bloody Wednesday '87
Blue Crush '02▸
Bobby '06
Brewster's Millions '45
Brewster's Millions '85
Bugsy '91▸
The Business of Strangers '01
Cedar Rapids '11▸
Chaos & Cadavers '03
Chelsea Walls '01
City of Ghosts '03
Come September '61
Computer Chess '13
Conversations with Other Women '05
Crackerjack '38
Crawlspace '86
Crocodile Dundee '86▸
Detective '85
Dirty Dancing '87▸
Dirty Pretty Things '03▸
The Double Hour '09
The Duchess of Buffalo '26

▸ = rated three bones or higher

The Duchess of Duke Street '78 ▶
Dunston Checks In '95
Eden '93
Eloise at the Plaza '03
The Fifth Element '97
Five Graves to Cairo '43 ▶
For Love or Money '93
Forgetting Sarah Marshall '08
40 Pounds of Trouble '62
Four Rooms '95
1408 '07
French Kiss '95
The Gay Bed and Breakfast of Terror '07
The Gay Deception '35
Ghosts of Goldfield '07
Girl in Black Stockings '57
The Girl with the Hungry Eyes '94
Give Us the Moon '44
The Grand Budapest Hotel '14 ▶
Grand Hotel '32 ▶
Happy Ever Afters '09
Her Highness and the Bellboy '45
Hit Me '96
Holiday Inn '42 ▶
Home Alone 2: Lost in New York '92
Hook, Line and Sinker '30
Hostage Hotel '00
Hot Tub Time Machine '10
Hotel '67
Hotel America '81
Hotel de Love '96
Hotel for Dogs '09
Hotel Imperial '27
Hotel Rwanda '04
Hotel Transylvania '12
I Served the King of England '07 ▶
It Could Happen to You '94
It Had to Be You '00
It Happened at Nightmare Inn '70
Italian for Beginners '01
Jet Lag '02
Jury Duty '95
Kiss Them for Me '57
The Lady From Lisbon '42
The Last Stop '99
The Longest Week '14
Lost in Translation '03 ▶
Mamma Mia! '08
The Man Who Lived at the Ritz '91
Mardi Gras: Spring Break '11
Meltdown '95
The Million Dollar Hotel '99
Mrs. Palfrey at the Claremont '05
Mistaken Identity '36
Morning '10
My Bodyguard '80 ▶
Mystery Train '89 ▶
New Rose Hotel '98
Nick of Time '95
Night at the Golden Eagle '02
A Night in Casablanca '46 ▶
The Night of the White Pants '06
The Night Porter '74
The Night We Called It a Day '03
Off Season '01
Old Mother Riley's New Venture '49
Open Windows '14
The Out-of-Towners '99
Paradise for Three '38
The Perfume of Yvonne '94
Plaza Suite '71 ▶
Pretty Woman '90 ▶
Priceless '06
Prom Night '08
Psycho '60 ▶
Psycho 2 '83
Psycho 3 '86
The Queen of Mean '90
The Red Inn '51
Roadside Prophets '92
Room Service '38
Room 314 '07
Rosebud Beach Hotel '85
The Second Best Exotic Marigold Hotel '15
Secret of the Black Trunk '62
See No Evil '06
Separate Tables '58 ▶
The Shining '80
A Single Girl '96
Smokin' Aces '07
The Snow Queen '02
Snowball Express '72
Some Girl(s) '13
Something Like Happiness '05
Somewhere '10
Somewhere in Time '80
Southside 1-1000 '50
Spare Parts '79
Suite 16 '94
Superman 2 '80 ▶
Sweet Lorraine '87 ▶
Ten Thousand Bedrooms '57
Terror at Red Wolf Inn '72
This Property Is Condemned '66
Three Strikes '00
3:10 to Yuma '57 ▶
Tower of Terror '97
The Trouble with Romance '09
28 Hotel Rooms '12
2046 '04
Twin Falls Idaho '99 ▶
Two Thousand Women '44
2:22 '08
Up in the Air '09 ▶
War Story '14
Weekend at the Waldorf '45 ▶
The White Cockatoo '35
Winter Sleep '14
Witchery '88

Grand Theft Auto

Auto Recovery '08
Banshee '06
Black Moon Rising '86
Corvette Summer '78
Crash and Burn '07
Eat My Dust '76
The Elder Son '06
The Fast and the Furious '01
The Fate of the Furious '17
Furious 7 '15
The Go-Getter '07
Gone in 60 Seconds '74
Gone in 60 Seconds '00
Grand Theft Auto '77
Hostage '05
Kiss of Death '94
Mad Bad '07
New Jersey Drive '95
No Man's Land '87
Rat Race '01
The Rookie '90
Sweet Revenge '76
Tsotsi '05 ▶

Grandparents

According to Greta '08
Adoration '08
Age of Consent '69
Alexandra '07 ▶
Aliens in the Attic '09
All I Want for Christmas '91
All Roads Lead Home '08
American Girl: Chrissa Stands Strong '09
American Gun '02 ▶
An American Rhapsody '01 ▶
American Wedding '03
American Woman '19
Anastasia '97
And So It Goes '14
Anne Frank: The Whole Story '01 ▶
Annie's Point '05
Another Happy Day '11
Arthur and the Invisibles '06
Arthur Christmas '11
Au Pair 2: The Fairy Tale Continues '01
Aurora Borealis '06
The Bad Mother's Handbook '07
Beautiful Wave '11
Beerfest '06
Big Eden '00
The Bird Can't Fly '07
Black Nativity '13
Black or White '14
Bloodworth '10
Boarding School '18
Boundaries '18
Bulletproof Monk '03
By Dawn's Early Light '00
Call of the Wild 3D '09
Captain Fantastic '16
The Caretaker '16
Carolina '03
The Chalk Garden '64 ▶
The Chamber '96
Charlie & Me '08
Charlie and the Chocolate Factory '05 ▶
Christmas in Canaan '09
Chronicle of the Raven '04
Clean '04
The Company of Wolves '85 ▶
Crackie '09
Crystal River '08
Cuban Blood '03
A Dad for Christmas '06
Dear Zachary: A Letter to a Son About His Father '08 ▶
Death Valley: The Revenge of Bloody Bill '04
Diary of a Mad Black Woman '05
Dirty Grandpa '16
A Dog of Flanders '99
Dolphin Tale '11
The Dynamiter '11
East Side Story '07
The Eddie Cantor Story '53
The Education of Little Tree '97 ▶
800 Bullets '02
18 Again! '88
Enchantment '48
The Etruscan Smile '19
Evergreen '04
Everything is Illuminated '05 ▶
Family Business '89
The Family Secret '24
Father's Little Dividend '51 ▶
Feed the Fish '09
The Fields '11
Final Assignment '80
5 Time Champion '11
The Flat '12 ▶
Flight of the Doves '71
Flowers in the Attic '87
Flowers in the Attic '14
Free Willy: Escape from Pirate's Cove '10
Georgia Rule '07
A Girl Like Me: The Gwen Araujo Story '06
The Grace Card '11
Gracie's Choice '04
Grandma '15 ▶
Grandma's Boy '06
A Grandpa for Christmas '07
The Green Years '46
The Greening of Whitney Brown '11
Hamlet & Hutch '14
Happenstance '00
Hard Four '07
Harvest '10
Hateship Loveship '13
The Heart Is Deceitful Above All Things '04
Heidi '37
Heidi '67
Heidi '93 ▶
Hereditary '18 ▶
Hesher '10
Hey Arnold! The Movie '02
The Hoodlum '19
Hoodwinked '05 ▶
Hoodwinked Too! Hood *vs.* Evil '11
How to Deal '03
I Wish '11 ▶
Ice Age: Continental Drift '12
I'll Follow You Down '13
I'll Take You There '99
I'm Going Home '00 ▶
In Her Shoes '05 ▶
In the Land of Women '06
Irina Palm '07
Jackass Presents: Bad Grandpa '13
Jersey Girl '04
Journey 2: The Mysterious Island '12
Joyful Noise '12
Just Henry '11
Keeping Up with the Steins '06
Knockout '11
Lady in a Jam '42
Language of the Enemy '07
Letters to Juliet '10
Life Support '07 ▶
Lifted '10
The Little Colonel '35 ▶
Little Miss Sunshine '06 ▶
The Looking Glass '16
The Lost Valentine '11
The Lottery Ticket '10
Love and Money '80
Lucky Grandma '20
Master of Disguise '02
Memorial Day '12
Midnight Bayou '09
Milton's Secret '16
Mrs. Palfrey at the Claremont '05
Misty '61
The Mother '03 ▶
Must Read After My Death '09
My Dog the Champion '14
My Louisiana Sky '02
A Night in Old Mexico '14
The Night of the Iguana '64 ▶
No More Orchids '32
The Notebook '13
The Old Curiosity Shop '07
On a Clear Day '05
On Borrowed Time '39 ▶
On My Way '14
Opposite Day '09
Out of the Woods '05
Owd Bob '97
Parental Guidance '12
Peace, Love & Misunderstanding '11
Pennies from Heaven '36
Persepolis '07 ▶
Petals on the Wind '14
Pete's Meteor '98
Pinky '49 ▶
Play the Game '09
Please Give '10
Poetry '10
Post Grad '09
Powder '95
The Princess Bride '87 ▶
The Princess Diaries 2: Royal Engagement '04
The Princess Diaries '01
A Princess for Christmas '11
The Proposal '09
Pure '02 ▶
Rain '06
Raising Victor Vargas '03
Red Clover '12
Red Hook Summer '12 ▶
Red Riding Hood '11
Red: Werewolf Hunter '10
Restless Spirits '99
River's End '05
Rumor Has It. . . '05
Santa and Pete '99
Saraband '03 ▶
Sci-Fighter '04
The Secret of Roan Inish '94 ▶
Shadow of the Hawk '76
The Shed '19
Sheeba '05
Sixteen Candles '84 ▶
Sleepwalking '08
The Smiling Ghost '41
Spy Kids 2: The Island of Lost Dreams '02 ▶
Spy Kids 3-D: Game Over '03
StarStruck '10
Storm Boy
Sunday Dinner for a Soldier '44
Super Buddies '13
Sword of Trust '19
Take a Giant Step '59
Tammy '14
Tammy and the Bachelor '57
Tartuffe '25
Tell Me a Riddle '80
Time to Leave '05 ▶
Toe to Toe '09
Treeless Mountain '08
The Triplets of Belleville '02 ▶
Two Bits '96
The Ultimate Gift '07
The Ultimate Life '13
The Vanished Empire '08
A Very Serious Person '06
The Visit '15
Walter and Henry '01 ▶
War Eagle, Arkansas '07
The Way Home '01
Wee Willie Winkie '37 ▶
Whale Rider '02 ▶
Where the Red Fern Grows: Part 2 '92
Wild Oranges '24
Willy Wonka & the Chocolate Factory '71 ▶
You Again '10
You Can't Take It With You '79
Young America '32
Zero Charisma '13

Great Britain

***See also** Ireland; London; Scotland*

Absolutely Anything '17
Adolf Hitler: My Part in His Downfall '74
The Affair '95
Alan Partridge '13 ▶
Alien Prey '78
All Is True '18
Amazing Mr. Blunden '72
American Friends '91
Among Giants '98
Angel '07
Angels and Insects '95 ▶
Angels One Five '54
Anne of the Thousand Days '69 ▶
Appropriate Adult '11
Asylum '05
August '95
An Awfully Big Adventure '94
The Bachelor Father '31
Back Home '90
Back to the Secret Garden '01
Band of Gold '95 ▶
The Bandit of Sherwood Forest '46
Bank Holiday '38
Barry Lyndon '75 ▶
Basil '98
Bean '97 ▶
Beast '17 ▶
Beau Brummell '54 ▶
Beau Brummell: This Charming Man '06
Becoming Jane '07
Belle '13
The Best of Men '12
The Big Scam '79
Billionaire Ransom '16
Billy Elliot '00 ▶
Birthday Girl '02
Black Death '10
Black Jack '79
Blinded by the Light '19 ▶
Blue Iguana '18
The Bookshop '18
Borg *vs.* McEnroe '17 ▶
The Borrowers '97
Borstal Boy '00
Boston Kickout '95
The Boy '16
Boy A '07
Brassed Off '96
Breaking the Bank '14
Brideshead Revisited '08
Brighton Rock '47 ▶
Brighton Rock '10
The Bronte Sisters '79
The Brontes of Haworth '73
Brothers of the Head '06
The Browning Version '94
The Buccaneers '95 ▶
Bullshot '83
Calendar Girls '03
Cambridge Spies '03
Camelot '67
The Canterville Ghost '86
The Canterville Ghost '96
Carrington '95
Catherine Cookson's Colour Blind '98
Catherine Cookson's The Black Velvet Gown '92
Catherine Cookson's The Cinder Path '94
Catherine Cookson's The Dwelling Place '94
Catherine Cookson's The Fifteen Streets '90
Catherine Cookson's Tilly Trotter '99
The Charge of the Light Brigade '68
Charles & Diana: A Palace Divided '93
Chicago Joe & the Showgirl '90
Chicken Run '00 ▶
Chicklit '16
Children of Men '06 ▶
Cider with Rosie '99
Circus '00
Cold Comfort Farm '94 ▶
Coming Home '98
A Congregation of Ghosts '09
The Constant Gardener '05 ▶
Control '07
The Corn Is Green '45 ▶
The Corn Is Green '79 ▶
Cranford '08
Crimson Peak '15 ▶
Cromwell '70
Crush '02
A Cry from the Streets '57
CSA: The Confederate States of America '04
Dad Savage '97
A Dance to the Music of Time '97
Danger UXB '81
Dark Blue World '01
Dark Horse '16
Darkest Hour '17 ▶
Dear Mr. Prohack '49
Deathwatch '02
Decline and Fall...of a Birdwatcher '68
The Deep Blue Sea '12
Deja Vu '98
Denial '16
Devices and Desires '91 ▶
Diana: Her True Story '93
Distant Voices, Still Lives '88 ▶
Don't Look Back '67
Doogal '05
Downton Abbey '19 ▶
Draw on Sweet Night '15
The Dresser '15 ▶
The Duke '99
The Eagle Has Landed '77 ▶
The Earl of Chicago '40
Eddie the Eagle '16
Edge of the World '37 ▶
Edie '19
Edward and Mrs. Simpson '80
Eliminators '16
Elizabeth R '72 ▶
Elizabeth: The Golden Age '07
Emma '96 ▶
Emma '97 ▶
Emma '09
Emma '20
Enduring Love '04
The Englishman Who Went up a Hill But Came down a Mountain '95 ▶
Enigma '01
Everybody Wins '90
Excalibur '81 ▶
FairyTale: A True Story '97
Far from the Madding Crowd '97 ▶
Far from the Madding Crowd '15
Farming '19
Feast of July '95
A Field in England '14 ▶
Fighter Squadron '48
Fighting with My Family '19
Film Stars Don't Die in Liverpool '17
The Final Cut '95 ▶
Final Score '18
Finding Neverland '04 ▶
Finding Your Feet '18
Firelight '97
Fisherman's Friends '19

Flambards '78
Flickers '80
For Love or Money '19
Forever and a Day '43 ▶
Formula 51 '01
The Four Feathers '02
Four Lions '10
Four Weddings and a Funeral '94 ▶
Framed '93 ▶
Frenchman's Creek '44
Frenchman's Creek '98
Funny Bones '94 ▶
Garfield: A Tail of Two Kitties '06
The Gathering '02
G.B.H. '91
The Gentlemen '20
The Girl with All the Gifts '17
Glorious 39 '09
Goal! The Dream Begins '06
God's Own Country '17 ▶
Goodbye, Mr. Chips '69
Goodbye, Mr. Chips '02
Goodnight, Mr. Tom '99
Gosford Park '01 ▶
The Great Muppet Caper '81 ▶
Greenfingers '00
The Guernsey Literary & Potato Peel Pie Society '18
Gulliver's Travels '95
Gwen '19
Harry Potter and the Goblet of Fire '05 ▶
The Hatching '16
Haunted '95
He Knew He Was Right '04
High Hopes '88 ▶
The Hireling '73
The History Boys '06
The History of Mr. Polly '07
The Holiday '06
Holy Matrimony '43 ▶
Home Again '13
Hope Gap '20
Hot Fuzz '07 ▶
The Hours '02 ▶
House of Cards '90 ▶
The House of Secrets '37
How Green Was My Valley '41 ▶
How I Live Now '13
How to Build a Girl '20
I Capture the Castle '02
I, Daniel Blake '16 ▶
I Remember Nelson '82
I'll Be There '03
Mission of Honor '19
Imagine Me & You '06
The Importance of Being Earnest '02
In His Life: The John Lennon Story '00
The Innocents '61 ▶
Inspector Clouseau '68
Into the Storm '09
The Invisible Woman '13 ▶
Iris '01 ▶
The Iron Lady '11
Jamaica Inn '82
Jane Eyre '96 ▶
Jane Eyre '97
Johnny English '03
Johnny English Strikes Again '18
Journey's End '18
Jude '96 ▶
Just Henry '11
The Keeper '18
The Kid Who Would Be King '19 ▶
The King '19 ▶
King Ralph '91
The King's Thief '55
Kingsman: The Golden Circle '17
Ladies in Lavender '04
Lady Chatterley '10 ▶
The Lady in the Van '15
Lady Jane '85 ▶
Lady Macbeth '17 ▶
The Lady's Not for Burning '87
Land Girls '09
Lara Croft: Tomb Raider '01
The Last of England '87 ▶
Lawless Heart '01
Legend '15
The Legend of Fritton's Gold '09
The Legend of Tarzan '16
The Libertine '05
Lillie '79 ▶
The Lion in Winter '68 ▶
The Little Stranger '18
Lloyds of London '36 ▶
Lock, Stock and 2 Smoking Barrels '98 ▶
The Long Day Closes '92 ▶
The Long Good Friday '80 ▶
Looking for Richard '96 ▶
Lorna Doone '34
Lorna Doone '90
Lorna Doone '01 ▶
Love & Friendship '16 ▶
Love for Lydia '79 ▶
Lucky Break '01
Madagascar Skin '95
Made in Dagenham '10 ▶
Made in Heaven '52
The Madness of King George '94 ▶
A Man for All Seasons '66 ▶
A Man for All Seasons '88 ▶
The Man in Grey '43 ▶
The Man Who Invented Christmas '17
The Man Who Knew Infinity '16
The Man Who Knew Too Little '97
Mary of Scotland '36 ▶
Me Before You '16
The Mercy '19
Merlin '98 ▶
The Mexican Spitfire Sees a Ghost '42
MI-5 '15
A Midwinter's Tale '95
The Mill on the Floss '39
The Mill on the Floss '97
Millions '05 ▶
A Mind to Murder '96
Miss Potter '06
Mrs. Brown '97 ▶
Mrs. Miniver '42 ▶
Mrs. Palfrey at the Claremont '05
Mr. Holmes '15
Mr. Toad's Wild Ride '96
Mr. Turner '14 ▶
The Mother '03 ▶
Munster, Go Home! '66
My Cousin Rachel '52
My Summer of Love '05
Dean Spanley '08
My Uncle Silas '01 ▶
Naked '93 ▶
The Naked Civil Servant '75 ▶
Nanny McPhee '06
National Lampoon's Van Wilder 2: The Rise of Taj '06
The New World '05 ▶
The Next of Kin '42
Night Must Fall '37 ▶
Nine Days a Queen '36 ▶
No Kidding '60
No Surrender '86 ▶
None But the Lonely Heart '44 ▶
Oasis: Supersonic '16 ▶
Of Time and the City '08 ▶
Official Secrets '19 ▶
Oh! What a Lovely War '69
Oliver Twist '05 ▶
The Omen '06
Once Upon a Time in the Midlands '02
One Chance '13
Oranges and Sunshine '10 ▶
Our Kind of Traitor '16
Pack of Lies '87
Pandaemonium '00
The Paranormal Diaries: Clophill '13
Passport to Pimlico '49
Persuasion '95 ▶
Peterloo '18
Pillars of the Earth '10
Pirate Radio '09
Plastic '14
Plenty '85
Poldark '75 ▶
Portrait of a Lady '96 ▶
Pride '14 ▶
Pride and Prejudice '95 ▶
Pride and Prejudice '05 ▶
Pride and Prejudice and Zombies '16
Prince of Poisoners: The Life and Crimes of William Palmer '98
Princess Caraboo '94
The Professor and the Madman '19
The Proposition '96
Pure '02 ▶
The Queen's Sister '05
A Question of Attribution '91
The Quiet Ones '14
Raffles '30 ▶
Raffles '39
The Railway Children '70 ▶
The Railway Children '00 ▶
Ray & Liz '19
Reckless '97 ▶
Reckless: The Sequel '98 ▶
The Reckoning '03 ▶
Red Riding, Part 1: 1974 '09
Red Riding, Part 2: 1980 '09
Red Riding, Part 3: 1983 '09
The Red Violin '98
A Respectable Trade '98
The Return of the Native '94
Return to Cranford '09
Reunion at Fairborough '85
Richard III '95 ▶
The Riddle of the Sands '79
Riders '88
Riff Raff '92 ▶
The Riot Club '15
The Rise of the Krays '16
Rocketman '19 ▶
Rogues of Sherwood Forest '50
A Royal Night Out '15 ▶
Royal Wedding '51 ▶
The Ruling Class '72 ▶
The Saint '97
Say Hello to Yesterday '71
Scandal '89 ▶
The Scarlet Tunic '97
Scoop '06
The Secret Diaries of Miss Anne Lister '10
The Secret Garden '49 ▶
Secret of the Black Trunk '62
Secret State '12
The Seeker: The Dark Is Rising '07
Sense and Sensibility '95 ▶
The Serpent's Kiss '97
The Servant '63 ▶
Shadowlands '93 ▶
Shanghai Knights '03
Shaun of the Dead '04 ▶
Shopping '93
Sightseers '12
Silver Dream Racer '83
Six Wives of Henry VIII '71 ▶
Son of Rambow '07
Sons and Lovers '60 ▶
Sorry We Missed You '20 ▶
The Special Relationship '10
Spectre '15
Speedy Death '99 ▶
Split Second '92
Starter for 10 '06
Station Jim '01
Stiff Upper Lips '96
Still Crazy '98 ▶
Stonehenge Apocalypse '10
Strange Relations '02
Summer in February '13
Sweet Revenge '98
Swept from the Sea '97
Sylvia '03
Tea with the Dames '18
Tess of the D'Urbervilles '08
Testament of Youth '79
That Sinking Feeling '79 ▶
They Shall Not Grow Old '19 ▶
Those Magnificent Men in Their Flying Machines '65 ▶
To Play the King '93 ▶
Tolkien '19
Tom Jones '98 ▶
A Touch of Class '73 ▶
The Trip '10 ▶
The Trip to Italy '14
Tristan & Isolde '06
Tristram Shandy: A Cock and Bull Story '05
Tunes of Glory '60 ▶
24 Hour Party People '01
2 Little Monsters '15
United '11
A United Kingdom '17
Vacuuming Completely Nude in Paradise '01
Valiant '05
Vanity Fair '04
Velvet Goldmine '98
A Very British Coup '88 ▶
Viceroy's House '17
A Village Affair '95
The Virgin Queen '55 ▶
Wallace & Gromit in The Curse of the Were-Rabbit '05 ▶
Warrior Queen '03
W.E. '11
The Wedding Guest '18
Weekend '11
We'll Meet Again '82
Whiskey Galore '48 ▶
The Whistle Blower '87 ▶
The White Cliffs of Dover '44 ▶
Wives and Daughters '01
The Wolves of Kromer '98
Woman in Black '89
A Woman of Substance '84
Wondrous Oblivion '06 ▶
Wuthering Heights '39 ▶
A Yank at Eton '42
Yanks '79
Year of the Comet '92
The Yellow Rolls Royce '64
Yesterday '19
The Young Americans '93
Young Bess '53 ▶
The Young Victoria '09 ▶
Young Winston '72 ▶

Great Death Scenes

See Death & Funerals

Great Depression

See also Hard Knock Life; Homeless

Ada '61
All the King's Men '49 ▶
American Madness '32
Angela's Ashes '99
Annie '99 ▶
Ask the Dust '06
The Ballad of the Sad Cafe '91
Big Bad Mama 2 '87
Big Bad Mama '74
Billy Bathgate '91
Bloody Mama '70
Bonnie & Clyde '67 ▶
Bonnie & Clyde '13
Bound for Glory '76 ▶
Boxcar Bertha '72
Catherine Cookson's The Man Who Cried '93
Charley and the Angel '73
Chinatown '74 ▶
Cinderella Man '05 ▶
The Cradle Will Rock '99
Dance Fools Dance '31 ▶
Dillinger '45 ▶
Dillinger '73
Dillinger and Capone '95
Dogville '03
Dream Chasers '82
Eleanor & Franklin '76 ▶
Emperor of the North Pole '73 ▶
Faithless '32
Falling for a Dancer '98
Four Deuces '75
Fresh Horses '88
The Funeral '96 ▶
The Grapes of Wrath '40 ▶
The Green Mile '99
The Group '66
Hallelujah, I'm a Bum '33
Hard Times '75 ▶
Henry & Verlin '94
Hidden Places '06
Hit the Dutchman '92
Homecoming: A Christmas Story '71
Honkytonk Man '82
Hoodlum '96
Hunter's Moon '97
The Inheritors '98
Inside Daisy Clover '65
The Iron Orchard '19
Ironweed '87 ▶
It Happened One Night '34 ▶
The Journey of Natty Gann '85 ▶
Just Around the Corner '38
Kansas City '95 ▶
King Kong '05 ▶
The King of Masks '99 ▶
Kings of the Evening '08
Kit Kittredge: An American Girl '08
Last Man Standing '96
Lawless '12
Life '99
The Life and Times of Hank Greenberg '99 ▶
Love on the Dole '41 ▶
Make Way for Tomorrow '37
Mary Poppins Returns '18
Melvin Purvis: G-Man '74
Merrily We Live '38 ▶
Mrs. Henderson Presents '05
Modern Times '36 ▶
Morning Glory '93
O Brother Where Art Thou? '00
Of Mice and Men '39 ▶
Of Mice and Men '81 ▶
Of Mice and Men '92 ▶
Oscar '91
Our Daily Bread '34 ▶
Paper Moon '73 ▶
Parachute Jumper '32
Pennies from Heaven '81 ▶
The Piano Lesson '94 ▶
Places in the Heart '84 ▶
Possessed '31
The Postman Always Rings Twice '46 ▶
The Postman Always Rings Twice '81
The Public Defender '31
Public Enemies '09
Rambling Rose '91 ▶
The Saddest Music in the World '03
Seabiscuit '03 ▶
Shadrach '98
Sounder '72 ▶
The Stars Fell on Henrietta '94
Street Scene '31 ▶
Sullivan's Travels '41 ▶
Sweet and Lowdown '99
Tenth Avenue Angel '47
They Shoot Horses, Don't They? '69 ▶
Thieves Like Us '74 ▶
Three-Cornered Moon '33
The Twelve Dogs of Christmas '05
Two Bits '96
Under Eighteen '32
Victor/Victoria '82 ▶
White Hot: The Mysterious Murder of Thelma Todd '91
Why Shoot the Teacher '79 ▶
Wild Boys of the Road '33
Wild Hearts Can't Be Broken '91 ▶
Wildflower '91 ▶
Winter People '89
The Yearling '94
You Only Live Once '37

Great Escapes

See also Men in Prison; POW/MIA; War, General; Women in Prison

Assassination '87
Austin Powers: International Man of Mystery '97 ▶
Bandits '99
Before Night Falls '00 ▶
Berlin Syndrome '17
Berlin Tunnel 21 '81
The Big Doll House '71
Blindness '08
Born to Be Wild '95
Breakout '75
Brute Force '47 ▶
Bus Driver '16
Butch Cassidy and the Sundance Kid '69 ▶
Captain Nemo and the Underwater City '69
The Ceremony '63
The Chase '66
Chasers '94
Chicken Run '00 ▶
Chronicle of an Escape '06
City of Fear '59
Colditz: Escape of the Birdmen '71
The Colditz Story '55
Con Air '97 ▶
Condition Red '95
The Cross of Lorraine '43
A Day in October '92
Deadly Mission '78
Deadly Target '94
The Deer Hunter '78 ▶
Desperate '47
Desperate Measures '98
Die Hard '88 ▶
Die Hard: With a Vengeance '95
Double Team '97
Down by Law '86 ▶
Era Notte a Roma '60 ▶
Escape '90
The Escape Artist '82 ▶
Escape from Alcatraz '79 ▶
Escape from Death Row '73
Escape from Fort Bravo '53
Escape from Hell '79
Escape from L.A. '96
Escape from New York '81
Escape from Sobibor '87 ▶
Escape: Human Cargo '98 ▶
Escape to Witch Mountain '75 ▶
The Escapist '08
Extremely Dangerous '99
Face/Off '97 ▶
Fantastic Voyage '66 ▶
The Fast Runner '01 ▶
Fast Walking '82
Feeling Minnesota '96
Flame Over India '59 ▶
Fled '96
Follow the River '95
Fortress 2: Re-Entry '99
Fortress '93
The Four Feathers '02
Frenchman's Creek '44
Frenchman's Creek '98
Gang Busters '55
The Grand Budapest Hotel '14 ▶
The Great Escape '63 ▶
The Great Train Robbery '79 ▶
Guardians of the Galaxy '14 ▶
Hangfire '91
Hannibal Brooks '69
Harold & Kumar Escape from Guantanamo Bay '08
Hart's War '02
Heaven '01
Heaven Ain't Hard to Find '10
Hellraiser 5: Inferno '00
Hide '08
Hitler: Beast of Berlin '39
The Horseman on the Roof '95
Houdini '53
Houdini '98
I Am David '04
The Ice Runner '93
In Hot Pursuit '77
The Inglorious Bastards '78
Inside Out '75
The Invisible Man '20 ▶
Iron Eagle '86
The Island '05
Jailbreakin' '72
Kidnapped '95
Ladyhawke '85
The Last Confederate: The Story of Robert Adams '05
Le Trou '59 ▶
Leaving Normal '92
Les Miserables '35 ▶
Les Miserables '57 ▶
Les Miserables '78 ▶
Lonely Are the Brave '62 ▶
The Long Riders '80 ▶
Lords of the Street '08
The Lovers and the Despot '16
Lucky Break '01
Madagascar '05
A Man Escaped '57 ▶
Man on a Tightrope '53
The Manhunt '86
McKenzie Break '70 ▶

Midnight Express '78 ▶
Missing in Action '84
Mrs. Soffel '84
The Mole People '56
Monte Cristo '22
Murder in the First '95
Murder One '88
The Muthers '76
Mysterious Island '61 ▶
Naked Youth '59
Night Crossing '81
No Escape '94
North by Northwest '59 ▶
Not Without My Daughter '90
On the Double '61
One That Got Away '57 ▶
Operation Thunderbolt '77
Pacific Inferno '85
Papillon '73 ▶
Parasomnia '08
Passage to Marseilles '44 ▶
The Password Is Courage '62
Paul '11
A Perfect World '93
Poseidon '06
Prison Break '38
Prison Break: The Final Break '09
The Prize '63 ▶
Public Enemies '09
Raiders of the Lost Ark '81 ▶
Raising Arizona '87 ▶
Raw Deal '48 ▶
Rescue Dawn '06 ▶
Ricochet '91 ▶
Rob Roy '95 ▶
The Rock '96 ▶
Romancing the Stone '84 ▶
Romeo Must Die '00
Runaway Train '85 ▶
The Saint '97
St. Ives '98
Samar '62
The Secret War of Harry Frigg '68
The Seventh Floor '93
The Shawshank Redemption '94 ▶
The Shining '80
Six: The Mark Unleashed '04
Skin Game '71 ▶
The Sound of Music '65 ▶
The Spy Who Came in from the Cold '65 ▶
Stalag 17 '53 ▶
Stalag Luft '93
Strange Cargo '40
The Sugarland Express '74 ▶
Tangled '10 ▶
Tequila Sunrise '88
Three Days of the Condor '75 ▶
Thunder County '74
To Catch a Thief '55 ▶
Torn Curtain '66
Toy Story '95 ▶
Toy Story 2 '99 ▶
The Truman Show '98 ▶
Two Fathers: Justice for the Innocent '94
UKM: The Ultimate Killing Machine '06
Venus Rising '95
Very Important Person '61
Victory '81
Von Ryan's Express '65 ▶
Wakefield '17
The Way Back '10
Welcome to Woop Woop '97
We're No Angels '55 ▶
White Nights '85
The Wild '06
The Wind Cannot Read '58
XXX: State of the Union '05
Zebra in the Kitchen '65

Greece--Ancient

Alexander '04
Alexander the Great '55
Atlantis, the Lost Continent '61
The Boys From Syracuse '40
Clash of the Titans '81
Clash of the Titans '10
The Colossus of Rhodes '61
Conquest of Mycene '63
Electra, My Love '74
Helen of Troy '56
Helen of Troy '03
Hellhounds '09
Hercules '14
Iphigenia '77 ▶
Jason and the Argonauts '63 ▶
Jason and the Argonauts '00
The Legend of Hercules '14
The Lion of Thebes '64 ▶
The Loves of Hercules '60
Medea '70
Medusa Against the Son of Hercules '62
Meet the Spartans '08
National Lampoon's The Legend of Awesomest Maximus '11
The Odyssey '97
300 '07
300: Rise of an Empire '13
The 300 Spartans '62
The Triumph of Hercules '66
The Trojan Horse '62
Trojan Women '71
Troy '04
Wrath of the Titans '12

Greece--Modern

Before Midnight '13 ▶
Captain Corelli's Mandolin '01
The Case of the Scorpion's Tail '71
Chevalier '16
Cliffs of Freedom '19
D'Agostino '12
Fedora '78
Fishtales '07
Forty Carats '73
I Live My Life '35
In the Cool of the Day '63
Island of Love '63
Mamma Mia! '08
The Mediterranean in Flames '72
Murderball '05 ▶
My Life in Ruins '09
Shirley Valentine '89 ▶
Signs & Wonders '00
The Sisterhood of the Traveling Pants '05
The Sisterhood of the Traveling Pants 2 '08
The Two Faces of January '14
Who's Got the Black Box? '67
Worlds Apart '17
Z '69 ▶

Grim Reaper

See also Death & the Afterlife

The Adventures of Baron Munchausen '89 ▶
The Belko Experiment '17
Bill & Ted's Bogus Journey '91
Death Takes a Holiday '34 ▶
El Crimen Perfecto '04
The Exorcist 2: The Heretic '77
Exorcist 3: Legion '90
Exorcist: The Beginning '04
Final Destination '00
Final Destination 2 '03
Final Destination 3 '06
The Frighteners '96
Last Action Hero '93
Meet Joe Black '98
Monty Python's The Meaning of Life '83 ▶
The Order '03
Riding the Bullet '04
The Seventh Seal '56 ▶
Soul Survivors '01

Growing Older

See also Death & Grandparents; Impending Retirement; Late Bloomin' Love

About Schmidt '02 ▶
Age Old Friends '89 ▶
Albert's Memorial '09
All Passion Spent '86
All the Light in the Sky '13 ▶
Amour '12 ▶
And So It Goes '14 ▶
The Angel Levine '70
Anglo-Saxon Attitudes '92
Anima '98
Anna '87 ▶
Another Lonely Hitman '95
Any Human Heart '11
Any Number Can Win '63
Apartment for Peggy '48
Around the Bend '04
As Young As You Feel '51 ▶
Atlantic City '81 ▶
Aurora Borealis '06
Away From Her '06 ▶
The Bachelor Father '31
The Ballad of Narayama '83 ▶
The Banger Sisters '02
*batteries not included '87
Before I Forget '07
Beginners '10 ▶
Belle Toujours '06 ▶
The Best Exotic Marigold Hotel '12 ▶
The Best of Times '86
Blackthorn '11
Blue Moon '00
Boardwalk '79
Bomber '09
The Boynton Beach Club '05
Bubba Ho-Tep '03 ▶
The Bucket List '07
Buena Vista Social Club '99 ▶
Camilla '94
Captain Kronos: Vampire Hunter '74 ▶
Casanova '05 ▶
The Cemetery Club '93
Central Station '98 ▶
Changing Times '04
The Cheyenne Social Club '70
Chicago Overcoat '09
Chimes at Midnight '67 ▶
Choices '86
The Christmas Box '95
Citizen Kane '41 ▶
City Slickers '91 ▶
Cloudburst '11 ▶
Clouds of Sils Maria '15
Cobb '94 ▶
Cocoon '85 ▶
Cocoon: The Return '88
The Congress '13
Crazy Heart '09
The Curious Case of Benjamin Button '08 ▶
Dad '89
Daddy Nostalgia '90 ▶
Danny Collins '15
Death Becomes Her '92 ▶
Death of a Salesman '86 ▶
The Death of Mr. Lazarescu '05
Diamonds '99
Don't Come Knocking '05
Dorian Gray '70
Dream a Little Dream '89
Dream Chasers '82
Driving Miss Daisy '89 ▶
Duck '05
Duplex '03
East of Fifth Avenue '33
Easy Living '49
Eating '90
Ebony Tower '86
Elaine Stritch: Shoot Me '14 ▶
Elegy '08
Elsa & Fred '14
Emma's Wish '98
The Enchanted Forest '45
Enemies of Laughter '00
An Englishman in New York '09
The Evening Star '96
Facing Windows '03
Fatal Trust '06
Father of the Bride Part 2 '95
The Field '90 ▶
The Final Hit '02
The Firemen's Ball '68 ▶
A Fish in the Bathtub '99
Folks! '92
For Love of the Game '99
A Foreign Field '93
Forever Young '92
Forget About It '06
Forty Carats '73
Forty Shades of Blue '05
Foxfire '87 ▶
From Above '13
The Gathering Storm '02 ▶
Gin Game '84 ▶
Ginger & Fred '86 ▶
The Girl from Paris '02 ▶
The Godfather, Part 3 '90 ▶
Gods and Monsters '98 ▶
Going in Style '79 ▶
Going in Style '17
The Golden Boys '08
The Good Guys and the Bad Guys '69
The Good Old Boys '95
The Good Thief '03 ▶
Goodbye Solo '08
Goodnight, Mr. Tom '99
Gran Torino '08 ▶
The Grandfather '98
The Great Beauty '13
Great Smokey Roadblock '76
Greedy '94
Grey Gardens '75 ▶
Grumpier Old Men '95
Grumpy Old Men '93 ▶
The Gun Hawk '63
Hamlet & Hutch '14
Hamsun '96
Hanging Up '99
Hannah Free '09
Happy Tears '09
Harakiri '62 ▶
Hard Labour '73
Hardbodies '84
Harry and Tonto '74 ▶
Harry Brown '09
Heading South '05 ▶
The Hitman Diaries '09
Hope Springs '12 ▶
Horton Foote's Alone '97
How About You '07
The Hunger '83
Hurry Up or I'll Be Thirty '73
Husbands '70
Hush, Hush, Sweet Charlotte '65 ▶
I Can't Sleep '93
Il Futuro '13
I'm Going Home '00 ▶
I'm Not Rappaport '96
In Custody '94
The Incredible Mrs. Ritchie '03
Innocent Bystanders '72
Iris '01 ▶
Iris Blond '98
Is Anybody There? '08
Jackass Presents: Bad Grandpa '13
Joan Rivers: A Piece of Work '10
Judy Berlin '99
King Lear '98 ▶
The King of Masks '99 ▶
Kotch '71 ▶
Lamerica '95 ▶
Land Ho! '14
Larry McMurtry's Streets of Laredo '95 ▶
The Last Brickmaker in America '01
The Last Days of Frankie the Fly '96
The Last Laugh '24 ▶
The Last Lieutenant '94
Last Love '13
The Last New Yorker '07
The Last Rites of Joe May '11
The Last Station '09
Last Vegas '13
The Last Word '17
Le Week-End '14
The Leech Woman '59
The Leisure Seeker '17
Lifeguard '76
Light Sleeper '92
Lightning Jack '94
Lilian's Story '95
Lilting '14 ▶
The Limey '99 ▶
Local Color '06
The Locket '02
The Long Way Home '98
Love '71 ▶
Love Comes Lately '07
Love Is Strange '14 ▶
Lovely, Still '08
Lucky '17 ▶
Ma Saison Preferee '93 ▶
Mafia! '98
The Magic Bubble '93
Make Way for Tomorrow '37
Mammuth '10
The Man on the Train '02 ▶
The Man on the Train '11
Marathon '80
Margot '09
Martin Chuzzlewit '94
Meet Joe Black '98
The Memory of a Killer '03
The Midwife '17 ▶
Mind the Gap '04
Miss Firecracker '89 ▶
Mrs. Dalloway '97
Mrs. Palfrey at the Claremont '05
Mr. Belvedere Rings the Bell '51
Mister 880 '50
Mr. Saturday Night '92
Monte Walsh '70 ▶
Monte Walsh '03
Moving Malcolm '03
My Afternoons with Margueritte '10 ▶
My Old Lady '14
Nebraska '13 ▶
Never Again '01
The Next Step '95
A Night in Old Mexico '14
No Sleep 'Til Madison '02
Nobody's Fool '94 ▶
The Notebook '04
The Odd Couple 2 '98
O'Horten '09 ▶
Old Goats '13
The Old Man and the Sea '58 ▶
The Old Man and the Sea '90
Olive Kitteridge '14 ▶
On Golden Pond '81 ▶
One Hundred and One Nights '95
Our Lady of the Assassins '01
Out of the Fog '41
The Out-of-Towners '99
Over the Hill '93
The Over-the-Hill Gang '69
The Over-the-Hill Gang Rides Again '70
Pals '87
Pastime '91 ▶
Pauline and Paulette '01
Pelle the Conqueror '88 ▶
The Pickle '93
Picture of Dorian Gray '45 ▶
Picture of Dorian Gray '74 ▶
A Place Called Home '04
Play Girl '41
Play the Game '09
Please Give '10
Poetry '10
The Private Life of Henry VIII '33 ▶
Pushing Hands '92
Quartet '12
Queens Logic '91
The Quiet American '02 ▶
Rabid Grannies '89
Ran '85 ▶
A Rather English Marriage '98
Reach for Me '08
RED 2 '13
RED '10
Renoir '12
Return of the Gunfighter '67
Return of the Rebels '81
Reunion at Fairborough '85
Rhapsody in August '91
Ride the High Country '62 ▶
Robot & Frank '12 ▶
Rocket Gibraltar '88 ▶
Rocky Balboa '06
Roommates '95
Rooster Cogburn '75
The Rounders '65
Run All Night '15
Safe House '99
The Savages '07 ▶
Sea People '00
The Set-Up '49 ▶
Seven Thieves '60 ▶
The Shell Seekers '89
The Shell Seekers '06
Shirley Valentine '89 ▶
A Shock to the System '90 ▶
The Shootist '76 ▶
A Short History of Decay '13
The Simple Life of Noah Dearborn '99
Soft for Digging '01
The Son of the Bride '01
A Song for Martin '01
The Sorcerers '67
Space Cowboys '00 ▶
Stand Up Guys '12
Standing in the Shadows of Motown '02 ▶
Star Trek: Insurrection '98
Starlet '12 ▶
Starting Out in the Evening '07
A Step Out of Line '71
Stephen King's Golden Years '91
The Stone Angel '07
The Straight Story '99 ▶
Strangers in Good Company '91 ▶
Summer Solstice '81
Summer Wishes, Winter Dreams '73
The Sunshine Boys '75 ▶
The Sunshine Boys '95
Tell Me a Riddle '80
Texas Guns '90
That Evening Sun '09 ▶
That's Life! '86
These Old Broads '01
Things Change '88 ▶
Three Days to Vegas '07
Three Strange Loves '49 ▶
Tish '42
To Dance with the White Dog '93 ▶
Tokyo Story '53 ▶
The Tomorrow Man '19
Toto le Heros '91 ▶
Tough Guys '86
Traveling Companion '96
The Trip to Bountiful '14 ▶
Trouble with the Curve '12
Tuesdays with Morrie '99
Twilight '98 ▶
Two for the Road '67 ▶
Two Weeks in Another Town '62
Umberto D '55 ▶
Unfinished Song '12
Unforgiven '92 ▶
Unhook the Stars '96
Up '09 ▶
Valley of the Sun '11
Venus '06 ▶
Voyage to the Beginning of the World '96 ▶
The Waiting Room '07
Waltzing Anna '06
The Wasp Woman '59
The Wendell Baker Story '05
The Whales of August '87 ▶
When a Woman Ascends the Stairs '60
Where the Money Is '00
The Whisperers '66
The Wild Bunch '69 ▶
Wild Grass '09
Wild River '60
Wild Strawberries '57 ▶
The World's Fastest Indian '05 ▶
Wrestling Ernest Hemingway '93
Young Adult '11
Young@Heart '07 ▶

Gunslingers

See also Pardners; Second Chance; Western Comedy; Westerns; Westrogens

Aces 'n Eights '08
Adios, Sabata '71
The Alamo '04
All Hell Broke Loose '09
Angel and the Badman '09
Appaloosa '08 ▶
The Assassination of Jesse James by the Coward Robert Ford '07 ▶

▶ = rated three bones or higher

Bad Men of Tombstone '49
The Ballad of Buster Scruggs '18 ▶
The Ballad of Lefty Brown '17
Black Patch '57
Blind Justice '94
Blue Story '20
Brimstone '17
Cat Ballou '65 ▶
Cjamango '67
A Cold Day in Hell '11
Cole Younger, Gunfighter '58
Cowboys & Aliens '11
Cowboys vs Dinosaurs '15
The Dark Tower '17
Dawn at Socorro '54
Dawn Rider '12
Day of the Evil Gun '68
Dear Wendy '05
Death of a Gunfighter '69
Death Rides a Horse '69
Decision at Sundown '57
The Desperadoes '43
Diablo '16
Django: Last Killer '67
Doc West '09
Dollar for the Dead '98
The Duelist '16
Dust '01
El Dorado '67 ▶
A Fistful of Dollars '64 ▶
Five Guns to Tombstone '60
For a Few Dollars More '65 ▶
Foresaken '16
Forsaken '15
Forty Guns '57
Four Fast Guns '59
From Noon Till Three '76
Frontier Marshal '39
The Gambler, the Girl and the Gunslinger '09
The Gun Hawk '63
Gun the Man Down '56
A Gunfight '71
Gunfight at the O.K. Corral '57 ▶
The Gunfighter '50 ▶
Gunfighter '98
Gunfighters '47
Gunfighter's Moon '96
Guns for Hire '15
Gunslinger '70
The Hanged Man '74
Hate for Hate '67
Heaven With a Gun '69
Hidden in the Woods '16
High Noon '52 ▶
High Noon '00
The Hunt '20
In a Valley of Violence '16
Johnny Yuma '66
Jonah Hex '10
The Kid '19
Kill Django '71
The Last Challenge '67
The Legend of Butch & Sundance '04
The Long Ride Home '01
The Magnificent Seven '60 ▶
The Magnificent Seven '16
Man from Del Rio '56
Man From God's Country '58
The Man Who Shot Liberty Valance '62 ▶
A Million Ways to Die In the West '14
More Dead Than Alive '68
My Darling Clementine '46 ▶
Never Grow Old '19
Noose for a Gunman '60
Once Upon a Time in the West '68 ▶
One After Another '68 ▶
One Fine Day, When Django Met Sartana '70
The Outsider '02
Panhandle '48
Piranhas '19
Polar '19
The Quick and the Dead '87
The Quick and the Dead '95
The Quick Gun '64
Raton Pass '51
Return of Sabata '71
Return of the Gunfighter '67
Rio Bravo '59 ▶
Roy Colt and Winchester Jack '70
Sabata '69
Shane '53 ▶
Shanghai Noon '00
The Sheepman '58
The Shootist '76 ▶
Short Grass '50
6 Guns '10
Son of a Gunfighter '65
Stagecoach: The Texas Jack Story '16
Standoff '16 ▶
Sukiyaki Western Django '08
Support Your Local Gunfighter '71 ▶
3:10 to Yuma '07 ▶
Tombstone '93 ▶
Top Gun '55
The Trail to Hope Rose '04
Triggerman '09
Unforgiven '92 ▶
Westworld '73 ▶
The Wonderful Country '59
Wyatt Earp '94

Gym Class

***See also** Elementary School/ Junior High; High School; School Daze*

Bad Teacher '11
Heaven Help Us '85
Mr. Woodcock '07
Porky's '82

Gymnastics

American Anthem '86
The Bronze '15
Dream to Believe '85
Full Out '15
The Gabby Douglas Story '14
The Gymnast '06
Nadia '84
Peaceful Warrior '06
Stick It '06

Gypsies

The Advocate '93 ▶
Animal Crackers '17
Babes in Toyland '61
The Bandits of Corsica '53
Born to Raise Hell '10
Caravan '46
Carmen '83 ▶
Carmen '03
Charge of the Lancers '54
Chocolat '00 ▶
A Ciambra '17
Drag Me to Hell '09
Hot Blood '56
The Hunchback '97
The Hunchback of Notre Dame '23 ▶
The Hunchback of Notre Dame '39 ▶
The Hunchback of Notre Dame '57
The Hunchback of Notre Dame '82 ▶
The Hunchback of Notre Dame '96 ▶
In the Arms of My Enemy '07
Incredibly Strange Creatures Who Stopped Living and Became Mixed-Up Zombies '63
Into the West '92 ▶
King of the Gypsies '78
Knuckle '11 ▶
Le Gitan '75
Little Minister '34 ▶
Love Potion #9 '92
Madonna of the Seven Moons '45
Man, Pride and Vengeance '67
The Man Who Cried '00
The Raggedy Rawney '90
Rascals '38
Roadkill '11
Sherlock Holmes: A Game of Shadows '11
The Sleeping Beauty '10
Snatch '00 ▶
Spring Parade '40
The Squall '29
Stephen King's Thinner '96
Time of the Gypsies '90 ▶
Triumph of the Spirit '89 ▶
The Wolf Man '41 ▶

Hackers

***See also** Computers*

Blackhat '15
Category 6: Day of Destruction '04
The Code Conspiracy '01
Code Hunter '02
Compadres '16
Confess '05
The Core '03
Cybergeddon '12
Demolition Man '93
Die Hard '88 ▶
Double Play '96
Ferris Bueller's Day Off '86 ▶
The Girl in the Spider's Web '18
The Girl Who Played With Fire '10
The Girl With the Dragon Tattoo '11 ▶
Hackers '95
Hellraiser: Hellworld '05
I.T. '16
Johnny English Strikes Again '18
Jumpin' Jack Flash '86
The Lather Effect '06
Live Free or Die Hard '07
Mission: Impossible '96 ▶
The Net '95
Nicotina '03
Noah's Ark '28
Real Genius '85 ▶
The Scratch '09
The Signal '14
Sneakers '92
Snowden '16
So Close '02
Summer Wars '09 ▶
Superman 3 '83
Swordfish '01
Underground: The Julian Assange Story '12
WarGames '83
WarGames: The Dead Code '08
Weird Science '85

Halloween

All Hallow's Eve 2 '15
All Hallow's Eve '13
American Nightmare '00
Boo 2! A Madea Halloween '17
Boo! '05
Boo! A Madea Halloween '16
The Caretaker '08
Casper '95 ▶
Clown Murders '83
The Dog Who Saved Halloween '11
Double Double Toil and Trouble '94
E.T.: The Extra-Terrestrial '82 ▶
The Fear: Halloween Night '99
Fun Size '12
The Ghost of Dragstrip Hollow '59
Girl *vs.* Monster '12
Goblin '10
Halloween '78 ▶
Halloween 2: The Nightmare Isn't Over! '81
Halloween 3: Season of the Witch '82
Halloween 4: The Return of Michael Myers '88
Halloween 5: The Revenge of Michael Myers '89
Halloween 6: The Curse of Michael Myers '95
Halloween '07
Halloween '18
Halloween: H20 '98 ▶
Halloween II '09
Halloweentown 2: Kalabar's Revenge '01
Halloweentown '98
Halloweentown High '04
Haunt '19
Hell Fest '18
Hellbent '04
Hellions '15
Hocus Pocus '93
The Hollywood Knights '80
House of 1000 Corpses '03
The Houses October Built '14
I Am Zozo '12
I Downloaded a Ghost '04
Idle Hands '99
I've Been Waiting for You '98
Jack-O '95
KISS Meets the Phantom of the Park '78
The Midnight Hour '86
Mischief Night '13
Mozart and the Whale '05
My Neighbor's Keeper '07
Night of the Demons 2 '94
Night of the Demons 3 '97
Night of the Demons '88
Night of the Demons '09
The Nightmare Before Christmas '93 ▶
November Christmas '10
Pay the Ghost '15
Return of the Living Dead: Rave to the Grave '05
Return to Halloweentown '06
Revenge of the Living Zombies '88
Satan's Little Helper '04
Scary Stories to Tell in the Dark '19
Spaced Invaders '90
Spooky Buddies '11
Stan Helsing '09
Tales of Halloween '15
31 '16
Trick or Treat '86
Trick 'r Treat '08 ▶
Twin Falls Idaho '99 ▶
When Good Ghouls Go Bad '01

Hallucinations/ Illusions

Aardvark '18
The Alphabet Killer '08
Angel of Death '09
The Art of Getting By '11
Baba Yaga '73
Bad Lieutenant: Port of Call New Orleans '09
A Beautiful Mind '01 ▶
Beneath '13
Between '05
Black Mountain Side '16
Blind Date '08
Bug '06
Buried Alive '90
Cake '14
The Caveman's Valentine '01
Confessions of an Opium Eater '62
The Congress '13
The Cradle '06
The Craft '96
Cria Cuervos '76 ▶
Crystal Fairy & the Magical Cactus '13
A Cure for Wellness '17
Dark Spirits '08
Dark Water '02
The Devil's Tomb '09
Diagnosis: Death '09
Dillinger Is Dead '69
Dolan's Cadillac '09
Don Peyote '14
Double Vision '02
The Dreaming '88
Escape From Tomorrow '13
Evil Eyes '04
The Eye '08
The Fever '04
Final '01
Frontier of Dawn '08
Ghost of the Needle '03
Ghost Ship '02
The Good Night '07
Gothika '03
Gradiva '06
The Haunted Airman '06
The Haunting of Molly Hartley '08
Hellraiser: Hellseeker '02
Hidden '09
Highly Dangerous '50
Hush Little Baby '07
Images '72
Impostor '02
Intruders '11
Invisible Child '99
Journey to the Seventh Planet '62
Judgementall Hai Kya '19
Killer Me '01
Klimt '06
Last Call: The Final Chapter of F. Scott Fitzgerald '02
The Last Man '19
The Last Will and Testament of Rosalind Leigh '12
The Letter '12
A Light in the Darkness '02
Max Payne '08
Memory '06
Monkeybone '01
Moon '09
The Mothman Prophecies '02
The Mystery of Edwin Drood '12
Naked Lunch '91 ▶
Nightwish '89
The Nines '07 ▶
Paranoia 1.0 '04
Peter Ibbetson '35
Phantasm: Ravager '16
Pi '98
Psychosis '10
Rapturious '07
Red 11 '19
Repulsion '65 ▶
The Return '06
S. Darko: A Donnie Darko Tale '09
Sanitarium '13
The Singing Detective '03
Soho Square '00
Solaris '02
Something Beneath '07
Stir of Echoes 2: The Homecoming '07
The Strange Case of Angelica '10
Trauma '04
Twixt '12
The Unborn '09
The Uninvited '09
Visitors '03
Waking Life '01
War Witch '12
Woodshock '17
Wrecked '10
Zero '97

Handyman Specials

***See also** Real Estate*

Are We Done Yet? '07
Awful Nice '14
Behind the Wall '08
Christmas Lodge '11
Cold Creek Manor '03
Don't Be Afraid of the Dark '11
Good People '14
The Good Witch's Garden '09
Greta '18
House of Sand and Fog '03 ▶
Ladies of the House '08
Life as a House '01
The March Sisters at Christmas '12
Mask Maker '10
Mr. Blandings Builds His Dream House '48 ▶
The Money Pit '86
Pacific Heights '90 ▶
Please Don't Eat the Daisies '60
The Tooth Fairy '06
Tribute '09
Under the Tuscan Sun '03

Hard Knock Life

***See also** Great Depression; Homeless*

After Tomorrow '32
Agnes Browne '99
Alambrista! '77
All or Nothing '02
Always Outnumbered Always Outgunned '98 ▶
American Buffalo '95
An American Crime '07
Angela's Ashes '99
The Baby Dance '98 ▶
Ballast '08
Beasts of the Southern Wild '12 ▶
Beggars in Ermine '34
Beijing Bicycle '01
Blondie Johnson '33
Boesman & Lena '00
Broken Blossoms '19 ▶
Brooklyn Castle '12 ▶
Cafe Express '83
Captain Scarlett '53
Carrie '52 ▶
Catherine Cookson's The Rag Nymph '96
Charlie and the Chocolate Factory '05 ▶
Chicago Calling '52
The Child '05 ▶
Child of God '14
Children of Heaven '98
Children of Invention '09
Christmas, Again '15
City of Joy '92
City Park '34
Claudelle Inglish '61
Clockers '95 ▶
Cocaine Angel '06
Code Unknown '00
Crackie '09
Crime in the Streets '56
Crisscross '92
Crows and Sparrows '49 ▶
The Damned Don't Cry '50
Dancing at Lughnasa '98
Daughters of the Sun '00
David Copperfield '70
David Copperfield '99
Devil's Island '96
A Dog of Flanders '99
Dolores Claiborne '94 ▶
The Dreamlife of Angels '98 ▶
The Dry Land '10
The Easiest Way '31
8 Mile '02 ▶
Elena and Her Men '56 ▶
Entertaining Angels: The Dorothy Day Story '96
Erin Brockovich '00 ▶
Even the Rain '10
Explicit Ills '08
Extreme Measures '96
Eye of God '97 ▶
Faithless '32
The Florida Project '17 ▶
Foolish '99
The Forbidden Street '49
Frozen River '08 ▶
The Full Monty '96 ▶
Get On Up '14
Gifted Hands: The Ben Carson Story '09
Going in Style '17
Gold Rush Maisie '40
The Good Earth '37 ▶
The Good Neighbor '16
Grbavica: The Land of My Dreams '06
Gridlock'd '96 ▶
The Grim Reaper '62 ▶
Hell's Kitchen '39
Here Comes Cookie '35
Heroes of the Heart '94
Hidden in America '96
Hideous Kinky '99
Hoax for the Holidays '10
Home By Christmas '06
A Home of Our Own '93
The Hoodlum '19
How to Be a Latin Lover '17
I Capture the Castle '02
In America '02 ▶
In Dubious Battle '17
The Inevitable Defeat of Mister & Pete '13
The Inheritors '98
The Intouchables '12
The Italian '15
Joe Dirt '01
Jolene '08
Jude '96 ▶
Jude the Obscure '71
Juke Girl '42
Juno and the Paycock '30
Kes '69 ▶
Killer of Sheep '77 ▶

▶ = rated three bones or higher

The King of Masks '99 ▶
Kings of the Evening '08
Kuhle Wampe, Or Who Owns the World? '32
La Boheme '26
La Vie en Rose '07
Lamerica '95 ▶
Laughing Sinners '31
Le Gitan '75
Les Miserables '35 ▶
Les Miserables '57 ▶
Les Miserables '78 ▶
Les Miserables '97 ▶
Les Miserables '12 ▶
Liam '00
Little Dorrit '08
Little Heroes '91
Little Women '94 ▶
Live-In Maid '04
Lolo '92
Lucky Star '29
Madame Sata '02
Mama Africa '02
Mama Flora's Family '98
Marius and Jeannette '97
The Match Factory Girl '90 ▶
Me Before You '16
Me You Them '00
Meantime '81
Metro Manila '13
Midnight Episode '50
Mrs. Wiggs of the Cabbage Patch '34
Moll Flanders '96
Monster's Ball '01 ▶
Monument Ave. '98
The Motel Life '12
Mother Teresa: In the Name of God's Poor '97
Mothers Cry '30
The Mustang '19 ▶
My Name Is Joe '98
Nicholas Nickleby '02 ▶
None But the Lonely Heart '44 ▶
Not One Less '99
The Old Curiosity Shop '94
The Old Curiosity Shop '07
An Old-Fashioned Thanksgiving '08
Oliver Twist '97
Oliver Twist '00 ▶
Oliver Twist '07
100 Streets '17
One Third of a Nation '39
The Optimists '73
Outside Bet '12
Paid in Full '02
Pay It Forward '00
Petits Freres '00
Pocketful of Miracles '61 ▶
The Pope of Greenwich Village '84
The Pursuit of Happyness '06
Ratcatcher '99
Restoration '94 ▶
Rich Hill '14 ▶
Riddler's Moon '98
The Road Home '01 ▶
Rosetta '99
Salaam Bombay! '88 ▶
Scrooged '88
Set It Off '96
7 Boxes '14 ▶
Shadrach '98
Shotgun Stories '07
Sixth and Main '77
Slumdog Millionaire '08 ▶
The Sorcerers '67
South Riding '11
Sparrows '26 ▶
Spider '02 ▶
Stakeout '62
The Stars Fell on Henrietta '94
Steel City '06
Stony Island '77
Stray Dogs '13
Street Scene '31 ▶
Sugar '09 ▶
Sunlight Jr. '13
The Super '91
Tenth Avenue Angel '47
Tess '79 ▶
Tess of the D'Urbervilles '98
Tess of the D'Urbervilles '08
Tess of the Storm Country '22

They Call Me Sirr '00
This Is My Father '99
Tobacco Road '41
Toe to Toe '09
Tokyo Sonata '09 ▶
Trash '14
Twinkletoes '26
Two Days, One Night '14 ▶
Una Noche '13
Under Eighteen '32
Union Depot '32
The Unseen '05
Up the Junction '68
Vagabond '85 ▶
Vanessa '07
A Way of Life '04
We the Animals '18 ▶
The Well-Digger's Daughter '11
Wendy and Lucy '08 ▶
Where the Hot Wind Blows '59
White Man's Burden '95
The White Ribbon '09
Who the Hell is Juliette? '98
The Wide Blue Road '57 ▶
Wild Boys of the Road '33
Willy Wonka & the Chocolate Factory '71 ▶
Winter's Bone '10 ▶
The World Made Straight '15
Woyzeck '94
Young Ones '14

Harlem

***See also** New York, New York*

American Gangster '07 ▶
Brother to Brother '04
A Brother's Kiss '97
The Cotton Club '84 ▶
For Colored Girls '10
Hoodlum '96
If Beale Street Could Talk '18 ▶
Never Die Alone '04
The Old Settler '01
Paid in Full '02
Preaching to the Choir '05
A Rage in Harlem '91 ▶
Ride '98
Twelve '10
Uncle Drew '18

Hawaii

***See also** Island Fare*

Acapulco Gold '78
Airplane vs. Volcano '14
The Big Bounce '04
The Black Camel '31
Blood and Orchids '86
Blue Crush '02 ▶
Blue Hawaii '62
Charlie Chan in Honolulu '38
The Descendants '11 ▶
50 First Dates '04
Flirting with Forty '09
Forgetting Sarah Marshall '08
Hawaii '66 ▶
Hell's Half Acre '54
Hercules '83
In God's Hands '98
In Love and War '58
Into the Blue 2: The Reef '09
Just Go With It '11
Kona Coast '68
Lilo & Stitch 2: Stitch Has a Glitch '05
Lilo & Stitch '02 ▶
Magnum P.I.: Don't Eat the Snow in Hawaii '80
Mike and Dave Need Wedding Dates '16
Miss Tatlock's Millions '48
Morning Light '08
Paradise, Hawaiian Style '66
Pearl '78
Pearl Harbor '01
A Perfect Getaway '09
Picture Bride '94
Princess Kaiulani '09
Punch-Drunk Love '02 ▶
Race the Sun '96
Riding Giants '04
Running for Grace '18
Sailor Beware '52
Soul Surfer '11

Tempted '03
A Very Brady Sequel '96
Waikiki Wedding '37 ▶

Heads!

***See also** Brains!; Ears!; Eyeballs!; Renegade Body Parts*

Azumi '03 ▶
Botched '07
The Brain that Wouldn't Die '63
Braveheart '95 ▶
8 Heads in a Duffel Bag '96
Four Skulls of Jonathan Drake '59
The Frozen Dead '66
Hereditary '18 ▶
Highlander 2: The Quickening '91
Highlander '86 ▶
Highlander: The Final Dimension '94
The Hitchhiker's Guide to the Galaxy '81 ▶
The Incredible Two-Headed Transplant '71
Lost Boys: The Tribe '08
The Mad Magician '54
The Man with Two Brains '83 ▶
Master of the Flying Guillotine '75
Mystery Men '99
The Skull '65
Tropic Thunder '08 ▶
The Voices '15

Hearts!

***See also** Eyeballs!; Renegade Body Parts*

An American Werewolf in Paris '97
Angel Heart '87
Apocalypto '06 ▶
Article 99 '92
Awake '07
Blood Work '02
Brainstorm '83
City of Angels '98
Crank: High Voltage '09
Dead in a Heartbeat '02
Dumb & Dumber '94
From Dusk Till Dawn '95
Heart '99
Heart of a Stranger '02
Indiana Jones and the Temple of Doom '84 ▶
The Intruder '04 ▶
John Q '02
The Last of the Mohicans '92 ▶
Legends of the Fall '94
The Magician '26
Mary Shelley's Frankenstein '94
My Bloody Valentine 3D '09
My Bloody Valentine '81
Operation Heartbeat '69
The Prophecy '95
The Prophecy 2: Ashtown '97
Pulp Fiction '94 ▶
Return to Me '00
Split Second '92
Tales from the Crypt '72 ▶
Tales from the Crypt Presents Bordello of Blood '96
The Terminator '84 ▶

Heaven Sent

***See also** Angels*

All Dogs Go to Heaven '89
All Dogs Go to Heaven 2 '95
All of Me '84
Almost an Angel '90
Always '89
Angel on My Shoulder '46 ▶
The Bishop's Wife '47 ▶
Brewster McCloud '70 ▶
Brother John '70 ▶
Bruce Almighty '03
Carousel '56 ▶
Chances Are '89 ▶
Charley and the Angel '73
Constantine '05
Date with an Angel '87
Defending Your Life '91 ▶
Dogma '99

Down to Earth '01
Family Man '00
Field of Dreams '89 ▶
For Heaven's Sake '50
Forever Darling '56
Ghost '90 ▶
Ghost Dad '90
He Sees You When You're Sleeping '02
Heading for Heaven '47
Heart Condition '90
Heaven '87
Heaven Can Wait '43 ▶
Heaven Can Wait '78 ▶
The Heavenly Kid '85
A Heavenly Vintage '09
Heaven's Door '12
Hello Again '87
Here Comes Mr. Jordan '41 ▶
The Horn Blows at Midnight '45 ▶
I Married an Angel '42
It Came Upon a Midnight Clear '84
It's a Wonderful Life '46 ▶
Kiss Me Goodbye '82
Liliom '30
Liliom '35 ▶
The Littlest Angel '69
The Lovely Bones '09
Made in Heaven '87
Miracle in Milan '51 ▶
Mr. Destiny '90
The Next Voice You Hear '50
No News from God '01
Oh, God! '77
Oh, God! Book 2 '80
Oh, God! You Devil '84
One Magic Christmas '85
The Preacher's Wife '96
Stairway to Heaven '46 ▶
Static '87
The Three Lives of Thomasina '63 ▶
Three Wise Women '11
To Gillian on Her 37th Birthday '96
Toothless '97
Truly, Madly, Deeply '91 ▶
Two of a Kind '83
What Dreams May Come '98
Wide Awake '97
Xanadu '80

Heists

***See also** Scams, Stings & Cons*

Age Out '19
Aladdin and the King of Thieves '96
The Anderson Tapes '71 ▶
The Apple Dumpling Gang '75
Army of One '94
Assault of the Rebel Girls '59
Bad Boys '95
Bad Santa 2 '16
Bad Santa '03
Bellman and True '88
Bells of Coronado '50
Belly '98
Best Men '98
The Bicycle Thief '48 ▶
Big Deal on Madonna Street '58 ▶
Blind Justice '94
The Bling Ring '13 ▶
Blood & Wine '96
The Boatniks '70
Body Count '97
Bonnie & Clyde '67 ▶
Born Bad '97
Bottle Rocket '95
Bound '96
The Brain '69
Breathing Fire '91
The Brooklyn Heist '08
Bullet Head '17
Butch and Sundance: The Early Days '79
The Captain Hates the Sea '34
Casino '95 ▶
The Catamount Killing '74
Cavalry Scout '51

C.I.A. 2: Target Alexa '94
City Unplugged '95
Cold Around the Heart '97
Collide '17
Corrupted Hands '00
Crime Broker '94
Crime Spree '03
Croupier '97 ▶
The Curse of the Jade Scorpion '01
Danger: Diabolik '68
Daring Dobermans '73
Dead Heat on a Merry-Go-Round '66 ▶
Dead Presidents '95
Decisions '10
Desperate Cargo '41
The Desperate Trail '94
Die Hard '88 ▶
Die Hard: With a Vengeance '95
Dog Eat Dog '64
The Dog Who Saved Christmas '09
Dollars '71 ▶
Double Trouble '91
Duffy '68
Dunston Checks In '95
11 Harrowhouse '74 ▶
Extreme Honor '01
Face '97
The Fall of the American Empire '19
Firetrap '01
Five Golden Dragons '67
French Kiss '95
Garage Sale Mystery '13
The Getaway '72
The Getaway '93
Getting Even with Dad '94
The Girl in the Spider's Web '18
Going in Style '79 ▶
Grand Larceny '92
Great Bank Hoax '78
The Green Glove '52
Grisbi '53
Gun Crazy '49 ▶
Guns Don't Argue '57
Gypsy '75
Hand Gun '93
Happy New Year '87
Happy, Texas '99 ▶
Hard Cash '01
Hard Hunted '92
The Hard Word '02
Harley Davidson and the Marlboro Man '91
The Heist '89
Hell Bound '57
High Risk '81
Hit Me '96
Holy Matrimony '94
The Horse Without a Head '63
How to Steal a Million '66 ▶
Hustlers '19 ▶
I Died a Thousand Times '55
Ice '93
The Immortals '95
Infamous '20
Inside Men '12
Interceptor '92
Kelly's Heroes '70
The Killing '56 ▶
Killing Them Softly '12
Killing Zoe '94
Lassiter '84
The Last Heist '16
The Last of Mrs. Cheyney '37 ▶
The Lavender Hill Mob '51 ▶
The League of Gentlemen '60 ▶
A Life Less Ordinary '97
Lightning Jack '94
Like a Fish Out of Water '99
Little Cigars '73
Lock, Stock and 2 Smoking Barrels '98 ▶
Logan Lucky '17 ▶
Loophole '83
Mad Money '08
A Man, a Woman, and a Bank '79
Man Trouble '92
Master Touch '74
The Million Dollar Rip-Off '76
Monster Party '18

Motorama '91
My Dog, the Thief '69
Normal Life '96
Now You See Me '13
Old Mother Riley's New Venture '49
On the Border '98
Once a Thief '96 ▶
Operation Condor 2: The Armour of the Gods '86
Out of Sight '98 ▶
Overdrive '17
The Padre '18
Palookaville '95 ▶
Pardon My Sarong '42
Parker '13
The Perfect Score '04
Persons Unknown '96
The Pink Panther 2 '09
Point Break '91
The Real McCoy '93
The Rebel Set '59
Reindeer Games '00
The Return of Boston Blackie '27
Rififi '54 ▶
The Rip Off '78
R.P.M. '97
Scarlet Street '45 ▶
The Score '01
Set It Off '96
Sexy Beast '00 ▶
The Slams '73
Sneakers '92
Solo: A Star Wars Story '18
The Song of Sway Lake '18
Spider's Web '01
The Split '68
The Squeaker '65
The Squeeze '87
Styx '00
They Met in Bombay '41
Thick as Thieves '99
Thief '81 ▶
Three Kings '99 ▶
To Catch a Thief '55 ▶
Too Many Crooks '59
Topkapi '64 ▶
Total Dhamaal '19
Tower Heist '11
Tracers '15
Track the Man Down '55
The Trail to Hope Rose '04
Trapped in Paradise '94
Triple Frontier '19
Triple 9 '15
Truth or Consequences, N.M. '97
Two If by Sea '95
2:22 '08
Two-Way Stretch '60
The Underneath '95 ▶
The Usual Suspects '95 ▶
Velocity Trap '99
Villain '71
Wasteland '13
Wheelman '17
Where the Money Is '00
White Fire '84
White Tiger '23
Who'll Stop the Rain? '78 ▶
The Wrong Arm of the Law '63 ▶
W.W. and the Dixie Dancekings '75

Heists: Armored Car

Armored '09
Armored Car Robbery '50
Burnt Money '00
Classe Tous Risque '60 ▶
Criss Cross '48 ▶
Firefight '03
Forfeit '07
Hard Rain '97
Heat '95 ▶
Heist '09
Kansas City Confidential '52 ▶
Le Deuxieme Souffle '66
Masterminds '16
Metro Manila '13
Raven's Ridge '97
Seven Seconds '05
Takers '10
They Came to Rob Las Vegas '68

▶ = *rated three bones or higher*

Heists: Art

American Animals '18 ▶
Art Heist '05
The Art of the Steal '13
Body Count '97
The Burnt Orange Heresy '20
Entrapment '99
Four Dogs Playing Poker '00
Framed '10
Gambit '66
Good Morning, Boys '37
The Good Thief '03 ▶
The Happy Thieves '61
Headhunters '11
Home Alone: The Holiday Heist '12
Just Business '08
Love Among Thieves '86
The Maiden Heist '08
The Monuments Men '13
My Mom's New Boyfriend '08
Once a Thief '90
Ordinary Decent Criminal '99
Our America '02
The Plot Thickens '36
Rome Express '32
Ruben Brandt, Collector '18
Running Out of Time 2 '06
St. Trinian's '07
The Thomas Crown Affair '68 ▶
The Thomas Crown Affair '99 ▶
Trance '13
Widows '02
Wild Target '10

Heists: Banks

Action Man '67
Along the Rio Grande '41
American Heist '15
American Madness '32
Baby Driver '17 ▶
Bandidas '06
Bandits '01
The Bank Dick '40 ▶
The Bank Job '07
The Bank Job '08 ▶
Bank Shot '74 ▶
Beverly Hills Chihuahua 2 '10
The Big Caper '57
The Big Scam '79
Boy Who Caught a Crook '61
Brave '07
Breaking News '04
Burning Life '94
Carnage Park '16
Cash on Demand '61
Catch That Kid '04
Children of Hannibal '98
Citizen Gangster '11
Crime Wave '54
Cut Off '06
The Dalton Girls '57
The Dark Knight '08 ▶
The Day They Robbed the Bank of England '60
Dead Birds '04
Dead Heist '07
Den of Thieves '18
The Desperadoes '43
Destroyer '18
Dillinger and Capone '95
Drive a Crooked Road '54
Drive Hard '14
Firewall '06
First Kill '17
Five Guns to Tombstone '60
Flypaper '11
44 Minutes: The North Hollywood Shootout '03
The Front Line '06
Fun With Dick and Jane '05
Going in Style '17
Goodnight for Justice: The Measure of a Man '12
Graduation '07
The Great St. Louis Bank Robbery '59
Gun Duel In Durango '57
Gun the Man Down '56
Hallelujah for Django '67
Hate for Hate '67
Heat '95 ▶
Heaven's Burning '97
Held Hostage '09
Hell or High Water '16 ▶
Hell's Heroes '30
Henry's Crime '10
Hero Wanted '08
High Life '09
Highway 301 '50
How to Rob a Bank '07
The Hurricane Heist '18
Inside Man '06 ▶
Inspector Gadget 2 '02
Intermission '03 ▶
Kidnapped '74
Kill Me Later '01
Larceny, Inc. '42
Living & Dying '07
The Lookout '07 ▶
Loophole '54
Lost '05
Love Is Colder Than Death '69
Malevolence '04
The Man on the Train '11
Marauders '16
Masterminds '16
Me and My Gal '32
The Moonlighter '53
A New Wave '07
No Good Deed '02
No Hands on the Clock '41
The Nut Job '14
Odds Against Tomorrow '59 ▶
The Old Man & the Gun '18 ▶
One Foot in Hell '60
The Outfit '73
Outlaws and Angels '16
The Perfect Host '10
Public Enemies '09
Pups '99
The Quick Gun '64
Radio Cab Murder '54
Raiders from Beneath the Sea '64
Reprisal '18
Ride a Crooked Trail '58
Ringo, the Lone Rider '68
The Robin Hood Gang '98
Robin's Hood '03
Sail a Crooked Ship '61
Saintly Sinners '62
Salt of the Sea '08
Scorched '02
The Set Up '95
The Shadow Laughs '33
Shakedown '02
Sidekicks '74
Skyway '33
Small Time Crooks '00
Son of Billy the Kid '49
The Spikes Gang '74
Stander '03
Stark Raving Mad '02
The Steel Trap '52
A Step Out of Line '71
The Stickup '01
Sugar & Spice '01 ▶
Swindle '02
Takers '10
Taxi '04
30 Minutes or Less '11
Three Godfathers '36
Thunderbirds '04
The Town '10 ▶
Transit '12
211 '18
Vault '19
Victoria '15
Violent Saturday '55
Wanda '70
Wyoming Renegades '55

Heists: Cars/Trucks

See also Grand Theft Auto; Motor Vehicle Dept.

The Con Artist '10
Corvette Summer '78
The Fate of the Furious '17
Gone in 60 Seconds '74
Gone in 60 Seconds '00
Grand Theft Auto '77
Great Smokey Roadblock '76
Pressed '11
Smokey Bites the Dust '81

Heists: Casinos

Any Number Can Win '63
The Aura '05 ▶
Bob le Flambeur '55 ▶
Carnival of Wolves '96
The Casino Job '08
5 Against the House '55
Get Lucky '13
Ghost of a Chance '01
The Good Thief '03 ▶
The Hollywood Sign '01
The Ladykillers '04
Machine Gun McCain '69
My Name is Modesty: A Modesty Blaise Adventure '04
Ocean's 11 '60
Ocean's Eleven '01 ▶
Ocean's Thirteen '07 ▶
The Outfit '73
Rip It Off '02
Seven Thieves '60 ▶
Stealing Las Vegas '12
Swelter '14
3000 Miles to Graceland '01

Heists: Gold/Precious Metals

Adios, Sabata '71
The Badlanders '58
The Black Dakotas '54
Border River '47
The Broken Star '56
Carson City '52
City Beneath the Sea '71
The Dukes '07
Exiled '06
The Five Man Army '69
Fool's Gold: The Story of the Brink's-Mat Robbery '92
Heist '01 ▶
High Tide '80
The Italian Job '69
The Italian Job '03 ▶
Low Tide '19
The Outriders '50
Plunder Road '57
Raiders of Ghost City '44
The Saint Meets the Tiger '43
Sam Whiskey '69
Setup '11
7 Men From Now '56
Son of a Gun '14
Son of Billy the Kid '49
24 Hours to Kill '65
When Eight Bells Toll '71
The Wrecking Crew '68
Yellow Sky '48 ▶

Heists: Jewels

Adventure in Manhattan '36
After the Sunset '04
Alias French Gertie '30
All About the Benjamins '02
And Now Ladies and Gentlemen '02
Arsene Lupin Returns '38
The Asphalt Jungle '50 ▶
Before the Devil Knows You're Dead '07 ▶
Berlin Job '12
Big Brown Eyes '36
The Black Bird '26
Bloodstone '88
Blue Iguana '18
Botched '07
Boys Will Be Boys '35
The Burglar '57
Cage of Evil '60
The Cats '68
City of Industry '96
City on Fire '87
The Code '09
The Collector '09
Columbus Day '08
Cool Breeze '72
Crackerjack '38
Cradle 2 the Grave '03
Crimson Gold '03
Deadly Isolation '05
Despicable Me 3 '17
Diamond Run '96
Dog Gone '08
The Dog Who Saved Christmas Vacation '10
Every Girl Should Have One '78
Fathom '67
Femme Fatale '02
Fish in a Barrel '01
Flawless '07
4.3.2.1 '10
The Frightened Man '52
The Gay Falcon '41
The Goose and the Gander '35
Grand Slam '67
The Great Diamond Robbery '53
The Hessen Conspiracy '09
High Flyers '37
The Hot Rock '70 ▶
Hot Tamale '06
The Hour of 13 '52
If Tomorrow Comes '86
Java Heat '13
Jewel Robbery '32
Jim Hanvey, Detective '37
Jr. Detective Agency '09
The Last Diamond '14
The Last of Mrs. Cheyney '29
Le Cercle Rouge '70 ▶
Lift '01
Lights in the Dusk '06
Little Man '06
The Lone Wolf Meets a Lady '40
The Love Punch '13
Mad Mission 3 '84
Modesty Blaise '66
Momentum '15
The Moonstone '72
Muppets Most Wanted '14
Murph the Surf '75
My Gun Is Quick '57
99 River Street '53
The Notorious Landlady '62
Ocean's 8 '18
Ocean's Twelve '04
Once Upon a Time in America '84 ▶
One More Time '70
Operation Amsterdam '60
Picture Claire '01
The Pink Panther '64 ▶
The Pink Panther '06
Place Vendome '98 ▶
Plastic '14
The Plot Thickens '36
Precious Cargo '16
Raffles '39
Recoil '53
Reservoir Dogs '92 ▶
Rope of Sand '49
Sandok '65
Score '95
The Sex Thief '74
Snatch '00 ▶
The Southern Star '69
The Squeeze '80
10 Minutes Gone '19
The Third Clue '34
Three Blondes in His Life '61
Trespass '11
Triplecross '95
The Walking Stick '70
Welcome to Collinwood '02
Whipsaw '35
You're Never Too Young '55

Heists: Stagecoach

See also Westerns

Along Came Jones '45 ▶
Cheyenne '47
The Dalton Girls '57
Gun Fury '53
Hard Ground '03
The Iron Sheriff '57
Oklahoma Kid '39 ▶
Outlaw's Son '57
The Over-the-Hill Gang Rides Again '70
Ringo's Big Night '66
The Silver Whip '53
The Tall T '57
3:10 to Yuma '57 ▶
3:10 to Yuma '07 ▶

Heists: Trains

The Biggest Bundle of Them All '68
Butch Cassidy and the Sundance Kid '69 ▶
Colorado Territory '49
The Great Train Robbery '79 ▶
House of Bamboo '55
Money Train '95
Night Passage '57
Pride of Africa '97
Railroad Tigers '17
Run for Cover '55
Tough Guys '86
Whispering Smith '48 ▶

Hell

See also Death & Devils; Religion; Satanism

All Dogs Go to Heaven '89
Bill & Ted's Bogus Journey '91
Bleach the Movie 4: Hell Verse '10
Constantine '05
Dark Angel: The Ascent '94
The Doorway '00
Faust: Love of the Damned '00
Freddy *vs.* Jason '03
Heaven Can Wait '43 ▶
Hellbound: Hellraiser 2 '88
Hellboy II: The Golden Army '08 ▶
Hellhounds '09
Hellraiser '87
Hellraiser 3: Hell on Earth '92
Hellraiser 4: Bloodline '95
Hellraiser 5: Inferno '00
Little Nicky '00
Rapturious '07
Silent Hill: Revelation 3D '12
South Park: Bigger, Longer and Uncut '99
Spawn '97 ▶
What Dreams May Come '98
Witchery '88
Wrath of the Titans '12

Hell High School

See also Cheerleaders; Dedicated Teachers; Errant Educators; High School; High School Reunions; Prom; School Daze

Afterschool '08
Angus '95
Animal Room '95
Anything for Love '93
Bad Reputation '05 ▶
Big Bully '95
Bill & Ted's Excellent Adventure '89
Billy Madison '94
Black Circle Boys '97
Blackboard Jungle '55 ▶
Blood of Dracula '57
Bloodmoon '90
Boltneck '98
Born Innocent '74
The Brady Bunch Movie '95 ▶
Buffy the Vampire Slayer '92 ▶
Cabin Fever 2: Spring Fever '08
Carrie '76 ▶
Carrie '02
Carrie '13
Cemetery High '89
Cheaters '00
Cherry Hill High '76
A Cinderella Story '04
Class '83
Class Act '91
Class of '44 '73
Class of 1984 '82
Class of 1999 2: The Substitute '93
Class of 1999 '90
Class of Nuke 'Em High 2: Subhumanoid Meltdown '91
Class of Nuke 'Em High 3: The Good, the Bad and the Subhumanoid '94
Class of Nuke 'Em High '86
Class Reunion Massacre '77
Clueless '95 ▶
Coach '78
Coneheads '93
Cooley High '75 ▶
The Craft '96
Creepers '85
Cruel Intentions 2 '99
Cry-Baby '90 ▶
Cutting Class '89
Dazed and Confused '93 ▶
Deadly Fieldtrip '74
Deal of a Lifetime '99
Demolition High '95
Detachment '12
Detention '03
Detention '11
Disturbing Behavior '98
Elephant '03 ▶
Evil '03 ▶
Excision '12
The Faculty '98
Fast Times at Ridgemont High '82 ▶
Fear '96
Ferris Bueller's Day Off '86 ▶
Finishing School '33
Ginger Snaps '01
Girl Fight '11
Girls in Chains '43
Girls Town '95
Graduation Day '81
Grease 2 '82
The Great St. Trinian's Train Robbery '66
Halloween: H20 '98 ▶
Hangman's Curse '03
Hard Knox '83
Hard Lessons '86
Heart of America '03
Heathers '89 ▶
Hell High '86
Hide and Go Shriek '87
Hiding Out '87
High School Caesar '60
High School Confidential '58
High School High '96
High School USA '84
Home Room '02 ▶
Homework '82
Hoosiers '86 ▶
Hostage High '97
I Was a Teenage Zombie '87
If. . . '69 ▶
Just One of the Girls '93
Kids in America '05
Killing Mr. Griffin '97
Light It Up '99
Little Witches '96
Loose Screws '85
Lust for a Vampire '71
Major Payne '95
The Majorettes '87
Making the Grade '84
Massacre at Central High '76
Mean Girls '04 ▶
Mirror, Mirror '90
Mr. Woodcock '07
Monster High '89
My Bodyguard '80 ▶
Napoleon Dynamite '04
National Lampoon's Senior Trip '95
Night Visitor '89
187 '97
Only the Strong '93
Peggy Sue Got Married '86
Pep Squad '98
Picture Day '13
Porky's 2: The Next Day '83
Porky's '82
The Positively True Adventures of the Alleged Texas Cheerleader-Murdering Mom '93 ▶
Pretty Persuasion '05
Prom Night 3: The Last Kiss '89
Prom Night 4: Deliver Us from Evil '91
Prom Night '80
Pump Up the Volume '90
The Quiet '05
The Rage: Carrie 2 '99
Return to Horror High '87
Rock 'n' Roll High School '79 ▶
Rock 'n' Roll High School Forever '91
Rock, Pretty Baby '56
Satan's Cheerleaders '77
Satan's School for Girls '73
School Ties '92 ▶
Screwballs '83
Senior Trip '81
Serial Killing 101 '04
Show Me Love '99

The Help: Female

The Help: Male

Hide the Dead Guy

High School

▶ = *rated three bones or higher*

Pretty Maids All In a Row '71
Princess Protection Program '09
The Principal '87
Project Almanac '15
Project X '11
Prom '11
Queen Sized '08
Radio '03
Radio Rebel '12
The Red Sneakers '01
The Restless Years '58
Rock 'n' Roll High School '79 ►
Rock 'n' Roll High School Forever '91
Rock the Paint '05
Rocket Science '07 ►
The Rookie '02 ►
Rushmore '98 ►
Rustin '01
Save the Last Dance '01
Saved! '04
Senior Skip Day '08
Seventeen Again '00
17 Again '09
The Shed '19
She's All That '99
She's Too Young '04
Sixteen Candles '84 ►
Sky High '05 ►
Slap Her, She's French '02
A Smile as Big as the Moon '12
Some Kind of Wonderful '87
A Song From the Heart '99
Spare Parts '15
The Spectacular Now '13 ►
Spider-Man: Homecoming '17 ►
Spork '10
Stand and Deliver '88 ►
Step '17
Step Up '06
Struck by Lightning '12
Student Seduction '03
The Substitute '96
Sugar & Spice '01 ►
Summer School '87
Sunday School Musical '08
Sundown '16
Surfacing '14
Swimfan '02
Take a Giant Step '59
Take the Lead '06
Teachers '84
Teen Spirit '11
Ten Things I Hate about You '99 ►
Terri '11
There Goes My Baby '92
They Call Me Sirr '00
Through the Fire '05 ►
Thunder Soul '10
Tiger Eyes '13
A Time for Dancing '00
To All the Boys I've Loved Before '18
To Be Fat Like Me '07
To Save a Life '10
Touchback '11
Tragedy Girls '17 ►
The Trotsky '09
21 Jump Street '12 ►
Twilight '08
The Twilight Saga: Eclipse '10
Undefeated '11
Under the Mistletoe '06
Underclassman '05
The Unguarded Moment '56
Valley Girl '20
Vampires Suck '10
Varsity Blood '14
Varsity Blues '98
Virgin '03
A Walk in My Shoes '10
Walking the Halls '12
War Eagle, Arkansas '07
A Warrior's Heart '11
Wasted on the Young '10
The Way Back '20
Weakness '10
What a Life '39
When the Game Stands Tall '14
Wild Cherry '09
Win Win '11
The Winning Season '09
Wish Upon '17
Young Adult '11
Your Name '17 ►
You're So Cupid '10
Zombi Child '20

High School Reunions

***See also** School Daze*

American Reunion '12
Back in the Day '14
Back to You and Me '05
Beautiful Girls '96 ►
Blue Jay '16 ►
Central Intelligence '16
Circle of Friends '06
Class Reunion Massacre '77
The D Train '15
Flying By '09
Grosse Pointe Blank '97 ►
Just Friends '05
National Lampoon's Class Reunion '82
Peggy Sue Got Married '86
Romy and Michele's High School Reunion '97
She Drives Me Crazy '07
Since You've Been Gone '97
Something Wild '86
Stay Cool '09
10 Years '12
Veronica Mars '14
Zack and Miri Make a Porno '08 ►

Hijacked!

Agent Red '00
Air Force One '97 ►
Airline Disaster '10
Airport '77 '77
Altitude '17
Appointment in Honduras '53
Code Two '53
Cotton Comes to Harlem '70 ►
Delta Force '86
Detour to Terror '80
Die Hard 2: Die Harder '90 ►
Drop Zone '94
15 Minutes of War '19
Final Approach '04
Final Approach '08
Fishing Without Nets '14
The Fourth Angel '01
The French Atlantic Affair '79
Greed in the Sun '64
The Hamburg Cell '04
Hi-Jacked '50
Hijacked '12
A Hijacking '13 ►
Hostage Flight '85
Low Heights '02
Maiden Voyage: Ocean Hijack '04
Maniac '77
The Mark '12
Non-Stop '14
Passenger 57 '92
7 Days in Entebbe '18
Skyjacked '72
Star Trek 5: The Final Frontier '89
The Taking of Pelham One Two Three '74 ►
The Taking of Pelham 123 '09
Under Siege 2: Dark Territory '95
United 93 '06 ►
Victory at Entebbe '76

Hinduism

Earth '98
Fire '96
Gandhi '82 ►
The Guru '02
The Mystic Masseur '01
Water '05

Hip-Hop/Rap

***See** Biopics: Musicians; Nashville Narratives; Rock Flicks; Struggling Musicians*

Hispanic America

American Fusion '05
Barrio Wars '02
The Burning Plain '08
Cellmates '12
Cesar Chavez '14
Chasing Papi '03
crazy/beautiful '01
The Dead One '07
Dragstrip Girl '94
East Side Story '07
The Fluffy Movie: Unity Through Laughter '14
Fools Rush In '97
From Prada to Nada '11
Gabriela '01
How the Garcia Girls Spent Their Summer '05
I Like It Like That '94 ►
Illegal Tender '07
La Mission '09
The Lawless '50
Lone Star '95 ►
Lotto Land '95
Love and Debate '06
Luminarias '99
Maid in Manhattan '02
The Maldonado Miracle '03
Mambo Cafe '00
Manito '03 ►
McFarland USA '15
Meddling Mom '13
Mexican Gangster '08
Mi Vida Loca '94
Miami Rhapsody '95
My Family '94 ►
My Man and I '52
Our Song '01 ►
Pinero '01
Quinceanera '06 ►
Race '99
Raising Victor Vargas '03
Real Women Have Curves '02 ►
Right Cross '50
The Ring '52
Roosters '95
Salsa '88
Selena '96
Spare Parts '15
Spin '04
Stand and Deliver '88 ►
Steal Big, Steal Little '95
The Street King '02
Sueno '05
Sugar '09 ►
Sweet 15 '90
Tortilla Heaven '07
Tortilla Soup '01
Trial '55
Wassup Rockers '06
The Wind That Shakes the Barley '06 ►
Zoot Suit '81 ►

Historical Comedy

Almost Heroes '97
Amreeka '09 ►
Caveman '81
The Death of Stalin '17 ►
Elvis & Nixon '16
The Favourite '18 ►
History of the World: Part 1 '81
Love and Death '75 ►
Monty Python and the Holy Grail '75 ►
Monty Python's Life of Brian '79 ►
1941 '79

Historical Detectives

The Adventures of Sherlock Holmes '39
The Alphabet Murders '65
The Crucifer of Blood '91
Death on the Nile '78
Dressed to Kill '46
Evil under the Sun '82
The Great Mouse Detective '86 ►
Hands of a Murderer '90
Heat of the Sun '99 ►
The Hound of the Baskervilles '39 ►
The Hound of the Baskervilles '59
The Hound of the Baskervilles '77
The Hound of the Baskervilles '83
The Hound of the Baskervilles '00
The Hound of the Baskervilles '02 ►
House of Fear '45
Motherless Brooklyn '19
Murder at the Baskervilles '37
Murder by Decree '79 ►
Murder on Approval '56
Murder on the Orient Express '74 ►
The Name of the Rose '86
The Pearl of Death '44
The Private Life of Sherlock Holmes '70 ►
Pursuit to Algiers '45
The Rose and the Jackal '90
Scarlet Claw '44 ►
The Seven-Per-Cent Solution '76 ►
Sherlock Holmes and the Deadly Necklace '62
Sherlock Holmes and the Incident at Victoria Falls '91
Sherlock Holmes and the Secret Weapon '42 ►
Sherlock Holmes Faces Death '43 ►
Sherlock Holmes in Washington '43
The Sign of Four '83
The Sign of Four '01
The Speckled Band '31 ►
A Study in Scarlet '33
A Study in Terror '66 ►
The Triumph of Sherlock Holmes '35
The Woman in Green '49
Young Sherlock Holmes '85

Historical Drama

***See also** Medieval Romps; Period Piece*

The Abdication '74
Abe Lincoln in Illinois '40 ►
Across the Wide Missouri '51
A.D. '85
The Affair of the Necklace '01
The Aftermath '19
The Agony and the Ecstasy '65
Agora '09
The Alamo '60 ►
The Alamo '04
The Alamo: Thirteen Days to Glory '87
Alexander '04
Alexander the Great '55
All Is True '18
Almayer's Folly '12
Almost Peaceful '02 ►
Alpha '18
Amadeus '84 ►
Amazing Grace '06 ►
Anastasia '56 ►
Anastasia: The Mystery of Anna '86
Andrei Rublev '66 ►
Anne of the Thousand Days '69 ►
Anonymous '11
Anthropoid '16
Antony and Cleopatra '73
Apocalypto '06 ►
April Morning '88
Aristocrats '99
Army of Shadows '69 ►
Arn: The Knight Templar '07
Artemisia '97
Assassination of Trotsky '72
The Attic: The Hiding of Anne Frank '88
Attila '54
Attila '01
The Autobiography of Miss Jane Pittman '74 ►
Backstabbing for Beginners '18
Backstairs at the White House '79 ►
The Ballad of Narayama '83 ►
Bang Rajan '00 ►
Barabbas '62
The Bastard '78
The Battle of Algiers '66 ►
Battle of Britain '69
Battle of the Bulge '65
The Battleship Potemkin '25 ►
Beatrice Cenci '69
Beau Brummell '54 ►
Becket '64 ►
The Beguiled '17
The Beloved Rogue '27 ►
Ben-Hur '26 ►
Ben-Hur '59 ►
Ben Hur '10
Ben-Hur '16
Beowulf '07 ►
Beowulf & Grendel '06
The Best of Enemies '19
Bet Your Life '04
Bhowani Junction '56
The Big Red One '80 ►
The Birth of a Nation '15 ►
The Birth of a Nation '16
Bisbee '17 '18
Bitter Harvest '17
Black Robe '91 ►
Blaise Pascal '71 ►
The Bounty '84
BPM (Beats Per Minute) '17
Braveheart '95 ►
Bridge of Spies '15 ►
A Bridge Too Far '77
Brigham Young: Frontiersman '40
Brother Sun, Sister Moon '73
The Bushido Blade '80
Cabeza de Vaca '90 ►
Cabiria '14
Caesar and Cleopatra '46
Caesar the Conqueror '63
California '63
Call of Heroes '16
Captain from Castile '47 ►
Carthage in Flames '60
Catherine Cookson's The Rag Nymph '96
Catherine the Great '34
Catherine the Great '95
Centennial '78 ►
Centurion '10
Chappaquiddick '17
The Charge of the Light Brigade '36 ►
The Charge of the Light Brigade '68
The Childhood of a Leader '16
Children of Paradise '44 ►
Christopher Columbus '49
Churchill '17
City of Life and Death '09
Cleopatra '34
Cleopatra '63
Cliffs of Freedom '19
Closed Curtain '13 ►
Condemned to Live '35
Conquest '37 ►
The Conspirator '10
Copperhead '13
Coriolanus '11 ►
The Court Martial of Billy Mitchell '55 ►
Creation '09
Cromwell '70
The Crossing '00
The Crucible '96 ►
The Crusades '35
The Current War: Director's Cut '19
Curse of the Golden Flower '06
Dances with Wolves '90 ►
A Dangerous Man: Lawrence after Arabia '91 ►
Danton '82 ►
Darkest Hour '17 ►
David and Bathsheba '51 ►
David Copperfield '35 ►
David Copperfield '70
David Copperfield '99
DC 9/11: Time of Crisis '04
Demetrius and the Gladiators '54
Denial '16
Desiree '54
Detroit '17 ►
The Devils '71 ►
Diane '55
The Divine Lady '29
Doctor Zhivago '65 ►
Doctor Zhivago '03
Downfall '04 ►
Dragon Blade '15
Draw on Sweet Night '15
Dream West '86
Druids '01
Drums in the Deep South '51
Dunkirk '17 ►
Dust of Life '95
Dynasty '76
The Eagle '11
Edward II '92
Effie Gray '15
Eight Men Out '88 ►
El Cid '61 ►
Eleanor & Franklin '76 ►
Eleanor: First Lady of the World '82
Elizabeth '98 ►
Elizabeth R '72 ►
Elizabeth: The Golden Age '07
Emperor '12
The Emperor and the Assassin '99
The Emperor's Shadow '96
The End of the Tour '15 ►
Erik, the Viking '65
Escape '12
The Exception '17
Experimenter '15
Fabiola '48 ►
FairyTale: A True Story '97
The Fall of the Roman Empire '64 ►
The Far Horizons '55
Farewell, My Queen '12 ►
The Favourite '18 ►
Fellini Satyricon '69 ►
The Fencer '15 ►
15 Minutes of War '19
The 15:17 to Paris '18
Finding Altamira '16
The Finest Hours '16
Fire Over England '37 ►
First Cow '20 ►
The First Olympics: Athens 1896 '84
The First Texan '56
The Flowers of War '11
Flyboys '06
Forever and a Day '43 ►
47 Ronin, Part 1 '42 ►
47 Ronin, Part 2 '42 ►
The Founder '17 ►
14 Blades '14
1492: Conquest of Paradise '92
Frantz '17 ►
Free State of Jones '16
Freedom Road '79
The Front Runner '18
Gallipoli '81 ►
Gangs of New York '02 ►
Gate of Hell '54 ►
Genghis Khan: To the Ends of the Earth and Sea '07
Genius '16
Geronimo: An American Legend '93
Gettysburg '93 ►
Giants of Rome '63
The Girl of Your Dreams '99
Gladiator of Rome '63
Glory '89 ►
Gods and Generals '03
Good Night, and Good Luck '05 ►
Goodbye Christopher Robin '17
The Gospel of John '03
The Gospel of John '15
Goya's Ghosts '06
The Great Commandment '41
The Greatest Game Ever Played '05
The Greatest Story Ever Told '65
The Guernsey Literary & Potato Peel Pie Society '18
Guilty by Suspicion '91
Gwen '19
Hamilton '20 ►
Harem '99
Harriet '19
Hatfields & McCoys '12 ►
Hawaii '66 ►
Henry V '44 ►

Henry V '89 ►
Hero '02 ►
Hidden Figures '17 ►
Hiroshima '95 ►
Hitler '62
The Horseman on the Roof '95
Hotel Mumbai '18
Hotel Rwanda '04
The Howards of Virginia '40
The Hunchback '97
The Hunchback of Notre Dame '57
The Hunchback of Notre Dame '82 ►
Hunter in the Dark '80
Hyde Park on Hudson '12
I Am Not Your Negro '17 ►
I Remember Nelson '82
I Shot Andy Warhol '96 ►
If They Tell You I Fell '89
Ike: Countdown to D-Day '04
Imperial Venus '63
In Dubious Battle '17
In Old Chicago '37 ►
Innocent Voices '04
The Innocents '16 ►
The Invaders '63
The Iron Orchard '19
Ironclad '11
Ironclad: Battle for Blood '14
Ivan the Terrible, Part 1 '44 ►
Ivan the Terrible, Part 2 '46 ►
Ivanhoe '52 ►
Ivanhoe '82
Ivanhoe '97 ►
J. Edgar '11
Jackie '16 ►
Jade Warrior '06
Jakob the Liar '99 ►
Jeanne la Pucelle '94
Jefferson in Paris '94
Jesus of Nazareth '77 ►
The Jewel in the Crown '84 ►
JFK '91 ►
Joan of Arc '48
Joan of Arc '99
John Adams '08
John Rabe '09
Johnny Tremain & the Sons of Liberty '58
Joyeux Noel '05 ►
Judith of Bethulia '14 ►
Julius Caesar '53 ►
Justin Morgan Had a Horse '81
Kama Sutra: A Tale of Love '96
Kaspar Hauser '93
The Keeping Room '15
Kesari '19
Khartoum '66
The Kid '19
Killing Lincoln '13
The King '19 ►
King David '85
King Richard and the Crusaders '54
Kingdom of Heaven '05 ►
The King's Speech '10 ►
Kolberg '45
Kundun '97 ►
La Marseillaise '37 ►
Labyrinth of Lies '14
The Lady and the Highwayman '89
Lady Godiva '55
Lady Jane '85 ►
Land of Mine '15
Last Days in the Desert '16 ►
Last Days of Pompeii '35
The Last Days of Pompeii '84
The Last Emperor '87 ►
Last Four Days '77
Last Knights '15
The Last Legion '07
The Last Station '09
The Last Valley '71
The Last Warrior '18
Lawrence of Arabia '62 ►
The Legend of Suriyothai '02
The Libertine '05
Lincoln '12 ►
The Lindbergh Kidnapping Case '76 ►
The Lion in Winter '68 ►
The Lion in Winter '03 ►
The Lion of Thebes '64 ►
Lionheart '87
A Little Chaos '14
Little House on the Prairie '74 ►
Lizzie '18
Lloyds of London '36 ►
Long Shadows '86
The Lost Bladesman '16
The Lost City '05
The Lost City of Z '17 ►
Loves of Three Queens '54
Loving '16 ►
Ludwig '72
Luther '74
Mahler '74 ►
A Man for All Seasons '66 ►
A Man for All Seasons '88 ►
Mandela '87 ►
Marie Antoinette '38
Marie Antoinette '06
Mark Felt: The Man Who Brought Down the White House '17
The Marquise of O '76
Martin Luther '53
Mary of Scotland '36 ►
Mary, Queen of Scots '71
Masada '81 ►
Mata Hari '85
Mayerling '68
The Meanest Man in Texas '19
Meek's Cutoff '10 ►
The Messenger: The Story of Joan of Arc '99
Michael Collins '96 ►
Missiles of October '74 ►
The Mission '86 ►
Mission Mangal '19
Mrs. Brown '97 ►
Mockery '27
Moll Flanders '96
Mongol '07 ►
Monsieur N. '03 ►
Moses '96
The Motorcycle Diaries '04 ►
Mountbatten: The Last Viceroy '86
Mozart's Sister '10
The Mudlark '50
Munich '05 ►
Mutiny on the Bounty '35 ►
Mutiny on the Bounty '62
Mysteries of Lisbon '10
Napoleon '03
Napoleon and Josephine: A Love Story '87
The Nativity Story '06
Nefertiti, Queen of the Nile '64
Never Look Away '18 ►
The New World '05 ►
Nicholas and Alexandra '71
Nicky's Family '13
The Nightingale '18 ►
Nightjohn '96
Nine Days a Queen '36 ►
9/11 '17
The Ninth Day '04 ►
Nixon '95 ►
No God, No Master '12
The North Star '16
Northman: A Viking Saga '15
O Jerusalem '07
Omar Khayyam '57
Operation Finale '18
Ophelia '19
The Ordeal of Dr. Mudd '80 ►
Orphans of the Storm '21 ►
Outlaw King '18
Outside the Law '10
Overlanders '46 ►
Padmaavat '18 ►
Passion in the Desert '97
Passion of Joan of Arc '28 ►
The Pathfinder '96
Pathfinder '07
The Patriot '00
Paul, Apostle of Christ '18
Pawn Sacrifice '15
Peter and Paul '81
Peterloo '18
Pharoah's Army '95
Portrait of a Lady '96 ►
Portrait of a Lady on Fire '19 ►
The Power of One '92
Pride and Prejudice '40 ►
Princess Kaiulani '09
The Private Life of Henry VIII '33 ►
The Private Lives of Elizabeth & Essex '39 ►
The Promise '17
Queen Christina '33 ►
Queen Margot '94 ►
Quo Vadis '51 ►
Ragtime '81 ►
Raintree County '57
Rasputin '85 ►
Rasputin and the Empress '33 ►
Red Cliff '08 ►
Reign of Terror '49
Resistance '20
A Respectable Trade '98
Restoration '94 ►
The Return of the Scarlet Pimpernel '37
Revolution '85
Richard III '55 ►
The Right Stuff '83 ►
Rikyu '90 ►
The Rise of Louis XIV '66 ►
Risen '16
Rob Roy-The Highland Rogue '53
The Robe '53
Robin and Marian '76
Robin Hood '10
Roots '77 ►
Roots: The Gift '88
Roots: The Next Generation '79 ►
Rosewood '96 ►
A Royal Affair '12 ►
Royal Deceit '94
Saint Joan '57
St. Michael Had a Rooster '72
St. Patrick: The Irish Legend '00
The Salem Witch Trials '02
Salome '53
Samson '18
Samson and Delilah '96
Samurai Banners '69
Samurai Reincarnation '81
Savannah '14
Scarlet Empress '34 ►
The Scarlet Letter '95
The Scarlet Pimpernel '99
The Scarlet Pimpernel 2: Mademoiselle Guillotine '99
The Scarlet Pimpernel 3: The Kidnapped King '99
The Scarlet Pimpernel '34 ►
The Scarlet Pimpernel '82 ►
The Scarlet Tunic '97
Sebastiane '79 ►
Senso '54 ►
Separate but Equal '91 ►
September Dawn '07
Shaka Zulu '83 ►
Shaka Zulu: The Last Great Warrior '01
Shenandoah '65 ►
Shin Heike Monogatari '55 ►
Shock and Awe '18
The Sicilian '87
The Sign of the Cross '33
Silence '16 ►
Sins of Rome '54
Six Wives of Henry VIII '71 ►
Soldier of Orange '78 ►
Son of Saul '15 ►
Song of Love '47 ►
Sophie Scholl: The Final Days '05 ►
Soul of the Game '96 ►
Spartacus '60 ►
Suez '38
Suffragette '15
Sunrise at Campobello '60 ►
Sunset Song '16
Surviving Picasso '96
Sword of War '09
Tai-Pan '86
A Tale of Two Cities '89 ►
A Taxi Driver '17 ►
The Ten Commandments '23
The Ten Commandments '56 ►
Ten Days That Shook the World '27 ►
Ten Who Dared '60
Testament of Youth '15 ►
That Hamilton Woman '41 ►
There Will Be Blood '07 ►
Therese '86 ►
They Died with Their Boots On '41 ►
Thirteen Days '00 ►
The Thorn Birds '83 ►
300 '07
300: Rise of an Empire '13
Three Kingdoms: Resurrection of the Dragon '08
Three Sovereigns for Sarah '85
To End All Wars '01
To Kill a King '03
The Tower of London '39
Tower of London '62
Transit '18
The Triangle Factory Fire Scandal '79
The Truce '96 ►
True Women '97
The Tunnel '01 ►
USS Indianapolis: Men of Courage '16
Vanina Vanini '61 ►
Vice '18
Viceroy's House '17
Victoria & Abdul '17
Vincere '09
The Virgin Queen '55 ►
Viva Zapata! '52 ►
The Wannsee Conference '84 ►
The War Lord '65 ►
Warlords '08 ►
Warrior Queen '03
The Warriors '55
The Watsons Go to Birmingham '13
The Winds of Kitty Hawk '78
The Winter War '89 ►
Wolf Totem '15
A Woman Called Golda '82 ►
A Woman Called Moses '78
Woman in Gold '15
Woman Walks Ahead '17
Young Bess '53 ►
Young Catherine '91 ►
Young Mr. Lincoln '39 ►
Zama '17
The Zookeeper's Wife '17

Historical Romance

See also Historical Drama

The Affair of the Necklace '01
The Agony and the Ecstasy '65
Alexander '04
Angelique '64
Angelique and the King '66
Angelique and the Sultan '68
Angelique: The Road to Versailles '65
Anne of the Thousand Days '69 ►
Barbara Frietchie '24
Becoming Jane '07
Bet Your Life '04
Braveheart '95 ►
Caesar and Cleopatra '46
Casanova '05
Catherine the Great '34
Catherine the Great '95
Clarissa '91 ►
Cleopatra '34
Cleopatra '63
Cleopatra '99
David and Bathsheba '51 ►
Doctor Zhivago '65 ►
Doctor Zhivago '03
Eleanor & Franklin '76 ►
The Exception '17
Frantz '17 ►
The Hunchback of Notre Dame '57
The Hunchback of Notre Dame '82 ►
The Hunchback of Notre Dame '96 ►
Ivanhoe '52 ►
Ivanhoe '82
Ivanhoe '97 ►
Jefferson in Paris '94
Kama Sutra: A Tale of Love '96
Love Happens '09
Mrs. Brown '97 ►
The New World '05 ►
Nicholas and Alexandra '71
The Other Boleyn Girl '08
Portrait of a Lady '67
Portrait of a Lady '96 ►
Pride and Prejudice '40 ►
The Princess of Montpensier '10 ►
The Private Life of Henry VIII '33 ►
The Private Lives of Elizabeth & Essex '39 ►
Ragtime '81 ►
Silk '07
Slow West '15
Southside with You '16 ►
A United Kingdom '17
Untamable Angelique '67

Hit Men/Women

See also Assassination; Organized Crime

African Rage '78
The Aggression Scale '12
Alex Cross '12
Amateur '94 ►
The American '10
Amores Perros '00 ►
Angel of Death '09
Angel's Dance '99
Asian Stories '06
The Assassin '15 ►
Assassin in Love '07
Assassination Tango '03 ►
Assassins '95
The Assassins '12
Back to Back '96
Bad Ass '09
Bad Country '14
Baja '95
Ballistic: Ecks vs. Sever '02
Bangkok Dangerous '00
Bangkok Dangerous '08
Big City Blues '99
The Big Hit '98
Big Trouble '02
Blackjack '97
Blast of Silence '61
Blonde and Blonder '07
Body Armour '07
Body Count '95
The Bodyguard '92
The Boss '73
The Bourne Identity '02 ►
Branded to Kill '67
Break '09
Brother '97
Bullet to the Head '12
Bulletproof Heart '95 ►
Bulworth '98 ►
The Casino Job '08
Cat Run '11
Certain Prey '11
Chain of Fools '00
Chicago Overcoat '09
Codename: Jaguar '98
Cold Sweat '93
Collateral '04 ►
The Collectors '99
Confessions of a Dangerous Mind '02
The Contract '98
The Contract '07
Contract Killer '98
Contract Killers '08
The Contractor '07
The Courier '12
Crank: High Voltage '09
Cybercity '99
Daredevil '03
DaVinci's War '92
Dead Fish '04
Dead Man Down '13
Deadlier Than the Male '67
Deliberate Intent '01
Desert Saints '01
Desperado '95 ►
Destination Vegas '95
Devils on the Doorstep '00
Diary of a Hitman '91
Dinner Rush '00 ►
Direct Hit '93
Dog Bite Dog '06
Dumb & Dumber '94
8 Heads in a Duffel Bag '96
El Mariachi '93 ►
Elmore Leonard's Gold Coast '97
Escape Clause '96
Exiled '06
Faithful '95
Fallen Angels '95
The Family '70
Faster '10
Fatal Justice '93
A Few Days in September '06
The Fifth Commandment '08
Fighting with Anger '07
Firepower '79
Fish in a Barrel '01
Formula 51 '01
Frenemy '09
Full Disclosure '00
Full Time Killer '01
The Funeral '96 ►
Game of Death '10
The Gene Generation '07
Ghost Dog: The Way of the Samurai '99
Gigli '03
Goodbye, Lover '99
Grosse Pointe Blank '97 ►
Guns, Girls and Gambling '11
Hail Mafia '65
Hanna '11
Hard-Boiled '92
Hard Contract '69
The Hatchet Man '32
Hidden Agenda '01
The Hit '01
The Hit List '11
Hit Parade '10
Hitman '07
Hitman's Journal '99
Hitman's Run '99
Hogfather '06
Hollow Point '95
Hotel '01
I Accidentally Domed Your Son '04
The Iceman '12
In Bruges '08
In the Name of the King 3: The Last Mission '14
In the Shadows '01
Interview With a Hitman '12
Intolerable Cruelty '03
The Irishman '19 ►
The Italian Connection '73
The Jackal '97
Jason Bourne '16
Jerry and Tom '98
Jesse Stone: Benefit of the Doubt '12
The Job '03
The Job '09
John Wick '14
John Wick: Chapter 2 '17 ►
John Wick: Chapter 3-Parabellum '19 ►
Johnny Cool '63
Johnny English Reborn '11
Joyride '97
The Kane Files '10
Kill Bill Vol. 1 '03 ►
Kill Bill Vol. 2 '04 ►
Kill 'Em All '12
The Killer '90 ►
Killer Elite '11
Killer Joe '11
The Killers '46 ►
Killers '10
Killing Emmett Young '02
The Killing Machine '09
Killing Them Softly '12
Killshot '09
King of the Ants '03
Kiss Me Deadly '08
The Korean '08
La Femme Nikita '91 ►
Lady Jayne Killer '03
Lansdown '01
Last Chance '07
The Last Hit Man '08
The Last Lullaby '08 ►
Le Choc '82
Le Samourai '67 ►
The Liability '12
Life Tastes Good '99
Life Without Dick '01
The Line '08
The Lineup '58
The Liquidator '65
Little Odessa '94

► = rated three bones or higher

The Locator 2: Braxton Returns '09
Looper '12 ►
The Lost Samaritan '08
Love '05
Love and Action in Chicago '99
Lucky Number Slevin '06
Made Men '99
The Man Who Knew Too Little '97
Man with a Gun '95
The Manchurian Candidate '62 ►
The Matador '06 ►
Max Payne '08
Mean Johnny Barrows '75
The Mechanic '72
The Mechanic '11
Mechanic: Resurrection '16
The Memory of a Killer '03
The Merry Gentleman '08
The Mexican '01
The Ministers '09
Mr. & Mrs. Smith '05 ►
Mongo's Back In Town '71
Murda Muzik '03
Murder by Contract '58
Murder C.O.D. '90
The Naked City '48 ►
Naked Weapon '03
Nemesis 4: Cry of Angels '97
Night of the Running Man '94
Ninja's Creed '09
No Witness '04
Nobody '07
Nurse Betty '00 ►
On the Edge '02
Once Upon a Time in Mexico '03 ►
One In the Chamber '12
One Night at McCool's '01
Operation: Endgame '10
Our Lady of the Assassins '01
Out of Line '00
Over the Wire '95
Overtime '11
The Pact '99
Paid '06
Paid to Kill '54
Pandora Machine '04
Panic '00
Perfect Killer '77
The Perfect Sleep '08
Pistol Whipped '08
The Pleasure Drivers '05
Point of No Return '93
Portrait of a Hitman '77
The Positively True Adventures of the Alleged Texas Cheerleader-Murdering Mom '93 ►
The Prince '14
Prisoner of Love '99
Prizzi's Honor '85 ►
The Professional '94
Project: Kill! '77
Pros and Ex-cons '05
Proud Mary '18
Puerto Vallarta Squeeze '04
Pulp Fiction '94 ►
Quick '93
Rain Fall '09
Raising Heroes '97
Razor Blade Smile '98
Real Time '08
Red Rock West '93 ►
Red Shadow '01
Red Siren '02
The Replacement Killers '98
R.I.C.C.O. '02
Rick '03
Ripley's Game '02 ►
Road of No Return '09
Road to Perdition '02 ►
Run All Night '15
Running with the Devil '19
Sabotage '96
Sanctuary '98
The Shadow Conspiracy '96
Shadowboxer '06
Shattered Image '98
Shoot 'Em Up '07
The Silencer '99
Sin City '05
Sin City: A Dame to Kill For '14
The Sisters Brothers '18
Sister's Keeper '07
Six Ways to Sunday '99
Sleepers '96
Smokin' Aces '07
Smokin' Aces 2: Assassins' Ball '10
Solo '06
The Specialist '75
The Specialist '94
Stiletto '08
Strangers on a Train '51 ►
Suddenly '54 ►
Ten 'Til Noon '06
Term Life '16
Terminal '18
The Tesseract '03
They Gave Him a Gun '37
Things to Do in Denver When You're Dead '95 ►
This Gun for Hire '42 ►
Three Came to Kill '61
The 3 Marias '03
Thrill Seekers '99
Triggermen '02
Triple Threat '19
29 Palms '03
Two Days in the Valley '96 ►
Two Tough Guys '03
U-Turn '97
Violet & Daisy '11
Viral Assassins '00
Wanted '08 ►
War '07
War, Inc. '08
Warm Blooded Killers '01
Whacked! '02
Who is Cletis Tout? '02
The Whole Nine Yards '00
The Whole Ten Yards '04
Wild Target '10
Wish You Were Dead '00
The Wrecking Crew '99
You Kill Me '07 ►

Hitchhikers

See ***Thumbs Up***

Hockey

See also ***Skating***
Bon Cop Bad Cop '06
The Boys '97
Breakfast With Scot '07
The Cutting Edge '92
D2: The Mighty Ducks '94
D3: The Mighty Ducks '96
Dutch Girls '87
Goon '12
Goon: Last of the Enforcers '17
Happy Gilmore '96
Hockey Night '84
The Ice Rink '99
It's a Pleasure '45
Jack Frost '98
Lethal Weapon 3 '92
The Love Guru '08
Love Story '70 ►
The Mighty Ducks '92
Miracle '04 ►
Miracle on Ice '81
Mr. Hockey: The Gordie Howe Story '13
MVP: Most Valuable Primate '00
Mystery, Alaska '99
No Sleep 'Til Madison '02
The Rocket '05 ►
Slap Shot '77 ►
Slap Shot 2: Breaking the Ice '02
Sticks and Stones '08
Strange Brew '83
Sudden Death '95
Tooth Fairy '10
Touch and Go '86
Waking Up Wally '05
Youngblood '86

Holidays

See also ***Christmas; Halloween; Horrible Holidays; New Year's Eve; Thanksgiving***
Adam Sandler's 8 Crazy Nights '02
An American Carol '08
Banner 4th of July '13
Be My Valentine '13
Believe '16
Boo 2! A Madea Halloween '17
Carry On Behind '75
Cupid '12
The Dog Who Saved Easter '15
Easter Parade '48 ►
Four '12
Groundhog Day '93 ►
Grown Ups '10
Holiday Breakup '16
Holidays '16
Hop '11
I Hate Valentine's Day '09
Jack Frost '97
Labor Day '13
The Lost Valentine '11
Love the Coopers '15
Mother's Day '16
Muck '15
The Oath '18
Smooch '11
Strange Days '95 ►
Take Me Home Tonight '11
Two Weeks with Love '50
A Valentine Carol '07
Valentine's Day '10
The White Balloon '95 ►
White Reindeer '13

The Holocaust

See also ***Germany; Judaism; Nazis & World War Two***
Adam Resurrected '08
Almost Peaceful '02 ►
Amen '02 ►
Anne Frank: The Whole Story '01 ►
Anthropoid '16
The Assisi Underground '84
The Attic: The Hiding of Anne Frank '88
Au Revoir les Enfants '87 ►
The Book Thief '13
The Boy in the Striped Pajamas '08 ►
Christabel '89
Conspiracy '01
The Counterfeiters '07 ►
The Cutter '05
A Day in October '92
Denial '16
The Devil's Arithmetic '99
The Diary of Anne Frank '59 ►
Dominion: Prequel to the Exorcist '05
Edges of the Lord '01
Enemies, a Love Story '89 ►
Era Notte a Roma '60 ►
Europa, Europa '91 ►
Everything is Illuminated '05 ►
The Execution '85
Facing Windows '03
Fateless '05 ►
A Film Unfinished '10
The Flat '12 ►
The Garden of the Finzi-Continis '71 ►
Generation War '13
Getting Away With Murder '96
The Girl of Your Dreams '99
God on Trial '08
The Goebbels Experiment '05
Good '08
Good Evening, Mr. Wallenberg '93
The Grey Zone '01
The Hiding Place '75
Hitler '62
The Holcroft Covenant '85
Holocaust '78 ►
Holocaust Survivors. . . Remembrance of Love '83
I Love You, I Love You Not '97
In a Glass Cage '86
In Darkness '11
In the Presence of Mine Enemies '97
Into the Arms of Strangers: Stories of the Kindertransport '00 ►
Jacob the Liar '74
Jakob the Liar '99 ►
Kanal '56 ►
Kapo '59 ►
The Last Butterfly '92
The Last Days '98 ►
The Last Metro '80 ►
The Last of the Unjust '13 ►
Lore '13 ►
The Murderers Are Among Us '46
Never Forget '91
The Ninth Day '04 ►
No Place on Earth '12
Operation Finale '18
Out of the Ashes '03
The Pawnbroker '65 ►
The Pianist '02 ►
Playing for Time '80 ►
Prisoner of Paradise '02 ►
The Rose Garden '89
Rosenstrasse '03 ►
Sarah's Key '10
Schindler's List '93 ►
A Secret '07 ►
The Serpent's Egg '78
Shoah '85 ►
The Shop on Main Street '65 ►
Sophie's Choice '82 ►
The Substance of Fire '96
Sunshine '99
This Must Be the Place '12
Triumph of the Spirit '89 ►
The Truce '96 ►
Uprising '01 ►
Verdict on Auschwitz: The Frankfurt Auschwitz Trial 1963-1965 '93 ►
Walking with the Enemy '13
Wallenberg: A Hero's Story '85 ►
The Wannsee Conference '84 ►

Home Alone

See also ***Childhood Visions***
Abner the Invisible Dog '13
Adventures in Babysitting '87
And You Thought Your Parents Were Weird! '91
The Apple Dumpling Gang '75
Baby's Day Out '94
The Blackcoat's Daughter '17
Blank Check '93
Bless the Beasts and Children '71
The Blue Lagoon '80
Boys Will Be Boys '97
Camp Nowhere '94
Children of Invention '09
Christina's House '99
Cloak & Dagger '84
Cohen and Tate '88
Cold Skin '18
Courage Mountain '89
Dirt Bike Kid '86
Don't Tell Mom the Babysitter's Dead '91
Duck Season '04 ►
Explorers '85
Fear of the Dark '02
Footsteps '03
Four Rooms '95
Gleaming the Cube '89
The Goonies '85
He Is My Brother '75
Home Alone '90 ►
Home Alone 2: Lost in New York '92
Home Alone 3 '97
Home Alone: The Holiday Heist '12
Home Invasion '16
Honey, I Shrunk the Kids '89
Honey, We Shrunk Ourselves '97
Hook '91
The Horse Without a Head '63
House Arrest '96
Intruders '16
Invaders from Mars '53
Invaders from Mars '86
Legend of Billie Jean '85
The Littlest Horse Thieves '76
Lord of the Flies '63 ►
Lord of the Flies '90
Mr. Wise Guy '42
Monkey Trouble '94
The Monster Squad '87
Nightwaves '03
Nobody Knows '04
Paradise '82
Phobia '13
The Rescue '88
Return to the Blue Lagoon '91
Scream '96 ►
The Secret Life of Pets '16
Shipwrecked '90
Shut In '16
Starfish '19
3 Ninjas '92
3 Ninjas Kick Back '94
Tideland '05
2 Brothers & a Bride '03
Wakefield '17
A Waltz Through the Hills '88
The Window '49 ►
The Wolf Hour '19
Young Sherlock Holmes '85

Home Invasion

See also ***Yuppie Nightmares***
Abner the Invisible Dog '13
The Aggression Scale '12
Annabelle '14
As Good As Dead '10
Better Watch Out '17
Borgman '13
Born Bad '11
Break-In '06
Breaking & Exiting '18
Breaking In '18
Cold in July '14 ►
Crime Wave '54
Cul de Sac '66 ►
Death Game '77
Desperate Hours '55 ►
Desperate Hours '90
Don't Breathe '16 ►
Door to Door Maniac '61
Elle '16 ►
The Fanatic '19
Fender Bender '16
Funny Games '97
Funny Games '07 ►
Heart of the Storm '04
Held Hostage '09
Hellions '15
Home Invasion '16
If I Die Before I Wake '98
I'll Sleep When I'm Dead '03 ►
In Their Skin '12
Intruder '16
Intruders '16
Kidnapped '10
The Killing Floor '06
Lady in a Cage '64 ►
The Last House on the Left '09
Mischief Night '13
Mother's Day '10
My Nanny's Secret '09
Open House '10
Outlaws and Angels '16
Outrage Born in Terror '09
Panic Room '02
Perfect Hideout '08
Phobia '13
The Purge '13
The Purge: Anarchy '14
The Purge: Election Year '16
Romper Stomper '92
Stash House '12
The Strangers '08
The Strangers: Prey at Night '18
Straw Dogs '72 ►
Straw Dogs '11
Trespass '11
The Truth '10
Villains '19
Wait until Dark '67 ►
You're Next '13

The Homefront: England

See also ***Great Britain; World War Two***
The Affair '95
Carrie's War '04
The Edge of Love '08
The Haunted Airman '06
Hope and Glory '87 ►
Joe Maddison's War '10
Land Girls '09
The Last of the Blonde Bombshells '00
Mrs. Henderson Presents '05
Mrs. Miniver '42 ►
Murder On the Home Front '13
Nanny McPhee Returns '10
The Song of Names '19
This Above All '42
Three Faces East '30
The Water Horse: Legend of the Deep '07
Waterloo Road '45
The White Cliffs of Dover '44 ►
The Woman in Black 2: Angel of Death '15

The Homefront: U.S./ Canada

See also ***World War Two***
Air Raid Wardens '43
Come See the Paradise '90 ►
Flags of Our Fathers '06 ►
For the Moment '94
Fort McCoy '11
The Home Front '02
The Human Comedy '43 ►
I'll Remember April '99
In Love and War '91
In the Mood '87
Ithaca '16
A League of Their Own '92 ►
The Messenger '09 ►
The More the Merrier '43 ►
1941 '79
The Pacific '10 ►
Racing with the Moon '84 ►
Raggedy Man '81 ►
Ride the Wild Fields '00
Saboteur '42 ►
Since You Went Away '44 ►
Stop-Loss '08 ►
Swing Shift '84
The War Bride '01
Wedding in White '72

Homeless

See also ***Great Depression; Hard Knock Life; Yuppie Nightmares***
Accatone! '61 ►
All Mine to Give '56
Almost Holy '16 ►
Amores Perros '00 ►
August Rush '07
Beyond the Blackboard '11
The Billion Dollar Hobo '78
Black Butterfly '17
The Book of Love '16
Borgman '13
Boy Who Caught a Crook '61
Breaking the Bank '14
Brother to Brother '04
Cardboard Boxer '16
Carpool Guy '05
Caught '96
The Caveman's Valentine '01
The Child '05
Children of Sanchez '79
Chloe & Theo '15
The Christmas Choir '08
A Christmas Tree Miracle '13
City Lights '31 ►
City Park '34
The Cold Lands '13
A Cross to Bear '12
Curly Sue '91
Dark Days '00
Dodes 'ka-den '70 ►
Drillbit Taylor '08
Duck '05
Duke '12
Eddie Presley '92
Emperor of the North Pole '73 ►
An Encounter with the Messiah '15
Entry Level '07
First, Last and Deposit '00
The Fisher King '91 ►

► = *rated three bones or higher*

Homicide

Homosexuality

See Bisexuality; Gays; Lesbians

Honeymoon

See also Marriage; Newlyweds; Wedding Bells

Hong Kong

See also Asia; China

▶ = rated three bones or higher

Gen-X Cops '99
Golden Needles '74
Hong Kong 1941 '84
In the Mood for Love '00
Infernal Affairs '02 ▶
Ip Man 2 '10
Kill a Dragon '67
Knock Off '98
Kung Fu Hustle '04 ▶
La Moustache '05
Love Is a Many-Splendored Thing '55
Man of Tai Chi '13
The Medallion '03
New Police Story '04
Noble House '88
Once a Thief '96 ▶
Push '09
Romeo Must Die '00
Rush Hour 2 '01
Silver Hawk '04
Tai-Pan '86
The Terror of the Tongs '61
That Man Bolt '73
TNT Jackson '75
Transformers: Age of Extinction '14
2046 '04
Twin Dragons '92
Vampire Effect '03
The White Storm '13 ▶

Horrible Holidays

***See also** Christmas; Halloween; Holidays; New Year's Eve; Thanksgiving; Vacation Hell*

American Gun '02 ▶
April Fool's Day '86
April Fool's Day '08
Asian Stories '06
ATM '12
Bad Santa '03
Better Watch Out '17
Black Christmas '75
Black Christmas '06
Bloody New Year '87
Body '15
Boo 2! A Madea Halloween '17
Chasing Christmas '05
The Children '08
Christmas Evil '80
Columbus Day '08
Days and Nights '14
The Devil's Teardrop '10
Don't Open Till Christmas '84
Dorm That Dripped Blood '82
Fall Down Dead '07
Gremlins '84 ▶
Halloween '78 ▶
Halloween 2: The Nightmare Isn't Over! '81
Halloween 3: Season of the Witch '82
Halloween 4: The Return of Michael Myers '88
Halloween 5: The Revenge of Michael Myers '89
Halloween 6: The Curse of Michael Myers '95
Halloween: H20 '98 ▶
Happy Birthday to Me '81
Happy Christmas '14
Home Sweet Home '80
I Still Know What You Did Last Summer '98
Independence Daysaster '13
Jack-O '95
Jam '06
Jersey Shore Shark Attack '12
Last Weekend '14
The Lottery Ticket '10
Mixed Nuts '94
Mother's Day '80
My Bloody Valentine 3D '09
My Bloody Valentine '81
The Myth of Fingerprints '97
The Night After Halloween '79
Night of the Demons 2 '94
Night of the Demons 3 '97
Night of the Demons '88
Piranha 3D '10
Pontypool '09
'R Xmas '01
Rare Exports: A Christmas Tale '10
The Ref '93 ▶
Resurrection '99
Sheitan '06
Silent Night '12
Silent Night, Bloody Night '73
Silent Night, Deadly Night '84
Silent Night, Deadly Night 2 '87
Silent Night, Deadly Night 3: Better Watch Out! '89
Silent Night, Deadly Night 4: Initiation '90
Silent Night, Deadly Night 5: The Toymaker '91
The Traveler '10
Uncertainty '08
Uncle Sam '96
Valentine '01
We're the Millers '13
What Love Is '07
When Do We Eat? '05

Horror Anthology

The ABCs of Death 2 '14
The ABCs of Death '12
Alien Massacre '67
All Hallow's Eve 2 '15
All Hallow's Eve '13
Asylum '72
The Basement '89
The Bay '12
Beneath the Flesh '09
Body Bags '93
Campfire Tales '98
A Christmas Horror Story '15
Creepshow '82
Creepshow 2 '87
Cremains '00 ▶
Dead of Night '45 ▶
Dead of Night '77
Deadtime Stories '86
Freakshow '95
Future Shock '93
Gallery of Horrors '67
Hellblock 13 '97
Holidays '16
The House that Dripped Blood '71
Into the Badlands '92
The Invoking 2 '15
The Monster Club '85
Necromentia '09
Night Gallery '69 ▶
Nightmare Cinema '19
Nightmares '83
The Offspring '87
Quicksilver Highway '98
Robinson Crusoe '54
Sanitarium '13
Scary Stories to Tell in the Dark '19
Southbound '16
Spirits of the Dead '68 ▶
Strange Frequency 2 '01
Tales from the Crypt '72 ▶
Tales from the Darkside: The Movie '90
Tales from the Hood '95
Tales of Halloween '15
Tales of Terror '62
Tales That Witness Madness '73
Terror Tract '00
Things '93
Three . . . Extremes '04
Torture Garden '67
Trilogy of Terror '75
Trilogy of Terror 2 '96
Twice-Told Tales '63 ▶
Twilight Zone: The Movie '83
Two Evil Eyes '90
V/H/S/2 '13 ▶
V/H/S '12
Vault of Horror '73
The Willies '90
XX '17
Zombieworld '15

Horror Comedy

Abraham Lincoln *vs.* Zombies '12
American Vampire '97
An American Werewolf in Paris '97
American Zombie '07
Amigo Undead '15
Andy Warhol's Dracula '74 ▶
Andy Warhol's Frankenstein '74
April Fool's Day '86
Arachnophobia '90
Army of Darkness '92 ▶
Assault of the Sasquatch '09
Astro-Zombies M4: Invaders from Cyberspace '12
Attack of the Herbals '11
Attack of the Killer Tomatoes '77
Attack of the Robots '66
The Attic Expeditions '01
Autopsy: A Love Story '02
The Babysitter '17
Bachelor Games '16
Bachelor Party in the Bungalow of the Damned '08
Bad Channels '92
Bad Meat '11
Bad Taste '88 ▶
Beauty Queen Butcher! '91
Beetlejuice '88 ▶
Behind the Mask: The Rise of Leslie Vernon '06
Bela Lugosi Meets a Brooklyn Gorilla '52
Beyond Re-Animator '03
Big Meat Eater '85
Bikini Bloodbath '06
Bikini Bloodbath Carwash '08
Bikini Bloodbath Christmas '09
Billy the Kid Versus Dracula '66
Biozombie '98
Bitter Feast '10
Black Sheep '06
Blood & Donuts '95
Blood Angels '05
Blood Hook '86
Bloodsucking Bastards '15
Body Bags '93
The Bogus Witch Project '00
The Bone Yard '90
Bonnie and Clyde *vs.* Dracula '08
Boo 2! A Madea Halloween '17
Boo! A Madea Halloween '16
The Boogie Man Will Get You '42
Botched '07
The Boy Who Cried Werewolf '10
Brain Damage '88
Bride of Chucky '98
Bride of Re-Animator '89
Bubba Ho-Tep '03 ▶
A Bucket of Blood '59 ▶
Bugged! '96
Burke & Hare '10
Burying the Ex '15
The Cabin in the Woods '12 ▶
Carry On Screaming '66
Christmas Evil '80
C.H.U.D. '84
Come to Daddy '20
The Comedy of Terrors '64 ▶
Cooties '14
Corporate Animals '19
Cottage Country '13
Creature from the Haunted Sea '60
The Creeps '97
Critters '86
Critters 2: The Main Course '88
Critters 3 '91
Critters 4 '91
Cruel Restaurant '08
Curse of the Queerwolf '87
Cutting Class '89
Dance of the Dead '08
Dark Shadows '12
Dead Alive '93
The Dead Don't Die '19
Dead Heat '88
Dead Snow '09
Dead Snow: Red *vs.* Dead '14 ▶
Deathgasm '15
Deep Murder '19
Detention '11
Diagnosis: Death '09
Dr. Jekyll and Sister Hyde '71
Dog Soldiers '01
Dolls '87
Don't Kill It '17
Doom Asylum '88
Dracula Blows His Cool '82
Dracula: Dead and Loving It '95
Dylan Dog: Dead of Night '11
Ed and His Dead Mother '93
Eddie the Sleepwalking Cannibal '12
Elvira, Mistress of the Dark '88
Elvira's Haunted Hills '02
Evil Spawn '87
Excision '12
Extra Ordinary '20
The Eye 3 '05
A Fantastic Fear of Everything '14
Father's Day '12
The Fearless Vampire Killers '67 ▶
Feast 2: Sloppy Seconds '08
Fido '06
The Final Girls '15
Flick '07
Frankenhooker '90
Frankenstein 1970 '58
Frankenstein's Great Aunt Tillie '83
Fraternity Massacre at Hell Island '07
Freaks of Nature '15
Fright Flick '10
Fright Night '11
The Frighteners '96
From Beyond '86 ▶
Funnyman '94
The Gay Bed and Breakfast of Terror '07
The Ghost Breakers '40 ▶
Ghoulies '84
Ghoulies 2 '87
Ghoulies 3: Ghoulies Go to College '91
Ghoulies 4 '93
Girl *vs.* Monster '12
Goblin '93
Goosebumps '15 ▶
Gremlins 2: The New Batch '90 ▶
Gremlins '84 ▶
Hansel & Gretel Get Baked '13
Hansel & Gretel: Witch Hunters '12
The Happiness of the Katakuris '01
The Hatching '16
A Haunted House 2 '14
A Haunted House '13
The Haunted Mansion '03
Head of the Family '96
Hellboy '04
Hillbillies in a Haunted House '67
Horns '13
The Horror of Frankenstein '70
House 2: The Second Story '87
House '86 ▶
Human Beasts '80
Hysterical '83
I Married a Vampire '87
I Sell the Dead '09
I Was a Teenage Zombie '87
Idle Hands '99
In Fabric '18
Incredibly Strange Creatures Who Stopped Living and Became Mixed-Up Zombies '63
Infestation '09
Insanitarium '08
Invasion for Flesh and Blood '94
Jack Frost 2: Revenge of the Mutant Killer Snowman '00
Jennifer's Body '09
Jesus Christ Vampire Hunter '01
John Dies at the End '12
Killer Klowns from Outer Space '88
Killer Movie '08
Killer Pad '06
Killer Tomatoes Eat France '91
Killer Tomatoes Strike Back '90
Killer Tongue '96
The Kingdom 2 '97 ▶
The Kingdom '95 ▶
Knights of Badassdom '13
Krampus '15
The Last Lovecraft: Relic of Cthulhu '09
Life After Beth '14
Little Monsters '19
Little Shop of Horrors '60 ▶
Little Shop of Horrors '86 ▶
Mama Dracula '80
A Man with a Maid '73
The Mask '94 ▶
Matinee '92
Mayhem '17
Microwave Massacre '83
Mr. Vampire '86
Mom '89
Monster in the Closet '86
Monster Man '03
The Monster of Phantom Lake '06
Motel Hell '80
Mummy's Boys '36
Munchies '87
My Bloody Banjo '15
My Boyfriend's Back '93
My Demon Lover '87
My Mom's a Werewolf '89
My Name Is Bruce '08
My Son, the Vampire '52
Nature of the Beast '07
Near Dark '87 ▶
Netherbeast Incorporated '07
Night of a Thousand Cats '72
Night of the Creeps '86
Night of the Living Deb '14
Nothing But Trouble '91
Nun of That '09
The Old Dark House '32 ▶
Old Mother Riley's Ghosts '41
Once Bitten '85
100 Bloody Acres '12
Otis '08
Out of the Dark '88
Overtime '11
Paranormal Movie '13
Pep Squad '98
Phantom Empire '87
Piranha '78
Piranha 2: The Spawning '82
Piranha 3DD '11
Pontypool '09
Psychos in Love '87
Q (The Winged Serpent) '82 ▶
Rabid Grannies '89
The Rambler '13
Rare Exports: A Christmas Tale '10
Re-Animator '84 ▶
Ready or Not '19 ▶
[REC] 3: Genesis '12
Redneck Zombies '88
Repo! The Genetic Opera '08
Return of the Killer Tomatoes! '88
Return of the Living Dead '85
Return of the Living Dead 2 '88
Return of the Living Dead 3 '93
The Return of the Swamp Thing '89
Return to Sleepaway Camp '08
Revenge of the Red Baron '93
Roman '06
Rosencrantz & Guildenstern Are Undead '10
Rubber '10
Satanic Panic '19
Saturday the 14th '81
Saturday the 14th Strikes Back '88
Scary Movie 2 '01
Scary Movie 3 '03
Scary Movie 4 '06
Scary Movie 5 '13
Schlock '73
Scout's Guide to the Zombie Apocalypse '15
Seed of Chucky '04
Septic Man '14
Severance '06
Sharknado 3: Oh Hell No! '15
Sharknado: The 4th Awakens '16
Shaun of the Dead '04 ▶
Sheitan '06
Skeleton Key 2: 667, the Neighbor of the Beast '08
Smiley '12
Son of Ingagi '40
Sorority Babes in the Slimeball Bowl-A-Rama '87
Spider Baby '64
Stage Fright '14
Stan Helsing '09
Strangers of the Evening '32
Street Trash '87
Student Bodies '81
The Stuff '85
Suck '09
The Taint '10
Tainted '98
Tales from the Crypt Presents Bordello of Blood '96
Tales from the Crypt Presents Demon Knight '94
Teenage Exorcist '93
Tequila Body Shots '99
Terror Tract '00
Terrorvision '86
Theatre of Blood '73 ▶
There's Nothing out There '90
They're Watching '16
The Thing with Two Heads '72
13 Sins '13
30 Nights of Paranormal Activity with the Devil Inside the Girl with the Dragon Tattoo '12
Three . . . Extremes '04
The Thrill Killers '65
Tone-Deaf '19
Tormented '09
The Toxic Avenger '86
The Toxic Avenger, Part 2 '89
The Toxic Avenger, Part 3: The Last Temptation of Toxie '89
Transylmania '09
Treasure of Fear '45
The Treat '98
Tremors 2: Aftershocks '96
Tremors 3: Back to Perfection '01
Tremors '89
The Tripper '06
The Troll Hunter '11
Tucker & Dale *vs.* Evil '10 ▶
Tusk '14
2001 Maniacs '05
2001 Maniacs: Field of Screams '10
Uncaged '16
Undead '05
The Undertaker and His Pals '67
Vamp '86
The Vampire Happening '71
Vampire in Brooklyn '95
Vampire Killers '09
Vampires of Sorority Row: Kickboxers From Hell '99
Vampires Suck '10
Villains '19
The Voices '15
Warm Bodies '13
What We Do in the Shadows '14
When Evil Calls '06
When Good Ghouls Go Bad '01
Wild Zero '00
Woke Up Dead '09
Wolfcop '15

▶ = *rated three bones or higher*

Yakuza Apocalypse '15
Yeti: A Love Story '08
Zombie Strippers '08
Zombieland: Double Tap '19 ▶
Zombies of Mass Destruction '10
Zombies on Broadway '44

Horse Racing

***See** Gambling; Horses; Jockeying for Position*

Horses

The Adventures of Gallant Bess '48
All Hat '07
All the Pretty Horses '00
And They're Off '11
The Appaloosa '66
April Love '57
Banjo Hackett '76
Ben-Hur '16
The Better 'Ole '26
Big Boy '30
Black Beauty '71
Black Beauty '94 ▶
The Black Stallion '79 ▶
The Black Stallion Returns '83
Blazing Saddles '74 ▶
Blue Fire Lady '78
The Bride Wore Boots '46
Broken Trail '06 ▶
Buck '11 ▶
By Dawn's Early Light '00
Call of the Forest '49
Casey's Shadow '78
Chino '75
City Slickers 2: The Legend of Curly's Gold '94
Cowgirls 'n Angels '12
Danielle Steel's Palomino '91
Danny '79
Dark Horse '92
Dark Horse '16
David Harum '34
The Devil Horse '26
Devil Horse '32
Dreamer: Inspired by a True Story '05
Eagle's Wing '79
The Electric Horseman '79
Emma's Chance '16
Envy '04
Equus '77
Far North '88
The First Auto '27
Flash '98
Flicka '06
Flicka: Country Pride '12
The Flying Deuces '39 ▶
Francis Goes to the Races '51
The Gentleman from Arizona '39
The Golden Stallion '49
The Great Mike '44
The Greening of Whitney Brown '11
Hair '79 ▶
Half-Baked '97
Harry and Snowman '16 ▶
Hell's Hinges '16
Home In Indiana '44
Horse Camp '14
Horse Girl '20
The Horse in the Gray Flannel Suit '68
A Horse Tale '15
The Horse Whisperer '97
The Horsemen '70
The Horses of McBride '12
Hot to Trot! '88
In Old Kentucky '35
In Pursuit of Honor '95
In the Arms of My Enemy '07
Indian Paint '64
International Velvet '78
Into the West '92 ▶
It Ain't Hay '43
Italian Straw Hat '27 ▶
Justin Morgan Had a Horse '81
King of the Wild Stallions '59
King of the Wind '93
Lean on Pete '17 ▶
The Littlest Horse Thieves '76
The Littlest Outlaw '54
The Long Shot '04
Lost Stallions:The Journey Home '08
Lotna '64
Lucky Luke '94
The Man from Snowy River '82
Meet Wally Sparks '97
Michael Shayne: Private Detective '40
The Miracle of the White Stallions '63
The Misfits '61 ▶
Misty '61
Moondance Alexander '07
The Mustang '19 ▶
My Friend Flicka '43 ▶
My Little Pony: The Movie '17
My Pal Trigger '46
National Lampoon's Animal House '78 ▶
Nico the Unicorn '98
Our Wild Hearts '13
Palio '15 ▶
Racing Stripes '05
The Red Fury '84
The Red Pony '49 ▶
Return to Snowy River '88 ▶
Ride a Wild Pony '75 ▶
The Rider '17
Riders '88
Riding High '50
Rolling Home '48
The Rounders '65
Running Free '00
Running Wild '73
Second Chances '98
Secretariat '10
Shannon's Rainbow '09
Shooting Fish '98
The Silver Stallion: King of the Wild Brumbies '93
Simpatico '99
Sing You Sinners '38
Something to Talk About '95
Speedy '28 ▶
Spirit: Stallion of the Cimarron '02
Sporting Blood '31
Stallion Road '47
Storm Rider '13
Texas Rein '16
That's My Man '47
Thunderhoof '48
Toy Story 2 '99 ▶
Treacherous Beauties '94
12 Strong '18
Two Bits & Pepper '95
The Undefeated '69
Urban Country '18
War Horse '11
Whisper 2: L'Aventure Continue '16
Wild Beauty '27
Wild Hearts Can't Be Broken '91 ▶
Wild Horse Hank '79
Wild Horses '82
Wild Horses '84
Wild Pony '83
Wild Stallion '52
The Wild Stallion '09
The Woman in Red '35

Hospitals & Medicine

***See also** Disease of the Week; Doctors & Emerging Viruses; Shrinks*

Abandoned '10
Against the Dark '08
Alive Inside '14 ▶
Article 99 '92
The Assignment '17
Asylum of the Damned '03
Autopsy '08
Awake '07
Awakenings '90 ▶
Bad Timing: A Sensual Obsession '80
The Barbarian Invasions '03 ▶
BASEketball '98
Beanpole '20 ▶
Between the Darkness and the Dawn '85
Between Two Women '45
Beyond the Black Rainbow '10
Boo! '05
Bringing Out the Dead '99
Britannia Hospital '82
Calendar Girls '03
Calling Dr. Gillespie '42
Carry On Matron '72
Carry On Nurse '59
The Cave '19 ▶
Cemetery of Splendor '15 ▶
The Children Act '18
City of Angels '98
City of Joy '92
The Clonus Horror '79
Cold Prey II '08
Coma '78 ▶
Coma '12
Come to the Stable '49 ▶
Crazy Eights '06
Critical Care '97
Critical Condition '86
Cry of the City '48
A Cure for Wellness '17
Dead Ringers '88 ▶
The Death of Dick Long '19
The Death of Mr. Lazarescu '05
Declaration of War '11
Desperate Measures '98
Diagnosis: Death '09
Disorderlies '87
Disorderly Orderly '64
Doctor at Large '57
Dr. Gillespie's Criminal Case '43
Dr. Gillespie's New Assistant '42
Doctor in Clover '66
Dr. Kildare's Strange Case '40
Dr. Kildare's Victory '42
Doctors' Wives '70
The Dresser '15 ▶
The Drone Virus '04
East of Kilimanjaro '57
The Egyptian '54
Eli '19
Evolution '16
Extreme Measures '96
Eyewitness '56
The Fall '06
FBI: Negotiator '05
Five '11 ▶
Five Feet Apart '19
For Roseanna '96
Fractured '19
Fragile '05
The Fugitive '93 ▶
Game of Death '10
Gifted Hands: The Ben Carson Story '09
The Girl in White '52
The Girl Who Kicked the Hornet's Nest '10
The Good Doctor '11
Green for Danger '47
The Green Light '37
Gross Anatomy '89
Halloween 2: The Nightmare Isn't Over! '81
Hannah Free '09
Hard-Boiled '92
Hard to Kill '89
The Healer '02
The Heart Specialist '06
The Hollars '16
Horror Hospital '73
The Hospital '71 ▶
Hospital of Terror '78
Hotel Artemis '18
Hours '13
If I Stay '14
In Love and War '96
Insidious '10
Intent to Kill '58
The Interns '62
John Q '02
Junior '94
Just Another Love Story '08
The Killing of a Sacred Deer '17
The Kingdom 2 '97 ▶
The Kingdom '95 ▶
The Lady With the Lamp '51
Lifespan '75
Like Father, Like Son '87
Louder Than Words '14
Maggie '15
The Man Who Shook the Hand of Vicente Fernandez '12 ▶
Memorial Day '12
Merrily We Go to Hell '32
The Midwife '17 ▶
The Mind of Mr. Soames '70
Miracle Dogs '03
Miracles From Heaven '16
Miss Evers' Boys '97
Motherland '17
My Year Without Sex '09
The National Health '73
National Lampoon Presents RoboDoc '08
Natural Selection '11
Nightmare Cinema '19
Nine Months '95
90 Minutes in Heaven '15
The 9th Life of Louis Drax '16
Nurse '80
Old Stone '16
One Flew Over the Cuckoo's Nest '75 ▶
Open Your Eyes '97 ▶
Operation Heartbeat '69
Ordinary Love '20
Painkillers '15
Patch Adams '98
Pathology '08
Planet Terror '07
Pride of the Marines '45 ▶
Psych: 9 '10
Range of Motion '00
Red 11 '19
Saturn in Opposition '07
A Shine of Rainbows '09
The Singing Detective '03
Something the Lord Made '04
State of Emergency '94
A Stolen Face '52
Stonehearst Asylum '13
A Stranger's Heart '07
Sublime '07
Such Good Friends '71
The Surgeon '94
Take Down '92
Tales from the Gimli Hospital '88
Talk to Her '02 ▶
Tender Loving Care '73
Terminator 2: Judgment Day '91 ▶
13 Moons '02
This Woman Is Dangerous '52
Three Men in White '44
The Tipping Point '07
12 Monkeys '95 ▶
28 Days '00
The Ugly '96
The Unknown Girl '17
Vigil in the Night '40
Vital Signs '90
The Void '17
Voodoo Possession '14
The Waiting Room '12
Welcome Stranger '47
Wetlands '13
Where Truth Lies '96
While You Were Sleeping '95 ▶
White Coats '04
Whose Life Is It Anyway? '81 ▶
Why I Wore Lipstick to My Mastectomy '06
Wildling '18
Young Dr. Kildare '38
Young Doctors in Love '82

Hostage!

***See also** Kidnapped!; Missing Persons*

The Abduction '96
Against the Wall '94 ▶
Air Force One '97 ▶
Air Rage '01
Airheads '94
Alan Partridge '13 ▶
Albino Alligator '96
Alien Raiders '08
Allie & Me '97
Ambush '50
Amos and Andrew '93
As Good As Dead '10
Attack the Gas Station '99
Auto Recovery '08
Bait '02
Bandits '01
Behind Your Eyes '11
Bel Canto '18
Berlin Syndrome '17
The Betrayed '08
Billionaire Ransom '16
Black Cobra 2 '89
Black Fox: Good Men and Bad '94
Blackout '78
Blues '08
Body Count '97
Born Bad '97
Born to Fight '07
Botched '07
The Boys Club '96
Brave '07
Breakaway '02
Breaking News '04
Cadillac Man '90
Captive '15
Captivity '07
Carjacked '11
Carnage Park '16
Carpool '96
The Chaos Experiment '09
Civic Duty '06
The Clearing '04 ▶
Close '19
Cold Sweat '71
The Collection '12
Command Performance '09
Cradle 2 the Grave '03
Cravings '06
Crime Wave '54
Crisis '50
Cry Terror! '58
Cube 2: Hypercube '02
Cube '98
Cul de Sac '66 ▶
Cyborg Soldier '08
Dark Heart '06
Dawning '09
Dead Silence '96
Deadlocked '00
Death and the Maiden '94 ▶
Demolition High '95
Desperate Hours '90
Dial 1119 '50
Die Hard '88 ▶
Die Hard 2: Die Harder '90 ▶
Diplomatic Siege '99
The Disappearance of Alice Creed '09
Dog Day Afternoon '75 ▶
Donald Cried '16
Door to Door Maniac '61
Edge of Eternity '59
Escape from New York '81
Face the Evil '97
Fall Time '94
Family Weekend '13
Fatal Mission '89
FBI: Negotiator '05
Firestorm '97
Firewall '06
First Sunday '08
Fishing Without Nets '14
Flypaper '11
Freezer '14
Friends and Family '01
Funny Games '97
Funny Games '07 ▶
Gigli '03
Gone Dark '03
Half Past Dead '02
Headless Body in Topless Bar '96
The Heist '96
Held Hostage '09
Held Up '00
A Hijacking '13 ▶
Homecoming '09
Hostage '05
Hostage High '97
Hostage Hotel '00
Hotel Mumbai '18
Housewife '72
The Human Centipede 2: Full Sequence '11
The Human Race '14
Hunt to Kill '10
If I Want to Whistle, I Whistle '10
In Her Line of Fire '06
Inside '06
Inside Man '06 ▶
Iron Eagle '86
Jeopardy '53
The Jesus Trip '71
John Q '02
Johnny 100 Pesos '93
Keyhole '11
Kidnapped '74
Kill Me Later '01
The Killing Jar '10
King of Comedy '82 ▶
Labor Day '13
Lace 2 '85
Last Day of Summer '10
The Last Mile '59
The Legend of Wolf Mountain '92
Light It Up '99
Living & Dying '07
Lockout '12
Mad City '97
The Marine 2 '09
The Marine '06
Mechanic: Resurrection '16
Meltdown '95
Miss Congeniality 2: Armed and Fabulous '05
Mistrial '96
Money Monster '16
Monos '19 ▶
Morgan's Ferry '99
Mother's Day '10
Munich '05 ▶
My Name is Modesty: A Modesty Blaise Adventure '04
My Son, My Son, What Have Ye Done '09
Mythica: The Necromancer '15
The Negotiator '98
Nick of Time '95
The Night Holds Terror '55
Nine Dead '10
No Contest '94
No Good Deed '02
No Good Deed '14
No Orchids for Miss Blandish '48
Nothing to Lose '96
Nothing to Lose '08
Olympus Has Fallen '13
One Way Out '95
Open House '10
Operation Thunderbolt '77
Outlaws and Angels '16
P2 '07
Pawn '13
Perfect Hideout '08
The Perfect Host '10
Perfect Strangers '03
A Perfect World '93
Peril '00
Petrified Forest '36 ▶
P.S. Your Cat is Dead! '02
Pups '99
Quick Change '90
Raiders of the Seven Seas '53
Raising the Heights '97
Rambo '08
Rampage: Capital Punishment '14
Red Mercury '05
Red State '11
The Ref '93 ▶
Repentance '14
Restraint '08
Roadside '15
Saw 2 '05
Saw 4 '07
Saw 5 '08
Scenes of the Crime '01
The Seventh Floor '93
Sex and the Other Man '95
S.F.W. '94
16 Blocks '06 ▶
Skyscraper '95
Something Wild '61
Special Forces '03
Speed 2: Cruise Control '97
Split Second '53
Stand Off '11
A Stranger Is Watching '82
The Strangers '08
Stranglehold '94
Stripteaser '95
Sudden Death '95
Suddenly '54 ▶
Summer's Moon '09

▶ = rated three bones or higher

Suspended Animation '02
SWAT: Unit 887 '15
Sweet Hostage '75
Take Down '92
The Taking of Pelham One Two Three '74 ▸
The Taking of Pelham 123 '09
This Gun for Hire '42 ▸
Three Came to Kill '61
3 from Hell '19
3 Ninjas: High Noon at Mega Mountain '97
Torn Apart '04
The Trap '59
Trespass '11
The Truth '10
Truth or Consequences, N.M. '97
Tube '03
12 Hours to Live '06
12 Monkeys '95 ▸
Uninvited Guest '99
Victoria '15
Victory at Entebbe '76
The Wedding Guest '18
Wild Oranges '24

Housekeepers
***See** The Help: Female*

Houston
***See also** Black Gold; Texas*
Apollo 13 '95 ▸
The Bad News Bears in Breaking Training '77
Brewster McCloud '70 ▸
Charlie Wilson's War '07
Dance with Me '98
Dancing in Twilight '05
Enron: The Smartest Guys in the Room '05 ▸
The Evening Star '96
Jason's Lyric '94
Lethal Force '00
Love and Mary '07
Mao's Last Dancer '09
Natural Selection '11
Puncture '11
Reality Bites '94
The Swarm '78
Terms of Endearment '83 ▸
Threshold '03
Thunder Soul '10
Towelhead '07
Urban Cowboy '80
Vietnam, Texas '90

Human Sacrifice
Apocalypto '06 ▸
Blood Feast '63
Borderland '07
Brides of the Beast '68
Children of the Corn '84
Children of the Corn 2: The Final Sacrifice '92
Children of the Corn 3: Urban Harvest '95
Children of the Corn 4: The Gathering '96
Children of the Corn 5: Fields of Terror '98
Children of the Corn 666: Isaac's Return '99
Children of the Corn: Revelation '01
Children of the Corn '09
Craze '74
Dance with the Devil '97
The Dead One '07
Eye of the Devil '67
Her Jungle Love '38
Indiana Jones and the Temple of Doom '84 ▸
Joe Versus the Volcano '90
She '25
She '83
The Snake People '68
Spellbinder '88
Talisman '98
The 13th Warrior '99
The Wicker Man '75 ▸
The Wicker Tree '10

Hunted!
***See also** Survival*
Apocalypto '06 ▸
Arctic Blue '93
Awaken '15
The Belko Experiment '17
Beyond Fear '93
Beyond Rangoon '95
Bigfoot: The Unforgettable Encounter '94
Black Rock '12
Bloody Homecoming '12
Brimstone '17
Carnage Park '16
Creature of Darkness '09
Cyborg 2 '93
Damned River '89
Death Hunt '81
Deep Dark Canyon '12
Deliverance '72 ▸
Desierto '16
Diary of a Hitman '91
Fortress '85
Freejack '92
The Frozen '12
The Good Guys and the Bad Guys '69
Hard Target 2 '16
Hard Target '93
The Hunt '20
The Hunted '94
The Hunted '03
The Hunters '11
Hydra '09
Hyenas '10
Johnny Allegro '49
Jumper '08
Jungleground '95
Killing Season '13
The Last of the Dogmen '95
Little Bigfoot '96
Maximum Risk '96
The Most Dangerous Game '32 ▸
The Naked Prey '66 ▸
Nightmare at Bittercreek '91
No Way Back '90
Only '20
Open Season '06
Our Kind of Traitor '16
Overkill '96
The Pest '96
Predators '10
Preservation '14
Primeval '07
Project Shadowchaser 3000 '95
The Reeds '09
Run for the Sun '56
Seraphim Falls '06
Severance '06
Shadowhunter '93
Shoot to Kill '88 ▸
Skinwalkers '07
Solo '96
Southern Comfort '81 ▸
Stag Night '08
Star Hunter '95
Storage 24 '12
Survival Quest '89
Surviving the Game '94
Tracked '98
Tracker '10
Wild Grizzly '99
Without Warning '80
Wolf Creek 2 '13
Wrong Turn '03

Hunting
***See also** Go Fish*
The Amazing Panda Adventure '95
Appetites '15
The Bear '89 ▸
Caddyshack '80 ▸
Dan Candy's Law '73
The Doe Boy '01
The Eagle Huntress '16 ▸
Escanaba in da Moonlight '01
First Blood '82
First Kill '17
Frostbiter: Wrath of the Wendigo '94
The Ghost and the Darkness '96
Hold the Dark '18
The Hunt '65 ▸
The Hunter '12
Ice Men '04
Iceman '19
Junglee '19
Lake Placid 3 '10
Lake Placid: The Final Chapter '12
The Last Dinosaur '77
The Last Hunt '56
The Lion Hunters '51
Mogambo '53 ▸
Night of the Grizzly '66
No Country for Old Men '07 ▸
Prey '10
Primal '19
Primeval '07
Rampage '63
The Revenant '15 ▸
Savannah '14
Tarzan and the Huntress '47
Those Calloways '65
Track of the Cat '54
Walking Out '17
White Hunter, Black Heart '90 ▸
Wind River '17 ▸

Hurricanes
***See also** Disaster Flicks; Flood*
Adrift '18
The Alamo '60 ▸
Bang '95
Bedtime Stories '08
Bend of the River '52 ▸
Break-In '06
Category 7: The End of the World '05
Crawl '19
The Curious Case of Benjamin Button '08 ▸
Dead Bodies '03
Dolphin Tale '11
500 MPH Storm '13
Fled '96
Flipper '63 ▸
Forces of Nature '99
Godzilla vs. Mothra '64
Gone Fishin' '97
Heart of the Storm '04
Hours '13
The Hurricane '37 ▸
Hurricane '79
The Hurricane Heist '18
Key Largo '48 ▸
The Killer Shrews '59
Knight Without Armour '37 ▸
Lassie, Come Home '43
The Layover '17
Long Lost Son '06
Marooned '69
My Best Friend's Girl '08
Nights in Rodanthe '08
Nuclear Hurricane '07
The Rig '10
Saw 6 '09
Sharknado 2: The Second One '14
Shutter Island '09 ▸
Slattery's Hurricane '49
Sleepy Hollow '99 ▸
Steamboat Bill, Jr. '28 ▸
Storm Tracker '99
Thunder Bay '53 ▸
The Toy '82
The Vessel '16

I Was a Teenage Criminal
***See also** Teen Comedy; Teen Drama; Teen Horror; Teen Musicals; Teen Romance*
Accused at 17 '09
Attack the Block '11
Bad Boys '83 ▸
Bad Turn Worse '14
Badlands '74 ▸
The Basketball Diaries '95
The Bling Ring '11
The Bling Ring '13 ▸
Blood Father '16 ▸
Bond of Silence '10
Boys in Brown '49
Brick '06 ▸
Chatroom '10
A Clockwork Orange '71 ▸
Coldwater '14
Crime and Punishment in Suburbia '00
Crime in the Streets '56
Criminal Lovers '99
Dead End Kids: Little Tough Guy '38
Devil's Knot '14
Dirty Little Billy '72
Dreams and Shadows '10
Drive By '01
Dummy '79
Family Weekend '13
Farming '19
Freeway 2: Confessions of a Trickbaby '99
Fugitive at 17 '12
Girl Fight '11
A Girl Like Me: The Gwen Araujo Story '06
Girlhood '14 ▸
God Bless America '11
Graduation '07
Guncrazy '92
Hell's House '32
High Life '18
High School Big Shot '59
If I Want to Whistle, I Whistle '10
The Interrogation of Michael Crowe '02
Jack of the Red Hearts '15 ▸
Jamesy Boy '14
Juice '92
Kid Cannabis '14
A Killer Among Friends '92
L.I.E. '01
Murder by Numbers '02
Naked Youth '59
The Outsiders '83
Paradise Lost: The Child Murders at Robin Hood Hills '95 ▸
Perfect Sisters '14
The Perfect Teacher '10
Pressed '11
Punk Love '06
Racing for Time '08
Riot in Juvenile Prison '59
7 Boxes '14 ▸
Shadow on the Window '57
Shank '09
Son of a Gun '14
The Spikes Gang '74
Starred Up '13 ▸
Tell Me No Lies '07
Tenderness '08
Treed Murray '01
Twelve '10
The Unguarded Moment '56
United States of Leland '03
Violet & Daisy '11
We Need to Talk About Kevin '11 ▸
Where Are Your Children? '44
While She Was Out '08
White Irish Drinkers '10
Wild Things 3: Diamonds in the Rough '05

Identity
***See** Amnesia; Mistaken Identity; Not-So-True Identity; Role Reversal; Torn in Two (or More)*

Illegal Immigration
Alambrista! '77
Aleksandr's Price '13
Around June '08
A Beautiful Life '08
Beneath Us '20
Bisbee '17 '18
The Border '82 ▸
Border Incident '49
Border Run '12
Born in East L.A. '87
Bowfinger '99 ▸
Bread and Roses '00
The Breaking Point '50 ▸
Cellmates '12
Crossing Over '09
Desierto '16
Dirty Pretty Things '03 ▸
El Norte '83 ▸
Frozen River '08 ▸
High Strung '16
Home Again '13
Hostile Border '16
Illegal '10
Immigration Tango '11
In America '02 ▸
La Promesse '96
A Lady Without Passport '50
The Last Enemy '08
Most Beautiful Island '17
No Boundaries '09
No Turning Back '01
Our Life '10
Samba '14
Sin Nombre '09 ▸
Stand Clear of the Closing Doors '13 ▸
Sweet 15 '90
The Visitor '07 ▸
Where the Road Meets the Sun '11
Which Way Home '09

I'm Not Dead, Yet!
American Violence '17
The Autopsy of Jane Doe '16
The Belko Experiment '17
Blackout '50
The Cats '68
Dawn of the Dead '04 ▸
Elektra '05
Euphoria '19
Happy Death Day '17
Hello Again '87
The Hero '17
Identicals '16
Incubus '05
The Jacket '05
Jason Bourne '16
The Lazarus Effect '15
Life After Beth '14
A Little Bit of Heaven '11
Lost Lagoon '58
Lucky '17 ▸
The Morgue '07
The Mountain Between Us '17
Move Over, Darling '63
My Favorite Wife '40 ▸
Poms '19
The Purge: Election Year '16
The Return of Martin Guerre '83 ▸
Seed '08
The Six Wives of Henry Lefay '09
Sommersby '93
Standoff '16 ▸
Stuck '07
Tamara '05
Three for the Show '55
A Very Brady Sequel '96

Immigration
America America '63
America So Beautiful '01
An American Rhapsody '01 ▸
An American Tail '86
Amexico '16
Amira & Sam '15 ▸
Appropriate Behavior '14
Ask the Dust '06
Avalon '90 ▸
The Beautiful Country '04
Blood Red '88
Blue Eyes '09
Border Blues '03
Border Incident '49
Borderline '80
Bread and Chocolate '73 ▸
Bread and Roses '00
Break of Dawn '88
Breaking and Entering '06
Brooklyn '15 ▸
Buck Privates Come Home '47 ▸
Bye-Bye '96
Cesar Chavez '14
Chasing Freedom '04
Children of Men '06 ▸
City of Gold '16 ▸
Code 46 '03
Code Unknown '00
Combination Platter '93
Coming to America '88 ▸
The Cowboy Way '94
Crossing Over '09
Crystal Swan '20 ▸
Dancer in the Dark '99
Dirty Pretty Things '03 ▸
East Is East '99 ▸
The Edge of Heaven '07 ▸
Enemies, a Love Story '89 ▸
ESL: English as a Second Language '05
Far and Away '92
Farming '19
Fast Food Nation '06 ▸
Fire at Sea '16 ▸
Four Sons '28
Frozen River '08 ▸
Gangs of New York '02 ▸
Gateway '38
The Glass Wall '53
Gran Torino '08 ▸
The Great New Wonderful '06
Green Card '90
Growing Up Smith '17
Happy End '17
Harry and Snowman '16 ▸
Heaven Before I Die '96
Hello Goodbye '08
Hester Street '75 ▸
Hold Back the Dawn '41
House of Sand and Fog '03 ▸
The Hundred-Foot Journey '14
I Can't Sleep '93
I Cover the Waterfront '33
I Do '13 ▸
The Immigrant '13 ▸
In America '02 ▸
The Infiltrators '20
The Intouchables '12
Island of the Hungry Ghosts '18
The Italian '15
It's a Big Country '51
Journey of Hope '90 ▸
Kill the Poor '03
A King in New York '57
Kings in Grass Castles '97
La Promesse '96
Late Marriage '01
Liam '00
Living on Tokyo Time '87
Low Heights '02
The Maldonado Miracle '03
Manhattan Merenque! '95
The Manions of America '81
Maryam '00
Miami Rhapsody '95
The Mistress of Spices '05
Monkey Business '31 ▸
Monsieur Lazhar '11
Morris from America '16 ▸
Moscow on the Hudson '84 ▸
Mother of George '13 ▸
The Namesake '06 ▸
Nanny Insanity '06
The New Land '72 ▸
No Turning Back '01
Out of the Ashes '03
Outside the Law '10
Pelle the Conqueror '88 ▸
Petty Crimes '02
The Polka King '18
Pulling Strings '13
Saint Judy '19
Saving Face '04
Spanglish '04
Sueno '05
The Sun Is Also a Star '19
Tarantella '95
The Terminal '04
The Three Burials of Melquiades Estrada '05 ▸
The Tiger Hunter '17
Under the Same Moon '07
Untamed '55
The Visitor '07 ▸
West Is West '87
Wetbacks '56
Where the Road Meets the Sun '11

Immortality
The Age of Adaline '15
Blade of the Immortal '17
Bram Stoker's Way of the Vampire '05
Cross '11
Doctor Sleep '19 ▸
The Final Patient '05
He Never Died '15
Highlander 2: The Quickening '91
Highlander '86 ▸
Highlander: Endgame '00
Highlander: The Final Dimension '94
Highlander: The Source '07
The Holy Mountain '73

▸ = rated three bones or higher

The Imaginarium of Doctor Parnassus '09
Immortal '04
Jungle Moon Men '55
The Man from Earth '07
The Man Who Turned to Stone '57
The Medallion '03
The Mummy: Tomb of the Dragon Emperor '08
The Seeker: The Dark Is Rising '07
She '35
She '65
The Spring '00
The Tomb '09
Tomie '99
Tuck Everlasting '02
Youth Without Youth '07

Impending Retirement

***See also** Growing Older; One Last Job*

Assault on Precinct 13 '05
Beyond '11
Bombers B-52 '57
Bright Lights '30
Brooklyn's Finest '09
Carry On Sergeant '58
Cellular '04
Chasing Ghosts '05
Colewell '19
Crackerjack 3 '00
Diamond Men '01►
Dying of the Light '14
Fallen Angels '95
Falling Down '93
Firetrap '01
The First Deadly Sin '80
The Flock '07
Growing Pains: Return of the Seavers '04
Half Broken Things '07
Hitman's Journal '99
K-9 3: P.I. '01
K-911 '99
Killer Instinct: From the Files of Agent Candice DeLong '03
Law and Order '53
Lethal Weapon '87►
Love to Kill '97
Loving Annabelle '06
The Lunchbox '13
Major League 3: Back to the Minors '98
The Man Who Shook the Hand of Vicente Fernandez '12►
The Mask of Zorro '98►
Mission: Impossible 3 '06►
Night Across the Street '12
O'Horten '09►
The Pledge '00►
The Princess Diaries 2: Royal Engagement '04
The Quickie '01
Santa Baby 2: Santa Maybe '09
Schultze Gets the Blues '03
Seven '95►
Sharpshooter '07
She Wore a Yellow Ribbon '49►
Silent Venom '08
A Simple Life '11►
Solo '06
Sonatine '96►
Spring Forward '99
Spy Game '01
Stone '10
To Live & Die in L.A. '85
The Wrestler '08►

Incest

***See also** Family Ties*

Against the Wind '90
An American Haunting '05
Andy Warhol's Frankenstein '74
Angels and Insects '95►
The Ballad of Jack and Rose '05►
Black Christmas '06
Born Killers '05
Brotherhood of the Wolf '01
Byleth: The Demon of Incest '72
The Cement Garden '93
The Cider House Rules '99►
Close My Eyes '91
Daniel & Ana '09
Downloading Nancy '08
Flowers in the Attic '87
Flowers in the Attic '14
Forbidden Relations '83
From Beginning to End '09
The Grifters '90►
Harry and Max '04
Hellraiser: Revelations '11
The House of Yes '97
I Stand Alone '98
Innocent Lies '95
Jug Face '13
The King '05
Little Boy Blue '97
Mad Cowgirl '06
Moebius '13
My Sister, My Love '78
Natural Born Killers '94
Novocaine '01
Outlaws and Angels '16
Petals on the Wind '14
Pola X '99
Precious: Based on the Novel 'Push' by Sapphire '09►
Ringmaster '98
Savage Grace '07
Say It Isn't So '01
Seducing Maarya '99
Sitcom '97
Spanking the Monkey '94►
The Sweet Hereafter '96►
Tarnation '03
The Thompsons '12
A Thousand Acres '97
'Tis a Pity She's a Whore '73
U-Turn '97
The Unspeakable Act '13
Visitor Q '01
The War Zone '98
Waterland '92
The Weight of Water '00
Wicked '98
Woman, Thou Art Loosed '04

India

***See also** Calcutta*

After the Wedding '19
American Chai '01
Aparajito '58►
Badla '19
Bandit Queen '94
Before the Rains '07
The Bengali Night '88
The Best Exotic Marigold Hotel '12►
Bhowani Junction '56
The Black Devils of Kali '55
Black Narcissus '47►
Bollywood Hero '09
Bombay Mail '34
Born Into Brothels: Calcutta's Red Light Kids '04
The Bourne Supremacy '04►
Bride & Prejudice '04
Carry On Up the Khyber '68
Charulata '64
The Cheetah Girls: One World '08
City of Joy '92
Clive of India '35
Conduct Unbecoming '75
Cotton Mary '99
The Courtesans of Bombay '85►
The Darjeeling Limited '07►
The Dead 2 '13
The Deceivers '88
Delhi Safari '12
Drums '38
Earth '98
Eat, Pray, Love '10
Ele, My Friend '93
Extraction '20
The Far Pavilions '84
Fire '96
Flame Over India '59►
Gandhi '82►
Gandu '10
Gunga Din '39►
Heat and Dust '82►
Hotel Mumbai '18
Hullabaloo over Georgie & Bonnie's Pictures '78
In Custody '94
In the Spider's Web '07
The Indian Tomb '21
Jalsaghar '58
The Jewel in the Crown '84►
Journey to the Lost City '58
Judgementall Hai Kya '19
Jungle Boy '96
Jungle Hell '55
Junglee '19
Kama Sutra: A Tale of Love '96
Kenner '73
Kesari '19
Kim '50►
Kim '84
King of the Khyber Rifles '53
Lagaan: Once upon a Time in India '01
The Letters '15
Lion '16►
The Lives of a Bengal Lancer '35►
Looking for Comedy in the Muslim World '06
Luka Chuppi '19
The Lunchbox '13
The Man Who Knew Infinity '16
The Man Who Would Be King '75►
Marigold '07
Masala '91
Million Dollar Arm '14
Mission Mangal '19
The Mistress of Spices '05
Monsoon '97
Monsoon Wedding '01►
Mother Teresa: In the Name of God's Poor '97
Mountbatten: The Last Viceroy '86
Mowgli: Legend of the Jungle '18
My Faraway Bride '06
The Namesake '06►
North West Frontier '59
Notebook '19
Octopussy '83
1000 Rupee Note '16►
The Other Side of the Door '16
Outsourced '06
Padmaavat '18►
A Passage to India '84►
Pather Panchali '54►
Photograph '19
The Rains Came '39
The Rains of Ranchipur '55
The Razor's Edge '46►
The River '51►
Rudyard Kipling's The Jungle Book '94
Sabaka '55
The Second Best Exotic Marigold Hotel '15
Shakespeare Wallah '65►
Sharpe's Challenge '06
Sharpe's Peril '08
Siddhartha '72
Slumdog Millionaire '08►
Staying On '80
Stiff Upper Lips '96
The Stranglers of Bombay '60
Such a Long Journey '98►
Tales of the Kama Sutra: The Perfumed Garden '98
Tarzan Goes to India '62
The Tiger Hunter '17
Tomorrow We Disappear '14
Total Dhamaal '19
Trishna '11
Uri: The Surgical Strike '19
Valley of Saints '12
Viceroy's House '17
War '19
The Warrior '01
Water '05
The Way Back '10
Wee Willie Winkie '37►
The World of Apu '59►
The Zoya Factor '19

Inheritance

All in a Night's Work '61
Almayer's Folly '12
Are You Here '13
The Aristocats '70►
Awful Nice '14
The Bachelor '99
The Back Trail '24
Bailey's Billion$ '05
Bed & Breakfast '10
Belle '13
The Best of Me '14
Beverly Lewis' The Confession '13
Billy Madison '94
Black Widow '87►
The Black Widow '05
Bleak House '05
A Blueprint for Murder '53
The Boy Who Cried Werewolf '10
Brewster's Millions '45
Brewster's Millions '85
Campbell's Kingdom '57
The Case of the Stuttering Bishop '37
Casper '95►
Cast a Long Shadow '59
The Cat and the Canary '39
Catherine Cookson's The Black Candle '92
The Chateau '01
The Chateau Meroux '11
The Cheyenne Social Club '70
Chilly Dogs '01
Chronicle of the Raven '04
Come Dance at My Wedding '09
Crimes of Fashion '04
Cutthroat Island '95
Daddy Issues '20
Daddy's Dyin'. . . Who's Got the Will? '90
Dark and Stormy Night '09
Dawg '02
Dear Mr. Prohack '49
Die Mommie Die! '03
Double or Nothing '37
Easy Money '83
Elena '11
Elvira, Mistress of the Dark '88
Emma '32
The Fighting Temptations '03
Finding Home '03
Fletch Lives '89
Flight of the Doves '71
Freaks '32►
Gaslight '44►
Ghost Cat '03
Ghost in the Invisible Bikini '66
The Glass House '01
Go for Zucker '05
Gold Diggers: The Secret of Bear Mountain '95
A Good Year '06
The Grand Budapest Hotel '14►
Great Expectations '11
Greedy '94
The Green Years '46
Growing the Big One '09
The Hardys Ride High '39
Has Anybody Seen My Gal? '52
The Hearse '80
The Hidden Hand '42
Hot to Trot! '88
I Capture the Castle '02
If I Had a Million '32
In Her Mother's Footsteps '06
The Inheritance '76
The Inheritance '97
Invisible Mom 2 '99
The Invoking '13
It's in the Bag! '45
It's Only Money '62
Jimmy the Gent '34
Johnny Yuma '66
Just Buried '07
Kidnapped '38
Kidnapped '48
Kidnapped '05►
King of Texas '02►
Knives Out '19►
La Cage aux Folles 3: The Wedding '86
Lake Dead '07
Larger Than Life '96
Las Vegas Nights '41
The Last of the Mobile Hot-shots '69
The Last Station '09
The Last Will and Testament of Rosalind Leigh '12
Lemony Snicket's A Series of Unfortunate Events '04
The List '07
Little Big League '94
Little Old New York '23
Loose Ankles '30
Lord of the Rings: The Fellowship of the Ring '01►
The Lost & Found Family '09
Love Kills '98
Love's Unfolding Dream '07
Mail Order Bride '63
The Making of a Lady '12
The Man From Toronto '32
The Man With a Cloak '51
Maya Dardel '17
Meet Mr. Callaghan '54
The Merry Frinks '34
The Merry Widow '25►
Milwaukee, Minnesota '03
Miss Pinkerton '32
Miss Tatlock's Millions '48
Mr. Deeds '02
Mr. Deeds Goes to Town '36►
Mr. Popper's Penguins '11
Modern Love '07
Montana Sky '07
Moon over Miami '41►
Mouse Hunt '97►
Murder by Invitation '41
My Cousin Rachel '52
My Old Lady '14
On Guard! '03►
Oriana '85
Outside of Paradise '38
Penny Princess '52
Phoenix '14►
Purlie Victorious '63
Rain or Shine '30
The Reception '05
Redemption Road '10
The Reunion '11
Rhubarb '51
Rushlights '13
The Saint in Palm Springs '41
The Sea '02
The Secrets of the Summer House '08
Seven Days' Leave '42
Shanghai Kiss '07
She Fell Among Thieves '78
She Played With Fire '57
She's Not Our Sister '11
Siblings '04
The Skeptic '09
Snow Dogs '02
Splitting Heirs '93
Summer Hours '08
Sundance and the Kid '69
Sword of Trust '19
Tartuffe '25
Texas Chainsaw 3D '13
13 Ghosts '01
Three Bad Sisters '56
Three Blind Mice '38
Three Little Girls In Blue '46
Time and Again '07
To Beat the Band '35
A Trick of the Mind '06
Trophy Wife '06
Two On a Guillotine '65
UHF '89
The Ultimate Gift '07
The Ultimate Life '13
The Unsuspected '47
Untamed '29
Value for Money '55
Violette '78►
Where There's a Will '55
The White Cockatoo '35
White Fang '36
Widow on the Hill '05
Wild Things 2 '04
A Woman's a Helluva Thing '01
The Working Man '33
You Never Can Tell '51
Zus & Zo '01

In-Laws

Affair in Trinidad '52
Ash Wednesday '02
August '95
Bag of Bones '11
Blood Relations '87
Brothers '09
Captain Fantastic '16
Commandments '96
Confessions of a Driving Instructor '76
Confessions of a Window Cleaner '74
Contraband '12
Cries in the Dark '06
Deadly Blessing '81
Death Comes to Pemberley '13
Deliver Us from Eva '03
Die! Die! My Darling! '65
Easy Virtue '08
The Eclipse '09
Every Day '10
The Ex '07
Five Nights in Maine '16
For Better or Worse '95
Four Mothers '41
Free Money '99
Girl with a Pearl Earring '03►
Grace '09
The Grandfather '98
Hateship Loveship '13
The Housemaid '10
Hurt '09
Hush '98
The In-Laws '79►
The In-Laws '03
In Secret '13
The Inheritance '76
The Inveterate Bachelor '58
Japanese War Bride '52
Junebug '05►
Keyhole '11
Kill the Umpire '50
Killers '10
Kiss the Bride '10
La Rupture '70
Land Ho! '14
The Last Letter '13
Lawless Heart '01
Le Divorce '03
Leila '97
A Little Help '11
Love '71►
Love Crazy '41►
Love Finds a Home '09
Love Liza '02
Love Songs '99
Madame X '37
The Man I Married '40
The Man with Two Faces '34
Meet the Fockers '04
Meet the Parents '00►
Melancholia '11►
Merry In-Laws '12
Monster-in-Law '05
Mother Didn't Tell Me '50
Mother of George '13►
Move Over, Darling '63
The Mugger '58
Mussolini & I '85
My Brother's Wife '89
Nearlyweds '13
A Night for Dying Tigers '10
Not Easily Broken '09
Onibaba '64►
The Over-the-Hill Gang '69
Petunia '13
Possession '08
Pride and Glory '08
Reign Over Me '07
Reykjavik-Rotterdam '08
Rio 2 '14
Rocky Balboa '06
The Santa Clause 3: The Escape Clause '06
Saving Christmas '14
Secrets of Women '52►
Shrek the Third '07
Silent Witness '85
So This Is New York '48
Son-in-Law '93
Steve Martini's Undue Influence '96
Stir of Echoes '99
Storm Warning '51
Together Again '43
The War Bride '01
The Weight of Water '00
You, Me and Dupree '06

► = rated three bones or higher

The Inquisition, What a Show!

See also *Period Piece: 15th Century*

Assassin's Creed '16
Captain from Castile '47 ▶
Fire Over England '37 ▶
Goya's Ghosts '06
History of the World: Part 1 '81
Man of La Mancha '72
The Mill and the Cross '11
The Pit and the Pendulum '61 ▶

Insects

See *Killer Bugs and Slugs*

Insomnia

See also *Up All Night*

Bringing Out the Dead '99
Dead Awake '01
Dream for an Insomniac '96
Fight Club '99 ▶
The Haunting '99
I Can't Sleep '93
Insomnia '97 ▶
Insomnia '02 ▶
The Machinist '04
Taxi Driver '76 ▶

Insurance

About Schmidt '02 ▶
The Adjuster '91
Alias Jesse James '59
Along Came Polly '04
Amnesia '96
The Apartment '60 ▶
Assignment to Kill '69
Beyond Suspicion '00
The Big Squeeze '96
Big Trouble '86
The Big White '05
The Black House '00
Black House '07
Burning Down the House '01
Carancho '10
The Case of the Scorpion's Tail '71
Cause of Death '00
Cedar Rapids '11 ▶
Changing Lanes '02 ▶
City of Ghosts '03
Coast of Skeletons '63
Code 46 '03
Counter Attack '84
Cover Up '49
Critical Care '97
The Crocodile Hunter: Collision Course '02
The Curse of the Jade Scorpion '01
Dangerous Summer '82
The Darwin Awards '06
Dead by Dawn '98
Dead Eyes of London '61
Deadlier Than the Male '67
Death Collector '89
Dillinger and Capone '95
Double Indemnity '44 ▶
Dying to Get Rich '98
The Electronic Monster '57
Enchanted Island '58
Entrapment '99
Escape Clause '96
Exit Plan '20
Firestarter 2: Rekindled '02
First Do No Harm '97
Flawless '07
Folks! '92
Four Dogs Playing Poker '00
Frank McKlusky, C.I. '02
Gambling Daughters '41
The Gay Falcon '41
Gold Diggers of 1937 '36
Gone in 60 Seconds '74
Goodbye, Lover '99
Hook, Line and Sinker '30
I Now Pronounce You Chuck and Larry '07
I Wonder Who's Killing Her Now? '76
If Tomorrow Comes '86
In the Mouth of Madness '95
The Insurance Man '86
John Grisham's The Rainmaker '97
The Killers '46 ▶
Lady Ice '73
The Last Adventure '67
The Laundromat '19
A Little Trip to Heaven '05
Lloyds of London '36 ▶
Lost Lagoon '58
Lush '01
Master Touch '74
A Monster with a Thousand Heads '15 ▶
Murder, He Says '45
National Lampoon's Gold Diggers '04
One Body Too Many '44
One Night in the Tropics '40
Paid to Kill '54
Prince of Poisoners: The Life and Crimes of William Palmer '98
Quick '93
Risk '00
Saint John of Las Vegas '09
Save the Tiger '73 ▶
Schemes '95
The Secret of the Purple Reef '60
The Settlement '99
She Played With Fire '57
Shed No Tears '48
Sicko '07
Sleep Easy, Hutch Rimes '00
Sleuth '72 ▶
The Suspect '05
Sweet Lies '88
Term Life '16
They Call It Murder '71
Thin Ice '12
Things Happen at Night '48
The Thomas Crown Affair '68 ▶
The Thomas Crown Affair '99 ▶
Three Blondes in His Life '61
A Touch of Class '73 ▶
Towards Darkness '07
Tropical Heat '93
The Truman Show '98 ▶
The Whole Nine Yards '00
Wild Oats '16
Wild Things 2 '04
Wish You Were Dead '00
A Woman of Independent Means '94 ▶

Internet Borne

See also *Computers; Hackers*

The Blair Witch Project '99
Catfish '10
Chatroom '10
Confess '05
Cyberbully '11
Dark House '09
Dee Snider's Strangeland '98
Defending Our Kids: The Julie Posey Story '03
Devour '05
Don't Hang Up '17
Dot.Kill '05
Family Weekend '13
Fatal Desire '05
Feardotcom '02
Feed '05
Friend Request '16
GhostWatcher '02
Girl Fight '11
Halloween: Resurrection '02
Hard Candy '06
Hellraiser: Hellworld '05
The Hunt '20
I Downloaded a Ghost '04
iCrime '11
Infamous '20
Jay and Silent Bob Strike Back '01
Killers '14
Lion '16 ▶
Lo and Behold: Reveries of the Connected World '16 ▶
Mail to the Chief '00
Murder.com '08
Must Love Dogs '05
Nancy '18
Nerve '16
The Net '95
Open Cam '05
Pulse '01
Pulse '06
Sexting '11
Sexting in Suburbia '12
Smiley '12
Snowden '16
Southland Tales '06
Suspicion '03
Talhotblond '12
3, 2, 1...Frankie Go Boom '12
To Be Takei '14
Tom Clancy's Netforce '98
Tragedy Girls '17 ▶
Turbulence 3: Heavy Metal '00
Unfriended: Dark Web '18
Untraceable '08
V/H/S '12
You've Got Mail '98
Zero Days '16

Interpol

The Art of the Steal '13
Assassins '95
Black Cobra 2 '89
Born to Raise Hell '10
The Case of the Scorpion's Tail '71
The Castle of Fu Manchu '68
Feed '05
Framed '90
Hitman '07
The International '09
Lord of War '05 ▶
The Medallion '03
Muppets Most Wanted '14
Nighthawks '81
Ninja Assassin '09
One More Time '70
Pickup Alley '57
Reflections '08
The Return of Dr. Mabuse '61
Soul Assassin '01
Street Fighter: The Legend of Chun-Li '09
Terror of Mechagodzilla '78
Tip On a Dead Jockey '57
The Tourist '10

Interracial Affairs

According to Greta '08
After the Rain '99
Ali: Fear Eats the Soul '74 ▶
All Night Long '62
Apache Rifles '64
The Banker '20
Barbershop 2: Back in Business '04 ▶
Beauty Shop '05 ▶
The Big Sick '17 ▶
Bird of Paradise '51
The Birth of a Nation '16
Bleeding Hearts '94
Bodied '17 ▶
The Bodyguard '92
Bridge to the Sun '61
Broken Blossoms '19 ▶
Bulworth '98 ▶
Cafe au Lait '94 ▶
Cake '05
Cape of Good Hope '04
Chaos '05
Chinese Box '97
Colorz of Rage '97
Come See the Paradise '90 ▶
Compulsion '08
Corrina, Corrina '94
Crash '05 ▶
The Crimson Kimono '59
Crown Heights '17
Dark Blue '03 ▶
Dear Wendy '05
The Delta '97
Detroit '17 ▶
Driving Miss Daisy '89 ▶
The Family Stone '05
The Family That Preys '08
Five Nights in Maine '16
Flame in the Streets '61
A Fond Kiss '04
The Forgiven '18
Freedomland '06
Get Out '17 ▶
Glory Road '06
The Grasshopper '69
Green Book '18 ▶
Guess Who '05
Guess Who's Coming to Dinner '67 ▶
Hairspray '07 ▶
The Hate U Give '18 ▶
Heaven and Earth '93
Hidden Figures '17 ▶
The Human Stain '03
Hustle & Flow '05 ▶
I Am Not Your Negro '17 ▶
In My Country '04
In the Mix '05
Iron Road '08
Japanese Story '03 ▶
Japanese War Bride '52
Jungle Fever '91 ▶
Kings '17
Lakeview Terrace '08 ▶
The Landlord '70
The Liberation of L.B. Jones '70
Love Field '91
Love Is a Many-Splendored Thing '55
Loving '16 ▶
Made in America '93
Make Your Move '13
Manderlay '05
Marci X '03
Melinda and Melinda '05
Miami Rhapsody '95
Misconceptions '08
Mississippi Masala '92 ▶
Mr. & Mrs. Loving '96 ▶
Monster's Ball '01 ▶
Morris from America '16 ▶
My Baby's Daddy '04
My Beautiful Laundrette '85 ▶
The Nephew '97
Never Die Alone '04
The New World '05 ▶
Norman, Is That You? '76
Not Easily Broken '09
November '05 ▶
Now & Forever '02
One Night Stand '97 ▶
Othello '22
Othello '52 ▶
Othello '65 ▶
Othello '95 ▶
Parallel Sons '95
Pariah '98
A Patch of Blue '65
The Pianist '91
Pieces of April '03
Pinky '49 ▶
The Pleasure Garden '25
Pocahontas '95 ▶
Rachel Getting Married '08 ▶
Relax. . . It's Just Sex! '98
A Respectable Trade '98
Restaurant '98
Romeo Must Die '00
The Royal Tenenbaums '01 ▶
Ruby's Bucket of Blood '01
Running for Grace '18
Save the Last Dance '01
The Second Chance '06
Shadowboxer '06
Shadows '60 ▶
Small Island '09
Snow Falling on Cedars '99
Soldiers of Change '06
Something New '06
The Story of a Three Day Pass '68
Storytelling '01 ▶
Taxi Blues '90 ▶
The Tenants '06
Three Stripes in the Sun '55
The Tic Code '99
A United Kingdom '17
Walking Tall '04
Wassup Rockers '06
The Watermelon Woman '97
The Wedding Banquet '93 ▶
Welcome II the Terrordome '95
The Wind Cannot Read '58
The Wrath of the Gods '14
Yes '04
Zebrahead '92 ▶

Interviews

See *This Is Your Life*

Inventors & Inventions

See also *Mad Scientists; Science & Scientists*

The Absent-Minded Professor '61 ▶
The American Side '16
Atlas Shrugged: Part 1 '11
Atlas Shrugged 3: Who Is John Galt? '14
Back to the Future '85 ▶
Blonde Comet '41
Breathe '17
A Bug's Life '98 ▶
Carbine Williams '52
Chairman of the Board '97
Chitty Chitty Bang Bang '68
C.H.O.M.P.S. '79
Cloudy with a Chance of Meatballs '09
The Current War: Director's Cut '19
Edison the Man '40
Envy '04
Excuse My Dust '51
Fast Life '32
Flash of Genius '08
Flubber '97
Flying High '31
The Great Moment '44
Gremlins '84 ▶
The Guilt Trip '12
Hello Down There '69
Honey, I Blew Up the Kid '92
Honey, I Shrunk the Kids '89
Honey, We Shrunk Ourselves '97
Horrible Bosses 2 '14
Invisible Mom '96
Iron Man '08 ▶
Iron Man 2 '10 ▶
Iron Man 3 '13 ▶
Jack Brown, Genius '94
The Jerk '79
Joy '15
Just My Luck '35
Lady of the Night '25 ▶
Like a Boss '20
Longitude '00 ▶
Looking for Love '64
The Man in the White Suit '51 ▶
The Man Who Fell to Earth '76 ▶
Mile a Minute Love '37
Mom's Outta Sight '01
The Mosquito Coast '86
Orgazmo '98
Pretty Bird '08
Primer '04 ▶
P.U.N.K.S. '98
Rememory '17
Robo-Dog '15
So Goes My Love '46
So This Is Washington '43
Son of Flubber '63
The Spanish Prisoner '97 ▶
Speed '36
Spitfire '42 ▶
Steamboy '05
The Story of Alexander Graham Bell '39 ▶
Strange Impersonation '46
Theremin: An Electronic Odyssey '95 ▶
Time After Time '79 ▶
Time Chasers '95
Tim's Vermeer '13 ▶
Tomorrowland '15
Uncanny '15
Up Goes Maisie '46
Up the Ladder '25
Village of the Giants '65
Where's Willie? '77
Witness for the Prosecution '57 ▶
The Young and Prodigious T.S. Spivet '15
Young Tom Edison '40

Invisibility

Abbott and Costello Meet the Invisible Man '51 ▶
Clash of the Titans '81
Dick Tracy vs. Crime Inc. '41
Doctor Faustus '68
Dr. Orloff and the Invisible Man '72
Forbidden Planet '56 ▶
Golden Voyage of Sinbad '73
Hollow Man 2 '06
Hollow Man '00
Invisible Agent '42
Invisible Dad '97
The Invisible Dr. Mabuse '62 ▶
Invisible Invaders '59
The Invisible Man '33 ▶
The Invisible Man '20 ▶
The Invisible Man Returns '40 ▶
The Invisible Man's Revenge '44
Invisible Mom 2 '99
Invisible Mom '96
The Invisible Monster '50
The Invisible Strangler '76
Invisible: The Chronicles of Benjamin Knight '93
The Invisible Woman '40 ▶
The League of Extraordinary Gentlemen '03
Mad Monster Party '68
The Man Who Wasn't There '83
Memoirs of an Invisible Man '92
Mr. Superinvisible '73
Mom's Outta Sight '01
My Magic Dog '97
Mystery Men '99
Now You See Him, Now You Don't '72
Orloff and the Invisible Man '70
The Phantom Creeps '39
Phantom from Space '53
Phantom 2040 Movie: The Ghost Who Walks '95
Predator '87
Return of Chandu '34
Sound of Horror '64
Time Warp '81

Iraq

See also *Civil War (non U.S.); Genocide/Ethnic Cleansing; Middle East; Persian Gulf/Iraq War*

The A-Team '10 ▶
American Sniper '14
Amira & Sam '15 ▶
Billy Lynn's Long Halftime Walk '16
Boys of Abu Ghraib '14
Buried '10
The Devil's Double '11
Generation Kill '08 ▶
Green Zone '10 ▶
The Ground Truth '06
House of Saddam '08
The Hurt Locker '08 ▶
Manticore '05
The Men Who Stare at Goats '09
No End in Sight '07 ▶
Official Secrets '19 ▶
Redacted '07
Seal Team '08
Semper Fi '19
Shock and Awe '18
Stop-Loss '08 ▶
Universal Squadrons '11
The Unknown Known '14 ▶
The Wall '17
War Dogs '16
War Tapes '06 ▶
The Yellow Birds '17

Ireland

See also *Belfast; Dublin*

American Women '00
Amongst Women '98
Angela's Ashes '99
The Bachelor Weekend '13
Bad Day for the Cut '17
Black '47 '18
Bloody Sunday '01 ▶
Blown Away '94
Bobbie's Girl '02
The Boxer '97
The Boys and Girl From County Clare '03
Breakfast on Pluto '05
Broken Harvest '94
Brooklyn '15 ▶
The Brylcreem Boys '96

▶ = rated three bones or higher

- The Butcher Boy '97 ▶
- Calvary '14 ▶
- Captain Boycott '47
- Captain Lightfoot '55
- Children in the Crossfire '84
- Conspiracy of Silence '03
- Cowboys & Angels '04 ▶
- The Crying Game '92 ▶
- Dancing at Lughnasa '98
- Danny Boy '82 ▶
- Darby O'Gill & the Little People '59 ▶
- Dark River '18
- The Dawning '88
- December Bride '91
- Don't Leave Home '18
- Driftwood '97
- Echoes '88
- The Eclipse '09
- The Eternal '99
- The External '99
- Extra Ordinary '20
- Falling for a Dancer '98
- Far and Away '92
- The Field '90 ▶
- The Fighting Prince of Donegal '66
- Five Minutes of Heaven '09
- Flight of the Doves '71
- 48 Angels '06
- The Guard '11 ▶
- Hangman's House '28
- Hard Times '09
- Hellboy II: The Golden Army '08 ▶
- The Hole in the Ground '19
- The Honeymooners '03
- How About You '07
- How Harry Became a Tree '01
- I See a Dark Stranger '46 ▶
- I Was Happy Here '66
- Images '72
- In Fear '13
- The Informer '29
- Intermission '03 ▶
- Irish Jam '05
- James Joyce: A Portrait of the Artist as a Young Man '77 ▶
- Lamb '85
- The Last of the High Kings '96
- The Last September '99
- Laws of Attraction '04
- Leap Year '10
- Legend of the Bog '08
- Leprechaun '93
- Life's a Breeze '14
- The Lodgers '17
- Love and Rage '99
- A Love Divided '01
- The Luck of the Irish '48
- The Magdalene Sisters '02 ▶
- The Magical Legend of the Leprechauns '99
- Man of Aran '34 ▶
- The Manions of America '81
- The Mapmaker '01
- The Matchmaker '97
- Middletown '06
- Miss Julie '14
- Moondance '95
- My Brother's War '97
- The Nephew '97
- Never Grow Old '19
- No Stone Unturned '17
- Nothing Personal '09
- Odd Man Out '47 ▶
- Ondine '09
- Ordinary Decent Criminal '99
- Outside of Paradise '38
- Parked '10
- Parnell '37
- The Playboys '92 ▶
- Poltergeist: The Legacy '96
- Prayer for the Dying '87
- P.S. I Love You '07
- The Quiet Man '52 ▶
- The Race '09
- Rawhead Rex '87
- The Real Charlotte '91
- The Rising of the Moon '57
- Roadkill '11
- Rory O'Shea Was Here '04
- Run & Jump '13
- The Run of the Country '95 ▶
- Ryan's Daughter '70
- St. Patrick: The Irish Legend '00
- Scarlett '94
- The Secret of Kells '09
- The Secret of Roan Inish '94 ▶
- Secret of the Cave '06
- The Seventh Stream '01
- She Creature '01
- A Shine of Rainbows '09
- Shrooms '07
- Sing Street '16 ▶
- Snatch '00 ▶
- Some Mother's Son '96 ▶
- Song o' My Heart '30
- Spectre '96
- Stay '13
- Stella Days '12
- Taffin '88
- This Is My Father '99
- Trojan Eddie '96 ▶
- Troubles '88
- Waiting for Dublin '07
- Waking Ned Devine '98 ▶
- War of the Buttons '95
- Widow's Peak '94
- The Wind That Shakes the Barley '06 ▶
- Wings of the Morning '37

Islam

***See also** Middle East*

- Among the Believers '15 ▶
- Beyond Honor '05
- The Big Sick '17 ▶
- Circumstance '11
- David & Layla '07
- Four Lions '10
- Hala '19
- He Named Me Malala '15
- In the Land of Blood and Honey '11
- The Infidel '10
- Jafar Panahi's Taxi '15 ▶
- Jinn '18
- The Keeper: The Legend of Omar Khayyam '05
- Leila '97
- Looking for Comedy in the Muslim World '06
- The Message '77
- Monsieur Ibrahim '03 ▶
- Mooz-Lum '10
- My Son the Fanatic '97 ▶
- The Oath '10 ▶
- Of Fathers and Sons '18 ▶
- Of Gods and Men '10 ▶
- Osama '03 ▶
- Paradise Now '05 ▶
- Persepolis '07 ▶
- Red Mercury '05
- Religulous '08 ▶
- The Road to Guantanamo '06
- Silent Waters '03
- Sorry, Haters '05
- The Space Between '10
- The Stoning of Soraya M. '08
- The Suitors '88
- Timbuktu '15 ▶
- Traitor '08
- The Trials of Muhammad Ali '13 ▶
- Wadjda '13 ▶
- The Wedding Guest '18
- The Wedding Song '09

Island Fare

***See also** Pacific Islands; Sex on the Beach*

- The Admirable Crichton '57
- The Adventures of Sadie '55
- Affair in Trinidad '52
- All the Brothers Were Valiant '53
- Alvin and the Chipmunks: Chipwrecked '11
- American Guerrilla in the Philippines '50
- Anthropophagus: The Grim Reaper '80
- Apostle '18
- Appointment With Venus '51
- Arachnid '01
- Atlantis, the Lost Continent '61
- Attack of the Sabretooth '05
- Au Pair 3: Adventure in Paradise '09
- The Ballad of Jack and Rose '05 ▶
- The Beach '00
- Beast of Blood '71
- Bees in Paradise '44
- Beneath the Blue '10
- The Bermuda Depths '78
- Bicycling With Moliere '13
- Bird of Paradise '32
- Bird of Paradise '51
- Black Rock '12
- The Black Waters of Echo's Pond '10
- Bleeders '97
- The Blue Lagoon '80
- Blue Lagoon: The Awakening '12
- Body Trouble '92
- Boot Camp '07
- The Bounty '84
- Brand Upon the Brain! '06 ▶
- The Breed '06
- The Bribe '48
- Cabin Boy '94
- Captain Corelli's Mandolin '01
- Captain Ron '92
- Cast Away '00 ▶
- The Castaway Cowboy '74
- Chandu on the Magic Island '34
- Cloudy with a Chance of Meatballs '09
- Club Dread '04
- Club Paradise '86
- Colossus and the Amazon Queen '60
- The Condemned '07
- Couples Retreat '09
- Crest of the Wave '54
- Crusoe '89
- Cthulhu '08
- Cutthroat Island '95
- Cyber Bandits '94
- Dark Harbor '98
- Dead of Night '99
- Dead Waters '94
- The Decoy Bride '11
- Deeply '99
- Dinotopia '02
- DOA: Dead or Alive '06
- Doomsdayer '00
- Dungeon of Harrow '64
- The Ebb-Tide '97
- Emmanuelle on Taboo Island '76
- Evolution '16
- Exit to Eden '94
- Eye of the Dolphin '06
- Far Cry '08
- The Fat Spy '66
- Father Goose '64
- Finding Home '03
- Fire at Sea '16 ▶
- Five Dolls for an August Moon '70
- Flipper '96 ▶
- Four Frightened People '34
- Four Last Songs '06
- F.P. 1 '33
- From Hell It Came '57
- Gale Force '01
- Ginger and Cinnamon '03
- Girl in Black '56
- The Girl With the Dragon Tattoo '09 ▶
- Growth '10
- The Guernsey Literary & Potato Peel Pie Society '18
- Gulliver's Travels '10
- Hack! '07
- Haven '04
- Head Above Water '96
- Heading South '05 ▶
- Heaven Knows, Mr. Allison '57 ▶
- Her Jungle Love '38
- Hero's Island '62
- House of the Dead '03
- How I Ended This Summer '10
- How to Train Your Dragon 2 '14
- How to Train Your Dragon '10
- Hurricane '79
- Hydra '09
- The Idol Dancer '20
- Impasse '69
- In Her Line of Fire '06
- In the Blood '13
- The Invitation '03
- The Island '80
- Island in the Sun '57
- The Island of Dr. Moreau '96
- Island of Lost Souls '32 ▶
- Island of the Dead '00
- Island of the Lost '68
- Islander '06
- Isle of Dogs '18 ▶
- Jack Frost 2: Revenge of the Mutant Killer Snowman '00
- Jacob Two Two Meets the Hooded Fang '99
- Joe Versus the Volcano '90
- Johnny Allegro '49
- Join the Marines '37
- Journey 2: The Mysterious Island '12
- Jules Verne's Mysterious Island '10
- Jurassic Park 3 '01
- Jurassic Park '93 ▶
- Kill a Dragon '67
- Kilma, Queen of the Amazons '75
- King Kong '05 ▶
- King of Devil's Island '10
- Kiss the Sky '98
- Kong: Skull Island '17
- The Kovak Box '06
- The Land That Time Forgot '09
- The Last Templar '09
- The Lighthouse '19 ▶
- A Little Piece of Sunshine '90
- Long Lost Son '06
- Lost Lagoon '58
- The Lost Medallion: The Adventures of Billy Stone '13
- The Lost World: Jurassic Park 2 '97
- The Lunatic '92
- Ma and Pa Kettle at Waikiki '55
- Madagascar '05
- Magic Magic '13
- Mamma Mia! '08
- A Man of Passion '88
- Mararia '98
- Matango '63
- McHale's Navy '97
- Men of War '94
- Mindhunters '05
- Mr. Art Critic '07
- Mr. Moto in Danger Island '39
- Moana '16 ▶
- Molokai: The Story of Father Damien '99
- Moonrise Kingdom '12 ▶
- Murder On a Honeymoon '35
- Mutiny on the Bounty '35 ▶
- Mutiny on the Bounty '62
- My Father the Hero '93
- My Little Assassin '99
- Mysterious Island '61 ▶
- Mysterious Island of Beautiful Women '79
- The Mystic Masseur '01
- The Natalee Holloway Story '09
- National Lampoon's Last Resort '94
- Nim's Island '08
- No Escape '94
- No Man Is an Island '62
- The Noah '75
- The Non-Stop Flight '26
- Northern Extremes '93
- Nuclear Hurricane '07
- Old Mother Riley's Jungle Treasure '51
- On an Island with You '48
- Once Upon a Wedding '05
- One Night in the Tropics '40
- Opa! '05
- The Other Side of Heaven '02
- The Others '01 ▶
- Owd Bob '97
- The Pagan '29
- Pagan Island '60
- Paradise '82
- The Passion of Anna '70 ▶
- Pearl of the South Pacific '55
- People '04
- Perfect Strangers '03
- Pippi in the South Seas '70
- Pirates of Blood River '62
- Pirates of the Caribbean: Dead Man's Chest '06
- The Postman '94 ▶
- The Prisoner of Shark Island '36
- PT 109 '63
- Pufnstuf '70
- The Quest '96
- Rapa Nui '93
- The Ravagers '65
- The Red Turtle '17 ▶
- Reel Paradise '05 ▶
- Rescue from Gilligan's Island '78
- Respiro '02
- Retreat '11
- Return to Nim's Island '13
- Return to Paradise '53
- Return to the Blue Lagoon '91
- Return to Treasure Island '54
- Rise of the Zombies '12
- Robinson Crusoe '54
- Robinson Crusoe '96
- The Rookie '59
- Rugrats Go Wild! '03
- Safe in Hell '31
- Savage Is Loose '74
- Savage Sisters '74
- The Secret of Monte Cristo '61
- The Secret of the Purple Reef '60
- The 7 Adventures of Sinbad '10
- The Seventh Dawn '64
- Sex and Lucia '01
- Shadow Warriors '97
- Shark Island '12
- Shelter Island '03
- A Shine of Rainbows '09
- Shockwave '06
- Signs of Life '68
- Sinbad and the Minotaur '11
- Six Days, Seven Nights '98
- The Sleeping Dictionary '02
- The Snake People '68
- Somewhere in Time '80
- Son of Fury '42 ▶
- Speed 2: Cruise Control '97
- Spy Kids 2: The Island of Lost Dreams '02 ▶
- Stephen King's The Storm of the Century '99
- Stranded '06
- The Stranger Within '13
- Submarine Base '43
- Summer Lover '08
- Surf's Up '07
- Survival Island '02
- Survival of the Dead '09
- Swept Away... '75 ▶
- Swept Away '02
- Tales of the Kama Sutra 2: Monsoon '98
- The Tempest '82 ▶
- The Tempest '10
- Third World Cop '99
- This Time for Keeps '47
- Treasure Island '12
- Trouble in Paradise '88
- Tyler Perry's Why Did I Get Married Too '10
- Undercurrent '99
- Unhappy Birthday '10
- Universal Soldiers '07
- Untamed Women '52
- Up Periscope '59
- Utopia '51
- Vanished '06
- Victory '95
- Vipers '08
- Waikiki Wedding '37 ▶
- Wake Me When It's Over '60
- Warbirds '08
- Week-End in Havana '41
- The Weight of Water '00
- We're Not Dressing '34 ▶
- When Time Ran Out '80
- Where the Wild Things Are '09
- Whispers and Lies '08
- The Wicker Man '06
- Wide Sargasso Sea '92
- Wide Sargasso Sea '06
- The Widow of Saint-Pierre '00 ▶
- The Wild Life '16
- Windbag the Sailor '36
- Witches of the Caribbean '05
- The Wizards of Waverly Place: The Movie '09
- Wonder Woman '17 ▶
- Xtro 3: Watch the Skies '95

Israel

***See also** The Holocaust; Judaism*

- Abe '20
- Adam Resurrected '08
- Ajami '09 ▶
- Ancient Relic '02
- The Attack '13 ▶
- The Band's Visit '07 ▶
- Bonjour Monsieur Shlomi '03 ▶
- Broken Wings '02 ▶
- The Bubble '06
- Cast a Giant Shadow '66
- Colombian Love '04
- Cup Final '92
- The Debt '10
- Diamonds '72
- Disengagement '07
- Don Verdean '15
- Eagles Attack at Dawn '70
- Exodus '60 ▶
- Fill the Void '12
- 5 Broken Cameras '11
- The Flat '12 ▶
- Foxtrot '18
- Free Zone '05
- The Gatekeepers '12 ▶
- The Gospel of John '15
- Hello Goodbye '08
- James' Journey to Jerusalem '03
- Japan Japan '07
- The Juggler '53
- Kippur '00 ▶
- Land of Plenty '04
- Late Marriage '01
- The Little Drummer Girl '84 ▶
- The Man Who Captured Eichmann '96
- Mother Night '96 ▶
- Munich '05 ▶
- O Jerusalem '07
- Omar '13 ▶
- Operation Finale '18
- Operation Thunderbolt '77
- The Operative '19
- The Other Son '12 ▶
- The Other Story '19
- Out in the Dark '12 ▶
- Paradise Now '05 ▶
- The Reports on Sarah and Saleem '19 ▶
- Salt of the Sea '08
- The Secrets '07
- The Seventh Coin '92
- Sufat Chol '16 ▶
- A Tale of Love and Darkness '16
- Time of Favor '00
- Under the Domim Tree '95
- Victory at Entebbe '76
- Wall '04 ▶
- You Don't Mess with the Zohan '08
- Zero Days '16

Istanbul, not Constantinople

- Climates '06 ▶
- The Edge of Heaven '07 ▶
- Fay Grim '06
- From Russia with Love '63 ▶
- L'Immortelle '63
- Kedi '17 ▶
- The Lark Farm '07
- The Mask of Dimitrios '44 ▶
- The Net 2.0 '06
- Steam: A Turkish Bath '96 ▶
- Taken 2 '12
- Topkapi '64 ▶

▶ = rated three bones or higher

The World Is Not Enough '99

Italy

See also Florence; Rome--Ancient; Rome--Modern; Venice

Accatone! '61 ▸
Afflicted '14
All Roads Lead to Rome '15
All Screwed Up '74 ▸
All the Money in the World '17
Amanda Knox: Murder on Trail in Italy '11
Amarcord '74 ▸
The American '10
And While We Were Here '13
Angela '02
Apocalypse Pompeii '14
The Assisi Underground '84
Avanti! '72
Baaria '09
Baba Yaga '73
Bambole '65
Beatrice Cenci '69
Berberian Sound Studio '12
Best of Youth '03 ▸
Beyond the Clouds '95
The Bicycle Thief '48 ▸
The Biggest Bundle of Them All '68
A Blade in the Dark '83
Blame It on the Bellboy '92
Blood Feud '79
Bright Star '09
The Burnt Orange Heresy '20
Call Me by Your Name '17 ▸
Captain Carey, U.S.A. '50
Catch-22 '70 ▸
Caterina in the Big City '03
Cemetery Man '95
Certified Copy '10
Christ Stopped at Eboli '79 ▸
A Ciambra '17
Ciao, Professore! '94
Cinema Paradiso '88 ▸
Cobra '25
Come September '61
The Conformist '71 ▸
Cry of a Prostitute: Love Kills '72
Curse of the Faceless Man '58
David's Birthday '09
Death Takes a Holiday '34 ▸
The Devil Inside '12
Diego Maradona '19 ▸
The Divine Lady '29
Divorce-Italian Style '62 ▸
Dondi '61
Don't Torture a Duckling '72
Double Team '97
Eat, Pray, Love '10
Eight Iron Men '52
The Eighteenth Angel '97
Enchanted April '92
Eros '04
Everyone Else '09
Excellent Cadavers '99
Executioner of Venice '63
The Face of an Angel '14
The Fallen '05 ▸
Fellini's Roma '72
Fiances '63
Final Justice '84
Fire at Sea '16 ▸
For Roseanna '96
Force of Arms '51
The 4th Tenor '02
Fragment of Fear '70
Francesco '93
The Garden of the Finzi-Continis '71 ▸
Giallo '09
Ginostra '02
The Glass Mountain '49
The Godfather, Part 3 '90 ▸
Gomorrah '08 ▸
A Good Woman '04
Happy as Lazzaro '18 ▸
The Haunting of Helena '12
Heaven '01
His Secret Life '01 ▸
Hornets' Nest '70
Hotel '01
I Am Love '09 ▸
Il Divo '08
I'm Not Scared '03
In Love and War '96
In Love and War '01
In Search of Fellini '17
Inferno '16
It Started in Naples '60 ▸
Italian for Beginners '01
The Italian Job '03 ▸
Kaos '85 ▸
La Chartreuse de Parme '48
La Dolce Vita '60 ▸
La Scorta '94 ▸
La Terra Trema '48 ▸
Laugh, Clown, Laugh '28 ▸
The Leopard '63 ▸
Letters to Juliet '10
The Lickerish Quartet '70
Life Is Beautiful '98 ▸
The Lizzie McGuire Movie '03
Loose Cannons '10
Loro '19
The Lost Moment '47
Love and Anarchy '73 ▸
The Love Light '21
The Luzhin Defence '00
Macaroni '85
Mafioso '62
Malena '00
Mamma Roma '62 ▸
A Man About the House '47
Massacre in Rome '73
Me, Myself and Her '16
Mediterranea '15 ▸
Meet Him and Die '76
Merry Andrew '58
Mia Madre '16
Miracle at St. Anna '08
A Month by the Lake '95
Mussolini & I '85
My Brother Is an Only Child '07
My House in Umbria '03 ▸
My Mother's Smile '02
Night Sun '90
1900 '76 ▸
Nora '00
Nostalghia '83
One Kiss '16
Only You '94
Open City '45 ▸
Orchestra Rehearsal '78
The Organizer '64
Ossessione '42 ▸
The Other Man '08
Our Life '10
Paisan '46 ▸
Palio '15 ▸
Pavarotti '19
Piranhas '19
The Pirates of Capri '49
Pompeii '14
The Postman '94 ▸
Prince of Foxes '49
The Red Violin '98
Ripley's Game '02 ▸
The Roman Spring of Mrs. Stone '03
Rome Adventure '62
Romeo & Juliet '13
St. Michael Had a Rooster '72
The Scent of a Woman '75
Screw Loose '99
The Secret of Santa Vittoria '69
The Seven Hills of Rome '58
Shoeshine '47 ▸
The Sicilian '87
The Sicilian Girl '09
The Skin '81
The Sky Is Falling '00
The Son's Room '00 ▸
Spice World: The Movie '97
Stealing Beauty '96
Stiff Upper Lips '96
The Stone Merchant '06
The Story of G.I. Joe '45 ▸
Stranger on the Prowl '52
Street Angel '28
A Summer in Genoa '08
Sword of War '09
Swordsman of Siena '62
The Talented Mr. Ripley '99
Three Coins in the Fountain '54
Three Peaks '19
Three Steps North '51
Too Bad She's Bad '54
The Tree of Wooden Clogs '78 ▸
The Trip to Italy '14
The Truce '96 ▸
The Twilight Saga: New Moon '09
Two Women '61 ▸
Uncle Nino '03
Under the Tuscan Sun '03
The Unknown Woman '06
Vincere '09
Voice from the Stone '17
Von Ryan's Express '65 ▸
Voyage in Italy '53
War Story '14
Welcome Home '18
What Did You Do in the War, Daddy? '66
Where Angels Fear to Tread '91 ▸
The White Sister '33
The Wide Blue Road '57 ▸
William Shakespeare's A Midsummer Night's Dream '99
Wolverine '96
Year of the Gun '91
The Yellow Rolls Royce '64
Zoolander 2 '16

It's the End of the World!

Doomsday Prophecy '11
4:44 Last Day on Earth '11
The Hitchhiker's Guide to the Galaxy '81 ▸
The Hitchhiker's Guide to the Galaxy '05 ▸
Melancholia '11 ▸
Seeking a Friend for the End of the World '12
When Worlds Collide '51

It's a Conspiracy, Man!

See also Capitol Capers

The Absence of Light '06
Absolute Power '97
Absolution '97
The Alchemists '99
All the President's Men '76 ▸
Anatomy '00 ▸
Android Cop '14
The Andromeda Strain '08
Apollo 18 '11
The Arrival 2 '98
The Arrival '96 ▸
Attack Force '06
Backlash '99
Backstabbing for Beginners '18
The Bank Job '08 ▸
Before I Say Goodbye '03
Blind Horizon '04
The Bourne Legacy '12 ▸
The Capitol Conspiracy '99
Central Intelligence '16
Chain Reaction '96
Circadian Rhythm '05
City Hall '95 ▸
The Clonus Horror '79
The Code Conspiracy '01
Company Business '91
Conspiracy Theory '97 ▸
The Constant Gardener '05 ▸
Cop Land '97 ▸
Crimson Rivers 2: Angels of the Apocalypse '05
Cyborg Soldier '08
The Da Vinci Code '06 ▸
A Dark Truth '12
Dead Bang '89
Deadly Game '77
Don Peyote '14
The Drone Virus '04
Echelon Conspiracy '09
Echo of Murder '00
Edge of Darkness '10
End Game '06
The End of Violence '97
Enemy of the State '98
Erased '12
Eraser '96
Executive Action '73
Eyeborgs '09
Fatal Deception: Mrs. Lee Harvey Oswald '93
The Fearmakers '58
Final Days of Planet Earth '06
Final Payback '99
Fire Serpent '07
Flashpoint '84
The Forgotten '04
The Fourth Protocol '87 ▸
The Game '97 ▸
The Girl With the Dragon Tattoo '11 ▸
Hell Swarm '00
Hidden '11
Hijacking Catastrophe: 9/11, Fear and the Selling of America '04
Inherent Vice '14 ▸
Interview with the Assassin '02
Jack Reacher: Never Go Back '16
The Jackal '97
Jason Bourne '16
JFK '91 ▸
Jimmy Vestvood: Amerikan Hero '16
Jurassic World: Fallen Kingdom '18
Kill the Messenger '14 ▸
The Kovak Box '06
The Last Templar '09
The Legend of Zorro '05
Lila & Eve '15
Looking for Richard '96 ▸
The Machinist '04
The Manchurian Candidate '62 ▸
The Manchurian Candidate '04 ▸
Marauders '16
Master '16
The Matrix '99 ▸
The Matrix Reloaded '03
The Matrix Revolutions '03 ▸
Meteor Apocalypse '10
Mr. Ricco '75
Mulholland Falls '95
Muppets from Space '99
Murder at 1600 '97
Nixon '95 ▸
No Way Out '87 ▸
The November Man '14
Oktober '98
Operation Avalanche '16
Our Kind of Traitor '16
The Package '89
Page Eight '11
Pandemic '09
The Parallax View '74 ▸
Patricia Cornwell's At Risk '10
Perfect Target '98
Pioneer '13
Pistol Whipped '08
Polar Storm '09
Poodle Springs '98
Power Play '02
The Prisoner '09
Proof of Lies '06
Psychotica '10
Rage '72
Rangers '00
Red Corner '97
Renaissance '06
Robin Cook's Terminal '96
Robin Hood '18
Rush Hour 2 '01
The Satan Bug '65
Secret State '12
Separate Lies '05
Seven Days in May '64 ▸
The Shadow Conspiracy '96
Shooter '07
16 Blocks '06 ▸
Sneakers '92
Southland Tales '06
The Speed of Thought '11
The Star Chamber '83
The State Within '06
Storm Catcher '99
Storm Tracker '99
Submerged '05
The Summit '08
They Are Among Us '04
They Crawl '01
They Live '88
31 North 62 East '09
Three Days of the Condor '75 ▸
Time Bomb '08
Tom Clancy's Netforce '98
Toxic Skies '08
Traitor '08
Transformers: Age of Extinction '14
Under the Silver Lake '18
Unholy '07
Venomous '01
WarGames: The Dead Code '08
Warning Shot '67
Watchmen '09
The Way of War '08
Wide Awake '07
Winter Kills '79 ▸
World for Ransom '54
World on a Wire '73
The X-Files '98

It's the End of the World!

Abolition '11
Asteroid *vs.* Earth '14
CAT. 8 '13
Cell '16
The Dark Tower '17
Daylight's End '16
Earth's Final Hours '12
End of the World '13
Eve of Destruction '13
Exploding Sun '13
Final Days of Planet Earth '06
40 Days and Nights '12
An Inconvenient Sequel: Truth to Power '17
Inferno '16
Into the Forest '16
It's a Disaster '12
Last Night '98 ▸
Legion '10
Pacific Rim '13
Parts Per Billion '14
Revelation Road: The Beginning of the End '13
Seeds of Destruction '11
Starfish '19
Summer Wars '09 ▸
10 Cloverfield Lane '16 ▸
This Is the End '13 ▸
12/12/12 '12
The World's End '13 ▸

Jail

See Alcatraz; Death Row; Great Escapes; Men in Prison; Women in Prison

Jamaica

See also Caribbean; Island Fare; Vacations

Belly '98
Captain Blood '35 ▸
Clara's Heart '88
Cocktail '88
Cool Runnings '93
Dr. No '62 ▸
The Harder They Come '72
Home Again '13
How Stella Got Her Groove Back '98
I Am Bolt '16 ▸
Marked for Death '90
The Mighty Quinn '89
Pirates of the Caribbean: Dead Man's Chest '06
Pirates of the Caribbean: The Curse of the Black Pearl '03 ▸
Rude Boy: The Jamaican Don '03
Swashbuckler '76
Third World Cop '99
White Squall '96
Wide Sargasso Sea '92

Japan

See also Asia; Tokyo

After the Storm '17 ▸
As You Like It '06
Azumi '03 ▸
The Ballad of Narayama '58 ▸
The Ballad of Narayama '83 ▸
Barbarian and the Geisha '58
Black Rain '88 ▸
Black Rain '89
Blood on the Sun '45
Blood: The Last Vampire '09
Bridge to the Sun '61
Bright Future '03 ▸
Cafe Lumiere '05
Captive Hearts '87
The Cove '09
Creepy '16 ▸
Demonlover '02
Destination Tokyo '43
Dr. Akagi '98
Dodes 'ka-den '70 ▸
Dolls '02 ▸
The Eel '96 ▸
Emperor '12
Extreme Private Eros: Love Song 1974 '74
Flight From Ashiya '64
Flight 7500 '16
The Forest '16
47 Ronin, Part 1 '42 ▸
47 Ronin, Part 2 '42 ▸
The Geisha Boy '58
Geisha Girl '52
Ghost in the Shell '17
Girls of the White Orchid '85
Gozu '03
The Grudge '04
Gung Ho '86
Hacksaw Ridge '16
Harakiri '62 ▸
Heaven & Earth '90 ▸
The Hidden Blade '04
Hiroshima '95 ▸
Hiroshima, Mon Amour '59 ▸
House Where Evil Dwells '82
The Hunted '94
The Idiot '51 ▸
Isle of Dogs '18 ▸
Jiro Dreams of Sushi '12 ▸
Kampai! For the Love of Sake '16 ▸
Kikujiro '99
Kubo and the Two Strings '16 ▸
The Last Samurai '03 ▸
Letters from Iwo Jima '06 ▸
Like Father, Like Son '13
Like Someone in Love '13
Lost in Translation '03 ▸
Madame Butterfly '95
A Majority of One '56
The Makioka Sisters '83 ▸
Memoirs of a Geisha '05
Midway '76
Mishima: A Life in Four Chapters '85 ▸
Miss Hokusai '16
Mr. Baseball '92
No Regrets for Our Youth '46 ▸
Objective, Burma! '45 ▸
Okinawa: The Afterburn '15
Okoge '93
Only Yesterday '16 ▸
Osaka Elegy '36
Otaku No Video '91 ▸
Our Little Sister '16
The Pillow Book '95
Pokemon the Movie: The Power of Us '18
Ponyo '08 ▸
Prisoners of the Sun '91 ▸
Promare '19
R100 '15
Ran '85 ▸
Rashomon '51 ▸
Red Beard '65 ▸
Resident Evil: Vendetta '17
Rikyu '90 ▸
Rising Sun '93 ▸
Samurai Banners '69
Samurai Rebellion '67 ▸
Samurai Reincarnation '81
Sansho the Bailiff '54 ▸
Sayonara '57 ▸
The Sea of Trees '16
Seven Samurai '54 ▸
Shall We Dance? '96 ▸
Shin Godzilla '16
Shin Heike Monogatari '55 ▸
Shogun '80 ▸
Shoplifters '18 ▸
Showdown in Little Tokyo '91
Silence '16 ▸
Silk '07
Sisters of the Gion '36
Sonatine '96 ▸

▸ = rated three bones or higher

The Sun '05
Taboo '99
Teenage Mutant Ninja Turtles 3 '93
13 Assassins '10
Thirty Seconds Over Tokyo '44 ▶
3 Ninjas Kick Back '94
Three Stripes in the Sun '55
To Be Takei '14
Tokyo-Ga '85 ▶
Tokyo Tribe '15
Tora! Tora! Tora! '70
Twenty-Four Eyes '54 ▶
The Twilight Samurai '02 ▶
Ugetsu '53 ▶
Under the Flag of the Rising Sun '72 ▶
Utamaro and His Five Women '46
Village of Dreams '97
Walk, Don't Run '66
What's Up, Tiger Lily? '66 ▶
The Wind Rises '13 ▶
The Wolverine '13
The Wolves '82 ▶
The Wrath of the Gods '14
The Yakuza '75
You Only Live Twice '67
Your Name '17 ▶
Zatoichi '03 ▶
Zatoichi *vs.* Yojimbo '70 ▶

Jazz & Blues

***See also** Price of Fame; Struggling Musicians*
All Night Long '62
Almost Blue '93
The Benny Goodman Story '55
Billy's Holiday '95
Bird '88 ▶
Birth of the Blues '41
Blueberry Hill '88
The Blues Brothers '80 ▶
Blues Brothers 2000 '98
Blues in the Night '41
The Cotton Club '84 ▶
Crossroads '86
Dingo '90
The Duke Is Tops '38
The Five Pennies '59
Forty Shades of Blue '05
The Gene Krupa Story '59
G.I. Blues '60
The Glenn Miller Story '54 ▶
Green Book '18 ▶
Guy and Madeline on a Park Bench '09 ▶
Jazz on a Summer's Day '59
The Jazz Singer '27
The Jazz Singer '80
Kansas City '95 ▶
Killer Diller '04
Lady Sings the Blues '72
Let's Get Lost '88 ▶
Lighting in a Bottle '04 ▶
Lost Highway '96
Miles Ahead '16 ▶
Mo' Better Blues '90
Moonlight Serenade '09
New Orleans '47
New York, New York '77 ▶
Paris Blues '61
Pete Kelly's Blues '55
Ragtime '81 ▶
Ray '04 ▶
Ring-a-Ding Rhythm '62
Round Midnight '86 ▶
Schultze Gets the Blues '03
Sepia Cinderella '47
Shadows '60 ▶
Silver Hawk '04
Some Like It Hot '59 ▶
A Song Is Born '48 ▶
The Song of Sway Lake '18
Stormy Monday '88
Sweet and Lowdown '99
Swing High, Swing Low '37
Syncopation '42
The Talented Mr. Ripley '99
Thunder Soul '10
Too Late Blues '61
Whiplash '14 ▶
Wild Orchid 2: Two Shades of Blue '92
Young Man with a Horn '50 ▶

Jealousy

All Night Long '62
Always Shine '16 ▶
Ambush '50
Amores Perros '00 ▶
Animals '08
As It Is In Heaven '04
Authors Anonymous '14
The Beguiled '17
Bending All the Rules '02
Between Love & Goodbye '08
Beyond All Limits '59
A Bigger Splash '15
The Black Bird '26
Black Swan '10 ▶
Blame '17
The Boxer and the Bombshell '08
The Break-Up '06
Claudia and David '46
Cold Showers '05
The Constant Nymph '43
Cracks '09
The Crimson Kimono '59
Crush '02
Curse of the Golden Flower '06
Daddy & Them '99
Daydream Nation '10
The Departure '20
Design for Living '33
The Devil and the Deep '32
The Devil's Backbone '01
Dirty Love '05
Do Not Disturb '65
Don't Think Twice '16
The Edge of Love '08
Elegy '08
Enchantment '48
The English Teacher '13
Enigma '01
Envy '04
Family Honeymoon '49
The Fast Runner '01 ▶
Fast Sofa '01
For Your Consideration '06
Frank & Lola '16
Getting Gertie's Garter '27
A Girl Cut in Two '07
The Girl in the Red Velvet Swing '55
Gosford Park '01 ▶
Gossip '00
Harry in Your Pocket '73
He Knew He Was Right '04
Heart '99
The Heavenly Body '44
Hellhounds '09
Her Cardboard Lover '42
The Housemaid '10
The Hypnotic Eye '60
I Declare War '12
In Her Skin '09
Inconceivable '17
The Inheritance '97
Jealousy '13 ▶
Jeanne Eagels '57
Julie '56
Kill Your Darlings '13
The King '05
Kiss Me Again '06
The Kreutzer Sonata '08
La Boheme '26
The Last Man '00
Le Donk & Scor-Zay-Zee '09
Leaving Metropolis '02
The Legend of Lylah Clare '68
Les Biches '68 ▶
Let's Do It Again '53
Lightning Strikes Twice '51
Like It Is '98 ▶
Little Black Book '04
Little Chenier: A Cajun Story '06
Lonely Hearts '06
The Loss of a Teardrop Diamond '08
Love Story '44
Lulu Belle '48
Mad Love '01
The Male Animal '42
Manpower '41
Mary Magdalene '19
Me Without You '01
Meet Me After the Show '51
Merci pour le Chocolat '00 ▶
The Merry Widow '25 ▶
Miranda '48
The Mississippi Gambler '53
The Moth Diaries '11
Murder in the Hamptons '05
My Wife is an Actress '01
No More Ladies '35
No Time For Love '43 ▶
Nora '00
Not Now Darling '73
Old Acquaintance '43
One Desire '55
Othello '01 ▶
The Other Man '08
Out of Time '03
Pandaemonium '00
The Passionate Plumber '32
Perfect Understanding '33
The Perfection '19
The Piano Teacher '01
Premature '20
The Prestige '06 ▶
The Price of Milk '00
Pumpkin '02
Rage in Heaven '41
Rampage '63
Revolutionary Road '08
Second Best '05
Seconds Apart '11
Sex and Breakfast '07
She's Working Her Way Through College '52
The Show '27
Signs & Wonders '00
Sleuth '07
Slow as Lightning '23
Sparkle '12
The Squall '29
A Star for Christmas '12
Sylvia '03
Taboo '99
This Woman Is Dangerous '52
Thunderhoof '48
Tiger Shark '32
Time '06
Trap for Cinderella '13
Unforgettable '17
The Valet '06
The Weather Man '05
The Weight of Water '00
When the Bough Breaks '16
Whiplash '48
White Wedding '10
Wife Versus Secretary '36 ▶
You Should Have Left '20

Jerusalem

Arn: The Knight Templar '07
Ben-Hur '59 ▶
Ben Hur '10
The Body '01
Countdown: Jerusalem '09
The Crusades '35
Eichmann '07
Every Time We Say Goodbye '86
Eyes Wide Open '09
Footnote '11
Hannah Arendt '12
Inch'Allah '12
Kadosh '99
Kingdom of Heaven '05 ▶
Language of the Enemy '07
Mary Magdalene '19
Miral '10
The Old Testament '62
The Silver Chalice '54
The Women's Balcony '16

Jockeying for Position

And They're Off '11
Archer's Adventure '85
The Bashful Bachelor '42
Big Boy '30
Bite the Bullet '75 ▶
The Black Stallion '79 ▶
Broadway Bill '34 ▶
Casey's Shadow '78
Champions '84
Cold Feet '89
The Cup '11
A Day at the Races '37 ▶
Dead Heat '01
Derby Day '52
Down Argentine Way '40 ▶
Dreamer: Inspired by a True Story '05
Duke of the Derby '62
Ex-Mrs. Bradford '36 ▶
Far and Away '92
50 to 1 '14
A Fine Mess '86
The First Saturday in May '08
Flicka: Country Pride '12
Francis Goes to the Races '51
The Gentleman from Arizona '39
Get a Job '16
Grand National Night '53
Great Dan Patch '49
Hidalgo '04
A Horse for Danny '95
Kentucky '38
Ladies Crave Excitement '35
Law of the Wild '34
The Lemon Drop Kid '51
Let It Ride '89
Lightning: The White Stallion '86
The Longshot '86
Ma and Pa Kettle at the Fair '52
Money from Home '53
Moon over Miami '41 ▶
My Brother Talks to Horses '47
My Old Man '79
National Velvet '44 ▶
Outside Bet '12
Palio '15 ▶
The Quiet Man '52 ▶
Riding High '50
Salty O'Rourke '45
Saratoga '37 ▶
Seabiscuit '03 ▶
Secretariat '10
Shooting Fish '98
Simpatico '99
Sing You Sinners '38
Sporting Blood '31
The Story of Seabiscuit '49
Swordsman of Siena '62
Sylvester '85
That's My Man '47
Thoroughbreds Don't Cry '37
Wall of Noise '63
Wild Beauty '27
Wings of the Morning '37

Joke and Dagger

***See also** Cold War Spies; Female Spies; Genre Spoofs; Satire & Spies & Spy Kids; World War One Spies; World War Two Spies*
The Accidental Spy '01
The Adventures of Rocky & Bullwinkle '00
Agent Cody Banks 2: Destination London '04
Agent Cody Banks '03
Austin Powers: International Man of Mystery '97 ▶
Austin Powers 2: The Spy Who Shagged Me '99 ▶
Austin Powers In Goldmember '02
Bang! Bang! You're Dead! '66
Call Me Bwana '63
Casino Royale '67
Code Name: The Cleaner '07
Condorman '81
Dead Men Don't Wear Plaid '82
D.E.B.S. '04
The Delphi Bureau: The Merchant of Death Assignment '72
Don't Raise the Bridge, Lower the River '68
Don't Worry, We'll Think of a Title '66
Duck Soup '33 ▶
G-Force '09
Get Smart '08
Get Smart, Again! '89
The Great Spy Chase '64
Hopscotch '80 ▶
Hot Enough for June '64
Hudson Hawk '91
I Dood It '43
I Spy '02
The In-Laws '79 ▶
The In-Laws '03
In Like Flint '67
Ishtar '87
Knight and Day '10
Knock on Wood '54
The Liquidator '65
Looney Tunes: Back in Action '03
The Man Who Knew Too Little '97
The Man with One Red Shoe '85
Max Rules '05
Memoirs of an Invisible Man '92
My Favorite Brunette '47
My Favorite Spy '51
A Night in Casablanca '46 ▶
The Nude Bomb '80
Operation: Endgame '10
OSS 117: Cairo, Nest of Spies '06
OSS 117: Lost in Rio '09
Otley '68
Our Man Flint '66
The Phynx '70
The President's Analyst '67 ▶
Real Men '87
RED '10
Salt & Pepper '68
The Shakiest Gun in the West '68
Spies Like Us '85
Spy Hard '96
Spy Kids 4: All the Time in the World '11
S*P*Y*S '74
13 Frightened Girls '63
Top Secret! '84 ▶
True Lies '94
Undercover Brother '02
What's Up, Tiger Lily? '66 ▶
Zoolander '01

Journalism

***See** Front Page; News at 11*

Judaism

***See also** The Holocaust; Israel; Rabbi*
Adam Sandler's 8 Crazy Nights '02
Address Unknown '44
Aimee & Jaguar '98
All My Loved Ones '00
Almost Peaceful '02 ▶
American Matchmaker '40
The Angel Levine '70
Angry Harvest '85 ▶
Anne Frank: The Whole Story '01 ▶
The Apprenticeship of Duddy Kravitz '74 ▶
The Assisi Underground '84
The Attic: The Hiding of Anne Frank '88
Au Revoir les Enfants '87 ▶
Autumn Sun '98 ▶
Barney's Version '10
Bee Season '05 ▶
The Believer '01
Ben-Hur '59 ▶
Ben-Hur '16
Black Book '06 ▶
The Book Thief '13
Bye Bye Braverman '67
The Chosen '81 ▶
Commissar '68 ▶
Conspiracy of Hearts '60 ▶
Counsellor-at-Law '33 ▶
Crossfire '47 ▶
Crossing Delancey '88 ▶
Dad On the Run '00
Daniel Deronda '02
David '97
David & Layla '07
A Day in October '92
Deconstructing Harry '97
Defiance '08
Demon '16 ▶
The Devil's Arithmetic '99
The Diary of Anne Frank '59 ▶
The Diary of Anne Frank '08
Disobedience '17
Disraeli '79 ▶
Divided We Fall '00
The Dybbuk '37 ▶
Enemies, a Love Story '89 ▶
Esther '98
Esther Kahn '00
Evan Almighty '07
Every Time We Say Goodbye '86
Everything is Illuminated '05 ▶
Exodus '60 ▶
Exodus: Gods and Kings '14
Eyes Wide Open '09
Fading Gigolo '13
Fateless '05 ▶
Fiddler on the Roof '71 ▶
Fill the Void '12
A Film Unfinished '10
The Flat '12 ▶
The Frisco Kid '79
Funny Girl '68 ▶
The Garden of the Finzi-Continis '71 ▶
Gentleman's Agreement '47 ▶
The Girl on the Train '09
Go for Zucker '05
God on Trial '08
The Golem '20 ▶
Golem: The Petrified Garden '93
Good Evening, Mr. Wallenberg '93
The Grand Role '04
Green Fields '37
The Grey Zone '01
The Harmonists '99
Hello Goodbye '08
Hester Street '75 ▶
Hitched for the Holidays '12
Holocaust '78 ▶
Holy Rollers '10
Home Before Dark '58
Homicide '91 ▶
I Love You, Alice B. Toklas! '68
I Love You, I Love You Not '97
I Love You Rosa '72
In Darkness '11
In the Presence of Mine Enemies '97
Indignation '16
The Infidel '10
The Infiltrator '95
Inglourious Basterds '09 ▶
Invincible '01
The Island on Bird Street '97
It Runs in the Family '03
Jacob the Liar '74
James' Journey to Jerusalem '03
The Jazz Singer '27
The Jazz Singer '52
The Jazz Singer '80
Jeremiah '98
Jewtopia '12
Jojo Rabbit '19 ▶
Jud Suess '40 ▶
The Juggler '53
Kadosh '99
Keeping the Faith '00
Keeping Up with the Steins '06
King David '85
King of the Corner '04 ▶
Kissing Jessica Stein '02
La Petite Jerusalem '05
Lansky '99
The Last Days '98 ▶
The Last Metro '80 ▶
The Last of the Unjust '13 ▶
The Last Winter '84
Late Marriage '01
Left Luggage '98
Leon the Pig Farmer '93
Let My People Go! '11
Liberty Heights '99
The Life and Times of Hank Greenberg '99 ▶
Life During Wartime '09
The Light Ahead '39
Love, Wedding, Marriage '11
Loving Leah '09
The Mad Adventures of Rabbi Jacob '73 ▶
Madman '79
The Man Who Captured Eichmann '96
The Man Who Cried '00
Masada '81 ▶
Max '02

▶ = rated three bones or higher

Menashe '17
The Merchant of Venice '04 ▸
Miracle at Midnight '98
Moses '96
Munich '05 ▸
The Murder of Mary Phagan '87 ▸
My Mother's Courage '95
The Nativity Story '06
Next Year in Jerusalem '98
1945 '17 ▸
No Place on Earth '12
No Way to Treat a Lady '68 ▸
Noa at Seventeen '82 ▸
Nora's Will '09
Norman '17
Nowhere in Africa '02
Once Upon a Time in America '84 ▸
One Day You'll Understand '08
One Night with the King '06
The Only Way '70
OSS 117: Lost in Rio '09
The Other Son '12 ▸
The Other Story '19
Oy Vey! My Son is Gay! '09
The Pawnbroker '65 ▸
Peep World '10
The Pianist '02 ▸
Playing Mona Lisa '00
Power '34
A Price Above Rubies '97
Prime '05
The Quarrel '93
The Rabbi's Cat '11
Radio Days '87 ▸
Religulous '08 ▸
Resistance '20
Safe Men '98
St. Urbain's Horseman '07
Sallah '63 ▸
Sarah's Key '10
Schindler's List '93 ▸
School Ties '92 ▸
A Secret '07 ▸
The Secrets '07
Septembers of Shiraz '16
A Serious Man '09 ▸
The Serpent's Egg '78
Shakespeare's Merchant '05
The Shop on Main Street '65 ▸
The Sky Is Falling '00
Snow in August '01
Sofie '92
Solomon '98
Solomon and Gaenor '98
The Sorrow and the Pity '71 ▸
Spring 1941 '08
Steel Toes '06
Stolen Summer '02
A Stranger Among Us '92
The Substance of Fire '96
Summer '03 '18
The Summer of Aviya '88
Sunshine '99
Symphony of Six Million '32
The Taxman '98
Then She Found Me '07
Time of Favor '00
To Dust '19
The Tollbooth '04
24 Days '14
The Twilight of the Golds '97
The Two of Us '68 ▸
Uncut Gems '19 ▸
Under the Domim Tree '95
Unstrung Heroes '95
Uprising '01 ▸
Used People '92
Voyage of the Damned '76 ▸
Wall '04 ▸
Wandering Jew '20
The Wedding Song '09
When Do We Eat? '05
Where's Poppa? '70 ▸
Will You Merry Me? '08
Wish I Was Here '14
The Women's Balcony '16
The Yankles '09
The Year My Parents Went on Vacation '07
Year One '09
Yentl '83 ▸
You Don't Mess with the Zohan '08
Zalmen or the Madness of God '75

Jungle Stories

***See also** Monkeyshines; Treasure Hunt*

Ace Ventura: When Nature Calls '95
Active Stealth '99
Africa Screams '49
African Treasure '52
Aguirre, the Wrath of God '72 ▸
All the Way, Boys '73
Amazon Jail '85
Anaconda '96
Anacondas: The Hunt for the Blood Orchid '04
The Art of Travel '08
Baby. . . Secret of the Lost Legend '85
Bat 21 '88
Bela Lugosi Meets a Brooklyn Gorilla '52
Beyond Rangoon '95
Black Cobra 3: The Manila Connection '90
The Black Devils of Kali '55
Bomba and the Hidden City '50
Bomba and the Jungle Girl '52
Bomba on Panther Island '49
Bomba, the Jungle Boy '49
Boy & the World '15 ▸
Brenda Starr '86
The Bride & the Beast '58
Bride of the Gorilla '51
Cannibal Holocaust '80
Cannibal Women in the Avocado Jungle of Death '89
Carry On Up the Jungle '70
Cobra Woman '44
Congo '95
Curious George '06
Death in the Garden '56
Death is Nimble, Death is Quick '67
Delta Force Commando '87
Devil Hunter '08
The Diamond of Jeru '01
DNA '97
Dr. Cyclops '40
Dr. Seuss' Horton Hears a Who! '08 ▸
Earth: One Amazing Day '17 ▸
East of Borneo '31
Elephant Boy '37 ▸
Elephant Stampede '51
Elephant Walk '54
The Emerald Forest '85 ▸
Emerald Jungle '80
Emmanuelle 6 '88
End of the Spear '06
Escape from Hell '79
Escape to Burma '55
Escape 2000 '81
Farewell to the King '89
Fatal Mission '89
Fire on the Amazon '93
Firewalker '86
Fitzcarraldo '82 ▸
Four Frightened People '34
The Further Adventures of Tennessee Buck '88
Fury '78
Fury of the Congo '51
George of the Jungle '97 ▸
Gold '16
Gold of the Amazon Women '79
The Golden Idol '54
Gorillas in the Mist '88 ▸
Green Fire '55
Green Inferno '72
The Green Inferno '14
Green Mansions '59
Greystoke: The Legend of Tarzan, Lord of the Apes '84
The Hive '08
How Tasty Was My Little Frenchman '71
Instinct '99
The Intended '02
Jane '17 ▸
Jane & the Lost City '87
Jumanji '95
Jumanji: The Next Level '19
Jumanji: Welcome to the Jungle '17
Jungle '52
Jungle '17
The Jungle Book 2 '03
The Jungle Book '42
The Jungle Book '67 ▸
The Jungle Book '16 ▸
Jungle Boy '96
Jungle Drums of Africa '53
Jungle Hell '55
Jungle Man-Eaters '54
Jungle Manhunt '51
Jungle Moon Men '55
Jungle Patrol '48
Jungle Warriors '84
Killer Leopard '54
Killers '88
Killing Heat '84
King Solomon's Treasure '76
Krippendorf's Tribe '98
The Land Unknown '57
The Legend of Tarzan '16
Liane, Jungle Goddess '56
The Lion Hunters '51
The Lion King '94 ▸
Lord of the Jungle '55
The Lost City '34
Lost City of the Jungle '45
The Lost City of Z '17 ▸
The Lost Continent '51
The Lost Jungle '34
Lost Treasure '03
The Lost Volcano '50
The Lost World '60
Mandrake '10
Mark of the Gorilla '58
Medicine Man '92
Merrill's Marauders '62
The Mighty Peking Man '77
Miraculous Journey '48
Missing in Action '84
The Mission '86 ▸
Mister Lonely '07
Mogambo '53 ▸
Monkey Kingdom '15 ▸
The Mosquito Coast '86
Mowgli: Legend of the Jungle '18
The Muthers '76
My Lucky Elephant '13
Mysterious Island of Beautiful Women '79
Nabonga '44
Naked Jungle '54 ▸
The Naked Prey '66 ▸
The New Adventures of Tarzan '35
Night Creature '79
No Man Is an Island '62
Objective, Burma! '45 ▸
Operation Dumbo Drop '95
Overkill '96
The Phantom '96
Predator '87
Predators '10
Prehistoric Women '67
Primal '19
Proof of Life '00
The Purple Plain '54
Pygmy Island '50
Queen of the Jungle '35
Rampage '63
The Real Glory '39 ▸
Red Dust '32 ▸
Rio 2 '14
Rise of the Dinosaurs '13
River of Death '90
River of Evil '64
The Road to Zanzibar '41 ▸
Romancing the Stone '84 ▸
Rudyard Kipling's The Jungle Book '94
Rudyard Kipling's the Second Jungle Book: Mowgli and Baloo '97
The Ruins '08
Run for the Sun '56
The Rundown '03
Safari Drums '53
Samar '62
Sandok '65
Sheena '84
Snakeman '05
Snatched '17
Sniper '92
Solo '96
Son of Kong '33
Sweet Revenge '87
Tarzan '99 ▸
Tarzan and His Mate '34 ▸
Tarzan and the Amazons '45
Tarzan and the Green Goddess '38
Tarzan and the Huntress '47
Tarzan and the Jungle Boy '68
Tarzan and the Leopard Woman '46
Tarzan and the Lost City '98
Tarzan and the Lost Safari '57
Tarzan and the She-Devil '53
Tarzan and the Slave Girl '50
Tarzan and the Trappers '58
Tarzan and the Valley of Gold '65
Tarzan Escapes '36 ▸
Tarzan Finds a Son '39 ▸
Tarzan, the Ape Man '32 ▸
Tarzan, the Ape Man '81
Tarzan the Fearless '33
Tarzan the Magnificent '60
Tarzan the Tiger '29
Tarzan Triumphs '43
Tarzan's Desert Mystery '43
Tarzan's Fight for Life '58
Tarzan's Greatest Adventure '59
Tarzan's Hidden Jungle '55
Tarzan's Magic Fountain '48
Tarzan's Peril '51
Tarzan's Revenge '38
Tarzan's Savage Fury '52
Tarzan's Secret Treasure '41
Tarzeena: Queen of Kong Island '08
Tears of the Sun '03
Terror in the Jungle '68
The Thin Red Line '98 ▸
The Thirsty Dead '74
The Treasure of the Amazon '85
Troma's War '88
Tropic Thunder '08 ▸
Tropical Heat '93
Tropical Malady '04
Turistas '06
Two Brothers '04
Virgin Sacrifice '59
Volunteers '85
Wages of Fear '55 ▸
Watchers 3 '94
Where the River Runs Black '86
White Huntress '57
The White Legion '36
The White Orchid '54
White Pongo '45
White Witch Doctor '53
White Woman '33
The World's Greatest Athlete '73
Yesterday's Enemy '59
Zombie Island Massacre '84

Junior Jocks

***See also** Baseball; Basketball; Childhood Buddies; Football; Hockey; Sports Comedy; Sports Drama*

Adam Sandler's 8 Crazy Nights '02
Amazing Grace & Chuck '87
The Bad News Bears '76 ▸
The Bad News Bears '05
Bad Parents '12
Benched '18
Bend It Like Beckham '02 ▸
The Big Green '95
D2: The Mighty Ducks '94
Dear Lemon Lima '09
The Great American Pastime '56
Gym Teacher: The Movie '08
Home Run Showdown '10
Kicking and Screaming '95 ▸
Ladybugs '92
Like Mike '02
Little Big League '94
Little Giants '94
The Longshots '08
Max Dugan Returns '83
The Mighty Ducks '92
The Perfect Game '09
Rebound '05
The Sandlot '93 ▸
The Sandlot 2 '05
The Sandlot 3: Heading Home '07
Stick It '06
Sticks and Stones '08
Underdog Kids '15

Justice Prevails...?

***See** Order in the Court*

Juvenile Delinquents

***See also** Gangs; Hell High School*

Angels with Dirty Faces '38 ▸
Bad Boys '83 ▸
Because They're Young '60
Blackboard Jungle '55 ▸
Boys Town '38 ▸
Capernaum '18 ▸
The Chorus '04
Coach Carter '05 ▸
Coldwater '14
Crime in the Streets '56
Crime School '38
The Day of the Outlaw '59
Detention '03
The Devil Is a Sissy '36
Flu Birds '08
Four Boys and a Gun '57
Gas House Kids '46
The Ghastly Love of Johnny X '12
Gridiron Gang '06
Hellion '13 ▸
High School Big Shot '59
Holes '03 ▸
Honey 2 '14
The Hoodlum Priest '61 ▸
Hope Ranch '02
Hot Rods to Hell '67
Hothead '63
Incident in an Alley '62
The Inevitable Defeat of Mister & Pete '13
Jack of the Red Hearts '15 ▸
The Kid From Cleveland '49
The Mayor of Hell '33
Night Comes On '18 ▸
Prey '19
Riot in Juvenile Prison '59
Rumble on the Docks '56
Safe Harbor '09
Schoolgirl Hitchhikers '73
See No Evil '06
Serious Charge '59
Shadow on the Window '57
Stealing Cars '16
Step Up '06
Susan Slept Here '54
13 West Street '62
Total Western '00
12 and Holding '05 ▸
2 Little Monsters '15
Urban Country '18
You Can't Get Away With Murder '39
Young America '32
The Young Savages '61
The Young Stranger '57

Karaoke

The Astronaut's Wife '99
The Cable Guy '96
College Road Trip '08
Crossroads '02
Duets '00
Glee: The 3D Concert Movie '11
High School Musical '06
I Still Know What You Did Last Summer '98
Jackpot '01
A Life Less Ordinary '97
Lost in Translation '03 ▸
Love, Honour & Obey '00
My Best Friend's Wedding '97
Once More With Feeling '08
Pushing Tin '99 ▸
Rush Hour 2 '01
Sex and the City 2 '10
A Smile Like Yours '96
The Watermelon Woman '97
When Harry Met Sally. . . '89 ▸

KGB

***See also** CIA/NSA; Cold War Spies; Russia/USSR*

Anna '19
Black Eagle '88
Cambridge Spies '03
Child 44 '15
The Company '07
Company Business '91
East-West '99
Enigma '82
Fair Game '95
Farewell '09
The Fourth Protocol '87 ▸
From Russia with Love '63 ▸
Gorky Park '83 ▸
Indiana Jones and the Kingdom of the Crystal Skull '08
The Killing Machine '09
The Living Daylights '87 ▸
Man On a String '60
Munich '05 ▸
No Way Out '87 ▸
Red Dawn '84
Red Scorpion '89
Red Serpent '02
Running Red '99
The Second Front '05
The Sellout '76
Sleepers '96
Smiley's People '82
Spy Hard '96
The Spy Who Loved Me '77
Subterfuge '98
Telefon '77
Tinker, Tailor, Soldier, Spy '80 ▸
Topaz '69 ▸
White Nights '85
The World Is Not Enough '99

Kiddie Viddy

***See** Animation & Cartoons*

Kidnapped!

***See also** Hostage!; Missing Persons*

Abandoned '47
Abducted: The Carlina White Story '12
Ace Ventura: Pet Detective '93
Act of Valor '12
Action Man '67
Acts of Violence '18
Adam '83 ▸
The Adventurer: The Curse of the Midas Box '13
African Rage '78
Against a Crooked Sky '75
Agent of Death '99
Air Bud 6: Air Buddies '06
An Alan Smithee Film: Burn, Hollywood, Burn '97
Alias Betty '01
All Superheroes Must Die '11
All the Money in the World '17
Almost Holy '16 ▸
Alone in the Woods '95
Along Came a Spider '01
Alpha Dog '06
American Fable '17
American Kickboxer 2: To the Death '93
Answers to Nothing '11
Apostle '18
Arsenal '17
The Art of War '00
Ashanti, Land of No Mercy '79
Assignment K '68
The Atomic City '52
Awaken '15
Baby's Day Out '94
Bad Samaritan '18
Ballistic: Ecks *vs.* Sever '02
Beach Blanket Bingo '65 ▸
Beer for My Horses '08
Beethoven's 2nd '93
Beethoven's Big Break '08
Behind Your Eyes '11
Believers '07
Belly of the Beast '03
Benji '74 ▸

▸ = *rated three bones or higher*

Berlin Syndrome '17
Beverly Hills Brats '89
Beverly Hills Chihuahua '08
Beyond Justice '92
Big Brother Trouble '00
The Big Hit '98
The Big Lebowski '97 ▸
Bigfoot '70
Bisbee '17 '18
Bitter Feast '10
Black Butterfly '17
Black Cat Run '98
Black Samurai '77
Bless the Child '00
Blind Heat '00
The Bodyguard 2 '07
Bone Dry '07
Bone Tomahawk '15
Borderland '07
Born of Earth '08
The Boss '73
Bound and Gagged: A Love Story '93
Brake '12
Brigsby Bear '17
Buffalo 66 '97▸
B.U.S.T.E.D. '99
Burial of the Rats '95
Buried '10
The Call '13
The Captive '14
Captivity '07
Carnage Park '16
Cash on Demand '61
Cecil B. Demented '00
Cellular '04
Celtic Pride '96
Charlie Chan at the Olympics '37
Charlie's Angels '00
The Chase '93
The Child Stealer '79
Chow Bella '98
The Chumscrubber '05
The City of Lost Children '95▸
The Clearing '04▸
Clifford's Really Big Movie '04
The Clinic '10
Close '19
Close Range '15
Close Your Eyes '02
Coffin '11
Cohen and Tate '88
Cold Blood '75
The Cold Light of Day '12
Collateral '04▸
The Collector '65▸
Collide '17
Commando '85▸
Contraband '40
The Coroner '98
Countdown '16
Crime Story '93
Crimebusters '79
Criminal Activities '15
A Crooked Somebody '18
The Crowd Roars '38
The Crying Game '92▸
The Cutter '05
Dance with the Devil '97
Daniel & Ana '09
A Date With the Falcon '42
Day of the Evil Gun '68
The Deal '08
Dean Koontz's Intensity '97
Decommissioned '16
The Deep End of the Ocean '98
The Defender '04
The Demons '19
Despicable Me 2 '13
The Devil on Horseback '36
Diablo '16
Dilili in Paris '18
The Disappearance of Alice Creed '09
Django and Sartana; It's the End '70
Django Strikes Again '87
Dog Eat Dog '16
Don't Say a Word '01
Door to Door Maniac '61
Double Play '96
Dumb & Dumber '94
Earthly Possessions '99
The Edukators '04
Elsewhere '09
The Emperor's Candlesticks '37
The End of Violence '97
Endure '10
The Entitled '11
Ernest Goes to Africa '97
Escape Plan 2: Hades '18
Everybody Knows '18
Everybody's Famous! '00
Evil Behind You '06
Excess Baggage '96
Executive Target '97
Extraction '15
Extraction '20
Extraordinary Rendition '07
Extreme Dating '04
Eye '96
Faceless '88
The Factory '10
Fargo '96 ▸
Final Justice '98
Final Score '18
Finn on the Fly '09
Fire in the Sky '93
Fireback '78
First Kill '17
Five Fingers '06
Flightplan '05
Flower & Snake '04
Follow the River '95
44 Inch Chest '09
Four Days in September '97
Four Warriors '15
Fugitive Champion '99
Game Night '18
The Gay Desperado '36
Getaway '13
The Gingerbread Man '97
A Girl, 3 Guys and a Gun '01
Go With God Gringo '66
The Gold Racket '37
The Golden Compass '07
Graceland '12
The Great Divide '29
Gringo '18
The Grissom Gang '71▸
Groupers '19
Guarding Tess '94
The Guilty '18▸
Gun Fury '53
Gun Shy '17
Hangfire '91
Happy as Lazzaro '18▸
Hate for Hate '67
The Heineken Kidnapping '11
Hey! Hey! USA! '38
Hickey & Boggs '72
Hidalgo '04
Hide and Seek '00
Holiday in Handcuffs '07
Hollywood Cop '87
Hollywood Wives: The New Generation '03
Honeybaby '74
Horrible Bosses 2 '14
House of Fury '05
iCrime '11
I'll Get You '53
I'm Not Scared '03
Implicated '98
In a Stranger's Hand '92
In Desert and Wilderness '01
In the Name of the King: A Dungeon Siege Tale '08
Inkheart '09
The Iron Petticoat '56
Island Monster '53
Jack the Giant Slayer '13
Java Heat '13
Judgment Day '99
Julia '08
Kansas City '95▸
Kentucky Jubilee '51
Kickboxer 3: The Art of War '92
Kid Colter '85
Kidnap '17
Kidnap Syndicate '76
Kidnapped '38
Kidnapped '48
Kidnapped '74
Kidnapped '95
Kidnapped '05▸
King's Ransom '05
Klown '12
Kung Fu Killer '08
La Femme Musketeer '03
Lake Consequence '92
Land of Death '03
The Last Assassins '96
The Last Hard Men '76
Last Lives '98
The Last Lullaby '08 ▸
Last Man Standing '11
A Life Less Ordinary '97
Life of Crime '13
The Lindbergh Kidnapping Case '76 ▸
Live Free or Die Hard '07
A Lonely Place to Die '11
Lorna Doone '22
Lost Treasure '03
The Lovers and the Despot '16
Lullaby '08
Ma and Pa Kettle at Waikiki '55
Macabre '58
Mad Dog Killer '77
Make Your Bets Ladies '65
Malibu's Most Wanted '03
Man on Fire '04
The Man Who Captured Eichmann '96
Mandy '18
Manipulator '71
Manny & Lo '96▸
Mansion of the Doomed '76
The Marine 3: Homefront '11
The Marked One '63
Mars Needs Moms '11
Master of Disguise '02
Maximum Impact '18
Mechanic: Resurrection '16
Mercy '96
Michael '11
The Mighty '98▸
A Mighty Heart '07▸
Misfire '14
Miss Congeniality 2: Armed and Fabulous '05
The Missing '03▸
Missing Girls '36
Mission: Impossible 3 '06▸
Mr. Nanny '93
The Money '75
Moran of the Lady Letty '22
Mother, May I Sleep With Danger? '96
The Mummy Returns '01
Munich '05▸
MXP: Most Xtreme Primate '03
My Gal Sunday '14
Mystery Men '99
Mystic River '03▸
Naked Weapon '03
Nancy '18
Nancy Steele Is Missing '37
National Lampoon's The Don's Analyst '97
Nature Calls '12
Navy Blues '37
Never Say Die '94
New Blood '99
Nick of Time '95
The Night of the Following Day '69
Night People '54
The Nightmare Before Christmas '93▸
No Deposit, No Return '76
No Orchids for Miss Blandish '48
No Way Back '96
Nobel Son '08
Nobody Lives Forever '46▸
Obsession '49
Of Gods and Men '10▸
Oldboy '03▸
Oldboy '13
Oliver Twist '05▸
The One-Armed Swordsman '67▸
101 Dalmatians '96
One Small Hero '99
Operation Abduction '58
Operation Condor 2: The Armour of the Gods '86
Operation Delta Force 2: Mayday '97
Orphans '87▸
Otis '08
Out of Reach '04
Out of Sight '98▸
Pain & Gain '13
Paper Bullets '99
Perfect Strangers '03
A Perfect World '93
Perpetrators of the Crime '98
The Phynx '70
Pirates of the Caribbean: The Curse of the Black Pearl '03 ▸
The Pirates Who Don't Do Anything: A VeggieTales Movie '08
The Pleasure Drivers '05
The President's Man '00
Priest '11
The Prince '14
Prince of Pennsylvania '88
Prisoners '13 ▸
Private Obsession '94
Professional Soldier '35
Proof of Life '00
Pulse '03
Queen's Messenger II '01
Quentin Durward '55
The Quest '96
'R Xmas '01
Rage '14
Raising Arizona '87▸
Rambo: Last Blood '19
Ransom! '56
Ransom '96▸
Rapt '09
The Real McCoy '93
Red Eye '05▸
Red Serpent '02
Reef 2: High Tide '12
Renaissance '06
Rendition '07
Reprisal '18
The Return of the Scarlet Pimpernel '37
Return to Never Land '02
The Revenger '90
Revolver '75
Ring of Fire 2: Blood and Steel '92
Ring of the Musketeers '93
Rio Diablo '93
Riot '96
The Road Killers '95
Robin-B-Hood '06
Room '15
Rumpelstiltskin '96
Running Scared '06
Rush Hour '98
The Russian Specialist '05
Ruthless People '86▸
Sandokan the Great '63
Savage Abduction '73
Savages '12
Saw '04
Scenes of the Crime '01
Screwed '00
Second Sight '89
Seven Hours to Judgment '88
Seven Psychopaths '12▸
Shadow Man '06
Shadow on the Window '57
Shanghai Noon '00
Sharpe's Challenge '06
Sharpe's Enemy '94
Shattered '07
Shattered Image '93
Show Me '04
The Shrine '10
Sicario: Day of the Soldado '18
The Signal '14
Silver Hawk '04
Singham '11
6 Bullets '12
600 Miles '16
Sky Captain and the World of Tomorrow '04
Sleepless Night '11▸
Sleight '17
The Smurfs 2 '13
Snatched '17
Snipes '01
Son of the Pink Panther '93
Spartan '04▸
Special Forces '11
Split '16
Spy School '08
The Squeeze '77
Stakeout '62
Starved '97
Stealing Candy '04
Stealing Sinatra '04
Stingaree '34
Stolen '12
Street Fighter '94
Suicide Kings '97
Sunchaser '96
Super 8 '11
Switchback '97
Sympathy for Mr. Vengeance '02 ▸
Taken 2 '12
Taken '99
Taken '08
Taken for Ransom '13
Taken in Broad Daylight '09
The Tale of Despereaux '08
Tar '97
The Target '15
Tarzan and the Slave Girl '50
Tarzan Triumphs '43
Tarzan's New York Adventure '42
Teaching Mrs. Tingle '99
Ted '12▸
Ten Canoes '06
10 Cloverfield Lane '16▸
That Darn Cat '96
Thin Air '00
31 '16
Thou Shalt Not Kill. . .Except '87
A Thousand Cuts '12
The Three Burials of Melquiades Estrada '05▸
3 Ninjas '92
3 Ninjas Knuckle Up '95
3-Way '04
Tie Me Up! Tie Me Down! '90
To Grandmother's House We Go '94
Tom & Thomas '02
Towards Darkness '07
Toy Story 2 '99▸
Trade '07
Traded '16
Transporter 2 '05
The Transporter '02
The Transporter Refueled '15
The Trap '22
Trapped '02
Trapped '06
TripFall '00
The Triplets of Belleville '02▸
Tropix '02
Tsotsi '05▸
Tuck Everlasting '02
12 Rounds '09
12 Years a Slave '13▸
24 Days '14
The 24th Day '04
23 Paces to Baker Street '56
Twinsitters '95
Two Bits & Pepper '95
Valley of the Heart's Delight '07
Vanished '06
The Vanishing '93
Violent Blue '10
Waikiki Wedding '37▸
Waist Deep '06
The Warrior '01
The Wash '01
Way of the Gun '00
We Have Your Husband '11
The Wedding Guest '18
What Lola Wants '15
Whiskey Tango Foxtrot '16
Whistling in the Dark '41▸
Who Is Clark Rockefeller? '10
The Whole Ten Yards '04
The Wild Card '03
Wild Ones on Wheels '62
The Wind and the Lion '75▸
Wolverine '96
The Woman '11
World for Ransom '54
The World in His Arms '52
Wrong Side of Town '10
You Were Never Really Here '17▸
Your Highness '11

Killer Apes and Monkeys

***See also** Monkeyshines*
A*P*E* '76
Battle for the Planet of the Apes '73
Beneath the Planet of the Apes '70
The Bride & the Beast '58
Congo '95
Conquest of the Planet of the Apes '72
Dawn of the Planet of the Apes '14 ▸
Dr. Orloff and the Invisible Man '72
Gorilla '56
King Kong '33 ▸
King Kong '76
King Kong '05 ▸
King Kong Lives '86
King Kong *vs.* Godzilla '63
King of Kong Island '78
King of the Lost World '06
Kong: Skull Island '17
The Legend of Tarzan '16
Link '86
Mighty Joe Young '49
Mighty Joe Young '98
The Mighty Peking Man '77
Monkey Shines '88
Night Fright '67
Planet of the Apes '68▸
Rat Pfink a Boo-Boo '66
Rise of the Planet of the Apes '11▸
Sands of the Kalahari '65
Son of Ingagi '40
Son of Kong '33
War for the Planet of the Apes '17▸

Killer Appliances

Final Destination 2 '03
Ghost in the Machine '93
The Mangler '94
Maximum Overdrive '86
Microwave Massacre '83

Killer Beasts

***See also** Killer Apes and Monkeys; Killer Dogs; Killer Kats; Killer Pigs; Killer Rodents*
The Abomination '88
Attack of the Gryphon '07
Beaks: The Movie '87
Behemoth '11
Black Zoo '63
Bog '84
The Cave '05
Chupacabra Terror '05
Chupacabra *vs.* the Alamo '13
Clash of the Titans '81
Creature '11
Creepshow '82
Day of the Animals '77
Food of the Gods '76
47 Meters Down: Uncaged '19
The Grey '12
Grizzly '76
Half-Caste '04
Hybrid '07
Hyenas '10
Jabberwocky '77
Jason and the Argonauts '63▸
Jason and the Argonauts '00
Jaws of Satan '81
Jurassic Park '93▸
The Legend of Tarzan '16
Life '17
The Lost World: Jurassic Park 2 '97
The Meg '18
The Monster '16
Monsterwolf '10
Monty Python and the Holy Grail '75▸
Night of the Grizzly '66
Panzer '13
Project Viper '02
A Quiet Place '18▸
Return to Boggy Creek '77
Rise of the Gargoyles '09
Rodan '56
Shakma '89

▸ = rated three bones or higher

Shin Godzilla '16
Shriek of the Mutilated '74
Sleepwalkers '92
The Slime People '63
Snowbeast '77
Subspecies '90
Trog '70
Winterbeast '92

Killer Brains

***See also** Renegade Body Parts*

Black Friday '40
Blood of Ghastly Horror '72
Boltneck '98
Brain Damage '88
The Brain from Planet Arous '57
Brain of Blood '71
The Brain that Wouldn't Die '63
Donovan's Brain '53 ▶
Fiend without a Face '58

Killer Bugs and Slugs

Absentia '11
Ants '77
Arachnid '01
Arachnophobia '90
AVH: Alien *vs.* Hunter '07
Beginning of the End '57
Bionicle 3: Web of Shadows '05
The Black Scorpion '57
Black Swarm '07
Blood Beast Terror '67
Bug '75
Bug Buster '99
Bugged! '96
Bugs '03
Camel Spiders '11
Centipede '05
Creepers '85
Creepshow '82
The Deadly Mantis '57
Destination: Infestation '07
DNA '97
Dragon Wasps '12
Earth *vs.* the Spider '58
Earth *vs.* the Spider '01
Eight Legged Freaks '02
Empire of the Ants '77
Evil Spawn '87
Food of the Gods '76
The Giant Spider Invasion '75
The Glass Trap '04
Godzilla *vs.* Megaguirus '00
Godzilla *vs.* Megalon '76
Godzilla *vs.* Mothra '64
Godzilla *vs.* Mothra '92
Growth '10
Highly Dangerous '50
The Hive '08
In the Spider's Web '07
Infestation '09
Infested: Invasion of the Killer Bugs '02
Insecticidal '05
Island of the Dead '00
Killer Bees '02
King of the Lost World '06
Kingdom of the Spiders '77
Kiss of the Tarantula '75
The Lair of the White Worm '88 ▶
Locusts: The 8th Plague '05
Lord of the Rings: The Return of the King '03 ▶
Man of the House '95
Mimic 2 '01
Mimic 3: Sentinel '03
The Mist '07 ▶
Mongolian Death Worm '10
Monster from Green Hell '58
The Monster That Challenged the World '57
Mosquito '95
Mosquito Man '05
Mothra '62 ▶
Mysterious Island '61 ▶
Mysterious Island '05
Naked Jungle '54 ▶
The Nest '88
Parasite '82
Phase 4 '74
Rebirth of Mothra 2 '97
Rebirth of Mothra '96
Return of the Fly '59
Sand Serpents '09
The Scorpion's Tail '71
Skeeter '93
Slither '06 ▶
Slugs '87
Son of Godzilla '66
Spiders '00
Spiders 2: Breeding Ground '01
Spiders '13
Squirm '76
Starship Troopers '97 ▶
Starship Troopers 2: Hero of the Federation '04
Starship Troopers 3: Marauder '08
Subhuman '04
The Swarm '78
Tarantula '55 ▶
Tarantulas: The Deadly Cargo '77
Tarzan's Desert Mystery '43
Terror Out of the Sky '78
The Thaw '09
Them! '54 ▶
They Came from Within '75
They Crawl '01
Ticks '93
Tremors 2: Aftershocks '96
Tremors 3: Back to Perfection '01
Tremors '89
The Wasp Woman '59
The Wasp Woman '96
World Without End '56
The Worm Eaters '77

Killer Cars & Trucks

***See also** Motor Vehicle Dept.*

Black Cadillac '03
The Car '77
The Cars That Ate Paris '74 ▶
Christine '84
Death Race '08
Death Race 2000 '75
Death Sport '78
Duel '71 ▶
The Hearse '80
Mad Max '80 ▶
Mad Max: Beyond Thunderdome '85
Maximum Overdrive '86
Phantom Racer '09
The Road Warrior '82 ▶
Super Hybrid '10
Trucks '97
The Wraith '87
Wrecker '15

Killer Clowns

***See also** Carnivals & Clowns*

Carnival of Souls '98
Clown '16
Clownhouse '88
The Devil's Rejects '05
Final Draft '07
Fraternity Massacre at Hell Island '07
Frayed '07
Haunt '19
Hellbreeder '04
House of 1000 Corpses '03
It '17 ▶
It Chapter Two '19
Killer Klowns from Outer Space '88
Killjoy '81
The Last Circus '10
S.I.C.K. Serial Insane Clown Killer '03
Spawn '97 ▶
Stephen King's It '90
31 '16
When Evil Calls '06

Killer Dogs

***See also** King of Beasts (Dogs)*

The Breed '06
Bullet Head '17
Cerberus '05
Cujo '83
Devil Dog: The Hound of Hell '78
Hellhounds '09
The Hound of the Baskervilles '39 ▶
The Hound of the Baskervilles '59
The Hound of the Baskervilles '00
The Hound of the Baskervilles '02 ▶
Man's Best Friend '93
Monster Dog '82
The Omen '76
The Pack '77
Pet Sematary 2 '92
Play Dead '81
Resident Evil '02
Revenge '86
Zoltan. . . Hound of Dracula '78

Killer Dreams

Alias John Preston '56
Bad Dreams '88
Beneath '07
Blood Rage '87
Chronicle of the Raven '04
Dario Argento's Trauma '93
Dark Corners '06
Dead of Night '45 ▶
Dream No Evil '70
The Dreaming '88
Evil Eyes '04
Freddy's Dead: The Final Nightmare '91
In Dreams '98
In Your Dreams '07
Inception '10 ▶
Intruders '11
Jack O'Lantern '04
Killer by Nature '10
The Lathe of Heaven '80
The Lathe of Heaven '02
A Lizard in a Woman's Skin '71
My Soul to Take '10
A Nightmare on Elm Street 2: Freddy's Revenge '85
A Nightmare on Elm Street 3: Dream Warriors '87
A Nightmare on Elm Street 4: Dream Master '88
A Nightmare on Elm Street 5: Dream Child '89
A Nightmare on Elm Street '84
A Nightmare on Elm Street '10
NightScreams '97
Paprika '06
Parasomnia '08
Past Tense '06
Phantasm '79
Premonition '07
Scream of the Banshee '11
Strange Impersonation '46
Waking Life '01
Wes Craven's New Nightmare '94 ▶
Witches of the Caribbean '05

Killer Kats

***See also** Cats*

Batman Returns '92
The Black Cat '81
Bomba on Panther Island '49
Call of the Wilderness '32
Cat People '42 ▶
Cat People '82
Cat Women of the Moon '53
The Corpse Grinders '71
Curse of the Cat People '44 ▶
The Leopard Man '43
Maneater '07
Night Creature '79
Night of a Thousand Cats '72
Pet Sematary '89
The Pyramid '14
Sandokan the Great '63
Seven Deaths in the Cat's Eye '72
The Tiger's Claw '51
Track of the Cat '54
The Uninvited '88

Killer Kiddies

***See also** Childhood Visions*

Alice Sweet Alice '76
Babysitter Wanted '08
The Bad Seed '56
The Bad Seed '85
Battle for Skyark '15
Before and After '95
Case 39 '10
The Child '76
The Children '80
The Children '08
Children of the Corn '84
Children of the Corn 2: The Final Sacrifice '92
Children of the Corn 3: Urban Harvest '95
Children of the Corn 5: Fields of Terror '98
Children of the Corn: Revelation '01
Children of the Corn '09
Children of the Corn: Genesis '11
Children of the Damned '63
Citadel '12
Daddy's Girl '96
Damien: Omen 2 '78
The Good Son '93
Goodnight Mommy '15
Grace '09
Gummo '97
Happy Death Day '17
Home Movie '08
Hurt '09
Hush Little Baby '07
Joshua '07 ▶
The Little Girl Who Lives down the Lane '76
Lizzie '18
Milo '98
The Omen '76
The Omen '06
Orphan '09
The Other '72 ▶
Red Riding Hood '03
A Reflection of Fear '73
Relative Fear '95
Seconds Apart '11
666: The Child '06
Soft for Digging '01
Tropic Thunder '08 ▶
12/12/12 '12
Village of the Damned '60 ▶
Village of the Damned '95
Wake Wood '10
Way Past Cool '00
Whisper '07
Wicked Little Things '07

Killer Pigs

***See also** Pigs*

The Amityville Horror '79
Evilspeak '82
Pigs '73
Prey '10
Razorback '84

Killer Plants

Attack of the Killer Tomatoes '77
Attack of the Moon Zombies '11
Body Snatchers '93
Day of the Triffids '63 ▶
The Freakmaker '73
From Hell It Came '57
Invasion of the Body Snatchers '56 ▶
Invasion of the Body Snatchers '78 ▶
Invasion of the Pod People '07
Killer Tomatoes Eat France '91
Killer Tomatoes Strike Back '90
Little Shop of Horrors '60 ▶
Little Shop of Horrors '86 ▶
Mandrake '10
Matango '63
The Monster of Phantom Lake '06
Navy *vs.* the Night Monsters '66
Please Don't Eat My Mother '72
Return of the Killer Tomatoes! '88
The Ruins '08
Seedpeople '92
Seeds of Evil '76
Swamp Devil '08
The Womaneater '59
Yog, Monster from Space '71

Killer Reptiles

Age of the Hobbits '12
Alligator '80 ▶
Alligator 2: The Mutation '90
Anaconda 3: The Offspring '08
The Big Alligator River '79
Black Water '07
Boa *vs.* Python '04
Crawl '19
Croc '07
Crocodile 2: Death Swamp '01
Crocodile '81
Crocodile '00
Croczilla '12
Destroy All Monsters '68
Dinocroc '04
Dinocroc Vs. Supergator '10
Dinosaurus! '60
Dragonslayer '81 ▶
Frogs '72
Gamera, the Invincible '66
Gamera *vs.* Barugon '66
Gamera *vs.* Gaos '67
Gamera *vs.* Guiron '69
Gamera *vs.* Zigra '71
Gator King '70
The Giant Behemoth '59
The Giant Gila Monster '59
Godzilla '98
Godzilla, King of the Monsters '56
Godzilla on Monster Island '72
Godzilla Raids Again '55
Godzilla 2000 '99 ▶
Godzilla *vs.* King Ghidora '91
Godzilla *vs.* Mechagodzilla II '93
Godzilla *vs.* Megalon '76
Godzilla *vs.* Monster Zero '68
Godzilla *vs.* Mothra '64
Godzilla *vs.* the Cosmic Monster '74
Godzilla *vs.* the Sea Monster '66
Godzilla *vs.* the Smog Monster '72
Godzilla's Revenge '69
The Great Wall '17
Hell Comes to Frogtown '88
Jurassic World: Fallen Kingdom '18
King Kong *vs.* Godzilla '63
King of the Lost World '06
Komodo '99
Komodo *vs.* Cobra '05
Lake Placid '99
Lake Placid 2 '07
Lake Placid 3 '10
Lake Placid: The Final Chapter '12
Mega Python Vs. Gatoroid '11
The Mole People '56
Mothra '62 ▶
Mysterious Island '05
Primeval '07
Pterodactyl '05
Q (The Winged Serpent) '82 ▶
Rana: The Legend of Shadow Lake '75
Rattlers '76
The Relic '96
Reptilian '99
Reptilicus '62
Return to Frogtown '92
Rogue '07
Stanley '72
Venom '82

Killer Rodents

***See also** Bats; Nice Mice*

The Bat '59
The Bat People '74
Bats '99
Burial of the Rats '95
The Devil Bat '41
Flushed Away '06 ▶
Food of the Gods '76
Food of the Gods: Part 2 '88
The Killer Shrews '59
Mulberry Street '06
Nezulla the Rat Monster '02
Night of the Lepus '72
Nightwing '79
Of Unknown Origin '83
The Rats '01
Trilogy of Terror 2 '96
Willard '03

Killer Sea Critters

***See also** Deep Blue; Go Fish; Killer Beasts*

Alligator '80 ▶
Around the World Under the Sea '65
Attack of the Jurassic Shark '12
Attack of the Swamp Creature '75
Barracuda '78
The Beach Girls and the Monster '65
The Beast '96
The Beast from 20,000 Fathoms '53
Beneath Loch Ness '01
The Bermuda Depths '78
Bermuda Tentacles '14
Beyond Atlantis '73
Blood Lake '14
Blood Surf '00
Bloodstalkers '76
The Cave '05
Creature from Black Lake '76
Creature from the Black Lagoon '54 ▶
Creature from the Haunted Sea '60
Creature of Destruction '67
The Creature Walks among Us '56
Creatures from the Abyss '94
Curse of the Swamp Creature '66
Dark Tide '12
Dark Waters '03
Deep Blue '03 ▶
Deep Blue Sea '99
Deep Rising '98
Deep Shock '03
Deepstar Six '89
Demon of Paradise '87
Devil Monster '46
Dinoshark '10
Eye of the Beast '07
Fer-De-Lance '74
Finding Nemo '03 ▶
The Flesh Eaters '64
47 Meters Down '17
Frankenfish '04
Godzilla '54
Godzilla *vs.* Mothra '64
Godzilla *vs.* the Sea Monster '66
Gorgo '61
The Great Alligator '81
Hello Down There '69
Horror of Party Beach '64
The Host '06 ▶
Humanoids from the Deep '80
Humanoids from the Deep '96
In the Heart of the Sea '15
Into the Blue '05
It Came from Beneath the Sea '55 ▶
Jason and the Argonauts '63 ▶
Jaws '75 ▶
Jaws 2 '78
Jaws 3 '83
Jaws of Death '76
Jaws: The Revenge '87
Jersey Shore Shark Attack '12
Kraken: Tentacles of the Deep '06
Legend of the Dinosaurs and Monster Birds '77
Loch Ness Terror '07
Malibu Shark Attack '09
The McConnell Story '55
Mean Streets '73 ▶
Mega Piranha '10
Mega Shark *vs.* Crocosaurus '10
Mega Shark Vs. Giant Octopus '09
Megalodon '03
Memphis Belle '90 ▶

▶ = rated three bones or higher

Moby Dick '11
Monster from the Ocean Floor '54
The Monster That Challenged the World '57
Mysterious Island '61 ▸
New York, New York '77 ▸
None But the Brave '65
Obsession '76
Octaman '71
Octopus 2: River of Fear '02
Octopus '00
Orca '77
Parasite '03
Penguins of Madagascar '14
The Phantom from 10,000 Leagues '56
Piranha '78
Piranha 2: The Spawning '82
Piranha 3D '10
Piranha 3DD '11
Piranha '95
Reap the Wild Wind '42
Red Water '01
The Reef '10
Revenge of the Creature '55
Scorpion with Two Tails '82
Sea Beast '08
Shark! '68
Shark Attack '99
Shark Attack 2 '00
Shark Attack 3: Megalodon '02
Shark Island '12
Shark Night 3D '11
Shark Swarm '08
Sharknado 2: The Second One '14
Sharknado 3: Oh Hell No! '15
Sharknado '13
Sharknado: The 4th Awakens '16
Sharktopus '10
The She-Creature '56
She Creature '01
Sherlock Holmes '10
Snakehead Terror '04
Snow Shark '11
Sphere '97
Swamp Shark '11
Swamp Thing '82
Tarzan and the Mermaids '48
Tentacles '77
Tiger Shark '32
20,000 Leagues under the Sea '54 ▸
20,000 Leagues Under the Sea '97
2-Headed Shark Attack '12
2010: Moby Dick '10
Up from the Depths '79
The Viking Women and the Sea Serpent '57
War of the Gargantuas '70

Killer Spouses

See also Wedding Hell

Black Widow '87 ▸
Blind Corner '63
Bluebeard '09
Body Heat '81 ▸
Catacombs '64
Collision '13
Cradle of Lies '06
Dead by Sunset '95
Deliberate Intent '01
Diabolique '55 ▸
Diabolique '96
The Disappearance of Vonnie '94
Double Cross '06
Double Jeopardy '99
Dragonwyck '46
Drew Peterson: Untouchable '12
Fatal Honeymoon '12
Four Flies on Grey Velvet '72
Fracture '07
High Stakes '93
Hit By Lightning '14
Julie '56
The Kreutzer Sonata '08
1922 '17
The Pastor's Wife '11
The Pleasure Garden '25
Proof of Lies '06
She Devil '57
Sleep, My Love '48
Sleeping with the Enemy '91
Souls for Sale '23
What Lies Beneath '00
White Oleander '02
A Woman, a Gun and a Noodle Shop '10
Woman in Hiding '49

Killer Teens

The Babysitter '17
Beautiful Boy '10
Brightburn '19
Devon's Ghost: Legend of the Bloody Boy '05
Disturbing Behavior '98
Happy Death Day '17
Heathers '89 ▸
I'm Not Ashamed '16
Little Sweetheart '90
River's Edge '87 ▸
Scream '96 ▸
Sins of Our Youth '16
Under One Roof '02
United States of Leland '03
We Monsters '15

Killer Toys

Amityville Dollhouse '96
Annabelle '14
Annabelle Comes Home '19
Bride of Chucky '98
Child's Play '88
Child's Play 2 '90
Child's Play 3 '91
Child's Play '19
Dance of Death '68
The Dead Pool '88
Dead Silence '07
Demonic Toys '90
Devil Doll '36 ▸
Devil Doll '64
Dollman vs Demonic Toys '93
Dolls '87
Dolly Dearest '92
Halloween 3: Season of the Witch '82
Magic '78
Pinocchio's Revenge '96
Poltergeist '82 ▸
The Preacher's Wife '96
Puppet Master '89
Puppet Master 2 '90
Puppet Master 3: Toulon's Revenge '90
Puppet Master 4 '93
Puppet Master 5: The Final Chapter '94
Puppet Master: The Littlest Reich '18
Retro Puppet Master '99
Seed of Chucky '04
Silent Night, Deadly Night 5: The Toymaker '91
Small Soldiers '98
Tales from the Hood '95
Trilogy of Terror '75
Trilogy of Terror 2 '96

Killing Sprees

The Act of Killing '13 ▸
Avengement '19
Beautiful Boy '10
Dark Places '15
Desierto '16
God Bless America '11
Green Room '15 ▸
Halloween '18
The Haunting of Sharon Tate '19
I'm Not Ashamed '16
Into the Abyss '11 ▸
John Doe: Vigilante '14 ▸
Killers Anonymous '19
Mechanic: Resurrection '16
Playback '12
The Purge: Election Year '16
Rampage '09
The Rig '10
Scream 4 '11
September Dawn '07
Sightseers '12
Sweet Virginia '17
3 from Hell '19
We Need to Talk About Kevin '11 ▸

King of Beasts (Dogs)

See also Killer Dogs

The Accidental Tourist '88 ▸
Ace of Hearts '08
Across the Bridge '57
The Adventures of Milo & Otis '89 ▸
After the Thin Man '36 ▸
Air Bud '97
Air Bud 2: Golden Receiver '98
Air Bud 3: World Pup '00
Air Bud 4: Seventh Inning Fetch '02
Air Bud 5: Buddy Spikes Back '03
All Dogs Go to Heaven '89
All Dogs Go to Heaven 2 '95
Alpha '18
Amores Perros '00 ▸
Annie '14
The Art of Racing in the Rain '19
As Good As It Gets '97 ▸
Aussie and Ted's Great Adventure '09
The Awful Truth '37 ▸
Babe '95 ▸
Babe: Pig in the City '98
The Back-Up Plan '10
Bad Moon '96
Balto '95
Bark! '02
Baxter '89
Beautiful Creatures '00
Because of Winn-Dixie '05
Beethoven '92
Beethoven's 2nd '93
Beethoven's 3rd '00
Beethoven's 4th '01
Beethoven's 5th '03
Beethoven's Christmas Adventure '11
Behave Yourself! '52
Benji '74 ▸
Benji: Off the Leash! '04
Benji the Hunted '87
Best in Show '00 ▸
Beverly Hills Chihuahua 2 '10
Beverly Hills Chihuahua 3: Viva La Fiesta! '12
Big Red '62
Bingo '91
Blondie Brings Up Baby '39
Blondie in Society '41
Bolt '08 ▸
The Boss Baby '17
A Boy and His Dog '75
Call of the Wild 3D '09
The Call of the Wild '35 ▸
Call of the Wild '72
Call of the Wild '93
The Case of the Howling Dog '34
Cats & Dogs '01
Cats & Dogs: The Revenge of Kitty Galore '10
Challenge To Be Free '76
Challenge to White Fang '86
Children of the Wild '37
Chilly Dogs '01
C.H.O.M.P.S. '79
A Christmas Wedding Tail '11
Clean Slate '94
Clifford's Really Big Movie '04
Closed Curtain '13 ▸
Cold Dog Soup '89
Cool Hand Luke '67 ▸
Courage of Lassie '46
Crackie '09
A Cry in the Dark '88 ▸
Cujo '83
Cybermutt '02
Danny Boy '46
Daring Dobermans '73
Dark Hazard '34
Darling Companion '12
Dead Dog '00
Deep Valley '47
Devil Dog: The Hound of Hell '78
Disgrace '08
Disney's Teacher's Pet '04 ▸
The Doberman Gang '72
Dr. Dolittle '98
Dr. Dolittle 4: Tail to the Chief '08
Dr. Dolittle: Million Dollar Mutts '09
Dr. Seuss' How the Grinch Stole Christmas '00
The Dog Lover '16
A Dog Named Christmas '09
A Dog of Flanders '59
A Dog of Flanders '99
Dog Park '98
Dog Pound Shuffle '75 ▸
The Dog Who Saved Christmas '09
The Dog Who Saved Christmas Vacation '10
The Dog Who Saved Easter '15
The Dog Who Saved Halloween '11
The Dog Who Saved the Holidays '12
The Dog Who Stopped the War '84
A Dog Year '09
The Dogfather '10
Dogville Shorts '30
Doogal '05
Down and Out in Beverly Hills '86
The Drop '14 ▸
The Duke '99
Duke '12
Dumb & Dumber '94
Eight Below '06
Eyes in the Night '42
Eyes of an Angel '91
Familiar Strangers '08
Fangs of the Wild '54
Far from Home: The Adventures of Yellow Dog '94
Finding Rin Tin Tin '07
First Dog '10
Fluke '95
For the Love of Benji '77
The Fox and the Hound '81 ▸
Frank '07
Frankenweenie '12 ▸
The Gay Dog '54
George! '70
Ghetto Dawg 2: Out of the Pits '05
Ghetto Dawg '02
Girl's Best Friend '08
The Gold Retrievers '10
A Golden Christmas 2: The Second Tail '11
A Golden Christmas '09
Good Boy! '03
Goodbye, My Lady '56
Goodbye to Language '14 ▸
A Goofy Movie '94
Great Adventure '75
Greyfriars Bobby '61
Hachiko: A Dog's Tale '09
Heavy Petting '07
Heck's Way Home '95
The Hills Have Eyes '77
Homeward Bound: The Incredible Journey '93 ▸
Homeward Bound 2: Lost in San Francisco '96
Hotel for Dogs '09
The Hound of the Baskervilles '59
I Am Legend '07 ▸
The Incredible Journey '63
Iron Will '93
Isle of Dogs '18 ▸
It Shouldn't Happen to a Dog '46
It's a Dog's Life '55
Jack London's The Call of the Wild '97
The Jerk '79
Jesse Stone: Innocents Lost '11
Jesse Stone: No Remorse '10
Jr. Detective Agency '09
Jury Duty '95
K-9 '89
K-911 '99
K-9000 '89
Kavik the Wolf Dog '80
Lady and the Tramp '55 ▸
Lady and the Tramp '19
Lassie '94
Lassie, Come Home '43
Lassie's Great Adventure '62
Legally Blonde 2: Red White & Blonde '03
Legally Blonde '01
Legend of the Northwest '78
Lightning Warrior '31
Little Heroes '91
Little Nicky '00
The Little Rascals '94
The Lone Defender '32
Look Who's Talking Now '93
Lost and Found '99
The Mad Room '69
Man Trouble '92
Man's Best Friend '93
Marley & Me '08
Marley & Me: The Puppy Years '11
Marmaduke '10
The Mask '94 ▸
Meet the Fockers '04
Men in Black 2 '02
The Mexican '01
Michael '96
Milo & Otis '89
Mrs. Brown, You've Got a Lovely Daughter '68
Mr. Peabody & Sherman '14
Mr. Superinvisible '73
Monster Dog '82
Monster-in-Law '05
More Dogs Than Bones '00
Must Love Dogs '05
My Dog Shep '46
My Dog Skip '99 ▸
My Dog, the Thief '69
My Magic Dog '97
Dean Spanley '08
Napoleon '96
Nikki, the Wild Dog of the North '61
Nutty Professor 2: The Klumps '00
Obsession '49
Oh, Heavenly Dog! '80
Old Yeller '57 ▸
Oliver & Company '88
101 Dalmatians '61 ▸
101 Dalmatians '96
Open Season 2 '08
Owd Bob '97
The Pack '77
The Painted Hills '51
Paranormal Activity 2 '10
Ping! '99
The Plague Dogs '82
Play Dead '81
Princess O'Rourke '43
Quigley '03
Rock Dog '17
Rough Magic '95
Rover Dangerfield '91
Rugrats Go Wild! '03
The Sandlot '93 ▸
Santa Buddies '09
Santa Paws 2: The Santa Pups '12
Savage Sam '63
Saving Shiloh '06
Scoob! '20
Scooby-Doo '02
Screwed '00
The Search for Santa Paws '10
The Secret Life of Pets 2 '19
Seven Psychopaths '12 ▸
Shadow of the Thin Man '41 ▸
The Shaggy D.A. '76
The Shaggy Dog '59
The Shaggy Dog '06
Sharpay's Fabulous Adventure '11
A Shaun the Sheep Movie: Farmageddon '19 ▸
Sherlock: Undercover Dog '94
Shiloh 2: Shiloh Season '99
Shiloh '97
Sleeping Dogs Lie '06
Snow Buddies '08
Snow Dogs '02
Soccer Dog: The Movie '98
Son of Lassie '45
Song of the Thin Man '47
Space Buddies '08
Spooky Buddies '11
Station Jim '01
Storm in a Teacup '37
The Stray '17
Super Buddies '13
Sweet November '01
There's Something about Mary '98 ▸
They Only Kill Their Masters '72
The Thin Man '34 ▸
The Thin Man Goes Home '44
Think Like a Dog '20
Three Wishes '95
Thunder In the Valley '47
To Dance with the White Dog '93 ▸
Toby McTeague '87
Togo '19 ▸
Tom and Jerry: The Movie '93
Top Dog '95
Tracked '98
The Triplets of Belleville '02 ▸
The Truth about Cats and Dogs '96 ▸
Turner and Hooch '89
12 Christmas Wishes For My Dog '11
The Twelve Dogs of Christmas '05
12 Dogs of Christmas: Great Puppy Rescue '12
The Ugly Dachshund '65
Umberto D '55 ▸
The Underdog '43
Up '09 ▸
Watchers 2 '90
Watchers '88
Watchers Reborn '98
Wendy and Lucy '08 ▸
What Happens Next '11
Where the Red Fern Grows '74
Where the Red Fern Grows: Part 2 '92
White Dog '82
White Fang 2: The Myth of the White Wolf '94
White Fang '36
White Fang and the Hunter '85
The Wizard of Oz '39 ▸
Wonder Boys '00 ▸
You Lucky Dog '10
You Never Can Tell '51
Zeus and Roxanne '96
Zoltan. . . Hound of Dracula '78

Kings

See Royalty; Royalty, British; Royalty, French; Royalty, Russian

Korean War

American Gun '02 ▸
Battle Circus '53
Battle Hymn '57
Battle of Jangsari '19
Battle Zone '52
Big Fish '03 ▸
The Bridges at Toko-Ri '55 ▸
Dragonfly Squadron '54
Fixed Bayonets! '51 ▸
For the Boys '91
The Glory Brigade '53
The Hook '63
The Hunters '58
Indignation '16
Iron Angel '64
The Last Picture Show '71 ▸
MacArthur '77
The Manchurian Candidate '62 ▸
Marines, Let's Go '61
M*A*S*H '70 ▸
M*A*S*H: Goodbye, Farewell & Amen '83 ▸
Men in War '57
Men of the Fighting Lady '54 ▸
The Nun and the Sergeant '62
One Minute to Zero '52
Pork Chop Hill '59 ▸
The Rack '56
Sayonara '57 ▸
The Steel Helmet '51 ▸
Target Zero '55
Time Limit '57
War Hunt '62

▸ = rated three bones or higher

Ku Klux Klan

BlacKkKlansman '18 ▶
Imperium '16

Kung Fu

See Martial Arts

L.A.

See also Earthquakes

Abandoned '10
Abbott and Costello in Hollywood '45
Act of Violence '48
Against the Law '98
Agent of Death '99
Akeelah and the Bee '06
An Alan Smithee Film: Burn, Hollywood, Burn '97
The Alarmist '98
All About Nina '18
All About You '01
All Nighter '17
All Over the Guy '01
Almighty Thor '11
Alvin and the Chipmunks '07
Always Outnumbered Always Outgunned '98 ▶
Amazing Grace '19 ▶
Ambushed '13
American East '07
An American Rhapsody '01 ▶
American Virgin '98
Americano '11
Amy's O '02
Android Cop '14
Angel's Dance '99
Annie Claus is Coming to Town '11
The Anniversary Party '01 ▶
Answers to Nothing '11
Apartment Troubles '15
The Apocalypse '07
Arc '06
Armored '09
Asian Stories '06
Ask the Dust '06
Assault on Precinct 13 '76 ▶
The Assistants '09
August '11
The Aviator '04 ▶
Baby Boy '01
Backfire '50
Bad Influence '90
Bad Reputation '18
Bad Words '13
A Bag of Hammers '11
Ballistica '10
Bandits '01
Bang '95
The Banker '20
Bar Hopping '00
Bark! '02
Barton Fink '91 ▶
Battle: Los Angeles '11
Battlefield America '12
Be Cool '05
Beach Patrol '79
Bean '97 ▶
The Beatnicks '00
Beatriz at Dinner '17
A Beautiful Life '08
Beefcake '99
Being Canadian '15 ▶
Being Charlie '16
Bellyfruit '99
Best of the Best: Without Warning '98
A Better Life '11 ▶
Between Midnight and Dawn '50
The Beverly Hillbillies '93
Beverly Hills Brats '89
Beverly Hills Ninja '96
Beyond Suspicion '00
The Big Bang '11
The Big Fall '96
Big Fat Liar '02
The Big Lebowski '97 ▶
Big Momma's House 2 '06
The Big Picture '89
The Big Take '18
The Big Tease '99
The Biggest Little Farm '18 ▶
Biker Boyz '03
Billy's Hollywood Screen Kiss '98
The Black Dahlia '06
Black Gunn '72
Black or White '14
Black Scorpion 2: Ground Zero '96
Blast from the Past '98
The Bling Ring '11
The Bling Ring '13 ▶
Blood & Concrete: A Love Story '91
Blow '01
Blue Streak '99
The Blue Tooth Virgin '09
Body Double '84 ▶
Border Blues '03
Born to Lose '99
Bottoms Up '06
Bowfinger '99 ▶
A Boy. A Girl. A Dream. '18
The Boys Next Door '85
Bram Stoker's Way of the Vampire '05
Bread and Roses '00
Break of Dawn '88
The Breaks '99
Brian Banks '18
Bright '17
The Broken Hearts Club '00 ▶
Broken Vessels '98 ▶
Brown's Requiem '98
Bruno '09
Bucky Larson: Born to Be a Star '11
Bulletproof '96
Bunco Squad '50
Burlesque '10
Cake '14
California Solo '12
Call Me: The Rise and Fall of Heidi Fleiss '04
Candyman 3: Day of the Dead '98
Capital Games '13
Cardboard Boxer '16
Carolina '03
Carpool Guy '05
Celebrity '98 ▶
Cement '99
Chain of Souls '00
Chandler '71
Changeling '08 ▶
The Chapman Report '62
Charlotte Sometimes '02
Chasing Papi '03
Chef '14 ▶
El Chicano '19
Christmas in Compton '12
A Cinderella Story '04
Circuit '02
City of Angels '98
City of Gold '16 ▶
City of Industry '96
The Clapper '18
Cleopatra's Second Husband '00
Code Two '53
Collateral '04 ▶
Collateral Damage '02
Color of a Brisk and Leaping Day '95
Come See the Paradise '90 ▶
Confidence '03
Constantine '05
Cool Blue '88
Cornered! '09
Cradle 2 the Grave '03
The Craft '96
Crank '06
Crank: High Voltage '09
Crash '05 ▶
crazy/beautiful '01
Crazy Eyes '12
Crimes of Passion '84 ▶
Criminal '04
The Crimson Kimono '59
Crocodile Dundee in Los Angeles '01
Cross '11
Crossing Over '09
The Crow 2: City of Angels '96
The Curse of La Llorona '19
Cursed '04
Cybernator '91
Cyxork 7 '06
The D Train '15
Daddy Issues '20
Dark Blue '03 ▶
Dark City '50
Dark Justice '00
Dark World '08
Darkwolf '03
David Crosby: Remember My Name '19
The Day After Tomorrow '04
The Day of the Locust '75 ▶
The Day the Earth Stopped '08
A Day Without a Mexican '04
Daybreak '01
Dead Again '91 ▶
Dead Air '08
Dead Bang '89
The Dead Girl '06
Dead Lenny '06
Dead Sexy '01
Dear God '96
Dear Santa '11
Death Among Friends '75
Death Wish 2 '82
Decisions '10
Defying Gravity '99
Delta Heat '92
Den of Thieves '18
The Dentist '96
The Departure '20
Destroyer '18
Devil in a Blue Dress '95 ▶
Devil's Knight '03
Die Hard '88 ▶
Digging for Fire '15
Dinner and Driving '97
Dirty '05
The Disaster Artist '17 ▶
Disney's The Kid '00
Doc Hollywood '91
Dog Days '18
The Dog Problem '06
Domino '05
Don't Be a Menace to South Central While Drinking Your Juice in the Hood '95
The Doom Generation '95 ▶
Dope '15 ▶
Dorfman in Love '11
Double Down '01
Douchebag '10
Down in the Valley '05
Drag Me to Hell '09
Drift '00
Drive '11 ▶
Dunston Checks In '95
East Side Story '07
Eastside '99
Echo in the Canyon '18
8mm '98
The Elder Son '06
Elektra Luxx '10
Ellie Parker '05 ▶
Encino Man '92
The End of Violence '97
End of Watch '12 ▶
Endings, Beginnings '20
Entertainment '15
Entourage '15
Escape from L.A. '96
ESL: English as a Second Language '05
An Evergreen Christmas '14
The Exiles '61
Exit Through the Gift Shop '10
The Face of Love '13
Face/Off '97 ▶
The Fall '06
Falling Down '93
Fast & Furious '09
The Fast and the Furious '01
Fast Lane '08
Fast Sofa '01
Fast Times at Ridgemont High '82 ▶
Female Perversions '96
52 Pick-Up '86
Filly Brown '12
Film Stars Don't Die in Liverpool '17
Final Combination '93
Finding Bliss '09
The First Time '12
Five Came Back '17 ▶
(500) Days of Summer '09
Fix '08
Flashbacks of a Fool '08
The Fluffer '01
Forfeit '07
44 Minutes: The North Hollywood Shootout '03
Foster '18
Four Dogs Playing Poker '00
Four Rooms '95
Fracture '07
Fragments '08
Frankie and Alice '10
Free Enterprise '98
Free Samples '12
The Freebie '10
Freeway '88
Frenemy '09
Friends with Money '06
Frisk '95
From Prada to Nada '11
Full Contact '93
Full Frontal '02
Funny People '09
The Future '11
The Gambler '14
Gang Boys '97
Gangster Squad '13
Garden of the Moon '38
Garden Party '08
Gemini '17
Get Him to the Greek '10
Get On the Bus '96 ▶
Get Shorty '95 ▶
Get Smart '08
Girl Meets Boy '13
Glam '97
The Glass House '01
The Glimmer Man '96
A Glimpse Inside the Mind of Charles Swan III '12
Gloria Bell '18
Go '99 ▶
Goal! The Dream Begins '06
Gods and Monsters '98 ▶
Going Clear: Scientology and the Prison of Belief '15 ▶
Going Shopping '05
Going to America '15
Good Dick '08
Goodbye, Lover '99
Gordon Glass '07
Grace of Monaco '14
Grace Unplugged '13
Grand Canyon '91 ▶
Grand Theft Parsons '03
The Green Hornet '11
Greenberg '10
Gridiron Gang '06
Grindin' '07
The Guardian '01
Guarding Eddy '04
Hail, Caesar! '16 ▶
Hair Show '04
Halls of Anger '70
Hancock '08
Hanging Up '99
Happy Endings '05
Hard As Nails '01
Hard Candy '06
Harsh Times '05
The Haunting of Sharon Tate '19
Havoc '05
He Walked by Night '48 ▶
Heart of Stone '01
Heat '95 ▶
Heaven Ain't Hard to Find '10
Hell Bound '57
Henry Poole Is Here '08 ▶
Hijacking Hollywood '97
The Hillside Stranglings '04
Hit and Run '12
Hit Man '72
Holding Trevor '07
The Holiday '06
Hollywood Homicide '03
Hollywood, Je T'Aime '09
Hollywoodland '06
Holy Hell '16
Home Again '17
Homicide '49
Hopelessly in June '11
Hostage '05
Hot Blood '56
Hot Tamale '06
The Hottie and the Nottie '08
How to Kill Your Neighbor's Dog '01
How to Lose Your Lover '04
How to Make Love to a Woman '09
Hugo Pool '97
Hurlyburly '98
Hustler White '96
I Am Omega '07
I Escaped from the Gestapo '43
I Love You, Alice B. Toklas! '68
I Love You, Don't Touch Me! '97
I Love Your Work '03
I Melt With You '11
iCrime '11
In a World... '13 ▶
The Informers '09
Ingrid Goes West '17
Inherent Vice '14 ▶
Internal Affairs '90
Intolerable Cruelty '03
The Invitation '16 ▶
Irene in Time '09
The Italian Job '03 ▶
It's a Disaster '12
It's My Party '95
Jack and Jill '11
Jackie Brown '97 ▶
Jay and Silent Bob Reboot '19
Jimmy Hollywood '94
johns '96
The Journey of Jared Price '00
Julia '08
Just Write '97
K-911 '99
Kate's Addiction '99
The Kid and I '05
The Kids Are All Right '10 ▶
Kill Bill Vol. 1 '03 ▶
Killer of Sheep '77 ▶
Kings '17
Kiss Kiss Bang Bang '05 ▶
Kiss Tomorrow Goodbye '00
Kitchen Privileges '00
Krews '10
LA Apocalypse '14
L.A. Confidential '97 ▶
L.A. Dicks '05
La La Land '16 ▶
An L.A. Minute '18
L.A. Story '91 ▶
L.A. Twister '04
L.A. Vice '89
Lady Jayne Killer '03
Lakeview Terrace '08 ▶
Land of Plenty '04
L.A.P.D.: To Protect and Serve '01
Last Call: The Final Chapter of F. Scott Fitzgerald '02
The Last Days of Frankie the Fly '96
Late Last Night '99
Latin Dragon '03
Laughing to the Bank '13
Laurel Canyon '02
Lawnmower Man 2: Beyond Cyberspace '95
The Learning Curve '01
Let the Devil Wear Black '99
Lethal Weapon 4 '98
Let's Be Cops '14
Liberty Stands Still '02
Lies & Alibis '06
Life Happens '11
Life of Lemon '11
Like Crazy '11 ▶
Lime Salted Love '06
The Limey '99 ▶
The Lincoln Lawyer '11
Linda Ronstadt: The Sound of My Voice '19 ▶
Living in Peril '97
The Lodger '09
Long-Term Relationship '06
Lost Angels '89
Love, Antosha '19 ▶
Love Don't Cost a Thing '03
The Loved One '65
Loveless in Los Angeles '07
The Low Life '95
Lowlife '17
Lowriders '17
Luminarias '99
Luster '02
The M Word '14
MacArthur Park '01
Madness in the Method '19
The Man from Elysian Fields '01 ▶
Man-Trap '61
Maneater '09
Maniac '12
Manpower '41
Maps to the Stars '14
Marriage Story '19 ▶
Matrimonium '05
Matter of Trust '98
Mayor of the Sunset Strip '03 ▶
The Meddler '15 ▶
Meet Market '08
Memento '00 ▶
Men '97
Mercy '09
The Mexican '01
Mexican Gangster '08
Michael Jackson's This Is It '09
Mid90s '18
Million Dollar Arm '14
Million Dollar Baby '04 ▶
The Missing Person '09
Mr. Roosevelt '17
The Mod Squad '99
Model Shop '69
Modern Vampires '98
Mojave '15
Mommie Dearest '81
More Dogs Than Bones '00
Mortal Challenge '97
Mother and Child '09
Ms. Purple '19
Mulholland Drive '01 ▶
The Muppets '11 ▶
Murder by Contract '58
The Muse '99
My Gun Is Quick '57
My Uncle: The Alien '96
Nancy Drew '07
National Lampoon Presents Cattle Call '06
National Security '03
The Neon Demon '16
Never Die Alone '04
Never Say Macbeth '07
The New Age '94
Next '07
The Next Best Thing '00
The Nice Guys '16 ▶
Nick of Time '95
The Nickel Children '05
The Nickel Ride '74
Night at the Golden Eagle '02
A Night at the Roxbury '98
Night Hunter '95
Night on Earth '91 ▶
Night Stalker '09
Nightcrawler '14 ▶
Nightstalker '02
The Nines '07 ▶
1941 '79
Obselidia '10
The Odd Couple 2 '98
On the Doll '07
Once Upon A Time... In Hollywood '19 ▶
187 '97
100 Mile Rule '02
100 Million BC '08
One Last Ride '03
Open House '10
The Outsider '14
Overnight '03 ▶
Pandemic '07
Paparazzi '04
Paper Bullets '99
Parental Guidance '98
Passenger Side '09
Paulie '98
Peep World '10
The Penthouse '10
People Like Us '12
The Perfect Host '10
Perfect Strangers '50
Permanent Midnight '98
Pete Smalls Is Dead '10
Phat Beach '96
Pie in the Sky '95
The Player '92 ▶
Point Blank '67
Pornography: A Thriller '10
A Portrait of James Dean: Joshua Tree, 1951 '12
Powder Blue '09
Predator 2 '90
Prey for Rock and Roll '03 ▶
The Prowler '51

P.S. Your Cat is Dead! '02
The Purge: Anarchy '14
Pursuit of Happiness '01
Quarantine '08
Quiet Days in Hollywood '97
Quinceanera '06 ▶
Race '99
Radio Stars on Parade '45
Raise Your Voice '04
Rampage: The Hillside Strangler Murders '04
Rampart '11
Real Women Have Curves '02 ▶
Recoil '97
Red Line '13
Redbelt '08 ▶
Relax. . . It's Just Sex! '98
Relentless '89
Remarkable Power '08
The Replacement Killers '98
Repo Chick '09
Repo Man '83 ▶
Resident Evil: Afterlife '10
Revenge Quest '96
The Rewrite '15
Right at Your Door '06
Riot '96
Riot in the Streets '96
Rize '05 ▶
Road Hard '15
Roadblock '51
Rock of Ages '12
Roman J. Israel, Esq. '17
Roman Polanski: Wanted and Desired '08
Ruby Sparks '12
Rules Don't Apply '16
Rumor Has It. . . '05
Rumpelstiltskin '96
Running Mates '00
Running Woman '98
Rush Hour '98
Ruthless People '86 ▶
Safe House '99
The Satan Bug '65
Save the Tiger '73 ▶
Scene of the Crime '49
The Scenesters '09
Scorcher '02
Scream 3 '00
Seamless '00
Seed of Chucky '04
Set It Off '96
Seven Psychopaths '12 ▶
Seven Stages to Achieve Eternal Bliss '20
Sex Tape '14
Sexy Evil Genius '13
Shadow of Doubt '98
Shakedown '02
Shakedown on the Sunset Strip '88
Sharknado '13
Shattered Innocence '87
Sherrybaby '06
Shopgirl '05 ▶
Short Cuts '93 ▶
Showtime '02
Shrink '09
Side by Side '12 ▶
Sing You Sinners '38
The Singing Detective '03
A Single Man '09 ▶
Sink or Swim '97
S.I.S. '08
Sister Aimee: The Aimee Semple McPherson Story '06
666: The Beast '07
Sixth and Main '77
Skyline '10
Skyscraper '95
Slaves of Hollywood '99
Sleeper Cell '05
SMART: Specialized Mobile Animal Rescue Team '16
Smiley Face '07
Smiling Fish & Goat on Fire '99
Sol Goode '01
The Soloist '09
Somebody to Love '94
Something New '06
Somewhere '10
Somewhere in the Night '46
The Souler Opposite '97
Sound of My Voice '11
South of Pico '07

Southland Tales '06
Southside 1-1000 '50
Spanglish '04
Spanish Judges '99
Special '06
Speed '94 ▶
Spent '00
Spin '07
Splendor '99
Splinter '06
The Split '68
Spread '09
Spun '02
The Spy Who Dumped Me '18
Stand and Deliver '88 ▶
Stand-Ins '97
Standing on Fishes '99
Standing Still '05
Star Maps '97
Starlet '12 ▶
Starry Night '99
StarStruck '10
Steel '97
The Steel Trap '52
Sticks '98
Still Breathing '97
Storm Tracker '99
Straight Outta Compton '15 ▶
Strange Days '95 ▶
Street Corner Justice '96
The Street King '02
Street Kings '08
Strictly Sexual '08
Stuber '19
Stuntmen '09
Sueno '05
Sugar Town '99
Sunset Boulevard '50 ▶
Sunset Rock '16
Sunset Strip '99
Suspense '46
S.W.A.T. '03
SWAT: Unit 887 '15
Swimming with Sharks '94 ▶
Swingers '96 ▶
Swordfish '01
Sympathy for Delicious '10
Tactical Force '11
Taken 3 '15
Takers '10
The Talent Given Us '04 ▶
Telling You '98
10 Items or Less '06
10,000 Km '14
The Terrorist Next Door '08
Testosterone '03
They Call Me Sirr '00
Thicker than Water '99
30 '59
30 Days of Night: Dark Days '10
This Christmas '07
This Is the End '13 ▶
Three Came to Kill '61
Three Strikes '00
Tickled '16 ▶
The Time Being '12
Time Code '00
To Live & Die in L.A. '85
Too Late Blues '61
Tortilla Soup '01
Totally F***ed Up '94
Touch '98
The Towering Inferno '74
Training Day '01
The Trigger Effect '96
The Trip '02
Trumbo '15
Trust Me '13
Twilight '98 ▶
Two Days in the Valley '96 ▶
2 Jacks '12
The Two Jakes '90
Unbroken: Path to Redemption '18
Under the Same Moon '07
Under the Silver Lake '18
Undercover Maisie '47
Underdog Kids '15
The Underground '97
Undiscovered '05
Unlawful Entry '92
Untogether '19
Unwed Mother '58
Up Goes Maisie '46
Valentine's Day '10
Valley Girl '20
Vampire Night '00

Velvet Buzzsaw '19
Vice Squad '53
Virtuosity '95
Volcano '97
Waist Deep '06
Walk of Shame '14
Walking the Halls '12
Warning Shot '67
The Wash '01
Wassup Rockers '06
We Are Your Friends '15
The Wedding Year '19
Welcome Says the Angel '01
What Just Happened '08
What Lola Wants '15
What We Do Is Secret '07
Whatever It Takes '00
What's Up, Scarlet? '05
Where the Road Meets the Sun '11
Where the Truth Lies '05
Where's Marlowe? '98
Whirlpool '49
Who Made the Potatoe Salad? '05
The Whole Ten Yards '04
Why Am I Doing This? '09
Wish I Was Here '14
Witchcraft 9: Bitter Flesh '96
Witness to Murder '54
Wonderland '03
Wrong Cops '13
Yellow '98
Yes Man '08
You Got Served '04
Young Man With Ideas '52

Labor & Unions

***See also** Miners & Mining*
American Dream '90 ▶
American Factory '19 ▶
An American Romance '44
Black Fury '35 ▶
Blue Collar '78 ▶
Boxcar Bertha '72
Bread and Roses '00
Brother John '70 ▶
Cesar Chavez '14
Chicago Confidential '57
Deadly Stranger '88
The Devil & Miss Jones '41 ▶
The Early Bird '25
The End of St. Petersburg '27 ▶
End of the Line '88
F.I.S.T. '78
The Garment Jungle '57
G.B.H. '91
Gung Ho '86
Harlan County, U.S.A. '76 ▶
Harlan County War '00
Hoffa '92 ▶
I Was a Communist for the FBI '51
I'm All Right Jack '59 ▶
In Dubious Battle '17
The Irishman '19 ▶
Joyride '77
Land of Promise '74
Last Exit to Brooklyn '90 ▶
Liam '00
Mac '93 ▶
Made in Dagenham '10 ▶
Man of Iron '81 ▶
Man of Marble '76 ▶
Matewan '87 ▶
The Molly Maguires '70
Moonlighting '82 ▶
New in Town '09
Newsies '92
Norma Rae '79 ▶
North Dallas Forty '79 ▶
On the Waterfront '54 ▶
The Organizer '64
The Pajama Game '57 ▶
Potiche '10 ▶
Pride '14 ▶
Riff Raff '92 ▶
Rumble on the Docks '56
Salt of the Earth '54 ▶
Silkwood '83 ▶
Singleton's Pluck '84 ▶
Strike '24 ▶
Take This Job & Shove It '81
Teamster Boss: The Jackie Presser Story '92 ▶
10,000 Black Men Named George '02

The Triangle Factory Fire Scandal '79
Which Way Is Up? '77
The Woman on Pier 13 '50

Lacrosse

Crooked Arrows '12
Toe to Toe '09
A Warrior's Heart '11

Las Vegas

***See** Viva Las Vegas!*

Late Bloomin' Love

***See also** Growing Older*
The African Queen '51 ▶
Ali: Fear Eats the Soul '74 ▶
Atlantic City '81 ▶
Autumn Sun '98 ▶
The Bridges of Madison County '95 ▶
Brief Encounter '46 ▶
Camilla '94
Cass Timberlane '47
Charly '68 ▶
The Christmas Wife '88
Circle of Two '80
Crazy from the Heart '91 ▶
Devil in the Flesh '46 ▶
Doctor in Distress '63
A Fine Romance '92
Forbidden Love '82
Forty Carats '73
Gin Game '84 ▶
Grumpier Old Men '95
Grumpy Old Men '93 ▶
Harold and Maude '71 ▶
How to Be a Latin Lover '17
Innocence '00 ▶
Ladies in Lavender '04
The Last New Yorker '07
Letters to Juliet '10
Lonely Hearts '82 ▶
The Lonely Passion of Judith Hearne '87 ▶
Lovely, Still '08
The Lovers '17 ▶
Macaroni '85
A Majority of One '56
A Man and a Woman '66 ▶
Manglehorn '15
A Month by the Lake '95
The Night of the Iguana '64 ▶
One Special Night '99
Other People's Money '91
Queen of the Stardust Ballroom '75 ▶
The Rainmaker '56 ▶
Roman Spring of Mrs. Stone '61 ▶
San Antonio '45
Shadowlands '93 ▶
Shirley Valentine '89 ▶
The Shock '23
The Shop Around the Corner '40 ▶
Shore Leave '25 ▶
Stroszek '77 ▶
Summertime '55 ▶
Twice in a Lifetime '85 ▶
Used People '92
With Six You Get Eggroll '68

Law & Lawyers

***See also** Order in the Court*
Adam's Rib '50 ▶
The Adderall Diaries '16
The Advocate '93 ▶
After Innocence '05 ▶
Afterburn '92 ▶
Afterwards '08
Alleged '10
Amanda Knox: Murder on Trail in Italy '11
American Tragedy '00
American Violet '09
Amistad '97 ▶
Anatomy of a Murder '59 ▶
And Justice for All '79
Andy Hardy Comes Home '58
Any Day Now '12 ▶
Badla '19
Beeswax '09 ▶
Before and After '95
Behind the Green Lights '35
Beyond a Reasonable Doubt '56

Beyond a Reasonable Doubt '09
Big Daddy '99
Black or White '14
Bleak House '85
Bleak House '05
Blind Faith '98
Blind Trust '06
Body Chemistry 4: Full Exposure '95
Body Language '95
Boomerang '47 ▶
Brain Donors '92
The Breaking Point '50 ▶
Breaking Point '09
Bringing Down the House '03
Brother's Keeper '92 ▶
The Candidate '72 ▶
Cape Fear '61 ▶
Cape Fear '91 ▶
Carancho '10
Career Woman '36
Carlito's Way '93 ▶
The Case for Christmas '11
The Case of the Black Cat '36
The Case of the Curious Bride '35
The Case of the Howling Dog '34
The Case of the Lucky Legs '35
The Case of the Stuttering Bishop '37
Castle on the Hudson '40 ▶
Cause of Death '00
Cell 2455, Death Row '55
Cell 213 '11
A Certain Justice '99
Certain Prey '11
Certain Women '16 ▶
Chains '49
The Chamber '96
Changeling '08 ▶
Changing Lanes '02 ▶
Character '97
Cherish '02
Chicago '27
Chicago '02 ▶
The Children Act '18
Chloe & Theo '15
Chosen '16
The Christmas Clause '08
A Christmas Proposal '08
Citizen Cohn '92
A Civil Action '98
Class Action '91 ▶
The Client '94
Closed Circuit '13
Compulsion '59 ▶
The Confession '98
Confusion of Genders '00
The Conqueror Worm '68 ▶
Conspiracy Theory '97 ▶
The Conspirator '10
Convicted '04
Conviction '10
The Coroner '98
Cosmos '16
Counsellor-at-Law '33 ▶
The Counselor '13
Criminal Intent '05
Criminal Justice '08
Criminal Law '89
Criminal Lawyer '51
Critical Care '97
Crude: The Real Price of Oil '09
Daddy's Little Girls '07
Danger: Love at Work '37
Dark Justice '91
Dark Waters '19 ▶
Dawg '02
Death and the Maiden '94 ▶
The Defense Rests '34
Degree of Guilt '95
Deliberate Intent '01
Denial '16
Destination Vegas '95
The Devil's Advocate '97
The Devil's Doorway '50
Dirty Mary Crazy Larry '74 ▶
Disorganized Crime '89
The Divorce of Lady X '38
Divorce Wars: A Love Story '82
Dr. Dolittle 2 '01
Dr. Jekyll and Mr. Hyde '08

Down the Drain '89
The Drag-Net '36
Dragons Forever '88
Dummy '79
El Paso '49
Enemy of the State '98
The Enforcer '51
Erin Brockovich '00 ▶
The Escape Artist '13 ▶
Evelyn '02 ▶
Evelyn Prentice '34
Exclusive Story '36
The Exorcism of Emily Rose '05 ▶
Eye Witness '49
Fair Game '95
The Family Secret '51
A Family Thanksgiving '10
Father's Day '96
Fear and Loathing in Las Vegas '98
Female Perversions '96
Fever '91
A Few Good Men '92 ▶
Final Justice '98
Final Verdict '91
Find Me Guilty '06 ▶
The Firm '93 ▶
First Monday in October '81
The First Texan '56
The Fixer '97
For Roseanna '96
Forbidden Sins '99
Force of Evil '49 ▶
Fracture '07
Frank McKlusky, C.I. '02
A Free Soul '31
From the Hip '86
Genealogies of a Crime '97
Getting Gotti '94
The Ghost of Spoon River '00
Ghosts of Mississippi '96
Gideon's Army '13
Gideon's Trumpet '80
The Girl From Monaco '08
The Girl in the News '41
The Girl on the Train '09
The Girl Who Kicked the Hornet's Nest '10
The Glass Shield '95
God's Not Dead: A Light in Darkness '18
The Good Fight '92
Goodnight for Justice '11
The Great American Sex Scandal '94
The Green '11
The Groom Wore Spurs '51
The Guilty '92
The Guilty '99
Guilty as Sin '93
Guilty Conscience '85 ▶
The Hard Word '02
Heaven Is a Playground '91
Heavens Fall '06
Her Fatal Flaw '06
Hidden '11
High Crimes '02
Home Again '13
Hostile Witness '68
I Am Sam '01
I Love You, Alice B. Toklas! '68
I Now Pronounce You Chuck and Larry '07
The Ice Harvest '05
Illegal '55
Illegal Affairs '96
I'm No Angel '33 ▶
In Pursuit '00
In the Family '11
In the Name of the Father '93 ▶
The Incident '89 ▶
Inherit the Wind '99
The Insult '17 ▶
The Interrogation of Michael Crowe '02
Intolerable Cruelty '03
The Island of Dr. Moreau '96
It Happened to Jane '59
It Runs in the Family '03
It's Only Money '62
It's the Rage '99
JAG '95
The Jagged Edge '85
John Grisham's The Rainmaker '97

▶ = rated three bones or higher

The Judge '49
The Judge '14
Judge Dredd '95
Judge Priest '34 ►
The Juror '96
Jury Duty '95
Just Cause '94
Just Mercy '19 ►
King and Country '64 ►
Lady from Louisiana '42
Lansdown '01
Last Dance '96
The Laundromat '19
Laws of Attraction '04
Lawyer Man '32
Legal Eagles '86
Legalese '98
Legally Blonde 2: Red White & Blonde '03
Legally Blonde '01
Legend of Billie Jean '85
Lemon Tree '08
Let Freedom Ring '39
Leviathan '14 ►
Liar Liar '97
Life & Times of Judge Roy Bean '72
The Lincoln Lawyer '11
A Little Help '11
Losing Isaiah '94 ►
Love Letters '99 ►
Love Stinks '99
Loving '16 ►
Lucky Seven '03
Luminarias '99
Madame X '29
Madame X '66
The Magnificent Yankee '50 ►
Man from Colorado '49
Man of the House '95
The Man Who Shot Liberty Valance '62 ►
The Man Who Sued God '01
Manhattan Melodrama '34 ►
Marked Woman '37 ►
Marriage on the Rocks '65
Marshall '17
Matter of Trust '98
Mayhem '17
The Merchant of Venice '04 ►
Michael Clayton '07 ►
Misconduct '16
Mister America '19
Mr. & Mrs. Loving '96 ►
Mr. Ricco '75
Molly's Game '17
Moonlight Mile '02 ►
Move Over, Darling '63
Muhammad Ali's Greatest Fight '13
Murder in the First '95
A Murder of Crows '99
My Cousin Rachel '52
My Cousin Vinny '92 ►
My Silent Partner '06
My Sister's Keeper '09
The Narrow Margin '52 ►
National Lampoon Presents RoboDoc '08
Night and the City '92 ►
Night Falls on Manhattan '96 ►
Nixon '95 ►
North Country '05
Nothing But the Truth '08 ►
The Nuisance '33
Nuremberg '00
Obsessed '02
On the Basis of Sex '18
Once Upon a Time in Anatolia '12 ►
One Angry Juror '10
One Night at McCool's '01
Operation Heartbeat '69
Orchids to You '35
Original Intent '91
The Other Woman '08
Our Mutual Friend '98
Out of the Woods '05
The Paper Chase '73 ►
Party Girl '58 ►
Past Sins '06
The Pelican Brief '93
Penthouse '33 ►
The People Against O'Hara '51
The People *vs.* Larry Flynt '96 ►
Perfect Witness '89
Perry Mason Returns '85 ►
Personal Effects '05
Phil Spector '13
Philadelphia '93 ►
Physical Evidence '89
Picture Windows '95
Pinocchio's Revenge '96
Plain Dirty '04
Plain Truth '04
Poor White Trash '00
Portraits of a Killer '95
Power of Attorney '94
Presumed Innocent '90 ►
Primal Fear '96
Prom Queen '04
Prosecuting Casey Anthony '13
Psychopath '97
Puncture '11
RBG '18 ►
The Reader '08
Reasonable Doubt '14
Red Corner '97
Red Riding, Part 3: 1983 '09
Reet, Petite and Gone '47 ►
Regarding Henry '91 ►
Reno '39
Restraining Order '99
Return to Paradise '98 ►
R.I.C.C.O. '02
The Right of the People '86
The Right of Way '31
Rio Rita '29
Roman J. Israel, Esq. '17
Roman Polanski: Wanted and Desired '08
Romance of the Limberlost '38
Rounders '98
Roxie Hart '42
Runaway Father '91
Runaway Jury '03 ►
Saint Judy '19
Scandal '50
The Sea Inside '04 ►
Separate Lies '05
Shadow of Doubt '98
The Shaggy Dog '06
Shakedown '88
Shakespeare's Merchant '05
Shall We Dance? '04
Sierra '50
A Simple Twist of Fate '94
The Skeleton Key '05
Sleepers '96
The Sleepy Time Gal '01
Slightly Honorable '40
Smart Woman '48
Society Lawyer '39
Something Borrowed '11
Split Second '99
The Star Chamber '83
State's Attorney '31
Steel Toes '06
Stephen King's Thinner '96
Steve Martini's The Judge '01
Steve Martini's Undue Influence '96
A Stranger in the Kingdom '98
Street Law '95
Stronger Than Desire '39
The Sun Shines Bright '53
The Sweet Hereafter '96 ►
Swing Vote '99
Swoon '91 ►
Ted 2 '15
They Call It Murder '71
This is Not a Film '10 ►
This Side of the Law '50
Three Brave Men '57
Three Strangers '46
Thurgood '11 ►
A Time to Kill '96 ►
To Kill a Mockingbird '62 ►
Too Young to Die '90
Torso '02
Town without Pity '61
Trial '55
The Trial '93
The Trial '10
Trial & Error '62
Trial and Error '96
Trial by Jury '94
The Trial of Old Drum '00
The Trials of Cate McCall '13
Trois Couleurs: Rouge '94 ►
True Believer '89
True Colors '91
True Confession '37
Truth or Die '86
Twelve Angry Men '57 ►
Twilight of Honor '63
Undermind '03
Up for Grabs '05
The Verdict '82 ►
Victim '61 ►
West of Memphis '12
What Color Is Love? '08
Where the Truth Lies '99
Wild Things '98
Win Win '11
The Winslow Boy '48 ►
The Winslow Boy '98 ►
The Wistful Widow of Wagon Gap '47
Witness for the Prosecution '57 ►
The Wives He Forgot '06
The Woman in Black '12
Woman of Desire '93
The World Was His Jury '58
The Wronged Man '10
You Don't Know Jack '10
Young Goethe in Love '11
Young Man With Ideas '52
The Young Philadelphians '59 ►
ZigZag '70

Leprechauns

Darby O'Gill & the Little People '59 ►
Finian's Rainbow '68 ►
Leprechaun '93
Leprechaun 2 '94
Leprechaun 3 '95
Leprechaun 4: In Space '96
Leprechaun 5: In the Hood '99
Leprechaun 6: Back 2 Tha Hood '03
The Luck of the Irish '48
The Magical Legend of the Leprechauns '99
Red Clover '12

Lesbians

See also Bisexuality; Gays; Gender Bending

Affinity '08
Aimee & Jaguar '98
Alien Prey '78
All Over Me '96 ►
And Then Came Lola '09
Another Way '82 ►
Antarctica '08
Appropriate Behavior '14
April's Shower '03
Baba Yaga '73
The Baby Formula '08
Bam Bam & Celeste '05 ►
Bar Girls '95
Better Than Chocolate '99
The Bitter Tears of Petra von Kant '72
Black Cobra '83
The Black Dahlia '06
The Blood Spattered Bride '72
Bloomington '10
Blow Dry '00
Blue is the Warmest Color '13 ►
Bobbie's Girl '02
Booksmart '19
Bound '96
Boys on the Side '94
Bug '06
But I'm a Cheerleader '99
Butterfly Kiss '94
Carol '15 ►
Cassanova Was a Woman '15
Catfight '17
The Celluloid Closet '95 ►
Chasing Amy '97
The Children's Hour '61
Chuck & Buck '00
Chutney Popcorn '99
Circumstance '11
Claire of the Moon '92
Cloudburst '11 ►
Colombiana '11
Concussion '13
Contracted '13
Daphne '07
Dark Town '04
Daughters of Darkness '71 ►
D.E.B.S. '04
Desert Hearts '86 ►
Devotion '95
Different Story '78
Disobedience '17
Do I Love You? '02
Double Face '70
The Duke of Burgundy '14 ►
The Edge of Heaven '07 ►
Elena Undone '10
Entre-Nous '83 ►
Eternal '04
Eulogy '04
Even Cowgirls Get the Blues '94
Everything Relative '96
Evil Remains '04
A Family Affair '01
The Favourite '18 ►
Fine Dead Girls '02
Fire '96
Fish Without a Bicycle '03
Foxfire '96
Freeheld '15
French Twist '95
Gaudi Afternoon '01
The Gay Bed and Breakfast of Terror '07
Ghosted '09
Gia '98
Gigli '03
The Girl '01
Girl Play '04
Gray Matters '06
The Gymnast '06
The Handmaiden '16 ►
Hannah Free '09
Happy Endings '05
He Died With a Falafel in His Hand '01
Head in the Clouds '04
High Art '98
Higher Learning '94
The Hours '02 ►
The Hunger '83
If These Walls Could Talk 2 '00
Imagine Me & You '06
In Her Line of Fire '06
The Incredibly True Adventure of Two Girls in Love '95
It's In the Water '96
Itty Bitty Titty Committee '07
I've Heard the Mermaids Singing '87 ►
Jack and Diane '12
The Jane Austen Book Club '07 ►
Just One Time '00
Kaboom '11
The Kids Are All Right '10 ►
The Killing of Sister George '69
Kiss Me Again '06
Kissing Jessica Stein '02
La Cucina '07
Late Bloomers '95
L'Auberge Espagnole '02 ►
Law of Desire '86 ►
Le Jupon Rouge '87
Leading Ladies '10
The Legend of Lylah Clare '68
Les Voleurs '96 ►
Lianna '83 ►
Life Blood '09
Life Partners '14
Little City '97
Lizzie '18
Lost and Delirious '01
Love on the Side '04
A Love to Keep '07
Lovesong '17
Loving Annabelle '06
A Marine Story '10
May '02
Me, Myself and Her '16
Memento Mori '00
The Miseducation of Cameron Post '18
The Monkey's Mask '00
My Baby's Daddy '04
My Mother Likes Women '02
My Sister, My Love '78
My Summer of Love '05
Nadja '95 ►
Nina's Heavenly Delights '06
On the Other Hand, Death '08
101 Reykjavik '00
Oranges Are Not the Only Fruit '89
Our Idiot Brother '11
Out at the Wedding '07
The Owls '09
Pariah '11 ►
The Perfect Family '11
The Perfection '19
Personal Best '82 ►
Pimp '18
Portrait of a Lady on Fire '19 ►
Possession '02
Pretty Persuasion '05
Prey for Rock and Roll '03 ►
The Rainbow '89 ►
Reaching for the Moon '13
Relax. . . It's Just Sex! '98
Rent '05
Robin's Hood '03
Russian Dolls '05
Saving Face '04
Schoolgirl Hitchhikers '73
The Secret Diaries of Miss Anne Lister '10
The Secrets '07
Seducers '77
Serving in Silence: The Margarethe Cammermeyer Story '95 ►
Set It Off '96
She Hate Me '04
Shelter Island '03
Show Me Love '99
The Silence '63 ►
Slaves to the Underground '96
Some Prefer Cake '97
The Souler Opposite '97
Standing Still '05
The Sticky Fingers of Time '97
Sugar Cookies '77
Sugar Sweet '02
Summertime '16
Tell It to the Bees '19
Tell No One '06 ►
That's Not Us '15
Thelma '17
Therese & Isabelle '67
Things You Can Tell Just by Looking at Her '00
Three of Hearts '93
Tick Tock '00 ►
Tick Tock Lullaby '07
Tipping the Velvet '02
Tokyo Cowboy '94
Totally F***ed Up '94
Trapped '06
The Truth About Jane '00
The Twilight Girls '57
Under the Tuscan Sun '03
An Unexpected Love '03
Vampire Killers '09
The Vampire Lovers '70
Vampyres '74
A Village Affair '95
Virgin Machine '88
Vita & Virginia '19
Walk on the Wild Side '62
The Watermelon Woman '97
What's Up, Scarlet? '05
When Love Comes '98
When Night Is Falling '95 ►
Wicked Lake '08
Wild Side '95
Windows '80
A Woman's a Helluva Thing '01
The World Unseen '07
X, Y & Zee '72
Your Sister's Sister '11

Libraries and Librarians

American Animals '18 ►
This Beautiful Fantastic '17
A Beautiful Life '08
Black Mask '96
The Boy Who Harnessed the Wind '19
The Breakfast Club '85 ►
City of Angels '98
Desk Set '57 ►
Foul Play '78 ►
Fright Night 2 '88
Ghostbusters '84 ►
Good News '47
Goodbye, Columbus '69 ►
The Gun in Betty Lou's Handbag '92
Hard-Boiled '92 ►
I Lost My Body '19 ►
It's a Wonderful Life '46 ►
Kicking and Screaming '95 ►
The Last Lullaby '08 ►
The Librarian: Curse of the Judas Chalice '08
The Librarian: Quest for the Spear '04
The Librarian: Return to King Solomon's Mines '06
The Mummy '99
The Music Man '62 ►
The Name of the Rose '86
No Man of Her Own '32
Obselidia '10
Ode to Joy '19
The Pagemaster '94
Party Girl '94
Robot & Frank '12 ►
7 Faces of Dr. Lao '63 ►
The Shawshank Redemption '94 ►
Shooting the Past '99
Something Wicked This Way Comes '83
Storm Center '56
The Time Traveler's Wife '09
Where the Heart Is '00
With Honors '94

Lifeguards

See also Beach Blanket Bingo; Swimming

Baywatch '17
Caddyshack '80 ►
Fun in Acapulco '63
Lifeguard '76
The Lifeguard '13
Malibu Shark Attack '09
The Sandlot '93 ►
The To Do List '13

Little People

Bad Santa 2 '16
Bad Santa '03
The Chronicles of Narnia: Prince Caspian '08
Foul Play '78 ►
Fred Claus '07
The Hobbit '78 ►
The Hobbit: An Unexpected Journey '12
The Hobbit: The Battle of the Five Armies '14
The Hot Flashes '13
In Bruges '08
It's a Small World '50
Jungle Moon Men '55
Kismet '44
Little Cigars '73
Little Man '06
Lord of the Rings: The Fellowship of the Ring '01 ►
Lord of the Rings: The Two Towers '02 ►
The Lord of the Rings '78
Lord of the Rings: The Return of the King '03 ►
Mirror Mirror '12
My Son, My Son, What Have Ye Done '09
Poltergeist '82 ►
Poltergeist 2: The Other Side '86
Poltergeist 3 '88
Santa Baby '06
The Secret of Loch Ness '08
Snow White and the Huntsman '12
Snow White and the Seven Dwarfs '37 ►
Snow White: The Fairest of Them All '02
The 3 Worlds of Gulliver '60
Time Bandits '81
Under the Rainbow '81
Willow '88
The Wizard of Oz '25
The Wizard of Oz '39 ►

► = rated three bones or higher

London

***See also** Great Britain; Royalty*

Abbott and Costello Meet Dr. Jekyll and Mr. Hyde *'52*
About a Boy *'02* ▶
An Adventure in Space and Time *'13*
The Aeronauts *'19*
Again, the Ringer *'64*
Agatha Christie's Murder is Easy *'82*
Agent Cody Banks 2: Destination London *'04*
AKA *'02*
Alfie *'66* ▶
All Night Long *'62*
All or Nothing *'02*
All Things to All Men *'13*
Almost Strangers *'01* ▶
Amazing Grace *'06* ▶
An American Werewolf in London *'81* ▶
Annie: A Royal Adventure *'95*
Another Life *'01*
Another Year *'10* ▶
Any Human Heart *'11*
Appointment in London *'53*
The Assassination Bureau *'69* ▶
Atonement *'07* ▶
Attack the Block *'11*
Austin Powers: International Man of Mystery *'97* ▶
The Avengers *'98*
B. Monkey *'97*
Bad Behavior *'92*
Ballet Shoes *'07*
The Bank Job *'08* ▶
Basic Instinct 2 *'06*
Beat Girl *'60*
Beautiful People *'99*
Beautiful Thing *'95* ▶
The Bed Sitting Room *'69*
Bedlam *'45* ▶
Bedrooms and Hallways *'98*
Before I Go to Sleep *'14*
Being Julia *'04* ▶
Bend It Like Beckham *'02* ▶
Berkeley Square *'98*
Berlin Job *'12*
The Best House in London *'69*
Beyond Borders *'03*
The Big I Am *'10*
The Black Bird *'26*
The Bletchley Circle *'13*
Blitz *'11*
Blue Story *'20*
Boogie Woogie *'09*
Born Romantic *'00*
The Bourne Ultimatum *'07* ▶
Breakfast on Pluto *'05*
Breaking and Entering *'06*
Breaking the Bank *'14*
Bridget Jones: The Edge of Reason *'04*
Bridget Jones's Baby *'16*
Bridget Jones's Diary *'01* ▶
Bright Star *'09*
Bright Young Things *'03*
The Broken *'08*
Broken Blossoms *'19* ▶
The Buddha of Suburbia *'92* ▶
Bunny Lake Is Missing *'65*
Caffeine *'06*
Call It a Day *'37*
A Certain Justice *'99*
Charlie *'04*
Charlie Chan in London *'34*
Charlie White *'04*
Chatroom *'10*
Chicago Joe & the Showgirl *'90*
Child in the House *'56*
The Children Act *'18*
The Chronicles of Narnia: The Lion, the Witch and the Wardrobe *'05*
Churchill *'17*
Clapham Junction *'07*
Clean *'04*
Cleanskin *'12*
Climbing High *'38*
Clive of India *'35*
Close My Eyes *'91*
Closer *'04* ▶
Cloudburst *'51*
Color Me Kubrick *'05*
Comic Act *'98* ▶
Compulsion *'08*
Confidential Agent *'45*
Confirm or Deny *'41*
The Conjuring 2 *'16*
The Constant Nymph *'43*
Contraband *'40*
The Contractor *'07*
The Cost of Love *'11*
Counter-Espionage *'42*
The Courier *'19*
Crackerjack *'38*
The Criminal *'00*
The Crimson Petal and the White *'12*
Croupier *'97* ▶
Danger UXB *'81*
The Day They Robbed the Bank of England *'60*
Dead Cert *'10*
Dead Cool *'04*
Dead Fish *'04*
Dead Gorgeous *'02*
Dead Man Running *'09*
Deadlier Than the Male *'67*
The Death of the Heart *'87*
Death on the Set *'35*
Denial *'16*
Devotion *'46*
Dick Barton, Special Agent *'48*
Die Another Day *'02*
Different for Girls *'96* ▶
Dirty Pretty Things *'03* ▶
The Disappeared *'08*
Disraeli *'79* ▶
Do I Love You? *'02*
Dom Hemingway *'13*
Dorian Gray *'09*
Dot the I *'03*
Dracula's Daughter *'36* ▶
Dream Street *'21*
The Duchess *'08* ▶
The Duchess of Duke Street *'78* ▶
Eagles Over London *'69*
Eastern Promises *'07* ▶
An Education *'09* ▶
An Egyptian Story *'82*
84 Charing Cross Road *'86* ▶
The Elephant Man *'80* ▶
11 Harrowhouse *'74* ▶
Elizabeth *'98* ▶
Enchantment *'48*
End of the Affair *'55*
The End of the Affair *'99* ▶
Endgame *'01*
Entrapment *'99*
The Escape *'18*
The Escapist *'08*
Esther Kahn *'00*
Esther Waters *'48*
Eurotrip *'04*
Exit Through the Gift Shop *'10*
Expresso Bongo *'59*
Extraordinary Rendition *'07*
Face *'97*
The Face of Fu Manchu *'65*
Faith *'94*
The Fan *'49*
Fanny Hill *'07*
A Fantastic Fear of Everything *'14*
Feedback *'20*
Fever Pitch *'96*
Fierce Creatures *'96*
The File of the Golden Goose *'69*
Filth *'08*
Filth and Wisdom *'08*
Flame in the Streets *'61*
Flawless *'07*
Flood *'07*
Flushed Away *'06* ▶
Fool's Gold: The Story of the Brink's-Mat Robbery *'92*
Footsteps in the Fog *'55*
The Forbidden Street *'49*
Foreign Correspondent *'40* ▶
The Foreigner *'17*
Forever and a Day *'43* ▶
Forget Me Not *'10*
Forgive and Forget *'99*
44 Inch Chest *'09*
Four in the Morning *'65*
4.3.2.1 *'10*
The Fourth Angel *'01*
Franklyn *'08*
Frenzy *'72* ▶
Friday the Thirteenth *'33*
Friends & Crocodiles *'05*
The Frightened City *'61*
The Frightened Man *'52*
From Hell *'01* ▶
Full Moon in Paris *'84*
The Gabby Douglas Story *'14*
The Gambler & the Lady *'52*
Gangster No. 1 *'00*
Gaslight *'40* ▶
The Gathering Storm *'02* ▶
The Gentlemen *'20*
Gentlemen's Relish *'01*
Get Him to the Greek *'10*
Get Lucky *'13*
The Giant Behemoth *'59*
Gideon's Daughter *'05*
Gideon's Day *'58*
Ginger & Rosa *'13*
Give Us the Moon *'44*
Going for Gold: The '48 Games *'12*
The Golden Bowl *'72* ▶
The Golden Bowl *'00*
Good People *'14*
Great Expectations *'81*
Great Expectations *'99*
Great Expectations *'11*
Great Expectations *'12*
The Great Muppet Caper *'81* ▶
The Green Cockatoo *'37*
Green Street Hooligans *'05* ▶
The Guilty *'92*
Hampstead *'19*
Hands of a Murderer *'90*
Hangover Square *'45*
Happy-Go-Lucky *'08* ▶
A Harlot's Progress *'06*
Harry Brown *'09*
Having a Wild Weekend *'65*
The Heart of Me *'02*
Heartless *'10*
Heaven's a Drag *'94*
The Heavy *'09*
Her Night of Romance *'24*
Hereafter *'10*
Hidden *'11*
High Heels and Low Lifes *'01*
Hope and Glory *'87* ▶
Horrors of the Black Museum *'59*
The Horse's Mouth *'58* ▶
Hostile Witness *'68*
The Hour of 13 *'52*
How to Be *'08*
The Human Centipede 2: Full Sequence *'11*
Husbands *'70*
Hysteria *'11*
I, Daniel Blake *'16* ▶
I Give It a Year *'13*
I, Monster *'71* ▶
I Really Hate My Job *'07*
I Sell the Dead *'09*
I Was Happy Here *'66*
An Ideal Husband *'47*
An Ideal Husband *'99* ▶
If I Were Free *'33*
If Only *'04*
I'll Never Forget You *'51*
I'll Sleep When I'm Dead *'03* ▶
Imagine Me & You *'06*
Immortality *'98*
In a Day *'06*
In Bruges *'08*
In the Loop *'09*
In the Name of the Father *'93* ▶
Incendiary *'08*
Incognito *'97*
The Infidel *'10*
The Infinite Worlds of H.G. Wells *'01*
The Innocent Sleep *'95*
Interview With a Hitman *'12*
Intimacy *'00*
Intruders *'11*
Irina Palm *'07*
The Iron Petticoat *'56*
It Always Rains on Sunday *'47*
It's Love Again *'36*
Janice Beard *'99*
Jimi: All Is by My Side *'14*
Johnny Was *'05*
Journey for Margaret *'42* ▶
Judy *'19* ▶
Kill Your Friends *'16*
Killing Me Softly *'01*
Kings *'07*
The Knack *'65* ▶
Lady L *'65*
The Lady With the Lamp *'51*
Lamb *'85*
Last Chance Harvey *'08*
Last Christmas *'19*
The Last Enemy *'08*
Last Orders *'01* ▶
Last Passenger *'14*
The Last Tree *'19*
Layer Cake *'05* ▶
The Leading Man *'96*
The League of Extraordinary Gentlemen *'03*
The Legend of Tarzan *'16*
The Liability *'12*
Like Crazy *'11* ▶
Like It Is *'98* ▶
The Limehouse Golem *'17*
The Line of Beauty *'06*
The Liquidator *'65*
The Little Princess *'39* ▶
London Boulevard *'10*
London Fields *'18*
London Has Fallen *'16*
London River *'09*
London Town *'46*
London Voodoo *'04*
The Long Good Friday *'80* ▶
A Long Way Down *'14*
The Look of Love *'13*
The Lost Boys *'78* ▶
Lost in Austen *'08*
The Lost Language of Cranes *'92* ▶
The Lost Son *'98*
Love Actually *'03*
Love and Death on Long Island *'97*
Love and Other Disasters *'06*
Love Is the Devil *'98* ▶
Lured *'47*
The Magician *'93*
Malice in Wonderland *'09*
Man Hunt *'41* ▶
Man in the Attic *'53*
The Man Who Knew Too Little *'97*
Mary Poppins *'64* ▶
Mary Poppins Returns *'18*
Mary Reilly *'95*
Match Point *'05* ▶
Maybe Baby *'99*
Me & Mrs. Jones *'02*
Me Without You *'01*
Meantime *'81*
Men in Black: International *'19*
A Merry War *'97* ▶
Metroland *'97*
MI-5 *'15*
Midnight Episode *'50*
Ministry of Fear *'44* ▶
Miranda *'48*
Miranda *'01*
Miss Conception *'08*
Miss London Ltd. *'43*
Miss Pettigrew Lives for a Day *'08* ▶
Mission: Impossible *'96* ▶
The Missionary *'82*
Mrs. Dalloway *'97*
Mrs. Henderson Presents *'05*
Mrs. Palfrey at the Claremont *'05*
Mr. Nice *'10*
Mr. Right *'06*
Moll Flanders *'96*
Molly Moon and The Incredible Book of Hypnotism *'15*
Moonlighting *'82* ▶
Moonwalkers *'16*
The Mother *'03* ▶
The Mudlark *'50*
The Mummy *'17*
The Mummy Returns *'01*
Murder On the Home Front *'13*
My Beautiful Laundrette *'85* ▶
My Brother the Devil *'12*
My Week With Marilyn *'11*
My Wife is an Actress *'01*
The Mysterious Magician *'65*
Naked *'93* ▶
The National Health *'73*
National Lampoon's European Vacation *'85*
Neil Gaiman's NeverWhere *'96*
Nicholas Nickleby *'02* ▶
Night and the City *'50* ▶
Night at the Museum: Secret of the Tomb *'14*
Night Junkies *'07*
Nighthawks *'78*
Nil by Mouth *'96*
Not Now Darling *'73*
Notes on a Scandal *'06* ▶
The Notorious Landlady *'62*
Notting Hill *'99* ▶
The Old Curiosity Shop *'94*
Old Mother Riley, MP *'39*
Oliver Twist *'85* ▶
Oliver Twist *'97*
Oliver Twist *'00* ▶
Oliver Twist *'05* ▶
Oliver Twist *'07*
Once More, With Feeling *'60*
100 Streets *'17*
101 Dalmatians *'96*
The Ones Below *'16*
Othello *'01* ▶
Otley *'68*
Our Kind of Traitor *'16*
Our Mother's House *'67*
Our Mutual Friend *'98*
Paddington 2 *'17* ▶
Paddington *'14* ▶
Page Eight *'11*
The Painted Lady *'97* ▶
The Parent Trap *'98*
P.D. James: The Murder Room *'04*
Penelope *'06*
Perfect Understanding *'33*
Peter Rabbit *'18*
Phantom Fiend *'35*
The Phantom of the Opera *'62*
Phantom Thread *'17* ▶
Photographing Fairies *'97*
Piccadilly *'29*
Pinochet's Last Stand *'06*
Plain Jane *'02*
Played *'06*
The Pleasure Garden *'25*
Plunkett & Macleane *'98*
Poldark *'96*
Possession *'02*
Postman's Knock *'62*
The Power and the Prize *'56*
Preaching to the Perverted *'97*
Priest *'94*
Psyche 59 *'64*
Pure *'02* ▶
Queen and Country *'14*
Radio Cab Murder *'54*
Rage in Heaven *'41*
Rancid Aluminium *'00*
Raw Meat *'72*
Razor Blade Smile *'98*
Red Mercury *'05*
Redemption *'13*
Reign of Fire *'02*
Return to Never Land *'02*
The Riddle *'07*
The Rise and Rise of Michael Rimmer *'70*
The Rise of the Krays *'16*
Robert Louis Stevenson's The Game of Death *'99*
RocknRolla *'08*
Romance and Rejection *'96*
Royal Wedding *'51* ▶
Ruby in the Smoke *'06*
Run, Fatboy, Run *'07*
Russian Dolls *'05*
Sabotage *'36* ▶
Sailing Along *'38*
The Saint in London *'39*
St. Urbain's Horseman *'07*
Salt & Pepper *'68*
Say Hello to Yesterday *'71*
Scenes of a Sexual Nature *'06*
The Search for John Gissing *'01*
The Secret Agent *'96*
The Secret Life of Mrs. Beeton *'06*
Secrets and Lies *'95*
The Sense of an Ending *'17*
Separate Lies *'05*
Sexy Beast *'00* ▶
The Shadow in the North *'07*
Shakespeare in Love *'98* ▶
Shanghai Knights *'03*
Shaun of the Dead *'04* ▶
She Played With Fire *'57*
Sherlock: Case of Evil *'02*
Sherlock Gnomes *'18*
Sherlock Holmes *'09*
Sherlock Holmes *'10*
Sherlock Holmes: A Game of Shadows *'11*
Sherlock Holmes and the Voice of Terror *'42*
Shine *'95* ▶
Shooters *'00*
Shooting Fish *'98*
Shooting the Past *'99*
The Siege of Sidney Street *'60*
Sirens *'02*
Sitting Target *'72*
Sliding Doors *'97*
Small Island *'09*
Snatch *'00* ▶
Soho Square *'00*
The Song of Names *'19*
The Sorcerers *'67*
Sorted *'04*
Sparkle *'07*
Spice World: The Movie *'97*
Spider *'02* ▶
Spin a Dark Web *'56*
Split Second *'92*
Stage Beauty *'04*
Stella Does Tricks *'96*
Storage 24 *'12*
Strange Bedfellows *'65*
Strapless *'90*
A Street Cat Named Bob *'16*
Success Is the Best Revenge *'84*
Sugarhouse *'07*
Sunday, Bloody Sunday *'71* ▶
Surveillance 24/7 *'07*
The Sweeney *'12*
Sweeney Todd: The Demon Barber of Fleet Street *'07*
Swinging With the Finkels *'11*
Tabloid *'10*
The Take *'09*
Take a Girl Like You *'70*
Tale of a Vampire *'92*
The Tall Guy *'89* ▶
Telstar: The Joe Meek Story *'08*
Their Finest *'17* ▶
These Foolish Things *'06*
They Made Me a Fugitive *'47*
13 Frightened Girls *'63*
This Above All *'42*
Three and Out *'08*
Three Strangers *'46*
Tick Tock Lullaby *'07*
Time After Time *'79* ▶
Tinker, Tailor, Soldier, Spy *'80* ▶
Tipping the Velvet *'02*
To Sir, with Love *'67*
Tom & Thomas *'02*
Topsy Turvy *'99* ▶
Touch of Pink *'04*
Touching Evil *'97* ▶
Trap for Cinderella *'13*
Trauma *'04*
Twenty8k *'12*
23 Paces to Baker Street *'56*
24 Hours in London *'00*
28 Days Later *'02*
28 Weeks Later *'07*
Twice upon a Yesterday *'98*
Twilight Women *'52*
Twinkletoes *'26*
Ultraviolet *'98*
Unfinished Song *'12*
A United Kingdom *'17*
Unknown White Male *'05* ▶
Unlocked *'17*
Unmade Beds *'09*
Unpublished Story *'42* ▶

Up the Junction '68
Upstairs Downstairs '11
The Upturned Glass '47
V for Vendetta '06
Vanity Fair '99
Venus '06 ▶
Vera Drake '04 ▶
The Verdict '46
The Very Thought of You '98
Victoria & Abdul '17
Vigil in the Night '40
Villain '71
Virtual Sexuality '99
The Waiting Room '07
The Walking Stick '70
A Waste of Shame '05
Water Babies '79
Waterloo Bridge '40 ▶
Waterloo Road '45
The Way We Live Now '02
The Weapon '56
The Wedding Date '05
Welcome to the Punch '13
Werewolf of London '35
What a Girl Wants '03
Wilde '97
Wimbledon '04
The Wings of the Dove '97 ▶
The Winslow Boy '98 ▶
Witchcraft 10: Mistress of the Craft '98
The Witness Vanishes '39
A Woman's Guide to Adultery '93
Wonderland '99
Wonderwall: The Movie '69
You Will Meet a Tall Dark Stranger '10
The Young Americans '93
The Young Poisoner's Handbook '94 ▶
Young Sherlock Holmes '85

Loneliness

See Only the Lonely

Loner Cops

See also Cops

Above the Law '88
Action Jackson '88
Bad Attitude '93
Bad Country '14
Bad Lieutenant '92 ▶
Blitz '11
The Breed '01
Code of Silence '85
Cop in Blue Jeans '78
Dead Bang '89
The Dead Pool '88
Die Hard '88 ▶
Die Hard 2: Die Harder '90 ▶
Die Hard: With a Vengeance '95
Dirty Harry '71 ▶
Dredd '12 ▶
The Enforcer '76
Excessive Force '93
Exit Wounds '01
Force of One '79
The Gauntlet '77
The Guilty '18 ▶
Hard-Boiled '92
Heat '87
Heat '95 ▶
In the Heat of the Night '67 ▶
Judge Dredd '95
Klute '71 ▶
Live Free or Die Hard '07
Magnum Force '73
Martial Outlaw '93
McQ '74
Minority Report '02 ▶
Mission of Death '97
Murder by Numbers '02
Navajo Blues '97
Northwest Trail '46
One Good Cop '91
The Pledge '00 ▶
Rent-A-Cop '88
RoboCop '87 ▶
Serpico '73 ▶
Sharky's Machine '81
Soho Square '00
Speed '94 ▶
Stick '85
Stone Cold '91
The Street King '02
Striking Distance '93
Sudden Impact '83
Ten to Midnight '83
Top Dog '95
Year of the Dragon '85

Long Distance Love

See also Road Trip; Romantic Adventure

Comet '14
Going the Distance '10
Hank and Asha '14
If Beale Street Could Talk '18 ▶
In Your Eyes '14
Like Crazy '11 ▶
More Than Friends '78
Nights and Weekends '08
10,000 Km '14
28 Hotel Rooms '12
What If '13

Long-Lost Relatives

Captain Fantastic '16
Despicable Me 3 '17
Edge of Winter '16
Our Little Sister '16
The Space Between Us '17

Look Ma! I'm on TV!

Almost Heaven '06
Are You Scared? '06
Auto Focus '02 ▶
Carolina '03
Cinema Verite '11
The Condemned '07
Confessions of a Dangerous Mind '02
Cruel World '05
Death Race 2 '10
Death to Smoochy '02
Dr. Dolittle: Million Dollar Mutts '09
Don't Think Twice '16
Eat Your Heart Out '96
EDtv '99
15 Minutes '01
Gale Force '01
Hairspray '07 ▶
Halloween: Resurrection '02
House of Bones '09
I-See-You.Com '06
Killer Cop '02
Killer Movie '08
Live! '07
Love or Money '01
Loveless in Los Angeles '07
Magnolia '99 ▶
Matrimonium '05
Monday Night Mayhem '02
My Best Friend '06
The New Gladiators '83
The Nines '07 ▶
Pleasantville '98 ▶
Ricky Nelson: Original Teen Idol '99
Say One for Me '59
Series 7: The Contenders '01
Showtime '02
Simon and Laura '55
Sink or Swim '97
Slumdog Millionaire '08 ▶
Starter for 10 '06
Stay Tuned '92
Strange Wilderness '08
Stuck On You '03
Sugar Sweet '02
The Three Stooges '12
The Truman Show '98 ▶
The TV Set '06
The 24 Hour Woman '99
Virtuality '09
War Tapes '06 ▶
Whatever You Say '02
A Woman, A Part '17
Woman on Top '00
Wrong Turn 2: Dead End '07

Lost Worlds

See also Parallel Universe

At the Earth's Core '76
Atragon '63
Beyond Atlantis '73
Brigadoon '54 ▶
Creatures the World Forgot '70
Gold of the Amazon Women '79
Jane & the Lost City '87
Journey to the Center of the Earth '59 ▶
Journey to the Center of the Earth '93
Journey to the Center of the Earth '99
Journey to the Center of the Earth '08
Jumanji '95
The Land That Time Forgot '75
The Land That Time Forgot '09
The Land Unknown '57
The Last Dinosaur '77
The Lost City of Z '17 ▶
The Lost Continent '51
Lost Horizon '37 ▶
The Lost World '25
The Lost World '60
The Mistress of Atlantis '32
Mysterious Island '61 ▶
Mysterious Island of Beautiful Women '79
The People That Time Forgot '77
Raptor Island '04
She '65
Smurfs: The Lost Village '17
Untamed Women '52
Warriors of Virtue '97
Where Time Began '77

Lottery Winners

Babette's Feast '87 ▶
Everything's Gone Green '06
Finder's Fee '01
Fox and His Friends '75 ▶
The Gay Deception '35
Highland Park '13
How Much Do You Love Me? '05
It Could Happen to You '94
Lady from Louisiana '42
Le Million '31 ▶
Loco Love '03
Lottery Bride '30
The Lottery Ticket '10
Lucky '11
Lucky Christmas '11
Lucky Day '91
Lucky Numbers '00
Lucky Partners '40
Mary Higgins Clark: Lucky Day '02
The Million Dollar Kid '99
Next Friday '00
The Squeeze '87
Sweepstake Annie '35
Three Strangers '46
29th Street '91
Uptown Saturday Night '74
Waking Ned Devine '98 ▶
Welcome to Me '15
The Wrong Box '66 ▶

Louisiana

See also American South; New Orleans; Southern Belles

All the King's Men '49 ▶
The Apostle '97 ▶
Beasts of the Southern Wild '12 ▶
The Best of Me '14
Blaze '89
Burning Cane '19
Divine Secrets of the Ya-Ya Sisterhood '02
Dream Boy '08
The Drowning Pool '75
Eve's Bayou '97 ▶
Evil Remains '04
The Final Project '16
Fletch Lives '89
For One Night '06
Forever My Girl '18
The Foxes of Harrow '47
Frankenfish '04
Heart of the Storm '04
Heaven's Prisoners '95
House of Wax '05
JFK '91 ▶
The Last Exorcism '10
Louisiana Purchase '41
Louisiana Story '48 ▶
Mammoth '06
Mask Maker '10
Monsterwolf '10
Navy Seals *vs.* Zombies '15
No Mercy '86
Passion Fish '92 ▶
Road House 2: Last Call '06
The Runner '15
Shark Night 3D '11
The Skeleton Key '05
A Soldier's Story '84 ▶
Sounder '72 ▶
Stay Alive '06
Steel Magnolias '89 ▶
Sugar Hill '74
Swamp Shark '11
Tigerland '00 ▶
The Toy Wife '38
Transit '12
Vampire Bats '05
Venom '05
Vincent N Roxxy '17
Wicked Blood '13
The Wronged Man '10

Lovable Loonies

See also Shrinks

Bean '97 ▶
Benny & Joon '93
Best in Show '00 ▶
Between Two Ferns '19
Beyond Therapy '86
Box of Moonlight '96
The Couch Trip '87
Crazy People '90
Crazylove '05
David and Lisa '62 ▶
The Fisher King '91 ▶
Ghost World '01 ▶
Gridlock'd '96 ▶
Guns for Hire '15
High-Rise '16
Julian Po '97
King of California '07
The King of Hearts '66 ▶
Lars and the Real Girl '07
Meet Wally Sparks '97
The Ninth Configuration '79 ▶
One Flew Over the Cuckoo's Nest '75 ▶
Patch Adams '98
The Ruling Class '72 ▶
Superstar '99
Toni Erdmann '16 ▶
What about Bob? '91 ▶

Lovers on the Lam

See also Fugitives

Badlands '74 ▶
Blood & Wine '96
Bobby Z '07
Bonnie & Clyde '67 ▶
Bonnie & Clyde '13
Boys '95
Criminal Lovers '99
Dust Be My Destiny '39
Equals '16
Feeling Minnesota '96
The Getaway '72
The Getaway '93
Ghost of a Chance '01
Gun Crazy '49 ▶
Guncrazy '92
Heaven's Burning '97
Helen of Troy '03
Hide '08
The Island '05
Jailbreakers '94
Jimmy & Judy '06
Johnny Cool '63
Kalifornia '93
Kill Me Later '01
Le Choc '82
Love and a .45 '94
Love Lies Bleeding '07
Machine Gun McCain '69
Mad Love '95
Man Who Loved Cat Dancing '73
Natural Born Killers '94
Niagara, Niagara '97
On the Run '73
Our Paradise '11
Perfect Hideout '08
River of Grass '94
The Road '00
Rough Magic '95
Shockproof '49
The Sugarland Express '74 ▶
Sun Don't Shine '12
Tomorrow Is Another Day '51
Trojan Eddie '96 ▶
True Romance '93
Two If by Sea '95
Underworld: Evolution '05
When Brendan Met Trudy '00 ▶
Where Danger Lives '50
Wild at Heart '90 ▶

Mad Scientists

See also Inventors & Science & Scientists

Alien Terminator '95
Alone in the Dark '05
The Animal '01
Astro-Zombies M3: Cloned '10
Atom Age Vampire '61
Attack of the Puppet People '58
Attack of the 60-Foot Centerfold '95
Attack of the Swamp Creature '75
The Attic Expeditions '01
The Avengers '98
Beast of Blood '71
Bela Lugosi Meets a Brooklyn Gorilla '52
The Belko Experiment '17
Beyond Re-Animator '03
The Black Sleep '56
The Blackout Experiments '16
Bloodlust '59
Bloodstorm: Subspecies 4 '98
Body Armor '96
The Body Shop '72
The Boogie Man Will Get You '42
The Brain that Wouldn't Die '63
Brainjacked '09
Brenda Starr '86
Bride of Re-Animator '89
Bride of the Monster '55
Bug Buster '99
Captain America '44
The Cars That Ate Paris '74 ▶
Castle of the Creeping Flesh '68
The City of Lost Children '95 ▶
Clockstoppers '02
The Cobweb '55
Colossus of New York '58
Creator '85
The Creeping Flesh '72
The Creeps '97
Crimes of Dr. Mabuse '32 ▶
A Cure for Wellness '17
Darkman '90 ▶
Darkman 2: The Return of Durant '94
Darkman 3: Die Darkman Die '95
The Dead Next Door '89
Dead Pit '89
Dead Sleep '91
Death Warmed Up '85
The Deathless Devil '05
Deep Red '94
Devil Doll '36 ▶
Disaster Zone: Volcano in New York '06
Dr. Black, Mr. Hyde '76
Doctor Blood's Coffin '62
Doctor Butcher M.D. '80
Dr. Cyclops '40
Dr. Death, Seeker of Souls '73
Dr. Frankenstein's Castle of Freaks '74
Dr. Goldfoot and the Bikini Machine '66
Dr. Jekyll and Mr. Hyde '20 ▶
Dr. Jekyll and Mr. Hyde '32 ▶
Dr. Jekyll and Mr. Hyde '41 ▶
Dr. Jekyll and Mr. Hyde '68
Dr. Jekyll and Mr. Hyde '73
Dr. Jekyll and Sister Hyde '71
Dr. Jekyll and the Wolfman '71
Dr. Jekyll's Dungeon of Death '82
Dr. No '62 ▶
Dr. Orloff's Monster '64
Doctor X '32
Donovan's Brain '53 ▶
Dracula 2: Ascension '03
The Eden Formula '06
Embryo '76
Faceless '88
Far Cry '08
The Fear Chamber '68
Firestarter 2: Rekindled '02
The Flesh Eaters '64
Frankenhooker '90
Frankenstein '31 ▶
Frankenstein '73
Frankenstein '93
Frankenstein and the Monster from Hell '74
Frankenstein '80 '79
Frankenstein Must Be Destroyed '69
Frankenstein Reborn '98
Frankenstein Unbound '90 ▶
Frankenstein's Daughter '58
Freaked '93
The Freakmaker '73
Geisha Girl '52
The Gene Generation '07
The German Doctor '14
The Giant Spider Invasion '75
Girl in His Pocket '57
The Glass Trap '04
Godsend '04
The Head '59
Hellmaster '92
Hideous Sun Demon '59
Higher Power '18
Hollow Man '00
House of Frankenstein '44
Hyena of London '62
I, Monster '71 ▶
Igor '08
The Immortalizer '89
The Incredible Two-Headed Transplant '71
The Indestructible Man '56
Invasion! '99
The Invisible Dr. Mabuse '62 ▶
The Invisible Man '33 ▶
The Invisible Man '20 ▶
The Invisible Ray '36
The Island of Dr. Moreau '77
The Island of Dr. Moreau '96
Island of Lost Souls '32 ▶
Island of Lost Women '59
Jekyll and Hyde '90
Jungle Manhunt '51
Jurassic Park '93 ▶
Kids in the Hall: Brain Candy '96
The Killing Device '92
King Kong Escapes '67
King of Kong Island '78
King of the Zombies '41
Lady Frankenstein '72
Lawnmower Man 2: Beyond Cyberspace '95
The Lawnmower Man '92
The Living Corpse '03
The Living Dead '33
The Lost City '34
The Lost Skeleton of Cadavra '01
The Magician '26
The Man They Could Not Hang '39
The Man Who Turned to Stone '57
The Man with Two Lives '42
Mandroid '93
Maniac '34
Mansion of the Doomed '76
The Manster '59
Mary Shelley's Frankenstein '94
Metamorphosis '90
Mom's Outta Sight '01
The Monster '25 ▶
The Monster Maker '44
The Munsters' Revenge '81
Mystery Science Theater 3000: The Movie '96
Naked Souls '95
Nightmare Castle '65
Nightmare Weekend '86
Orloff and the Invisible Man '70
Patrick '13
The Phantom '09
Philadelphia Experiment 2 '93

▶ = *rated three bones or higher*

Piano Tuner of Earthquakes '05
The Pink Panther Strikes Again '76 ▶
The Pit and the Pendulum '09
Proteus '95
Puzzlehead '05
The Rage '07
Re-Animator '84 ▶
Red Blooded American Girl '90
Repo! The Genetic Opera '08
Retroactive '97
Return of the Killer Tomatoes! '88
Revolt of the Zombies '36
Rites of Frankenstein '72
Rubber's Lover '97
Sabretooth '01
Samson in the Wax Museum '63
The Satan Bug '65
Screamers '80
Shadow of Chinatown '36
She Demons '58
Shock Waves '77
Sky Captain and the World of Tomorrow '04
The Song of Sway Lake '18
Sonic the Hedgehog '20
Species 3 '04
Spider-Man '02 ▶
Spider-Man 2 '04 ▶
Spy Kids 3-D: Game Over '03
Star Trek: Generations '94 ▶
Strange Behavior '81
Strange Case of Dr. Jekyll & Mr. Hyde '68
Superargo '67
Supersonic Man '78
Tarzeena: Queen of Kong Island '08
Teenage Zombies '58
Terror Is a Man '59
Testament of Dr. Mabuse '62
Three Identical Strangers '18 ▶
The Tingler '59 ▶
Underdog '07
The Unearthly '57
The Vampire Bat '32
Victor Frankenstein '15
The Wasp Woman '96
The Werewolf '56
Werewolf of London '35
Wes Craven Presents Mind Ripper '95
Wild Wild West '99

Madrid

***See also** Barcelona; Spain*
All About My Mother '99 ▶
The Barefoot Contessa '54 ▶
Boystown '07
Chef's Special '08
Goal 2: Living the Dream '07
The Happy Thieves '61
Intruders '11
Kidnapped '10
Km. 0 '00
Little Ashes '09
Live Flesh '97 ▶
Martin (Hache) '97
The Method '05 ▶
Tip On a Dead Jockey '57
What Have I Done to Deserve This? '85 ▶
Women on the Verge of a Nervous Breakdown '88 ▶

Mafia

***See** Organized Crime*

Magic

***See also** Genies; Magic Carpet Rides; Occult*
Aladdin '19
The Alchemist '81
Animal Crackers '17
Arabian Nights '00
Balloon Farm '97
Bedknobs and Broomsticks '71
Bewitched '05
The Black Cauldron '85
Black Magic Terror '79
Bogus '96
The Brothers Grimm '05
The Butcher's Wife '91
Chandu on the Magic Island '34
Chandu the Magician '32
The Chronicles of Narnia: The Lion, the Witch and the Wardrobe '05
The Color of Magic '08
The Craft '96
The Day the Earth Froze '59
Death Defying Acts '07
Deceptive Practice: The Mysteries and Mentors of Ricky Jay '12
Deceptive Practice: The Mysteries and Mentors of Ricky Jay '13 ▶
Doctor Mordrid: Master of the Unknown '90
Doctor Strange '16 ▶
Don't Torture a Duckling '72
Doogal '05
Dream a Little Dream 2 '94
Dungeons and Dragons '00
Ella Enchanted '04 ▶
Enchanted '07
Escape to Witch Mountain '75 ▶
Eternally Yours '39
FairyTale: A True Story '97
Fantastic Beasts and Where to Find Them '16
Frozen '13 ▶
Frozen II '19 ▶
The Geisha Boy '58
Get to Know Your Rabbit '72
Goosebumps 2: Haunted Halloween '18
The Great Buck Howard '09 ▶
The Great Magician '11
Grimm's Snow White '12
Happily N'Ever After '07
Harry Potter and the Chamber of Secrets '02 ▶
Harry Potter and the Deathly Hallows, Part 1 '10 ▶
Harry Potter and the Deathly Hallows, Part 2 '11 ▶
Harry Potter and the Goblet of Fire '05 ▶
Harry Potter and the Half-Blood Prince '09
Harry Potter and the Order of the Phoenix '07
Harry Potter and the Prisoner of Azkaban '04
Harry Potter and the Sorcerer's Stone '01 ▶
The Hobbit: An Unexpected Journey '12
The Hobbit: The Battle of the Five Armies '14
The Holy Mountain '73
Houdini '53
Houdini '98
Houdini '14
The House with a Clock in Its Walls '18
The Illusionist '06
The Illusionist '10 ▶
The Immigrant '13 ▶
The Incredible Burt Wonderstone '13
Is Anybody There? '08
Kids of the Round Table '96
Klaus '19 ▶
Knights of Bloodsteel '09
Kongo '32
The Linguini Incident '92
Long Life, Happiness and Prosperity '02
Lord of Illusions '95
Lord of the Rings: The Fellowship of the Ring '01 ▶
Lord of the Rings: The Two Towers '02 ▶
Lord of the Rings: The Return of the King '03 ▶
The Mad Magician '54
Magic in the Moonlight '14
Magic Man '10
The Magician '58 ▶
Merlin '98 ▶
Merlin's Apprentice '06
Miracles for Sale '39
Mr. Magorium's Wonder Emporium '07
The Mistress of Spices '05
More Than a Miracle '67
My Chauffeur '86
Mythica: A Quest for Heroes '15
Nanny McPhee '06
Next '07
Night Across the Street '12
Now You See Me 2 '16
Now You See Me '13
The Nutcracker and the Four Realms '18
Onward '20 ▶
Oz the Great and Powerful '13
Penelope '06
Penn and Teller Get Killed '90
Practical Magic '98
The Prestige '06 ▶
Prospero's Books '91 ▶
Pufnstuf '70
Ratz '99
Rough Magic '95
Scoop '06
The Secret of Moonacre '08
The Seeker: The Dark Is Rising '07
7 Faces of Dr. Lao '63 ▶
Shorts: The Adventures of the Wishing Rock '09
A Simple Wish '97
The Sleeping Beauty '10
Sleight '17
Snow White and the Huntsman '12
The Sorcerer's Apprentice '10
Stardust '07 ▶
Stephen King's Thinner '96
Strange Magic '15
The Swan Princess 2: Escape from Castle Mountain '97
Sword & the Sorcerer '82
Teen Witch '89
The Tempest '10
13 Going on 30 '04
Three . . . Extremes '04
Tomorrow We Disappear '14
Tooth Fairy '10
Two On a Guillotine '65
Willow '88
The Wizard of Gore '70
The Wizard of Gore '07
Wizards of the Demon Sword '94
The Wizards of Waverly Place: The Movie '09
Zotz! '62

Magic Carpet Rides

***See also** Genies*
Aladdin '92 ▶
Aladdin and the King of Thieves '96
Arabian Nights '00
Golden Voyage of Sinbad '73
The Magic Carpet '51
1001 Arabian Nights '59
The Seventh Voyage of Sinbad '58 ▶
Sinbad and the Eye of the Tiger '77
Sinbad of the Seven Seas '89
Sinbad, the Sailor '47 ▶
The Thief of Bagdad '40 ▶
The Thief of Baghdad '24 ▶
The Thief of Baghdad '78

Mail-Order Brides

***See also** Marriage; Wedding Bells*
Birthday Girl '02
Mail Order Bride '63
Mail Order Bride '08
Mail Order Wife '04
Mississippi Mermaid '69 ▶
Naked Jungle '54 ▶
Naughty Marietta '35
Original Sin '01
Prairie Fever '08
The Purchase Price '32
Sweet Land '05
2 Brothers & a Bride '03
Zandy's Bride '74

Makeovers

Another Cinderella Story '08
Beauty and the Boss '33
The Church Mouse '34
Cinderella '50 ▶
A Cinderella Story '04
Clueless '95 ▶
The Courtship of Andy Hardy '42
Crazy, Stupid, Love. '11 ▶
Do You Love Me? '46
Dorfman in Love '11
The DUFF '15
Enchanted '07
Ever After: A Cinderella Story '98 ▶
Fifty Shades of Grey '15
Fine Manners '26
G.B.F. '13
Geek Charming '11
Gigi '58 ▶
The Girl Most Likely to. . . '73
The Glass Slipper '55
Grease '78 ▶
Heartless '10
Her Sister from Paris '25
Hostile Makeover '09
In a Day '06
The Iron Petticoat '56
Kate Plays Christine '16 ▶
Kingsman: The Secret Service '15
La Femme Nikita '91 ▶
Lady for a Day '33 ▶
Last Holiday '06
Let Us Be Gay '30
Love Hurts '09
Made On Broadway '33
The Makeover '13
Making Mr. Right '08
The Mirror Has Two Faces '96
Miss Congeniality '00
Miss Pettigrew Lives for a Day '08 ▶
More Than A Secretary '36
Muriel's Wedding '94 ▶
My Big Fat Greek Wedding '02
My Brilliant Career '79 ▶
My Fair Lady '64 ▶
The Princess Diaries '01
Pygmalion '38 ▶
Sabrina '54 ▶
Sabrina '95
She's All That '99
Slightly Dangerous '43
Stolen Face '52
Teen Spirit '11
This Is the Night '32
Trap for Cinderella '13
Tricks of a Woman '08
Undercover Bridesmaid '12
Union Depot '32
Vacation from Marriage '45
Vertigo '58 ▶

Making Friends

***See also** Mad Scientists; Renegade Body Parts*
The Addams Family '19
Andy Warhol's Frankenstein '74
A Beautiful Day in the Neighborhood '19 ▶
Bill & Ted's Bogus Journey '91
Deadly Friend '86
Frankenhooker '90
Frankenstein '31 ▶
Frankenstein '73
Frankenstein '93
Frankenstein Created Woman '66 ▶
Frankenstein Must Be Destroyed '69
Frankenstein Reborn '98
Frankenstein Unbound '90 ▶
Frankenstein's Daughter '58
Frankenweenie '12 ▶
I, Daniel Blake '16 ▶
In the Aisles '19
Like Someone in Love '13
Little Men '16 ▶
The Little Prince '16 ▶
Lost in Space '98
Making Mr. Right '86
Mary Shelley's Frankenstein '94
Multiplicity '96
Neighbors 2: Sorority Rising '16
Nina '16
Picture Day '13
Repli-Kate '01
Standing Up '13
Swiss Army Man '16
Young Frankenstein '74 ▶

Marriage

***See also** Divorce; In-Laws; Killer Spouses; Marriage Hell; Marriages of Convenience; Otherwise Engaged; War Between the Sexes; Wedding Bells; Wedding Hell*

Marriage Hell

***See also** Divorce; Domestic Abuse; Killer Spouses; Marriages of Convenience*
Abraham's Valley '93
Acrimony '18
Adopt a Sailor '08
Affairs of Anatol '21
After Sex '97
Afterglow '97
All Things Fair '95
American Beauty '99 ▶
Amnesia '96
Angel '37
Angels in America '03 ▶
Anglo-Saxon Attitudes '92
Anna Karenina '96
Another Woman '94
Antichrist '09
Attack of the 50 Ft. Woman '93
Autumn Hearts: A New Beginning '07
The Backwoods '06
Bad Manners '98
Band Aid '17
The Beaver '11
Behind That Curtain '29
The Best Intentions '92 ▶
Between Us '12
Beyond Betrayal '94
B.F.'s Daughter '48
Big Eyes '14
The Big Squeeze '96
The Bigamist '53
Blanche Fury '48
Blind Date '08
Blonde Venus '32 ▶
The Blood Oranges '97
Blood Wedding '81 ▶
The Blue Tooth Virgin '09
Blue Valentine '10
Bluebeard '09
The Box '09
Bright Leaf '50
The Buccaneers '95 ▶
The Burning Bed '85 ▶
A Burning Hot Summer '11
The Buttercup Chain '70
The Captive '14
Car Trouble '86
Carry On Cabby '63
Cast a Dark Shadow '55 ▶
Catherine Cookson's The Man Who Cried '93
Cause for Alarm '51
Chained '34
A Change of Seasons '80
Charles & Diana: A Palace Divided '93
Charulata '64
Cheaters '84
Cheatin' Hearts '93
Child Bride of Short Creek '81
Chinese Roulette '86
Clash by Night '52 ▶
Cold Heaven '92
Come Back, Little Sheba '52 ▶
The Comfort of Strangers '91 ▶
Committed '99
Conflict '45 ▶
Consinsual '10
Cool and the Crazy '94
Cotton Mary '99
Country Girl '54 ▶
Cover '08
Crazy Love '07 ▶
Crime & Passion '75
The Crimson Petal and the White '12
Cul de Sac '66 ▶
Damage '92 ▶
Dangerous Game '93
Dangerous Liaisons '60
Daniel Deronda '02
Day-Time Wife '39
Dead in the Water '91
Dead Mate '88
Death Kiss '74
Desire and Hell at Sunset Motel '92
Desire Under the Elms '58
The Details '11
Dial 'M' for Murder '54 ▶
Diary of a Mad Black Woman '05
The Diary of Ellen Rimbauer '03
Did You Hear About the Morgans? '09
The Dish & the Spoon '11
Divorce Wars: A Love Story '82
The Divorcee '30
A Doll's House '73
A Doll's House '73 ▶
Dominique '79
The Door in the Floor '04 ▶
Double Indemnity '44 ▶
Downloading Nancy '08
Dream Lover '93
Drew Peterson: Untouchable '12
Drowning by Numbers '87 ▶
The Duchess '08 ▶
Easy Living '49
The Edge of Love '08
Effi Briest '74 ▶
Element of Doubt '96
Ellie '84
Emmanuelle, the Queen '79
Enough '02
The Entertainer '60 ▶
Ethan Frome '92
Everlasting Moments '08
Faithful '95
Faithless '00 ▶
Falling for a Dancer '98
The Family Tree '10
Far from Heaven '02 ▶
5x2 '04
The Flower of My Secret '95 ▶
Four Corners of Suburbia '05
French Twist '95
Gaslight '40 ▶
Gaslight '44 ▶
The Girl in the Red Velvet Swing '55
The Golden Bowl '72 ▶
The Golden Bowl '00
Gone Girl '14 ▶
Good '08
A Good Marriage '14
The Good Wife '86
Grindstone Road '07
Gun Hill Road '11
Happy, Happy '10
The Hawk '93
Haywire '80
Head Above Water '96
The Heart of Me '02
Heartburn '86 ▶
Heaven '99
Heroes of the East '08 ▶
He's Just Not That Into You '09
Hitched '01
Hollywood Wives: The New Generation '03
Home Before Dark '58
The Horrible Dr. Hichcock '62
Hot Blood '56
Hurry Sundown '67
Husbands and Wives '92 ▶
Hush '98
I Do & I Don't '07
I Smile Back '15
I Was Happy Here '66
Ice Follies of 1939 '39
If I Were Free '33
If Winter Comes '41
Illicit '31
In Name Only '39

▶ = rated three bones or higher

The Innocent '76
Innocents with Dirty Hands '76
Intent to Kill '58
The Intervention '16
The Inveterate Bachelor '58
Invisible '06
The Invisible Woman '13 ▶
The Jane Austen Book Club '07 ▶
Ju Dou '90 ▶
Jude the Obscure '71
Keyhole '11
The Kill-Off '89
Killing Me Softly '01
La Bete Humaine '38 ▶
Lantana '01 ▶
Lea '96
L'Enfer '93 ▶
Let's Kill Ward's Wife '14
Lies My Mother Told Me '05
Life During Wartime '09
Little Devil '07
Lost Holiday: The Jim & Suzanne Shemwell Story '07
Loulou '80 ▶
A Love Divided '01
The Love Guru '08
The Love Parade '29
The Lovers '59 ▶
The Lovers '17 ▶
Lured Innocence '97
Lymelife '08
Mad Love '01
Madame Bovary '91 ▶
Madame Butterfly '95
Maggie's Plan '16
Mail Order Wife '04
The Man I Married '40
The Man in the Net '59
Man-Trap '61
Maneater '09
Marie and Bruce '04
Married Life '07 ▶
A Matter of Dignity '57
Merrily We Go to Hell '32
Moon over Harlem '39
Moscow, Belgium '08
Mouth to Mouth '95
My Blueberry Nights '07
My Husband's Double Life '01
The Nanny Diaries '07
Nature's Grave '08
Necessity '88
Nevermore '07
99 River Street '53
No Down Payment '57
Nora '00
Normal Life '96
Not Easily Broken '09
The One I Love '14
One Trick Pony '80
Overboard '18
The Painted Veil '34
The Painted Veil '06
Paradise: Faith '12
Payment on Demand '51
A Perfect Man '13
A Perfect Murder '98
Personal Vendetta '96
Petulia '68 ▶
Petunia '13
Portrait of a Lady '67
Portrait of an Assassin '49
The Pumpkin Eater '64 ▶
Queen Bee '55
Rabbit, Run '70
Rage in Heaven '41
A Rage to Live '65
Raise the Red Lantern '91 ▶
Raton Pass '51
Reversal of Fortune '90 ▶
Revolutionary Road '08
The Rich Man's Wife '96
Romance & Cigarettes '05
Rose of Washington Square '39
Roses Are for the Rich '87
The Salesman '16 ▶
The Scar of Shame '27
Scenes from a Mall '91
Scenes from a Marriage '73 ▶
Scorchers '92
The Sea of Grass '47
Second Skin '99
Secret Beyond the Door '48
The Secret Life of Girls '99
Separate Lies '05
A Separation '11
Serena '14
Serious Moonlight '09
7 Days to Live '00
Seventh Heaven '98
She-Devil '89
Shed No Tears '48
Shoot the Moon '82
Silent Victim '92
Simon and Laura '55
Sleep, My Love '48
Sleeping with the Enemy '91
Slippery Slope '06
Snow Angels '07 ▶
So Well Remembered '47
The Stepford Wives '75 ▶
The Stepford Wives '04
Stolen Face '52
The Stone Angel '07
The Stone Merchant '06
The Stoning of Soraya M. '08
Story of a Love Affair '50
Straw Dogs '11
Sudden Fear '52 ▶
Summer in February '13
Suspicion '41 ▶
The Taste of Money '12
Ten Cents a Dance '31
Tender Is the Night '62
Tension '50
Term of Trial '63
3 Backyards '10
Till Murder Do Us Part '92
Timbuktu '59
Tom & Viv '94 ▶
Too Far to Go '79 ▶
Tornado '43
Town and Country '01
The Toy Wife '38
Twinkletoes '26
Two for the Road '67 ▶
The Two Mr. Kissels '08
Tyler Perry's Hell Hath No Fury Like a Woman Scorned: The Play '14
Tyrannosaur '11
Under Capricorn '49
Under Still Waters '08
Undercurrent '46
Up the Ladder '25
Vacancy '07
Valerie '57
The Waiting City '09
The War of the Roses '89 ▶
Water for Elephants '11
We Don't Live Here Anymore '04
Weakness '10
Welcome to the Rileys '10
What Happens in Vegas '08
When the Bough Breaks '16
Where Hearts Lie '16
White Woman '33
The Whole Truth '16
Who's Afraid of Virginia Woolf? '66 ▶
The Widowing of Mrs. Holroyd '95
Wildlife '18 ▶
With a Song in My Heart '52 ▶
The Woman on the Beach '47
Wuthering Heights '09
You Will Meet a Tall Dark Stranger '10
Young Man With Ideas '52

Marriages of Convenience

Angelique '64
August '11
Between Love & Goodbye '08
Boulevard '15
Brokeback Mountain '05 ▶
The Canadian '26
Come Live With Me '40
The Crown Prince '06
De-Lovely '04
Design for Living '33
Fall Guy '82
Flickers '80
Float '08
The Golden Arrow '36
The Great McGinty '40 ▶
Green Card '90
The Groom Wore Spurs '51
Head On '04
I Do '13 ▶
I Now Pronounce You Chuck and Larry '07
Immigration Tango '11
Kill the Poor '03
The Last of the Mobile Hotshots '69
Loco Love '03
Lorna's Silence '08
Love for Rent '05
Love or Money '01
Loving Leah '09
Lucky '11
Mail Order Wife '04
Never Say Die '39
A Paper Wedding '89 ▶
The Princess of Montpensier '10 ▶
The Proposal '09
Seducing Maarya '99
Small Island '09
Sunny '30
Therese '12
Tim Burton's Corpse Bride '05 ▶
2 Brothers & a Bride '03
The Wedding Banquet '93 ▶
Wild Is the Wind '57
You May Not Kiss the Bride '12

Mars

***See also** Space Operas*

Abbott and Costello Go to Mars '53
The Angry Red Planet '59
Approaching the Unknown '16
Buck Rogers in the 25th Century '79
Capricorn One '78 ▶
Cave Women on Mars '08
Christmas on Mars '08
Crimson Force '05
Destination Mars '06
Doom '05
Flight to Mars '52
Frankenstein Meets the Space Monster '65
The Invader '96
It! The Terror from Beyond Space '58
John Carpenter's Ghosts of Mars '01
John Carter '12
The Last Days on Mars '13
Life '17
Mars Attacks! '96
Mars Needs Moms '11
The Martian '15 ▶
The Martian Chronicles: Part 1 '79
The Martian Chronicles: Part 2 '79
The Martian Chronicles: Part 3 '79
Mission to Mars '00
My Favorite Martian '98
Planet of Blood '66
Project Shadowchaser 3000 '95
Queen of Blood '66
Red Faction: Origins '11
Red Planet '00
Red Planet Mars '52
RocketMan '97
Rocketship X-M '50
Santa Claus Conquers the Martians '64
Species 2 '98
Total Recall '90 ▶
The War of the Planets '65
War of the Worlds 2: The Next Wave '08
Zombies of the Stratosphere '52

Martial Arts

***See also** Ninjas; Supernatural Martial Arts*

Above the Law '88
Aeon Flux '05
Alley Cat '84
Altitude '17
American Chinatown '96
American Kickboxer 1 '91
American Kickboxer 2: To the Death '93
American Ninja 2: The Confrontation '87
American Ninja 3: Blood Hunt '89
American Ninja 4: The Annihilation '91
American Ninja '85
American Samurai '92
American Streetfighter '96
The Amsterdam Connection '78
Angel Town '89
The Art of Self-Defense '19 ▶
Ashes of Time '94 ▶
Ashes of Time Redux '08
The Assassin '15 ▶
The Assassin's Blade '08
Azumi 2 '05
Azumi '03 ▶
Back in Action '94
Balls of Fury '07
Bat Without Wings '80
Battle Creek Brawl '80
Beatdown '10
The Bells of Death '68
Belly of the Beast '03
Best of the Best 2 '93
Best of the Best 3: No Turning Back '95
Best of the Best '89
Best of the Best: Without Warning '98
Beverly Hills Ninja '96
The Big Brawl '80
Big Stan '07
Big Trouble in Little China '86
Black Belt '92
Black Belt Jones '74
Black Eagle '88
Black Mask 2: City of Masks '02
Black Mask '96
Black Samurai '77
Blackbelt 2: Fatal Force '93
Blind Fury '90
Bloodfist '89
Bloodfist 2 '90
Bloodfist 3: Forced to Fight '92
Bloodfist 4: Die Trying '92
Bloodfist 5: Human Target '93
Bloodfist 6: Ground Zero '94
Bloodfist 7: Manhunt '95
Bloodfist 8: Hard Way Out '96
Bloodsport 4: The Dark Kumite '98
Bloodsport '88
The Bodyguard 2 '07
The Bodyguard '76
The Bodyguard '04
Born Losers '67
Born to Fight '07
Born to Raise Hell '10
Braddock: Missing in Action 3 '88
Brave '07
The Brave Archer '77
The Brave Archer and His Mate '82
Breaker! Breaker! '77
Breathing Fire '91
The Bride with White Hair '93
The Bride with White Hair 2 '93
The Bronx Executioner '86
Bruce Lee Fights Back from the Grave '76
Bulletproof Monk '03
The Bushido Blade '80
Butterfly Sword '93
Capital Punishment '96
Catch the Heat '87
The Cave of the Silken Web '67
China O'Brien '88
The Chinatown Kid '78
Chinese Connection 2 '77
Chinese Connection '73
Chinese Odyssey 2002 '02
Circle of Iron '78
The Circuit 2 '02
The City of Violence '06
Cleopatra Jones '73
Cleopatra Jones & the Casino of Gold '75
The Cobra '68
Come Drink with Me '65 ▶
Counter Attack '84
Cradle 2 the Grave '03
Crime Story '93
The Crippled Masters '82
Crouching Tiger, Hidden Dragon '00 ▶
Crouching Tiger, Hidden Dragon: Sword of Destiny '16
Curse of the Golden Flower '06
A Dangerous Place '94
Day of the Panther '88
Deadly Bet '91
Deadly Target '94
Death Machines '76
Death Ring '93
Death Trance '05
Death Warrant '90
The Delightful Forest '72
DOA: Dead or Alive '06
Dolemite '75
Double Dragon '94
Double Impact '91
Dragon Eyes '12
Dragon Lord '82
Dragon: The Bruce Lee Story '93 ▶
Dragon Tiger Gate '07
Dragons Forever '88
Duel of Fists '71
The Duel of the Century '81
Duel to the Death '82
The Dynamite Brothers '74
Eagle's Shadow '84
8 Diagram Pole Fighter '84 ▶
18 Fingers of Death '05
Elektra '05
Empire of Assassins '11
An Empress and the Warriors '08
Enter the Dragon '73 ▶
Enter the Ninja '81
Enter the Warriors Gate '17
The Executioners '93
An Eye for an Eye '81
Fantasy Mission Force '84
Fearless Tiger '94
Ferocious Female Freedom Fighters '88
The Fight Within '16
Final Impact '91
Firecracker '81
Firewall '06
Fist of Fear, Touch of Death '80
Fist of Legend '94
Fists of Fury '73 ▶
Five Deadly Venoms '78 ▶
Five Element Ninjas '82
Flash Point '07
The Foot Fist Way '08
The Forbidden Kingdom '08
Force of One '79
Forced to Fight '11
Forced Vengeance '82
Full Contact '93
Futurekick '91
G2: Mortal Conquest '99
Game of Death '79
Gang Justice '94
Ghostwarrior '86
Gladiator Cop: The Swordsman 2 '95
The Glimmer Man '96
Golden Swallow '68 ▶
Goldfinger '64 ▶
Good Guys Wear Black '78
The Grandmaster '13
The Great Challenge '04
Guardian Angel '94
The Guardsman '15
Gymkata '85
Half a Loaf of Kung Fu '78
Hard Target 2 '16
Hard to Kill '89
Have Sword, Will Travel '69
Hawk's Vengeance '96
Heart of Dragon '85
Heatseeker '95
Heaven & Hell '78
Here Comes the Boom '12
Hero '02 ▶
Hero and the Terror '88
Heroes of the East '08 ▶
Heroes Two '73
The Heroic Ones '70
The Heroic Trio '93
Honor '06
Hot Potato '76
House of Flying Daggers '04 ▶
House of Fury '05
House of Traps '81
Ichi '08
Immortal Combat '94
In Your Face '77
Infra-Man '76
Intimate Confessions of a Chinese Courtesan '72
Invasion U.S.A. '85
Ip Man 2 '10
Ip Man 3 '16
Ip Man 4: The Finale '19
Ip Man '08
Iron Monkey '93
Jackie Chan's First Strike '96 ▶
Jackie Chan's The Myth '05
Jade Warrior '06
Jaguar Lives '79
Jet Li's Fearless '06
Jet Li's The Enforcer '95
Joe Somebody '01
Journey of the Doomed '85
Journey to the West '14
Karate Cop '91
The Karate Kid '84 ▶
The Karate Kid '10
The Karate Kid: Part 2 '86
The Karate Kid: Part 3 '89
Kentucky Fried Movie '77 ▶
Kickboxer '89
Kickboxer 2: The Road Back '90
Kickboxer 3: The Art of War '92
Kickboxer 4: The Aggressor '94
Kickboxer: Vengeance '16
Kill! '68
Kill and Kill Again '81
Kill Bill Vol. 1 '03 ▶
Kill Bill Vol. 2 '04 ▶
Kill 'Em All '12
Kill Line '91
Kill or Be Killed '66
King Boxer '72
Kingdom of Blood: The Final Battle '16
Kiss of the Dragon '01
Knock Off '98
Knucklehead '10
The Kumite '03
Kung Fu '72
Kung Fu Hustle '04
Kung Fu Panda '08 ▶
Kung Fu Panda 2 '11 ▶
Kung Fu Panda 3 '16 ▶
Kung Fu: The Movie '86
Kung Pow! Enter the Fist '02
Lady Dragon '92
Lady Snowblood: Love Song of Vengeance '74
The Last Airbender '10
The Last Dragon '85
Last Hurrah for Chivalry '78
Latin Dragon '03
Legacy of Rage '86
The Legend of Drunken Master '94 ▶
Legend of the Liquid Sword '93
The Legend of the 7 Golden Vampires '73
The Legend of the Shadowless Sword '08
Lethal Ninja '93
Lionheart '90
Little Dragons '80
Lone Tiger '94
Lone Wolf and Cub '72
Lone Wolf and Cub: Baby Cart at the River Styx '72
The Magic Blade '08
Magic Kid 2 '94
Magic Kid '92
The Magnificent Trio '66
Man of Tai Chi '13
The Man with the Iron Fists '12
Marked for Death '90
Martial Outlaw '93
The Master '80
Master of the Flying Guillotine '75

▶ = rated three bones or higher

Master with Cracked Fingers '71
Maximum Risk '96
The Medallion '03
Meltdown '95
Miami Connection '87
The Millionaire's Express '86
Mr. Nice Guy '98
Mortal Kombat 1: The Movie '95
Mortal Kombat 2: Annihilation '97
Moving Target '00
Negative Happy Chainsaw Edge '08
Never Back Down 2: The Beatdown '11
Never Back Down '08
Never Back Down: No Surrender '16
Never Surrender '09
New Fist of Fury '76
New York Cop '94
The Next Karate Kid '94
Night Hunter '95
Night Master '87
Night of the Warrior '91
9 1/2 Ninjas '90
Nine Deaths of the Ninja '85
Ninja Academy '90
Ninja Assassin '09
Ninja Connection '90
Ninja in the U.S.A. '88
Ninja the Battalion '90
Ninja's Creed '09
Octagon '80
Omega Cop '90
Once Upon a Time in China '91 ▶
Once Upon a Time in China II '92 ▶
Once Upon a Time in China III '93 ▶
The One '01
The One-Armed Swordsman '67 ▶
One Down, Two to Go! '82
One Man Army '93
Ong Bak 2 '08
Ong-Bak '03 ▶
Only the Strong '93
Operation Condor '91
Opium and Kung-Fu Master '84 ▶
Out for Blood '93
Out for Justice '91
The Perfect Weapon '91
Pit Fighter '05
The Power Within '95
Pray for Death '85
The President's Man 2: A Line in the Sand '02
The President's Man '00
The Princess Blade '02
The Prisoner '90
The Prodigal Son '82
Project A '83
Project A: Part 2 '87 ▶
The Promise '05
Protector '85
The Purifiers '04
Pushed to the Limit '92
The Quest '96
Rage and Honor '92
Rage and Honor 2: Hostile Takeover '93
Rage of Honor '87
Ragin' Cajun '90
Raging Phoenix '09
The Raid: Redemption '11 ▶
Rapid Fire '92
Raw Force '81
Raw Target '95
The Rebel '08 ▶
Red Shadow '01
Redbelt '08 ▶
Redemption: Kickboxer 5 '95
Reign of Assassins '10
Remo Williams: The Adventure Begins '85
Retrievers '82
Return of the Dragon '73
Return of the Street Fighter '74
Revenge of the Ninja '83
Rica 2: Lonely Wanderer '73
Rica 3: Juvenile's Lullaby '73
Rica '72
Ring of Fire 2: Blood and Steel '92
Ring of Fire 3: Lion Strike '94
Ring of Fire '91
Riot '96
Romeo Must Die '00
Rumble in the Bronx '96
Running on Karma '03
Samurai Cop '89
The Sanctuary '09
Sanshiro Sugata '43 ▶
Sci-Fighter '04
Scorpion '86
7 Grand Masters '04 ▶
Seven Swords '07
Shanghai Express '86
Shanghai Knights '03
Shaolin & Wu Tang '81 ▶
Shaolin Soccer '01
The Shepherd: Border Patrol '08
Showdown in Little Tokyo '91
Silent Rage '82
Silver Hawk '04
Sister Street Fighter 2: Hanging by a Thread '74
Sister Street Fighter '76
The Sorcerer and the White Snake '13
The Spy Next Door '10
Stranglehold '94
The Street Fighter '74
Street Fighter: The Legend of Chun-Li '09
The Street Fighter's Last Revenge '74
Supercop 2 '93
Supercop '92
Surf Ninjas '93
Sword Masters: Brothers Five '70
Sword Masters: Two Champions of Shaolin '80
Sword Masters: Web of Death '76
Sword of Doom '67 ▶
Sword of Honor '94
Swordsmen in Double Flag Town '91
Sworn to Justice '97
Talons of the Eagle '92
Teenage Mutant Ninja Turtles: The Movie '90
Teenage Mutant Ninja Turtles 2: The Secret of the Ooze '91
Teenage Mutant Ninja Turtles 3 '93
Teenage Mutant Ninja Turtles '14
The 36th Chamber of Shaolin '78 ▶
3 Ninjas '92
3 Ninjas: High Noon at Mega Mountain '97
3 Ninjas Kick Back '94
3 Ninjas Knuckle Up '95
Throw Down '00
Tiger Claws '91
Tiger Heart '96
Timecop 2: The Berlin Decision '03
Timecop '94
TKO '06
TNT Jackson '75
To Be the Best '93
Tokyo Raiders '00 ▶
Top Dog '95
Trancers 3: Deth Lives '92
Transformed '05
Triple Threat '19
Tube '03
Twin Dragons '92
Twin Warriors '93
Ultraviolet '06
Undefeatable '94
Unleashed '05
Vampire Assassin '05
Vampire Effect '03
The Vanquisher '10
Versus '00
Warrior '11 ▶
Warrior of Justice '96
The Way To Fight '96
White Tiger '95
Wing Chun '94
Young Master '80
Young Tiger '74
Zatoichi: Master Ichi and a Chest of Gold '64
Zatoichi: The Blind Swordsman and the Chess Expert '65
Zatoichi: The Blind Swordsman's Vengeance '66
Zatoichi vs. Yojimbo '70 ▶
Zu Warriors '01

Mass Media

***See** Front Page; Radio*

Masseurs

At First Sight '98
Happy Times '00
Living Out Loud '98
Love Kills '98
The Mystic Masseur '01
Never Say Never Again '83
Winter of Frozen Dreams '08

Matchmakers & Matchmaking

A Christmas Wedding Tail '11
Crossing Delancey '88 ▶
Cupid '12
Fiddler on the Roof '71 ▶
A Golden Christmas 2: The Second Tail '11
Hello, Dolly! '69
Junior Miss '45
Love & Friendship '16 ▶
Love Is a Ball '63
The Matchmaker '58 ▶
The Matchmaker '97
The Model and the Marriage Broker '51
Straight from the Heart '03
Tish '42

Mathemagicians

Agatha Christie's Murder is Easy '82
The Bank '01
A Beautiful Mind '01 ▶
Beautiful Ohio '06
A Brilliant Young Mind '14
The Computer Wore Tennis Shoes '69
Conceiving Ada '97
Cube '98
Dear Brigitte '65
Domain '09
Enigma '01
Gifted '17
Good Will Hunting '97
Hidden Figures '17 ▶
The Imitation Game '14 ▶
An Invisible Sign '11
The Last Enemy '08
The Oxford Murders '08
Pi '98
Proof '91 ▶
Proof '05 ▶
Rain Man '88 ▶
Raising Genius '04
Real Genius '85 ▶
Sphere '97
Stand and Deliver '88 ▶
Stand-In '37 ▶
21 '08
21 Grams '03 ▶

May-December Romance

***See also** Coming of Age; Growing Older; Romantic Adventure*

Adore '13
After Sex '97
All That Heaven Allows '55 ▶
Atlantic City '81 ▶
Autumn in New York '00
The Best Offer '13
Bright Days Ahead '14
Cass Timberlane '47
The Cat's Meow '01
Cheri '09
Compulsion '08
Crash Pad '17
Crush '02
Elegy '08
A Fantastic Woman '18
Fascination '04
Film Stars Don't Die in Liverpool '17
Flirting with Forty '09
Forty Shades of Blue '05
The Gang's All Here '43
Georgy Girl '66 ▶
Girl with Green Eyes '64
Girl's Dormitory '36
The Graduate '67 ▶
Guinevere '99 ▶
Harold and Maude '71 ▶
Home Again '17
The Housekeeper '02
How to Be a Latin Lover '17
The Human Stain '03
I Heart Huckabees '04
Interlude '68
Intermission '03 ▶
The Invisible Woman '13 ▶
The Last of Robin Hood '13
Lolita '62 ▶
Lolita '97
Love and Pain and the Whole Damn Thing '73
Love in the Afternoon '57
The Love Letter '99
Love Ranch '10
Lured Innocence '97
Middle of the Night '59
The Mother '03 ▶
Nelly et Monsieur Arnaud '95 ▶
The New Romantic '18
Our Lady of the Assassins '01
The Pallbearer '95
Perfect Love '96
Phantom Thread '17 ▶
Prime '05
P.S. '04
The Quiet American '02 ▶
Reckless '97 ▶
Reckless: The Sequel '98 ▶
Roman Spring of Mrs. Stone '61 ▶
Rumor Has It. . . '05
Sabrina '54 ▶
Seducing Maarya '99
Shopgirl '05 ▶
Six Days, Seven Nights '98
Slogan '69
Some Kind of Beautiful '15
Stay '13
Suburban Girl '07
That Obscure Object of Desire '77 ▶
Tim '79
Trojan Eddie '96 ▶
Venus '06 ▶
Whatever Works '09
Widow on the Hill '05

The Meaning of Life

The Apostle '97 ▶
Being Human '94
Bless Me, Ultima '13
Brad's Status '17
The Designated Mourner '97
Do You Believe? '15
Don't Think Twice '16
Emma's Chance '16
End of the Road '70
Field of Dreams '89 ▶
The French Lieutenant's Woman '81 ▶
Funny Face '57 ▶
Gospa '94
Healing '15
Heaven Can Wait '43 ▶
Heaven Can Wait '78 ▶
Here Comes Mr. Jordan '41 ▶
The Hitchhiker's Guide to the Galaxy '05 ▶
Home Run '13
I Am Potential '15
It's All So Quiet '13
Jeff, Who Lives at Home '12
Julian Po '97
The Late Bloomer '16
The Letters '15
The Longest Week '14
Love and Death '75 ▶
Lucky '17 ▶
The Meddler '15 ▶
Monty Python's The Meaning of Life '83 ▶
My Life '93
My Own Private Idaho '91 ▶
Night Across the Street '12
Nina '16
October Baby '12
Off the Lip '04
Prince Avalanche '13
Pygmy Island '50
The Razor's Edge '46 ▶
The Razor's Edge '84
The Remains of the Day '93 ▶
Searching For Wooden Watermelons '01
Seven Days in Utopia '11
Shadowlands '93 ▶
The Sheltering Sky '90 ▶
Tattoo, a Love Story '02
The Trial '93
Where Hope Grows '15
Why Has Bodhi-Darma Left for the East '89
Wings of Desire '88 ▶
A Woman's a Helluva Thing '01
Zabriskie Point '70 ▶
Zero Charisma '13

Medieval Romps

***See also** Camelot (Old); Historical Drama; Period Piece; Swashbucklers*

The Adventures of Marco Polo '38
The Adventures of Robin Hood '38 ▶
Age of the Dragons '11
Army of Darkness '92 ▶
Assassin's Creed '16
Becket '64 ▶
Being Human '94
Black Death '10
Black Knight '01
The Black Rose '50
Braveheart '95 ▶
Camelot '67
The Canterbury Tales '71
The Castilian '63
Choice of Weapons '76
Chunhyang '00
The Company of Wolves '85 ▶
Conquest of the Normans '62
Crusade: A March through Time '06
Deathstalker 2: Duel of the Titans '87
Deathstalker '83
The Decameron '70 ▶
Decameron Nights '53
Destiny '97
Diane '55
Don Quixote '57 ▶
Donkey Skin '70 ▶
Dragon Storm '04
Dragonheart '96
Dragonheart: A New Beginning '00
Dragonslayer '81 ▶
El Cid '61 ▶
Excalibur '81 ▶
The Fighting Prince of Donegal '66
First Knight '95
The Flame & the Arrow '50 ▶
Flesh and Blood '85
Francesco '93
Gate of Hell '54 ▶
George and the Dragon '04
The Great Wall '17
Hamlet '90 ▶
Hawk the Slayer '81
In the Name of the King: A Dungeon Siege Tale '08
Inquisition '76
Ironclad '11
Ivanhoe '52 ▶
Ivanhoe '82
Ivanhoe '97 ▶
Jabberwocky '77
Jack the Giant Killer '62 ▶
The Juniper Tree '87
Just Visiting '01
King Arthur: Legend of the Sword '17
King Arthur, the Young Warlord '75
Kingdom of Heaven '05 ▶
A Knight in Camelot '98
Knights of the Round Table '53
A Knight's Tale '01
Ladyhawke '85
The Lady's Not for Burning '87
Lancelot of the Lake '74
Legend '86
The Lion in Winter '68 ▶
The Lion in Winter '03 ▶
Lionheart '87
The Little Hours '17 ▶
The Magic Stone '95
The Magic Sword '62
Mark of the Devil 2 '72
Mark of the Devil '69
Masque of the Red Death '65 ▶
The Mongols '60
Monty Python and the Holy Grail '75 ▶
The Name of the Rose '86
The Navigator '88 ▶
Omar Khayyam '57
Onibaba '64 ▶
Outlaw King '18
Passion of Joan of Arc '28 ▶
Perceval '78
Pied Piper '72
Pillars of the Earth '10
Pippin '81 ▶
The Prince of Thieves '48
Princess of Thieves '01
Quest for Camelot '98
Ran '85 ▶
Rashomon '51 ▶
The Return of Martin Guerre '83 ▶
Richard III '55 ▶
Robin and Marian '76
Robin Hood '22 ▶
Robin Hood '73 ▶
Robin Hood '91 ▶
Robin Hood '10
Robin Hood: Men in Tights '93
Robin Hood: Prince of Thieves '91
Robin Hood. . . The Legend: Robin Hood and the Sorcerer '83
Sansho the Bailiff '54 ▶
Season of the Witch '10
Seven Samurai '54 ▶
The Seventh Seal '56 ▶
Sorceress '88 ▶
Star Knight '85
Sword & the Sorcerer '82
The Sword in the Stone '63 ▶
Sword of Lancelot '63
Sword of Sherwood Forest '60
Sword of the Valiant '83
Temptation of a Monk '94
The 13th Warrior '99
Throne of Blood '57 ▶
Time Bandits '81
Timeline '03
Transformers: The Last Knight '17
Tristan & Isolde '06
The Undead '57
Unidentified Flying Oddball '79
The Vikings '58
The Warrior & the Sorceress '84
Wholly Moses! '80
Wizards of the Demon Sword '94
Young Ivanhoe '95
Young Warlord '75
Your Highness '11

Meltdown

***See also** Disaster Flicks*

Above and Beyond '53 ▶
Amazing Grace & Chuck '87
American Meltdown '04
The Atomic Cafe '82 ▶
The Atomic Kid '54
Bad Moms '16
Beneath the Planet of the Apes '70
Black Rain '88 ▶
Bloodfist 6: Ground Zero '94
Bomb Squad '97
Broken Arrow '95
The Caretaker '16
Chain Reaction '80
Chernobyl Diaries '12
The China Syndrome '79 ▶

▶ = rated three bones or higher

Cloak and Dagger '46
Countdown to Zero '10
Crimson Tide '95 ▶
Critical Mass '00
Danger Beneath the Sea '02
The Day After '83 ▶
The Day the Earth Caught Fire '61 ▶
The Death Merchant '91
Desert Bloom '86 ▶
Disorder '16
Dr. Strangelove, or: How I Learned to Stop Worrying and Love the Bomb '64 ▶
Doomsdayer '00
Fail-Safe '64 ▶
Fat Man and Little Boy '89
First Spaceship on Venus '60 ▶
First Strike '85
Flight of Black Angel '91
The Fourth Protocol '87 ▶
Freedom Strike '98
Future Kill '85
Gangland '00
Geisha Girl '52
Glen and Randa '71
H-Man '59
Hiroshima '95 ▶
I Live in Fear '55 ▶
Interceptor Force 2 '02
Invasion U.S.A. '52
Jackie Chan's First Strike '96 ▶
MacGruber '10
The Manhattan Project '86
Massive Retaliation '85
Miracle Mile '89 ▶
Modern Problems '81
Night Siege Project: Shadowchaser 2 '94
Nuclear Hurricane '07
A Nymphoid Barbarian in Dinosaur Hell '94
Omega Man '71
On the Beach '59 ▶
On the Beach '00
Panic in Year Zero! '62
The Patriot '86
The Peacekeeper '98
The Peacemaker '97
Prisoner in the Middle '74
Reactor '78
The Reflecting Skin '91
Rhapsody in August '91
Rocket Attack U.S.A. '58
The Sacrifice '86 ▶
Scorcher '02
Seven Days in May '64 ▶
The Shoes of the Fisherman '68
Silkwood '83 ▶
Slugs '87
Southland Tales '06
Special Bulletin '83 ▶
Split Second '53
The Spy Who Loved Me '77
Sun Choke '16
Superman 4: The Quest for Peace '87
The Terminators '09
Testament '83 ▶
Thirst Street '17
This Is Not a Test '62
True Lies '94
The 27th Day '57
U.S. Seals 2 '01
Universal Soldier: Regeneration '09
Unknown World '51
Utopia '51
Voyage to the Bottom of the Sea '61 ▶
WarGames '83
Warhead '96
When the Wind Blows '86 ▶
The World Is Not Enough '99
Young Lady Chatterly 2 '85

Memphis

See also American South; Nashville Narratives

The Blind Side '09
The Client '94
Elvis: The Movie '79
Finding Graceland '98
The Firm '93 ▶
Forty Shades of Blue '05
The Grace Card '11
Hustle & Flow '05 ▶
John Grisham's The Rainmaker '97
Kill Switch '08
The Loss of a Teardrop Diamond '08
My Blueberry Nights '07
Mystery Train '89 ▶
Porto '17
The Silence of the Lambs '91 ▶
Undefeated '11
Walk the Line '05 ▶

Men

See also Dads; Repressed Men; War Between the Sexes

Men in Prison

See also Fugitives; Great Escapes; POW/MIA; Women in Prison

Adam's Woman '70
After Innocence '05 ▶
Against the Wall '94 ▶
All the Pretty Horses '00
American History X '98
American Me '92 ▶
American Violence '17
Andersonville '95 ▶
Angels with Dirty Faces '38 ▶
Animal 2 '07
Animal '05
Animal Factory '00
Appointment with Crime '45
Bad Boys '83 ▶
Bait '00
Band of the Hand '86
Beaumarchais the Scoundrel '96
Before Night Falls '00 ▶
Beggar's Opera '54
Beyond Re-Animator '03
Beyond the Call '96
Beyond the Walls '12
Big House, U.S.A. '55
Big Stan '07
Birdman of Alcatraz '62 ▶
Black Lemons '70
Blackwell's Island '39
Bloodsport 4: The Dark Kumite '98
Blow '01
Blues Brothers 2000 '98
The Boston Strangler: The Untold Story '08
Boys of Abu Ghraib '14
Boys Will Be Boys '35
Break of Dawn '88
Breaker Morant '80 ▶
Breakout '75
Broken Hill '09
Bronson '09
Brubaker '80 ▶
Brute Force '47 ▶
Bundy: A Legacy of Evil '08
Buried Alive '39
The Cable Guy '96
Caged Animal '10
Call Northside 777 '48 ▶
Camp X-Ray '14
Captives '94
Carandiru '03
Carbine Williams '52
Castle on the Hudson '40 ▶
Catch a Fire '06
Catch Me If You Can '02
Cell 2455, Death Row '55
Cell 211 '09
Cell 213 '11
Cellmates '12
The Chamber '96
Chopper '00
City Without Men '43
Club Fed '90
The Color of Freedom '07
Con Air '97 ▶
Con Games '02
Confusion of Genders '00
Convict Cowboy '95
Convicted '50
Conviction '02
Conviction '10
Cool Hand Luke '67 ▶
The Count of Monte Cristo '12
The Count of Monte Cristo '34 ▶
The Count of Monte Cristo '99
The Count of Monte Cristo '02
The Craigslist Killer '11
The Criminal Code '31
Criminal Justice '08
Cry Danger '51 ▶
Dangerous Relations '93
Dante 01 '08
The Daring Young Man '35
Dark Blue World '01
Darkdrive '98
Day of Reckoning '33
Deadlock '91
Death House '88
Death Race '08
Death Race 2 '10
Death Warrant '90
Deathrow Gameshow '88
The Defiant Ones '58 ▶
The Delightful Forest '72
The Dirty Dozen '67 ▶
The Dirty Dozen: The Deadly Mission '87
The Dirty Dozen: The Fatal Mission '88
The Dirty Dozen: The Next Mission '85
Doin' Time '85
Doing Time '02
Doing Time for Patsy Cline '97
The Domino Principle '77
Double Team '97
Down by Law '86 ▶
Drifter '09
Duffy of San Quentin '54
Each Dawn I Die '39
Eagles Attack at Dawn '70
Edmond '05
Embassy '72
Empire of the Sun '87 ▶
Ernest Goes to Jail '90
Escape from Alcatraz '79 ▶
Escape from Death Row '73
Escape from New York '81
Escape Plan '13
The Escapist '08
Everyday '12
Execution of Raymond Graham '85
The Executioner's Song '82
The Experiment '01
The Experiment '10
Face/Off '97 ▶
The Family Secret '24
Fast Walking '82
Felon '08
The Fence '94
The Fiend Who Walked the West '58
First Time Felon '97
Fled '96
Fortress 2: Re-Entry '99
Fortress '93
Framed '75
Gang Busters '55
Get the Gringo '12
Gideon's Trumpet '80
The Glass House '72 ▶
The Great O'Malley '36
The Green Mile '99
Green Street Hooligans 2 '09
Greenfingers '00
Guantanamero '07
Half-Baked '97
Half Past Dead '02
Hangfire '91
Hard Justice '95
The Hard Word '02
He Got Game '98
Healing '15
Heaven Ain't Hard to Find '10
Hellgate '52
The Hill '65
Hold 'Em Jail '32
House Across the Bay '40
House of Bodies '13
Hunger '08
The Hurricane '99 ▶
I Am a Fugitive from a Chain Gang '32 ▶
I Killed That Man '42
I Love You Phillip Morris '10
If Beale Street Could Talk '18 ▶
If I Want to Whistle, I Whistle '10
In God's Hands '98
In Hell '03
In Hot Pursuit '77
In the Name of the Father '93 ▶
An Innocent Man '89
Inside '96 ▶
Inside the Walls of Folsom Prison '51
Instinct '99
The Invisible Strangler '76
Jailbreakin' '72
Jailhouse Rock '57 ▶
Jamesy Boy '14
John Carpenter's Ghosts of Mars '01
Johnny Handsome '89 ▶
K-11 '11
Kabei: Our Mother '08
Kansas City Confidential '52 ▶
The Keeper '96
Keillers Park '05
Killer: A Journal of Murder '95
Kiss of the Spider Woman '85 ▶
Land of the Blind '06
The Last Castle '01
The Last Detail '73 ▶
The Last Mile '32
The Last Mile '59
Law Abiding Citizen '09
Le Trou '59 ▶
Leo '02
Les Miserables '97 ▶
A Lesson Before Dying '99 ▶
Let's Go to Prison '06
Life '99
The Life of David Gale '03
The Life of Emile Zola '37 ▶
Lilies '96
Lock Up '89
Lockdown '00
Locked Down '10
Lockout '12
The Longest Yard '74 ▶
The Longest Yard '05
Lost Behind Bars '06
Lost Highway '96
Lucky Break '01
A Man Escaped '57 ▶
A Man Named Rocca '61
Man of La Mancha '72
Mandela: Long Walk to Freedom '13
Maximum Security '87
McKenzie Break '70 ▶
Mean Frank and Crazy Tony '75
Mean Machine '01
Memron '04
Middle of Nowhere '12
Midnight Express '78 ▶
Mrs. Soffel '84
Monster's Ball '01 ▶
Monte Cristo '22
Moon 44 '90
Most Wanted '97
Murder in the First '95
The Mustang '19 ▶
Mutiny in the Big House '39
My Boys Are Good Boys '78
My Cousin Vinny '92 ▶
New Crime City: Los Angeles 2020 '94
The New Guy '02
The Night and the Moment '94
The Night Visitor '70
No Escape '94
Noble Things '08
Ocean's Eleven '01 ▶
On the Yard '79
One Sunday Afternoon '33
Out in Fifty '99
Out of Sight '98 ▶
Papillon '73 ▶
Paradise Lost 3: Purgatory '11
Pardon Us '31
Penitentiary 2 '82
Penitentiary '79
Peter Ibbetson '35
Phantom Empire '87
Pressure Point '62 ▶
The Prey '11
Prison Break '38
Prison on Fire 2 '91
Prison on Fire '87
Prison Train '38
The Prisoner '90
Prisoner '07
The Prisoner of Shark Island '36
The Prisoner of Zenda '22
A Prophet '09 ▶
Pros & Cons '99
Proximity '00
The Pursuit of Happiness '70
The Quare Fellow '62
Red Dragon '02
Redeemer '02
Return to Paradise '98 ▶
Revolt in the Big House '58
Ring of Death '08
Riot '69
Riot in Cell Block 11 '54 ▶
Riot in Juvenile Prison '59
The Road to Guantanamo '06
The Rock '96 ▶
Rosewater '14
Runaway Train '85 ▶
Sade '00
St. Michael Had a Rooster '72
Samar '62
San Quentin '37
The Santa Trap '02
Say It With Songs '29
Scum '79 ▶
The Shawshank Redemption '94 ▶
Shoeshine '47 ▶
Shooting Fish '98
Short Eyes '79 ▶
Shot in the Heart '01 ▶
Six: The Mark Unleashed '04
Slam '98
The Slams '73
A Slipping Down Life '99
Some Mother's Son '96 ▶
Soul Vengeance '75
Southside 1-1000 '50
Spy Game '01
Standard Operating Procedure '08 ▶
Starred Up '13 ▶
Steel City '06
Stir Crazy '80
Stone '10
Sullivan's Travels '41 ▶
The Take '09
Taking Care of Business '90
Tank '83
Tempest '28
Terminal Island '73
There Was a Crooked Man '70 ▶
There's Something about Mary '98 ▶
They Went That-a-Way & That-a-Way '78
33 Postcards '11
This is Not a Film '10 ▶
Timelock '99
Tracked '98
Tracks '05
Trading Places '83
Traitor '08
Triumph of the Spirit '89 ▶
The Truce '96 ▶
True Crime '99
Truth or Die '86
20,000 Years in Sing Sing '33
Two-Way Stretch '60
Ulee's Gold '97 ▶
Underworld U.S.A. '61 ▶
Undisputed 2: Last Man Standing '06
Undisputed '02
Unshackled '00
Up the River '30
The Valachi Papers '72
The Visit '00 ▶
The Way Back '10
Weary River '29
Who is Cletis Tout? '02
Winnie Mandela '13
Wishmaster 2: Evil Never Dies '98
Without Evidence '96
The Wronged Man '10
XXX: State of the Union '05
You Can't Get Away With Murder '39
You Don't Know Jack '10

Mental Hospitals

See also Doctors & Shrinks

About Scout '15 ▶
Adam Resurrected '08
Amputee with an Axe '73
Angel Dusted '81
Asylum '05
The Attic Expeditions '01
Augustine '12 ▶
Backtrack '16
Basketweave '06
Beg! '94
Beyond the Dunwich Horror '08
Beyond the Wall of Sleep '06
Boogeyman 2 '07
Captive '98
The Caretakers '63
Choke '08
Crazy as Hell '02
Crazylove '05
The Dark Horse '14 ▶
Deadgirl '08
The Devil Inside '12
Elling '01
Final '01
Frankie and Alice '10
Frayed '07
Freaky Faron '06
Girl, Interrupted '99
Glass '19
God Help the Girl '14
Gothika '03
Grave Encounters 2 '12
Halloween: Resurrection '02
Happy Hell Night '92
Helen '09
High Wall '47
House of Fools '02
Hunger Point '03
Insanitarium '08
It's Kind of a Funny Story '10
The Jacket '05
Killer Instinct '00
Kings and Queen '04 ▶
Kisses in the Dark '97
The Lazarus Project '08
A Light in the Darkness '02
A Love to Keep '07
Madhouse '04
Manic '01
Mercy Black '19
The Moment '13
Murder Without Conviction '04
Neo Ned '05
Night of the Hunted '80
Nothing to Lose '08
On the Edge '00
On the Inside '11
Opium: Diary of a Madwoman '07
Parasomnia '08
Patrick '13
The Professor and the Madman '19
Rage in Heaven '41
Reprise '06
Revolution #9 '01
Sanitarium '13
Screaming Dead '03
The Scribbler '14
Session 9 '01
Shoot or Be Shot '02
Short Term 12 '13 ▶
Shutter Island '09 ▶
Skeleton Crew '09
Stateside '04
Sucker Punch '11
Tarnation '03
13th Child: Legend of the Jersey Devil '02
Touched With Fire '16
Unsane '18
Valley of the Sun '11
Veronika Decides to Die '15
Vincere '09
The Ward '10
Ward No. 6 '09

▶ = rated three bones or higher

Wrong Turn 4: Bloody Beginnings '11
You Wont Miss Me '09

Mental Retardation

***See also** Physical Problems; Savants*

All the Little Animals '98
Behind the Mask '99
Bill '81 ►
Bill: On His Own '83 ►
Charly '68 ►
Dark Night of the Scarecrow '81
A Day in the Death of Joe Egg '71 ►
Digging to China '98
A Dog Named Christmas '09
Dominick & Eugene '88 ►
Dreamcatcher '03
Family Pictures '93 ►
Flowers for Algernon '00
Gigli '03
Guarding Eddy '04
Harlem Aria '99
Heart of Dragon '85
Hit Me '96
Homer and Eddie '89
House of D '04
I Am Sam '01
It Came from the Sky '98
King of the Jungle '01
Knucklehead '15►
Light in the Piazza '61
Little Chenier: A Cajun Story '06
The Lookout '07►
Lucky Day '91
Madeo '09
Malcolm '86
Mifune '99
Milwaukee, Minnesota '03
Molly '99
My Brother '06
My Louisiana Sky '02
Of Mice and Men '39►
Of Mice and Men '81►
Of Mice and Men '92►
The Other Sister '98
Pauline and Paulette '01
The Peanut Butter Falcon '19
Radio '03
Rain Man '88►
The Rain People '69►
The Ringer '05
Shooting Fish '98
Sling Blade '96►
Square Dance '87
Sweetie '89►
There's Something about Mary '98►
Tim '79
The Village '04
What's Eating Gilbert Grape '93►
Where Hope Grows '15
The Wizard '89
The Yarn Princess '94
Yonkers Joe '08
ZigZag '02►

Mercenaries

The A-Team '10►
Airboss '97
Anaconda 3: The Offspring '08
Anti-Terrorist Cell: Manhunt '01
Babylon A.D. '08
Barb Wire '96
Billionaire Ransom '16
Black Death '10
Blast '04
Blood, Guts, Bullets and Octane '99
Bridge of Dragons '99
A Bullet for the General '68
The Chronicles of Riddick '04
Code Name: Wild Geese '84
Codename: Wildgeese '84
Confessions of an Opium Eater '62
Congo '95
Dark of the Sun '68
Deadpool '16
Death Squad '14
The Devil's Tomb '09
Diamond Dogs '07
The Dogs of War '81
Elephant White '11
Encrypt '03
The Expendables 2 '12
The Expendables 3 '14
The Expendables '10
Extraction '20
Far Cry '08
The Five Man Army '69
The Foreigner '03
The General Died at Dawn '36 ►
George A. Romero's Land of the Dead '05 ►
Golden Needles '74
Green Inferno '72
Hardcore Henry '15
Hercules '14
Heroes Shed No Tears '86
Hired to Kill '91
Honeybaby '74
Honor Among Thieves '68
The Hunter '12
I Am Vengeance '18
I Am Vengeance: Retaliation '20
Ironclad '11
Ironclad: Battle for Blood '14
Kill a Dragon '67
The Last Grenade '70
Last Man Standing '96
Lethal Weapon '87►
The Lost World: Jurassic Park 2 '97
The Magnificent Seven '60►
The Magnificent Seven '16
Maximum Conviction '12
The Mercenaries '62
The Mercenaries '80
Mercenaries '11
Mercenary '96
Mercenary: Absolution '15
Mission. . . Kill '85
The Outsider '14
The Peacekeeper '98
Perfect Target '98
The Planet '06
Predators '10
Proof of Life '00
Rambo '08
Riddick '13
Robin Hood '10
RoboCop 3 '91
Ronin '98
The Scorpion King 3: Battle for Redemption '11
Sea Wolf: The Pirate's Curse '05
Sharktopus '10
Skeleton Coast '89
Streets of Fire '84
The Substitute 2: School's Out '97
The Substitute 3: Winner Takes All '99
The Substitute '96
Survival of the Dead '09
Swordsman of Siena '62
Tales of an Ancient Empire '11
The Target '02
The Transporter '02
211 '18
The Ultimate Weapon '97
Wild Geese '78
Yojimbo '61►

Mermaids

***See also** Folklore & Legends*

Aquamarine '06
Beach Blanket Bingo '65►
The Fat Spy '66
Fishtales '07
Lady in the Water '06
The Lighthouse '19►
The Little Mermaid '75
The Little Mermaid '89►
The Little Mermaid '18
Mad About Men '54
The Mermaid '16►
Miranda '48
Night Tide '61
Sea People '00
She Creature '01
Splash '84

Metamorphosis

***See also** Genetics; Werewolves*

An American Werewolf in London '81 ►
Boogie Nights '97 ►
Cat People '42 ►
Cat People '82
Catwoman '04
The Company of Wolves '85 ►
The Curse of the Werewolf '61
Earth *vs.* the Spider '01
The Fly '86 ►
The Fly 2 '89
The Fly '58 ►
The Howling '81 ►
Jack Frost '98
The Lair of the White Worm '88 ►
Marker '05
Miss Congeniality '00
Naked Lunch '91 ►
Nine Lives '16
Nutty Professor 2: The Klumps '00
The Nutty Professor '96►
Silver Bullet '85
Slither '06►
Species '95
Stephen King's Thinner '96
Uzumaki '00
Vampire in Brooklyn '95
The Wasp Woman '96
Wolfen '81►
The Wolfman '82
A Woman, A Part '17
Zero '97

Meteors, Asteroids, and Comets

***See also** Alien Beings--Vicious; Disaster Flicks; Space Operas*

Alien Dead '79
Anna's Storm '07
The Apocalypse '07
Armageddon '98
Asteroid *vs.* Earth '14
Black Horizon '01
The Blob '58
The Blob '88►
City Beneath the Sea '71
Coherence '13
Creepshow '82
The Day It Came to Earth '77
Day of the Triffids '63►
Deep Impact '98
Die, Monster, Die! '65
Dinosaur '00
Disaster Movie '08
Dragon Storm '04
Falling Fire '97
H. '15►
Ice Age: Collision Course '16
Impact '09
The Invisible Ray '36
It Came From Another World '07
Judgment Day '99
Lifeforce '85
The Lost Skeleton of Cadavra '01
Mammoth '06
Meteor '79
Meteor '09
Meteor Apocalypse '10
The Meteor Man '93
Meteor Storm '10
The Monolith Monsters '57
Moon Zero Two '70
Night of the Comet '84
Only '20
The Phantom Creeps '39
The Pink Chiquitas '86
Polar Storm '09
Return of the Aliens: The Deadly Spawn '83
Rock Jocks '12
S. Darko: A Donnie Darko Tale '09
Seeking a Friend for the End of the World '12
Solid State '12
Stalker '79►
Supernova '09
Tycus '98
Valley of the Dragons '61

Mexico

***See also** Central America*

The A-Team '10 ►
Across the Bridge '57
Across the Line: The Exodus of Charlie Wright '10
Act of Valor '12
Adios, Sabata '71
Against All Odds '84
The Alamo '04
All Souls Day '05
All the Pretty Horses '00
Americano '11
Amexico '16
Amores Perros '00 ►
And Starring Pancho Villa as Himself '03 ►
Babel '06 ►
The Bad Man '41
Bandolero! '68
Beat '00
Beautiful Wave '11
Between '05
Beverly Hills Chihuahua '08
Big Steal '49►
The Black Scorpion '57
Bloody Proof '99►
The Border '82►
Border Lost '08
Border River '47
Border Run '12
Borderland '07
Borderline '80
Bordertown '06
Breakout '75
The Broken Tower '11
A Bullet for the General '68
Bullfighter & the Lady '50
Cannon for Cordoba '70
Captain from Castile '47►
The Careless Years '57
Casa de mi Padre '12
The Chambermaid '19
The Cisco Kid '94
Club Med '86
Compadres '16
Companeros '70
Contract to Kill '16
The Counselor '13
Crazy from the Heart '91►
The Crime of Father Amaro '02►
Crocodile 2: Death Swamp '01
Dance with the Devil '97
Daniel & Ana '09
Deep Crimson '96
Delta Farce '07
Desierto '16
Desperado '95►
The Devil's in the Details '13
Devoured '14
Dinoshark '10
Django '68
Double Take '01
Drug Wars: The Camarena Story '90►
Duck Season '04►
Dust to Glory '05►
8 Heads in a Duffel Bag '96
Eisenstein in Guanajuato '15
El Gringo '12
El Mariachi '93►
Everybody Loves Somebody '17►
Expecting a Miracle '09
The Falcon in Mexico '44
The Five Man Army '69
For Greater Glory '12
Frida '84
Frida '02
From Dusk Till Dawn '95
From Dusk Till Dawn 3: The Hangman's Daughter '99
Fun in Acapulco '63
Get the Gringo '12
Glory Road '06
Go for Sisters '13
The Go-Getter '07
Goal! The Dream Begins '06
The Gold Racket '37
Gringo '18
The Heartbreak Kid '07
Highway Patrolman '91
His Kind of Woman '51►
Hold Back the Dawn '41
Holiday in Mexico '46
The Hollow Point '16
A Home of Our Own '75
Honeymoon '47
Hostile Border '16
The Hottest State '06
I Witness '03
In Caliente '35
In Pursuit '00
In the Pit '06
Inhale '10
Jeopardy '53
John Carpenter Presents Vampires: Los Muertos '02
Juarez '39
Kid from Spain '32
Kill Bill Vol. 2 '04 ►
Kings of the Sun '63
La Cucaracha '99
Ladrones '15
The Last Rites of Ransom Pride '09
Like A Bride '94►
The Line '08
Linewatch '08
Lolo '92
Los Olvidados '50►
Love Among Thieves '86
Love Has Many Faces '65
Lucia, Lucia '03
Machete '10
Machete Kills '13
The Magnificent Seven '60►
Man on Fire '04
Marriage on the Rocks '65
Massacre '56
The Matador '06►
Mercury Plains '16
The Mexican '01
Mexican Hayride '48
Mexico City '00
Midaq Alley '95►
Misfire '14
Miss Bala '12
Miss Bala '19
A Monster with a Thousand Heads '15►
Monsters '10
The Mule '18►
My Father, My Mother, My Brothers and My Sisters '99
Nacho Libre '06
Narco Cultura '13►
Nicotina '03
A Night in Old Mexico '14
The Night of the Iguana '64►
Not Forgotten '09
Octaman '71
Old Gringo '89
On the Line '84
On the Road '12
Once Upon a Time in Mexico '03►
One Long Night '07
One Man's Hero '98
Out of the Past '47►
Out to Sea '97
Outta Time '01
The Perfect Game '09
Post Tenebras Lux '12
The Professionals '66►
Puerto Vallarta Squeeze '04
Pulling Strings '13
Pure Luck '91
Que Viva Mexico '32►
Rambo: Last Blood '19
Rio Rita '29
The Road to El Dorado '00
Roma '18►
Rough Magic '95
Rudo y Cursi '09
The Ruins '08
Run for the Sun '56
Rx '06
Savages '12
The Scout '94
Selena '96
Serenade '56
Sex and the City: The Movie '08
The Shallows '16
Shark Attack 3: Megalodon '02
Sharktopus '10
Sicario '15►
Sicario: Day of the Soldado '18
Sin Nombre '09 ►
600 Miles '16
Sonny and Jed '73
Spanglish '04
Sugar Kisses '13
Sundown '16
They Came to Cordura '59
Three Amigos '86
The Three Burials of Melquiades Estrada '05 ►
Thunder at the Border '66
Tigers Are Not Afraid '19 ►
Tod@s Caen '19
The Torch '50
Touch of Evil '58 ►
Trade '07
Traffic '00 ►
Treasure of the Sierra Madre '48 ►
2012: Doomsday '08
Two Mules for Sister Sara '70►
Under the Volcano '84►
Valdez Is Coming '71
Vera Cruz '53
Villa Rides '68
Vintage Model '92
Viva Knievel '77
Viva Zapata! '52►
The Wailer '06
Way of the Gun '00
We Are What We Are '11
We Have Your Husband '11
Welcome to Acapulco '19
We're the Millers '13
Which Way Home '09
The White Orchid '54
The Whole Ten Yards '04
Wild Rovers '71
The Wonderful Country '59
Y Tu Mama Tambien '01

Miami

***See also** American South*

Absolute Zero '05
Ace Ventura: Pet Detective '93
All About the Benjamins '02
Analyze This '98►
Any Given Sunday '99►
Bachelor Party 2: The Last Temptation '08
Bad Boys '95
Bad Boys 2 '03
Bad Boys for Life '20
Band of the Hand '86
Big Trouble '02
The Birdcage '95►
The Blackout '97
Blood & Wine '96
Chasing Papi '03
Chef '14
The Crew '00
Cronicas '04
Curdled '95
The Day Shall Come '19
The Devil Incarnate '13
Elmore Leonard's Gold Coast '97
Fair Game '95
Final Engagement '07
Fires Within '91
Forever Mine '99
Get Shorty '95►
Holiday Spin '12
Immigration Tango '11
In the Shadows '01
Instinct '99
Kings of South Beach '07
Lansky '99
The Last Marshal '99
Life During Wartime '09
Meet Me After the Show '51
Miami Beach Cops '93
Miami Blues '90
Miami Hustle '95
Miami Rhapsody '95
The Miami Story '54
Miami Vice '84
Miami Vice '06
Moon over Miami '41►
Nothing But the Truth '41
Notorious '46►
Out of Sight '98►
Percentage '13
The Perez Family '94
The Pest '96
The Prince and the Pauper '07

Push *'06*
Red Eye *'05* ▶
Reno 911! Miami *'07*
Ride *'98*
Rough Night *'17*
Scarface *'83* ▶
Second Honeymoon *'37*
Six-Pack Annie *'75*
The Slammin' Salmon *'09*
Step Up Revolution *'12*
Stick *'85*
There's Something about Mary *'98* ▶
Tony Rome *'67*
Transporter 2 *'05*
2 Fast 2 Furious *'03*
Two Much *'96*
Wild Things *'98*

Michigan

Aliens in the Attic *'09*
American Pie *'99* ▶
American Pie 2 *'01*
American Pie Presents: Beta House *'07*
American Reunion *'12*
American Wedding *'03*
Anatomy of a Murder *'59* ▶
Answer This *'10*
Family Weekend *'13*
Glory Daze *'96*
Going Back *'83*
Grosse Pointe Blank *'97* ▶
Hide Away *'11*
Highland Park *'13*
Jumper *'08*
The Myth of the American Sleepover *'10*
Roger & Me *'89* ▶
Semi-Pro *'08*
Seven Sweethearts *'42*
Tape *'01* ▶
The Virgin Suicides *'99*
Winter Passing *'05*
You Don't Know Jack *'10*

Middle East

***See also** Desert War/Foreign Legion; Deserts; Genies; Islam; Israel; Persian Gulf/Iraq War; Terrorism*

Abbott and Costello Meet the Mummy *'55*
Abe *'20*
Action in Arabia *'44*
A.D. *'85*
Afghan Knights *'07*
Ajami *'09* ▶
Ali Baba and the Forty Thieves *'43*
All the King's Men *'99*
The Ambassador *'84*
Among the Believers *'15* ▶
Appointment With Death *'10*
The Arab Conspiracy *'76*
Arabian Adventure *'79*
Arabian Nights *'42*
Arabian Nights *'00*
Armadillo *'11*
Army of One *'16*
The Assignment *'97*
The Attack *'13* ▶
Beaufort *'07* ▶
Beirut *'18*
Bitter Victory *'58*
Black Thunder *'98*
Bloodstone *'88*
Body of Lies *'08*
Boutique *'04*
Brothers *'04* ▶
Cairo Time *'09*
Candlelight in Algeria *'44*
Caramel *'07* ▶
The Cave *'19* ▶
The Ceremony *'63*
Chain of Command *'95*
Chicken With Plums *'11*
Citizen Soldier *'16*
Closed Curtain *'13* ▶
Collision *'13*
Control Room *'04* ▶
Corrupted Hands *'00*
The Crusades *'35*
Cup Final *'92*
Day of the Falcon *'11*
Desert Thunder *'99*
The Dictator *'12*
A Different Loyalty *'04* ▶
Dirty Wars *'13*
Dream Wife *'53*
Drone *'17*
Eagles Attack at Dawn *'70*
The Egyptian *'54*
Escape From Zahrain *'62*
Escape: Human Cargo *'98* ▶
Exorcist: The Beginning *'04*
Fahrenheit 9/11 *'04* ▶
5 Broken Cameras *'11*
Five Fingers *'06*
Five Graves to Cairo *'43* ▶
Flanders *'06*
The Flight of the Phoenix *'65* ▶
For Sama *'19* ▶
Foxtrot *'18*
Gabbeh *'96* ▶
The Girl in the Sneakers *'99*
A Girl Walks Home Alone at Night *'14*
The Glory Boys *'84*
The Gospel of John *'15*
Gradiva *'06*
Gunner Palace *'04* ▶
Halfmoon *'95*
Harem *'99*
Harum Scarum *'65*
Held Hostage *'91*
Hidalgo *'04*
Hijacking Catastrophe: 9/11, Fear and the Selling of America *'04*
A Hologram for the King *'16*
Honeybaby *'74*
Hyena Road *'16*
I Am Vengeance *'18*
The Idol *'15* ▶
Ilsa, Harem Keeper of the Oil Sheiks *'76*
Incendies *'10* ▶
The Insult *'17* ▶
Iron Eagle *'86*
Iron Eagle 2 *'88*
Iron Man *'08* ▶
Ishtar *'87*
Jafar Panahi's Taxi *'15* ▶
Jarhead *'05*
The Jewel of the Nile *'85*
Jirga *'19*
Joseph *'95*
Kandahar *'01*
Keep Walking *'82* ▶
The Keeper: The Legend of Omar Khayyam *'05*
Khartoum *'66*
King Richard and the Crusaders *'54*
The Kingdom *'07*
Land of Plenty *'04*
Last Men In Aleppo *'17* ▶
Lawrence of Arabia *'62* ▶
Lebanon *'09*
Legend of the Lost Tomb *'97*
Leila *'97*
Lemon Tree *'08*
Life and Nothing More . . . *'92*
The Lone Runner *'88*
Lone Survivor *'13*
Looking for Comedy in the Muslim World *'06*
Low Heights *'02*
Marooned in Iraq *'02*
Mary Magdalene *'19*
A Matter of WHO *'62*
May in the Summer *'13*
Mercenary *'96*
A Mighty Heart *'07* ▶
Monsters: Dark Continent *'15*
Moses *'96*
Mustang *'15* ▶
My Favorite Spy *'51*
The Nativity Story *'06*
Neither Heaven Nor Earth *'16*
The Objective *'08*
Occupation: Dreamland *'05* ▶
Of Fathers and Sons *'18* ▶
Omar *'13* ▶
Only Lovers Left Alive *'13*
The Operative *'19*
Orde Wingate *'76*
Osama *'03* ▶
Our Music *'04*
Painkillers *'15*
Paradise *'82*
Paradise Now *'05* ▶
Passion in the Desert *'97*
The Passion of the Christ *'04* ▶
Passport to Suez *'43*
The Past *'13* ▶
The Patience Stone *'13* ▶
Paul, Apostle of Christ *'18*
Peace, Propaganda & the Promised Land *'04*
A Private War *'18*
The Pyramid *'14*
Raiders of the Lost Ark *'81* ▶
The Reports on Sarah and Saleem *'19* ▶
The Road to Guantanamo *'06*
The Road to Morocco *'42* ▶
The Robe *'53*
Rock the Kasbah *'15*
Rosewater *'14*
Saadia *'53*
The Salesman *'16* ▶
Salmon Fishing in the Yemen *'11*
Septembers of Shiraz *'16*
Sex and the City 2 *'10*
The Sheik *'21* ▶
Shirin *'09*
Silent Waters *'03*
Sirocco *'51*
Sniper: Special Ops *'16*
Son of Ali Baba *'52*
Spartan *'04* ▶
The Spy Who Loved Me *'77*
The Square *'13*
Steel Sharks *'97*
The String *'09*
Suez *'38*
Syriana *'05* ▶
Team America: World Police *'04* ▶
The Tiger and the Snow *'05*
Torn Apart *'89*
Traitor *'08*
Turtles Can Fly *'04* ▶
24 Hours to Kill *'65*
Uncovered: The War on Iraq *'04*
Under the Shadow *'16* ▶
Voices of Iraq *'04* ▶
Wadjda *'13* ▶
Wall *'04* ▶
Waltz with Bashir *'08* ▶
A War *'15* ▶
War Dogs *'16*
War, Inc. *'08*
The War Within *'05*
A Wedding in Galilee *'87* ▶
The Wedding Song *'09*
West Beirut *'98*
Where the Spies Are *'65*
Whiskey Tango Foxtrot *'16*

Midlife Crisis

***See also** Adultery; Growing Older; Strained Suburbia*

About Fifty *'11*
After Fall, Winter *'11*
American Beauty *'99* ▶
At Middleton *'13*
The Babysitters *'07*
Bad Words *'13*
Being Julia *'04* ▶
The Black Marble *'79* ▶
Blue Jasmine *'13* ▶
Bob Funk *'09*
Box of Moonlight *'96*
Brad's Status *'17*
Broken Flowers *'05*
California Solo *'12*
Change of Plans *'09*
City Slickers *'91* ▶
Clouds of Sils Maria *'15*
Colewell *'19*
Cyrus *'10*
Dear Heart *'64* ▶
Dirty 30 *'16*
Edmond *'05*
The English Teacher *'13*
Every Day *'10*
Everything Must Go *'10*
Falling in Love Again *'80*
Float *'08*
Flying By *'09*
Fortunes *'05*
Full Moon in Blue Water *'88*
Goodbye to All That *'14*
The Hammer *'07*
Handsome Harry *'09*
Hello Goodbye *'08*
High Time *'60*
Hit By Lightning *'14*
The Hot Flashes *'13*
I Dream of Murder *'06*
I Love You, Alice B. Toklas! *'68*
I Think I Love My Wife *'07*
If Winter Comes *'41*
The Internship *'13*
It's Complicated *'09*
Jack Goes Boating *'10*
King of the Corner *'04* ▶
Kings *'07*
The Land of Steady Habits *'18*
Larry Crowne *'11*
Lebanon, PA *'10*
Len & Company *'16*
L'Ennui *'98*
The Long Summer of George Adams *'82*
Looking for Eric *'09*
Loving *'70*
Lucky Them *'13*
The Man of My Life *'06*
The Matador *'06* ▶
Meet Bill *'07*
The Mermaid Chair *'06*
Milk and Honey *'03*
Mrs. Washington Goes to Smith *'09*
Multiple Sarcasms *'10*
Nights in Rodanthe *'08*
Non-Fiction *'18*
Notre Histoire *'84*
On a Clear Day *'05*
Once More With Feeling *'08*
The Oranges *'12*
The Owls *'09*
Paper Man *'09*
A Perfect Ending *'12*
The Private Lives of Pippa Lee *'09*
Queen to Play *'09*
Roadie *'11*
The Savages *'07* ▶
Shall We Dance? *'04*
Shirley Valentine *'89* ▶
Sideways *'04* ▶
Six Strong Guys *'04*
Somewhere Slow *'14*
The Space Between *'10*
States of Control *'98*
Step Brothers *'08*
Talhotblond *'12*
Tammy *'14*
The Tempest *'82* ▶
There's Always Tomorrow *'56*
Things to Come *'16* ▶
35 Shots of Rum *'08*
This Is 40 *'12*
The Trouble With Bliss *'11*
Turn Back the Clock *'33*
Two Tickets to Paradise *'06*
Unanswered Prayers *'10*
Under the Eiffel Tower *'18*
Undertaking Betty *'02*
Up in the Air *'09* ▶
The Weather Man *'05*
When a Man Falls in the Forest *'07*
When Did You Last See Your Father? *'07*
While We're Young *'14*
Whole New Thing *'05*
Wild Hogs *'07*
Wonderful World *'09*

Military: Air Force

***See also** Airborne*

Above and Beyond *'06*
Afterburn *'92* ▶
Air Force *'43* ▶
Aloha *'15*
Area 51 *'11*
Battle Hymn *'57*
Black Thunder *'98*
Bombers B-52 *'57*
Desert Thunder *'99*
The Devil Makes Three *'52*
Fighter Squadron *'48*
The Flemish Farm *'43*
Flight From Ashiya *'64*
God is My Co-Pilot *'45*
Good Kill *'15*
The Haunted Airman *'06*
Hot Shots! *'91* ▶
Hot Shots! Part Deux *'93*
Mach 2 *'00*
Memphis Belle *'90* ▶
Mosquito Squadron *'70*
1,000 Plane Raid *'69*
Operation Haylift *'50*
The Pentagon Wars *'98*
Pilot No. 5 *'43*
Rally 'Round the Flag, Boys! *'58*
Red Sky *'14*
Rescue Dawn *'06* ▶
Sergeant Deadhead *'65*
The Space Children *'58*
Space Cowboys *'00* ▶
Starlift *'51*
Storm Catcher *'99*
Strategic Air Command *'55*
Tactical Assault *'99*
Terminator 3: Rise of the Machines *'03* ▶
Terror Street *'54*
Toward the Unknown *'56*
Two Thousand Women *'44*
Valiant *'05*
Wake Me When It's Over *'60*
War Lover *'62*
The Way to the Stars *'45*

Military: Army

The A-Team *'10* ▶
Active Stealth *'99*
Adolf Hitler: My Part in His Downfall *'74*
Advance to the Rear *'64*
After the Rain *'99*
American Soldiers *'05*
Arizona *'31*
Backfire *'50*
Band of Brothers *'01* ▶
The Base 2: Guilty as Charged *'00*
The Base *'99*
Basic *'03*
Battle at Bloody Beach *'61*
Battle of the Bulge *'65*
Behind the Lines *'97*
Bennett's War *'19*
The Better 'Ole *'26*
Beyond Victory *'31*
Big Bear *'98*
The Big Red One *'80* ▶
Big Steal *'49* ▶
Billy Lynn's Long Halftime Walk *'16*
Bitter Victory *'58*
Black Hawk Down *'01* ▶
Black Ops *'20*
Bloody Sunday *'01* ▶
Boys of Abu Ghraib *'14*
Breakthrough *'50*
Buffalo Soldiers *'97* ▶
Buffalo Soldiers *'01*
Camel Spiders *'11*
Camp X-Ray *'14*
Canal Zone *'42*
Cannon for Cordoba *'70*
Captain America: The First Avenger *'11*
Captain America: The Winter Soldier *'14* ▶
Casualties of War *'89* ▶
Cavalry Scout *'51*
Chain of Command *'15*
Chaos Factor *'00*
Citizen Soldier *'16*
The Command *'54*
Company of Heroes *'13*
Copperhead *'13*
Courage Under Fire *'96* ▶
The Court Martial of Billy Mitchell *'55* ▶
The Crossing *'00*
Cry Havoc *'43*
The Day the Earth Stopped *'08*
Dead Men Can't Dance *'97*
Deadly Game *'77*
Dear John *'10*
The Devil Horse *'26*
The Devil's Double *'11*
D.I. *'57*
The Dirty Dozen *'67* ▶
The Dirty Dozen: The Deadly Mission *'87*
The Dirty Dozen: The Fatal Mission *'88*
The Dirty Dozen: The Next Mission *'85*
A Distant Trumpet *'64*
Dondi *'61*
The Duchess of Buffalo *'26*
Eight Iron Men *'52*
Elvira Madigan *'67* ▶
Emperor *'12*
Ernest in the Army *'97*
Everyman's War *'09*
Evolution *'01*
Fatal Error *'99*
Fearless Fagan *'52*
The Fighting Eagle *'27*
Flesh Wounds *'10*
Flight Angels *'40*
Florence Nightingale *'85*
Florence Nightingale *'08*
Fort McCoy *'11*
40 Guns to Apache Pass *'67*
Francis Joins the WACs *'54*
Fury *'14*
The Gambler from Natchez *'54*
Garrison *'07*
The Gay Deceivers *'69*
The General's Daughter *'99*
Geronimo: An American Legend *'93*
Gettysburg *'93* ▶
G.I. Blues *'60*
G.I. Joe: The Rise of Cobra *'09*
G.I. Joe: Retaliation *'13*
The Girl He Left Behind *'56*
The Glory Brigade *'53*
Gods and Generals *'03*
Godzilla *'98*
The Good German *'06*
A Good Man *'14*
The Great Raid *'05*
The Green Berets *'68*
Hacksaw Ridge *'16*
Hart's War *'02*
Hellgate *'52*
The Hessen Conspiracy *'09*
Home of the Brave *'06*
Hornets' Nest *'70*
Hostiles *'17*
The Hunt for Eagle One: Crash Point *'06*
The Hunted *'03*
The Hurt Locker *'08* ▶
Hyena Road *'16*
Ice Quake *'10*
Idol on Parade *'59*
Ignition *'01*
Imitation General *'58*
In Pursuit of Honor *'95*
In the Army Now *'94*
In the Meantime, Darling *'44*
In the Valley of Elah *'07* ▶
Independence Day *'96* ▶
Invasion of the Star Creatures *'63*
The Iron Petticoat *'56*
Keep Your Powder Dry *'45*
The Last Castle *'01*
The Last Full Measure *'19*
Lost Battalion *'01*
The Lucky Ones *'08*
MacArthur *'77*
The Major and the Minor *'42* ▶
M*A*S*H *'70* ▶
M*A*S*H: Goodbye, Farewell & Amen *'83* ▶
Massacre River *'49*
The Master Plan *'55*
The Men Who Stare at Goats *'09*
The Messenger *'09* ▶
A Midnight Clear *'92* ▶
Military Intelligence and You! *'06*
The Missing *'03* ▶
The Monuments Men *'13*
Neither Heaven Nor Earth *'16*
Never Wave at a WAC *'52*
New World *'95*
Night People *'54*
1915 *'82*
1941 *'79*
The Nun and the Sergeant *'62*
Occupation: Dreamland *'05* ▶
Once an Eagle *'76*
One Little Indian *'73*
One Man's Hero *'98*
Only the Brave *'06*
Operation Dumbo Drop *'95*
Operation Mad Ball *'57*

▶ = rated three bones or higher

Operation Valkyrie '04
Organizm '08
Over 21 '45
Pandemic '09
Passchendaele '10
Patton '70 ▶
The Peacemaker '97
The Perfect Furlough '59
Pillars of the Sky '56
Platoon '86 ▶
Private Benjamin '80
The Rack '56
Rage '72
The Railway Man '13
Rangers '00
Ravenous '99
Red Sands '09
Redacted '07
Rendezvous '35
Restrepo '10
The Revengers '72
Saints and Soldiers: Airborne Creed '12
Saving Private Ryan '98 ▶
The Scarlet Coat '55
Screaming Eagles '56
See Here, Private Hargrove '44
Seminole '53
The Sergeant '68
Serving in Silence: The Margarethe Cammermeyer Story '95 ▶
Seven Days' Leave '42
The Siege '98
Siege at Red River '54
Silent Night '02
The Skin '81
Slayer '06
Sniper: Ghost Shooter '16
Sniper: Special Ops '16
Soldier '98
Soldier Love Story '10
Soldier's Girl '03 ▶
A Soldier's Story '84 ▶
Something for the Boys '44
Special Forces '03
Spirit: Stallion of the Cimarron '02
Spring Parade '40
Standard Operating Procedure '08 ▶
Starship Troopers '97 ▶
Steel '97
Stop-Loss '08 ▶
The Story of a Three Day Pass '68
The Story of G.I. Joe '45 ▶
Stripes '81
Sunday Dinner for a Soldier '44
Taking Sides '01 ▶
The Tanks Are Coming '51
Target Zero '55
Thank You for Your Service '17 ▶
There's Something About a Soldier '43
The Thin Red Line '64
The Thin Red Line '98 ▶
Three Kings '99 ▶
A Thunder of Drums '61
Tigerland '00 ▶
The Tillman Story '10 ▶
Time Limit '57
To End All Wars '01
Tomahawk '51
Tomorrow We Live '42
Top Secret Affair '57
Transformers: Revenge of the Fallen '09
The Trench '99
Trooper Hook '57
Tunnel Rats '08
12 Strong '18
28 Days Later '02
28 Weeks Later '07
UKM: The Ultimate Killing Machine '06
Underground '70
The WAC From Walla Walla '52
Wackiest Ship in the Army '61
The Wall '99 ▶
War Horse '11
War Machine '17
War Paint '53
Waterloo Road '45
Way of a Gaucho '52
The Weapon '56
We'll Meet Again '82
West Point '27
Westbound '58
When Trumpets Fade '98
When Willie Comes Marching Home '50 ▶
The White Sister '33
The Wonderful Country '59
X-Men Origins: Wolverine '09
X2: X-Men United '03 ▶
XXX: State of the Union '05
Yossi & Jagger '02
You Must Be Joking! '65

Military Comedy

***See also** Comedy; War, General*

Abbott and Costello in the Foreign Legion '50
Adolf Hitler: My Part in His Downfall '74
Advance to the Rear '64
All Hands on Deck '61
Appointment With Venus '51
Article 99 '92
At War with the Army '50
Basic Training '86
Before Winter Comes '69
Best Defense '84
Best Foot Forward '43
Biloxi Blues '88
Black and White in Color '76 ▶
Carbide and Sorrel '63
Caught in the Draft '41 ▶
Chesty Anderson USN '76
Dad's Army '16
Delta Farce '07
Don't Go Near the Water '57
Down Periscope '96
Ensign Pulver '64
Ernest in the Army '97
Everything's Ducky '61
Fearless Fagan '52
The Fighting Eagle '27
The Flying Deuces '39 ▶
Follow That Camel '67
Francis Goes to West Point '52
Francis in the Navy '55
Francis Joins the WACs '54
Getting Wasted '80
G.I. Blues '60
The Girl He Left Behind '56
Going Under '91
Here Comes the Navy '34
Hot Shots! '91 ▶
Hot Shots! Part Deux '93
Imitation General '58
In the Army Now '94
In the Meantime, Darling '44
Invasion Quartet '61
The Iron Petticoat '56
Johnny Doesn't Live Here Any More '44
Jumping Jacks '52
Kiss Them for Me '57
Major Payne '95
A Man Called Sarge '90
Marines, Let's Go '61
M*A*S*H '70 ▶
M*A*S*H: Goodbye, Farewell & Amen '83 ▶
McHale's Navy '64
McHale's Navy '97
Military Intelligence and You! '06
Miracle of Morgan's Creek '44 ▶
The Mouse That Roared '59 ▶
Navy Blues '37
Never Wave at a WAC '52
1941 '79
No Time for Sergeants '58 ▶
Off Limits '53
On the Double '61
Onionhead '58
Operation Mad Ball '57
Over 21 '45
The Perfect Furlough '59
Private Benjamin '80
Private Navy of Sgt. O'Farrell '68
Private Valentine: Blonde & Dangerous '08
Privates on Parade '84
Renaissance Man '94
The Rookie '59
The Sad Sack '57
See Here, Private Hargrove '44
Sgt. Bilko '95
Sergeant Deadhead '65
Seven Days' Leave '42
Snuffy Smith, Yard Bird '42
Soldier in the Rain '63
The Square Peg '58
Stripes '81
Suppose They Gave a War and Nobody Came? '70
23 1/2 Hours Leave '37
The Virgin Soldiers '69
Viva Max '69
Waiting for Dublin '07
Wake Me When It's Over '60
Weekend Pass '84
The West Point Story '50
You Know What Sailors Are '59
You're In the Navy Now '51

Military Crimes & Trials

***See also** Foreign Intrigue; Military: Air Force; Military: Army; Military Comedy; Military: Foreign; Military: Marines; Military: Navy; Order in the Court*

Buffalo Soldiers '01
The Caine Mutiny '54 ▶
The Caine Mutiny Court Martial '88 ▶
Call of Heroes '16
Casualties of War '89 ▶
The Conspirator '10
The Court Martial of Billy Mitchell '55 ▶
A Few Good Men '92 ▶
A Glimpse of Hell '01
Hart's War '02
High Crimes '02
The Hill '65
I Am Vengeance: Retaliation '20
Ignition '01
The Last Castle '01
Paths of Glory '57 ▶
The Rack '56
Rules of Engagement '00
Seminole '53
Sergeant Rutledge '60 ▶
South Sea Woman '53
Time Limit '57
Under the Flag of the Rising Sun '72 ▶

Military: Foreign

The Aftermath '19
Alexandra '07 ▶
All Quiet on the Western Front '30 ▶
All Quiet on the Western Front '79
All the King's Men '99
Ambush '99 ▶
Appointment in London '53
The Ascent '76 ▶
Atonement '07 ▶
Battle of Britain '69
The Beast '88
Beaufort '07 ▶
Bees in Paradise '44
Before Winter Comes '69
Beneath Hill 60 '10
Bitter Victory '58
Black and White in Color '76 ▶
Black '47 '18
Breaker Morant '80 ▶
The Brylcreem Boys '96
California '63
Captain Corelli's Mandolin '01
Captains of the Clouds '42
Captive Heart '47 ▶
Carry On Sergeant '58
Carry On Up the Khyber '68
Charge of the Lancers '54
The Charge of the Light Brigade '36 ▶
The Charge of the Light Brigade '68
City of Life and Death '09
Cliffs of Freedom '19
Counter-Attack '45
The Cuckoo '02
Cup Final '92
Danger Close '19
Das Boot '81 ▶
The Dawn Patrol '30 ▶
Days of Glory '06
Deserter '02
The Devil Is a Woman '35 ▶
Devils on the Doorstep '00
Die Another Day '02
Disorder '16
Dog Soldiers '01
Doomsday '08
Dresden '06
The Duchess of Langeais '07 ▶
Eagles Over London '69
East of Sudan '64
Enemy at the Gates '00
Escape from Sobibor '87 ▶
Eye in the Sky '15 ▶
The Fighting Rats of Tobruk '44
Five Graves to Cairo '43 ▶
Flags of Our Fathers '06 ▶
Flanders '06
The Flowers of War '11
For the Moment '94
The Four Feathers '02
Four Sons '40
Foxtrot '18
Gallipoli '81 ▶
Generation War '13
The Glory Brigade '53
The High Bright Sun '65
The Hill '65
Hostile Waters '97
Hungarian Rhapsody '28
The Hunt for Red October '90 ▶
Ice Soldiers '13
I'll Remember April '99
Mission of Honor '19
In the Land of Blood and Honey '11
In Which We Serve '43 ▶
The Indian Tomb '21
Into the White '12
Jack Ryan: Shadow Recruit '14
The Journey '59
Journey's End '18
Jump Into Hell '55
Katyn '07
King and Country '64 ▶
King of the Khyber Rifles '53
Kippur '00 ▶
La France '07
The Lady '11
Lagaan: Once upon a Time in India '01
The Lark Farm '07
The Last Lieutenant '94
The Last Outpost '35
The Last September '99
Lebanon '09
Lemon Tree '08
Letters from Iwo Jima '06 ▶
Madame Sans-Gene '62
The Marquise of O '76
Midway '19
Miss London Ltd. '43
Neither Heaven Nor Earth '16
Night of the Generals '67 ▶
1917 '19 ▶
1911 '11
No Man's Land '01
Notebook '19
Of Gods and Men '10 ▶
The One That Got Away '96
Osombie '12
Passion in the Desert '97
Peterloo '18
Pretty Village, Pretty Flame '96 ▶
Prisoner of the Mountains '96 ▶
The Red Baron '08
The Red Danube '50
The Redemption of General Butt Naked '11
The Road to Glory '36
Savior '98 ▶
The Scarlet Tunic '97
Sergeant Klems '71
'71 '14 ▶
Shake Hands With the Devil '07
Sharpe's Challenge '06
Sharpe's Peril '08
Silent Night '02
633 Squadron '64
Soldier of Orange '78 ▶
Stairway to Heaven '46 ▶
Stalingrad '94
Storm Over the Nile '55
Sword of Honour '01
Sword of War '09
Taxi for Tobruk '60 ▶
Tempest '28
31 North 62 East '09
The 300 Spartans '62
Time of Favor '00
To End All Wars '01
Tracker '10
Traffic '00 ▶
Troubles '88
Tunes of Glory '60 ▶
Two Men Went to War '02
The Unknown Soldier '98
Uri: The Surgical Strike '19
Victory at Entebbe '76
Waltz with Bashir '08 ▶
A War '15 ▶
War '19
The Water Horse: Legend of the Deep '07
The Way Ahead '44
The Way Back '10
The Way to the Stars '45
The Widow of Saint-Pierre '00 ▶
The Wind Cannot Read '58
The Wind That Shakes the Barley '06 ▶
Woyzeck '78 ▶
Wozzeck '47
Yesterday's Enemy '59
Zama '17
Zarak '56
Zone 39 '96

Military: Marines

American Son '08
Annapolis '06
Back to Bataan '45
Bataan '43
Battle Cry '55 ▶
Battle: Los Angeles '11
Battle Zone '52
Black Ops '07
Brothers '09
California Dreamin' '07
Dangerous Evidence: The Lori Jackson Story '99
Death Before Dishonor '87
Doom '05
A Family of Spies '90
A Few Good Men '92 ▶
First to Fight '67
Flags of Our Fathers '06 ▶
Flying Leathernecks '51 ▶
Full Metal Jacket '87 ▶
Generation Kill '08 ▶
Guadalcanal Diary '43
The Halls of Montezuma '50
Heartbreak Ridge '86 ▶
Hell and Back Again '11
High Crimes '02
In Love and War '58
Jarhead 2: Field of Fire '14
Jarhead '05
Johnny Doesn't Live Here Any More '44
Join the Marines '37
Leprechaun 4: In Space '96
Lifted '10
The Lucky One '12
Man Down '16
The Marine 2 '09
The Marine 3: Homefront '11
The Marine '06
A Marine Story '10
Marines, Let's Go '61
Max '15
Megan Leavey '17
Most Wanted '97
Painkillers '15
Platoon '86 ▶
Pork Chop Hill '59 ▶
Pride of the Marines '45 ▶
The Proud and Profane '56
Purple Heart '05
Quicksand '01
The Real Glory '39 ▶
The Rock '96 ▶
Rules of Engagement '00
Salute to the Marines '43
Sand Serpents '09
Sands of Iwo Jima '49 ▶
Second in Command '05
Semper Fi '19
The Siege of Firebase Gloria '89
Sniper 2 '02
Sniper Reloaded '11
South Sea Woman '53
Spartan '04 ▶
Stateside '04
Taking Chance '09
Tarawa Beachhead '58
Tell It to the Marines '26
Universal Soldiers '07
A Warm Wind '11
The Wind and the Lion '75 ▶
Windtalkers '02

Military: Navy

***See also** Sail Away*

Act of Valor '12
Adopt a Sailor '08
Agent Red '00
All Ashore '53
All Hands on Deck '61
American Sniper '14
American Warship '12
American Warships '01
Anchors Aweigh '45 ▶
Annapolis '06
Antwone Fisher '02 ▶
Appointment With Venus '51
Battle of the Coral Sea '59
Battleship '12
Behind Enemy Lines 2: Axis of Evil '06
Behind Enemy Lines 3: Colombia '08
Behind Enemy Lines '01
Beneath the Blue '10
Bermuda Tentacles '14
Black Ops '07
The Bridges at Toko-Ri '55 ▶
Burning Blue '14
The Caine Mutiny '54 ▶
Chasers '94
Crest of the Wave '54
Crimson Tide '95 ▶
The Crowded Sky '60
Danger Beneath the Sea '02
David Harding, Counterspy '50
Depth Charge '08
Destination Gobi '53
Dive Bomber '41 ▶
The Divine Lady '29
Down Periscope '96
The Eleventh Hour '08
Enemy Below '57 ▶
Everything's Ducky '61
A Few Good Men '92 ▶
Fighting Seabees '44
The Fighting Sullivans '42 ▶
Flags of Our Fathers '06 ▶
Flight Command '40
The Flying Fleet '29
Follow the Boys '63
Francis in the Navy '55
Freedom Strike '98
Further Up the Creek '58
The Gallant Hours '60 ▶
G.I. Jane '97
A Glimpse of Hell '01
Handsome Harry '09
Hell Boats '70
Hell Divers '31
Hellcats of the Navy '57
Here Come the Waves '45 ▶
Here Comes the Navy '34
High Barbaree '47
The Honeymoon Machine '61
Horatio Hornblower '99 ▶
Horatio Hornblower: The Adventure Continues '01 ▶
Hostile Waters '97
The Hunt for Red October '90 ▶
Hunter Killer '18
In Love and War '91
It's Tough to Be Famous '32
Jack Ryan: Shadow Recruit '14
Jarhead 2: Field of Fire '14
The King '05
Kiss Them for Me '57
The Last Detail '73 ▶

▶ = rated three bones or higher

- The Lost Valentine '11
- Master and Commander: The Far Side of the World '03 ▶
- McHale's Navy '64
- McHale's Navy '97
- Men of Honor '00
- Men of the Sea '35
- Midway '19
- Mission of the Shark '91 ▶
- Mister Roberts '55 ▶
- Navy Blue and Gold '37
- Navy Blues '29
- Navy Blues '37
- Navy SEALS '90
- Navy *vs.* the Night Monsters '66
- Navy Way '44
- No Man Is an Island '62
- No Way Out '87 ▶
- The Non-Stop Flight '26
- An Officer and a Gentleman '82 ▶
- On the Town '49 ▶
- 100 Million BC '08
- Onionhead '58
- Operation Bikini '63
- Operation Petticoat '59 ▶
- The Pacifier '05
- Pearl '78
- Pearl Harbor '01
- Private Navy of Sgt. O'Farrell '68
- PT 109 '63
- Raptor Island '04
- Renegades '17
- Ride for Lance '14
- Rodgers & Hammerstein's South Pacific '01
- Run Silent, Run Deep '58 ▶
- Sabotage '96
- Sailor Beware '52
- Sailor of the King '53
- The Sand Pebbles '66 ▶
- The Sea Ghost '31
- Seal Team 8: Behind Enemy Lines '14
- Seal Team Six: The Raid on Osama Bin Laden '12
- Seas Beneath '31
- The Sender '98
- Shadow Warriors '97
- Shipmates '31
- Shipmates Forever '35
- Silent Venom '08
- Skirts Ahoy! '52
- South Pacific '58 ▶
- Stand by for Action '42
- Stateside '04
- Stealth '05
- Stealth Fighter '99
- Steel Sharks '97
- Submerged '00
- Tears of the Sun '03
- They Were Expendable '45 ▶
- Three Brave Men '57
- Three Sailors and a Girl '53
- Top Gun '86
- 2 Guns '13
- U-571 '00
- Under Siege '92
- U.S. Seals 2 '01
- U.S. Seals '98
- U.S. SEALs: Dead or Alive '02
- USS Indianapolis: Men of Courage '16
- Vacation from Marriage '45
- Wake Up and Dream '46
- Wings of the Navy '39
- Wolverine '96
- The Woman From Monte Carlo '31
- XXX: State of the Union '05
- Yankee Buccaneer '52
- You Know What Sailors Are '59
- You're In the Navy Now '51
- Zero Dark Thirty '12 ▶

Military Romance

- Annapolis '06
- Brothers '04 ▶
- The Christmas Card '06
- Cold Mountain '03 ▶
- Darby's Rangers '58
- Dear John '10
- The English Patient '96 ▶
- A Farewell to Arms '32 ▶
- A Farewell to Arms '57
- Force of Arms '51
- From Here to Eternity '53 ▶
- G.I. Blues '60
- In Harm's Way '65
- In Love and War '96
- Joyeux Noel '05 ▶
- The Life and Death of Colonel Blimp '43 ▶
- An Officer and a Gentleman '82 ▶
- Purple Hearts '84
- She Wore a Yellow Ribbon '49 ▶
- Shipmates Forever '35
- South Pacific '58 ▶
- The Tiger and the Snow '05
- Top Gun '86
- A Very Long Engagement '04 ▶
- West Point '27
- Wings '27

Military School

- Brother Rat '38
- Child's Play 3 '91
- Damien: Omen 2 '78
- Dress Gray '86 ▶
- Dress Parade '27
- Evilspeak '82
- Field of Lost Shoes '14
- The Long Gray Line '55 ▶
- The Lords of Discipline '83
- The Major and the Minor '42 ▶
- Major Payne '95
- Private Romeo '11
- Renaissance Man '94
- Taps '81
- Toy Soldiers '84
- Up the Academy '80

Military Westerns

***See also** Military: Army; Westerns*

- The Alamo '60 ▶
- Ambush '50
- Cavalry Charge '51
- Cavalry Command '63
- The Command '54
- A Distant Trumpet '64
- Escape from Fort Bravo '53
- Fort Bowie '58
- Fort Massacre '58
- 40 Guns to Apache Pass '67
- Hawmps! '76
- Hellgate '52
- Hondo '53 ▶
- The Horse Soldiers '59
- In Pursuit of Honor '95
- Pharoah's Army '95
- Rio Grande '50 ▶
- Sergeant Rutledge '60 ▶
- Sergeants 3 '62
- She Wore a Yellow Ribbon '49 ▶
- Shenandoah '65 ▶
- Soldier Blue '70
- Taza, Son of Cochise '54
- They Died with Their Boots On '41 ▶
- A Thunder of Drums '61
- Virginia City '40 ▶
- Westbound '58

Milwaukee

***See also** America's Heartland*

- American Movie '99 ▶
- BASEketball '98
- Dawn of the Dead '04 ▶
- The Giant Spider Invasion '75
- Mr. 3000 '04

Miners & Mining

- Ace in the Hole '51 ▶
- The Adventures of Bullwhip Griffin '66
- Against the Wild '14
- Angels Die Hard '70
- Apache Rifles '64
- Araya '59
- Backlash: Oblivion 2 '95
- Bad for Each Other '53
- The Badlanders '58
- Bait '54
- Ballad of Cable Hogue '70 ▶
- Barricade '49
- Beneath '13
- Beneath Hill 60 '10
- The Big Man: Crossing the Line '91 ▶
- Billy Elliot '00 ▶
- The Bird Can't Fly '07
- Bisbee '17 '18
- Black Fury '35 ▶
- Blood Diamond '06
- Brassed Off '96
- Burning Rage '84
- Call of the Coyote '34
- The Call of the Wild '35 ▶
- Cannibal! The Musical '96
- Chained Heat 3: Hell Mountain '98
- Challenge to White Fang '86
- The Cisco Kid and the Lady '39
- The Claim '00
- Coal Miner's Daughter '80 ▶
- The Corn Is Green '79 ▶
- Dark Descent '02
- Dear Wendy '05
- Drums Across the River '54
- The Dude Goes West '48
- Dudley Do-Right '99
- Edge of Eternity '59
- Fire Down Below '97
- Flaming Frontiers '38
- Garden of Evil '54
- Gold for the Caesars '63
- Gold Is Where You Find It '38
- Gold Rush Maisie '40
- The Golden Eye '48
- Goldrush: A Real Life Alaskan Adventure '98
- Grand Canyon Trail '48
- Green Fire '55
- Gwen '19
- The Hallelujah Trail '65
- Harlan County, U.S.A. '76 ▶
- Harlan County War '00
- How Green Was My Valley '41 ▶
- It All Starts Today '99
- Jack London's The Call of the Wild '97
- The Jackals '67
- Jungle Man-Eaters '54
- Jungle Manhunt '51
- Kill Django '71
- King Solomon's Mines '85
- Lady in a Jam '42
- The Legend of Tarzan '16
- Little Accidents '14
- Little Church Around the Corner '23
- Margaret's Museum '95 ▶
- Matewan '87 ▶
- McCabe & Mrs. Miller '71 ▶
- The Molly Maguires '70
- Moon '09
- Moon Zero Two '70
- Naked Hills '56
- No Man's Law '27
- North Country '05
- North Star '96
- North to Alaska '60 ▶
- The Nugget '02
- October Sky '99 ▶
- Out of the Black '01
- Paint Your Wagon '69
- Pale Rider '85 ▶
- Picture Windows '95
- Poldark 2 '75 ▶
- Poldark '75 ▶
- Poldark '96
- Pride '14 ▶
- Re-Generation '04
- Ride the High Country '62 ▶
- The Rider of Death Valley '32
- Rider on a Dead Horse '62
- Rope of Sand '49
- The Rundown '03
- Salt of the Earth '54 ▶
- A Sierra Nevada Gunfight '13
- Smilla's Sense of Snow '96
- Solomon and Gaenor '98
- Sons and Lovers '60 ▶
- The Spoilers '42 ▶
- The Stars Look Down '39 ▶
- Tarzan and the Valley of Gold '65
- The 33 '15
- Tide of Empire '29
- Tornado '43
- The Trail of '98 '28
- The Trail to Hope Rose '04
- Tremors 4: The Legend Begins '04
- Wanda Nevada '79
- War Drums '57
- The War Wagon '67 ▶
- Way Out West '37 ▶
- Where the Green Ants Dream '84
- White Fang '36
- Wicked Little Things '07
- The Widowing of Mrs. Holroyd '95
- Within the Rock '96

Minnesota

***See also** America's Heartland*

- Aurora Borealis '06
- Beautiful Girls '96 ▶
- Best Man Down '12
- Contagion '11 ▶
- D2: The Mighty Ducks '94
- D3: The Mighty Ducks '96
- Dawning '09
- Far North '88
- Fargo '96 ▶
- Feeling Minnesota '96
- The Good Son '93
- Grace Is Gone '07 ▶
- Graffiti Bridge '90
- The Great Northfield Minnesota Raid '72
- Grumpier Old Men '95
- Grumpy Old Men '93 ▶
- The Heartbreak Kid '72 ▶
- Ice Castles '79
- Into Temptation '09
- Iron Will '93
- Jingle All the Way '96
- Joe Somebody '01
- Kumiko the Treasure Hunter '14 ▶
- Leatherheads '08
- Little Big League '94
- A Little Trip to Heaven '05
- The Long Riders '80 ▶
- The Mighty Ducks '92
- Milwaukee, Minnesota '03
- New in Town '09
- The New Land '72 ▶
- North Country '05
- Older Than America '08
- The Personals '83
- A Prairie Home Companion '06
- Purple Rain '84
- Regression '16
- Scared Silent '02
- A Serious Man '09 ▶
- A Simple Plan '98 ▶
- Slaughterhouse Five '72
- Stuck Between Stations '11
- That Was Then. . . This Is Now '85
- Untamed Heart '93
- Young Adult '11

Missing Persons

***See also** Hostage!; Kidnapped!*

- Abandon '02
- Abandoned '47
- Abandoned '10
- Absentia '11
- Adam '83 ▶
- The Adventurer: The Curse of the Midas Box '13
- Agatha '79
- Agatha Christie: A Life in Pictures '04
- All Good Things '10
- All Nighter '17
- The Amazing Spider-Man '12 ▶
- American Son '19
- American Woman '19
- Anastasia '56 ▶
- Anastasia: The Mystery of Anna '86
- And Never Let Her Go '01
- And Soon the Darkness '10
- AngKor: Cambodia Express '81
- Answers to Nothing '11
- Arc '06
- Assassination in Rome '65
- Atlas Shrugged: Part 1 '11
- Bag of Bones '11
- Beautiful '09
- Beneath the Mississippi '08
- Between '05
- Between Truth and Lies '06
- Beyond '11
- Beyond the Gates '16
- The Big Bang '11
- Big Jake '71
- Blade Runner 2049 '17
- Blind Eye '06
- Border Run '12
- Born of Earth '08
- The Bravos '72
- Breakdown '96 ▶
- Bringing Ashley Home '11
- Bunny Lake Is Missing '65
- Bureau of Missing Persons '33
- Burning '18 ▶
- Cavalcade of the West '36
- Chain of Souls '00
- Changeling '08 ▶
- Chasing Sleep '00
- Cocaine and Blue Eyes '83
- Come and Find Me '16
- Compulsion '13
- Conspiracy '08
- Countdown: Jerusalem '09
- Creepy '16 ▶
- Cries in the Dark '06
- Criminal Desire '98
- Cropsey '10
- The Crow Road '96
- The Cry: La Llorona '07
- The Cry of the Owl '09
- Curse of the Pink Panther '83
- Dangerous Crossing '53
- Dark World '08
- Deadly Honeymoon '10
- Death and Cremation '10
- The Descent 2 '09
- Direct Contact '09
- The Disappearance of Vonnie '94
- The Disappeared '08
- Domain '18
- Don't Knock Twice '17
- Don't Look Up '08
- Drew Peterson: Untouchable '12
- Dying Room Only '73
- Earthquake Bird '19
- Eight Days to Live '06
- Elsewhere '09
- The Emerald Forest '85 ▶
- The Empty Acre '07
- Equinox '71 ▶
- Every Secret Thing '15
- Experiment in Terror '62 ▶
- Eye Witness '49
- Face of Terror '04
- The Falcon in Danger '43
- The Family Fang '16
- Final Cut '88
- Five Days '07
- Flesh Wounds '10
- The Flock '07
- Forget Me Not '09
- Fractured '19
- Frantic '88 ▶
- Freedomland '06
- From Hollywood to Deadwood '89
- The Frozen '12
- Garrison '07
- Get a Clue '02
- The Girl Hunters '63
- Girl Missing '33
- The Girl on the Train '16
- The Girl With the Dragon Tattoo '09 ▶
- The Girl With the Dragon Tattoo '11 ▶
- Give Me Your Hand '09
- Gone '12
- Gone Baby Gone '07 ▶
- Gone Girl '14 ▶
- The Good German '06
- The Good Student '08
- Grayeagle '77
- The Hangover '09
- Harem '85
- Harper '66 ▶
- Harrison's Flowers '02
- The Haunting of Winchester House '09
- Heading for Heaven '47
- Hell Squad '85
- Her Sister's Keeper '06
- Hidden '09
- Hide in Plain Sight '80 ▶
- High Road to China '83
- Hogfather '06
- Home for Christmas '93
- Hoodwinked Too! Hood *vs.* Evil '11
- House of Bones '09
- The Hungry Ghosts '09
- The Hunter '12
- The Hunters '13
- Hurricane Smith '92
- Imagining Argentina '04
- In Her Skin '09
- In the Blood '13
- In the Mouth of Madness '95
- Inherent Vice '14 ▶
- Into Thin Air '85 ▶
- The Invisible '07
- The Iris Effect '04
- The Irishman '19 ▶
- The Island at the Top of the World '74
- It Chapter Two '19
- Jesse Stone: Thin Ice '09
- Journey to the Center of the Earth '08
- Julieta '16
- Just Another Secret '89
- Just Business '08
- Justice for Natalee '11
- Kalamity '10
- Katyn '07
- Keane '04 ▶
- Kentucky Jubilee '51
- Kidnap Syndicate '76
- Killer Leopard '54
- The Lady Vanishes '38 ▶
- The Lady Vanishes '79
- The Lady Vanishes '13
- Larceny in Her Heart '46
- The Last Time I Saw Macao '13
- The Last Winter '84
- The Least of These '08
- Left Bank '08
- Left Behind '14
- The Levenger Tapes '16
- Lies and Illusions '09
- LIP Service '99
- Little Girl Lost: The Delimar Vera Story '08
- London River '09
- Long Time Since '97
- Looking for Kitty '04
- Lost in Paris '17
- Lost Treasure of the Maya '08
- Love Me '12
- Loveless '18 ▶
- Love's Christmas Journey '11
- A Low Down Dirty Shame '94
- Lucky Number Slevin '06
- The Man in the Net '59
- Mannaja: A Man Called Blade '77
- Maya Dardel '17
- Meadowland '15
- Megan Is Missing '11
- A Memory In My Heart '99
- The Men Who Stare at Goats '09
- Mexico City '00
- Misery '90 ▶
- Miss Tatlock's Millions '48
- Missing '82 ▶
- Missing Brendan '03
- The Missing Person '09
- Mr. District Attorney '41
- The Moment '13
- Moon Zero Two '70
- Murder, My Sweet '44 ▶
- Murder on Pleasant Drive '06
- My Baby Is Missing '07
- The Mystery of Edwin Drood '12
- Nancy Steele Is Missing '37
- Neither Heaven Nor Earth '16
- Never Take Candy From a Stranger '60
- A Nightmare Come True '97
- Nim's Island '08
- 99 Pieces '07

No Hands on the Clock '41
The Norliss Tapes '73
Not Forgotten '09
Oh Lucy! '17
Old Gringo '89
The Operative '19
The Orphanage '07 ▶
The Outsider '14
The Owls '09
Passengers '08
Pay the Ghost '15
Percy Jackson & The Olympians: The Lightning Thief '10
Personal Effects '05
Phoenix Forgotten '17
Picnic at Hanging Rock '75 ▶
The Poison Rose '19
Pokémon Detective Pikachu '19
Pornography: A Thriller '10
Presumed Dead '06
Prisoner of Zenda '37 ▶
The Professionals '66 ▶
Psych-Out '68
Pure Luck '91
The Questor Tapes '74
Raising Arizona '87 ▶
Rare Exports: A Christmas Tale '10
The Reckoning '14
Red Riding, Part 1: 1974 '09
Red Riding, Part 3: 1983 '09
Red White & Blue '10
Returned '15
Riddle '13
The Rig '10
Romancing the Stone '84 ▶
Seance on a Wet Afternoon '64 ▶
The Search for One-Eye Jimmy '94
The Searchers '56 ▶
Searching '18 ▶
Seventeen and Missing '06
Shoplifters '18 ▶
Short Night of Glass Dolls '71
The Shortcut '09
The Shrine '10
Shutter Island '09 ▶
A Simple Favor '18 ▶
Sin '02
Sister's Keeper '07
Skeletons '10
Slender Man '18
Snow 2: Brain Freeze '08
Sometimes Always Never '19
The Song of Names '19
Spinning Man '18
Spy in the Sky '58
Stand Clear of the Closing Doors '13 ▶
Stolen '09
Stranded '06
Strangerland '15
Street Girls '75
Suspense '46
Talking to Heaven '02
The Tall Man '12
Tarzan the Fearless '33
Terminal Force '88
Texas Killing Fields '11
The Theory of the Leisure Class '01
Thin Air '00
30 '59
Threat of Exposure '02
Time Trap '17
Tokyo Joe '49
Tony Rome '67
Top of the Lake '13 ▶
Tower of the Firstborn '98
The Tracey Fragments '07
Twenty Plus Two '61
2 Minutes Later '07
Unforgivable '11
Vampire Night '00
The Vanishing '88 ▶
The Vanishing '19
The Vanishing of Sidney Hall '17
The Viking Women and the Sea Serpent '57
Voodoo Possession '14
Wakefield '17
Wallenberg: A Hero's Story '85 ▶

Wanted: Babysitter '75
Warp Speed '81
We Don't Belong Here '17
Where Are the Children? '85
Whispers and Lies '08
White Bird in a Blizzard '14
White Fire '53
Who Is Simon Miller? '11
Who Saw Her Die? '72
The Wicker Man '75 ▶
The Wicker Man '06
Winter's Bone '10 ▶
Wish You Were Here '12
Without a Trace '83
The Wolfman '09
The World of Kanako '15
A Wrinkle in Time '18
The X Files: I Want to Believe '08

Missionaries

See also Nuns & Religion; Religious Epics

The African Queen '51 ▶
Beyond the Next Mountain '87
Black Robe '91 ▶
End of the Spear '06
The Falls: Covenant of Grace '16
The Falls: Testament of Love '13
Hawaii '66 ▶
The Inn of the Sixth Happiness '58 ▶
The Keys of the Kingdom '44 ▶
The Mission '86 ▶
Mission to Glory '80
The Missionary '82
The Other Side of Heaven 2: Fire of Faith '19
The Other Side of Heaven '02
Paradise Road '97
Rambo '08
The Wicker Tree '10

Mistaken Identity

See also Amnesia; Gender Bending; Role Reversal

Across the Bridge '57
The Adventures of Bullwhip Griffin '66
Allied '16
Along Came Jones '45 ▶
Amos and Andrew '93
Another You '91
Apres-Vous '03
As You Like It '36
As You Like It '06
As Young As You Feel '51 ▶
The Assignment '97
The Associate '79
The Aura '05 ▶
Author: The JT LeRoy Story '16
Bachelor Flat '62
Bachelor Mother '39 ▶
The Ballad of Little Jo '93
Barocco '76
The Beautician and the Beast '97
The Beautiful Blonde from Bashful Bend '49
Being There '79 ▶
Betrayed '54 ▶
A Better Way to Die '00
Beyond Suspicion '00
The Big Lebowski '97 ▶
The Big Picture '10
Black Glove '54
Blame It on the Bellboy '92
Bobby Z '07
Body Snatchers '93
Borderline '50
The Boss of It All '06
Breakin' All The Rules '04
Broadway Limited '41
Bullets or Ballots '38 ▶
Bullseye! '90
Bundle of Joy '56
Bushwhacked '95
Camp Cucamonga: How I Spent My Summer Vacation '90
Captain Underpants: The First Epic Movie '17
The Capture '50 ▶

Carry On Admiral '57
CB4: The Movie '93
Center of the Web '92
The Central Park Five '12 ▶
Chameleon Street '89 ▶
Changeling '08 ▶
Charade '63 ▶
The Chase '66
Christmas in the Clouds '01
City of Ghosts '03
The Closet '00
Codename: Jaguar '98
Company Man '00
Complete Unknown '16
Cornbread, Earl & Me '75
A Couch in New York '95
The Couch Trip '87
Counterblast '48
The Court Jester '56 ▶
Date Night '10
Daughters of the Sun '00
Dave '93 ▶
Deadwood '65
The Desert Song '53
Dog Gone Love '03
Don Juan DeMarco '94
Don't Tell Her It's Me '90
Don't Worry, We'll Think of a Title '66
Double Identity '10
Double Play '96
Double Take '01
Double Wedding '10
The Duchess of Buffalo '26
El Mariachi '93 ▶
The Emperor's Candlesticks '37
Ernest Goes to Jail '90
Everybody Wants to Be Italian '08
Execution of Raymond Graham '85
F/X 2: The Deadly Art of Illusion '91
Falling for Grace '06
The Family Plan '05
Feet First '30
Five Graves to Cairo '43 ▶
The Flame of New Orleans '41 ▶
Flightplan '05
Focus '01
Gangway '37
Garfield: A Tail of Two Kitties '06
The Gay Divorcee '34 ▶
Generale Della Rovere '09 ▶
The Glass Bottom Boat '66
Going Wild '30
Good Neighbor Sam '64 ▶
The Great Dictator '40 ▶
Grosse Fatigue '94 ▶
The Gun in Betty Lou's Handbag '92
Happy Go Lovely '51
Her Highness and the Bellboy '45
Her Night of Romance '24
Hero '92 ▶
High & Low '62 ▶
High Lonesome '50
Holy Matrimony '43 ▶
Honolulu '39
Houseguest '94
The Hustle '08
I Want to Live! '58 ▶
I Will, I Will...for Now '76
Identity Thief '13
If Looks Could Kill '91
The Imposters '98
In Society '44
The Inspector General '49 ▶
Intimate Strangers '04 ▶
Invasion of the Body Snatchers '78 ▶
Irene '40
It Started with Eve '41 ▶
It Takes Two '95
It! The Terror from Beyond Space '58
Jade '95
Johnny Handsome '89 ▶
Just Write '97
Kansas City Confidential '52 ▶
Keaton's Cop '90
Kid from Spain '32
Killer Dill '47
The Killing Time '87
The King of Masks '99 ▶

A Kiss Before Dying '91
Km. 0 '00
Lady Killer '97
The Last Winter '84
Let It Shine '12
Like Father, Like Son '13
Like Someone in Love '13
The Little Drummer Girl '84 ▶
Little Man '06
The Lizzie McGuire Movie '03
Lolly-Madonna XXX '73
Lost Highway '96
Love at Large '89 ▶
Lucky Number Slevin '06
Mad About Music '38 ▶
Made in America '93
The Magnificent Two '67
The Majestic '01
Mamma Mia! '08
The Man '05
Man From God's Country '58
The Man Who Knew Too Little '97
The Man with One Red Shoe '85
The Mark of Zorro '40 ▶
Meet the Deedles '98
Memento '00 ▶
Merrily We Live '38 ▶
Miami Hustle '95
Mickey Blue Eyes '99
Mississippi Mermaid '69 ▶
Mistaken Identity '36
Mr. Klein '76 ▶
Monsieur Beaucaire '46 ▶
The Monster '96
Muppets Most Wanted '14
My Favorite Spy '51
My Geisha '62
My Man Godfrey '36 ▶
My Outlaw Brother '51
Mystery Date '91
Naughty Marietta '35
Never a Dull Moment '68
Next of Kin '84
The Night We Never Met '93
Nightfall '56 ▶
Nine Lives '16
Nobody's Perfect '90
North by Northwest '59 ▶
The Nutt House '95
Obsession '76
Off Season '01
On the Double '61
One Body Too Many '44
Only You '94
Opportunity Knocks '90
Oscar '91
The Over-the-Hill Gang Rides Again '70
Pale Saints '97
Paper Mask '91
Paradise for Three '38
Pardon My Sarong '42
The Parent Trap '61
The Parent Trap '98
The Parent Trap II '86
The Passenger '75 ▶
The Perfect Man '05
Phantom Fiend '35
Picture Perfect '96
The Player '92 ▶
Prelude to a Kiss '92
Priceless '06
Prime '05
The Princess Comes Across '36 ▶
Princess O'Rourke '43
Private Life of Don Juan '34
Purple Noon '60 ▶
Ranson's Folly '26
Red Firecracker, Green Firecracker '93
Red Heat '85
Red Rock West '93 ▶
Reindeer Games '00
The Reluctant Agent '89
The Reluctant Astronaut '67
Return of Jesse James '50
The Return of Martin Guerre '83 ▶
The Road to Guantanamo '06
Romance on the High Seas '48 ▶
Running Hot '83
Safe Men '98

St. Benny the Dip '51
The Santa Clause '94
Say It Isn't So '01
The Scapegoat '59
The Scar '48
Scream of Fear '61 ▶
Seconds '66 ▶
The Secret of My Success '87
Sergeant Deadhead '65
The 7th Commandment '61
She's the Man '06
Sister Act '92
Sister Act 2: Back in the Habit '93
Sister's Keeper '07
The Sleepy Time Gal '01
Smokey and the Bandit, Part 3 '83
Something in the Wind '47
Son of Gascogne '95
South of Panama '41
Splitting Heirs '93
The Square Peg '58
A Stolen Life '46
Straight Talk '92
The Stupids '95
The Suitors '88
Sunday '96
Support Your Local Gunfighter '71 ▶
Suture '93
Swing Hostess '44
10 Rillington Place '71 ▶
The Tenth Man '88
Texas Carnival '51
The Thin Blue Line '88 ▶
Things Change '88 ▶
Things I Never Told You '96
The 39 Steps '35 ▶
Toni Erdmann '16 ▶
Top Hat '35 ▶
Toto le Heros '91 ▶
The Tourist '10
Tropic Thunder '08 ▶
The Truth about Cats and Dogs '96 ▶
Twelfth Night '96
Twin Dragons '92
Two Much '96
The Unholy Three '30 ▶
The Well '51 ▶
We're No Angels '89
West of the Pecos '45
Westward Bound '30
While You Were Sleeping '95 ▶
Who's Harry Crumb? '89
Wings of the Morning '37
Withnail and I '87 ▶
The Wrong Guys '88
You Said a Mouthful '32
Young Master '80

Mockumentary

See also Documentary; Genre Spoofs

Acapulco Gold '78
All You Need Is Cash '78 ▶
American Zombie '07
. . .And God Spoke '94
The Baby Formula '08
The Bay '12
Behind the Mask: The Rise of Leslie Vernon '06
Believe '07
Best in Show '00 ▶
Big Man Japan '07
Bigfoot: The Lost Coast Tapes '12
The Blair Witch Project '99
Bob Roberts '92 ▶
Borat: Cultural Learnings of America for Make Benefit Glorious Nation of Kazakhstan '06 ▶
Born to Lose '99
Brother's Justice '11
Brothers of the Head '06
Comic Book: The Movie '04 ▶
Computer Chess '13
Confetti '06
CSA: The Confederate States of America '04
Danny Roane: First Time Director '06
A Day Without a Mexican '04
Drop Dead Gorgeous '99

8213: Gacy House '10
Fear of a Black Hat '94
Flyboys '06
For Your Consideration '06
Forgotten Silver '96 ▶
Gamers '06
Glen or Glenda? '53
Hard Core Logo 2 '10
Hard Core Logo '96
Incident at Loch Ness '04 ▶
Invasion '07
It's All Gone, Pete Tong '04
Jackie's Back '99
Killing Gunther '17
The Last Broadcast '98 ▶
Lisa Picard Is Famous '01
Live! '07
Mail Order Wife '04
Mascots '16
Memron '04
A Mighty Wind '03 ▶
Never Been Thawed '05
No Men Beyond This Point '15
On Edge '03
Operation Avalanche '16
The Other Side of the Wind '18
Pittsburgh '06
Pygmy Island '50
Real Time: Siege at Lucas Street Market '00
Rescue Dawn '06 ▶
The Return of Spinal Tap '92
Shadow People '13
Stardom '00
SuperGuy: Behind the Cape '02
This Is Spinal Tap '84 ▶
Tristram Shandy: A Cock and Bull Story '05
2001 Maniacs: Field of Screams '10
Waiting for Guffman '96
Walk Hard: The Dewey Cox Story '07
Zelig '83 ▶

Model Citizens

Abdulla the Great '56
Artists and Models '37
Artists and Models Abroad '38
Blackjack '97
Captivity '07
The Case of the Bloody Iris '72
A Change of Place '94
Cover Girl '44 ▶
Cover Girl Models '75
Daniella by Night '61
Darling '65 ▶
Designing Woman '57 ▶
Domino '05
D.R.E.A.M. Team '99
Drop Dead Gorgeous '10
Eight Miles High '07
The Eighteenth Angel '97
Eyes of Laura Mars '78
Face of Terror '04
Faceless '88
Fall '97
Funny Face '57 ▶
Gia '98
Giving It Up '99
Head Over Heels '01
Human Desires '97
I Can Get It For You Wholesale '51
In and Out '97 ▶
The Invisibles '99
The Last International Playboy '08
Looker '81
Mahogany '75
Making of a Male Model '83
The Model and the Marriage Broker '51
Model Shop '69
One Last Thing '05
Raising Helen '04
Ready to Wear '94
The Reckless Hour '31
Screaming Dead '03
Shattered Innocence '87
Slaves of New York '89
So Fine '81
Stardom '00
Stolen Holiday '37

▶ = rated three bones or higher

Storm Warning '51
The System '64
Taxi '04
30 Years to Life '01
Tricks of a Woman '08
The Unbelievable Truth '90
Unzipped '94 ▶
The Valet '06
What's New Pussycat? '65 ▶
Wonderwall: The Movie '69
You and I '11
Zoolander '01

Modern Cowboys

***See also** Western Comedy; Westerns*

All the Pretty Horses '00
Another Pair of Aces: Three of a Kind '91 ▶
Barbarosa '82 ▶
The Big Empty '04
Brokeback Mountain '05 ▶
Bronco Billy '80
Buck '11 ▶
By Dawn's Early Light '00
City Slickers 2: The Legend of Curly's Gold '94
City Slickers '91 ▶
Coogan's Bluff '68 ▶
Cowboy Up '00
The Cowboy Way '94
Don't Come Knocking '05
Down in the Valley '05
Edge of Eternity '59
8 Seconds '94
The Electric Horseman '79
Fool for Love '86
The Hi-Lo Country '98
Hope Ranch '02
The Horse Whisperer '97
The Last Cowboy '03
The Last of the Dogmen '95
Lonely Are the Brave '62 ▶
The Magnificent Seven '16
A Prairie Home Companion '06
Rhinestone '84
Toy Story '95 ▶
Toy Story 2 '99 ▶
An Unfinished Life '05
Wild Horses '84

Modern Shakespeare

All Night Long '62
Chimes at Midnight '67 ▶
Cymbeline '15
A Double Life '47 ▶
Forbidden Planet '56 ▶
Gnomeo & Juliet '11
The Godfather '72 ▶
The Godfather, Part 2 '74 ▶
The Godfather, Part 3 '90 ▶
Hamlet 2 '08 ▶
Hamlet '00 ▶
Jubal '56
The King Is Alive '00
King of Texas '02 ▶
Kiss Me Kate '53 ▶
Let the Devil Wear Black '99
The Lion King 1 1/2 '04 ▶
Looking for Richard '96 ▶
Love Is All There Is '96
Macbeth '06
Men of Respect '91
A Midsummer Night's Sex Comedy '82 ▶
Much Ado About Nothing '13 ▶
My Own Private Idaho '91 ▶
O '01 ▶
Otello '86 ▶
Othello '01 ▶
Private Romeo '11
Prospero's Books '91 ▶
Ran '85 ▶
Richard III '95 ▶
Ring of Fire '91
Ronnie and Julie '97
Rosencrantz & Guildenstern Are Dead '90 ▶
Rosencrantz & Guildenstern Are Undead '10
Scotland, PA '02
Shakespeare Wallah '65 ▶
Shakespeare's Merchant '05
She's the Man '06
Shiner '00
Siberian Lady Macbeth '61 ▶
The Street King '02
The Tempest '82 ▶
Ten Things I Hate about You '99 ▶
Theatre of Blood '73 ▶
The Three Weird Sisters '48
Throne of Blood '57 ▶
Tromeo & Juliet '95
West Side Story '61 ▶
William Shakespeare's Romeo and Juliet '96 ▶

Moms

***See** Bad Dads; Dads; Monster Moms; Parenthood; Stepparents*

Monkeyshines

***See also** Jungle Stories; Killer Apes and Monkeys; Wild Kingdom*

Babe: Pig in the City '98
The Barefoot Executive '71
Bedtime for Bonzo '51
Black Zoo '63
Blood Monkey '07
Born to Be Wild '95
The Bride & the Beast '58
Buddy '97
Carry On Up the Jungle '70
Cloudy with a Chance of Meatballs '09
Congo '95
Curious George '06
Curtain at Eight '33
Dawn of the Planet of the Apes '14 ▶
Die Laughing '80
Dr. Dolittle '98
Dunston Checks In '95
Ed '96
George of the Jungle '97 ▶
The Hangover, Part 2 '11
Ice Age: Continental Drift '12
Instinct '99
Jane '17 ▶
Jay and Silent Bob Strike Back '01
King Kong '33 ▶
King Kong '76
Mark of the Gorilla '58
Mom, Can I Keep Her? '98
Monkey Business '52 ▶
Monkey Shines '88
Monkey Trouble '94
Monkeybone '01
MVP: Most Valuable Primate '00
MVP2: Most Vertical Primate '01
MXP: Most Xtreme Primate '03
Outbreak '94 ▶
Planet of the Apes '01 ▶
The Powerpuff Girls Movie '02 ▶
Project Nim '11 ▶
Race to Space '01
Rise of the Planet of the Apes '11 ▶
The Rundown '03
Sergeant Deadhead '65
The Sisters '05
Space Chimps '08
Spark: A Space Tail '17
Speed Racer '08
Summer of the Monkeys '98
Tarzan '99 ▶
Tarzan and the Leopard Woman '46
Tarzan Triumphs '43
Terror Tract '00
Treasure Buddies '12
Upstairs Downstairs '11
War for the Planet of the Apes '17 ▶
Who's Your Monkey '07
The Wild Thornberrys Movie '02 ▶

Monks

***See also** Clergymen; Martial Arts*

Black Death '10
The Da Vinci Code '06 ▶
The Forbidden Kingdom '08
Hitman '07
Kundun '97 ▶
Lost Horizon '73
The Mermaid Chair '06
Monty Python and the Holy Grail '75 ▶
Nacho Libre '06
The Name of the Rose '86
Of Gods and Men '10 ▶
Rasputin '85 ▶
Rasputin and the Empress '33 ▶
The Secret of Kells '09
The 36th Chamber of Shaolin '78 ▶
Van Helsing '04 ▶

Monster Moms

***See also** Bad Dads; Dads; Moms; Parenthood*

Alias Betty '01
Almost Dead '94
The American '01
American Venus '07
Animal Kingdom '09 ▶
The Anniversary '68
The Baby '72
Bad Boy Bubby '93
The Bad Son '07
Bellissima '51 ▶
Beowulf '07 ▶
Berlinguer I Love You '77
Beyond the Door '75
Big Bad Mama 2 '87
Big Bad Mama '74
Blood and Orchids '86
Bloody Mama '70
Boystown '07
Brand Upon the Brain! '06 ▶
Carrie '76 ▶
Carrie '02
Carrie '13
Catfish in Black Bean Sauce '00
The Cats '68
Chutney Popcorn '99
Cop Au Vin '85
Cora Unashamed '00
Dead Alive '93
Dead Pet '01
Deadly Advice '93
Death in Love '08
Die! Die! My Darling! '65
Die Mommie Die! '03
Divine Secrets of the Ya-Ya Sisterhood '02
Dogtooth '09
Dolores Claiborne '94 ▶
East of Eden '54 ▶
East of Eden '80
Ed and His Dead Mother '93
Excision '12
Felicia's Journey '99 ▶
Fiona '98
Flesh Eating Mothers '89
Flowers in the Attic '14
From Dusk Till Dawn 3: The Hangman's Daughter '99
Ghosts Never Sleep '05
Glass House: The Good Mother '06
Gone Baby Gone '07 ▶
Gorgo '61
Gracie's Choice '04
The Grifters '90 ▶
Hard, Fast and Beautiful '51
Hard to Handle '33
Harm's Way '07
Hidden '09
His Greatest Gamble '34
Hunger Point '03
Hush '98
Hush Little Baby '93
Ice Princess '05
Inconceivable '17
The Intended '02
Introducing the Dwights '07
Invaders from Mars '53
Invaders from Mars '86
Jug Face '13
The Last of Robin Hood '13
Leading Ladies '10
A Light in the Darkness '02
Listen to Your Heart '10
A Little Thing Called Murder '06
Little Voice '98 ▶
The Locusts '97
Love at First Kill '08
Lucky Day '91
Ma Barker's Killer Brood '60
The Manchurian Candidate '62 ▶
A Matter of Dignity '57
Medea '70
Mom '89
Mommie Dearest '81
Mommy 2: Mommy's Day '96
Mommy '95
Monster-in-Law '05
Monster's Ball '01 ▶
Mother '94
Mother's Boys '94
Mother's Day '80
Mother's Day '10
The Nightman '93
Nobody's Children '52
Nutcracker: Money, Madness & Murder '87 ▶
Only God Forgives '13
Parents '89 ▶
Passion '99
Perfect Sisters '14
Picture Mommy Dead '66
Pilgrimage '33
The Positively True Adventures of the Alleged Texas Cheerleader-Murdering Mom '93 ▶
Possessing Piper Rose '11
Precious: Based on the Novel 'Push' by Sapphire '09 ▶
Psycho '60 ▶
Psycho 2 '83
Psycho 3 '86
Queen of Hearts '19
Rosetta '99
Running with Scissors '06
Santa Sangre '90 ▶
Savage Grace '07
Say It Isn't So '01
Serial Mom '94 ▶
Shopworn '32
Six Ways to Sunday '99
Sleepwalkers '92
Sleepwalking '08
Sonny '02
Spanglish '04
Spanking the Monkey '94 ▶
The Star '52 ▶
The Stepmother '71
Sybil '76 ▶
Touch of Pink '04
Track of the Cat '54
Trilogy of Terror 2 '96
The Ugly '96
Unforgettable '17
White Oleander '02
Wild at Heart '90 ▶
Willard '03

Monster Yuks

Abbott and Costello Meet Dr. Jekyll and Mr. Hyde '52
Abbott and Costello Meet Frankenstein '48 ▶
Abbott and Costello Meet the Killer, Boris Karloff '49
Abbott and Costello Meet the Mummy '55
The Addams Family '91
Addams Family Values '93
Boo 2! A Madea Halloween '17
Boo! A Madea Halloween '16
The Calamari Wrestler '04
Drop Dead Fred '91
Girl vs. Monster '12
Goobers! '97
Gooby '09
Hotel Transylvania 3: Summer Vacation '18
Little Monsters '89
A Monster in Paris '11
Monster Trucks '16
Monsters, Inc. '01 ▶
Monsters University '13
Munster, Go Home! '66
Pokémon Detective Pikachu '19
Pom Poko '94
Scooby-Doo 2: Monsters Unleashed '04
The Water Horse: Legend of the Deep '07
What's Up, Hideous Sun Demon? '83

Monsters, General

***See** Bigfoot/Yeti; Ghosts, Ghouls, & Giants; Killer Beasts; Killer Bugs and Slugs; Killer Plants; Killer Reptiles; Killer Sea Critters; Killer Toys; Mad Scientists; Mummies; Robots, Cyborgs & Vampires; Werewolves; Zombies*

Montana

Almost Heroes '97
Always '89
Amazing Grace & Chuck '87
The Ballad of Little Jo '93
Big Eden '00
Bright Angel '91
Bustin' Loose '81 ▶
Cattle Queen of Montana '54
Certain Women '16 ▶
Clay Pigeons '98
Cold Feet '89
Cowboys vs Dinosaurs '15
Disorganized Crime '89
Evel Knievel '72
Fear X '03 ▶
Forrest Gump '94 ▶
The Horse Whisperer '97
Jeremiah Johnson '72 ▶
Juanita '19
The Killer Inside Me '76
Legends of the Fall '94
Little Big Man '70 ▶
Lonesome Dove '89 ▶
Me & Will '99
Missouri Breaks '76
The Patriot '99
Rancho Deluxe '75 ▶
Return to Lonesome Dove '93
A River Runs Through It '92 ▶
The River Wild '94
Season of Change '94
The Slaughter Rule '01
Star Trek: First Contact '96 ▶
Stay Away, Joe '68
The Stone Boy '84 ▶
They Died with Their Boots On '41 ▶
Thunderbolt & Lightfoot '74 ▶
Under Siege 2: Dark Territory '95
Walking Out '17

Monte Carlo/Monaco

Cash '08
Charlie Chan at Monte Carlo '37
The Counterfeiters '07 ▶
Easy Virtue '08
The Garden of Eden '28 ▶
The Girl From Monaco '08
Grand Prix '66
Heartbreaker '10
Herbie Goes to Monte Carlo '77
Monte Carlo '30
Monte Carlo '86
Monte Carlo '11
Priceless '06
Rebecca '40 ▶
Rebecca '97 ▶
The Red Shoes '48 ▶
Seven Thieves '60 ▶
Strike It Rich '90
Those Daring Young Men in Their Jaunty Jalopies '69

Montreal

***See also** Canada*

The Apprentice '71
The Apprenticeship of Duddy Kravitz '74 ▶
The Barbarian Invasions '03 ▶
Barney's Version '10
Because Why? '93
Bon Cop Bad Cop '06
A Bullet for Joey '55
Come As You Are '20
The Double Life of Eleanor Kendall '08
Eddie and the Cruisers 2: Eddie Lives! '89
Eliza's Horoscope '70
Eternal '04
Familia '05
Funkytown '11
Gabrielle '13 ▶
Good Neighbors '10
Heartbeats '11
I Killed My Mother '09
Intent to Kill '58
Jesus of Montreal '89 ▶
Laurence Anyways '12
Leolo '92 ▶
Love and Human Remains '93 ▶
Malarek '89
Mambo Italiano '03
Monsieur Lazhar '11
The Pact '99
Pale Saints '97
The Quarrel '93
The Red Violin '98
St. Urbain's Horseman '07
The Score '01
Seducing Doctor Lewis '03
Seducing Maarya '99
Stay '13
Steel Toes '06
Taking Lives '04
The Trotsky '09
The Victory '81
The Whole Nine Yards '00
A Wind from Wyoming '94

Moonshiners

The Dukes of Hazzard '05
The Dukes of Hazzard: The Beginning '06
Fireball 500 '66
The Last American Hero '73 ▶
Monsieur Gangster '63
Moonshine Mountain '64
My Dog Skip '99 ▶
Snuffy Smith, Yard Bird '42
This Stuff'll Kill Ya! '71
Thunder Road '58 ▶

Mormons

***See also** Religion*

Angels in America '03 ▶
The Avenging Angel '95
Babyteeth '20 ▶
Bonneville '06
Brigham City '01
Brigham Young: Frontiersman '40
The Falls: Covenant of Grace '16
The Falls: Testament of Love '13
Georgia Rule '07
Latter Days '04
Lies & Alibis '06
Messenger of Death '88
Mitt '14
A Mormon Maid '17
Orgazmo '98
The Other Side of Heaven '02
Outlaw Prophet: Warren Jeffs '14
September Dawn '07
Virginia '10
Wagon Master '50 ▶

Morticians & Undertakers

After.life '10
Beneath the Darkness '12
Bernie '12 ▶
The Embalmer '03 ▶
I'll Bury You Tomorrow '02
Just Buried '07
The Loved One '65
The Mortician '11
Mortuary Academy '91
My Girl '91
Scar '07
The Undertaker and His Pals '67
The Undertaker's Wedding '97
Undertaking Betty '02
You Kill Me '07 ▶

Moscow

***See also** Russia/USSR*

Botched '07
The Bourne Ultimatum '07 ▶
Clear All Wires! '33
Command Performance '09
Comrade X '40
The Darkest Hour '11

Day Watch '06 ▸
Elena '11
Farewell '09
Get Smart '08
Gorky Park '83 ▸
The Iron Petticoat '56
The Kremlin Letter '70
Man On a String '60
Mission: Impossible-Ghost Protocol '11 ▸
Mission to Moscow '43
Moscow Does Not Believe in Tears '80 ▸
Moscow on the Hudson '84 ▸
Moscow Zero '06
Mute Witness '95
Night Watch '04
Our Kind of Traitor '16
The Outskirts '98 ▸
Perestroika '09
Police Academy 7: Mission to Moscow '94
PU-239 '06
Red Heat '88
Redline '97
The Russia House '90
The Saint '97
Silent Partner '05
Taxi Blues '90 ▸
12 '07
The Vanished Empire '08
You and I '11

Moscow Mafia

***See also** Gangs; Organized Crime; Russia/USSR*

Berlin Job '12
Birthday Girl '02
Born to Raise Hell '10
Brother '97
City Unplugged '95
The Code '09
Crimes of the Past '09
The Diplomat '08
Double Identity '10
Eastern Promises '07 ▸
The Equalizer '14
Goldeneye '95 ▸
Hard As Nails '01
The Jackal '97
John Wick '14
The Killing Machine '09
Lethal '04
Little Odessa '94
Middle Men '10
One In the Chamber '12
Our Kind of Traitor '16
PU-239 '06
Rage '14
Red Heat '88
Remarkable Power '08
Ripley's Game '02 ▸
RocknRolla '08
Rounders '98
Ruslan '09
Setup '11
The Stranger '10
Takedown '10
We Own the Night '07
What Comes Around '06

Motor Vehicle Dept.

***See also** Big Rigs; Bikers; Checkered Flag; Killer Cars & Motorcycles*

Action Jackson '88
The Adventures of Ford Fairlane '90
American Graffiti '73 ▸
L'Automobile '71
Back to the Future '85 ▸
Bail Out '90
The Betsy '78
Black Cat Run '98
Black Moon Rising '86
Blitz '85
Blood, Guts, Bullets and Octane '99
The Blues Brothers '80 ▸
Cadillac Man '90
Captured '99
The Car '77
Car Babes '06
Car Trouble '86
Car Wash '76
Carpool '96
Carpool Guy '05
Cars 2 '11
The Chase '93
Chitty Chitty Bang Bang '68
Collision '09
Coneheads '93
Corvette Summer '78
Coupe de Ville '90
Crash '95
Crazy for Christmas '05
Cry Panic '74
Dangerous Curves '88
D.C. Cab '84
Death Proof '07
Death Race 2 '10
Devil's Knight '03
Dolan's Cadillac '09
Drive '11 ▸
Drive a Crooked Road '54
Drive Angry '11
Drive-In '76
Drive-In Massacre '74
The Driver '78
Duel '71 ▸
The Dukes of Hazzard '05
The Dukes of Hazzard: The Beginning '06
Dumb & Dumber '94
Excuse My Dust '51
Fast & Furious 6 '13 ▸
Fast & Furious '09
The Fast and the Furious '01
Fast Five '11
Fast Lane '08
Ferris Bueller's Day Off '86 ▸
The First Auto '27
Flash of Genius '08
Follow That Car '80
Ford: The Man & the Machine '87
Freeway '88
Furious 7 '15
Getaway '13
The Goddess of 1967 '00
Gone in 60 Seconds '74
Gone in 60 Seconds '00
The Goods: Live Hard, Sell Hard '09
Gran Torino '08 ▸
Gung Ho '86
The Hearse '80
Herbie: Fully Loaded '05
Herbie Rides Again '74
High Rolling in a Hot Corvette '77
Highway Patrolman '91
Highwaymen '03
The Hollywood Knights '80
Hometown U.S.A. '79
Jade '95
Joyride '97
The Karate Kid '84 ▸
Kidnapped '74
Landspeed '01
The Last Run '71
License to Drive '88
The Lincoln Lawyer '11
The Lively Set '64
The Love Bug '68
Maximum Overdrive '86
Mr. Toad's Wild Ride '96
Motorama '91
Moving Violations '85
My Chauffeur '86
National Lampoon's Vacation '83 ▸
Nick & Norah's Infinite Playlist '08 ▸
Night on Earth '91 ▸
Octane '07
Pepper and His Wacky Taxi '72
Pie in the Sky '95
Repo Jake '90
Repo Man '83 ▸
Roger & Me '89 ▸
R.P.M. '97
Sex Drive '08
Silkwood '83 ▸
Stephen King's Thinner '96
Stingray '78
Sunset Limousine '83
Superbug Super Agent '76
Swedish Auto '06
Tail Lights Fade '99
This Man Must Die '70 ▸
Tomboy '85
Traffic '71
Transporter 3 '08
True Lies '94
Tucker: The Man and His Dream '88 ▸
Two Lane Blacktop '71 ▸
Uncle Buck '89 ▸
Used Cars '80 ▸
The Van '77
Vanishing Point '71
Wrecked '10
The Yellow Rolls Royce '64

Motorcycles

Angel Unchained '70
Angels Die Hard '70
Angels from Hell '68
Angels Hard As They Come '71
Angels' Wild Women '72
Bennett's War '19
Beyond the Law '92
Biker Boyz '03
Born Losers '67
Born to Ride '91
The Brown Bunny '03
Bury Me an Angel '71
C.C. & Company '70
Chopper Chicks in Zombietown '91
Chrome and Hot Leather '71
City Limits '85
Code Two '53
The Courier '19
Crossing the Line '90
Cycle Psycho '72
Cyclone '87
Death Sport '78
Devil's Angels '67
Dirt Bike Kid '86
Easy Rider '69 ▸
Easy Wheels '89
Electra Glide in Blue '73 ▸
Evel Knievel '72
Every Which Way But Loose '78
Eye of the Tiger '86
Fugitive Champion '99
The Great Escape '63 ▸
The Hard Ride '71
Harley Davidson and the Marlboro Man '91
Hellcats '68
Hell's Angels on Wheels '67
Hell's Angels '69 '69
Hell's Belles '69
In Your Face '77
The Indian '07
The Jesus Trip '71
Knightriders '81
The Losers '70
Loveless '83
Mad Max '80 ▸
Motor Psycho '65
The Motorcycle Diaries '04 ▸
Murdercycle '99
The Naked Angels '69
Nam Angels '88
Northville Cemetery Massacre '76
On Any Sunday: The Next Chapter '14
The Place Beyond the Pines '13 ▸
Planet Terror '07
Psychomania '73
Raising Arizona '87 ▸
Rebel Rousers '69
Rebel Run '94
Return of the Rebels '81
Ride for Lance '14
Road to Paloma '14
Run, Angel, Run! '69
Savage Dawn '84
She-Devils on Wheels '68
The Sidehackers '69
Sidewinder One '77
Silver Dream Racer '83
Spetters '80
Stone Cold '91
Streets of Fire '84
Supercross: The Movie '05
Then Came Bronson '68
Timerider '83
Torque '04
Viva Knievel '77
Werewolves on Wheels '71
The Wild Angels '66
Wild Guitar '62
The Wild One '54 ▸
Wild Wheels '69
Winners Take All '87
The World's Fastest Indian '05 ▸

Mountaineering

The Abominable Snowman '57
Blindsight '06 ▸
Bushwhacked '95
The Challenge '38 ▸
Cliffhanger '93 ▸
The Climbers '19
Courage Mountain '89
Edie '19
The Eiger Sanction '75
Everest '07
Everest '15
Extreme Ops '02
Five Days One Summer '82
Free Solo '18 ▸
Heidi '67
Into Thin Air: Death on Everest '97
K2: The Ultimate High '92
A Lonely Place to Die '11
The Mountain '56
The Mountain Between Us '17
My Side of the Mountain '69
North Face '08 ▸
127 Hours '10 ▸
The Passage '79
Seven Years in Tibet '97
Sherpa '15 ▸
Storm and Sorrow '90
The Summit '13
Third Man on the Mountain '59
Touch the Top of the World '06
Touching the Void '03
Vertical Limit '00
A Walk in the Woods '15
The White Tower '50 ▸
The Wildest Dream: The Conquest of Everest '10

Mummies

***See also** Zombies*

Abbott and Costello Meet the Mummy '55
All New Adventures of Laurel and Hardy: For Love or Mummy '98
Ancient Evil: Scream of the Mummy '00
The Awakening '80
Belphegor: Phantom of the Louvre '01
Blood from the Mummy's Tomb '71
Bram Stoker's The Mummy '97
Bubba Ho-Tep '03 ▸
Castle of the Living Dead '64
The Creeps '97
The Curse of King Tut's Tomb '06
Dawn of the Mummy '82
Day of the Mummy '14
The External '99
The Fallen Ones '05
Legend of the Bog '08
Mad Monster Party '68
The Monster Squad '87
The Mummy '32 ▸
The Mummy '59 ▸
The Mummy '99
The Mummy '17
The Mummy Lives '93
The Mummy Returns '01
The Mummy: Tomb of the Dragon Emperor '08
Mummy's Boys '36
The Mummy's Hand '40
The Mummy's Shroud '67
The Mummy's Tomb '42
Relative Stranger '09
Russell Mulcahy's Tale of the Mummy '99
7 Mummies '06
Sphinx '81

Museums

Abbott and Costello Meet Frankenstein '48 ▸
All New Adventures of Laurel and Hardy: For Love or Mummy '98
Belphegor: Phantom of the Louvre '01
Blood Relic '05
The Chaperone '11
Crucible of Terror '72
Curious George '06
The Da Vinci Code '06 ▸
Dirty Pictures '00
Exotic House of Wax '97
From the Mixed-Up Files of Mrs. Basil E. Frankweiler '95
Ghostbusters 2 '89
The Goldfinch '19
The Hideaways '73
House of Wax '53 ▸
House of Wax '05
Mad City '97
The Maiden Heist '08
Mammoth '06
Manticore '05
The Mummy Returns '01
Museum Hours '13 ▸
Mystery of the Wax Museum '33 ▸
Night at the Museum '06
Night at the Museum: Battle of the Smithsonian '09
Night at the Museum: Secret of the Tomb '14
Nightmare in Wax '69
P.D. James: The Murder Room '04
The Pick-Up Artist '87
The Relic '96
Ruben Brandt, Collector '18
Scooby-Doo 2: Monsters Unleashed '04
The Shape of Things '03
The Silence '06
The Square '17
Tenacious D in the Pick of Destiny '06
The Thomas Crown Affair '99 ▸
Topkapi '64 ▸
Vibes '88
Waxwork 2: Lost in Time '91
Waxwork '88
The Witness '99
Wonderstruck '17

Music

***See** Biopics: Musicians; Nashville Narratives; Rock Flicks; Struggling Musicians*

Musical Comedy

The Adventures of Priscilla, Queen of the Desert '94 ▸
The Affairs of Dobie Gillis '53
All Ashore '53
Almost Angels '62
Alvin and the Chipmunks: The Squeakuel '09
Andy Hardy Meets Debutante '40
Anything Goes '56
April in Paris '52
Artists and Models '37
Artists and Models '55
Artists and Models Abroad '38
Athena '54
Babes in Arms '39
Babes on Broadway '41
Band Aid '17
Bathing Beauty '44
Be Yourself '30
Beach Blanket Bingo '65 ▸
Beach Party '63
Because You're Mine '52
Beggar's Opera '54
Bert Rigby, You're a Fool '89
Best Foot Forward '43
The Best Little Whorehouse in Texas '82
The Big Broadcast of 1938 '38
Bikini Beach '64
Billy Rose's Jumbo '62 ▸
Birth of the Blues '41
The Blues Brothers '80 ▸
Blues Brothers 2000 '98
Boardinghouse Blues '48
Bodied '17 ▸
The Boy Friend '71 ▸
The Boys and Girl From County Clare '03
The Boys From Syracuse '40
Bride & Prejudice '04
Broadway Melody of 1936 '35 ▸
Broadway Rhythm '44
Bundle of Joy '56
Bye, Bye, Birdie '63 ▸
Cairo '42
Campus Rhythm '43
Cannibal! The Musical '96
Captain January '36
Carefree '38 ▸
Chasing Rainbows '30
The Cocoanuts '29
Colleen '36
College Humor '33
College Swing '38
Coney Island '43 ▸
Copacabana '47
The Court Jester '56 ▸
Cover Girl '44 ▸
Cowboy from Brooklyn '38
Cry-Baby '90 ▸
Dames '34 ▸
Dance, Girl, Dance '40
Dangerous When Wet '53
Darling Lili '70
The Daughter of Rosie O'Grady '50
Delightfully Dangerous '45
The Devil's Brother '33
Disorderlies '87
Dixiana '30
Dixie Jamboree '44
Do You Love Me? '46
Doll Face '46
Double or Nothing '37
Du Barry Was a Lady '43
The Duchess of Idaho '50
Easy Come, Easy Go '67
Easy to Wed '46
The Eddie Cantor Story '53
Everybody Sing '38
Everyone Says I Love You '96 ▸
Excuse My Dust '51
Fashions of 1934 '34
Father Is a Bachelor '50
Feudin', Fussin', and A-Fightin' '48
Finian's Rainbow '68 ▸
The First Nudie Musical '75
Flirtation Walk '34
Flower Drum Song '61
Flying High '31
Follow That Dream '61
Follow the Boys '63
Follow Your Heart '36
Four Jills in a Jeep '44
Frankie and Johnny '65
Frolics on Ice '39
Fun in Acapulco '63
Funny Face '57 ▸
A Funny Thing Happened on the Way to the Forum '66 ▸
Garden of the Moon '38
The Gay Desperado '36
The Gay Divorcee '34 ▸
Gentlemen Prefer Blondes '53 ▸
George White's Scandals of 1935 '35
Get Yourself a College Girl '64
The Ghastly Love of Johnny X '12
G.I. Blues '60
Gigi '58 ▸
The Girl Can't Help It '56
Girl Crazy '43 ▸
Girl Happy '65
Girl of the Golden West '38
Girls! Girls! Girls! '62
Give a Girl a Break '53
Give Me a Sailor '38
Glee: The 3D Concert Movie '11
Glorifying the American Girl '30
Godspell '73
Going Hollywood '33 ▸
Going My Way '44 ▸
Gold Diggers of 1933 '33 ▸
Gold Diggers of 1935 '35 ▸
Gold Diggers of 1937 '36
The Goldwyn Follies '38

Musical

Good News '47
Grease 2 '82
Grease '78 ▸
The Great American Broadcast '41 ▸
The Grinch '18
Guys and Dolls '55 ▸
Gypsy '62 ▸
Gypsy '93
Hairspray '88 ▸
Hairspray '07 ▸
Hallelujah, I'm a Bum '33
The Happiest Millionaire '67
The Happiness of the Katakuris '01
Happy Go Lovely '51
The Harvey Girls '46 ▸
Head '68 ▸
Hearts Beat Loud '18
Hello, Dolly! '69
Help! '65 ▸
Here Come the Girls '53
Here Come the Waves '45 ▸
Here Comes the Groom '51
Here is My Heart '34
High Society '56 ▸
His Butler's Sister '44
Hit the Deck '55
Hold On! '66
Holiday in Mexico '46
Holiday Inn '42 ▸
Hollywood Canteen '44 ▸
Honolulu '39
Hooray for Love '35
Hot Blood '56
How to Stuff a Wild Bikini '65
How to Succeed in Business without Really Trying '67 ▸
How To Talk To Girls At Parties '17
Huckleberry Finn '74
Hullabaloo '40
I Dood It '43
I Dream of Jeannie '52
I Love Melvin '53
I Married an Angel '42
In Caliente '35
In the Good Old Summertime '49 ▸
In the Navy '41
International House '33
Irene '40
It All Came True '40
It Happened in Brooklyn '47
It's a Great Feeling '49
It's Love Again '36
Jesus Christ Vampire Hunter '01
Jupiter's Darling '55
Just for You '52
Keep 'Em Flying '41
Kid from Spain '32
Kid Galahad '62
Kid Millions '34
Kiss Me Kate '53 ▸
Kissin' Cousins '64
Lady Be Good '41
Le Million '31 ▸
Les Girls '57
Let's Dance '50
Let's Do It Again '53
Life Begins for Andy Hardy '41 ▸
Li'l Abner '59
Lili '53 ▸
Linda Linda Linda '05 ▸
Little Nellie Kelly '40
Little Shop of Horrors '86 ▸
Live a Little, Love a Little '68
London Town '46
Looking for Love '64
Louisiana Purchase '41
Love Me Tonight '32 ▸
The Love Parade '29
Lovely to Look At '52 ▸
Lucky Me '54
Lullaby of Broadway '51
Luxury Liner '48
Make a Wish '37
Mame '74
Mamma Mia! '08
Mamma Mia! Here We Go Again '18
Meet Me After the Show '51
The Merry Widow '34 ▸
Miss London Ltd. '43
Mississippi '35
Money from Home '53
Monte Carlo '30
The Muppet Christmas Carol '92
The Muppet Movie '79 ▸
The Muppets Take Manhattan '84 ▸
Muscle Beach Party '64
My Blue Heaven '50
My Dream Is Yours '49
My Love Came Back '40
My Sister Eileen '55 ▸
Nancy Goes to Rio '50
Naughty Marietta '35
Neptune's Daughter '49
New Faces of 1937 '37
New Faces of 1952 '54
Newsies '92
Old Man Rhythm '35
On a Clear Day You Can See Forever '70
On the Avenue '37 ▸
On with the Show '29
One from the Heart '82
One Hour with You '32
One in a Million '36 ▸
One Night in the Tropics '40
One Touch of Venus '48
The Opposite Sex '56
Paint Your Wagon '69
Painting the Clouds With Sunshine '51
The Pajama Game '57 ▸
Pajama Party '64
Pal Joey '57 ▸
Panama Hattie '42
The Perils of Pauline '47
Phantom of the Paradise '74
Pigskin Parade '36
Pin-Up Girl '44
The Pirate '48 ▸
The Pirates of Penzance '83
Pitch Perfect 2 '15
Pitch Perfect '12
Pittsburgh '06
Popeye '80
Presenting Lily Mars '43
The Producers '05
Radio Stars on Parade '45
Rebecca of Sunnybrook Farm '38
Rhythm on the Range '36
Rhythm on the River '40
Riding High '50
Rio Rita '29
The Road to Bali '53 ▸
The Road to Morocco '42 ▸
Road to Nashville '67
The Road to Rio '47 ▸
The Road to Singapore '40
The Road to Utopia '46 ▸
The Road to Zanzibar '41 ▸
Roadie '80
Roberta '35 ▸
Robin and the 7 Hoods '64
Rock Dog '17
Rock 'n' Roll High School '79 ▸
Rock 'n' Roll High School Forever '91
Romance & Cigarettes '05
Romance on the High Seas '48 ▸
Royal Wedding '51 ▸
The Saddest Music in the World '03
Sally '29
Sally, Irene and Mary '38
Sarah Silverman: Jesus Is Magic '05
Say One for Me '59
Sensations of 1945 '44
Sgt. Pepper's Lonely Hearts Club Band '78
Seven Brides for Seven Brothers '54 ▸
Seven Days' Leave '42
The Seven Little Foys '55 ▸
1776 '72 ▸
Sextette '78
Shake, Rattle and Rock '57
Shake, Rattle & Rock! '94
Shall We Dance '37 ▸
She's Working Her Way Through College '52
Ship Ahoy '42
Shock Treatment '81
The Shocking Miss Pilgrim '47
Show Business '44 ▸
Silk Stockings '57 ▸
Sing '16
Sing, Baby, Sing '36
Singin' in the Rain '52 ▸
The Singing Kid '36
Sioux City Sue '46
Sitting On the Moon '36
The Sky's the Limit '43
Slightly French '49
Small Town Girl '53
The Smiling Lieutenant '31
A Song Is Born '48 ▸
Speedway '68
Spice World: The Movie '97
Spinout '66
Spotlight Scandals '43
Springtime in the Rockies '42
Star Spangled Rhythm '42 ▸
Starlift '51
Starstruck '82
State Fair '45 ▸
State Fair '62
Step Lively '44
The Stooge '51
The Stork Club '45
Strike Up the Band '40
Summer Holiday '48
Summer Stock '50 ▸
Sunny '30
Sunny '41
Sunny Skies '30
Sweethearts '38 ▸
Swing Time '36 ▸
Take Me Out to the Ball Game '49
Tea for Two '50 ▸
Texas Carnival '51
Thanks a Million '35
That Certain Age '38
There's No Business Like Show Business '54 ▸
Thin Ice '37 ▸
Thoroughly Modern Millie '67
Three Daring Daughters '48
Three for the Show '55
Three Little Girls In Blue '46
The Three Musketeers '39
Three Sailors and a Girl '53
Three Smart Girls '36 ▸
Tickle Me '65
To Beat the Band '35
Too Many Girls '40
Top Banana '54
Top Hat '35 ▸
23 1/2 Hours Leave '37
Two Girls and a Sailor '44 ▸
Two Sisters From Boston '46
Two Tickets to Broadway '51
Two Weeks with Love '50
UglyDolls '19
The Unsinkable Molly Brown '64 ▸
Up in Arms '44
Up in Central Park '48
Valley Girl '20
Wabash Avenue '50
Waikiki Wedding '37 ▸
Wake Up and Live '37
We're Not Dressing '34 ▸
The West Point Story '50
When the Boys Meet the Girls '65
White Christmas '54 ▸
Whoopee! '30
Wild On the Beach '65
A Woman Is a Woman '60 ▸
Wonder Man '45
Yes, Giorgio '82
Yesterday '19
Yolanda and the Thief '45
You Can't Have Everything '37
You Were Never Lovelier '42 ▸
You'll Find Out '40
You'll Never Get Rich '41 ▸
Ziegfeld Follies '46

Musical Drama

Across the Universe '07
Band Aid '17
The Band Wagon '53 ▸
The Barkleys of Broadway '49 ▸
Battle of the Year '13
Battlefield America '12
The Belle of New York '52
Bells Are Ringing '60 ▸
Beloved '11
Beyond the Lights '14
Big Fella '37
Black Nativity '13
Blaze '18 ▸
Blonde Venus '32 ▸
Blue Hawaii '62
Body Rock '84
Bright Lights '30
Broadway '42
Broadway Serenade '39
The Broken Circle Breakdown '12
Broken Hill '09
The Buddy Holly Story '78 ▸
Burlesque '10
Cabaret '72 ▸
Cadillac Records '08 ▸
Camelot '67
Can-Can '60
Carmen: A Hip Hopera '01
Carmen Jones '54 ▸
Carnegie Hall '47
Carnival Rock '57
The Cat and the Fiddle '34 ▸
The Chocolate Soldier '41
Clambake '67
Coal Miner's Daughter '80 ▸
Cold War '18 ▸
The Constant Nymph '43
The Cotton Club '84 ▸
Crossover Dreams '85
Curly Top '35
Daddy Long Legs '55 ▸
A Damsel in Distress '37 ▸
Dance Hall '41
Dancing Lady '33
Dancing Pirate '36
Dark Streets '08
A Date with Judy '48
De-Lovely '04
The Desert Song '43
Devdas '55 ▸
Devdas '02 ▸
Dimples '36
Dogs in Space '87
Don Quixote '35 ▸
Double Trouble '67
Down Argentine Way '40 ▸
Dreamgirls '06 ▸
The Duke Is Tops '38
Evita '96
Expresso Bongo '59
Fast Forward '84
Feel the Noise '07
Fiddler on the Roof '71 ▸
The Firefly '37
Fisherman's Wharf '39
The Five Pennies '59
Flashdance '83
Footloose '84
The Forbidden Dance '90
Forever My Girl '18
42nd Street '33 ▸
Funny Girl '68 ▸
Funny Lady '75
Gangway '37
George Balanchine's The Nutcracker '93
Get On Up '14
The Glass Mountain '49
The Glenn Miller Story '54 ▸
Go Into Your Dance '35
Go, Johnny Go! '59
God Help the Girl '14
Golden Dawn '30
Goodbye, Mr. Chips '69
Grace Unplugged '13
Graffiti Bridge '90
Great Balls of Fire '89
The Great Caruso '51
The Great Waltz '38 ▸
The Great Ziegfeld '36 ▸
The Greatest Showman '17
Hamilton '20 ▸
Hard to Hold '84
The Harder They Come '72
Harmony Lane '35
Harum Scarum '65
Hearts Beat Loud '18
Hello, Frisco, Hello '43
High, Wide and Handsome '37
Hit Parade of 1937 '37
Honeysuckle Rose '80
The House of Tomorrow '18
How She Move '08
Hustle & Flow '05 ▸
I Could Go on Singing '63
The Identical '14
Idolmaker '80
If You Knew Susie '48
I'll Cry Tomorrow '55 ▸
I'll See You in My Dreams '51
I'm Not There '07 ▸
The In Crowd '88
Inside Llewyn Davis '13 ▸
It Happened at the World's Fair '63
It's Always Fair Weather '55
Jailhouse Rock '57 ▸
The Jazz Singer '27
The Jazz Singer '52
The Jazz Singer '80
Jeanne and the Perfect Guy '98
Jersey Boys '14
Jesus Christ, Superstar '73 ▸
Jesus Christ Superstar '00
Jimi: All Is by My Side '14
Jolson Sings Again '49
The Jolson Story '46 ▸
The Josephine Baker Story '90 ▸
Joyful Noise '12
Jungle Patrol '48
Just Around the Corner '38
The King and I '56 ▸
King Creole '58
La Bamba '87 ▸
Lady and the Tramp '19
Lady Sings the Blues '72
Lagaan: Once upon a Time in India '01
Lambada '89
The Last Five Years '14 ▸
A Late Quartet '12
Les Miserables '12 ▸
The Little Colonel '35 ▸
Little Miss Broadway '38
The Littlest Angel '69
The Littlest Rebel '35
Living In a Big Way '47
Lottery Bride '30
Love Me or Leave Me '55 ▸
Love Me Tender '56
Love Songs '07
The Mambo Kings '92 ▸
The Man I Love '46 ▸
Man of La Mancha '72
Marco '73
Marguerite '16 ▸
A Matter of Time '76
Meet the People '44
Melody Master '41
Miss Sadie Thompson '53 ▸
MTV's Wuthering Heights '03
Murder at the Vanities '34
Music For Millions '44
The Music Man '62 ▸
My Fair Lady '64 ▸
New Moon '40
New Orleans '47
New York, New York '77 ▸
Night and Day '46
Night Song '47
Nine '09
No, No Nanette '40
Oliver! '68 ▸
Once '06
The One and Only, Genuine, Original Family Band '68 ▸
One Trick Pony '80
Orchestra Wives '42 ▸
Orfeu '99
Paradise, Hawaiian Style '66
Paradise in Harlem '40
Paradise Island '30
Paris Blues '61
Paris 36 '08
Pennies from Heaven '36
Pennies from Heaven '81 ▸
Pete Kelly's Blues '55
The Phantom of the Opera '04
A Prairie Home Companion '06
Princess Tam Tam '35 ▸
Purple Rain '84
Quadrophenia '79 ▸
Rappin' '85
Reckless '35
The Red Shoes '48 ▸
Rent '05
Rhapsody in Blue '45 ▸
Rock, Baby, Rock It '57
Rock, Rock, Rock '56
Rocketman '19 ▸
Rooftops '89
The Rose '79 ▸
Rose Marie '36 ▸
Rose Marie '54 ▸
Rose of Washington Square '39
Roustabout '64
Rudderless '14
Sailing Along '38
Salsa '88
Sarafina! '92 ▸
Satisfaction '88
Say It With Songs '29
Scrooge '70
Serenade '56
She's Back on Broadway '53
Shining Star '75
Shipmates Forever '35
Shout '91
Show Boat '36 ▸
Show Boat '51
Sincerely Yours '55
The Singing Detective '86 ▸
Smilin' Through '41
So This Is Love '53
Something to Sing About '36
Song o' My Heart '30
Song of Freedom '36
Song to Song '17
Song Without End '60
Songwriter '84
The Sound of Music '65 ▸
Sparkle '76
Sparkle '12
Star! '68
Stars and Stripes Forever '52 ▸
State Property 2 '05
Stay Away, Joe '68
Step Up 3D '10
Step Up: All In '14
Step Up Revolution '12
Step Up 2 the Streets '08
Stony Island '77
Stowaway '36 ▸
Sueno '05
Sunday in the Park with George '86 ▸
Swanee River '39
Sweeney Todd: The Demon Barber of Fleet Street '07
Sweet Charity '69 ▸
Sweet Dreams '85
Syncopation '42
Tap '89
Tapped Out '03
Teen Spirit '18
That's My Baby! '44
They Shall Have Music '39
This Is the Army '43
Tommy '75
Umbrellas of Cherbourg '64 ▸
Uncle Joe Shannon '78
Vox Lux '18
Waltz King '63
West Side Story '61 ▸
What's Love Got to Do with It? '93
Whiplash '14 ▸
Wonder Bar '34
Yankee Doodle Dandy '42 ▸
Yentl '83
Young at Heart '54
Young Caruso '51
Young Man with a Horn '50 ▸
Ziegfeld Girl '41 ▸
Zoot Suit '81 ▸
Zou Zou '34

Musical Fantasy

Alice '86
Anything But Love '02
Babes in Toyland '61
Beauty and the Beast '17
Bedknobs and Broomsticks '71
Brigadoon '54 ▸
Butterfly Ball '76
Cabin in the Sky '43 ▸
Carousel '56 ▸
Chitty Chitty Bang Bang '68
Cinderella '64
Cinderella '97
Cinderella III: A Twist in Time '07
Cinderella 2000 '78

A Connecticut Yankee in King Arthur's Court '49
Damn Yankees '58 ▶
Dancer in the Dark '99
Doctor Dolittle '67
Down to Earth '47
8 Women '02 ▶
Fairy Tales '76
The 5000 Fingers of Dr. T '53 ▶
Gepetto '00
High School Musical '06
Into the Woods '14
Kismet '55
Labyrinth '86 ▶
The Little Prince '74
The Living Corpse '03
Lost Horizon '73
March of the Wooden Soldiers '34 ▶
Mary Poppins '64 ▶
Mary Poppins Returns '18
Moulin Rouge '01 ▶
Neapolitan Carousel '54
The New Adventures of Pippi Longstocking '88
Once Upon a Brothers Grimm '77
Peter Pan '60 ▶
Princess Raccoon '05
Purana Mandir '84 ▶
Repo! The Genetic Opera '08
Return to Waterloo '85
Rocketman '19 ▶
Rumpelstiltskin '86
The Singing Detective '03
Sleeping Beauty '89
The Slipper and the Rose '76
Strange Frequency 2 '01
Willy Wonka & the Chocolate Factory '71 ▶
The Wizard of Oz '39 ▶
Wonderwall: The Movie '69
Xanadu '80
Zero Patience '94

Musicals

See *Animated Musicals; Disco Musicals; Musical Comedy; Musical Drama; Musical Fantasy*

Mutiny

See also *Deep Blue; Sail Away; Sea Disasters; Shipwrecked*
All the Brothers Were Valiant '53
Amistad '97 ▶
The Bounty '84
The Caine Mutiny '54 ▶
The Caine Mutiny Court Martial '88 ▶
Crimson Tide '95 ▶
Mutiny '52
The Mutiny of the Elsinore '39
Mutiny on the Bounty '35 ▶
Mutiny on the Bounty '62

Mystery & Suspense

See *Contemporary Noir; Crime Drama; Film Noir; Serial Killers; Spies & Espionage*

Mythology

See also *Folklore & Legends*
Aswang '03
Atlantis, the Lost Continent '61
Attack of the Gryphon '07
Ba'al: The Storm God '08
Banshee!!! '08
Beowulf '07 ▶
The Cave of the Silken Web '67
Cerberus '05
Chupacabra Terror '05
Clash of the Titans '81
Clash of the Titans '10
Colossus and the Amazon Queen '60
Conquest of Mycene '63
Damon and Pythias '62
Dark Kingdom: The Dragon King '04
Death Kappa '10
Dragon Wars '07
Electra, My Love '74
Fury of Achilles '62
The Fury of Hercules '61
Gods of Egypt '16
The Gorgon '64
The Great Yokai War '05
Helen of Troy '03
Hellhounds '09
Hercules '58
Hercules '83
Hercules '97 ▶
Hercules against the Moon Men '64
Hercules and the Captive Women '63
Hercules in New York '70
Hercules in the Haunted World '64
Hercules, Prisoner of Evil '64
Hercules Unchained '59
Hercules *vs.* the Sons of the Sun '64
How to Train Your Dragon: The Hidden World '19 ▶
Immortals '11
Jason and the Argonauts '00
The Kid Who Would Be King '19 ▶
King Arthur: Legend of the Sword '17
Lady Terminator '89 ▶
The Legend of Hercules '14
The Loves of Hercules '60
The Maid '05
Medusa Against the Son of Hercules '62
Onmyoji 2 '03
Onmyoji '01
Percy Jackson: Sea of Monsters '13
Sinbad and the Eye of the Tiger '77
Sinbad: Legend of the Seven Seas '03
Sinbad of the Seven Seas '89
Sinbad, the Sailor '47 ▶
Son of Hercules in the Land of Darkness '63
Thor: The Dark World '13
300: Rise of an Empire '13
Transformers: The Last Knight '17
The Triumph of Hercules '66
Troy '04
Wonder Woman '17 ▶
Wrath of the Titans '12
You're So Cupid '10

Nannies & Governesses

See also *Babysitting; Bringing Up Baby; The Help: Female; Parenthood*
Adam Had Four Sons '41
Addams Family Values '93
All This and Heaven Too '40 ▶
Anna and the King of Siam '46 ▶
Appointment With Death '10
At the Midnight Hour '95
Au Pair 2: The Fairy Tale Continues '01
Au Pair '99
Becky Sharp '35
Berkeley Square '98
Big Momma's House 2 '06
Blanche Fury '48
The Boy '16
A Cat in Paris '11
The Chalk Garden '64 ▶
Corrina, Corrina '94
Cousin Bette '97
The Crimson Petal and the White '12
Dark Shadows '12
The Devil's Own '96 ▶
East of Sudan '64
Eloise at the Plaza '03
Emma's Wish '98
The Family Holiday '07
Flame Over India '59 ▶
Flight of the Red Balloon '08
Friend of the Family 2 '96
The Governess '98
The Hand that Rocks the Cradle '92
The Haunting of Morella '91
Heidi '37
Inconceivable '17
The Innocents '61 ▶
Invisible Child '99
Jack and Sarah '95
Jane Eyre '34
Jane Eyre '44 ▶
Jane Eyre '83 ▶
Jane Eyre '96 ▶
Jane Eyre '97
Jane Eyre '06
Kathleen '41
The King and I '56 ▶
The King and I '99
Lady Audley's Secret '00
Left Luggage '98
Mammoth '09
Mary Poppins '64 ▶
Mary Poppins Returns '18
Midnight's Child '93
Mrs. Doubtfire '93
Mrs. Miracle '09
Mr. Nanny '93
My Nanny's Secret '09
The Nanny '65
The Nanny Diaries '07
The Nanny Express '08
A Nanny for Christmas '10
Nanny Insanity '06
Nanny McPhee '06
Nanny McPhee Returns '10
The Nightcomers '72
Paranormal Activity 2 '10
The Perfect Nanny '00
Peter Pan '53 ▶
Peter Pan '60 ▶
Provocateur '96
Roma '18 ▶
The Second Mother '15 ▶
The Secret Life of Bees '08 ▶
666: The Child '06
The Sound of Music '65 ▶
The Story of Three Loves '53
The Stranger Game '06
Sun Choke '16
Tempted '03
Tully '18
The Turn of the Screw '74
The Turn of the Screw '92
The Turn of the Screw '99
The Unknown Woman '06
Uptown Girls '03
Vanity Fair '99

Nashville

See also *American South; Nashville Narratives*
Blue Valley Songbird '99
Concrete Cowboys '79
Doing Time for Patsy Cline '97
Honkytonk Man '82
The Last Movie Star '17
Nashville '75 ▶
Neil Young: Heart of Gold '06 ▶
The Night the Lights Went Out in Georgia '81
Sweet Country Road '83
The Thing Called Love '93
W.W. and the Dixie Dancekings '75

Nashville Narratives

See also *American South; Biopics: Musicians; Southern Belles*
Coal Miner's Daughter '80 ▶
The Country Bears '02
Country Strong '10
Crazy '08
Crazy Heart '09
Doing Time for Patsy Cline '97
Falling from Grace '92
Following Her Heart '94
Honeysuckle Rose '80
Honkytonk Man '82
Jackpot '01
The Last Ride '12
Nashville '75 ▶
The Night the Lights Went Out in Georgia '81
Payday '73
Pure Country '92
Pure Country 2: The Gift '10
Rhinestone '84
Rikky and Pete '88
Ring of Fire '13
Road to Nashville '67
Saturday Night Special '92
Songwriter '84
Strawberry Summer '12
Sweet Dreams '85
Tender Mercies '83 ▶
The Thing Called Love '93
W.W. and the Dixie Dancekings '75
Your Cheatin' Heart '64

National Guard

See also *Military: Army; Persian Gulf/Iraq War*
Allegiance '12
Attack! '56 ▶
Beginning of the End '57
Between Heaven and Hell '56 ▶
Delta Farce '07
First Blood '82
The Ground Truth '06
The Hills Have Eyes 2 '07
Maneater '07
Night of the Lepus '72
Return '11
Southern Comfort '81 ▶
Viva Max '69

Native America

Across the Wide Missouri '51
Alone Yet Not Alone '13
Ambush '50
American Mystic '10
Angry Joe Bass '76
Apache Blood '75
Apache Rifles '64
Battle of Rogue River '54
Battles of Chief Pontiac '52
The Bears & I '74
Big Bear '98
Big Eden '00
Billy Jack '71
Billy Two Hats '74
Birds of Passage '18 ▶
Black Cloud '04
The Black Dakotas '54
Black Fox: The Price of Peace '94
Black Robe '91 ▶
Bone Eater '07
Born Losers '67
Broken Arrow '50
Brother Bear 2 '06
Brother Bear '03
Brotherhood of the Wolf '01
Buffalo Bill Rides Again '47
Buffalo Soldiers '97 ▶
Bury My Heart at Wounded Knee '07
The Business of Fancydancing '02
Call Her Savage '32
Canyon Passage '46 ▶
Captain Apache '71
Carry On Columbus '92
Cavalier of the West '31
Cavalry Charge '51
Cavalry Scout '51
Centennial '78 ▶
Chato's Land '71
Cheyenne Autumn '64
Cheyenne Warrior '94
Christmas in the Clouds '01
Chuka '67
Comanche Moon '08
The Comancheros '61 ▶
The Command '54
Conquest of Cochise '53
Cotter '72
Coyote Waits '03
Crazy Horse and Custer: 'The Untold Story' '90
Crooked Arrows '12
Crypt of Dark Secrets '76
Dakota Incident '56
Dalva '95
Dan Candy's Law '73
Dance Me Outside '95
Dances with Wolves '90 ▶
The Dark Wind '91
Davy Crockett, Indian Scout '50
Day of the Evil Gun '68
Dead Man '95
The Devil Horse '26
The Devil's Doorway '50
A Distant Trumpet '64
The Doe Boy '01
Drums Across the River '54
The Education of Little Tree '97 ▶
Escape from Fort Bravo '53
The Exiles '61
The Far Horizons '55
Fish Hawk '79
Flags of Our Fathers '06 ▶
Flaming Star '60 ▶
Flap '70
Fleshburn '84
Follow the River '95
Fort Bowie '58
Fort Defiance '51
Fort Dobbs '58
Fort Massacre '58
Fort Osage '51
Fort Vengeance '53
Fort Yuma '55
40 Guns to Apache Pass '67
Four Sheets to the Wind '07
From Above '13
Frozen River '08 ▶
The Gatling Gun '72
Geronimo '93 ▶
Geronimo: An American Legend '93
Ghost Dance '83
A Good Day to Die '95
The Gun That Won the West '55
Guns, Girls and Gambling '11
Hiawatha '52
Hondo '53 ▶
Hostiles '17
Hybrid '07
I Will Fight No More Forever '75 ▶
Incident at Oglala: The Leonard Peltier Story '92 ▶
The Indian Fighter '55 ▶
The Indian in the Cupboard '95
Jim Thorpe: All American '51
Jimmy P. '13
Joe Panther '76 ▶
Johnny Firecloud '75
The Last of His Tribe '92
The Last of the Dogmen '95
The Last of the Mohicans '20 ▶
The Last of the Mohicans '32
The Last of the Mohicans '36
The Last of the Mohicans '92 ▶
The Legend of Wolf Mountain '92
Little Big Man '70 ▶
The Lone Ranger '13
The Lost Child '00
Lost Colony: The Legend of Roanoke '07
The Magic Stone '95
The Magnificent Seven '98
A Man Called Horse '70 ▶
Man of the House '95
The Manitou '78
Map of the Human Heart '93
Massacre '34
Massacre River '49
Meek's Cutoff '10 ▶
Miracle at Sage Creek '05
The Missing '03 ▶
Mission to Glory '80
Monsterwolf '10
A Mormon Maid '17
Navajo Blues '97
Neverland '11
The New World '05 ▶
Not Like Everyone Else '06
Older Than America '08
One Little Indian '73
The Pathfinder '96
Pathfinder '07
Pillars of the Sky '56
Pocahontas '95 ▶
Pocahontas: The Legend '95
Poltergeist 2: The Other Side '86
Powwow Highway '89 ▶
The Prophecy '95
Quincannon, Frontier Scout '56
Ramona '36
Rebel Run '94
The Red Fury '84
Renegades '89
Requiem for a Heavyweight '56 ▶
Requiem for a Heavyweight '62 ▶
Ricochet River '98
Rites of Passage '12
Road to Paloma '14
Running Brave '83
Saskatchewan '54
Savage Sam '63
Savage Wilderness '55
The Secret of Navajo Cave '76
Seminole '53
Seminole Uprising '55
Sergeants 3 '62
Shadow of the Hawk '76
Shadowhunter '93
Siege at Red River '54
Silent Tongue '92
Sioux City '94
Sitting Bull '54
Skins '02
Skinwalker '02
Skipped Parts '00
Smith! '69
Smoke Signals '98
The Song of Hiawatha '97
Songs My Brother Taught Me '15 ▶
Southwest Passage '54
Spirit Rider '93 ▶
Spirit: Stallion of the Cimarron '02
Spoilers of the North '47
Squanto: A Warrior's Tale '94 ▶
The Squaw Man '14
The Squaw Man '31
Stolen Women, Captured Hearts '97
Sunchaser '96
Taking Chances '09
Taza, Son of Cochise '54
Tell Them Willie Boy Is Here '69 ▶
Terror in the Jungle '68
A Thief of Time '04
This May Be the Last Time '14
3 Ninjas Knuckle Up '95
Three Warriors '77
Thunder at the Border '66
A Thunder of Drums '61
Thunderheart '92 ▶
Tiger Eyes '13
Tomahawk '51
Tonka '58
Track of the Moonbeast '76
The Trail to Hope Rose '04
Trooper Hook '57
True Heart '97
True Women '97
The Twilight Saga: Eclipse '10
The Twilight Saga: New Moon '09
Unconquered '47
Undead or Alive '07
Uninvited '93
The Vanishing American '25
The Villain '79
Wagons West '52
War Drums '57
War Paint '53
A Warrior's Heart '11
When Two Worlds Collide '16 ▶
White Comanche '68
White Fang 2: The Myth of the White Wolf '94
The White Squaw '56
Wind River '98
Wind River '17 ▶
Windrunner '94
Windtalkers '02
Windwalker '81 ▶
Woman Walks Ahead '17
The Wonderful Country '59
Zoe '01

▶ = rated three bones or higher

Nazis & Other Paramilitary Slugs

***See also** Germany; The Holocaust; Judaism; World War Two*

Adam Resurrected '08
Address Unknown '44
All the Queen's Men '02
All Through the Night '42 ▶
Allied '16
Amen '02 ▶
Angel of Death '86
Angel with the Trumpet '50
Angry Harvest '85 ▶
Anima '98
Anthropoid '16
Any Man's Death '90
Apt Pupil '97
Ark of the Sun God '82
The Army of Crime '10
Army of Shadows '69 ▶
The Assisi Underground '84
Attack of the Herbals '11
Attack on Leningrad '09
Background to Danger '43 ▶
Bedknobs and Broomsticks '71
Berlin Correspondent '42
Berlin Express '48 ▶
Betrayed '54 ▶
Beyond Valkyrie: Dawn of the Fourth Reich '16
Black Book '06 ▶
The Black Klansman '66
Blood Creek '09
Bloodrayne: The Third Reich '11
Blubberella '11
The Blues Brothers '80 ▶
Bon Voyage '03 ▶
The Boy in the Striped Pajamas '08 ▶
The Boys from Brazil '78
Bulletproof Monk '03
Cabaret '72 ▶
Cabo Blanco '81
Candlelight in Algeria '44
Captain America: The First Avenger '11
Casablanca '42 ▶
Casablanca Express '89
Chosen '16
Christopher and His Kind '11 ▶
Close-Up '48
Colditz: Escape of the Birdmen '71
Commandos Strike at Dawn '43
Confessions of a Nazi Spy '39
The Conformist '71 ▶
Conspiracy '01
The Conspirators '44
Contraband '40
Cottage to Let '41
Counter-Espionage '42
Counterblast '48
The Counterfeit Traitor '62 ▶
The Counterfeiters '07 ▶
Counterpoint '67
The Cross of Lorraine '43
Dam Busters '55 ▶
Dangerously We Live '41
A Day in October '92
Dead Bang '89
Dead Snow '09
Dead Snow: Red vs. Dead '14 ▶
Death in Love '08
The Death of Adolf Hitler '84
The Debt '07
The Debt '10
Defiance '08
Denial '16
Descending Angel '90 ▶
Desert Commandos '67
The Desert Fox '51 ▶
The Desert Song '43
Despair '78 ▶
The Devil Makes Three '52
The Devil's Brigade '68
The Diary of Anne Frank '59 ▶
The Dirty Dozen '67 ▶
The Dirty Dozen: The Deadly Mission '87
The Dirty Dozen: The Fatal Mission '88
The Dirty Dozen: The Next Mission '85
Divided We Fall '00
Dominion: Prequel to the Exorcist '05
Downfall '04 ▶
Edge of Darkness '43 ▶
Eichmann '07
The Empty Mirror '99
Enemy at the Gates '00
Enemy of Women '44
Enigma Secret '79
Escape '40
Escape from Sobibor '87 ▶
Europa, Europa '91 ▶
The Exception '17
The Execution '85
Eye of the Needle '81
Eyes in the Night '42
The Fallen '05 ▶
The Fallen Sparrow '43 ▶
Fateless '05 ▶
The Fifth Horseman Is Fear '64
A Film Unfinished '10
Firewalker '86
Five Fingers '52 ▶
Five Graves to Cairo '43 ▶
The Flesh Eaters '64
Flesh Feast '69
Force 10 from Navarone '78
Foreign Correspondent '40 ▶
The Forty-Ninth Parallel '41 ▶
Four Bags Full '56
The Four Horsemen of the Apocalypse '62
Four Sons '40
The Frozen Dead '66
Generation War '13
The German Doctor '14
Germany Year Zero '48 ▶
Getting Away With Murder '96
The Girl of Your Dreams '99
The Gleiwitz Case '61
The Goebbels Experiment '05
Good '08
Good Evening, Mr. Wallenberg '93
The Great Dictator '40 ▶
The Great Escape '63 ▶
The Grey Zone '01
Hamsun '96
Hangmen Also Die '42
Hannah Arendt '12
The Harmonists '99
Hart's War '02
The Haunted World of El Superbeasto '09
Head in the Clouds '04
Hearts of War '07
Hell Commandos '69
Hellboy '04
Hell's Bloody Devils '70
The Heroes of Telemark '65
Hidden in Silence '96
A Hidden Life '19
The Hiding Place '75
Higher Learning '94
Hitler '62
Hitler: Beast of Berlin '39
Hitler: The Last Ten Days '73
Hitler: The Rise of Evil '03
Holocaust '78 ▶
The Home Front '02
Hornets' Nest '70
The House on Carroll Street '88
The House on Garibaldi Street '79
House on 92nd Street '45 ▶
I Escaped from the Gestapo '43
Ill Met By Moonlight '57
Ilsa, Harem Keeper of the Oil Sheiks '76
Imperium '16
In a Glass Cage '86
In the Presence of Mine Enemies '97
The Incredible Mr. Limpet '64
Indiana Jones and the Last Crusade '89 ▶
Indiana Jones and the Temple of Doom '84 ▶
The Infiltrator '95
Inglourious Basterds '09 ▶
Inside Out '75
Invincible '01
Invisible Agent '42
The Island on Bird Street '97
Jacob the Liar '74
Jakob the Liar '99 ▶
Joe and Max '02 ▶
Jojo Rabbit '19 ▶
Judgment at Nuremberg '61 ▶
Julia '77 ▶
Kanal '56 ▶
Kapo '59 ▶
The Klansman '74
Labyrinth of Lies '14
Lassiter '84
The Last Butterfly '92
The Last Drop '05
The Last Metro '80 ▶
The Last Train '74
Life Is Beautiful '98 ▶
Lifeboat '44 ▶
Lilli Marlene '50
Lisa '62
The Longest Day '62 ▶
The Lucifer Complex '78
A Man Escaped '57 ▶
Man Hunt '41 ▶
The Man I Married '40
The Man in the Glass Booth '75 ▶
The Man Who Captured Eichmann '96
The Man Who Lived at the Ritz '91
Manborg '11
Marathon Man '76 ▶
Margin for Error '43
Massacre in Rome '73
Master Key '44
The Master Race '44
Max Manus: Man of War '08
The Mediterranean in Flames '72
Mephisto '81 ▶
Ministry of Fear '44 ▶
Miracle at Midnight '98
Missiles from Hell '58
Mr. Klein '76 ▶
Monarch of the Moon '05
The Monuments Men '13
The Moon is Down '43
The Mortal Storm '40 ▶
Mosquito Squadron '70
Mother Night '96 ▶
Music Box '89
My Mother's Courage '95
The Nasty Girl '90 ▶
Neo Ned '05
Never Look Away '18 ▶
The Next of Kin '42
Night Ambush '57
A Night in Casablanca '46 ▶
Night of the Fox '90
Night of the Generals '67 ▶
The Night Porter '74
Night Train to Munich '40 ▶
Night Train to Venice '93
The Ninth Day '04 ▶
No Dead Heroes '87
The North Star '43 ▶
Northern Pursuit '43
Notorious '46 ▶
Nuremberg '00
Oasis of the Zombies '82
The Odessa File '74
The Ogre '96
On the Double '61
Once Upon a Honeymoon '42
One of Our Aircraft Is Missing '41 ▶
The Only Way '70
Open City '45 ▶
Operation Daybreak '75
Operation Eichmann '61
Operation Finale '18
Out of the Ashes '03
Outpost '07
Outpost: Black Sun '12
Overlord '18
Panzer '13
Pariah '98
Paris After Dark '43
The Passage '79
Passage to Marseilles '44 ▶
Passport to Suez '43
The Pianist '02 ▶
Porcile '69
Prayer of the Rollerboys '91
Pressure Point '62 ▶
Prisoner of Paradise '02 ▶
Puppet Master 3: Toulon's Revenge '90
Puppet Master: The Littlest Reich '18
The Quiller Memorandum '66 ▶
Raid on Rommel '71
Raiders of the Lost Ark '81 ▶
Remember '15
Reunion in France '42
Richard III '95 ▶
Rio Rita '42
River of Death '90
Robinson Crusoe: The Great Blitzkrieg '08
The Rocketeer '91 ▶
The Rose Garden '89
Rosenstrasse '03 ▶
Safe Conduct '01 ▶
The Scarlet & the Black '83
Schindler's List '93 ▶
Schtonk '92
Scream and Scream Again '70
Sea of Sand '58
The Secret War of Harry Frigg '68
She Demons '58
Sherlock Holmes and the Voice of Terror '42
Shining Through '92
Shock Waves '77
The Silver Fleet '43
633 Squadron '64
Sky Murder '40
So Ends Our Night '41 ▶
Soldier of Orange '78 ▶
A Soldier's Tale '91
Son of Lassie '45
Sophie Scholl: The Final Days '05 ▶
The Sorrow and the Pity '71 ▶
The Sound of Music '65 ▶
The Square Peg '58
Stalag 17 '53 ▶
Stalag Luft '93
The Statement '03
The Stranger '46 ▶
Strayed '03 ▶
Submarine Base '43
Sundown '41
Surf Nazis Must Die '87
Swing Kids '93
Tarzan's Desert Mystery '43
They Came to Blow Up America '43
They Saved Hitler's Brain '64
13 Minutes '17
13 Rue Madeleine '46 ▶
This Land Is Mine '43 ▶
To Be or Not to Be '42 ▶
To Be or Not to Be '83
To Catch a King '84
Tomorrow the World '44
Tonight We Raid Calais '43
Top Dog '95
Top Secret! '84 ▶
The Tormentors '71
Transit '18
Triumph of the Spirit '89 ▶
Triumph of the Will '34 ▶
The 25th Hour '67
Underground '41
Underground '70
Unpublished Story '42 ▶
Uprising '01 ▶
Valkyrie '08
Wallenberg: A Hero's Story '85 ▶
War & Remembrance '88
War & Remembrance: The Final Chapter '89
Watch on the Rhine '43 ▶
Waterfront '44
The Wedding Song '09
Where Eagles Dare '68 ▶
The Winds of War '83
Winter in Wartime '10
Wizards '77
Woman in Gold '15
Women in Bondage '43
X-Men: First Class '11 ▶
Yank in Libya '42
The Yesterday Machine '63
Yoga Hosers '16
Zelary '03 ▶
Zentropa '92
Zombie Lake '80
Zone Troopers '84
The Zookeeper's Wife '17

Near-Death Experiences

***See also** Death & the Afterlife*

Dead Zone '83 ▶
Downhill '20
Fearless '93 ▶
The Final Destination '09
Final Destination 5 '11
Flatliners '90
Flatliners '17
Fugly! '14
Ghost Town '08 ▶
Heaven Is for Real '14
Hereafter '10
I Spit on Your Grave 2 '13
Let There Be Light '17
Muck '15
A Near-Death Experience '08
The 9th Life of Louis Drax '16
The Princess and the Warrior '00 ▶
The Purge: Election Year '16
Urban Ghost Story '98
Violent Blue '10

Negative Utopia

***See also** Paradise Gone Awry; Post-Apocalypse*

Alphaville '65 ▶
Animal Farm '55 ▶
The Bad Batch '17
Brazil '85 ▶
Code 46 '03
El Norte '83 ▶
Equals '16
Futureworld '76
Gattaca '97 ▶
Homo Sapiens '16
The Island '05
Maze Runner: The Death Cure '18
Metropolis '26 ▶
Moonraker '79
The Mosquito Coast '86
1984 '56 ▶
1984 '84 ▶
Ready Player One '18
Rollerball '75
Rollerball '02
Soylent Green '73
10th Victim '65 ▶
THX 1138 '71 ▶
V for Vendetta '06
Zardoz '73

Netherlands

***See also** Amsterdam; Europe*

Antonia's Line '95
The Audrey Hepburn Story '00
Black Book '06 ▶
A Bridge Too Far '77
Dutch Girls '87
For a Lost Soldier '93
The Hiding Place '75
The House of the Seven Hawks '59
The Last Drop '05
The Red Mill '27
The Silver Fleet '43
Spetters '80
Tulip Fever '17
Turkish Delight '73
Winter in Wartime '10

New Black Cinema

***See** African America; Blaxploitation*

New Jersey

***See also** New York, New York*

Above Suspicion '00
American Chai '01
American Gangster '07 ▶
Aqua Teen Hunger Force Colon Movie Film for Theaters '07
Atlantic City '81 ▶
Baby It's You '82 ▶
Bad Parents '12
Bandslam '09
Be Kind Rewind '08
Beer League '06
Blues in the Night '41
Bogus '96
Bought and Sold '03
Camp Hell '10
Cannibal Campout '88
Chasing Amy '97
Cheaper by the Dozen '50 ▶
Chuck '17
Cinderella Man '05 ▶
Cleaner '07
Clerks 2 '06 ▶
Clerks '94 ▶
Cold Hearts '99
Confessions of a Teenage Drama Queen '04
The Cookout '04
Cop Land '97 ▶
Coyote Ugly '00
The Day the Earth Stood Still '08
Dogma '99
Down the Shore '11
Eddie and the Cruisers '83
Family Man '00
Freedomland '06
Garden State '04 ▶
Girl Most Likely '12
Glass Chin '14
Harold and Kumar Go to White Castle '04
Hysterical Blindness '02
In the Mix '05
Jersey Boys '14
Jersey Girl '92
Jersey Girl '04
Jersey Shore Shark Attack '12
Just Friends '05
The Last Broadcast '98 ▶
Lean on Me '89 ▶
Low Tide '19
Mallrats '95
Moving '88
Nearing Grace '05
New Jersey Drive '95
Not Fade Away '12
Now You Know '02
On the Outs '05
One for the Money '12
The Oranges '12
Palindromes '04 ▶
Paterson '16 ▶
Patti Cake$ '17
Paul Blart: Mall Cop '09
The Purple Rose of Cairo '85 ▶
Return of the Secaucus 7 '80 ▶
Rocket Science '07 ▶
Second Best '05
The Station Agent '03 ▶
The Sweeter Side of Life '13
This Thing of Ours '03
The Toxic Avenger '86
Tracks '05
Trade '07
War of the Worlds '05 ▶
The War Within '05
The Whole Shebang '01
Win Win '11
Winter Solstice '04 ▶
Zombie Honeymoon '04

New Orleans

***See also** American South*

Albino Alligator '96
American Virgin '09
Angel Heart '87
Anne Rice's The Feast of All Saints '01
Bad Lieutenant: Port of Call New Orleans '09
Band of Angels '57
Bending the Rules '12
The Big Easy '87 ▶
Birth of the Blues '41
Blues Brothers 2000 '98
Broken Vows '16
Buccaneer's Girl '50
Candyman 2: Farewell to the Flesh '94
The Chaperone '11
Child of Glass '78

▶ = rated three bones or higher

New Year's Eve

New York, New York

▶ = rated three bones or higher

Falling in Love '84
Falling Up '08
Fame '80 ▶
Fame '09
Fantastic Beasts and Where to Find Them '16
Fantastic Four '05
Fatal Attraction '87 ▶
Feardotcom '02
Feel the Noise '07
Fever '99
15 Minutes '01
The Fifth Element '97
54 '98
Fighting '09
Finder's Fee '01
Finding Forrester '00
A Fine Madness '66 ▶
Fingers '78 ▶
Fiona '98
First Love '39
The First Purge '18
The First Wives Club '96
The Fisher King '91 ▶
The Fitzgerald Family Christmas '12
Five and Ten '31
5 Flights Up '15
Flannel Pajamas '06
Flawless '99
Florence Foster Jenkins '16
Focus '01
Food of Love '02
For a Good Time, Call... '12
For Heaven's Sake '50
For Love or Money '93
For Pete's Sake '74
The Foreigner '78
Fort Apache, the Bronx '81 ▶
Forty Naughty Girls '37
42nd Street '33 ▶
.45 '06
Four and a Half Women '05
4:44 Last Day on Earth '11
A Four Letter Word '07
4 Single Fathers '09
4.3.2.1 '10
Frances Ha '13 ▶
Frankie and Johnny '91 ▶
Freelancers '12
The French Connection '71 ▶
The French Minister '13
Frequency '00
The Freshman '90
Friends and Family '01
Friends With Benefits '11
Frogs for Snakes '98
Fuel '08 ▶
The Funeral '96 ▶
Funny Girl '68 ▶
Funny Valentine '05
Fur: An Imaginary Portrait of Diane Arbus '06
Furlough '18
G '02
Game 6 '05
Games '67
Gangs of New York '02 ▶
The Garment Jungle '57
Gas House Kids '46
The Gay Deception '35
Gayby '12
Generation Um... '13
George White's Scandals of 1935 '35
Georgia O'Keefe '09
Get a Clue '02
Get Rich or Die Tryin' '05
Get Well Soon '01
Getting High '06
Ghost '90 ▶
Ghost Town '08 ▶
Ghostbusters 2 '89
Ghostbusters '84 ▶
Ghostbusters '16
Gildersleeve on Broadway '43
Gimme the Loot '12
The Girl From Mexico '39
The Girl in the Book '15
The Girl in the Red Velvet Swing '55
The Girl in White '52
Girl of the Night '60
The Girlfriend Experience '09
Giuliani Time '05
Give Me Your Heart '36
Giving It Up '99

The Glass Wall '53
Glitter '01
Gloria '98
Go Into Your Dance '35
The Godfather '72 ▶
The Godfather, Part 2 '74 ▶
The Godfather, Part 3 '90 ▶
Godspell '73
Godzilla '98
Going the Distance '10
Golden Exits '17
The Golden Spiders: A Nero Wolfe Mystery '00
The Goldfinch '19
The Good Guy '10
The Good Heart '09
The Good Night '07
Good Time '17 ▶
The Goodbye Girl '77 ▶
Goodfellas '90 ▶
Gossip '99
Gotti '96
Grace of My Heart '96
Grand Central Murder '42
Gravesend '97
Gray Matters '06
The Great Diamond Robbery '53
Great Expectations '97
The Great Gatsby '74
The Great Gatsby '13
The Great New Wonderful '06
Green Card '90
Greenwich Village '44
Greetings '68 ▶
Greetings from Tim Buckley '12
Greta '18
The Guilty Generation '31
The Guitar '08
Gun Hill Road '11
The Guys '02 ▶
Guys and Dolls '55 ▶
Gypsy 83 '01
Habit '97
Hair '79 ▶
Half a Hero '53
Half Nelson '06 ▶
Hamlet '00 ▶
Hangin' with the Homeboys '91 ▶
Hanging Up '99
Hannah and Her Sisters '86 ▶
Hannah Arendt '12
Happy Accidents '00
Happy Hour '03
Happythankyoumoreplease '10
Harlem Aria '99
Harlem Nights '89
Harry and Tonto '74 ▶
A Hatful of Rain '59
Hav Plenty '97 ▶
Head Over Heels '01
Headless Body in Topless Bar '96
Heartburn '86 ▶
Hearts Beat Loud '18
Heaven Help Us '85
Heights '04
Hellboy II: The Golden Army '08 ▶
Hello Again '87
Hell's Kitchen '39
Henry Fool '98 ▶
The Hessen Conspiracy '09
Hester Street '75 ▶
Hi-Life '98
Hi, Mom! '70 ▶
Hide and Seek '05
High Art '98
High Strung '16
Highlander '86 ▶
Highlander: Endgame '00
His Butler's Sister '44
His Girl Friday '40 ▶
Hit and Runway '01
Hitch '05
Hitched for the Holidays '12
The Hoarder '15
The Hoax '06
Holy Rollers '10
Home Alone 2: Lost in New York '92
A Home at the End of the World '04
Homeless to Harvard: The Liz Murray Story '03

Honey 2 '14
Honey '03
The Hoodlum '19
Hoodlum '96
The Hottest State '06
The Hours '02 ▶
House of D '04
House of Mirth '00 ▶
The House on 56th Street '33
How I Got Lost '09
How to Be Single '16
How to Lose a Guy in 10 Days '03
How to Lose Friends & Alienate People '08
The Hunger '83
The Hungry Ghosts '09
Hurricane Streets '96
Husbands and Wives '92 ▶
I Am Legend '07 ▶
I Can Get It For You Wholesale '51
I Do '13 ▶
I Don't Know How She Does It '11
I Hate Valentine's Day '09
I Spit on Your Grave 2 '13
I Think I Love My Wife '07
The Iceman Cometh '60 ▶
The Iceman Cometh '73
If Beale Street Could Talk '18 ▶
If I Had My Way '40
If You Only Knew '00
Igby Goes Down '02 ▶
I'll Take You There '99
Illuminata '98
I'm Not Rappaport '96
The Immigrant '13 ▶
Immortal '04
In America '02 ▶
In Good Company '04 ▶
In the Cut '03
In the Mix '05
In the Weeds '00
Indian Point '16
The Inevitable Defeat of Mister & Pete '13
Inside Llewyn Davis '13 ▶
Inside Man '06 ▶
Intern '00
The Interpreter '05 ▶
Interview '07 ▶
Into the Fire '05
Ira & Abby '06
Irish Eyes Are Smiling '44
The Irish in Us '35
The Irishman '19 ▶
Irreplaceable You '18
It Could Happen to You '94
It Felt Like Love '14
It Had to Be You '00
It Happened in Brooklyn '47
It Happened on 5th Avenue '47
It Runs in the Family '03
It Should Happen to You '54 ▶
Italian Movie '93
It's All About Love '03
It's My Turn '80
Jack and Diane '12
Jack and Jill vs. the World '08
Jack Goes Boating '10
James White '15 ▶
Jane Doe '96
The January Man '89
The Jazz Singer '52
Jean-Michel Basquiat: The Radiant Child '10 ▶
Jeffrey '95
Jennifer On My Mind '71
Jesse '11
Jimi: All Is by My Side '14
Joe '70
Joe Gould's Secret '00
Joe's Apartment '96
Johnny Suede '92
Joshua '07 ▶
Juice '92
Julie & Julia '09 ▶
Jumpin' Jack Flash '86
Jungle Fever '91 ▶
Jungle 2 Jungle '96
Junior Miss '45
Just a Kiss '02
Just My Luck '06
Just One Time '00

Just the Ticket '98
K-PAX '01
Kate & Leopold '01
Keane '04 ▶
Keep the Lights On '12 ▶
Keeping the Faith '00
Kentucky Moonshine '38
Kick-Ass '10 ▶
Kicked in the Head '97
Kids '95
Kilimanjaro '13
Kill by Inches '99
Kill the Poor '03
Kill Your Darlings '13
Killerman '19
The Killing Gene '07
King Kong '33 ▶
King Kong '05 ▶
King of Comedy '82 ▶
King of New York '90 ▶
King of the Gypsies '78
King of the Jungle '01
Kiss Me Again '06
Kiss Me, Guido '97
Kissing Jessica Stein '02
The Kitchen '19
Klute '71 ▶
Knights of the South Bronx '05
Knock Down the House '19
Koch '13 ▶
Kramer vs. Kramer '79 ▶
Labor Pains '09
Lady on a Train '45 ▶
The Landlord '70
The Last Days of Disco '98 ▶
Last Exit to Brooklyn '90 ▶
The Last Five Years '14 ▶
The Last International Playboy '08
The Last New Yorker '07
Last Night '10
The Last Seduction '94 ▶
The Last Time '06
The Last Witch Hunter '15
A Late Quartet '12
Laws of Gravity '92 ▶
Lay the Favorite '12
Legal Eagles '86
Let It Snow '99
Let's Do It Again '53
The Letter '12
The Life and Times of Hank Greenberg '99 ▶
Life Begins at Eight-Thirty '42
Life Itself '18
A Life of Her Own '50
Life Support '07 ▶
The Light of the Moon '17 ▶
Light Sleeper '92
Lily & Kat '15
Limitless '11
Liquid Sky '83 ▶
Lisa Picard Is Famous '01
Listen to Your Heart '10
Little Manhattan '05
Little Men '16 ▶
Little Miss Marker '34 ▶
Little Nicky '00
Little Old New York '23
Living in Oblivion '94 ▶
Living It Up '54
Living Out Loud '98
London '05
Lonely Hearts '06
Long Time Since '97
The Longest Week '14
Look Who's Talking, Too '90
Looking for Kitty '04
Looking for Richard '96 ▶
Loosies '11
Lord of War '05 ▶
The Lords of Flatbush '74
Loser '00
Lost Angel '43
Lost in Yonkers '93
Lotto Land '95
Love '05
Love Affair '94
Love at First Bite '79
Love in the Time of Money '02
Love Is Better Than Ever '52
Love Is Strange '14 ▶
Love Story '70 ▶
Love the Hard Way '01
The Love Trap '29
A Lovely Way to Die '68

Loving '70
The Luck of the Irish '48
Lucky Number Slevin '06
Lullaby of Broadway '51
Lulu on the Bridge '98
Ma and Pa Kettle Go to Town '50
Mad Dog Coll '61
Mad Hot Ballroom '05 ▶
Made '01
Made On Broadway '33
Mafia '11
Maid in Manhattan '02
Mail Order Wife '04
Make Your Move '13
Making Mr. Right '08
Maladies '13
Malcolm X '92 ▶
Mambo Cafe '00
Mammoth '09
The Man in 3B '16
Man of the Century '99
Man on a Ledge '12
Man on Wire '08
The Man Who Played God '32
The Man With a Cloak '51
The Manchurian Candidate '62 ▶
Manhattan '79 ▶
Manhattan Love Song '34
Manhattan Melodrama '34 ▶
Manhattan Merenque! '95
Manhattan Merry-Go-Round '37
Manhattan Murder Mystery '93 ▶
Manito '03 ▶
Marathon Man '76 ▶
Margaret '11
Margarita Happy Hour '01
Margin Call '11 ▶
Margin for Error '43
Maria Full of Grace '04 ▶
Marie and Bruce '04
Marriage Story '19 ▶
Marty '55 ▶
Mary, Mary '63
Max Payne '08
Maximum Risk '96
The Mayor of 44th Street '42
Maze '01
Me and Orson Welles '09
Mean Streets '73 ▶
Meet Dave '08
Meeting Spencer '11
Melinda and Melinda '05
Melvin Goes to Dinner '03
Men in Black 2 '02
Men in Black '97 ▶
Menashe '17
The Mend '15 ▶
Mercy '96
The Merry Frinks '34
Metropolitan '90 ▶
Michael Clayton '07 ▶
Mickey Blue Eyes '99
Middle of the Night '59
Midnight Cowboy '69 ▶
Mighty Aphrodite '95
Milk and Honey '03
Mimic '97
Mimic 2 '01
Mind the Gap '04
The Minion '98
The Ministers '09
Minnie and Moskowitz '71
Miracle on 34th Street '47 ▶
Miracle on 34th Street '94
Miracles for Sale '39
The Mirror Has Two Faces '96
Misery '90 ▶
Missing Girls '36
Mrs. Parker and the Vicious Circle '94
Mrs. Santa Claus '96
Mr. Blandings Builds His Dream House '48 ▶
Mister Buddwing '66
Mr. Jealousy '98
Mr. Popper's Penguins '11
Mistletoe Over Manhattan '11
Mistress America '15
Mixing Nia '98
Mo' Better Blues '90
Money Train '95
The Money Trap '65

Monogamy '10
Monsters and Men '18
Moon over Broadway '98 ▶
More Than Friends '78
Morning Glory '33
Morning Glory '10
The Mortal Instruments: City of Bones '13
Mortal Thoughts '91
Moscow on the Hudson '84 ▶
Most Beautiful Island '17
A Most Violent Year '14 ▶
Motherhood '09
Motherless Brooklyn '19
Mudbloods: A Movie About Quidditch '14
Mulberry Street '06
Multiple Sarcasms '10
The Muppets Take Manhattan '84 ▶
Murda Muzik '03
Murder, Inc. '60
The Murder Man '35
Murder On a Bridle Path '36
Music & Lyrics '07
Music of the Heart '99
My Blueberry Nights '07
My Favorite Year '82 ▶
My Gal Sal '42
My Little Assassin '99
My Man Godfrey '36 ▶
My Sister Eileen '42
My Sister Eileen '55 ▶
My Super Ex-Girlfriend '06
Mysterious Skin '04 ▶
Nadja '95 ▶
The Naked City '48 ▶
Naked in New York '93
The Namesake '06 ▶
The Nanny Diaries '07
The Narrows '08
National Treasure '04
The Natural '84 ▶
Network '76 ▶
Never Again '01
Never Forever '07
Never Rarely Sometimes Always '20 ▶
New Jack City '91
New York Cop '94
New York, I Love You '09
New York Minute '04
New York, New York '77 ▶
New York Ripper '82
New York Stories '89 ▶
The New Yorker '98
Newlyweds '11
News from Home '76
The Next Big Thing '02 ▶
Next Stop, Greenwich Village '76 ▶
Next Time We Love '36
Next Year in Jerusalem '98
Nice Guy Johnny '10
Nick & Norah's Infinite Playlist '08 ▶
Nico Icon '95 ▶
Night and the City '92 ▶
Night at the Museum '06
The Night Before '15
Night Editor '46
Night Falls on Manhattan '96 ▶
Night Has Settled '14
Night on Earth '91 ▶
Night Shift '82
The Night They Raided Minsky's '69 ▶
The Night We Never Met '93
Nights and Weekends '08
9 1/2 Weeks '86
9/11 '17
1931: Once Upon a Time in New York '72
The Ninth Gate '99
No More Orchids '32
No Orchids for Miss Blandish '48
No Reservations '07
No Such Thing '01
No Time For Comedy '40
No Time For Love '43 ▶
Noel '04
Noise '07
Nora Prentiss '47
Norman '17
Notorious '09
A Novel Romance '11
Nutcracker: Money, Madness & Murder '87 ▶

▶ = rated three bones or higher

NYC: Tornado Terror '08
NYC Underground '13
The Object of My Affection '98
Ocean's 8 '18
Octopus 2: River of Fear '02
The Odd Couple '68 ▸
Oh Christmas Tree! '13
Okja '17 ▸
The Old Homestead '35
Olga's Girls '64
Oliver & Company '88
On the Town '49 ▸
On the Waterfront '54 ▸
Once in the Life '00
Once More With Feeling '08
The One '11
One Fine Day '96
100 Feet '08
One Last Thing '05
1,000 Years From Now '52
One Tough Cop '98
On_Line '01
The Only Living Boy in New York '17
Only When I Laugh '81 ▸
The Other Guys '10
Our Italian Husband '04
Our Song '01 ▸
Out at the Wedding '07
The Out-of-Towners '70 ▸
The Out-of-Towners '99
Outrageous! '77 ▸
Over-Exposed '56
Paddy O'Day '35
The Painted Lady '97 ▸
Panic in Needle Park '71 ▸
Panic Room '02
The Paper '94 ▸
Paradise Alley '78
Paradise in Harlem '40
Pariah '11 ▸
Paris Is Burning '91 ▸
The Park Is Mine '85
Park Row '52
Party Girl '94
Party Monster '03
Passion of Mind '00
Path to Paradise '97
The Peacemaker '97
Penguin Pool Murder '32
People I Know '02
People Places Things '15
Perception '06
A Perfect Murder '98
Perfect Stranger '07
Personals '00
Peter and Vandy '09
Petty Crimes '02
Petunia '13
The Phantom '96
Phantom Boy '16
Phoebe in Wonderland '08
Phone Booth '02
Pi '98
The Pick-Up Artist '87
Pickup Alley '57
Pieces of April '03
Pillow Talk '59 ▸
Pinero '01
Pipe Dream '02
Pirate Radio '09
Playmobil: The Movie '19
Plaza Suite '71 ▸
Please Give '10
Pollock '00 ▸
The Pompatus of Love '95
The Pope of Greenwich Village '84
Pornography: A Thriller '10
Portrait of Jennie '48 ▸
Postcards from America '95
Premature '20
Premium Rush '12 ▸
Pretty Baby '50
A Price Above Rubies '97
Pride and Glory '08
Prime '05
The Prince of Central Park '77 ▸
Prince of Central Park '00
Prince of the City '81 ▸
The Prince of Tides '91 ▸
The Princess & the Call Girl '84
Princess O'Rourke '43
Prisoner of Second Avenue '74
Private Parts '96
The Producers '05
The Proposal '09
P.S. I Love You '07
The Public Eye '92 ▸
Puccini for Beginners '06
Purple Violets '07
Pushing Tin '99 ▸
The Quare Fellow '62
The Quest '96
Quick Change '90
Quid Pro Quo '08
'R Xmas '01
Radio Days '87 ▸
Rafter Romance '33
A Rage in Harlem '91 ▸
Raging Bull '80 ▸
Ragtime '81 ▸
A Raisin in the Sun '61 ▸
A Raisin in the Sun '89 ▸
Raising Helen '04
Raising Victor Vargas '03
Ransom '96 ▸
The Rat Race '60 ▸
The Rats '01
Ratter '16
Ready to Wear '94
The Real Blonde '97
Rear Window '54 ▸
The Rebound '09
The Reckless Hour '31
Red Hook Summer '12 ▸
Reducing '31
Reign Over Me '07
Remedy '05
Rent '05
Report to the Commissioner '75 ▸
Resident Evil: Vendetta '17
Return to Paradise '98 ▸
Revenge of the Green Dragons '14
Revolution #9 '01
Ride '98
Righteous Kill '08
Riot on 42nd Street '87
The Ritz '76 ▸
Roadie '11
The Roaring Twenties '39 ▸
Rob the Mob '14
Roger Dodger '02 ▸
Romance & Cigarettes '05
Rosemary's Baby '68 ▸
Rosencrantz & Guildenstern Are Undead '10
Rounders '98
The Royal Tenenbaums '01 ▸
Rudy: The Rudy Giulani Story '03
Rumble in the Bronx '96
Rumble on the Docks '56
Runaway Bride '99 ▸
A Safe Place '71
Sally, Irene and Mary '38
Saturday Night at the Baths '75
Saturday Night Fever '77
Save the Last Dance 2 '06
Saving Face '04
Say One for Me '59
Scandal Sheet '52
Scent of a Woman '92 ▸
School for Scoundrels '06
Scrooged '88
The Search for One-Eye Jimmy '94
The Search for Santa Paws '10
Searching for Bobby Fischer '93 ▸
Searching for Paradise '02
The Secret Life of Pets '16
The September Issue '09
Serendipity '01
Serpico '73 ▸
Seven '95 ▸
The Seven-Ups '73
The Seven Year Itch '55 ▸
Sex and the City: The Movie '08
Sex and the City 2 '10
Sex Positive '09
Shadow of Doubt '35
Shadows and Fog '92
Shadows and Lies '10
ShadowZone: The Undead Express '96
Shaft '00 ▸
Shaft '19
Shame '11 ▸
Sharknado 2: The Second One '14
Sharpay's Fabulous Adventure '11
Shattered Glass '03 ▸
She-Devil '89
Shelter '15
Shelter Island '03
She's Back on Broadway '53
She's Gotta Have It '86 ▸
She's the One '96
Shine a Light '08
Shining Star '75
Shutterbug '10
Sidewalks of New York '01
The Siege '98
Sing, Baby, Sing '36
Single White Female '92
The Sisters '05
The Sitter '11
Six Days, Six Nights '94
Six Degrees of Separation '93
16 Blocks '06 ▸
61* '01 ▸
Sky Captain and the World of Tomorrow '04
Slaves of New York '89
Sleepers '96
Slightly Dangerous '43
Slippery Slope '06
Sliver '93
Small Time Crooks '00
Smart Blonde '37
Smithereens '82
The Smurfs '11
So This Is Love '53
So This Is New York '48
Someday This Pain Will Be Useful to You '11
Someone Great '19
Someone Like You '01
Something Borrowed '11
Something Short of Paradise '79
Something to Live For '52
Something Wild '61
Something Wild '86
Somewhere in the City '97
The Son of No One '11
Son of Sam '08
Sophie's Choice '82 ▸
The Sorcerer's Apprentice '10
Sorry, Haters '05
Soul Men '08
The Sound of Silence '19
The Spanish Prisoner '97 ▸
Sparks '13
Speedy '28 ▸
Spider-Man '02 ▸
Spider-Man 2 '04 ▸
Spider-Man 3 '07
Splash '84
The Squid and the Whale '05 ▸
Stag Night '08
Stage Door '37 ▸
Stand Clear of the Closing Doors '13 ▸
A Stand Up Guy '16
Starting Out in the Evening '07
State of Grace '90 ▸
Staten Island '09
Stay '05
Staying Alive '83
Step Lively '44
Step Up 3D '10
Stepmom '98 ▸
The Sticky Fingers of Time '97
Still of the Night '82
Stir Crazy '80
Stonewall '95 ▸
Straight from the Heart '03
Straight out of Brooklyn '91
Stranger than Paradise '84 ▸
Street Scene '31 ▸
Street Smart '87
Street Trash '87
Streetwalkin' '85
The Strike '16
Stuart Little 2 '02 ▸
The Substance of Fire '96
The Substitute 2: School's Out '97
Suburban Girl '07
Subway Stories '97
Such Good Friends '71
Sudden Manhattan '96
Sugar '09 ▸
Sugar Hill '94
Sully '16
Summer of Sam '99
The Sun Is Also a Star '19
Sunday '96
Sunday in New York '63
Sundays at Tiffany's '10
Sunny '30
The Sunset Limited '11
Sunset Park '96
The Super '91
The Super Cops '74
Superfly '72
Supporting Characters '13
Sweet and Low-Down '44
Sweet Charity '69 ▸
Sweet Home Alabama '02
Sweet Smell of Success '57 ▸
Swindle '02
Swing Hostess '44
The Switch '10
Symphony of Six Million '32
Table One '00
Tadpole '02
Take the Lead '06
The Taking of Pelham One Two Three '74 ▸
The Taking of Pelham 123 '09
A Tale of Two Pizzas '03
The Talent Given Us '04 ▸
Tart '01
Tarzan's New York Adventure '42
The Tavern '00
Taxi! '32
Taxi '04
Taxi Driver '76 ▸
Ten Thousand Saints '15
The Tenants '06
The Tender Trap '55
The Tenderfoot '32
Tenth Avenue Angel '47
The 10th Kingdom '00
That Awkward Moment '14
That's What She Said '12
Then She Found Me '07
They Call It Sin '32
They Came Together '14
They Gave Him a Gun '37
The Thing About My Folks '05
The Third Girl from the Left '73
Third Person '13
Thirteen Conversations About One Thing '01 ▸
Thirty Day Princess '34
30 Years to Life '01
This Must Be the Place '12
This Revolution '05
The Thomas Crown Affair '99 ▸
3 A.M. '01 ▸
Three Days of the Condor '75 ▸
Three Men and a Baby '87 ▸
Three Sailors and a Girl '53
Three Wise Girls '32
Through the Fire '05 ▸
The Tic Code '99
Timeless '96
Times Square '80
Tiny Furniture '10 ▸
TMNT: Teenage Mutant Ninja Turtles '07
Today's Special '09 ▸
The Tollbooth '04
Tony n' Tina's Wedding '07
Tootsie '82 ▸
Top Five '14 ▸
Torch Singer '33
Torch Song Trilogy '88
Tower Heist '11
Town and Country '01
Tracers '15
The Trade '03
Transamerica '05 ▸
Trash '70
The Treatment '06
A Tree Grows in Brooklyn '45 ▸
Trick '99 ▸
A Troll in Central Park '94
True Blue '01
Trust the Man '06
Turn the River '07
25th Hour '02
21 Bridges '19
The 24 Hour Woman '99
29th Street '91
Twisted '96
2 by 4 '98
Two for the Money '05
Two Girls and a Guy '98 ▸
200 Cigarettes '98
Two Lovers '09 ▸
Two Night Stand '14
Two Ninas '00
Two of Us '00
Two Sisters From Boston '46
Two Weeks Notice '02
Ultrachrist! '03
Uncertainty '08
Uncle Drew '18
Uncut Gems '19 ▸
Under Eighteen '32
Under Hellgate Bridge '99
Unfaithful '02 ▸
Unknown White Male '05 ▸
An Unmarried Woman '78 ▸
Untamed '29
Untamed Heart '93
(Untitled) '09
Unzipped '94 ▸
Up in Central Park '48
Upperworld '34
Uptown Girls '03
Uptown New York '32
Urbania '00
Vampire in Brooklyn '95
Vanilla Sky '01
Vanya on 42nd Street '94 ▸
Variety '83
Varsity Show '37
The Velocity of Gary '98
Very Good Girls '13
A Very Harold & Kumar Christmas '11
A Very Natural Thing '73
Very Semi-Serious: A Partially Thorough Portrait of New Yorker Cartoonists '15
A Very Special Favor '65
Violet Tendencies '10
Virtue '32
Visions of Sugarplums '99
The Visitor '07 ▸
The Voice of the Turtle '47
The Wackness '08
The Waiting Game '99
The Walk '15
A Walk Among the Tombstones '14
Walking and Talking '96
Wall Street 2: Money Never Sleeps '10
Wall Street '87 ▸
Walls of Glass '85
Wanderlust '12
Wannabes '01
The War Within '05
Washington Heights '02
Washington Square '97 ▸
The Way We Were '73 ▸
W.E. '11
The Wedding Party '69
We're Back! A Dinosaur's Story '93
West Side Story '61 ▸
The Wet Parade '32
What Happens in Vegas '08
What Happens Next '11
What Maisie Knew '12 ▸
Whatever Works '09
When Harry Met Sally. . . '89 ▸
When Will I Be Loved '04
Where God Left His Shoes '07
Where Is Kyra? '17
Whiplash '48
Whipped '00
Whirlygirl '04
White Girl '16
Who Gets to Call It Art? '05
Who's That Knocking at My Door? '68 ▸
Why Stop Now '12
Wife, Husband and Friend '39
The Wild '06
Wild Boys of the Road '33
Wild Style '83
Winner Take All '32
Winter Passing '05
Winter's Tale '14
Wirey Spindell '99
Wise Guys '86
Wisegal '08
Wisegirls '02
The Witches of Oz '11
Within the Law '23
Witness to the Mob '98
Wolf '94
The Wolf Hour '19
Wolfen '81 ▸
A Woman, A Part '17
The Woman Between '31
The Women '08
Wonderful World '09
Wonderstruck '17
Working Girl '88 ▸
World Trade Center '06 ▸
X-Men '00
XX/XY '02
The Yards '00
Year of the Dragon '85
Yellow '06
You Belong to Me '07
You Can't Have Everything '37
You Don't Mess with the Zohan '08
You Stupid Man '02
You Tell Me '06
You Wont Miss Me '09
Young Dr. Kildare '38
The Young Girl and the Monsoon '99
The Young Savages '61
Youngblood Hawke '64
The Youngest Profession '43
You've Got Mail '98

New Zealand

***See** Down Under*

Newlyweds

***See also** Wedding Bells*

Are We Done Yet? '07
Barefoot in the Park '67 ▸
Best Man Down '12
The Blood Spattered Bride '72
The Canyon '09
Chunhyang '00
Claudia '43
Crossroads '42
Dark Country '09
The Devil Incarnate '13
Devil's Pond '03
Doorway to Hell '30
Family Honeymoon '49
Flight Angels '40
Gasoline Alley '51
Gidget Gets Married '72
Gift of the Magi '10
Girl Missing '33
A Good Woman '04
The Guilty Generation '31
A Haunted House '13
The Heartbreak Kid '72 ▸
Highball '97 ▸
Honeymoon '14
Hungry Hearts '15
I Give It a Year '13
I Married a Monster from Outer Space '58
Identity '03
It's Tough to Be Famous '32
Just Married '03
Lakeview Terrace '08 ▸
The Land That Time Forgot '09
The Long, Long Trailer '54
Love Actually '03
Love, Wedding, Marriage '11
Machine Gun McCain '69
Made for Each Other '39 ▸
Made in Heaven '52
Mail Order Bride '63
Mail Order Wife '04
Mannequin '37
Meet the Stewarts '42
Mexican Spitfire '40
Mr. & Mrs. Loving '96 ▸
Montana Moon '30
Mother Didn't Tell Me '50
Move Over, Darling '63
My Week With Marilyn '11

National Lampoon's Gold Diggers '04
Nearlyweds '13
Newlyweds '11
Nightmare Honeymoon '73
No Down Payment '57
No Room for the Groom '52
On the Line '84
A Perfect Getaway '09
Petunia '13
Playing House '10
Polly of the Circus '32
Prelude to a Kiss '92
The Reception '05
The Secret Bride '35
She's Having a Baby '88
Shrek 2 '04 ▸
Snow 2: Brain Freeze '08
So I Married an Axe Murderer '93
Stop Me Before I Kill! '60
10 '79
To Rome with Love '12
The Twilight Saga: Breaking Dawn, Part 1 '11
Upstairs and Downstairs '59
Voulez-Vous Danser avec Moi? '59
The Vow '12
West of Broadway '31
Wide Sargasso Sea '06
The Wyvern Mystery '00
You May Not Kiss the Bride '12
You, Me and Dupree '06
Young Ideas '43
Zombie Honeymoon '04

News at 11

***See also** Front Page; Look Ma! I'm on TV!; Mass Media*

All About Steve '09
American Crime '04
Anchorman: The Legend of Ron Burgundy '04
Anchorman 2: The Legend Continues '13
Bombshell '19
Broadcast News '87▸
Bruce Almighty '03
The China Syndrome '79▸
Christine '16
The Clearstream Affair '15
Control Room '04▸
The Dead Pool '88
Dead Rising: End Game '16
Dog Days '18
Eyewitness '81
A Face in the Crowd '57▸
15 Minutes '01
Good Night, and Good Luck '05▸
Hot Type: 150 Years of The Nation '15
The Hunting Party '07
If There's a Hell Below '16
The Insider '99▸
Joseph Pulitzer: Voice of the People '18
Kate Plays Christine '16▸
Life or Something Like It '02
Little Black Book '04
Live from Baghdad '03▸
Mike Wallace Is Here '19▸
Morning Glory '10
Much Ado About Nothing '05
Natural Born Killers '94
Network '76▸
News at Eleven '86
The Night We Called It a Day '03
Outfoxed: Rupert Murdoch's War on Journalism '04▸
Peterloo '18
The Post '17▸
A Private War '18
Quarantine '08
[Rec] '07
Richard Jewell '19▸
The Scenesters '09
Special Bulletin '83▸
Switching Channels '88
This Revolution '05
To Die For '95▸
Truth '15
Up Close and Personal '96▸
Vantage Point '08

Weapons of Mass Distraction '97

Newspapers

***See** Front Page*

Niagara Falls

The Art of the Steal '13
A Beginner's Guide to Endings '10
Bruce Almighty '03
Emma '32
I Now Pronounce You Chuck and Larry '07
The Long Kiss Goodnight '96
Niagara '52
Niagara Motel '06
Niagara, Niagara '97
Superman 2 '80 ▸
Tammy '14

Nice Mice

***See also** Killer Rodents*

An American Tail '86
An American Tail: Fievel Goes West '91
Babe '95▸
Babe: Pig in the City '98
The Chronicles of Narnia: The Voyage of the Dawn Treader '10
Dr. Seuss' Horton Hears a Who! '08▸
Ernest & Celestine '13
Escape from Alcatraz '79▸
Flowers for Algernon '00
Flushed Away '06▸
The Great Mouse Detective '86▸
The Green Mile '99
The Hitchhiker's Guide to the Galaxy '05▸
The Island on Bird Street '97
Mouse Hunt '97▸
Ratatouille '07▸
Ratz '99
The Rescuers '77▸
The Rescuers Down Under '90
Road Trip '00
The Secret of NIMH 2 '98
The Secret of NIMH '82▸
Sitcom '97
Stuart Little '99
Stuart Little 2 '02▸
Stuart Little 3: Call of the Wild '06
The Tale of Despereaux '08

Nightclubs

The Adventures of Pluto Nash '02
All Night Long '62
America So Beautiful '01
American Swing '08
Animal Instincts '92
Anything But Love '02
Backbeat '94▸
The Bamboo Blonde '46
Be Yourself '30
Berlin Blues '89
Better Than Chocolate '99
Birth of the Blues '41
Black Angel '46▸
Black Glove '54
Blood Brothers '07
The Blue Angel '30▸
Blues '08
Body Shots '99
Bonded by Blood '09
Bordertown '35
Born Romantic '00
The Bride Wore Red '37
Bus Stop '56▸
Cabaret '72▸
Cabaret Balkan '98
Cafe Society '97
Café Society '16
Can-Can '60
Carnival Rock '57
Casablanca '42▸
CB4: The Movie '93
CBGB '13
Charlie Chan on Broadway '37
Christopher and His Kind '11▸
City of Ghosts '03
Copacabana '47

The Cotton Club '84 ▸
The Cyberstalking '99
Dance, Girl, Dance '40
Dancing at the Blue Iguana '00
A Dangerous Profession '49
Dark Secrets '95
Dark Streets '08
Dead Cert '10
The Desert Song '43
Desperate Cargo '41
Destination Murder '50
Dick Tracy '90 ▸
Double or Nothing '37
Dracula Blows His Cool '82
The Drag-Net '36
The Dreamlife of Angels '98 ▸
Eden '14
Enter the Void '09
The Fabulous Baker Boys '89 ▸
Fake Out '82
54 '98
Fog Over Frisco '34
Folies Bergere de Paris '35
Framed '30
Framed '75
French Can-Can '55▸
Fun in Acapulco '63
Funkytown '11
Garden of the Moon '38
G.I. Blues '60
The Girl '01
Girls! Girls! Girls! '62
Go Into Your Dance '35
The Gold Racket '37
Goodbye Baby '07
The Green Cockatoo '37
Green Room '15▸
Greenwich Village '44
Harlem Nights '89
He Found a Star '41
The Helen Morgan Story '57
Honeydripper '07▸
House of the Rising Sun '11
I Can Do Bad All By Myself '09
I Walk Alone '48
I Was an American Spy '51
Idlewild '06
If I Had My Way '40
In the Mix '05
Invincible '01
Irish Eyes Are Smiling '44
Irreversible '02
It All Came True '40
It Started in Naples '60▸
It's All Gone, Pete Tong '04
The Killing of a Chinese Bookie '76
King Creole '58
Kings of South Beach '07
La Cage aux Folles '78▸
La Cage aux Folles 2 '81
La Cage aux Folles 3: The Wedding '86
Lady on a Train '45▸
Lambada '89
Las Vegas Nights '41
The Last Days of Disco '98▸
Le Samourai '67▸
Lenny '74▸
Like It Is '98▸
Liquid Dreams '92
Little Shots of Happiness '97
Lola '81
The Lost City '05
Love Come Down '00
Love Goggles '99
Love Jones '96▸
Lullaby of Broadway '51
Lured '47
Mad Dog and Glory '93▸
Madame Sata '02
Magic Mike '12
Maisie Goes to Reno '44
Make Your Move '13
The Mambo Kings '92▸
Manpower '41
Marked Woman '37▸
The Mask '94▸
Mickey One '65
Midnight Warrior '89
Mighty Joe Young '49
Miracles '89
Miss Pettigrew Lives for a Day '08▸
Moonlight Serenade '09

Morocco '30 ▸
Moulin Rouge '01 ▸
New Orleans '47
Night After Night '32
A Night at the Roxbury '98
Night Cargo '36
A Night in Heaven '83
Night of the Living Deb '14
The Night They Raided Minsky's '69 ▸
No Surrender '86 ▸
Nora Prentiss '47
The Nude Set '57
The Nutty Professor '63 ▸
Outside of Paradise '38
Pandora and the Flying Dutchman '51
Party Girl '58 ▸
Party Girl '94
Party Monster '03
Pecker '98
People '04
Pete Kelly's Blues '55
Piccadilly '29
Playing by Heart '98
Preaching to the Perverted '97
The Public Eye '92▸
Rebel '85
Roger Dodger '02▸
Ruby '92
Ruby's Dream '82
St. Louis Woman '34
Sally, Irene and Mary '38
Salt & Pepper '68
The Score '01
Shanghai Triad '95▸
The Shining Hour '38
Shopworn '32
Showgirls '95
Sleepless Night '11▸
Smash-Up: The Story of a Woman '47▸
Somewhere in the Night '46
Sorted '04
Speed-Dating '10
Spin '07
Stage Struck '48
Stark Raving Mad '02
Stonewall '95▸
Sweet Evil '98
Swindle '02
Swing Fever '43
Swingers '96▸
The Talented Mr. Ripley '99
That Naughty Girl '58
The Third Girl from the Left '73
Tiger Bay '33
Time Out for Rhythm '41
To Catch a King '84
Tomorrow We Live '42
Too Late Blues '61
Torch Singer '33
Trigger Happy '96
The Truth About Youth '30
24 Hour Party People '01
200 Cigarettes '98
Undercurrent '99
Uptown Saturday Night '74
Urge '16
Vamp '86
We Are the Hartmans '11
We Own the Night '07
Whiplash '48
Whirlpool '34
Whistle Stop '46
The White Angel '55
Who Do You Love '08
Why Be Good? '29
A Woman Is a Woman '60▸
Wonder Bar '34
Woo '97
Xanadu '80

Ninjas

***See also** Martial Arts*

Azumi 2 '05
Azumi '03▸
Batman Begins '05▸
Black Tight Killers '66▸
Elektra '05
Five Element Ninjas '82
Heroes of the East '08▸
Kill 'Em All '12
The LEGO Ninjago Movie '17
Miami Connection '87
Ninja Assassin '09

Ninja in the U.S.A. '88
Red Shadow '01
RoboCop 3 '91
Shinobi '05 ▸
Shinobi no Mono '62 ▸
Shinobi no Mono 2: Vengeance '63 ▸
Shinobi No Mono 3: Resurrection '09
Shrink '09
3 Ninjas Kick Back '94
TMNT: Teenage Mutant Ninja Turtles '07

Ninjitsu

***See** Martial Arts*

No-Exit Motel

***See also** Grand Hotel*

Axe '06
The Bag Man '14
Beneath the Dark '10
Bug '06
Dead Simple '01
Eaten Alive '76
Identity '03
In the Tall Grass '19
The Innkeepers '11
Interstate '07
Lake Dead '07
Memento '00▸
Motel Hell '80
Mountaintop Motel Massacre '86
The Newlydeads '87
Poor Pretty Eddie '73
Psycho '60▸
Psycho 2 '83
Psycho 3 '86
Psycho 4: The Beginning '90
Psycho '98
Rubber '10
Slaughter Hotel '71
Tape '01▸
Terror Trap '10
Vacancy 2: The First Cut '08
Vacancy '07

Not-So-True Identity

Abduction '11
Above Suspicion '00
Adoration '08
Adventure in Manhattan '36
AKA '02
Albert Nobbs '11
Albino Alligator '96
Alias the Doctor '32
Allied '16
The Amazing Mrs. Holiday '43
The Amazing Spider-Man 2 '14
The Amazing Spider-Man '12▸
Anonymous Rex '04
Apt Pupil '97
Armistead Maupin's Tales of the City '93
The Associate '96
The Australian Story '52
Autumn Sun '98▸
Bad Santa '03
Batman Begins '05▸
Beggars of Life '28
Beverly Lewis' The Confession '13
Beyond Betrayal '94
The Big Caper '57
Big Momma's House 2 '06
Big Momma's House '00
The Black Bird '26
Black Book '06▸
Black Like Me '64
The Black Tulip '64
Blue Streak '99
Boat Trip '03
A Boyfriend for Christmas '04
Boys Don't Cry '99▸
The Breaks '99
Bride by Mistake '44
Bubba Ho-Tep '03▸
Buccaneer's Girl '50
Buster's Mal Heart '17
Cafe Metropole '37
Campus Rhythm '43
Captain Kidd and the Slave Girl '54
Catch Me If You Can '02

Cell 211 '09
Certified Copy '10
Chain Gang '50
Charley's Aunt '41 ▸
Charlotte Gray '01
Chase a Crooked Shadow '58
Chasing Liberty '04
Cheyenne '47
Chicklit '16
The Claim '00
Clancy Street Boys '43
Code Name: The Cleaner '07
Color Me Kubrick '05
The Company You Keep '12
Complete Unknown '16
The Concert '09
Corky Romano '01
The Cotton Club '84 ▸
The Count of Monte Cristo '99
Cowboy from Brooklyn '38
Crossroads '42
Cymbeline '15
Daniel Deronda '02
Dear Frankie '04
Deceived '91
Deception '08
Defying Gravity '99
The Departed '06▸
Destination Murder '50
Devil in the Flesh 2 '00
The Devil's Double '11
A Different Loyalty '04▸
Disappearing in America '08
Don't Lose Your Head '66
The Double Life of Eleanor Kendall '08
The East '13
Easy Money '10▸
Easy to Wed '46
The Elder Son '06
Elf '03▸
The Emperor's New Clothes '01
Empire of the Wolves '05
Europa, Europa '91▸
Exit Through the Gift Shop '10
Exit Wounds '01
Extasis '96
Face/Off '97▸
Face the Music '00
Failure to Launch '06
Felt '15
Femme Fatale '02
A Fig Leaf for Eve '44
The Flowers of War '11
Folies Bergere de Paris '35
For Richer or Poorer '97
Forever Mine '99
Freshman Orientation '04
Gattaca '97▸
The Gay Deception '35
Gentleman's Agreement '47▸
George White's Scandals '45
Going Postal '10
The Golden Arrow '36
Good Advice '01
The Good Fairy '35▸
Gosford Park '01▸
The Governess '98
The Green Hornet '11
Grey Owl '99
Gun Shy '00
The Guru '02
Hannah Montana: The Movie '09
Happiness Ahead '34
Happy, Texas '99▸
Hard to Forget '98
Head Over Heels '01
Hell Is Sold Out '51
Hidden Away '13
High Crimes '02
The History of Mr. Polly '07
A History of Violence '05▸
Holiday Engagement '11
Holy Motors '12▸
Homegrown '97
The Human Stain '03
I Now Pronounce You Chuck and Larry '07
Ida '13▸
Identicals '16
Identity Theft: The Michelle Brown Story '04

▸ = rated three bones or higher

If a Man Answers '62
If You Could Only Cook '36
If You Only Knew '00
I'll Wait for You '41
Imitation General '58
Imitation of Life '34
Imitation of Life '59 ▸
The Importance of Being Earnest '02
Impostor '02
Infernal Affairs '02 ▸
The Infidel '10
Iron Road '08
It's Love Again '36
Jewtopia '12
The Joneses '09
The Journey '59
Just Another Love Story '08
Just My Luck '06
Juwanna Mann '02
Kentucky '38
Key Witness '47
Kill Me Quick, I'm Cold '67
The Killing Machine '09
Kismet '44
A Knight's Tale '01
La France '07
The Lady Eve '41 ▸
The Law and the Lady '51
The Legend of Rita '99
Les Miserables '97 ▸
Let's Be Cops '14
Libel '59
Lip Service '00
Little Man '06
Little Old New York '23
The Long Kiss Goodnight '96
Long Lost Son '06
The Lookalike '14
Lost Boundaries '49
Love Me Tonight '32 ▸
Mad About Men '54
The Mad Adventures of Rabbi Jacob '73 ▸
Maid in Manhattan '02
The Major and the Minor '42 ▸
Malibu's Most Wanted '03
The Man From Toronto '32
The Man in Possession '31
The Man Who Lies '68
The Man with Two Faces '34
Mask of Death '97
The Mask of Zorro '98 ▸
Master of Disguise '02
The Master Race '44
Me & Mrs. Jones '02
The Mexican Spitfire Out West '40
The Mexican Spitfire Sees a Ghost '42
Miss Tatlock's Millions '48
Mrs. Palfrey at the Claremont '05
Mrs. Winterbourne '96
Mr. & Mrs. Smith '05 ▸
Mr. Belvedere Rings the Bell '51
Mister Cinderella '36
Mister Lonely '07
Monte Carlo '30
Monte Carlo '11
Monte Cristo '22
Moon over Miami '41 ▸
Mother Night '96 ▸
Mulan '98
Mulholland Drive '01 ▸
Mumford '99 ▸
My First Wedding '04
My Friend from India '27
My Name Is Sarah '07
Nancy Steele Is Missing '37
Never Been Kissed '99
Nevil Shute's The Far Country '85
The Next Big Thing '02
Night Cargo '36
Nobody's Baby '37
Nora Prentiss '47
One More Time '70
Open Season 3 '10
Orlando '92 ▸
The Other Man '08
Our Man in Havana '59 ▸
Our Mutual Friend '98
Out at the Wedding '07
Out to Sea '97
The Painted Lady '97 ▸
Painting the Clouds With Sunshine '51
The Parent Trap '98
Perfect Stranger '07
The Phantom of Santa Fe '36
Pinky '49 ▸
Pipe Dream '02
The Pirates of Capri '49
The Pretty One '14
The Prince & Me '04
The Prince and the Pauper '07
The Prince and the Surfer '99
Princess of Thieves '01
Princess Protection Program '09
The Prisoner of Zenda '22
The Public Defender '31
The Quarry '98
Radio Rebel '12
The Red Danube '50
Redemption '13
Ride a Crooked Trail '58
The Ringer '05
Road to Paradise '30
Rock My World '02
The Rowdy Girls '00
Rushlights '13
The Saint '97
Sally '29
The Scapegoat '12
Scaramouche '23
The Scarlet Pimpernel '99
The Scarlet Pimpernel 2: Mademoiselle Guillotine '99
The Scarlet Pimpernel 3: The Kidnapped King '99
The Scarlet Pimpernel '34 ▸
The Scarlet Pimpernel '82 ▸
The Secret Agent '96
The Secret Invasion '64
Shadows '60 ▸
Shallow Hal '01
The Sheepman '58
The Silencer '99
Silver Hawk '04
Ski Party '65
Slightly Dangerous '43
Slightly French '49
So Undercover '13
Soccer Mom '08
Somewhere in the Night '46
Son of the Gods '30
Soul Man '86
Southside 1-1000 '50
Spring in Park Lane '48
Storm Over the Nile '55
Strange Bedfellows '04
Stranger in My Bed '05
Super '10
Sweet Revenge '76
The Tailor of Panama '00 ▸
Taking Care of Business '90
Taking Lives '04
The Talented Mr. Ripley '99
Tartuffe '25
Tension '50
That Funny Feeling '65
That Night in Rio '41
They Came to Blow Up America '43
The Thief '97
Third Finger, Left Hand '40
Thirty Day Princess '34
This Side of the Law '50
Three Blind Mice '38
Three Identical Strangers '18 ▸
Three to Tango '99
Through the Back Door '21
Tonight We Raid Calais '43
Too Young to Kiss '51
Tooth Fairy 2 '12
Tooth Fairy '10
Total Recall '12
Trial and Error '96
The Triumph of Love '01
True Story '15
The Truman Show '98 ▸
The Truth About Charlie '02
Truth Be Told '11
Twenty Plus Two '61
Twin Dragons '92
Two of a Kind '51
Two Shades of Blue '98
Uniform '03
The Valet '06
Virtual Sexuality '99
Wake '09
Walking with the Enemy '13
The Wedding Ringer '15
We're the Millers '13
What the Deaf Man Heard '98 ▸
Who is Cletis Tout? '02
Who Was That Lady? '60
The Witness Files '00
The Woman Between '31
Woman On the Run '50
The Wrath of God '72
You Don't Mess with the Zohan '08
You're Never Too Young '55
Youth in Revolt '10

Nuclear Disaster

See Disaster Flicks; Meltdown

Nuclear Energy

The Abyss '89 ▸
Atomic Rulers of the World '65
The Chosen '77
Class of Nuke 'Em High 2: Subhumanoid Meltdown '91
Class of Nuke 'Em High 3: The Good, the Bad and the Subhumanoid '94
Class of Nuke 'Em High '86
Devices and Desires '91 ▸
Die, Monster, Die! '65
Dirty Games '89
Godzilla '98
Indian Point '16
Island of Lost Women '59
Journey to the Center of Time '67
The Man from U.N.C.L.E. '15
Most Dangerous Man Alive '61
Pandora's Promise '13
Panic in the City '68
Phantom '13
The President's Man 2: A Line in the Sand '02
PU-239 '06
Return from Witch Mountain '78
The Return of Dr. Mabuse '61
The Russian Woodpecker '15 ▸
Zero Days '16

Nuns & Priests

See also Missionaries; Religion; Religious Epics

Absolution '81
Absolution '05
Agnes of God '85
The Agony and the Ecstasy '65
All About My Mother '99 ▸
All Saints '17
Amateur '94 ▸
Amen '02 ▸
The American '01
The American '10
Angels with Dirty Faces '38 ▸
Annabelle '14
The Apostate '98
Appointment With Danger '51
Arn: The Knight Templar '07
The Assisi Underground '84
The Atonement of Gosta Berling '24 ▸
Bad Education '04 ▸
The Barbarian Invasions '03 ▸
Beavis and Butt-Head Do America '96
Becket '64 ▸
Bedevilled '55
Behind the Wall '08
The Bells of St. Mary's '45 ▸
The Big Wedding '13
Black Narcissus '47 ▸
Black Robe '91 ▸
The Blackcoat's Daughter '17
The Bloodstained Shadow '78
The Blues Brothers '80 ▸
Blues Brothers 2000 '98
The Body '01
Body & Soul '93 ▸
The Boys of St. Vincent '93 ▸
Boys Town '38 ▸
Brand New Day '10
Breakfast on Pluto '05
Brides of Christ '91
The Bridge of San Luis Rey '44 ▸
The Bridge of San Luis Rey '05
Calvary '14 ▸
Camila '84 ▸
Camp Hell '10
The Cardinal '63
Cardinal Richelieu '35
Change of Habit '69
Changing Habits '96
Child's Play '72
Chocolat '00 ▸
The Christmas Choir '08
Come to the Stable '49 ▸
The Confession '20
The Confessional '75
The Confessor '04
Conspiracy of Hearts '60 ▸
Conspiracy of Silence '03
Corpus Christi '19 ▸
The Crime of Father Amaro '02 ▸
The Cross & the Switchblade '72
Cry, the Beloved Country '95 ▸
The Dangerous Lives of Altar Boys '02 ▸
Daredevil '03
Dead Man Walking '95 ▸
Dead Waters '94
Deliver Us From Evil '14
Demonia '90
The Devils '71 ▸
The Devil's Playground '76 ▸
Diary of a Country Priest '50 ▸
Dixie: Changing Habits '85 ▸
Dominion: Prequel to the Exorcist '05
Doubt '08 ▸
Dracula 2: Ascension '03
Dracula 3: Legacy '05
The Duchess of Langeais '07 ▸
Edges of the Lord '01
The Eighteenth Angel '97
Elmer Gantry '60 ▸
End of Days '99
The End of the Affair '99 ▸
End of the World '76
The Exorcism of Emily Rose '05 ▸
The Exorcist '73 ▸
The Exorcist 2: The Heretic '77
Exorcist: The Beginning '04
Expecting a Miracle '09
The Father Clements Story '87
Father's Day '12
The Fifth Element '97
Final Engagement '07
The Fireball '50
Flexing with Monty '10
The Flowers of War '11
The Fog '78
For Greater Glory '12
Forever Young '85
40 Days and 40 Nights '02
The Fugitive '48 ▸
Going My Way '44 ▸
The Good Catholic '17
Gospa '94
Goya's Ghosts '06
Happy Hell Night '92
The Haunting of Lisa '96
Heaven Knows, Mr. Allison '57 ▸
Henry Poole Is Here '08 ▸
Hideous Kinky '99
Hoax for the Holidays '10
A Home of Our Own '75
The Hoodlum Priest '61 ▸
Hunger '08
I Confess '53
I Do & I Don't '07
I, the Worst of All '90
Ida '13 ▸
In This House of Brede '75 ▸
The Innocents '16 ▸
Into Temptation '09
Jesus of Montreal '89 ▸
John Carpenter Presents Vampires: Los Muertos '02
Joshua '02
Joyeux Noel '05 ▸
Judgment '90 ▸
Keeping the Faith '00
Kid Monk Baroni '52
Lamb '85
The Last Don 2 '98
The Last Mile '59
The Last Request '06
Last Rites '88
The Last Templar '09
The Least of These '08
The Left Hand of God '55 ▸
Leon Morin, Priest '61
Liam '00
License to Wed '07
Lilies of the Field '63 ▸
The Little Hours '17 ▸
Little Sister '16 ▸
Lost City Raiders '08
Loving Annabelle '06
Machete '10
Madeline '98
The Magdalene Sisters '02 ▸
The Maldonado Miracle '03
Manna from Heaven '02
Mass Appeal '84
Massacre in Rome '73
The Mighty Macs '09
Mission to Glory '80
Mister Lonely '07
Molokai: The Story of Father Damien '99
Monsignor '82
More Than a Miracle '67
Mother Joan of the Angels '60 ▸
My First Wedding '04
My Mother's Smile '02
Mysteries of Lisbon '10
Nacho Libre '06
The Name of the Rose '86
Nasty Habits '77
Night of the Assassin '70
Night of the Demons 2 '94
Night Sun '90
The Ninth Day '04 ▸
Nobody's Children '52
Noel '04
Northfork '03
Not of This World '99
Novitiate '17
The Nun '18
The Nun and the Sergeant '62
Nuns on the Run '90
The Nun's Story '59 ▸
The Omen '76
The Order '03
Oscar and Lucinda '97
Pale Rider '85 ▸
Passing Glory '99 ▸
The Perfect Game '09
Phantom Punch '09
Philomena '13
Pieces of Dreams '70
The Possessed '77
Possessed '00
Prayer for the Dying '87
Priest '94
Priest '11
The Priest's Wife '71
Primal Fear '96
Prince of Darkness '87
The Prisoner '55 ▸
The Proposition '97
The Ravagers '65
Ready? OK! '08
The Reaping '07
The Reckoning '03 ▸
The Red Danube '50
The Red Inn '51
Redemption '13
Revenge of the Musketeers '94
Rise of the Gargoyles '09
The Rite '11
Romance '30
Sacrifice '11
Saintly Sinners '62
Salem's Lot '04
Sanctuary '98
Say One for Me '59
The Scarlet & the Black '83
Scary Movie 2 '01
Sea Wife '57
Second Sight '89
The Sessions '12 ▸
The Shoes of the Fisherman '68
Shooting Dogs '05
Silver Bullet '85
The Singing Nun '66
Sinner '07
Sister Act '92
Sister Act 2: Back in the Habit '93
Sisters of War '10
666: The Beast '07
Sleepers '96
The Song of Hiawatha '97
Sorceress '88 ▸
Soul Survivors '01
The Sound of Music '65 ▸
Stella Days '12
Stigmata '99
Stolen Summer '02
Sympathy for Delicious '10
There Be Dragons '11
Therese '86 ▸
Therese: The Story of Saint Therese of Lisieux '04
The Third Miracle '99
Thirst '09 ▸
The Three Stooges '12
Thunder on the Hill '51
To Kill a Priest '89
To the Wonder '12
Trouble along the Way '53
The Trouble with Angels '66
True Confessions '81 ▸
Under the Red Robe '36
The Unholy '88
Wanted '98
Way of the Wicked '14
We're No Angels '89
Where Angels Go, Trouble Follows '68
The White Angel '55 ▸
The White Sister '23 ▸
The White Sister '33
Wide Awake '97
The Winter Light '62 ▸
The Wrath of God '72
The X Files: I Want to Believe '08

Nuns with Guns

The Enforcer '76
The Mighty Macs '09
Ms. 45 '81 ▸
Nun of That '09
Nuns on the Run '90
Offensive Behaviour '04
Two Mules for Sister Sara '70 ▸
Vision '09
We're No Angels '89
Wuthering Heights '09

Nursploitation!

See also Doctors & Nurses

Born for Hell '76
Candy Stripe Nurses '74
Countdown '79
Emmanuelle in the Country '78
Hospital of Terror '78
Inner Sanctum '91
Night Call Nurses '72
Private Duty Nurses '71
The Sensuous Nurse '76
The Student Nurses '70
Tender Loving Care '73
The Young Nurses '73

Obsessive Love

Aaron Loves Angela '75
Addicted to Her Love '06
Addicted to Love '96
After Sex '97
Against All Odds '84
All I See Is You '17
Alone With Her '07
And Never Let Her Go '01
Anna Karenina '35 ▸
Anna Karenina '48
Anna Karenina '96
Anna Karenina '00
Anna Karenina '12
The Aviator's Wife '80 ▸
Bad Timing: A Sensual Obsession '80
Barney's Version '10

▸ = rated three bones or higher

The Best Man '97
The Best Offer '13
Betty Blue '86 ▸
Beyond the Clouds '95
Borderline '02 ▸
The Bridesmaid '04
Brief Encounter '46 ▸
Can't Buy Me Love '87
Carmen '03
Cause Celebre '87 ▸
The Center of the World '01
Changing Times '04
Chungking Express '95 ▸
The Climax '44
The Constant Nymph '43
Crazy Love '07 ▸
The Crown Prince '06
The Crush '93
Crush '09
Crush '13
Cyrano de Bergerac '25 ▸
Cyrano de Bergerac '50 ▸
Cyrano de Bergerac '90 ▸
Damage '92 ▸
Death and Desire '97
Deep Crimson '96
Devil in the Flesh 2 '00
Devil in the Flesh '87
Devil in the Flesh '98
Doctor Zhivago '03
Driftwood '97
The Duchess of Langeais '07 ▸
Eccentricities of a Blonde-Haired Girl '10 ▸
8 1/2 Women '99
Emily Bronte's Wuthering Heights '92
End of the Affair '55
The End of the Affair '99 ▸
Endless Love '81
Enduring Love '04
The English Patient '96 ▸
Eros '04
Eva '62
Eye of God '97 ▸
Eye of the Beholder '99
The Face of Love '13
Far from the Madding Crowd '97 ▸
Fatal Attraction '87 ▸
Fear '96
Fever Pitch '05
The File on Thelma Jordon '50 ▸
Film Geek '06
For Sale '98
Frank & Lola '16
G '02
Ghost '90 ▸
A Girl Cut in Two '07
Going Postal '98
The Good Girl '02 ▸
The Good Night '07
Goodbye, Dragon Inn '03
The Great Gatsby '13
Grimm Love '06
He Loves Me . . . He Loves Me Not '02
The Heartbreak Kid '72 ▸
Homage '95
House of Women '62
Hush '98
L'Immortelle '63
Intimate Stranger '06
Jealousy '99
Julie '56
Kama Sutra: A Tale of Love '96
Kill Your Darlings '13
Last Breath '96
Laurence Anyways '12
L'Ennui '98
Les Biches '68 ▸
Letter from an Unknown Woman '48 ▸
Letters from a Killer '98
Live Flesh '97 ▸
Lost and Delirious '01
Love and Death on Long Island '97
Love and Rage '99
Loverboy '05
Lust, Caution '07
Mad Love '95
Mad Love '01
Mararia '98
Miss Monday '98
Mr. Wrong '95
My Cousin Rachel '52
The Mystery of Edwin Drood '35
Not My Life '06
Notre Histoire '84
Obsessed '09
Obsession '97
The Obsession '06
Only Love '98
Our Mutual Friend '98
Perfect Sense '11
Perfect Strangers '03
The Perfect Teacher '10
Phantom '22
The Phantom of the Opera '25 ▸
The Phantom of the Opera '43 ▸
The Phantom of the Opera '62
The Phantom of the Opera '89
The Phantom of the Opera '90
The Phantom of the Opera '98
A Place in the Sun '51 ▸
Plain Jane '02
The Prowler '51
Punch-Drunk Love '02 ▸
Rage in Heaven '41
The Reader '08
Romeo and Juliet '36 ▸
Romeo and Juliet '54
Romeo and Juliet '68 ▸
Roxanne '87 ▸
The Rum Diary '11
Sabrina '54 ▸
Sabrina '95
Say Nothing '01
Sea of Love '89 ▸
Show Boat '36 ▸
Show Boat '51
Silent Cry Aloud '16
A Slipping Down Life '99
Some Kind of Wonderful '87
Something Wild '61
The Sterile Cuckoo '69 ▸
Strangers May Kiss '31
Summer Storm '44
Sun Choke '16
Swimfan '02
Sylvia '03
Talhotblond '12
Temptress Moon '96
10 '79
Testosterone '03
There's Something about Mary '98 ▸
A Thin Line Between Love and Hate '96
XIII '08
A Thousand Kisses Deep '11
Time '06
To Gillian on Her 37th Birthday '96
The Traveling Executioner '70
Truly, Madly, Deeply '91 ▸
Tulip Fever '17
Twisted Obsession '90
Una '17
Vincere '09
Virtual Obsession '98
Walk the Line '05 ▸
West Side Story '61 ▸
When the Bough Breaks '16
Wicker Park '04
Wild Grass '09
Wilde '97
Wuthering Heights '39 ▸
Wuthering Heights '70
Wuthering Heights '98
Wuthering Heights '12

Occult

***See also** Demons & Satanism; Witchcraft*

Alone in the Dark '05
The Amazing Mr. X '48
Amityville Dollhouse '96
Apostle '18
Army of Darkness '92 ▸
Bad Dreams '88
Barbarian Queen '85
The Believers '87
Beyond Dream's Door '88
Beyond Evil '80
Beyond the Door 3 '91
The Black Cat '81
Black Circle Boys '97
Black Magic Terror '79
Blackbeard's Ghost '67
Bless the Child '00
Blood Creek '09
Blood Diner '87
Blood Orgy of the She-Devils '74
Bloodspell '87
Born of Fire '87
Brimstone & Treacle '82 ▸
The Brotherhood 3: The Young Demons '02
The Brotherhood of Satan '71
Brotherhood of the Wolf '01
Burn, Witch, Burn! '62
The Burning Court '62
Cabin in the Sky '43 ▸
The Canal '14
Cat in the Cage '68
Chandu on the Magic Island '34
Child of Glass '78
Children Shouldn't Play with Dead Things '72
Chill '06
Close Your Eyes '02
The Craft '96
Craze '74
The Crow: Wicked Prayer '05
Curse of the Demon '57 ▸
Curse of the Devil '73
Damien: Omen 2 '78
Damn Yankees '58 ▸
Dance with the Devil '97
Darkness '02
Dead Men Don't Die '91
Deathstalker 4: Match of Titans '92
Deep Red: Hatchet Murders '75
Demon Rage '82
Demonoid, Messenger of Death '81
Demons 2 '87
Demons of Ludlow '75
The Devil & Daniel Webster '41 ▸
Devil Dog: The Hound of Hell '78
Devil Doll '64
The Devils '71 ▸
The Devil's Candy '17
The Devil's Hand '61
The Devil's Nightmare '71
Devil's Rain '75
Devil's Son-in-Law '77
Diary of a Madman '63
Doctor Faustus '68
Dominique '79
Dona Flor and Her Two Husbands '78 ▸
Donovan's Brain '53 ▸
Don't Be Afraid of the Dark '73
Dream Man '94
Dreamscape '84
The Dunwich Horror '70
The Dybbuk '37 ▸
Encounter with the Unknown '75
The Entity '83
Equinox '71 ▸
Eternal Evil '87
The Evil '78
Evil Dead '83
Evil Dead 2: Dead by Dawn '87
Evil Dead '13
The Evil Mind '34
Evilspeak '82
Excalibur '81 ▸
Exorcism '74
The Exorcist '73 ▸
The Exorcist 2: The Heretic '77
Exorcist 3: Legion '90
Eye of the Demon '87
Fallen '97
The Final Conflict '81
The First Power '89
The Fish that Saved Pittsburgh '79
Gates of Hell 2: Dead Awakening '96
The Girl in a Swing '89
God Told Me To '76
The Guardian '90
Haxan: Witchcraft through the Ages '22 ▸
The Hearse '80
Horror Hotel '60
The House on Skull Mountain '74
I Am Zozo '12
I Don't Want to Be Born '75
Inferno '80
Into the Badlands '92
The Invasion of Carol Enders '74
Invasion of the Blood Farmers '72
Kill, Baby, Kill '66 ▸
Killing Hour '84
The Kingdom 2 '97 ▸
The Kingdom '95 ▸
The Kiss '88
KISS Meets the Phantom of the Park '78
Lady Terminator '89 ▸
Land of the Minotaur '77
The Legacy '79
The Legend of Bloody Mary '08
The Legend of Hell House '73 ▸
Life-Size '00
Lost Souls '00
The Magician '58 ▸
Making Contact '86
The Mangler '94
Manos, the Hands of Fate '66
Mardi Gras for the Devil '93
Mardi Gras Massacre '78
Medea '70
Midnight '81
Mirror, Mirror 2: Raven Dance '94
Mirror, Mirror '90
Mirror of Death '87
Mists of Avalon '01 ▸
Moscow Zero '06
Mystic Circle Murder '39
Necromancer: Satan's Servant '88
Necropolis '87
The Night Stalker '71
The Night Strangler '72
The Occultist '89
Only You '94
The Oracle '85
Orgy of the Dead '65
Ouija: Origin of Evil '16
Phantasm '79
Phantasm 2 '88
Phantasm 3: Lord of the Dead '94
Poltergeist '82 ▸
Poltergeist 2: The Other Side '86
Poltergeist 3 '88
The Psychic '68
Psychic '91
Psychic Killer '75
Psychomania '73
Puppet Master '89
Race with the Devil '75
The Raven '63 ▸
A Reflection of Fear '73
The Reincarnate '71
Repossessed '90
Retribution '88
Return from Witch Mountain '78
Return of Chandu '34
Rosemary's Baby '68 ▸
Ruby '77
Run If You Can '87
Sabaka '55
The Sacrifice '05
Season of the Witch '73
Second Sight '89
Seizure '74
Sensation '94
The Sentinel '76
The Seventh Sign '88
The Seventh Victim '43 ▸
Shock 'Em Dead '90
Silent Night, Deadly Night 3: Better Watch Out! '89
Sinister Hands '32
The Spaniard's Curse '58
Spellbinder '88
Spellbound '41
Summer of Fear '78
Supergirl '84
Teen Witch '89
Terror Creatures from the Grave '66
Three Sovereigns for Sarah '85
To the Devil, a Daughter '76
The Torture Chamber of Dr. Sadism '69
The Touch of Satan '70
The Undead '57
Unknown Powers '80
Venus in Furs '70
Vibes '88
The Visitor '80
Warlock Moon '73
The Wicker Man '75 ▸
The Wicker Tree '10
Wishmaster 4: The Prophecy Fulfilled '02
Wishmaster '97
Witch Who Came from the Sea '76
Witchboard '87
Witchboard 3: The Possession '95
Witchcraft 2: The Temptress '90
Witchcraft 4: Virgin Heart '92
The Witches of Eastwick '87
The Witching '72
The Witchmaker '69
The Witch's Mirror '60
The Wizard of Oz '39 ▸
Wizards '77
The Woman Who Came Back '45
Zapped Again '89
The Zodiac Killer '71

Oceans

***See** Deep Blue; Go Fish; Killer Sea Critters; Mutiny; Scuba; Shipwrecked; Submarines*

Office Surprise

The Belko Experiment '17
Can You Keep a Secret? '19
Casino '95 ▸
Control Alt Delete '08
Daredevil '03
Dead Again '91 ▸
Dial 'M' for Murder '54 ▸
Die Hard '88 ▸
Goldeneye '95 ▸
Grosse Pointe Blank '97 ▸
Henry: Portrait of a Serial Killer '90 ▸
Inhuman Resources '12
A Job to Kill For '06
La Femme Nikita '91 ▸
Misery '90 ▸
Miss Nobody '10
Mission: Impossible '96 ▸
My Bloody Banjo '15
9 to 5 '80
Office Christmas Party '16
Office Killer '97
Operation: Endgame '10
Point of No Return '93
Septic Man '14
The Temp '93

Ohio

***See also** America's Heartland; Cincinnati*

Absolution '05
Against the Ropes '04
Air Force One '97 ▸
American Factory '19 ▸
American Splendor '03 ▸
Antwone Fisher '02 ▸
Beautiful Ohio '06
Beyond Dream's Door '88
Brubaker '80 ▸
Bubble '06
Chicken People '16 ▸
A Christmas Story '83 ▸
Dahmer '02
Dirty Pictures '00
Edge of Seventeen '99
The Faculty '98
Finding Steve McQueen '19
The Fits '16
The Fortune Cookie '66 ▸
Guarding Tess '94
Gummo '97
A Home at the End of the World '04
Howard the Duck '86
The Ides of March '11
Kit Kittredge: An American Girl '08
The Knight Before Christmas '19
The Land '16
Little Man Tate '91 ▸
Major League '89
Major League 2 '94
The Prize Winner of Defiance, Ohio '05 ▸
Rain Man '88 ▸
Reckless '97 ▸
Return '11
The Rocker '08
The Shawshank Redemption '94 ▸
The Silence of the Lambs '91 ▸
The Soloist '09
Stranger than Paradise '84 ▸
Take Shelter '11 ▸
Tango and Cash '89
Teachers '84
That Hagen Girl '47
Traffic '00 ▸
Trick 'r Treat '08 ▸
Welcome to Collinwood '02

Oil

***See** Black Gold*

Oldest Profession

***See also** Gigolos; Women in Prison*

Accatone! '61 ▸
Ada '61
Adua and Her Friends '60
Aleksandr's Price '13
Alexander: The Other Side of Dawn '77
The Allnighter '87
American Gigolo '79
American Heart '92 ▸
American Justice '86
American Psycho '99
The Amsterdam Connection '78
Angel 3: The Final Chapter '88
Angel '84
Anna Christie '23 ▸
Anna Christie '30
Another Lonely Hitman '95
Armistead Maupin's More Tales of the City '97
Aroused '66
L'Automobile '71
Avenging Angel '85
The Babysitters '07
Back Roads '81
Bad Girls '94
Bad Lieutenant: Port of Call New Orleans '09
The Bag Man '14
The Balcony '63 ▸
Band of Gold '95 ▸
Before I Forget '07
Belle de Jour '67 ▸
Beloved '11
Beloved/Friend '99
The Best House in London '69
The Best Little Whorehouse in Texas '82
Between Something & Nothing '08
Beverly Hills Vamp '88
Beyond Desire '94
Big City Blues '99
Blood Money: The Story of Clinton and Nadine '88
Blow Out '81 ▸
The Blue Hour '91
Boiling Point '93
The Book of Stars '99
Born Into Brothels: Calcutta's Red Light Kids '04
The Bridge to Nowhere '09
Broken Trail '06 ▸
Business is Business '71
Butterfield 8 '60 ▸
Byzantium '12
Cafe Society '97
Call Me: The Rise and Fall of Heidi Fleiss '04

▸ = *rated three bones or higher*

The Olympics

On the Rocks

▶ = rated three bones or higher

Jesse Stone: Benefit of the Doubt '12
Jesse Stone: Death in Paradise '06
Jesse Stone: Night Passage '06
Jesse Stone: No Remorse '10
Jesse Stone: Stone Cold '05
Jesse Stone: Thin Ice '09
Jiminy Glick in LaLa Wood '05
Joe '13 ►
Joe the King '99
Julia '08 ►
Kill Cruise '90
Killer McCoy '47
La Cucaracha '99
The Last American Hero '73 ►
Last Call: The Final Chapter of F. Scott Fitzgerald '02
The Last of Robin Hood '13
The Last Posse '53
The Last Ride '12
Le Beau Serge '58 ►
Leaving Las Vegas '95 ►
The Lena Baker Story '08
Let It Ride '89
License to Kill '84
Lies My Mother Told Me '05
Life Begins at Eight-Thirty '42
Like Dandelion Dust '09
Little Boy Blue '97
The Little Foxes '41 ►
Little Voice '98 ►
The Living Wake '07
Long Day's Journey into Night '62 ►
Long Day's Journey into Night '88
The Lost Weekend '45 ►
Love on a Pillow '62
A Love Song for Bobby Long '04
Lucky Day '91
Lush '01
Maisie Was a Lady '41
The Man in the Net '59
Man-Trap '61
The Master '12 ►
Matter of Trust '98
Merrily We Go to Hell '32
The Missing Person '09
Mrs. Parker and the Vicious Circle '94
The Morning After '86
My Favorite Year '82 ►
My Name Is Joe '98
My Name Is Sarah '07
My Old Lady '14
My Zinc Bed '08
National Lampoon's Animal House '78 ►
Nebraska '13 ►
Nightmare Alley '47
No Down Payment '57
No Such Thing '01
Non-Stop '14
Notre Histoire '84
The Off Hours '11
Office Christmas Party '16
Once Were Warriors '94 ►
One for the Road '82
One Too Many '51
Only When I Laugh '81 ►
Orphan '09
Papa: Hemingway in Cuba '16
Papa's Delicate Condition '63 ►
The Party Never Stops '07
The People Against O'Hara '51
People Like Us '12
Perfect Sisters '14
The Phantom Carriage '21 ►
The Pick-Up Artist '87
Place Vendome '98 ►
Pollock '00 ►
Prairie Fever '08
Prozac Nation '01
Pushing Tin '99 ►
Rabbit, Run '70
Reaching for the Moon '13
Red Lights '04 ►
Revenge of the Nerds '84
Rio Bravo '59 ►
River Red '98
The Robe '53
Rosetta '99
Rough Night '17
Run All Night '15
Running From Crazy '13
Scent of a Woman '92 ►
The Secret Rapture '94
Shakes the Clown '92
She's So Lovely '97
A Shot at Glory '00
Shrink '09
The Sin of Harold Diddlebock '47
The Singing Blacksmith '38
A Single Man '09 ►
16 Years of Alcohol '03
Skin Deep '89
Skins '02
Sling Blade '96 ►
Smash-Up: The Story of a Woman '47 ►
Snow Angels '07 ►
Something to Live For '52
Something Wild '61
Son-in-Law '93
The Spectacular Now '13 ►
Spent '00
The Star '52 ►
A Star Is Born '54 ►
A Star Is Born '76
Strange Brew '83
Street Kings '08
Struggle '31
Stuart Saves His Family '94
Submarino '10
Sunset Strip '99
Swanee River '39
Take Me Home: The John Denver Story '00
Taken for Ransom '13
Tales of Ordinary Madness '83
Ten Nights in a Barroom '13
The Tenant of Wildfell Hall '96
Tender Is the Night '62
Tennessee '08
Term of Trial '63
Thirteen '03 ►
Too Much, Too Soon '58
Touching Home '08
Tree's Lounge '96
The Trials of Cate McCall '13
True Crime '99
Tugboat Annie '33 ►
Turning Paige '01
28 Days '00
Twisted '04
Tyrannosaur '11
Under Capricorn '49
Under the Volcano '84 ►
Unearthed '07
The Verdict '82 ►
Wagons East '94
The Wet Parade '32
What Price Hollywood? '32 ►
When a Man Loves a Woman '94
When Love Is Not Enough: The Lois Wilson Story '10
Whiskey Galore '48 ►
White Irish Drinkers '10
White Lightning '73
The Winning Team '52
Winter Passing '05
Words and Pictures '13
You Kill Me '07 ►
Your Cheatin' Heart '64

One Last Job

***See also** Crime Drama; Heists; Hit Men/Women; Organized Crime; Scams, Stings & Cons*

Action Man '67
The Art of the Steal '13
The Asphalt Jungle '50 ►
Assassins '95
Baby Driver '17 ►
The Brothers Bloom '09
Carnival of Wolves '96
The Chaperone '11
Chicago Overcoat '09
City of Industry '96
City on Fire '87
Collide '17
Columbus Day '08
Contraband '12
The Crew '08
Crime Wave '54
Dead or Alive '02
The Debt '03
Despicable Me 3 '17
Dillinger and Capone '95
Entrapment '99
Exiled '06
Fast Five '11
Fitzwilly '67
Ghetto Dawg 2: Out of the Pits '05
Going in Style '79 ►
Gone in 60 Seconds '00
The Good Samaritan '12
The Hard Word '02
Heat '95 ►
Heist '01 ►
In the Name of the King 3: The Last Mission '14
Innocent Bystanders '72
Jason Bourne '16
The Job '03
The Kane Files '10
The Killer '90 ►
Killer Instinct: From the Files of Agent Candice DeLong '03
The Last Lullaby '08 ►
The Last Run '71
Layer Cake '05 ►
Le Choc '82
Mechanic: Resurrection '16
The Mummy: Tomb of the Dragon Emperor '08
The November Man '14
The Old Man & the Gun '18 ►
Once a Thief '90
Out of Sight '98 ►
Predestination '15 ►
The Ref '93 ►
Reindeer Games '00
Reykjavik-Rotterdam '08
The Rundown '03
The Score '01
Seven Thieves '60 ►
Sexy Beast '00 ►
Sharpshooter '07
Shooters '00
The Sisters Brothers '18
Sister's Keeper '07
Small Time Crooks '00
Sniper 2 '02
Solo '06
The Squeeze '80
The Star '52 ►
Stash House '12
Takers '10
Thief '81 ►
Things to Do in Denver When You're Dead '95 ►
3 Days to Kill '14
Today You Die '05
Tough Guys '86
Two If by Sea '95
The Usual Suspects '95 ►

Only the Lonely

Adrift in Manhattan '07
The Adventures of Sharkboy and Lavagirl in 3-D '05
After the Wedding '06 ►
Alarm '08
All or Nothing '02
All That Heaven Allows '55 ►
Amelie '01 ►
The American '10
American Splendor '03 ►
Americano '11
Another Year '10 ►
The Art of Getting By '11
As It Is In Heaven '04
Audition '99
An Autumn Afternoon '62 ►
Avenue Montaigne '06
The Ballad of Little Jo '93
Barstool Cowboy '08
Beautiful Something '16
Bed of Roses '95
Besieged '98
Betrayal '74
Bird People '14
Birdman of Alcatraz '62 ►
The Body Shop '72
Born Romantic '00
Bossa Nova '99
Bread and Tulips '01 ►
Broken English '07
Broken Flowers '05
The Browning Version '51 ►
Buddy Boy '99
The Business of Strangers '01
Casual Encounters '16
The Cemetery Club '93
The Center of the World '01
Central Station '98 ►
Change My Life '01
Charlotte Sometimes '02
Choose Me '84 ►
A Chorus of Disapproval '89
A Christmas Without Snow '80
Citizen Kane '41 ►
The Closet '00
Conversations with Other Women '05
Cotter '72
Cowboys Don't Cry '88
Cyrano de Bergerac '25 ►
Cyrano de Bergerac '50 ►
Cyrano de Bergerac '90 ►
Dark Horse '11
Day Night Day Night '06 ►
Dead Letter Office '98
Deep Valley '47
Delirious '06
Desperately Seeking Susan '85
Distant Thunder '88
A Doll's House '73
A Doll's House '73 ►
Don McKay '09
Eagle *vs.* Shark '07
Easier With Practice '10
Eat Drink Man Woman '94 ►
The Eclipse '62 ►
Eighth Grade '18 ►
84 Charing Cross Road '86 ►
The Enchanted Cottage '45
E.T.: The Extra-Terrestrial '82 ►
Every Man for Himself & God Against All '75 ►
Expired '07
The Extra Man '10
Eye of the Needle '81
The Face of Love '13
Fallen Angel '45
Fanatic '82
Fat Kid Rules the World '12
Felicia's Journey '99 ►
Fever '99
Fiances '63
Fire '96
Forget Me Not '10
Full Moon in Blue Water '88
Full Moon in Paris '84
The Giant Mechanical Man '12
Ginger Snaps '01
God's Lonely Man '96
The Gun in Betty Lou's Handbag '92
Half Broken Things '07
Happy Endings '05
Hard Pill '05
Harold and Maude '71 ►
Hateship Loveship '13
The Heart Is a Lonely Hunter '68 ►
Heavy '94 ►
Henry Poole Is Here '08 ►
High School Big Shot '59
Hiroshima, Mon Amour '59 ►
Hit By Lightning '14
Hoffman '70
The Human Stain '03
The Hunchback of Notre Dame '39 ►
The Hunchback of Notre Dame '57
The Hunter '12
Husbands and Wives '92 ►
I Take This Woman '40
I Want Someone to Eat Cheese With '06
I Was Happy Here '66
In the Winter Dark '98
Internet Dating '08
An Invisible Sign '11
Is Anybody There? '08
I've Loved You So Long '08 ►
Jack Goes Boating '10
Joshy '16
Kaspar Hauser '93
Kumiko the Treasure Hunter '14 ►
La Leon '07
Labor Day '13
Lars and the Real Girl '07
The Last Best Year '90
Last Chance Harvey '08
The Legend of 1900 '98
Les Voleurs '96 ►
Let the Right One In '08
The Locket '02
The Lonely Guy '84
Lonely Hearts '82 ►
Lonely Hearts '06
The Lonely Passion of Judith Hearne '87 ►
Looking for Kitty '04
Lost in Translation '03 ►
Lovely, Still '08
Lovesong '17
Lulu on the Bridge '98
The Lunchbox '13
Luther the Geek '90
Madagascar Skin '95
Man of Flowers '84
Marty '55 ►
The Match Factory Girl '90 ►
Maudie '17 ►
Men Don't Leave '89
The Merry Gentleman '08
Middle of the Night '59
Midnight Clear '06
The Milk of Sorrow '09
Mind the Gap '04
Minnie and Moskowitz '71
Mrs. Palfrey at the Claremont '05
Moon '09
Mouchette '67 ►
Moving Malcolm '03
My First Mister '01
The New Romantic '18
The Night Digger '71
976-EVIL '88
Ninotchka '39 ►
The Noah '75
Noel '04
None But the Lonely Heart '44 ►
Not of This World '99
Notes from Underground '95
Nothing Personal '09
O Fantasma '00
Olive Kitteridge '14 ►
Once Around '91
Only the Lonely '91
Only You '92
Our Miss Brooks '56
Pan's Labyrinth '06 ►
Paper Man '09
The Passion of Anna '70 ►
Persona '66 ►
Pi '98
A Price Above Rubies '97
Priest of Love '81
Primal Secrets '94
The Prime of Miss Jean Brodie '69 ►
The Prince of Central Park '77 ►
Private Fears in Public Places '06
The Pursuit of Happiness '70
Queen of the Stardust Ballroom '75 ►
The Rachel Papers '89 ►
Rachel, Rachel '68 ►
Rapture '65
The Red Desert '64 ►
Red Kimono '25
Remember Sunday '13
Rhythm Thief '94
Richie Rich '94
Robinson Crusoe '54
Roman '06
Romantics Anonymous '10
Roseland '77 ►
Safety Not Guaranteed '12 ►
Samurai 2: Duel at Ichijoji Temple '55 ►
Scene of the Crime '87 ►
The Seagull '75
Seize the Day '86 ►
Separate Tables '58 ►
September '88
The Sergeant '68
7 Below '11
Sherman's March '86 ►
A Single Man '09 ►
A Single Shot '13
Sister '12
Sleepless in Seattle '93 ►
Snow Cake '06
Some Days Are Better Than Others '10
Someone to Love '87
Somersault '04
Something Wild '61
The Spectator '04
Speed Dating '07
Spider '02 ►
The Station Agent '03 ►
Stranger on the Prowl '52
Stuart Saves His Family '94
Summer '86 ►
Sunday '96
Sunday, Bloody Sunday '71 ►
Swedish Auto '06
Synecdoche, New York '08 ►
Terri '11
That Cold Day in the Park '69
That Evening Sun '09 ►
Til There Was You '96
Tomorrow '72 ►
12 and Holding '05 ►
Twin Falls Idaho '99 ►
The Undying '09
Unmade Beds '09
Vagabond '85 ►
The Village Barbershop '08
The Visitor '07 ►
Wakefield '17
The War Zone '98
Ward No. 6 '09
Waterloo Road '45
What Happened Was. . . '94
Where Are Your Children? '44
While You Were Sleeping '95 ►
The Whisperers '66
Willard '03
Wilson '17
Woman in the Shadows '34
World Traveler '01
The Young in Heart '38 ►

Opera

***See also** Musicals*

Bel Canto '18
Callas Forever '02
The Climax '44
Cosi '95 ►
Farinelli '94
The Fifth Element '97
Florence Foster Jenkins '16
Follow Your Heart '36
Foul Play '78 ►
The Glass Mountain '49
Harlem Aria '99
Interrupted Melody '55 ►
Joyeux Noel '05 ►
Madame Butterfly '95
The Man Who Cried '00
Marguerite '16 ►
Merci Docteur Rey '04 ►
Naughty Marietta '35
A Night at the Opera '35 ►
One Chance '13
Opera '88
Pavarotti '19
The Perfect Husband '92
The Phantom of the Opera '62
The Phantom of the Opera '90
The Phantom of the Opera '98
The Phantom of the Opera '04
Piano Tuner of Earthquakes '05
Puccini for Beginners '06
Quartet '12
Rhapsody of Spring '98
Riding Alone for Thousands of Miles '05
Romance '30
Serenade '56
So This Is Love '53
Stingaree '34
This Time for Keeps '47
To Rome with Love '12
Tonight or Never '31
Torrent '26

► = rated three bones or higher

- Two Sisters From Boston '46
- Wife, Husband and Friend '39

Orchestra Conductors

- The Concert '09
- Counterpoint '67
- Fantasia '40 ►
- Interlude '68
- I've Always Loved You '46
- The Red Shoes '48 ►
- Unfaithfully Yours '48 ►
- Unfaithfully Yours '84
- Youth '15

Order in the Court

See also Justice Prevails...?; Law & Military Crimes & Trials

- Absence of Malice '81
- The Accused '88 ►
- Adam's Rib '50 ►
- Alimony Madness '33
- Alleged '10
- Amanda Knox: Murder on Trail in Italy '11
- Amazing Dr. Clitterhouse '38 ►
- The Ambush Murders '82
- An American Crime '07
- An American Tragedy '31
- American Tragedy '00
- Anatomy of a Murder '59 ►
- And Justice for All '79
- The Andersonville Trial '70 ►
- Angel Face '52 ►
- Artemisia '97
- Bee Movie '07
- Beefcake '99
- Before and After '95
- Beyond a Reasonable Doubt '56
- Big Daddy '99
- The Black Legion '37 ►
- Blind Faith '98
- Blind Trust '06
- Blood and Orchids '86
- Blue-Eyed Butcher '12
- Body Chemistry 4: Full Exposure '95
- Body of Evidence '92
- Boomerang '47 ►
- Bordertown '35
- Bounce '00
- Breaker Morant '80 ►
- Broken Trust '95
- The Burning Bed '85 ►
- The Caine Mutiny Court Martial '88 ►
- Career Woman '36
- The Case for Christmas '11
- The Case of the Curious Bride '35
- The Castle '97
- Cause Celebre '87 ►
- Chains '49
- The Chamber '96
- The Chatterley Affair '06
- The Cheat '31
- Chicago '27
- Chicago 10 '07 ►
- Citizen Jane '09
- A Civil Action '98
- Class Action '91 ►
- The Client '94
- Closed Circuit '13
- Cole Younger, Gunfighter '58
- Comedy of Power '06
- Compulsion '59 ►
- Conduct Unbecoming '75
- The Confession '98
- Conspiracy: The Trial of the Chicago Eight '87 ►
- The Conspirator '10
- The Court Martial of Billy Mitchell '55 ►
- A Covenant With Death '67
- Crazy in Alabama '99
- Crime Broker '94
- Crimebroker '93
- Criminal Intent '05
- Criminal Lawyer '51
- Crossroads '42
- The Crucible '96 ►
- A Cry in the Dark '88 ►
- Cry Rape! '73
- A Dad for Christmas '06
- Dancer in the Dark '99
- Dangerous Beauty '98 ►
- Dangerous Evidence: The Lori Jackson Story '99
- A Date With Darkness '03
- Deacon Brodie '98
- Dead by Sunset '95
- Deadlocked '00
- Dear God '96
- A Death in California '85
- Death Sentence '74
- The Defense Rests '34
- Defenseless '91
- Degree of Guilt '95
- Deliberate Intent '01
- Denial '16
- Design for Scandal '41
- The Devil & Daniel Webster '41 ►
- The Devil's Advocate '97
- Devil's Knot '14
- Dirty Pictures '00
- The Disappearance of Vonnie '94
- Disclosure '94
- Dishonored Lady '47
- Dr. Jekyll and Mr. Hyde '08
- A Dry White Season '89 ►
- The Earl of Chicago '40
- Emma '32
- Ernest Goes to Jail '90
- The Escape Artist '13 ►
- Eureka! '81
- Evelyn '02 ►
- Evelyn Prentice '34
- The Exorcism of Emily Rose '05 ►
- Extremely Wicked, Shockingly Evil and Vile '19
- The Family Secret '51
- A Fever In the Blood '61
- A Few Good Men '92 ►
- Final Justice '98
- Final Verdict '91
- Find Me Guilty '06 ►
- Flash of Genius '08
- A Free Soul '31
- From the Hip '86
- Getting Gotti '94
- Ghosts of Mississippi '96
- Gideon's Trumpet '80
- The Gift '00
- A Girl Cut in Two '07
- The Girl in the News '41
- The Girl in the Red Velvet Swing '55
- A Girl Like Me: The Gwen Araujo Story '06
- The Girl Who Kicked the Hornet's Nest '10
- God on Trial '08
- The Good Father '87 ►
- The Good Fight '92
- The Good Mother '88
- Gospa '94
- The Great American Sex Scandal '94
- Guilty as Sin '93
- Hannah Arendt '12
- Heart of the Beholder '05 ►
- Held Hostage '09
- Her Fatal Flaw '06
- Hostile Witness '68
- How Many Miles to Babylon? '82
- Howl '10
- The Hurricane '99 ►
- I Want to Live! '58 ►
- Illegally Yours '87
- In the Name of the Father '93 ►
- InAlienable '08
- Incident in an Alley '62
- Indictment: The McMartin Trial '95 ►
- Inherit the Wind '60 ►
- Inherit the Wind '99
- The Inveterate Bachelor '58
- Jaded '96
- The Jagged Edge '85
- Jailbait: Betrayed By Innocence '86
- Jasper, Texas '03
- Jeanne la Pucelle '94
- Joan of Arc '99
- John Grisham's The Rainmaker '97
- The Judge '49
- The Judge '14
- Judgment at Nuremberg '61 ►
- Judgment in Berlin '88
- Judicial Indiscretion '07
- The Juror '96
- Jury Duty '95
- A Killing in a Small Town '90 ►
- King and Country '64 ►
- Knock on Any Door '49
- Knots '05
- The Last Letter '04
- The Last Wave '77 ►
- Legalese '98
- Legally Blonde '01
- The Legend of Lizzie Borden '75 ►
- The Letter '29
- Liar Liar '97
- Libel '59
- The Lincoln Lawyer '11
- The List '99
- A Little Thing Called Murder '06
- Lizzie Borden Took an Ax '14
- The Long Dark Hall '51
- The Love God? '70
- Loving '16 ►
- Lucky Partners '40
- Lured Innocence '97
- Madame X '29
- Madame X '37
- Madame X '66
- Made On Broadway '33
- Madeleine '50
- Maid of Salem '37
- The Man in the Glass Booth '75 ►
- A Map of the World '99
- The Merchant of Venice '04 ►
- Midnight '34
- Midnight in the Garden of Good and Evil '97
- Midnight Mary '33
- Miracle on 34th Street '47 ►
- Miracle on 34th Street '94
- Mrs. Harris '05
- Mr. Deeds Goes to Town '36 ►
- Mistrial '96
- Monsieur Beaucaire '24
- Moonlight Mile '02 ►
- Move Over, Darling '63
- Muhammad Ali's Greatest Fight '13
- Murder '30 ►
- Murder in the First '95
- Music Box '89
- My Cousin Vinny '92 ►
- My Sister's Keeper '09
- Naked Lie '89
- Never Forget '91
- Never Take Candy From a Stranger '60
- The Next Best Thing '00
- Night Falls on Manhattan '96 ►
- The Notorious Landlady '62
- Nuremberg '00
- Nutcracker: Money, Madness & Murder '87 ►
- Nuts '87 ►
- Obsessed '02
- On the Basis of Sex '18
- One Angry Juror '10
- One Way '06
- Operation Secret '52
- Orchids to You '35
- The Other Woman '08
- Painted Faces '29
- The Paradine Case '47
- Passion of Joan of Arc '28 ►
- The Pastor's Wife '11
- The People Against O'Hara '51
- The People *vs.* Dr. Kildare '41
- The People *vs.* Larry Flynt '96 ►
- Perfect Strangers '50
- Perry Mason Returns '85 ►
- Phil Spector '13
- Philadelphia '93 ►
- Piccadilly '29
- Presumed Innocent '90 ►
- Primal Fear '96
- Prisoners of the Sun '91 ►
- Prosecuting Casey Anthony '13
- Psychopath '97
- Rampage '87
- The Reader '08
- Red Corner '97
- Red Kimono '25
- Remember the Night '40 ►
- Return to Paradise '98 ►
- Reversal of Fortune '90 ►
- The Rite '69
- River Red '98
- Romance of the Limberlost '38
- The Rose Garden '89
- Roses Are for the Rich '87
- Roxie Hart '42
- Rules of Engagement '00
- Runaway Jury '03 ►
- Sacco & Vanzetti '71
- See No Evil: The Moors Murders '06
- The Sellout '51
- Seminole '53
- Separate but Equal '91 ►
- A Separation '11
- Sergeant Rutledge '60 ►
- Sex & Lies in Sin City: The Ted Binion Scandal '08
- Shadow of Doubt '98
- The Shaggy Dog '06
- Shattered City: The Halifax Explosion '03
- Silent Victim '92
- A Simple Twist of Fate '94
- Sleepers '96
- Smart Woman '48
- Snow Falling on Cedars '99
- The Social Network '10 ►
- Souls at Sea '37
- Stairway to Heaven '46 ►
- The Star Chamber '83
- State's Attorney '31
- Steve Martini's The Judge '01
- Story of Mankind '57
- A Stranger in the Kingdom '98
- Stranger on Horseback '55
- Stronger Than Desire '39
- Stuck on You '84
- Suspect '87
- Swing Vote '99
- Swoon '91 ►
- Tammy Tell Me True '61
- Term of Trial '63
- They Won't Believe Me '47 ►
- Three Brave Men '57
- A Time to Kill '96 ►
- To Kill a Mockingbird '62 ►
- Tom and Huck '95 ►
- Too Young to Die '90
- Torso '02
- Town without Pity '61
- Trial '55
- The Trial '63 ►
- The Trial '93
- The Trial '10
- Trial & Error '62
- Trial and Error '96
- Trial by Jury '94
- The Trial of Lee Harvey Oswald '77
- The Trial of Old Drum '00
- The Trials of Cate McCall '13
- The Trials of Oscar Wilde '60 ►
- True Confession '37
- 12 '07
- Twelve Angry Men '57 ►
- 22 July '18
- Twilight of Honor '63
- Unthinkable '07
- Upperworld '34
- Valerie '57
- The Verdict '82 ►
- Verdict on Auschwitz: The Frankfurt Auschwitz Trial 1963-1965 '93 ►
- We Live Again '34
- The Weight of Water '00
- Welcome to Marwen '18
- What Color Is Love? '08
- When Every Day Was the Fourth of July '78
- Where Love Has Gone '64
- Where the Truth Lies '99
- White Mischief '88 ►
- White Squall '96
- The Whole Truth '16
- Why Do Fools Fall in Love? '98
- Wild Boys of the Road '33
- Wilde '97
- The Winslow Boy '48 ►
- Witness for the Prosecution '57 ►
- The Wives He Forgot '06
- Wives under Suspicion '38
- The Woman From Monte Carlo '31
- Woman in Brown '48
- The Woman in Red '35
- A Woman's Face '38 ►
- A Woman's Face '41 ►
- The World Was His Jury '58
- You Don't Know Jack '10
- The Young Philadelphians '59 ►
- The Young Savages '61
- ZigZag '70

Organ Transplants

See also Disease of the Week; Doctors & Hospitals & Second Chance

- Abduction '07
- The Awful Dr. Orloff '62
- Black Friday '40
- Blood Work '02
- Brain of Blood '71
- The Brain that Wouldn't Die '63
- Brainwaves '82
- Clone Hunter '09
- Dead Man's Eyes '44
- The Eye '08
- The 5th Quarter '10
- Ghost in the Shell '17
- Heart '99
- Heart of a Stranger '02
- The House of Tomorrow '18
- Hybrid '07
- I'll Bury You Tomorrow '02
- In the Eyes of a Killer '09
- The Incredible Two-Headed Transplant '71
- The Indian '07
- Inhale '10
- The Intruder '04 ►
- John Q '02
- Killer Deal '99
- Lowlife '18
- The Man with Two Brains '83 ►
- New Blood '99
- Night of the Bloody Apes '68
- Operation Heartbeat '69
- Paris '08
- Race Against Time '00
- Repo Men '10
- Repo! The Genetic Opera '08
- Return to Me '00
- A Stranger's Heart '07
- 13 Moons '02
- Train '08
- 21 Grams '03 ►
- Untamed Heart '93
- Young Frankenstein '74 ►

Organized Crime

See also Crimedy; Disorganized Crime; Gangs; Moscow Mafia; Triads; Urban Gangstas; Yakuza

- Absence of Malice '81
- The Accountant '16
- Across 110th Street '72
- Across the Line: The Exodus of Charlie Wright '10
- Acts of Violence '18
- The Aggression Scale '12
- Alibi '29
- All the Money in the World '17
- Alphabet City '84
- American Born '89
- American Chinatown '96
- American Cousins '02
- American Hustle '13 ►
- American Justice '86
- The American Soldier '70
- American Yakuza '94
- Analyze That '02
- Analyze This '98 ►
- Angel's Dance '99
- Angels Wash Their Faces '39
- Angels with Dirty Faces '38 ►
- Another Stakeout '93
- Armed Response '86
- Arsenal '17
- As Tears Go By '88 ►
- Ash Is Purest White '18 ►
- Atlantic City '81 ►
- Avenging Disco Godfather '76
- Back to Back '96
- Backtrack '89 ►
- Bad Ass '09
- Bad Boys for Life '20
- Bad Day for the Cut '17
- Ball of Fire '41 ►
- The Bannen Way '10
- Batman Begins '05 ►
- Be Cool '05
- The Beast of the City '32
- Beautiful Joe '00
- Bedevilled '55
- Best of the Best: Without Warning '98
- A Better Way to Die '00
- Beverly Hills Cop 3 '94
- Beyond the Trophy '12
- Big Bad Mama 2 '87
- The Big Caper '57
- Big Combo '55 ►
- The Big Hit '98
- The Big I Am '10
- Big News '29
- The Big Slice '90
- Billy Bathgate '91
- Birds of Prey: And the Fantabulous Emancipation of One Harley Quinn '20
- Birth of the Blues '41
- Bitter Sweet '98
- Black Belt Jones '74
- Black Caesar '73
- Black Godfather '74
- Black Gunn '72
- Black Lemons '70
- Black Mass '15
- Black Shampoo '76
- Blackway '16
- Blank Check '93
- Blind Fury '90
- Blood & Concrete: A Love Story '91
- Blood Money '98
- Blood Money '99
- Blood Vows: The Story of a Mafia Wife '87
- Blues in the Night '41
- Body Trouble '92
- Bonanno: A Godfather's Story '99
- Bonded by Blood '09
- Bookies '03
- Boondock Saints '99
- The Boss '56
- The Boss '73
- Boss of Bosses '99
- Bought and Sold '03
- Bound '96
- The Box '03
- The Boys '97
- Branded to Kill '67
- The Breaking Point '50 ►
- Brighton Rock '47 ►
- A Bronx Tale '93 ►
- Brooklyn Rules '07
- A Brooklyn State of Mind '97
- Brother '97
- The Brotherhood '68
- The Brothers Rico '57
- Bugsy '91 ►
- Bugsy Malone '76
- A Bullet for Joey '55
- Bullets over Broadway '94 ►
- B.U.S.T.E.D. '99
- The Busy Body '67
- The Butcher '07
- BuyBust '18
- By the Gun '14
- Caliber 9 '72
- Capone '89
- Capone '20
- The Captive City '52
- Car 54, Where Are You? '94
- Ca$h '06
- Casino '95 ►
- A Cat in Paris '11
- Chandler '71
- Charlie Countryman '13
- Chasing Ghosts '05
- Chicago Confidential '57
- The Chinatown Murders: Man against the Mob '89
- Chow Bella '98

► = rated three bones or higher

City Hall '95 ▶
City Unplugged '95
Cleaverville '07
The Client '94
Cocaine and Blue Eyes '83
Code of Honor '16
Cohen and Tate '88
Coldblooded '94
The Collectors '99
Connie and Carla '04
Contraband '12
Contract on Cherry Street '77
Cookie '89
Cop in Blue Jeans '78
Cops and Robbersons '94
Corky Romano '01
The Corruptor '99 ▶
The Cotton Club '84 ▶
Crazy Six '98
The Crew '00
The Crew '08
Crime Boss '72
Crime Spree '03
Crimes of Fashion '04
The Crowd Roars '38
Crypto '19
Dangerous Charter '62
Darkman 3: Die Darkman Die '95
Day at the Beach '98
Dead Cert '10
Dead Heat '01
Dead Lenny '06
Dead Pigeon on Beethoven Street '72
Dead Silent '99
Deadly Game '98
Deadly Target '94
Deadly Weapons '70
Death Force '78
Death to Smoochy '02
Death Wish 5: The Face of Death '94
The Debt '98
Decisions '10
The Departed '06 ▶
Desperate '47 ▶
Desperate Crimes '93
Deuces Wild '02
The Devil's Dominoes '07
The Devil's in the Details '13
Dick Tracy '90 ▶
Dinner Rush '00 ▶
Dirty Deeds '02 ▶
District 13: Ultimatum '09
Doctor Detroit '83
Dog Eat Dog '16
The Dogfather '10
Dolan's Cadillac '09
The Don Is Dead '73
Donnie Brasco '96 ▶
Doorway to Hell '30
Double Bang '01
Doughboys '08
The Drag-Net '36
Dress to Kill '07
The Drop '14 ▶
Drunken Angel '48 ▶
The Earl of Chicago '40
Eastside '99
Easy Money '10 ▶
Easy Money: Hard to Kill '12
El Padrino '04
Elmore Leonard's Gold Coast '97
The Embalmer '03 ▶
Empire of the Wolves '05
The Enforcer '51
Ernest Goes to Jail '90
Escobar: Paradise Lost '15
Essex Boys '99
Eureka! '81
Excellent Cadavers '99
Excessive Force '93
Exclusive Story '36
The Executioner, Part 2: Frozen Scream '84
Exiled '06
Extremely Dangerous '99
An Eye for an Eye '81
Fake '10
Fake Out '82
The Fall of the American Empire '19
The Family '70
The Family '13
Family of Cops 2: Breach of Faith '97
Federal Protection '02
Final Justice '84
Fingers '78 ▶
Fireback '78
The Firm '93 ▶
First Degree '95
Fist of Honor '92
The Fixer '97
Flash Point '07
Fled '96
Fog Over Frisco '34
Force of Evil '49 ▶
Force of Execution '13
Forced to Fight '11
Freezer '14
The Freshman '90
Friends and Family '01
The Frightened City '61
Frogs for Snakes '98
Fugitive Rage '96
The Funeral '96 ▶
The Gambler '14
Gangster No. 1 '00
Gangster Squad '13
The Garment Jungle '57
The George Raft Story '61
Get Rita '75
Getting Gotti '94
Ghetto Dawg 2: Out of the Pits '05
Ghetto Dawg '02
Ghost Dog: The Way of the Samurai '99
Gigli '03
Ginostra '02
The Girl Who Had Everything '53
The Girl Who Knew Too Much '69
Give 'Em Hell Malone '09
Gloria '80
Gloria '98
Go Into Your Dance '35
The Godfather '72 ▶
The Godfather, Part 2 '74 ▶
The Godfather, Part 3 '90 ▶
The Godson '98
Gomorrah '08 ▶
The Good Samaritan '12
Goodfellas '90 ▶
Gotti '96
Gozu '03
The Guilty Generation '31
Gun Shy '00
Gunshy '98 ▶
Hail Mafia '65
The Hangover, Part III '13
Hard-Boiled '92
The Harder They Fall '56 ▶
Harlem Nights '89
Harvard Man '01
Hawk's Vengeance '96
He Sees You When You're Sleeping '02
Headshot '17
Heat '87
Hell Up in Harlem '73
Hey! Hey! USA! '38
Hiding Out '87
High Heels and Low Lifes '01
High Voltage '98
Highway '01
Hijack Highway '55
Hired to Kill '73
A History of Violence '05 ▶
Hit Lady '74
Hit the Dutchman '92
The Hitman Diaries '09
Hitman's Journal '99
Hitman's Run '99
The Hollow Point '16
Hollywood Cop '87
Hollywood Man '76
The Hollywood Sign '01
Homicide '49
Honor Thy Father '73
Hoodlum '96
Hoodlum & Son '03
Hoods '98
Hot Cars '56
House of the Rising Sun '11
How to Kill a Judge '75
Hurricane Smith '92
The Hustle '08
I Accidentally Domed Your Son '04
I Died a Thousand Times '55
I, Mobster '58
Ice '93
The Ice Harvest '05
Il Divo '08
I'll Sleep When I'm Dead '03 ▶
I'll Wait for You '41
Illegal Business '06
Illegal Tender '07
In Bruges '08
In Order of Disappearance '14
In the Electric Mist '08
In the Mix '05
Infernal Affairs '02 ▶
Infernal Affairs 2 '03
Infernal Affairs 3 '03
The Infiltrator '16
Innocent Blood '92
Inside Out '11
Internes Can't Take Money '37
Island of Love '63
It All Came True '40
The Italian Connection '73
I've Got Your Number '34
Jersey Boys '14
Jesse Stone: No Remorse '10
Johnny Cool '63
The Juror '96
Just Getting Started '17
Kansas City '95 ▶
Keaton's Cop '90
Keyhole '11
Kid Monk Baroni '52
Kill Me Again '89
Kill the Irishman '11
The Killer '90 ▶
The Killers '46 ▶
The Killing Man '94
The Killing of a Chinese Bookie '76
Killing Them Softly '12
The King '18
The King of the Roaring '20s: The Story of Arnold Rothstein '61
King of the Underworld '39
Kings of South Beach '07
Kiss of Death '94
Kiss Toledo Goodbye '00
Kiss Tomorrow Goodbye '50
The Kitchen '19
Knockaround Guys '01
Knucklehead '10
La Scorta '94 ▶
Lady Jayne Killer '03
Lady of the Evening '75
Lansky '99
The Last Days of Frankie the Fly '96
The Last Don 2 '98
The Last Don '97
Last Exit to Brooklyn '90 ▶
The Last Godfather '10
Last Rites '88
The Last Run '71
The Last Shot '04
The Last Word '95
Lawless '12
Layer Cake '05 ▶
Leaves of Grass '09
Lepke '75
Life Tastes Good '99
Lila & Eve '15
The Line '08
Little Caesar '30 ▶
Little Cigars '73
Little Odessa '94
Live by Night '16
Loan Shark '52
Logan's War: Bound by Honor '98
London Boulevard '10
The Long Good Friday '80 ▶
The Lookalike '14
Looper '12 ▶
Lorna's Silence '08
The Lost Capone '90 ▶
Lost Highway '96
Love, Honour & Obey '00
Love That Brute '50
Love to Kill '97
Luck of the Draw '00
Lucky Grandma '20
Lucky Luciano '74
Lucky Number Slevin '06
Ma and Pa Kettle Go to Town '50
Macbeth '06
Machine Gun McCain '69
Mad Dog and Glory '93 ▶
Mad Dog Coll '61
Made '01
Madea's Witness Protection '12
Madigan's Millions '67
Mafia! '98
Mafioso '62
Magic Kid '92
Making the Grade '84
Mambo Cafe '00
The Man I Love '46 ▶
Man in the Vault '56
Man with a Gun '95
Manderlay '05
Manhunt '73
Married to the Mob '88 ▶
Mauvais Sang '86
The Mayor of Hell '33
Me and the Mob '94
Mean Machine '73
Mean Streets '73 ▶
The Mechanic '72
Meet Him and Die '76
Melvin Purvis: G-Man '74
Men of Respect '91
Mercenary: Absolution '15
Miami Connection '87
The Miami Story '54
Mickey Blue Eyes '99
Mickey One '65
Middle Men '10
Mikey & Nicky '76
Miller's Crossing '90 ▶
Miracles '89
Miss Bala '12
Missing Girls '36
The Mission '99
Mr. Majestyk '74
Mr. Soft Touch '49
The Mob '51
Mobsters '91
Money Kings '98
Monsieur Gangster '63
Moon over Harlem '39
Moscow Heat '04
Moving Target '89
Moving Target '96
Mulholland Falls '95
Murder, Inc. '60
My Blue Heaven '90
My Silent Partner '06
The Mysteries of Pittsburgh '08
The Narrow Margin '52 ▶
The Narrows '08
National Lampoon's The Don's Analyst '97
Necessity '88
The Nest '02
New Blood '99
New Mafia Boss '72
New Orleans Uncensored '55
Next of Kin '89
The Nickel Ride '74
1931: Once Upon a Time in New York '72
Nitti: The Enforcer '88
No Blood No Tears '02 ▶
No Way Back '96
Nowhere Land '98
No. 3 '97
Odd Jobs '85
Offensive Behaviour '04
Once a Thief '96 ▶
Once Upon a Time in America '84 ▶
Once Upon a Time in Brooklyn '13
Organized Crime & Triad Bureau '93
Osso Bucco '08
Our Kind of Traitor '16
Out for Justice '91
The Outfit '73
Over-Exposed '56
Overdrive '17
Paid '30
Panic Button '62
Paper Bullets '41
Paper Bullets '99
Party Girl '58 ▶
Passion Play '10
Penthouse '33 ▶
Perfect Killer '77
Perfect Witness '89
Perrier's Bounty '09
The Phantom '09
The Phenix City Story '55
The Pick-Up Artist '87
Pieta '13 ▶
Piranhas '19
Played '06
Players '03
The Plot Against Harry '69 ▶
Point Blank '67
Police Academy 7: Mission to Moscow '94
Politics '31
Port of New York '49
Portland Expose '57
Power and Beauty '02
Power of Attorney '94
Pray for Death '85
Prime Target '91
Prizzi's Honor '85 ▶
The Proposal '00
Proud Mary '18
The Public Eye '92 ▶
Public Menace '35
Pulp Fiction '94 ▶
Quick '93
The Quickie '01
Race Street '48
Rancid Aluminium '00
Rapid Fire '92
Raw Deal '86
Recoil '97
The Red-Haired Alibi '32
Red Heat '88
Red Line '96
The Replacement Killers '98
The Return of Joe Rich '11
The Revenger '90
Ricco '74
Ring of Fire 3: Lion Strike '94
Ring of the Musketeers '93
Riot on 42nd Street '87
Ripley's Game '02 ▶
The Rise and Fall of Legs Diamond '60
The Rise of the Krays '16
Road to Perdition '02 ▶
The Roaring Twenties '39 ▶
Rob the Mob '14
Rock, Baby, Rock It '57
RocknRolla '08
Romeo Is Bleeding '93
Romeo Must Die '00
Ruby '92
Rude Boy: The Jamaican Don '03
Rulers of the City '76
Rulers of the City '77
The Runner '99
Running Scared '06
Rush Hour 3 '07
Ruslan '09
Safe Men '98
Samurai Cop '89
Scarface '31 ▶
A Score to Settle '19
The Secret Six '31 ▶
Secrets of an Undercover Wife '07
Setup '11
Shade '03
Shadows and Lies '10
Shaft's Big Score '72
Shoot First, Die Later '74
Showdown '94
Shut-Eye '03
The Sicilian Girl '09
Sister Street Fighter 2: Hanging by a Thread '74
Sitting Ducks '80 ▶
600 Miles '16
Skidoo '68
The Slams '73
Slaughter '72
Slaughter's Big Ripoff '73
Sleepers '96
Sleepless '17
A Slight Case of Murder '38
Smalltime '96
Smart Blonde '37
Smashing the Rackets '38
Smokin' Aces '07
Snatch '00 ▶
Society Lawyer '39
Solo '06
Soul Survivor '95
Southie '98
Speed Kills '18
Spin a Dark Web '56
Stand-In '85
Stand Off '11
A Stand Up Guy '16
Stark Raving Mad '02
State of Grace '90 ▶
Staten Island '09
State's Attorney '31
Stephen King's Thinner '96
Sticks '98
Stiletto '08
Stiletto Dance '01
The Stone Killer '73
Stonebrook '98
Street Boss '09
Street Gun '96
Street People '76
Street War '76
Sugartime '95
The System '53
T-Men '47 ▶
The Take '74
The Take '09
Target for Killing '66
Taxi! '32
The Taxman '98
Temptress Moon '96
The Tenderfoot '32
10th & Wolf '06
Terminal Force '88
The Terror of the Tongs '61
Thick as Thieves '99
Thief '81 ▶
Things Change '88 ▶
Third World Cop '99
This Day and Age '33
The Threepenny Opera '31
Thugs '96
Ticket of Leave Man '37
TKO '06
To Die For '95 ▶
To the Limit '95
Tomorrow We Live '42
Tony Rome '67
Total Western '00
The Trap '59
Trespass Against Us '16
Trial by Jury '94
The Tribe '15 ▶
Trigger Happy '96
Trojan Eddie '96 ▶
True Romance '93
24 Hours in London '00
Ultimate Heist '09
Under Hellgate Bridge '99
The Undertaker's Wedding '97
Underworld '96
Underworld U.S.A. '61 ▶
Undisputed 2: Last Man Standing '06
Unleashed '05
The Untouchables '87 ▶
The Valachi Papers '72
Vault '19
Velvet Smooth '76
Venus and Vegas '10
Veronica Guerin '03
Vice Raid '60
The Voice of the City '29
Wannabes '01
Wanted '98
Weary River '29
West New York '96
Whacked! '02
What Doesn't Kill You '08
What Up? '08
Where the Hot Wind Blows '59
Where the Sidewalk Ends '50
White Heat '49 ▶
White Hot: The Mysterious Murder of Thelma Todd '91
White Sands '92
The Whole Ten Yards '04
Who's Got the Action? '63
The Wild Card '03
Wild Card '15
Wiretapper '55
Wise Guys '86
Wisegal '08
Wisegirls '02
Witness Protection '99 ▶
Witness to the Mob '98
Wolves in the Snow '02
The Woman Racket '30
The Wrestler '73

▶ = rated three bones or higher

Wrong Side of Town '10
Wrong Turn at Tahoe '09
The Yellow Rolls Royce '64
You Can't Escape Forever '42
Young Man With Ideas '52
Zatoichi: The Life and Opinion of Masseur Ichi '62
Zatoichi: Zatoichi's Flashing Sword '64
Zebra Force '76

Ostracism

Disobedience '17

Otherwise Engaged

***See also** Romantic Triangles; Wedding Bells; Wedding Hell*

ABCD '99
The Accidental Husband '08
Across the Hall '09
Across to Singapore '28
An Affair to Remember '57
After Tomorrow '32
The Age of Innocence '34
The Age of Innocence '93▶
Air Eagles '31
Aladdin '92▶
Alibi Ike '35
Alleged '10
An Alligator Named Daisy '55
Always Goodbye '38
American Crude '07
Arthur '81▶
Au Pair '99
The Bachelor '99
Bachelor Flat '62
The Bachelor Weekend '13
Baggage Claim '13
Ball & Chain '04
The Barbarian '33
The Battle of Shaker Heights '03
The Baxter '05
Bell, Book and Candle '58
Belladonna '08
Best Friends '75
The Big Hit '98
The Birdcage '95▶
Bitter/Sweet '09
Black Widow Murders: The Blanche Taylor Moore Story '93
Blind Date '87
Blind Dating '06
Breakfast for Two '37
The Breakup Artist '04
Bridesmaids '11▶
The Brothers '01▶
Bubble Boy '01
Calcutta '47
Captain Corelli's Mandolin '01
The Careless Years '57
Catherine Cookson's The Black Candle '92
Catherine Cookson's The Wingless Bird '97
Chicken Tikka Masala '05
Christina '10
A Christmas Wedding '06
Clarissa '91▶
Clerks 2 '06▶
Come as You Are '05
Come Dance at My Wedding '09
Come September '61
Coming to America '88▶
Confessions of an American Bride '05
Congratulations '13
Cracked Nuts '31
The Craigslist Killer '11
Cupid & Cate '00
Curse of the Faceless Man '58
A Date With the Falcon '42
Daughters Courageous '39
Dear Heart '64▶
The Decoy Bride '11
Deep Waters '48
Dinner and Driving '97
Divine Secrets of the Ya-Ya Sisterhood '02
Dr. Kildare's Crisis '40
A Dog's Breakfast '07
Dot the I '03
Douchebag '10
Dream Wife '53
East of the River '40
East Side of Heaven '39
Easy to Wed '46
8mm 2 '05
Emma '97▶
Eva '62
Everyone Says I Love You '96▶
Faithless '32
The Falcon in Danger '43
The Family Stone '05
Fandango '85
Fantastic Four '05
The Fiance '96
Fiances '63
Fill the Void '12
Final Engagement '07
The Finances of the Grand Duke '24
Firefall '94
The First to Go '97
The Five-Year Engagement '12
Flame in the Streets '61
The Florentine '98
Fog Over Frisco '34
For the Love of Grace '08
Forces of Nature '99
The Four Feathers '02
A Four Letter Word '07
Four Weddings and a Funeral '94▶
Four Wives '39
Four's a Crowd '38
Frankenhooker '90
Frat Party '09
French Kiss '95
Friends and Family '01
Gabriela '01
The Gay Falcon '41
George of the Jungle '97▶
George White's Scandals '45
Getting Gertie's Garter '27
Gildersleeve on Broadway '43
Goal 2: Living the Dream '07
A Golden Christmas 2: The Second Tail '11
Gone with the Wind '39▶
The Graduate '67▶
Gray Matters '06
Guess Who '05
A Guy Thing '03
The Hangover, Part 2 '11
Happy Times '00
Hard to Handle '33
Heartbreaker '10
Heights '04
Held Up '00
Her Fatal Flaw '06
High Society '56▶
His Girl Friday '40▶
Holiday Baggage '08
Holiday Engagement '11
Honeymoon '47
Hopelessly in June '11
Hotel de Love '96
The House of Yes '97
How to Deal '03
I Capture the Castle '02
I Do & I Don't '07
I Do (But I Don't) '04
I Hope They Serve Beer in Hell '09
I Love You, Man '09▶
The Illusionist '06
I'm Reed Fish '06
In and Out '97▶
In the Eyes of a Killer '09
The Infidel '10
The Intended '02
Intimate Betrayal '96
I.Q. '94
It Had to Be You '00
It Takes Two '95
It's Love I'm After '37
Jealousy '99
John Loves Mary '48
The Jolly Boys' Last Stand '00
Just One Night '00
Just One Time '00
Kathleen '41
The King's Guard '01
Kiss the Bride '07
Kiss Them for Me '57
Kiss Toledo Goodbye '00
Kissing a Fool '98
Laggies '13
The Last Time '06
Last Vegas '13
Laurel Canyon '02
Law and Order '53
Legally Blonde '01
Let Us Live '39
Letters to Juliet '10
License to Wed '07
Lies and Illusions '09
Lies and Whispers '98
Light in the Piazza '61
The Lively Set '64
The Locket '46
The Lone Wolf Meets a Lady '40
The Loneliest Planet '12
Lorna Doone '01▶
Love Affair '39▶
Love Affair '94
Love and Basketball '00▶
Love and Mary '07
Love Before Breakfast '36
Love Is News '37▶
The Love Letter '98
Lovers Courageous '32
Lucky Partners '40
Lucky Star '29
Made of Honor '08
Madea Goes to Jail '09
Maisie Was a Lady '41
Mama's Boy '07
Man of the World '31
The Man Who Played God '32
Marigold '07
Marry Me '10
Match Point '05▶
May in the Summer '13
Men in White '34
Merry Andrew '58
Merry In-Laws '12
Miami Rhapsody '95
Middle of the Night '59
Midnight in Paris '11▶
Miss Julie '99
Mission: Impossible 3 '06▶
Mississippi '35
Monogamy '10
Monster-in-Law '05
Moonstruck '87▶
More Sex and the Single Mom '05
Mulan 2 '04
Music from Another Room '97
My Best Friend's Wedding '97
My Best Girl '27▶
My Big Fat Greek Wedding '02
My Fake Fiance '09
My Faraway Bride '06
My Girlfriend's Back '10
My Mom's New Boyfriend '08
My Son, My Son, What Have Ye Done '09
The Mystery of Edwin Drood '12
Nature of the Beast '07
The New Twenty '08
Nice Guy Johnny '10
Night Shift '82
No Looking Back '98
The Note 2: Taking a Chance on Love '09
Oh, Men! Oh, Women! '57
The Old Settler '01
Older Than America '08
Once Upon a Time in China III '93▶
Once Upon a Wedding '05
One Way '06
One Week '08
One Wonderful Sunday '47
Onegin '99
Only You '94
Open Window '06
Our Mutual Friend '98
Out at the Wedding '07
Over Her Dead Body '08
The Overbrook Brothers '09
Paperback Romance '96
Peeples '13
The Perfect Wedding '12
Persuasion '71
The Philadelphia Story '40▶
Picture Perfect '96
The Price of Milk '00
Pride and Prejudice '95▶
Pride of the Marines '45▶
The Princess & the Call Girl '84
The Princess Bride '87▶
The Princess Diaries 2: Royal Engagement '04
The Proposal '09
Quentin Durward '55
Rachel Getting Married '08▶
Raiders of the Seven Seas '53
Rascals '38
The Reception '05
Red Ensign '34
Red: Werewolf Hunter '10
Relative Strangers '06
Relative Values '99
Revolution #9 '01
Ride Clear of Diablo '54
Rings on Her Fingers '42
River Street '95
The River Within '09
Robin Hood: Prince of Thieves '91
Romance of the Limberlost '38
The Romantics '10
The Room '03
The Rough and the Smooth '59
Rough Magic '95
A Royal Christmas '14
The Rum Diary '11
Rumor Has It. . . '05
Runaway Bride '99▶
Ruslan '09
Ruthless '48
Sabrina '95
Saving Silverman '01
Say It Isn't So '01
The Scarlet Tunic '97
A Secret Affair '99
Seeing Other People '04
Serendipity '01
Sergeant Deadhead '65
Seven Days' Leave '42
Shag: The Movie '89▶
Shakespeare in Love '98▶
Sharpe's Peril '08
Shooting Fish '98
Shopworn '32
Sideways '04▶
Silver Skates '43
Six Days, Seven Nights '98
Slave '09
Sleeping Dogs Lie '06
Sleepless in Seattle '93▶
The Smiling Ghost '41
Something Borrowed '11
Son-in-Law '93
Speechless '94
Speedy Death '99▶
Stealing Harvard '02
Storm Over the Nile '55
The Strangers '08
Sufat Chol '16▶
Sunday in New York '63
Sundays at Tiffany's '10
Sunny '30
Sweet Home Alabama '02
Swordsman of Siena '62
Swordsmen in Double Flag Town '91
Tarzan and the Lost City '98
10 Rules for Sleeping Around '13
Ten Thousand Bedrooms '57
The Tender Trap '55
That Old Feeling '96
That's My Boy '12
Their Own Desire '29
There Goes the Bride '32
13 Going on 30 '04
This Modern Age '31
Three Loves Has Nancy '38
Three Wise Women '11
To Rome with Love '12
Trial and Error '96
The Truth About Youth '30
27 Dresses '08
Tyler Perry's Good Deeds '12
Under the Yum-Yum Tree '63
The Uninvited '09
Unthinkable '07
Value for Money '55
A Very Long Engagement '04▶
A Very Special Favor '65
Wall Street 2: Money Never Sleeps '10
We Were Dancing '42
Wedding Crashers '05▶
Wedding Daze '06
The Wedding Director '06
The Wedding Night '35
The Wedding Planner '01
The Wedding Singer '97
The Wedding Song '09
Welcome Home Roscoe Jenkins '08
White Wedding '10
Who Made the Potatoe Salad? '05
A Wild Affair '63
Will You Merry Me? '08
William & Catherine: A Royal Romance '11
William & Kate '11
Window Theory '04
Wirey Spindell '99
The Wolfman '09
Working Miracles '10
You Again '10
You Can't Get Away With Murder '39
You Can't Take It With You '79
You Gotta Stay Happy '48
You Never Can Tell '51

Out of Order

***See also** Flashback*

Across the Hall '09
Always Will '06
Before the Devil Knows You're Dead '07▶
Big Fish '03▶
The Blackcoat's Daughter '17
Ca$h '06
Cashback '06
Deja Vu '06
Dunkirk '17▶
Following '99
The Fountain '06
Franklyn '08
Hero '02▶
Irreversible '02
Kill Bill Vol. 1 '03▶
Kill Bill Vol. 2 '04▶
The Killing '56▶
The Lake House '06
Memento '00▶
Peter and Vandy '09
Pinero '01
Premonition '07
Pulp Fiction '94▶
Reservoir Dogs '92▶
Staten Island '09
Submergence '18
Ten 'Til Noon '06
Tick Tock '00▶
Triangle '09
21 Grams '03▶
Vantage Point '08
What We Become '16
Wonderstruck '17

Out of This World Sex

***See also** Alien Babes; Alien Beings--Benign; Alien Beings--Vicious; Aliens Are People, Too; Space Operas*

Alien Visitor '95
Breeders '86
Decoys '04
Decoys: The Second Seduction '07
High Life '18
Species '95
Species 2 '98
The Twilight Saga: Breaking Dawn, Part 1 '11
2069: A Sex Odyssey '78

Pacific Islands

***See also** Island Fare*

Balboa '82
Battle at Bloody Beach '61
Blue Hawaii '62
BuyBust '18
Carlton Browne of the F.O. '59
Castaway '87
Cry Havoc '43
Cry of Battle '63
Danger Close '19
Don't Go Near the Water '57
Enchanted Island '58
Fighting Marines '36
First to Fight '67
Flags of Our Fathers '06▶
Fog Island '45
Food of the Gods '76
From Here to Eternity '53▶
Graceland '12
The Great Raid '05
Hell in the Pacific '69▶
His Majesty O'Keefe '53
The Island of Dr. Moreau '77
Island of the Hungry Ghosts '18
Jirga '19
The Kingmaker '19▶
The Last Flight of Noah's Ark '80
The Last Warrior '89
The Legend of Johnny Lingo '03
Letters from Iwo Jima '06▶
Lt. Robin Crusoe, U.S.N. '66
Mad Doctor of Blood Island '68
Malay Nights '32
The Mermaids of Tiburon '62
Midway '19
Miss Sadie Thompson '53▶
Mission Manila '87
Mr. Robinson Crusoe '32
Moana '16▶
Mysterious Island '61▶
The Nightingale '18▶
Noon Sunday '75
Operation Bikini '63
The Other Side of Heaven 2: Fire of Faith '19
The Pacific '10▶
Paradise, Hawaiian Style '66
Paradise Road '97
Pardon My Sarong '42
Pilot No. 5 '43
Pride of the Marines '45▶
The Proud and Profane '56
Rain '32
Reel Paradise '05▶
Rodgers & Hammerstein's South Pacific '01
Sailor of the King '53
Salute to the Marines '43
Sisters of War '10
South Pacific '58▶
South Sea Woman '53
Stand by for Action '42
Storm Boy
Tabu: A Story of the South Seas '31▶
Tora! Tora! Tora! '70
True History of the Kelly Gang '20
Unbroken '14
Wackiest Ship in the Army '61
Wake Island '42▶
White Shadows in the South Seas '29
Windtalkers '02
The Year of Living Dangerously '82▶

Painting

***See** Art & Artists*

Paperboys

The Benchwarmers '06
Better Off Dead '85
The Brady Bunch Movie '95▶
Newsies '92
The Paperboy '12
While You Were Sleeping '95▶
Willy Wonka & the Chocolate Factory '71▶

Parades & Festivals

***See also** Carnivals & Circuses*

Barney's Great Adventure '98
Doc Hollywood '91
Easter Parade '48▶
Ferris Bueller's Day Off '86▶
Festival Express '03▶

▶ = rated three bones or higher

The Fugitive '93 ▸
Groundhog Day '93 ▸
Jingle All the Way '96
Love at the Thanksgiving Day Parade '12
The Matchmaker '97
Miracle on 34th Street '47 ▸
Miracle on 34th Street '94
National Lampoon's Animal House '78 ▸
Pokemon the Movie: The Power of Us '18
State of Grace '90 ▸
Waiting for Guffman '96

Paradise Gone Awry

The Beach '00
Club Paradise '86
Dead Water '19
Kiss the Sky '98
Mary '19
The Mosquito Coast '86
Six Days, Seven Nights '98
Welcome to the Jungle '13

Parallel Universe

***See also** Lost Worlds*
Alice '09
Alice in Wonderland '50
Alice in Wonderland '51 ▸
Alice in Wonderland '99
Blue Flame '93
The Butterfly Effect '04
The Chronicles of Narnia: The Lion, the Witch and the Wardrobe '05
Citizen Toxie: The Toxic Avenger 4 '01
Coherence '13
Comfort and Joy '03
Cool World '92
Coraline '09 ▸
Crossworlds '96
Dark City '97
Doctor Strange '16 ▸
A Family Thanksgiving '10
Ferocious Planet '11
Holiday Switch '07
Identicals '16
The Imaginarium of Doctor Parnassus '09
Inland Empire '06
Isn't It Romantic '19
Journey to the Center of the Earth '59 ▸
Journey to the Center of the Earth '88
Jumanji '95
Land of the Lost '09
Last Action Hero '93
Last Lives '98
The Little Mermaid '89 ▸
Logan's Run '76
Me Myself I '99
MirrorMask '05
The Mortal Instruments: City of Bones '13
Mortal Kombat 2: Annihilation '97
Neil Gaiman's NeverWhere '96
Never Let Me Go '10
9 '09 ▸
The One '01
Out of Blue '19
Passion of Mind '00
Possible Loves '00 ▸
The Purple Rose of Cairo '85 ▸
Re-Cycle '06
Silent Hill '06
Splash '84
Stargate: Continuum '08
Super Mario Bros. '93
The 10th Kingdom '00
The Thirteenth Floor '99
Tin Man '07
Twisted '96
Uncertainty '08
Undermind '03
Webs '03
Who Framed Roger Rabbit '88 ▸

Paramedics

Bringing Out the Dead '99
Broken Vessels '98 ▸
Mother, Jugs and Speed '76
The Sweetest Thing '02
There's Something about Mary '98 ▸

Pardners

***See also** Buddies; Westerns*
Appaloosa '08 ▸
Becoming Mike Nichols '16
Butch and Sundance: The Early Days '79
Butch Cassidy and the Sundance Kid '69 ▸
The Cowboy Way '94
Hell or High Water '16 ▸
The Magnificent Seven '16
Open Range '03 ▸
Pardners '56
Shanghai Noon '00
Silverado '85 ▸
Texas Rangers '01
Tombstone '93 ▸
Wyatt Earp '94
Young Guns 2 '90
Young Guns '88

Parenthood

***See also** Adoption & Bad Dads; Bringing Up Baby; Custody Battles; Dads; Moms; Monster Moms; Single Parents; Stepparents*
About Sunny '12 ▸
Adam '83 ▸
Addams Family Values '93
The Adventures of Sebastian Cole '99
Afraid of the Dark '92
Aliens '86 ▸
All Roads Lead to Rome '15
All the Kind Strangers '74
Almayer's Folly '12
Amazing Grace '74
American Heart '92 ▸
American Woman '19
Any Day Now '12 ▸
As Cool As I Am '13
At Middleton '13
An Autumn Afternoon '62 ▸
Away We Go '09
Babel '06 ▸
Babies '10 ▸
Baby Boom '87
Baby Girl Scott '87
The Babymakers '12
Bachelor Mother '39 ▸
Back to the Beach '87
Backfield in Motion '91
Bad Bush '09
Bad Moms '16
A Bad Moms Christmas '17
Bad Parents '12
The Ballad of Narayama '83 ▸
The Banger Sisters '02
Barry Munday '10
Basket Case 3: The Progeny '92
Battling for Baby '92
The Beach Bum '19
Beautiful Boy '10
Beyond Silence '96
Big Daddy '99
Big Fella '37
Big Girls Don't Cry. . . They Get Even '92
The Big Wheel '49
Blockers '18
Blow '01
Bobbie's Girl '02
Boyhood '14 ▸
The Boys Are Back '09
Boys Town '38 ▸
Brad's Status '17
Breakfast With Scot '07
Bringing Up Bobby '11
Broken Wings '02 ▸
Bye Bye, Love '94
Cahill: United States Marshal '73
Captain Fantastic '16
Careful, He Might Hear You '84 ▸
Carnage '11
Casanova Brown '44
Casey's Shadow '78
Cheaper by the Dozen '50 ▸
Cheaper by the Dozen '03
Cherry Blossoms '08
The Child '05
The Children of Times Square '86
Chinese Puzzle '13
The Christmas Hope '09
Cold River '81
Commissar '68 ▸
The Confirmation '16
A Cool, Dry Place '98
The Courtship of Eddie's Father '62 ▸
Cowboys Don't Cry '88
Crisscross '92
Crooklyn '94 ▸
A Cry in the Dark '88 ▸
Cyrus '10
Daddy Nostalgia '90 ▸
Danielle Steel's Daddy '91
Danielle Steel's Fine Things '90
The Day My Parents Ran Away '93
The Deep End of the Ocean '98
Delivery Man '13
The Descendants '11 ▸
Diane '18
The Dinner '17
Distant Voices, Still Lives '88 ▸
Dona Herlinda & Her Son '86
Drunk Parents '19
Dutch '91
Eat Drink Man Woman '94 ▸
Edge of Winter '16
The Emerald Forest '85 ▸
Endless Love '81
Enough Said '13 ▸
The Etruscan Smile '19
Familia '05
Family Honeymoon '49
Family Weekend '13
Father and Son '03
Father of My Children '09
Father of the Bride '50 ▸
Father of the Bride Part 2 '95
51 Birch Street '05 ▸
Firelight '97
Five Finger Exercise '62
Flirting with Disaster '95 ▸
Follow the Stars Home '01
For Sama '19 ▸
Forbidden Planet '56 ▸
The Forgotten '04
40 Pounds of Trouble '62
The Future of Emily '85
Gallant Lady '33
The Game Plan '07
Get a Job '16
Ghost Dad '90
Gifted '17
Gleason '16 ▸
God Bless the Child '88 ▸
Godsend '04
The Good Father '87 ▸
The Good Mother '88
A Goofy Movie '94
Grace Is Gone '07 ▸
Graduation '17
Grey Gardens '09 ▸
Grown Ups 2 '13
Grown Ups '10
Guess What We Learned in School Today? '70
Gypsy '62 ▸
Gypsy '93
Happiness Runs '10
Happy, Happy '10
The Happy Road '57
Harry & Son '84
Held for Murder '32
Hemel '14
High Life '18
High Tide '87 ▸
A Hole in the Head '59
Holiday for Lovers '59
Holiday Heart '00
Home Again '13
Home from the Hill '60 ▸
A Home of Our Own '93
Honey Boy '19 ▸
Hope Floats '98
The House '17
House Arrest '96
House of Sand '05 ▸
Houseboat '58
The Hungry Ghosts '09
Hungry Hearts '15
The Hybrids Family '16
I Accuse My Parents '45
I Am Potential '15
I Never Sang for My Father '70 ▸
I Remember Mama '48 ▸
I'll Do Anything '93
I'll Take Sweden '65
Immediate Family '89
In Love We Trust '07
In the Bedroom '01 ▸
In the Family '11
Infinitely Polar Bear '14
Insidious: Chapter 2 '13
Instant Family '18
Intruders '11
Irreconcilable Differences '84
Jack and Sarah '95
Janie Jones '10
Jersey Girl '04
Jesus Henry Christ '12
Jinn '18
Joshua '07 ▸
Journey for Margaret '42 ▸
The Journey Home '14
Judy Berlin '99
Jungle 2 Jungle '96
Jurassic Park 3 '01
The Kids Are All Right '10 ▸
Kiss Daddy Goodbye '81
Kolya '96 ▸
Lady Bird '17 ▸
Ladybird, Ladybird '93 ▸
The Last Gangster '37
Leave No Trace '18 ▸
Liar Liar '97
Life, Animated '16 ▸
Life as a House '01
Life As We Know It '10
Life Itself '18
Little Children '06 ▸
A Little Help '11
Little Men '16 ▸
London River '09
Long Lost Son '06
Losing Isaiah '94 ▸
Lost Angels '89
Louder Than Words '14
Love Is All There Is '96
Ma and Pa Kettle Back On the Farm '51
Ma Barker's Killer Brood '60
Magic in the Water '95
Magical Girl '14 ▸
Mama Flora's Family '98
Mamma Roma '62 ▸
Mammoth '09
Manchester by the Sea '16 ▸
Matilda '96 ▸
Max Dugan Returns '83
The Meddler '15 ▸
The Memory Keeper's Daughter '08
Men Don't Leave '89
Men, Women & Children '14
Menashe '17
Mermaids '90 ▸
Miracle on 34th Street '94
Mrs. Doubtfire '93
Mr. Mom '83 ▸
Mom '89
Mom & Dad '47
Moms' Night Out '14
More Sex and the Single Mom '05
Mother of George '13 ▸
My Baby's Daddy '04
My Life '93
My Mom's a Werewolf '89
My Neighbor's Keeper '07
Mysterious Ways '15
The Namesake '06 ▸
National Lampoon's European Vacation '85
Neighbors 2: Sorority Rising '16
The New Daughter '10
The Next Best Thing '00
Next of Kin '84
The Nice Guys '16 ▸
Nine Lives '16
No Dessert Dad, 'Til You Mow the Lawn '94
Not Suitable for Children '12
The Note '07
Nothing in Common '86
The Odd Life of Timothy Green '12
On Golden Pond '81 ▸
One Fine Day '96
One Man's War '90
One More Time '15
The Ones Below '16
Only the Lonely '91
Only When I Laugh '81 ▸
The Other Story '19
Otherhood '19
The Others '01 ▸
The Pacifier '05
Padre Padrone '77 ▸
Pampered Youth '25
The Parent Trap '98
Parental Guidance '12
Parenthood '89 ▸
Parents '89 ▸
Paris, Texas '83 ▸
Pay the Ghost '15
Penny Serenade '41 ▸
People Places Things '15
The Perfect Family '11
Perfect Parents '06
Poil de Carotte '31
Prisoners '13 ▸
Proxy '13
Psycho 4: The Beginning '90
Queen of Hearts '19
Queens of the Ring '13
A Question of Faith '17
The Quiet Room '96
Quitters '16
Rabbit Hole '10 ▸
Rage '14
Raising Arizona '87 ▸
Raising Genius '04
Raising Helen '04
Ray & Liz '19
Red Doors '05
The Red House '47 ▸
Red River '48 ▸
Relative Strangers '06
The Reluctant Debutante '58 ▸
The Remarkable Mr. Pennypacker '59
Revenge '71
Riding in Cars with Boys '01
Road Hard '15
Room for One More '51
Runaway Father '91
The Sandy Bottom Orchestra '00
The Santa Clause '94
Sarah's Child '96
Say It With Songs '29
The Second Mother '15 ▸
Secrets and Lies '95
The Shaggy D.A. '76
She Hate Me '04
Sherrybaby '06
Shut In '16
Silence of the Heart '84 ▸
Silent Cry Aloud '16
Silent Witness '99
A Simple Twist of Fate '94
The Singing Fool '28
Sinister 2 '15
A Slightly Pregnant Man '79
Small Town Saturday Night '10
Some Kind of Beautiful '15
Somewhere '10
Son of Godzilla '66
Star Wars: The Force Awakens '15 ▸
Steel Magnolias '89 ▸
Stella '89
Stella Dallas '37 ▸
The Strange Love of Molly Louvain '32
Superdad '73
Surprise, Surprise '09
The Switch '10
Target '85
Tea with Mussolini '99
Teenage Bad Girl '59
Teenage Rebel '56
Tequila Sunrise '88
Term Life '16
Terminator 2: Judgment Day '91 ▸
Terms of Endearment '83 ▸
Thank You for Smoking '06
There Will Be Blood '07 ▸
This Is 40 '12
This Property Is Condemned '66
Those We Love '32
Three Fugitives '89
Three Men and a Baby '87 ▸
Three Men and a Cradle '85 ▸
Throw Momma from the Train '87 ▸
Times Have Been Better '06
Toni Erdmann '16 ▸
Trading Mom '94
Trucker '08
Tumbleweeds '98
The Turning Point '77
20th Century Women '17
The Twilight Saga: Breaking Dawn, Part 2 '12
Ulee's Gold '97 ▸
The Unborn 2 '94
Under the Mistletoe '06
Undercover Blues '93
Valentin '02
Valley of the Sun '11
We Monsters '15
What Maisie Knew '12 ▸
What We Did on Our Holiday '15
Where Are the Children? '85
Where's Poppa? '70 ▸
Wild Rose '18 ▸
Wish I Was Here '14
With Six You Get Eggroll '68
Without a Trace '83
Yours, Mine & Ours '68
The Zodiac '05

Paris

***See also** France*
Accused '36
An Affair of Love '99
After Fall, Winter '11
After Sex '97
AKA '02
Alias Betty '01
Almost Peaceful '02 ▸
Alphaville '65 ▸
The Ambassador's Daughter '56
Amelie '01 ▸
The American '01
American Dreamer '84
An American in Paris '51 ▸
An American Werewolf in Paris '97
Amour '12 ▸
Angel '37
Angel-A '05
Angelique: The Road to Versailles '65
Another 9 1/2 Weeks '96
Apres-Vous '03
April in Paris '52
Arch of Triumph '48 ▸
Arch of Triumph '85
The Army of Crime '10
Artists and Models Abroad '38
As Above, So Below '14
The Assignment '97
Assignment: Paris '52
Au Pair '99
Avenue Montaigne '06
The Aviator's Wife '80 ▸
Baise Moi '00
Ballets Russes '05 ▸
Balzac: A Life of Passion '99 ▸
The Beat My Heart Skipped '05 ▸
Beau Pere '81 ▸
Beaumarchais the Scoundrel '96
The Beautiful Person '08
Bed and Board '70 ▸
Bedevilled '55
Before I Forget '07
Before Sunset '04 ▸
Bel Ami '12
Belle Toujours '06 ▸
Belphegor: Phantom of the Louvre '01
Beyond the Clouds '95
Bird People '14
Blame It on Fidel '06
Boarding Gate '07
Boeing Boeing '65
Born in 68 '08
The Bourne Identity '02 ▸
Boy Meets Girl '84 ▸
BPM (Beats Per Minute) '17
Breathless '59 ▸
Brigands: Chapter VII '97
Broken English '07
The Broken Tower '11
The C-Man '49
Cafe Metropole '37
Camille '36 ▸
Camille '84

▸ = rated three bones or higher

Cartouche '62 ►
Cash '08
Casque d'Or '52 ►
A Cat in Paris '11
Catacombs '07
Celestial Clockwork '94
Change My Life '01
A Change of Place '94
Change of Plans '09
Chaos '01
Charade '63 ►
Chariots of Fire '81 ►
Charlie Chan in City of Darkness '39
Charlie Chan in Paris '35
Cheri '09
Children of Paradise '44 ►
Children of the Century '99
Circle of Love '64
Circle of Passion '97
The Class '08
Clean '04
Cleo from 5 to 7 '61 ►
Coco Chanel & Igor Stravinsky '09
Code Unknown '00
Comedy of Innocence '00
The Concert '09
Confusion of Genders '00
Cousin Bette '97
The Cousins '59 ►
CQ '01
Crazy Horse '12 ►
Crime Spree '03
Crimson Rivers 2: Angels of the Apocalypse '05
Crossroads '42
The Da Vinci Code '06 ►
Dad On the Run '00
Daguerreotypes '75 ►
Dangerous Liaisons '03
A Dangerous Man: Lawrence after Arabia '91 ►
Daniella by Night '61
Dear Brigitte '65
Delicacy '12
Delicatessen '92 ►
Delta of Venus '95
Demonlover '02
Design for Living '33
The Destructors '74
Detective '85
The Devil, Probably '77
The Devil Wears Prada '06
Dheepan '16
Dilili in Paris '18
Dingo '90
The Dirty Girls '64
The Disenchanted '90
District B13 '04
District 13: Ultimatum '09
Diva '82 ►
The Dreamers '03
The Duchess of Langeais '07 ►
Elles '11
The Emperor's New Clothes '01
Empire of the Wolves '05
The Escape '18
Everyone Says I Love You '96 ►
The Face at the Window '39
Faithless '00 ►
The Fall '98
The Fantastic Night '42 ►
Fashions of 1934 '34
The Fatal Image '90
Father of My Children '09
The Favor, the Watch, & the Very Big Fish '92
Fay Grim '06
Femme Fatale '02
A Few Days in September '06
The 15:17 to Paris '18
A Fine Romance '92
Flight of the Red Balloon '08
Folies Bergere de Paris '35
Forget Paris '95
Frank & Lola '16
Frantic '88 ►
Free Men '12
French Can-Can '55 ►
A French Gigolo '08
French Kiss '95
The French Minister '13
French Postcards '79
The French Touch '54
Friday Night '02
From Hell to Victory '79
From Paris With Love '10
Frontier of Dawn '08
Funny Face '57 ►
Gabrielle '05
Gainsbourg: A Heroic Life '10
Games of Love and Chance '03
Gentlemen Prefer Blondes '53 ►
G.I. Joe: The Rise of Cobra '09
Gigi '58 ►
The Girl '01
The Girl on the Bridge '98 ►
The Girl on the Train '09
Girlhood '14 ►
God's Gift to Women '31
Gold Diggers in Paris '38
Good Morning, Boys '37
The Grand Role '04
The Great Garrick '37
Half-Shot at Sunrise '30
Hannibal Rising '07
Happenstance '00
Happily Ever After '04
The Happy Road '57
Head in the Clouds '04
Head Over Heels '37
Heartbeat '46
Heartbeat Detector '07
Henri Langlois: The Phantom of the Cinematheque '04 ►
Henry & June '90 ►
Hereafter '10
Hidden '05 ►
The Holes '72
Hollywood, Je T'Aime '09
Holy Motors '12 ►
House of D '04
The Housekeeper '02
How to Steal a Million '66 ►
Hugo '11 ►
The Hunchback '97
The Hunchback of Notre Dame '39 ►
The Hunchback of Notre Dame '57
The Hunchback of Notre Dame '82 ►
The Hunchback of Notre Dame '96 ►
I Can't Sleep '93
I Don't Kiss '91
I Lost My Body '19 ►
I Met Him in Paris '37
I Want to Go Home '89
If Looks Could Kill '91
I'm Going Home '00 ►
In Praise of Love '01
In Secret '13
In the French Style '63
Incognito '97
Inglourious Basterds '09 ►
Inside Paris '06
Interview with the Vampire '94
Intimate Strangers '04 ►
Intolerance '16 ►
The Intouchables '12
Invisible Circus '00
The Invisibles '99
Irma Vep '96
Is Paris Burning? '66 ►
Jeanne and the Perfect Guy '98
Jefferson in Paris '94
Julie & Julia '09 ►
Kiki '26
Killing Zoe '94
Kiss of the Dragon '01
La Boheme '26
La Boum '81
La Chinoise '67
La Marseillaise '37 ►
La Moustache '05
La Petite Jerusalem '05
La Sentinelle '92
La Separation '98 ►
La Vie en Rose '07
The Lady and the Duke '01
Lady L '65
The Last Flight '31
Last Love '13
The Last Metro '80 ►
Last Tango in Paris '73 ►
The Last Time I Saw Paris '54
Le Cercle Rouge '70 ►
Le Deuxieme Souffle '66
Le Divorce '03
Le Petit Lieutenant '05
Le Samourai '67 ►
Le Trou '59 ►
Le Week-End '14
Les Cousins '59
Les Miserables '97 ►
Les Miserables '12 ►
Les Misérables '19
Les Vampires '15 ►
Let My People Go! '11
Let the Sunshine In '17
Little Ashes '09
A Little Romance '79 ►
Look at Me '04 ►
Lost in Paris '17
Love After Love '94
Love Me Tonight '32 ►
The Love Punch '13
Love Songs '07
The Lovers on the Bridge '91
Lucy '14
Ma and Pa Kettle on Vacation '53
Ma Vie en Rose '97 ►
The Mad Adventures of Rabbi Jacob '73 ►
Madame X '37
Made in Paris '65
Madeline '98
The Madwoman of Chaillot '69
Making Plans for Lena '09
The Man in the Iron Mask '98 ►
Man of the World '31
The Man Who Could Cheat Death '59
The Man Who Cried '00
The Man Who Lived at the Ritz '91
Marguerite '16 ►
Marquis de Sade '96
The Matrimonial Bed '30
Mauvaise Graine '33
Max, Mon Amour '86
Melo '86
Mesmer '94
Mesrine: Part 1-Killer Instinct '08
Mesrine: Part 2-Public Enemy Number 1 '08
Metroland '97
Micmacs '09
Midnight in Paris '11 ►
The Moderns '88 ►
Modigliani '04
Mon Oncle d'Amerique '80 ►
Monsieur Ibrahim '03 ►
Monsieur N. '03 ►
Monte Carlo '11
The Monuments Men '13
Mood Indigo '13
Mortal Transfer '01
Moulin Rouge '01 ►
The Murderer Lives at Number 21 '42
Murders in the Rue Morgue '71
The Murders in the Rue Morgue '86 ►
My Best Friend '06
My Life and Times with Antonin Artaud '93 ►
My Old Lady '14
My Piece of the Pie '11
My Sex Life. . . Or How I Got into an Argument '96
My Wife is an Actress '01
My Worst Nightmare '11
The Mystery of Marie Roget '42
The Names of Love '10
Napoleon '03
Nelly et Monsieur Arnaud '95 ►
The New Eve '98 ►
A New Kind of Love '63
New Morals for Old '32
Night on Earth '91 ►
Ninotchka '39 ►
Nocturama '17
Non-Fiction '18
Now and Forever '34
The Nude Set '57
Old Mother Riley in Paris '38
Oliver Twist '33
One Day You'll Understand '08
One Hour with You '32
Orpheus '49
Our Paradise '11
Outside the Law '10
Paris '08
Paris After Dark '43
Paris Blues '61
Paris Holiday '57
Paris, je t'aime '06
Paris 36 '08
Paris When It Sizzles '64
A Parisian Romance '32
The Passionate Plumber '32
The Perfect Furlough '59
Perfume: The Story of a Murderer '06
Personal Shopper '17 ►
Petits Freres '00
The Phantom of Paris '31
The Phantom of the Opera '25 ►
The Phantom of the Opera '43 ►
The Phantom of the Opera '90
The Phantom of the Opera '98
The Phantom of the Opera '04
Pigalle '95
The Pink Panther 2 '09
The Pink Panther '06
Place Vendome '98 ►
Plucking the Daisy '56
Point Blank '10
Pola X '99
Polisse '11 ►
Portraits Chinois '96
The Private Affairs of Bel Ami '47 ►
Private Fears in Public Places '06
Puerto Ricans in Paris '16
Rage in Heaven '41
Rapt '09
Rapture '65
Ratatouille '07 ►
Ready to Wear '94
Red Lights '04 ►
The Red Lily '24
Renaissance '06
The Return of the Scarlet Pimpernel '37
The Rich Are Always With Us '32
Rich, Young and Pretty '51
Ridicule '96 ►
Rise of the Gargoyles '09
Ronin '98
Rosemary's Baby '14
Round Midnight '86 ►
Rugrats in Paris: The Movie '00 ►
Rush Hour 3 '07
Russian Dolls '05
Safe Conduct '01 ►
Sarah's Key '10
A Scandal in Paris '46
Scaramouche '23
The Science of Sleep '06
7th Heaven '27
Sex & Mrs. X '00
Shall We Kiss? '07
Shoot the Piano Player '62 ►
The Sin of Madelon Claudet '31 ►
Sin Takes a Holiday '30
Since Otar Left. . . '03
A Single Girl '96
Siren of the Tropics '27
Six in Paris '68
Sleepless Night '11 ►
Something's Gotta Give '03 ►
Son of Gascogne '95
Special Treatment '10
The Story of a Three Day Pass '68
Subway '85
Summer '86 ►
The Sun Also Rises '57
Take Her, She's Mine '63
Taken '08
The Tango Lesson '97
Target '85
Team America: World Police '04 ►
Tell No One '06 ►
The Temptress '26
The Testament of Dr. Cordelier '59 ►
Theatre of Death '67
They Had to See Paris '29
Things to Come '16 ►
Third Person '13
Thirst Street '17
13 Rue Madeleine '46 ►
The 36th Precinct '04 ►
This Is the Night '32
This Modern Age '31
3 Days to Kill '14
The Three Musketeers '11
To Paris with Love '55
Torrent '26
Total Eclipse '95
The Tourist '10
Transporter 3 '08
Triple Agent '04
The Triplets of Belleville '02 ►
Tropic of Cancer '70 ►
The Truth About Charlie '02
24 Days '14
2 Days in Paris '07 ►
Two or Three Things I Know about Her '66
Under the Eiffel Tower '18
Under the Roofs of Paris '29 ►
Under the Sand '00 ►
Unlocked '17
Until September '84
Va Savoir '01
The Valet '06
Venus Beauty Institute '98
Venus in Fur '13 ►
A Very Long Engagement '04 ►
Victor/Victoria '82 ►
Victory '81
View from the Top '03
What Time Is It There? '01
The Woman in the Fifth '11
The Women on the Sixth Floor '10
Wonder Bar '34
Young & Beautiful '13
Zazie dans le Metro '61 ►

Party Hell

***See also** Slasher Flicks*

All Out Dysfunktion! '16
The Anniversary Party '01 ►
April Fool's Day '86
Beatriz at Dinner '17
Bel Canto '18
Body '15
Boo 2! A Madea Halloween '17
Carrie '76 ►
Carrie '02
Climax '18
Death Do Us Part '14
The Death of Dick Long '19
The Dinner Party '20
Dirty 30 '16
The Final '10
Good Boys '19
Happy Birthday to Me '81
Hell Night '81
Hello Mary Lou: Prom Night 2 '87
Home '05
The Invitation '16 ►
Joshy '16
Killer Party '86
Lazer Team '16
Life of the Party '18
London '05
Ma '19
Meet Wally Sparks '97
Mike and Dave Need Wedding Dates '16
Mimesis '11
Night of the Demons '88
Office Christmas Party '16
Old School '03
Ordinary World '16
The Party '17
Prom Night 3: The Last Kiss '89
Prom Night 4: Deliver Us from Evil '91
Prom Night '80
Rabid Grannies '89
The Rage: Carrie 2 '99
The Raven '07
Rough Night '17
6 Plots '12
Slumber Party Massacre '82
Slumber Party Massacre 2 '87
Slumber Party Massacre 3 '90
Twilight Zone: The Movie '83
Varsity Blood '14

Patriotism & Paranoia

Billy Lynn's Long Halftime Walk '16
Body of Lies '08
Born on the Fourth of July '89 ►
The Chase '66
Civic Duty '06
The Congressman '16
The Cosmic Man '59
Cuck '19
Dangerously We Live '41
Day Zero '07
Delta Force '86
Dress Gray '86 ►
F/X '86 ►
Fahrenheit 9/11 '04 ►
The Fallen '05 ►
Firefox '82
First Blood '82
Good Night, and Good Luck '05 ►
The Good Shepherd '06
Green Zone '10 ►
Guilty by Suspicion '91
Harry's War '84
Heroes for Sale '33 ►
I Was a Communist for the FBI '51
The Insurgents '06
Ivan the Terrible, Part 1 '44 ►
Ivan the Terrible, Part 2 '46 ►
Keeper of the Flame '42
The Last Enemy '08
Missing in Action '84
Mission to Moscow '43
Mom & Dad '47
My Son John '52
Nixon '95 ►
The Oath '18
Outlaw King '18
Paranoia 1.0 '04
Patton '70 ►
The Prisoner '55 ►
The Purge: Election Year '16
Rambo: First Blood, Part 2 '85
Rambo 3 '88
Red Dawn '84
The Red Menace '49
Rendition '07
Reunion in France '42
The Sea Hawk '40 ►
Shooter '07
The Siege '98
So Proudly We Hail '43 ►
Spartan '04 ►
Taps '81
Thirty Seconds Over Tokyo '44 ►
The 27th Day '57
XXX: State of the Union '05
Zero Days '16

Peace

Call Me Lucky '15 ►
The Day the Earth Stood Still '51 ►
The Deserters '83
Destry Rides Again '39 ►
Firehead '90
Friendly Persuasion '56 ►
Gandhi '82 ►
Joyeux Noel '05 ►
A Midnight Clear '92 ►
Sophie Scholl: The Final Days '05 ►
War and Peace '56
War and Peace '68 ►

Peculiar Partners

***See also** Buddies; Buddy Cops; Cops*

Alien Nation '88
Alien Nation: Dark Horizon '94
Alpha '18
The Beautician and the Beast '97

► = rated three bones or higher

Bending the Rules '12
The BFG '16
Blades of Glory '07
Bonnie and Clyde *vs.* Dracula '08
Cop and a Half '93
Cop Dog '08
Dead Heat '88
Dollman '90
Dream with the Fishes '97
The Forbidden Kingdom '08
Ghost Team '16
The Glimmer Man '96
Gridlock'd '96 ►
The Hard Way '91 ►
The Hidden 2 '94
The Hidden '87 ►
Judge Dredd '95
Judgementall Hai Kya '19
K-9 '89
K-911 '99
Miss Peregrine's Home for Peculiar Children '16
Phantom Boy '16
Puzzle '18
Stop! or My Mom Will Shoot '92
Theodore Rex '95
Top Dog '95
Turner and Hooch '89
Under Siege '92

Pen Pals

See also Going Postal
Bell, Book and Candle '58
Christmas in Boston '05
Convicted '04
Dear Dictator '18
Dear John '10
Eurotrip '04
Everyman's War '09
Eye of God '97 ►
Leo '02
The Letter '29
Letters to Juliet '10
Love Letters '99 ►
The Lunchbox '13
Mary and Max '09
Never Say Goodbye '46
Nights in Rodanthe '08
The Paperboy '12
Reindeer Games '00
Shadows and Lies '10
The Shop Around the Corner '40 ►
Signed, Sealed, Delivered for Christmas '14
Soldier Love Story '10
Strong Man '26 ►
The Wildest Dream: The Conquest of Everest '10
You've Got Mail '98

Penguins

See also Cold Spots; Wild Kingdom
Batman Returns '92
Billy Madison '94
Earth: One Amazing Day '17 ►
Encounters at the End of the World '07 ►
Happy Feet '06 ►
Happy Feet Two '11
Madagascar: Escape 2 Africa '08
Madagascar 3: Europe's Most Wanted '12
Madagascar '05
March of the Penguins '05 ►
Mr. Popper's Penguins '11
My Favorite Blonde '42 ►
Penguins '19 ►
Penguins of Madagascar '14
Surf's Up '07
Toy Story 2 '99 ►
The Wild '06

Period Piece

See also Historical Drama; Medieval Romps; Royalty
Alexander '04
Ashura '05
The Assassin '15 ►
The Assassins '12
The Assassin's Blade '08
The Ballad of Lefty Brown '17
The Ballad of Narayama '58 ►
Battle of the Warriors '06
A Beautiful Day in the Neighborhood '19 ►
Ben-Hur '16
Birds of Passage '18 ►
Blade of the Immortal '17
Blind Woman's Curse '70
Blood and Bones '04
Bushido: The Cruel Code of the Samurai '63 ►
Capone '20
Curse of the Golden Flower '06
David and Goliath '61
Dragon Blade '15
Draw on Sweet Night '15
Duel to the Death '82
Early Man '18
Effie Gray '15
8 Diagram Pole Fighter '84 ►
An Empress and the Warriors '08
Escape '12
14 Blades '14
Genghis Khan: To the Ends of the Earth and Sea '07
Genius '16
The Greatest Showman '17
The Guardsman '15
Guinevere '94
Hard to Be a God '13
Heroes Two '73
Holmes & Watson '18
House of Flying Daggers '04 ►
Iceman '19
Ichi '08
I'm Not Here '19
Mission of Honor '19
Ip Man 4: The Finale '19
Ironclad: Battle for Blood '14
Judy & Punch '20
Keep Walking '82 ►
The Keeper: The Legend of Omar Khayyam '05
Kill! '68
La Femme Musketeer '03
Lady Macbeth '17 ►
LBJ '17
The Little Hours '17 ►
Love & Mercy '15 ►
The Magnificent Trio '66
Marco Polo '07
Mary Magdalene '19
Mary Shelley '17
The Meanest Man in Texas '19
Mongol '07 ►
Musa: The Warrior '01 ►
My Golden Days '15 ►
Dean Spanley '08
Never Look Away '18 ►
Northman: A Viking Saga '15
One Night with the King '06
Operation Finale '18
Outlaw King '18
The Outsider '19
Padmaavat '18 ►
Pathfinder '07
The Phantom of the Opera '04
The Promise '05
Rebel in the Rye '17
The Reckoning '03 ►
Robin Hood '18
The Romance of Astrea and Celadon '07
A Royal Scandal '45
Run This Town '20
Samson '18
Samurai Fiction '99 ►
The Sea is Watching '02 ►
Season of the Witch '10
Shadow '18 ►
Shock and Awe '18
Suffragette '15
Sword of the Beast '65 ►
A Tale of Love and Darkness '16
Tristan & Isolde '06
Troy '04
Underworld: Rise of the Lycans '09
The Young Messiah '16

Period Piece: 15th Century

The Advocate '93 ►
The Beloved Rogue '27 ►
Carry On Columbus '92
Christopher Columbus '49
Dracula: The Dark Prince '01
Jeanne la Pucelle '94
Joan of Arc '48
Joan of Arc '99
The King '19 ►
Mad Love '01
The Messenger: The Story of Joan of Arc '99
Quentin Durward '55
The Warrior '01

Period Piece: 16th Century

Aguirre, the Wrath of God '72 ►
Anonymous '11
Apocalypto '06 ►
Beatrice Cenci '69
Caravaggio '07
The Countess '09
Dangerous Beauty '98 ►
Day of Wrath '06
The Devil-Ship Pirates '64
Elizabeth '98 ►
Elizabeth I '05 ►
Elizabeth: The Golden Age '07
The Fountain '06
Henry V '44 ►
Henry V '89 ►
Highlander: Endgame '00
Ivan the Terrible, Part 1 '44 ►
Ivan the Terrible, Part 2 '46 ►
Kagemusha '80 ►
Kama Sutra: A Tale of Love '96
Lost Colony: The Legend of Roanoke '07
Luther '03
Mad Love '01
A Man for All Seasons '66 ►
A Man for All Seasons '88 ►
Mary of Scotland '36 ►
Mary Queen of Scots '18
The Merchant of Venice '04 ►
The Mill and the Cross '11
Mysterious Museum '99
Orlando '92 ►
The Other Boleyn Girl '03
The Other Boleyn Girl '08
Pirates of Tortuga '61
The Prince and the Pauper '01
Prince of Foxes '49
The Princess of Montpensier '10 ►
The Private Life of Henry VIII '33 ►
The Private Lives of Elizabeth & Essex '39 ►
Queen Margot '94 ►
Rikyu '90 ►
The Road to El Dorado '00
Samurai Banners '69
The Sea Hawk '24
The Sea Hawk '40 ►
Seven Samurai '54 ►
Seven Seas to Calais '62
Shakespeare in Love '98 ►
Shinobi no Mono '62 ►
Shinobi no Mono 2: Vengeance '63 ►
Swordsman of Siena '62
Taras Bulba '62
The Virgin Queen '55 ►
A Waste of Shame '05
Young Bess '53 ►

Period Piece: 17th Century

The Abdication '74
All Is True '18
Angelique '64
Angelique and the King '66
Angelique and the Sultan '68
Angelique: The Road to Versailles '65
At Sword's Point '51
Bardelys the Magnificent '26
Black Robe '91 ►
Black Torment '64
Blackbeard '06
Bluebeard '09
Cardinal Richelieu '35
The Conqueror Worm '68 ►
The Crucible '96 ►
The Deluge '73
Delusions of Grandeur '76
The Devils '71 ►
Draw on Sweet Night '15
Ever After: A Cinderella Story '98 ►
A Field in England '14 ►
Forever Amber '47
The Four Musketeers '75 ►
Frenchman's Creek '44
Frenchman's Creek '98
Girl with a Pearl Earring '03 ►
Harakiri '62 ►
Highlander: Endgame '00
Hudson's Bay '40
I, the Worst of All '90
The Iron Mask '29
Kidnapped '05 ►
The King's Thief '55
The King's Whore '90
The Libertine '05
A Little Chaos '14
Lorna Doone '22
Lorna Doone '34
Lorna Doone '90
Lorna Doone '01 ►
Maid of Salem '37
The Man in the Iron Mask '39 ►
The Man in the Iron Mask '77 ►
The Man in the Iron Mask '97
The Man in the Iron Mask '98 ►
Marquis de Sade '96
Moliere '07
Monsieur Vincent '47 ►
More Than a Miracle '67
Mother Joan of the Angels '60 ►
The Musketeer '01
The New World '05 ►
The Night and the Moment '94
Nightwatching '07
Pirates of the Caribbean: The Curse of the Black Pearl '03 ►
The Pirates Who Don't Do Anything: A VeggieTales Movie '08
Queen Christina '33 ►
Rapa Nui '93
Rembrandt '36 ►
Restoration '94 ►
Revenge of the Musketeers '94
Robinson Crusoe '54
The Salem Witch Trials '02
Samurai Reincarnation '81
The Scarlet Letter '34
The Scarlet Letter '73 ►
The Scarlet Letter '79 ►
The Scarlet Letter '95
The Serpent's Kiss '97
Silence '16 ►
Squanto: A Warrior's Tale '94 ►
Stage Beauty '04
The Three Musketeers '21 ►
The Three Musketeers '39
The Three Musketeers '48
The Three Musketeers '74 ►
The Three Musketeers '93
The Three Musketeers '11
To Kill a King '03
Tous les Matins du Monde '92 ►
Untamable Angelique '67
Vatel '00
The Wicked Lady '45
Zemsta '02

Period Piece: 18th Century

The Affair of the Necklace '01
Alone Yet Not Alone '13
Amadeus '84 ►
Amazing Grace '06 ►
The Amorous Adventures of Moll Flanders '65
April Morning '88
Aristocrats '99
The Aristocrats '99
As You Like It '06
The Awakening Land '78
Bang Rajan '00 ►
Barry Lyndon '75 ►
Beau Brummell: This Charming Man '06
Beaumarchais the Scoundrel '96
Becoming Jane '07
Beggar's Opera '54
Belle '13
Beloved Sisters '14 ►
The Black Castle '52
Black Jack '79
The Black Tulip '64
Bleak House '05
BloodRayne '06
The Bounty '84
The Bridge of San Luis Rey '05
Brotherhood of the Wolf '01
Cartouche '62 ►
Casanova '05
Casanova '05 ►
Casanova's Big Night '54
Catherine the Great '34
Catherine the Great '95
The Chess Player '27
Clive of India '35
The Crossing '00
Dangerous Liaisons '88 ►
Danton '82 ►
Deacon Brodie '98
The Divine Lady '29
Don't Lose Your Head '66
Du Barry Was a Lady '43
The Duchess '08 ►
Fanny Hill '07
Farewell, My Queen '12 ►
Farinelli '94
The Favourite '18 ►
Follow the River '95
Goya's Ghosts '06
The Great Garrick '37
Gulliver's Travels '39
Gulliver's Travels '77
Gulliver's Travels '95
Hamilton '20 ►
A Harlot's Progress '06
Hero's Island '62
Highlander: Endgame '00
I'll Never Forget You '51
Immortal Beloved '94
The Incredible Journey of Mary Bryant '05
Interview with the Vampire '94
John Adams '08
Joseph Andrews '77
Kidnapped '38
Kidnapped '95
La Marseillaise '37 ►
The Lady and the Duke '01
The Last of the Mohicans '20 ►
The Last of the Mohicans '32
The Last of the Mohicans '36
The Last of the Mohicans '92 ►
The Last Supper '76 ►
Les Miserables '35 ►
Les Miserables '52
Les Miserables '57 ►
Les Miserables '78 ►
Les Miserables '97 ►
Longitude '00 ►
Loves & Times of Scaramouche '76
Madame Bovary '15
Madame Sans-Gene '62
The Madness of King George '94 ►
Marie Antoinette '38
Marie Antoinette '06
The Marquise of O '76
Men of the Sea '35
Mesmer '94
Moll Flanders '96
Monsieur Beaucaire '46 ►
Mozart's Sister '10
Mutiny on the Bounty '35 ►
Mutiny on the Bounty '62
Napoleon '03
Night Sun '90
Oklahoma! '99 ►
On Guard! '03 ►
Orlando '92 ►
Pandaemonium '00
Passion '19
The Patriot '00
Perfume: The Story of a Murderer '06
The Pirates of Capri '49
Plunkett & Macleane '98
Poldark 2 '75 ►
Poldark '75 ►
Portrait of a Lady on Fire '19 ►
Power '34
Prince Brat and the Whipping Boy '95 ►
Ridicule '96 ►
The Road to Yesterday '25
Rob Roy '95 ►
Rob Roy-The Highland Rogue '53
A Royal Affair '12 ►
Sade '00
Sally Hemings: An American Scandal '00
Samurai Rebellion '67 ►
Scaramouche '23
The Scarlet Pimpernel '99
The Scarlet Pimpernel 2: Mademoiselle Guillotine '99
The Scarlet Pimpernel 3: The Kidnapped King '99
The Scarlet Pimpernel '34 ►
The Scarlet Pimpernel '82 ►
Seraphim Falls '06
Shogun '80 ►
Sleepy Hollow '99 ►
Son of Fury '42 ►
The Swordsman '47
A Tale of Two Cities '36 ►
A Tale of Two Cities '58 ►
A Tale of Two Cities '80
A Tale of Two Cities '89 ►
Tom Jones '63 ►
Tom Jones '98 ►
The Triumph of Love '01
Valmont '89 ►
When a Man Loves '27
Wuthering Heights '12
Yellow Sky '48 ►
Young Goethe in Love '11
Zama '17

Period Piece: 19th Century

Abraham Lincoln: Vampire Hunter '12
Abraham Lincoln *vs.* Zombies '12
Across to Singapore '28
Adam's Woman '70
Adios, Sabata '71
The Adventures of Mark Twain '44 ►
The Aeronauts '19
Affinity '08
The Age of Innocence '34
The Age of Innocence '93 ►
The Alamo '04
Albert Nobbs '11
All the Brothers Were Valiant '53
America America '63
The American '01
An American Haunting '05
American Outlaws '01
Angels and Insects '95 ►
Anna and the King '99
Anna and the King of Siam '46 ►
Anna Karenina '35 ►
Anna Karenina '48
Anna Karenina '96
Anna Karenina '00
Anna Karenina '12
Anne Rice's The Feast of All Saints '01
Anthony Adverse '36
Anton Chekhov's The Duel '09
Appaloosa '08 ►
The Assassination Bureau '69 ►
The Assassination of Jesse James by the Coward Robert Ford '07 ►
August '95
Augustine '12
The Avenging Angel '95

► = rated three bones or higher

▶ = rated three bones or higher

A Scandal in Paris '46
Scarlett '94
The Scent of Rain & Lightening '17
Sea Devils '53
The Secret Diaries of Miss Anne Lister '10
The Secret Garden '49 ▸
The Secret Garden '84
The Secret Garden '87 ▸
The Secret Garden '93
The Secret Life of Mrs. Beeton '06
The Secret of Monte Cristo '61
Seminole '53
Sense & Sensibility '85
Sense and Sensibility '95 ▸
Sense & Sensibility '07
Senso '54 ▸
September Dawn '07
Sergeant Rutledge '60 ▸
Seven Angry Men '55
The Shadow in the North '07
Shanghai Knights '03
Shanghai Noon '00
Sharpe's Battle '94
Sharpe's Challenge '06
Sharpe's Company '94
Sharpe's Eagle '93
Sharpe's Enemy '94
Sharpe's Gold '94
Sharpe's Honour '94
Sharpe's Justice '97
Sharpe's Legend '97
Sharpe's Mission '96
Sharpe's Peril '08
Sharpe's Regiment '96
Sharpe's Revenge '97
Sharpe's Rifles '93
Sharpe's Siege '96
Sharpe's Sword '94
Sharpe's Waterloo '97
Sherlock: Case of Evil '02
Sherlock Holmes '09
Sherlock Holmes '10
Sherlock Holmes: A Game of Shadows '11
The Shocking Miss Pilgrim '47
Show Boat '36 ▸
Show Boat '51 ▸
The Sign of Four '83
The Sign of Four '01
Silas Marner '85 ▸
Silk '07
Sinful Davey '69
The Sisters Brothers '18
Sitting Bull '54
Sixty Glorious Years '38
Skin Game '71 ▸
Slow West '15 ▸
Snow Flower and the Secret Fan '11
So Goes My Love '46
Sofie '92
Sommersby '93
A Song of Innocence '05
A Song to Remember '45 ▸
Song Without End '60
Souls at Sea '37
Spirit: Stallion of the Cimarron '02
Spring Symphony '86
Stand Up and Fight '39
Station Jim '01
Steamboy '05
Stolen Women, Captured Hearts '97
Stonehearst Asylum '13
The Story of Alexander Graham Bell '39 ▸
The Story of an African Farm '04
Strange Lady in Town '55
The Stranglers of Bombay '60
The Strauss Family '73
The Substitute Wife '94
Suez '38
Sukiyaki Western Django '08
Sweeney Todd: The Demon Barber of Fleet Street '07
Swept from the Sea '97
Taboo '99
Tai-Pan '86
The Tall Target '51
Taza, Son of Cochise '54
The Tenant of Wildfell Hall '96
Tess '79 ▸
Tess of the D'Urbervilles '98
Tess of the D'Urbervilles '08
Testimony of Two Men '77
The Texans '38
Texas Rangers '01
That Forsyte Woman '50
Therese Raquin '80
Therese: The Story of Saint Therese of Lisieux '04
13 Assassins '10
The Thorn Birds: The Missing Years '96 ▸
Three Men in a Boat '56
Tide of Empire '29
Tim Burton's Corpse Bride '05 ▸
Tipping the Velvet '02
Tom and Huck '95 ▸
Tom Sawyer '73
Tommy's Honour '17
Topsy Turvy '99 ▸
Torrents of Spring '90
Total Eclipse '95
The Toy Wife '38
The Trail of '98 '28
Treasure Island '12
Tremors 4: The Legend Begins '04
True History of the Kelly Gang '20
The True Story of Jesse James '57
Twelfth Night '96
12 Years a Slave '13 ▸
The Twilight Samurai '02 ▸
Two Sisters From Boston '46
Under Capricorn '49
Under the Greenwood Tree '05
Untamed '55
Utamaro and His Five Women '46
Vacas '91
The Valley of Decision '45 ▸
Van Gogh '92 ▸
Vanity Fair '32
Vanity Fair '99
Vanity Fair '04
The Verdict '46
Victoria & Abdul '17
Victoria & Albert '01
Victoria the Great '37
The Village '04
Vincent & Theo '90 ▸
Wabash Avenue '50
Waltz King '63
War and Peace '56
War and Peace '68 ▸
War and Peace '73
Warlords '08 ▸
Washington Square '97 ▸
Way of a Gaucho '52
The Way of the West '11
The Way We Live Now '02
The Weight of Water '00
Werewolf: The Beast Among Us '12
The Whale '13
What Katy Did '99
When Calls the Heart '13
When the Last Sword is Drawn '02 ▸
Wide Sargasso Sea '92
Wide Sargasso Sea '06
The Widow of Saint-Pierre '00 ▸
Wild Bill '95
Wild Wild West '99
Wilde '97
Winchester '18
The Wind '19
Wind River '98
Wives and Daughters '01
The Woman in Black '12
The Woman in White '97
A Woman Rebels '36
The World in His Arms '52
The World Moves On '34
Wuthering Heights '09
The Wyvern Mystery '00
Young Sherlock Holmes '85
The Young Victoria '09 ▸
Zarak '56
Zatoichi '03 ▸

Period Piece: 20th Century

America's Dream '95 ▸
Any Human Heart '11
The Babe '92
Beloved '11
Bride of the Wind '01
Carrington '95
Cloudstreet '11
Cobb '94 ▸
Coco Before Chanel '09
Coco Chanel '08
Coming Through '85
The Conquerors '32
Cranford '08
A Dance to the Music of Time '97
Dust '01
Everlasting Moments '08
Frida '02
Georgia O'Keefe '09
Gypsy '62 ▸
Gypsy '93
Hold the Dream '86
Houdini '14
House of Sand '05 ▸
Indochine '92 ▸
Interview with the Vampire '94
Iris '01 ▸
JFK: Reckless Youth '93
Lagaan: Once upon a Time in India '01
Lansky '99
The Last Emperor '87 ▸
Lee Daniels' The Butler '13
The Legend of 1900 '98
Legends of the Fall '94
Lillie '79 ▸
Malcolm X '92 ▸
Mama Flora's Family '98
Mandela: Long Walk to Freedom '13
Me Without You '01
Nanny McPhee '06
Nicholas and Alexandra '71
Nuts! '16 ▸
O Pioneers! '91
Orlando '92 ▸
Our Town '03
Outside the Law '10
Princess Kaiulani '09
Rasputin '85 ▸
Rasputin and the Empress '33 ▸
Rasputin the Mad Monk '66
Rich Man, Poor Man '76 ▸
Savage Grace '07
Savannah '14
Scott Joplin '77
Simon and the Oaks '12
The Song of the Lark '01
Star! '68
Sunshine '99
There Will Be Blood '07 ▸
Tom & Viv '94 ▸
Two Brothers '04
The Vanishing Virginian '41
Vincere '09
Winchell '98
A Woman of Substance '84
The World Moves On '34
Youth Without Youth '07

Period Piece: 1900s

Adventure in Baltimore '49
Angel '07
Anne of Green Gables '85 ▸
Apostle '18
Back Street '41
Berkeley Square '98
The Best Intentions '92 ▸
Beyond the Wall of Sleep '06
Call of the Yukon '38
Cheaper by the Dozen '50 ▸
Cheri '09
The Cherry Orchard '99
City Boy '93 ▸
Colonel Redl '84 ▸
Daughters of the Dust '91 ▸
The Day They Robbed the Bank of England '60
The Dead '87 ▸
December Bride '91
The Dolly Sisters '46
Fanny and Alexander '83 ▸
Fiddler on the Roof '71 ▸
55 Days at Peking '63 ▸
Finding Neverland '04 ▸
The Forbidden Quest '93
Gentlemen's Relish '01
The Girl in White '52
The Go-Between '71 ▸
The Golden Bowl '00
The Golden Boys '08
The Good Old Boys '95
Hamlet '01
Hangover Square '45
The Happy Years '50
Hester Street '75 ▸
House of Mirth '00 ▸
The House on 56th Street '33
I Remember Mama '48 ▸
Illuminata '98
The Illusionist '06
The Imported Bridegroom '89
Institue Benjamenta or This Dream People Call Human Life '95
It's a Dog's Life '55
Jet Li's Fearless '06
Kill or Be Killed '15
Klimt '06
La Ronde '51 ▸
Lady L '65
Land of Promise '74
Legendary Weapons of China '82
Les Destinees '00
Like Water for Chocolate '93 ▸
The Lost Boys '78 ▸
Madame Butterfly '95
The Magnificent Ambersons '42 ▸
The Magnificent Ambersons '02
Man of Evil '48
Meet Me in St. Louis '44 ▸
A Midsummer Night's Sex Comedy '82 ▸
Miss Potter '06
Mrs. Soffel '84
Mr. Toad's Wild Ride '96
Mother Wore Tights '47 ▸
My Fair Lady '64 ▸
My Uncle Silas '01 ▸
Neverland '11
Nora '00
Old San Francisco '27
One Sunday Afternoon '48
Our Town '40 ▸
Our Town '77 ▸
Our Town '89
Over the Waves '49
Papa's Delicate Condition '63 ▸
Ragtime '81 ▸
The Railway Children '70 ▸
The Railway Children '00 ▸
A River Runs Through It '92 ▸
The Road to Wellville '94
A Room with a View '86 ▸
A Room With a View '08
San Francisco '36 ▸
Shadow Magic '00
She Creature '01
A Summer Story '88 ▸
Tales from the Gimli Hospital '88
The Vanishing '19
Viva Zapata! '52 ▸
We of the Never Never '82 ▸
Where Angels Fear to Tread '91 ▸
White Witch Doctor '53
The Widowing of Mrs. Holroyd '95
William Shakespeare's A Midsummer Night's Dream '99
Woman in Gold '15
Yentl '83

Period Piece: 1910s

Abbott and Costello Meet the Keystone Kops '54
The Actress '53
And Starring Pancho Villa as Himself '03 ▸
Angel '07
Anglo-Saxon Attitudes '92
Anne of Avonlea '87 ▸
Atlantic City '44
Atlantis: The Lost Empire '01
The Basket '99
Birdsong '12
Bisbee '17 '18
Britannic '00
British Agent '34
Cannon for Cordoba '70
Catherine Cookson's Colour Blind '98
The Chambermaid on the Titanic '97
Chicken Every Sunday '48
Choices of the Heart: The Margaret Sanger Story '95
Christy '94
Cider with Rosie '99
Coco Chanel & Igor Stravinsky '09
Cold Skin '18
Country Life '95
Courage Mountain '89
A Death in the Family '02
Doctor Zhivago '65 ▸
Eight Men Out '88 ▸
The Englishman Who Went up a Hill But Came down a Mountain '95 ▸
FairyTale: A True Story '97
The Fall '06
Flambards '78
The Flame Trees of Thika '81 ▸
Flickers '80
Frantz '17 ▸
From Dusk Till Dawn 3: The Hangman's Daughter '99
Gabrielle '05
The Girl in the Red Velvet Swing '55
The Greatest Game Ever Played '05
Grizzly Falls '99
Heartland '81 ▸
Hole in the Sky '95
Howard's End '92 ▸
The I Don't Care Girl '53
The Iceman Cometh '60 ▸
The Iceman Cometh '73
Iron Will '93
Jet Li's Fearless '06
Journey's End '18
King of Devil's Island '10
Klimt '06
Lady Chatterley '92
Lady Chatterley's Lover '55
Lady Chatterley's Lover '81
The Lark Farm '07
The Last of His Tribe '92
The Last Place on Earth '85
The Last Rites of Ransom Pride '09
The Last Station '09
The Lightkeepers '09
Lily Dale '96
A Little Princess '95 ▸
The Lost World '02
Lure of the Wilderness '52
The Man Who Knew Infinity '16
Max '02
Michael Collins '96 ▸
Mrs. Santa Claus '96
Modigliani '04
A Monster in Paris '11
The Murder of Mary Phagan '87 ▸
My Brother Talks to Horses '47
Nickelodeon '76
1917 '19 ▸
1911 '11
No God, No Master '12
Old Gringo '89
On Moonlight Bay '51
On Valentine's Day '86
Opium: Diary of a Madwoman '07
Picture Bride '94
Plain Jane '02
A Promise '13
The Promise '17
Red Firecracker, Green Firecracker '93
Remember the Day '41
Renoir '12
Sarah, Plain and Tall '91 ▸
Sarah, Plain and Tall: Skylark '93
Sarah, Plain and Tall: Winter's End '99 ▸
Savage Messiah '72 ▸
Seraphine '08 ▸
Shackleton '02 ▸
Shattered City: The Halifax Explosion '03
She '65
The Shooting Party '85 ▸
Shopworn Angel '38 ▸
The Siege of Sidney Street '60
Solomon and Gaenor '98
Sons and Lovers '60 ▸
Stiff Upper Lips '96
Summer in February '13
Summer Storm '44
Sunset '18
Sunset Song '16
They Came to Cordura '59
They Shall Not Grow Old '19 ▸
Titanic '12
Tracker '10
The Traveling Executioner '70
Troubles '88
Tuck Everlasting '02
An Unfinished Piece for a Player Piano '77 ▸
A Very Long Engagement '04 ▸
Victory '95
The Well-Digger's Daughter '11
When Calls the Heart '13
The White Ribbon '09
The Wings of the Dove '97 ▸
The Winslow Boy '98 ▸
Women in Love '11
Wonder Woman '17 ▸

Period Piece: 1920s

Agatha Christie: A Life in Pictures '04
The Age of Shadows '16
Al Capone '59 ▸
Alleged '10
Amelia '09
Another Life '01
The Artist '11 ▸
The Aviator '04 ▸
Balto '95
Belles on Their Toes '52
Black Gold '62 ▸
Blackthorn '11
Bobby Jones: Stroke of Genius '04
The Boxer and the Bombshell '08
The Bretts '88 ▸
Brideshead Revisited '08
Bright Young Things '03
Broadway '42
The Broken Tower '11
Bullets over Broadway '94 ▸
Burning Daylight '10
By the Light of the Silvery Moon '53
The Cat's Meow '01
Changeling '08 ▸
Character '97
Chicago '02 ▸
Coco Chanel & Igor Stravinsky '09
Cold Comfort Farm '94 ▸
The Cotton Club '84 ▸
A Covenant With Death '67
De-Lovely '04
Death Defying Acts '07
Don't Look Up '08
Downton Abbey '19 ▸
Easy Virtue '08
Ele, My Friend '93
Enchanted April '92
Entertaining Angels: The Dorothy Day Story '96
Fantastic Beasts and Where to Find Them '16
Fantastic Beasts: The Crimes of Grindelwald '18
The Five Man Army '69
For Greater Glory '12
The Front Page '74
The Great Gatsby '74
The Great Gatsby '01
The Great Gatsby '13
The Great Magician '11
The Great Waldo Pepper '75 ▸
Greenwich Village '44
The Grissom Gang '71 ▸

▸ = rated three bones or higher

The Harmonists '99
Has Anybody Seen My Gal? '52
Haunted '95
The Helen Morgan Story '57
Hemingway's Garden of Eden '08
High Road to China '83
The Hireling '73
Hit the Dutchman '92
Hollywood Cavalcade '39
The House on 56th Street '33
I'll See You in My Dreams '51
The Immigrant '13 ▶
Incantato '03
Inherit the Wind '99
Inside the Walls of Folsom Prison '51
The Intended '02
Intimate Affairs '01
The Jazz Singer '80
Jeanne Eagels '57
Johnny Dangerously '84
Killer: A Journal of Murder '95
Kung Fu Killer '08
Lady Chatterley '10 ▶
The Last Flight '31
The Last September '99
Leatherheads '08
The Legend of Bagger Vance '00
Legend of Valentino '75
Legionnaire '98
Les Destinees '00
The Light Between Oceans '16
Little Ashes '09
Live by Night '16
The Lodgers '17
Longitude '00 ▶
The Loss of a Teardrop Diamond '08
The Lost City of Z '17 ▶
Love for Lydia '79 ▶
Love That Brute '50
The Lover '92
The Luzhin Defence '00
Mad Dog Coll '61
Magic in the Moonlight '14
Maids of Wilko '79
Man of the Century '99
Marguerite '16 ▶
Mary Poppins Returns '18
Melo '86
Memoirs of a Geisha '05
Mrs. Dalloway '97
Mrs. Parker and the Vicious Circle '94
Mister Johnson '91 ▶
The Moderns '88 ▶
The Mummy '99
My Life So Far '98
The Newton Boys '97
Once Upon a Time in America '84 ▶
The Painted Veil '06
Party Girl '58 ▶
A Passage to India '84 ▶
The Princess and the Frog '09 ▶
The Quest '96
The Rabbi's Cat '11
The Rebel '08 ▶
Return to Paradise '53
The Roaring Twenties '39 ▶
Robin and the 7 Hoods '64
Rosewood '96 ▶
Roxie Hart '42
Running for Grace '18
The St. Valentine's Day Massacre '67
Seraphine '08 ▶
Serena '14
Shadow of the Vampire '00 ▶
She Fell Among Thieves '78
Sister Aimee: The Aimee Semple McPherson Story '06
The Slingshot '93 ▶
Speedy Death '99 ▶
Splendor in the Grass '61 ▶
The Stationmaster's Wife '77
Studs Lonigan '60
Summer Lover '08
The Sun Also Rises '57
Sweet Land '05

Swoon '91 ▶
Temptress Moon '96
10,000 Black Men Named George '02
Tender Is the Night '62
Tenderness of the Wolves '73
Theremin: An Electronic Odyssey '95 ▶
Therese '12
Thoroughly Modern Millie '67
Those Daring Young Men in Their Jaunty Jalopies '69
The Tigress '93
Togo '19 ▶
Twenty-Four Eyes '54 ▶
Under the Biltmore Clock '85
The Untouchables '87 ▶
Valentino '77
Vita & Virginia '19
Where the Rivers Flow North '94
Wild Party '74
The Wildest Dream: The Conquest of Everest '10
The Wind Rises '13 ▶
The Wind That Shakes the Barley '06 ▶
The Wolves '82 ▶
Woman in Black '89
Wonderstruck '17
The Wooden Man's Bride '94
You Know My Name '99 ▶
Young Cassidy '65

Period Piece: 1930s

All My Loved Ones '00
Amelia '09
Amelia Earhart: The Final Flight '94
Appointment With Death '10
Ask the Dust '06
Atonement '07 ▶
The Aviator '04 ▶
Ballet Shoes '07
Barefoot Boy '38
Before the Rains '07
Being Julia '04 ▶
Belle Epoque '92 ▶
B.F.'s Daughter '48
Bitter Harvest '17
Blood and Orchids '86
Blood Brothers '07
Blood Creek '09
Booky's Crush '09
Borstal Boy '00
Break of Dawn '88
Brideshead Revisited '08
Burnt by the Sun '94 ▶
Butterfly '98 ▶
Café Society '16
Cambridge Spies '03
Captain Calamity '36
Cause Celebre '87 ▶
The Charmer '87
Cheerful Weather for the Wedding '12
Child Star: The Shirley Temple Story '01
The Children of Huang Shi '08
Christopher and His Kind '11 ▶
City of Life and Death '09
Cora Unashamed '00
Cracks '09
The Dance of Reality '14
Dancing at Lughnasa '98
Dangerous Liaisons '12
Dark and Stormy Night '09
Dark Streets '08
Day of the Falcon '11
Dead End Kids: Little Tough Guy '38
The Death of the Heart '87
The Devil's Backbone '01
Disappearances '06
Dogville '03
Doktor Faustus '82
The Education of Little Tree '97 ▶
Eva '09
Everyone's Hero '06
The Field '90 ▶
The Final Master '16
The Flowers of War '11
The Gathering Storm '02 ▶
Get Low '09 ▶

Gilles' Wife '04
Glorious 39 '09
Go Tell It on the Mountain '84
Good '08
A Good Woman '04
Gosford Park '01 ▶
The Grand Budapest Hotel '14 ▶
The Grass Harp '95
The Great Debaters '07 ▶
Grey Gardens '09 ▶
The Handmaiden '16 ▶
The Harmonists '99
Head in the Clouds '04
The Heart of Me '02
Heat of the Sun '99 ▶
Heavens Fall '06
The Helen Morgan Story '57
The Highwaymen '19
The Hindenburg '75
Hoodlum & Son '03
Houdini '53
Hugo '11 ▶
Hyde Park on Hudson '12
I Capture the Castle '02
I Don't Want to Talk About It '94
I Served the King of England '07 ▶
Idlewild '06
The Imposters '98
In Dubious Battle '17
In Pursuit of Honor '95
In the Realm of the Senses '76 ▶
The Inheritors '82
Innocent Lies '95
Invincible '01
Ip Man '08
The Iron Orchard '19
Joe and Max '02 ▶
John Rabe '09
King Kong '05 ▶
The King's Speech '10 ▶
Ladies in Lavender '04
The Lady Vanishes '13
Lassie '05
Last Call: The Final Chapter of F. Scott Fitzgerald '02
Liam '00
The Little Mermaid '18
Lost Horizon '73
Love's Labour's Lost '00
Mad Dog Coll '61
Madame Sata '02
The Man I Married '40
The Man Who Cried '00
Manderlay '05
Me and Orson Welles '09
Memoirs of a Geisha '05
A Merry War '97 ▶
Mildred Pierce '11
Miracles '89
Miss Pettigrew Lives for a Day '08 ▶
Mrs. Henderson Presents '05
The Moon & the Stars '07
The Moonshine War '70
Mrs. Lowry & Son '19
The Mummy Returns '01
Murder in a Small Town '99
Murder, Inc. '60
Murder on the Orient Express '10 ▶
Murderous Maids '00
North Face '08 ▶
Nothing Too Good for a Cowboy '98
Nowhere in Africa '02
The Oil Raider '34
Out of the Cold '99
Pandora and the Flying Dutchman '51
Paris 36 '08
Pavilion of Women '01
The Phantom Lover '95
Pride of Africa '97
The Prime of Miss Jean Brodie '69 ▶
The Prime of Miss Jean Brodie '78
The Proposition '97
Public Enemies '09
Purple Butterfly '03 ▶
Quiet Days in Clichy '90
Rabbit-Proof Fence '02 ▶
Radioland Murders '94

Ray '04 ▶
The Remains of the Day '93 ▶
Respire '09
Richard III '95 ▶
Road to Perdition '02 ▶
The Rocketeer '91 ▶
The Saddest Music in the World '03
Shanghai Triad '95 ▶
Sirens '94
Sky Captain and the World of Tomorrow '04
The Sleeping Dictionary '02
South Riding '11
Spies of Warsaw '13
Stargate: Continuum '08
Swing Kids '93
Tall, Dark and Handsome '41
Tea with Mussolini '99
There Be Dragons '11
These Foolish Things '06
The Thirteenth Floor '99
This Is My Father '99
Three Strangers '46
Triple Agent '04
Under the Volcano '84 ▶
Up at the Villa '00
Upstairs Downstairs '11
Valley of the Heart's Delight '07
Walk on the Wild Side '62
Water for Elephants '11
W.E. '11
The White Countess '05 ▶
The Whole Wide World '96 ▶
Wild River '60
The Wind Rises '13 ▶
The Yellow Rolls Royce '64

Period Piece: 1940s

The Aftermath '19
Aimee & Jaguar '98
All the King's Men '06
All the Pretty Horses '00
All Things Fair '95
Allied '16
Almost Peaceful '02 ▶
Anthropoid '16
Australia '08
The Aviator '04 ▶
Back Home '90
Back to the Secret Garden '01
Barton Fink '91 ▶
Batman: Mask of the Phantasm '93
Beanpole '20 ▶
Before the Fall '04
The Best of Men '12
The Black Dahlia '06
Bon Voyage '03 ▶
Broken Silence '01 ▶
Bugsy '91 ▶
The Caller '08
Carry Me Home '04
Charms for the Easy Life '02
Children On Their Birthdays '02
The Chorus '04
The Chosen '81 ▶
Christina '10
The Chronicles of Narnia: The Lion, the Witch and the Wardrobe '05
The Cider House Rules '99 ▶
Color of a Brisk and Leaping Day '95
The Counterfeiters '07 ▶
The Curse of the Jade Scorpion '01
Daphne '07
Darkest Hour '17 ▶
Dead Gorgeous '02
Deep Crimson '96
Delta of Venus '95
Devil in a Blue Dress '95 ▶
The Diary of Anne Frank '08
Doktor Faustus '82
The Doorbell Rang: A Nero Wolfe Mystery '01
Downfall '04 ▶
Dunkirk '17 ▶
Earth '98
East-West '99
The Edge '10
The Exception '17
Exorcist: The Beginning '04

The Fallen '05 ▶
Farewell, My Lovely '75 ▶
15 Amore '98
The Fifth Horseman Is Fear '64
A Film Unfinished '10
Florence Foster Jenkins '16
Focus '01
For a Lost Soldier '93
The Forbidden Quest '93
Fort McCoy '11
42 '13 ▶
Gainsbourg: A Heroic Life '10
Gate of Flesh '64
Going for Gold: The '48 Games '12
The Golden Spiders: A Nero Wolfe Mystery '00
Good Evening, Mr. Wallenberg '93
The Good German '06
The Good Shepherd '06
The Good, the Bad, the Weird '08
Goodbye, Mr. Chips '69
Goodnight, Mr. Tom '99
The Grass Harp '95
The Grey Zone '01
Hacksaw Ridge '16
Hannibal Rising '07
Head in the Clouds '04
The Heart of Me '02
Hong Kong 1941 '84
The Hours '02 ▶
The Human Stain '03
In the Mood '87
The Infinite Worlds of H.G. Wells '01
The Innocents '16 ▶
Ip Man 2 '10
Ithaca '16
Jimmy P. '13
Joe Gould's Secret '00
Julie & Julia '09 ▶
Kabei: Our Mother '08
Keep the Faith, Baby '02
Kill Your Darlings '13
A Killing Affair '85
Kinsey '04 ▶
Kon-Tiki '12
Kung Fu Hustle '04
La Vie en Rose '07
Land of Mine '15
The Last Time I Committed Suicide '96
A League of Their Own '92 ▶
The Lena Baker Story '08
A Lesson Before Dying '99 ▶
The Little Stranger '18
Lonely Hearts '06
The Lost City '05
Lost in Yonkers '93
Malena '00
The Man Who Wasn't There '01 ▶
Mararia '98
Margaret's Museum '95 ▶
Married Life '07 ▶
A Matador's Mistress '08
The McCullochs '75
The Member of the Wedding '52 ▶
Memoirs of a Geisha '05
Miral '10
Mrs. Henderson Presents '05
Mountbatten: The Last Viceroy '86
The Mummy: Tomb of the Dragon Emperor '08
My Dog Skip '99 ▶
The Mystery of Rampo '94 ▶
The Mystic Masseur '01
The Neon Bible '95
Neruda '16
The Ninth Day '04 ▶
The Notebook '04
Nowhere in Africa '02
Nuremberg '00
O Jerusalem '07
The Old Settler '01
On the Road '12
Orde Wingate '76
Other Voices, Other Rooms '95
The Others '01 ▶
Pan's Labyrinth '06 ▶
Partition '07

The Pianist '02 ▶
Pollock '00 ▶
Possessed '00
The Power of One '92
Professor Marston and the Wonder Women '17
The Public Eye '92 ▶
The Quarrel '93
Racing with the Moon '84 ▶
Railroad Tigers '17
Ray '04 ▶
Resistance '20
The Return of Eliot Ness '91
Ride the Wild Fields '00
The Rising Place '02
RKO 281 '99 ▶
The Road from Coorain '02
The Rocket '05 ▶
Rocky Marciano '99
Rosenstrasse '03 ▶
A Royal Night Out '15 ▶
The Runaway '00
Sarah's Key '10
Season of Change '94
A Secret '07 ▶
A Separate Peace '04
The Seventh Dawn '64
The Shadow Within '07
Shakedown on the Sunset Strip '88
Shanghai '09 ▶
The Shell Seekers '06
The Sins of Rachel Cade '61
Snow Falling on Cedars '99
Snow in August '01
Something the Lord Made '04
Sophie Scholl: The Final Days '05 ▶
Spring 1941 '08
Stand-Ins '97
Strayed '03 ▶
Sudie & Simpson '90 ▶
Surviving Picasso '96
Swing Shift '84
Three Comrades '38 ▶
Three Stripes in the Sun '55
Timbuktu '59
Torso '02
Trumbo '07 ▶
The Two Jakes '90
Under the Piano '95
A United Kingdom '17
Viceroy's House '17
Village of Dreams '97
The Water Horse: Legend of the Deep '07
The Way Back '10
W.E. '11
The Wedding Song '09
With a Song in My Heart '52 ▶
The Woman in Black 2: Angel of Death '15
The Yellow Rolls Royce '64
Your Cheatin' Heart '64
Zelary '03 ▶
The Zookeeper's Wife '17

Period Piece: 1950s

Absolute Beginners '86
The Affairs of Dobie Gillis '53
Alien Trespass '09
All the King's Men '06
Almayer's Folly '12
An American Rhapsody '01 ▶
Amongst Women '98
Anglo-Saxon Attitudes '92
The Audrey Hepburn Story '00
Austin Powers In Goldmember '02
Back to the Future '85 ▶
Back to the Future, Part 2 '89
Badlands '74 ▶
The Banker '20
Battle of Jangsari '19
A Beautiful Mind '01 ▶
Beefcake '99
Beyond the Sea '04
Big Eyes '14
Big Night '95
Big Town '87
The Bletchley Circle '13
Blind Faith '98
The Blue Kite '93 ▶
Bluebeard '09

▶ = rated three bones or higher

Book of Love '91
The Bookshop '18
Born Reckless '59
Boycott '02 ▶
Bride Flight '08
The Buddy Holly Story '78 ▶
Bye, Bye, Birdie '63 ▶
Cadillac Records '08 ▶
Cafe Society '97
The California Kid '74
Capote '05 ▶
Carol '15 ▶
Che '08
Chicken Run '00 ▶
Chicken With Plums '11
Child Bride of Short Creek '81
Chocolat '00 ▶
The Christine Jorgensen Story '70
Circle of Friends '94
Citizen Gangster '11
The Climb '97
Cold War '18 ▶
The Company '07
Cool and the Crazy '94
Corrina, Corrina '94
Cotton Mary '99
Crazy '08
Crazy Love '07 ▶
Crazy Mama '75
Cry-Baby '90 ▶
Cuban Blood '03
Dance with a Stranger '85 ▶
Dark Blue World '01
Dark Fields '09
Dark of the Sun '68
Dead Poets Society '89 ▶
The Death of Stalin '17 ▶
Desire and Hell at Sunset Motel '92
Deuces Wild '02
Devil's Island '96
Diner '82 ▶
Dirty Dancing '87 ▶
Dirty Dancing: Havana Nights '04
The Door in the Floor '04 ▶
Dreaming of Joseph Lees '99
Echoes '88
Elvis: The Movie '79
End of the Spear '06
Eros '04
Evelyn '02 ▶
Evening '07
Evil '03 ▶
Fall Time '94
Far from Heaven '02 ▶
Father of the Bride '50 ▶
Fences '16 ▶
Flick '07
Flowers in the Attic '14
For the Boys '91
The Founder '17 ▶
The Front '76 ▶
Fur: An Imaginary Portrait of Diane Arbus '06
The Game of Their Lives '05
The Ghastly Love of Johnny X '12
Going All the Way '97
Golden Gate '93
Good Night, and Good Luck '05 ▶
The Good Shepherd '06
Grease 2 '82
Grease '78 ▶
Guilty by Suspicion '91
A Gun, a Car, a Blonde '97
Hannibal Rising '07
Haywire '80
The Heart of Dixie '89
Hello, Hemingway '90
Her Majesty '01
Hey Good Lookin' '82
The High Bright Sun '65
A Hole in One '04
Hollywoodland '06
Hometown U.S.A. '79
Honeydripper '07
Hounddog '08
The Hours '02 ▶
The House on Carroll Street '88
Housekeeping '87 ▶
Howl '10
The Hudsucker Proxy '93 ▶
I Am David '04
I Served the King of England '07 ▶
The Imitation Game '14 ▶
In His Life: The John Lennon Story '00
Indiana Jones and the Kingdom of the Crystal Skull '08
Indignation '16
Introducing Dorothy Dandridge '99 ▶
Inventing the Abbotts '97
I.Q. '94
Jailbreakers '94
James Dean '76
James Dean '01
James Dean: Live Fast, Die Young '97
Julie & Julia '09 ▶
Jump Into Hell '55
Just Henry '11
Just Looking '99
A King in New York '57
Kinsey '04 ▶
Kitchen Stories '03
The Kitchen Toto '87 ▶
La Bamba '87 ▶
L.A. Confidential '97 ▶
La Vie en Rose '07
Labyrinth of Lies '14
Last Exit to Brooklyn '90 ▶
The Last Godfather '10
The Last of Robin Hood '13
The Last Picture Show '71 ▶
The Last Ride '12
Liberty Heights '99
Life '15 ▶
Little Richard '00
Lola '81
The Long Day Closes '92 ▶
The Long Summer of George Adams '82
The Long Walk Home '89 ▶
The Lords of Flatbush '74
The Lost City '05
Lost, Lonely, and Vicious '59
A Love Divided '01
Loveless '83
Loving '16 ▶
Mac '93 ▶
The Majestic '01
The Mambo Kings '92 ▶
The Man in the Moon '91 ▶
The Master '12 ▶
Mischief '85
Mr. Rock 'n' Roll: The Alan Freed Story '99
Mona Lisa Smile '03
Moscow Does Not Believe in Tears '80 ▶
Motherless Brooklyn '19
The Motorcycle Diaries '04 ▶
The Mountain '19
Mulholland Falls '95
My American Cousin '85 ▶
My Favorite Year '82 ▶
My Louisiana Sky '02
My One and Only '09
My Week With Marilyn '11
The Mystic Masseur '01
New World '95
Newsfront '78 ▶
Northfork '03
The Notorious Bettie Page '06
Nowhere Boy '09
Once Upon a Time . . . When We Were Colored '95 ▶
One Plus One '61
OSS 117: Cairo, Nest of Spies '06
The Other Side of Heaven '02
The Other Side of Sunday '96
Our Time '74
A Painted House '03
Papa: Hemingway in Cuba '16
Parents '89 ▶
The Passion of Ayn Rand '99
Peacock '09
Peggy Sue Got Married '86
The Perfect Game '09
Perfect Harmony '91
The Perfume of Yvonne '94
Phantom Thread '17 ▶
The Phenix City Story '55 ▶
Pillow Talk '59 ▶
The Playboys '92 ▶
Pollock '00 ▶
Porky's '82
A Portrait of James Dean: Joshua Tree, 1951 '12
The Prize Winner of Defiance, Ohio '05 ▶
The Producers '05
Queen and Country '14
The Quiet American '02 ▶
Quiz Show '94 ▶
A Rage in Harlem '91 ▶
A Raisin in the Sun '89 ▶
A Raisin in the Sun '08
Ray '04 ▶
Reaching for the Moon '13
The Reader '08
The Reflecting Skin '91
Relative Values '99
Revolutionary Road '08
The Road Home '01 ▶
Roadracers '94
Rock, Baby, Rock It '57
The Rocket '05 ▶
Rocky Marciano '99
The Rosa Parks Story '02
Round Midnight '86 ▶
Rules Don't Apply '16
The Rum Diary '11
Saint Ralph '04
Saving Grace B. Jones '09
The Scapegoat '12
The Scent of Green Papaya '93 ▶
School Ties '92 ▶
A Secret '07 ▶
Shadowlands '93 ▶
Shake, Rattle and Rock '57
Shake, Rattle & Rock! '94
Shout '91
Shutter Island '09 ▶
The Singing Detective '03
Snow Falling on Cedars '99
Sparkle '76
Stan & Ollie '18 ▶
The Star Maker '95
Starkweather '04
Stella Days '12
The Sticky Fingers of Time '97
Stolen '09
Strange Invaders '83 ▶
A Stranger in the Kingdom '98
Suburbicon '17
Superdad '73
Swimming Upstream '03
Sylvia '03
The Talented Mr. Ripley '99
Teenage Doll '57
Tell It to the Bees '19
Terranova '91
That'll Be the Day '73
The Thief '97
This Boy's Life '93 ▶
Though None Go With Me '06
Three Wishes '95
Tito and Me '92 ▶
The Tournament '09
The Tree of Life '11 ▶
The Trial of Old Drum '00
Trumbo '07 ▶
Tune in Tomorrow '90
Two Family House '99
United '11
The Vast of Night '20 ▶
Vera Drake '04 ▶
Voice from the Stone '17
Walk the Line '05 ▶
Walker Payne '06
The War of the Worlds '53 ▶
The Way We Were '73 ▶
When Father Was Away on Business '85 ▶
Where the Truth Lies '05
Who Do You Love '08
Who Shot Pat? '92
The Wild One '54 ▶
Women Without Men '09
Wonder Wheel '17
The World Unseen '07
Wrestling with Alligators '98
W.W. and the Dixie Dancekings '75
Your Cheatin' Heart '64
You've Ruined Me, Eddie '58

Period Piece: 1960s

***See also** Boomer Reunions*

Across the Universe '07
Adam at 6 a.m. '70
Adam Resurrected '08
An Adventure in Space and Time '13
Agatha Christie: A Life in Pictures '04
Agnes Browne '99
Ali '01
Alice's Restaurant '69
All I Wanna Do '98
An American Affair '09
An American Crime '07
American Gangster '07 ▶
American Graffiti '73 ▶
American Pastoral '16
Angels Hard As They Come '71
Apollo 11 '19 ▶
Asylum '05
Austin Powers 2: The Spy Who Shagged Me '99 ▶
Auto Focus '02 ▶
Awakenings of the Beast '68
The Baader Meinhof Complex '08
Backbeat '94 ▶
Bad Education '04 ▶
Bad Times at the El Royale '18
The Banker '20
The Beautiful, the Bloody and the Bare '64
Believe in Me '06
Berkeley '05
Best of Youth '03 ▶
Betty & Coretta '13
Beyond the Sea '04
The Big Chill '83 ▶
Big Eyes '14
Big Sur '13
Blast-Off Girls '67
The Blue Kite '93 ▶
Blue Sky '91 ▶
Bob & Carol & Ted & Alice '69
Bobby '06
Born in 68 '08
Born on the Fourth of July '89 ▶
The Boston Strangler: The Untold Story '08
The Boys and Girl From County Clare '03
The Boys of 2nd Street Park '03 ▶
Brand New Day '10
Brian's Song '01
The Bridges of Madison County '95 ▶
Brighton Rock '10
Brokeback Mountain '05 ▶
A Bronx Tale '93 ▶
Burnt Money '00
Capote '05 ▶
Catch Me If You Can '02
Cesar Chavez '14
Chappaquiddick '17
Charlie '04
Chasing Christmas '05
The Chatterley Affair '06
Che '08
Chicago 10 '07 ▶
Child of God '14
Children Shouldn't Play with Dead Things '72
Christmas in Canaan '09
City of God '02
The Climbers '19
The Company '07
Company Man '00
Confessions of a Dangerous Mind '02
Confessions of Sorority Girls '94
Conspiracy: The Trial of the Chicago Eight '87 ▶
CQ '01
Crazy in Alabama '99
The Crimson Cult '68
Dangerous Liaisons '03
Dead Beat '94
Dead Presidents '95
Dear Eleanor '16
The Debt '07
The Debt '10
December Boys '07
Deserter '02
Detroit '17 ▶
Digging to China '98
Dirty Deeds '02 ▶
The Dish '00 ▶
Dogfight '91 ▶
The Doors '91
Doubt '08 ▶
Down With Love '03
The Dreamers '03
Dreamgirls '06 ▶
Dynamite Chicken '70
Easy Rider '69 ▶
An Education '09 ▶
Eichmann '07
Eight Miles High '07
El Cantante '06
Eros '04
Even Cowgirls Get the Blues '94
The Express '08
Factory Girl '06
Falling Angels '03
A Family of Spies '90
Fatal Deception: Mrs. Lee Harvey Oswald '93
Filth '08
Final Portrait '17
First Love and Other Pains / One of Them '99
First Man '18
Five Corners '88 ▶
Flash of Genius '08
Flashback '89 ▶
Flawless '07
Flipped '10
Ford v Ferrari '19 ▶
Four Friends '81 ▶
Free to Run '16
Freedom Song '00 ▶
Freedom Summer '14
Fritz the Cat '72 ▶
From the Earth to the Moon '98 ▶
Gainsbourg: A Heroic Life '10
Gangster No. 1 '00
Gimme Shelter '70
The Girl '12
Girl, Interrupted '99
Glory Road '06
The Glory Stompers '67
Godspell '73
The Good Shepherd '06
Grace of Monaco '14
Grace of My Heart '96
Green Book '18 ▶
Greetings '68 ▶
Greetings from Tim Buckley '12
Hair '79 ▶
Hairspray '07 ▶
Hannah Arendt '12
The Haunting of Sharon Tate '19
Head '68 ▶
Hearts in Atlantis '01
The Help '11 ▶
Help Wanted Female '68
Hendrix '00
Hidden Figures '17 ▶
Hideous Kinky '99
High Hopes '88 ▶
Hitchcock '12
The Hollywood Knights '80
Hula Girls '06
I Am Not Your Negro '17 ▶
I Drink Your Blood '71
I Love You, Alice B. Toklas! '68
I Shot Andy Warhol '96 ▶
Ida '13 ▶
The Identical '14
If These Walls Could Talk 2 '00
Imaginary Crimes '94 ▶
In His Father's Shoes '97
In His Life: The John Lennon Story '00
In the Mood for Love '00
Infamous '06
Inside Llewyn Davis '13 ▶
The Irishman '19 ▶
Isn't She Great '00
Jackie '16 ▶
Jackie Bouvier Kennedy Onassis '00
Jayne Mansfield's Car '13
Jersey Boys '14
Jimi: All Is by My Side '14
John John in the Sky '00
Judy '19 ▶
K-19: The Widowmaker '02
The Kennedys '11
Killing Kennedy '13
A Kind of Murder '16
The Least Among You '09
Lennon Naked '10
Like A Bride '94 ▶
Liz & Dick '12
The Locusts '97
Longford '06
The Look of Love '13
The Lords of Discipline '83
Love Field '91
Loving '16 ▶
Lumumba '01 ▶
M. Butterfly '93
Made in Dagenham '10 ▶
The Magdalene Sisters '02 ▶
Magic Trip: Ken Kesey's Search for a Kool Place '11
Maladies '13
The Manson Family '04
Mantis in Lace '68
Margot '09
Married to It '93
Matinee '92
Men in Black 3 '12
The Mercy '19
Mesrine: Part 1-Killer Instinct '08
Metroland '97
Middletown '06
Miral '10
Mr. Church '16
Monsieur Ibrahim '03 ▶
Moonrise Kingdom '12 ▶
Moonwalkers '16
More '69
More American Graffiti '79
My Brother Is an Only Child '07
My Little Assassin '99
Not Fade Away '12
Novitiate '17
Odd Birds '85
Off Limits '87
On Chesil Beach '17
Once Upon A Time... In Hollywood '19 ▶
The Only Thrill '97
Only Yesterday '16 ▶
Operation Avalanche '16
OSS 117: Lost in Rio '09
The Other Side of Heaven 2: Fire of Faith '19
Ouija: Origin of Evil '16
Out '82
Pack of Lies '87
The Paperboy '12
Parkland '13
Passing Glory '99 ▶
Path to War '02 ▶
A Perfect World '93
Phantom Punch '09
Pirate Radio '09
Place of Execution '09
A Plumm Summer '08
Poodle Springs '98
Power and Beauty '02
The Private Lives of Pippa Lee '09
Psych-Out '68
Psycho Beach Party '00
Race to Space '01
Rainbow Bridge '71
Ray '04 ▶
Reaching for the Moon '13
The Reader '08
The Rebel Set '59
Rescue Dawn '06 ▶
RFK '02
Rhapsody of Spring '98
Riding in Cars with Boys '01
Riding the Bullet '04
The Road to Coronation Street '10
Romulus, My Father '07 ▶
R.P.M.* (*Revolutions Per Minute) '70
Ruby Bridges '98
Ruby's Bucket of Blood '01

▶ = rated three bones or higher

The Sandlot '93 ▶
The Sandpiper '65
Satan's Sadists '69
Seberg '19
Second Thoughts '83
The Secret Life of Bees '08 ▶
See No Evil: The Moors Murders '06
Selma '14 ▶
Selma, Lord, Selma '99
A Serious Man '09 ▶
Sex & Drugs & Rock & Roll '10
Shag: The Movie '89 ▶
The Shape of Water '17 ▶
A Single Man '09 ▶
The '60s '99
61* '01 ▶
Skipped Parts '00
Slashed Dreams '74
A Small Circle of Friends '80
Snake & Mongoose '13
The Snake People '68
Soldiers of Change '06
Sparkle '12
The Speed Lovers '68
Steal This Movie! '00
Stoned '05
The Stoned Age '94
Stonewall '15
The Strawberry Statement '70
Sugartime '95
Surfwise '07 ▶
Swimming Upstream '03
Sylvia '03
Taking Woodstock '09
Talk to Me '07
Teen Beach Movie '13
Telling Lies in America '96
Telstar: The Joe Meek Story '08
A Texas Funeral '99
That Night '93
That Thing You Do! '96 ▶
That's What I Am '11
The Theory of Everything '14
There Goes My Baby '92
There's a Girl in My Soup '70
Thirteen Days '00 ▶
Thumb Tripping '72
Tin Men '87
To the Stars '20
Toast '10
Tower '16 ▶
The Trip '67
The Tunnel '01 ▶
Tunnel Rats '08
The 24 Hour War '16
The Two Faces of January '14
Undercover With the KKK '78
Used People '92
Valentin '02
Wah-Wah '05
Waiting for the Light '90
Walk Hard: The Dewey Cox Story '07
A Walk on the Moon '99
Walk the Line '05 ▶
The Ward '10
The Watsons Go to Birmingham '13
The Weather Underground '02 ▶
When I Find the Ocean '06
Where Angels Go, Trouble Follows '68
Where the Truth Lies '05
The White Crow '18
Who Do You Love '08
Who'll Stop the Rain? '78 ▶
Wild in the Streets '68
Wild Reeds '94 ▶
Wildlife '18 ▶
Wolf Totem '15
The Women on the Sixth Floor '10
Wondrous Oblivion '06 ▶
Won't You Be My Neighbor? '18 ▶
The Woods '03
Woodstock '70 ▶
The World's Fastest Indian '05 ▶

X-Men: First Class '11 ▶
Yellow Submarine '68 ▶
Zeroville '19
The Zodiac '05
Zodiac '07
Zombi Child '20

Period Piece: 1970s

Action Point '18
After the Rain '99
Ali '01
All Good Things '10
Almost Famous '00 ▶
American Gangster '07 ▶
American Hustle '13 ▶
American Made '17
Anchorman: The Legend of Ron Burgundy '04
Ann Rule Presents: The Stranger Beside Me '03
Apollo 18 '11
Argo '12 ▶
Armistead Maupin's More Tales of the City '97
Armistead Maupin's Tales of the City '93
The Assassination of Richard Nixon '05
Austin Powers In Goldmember '02
Auto Focus '02 ▶
Baadasssss! '03 ▶
The Baader Meinhof Complex '08
The Backwoods '06
Bad Education '04 ▶
Balzac and the Little Chinese Seamstress '02
The Bank Job '08 ▶
Barney's Version '10
Battle of the Sexes '17
Beautiful Ohio '06
Behind the Candelabra '13
The Best of Enemies '19
Best of Youth '03 ▶
The Betty Ford Story '87 ▶
Blame It on Fidel '06
Blood Done Sign My Name '10
Blood Ties '13
Bloody Sunday '01 ▶
Blow '01
Blue Hill Avenue '01
Bohemian Rhapsody '18
Boogie Nights '97 ▶
Boogie Vision '77
Breakfast on Pluto '05
The Bronx Is Burning '07
Brothers of the Head '06
Bundy: A Legacy of Evil '08
Callas Forever '02
Carlito's Way: Rise to Power '05
Carlos '10
Carnage Park '16
Casino '95 ▶
Catch Me If You Can '02
CBGB '13
Cellmates '12
Cemetery Junction '10
Cesar Chavez '14
Chasing 3000 '07
Children of the Corn '09
Chopper '00
Christine '16
Chronicle of an Escape '06
Chuck '17
Cinema Verite '11
City of God '02
The Clinic '10
Coming Home '14
Concerning Violence '14
Confessions of a Dangerous Mind '02
Control '07
Creatures from the Pink Lagoon '07
Crooklyn '94 ▶
Crossing the Bridge '92
The Curse of La Llorona '19
The Damned United '09
The Dangerous Lives of Altar Boys '02 ▶
Dark Shadows '12
Dazed and Confused '93 ▶
A Decade Under the Influence '02 ▶
Detroit Rock City '99
Dick '99 ▶

Diggers '06
Dolemite Is My Name '19 ▶
Donnie Brasco '96 ▶
Dreamgirls '06 ▶
Drugstore Cowboy '89 ▶
East Is East '99 ▶
Eaters '15
El Cantante '06
Elvis & Nixon '16
The Emperor's Club '02
Escape from Pretoria '20
Escape: Human Cargo '98 ▶
Extremely Wicked, Shockingly Evil and Vile '19
Fear and Loathing in Las Vegas '98
The Fields '11
15 Minutes of War '19
54 '98
Film Stars Don't Die in Liverpool '17
Finding Steve McQueen '19
First They Killed My Father '17
Five Minutes of Heaven '09
Flashbacks of a Fool '08
Forever Mine '99
Frailty '02 ▶
Frankie and Alice '10
Freaky Deaky '12
Free Fire '17
Free Ride '13
From the Earth to the Moon '98 ▶
Frost/Nixon '08 ▶
Funkytown '11
Gia '98
Good Fences '03
The Good Humor Man '05
Gracie '07
Grand Theft Parsons '03
Green Dragon '01
Green Plaid Shirt '96
Grey Gardens '09 ▶
Heading South '05 ▶
Hedwig and the Angry Inch '00 ▶
Hideous Kinky '99
Higher Ground '11 ▶
The Hillside Stranglings '04
The Hoax '06
House of D '04
How To Talk To Girls At Parties '17
H.P. Lovecraft's The Color Out of Space '10
I Know My First Name Is Steven '89
The Ice Storm '97 ▶
If Beale Street Could Talk '18 ▶
If These Walls Could Talk 2 '00
I'm Not Scared '03
Imagining Argentina '04
Inherent Vice '14 ▶
The Inkwell '94
Invincible '06 ▶
Invisible Circus '00
The Irishman '19 ▶
Isn't She Great '00
Jacob '11
Jesus' Son '99
Jill the Ripper '00
Joe the King '99
Kate Plays Christine '16 ▶
Kill the Irishman '11
Killing Bono '11
Kippur '00 ▶
The Kitchen '19
The Kite Runner '07 ▶
The Ladies Man '00
The Last Circus '10
The Last King of Scotland '06 ▶
The Last of the High Kings '96
Last Rampage '17
Left Luggage '98
The Legend of Rita '99
Lennon Naked '10
Life of Crime '13
Local Color '06
Long Time Since '97
The Look of Love '13
Lords of Dogtown '05
Love Ranch '10
A Love to Keep '07
The Lovely Bones '09

The Lovers and the Despot '16
Mafia '11
Man on the Moon '99
Man on Wire '08
Mao's Last Dancer '09
Mark Felt: The Man Who Brought Down the White House '17
Maryam '00
Mesrine: Part 1-Killer Instinct '08
Mesrine: Part 2-Public Enemy Number 1 '08
Metroland '97
Mighty Fine '12
The Mighty Macs '09
Miles Ahead '16 ▶
Milk '08 ▶
Miracle '04 ▶
The Missing Picture '13
Mr. Nice '10
Moonlight Mile '02 ▶
Muhammad Ali's Greatest Fight '13
Multiple Sarcasms '10
Munich '05 ▶
Murder in Greenwich '02
Music Within '07
My Friend Dahmer '17
Nearing Grace '05
Never Let Me Go '10
New Waterford Girl '99
The Nice Guys '16 ▶
Night Catches Us '10
The Night We Called It a Day '03
North Country '05
Of Love and Shadows '94
Off the Map '03 ▶
On the Basis of Sex '18
The Other Side of the Wind '18
Persepolis '07 ▶
Pinero '01
The Poker House '09
The Post '17 ▶
Prefontaine '96
Pride '07
Protecting the King '07
The Quiet Ones '14
Radio '03
Rain '01
Rampage: The Hillside Strangler Murders '04
Ratcatcher '99
Rated X '00
Red Riding, Part 1: 1974 '09
Rhapsody of Spring '98
Riding in Cars with Boys '01
Rise of the Footsoldier '07
Roll Bounce '05 ▶
Rolling Thunder Revue: A Bob Dylan Story by Martin Scorsese '19 ▶
Roma '18 ▶
Roman Polanski: Wanted and Desired '08
The Royal Tenenbaums '01 ▶
The Runaways '10
Running with Scissors '06
Rush '13 ▶
Sal '11
The Sandlot 2 '05
The Sandlot 3: Heading Home '07
Scotland, PA '02
Secretariat '10
Semi-Pro '08
Septembers of Shiraz '16
The '70s '00
'71 '14 ▶
Sex & Drugs & Rock & Roll '10
Shot in the Heart '01 ▶
Silent Waters '03
Slums of Beverly Hills '98 ▶
Son of Sam '08
Soul Power '08
The Source Family '13
Spirit of '76 '91
Spy Game '01
Stander '03
Starsky & Hutch '04
Steal This Movie! '00
Stolen Summer '02
Strawberry and Chocolate '93 ▶
Street Boss '09

Such a Long Journey '98 ▶
Summer of Sam '99
Sunset Strip '99
Surfwise '07 ▶
Suspiria '18
Swinging Safari '19
Tabloid '10
Take Me Home: The John Denver Story '00
That's the Way I Like It '99
The Thin Blue Lie '00
The Third Miracle '99
31 '16
Thunder Soul '10
The Tiger Hunter '17
Tigerland '00 ▶
Torremolinos 73 '03
Tracks '14
The Trip '02
20th Century Women '17
24 Hour Party People '01
Two of Us '00
The U.S. Vs. John Lennon '06
The Vanished Empire '08
Vault '19
Velvet Goldmine '98
The Virgin Suicides '99
Waking the Dead '00
Walk Hard: The Dewey Cox Story '07
The War '94
Water Drops on Burning Rocks '99
We Are Marshall '06
The Weather Underground '02 ▶
West Beirut '98
What We Do Is Secret '07
Where the Truth Lies '05
White Irish Drinkers '10
Winter of Frozen Dreams '08
Without Limits '97 ▶
The Wolf Hour '19
Wonderstruck '17
Won't You Be My Neighbor? '18 ▶
The World Made Straight '15
X-Men: Days of Future Past '14 ▶
Xiu Xiu: The Sent Down Girl '97 ▶
The Year Dolly Parton Was My Mom '11
The Year My Parents Went on Vacation '07
You've Got a Friend '07
Zodiac '07

Period Piece: 1980s

Adventureland '09 ▶
The Adventures of Sebastian Cole '99
American Fable '17
American Psycho '99
Anchorman 2: The Legend Continues '13
Angela '02
Anvil! The Story of Anvil '09
Apt Pupil '97
Ash Wednesday '02
The Assignment '97
Atomic Blonde '17
Autumn Hearts: A New Beginning '07
Bad Country '14
Bad Education '04 ▶
Best of Youth '03 ▶
Beyond Borders '03
Beyond the Blackboard '11
Billionaire Boys Club '18
Billy Elliot '00 ▶
Bleed for This '16
Blinded by the Light '19 ▶
Blow '01
Borg vs. McEnroe '17 ▶
Born in 68 '08
Brooklyn Rules '07
Buffalo Soldiers '01
Bumblebee '18 ▶
Burton and Taylor '13
The Business '05
Call Me by Your Name '17 ▶
The Capture of the Green River Killer '08
Capturing the Friedmans '03 ▶
Carlos '10
Catch a Fire '06

Chapter 27 '07
Charlie Wilson's War '07
City of God '02
Cold in July '14 ▶
Computer Chess '13
Cropsey '10
Crown Heights '17
Cruise '18
Dallas Buyers Club '13 ▶
Dangerous Evidence: The Lori Jackson Story '99
The Day Reagan Was Shot '01
Days and Nights '14
Decoding Annie Parker '13
The Devil's Double '11
Dirty Girl '10
The Disappearance of Vonnie '94
Disco and Atomic War '14
District 9 '09 ▶
Donnie Darko '01 ▶
Drug Wars: The Camarena Story '90 ▶
Dumb and Dumberer: When Harry Met Lloyd '03
Earthquake Bird '19
Edge of Seventeen '99
Endgame '09
An Englishman in New York '09
Everest '07
An Everlasting Piece '00
Extremely Wicked, Shockingly Evil and Vile '19
Falco '08
Farewell '09
Fever Pitch '96
Fierce People '05
Fifty Dead Men Walking '08
The Final Girls '15
Find Me Guilty '06 ▶
Fool's Gold: The Story of the Brink's-Mat Robbery '92
Forever Mine '99
Formosa Betrayed '09
4 Months, 3 Weeks and 2 Days '07 ▶
Foxcatcher '14 ▶
Friday Night Lights '04 ▶
Friends & Crocodiles '05
The Front Runner '18
Game 6 '05
G.B.H. '91
Ghostboat '06
Gifted Hands: The Ben Carson Story '09
Good Bye, Lenin! '03 ▶
Green Plaid Shirt '96
A Guide to Recognizing Your Saints '06
Hands of Stone '16
Happiness Runs '10
Haunter '13
Heart of the Beholder '05 ▶
The Heineken Kidnapping '11
High Life '09
The History Boys '06
Hollywood North '03
House of Saddam '08
The House of the Devil '09 ▶
Hunger '08
The Hunt for the I-5 Killer '11
Hurlyburly '98
Hustle '04
Hysterical Blindness '02
The Iceman '12
In America '02 ▶
The Infiltrator '16
The Informers '09
Innocent Voices '04
The Iron Lady '11
It '17 ▶
Jackie Bouvier Kennedy Onassis '00
Jean-Michel Basquiat: The Radiant Child '10 ▶
Joker '19 ▶
Just Ask My Children '01
Kill the Poor '03
Killing Bono '11
Labor Day '13
The Lady '11
Lan Yu '01
Last Days in Vietnam '14
The Last Days of Disco '98 ▶
The Last Shot '04

▶ = rated three bones or higher

Lebanon '09
The Legend of Rita '99
Leto '19
The Line of Beauty '06
The Lives of Others '06 ▶
The Lovers on the Bridge '91
Low Tide '19
The Magician '93
Maiden '18 ▶
Man on the Moon '99
Mandy '18
Mao's Last Dancer '09
Marathon '09
McFarland USA '15
MDMA '18
Memories of Murder '03
Miracle '04 ▶
Mrs. Harris '05
The Mistake '91
Mr. Nice '10
Monster '03▶
A Most Violent Year '14▶
The Music Never Stopped '11
My Brothers '10
The Mysteries of Pittsburgh '08
Night Stalker '09
Nightstalker '02
1982 '16
No '12
No Country for Old Men '07▶
The Normal Heart '14▶
North Country '05
One Day You'll Understand '08
Only Yesterday '16▶
Oranges and Sunshine '10▶
Outside Bet '12
Overtime '11
Owning Mahowny '03
Paid in Full '02
Paranormal Activity 3 '11
Party Monster '03
The Perez Family '94
The Perfect Age of Rock 'n' Roll '10
Permanent '17
Persepolis '07▶
Pinero '01
Ping Pong Summer '14
Point of Origin '02
Precious: Based on the Novel 'Push' by Sapphire '09▶
Pride '14▶
The Pursuit of Happyness '06
The Railway Man '13
Ready Player One '18
Red Riding, Part 2: 1980 '09
Red Riding, Part 3: 1983 '09
Rent '05
The Replacements '00
Revenge of the Green Dragons '14
Ricky Nelson: Original Teen Idol '99
Riding in Cars with Boys '01
Riot on 42nd Street '87
Rise of the Footsoldier '07
The Riverman '04
Rock of Ages '12
Rock Star '01
Safe Men '98
A Season on the Brink '02
A Secret '07▶
Selling Hitler '91
The Sessions '12▶
Sex & Drugs & Rock & Roll '10
The Shell Seekers '06
Skateland '10
SLC Punk! '99
A Smile as Big as the Moon '12
The Son of No One '11
Son of Rambow '07
Sonny '02
Southside with You '16▶
The Souvenir '19▶
Spider '02▶
Spy Game '01
The Squid and the Whale '05▶
Stander '03
Starter for 10 '06
Stateside '04
Summer of 84 '18
Summer Palace '06 ▶
Summer's End '99
The Take '09
Take Me Home Tonight '11
A Taxi Driver '17 ▶
Ten Thousand Saints '15
This Is England '06
Three Identical Strangers '18 ▶
To Walk with Lions '99
Triage '09
The Trip '02
24 Hour Party People '01
Twice Born '12
200 Cigarettes '98
Typhoon '06
Under the Shadow '16 ▶
Underground: The Julian Assange Story '12
Valentine '01
Valley Girl '20
Velvet Goldmine '98
Waking the Dead '00
Watchmen '09
We Are the Best! '13▶
We Own the Night '07
The Wedding Singer '97
Wet Hot American Summer '01▶
What Goes Up '09
White Bird in a Blizzard '14
White Boy Rick '18
The Witnesses '07
Wonderland '03
The Wood '99

Period Piece: 1990s

Amelie '01▶
Among Brothers '05
Appropriate Adult '11
The Bang Bang Club '10
Battle in Seattle '07
Before You Say 'I Do' '09
Behind the Red Door '02
Being Frank '19
Beyond Borders '03
Big Shot: Confessions of a Campus Bookie '02
Black Hawk Down '01▶
Bleed for This '16
Bonded by Blood '09
BPM (Beats Per Minute) '17
The Brittany Murphy Story '14
Bully '01
Burning Blue '14
California Dreamin' '07
Can You Ever Forgive Me? '18▶
The Capture of the Green River Killer '08
Chasing Mavericks '12
Chasing the Green '09
Climax '18
Closing the Ring '07
Color Me Kubrick '05
Control Alt Delete '08
Crystal Swan '20▶
Dark Blue '03▶
Dark Matter '07
The Debt '07
The Debt '10
Decoding Annie Parker '13
Definitely, Maybe '08▶
Devil's Knot '14
The Diving Bell and the Butterfly '07▶
Eden '14
An Englishman in New York '09
Escobar: Paradise Lost '15
Exiled '06
Fanboys '09
The Final Season '07
Five Minutes of Heaven '09
44 Minutes: The North Hollywood Shootout '03
Foxcatcher '14▶
Freedom Writers '07
Friends & Crocodiles '05
Go West '05
Good Neighbors '10
Greetings from Tim Buckley '12
Hachiko: A Dog's Tale '09
Highway '01
Holy Rollers '10
House of Fools '02
House of Versace '13
How I Married My High School Crush '07
The Human Stain '03
The Hunting Party '07
I'm Not Ashamed '16
In the Land of Blood and Honey '11
The Informant! '09
The Interrogation of Michael Crowe '02
Into the Wild '07 ▶
Invictus '09 ▶
Jasper, Texas '03
Kandahar '01
Kill the Messenger '14 ▶
Kill Your Friends '16
Kings '17
Kings of South Beach '07
The Lady '11
Landline '17
Laurence Anyways '12
A Life Interrupted '07
The Listening '06
Live from Baghdad '03▶
Lords of Soaptown: The True Story of Freestyle Walking '16
Man of the Century '99
Marooned in Iraq '02
Masterminds '16
Memorial Day '12
Mid90s '18
The Miseducation of Cameron Post '18
Moneyball '11▶
Murder in the Hamptons '05
Murderland '09
The Navigators '01
No Man's Land '01
Notorious '09
Of Gods and Men '10▶
One Long Night '07
Our America '02
Party Monster '03
Perestroika '09
The Perfect Age of Rock 'n' Roll '10
Pinochet's Last Stand '06
PU-239 '06
The Queen '06▶
'R Xmas '01
Rampart '11
Remember the Daze '07
Richard Jewell '19▶
Rob the Mob '14
Shadow Dancer '12▶
Shake Hands With the Devil '07
Shattered Glass '03▶
Shooting Dogs '05
The Sicilian Girl '09
The Special Relationship '10
Spy Game '01
Summer Palace '06▶
Super Dark Times '17
10th & Wolf '06
The Terrorist Next Door '08
Three Kings '99▶
The To Do List '13
Touchback '11
21 '08
Underground: The Julian Assange Story '12
Vice '18
The Wackness '08
Waking Up Wally '05
Wasted '06
W.E. '11
When Did You Last See Your Father? '07
The Whistleblower '11▶
Whitney '15
Wild '14▶
The Wildest Dream: The Conquest of Everest '10
You Don't Know Jack '10

Persian Gulf/Iraq War

***See also** Desert War/Foreign Legion*

Afghan Luke '11
American Soldiers '05
American Son '08
Backstabbing for Beginners '18
Courage Under Fire '96▶
The Dry Land '10
Generation Kill '08▶
Grace Is Gone '07 ▶
Green Zone '10 ▶
Home of the Brave '06
House of Saddam '08
The Hurt Locker '08 ▶
The Jacket '05
Jarhead 2: Field of Fire '14
Jarhead '05
Lions for Lambs '07
Live from Baghdad '03 ▶
The Lucky Ones '08
Memorial Day '12
The Messenger '09 ▶
Official Secrets '19 ▶
The One That Got Away '96
Redacted '07
Seal Team '08
The Situation '06
Standard Operating Procedure '08 ▶
Stir of Echoes 2: The Homecoming '07
Stop-Loss '08▶
Tactical Assault '99
Three Kings '99▶
Time Bomb '08
Zero Dark Thirty '12▶

Philadelphia

The Answer Man '09
Baby Mama '08
Backwards '12
Birdy '84▶
Blow Out '81▶
The Burglar '57
Cafe '10
Cover '08
Devil '10
Downtown '89
Explicit Ills '08
Fat Albert '04
Fugitive at 17 '12
God's Pocket '14
A History of Violence '05▶
I Don't Buy Kisses Anymore '92
In Her Shoes '05▶
In the Shadow of the Moon '19
Invincible '06▶
The Jazz Singer '52
King of the Corner '04▶
Kitty Foyle '40▶
Law Abiding Citizen '09
Like Mike '02
Little Girl Lost: The Delimar Vera Story '08
Love N' Dancing '09
Mannequin 2: On the Move '91
Mannequin '87
Marnie '64▶
McCanick '14
Money for Nothing '93
My Baby's Daddy '04
Nasty Habits '77
National Treasure '04
Next Day Air '09
Night Catches Us '10
1982 '16
No Boundaries '09
Philadelphia '93▶
The Philadelphia Story '40▶
Pride '07
Quest '17
The Remarkable Mr. Pennypacker '59
Rock School '05▶
Rocky '76▶
Rocky 2 '79
Rocky 3 '82
Rocky 4 '85
Rocky 5 '90
Rocky Balboa '06
A Secret Affair '99
Shazam! '19
Silver Linings Playbook '12▶
The Sixth Sense '99▶
Snipes '01
State Property 2 '05
Stonewall '95▶
The Thin Blue Lie '00
Trading Places '83
12 Monkeys '95▶
Two Bits '96
2 Minutes Later '07
Unbreakable '00
Up Close and Personal '96▶
Waiting '00
The Watermelon Woman '97
Winter Kills '79 ▶
Witness '85 ▶
The Young Philadelphians '59 ▶

Phobias!

Arachnophobia '90
As Good As It Gets '97 ▶
Beneath the Flesh '09
Blackjack '97
The Blackout Experiments '16
Body Double '84 ▶
Citadel '12
Copycat '95
GhostWatcher '02
High Anxiety '77
Phobia '13
Phobic '02
Pontiac Moon '94
Pretty Woman '90 ▶
Vertigo '58▶
The Wedding Year '19
What about Bob? '91▶

Phone Sex

***See also** Sex & Sexuality*

Easier With Practice '10
Girl 6 '96
Happiness '98▶
Love in the Time of Money '02
Mouth to Mouth '95
Punch-Drunk Love '02▶
Short Cuts '93▶
The Telephone Book '71
The Truth about Cats and Dogs '96▶
Walking and Talking '96

Phone Terror

Black Christmas '06
Black Sabbath '64▶
The Caller '11
Cell '16
Cellular '04
Dead Tone '07
Don't Answer the Phone '80
Eagle Eye '08
Echelon Conspiracy '09
88 Minutes '08
The Jerky Boys '95
Jexi '19
Liberty Stands Still '02
The Night Caller '97
976-EVIL 2: The Astral Factor '91
976-EVIL '88
Non-Stop '14
One Missed Call '08
Party Line '88
Phone Booth '02
Scream '96▶
Scream 2 '97▶
Scream 3 '00
6 Plots '12
Sorry, Wrong Number '48▶
Telefon '77
13 Sins '13
Thr3e '07
Vehicle 19 '13
When a Stranger Calls '79
When a Stranger Calls '06
When a Stranger Calls Back '93

Photography

***See** Shutterbugs*

Physical Problems

***See also** Blindness; Deafness; Mental Retardation; Savants*

Act of Violence '48
The Affair '73▶
An Affair to Remember '57
Alien: Resurrection '97▶
American Loser '07
Amour '12▶
Amy '81
Answers to Nothing '11
The Aura '05▶
Autumn Sonata '78▶
Avatar '09▶
The Baytown Outlaws '12
Beastly '11
The Best of Men '12
The Big Lebowski '97▶
Big Street '42
Blankman '94
Bleed for This '16
The Bone Collector '99
Born on the Fourth of July '89 ▶
Breaking the Waves '95 ▶
A Broken Life '07
Brotherhood of the Wolf '01
Catherine Cookson's The Wingless Bird '97
Chained for Life '51
Charlie & Me '08
Chasing 3000 '07
Chinese Roulette '86
Choices '81
Christmas Comes Home to Canaan '11
City Streets '38
Closer and Closer '96
Coming Home '78 ▶
Cop Au Vin '85
The Craft '96
Crazy '08
The Crippled Masters '82
Crossbar '79
A Day in the Death of Joe Egg '71▶
Dead Silent '99
The Debt '10
Declaration of War '11
Deuce Bigalow: Male Gigolo '99
Diamonds '99
The Dive from Clausen's Pier '05
The Diving Bell and the Butterfly '07▶
Dolphin Tale '11
Don't Say a Word '01
Double Parked '00
Dracula 2: Ascension '03
Dreams and Shadows '10
The Duchess of Langeais '07▶
Easy Money: Hard to Kill '12
Eden '98
El Cochecito '60▶
The Elephant Man '80▶
Even Cowgirls Get the Blues '94
Event Horizon '97
The Ex '07
Expecting a Miracle '09
The Exploding Girl '09
Face of Fire '59
Faces in the Crowd '11
The Fall '06
Fallen Angels '95
Fireworks '97
Flawless '99
Flight Angels '40
Floating '97
Follow the Stars Home '01
Four Fast Guns '59
Freddy Got Fingered '01
The Fugitive '93▶
George Wallace '97
Give Me Liberty '19
The Glass Menagerie '87▶
Good Luck '96
Good Neighbors '10
Goodbye, Dragon Inn '03
The Goonies '85
Gray's Anatomy '96
The Great O'Malley '36
Grown Up Movie Star '10
A Gun, a Car, a Blonde '97
Harold '08
The Haunted Airman '06
He Was a Quiet Man '07
Hell and Back Again '11
Holy Motors '12▶
Home of the Brave '06
Hugo Pool '97
Humble Pie '07
The Hunchback '97
The Hunchback of Notre Dame '23▶
The Hunchback of Notre Dame '39▶
The Hunchback of Notre Dame '57
The Hunchback of Notre Dame '96▶
Hunger Point '03
I Don't Want to Talk About It '94
I Know Who Killed Me '07

 ▶ *= rated three bones or higher*

Inside Moves '80
The Intouchables '12
Invasion Quartet '61
It Runs in the Family '03
It's Good to Be Alive '74
Jack and Jill *vs.* the World '08
Jackass Presents: Bad Grandpa '13
Joni '79
Just Wright '10
Kate's Secret '86
The Kid and I '05
Kingpin '96
The King's Speech '10 ▸
Kongo '32
Lady Chatterley '10 ▸
Lea '96
Lewis and Clark and George '97
Lightning Jack '94
Live Flesh '97 ▸
Looking for Richard '96 ▸
Love Affair '39 ▸
Love Affair '94
Lovely, Still '08
The Lucky Ones '08
Lucky Star '29
Mac and Me '88
The Magic of Belle Isle '12
The Man with the Golden Arm '55 ▸
The Man Without a Face '93
Mannaja: A Man Called Blade '77
Marathon '09
Mask '85 ▸
The Men '50 ▸
Micmacs '09
Million Dollar Baby '04 ▸
Miracle in Lane Two '00
The Miracle Worker '62 ▸
The Miracle Worker '79 ▸
The Miracle Worker '00
Monkey Shines '88
Morgan '12
Murderball '05 ▸
Music Within '07
Mute Witness '95
My Left Foot '89 ▸
My Own Love Song '10
Natural Selection '11
Niagara, Niagara '97
Night Monster '42
Night Must Fall '37 ▸
Night Must Fall '64
Not Suitable for Children '12
November Christmas '10
Of Human Bondage '34 ▸
Once a Thief '90
Once Upon a Spy '80
Ondine '09
One Way to Valhalla '09
Orphans '97
The Other Side of the Mountain '75
The Other Side of the Mountain, Part 2 '78
Out of the Black '01
Outside Providence '99
Paperback Romance '96
Paradise: Faith '12
Passion Fish '92 ▸
The Passion of Anna '70 ▸
Passion Play '10
Paula '52
The Penalty '20
Penelope '06
The People *vs.* Larry Flynt '96 ▸
Perception '06
Persons Unknown '96
The Phantom of the Opera '25 ▸
The Phantom of the Opera '43 ▸
Phantom Pain '09
The Pit '81
Portrait of an Assassin '49
Powder '95
Pumpkin '02
Quid Pro Quo '08
Ratboy '86
Re-Generation '04
Reach for the Sky '56
Rear Window '54 ▸
The Red Dwarf '99
Regarding Henry '91 ▸
Remember Sunday '13
Renoir '12
Richard III '55 ▸
Riddler's Moon '98
Ride a Wild Pony '75 ▸
The Right to Live '35
Ripple Effect '07
The River '51 ▸
Robbers' Roost '55
Rocket Science '07 ▸
Rory O'Shea Was Here '04
Roxanne '87 ▸
Rumble in the Bronx '96
Run for Cover '55
Rust and Bone '12 ▸
Saved! '04
Scent of a Woman '92 ▸
The Sea Inside '04 ▸
Second Chances '98
The Secret '93
The Sessions '12 ▸
Sex & Drugs & Rock & Roll '10
Shallow Hal '01
Short Night of Glass Dolls '71
Shutterbug '10
Silence '73
Silent Witness '99
Silver Bullet '85
Sitcom '97
Skeletons '10
The Small Back Room '49 ▸
The Son of the Bride '01
Soul Surfer '11
Speak '04 ▸
The Spiral Staircase '46 ▸
Spiral Staircase '75
The Station Agent '03 ▸
Steel '97
The Steel Claw '61
Stella Maris '18 ▸
The Stone Merchant '06
The Stratton Story '49 ▸
Suite 16 '94
The Sum of Us '94 ▸
The Sun Also Rises '57
Sunlight Jr. '13
Surprise, Surprise '09
Sweet and Lowdown '99
Sympathy for Delicious '10
Symphony of Six Million '32
Synecdoche, New York '08 ▸
The Theory of Everything '14
There's Something about Mary '98 ▸
Things to Do in Denver When You're Dead '95 ▸
To All My Friends on Shore '71 ▸
Touched '05
Trouble with the Curve '12
Tusk '14
12 Hours to Live '06
Twin Falls Idaho '99 ▸
Uncle Joe Shannon '78
Under the Piano '95
Untamed Heart '93
Very Annie Mary '00
Vibrations '94
The Walking Stick '70
War Eagle, Arkansas '07
A Warm Wind '11
The Waterdance '91 ▸
What Ever Happened to Baby Jane? '62 ▸
What the Deaf Man Heard '98 ▸
What's Eating Gilbert Grape '93 ▸
Whiplash '48
Whose Life Is It Anyway? '81 ▸
Wild Wild West '99
A Woman's Face '38 ▸
A Woman's Face '41 ▸
Wonder '17
Words and Pictures '13
Working Miracles '10
Wrecked '10
X-Men '00
X2: X-Men United '03 ▸
The Year of Getting to Know Us '08

Pigs

See also Killer Pigs

The Advocate '93 ▸
The Angry Birds Movie '16
The Angry Birds Movie 2 '19
Animal Farm '99
Arlo the Burping Pig '16
Babe '95 ▸
Babe: Pig in the City '98
The Biggest Little Farm '18 ▸
The Black Cauldron '85
Charlotte's Web '73
Charlotte's Web '06 ▸
College Road Trip '08
Doc Hollywood '91
Gordy '95
Leon the Pig Farmer '93
Nanny McPhee Returns '10
Okja '17 ▸
A Private Function '84
The Simpsons Movie '07 ▸
Spark: A Space Tail '17
Toy Story '95 ▸
Toy Story 2 '99 ▸
Upstream Color '13 ▸
Waikiki Wedding '37 ▸

Pirates

See also Island Fare; Sail Away; Swashbucklers

Abbott and Costello Meet Captain Kidd '52
Against All Flags '52 ▸
The Black Pirate '26 ▸
The Black Swan '42 ▸
Blackbeard '06
Blackbeard the Pirate '52
Blackbeard's Ghost '67
The Buccaneer '58
Buccaneer's Girl '50
Captain Blood '35 ▸
Captain Calamity '36
Captain Kidd '45
Captain Kidd and the Slave Girl '54
Captain Phillips '13 ▸
Captain Ron '92
Carry On Jack '63
Cinderella '12
Colossus and the Amazon Queen '60
Crimson Pirate '52 ▸
Cutthroat Island '95
Dancing Pirate '36
Dead Water '19
The Devil-Ship Pirates '64
Double Crossbones '51
Frenchman's Creek '44
Frenchman's Creek '98
The Golden Hawk '52
Gun Shy '17
Hercules and the Black Pirate '60
Hero's Island '62
His Majesty O'Keefe '53
Hook '91
Ice Age: Continental Drift '12
Ice Pirates '84
Labou '07
Long John Silver '54
The Master of Ballantrae '53
Muppet Treasure Island '96
Mysterious Island '05
Naughty Marietta '35
Neverland '11
New Moon '40
Peter Pan '53 ▸
Peter Pan '60 ▸
Peter Pan '03
The Phantom '96
Phantom Raiders '40
The Pirate '48 ▸
Pirate Movie '82
The Pirates! Band of Misfits '12
Pirates of Blood River '62
The Pirates of Capri '49
The Pirates of Penzance '83
Pirates of the Caribbean: At World's End '07
Pirates of the Caribbean: Dead Man's Chest '06
Pirates of the Caribbean: Dead Men Tell No Tales '17
Pirates of the Caribbean: On Stranger Tides '11
Pirates of the Caribbean: The Curse of the Black Pearl '03 ▸
Pirates of Tortuga '61
Pirates of Treasure Island '06
The Pirates Who Don't Do Anything: A VeggieTales Movie '08
The Princess and the Pirate '44 ▸
The Princess Bride '87 ▸
Raiders of the Seven Seas '53
Return to Never Land '02
Sandokan the Great '63
The Sea Hawk '24
The Sea Hawk '40 ▸
Sea Wolf: The Pirate's Curse '05
Shipwrecked '90
Six Days, Seven Nights '98
Space Truckers '97
The Spanish Main '45
The SpongeBob Movie: Sponge Out of Water '15
Stardust '07 ▸
Swashbuckler '76
The Swiss Family Robinson '60 ▸
Tiger of the Seven Seas '62
Treasure Island '34 ▸
Treasure Island '50 ▸
Treasure Island '72
Treasure Island '89
Treasure Island '99
Treasure Island '12
Treasure Planet '02
Untamable Angelique '67
Yankee Buccaneer '52
Yellowbeard '83

Pittsburgh

Alone in the Neon Jungle '87
Angels in the Outfield '51 ▸
Angels in the Outfield '94
Bad for Each Other '53
Bloodsucking Pharoahs of Pittsburgh '90
Bob Roberts '92 ▸
The Bread, My Sweet '01
The Bridge to Nowhere '09
The Cemetery Club '93
Chasing 3000 '07
The D Train '15
Diabolique '96
Dominick & Eugene '88 ▸
Fatal Desire '05
Fences '16 ▸
The Fish that Saved Pittsburgh '79
Flashdance '83
Happy Tears '09
Houseguest '94
I Was a Communist for the FBI '51
Innocent Blood '92
Mrs. Soffel '84
The Mysteries of Pittsburgh '08
The Piano Lesson '94 ▸
Pittsburgh '06
Roommates '95
Silent Witness '85
Smart People '08
Stigmata '99
Striking Distance '93
Sudden Death '95
10th & Wolf '06
The Valley of Decision '45 ▸
Warrior '11 ▸
Wonder Boys '00 ▸
Zack and Miri Make a Porno '08 ▸

Plastic Surgery

Ash Wednesday '73
Behind the Candelabra '13
Breast Men '97
Circus of Horrors '60
Dark Passage '47
Death Becomes Her '92 ▸
Face/Off '97 ▸
Faceless '88
Fallen Angel '99
The Girl Most Likely to. . . '73
Goodnight Mommy '15
I Accidentally Domed Your Son '04
The Man with Bogart's Face '80
Nightmare Cinema '19
Nora Prentiss '47
The Promise '79
Rabid '77
The Skin I Live In '11
A Stolen Face '52
Stolen Face '52
Strange Impersonation '46
30 Years to Life '01
Time '06

Poetry

Adult World '13
The Barretts of Wimpole Street '34 ▸
The Beach Bum '19
Before Night Falls '00 ▸
Blue Car '03 ▸
Bright Star '09
The Broken Tower '11
The Business of Fancydancing '02
Byron '03
The Color of Pomegranates '69 ▸
A Fine Madness '66 ▸
For Colored Girls '10
Groundhog Day '93 ▸
Henry Fool '98 ▸
Hunt for the Wilderpeople '16 ▸
I Heart Huckabees '04
I, the Worst of All '90
In Custody '94
The Ister '04 ▸
Kahlil Gibran's The Prophet '15 ▸
Louder Than a Bomb '10
Marathon '09
Marianne & Leonard: Words of Love '19
My Life and Times with Antonin Artaud '93 ▸
Neruda '16
Paterson '16 ▸
Pinero '01
Poetic Justice '93
Poetry '10
Possession '02
The Postman '94 ▸
A Quiet Passion '17
Reaching for the Moon '13
Satan's Brew '76
Shirin '09
So I Married an Axe Murderer '93
Some Kind of Beautiful '15
Summer Lover '08
Sylvia '03
Tales of Ordinary Madness '83
Till Human Voices Wake Us '02
Tom & Viv '94 ▸
Total Eclipse '95
Touched With Fire '16

Poisons

Agatha Christie's Sparkling Cyanide '83
Arsenic and Old Lace '44 ▸
Barracuda '78
Batman and Robin '97
The Courier '19
The Crazies '73
D.O.A. '49 ▸
D.O.A. '88
Doomwatch '72
The Emperor's New Groove '00 ▸
Kiss and Kill '68
My Cousin Rachel '17
Safe '95 ▸
Snow White and the Seven Dwarfs '37 ▸
The Young Poisoner's Handbook '94 ▸

Poker

See also Gambling

All Things to All Men '13
Angels Over Broadway '40 ▸
A Big Hand for the Little Lady '66
Casino Royale '06 ▸
The Cincinnati Kid '65
Cornered! '09
Cowboy '58 ▸
Dark City '50
Deal '08
Destry Rides Again '39 ▸
Finder's Fee '01
The Gambler Returns: The Luck of the Draw '93
Havana '90
Hit Me '96
Honeymoon in Vegas '92
House of Games '87 ▸
It Happened at the World's Fair '63
Kenny Rogers as the Gambler '80
Kenny Rogers as the Gambler, Part 2: The Adventure Continues '83
Kenny Rogers as the Gambler, Part 3: The Legend Continues '87
The Killing of a Chinese Bookie '76
Killing Them Softly '12
Knock Outs '92
Les Biches '68 ▸
Lucky You '07
Maverick '94
Mississippi Grind '15 ▸
Mr. Mom '83 ▸
Molly's Game '17
The Music of Chance '93
Ocean's Eleven '01 ▸
Poker Alice '87
The Poker Club '08
The Poker House '09
Red Shoe Diaries: Strip Poker '96
Rounders '98
Ruggles of Red Gap '35 ▸
Shade '03
The Showdown '40
Sink or Swim '97
Smart Money '31
Triggerman '09
Wanda Nevada '79
Wild Bill '95

Police Detectives

Abandon '02
Abandoned '10
Above the Law '88
Accused at 17 '09
Alex Cross '12
All-American Murder '91
Along Came a Spider '01
The Alphabet Killer '08
The American Side '16
Anamorph '07
And Never Let Her Go '01
Angel of Death '02
Angels Don't Sleep Here '00
Another Stakeout '93
Another Woman '94
Answers to Nothing '11
Arbitrage '12 ▸
Bad Lieutenant: Port of Call New Orleans '09
The Bad Son '07
Bad Timing: A Sensual Obsession '80
Batman Begins '05 ▸
Beautiful Creatures '00
Behind the Green Lights '35
Belphegor: Phantom of the Louvre '01
Betrayed '44
Between '05
Between Your Legs '99
Beyond '11
Beyond the Trophy '12
Big Brown Eyes '36
The Black Belly of the Tarantula '71
Black Heat '76
Black Widow '54
BlacKkKlansman '18 ▸
Blackmail '29 ▸
Blind Trust '06
The Bling Ring '11
Blink '93
Blitz '11
Blood '09
Blood & Concrete: A Love Story '91
Blood Out '10
Bloody Proof '99 ▸
A Blueprint for Murder '53
Bon Cop Bad Cop '06
Bond of Silence '10
Borderline '02 ▸
The Boston Strangler: The Untold Story '08

Bound by Lies '05
The Box '07
Boy Wonder '10
The Brave One '07
Brother's Keeper '02
Bubble '06
A Bullet for Joey '55
Bullitt '68 ▸
Bunco Squad '50
Butterfly Collectors '99
Cage of Evil '60
The Calling '14
The Captive '14
Carrie '02
Catwoman '04
Caught in the Crossfire '10
Chain of Fools '00
The Chaos Experiment '09
Charlie Chan at Treasure Island '39
Charlie Chan in Honolulu '38
Cheaters' Club '06
Chicago Overcoat '09
Chill '06
Christina '10
ChromeSkull: Laid to Rest 2 '11
Citizen Jane '09
City by the Sea '02
Cold and Dark '05
Collision '09
The Color of Lies '99
Columbo: Murder by the Book '71
Columbo: Prescription Murder '67
Columbus Circle '10
Compulsion '13
Contract on Cherry Street '77
Cookie's Fortune '99 ▸
Cop Hater '58
Corpse Mania '81
Counterspy Meets Scotland Yard '50
Cover '08
Coyote Waits '03
The Cradle of Courage '20
The Craigslist Killer '11
Crash '05 ▸
Crime and Punishment, USA '59
Crime Wave '54
The Criminal '00
Criminal Justice '08
Criminals Within '41
The Crimson Kimono '59
Crimson Rivers 2: Angels of the Apocalypse '05
The Cry: La Llorona '07
Cry Rape! '73
Cure '97 ▸
Curse of the Pink Panther '83
Cyberstalker '96
The Dalton Girls '57
The Dancer Upstairs '02
Dangerous Money '46
Darkness Falls '20
Darkwolf '03
Dead in a Heartbeat '02
Dead Sexy '01
Dead Silence '07
Dead Tone '07
Death Among Friends '75
Death and Cremation '10
Death from a Distance '36
The Deep End of the Ocean '98
Destroyer '18
The Detective '68 ▸
Detective '85
Detective Bureau 2-3: Go to Hell Bastards! '63
Detective Story '51 ▸
Devil '10
Diamond Run '96
Dick Tracy '37
Dick Tracy '90 ▸
Dick Tracy Meets Gruesome '47
Dick Tracy Returns '38
Dick Tracy vs. Crime Inc. '41
Dirty Tricks '00
Dogwatch '97
Dot.Kill '05
Double Cross '06
Double Vision '02
Double Whammy '01
Dragged Across Concrete '18
Dragnet '54
Dragnet '87
Ed McBain's 87th Precinct: Heatwave '97
Ed McBain's 87th Precinct: Lightning '95
Edge of Darkness '86
Edge of Darkness '10
The Element of Crime '84
Empire of the Wolves '05
End Game '09
Endure '10
The Enforcer '76
Escape Clause '96
Eternal '04
Exposed '16
Faces in the Crowd '11
The Fall of the American Empire '19
Fallen Angel '99
Falling Down '93
Fear X '03 ▸
Feardotcom '02
Felony '13
15 Minutes '01
Filth '13
Final Move '06
The First Deadly Sin '80
Five Days '07
Flick '07
Formula 51 '01
Forty Naughty Girls '37
Foul Play '78 ▸
Framed '30
Freaky Deaky '12 ▸
Freedomland '06
From Hell '01 ▸
Fugitive Among Us '92
Fugitive at 17 '12
Gambler's Choice '44
Gangster Squad '13
Gemini '17
Ghost Image '07
Giallo '09
The Girl by the Lake '07
Girl Missing '33
The Girl Most Likely to... '73
Goldstone '18
Gone Baby Gone '07 ▸
Gone Girl '14 ▸
The Good Thief '03 ▸
The Gore-Gore Girls '72
Grand National Night '53
Green Eyes '34
Green for Danger '47
The Guardian '01
Guardian Angel '94
Gun '10
The Gunman '03
Guns for Hire '15
Hangman '17
Hard As Nails '01
Heat '95 ▸
The Heat '13
Hellraiser 5: Inferno '00
Hero Wanted '08
The Highwaymen '19
The Hit List '11
Hitched '01
Home Room '02 ▸
Hostage '05
House of Bodies '13
The House of the Arrow '53 ▸
The House of the Seven Hawks '59
The Human Monster '39
The Hunted '48
The Hustle '75
The Hypnotic Eye '60
I Dream of Murder '06
Impact Point '08
In the Cut '03
In the Electric Mist '08
In the Valley of Elah '07 ▸
Infernal Affairs '02 ▸
Infernal Affairs 2 '03
Infernal Affairs 3 '03
Innocent Lies '95
InSight '11
Insomnia '97 ▸
Insomnia '02 ▸
Inspector Bellamy '09 ▸
The Interrogation of Michael Crowe '02
It Shouldn't Happen to a Dog '46
Jesse '11
Jesse Stone: Innocents Lost '11
Jill the Ripper '00
Jim Hanvey, Detective '37
Julie '56
Jr. Detective Agency '09
K-9 3: P.I. '01
K-9 '89
K-911 '99
Karate Dog '04
Kept '01
Kill Switch '08
Killer Deal '99
The Killer Is Loose '56
Killing Emmett Young '02
A Killing Spring '02
Kiss Me...Kill Me '76
Kiss the Girls '97
Knives Out '19 ▸
L.A. Confidential '97 ▸
Lantana '01 ▸
Last Hour '08
The Last Trimester '06
Laura '44 ▸
Le Petit Lieutenant '05
The Ledge '11
Legacy '08
Legacy of Fear '06
Let Us Live '39
Lies & Alibis '06
The Limehouse Golem '17
Little Girl Lost: The Delimar Vera Story '08
A Lizard in a Woman's Skin '71
The Lodger '09
Lonely Hearts '06
Loose Cannons '90
Loosies '11
The Lost Angel '04
Lost Behind Bars '06
Love and Bullets '79
Lucky '11
Lulu '02
The Mad Bomber '72
Mafia '11
Magic Man '10
The Magician '93
Magnum Force '73
Man on the Eiffel Tower '48 ▸
The Man Who Cheated Himself '50
Mary Higgins Clark: Lucky Day '02
Max Payne '08
Medium Raw: Night of the Wolf '10
Memories of Murder '03
The Memory of a Killer '03
Mercy '00
Meskada '10
Midnight 2: Sex, Death, and Videotape '93
The Million Dollar Hotel '99
A Mind to Murder '96
The Ministers '09
Mirrors 2 '10
Miss Nobody '10
Miss Pinkerton '32
Mr. Brooks '07
The Money Trap '65
Mongo's Back In Town '71
Mortal Transfer '01
Mother, May I Sleep With Danger? '96
Murder at 1600 '97
Murder at the Vanities '34
Murder by Numbers '02
Murder C.O.D. '90
Murder in Greenwich '02
Murder On a Bridle Path '36
Murder On a Honeymoon '35
Murder on Pleasant Drive '06
Murder On the Blackboard '34
Murderland '09
My Neighbor's Keeper '07
My Son, My Son, What Have Ye Done '09
My Soul to Take '10
The Mystery of a Hansom Cab '12
The Mystery of Marie Roget '42
Mystery Street '50
Mystic River '03 ▸
The Natalee Holloway Story '09
Nick Knight '89
Night Editor '46
Night School '81
Night Stalker '87
Nightwatch '96
No One Sleeps '01
No Way to Treat a Lady '68 ▸
Nocturne '46
November '05 ▸
Number One with a Bullet '87
Observe and Report '09
On Dangerous Ground '51 ▸
Once Upon a Time in Anatolia '12 ▸
One Good Cop '91
One Missed Call '08
One Night at McCool's '01
Open Cam '05
The Organization '71 ▸
Osso Bucco '08
The Other Guys '10
Out of Blue '19
Out of Time '03
Partners '09
Partners in Crime '99
Patricia Cornwell's At Risk '10
Patricia Cornwell's The Front '10
Paula '52
P.D. James: Death in Holy Orders '03
Penguin Pool Murder '32
The Perfect Host '10
The Phantom Light '35
The Phantom of Soho '64
Phone Booth '02
The Pink Panther 2 '09
The Pink Panther '06
Place of Execution '09
Play Nice '92
The Plot Thickens '36
Postmark for Danger '56
Pound of Flesh '10
The Power '68
Practical Magic '98
The Presidio '88
Presumed Dead '06
Pretty Maids All In a Row '71
The Prey '11
Pride and Glory '08
Prisoners '13 ▸
Private Hell 36 '54
The Prophet's Game '99
Psych: 9 '10
The Psychopath '66
Puerto Ricans in Paris '16
Pushover '54
Race Street '48
The Raven '12
Recipe for Revenge '98
The Reckoning '14
Red Riding, Part 1: 1974 '09
Red Riding, Part 2: 1980 '09
Red Riding, Part 3: 1983 '09
Relentless '89
Relentless 2: Dead On '91
Relentless 3 '93
Relentless 4 '94
Resurrection '99
The Return of Dr. Mabuse '61
Revenge Quest '96
Ricochet '91 ▸
Ride Along 2 '16
Righteous Kill '08
Ring of Death '69
The River King '05
The River Murders '11
The Riverman '04
Rome Express '32
Rush Hour 3 '07
Sabotage '14
Safe Harbor '06
Sanctimony '01
Sapphire '59 ▸
Saw 2 '05
Saw 5 '08
Scene of the Crime '49
The Scent of Rain & Lightening '17
Scotland, PA '02
Sea of Love '89 ▸
Searching '18 ▸
Second Sight '99 ▸
Seconds Apart '11
Secrets of Eden '12
Seduced: Pretty When You Cry '01
Seven '95 ▸
Seven Blood-Stained Orchids '72
The Seven-Ups '73
Shoot First, Die Later '74
Showtime '02
The Silence '06
Sin City '05
Sinister Hands '32
Sinners and Saints '10
Sitting Target '72
16 Blocks '06 ▸
Skinwalker '02
Sleepless '01
Smart Blonde '37
Smoke Screen '10
The Sniper '52
So Dark the Night '46
Someone to Watch Over Me '87 ▸
Somewhere in the Night '46
The Son of No One '11
Speed Dating '07
The Spirit '87
Splinter '06
The Squeeze '77
Stage Struck '48
Stakeout '87
Stiletto '08
Stolen '09
The Strange Case of Dr. Jekyll and Mr. Hyde '06
Stray '19
Stray Dog '49 ▸
Street Fighter: The Legend of Chun-Li '09
Street Kings '08
Street Kings 2: Motor City '11
Streets of Blood '09
Strike a Pose '93
Stuber '19
Suicide Club '02
Surrogates '09
Takers '10
Tales from the Crypt Presents Bordello of Blood '96
Talking to Heaven '02
Tangled '01
Teeth and Blood '15
Tell No One '06 ▸
Telling Lies '06
Tenderness '08
Tension '50
Texas Killing Fields '11
That Beautiful Somewhere '06
They Call Me Mr. Tibbs! '70
Third World Cop '99
The 36th Precinct '04 ▸
The Thomas Crown Affair '99 ▸
Ticker '01
To Catch a Killer '92 ▸
Tomorrow Is Another Day '51
Top of the Lake '13 ▸
Torso '02
Touching Evil '97 ▸
Towards Zero '07
Transfixed '01
Trauma '04
True Blue '01
True Romance '93
12 Rounds 3: Lockdown '15
12 Rounds '09
24 Days '14
21 Bridges '19
Twisted '04
2:13 '09
Ultimate Heist '09
Undercover Maisie '47
The Unguarded Moment '56
Unthinkable '07
V for Vendetta '06
Vampire Assassin '05
Vendetta '15
Vertigo '58 ▸
The Voice of the City '29
War on Everyone '17
Wasabi '01
We Are What We Are '11
Weaponized '16
Welcome to the Punch '13
What to Do in Case of Fire '02
What Your Eyes Don't See '99
When the Sky Falls '99
Where the Sidewalk Ends '50
Whirlpool '49
Whispering Smith '48 ▸
The Wicker Man '75 ▸
Wild Things 3: Diamonds in the Rough '05
Wild Things '98
Wild Things: Foursome '10
Wilder '00
Winter of Frozen Dreams '08
Witchcraft 10: Mistress of the Craft '98
Witness '85 ▸
Witness to Murder '54
World of the Depraved '67
Zodiac '07

Politics

See also Capitol Capers; Presidency; Vote for Me!

Absolute Power '97
The Act of Killing '13 ▸
Ada '61
Adventure in Washington '41
An African Election '11
All the King's Men '06
Amazing Grace '06 ▸
The Ambassador '11
America: Imagine the World Without Her '14
American Dharma '18
American Hustle '13 ▸
American Pastoral '16
The American President '95 ▸
Americathon '79
And the Band Played On '93 ▸
Angels in America '03 ▸
Animal Instincts '92
Archangel '05
Art of War 2: The Betrayal '08
The Art of War '00
Article 99 '92
As Goes Janesville '12
The Assassination of Richard Nixon '05
Atlas Shrugged 2: The Strike '12
Atlas Shrugged 3: Who Is John Galt? '14
Attila '01
Baaria '09
Backstabbing for Beginners '18
The Baroness and the Butler '38
Battle in Seattle '07
Beggars in Ermine '34
Being There '79 ▸
Bel Canto '18
Best of Enemies '15 ▸
Beyond Obsession '82
Beyond Rangoon '95
The Big Boss '41
The Big Brass Ring '99
Billy Jack Goes to Washington '77
The Birdcage '95 ▸
Bitter Sugar '96 ▸
Black Jesus '68
The Black Panthers: Vanguard of the Revolution '15 ▸
Black Sheep '96
Blame It on Fidel '06
Blaze '89
Blood Money: The Story of Clinton and Nadine '88
The Blue Kite '93 ▸
Bob Roberts '92 ▸
Bopha! '93 ▸
The Boss '56
BPM (Beats Per Minute) '17
Break of Dawn '88
Broken City '13
Bulworth '98 ▸
Buried Alive '39
Burnt by the Sun '94 ▸
Bush's Brain '04
Call Him Mr. Shatter '74
The Campaign '12
Canadian Bacon '94

▸ = rated three bones or higher

The Candidate '72 ►
Cape of Good Hope '04
Carla's Song '97
Carry On Emmanuelle '78
Casino '95 ►
Casino Jack and the United States of Money '10
Caterina in the Big City '03
Chain of Command '95
Charlie Wilson's War '07
Chasing Freedom '04
Chicago 10 '07 ►
Children of Men '06 ►
Children of the Revolution '95
China Gate '57 ►
Choose Connor '07
Citizen Cohn '92
Citizen K '19
City Hall '95 ►
Clear and Present Danger '94
Client 9: The Rise and Fall of Eliot Spitzer '10
Colonel Effingham's Raid '45
The Comedians '67
The Congressman '16
Conspiracy: The Trial of the Chicago Eight '87 ►
The Contender '00
Conventioneers '05
Coronado '03
Corporate Affairs '90
Corruption '33
Country '84 ►
Country Life '95
The Cradle Will Rock '99
crazy/beautiful '01
The Crooked Road '65
CSA: The Confederate States of America '04
A Dangerous Man: Lawrence after Arabia '91 ►
Dave '93 ►
The Day Shall Come '19
A Day Without a Mexican '04
DC 9/11: Time of Crisis '04
The Dead Zone '02
The Deal '05
Dear Dictator '18
Dear Wendy '05
Death and the Maiden '94 ►
Death of a Nation '18
The Death of Stalin '17 ►
Defense of the Realm '85 ►
Devil in a Blue Dress '95 ►
The Devils '71 ►
The Dictator '12
The Dinner '17
The Disappearance of Garcia Lorca '96
Disraeli '79 ►
The Distinguished Gentleman '92
Don's Party '76 ►
The Duchess '08 ►
The Edge of Democracy '19
The Edukators '04
The Eleventh Hour '08
Elizabeth '98 ►
Elizabeth R '72 ►
The Emperor and the Assassin '99
The Emperor's New Clothes '01
Endgame '09
Enemies Among Us '10
The Enemy Within '94
Enron: The Smartest Guys in the Room '05 ►
An Everlasting Piece '00
Evita '96
Eye of the Stranger '93
Fahrenheit 11/9 '18
Fahrenheit 9/11 '04 ►
Fair Game '10 ►
Faith '94
Fatwa '06
Fever Mounts at El Pao '59
Fidel '02 ►
The Final Cut '95 ►
Fires Within '91
First Daughter '04
First Family '80
First Lady '20
First Monday in October '81
The First Purge '18
A Flash of Green '85
Flirting With Danger '35
The Fog of War: Eleven Lessons from the Life of Robert S. McNamara '03 ►
For Greater Glory '12
Forbidden '32
Foreplay '75
Formosa Betrayed '09
Four Days in September '97
Four More Years '10
The French Minister '13
The French Woman '79
Friday Foster '75
Gabriel Over the White House '33 ►
Game Change '12
Gangs of New York '02 ►
G.B.H. '91
George Wallace '97
Germany in Autumn '78
The Ghost Writer '10
G.I. Jane '97
The Girl in the Cafe '05
The Girl On the Train '13
Giuliani Time '05
Gladiator '00 ►
Glorious 39 '09
Go Further '03
Going Upriver: The Long War of John Kerry '04
Golem: The Petrified Garden '93
A Good Man in Africa '94
Good Night, and Good Luck '05 ►
The Gorgeous Hussy '36
The Great Hack '19 ►
The Great Man's Lady '42
The Great McGinty '40 ►
The Great Water '04
Guilty by Suspicion '91
Hail Satan? '19 ►
Hamilton '20 ►
Hangar 18 '80
Her Forgotten Past '33
Hidden '11
Hijacking Catastrophe: 9/11, Fear and the Selling of America '04
Hillary's America: The Secret History of the Democratic Party '16
Hombres Armados '97 ►
Hoodlum Empire '52
House of Cards '90 ►
The House of the Spirits '93
How to Frame a Figg '71
Hunger '08
The Hunger Games: Catching Fire '13 ►
The Hunting of the President '04
I Am Cuba '64
An Ideal Husband '47
An Ideal Husband '99 ►
Il Divo '08
In My Country '04
In the Lake of the Woods '96
In the Line of Duty: Ambush in Waco '93
In the Line of Fire '93 ►
In the Loop '09
In the Name of the Father '93 ►
An Inconvenient Sequel: Truth to Power '17
An Inconvenient Truth '06 ►
Indochine '92 ►
Inequality For All '13 ►
The Infiltrators '20
Inside Job '10 ►
The Interpreter '05 ►
Into the Storm '09
The Iron Lady '11
Irresistible '20
J. Edgar '11
Jackie, Ethel, Joan: The Kennedy Women '01
Jefferson in Paris '94
The Jesse Ventura Story '99
JFK '91 ►
Journeys with George '02
Kansas City '95 ►
The Keeper: The Legend of Omar Khayyam '05
Key to the City '50
Kichiku: Banquet of the Beasts '04
Killer Image '92
The Killing Device '92
The King '18
The Kingmaker '19 ►
Knife Fight '13
Knock Down the House '19
Koch '13 ►
Kundun '97 ►
The Lady '11
Lamerica '95 ►
Land of the Blind '06
Land of the Free '98
The Last Full Measure '19
The Last Supper '96
LBJ '17
Les Miserables '97 ►
Lincoln '12 ►
A Lion Is in the Streets '53 ►
Lions for Lambs '07
A Little Bit of Soul '97
The Little Drummer Girl '84 ►
Little Mother '71
Long Shot '19
Looking for Comedy in the Muslim World '06
Loro '19
The Lost City '05
Louisiana Purchase '41
Love Actually '03
Love Letters '99 ►
Lumumba '01 ►
M. Butterfly '93
Machete '10
Magnificent Doll '46
The Man Who Shot Liberty Valance '62 ►
The Manchurian Candidate '62 ►
The Manchurian Candidate '04 ►
Mandela '87 ►
Mandela and de Klerk '97
Mandela: Long Walk to Freedom '13
Manderlay '05
Maryam '00
The Matchmaker '97
The Mating Game '59 ►
Max '02
Mayerling '68
Mayor Cupcake '11
Medium Cool '69 ►
Meet Wally Sparks '97
Meeting Venus '91
Michael Collins '96 ►
Miral '10
Miss Sloane '16
Missiles of October '74 ►
Mission to Moscow '43
Mister America '19
Mr. Smith Goes to Washington '39 ►
Mitt '14
Money for Nothing: Inside the Federal Reserve '13
Mountbatten: The Last Viceroy '86
My Brother's War '97
My Little Assassin '99
The Mystic Masseur '01
The Names of Love '10
National Lampoon's Senior Trip '95
Neruda '16
Nick of Time '95
Nixon '95 ►
No '12
No End in Sight '07 ►
No Witness '04
Norman '17
Northern Extremes '93
The Oath '18
Of Love and Shadows '94
Official Secrets '19 ►
The Omen '06
1000 Rupee Note '16 ►
Ophelia '19
Orwell Rolls in His Grave '03
Our Brand Is Crisis '05 ►
Our Brand is Crisis '15
Our Kind of Traitor '16
Outfoxed: Rupert Murdoch's War on Journalism '04 ►
Outrage '09
The Outskirts '98 ►
Page Eight '11
Paradise Now '05 ►
Paris 36 '08
Parnell '37
The Party '17
Peace, Propaganda & the Promised Land '04
The Pelican Brief '93
People I Know '02
The Perez Family '94
The Phenix City Story '55 ►
Pizza Man '91
A Place in the World '92 ►
Poldark '96
Poverty, Inc. '14
Presumed Innocent '90 ►
Primary Colors '98
The Purge: Election Year '16
Purple Butterfly '03 ►
The Queen '06 ►
Quiet Fire '91
Rain Without Thunder '93
Recount '08
Rendition '07
Report to the Commissioner '75 ►
The Reports on Sarah and Saleem '19 ►
Richard III '95 ►
Robert Kennedy and His Times '90
Ronnie and Julie '97
Roseanne for President! '16
Run This Town '20
The Runner '15
Running Mates '92 ►
Running Mates '00
St. Michael Had a Rooster '72
Salt of the Earth '54 ►
Samaritan: The Mitch Snyder Story '86 ►
The San Francisco Story '52
The Sea Inside '04 ►
Seberg '19
The Second Civil War '97
The Secret '93
The Secret Bride '35
The Secret Four '39
Secret State '12
Seduced '85
The Seduction of Joe Tynan '79
The '70s '00
The Shadow Conspiracy '96
Shock and Awe '18
Silver City '04
Some Mother's Son '96 ►
Something for the Birds '52
Something in the Air '13
Sophie Scholl: The Final Days '05 ►
South of the Border '09
Southside with You '16 ►
Spartan '04 ►
The Special Relationship '10
Speechless '94
The Square '13
Star Wars: Episode 3-Revenge of the Sith '05 ►
State of Play '03 ►
State of Play '09 ►
State of the Union '48 ►
The State Within '06
Stop-Loss '08 ►
Storyville '92
Strawberry and Chocolate '93 ►
Striptease '96
Subversion '79
Supreme Sanction '99
Syriana '05 ►
The System '53
Tanner '88 '88 ►
Tanner on Tanner '04
Taxi Blues '90 ►
Temptation of a Monk '94
This is Not a Film '10 ►
This Revolution '05
Timecop '94
Tito and Me '92 ►
To Live '94 ►
To Play the King '93 ►
Too Big to Fail '11
Trial by Media '00
The Trojan Horse '08
Truman '95
Truth '15
The Tunnel '01 ►
Two Deaths '94
2016: Obama's America '12
Typhoon '06
Uncovered: The War on Iraq '04
The Undefeated '11
Under Western Stars '38
The U.S. Vs. John Lennon '06
Unnatural Causes '86 ►
Up at the Villa '00
Up in Central Park '48
Upstairs Downstairs '11
V for Vendetta '06
The Vector File '03
A Very British Coup '88 ►
The Veteran '06
Vice '18
Vincere '09
Viva Zapata! '52 ►
W. '08 ►
Wag the Dog '97
Wall '04 ►
The War Room '93 ►
Washington: Behind Closed Doors '77
The Weather Underground '02 ►
Wedding Wars '06
Welcome to Mooseport '04
Welcome to New York '15
Werewolf of Washington '73
Who Killed the Electric Car? '06
Wild in the Streets '68
Wild Reeds '94 ►
The Wind That Shakes the Barley '06 ►
World War II: When Lions Roared '94
XXX: State of the Union '05
The Yes Men '03
Zero Days '16
Zero Population Growth '72
Zipper '15

Polygamy

***See also** Adultery; Marriage*

Brigham Young: Frontiersman '40
Captain's Paradise '53 ►
Deceived '91
Enemies, a Love Story '89 ►
In God's Country '07
The Last King of Scotland '06 ►
Me You Them '00
Monsieur Verdoux '47 ►
Moolaade '04
My 5 Wives '00
The 19th Wife '10
Relative Strangers '99
Sufat Chol '16 ►
The Wives He Forgot '06

Pool

***See also** Gambling*

Albino Alligator '96
The American President '95 ►
The Baron and the Kid '84
The Color of Money '86 ►
Groupers '19
The Hustler '61 ►
Kiss Shot '89
The Last Time I Committed Suicide '96
The Music Man '62 ►
Poolhall Junkies '02
Stickmen '01
Think Tank '06
Turn the River '07
Up Against the Eight Ball '04

Pornography

***See also** Sex & Sexuality*

About Cherry '12
Absolution '03
Adult World '13
Amateur '94 ►
Auto Focus '02 ►
Back Against the Wall '00
Beyond Justice '01
Body Double '84 ►
Boogie Nights '97 ►
Bucky Larson: Born to Be a Star '11
Come as You Are '05
Cuck '19
Cyber Seduction: His Secret Life '05
Daniel & Ana '09
Deep Murder '19
Defenseless '91
Demonlover '02
Dirty Pictures '00
Don Jon '13
8mm '98
Elektra Luxx '10
Finding Bliss '09
The Fluffer '01
Frisk '95
Gandu '10
Gardens of the Night '08
Gentlemen's Relish '01
The Girl Next Door '04
The Guru '02
Hammerhead '68
Hardcore '79
Heavy Traffic '73 ►
Hi, Mom! '70 ►
Hit Man '72
Hollywood Vice Squad '86
Humpday '09
I Want Candy '07
Inserts '76
Inside Deep Throat '05 ►
King Cobra '16
Knocked Up '07
The Last Porno Flick '74
The Look of Love '13
The Love God? '70
Lovelace '13
Meet Monica Velour '10
Men, Women & Children '14
Middle Men '10
The Moguls '05
Mope '19
Orgazmo '98
The People *vs.* Larry Flynt '96 ►
The Pornographer '00
The Pornographers '66 ►
Pornography: A Thriller '10
Pretty Dead Things '06
Rated X '00
Running Scared '06
Shattered Innocence '87
The Silence '10 ►
The Sinister Urge '60
Slippery Slope '06
Snap Decision '01
South Bronx Heroes '85
Starlet '12 ►
States of Control '98
This Girl's Life '03
Torremolinos 73 '03
Variety '83
Who's Your Monkey '07
The Woman '11
Women in Trouble '09
Wonderland '03
Zack and Miri Make a Porno '08 ►

Portland (Oregon, not Maine)

Bigger Than the Sky '05
Body of Evidence '92
The Burning Plain '08
Drugstore Cowboy '89 ►
Elephant '03 ►
Feast of Love '07
The Hunted '03
Lean on Pete '17 ►
Leave No Trace '18 ►
Magnificent Obsession '54
Mr. Brooks '07
My Own Private Idaho '91 ►
Paranoid Park '07
Portland Expose '57
Saving Sarah Cain '07
Spiral '07
The Stepfather '09
Stranger in My Bed '05
Timmy Failure: Mistakes Were Made '20
Untraceable '08
Zero Effect '97

Possession

Along Came the Devil '18
The Amityville Horror '05
Annabelle Comes Home '19
Annabelle: Creation '17
Army of Darkness '92 ►
Burnt Offerings '76
The Conjuring 2 '16
The Covenant '06
Demon '16 ►
Demons 2 '87

► = rated three bones or higher

Demons '86
The Devil's Candy '17
Evil Dead '83
Evil Dead 2: Dead by Dawn '87
Evil Dead '13
Fallen '97
In Fabric '18
Isabelle '19
Jennifer's Body '09
Mirrors '08
Night of the Demons 2 '94
Night of the Demons 3 '97
Night of the Demons '88
Night of the Demons '09
Nightmare Cinema '19
Ouija: Origin of Evil '16
Prince of Darkness '87
The Prodigy '19
Session 9 '01
The Shining '80
Under the Shadow '16►

Post-Apocalypse

See also Negative Utopia

A. I.: Artificial Intelligence '01
Abe's Tomb '07
After Earth '13
After the Fall of New York '85
Aftermath '85
Aftermath '12
Against the Dark '09
Alien Apocalypse '05
Automatons '06
Babylon A.D. '08
Battle for the Planet of the Apes '73
Battle Queen 2020 '99
The Bed Sitting Room '69
Beneath the Planet of the Apes '70
The Blood of Heroes '89
The Book of Eli '10
Bounty Killer '13
A Boy and His Dog '75
Bridge of Dragons '99
Bunraku '10
Chained Heat 3: Hell Mountain '98
Circuitry Man '90
City Limits '85
Class of 1999 '90
Clone '05
Cold Harvest '98
Crash and Burn '90
Creation of the Humanoids '62
The Cured '18
Cyborg '89
The Dalmarian Chronicles '03
Damnation Alley '77
Dawn of the Planet of the Apes '14►
The Day '11
Day of the Dead '85
Day the World Ended '55
Daybreak '93
Daylight's End '16
Death Games '02
Death Racers '08
Deathlands: Homeward Bound '03
Def-Con 4 '85
Domain '18
Doomsday '08
Double Dragon '94
Dredd '12►
The Element of Crime '84
Encrypt '03
Equilibrium '02
The Final Storm '09
First Spaceship on Venus '60►
Five '51
Fortress of Amerikka '89
Future Kill '85
Future World '18
Genesis II '73
Glen and Randa '71
Goodbye World '14
The Handmaid's Tale '90
Hardware '90
Hell Comes to Frogtown '88
Hey, Happy! '01
How I Live Now '13
The Hunger Games '12►
The Hunger Games: Catching Fire '13 ►
The Hungover Games '14
Hybrid '97
I Am Legend '07 ►
I Think We're Alone Now '18
Infected '13
IO '19
It Comes at Night '17
Judge Dredd '95
Karate Cop '91
Land of Doom '84
The Last Eve '05
The Last Man '00
The Last Man on Earth '64
Last Stand '00
Le Dernier Combat '84 ►
Lord of the Flies '63 ►
The Lost Future '10
The Machine '13
Mad Max '80 ►
Mad Max: Beyond Thunderdome '85
Mad Max: Fury Road '15►
Maggie '15
Man Down '16
The Mark 2: Redemption '13
The Matrix '99►
The Matrix Reloaded '03
The Matrix Revolutions '03►
Maze Runner: The Death Cure '18
Mortal Engines '18
Natural City '03
Nautilus '99
Nemesis '93
Night of the Comet '84
9 '09►
1990: The Bronx Warriors '83
The Noah '75
Oblivion '13
Omega Cop '90
Omega Doom '96
Omega Man '71
On the Beach '59►
On the Beach '00
1,000 Years From Now '52
Only '20
Panic in Year Zero! '62
Patient Zero '18
Phoenix the Warrior '88
Planet Earth '74
Planet of the Apes '68►
Plughead Rewired: Circuitry Man 2 '94
Post Impact '04
The Postman '97
Prayer of the Rollerboys '91
Priest '11
Pulse '01
The Quiet Earth '85►
Quintet '79
Raiders of the Sun '92
Reign of Fire '02
Resident Evil: The Final Chapter '16
Resistance '92
Rise of the Zombies '12
The Road '09
The Road Warrior '82►
RoboCop '87►
Screamers '96
7 Angels in Eden '07
The Seventh Sign '88
She '83
Shepherd '99
Silent Running '71►
Six-String Samurai '98
The Slime People '63
Soldier '98
Southland Tales '06
Stake Land '10
Star Quest '94
The Starving Games '13
Steel Dawn '87
Steel Frontier '94
Stephen King's The Stand '94
Tank Girl '94
Teenage Caveman '58
Teenage Caveman '01
10,000 A.D.: The Legend of the Black Pearl '08
Terminator 2: Judgment Day '91►
Terminator Salvation '09
Testament '83►
Things to Come '36►
The Time Machine '02
Time of the Wolf '03 ►
Titan A.E. '00
Tooth and Nail '07
Turbo Kid '15
12 Monkeys '95 ►
20 Years After '08
28 Days Later '02
28 Weeks Later '07
Ultraviolet '06
The Vanguard '08
Virus '82
Walking Deceased '15
War for the Planet of the Apes '17 ►
Warlords '88
Warlords of the 21st Century '82
Warriors of the Wasteland '83
Waterworld '95
Welcome II the Terrordome '95
Where Have All the People Gone? '74
Z for Zachariah '15
Zombieworld '15
Zone 39 '96

Postwar

See also Veterans

Act of Violence '48
Americana '81
Apartment for Peggy '48
An Awfully Big Adventure '94
Baaria '09
Back Home '90
Baltic Deputy '37►
Before Winter Comes '69
Behold a Pale Horse '64
Berlin Express '48►
The Best Years of Our Lives '46►
Bitter Rice '49►
Black Rain '88►
The Bletchley Circle '13
Born on the Fourth of July '89►
Bridge to the Sun '61
Buffalo Soldiers '97►
The Burmese Harp '56►
The Bushwackers '52
Cabo Blanco '81
Captain Carey, U.S.A. '50
Carbide and Sorrel '63
Chattahoochee '89
Cinema Paradiso '88►
Close-Up '48
Courage Under Fire '96►
A Dangerous Man: Lawrence after Arabia '91►
Dear Mr. Prohack '49
Desire Me '47
Deutschland im Jahre Null '47►
The Devil Makes Three '52
The Devil's Doorway '50
Distant Thunder '88
Distant Voices, Still Lives '88►
Dixie Lanes '88
Early Summer '51►
Eat a Bowl of Tea '89►
Exodus '60►
Father '67►
The Fighting Kentuckian '49
First Blood '82
Foolish Wives '22►
Four in a Jeep '51
Fraulein '58
Gate of Flesh '64
Germany Year Zero '48►
Going for Gold: The '48 Games '12
The Good German '06
Grave of the Fireflies '88►
Grbavica: The Land of My Dreams '06
The Guilt of Janet Ames '47
Gun Fury '53
Heroes '77
The Hi-Lo Country '98
The Hills Run Red '67
Hiroshima, Mon Amour '59►
Horizons West '52
House '86►
Hurry Sundown '67
I Am a Fugitive from a Chain Gang '32►
The Impatient Years '44
In a Glass Cage '86
The Indian Runner '91
The Innocent '93
Inside Out '75
It Always Rains on Sunday '47
It Happened in New Orleans '36
It Happened on 5th Avenue '47
Jacob's Ladder '90
Judgment at Nuremberg '61 ►
Killing Down '06
The Last Flight '31
The Last Reunion '80
The Last Time I Saw Paris '54
Le Dernier Combat '84 ►
The Left Hand of God '55 ►
Les Rendez-vous D'Anna '78
Lilies of the Field '63►
The Limping Man '53
Lisa '62
Living In a Big Way '47
Lone Rider '08
Love Is a Many-Splendored Thing '55
Love Nest '51
The Man in the Glass Booth '75►
Man of Marble '76►
Maria's Lovers '84
The Marriage of Maria Braun '79►
The Master Plan '55
Max '02
Mine Own Executioner '47►
The Miniver Story '50
Mrs. Dalloway '97
A Month in the Country '87►
Mother Night '96►
Mudbound '17►
The Murderers Are Among Us '46
My Life and Times with Antonin Artaud '93►
Nevil Shute's The Far Country '85
New World '95
1945 '17►
1900 '76►
Nobody Lives Forever '46►
Notorious '46►
The Odessa File '74
One Wonderful Sunday '47
Photographing Fairies '97
Plenty '85
A Private Function '84
QB VII '74►
Quality Street '37
Rambo: First Blood, Part 2 '85
Random Harvest '42►
The Razor's Edge '46►
The Reader '08
Rebel in Town '56
The Red Danube '50
Rich Man, Poor Man '76►
Ride the Pink Horse '47►
Rio Conchos '64►
The Romance of Rosy Ridge '47
The Rose Garden '89
Savage Dawn '84
The Search '48►
Seraphim Falls '06
The Sergeant '68
Shoeshine '47►
Small Island '09
Sommersby '93
Sophie's Choice '82►
Souvenir '88
Stranger on the Prowl '52
Strategic Air Command '55
The Subject Was Roses '68►
Sunshine '99
Taking Sides '01►
The Teahouse of the August Moon '56
The Texans '38
Thank You for Your Service '17►
They Gave Him a Gun '37
They Made Me a Fugitive '47
The Third Man '49►
Three Comrades '38►
Three Steps North '51
Three Stripes in the Sun '55
Till the End of Time '46
Trained to Kill, U.S.A. '75
The Truce '96 ►
Verboten! '59
Vietnam, Texas '90
A Walk in the Clouds '95
We All Loved Each Other So Much '77 ►
The Weapon '56
The Whistleblower '11 ►
Who'll Stop the Rain? '78 ►
Wish You Were Here '87 ►
World for Ransom '54
The Yakuza '75
Year of the Quiet Sun '84 ►
Zentropa '92

POW/MIA

See also Vietnam War; War, General; World War Two

Against the Wind '48
American Commandos '84
Andersonville '95►
The Andersonville Trial '70►
Au Revoir les Enfants '87►
Bat 21 '88
Battle of the Coral Sea '59
The Beast '88
The Beasts of Marseilles '57
Blockhouse '73
The Bridge on the River Kwai '57►
Bridge to Hell '87
The Brylcreem Boys '96
Captive Heart '47►
Captive Hearts '87
Colditz: Escape of the Birdmen '71
The Colditz Story '55
Come See the Paradise '90►
Cornered '45►
The Cross of Lorraine '43
Devils on the Doorstep '00
The Elusive Corporal '62►
Empire of the Sun '87►
Era Notte a Roma '60►
Escape '90
Escape from Fort Bravo '53
Escape from Sobibor '87►
Escape to Athena '79
15 Amore '98
Fighting Mad '77
Force of Arms '51
Fort McCoy '11
Generale Della Rovere '09►
Grand Illusion '37►
The Great Escape '63►
The Great Raid '05
Hannibal Brooks '69
Hanoi Hilton '87
Hart's War '02
Hell to Eternity '60
The Hook '63
The Human Condition: A Soldier's Prayer '61►
In Enemy Hands '04
In Love and War '91
In Love and War '01
In Tranzit '07
The Incident '89►
The Iron Triangle '89
The Keeper '18
King Rat '65►
Land of Mine '15
The Lost Valentine '11
The Master Race '44
McKenzie Break '70►
Merry Christmas, Mr. Lawrence '83►
Mine Own Executioner '47►
Missing in Action '84
Nam Angels '88
Objective, Burma! '45►
One That Got Away '57►
Pacific Inferno '85
Paradise Road '97
The Password Is Courage '62
Porridge '91
Prisoners of the Sun '91►
The Purple Heart '44
The Rack '56
Raiders of Leyte Gulf '63
The Railway Man '13
Rescue Dawn '06►
The Road to Guantanamo '06
Rolling Thunder '77
St. Ives '98
Seven Years in Tibet '97
Sisters of War '10
Some Kind of Hero '82
Stalag 17 '53 ►
Stalag Luft '93
Three Came Home '50 ►
Three Wishes '95
Time Limit '57
To End All Wars '01
A Town Like Alice '56
Two Thousand Women '44
Unbroken '14
Very Important Person '61
Victory '81
Von Ryan's Express '65 ►
Wake Up and Dream '46
The Wind Cannot Read '58
Women of Valor '86

Pregnant Men

Enemy Mine '85
InAlienable '08
Junior '94
A Slightly Pregnant Man '79

Pregnant Pauses

See also Bringing Up Baby

Alien 3 '92
All About My Mother '99►
The All-American Boy '73
All Neat in Black Stockings '69
Angel Rodriguez '05
Angie '94
Annabelle '14
Apartment for Peggy '48
Are We Done Yet? '07
Armistead Maupin's More Tales of the City '97
Arn: The Knight Templar '07
The Astronaut's Wife '99
Aswang '03
Away We Go '09
The Baby Dance '98►
The Baby Formula '08
The Baby Maker '70
Baby Mama '08
Baby of the Bride '91
Baby on Board '08
Babyfever '94
Babylon A.D. '08
The Back-Up Plan '10
Bad Girl '31
The Bad Mother's Handbook '07
Barbershop '02►
Barry Munday '10
Beautiful People '99
Bed and Board '70►
The Bed Sitting Room '69
Bella '06
Bellyfruit '99
Beloved/Friend '99
Beneath the Harvest Sky '14
Beyond the Blackboard '11
Big City '37
Black Irish '07
Bleeding Hearts '94
The Book of Love '16
Born Bad '11
Boys on the Side '94
Brand New Life '72
Bride Flight '08
Bridget Jones's Baby '16
Brink of Life '57
Brother Rat '38
The Brothers Solomon '07
Cafe au Lait '94►
Cafe Lumiere '05
Caged '50►
Catherine Cookson's The Dwelling Place '94
Catherine Cookson's The Wingless Bird '97
Cell 211 '09
Cheyenne Warrior '94
Children of Men '06►
Children of the Corn: Genesis '11
Chinese Puzzle '13
Choices '86
Chutney Popcorn '99
The Circle '00
Citizen Ruth '96
The Clinic '10
Cocktail '88
Coming Out '89

► = *rated three bones or higher*

Coal Miner's Daughter '80 ▶
Comeback '83
The Comic '69 ▶
The Commitments '91 ▶
Control '07
The Cotton Club '84 ▶
Crossover Dreams '85
Darling '65 ▶
Dead Ringers '88 ▶
Don't Think Twice '16
Dreamgirls '06 ▶
Echo Park '86
Eddie and the Cruisers 2: Eddie Lives! '89
Eddie and the Cruisers '83
Edie in Ciao! Manhattan '72
EDtv '99
Elmer Gantry '60 ▶
Elvis: The Movie '79
Eureka! '81
Extra Girl '23
Factory Girl '06
Falco '08
Fame '80 ▶
The Fan '81
Feel the Noise '07
The Five Heartbeats '91 ▶
Flashdance '83
Forbidden Relations '83
Forever My Girl '18
Frances '82 ▶
The Gene Krupa Story '59
George White's Scandals of 1935 '35
The Goddess '58 ▶
Goodbye, Norma Jean '75
Gore Vidal's Lincoln '88
Grosse Fatigue '94 ▶
The Gunfighter '50 ▶
Hail Caesar '94
A Hard Day's Night '64 ▶
Her Smell '19
Hero at Large '80
Idolmaker '80
I'll Cry Tomorrow '55 ▶
I'm Not There '07 ▶
Imitation of Life '34
Imitation of Life '59 ▶
Inside Daisy Clover '65
Irreconcilable Differences '84
It Could Happen to You '94
It Should Happen to You '54 ▶
It's Tough to Be Famous '32
The Jacksons: An American Dream '92
James Dean '76
The Jayne Mansfield Story '80
The Jazz Singer '80
Jersey Boys '14
Jimmy Hollywood '94
Jo Jo Dancer, Your Life Is Calling '86
King of Comedy '82 ▶
La Bamba '87 ▶
La Dolce Vita '60 ▶
Ladies and Gentlemen, the Fabulous Stains '82
Lady Jane '85 ▶
Lady Sings the Blues '72
Lenny '74 ▶
Little Caesar '30 ▶
Lords of Dogtown '05
Love Me or Leave Me '55 ▶
The Magnificent Ambersons '42 ▶
The Magnificent Ambersons '02
Mahogany '75
The Main Event '79
Man in the Mirror: The Michael Jackson Story '04
The Man Who Would Be King '75 ▶
Mephisto '81 ▶
Miss All-American Beauty '82
Mistress '91
Mommie Dearest '81
Music & Lyrics '07
My Fair Lady '64 ▶
My Favorite Year '82 ▶
Naked in New York '93
Oh, God! You Devil '84
The One and Only '78
One Trick Pony '80
Payday '73
Pecker '98
A Perfect Day '06
Postcards from the Edge '90 ▶
Pure Country '92
Purple Rain '84
The Queen of Mean '90
Raging Bull '80 ▶
Ransom '96 ▶
Rocky '76 ▶
Rocky 2 '79
Rocky 3 '82
Rocky 4 '85
Rocky 5 '90
The Rose '79 ▶
Scarlet Diva '00
The Seduction '82
Shakes the Clown '92
Show People '28 ▶
Sins '85
Smash-Up: The Story of a Woman '47 ▶
Smithereens '82
S.O.B. '81
Sparkle '12
Star 80 '83
A Star Is Born '37 ▶
A Star Is Born '54 ▶
A Star Is Born '18 ▶
Stardom '00
Stardust Memories '80
Stoned '05
Sunset Boulevard '50 ▶
Svengali '83
Sweet Dreams '85
Sweet Perfection '90
Sweethearts '38 ▶
The Thing Called Love '93
The Tiger Woods Story '98
Too Late Blues '61
Tragedy Girls '17 ▶
True Colors '91
Tucker: The Man and His Dream '88 ▶
Two Weeks in Another Town '62
Undiscovered '05
Valley of the Dolls '67
Velvet Goldmine '98
Vox Lux '18
What Ever Happened to Baby Jane? '62 ▶
What Price Hollywood? '32 ▶
What's Love Got to Do with It? '93
While the City Sleeps '56 ▶
Winning '69 ▶
You Light Up My Life '77
Youngblood Hawke '64
Your Cheatin' Heart '64
Ziegfeld Girl '41 ▶

Princes/Princesses

See Royalty; Royalty, British; Royalty, French; Royalty, Russian

Prison

See also Alcatraz; Devil's Island; Escaped Cons; Great Escapes; Men in Prison; POW/MIA; Women in Prison

Prison Breaks

See also Great Escapes; Men in Prison; Women in Prison

Alien Invasion Arizona '07
The Big Bird Cage '72
The Big Doll House '71
The Big House '30 ▶
Big House, U.S.A. '55
The Big Shot '42
Caged Fury '90
Captive '15
Citizen Gangster '11
The Confession '20
Cool Hand Luke '67 ▶
Eddie Macon's Run '83
Escape from Alcatraz '79 ▶
Escape from Death Row '73
Escape from Hell '79
Escape from Pretoria '20
Escape Plan 2: Hades '18
Escape Plan '13
Extremely Dangerous '99
Fast Five '11
For You I Die '47
Gang Busters '55
A Good Day to Die Hard '13
Hate for Hate '67
A Horrible Way to Die '10
I Am a Fugitive from a Chain Gang '32 ▶
I Love You Phillip Morris '10
The Infiltrators '20
Jailbreakers '94
Jailbreakin' '72
A Killer in the Family '83
The Killer Is Loose '56
Kiss Tomorrow Goodbye '50
Last Rampage '17
Lucky Break '01
Me and My Gal '32
Mesrine: Part 2-Public Enemy Number 1 '08
Midnight Express '78 ▶
The Mind's Eye '16
Murder One '88
Naked Youth '59
The Next Three Days '10
The Old Man & the Gun '18 ▶
Papillon '17
A Perfect World '93
Point Blank '98
Prison Break '38
Prison Break: The Final Break '09
Revolt in the Big House '58
Semper Fi '19
Sitting Target '72
Skidoo '68
The Slams '73
Son of a Gun '14
Stander '03
The Sugarland Express '74 ▶
Swelter '14
They Gave Him a Gun '37
3 from Hell '19
Thunder County '74
We're No Angels '55 ▶
We're No Angels '89
You Can't Get Away With Murder '39

Private Eyes

Abbott and Costello Meet the Invisible Man '51 ▶
Alone in the Dark 2 '08
Alone in the Dark '05
Alphaville '65 ▶
Angel Heart '87
Anonymous Rex '04
Bad Seed '00
Beyond Justice '01
The Big Bang '11
The Big Empty '98 ▶
The Big Fall '96
The Big Sleep '46 ▶
The Big Sleep '78
Big Store '41
The Big Take '18
Billion Dollar Brain '67
The Black Camel '31
The Black Doll '38
Black Eye '74
Blackout '54
Blonde for a Day '46
Blue Blood '07
Blue, White and Perfect '42
Breathless '12
Brown's Requiem '98
Bulldog Drummond Comes Back '37
Bulldog Drummond Escapes '37
Bulldog Drummond's Bride '39
Bulldog Drummond's Peril '38
The Caller '08
Camouflage '00
The Captain Hates the Sea '34
Cat City '08
Cat Run '11
Caught in the Act '04
Chandler '71
Charlie Chan and the Curse of the Dragon Queen '81
Charlie Chan at Monte Carlo '37
Charlie Chan at the Circus '36
Charlie Chan at the Olympics '37
Charlie Chan at the Opera '36 ▶
Charlie Chan at the Race Track '36
Charlie Chan in Egypt '35
Charlie Chan in London '34
Charlie Chan in Paris '35
Charlie Chan in Shanghai '35
Charlie Chan on Broadway '37
Charlie Chan's Secret '35
Chinatown '74 ▶
The Chinese Cat '44
The Chinese Ring '47
Clean Slate '94
Cocaine and Blue Eyes '83
Cold in July '14 ▶
Concrete Cowboys '79
Counterspy Meets Scotland Yard '50
Criminal Desire '98
Cry Uncle '71
The Curse of the Jade Scorpion '01
Curtain at Eight '33
The Dain Curse '78
Dark Corner '46 ▶
The Dark Hour '36
Dark Side of Midnight '86
Dead Again '91 ▶
Dead Evidence '00
Dead Men Don't Wear Plaid '82
Dead Pigeon on Beethoven Street '72
Detective Sadie & Son '84
Devil in a Blue Dress '95 ▶
Diabolique '96
Dilili in Paris '18
The Doorbell Rang: A Nero Wolfe Mystery '01
The Drowning Pool '75
Dylan Dog: Dead of Night '11
8mm '98
The End of the Affair '99 ▶
Everybody Wins '90
Eye of the Killer '99
Eyes in the Night '42
Faceless '88
The Falcon in Mexico '44
Farewell, My Lovely '75 ▶
Fearless '77
For Sale '98
Forbidden Games '95
From Hollywood to Deadwood '89
Ginger '72
The Girl Hunters '63
Give 'Em Hell Malone '09
The Golden Spiders: A Nero Wolfe Mystery '00
Gone Baby Gone '07 ▶
Gotham '88 ▶
Grand Central Murder '42
A Gun, a Car, a Blonde '97
Gunfight at Comanche Creek '64
The Happytime Murders '18
Hard to Forget '98
Hickey & Boggs '72
Hollywood Confidential '97
Hollywood Wives: The New Generation '03
Hollywoodland '06
Human Desires '97
Hustle '04
I Heart Huckabees '04
I, the Jury '82
Ice Blues: A Donald Strachey Mystery '08
In the Deep Woods '91
Inherent Vice '14 ▶
Intolerable Cruelty '03
It's a Wonderful World '39
The Jade Mask '45
Jimmy Vestvood: Amerikan Hero '16
Jr. Detective Agency '09
Just Off Broadway '42
The Kennel Murder Case '33
Kill Me Again '89
Kill or Cure '62
Kiss Kiss Bang Bang '05 ▶
Kiss Me Deadly '55 ▶
Knives Out '19 ▶
L.A. Dicks '05
La Rupture '70
Lady in Cement '68
Lady in the Lake '46
Larceny in her Heart '46
Last Days '05
The Late Show '77 ▶
LIP Service '99
The Long Goodbye '73 ▶
The Long Kiss Goodnight '96
Looking for Kitty '04
Lord of Illusions '95
The Lost Son '98
Love at Large '89 ▶
Love Walked In '97
A Low Down Dirty Shame '94
Magnum P.I.: Don't Eat the Snow in Hawaii '80
The Maltese Falcon '31 ▶
The Maltese Falcon '41 ▶
The Man with Bogart's Face '80
Marlowe '69
Meet Mr. Callaghan '54
Meet Nero Wolfe '36
Meeting at Midnight '44
Michael Shayne: Private Detective '40
Mindstorm '01
The Missing Person '09
Mr. Moto in Danger Island '39
Mr. Moto's Gamble '38
Mr. Moto's Last Warning '39 ▶
Mr. Wong, Detective '38
Mr. Wong in Chinatown '39
The Monkey's Mask '00
Moonlighting '85
Motherless Brooklyn '19
Murder by Death '76
Murder, My Sweet '44 ▶
Murder on the Orient Express '01
Murder on the Orient Express '10 ▶
Murder over New York '40
My Gal Sunday '14
My Gun Is Quick '57
Mystery of Mr. Wong '39
The Next Big Thing '02
The Nice Guys '16 ▶
Nick Carter, Master Detective '39
Night Moves '75 ▶
No Hands on the Clock '41
Not My Life '06
The Nuisance '33
On the Other Hand, Death '08
One of My Wives Is Missing '76
One Shoe Makes It Murder '82
Out of the Past '47 ▶
The Outsider '14
The Panther's Claw '42
Peter Gunn '89
The Poison Rose '19
Pokémon Detective Pikachu '19
Poodle Springs '98
A Prairie Home Companion '06
Remarkable Power '08
The Return of Boston Blackie '27
The Right Temptation '00
Rock Slyde: Private Eye '09
Ryder P.I. '86
San Saba '08
Satan Met a Lady '36
The Scarlet Clue '45
The Scratch '09
Sexton Blake and the Hooded Terror '38
Shaft '71 ▶
Shaft '00 ▶
Shaft '19
Shaft in Africa '73
Shaft's Big Score '72
Shall We Dance? '04
Shamus '73
Sheba, Baby '75
Shock to the System '06
Silver City '04
Sin City '05
The Sin Seer '15
The Singing Detective '86 ▶
The Singing Detective '03
Sky Murder '40
Sleepers West '41
Smile Jenny, You're Dead '74
The Smiling Ghost '41
So Undercover '13
The Soft Kill '94
South Beach '92
Spenser: A Savage Place '94
Spenser: Ceremony '93
Spenser: Pale Kings & Princes '94
Spenser: The Judas Goat '94
Stolen Kisses '68 ▶
Story of a Love Affair '50
The Strange Case of Dr. Rx '42
Sunset Grill '92
Suspicious Minds '96
Sweet Lies '88
TekWar '94
Thank you, Mr. Moto '37
There's Something about Mary '98 ▶
They All Laughed '81 ▶
Thin Air '00
Think Fast, Mr. Moto '37
Third Man Out: A Donald Strachey Mystery '05
Tick Tock '00 ▶
Tony Rome '67
The Trap '46
A Trick of the Mind '06
Trixie '00
Trouble Man '72
Twenty Plus Two '61
Twilight '98 ▶
The Two Jakes '90
2 Minutes Later '07
Under Suspicion '92 ▶
Unforgivable '11
V/H/S/2 '13 ▶
Vegas '78
V.I. Warshawski '91
A Walk Among the Tombstones '14
Where's Marlowe? '98
Who Framed Roger Rabbit '88 ▶
World for Ransom '54
Zero Effect '97

Prohibition Gangs

See also Gangs; Organized Crime; Period Piece: 1920s

Al Capone '59 ▶
City Heat '84
Corsair '31
The King of the Roaring '20s: The Story of Arnold Rothstein '61
Lady Killer '33 ▶
Lawless '12
Live by Night '16
Miller's Crossing '90 ▶
Mobsters '91
Nitti: The Enforcer '88
Once Upon a Time in America '84 ▶
Public Enemy '31 ▶
The Purple Gang '59
The Roaring Twenties '39 ▶
Robin and the 7 Hoods '64
The St. Valentine's Day Massacre '67
The Untouchables '87 ▶
The Wet Parade '32

Prom

See also Hell High School; School Daze

Bart Got a Room '08
Blockers '18
Cabin Fever 2: Spring Fever '08
Carrie '76 ▶
Carrie '02
Carrie '13
Cynthia '47
Detention '11
Drive Me Crazy '99
Footloose '84
For One Night '06
G.B.F. '13
Hello Mary Lou: Prom Night 2 '87
High School Musical 3: Senior Year '08

▶ = rated three bones or higher

Jawbreaker '98
My Big Fat Greek Wedding 2 '16
Never Been Kissed '99
The Night Before '88
Night School '18
Peggy Sue Got Married '86
Pretty in Pink '86
Prom '11
Prom Night 3: The Last Kiss '89
Prom Night 4: Deliver Us from Evil '91
Prom Night '80
Prom Night '08
Prom Queen '04
Prom Wars '08
Queen Sized '08
Radio Rebel '12
The Rage: Carrie 2 '99
Rock, Rock, Rock '56
The Rocker '08
Saved! '04
She's All That '99
Teen Spirit '11
The Texas Chainsaw Massacre 4: The Next Generation '95
Trippin' '99
Urban Legends: Bloody Mary '05
Whatever It Takes '00

Propaganda

See *Patriotism & Politics*

Prostitutes

See *Gigolos; Oldest Profession*

Protests

See also *Rebel With a Cause*
American Zombie '07
Born on the Fourth of July '89►
Clemency '19
The Dog Lover '16
The Edge of Democracy '19
Forrest Gump '94►
Hairspray '88►
How to Survive a Plague '12►
In the Name of the Father '93►
Jojo Rabbit '19►
The Long Walk Home '89►
Malcolm X '92►
Matewan '87►
Michael Collins '96►
Norma Rae '79►
Panther '95
Peterloo '18
Pride '14►
The Professor '19
Radio Rebel '12
Silkwood '83►
Winter on Fire: Ukraine's Fight for Freedom '15►

Psychiatry

See *Shrinks*

Psychic Abilities

See also *Mystery & Supernatural Comedy; Supernatural Horror*
Affinity '08
After Midnight '89
The Bandits of Corsica '53
Beyond '11
Beyond the Black Rainbow '10
The Black Camel '31
Carolina Moon '07
Carrie '76►
Carrie '02
The Cell 2 '09
Cemetery of Splendor '15►
Clive Barker's Book of Blood '08
Close Your Eyes '02
A Crooked Somebody '18
The Dark '79
Dead Zone '83►
The Dead Zone '02
Death Defying Acts '07
Deathtrap '82
Distorted '18
Donovan's Echo '11
Don't Look Now '73►
Dream Man '94
Dreamscape '84
Everybody Says I'm Fine! '06
The Eyes of Charles Sand '74
Fear '90
Final Destination '00
Final Move '06
Firestarter 2: Rekindled '02
Firestarter '84
First Snow '07
Forbidden Games '95
Friday the 13th, Part 7: The New Blood '88
The Frighteners '96
From Hell '01►
The Frozen Dead '66
Ghost '90►
The Gift '00
The Haunting '63►
The Haunting of Lisa '96
Hearts in Atlantis '01
Hereafter '10
House of Bones '09
Imagining Argentina '04
In Her Mother's Footsteps '06
In the Blood '06
In Your Eyes '14
Initiation '87
Insidious: Chapter 3 '15
Insidious: The Last Key '18
Jonathan '19
Kaboom '11
L.A. Dicks '05
Lake Mungo '08
The Legend of Hell House '73►
Life Without Dick '01
London Fields '18
Love and Human Remains '93►
Magic in the Moonlight '14
Man on a Swing '74
The Men Who Stare at Goats '09
The Mind Reader '33
Mindstorm '01
Momentum '03
Mother of Tears '08
The Mothman Prophecies '02
Next '07
The Orphanage '07►
Over Her Dead Body '08
Patrick '13
Poltergeist '82►
Poltergeist 2: The Other Side '86
Poltergeist 3 '88
The Power '68
The Psychic '68
Psychic Experiment '10
Push '09
The Quiet Ones '14
Red Lights '12
Ringu '98►
Running on Karma '03
Scanners '81
Scanners: The Showdown '94
Seance on a Wet Afternoon '64►
Second Sight '89
Second Sight '07
Serenity '05►
Seventeen and Missing '06
The Shadow Within '07
The Shining '80
6 Degrees of Hell '12
The Sixth Sense '99►
Skeletons '10
The Skeptic '09
Solace '16
Stephen King's Rose Red '02
Sworn to Justice '97
Talking to Heaven '02
Thelma '17
Thicker than Water '99
Trancers '84
Trancers 6: Life After Deth '02
Vibes '88
Visions '16
Visions of Murder '93
Voodoo Moon '05
Warp Speed '81
What Women Want '00
The X Files: I Want to Believe '08
You Will Meet a Tall Dark Stranger '10

Psycho-Thriller

See *Mystery & Suspense*

Psychotics/Sociopaths

See also *Roommates from Hell*
Albino Alligator '96
Alex Cross '12
Angel Face '52►
Apartment Zero '88►
Appointment With Danger '51
The Assassination of Jesse James by the Coward Robert Ford '07►
The Assassination of Richard Nixon '05
The Avenger '60
Bad Bush '09
Bad Ronald '74►
The Bad Seed '56
Badlands '74►
Ball of Wax '03
Basement Jack '09
Bereavement '10
Berserk! '67
Black Eliminator '78
Blind Side '93
Bloodmyth '09
Blue Steel '90
Body Bags '93
Bone Daddy '97
Born Bad '11
Born for Hell '76
Born Killers '05
The Boston Strangler '68
Boxing Helena '93
The Boys Next Door '85
Breakdown '96►
Broken Arrow '95
Broken Vows '16
The Butcher Boy '97►
The Cable Guy '96
The Canal '14
Cape Fear '61►
Cape Fear '91►
Carnage Park '16
The Centerfold Girls '74
The Childhood of a Leader '16
Citadel '12
Clay Pigeons '98
Cold Creek Manor '03
Cold Eyes of Fear '70
Cold Steel '87
Con Air '97►
Consenting Adults '92
Corpse Mania '81
Countdown '16
Cries in the Dark '06
Crimes of Dr. Mabuse '32►
The Crush '93
Curve '16
Damned River '89
Dario Argento's Trauma '93
Dark City '50
The Dark Knight '08►
The Dark Ride '78
A Date With Darkness '03
Dead by Sunset '95
Deadbolt '92
Deadly Daphne's Revenge '93
Death and Cremation '10
A Death in California '85
Death Sentence '74
Dee Snider's Strangeland '98
Demolition Man '93
The Dentist '96
Deranged '74►
Deranged '87
Desperate Measures '98
Dr. Giggles '92
Don't Answer the Phone '80
Doppelganger: The Evil Within '90
Dot.Kill '05
Down in the Valley '05
The Drifter '88
Escape Velocity '99
Eye of God '97►
The Eyes of My Mother '16
Fade to Black '80
Falling Down '93
The Fan '81
The Fan '96
Fatal Attraction '87►
Fatal Secrets '09
Fear '88
Fear '96
Fear City '85
The Fiance '96
The Fiend Who Walked the West '58
The Final Storm '09
Fireball '09
Frayed '07
From Dusk Till Dawn '95
The Front Line '06
Funny Games '07►
The Gingerbread Man '97
Girl in Black Stockings '57
The Glimmer Man '96
Gloria '98
Guardian Angel '94
The Guest '14
Guilty as Sin '93
Halloween: H20 '98►
Haunt '19
Headless Body in Topless Bar '96
Heat '95►
Helter Skelter '76
Helter Skelter Murders '71
Hide '08
High Tension '03
Highway Hitcher '98
The Hitcher '07
Homage '95
Homer and Eddie '89
A Horrible Way to Die '10
The Hostage '67
Hot Potato '76
The House That Jack Built '18
Hunting Humans '02
Hush '98
I Am Not A Serial Killer '16
I Know What You Did Last Summer '97►
I Still Know What You Did Last Summer '98
Ichi the Killer '01
In Dreams '98
In the Lake of the Woods '96
In the Line of Fire '93►
In the Mouth of Madness '95
The Intruder '19
Joy Ride 2: Dead Ahead '08
Kalifornia '93
Keys to Tulsa '96
The Killer Inside Me '76
The Killer Inside Me '10
The Killer Is Loose '56
Killing Obsession '94
Killing Zoe '94
The King '05
Kiss the Girls '97
Knock Knock '15
The Last House on the Left '09
Letting Go '12
Lightning Bolt '67
The Lightship '86
The Little Girl Who Lives down the Lane '76
Live Wire '92
Lonely Hearts '06
Love & Mercy '15►
Lovesick '14
The Mad Bomber '72
Mad Dog Coll '61
Mad Dog Killer '77
The Mad Executioners '65
Mademoiselle '66
A Man in Uniform '93
Maniac '12
Meet the Deedles '98
Meeting Evil '12
Metro '96
Midnight 2: Sex, Death, and Videotape '93
Mimesis '11
Misbegotten '98
Mommie Dearest '81
Monster Party '18
Morgan '16
Mother's Boys '94
Motor Home Massacre '05
Moving Targets '87
Murder by Numbers '02
Murder C.O.D. '90
The Naked Flame '68
Natural Enemy '96
The Neighbor '93
Night Must Fall '64
No Brother of Mine '07
No Country for Old Men '07►
Office Killer '97
Once Upon A Time... In Hollywood '19►
One Good Turn '95
Open House '10
Pacific Heights '90►
The Paperboy '94
Past Midnight '92
The Perfect Teacher '10
Perfume: The Story of a Murderer '06
Piercing '18
Play Nice '92
Playgirl Killer '66
Poison Ivy '92
Pretty Poison '68►
Prime Time Murder '92
Prom Night '08
Psycho '60►
Psycho 2 '83
Psycho 3 '86
Psycho 4: The Beginning '90
The Psychopath '66
Psychos in Love '87
Pulse '03
The Rage '96
Rampage '87
Relentless '89
Repulsion '65►
Reservoir Dogs '92►
Retroactive '97
The Rich Man's Wife '96
Ricochet '91►
Ripley's Game '02►
Rites of Passage '12
The River Wild '94
The Road Killers '95
Roadkill '89
The Sadist '63
Sarah's Child '96
Savage Abduction '73
Saw 2 '05
Saw 3 '06
Scream '96►
Scream 2 '97►
Scream 3 '00
Secret Smile '05
Secret Window '04
The Seduction '82
See No Evil '06
Seven '95►
Seven Hours to Judgment '88
Seven Psychopaths '12►
The Seventh Floor '93
Shark Island '12
Shattered '07
The Shining '80
Shutter Island '09►
Shuttle '09
The Silencer '92
Single White Female '92
Single White Female 2: The Psycho '05
The Sitter '07
Skinner '93
Someone Behind the Door '71
Speed '94►
Speed 2: Cruise Control '97
Stalked at 17 '12
Starved '97
The Stepfather '87►
Stepfather 2: Make Room for Daddy '89
Stepfather 3: Father's Day '92
The Stepfather '09
Stripped to Kill '87
Stripteaser '95
Sugarhouse '07
Suicide Squad '16
Suspect Zero '04
Suspicious River '00
Sweet Hostage '75
The Take '09
Taking Lives '04
The Talented Mr. Ripley '99
Ted & Venus '93
The Temp '93
The Tenant '76►
Tetsuo: The Iron Man '92
Texas Chainsaw 3D '13
A Thin Line Between Love and Hate '96
Three the Hard Way '74
3000 Miles to Graceland '01
To Die For '95►
To Have and to Hold '06
Tone-Deaf '19
The Tripper '06
Truth or Consequences, N.M. '97
Turbulence '96
Twin Peaks: Fire Walk with Me '92
The Two Mrs. Carrolls '47
U-Turn '97
Unlawful Entry '92
Unspeakable '02
Urban Legend '98
The Vanishing '93
The Vanquished '52
Vice Squad '82
Violence at Noon '66►
What Ever Happened to Baby Jane? '62►
When a Stranger Calls '06
When a Stranger Calls Back '93
Whispers '89
White Heat '49►
With a Friend Like Harry '00►
The Witness '99
Wolf Creek '05
The Young Poisoner's Handbook '94►
Zero Degrees Kelvin '95

Publicists

See also *Behind the Scenes*
Amelia Earhart: The Final Flight '94
America's Sweethearts '01
The Big Circus '59
Breaking News '04
Christmas Cupid '10
Cursed '04
Dancing Co-Ed '39
The Fearmakers '58
For Your Consideration '06
Four's a Crowd '38
Gideon's Daughter '05
A Girl Cut in Two '07
Go West, Young Man '36
The Great Buck Howard '09►
Hancock '08
The Harder They Fall '56►
It's Tough to Be Famous '32
Jersey Girl '04
Jiminy Glick in LaLa Wood '05
Life '15►
Looking for Love '64
Loving You '57
Mad About Music '38►
Made On Broadway '33
The Nines '07►
The Parent Trap '98
People I Know '02
Phone Booth '02
Sparkle '07
Sweet Smell of Success '57►
12 Men of Christmas '09
Win a Date with Tad Hamilton! '04

Puerto Rico

The Apostate '98
Assassins '95
The Caller '11
Counterplot '59
D.R.E.A.M. Team '99
Feel the Noise '07
Frankenstein Meets the Space Monster '65
Illegal Tender '07
Nanny McPhee Returns '10
The Pirates! Band of Misfits '12
Puerto Ricans in Paris '16
The Rum Diary '11
Ship Ahoy '42
Sunstorm '01

Punk Rock

See also *Rock Flicks*
Born to Lose '99
Broadway Idiot '13

CBGB '13
Control '07
End of the Century: The Story of the Ramones '03 ►
The Filth and the Fury '99
Green Room '15 ►
Hard Core Logo '96
Her Smell '19
The House of Tomorrow '18
Ladies and Gentlemen, the Fabulous Stains '82
Len & Company '16
Native Son '19
Repo Man '83 ►
Rock 'n' Roll High School '79 ►
Rock 'n' Roll High School Forever '91
Sex & Drugs & Rock & Roll '10
Sid & Nancy '86 ►
Times Square '80
24 Hour Party People '01
We Are the Best! '13►
What We Do Is Secret '07

Puppets

See also Killer Toys; Toys

Actium Maximus: War of the Alien Dinosaurs '05
The Adventures of Pinocchio '96
Alice in Wonderland '50
Along with Ghosts '69
Arachnia '03
The Beaver '11
Being Elmo: A Puppeteer's Journey '11
Curse of the Puppet Master: The Human Experiment '98
The Dark Crystal '82►
Devil Doll '64
Dolls '02►
Extreme Movie '08
The Forbidden Street '49
Gepetto '00
The Great Gabbo '29
The Great Rupert '50►
The Happytime Murders '18
Judy & Punch '20
Lili '53►
Magic '78
Meet the Feebles '89
MirrorMask '05
The Muppets' Wizard of Oz '05
100 Monsters '68
The Oogieloves in the Big Balloon Adventure '12
Paper Heart '09
Pinocchio '40►
Pinocchio '02
Puppet Master '89
Puppet Master 2 '90
Puppet Master 4 '93
Puppet Master 5: The Final Chapter '94
Puppet Master: The Littlest Reich '18
Retro Puppet Master '99
Saw '04
Shanks '74
The Sound of Music '65►
Team America: World Police '04►
Tomorrow We Disappear '14
Won't You Be My Neighbor? '18►

Queens

See Royalty; Royalty, British; Royalty, French; Royalty, Russian

Rabbi

See also Clergymen; Judaism

Before the Rain '94►
Bulletproof Monk '03
The Chosen '77
David & Layla '07
The Deal '08
Enemies, a Love Story '89►
Fill the Void '12
The Frisco Kid '79
God on Trial '08
Hearts of War '07
Hello Goodbye '08
In the Presence of Mine Enemies '97
Loving Leah '09
Lucky Number Slevin '06
Mitch Albom's Have a Little Faith '11
Nora's Will '09
The Quarrel '93
Rasputin '85 ►
Rasputin and the Empress '33 ►
The Secrets '07
A Serious Man '09 ►
Stolen Summer '02
Time of Favor '00
The Unborn '09
The Yankles '09

Rabbits

Alice '88 ►
Alice in Wonderland '51 ►
Alice in Wonderland '99
Bambi '42►
Bunny Whipped '06
Donnie Darko '01►
Fatal Attraction '87►
The Geisha Boy '58
Get to Know Your Rabbit '72
Hank and Mike '08
Harvey '50►
Hoodwinked '05►
Hop '11
Igor '08
Inland Empire '06
The Last Mimzy '07
Mona Lisa '86►
Monty Python and the Holy Grail '75►
Nasty Rabbit '64
Night of the Lepus '72
Peter Rabbit '18
Phenomenon '96
Roger & Me '89►
Space Jam '96
Wallace & Gromit in The Curse of the Were-Rabbit '05►
Watership Down '78
Who Framed Roger Rabbit '88►

Raccoons

Ace Ventura: Pet Detective '93
Air Bud 4: Seventh Inning Fetch '02
Furry Vengeance '10
Guardians of the Galaxy '14►
Guardians of the Galaxy Vol. 2 '17►
Harold and Kumar Go to White Castle '04
Hoodwinked '05►
Over the Hedge '06►
Pocahontas '95►
Where the Red Fern Grows '74

Race Against Time

Alien Invasion Arizona '07
All the Money in the World '17
The Andromeda Strain '71
Andromedia '00
Angels & Demons '09
Apollo 13 '95►
Arctic '18
Around the World in 80 Days '04
Balto '95
The Bay '12
Bitter Harvest '81►
Black Dawn '05
Blown Away '94
The Borrowers '97
Broken Arrow '95
Bronson '09
Cellular '04
Chain Letter '10
Chain Reaction '80
The China Syndrome '79►
Collateral '04►
Coma '78►
The Commuter '18
Convicted '04
Daylight '96
The Dead 2 '13
Death Note 3: L Change the World '08
Death Trance '05
Deja Vu '06
D.O.A. '49 ►
D.O.A. '88
Eagle Eye '08
88 Minutes '08
Escape from L.A. '96
Escape from Pretoria '20
Fail-Safe '64 ►
Free Willy 2: The Adventure Home '95
Free Willy 3: The Rescue '97
Grand Tour: Disaster in Time '92
Held Hostage '09
Hell Commandos '69
Hidden Figures '17 ►
High Flying Bird '19
The Huntsman: Winter's War '16
Hypersonic '02
I Wouldn't Be in Your Shoes '48
I'll Be Home for Christmas '98
In Pursuit of Honor '95
In the Tall Grass '19
In Time '11
Independence Day '96►
Inferno '16
Interception '08
Interrogation '16
The Killer That Stalked New York '47
Kung Fu Killer '08
Last Dance '96
Last Stand '00
Lightning: Fire from the Sky '00
The Limehouse Golem '17
Logan Lucky '17►
Lorenzo's Oil '92►
The Magnetic Monster '53
Making Babies '19
Mechanic: Resurrection '16
Mile 22 '18
Moscow Heat '04
Nezulla the Rat Monster '02
Nick of Time '95
Non-Stop '14
Octopussy '83
Once Upon a Forest '93
Onward '20►
Outbreak '94►
Panic in Echo Park '77
Panic in the City '68
Panic in the Streets '50►
The Paradise Virus '03
The Peacemaker '97
A Perfect Day '16
The Princess Diaries 2: Royal Engagement '04
Prisoner in the Middle '74
Pursuit '72►
Race Against Time '00
Rattlesnake '19
Recon 2023: The Gauda Prime Conspiracy '08
Retrograde '03
Return to Paradise '98►
Saigon '47
The Sanctuary '09
The Satan Bug '65
Satellite in the Sky '56
Saw '04
The Silver Streak '34
Skyjacked '72
Solar Attack '06
Somebody Has to Shoot the Picture '90►
Sudden Death '95
Sunset '18
Supernova '05
Terror on a Train '53
Terror Street '54
Things to Do in Denver When You're Dead '95►
A Thousand Cuts '12
3 Days Gone '08
Time Lock '57
Time Without Pity '57
Tramp, Tramp, Tramp '26
Trapped: Buried Alive '02
TripFall '00
True Crime '99
Twister '96
The Two Mr. Kissels '08
Tycus '98
Virus X '10
WarGames '83
The Wave '15 ►
xXx: Return of Xander Cage '17

Radio

See also Mass Media

The Accidental Husband '08
Acts of Contrition '95
The Adventures of Ford Fairlane '90
Airheads '94
Alan Partridge '13 ►
American Graffiti '73 ►
American Nightmare '00
Amy's O '02
Are You Listening? '32
Bad Channels '92
The Bounce Back '16
The Brave One '07
Break of Dawn '88
Breakfast in Hollywood '46
Buck Benny Rides Again '40
Buster's Mal Heart '17
Bye Bye, Love '94
Cadillac Records '08►
Campus Rhythm '43
Carefree '38►
Choose Me '84►
Citizens Band '77►
City in Panic '86
The Couch Trip '87
Daddy's Home '15
Danger on the Air '38
Dead Air '08
Dear White People '14►
Dirty Mind of Young Sally '72
Feedback '20
The Fisher King '91►
FM '78
The Fog '78
Freeway '88
Frequency '00
The Girl From Mexico '39
Girls Night Out '83
Good Morning, Vietnam '87►
The Great American Broadcast '41►
Grosse Pointe Blank '97►
Hit Parade of 1937 '37
Holiday Rush '19
Hollywood Hotel '37
The Hucksters '47►
Hullabaloo '40
I'll Believe You '07
The Jackpot '50
Joe Dirt '01
Kentucky Moonshine '38
Laser Moon '92
Lilli Marlene '50
Look Who's Laughing '41
Love Serenade '96
The Man Who Came to Dinner '41►
Midnight Confessions '95
Mr. Rock 'n' Roll: The Alan Freed Story '99
My Blue Heaven '50
My Dream Is Yours '49
The Next Voice You Hear '50
The Night Caller '97
The Night Listener '06
No Trace '50
Nuts! '16►
The Old Homestead '35
Once Upon a Honeymoon '42
Open House '86
Our America '02
People Are Funny '46
Pirate Radio '09
Play Misty for Me '71►
Pontypool '09
Pot o' Gold '41
A Prairie Home Companion '06
Private Parts '96
Psycho 4: The Beginning '90
Pump Up the Volume '90
Radio Days '87►
Radio Rebel '12
Radio Stars on Parade '45
Radioland Murders '94
Rebecca of Sunnybrook Farm '38
The Republic of Love '03
Requiem for Murder '99
Rude '96
Say It With Songs '29
Shadow People '13
Sherlock Holmes and the Voice of Terror '42
The Singing Kid '36
Sleepless in Seattle '93 ►
The Sleepy Time Gal '01
Straight Talk '92
Strictly Dynamite '34
Strike Up the Band '40
Talk Radio '88 ►
Talk to Me '07
Telling Lies in America '96
Torch Singer '33
The Truth about Cats and Dogs '96 ►
Tune in Tomorrow '90
The Twenty Questions Murder Mystery '50
20 Years After '08
Under the Mistletoe '06
The Unsuspected '47
A Valentine Carol '07
The Vast of Night '20►
Wake Up and Live '37
The Warriors '79
Whispering Ghosts '42
Whistling in Brooklyn '43
Who Done It? '42
Winchell '98
WUSA '70

Rags to Riches

See also Cinderella Stories; Price of Fame; Wrong Side of the Tracks

Aladdin '92►
All the King's Men '49►
The Amorous Adventures of Moll Flanders '65
Anna Nicole '13
Annie '82
B.A.P.'s '97
Bernie '12►
The Beverly Hillbillies '93
Blank Check '93
Blue Jasmine '13►
Body Slam '87
Boogie Nights '97►
Breaking Glass '80
Brewster's Millions '85
The Buddy Holly Story '78►
Callie and Son '81
Christmas in July '40►
Cinderella Man '05►
Citizen Kane '41►
Coal Miner's Daughter '80►
The Cookout '04
Daddy Long Legs '55►
The Damned Don't Cry '50
Dangerous When Wet '53
Darling '65►
Dead by Dawn '98
Dodsworth '36►
EDtv '99
Emperor Jones '33
Envy '04
Evita '96
Fifth Avenue Girl '39
Film Geek '06
Footlight Parade '33►
For Richer, for Poorer '92
Forever Amber '47
G '02
Give a Girl a Break '53
Goal! The Dream Begins '06
Going in Style '17
Great Expectations '97
The Great Rupert '50►
Hero '92►
How to Be a Latin Lover '17
The Hudsucker Proxy '93►
I Love Melvin '53
It Could Happen to You '94
Jailhouse Rock '57►
The Jerk '79
Jimmy Hollywood '94
Joseph Andrews '77
Kept Husbands '31
King Arthur: Legend of the Sword '17
Lady for a Day '33►
The Last American Hero '73►
The Last Laugh '24►
Lenny '74 ►
Lili '53 ►
Little Lord Fauntleroy '36 ►
Little Lord Fauntleroy '95
Livin' Large '91
Love Nest '51
Lucky Partners '40
Magic Beyond Words: The JK Rowling Story '11
The Mambo Kings '92 ►
The Manions of America '81
Mannequin '37
McQueen '18 ►
Meet John Doe '41 ►
Memoirs of a Geisha '05
Million Dollar Baby '04 ►
A Million to Juan '94
Mrs. Parkington '44
Mrs. Winterbourne '96
Mr. Billion '77
Money for Nothing '93
My Fair Lady '64►
The Object of Beauty '91►
Overnight '03►
The Patsy '64
Possessed '31
Power '34
Pride of the Clan '18
The Prince and the Pauper '37►
The Prince and the Pauper '78
The Prince and the Pauper '01
The Prince and the Showgirl '57
Princess Tam Tam '35►
Pygmalion '38►
Rebecca of Sunnybrook Farm '17
The Return of the Beverly Hillbillies '81
Rocky '76►
Rudo y Cursi '09
Scruples '80
The Secret of My Success '87
Sepia Cinderella '47
The Sin of Harold Diddlebock '47
The Sin of Madelon Claudet '31►
Slumdog Millionaire '08►
Speak Easily '32
The Stars Fell on Henrietta '94
The Stork Club '45
Straight Talk '92
Sweet Hearts Dance '88
The Tall Guy '89►
Tapped Out '03
There Will Be Blood '07►
They Had to See Paris '29
Three Coins in the Fountain '54
The Toast of New Orleans '50
Toast of New York '37►
Trading Places '83
Trois Couleurs: Blanc '94►
The Unsinkable Molly Brown '64►
Up Close and Personal '96►
Vanity Fair '04
What Price Hollywood? '32►
Willy Wonka & the Chocolate Factory '71►
A Woman of Substance '84
Working Girl '88►
Ziegfeld Girl '41►

Rape

See also Sexual Abuse

The Accused '88►
The Adventurers '70
Aftershock '12
All About Lily Chou-Chou '01►
American Commandos '84
American Gun '05
And Justice for All '79
Autumn Blood '14
Bad Lieutenant '92►
Baise Moi '00
Bandit Queen '94
Bastard out of Carolina '96
The Beast Within '82
Black Heat '76
Blackrock '97
Blue Desert '91►

Body Shots '99
Bordertown '06
Born Innocent '74
Boys Don't Cry '99 ▶
Broken Badge '85 ▶
A Brother's Kiss '97
Bullies '86
Caged Terror '72
Cannibal Holocaust '80
The Casino Job '08
Casualties of War '89 ▶
The Center of the World '01
The Central Park Five '12 ▶
Chain Gang Women '72
Chaos '05
The Circuit 2 '02
Class of 1984 '82
A Clockwork Orange '71 ▶
Code of Honor '82
Consinsual '10
Corrupted Minds '06
Coward of the County '81
Cracker: Men Should Weep '94
Cronicas '04
Cry Rape! '73
The Curse of Downers Grove '15
A Date With Darkness '03
Dead Man Walking '95 ▶
Deadly Daphne's Revenge '93
Death and the Maiden '94 ▶
Death Blow '87
A Death in California '85
Death Wish '74
Deep in the Heart '83
Deliverance '72 ▶
Demon Seed '77 ▶
Derailed '05
Descent '07
Desolation Angels '95
The Desperados '70
Devil Hunter '08
Diary of a Lost Girl '29 ▶
Divided We Stand '00
Dogville '03
Ed McBain's 87th Precinct: Heatwave '97
Elle '16 ▶
Emmanuelle's Daughter '79
The Entity '83
Extremities '86
An Eye for an Eye '95
Felt '15
Final Justice '94
Flesh and Blood '85
The Flowers of War '11
Forbidden Sun '89
Free, White, and 21 '62
From the Life of the Marionettes '80 ▶
Fugitive Among Us '92
The General's Daughter '99
The Girl Who Played With Fire '10
The Girl With the Dragon Tattoo '11 ▶
Girls Against Boys '12
Girls Town '95
Gonin 2 '96
Gossip '99
The Gravedancers '06
The Guilty '92
Guncrazy '92
Hannie Caulder '72
Havoc '05
The Heart Is Deceitful Above All Things '04
His Name Was King '71
Home Before Midnight '84
The Hooked Generation '69
Hornets' Nest '70
The Hotel New Hampshire '84
Hounddog '08
The Hunting Ground '15 ▶
I Spit on Your Grave 2 '13
I Spit on Your Grave '77
I Spit on Your Grave '10
I Spit on Your Grave: Vengeance Is Mine '15
Ichi the Killer '01
I'll Sleep When I'm Dead '03 ▶
In the Land of Blood and Honey '11
Incognito '99
The Innocents '16 ▶
Irreversible '02
It's Alive '74 ▶
Jackson County Jail '76
Jaded '96
Jailbait: Betrayed By Innocence '86
Jodi Picoult's Salem Falls '11
Kika '94
The Kite Runner '07 ▶
Knock Knock '15
Lady Snowblood '73 ▶
Landscape in the Mist '88 ▶
The Last House on the Left '09
Lesser Evil '06
Lethal Victims '87
A Life Interrupted '07
The Light of the Moon '17 ▶
Lipstick '76
Liquid Sky '83 ▶
Lost in Beijing '07
Love and Debate '06
The Marquise of O '76
Memoirs of a Geisha '05
Memories of Murder '03
Ms. 45 '81 ▶
Motor Psycho '65
The Mudge Boy '03
Mysterious Skin '04 ▶
Necromancer: Satan's Servant '88
Never Rarely Sometimes Always '20 ▶
Night of the Demon '80
The Nightingale '18 ▶
Nightmare Honeymoon '73
No Down Payment '57
NoNames '10
Northville Cemetery Massacre '76
Once Upon a Time in America '84 ▶
One Tough Cop '98
One Way '06
Open Window '06
The Outrage '64
Outrage '93
Palindromes '04 ▶
Pariah '98
A Passage to India '84 ▶
The Phantom of Soho '64
Poetry '10
Positive I.D. '87
Postcards from America '95
Precious: Based on the Novel 'Push' by Sapphire '09 ▶
The Principal '87
Quiet Days in Hollywood '97
Rashomon '51 ▶
A Reason to Believe '95
The Reckoning '03 ▶
Redacted '07
Return to Sender '15
Revenge '17
Rica '72
Rider on the Rain '70 ▶
Riot on Sunset Strip '67
Rob Roy '95 ▶
Room '15
The Salesman '16 ▶
Scared Silent '02
Sci-Fighters '96
Seeking Justice '12
Sex Crimes '92
Showgirls '95
The Sidehackers '69
Silent Witness '85
Sirens '02
Slashed Dreams '74
Something Wild '61
Speak '04 ▶
A Stranger Is Watching '82
Straw Dogs '72 ▶
Streets '90
Studs Lonigan '60
Sudden Impact '83
Suspicious River '00
Tainted '88
The Tale '18 ▶
Talk to Her '02 ▶
Tarnation '03
The Tenth Circle '08
Terror Among Us '81
Things Behind the Sun '01
The Thompsons '12
Three Billboards Outside Ebbing, Missouri '17 ▶
Time to Kill '89
A Time to Kill '96 ▶
Titus '99
To Kill a Mockingbird '62 ▶
To Kill a Stranger '84
The Tormentors '71
Town without Pity '61
Trade '07
Trust '10
Violent Ones '68
Virgin '03
The Virgin Spring '59 ▶
Wasted on the Young '10
When He's Not a Stranger '89 ▶
When Justice Fails '98
Wild Boys of the Road '33
Wild Riders '71
Wind River '17 ▶
Within Our Gates '20
Woman, Thou Art Loosed '04
The Young One '61

Rats!

See also Killer Rodents; Nice Mice

Beverly Hills Chihuahua '08
Beyond Re-Animator '03
Burial of the Rats '95
Charlotte's Web '73
Charlotte's Web '06 ▶
Chicken Run '00 ▶
Enchanted '07
Flushed Away '06 ▶
Food of the Gods '76
Food of the Gods: Part 2 '88
The Great Mouse Detective '86 ▶
Insanitarium '08
Mulberry Street '06
Muppets from Space '99
The Muppets Take Manhattan '84 ▶
1922 '17
Pied Piper '72
The Pied Piper of Hamelin '57
Ratatouille '07 ▶
The Rats '01
The Secret of NIMH 2 '98
The Secret of NIMH '82 ▶
The Tale of Despereaux '08
Teenage Mutant Ninja Turtles: The Movie '90
Teenage Mutant Ninja Turtles 2: The Secret of the Ooze '91
Teenage Mutant Ninja Turtles 3 '93
TMNT: Teenage Mutant Ninja Turtles '07
Wanted '08 ▶
Willard '03

Real Estate

All Good Things '10
All We Had '16
Aquarius '16 ▶
Are We Done Yet? '07
Arizona '18
The Banker '20
Barbershop 2: Back in Business '04 ▶
*batteries not included '87
Battle of the Sexes '28
The Beat My Heart Skipped '05 ▶
The Big Bounce '04
Boy, Did I Get a Wrong Number! '66
Boys on the Side '94
Boystown '07
A Bread Factory, Part Two '18 ▶
A Brooklyn State of Mind '97
Burning Daylight '28
Career Girls '97 ▶
Cat City '08
Clean and Sober '88 ▶
Confidentially Yours '83 ▶
Different Story '78
District 13: Ultimatum '09
Duplex '03
Empire of the Ants '77
Family Reunion '81
5 Flights Up '15
For Love or Money '93
Four Mothers '41
Furry Vengeance '10
Garden Party '08
Glengarry Glen Ross '92 ▶
A Good Year '06
The Haunted Mansion '03
Hollywood Homicide '03
Hurry Sundown '67
Just Add Water '07
Kill the Poor '03
Killer Instinct '00
Ladrones '15
Last Call '90
Little Men '16 ▶
Love on the Side '04
Meatballs 4 '92
Messenger of Death '88
Miranda '01
Mr. Popper's Penguins '11
Moonlight Mile '02 ▶
My 5 Wives '00
99 Homes '14 ▶
Norm of the North '16
Open House '86
Protection '01
Read My Lips '01
Remedy for Riches '40
River Street '95
RocknRolla '08
Skin Game '31
Smart Cookies '13
The Sound of Silence '19
Stay Hungry '76 ▶
Stormy Monday '88
Sunshine State '02 ▶
Teenage Exorcist '93
Terror Tract '00
To Die For '89
Tomorrow We Disappear '14
The Two Jakes '90
The Two Mr. Kissels '08
Two Weeks Notice '02
The Unforeseen '07
Where Hearts Lie '16
Wild Orchid '90

Reality TV

Apartment Troubles '15
Camp Dread '14
Christine '16
Kate Plays Christine '16 ▶
Nerve '16
The One I Wrote For You '14
The Wonders '15

REALLY Bad TV

Poltergeist '82 ▶
The Ring '02
Terrorvision '86
The Video Dead '87
Videodrome '83

Rebel With a Cause

See also Rebel Without a Cause; The Resistance

The Accused '88 ▶
Ace High '68
Aeon Flux '05
Afterburn '92 ▶
Alice's Restaurant '69
All Eyez on Me '17
And Starring Pancho Villa as Himself '03 ▶
Aquarius '16 ▶
As Young As You Feel '51 ▶
The Attic: The Hiding of Anne Frank '88
Basquiat '96 ▶
Battle for Skyark '15
Billy Jack '71
Billy Jack Goes to Washington '77
The Birth of a Nation '16
The Blob '58
Blue Collar '78 ▶
Born Losers '67
Boyz N the Hood '91 ▶
Braveheart '95 ▶
Broken Silence '01 ▶
Brubaker '80 ▶
Burglar '87 ▶
The Burmese Harp '56 ▶
Captain Fantastic '16
The China Syndrome '79 ▶
Courage '86 ▶
Courageous Dr. Christian '40
Daybreak '93
Dead Poets Society '89 ▶
Deadly Stranger '88
Demolition High '95
Die Hard '88 ▶
Die Hard 2: Die Harder '90 ▶
Disturbing Behavior '98
Dragon Blade '15
The Eagle Huntress '16 ▶
East of Eden '54 ▶
East of Eden '80
Easy Wheels '89
The Edukators '04
The Fighter '52 ▶
The Firing Line '91
Flesh and the Spur '57
Flight of the Intruder '90
Foxfire '96
Free State of Jones '16
The Fugitive '48 ▶
Gandhi '82 ▶
The Girl in the Sneakers '99
Go Further '03
Gorillas in the Mist '88 ▶
Guess Who's Coming to Dinner '67 ▶
Hacksaw Ridge '16
Hair '79 ▶
Hardcore '79
Hidden City '87
Hunt for the Wilderpeople '16 ▶
In the Name of the Father '93 ▶
James Dean: Live Fast, Die Young '97
Joe Kidd '72
Johnny Firecloud '75
Katherine '75
Kidnapped '95
Kung Fu '72
La Marseillaise '37 ▶
The Last American Hero '73 ▶
Lawrence of Arabia '62 ▶
Legend of Billie Jean '85
Legend of the Lone Ranger '81
Light It Up '99
Little Tough Guy '38
The Lobster '16
Lois Gibbs and the Love Canal '82
The Loneliness of the Long Distance Runner '62 ▶
Lust for Life '56 ▶
Luther '74
Man of Marble '76 ▶
The Manhattan Project '86
Marie '85 ▶
Michael Collins '96 ▶
Middle School: The Worst Years of My Life '16
Mr. Smith Goes to Washington '39 ▶
A Monster with a Thousand Heads '15 ▶
Network '76 ▶
Night of Evil '62
Norma Rae '79 ▶
Odd Man Out '47 ▶
One-Eyed Jacks '61 ▶
One Man's War '90
Original Intent '91
Outbreak '94 ▶
Outlaw King '18
Patch Adams '98
Paths of Glory '57 ▶
Patty Hearst '88
Plutonium Baby '87
Prefontaine '96 ▶
The Principal '87
Private Parts '96
The Professor '19
Project X '87
A Raisin in the Sun '61 ▶
A Raisin in the Sun '89 ▶
The Rebel '08 ▶
Rob Roy '95 ▶
Robin Hood: Prince of Thieves '91
The Rock '96 ▶
Rogue One: A Star Wars Story '16 ▶
Runaway Daughters '94
Samaritan: The Mitch Snyder Story '86 ▶
The Sand Pebbles '66 ▶
Sansho the Bailiff '54 ▶
The Scarlet Pimpernel '99
The Scarlet Pimpernel 2: Mademoiselle Guillotine '99
The Scarlet Pimpernel 3: The Kidnapped King '99
The Scarlet Pimpernel '34 ▶
The Scarlet Pimpernel '82 ▶
The Secret Agent '96
Secret of Stamboul '36
Serpico '73 ▶
The Shock '23
Silkwood '83 ▶
Sins of Rome '54
Snowden '16
Solo '96
Somebody Has to Shoot the Picture '90 ▶
Stay Away, Joe '68
Steel Frontier '94
The Stranger Wore a Gun '53
Sympathy for the Devil '70
Taffin '88
Tank Girl '94
Teenage Mutant Ninja Turtles: Out of the Shadows '16
The Texican '66
This Land Is Mine '43 ▶
The Tin Star '57 ▶
To Kill a Priest '89
True Believer '89
Under Western Stars '38
V: The Final Battle '84
WarGames '83
The Westerner '40 ▶
Wisdom '87
Without Limits '97 ▶

Rebel Without a Cause

See also Rebel With a Cause

Across the Tracks '89
After '19
All Night Long '81 ▶
Badlands '74 ▶
A Boy and His Dog '75
The Boys Next Door '85
Breathless '59 ▶
Breathless '83
Charlie Bartlett '07 ▶
Cheech and Chong's Up in Smoke '79
A Clockwork Orange '71 ▶
Cool As Ice '91
Dino '57
Easy Rider '69 ▶
The Electric Horseman '79
The Fence '94
Ferris Bueller's Day Off '86 ▶
Five Easy Pieces '70 ▶
The Fugitive Kind '60
Fury to Freedom: The Life Story of Raul Ries '85
Gandu '10
Going Places '74 ▶
Guncrazy '92
Heart Beat '80
Hud '63 ▶
If. . . '69 ▶
Inventing the Abbotts '97
Just for the Hell of It '68
Kicked in the Head '97
Leather Jackets '90
Loser '97
Lost Angels '89
Niagara, Niagara '97
Over the Edge '79 ▶
Presumed Guilty '91
Pump Up the Volume '90
Rambo: First Blood, Part 2 '85
Rambo 3 '88
Rebel Rousers '69
Rebel Run '94
Rebel without a Cause '55 ▶
Reckless '84
Road House '89
Roadracers '94
Rocky 4 '85
September 30, 1955 '77
sex, lies and videotape '89 ▶
Shopping '93
SLC Punk! '99
Stealing Cars '16
Suburbia '83
That Was Then. . . This Is Now '85
3:15: The Moment of Truth '86
Thunder Road '58 ▶
Top Gun '86
West Side Story '61 ▶

▶ = rated three bones or higher

The Wild Angels '66
The Wild One '54 ►
Youth in Revolt '10

Red Cross
The Innocents '16 ►
The Proud and Profane '56
So Proudly We Hail '43 ►
The White Cliffs of Dover '44 ►

Red Scare
See also Cold War Spies; Communists & Foreign Intrigue; Politics; Russia/USSR
Arsenal '29 ►
Assignment: Paris '52
Baltic Deputy '37 ►
The Bamboo Saucer '68
Battle Beneath the Earth '68
A Beautiful Mind '01 ►
Big Jim McLain '52
A Bullet for Joey '55
Chapayev '34 ►
China Cry '91
Commissar '68 ►
Comrade X '40
Conspirator '49
Earth '30 ►
Golden Gate '93
Guilty by Suspicion '91
Guilty of Treason '50
I Was a Communist for the FBI '51
Indochine '92 ►
The Inner Circle '91 ►
Invasion U.S.A. '52
Invasion U.S.A. '85
Jet Pilot '57
Man of Iron '81 ►
Man of Marble '76 ►
The Manchurian Candidate '62 ►
Mandela '87 ►
The Master Plan '55
Missiles of October '74 ►
Mother Kusters Goes to Heaven '76 ►
My Son John '52
Never Let Me Go '53
Nicholas and Alexandra '71
Night Crossing '81
Night Flight from Moscow '73
The Red Danube '50
Red Dawn '84
The Red Menace '49
Reds '81 ►
Running Red '99
The She-Beast '65
Storm Center '56
Strike '24 ►
Three Brave Men '57
Tito and Me '92 ►
Tobor the Great '54
The Ugly American '63
Walk a Crooked Mile '48
Walk East on Beacon '52
When Father Was Away on Business '85 ►
The Woman on Pier 13 '50

Reefer Madness
Alpha Dog '06
Angel Dusted '81
Cash Crop '98
Cheech and Chong's Next Movie '80
Cheech and Chong's Nice Dreams '81
Cheech and Chong's Up in Smoke '79
Dead Man on Campus '97
Dealing: Or the Berkeley-to-Boston Forty-Brick Lost-Bag Blues '72
Fix '08
Free Ride '13
Friday '95
Garden Party '08
Goats '12
The Good Girl '02 ►
Grandma's Boy '06
The Greatest '09
Gringo '18
Half-Baked '97
Hansel & Gretel Get Baked '13
Harold & Kumar Escape from Guantanamo Bay '08
Harold and Kumar Go to White Castle '04
High School '10
How High '01
Humboldt County '08
I Love You, Alice B. Toklas! '68
Inherent Vice '14 ►
Jewel Robbery '32
Kid Cannabis '14
Knocked Up '07
The Lifeguard '13
Next Day Air '09
Peace, Love, & Misunderstanding '11
Pineapple Express '08 ►
Police, Adjective '09
Puff, Puff, Pass '06
Reefer Madness '38
Saving Grace '00
Shrink '09
The Sitter '11
Smiley Face '07
Strange Wilderness '08
Surfer, Dude '08
Ted '12 ►
This Is the End '13 ►
A Very Harold & Kumar Christmas '11
The Wackness '08
The Wash '01
We're the Millers '13
The World Made Straight '15

Refugees
All Saints '17
The Bad Batch '17
The Best of Men '12
Dheepan '16
The Good Lie '14
The Insult '17 ►
Lore '13 ►
Mediterranea '15 ►
The Other Side of Hope '17
The Power and the Prize '56
So Ends Our Night '41 ►
The Song of Names '19
Transit '18
War Story '14

Reggae
See also Jamaica; Rock Flicks
Dancehall Queen '97
The Harder They Come '72
Rude Boy: The Jamaican Don '03
Soul Survivor '95

Rehab
See also Drug Use & On the Rocks
Being Charlie '16
Bounce '00
Clean '04
Clean and Sober '88 ►
Crutch '04
Down to the Bone '04
Excuse Me for Living '12
Eye See You '01
Fix '08
Gridlock'd '96 ►
Honey Boy '19 ►
House of Versace '13
The Hungry Ghosts '09
In My Pocket '11
Janie Jones '10
Jesse Stone: Innocents Lost '11
Jesus' Son '99
Oslo, August 31st '11
Rachel Getting Married '08 ►
Save Me '07
The Secret of Zoey '02
Slums of Beverly Hills '98 ►
Synanon '65
To Write Love On Her Arms '14
True Confessions of a Hollywood Starlet '08
28 Days '00
Welcome to Marwen '18
When a Man Loves a Woman '94
Why Stop Now '12
The Work '17 ►

Reincarnation
See also Death & the Afterlife
Andromedia '00
Angel on My Shoulder '46 ►
Audrey Rose '77
Belladonna '08
Birth '04
Bram Stoker's The Mummy '97
The Calamari Wrestler '04
Cats '19
Chances Are '89 ►
Colorful: The Motion Picture '10 ►
Creature of Destruction '67
Curse of the Faceless Man '58
Dead Again '91 ►
Devi '60 ►
A Dog's Journey '19
A Dog's Purpose '17
Down to Earth '01
The Fallen Ones '05
Flatland '02
Fluke '95
Heart and Souls '93
Heaven Can Wait '78 ►
Here Comes Mr. Jordan '41 ►
Jade Warrior '06
Little Buddha '93
The Mummy '99
The Mummy Lives '93
The Mummy Returns '01
My Blood Runs Cold '65
Dean Spanley '08
Nightmare at the End of the Hall '08
Oh, Heavenly Dog! '80
On a Clear Day You Can See Forever '70
P.S. '04
Quigley '03
Racing Daylight '07
Rapturious '07
Rasen '98
The Search for Bridey Murphy '56
She '65
Switch '91 ►
Tales of the Kama Sutra 2: Monsoon '98
Tequila Body Shots '99
Uncle Boonmee Who Can Recall His Past Lives '10
The Unmistaken Child '08
The Vengeance of She '68
Winter's Tale '14
You Never Can Tell '51
Youth Without Youth '07

Religion
See also Buddhism; Islam; Judaism; Missionaries; Nuns & Religious Epics; Saints
The Abdication '74
Absolution '81
Adam's Apples '05
Agora '09
Alice Sweet Alice '76
All Saints '17
Alone Yet Not Alone '13
Along Came the Devil 2 '19
Amazing Grace '06 ►
Amazing Grace '19 ►
American Mystic '10
Ancient Relic '02
Androcles and the Lion '52
Angel Baby '61
Angel of Death '02
Angela '94
Angels & Demons '09
Angels in America '03 ►
The Apostle '97 ►
Apostle '18
The Avenging Angel '95
Bad Education '04 ►
Badge of Faith '15
Before the Rain '94 ►
Believe '16
Bernadette '90
Beyond the Hills '13
The Big Squeeze '96
Black Death '10
Black Nativity '13
Blackbird '14
The Blackcoat's Daughter '17
Bless Me, Ultima '13
Blue Like Jazz '12
The Body '01
Body and Soul '24
Born to Win '16
The Brand New Testament '15 ►
Breaking the Waves '95 ►
Breakthrough '19
Brides of Christ '91
Brigham City '01
Brigham Young: Frontiersman '40
Broken Vows '87
Brother Sun, Sister Moon '73
Brotherhood of the Wolf '01
Burning Cane '19
The Butcher Boy '97 ►
Camila '84 ►
The Case for Christ '17
Catching Faith '15
Catholics '73 ►
Chariots of Fire '81 ►
The Children Act '18
Child's Play '72
Chocolat '00 ►
The Chronicles of Narnia: The Lion, the Witch and the Wardrobe '05
The Church '98 ►
Citizen Ruth '96
The Club '16 ►
The Code Conspiracy '01
C.O.G. '13
Come to the Stable '49 ►
Commandments '96
Conquest of Space '55
Conspiracy of Silence '03
Contact '97
The Convent '95
Corpus Christi '19 ►
Courageous '11
Cracker: The Big Crunch '94
Crazy Wisdom: The Life & Times of Chogyam Trungpa Rinpoche '11
Creation '09
Crimes of Passion '84 ►
A Cross to Bear '12
The Curse of La Llorona '19
The Da Vinci Code '06 ►
Dead Man Walking '95 ►
Def by Temptation '90
Destiny '97
Devi '60 ►
The Devil at 4 O'Clock '61
The Devil's Candy '17
Divine Intervention '07
Do You Believe? '15
Dr. Syn '37
Dr. Syn, Alias the Scarecrow '64
Dogma '99
Don Jon '13
Don Verdean '15
Don't Leave Home '18
The Duel '16
Earth '98
El Cid '61 ►
Elizabeth '98 ►
An Encounter with the Messiah '15
The End of the Affair '99 ►
End of the Spear '06
Entertaining Angels: The Dorothy Day Story '96
An Everlasting Piece '00
The Exorcism of Emily Rose '05 ►
Eye of God '97 ►
False Prophets '06
Father of Lies '07
The Favor, the Watch, & the Very Big Fish '92
The Fiend '71
The Fight Within '16
Finding Altamira '16
First Reformed '17
The Flowers of St. Francis '50 ►
A Fond Kiss '04
A Fool and His Money '88
For Colored Girls '10
Foresaken '16
The Forgiven '18
Forgiveness '15
Francesco '93
Freak Show '18
Freedom '14
Friendly Persuasion '56 ►
From a Far Country: Pope John Paul II '81
The Gathering '02
The Gaucho '27 ►
The Ghoul '75
Girl Rising '13 ►
God Bless the Broken Road '18
The Godfather, Part 3 '90 ►
God's Gun '75
God's Not Dead 2 '16
God's Not Dead '14
God's Not Dead: A Light in Darkness '18
Godspell '73
Going Clear: Scientology and the Prison of Belief '15 ►
The Good Catholic '17
Gospa '94
The Gospel '05 ►
The Gospel of John '15
Greaser's Palace '72
The Greatest Story Ever Told '65
The Green Pastures '36 ►
The Guyana Tragedy: The Story of Jim Jones '80
Hail Mary '85
Hail Satan? '19 ►
Hala '19
Hallelujah! '29 ►
Harvest of Fire '95
The Harvesters '19
Hate Crime '05
The Healer '02
The Heart Is Deceitful Above All Things '04
Heart of the Beholder '05 ►
Heaven Ain't Hard to Find '10
Heavens Above '63 ►
Heaven's Door '12
Helas pour Moi '94
Henry Poole Is Here '08 ►
Holy Girl '04 ►
Holy Hell '16
Holy Man '98
Holy Matrimony '94
Horror in the Wind '08
Hors Satan '11
The Hunchback '97
I Am Michael '17
I Can Only Imagine '18
I Origins '14
I, the Worst of All '90
I'd Climb the Highest Mountain '51 ►
In the Line of Duty: Ambush in Waco '93
Inherit the Wind '60 ►
The Innocents '16 ►
Invasion of the Space Preachers '90
Island of the Hungry Ghosts '18
Jada '08
Jeanne la Pucelle '94
Jesus Christ, Superstar '73 ►
Jesus Christ Superstar '00
Jesus of Nazareth '77 ►
The Jesus Trip '71
Joan of Arc '48
Joan of Arc '99
Joni '79
Joshua '02
The Judas Project: The Ultimate Encounter '94
Keep Walking '82 ►
The Keeper: The Legend of Omar Khayyam '05
Keeping Mum '05
Kesari '19
Kingdom of Heaven '05 ►
Klondike Annie '36
La Chartreuse de Parme '48
La Petite Jerusalem '05
Last Days in the Desert '16 ►
The Last Eve '05
Last Ounce of Courage '12
The Last Temptation of Christ '88 ►
Latter Days '04
Laughing Sinners '31
Leap of Faith '92
Leaves from Satan's Book '21
The Ledge '11
Left Behind '14
Left Behind: The Movie '00
Les Destinees '00
Let There Be Light '17
The Letter Writer '11
The Letters '15
Levity '03
Lilies '96
Little Buddha '93
Little Church Around the Corner '23
Little Richard '00
The Littlest Angel '69
Loggerheads '05 ►
Lonesome Dove Church '14
Looking for Comedy in the Muslim World '06
The Loss of Sexual Innocence '98
A Love Divided '01
Luther '74
Major Barbara '41 ►
The Maldonado Miracle '03
A Man Called Peter '55 ►
A Man for All Seasons '66 ►
A Man for All Seasons '88 ►
The Man Who Sued God '01
Marjoe '72
The Mark 2: Redemption '13
Martin Luther '53
Mary Magdalene '19
Mary, Mother of Jesus '99
Mary, Queen of Scots '71
The Masked Saint '16
Mea Maxima Culpa: Silence in the House of God '12
Menashe '17
The Message '77
The Milky Way '68 ►
The Mill and the Cross '11
The Miracle of Marcelino '55
Miracle of Our Lady of Fatima '52
The Miracle Woman '31
Miracles From Heaven '16
The Miseducation of Cameron Post '18
Mitch Albom's Have a Little Faith '11
Monsieur Vincent '47 ►
Monty Python's Life of Brian '79 ►
A Mormon Maid '17
mother! '17
Mother Joan of the Angels '60 ►
Mother Teresa: In the Name of God's Poor '97
My Mother's Smile '02
Mysterious Ways '15
Natural Selection '11
The Neon Bible '95
New York Doll '05 ►
The Next Voice You Hear '50
The Night of the Iguana '64 ►
90 Minutes in Heaven '15
The Ninth Day '04 ►
Nostalghia '83
Novitiate '17
Oh, God! '77
The Omen '06
One Man's Way '63
Oranges Are Not the Only Fruit '89
Ordet '55 ►
Ordinary Sinner '02
The Other Side of Heaven 2: Fire of Faith '19
The Other Side of Heaven '02
The Other Side of Sunday '96
The Other Story '19
Outlaw Prophet '01
Overcomer '19
The Overnighters '14 ►
Paradise: Faith '12
Paradise Now '05 ►
The Paranormal Diaries: Clophill '13
Partition '07
The Passion of Darkly Noon '95
Passion of Joan of Arc '28 ►
Paul, Apostle of Christ '18

P.D. James: Death in Holy Orders '03
Pearl Diver '04
The Perfect Family '11
Peter and Paul '81
Philomena '13
Pi '98
Picking Up the Pieces '99
Pillars of the Earth '10
Pray TV '80
Prayers for Bobby '09 ▶
Preacherman '83
The Preacher's Wife '96
Priceless '16
Priest '94
The Prodigal Planet '88
The Quarry '98
Queen Margot '94 ▶
A Question of Faith '17
Quo Vadis '51 ▶
Rain '32
The Rapture '91
The Reckoning '03 ▶
The Rector's Wife '94
Red Hook Summer '12 ▶
Red Planet Mars '52
The Red Tent '14
The Redemption of General Butt Naked '11
Religulous '08 ▶
Resurrection '80 ▶
Resurrection '99
The Resurrection of Gavin Stone '17
Return to Paradise '53
Revelation '00
Revelation Road: The Beginning of the End '13
Ring the Bell '13
Risen '16
Rock Haven '07
Romero '89
The Rook '99
Rules Don't Apply '16
St. Benny the Dip '51
Saint Joan '57
St. Patrick: The Irish Legend '00
Saint Ralph '04
Saints and Soldiers '03
Satanic Panic '19
Saved! '04
Saving Christmas '14
Scandal at Scourie '53
The Scarlet Letter '79 ▶
Sebastiane '79 ▶
The Second Chance '06
The Shack '17
Shadowlands '93 ▶
Silence '16 ▶
Simon and the Oaks '12
Small Town Murder Songs '10
Son of God '14
Son of Morning '11
Son of Rambow '07
The Song of Bernadette '43 ▶
Spotlight '15 ▶
Stigmata '99
Stolen Summer '02
A Stranger in the Kingdom '98
The Stray '17
Summer '03 '18
Susan and God '40 ▶
Tales from the Crypt Presents Bordello of Blood '96
Them That Follow '19
There Be Dragons '11
There Will Be Blood '07 ▶
They're Watching '16
The Third Miracle '99
This May Be the Last Time '14
This Stuff'll Kill Ya! '71
360 '12
Through a Glass Darkly '61 ▶
Timbuktu '15 ▶
To Dust '19
The Tollbooth '04
Touch '96
Trapped by the Mormons '22
Tribulation '00
21 Grams '03 ▶
2012: Doomsday '08
The Two Popes '19 ▶
Tyrannosaur '11
Ultrachrist! '03
Unbroken: Path to Redemption '18
Unplanned '19
Untogether '19
Vanished-Left Behind: Next Generation '16
The Vessel '16
Virgin '03
A Walk to Remember '02
Wall '04 ▶
War Room '15
The Way '10
Welcome to Paradise '07
West Beirut '98
When Night Is Falling '95 ▶
Where Angels Go, Trouble Follows '68
Whistling in the Dark '41 ▶
Wholly Moses! '80
Why Has Bodhi-Darma Left for the East '89
The Wicker Man '06
Wide Awake '97
The Winter Light '62 ▶
Wise Blood '79 ▶
Witness '85 ▶
Woman, Thou Art Loosed '04
Worth: The Testimony of Johnny St. James '12

Religious Epics

***See also** Christianity; Judaism; Religion*

Abraham '94
A.D. '85
The Agony and the Ecstasy '65
. . .And God Spoke '94
Barabbas '62
Ben-Hur '26 ▶
Ben-Hur '59 ▶
Ben-Hur '16
The Bible '66
Cleopatra '63
David '97
David and Bathsheba '51 ▶
David and Goliath '61
Demetrius and the Gladiators '54
The Egyptian '54
El Cid '61 ▶
From the Manger to the Cross '12
The Gospel According to St. Matthew '64 ▶
The Gospel of John '03
Jacob '94
Jesus '00
Joseph '95
Judith of Bethulia '14 ▶
Keep Walking '82 ▶
The King of Kings '61 ▶
Kingdom of Heaven '05 ▶
Moses '76
Moses '96
The Nativity Story '06
Noah's Ark '99
The Old Testament '62
One Night with the King '06
The Passion of the Christ '04 ▶
Prince of Egypt '98 ▶
The Prodigal '55
The Robe '53
Samson and Delilah '96
The Sign of the Cross '33
Sodom and Gomorrah '62
Son of God '14
The Song of Bernadette '43 ▶
The Story of David '76 ▶
The Story of Jacob & Joseph '74 ▶
The Story of Ruth '60
The Ten Commandments '23
The Ten Commandments '56 ▶
The Young Messiah '16

Renegade Body Parts

***See also** Killer Brains*

The Addams Family '91
Addams Family Values '93
And Now the Screaming Starts '73
The Animal '01
The Beast with Five Fingers '46
Blood of Ghastly Horror '72
Body Parts '91
Body Parts '94
The Brain that Wouldn't Die '63
Careless '07
The Crawling Eye '58
The Crawling Hand '63
Crazy in Alabama '99
Demonoid, Messenger of Death '81
Doctor Butcher M.D. '80
Dororo '07
8 Heads in a Duffel Bag '96
Evil Dead 2: Dead by Dawn '87
Gravesend '97
The Hand '81 ▶
Hands of a Stranger '62
The Hands of Orlac '25
The Hands of Orlac '60
How to Get Ahead in Advertising '89 ▶
Idle Hands '99
In the Eyes of a Killer '09
The Incredible Two-Headed Transplant '71
Killer Tongue '96
The Kingdom 2 '97 ▶
The Kingdom '95 ▶
Machined '06
Mad Love '35 ▶
The Man with Two Brains '83 ▶
Picking Up the Pieces '99
Planet Terror '07
Quicksilver Highway '98
The Thing with Two Heads '72
Tomcats '01
Virus '98
Waxwork 2: Lost in Time '91

Rent-a-Cop

Above the Rim '94
Armed and Dangerous '86
The Cookout '04
Critical Mass '00
Cyber-Tracker '93
Devil '10
Disorder '16
Eddie Presley '92
End of Days '99
Fear X '03 ▶
Friday After Next '02
Gordon Glass '07
The Heist '89
Hobgoblins '87
House of the Rising Sun '11
Inspector Gadget '99
Light It Up '99
Looney Tunes: Back in Action '03
The Maiden Heist '08
Mannequin '87
Mirrors 2 '10
Mirrors '08
Museum Hours '13 ▶
National Security '03
Night at the Museum '06
Night at the Museum: Battle of the Smithsonian '09
Night at the Museum: Secret of the Tomb '14
Observe and Report '09
P2 '07
Paul Blart: Mall Cop 2 '15
Paul Blart: Mall Cop '09
Rent-A-Cop '88
The Shape of Things '03
Star Spangled Rhythm '42 ▶
Takedown '10
Tapeheads '89
The Texas Streak '26
Trixie '00
Unbreakable '00
Underdog '07
Urban Legend '98
Walking the Halls '12

Repressed Men

***See also** Men*

The Age of Innocence '93 ▶
American Beauty '99 ▶
Beloved/Friend '99
Bitter Moon '92
Bleak Moments '71
The Bodyguard '92
Box of Moonlight '96
Changing Times '04
Falling Down '93
Far Side of the Moon '03
Felicia's Journey '99 ▶
Fight Club '99 ▶
The Game '97 ▶
The Good Shepherd '06
The Hawk Is Dying '06
Howard's End '92 ▶
I'm Not Here '19
In and Out '97 ▶
Kiss the Sky '98
Like It Never Was Before '95
Little Children '06 ▶
The Little Kidnappers '90
Love and Death on Long Island '97
Maurice '87 ▶
My Best Friend '06
On a Clear Day '05
The Preacher's Wife '96
A Rather English Marriage '98
The Red Dwarf '99
The Remains of the Day '93 ▶
Shadowlands '93 ▶
Sirens '94
Split Second '99
Till Human Voices Wake Us '02
When Did You Last See Your Father? '07
Yi Yi '00
Zero Degrees Kelvin '95

Rescue Missions

***See also** Rescue Missions Involving Time Travel*

Agent of Death '99
Air Rage '01
Alaska '96
Alone in the Woods '95
The Amazing Panda Adventure '95
Angelique and the Sultan '68
Apocalypse Pompeii '14
Apollo 13 '95 ▶
Argo '12 ▶
Balto '95
Battle of the Damned '14
Beer for My Horses '08
Behind Enemy Lines '96
Behind Enemy Lines '01
Berlin Tunnel 21 '81
Beverly Hills Chihuahua '08
Beyond Borders '03
Big Miracle '12
Bionicle 3: Web of Shadows '05
Black Dawn '05
Black Hawk Down '01 ▶
Blade 2 '02
Blind Heat '00
Bolt '08 ▶
Bone Tomahawk '15
The Book of Henry '17
Born to Be Wild '95
Breakout '75
A Bug's Life '98 ▶
Canal Zone '42
The Chamber '96
The City of Lost Children '95 ▶
Close Range '15
Collide '17
Comanche Station '60
Commando '85 ▶
Company of Heroes '13
Con Air '97 ▶
Courage Under Fire '96 ▶
Dante's Peak '97
The Day After Tomorrow '04
Daylight '96
The Dead 2 '13
Death is Nimble, Death is Quick '67
Decommissioned '16
Delta Force One-The Lost Patrol '99
Desperate Search '52
The Diamond of Jeru '01
Die Hard '88 ▶
Die Hard 2: Die Harder '90 ▶
Die Hard: With a Vengeance '95
The Dirty Dozen: The Deadly Mission '87
Django and Sartana; It's the End '70
Django Strikes Again '87
Dunkirk '17 ▶
Eight Below '06
End of a Gun '16
Ernest Scared Stupid '91
Escape from L.A. '96
Escape From Planet Earth '13
Event Horizon '97
The Ewok Adventure '84
Executioner of Venice '63
Executive Decision '96
Expect No Mercy '95
Far from Home: The Adventures of Yellow Dog '94
Fever '91
15 Minutes of War '19
Finding Nemo '03 ▶
First Kill '17
Flight From Ashiya '64
Force: Five '81
Free Willy '93
Free Willy 2: The Adventure Home '95
Free Willy 3: The Rescue '97
The Golden Compass '07
The Great Raid '05
Grizzly Mountain '97
The Guardian '06
Hard Ticket to Hawaii '87
Hellhounds '09
The Hidden Fortress '58 ▶
The Hills Have Eyes 2 '07
Hired to Kill '91
Honeybaby '74
Hoodwinked Too! Hood vs. Evil '11
Hoot '06
Ice Age '02 ▶
Ice Age: Dawn of the Dinosaurs '09
In Her Line of Fire '06
In the Tall Grass '19
Independence Day '96 ▶
Inkheart '09
The Inn of the Sixth Happiness '58 ▶
Island in the Sky '53 ▶
Jack the Giant Slayer '13
Jeopardy '53
Joey '98
Journey 2: The Mysterious Island '12
Journey to the Center of the Earth '99
Jupiter Ascending '15
Jurassic Park 3 '01
Kids of the Round Table '96
Killer Elite '11
Kung Fu Killer '08
La Femme Musketeer '03
Land of Death '03
The Last Descent '16
The Last Hard Men '76
Legend of the Lost Tomb '97
Lockout '12
Lola Colt '67
The Lone Runner '88
The Losers '70
Losing Isaiah '94 ▶
The Lost Treasure of the Grand Canyon '08
The Magnificent Seven '60 ▶
The Marine 3: Homefront '11
The Marine '06
Master of Disguise '02
The Matrix Revolutions '03 ▶
Mercenaries '11
Mercy Mission '93
Miracle at Midnight '98
The Missing '03 ▶
Missing in Action 2: The Beginning '85
Missing in Action '84
Mission: Impossible 3 '06 ▶
Mission to Mars '00
Morning Departure '50
Moscow Zero '06
Naked Souls '95
Navy SEALS '90
North West Frontier '59
Okja '17 ▶
Oliver & Company '88
One Small Hero '99
Operation Cross Eagles '69
Operation Delta Force 2: Mayday '97
Operation Delta Force 5: Random Fire '00
Operation Dumbo Drop '95
Ordeal in the Arctic '93
Outbreak '94 ▶
The Phynx '70
Pirates of the Caribbean: At World's End '07
Pirates of the Caribbean: The Curse of the Black Pearl '03 ▶
Playing with Fire '19
Playmobil: The Movie '19
Pray for Death '85
The President's Man '00
Queen of Blood '66
Raid on Entebbe '77 ▶
Rambo: First Blood, Part 2 '85
Red Planet '00
The Rescue '88
The Rescuers '77 ▶
The Rescuers Down Under '90
Return of Chandu '34
The Return of the Scarlet Pimpernel '37
Revenge of the Barbarians '60
Revenge of the Musketeers '94
Riot '96
The Rock '96 ▶
Rules of Engagement '00
Sasquatch '02
Saving Private Ryan '98 ▶
Saving Shiloh '06
Screamers: The Hunting '09
The Searchers '56 ▶
The Secret Agent Club '96
The Secret Invasion '64
The Secret of NIMH 2 '98
7 Days in Entebbe '18
Seven Samurai '54 ▶
Seven Seconds '05
Shadow Warriors 2: Hunt for the Death Merchant '97
Shanghai Noon '00
Shrek '01 ▶
Silver Hawk '04
The Sinking of the Laconia '10
6 Bullets '12
The Slender Thread '65 ▶
SMART: Specialized Mobile Animal Rescue Team '16
The Smurfs 2 '13
Sniper: Special Ops '16
S.O.S. Iceberg '33
Special Forces '03
Special Forces '11
Spy Game '01
Spy Kids '01 ▶
Star Trek: Insurrection '98
Starship Troopers 3: Marauder '08
Steel Sharks '97
Stranglehold '94
Street Fighter '94
Submarine Attack '54
Submerged '00
Sudden Death '95
Supernova '99
Taken '08
The Tale of Despereaux '08
Tarzan Triumphs '43
Tears of the Sun '03
Tell It to the Marines '26
Terror Peak '03
Three Bad Men '05
Thunder in Paradise 2 '94
Thunder in Paradise '93
Toy Story '95 ▶
Toy Story 2 '99 ▶
Trolls '16
Tugboat Annie '33 ▶
The Tunnel '01 ▶
Two Bits & Pepper '95
2001: A Space Travesty '00
Uncommon Valor '83
Valiant '05
Varian's War '01
Vertical Limit '00
Victory at Entebbe '76
Volcano '97
Waikiki Wedding '37 ▶
Welcome to Sarajevo '97 ▶
The Wild '06
Wings in the Dark '35
Wolverine '96
The World in His Arms '52

▶ = rated three bones or higher

The World Is Not Enough '99
World Trade Center '06 ▶
Wrath of the Titans '12
X2: X-Men United '03 ▶
The Yakuza '75
Yankee Buccaneer '52
Your Highness '11
Zathura '05 ▶

Rescue Missions Involving Time Travel

***See also** Rescue Missions; Time Travel; Time Warped*

Back to the Future '85 ▶
Back to the Future, Part 2 '89
Back to the Future, Part 3 '90 ▶
Bill & Ted's Excellent Adventure '89
Deja Vu '06
Disney's The Kid '00
Frequency '00
Hot Tub Time Machine 2 '15
Jumanji '95
Lost in Space '98
Millennium '89
The Navigator '88 ▶
100 Million BC '08
Star Trek 4: The Voyage Home '86 ▶
Star Trek: First Contact '96 ▶
Superman: The Movie '78 ▶
Terminator 2: Judgment Day '91 ▶
Terminator 3: Rise of the Machines '03 ▶
The Terminator '84 ▶
Time After Time '79 ▶
Timeline '03
Timemaster '95
Trancers 2: The Return of Jack Deth '90
When Time Expires '97
Zathura '05 ▶

The Resistance

***See also** World War Two; World War Two Spies*

Action in the North Atlantic '43
The Age of Shadows '16
Alien Siege '05
American Guerrilla in the Philippines '50
The Army of Crime '10
Army of Shadows '69 ▶
Black Book '06 ▶
Bloodrayne: The Third Reich '11
Blubberella '11
Carve Her Name with Pride '58
Casablanca '42 ▶
Charlotte Gray '01
The Conspirators '44
The Cross of Lorraine '43
A Day in October '92
Defiance '08
Edge of Darkness '43 ▶
Equilibrium '02
Four Sons '40
Free Men '12
A Generation '54 ▶
Hangmen Also Die '42
The Heroes of Telemark '65
Holocaust '78 ▶
Ill Met By Moonlight '57
In Dubious Battle '17
Invasion Quartet '61
Julia '77 ▶
The Last Lieutenant '94
The Last Metro '80 ▶
Max Manus: Man of War '08
Missiles from Hell '58
The Moon is Down '43
Operation Daybreak '75
Operation Secret '52
Outlaw King '18
Paris After Dark '43
Passage to Marseilles '44 ▶
Resistance '03
Rogue One: A Star Wars Story '16 ▶
Safe Conduct '01 ▶
The Silver Fleet '43
Soldier of Orange '78 ▶
Sophie Scholl: The Final Days '05 ▶
The Square Peg '58
This Land Is Mine '43 ▶
To Be or Not to Be '42 ▶
To Be or Not to Be '83
The Train '65 ▶
Underground '41
Underground '70
Watch on the Rhine '43 ▶
When Willie Comes Marching Home '50 ▶
Whose Streets? '17
Winter in Wartime '10
The Yellow Rolls Royce '64

Reunited

***See also** Amnesia; I'm Not Dead, Yet!; Island Fare; Missing Persons*

About Alex '14
Amnesiac '15
Autumn Hearts: A New Beginning '07
Before Sunset '04 ▶
Blue Jay '16 ▶
Cast Away '00 ▶
The Deep End of the Ocean '98
The End of the Affair '99 ▶
Garden State '04 ▶
Goodbye World '14
The Groomsmen '06
Hard to Kill '89
Hired Hand '71
Homecoming '13
Johnson Family Vacation '04
Keeping Up with the Steins '06
Last Flag Flying '17
Love '05
Magnolia '99 ▶
Marilyn Hotchkiss' Ballroom Dancing & Charm School '06
Matchstick Men '03 ▶
Mrs. Wiggs of the Cabbage Patch '34
Move Over, Darling '63
My Favorite Wife '40 ▶
The Parent Trap '61
The Parent Trap '98
Pitch Perfect 3 '17
Riding Alone for Thousands of Miles '05
Rude '96
Second Honeymoon '37
A Simple Twist of Fate '94
Sin Nombre '09 ▶
Sometimes Always Never '19
Story of a Love Affair '50
The Sunshine Boys '95
T2 Trainspotting '17
10 Years '12

Revenge

***See** Vigilantes*

Revolutionary War

America '24
April Morning '88
The Bastard '78
Benedict Arnold: A Question of Honor '03
The Crossing '00
The Howards of Virginia '40
Johnny Tremain & the Sons of Liberty '58
Papa: Hemingway in Cuba '16
The Patriot '00
Revolution '85
The Scarlet Coat '55
1776 '72 ▶
Something in the Air '13
Sweet Liberty '86
The Time of Their Lives '46

Rio

Before the Devil Knows You're Dead '07 ▶
Black Orpheus '58 ▶
Blame It on Rio '84
Bossa Nova '99
Central Station '98 ▶
City of God '02
City of Men '07 ▶
Fast Five '11
Flying Down to Rio '33
Focus '15
From Beginning to End '09
Grand Slam '67
Herbie Goes Bananas '80
Holiday for Lovers '59
Kickboxer 3: The Art of War '92
Madame Sata '02
Notorious '46 ▶
Orfeu '99
OSS 117: Lost in Rio '09
Party Girls for Sale '54
Possible Loves '00 ▶
Reaching for the Moon '13
Rio 2 '14
Rio '11
Rio, I Love You '14
Rio Sex Comedy '10
The Road to Rio '47 ▶
That Night in Rio '41
Trash '14
Venus in Furs '70
Wild Orchid '90

A River Runs Through the Plot

***See also** Sail Away; Whitewater Rafting*

The Adventures of Huck Finn '93 ▶
The Adventures of Huckleberry Finn '39 ▶
The Adventures of Huckleberry Finn '60
The Adventures of Huckleberry Finn '85
The African Queen '51 ▶
Anacondas: The Hunt for the Blood Orchid '04
Apocalypse Now '79 ▶
Bend of the River '52 ▶
Beneath the Mississippi '08
Beyond the Call of Duty '92
Black Box '12
The Bridge at Remagen '69
The Bridge on the River Kwai '57 ▶
Cape Fear '91 ▶
Death on the Nile '78
East of Sudan '64
The Edge '97
The Far Horizons '55
Lord of the Rings: The Fellowship of the Ring '01 ▶
Lord of the Rings: The Return of the King '03 ▶
Mean Creek '04 ▶
Missouri Breaks '76
Mystic River '03 ▶
The Outlaw Josey Wales '76 ▶
The River '51 ▶
The River '84
River of No Return '54
A River Runs Through It '92 ▶
The River Wild '94
River's Edge '87 ▶
Rooster Cogburn '75
Striking Distance '93
Sully '16
White River '99
Without a Paddle '04

Road Trip

***See also** Bikers; Checkered Flag; Motor Vehicle Dept.*

Aberdeen '00
About Schmidt '02 ▶
About Scout '15 ▶
Across the Great Divide '76
Across the Moon '94
Adrenaline Drive '99
The Adventures of Huck Finn '93 ▶
The Adventures of Milo & Otis '89 ▶
The Adventures of Priscilla, Queen of the Desert '94 ▶
Albert's Memorial '09
Alice Doesn't Live Here Anymore '74
All About Steve '09
All Roads Lead to Rome '15
Alligator Eyes '90
Almost Famous '00 ▶
Aloha, Bobby and Rose '74
Along for the Ride '00
Alpha and Omega '10
American Gun '02 ▶
American Virgin '09
Annie's Point '05
Another Day in Paradise '98
The Apocalypse '07
Are We There Yet? '05
Ariel '89 ▶
Around the Bend '04
Around the World in 80 Days '56 ▶
Around the World in 80 Days '89
Around the World in 80 Days '04
The Art of Travel '08
As Good As It Gets '97 ▶
Ashik Kerib '88 ▶
Ass Backwards '13
Away We Go '09
Babel '06 ▶
Babylon A.D. '08
Bachelor Games '16
Back Road Diner '99
Bad Company '72 ▶
Bad Times at the El Royale '18
Badland '07
Bam Bam & Celeste '05 ▶
Bandwagon '95
Barefoot '14
The Beautiful Country '04
Beautiful Joe '00
Beautiful Wave '11
Beavis and Butt-Head Do America '96
Because of You '95
Beethoven's 3rd '00
Beggars of Life '28
Behind Your Eyes '11
Benny Bliss & the Disciples of Greatness '07
Best Friends '75
Betty '97
Between Two Ferns '19
The Big Empty '04
Big Fish '03 ▶
Bingo '91
Bird on a Wire '90
A Birder's Guide to Everything '14
Black Day Blue Night '95
Black Dog '98
The Black Rose '50
Blue Murder at St. Trinian's '56 ▶
Blue State '07
The Blues Brothers '80 ▶
Blues Brothers 2000 '98
Bolero '84
Bomber '09
Bond of Fear '56
Bonneville '06
Boogie Boy '98
Borat: Cultural Learnings of America for Make Benefit Glorious Nation of Kazakhstan '06 ▶
Born to Be Wild '95
Born to Ride '11
Bound for Glory '76 ▶
Boundaries '18
The Bounty Hunter '10
The Bourne Ultimatum '07 ▶
Box of Moonlight '96
A Boy. A Girl. A Dream. '18
Boys on the Side '94
Brand New Day '10
Bright Angel '91
Broken Flowers '05
The Brothers Grimm '05
The Brown Bunny '03
Bubble Boy '01
Buck and the Preacher '72
The Bucket List '07
Bunny and the Bull '09
Bustin' Loose '81 ▶
Butch Cassidy and the Sundance Kid '69 ▶
Butterfly Kiss '94
By Dawn's Early Light '00
Bye Bye Brazil '79
California Dreaming '07
Camilla '94
Camille '07
Cannonball '76
Cannonball Run 2 '84
Cannonball Run '81
A Canterbury Tale '44 ▶
Carbide and Sorrel '63
Carjacked '11
Cas & Dylan '15
Catfish '10
Central Station '98 ▶
Certified Copy '10
The Chase '93
Chasers '94
Chasing Liberty '04
Chasing 3000 '07
Cheech and Chong: Things Are Tough All Over '82
Chef '14
Children of Hannibal '98
The Children of Huang Shi '08
Cirque du Freak: The Vampire's Assistant '09
Cloudburst '11 ▶
Coast to Coast '04
Cold Around the Heart '97
Cold Mountain '03 ▶
College Road Trip '08
The Color Wheel '11
Come As You Are '20
Committed '99
Country Strong '10
Coupe de Ville '90
Crazy in Alabama '99
Crazy Mama '75
The Croods '13
Crossroads '86
Crossroads '02
Crystal Fairy & the Magical Cactus '13
The Cure '95
Daddy & Them '99
Damnation Alley '77
The Darjeeling Limited '07 ▶
Dark Country '09
Dark House '14
Daughter of Keltoum '01
The Daytrippers '96
The Dead Don't Die '19
Dear Eleanor '16
The Delivery '99
Destination Wedding '18
Detour '46 ▶
Detour '17
The Devil Incarnate '13
Diamond Men '01 ▶
Diamonds '99
Diary of a Wimpy Kid: The Long Haul '17
Diminished Capacity '08
Dirty Girl '10
Disappearances '06
The Dish & the Spoon '11
Disney's Teacher's Pet '04 ▶
Doctor Chance '97
Dogma '99
Doing Time for Patsy Cline '97
Don't Come Knocking '05
The Doom Generation '95 ▶
Douchebag '10
Down by Law '86 ▶
The Dream Catcher '99
Dream with the Fishes '97
Drive '96
Driveways '19 ▶
Driving Lessons '06
Drowning on Dry Land '00
Due Date '10
Dumb & Dumber '94
Dumb and Dumber To '14
Dutch '91
Earthly Possessions '99
Easy Rider '69 ▶
Eat, Pray, Love '10
Eaters '15
El Camino '08
Elopement '51
Elvis Has Left the Building '04
End of a Gun '16
End of the Line '88
Eternity and a Day '97
Eurotrip '04
Every Which Way But Loose '78
Everybody's Fine '09
Everything, Everything '17
Everything is Illuminated '05 ▶
Extremedays '01
Eye of the Beholder '99
Fandango '85
Far Out Man '89
Fast Sofa '01
Fat, Sick & Nearly Dead '11
Father Figures '17
Father Hood '93
Fear and Loathing in Las Vegas '98
Finding Graceland '98
Finding North '97
First Dog '10
$5 a Day '08
Flight of the Innocent '93
Flim-Flam Man '67
Flirting with Disaster '95 ▶
Follow the Boys '63
Forces of Nature '99
The Forsaken '01
Fort Tilden '14
Free Zone '05
Freeway 2: Confessions of a Trickbaby '99
From Dusk Till Dawn '95
The Fundamentals of Caring '16
Furlough '18
Get On the Bus '96 ▶
Girl's Best Friend '08
Give Me Liberty '19
Give Me Your Hand '09
Go Further '03
The Go-Getter '07
The Goddess of 1967 '00
The Good Companions '33
Goodbye Pork Pie '81
A Goofy Movie '94
Grace Is Gone '07 ▶
Grand Theft Parsons '03
The Grapes of Wrath '40 ▶
The Great Buck Howard '09 ▶
Great Smokey Roadblock '76
The Great Texas Dynamite Chase '76
Green Book '18 ▶
Guantanamera '95 ▶
The Guilt Trip '12
Gypsy 83 '01
Handsome Harry '09
The Hangover, Part III '13
The Happening '08
The Happy Road '57
Hard Core Logo '96
Hard Luck '01
Harold and Kumar Go to White Castle '04
Harry and Tonto '74 ▶
Heart Beat '80
Heaven's Burning '97
Heck's Way Home '95
Hector and the Search for Happiness '14
Hedwig and the Angry Inch '00 ▶
Hell's Angels on Wheels '67
Here '12
High Rolling in a Hot Corvette '77
Highway '01
Highway Hitcher '98
The Highway Man '99
Highway 61 '91
Highwaymen '03
Hit and Run '12
The Hitcher 2: I've Been Waiting '03
The Hitcher '86
The Hitcher '07
The Hitman's Bodyguard '17
The Hobbit: An Unexpected Journey '12
Hold On! '66
Hollywood or Bust '56
Homecoming '96
Homer and Eddie '89
The Homesman '14
Homeward Bound: The Incredible Journey '93 ▶
Homeward Bound 2: Lost in San Francisco '96
Honky Tonk Freeway '81
Honkytonk Man '82
Hot Blooded '98
Hot Pursuit '15
Hot Rods to Hell '67
House of Wax '05
The Houses October Built '14
How I Got Lost '09
Huck and the King of Hearts '93
Hunted '52

▶ = rated three bones or higher

I Accidentally Domed Your Son '04
I Am David '04
I Got Five on It '05
Ice Age: The Meltdown '06
Identity Thief '13
Il Sorpasso '63
I'll Be Home for Christmas '98
I'll Take You There '99
In Fear '13
In This World '03
The Incredible Journey '63
Infamous '20
Innocents '00
Interstate 60 '02
Interstate '07
Into the Night '85
Into the West '92 ▶
Into the Wild '07 ▶
The Intruder '04 ▶
The Invoking '13
Is Anybody There? '08
The Italian '05
It's a Mad, Mad, Mad, Mad World '63
Jackass Presents: Bad Grandpa '13
Jackie '12
Jackpot '01
Jam '06
James' Journey to Jerusalem '03
Janie Jones '10
Jay and Silent Bob Reboot '19
Jay and Silent Bob Strike Back '01
Jeepers Creepers '01
Jerome '98 ▶
Jiminy Glick in LaLa Wood '05
Joe Dirt '01
Johnson Family Vacation '04
Josh and S.A.M. '93
The Journey of Natty Gann '85 ▶
Joy Ride 3: Road Kill '14
Joy Ride '01 ▶
Joyride '77
The Judge Steps Out '49
Just Like a Woman '13
Just Like the Son '06
Kalifornia '93
Kandahar '01
Keepin' It Real '01
Kikujiro '99
Kill Your Darlings '06
Killer Bud '00
Kingpin '96
Kumiko the Treasure Hunter '14 ▶
La Strada '54 ▶
La Vie Promise '02
Ladies and Gentlemen, the Fabulous Stains '82
Lady Jayne Killer '03
Lamb '16
Lamerica '95 ▶
Landscape in the Mist '88 ▶
Larger Than Life '96
Lassie '05
The Last Legion '07
The Last Movie Star '17
Last Orders '01 ▶
Last Ride '09
The Last Ride '12
Last Stop for Paul '08
The Layover '17
Lean on Pete '17 ▶
Leap Year '10
Leaving Normal '92
The Leisure Seeker '17
Les Rendez-vous D'Anna '78
Letters to Juliet '10
Lewis and Clark and George '97
A Life Less Ordinary '97
Life's a Breeze '14
The Limits of Control '09
Lisboa '99
Little Miss Sunshine '06 ▶
The Living End '92
Locke '13
Lolita '97
The Long Dumb Road '19
The Long Haul '57
The Long, Long Trailer '54
The Long Way Home '98
Lord of the Rings: The Fellowship of the Ring '01 ▶
Lord of the Rings: The Two Towers '02 ▶
Lord of the Rings: The Return of the King '03 ▶
Lost '05
Lost in America '85 ▶
Love and a .45 '94
Love on a Bet '36
Lovesong '17
A Loving Father '02
The Lucky Ones '08
Lucky Them '13
Luminous Motion '00
Mad Love '95
Magic Trip: Ken Kesey's Search for a Kool Place '11
Mammuth '10
Marooned in Iraq '02
Me and the Kid '93
Me & Will '99
Me, Myself, and Irene '00 ▶
Meet the Fockers '04
Meet the Guilbys '15
The Mexican '01
Michael '96
Midnight Run '88 ▶
Miss Stevens '16
Missing Link '19
Mob Story '90
Monsieur Ibrahim '03 ▶
Monster Man '03
More '69
The Motel Life '12
The Motorcycle Diaries '04 ▶
The Mountain '19
Moving McAllister '07
Mulan 2 '04
The Muppet Movie '79 ▶
Music For Millions '44
The Music of Chance '93
My Blueberry Nights '07
My Brothers '10
My Fellow Americans '96
My Life in Ruins '09
My One and Only '09
My Own Love Song '10
My Own Private Idaho '91 ▶
National Lampoon Presents: Endless Bummer '09
National Lampoon's Vacation '83 ▶
The National Tree '09
Natural Born Killers '94
Natural Selection '11
Natural Selection '12
Nebraska '13 ▶
Neon Signs '96
Never Goin' Back '18
Never on Tuesday '88
Never Rarely Sometimes Always '20 ▶
Niagara, Niagara '97
A Night in Old Mexico '14
Night on Earth '91 ▶
No Blade of Grass '70
No Sleep 'Til Madison '02
Nurse Betty '00 ▶
Obselidia '10
The Odd Couple 2 '98
The Odd Way Home '13
The Odyssey '97
Oh Lucy! '17
The Old-Fashioned Way '34
On My Way '14
On the Road '12
On Tour '10
One Way Out '95
One Week '08
The Open Road '09
Open Road '13
The Opposite of Sex '98
Otherhood '19
Out '82
Over the Hill '93
The Overbrook Brothers '09
Overnight Delivery '96
Paddleton '19
Palindromes '04 ▶
Paper Heart '09
Paper Moon '73 ▶
Paper Towns '15
Paris Can Wait '17
Passenger Side '09
The Passing of Evil '70
Paul '11
Paulie '98
The Peanut Butter Falcon '19
Pee-wee's Big Adventure '85 ▶
The Perfect Age of Rock 'n' Roll '10
The Perfect Game '09
Phat Beach '96
Philomena '13
The Picasso Summer '69
Pieces of April '03
Pierrot le Fou '65 ▶
Pink Cadillac '89
Pinocchio '02
Planes, Trains & Automobiles '87
Play for Me '01
Play It to the Bone '99
Please Stand By '17
The Pleasure Drivers '05
Pontiac Moon '94
Powwow Highway '89 ▶
Preacher's Kid '10
Priceless '16
Prime Target '91
Prison Train '38
Pulse '03
Queen & Slim '19 ▶
Rain Man '88 ▶
The Rain People '69 ▶
Rainbow Bridge '71
The Rambler '13
Rat Race '01
Rattlesnake '19
Red Lights '04 ▶
Redemption Road '10
The Reivers '69 ▶
Remember '15
Retroactive '97
Ride '98
Ride for Lance '14
Ride in the Whirlwind '66
Riding Alone for Thousands of Miles '05
The Road '00
The Road '09
Road Games '81
Road Hard '15
The Road Killers '95
Road Movie '72
The Road to Bali '53 ▶
The Road to El Dorado '00
The Road to Hong Kong '62
The Road to Morocco '42 ▶
Road to Perdition '02 ▶
The Road to Rio '47 ▶
The Road to Singapore '40
The Road to Utopia '46 ▶
The Road to Zanzibar '41 ▶
Road Trip '00
Road Trip: Beer Pong '09
The Road Warrior '82 ▶
Roadie '80
Roadkill '89
Roadkill '11
Roadside '15
Roadside Prophets '92
The Rocker '08
Rockin' Road Trip '85
Rolling Family '04
Rolling Thunder Revue: A Bob Dylan Story by Martin Scorsese '19 ▶
Rough Magic '95
The Rover '14
Run Hide Die '15
The Runaway Bus '54
Runaway Daughters '94
Running Hot '83
Rust Creek '19
RV '06
Rx '06
Safelight '15
The Saragossa Manuscript '65
Satanic '15
Sawdust & Tinsel '53 ▶
Say It Isn't So '01
Scarecrow '73
Schultze Gets the Blues '03
Searching for Bobby D '05
Second-Hand Hearts '81
Secret Ballot '01 ▶
Seeking a Friend for the End of the World '12
Serving Sara '02
Sesame Street Presents: Follow That Bird '85
Seventeen Years '99 ▶
Sex Drive '08
A Shadow You Soon Will Be '94
She Drives Me Crazy '07
Sherman's March '86 ▶
Sherman's Way '08
Shrek the Third '07
Siddhartha '72
Sideways '04 ▶
Sightseers '12 ▶
Silk '07
The Simpsons Movie '07 ▶
Sin Nombre '09 ▶
600 Miles '16
Six-String Samurai '98
Slither '73 ▶
Smoke Signals '98
So B. It '17
Some Girl(s) '13
Someone Great '19
Something Wild '86
Sonic the Hedgehog '20
Sorcerer '77
Soul Men '08
The Space Between '10
Sparkler '99
Speed Racer '08
Spies Like Us '85
Spree '79
The Spy Who Dumped Me '18
Stake Land '10
The Star '17
Starman '84 ▶
Stir Crazy '80
Stoned Bros. '09
Stop-Loss '08 ▶
The Straight Story '99 ▶
Strawberry Fields '97
Summer City '77
Sun Don't Shine '12
Sunchaser '96
The Sure Thing '85 ▶
Surfwise '07 ▶
The Sweetest Thing '02
Take Me Home '11
Taking Chance '09
The Talent Given Us '04 ▶
Tammy '14
A Taxi Driver '17 ▶
Tenacious D in the Pick of Destiny '06
Tennessee '08
Testosterone '03
Thelma & Louise '91 ▶
Then Came Bronson '68
The Thing About My Folks '05
The Thompsons '12
Those Magnificent Men in Their Flying Machines '65 ▶
The Three Burials of Melquiades Estrada '05 ▶
Three Days to Vegas '07
Thumb Tripping '72
Time of the Wolf '03 ▶
Time Out '01
To Wong Foo, Thanks for Everything, Julie Newmar '95
Tommy Boy '95
Tomorrow You're Gone '12
Torque '04
Toy Story 4 '19 ▶
The ToyBox '18
Transamerica '05 ▶
Transit '12
Traveling Man '89
The Trip '10 ▶
The Trip to Bountiful '14 ▶
The Trip to Italy '14
The Trip to Spain '17
Trouble Bound '92
The Truce '96 ▶
True Romance '93
Truth or Consequences, N.M. '97
Twentieth Century '34 ▶
28 Days Later '02
Twentynine Palms '03
Twins '88
Two for the Road '67 ▶
Two Tickets to Paradise '06
2: Voodoo Academy '12
Under the Same Moon '07
Until the End of the World '91 ▶
Vacation '15
Valhalla Rising '09
Vince Vaughn's Wild West Comedy Show '06
Violent Road '58
Voyage in Italy '53
Wagons East '94
Waking Up in Reno '02
The Watsons Go to Birmingham '13
The Way '10
The Way West '67
The Wayward Bus '57
Wedding Bell Blues '96
Weekend '67 ▶
Welcome Home, Soldier Boys '72
We're the Millers '13
West of Here '02
Western '96
Where the Heart Is '00
White Line Fever '75
White River '99
White Wedding '10
Wieners '08
Wild America '97 ▶
Wild at Heart '90 ▶
Wild Boys of the Road '33
Wild Hogs '07
The Wizard '89
The Wizard of Oz '39 ▶
World Traveler '01
Wrecker '15
Wristcutters: A Love Story '06
xXx: Return of Xander Cage '17
Y Tu Mama Tambien '01
The Yellow Handkerchief '08 ▶
The Young and Prodigious T.S. Spivet '15
The Young Kieslowski '15
Zoe '01
Zombieland '09 ▶

Robots, Cyborgs & Androids

A. I.: Artificial Intelligence '01
The Absence of Light '06
Alien '79 ▶
Alien Chaser '96
Alien Factor 2: The Alien Rampage '01
Alien: Resurrection '97 ▶
Aliens '86 ▶
Alita: Battle Angel '19
American Cyborg: Steel Warrior '94
And You Thought Your Parents Were Weird! '91
Android '82
The Android Affair '95
Android Cop '14
Assassin '86
Astro Boy '09
The Astro-Zombies '67
Atom Nine Adventures '07
Atomic Rulers of the World '65
Automatons '06
A-X-L '18
Battle of the Damned '14
Battlestar Galactica: The Plan '09
The Beast in Space '80
Bicentennial Man '99
Big Hero 6 '14
Bill & Ted's Bogus Journey '91
The Black Hole '79
Blade Runner '82 ▶
Blade Runner 2049 '17
Bumblebee '18 ▶
Caprica '09
Carver's Gate '96
Casshern '04
Chappie '15
The Chess Player '27
Chicken Little '05
Chopping Mall '86
Circuitry Man '90
Class of 1999 2: The Substitute '93
Class of 1999 '90
Colossal '17
Colossus of New York '58
Creation of the Humanoids '62
Cyber-Tracker 2 '95
Cyber-Tracker '93
Cybernator '91
Cyborg '89
Cyborg 2 '93
Cyborg 3: The Recycler '95
Cyborg Conquest '09
Cyborg Soldier '94
Cyborg Soldier '08
Daleks-Invasion Earth 2150 A.D. '66
The Dalmarian Chronicles '03
D.A.R.Y.L. '85
The Day the Earth Stood Still '51 ▶
The Day the Earth Stopped '08
Dead or Alive: Final '02
Death Racers '08
The Deathless Devil '05
Destination Mars '06
Destination: Outer Space '10
Devil Girl from Mars '54
Digital Man '94
Dr. Goldfoot and the Bikini Machine '66
Edward Scissorhands '90 ▶
The Empire Strikes Back '80 ▶
Eve of Destruction '90
Evil Brain from Outer Space '65
Evolver '94
Ex Machina '15 ▶
Eyeborgs '09
The Fifth Element '97
Forbidden Planet '56 ▶
Future World '18
G-Force '09
Ghost in the Shell '95 ▶
Ghost in the Shell '17
Godzilla *vs.* SpaceGodzilla '94
GOG '54
Hands of Steel '86
The Haunted World of El Superbeasto '09
Heartbeeps '81
Heatseeker '95
The Hitchhiker's Guide to the Galaxy '81 ▶
The Hitchhiker's Guide to the Galaxy '05 ▶
The Human Duplicators '64
I, Robot '04
Impostor '02
The Iron Giant '99 ▶
Jack the Giant Killer '13
K-9000 '89
King Kong Escapes '67
Kronos '57
Lost in Space '98
Mac and Me '88
The Machine '13
Manborg '11
Mandroid '93
Meet Dave '08
Message from Space '78
Metal Shifters '11
Metropolis '26 ▶
Monsters *vs.* Aliens '09
Moon '09
Mortal Challenge '97
Mystery Science Theater 3000: The Movie '96
National Lampoon Presents RoboDoc '08
Natural City '03
Negadon: The Monster from Mars '05
Nemesis '93
Night Siege Project: Shadowchaser 2 '94
Omega Doom '96
Outerworld '87
Pacific Rim '13
Pacific Rim: Uprising '18
Pandora Machine '04
Piano Tuner of Earthquakes '05
Plughead Rewired: Circuitry Man 2 '94
Postman Pat: The Movie '14
Project Shadowchaser 3000 '95
Prometheus '12
Prototype '83 ▶
Puzzlehead '05
The Questor Tapes '74
Real Steel '11

▶ = *rated three bones or higher*

Recon 2023: The Gauda Prime Conspiracy '08
Return of the Jedi '83 ►
RoboCop '87 ►
RoboCop 2 '90
RoboCop 3 '91
RoboCop '14
RoboGeisha '06
Robot & Frank '12 ►
Robot Jox '90
Robot Monster '53
Robot Stories '03
Robot Wars '93
Robots '05
Runaway '84
Serenity '05 ►
Shadow Warriors '95
Shockwave '06
Short Circuit 2 '88
Short Circuit '86
Silent Running '71 ►
Sky Captain and the World of Tomorrow '04
Solo '96
Space Truckers '97
Star Crash '78
Star Trek: First Contact '96 ►
Star Trek: Generations '94 ►
Star Trek: Nemesis '02
Star Wars '77 ►
Star Wars: Episode 1-The Phantom Menace '99 ►
Star Wars: Episode 2-Attack of the Clones '02 ►
Star Wars: Episode 3-Revenge of the Sith '05 ►
Star Wars: The Clone Wars '08
Star Wars: The Force Awakens '15 ►
Star Wars: The Last Jedi '17 ►
The Stepford Wives '04
Storm Trooper '98
Superman: Unbound '13
Surrogates '09
T-Force '94
Terminator 2: Judgment Day '91 ►
Terminator 3: Rise of the Machines '03 ►
The Terminator '84 ►
Terminator: Dark Fate '19
Terminator Genisys '15
Terminator Salvation '09
The Terminators '09
Terror of Mechagodzilla '78
Tobor the Great '54
Total Recall 2070: Machine Dreams '99
Transformers '07
Transformers: Age of Extinction '14
Transformers: Dark of the Moon '11
Transformers: Revenge of the Fallen '09
Transformers: The Last Knight '17
Transmorphers '07
Transmorphers: Fall of Man '09
Treasure Planet '02
Uncanny '15
Universal Soldier: Day of Reckoning '12
Universal Soldier: The Return '99
Universal Soldiers '07
Vice '15
Virus '98
Virus X '10
Voyage of the Rock Aliens '87
WALL-E '08 ►
Westworld '73 ►
Zathura '05 ►

Rock Flicks

The Adventures of Buckaroo Banzai Across the Eighth Dimension '84 ►
Almost Famous '00 ►
Alvin and the Chipmunks '07
American Pop '81
Anvil! The Story of Anvil '09
Awesome! I F***in' Shot That! '06 ►
Backbeat '94 ►
Bad Reputation '18
Beat Street '84
Beyond the Valley of the Dolls '70
Big Star: Nothing Can Hurt Me '13 ►
Blame It on the Night '84
The Blues Brothers '80 ►
Blues Brothers 2000 '98
Born to Boogie '72
Brothers of the Head '06
Bummer '73
Burglar '87 ►
Chuck Berry: Hail! Hail! Rock 'n' Roll '87 ►
The Commitments '91 ►
Confessions of a Teenage Drama Queen '04
The Cool Ones '67
Cry-Baby '90 ►
David Crosby: Remember My Name '19
Detroit Rock City '99
DIG! '04 ►
Disorderlies '87
The Doors '91
Double Trouble '67
Echo in the Canyon '18
Eddie and the Cruisers 2: Eddie Lives! '89
Eddie and the Cruisers '83
Elvis: The Movie '79
End of the Century: The Story of the Ramones '03 ►
Face the Music '00
Festival Express '03 ►
The Filth and the Fury '99
The Five Heartbeats '91 ►
FM '78
Follow That Dream '61
Frankie and Johnny '65
Garage Days '03
George Harrison: Living in the Material World '11
Get Crazy '83
Get Him to the Greek '10
Gimme Shelter '70
The Girl Can't Help It '56
Give My Regards to Broad Street '84
Grace of My Heart '96
Grand Theft Parsons '03
Great Balls of Fire '89
Gypsy 83 '01
Hail Caesar '94
Hard Core Logo '96
A Hard Day's Night '64 ►
The Harder They Come '72
Head '68 ►
Hedwig and the Angry Inch '00 ►
Help! '65 ►
Her Smell '19
Horsey '99
The House of Tomorrow '18
How to Build a Girl '20
The Identical '14
I'll Be There '03
In His Life: The John Lennon Story '00
It Might Get Loud '09
The Jacksons: An American Dream '92
Jailhouse Rock '57 ►
Janie Jones '10
Jimi: All Is by My Side '14
Johnny Suede '92
Jonas Brothers: The 3D Concert Experience '09
Josie and the Pussycats '01
Juliet, Naked '18
The Kids Are Alright '79 ►
Killing Bono '11
KISS Meets the Phantom of the Park '78
La Bamba '87 ►
The Lady Is a Square '58
Last Days '05
The Last Waltz '78 ►
Laurel Canyon '02
Let It Be '70
Leto '19
Lip Service '00
Little Richard '00
Loving You '57
Masked and Anonymous '03
Mayor of the Sunset Strip '03 ►
Metallica: Some Kind of Monster '04 ►
Metallica Through the Never '13
Monterey Pop '68 ►
Muscle Shoals '13 ►
Music & Lyrics '07
The Music Never Stopped '11
Neil Young: Heart of Gold '06 ►
Netherworld '90
Nico Icon '95 ►
1991: The Year Punk Broke '92
Oasis: Supersonic '16 ►
Pearl Jam Twenty '11
The Perfect Age of Rock 'n' Roll '10
The Phynx '70
Plush '13
Popstar: Never Stop Never Stopping '16 ►
Prey for Rock and Roll '03 ►
Privilege '67
Quadrophenia '79 ►
Queen of the Damned '02
The Return of Spinal Tap '92
Ring-a-Ding Rhythm '62
Rock & Rule '83
Rock, Baby, Rock It '57
Rock Dog '17
Rock My World '02
Rock 'n' Roll High School '79 ►
Rock 'n' Roll High School Forever '91
Rock 'n' Roll Nightmare '85
Rock, Pretty Baby '56
Rock Star '01
The Rocker '08
Rolling Thunder Revue: A Bob Dylan Story by Martin Scorsese '19 ►
The Runaways '10
Satisfaction '88
Scenes from the Goldmine '87
School of Rock '03 ►
Sex & Drugs & Rock & Roll '10
Shock 'Em Dead '90
Shooting Livien '05
Shout '91
Sid & Nancy '86 ►
Six-String Samurai '98
Song to Song '17
Spice World: The Movie '97
Still Crazy '98 ►
Streets of Fire '84
The Suburbans '99
Suck '09
Sugar Town '99
Sunset Strip '99
Sympathy for Delicious '10
Taking Woodstock '09
The T.A.M.I. Show '64 ►
Tapeheads '89
Telstar: The Joe Meek Story '08
Tenacious D in the Pick of Destiny '06
That Thing You Do! '96 ►
Theremin: An Electronic Odyssey '95 ►
This Is Elvis '81
This Is Spinal Tap '84 ►
Tommy '75
Tonight You're Mine '11
Trick or Treat '86
Trigger '10
24 Hour Party People '01
U2: Rattle and Hum '88
Velvet Goldmine '98
Vibrations '94
Voyage of the Rock Aliens '87
Walk Hard: The Dewey Cox Story '07
Western Stars '19 ►
What We Do Is Secret '07
When Love Comes '98
Wild Guitar '62
Wild Rose '18 ►
Woodstock '70 ►
Yellow Submarine '68 ►
Yesterday '19

Rock Stars on Film

See Biopics: Musicians; Rock Flicks

Rodeos

See also Westerns

The Adventures of Gallant Bess '48
Born Reckless '59
Convict Cowboy '95
Cowboy from Brooklyn '38
Cowboy Up '00
The Cowboy Way '94
Cowgirls 'n Angels '12
8 Seconds '94
Every Second Counts '08
Girl from Calgary '32
Junior Bonner '72 ►
Lady Takes a Chance '43 ►
The Last Ride '94
Lights of Old Santa Fe '47
The Longest Ride '15
The Lusty Men '52 ►
The Misfits '61 ►
Painted Hero '95
Pee-wee's Big Adventure '85 ►
Rhythm on the Range '36
The Rider '17
Rodeo Girl '80
Rodeo Rhythm '42
Rolling Home '48
Stir Crazy '80
The Story of Will Rogers '52
Valley Inn '14

Rogue Cops

See also Crime Drama; Organized Crime

Ambushed '13
Android Cop '14
Armed and Dangerous '86
Assault on Precinct 13 '05
Back in Business '96
Bad Lieutenant '92 ►
Bad Lieutenant: Port of Call New Orleans '09
Beast Cops '98 ►
Beyond Betrayal '94
Big Momma's House 2 '06
Blood Out '10
The Broken Star '56
The Burglar '57
Cage of Evil '60
Captive '98
The Case Against Brooklyn '58
Caught in the Crossfire '10
Changeling '08 ►
Chasing Ghosts '05
Contract on Cherry Street '77
Cop Land '97 ►
Cops vs. Thugs '75
Corrupt '84 ►
Dark Blue '03 ►
Dealing: Or the Berkeley-to-Boston Forty-Brick Lost-Bag Blues '72
Decisions '10
Defendor '09
Detroit '17 ►
Dirty '05
District 13: Ultimatum '09
Dogwatch '97
Double Bang '01
Dragon Eyes '12
Endgame '01
Enemies Among Us '10
Enough '02
Eraser '96
Exit Wounds '01
Family in Hiding '06
Filth '13
Final Payback '99
Fish in a Barrel '01
Flashfire '94
Freelancers '12
Full Clip '06
Gang Related '96
The Gauntlet '77
The Glass Shield '95
Goodbye South, Goodbye '96
The Guard '11 ►
Hard to Kill '89
Harsh Times '05
Heaven '01
The Heavy '09
I Saw the Devil '10
Internal Affairs '90
Johnny O'Clock '47
The Kane Files '10
Killer Cop '02
Kiss of the Dragon '01
L.A. Confidential '97 ►
Lakeview Terrace '08 ►
L.A.P.D.: To Protect and Serve '01
Last Chance Cafe '06
Last Man Standing '96
Lethal Force '00
Lethal Weapon 3 '92
Lone Star '95 ►
Magnum Force '73
McCanick '14
The Mod Squad '99
The Money Trap '65
Narc '02 ►
The Negotiator '98
New Jersey Drive '95
Night Falls on Manhattan '96 ►
One Way Out '02
Our Man in Havana '59 ►
Pawn '13
Payback '98 ►
Point Blank '10
Premium Rush '12 ►
Pressure '02
Pride and Glory '08
The Professional '94
The Prowler '51
Rampart '11
Red Riding, Part 1: 1974 '09
Red Riding, Part 2: 1980 '09
Red Riding, Part 3: 1983 '09
Rent-A-Cop '88
Rip It Off '02
Romeo Is Bleeding '93
Sabotage '14
The Salton Sea '02
Samaritan Girl '04
Serpico '73 ►
Shaft '00 ►
Shakedown '88
Sin City '05
Sin City: A Dame to Kill For '14
16 Blocks '06 ►
Sleepless Night '11 ►
The Split '68
Stander '03
Steve Martini's The Judge '01
The Stickup '01
Stiletto '08
Street Kings 2: Motor City '11
Striking Distance '93
Super Troopers '01
S.W.A.T. '03
The Take '74
Tales from the Hood '95
The Thin Blue Lie '00
Things to Do in Denver When You're Dead '95 ►
Touch of Evil '58 ►
Training Day '01
Trash '14
The Trial Begins '07
Twelve Hours to Kill '60
Twenty8k '12
2 Fast 2 Furious '03
Unlawful Entry '92
Vehicle 19 '13
Violent Cop '89
War on Everyone '17
Witness '85 ►
Would Be Kings '08

Role Reversal

See also Gender Bending

All of Me '84
Anastasia '56 ►
Anastasia: The Mystery of Anna '86
Angel '84
Angel on My Shoulder '46 ►
Babe '95 ►
The Bank Dick '40 ►
Big '88 ►
Biggles '85
Billy Madison '94
Blood of Dracula '57
Captive Heart '47 ►
Catfight '17
The Change-Up '11
Cheech and Chong's The Corsican Brothers '84
Christmas in Connecticut '45 ►
Cinderfella '60
Clambake '67
Class Act '91
Coming to America '88 ►
Condorman '81
The Couch Trip '87
Courage '86 ►
Dave '93 ►
Desperately Seeking Susan '85
Dr. Black, Mr. Hyde '76
Doctor Detroit '83
Doctor Dolittle '67
Dr. Jekyll and Mr. Hyde '20 ►
Dr. Jekyll and Mr. Hyde '32 ►
Dr. Jekyll and Mr. Hyde '41 ►
Dr. Jekyll and Mr. Hyde '68
Dr. Jekyll and Mr. Hyde '73
Down and Out in Beverly Hills '86
Dream a Little Dream '89
The Eagle Huntress '16 ►
18 Again! '88
Extremities '86
48 Hrs. '82 ►
Freaky Friday '76
Freaky Friday '03 ►
Garfield: A Tail of Two Kitties '06
The Great Gabbo '29
Greystoke: The Legend of Tarzan, Lord of the Apes '84
Guest Wife '45
Heart Like a Wheel '83
Hero '92 ►
Hiding Out '87
Holiday Wishes '06
The Hot Chick '02
Identity Crisis '90
The Incredible Mr. Limpet '64
Incredibles 2 '18 ►
Iron Maze '91
It's a Boy Girl Thing '06
Jekyll and Hyde '90
Johnny Guitar '53 ►
Junior '94
Just One of the Guys '85
Kagemusha '80 ►
Kim '50 ►
La Femme Nikita '91 ►
La Ronde '51 ►
The Lady Vanishes '38 ►
The Lady Vanishes '79
Ladybugs '92
The Legend of Tarzan '16
Liane, Jungle Goddess '56
Like Father, Like Son '87
Liquid Sky '83 ►
Lonely Wives '31
Maid to Order '87
Male and Female '19 ►
The Man Who Haunted Himself '70
Mrs. Winterbourne '96
Mr. Fix It '06
Monkey Business '52 ►
Moon over Parador '88
My Blue Heaven '90
My Fair Lady '64 ►
Naked Souls '94
Now, Voyager '42 ►
Opportunity Knocks '90
Opposite Day '09
Overboard '87
Paris When It Sizzles '64
Performance '70 ►
Persona '66 ►
Pocketful of Miracles '61 ►
Point of No Return '93
Posse '75 ►
The Prince and the Pauper '37 ►
The Prince and the Pauper '62
The Prince and the Pauper '78
The Prince and the Pauper '01
Prisoner of Zenda '37 ►
Prisoner of Zenda '52
Prisoner of Zenda '79
Psycho '60 ►
Quicksilver '86
The Raggedy Rawney '90
Raid on Rommel '71
Red Lion '69
The Road to Yesterday '25
Roman Holiday '53 ►

A Saintly Switch '99
Savages '72
The Scarlet Pimpernel '82 ▶
The Secret '07
September Affair '50
The Shaggy D.A. '76
The Shaggy Dog '59
Showdown in Little Tokyo '91
Silent Night, Deadly Night '84
A Slightly Pregnant Man '79
Sommersby '93
A Stolen Face '52
Straight Talk '92
Summer Night with Greek Profile, Almond Eyes & Scent of Basil '87
Sweet Revenge '90
Switch '91 ▶
Sylvia Scarlett '35
Taking Care of Business '90
A Tale of Two Cities '89 ▶
The Tango Lesson '97
Tomboy '40
Tootsie '82 ▶
Trading Places '83
The Two Faces of Dr. Jekyll '60
Vice Versa '88 ▶
Victor/Victoria '82 ▶
A Walk in My Shoes '10
Watermelon Man '70
White Man's Burden '95
White Sands '92
Wish upon a Star '96
Wonder Man '45
Yankee Zulu '95
Yentl '83

Roller Skating

Boogie Nights '97 ▶
Derby '71 ▶
The Fireball '50
Kansas City Bomber '72
Prayer of the Rollerboys '91
Roll Bounce '05 ▶
Roller Boogie '79
Rollerball '75
Rollerball '02
Skateland '10
Solarbabies '86
Unholy Rollers '72
Whip It '09 ▶
Xanadu '80

Romance

***See also** Late Bloomin' Love; Lovers on the Lam; Romantic Adventure; Romantic Triangles; Teen Romance*
A Late Quartet '12

Romantic Adventure

Above Suspicion '43 ▶
The African Queen '51 ▶
Allied '16
The American '10
Antz '98 ▶
Arabian Nights '42
Arabian Nights '00
As You Like It '06
The Awakening '95
Away We Go '09
Baby. . . Secret of the Lost Legend '85
The Barbarian '33
Beau Ideal '31
Beautiful Creatures '13
The Bounty Hunter '10
Brigham Young: Frontiersman '40
Broken Lullaby '94
Caprice '67
Captain Calamity '36
Captain from Castile '47 ▶
Casanova '05
Casanova '05 ▶
Chasing Liberty '04
China Seas '35 ▶
Cirque du Soleil: Worlds Away '12
Crouching Tiger, Hidden Dragon '00 ▶
Down Argentine Way '40 ▶
Duplicity '09
Ever After: A Cinderella Story '98 ▶
Fanfan la Tulipe '51 ▶
Fool's Gold '08
Frenchman's Creek '44
Frenchman's Creek '98
Going to America '15
Gun Crazy '49 ▶
Guncrazy '92
Her Jungle Love '38
The Indian Fighter '55 ▶
International Settlement '38
Invisible Agent '42
It's a Wonderful World '39
The Jewel of the Nile '85
Joe Versus the Volcano '90
Knight and Day '10
A Knight's Tale '01
The Last of the Mohicans '92 ▶
The Last Templar '09
The Mask of Zorro '98 ▶
Mr. Right '16
The Mistress of Atlantis '32
Mogambo '53 ▶
The Mountain Between Us '17
Mutiny Ahead '35
Negative Happy Chainsaw Edge '08
Oscar and Lucinda '97
Painted Skin: The Resurrection '12
Paris Can Wait '17
Passengers '16
Pocahontas '95 ▶
Princess of the Nile '54
The Proposition '96
The Rains of Ranchipur '55
Red Dust '32 ▶
Rio, I Love You '14
Robot Pilot '41
The Rocketeer '91 ▶
Romancing the Stone '84 ▶
Rough Magic '95
Russian Dolls '05
The Seventh Dawn '64
The Shape of Water '17 ▶
Sideways '04 ▶
Six Days, Seven Nights '98
Son of Ali Baba '52
The Space Between Us '17
Sparks '13
Spider-Man 3 '07
The Tempest '10
The Thomas Crown Affair '99 ▶
The Truth About Charlie '02
Untamed '55

Romantic Mystery

***See also** Mystery & Psycho-Thriller*
American Dreamer '84
Angels Fall '07
Another Woman '94
At the Midnight Hour '95
Beast '17 ▶
The Black Widow '05
Blue Smoke '07
Carnal Innocence '11
Carolina Moon '07
A Change of Place '94
Charade '63 ▶
Come and Find Me '16
Every Woman Knows a Secret '99
Hard to Forget '98
High Noon '09
Laura '44 ▶
Loving Evangeline '98
Married Life '07 ▶
Midnight Bayou '09
Montana Sky '07
The Moon-Spinners '64
Moontide '42
My Cousin Rachel '52
Northern Lights '09
Notorious '46 ▶
Rear Window '54 ▶
Recipe for Revenge '98
The Romantics '10
Secret Smile '05
The Thin Man '34 ▶
To Catch a Thief '55 ▶
To Have & Have Not '44 ▶
Treacherous Beauties '94
Tribute '09
The Waiting Game '98

Romantic Triangles

***See also** Otherwise Engaged*
The Accompanist '20
Across to Singapore '28
The Aftermath '19
The Age of Innocence '93 ▶
Aladdin '92 ▶
Alexander the Last '09
All the Brothers Were Valiant '53
All Things Fair '95
Almost Friends '17
Amateur '94 ▶
Ambush '50
Amnesia '96
Among Giants '98
Amores Perros '00 ▶
Angie '94
Another Dawn '37
Another Woman's Husband '00
Answer This '10
Anything But Love '02
The Apprentice '71
Apres-Vous '03
The Art of Murder '99
Ash Wednesday '02
Atlantics '19 ▶
August '11
Autopsy: A Love Story '02
The Aviator's Wife '80 ▶
Bait '54
Baja '95
Balzac and the Little Chinese Seamstress '02
Bandits '01
Battle Zone '52
The Baxter '05
Be My Valentine '13
Belladonna '08
Beloved Sisters '14 ▶
Bending All the Rules '02
The Best Man '97
Betrayed '44
A Better Tomorrow, Part 3 '89
Beyond the Rocks '22
The Big Bounce '69
The Big Shot '42
Big Stone Gap '15
Bitter Moon '92
Bitter/Sweet '09
The Black Bird '26
The Black Dahlia '06
Black Day Blue Night '95
Blue Skies '46 ▶
Blue Valley Songbird '99
Body Heat '81 ▶
Bon Voyage '03 ▶
The Book of Life '14
Book of Love '04
Boom Town '40
Bordertown '35
Bottled Up '13
The Boxer and the Bombshell '08
The Boys and Girl From County Clare '03
Bread, Love and Dreams '53
Breakin' All The Rules '04
Breaking Wind '12
The Bride Comes Home '35
Bride of the Wind '01
Bridget Jones: The Edge of Reason '04
Bridget Jones's Baby '16
Brightest Star '14
Broadcast News '87 ▶
Brooklyn '15 ▶
Brothers '04 ▶
Brothers '09
The Brylcreem Boys '96
Bubble '06
Bull Durham '88 ▶
Burying the Ex '15
A Business Affair '93
Butterfly Sword '93
Cactus Flower '69
Cafe au Lait '94 ▶
Cake '05
Calendar '93 ▶
Call of the Yukon '38
Canyon Passage '46 ▶
Captain Corelli's Mandolin '01
Caravan '46
Carnal Knowledge '71 ▶
Carny '80 ▶
Carried Away '95
Carrington '95
Casa de mi Padre '12
Casablanca '42 ▶
Casino '95 ▶
Caught '96
Central Airport '33
The Ceremony '63
Ceremony '10
Chance at Heaven '33
Cheerful Weather for the Wedding '12
Children of the Century '99
The Choice '16
Circle of Passion '97
Cleopatra's Second Husband '00
Closer '04 ▶
Coastlines '02
Coco Before Chanel '09
A Coeur Joie '67
Come Live With Me '40
Coming Out '89
Condition Red '95
Coney Island '43 ▶
The Constant Nymph '43
The Cook, the Thief, His Wife & Her Lover '90 ▶
Corrupted Hands '00
Country Life '95
Cowboy Up '00
Cowboys and Angels '00
Crashing '07
The Crucible '96 ▶
Cruel Intentions 3 '04
The Cuckoo '02
Daisy Kenyon '47
Dalva '95
Damage '92 ▶
Dangerous Cargo '96
Dangerous Passion '95
Dark Blue World '01
Dark Harbor '98
Dark Hearts '12
Dawn Rider '12
Day of Reckoning '33
Daydream Nation '10
Days '02
Days of Being Wild '91 ▶
Dead Beat '94
Dead in the Water '01
Dead Ringers '88 ▶
Dear Heart '64 ▶
Dear John '10
Dear Wendy '05
The Debt '10
Deceit '06
December Bride '91
A Decent Proposal '06
The Decoy Bride '11
The Deep Blue Sea '12
Design for Living '33
Desire Me '47
The Devil Is a Woman '35 ▶
Devotion '46
Devotion '95
Diabolique '96
Dinner and Driving '97
Don't Make Waves '67
The Doom Generation '95 ▶
Dot the I '03
The Dreamers '03
Dreaming of Joseph Lees '99
Dreamland '06 ▶
Drift '00
Driven '01
Dry Cleaning '97
The Dying Gaul '05 ▶
Earthquake Bird '19
East of the River '40
East Side Story '07
The Edge of Love '08
The Edukators '04
Elephant Walk '54
The Embalmer '03 ▶
Emma '96 ▶
An Empress and the Warriors '08
End of the Affair '55
The End of the Affair '99 ▶
Endings, Beginnings '20
Enduring Love '04
The English Patient '96 ▶
Eros '04
Ethan Frome '92
Everybody Loves Somebody '17 ▶
Everyone Says I Love You '96 ▶
Evil Dead Trap 2: Hideki '91
Facing Windows '03
Faithless '00 ▶
A Family Affair '01
The Fan '49
Far from Heaven '02 ▶
Far North '07
Fast Workers '33
The Favor '92
The Favourite '18 ▶
Feast of July '95
Feast of Love '07
Fever '91
Fidelio: Alice's Odyssey '14
Finding Your Feet '18
First Knight '95
The First Wives Club '96
The Flame of New Orleans '41 ▶
Flesh '32
Flowing Gold '40
The Fluffer '01
The Flying Fleet '29
For the Love of Grace '08
For You I Die '47
Forever Mine '99
Forty Shades of Blue '05
Foxfire Light '82
French Film '08
French Kiss '95
French Twist '95
Frontier Marshal '39
Frontier of Dawn '08
Full Time Killer '01
The Future '11
G '02
Garage Days '03
The Getaway '72
The Getaway '93
Gilles' Wife '04
A Girl Cut in Two '07
The Girl from 10th Ave. '35
Girl Loves Boy '37
The Girl Said No '30
The Girl with a Suitcase '60
Girl's Dormitory '36
The Glass Mountain '49
Gloomy Sunday '02 ▶
God's Gift to Women '31
The Golden Bowl '72 ▶
The Golden Bowl '00
The Good Guy '10
The Good Heart '09
Goodbye Baby '07
Goodbye, Lover '99
Goodbye My Fancy '51
Gray Matters '06
The Great Gatsby '74
The Great Gatsby '13
Grind '96
Gunshy '98 ▶
Guy and Madeline on a Park Bench '09 ▶
Hana & Alice '04 ▶
Happily Ever After '04
Have Sword, Will Travel '69
Head in the Clouds '04
Head Over Heels '37
The Heart of Me '02
Heartbeats '11
Hearts of War '07
Hell Boats '70
Hemingway's Garden of Eden '08
Henry & June '90 ▶
Her Cardboard Lover '42
Her Secret '33
Here on Earth '00
Hero '02 ▶
The Hi-Lo Country '98
High Art '98
High Society '56 ▶
Hilary and Jackie '98 ▶
Hollywoodland '06
Homage '95
A Home at the End of the World '04
Honey 3: Dare to Dance '16
Hong Kong 1941 '84
The Host '13
Hot Saturday '32
Housewife '34
How Do You Know '10
I Love You Baby '01
I Met Him in Paris '37
I Take This Woman '40
If I Were You '12
If Winter Comes '41
Imagine Me & You '06
In the Shadows '98
Indecent Proposal '93
Inside Out '11
Interlocked '98
Intermission '03 ▶
Intersection '93
Intimate Betrayal '96
Intruso '93
The Irish in Us '35
Irreversible '02
It Could Happen to You '94
It's Complicated '09
J'accuse! '19 ▶
Jason's Lyric '94
Jerichow '15 ▶
Johnny Doesn't Live Here Any More '44
Jonathan '19
Josette '38
Jules and Jim '62 ▶
Juliet, Naked '18
Just Another Love Story '08
Just Go With It '11
Kaaterskill Falls '01
The Keeper: The Legend of Omar Khayyam '05
Keeping the Faith '00
Kiss the Sky '98
Kissing a Fool '98
La Petite Lili '03
La Piscine '69
La Roue '23 ▶
Ladies in Lavender '04
The Ladies of the Bois de Bologne '44
Lady Chatterley '92
Lady of the Night '25 ▶
Laila '29
The Last Kiss '01
The Last Man '00
The Last of the Mohicans '92 ▶
The Last Outpost '35
The Last Time '06
The Layover '17
Le Jupon Rouge '87
The Leading Man '96
Leaving Metropolis '02
The Ledge '11
Legends of the Fall '94
Les Biches '68 ▶
Les Voleurs '96 ▶
Let It Shine '12
Leto '19
Let's Do It Again '53
Lily & Kat '15
Little Monsters '19
Lives of Performers '72
Lloyds of London '36 ▶
The Lost Zeppelin '29
Love Actually '03
Love Affair '32
Love Before Breakfast '36
Love, etc. '96
Love Serenade '96
Love Songs '07
Love Thy Neighbor '02
Love Walked In '97
The Lovers '59 ▶
Lovers of Hate '10
Lucky Seven '03
Lucky Star '29
Lured Innocence '97
Made in Paris '65
Made of Honor '08
Maggie's Plan '16
Making Love '82
Making the Rules '14
The Man From Yesterday '32
The Man I Love '97
Man in the Saddle '51
Manpower '41
Mararia '98
Married Life '07 ▶
The Married Virgin '18
Massacre River '49
Match Point '05 ▶
Matter of Trust '98
Maze '01
Me, Myself and Her '16
Melinda and Melinda '05
Melo '86
The Men Next Door '12
Men with Wings '38
The Merry Widow '25 ▶
Middle of Nowhere '12

Mildred Pierce '45 ▶
Miller's Crossing '90 ▶
The Mississippi Gambler '53
Mr. Jealousy '98
Mists of Avalon '01 ▶
Mo' Better Blues '90
Mogambo '53 ▶
Mojave Moon '96
Money Train '95
Moondance '95
Moonlight Whispers '99
Moscow, Belgium '08
The Mother '03 ▶
Mouth to Mouth '95
My Best Friend's Girl '08
My Best Friend's Wedding '97
My Blind Brother '16
My Brother Is an Only Child '07
My Favorite Wife '40 ▶
My Girlfriend's Back '10
My Girlfriend's Boyfriend '10
My Side Piece '16
My Worst Nightmare '11
My Zinc Bed '08
The Mysteries of Pittsburgh '08
Never Let Me Go '10
Never Say Die '39
The New Twenty '08
Next Time We Love '36
Night Cargo '36
Night Train to Lisbon '13
No Strings Attached '11
No Way Home '96
Nob Hill '45 ▶
Not Since You '09
A Novel Romance '11
Obsession '97
On the Beach '00
Once a Thief '96 ▶
Once More, With Feeling '60
Once Upon a Time in the Midlands '02
The One '11
One Desire '55
100 Bloody Acres '12
One Night Stand '97 ▶
One Sunday Afternoon '33
One Sunday Afternoon '48
Only You '94
The Opposite of Sex '98
Orchids to You '35
Ordinary Sinner '02
The Other Boleyn Girl '08
Other Men's Women '31
The Other Woman '08
Out of Africa '85 ▶
Outside In '17
Paint and Powder '25
The Pallbearer '95
Palmetto '98
A Parisian Romance '32
Party Husband '31
The Passionate Plumber '32
The Patsy '28
Pearl Harbor '01
Perfect Victims '08
The Perfect Wedding '12
Perhaps Love '05
The Philadelphia Story '40 ▶
Phoenix '06
The Pianist '91
Plain Dirty '04
Plain Jane '02
Play It to the Bone '99
Playing by Heart '98
Polish Wedding '97
Portrait in Black '60
Portraits Chinois '96
Potiche '10 ▶
Power and Beauty '02
Power Dive '41
Pretenders '19
A Price Above Rubies '97
Private Peaceful '12
Professor Marston and the Wonder Women '17
The Promise '05
A Promise '13
Puccini for Beginners '06
Pushing Tin '99 ▶
Puzzlehead '05
Queer Duck: The Movie '06
The Quiet American '02 ▶
Quiet Days in Hollywood '97
Radio Inside '94
Rancid '04
Reaching for the Moon '13
Reality Bites '94
Reckless '97 ▶
Reckless: The Sequel '98 ▶
Red Riding Hood '11
Reducing '31
Restoration '94 ▶
Revenge '90
The Rich Are Always With Us '32
Riders '88
The Right Kind Of Wrong '13
The Right to Live '35
Risk '00
Road House '48
Road to Riches '01 ▶
Roadie '11
Robin Hood: Prince of Thieves '91
A Room with a View '86 ▶
Rory O'Shea Was Here '04
A Royal Affair '12 ▶
Rumor Has It. . . '05
Saadia '53
Sabrina '54 ▶
Sabrina '95
Salty O'Rourke '45
Samurai Banners '69
Saturday Night and Sunday Morning '60 ▶
Saturday Night Special '92
Savages '12
Scorned 2 '96
The Sea Gull '68
The Second Front '05
Second Skin '99
Secret Lives of Second Wives '08
Separate Lies '05
The Separation '94
September '96
Serenade '56
The Serpent's Kiss '97
Sex and the Other Man '95
The Sex Monster '99
She's Gotta Have It '86 ▶
She's So Lovely '97
Shopgirl '05 ▶
The Show '27
Silk '07
Silver Skates '43
Simpatico '99
Sing Street '16 ▶
The Situation '06
Six Days, Six Nights '94
Sky Captain and the World of Tomorrow '04
Slattery's Hurricane '49
Slaves to the Underground '96
Sleep with Me '94
Sleepless in Seattle '93 ▶
Sliding Doors '97
Slogan '69
The Smiling Lieutenant '31
Something Borrowed '11
Something More '99
Something's Gotta Give '03 ▶
Sommersby '93
The Song of Songs '33
Sparkle '07
The Spectator '04
Speed '36
Splendor '99
Spring 1941 '08
Stallion Road '47
Stella '55
Stella Maris '18 ▶
Stolen Face '52
Stonewall '95 ▶
Strictly Dynamite '34
Sueno '05
Suez '38
Summer Catch '01
Summer in February '13
Summer Lover '08
Summer Lovers '82
Superman Returns '06
Susan Slade '61
Sweet Home Alabama '02
The Sweet Life '03
Swing Shift Maisie '43
Take This Waltz '11
Talhotblond '12
Talk of Angels '96
Tangled '01
Tango '98
Tape '01 ▶
Tell It to the Marines '26
Tempted '01
Ten Cents a Dance '31
The Tenant of Wildfell Hall '96
The Tenants '06
Tequila Sunrise '88
Tess '79 ▶
Tess of the D'Urbervilles '98
There Be Dragons '11
There's Something About a Soldier '43
There's Something about Mary '98 ▶
These Foolish Things '06
They Gave Him a Gun '37
A Thin Line Between Love and Hate '96
The Third Girl from the Left '73
This Is the Night '32
This Means War '12
Though None Go With Me '06
3 '10
Three for the Show '55
Three of Hearts '93
Three to Tango '99
3-Way '04
Threesome '94
A Throw of Dice '29 ▶
Thunder Birds '42
Thunder in Carolina '60
Thunderhoof '48
The Tiger's Claw '51
Time of Favor '00
Tin Cup '96 ▶
To Rome with Love '12
To the Wonder '12
Torrents of Spring '90
Torrid Zone '40
Totally Blonde '01
Town and Country '01
The Toy Wife '38
The Trio '97
Triplecross '95
Trojan War '97
Trouble in Paradise '32 ▶
The Truth about Cats and Dogs '96 ▶
The Truth About Youth '30
Twice upon a Yesterday '98
The Twilight Saga: New Moon '09
Twister '96
The Two Faces of January '14
Two Girls and a Guy '98 ▶
Two Girls on Broadway '40
Two Lovers '09 ▶
Two Minutes to Play '37
Two Much '96
Two Ninas '00
Two Shades of Blue '98
U-Turn '97
Unanswered Prayers '10
The Unbearable Lightness of Being '88 ▶
Uncanny '15
Under Hellgate Bridge '99
The Underneath '95 ▶
Undertaking Betty '02
Unfaithful '02 ▶
The Unknown Soldier '98
The Unspeakable Act '13
Vagabond Lady '35
The Valet '06
Value for Money '55
The Velocity of Gary '98
Very Good Girls '13
A Very Merry Mix-Up '13
Vicky Cristina Barcelona '08
The Viking '28
A Village Affair '95
Wabash Avenue '50
Waiting to Exhale '95 ▶
A Walk on the Moon '99
Wall of Noise '63
Warlords '08 ▶
A Waste of Shame '05
Waterloo Road '45
We All Fall Down '00
We Are Your Friends '15
We Don't Live Here Anymore '04
The Wedding Banquet '93 ▶
The Wedding Singer '97
Welcome to Mooseport '04
The West Wittering Affair '05
What If '13
When the Bough Breaks '16
When Will I Be Loved '04
While You Were Sleeping '95 ▶
Whiplash '48
White Mischief '88 ▶
The Whole Nine Yards '00
Wild Is the Wind '57
Wild Things '98
A Wind from Wyoming '94
The Wings of the Dove '97 ▶
Wings of the Navy '39
Winner Take All '32
The Winning of Barbara Worth '26
Wishful Thinking '96
The Woman Between '31
Woman Is the Future of Man '04 ▶
The Woman on the Beach '47
Woman Wanted '98
A Woman's a Helluva Thing '01
Women Who Kill '17
Wonder Bar '34
X, Y & Zee '72
XX/XY '02
Yes '04
You and Me '06
You Can't Have Everything '37
You Gotta Stay Happy '48
You Stupid Man '02
You Will Meet a Tall Dark Stranger '10
Your Sister's Sister '11
Z for Zachariah '15
Zero '18
Zhou Yu's Train '02

Rome--Ancient

***See also** Historical Drama; Italy*

A.D. '85
Amazons and Gladiators '01
Attila '54
Attila '01
Ben-Hur '26 ▶
Ben-Hur '59 ▶
Ben Hur '10
Ben-Hur '16
Caesar and Cleopatra '46
Caesar the Conqueror '63
Caligula '80
Cleopatra '34
Cleopatra '63
Cleopatra '99
Coriolanus '11 ▶
Cyclops '08
Demetrius and the Gladiators '54
Druids '01
Duel of Champions '61
The Eagle '11
Fabiola '48 ▶
The Fall of the Roman Empire '64 ▶
Fellini Satyricon '69 ▶
A Funny Thing Happened on the Way to the Forum '66 ▶
Gladiator '00 ▶
Julius Caesar '53 ▶
Julius Caesar '70
Jupiter's Darling '55
King Arthur '04
Last Days of Pompeii '35
The Last Days of Pompeii '60
The Last Days of Pompeii '84
The Last Legion '07
Quo Vadis '51 ▶
The Robe '53
The Sign of the Cross '33
Spartacus '60 ▶
Titus '99
Troy '04
Two Gladiators '64

Rome--Modern

***See also** Italy*

The Abdication '74
Adua and Her Friends '60
And the Wild, Wild Women '59
Angels & Demons '09
Artemisia '97
Assassination in Rome '65
Barney's Version '10
Bellissima '51 ▶
The Belly of an Architect '91 ▶
Besieged '98
A Burning Hot Summer '11
Camille 2000 '69
Caterina in the Big City '03
Daniella by Night '61
Days '02
Death Has a Bad Reputation '90
Death Will Have Your Eyes '74
Don't Tell '05
Facing Windows '03
Fellini's Roma '72
Four Flies on Grey Velvet '72
The Frightened Woman '71
Ginger & Fred '86 ▶
The Godfather, Part 3 '90 ▶
The Great Beauty '13
Hudson Hawk '91
Il Futuro '13
La Dolce Vita '60 ▶
The Last Kiss '01
The Listening '06
Live Like a Cop, Die Like a Man '76
Madonna of the Seven Moons '45
The Moon & the Stars '07
My Own Private Idaho '91 ▶
National Lampoon's European Vacation '85
Night on Earth '91 ▶
Ocean's Twelve '04
The Omen '06
The Order '03
Portrait of a Lady '96 ▶
The Priest's Wife '71
Quiet Chaos '08
Red Riding Hood '03
The Rite '11
Roman Holiday '53 ▶
Roman Spring of Mrs. Stone '61 ▶
The Scarlet & the Black '83
A Special Day '77 ▶
The Spectator '04
Steam: A Turkish Bath '96 ▶
The Stendahl Syndrome '95
The Talented Mr. Ripley '99
Ten Thousand Bedrooms '57
Third Person '13
To Rome with Love '12
Traveling Companion '96
The Trial Begins '07
The Two Popes '19 ▶
Valentino: The Last Emperor '08
When in Rome '09
The White Sheik '52 ▶

Roommates from Hell

***See also** Psychotics/ Sociopaths*

All Out Dysfunktion! '16
Baked in Brooklyn '16
Black Butterfly '17
Condemned '15
Deadbolt '92
Dirty Lies '16
Everybody Wants Some!! '16
For a Good Time, Call... '12
He Died With a Falafel in His Hand '01
Kill for Me '12
The Last Supper '96
Lip Service '00
Malice '93
Man in the Attic '53
The Night We Never Met '93
Pacific Heights '90 ▶
Perfect Tenant '99
The Roommate '11
The Secret Life of Pets '16
Shallow Grave '94
Single White Female '92
Single White Female 2: The Psycho '05
Sun Choke '16
Table for Three '09
Ties That Bind '06
When the Bough Breaks '16
Zero Degrees Kelvin '95

Royalty

***See also** Historical Drama; Medieval Romps; Period Piece; Royalty, British; Royalty, Russian*

Abdulla the Great '56
The Adventures of Marco Polo '38
Aladdin '92 ▶
Ali Baba and the Forty Thieves '43
Alice '09
Alice in Wonderland '10
Alice Through the Looking Glass '16
Angelique and the Sultan '68
Anna and the King '99
Anna and the King of Siam '46 ▶
Annie: A Royal Adventure '95
Arabian Nights '42
Arabian Nights '00
Atlantis: The Lost Empire '01
Balalaika '39
Barbarian Queen 2: The Empress Strikes Back '89
The Baroness and the Butler '38
The Beautician and the Beast '97
Beauty and the Beast: A Dark Tale '10
Beowulf '07 ▶
Beowulf & Grendel '06
The Black Cauldron '85
Brave '12
Caligula '80
Camelot '67
Carlton Browne of the F.O. '59
Carry On Columbus '92
Carry On Henry VIII '71
Charles & Diana: A Palace Divided '93
Children of Dune '03
Chimes at Midnight '67 ▶
Chinese Odyssey 2002 '02
The Chronicles of Narnia: Prince Caspian '08
The Chronicles of Narnia: The Voyage of the Dawn Treader '10
Cinderella '97
Cinderella '15
Cleopatra '34
Cleopatra '63
Cleopatra '99
Cobra Woman '44
Coming to America '88 ▶
Conquest of the Normans '62
The Court Jester '56 ▶
Cracked Nuts '31
The Crown Prince '06
The Crusades '35
Curse of the Golden Flower '06
Damon and Pythias '62
David '97
Delgo '08
The Divine Lady '29
Dr. Syn, Alias the Scarecrow '64
Donkey Skin '70 ▶
Dracula: The Dark Prince '01
Dragonheart '96
Dream Wife '53
Du Barry Was a Lady '43
Dune '84
Dune '00
East Meets West '36
East of Borneo '31
The Egyptian '54
Elena and Her Men '56 ▶
Ella Enchanted '04 ▶
Emperor '12
The Emperor and the Assassin '99
Emperor Jones '33
Emperor Waltz '48
The Emperor's New Groove '00 ▶
The Emperor's Shadow '96
Enchanted '07
Eragon '06

Esther '98
Ever After: A Cinderella Story '98 ▸
Excalibur '81 ▸
Fairy Tales '76
Farinelli '94
The Favourite '18 ▸
The Fighting Prince of Donegal '66
The Finances of the Grand Duke '24
Fire & Ice: The Dragon Chronicles '08
First Knight '95
First Lady '20
Fit for a King '37
Forever Amber '47
The Fountain '06
14 Blades '14
The Gay Deception '35
Gladiator '00 ▸
Goya's Ghosts '06
Grace Kelly '83
Grace of Monaco '14
Grimm's Snow White '12
Hamlet '96▸
Hamlet '01
Harem '99
Harem Girl '52
Helen of Troy '03
Hellboy II: The Golden Army '08▸
Hennessy '75
Her Highness and the Bellboy '45
Hercules '14
Hercules, Samson and Ulysses '64
Hercules the Legendary Journeys, Vol. 2: The Lost Kingdom '94
Hero '02▸
His Majesty, the American '19
A Hologram for the King '16
The Huntsman: Winter's War '16
The Illusionist '06
Immortals '11
In the Name of the King: A Dungeon Siege Tale '08
In the Name of the King 3: The Last Mission '14
The Indian Tomb '21
Jack the Giant Slayer '13
Jason and the Argonauts '00
Java Heat '13
Joseph '95
Journey to Promethea '10
Julius Caesar '53▸
Julius Caesar '70
Kama Sutra: A Tale of Love '96
Kaspar Hauser '93
A Kid in Aladdin's Palace '97
A Kid in King Arthur's Court '95
Kind Hearts and Coronets '49▸
The King '19▸
The King and I '56▸
The King and I '99
King Arthur: Legend of the Sword '17
A King in New York '57
King Ralph '91
Kingdom of Blood: The Final Battle '16
The King's Guard '01
Kings of the Sun '63
The King's Thief '55
The King's Whore '90
Kismet '44
Lace 2 '85
Lace '84
The Lady and the Duke '01
Lancelot of the Lake '74
The Last Emperor '87▸
The Legend of Hercules '14
The Legend of Suriyothai '02
The Leopard '63▸
Lillie '79▸
The Little Prince '16▸
Lorna Doone '22
Lost in a Harem '44
The Love Parade '29
Love's Labour's Lost '00
Ludwig '72
Macbeth '48 ▸
Macbeth '70 ▸
Macbeth '71 ▸
Macbeth '15
Mad Love '01
The Magic Carpet '51
Maleficent '14
The Man Who Would Be King '75 ▸
Mannequin 2: On the Move '91
The Master of Ballantrae '53
Mayerling '36 ▸
Mayerling '68
Medea '88
Meet the Spartans '08
The Merry Widow '25 ▸
Metamorphosis '07
A Midsummer Night's Dream '35 ▸
A Midsummer Night's Dream '96
Mirror Mirror '12
Mr. Imperium '51
Mom and Dad Save the World '92
Monsieur Beaucaire '24
Monsieur Beaucaire '46▸
Monte Carlo '30
More Than a Miracle '67
Moses '96
Mulan '98
My Friend from India '27
Mysteries of Lisbon '10
Mythica: A Quest for Heroes '15
National Lampoon's The Legend of Awesomest Maximus '11
Northman: A Viking Saga '15
One Night with the King '06
One Romantic Night '30
Ophelia '19
Outlaw King '18
Passion '19
The Pharaoh's Curse '57
Phedre '68
Phoenix '78
The Pirates of Capri '49
The Pirates Who Don't Do Anything: A VeggieTales Movie '08
The Polar Bear King '94
Ponyo '08▸
Power '34
The Prince & Me 2: Royal Wedding '06
The Prince & Me 3: A Royal Honeymoon '08
The Prince & Me 4: The Elephant Adventure '10
The Prince & Me '04
The Prince and the Pauper '37▸
The Prince and the Pauper '62
The Prince and the Pauper '78
The Prince and the Showgirl '57
The Prince and the Surfer '99
Prince Brat and the Whipping Boy '95▸
Prince of Persia: The Sands of Time '10
Princess: A Modern Fairytale '08
Princess Caraboo '94
The Princess Comes Across '36▸
The Princess Diaries 2: Royal Engagement '04
The Princess Diaries '01
Princess Kaiulani '09
Princess of Mars '09
Princess of the Nile '54
Princess O'Rourke '43
Princess Protection Program '09
Princess Raccoon '05
Princess Tam Tam '35▸
Prisoner of Zenda '37▸
Prisoner of Zenda '52
Prisoner of Zenda '79
Professional Soldier '35
The Promise '05
Queen Christina '33▸
Queen Kelly '29▸
Quest for Camelot '98
The Rape of the Sabines '61
Red Cliff '08 ▸
Return to Oz '85
Roman Holiday '53 ▸
A Royal Affair '12 ▸
The Royal Bed '31
A Royal Christmas '14
Royal Deceit '94
A Royal Night Out '15 ▸
The Saragossa Manuscript '65
The Scorpion King 2: Rise of a Warrior '08
The Scorpion King 3: Battle for Redemption '11
Shadow '18 ▸
Shanghai Noon '00
Sharpe's Challenge '06
Shin Heike Monogatari '55 ▸
Shrek 2 '04 ▸
Shrek '01▸
Shrek Forever After '10
Shrek the Third '07
The Sign of the Cross '33
The Singing Princess '49
The Smiling Lieutenant '31
Smooch '11
Snow White and the Huntsman '12
Snow White and the Seven Dwarfs '37▸
Snow White: The Fairest of Them All '02
Solomon '98
Solomon and Sheba '59
Son of Ali Baba '52
Splitting Heirs '93
Spring Parade '40
Star Knight '85
Stardust '07▸
Start the Revolution without Me '70▸
Storm over Asia '28▸
The Story of David '76▸
Storybook '95
The Sun '05
Surf Ninjas '93
The Swan '56▸
The Swan Princess 2: Escape from Castle Mountain '97
The Sword & the Rose '53
Sword & the Sorcerer '82
Sword of War '09
The Tale of Despereaux '08
Tale of Tales '15
The Tale of the Princess Kaguya '13▸
Tangled '10▸
Tarzan and the Huntress '47
Tarzan Goes to India '62
Tarzan's Peril '51
The Tempest '10
The 10th Kingdom '00
The Thief and the Cobbler '96▸
Thirty Day Princess '34
Throne of Blood '57▸
Titus '99
To Play the King '93▸
The Tower of London '39
Tower of London '62
The Triumph of Love '01
Two Nights with Cleopatra '54
A United Kingdom '17
Vatel '00
Victoria & Abdul '17
The War Lord '65▸
The Warriors '55
Where There's Life '47
Willow '88
Witchville '10
Wonder Woman '17▸
Your Highness '11

Royalty, British

See also ***Great Britain; Historical Drama; Medieval Romps; Period Piece; Royalty***

The Adventures of Robin Hood '38▸
Agent Cody Banks 2: Destination London '04
All the King's Men '99
Anne of the Thousand Days '69▸
Anonymous '11
Beau Brummell: This Charming Man '06
Becket '64 ▸
Black Knight '01
The Black Shield of Falworth '54
Braveheart '95 ▸
Diana '13
Diana: Her True Story '93
Downton Abbey '19 ▸
The Duchess '08 ▸
The Earl of Chicago '40
Edward and Mrs. Simpson '80
Edward II '92
Edward the King '75
Elizabeth '98 ▸
Elizabeth R '72 ▸
Elizabeth I '05 ▸
Elizabeth: The Golden Age '07
George and the Dragon '04
Henry IV '85
Henry V '44▸
Henry V '89▸
Her Majesty '01
Hudson's Bay '40
Hyde Park on Hudson '12
Ironclad '11
Ivanhoe '97▸
The King '05
King Lear '98▸
King Richard and the Crusaders '54
The King's Speech '10▸
A Knight in Camelot '98
Lady Godiva '55
Lady Jane '85▸
The Libertine '05
The Lion in Winter '68▸
The Lion in Winter '03▸
Looking for Richard '96▸
The Madness of King George '94▸
A Man for All Seasons '66▸
A Man for All Seasons '88▸
Mary of Scotland '36▸
Mary, Queen of Scots '71
Mary Queen of Scots '18
Merlin '98▸
Mrs. Brown '97▸
Mists of Avalon '01▸
The Mudlark '50
Nine Days a Queen '36▸
Orlando '92▸
The Other Boleyn Girl '03
The Other Boleyn Girl '08
Pillars of the Earth '10
The Prince and the Pauper '01
A Princess for Christmas '11
Princess of Thieves '01
The Private Life of Henry VIII '33▸
The Private Lives of Elizabeth & Essex '39▸
The Queen '06▸
Restoration '94▸
Revenge of the Musketeers '63
Richard III '55▸
Richard III '95▸
Robin Hood '10
Seven Seas to Calais '62
Shakespeare in Love '98▸
Shanghai Knights '03
Six Wives of Henry VIII '71▸
Sixty Glorious Years '38
The Squaw Man '14
The Squaw Man '31
To Kill a King '03
Tristan & Isolde '06
Victoria & Albert '01
Victoria the Great '37
The Virgin Queen '55▸
W.E. '11
William & Catherine: A Royal Romance '11
William & Kate '11
Young Bess '53▸
The Young Victoria '09▸
Youth '15

Royalty, French

See also ***France; Paris; Royalty; Royalty, British***

The Affair of the Necklace '01
Angelique '64
Angelique and the King '66
Angelique: The Road to Versailles '65
At Sword's Point '51
Bardelys the Magnificent '26
Beaumarchais the Scoundrel '96
The Beloved Rogue '27 ▸
Brotherhood of the Wolf '01
Cardinal Richelieu '35
Desiree '54
Fanfan la Tulipe '51 ▸
Farewell, My Queen '12 ▸
The Fifth Musketeer '79
The 4 Musketeers '05
Imperial Venus '63
The Iron Mask '29
Jeanne la Pucelle '94
Joan of Arc '48
Joan of Arc '99
The Lion in Winter '03▸
A Little Chaos '14
Love Me Tonight '32▸
Madame Sans-Gene '62
The Man in the Iron Mask '39▸
The Man in the Iron Mask '77▸
The Man in the Iron Mask '97
The Man in the Iron Mask '98▸
Marie Antoinette '38
Marie Antoinette '06
Mozart's Sister '10
Napoleon '03
Napoleon and Josephine: A Love Story '87
The Princess of Montpensier '10▸
Queen Margot '94▸
Quentin Durward '55
Revenge of the Musketeers '63
Revenge of the Musketeers '94
Ridicule '96▸
The Rise of Louis XIV '66▸
Suez '38
The Three Musketeers '21▸
The Three Musketeers '33
The Three Musketeers '39
The Three Musketeers '48
The Three Musketeers '74▸
The Three Musketeers '93
The Three Musketeers '11

Royalty, Russian

See also ***Historical Drama; Medieval Romps; Period Piece; Royalty; Russia/USSR***

Alexander Nevsky '38▸
Anastasia '56▸
Anastasia '97
Anastasia: The Mystery of Anna '86
Catherine the Great '34
Catherine the Great '95
The Chess Player '27
Clear All Wires! '33
The Duchess of Buffalo '26
The Emperor's Candlesticks '37
Ivan the Terrible, Part 1 '44▸
Ivan the Terrible, Part 2 '46▸
Never Say Die '39
Nicholas and Alexandra '71
The Prisoner of Zenda '22
Rasputin '85▸
Rasputin and the Empress '33▸
Rasputin the Mad Monk '66
Scarlet Empress '34▸
Tempest '28
We Live Again '34
The White Countess '05▸
Young Catherine '91▸

Runaways

American Gun '02▸
American Honey '16
At First Light '18
Bandits '01
A Beautiful Life '08
Being Charlie '16
Born Innocent '74
The Capture of the Green River Killer '08
Children of the Night '85
The Chronicles of Riddick '04
Escape from L.A. '96
Flight of the Doves '71
The Green '11
Happy Feet Two '11
The Happy Road '57
Hick '11
Hunt for the Wilderpeople '16 ▸
Hunted '52
The Hybrids Family '16
Jimmy Zip '00
The Kings of Summer '13
Kisses '08 ▸
Leap! '16
Little Ladies of the Night '77
Lost Angel '43
Maybe I'll Come Home in the Spring '71
Mean Dreams '17
The Mind of Mr. Soames '70
Missing Girls '36
Mokey '42
Moonrise Kingdom '12▸
My Own Private Idaho '91▸
Nerve '16
The Nickel Children '05
The North Star '16
Odongo '56
The Padre '18
Pixote '81▸
Please Stand By '17
The Private Lives of Pippa Lee '09
Psych-Out '68
Quitters '16
River: The Legend of La Llorona '06
Runaway '05
Saddle Tramp '47
Safelight '15
Spenser: Ceremony '93
The Spikes Gang '74
Standing Up '13
Suburbia '83
Summer With Monica '53
Una '17
Welcome to the Rileys '10
What Lola Wants '15
Where the Day Takes You '92
Win Win '11
The Year Dolly Parton Was My Mom '11

Running

Across the Tracks '89
Billie '65
Brittany Runs a Marathon '19
Chariots of Fire '81▸
Forrest Gump '94▸
The Four Minute Mile '88
Free to Run '16
Freerunner '10
I Am Bolt '16▸
The Jesse Owens Story '84
Jim Thorpe: All American '51
The Loneliness of the Long Distance Runner '62▸
Marathon '80
Marathon Man '76▸
Meatballs '79
Miles from Nowhere '09
On the Edge '86
Overcomer '19
Patriots Day '17
Prefontaine '96
Race '16
Racing for Time '08
Run, Fatboy, Run '07
Run the Race '19
Running Brave '83
Saint Ralph '04
Wildcats '86
Without Limits '97▸

Russian Revolution

See also ***Red Scare; Russia/USSR; World War One***

Anastasia '56▸
Anastasia '97
Anastasia: The Mystery of Anna '86
Ballets Russes '05▸

▸ = rated three bones or higher

The Battleship Potemkin '25 ►
British Agent '34
Doctor Zhivago '65 ►
Doctor Zhivago '03
Nicholas and Alexandra '71
Rasputin '85 ►
Rasputin and the Empress '33 ►
Rasputin the Mad Monk '66
Reds '81 ►
Tempest '28
Ten Days That Shook the World '27 ►

Russia/USSR

***See also** Moscow; Red Scare*

Almost Holy '16 ►
Anastasia '56 ►
Anastasia '97
Anastasia: The Mystery of Anna '86
Anna '19
Anna Karenina '12
Anton Chekhov's The Duel '09
Archangel '05
The Ascent '76 ►
Assassination of Trotsky '72
Attack on Leningrad '09
Balalaika '39
Ballets Russes '05 ►
Baltic Deputy '37 ►
The Battleship Potemkin '25 ►
Beanpole '20 ►
Beyond Borders '03
Bitter Harvest '17
BloodRayne '06
The Bourne Supremacy '04 ►
Bridge of Spies '15 ►
Brigands: Chapter VII '97
The Brothers Karamazov '58 ►
Burglar '87 ►
Burnt by the Sun '94 ►
Chernobyl Diaries '12
The Cherry Orchard '99
Child 44 '15
Children of the Revolution '95
Citizen K '19
Citizen X '95 ►
Come and See '85 ►
Commissar '68 ►
Comrade X '40
Crimson Tide '95 ►
Days of Glory '43
The Deal '05
The Death of Mr. Lazarescu '05
The Death of Stalin '17 ►
Dersu Uzala '75 ►
Devil's Pass '13
A Different Loyalty '04 ►
Direct Contact '09
Disco and Atomic War '14
Doctor Zhivago '65 ►
Doctor Zhivago '03
Don't Drink the Water '69
The Double Man '67
Drums of Jeopardy '31
The Duchess of Buffalo '26
The Duelist '16
The Eagle '25 ►
East-West '99
The Edge '10
Eisenstein in Guanajuato '15
The Emperor's Candlesticks '37
The End of St. Petersburg '27 ►
Enemy at the Gates '00
Final Assignment '80
Final Score '18
First Strike '85
Frederick Forsyth's Icon '05
Freezer '14
The Gambler '97
The Girl from Petrovka '74
Goldeneye '95 ►
Golem: The Petrified Garden '93
A Good Day to Die Hard '13
Gorky Park '83 ►
Happy People: A Year in the Taiga '13 ►
Hardcore Henry '15
Hitman '07
House of Fools '02
How I Ended This Summer '10
The Hunt for Red October '90 ►
The Ice Runner '93
In Hell '03
In Tranzit '07
The Inner Circle '91 ►
The Ister '04 ►
The Italian '05
Ivan the Terrible, Part 1 '44 ►
Ivan the Terrible, Part 2 '46 ►
Jack Ryan: Shadow Recruit '14
The Jackal '97
K-19: The Widowmaker '02
Laser Mission '90
The Last Command '28 ►
The Last Station '09
Leto '19
Leviathan '14 ►
The Light Ahead '39
Little Vera '88 ►
The Loneliest Planet '12
Love and Death '75 ►
Loveless '18 ►
The Man with the Movie Camera '29 ►
Maximum Impact '18
The Mirror '75 ►
Mistresses '19
Mobius '13
Moscow Does Not Believe in Tears '80 ►
Mother '26 ►
Mother and Son '97
Mute Witness '95
My Name Is Ivan '62 ►
Never Let Me Go '53
Nicholas and Alexandra '71
Night Watch '04
No Place on Earth '12
Nostalghia '83
Our Kind of Traitor '16
The Outskirts '98 ►
Pawn Sacrifice '15
The Peacemaker '97
Phantom '13
Prisoner of the Mountains '96 ►
Rasputin '85 ►
Rasputin and the Empress '33 ►
Rasputin the Mad Monk '66
The Red and the White '68 ►
Red Heat '88
Red Joan '19
Red Sparrow '18
Reds '81 ►
A Royal Scandal '45
The Russia House '90
Russian Dolls '05
Russian Roulette '93
The Russian Woodpecker '15 ►
The Saint '97
Scarlet Empress '34 ►
Schizo '04
The Sea Gull '68
Siberia '18
Siberiade '79 ►
Since Otar Left. . . '03
A Slave of Love '78 ►
Stalingrad '94
Summer Storm '44
Taxi Blues '90 ►
Terminal Velocity '94
Theremin: An Electronic Odyssey '95 ►
The Thief '97
Torrents of Spring '90
The Truce '96 ►
2 Brothers & a Bride '03
War and Peace '56
War and Peace '68 ►
War and Peace '73
The Way Back '10
We the Living '42
The White Crow '18
White Nights '85
Window to Paris '95
The Winter War '89 ►
World War III '86
Young Catherine '91 ►

Rwanda

***See also** Africa*

Gorillas in the Mist '88 ►
Hotel Rwanda '04
Shake Hands With the Devil '07
Shake Hands With the Devil: The Journey of Romeo Dallaire '04 ►
Shooting Dogs '05
Sometimes in April '05 ►

Sail Away

***See also** Deep Blue; Go Fish; Killer Sea Critters; Mutiny; Scuba; Shipwrecked; Submarines*

Across to Singapore '28
The Adventures of Huckleberry Finn '39 ►
An Affair to Remember '57
The African Queen '51 ►
Against the Sun '15
All at Sea '57
All is Lost '13 ►
All the Brothers Were Valiant '53
America America '63
American Warship '12
And the Ship Sails On '83 ►
Anna Christie '30
Anything Goes '56
Assault on a Queen '66
Assignment to Kill '69
Atlantics '19 ►
Away All Boats '56
The Battleship Potemkin '25 ►
Beat the Devil '53 ►
Between Two Worlds '44
Beyond the Poseidon Adventure '79
The Big Broadcast of 1938 '38
The Big Game '72
Billy Budd '62 ►
Bitter Moon '92
Black Ops '07
Blast '04
Blondie Goes Latin '42
Blood Work '02
Blue, White and Perfect '42
A Blueprint for Murder '53
Boat Trip '03
The Boatniks '70
The Book of Love '16
The Bounty '84
Boy in Blue '86
Breakfast for Two '37
The Breaking Point '50 ►
Brideshead Revisited '08
Britannic '00
Cabin Boy '94
The Caine Mutiny Court Martial '88 ►
The Captain Hates the Sea '34
Captain Horatio Hornblower '51 ►
Captain Jack '98
Captain Phillips '13 ►
Captain Ron '92
Captain Salvation '27
Captains Courageous '37 ►
Captains Courageous '95
Captain's Paradise '53 ►
The Captain's Table '60
Carry On Admiral '57
Carry On Cruising '62
Carry On Jack '63
The Cat's Meow '01
Charlie Chan in Honolulu '38
Charlie Chan's Murder Cruise '40
China Seas '35 ►
Christmas in Paradise '07
The Chronicles of Narnia: The Voyage of the Dawn Treader '10
Chupacabra Terror '05
Colleen '36
Convoy '40
Counterstrike '03
A Countess from Hong Kong '67
The Crew '95
Crimson Tide '95 ►
The Curious Case of Benjamin Button '08 ►
Damn the Defiant '62 ►
Danger Beneath the Sea '02
Dangerous Charter '62
Dangerous Crossing '53
Dangerous Money '46
Das Boot '81 ►
Dead Calm '89 ►
Dead in the Water '01
Deadly Honeymoon '10
Deadly Voyage '96
The Decks Ran Red '58
The Deep '77
Deep Rising '98
Deep Waters '48
Destroyer '43 ►
Diary of a Suicide '73
Die Hard: With a Vengeance '95
Dixie Jamboree '44
Doctor at Sea '56
Dolittle '20
Don Winslow of the Coast Guard '43
Donkey Punch '08
The Dove '74
Down Periscope '96
Down to the Sea in Ships '22
Duffy '68
East of Sudan '64
The Ebb-Tide '97
Ensign Pulver '64
Erik, the Viking '65
Escape under Pressure '00
Exclusive Story '36
Failure to Launch '06
Far from Home: The Adventures of Yellow Dog '94
Fast Life '32
Feet First '30
Ferry to Hong Kong '59
Fidelio: Alice's Odyssey '14
The Fighting Sullivans '42 ►
Film Socialisme '10
The Final Countdown '80 ►
Final Voyage '99
Flat Top '52
Flight From Ashiya '64
Flight of the Intruder '90
Flipper '96 ►
Fool's Gold '08
Francis in the Navy '55
The French Atlantic Affair '79
Friday the 13th, Part 8: Jason Takes Manhattan '89
Further Up the Creek '58
Gangway '37
Gateway '38
The Ghost Ship '43
Ghost Ship '53
Ghost Ship '02
Give Me a Sailor '38
Going Overboard '89
Going Under '91
Gone Fishin' '97
Gray Lady Down '77
The Great Lover '49
The Gun Runners '58
The Hairy Ape '44
The Haunted Sea '97
Hawaii Calls '38
He Is My Brother '75
Hey! Hey! USA! '38
History Is Made at Night '37 ►
Horatio Hornblower '99 ►
Horatio Hornblower: The Adventure Continues '01 ►
The House of the Seven Hawks '59
The Hunt for Red October '90 ►
The Imposters '98
In Which We Serve '43 ►
The Incredible Mr. Limpet '64
The Incredible Petrified World '58
Isle of Forgotten Sins '43
The Jack of Diamonds '49
JAG '95
Jason and the Argonauts '00
Jaws '75 ►
Jaws 2 '78
The Jewel of the Nile '85
Juggernaut '74 ►
Kill Cruise '90
Knife in the Water '62 ►
Kon-Tiki '12
Lakeboat '00
The Last Lovecraft: Relic of Cthulhu '09
The Last of Sheila '73
The Last Voyage '60
The Legend of 1900 '98
The Legend of Sea Wolf '75
Life of Pi '12 ►
Lifeboat '44 ►
Light at the Edge of the World '71
The Lightship '86
Like Father '18
Live and Let Die '73
Loch Ness '95
Long John Silver '54
The Long Ships '64
The Long Voyage Home '40 ►
Longitude '00 ►
Lord Jim '65 ►
Lost Voyage '01
Love Affair '39 ►
Luxury Liner '48
Madison '01
The Magic Stone '95
Maiden '18 ►
Maiden Voyage: Ocean Hijack '04
A Majority of One '56
Manfish '56
Mara Maru '52
Master and Commander: The Far Side of the World '03 ►
McHale's Navy '64
Mean Creek '04 ►
Men of the Sea '35
The Mercy '19
The Mermaids of Tiburon '62
Message in a Bottle '98
Mile a Minute Love '37
Mister Roberts '55 ►
Moby Dick '11
Monkey Business '31 ►
Moran of the Lady Letty '22
Morituri '65 ►
Morning Light '08
Muppet Treasure Island '96
Mutiny '52
The Mutiny of the Elsinore '39
Mutiny on the Bounty '35 ►
Mutiny on the Bounty '62
New Moon '40
A Night to Remember '58 ►
The Odyssey '97
One Crazy Summer '86
One Way Passage '32
Operation Petticoat '59 ►
Out to Sea '97
Oxford Blues '84
The Perfect Storm '00
Pirate Radio '09
Pirates of the Caribbean: At World's End '07
Pirates of the Caribbean: On Stranger Tides '11
Pirates of the Caribbean: The Curse of the Black Pearl '03 ►
The Poseidon Adventure '72
The Poseidon Adventure '05
The Princess Comes Across '36 ►
Pursuit of the Graf Spee '57
Reap the Wild Wind '42
[REC] 4: Apocalypse '14
Red Ensign '34
The Reef '10
Rich and Strange '32
Romancing the Stone '84 ►
Run Silent, Run Deep '58 ►
Safe Harbor '09
Sail a Crooked Ship '61
The Sand Pebbles '66 ►
Sea Chase '55
The Sea Ghost '31
Seven Seas to Calais '62
Seven Were Saved '47
Shades of Fear '93
She Creature '01
Ship Ahoy '42
Ship of Fools '65 ►
Sinbad: Legend of the Seven Seas '03
Sinbad, the Sailor '47 ►
Sink the Bismarck '60 ►
Slave '09
Slave Ship '37
Souls at Sea '37
Speed 2: Cruise Control '97
Spiders 2: Breeding Ground '01
Stand by for Action '42
Stargate: Continuum '08
Steamboat Bill, Jr. '28 ►
Steamboat Round the Bend '35
The Story of Three Loves '53
Swashbuckler '76
The Talented Mr. Ripley '99
Tampico '44
Task Force '49
Their Own Desire '29
They Were Expendable '45 ►
Think Fast, Mr. Moto '37
The 13th Warrior '99
Three Daring Daughters '48
Three Men in a Boat '56
Thunder in Paradise '93
Tiger Shark '32
Titanic 2 '10
Titanic '53 ►
Titanic '96
Titanic '97 ►
To Gillian on Her 37th Birthday '96
To Have & Have Not '44 ►
Today We Live '33
Torpedo Run '58
Treasure Island '12
The Treasure of Jamaica Reef '74
Treasure Planet '02
The Triangle '01
Triangle '09
Tugboat Annie '33 ►
2103: Deadly Wake '97
Under Siege '92
The Unsinkable Molly Brown '64 ►
Up the Creek '84
Valhalla Rising '09
The Viking '28
Virus '98
Visitors '03
Voyage of the Damned '76 ►
Wake of the Red Witch '49
Wake Up and Dream '46
Waterworld '95
The Weight of Water '00
We're Not Dressing '34 ►
Wetbacks '56
White Squall '96
The Wild Life '16
Wild Oranges '24
Wild Orchids '28
Wind '92
Windbag the Sailor '36
Windjammer '37
Winds of Terror '01
Witch Who Came from the Sea '76
The Woman Between '31
Woman of Desire '93
The World in His Arms '52
The Wreck of the Mary Deare '59
Yankee Clipper '27

St. Peterburg (Russia)

***See** Russia/USSR*

St. Petersburg (Russia)

Anastasia '97
Anna Karenina '35 ►
Anna Karenina '48
Anna Karenina '96
Anna Karenina '00
Brother '97
Cold Souls '09
The Iris Effect '04
Onegin '99
2 Brothers & a Bride '03
Water '05

Saints

***See also** Religion*

Bernadette '90
Brother Sun, Sister Moon '73
The Flowers of St. Francis '50 ►
Francesco '93
Joan of Arc '48
Millions '05 ►
Miracle of Our Lady of Fatima '52
My Mother's Smile '02
Passion of Joan of Arc '28 ►

► = rated three bones or higher

Saint Joan '57
St. Patrick: The Irish Legend '00
Sebastiane '79 ▶
The Song of Bernadette '43 ▶
Therese '86 ▶
Therese: The Story of Saint Therese of Lisieux '04
A Time for Miracles '80

Salespeople

See also Corporate Shenanigans

Adventures in Babysitting '87
The Alarmist '98
Alien Trespass '09
American Honey '16
The Assassination of Richard Nixon '05
Bathtubs Over Broadway '18 ▶
Believe '07
Betrayed '44
Big Fish '03 ▶
The Big Kahuna '00
Breakfast of Champions '98
Cadillac Man '90
Call Me Mrs. Miracle '10
Car Babes '06
Cedar Rapids '11 ▶
Death of a Salesman '51 ▶
Death of a Salesman '86 ▶
Demoted '11
Diamond Men '01 ▶
El Crimen Perfecto '04 ▶
Failure to Launch '06
The Fan '96
Feudin', Fussin', and A-Fightin' '48
First Snow '07
The First Time '52
Foul Play '78 ▶
The Founder '17 ▶
Gigantic '08
Glengarry Glen Ross '92 ▶
A Good Baby '99
The Good Girl '02 ▶
The Goods: Live Hard, Sell Hard '09
Great World of Sound '07
Grilled '06
Happily Ever After '04
Hot Cars '56
The Iceman Cometh '60 ▶
The Iceman Cometh '73
In Fabric '18
Jingle All the Way '96
The Joneses '09
Last Holiday '06
Lisboa '99
Love and Other Drugs '10
The Magnificent Two '67
The Man '05
Me and You and Everyone We Know '05 ▶
Meet Bill '07
Moscow on the Hudson '84 ▶
The Music Man '62 ▶
My First Mister '01
Nathalie Granger '72
Night School '18
100 Mile Rule '02
The Other Side of Hope '17
Our Man in Havana '59 ▶
Pennies from Heaven '81 ▶
Penny Princess '52
Phat Girlz '06
Prescription Thugs '16
Pretty Woman '90 ▶
The Rainmaker '56 ▶
Re-Generation '04
Risk '00
Role Models '08 ▶
The Sensation of Sight '06
Side Effects '05
Small Time '14
The Smell of Success '09
Spooner '08
Suckerfish '99
Super Sucker '03
Terror Tract '00
Thin Ice '12
Tin Men '87
Torremolinos 73 '03
Trojan Eddie '96 ▶
Valley Inn '14

Salvation Army

Guys and Dolls '55 ▶
Major Barbara '41 ▶

Samurai

See also Japan

The Adventures of Buckaroo Banzai Across the Eighth Dimension '84 ▶
American Samurai '92
Ashura '05
Azumi '03 ▶
Blade of the Immortal '17
Blind Fury '90
Blood: The Last Vampire '09
The Bushido Blade '80
Bushido: The Cruel Code of the Samurai '63 ▶
Dororo '07
Five Element Ninjas '82
47 Ronin '13
47 Ronin, Part 1 '42 ▶
47 Ronin, Part 2 '42 ▶
Ghost Dog: The Way of the Samurai '99
Ghostwarrior '86
Goyokin '69 ▶
Hana: The Tale of a Reluctant Samurai '07
Hara-Kiri: Death of a Samurai '11
Harakiri '62 ▶
Heaven & Earth '90 ▶
The Hidden Blade '04
House Where Evil Dwells '82
Hunter in the Dark '80
Ichi '08
Kibakichi 2 '04
Kibakichi '04
Kill! '68
Kill Bill Vol. 1 '03 ▶
Kubo and the Two Strings '16 ▶
Kuroneko '68 ▶
The Last Samurai '03 ▶
Lone Wolf and Cub '72
Lone Wolf and Cub: Baby Cart to Hades '72
Moon over Tao '97 ▶
The Princess Blade '02
Rashomon '51 ▶
Red Sun '71
Revenge '64
Ronin Gai '90
Samurai Banners '69
Samurai Fiction '99 ▶
Sanjuro '62 ▶
The Sea is Watching '02 ▶
Seven Samurai '54 ▶
Shinobi '05 ▶
Shogun '80 ▶
Shogun Assassin 2: Lightning Swords of Death '73 ▶
Shogun Assassin '80
Sukiyaki Western Django '08
Sword of Doom '67 ▶
Sword of the Beast '65 ▶
Taboo '99
Throne of Blood '57 ▶
The Twilight Samurai '02 ▶
When the Last Sword is Drawn '02 ▶
The Wolverine '13
Yojimbo '61 ▶
Zatoichi '03 ▶
Zatoichi: Master Ichi and a Chest of Gold '64
Zatoichi: The Blind Swordsman and the Chess Expert '65
Zatoichi: The Blind Swordsman's Vengeance '66
Zatoichi: The Life and Opinion of Masseur Ichi '62
Zatoichi *vs.* Yojimbo '70 ▶

San Diego

Anchorman: The Legend of Ron Burgundy '04
Antwone Fisher '02 ▶
The Cat's Meow '01
Chubasco '67
Dive Bomber '41 ▶
Flight Command '40
Flirting with Disaster '95 ▶
Gardens of the Night '08
In the Navy '41
My Blue Heaven '90
My Son, My Son, What Have Ye Done '09
Ready? OK! '08
Sideways '04 ▶
Tiger Shark '32
Top Gun '86
Traffic '00 ▶
Tumbleweeds '98
29th & Gay '05

San Francisco

See also Earthquakes

Address Unknown '44
Against the Wall '04
All About You '01
All Dogs Go to Heaven 2 '95
Always Be My Maybe '19
The Amazing Mrs. Holiday '43
And Then Came Lola '09
Armistead Maupin's More Tales of the City '97
Armistead Maupin's Tales of the City '93
Around June '08
Aussie and Ted's Great Adventure '09
Babies '10 ▶
The Bachelor '99
Barbary Coast '35 ▶
Basic Instinct '92
Behind That Curtain '29
Beyond the Door '75
Big Trouble in Little China '86
Blonde Ice '48
Blue Jasmine '13 ▶
Bullitt '68 ▶
Cardiac Arrest '74
Chan Is Missing '82 ▶
Charlie Chan at Treasure Island '39
Cherish '02
The Chinatown Kid '78
The Chinese Ring '47
Christmas Comes Home to Canaan '11
Cocaine and Blue Eyes '83
Confessions of a Sociopathic Social Climber '05
Confessions of an Opium Eater '62
The Conversation '74 ▶
Copycat '95
The Cradle of Courage '20
Dawn of the Planet of the Apes '14 ▶
Days of Wine and Roses '62 ▶
The Dead Pool '88
Dealing: Or the Berkeley-to-Boston Forty-Brick Lost-Bag Blues '72
Desperate Measures '98
Dim Sum: A Little Bit of Heart '85 ▶
Dirty Harry '71 ▶
Disappearing in America '08
Dr. Dolittle '98
Dr. Jekyll's Dungeon of Death '82
Doctor Who '96
Dogfight '91 ▶
Dogwatch '97
Dopamine '03
Dream for an Insomniac '96
Dream with the Fishes '97
The Enforcer '76
The Etruscan Smile '19
An Eye for an Eye '81
The Fan '96
Final Analysis '92
Fisherman's Wharf '39
The Five-Year Engagement '12
Flame of the Barbary Coast '45
Flower Drum Song '61
Fog Over Frisco '34
Fools '70
40 Days and 40 Nights '02
48 Hrs. '82 ▶
Foul Play '78 ▶
Four Christmases '08
Freebie & the Bean '74
Frisco Jenny '32
Frisco Kid '35
The Frisco Kid '79
The Game '97 ▶
George of the Jungle '97 ▶
Going the Distance '10
Golden Gate '93
Groove '00 ▶
Guinevere '99 ▶
Haiku Tunnel '00
The Hatchet Man '32
Hello, Frisco, Hello '43
Hereafter '10
His and Her Christmas '05
Homeward Bound 2: Lost in San Francisco '96
I Remember Mama '48 ▶
The Impatient Years '44
Inside Out '15 ▶
Invasion of the Body Snatchers '78 ▶
Ip Man 4: The Finale '19
It Came from Beneath the Sea '55 ▶
Jade '95
Just like Heaven '05
Just One Night '00
Key to the City '50
Kiss Them for Me '57
Kuffs '92
La Mission '09
The Last Black Man in San Francisco '19 ▶
The Laughing Policeman '74
The Law and the Lady '51
Life Tastes Good '99
The Lineup '58
Little City '97
The Lively Set '64
Magnum Force '73
The Maltese Falcon '41 ▶
The Man Who Cheated Himself '50
MDMA '18
Medicine for Melancholy '08
Mega Shark Vs. Giant Octopus '09
Memoirs of an Invisible Man '92
The Men's Club '86
Meteor Storm '10
Metro '96
Milk '08 ▶
Mission '00
Mr. Ricco '75
The Mistress of Spices '05
Monster in the Closet '86
My Silent Partner '06
Nightmare in Blood '75
Nim's Island '08
Nina Takes a Lover '94
Nine Months '95
No Escape '53
No One Sleeps '01
Nob Hill '45
Nora Prentiss '47
Old San Francisco '27
On the Road '12
The Other End of the Line '08
Pacific Heights '90 ▶
Playing Mona Lisa '00
Poltergeist: The Legacy '96
The Presidio '88
The Princess Diaries '01
The Princess of Nebraska '07
The Pursuit of Happyness '06
Quitters '16
Race Street '48
Rated X '00
Rise of the Planet of the Apes '11 ▶
The Rock '96 ▶
The Saint Strikes Back '39
San Francisco '36 ▶
The San Francisco Story '52
San Franpsycho '06
Screaming Mimi '58
Serendipity '01
Serial '80 ▶
Shadows Over Chinatown '46
The Shock '23
Shut Up Little Man! An Audio Misadventure '11
The Single Standard '29
The Sisters '38 ▶
Skidoo '68
A Smile Like Yours '96
Smooch '11
The Sniper '52
So I Married an Axe Murderer '93
Some Prefer Cake '97
Someone Great '19
Starlift '51
Stranded '35
Sucker Free City '05 ▶
Sudden Impact '83
Sweet November '01
The Sweetest Thing '02
Ticker '01
Time After Time '79 ▶
Times of Harvey Milk '83 ▶
True Crime '99
Tweek City '05
Twisted '04
Under One Roof '02
Up for Grabs '05
Vertigo '58 ▶
Visions of Murder '93
Walk a Crooked Mile '48
War '07
Waterfront '44
We Were Here '11
The Wedding Planner '01
West Is West '87
What's Up, Doc? '72 ▶
The Wild Parrots of Telegraph Hill '03 ▶
Wildflowers '99
The Woman on Pier 13 '50
Woman On the Run '50
Woman on Top '00
You Kill Me '07 ▶
The Zodiac '05
Zodiac '07
The Zodiac Killer '71

Sanity Check

See Doctors & Hospitals & Shrinks

Satanism

See also Demons & Devils; Occult

Amazon Jail '85
Asylum of Satan '72
The Babysitter '17
Bad Dreams '88
Beast of the Yellow Night '70
Beyond the Door 3 '91
The Black Cat '34 ▶
Black Roses '88
Black Sunday '60 ▶
Bless the Child '00
Blood Orgy of the She-Devils '74
The Bloodsuckers '70
The Brotherhood of Satan '71
The Chosen '77
The Convent '00
The Crimson Cult '68
The Crow: Wicked Prayer '05
Damien: Omen 2 '78
The Demon Lover '77
Demonoid, Messenger of Death '81
The Devil & Daniel Webster '41 ▶
The Devil Rides Out '68 ▶
The Devils '71 ▶
The Devil's Daughter '91
Devil's Due '14
The Devil's Nightmare '71
The Devil's Partner '58
The Devil's Possessed '74
The Devil's Prey '01
Devil's Rain '75
Devil's Son-in-Law '77
Disciple of Death '72
Doctor Faustus '68
Dominion: Prequel to the Exorcist '05
Equinox '71 ▶
Eternal Evil '87
Evilspeak '82
Exorcism '74
The Exorcist '73 ▶
The Exorcist 2: The Heretic '77
Eye of the Demon '87
Family Reunion '79
Fear No Evil '80
The Final Conflict '81
Ghoulies 4 '93
Hail Satan? '19 ▶
Hors Satan '11
House of the Black Death '65
I Don't Want to Be Born '75
I Drink Your Blood '71
Inferno '80
Invitation to Hell '82
Invitation to Hell '84
Jaws of Satan '81
Jezebeth '11
Land of the Minotaur '77
Leaves from Satan's Book '21
A Little Bit of Soul '97
Lost Souls '00
The Man and the Monster '65
The Mangler '94
The Mephisto Waltz '71 ▶
Midnight '81
Midnight's Child '93
Mind, Body & Soul '92
Necromancer: Satan's Servant '88
Night Visitor '89
976-EVIL 2: The Astral Factor '91
976-EVIL '88
The Ninth Gate '99
The Occultist '89
Oh, God! You Devil '84
The Omen '76
One of Them '03
Prime Evil '88
Prince of Darkness '87
The Pyx '73 ▶
Race with the Devil '75
Ready or Not '19 ▶
The Relic '96
Revenge '86
Rosemary's Baby '68 ▶
Rosemary's Baby '14
Satanic Panic '19
The Satanic Rites of Dracula '73
Satan's Cheerleaders '77
Satan's School for Girls '73
The Sentinel '76
Servants of Twilight '91
The Seventh Victim '43 ▶
Sheitan '06
Shock 'Em Dead '90
The Soul Guardians '98
Spellbinder '88
Sugar Cookies '77
To the Devil, a Daughter '76
12/12/12 '12
Vampire Clan '02
The Visitor '80
Warlock '91
Warlock: The Armageddon '93
Weirdsville '07
Witchcraft 6: The Devil's Mistress '94
Witchcraft 10: Mistress of the Craft '98
Witchcraft '88

Satire & Parody

See also Black Comedy; Comedy; Genre Spoofs

Abbott and Costello Go to Mars '53
The Adventures of Sherlock Holmes' Smarter Brother '78 ▶
Aftershock '88
Airplane 2: The Sequel '82
Airplane! '80 ▶
An Alan Smithee Film: Burn, Hollywood, Burn '97
Alex in Wonderland '70
Alien Trespass '09
All Out Dysfunktion! '16
All Through the Night '42 ▶
All You Need Is Cash '78 ▶
The Alphabet Murders '65
Amazing Dr. Clitterhouse '38 ▶
Amazon Women on the Moon '87
An American Carol '08
American Dreamz '06
American Psycho '99
Americathon '79
. . .And God Spoke '94
And Now a Word From Our Sponsor '13
Andy Warhol's Dracula '74 ▶

- Andy Warhol's Frankenstein '74
- Animal Farm '55 ►
- Animal Farm '99
- Any Wednesday '66
- The Apartment '60 ►
- Arizona '18
- As Young As You Feel '51 ►
- The Associate '79
- Attack of the Robots '66
- Attack the Gas Station '99
- Auntie Mame '58 ►
- Austin Powers: International Man of Mystery '97 ►
- Austin Powers 2: The Spy Who Shagged Me '99 ►
- Baberellas '03
- Bad Medicine '85
- Bad Parents '12
- Bamboozled '00
- Bananas '71 ►
- Barney's Version '10
- Barry McKenzie Holds His Own '74
- Basic Training '86
- Beatriz at Dinner '17
- Beautiful '00
- Behind the Mask: The Rise of Leslie Vernon '06
- Being There '79 ►
- Best in Show '00 ►
- The Best Man '64 ►
- Beyond the Valley of the Dolls '70
- Beyond Therapy '86
- B.F.'s Daughter '48
- The Big Bus '76
- Big Deal on Madonna Street '58 ►
- The Big Picture '89
- The Big Tease '99
- Big Trouble in Little China '86
- Black and White in Color '76 ►
- Bob & Carol & Ted & Alice '69
- Bob Roberts '92 ►
- Bodied '17 ►
- The Bogus Witch Project '00
- The Bonfire of the Vanities '90
- Boogie Vision '77
- Born in East L.A. '87
- Boss '74
- Boy Meets Girl '38 ►
- The Brady Bunch Movie '95 ►
- Bread and Chocolate '73 ►
- Breakfast of Champions '98
- Breaking Wind '12
- Bring It On '00
- Britannia Hospital '82
- Buffalo Soldiers '01
- Bullshot '83
- Bulworth '98 ►
- The 'Burbs '89
- But I'm a Cheerleader '99
- Butter '12
- Call Me Lucky '15 ►
- Camera Buff '79
- Canadian Bacon '94
- The Candidate '72 ►
- Candy '68
- Carry On Cleo '65
- Carry On Dick '75
- Casa de mi Padre '12
- Casino Royale '67
- Cave Women on Mars '08
- Caveman '81
- CB4: The Movie '93
- Cecil B. Demented '00
- Champagne for Caesar '50 ►
- Chaos Theory '08
- The Cheap Detective '78 ►
- Cherry Falls '00
- Children of the Revolution '95
- Chronically Unfeasible '00
- Citizen Ruth '96
- Clockwise '86
- A Clockwork Orange '71 ►
- Club Dread '04
- The Coca-Cola Kid '84 ►
- Cold Turkey '71 ►
- Coup de Grace '78
- Creature from the Haunted Sea '60
- Dark Habits '84
- Dark Star '74 ►
- Darling Lili '70
- Date Movie '06
- The Day Shall Come '19
- A Day Without a Mexican '04
- Dead Men Don't Die '91
- Dead Men Don't Wear Plaid '82
- The Deal '08
- Deal of the Century '83
- The Death of Stalin '17 ►
- Deathrow Gameshow '88
- Decline and Fall...of a Birdwatcher '68
- Destination Mars '06
- Destination: Outer Space '10
- Diary of a Chambermaid '64 ►
- Dick '99 ►
- The Discreet Charm of the Bourgeoisie '72 ►
- Don't Be a Menace to South Central While Drinking Your Juice in the Hood '95
- Down and Out in Beverly Hills '86
- Down to Earth '47
- Down Under '86
- Downsizing '17
- Dracula: Dead and Loving It '95
- Dragnet '87
- Drop Dead Gorgeous '99
- Easy Wheels '89
- EDtv '99
- Election '99 ►
- 11 Harrowhouse '74 ►
- Erik the Viking '89
- Evil Roy Slade '71 ►
- Executive Koala '06 ►
- Exposed '03
- The Family Game '83 ►
- The Fat Spy '66
- Fatal Instinct '93
- Fay Grim '06
- Fear of a Black Hat '94
- Ferocious Female Freedom Fighters '88
- Fido '06
- The Final Girls '15
- First Family '80
- The Flaming Teen-Age '56
- Flesh Gordon '72
- Floundering '94
- Forgotten Silver '96 ►
- The Fortune Cookie '66 ►
- Four Lions '10
- The French Minister '13
- The French Touch '54
- The Freshman '90
- The Front '76 ►
- Fuse '03
- Gabriel Over the White House '33 ►
- Galactic Gigolo '87
- Galaxina '80
- Geek Maggot Bingo '83
- Genevieve '53 ►
- Gentlemen Prefer Blondes '53 ►
- Get to Know Your Rabbit '72
- Girls in Prison '94
- Go for Zucker '05
- God Bless America '11
- Going Berserk '83
- Going Places '74 ►
- Going Postal '98
- Gosford Park '01 ►
- Greaser's Palace '72
- The Great Dictator '40 ►
- The Great White Hype '96
- Greener Grass '19
- The Groove Tube '72
- Gulliver's Travels '95
- Gumshoe '72
- Gypsy '75
- Hail the Conquering Hero '44 ►
- Hairspray '88 ►
- Half a Sixpence '67
- Hamlet 2 '08 ►
- Happiness '32
- Hard Core Logo '96
- A Haunted House '13
- The Haunted World of El Superbeasto '09
- Heaven Can Wait '43 ►
- Heavens Above '63 ►
- Heckler '08
- Hexed '93
- High Anxiety '77
- High Hopes '88 ►
- High School High '96
- High Season '88
- Hijacking Hollywood '97
- History of the World: Part 1 '81
- Hollywood North '03
- Home Movies '79
- Horror in the Wind '08
- The Horror of Frankenstein '70
- The Hospital '71 ►
- Hot Shots! '91 ►
- Hot Shots! Part Deux '93
- The Hound of the Baskervilles '77
- How I Got into College '89
- The Hungover Games '14
- I Feel Pretty '18
- I Love You, Alice B. Toklas! '68
- I Married a Vampire '87
- I Was a Zombie for the FBI '82
- I Was Born But. . . '32 ►
- Idiocracy '06
- I'll Do Anything '93
- I'm All Right Jack '59 ►
- I'm Gonna Git You Sucka '88 ►
- I'm So Excited '13
- In a World... '13 ►
- In the Loop '09
- The Incredible Shrinking Woman '81
- Incredibly Strange Creatures Who Stopped Living and Became Mixed-Up Zombies '63
- Intern '00
- The Interview '14
- Invasion Earth: The Aliens Are Here! '87
- Irma Vep '96
- Is There Sex After Death? '71 ►
- J-Men Forever! '79 ►
- Jabberwocky '77
- Jail Party '04
- Jailbait! '00
- Jay and Silent Bob Strike Back '01
- Jekyll & Hyde. . . Together Again '82
- Jesus Christ Vampire Hunter '01
- Jimmy Vestvood: Amerikan Hero '16
- Johnny Dangerously '84
- The Joneses '09
- Kentucky Fried Movie '77 ►
- Kids in the Hall: Brain Candy '96
- The King of Hearts '66 ►
- An L.A. Minute '18
- The Ladies' Man '61
- The Landlord '70
- Lawn Dogs '96
- Legalese '98
- Leon the Pig Farmer '93
- Leviathan '14 ►
- The Lobster '16
- Lola Colt '67
- Lord Love a Duck '66
- Love and a .45 '94
- Love and Death '75 ►
- Love at Stake '87
- The Loved One '65
- MacGruber '10
- Mad City '97
- Mad Mission 3 '84
- Mad Monster Party '68
- Malibu's Most Wanted '03
- Mammuth '10
- Man Bites Dog '91
- The Man in the White Suit '51 ►
- The Man Who Came to Dinner '41 ►
- The Man with Bogart's Face '80
- The Man with Two Brains '83 ►
- Maps to the Stars '14
- Mars Attacks! '96
- The Men Who Stare at Goats '09
- The Meteor Man '93
- Mickey '17
- A Mighty Wind '03 ►
- The Milky Way '68 ►
- Miss Cast Away '04
- The Missionary '82
- Mr. Write '92
- Modern Times '36 ►
- Monarch of the Moon '05
- Monster in a Box '92 ►
- A Monster in Paris '11
- The Monster of Phantom Lake '06
- Monty Python and the Holy Grail '75 ►
- Monty Python's Life of Brian '79 ►
- Monty Python's The Meaning of Life '83 ►
- More Wild, Wild West '80
- The Mouse on the Moon '62 ►
- The Mouse That Roared '59 ►
- Movers and Shakers '85
- Movie, Movie '78
- Murder by Death '76
- My Best Friend Is a Vampire '88
- My Best Girl '27 ►
- My Piece of the Pie '11
- Myra Breckinridge '70
- Mystery Science Theater 3000: The Movie '96
- The Naked Gun: From the Files of Police Squad '88 ►
- Naked in New York '93
- Nasty Habits '77
- The National Health '73
- National Lampoon Goes to the Movies '81
- National Lampoon's Animal House '78 ►
- National Lampoon's Loaded Weapon 1 '93
- Natural Born Killers '94
- Night Patrol '85
- 99 & 44/100 Dead '74
- No News from God '01
- Northanger Abbey '87
- No. 3 '97
- The Nutty Professor '63 ►
- The Oath '18
- Office Space '98
- On the Avenue '37 ►
- Open Season '95
- Orchestra Rehearsal '78
- Oscar '91
- The Other Side of the Wind '18
- Outlaw Prophet '01
- Over 21 '45
- Paranormal Movie '13
- Parasite '19 ►
- Pardners '56
- Partners '82
- P.C.U. '94
- The Pentagon Wars '98
- Personal Services '87
- Petticoat Planet '96
- Phantom of Liberty '74 ►
- The Pink Chiquitas '86
- Pipe Dream '02
- The Player '92 ►
- Polyester '81
- The Positively True Adventures of the Alleged Texas Cheerleader-Murdering Mom '93 ►
- Pray TV '80
- The President's Analyst '67 ►
- Primary Colors '98
- Prime Time '77
- The Princess Bride '87 ►
- A Private Function '84
- The Producers '68 ►
- Purana Mandir '84 ►
- Putney Swope '69 ►
- The Rage In Placid Lake '03
- Rat Pfink a Boo-Boo '66
- Ready to Wear '94
- Real Men '87
- Red Garters '54
- Red Shadow '01
- Reno 911! Miami '07
- Rentadick '72
- Repentance '87 ►
- Repossessed '90
- Return of Captain Invincible '83
- The Return of Spinal Tap '92
- Ricky 1 '88
- Ring of the Musketeers '93
- The Riot Club '15
- The Rise and Rise of Michael Rimmer '70
- Robin Hood: Men in Tights '93
- The Rocky Horror Picture Show '75 ►
- Romeo Is Bleeding '93
- Rosalie Goes Shopping '89 ►
- The Royal Bed '31
- The Ruling Class '72 ►
- Running Mates '92 ►
- Running Mates '00
- Sallah '63 ►
- Salvation Boulevard '11
- Samurai Fiction '99 ►
- Saved! '04
- Scary Movie '00
- Scary Movie 4 '06
- Scary Movie 5 '13
- Schizopolis '97
- School for Scoundrels '60 ►
- Scream '96 ►
- Scream 2 '97 ►
- Scream 3 '00
- Scrooged '88
- Search and Destroy '94
- The Second Civil War '97
- Second Time Lucky '84
- Seduction of Mimi '72 ►
- Serial '80 ►
- Serial Mom '94 ►
- Series 7: The Contenders '01
- A Session with The Committee '68
- Shampoo '75
- A Shock to the System '90 ►
- Shoot or Be Shot '02
- Shriek If You Know What I Did Last Friday the 13th '00
- Sidekick '05
- Silent Movie '76
- Silver Case '11
- Silver City '04
- Sink or Swim '97
- Slammer Girls '87
- Slap Her, She's French '02
- Sleeper '73 ►
- Smile '75 ►
- S.O.B. '81
- Son of Morning '11
- Sorry to Bother You '18
- Soul Plane '04
- Spaceballs '87
- Spaced Out '80
- Spaceship '81
- The Specials '00 ►
- Spirit of '76 '91
- Spy Hard '96
- Stan Helsing '09
- Starsky & Hutch '04
- The Starving Games '13
- Stay Tuned '92
- Stiff Upper Lips '96
- Straight to Hell '87
- Strange Invaders '83 ►
- Streetfight '75
- Subversion '79
- Sullivan's Travels '41 ►
- Sunset '88
- SuperGuy: Behind the Cape '02
- Suppose They Gave a War and Nobody Came? '70
- Surf Nazis Must Die '87
- Surge of Power: The Stuff of Heroes '04
- Swimming with Sharks '94 ►
- Sympathy for the Devil '70
- Tamara Drewe '10
- Tanner '88 '88 ►
- Tanner on Tanner '04
- Tapeheads '89
- Tarzeena: Queen of Kong Island '08
- Team America: World Police '04 ►
- Thank You for Smoking '06
- Thanks a Million '35
- They Came Together '14
- They Live '88
- 30 Nights of Paranormal Activity with the Devil Inside the Girl with the Dragon Tattoo '12
- This Is Spinal Tap '84 ►
- The Thrill of It All! '63
- Tim and Eric's Billion Dollar Movie '12
- To Be or Not to Be '83
- Tom and Francie '05 ►
- Too Many Crooks '59
- Top Secret! '84 ►
- Trailer, the Movie '99
- Transylvania 6-5000 '85
- Trash '70
- Trial & Error '62
- Tropic Thunder '08 ►
- True Stories '86 ►
- Trust Me '13
- Tunnelvision '76
- The TV Set '06
- 2001: A Space Travesty '00
- UHF '89
- Ultrachrist! '03
- Undercover Brother '02
- (Untitled) '09
- Up from the Depths '79
- Up the Academy '80
- Vacuuming Completely Nude in Paradise '01
- Vanity Fair '99
- Velvet Buzzsaw '19
- A Very Brady Sequel '96
- Very Important Person '61
- The Villain Still Pursued Her '41
- Virgin High '90
- Voyage of the Rock Aliens '87
- Waiting for Guffman '96
- Walker '87
- Walking Deceased '15
- War, Inc. '08
- War Machine '17
- Watermelon Man '70
- Weapons of Mass Distraction '97 ►
- What to Do in Case of Fire '02
- What's Up, Hideous Sun Demon? '83
- What's Up, Tiger Lily? '66 ►
- The Wheeler Dealers '63 ►
- When Nature Calls '85
- When Willie Comes Marching Home '50 ►
- Where in the World Is Osama Bin Laden? '06
- Where the Buffalo Roam '80
- Where's Marlowe? '98
- The White Sheik '52 ►
- Wholly Moses! '80
- Who's Who '78
- Wild, Wild West Revisited '79
- Will Success Spoil Rock Hunter? '57
- Window to Paris '95
- Without a Clue '88
- The Worm Eaters '77
- Xala '75 ►
- You'll Find Out '40
- Young Doctors in Love '82
- Young Frankenstein '74 ►
- Zachariah '70
- Zarkorr! The Invader '96
- Zelig '83 ►
- Zeta One '69
- Zoolander '01
- Zorro, the Gay Blade '81

Savannah

See also American South

- Crime and Punishment in Suburbia '00
- Forces of Nature '99
- The Gingerbread Man '97
- The Legend of Bagger Vance '00
- Midnight in the Garden of Good and Evil '97
- Scarlett '94

Savants

See also Mental Retardation

- Being There '79 ►
- Champagne for Caesar '50 ►
- Charly '68 ►
- Doctor Dolittle '67

► = rated three bones or higher

Forrest Gump '94 ▶
Malcolm '86
Mercury Rising '98
Rain Man '88 ▶
Tony Draws a Horse '51

Scams, Stings & Cons

See also Heists

Abbott and Costello Meet the Keystone Kops '54
Adios Amigo '75
After the Fox '66
The Amazing Mr. X '48
American Buffalo '95
American Hustle '13 ▶
Angel-A '05
Another You '91
The Art of the Steal '13
Assault on a Queen '66
Back in Business '06
Backflash '01
Bad Company '02
A Bag of Hammers '11
The Bannen Way '10
Beautiful Joe '00
Bedtime Story '63
Best Laid Plans '99
Best of the Badmen '50
Beyond a Reasonable Doubt '56
The Big Bounce '04
The Big Lebowski '97 ▶
The Big Squeeze '96
Big Trouble '86
Billionaire Boys Club '87
Billionaire Boys Club '18
Birds & the Bees '56
Birthday Girl '02
Blackheart '98
Blackout '54
Blonde Crazy '31
Blue Murder at St. Trinian's '56 ▶
Bottle Rocket '95
The Bride Goes Wild '48
Bringing Up Bobby '11
The Brothers Bloom '09
The Brothers Grimm '05
Brown's Requiem '98
Buffaloed '20
Bunco Squad '50
Burning Down the House '01
Butterfly Affair '71
Candleshoe '78
Capital '12
Capricorn One '78 ▶
Carancho '10
Cartier Affair '84
Casino '95 ▶
Catch Me a Spy '71
Catch Me If You Can '02
Cause for Alarm '51
Chameleon Street '89 ▶
The Charmer '87
Cheech and Chong: Things Are Tough All Over '82
Children On Their Birthdays '02
Chinatown '74 ▶
Choke '08
Circus '00
City of Ghosts '03
Cleaverville '07
Club Fed '90
Color Me Kubrick '05
The Color of Money '86 ▶
The Con Artists '80
Confidence '03
Consenting Adults '92
The Conversation '74 ▶
Cops and Robbers '73
Cotton Comes to Harlem '70 ▶
Crack-Up '46
Criminal '04
The Crooked Web '55
Croupier '97 ▶
Curly Sue '91
Dangerous Summer '82
Dark City '50
Dead Heat on a Merry-Go-Round '66 ▶
The Dead Pool '88
Deadfall '93
The Deal '05
The Deal '08
Dear God '96
Death Defying Acts '07
Deception '92
Deception '08
Deep Crimson '96
Dennis the Menace Strikes Again '98
The Desperate Trail '94
Diggstown '92
Dirty Rotten Scoundrels '88 ▶
The Distinguished Gentleman '92
Dudley Do-Right '99
Elmer Gantry '60 ▶
Every Day's a Holiday '38
Everything's Gone Green '06
F/X 2: The Deadly Art of Illusion '91
F/X '86 ▶
Fakers '04
False Pretenses '04
The Family Holiday '07
Fargo '96 ▶
Female On the Beach '55
Fierce Creatures '96
A Fish Called Wanda '88 ▶
Fitzwilly '67
$5 a Day '08
Fix '08
Flim-Flam Man '67
Focus '15
For Better or Worse '95
The Fortune Cookie '66 ▶
The Fourth Protocol '87 ▶
The 4th Tenor '02
Framed '90
The Frighteners '96
Gambit '12
Gang Related '96
The Gay Falcon '41
Get Shorty '95 ▶
Glengarry Glen Ross '92 ▶
Going Postal '10
Gone Fishin' '97
Good Neighbor Sam '64 ▶
The Good Samaritan '12
Goodbye, Lover '99
Goodnight for Justice: Queen of Hearts '13
Great Bank Hoax '78
The Great Diamond Robbery '53
The Great White Hype '96
Great World of Sound '07
Green Card '90
The Grifters '90 ▶
The Handmaiden '16 ▶
Hard to Handle '33
Harry & Walter Go to New York '76
Heartbreakers '01
Hi Diddle Diddle '43
The Hoax '06
Hold Your Man '33 ▶
The Honeymoon Machine '61
Hooray for Love '35
Hopscotch '80 ▶
The Hot Rock '70 ▶
House of Games '87 ▶
Housesitter '92
The Hustle '19
I Got the Hook-Up '98
I Love Melvin '53
I Love You Again '40 ▶
I Love You Phillip Morris '10
Il Bidone '55
In the Soup '92
The Inspectors 2: A Shred of Evidence '00
Invasion of the Space Preachers '90
Irish Jam '05
Island of Love '63
Jackie Brown '97 ▶
Just the Ticket '98
Kill Me Quick, I'm Cold '67
The Killing '56 ▶
Kind Hearts and Coronets '49 ▶
The King and Four Queens '56
The King of Marvin Gardens '72
King's Ransom '05
The Lady Eve '41 ▶
A Lady of Chance '28
The Ladykillers '04
Lamerica '95 ▶
The Last Adventure '67
The Last Exorcism '10
The Last of Mrs. Cheyney '37 ▶
The Last Seduction 2 '98
The Law and the Lady '51
Leap of Faith '92
The Learning Curve '01
The Lemon Drop Kid '51
Let's Do It Again '75
Lies My Mother Told Me '05
Life Stinks '91
Like a Fish Out of Water '99
The Little Giant '33
A Little Thing Called Murder '06
Lock, Stock and 2 Smoking Barrels '98 ▶
Lonely Hearts '91
Lonely Hearts '06
Love Kills '98
Love the Hard Way '01
The Madwoman of Chaillot '69
Mail Order Bride '08
Maisie Gets Her Man '42
Maisie Goes to Reno '44
Malone '87
The Man '05
Man of the World '31
Manhattan Melodrama '34 ▶
The Mask of Diijon '46
Matchstick Men '03 ▶
Maverick '94
McHale's Navy '64
McHale's Navy '97
Me and the Kid '93
Mexican Hayride '48
Mexican Spitfire at Sea '42
Miami Hustle '95
Millions '90
Milwaukee, Minnesota '03
The Mind Reader '33
The Miracle Woman '31
Miranda '01
Mistaken Identity '36
Mr. Lucky '43 ▶
Mo' Money '92
The Monster '96
Mortdecai '15
Murder on Approval '56
The Music Man '62 ▶
National Lampoon Presents Cattle Call '06
National Lampoon's Gold Diggers '04
Never Give a Sucker an Even Break '41 ▶
Never Say Never Again '83
The Next Big Thing '02
Night and the City '50 ▶
Night and the City '92 ▶
Nightmare Alley '47
Nine Queens '00
No Way Out '87 ▶
Nobody Lives Forever '46 ▶
None But the Lonely Heart '44 ▶
Nothing Sacred '37 ▶
Now and Forever '34
The Nuisance '33
Ocean's Thirteen '07 ▶
Office Space '98
One Christmas '95
100 Mile Rule '02
One of My Wives Is Missing '76
One Way Passage '32
Opportunity Knocks '90
Ossessione '42 ▶
Out to Sea '97
Pale Saints '97
Palmetto '98
Panic Button '62
Paper Man '71
Paper Moon '73 ▶
The Parallax View '74 ▶
Parasite '19 ▶
Parole, Inc. '49
Percentage '13
The Pest '96
Piece of the Action '77
Play Girl '41
Popi '69 ▶
Portrait of a Lady '96 ▶
The Prime Gig '00
Prime of Your Life '10
The Producers '68 ▶
The Producers '05
The Promoter '52 ▶
Purlie Victorious '63
The Quest '96
Quiz Show '94 ▶
Reborn '81
Reclaim '14
Remedy for Riches '40
The Ringer '05
Rings on Her Fingers '42
Risk '00
Risky Business '83 ▶
The Road to El Dorado '00
The Road to Zanzibar '41 ▶
Rushlights '13
Ruthless People '86 ▶
Save the Tiger '73 ▶
The Scapegoat '59
Schemes '95
Schtonk '92
Search for Beauty '34
The Secret of the Purple Reef '60
Sgt. Bilko '95
The Settlement '99
Shade '03
Shattered Image '93
Shed No Tears '48
Shooting Fish '98
Sidekicks '74
Silk 'n' Sabotage '94
Simpatico '99
Sinner '07
Six Degrees of Separation '93
Skin Game '71 ▶
Slackers '02
Slither '73 ▶
Southern Belles '05
The Spanish Prisoner '97 ▶
Spenser: A Savage Place '94
Splinterheads '09
The Squeeze '80
The Squeeze '87
Stacy's Knights '83
The Star Maker '95
Stavisky '74 ▶
Still Breathing '97
The Sting '73 ▶
The Sting 2 '83
Stolen Hearts '95
Stolen Holiday '37
The Story of a Cheat '36 ▶
Suicide Kings '97
Support Your Local Gunfighter '71 ▶
Sweet Talker '91
The Swindle '97
Swindled '04
The Switch '76
Tall in the Saddle '44
A Taste for Killing '92
The Taxman '98
Tequila Sunrise '88
Thin Ice '12
Things Change '88 ▶
Things to Do in Denver When You're Dead '95 ▶
36 Hours '64 ▶
365 Nights in Hollywood '34
Thrilled to Death '88
Ticket of Leave Man '37
The Tigress '93
Too Bad She's Bad '54
Tootsie '82 ▶
Touch '96
Train Robbers '73
Traveller '96 ▶
Tricheurs '84
Trick Baby '72
Trojan Eddie '96 ▶
Trouble in Paradise '32 ▶
The Two Faces of January '14
Two Much '96
Two of a Kind '51
Two Smart People '46
Undercover Maisie '47
The Unholy Three '30 ▶
Union Depot '32
Virtue '32
The Warrior & the Sorceress '84
Watch the Birdie '50
We Were Dancing '42
The Wendell Baker Story '05
Whacked! '02
When Will I Be Loved '04
Where the Money Is '00
White Men Can't Jump '92
White River '99
Who Is Clark Rockefeller? '10
Wife Wanted '46
Wild Things 3: Diamonds in the Rough '05
Wild Things '98
Wild Things: Foursome '10
Windbag the Sailor '36
The Winner '96
Wish You Were Dead '00
Within the Law '23
Yonkers Joe '08

Scared 'Chuteless

See also Airborne; Skydiving

Con Air '97 ▶
Double Team '97
Eraser '96
Firehouse Dog '07
Goldeneye '95 ▶
Point Break '91
Terminal Velocity '94

School Daze

See also Campus Capers; Hell High School

Absolution '81
Accident '67
Acts of Death '07
The Adventures of Sebastian Cole '99
All I Wanna Do '98
All Things Fair '95
American Friends '91
Amy '81
Angels in the Endzone '98
Anna and the King of Siam '46 ▶
Around the Fire '98
Art School Confidential '06
Attack of the 50 Foot Cheerleader '12
Au Revoir les Enfants '87 ▶
Back to School '86
Backfield in Motion '91
The Basket '99
Battle Royale '00
Before the Fall '04
The Beguiled '70 ▶
The Belles of St. Trinian's '53 ▶
The Bells of St. Mary's '45 ▶
The Best of Enemies '19
Big and Hairy '98
Big Bully '95
Billy Madison '94
Black Narcissus '47 ▶
Black Rat '10
Blame '17
Blue Ridge Fall '99
Blue Spring '01
Boarding School '83
Born to Race: Fast Track '14
Born to Win '16
Boys '95
The Browning Version '51 ▶
The Browning Version '94
Buffaloed '20
Buried Alive '89
Centerstage: On Pointe '16
Cheaters '00
Cheers for Miss Bishop '41
Children of a Lesser God '86 ▶
The Children's Hour '61
The Chocolate War '88 ▶
Christy '94
Ciao, Professore! '94
Clueless '95 ▶
The Convent '00
The Corn Is Green '45 ▶
crazy/beautiful '01
Crazy from the Heart '91 ▶
Cruel Intentions '98
D3: The Mighty Ducks '96
The Dangerous Lives of Altar Boys '02 ▶
Dead Poets Society '89 ▶
Death Tunnel '05
Detachment '12
The Devil's Backbone '01
The Devil's Playground '76 ▶
Diabolique '96
Diary of a Wimpy Kid '10
Doctor Dolittle '67
The Dog Who Saved Summer '15
Dream to Believe '85
Dress Gray '86 ▶
Drive Me Crazy '99
Eden '98
Educating Rita '83 ▶
Europa, Europa '91 ▶
The Faculty '98
Fallen '17
Fame '80 ▶
Fast Times at Ridgemont High '82 ▶
The Final Master '16
Finding a Family '10
Finding Forrester '00
Fist Fight '17
Flirting '89 ▶
Flubber '97
Free of Eden '98
French Postcards '79
Games Girls Play '75
Get Real '99
Getting It On '83
The Getting of Wisdom '77
Getting Straight '70
Getting Wasted '80
Goodbye, Mr. Chips '39 ▶
Goodbye, Mr. Chips '69
Grown Ups '80
Guess What We Learned in School Today? '70
Half Nelson '06 ▶
Hard Knox '83
Hard Lessons '86
Harry Potter and the Half-Blood Prince '09
Heavenly Creatures '94 ▶
Here Come the Co-Eds '45
High Strung '16
The History Boys '06
Homecoming '13
Homeless to Harvard: The Liz Murray Story '03
Homework '82
Honey 3: Dare to Dance '16
How I Got into College '89
How to Eat Fried Worms '06
The Hunt '13 ▶
The Hunting Ground '15 ▶
Idle Hands '99
In a Class of His Own '99
Iron & Silk '91
Is There Life Out There? '94
Jack '96
Judy Berlin '99
Kindergarten Cop 2 '16
Kindergarten Cop '90
Lambada '89
Late Bloomers '95
Liberty Heights '99
Life of the Party '18
Little Men '98
The Little Princess '39 ▶
A Little Princess '95 ▶
Lloyd '00
The Long Gray Line '55 ▶
The Lords of Discipline '83
Love Me if You Dare '03
The Major and the Minor '42 ▶
Major Payne '95
Married to It '93
Matilda '96 ▶
Max Keeble's Big Move '01
Mean Girls '04 ▶
Memento Mori '00
Middle School: The Worst Years of My Life '16
Morris from America '16 ▶
Mudbloods: A Movie About Quidditch '14
A Murder of Quality '90
Murder 101 '91
Music of the Heart '99
My Teacher Ate My Homework '98
My Teacher's Wife '95
National Lampoon's Class Reunion '82
National Lampoon's Senior Trip '95
Neighbors 2: Sorority Rising '16
The NeverEnding Story '84 ▶
Nighthawks '78
Notebook '19
Old Mother Riley, Headmistress '50
Oleanna '94
Our Time '74
Outside Providence '99
Oxford Blues '84
Passing Glory '99 ▶

▶ = rated three bones or higher

The People '71
The Perfect Date '19
Perfect Harmony '91
Permanent '17
Porky's '82
Powder '95
Pride of Jesse Hallum '81
The Prime of Miss Jean Brodie '69 ▶
The Pure Hell of St. Trinian's '61
Rachel, Rachel '68 ▶
The Rage: Carrie 2 '99
Real Genius '85 ▶
Remember the Daze '07
Renaissance Man '94
Ricochet River '98
The Riot Club '15
Robin of Locksley '95
Ruby Bridges '98
Sabrina the Teenage Witch '96
The St. Tammany Miracle '94
The Sandpiper '65
Satan's School for Girls '73
School for Scoundrels '60 ▶
School of Life '06
Sex Ed '14
Shout '91
The Sixth Sense '99 ▶
Stanley and Iris '90
Star Kid '97 ▶
Starter for 10 '06
The Strange One '57
Student Confidential '87
The Student Teachers '73
The Substitute 2: School's Out '97
The Substitute 4: Failure is Not an Option '00
The Substitute '93
Summer School Teachers '75
Tea and Sympathy '56 ▶
To Sir, with Love '67
Tolkien '19
Tom Brown's School Days '40
Tom Brown's School Days '51 ▶
Tommy Boy '95
Toy Soldiers '91
Treehouse Hostage '99
Trippin' '99
The Trouble with Angels '66
Twenty-Four Eyes '54 ▶
The Twilight Girls '57
Up the Academy '80
Up the Down Staircase '67 ▶
Virgin Queen of St. Francis High '88
Vital Signs '90
Waiting for Superman '10
Waterland '92
The Wave '08 ▶
Whatever It Takes '00
Where Is My Friend's House? '87
Why Shoot the Teacher '79 ▶
Wild Reeds '94 ▶
The Winslow Boy '48 ▶
With Honors '94
The Worst Witch '86
Yentl '83
You Are Not Alone '78
Zebrahead '92 ▶

Sci Fi

***See** Alien Babes; Alien Beings--Benign; Alien Beings--Vicious; Alien Cops; Aliens Are People, Too; Animated Sci-Fi; Cloning Around; Comedy Sci-Fi; Fantasy; Future Cop; Future Shock; Out of This World Sex; Sci-Fi Westerns; Space Operas*

Science & Scientists

***See also** Genetics; Inventors & Mad Scientists*

Absolute Zero '05
The Aeronauts '19
After Innocence '05 ▶
Agent Cody Banks '03
Air Hawks '35
Alien Nation: Body and Soul '95
Alien Raiders '08
Alien: Resurrection '97 ▶
Alien vs. Predator '04
Alive Inside '14 ▶
Altered States '80 ▶
The Amazing Captain Nemo '78
Anacondas: Trail of Blood '09
Android '82
The Andromeda Strain '71
The Andromeda Strain '08
Annihilation '18
Another Earth '11
Around the World Under the Sea '65
Arrowsmith '31
Assassin '86
Astro Boy '09
The Atomic City '52
The Atomic Man '56
Attack of the Robots '66
AVH: Alien vs. Hunter '07
Ballistica '10
Beach Party '63
A Beautiful Mind '01 ▶
Before the Flood '16
Behemoth '11
Beneath the Blue '10
The Big Game '72
Black Swarm '07
Bombshell '97
The Boy Who Harnessed the Wind '19
Brotherhood of the Wolf '01
A Bullet for Joey '55
Captain America: The First Avenger '11
Captain America: The Winter Soldier '14 ▶
CAT. 8 '13
Chain Reaction '96
Chasing Ice '12 ▶
Children of the Damned '63
Chill Factor '99
Chimera Strain '19
Clara '19
Colditz: Escape of the Birdmen '71
Collision Earth '11
Colony: The Endangered World of Bees '11
Contact '97
The Core '03
Corn '04
Crack in the World '65
Creation '09
Crest of the Wave '54
Cybermutt '02
The Dallas Connection '94
Dam Busters '55 ▶
Dark Matter '07
Dark Star '74 ▶
A Dark Truth '12
Darkman '90 ▶
Darwin's Darkest Hour '09
A Date With the Falcon '42
Dawn of the Planet of the Apes '14 ▶
The Day After Tomorrow '04
The Day of the Dolphin '73
Day One '89 ▶
The Day the Earth Stood Still '08
Dead Men Don't Wear Plaid '82
The Dead Next Door '89
Deadly Friend '86
Deadly Shift '08
Deep Blue Sea '99
Deep Core '00
The Defector '66
Demon Seed '77 ▶
Destination: Infestation '07
Destination Inner Space '66
Dick Barton, Special Agent '48
Die Laughing '80
Die, Monster, Die! '65
Dinocroc Vs. Supergator '10
Dirty Games '89
The Discovery '17
The Dish '00 ▶
Dr. Alien '88
Doctor Dolittle '67
Dr. Ehrlich's Magic Bullet '40
Dr. Jekyll and Ms. Hyde '95
Dolphin Tale '11
Earth II '71
Earth's Final Hours '12
Eight Below '06
Embrace of the Serpent '15
Encounters at the End of the World '07 ▶
Europa Report '13 ▶
Eve of Destruction '13
Evolution '01
The Experiment '10
Exploding Sun '13
Eye of the Beast '07
Fantastic Voyage '66 ▶
Fat Man and Little Boy '89
The Female Brain '18
Ferocious Planet '11
Finn on the Fly '09
The Fly '86 ▶
The Fly 2 '89
The Fly '58 ▶
Forbidden World '82
Forever Darling '56
Four Sided Triangle '53
The 4D Man '59
The Frankenstein Syndrome '10
Frankenweenie '12 ▶
From Hell It Came '57
Gattaca '97 ▶
The Gene Generation '07
Genesis II '73
Griff the Invisible '10
Habitat '97
Hard to Be a God '13
The Henderson Monster '80
Hold On! '66
How I Ended This Summer '10
Hulk '03
Human Nature '02
I Origins '14
Ice Twisters '09
I'll Follow You Down '13
I'll Get You '53
Impact '09
An Inconvenient Sequel: Truth to Power '17
An Inconvenient Truth '06 ▶
The Incredible Hulk '08
The Incredible Hulk Returns '88
Independence Day: Resurgence '16
Infinity '96
International House '33
Interstellar '14
The Invisible Man '20 ▶
The Invisible Man Returns '40 ▶
IO '19
I.Q. '94
The Ister '04 ▶
It Came From Another World '07
Jane '17 ▶
The Jensen Project '10
Journey to the Center of the Earth '93
Journey to the Center of the Earth '08
Junior '94
Jurassic Park '93 ▶
Just Eat It '14
Kate & Leopold '01
Killer Wave '07
The Killing Room '09
Kinsey '04 ▶
Kitchen Stories '03
Land of the Lost '09
The Last Days on Mars '13
The Lazarus Effect '15
Link '86
A Little Bit of Soul '97
Little Joe '19
Lo and Behold: Reveries of the Connected World '16 ▶
Lost Angel '43
The Lost Skeleton of Cadavra '01
The Lost World '92
The Lost World: Jurassic Park 2 '97
Love Potion #9 '92
Magma: Volcanic Disaster '06
The Magnetic Monster '53
The Man with Two Brains '83 ▶
Mary Reilly '95
Medicine Man '92
Mega Piranha '10
Megafault '09
Metal Tornado '11
Meteor '09
Mimic '97
The Mind Benders '63
Miracle Mile '89 ▶
Mission Mangal '19
Mr. Superinvisible '73
Monkey Business '52 ▶
Monkey's Uncle '65
Morgan '16
Mosquito Man '05
My Science Project '85
My Stepmother Is an Alien '88
Nautilus '99
Neptune Factor '73
No Smoking '55
October Sky '99 ▶
100 Million BC '08
Out of Blue '19
Outbreak '94 ▶
Pandora's Promise '13
Patient Zero '18
Perestroika '09
Perfect Sense '11
Pete's Meteor '98
Phantom Empire '87
Polar Storm '09
The Power '68
Project Nim '11 ▶
Project X '87
Prometheus '12
Proof of Lies '06
The Questor Tapes '74
The Quiet Earth '85 ▶
Rampage '18
Re-Generation '04
Real Genius '85 ▶
The Reaping '07
Red 11 '19
Red Lights '12
The Relic '96
Rememory '17
Replicas '18
Return of Captain Invincible '83
Return of the Fly '59
Rise of the Planet of the Apes '11 ▶
RoboCop '14
The Rocky Horror Picture Show '75 ▶
The Saint '97
Salmon Fishing in the Yemen '11
Seattle Superstorm '12
Senseless '98
Shaker Run '85
Shakma '89
Sharktopus '10
Simon '80
Smilla's Sense of Snow '96
Solar Attack '06
Son of Flubber '63
A Sound of Thunder '05
The Space Children '58
Space Master X-7 '58
Spaceways '53
Species '95
Sphere '97
Splice '10
Spy in the Sky '58
Stephen King's Golden Years '91
Stonehenge Apocalypse '10
The Storm '09
Sub Down '97
Sunshine '07
Super Eruption '11
Supernova '05
Swamp Thing '82
Tarantula '55 ▶
Termination Point '07
These Are the Damned '63
The Thing '82
The Thing '11
Things to Come '36 ▶
This Island Earth '55
Threshold '03
Time to Choose '16 ▶
Timeline '03
To Commit a Murder '67
To Dust '19
Tomorrowland '15
12:01 '93
2012: Doomsday '08
Ultraviolet '98
Underwater '20
Unforgettable '96
Universal Soldiers '07
Unknown Island '48
Unknown World '51
Virus '98
The Void '01
Walk East on Beacon '52
War of the Satellites '58
What the #$*! Do We Know? '04
Where Time Began '77
Wide Awake '07
Woman in the Dunes '64 ▶
Yes '04
The Yesterday Machine '63

Sci-Fi Romance

Alita: Battle Angel '19
Avatar '09 ▶
The Bad Batch '17
Blade Runner '82 ▶
The Empire Strikes Back '80 ▶
Equals '16
Her '13 ▶
The Host '13
How To Talk To Girls At Parties '17
The Infinite Worlds of H.G. Wells '01
The Last Vampire on Earth '10
Logan's Run '76
Mr. Nobody '13
1,000 Years From Now '52
Passengers '16
Perfect Sense '11
Return of the Jedi '83 ▶
The Speed of Thought '11
Star Wars: Episode 1-The Phantom Menace '99 ▶
Star Wars: Episode 2-Attack of the Clones '02 ▶
Star Wars: Episode 3-Revenge of the Sith '05 ▶
Star Wars: The Clone Wars '08
The Terminator '84 ▶
Upside Down '13

Sci-Fi Westerns

***See also** Sci Fi; Supernatural Westerns; Westerns*

Alien Outlaw '85
Back to the Future, Part 3 '90 ▶
Backlash: Oblivion 2 '95
Battle Beyond the Stars '80
The Dark Tower '17
High Plains Invaders '09
Oblivion '94
Outland '81
The Phantom Empire '35
Westworld '73 ▶
Young Ones '14

Scotland

***See also** Edinburgh; Glasgow*

Aberdeen '00
The Acid House '98
Almost Heaven '06
Attack of the Herbals '11
Behind the Lines '97
Beneath Loch Ness '01
The Big Man: Crossing the Line '91 ▶
Bonnie Scotland '35
Brave '12
Braveheart '95 ▶
Breaking the Waves '95 ▶
Brigadoon '54 ▶
Deacon Brodie '98
Dear Frankie '04
The Decoy Bride '11
Devil Girl from Mars '54
Dr. Bell and Mr. Doyle: The Dark Beginnings of Sherlock Holmes '00
Dog Soldiers '01
Dreams Lost, Dreams Found '87
The Eagle '11
Edie '19
Entrapment '99
Escape '90
The Etruscan Smile '19
The Flying Scotsman '06
Geordie '55
God Help the Girl '14
Golf in the Kingdom '10
The Governess '98
The Green Years '46
Gregory's Girl '80 ▶
Greystoke: The Legend of Tarzan, Lord of the Apes '84
Happy Go Lovely '51
Highlander: Endgame '00
Hunted '52
I Know Where I'm Going '45 ▶
Incident at Loch Ness '04 ▶
Joyeux Noel '05 ▶
Kidnapped '38
Kidnapped '48
Kidnapped '95
Kidnapped '05 ▶
The Last Musketeer '00
Little Minister '34 ▶
Local Hero '83 ▶
Loch Ness '95
A Lonely Place to Die '11
Macbeth '15
Made of Honor '08
Madeleine '50
Mary of Scotland '36 ▶
Mary, Queen of Scots '71
The Master of Ballantrae '53
Mister Lonely '07
Morvern Callar '02
My Life So Far '98
No Blade of Grass '70
Northman: A Viking Saga '15
One More Kiss '99
Outlaw King '18
Pride of the Clan '18
Princess Kaiulani '09
Ratcatcher '99
Ring of Bright Water '69 ▶
Rob Roy '95 ▶
Rob Roy-The Highland Rogue '53
St. Ives '98
The Secret of Loch Ness '08
September '96
A Shot at Glory '00
Sinful Davey '69
Sunset Song '16
Sweet Sixteen '02 ▶
The Swordsman '47
T2 Trainspotting '17
The 39 Steps '09
This Is Not a Love Song '02
The Three Lives of Thomasina '63 ▶
Thunder In the Valley '47
Tommy's Honour '17
Tonight You're Mine '11
The Tournament '09
Trouble in the Glen '54
Under the Skin '13 ▶
Urban Ghost Story '98
Valhalla Rising '09
The Vanishing '19
The Water Horse: Legend of the Deep '07
What We Did on Our Holiday '15
When Eight Bells Toll '71
Whiskey Galore '48 ▶
The Wicker Tree '10
Wilbur Wants to Kill Himself '02 ▶
Wild Country '05
Wild Rose '18 ▶
Year of the Comet '92
Young Adam '03 ▶

Scotland Yard

***See also** Foreign Cops*

Across the Bridge '57
The Adventures of Sherlock Holmes '39
Again, the Ringer '64
Agatha Christie's Murder is Easy '82
Agent Cody Banks 2: Destination London '04
The Arsenal Stadium Mystery '39
Basic Instinct 2 '06
Behind That Curtain '29
The Black Cat '81
The Black Sleep '56

▶ = rated three bones or higher

Blackmail '29 ►
Brides of Fu Manchu '66
Bulldog Drummond's Bride '39
Bulldog Drummond's Peril '38
Bunny Lake Is Missing '65
A Certain Justice '99
Charlie Chan's Murder Cruise '40
Circus of Fear '67
Close Your Eyes '02
Cloudburst '51
Cottage to Let '41
Counter-Espionage '42
Crackerjack '38
The Day of the Jackal '73 ►
The Diplomat '08
Dr. Mabuse *vs.* Scotland Yard '64
Don't Open Till Christmas '84
Dracula's Daughter '36►
Dressed to Kill '46
Drums of Fu Manchu '40►
Eastern Promises '07►
The Face of Fu Manchu '65
The Fiendish Plot of Dr. Fu Manchu '80
The File of the Golden Goose '69
Foreign Correspondent '40►
The Fourth Angel '01
Frenzy '72►
From Hell '01►
Gallery of Horrors '67
Gaslight '44►
Gideon's Day '58
Green for Danger '47
Hangover Square '45
Horrors of the Black Museum '59
The Hound of the Baskervilles '39►
The Hound of the Baskervilles '59
The Hound of the Baskervilles '77
The Hound of the Baskervilles '83
The Hound of the Baskervilles '00
The Hound of the Baskervilles '02►
The Hour of 13 '52
The House of Secrets '37
The House that Dripped Blood '71
The Invisible Man Returns '40►
Kaleidoscope '66
Kill Me Tomorrow '57
The Lavender Hill Mob '51►
A Little Piece of Sunshine '90
The Man from Planet X '51
The Man Who Knew Too Much '34►
The Medusa Touch '78
A Mind to Murder '96
Ministry of Fear '44►
The Moonstone '72
The Moonstone '97►
Obsession '49
P.D. James: Death in Holy Orders '03
Raffles '39
Raw Meat '72
Razor Blade Smile '98
Return of the Vampire '43
The Runaway Bus '54
Sabotage '36►
The Saint in London '39
The Satanic Rites of Dracula '73
Shanghai Knights '03
Sherlock Holmes and the Secret Weapon '42►
Shiner '00
The 39 Steps '35►
The Tourist '10
The Vengeance of Fu Manchu '67
The Verdict '46
Villain '71
The Voice of Merrill '52
Walk a Crooked Mile '48
The Wolfman '09
The Woman in Green '49

Screwball Comedy

***See also** Comedy; Slapstick Comedy*

All in a Night's Work '61
Ambassador Bill '31
And Baby Makes Six '79
Antonio '73
As You Like It '36
Assault of the Party Nerds '89
Attention Shoppers '99
The Awful Truth '37 ►
The Bachelor and the Bobby-Soxer '47 ►
Bachelor Mother '39 ►
Back to School '86
Bank Shot '74 ►
Bedazzled '68 ►
Bedtime Story '63
Beer '85
Big Brown Eyes '36
Big Business '88
Blame It on the Bellboy '92
The Bliss of Mrs. Blossom '68►
Blue Murder at St. Trinian's '56►
Boeing Boeing '65
Boogie Vision '77
The Break-Up '06
Breakfast for Two '37
The Bride Came C.O.D. '41
The Bride Comes Home '35
The Bride Wore Boots '46
Bringing Down the House '03
Bringing Up Baby '38►
Bullseye! '90
The Calamari Wrestler '04
Camp Cucamonga: How I Spent My Summer Vacation '90
Carry On Admiral '57
The Chaplin Revue '58
Christmas in the Clouds '01
The Circus '28►
Connie and Carla '04
The Couch Trip '87
Crackers '84
Danger: Love at Work '37
Doctor in the House '53►
Dr. Otto & the Riddle of the Gloom Beam '86
Doctor Takes a Wife '40►
Double Wedding '37►
Doubting Thomas '35
Down Among the Z Men '52
Down the Drain '89
Due Date '10
Easy Living '37►
Easy Money '83
Egg and I '47►
El Matador '03
Everything You Always Wanted to Know about Sex (But Were Afraid to Ask) '72►
The Family Stone '05
The Favor, the Watch, & the Very Big Fish '92
Fist Fight '17
Fit for a King '37
Forces of Nature '99
Forever Darling '56
Forsaking All Others '35
Four's a Crowd '38
The Gay Deceivers '69
The Geisha Boy '58
Get Crazy '83
The Gilded Lily '35
Gray Matters '06
Hands Across the Table '35►
A Hard Day's Night '64►
Hard to Get '38
Harvey '50►
Her Husband's Affairs '47
He's My Girl '87
Holiday '38►
How Sweet It Is! '68
I Heart Huckabees '04
I Love You Again '40►
Identity Thief '13
If You Could Only Cook '36
Inspector Hornleigh '39
Intolerable Cruelty '03
Italian Straw Hat '27►
It's a Wonderful World '39
It's Love I'm After '37
It's the Old Army Game '26 ►
Joy of Living '38 ►
La Chevre '81 ►
The Ladies Man '00
The Lady Eve '41 ►
Lady in a Jam '42
Laws of Attraction '04
Leatherheads '08
Libeled Lady '36 ►
A Life Less Ordinary '97
Life Stinks '91
Live, Love and Learn '37
Lobster Man from Mars '89
The Long, Long Trailer '54
Love Before Breakfast '36
The Love Bug '68
Love Crazy '41 ►
Love Is News '37 ►
Love on a Bet '36
Lucky Partners '40
The Major and the Minor '42 ►
Make Mine Mink '60►
Malibu Beach '78
The Marriage Circle '24►
Marriage on the Rocks '65
Mascots '16
Masterminds '16
The Mating Game '59►
Meatballs 2 '84
Meet the Parents '00►
Merrily We Live '38►
A Midsummer Night's Sex Comedy '82►
Miracle of Morgan's Creek '44►
Miss Tatlock's Millions '48
Mr. & Mrs. Smith '41►
Modern Girls '86
The Money Pit '86
Monkey Business '52►
Monkeys, Go Home! '66
The Moon's Our Home '36
The More the Merrier '43►
Morons from Outer Space '85
The Munsters' Revenge '81
My American Cousin '85►
My Chauffeur '86
My Favorite Brunette '47
My Favorite Wife '40►
My Man Godfrey '36►
My Mother Likes Women '02
National Lampoon's Christmas Vacation 2: Cousin Eddie's Big Island Adventure '03
National Lampoon's Christmas Vacation '89
National Lampoon's European Vacation '85
National Lampoon's Vacation '83►
Nervous Ticks '93
No Time For Love '43►
No Vacancy '99
Noises Off '92
Not for Publication '84
Nothing Sacred '37►
The Nude Bomb '80
Overboard '18
The Palm Beach Story '42►
Pink Flamingos '72
Platinum Blonde '31►
Police Academy 3: Back in Training '86
Polyester '81
The Saddest Music in the World '03
See No Evil, Hear No Evil '89
Shoot or Be Shot '02
Simon '80
The Smallest Show on Earth '57►
Social Intercourse '01
Some Like It Hot '59►
Somewhere in the City '97
A Southern Yankee '48
Spaced Invaders '90
Spring Break '83
Start the Revolution without Me '70►
Stir Crazy '80
Stroker Ace '83
The Student Teachers '73
Summer School Teachers '75
Superdad '73
Sweet Revenge '90
The Swinging Cheerleaders '74
Switching Channels '88
Talk of the Town '42 ►
Teen Witch '89
Tell It to the Judge '49
That Naughty Girl '58
That Wonderful Urge '48
They Went That-a-Way & That-a-Way '78
Three Loves Has Nancy '38
Together Again '43
Too Many Husbands '40
Tricks of the Trade '88
The Twist '76
Uncle Drew '18
Vibes '88
Vice Versa '88 ►
Waitress '81
Waltz of the Toreadors '62 ►
Watch the Birdie '50
Wedding Present '36
What's Up, Doc? '72►
When Women Had Tails '70
When Women Lost Their Tails '75
Which Way Is Up? '77
Who's That Girl? '87
Wild Women of Wongo '59
Wonder Boys '00►
World's Greatest Lover '77
You Can't Cheat an Honest Man '39►
You Can't Take It with You '38►
Zotz! '62

Scuba

***See also** Deep Blue*

The Abyss '89►
Beneath the 12-Mile Reef '53
The Big Blue '88
The Cave '05
The Deep '77
Easy Come, Easy Go '67
ffolkes '80
Flipper '63►
Flipper's New Adventure '64►
Fool's Gold '08
47 Meters Down '17
Into the Blue 2: The Reef '09
Into the Blue '05
Isle of Forgotten Sins '43
Leviathan '89
The Life Aquatic with Steve Zissou '04
Men of Honor '00
Navy SEALS '90
Neptune Factor '73
Never Say Never Again '83
Night of the Sharks '87
Oceans of Fire '86
Open Water '03►
Thunderball '65

Sculptors

***See also** Art & Artists*

The Agony and the Ecstasy '65
Beautiful Something '16
Before and After '95
A Bucket of Blood '59►
Camille Claudel '89►
Fly Away Home '96►
House of Wax '53►
The Juror '96
The Silver Chalice '54
The Song of Songs '33
Together Again '43
Voice from the Stone '17

Sea Disasters

***See also** Air Disasters; Deep Blue; Disaster Flicks; Shipwrecked*

The Abyss '89►
Adrift '18
Airport '77 '77
Beyond the Poseidon Adventure '79
Black Ops '07
Das Boot '81►
Deep Rising '98
Deep Water '06►
Deepstar Six '89
Deepwater Horizon '16
Far from Home: The Adventures of Yellow Dog '94
The Fog '05
47 Meters Down: Uncaged '19
The Ghost Ship '43
Guerillas in Pink Lace '64
In the Heart of the Sea '15
Juggernaut '74 ►
K-19: The Widowmaker '02
Killer Wave '07
The Last Voyage '60
Leviathan '89
Life of Pi '12 ►
Mary '19
Men of Honor '00
A Night to Remember '58 ►
Open Water '03 ►
Poseidon '06
The Poseidon Adventure '72
The Poseidon Adventure '05
Primal '19
Raise the Titanic '80
The Sinking of the Laconia '10
S.O.S. Titanic '79
Souls at Sea '37
Titanic '53►
Titanic '97►
Titanic '12
Underwater '20
The Unsinkable Molly Brown '64►
Waterworld '95

Seattle

Agent Cody Banks '03
Ann Rule Presents: The Stranger Beside Me '03
The Art of Racing in the Rain '19
The Bad Son '07
Battle in Seattle '07
Boy Culture '06
Dead in a Heartbeat '02
The Diary of Ellen Rimbauer '03
Dim Sum Funeral '08
Divorce Wars: A Love Story '82
Dream Man '94
88 Minutes '08
Fat Kid Rules the World '12
Georgia '95►
Girl in Progress '12
Greenmail '01
A Guy Thing '03
The Heart of the Game '05
The Hitman '91
Humpday '09
It Happened at the World's Fair '63
Judicial Indiscretion '07
The Last Mimzy '07
Life or Something Like It '02
Little Buddha '93
Love Happens '09
Lucky Seven '03
Lucky Them '13
Midnight Sun '18
My Own Private Idaho '91►
Pearl Jam Twenty '11
Ray '04►
Seattle Superstorm '12
Shattered Image '98
Singles '92►
Slaves to the Underground '96
Sleepless in Seattle '93►
The Slender Thread '65►
Stakeout '87
Storm Cell '08
Things We Lost in the Fire '07
Thr3e '07
A Valentine Carol '07
Weather Girl '09
Where'd You Go, Bernadette '19
World's Greatest Dad '09►

Second Chance

Another Earth '11
Audrey's Rain '03
The Beaver '11
Before Sunset '04►
Begin Again '13
The Best of Me '14
Between Two Worlds '44
Bleed for This '16
Blind Date '08
Blood Ties '13
Broken Hill '09
Chances Are '89 ►
City Island '09
City of Bad Men '53
The Clown '53
Complete Unknown '16
The Concert '09
The Confirmation '16
Dangerous '35
Danny Collins '15
Donna on Demand '09
Don't Let Go '19
Enough Said '13 ►
Florence Foster Jenkins '16
Gloria '13 ►
Gossip '08
Gridiron Gang '06
The Hangman '59
Hard Contract '69
Harry and Snowman '16►
Hell's Kitchen NYC '97
Hope Ranch '02
How to Make Love to a Woman '09
Hysterical Blindness '02
If Only '04
Islander '06
Juanita '19
Judas Kiss '11
Knuckle Sandwich '04
Lady in a Jam '42
Last Chance Cafe '06
Last Chance Harvey '08
Leo '02
Letters to Juliet '10
Levity '03
Life as a House '01
A Little Inside '01
The Long Memory '53
Looking for Eric '09
Lord Jim '65►
Louder Than Bombs '16
Love Happens '09
Marjorie Prime '17
Merrily We Go to Hell '32
Mr. Destiny '90
Mr. 3000 '04
Nights in Rodanthe '08
Nine Lives '16
Once Upon a Time in the Midlands '02
One Desire '55
Paint and Powder '25
Payment on Demand '51
The Perfect Age of Rock 'n' Roll '10
Place Vendome '98►
The Princess and the Warrior '00►
Real Steel '11
Reunion at Fairborough '85
The Rookie '02►
The Second Time Around '61
Seventeen Again '00
Shadowheart '09
She '65
She Played With Fire '57
She's Back on Broadway '53
Snapshots '02
Soda Springs '11
Solaris '02
Suicide Squad '16
Sweet and Low-Down '44
Their Own Desire '29
This Woman Is Dangerous '52
Touchback '11
Undertow '49
Unshackled '00
The Vow '12
Wall Street 2: Money Never Sleeps '10
We Live Again '34
The Wedding Chapel '13
White Night Wedding '08
The Yankles '09

Secret Service

***See also** Capitol Capers; Funny Money*

Absolute Power '97
Agent of Death '99
Air Force One '97►
Along Came a Spider '01
Angel Has Fallen '19

September

Assassination '87
Boiling Point '93
Brake '12
Chain of Command '00
Chasing Liberty '04
Cleanskin '12
Counterstrike '03
Dave '93 ▸
D.E.B.S. '04
End Game '06
First Daughter '04
First Kid '96
Guarding Tess '94
Hackers '95
Highly Dangerous '50
Holt of the Secret Service '42
In Her Line of Fire '06
In the Line of Fire '93 ▸
The Interpreter '05 ▸
Johnny English Strikes Again '18
The Kidnapping of the President '80
The League of Extraordinary Gentlemen '03
Mach 2 '00
Maximum Impact '18
Murder at 1600 '97
Olympus Has Fallen '13
Parkland '13
Raiders of Ghost City '44
The Sentinel '06
The Silencers '96
Spartan '04 ▸
T-Men '47 ▸
To Live & Die in L.A. '85
Under the Rainbow '81
Vantage Point '08
White House Down '13

September 11th

DC 9/11: Time of Crisis '04
Extremely Loud and Incredibly Close '11
A Few Days in September '06
Giuliani Time '05
The Great New Wonderful '06
The Hamburg Cell '04
Hijacking Catastrophe: 9/11, Fear and the Selling of America '04
A Little Help '11
Mooz-Lum '10
9/11 '17
Reign Over Me '07
Sheeba '05
The Space Between '10
United 93 '06 ▸
Where in the World Is Osama Bin Laden? '06
World Trade Center '06 ▸

Serial Killers

***See also** Crime Sprees; Slasher Flicks*

Acolytes '08
Addams Family Values '93
Addicted to Murder '95
Addicted to Murder 2: Tainted Blood '97
Addicted to Murder 3: Bloodlust '99
Aileen: Life and Death of a Serial Killer '03 ▸
Along Came a Spider '01
The Alphabet Killer '08
American Crime '04
American Nightmare '00
American Psycho 2: All American Girl '02
American Psycho '99
American Strays '96
American Streetfighter 2: The Full Impact '97
Anamorph '07
Angel of Death '02
Ann Rule Presents: The Stranger Beside Me '03
Antibodies '05
The Apostate '98
Appropriate Adult '11
Aroused '66
The Arousers '70
Art School Confidential '06
Awake '19
Awakening the Zodiac '17
The Awful Dr. Orloff '62
The Bad Son '07
Band of Gold '95 ▸
Banshee '06
Barking Dogs Never Bite '00 ▸
Baseline Killer '08
Basement Jack '09
Basketweave '06
Bereavement '10
Beyond Redemption '99
Black & White '99
The Black Belly of the Tarantula '71
Black House '07
Black Widow Murders: The Blanche Taylor Moore Story '93
The Bletchley Circle '13
Blitz '11
Blondes Have More Guns '95
Blood Work '02
Bloodline '19
Bloodmoon '97
Bloody Proof '99 ▸
Blowback '99
Body Parts '91
Bon Cop Bad Cop '06
The Bone Collector '99
The Boston Strangler '68
The Boston Strangler: The Untold Story '08
Bound by Lies '05
Boystown '07
Bride of Chucky '98
The Bride of Frank '96
Brigham City '01
BTK Killer '06
Bundy: A Legacy of Evil '08
Butterfly Kiss '94
Cabin by the Lake '00
The Calling '14
Captivity '07
The Capture of the Green River Killer '08
Carnal Innocence '11
Carolina Moon '07
The Cell 2 '09
The Cell '00
Chaos '05
Cherry Falls '00
Child of God '14
ChromeSkull: Laid to Rest 2 '11
Citizen X '95 ▸
Clay Pigeons '98
Close Your Eyes '02
Closer and Closer '96
Club Dread '04
Cold Blooded '00
Cold Prey II '08
The Collection '12
Con Air '97 ▸
Cop '88
Copycat '95
Cornered! '09
The Coroner '98
Corpse Mania '81
Cosh Boy '52
Crimetime '96
The Crimson Code '99
The Crimson Rivers '01
Cronicas '04
Cruel and Unusual '01
Curdled '95
Cure '97 ▸
Cyberstalker '96
Dahmer '02
Dark Asylum '01
Dark Corners '06
The Dark Ride '78
Darkness Falls '20
The Darwin Awards '06
Dead Certain '92
Dead Evidence '00
Deadly Neighbor '91
Dean Koontz's Intensity '97
The Deliberate Stranger '86 ▸
Delivered '98
A Demon in My View '92
Detention '11
Diary of a Serial Killer '97
Dirt Boy '01
Dirty Harry '71 ▸
Disturbia '07
Dr. Jekyll and Mr. Hyde '08
Dot.Kill '05
Double Vision '02
Drifter '09
Ed Gein '01
Ed McBain's 87th Precinct: Lightning '95
8213: Gacy House '10
88 Minutes '08
The Element of Crime '84
The Eleventh Victim '12
End Game '09
Endangered Species '02
Evil Dead Trap 2: Hideki '91
Evil Laugh '86
Exorcist 3: Legion '90
Extremely Wicked, Shockingly Evil and Vile '19
Eye of the Beholder '99
Eye of the Killer '99
Eye See You '01
Eyes of a Stranger '81
Eyes of Laura Mars '78
Faces in the Crowd '11
Fall Down Dead '07
Fallen '97
Fallen Angel '99
Fatal Charm '92
Father's Day '12
Fear '90
The Fear: Halloween Night '99
Feardotcom '02
Felicia's Journey '99 ▸
Fender Bender '16
Final Combination '93
Final Move '06
The First Power '89
Five Dolls for an August Moon '70
For Sale By Owner '05
Frailty '02 ▸
Freeway 2: Confessions of a Trickbaby '99
Freeway '95
Frequency '00
The Frighteners '96
The Frozen Ground '13
Ghost in the Machine '93
Ghost of the Needle '03
Giallo '09
The Girl Who Knew Too Much '63
The Girl With the Dragon Tattoo '11 ▸
The Glimmer Man '96
Gone '12
A Good Marriage '14
Good Neighbors '10
The Greasy Strangler '16
The Gunman '03
Hangman '00
Hangman '17
Hannibal '01
Haunter '13
The Hawk '93
Hell Fest '18
Hellbent '04
Henry: Portrait of a Serial Killer 2: Mask of Sanity '96
Henry: Portrait of a Serial Killer '90 ▸
Hideaway '94
Highwaymen '03
The Hills Have Eyes '06
The Hillside Stranglings '04
Honeymoon Killers '70 ▸
A Horrible Way to Die '10
The Horror Show '89
Horrors of the Black Museum '59
The Hour of 13 '52
House of Bodies '13
The House That Jack Built '18
How to be a Serial Killer '08
The Hunt for the I-5 Killer '11
Hunting Humans '02
I Am Not A Serial Killer '16
I Can't Sleep '93
I Know Who Killed Me '07
I Saw the Devil '10
Identity '03
Impulse '74
iMurders '08
In Dreams '98
In the Blood '06
In the Deep Woods '91
In the Shadow of the Moon '19
Inhuman Resources '12
Inhumanity '00
Inn on the River '62
The Invisible Strangler '76
Iris Johansen's The Killing Game '11
Jack Frost '97
Jack the Ripper '76
Jack the Ripper '88 ▸
The January Man '89
Jason X '01
Jennifer 8 '92
Joy Ride 3: Road Kill '14
Kalifornia '93
Karla '06
Kill Switch '08
Killer by Nature '10
Killer Instinct: From the Files of Agent Candice DeLong '03
Killer Me '01
Killers '14
The Killing Gene '07
Kiss the Girls '97
Kontroll '03 ▸
Lady Killer '97
Laid to Rest '09
Laser Moon '92
The Last Heist '16
The Last Letter '04
The Laughing Policeman '74
Le Boucher '69 ▸
Legacy of Fear '06
The Limehouse Golem '17
The Lodger '09
The Lost Angel '04
Love and Human Remains '93 ▸
Lucky '11
Lured '47
M '31 ▸
Machined '06
The Mad Executioners '65
Malevolence '04
Man Bites Dog '91
Man in the Attic '53
Maniac Cop '88
Massage Parlor Murders '73
Medium Raw: Night of the Wolf '10
Memories of Murder '03
Mercy '00
The Midnight Meat Train '08
Mindhunters '05
The Minus Man '99
Mr. Brooks '07
Mixed Nuts '94
The Monster '96
Monster '03 ▸
Murder On the Home Front '13
The Murderer Lives at Number 21 '42
My Friend Dahmer '17
My Soul to Take '10
Natural Born Killers '94
Nature of the Beast '94
Never Talk to Strangers '95
The Night Digger '71
Night Divides the Day '01
Night Hunter '19
Night Shadow '90
Night Stalker '87
Night Stalker '09
Night Vision '97
Nightmare Detective '06
A Nightmare on Elm Street '10
Nightscare '93
Nightstalker '02
Nightwatch '96
99 Pieces '07
Ninja's Creed '09
No One Sleeps '01
No Way to Treat a Lady '68 ▸
Nurse 3D '13
Office Killer '97
Open Cam '05
Otis '08
The Pact '12
Parasomnia '08
The Perfect Witness '07
Phobic '02
Piano Man '96
The Pledge '00 ▸
Portraits of a Killer '95
Postmortem '98
The Prey '11
Prey of the Chameleon '91
Prime Suspect '92 ▸
Probable Cause '95
The Prophet's Game '99
Psych: 9 '10
Psychic '91
Psychopath '97
Rampage: The Hillside Strangler Murders '04
The Raven '12
Ravenous '99
The Reaper '97
Red Dragon '02
Red Riding, Part 1: 1974 '09
Red Riding, Part 2: 1980 '09
Reflections '08
Relentless '89
Relentless 3 '93
Relentless 4 '94
Replicant '01
Rest Stop '06
Resurrection '99
Retribution '98
Return to Cabin by the Lake '01
Revenge Quest '96
Righteous Kill '08
Rites of Frankenstein '72
The Riverman '04
Roman de Gare '07
Sacrifice '00
Salvage '06
San Franpsycho '06
Sanctimony '01
Satan's Little Helper '04
Saw '04
Saw 2 '05
Saw 4 '07
Saw 6 '09
Scar '07
Scary Movie '00
The Scenesters '09
Scoop '06
Scream '96 ▸
Scream 2 '97 ▸
Scream 3 '00
Serial Killer '95
Serial Killing 101 '04
Serial Mom '94 ▸
Serial Slayer '03
Seven '95 ▸
Seven Blood-Stained Orchids '72
Shallow Ground '04
The Silence of the Lambs '91 ▸
Silent Night '12
Skeleton Crew '09
Skinned Alive '08
Slaughter of the Innocents '93
Sleepless '01
Sleepstalker: The Sandman's Last Rites '94
Snapdragon '93
The Snowman '17
The Snowtown Murders '12 ▸
So I Married an Axe Murderer '93
Soho Square '00
Solace '16
Son of Sam '08
Split '16
Split Second '92
Stagefright '87
Starkweather '04
The Stendahl Syndrome '95
The Strange Case of Dr. Jekyll and Mr. Hyde '06
The Strange Case of Dr. Rx '42
Stranger by Night '94
Strangler of Blackmoor Castle '63
Striking Distance '93
Summer of 84 '18
Summer of Sam '99
Surveillance '08
Suspect Zero '04
Sweeney Todd: The Demon Barber of Fleet Street '07
Switchback '97
Taking Lives '04
10 Rillington Place '71 ▸
Ten to Midnight '83
Tenderness of the Wolves '73
There's Something about Mary '98 ▸
Thirst '09 ▸
13 Gantry Row '98
Thr3e '07
3 A.M. '01 ▸
Ticking Clock '10
To Catch a Killer '92 ▸
The Todd Killings '71
Trail of a Serial Killer '98
Transfixed '01
True Crime '95
Tunnel Vision '95
Turbulence '96
Twisted '04
2:13 '09
The Ugly '96
Unconditional Love '03
Uncovered '94
Undefeatable '94
Unspeakable '02
Untraceable '08
Urban Menace '99
V/H/S '12
Vacancy 2: The First Cut '08
Valentine '01
Vegas Vice '94
Vice Girls '96
The Watcher '00
When a Stranger Calls '06
When the Bough Breaks '93
While the City Sleeps '56 ▸
White River '99
Winter Kill '74
Witchcraft 10: Mistress of the Craft '98
Wolf Creek 2 '13
Wolf Creek '05
Women Who Kill '17
Zipperface '92
The Zodiac '05
Zodiac '07

Sex & Sexuality

***See also** Crimes of Passion; Erotic Thrillers; Pornography; Sex on the Beach*

About Adam '00
About Last Night '14
Accident '67
Accidental Love '15
The Adjuster '91
Adore '13
The Adventures of Sadie '55
The Advocate '93 ▸
An Affair of Love '99
Affairs of Anatol '21
After '19
After Tomorrow '32
Afterglow '97
Afternoon Delight '13
Alfie '66 ▸
Alfie '04
Alien Nation: Body and Soul '95
All Neat in Black Stockings '69
All Things Fair '95
The Allnighter '87
Amateur Night '16
The Amazing Transplant '70
American Beauty '99 ▸
American Gigolo '79
American Pie '99 ▸
American Pie 2 '01
American Reunion '12
American Swing '08
American Virgin '98
The Amorous Adventures of Moll Flanders '65
The Amy Fisher Story '93
Anatomy of Hell '04
And God Created Woman '57
And God Created Woman '88
And Then We Danced '20 ▸
Angel Blue '97
Angel of H.E.A.T. '82
Angels and Insects '95 ▸
Angels in America '03 ▸
Animal Instincts '92
Animal Instincts 2 '94
Animal Instincts 3: The Seductress '95
Anne Rice's The Feast of All Saints '01
Anomalisa '16 ▸
Antarctica '08
Any Wednesday '66
The Apartment '60 ▸

▸ = rated three bones or higher

▸ = rated three bones or higher

Men, Women & Children '14
Menage '86 ▶
Mercy '00
Metroland '97
Midnight Tease '94
Midsommar '19
A Midsummer Night's Sex Comedy '82 ▶
Migrating Forms '00
Millions '90
Mirror Images '91
Mirror, Mirror 3: The Voyeur '96
Miss Julie '50
Miss Julie '99
Miss Julie '14
Miss Right '81
Miss Sadie Thompson '53 ▶
Mo' Better Blues '90
Monsieur Hire '89 ▶
Monster's Ball '01 ▶
Montenegro '81 ▶
Monty Python's The Meaning of Life '83 ▶
The Moon Is Blue '53
Moonlight '16 ▶
Moonlight Whispers '99
More Sex and the Single Mom '05
Motel Blue '98
The Mother '03 ▶
Mouth to Mouth '95
Movers and Shakers '85
My Chauffeur '86
My Demon Lover '87
My Life to Live '62 ▶
My Sex Life. . . Or How I Got into an Argument '96
My Teacher's Wife '95
Myra Breckinridge '70
Naked Lie '89
The Names of Love '10
National Lampoon's Adam & Eve '05
Natural Born Pranksters '16
Nea '78
Nekromantik 2 '91
Nekromantik '87
Nenette and Boni '96 ▶
Nerolio '96
Never Forever '07
Never Talk to Strangers '95
New Rose Hotel '98
Night Fire '94
Night Has Settled '14
Night of the Living Deb '14
Night Owls '15
The Nightman '93
No Men Beyond This Point '15
No Sex Please-We're British '73
No Strings Attached '11
No Vacancy '99
Nobody Walks '12
Norma Jean and Marilyn '95
The Notorious Bettie Page '06
Novel Desires '92
Novitiate '17
Nurse 3D '13
Nymphomaniac: Volume II '14
O Fantasma '00
The Off Hours '11
Oh! Calcutta! '72
On the Basis of Sex '18
On the Road '12
Once Is Not Enough '75
One Day '11
100 Girls '00
One Night Stand '95
One Night Stand '97 ▶
One Plus One '61
The Other Side of Midnight '77
Over the Wire '95
The Overnight '15
The Painted Lady '97 ▶
The Paperboy '12
Paradise: Hope '13
Paranoia '69
Party Animal '83
Passion '82
Passion '99
The Passion of Ayn Rand '99
The Passion of Darkly Noon '95
Pauline at the Beach '83 ▶
A Perfect Ending '12
The Perfect Guy '15
Perfect Sense '11
The Perfection '19
Performance '70 ▶
The Perils of Gwendoline '84
Permission '18
Petticoat Planet '96
Peyton Place '57 ▶
The Photograph '20
Picnic '55 ▶
Picture Day '13
Pigalle '95
Pimp '18
Pinero '01
Play the Game '09
Play Time '94
Playgirl Killer '66
Point of Terror '71
Poison Ivy '92
Poison Ivy 2: Lily '95
Poison Ivy 3: The New Seduction '97
The Pornographers '66 ▶
Portrait of a Lady on Fire '19 ▶
The Postman Always Rings Twice '46 ▶
The Postman Always Rings Twice '81
Power, Passion & Murder '83
Praise '98 ▶
Preacherman '83
Premature '20
Pretenders '19
Pretty Baby '78 ▶
Pretty Woman '90 ▶
The Princess & the Call Girl '84
Private Lessons '75
Queen & Slim '19 ▶
Queen of Hearts '19
Quid Pro Quo '08
Quiet Days in Hollywood '97
R100 '15
Rain '32
Rain '01
Raising Cain '92
Rambling Rose '91 ▶
A Real Young Girl '75
Reckless '97 ▶
Reckless: The Sequel '98 ▶
Red Meat '98
Red Shoe Diaries '92
Red Shoe Diaries 2: Double Dare '92
Red Shoe Diaries 3: Another Woman's Lipstick '93
Red Shoe Diaries 4: Auto Erotica '93
Red Shoe Diaries 5: Weekend Pass '95
Red Shoe Diaries 6: How I Met My Husband '95
Red Shoe Diaries 7: Burning Up '96
Red Shoe Diaries 8: Night of Abandon '97
Red Shoe Diaries: Four on the Floor '96
Red Shoe Diaries: Luscious Lola '00
Red Shoe Diaries: Strip Poker '96
Red Shoe Diaries: Swimming Naked '00
The Red Violin '98
Rendez-vous '85 ▶
Repo Jake '90
Repulsion '65 ▶
Return to Peyton Place '61
Riders '88
The Right Temptation '00
Rio Sex Comedy '10
Ripe '97
Rita, Sue & Bob Too '87 ▶
Rites of Frankenstein '72
The Road to Wellville '94
The Rocky Horror Picture Show '75 ▶
Roger Dodger '02 ▶
Romance '99
Rosebud Beach Hotel '85
The Rowdy Girls '00
The Rue Morgue Massacres '73
The Runner '15
Running with the Devil '19
Russian Dolls '05
The Sailor Who Fell from Grace with the Sea '76
Saints and Sinners '95
Salmonberries '91
Satanic Panic '19
The Scarlet Letter '79 ▶
Scene of the Crime '87 ▶
Score '72
Scorned 2 '96
Scrubbers '82
Sea of Love '89 ▶
Secret Games 3 '94
Secrets '71
The Seduction of Joe Tynan '79
Seduction: The Cruel Woman '89
The Seductress '00
Seeing Other People '04
The Seniors '78
The Sessions '12 ▶
Seven Deadly Sins '10
The '70s '00
Sex '20
Sex and Breakfast '07
Sex and Lucia '01
Sex & Mrs. X '00
Sex and the Other Man '95
Sex and the Single Mom '03
Sex Crimes '92
Sex Ed '14
Sex is Comedy '02
Sex Kittens Go to College '60
Sex on the Run '78
Sex Tape '14
Sextette '78
Sexting '11
Sexual Malice '93
Sexual Roulette '96
Shampoo '75
Sherrybaby '06
She's Gotta Have It '86 ▶
She's Too Young '04
Shopgirl '05 ▶
Showgirls '95
Sibling Rivalry '90
Siddhartha '72
Silk 'n' Sabotage '94
Sirens '94
The Sister-in-Law '74
Six Days, Six Nights '94
Ski School '91
Skin Deep '89
Sliver '93
Snapdragon '93
Some Velvet Morning '13
Somersault '04
Something About Sex '98
Something in the Air '13
Somewhere in the City '97
Sons and Lovers '60 ▶
Sooner or Later '78
The Souvenir '19 ▶
Space Station 76 '14
Species 3 '04
Spirit Lost '96
Splendor in the Grass '61 ▶
Spring Breakers '13 ▶
Sprung '96
The Squall '29
Star 80 '83
The Stationmaster's Wife '77
Stepping Out '31
Stiff Upper Lips '96
Stone '10
Stormswept '95
Storyville '92
The Strangers '98
Strictly Sexual '08
Strike a Pose '93
Stripped to Kill '87
The Stud '78
Summer Heat '87
Summer Lovers '82
Summer of '04 '06
Summer School Teachers '75
Summer With Monica '53
Summertime '16
Super Bitch '73
Superbad '07 ▶
Supervixens '75
Susan Slept Here '54
Susana '51 ▶
Sweet Ecstasy '62
Sweet Evil '98
Sweet Lies '88
Sweet Movie '75
The Sweet Ride '68
Sweet Spirits '71
Swimming Pool '70
Swimming Pool '03 ▶
Swingers '96 ▶
Swinging Safari '19
Sylvia '03
Tabloid '10
Take a Girl Like You '70
Tale of Two Sisters '89
Tales of Erotica '93
Tales of the Kama Sutra: The Perfumed Garden '98
Talkin' Dirty after Dark '91
The Taste of Money '12
The Taste of Others '00 ▶
Tea and Sympathy '56 ▶
Teach Me '97
Tempted '01
Temptress Moon '96
Ten Inch Hero '07
10,000 Km '14
Teorema '68
Terrified '94
The Terror Within '88
Test Tube Babies '48
Texasville '90
Thanks for Sharing '13
That Obscure Object of Desire '77 ▶
Therese & Isabelle '67
Thief of Hearts '84
Things You Can Tell Just by Looking at Her '00
Thirteen '03 ▶
36 Fillete '88 ▶
This Property Is Condemned '66
3 Generations '17
360 '12
3-Way '04
The Tigress '93
'Tis a Pity She's a Whore '73
The To Do List '13
To Sleep with a Vampire '92
To the Stars '20
Toe to Toe '09
Tom Jones '63 ▶
Tom Jones '98
Traded '16
Trainwreck '15 ▶
Trash '70
Trishna '11
Trojan War '97
Tropic of Cancer '70 ▶
Tropical Heat '93
The Trouble With Bliss '11
Turkish Delight '73
28 Hotel Rooms '12
Twentynine Palms '03
Twin Peaks: Fire Walk with Me '92
Twins of Evil '71
The Twist '76
2 by 4 '98
2 Days in Paris '07 ▶
Two Days in the Valley '96 ▶
Two Deaths '94
Two Night Stand '14
Una '17
Una Noche '13
The Unbearable Lightness of Being '88 ▶
Uncut Gems '19 ▶
Under Suspicion '92
Under the Yum-Yum Tree '63
The Unspeakable Act '13
Untogether '19
Up in the Air '09 ▶
Vacuuming Completely Nude in Paradise '01
The Valley Obscured by the Clouds '70
Valley of the Sun '11
Valmont '89 ▶
Vanilla Sky '01
Variety '83
Venus in Fur '13 ▶
A Very Special Favor '65
The Vicious Kind '09
A View to a Kill '85
Virgin Queen of St. Francis High '88
The Virgin Soldiers '69
Virtual Encounters '96
Virtual Girl '00
Virtual Sexuality '99
The Voyeur '94
Waiting '05
Watch Me '96
Water Drops on Burning Rocks '99
We Don't Live Here Anymore '04
Wedding in Blood '74 ▶
Weekend '11 ▶
Weekend Pass '84
Wetlands '13
What Men Want '19
What Planet Are You From? '00
Whatever You Say '02
What's Good for the Goose '69
What's Your Number? '11
When Will I Be Loved '04
When Women Had Tails '70
Where the Boys Are '84 '84
Where the Hot Wind Blows '59
Where the Truth Lies '05
Whispers in the Dark '92
White Bird in a Blizzard '14
Wide Sargasso Sea '92
A Wild Affair '63
Wild at Heart '90 ▶
Wild Oats '16
Wild Things '98
The Wilde Wedding '17
Winter Sleepers '97
Wish You Were Here '87 ▶
The Witches of Eastwick '87
A Woman, Her Men and Her Futon '92
The Woman Next Door '81 ▶
Woman of Desire '93
Woman Times Seven '67
Women in Love '70 ▶
Women on the Verge of a Nervous Breakdown '88 ▶
Working Girls '75
Working Girls '87 ▶
X, Y & Zee '72
Yanks '79
Yesterday, Today and Tomorrow '64 ▶
You Don't Mess with the Zohan '08
Young Adam '03 ▶
Young & Beautiful '13
The Young Kieslowski '15
Young Lady Chatterly 2 '85
Your Friends & Neighbors '98 ▶
Youth in Revolt '10
The Yum-Yum Girls '78
Zabriskie Point '70 ▶
Zandalee '91
Zapped! '82
Zero '97
Zipper '15
Zombie Island Massacre '84

Sex on the Beach

***See also** Island Fare*

Against All Odds '84
Airplane! '80 ▶
The Beach '00
The Blue Lagoon '80
Come Undone '00
Cote d'Azur '05
Everything, Everything '17
The Firm '93 ▶
From Here to Eternity '53 ▶
Heading South '05 ▶
Kiss Tomorrow Goodbye '00
Maslin Beach '97
Memoirs of an Invisible Man '92
Mixed Nuts '94
Phat Beach '96
Sweet Ecstasy '62
Swept Away. . . '75 ▶
Swept from the Sea '97
Tales of the Kama Sutra 2: Monsoon '98
Young Adam '03 ▶

Sexploitation

***See** Erotic Thrillers*

Sexual Abuse

***See also** Domestic Abuse; Rape*

The Accused '88 ▶
All About Lily Chou-Chou '01 ▶
Bad Education '04 ▶
The Bed You Sleep In '93
The Book of Henry '17
Boxing Helena '93
The Boys of St. Vincent '93 ▶
The Club '16 ▶
Compliance '12 ▶
The Devils '71 ▶
Dream Boy '08
Hard Candy '06
Heart of the Stag '84 ▶
High Life '18
Ilsa, Harem Keeper of the Oil Sheiks '76
Invisible Scars '15
The Lena Baker Story '08
A Long Way Home '01
Mea Maxima Culpa: Silence in the House of God '12
Mesmerized '84
Mysterious Skin '04 ▶
Mystic River '03 ▶
The Night Porter '74
The Notorious Bettie Page '06
Nymphomaniac, Volume 1 '13
Outlaw Prophet: Warren Jeffs '14
The Perfection '19
Priest '94
Red Hook Summer '12 ▶
Regression '16
Romper Stomper '92
Southern Man '99
Spotlight '15 ▶
Sucker Punch '11
Trade '07
Traffik '18
Twin Peaks: Fire Walk with Me '92
Woman, Thou Art Loosed '04
You Were Never Really Here '17 ▶

Sexual Harassment

Bombshell '19
Disclosure '94
Foxfire '96
G.I. Jane '97
9 to 5 '80
North Country '05
Obsessed '02
Oleanna '94

Ships

***See** Deep Blue; Mutiny; Sail Away; Shipwrecked; Submarines*

Shipwrecked

***See also** Sea Disasters*

AE: Apocalypse Earth '13
Alvin and the Chipmunks: Chipwrecked '11
Benji the Hunted '87
The Black Pirate '26 ▶
The Black Stallion '79 ▶
Blue Fin '78
The Blue Lagoon '80
Cabeza de Vaca '90 ▶
Chevalier '16
Courage '09
Dead of Night '99
Dungeon of Harrow '64
Eye of the Needle '81
Far from Home: The Adventures of Yellow Dog '94
Greystoke: The Legend of Tarzan, Lord of the Apes '84
He Is My Brother '75
Hercules, Samson and Ulysses '64
Humongous '82
The Island of Dr. Moreau '77
Island of Lost Souls '32 ▶
Island of the Lost '68
Kilma, Queen of the Amazons '75
The Last Templar '09
Light at the Edge of the World '71
Madagascar '05
Male and Female '19 ▶
Matango '63

▶ = rated three bones or higher

► = rated three bones or higher

You Ain't Seen Nothin' Yet '12
Your Cheatin' Heart '64
Zeroville '19

Showbiz Horror

***See also** Behind the Scenes; Showbiz Dramas; Showbiz Thrillers*

Audition '99
A Blade in the Dark '83
Bleading Lady '10
Cut '00
Don't Look Up '08
Fright Flick '10
Hollywood Kills '06
House of Bones '09
The Hypnotic Eye '60
Madhouse '74
The Phantom of Hollywood '74
Popcorn '89
Prisoner '07
Scream 2 '97▶
Shadow of the Vampire '00▶
Skeleton Crew '09
Theatre of Blood '73▶
13 Seconds '03

Showbiz Musicals

***See also** Musical Fantasy; Musicals; Showbiz Comedies*

All That Jazz '79▶
Bloodhounds of Broadway '89
Broadway Serenade '39
Bye Bye Birdie '95
Camp Rock 2: The Final Jam '10
Career Girl '44
Cats Don't Dance '97
Chasing Rainbows '30
Chicago '02▶
A Chorus Line '85
The Devil on Horseback '36
The Eddie Cantor Story '53
George White's Scandals '45
Get On Up '14
Glitter '01
Gold Diggers in Paris '38
Golden Girl '51
The Good Companions '33
The Greatest Showman '17
Greenwich Village '44
Hedwig and the Angry Inch '00▶
The Helen Morgan Story '57
Hollywood Hotel '37
The I Don't Care Girl '53
Idlewild '06
Idol on Parade '59
If I'm Lucky '46
Irish Eyes Are Smiling '44
It's a Great Life '29
Jersey Boys '14
Kiss Me Kate '53▶
La La Land '16▶
Lord Byron of Broadway '30
Moulin Rouge '01▶
My Gal Sal '42
My Wild Irish Rose '47
Nine '09
Noises Off '92
The Old Homestead '35
On with the Show '29
Rock of Ages '12
Sailing Along '38
Sally '29
Sally, Irene and Mary '38
Sing, Baby, Sing '36
Singin' in the Rain '52▶
Something for the Boys '44
Step Lively '44
The Suburbans '99
Sweet and Low-Down '44
The Temptations '98
There's No Business Like Show Business '54▶
Three for the Show '55
Three Little Words '50
Till the Clouds Roll By '46
Time Out for Rhythm '41
Varsity Show '37
Wake Up and Live '37
Wonder Bar '34
Yankee Doodle Dandy '42▶

Showbiz Thrillers

Broken Embraces '09▶
Children Shouldn't Play with Dead Things '72
Dead of Winter '87▶
The Dead Pool '88
Death on the Set '35
F/X 2: The Deadly Art of Illusion '91
F/X '86▶
Hollywood Story '51
The House of Seven Corpses '73
I Wake Up Screaming '41▶
iCrime '11
Kiss Tomorrow Goodbye '00
Lady of Burlesque '43
Number One Fan '94
Return to Cabin by the Lake '01
Return to Horror High '87
The Salesman '16▶
Satan in High Heels '61
The Stunt Man '80▶
A Thousand Cuts '12
What Ever Happened To. . . '93
What Ever Happened to Baby Jane? '62▶

Shrinkage

***See also** Metamorphosis*

The Ant Bully '06
Arthur and the Invisibles '06
Attack of the Puppet People '58
Bad Channels '92
Dr. Cyclops '40
Honey, I Shrunk the Kids '89
Honey, We Shrunk Ourselves '97
The Incredible Shrinking Man '57▶
The Incredible Shrinking Woman '81
Meet Dave '08
Once Upon a Spy '80
Phantasm '79
The Seventh Voyage of Sinbad '58▶

Shrinks

***See also** Doctors & Nurses*

Abandoned '10
The Accidental Husband '08
Agnes of God '85
Almost Dead '94
America '09
Analyze That '02
Analyze This '98▶
Angel Dusted '81
Anger Management '03
Answers to Nothing '11
Antwone Fisher '02▶
Assassin's Bullet '12
Assault on Precinct 13 '05
Bark! '02
Basic Instinct 2 '06
Batman Forever '95▶
A Beautiful Mind '01▶
Before I Go to Sleep '14
Behind the Lines '97
Betrayal '78
Betty '97
Between Truth and Lies '06
Beyond Therapy '86
Big Jim McLain '52
Bliss '96
Body Chemistry 2: Voice of a Stranger '91
Body of Influence 2 '96
Body of Influence '93
Borderline '02▶
Calling Dr. Gillespie '42
Captain Newman, M.D. '63
The Caretakers '63
The Cell '00
Charlie Bartlett '07▶
Cheaters' Club '06
The Cobweb '55
Color of Night '94
Coming Apart '69
Conspiracy Theory '97▶
The Couch '62
A Couch in New York '95
The Couch Trip '87
Couples Retreat '09
Cracker: Brotherly Love '95▶
Cracker: Men Should Weep '94
Cracker: The Big Crunch '94
Cracker: To Be a Somebody '94
Cravings '06
Crazy as Hell '02
Cruel Intentions '98
Dallas 362 '03
A Dangerous Method '11
Dangerously We Live '41
Dark Asylum '01
Dark Mirror '46▶
The Day the World Ended '01
Deconstructing Harry '97
Defendor '09
Desire Me '47
Dial 1119 '50
Disney's The Kid '00
Disturbing Behavior '98
The Dog Problem '06
Don Juan DeMarco '94
Don't Look Down '98
Don't Say a Word '01
Downloading Nancy '08
The Dream Team '89
Dressed to Kill '80
88 Minutes '08
Eros '04
The Evening Star '96
The Eye '02
Face to Face '76▶
Faithful '95
Fear '90
The Fear '94
Female Perversions '96
Final '01
Final Analysis '92
A Fine Madness '66▶
The Fourth Kind '09
Frankie and Alice '10
Future Shock '93
Genealogies of a Crime '97
Girl of the Night '60
A Girl Thing '01
Good Will Hunting '97
Gothika '03
Grosse Pointe Blank '97▶
The Grudge 3 '09
Gun Shy '00
Halloween '78▶
Halloween II '09
Hangman '00
Happiness '98▶
He Loves Me '11
Heaven '99
Hector and the Search for Happiness '14
Hell's Gate '01
High Anxiety '77
High Wall '47
The Hole '01
Holiday for Lovers '59
Home Movie '08
Home Movies '79
Hope Springs '12▶
House of Games '87▶
I Don't Buy Kisses Anymore '92
I Dream of Murder '06
I Never Promised You a Rose Garden '77▶
I, Robot '04
If Lucy Fell '95
The Impossible Years '68
Indecent Behavior 2 '94
Inside Out '05
Instinct '99
Intimate Strangers '04▶
The Invasion '07
Jade '95
Jesse Stone: No Remorse '10
Jimmy P. '13
K-PAX '01
Karla '06
Kate's Secret '86
Kill Your Darlings '06
Killer by Nature '10
Knock on Wood '54
The Lady Gambles '49
Lady in a Jam '42
Lantana '01▶
Lies and Whispers '98
A Lizard in a Woman's Skin '71
The Locket '46
Lovesick '83
The Man Who Loved Women '83
Manic '01
Matchstick Men '03▶
Merci Docteur Rey '04▶
Mercy '00
A Mind to Murder '96
Mine Own Executioner '47▶
Mr. Jones '93
The Moment '13
Monkeybone '01
Mortal Transfer '01
The Mugger '58
Mulholland Falls '95
Mumford '99▶
Murderland '09
Murderous Intent '06▶
Must Read After My Death '09
The Myth of Fingerprints '97
National Lampoon's The Don's Analyst '97
Nell '94
The Night Caller '97
Nightmare Alley '47
Numb '07
Oh, Men! Oh, Women! '57
On a Clear Day You Can See Forever '70
On the Edge '00
Once More With Feeling '08
Once You Kiss a Stranger '69
One Fine Day '96
One Flew Over the Cuckoo's Nest '75▶
Open Your Eyes '97▶
Panic '00
Passion of Mind '00
The Penitent Man '10
Pilot X '37
The President's Analyst '67▶
Pressure Point '62▶
Primal Fear '96
Prime '05
The Prince of Tides '91▶
Progeny '98
Prozac Nation '01
Pussycat, Pussycat, I Love You '70
Quicksand '01
Rampage: The Hillside Strangler Murders '04
Reflections '08
Reign Over Me '07
Riot in Juvenile Prison '59
The Royal Tenenbaums '01▶
Ruby Sparks '12
Running with Scissors '06
The Scar '48
Screaming Mimi '58
The Secret Heart '46
Seventh Heaven '98
A Severed Head '70
She Wouldn't Say Yes '45
Shock! '46
Shrink '09
Side Effects '13▶
Silent Fall '94
6 Souls '13
The Sixth Sense '99▶
The Sleeping Tiger '54
Solaris '02
Sometimes They Come Back. . . Again '96
The Son's Room '00▶
Special Treatment '10
Spellbound '45▶
Sphere '97
Stephanie Daley '06
Still of the Night '82
Stop Me Before I Kill! '60
Strange Relations '02
The Stranger '87▶
The Stranger '10
Stranger Than Fiction '06
The Stranger Within '13
Streets of Blood '09
Stuart Saves His Family '94
Sworn to Justice '97
Sybil '76▶
Tender Is the Night '62
They Come Back '07
They Might Be Giants '71▶
36 Hours '64▶
The Three Faces of Eve '57
Through a Glass Darkly '61▶
Till Human Voices Wake Us '02
Tin Cup '96▶
The Treatment '06
Triage '09
Trust '10
12 Monkeys '95▶
Twisted '04
The Ugly '96
Uncaged Heart '07
Underworld '96
The Unsaid '01
Veronika Decides to Die '15
A Very Special Favor '65
Victim of Love '91
Visions of Murder '93
The Visit '00▶
The Voices '15
The Wackness '08
Waking Madison '10
The Watcher '00
Wes Craven Presents: They '02
What Lies Beneath '00
What's New Pussycat? '65▶
Where Truth Lies '96
Whirlpool '49
Whispers in the Dark '92
The Wife '95
Wild in the Country '61
Wilderness '96
You Must Be Joking! '65
You Wont Miss Me '09
The Young Poisoner's Handbook '94▶

Shutterbugs

***See also** Front Page*

Addicted to Love '96
Adrift in Manhattan '07
Amelie '01▶
And Then Came Lola '09
Austin Powers: International Man of Mystery '97▶
Austin Powers 2: The Spy Who Shagged Me '99▶
Baba Yaga '73
Backbeat '94▶
The Bang Bang Club '10
Battle Zone '52
The Beautiful, the Bloody and the Bare '64
Beefcake '99
Bending All the Rules '02
Bill Cunningham New York '10
Billy's Hollywood Screen Kiss '98
Blondie Meets the Boss '39
Blood Gnome '02
Blow-Up '66▶
The Blue Gardenia '53▶
Body Shot '93
Bound by Lies '05
The Bridges of Madison County '95▶
Calendar '93▶
Camera Buff '79
The Caveman's Valentine '01
China Girl '42
Close-Up '48
Closer '04▶
Dark Mirror '07
Darkroom '90
Death and Desire '97
Delirious '06
Dirty Love '05
Dr. Mabuse *vs.* Scotland Yard '64
Don't Answer the Phone '80
Double Exposure '82
Down in the Delta '98▶
Easy Money '83
Everlasting Moments '08
Eyes Behind the Stars '72
Eyes of Laura Mars '78
The Family Jewels '65
The Favor, the Watch, & the Very Big Fish '92
Femme Fatale '02
Fire on the Amazon '93
Firefall '94
Footsteps '98
The Front Runner '18
Funny Face '57▶
Garden Party '08
Georgia O'Keefe '09
The Governess '98
Guinevere '99▶
Hard Candy '06
Harrison's Flowers '02
Head in the Clouds '04
Heat and Sunlight '87
Heights '04
Here '12
High Art '98
High Season '88
Hope Floats '98
I Love Melvin '53
Joe Gould's Secret '00
Johnny Skidmarks '97
Killer Image '92
Love Is a Gun '94
Mad Dog and Glory '93▶
Madame Claude '77
Memento '00▶
The Midnight Meat Train '08
Mr. Brooks '07
Monogamy '10
Murder With Pictures '36
Nightcrawler '14▶
No Time For Love '43▶
Not for Publication '84
The Notorious Bettie Page '06
November '05▶
Of Love and Shadows '94
On Each Side '07
One Hour Photo '02▶
The Orgasm Diaries '10
Over-Exposed '56
Paparazzi '04
Pecker '98
Peeping Tom '60▶
Perfume '01
The Photograph '20
Photographing Fairies '97
Picture Snatcher '33
Polisse '11▶
The Portrait '99
Portraits of a Killer '95
Pretty Baby '78▶
Proof '91▶
The Public Eye '92▶
Rear Window '54▶
Return to Boggy Creek '77
The Salt of the Earth '14▶
Screaming Dead '03
Secret File of Hollywood '62
Shadow Magic '00
Shooting the Past '99
Shot '01
Shutter '05
Shutter '08
Shutterbug '10
Smoke '95
Snap Decision '01
Snapshot '77
Somebody Has to Shoot the Picture '90▶
Spice World: The Movie '97
Stephen King's The Night Flier '96
Stepmom '98▶
Sunset Strip '99
The System '64
A Time to Die '91
Time to Leave '05▶
Triage '09
Tricks of a Woman '08
The Truth about Cats and Dogs '96▶
2 Minutes Later '07
The Unbearable Lightness of Being '88▶
Until the End of the World '91▶
Visitors '13
War Story '14
Watch Me '96
Watch the Birdie '50
The Watcher '00
The Weight of Water '00
Where the Heart Is '00
Wild America '97▶
The Wild Stallion '09
The Winter Guest '97▶

Sibling Rivalry

***See also** Brothers & Sisters*

Aardvark '18
Across the Tracks '89
All the Brothers Were Valiant '53
American Flyers '85
America's Sweethearts '01
Awful Nice '14
Beautiful Ohio '06

Before the Devil Knows You're Dead '07 ▶
Ben-Hur '16
Big Brother Trouble '00
Blood Ties '13
The Boss Baby '17
The Boys and Girl From County Clare '03
The Brotherhood '68
Brothers '09
A Brother's Kiss '97
The Brothers McMullen '94 ▶
Brothers of the Head '06
Cadillac Ranch '96
Centerstage: On Pointe '16
Central Airport '33
The Color Wheel '11
The Crowd Roars '32
Dead Ringer '64
Defiance '08
Despicable Me 3 '17
Diary of a Wimpy Kid 2: Rodrick Rules '11
The Do-Deca-Pentathlon '12
A Dog's Breakfast '07
Douchebag '10
East of Eden '54 ▶
East of Eden '80
Fighting with My Family '19
Fred Claus '07
Georgia '95 ▶
Go for Zucker '05
Hair Show '04
Harvest '10
Haywire '80
Hilary and Jackie '98 ▶
Home Run Showdown '10
King Lear '98 ▶
The Little Foxes '41 ▶
Little Women '18
Lovers of Hate '10
My Blind Brother '16
My Brother Is an Only Child '07
My Sister's Keeper '02
Nature Calls '12
Newcastle '08
Office Christmas Party '16
The Overbrook Brothers '09
Peep World '10
The Perfect Son '00
Ricky '09
Scout's Honor: Badge to the Bone '09
A Short History of Decay '13
Sibling Rivalry '90
Six Days, Six Nights '94
Summer Hours '08
The Sweet Life '03
This Is Where I Leave You '14
A Thousand Acres '97
Three Priests '08
3, 2, 1...Frankie Go Boom '12
The Two Mr. Kissels '08
(Untitled) '09
We Are What We Are '11
Wicked Blood '13
Yours, Mine & Ours '05
Zus & Zo '01

Sieges & Standoffs

***See also** Big Battles; Hostage!; Trapped with a Killer!*

The Alamo '60 ▶
The Alamo '04
Aquarius '16 ▶
Assault on Precinct 13 '76 ▶
Assault on Precinct 13 '05
Battleground '49 ▶
Braveheart '95 ▶
Bury My Heart at Wounded Knee '07
Dawn of the Dead '78 ▶
Dawn of the Dead '04 ▶
Day of the Dead '85
Dog Day Afternoon '75 ▶
El Cid '61 ▶
El Dorado '67 ▶
Evil Dead '83
Excalibur '81 ▶
Family Weekend '13
The Four Feathers '39 ▶
The Four Feathers '78
The Four Feathers '02
From Dusk Till Dawn '95
The Great Wall '17
Inside Man '06 ▶
Khartoum '66
Kingdom of Heaven '05 ▶
The Last of the Mohicans '92 ▶
Legion '10
Light It Up '99
Lord of the Rings: The Two Towers '02 ▶
Lord of the Rings: The Return of the King '03 ▶
The Nest '02
Night of the Living Dead '68 ▶
Return of the Living Dead '85
Rio Bravo '59 ▶
The Road Warrior '82 ▶
Scarface '31 ▶
Scenes of the Crime '01
Shaun of the Dead '04 ▶
The Siege '98
Siege at Red River '54
The Siege of Firebase Gloria '89
S.W.A.T. '03
300 '07
300: Rise of an Empire '13
Tomorrow Never Comes '77
The Town '10 ▶
Treed Murray '01
Troy '04
Zulu '64

Silent Films

The Ace of Hearts '21
Across to Singapore '28
The Adorable Cheat '28
The Adventures of Tarzan '21
Aelita: Queen of Mars '24
Amarilly of Clothesline Alley '18
American Pluck '25
Anna Christie '23 ▶
Arsenal '29 ▶
The Artist '11 ▶
The Atonement of Gosta Berling '24 ▶
Avenging Conscience '14
The Back Trail '24
Barbara Frietchie '24
Bardelys the Magnificent '26
The Bat '26 ▶
The Battleship Potemkin '25 ▶
Battling Butler '26
Beau Brummel '24
Bed and Sofa '27 ▶
Beggars of Life '28
The Bells '26 ▶
The Beloved Rogue '27 ▶
Ben-Hur '26 ▶
The Better 'Ole '26
Beyond the Rocks '22
The Big Parade '25 ▶
The Birth of a Nation '15 ▶
The Black Bird '26
The Black Pirate '26 ▶
Blind Husbands '19 ▶
Blood and Sand '22
Body and Soul '24
Brand Upon the Brain! '06 ▶
Broken Blossoms '19 ▶
Broken Hearts of Broadway '23
Burning Daylight '28
The Cabinet of Dr. Caligari '19 ▶
Cabiria '14
California Straight Ahead '25
The Cameraman '28 ▶
The Canadian '26
Captain Salvation '27
The Cat and the Canary '27 ▶
Champagne '28
The Chaplin Revue '58
The Chess Player '27
Chicago '27
The Cigarette Girl of Mosselprom '24
The Circus '28 ▶
City Girl '30
City Lights '31 ▶
Civilization '16 ▶
Cobra '25
Conductor 1492 '24
The Confession '20
The Count of Monte Cristo '12
The Cradle of Courage '20
Daddy Long Legs '19
Dancing Mothers '26
Destiny '21 ▶
The Devil Horse '26
Diary of a Lost Girl '29 ▶
The Divine Lady '29
Dr. Jekyll and Mr. Hyde '20 ▶
Dr. Mabuse, The Gambler '22 ▶
Dog Star Man '64 ▶
Don Juan '26 ▶
Don Q., Son of Zorro '25
Down to the Sea in Ships '22
Dream Street '21
Dress Parade '27
The Duchess of Buffalo '26
The Eagle '25 ▶
Earth '30 ▶
Easy Virtue '27
The End of St. Petersburg '27 ▶
Evangeline '29
Exit Smiling '26
Extra Girl '23
The Eyes of Youth '19
The Family Secret '24
The Farmer's Wife '28
Faust '26 ▶
Feel My Pulse '28
The Fighting Eagle '27
The Finances of the Grand Duke '24
Fine Manners '26
Flesh and Blood '22
The Flesh and the Devil '27 ▶
The Flying Fleet '29
A Fool There Was '14
Foolish Wives '22 ▶
The Forbidden City '18
The Four Horsemen of the Apocalypse '21 ▶
Four Sons '28
The Freshman '25 ▶
From the Manger to the Cross '12
The Garden of Eden '28 ▶
The Gaucho '27 ▶
The General '26 ▶
Getting Gertie's Garter '27
Girl Shy '24 ▶
Go West '25 ▶
The Gold Rush '25 ▶
The Golem '20 ▶
The Greatest Question '19
Gypsy Blood '18
The Hands of Orlac '25
Hangman's House '28
Happiness '32
Haxan: Witchcraft through the Ages '22 ▶
He Who Gets Slapped '24 ▶
Heart o' the Hills '19
Her Night of Romance '24
Her Sister from Paris '25
Hindle Wakes '27
His Majesty, the American '19
His Picture in the Papers '16
The Hoodlum '19
Hotel Imperial '27
The Houdini Serial '20
The Hunchback of Notre Dame '23 ▶
Hungarian Rhapsody '28
I Was Born But. . . '32 ▶
The Idol Dancer '20
In the Days of the Thundering Herd & the Law & the Outlaw '14
Intolerance '16 ▶
The Iron Horse '24 ▶
The Iron Mask '29
It '27
The Italian '15
Italian Straw Hat '27 ▶
It's the Old Army Game '26 ▶
J'accuse! '19 ▶
The Jazz Singer '27
Joyless Street '25 ▶
Judex '16
Judith of Bethulia '14 ▶
The Kid Brother '27 ▶
Kiki '26
King of Kings '27
King of the Wild Stallions '59
Kismet '20 ▶
The Kiss '29 ▶
Kriemhilde's Revenge '24 ▶
La Boheme '26
La Roue '23 ▶
A Lady of Chance '28
Lady of the Night '25 ▶
Lady Windermere's Fan '25
Laila '29
The Last Command '28 ▶
The Last Laugh '24 ▶
The Last of the Mohicans '20 ▶
Laugh, Clown, Laugh '28 ▶
Lazybones '25
Leaves from Satan's Book '21
Les Vampires '15 ▶
Lightning Hutch '26
The Little American '17
Little Church Around the Corner '23
Little Old New York '23
The Lodger '26 ▶
The Lost World '25
The Love Flower '20
The Love of Jeanne Ney '27
Lucky Star '29
The Magician '26
Male and Female '19 ▶
The Man Who Had Everything '20
The Man Who Laughs '27 ▶
The Man with the Movie Camera '29 ▶
The Manxman '29
Mark of Zorro '20 ▶
The Marriage Circle '24 ▶
Master of the House '25 ▶
Merry-Go-Round '23 ▶
The Merry Widow '25 ▶
Metropolis '26 ▶
Mickey '17
Midnight Faces '26
Mr. Wu '27
Modern Times '36 ▶
Monsieur Beaucaire '24
Monte Cristo '22
Moran of the Lady Letty '22
A Mormon Maid '17
Mother '26 ▶
My Best Girl '27 ▶
My Friend from India '27
The Mysterious Lady '28
Nanook of the North '22 ▶
No Man's Law '27
Noah's Ark '28
Nomads of the North '20
The Non-Stop Flight '26
The Notorious Lady '27
Old San Francisco '27
Oliver Twist '22 ▶
One Arabian Night '20 ▶
Orphans of the Storm '21 ▶
Othello '22
Our Dancing Daughters '28
Our Hospitality '23 ▶
The Outlaw and His Wife '17
Outside the Law '21
Pace That Kills '28
The Pagan '29
Paint and Powder '25
Pampered Youth '25
Pandora's Box '28 ▶
Passion '19
Passion of Joan of Arc '28 ▶
Patchwork Girl of Oz '14
Paths to Paradise '25 ▶
The Patsy '28
Peter Pan '24
Phantom '22
The Phantom Carriage '21 ▶
The Phantom Chariot '20
The Phantom of the Opera '25 ▶
The Plastic Age '25
The Pleasure Garden '25
The Plunderers '60
Pride of the Clan '18
The Primitive Lover '22
The Prisoner of Zenda '22
Queen Kelly '29 ▶
Ranson's Folly '26
The Raven '15
Rebecca of Sunnybrook Farm '17
Red Kimono '25
The Red Lily '24
The Red Mill '27
Regeneration '15
The Return of Boston Blackie '27
The Ring '27
The Road to Yesterday '25
Robin Hood '22 ▶
Romola '25
Sadie Thompson '28 ▶
Safety Last '23 ▶
Sally of the Sawdust '25
The Saphead '21
The Scar of Shame '27
Scaramouche '23
Secrets of a Soul '25
Seven Years Bad Luck '21 ▶
7th Heaven '27
Sex '20
Shadows '22
She '25
The Sheik '21 ▶
Sherlock Holmes '22
The Shock '23
The Show '27
Show People '28 ▶
Siegfried '24 ▶
Silent Movie '76
The Single Standard '29
Siren of the Tropics '27
Skinner's Dress Suit '26
Slow as Lightning '23
The Smart Set '28
Soul of the Beast '23
Souls for Sale '23
Sparrows '26 ▶
Speedway '29
Speedy '28 ▶
Spiders '18 ▶
Spies '28 ▶
Spite Marriage '29 ▶
Spring Fever '27
The Squaw Man '14
Steamboat Bill, Jr. '28 ▶
Stella Maris '18 ▶
Storm over Asia '28 ▶
Street Angel '28
Strike '24 ▶
Suds '20
Sunrise '27 ▶
Tabu: A Story of the South Seas '31 ▶
Tartuffe '25
Tarzan the Tiger '29
Tell It to the Marines '26
Tempest '28
The Temptress '26
The Ten Commandments '23
Ten Days That Shook the World '27 ▶
Ten Nights in a Barroom '13
Tess of the Storm Country '22
The Texas Streak '26
That Certain Thing '28
The Thief '52
The Thief of Baghdad '24 ▶
The Three Musketeers '21 ▶
Three Word Brand '21
Through the Back Door '21
A Throw of Dice '29 ▶
Tide of Empire '29
Tillie's Punctured Romance '14
Tol'able David '21
The Toll Gate '20
Torrent '26
Traffic in Souls '13 ▶
The Trail of '98 '28
Tramp, Tramp, Tramp '26
The Trap '22
Trapped by the Mormons '22
Treasure of Arne '19
True Heart Susie '19
Tumbleweeds '25 ▶
20,000 Leagues under the Sea '16 ▶
Twinkletoes '26
Uncle Tom's Cabin '27
The Unholy Three '25 ▶
Up the Ladder '25
The Vanishing American '25
Variety '25 ▶
The Viking '28
Warning Shadows '23 ▶
Way Down East '20 ▶
West-Bound Limited '23
West Point '27
When a Man Loves '27
When the Clouds Roll By '19 ▶
Where the North Begins '23
White Gold '28 ▶
The White Sin '24
The White Sister '23 ▶
White Tiger '23
Why Be Good? '29
Why Change Your Wife? '20
Wild Beauty '27
Wild Horse Canyon '25
Wild Oranges '24
Wild Orchids '28
Wings '27
Within Our Gates '20
Within the Law '23
The Wizard of Oz '25
Wolf Blood '25
Woman in the Moon '29
A Woman of the World '25
The Wrath of the Gods '14
Yankee Clipper '27
Zvenigora '28 ▶

Silent Horror/Fantasy Classics

***See** Silent Films*

Single Parents

***See also** Bringing Up Baby; Parenthood*

About a Boy '02 ▶
About Sunny '12 ▶
Air Bud 2: Golden Receiver '98
Akeelah and the Bee '06
Alias Betty '01
All About My Mother '99 ▶
An American Crime '07
American Gun '05
American History X '98
American Violet '09
Amreeka '09 ▶
And Now a Word From Our Sponsor '13
And So They Were Married '36
And Then Came Love '07
Annie Claus is Coming to Town '11
The Answer Man '09
Any Day '15
Anywhere But Here '99
Are We There Yet? '05
Arizona '18
As Good As It Gets '97 ▶
Baby Boom '87
The Bad Mother's Handbook '07
Bag of Bones '11
A Bag of Hammers '11
Bandslam '09
Be My Valentine '13
Beautiful '00
Because I Said So '07
Because of Winn-Dixie '05
Black Nativity '13
Blended '14
Blue Car '03 ▶
Bogus '96
Bon Cop Bad Cop '06
The Boys Are Back '09
Brave New Girl '04
Bringing Up Bobby '11
Broken Wings '02 ▶
Bunny Lake Is Missing '65
Burning Man '11
Bye Bye, Love '94
Cape of Good Hope '04
Captain Fantastic '16
Captive '15
The Case for Christmas '11
Casper '95 ▶
Catch and Release '07
The Chambermaid '19
Changeling '08 ▶
Charlie St. Cloud '10
Chasing 3000 '07
Chicken Little '05
Children of Invention '09
Chitty Chitty Bang Bang '68
Christmas Lodge '11
The Christmas Pageant '11
Christmas Town '08
A Christmas Wedding Tail '11
Citadel '12
Cold Comes the Night '14
Cowgirls 'n Angels '12
Crazy for Christmas '05
Crazy on the Outside '10

▶ = rated three bones or higher

Crimes of the Past '09
The Cry: La Llorona '07
Cybermutt '02
Cyrus '10
Daddy's Little Girls '07
Daltry Calhoun '05
Dancehall Queen '97
Dancer in the Dark '99
Dark Water '02
A Deadly Encounter '04
Dear Frankie '04
Dolphin Tale '11
Double Parked '00
Edge of Winter '16
Eighth Grade '18 ▶
Enchanted '07
Erin Brockovich '00 ▶
E.T.: The Extra-Terrestrial '82 ▶
Evelyn '02 ▶
Evergreen '04
Family in Hiding '06
Father and Son '03
Fay Grim '06
Fierce People '05
Finding a Family '10
First, Last and Deposit '00
Fish Tank '09 ▶
5 Time Champion '11
Flight of the Red Balloon '08
Flightplan '05
Flirting with Forty '09
The Florida Project '17 ▶
Forever My Girl '18
4 Single Fathers '09
Free Ride '13
Free Style '09
Gifted Hands: The Ben Carson Story '09
Girl in Progress '12
A Girl Like Me: The Gwen Araujo Story '06
The Girl Next Door '53
Girlfight '99 ▶
God Bless the Broken Road '18
A Golden Christmas '09
The Goodbye Girl '77 ▶
Goodbye to All That '14
Grbavica: The Land of My Dreams '06
The Green Promise '49
The Haunting of Helena '12
Hearts Beat Loud '18
Hearts in Atlantis '01
Hide and Seek '05
Hideous Kinky '99
High Noon '09
The Hole in the Ground '19
Home Again '17
House of D '04
How I Killed My Father '03 ▶
How Stella Got Her Groove Back '98
Hysterical Blindness '02
I Am Sam '01
I Could Never Be Your Woman '06
I Now Pronounce You Chuck and Larry '07
Ice Princess '05
I'll Be There '03
I'm Glad My Mother Is Alive '09
In the Valley of Elah '07 ▶
Intimate Stranger '06
Introducing the Dwights '07
Jerry Maguire '96 ▶
Jersey Girl '04
Kansas City Bomber '72
The Karate Kid '84 ▶
The Karate Kid '10
Kenner '73
Knowing '09
Kramer *vs.* Kramer '79 ▶
La Mission '09
The Last Cowboy '03
The Last Rites of Joe May '11
Leaving Barstow '08
Let the Sunshine In '17
Limbo '99
A Little Inside '01
LOL '12
Long Life, Happiness and Prosperity '02
The Long Shot '04
Loverboy '05
Love's Kitchen '11
Lucky Christmas '11
Magic Beyond Words: The JK Rowling Story '11
The Magic of Belle Isle '12
Maid in Manhattan '02
Margarita Happy Hour '01
Martian Child '07
Me and You and Everyone We Know '05 ▶
Meet Dave '08
Message in a Bottle '98
The Midwife '17 ▶
The Mighty Celt '05
Mildred Pierce '11
Millions '05 ▶
Mind the Gap '04
Miracle Run '04
Mrs. Wiggs of the Cabbage Patch '34
Mommy '14 ▶
More Sex and the Single Mom '05
Morris from America '16 ▶
The Most Wonderful Time of the Year '08
The Mother '03 ▶
The Mudge Boy '03
Music of the Heart '99
Must Love Dogs '05
My Baby's Daddy '04
My Piece of the Pie '11
Nanny McPhee '06
Never Back Down '08
The New Daughter '10
No Reservations '07
Northpole '14
Novel Romance '06
One Fine Day '96
The Pacifier '05
Paul Blart: Mall Cop '09
Pay It Forward '00
People Like Us '12
The Perfect Holiday '07
The Perfect Man '05
A Place Called Home '04
The Players Club '98 ▶
Portrait of an Escort '80
The Principal '87
Private Property '06
Pulling Strings '13
Pure '02 ▶
Quiet Chaos '08
Rattlesnake '19
Ready? OK! '08
The Rewrite '15
Ricky '09
The Ring '02
Row Your Boat '98
Rugrats in Paris: The Movie '00 ▶
Rust and Bone '12 ▶
Sabotage '96
Safe Haven '13
St. Vincent '14
The Santa Incident '10
Secrets in the Walls '10
Secrets of the Mountain '10
Sex and the Single Mom '03
The Shipping News '01
The Sixth Sense '99 ▶
Skeletons in the Closet '00
Sleepless in Seattle '93 ▶
Sleepless Night '11 ▶
Sleepwalking '08
Small Town Saturday Night '10
Soldier Love Story '10
Something Like Happiness '05
Son of Rambow '07
The Spiderwick Chronicles '08 ▶
The Spring '00
Stolen '09
A Summer in Genoa '08
Sunshine Cleaning '09 ▶
Sweet Sixteen '02 ▶
Swing Vote '08
A Taste of Romance '12
Ten Things I Hate about You '99 ▶
Things You Can Tell Just by Looking at Her '00
Think of Me '11
Thirteen '03 ▶
The Tic Code '99
Time to Leave '05 ▶
The Town Is Quiet '00
Trucker '08
Turning Paige '01
20th Century Women '17
Twice Born '12
Twilight '08
Tyler Perry's Good Deeds '12
Tyler Perry's Meet the Browns '08
Tyler Perry's The Single Moms' Club '14
The Ultimate Gift '07
Uncaged Heart '07
Undertow '04
An Unfinished Life '05
Untraceable '08
Virginia '10
Waist Deep '06
The Waiting Room '07
A Walk in My Shoes '10
A Walk to Remember '02
Welcome to Paradise '07
What a Girl Wants '03
Where Are My Children? '94
Where the Heart Is '00
Where the Wild Things Are '09
The White Countess '05 ▶
Wilbur Wants to Kill Himself '02 ▶
Wild Rose '18 ▶
Wilderness Love '02
Wildflowers '99
Winter Solstice '04 ▶
Won't Back Down '12
World's Greatest Dad '09 ▶
You Can Count On Me '99 ▶
Yours, Mine & Ours '05
Zeus and Roxanne '96

Singles

***See also** Dates from Hell*

About a Boy '02 ▶
About Fifty '11
About Last Night. . . '86 ▶
Bar Hopping '00
Beautiful Girls '96 ▶
Before Sunrise '94
Beginners '10 ▶
A Bet's a Bet '14
Boys' Night Out '62 ▶
Breakfast at Tiffany's '61 ▶
Bridal Fever '08
Bridget Jones's Baby '16
Bridget Jones's Diary '01 ▶
Bye Bye, Love '94
Christmas Angel '09
Crazy, Stupid, Love. '11 ▶
Crossing Delancey '88 ▶
Dirty 30 '16
Everybody Loves Somebody '17 ▶
Everyone Says I Love You '96 ▶
Everything Relative '96
Extreme Dating '04
A Family Thanksgiving '10
Forget Paris '95
Funny Valentine '05
He Said, She Said '91
He's Just Not That Into You '09
How to Be Single '16
How to Fall in Love '12
Jack Goes Boating '10
Kicking and Screaming '95 ▶
The Land of Steady Habits '18
Let the Sunshine In '17
Life As We Know It '10
Love & Sex '00
Management '09
Meet Market '08
Metropolitan '90 ▶
Mr. Wonderful '93
Mr. Wrong '95
Mystic Pizza '88 ▶
The Opposite Sex and How to Live With Them '93
The Personals '98
Pillow Talk '59 ▶
Pirate Radio '09
Reality Bites '94
St. Elmo's Fire '85
Singles '92 ▶
Sleepless in Seattle '93 ▶
Sliding Doors '97
Someone Marry Barry '12
Something Borrowed '11
Speed Dating '07
Speed-Dating '10
Spin '07
That Touch of Mink '62
The Thing Called Love '93
35 and Ticking '10
Timer '09
Trial and Error '96
Wedding Bell Blues '96
When Harry Met Sally. . . '89 ▶
Wild Grass '09
Zookeeper '11

Sixties

***See** Period Piece: 1960s*

Skateboarding

Above and Beyond '53 ▶
Back to the Future '85 ▶
Beautiful Losers '08
Boxboarders! '07
Clueless '95 ▶
Dishdogz '05
Gleaming the Cube '89
Grind '03
Gummo '97
Kids '95
The Land '16
The Last Drop '05
Lords of Dogtown '05
Mid90s '18
Minding the Gap '18 ▶
MVP2: Most Vertical Primate '01
Paranoid Park '07
Skateboard '77
The Skateboard Kid 2 '94
Wassup Rockers '06

Skating

***See also** Hockey*

Airborne '93
American Venus '07
ATL '06
Blades of Glory '07
Champions: A Love Story '78
The Cutting Edge 3: Chasing the Dream '08
The Cutting Edge '92
The Cutting Edge: Fire and Ice '10
The Cutting Edge: Going for the Gold '05
Death to Smoochy '02
Frolics on Ice '39
Hans Brinker '69
Happy Landing '38
I, Tonya '17 ▶
Ice Castles '79
Ice Castles '10
Ice Follies of 1939 '39
Ice Princess '05
The Ice Rink '99
Iceland '42
It's a Pleasure '45
It's All About Love '03
My Life on Ice '02
My Lucky Star '38
On Edge '03
One in a Million '36 ▶
Schizo '77
Silver Skates '43
Suspense '46
Wintertime '43

Skiing

Aspen Extreme '93
Assignment K '68
Avalanche '78
Better Off Dead '85
Christmas in the Clouds '01
Deep Winter '08
Downhill '20
Downhill Racer '69
Downhill Willie '96
Dumb & Dumber '94
Extreme Ops '02
Fire and Ice '87
For Your Eyes Only '81 ▶
Force Majeure '14 ▶
Hot Dog. . . The Movie! '83
Hot Tub Time Machine '10
Ice Spiders '07
Lost and Found '79
On Her Majesty's Secret Service '69 ▶
The Other Side of the Mountain '75
The Other Side of the Mountain, Part 2 '78
Out Cold '01
Red Snow '91
Ski Party '65
Ski Patrol '89
Ski School '91
Ski School 2 '94
Snowball Express '72
Snowballin' '71
Snowballing '85
Snowblind '78
True Lies '94
Winter a Go-Go '65

Skinheads

***See also** Nazis & Other Paramilitary Slugs*

Adam's Apples '05
American History X '98
An American Werewolf in Paris '97
The Believer '01
Brotherhood of Murder '99
Cracker: To Be a Somebody '94
Farming '19
Green Room '15 ▶
Imperium '16
The Infiltrator '95
Lola and Billy the Kid '98
Meantime '81
Romper Stomper '92
Skin '18 ▶
Steel Toes '06
The Substitute 4: Failure is Not an Option '00
Surf Nazis Must Die '87
This Is England '06
The Turning '92
White Lies '98

Skydiving

***See also** Scared 'Chuteless*

Cutaway '00
Drop Zone '94
Fandango '85
The Gypsy Moths '69
Honeymoon in Vegas '92
Point Break '91
Terminal Velocity '94

Slapstick Comedy

***See also** Comedy; Screwball Comedy*

Abbott and Costello Go to Mars '53
Abbott and Costello in Hollywood '45
Abbott and Costello in the Foreign Legion '50
Abbott and Costello Meet Captain Kidd '52
Abbott and Costello Meet Dr. Jekyll and Mr. Hyde '52
Abbott and Costello Meet Frankenstein '48 ▶
Abbott and Costello Meet the Invisible Man '51 ▶
Abbott and Costello Meet the Keystone Kops '54
Abbott and Costello Meet the Killer, Boris Karloff '49
Abbott and Costello Meet the Mummy '55
Ace Ventura: Pet Detective '93
Ace Ventura: When Nature Calls '95
Action Point '18
The Adventures of Buckaroo Banzai Across the Eighth Dimension '84 ▶
Africa Screams '49
After the Fox '66
Air Raid Wardens '43
All New Adventures of Laurel and Hardy: For Love or Mummy '98
All of Me '84
American Pluck '25
Amos and Andrew '93
Anchorman 2: The Legend Continues '13
Animal Crackers '30 ▶
Any Which Way You Can '80
Armed and Dangerous '86
Around the World in a Daze '63
At the Circus '39
At War with the Army '50
Baby's Day Out '94
The Bad News Bears '76 ▶
The Bad News Bears Go to Japan '78
The Bad News Bears in Breaking Training '77
The Bank Dick '40 ▶
The Barefoot Executive '71
Bean '97 ▶
Bedtime for Bonzo '51
Beethoven '92
Beethoven's 2nd '93
The Bellboy '60
Big Store '41
Block-heads '38 ▶
Bohemian Girl '36 ▶
Bonnie Scotland '35
Boy, Did I Get a Wrong Number! '66
Boys Will Be Boys '97
Brain Donors '92
Buck Privates '41
Buck Privates Come Home '47 ▶
The Caddy '53
The Campaign '12
Candleshoe '78
Carry On Abroad '72
Carry On at Your Convenience '71
Carry On Behind '75
Carry On Cabby '63
Carry On Camping '71
Carry On Columbus '92
Carry On Constable '60
Carry On Cruising '62
Carry On Doctor '68 ▶
Carry On Emmanuelle '78
Carry On England '76
Carry On Henry VIII '71
Carry On Jack '63
Carry On Loving '70
Carry On Matron '72
Carry On Nurse '59
Carry On Regardless '61
Carry On Spying '64
Carry On Up the Jungle '70
Carry On Up the Khyber '68
Casanova's Big Night '54
Caught Plastered '31
Cheech and Chong: Still Smokin' '83
Cheech and Chong: Things Are Tough All Over '82
Cheech & Chong's Animated Movie! '13
Cheech and Chong's Next Movie '80
Cheech and Chong's The Corsican Brothers '84
Cheech and Chong's Up in Smoke '79
Christmas in July '40 ▶
Cinderfella '60
Comin' Round the Mountain '51
Corky Romano '01
Cracked Nuts '31
Cracking Up '83
Dad's Army '16
Dance with Me, Henry '56
Date Movie '06
A Day at the Races '37 ▶
The Delicate Delinquent '56
Detective School Dropouts '85
Disorderly Orderly '64
Don't Lose Your Head '66
Don't Raise the Bridge, Lower the River '68
Doughboys '30
Dragons Forever '88
Duck Soup '33 ▶
Ernest Goes to Africa '97
Ernest Goes to Camp '87
Ernest Goes to Jail '90
Ernest Scared Stupid '91
The Errand Boy '61
The Family Jewels '65
Feudin', Fussin', and A-Fightin' '48
A Fine Mess '86
Flim-Flam Man '67
Flubber '97
The Flying Deuces '39 ▶

▶ = rated three bones or higher

▶ = rated three bones or higher

Andy Hardy's Private Secretary '41
Angie '94
Another Year '10 ▶
Any Human Heart '11
Arizona Dream '94
Autumn Moon '92
Avalon '90 ▶
Babycakes '89
Bad Behavior '92
The Ballad of Andy Crocker '69
Ballast '08
The Basketball Diaries '95
Before Midnight '13 ▶
Before Sunrise '94
Believe '16
The Bicycle Thief '48 ▶
Big Fan '09
Big Stone Gap '15
Billy Galvin '86
Bleak Moments '71
Bloodbrothers '78
Blueberry Hill '88
Bodies, Rest & Motion '93
A Bread Factory, Part One '18 ▶
A Bread Factory, Part Two '18 ▶
Breaking In '89 ▶
Bright Angel '91
The Brothers McMullen '94 ▶
Bus Stop '56 ▶
Camilla '94
Captains Courageous '37 ▶
Captains Courageous '95
Car Wash '76
Cesar '36 ▶
The Chambermaid '19
Christy '94
Circle of Friends '94
Citizens Band '77 ▶
Cock & Bull Story '03
Cotter '72
Courtship '87 ▶
Creep '15
Crisscross '92
Crooklyn '94 ▶
Cross Creek '83
Crossing Delancey '88 ▶
Crows and Sparrows '49 ▶
Crystal River '08
Cupid & Cate '00
Cyclo '95
Dance Me Outside '95
Dancer, Texas-Pop. 81 '98 ▶
Days of Heaven '78 ▶
Delicatessen '92 ▶
Desperate Characters '71 ▶
Diamond Men '01 ▶
Dim Sum: A Little Bit of Heart '85 ▶
Diner '82 ▶
Dinner at Eight '89
Dodes 'ka-den '70 ▶
A Dog Year '09
Donnybrook '18
Double Happiness '94 ▶
Double Parked '00
Down the Shore '11
Driveways '19 ▶
Drunk Parents '19
Early Summer '51 ▶
Eat a Bowl of Tea '89 ▶
Eat Drink Man Woman '94 ▶
Eating '90
Echo Park '86
Edge of the World '37 ▶
The Eel '96 ▶
An Egyptian Story '82
End of the Line '88
The Englishman Who Went up a Hill But Came down a Mountain '95 ▶
Entertaining Angels: The Dorothy Day Story '96
Every Day '10
Every Man for Himself & God Against All '75 ▶
Everybody's All American '88
The Exiles '61
The Family Game '83 ▶
Fanny and Alexander '83 ▶
Federal Hill '94
Five Corners '88 ▶
Four in the Morning '65
Fragments '08
Frances Ha '13 ▶
The Freebie '10
Fried Green Tomatoes '91 ▶
The Funeral '84 ▶
Gimme the Loot '12
Girlfriends '78 ▶
A Glimpse Inside the Mind of Charles Swan III '12
Go Fish '94 ▶
God's Little Acre '58 ▶
Gomorrah '08 ▶
The Good Life '07
The Graduate '67 ▶
Grand Canyon '91 ▶
Gregory's Girl '80 ▶
The Group '66
Gummo '97
Hale County This Morning, This Evening '18 ▶
Hannah and Her Sisters '86 ▶
Hannah Takes the Stairs '07
Happy-Go-Lucky '08 ▶
Happy Together '96
Heavy Traffic '73 ▶
Hello, Hemingway '90
Henry & Verlin '94
Henry Hill '00
Hester Street '75 ▶
Hide Away '11
The High Cost of Living '10
High Hopes '88 ▶
Honor Thy Father '73
How to Be '08
How U Like Me Now? '92 ▶
Humanity '99
Hurricane Streets '96
I Don't Buy Kisses Anymore '92
I Like It Like That '94 ▶
I Love Budapest '01
I Remember Mama '48 ▶
I Wanna Hold Your Hand '78
I Was Happy Here '66
I'd Climb the Highest Mountain '51 ▶
The Idiots '99
The Inheritors '82
Innocent Sorcerers '60
Inventing the Abbotts '97
Ironweed '87 ▶
It All Starts Today '99
I've Loved You So Long '08 ▶
Jacknife '89 ▶
Jalsaghar '58
Jerome '98 ▶
The Jimmy Show '01
The Joe McDoakes Collection '42
Joyless Street '25 ▶
Jude '96 ▶
Judge Priest '34 ▶
Just About Famous: A Film About Celebrity Impersonators '15
The Keeper of the Bees '35
The Kid with a Bike '11
Kings Row '41 ▶
La Terra Trema '48 ▶
Ladybird, Ladybird '93 ▶
The Last New Yorker '07
The Last Picture Show '71 ▶
The Last Rites of Joe May '11
Last Summer In the Hamptons '96 ▶
Late Spring '49 ▶
L'Auberge Espagnole '02 ▶
Laws of Gravity '92 ▶
Learning to Drive '15
The Leather Boys '63
Life Begins for Andy Hardy '41 ▶
Life of Lemon '11
Life with Father '47 ▶
Light of My Eyes '01
Lily Dale '96
Little Women '33 ▶
Little Women '49 ▶
Little Women '78
Living on Tokyo Time '87
Local Hero '83 ▶
Look Back in Anger '58 ▶
The Lords of Flatbush '74
Lost Dream '09
Louder than Bombs '01
Love Is Strange '14 ▶
Love on the Run '78 ▶
Lucky Days '08
Ma Saison Preferee '93 ▶
Mac '93 ▶
Madame Sousatzka '88 ▶
Mamma Roma '62 ▶
Manito '03 ▶
Marius '31 ▶
The Mayor of Casterbridge '03
Mean Streets '73 ▶
Medicine for Melancholy '08
Meet Me in St. Louis '44 ▶
Metal Skin '94
Metropolitan '90 ▶
Middlemarch '93 ▶
Mississippi Masala '92 ▶
Mitch Albom's Have a Little Faith '11
Moonstruck '87 ▶
More American Graffiti '79
The Music Man '62 ▶
My Afternoons with Marguerite '10 ▶
My Family '94 ▶
My Sister Eileen '55 ▶
My Summer Story '94
My Year Without Sex '09
Mystic Pizza '88 ▶
Naked '93 ▶
Nashville '75 ▶
Nathalie Granger '72
The New Age '94
New Waterford Girl '99
Night Catches Us '10
Nightjohn '96
1918 '85
Nobody's Fool '86
Nobody's Fool '94 ▶
NoNames '10
Now and Then '95
The Off Hours '11
Oklahoma! '55 ▶
Old Swimmin' Hole '40
Once Were Warriors '94 ▶
One Day '11
One Third of a Nation '39
One Way to Valhalla '09
Our Town '40 ▶
Our Town '77 ▶
Our Town '89
Our Vines Have Tender Grapes '45 ▶
The Out-of-Towners '70 ▶
Papa's Delicate Condition '63 ▶
The Paper Chase '73 ▶
The Patriots '33 ▶
Pete 'n' Tillie '72
Phenomenon '96
The Playboys '92 ▶
The Pope of Greenwich Village '84
Praise '98 ▶
Priest '94
Prisoner of Second Avenue '74
Queens Logic '91
The Quiet Room '96
Raggedy Man '81 ▶
Raging Bull '80 ▶
Rambling Rose '91 ▶
Real Life '79 ▶
The Reckoning '69
Return '11
Return of the Secaucus 7 '80 ▶
Return to Cranford '09
Return to Mayberry '85
Rhythm Thief '94
Riff Raff '92 ▶
A River Runs Through It '92 ▶
The River Why '10
Room at the Top '59 ▶
Roommates '95
Rosalie Goes Shopping '89 ▶
Roughly Speaking '45
The Rules of the Game '39 ▶
Same Time, Next Year '78 ▶
Saturday Night and Sunday Morning '60 ▶
The Search for One-Eye Jimmy '94
September '96
7 Boxes '14 ▶
Short Cuts '93 ▶
A Single Girl '96
Sinners '89
Sister '12
Sisters of the Gion '36
The Smallest Show on Earth '48
The Smallest Show on Earth '57 ▶
Smiling Fish & Goat on Fire '99
Smithereens '82
Smoke '95
Some Came Running '58 ▶
Something Like Happiness '05
The Song of Sparrows '08
The Southerner '45 ▶
Speed of Life '99
The Star Maker '95
State Fair '45 ▶
State Fair '62
Steam: A Turkish Bath '96 ▶
Steamboat Bill, Jr. '28 ▶
Steel Magnolias '89 ▶
Stranger than Paradise '84 ▶
Stroszek '77 ▶
Sufat Chol '16 ▶
The Sun Shines Bright '53
Sweet Jane '98
Tex '82
That Sinking Feeling '79 ▶
Thirteen Conversations About One Thing '01 ▶
35 and Ticking '10
The Time of Your Life '48 ▶
Tin Men '87
To Kill a Mockingbird '62 ▶
Tonio Kroger '65
Tortilla Heaven '07
A Touch of Class '73 ▶
The Tree of Wooden Clogs '78 ▶
Tree's Lounge '96
Trouble in the Glen '54
True Love '89 ▶
Twenty Bucks '93 ▶
29th Street '91
Twice in a Lifetime '85 ▶
Twist & Shout '84 ▶
Two Days in the Valley '96 ▶
Tyrannosaur '11
Unhook the Stars '96
Urban Cowboy '80
Used People '92
Valley Inn '14
Waiting for Guffman '96
Walls of Glass '85
Wanderers '79 ▶
Washington Heights '02
Weakness '10
A Wedding '78
When the Party's Over '91
The White Balloon '95 ▶
Who's That Knocking at My Door? '68 ▶
Why Shoot the Teacher '79 ▶
Wild Style '83
Wish You Were Here '87 ▶
Women from the Lake of Scented Souls '94 ▶
Wonderful World '09
Wonderland '99
World Traveler '01
The Year My Parents Went on Vacation '07
Yi Yi '00
You Are Here * '00
You Can Count On Me '99 ▶
Zorba the Greek '64 ▶

Slob Comedy

***See also** Slapstick Comedy; Stupid Is...*

Accepted '06
Airheads '94
Anger Management '03
The Animal '01
Bachelor Party '84
Bait Shop '08
Beer League '06
Beerfest '06
The Benchwarmers '06
Better Off Dead '85
Beverly Hills Ninja '96
Big Daddy '99
Bill & Ted's Bogus Journey '91
Bill & Ted's Excellent Adventure '89
Billy Madison '94
Bio-Dome '96
Black Sheep '96
The Blues Brothers '80 ▶
Blues Brothers 2000 '98
Bob the Butler '05
Caddyshack 2 '88
Caddyshack '80 ▶
Dead Man on Campus '97
Delta Farce '07
Deuce Bigalow: Male Gigolo '99
Dirty Work '97
Dodgeball: A True Underdog Story '04
Dude, Where's My Car? '00
Dumb & Dumber '94
Employee of the Month '06
Friday '95
Friday After Next '02
Grandma's Boy '06
Grind '03
Half-Baked '97
Happy Gilmore '96
Harold and Kumar Go to White Castle '04
The Hollywood Knights '80
The Hot Chick '02
How High '01
Idiocracy '06
In the Army Now '94
Jackass Number Two '06
Jackass: The Movie '02
Joe Dirt '01
Kangaroo Jack '02
Knocked Up '07
Let's Go to Prison '06
Little Athens '05
Little Nicky '00
Making the Grade '84
Malibu's Most Wanted '03
Meatballs '79
Mr. Deeds '02
The Moguls '05
My Baby's Daddy '04
Nacho Libre '06
National Lampoon's Animal House '78 ▶
National Lampoon's Holiday Reunion '03
National Lampoon's Van Wilder 2: The Rise of Taj '06
National Lampoon's Van Wilder '02
The New Guy '02
Next Friday '00
Night Shift '82
The Nugget '02
Old School '03
One Crazy Summer '86
P.C.U. '94
Police Academy '84
Porky's 2: The Next Day '83
Porky's '82
Porky's Revenge '85
Postal '07
Road Trip '00
School of Rock '03 ▶
Screwed '00
Shakes the Clown '92
Son-in-Law '93
Sorority Boys '02
Spies Like Us '85
Step Brothers '08
Strange Brew '83
Strange Wilderness '08
Stripes '81
Super Troopers '01
Tomcats '01
Tommy Boy '95
Waiting '05
The Wash '01
The Waterboy '98
Wayne's World 2 '93
Wayne's World '92 ▶
The Wedding Singer '97
White Coats '04
The Whoopee Boys '86
Wieners '08
Without a Paddle '04

Small-Town Sheriffs

Ace in the Hole '51 ▶
Angels Fall '07
Back Road Diner '99
The Badge '02
Beer for My Horses '08
Best Men '98
Billy the Kid '30
Black Cadillac '03
Black Swarm '07
Blood Crime '02
Blood Out '10
Blue Ridge Fall '99
Bone Eater '07
Born of Earth '08
The Boy From Oklahoma '54
The Brass Legend '56
Breathless '12
Brigham City '01
Bubble '06
The California Kid '74
Camel Spiders '11
Camille '07
Carny '09
Cash Crop '98
Cherry Falls '00
Children On Their Birthdays '02
Christmas Caper '07
A Christmas Wish '11
Coastlines '02
Cop Land '97 ▶
Cover Up '49
The Day of the Wolves '71
The Dead Don't Die '19
Deadly Game '77
Dear Wendy '05
Death of a Gunfighter '69
The Death of Dick Long '19
The Descent 2 '09
The Desperadoes '43
The Devil's Dominoes '07
The Devil's Rejects '05
Doc West '09
Down in the Valley '05
The Dukes of Hazzard '05
The Dukes of Hazzard: The Beginning '06
Edge of Eternity '59
Eight Legged Freaks '02
El Dorado '67 ▶
El Gringo '12
El Paso '49
Eye of the Storm '98
Feed the Fish '09
Feudin', Fussin', and A-Fightin' '48
First Kill '17
Flame of the West '45
Forty Guns '57
Frayed '07
The Girl in the Empty Grave '77
Good Intentions '10
The Good Witch '08
The Good Witch's Garden '09
The Good Witch's Gift '10
Gospel Hill '08
Gun for 100 Graves '68
The Gunfight at Dodge City '59
Gunfight in Abilene '67
Halloween II '09
Happy, Texas '99 ▶
Hard Ground '03
Hard Luck '01
Hard Rain '97
Hell or High Water '16 ▶
A History of Violence '05 ▶
Hold the Dark '18
The Hollow Point '16
Hurry Sundown '67
I Walk the Line '70
In a Valley of Violence '16
In the Heat of the Night '67 ▶
The Iron Sheriff '57
Jesse Stone: Death in Paradise '06
Jesse Stone: Innocents Lost '11
Jesse Stone: Night Passage '06
Jesse Stone: No Remorse '10
Jesse Stone: Sea Change '07
Jesse Stone: Stone Cold '05
Jesse Stone: Thin Ice '09
The Killer Inside Me '10
Knockaround Guys '01
Lake Placid 3 '10
Lake Placid: The Final Chapter '12
The Last Hard Men '76
The Last Posse '53
The Last Stand '13
The Levenger Tapes '16
Life Blood '09
Little Chenier: A Cajun Story '06

▶ = rated three bones or higher

A Lobster Tale '06
Lone Star '95 ►
Long Days of Revenge '67
The Lost Capone '90 ►
Man from Del Rio '56
Maneater '07
A Marine Story '10
Miss Meadows '14
Monsterwolf '10
The Mothman Prophecies '02
My Bloody Valentine 3D '09
No Country for Old Men '07 ►
Northern Lights '09
One Foot in Hell '60
Pardners '56
Piranha 3D '10
Planet Terror '07
Powder River '53
Rampage '09
A Real American Hero '78
Red Clover '12
Red Hill '10
Red Rock West '93 ►
Red State '11
Retribution Road '07
Riddle '13
Rio Bravo '59 ►
Run for Cover '55
Running Target '56
Rushlights '13
Rustin '01
Scream 4 '11
The Second Time Around '61
The Secret of Hidden Lake '06
The Secrets of Comfort House '06
The Sellout '51
Shallow Ground '04
Shark Night 3D '11
The Sheriff of Fractured Jaw '59
Silent Night '12
Silverado '85 ►
Six-Pack Annie '75
Slither '06 ►
A Small Town in Texas '76
Small Town Santa '14
Small Town Saturday Night '10
Snakehead Terror '04
Strange Fruit '04
Sudden Impact '83
Sundown: The Vampire in Retreat '08
The Suspect '14
Swamp Devil '08
Swamp Shark '11
Swelter '14
Switchback '97
Taking Chances '09
Terror Trap '10
The Texas Chainsaw Massacre '03
The Texas Chainsaw Massacre: The Beginning '06
30 Days of Night '07
Three Billboards Outside Ebbing, Missouri '17 ►
Tick... Tick... Tick '70
Top Gun '55
The Trip to Bountiful '14 ►
Twilight '08
Unearthed '07
An Unfinished Life '05
Valley of the Heart's Delight '07
Vampires Suck '10
Veronica Mars '14
Walking Tall '73
Walking Tall '04
Walking Tall: Lone Justice '07
Walking Tall: Part 2 '75
Walking Tall: The Final Chapter '77
Water's Edge '03
The Werewolf '56
Winter Kill '74
Witless Protection '08
Wolf Moon '09

Smuggler's Blues

***See also** Crime & Drug Use & Abuse*

Acapulco Gold '78
Addicted to Her Love '06
Afterschool '08
American Gangster '07 ►
Arc '06
Ask a Policeman '38
Bad Boys 2 '03
Bad Lieutenant: Port of Call New Orleans '09
Barrier of the Law '54
Beneath the Harvest Sky '14
Better Luck Tomorrow '02 ►
The Big Turnaround '88
The Blonde '92
Blow '01
Blue, White and Perfect '42
Boarding Gate '07
Bobby Z '07
Bonded by Blood '09
Breaking Point '09
The Bribe '48
Brick '06 ►
Brooklyn's Finest '09
Brother '00 ►
The Business '05
Cafe '10
The Carey Treatment '72
Casa de mi Padre '12
Charlie Bartlett '07 ►
Charlie Chan in Shanghai '35
City of God '02
Cocaine and Blue Eyes '83
Codename: Wildgeese '84
Collision '09
Contraband '12
Contract to Kill '16
The Corner '00
The Crew '08
Cutaway '00
Dead Drop '13
Dealing: Or the Berkeley-to-Boston Forty-Brick Lost-Bag Blues '72
Detention '03
Deuces Wild '02
The Devil Makes Three '52
The Devil's in the Details '13
Disappearing in America '08
Down Terrace '10
Dredd '12 ►
Drug Wars: The Camarena Story '90 ►
El Padrino '04
Empire '02
End of Watch '12 ►
Enemies Closer '14
Enter the Void '09
Essex Boys '99
Everyday Black Man '10
Exit Wounds '01
Face of Terror '04
Fast & Furious '09
Final Engagement '07
Finish Line '08
Fix '08
Formula 51 '01
Free Ride '13
Frozen River '08 ►
The Gold Racket '37
Gone Baby Gone '07 ►
The Guard '11 ►
The Guardian '01
Half-Baked '97
Harry Brown '09
Her Sister's Keeper '06
Heroes Shed No Tears '86
The High Cost of Living '10
High School Confidential '58
Holy Rollers '10
Hostile Border '16
How It All Went Down '03
Humboldt County '08
Illegal Business '06
In Too Deep '99
The Infiltrator '16
The Informers '09
Jimmy Zip '00
Journey to the End of the Night '06
Jungle Man-Eaters '54
Just Add Water '07
Kill the Messenger '14 ►
Kona Coast '68
The Last Minute '01
Leaves of Grass '09
Lethal Weapon 2 '89 ►
Lies and Crimes '07
Lies and Illusions '09
The Line '08
The Lineup '58
Linewatch '08
A Little Piece of Sunshine '90
The Living Daylights '87 ►
Loaded '08
Mad Bad '07
A Man Apart '03
Maria Full of Grace '04 ►
A Marine Story '10
Martial Outlaw '93
Memento '00 ►
Mexican Blow '02
Mexican Gangster '08
The Mexican Spitfire Sees a Ghost '42
Miami Vice '06
Mr. Nice '10
The Money Trap '65
Next Day Air '09
The Non-Stop Flight '26
Of Boys and Men '08
On the Edge '02
On Thin Ice '03
Once in the Life '00
Only God Forgives '13
Our Lady of the Assassins '01
Out For a Kill '03
Outta Time '01
Paid '06
Paid in Full '02
Party Monster '03
Penny Princess '52
Pickup Alley '57
Pineapple Express '08 ►
Play Dead '09
The Raid: Redemption '11 ►
Rare Birds '01
Red Serpent '02
Requiem for a Dream '00 ►
Return of the Living Dead: Rave to the Grave '05
Reykjavik-Rotterdam '08
Rise of the Footsoldier '07
Rude Boy: The Jamaican Don '03
The Rules of Attraction '02
Sacrifice '11
Shaft '00 ►
The Shepherd: Border Patrol '08
Sherlock: Case of Evil '02
Shifty '08
Shut-Eye '03
600 Miles '16
Snitch '13
Spun '02
Starsky & Hutch '04
The Street Fighter's Last Revenge '74
Street Vengeance '95
Subterfuge '98
Sugar Hill '94
Sunstorm '01
Super Troopers '01
Sweet Sixteen '02 ►
Tarzan's Greatest Adventure '59
The Taste of Others '00 ►
Tequila Sunrise '88
Time and Tide '00
Tip On a Dead Jockey '57
Torque '04
Training Day '01
Transsiberian '08 ►
True Romance '93
Tweek City '05
Twelve '10
25th Hour '02
Under Hellgate Bridge '99
Up and Down '04
Venice Underground '05
Veronica Guerin '03
Vice '08
Viva Knievel '77
The Wackness '08
War Dogs '16
The Way of the West '11
We Own the Night '07
Weirdsville '07
We're the Millers '13
Winter's Bone '10 ►
Would Be Kings '08
Wrong Turn at Tahoe '09

Snakes

***See also** Killer Reptiles; Wild Kingdom*

Anaconda '96
Anacondas: The Hunt for the Blood Orchid '04
Anacondas: Trail of Blood '09
Black Cobra '83
Boa '02
Boa *vs.* Python '04
The Craft '96
Curse 2: The Bite '88
Fer-De-Lance '74
Fools Rush In '97
Foul Play '78 ►
Green Snake '93
Halfmoon '95
Harry Potter and the Chamber of Secrets '02 ►
Hounddog '08
Hydra '09
Indiana Jones and the Last Crusade '89 ►
Indiana Jones and the Temple of Doom '84 ►
Jackass 3D '10
Journey to the Lost City '58
The Jungle Book '67 ►
Kill Bill Vol. 2 '04 ►
King Cobra '98
Lewis and Clark and George '97
Mega Python Vs. Gatoroid '11
Megasnake '07
Natural Born Killers '94
Python '00
Python 2 '02
Raiders of the Lost Ark '81 ►
Rattlers '76
The Reptile '66
The Road Warrior '82 ►
Silent Predators '99
Silent Venom '08
The Snake People '68
Snakeman '05
Snakes on a Plane '06
Sssssss '73
Stanley '72
Them That Follow '19
Venom '05
Venomous '01
Vipers '08
The Wild '06
Women's Prison Escape '74

Sniper

***See also** Crime Sprees; Hit Men/Women; Military: Army*

American Sniper '14
Bone Dry '07
Brigands: Chapter VII '97
Carnage Park '16
Conspiracy '08
Dirty Harry '71 ►
Enemy at the Gates '00
Grand Piano '13
Hyena Road '16
Jack Reacher '12
Jarhead '05
Liberty Stands Still '02
The Manchurian Candidate '04 ►
The Marine 2 '09
The Musketeer '01
Outrage Born in Terror '09
Phone Booth '02
Point Break '91
Purple Heart '05
Sharpshooter '07
Shooter '07
Shot Through the Heart '98 ►
Sniper '92
Sniper 2 '02
The Sniper '52
Sniper '75 ►
Sniper: Ghost Shooter '16
Sniper: Legacy '14
Sniper Reloaded '11
Tower '16 ►
Two Minute Warning '76
The Wall '17
Winter Kills '79 ►

Snowboarding

***See also** Skiing*

Agent Cody Banks '03
Chalet Girls '11
Extreme Ops '02
First Descent '05
Frozen '10
Out Cold '01
6 Below: Miracle on the Mountain '17

Soccer

Air Bud 3: World Pup '00
Bad Parents '12
Bend It Like Beckham '02 ►
Big Brother Trouble '00
The Big Green '95
Bossa Nova '99
The Club '81 ►
Coach '10
Cracker: To Be a Somebody '94
The Cup '99
Cup Final '92
The Damned United '09
Diego Maradona '19 ►
Early Man '18
Fever Pitch '96
The Final Goal '94
Final Score '18
The Game of Their Lives '05
Goal 2: Living the Dream '07
Goal! The Dream Begins '06
Golden Shoes '15
Gracie '07
Green Street Hooligans '05 ►
Greener Grass '19
Gregory's Girl '80 ►
Guys and Balls '04
Her Best Move '07
Home Team '98
Hot Shot '86
Joyeux Noel '05 ►
The Keeper '18
Kicking & Screaming '05
Kicking It '08
Ladybugs '92
Looking for Eric '09
Mean Machine '01
One Fine Day '96
The Other Half '06
The Pink Panther '06
Playing for Keeps '12
Rudo y Cursi '09
Shaolin Soccer '01
She's the Man '06
A Shot at Glory '00
Soccer Dog: The Movie '98
Soccer Mom '08
Stuart Little 2 '02 ►
Those Glory, Glory Days '83
United '11
Victory '81

Softball

***See also** Baseball; Sports Comedy; Sports Documentaries; Sports Drama*

Beer League '06
The Broken Hearts Club '00 ►
A League of Their Own '92 ►
To Be Fat Like Me '07

South America

***See also** Central America*

Aftershock '12
Aguirre, the Wrath of God '72 ►
American Made '17
Americano '55
Anacondas: The Hunt for the Blood Orchid '04
And Soon the Darkness '10
Apartment Zero '88 ►
Araya '59
Assassination Tango '03 ►
Bacurau '20
Bananas '71 ►
Behind Enemy Lines 3: Colombia '08
Behind the Sun '01
Bel Canto '18
Birds of Passage '18 ►
Black Orpheus '58 ►
Blackthorn '11
Blue Eyes '09
Boy & the World '15 ►
The Bridge of San Luis Rey '05
Burden of Dreams '82 ►
Burnt Money '00
Butch Cassidy and the Sundance Kid '69 ►
Bye Bye Brazil '79
Carandiru '03
Carnival of Crime '62
Casa de los Babys '03 ►
Catch the Heat '87
The Celestine Prophecy '06
Che '08
Chronically Unfeasible '00
Chronicle of an Escape '06
Chronicle of the Raven '04
The City of Your Final Destination '09
Clear and Present Danger '94
The Club '16 ►
Cobra Verde '88
Collateral Damage '02
Crisis '50
Cronicas '04
Crystal Fairy & the Magical Cactus '13
The Dance of Reality '14
The Dancer Upstairs '02
The Dark Side of the Heart '92
Death and the Maiden '94 ►
Death in the Garden '56
The Devil on Horseback '36
Doctor Chance '97
Down Argentine Way '40 ►
Earthquake in Chile '74
The Edge of Democracy '19
800 Leagues Down the Amazon '93
El Carro '04
Embrace of the Serpent '15
The Emerald Forest '85 ►
End of the Spear '06
Even the Rain '10
Evita '96
The Expendables '10
Felicidades '00
Fitzcarraldo '82 ►
Flirting With Danger '35
Four Days in September '97
The Fugitive '48 ►
Funny, Dirty Little War '83
Fury '78
The German Doctor '14
Gloria '13 ►
Green Fire '55
Green Mansions '59
Gun Shy '17
Guns of Darkness '62
Happy Together '96
Hercules *vs.* the Sons of the Sun '64
Hidden in the Woods '16
Holy Girl '04 ►
The Hour of the Star '85 ►
House of Sand '05 ►
The House of the Spirits '93
I Don't Want to Talk About It '94
Imagining Argentina '04
Indiana Jones and the Kingdom of the Crystal Skull '08
The Infiltrator '16
Innocent Voices '04
It's All True '93
Johnny 100 Pesos '93
Journey to the End of the Night '06
Jungle '17
La Leon '07
Let's Get Harry '87
The Liberator '13
Little Mother '71
Looking for Palladin '08
The Lost City of Z '17 ►
Lost Embrace '04
Lost Treasure of the Maya '08
Love and Money '80
Magic Magic '13
The Magnificent Two '67
Manos sucias '15 ►
Maria Full of Grace '04 ►
Me You Them '00
Mega Piranha '10
Missing '82 ►
The Mission '86 ►

Mission. . . Kill '85
Monos '19 ►
Monster '78
Moon over Parador '88
The Motorcycle Diaries '04 ►
The Muthers '76
Naked Jungle '54 ►
Nancy Goes to Rio '50
Night Flight '33
Night Gallery '69 ►
Nine Queens '00 ►
No '12
Of Love and Shadows '94
Only Angels Have Wings '39 ►
Oriana '85
Our Brand Is Crisis '05 ►
Our Brand is Crisis '15
Our Lady of the Assassins '01
Overkill '96
The Padre '18
The Paranoids '08
A Place in the World '92 ►
Play for Me '01
Primal '19
Quilombo '84
Rise of the Dinosaurs '13
Rolling Family '04
Romancing the Stone '84 ►
The Savage '75
The Second Mother '15 ►
Secre of the Andes '98
The Secret in Their Eyes '09 ►
Senna '11
A Shadow You Soon Will Be '94
Shoot to Kill '90
Slayer '06
Snatched '17
Socrates '18 ►
The Son of the Bride '01
South of the Border '09
Submarine Base '43
Tango '98
Tarzan and the Great River '67
The Temptress '26
Terranova '91
Terror in the Jungle '68
Testosterone '03
Tetro '09
The 33 '15
The Three Caballeros '45
Tiger Bay '33
To Kill a Stranger '84
Towards Darkness '07
Triple Frontier '19
Turistas '06
Up '09 ►
Valentin '02
Veronico Cruz '87
Violeta Went to Heaven '13 ►
Waste Land '10
Way of a Gaucho '52
What Your Eyes Don't See '99
When Two Worlds Collide '16 ►
The White Diamond '04 ►
Wild Orchid '90
The Year My Parents Went on Vacation '07
You Were Never Lovelier '42 ►
Zama '17

Southern Belles

***See also** American South; Nashville Narratives; Women*

Blaze '89
Cat on a Hot Tin Roof '58 ►
Cat on a Hot Tin Roof '84
Children On Their Birthdays '02
Crimes of the Heart '86
Dear Dead Delilah '72
Driving Miss Daisy '89 ►
Forever My Girl '18
The Glass Menagerie '87 ►
Gone with the Wind '39 ►
Hush, Hush, Sweet Charlotte '65 ►
Jezebel '38 ►
The Little Foxes '41 ►
Miss Firecracker '89 ►
Nashville '75 ►
North and South Book 1 '85 ►
North and South Book 2 '86 ►
The Notebook '04
Other Voices, Other Rooms '95
Queen Bee '55
Rich in Love '93
Scarlett '94
Scorchers '92
Southern Belles '05
Steel Magnolias '89 ►
A Streetcar Named Desire '51 ►
A Streetcar Named Desire '95
The Trip to Bountiful '85 ►

Space Operas

***See also** Alien Beings--Benign; Alien Beings--Vicious*

Alien '79 ►
The Apocalypse '96
Apollo 13 '95 ►
Approaching the Unknown '16
Assignment Outer Space '61
Avatar '09 ►
Battle Beyond the Stars '80
Battle Beyond the Sun '63
Battlestar Galactica '78
Battlestar Galactica: The Plan '09
The Black Hole '79
Black Horizon '01
Buck Rogers Conquers the Universe '39
Capricorn One '78 ►
Cat Women of the Moon '53
The Cold Equations '96
Conquest of Space '55
Contact '97
Countdown '68
Creature '85
Crimson Force '05
Dante 01 '08
Dark Breed '96
Dark Star '74 ►
The Day the Sky Exploded '57
Dead Fire '98
Destination Moon '50
Destination Moonbase Alpha '75
Destination Saturn '39
The Dish '00 ►
Earth II '71
Earthstorm '06
Escape from Planet Earth '67
Escape Velocity '99
Europa Report '13 ►
Event Horizon '97
Explorers '85
Fire Maidens from Outer Space '56
First Men in the Moon '64
First Spaceship on Venus '60 ►
Flight to Mars '52
Fly Me to the Moon '08
Forbidden Planet '56 ►
From the Earth to the Moon '98 ►
Galaxy of Terror '81
Gattaca '97 ►
Gravity '13 ►
The Green Slime '68
Guardians of the Galaxy '14 ►
Hangar 18 '80
Have Rocket Will Travel '59
Heavens Above '63 ►
Hellraiser 4: Bloodline '95
Horrors of the Red Planet '64
In the Dead of Space '99
In the Shadow of the Moon '07 ►
Inseminoid '80
Interstellar '14
John Carpenter's Ghosts of Mars '01
Journey to the Far Side of the Sun '69 ►
Laser Mission '90
The Last Starfighter '84
Lifepod '93
Lockout '12
Lost in Space '98
Marooned '69
Message from Space '78
Mission to Mars '00
Mom and Dad Save the World '92
Monarch of the Moon '05
Moon 44 '90
Moon Zero Two '70
Moonraker '79
The Mouse on the Moon '62 ►
Mystery Science Theater 3000: The Movie '96 ►
Nude on the Moon '61
Outland '81
Pandorum '09
Passengers '16
Planet Burg '62
Planet of the Apes '68 ►
Planet of the Apes '01 ►
Planet of the Dinosaurs '80
Planet of the Vampires '65
Prometheus '12
Race to Space '01
Red Planet '00
The Reluctant Astronaut '67
Return of the Jedi '83 ►
Riddick '13
The Right Stuff '83 ►
Robinson Crusoe on Mars '64
Robot World '15
RocketMan '97
Rocketship X-M '50
Satellite in the Sky '56
Saturn 3 '80
Scorpio One '97
Serenity '05 ►
Silent Running '71 ►
Solar Crisis '92
Solaris '72
Solaris '02
Space Buddies '08
Space Chimps '08
Space Cowboys '00 ►
Space Mutiny '88
Space Station 76 '14
Space Warriors '13
Spaceballs '87
SpaceCamp '86
Spacejacked '98
Star Crash '78
Star Slammer '87
Star Trek: The Motion Picture '79
Star Trek 2: The Wrath of Khan '82 ►
Star Trek 3: The Search for Spock '84
Star Trek 4: The Voyage Home '86 ►
Star Trek 5: The Final Frontier '89
Star Trek 6: The Undiscovered Country '91
Star Trek '09 ►
Star Trek: First Contact '96 ►
Star Trek: Generations '94 ►
Star Trek: Insurrection '98
Star Trek: Into Darkness '13 ►
Star Trek: Nemesis '02
Star Wars '77 ►
Star Wars: Episode 2-Attack of the Clones '02 ►
Star Wars: Episode 3-Revenge of the Sith '05 ►
Star Wars: The Clone Wars '08
Star Wars: The Force Awakens '15 ►
Star Wars: The Last Jedi '17 ►
Star Wars: The Rise of Skywalker '19
Stargate: The Ark of Truth '08
Sunshine '07
Supernova '99
Three Stooges in Orbit '62
Titan A.E. '00
Transformers: The Last Knight '17
Treasure Planet '02
12 to the Moon '60
2001: A Space Odyssey '68 ►
2001: A Space Travesty '00
2010: The Year We Make Contact '84 ►
Valerian and the City of a Thousand Planets '17
Vegas in Space '94
Velocity Trap '99
Virtuality '09
Voyage to the Planet of Prehistoric Women '68
Voyage to the Prehistoric Planet '65
WALL-E '08 ►
Warlords of the 21st Century '82
Wing Commander '99
Woman in the Moon '29

Spaghetti Western

***See also** Western Comedy; Westerns*

Ace High '68
Adios, Sabata '71
And God Said to Cain '69
Any Gun Can Play '67
Apache's Last Battle '64
The Ballad of Buster Scruggs '18 ►
Belle Starr '79
Beyond the Law '68
The Big Gundown '66
Boot Hill '69
Bullet for Sandoval '70
A Bullet for the General '68
California '77
Chino '75
Cjamango '67
Dead Man's Bounty '06
Death Rides a Horse '69
Django and Sartana; It's the End '70
Django: Last Killer '67
Django Shoots First '74
Doc West '09
Dollar for the Dead '98
800 Bullets '02
Execution '68
A Fistful of Dollars '64 ►
A Fistful of Dynamite '72 ►
Fistful of Lead '70
The Five Man Army '69
For a Few Dollars More '65
Fort Yuma Gold '66
Four Dollars of Revenge '66
Go With God Gringo '66
The Good, the Bad and the Ugly '67 ►
The Grand Duel '73
Gun for 100 Graves '68
Gunfight at Red Sands '63
Gunfire '78
Gunslinger '70
Hallelujah for Django '67
Hang 'Em High '67
Hate for Hate '67
Hellbenders '67
The Hills Run Red '67
His Name Was King '71
Johnny Yuma '66
Kill Django '71
Lola Colt '67
Long Days of Revenge '67
A Long Ride From Hell '68
Man, Pride and Vengeance '67
Mannaja: A Man Called Blade '77
Minnesota Clay '65
A Minute to Pray, a Second to Die '67
My Name Is Nobody '74
Navajo Joe '67
Once Upon a Time in the West '68 ►
One After Another '68 ►
One Fine Day, When Django Met Sartana '70
Red Sun '71
Return of Sabata '71
Revenge of Sartana '65
Ringo, the Lone Rider '68
Ringo's Big Night '66
Ringo's Mark of Vengeance '67
Roy Colt and Winchester Jack '70
Sabata '69
Shoot the Living, Pray for the Dead '70
Sukiyaki Western Django '08
Sundance and the Kid '69
Take a Hard Ride '75
Trinity Is Still My Name '75
Twice a Judas '69
White Comanche '68

Spain

***See also** Barcelona; Madrid; Spanish Civil War*

Against the Wind '90
Americano '05
Angel of Death '02
The Backwoods '06
Bad Education '04 ►
Barcelona '94 ►
Behold a Pale Horse '64
Belle Epoque '92 ►
Blood and Sand '41 ►
Broken Silence '01 ►
Bunny and the Bull '09
The Business '05
Butterfly '98 ►
Carmen, Baby '66
Carnage '02
Carry On Abroad '72
The Castilian '63
The Cold Light of Day '12
Day of Wrath '06
Destiny '97
The Devil Is a Woman '35 ►
The Devil's Backbone '01
The Disappearance of Garcia Lorca '96
Donkey Punch '08
800 Bullets '02
El Bulli: Cooking in Progress '11
El Crimen Perfecto '04
11-11-11 '11
Everybody Knows '18
Ferdinand '17
Finding Altamira '16
Food of Love '02
For Whom the Bell Tolls '43 ►
Gaudi Afternoon '01
The Grandfather '98
Guernica '16
Hard Contract '69
Intacto '01
It's All Gone, Pete Tong '04
Julieta '16
Kevin & Perry Go Large '00
Km. 0 '00
The Last Run '71
The Last Seduction 2 '98
L'Auberge Espagnole '02 ►
The Limits of Control '09
Love and Pain and the Whole Damn Thing '73
Love Can Seriously Damage Your Health '96
A Love to Keep '07
Mad Love '01
Magical Girl '14 ►
A Matador's Mistress '08
Mondays in the Sun '02
Morvern Callar '02
Most Beautiful Island '17
My Mother Likes Women '02
Nico and Dani '00
Open Graves '09
The Orphanage '07 ►
Pain and Glory '19 ►
Pandora and the Flying Dutchman '51
Pan's Labyrinth '06 ►
The Pride and the Passion '57
Running Out of Time '94
The Sea Inside '04 ►
Second Skin '99
Sexy Beast '00 ►
Slave '09
The Spanish Gardener '57 ►
Summer Camp '16
The Sun Also Rises '57
Take My Eyes '03
Talk of Angels '96
Talk to Her '02 ►
10,000 Km '14
Things I Left in Havana '97
Tierra '95
Torremolinos 73 '03
Torrent '26
A Touch of Class '73 ►
The Trip to Spain '17
Vacas '91
Vantage Point '08
Volver '06 ►
The Way '10
Wild Oats '16

Spanish Civil War

Behold a Pale Horse '64
Broken Silence '01 ►
Confidential Agent '45
The Devil's Backbone '01
The Disappearance of Garcia Lorca '96
The Fallen Sparrow '43 ►
For Whom the Bell Tolls '43 ►
The Girl of Your Dreams '99
Head in the Clouds '04
Hemingway & Gelhorn '12
If They Tell You I Fell '89
The Last Circus '10
The Night Has Eyes '42
There Be Dragons '11
Vacas '91

Spiders

***See also** Killer Bugs and Slugs*

Age of the Hobbits '12
The Angry Red Planet '59
Arachnia '03
Arachnophobia '90
Charlotte's Web '73
Charlotte's Web '06 ►
Cirque du Freak: The Vampire's Assistant '09
The Covenant '06
Earth *vs.* the Spider '58
Eight Legged Freaks '02
Fury of the Congo '51
The Giant Spider Invasion '75
Ice Spiders '07
In the Spider's Web '07
Infestation '09
James and the Giant Peach '96 ►
Kingdom of the Spiders '77
Kiss of the Tarantula '75
Lord of the Rings: The Return of the King '03 ►
Lost in Space '98
Microcosmos '96 ►
Spider-Man: Homecoming '17 ►
Tarantulas: The Deadly Cargo '77
Webs '03

Spies & Espionage

***See also** CIA/NSA; Cold War Spies; Foreign Intrigue; Joke and Dagger; Spy Kids; Terrorism; World War One Spies; World War Two Spies*

Abduction '11
Above Suspicion '43 ►
The Accidental Spy '01
Advance to the Rear '64
The Adventures of Rocky & Bullwinkle '00
The Adventures of Tartu '43
Aeon Flux '05
Agent Cody Banks 2: Destination London '04
Allied '16
American Assassin '17
Anthropoid '16
The Apocalypse Watch '97
Arabesque '66
The Art of War '00
Artists and Models '55
Assignment K '68
Assignment: Paris '52
Atomic Blonde '17
The Atomic Kid '54
Attack of the Robots '66
Austin Powers: International Man of Mystery '97 ►
Austin Powers 2: The Spy Who Shagged Me '99 ►
Austin Powers In Goldmember '02
The Avengers '98
Bad Company '94
Ballistic: Ecks *vs.* Sever '02
Balls of Fury '07
Bang! Bang! You're Dead! '66
The Bank Job '08 ►
Barely Lethal '15
Beaumarchais the Scoundrel '96

► *= rated three bones or higher*

Behind Enemy Lines '85
The Big Game '72
The Big Lift '50
Billion Dollar Brain '67
Birds Do It '66
Black Brigade '69
Black Eagle '88
Blue Ice '92
Blue, White and Perfect '42
The Bourne Identity '88 ▶
The Bourne Identity '02 ▶
The Bourne Supremacy '04 ▶
The Bourne Ultimatum '07 ▶
Breach '07
The Brothers Grimsby '16
Bulldog Drummond Escapes '37
Bulletproof '88
Cambridge Spies '03
Candlelight in Algeria '44
Captain Carey, U.S.A. '50
Carry On Spying '64
Cars 2 '11
Casablanca '42 ▶
Casino Royale '67
Casino Royale '06 ▶
The Catcher Was a Spy '18
Cats & Dogs: The Revenge of Kitty Galore '10
Charge of the Model T's '76
Charlie Chan at the Olympics '37
Charlie Chan in Panama '40
China Girl '42
Clear and Present Danger '94
Codename: Icarus '85
Codename: Wildgeese '84
The Cold Light of Day '12
Confessions of a Nazi Spy '39
Confidential Agent '45
The Conspirators '44
Contraband '40
Counter-Espionage '42
Cradle 2 the Grave '03
Crimes of the Past '09
Criminals Within '41
Dandy in Aspic '68
Dangerously We Live '41
Daniel '83
Daniella by Night '61
Dark Journey '37 ▶
Darling Lili '70
The Day of the Dolphin '73
The Day of the Jackal '73 ▶
Deadly Reckoning '01
Death Has a Bad Reputation '90
Death is Nimble, Death is Quick '67
Death Ray 2000 '81
The Debt '07
The Debt '10
The Delphi Bureau: The Merchant of Death Assignment '72
Derailed '02
Desperate Cargo '41
Despicable Me 2 '13
Diamonds Are Forever '71 ▶
Die Another Day '02
A Different Loyalty '04 ▶
The Diplomat '08
Dishonored '31
Dr. No '62 ▶
The Doll Squad '73
Don't Drink the Water '69
Doomsday Gun '94
The Double '11
Double Agents '59
Double Identity '10
The Double Man '67
Down Among the Z Men '52
Edge of Darkness '86
Elizabeth '98 ▶
The Emperor's Candlesticks '37
Escape from Fort Bravo '53
Espionage in Tangiers '65
The Exception '17
The Executioner '70
Exile Express '39
Extremely Dangerous '99
Eyewitness '81
A Family of Spies '90
Farewell '09
Fathom '67
Fay Grim '06
A Few Days in September '06
Fire Over England '37 ▶
Firefall '94
Flight to Nowhere '46
Flying Blind '41
The Foreigner '78
The Formula '80
From Paris With Love '10
The General Died at Dawn '36 ▶
Get Smart '08
Get Smart, Again! '89
G.I. Joe: Retaliation '13
Girls Are for Loving '73
The Glass Bottom Boat '66
Golden Earrings '47
Golden Girl '51
Goldeneye '95 ▶
Goldfinger '64 ▶
The Great Spy Chase '64
The Groundstar Conspiracy '72 ▶
The Gunman '15
The Hades Factor '06
Hammerhead '68
Hanky Panky '82
Hanna '11
Hard Ticket to Hawaii '87
Haywire '12 ▶
Head Over Heels '01
Hidden Agenda '99
Highly Dangerous '50
Hillbillies in a Haunted House '67
The Holcroft Covenant '85
The House on Garibaldi Street '79
House on 92nd Street '45 ▶
The Hunt for Red October '90 ▶
I Stand Condemned '36
The Impossible Spy '87 ▶
Innocent Bystanders '72
Inside the Lines '30
Internecine Project '73
J-Men Forever! '79 ▶
Jack Ryan: Shadow Recruit '14
Jackie Chan's First Strike '96 ▶
Jason Bourne '16
Joan of Paris '42 ▶
Johnny English '03
Johnny English Reborn '11
Jungle Drums of Africa '53
Just Another Secret '89
Keeping Up with the Joneses '16
Kill Factor '78
Kim '50 ▶
Kingsman: The Golden Circle '17
Kingsman: The Secret Service '15
Kiss Kiss Kill Kill '66
Kiss Me Deadly '08
Knight and Day '10
Knock on Wood '54
The Kremlin Letter '70
La Cage aux Folles 2 '81
Ladies' Man '62
Last Embrace '79 ▶
Last Man Standing '11
Last Run '01
Le Magnifique '76
Le Professionnel '81 ▶
License to Kill '64
License to Kill '89 ▶
Lightning Bolt '67
Lipstick Camera '93
The Liquidator '65
The Little Drummer Girl '84 ▶
A Little Piece of Sunshine '90
Live and Let Die '73
The Lives of Others '06 ▶
Loaded Guns '75
The Love Light '21
Love on the Run '36
Ma and Pa Kettle on Vacation '53
Mad Mission 3 '84
Madame Sin '71
Make Your Bets Ladies '65
Malone '87
The Man from U.N.C.L.E. '15
Man Hunt '41 ▶
Man on a Tightrope '53
The Man Outside '68
The Man Who Wasn't There '83
The Man with the Golden Gun '74
Marie Galante '34 ▶
Maroc 7 '67
The Mask of Dimitrios '44 ▶
The Master Plan '55
Master Spy: The Robert Hanssen Story '02
Mata Hari '32 ▶
Mata Hari '85
The Medallion '03
The Mind Benders '63
Mission: Impossible 2 '00 ▶
Mission: Impossible 3 '06 ▶
Mission: Impossible '96 ▶
Mission: Impossible Rogue Nation '15 ▶
Mission: Impossible-Fallout '18 ▶
Mission to Venice '63
Mr. Superinvisible '73
Modesty Blaise '66
The Monocle '64
Moonraker '79
A Most Wanted Man '14
Murder on the Midnight Express '74
Murderers' Row '66
The Mysterious Lady '28
Navy Blues '37
Never Say Never Again '83
Nick Carter, Master Detective '39
North by Northwest '59 ▶
The November Man '14
The Odessa File '74
Old Mother Riley in Paris '38
Old Mother Riley's Ghosts '41
On Her Majesty's Secret Service '69 ▶
Once Upon a Spy '80
One Armed Executioner '80
One of Our Dinosaurs Is Missing '75
Operation Abduction '58
Operation Avalanche '16
The Operative '19
Operator 13 '34
OSS 117: Cairo, Nest of Spies '06
OSS 117: Lost in Rio '09
Our Kind of Traitor '16
Pack of Lies '87
Page Eight '11
Panic in the City '68
Passport to Suez '43
Patriot Games '92 ▶
Picasso Trigger '89
Pirates of Tortuga '61
The Price of the Bride '90
Pride and Extreme Prejudice '90
Project X '68
Protocol '84
Quantum of Solace '08
The Quiller Memorandum '66 ▶
The Recruit '03
RED 2 '13
Red Joan '19
Red Sparrow '18
Reilly: Ace of Spies '87 ▶
Rendezvous '35
Rescue from Gilligan's Island '78
Retrievers '82
Return of the Man from U.N.C.L.E. '83
Return to Savage Beach '97
Robinson Crusoe of Clipper Island '36
Ronin '98
The Rose and the Jackal '90
Sabotage '36 ▶
The Saint '97
Salt '10 ▶
Salt & Pepper '68
The Scarlet Coat '55
Sea Devils '53
The Secret Agent '36 ▶
The Secret Agent '96
Secret Agent of Japan '42
Secret Agent Super Dragon '66
The Sellout '76
Seoul Raiders '05
Shadow Dancer '12 ▶
A Show of Force '90
The Silencers '66
Skyfall '12 ▶
Smiley's People '82
Sneakers '92
Snowden '16
South of Panama '41
A Southern Yankee '48
The Spanish Prisoner '97 ▶
Spartan '04 ▶
Spectre '15
Spies '28 ▶
Spies in Disguise '19
Spies, Lies and Naked Thighs '91
Spies of Warsaw '13
Spy Game '01
Spy in Black '39 ▶
Spy in the Sky '58
Spy Kids 4: All the Time in the World '11
The Spy Next Door '10
The Spy Who Dumped Me '18
The Spy Who Loved Me '77
The Spy Within '94
State Department File 649 '49
Submergence '18
Swing Shift Maisie '43
Swordfish '01
Syriana '05 ▶
The Tailor of Panama '00 ▶
Taken 2 '12
Taken '08
The Tall Blond Man with One Black Shoe '72 ▶
Target for Killing '66
Target of Opportunity '04
Terminal Velocity '94
They Came to Blow Up America '43
They Got Me Covered '43
The Third Man '49 ▶
XIII '08
13 Frightened Girls '63
The 39 Steps '35 ▶
The Thirty-Nine Steps '79
Three Days of the Condor '75 ▶
Thunderball '65
Tinker, Tailor, Soldier, Spy '80 ▶
Tinker Tailor Soldier Spy '11 ▶
To Commit a Murder '67
Tokyo Joe '49
Tomorrow Never Dies '97
Total Recall '12
Traitor '08
Trenchcoat '83
Triple Agent '04
The Tuxedo '02
Undeclared War '91
Under the Rainbow '81
Undercover Blues '93
Undercover Brother '02
The Uranium Conspiracy '78
The Venetian Affair '67
A View to a Kill '85
Viper '88
Virginia City '40 ▶
The WAC From Walla Walla '52
The Waiting Time '99
Walk a Crooked Mile '48
Walk East on Beacon '52
Wanted Dead or Alive '86
When Eight Bells Toll '71
Where the Spies Are '65
WhiteForce '88
Who Is Simon Miller? '11
Who Was That Lady? '60
Who's Got the Black Box? '67
Wild Wild West '99
Wonder Woman '74
The Wrecking Crew '68
XXX '02
You Only Live Twice '67
Your Turn Darling '63
Zeppelin '71
Zero Days '16
Zeta One '69
Zotz! '62

Sports

***See also** Baseball; Basketball; Bicycling; Boxing; Football; Golf; Hockey; The Olympics; Running; Scuba; Skating; Skiing; Skydiving; Soccer; Sports Comedy; Sports Drama; Surfing; Swimming; Tennis; Volleyball*

Sports Comedy

Air Bud '97
Air Bud 2: Golden Receiver '98
Air Bud 3: World Pup '00
Air Bud 4: Seventh Inning Fetch '02
Air Bud 5: Buddy Spikes Back '03
The Air Up There '94
Alibi Ike '35
Angels in the Infield '00
Angels in the Outfield '94
The Art of Self-Defense '19 ▶
The Bad News Bears '76 ▶
The Bad News Bears '05
The Bad News Bears Go to Japan '78
The Bad News Bears in Breaking Training '77
Bad Parents '12
Balls of Fury '07
Balls Out: Gary the Tennis Coach '09
BASEketball '98
Beer League '06
Benched '18
The Benchwarmers '06
Bend It Like Beckham '02 ▶
The Best of Times '86
Big and Hairy '98
The Big Green '95
Billie '65
Bingo Long Traveling All-Stars & Motor Kings '76 ▶
Blades of Glory '07
Blue Juice '95
Body Slam '87
Boxboarders! '07
The Boys '97
Bring It On: Fight to the Finish '09
The Bronze '15
Bull Durham '88 ▶
Cars '06 ▶
Celtic Pride '96
Coach '10
The Comebacks '07
Cool Runnings '93
The Cup '99
D2: The Mighty Ducks '94
D3: The Mighty Ducks '96
Diggstown '92
The Do-Deca-Pentathlon '12
Dodgeball: A True Underdog Story '04
Downhill Willie '96
Draft Day '14
Ed '96
Eddie '96
Eleven Men and a Girl '30
Elmer the Great '33
Everybody Wants Some!! '16
Fast Break '79
Fever Pitch '96
Fever Pitch '05
The Fish that Saved Pittsburgh '79
The Foul King '00
The Freshman '25 ▶
The Game Plan '07
Game 6 '05
Geordie '55
Goon '12
Goon: Last of the Enforcers '17
The Great American Pastime '56
The Great White Hype '96
Gus '76
Guys and Balls '04
Gym Teacher: The Movie '08
The Hammer '07
Happy Gilmore '96
Her Best Move '07
Hold 'Em Jail '32
Home Run Showdown '10
Home Team '98
Hot Dog. . . The Movie! '83
The Hot Flashes '13
How Do You Know '10
The Iron Ladies 2 '03
The Iron Ladies '00
Jerry Maguire '96 ▶
Jocks '87
Johnny Be Good '88
Kicking & Screaming '05
Kill the Umpire '50
Kingpin '96
Knucklehead '10
Ladybugs '92
A League of Their Own '92 ▶
Leatherheads '08
Little Big League '94
Little Giants '94
The Longest Yard '74 ▶
The Longshot '86
The Longshots '08
Looking for Eric '09
Lords of Soaptown: The True Story of Freestyle Walking '16
Love in the Rough '30
Major League '89
Major League 2 '94
Major League 3: Back to the Minors '98
Mascots '16
Men with Brooms '02
The Mighty Ducks '92
Mr. Baseball '92
Mr. 3000 '04
Monty Python's The Meaning of Life '83 ▶
MVP: Most Valuable Primate '00
Mystery, Alaska '99
Nacho Libre '06
National Lampoon's Golf Punks '99
Necessary Roughness '91
North Dallas Forty '79 ▶
The One and Only '78
Paper Lion '68
Pat and Mike '52 ▶
Perfect Game '00
Ping Pong '02 ▶
Playin' For Love '15 ▶
Playing for Keeps '12
Possums '99
Prize Fighter '79
Queens of the Ring '13
Rebound '05
The Replacements '00
Rhubarb '51
The Ringer '05
Rookie of the Year '93
Rudo y Cursi '09
Run, Fatboy, Run '07
The St. Tammany Miracle '94
The Sandlot '93 ▶
The Sandlot 2 '05
The Sandlot 3: Heading Home '07
The Scout '94
Semi-Pro '08
Semi-Tough '77
Shaolin Soccer '01
Sit Tight '31
The Sixth Man '97
Ski School '91
Slam Dunk Ernest '95
Slap Shot '77 ▶
Slap Shot 2: Breaking the Ice '02
The Smart Set '28
Soccer Dog: The Movie '98
Soccer Mom '08
Space Jam '96
Speedway '29
Splitz '84
Spring Fever '27
The Squeeze '15
Squeeze Play '79
Stick It '06
Sunset Park '96
Thunderstruck '12
Tin Cup '96 ▶
Uncle Drew '18
Undrafted '16
The Waterboy '98
White Men Can't Jump '92
Who's Your Caddy? '07

▶ = rated three bones or higher

Wildcats '86
Wimbledon '04
Win Win '11
The Winning Season '09
The World's Greatest Athlete '73

Sports Documentaries

The Armstrong Lie '13 ▶
Bigger Stronger Faster '08
Champs '15 ▶
The Eagle Huntress '16 ▶
The First Saturday in May '08
Free to Run '16
Generation Iron '13 ▶
Gleason '16 ▶
The Great Alone '15
Harry and Snowman '16 ▶
The Heart of the Game '05
Hoop Dreams '94 ▶
I Am Bolt '16 ▶
In Search of Greatness '18 ▶
The Life and Times of Hank Greenberg '99 ▶
Linsanity '13
More Than a Game '08
Morning Light '08
Mudbloods: A Movie About Quidditch '14
Murderball '05 ▶
On Any Sunday: The Next Chapter '14
Senna '11
Through the Fire '05 ▶
The 24 Hour War '16
Tyson '08
Undefeated '11
Up for Grabs '05
When We Were Kings '96 ▶
Winning: The Racing Life of Paul Newman '15

Sports Drama

Above the Rim '94
Airborne '93
The All-American Boy '73
All the Right Moves '83
American Anthem '86
American Flyers '85
American Kickboxer 1 '91
Annapolis '06
Any Given Sunday '99 ▶
The Art of Racing in the Rain '19
Babe! '75 ▶
The Babe '92
Babe Ruth Story '48
Backwards '12
Ball of Wax '03
Bang the Drum Slowly '73 ▶
Bare Knuckles '10
Battle of the Sexes '17
Beach Kings '08
Beatdown '10
Believe in Me '06
Bennett's War '19
The Big Blue '88
Big Leaguer '53
Black Cloud '04
The Blind Side '09
Blonde Comet '41
Blue Chips '94
Bobby Jones: Stroke of Genius '04
Body and Soul '47 ▶
Body & Soul '81
Born to Race: Fast Track '14
Boy in Blue '86
The Break '95
Breaking Away '79 ▶
Brian Banks '18
Brian's Song '71 ▶
The Bronx Is Burning '07
Calvin Marshall '09
Carnera: The Walking Mountain '08
Carter High '15
Catching Faith '15
Champion '49 ▶
Champions '84
Chariots of Fire '81 ▶
Chasing Mavericks '12
Chasing 3000 '07
Chuck '17
The Club '81 ▶
Coach '78
Coach Carter '05 ▶
Cobb '94 ▶
The Color of Money '86 ▶
Concussion '15
Creed '15 ▶
Creed II '18
Crooked Arrows '12
Crossbar '79
Crossover '06
The Crowd Roars '38
The Cup '11
Curveball '15
The Cutting Edge '92
The Cutting Edge: Fire and Ice '10
The Damned United '09
Days of Thunder '90
Deep Winter '08
Dempsey '83
Downhill Racer '69
Draft Day '14
Dream to Believe '85
Dreamer: Inspired by a True Story '05
Eight Men Out '88 ▶
8 Seconds '94
Emma's Chance '16
The Express '08
The Fan '96
Fat City '72 ▶
The Fencer '15 ▶
Field of Dreams '89 ▶
The 5th Quarter '10
Fight to the Finish '16
The Fight Within '16
The Fighter '10 ▶
A Fighting Man '14
The Final Season '07
Final Shot: The Hank Gathers Story '92
The Fireball '50
The First Olympics: Athens 1896 '84
The Flying Scotsman '06
For Love of the Game '99
Ford v Ferrari '19 ▶
Forever Strong '08
40 Love '15
42 '13 ▶
The Four Minute Mile '88
Free Style '09
Friday Night Lights '04 ▶
From Mexico With Love '09
Full Out '15
Full Ride '02
Futuresport '98
The Gabby Douglas Story '14
The Game of Their Lives '05
Game 6 '05
Game Time: Tackling the Past '11
Gentleman Jim '42 ▶
Girlfight '99 ▶
Gladiator '92
Glory Road '06
Goal 2: Living the Dream '07
Goal! The Dream Begins '06
Going for Gold: The '48 Games '12
Golf in the Kingdom '10
Gracie '07
Grambling's White Tiger '81
The Greatest Game Ever Played '05
Green Street Hooligans '05 ▶
Gridiron Gang '06
Guarding Eddy '04
The Hammer '11
Hands of Stone '16
Hard, Fast and Beautiful '51
He Got Game '98
Heart Like a Wheel '83
Heaven Is a Playground '91
High Flying Bird '19
Hockey Night '84
Home of the Giants '07
Home Run '13
Hoosiers '86 ▶
Hot Shot '86
Huddle '32
Hurricane Season '09
The Hustler '61 ▶
I, Tonya '17 ▶
Ice Castles '79
Ice Princess '05
International Velvet '78
Invictus '09 ▶
Invincible '06 ▶
The Jesse Owens Story '84
Jim Thorpe: All American '51
The Joe Louis Story '53
Kansas City Bomber '72
The Kid From Cleveland '49
Kid Galahad '37 ▶
Kid Monk Baroni '52
Knockdown '11
Knockout '11
Knute Rockne: All American '40 ▶
Lagaan: Once upon a Time in India '01
Landspeed '01
The Last American Hero '73 ▶
The Legend of Bagger Vance '00
Legendary '10
The Longshots '08
Love and Basketball '00 ▶
Madison '01
McFarland USA '15
The Mighty Macs '09
Million Dollar Arm '14
Miracle '04 ▶
Miracle on Ice '81
The Miracle Season '18
Mr. Hockey: The Gordie Howe Story '13
Moneyball '11 ▶
My All American '15
Nadia '84
The Natural '84 ▶
Never Back Down 2: The Beatdown '11
O '01 ▶
The Oklahoma City Dolls '81
On the Edge '86
One on One '77
Over the Top '86
Overcomer '19
Passing Glory '99 ▶
Pastime '91 ▶
Peaceful Warrior '06
The Perfect Game '09
Personal Best '82 ▶
Phantom Punch '09
The Phenom '16
The Philly Kid '12
Ping Pong '02 ▶
Pistol: The Birth of a Legend '90
Prefontaine '96
Price of Glory '00
Pride '07
Pride of St. Louis '52
The Pride of the Yankees '42 ▶
The Program '93
The Program '15
Race '16
Radio '03
Raging Bull '80 ▶
Rebound: The Legend of Earl 'The Goat' Manigault '96
Red Line 7000 '65
Red Surf '90
Remember the Titans '00 ▶
Requiem for a Heavyweight '56 ▶
Requiem for a Heavyweight '62 ▶
Resurrecting the Champ '07
Right Cross '50
Ring the Bell '13
Rock the Paint '05
The Rocket '05 ▶
Rocky '76 ▶
Rocky 2 '79
Rocky 3 '82
Rocky 4 '85
Rocky 5 '90
Rocky Marciano '99
Rollerball '02
Rowing Through '96
Rudy '93
Run the Race '19
Running Brave '83
Rush '13 ▶
Saint Ralph '04
A Scene at Sea '92
School Ties '92 ▶
A Season on the Brink '02
Secretariat '10
Seven Days in Utopia '11
Shiner '00
A Shot at Glory '00
Side Out '90
61* '01 ▶
Snake & Mongoose '13
Soul of the Game '96 ▶
Soul Surfer '11
Southpaw '15
Sporting Blood '31
The Squeeze '15
Sticks and Stones '08
The Stratton Story '49 ▶
Sugar '09 ▶
Summer Catch '01
Supercross: The Movie '05
Swimming Upstream '03
Talent for the Game '91
That Championship Season '82
They Call Me Sirr '00
This Sporting Life '63 ▶
Thunder in Dixie '65
Tiger Town '83
The Tiger Woods Story '98
Touch and Go '86
Touchback '11
Trading Paint '19
Trouble with the Curve '12
21 Hours at Munich '76 ▶
Two for the Money '05
Two Minutes to Play '37
Underdog Kids '15
United '11
Varsity Blues '98
Victory '81
Vision Quest '85
A Warrior's Heart '11
The Way Back '20
We Are Marshall '06
When the Game Stands Tall '14
Wilma '77
Wind '92
The Winning Team '52
Without Limits '97 ▶
Wondrous Oblivion '06 ▶
The World's Fastest Indian '05 ▶
The Wrestler '08 ▶
The Yankles '09
Youngblood '86

Sports Romance

***See also** Baseball; Basketball; Football; Hockey; Romantic Triangles; Skating; Soccer; Sports Comedy; Sports Drama*

All the Right Moves '83
Bend It Like Beckham '02 ▶
Bull Durham '88 ▶
The Cutting Edge 3: Chasing the Dream '08
The Cutting Edge '92
The Cutting Edge: Fire and Ice '10
The Cutting Edge: Going for the Gold '05
Days of Thunder '90
Everybody's All American '88
Gregory's Girl '80 ▶
Happy Landing '38
Heaven Can Wait '78 ▶
Ice Castles '79
Ice Castles '10
It's a Pleasure '45
Just Wright '10
Love and Basketball '00 ▶
My Blind Brother '16
The Natural '84 ▶
Ronnie and Julie '97
She's the Man '06
Silver Skates '43
Summer Catch '01
Thin Ice '37 ▶
Youngblood '86
The Zoya Factor '19

Spring Break

***See also** Vacations*

Being Frank '19
From Justin to Kelly '03
Lauderdale '89
Mardi Gras: Spring Break '11
Palm Springs Weekend '63
Spring Break '83
Spring Breakdown '08
Spring Breakers '13 ▶
Sundown '16
There's Nothing out There '90
22 Jump Street '14
Where the Boys Are '60
Wild On the Beach '65

Spy Kids

***See also** Childhood Visions; Spies & Espionage*

Agent Cody Banks 2: Destination London '04
Agent Cody Banks '03
Alex Rider: Operation Stormbreaker '06
The Boss Baby '17
Cloak & Dagger '84
Codename: Icarus '85
Hangman's Curse '03
Harriet the Spy '96
If Looks Could Kill '91
The Kid with the X-Ray Eyes '99
Kim '84
Max Rules '05
My Name Is Ivan '62 ▶
My Spy '19
The Secret Agent Club '96
Spy Kids 2: The Island of Lost Dreams '02 ▶
Spy Kids 3-D: Game Over '03
Spy Kids 4: All the Time in the World '11
Spy Kids '01 ▶
Spy School '08
Thunderbirds '04

Stagestruck

***See also** Showbiz Comedies; Showbiz Dramas; Showbiz Thrillers*

The Actress '53
Adventure in Manhattan '36
Alexander the Last '09
All About Eve '50 ▶
Anna Karenina '12
Applause '29 ▶
Because of Him '45
Becoming Mike Nichols '16
Being Julia '04 ▶
Bicycling With Moliere '13
Bigger Than the Sky '05
Birdman, or (The Unexpected Virtue of Ignorance) '14 ▶
Black Widow '54
Blame '17
Bloodhounds of Broadway '52
Bloodhounds of Broadway '89
Bright Lights '30
Broadway Damage '98
Broadway Danny Rose '84 ▶
Broadway Idiot '13
Broadway Limited '41
Broadway Melody '29
Broadway Melody of 1938 '37
Broadway Rhythm '44
Bullets over Broadway '94 ▶
Burlesque '10
Burton and Taylor '13
Cain and Mabel '36
Career Girl '44
Carnegie Hall '47
Chasing Rainbows '30
The Christmas Pageant '11
Cirque du Soleil: Worlds Away '12
Cold Souls '09
Coney Island '43 ▶
The Cradle Will Rock '99
Critic's Choice '63
Curtain at Eight '33
Dames '34 ▶
Dancing Lady '33
Dangerous '35
Dare '09
The Daughter of Rosie O'Grady '50
The Dolly Sisters '46
The Dresser '15 ▶
Eating Out 4: Drama Camp '11
The Eddie Cantor Story '53
Elaine Stritch: Shoot Me '14 ▶
The English Teacher '13
An Englishman in New York '09
Esther Kahn '00
Every Little Step '08
Everything I Have is Yours '52
Exit Smiling '26
Fame '80 ▶
First a Girl '35
Fish Without a Bicycle '03
Florence Foster Jenkins '16
For Heaven's Sake '50
Forty Naughty Girls '37
Frogs for Snakes '98
Gallant Sons '40
The Gallows Act II '19
George White's Scandals '45
George White's Scandals of 1935 '35
Go Into Your Dance '35
Gold Diggers of 1937 '36
The Good Companions '33
Goodbye Baby '07
Grand Piano '13
The Great Garrick '37
The Great Ziegfeld '36 ▶
Gypsy '62 ▶
Gypsy '93
Hamlet 2 '08 ▶
The Hard Way '43
Heights '04
The Helen Morgan Story '57
Henry's Crime '10
Hooray for Love '35
Illuminata '98
I'm Going Home '00 ▶
Interview with the Vampire '94
Introducing the Dwights '07
It's Love I'm After '37
The Jazz Singer '52
Jeanne Eagels '57
Jesus of Montreal '89 ▶
Kevin Hart: Let Me Explain '13
Kevin Hart: What Now? '16
Kiki '26
The King of Masks '99 ▶
Kiss Me, Guido '97
La Boheme '26
La La Land '16 ▶
The Last Metro '80 ▶
The Leading Man '96
Let's Make Love '60
The Letter '12
Life Begins at Eight-Thirty '42
Lillian Russell '40
Lillie '79 ▶
London Town '46
Look for the Silver Lining '49
Lord Byron of Broadway '30
Lucky Break '01
The Mad Magician '54
Madeline's Madeline '18
The Man with Two Faces '34
Me and Orson Welles '09
Meet the People '44
Meeting Spencer '11
A Midwinter's Tale '95
Mrs. Henderson Presents '05
Moon over Broadway '98 ▶
Morning Glory '33
Mother Wore Tights '47 ▶
The Muppets '11 ▶
My Gal Sal '42
My Wild Irish Rose '47
Never Say Macbeth '07
New Faces of 1937 '37
The Next Step '95
Next Time We Love '36
Nicholas Nickleby '02 ▶
No Time For Comedy '40
NOW: In the Wings on a World Stage '14
The Old-Fashioned Way '34
On with the Show '29
Paint and Powder '25
Paris 36 '08
The Phantom Lover '95
Presenting Lily Mars '43
The Producers '05
The Reckoning '03 ▶
Rosencrantz & Guildenstern Are Undead '10
Sally '29
The Sea Gull '68

▶ = *rated three bones or higher*

Shakespeare in Love '98 ▶
Sharpay's Fabulous Adventure '11
She's Back on Broadway '53
The Singing Fool '28
The Singing Kid '36
Something to Live For '52
Stage Door '37 ▶
Stagefright '87
Star! '68
Success Is the Best Revenge '84
Sundays at Tiffany's '10
Synecdoche, New York '08 ▶
Tea for Two '50 ▶
The Tenderfoot '32
These Foolish Things '06
Three Sailors and a Girl '53
Tipping the Velvet '02
Topsy Turvy '99 ▶
Two Girls on Broadway '40
Va Savoir '01
Vanya on 42nd Street '94 ▶
Varsity Show '37
Venus in Fur '13 ▶
William Shakespeare's A Midsummer Night's Dream '99
Witchcraft 11: Sisters in Blood '00
Yankee Doodle Dandy '42 ▶
You Ain't Seen Nothin' Yet '12
You Can't Have Everything '37
Young Cassidy '65

Stalked!

See also Obsessive Love

Addicted to Love '96
All Hallow's Eve 2 '15
Alone With Her '07
Backwoods '87
Baghead '08
Black Christmas '19
Blackway '16
Blood Trails '06
The Bottom of the Sea '03 ▶
The Boy Next Door '15
Broken Vows '16
Buddy Boy '99
The Cable Guy '96
Carnage Park '16
The Case of the Bloody Iris '72
Cherish '02
Christina's House '99
Chuck & Buck '00
Copycat '95
A Deadly Encounter '04
Enduring Love '04
The Fan '81
The Fan '96
Fatal Attraction '87 ▶
Feedback '20
The Gingerbread Man '97
Greener Grass '19
Greta '18
He Loves Me . . . He Loves Me Not '02
Hoot '06
I Love Your Work '03
Impulse '08
Incognito '99
Ingrid Goes West '17
Intruder '16
Irresistible '06
I.T. '16
The Killing Floor '06
Klute '71 ▶
Living in Peril '97
Ma '19
Mr. Wrong '95
Night Watcher '08
Number One Fan '94
O Fantasma '00
Obsessed '09
P2 '07
A Perfect Getaway '09
The Perfect Guy '15
Perfect Strangers '03
Personal Effects '05
Portrait of an Escort '80
Prom Night '08
Ratter '16
Red Road '06
The Rendering '02
The Resident '10
Secret Window '04
The Seduction '82
Shadow of Fear '12
Sleep Tight '11
Stalked '99
Stalked at 17 '12
Stalker '98
Stalking Laura '93
Sunlight Jr. '13
Taxi Driver '76 ▶
Turn of the Blade '97
The Unguarded Moment '56
Unsane '18
Waiting for Forever '11
Welcome Home '18
Wicker Park '04
Yella '07 ▶

Star Gazing

The Arrival '96
The Death and Life of John F. Donovan '19
Deep Impact '98
Eliza's Horoscope '70
The Fish that Saved Pittsburgh '79
The Heavenly Body '44
Local Hero '83 ▶
My Stepmother Is an Alien '88
Out of Blue '19
Popstar: Never Stop Never Stopping '16 ▶
The Resurrection of Gavin Stone '17
Roxanne '87 ▶

Stay-at-Home Dads

See also Dads; Doofus Dads

The Ballad of Jack and Rose '05 ▶
Captain Fantastic '16
Daddy Day Care '03
Incredibles 2 '18 ▶
Kramer vs. Kramer '79 ▶
Mr. Mom '83 ▶
Ramona and Beezus '10
Signs '02 ▶

Stepparents

See also Family Ties; Parenthood

The Adventures of Sebastian Cole '99
All the Little Animals '98
The Amityville Horror '05
Angel Face '52 ▶
Another Cinderella Story '08
Ararat '02 ▶
Are We Done Yet? '07
Are You Here '13
Beat Girl '60
Beau Pere '81 ▶
Benji: Off the Leash! '04
Big Girls Don't Cry. . . They Get Even '92
Big Mommas: Like Father, Like Son '11
A Blueprint for Murder '53
Born Bad '11
Cafe Lumiere '05
Cinderella '50 ▶
Cinderella '15
A Cinderella Story '04
A Cinderella Story: Once Upon a Song '11
Courage '09
Daddy's Home 2 '17
Daddy's Home '15
The Day the Earth Stood Still '08
Dead Cool '04
Deathlands: Homeward Bound '03
Domestic Disturbance '01
Don't Cry Now '07
Ellie '84
Enchanted '07
Ever After: A Cinderella Story '98 ▶
Everyone Says I Love You '96 ▶
Eyes in the Night '42
Fascination '04
Fear '96
Fog Over Frisco '34
The Furies '50
Georgia Rule '07
God's Pocket '14
The Good Witch's Charm '12
The Good Witch's Family '11
Happily N'Ever After '07
Happy Times '00
Home Before Dark '58
Home for Christmas '93
Hot Rod '07
House of Darkness '48
I Capture the Castle '02
I-See-You.Com '06
Imaginary Playmate '06
Jingle All the Way 2 '14
Journey 2: The Mysterious Island '12
Just Henry '11
Kangaroo Jack '02
Lassie '94
Life, Above All '10
The Lodge '19
Look at Me '04 ▶
Looking for Eric '09
Looking for Palladin '08
Love Actually '03
Maleficent '14
Merci pour le Chocolat '00 ▶
Mokey '42
Mom, Dad and Her '08
Night of the Twisters '95
One Way to Valhalla '09
The Orphan '79
Pan's Labyrinth '06 ▶
Petits Freres '00
Place of Execution '09
Private Passions '85
Queen of Hearts '19
Radio Rebel '12
Rags '12
The Return of the Swamp Thing '89
Rivals '72
Running Scared '06
Second Sight '99 ▶
The Secret Heart '46
Seventeen Years '99 ▶
Shadowboxer '06
She Fell Among Thieves '78
Siblings '04
The Snorkel '58
Snow White: A Deadly Summer '12
Snow White: A Tale of Terror '97
Snow White: The Fairest of Them All '02
Spy Kids 4: All the Time in the World '11
Step Brothers '08
Step Dogs '13
The Stepdaughter '00
The Stepfather '87 ▶
Stepfather 2: Make Room for Daddy '89
Stepfather 3: Father's Day '92
The Stepfather '09
Stepmom '98 ▶
The Stepmother '71
Sucker Punch '11
A Summer to Remember '61 ▶
Tadpole '02
This Boy's Life '93 ▶
Thoroughbreds '17
Time Regained '99
Toast '10
Transamerica '05 ▶
Unforgettable '17
Unleashed '05
The Wackness '08
Wah-Wah '05
Whirlpool '34
Wild Things 3: Diamonds in the Rough '05
The Woman Between '31
A Yank at Eton '42
Yours, Mine & Ours '05

Stewardesses

See also Airborne

Airplane! '80 ▶
Black Tight Killers '66 ▶
Blazing Stewardesses '75
Boeing Boeing '65
Elizabethtown '05
Executive Decision '96
Jackie Brown '97 ▶
Passenger 57 '92
The Terminal '04
Thirst Street '17
Three Guys Named Mike '51
Turbulence '96
View from the Top '03
Zero Hour! '57

Storytelling

See also Family Viewing

American Fable '17
Babyfever '94
Big Fish '03 ▶
Brigsby Bear '17
The Company of Wolves '85 ▶
Hitchcock '12
Lakeboat '00
The Little Prince '16 ▶
Monster in a Box '92 ▶
My Dinner with Andre '81 ▶
The NeverEnding Story 3: Escape from Fantasia '94
The Princess Bride '87 ▶
The Story Lady '93
A Tale of Love and Darkness '16
Ten Canoes '06
The Willies '90
Windwalker '81 ▶

Strained Suburbia

See also Yuppie Nightmares

The Addams Family '19
Alpha Dog '06
American Beauty '99 ▶
The Amityville Horror '79
Amongst Friends '93
Amos and Andrew '93
Arlington Road '99
Beavis and Butt-Head Do America '96
Betrayed: A Story of Three Women '95
Blue Velvet '86 ▶
The Brady Bunch Movie '95 ▶
The 'Burbs '89
Catch Me If You Can '02
The Chapman Report '62
Chlorine '13
Christmas With the Kranks '04
The Chumscrubber '05
Civic Duty '06
Clownhouse '88
Coherence '13
Cold Turkey '71 ▶
Coneheads '93
Confined '10
Consenting Adults '92
The Cookout '04
Crime and Punishment in Suburbia '00
Dark Horse '11
Dark Skies '13
Deadly Neighbor '91
Deck the Halls '06
Dennis the Menace '93
Dennis the Menace Strikes Again '98
Desperate Hours '55 ▶
Desperate Hours '90
The Details '11
Disturbia '07 ▶
Don't Tell Mom the Babysitter's Dead '91
Down to the Bone '04
Drone '17
Edward Scissorhands '90 ▶
Elephant '03 ▶
11:14 '03
Envy '04
Faithful '95
Flipped '10
The Girl Next Door '04
Godmoney '97
Good Fences '03
The Graduate '67 ▶
Grand Canyon '91 ▶
The Green '11
Gummo '97
Half a Hero '53
Hidden '05 ▶
Hocus Pocus '93
Home Alone '90 ▶
Home Alone 3 '97
House '86 ▶
How to Beat the High Cost of Living '80
Hugo Pool '97
Imaginary Heroes '05
Inside Out '05
Jaws '75 ▶
Jaws 2 '78
Just Before Nightfall '71
Kate's Secret '86
Keeping Up with the Joneses '16
Killers '10
Krippendorf's Tribe '98
Little Children '06 ▶
Little Man '06
Look in Any Window '61
Loving '70
Marked for Death '90
Michael '11
Milton's Secret '16
Mr. & Mrs. Smith '05 ▶
Mr. Blandings Builds His Dream House '48 ▶
The Money Pit '86
Monster House '06 ▶
Murder of a Cat '14
My Blue Heaven '90
My New Gun '92
Neighbors '81
Next Friday '00
1941 '79
No Down Payment '57
101 Ways (The Things a Girl Will Do to Keep Her Volvo) '00
Opportunity Knocks '90
The Oranges '12
The Osterman Weekend '83
Over the Edge '79 ▶
Over the Hedge '06 ▶
A Packing Suburbia '99
Palindromes '04 ▶
Paranormal Activity 2 '10
Paranormal Activity 5: The Ghost Dimension '15
Parents '89 ▶
Please Don't Eat the Daisies '60
Polyester '81
The Positively True Adventures of the Alleged Texas Cheerleader-Murdering Mom '93 ▶
Premonition '07
The Prize Winner of Defiance, Ohio '05 ▶
Puzzle '18
Rabbit, Run '70
Rally 'Round the Flag, Boys! '58
Red Doors '05
Return of the Living Dead 2 '88
Revolutionary Road '08
Serial Mom '94 ▶
Serial Slayer '03
Sexting in Suburbia '12
Shattered Spirits '86
Short Cuts '93 ▶
The Stepford Wives '75 ▶
The Stepford Wives '04
The Stranger '46 ▶
The Swimmer '68 ▶
Terrorvision '86
There's Always Tomorrow '56
3 Backyards '10
Three Wishes '95
The Trigger Effect '96
12 and Holding '05 ▶
Twice in a Lifetime '85 ▶
The Underworld Story '50
The Unguarded Moment '56
A Very Brady Sequel '96
The Virgin Suicides '99
Wakefield '17
The War of the Roses '89 ▶
We Need to Talk About Kevin '11 ▶
When Every Day Was the Fourth of July '78
The Whole Nine Yards '00
Winter Solstice '04 ▶
Your Friends & Neighbors '98 ▶

Strippers

Afternoon Delight '13
American Wedding '03
Americano '11
Anna Nicole '13
The Badge '02
A Beautiful Life '08
The Big Bang '11
Blaze '89
Blood Money '98
Body Language '95
The Box '03
Breakdown '96 ▶
Cadillac Ranch '96
The Casino Job '08
The Center of the World '01
Choke '08
City Island '09
Closer '04 ▶
Club Vampire '98
Crazy Horse '12 ▶
Dancing at the Blue Iguana '00
Dangerous Ground '96
Day of the Warrior '96
Devil's Den '06
Dirty Girl '10
A Dirty Shame '04
Doctor in Love '60
The Dog Problem '06
Dogma '99 ▶
End Game '09
ESL: English as a Second Language '05
Exotica '94 ▶
The Fluffer '01
Frankie and Alice '10
From Dusk Till Dawn '95
The Frozen Ground '13
The Full Monty '96 ▶
The G-String Horror '12
A Good Marriage '14
Gypsy '62 ▶
Gypsy '93
The Hangover '09
Hard As Nails '01
Headless Body in Topless Bar '96
The Heart Is Deceitful Above All Things '04
Heaven '99
Hey Hey It's Esther Blueberger '08
Hustle & Flow '05 ▶
Hustlers '19 ▶
I Hope They Serve Beer in Hell '09
I Know Who Killed Me '07
Joint Body '11
Keys to Tulsa '96
Kiss of Death '94
Kiss of Fire '98
Lady of Burlesque '43
Lap Dancing '95
The Last Word '95
Lenny '74 ▶
Love and Other Four Letter Words '07
Made '01
Magic Mike '12
Magic Mike XXL '15
Master Spy: The Robert Hanssen Story '02
Miami Hustle '95
Midnight Tease 2 '95
Midnight Tease '94
Mrs. Henderson Presents '05
A Night in Heaven '83
Night Junkies '07
The Nude Set '57
#1 Cheerleader Camp '10
On Tour '10
Overnight Delivery '96
Pecker '98
Pigalle '95
Planet Terror '07
The Players Club '98 ▶
Plucking the Daisy '56
Powder Blue '09
Rough Night '17
St. Vincent '14
Screaming Mimi '58
Seven Thieves '60 ▶
Sex & Lies in Sin City: The Ted Binion Scandal '08
The Showgirl Murders '95
Showgirls '95
Sin City '05
Sin City: A Dame to Kill For '14
Sparkler '99
Stag '97
Strip Search '97
Stripshow '95
Striptease '96
Stripteaser '95

Studs Lonigan '60
Sweet Evil '98
13 Moons '02
Tin Cup '96 ▶
True Lies '94
Tully '00 ▶
Under Siege '92
Vacuuming Completely Nude in Paradise '01
Welcome to the Rileys '10
We're the Millers '13
Whirlygirl '04
Working Girls '75
The Wrestler '08 ▶
Yellow '06
Zombie Strippers '08

Struggling Artists

***See also** Art & Biopics: Artists*

Apartment 12 '06
Art School Confidential '06
At Eternity's Gate '18
Basquiat '96 ▶
Before Night Falls '00 ▶
Brother to Brother '04
Catfight '17
Dark Hearts '12
The Devil's Candy '17
Don't Think Twice '16
Don't Worry, He Won't Get Far on Foot '18
Fake '10
Heights '04
In the Realms of the Unreal '04 ▶
Jealousy '13 ▶
La La Land '16 ▶
Lemon '17
Live, Love and Learn '37
Love in Pawn '53
Love Letters '99 ▶
Mesrine: Part 1-Killer Instinct '08
Photograph '19
Shopgirl '05 ▶
A Simple Promise '07
Standing on Fishes '99
The Time Being '12
The Tollbooth '04
Vincent & Theo '90 ▶

Struggling Musicians

***See also** Biopics: Musicians; Music*

The Adventures of Buckaroo Banzai Across the Eighth Dimension '84 ▶
All You Need Is Cash '78 ▶
Backbeat '94 ▶
The Beat My Heart Skipped '05 ▶
Beyond the Valley of the Dolls '70
Bikini Summer '91
Billy's Holiday '95
Blast-Off Girls '67
Blaze '18 ▶
Blues in the Night '41
The Brady Bunch Movie '95 ▶
Breaking Glass '80
Cheech and Chong's Up in Smoke '79
The Competition '80 ▶
Crossover Dreams '85
Crossroads '86
Departures '08
Dogs in Space '87
Doing Time for Patsy Cline '97
Eddie and the Cruisers 2: Eddie Lives! '89
Eddie and the Cruisers '83
The Fabulous Dorseys '47
Falling from Grace '92
Fear of a Black Hat '94
The Five Heartbeats '91 ▶
Florence Foster Jenkins '16
Frank '14 ▶
Ganked '05
Garden Party '08
Gold Star '17
Gridlock'd '96 ▶
Hustle & Flow '05 ▶
Jack Frost '98
A Man Called Adam '66
Mo' Better Blues '90
Morris from America '16 ▶
Murder Rap '87
Oh, God! You Devil '84
One Trick Pony '80
The Pacific and Eddy '07
Punk Love '06
Purple Rain '84
The Return of Spinal Tap '92
Rhinestone '84
Rock & Rule '83
Rock School '05 ▶
Rock Star '01
The Rose '79 ▶
Satisfaction '88
School of Rock '03 ▶
A Simple Promise '07
A Slipping Down Life '99
Sparkle '76
A Star Is Born '76
A Star Is Born '18 ▶
Streets of Fire '84
Sueno '05
Sunset Strip '99
Tender Mercies '83 ▶
This Is Spinal Tap '84 ▶
Too Young to Kiss '51
Vibrations '94
You Light Up My Life '77

Stuntmen

Death Proof '07
Drive '11 ▶
800 Bullets '02
The Fall '06
Ghost Rider '07
Having a Wild Weekend '65
Hooper '78
Hot Rod '07
Looney Tunes: Back in Action '03
Miss Tatlock's Millions '48
Slogan '69
The Stunt Man '80 ▶
Stuntmen '09
Vendetta '85

Stupid Is...

Adopted '09
American Pie Presents Band Camp '05
Ass Backwards '13
Awful Nice '14
Be Kind Rewind '08
Bean '97 ▶
Beavis and Butt-Head Do America '96
Being There '79 ▶
The Benchwarmers '06
Big Top Pee-wee '88
Bill & Ted's Bogus Journey '91
Bill & Ted's Excellent Adventure '89
Billy Madison '94
Bio-Dome '96
Black Sheep '96
Blonde and Blonder '07
Caddyshack '80 ▶
Chairman of the Board '97
The Dinner Game '98
Drowning Mona '00
Dudley Do-Right '99
Dumb & Dumber '94
Dumb and Dumber To '14
Dumb and Dumberer: When Harry Met Lloyd '03
Employee of the Month '06
The Extreme Adventures of Super Dave '98
Fast Times at Ridgemont High '82 ▶
Forrest Gump '94 ▶
Frank McKlusky, C.I. '02
Get Smart '08
Half-Baked '97
The Hangover, Part III '13
Happy Gilmore '96
Hot Rod '07
Housebroken '09
Idiot Box '97
Idle Hands '99
Jackass 3D '10
Jackass Number Two '06
The Jerk '79
The Jerky Boys '95
Joe Dirt '01
Kickin' It Old Skool '07
Killer Bud '00
Let's Go to Prison '06
The Life of Lucky Cucumber '08
Little Nicky '00
Lock, Stock and 2 Smoking Barrels '98 ▶
Masterminds '16
Meet the Deedles '98
Mr. Accident '99
Mr. Bean's Holiday '07
National Lampoon's Animal House '78 ▶
National Lampoon's Ratko: The Dictator's Son '09
The Nutty Professor '63 ▶
Orgazmo '98
Pee-wee's Big Adventure '85 ▶
The Penthouse '10
The Pink Panther 2 '09
Ready to Rumble '00
Road Trip '00
Romy and Michele's High School Reunion '97
The Sasquatch Gang '06
Scary Movie 4 '06
Son-in-Law '93
Stealing Harvard '02
Step Brothers '08
Strange Wilderness '08
The Stupids '95
30 Minutes or Less '11
Tommy Boy '95
Venus and Vegas '10
The Waterboy '98
Wayne's World '92 ▶
What Up? '08
White Mile '94
Witless Protection '08
Young Einstein '89
Zoolander '01

Submarines

***See also** Deep Blue*

Above Us the Waves '55 ▶
The Abyss '89 ▶
Action in the North Atlantic '43
Agent Red '00
The Amazing Captain Nemo '78
Assault on a Queen '66
Atlantis: The Lost Empire '01
Atomic Submarine '59
Atragon '63
Battle of the Coral Sea '59
Below '02
Black Sea '14
Black Water '18
Captain Nemo and the Underwater City '69
Counter Measures '99
Crash Dive '43
Crash Dive '96
Crimson Tide '95 ▶
Danger Beneath the Sea '02
Das Boot '81 ▶
Deep Shock '03
Depth Charge '08
Destination Tokyo '43
The Devil and the Deep '32
Down Periscope '96
Enemy Below '57 ▶
The Fate of the Furious '17
Fer-De-Lance '74
First Strike '85
For Your Eyes Only '81 ▶
Ghostboat '06
Going Under '91
Hostile Waters '97
The Hunley '99
The Hunt for Red October '90 ▶
Hunter Killer '18
Ice Station Zebra '68
In Enemy Hands '04
The Incredible Mr. Limpet '64
The Inside Man '84
K-19: The Widowmaker '02
Latitude Zero '69
The League of Extraordinary Gentlemen '03
Leviathan '89
Magma: Volcanic Disaster '06
Mega Shark Vs. Giant Octopus '09
Morning Departure '50
Mysterious Island '61 ▶
Nautilus '99
1941 '79
Octopus '00
On the Beach '00
Operation Bikini '63
Operation Delta Force 2: Mayday '97
Operation Delta Force 3: Clear Target '98
Operation Petticoat '59 ▶
Phantom '13
Raise the Titanic '80
Run Silent, Run Deep '58 ▶
Sailor Beware '52
The Sea Ghost '31
Silent Venom '08
The Silver Fleet '43
The Spy Who Loved Me '77
Stargate: Continuum '08
Steel Sharks '97
Sub Down '97
Submarine Attack '54
Submarine Base '43
Submerged '05
30,000 Leagues Under the Sea '07
Three Sailors and a Girl '53
Torpedo Run '58
20,000 Leagues under the Sea '16 ▶
20,000 Leagues under the Sea '54 ▶
20,000 Leagues Under the Sea '97
2010: Moby Dick '10
U-571 '00
Up Periscope '59
USS Indianapolis: Men of Courage '16
Voyage to the Bottom of the Sea '61 ▶
We Dive at Dawn '43 ▶
Yellow Submarine '68 ▶
You Only Live Twice '67

Subways

***See also** Trains*

Adventures in Babysitting '87
The Amazing Spider-Man '12 ▶
Bugs '03
Bulletproof Monk '03
Carlito's Way '93 ▶
Cry Terror! '58
Daybreak '01
Die Hard: With a Vengeance '95
Eve of Destruction '90
The French Connection '71 ▶
Fruitvale Station '13
The Fugitive '93 ▶
Greta '18
High Strung '16
Highlander 2: The Quickening '91
The Italian Job '03 ▶
The Jackal '97
Kontroll '03 ▶
Lethal Weapon 3 '92
Man Hunt '41 ▶
The Midnight Meat Train '08
The Million Dollar Rip-Off '76
Mimic '97
Money Train '95
Next Stop, Wonderland '98
NYC Underground '13
On the Line '01
Predator 2 '90
Pretty Baby '50
Raw Meat '72
Reconstruction '03
Red Line '13
Risky Business '83 ▶
ShadowZone: The Undead Express '96
Sliding Doors '97
Speed '94 ▶
Stag Night '08
Stand Clear of the Closing Doors '13 ▶
Subway '85
Subway Stories '97
The Taking of Pelham One Two Three '74 ▶
The Taking of Pelham 123 '09
Three and Out '08
Trick '99 ▶
Tube '03
The Warriors '79
Zazie dans le Metro '61 ▶

Suicide

***See also** Death & the Afterlife*

About Alex '14
Absence of Malice '81
According to Greta '08
Against the Current '09
Alien 3 '92
Alive or Dead '08
All About Lily Chou-Chou '01 ▶
The American Side '16
American Strays '96
And Everything Is Going Fine '10
Angels Over Broadway '40 ▶
Anna Karenina '12
The Apartment '60 ▶
Apartment 1303 '07
Apres-Vous '03
Ararat '02 ▶
The Arrangement '69
Autopsy '75
Bad Girls Dormitory '84
Bad Timing: A Sensual Obsession '80
Ballast '08
Beautiful Kate '09 ▶
Bedazzled '68 ▶
Believers '07
The Bell Jar '79
Betrayed at 17 '11
Better Off Dead '85
Between Two Worlds '44
The Big Chill '83 ▶
Black Heaven '10
The Black House '00
Body & Soul '93 ▶
Boogeyman 3 '08
Breaking & Exiting '18
A Broken Life '07
The Broken Tower '11
Brute Force '47 ▶
Bully '11 ▶
The Bye Bye Man '17
Cake '14
Cas & Dylan '15
Cause Celebre '87 ▶
Change My Life '01
Christie's Revenge '07
Christine '16
The Chumscrubber '05
Cobain: Montage of Heck '15 ▶
Colorful: The Motion Picture '10 ▶
Come Undone '00
The Confessor '04
Conspiracy of Silence '03
Control '07
Cookie's Fortune '99 ▶
Courage Under Fire '96 ▶
Crimes of the Heart '86
The Crown Prince '06
Crumb '94 ▶
The Curve '97
Cyberbully '11
Dark City '50
Dark Remains '05
Dark Side '02
Darkness Falls '20
The Daughter '15
Dead Man on Campus '97
Dead Poets Society '89 ▶
The Debt '10
Deep Water '06 ▶
Delicatessen '92 ▶
Delinquent Daughters '44
The Departure '17
Deutschland im Jahre Null '47 ▶
Devil '10
The Discovery '17
Dolls '02 ▶
Dominique '79
Double Suicide '69 ▶
Downloading Nancy '08
Dream with the Fishes '97
The Eagle and the Hawk '33 ▶
East of Fifth Avenue '33
Elizabethtown '05
The End '78 ▶
Eva '62
The Event '03
Event Horizon '97
Excuse Me for Living '12
Exit Plan '20
The Eye 2 '04
Faithful '95
False Pretenses '04
Fat Kid Rules the World '12
Father of My Children '09
Father's Day '96
Fedora '78
The Fire Within '64 ▶
First Reformed '17
The First Wives Club '96
Five Star Final '31
For One More Day '07
The Forest '16
Free Fall '14
From the Journals of Jean Seberg '95
Frontier of Dawn '08
Full Metal Jacket '87 ▶
Fuzz '72
Germany Year Zero '48 ▶
The Girl on the Bridge '98 ▶
Golden Gate '93
Gonin 2 '96
Goodbye, Raggedy Ann '71
Goodbye Solo '08
The Guyana Tragedy: The Story of Jim Jones '80
Hamlet '96 ▶
The Hanging Garden '97
Hangman's Curse '03
The Happening '08
Happiness Runs '10
The Hard Way '43
Harold and Maude '71 ▶
Haywire '80
Head On '04
Heading for Heaven '47
Heat '95 ▶
Heathers '89 ▶
Hide and Seek '05
Hollow '11
Hollywoodland '06
The Hours '02 ▶
The Hudsucker Proxy '93 ▶
The Hustle '75
The Iceman Cometh '73
Imaginary Heroes '05
The Internet's Own Boy: The Story of Aaron Swartz '14 ▶
The Isle '01
It's a Wonderful Life '46 ▶
Julian Po '97
Julia's Eyes '10
Just Before I Go '15
Kate Plays Christine '16 ▶
Kill Me Later '01
Kill Your Darlings '06
Kings and Queen '04 ▶
The Kovak Box '06
Last Days '05
Last Love '13
Last Tango in Paris '73 ▶
The Last Time I Committed Suicide '96
The Last Word '08
Le Corbeau '43 ▶
Leaving Las Vegas '95 ▶
A Long Way Down '14
Love Is Blind '19
Love Liza '02
Love on a Pillow '62
Maborosi '95 ▶
M*A*S*H '70 ▶
Maya Dardel '17
Melo '86
Mrs. Dalloway '97
Mixed Nuts '94
Monsieur Lazhar '11
Monster's Ball '01 ▶
Morvern Callar '02
Mother Kusters Goes to Heaven '76 ▶
Mouchette '67 ▶
My Sweet Suicide '98
'night, Mother '86
Night Owls '15
Nightmare at the End of the Hall '08
Nightmare Detective '06
No More Orchids '32
Nora's Will '09
Now & Forever '02
Ode to Billy Joe '76
Old English '30
Olive Kitteridge '14 ▶
On Body and Soul '17 ▶
On the Edge '00

▶ = rated three bones or higher

▸ = rated three bones or higher

Supernatural

Cthulhu '08
Cult '07
The Curse of King Tut's Tomb '06
The Curse of La Llorona '19
Curse of the Demon '57 ▶
Curse of the Headless Horseman '72
Curse of the Living Corpse '64
The Curse of the Werewolf '61
Damien: Omen 2 '78
Dance of Death '68
The Dark '79
Dark Fields '09
The Dark Myth '90
Dark Remains '05
Dark Spirits '08
Dark Water '02
Darklight '04
The Darkness '16
Darkness Falls '03
The Daughter of Dr. Jekyll '57
Daughters of Satan '72
Dawn of the Mummy '82
Day Watch '06 ▶
Dead and Buried '81
Dead Are Alive '72
Dead Collections '12
Dead Mine '12
Dead Waves '06
The Death Curse of Tartu '66
Death Mask '98
Death Tunnel '05
Death Valley: The Revenge of Bloody Bill '04
Deathdream '72
Deathwatch '02
Deep Red: Hatchet Murders '75
Def by Temptation '90
Deliver Us From Evil '14
The Demon Lover '77
Demon of Paradise '87
Demon Rage '82
Demonia '90
Demonoid, Messenger of Death '81
Demons 2 '87
Demons '86
Demons of Ludlow '75
Demonstone '89
Despiser '03
Devil '10
Devil Dog: The Hound of Hell '78
Devil Doll '64
The Devil Inside '12
The Devil Rides Out '68 ▶
The Devil's Candy '17
The Devil's Daughter '91
The Devil's Hand '61
The Devil's Nightmare '71
The Devil's Partner '58
The Devil's Possessed '74
Devil's Rain '75
Devil's Wedding Night '73
Devonsville Terror '83
Devour '05
The Diabolical Dr. Z '65
Diary of a Madman '63
Die, Monster, Die! '65
Disciple of Death '72
The Doctor and the Devils '85
Doctor Butcher M.D. '80
Dr. Frankenstein's Castle of Freaks '74
Doctor Phibes Rises Again '72
Doctor Sleep '19 ▶
Dr. Tarr's Torture Dungeon '75
Dominion: Prequel to the Exorcist '05
Don't Be Afraid of the Dark '73
Don't Be Afraid of the Dark '11
Dororo '07
Down a Dark Hall '18
Drag Me to Hell '09
The Dreaming '88
The Drop '06
The Dunwich Horror '70
Dust Devil '93
Echoes '15
Edge of Sanity '89
The Eighteenth Angel '97
11-11-11 '11
Embrace of the Vampire '95
Endangered Species '02
Equinox '71 ▶
The Evil '78
Evil Dead Trap 2: Hideki '91
Evil Dead Trap '88 ▶
Evilspeak '82
Exorcism '74
The Exorcism of Emily Rose '05 ▶
The Exorcist '73 ▶
The Exorcist 2: The Heretic '77
The Eye 2 '04
The Eye '08
Fallen '97
The Fallen Ones '05
Farmhouse '08
Female Vampire '73
The Final Conflict '81
The Final Patient '05
Firestarter '84
The First Power '89
Flight 7500 '16
The Fog '05
The Forest '16
1408 '07
The Fourth Kind '09
Freaky Faron '06
From Beyond the Grave '73
From Dusk Till Dawn '95
The G-String Horror '12
The Gallows Act II '19
Gate 2 '92
The Gate '87
Gates of Hell 2: Dead Awakening '96
George A. Romero's Land of the Dead '05 ▶
The Ghastly Ones '68
The Ghost '63
The Ghost '04
The Ghost Brigade '93
Ghost Dance '83
Ghost Rider '07
Ghost Rider: Spirit of Vengeance '12
Ghost Story '81
The Ghosts of Hanley House '68
GhostWatcher '02
Ghouls '07
Giant from the Unknown '58
Ginger Snaps Back: The Beginning '04
Ginger Snaps: Unleashed '04
Goblin '10
God Told Me To '76
Godsend '04
Grave Encounters 2 '12
Grave Secrets: The Legacy of Hilltop Drive '92
The Gravedancers '06
The Grudge '04
Half-Caste '04
Half Light '05
The Happiness of the Katakuris '01
Haunted Highway '05
The Haunted Palace '63
Haunter '13
The Haunting in Connecticut 2: Ghosts of Georgia '13
The Haunting in Connecticut '09
The Haunting of Molly Hartley '08
Haunting Sarah '05
The Hazing '04
Headless Horseman '07
Headspace '02
The Hearse '80
Heaven & Hell '78
Hellbound: Hellraiser 2 '88
Hellions '15
Hellraiser '87
Hellraiser 3: Hell on Earth '92
Hellraiser 4: Bloodline '95
Hellraiser: Deader '05
Hellraiser: Hellseeker '02
Hellraiser: Hellworld '05
Hellraiser: Revelations '11
Hell's Ground '08
Hereditary '18 ▶
Hide and Seek '05
Hold Your Breath '12
Hollow '11
Home Sick '08
Horns '13
The Horrible Dr. Bones '00
The Horrible Dr. Hichcock '62
The Horror at 37,000 Feet '73
Horror Express '72
Horror Hotel '60
Horror of the Blood Monsters '70
Horror Rises from the Tomb '72
The House by the Cemetery '83
The House of Seven Corpses '73
House of the Dead '03
The House on Skull Mountain '74
House Where Evil Dwells '82
The Howling '81 ▶
Howling 2: Your Sister Is a Werewolf '85
Howling 3: The Marsupials '87
Howling 4: The Original Nightmare '88
Howling 5: The Rebirth '89
Howling 6: The Freaks '90
I Am Not A Serial Killer '16
I Am Zozo '12
In Fabric '18
The Indestructible Man '56
Inferno '80
The Inheritance '10
Initiation of Sarah '78
The Innkeepers '11
The Innocents '61 ▶
Inquisition '76
Insidious '10
Insidious: The Last Key '18
Inugami '01 ▶
Invasion of the Blood Farmers '72
The Invisible '07
Invitation to Hell '82
Isabelle '19
It Follows '15 ▶
It's Alive! '68
Jack O'Lantern '04
Jacob '11
Jaws of Satan '81
J.D.'s Revenge '76
Jennifer's Body '09
Jezebeth '11
Ju-On: The Grudge '03
Ju-On 2 '00
Kill, Baby, Kill '66 ▶
Kill Katie Malone '10
The Kiss '88
Kiss Daddy Goodbye '81
Kiss of the Damned '12
Knocking on Death's Door '99
Kwaidan '64 ▶
Lady Terminator '89 ▶
Land of the Minotaur '77
The Last Broadcast '98 ▶
The Last Lovecraft: Relic of Cthulhu '09
The Last Man on Earth '64
Left Bank '08
Left in Darkness '06
The Legacy '79
The Legend of Bloody Mary '08
The Legend of Hell House '73 ▶
The Legend of Lucy Keyes '06
Lethal Dose '03
Let's Scare Jessica to Death '71
Life Blood '09
Lights Out '16
Lisa and the Devil '75
The Living Corpse '03
Living Doll '90
Lord of Illusions '95
Lost Colony: The Legend of Roanoke '07
Lost Souls '98
Lost Souls '00
Lurkers '88
Lust for a Vampire '71
The Maid '05
Mama '13 ▶
The Man and the Monster '65
Manhattan Baby '82
Maniac '34
The Manitou '78
Manos, the Hands of Fate '66
Manticore '05
Mardi Gras for the Devil '93
Mardi Gras Massacre '78
Mark of the Devil 2 '72
Mark of the Devil '69
Mark of the Witch '70
Marked '07
Mary, Mary, Bloody Mary '76
The Medusa Touch '78
Megalodon '03
Memento Mori '00
The Mephisto Waltz '71 ▶
Mercy Black '19
Messengers 2: The Scarecrow '09
The Messengers '07
Messiah of Evil '74
Midnight '81
Midnight's Child '93
The Mind's Eye '16
Mirror, Mirror '90
Mirror of Death '87
Mirrors 2 '10
Mirrors '08
The Mist '07 ▶
The Morgue '07
Mother of Tears '08
Mothman '10
The Mummy's Shroud '67
Necromancer: Satan's Servant '88
Necromentia '09
Necropolis '87
Needle '10
Negative Happy Chainsaw Edge '08
Neon Maniacs '86
The Nesting '80
Netherworld '90
The New Daughter '10
The Night Evelyn Came Out of the Grave '71
Night Nurse '77
Night of the Death Cult '75
Night of the Demons 2 '94
Night of the Demons '88
Night of the Demons '09
The Night of the Devils '72
Night of the Ghouls '59
Night of the Sorcerers '70
Night Orchid '97 ▶
The Night Stalker '71
The Night Strangler '72
Night Visitor '89
Night Watch '04
Nightmare '07
Nightmare Castle '65
Nightmare Detective '06
Nightmare in Blood '75
Nightmare Sisters '87
Nightmare Weekend '86
Nightstalker '81
Nightwish '89
Nomads '86
The Norliss Tapes '73
Nothing But the Night '72
The Nun '18
The Objective '08
The Occultist '89
Odd Thomas '13
Of Unknown Origin '83
The Offspring '87
Omen 4: The Awakening '91
The Omen '76
The Omen '06
100 Feet '08
100 Monsters '68
One Missed Call 2 '05
One Missed Call 3: Final '06
One Missed Call '03 ▶
Onmyoji 2 '03
Onmyoji '01
The Oracle '85
The Order '03
Orgy of the Dead '65
Orgy of the Vampires '73
The Orphanage '07 ▶
The Other '72 ▶
The Other Side of the Door '16
The Others '01 ▶
Ouija '14
Ouija: Origin of Evil '16
Outpost '07
Outpost: Black Sun '12
Outpost: Rise of the Spetsnaz '13
Overlord '18
The Pact '12
Pan's Labyrinth '06 ▶
Paranormal Activity '09 ▶
Paranormal Activity 2 '10
Paranormal Activity 3 '11
Paranormal Activity 4 '12
Paranormal Activity 5: The Ghost Dimension '15
Paranormal Activity: The Marked Ones '14
The Paranormal Diaries: Clophill '13
Parasite '03
Patrick '78
Pet Sematary '89
Pet Sematary 2 '92
Pet Sematary '19
Phantasm '79
Phantasm 2 '88
Phantoms '97
The Pharaoh's Curse '57
Poltergeist '82 ▶
Poltergeist 2: The Other Side '86
Poltergeist 3 '88
Poltergeist: The Legacy '96
The Possessed '77
Possessing Piper Rose '11
Possession '08
The Possession '12
The Possession of Joel Delaney '72
The Possession of Michael King '14
The Premonition '75
Premonition '98
The Prodigy '19
The Prophecy '95
The Psychic '68
Psychomania '73
Pulse '01
Pulse '06
Pumpkinhead 3: Ashes to Ashes '06
Pumpkinhead 4: Blood Feud '07
Pumpkinhead '88
Purana Mandir '84 ▶
Quarantine '08
Rapturious '07
Rasen '98
Rawhead Rex '87
Re-Cycle '06
Reaper '15
The Reaping '07
[REC] 4: Apocalyse '14
Red Lights '12
Red Sands '09
The Red Shoes '05
The Relic '96
Respire '09
Rest Stop: Don't Look Back '08
Return to House on Haunted Hill '07
Revolt of the Zombies '36
The Ring 2 '05
The Ring '02
The Ring Virus '99
Rings '17
Ringu 0 '01
Ringu 2 '99
Ringu '98 ▶
The Rite '11
Route 666 '01
Salem's Lot '04
Salvage '06
Sarah's Child '96
Satanic '15
Savage Harvest 2: October Blood '06
Scream of the Banshee '11
Scream of the Wolf '74
Seance '06
Seeding of a Ghost '86
Session 9 '01
7 Days to Live '00
7 Mummies '06
7500 '12
Shadow of the Hawk '76
Shadow People '13
The Shadow Within '07
Shallow Ground '04
Shock 'Em Dead '90
Shutter '08
Signs '02 ▶
Silent Hill '06
Silent House '12
Sinister '12
6 Degrees of Hell '12
666: The Beast '07
666: The Child '06
The Skeleton Key '05
The Skeptic '09
The Skull '65
Sleepstalker: The Sandman's Last Rites '94
Sorceress '94
The Soul Guardians '98
Soul Survivors '01
Space Master X-7 '58
Spooky Encounters '80
Spring '15 ▶
Stephen King's Rose Red '02
Stephen King's The Storm of the Century '99
Stephen King's Thinner '96
Stir of Echoes '99
Stitches '12
The Stranger '15
Sugar Hill '74
Sundown: The Vampire in Retreat '08
Supernatural '33
Tales from the Crypt Presents Ritual '02
Tamara '05
Terror Creatures from the Grave '66
They Come Back '07
13 Ghosts '60
13 Ghosts '01
13 Seconds '03
The Tomb '09
The Tooth Fairy '06
The Traveler '10
The Turn of the Screw '74
The Turn of the Screw '92
The Turn of the Screw '99
12/12/12 '12
The Twilight Saga: Breaking Dawn, Part 1 '11
Twixt '12
The Unborn '09
Under the Shadow '16 ▶
Underworld: Awakening '12
The Undying '09
The Uninvited '09
The Unquiet '08
Unseen Evil '99
Unspeakable '00
Urban Ghost Story '98
Uzumaki '00
Vanishing on 7th Street '10
The Vault '00
Velvet Buzzsaw '19
Versus '00
The Village '04
Visions '16
Vlad '03
Voices from Beyond '90
Voodoo Academy '00
Vulture's Eye '04
The Wailing '16
Wake Wood '10
We are Still Here '15
Wendigo '01
Wes Craven Presents: They '02
The Whip and the Body '63
White Noise 2: The Light '07
White Noise '05
Wicked Lake '08
Wicked Little Things '07
The Wind '19
Wind Chill '07
Wish Upon '17
Witchcraft 4: Virgin Heart '92
Witchcraft 10: Mistress of the Craft '98
The Witches '66
The Woman in Black 2: Angel of Death '15
The Woman in Black '12
The Wraith '87
The Wretched '08

▶ = rated three bones or higher

Supernatural Martial Arts

The Crow '93
The Four '12
Hellbound '94
The Heroic Trio '93
Holy Flame of the Martial World '83
Jesus Christ Vampire Hunter '01
The Last Eve '05
The Legend of the 7 Golden Vampires '73
Legendary Weapons of China '82
Lone Wolf and Cub: Baby Cart at the River Styx '72
Lone Wolf and Cub: Baby Cart to Hades '72
Mercury Man '06
The Mummy: Tomb of the Dragon Emperor '08
Remo Williams: The Adventure Begins '85
Sgt. Kabukiman N.Y.P.D. '94
Sword Masters: The Battle Wizard '77
TMNT: Teenage Mutant Ninja Turtles '07
Wind and Cloud: The Storm Riders '04
Zu: Warriors from the Magic Mountain '83

Supernatural Westerns

Billy the Kid Versus Dracula '66
BloodRayne 2: Deliverance '07
Dead Birds '04
The Hitcher '86
Into the Badlands '92
Jesse James Meets Frankenstein's Daughter '65
John Carpenter's Vampires '97
Jonah Hex '10
Near Dark '87▸
Sundown '91
Sundown: The Vampire in Retreat '08
Timerider '83

Surfing

See also *Beach Blanket Bingo*

Beach Blanket Bingo '65▸
Beach Party '63
Beautiful Wave '11
Big Wednesday '78
Bikini Beach '64
Blackrock '97
Blood Surf '00
Blue Crush 2 '11
Blue Crush '02▸
Blue Juice '95
Bra Boys '07
California Dreaming '79
Chairman of the Board '97
Chasing Mavericks '12
The Endless Summer 2 '94▸
The Endless Summer '66▸
Escape from L.A. '96
Fantastic Four: Rise of the Silver Surfer '07
Flirting with Forty '09
Follow Me '69
Gidget '59
How to Stuff a Wild Bikini '65
In God's Hands '98
Lauderdale '89
Lilo & Stitch '02▸
Local Boys '02
Marmaduke '10
Meet the Deedles '98
Muscle Beach Party '64
National Lampoon Presents: Endless Bummer '09
Newcastle '08
North Shore '87
Off the Lip '04
Point Break '91
Psycho Beach Party '00
Red Surf '90
Ride the Wild Surf '64
Riding Giants '04
A Scene at Sea '92
The Shallows '16▸
Shelter '07
Soul Surfer '11
South Beach Academy '96
Step Into Liquid '03▸
Summer City '77
Surf Nazis Must Die '87
Surfer, Dude '08
Surf's Up '07
Surfwise '07▸
Teen Beach Movie '13

Survival

See also *Hunted!; Negative Utopia; Post-Apocalypse*

Absolution '97
Ad Astra '19▸
Adam Resurrected '08
The Admirable Crichton '57
Adrift '18
After Earth '13
Aftermath '12
Aftershock '12
Against the Sun '15
Against the Wild '14
Against the Wild II: Survive the Seregenti '16
Age Out '19
Alien Uprising '12
Alive '93
All is Lost '13▸
Alpha '18
Amerigeddon '16
Amusement '08
Andron: The Black Labyrinth '16
Angel Has Fallen '19
The Angry Birds Movie 2 '19
Arctic '18
Arctic Blue '93
Arctic Tale '07
Attack on Leningrad '09
Autumn Blood '14
The Aviator '85
Bad Times at the El Royale '18
Bat 21 '88
Battle for Terra '09▸
Battle of Jangsari '19
Battle of the Damned '14
Battlefield Earth '00
Beanpole '20▸
The Bed Sitting Room '69
The Belko Experiment '17
Beyond the Call to Duty '16
Billionaire Ransom '16
Bio-dead '09
Black Book '06▸
Black Ops '20
Black Rain '88▸
Blood Father '16▸
Bloodmyth '09
Blue Lagoon: The Awakening '12
The Book of Eli '10
A Bread Factory, Part One '18▸
A Bread Factory, Part Two '18▸
The Bridge on the River Kwai '57▸
A Bullet Is Waiting '54
The Canyon '09
Captain January '36
Captain Phillips '13▸
Carriers '09
Cast Away '00▸
Cell '16
Centurion '10
Challenge To Be Free '76
Cheyenne Warrior '94
City of Ember '08
Cliffhanger '93▸
Close Range '15
The Cold Lands '13
Cold Mountain '03▸
Cold River '81
Coldwater '14
The Colony '98
Cool Hand Luke '67▸
The Core '03
Courage '09
Courage Under Fire '96▸
The Courier '19
Crawl '19
Curve '16
Damned River '89
Dark Metropolis '10
The Darkest Hour '11
Das Boot '81▸
Dawn of the Planet of the Apes '14▸
The Day After '83▸
Daylight '96
Dead Calm '89▸
Dead Water '19
Deadly Harvest '72
Death Hunt '81
Death Valley '04
The Decks Ran Red '58
Deep Murder '19
Def-Con 4 '85
Deliverance '72▸
Delos Adventure '86
The Descent '05
Desert Migration '16▸
Desperate Search '52
The Devil at 4 O'Clock '61
Divergent '14
Domain '18
The Donner Party '09
Dust Devil '93
Edge of Honor '91
Eight Below '06
Eight Days to Live '06
Empire of the Sun '87▸
Enemy Mine '85
Escape from Hell '79
Escape from Wildcat Canyon '99
Exit Speed '08
Far from Home: The Adventures of Yellow Dog '94
Far North '07
Fateless '05▸
Fight for Your Life '77
The Final Destination '09
The First Purge '18
Five '51
Fixed Bayonets! '51▸
Flags of Our Fathers '06▸
Flight from Glory '37
The Flight of the Phoenix '65▸
Flight of the Phoenix '04
The Forbidden Quest '93
Fortress '85
47 Meters Down '17
Four Frightened People '34
Fragments '08
Free Fire '17
Gangland '00
Gas-s-s-s! '70
Germany, Pale Mother '80
Germany Year Zero '48▸
Gerry '02
Ghost Town '56
Godzilla: King of the Monsters '19
Grave of the Fireflies '88▸
Gravity '13▸
The Grey '12
He Is My Brother '75
Heaven and Earth '93
Heaven Knows, Mr. Allison '57▸
Heck's Way Home '95
Hell Fest '18
Heroes for Sale '33▸
High Barbaree '47
High Life '18
High Noon '52▸
High Noon '00
High Plains Invaders '09
Honeyland '19▸
House of 9 '05
House of Sand '05▸
How I Ended This Summer '10
How I Live Now '13
The Human Race '14
The Hunger Games '12▸
The Hunger Games: Catching Fire '13▸
The Hunger Games: Mockingjay--Part 1 '14
I Am Legend '07▸
I Am Omega '07
I Think We're Alone Now '18
The Impossible '12▸
In Darkness '11▸
In Desert and Wilderness '01
In the Heart of the Sea '15
The Incredible Journey '63
Intacto '01
Into the Forest '16
Into the White '12
Into Thin Air: Death on Everest '97
IO '19
Isabelle '19
The Island at the Top of the World '74
Island of the Hungry Ghosts '18
Island of the Lost '68
The Island on Bird Street '97
Jeremiah Johnson '72▸
Jojo Rabbit '19▸
The Journey Home '14
Jules Verne's Mysterious Island '10
Just Before Dawn '80
Killer Deal '99
The Killing Fields '84▸
King Rat '65▸
Kon-Tiki '12
The Land That Time Forgot '75
The Lark Farm '07
The Last Chance '45▸
Last Exit to Brooklyn '90▸
The Last Flight of Noah's Ark '80
The Last of the Dogmen '95
Le Dernier Combat '84▸
Legend of Alfred Packer '80
The Legend of Wolf Mountain '92
Legion '10
Legionnaire '98
The Life and Death of Colonel Blimp '43▸
Life of Pi '12▸
Lifeboat '44▸
Limbo '99
Lisa '62
Lord of the Flies '63▸
Lord of the Flies '90
Lore '13▸
The Lost Future '10
Lost Holiday: The Jim & Suzanne Shemwell Story '07
The Lost Zeppelin '29
Love on the Dole '41▸
Male and Female '19▸
Man in the Wilderness '71
Marooned in Iraq '02
Mean Dreams '17
Melody '71
Merry Christmas, Mr. Lawrence '83▸
Miraculous Journey '48
Mischief Night '13
Mr. Robinson Crusoe '32
Monos '19▸
Monster Party '18
Morning Departure '50
The Mosquito Coast '86
Most Beautiful Island '17
The Most Dangerous Game '32▸
The Mountain Between Us '17
My Entire High School Sinking Into the Sea '17
My Side of the Mountain '69
Mysterious Island '61▸
The Naked Prey '66▸
Nanook of the North '22▸
Night of the Living Deb '14
Nightmare at Bittercreek '91
Nightmare at Noon '87
9 '09▸
No Blade of Grass '70
North Face '08▸
The Notebook '13
Objective, Burma! '45▸
On the Beach '59▸
On the Beach '00
Once Before I Die '65
127 Hours '10▸
1,000 Years From Now '52
Ordeal in the Arctic '93
Ordinary Love '20
The Owl and the Sparrow '07
Pagan Island '60
Panic in Year Zero! '62
Panic Room '02
Paradise '82
Passion in the Desert '97
Perfect Witness '89
Phone Call from a Stranger '52
The Pianist '02▸
Pioneer Woman '73
Pitch Black '00▸
Poseidon '06
The Poseidon Adventure '72
The Poseidon Adventure '05
Predators '10
Preservation '14
Prey '19
Project Solitude: Buried Alive '09
A Prophet '09▸
Proteus '95
Prowl '10
Pulse 2: Afterlife '08
The Purge: Anarchy '14
The Purge: Election Year '16
Quest for Fire '82▸
The Red Turtle '17▸
The Reef '10
Resident Evil: Afterlife '10
Resident Evil: Apocalypse '04
Resident Evil: Extinction '07
Retreat '11
Return of the Jedi '83▸
The Ride Back '57
The Road '09
Robinson Crusoe '54
The Rover '14
Rust Creek '19
Sahara '43▸
Sanctum '11
Sands of the Kalahari '65
Satanic Panic '19
Savage Is Loose '74
Saw 3D: The Final Chapter '10
Scenic Route '13
Sea Gypsies '78
Sea Wife '57
Seven Days in May '64▸
Seven Were Saved '47
Severed Ways '09
Shackleton '02▸
Sharpe's Peril '08
She'll Be Wearing Pink Pajamas '84
A Sierra Nevada Gunfight '13
Silence '73
Sister '12
6 Below: Miracle on the Mountain '17
Six Days, Seven Nights '98
The Skin '81
Skyline '10
Sniper '92
The Snow Walker '03
Snowbound: The Jim and Jennifer Stolpa Story '94
Snowpiercer '14▸
Socrates '18▸
S.O.S. Pacific '60
SpaceCamp '86
Spree '79
Stagecoach '39▸
Stagecoach '66
Starfish '19
The Steel Lady '53
Storm and Sorrow '90
The Strangers '08
Stronger '17▸
Sub Down '97
Survival Quest '89
Sweet Sweetback's Baadasssss Song '71▸
Swept Away '02
The Swiss Family Robinson '60▸
Taxi for Tobruk '60▸
The Terminators '09
The Terror '63
Testament '83▸
Thief '81▸
The Thing '11
3022 '19
This Is the End '13▸
Three Came Home '50▸
Tigers Are Not Afraid '19▸
Titanic '96
Tooth and Nail '07
Touching the Void '03
The ToyBox '18
The Trail of '98 '28
Tremors 5: Bloodlines '15
Trouble in Paradise '88
Trucks '97
True Heart '97
Tundra '36
20 Years After '08
28 Days Later '02
Two Women '61▸
Two Years at Sea '12
The Voyage of the Yes '72
Wagon Master '50▸
Walkabout '71▸
Walking Deceased '15
Walking Thunder '94
The Wall '13
The Wandering Earth '19
War Witch '12
Warm Bodies '13
Waterworld '95
The Way Back '10
We Are What We Are '11
The Whale '13
Wheelman '17
When Trumpets Fade '98
The White Dawn '75
White Fang and the Hunter '85
White Water Summer '87
White Wolves 3: Cry of the White Wolf '98
Wild America '97▸
World Trade Center '06▸
The World's End '13▸
Yeti '08
You Should Have Left '20
Z for Zachariah '15
Zarkorr! The Invader '96
Zombieland '09▸

Suspended Animation

Alien 3 '92
Aliens '86▸
Austin Powers: International Man of Mystery '97▸
Batman and Robin '97
Buck Rogers in the 25th Century '79
Chances Are '89▸
Coma '78▸
Demolition Man '93
Encino Man '92
Forever Young '92
Genesis II '73
Late for Dinner '91
Planet of the Apes '68▸
Strange New World '75

Suspense

See *Mystery & Suspense*

Swashbucklers

See also *Action-Adventure; Fencing; Medieval Romps*

Abbott and Costello Meet Captain Kidd '52
Adventures of Don Juan '49▸
The Adventures of Robin Hood '38▸
Against All Flags '52▸
Ali Baba and the Forty Thieves '43
Anthony Adverse '36
Arabian Nights '42
At Sword's Point '51
The Bandit of Sherwood Forest '46
The Bandits of Corsica '53
Bardelys the Magnificent '26
The Beloved Rogue '27▸
The Black Pirate '26▸
The Black Rose '50
The Black Shield of Falworth '54
The Black Swan '42▸
The Black Tulip '64
Blackbeard '06
Blackbeard the Pirate '52
Blackbeard's Ghost '67
Bluebeard '72
The Bold Caballero '36
The Buccaneer '58
Buccaneer's Girl '50
Captain Blood '35▸
Captain Calamity '36
Captain Horatio Hornblower '51▸
Captain Kidd '45
Captain Kidd and the Slave Girl '54
Captain Kronos: Vampire Hunter '74▸
Captain Lightfoot '55
Captain Ron '92
Carry On Jack '63

▸ = rated three bones or higher

Cartouche '62 ▸
Casanova '05
Cheech and Chong's The Corsican Brothers '84
China Seas '35 ▸
Corsair '31
The Corsican Brothers '42
The Count of Monte Cristo '12
The Count of Monte Cristo '34 ▸
The Count of Monte Cristo '99
The Count of Monte Cristo '02
The Court Jester '56 ▸
Crimson Pirate '52 ▸
Cutthroat Island '95
Dancing Pirate '36
The Devil-Ship Pirates '64
Dr. Syn '37
Dr. Syn, Alias the Scarecrow '64
Don Juan DeMarco '94
Don Q., Son of Zorro '25
Double Crossbones '51
Executioner of Venice '63
Fanfan la Tulipe '51 ▸
The Fifth Musketeer '79
Fighting Marines '36
The Fighting Prince of Donegal '66
The Flame & the Arrow '50 ▸
The Four Musketeers '75 ▸
The 4 Musketeers '05
Frenchman's Creek '44
Frenchman's Creek '98
The Golden Hawk '52
Gypsy '75
Hell Ship Mutiny '57
Hercules and the Black Pirate '60
Hero's Island '62
Highlander: The Gathering '92
His Majesty O'Keefe '53
Hook '91
The Iron Mask '29
The Island '80
Kidnapped '05 ▸
The King's Guard '01
The King's Thief '55
La Femme Musketeer '03
The Lady and the Highwayman '89
The Legend of Zorro '05
The Lives of a Bengal Lancer '35 ▸
Long John Silver '54
The Lost Princess '05
The Man in the Iron Mask '39 ▸
The Man in the Iron Mask '77 ▸
The Man in the Iron Mask '97
The Man in the Iron Mask '98 ▸
Mark of Zorro '20 ▸
The Mark of Zorro '40 ▸
The Mask of Zorro '98 ▸
The Master of Ballantrae '53
Master of Dragonard Hill '89
Men of the Sea '35
Mickey, Donald, Goofy: The Three Musketeers '04
Monty Python's The Meaning of Life '83 ▸
Moonfleet '55
Moran of the Lady Letty '22
Muppet Treasure Island '96
The Musketeer '01
My Favorite Year '82 ▸
Nate and Hayes '83
Naughty Marietta '35
New Moon '40
On Guard! '03 ▸
The Phantom '96
The Pirate '48 ▸
Pirate Movie '82
Pirates of Blood River '62
The Pirates of Capri '49
The Pirates of Penzance '83
Pirates of the Caribbean: At World's End '07
Pirates of the Caribbean: On Stranger Tides '11
Pirates of the Caribbean: The Curse of the Black Pearl '03 ▸
Pirates of the Coast '61
Pirates of the Seven Seas '62
Pirates of Tortuga '61
Pirates of Treasure Island '06
Prince of Foxes '49
The Princess and the Pirate '44 ▸
The Princess Bride '87 ▸
Princess of Thieves '01
Prisoner of Zenda '37 ▸
Prisoner of Zenda '52
Prisoner of Zenda '79
Project A '83
Project A: Part 2 '87
Quentin Durward '55
Raiders of the Seven Seas '53
Revenge of the Musketeers '63
Revenge of the Musketeers '94
Ring of the Musketeers '93
Robin Hood '73 ▸
Rogues of Sherwood Forest '50
Romola '25
Royal Flash '75 ▸
Scaramouche '52 ▸
The Scarlet Pimpernel '99
The Scarlet Pimpernel 2: Mademoiselle Guillotine '99
The Scarlet Pimpernel 3: The Kidnapped King '99
The Scarlet Pimpernel '34 ▸
The Scarlet Pimpernel '82 ▸
The Sea Hawk '24
The Sea Hawk '40 ▸
The Secret of Monte Cristo '61
Seven Seas to Calais '62
Shipwrecked '90
The Sign of Zorro '60
Sinbad and the Eye of the Tiger '77
Sinbad, the Sailor '47 ▸
Son of Ali Baba '52
Son of Fury '42 ▸
The Son of Monte Cristo '40
The Spanish Main '45
The Story of Robin Hood & His Merrie Men '52 ▸
Swashbuckler '76
The Swiss Family Robinson '60 ▸
Sword & the Sorcerer '82
Sword of Sherwood Forest '60
The Swordsman '47
The Swordsman '92
Swordsman of Siena '62
Three Amigos '86
The Three Musketeers '21 ▸
The Three Musketeers '33
The Three Musketeers '39
The Three Musketeers '48
The Three Musketeers '74 ▸
The Three Musketeers '93
The Three Musketeers '11
Tiger of the Seven Seas '62
Treasure Island '34 ▸
Treasure Island '50 ▸
Treasure Island '72
Treasure Island '89
Treasure Island '99
Under the Red Robe '36
Virgin Territory '07
The Warriors '55
Yankee Buccaneer '52
Yellowbeard '83
Zorro '74
Zorro, the Gay Blade '81

Swimming

***See also** Deep Blue; Go Fish; Island Fare; Killer Sea Critters; Lifeguards; Pacific Islands*

Against the Current '09
Back to School '86
Barracuda '78
Bathing Beauty '44
The Big Bad Swim '06
The Bridges at Toko-Ri '55 ▸
Cocoon '85 ▸
Dangerous When Wet '53
Easy to Love '53
Fast Times at Ridgemont High '82 ▸
Giulia Doesn't Date at Night '09
Gremlins '84 ▸
The Guardian '06
Imaginary Heroes '05
Jaws '75 ▸
Million Dollar Mermaid '52
Neptune's Daughter '49
On a Clear Day '05
Pride '07
Sea People '00
Sleeping with the Enemy '91
Splash '84 ▸
Surfacing '14
Swimfan '02
The Swimmer '68 ▸
Swimming Upstream '03
This Time for Keeps '47
Thrill of a Romance '45
The Tunnel '01 ▸
Unbreakable '00
Under the Silver Lake '18
You Said a Mouthful '32

Swingers

American Swing '08
Barfly '87 ▸
Bob & Carol & Ted & Alice '69
A Change of Seasons '80
Eating Raoul '82 ▸
Invasion of the Bee Girls '73 ▸
9 1/2 Weeks '86
The Party '68 ▸
The Swap '71
The Swinging Cheerleaders '74
Swinging Safari '19
Your Friends & Neighbors '98 ▸

Sword & Sandal

Alexander '04
Ali Baba and the Forty Thieves '43
Ali Baba and the Seven Saracens '64
Amazons and Gladiators '01
Arabian Nights '42
Ashes of Time '94 ▸
The Avenger '62
The Beast of Babylon Against the Son of Hercules '63
Ben-Hur '16
Caesar the Conqueror '63
Challenge of the Gladiator '65
Clash of the Titans '10
Colossus and the Amazon Queen '60
The Colossus of Rhodes '61
Colossus of the Arena '62
Conan the Barbarian '11
Cyclops '08
Damon and Pythias '62
David and Goliath '61
Duel of Champions '61
Fabiola '48 ▸
Fire Monsters Against the Son of Hercules '62
Four Warriors '15
Fury of Achilles '62
Giants of Rome '63
Gladiator '00 ▸
Gladiator of Rome '63
Gladiators 7 '62
Gold for the Caesars '63
Goliath Against the Giants '63
Goliath and the Barbarians '60
Goliath and the Dragon '61
Goliath and the Sins of Babylon '64
Gor '88
Hellhounds '09
Hercules '58
Hercules '14
Hercules against the Moon Men '64
Hercules and the Captive Women '63
Hercules and the Tyrants of Babylon '64
Hercules in the Haunted World '64
Hercules, Prisoner of Evil '64
Hercules, Samson and Ulysses '64
Hercules Unchained '59
Hercules *vs.* the Sons of the Sun '64
Hero of Rome '63
The Invincible Gladiator '62
Journey to Promethea '10
The Last Days of Pompeii '60
Last Knights '15
The Mighty Ursus '61
National Lampoon's The Legend of Awesomest Maximus '11
Pompeii '14
Revak the Rebel '60
Revenge of the Barbarians '60
Samson '61
Samson and His Mighty Challenge '64
Samson and the 7 Miracles of the World '62
The Scorpion King '02
The Scorpion King 2: Rise of a Warrior '08
The Scorpion King 3: Battle for Redemption '11
The Scorpion King 4: Quest for Power '15
Sins of Rome '54
The Slave '62
Son of Ali Baba '52
Son of Hercules in the Land of Darkness '63
Sword of Venus '53
Thor and the Amazon Women '60
Three Avengers '64
300 '07
300: Rise of an Empire '13
The 300 Spartans '62
Tristan & Isolde '06
The Triumph of Hercules '66
The Trojan Horse '62
Troy '04
Two Gladiators '64
Ulysses Against the Son of Hercules '61
Ursus in the Land of Fire '63
War Goddess '74

Sydney

***See also** Down Under*

Around the Block '13
Better Than Sex '00
The Boxer and the Bombshell '08
Bra Boys '07
Burning Man '11
Cosi '95 ▸
Danny Deckchair '03
The Diplomat '08
Dirty Deeds '02 ▸
Doing Time for Patsy Cline '97
Don's Party '76 ▸
He Died With a Falafel in His Hand '01
Introducing the Dwights '07
Joey '98
The Last Wave '77 ▸
Lilian's Story '95
Little Fish '05 ▸
Me Myself I '99
Napoleon '96
$9.99 '08
Not Suitable for Children '12
Over the Hill '93
The Road from Coorain '02
The Silence '06
Solo '06
The Square '08
The Sum of Us '94 ▸
Young Einstein '89

Tale of the Tape

Afflicted '14
Afterschool '08
All Hallow's Eve 2 '15
All Hallow's Eve '13
Alone With Her '07
American Virgin '09
Apollo 18 '11
As Above, So Below '14
Auto Focus '02 ▸
Awakening the Zodiac '17
Be Kind Rewind '08
Benny's Video '92
Betrayed at 17 '11
The Big Hit '98
Blair Witch '16
The Blair Witch Project '99
Born to Ride '11
A Broken Life '07
Capturing the Friedmans '03 ▸
Cat Run '11
Christine '16
Circumstance '11
Cloverfield '08
Coffin '11
Comedy of Innocence '00
The Darwin Awards '06
Deadline '09
The Devil Inside '12
Devil's Due '14
Devil's Pass '13
Diary of the Dead '07
Donkey Punch '08
Dread '09
Earth to Echo '14
8mm 2 '05
Enemy of the State '98
Evil Dead '83
Felony '95
Final Assignment '80
Final Cut '98
The Fourth Kind '09
The Frankenstein Theory '13
Freeze Frame '04
Fright Flick '10
Generation Um... '13
Ghost Image '07
Hank and Asha '14
Hard to Kill '89
Home Movie '08
Homework '90
iCrime '11
I'm Reed Fish '06
The Interrogation of Michael Crowe '02
Interview with the Assassin '02
Into the Storm '14
Invasion '07
Janice Beard '99
Jimmy & Judy '06
The Jolly Boys' Last Stand '00
Judicial Indiscretion '07
Kate Plays Christine '16 ▸
Laid to Rest '09
Lake Mungo '08
The Last Will and Testament of Rosalind Leigh '12
Love or Money '01
Megan Is Missing '11
Mr. Nice Guy '98
Monster '08
My Life on Ice '02
My Neighbor's Secret '09
Night Watcher '08
Nightcrawler '14 ▸
Once You Kiss a Stranger '69
100 Mile Rule '02
Operation Avalanche '16
The Other Side of the Wind '18
Paranormal Activity 2 '10
Paranormal Activity 3 '11
Paranormal Activity 4 '12
Paranormal Activity 5: The Ghost Dimension '15
Paranormal Activity: The Marked Ones '14
The Perfect Witness '07
Playback '12
The Possession of Michael King '14
Prisoner '07
Project Almanac '15
The Pyramid '14
Quarantine '08
The Quiet Ones '14
Rampart '11
Rasen '98
[Rec] 2 '09
Red Road '06
Red Roses and Petrol '03
The Ring Virus '99
Rings '17
Ringu 0 '01
Ringu 2 '99
Ringu '98 ▸
Road Trip '00
Run This Town '20
The Sacrament '13
Savage Harvest 2: October Blood '06
Scary Movie 5 '13
The Scenesters '09
sex, lies and videotape '89 ▸
Sex Tape '14
Shredderman Rules '07
Sinister '12
Sky High '84
Sliver '93
Son of Rambow '07
Spy Games '99
Tell Me No Lies '07
Terror Trap '10
The Time Being '12
The Troll Hunter '11
Two Weeks '06
V/H/S/2 '13 ▸
V/H/S '12
Vacancy 2: The First Cut '08
Vacancy '07
Video Violence '87
The Virginity Hit '10
Waking Madison '10
Warm Blooded Killers '01
The Wedding Bros. '08
Willow Creek '13

Talking Animals

***See also** Wild Kingdom*

Absolutely Anything '17
Air Bud 6: Air Buddies '06
Alice in Wonderland '33
Alice in Wonderland '10
Animal Farm '99
The Ape '05
Aussie and Ted's Great Adventure '09
Babe '95 ▸
Babe: Pig in the City '98
Barnyard '06
Beethoven's Christmas Adventure '11
Beverly Hills Chihuahua 2 '10
Beverly Hills Chihuahua 3: Viva La Fiesta! '12
Beverly Hills Chihuahua '08
Big Top Pee-wee '88
Brother Bear 2 '06
Cats & Dogs '01
Charlotte's Web '06 ▸
Chicken Little '05
A Christmas Wedding Tail '11
The Chronicles of Narnia: The Lion, the Witch and the Wardrobe '05
Clifford's Really Big Movie '04
Cloudy with a Chance of Meatballs '09
Delhi Safari '12
Dinotopia '02
Dr. Dolittle '98
Dr. Dolittle 2 '01
Dr. Dolittle 3 '06
Dr. Dolittle 4: Tail to the Chief '08
Doctor Dolittle '67
Dr. Dolittle: Million Dollar Mutts '09
Dr. Seuss' Horton Hears a Who! '08 ▸
The Dog Who Saved Easter '15
The Dog Who Saved Halloween '11
A Dog's Purpose '17
Dolittle '20
Everything's Ducky '61
Flushed Away '06 ▸
Francis Covers the Big Town '53
Francis Goes to the Races '51
Francis Goes to West Point '52
Francis in the Haunted House '56
Francis in the Navy '55

▸ = rated three bones or higher

Francis Joins the WACs '54
Francis the Talking Mule '49 ▶
G-Force '09
Garfield: A Tail of Two Kitties '06
George of the Jungle '97 ▶
The Golden Compass '07
Good Boy! '03
Guardians of the Galaxy '14 ▶
Guardians of the Galaxy Vol. 2 '17 ▶
Guardians of the Lost Code '10
Harvey '50 ▶
Home on the Range '04
Homeward Bound: The Incredible Journey '93 ▶
Homeward Bound 2: Lost in San Francisco '96
Hoodwinked '05 ▶
Ice Age: Collision Course '16
Ice Age: Continental Drift '12
Inland Empire '06
Karate Dog '04
Kung Fu Panda '08 ▶
Little Nicky '00
Madagascar: Escape 2 Africa '08
Madagascar 3: Europe's Most Wanted '12
Madagascar '05
Malibu's Most Wanted '03
Marley & Me: The Puppy Years '11
Marmaduke '10
Men in Black 2 '02
Men in Black '97 ▶
The Nut Job '14
Over the Hedge '06 ▶
Paddington 2 '17 ▶
Paddington '14 ▶
Paulie '98
Peter Rabbit '18
The Princess and the Frog '09 ▶
The Rabbi's Cat '11
Racing Stripes '05
Rango '11 ▶
Santa Buddies '09
Santa Paws 2: The Santa Pups '12
The Search for Santa Paws '10
The Secret Life of Pets '16
Sherlock: Undercover Dog '94
Shrek the Third '07
Sing '16
The SpongeBob SquarePants Movie '04
Spooky Buddies '11
Stuart Little '99
Super Buddies '13
Tommy and the Cool Mule '09
Up '09 ▶
The Voices '15
Winnie the Pooh '11 ▶
Zookeeper '11

Tanks

***See also** Military: Army*
The A-Team '10 ▶
Battle of the Bulge '65
The Beast '88
The Big Red One '80 ▶
A Bridge Too Far '77
Courage Under Fire '96 ▶
Cross of Iron '76
The Fate of the Furious '17
Fury '14
Indiana Jones and the Last Crusade '89 ▶
Kelly's Heroes '70
Lion of the Desert '81 ▶
Patton '70 ▶
Sahara '95
The Steel Lady '53
Tank '83
Tank Girl '94

Tattoos

Beastly '11
Blue Tiger '94
The Broken Circle Breakdown '12
Cape Fear '91 ▶
The Crow 2: City of Angels '96
Cyber Bandits '94
Double Team '97
Down Periscope '96
Eastern Promises '07 ▶
Escape from L.A. '96
The Expendables '10
Foxfire '96
The Girl With the Dragon Tattoo '09 ▶
The Girl With the Dragon Tattoo '11 ▶
The Hangover, Part 2 '11
Hesher '10
Hitman '07
Horsemen '09
Houseguest '94
The Illustrated Man '69 ▶
In the Cut '03
In the Name of the King 3: The Last Mission '14
The King of Staten Island '20
The Last Airbender '10
Lust in the Dust '85 ▶
Memento '00 ▶
The Mortician '11
Necromentia '09
The Night of the Hunter '55 ▶
Prey for Rock and Roll '03 ▶
Skin '18 ▶
Son-in-Law '93
Starship Troopers '97 ▶
Stir Crazy '80
The Taking of Pelham 123 '09
Tattoo, a Love Story '02
The Tattooist '07
XIII '08
Waterworld '95
The Yakuza '75

Taxing Situations

The Accountant '16
As Goes Janesville '12
The Brady Bunch Movie '95 ▶
Dinner for Schmucks '10
Exotica '94 ▶
Goyokin '69 ▶
Hair Show '04
Lagaan: Once upon a Time in India '01
Mary, Mary '63
The Mating Game '59 ▶
Off the Map '03 ▶
Order of Chaos '10
Rogues of Sherwood Forest '50
Seven Pounds '08
Speedway '68
Strange Bedfellows '04
Stranger Than Fiction '06
A Taxing Woman '87 ▶
The Taxman '98
The Trial Begins '07
The Undercover Man '49

Technicolor Yawn

Ace Ventura: When Nature Calls '95
Anaconda '96
Bachelorette '12
BASEketball '98
Blood Simple '85 ▶
Boat Trip '03
Car Wash '76
The Crying Game '92 ▶
The Cutting Edge '92
Dogfight '91 ▶
Eating Raoul '82 ▶
The Exorcist '73 ▶
Fear and Loathing in Las Vegas '98
52 Pick-Up '86
Fred: The Movie '10
Get Him to the Greek '10
Heathers '89 ▶
Jackass 3D '10
Jackass Number Two '06
Jaws '75 ▶
Kingpin '96
Larry the Cable Guy: Health Inspector '06
Monty Python's The Meaning of Life '83 ▶
My Giant '98
National Lampoon's Animal House '78 ▶
Osmosis Jones '01
Parenthood '89 ▶
Poltergeist 2: The Other Side '86
The Sandlot '93 ▶
Sirens '94
Stand by Me '86 ▶
That's What She Said '12
This Is Spinal Tap '84 ▶
The Verdict '82 ▶
The Witches of Eastwick '87

Technology Rampant

A Nous la Liberte '31 ▶
Age of Dinosaurs '13
Alien 51 '04
Alien Lockdown '04
Anatomy 2 '03
The Android Affair '95
Assassin '86
Astro-Zombies M4: Invaders from Cyberspace '12
Attack of the Robots '66
Automatons '06
Baby Girl Scott '87
Back to the Future '85 ▶
Batman Forever '95 ▶
Benny Bliss & the Disciples of Greatness '07
Best Defense '84
Bicentennial Man '99
Billion Dollar Brain '67
Black Cobra 3: The Manila Connection '90
The Black Hole '79
Black Mask 2: City of Masks '02
Blade Runner '82 ▶
Blades '89
Bloodlust '59
Bloodshot '20
Brainscan '94
Breakout '98
Catfish '10
Cell '16
Chandu the Magician '32
Charlie's Angels '19
Charly '68 ▶
Child's Play '19
Chopping Mall '86
The Circle '17
Circuitry Man '90
Colossus: The Forbin Project '70 ▶
Computer Wizard '77
Confess '05
The Congress '13
Countdown '19
Crash and Burn '90
Creation of the Humanoids '62
Cyber Bandits '94
Cyber-Tracker 2 '95
The Cyberstalking '99
Dean Koontz's Black River '01
Dean Koontz's Mr. Murder '98
Death Ray 2000 '81
Deep Evil '04
Demon Seed '77 ▶
Demonlover '02
Descent '05
Detonator 2: Night Watch '95
Devour '05
Diamonds Are Forever '71 ▶
Digital Man '94
Dr. Goldfoot and the Bikini Machine '66
Doomsdayer '00
Dragon Wasps '12
Dredd '12 ▶
Dungeonmaster '83
The Emoji Movie '17
Encrypt '03
Enemy of the State '98
Eve of Destruction '90
Evolver '94
Ex Machina '15 ▶
Eyeborgs '09
Fail-Safe '64 ▶
Fair Game '95
Family Viewing '87 ▶
Fast & Furious Presents: Hobbs & Shaw '19
Fatal Error '99
Feardotcom '02
The Fifth Element '97
The Fifth Estate '13
Final Mission '93
The Final Programme '73
500 MPH Storm '13
The Fly '86 ▶
The Fly 2 '89
The Fly '58 ▶
Four Boxes '09
Fugitive Mind '99
Futureworld '76
Geostorm '17
Ghost in the Machine '93
Ghost Machine '09
Goldeneye '95 ▶
The Good Neighbor '16
The Great Hack '19 ▶
Hackers '95
Her '13 ▶
Hologram Man '95
Horror in the Wind '08
Hostile Intent '97
How to Make a Monster '01
I, Robot '04
iMurders '08
Interception '08
The Internship '13
Island of Lost Women '59
Jexi '19
Jobs '13
Johnny Mnemonic '95
Johnny 2.0 '99
Judge Dredd '95
A King in New York '57
Komodo *vs.* Cobra '05
Lawnmower Man 2: Beyond Cyberspace '95
Live Free or Die Hard '07
Live Wire: Human Timebomb '95
Lo and Behold: Reveries of the Connected World '16 ▶
Lost in Space '98
Lucy '14
The Magnetic Monster '53
Marjorie Prime '17
The Mark '12
The Matrix '99 ▶
The Matrix Reloaded '03
The Matrix Revolutions '03 ▶
Maximum Overdrive '86
Men, Women & Children '14
Metropolis '26 ▶
Microwave Massacre '83
Mr. Toad's Wild Ride '96
Modern Times '36 ▶
Mon Oncle '58 ▶
Moonraker '79
Morgan '16
The Munsters' Revenge '81
Mutant Hunt '87
Natural City '03
Nerve '16
The Net '95
Net Games '03
New Crime City: Los Angeles 2020 '94
On_Line '01
Paranoia '13
The Perfect Date '19
Perfect Stranger '07
The Philadelphia Experiment '84
The Pirates of Silicon Valley '99
Plughead Rewired: Circuitry Man 2 '94
Project: Eliminator '91
Project Viper '02
Pulse 2: Afterlife '08
Pulse '06
The Quiet Earth '85 ▶
Rage '95
Redline '97
Replikator: Cloned to Kill '94
Resident Evil '02
RoboCop '87 ▶
RoboCop 2 '90
RoboCop 3 '91
RoboCop '14
Robot & Frank '12 ▶
Robot Jox '90
The Rocket Man '54
Runaway '84
Saturn 3 '80
Screamers '96
Search and Destroy '88
Searching '18 ▶
Seeds of Destruction '11
The Seventh Floor '93
Shadowzone '89
Shaker Run '85
Shocker '89
Shockwave '06
Short Circuit 2 '88
Short Circuit '86
Silicon Cowboys '16
Simone '02
Small Soldiers '98
Smart House '00
Sneakers '92
The Social Network '10 ▶
Soldier '98
Solo '96
Speaking Parts '89 ▶
Speed 2: Cruise Control '97
The Spy Who Loved Me '77
Stay Tuned '92
Stealth '05
Terminal Impact '95
The Terminal Man '74
Terminator 2: Judgment Day '91 ▶
Terminator 3: Rise of the Machines '03 ▶
The Terminator '84 ▶
Terminator Genisys '15
The Terminators '09
Terrorvision '86
Things to Come '36 ▶
Think Like a Dog '20
The Thirteenth Floor '99
Three Blind Mice '02
Timer '09
Tom Clancy's Netforce '98
Transcendence '14
Transmorphers '07
Transmorphers: Fall of Man '09
Tron '82
Turbulent Skies '10
12:01 '93
2001: A Space Odyssey '68 ▶
The Unborn '91
Under Siege 2: Dark Territory '95
Virtual Obsession '98
Virtual Sexuality '99
Virtuosity '95
Visitors '13
WarGames '83
Warning Sign '85
Weaponized '16
Weather Wars '11
Weird Science '85
Westworld '73 ▶
What's Up, Hideous Sun Demon? '83
Wild Palms '93
xXx: Return of Xander Cage '17
Zardoz '73
Zero Days '16
The Zero Theorem '13
Zombie Strippers '08

Technology-Rampant

***See** Computers; Killer Appliances; Robots, Cyborgs & Androids*

Teen Adventure

***See also** Adventure Drama; High School; Teen Drama; Teen Horror; Teen Romance*
Abominable '19
The Adventurer: The Curse of the Midas Box '13
The Amazing Spider-Man '12 ▶
American Honey '16
Area 51 '15
A-X-L '18
A Birder's Guide to Everything '14
Chasing 3000 '07
Crank: High Voltage '09
Dear Eleanor '16
Dragonball: Evolution '09
Dreamgirls '06 ▶
Enter the Warriors Gate '17
Eragon '06
Fallen '17
Finding Bliss '09
Ghosts of Girlfriends Past '09
Gone Fishin' '97
Hairspray '07 ▶
Harry Potter and the Half-Blood Prince '09
Harry Potter and the Order of the Phoenix '07
How to Train Your Dragon '10
The Hunger Games '12 ▶
I Love You Phillip Morris '10
The Jensen Project '10
Journey 2: The Mysterious Island '12
Jumanji: Welcome to the Jungle '17
Kick-Ass '10 ▶
Kicks '16
Kim Possible '19
Kin '18
Life of Pi '12 ▶
Mr. Brooks '07
Mulan '98
Nancy Drew '07
Octopussy '83
The Skeleton Key '05
Sky High '05 ▶
The Space Between Us '17
Space Warriors '13
Spooky Stakeout '16
That Darn Cat '96
13 Frightened Girls '63
The 13th Warrior '99
WarGames '83
Whisper 2: L'Aventure Continue '16

Teen Angst

***See** Coming of Age; Hell High School; Teen Adventure; Teen Comedy; Teen Drama; Teen Horror; Teen Musicals; Teen Romance*

Teen Comedy

***See also** High School*
Agent Cody Banks 2: Destination London '04
Agent Cody Banks '03
Ah, Wilderness! '35 ▶
American Pie '99 ▶
American Pie Presents: Book of Love '09
American Pie Presents: The Naked Mile '06
Angus '95
Angus, Thongs and Perfect Snogging '08
Aquamarine '06
Assassination of a High School President '08
Attack of the 50 Foot Cheerleader '12
The Baby-Sitters' Club '95
Balls Out: Gary the Tennis Coach '09
Barely Lethal '15
Bart Got a Room '08
Better Off Dead '85
Big Fat Liar '02
Big Time Adolescence '20
The Biggest Fan '02
Bill & Ted's Bogus Journey '91
Bill & Ted's Excellent Adventure '89
Blockers '18
Book of Love '91
Booksmart '19
Boxboarders! '07
The Brady Bunch Movie '95 ▶
Bring It On '00
Bring It On: Fight to the Finish '09
Camp '03
Can't Hardly Wait '98
Charlie Bartlett '07 ▶
Citizen Duane '06
Clueless '95 ▶
College '08
Confessions of a Teenage Drama Queen '04
Cop Dog '08
Cougars, Inc. '10
Cow Belles '06
The Curiosity of Chance '06
Dear Dictator '18
Dear Lemon Lima '09
D.E.B.S. '04

▶ = rated three bones or higher

Don't Tell Mom the Babysitter's Dead '91
Drillbit Taylor '08
Duck Season '04 ►
The DUFF '15
Easy A '10 ►
Eighth Grade '18 ►
Everybody Wants Some!! '16
Extreme Movie '08
Family Weekend '13
Fast Times at Ridgemont High '82 ►
Fat Albert '04
Fat Kid Rules the World '12
Ferris Bueller's Day Off '86 ►
Fired Up! '09
First Daughter '04
Flower '18
Foreign Exchange '08
Fred: The Movie '10
From Prada to Nada '11
Full of It '07
Fun Size '12
G.B.F. '13
Geek Charming '11
Getting It '06
The Ghost of Dragstrip Hollow '59
The Girl Next Door '04
Good Boys '19
Good Kids '16
Hannah Montana: The Movie '09
Happy Campers '01
Harold '08
Harriet the Spy: Blog Wars '10
Heavyweights '94
Her Best Move '07
High School '10
Hoot '06
House Party '90 ►
How to Build a Girl '20
I Love You, Beth Cooper '09
Initiation '87
It's a Boy Girl Thing '06
It's Kind of a Funny Story '10
The Jerk Theory '11
John Tucker Must Die '06
Jump In! '07
Jr. Detective Agency '09
Just One of the Girls '93
Kamikaze Girls '04
Kevin & Perry Go Large '00
Kick-Ass '10 ►
Kids in America '05
The Legend of Fritton's Gold '09
Linda Linda Linda '05 ►
The Lizzie McGuire Movie '03
Love Laughs at Andy Hardy '46
Mean Girls 2 '11
Mean Girls '04 ►
Meet Monica Velour '10
Minutemen '08
Miss Stevens '16
Modern Girls '86
Monte Carlo '11
My Father the Hero '93
The Myth of the American Sleepover '10
New Waterford Girl '99
New York Minute '04
Nick & Norah's Infinite Playlist '08 ►
Not Another Teen Movie '01
One Crazy Summer '86
One Last Thing '05
Orange County '02
The Perfect Man '05
The Perfect Score '04
Picture This! '08
Ping Pong '02 ►
Ping Pong Summer '14
Porky's 2: The Next Day '83
Porky's '82
Porky's Revenge '85
The Prankster '10
Project X '11
Prom '11
Prom Wars '08
Radio Rebel '12
The Rage In Placid Lake '03
Raging Hormones '99
Raising Genius '04
The Red Sneakers '01
Remember the Daze '07
Risky Business '83 ►
Rock 'n' Roll High School '79 ►
Rock 'n' Roll High School Forever '91
Rock, Rock, Rock '56
Senior Skip Day '08
17 Again '09
Sex Drive '08
She's All That '99
Shredderman Rules '07
The Sisterhood of the Traveling Pants '05
Sixteen Candles '84 ►
16 Wishes '10
Sky High '05 ►
Slash '16
Sleepover '04
Stick It '06
Struck by Lightning '12
Submarine '10 ►
Sugar & Spice '01 ►
Sundown '16
Superbad '07 ►
Sydney White '07
Teen Spirit '11
These Girls '05
Thumbsucker '05 ►
To All the Boys I've Loved Before '18
The To Do List '13
Too Cool for Christmas '04
The Trotsky '09
True Confessions of a Hollywood Starlet '08
Unaccompanied Minors '06
Vampires Suck '10
The Virginity Hit '10
Wassup Rockers '06
Wild Cherry '09
Wild Child '08
The Winning Season '09
Yoga Hosers '16
The Youngest Profession '43
Youth in Revolt '10

Teen Drama

See also Hell High School; High School; Teen Comedy; Teen Horror; Teen Romance

Abel's Field '12
Accidents Happen '09
Addicted to Her Love '06
After '19
Alex Rider: Operation Stormbreaker '06
All About Lily Chou-Chou '01 ►
America '09
An American Affair '09
Angel Rodriguez '05
The Art of Getting By '11
As Cool As I Am '13
ATL '06
Beach Rats '17
Beautiful '09
Beautiful Wave '11
Because They're Young '60
Before I Fall '17
Being Charlie '16
Beneath the Harvest Sky '14
Betrayed at 17 '11
The Big Night '51
The Black Balloon '09
Blame '17
Blue Story '20
Bomb the System '05
Boot Camp '07
Born 2 Race '11
Boys in Brown '49
Brick '06 ►
Call Me by Your Name '17 ►
Camp Hell '10
Chronicle '12 ►
The Chumscrubber '05
A Ciambra '17
The Class '08
Clip '13
Coldwater '14
Contest '13
Crackie '09
Crows Zero '07
Crusade: A March through Time '06
Curveball '15
Cyber Seduction: His Secret Life '05
Cyberbully '11
A Dad for Christmas '06
Dare '09
Daydream Nation '10
The Diary of a Teenage Girl '15 ►
Dirty Girl '10
The Disappeared '08
The Dynamiter '11
Eden '14
800 Bullets '02
Elsewhere '09
Emma's Chance '16
Every Day '18
Every Second Counts '08
Evil '03 ►
The Fast and the Furious: Tokyo Drift '06
The Fault In Our Stars '14
Fighting the Odds: The Marilyn Gambrell Story '05
Finding a Family '10
First Light '10
Fish Tank '09 ►
Five Feet Apart '19
Flicka: Country Pride '12
The Forbidden Kingdom '08
47 Meters Down: Uncaged '19
Freedom Writers '07
Freeway '95
Fugitive at 17 '12
Full Count '06
Gallant Sons '40
Game of Your Life '11
Gangster's Boy '38
Gardens of the Night '08
Giant Little Ones '19
Ginger & Rosa '13
Girl '18 ►
Girl Fight '11
Girl in Progress '12
The Girl in the Sneakers '99
A Girl Like Her '15
A Girl of the Limberlost '90 ►
Girl, Positive '07
Girlhood '14 ►
Goats '12
The Good Humor Man '05
Grace Unplugged '13
Gracie '07
Graduation '07
Grown Up Movie Star '10
Gun Hill Road '11
Hala '19
Hanna '11
Happiness Runs '10
Hard Candy '06
Harvest '11
The Hate U Give '18 ►
Havoc 2: Normal Adolescent Behavior '07
Havoc '05
Heart of America '03
Hellion '13 ►
Hey Hey It's Esther Blueberger '08
Hick '11
High School '40
The History Boys '06
Holy Girl '04 ►
Home of the Giants '07
Homeless to Harvard: The Liz Murray Story '03
Horse Camp '14
How I Live Now '13
I Killed My Mother '09
If. . . '69 ►
If I Stay '14
It Felt Like Love '14
It's Kind of a Funny Story '10
Janie Jones '10
Japan Japan '07
Jitters '10
Keith '08
Kes '69 ►
King of Devil's Island '10
Knockout '11
Ladies and Gentlemen, the Fabulous Stains '82
The Land '16
The Last Song '10
The Last Tree '19
Lean on Pete '17 ►
The Letter Writer '11
Linda Linda Linda '05 ►
Lisa, Bright and Dark '73
LOL '12
Lost Stallions: The Journey Home '08
Low Tide '19
Margaret '11
Me and Earl and the Dying Girl '15 ►
Me and You '12
Megan Is Missing '11
Mid90s '18
The Miseducation of Cameron Post '18
Mom at Sixteen '05
Mom, Dad and Her '08
Morris from America '16 ►
Mother '13
Murderous Intent '06 ►
My Brother the Devil '12
My Dog the Champion '14
Never Back Down '08
Never Goin' Back '18
Never Rarely Sometimes Always '20 ►
The Nickel Children '05
Night Comes On '18 ►
Not Like Everyone Else '06
Now Is Good '12
On the Outs '05
One Kiss '16
One Last Thing '05
One Perfect Day '04
Our America '02
A Packing Suburbia '99
Palo Alto '07
Palo Alto '14
Paranoid Park '07
Pariah '11 ►
The Party Never Stops '07
The Perks of Being a Wallflower '12 ►
Ping Pong '02 ►
Piranhas '19
The Pregnancy Pact '10
The Pregnancy Project '12
Pretty Persuasion '05
Prom Queen '04
Queen Sized '08
The Quiet '05
Quinceanera '06 ►
Quitters '16
Reviving Ophelia '10
Riot on Sunset Strip '67
River's End '05
Rock the Paint '05
Rocket Science '07 ►
Running with Scissors '06
Ryna '05
Safelight '15
Samaritan Girl '04
Saving Zoe '19
Say Anything '89 ►
The Secret of Zoey '02
Seven Deadly Sins '10
Sexting in Suburbia '12
She's Too Young '04
Silence of the Heart '84 ►
Sin Nombre '09 ►
Sing Street '16 ►
Sins of Our Youth '16
Skateland '10
Somersault '04
Spare Parts '15
Spirit Bear: The Simon Jackson Story '05
Stalked at 17 '12
Stealing Cars '16
Stephanie Daley '06
Still Green '07
Sugar Kisses '13
Summer of 84 '18
Super Dark Times '17
Surfacing '14
Take a Giant Step '59
Take the Lead '06
Tanner Hall '09
Teen Spirit '18
Teenage Mutant Ninja Turtles 2: The Secret of the Ooze '91
Teenage Rebel '56
Terri '11
3 Generations '17
Tiger Eyes '13
To Be Fat Like Me '07
To Save a Life '10
To the Stars '20
To Write Love On Her Arms '14
Toe to Toe '09
Too Soon to Love '60
Too Young to Be a Dad '02
Too Young to Marry '07
Towelhead '07
Trash '14
The Tribe '15 ►
Triple Dog '09
True Crime '95
The Truth About Emanuel '13
Turning Paige '01
20th Century Women '17
Una Noche '13
Underground: The Julian Assange Story '12
Unwed Mother '58
Vanished-Left Behind: Next Generation '16
Wah-Wah '05
Walking the Halls '12
War Eagle, Arkansas '07
War Horse '11
A Warrior's Heart '11
Wassup Rockers '06
Wasted on the Young '10
Waves '19 ►
Welcome to the Rileys '10
White Frog '12
White Squall '96
Wild Boys of the Road '33
The Wild Stallion '09
Winter's Bone '10 ►
The Witness '99
The World Made Straight '15
Yelling to the Sky '11
The Young Stranger '57

Teen Horror

See also Hell High School; Horror Comedy; Teen Angst

The Absent '11
Acolytes '08
Acts of Death '07
Albino Farm '09
Alien Trespass '09
All the Boys Love Mandy Lane '06
April Fools '07
Attack of the Jurassic Shark '12
Automaton Transfusion '06
Autopsy '08
The Babysitter '17
Babysitter Wanted '08
Backslash '05
Bad Meat '11
Beastly Boyz '06
Beauty Queen Butcher! '91
Beneath the Darkness '12
Bereavement '10
Big Bad Wolf '06
Bikini Bloodbath '06
Black Christmas '19
Black Rat '10
Blood & Chocolate '07
Blood Lake '14
Blood Night: The Legend of Mary Hatchet '09
Bloody Homecoming '12
Boarding School '18
Boogeyman 3 '08
Born Bad '11
Brightburn '19
The Brotherhood 3: The Young Demons '02
The Caretaker '08
Carrie '13
Centipede '05
Chain Letter '10
Chaos '05
Cherry Falls '00
Children of the Corn 2: The Final Sacrifice '92
Child's Play '19
Chronicle '12 ►
Countdown '19
Crush '13
Cry Wolf '05
Cursed '04
Dance of the Dead '08
Dead Silence '98
Deadgirl '08
Decoys '04
Decoys: The Second Seduction '07
Detention '11
Devon's Ghost: Legend of the Bloody Boy '05
Devour '05
Disturbing Behavior '98
Don't Hang Up '17
Don't Knock Twice '17
Down a Dark Hall '18
Excision '12
The Eye 3 '05
Fading of the Cries '10
Fear of the Dark '02
Fender Bender '16
The Final '10
Final Destination 3 '06
Flu Birds '08
Forget Me Not '09
47 Meters Down: Uncaged '19
Freaks of Nature '15
Freddy *vs.* Jason '03
Fright Night 2: New Blood '13
The Gallows Act II '19
Ginger Snaps '01
Girl *vs.* Monster '12
The Glass House '01
Grizzly Rage '07
Hangman's Curse '03
Hansel & Gretel Get Baked '13
Happy Death Day 2U '19
Happy Hell Night '92
Haunt '19
Haunter '13
The Haunting of Molly Hartley '08
Headless Horseman '07
The Hitcher '07
The Hollow '04
Home Sick '08
Hostel '06
House at the End of the Street '12
I Know What You Did Last Summer '97 ►
I Still Know What You Did Last Summer '98
The Initiation of Sarah '06
Invasion '07
The Invisible '07
Jack and Diane '12
Jamie Marks is Dead '13
Jennifer's Body '09
Killer Instinct '00
Lake Placid: The Final Chapter '12
Look Away '18
Ma '19
Marker '05
Monster Party '18
The Moth Diaries '11
My Soul to Take '10
Never Cry Werewolf '08
A Nightmare on Elm Street '10
One Missed Call 3: Final '06
One of Them '03
Ouija '14
Playback '12
The Poltergeist of Borley Forest '13
Predator Island '05
Prey '19
Prom Night '08
Prowl '10
Psychotica '10
Pulse '01
Rabies '10
Red Clover '12
Red Riding Hood '03
Return to Sleepaway Camp '08
R.L. Stine's The Haunting Hour: Don't Even Think About It '07
The Sacrifice '05
Satanic '15
Scary Stories to Tell in the Dark '19
Scream '96 ►
Scream 4 '11
Serial Killing 101 '04
The Shortcut '09
Slender Man '18
Snow White: A Deadly Summer '12
Some Kind of Hate '15
Spliced '03
Stay Alive '06
Stitches '12
Student Bodies '81
Summer's Moon '09
Superhero Movie '08

► = rated three bones or higher

Sweet Insanity '06
Swimfan '02
Talisman '98
Tamara '05
Tormented '09
Truth or Dare '18
2: Voodoo Academy '12
Uncaged '16
Vampire Academy '14
Varsity Blood '14
Venom '05
Viral '16
Way of the Wicked '14
When a Stranger Calls '06
When Evil Calls '06
Wild Country '05
Wildling '18
Wishmaster 3: Beyond the Gates of Hell '01
Witches of the Caribbean '05
Without Warning '80

Teen Musicals

Absolute Beginners '86
The American Mall '08
Another Cinderella Story '08
April Love '57
Bandslam '09
Beach Blanket Bingo '65▶
Beach Party '63
Bikini Beach '64
Brand New Day '10
Camp Rock 2: The Final Jam '10
Camp Rock '08
The Cheetah Girls 2 '06
The Cheetah Girls '03
The Cheetah Girls: One World '08
A Cinderella Story: Once Upon a Song '11
Cry-Baby '90▶
Fame '80▶
Fame '09
Footloose '11
Glee: The 3D Concert Movie '11
Go For It! '10
Grease 2 '82
Grease '78▶
Hairspray '88▶
High School Musical '06
High School Musical 2 '07
High School Musical 3: Senior Year '08
How She Move '08
How to Stuff a Wild Bikini '65
Josie and the Pussycats '01
Just for Fun '63
Justin Bieber: Never Say Never '11
Lemonade Mouth '11
Let It Shine '12
Not Fade Away '12
Pajama Party '64
Rags '12
Ring-a-Ding Rhythm '62
Rock 'n' Roll High School '79▶
Rock 'n' Roll High School Forever '91
Rock, Pretty Baby '56
Sharpay's Fabulous Adventure '11
Spectacular '09
StarStruck '10
Step Up 2 the Streets '08
Sunday School Musical '08
Teen Beach Movie '13
Untamed Youth '57
Valley Girl '20
We Are the Best! '13▶
Were the World Mine '08

Teen Romance

***See also** Cinderella Stories; High School; Teen Angst; Teen Comedy*

Aaron Loves Angela '75
According to Greta '08
After '19
American Honey '16
The American Mall '08
Another Cinderella Story '08
April Love '57
Aquamarine '06
Babyteeth '20▶
Beastly '11
Beautiful Creatures '13
The Beautiful Person '08
Beautiful Thing '95▶
Beyond Clueless '14
The Biggest Fan '02
The Blue Lagoon '80
Blue Lagoon: The Awakening '12
Book of Love '04
Boys '95
Boys and Girls '00
Call Me by Your Name '17▶
Camp Rock 2: The Final Jam '10
Can't Buy Me Love '87
The Careless Years '57
Chalet Girls '11
Cherry Crush '07
Circumstance '11
Closet Monster '16
Cold Showers '05
crazy/beautiful '01
Cynthia '47
Down in the Valley '05
Dream Boy '08
Dreaming About You '92
Drive Me Crazy '99
The Edge of Seventeen '16▶
An Education '09▶
Ella Enchanted '04▶
Endless Love '81
Endless Love '14
Every Day '18
Everything, Everything '17
The Fault In Our Stars '14
First Daughter '04
The First Time '12
Five Feet Apart '19
Flipped '10
Flirting '89▶
Footloose '11
Full Ride '02
Games of Love and Chance '03
Get Over It! '01
Gregory's Girl '80▶
Harry Potter and the Half-Blood Prince '09
Here on Earth '00
High School Musical '06
High School Musical 2 '07
High School Musical 3: Senior Year '08
Hotel Transylvania '12
I Love You, I Love You Not '97
If I Stay '14
The Incredibly True Adventure of Two Girls in Love '95
Jack and Diane '12
The Jerk Theory '11
John Tucker Must Die '06
Joyful Noise '12
Keith '08
Kids in America '05
The Last Vampire on Earth '10
Let It Snow '19
Lila Says '04
Love Me '12
Love, Simon '18▶
Mad Love '95
The Man in the Moon '91▶
Marking Time '03
Mean Dreams '17
Midnight Sun '18
The Miseducation of Cameron Post '18
Moonlight Whispers '99
Morris from America '16▶
My Dog the Champion '14
My Summer of Love '05
Now Is Good '12
O '01▶
Ode to Billy Joe '76
The Perfect Date '19
Pizza '05
Pope Dreams '06
Premature '20
Pretty in Pink '86
Punk Love '06
Raise Your Voice '04
Rapture '65
Restless '11
The Restless Years '58
Romeo and Juliet '68▶
Romeo & Juliet '13
Ronnie and Julie '97
Safelight '15
Sixteen Candles '84▶
Slash '16
Snow Angels '07▶
Some Kind of Wonderful '87
The Space Between Us '17
The Spectacular Now '13▶
StarStruck '10
The Starving Games '13
Step Up '06
Ten Things I Hate about You '99▶
Time Freak '18
To All the Boys: P.S. I Still Love You '20
To All the Boys I've Loved Before '18
Twilight '08
The Twilight Saga: Breaking Dawn, Part 1 '11
The Twilight Saga: Eclipse '10
The Twilight Saga: New Moon '09
Valley Girl '83
Very Good Girls '13
The Wackness '08
A Walk to Remember '02
What Lola Wants '15
What Matters Most '01
Whatever It Takes '00
William Shakespeare's Romeo and Juliet '96▶
Young Adult '11
You're So Cupid '10
Zebrahead '92▶

Teen Sci Fi/Fantasy

After Earth '13
At First Light '18
Beastly '11
The Darkest Minds '18
Divergent '14
Earth to Echo '14
The Giver '14
The Golden Compass '07
Harry Potter and the Deathly Hallows, Part 1 '10▶
Harry Potter and the Deathly Hallows, Part 2 '11▶
Harry Potter and the Half-Blood Prince '09
The Hunger Games '12▶
The Hunger Games: Mockingjay--Part 1 '14
I Am Number Four '11
Insurgent '15
The Maze Runner '14
Maze Runner: The Death Cure '18
The Mortal Instruments: City of Bones '13
Neverland '11
Percy Jackson: Sea of Monsters '13
Power Rangers '17
Project Almanac '15
Starfish '19
Super Storm '12
Teenage Space Vampires '99
Yoga Hosers '16

Televangelists

***See also** Look Ma! I'm on TV!; Mass Media; Religion*

Almost an Angel '90
Devil in the Flesh '98
The Eyes of Tammy Faye '00
Fletch Lives '89
Forfeit '07
Gospel of Deceit '06
Jesus Camp '06
License to Kill '89▶
Lost '05
Repo Man '83▶
Repossessed '90
Tales from the Crypt Presents Bordello of Blood '96
Wiretapper '55

Television

***See** Look Ma! I'm on TV!; Mass Media*

Tennis

Balls Out: Gary the Tennis Coach '09
Battle of the Sexes '17
Borg *vs.* McEnroe '17▶
The Break '95
Fletch '85
40 Love '15
Hard, Fast and Beautiful '51
Jocks '87
Match Point '05▶
Nobody's Perfect '90
The Squid and the Whale '05▶
Wimbledon '04
The Witches of Eastwick '87

Terminal Confusion

Beavis and Butt-Head Do America '96
Big Trouble '02
Dumb & Dumber '94
8 Heads in a Duffel Bag '96
Home Alone 2: Lost in New York '92
Home Alone 3 '97
Jet Lag '02
Knockaround Guys '01
More Dogs Than Bones '00
The Out-of-Towners '99
Terminal Invasion '02
Unaccompanied Minors '06
Up in the Air '09▶
Wait until Dark '67▶
What's Up, Doc? '72▶

Terminal Illness

***See also** Disease of the Week*

The Angriest Man in Brooklyn '14
Antiviral '12
Ba'al: The Storm God '08
The Barbarian Invasions '03▶
Beaches '88▶
Beautiful Kate '09▶
Because of You '95
Beginners '10▶
A Beginner's Guide to Endings '10
Behind the Red Door '02
Beverly Lewis' The Confession '13
Beverly Lewis' The Shunning '11
Big Bad Love '02
Big Fish '03▶
Biutiful '10
Blow Dry '00
The Blue Butterfly '04
Blue Eyes '09
Bound by a Secret '09
The Bread, My Sweet '01
Break '09
Bright Star '09
The Broken Circle Breakdown '12
The Bucket List '07
The Bumblebee Flies Anyway '98
Burning Man '11
The Cake Eaters '07
Camille '84
Cherry Blossoms '08
Chinese Box '97
Christmas In Conway '13
The Christmas Shoes '02
A Christmas Tale '08▶
Chronic '16
The Claim '00
Claudia '43
Crack in the World '65
Crank '06
Cria Cuervos '76▶
Cries and Whispers '72▶
The Dark Side of the Sun '88
A Day Late and a Dollar Short '14
The Death of Mr. Lazarescu '05
Devotion '46
Dying of the Light '14
Dying Young '91
The End of the Affair '99▶
The Etruscan Smile '19
Evening '07
Every Day '10
Everything, Everything '17
Fanboys '09
The Fault In Our Stars '14
A Fighting Man '14
The Fitzgerald Family Christmas '12
48 Angels '06
The Fountain '06
From Above '13
Funny People '09
Gabriel & Me '01
Gleason '16▶
God Bless America '11
The Grand Role '04
Griffin & Phoenix '06
Groom Lake '02
The Guitar '08
Hard Luck '01
Harvest '10
Henry Poole Is Here '08▶
Here on Earth '00
Hong Kong 1941 '84
If I Had a Million '32
Igby Goes Down '02▶
In America '02▶
In Love We Trust '07
In the Shadows '98
Inhale '10
Juncture '07
Keith '08
Klimt '06
La Boheme '26
The Lady '11
The Last Hit Man '08
Last Holiday '06
The Last of the Mobile Hot-shots '69
The Last Request '06
Late August, Early September '98
A Late Quartet '12
Life as a House '01
Life Itself '14▶
The Line '08
Listen to Your Heart '10
A Little Bit of Heaven '11
The Living Wake '07
Love and Pain and the Whole Damn Thing '73
Love Story '44
Magnolia '99▶
Marion Bridge '02
The Medicine Show '01
Missing Brendan '03
Mrs. Wiggs of the Cabbage Patch '34
Mr. Rice's Secret '00
Mood Indigo '13
Moulin Rouge '01▶
My Brother '06
My First Mister '01
My Life Without Me '03
Never Say Die '39
Next Time We Love '36
The Night Listener '06
No Sad Songs For Me '50
The Normal Heart '14▶
Norman '10
Now Is Good '12
One Last Thing '05
One More Kiss '99
One True Thing '98▶
One Way Passage '32
One Week '08
The Other Love '47
Other People '16
Paddleton '19
Parting Shots '98
The Perfect Son '00
Perfume '01
Pieces of April '03
Pope Dreams '06
Pride and Glory '08
The Professor '19
Promises to Keep '85
Rage '72
Rails & Ties '07
Reach for Me '08
Red Meat '98
Respire '09
Restless '11
Ripley's Game '02▶
The Secret of Dr. Kildare '39
The Secrets '07
The Settlement '99
Seven Pounds '08
Shadowboxer '06
She Drives Me Crazy '07
A Short Stay in Switzerland '09
The Singing Fool '28
The Sleepy Time Gal '01
Snowmen '10
Speed of Life '99
Stealing Beauty '96
Stepmom '98▶
Sweet November '68
Sweet November '01
Tennessee '08
Terms of Endearment '83▶
Things You Can Tell Just by Looking at Her '00
13 Moons '02
3 Days to Kill '14
Time to Leave '05▶
The Tomb '09
Transcendence '14
Tuesdays with Morrie '99
21 Grams '03▶
Two Weeks '06
The Ultimate Gift '07
Uncle Boonmee Who Can Recall His Past Lives '10
Under the Lighthouse Dancing '97
Unfinished Song '12
Vernie '04
Veronika Decides to Die '15
A Very Serious Person '06
Vintage Model '92
Virtual Obsession '98
The Visit '00▶
Waiting for Forever '11
A Walk to Remember '02
What If God Were the Sun? '07
When Did You Last See Your Father? '07
The Wings of the Dove '97▶
Winter's Tale '14
Wit '01▶
With Honors '94
ZigZag '70

Terror in Tall Buildings

***See also** Elevators; Mystery & Suspense*

The Belko Experiment '17
Blackout '78
Botched '07
The Dark Tower '17
Devil '10
Die Hard '88▶
Firetrap '01
George A. Romero's Land of the Dead '05▶
The Glass Trap '04
Hotel Mumbai '18
9/11 '17
Poltergeist 3 '88
Skyscraper '95
Skyscraper '18
Speed '94▶
Terror on the 40th Floor '74
Tower '16▶
The Towering Inferno '74
Wish I Was Here '14
World Trade Center '06▶

Terrorism

***See also** Crime & Foreign Intrigue; Spies & Espionage*

Absolution '03
Act of Valor '12
Act of War '96
Action Force: The Movie '87
Active Stealth '99
Agent Red '00
Air Force One '97▶
Airborne '98
Airboss '97
Airline Disaster '10
The Amateur '82
American Assassin '17
American Dreamz '06
American Meltdown '04
American Pastoral '16
Amerigeddon '16
Among the Believers '15▶
Antibody '02
Arlington Road '99
Army of One '16
The Art of War 3: Retribution '08
The Assignment '97
Atom Nine Adventures '07
The Attack '13▶
Auto Recovery '08
The Baader Meinhof Complex '08
Bad Company '02

▶ = *rated three bones or higher*

Ballistica '10
Barcelona '94 ▸
Battle Planet '08
Belly of the Beast '03
Bio-dead '09
Black Cobra 2 '89
Black Cobra 3: The Manila Connection '90
Black Dawn '05
Black Sunday '77
Blast '04
Bloodfist 6: Ground Zero '94
Blown Away '94
Body of Lies '08
Bomb Squad '97
Bombshell '97
Brake '12
Breakfast on Pluto '05
Buried '10
Camp X-Ray '14
Captain America 2: Death Too Soon '79
Captive '87
Carlos '10
The Cassandra Crossing '76
Chasing Freedom '04
Children of Men '06▸
C.I.A. 2: Target Alexa '94
Circle of Deceit '94
Civic Duty '06
Cleanskin '12
Collateral Damage '02
Command Performance '09
Commando '85▸
A Common Man '12
Contaminated Man '00
Contract to Kill '16
Counter Measures '99
Counterstrike '03
Cover-Up '91
Covert Assassin '94
Crash and Burn '90
Crash & Byrnes '99
Crash Dive '96
Criminal '16
Critical Mass '00
Cry of the Innocent '80▸
The Crying Game '92▸
The Dancer Upstairs '02
The Dark Knight Rises '12▸
Day Night Day Night '06▸
DC 9/11: Time of Crisis '04
Dead Air '08
Dead in a Heartbeat '02
Dead or Alive '02
Deadline '87
Deadly Reckoning '01
Death Before Dishonor '87
Death Has a Bad Reputation '90
The Death Merchant '91
Death Merchants '73
Death Note 3: L Change the World '08
Death of the Incredible Hulk '90
The Defender '04
Delta Force 3: The Killing Game '91
Delta Force '86
Delta Force Commando '87
Delta Force One-The Lost Patrol '99
Demolition High '95
Desert Thunder '99
The Devil's Own '96▸
Dick Barton, Special Agent '48
Die Hard '88▸
Die Hard 2: Die Harder '90▸
Die Hard: With a Vengeance '95
Diplomatic Siege '99
Dirty Games '89
Dr. Otto & the Riddle of the Gloom Beam '86
Dog Day Afternoon '75▸
Domino '19
Doomsdayer '00
Double Team '97
D.R.E.A.M. Team '99
Drone '17
Dying of the Light '14
The Enforcer '76
Eraser '96
Escape under Pressure '00
Evil Behind You '06
The Evil That Men Do '84
Executive Decision '96
Extraction '15
Extreme Limits '01
Extreme Ops '02
Eye in the Sky '15 ▸
Face of Terror '04
Face/Off '97 ▸
Fahrenheit 9/11 '04 ▸
Falling Fire '97
The Fate of the Furious '17
A Father's Revenge '88
Fatwa '06
ffolkes '80
The 15:17 to Paris '18
Final Score '18
Final Voyage '99
Five Fingers '06
The Foreigner '17
Fortress of Amerikka '89
Four Lions '10
The Fourth Angel '01
Freedom Strike '98
From Paris With Love '10
Full Disclosure '00
Futuresport '98
The Gatekeepers '12▸
G.I. Joe: The Rise of Cobra '09
The Glory Boys '84
The Great New Wonderful '06
Harold & Kumar Escape from Guantanamo Bay '08
He Named Me Malala '15
Heaven '01
Held Hostage '91
Hell Squad '85
Hidden Agenda '90
Hologram Man '95
Hostage Flight '85
The Hunt for Eagle One: Crash Point '06
Hunter Killer '18
Hyena Road '16
If a Tree Falls: A Story of the Earth Liberation Front '11
Imperium '16
The Impostors '98
In the Name of the Father '93▸
Incendiary '08
The Insurgents '06
Interception '08
Invasion U.S.A. '85
Invisible Circus '00
Iron Man '08▸
Jirga '19
Judgment in Berlin '88
Juggernaut '74▸
Katherine '75
Kichiku: Banquet of the Beasts '04
The Kidnapping of the President '80
The Kingdom '07
Knock Off '98
Land of Plenty '04
Land of the Blind '06
Land of the Free '98
L'Annee Sainte '76
Last Stand '00
The Legend of Rita '99
The Little Drummer Girl '84▸
Live Free or Die Hard '07
Live Wire '92
The Locator 2: Braxton Returns '09
London Has Fallen '16
The Lost Command '66
The Mad Bomber '72
Maiden Voyage: Ocean Hijack '04
The Man Who Knew Too Little '97
The Marine 2 '09
The Marine 3: Homefront '11
McHale's Navy '97
Merchants of War '90
MI-5 '15
Michael Collins '96▸
Mile 22 '18
The Molly Maguires '70
A Most Wanted Man '14
Munich '05▸
Murder on Flight 502 '75
My Brother's War '97
Naked Gun 33 1/3: The Final Insult '94
Navy SEALS '90
Newtown '16▸
Next '07
Night of the Assassin '70
Nighthawks '81
9/11 '17
Ninja Connection '90
Ninja the Battalion '90
No Contest '94
No Dead Heroes '87
Nocturama '17
Non-Stop '14
The Oath '10 ▸
Odd Man Out '47 ▸
Oklahoma City '17
Olympus Has Fallen '13
Once Upon a Time in China II '92 ▸
Operation Delta Force 5: Random Fire '00
Operation Thunderbolt '77
Osombie '12
Panic in the Streets '50 ▸
Paradise Now '05▸
The Passenger '75▸
Passenger 57 '92
Path to Paradise '97
The Patriot '86
Patriot Games '92▸
Patriots Day '17
Patty Hearst '88
The Peacekeeper '98
The Peacemaker '97
The Poseidon Adventure '05
Postal '07
The President's Man 2: A Line in the Sand '02
The President's Man '00
Pursuit '72▸
Rachida '05▸
Raid on Entebbe '77▸
Rangers '00
Rapid Assault '99
Red Line '13
Red Mercury '05
Rendition '07
Repo Chick '09
Riot '96
The Rock '96▸
Rollercoaster '77
Royal Warriors '86
Running Out of Time '94
Saint Judy '19
Seal Team Six: The Raid on Osama Bin Laden '12
The Secret Agent '96
Secret Agent Super Dragon '66
Shakedown '02
Shock and Awe '18
Sicario: Day of the Soldado '18
The Siege '98
Skeleton Coast '89
Sleeper Cell '05
Sniper 3 '04
Sniper: Ghost Shooter '16
Source Code '11▸
Special Bulletin '83▸
Special Forces '11
Stalking Danger '86
Standard Operating Procedure '08▸
Star Trek: Into Darkness '13▸
The State Within '06
The Stone Merchant '06
Stronger '17▸
Stuber '19
Submerged '00
Sudden Death '95
The Sum of All Fears '02
SWAT: Unit 887 '15
Sweepers '99
Swordfish '01
Syriana '05▸
The Take '16
The Taking of Pelham One Two Three '74▸
Team America: World Police '04▸
Terminal Rush '96
Termination Man '97
The Terrorist '98
The Terrorist Next Door '08
The Terrorists '74
3 Days to Kill '14
Thunderball '65
Time of Favor '00
A Town Called Hell '72
Toy Soldiers '91
Trained to Kill, U.S.A. '75
Traitor '08
Troma's War '88
True Lies '94
Tube '03
Turbulence 2: Fear of Flying '99
Turk 182! '85
12 Strong '18
22 July '18
21 Hours at Munich '76 ▸
Typhoon '06
Undeclared War '91
Under Siege '92
United 93 '06 ▸
U.S. SEALs: Dead or Alive '02
Universal Soldier: Regeneration '09
Unlocked '17
Unthinkable '10
Uri: The Surgical Strike '19
V for Vendetta '06
The Vanquisher '10
The Vector File '03
The Vernonia Incident '89
Victory at Entebbe '76
Viper '88
Vox Lux '18
Wanted Dead or Alive '86
The War Within '05
The Way of War '08
Weaponized '16
The Weather Underground '02▸
Where in the World Is Osama Bin Laden? '06
The White Lioness '96
Winds of Terror '01
Women on the Verge of a Nervous Breakdown '88▸
The World Is Not Enough '99
World Trade Center '06▸
Wrong Is Right '82
Year of the Gun '91
You Don't Mess with the Zohan '08
You Only Live Twice '67
Zero Dark Thirty '12▸
Zero Days '16

Texas

***See also** American South; Dallas; Houston; Westerns*

About Scout '15▸
Age Out '19
Ain't Them Bodies Saints '13▸
The Alamo '60▸
The Alamo '04
Alamo Bay '85
All the Boys Love Mandy Lane '06
All the Pretty Horses '00
American Violet '09
Angels Sing '13
The Astronaut Farmer '07
At the Death House Door '08▸
Bad Turn Worse '14
Barracuda '17
The Baytown Outlaws '12
Beeswax '09▸
Beneath the Darkness '12
Bernie '12▸
The Big Gundown '66
Blaze '18▸
Blood Simple '85▸
Boom Town '40
Breathless '12
Brotherhood '10
Call Her Savage '32
Cattle Town '52
Christmas Child '03
Christmas Comes Home to Canaan '11
Christmas in Canaan '09
Chupacabra *vs.* the Alamo '13
The Client List '10
Cold in July '14
The Comebacks '07
Corky '72
Dancer, Texas-Pop. 81 '98▸
Days of Heaven '78▸
Dazed and Confused '93▸
The Deadbeat Club '04
The Devil's Candy '17
Dr. T & the Women '00▸
Drop Dead Sexy '05
The Dry Land '10
The Duel '16
Duel in the Sun '46 ▸
Elvis and Annabelle '07
Exit Speed '08
F6 Twister '12
False Pretenses '04
Fatal Deception: Mrs. Lee Harvey Oswald '93
The First Texan '56
$5 a Day '08
5 Time Champion '11
For Sale By Owner '05
Friday Night Lights '04 ▸
From Mexico With Love '09
Giant '56 ▸
Glory Road '06
The Great Debaters '07 ▸
Happy, Texas '99 ▸
Hell or High Water '16 ▸
High School '40
The Highwaymen '19
The Hills Run Red '67
Hope Floats '98
The Hot Flashes '13
The Hot Spot '90
I'll Be Seeing You '44
The Imposter '12▸
In a Valley of Violence '16
Into the Abyss '11▸
The Iron Orchard '19
It's a Big Country '51
JFK '91▸
Joe '13▸
The Keeper '09
Kill or Be Killed '15
Kill the Umpire '50
The Killer Inside Me '10
Killer Joe '11
Killing Kennedy '13
The King '05
Larry McMurtry's Streets of Laredo '95▸
The Last Cowboy '03
The Last Picture Show '71▸
The Last Sunset '61
LBJ '17
The Life of David Gale '03
Life on the Line '16
Little Boy Blue '97
Lonesome Dove '89▸
Lonesome Dove Church '14
Love and a .45 '94
Love & Air Sex '14
Man of the House '05
Mr. Roosevelt '17
My All American '15
Nadine '87
Never Goin' Back '18
No Country for Old Men '07▸
Noble Things '08
Not Forgotten '09
Open Windows '14
Paradise, Texas '05
Paris, Texas '83▸
Parkland '13
A Perfect World '93
Places in the Heart '84▸
Planet Terror '07
The Positively True Adventures of the Alleged Texas Cheerleader-Murdering Mom '93▸
Racing for Time '08
Raggedy Man '81▸
Retribution Road '07
The Return '06
Return to Lonesome Dove '93
Rio Lobo '70
River's End '05
Rushlights '13
The Searchers '56▸
Seven Days in Utopia '11
75 Degrees '00
Skateland '10
Song to Song '17
Sons of Katie Elder '65▸
Soul's Midnight '06
Spring Breakdown '08
The Stars Fell on Henrietta '94
Stop-Loss '08▸
The Sugarland Express '74▸
Tarnation '03
Terror in a Texas Town '58
Texas Chainsaw 3D '13
The Texas Chainsaw Massacre: The Beginning '06
Texas Killing Fields '11
The Texas Streak '26
There Will Be Blood '07 ▸
The Three Burials of Melquiades Estrada '05 ▸
Tin Cup '96 ▸
Tower '16 ▸
The Town That Dreaded Sundown '14
The Trip to Bountiful '85 ▸
The Trip to Bountiful '14 ▸
True Stories '86 ▸
Undercover Bridesmaid '12
The Unforeseen '07
Universal Squadrons '11
Varsity Blues '98
Vietnam, Texas '90
The Wendell Baker Story '05
What Matters Most '01
Whip It '09 ▸
The Wild Man of the Navidad '08
The Windsplitter '71
Young Guns of Texas '62
Your Love Never Fails '11

Thanksgiving

***See also** Holidays*

American Son '08
Avalon '90▸
Cold Turkey '13
A Day for Thanks on Walton's Mountain '82
Deadfall '12
Eat, Pray, Love '10
Familiar Strangers '08
A Family Thanksgiving '10
Free Birds '13
Hannah and Her Sisters '86▸
Holiday Engagement '11
Home for the Holidays '95
The House of Yes '97
The Ice Storm '97▸
Jack and Jill '11
Krisha '15
Love at the Thanksgiving Day Parade '12
Mrs. Wiggs of the Cabbage Patch '34
The Myth of Fingerprints '97
National Lampoon's Holiday Reunion '03
The Oath '18
An Old-Fashioned Thanksgiving '08
Palo Alto '07
Peter and Vandy '09
Pieces of April '03
Planes, Trains & Automobiles '87
Prisoners '13▸
Squanto: A Warrior's Tale '94▸
Tadpole '02
A Time to Remember '03
The Vicious Kind '09
The War at Home '96
What's Cooking? '00▸
Who Made the Potatoe Salad? '05

There Goes the Neighborhood

***See also** Apartments & Real Estate; Strained Suburbia; Yuppie Nightmares*

American Beauty '99▸
Arlington Road '99
Beautiful '09
Boo! A Madea Halloween '16
The Boy Next Door '15
The 'Burbs '89
Cell '16
Civic Duty '06
Confined '10
Creepy '16▸
The Damned '06
Despicable Me '10
Disturbia '07
Drunk Parents '19
Fright Night '85
Fright Night '11
Ghostbusters '16
Good Neighbors '10
House at the End of the Street '12
The House Next Door '06

▸ = rated three bones or higher

▶ = rated three bones or higher

Star Trek 4: The Voyage Home '86 ▸
Star Trek '09 ▸
Star Trek: First Contact '96 ▸
Stargate '94
Stargate: Continuum '08
The Sticky Fingers of Time '97
The Swordsman '92
Synchronicity '16
Teenage Mutant Ninja Turtles 3 '93
Termination Point '07
Terminator 2: Judgment Day '91 ▸
Terminator 3: Rise of the Machines '03 ▸
The Terminator '84 ▸
Terminator: Dark Fate '19
Terminator Genisys '15
Test Tube Teens from the Year 2000 '93
The Thirteenth Floor '99
A Thousand Kisses Deep '11
The Three Stooges Meet Hercules '61
Thrill Seekers '99
Ticking Clock '10
Time After Time '79 ▸
Time and Again '07
Time Bandits '81
Time Barbarians '90
Time Chasers '95
Time Freak '18
The Time Machine '60 ▸
The Time Machine '02
Time Runner '92
The Time Traveler's Wife '09
Timecop 2: The Berlin Decision '03
Timecop '94
Timekeeper '98
Timeline '03
Timemaster '95
Timerider '83
Timestalkers '87
The Tomorrow Man '01
Total Reality '97
Trancers '84
Trancers 2: The Return of Jack Deth '90
Trancers 3: Deth Lives '92
Trancers 4: Jack of Swords '93
Trancers 5: Sudden Deth '94
Trancers 6: Life After Deth '02
12 Monkeys '95 ▸
12:01 '93
Twice upon a Yesterday '98
Unidentified Flying Oddball '79
The Visitors '95
Vlad '03
Warlock '91
Waxwork 2: Lost in Time '91
When Time Expires '97
A Wrinkle in Time '18
X-Men: Days of Future Past '14 ▸
Yor, the Hunter from the Future '83

Time Warped

Austin Powers: International Man of Mystery '97 ▸
Austin Powers 2: The Spy Who Shagged Me '99 ▸
Black Knight '01
Blast from the Past '98
The Brady Bunch Movie '95 ▸
Comet '14
Demolition Man '93
Disney's The Kid '00
Edge of Tomorrow '14 ▸
Encino Man '92
Forever Young '92
Genesis II '73
Groundhog Day '93 ▸
Happy Death Day 2U '19
Haunter '13
I'm Not Here '19
Jimmy, the Boy Wonder '66
Kate & Leopold '01
Kickin' It Old Skool '07
La Vie en Rose '07
The Last Five Years '14 ▸
Late for Dinner '91
Leave It to Beaver '97
Mr. Nobody '13
The One I Love '14
Paycheck '03
Peggy Sue Got Married '86
Phantasm: Ravager '16
Pleasantville '98 ▸
Retroactive '97
Teen Beach Movie '13
13 Going on 30 '04
Time Warp '81
Touchback '11
Triangle '09
Turn Back the Clock '33
The Two Worlds of Jenny Logan '79
A Very Brady Sequel '96
Wonderstruck '17
Zathura '05 ▸

Titanic

The Chambermaid on the Titanic '97
A Night to Remember '58 ▸
Raise the Titanic '80
S.O.S. Titanic '79
Titanic '53 ▸
Titanic '96
Titanic '97 ▸
The Unsinkable Molly Brown '64 ▸

To the Moon!

***See also** Space Operas*

The Adventures of Baron Munchausen '89 ▸
The Adventures of Pluto Nash '02
Apollo 13 '95 ▸
Apollo 18 '11
Apollo 11 '19 ▸
Armstrong '19
Attack of the Moon Zombies '11
Beyond the Stars '89
Cat Women of the Moon '53
Countdown '68
Despicable Me '10
Destination Moon '50
Destination Moonbase Alpha '75
The Dish '00 ▸
First Men in the Moon '64
Fly Me to the Moon '08
From the Earth to the Moon '98 ▸
The Future '11
Hidden Figures '17 ▸
In the Shadow of the Moon '07 ▸
Jungle Moon Men '55
Missile to the Moon '59
Moon '09
Moon Pilot '62
Moon Zero Two '70
The Mouse on the Moon '62 ▸
Operation Avalanche '16
Quatermass 2 '57 ▸
Radar Men from the Moon '52
The Secret of Moonacre '08
They Came from Beyond Space '67
Transformers: Dark of the Moon '11
12 to the Moon '60

Toilets

***See** Bathroom Scenes*

Tokyo

***See also** Japan*

Austin Powers In Goldmember '02
An Autumn Afternoon '62 ▸
Babel '06 ▸
Babies '10 ▸
The Bad News Bears Go to Japan '78
Big Man Japan '07
Black Rain '89
Bright Future '03 ▸
Cafe Lumiere '05
Call Me Mister '51
Cherry Blossoms '08
Dodes 'ka-den '70 ▸
Earthquake Bird '19
Enter the Void '09
The Fast and the Furious: Tokyo Drift '06
Gamera vs. Barugon '66
Gappa the Trifibian Monster '67
Ghidrah the Three Headed Monster '65
Godzilla '54
Godzilla '14 ▸
Godzilla, King of the Monsters '56
Godzilla 2000 '99 ▸
Godzilla vs. King Ghidora '91
Godzilla vs. Megalon '76
The Grudge 2 '06
H-Man '59
House of Bamboo '55
Ju-On: The Grudge '03
Kabei: Our Mother '08
Kill Bill Vol. 1 '03 ▸
Kumiko the Treasure Hunter '14 ▸
Marines, Let's Go '61
Mega Shark Vs. Giant Octopus '09
Monster '08
Mothra '62 ▸
Nobody Knows '04
Okoge '93
One Wonderful Sunday '47
Only Yesterday '16 ▸
Otaku No Video '91 ▸
Outrage '10
Pale Flower '64
Pulse '01
Rain Fall '09
The Ramen Girl '08
Running Brave '83
Shin Godzilla '16
Shoplifters '18 ▸
Shutter '08
Stopover Tokyo '57
Street of Shame '56 ▸
Suicide Club '02
Thirty Seconds Over Tokyo '44 ▸
Tokyo! '09
Tokyo-Ga '85 ▸
Tokyo Joe '49
Tokyo Sonata '09 ▸
Tokyo Story '53 ▸
War of the Gargantuas '70
Wasabi '01

Torn in Two (or More)

Abbott and Costello Meet Dr. Jekyll and Mr. Hyde '52
Ashes of Time '94 ▸
Batman Forever '95 ▸
Carbon Copy '69
Color of Night '94
The Dark Knight '08 ▸
Dr. Jekyll and Ms. Hyde '95
Dr. Jekyll and Mr. Hyde '20 ▸
Dr. Jekyll and Mr. Hyde '32 ▸
Dr. Jekyll and Mr. Hyde '41 ▸
Dr. Jekyll and Mr. Hyde '68
Dr. Jekyll and Mr. Hyde '73
Dr. Jekyll and Sister Hyde '71
Edge of Sanity '89
Exorcist 3: Legion '90
The Eyes of My Mother '16
Fight Club '99 ▸
Frankie and Alice '10
Hulk '03
I, Monster '71 ▸
The Incredible Hulk '08
Jekyll '07 ▸
Jekyll and Hyde '90
Jekyll & Hyde. . . Together Again '82
The League of Extraordinary Gentlemen '03
Madonna of the Seven Moons '45
Mary Reilly '95
Me, Myself, and Irene '00 ▸
More of Me '07
Multiplicity '96
Never Talk to Strangers '95
Nutty Professor 2: The Klumps '00
The Nutty Professor '63 ▸
The Nutty Professor '96 ▸
Passion of Mind '00
Peacock '09
Primal Fear '96
Psycho Beach Party '00
Raising Cain '92
A Scanner Darkly '06
The Scribbler '14
Separate Lives '94
Shattered Image '98
6 Souls '13
So Dark the Night '46
Spider-Man '02 ▸
The Strange Case of Dr. Jekyll and Mr. Hyde '06
Sybil '76 ▸
The Three Faces of Eve '57
Tierra '95
Waking Madison '10

Toronto

***See also** Canada*

Anvil! The Story of Anvil '09
Ararat '02 ▸
The Baby Formula '08
Between Strangers '02
Bon Cop Bad Cop '06
Booky's Crush '09
Breakfast With Scot '07
Chloe '09
Citizen Gangster '11
Decoding Annie Parker '13
Enemy '13
Exotica '94 ▸
The Good Samaritan '12
Hollywood North '03
How She Move '08
Jiminy Glick in LaLa Wood '05
Last Night '98 ▸
The Life Before This '99
The Man From Toronto '32
The Newton Boys '97
One Week '08
Owning Mahowny '03
Paris, France '94
Picture Claire '01
The Republic of Love '03
Rude '96
Run This Town '20
Scott Pilgrim vs. the World '10
Siblings '04
Sidekick '05
Soul Survivor '95
Spenser: A Savage Place '94
Take This Waltz '11
Treed Murray '01
Trigger '10
Twist '03 ▸

Torrid Love Scenes

***See** Sex & Sex on the Beach; Sexploitation*

Toys

***See also** Killer Toys*

Annabelle Comes Home '19
Aussie and Ted's Great Adventure '09
Babes in Toyland '61
Big '88 ▸
The Boy '16
Brahms: The Boy II '19
Child's Play '88
Child's Play 2 '90
Child's Play '19
Christopher Robin '18
Curse of Chucky '13
Dance of Death '68
Demonic Toys '90
Dolls '87
Dolly Dearest '92
Home Alone 3 '97
Hugo '11 ▸
Jingle All the Way '96
Josh Kirby. . . Time Warrior: Chapter 3, Trapped on Toyworld '95
Klaus '19 ▸
A Lego Brickumentary '15
The LEGO Movie 2: The Second Part '19
Life-Size '00
Mr. Magorium's Wonder Emporium '07
9 '09 ▸
Playmobil: The Movie '19
Postal '07
Puzzle '18
Silent Night, Deadly Night 5: The Toymaker '91
There's Always Tomorrow '56
The Toy '82
Toy Story '95 ▸
Toy Story 2 '99 ▸
Toy Story 3 '10 ▸
Toy Story 4 '19 ▸
Toys '92
Trolls World Tour '20
UglyDolls '19
Zathura '05 ▸

Tragedy

***See** Drama*

Trailer Parks

8 Mile '02 ▸
Far from Home '89
Going Home '71
High Tide '87 ▸
Killer Joe '11
The Last Starfighter '84
Love and a .45 '94
Meet Monica Velour '10
Mobile Homes '19
Poor White Trash '00
Raising Arizona '87 ▸
Spork '10
The Strangers: Prey at Night '18
A Very Mary Christmas '10

Trains

***See also** Heists: Trains; Subways*

Across the Bridge '57
Agatha Christie's Murder is Easy '82
Around the World in 80 Days '04
Atlas Shrugged: Part 1 '11
Atomic Train '99
Avalanche Express '79
Back to the Future, Part 3 '90 ▸
Before Sunrise '94
Before We Go '14
Berlin Express '48 ▸
Bombay Mail '34
Boxcar Bertha '72
The Brain '69
Breakheart Pass '76
Broken Arrow '95
Cafe Express '83
Cafe Lumiere '05
California Dreamin' '07
Carson City '52
The Cassandra Crossing '76
Closely Watched Trains '66 ▸
Color of a Brisk and Leaping Day '95
The Commuter '18
Courage Under Fire '96 ▸
Dakota '45
Danger Lights '30
The Darjeeling Limited '07 ▸
Denver and the Rio Grande '52
Derailed '02
Detonator '93
The Dirty Dozen: The Fatal Mission '88
The Edge '10
Emperor of the North Pole '73 ▸
End of the Line '88
Eurotrip '04
Exile Express '39
The 15:17 to Paris '18
The Five Man Army '69
Flame Over India '59 ▸
Free Money '99
From Russia with Love '63 ▸
The Fugitive '93 ▸
The General '26 ▸
The Ghost and the Darkness '96
The Ghost Train '41
The Girl on the Train '09
The Girl On the Train '13
The Girl on the Train '16
Go Kill and Come Back '68
Grand Central Murder '42
The Great Locomotive Chase '56
The Great Train Robbery '79 ▸
The Greatest Show on Earth '52 ▸
The Gun That Won the West '55
Hachiko: A Dog's Tale '09
The Harvey Girls '46 ▸
Horror Express '72
Hot Lead & Cold Feet '78
Hugo '11 ▸
I Wish '11 ▸
The Inglorious Bastards '78
Interrupted Journey '49
The Iron Horse '24 ▸
Iron Road '08
It Happened to Jane '59
It's a Big Country '51
The Journey of Natty Gann '85 ▸
La Bete Humaine '38 ▸
La Roue '23 ▸
The Lady Eve '41 ▸
Lady on a Train '45 ▸
The Lady Vanishes '38 ▸
The Lady Vanishes '79
The Lady Vanishes '13
Last Passenger '14
The Legend of Zorro '05
Liliom '30
The Long Summer of George Adams '82
The Lost Valentine '11
The Major and the Minor '42 ▸
Malcolm '86
Man Who Loved Cat Dancing '73
Man Without a Star '55 ▸
The Millionaire's Express '86
The Missing Person '09
Mission: Impossible '96 ▸
Mrs. Winterbourne '96
Murder on the Midnight Express '74
Murder on the Orient Express '74 ▸
Murder on the Orient Express '01
Murder on the Orient Express '10 ▸
Murder on the Orient Express '17 ▸
My Friend Irma Goes West '50
My House in Umbria '03 ▸
Mystery Mountain '34
Narrow Margin '90
The Navigators '01
The Newton Boys '97
Night Passage '57
Night Train '09
Night Train Murders '75
Night Train to Lisbon '13
Night Train to Munich '40 ▸
Night Train to Terror '84
Night Train to Venice '93
The Odyssey of the Pacific '82
The Old-Fashioned Way '34
Once Upon a Time in the West '68 ▸
Other Men's Women '31
The Out-of-Towners '99
The Peacemaker '97
Plunder Road '57
The Polar Express '04
Pride of Africa '97
Prison Train '38
Railroad Tigers '17
Rails & Ties '07
The Railway Man '13
The Rainmakers '35
Red Lights '04 ▸
Repo Chick '09
Return to Cranford '09
Return to Waterloo '85
Rhythm on the Range '36
The Road to Yesterday '25
Rome Express '32
Runaway Train '85 ▸
Running Scared '86
Saratoga Trunk '45
Shanghai Express '32 ▸
Shanghai Express '86
The Silver Streak '34
Silver Streak '76 ▸
Sleepers West '41
Snowpiercer '14 ▸
Some Like It Hot '59 ▸
Source Code '11 ▸
Stand Up and Fight '39
Starman '84 ▸
The Station Agent '03 ▸

Station Jim '01
Strangers on a Train '51 ►
Subway '85
Switchback '97
The Tall Target '51
10,000 Black Men Named George '02
Terror on a Train '53
Terror Train '80
There Goes the Bride '32
Thomas and the Magic Railroad '00
Those Who Love Me Can Take the Train '98
3:10 to Yuma '57 ►
Throw Momma from the Train '87 ►
Tough Guys '86
The Tourist '10
Tracks '76
Trading Places '83
The Trail of the Lonesome Pine '36►
The Train '65►
Train '08
The Train Killer '83
Train Robbers '73
Transsiberian '08►
The Truce '96►
Tube '03
Two Smart People '46
Unbreakable '00
Under Siege 2: Dark Territory '95
Union Depot '32
Union Pacific '39►
Unstoppable '10►
Von Ryan's Express '65►
The Waiting Room '07
Which Way Home '09
While You Were Sleeping '95►
Wild Boys of the Road '33
Without Reservations '46
Zentropa '92
Zhou Yu's Train '02

Transvestites & Transsexuals

See Gender Bending

Trapped with a Killer!

See also Psychotics/Sociopaths

Air Force One '97►
Alien Terminator '95
Alpha Alert '13
Are You Scared 2 '09
ATM '12
Blackout '07
Blind Witness '89
Blink '93
The Butcher '07
BuyBust '18
The Call '13
Clue '85
The Collection '12
Con Air '97►
Condemned '15
Copycat '95
Curve '16
Dead Calm '89►
Deadbolt '92
Devil '10
Don't Breathe '16►
Extremities '86
Eye of the Needle '81
Fall Down Dead '07
Fatal Attraction '87►
Fever '91
Final Justice '94
For Sale By Owner '05
Headless Body in Topless Bar '96
High Tension '03
The Hills Have Eyes '06
The Hoarder '15
The Hunt '20
The Impostors '98
Intruder '16
Kalifornia '93
The Killing Room '09
Kiss the Girls '97
Last Hour '08
Last Passenger '14
Lifepod '93
Lost in the Dark '07
Love Sick Love '12
Malevolence '04
Manhunter '86 ►
Medium Raw: Night of the Wolf '10
Mindhunters '05
Misery '90 ►
Mute Witness '95
Narrow Margin '90
No Way Back '90
Pacific Heights '90 ►
The Penthouse '89
Perfect Hideout '08
Rest Stop '06
Saw '04
See No Evil '06
Serial Slayer '03
The Shallows '16 ►
The Shining '80
The Silence of the Lambs '91 ►
Slaughter of the Innocents '93
Sleep Tight '11
Standoff '16►
Ten Little Indians '75
The Terror '63
Terror in the Mall '98
Terror Train '80
Texas Chainsaw 3D '13
The Texas Chainsaw Massacre: The Beginning '06
31 '16
A Thousand Cuts '12
The Tie That Binds '95
Turbulence '96
Virus '98
Wait until Dark '67►
What's the Matter with Helen? '71
When a Stranger Calls '79
When a Stranger Calls '06
When a Stranger Calls Back '93
Whiteout '09
Witness to Murder '54
You're Next '13

Treasure Hunt

Abbott and Costello Meet the Mummy '55
The Adventures of Tintin '11
After the Storm '01
All the Brothers Were Valiant '53
Allan Quartermain and the Temple of Skulls '08
Alvin and the Chipmunks: Chipwrecked '11
Are You Scared 2 '09
Army of the Dead '08
Arthur and the Invisibles '06
Beethoven's 5th '03
Black Sea '14
Blood Money '17
Cabo Blanco '81
Call of the Wild '93
Captain Calamity '36
Captain Kidd and the Slave Girl '54
City Slickers 2: The Legend of Curly's Gold '94
Coast of Skeletons '63
Comin' Round the Mountain '51
Croczilla '12
Cutthroat Island '95
Dead Mine '12
Diamond Dogs '07
The Diamond of Jeru '01
Diamonds '99
Dollar for the Dead '98
Enemy Gold '93
Escape under Pressure '00
The Fat Spy '66
A Field in England '14►
The Fiend Who Walked the West '58
Fool's Gold '08
Forgotten City '98
Gold '16
Gold Diggers: The Secret of Bear Mountain '95
The Gold Retrievers '10
The Good, the Bad, the Weird '08
The Goonies '85
Greedy '94
Green Fire '55
The Haunted Sea '97
Hear No Evil '93
Holes '03 ►
The House of the Seven Hawks '59
Impasse '69
Inside Out '75
Into the Blue 2: The Reef '09
Into the Blue '05
It's a Mad, Mad, Mad, Mad World '63
The Jack of Diamonds '49
The Jewel of the Nile '85
Kelly's Heroes '70
The Killing Grounds '97
King of California '07
Klondike Fever '79
Kraken: Tentacles of the Deep '06
Kull the Conqueror '97
Kumiko the Treasure Hunter '14►
Labou '07
Lara Croft: Tomb Raider '01
Lara Croft Tomb Raider: The Cradle of Life '03
The Last Adventure '67
The Last Templar '09
The Legend of Fritton's Gold '09
Lewis and Clark and George '97
The Librarian: Curse of the Judas Chalice '08
The Librarian: Quest for the Spear '04
The Librarian: Return to King Solomon's Mines '06
Lost City Raiders '08
Lost Treasure '03
The Lost Treasure of Sawtooth Island '99
The Lost Treasure of the Grand Canyon '08
Lost Treasure of the Maya '08
The Lost Volcano '50
Lust in the Dust '85►
The Man with the Iron Fists '12
Mandrake '10
Mara Maru '52
Mark of the Gorilla '58
The Mermaids of Tiburon '62
Million Dollar Mystery '87
Mortdecai '15
The Mummy '99
Muppet Treasure Island '96
Mutiny Ahead '35
Naked Hills '56
National Treasure '04
National Treasure: Book of Secrets '07
Old Mother Riley's Jungle Treasure '51
One-Eyed Soldiers '67
Operation Condor '91
Pattern for Plunder '62
Pirates of Blood River '62
Pirates of the Caribbean: On Stranger Tides '11
Pirates of Treasure Island '06
Rat Race '01
The Ravagers '65
Red Water '01
Renegades '17
Return to Treasure Island '54
Ringo's Mark of Vengeance '67
Romancing the Stone '84►
Roy Colt and Winchester Jack '70
Rudyard Kipling's The Jungle Book '94
The Rundown '03
Russell Mulcahy's Tale of the Mummy '99
Sahara '05
The Sanctuary '09
Sea Wolf: The Pirate's Curse '05
Secre of the Andes '98
The Secret of Loch Ness '08
The Secret of Monte Cristo '61
Secrets of the Mountain '10
7 Mummies '06
Shadow of Chikara '77
Sinbad and the Minotaur '11
Sinbad, the Sailor '47 ►
Sleepover '04
Slow Burn '00
Tarzan's Secret Treasure '41
Thank you, Mr. Moto '37
There Goes the Neighborhood '92
Thieves of Fortune '89
Tom and Huck '95 ►
Total Dhamaal '19
Treasure Buddies '12
Treasure Guards '11
Treasure Island '34 ►
Treasure Island '50 ►
Treasure Island '72
Treasure Island '89
Treasure Island '99
Treasure Island '12
The Treasure of Jamaica Reef '74
The Treasure of Matecumbe '76
The Treasure of the Amazon '85
Treasure of the Sierra Madre '48►
Treasure of the Yankee Zephyr '83
Treasure Planet '02
Treasure Raiders '07
Trespass '92
The Triangle '01
Undertow '04
Uninvited '93
Whistling in Dixie '42
Wild Ones on Wheels '62
Without a Paddle '04

Trees & Forests

See also Good Earth; Wilderness

Adam's Apples '05
The Adventures of Robin Hood '38►
Alien 3000 '04
Antichrist '09
As You Like It '06
Avatar '09►
The Backwoods '06
Backwoods '08
Bambi II '06
Beauty and the Beast: A Dark Tale '10
Big Trees '52►
Blackwoods '02
Blair Witch '16
Blood Crime '02
Blood Trails '06
The Brothers Grimm '05
The Contract '07
A Crack in the Floor '00
Creep '15
Criminal Lovers '99
Curse of the Witching Tree '15
Dead in the Water '06
Dead Snow '09
Defiance '08
Delhi Safari '12
Deliver Us From Evil '73
Dr. Dolittle 2 '01
Dr. Seuss' The Lorax '12
Dr. Tarr's Torture Dungeon '75
Equinox '71►
Evil Dead '83
Fatal Passion '94
Fear Runs Silent '99
Ferngully: The Last Rain Forest '92
Flu Birds '08
Forest Warrior '95
Frayed '07
The Frozen '12
Furry Vengeance '10
Grizzly Rage '07
Heartwood '98
The Hole in the Ground '19
Hole in the Sky '95
Hoodwinked '05►
The Hunted '03
The Hunter '12
Inferno '01
Into the Forest '16
Invisible '06
It Comes at Night '17
It Waits '05
The Last Broadcast '98 ►
The Legend of Bloody Jack '07
Lemon Tree '08
Lost Holiday: The Jim & Suzanne Shemwell Story '07
The Many Adventures of Winnie the Pooh '77
Mirror Mirror '12
The Monster '16
Motor Home Massacre '05
Murder at Devil's Glen '99
The National Tree '09
Nightmare Man '06
Old Joy '06 ►
Open Season 2 '08
Open Season '06
Out of Time '00
The Passion of Darkly Noon '95
Pete's Dragon '16
Piglet's Big Movie '03
Pokemon the Movie: The Power of Us '18
Poltergeist 2: The Other Side '86
The Poltergeist of Borley Forest '13
A Quiet Place '18►
Rabies '10
Return of the Jedi '83►
Robin Hood: Prince of Thieves '91
The Romance of Astrea and Celadon '07
Rust Creek '19
Sasquatch '02
The Sea of Trees '16
The Secret of Kells '09
Severance '06
Shrooms '07
Simon Says '07
Slender Man '18
Smoke Jumpers '08
Smurfs: The Lost Village '17
Snow White and the Huntsman '12
Soft for Digging '01
Staten Island '09
SuperFire '02
Surviving the Game '94
Tell No One '06►
The Tripper '06
Two Years at Sea '12
Vertigo '58►
The Village '04
The Watch '08
The Watcher in the Woods '81
Where the Rivers Flow North '94
Where the Wild Things Are '09
Wildfire 7: The Inferno '02
Wildling '18
William Shakespeare's A Midsummer Night's Dream '99
Winnie the Pooh '11►
Witchslayer Gretl '12
Without a Paddle: Nature's Calling '09
The Wizard of Oz '39►
The Woods '03
The Woods Have Eyes '07
Wrong Turn '03

Triads

See also China; Gangs

The Art of War '00
Battle Creek Brawl '80
Burning '18►
The Corruptor '99►
Dogwatch '97
The Greasy Strangler '16
Hard-Boiled '92
Infernal Affairs '02►
The Killer '90►
Lethal Weapon 4 '98
The Promise '17
Robin-B-Hood '06
Rush Hour 2 '01
Song to Song '17
Sun Choke '16
Three Identical Strangers '18►
Time and Tide '00
War '07

True Crime

See also Crime & This Is Your Life; True Stories

Abducted: The Carlina White Story '12
Abduction '11
The Adderall Diaries '16
Aileen: Life and Death of a Serial Killer '03 ►
Alpha Dog '06
Amanda Knox: Murder on Trail in Italy '11
American Animals '18 ►
An American Crime '07
American Gangster '07 ►
American Tragedy '00
Amish Grace '10
Among Brothers '05
And Never Let Her Go '01
Angela '02
Ann Rule Presents: The Stranger Beside Me '03
Another Life '01
Appropriate Adult '11
The Assassination of Richard Nixon '05
At Close Range '86►
Awakening the Zodiac '17
The Bank Job '08►
Baseline Killer '08
Beatrice Cenci '69
Bernie '12►
Big Shot: Confessions of a Campus Bookie '02
Billionaire Boys Club '87
Billionaire Boys Club '18
The Black Dahlia '06
Black Widow Murders: The Blanche Taylor Moore Story '93
Blackrock '97
Blackwater Valley Exorcism '06
Blanche Fury '48
The Bling Ring '11
The Bling Ring '13►
Blood and Orchids '86
Blue-Eyed Butcher '12
Bond of Silence '10
Bonded by Blood '09
Bonnie & Clyde '13
Boomerang '47►
Borderland '07
Bordertown '06
The Boston Strangler '68
The Boston Strangler: The Untold Story '08
Boys Don't Cry '99►
BTK Killer '06
Bully '01
Burke & Hare '10
Burnt Money '00
Capote '05►
The Capture of the Green River Killer '08
Capturing the Friedmans '03►
The Case Against Brooklyn '58
Casino Jack and the United States of Money '10
Catch Me If You Can '02
The Cat's Meow '01
Cause Celebre '87►
The Central Park Five '12►
Changeling '08►
Chapter 27 '07
Chicago Joe & the Showgirl '90
Chopper '00
Citizen Gangster '11
Citizen Jane '09
Citizen X '95►
City by the Sea '02
City of God '02
Color Me Kubrick '05
Compliance '12►
Compulsion '59►
Confessions of a Nazi Spy '39
The Craigslist Killer '11
Crazy Love '07►
Crimson Gold '03
Cropsey '10
Crown Heights '17
Dahmer '02
Dark Crimes '16
A Date With Darkness '03

► = rated three bones or higher

The Day They Robbed the Bank of England '60
Deadly Relations '93
Deadly Voyage '96
A Death in California '85
Deep Crimson '96
The Deliberate Stranger '86 ▶
Devil's Knot '14
Dillinger '73
The Disappearance of Vonnie '94
The Dog '14 ▶
Drew Peterson: Untouchable '12
Drug Wars: The Camarena Story '90 ▶
Dummy '79
Echo of Murder '00
Ed Gein '01
Eichmann '07
Escape from Pretoria '20
Essex Boys '99
Excellent Cadavers '99
The Executioner's Song '82
Extremely Wicked, Shockingly Evil and Vile '19
The Face of an Angel '14
The Falcon and the Snowman '85 ▶
A Family of Spies '90
Fatal Desire '05
Fatal Honeymoon '12
Fool's Gold: The Story of the Brink's-Mat Robbery '92
The Forgiven '18
44 Minutes: The North Hollywood Shootout '03
Foxcatcher '14 ▶
From Hell '01 ▶
The General '98 ▶
Getting Gotti '94
The Girl in the Red Velvet Swing '55
A Girl Like Me: The Gwen Araujo Story '06
Gone '10
Gotti '96
Gotti '18
The Great St. Louis Bank Robbery '59
Grimm Love '06
Headless Body in Topless Bar '96
Heavens Fall '06
The Heineken Kidnapping '11
Helter Skelter '76
Helter Skelter Murders '71
The Hillside Stranglings '04
Hollywoodland '06
Holy Rollers '10
The Hunt for the I-5 Killer '11
Hustlers '19 ▶
I Can't Sleep '93
I Know My First Name Is Steven '89
The Iceman '12
Identity Theft: The Michelle Brown Story '04
Imperium '16
The Imposter '12 ▶
In Cold Blood '96
In Her Skin '09
The Infiltrator '16
Intimate Stranger '06
Into the Abyss '11 ▶
The Irishman '19 ▶
Jasper, Texas '03
Johnny 100 Pesos '93
Justice for Natalee '11
Karla '06
Keillers Park '05
Kid Cannabis '14
Kill the Irishman '11
Kill Your Darlings '13
Killer: A Journal of Murder '95
A Killer Among Friends '92
A Killer in the Family '83
Killer Instinct: From the Files of Agent Candice DeLong '03
Kings of South Beach '07
Ladies in Retirement '41
L'Appat '94
The Laramie Project '02 ▶
Lawless '12
The Legend of Lizzie Borden '75 ▶
Let Him Have It '91 ▶
Lies My Mother Told Me '05
The Life Before This '99
A Life Interrupted '07
A Little Thing Called Murder '06
Lizzie '18
Lizzie Borden Took an Ax '14
Lonely Hearts '06
Mad Dog Morgan '76
The Magician '93
The Manson Family '04
Master Spy: The Robert Hanssen Story '02
Masterminds '16
Matthew Shepard Is a Friend of Mine '14
Mesrine: Part 1-Killer Instinct '08
Mesrine: Part 2-Public Enemy Number 1 '08
Midnight in the Garden of Good and Evil '97
Milk '08 ▶
Mrs. Harris '05
Mrs. Soffel '84
Monster '03 ▶
The Mule '18 ▶
Murder in Coweta County '83
Murder in Greenwich '02
Murder in New Hampshire: The Pamela Smart Story '91
Murder in the Hamptons '05
Murder, Inc. '60
Murder on Pleasant Drive '06
Murderous Maids '00
Murph the Surf '75
My Son, My Son, What Have Ye Done '09
The Natalee Holloway Story '09
Neruda '16
The Newton Boys '97
Newtown '16 ▶
Night Stalker '09
Nightstalker '02
Normal Life '96
Nutcracker: Money, Madness & Murder '87 ▶
Obsessed '02
The Old Man & the Gun '18 ▶
On Thin Ice '03
The Onion Field '79 ▶
Operation Eichmann '61
Outlaw Prophet: Warren Jeffs '14
Owning Mahowny '03
Pain & Gain '13
Paradise Lost: The Child Murders at Robin Hood Hills '95 ▶
Paradise Lost 2: Revelations '99 ▶
Paradise Lost 3: Purgatory '11
Party Monster '03
The Pastor's Wife '11
Path to Paradise '97
Patriots Day '17
The People *vs.* Jean Harris '81 ▶
Perfect Murder, Perfect Town '00
Perfect Sisters '14
Phil Spector '13
The Phenix City Story '55 ▶
Point of Origin '02
Prince of Poisoners: The Life and Crimes of William Palmer '98
Prince of the City '81 ▶
Prosecuting Casey Anthony '13
Rampage '87
Rampage: The Hillside Strangler Murders '04
Rapt '09
Rise of the Footsoldier '07
The Riverman '04
Rob the Mob '14
Savage Grace '07
See No Evil: The Moors Murders '06
Sex & Lies in Sin City: The Ted Binion Scandal '08
Shakedown on the Sunset Strip '88
The Sicilian Girl '09
Sister My Sister '94
Snowden '16
The Snowtown Murders '12 ▶
Soldier's Girl '03 ▶
Son of Sam '08
Stalking Laura '93
Stander '03
Starkweather '04
Stolen Holiday '37
Street Boss '09
Strong Island '17 ▶
Student Seduction '03
Summer of Sam '99
Swoon '91 ▶
Taken in Broad Daylight '09
Talhotblond '12
The Terrorist Next Door '08
The Theory of the Leisure Class '01
Till Murder Do Us Part '92
Too Young to Die '90
Torso '02
Tracks '05
Trial by Fire '18
Triple Agent '04
Triple Cross '67 ▶
22 July '18
211 '18
Unthinkable '07
The Untold Story of Emmett Louis Till '05 ▶
Valley of the Heart's Delight '07
Vampire Clan '02
Verdict on Auschwitz: The Frankfurt Auschwitz Trial 1963-1965 '93 ▶
Veronica Guerin '03
We Have Your Husband '11
West of Memphis '12
When the Sky Falls '99
Who Is Clark Rockefeller? '10
Widow on the Hill '05
Winter of Frozen Dreams '08
Wisegal '08
Without Evidence '96
Witness to the Mob '98
Wolf Creek '05
Wonderland '03
The Zodiac '05
Zodiac '07
The Zodiac Killer '71

True Stories

See also This Is Your Life; True Crime

Abandoned and Deceived '95
The Abduction '96
Above and Beyond '53 ▶
The Accused '88 ▶
Adam '83 ▶
Adrift '18
An Adventure in Space and Time '13
The Affair of the Necklace '01
Afterburn '92 ▶
Aftermath '17
Against the Wall '94 ▶
Aileen: Life and Death of a Serial Killer '03 ▶
Aimee & Jaguar '98
AKA '02
Al Capone '59 ▶
The Alamo '60 ▶
Alamo Bay '85
Alive '93
All Eyez on Me '17
All Mine to Give '56
All My Loved Ones '00
All Saints '17
All the King's Men '99
All the President's Men '76 ▶
Alvarez Kelly '66
Amazing Grace '06 ▶
The Ambush Murders '82
Amelia Earhart: The Final Flight '94
An American Haunting '05
American Sniper '14
American Violet '09
The Amityville Horror '79
The Amy Fisher Story '93
And the Band Played On '93 ▶
Andersonville '95 ▶
Andre '94
The Ann Jillian Story '88
Anna and the King of Siam '46 ▶
Anthropoid '16
Antwone Fisher '02 ▶
Any Day Now '12 ▶
Apollo 13 '95 ▶
Archer's Adventure '85
Argo '12 ▶
The Aristocrats '99
The Army of Crime '10
Artemisia '97
The Assassination of Richard Nixon '05
The Assisi Underground '84
At Eternity's Gate '18
Attack on Leningrad '09
The Attic: The Hiding of Anne Frank '88
Au Revoir les Enfants '87 ▶
The Aviator '04 ▶
Awakenings '90 ▶
Away All Boats '56
Baadasssss! '03 ▶
The Baader Meinhof Complex '08
Back to 1942 '12
Backbeat '94 ▶
Bad Blood '81
Bad Bush '09
Badlands '74 ▶
Ballad in Blue '66
The Ballad of Little Jo '93
Balto '95
The Bang Bang Club '10
The Banker '20
The Basketball Diaries '95
Bataan '43
Batkid Begins '15
Battle Hymn '57
Battle in Seattle '07
Battle of the Eagles '79
Battle of the Sexes '17
Beaufort '07 ▶
Beautiful Boy '18
Beautiful Dreamers '92
Behind the Mask '99
Believe in Me '06
The Believer '01
Belle '13
Beloved Infidel '59
Beneath '13
The Bengali Night '88
Bernard and Doris '08 ▶
The Best of Men '12
The Betty Ford Story '87 ▶
Beyond the Blackboard '11
Beyond the Next Mountain '87
Beyond the Sea '04
Big Eyes '14
Big Miracle '12
The Big Red One '80 ▶
The Big Sick '17 ▶
Bill '81 ▶
Bill: On His Own '83 ▶
The Birth of a Nation '16
Bisbee '17 '18
Bitter Harvest '81 ▶
Black Hawk Down '01 ▶
Blaze '18 ▶
Bleed for This '16
The Blind Side '09
Blood Done Sign My Name '10
Bloody Sunday '01 ▶
Blow '01
The Blue Butterfly '04
Bohemian Rhapsody '18
Bombshell '19
Bonanno: A Godfather's Story '99
Bonnie & Clyde '67 ▶
The Boston Strangler '68
The Bounty '84
Boy Erased '18
The Boy Who Harnessed the Wind '19
The Boys of St. Vincent '93 ▶
Breach '07
Breast Men '97
Brian's Song '71 ▶
The Bridge '59
The Bridge at Remagen '69
Bridge to the Sun '61
Bringing Ashley Home '11
Brink's Job '78 ▶
Britannic '00
The Bronx Is Burning '07
Brotherhood of Murder '99
Buddy '97
The Burning Bed '85 ▶
Cabeza de Vaca '90 ▶
Cafe Society '97
Calendar Girls '03
California Dreamin' '07
Call Me: The Rise and Fall of Heidi Fleiss '04
Call Northside 777 '48 ▶
Cambridge Spies '03
Camila '84 ▶
Captain Phillips '13 ▶
Carandiru '03
Carbine Williams '52
Carve Her Name with Pride '58
Castaway '87
Casualties of War '89 ▶
Catch a Fire '06
The Catcher Was a Spy '18
Chameleon Street '89 ▶
Champions '84
Chariots of Fire '81 ▶
Charlie Wilson's War '07
The Chase '91
Chasing Mavericks '12
Chasing the Green '09
Chasing 3000 '07
Chattahoochee '89
Cheaper by the Dozen '50 ▶
Cheaters '00
Cheyenne Autumn '64
The Children Nobody Wanted '81 ▶
The Children of Huang Shi '08
Children of the Night '85
China Cry '91
Choices of the Heart: The Margaret Sanger Story '95
Christabel '89
Christian the Lion '76
Christiane F. '82 ▶
The Christine Jorgensen Story '70
Chronicle of an Escape '06
Chuck '17
Churchill '17
Cinderella Man '05 ▶
Citizen X '95 ▶
City of Life and Death '09
A Civil Action '98
Coach Carter '05 ▶
Coming Through '85
Communion '89
Conspiracy '12 ▶
A Congregation of Ghosts '09
The Conjuring '13 ▶
The Conspirator '10
Conviction '02
Conviction '10
Cool Runnings '93
The Counterfeit Traitor '62 ▶
The Counterfeiters '07 ▶
Courage '86 ▶
The Courage to Love '00
The Court Martial of Billy Mitchell '55 ▶
Cowboy '58 ▶
The Cradle Will Rock '99
Crash Course '00
Crimson Gold '03
The Crossing '00
The Crown Prince '06
Cry Freedom '87
A Cry in the Dark '88 ▶
The Cup '11
The Current War: Director's Cut '19
Dallas Buyers Club '13 ▶
Dance with a Stranger '85 ▶
A Dangerous Method '11
Dangerous Minds '95
Dark Matter '07
Dark Waters '19 ▶
David and Lisa '62 ▶
Day One '89 ▶
The Day Reagan Was Shot '01
Days of Glory '06
DC 9/11: Time of Crisis '04
Dead Ringers '88 ▶
Death of a Centerfold '81
The Death of Adolf Hitler '84
The Death of Richie '76
Declaration of War '11
Decoding Annie Parker '13
Deepwater Horizon '16
Defending Our Kids: The Julie Posey Story '03
Defiance '08
The Deliberate Stranger '86 ▶
Delta Force '86
Denial '16
Deranged '74 ▶
The Devil's Double '11
The Diary of Anne Frank '59 ▶
The Diary of Anne Frank '08
A Different Loyalty '04 ▶
Dillinger '45 ▶
Dillinger '73
Dirty Pictures '00
The Disappointments Room '16
The Dish '00 ▶
The Diving Bell and the Butterfly '07 ▶
The Doctor '91
Dr. Ehrlich's Magic Bullet '40
Dog Day Afternoon '75 ▶
Dolphin Tale '11
Domino '05
Donnie Brasco '96 ▶
Don't Worry, He Won't Get Far on Foot '18
Doomsday Gun '94
The Dove '74
Dreamer: Inspired by a True Story '05
Drugstore Cowboy '89 ▶
Drum Beat '54
The Duchess '08 ▶
Duke '12
Duma '05 ▶
Dunkirk '17 ▶
East-West '99
Eddie Macon's Run '83
Edie in Ciao! Manhattan '72
Edison the Man '40
The Education of Sonny Carson '74
Edward and Mrs. Simpson '80
Egg and I '47 ▶
Eight Below '06
Eight Days to Live '06
Eight Men Out '88 ▶
8 Seconds '94
84 Charing Cross Road '86 ▶
The Elephant Man '80 ▶
Elvira Madigan '67 ▶
Elvis: The Movie '79
The Emerald Forest '85 ▶
Emperor '12
Empire of the Sun '87 ▶
Encounter with the Unknown '75
End of the Spear '06
The End of the Tour '15 ▶
Endangered Species '82
Enemy at the Gates '00
Enemy of Women '44
The Enforcer '51
Enigma Secret '79
Entertaining Angels: The Dorothy Day Story '96
The Entity '83
Erin Brockovich '00 ▶
Escape from Pretoria '20
Escape from Sobibor '87 ▶
Escape: Human Cargo '98 ▶
Europa, Europa '91 ▶
Evel Knievel '72
Evelyn '02 ▶
Everest '07
Every Man for Himself & God Against All '75 ▶
Everyman's War '09
Evil '03 ▶
Execution of Raymond Graham '85
The Executioner's Song '82
Exodus '60 ▶
Experimenter '15
The Explosive Generation '61
The Express '08

▶ = rated three bones or higher

Extraordinary Measures '10
Extreme Justice '93
Fair Game '10 ▶
The Falcon and the Snowman '85 ▶
False Arrest '92
Farewell '09
Farinelli '94
Fast Company '78
Fat Man and Little Boy '89
The Father Clements Story '87
The FBI Story '59 ▶
Fear Strikes Out '57 ▶
Fearless Fagan '52
The Fencer '15 ▶
Fifth Day of Peace '72
Fifty Dead Men Walking '08
50 to 1 '14
The Fighter '10 ▶
Fighting Seabees '44
The Fighting Sullivans '42 ▶
Fighting the Odds: The Marilyn Gambrell Story '05
Filth '08
The Final Season '07
Find Me Guilty '06 ▶
Finding a Family '10
Fire in the Sky '93
Firefighter '86
First Man '18
First Time Felon '97
Fisherman's Friends '19
Fitzcarraldo '82 ▶
Five Minutes of Heaven '09
Flash of Genius '08
The Flemish Farm '43
Florence Nightingale '85
Florence Nightingale '08
The Flowers of War '11
Flyboys '06
The Flying Scotsman '06
For Greater Glory '12
For Love or Country: The Arturo Sandoval Story '00
For One Night '06
Ford v Ferrari '19 ▶
Forever Love '98
Forever Strong '08
Fort McCoy '11
42 '13 ▶
The Founder '17 ▶
Four Days in September '97
Frances '82 ▶
Frankie and Alice '10
Freedom Writers '07
Freeheld '15
Friday Night Lights '04 ▶
The Front Runner '18
Frost/Nixon '08 ▶
Fruitvale Station '13
The Gabby Douglas Story '14
The Game of Their Lives '05
George Wallace '97 ▶
Geronimo '93 ▶
Get Rich or Die Tryin' '05
The Ghost and the Darkness '96
Ghosts of Mississippi '96
Gia '98
Gideon's Trumpet '80
Gifted Hands: The Ben Carson Story '09
Girl Fight '11
The Girl in White '52
The Girl on the Train '09
Girls of the White Orchid '85
The Gleiwitz Case '61
Glory Road '06
Going for Gold: The '48 Games '12
Gold '16
Goldrush: A Real Life Alaskan Adventure '98
Good Evening, Mr. Wallenberg '93
The Good Lie '14 ▶
Good Night, and Good Luck '05 ▶
Goodfellas '90 ▶
Gospa '94
Gracie '07
Gracie's Choice '04
Grambling's White Tiger '81
Grand Theft Parsons '03
Grave Secrets: The Legacy of Hilltop Drive '92
The Great Debaters '07 ▶
The Great Escape '63 ▶
The Great Locomotive Chase '56
The Great Raid '05
The Great Train Robbery '79 ▶
The Greatest Game Ever Played '05
The Greek Tycoon '78
Green Book '18 ▶
Greenfingers '00
Grey Gardens '09 ▶
Grey Owl '99
The Grey Zone '01
Gridiron Gang '06
Guarding Eddy '04
The Guyana Tragedy: The Story of Jim Jones '80
The Guys '02 ▶
Hachiko: A Dog's Tale '09
Hacksaw Ridge '16
Hampstead '19
Hannah Arendt '12
Hard Choices '84 ▶
Hard Lessons '86
Harlan County War '00
The Harmonists '99
The Haunting in Connecticut '09
He Named Me Malala '15
He Walked by Night '48 ▶
The Heart Is Deceitful Above All Things '04
Heart Like a Wheel '83
Heart of a Stranger '02
Heart of the Beholder '05 ▶
Heartland '81 ▶
Heaven Is for Real '14
Heaven Knows What '15 ▶
Heavenly Creatures '94 ▶
Held Hostage '91
Hell to Eternity '60
Hellcats of the Navy '57
Helter Skelter '76
Helter Skelter Murders '71
Henry & June '90 ▶
Henry: Portrait of a Serial Killer '90 ▶
Hidden Figures '17 ▶
Hidden in Silence '96
A Hidden Life '19
Hide in Plain Sight '80 ▶
The Hiding Place '75
Hilary and Jackie '98 ▶
The Hindenburg '75
The Hoax '06
A Home of Our Own '75
A Home of Our Own '93
Homeless to Harvard: The Liz Murray Story '03
Honeymoon Killers '70 ▶
Honor Thy Father '73
Hoodlum Empire '52
The Hoodlum Priest '61 ▶
The Hook '63
The Horse Soldiers '59
The Horses of McBride '12
Hostage High '97
Hostile Waters '97
Hotel Mumbai '18
Hotel Rwanda '04
House of Versace '13
The House on Garibaldi Street '79
How to Lose Friends & Alienate People '08
Howl '10
Hula Girls '06
The Hummingbird Project '18
Hunger '08
The Hunley '99
The Hunter '80
The Hurricane '99 ▶
Hurricane Season '09
Hyde Park on Hudson '12
I Am a Fugitive from a Chain Gang '32 ▶
I Am Michael '17
I Can Only Imagine '18
I Dreamed of Africa '00
I Love You Phillip Morris '10
I Love You to Death '90
I Only Want You to Love Me '76
I Shot Andy Warhol '96 ▶
I, the Worst of All '90
I Was an American Spy '51
I Will Fight No More Forever '75 ▶
Il Divo '08
I'm Dancing as Fast as I Can '82
Mission of Honor '19
The Imitation Game '14 ▶
The Impossible '12 ▶
The Impossible Spy '87 ▶
In a Class of His Own '99
In Cold Blood '67 ▶
In Darkness '11
In Love and War '01
In Pursuit of Honor '95
In the Heart of the Sea '15
In the Line of Duty: Ambush in Waco '93
In the Line of Duty: The FBI Murders '88 ▶
In the Mood '87
In the Name of the Father '93 ▶
In the Time of the Butterflies '01
In Which We Serve '43 ▶
The Incredible Journey of Mary Bryant '05
Indictment: The McMartin Trial '95 ▶
The Infiltrator '95
The Infiltrators '20
Infinity '96
The Informant! '09
Inherit the Wind '60 ▶
Inherit the Wind '99
The Inn of the Sixth Happiness '58 ▶
The Inner Circle '91 ▶
The Innocents '16 ▶
The Insider '99 ▶
The Interrogation of Michael Crowe '02
Interrupted Melody '55 ▶
Into the White '12
Into the Wild '07 ▶
Into Thin Air: Death on Everest '97
The Intouchables '12
Invictus '09 ▶
Invincible '01
Invincible '06 ▶
Iron Will '93
It's Good to Be Alive '74
It's My Party '95
Izzy & Moe '85
Jackie '16 ▶
The Jayne Mansfield Story '80
The Jesse Owens Story '84
The Jesse Ventura Story '99
Jesus Christ, Superstar '73 ▶
JFK '91 ▶
Jimmy P. '13
Jo Jo Dancer, Your Life Is Calling '86
John Rabe '09
Johnson County War '02
Joni '79
Journey of Hope '90 ▶
Joyeux Noel '05 ▶
Judgment in Berlin '88
Julia '77 ▶
Julie & Julia '09 ▶
Just Ask My Children '01
Just Mercy '19 ▶
Justin Morgan Had a Horse '81
K-19: The Widowmaker '02
Kaspar Hauser '93
Katyn '07
The Kid and I '05
Kidco '83
Kill the Messenger '14 ▶
Killer: A Journal of Murder '95
The Killing Fields '84 ▶
A Killing in a Small Town '90 ▶
King of Devil's Island '10
King of the Wind '93
The King's Speech '10 ▶
Kinky Boots '06
Knights of the South Bronx '05
Knute Rockne: All American '40 ▶
Kon-Tiki '12
Kundun '97 ▶
Lady Jane '85 ▶
Ladybird, Ladybird '93 ▶
Land of Mine '15
The Last American Hero '73 ▶
Last Call: The Final Chapter of F. Scott Fitzgerald '02
The Last Place on Earth '85
The Last Shot '04
The Last Supper '76 ▶
The Late Shift '96
Lean on Me '89 ▶
The Least Among You '09
Lee Daniels' The Butler '13
Left to Die: The Sandra and Tammi Chase Story '12
Legend of Boggy Creek '75
The Lena Baker Story '08
Let Him Have It '91 ▶
Lethal Lolita-Amy Fisher: My Story '92
The Libertine '05
Life of a King '13
Life Support '07 ▶
Lightning Bug '04
Lion '16 ▶
Little Boy Lost '78
Little Girl Lost: The Delimar Vera Story '08
Little Heroes '91
Little Laura & Big John '73
Live from Baghdad '03 ▶
Living Proof '08
Longford '06
Longitude '00 ▶
The Longshots '08
Lords of Dogtown '05
Lorenzo's Oil '92 ▶
Lost Battalion '01
Lost Boundaries '49
The Lost Boys '78 ▶
The Lost Child '00
The Lost City of Z '17 ▶
Lost Holiday: The Jim & Suzanne Shemwell Story '07
Love and Rage '99
A Love Divided '01
Love Ranch '10
The Lovers and the Despot '16
Loving '16 ▶
Lumumba '01 ▶
Luna: Spirit of the Whale '07
M. Butterfly '93
Ma Barker's Killer Brood '60
Machine Gun Preacher '11
Mad Dog Morgan '76
Madame Claude '77
Made in Dagenham '10 ▶
Madeleine '50
Madison '01
Madman '79
The Magdalene Sisters '02 ▶
Malaya '49
A Man Escaped '57 ▶
Man On a String '60
The Man Who Captured Eichmann '96
The Man Who Never Was '55 ▶
Mandela and de Klerk '97
The Manson Family '04
Marathon '09
Marie '85 ▶
Marked Woman '37 ▶
Mary Queen of Scots '18
Mary White '77
Mask '85 ▶
Massacre in Rome '73
Mata Hari '32 ▶
Matewan '87 ▶
Max Manus: Man of War '08
Mayerling '36 ▶
Mayerling '68
The McConnell Story '55
McFarland USA '15
Mediterranea '15 ▶
Meek's Cutoff '10 ▶
Megan Leavey '17
Melvin and Howard '80 ▶
Memphis Belle '90 ▶
Men of Honor '00
A Message to Garcia '36
Michael Collins '96 ▶
Midnight Express '78 ▶
A Mighty Heart '07 ▶
The Mighty Macs '09
Million Dollar Arm '14
Miracle '04 ▶
Miracle in Lane Two '00
Miracle of Our Lady of Fatima '52
Miracle Run '04
The Miracle Season '18
The Miracle Worker '62 ▶
The Miracle Worker '79 ▶
The Miracle Worker '00
Miracles From Heaven '16
Miss Evers' Boys '97
Missing '82 ▶
Mission of the Shark '91 ▶
Mrs. Soffel '84
Mr. & Mrs. Loving '96 ▶
Mr. Nice '10
Mockingbird Don't Sing '01
The Molly Maguires '70
Molly's Game '17
Molokai: The Story of Father Damien '99
Money for Nothing '93
Moneyball '11 ▶
The Monuments Men '13
Mope '19
The Morrison Murders '96
Mother Joan of the Angels '60 ▶
Mother of Mine '05 ▶
Mother Teresa: In the Name of God's Poor '97
The Mothman Prophecies '02
Mozart and the Whale '05
Muhammad Ali's Greatest Fight '13
Murder in Coweta County '83
Murder in the First '95
Murder in the Old Red Barn '36
The Murder of Mary Phagan '87 ▶
Murder One '88
Murph the Surf '75
Music of the Heart '99
Music Within '07
Mutiny on the Bounty '35 ▶
Mutiny on the Bounty '62
My Darling Clementine '46 ▶
My Husband's Double Life '01
My Left Foot '89 ▶
My Mother's Courage '95
My Name Is Bill W. '89 ▶
My Own Country '98
My Sister's Keeper '02
My Son, My Son, What Have Ye Done '09
My Week With Marilyn '11
The Nasty Girl '90 ▶
Ned Kelly '03
The New World '05 ▶
The Newton Boys '97
Night Ambush '57
Night Crossing '81
A Night to Remember '58 ▶
The Night We Called It a Day '03
Nightmare at 43 Hillcrest '74
90 Minutes in Heaven '15
96 Minutes '11
The Ninth Day '04 ▶
Nitti: The Enforcer '88
No God, No Master '12
No Man Is an Island '62
Norma Rae '79 ▶
Normal Life '96
North Country '05
North Face '08 ▶
Not Like Everyone Else '06
Not Without My Daughter '90
Nuremberg '00
Nurse Edith Cavell '39 ▶
October Sky '99 ▶
Ode to Joy '19
Of Gods and Men '10 ▶
Official Secrets '19 ▶
Old Gringo '89
On the Basis of Sex '18
On the Outs '05
One Chance '13
127 Hours '10 ▶
One Man's Hero '98
One That Got Away '57 ▶
The One That Got Away '96
The Onion Field '79 ▶
Only the Brave '06
Operation Daybreak '75
Operation Haylift '50
Operation Thunderbolt '77
Operation Valkyrie '04
Opposing Force '87
Oranges and Sunshine '10 ▶
The Ordeal of Dr. Mudd '80 ▶
The Other Side of the Mountain '75
The Other Side of the Mountain, Part 2 '78
Our America '02
Our Brand is Crisis '15
Out of the Ashes '03
Outlaw King '18
The Ox '91
Pack of Lies '87
Papa: Hemingway in Cuba '16
Parkland '13
Passion of Joan of Arc '28 ▶
The Password Is Courage '62
Pat Garrett & Billy the Kid '73 ▶
Paths of Glory '57 ▶
Patton '70 ▶
Patty Hearst '88
The Pentagon Wars '98
The People *vs.* Larry Flynt '96 ▶
The Perfect Game '09
The Perfect Storm '00
The Phenix City Story '55
Philby, Burgess and MacLean: Spy Scandal of the Century '84
Philomena '13
The Pianist '02 ▶
Pinochet's Last Stand '06
Playing for Time '80 ▶
The Plot to Kill Hitler '90
The Positively True Adventures of the Alleged Texas Cheerleader-Murdering Mom '93 ▶
Possessed '00
Prayers for Bobby '09 ▶
The Pregnancy Pact '10
The Pregnancy Project '12
Pressure Point '62 ▶
Pretty Village, Pretty Flame '96 ▶
Prick Up Your Ears '87 ▶
Pride '07
Pride '14 ▶
Pride of the Marines '45 ▶
Primeval '07
Prince of the City '81 ▶
Princess Caraboo '94
The Prisoner of Shark Island '36
A Private Matter '92 ▶
The Prize Pulitzer '89
The Prize Winner of Defiance, Ohio '05 ▶
Prom Queen '04
The Promise '17
Protecting the King '07
PT 109 '63
Puncture '11
The Pursuit of Happyness '06
The Queen '06 ▶
Queen of Katwe '16 ▶
A Question of Attribution '91
Quilombo '84
Rabbit-Proof Fence '02 ▶
Racing for Time '08
Radio '03
Raid on Entebbe '77 ▶
The Railway Man '13
Rated X '00
Reach for the Sky '56
A Real American Hero '78
Rebound: The Legend of Earl 'The Goat' Manigault '96
Recount '08
Red Cliff '08 ▶
Red Dog '11
Red Joan '19
Red Riding, Part 1: 1974 '09
Red Riding, Part 2: 1980 '09
Redacted '07
Reds '81 ▶
Reilly: Ace of Spies '87 ▶
The Report '19
Rescue Dawn '06 ▶

The Return of Martin Guerre '83 ►
Return to Zero '14
Reversal of Fortune '90 ►
Richard Jewell '19 ►
Riding in Cars with Boys '01
Ring of Bright Water '69 ►
Ring of Terror '62
Riot in Cell Block 11 '54 ►
Riot in the Streets '96
River's Edge '87 ►
The Road to Coronation Street '10
Rodeo Girl '80
Rogue Trader '98
Room for One More '51
Rosewater '14
Rosewood '96 ►
Roswell: The U.F.O. Cover-Up '94
Rough Riders '97
Ruby '92
Ruby Bridges '98
Rudy '93
The Rumor Mill '86
Run This Town '20
Runaway Father '91
The Runaways '10
Running Brave '83
Rush '13 ►
Sacco & Vanzetti '71
Safe Conduct '01 ►
Safe Harbor '09
St. Helen's, Killer Volcano '82
The St. Valentine's Day Massacre '67
The Salem Witch Trials '02
Samaritan: The Mitch Snyder Story '86 ►
Same Kind of Different as Me '17
Samurai 1: Musashi Miyamoto '55 ►
Samurai 2: Duel at Ichijoji Temple '55 ►
Samurai 3: Duel at Ganryu Island '56 ►
Savage Messiah '02
Savannah '14
Scandal '89 ►
A Scandal in Paris '46
Scared Silent '02
The Scarlet & the Black '83
Schindler's List '93 ►
Sea Gypsies '78
The Sea Inside '04 ►
Sea Wolves '81
The Search for Bridey Murphy '56
Searching for Bobby Fischer '93 ►
Searching For Sugar Man '12 ►
Seberg '19
The Secret Diaries of Miss Anne Lister '10
Secretariat '10
Selena '96
Selling Hitler '91
Selma '14 ►
Selma, Lord, Selma '99
Separate but Equal '91 ►
Septembers of Shiraz '16
Sergeant York '41 ►
Serpico '73 ►
Serving in Silence: The Margarethe Cammermeyer Story '95 ►
The Sessions '12 ►
Seven Years in Tibet '97
Sgt. Stubby: An American Hero '18
Shackleton '02 ►
Shadow of Fear '12
Shadowlands '93 ►
Shake Hands With the Devil '07
Shake Hands With the Devil: The Journey of Romeo Dallaire '04 ►
Shattered City: The Halifax Explosion '03
Shattered Dreams '90
Shattered Glass '03 ►
Shine '95 ►
Shock and Awe '18
Shooting Dogs '05
A Short Stay in Switzerland '09
Shot in the Heart '01 ►
Shot Through the Heart '98 ►
The Sicilian '87
Sid & Nancy '86 ►
The Siege of Sidney Street '60
Silent Night '02
Silent Victim '92
Silkwood '83 ►
The Singing Nun '66
Sins of the Father '01 ►
Sister Aimee: The Aimee Semple McPherson Story '06
Sisters of War '10
Six Degrees of Separation '93
633 Squadron '64
The Slender Thread '65 ►
Smile '05
A Smile as Big as the Moon '12
Snap Decision '01
Sniper '75 ►
Snowbound: The Jim and Jennifer Stolpa Story '94
So Proudly We Hail '43 ►
The Social Network '10 ►
Soldier Blue '70
The Soloist '09
Something the Lord Made '04
Sophie Scholl: The Final Days '05 ►
Soul of the Game '96 ►
Soul Surfer '11
The Sound of Music '65 ►
Spare Parts '15
Spartacus '60 ►
Spirit Bear: The Simon Jackson Story '05
Spirit of St. Louis '57 ►
Spotlight '15 ►
Springfield Rifle '52
Stan & Ollie '18 ►
Stand and Deliver '88 ►
The Stanford Prison Experiment '15
Star 80 '83
Starved '97
Steve Jobs: The Man in the Machine '15
Stonewall '95 ►
The Stoning of Soraya M. '08
Storm and Sorrow '90
The Straight Story '99 ►
The Stratton Story '49 ►
The Stray '17
Street Smart '87
Stronger '17 ►
Stuck '07
The Sugarland Express '74 ►
Sugartime '95
Sully '16
The Super Cops '74
Swimming Upstream '03
Tag '18
Take the Lead '06
Taken From Me: The Tiffany Rubin Story '10
Taking Chance '09
Taking Sides '01 ►
The Tale '18 ►
Talk to Me '07
Taming Andrew '00
Teamster Boss: The Jackie Presser Story '92 ►
Temple Grandin '10 ►
The Wedding Gift '93 ►
10 Rillington Place '71 ►
Ten Who Dared '60
Tenderness of the Wolves '73
Testament of Youth '15 ►
They Call Me Sirr '00
The Thin Blue Lie '00
The Thin Blue Line '88 ►
Thirteen Days '00 ►
Thirty Seconds Over Tokyo '44 ►
Three Brave Men '57
Three Came Home '50 ►
The Three Faces of Eve '57
The 300 Spartans '62
Three Identical Strangers '18 ►
Three Stripes in the Sun '55
The Tiger Woods Story '98
Time Out '01
Titanic '53 ►
Titanic '96
Titanic '97 ►
To Catch a Killer '92 ►
To End All Wars '01
To Kill a Priest '89
To Write Love On Her Arms '14
Toast of New York '37 ►
Togo '19 ►
Touch the Top of the World '06
Touching the Void '03
Tracks '14
Trial by Fire '18
The Trial of Old Drum '00
The Triangle Factory Fire Scandal '79
Triple Cross '67 ►
Triumph of the Spirit '89 ►
True Confessions '81 ►
True Story '15
Truth '15
The Truth About Jane '00
Tuesdays with Morrie '99
The Tunnel '01 ►
The Tuskegee Airmen '95 ►
12 Strong '18
12 Years a Slave '13 ►
21 '08
24 Hour Party People '01
29th Street '91
Two Came Back '97
Two Men Went to War '02
The Two Popes '19 ►
Unbroken '14
Unconditional '12
Under the Lighthouse Dancing '97
Undercover With the KKK '78
United '11
A United Kingdom '17
United 93 '06 ►
Unknown White Male '05 ►
Unplanned '19
Unshackled '00
The Untold Story of Emmett Louis Till '05 ►
The Upside '17
Valentin '02
Valkyrie '08
Varian's War '01
Vendetta '99
Vengeance Is Mine '79 ►
Vice '18
Victoria & Abdul '17
Victory at Entebbe '76
Video Voyeur: The Susan Wilson Story '02
Violette '78 ►
Voyage of the Damned '76 ►
Waking Up Wally '05
Walking Tall '73
Walking Tall: Part 2 '75
Walking Tall: The Final Chapter '77
Walking with the Enemy '13
The Wall '83 ►
Wallenberg: A Hero's Story '85 ►
The Wannsee Conference '84 ►
War Dogs '16
War Machine '17
The Wave '08 ►
We Are Marshall '06
We Bought a Zoo '11
The Wedding Gift '93 ►
Wedding in Blood '74 ►
Welcome to Marwen '18
Welcome to Sarajevo '97 ►
The Whale '13
What Color Is Love? '08
What's Love Got to Do with It? '93
When Love Is Not Enough: The Lois Wilson Story '10
When the Game Stands Tall '14
Where Are My Children? '94
Whirlygirl '04
The Whistleblower '11 ►
The White Crow '18
White Mile '94
White Mischief '88 ►
The Whole Wide World '96 ►
Why I Wore Lipstick to My Mastectomy '06
Wild '14 ►
Wild America '97 ►
The Wild Child '70 ►
Wild Hearts Can't Be Broken '91 ►
The Wildest Dream: The Conquest of Everest '10
William & Catherine: A Royal Romance '11
William & Kate '11
Winchester '18
With a Song in My Heart '52 ►
Without a Trace '83
A Woman Called Golda '82 ►
Won't You Be My Neighbor? '18 ►
A World Apart '88 ►
World Trade Center '06 ►
The World's Fastest Indian '05 ►
The Wrong Man '56 ►
The Wronged Man '10
You Don't Know Jack '10
You Know My Name '99 ►
The Young Poisoner's Handbook '94 ►
Yours, Mine & Ours '68
Yuri Nosenko, KGB '86
The Zodiac Killer '71
The Zookeeper's Wife '17
Zoot Suit '81 ►
Zulu '64

Twins

See also Brothers & Family Ties

The Absent '11
Adaptation '02 ►
Angels Don't Sleep Here '00
The Attic '06
Bad Company '02
The Bandits of Corsica '53
Basket Case '82 ►
Basket Case 2 '90
Basket Case 3: The Progeny '92
Beautiful Kate '09 ►
Beeswax '09 ►
Big Business '88
Billboard Dad '98
The Boys From Syracuse '40
The Bride with White Hair '93
Brotherly Love '85
Brothers of the Head '06
Chained for Life '51
A Change of Place '94
El Chicano '19
Children of Dune '03
A Cinderella Story '04
Citizen Toxie: The Toxic Avenger 4 '01
Class of Nuke 'Em High 3: The Good, the Bad and the Subhumanoid '94
Cobra Woman '44
Coffee and Cigarettes '03 ►
The Corsican Brothers '42
The Crazysitter '94
Crescendo '69
Dark Side '02
Dead Men Walk '43
Dead Ringer '64
Dead Ringers '88 ►
Despicable Me 3 '17
Devil's Wedding Night '73
Double Double Toil and Trouble '94
Double Impact '91
The Double Life of Veronique '91
Double Trouble '91
Double Wedding '10
The Dreamers '03
The Fat Spy '66
Father Figures '17
The Fifth Musketeer '79
The Forest '16
Freaks '32 ►
Give Me Your Hand '09
The Good Thief '03 ►
Hangman's Curse '03
Haunting Sarah '05
Her Sister from Paris '25
Here Come the Waves '45 ►
Hotel de Love '96
House of Wax '05
How the West Was Fun '95
The Identical '14
Incendies '10 ►
Into the Fire '05
It Takes Two '95
Jack and Jill '11
Jackie '12
Julia's Eyes '10
Leaves of Grass '09
Legally Blondes '09
The Lodgers '17
Look Away '18
Looney Tunes: Back in Action '03
Lost Honeymoon '47
Love and Mary '07
Love! Valour! Compassion! '96
Major League 3: Back to the Minors '98
The Man in the Iron Mask '39 ►
The Man in the Iron Mask '77 ►
The Man in the Iron Mask '97
The Man in the Iron Mask '98 ►
Man with a Gun '95
Maximum Risk '96
Mercy Streets '00
Miracle Run '04
Mirror Images '91
Mrs. Miracle '09
Mother Lode '82
My Guardian Angel '16
The Mystery of Edwin Drood '12
The Myth of the American Sleepover '10
New York Minute '04
Newcastle '08
The Notebook '13
The Nutt House '95
One More Time '70
The Other '72 ►
The Parent Trap '61
The Parent Trap '98
The Parent Trap II '86
Personal Shopper '17 ►
Preaching to the Choir '05
The Pretty One '14
The Prince and the Pauper '07
The Prince and the Surfer '99
Private Property '06
Raising Cain '92
Rebirth of Mothra 2 '97
Rebirth of Mothra '96
Reflections '08
The Reluctant Agent '89
Ripe '97
The Rise of the Krays '16
Road to Paradise '30
Schizopolis '97
Second Sight '99 ►
Seconds Apart '11
Seed of Chucky '04
Simon Says '07
Sinister 2 '15
Sisters '73 ►
The Skeleton Twins '14 ►
The Spiderwick Chronicles '08 ►
Start the Revolution without Me '70 ►
Steal Big, Steal Little '95
A Stolen Life '46
Stuck On You '03
Suburbicon '17
Take Me Home Tonight '11
Take My Advice: The Ann & Abby Story '99
Thicker Than Water '93
Three . . . Extremes '04
Three Identical Strangers '18 ►
The Tiger's Tale '06
To Grandmother's House We Go '94
Tom & Thomas '02
Touching Home '08
12 and Holding '05 ►
Twin Dragons '92
Twin Falls Idaho '99 ►
Twin Sisters '91
Twins '88
Twins of Evil '71
Twinsitters '95
Twitches '05
Twitches Too '07
2 Minutes Later '07
Two Much '96
Una Noche '13
Urban Legends 2: Final Cut '00
Vampire Effect '03
Village of Dreams '97
Wagons Westward '40
White Comanche '68
Wonder Man '45
The Woods Have Eyes '07
The Young Girls of Rochefort '68
You're So Cupid '10

Twister!

See also Disaster Flicks

Alien Storm '12
Category 7: The End of the World '05
Category 6: Day of Destruction '04
The Day After Tomorrow '04
Eye of the Storm '98
F6 Twister '12
Ice Twisters '09
Into the Storm '14
Metal Tornado '11
Night of the Twisters '95
NYC: Tornado Terror '08
Oz the Great and Powerful '13
Places in the Heart '84 ►
Sharknado 2: The Second One '14
Stonados '13
Storm Cell '08
Storm Chasers: Revenge of the Twister '98
Storm Tracker '99
Tornado '43
Tornado! '96
Tornado Valley '09
Twister '96
Where the Heart Is '00
The Wizard of Oz '25
The Wizard of Oz '39 ►

UFOs

See Alien Beings--Benign; Alien Beings--Vicious; Space Operas

Under My Skin

Antibody '02
Eccentricities of a Blonde-Haired Girl '10 ►
Fantastic Voyage '66 ►
Indignation '16
Innerspace '87
A Kind of Murder '16
Osmosis Jones '01
The Rewrite '15
Zero '97

Undercover Cops

See also Crime Drama; Organized Crime

Angel of Destruction '94
Appointment With Danger '51
Assault on Precinct 13 '05
Bad Boys 2 '03
Barrier of the Law '54
The Base 2: Guilty as Charged '00
Beyond Suspicion '00
Beyond the Law '92
Big Momma's House 2 '06
Big Momma's House '00
The Bodyguard 2 '07
Border Incident '49
Break a Leg '03
Brick Mansions '14
Brooklyn's Finest '09
Bullets or Ballots '38 ►
The Case Against Brooklyn '58
City on Fire '87
The Code '09
Con Games '02
The Crooked Web '55
Cruising '80
Cutaway '00

 ► = rated three bones or higher

► = rated three bones or higher

Sucker Free City '05 ▶
Sugar Hill '94
Take the Lead '06
Tapped Out '03
Tar '97
Ten Benny '98
13 Moons '02
This Revolution '05
TKO '06
Training Day '01
Treed Murray '01
Turn It Up '00
Twist '03 ▶
Underground President '07
Urban Crossfire '94
Waist Deep '06
Wassup Rockers '06
Way Past Cool '00
We All Fall Down '00
What About Your Friends: Weekend Getaway '02
White Man's Burden '95
Yelling to the Sky '11
Zebrahead '92 ▶

Urban Gangstas

See also Gangs; Urban Drama

All Eyez on Me '17
Animal '05
Back in the Day '05
Better Dayz '02
Black Dynamite '09
Blood Billz '03
Blood Out '10
Blues '08
Breaking Point '09
Carlito's Way: Rise to Power '05
Charlie '04
Colors '88 ▶
Cradle 2 the Grave '03
A Day in the Life '09
Death Toll '07
The FP '12
Get Rich or Die Tryin' '05
Ghetto Dawg 2: Out of the Pits '05
Ghetto Dawg '02
Guilty by Association '03
Gun '10
Havoc '05
Honor '06
Hood Vengeance '09
In Too Deep '99
Jacked Up '01
Keepin' It Real '01
Krews '10
The Mortician '11
The Next Hit '08
On the Edge '02
Paid in Full '02
Percentage '13
Pimp '18
Rhapsody '01
R.I.C.C.O. '02
Saving God '08
Shot '01
Sin Nombre '09 ▶
Snipes '01
State Property 2 '05
Stryker '04
The Substitute 2: School's Out '97
Thugz '04
Training Day '01
Urban Justice '07
Vincent N Roxxy '17
Waist Deep '06
Wassup Rockers '06
Way Past Cool '00

Urban Legends

The Barrens '12
The Blair Witch Project '99
Blood Night: The Legend of Mary Hatchet '09
Bloody Murder '99
The Bye Bye Man '17
Campfire Tales '98
Candyman 2: Farewell to the Flesh '94
Candyman '92
The Caretaker '08
Cropsey '10
The Curve '97
Dead Man on Campus '97
Don't Leave Home '18
Fragile '05
I Know What You Did Last Summer '97 ▶
I Still Know What You Did Last Summer '98
Nightmares '83
One Missed Call '03 ▶
The Ring '02
Ringu 2 '99
Ringu '98 ▶
River: The Legend of La Llorona '06
Slender Man '18
The Tall Man '12
Urban Legend '98
Urban Legends 2: Final Cut '00
Urban Legends: Bloody Mary '05
Willow Creek '13
The Woods Have Eyes '07

U.S. Marshals

See also Loner Cops; Westerns

American Bandits: Frank and Jesse James '10
Black Patch '57
Burn After Reading '08
Cahill: United States Marshal '73
Circle '10
A Cold Day in Hell '11
Colorado Territory '49
Con Air '97 ▶
Dear Wendy '05
Did You Hear About the Morgans? '09
Eraser '96
The Fighting Lawman '53
Frontier Marshal '39
The Fugitive '93 ▶
Gunfight at the O.K. Corral '57 ▶
Hang 'Em High '67
The Hangman '59
Heaven's Gate '81
High Noon '52 ▶
The Kansan '43
The Last Challenge '67
Law and Order '53
My Darling Clementine '46 ▶
Noose for a Gunman '60
Out of Sight '98 ▶
Outland '81
Ride a Crooked Trail '58
Rooster Cogburn '75
Shutter Island '09 ▶
South of Heaven, West of Hell '00
Texas Rangers '01
Tombstone '93 ▶
True Grit '69 ▶
True Grit '10 ▶
U.S. Marshals '98
The Usual Suspects '95 ▶
Wagons Westward '40
Whiteout '09
Witness Protection '99 ▶
Wyatt Earp '94

USO

See also World War Two

For the Boys '91
Four Jills in a Jeep '44
Pitch Perfect 3 '17
Rock the Kasbah '15
Stage Door Canteen '43

Vacation Hell

Afflicted '14
Aftershock '12
Alive or Dead '08
An American Werewolf in London '81 ▶
And Soon the Darkness '10
Back Road Diner '99
Backwoods '87
Barricade '12
The Beach '00
Berlin Syndrome '17
The Big Alligator River '79
Big Bad Wolf '06
A Bigger Splash '15
Black Demons '91
Black Heaven '10
The Black Waters of Echo's Pond '10
Bond of Fear '56
The Breed '06
Brokedown Palace '99
Bunny and the Bull '09
Burnt Offerings '76
The Cabin in the Woods '12 ▶
Charlie Countryman '13
Chernobyl Diaries '12
Chicago '27
The Cold Light of Day '12
The Comfort of Strangers '91 ▶
Cosmos '16
Crisis '50
Dead in the Water '06
Dead Water '19
Death Do Us Part '14
Deliverance '72 ▶
Devil Wears White '86
Disappearance '02
Donkey Punch '08
Downhill '20
8 Heads in a Duffel Bag '96
Escape From Tomorrow '13
Everyone Else '09
Extraterrestrial '14
The Eye 3 '05
Fantasy Island '20
The Fatal Image '90
The Five '10
Force Majeure '14 ▶
47 Meters Down '17
Frantic '58 ▶
Grotesque '87
The Hills Have Eyes '77
Hollow '11
Hostel '06
Hostel: Part 2 '07
The Impossible '12 ▶
Jack Frost 2: Revenge of the Mutant Killer Snowman '00
Jeopardy '53
Jindabyne '06
Lies I Told My Little Sister '14
The Lodge '19
Magic Magic '13
The Man Who Knew Too Much '34 ▶
The Marine 2 '09
Mary '19
Midnight Express '78 ▶
Midsommar '19
Mr. Bean's Holiday '07
Muck '15
Nature's Grave '08
Nightmare at Bittercreek '91
100 Bloody Acres '12
The One I Love '14
Open Water '03 ▶
Red Lights '04 ▶
Rest Stop '06
Ring of Fire 3: Lion Strike '94
The River Wild '94
The Ruins '08
Run Hide Die '15
Russian Roulette '93
Shark Attack 3: Megalodon '02
Six Days, Seven Nights '98
Snatched '17
Stranded '06
The Stranger Within '13
Summer Camp '16
Taken 2 '12
Target '85
Terror at Red Wolf Inn '72
Terror at Tenkiller '86
Three Peaks '19
Tone-Deaf '19
TripFall '00
Tucker & Dale *vs.* Evil '10 ▶
Turistas '06
Twitch of the Death Nerve '71
2001 Maniacs '05
Urge '16
Us '19 ▶
Vacancy '07
Vanished '06
The Wailer '06
Welcome Home '18
Whispers and Lies '08
Wicked Lake '08
The Willoughbys '20
Wish You Were Here '12
Witchery '88
Worlds Apart '17
You May Not Kiss the Bride '12
You Should Have Left '20

Vacations

The Adventures of Sharkboy and Lavagirl in 3-D '05
Agatha Christie's A Caribbean Mystery '83
Alexandra '07 ▶
American Gothic '88
American Pie 2 '01
An American Werewolf in London '81 ▶
Assassination in Rome '65
Au Pair 3: Adventure in Paradise '09
Babel '06 ▶
Backwoods '87
Bank Holiday '38
Beethoven's 3rd '00
Before Midnight '13 ▶
Beneath the Blue '10
Beyond the Door 3 '91
Blame It on Rio '84
Blended '14
Blondie Takes a Vacation '39
Body Trouble '92
Bread and Tulips '01 ▶
Brokedown Palace '99
Cabin Boy '94
Cairo Time '09
California Dreaming '07
California Suite '78 ▶
Camilla '94
Cancel My Reservation '72
Captain Ron '92
Carry On Abroad '72
Casual Sex? '88
Charlie Chan at the Circus '36
Cheaper by the Dozen 2 '05
Cherry Blossoms '08
Chevalier '15
City Slickers '91 ▶
Claire's Knee '71 ▶
Club Dread '04
Club Med '86
Come September '61
The Comfort of Strangers '91 ▶
Cote d'Azur '05
Couples Retreat '09
The Darkness '16
David's Birthday '09
December Boys '07
Deliverance '72 ▶
Devil Wears White '86
Diary of a Wimpy Kid: Dog Days '12
Dirty Dancing '87 ▶
Dirty Grandpa '16
Disappearance '02
Dodson's Journey '01
The Dog Who Saved Christmas Vacation '10
Don't Drink the Water '69
Don't Make Waves '67
Eating Out: The Open Weekend '11
8 Heads in a Duffel Bag '96
Enchanted April '92
Eurotrip '04
Family Reunion '79
Far from Home '89
A Far Off Place '93
Fast and Furious '39
The Fatal Image '90
Feeders '96
The First to Go '97
Fisherman's Friends '19
Forgetting Sarah Marshall '08
Frank '07
Frankie '19
Frantic '88 ▶
Fraternity Vacation '85
French Fried Vacation '79
From Justin to Kelly '03
Funny Games '97
Gidget Goes Hawaiian '61
Gidget Goes to Rome '63
Ginger and Cinnamon '03
The Girl Getters '66
Girls Can't Swim '99
Girls Trip '17 ▶
A Good Old Fashioned Orgy '11
The Great Outdoors '88
Grotesque '87
Grown Ups '10
Harry and the Hendersons '87
Head Above Water '96
Heading South '05 ▶
The Hills Have Eyes '77
The Hills Have Eyes '06
Hindle Wakes '27
Holiday for Lovers '59
Hollywood, Je T'Aime '09
Home Alone '90 ▶
Home Alone 2: Lost in New York '92
Hot Pursuit '87
Hotel Transylvania 3: Summer Vacation '18
Housebroken '09
The Housekeeper '02
How Stella Got Her Groove Back '98
I Met Him in Paris '37
In the City of Sylvia '07
In the Cool of the Day '63
The Inkwell '94
Inspector Bellamy '09 ▶
Jack Frost 2: Revenge of the Mutant Killer Snowman '00
Just Go With It '11
Just Looking '99
Kevin & Perry Go Large '00
The King Is Alive '00
La Collectionneuse '67
La Piscine '69
Land Ho! '14
Last Holiday '06
The Last of the High Kings '96
Last Summer In the Hamptons '96 ▶
Le Week-End '14
Lena's Holiday '90
Lie Down with Dogs '95
Lies I Told My Little Sister '14
Like It Never Was Before '95
Little Bigfoot '96
Little White Lies '10
The Loneliest Planet '12
The Long, Long Trailer '54
Love and Pain and the Whole Damn Thing '73
Love! Valour! Compassion! '96
The Lunatic '92
Mafioso '62
Magic in the Water '95
Magic Kid '92
Maisie Goes to Reno '44
The Man of My Life '06
The Man Who Knew Too Much '34 ▶
The Man Who Knew Too Much '56
The Mask of Dimitrios '44 ▶
Mr. Hobbs Takes a Vacation '62 ▶
Mr. Hulot's Holiday '53 ▶
Monte Carlo '11
A Month by the Lake '95
Morvern Callar '02
The Muppets '11 ▶
Murder On a Honeymoon '35
My Father, My Mother, My Brothers and My Sisters '99
My Father the Hero '93
My Life in Ruins '09
My Uncle Silas '01 ▶
National Lampoon's Christmas Vacation '89
National Lampoon's Dad's Week Off '97
National Lampoon's European Vacation '85
National Lampoon's Vacation '83 ▶
Nico and Dani '00
Nightmare at Bittercreek '91
Nights in Rodanthe '08
Off Season '01
The One I Love '14
Open Water '03 ▶
The Out-of-Towners '70 ▶
Overkill '96
Paradise for Three '38
Pauline at the Beach '83 ▶
Phat Girlz '06
Ping Pong Summer '14
Queen of Earth '15 ▶
Rain '01
Raising Victor Vargas '03
Red Lights '04 ▶
Ring of Fire 3: Lion Strike '94
The River Wild '94
Rugrats Go Wild! '03
Russian Roulette '93
RV '06
Sex and the City 2 '10
Shark Attack 3: Megalodon '02
Siam Sunset '99
The Sisterhood of the Traveling Pants '05
The Sisterhood of the Traveling Pants 2 '08
Six Days, Seven Nights '98
So This Is New York '48
Someone Great '19
Spider-Man: Far from Home '19 ▶
Spring Break '83
Spring Breakdown '08
Stealing Beauty '96
Still Green '07
Summer Eleven '10
Summer of '04 '06
Summer Rental '85
A Summer's Tale '96
Swimming Pool '03 ▶
The System '64
Target '85
Terror at Red Wolf Inn '72
Terror at Tenkiller '86
That's Not Us '15
Their Own Desire '29
This Time for Keeps '47
To Rome with Love '12
TripFall '00
Twitch of the Death Nerve '71
2 Days in Paris '07 ▶
Two for the Road '67 ▶
Two If by Sea '95
Tyler Perry's Why Did I Get Married? '07
Tyler Perry's Why Did I Get Married Too '10
Under the Eiffel Tower '18
Urge '16
Us '19 ▶
Vegas Vacation '96
Vicky Cristina Barcelona '08
The Wailer '06
A Walk on the Moon '99
The Way Way Back '13 ▶
Week-End in Havana '41
Weekend at Bernie's '89
Welcome to Spring Break '88
Where the Boys Are '84 '84
Where the Boys Are '60
Witchery '88
With a Friend Like Harry '00 ▶
The Wizards of Waverly Place: The Movie '09
You're Only Young Once '37

Vampire Babes

See also Up All Night; Vampires

Addicted to Murder '95
Addicted to Murder 2: Tainted Blood '97
Addicted to Murder 3: Bloodlust '99
American Vampire '97
Argento's Dracula 3D '13
Blade 2 '02
Blood Angels '05
The Blood Spattered Bride '72
Blood: The Last Vampire '09
BloodRayne '06
Bloodrayne: The Third Reich '11
The Brides of Dracula '60
Buffy the Vampire Slayer '92 ▶
Byzantium '12
Captain Kronos: Vampire Hunter '74 ▶
Cold Hearts '99
Count Dracula '77
The Craving '80
Crypt of the Living Dead '73

▶ = *rated three bones or higher*

Daughters of Darkness '71 ►
Dracula's Daughter '36 ►
Elvira's Haunted Hills '02
Eternal '04
Fangs of the Living Dead '68
The Fearless Vampire Killers '67 ►
The Forsaken '01
Fright Night 2: New Blood '13
Fright Night '85
From Dusk Till Dawn '95
From Dusk Till Dawn 3: The Hangman's Daughter '99
A Girl Walks Home Alone at Night '14
The Girl with the Hungry Eyes '94
Habit '97
The Insatiable '06
Interview with the Vampire '94
Jezebeth '11
John Carpenter Presents Vampires: Los Muertos '02
John Carpenter's Vampires '97
The Kiss '88
Kiss of the Damned '12
The League of Extraordinary Gentlemen '03
Lemora, Lady Dracula '73
The Librarian: Curse of the Judas Chalice '08
Life Blood '09
Lips of Blood '75
Lust for a Vampire '71
Lust for Dracula '04
Mary, Mary, Bloody Mary '76
Metamorphosis '07
The Midnight Hour '86
The Moth Diaries '11
Nadja '95 ►
Night Junkies '07
Night of the Sorcerers '70
Once Bitten '85
Prowl '10
Queen of Blood '66
Queen of the Damned '02
Razor Blade Smile '98
Rise: Blood Hunter '07
Samson *vs.* the Vampire Women '61
Saturday the 14th Strikes Back '88
Sergio Lapel's Drawing Blood '99
Sorority House Vampires '95
Stephen King's The Night Flier '96
Suck '09
Tales from the Crypt Presents Bordello of Blood '96
The Thirst '06
30 Days of Night: Dark Days '10
Twins of Evil '71
Ultraviolet '06
Underworld: Evolution '05
Vamp '86
Vampire Academy '14
Vampire Killers '09
The Vampire Lovers '70
Vampire Night '00
Vampires of Sorority Row: Kickboxers From Hell '99
Vamps '12
Vampyres '74
Van Helsing '04 ►
The Velvet Vampire '71
Witchcraft 10: Mistress of the Craft '98
The Witches Hammer '06
Wolvesbayne '09

Vampire Spoof

***See also** Horror Comedy; Vampires*

Andy Warhol's Dracula '74 ►
Beverly Hills Vamp '88
Bloodsucking Bastards '15
Breaking Wind '12
Buffy the Vampire Slayer '92 ►
Dracula Blows His Cool '82
Dracula: Dead and Loving It '95
Dracula *vs.* Frankenstein '71
Elvira's Haunted Hills '02
The Fearless Vampire Killers '67 ►
Hotel Transylvania '12
I Married a Vampire '87
Jesus Christ Vampire Hunter '01
The Little Vampire '00
Love at First Bite '79
The Malibu Beach Vampires '91
Mr. Vampire '86
My Best Friend Is a Vampire '88
Near Dark '87 ►
Netherbeast Incorporated '07
Once Bitten '85
A Polish Vampire in Burbank '80
Pretty Dead Things '06
Rockula '90
Rosencrantz & Guildenstern Are Undead '10
Skeleton Key 2: 667, the Neighbor of the Beast '08
Suck '09
Sundown: The Vampire in Retreat '08
Transylmania '09
Vamp '86
The Vampire Happening '71
Vampire Killers '09
Vampires Suck '10
What We Do in the Shadows '14
Yakuza Apocalypse '15

Vampires

***See also** Up All Night; Vampire Babes; Vampire Spoof*

Abe's Tomb '07
Abraham Lincoln: Vampire Hunter '12
The Absence of Light '06
Addicted to Murder '95
Addicted to Murder 2: Tainted Blood '97
Addicted to Murder 3: Bloodlust '99
Afflicted '14
After Sundown '06
Against the Dark '08
Alien Massacre '67
Alucard '08
Angel of the Night '98
Argento's Dracula 3D '13
Aswang '03
Attack from Mars '88
Avia: Vampire Hunter '05
The Bat People '74
Beast of Morocco '66
Billy the Kid Versus Dracula '66
The Black Room '82
Black Sabbath '64 ►
Blacula '72
Blade 2 '02
Blade '98
Blade: Trinity '04
The Bleeding '09
Blood '09
Blood & Donuts '95
Blood and Roses '61
Blood Freak '72
Blood of Dracula's Castle '69
Blood of the Vampire '58
The Blood Spattered Bride '72
Blood Thirst '65
Blood Ties '92
Bloodlust: Subspecies 3 '93
BloodRayne 2: Deliverance '07
BloodRayne '06
Bloodrayne: The Third Reich '11
Bloodstone: Subspecies 2 '92
Bloodstorm: Subspecies 4 '98
The Bloodsuckers '70
Bloodsuckers from Outer Space '83
Blubberella '11
Bram Stoker's Dracula '92
The Breed '01
The Brides of Dracula '60
Brotherhood of Blood '08
Buffy the Vampire Slayer '92 ►
Byzantium '12
Captain Kronos: Vampire Hunter '74 ►
Children of the Night '92
Cirque du Freak: The Vampire's Assistant '09
Club Vampire '98
Condemned to Live '35
Count Dracula '71
Count Dracula '77
Count Yorga, Vampire '70
The Craving '80
Cronos '94
Crypt of the Living Dead '73
Da Sweet Blood of Jesus '14
The Damned '06
Dark Shadows '12
Dark Town '04
Daughters of Darkness '71 ►
Day Watch '06 ►
Daybreakers '09
Dead Cert '10
Dead Men Walk '43
The Devil Bat '41
The Devil Bat's Daughter '46
Devil's Wedding Night '73
Dracula '31 ►
Dracula Spanish Version '31
Dracula '73
Dracula '79
Dracula A.D. 1972 '72
Dracula: Dead and Loving It '95
Dracula Has Risen from the Grave '68
Dracula Rising '93
Dracula 2000 '00
Dracula Untold '14
Dracula *vs.* Frankenstein '69
Dracula's Daughter '36 ►
Dracula's Great Love '72
Dracula's Last Rites '79
Dracula's Widow '88
Dylan Dog: Dead of Night '11
Elvira, Mistress of the Dark '88
Embrace of the Vampire '95
Evils of the Night '85
Fangs of the Living Dead '68
Female Vampire '73
The Forsaken '01
Freaks of Nature '15
Fright Night 2 '88
Fright Night '85
Fright Night '11
From Dusk Till Dawn '95
From Dusk Till Dawn 2: Texas Blood Money '98
Ganja and Hess '73
Grave of the Vampire '72
Graveyard Shift '87
Habit '97
Heartstopper '92
The Horror of Dracula '58 ►
Horror of the Blood Monsters '70
Hotel Transylvania 2 '15
Hotel Transylvania 3: Summer Vacation '18
House of Dark Shadows '70 ►
House of Dracula '45
House of Frankenstein '44
The House that Dripped Blood '71
Howling 6: The Freaks '90
The Hunger '83
I, Vampiri '56
Immortality '98
Innocent Blood '92
Interview with the Vampire '94
Isle of the Dead '45
John Carpenter's Vampires '97
Kiss of the Vampire '62
The Last Man on Earth '64
The Last Vampire on Earth '10
Legend of the Liquid Sword '93
The Legend of the 7 Golden Vampires '73
Lemora, Lady Dracula '73
Les Vampires '15 ►
Let Me In '10
Let the Right One In '08
Let's Scare Jessica to Death '71
Lifeforce '85
Lips of Blood '75
The Lost Boys '87
Lost Boys: The Thirst '10
Lost Boys: The Tribe '08
Lust for a Vampire '71
Made in Dagenham '10 ►
Manborg '11
Martin '77 ►
Mary, Mary, Bloody Mary '76
Metamorphosis '07
The Midnight Hour '86
Midnight Kiss '93
Modern Vampires '98
The Monster Club '85
The Monster Squad '87
My Son, the Vampire '52
Nadja '95 ►
Near Dark '87 ►
Nick Knight '89
Night Hunter '95
Night Junkies '07
Night of Dark Shadows '71 ►
The Night of the Devils '72
Night of the Sorcerers '70
The Night Stalker '71
Night Watch '04
Nightmare in Blood '75
Nosferatu the Vampyre '79
Not of This Earth '88
Not of This Earth '96
Once Bitten '85
Only Lovers Left Alive '13
Orgy of the Vampires '73
Planet of Blood '66
Planet of the Vampires '65
Priest '11
Project Vampire '93
Prowl '10
Pulse '03
Queen of the Damned '02
Rabid '77
Red Blooded American Girl '90
The Reflecting Skin '91
The Return of Count Yorga '71
Return of the Vampire '43
Return to Salem's Lot '87
Rise: Blood Hunter '07
Rosencrantz & Guildenstern Are Undead '10
Salem's Lot '79
Salem's Lot '04
Samson *vs.* the Vampire Women '61
The Satanic Rites of Dracula '73
The Scars of Dracula '70
Scream Blacula Scream '73
7 Mummies '06
Shadow of the Vampire '00 ►
ShadowZone: The Undead Express '96
The Shed '19
Slayer '06
Sleepwalkers '92
Son of Dracula '43 ►
Sorority House Vampires '95
Stake Land '10
Stephen King's The Night Flier '96
The Stranger '15
Subspecies '90
Suck '09
Sundown '91
Tainted '98
Tale of a Vampire '92
Tales from the Crypt Presents Bordello of Blood '96
Tales of an Ancient Empire '11
A Taste of Blood '67
Taste the Blood of Dracula '70
Teenage Space Vampires '99
Teeth and Blood '15
Theatre of Death '67
Thirst '79
The Thirst '06
Thirst '09 ►
The Thirsty Dead '74
30 Days of Night '07
30 Days of Night: Dark Days '10
The Thompsons '12
To Die For '89
To Sleep with a Vampire '92
Track of the Vampire '66
Transylvania Twist '89
Twilight '08
The Twilight Saga: Breaking Dawn, Part 1 '11
The Twilight Saga: Breaking Dawn, Part 2 '12
The Twilight Saga: Eclipse '10
The Twilight Saga: New Moon '09
Twins of Evil '71
Ultraviolet '98
Uncle Was a Vampire '59
Underworld '03
Underworld: Awakening '12
Underworld: Blood Wars '16
Underworld: Evolution '05
Underworld: Rise of the Lycans '09
The Unearthing '93
Vamp '86
Vampire Academy '14
Vampire Assassin '05
Vampire at Midnight '88
The Vampire Bat '32
Vampire Circus '71
Vampire Effect '03
The Vampire Happening '71
The Vampire Hookers '78
Vampire in Brooklyn '95
Vampire Journals '96
The Vampire Lovers '70
Vampirella '96
Vampire's Kiss '88 ►
Vampyr '31 ►
Vampyres '74
Van Helsing '04 ►
The Velvet Vampire '71
Vlad '03
The Werewolf *vs.* the Vampire Woman '70
What We Do in the Shadows '14
The Wicked '89
Witchcraft 7: Judgement Hour '95
The Witches Hammer '06
Wolvesbayne '09
Zoltan. . . Hound of Dracula '78

Vaudeville

Babes in Arms '39
Broadway Melody '29
Chicago '02 ►
The Daughter of Rosie O'Grady '50
The Dolly Sisters '46
For Me and My Gal '42
Gypsy '62 ►
Harry & Walter Go to New York '76
Holiday Inn '42 ►
The I Don't Care Girl '53
Look for the Silver Lining '49
Mother Wore Tights '47 ►
The Seven Little Foys '55 ►
Show Business '44 ►
The Sunshine Boys '75 ►
Variety Lights '51 ►
Yankee Doodle Dandy '42 ►

Venice

***See also** Italy*

Assassination in Rome '65
Blame It on the Bellboy '92
The Bloodstained Shadow '78
Bread and Tulips '01 ►
Brideshead Revisited '08
Casanova '05 ►
Casanova '05
Children of the Century '99
The Comfort of Strangers '91 ►
Dangerous Beauty '98 ►
Death in Venice '71 ►
Don't Look Now '73 ►
Eternal '04
Everyone Says I Love You '96 ►
A Few Days in September '06
The Honeymoon Machine '61
Indiana Jones and the Last Crusade '89 ►
The Italian Job '03 ►
The League of Extraordinary Gentlemen '03
A Little Romance '79 ►
Marco Polo '07
The Merchant of Venice '04 ►
Night Train to Venice '93
Only You '94
Othello '65 ►
Othello '95 ►
Panic Button '62
A Secret Affair '99
Summertime '55 ►
The Thief Lord '06
This Is the Night '32
Tonight or Never '31
The Tourist '10
2 Days in Paris '07 ►
Unforgivable '11
The Venetian Affair '67
Venice, Venice '92
Walk, Don't Run '66
Who Saw Her Die? '72
The Wings of the Dove '97 ►

Veterans

***See also** Postwar*

The A-Team '10 ►
The Accursed '57
Act of Violence '48
Acts of Violence '18
Air Force One '97 ►
Alamo Bay '85
Alpha Alert '13
American Eagle '90
Americana '81
Amira & Sam '15 ►
Angels from Hell '68
Apartment for Peggy '48
Armored '09
Article 99 '92
Ashes and Embers '82
Avatar '09 ►
The Back Trail '24
Backfire '50
Backfire '88
Bad Company '72 ►
The Ballad of Andy Crocker '69
The Best of Men '12
The Best Years of Our Lives '46 ►
Billy Jack '71
Birds of Prey '72
Birdy '84 ►
Black Rock '12
The Black Six '74
Born for Hell '76
Born to Ride '11
The Boss '56
Braddock: Missing in Action 3 '88
Brothers '09
Bug '06
The Bushwackers '52
Bushwick '17
The Cage '89
Cannibal Apocalypse '80
Charms '73
Chattahoochee '89
Child Bride of Short Creek '81
Children of the Corn '09
Citizen Gangster '11
Colonel Effingham's Raid '45
Combat Shock '84
Conspiracy '08
Crimson Gold '03
The Crooked Web '55
Cry of the Innocent '80 ►
Da 5 Bloods '20
Dark Heart '06
Diablo '16
Disorder '16
Distant Thunder '88
A Dog Named Christmas '09
Donnybrook '18
The Dry Land '10
The Duelist '16
Duke '12
The Enchanted Cottage '45
Fear '88
The Fearmakers '58
Fireback '78

► = rated three bones or higher

Veterinarians

See also Cats; Doctors & Farm Livin'; King of Beasts (Dogs)

Videogames

Vietnam War

See also Postwar; POW/MIA

Vigilantes

See also Revenge

Vikings

Virtual Reality

See also Computers; Technology-Rampant

Viva Las Vegas!

See also Gambling

▸ = rated three bones or higher

Miss Congeniality 2: Armed and Fabulous *'05*
My Blueberry Nights *'07*
My Friend Irma Goes West *'50*
Nature of the Beast *'94*
The Night Stalker *'71*
Ocean's 11 *'60*
Ocean's Eleven *'01* ▶
Painting the Clouds With Sunshine *'51*
Paul Blart: Mall Cop 2 *'15*
Play It to the Bone *'99*
Player 5150 *'08*
Rain Man *'88* ▶
The Rat Pack *'98*
Rat Race *'01*
Rock-a-Doodle *'92*
R.S.V.P. *'02*
The Runner *'99*
Rush Hour 2 *'01*
Saint John of Las Vegas *'09*
Sex & Lies in Sin City: The Ted Binion Scandal *'08*
The Showgirl Murders *'95*
Showgirls *'95*
Sister Act *'92*
Six-String Samurai *'98*
Sky Full of Moon *'52*
Sparkler *'99*
Speedway Junky *'99*
Starman *'84* ▶
Stealing Las Vegas *'12*
Step Up: All In *'14*
Stripshow *'95*
Sugartime *'95*
Swingers *'96* ▶
Sword of Honor *'94*
They Came to Rob Las Vegas *'68*
Think Like a Man Too *'14*
Think of Me *'11*
Three Days to Vegas *'07*
3000 Miles to Graceland *'01*
Tomcats *'01*
21 *'08*
Two for the Money *'05*
Up Against the Eight Ball *'04*
Vampirella *'96*
The Vegas Strip Wars *'84*
Vegas Vacation *'96*
Vegas Vice *'94*
Venus and Vegas *'10*
Very Bad Things *'98*
Viva Las Vegas *'63*
Wedding Bell Blues *'96*
What Happens in Vegas *'08*
Where It's At *'69*
The Wild Card *'03*
Wild Card *'15*
The Winner *'96*
Yonkers Joe *'08*

Volcanos

***See also** Disaster Flicks*

Alvin and the Chipmunks: Chipwrecked *'11*
Apocalypse Pompeii *'14*
Behemoth *'11*
Bird of Paradise *'51*
Dante's Peak *'97*
Descent *'05*
The Devil at 4 O'Clock *'61*
Disaster Zone: Volcano in New York *'06*
Ginostra *'02*
The Happiness of the Katakuris *'01*
Her Jungle Love *'38*
Into the Inferno *'16* ▶
Joe Versus the Volcano *'90*
Journey 2: The Mysterious Island *'12*
Journey to the Center of the Earth *'93*
Jules Verne's Mysterious Island *'10*
Jurassic World: Fallen Kingdom *'18*
Krakatoa East of Java *'69*
Last Days of Pompeii *'35*
The Last Days of Pompeii *'60*
The Last Days of Pompeii *'84*
The Lost Volcano *'50*
Magma: Volcanic Disaster *'06*
Miami Magma *'11*
Pompeii *'14*
Pterodactyl *'05*
St. Helen's, Killer Volcano *'82*
The Skin *'81*
Super Eruption *'11*
Terror Peak *'03*
Untamed Women *'52*
Volcano *'97*
Waikiki Wedding *'37* ▶
When Time Ran Out *'80*
The Wrath of the Gods *'14*

Volleyball

Air Bud 5: Buddy Spikes Back *'03*
Airplane *vs.* Volcano *'14*
Beach Kings *'08*
Cast Away *'00* ▶
Impact Point *'08*
The Iron Ladies 2 *'03*
The Iron Ladies *'00*
Meet the Parents *'00* ▶
Miles *'17*
The Miracle Season *'18*
Side Out *'90*
South Beach Academy *'96*
Superdad *'73*
Top Gun *'86*

Voodoo

***See also** Occult*

Angel Heart *'87*
Asylum *'72*
Black Demons *'91*
Blues Brothers 2000 *'98*
Caribe *'87*
Eve's Bayou *'97* ▶
Hatchet 2 *'10*
The House on Skull Mountain *'74*
How to Stuff a Wild Bikini *'65*
I Eat Your Skin *'64*
I Walked with a Zombie *'43* ▶
Jonah Hex *'10*
Jungle Drums of Africa *'53*
Live and Let Die *'73*
London Voodoo *'04*
Marked for Death *'90*
Naked Evil *'66*
Needle *'10*
The Offspring *'87*
Plague of the Zombies *'66*
The Possession of Joel Delaney *'72*
Scream Blacula Scream *'73*
The Serpent and the Rainbow *'87*
The Snake People *'68*
Sugar Hill *'74*
Tales from the Crypt Presents Ritual *'02*
Tales from the Hood *'95*
Theatre of Death *'67*
Vanished *'06*
Venom *'05*
Voodoo *'95*
Voodoo Academy *'00*
Voodoo Dawn *'89*
Voodoo Dawn *'99*
Voodoo Possession *'14*
Weekend at Bernie's 2 *'93*
Zombi Child *'20*

Vote for Me!

***See also** Capitol Capers*

Ada *'61*
The Adjustment Bureau *'11*
An African Election *'11*
All the King's Men *'06*
Annie *'14*
The Big Brass Ring *'99*
Bobby *'06*
Bulworth *'98* ▶
The Campaign *'12*
The Candidate *'72* ▶
Choose Connor *'07*
Citizen Duane *'06*
The Contract *'98*
Dark Metropolis *'10*
Definitely, Maybe *'08* ▶
Deterrence *'00*
Election *'99* ▶
Fairfield Road *'10*
A Family Affair *'37*
A Fever In the Blood *'61*
Four More Years *'10*
The Front Runner *'18*
Game Change *'12*
G.B.H. *'91*
Get Yourself a College Girl *'64*
Girl Crazy *'32*
The Good Witch's Family *'11*
Goodbye My Fancy *'51*
The Growing Pains Movie *'00*
Hard to Kill *'89*
Head of State *'03*
Homicide: The Movie *'00*
The Ides of March *'11*
If I'm Lucky *'46*
JFK: Reckless Youth *'93*
Just for Fun *'63*
The Kennedys *'11*
The Last Debate *'00*
Legacy *'10*
Life Begins at Forty *'35*
A Lion Is in the Streets *'53* ▶
Long Shot *'19*
Machete *'10*
Maid in Manhattan *'02*
Mail to the Chief *'00*
The Makeover *'13*
Malibu's Most Wanted *'03*
Man of the Year *'06*
The Manchurian Candidate *'62* ▶
Me & Mrs. Jones *'02*
Menno's Mind *'96*
No *'12*
Old Mother Riley, MP *'39*
Politics *'31*
Poster Boy *'04*
Primary Colors *'98*
The Purge: Election Year *'16*
Race *'99*
Random Hearts *'99*
Recount *'08*
Reform Girl *'33*
The Reformer and the Redhead *'50*
Remember the Day *'41*
The Rise and Rise of Michael Rimmer *'70*
Running Mates *'00*
The Seduction of Joe Tynan *'79*
Slow Burn *'05*
Southland Tales *'06*
Swing Vote *'08*
Thanks a Million *'35*
31 North 62 East *'09*
The Trojan Horse *'08*
An Unreasonable Man *'06* ▶
Waking the Dead *'00*

Wagon Train

***See also** Military Westerns; Westerns*

Bend of the River *'52* ▶
The Big Trail *'30* ▶
The Command *'54*
Davy Crockett, Indian Scout *'50*
The Donner Party *'09*
Fighting Caravans *'31*
Fort Osage *'51*
The Hallelujah Trail *'65*
The Indian Fighter *'55* ▶
Kit Carson *'40*
Meek's Cutoff *'10* ▶
The Outriders *'50*
The Paleface *'48* ▶
September Dawn *'07*
Seven Alone *'75*
Silverado *'85* ▶
Solaris *'02*
Stolen Women, Captured Hearts *'97*
Wackiest Wagon Train in the West *'77*
Wagon Master *'50* ▶
Wagons East *'94*
Wagons West *'52*

Waiters & Waitresses

About Adam *'00*
According to Greta *'08*
Alice Doesn't Live Here Anymore *'74*
Alien Trespass *'09*
All We Had *'16*
Along Came Polly *'04*
Amelie *'01* ▶
Anything But Love *'02*
Apres-Vous *'03*
Arthur *'81* ▶
As Good As It Gets *'97* ▶
Ask the Dust *'06*
Atlantic City *'81* ▶
Avenue Montaigne *'06*
Betrayed *'44*
Bikini Bistro *'94*
Brighton Rock *'10*
Bug *'06*
Burlesque *'10*
Caffeine *'06*
Celebrity *'98* ▶
A Christmas Wish *'11*
Code Name: The Cleaner *'07*
Coffee and Cigarettes *'03* ▶
The Cooler *'03* ▶
Coyote Ugly *'00*
Dancer, Texas-Pop. 81 *'98* ▶
Dream for an Insomniac *'96*
Duets *'00*
East Side Story *'07*
Edmond *'05*
The Embalmer *'03* ▶
Eye of God *'97* ▶
Fallen Angel *'45*
Fear and Loathing in Las Vegas *'98*
Feed the Fish *'09*
Feeling Minnesota *'96*
Five Easy Pieces *'70* ▶
The 4th Tenor *'02*
Fragments *'08*
Frankie and Johnny *'91* ▶
Gloomy Sunday *'02* ▶
God Bless the Broken Road *'18*
Goodbye Baby *'07*
Hard Eight *'96* ▶
Having a Wonderful Time *'38*
Heavy *'94* ▶
Hide Away *'11*
Highway Hitcher *'98*
Holiday in Handcuffs *'07*
A Horrible Way to Die *'10*
Hysterical Blindness *'02*
I Served the King of England *'07* ▶
In the Weeds *'00*
It Could Happen to You *'94*
Just a Kiss *'02*
The Killing Jar *'10*
Legion *'10*
Love on the Side *'04*
The Machinist *'04*
Million Dollar Baby *'04* ▶
Monster Party *'18*
Monster's Ball *'01* ▶
Moon over Miami *'41* ▶
Moontide *'42*
The Muppets Take Manhattan *'84* ▶
My Blueberry Nights *'07*
My Girlfriend's Boyfriend *'10*
Mystic Pizza *'88* ▶
No Looking Back *'98*
Not Another B Movie *'10*
Nurse Betty *'00* ▶
The Off Hours *'11*
Office Space *'98*
One Girl's Confession *'53*
Osso Bucco *'08*
The Postman Always Rings Twice *'46* ▶
The Postman Always Rings Twice *'81*
Protocol *'84*
Pure Danger *'96*
The Purple Rose of Cairo *'85* ▶
Quiet Days in Hollywood *'97*
The Red Mill *'27*
Remember Sunday *'13*
Restaurant *'98*
Return to Me *'00*
The Runner *'99*
Salem's Lot *'04*
A Season for Miracles *'99*
The Secret Six *'31* ▶
Sex and Lucia *'01*
Shadow of Fear *'12*
Shaft *'00* ▶
Shopworn *'32*
Skipped Parts *'00*
The Slammin' Salmon *'09*
Sliding Doors *'97*
Spin *'07*
The Spitfire Grill *'95*
Still Waiting *'08*
A Summer's Tale *'96*
Support the Girls *'18*
Swedish Auto *'06*
Swimming *'00*
Tennessee *'08*
Thelma & Louise *'91* ▶
Time to Leave *'05* ▶
Unbeatable Harold *'06*
Untamed Heart *'93*
Waiting *'00*
Waiting *'05*
The Waiting Game *'99*
Waitress *'81*
Waitress *'07* ▶
Weather Girl *'09*
Wedding Daze *'06*
The Wedding Singer *'97*
White Palace *'90*
Wisegirls *'02*

Wall Street

***See also** Corporate Shenanigans*

American Psycho *'99*
Arbitrage *'12* ▶
The Big Short *'15* ▶
Boiler Room *'00* ▶
The Bonfire of the Vanities *'90*
Clancy in Wall Street *'30*
Cosmopolis *'12* ▶
Criminal Activities *'15*
Equity *'16*
Family Man *'00*
For Pete's Sake *'74*
From the Terrace *'60*
The Good Guy *'10*
Limitless *'11*
Nothing But the Truth *'41*
Toast of New York *'37* ▶
Trading Places *'83*
The Two Mr. Kissels *'08*
Wall Street *'87* ▶
The Wheeler Dealers *'63* ▶
The Wolf of Wall Street *'13* ▶
The Women on the Sixth Floor *'10*
Working Girl *'88* ▶

War Between the Sexes

***See also** Divorce; Marriage; Singles*

About Last Night. . . *'86* ▶
Adam's Rib *'50* ▶
Addicted to Love *'96*
The African Queen *'51* ▶
All of Me *'84*
All Tied Up *'92*
Always *'85* ▶
Anchorman: The Legend of Ron Burgundy *'04*
Anchorman 2: The Legend Continues *'13*
Annie Hall *'77* ▶
Around the World Under the Sea *'65*
The Awful Truth *'37* ▶
Baby on Board *'08*
The Ballad of the Sad Cafe *'91*
Basic Training *'86*
Battle of the Sexes *'28*
The Beguiled *'17*
Behind Office Doors *'31*
Berlin Syndrome *'17*
The Best Intentions *'92* ▶
The Bigamist *'53*
Black Moon *'75*
Blood and Sand *'41* ▶
The Bodyguard *'92*
Bonnie's Kids *'73*
Boomerang *'92*
The Bride Walks Out *'36*
Brief Interviews With Hideous Men *'09*
Bringing Up Baby *'38* ▶
Buffalo Jump *'90* ▶
Bull Durham *'88* ▶
Cannibal Women in the Avocado Jungle of Death *'89*
Carmen *'83* ▶
Carmen Jones *'54* ▶
Carry On Cabby *'63*
Carry On Nurse *'59*
Casablanca *'42* ▶
Casanova's Big Night *'54*
Castaway *'87*
Casual Sex? *'88*
Chained *'34*
Cruel Intentions *'98*
The Cry of the Owl *'87*
The Cutting Edge *'92*
Dangerous Liaisons *'60*
Def Jam's How to Be a Player *'97*
Designing Woman *'57* ▶
Disclosure *'94*
Divorce His, Divorce Hers *'72*
Divorce-Italian Style *'62* ▶
Dogfight *'91* ▶
Dream Wife *'53*
Easy Wheels *'89*
Far and Away *'92*
The Favor *'92*
Fever *'91*
First Monday in October *'81*
The First to Go *'97*
The First Wives Club *'96*
Forever Darling *'56*
Forget Paris *'95*
Frankie and Johnny *'91* ▶
Front Page Woman *'35*
Gone with the Wind *'39* ▶
The Good Father *'87* ▶
Goodbye Love *'34*
Guarding Tess *'94*
The Happy Ending *'69*
He Said, She Said *'91*
Heartburn *'86* ▶
His Girl Friday *'40* ▶
Housesitter *'92*
I Live My Life *'35*
I Love Trouble *'94*
In the Good Old Summertime *'49* ▶
In the Line of Fire *'93* ▶
Irreconcilable Differences *'84*
It Happened One Night *'34* ▶
The Jewel of the Nile *'85*
Juliet of the Spirits *'65* ▶
Just Tell Me What You Want *'80*
The King and I *'56* ▶
Kiss Me Kate *'53* ▶
Kramer *vs.* Kramer *'79* ▶
L.A. Story *'91* ▶
The Lady Says No *'51*
The Last Woman on Earth *'61*
Legion of Iron *'90*
Lily in Love *'85*
The Lion in Winter *'68* ▶
Love Crazy *'41* ▶
Love in the Afternoon *'57*
Love Nest *'51*
Lover Come Back *'61*
Lucky Partners *'40*
Manhattan *'79* ▶
Many Rivers to Cross *'55*
Maria's Lovers *'84*
The Marriage of Maria Braun *'79* ▶
The Marrying Man *'91*
Maverick *'94*
McLintock! *'63* ▶
A Midsummer Night's Dream *'35* ▶
A Midsummer Night's Dream *'96*
Mike and Dave Need Wedding Dates *'16*
Moonlighting *'85*
Moonstruck *'87* ▶
Mortal Thoughts *'91*
Much Ado about Nothing *'93* ▶
Murphy's Law *'86*
My Brilliant Career *'79* ▶
A New Leaf *'71*
9 to 5 *'80*
Nothing in Common *'86*
The Opposite Sex and How to Live With Them *'93*
Pat and Mike *'52* ▶
Pauline at the Beach *'83* ▶
A Piece of Pleasure *'74* ▶
Pillow Talk *'59* ▶
Places in the Heart *'84* ▶
Private Lives *'31* ▶
Prizzi's Honor *'85* ▶
Public Enemy *'31* ▶
Queen of Outer Space *'58*
The Quiet Man *'52* ▶
Ramrod *'47*
The Ref *'93* ▶

▶ = *rated three bones or higher*

Romancing the Stone '84 ►
Rooster Cogburn '75
Running Mates '92 ►
Sabrina '54 ►
Sabrina '95
Scenes from a Mall '91
Seance on a Wet Afternoon '64 ►
Serious Moonlight '09
She-Devil '89
Shore Leave '25 ►
Siberian Lady Macbeth '61 ►
The Single Standard '29
Someone Like You '01
Speechless '94
Spies, Lies and Naked Thighs '91
Star 80 '83
Sufat Chol '16 ►
Summer Night with Greek Profile, Almond Eyes & Scent of Basil '87
Swept Away '02
Switch '91 ►
Switching Channels '88
The Taint '10
The Taming of the Shrew '29
The Taming of the Shrew '67 ►
A Taxing Woman '87 ►
Teacher's Pet '58 ►
Ted & Venus '93
That Awkward Moment '14
That Old Feeling '96
Thelma & Louise '91 ►
The Thing '51 ►
Thor and the Amazon Women '60
Three of Hearts '93
Tiger and the Pussycat '67
To Have & Have Not '44 ►
To Wong Foo, Thanks for Everything, Julie Newmar '95
Tony Draws a Horse '51
True Love '89 ►
Two Weeks Notice '02
The Ugly Truth '09
The War of the Roses '89 ►
What Women Want '10
When Harry Met Sally. . . '89 ►
When Ladies Meet '41
When Women Lost Their Tails '75
Who's Afraid of Virginia Woolf? '66 ►
Wife Versus Secretary '36 ►
The Witches of Eastwick '87
Without Love '45
Without Men '11
Woman of the Year '42 ►
Women & Men: In Love There Are No Rules '91
Women & Men: Stories of Seduction '90
Women on the Verge of a Nervous Breakdown '88 ►
Women *vs.* Men '02
The World According to Garp '82 ►
Year of the Comet '92
Yesterday, Today and Tomorrow '64 ►
Your Friends & Neighbors '98 ►
You're a Big Boy Now '66 ►

War Brides

See also *Marriage; Marriages of Convenience; Vietnam War; World War One; World War Two*

Bride Flight '08
Heaven and Earth '93
I Was a Male War Bride '49 ►
Japanese War Bride '52
John Loves Mary '48
Sayonara '57 ►
The War Bride '01

War, General

See also *Anti-War War Movies; Big Battles; Civil War; Korean War; Persian Gulf/Iraq War; Postwar; POW/MIA; Revolutionary War; Terrorism; Veterans; Vietnam War; World War One; World War Two*

The Alamo '60 ►
The Alamo: Thirteen Days to Glory '87
Alexander '04
Alexander Nevsky '38 ►
Alexander the Great '55
Alexandra '07 ►
And Starring Pancho Villa as Himself '03 ►
Anna Karenina '48
Armadillo '11
Atlas '60
The Avenger '62
Ballad of a Soldier '60 ►
Bang Rajan '00 ►
Barb Wire '96
The Battle of Algiers '66 ►
Battle of Jangsari '19
Battle of the Warriors '06
The Beast '88
Beasts of No Nation '15
Beau Geste '39 ►
Before the Rain '94 ►
Bet Your Life '04
Billy Lynn's Long Halftime Walk '16
Bitter Harvest '17
The Bitter Tea of General Yen '33 ►
Blood Diamond '06
Bloodshot '20
Bounty Killer '13
Braveheart '95 ►
Brothers '04 ►
The Buccaneer '58
A Bullet for the General '68
Bushido: The Cruel Code of the Samurai '63 ►
By Dawn's Early Light '89
Captain America: Civil War '16 ►
Captain Horatio Hornblower '51 ►
Carthage in Flames '60
Cast a Giant Shadow '66
Cavalry Command '63
The Cave '19 ►
Chapayev '34 ►
Charge of the Lancers '54
The Charge of the Light Brigade '36 ►
The Charge of the Light Brigade '68
Citizen Soldier '16
Civilization '16 ►
Cliffs of Freedom '19
Concerning Violence '14
The Conqueror '56
Conquest of the Normans '62
Control Room '04 ►
Coup de Grace '78
The Court Martial of Billy Mitchell '55 ►
Cromwell '70
Cup Final '92
Danger Close '19
Deadline '87
The Deluge '73
The Desert of the Tartars '76
The Devil Came on Horseback '07 ►
Devil Wears White '86
Dheepan '16
Dirty Wars '13
Distant Drums '51
Dragon Blade '15
Dragon Seed '44
Drone '17
Eagles Attack at Dawn '70
El Cid '61 ►
An Empress and the Warriors '08
The Enchanted Cottage '45
The End of St. Petersburg '27 ►
Ender's Game '13
Eye in the Sky '15 ►
Fahrenheit 9/11 '04 ►
The Fall of the Roman Empire '64 ►
Field of Lost Shoes '14
The Fighter '52 ►
Fighting Marines '36
The Fighting Prince of Donegal '66
The Finest Hour '91
Fire Over England '37 ►
The Firing Line '91
5 Days of War '11
For Sama '19 ►
Forever and a Day '43 ►
Fort Apache '48 ►
47 Ronin '13
The Four Feathers '39 ►
The Four Feathers '78
F.P. 1 '33
Free State of Jones '16
Funny, Dirty Little War '83
Garm Wars: The Last Druid '15
Good Kill '15
The Grandmaster '13
The Great Wall '17
Guernica '16
Gunga Din '39 ►
Gunner Palace '04 ►
Guns at Batasi '64
Hail the Conquering Hero '44 ►
Harry's War '84
Heart of a Nation '43 ►
Heartbreak Ridge '86 ►
Heaven & Earth '90 ►
Hell in the Pacific '69 ►
Henry V '89 ►
The Hidden Fortress '58 ►
A Hidden Life '19
High-Rise '16
Hijacking Catastrophe: 9/11, Fear and the Selling of America '04
Hombres Armados '97 ►
Hotel Rwanda '04
House of Fools '02
How I Won the War '67
Howl's Moving Castle '04
Hyena Road '16
Independence Day: Resurgence '16
The Informer '35 ►
Innocent Voices '04
The Invincible Gladiator '62
Ip Man '08
Jarhead '05
Jirga '19
Johnny Got His Gun '71 ►
Jojo Rabbit '19 ►
Journey's End '18
Judith of Bethulia '14 ►
Kesari '19
Khartoum '66
Killers '88
The King '19 ►
King Arthur '04
Kingdom of Heaven '05 ►
Kippur '00 ►
Kolberg '45
La Marseillaise '37 ►
The Last Face '17
Last Flag Flying '17
The Last Full Measure '19
The Last Grenade '70
Last Men In Aleppo '17 ►
The Last of the Mohicans '20 ►
The Last of the Mohicans '32
The Last of the Mohicans '36
The Last of the Mohicans '92 ►
The Last Valley '71
The Last Warrior '18
Latino '85
Laughing at Life '33
Le Petit Soldat '60 ►
The Legend of Suriyothai '02
The Life and Death of Colonel Blimp '43 ►
Lion of the Desert '81 ►
Lone Survivor '13
The Longest Day '62 ►
The Lost Command '66
Louder Than Bombs '16
Macbeth '15
Man Down '16
Man from the Alamo '53 ►
Manos sucias '15 ►
Massive Retaliation '85
Megan Leavey '17
A Message to Garcia '36
Midway '19
Mission to Glory '80
The Mongols '60
Monos '19 ►
Monsters: Dark Continent '15
Mother '26 ►
The Mouse That Roared '59 ►
Mulan '98
Musa: The Warrior '01 ►
Navy Seals *vs.* Zombies '15
Neither Heaven Nor Earth '16
The Nightingale '18 ►
1917 '19 ►
1911 '11
No Man's Land '01
Occupation: Dreamland '05 ►
Of Fathers and Sons '18 ►
Old Gringo '89
An Ordinary Man '18
Orphans of the Storm '21 ►
Our Music '04
Out of the Furnace '13
Outlaw King '18
The Patience Stone '13 ►
Peace, Propaganda & the Promised Land '04
A Perfect Day '16
The Phantom Planet '61
Planet of the Apes '01 ►
Prehistoric Bimbos in Armageddon City '93
The Pride and the Passion '57
Prisoner of the Mountains '96 ►
A Private War '18
The Promise '17
Purple Butterfly '03 ►
Railroad Tigers '17
The Rape of the Sabines '61
The Real Glory '39 ►
A Reason to Live, a Reason to Die '73
The Red and the White '68 ►
Red Dawn '84
Red Joan '19
Revenge of the Barbarians '60
Revolt '17
Richard III '95 ►
Ride to Glory '71
The Road to Guantanamo '06
Rogue One: A Star Wars Story '16 ►
Rough Riders '97
The Russian Woodpecker '15 ►
Ryan's Daughter '70
Samson '18
Sanders of the River '35 ►
Santiago '56
Seminole Uprising '55
Semper Fi '19
Senso '54 ►
The Seventeenth Bride '84
Shadow '18 ►
Shaka Zulu: The Last Great Warrior '01
Shake Hands With the Devil: The Journey of Romeo Dallaire '04 ►
The Shame '68 ►
Sharpe's Battle '94
Sharpe's Company '94
Sharpe's Eagle '93
Sharpe's Enemy '94
Sharpe's Gold '94
Sharpe's Honour '94
Sharpe's Justice '97
Sharpe's Legend '97
Sharpe's Mission '96
Sharpe's Regiment '96
Sharpe's Revenge '97
Sharpe's Rifles '93
Sharpe's Siege '96
Sharpe's Sword '94
Sharpe's Waterloo '97
Shock and Awe '18
Shot Through the Heart '98 ►
Smugglers '75
Sniper: Ghost Shooter '16
Sniper: Special Ops '16
Something of Value '57 ►
South Park: Bigger, Longer and Uncut '99
Star Wars: The Rise of Skywalker '19
Starship Troopers '97 ►
Storm over Asia '28 ►
Taras Bulba '62
Teeth and Blood '15
Thank You for Your Service '17 ►
They Shall Not Grow Old '19 ►
They Will Have to Kill Us First: Malian Music in Exile '15
13 Hours: The Secret Soldiers of Benghazi '16
This Island Earth '55
Time to Kill '89
Tolkien '19
The Torch '50
Tristan & Isolde '06
The Troubles We've Seen '94
Troy '04
Turtles Can Fly '04 ►
12 Strong '18
The Ugly American '63
Ulysses' Gaze '95
Uncovered: The War on Iraq '04
Under Fire '83 ►
The Unknown Known '14 ►
Uri: The Surgical Strike '19
Vera Cruz '53
Villa Rides '68
Voices of Iraq '04 ►
Walker '87
The Wall '17
A War '15 ►
War and Peace '56
War and Peace '68 ►
War and Peace '73
War Dogs '16
War for the Planet of the Apes '17 ►
War Machine '17
War Witch '12
Warcraft '16
Warlords '08 ►
We Come As Friends '14
Welcome to Sarajevo '97 ►
Whiskey Tango Foxtrot '16
Wing Commander '99
World War III '86
Yank in Libya '42
The Yellow Birds '17
Young Winston '72 ►
Zulu Dawn '79 ►

Washington, DC

See *Capitol Capers*

Weathermen

See also *News at 11*

The 4th Floor '99
Groundhog Day '93 ►
L.A. Story '91 ►
Lucky Numbers '00
NYC: Tornado Terror '08
The Perfect Storm '00
Storm Seekers '08
Tornado Valley '09
Twister '96
The Weather Man '05

Wedding Bells

See also *Marriage; Otherwise Engaged; Wedding Hell*

About Schmidt '02 ►
After the Wedding '06 ►
After the Wedding '19
Aladdin and the King of Thieves '96
Alvin and the Chipmunks: Road Chip '15
American Wedding '03
Anne of Green Gables: The Continuing Story '99
Another Happy Day '11
April's Shower '03
The Arrangement '99 ►
The Bachelor '99
Bachelorette '12
Badge of Faith '15
The Baxter '05
The Beach Bum '19
Because I Said So '07
Before You Say 'I Do' '09
Bend It Like Beckham '02 ►
The Benefactor '16
The Best Man '99 ►
Betsy's Wedding '90
The Big Wedding '13
Bite '16
Blind Date '87
The Bread, My Sweet '01
Bridal Fever '08
The Bride Came C.O.D. '41
The Bride Goes Wild '48
The Bride Walks Out '36
Bride Wars '09
Bridesmaids '11 ►
Broken Vows '16
Buying the Cow '02
Cake '05
Ceremony '10
Chaos Theory '08
Cheerful Weather for the Wedding '12
A Christmas Wedding '06
A Christmas Wedding Tail '11
Come Dance at My Wedding '09
Confessions of a Window Cleaner '74
Confessions of an American Bride '05
Confusion of Genders '00
Conversations with Other Women '05
Corrupted Hands '00
Cowboys and Angels '00
Curve '16
Dan in Real Life '07
The Daring Young Man '35
Date Bait '60
Death Do Us Part '14
The Decoy Bride '11
Demon '16 ►
Destination Wedding '18
Dina '17 ►
Dirty Grandpa '16
The Duke '99
Easy Money '83
Easy Virtue '08
Eat, Pray, Love '10
8 Seconds '94
Emma '96 ►
Emma '97 ►
Esmeralda Comes by Night '98
Evening '07
Everybody Knows '18
Everybody Loves Somebody '17 ►
Everyone Says I Love You '96 ►
Fandango '85
Fantastic Four: Rise of the Silver Surfer '07
The Farewell '19 ►
Father of the Bride '50 ►
Father of the Bride '91
A Few Best Men '11
Fiddler on the Roof '71 ►
For Love or Money '19
Forget Paris '95
Four Weddings and a Funeral '94 ►
Freaky Friday '03 ►
Full of Life '56
Ghosts of Girlfriends Past '09
Gidget Gets Married '72
The Girl Said No '30
Give Me a Sailor '38
The Godfather '72 ►
Good Luck Chuck '07
The Good Witch's Gift '10
The Groomsmen '06
Happy Ever Afters '09
Hard Promises '92
Heartbreakers '01
Holy Matrimony '94
Honeymoon in Vegas '92
House Party 3 '94
Housesitter '92
How I Married My High School Crush '07
I Do '06
I Do & I Don't '07
I Do (But I Don't) '04
I Me Wed '07
I Want to Get Married '11
I'm with Lucy '02
Imagine Me & You '06
Intolerable Cruelty '03
Invitation '51
It Started with Eve '41 ►
Jack and Sarah '95
Jerry Maguire '96 ►
The Jewel of the Nile '85
John Loves Mary '48

Jumping the Broom '11
Kiss the Bride '10
Kissing a Fool '98
Knight and Day '10
Last Wedding '01
Lola Versus '12
Love and Other Four Letter Words '07
Love, etc. '96
The Love Punch '13
Lovers and Other Strangers '70 ▶
Ma Vie en Rose '97 ▶
Maleficent: Mistress of Evil '19
Mamma Mia! '08
Margot at the Wedding '07
The Marrying Man '91
Matrimonium '05
May in Summer '13
Meet the Fockers '04
Melancholia '11▶
Miami Rhapsody '95
Mickey Blue Eyes '99
Minnie and Moskowitz '71
The Mirror Has Two Faces '96
Mrs. Winterbourne '96
Monsoon Wedding '01▶
Moonstruck '87▶
Much Ado About Nothing '13▶
Muriel's Wedding '94▶
My Best Friend's Wedding '97
My Big Fat Greek Wedding '02
My Favorite Wife '40▶
My First Wedding '04
Nanny McPhee '06
The Neighbor '07
Nine Months '95
Noah's Arc: Jumping the Broom '08
Not Since You '09
Notting Hill '99▶
Nutty Professor 2: The Klumps '00
The Odd Couple 2 '98
The One '11
Only You '94
Open Season 2 '08
The Other Story '19
Our Family Wedding '10
Out at the Wedding '07
Painting the Clouds With Sunshine '51
The Perfect Wedding '12
The Philadelphia Story '40▶
Photograph '19
Pirates of the Caribbean: Dead Man's Chest '06
Plus One '19
Polish Wedding '97
Prelude to a Kiss '92
The Prince & Me 2: Royal Wedding '06
The Prince & Me 4: The Elephant Adventure '10
Princess O'Rourke '43
The Proposal '09
Ready or Not '19▶
Reckless: The Sequel '98▶
Revenge of the Bridesmaids '10
Revenge of the Nerds 4: Nerds in Love '94
Rhythm on the Range '36
Ride with the Devil '99
The Right Kind Of Wrong '13
The Romantics '10
Roommates '95
Royal Wedding '51▶
Save the Date '12
The Second Best Exotic Marigold Hotel '15
Seven Sweethearts '42
Sex and the City: The Movie '08
She's Having a Baby '88
Christmas All Over Again '16
Sixteen Candles '84▶
The Son of the Bride '01
The Sound of Music '65▶
Splendor '99
Standing Still '05
Star Trek: Nemesis '02
Steel Magnolias '89▶
Sufat Chol '16▶
The Tender Trap '55
That Old Feeling '96
Them That Follow '19
The Theory of Everything '14
Think Like a Man Too '14
The 30-Foot Bride of Candy Rock '59
Three Men and a Little Lady '90
Three Smart Girls Grow Up '39 ▶
Tim Burton's Corpse Bride '05 ▶
27 Dresses '08
The Twilight Saga: Breaking Dawn, Part 1 '11
Two Moon Junction '88
Two Weeks Notice '02
Tyler Perry's Hell Hath No Fury Like a Woman Scorned: The Play '14
Under the Eiffel Tower '18
Undercover Bridesmaid '12
Up in the Air '09▶
A Valentine Carol '07
A Very Merry Daughter of the Bride '08
Waikiki Wedding '37▶
A Wedding '78
Wedding Bell Blues '96
The Wedding Bros. '08
Wedding Crashers '05▶
The Wedding Date '05
The Wedding Guest '18
The Wedding Party '69
The Wedding Party '97
The Wedding Plan '17
Wedding Present '36
The Wedding Ringer '15
Wedding Wars '06
The Wedding Year '19
West Is West '87
When Harry Met Sally. . . '89▶
Where the Heart Is '00
Where There's Life '47
White Night Wedding '08
White Wedding '10
The Wilde Wedding '17
The Wood '99
You Again '10

Wedding Hell

See also Marriage; Marriage Hell; Otherwise Engaged; Wedding Bells

Analyze This '98▶
Arthur '81▶
The Best Man '97
Best Men '98
The Big Day '99
Bite '16
The Blood Spattered Bride '72
The Bride '85
The Bride of Frankenstein '35▶
Bride of Killer Nerd '91
Bride of Re-Animator '89
Bride of the Gorilla '51
Bride of the Monster '55
The Bride with White Hair '93
The Bride Wore Black '68▶
Brides of the Beast '68
Cake: A Wedding Story '07
Captive '98
The Catered Affair '56▶
Cheatin' Hearts '93
Confetti '06
Death Do Us Part '14
Dr. T & the Women '00▶
Feeling Minnesota '96
The Five-Year Engagement '12
The Flame of New Orleans '41▶
Forces of Nature '99
Ganja and Hess '73
A Girl Cut in Two '07
The Graduate '67▶
The Hanging Garden '97
Hangman's House '28
He Knows You're Alone '80
Hellhounds '09
Honeymoon Killers '70▶
I Married a Monster from Outer Space '58
I Think I Do '97
In and Out '97 ▶
The In-Laws '03
Kill Bill Vol. 1 '03 ▶
Kill Bill Vol. 2 '04 ▶
Last Chance Harvey '08
Last Lives '98
Late Marriage '01
Like Father '18
Love Stinks '99
Meet the Parents '00 ▶
Mike and Dave Need Wedding Dates '16
Monster-in-Law '05
My New Gun '92
Niagara '52
Norbit '07
Old School '03
On Chesil Beach '17
[REC] 3: Genesis '12
Riding in Cars with Boys '01
River Street '95
Runaway Bride '99▶
Saving Silverman '01
The Sweetest Thing '02
Table 19 '17
That Old Feeling '96
Tim Burton's Corpse Bride '05▶
Tomcats '01
Tony n' Tina's Wedding '07
Trojan Eddie '96▶
True Love '89▶
28 Days '00
The Undertaker's Wedding '97
Very Bad Things '98
The Wedding Banquet '93▶
Wedding in Blood '74▶
Wedding in White '72
The Wedding Planner '01
The Wedding Singer '97
You and Me '38

Werewolves

See also Metamorphosis

An American Werewolf in London '81▶
An American Werewolf in Paris '97
Animals '08
Bad Moon '96
The Beast Must Die '75
Big Bad Wolf '06
Big Fish '03▶
Blood & Chocolate '07
Blood of Dracula's Castle '69
The Boy Who Cried Werewolf '10
Bride of the Gorilla '51
The Company of Wolves '85▶
The Craving '80
The Creeps '97
Curse of the Devil '73
Curse of the Queerwolf '87
The Curse of the Werewolf '61
Cursed '04
Darkwolf '03
Dr. Jekyll and the Wolfman '71
Dog Soldiers '01
Dracula *vs.* Frankenstein '69
Dylan Dog: Dead of Night '11
Frankenstein Meets the Wolfman '42▶
Full Eclipse '93
The Fury of the Wolfman '70
Ginger Snaps '01
Ginger Snaps Back: The Beginning '04
Ginger Snaps: Unleashed '04
Harry Potter and the Prisoner of Azkaban '04
Hercules, Prisoner of Evil '64
House of Dracula '45
House of Frankenstein '44
The Howling '81▶
Howling 2: Your Sister Is a Werewolf '85
Howling 3: The Marsupials '87
Howling 4: The Original Nightmare '88
Howling 6: The Freaks '90
Kibakichi 2 '04
Kibakichi '04
The Legend of the Wolf Woman '77
The Mad Monster '42
Mating Dance '08
Monster Dog '82
The Monster Squad '87
Moon of the Wolf '72
My Mom's a Werewolf '89
Nature of the Beast '07
Never Cry Werewolf '08
Orgy of the Dead '65
Red Riding Hood '11
Red: Werewolf Hunter '10
Return of the Vampire '43
Scream of the Wolf '74
Silver Bullet '85
Skinwalkers '07
The Strangers '98
Teen Wolf '85
Teen Wolf Too '87
The Twilight Saga: Breaking Dawn, Part 1 '11
The Twilight Saga: Breaking Dawn, Part 2 '12
The Twilight Saga: Eclipse '10
The Twilight Saga: New Moon '09
Uncaged '16
Underworld '03
Underworld: Awakening '12
Underworld: Blood Wars '16
Underworld: Evolution '05
Underworld: Rise of the Lycans '09
Van Helsing '04▶
Waxwork '88
The Werewolf '56
Werewolf '95
Werewolf of London '35
Werewolf of Washington '73
Werewolf: The Beast Among Us '12
The Werewolf *vs.* the Vampire Woman '70
Werewolves on Wheels '71
Wilderness '96
Wolf '94
Wolf Blood '25
The Wolf Man '41▶
Wolf Moon '09
Wolfen '81▶
The Wolfman '82
The Wolfman '09
The Wolves of Kromer '98
Wolvesbayne '09

West Virginia

Arlington Road '99
Big Business '88
The Big Clock '48▶
Boa *vs.* Python '04
Coal Miner's Daughter '80▶
Dead Leaves '98
The Devil and Daniel Johnston '05▶
Gods and Generals '03
The Happening '08
Hatfields & McCoys '12▶
Heroes of the Heart '94
A Killing Affair '85
Matewan '87▶
Medium Cool '69▶
The Mothman Prophecies '02
Mumford '99▶
The Night of the Hunter '55▶
October Sky '99▶
The Silence of the Lambs '91▶
Silent Hill '06
Silent Hill: Revelation 3D '12
Sweet Dreams '85
Tumbleweeds '98
We Are Marshall '06
When Willie Comes Marching Home '50▶
Win a Date with Tad Hamilton! '04
Wrong Turn '03
Wrong Turn 2: Dead End '07
Wrong Turn 3: Left for Dead '09
Wrong Turn 4: Bloody Beginnings '11
The X Files: I Want to Believe '08

Western Comedy

See also Comedy; Westerns

Adios Amigo '75
Alias Jesse James '59
Along Came Jones '45 ▶
The Apple Dumpling Gang '75
The Apple Dumpling Gang Rides Again '79
The Bad Man '41
Bad Man's River '72
The Ballad of Buster Scruggs '18 ▶
Ballad of Cable Hogue '70 ▶
The Ballad of Josie '67
Bandidas '06
Bang Bang Kid '67
The Beautiful Blonde from Bashful Bend '49
Blazing Saddles '74 ▶
Boss '74
Bronco Billy '80
Brothers O'Toole '73
Buck Benny Rides Again '40
Bus Stop '56▶
Carry On Cowboy '66
Cat Ballou '65▶
Catlow '71
Check & Double Check '30
The Cherokee Kid '96
The Cheyenne Social Club '70
The Cisco Kid '94
City Slickers 2: The Legend of Curly's Gold '94
City Slickers '91▶
Cold Feet '89
Companeros '70
The Cowboy Way '94
Damsel '18
Destry Rides Again '39▶
The Duchess and the Dirtwater Fox '76
The Dude Goes West '48
800 Bullets '02
Evil Roy Slade '71▶
Four for Texas '63
The Frisco Kid '79
From Noon Till Three '76
Go West '40
Goin' South '78▶
The Good Guys and the Bad Guys '69
Greaser's Palace '72
Great Scout & Cathouse Thursday '76
The Hallelujah Trail '65
Hangman's Knot '52
Hawmps! '76
Hearts of the West '75▶
Home on the Range '04
How the West Was Fun '95
I'm from Arkansas '44
The Kid Brother '27▶
Lemonade Joe '64
Life & Times of Judge Roy Bean '72
Lightning Jack '94
Lucky Luke '94
Mail Order Bride '63
Many Rivers to Cross '55
Maverick '94
McLintock! '63▶
A Million Ways to Die In the West '14
Montana Moon '30
More Wild, Wild West '80
Oklahoma Kid '39▶
The Outlaws Is Coming! '65
The Over-the-Hill Gang '69
The Over-the-Hill Gang Rides Again '70
The Paleface '48▶
Pardners '56
Pocket Money '72
Rancho Deluxe '75▶
Red Garters '54
Rhythm on the Range '36
Ride 'Em Cowboy '42
The Rounders '65
Roy Colt and Winchester Jack '70
Rustler's Rhapsody '85
Sam Whiskey '69
The Scalphunters '68
Scandalous John '71
The Second Time Around '61
Sergeants 3 '62
The Shakiest Gun in the West '68
Shanghai Knights '03
Shanghai Noon '00
The Sheepman '58
The Sheriff of Fractured Jaw '59
Sidekicks '74
Sky Full of Moon '52
Son of Paleface '52 ▶
Sons of Trinity '95
Straight to Hell '87
Sundance and the Kid '69
Sunset '88
Support Your Local Gunfighter '71 ▶
Support Your Local Sheriff '69 ▶
Texas '41 ▶
Texas Across the River '66
There Was a Crooked Man '70▶
They Call Me Trinity '72
Three Godfathers '48▶
Trinity Is Still My Name '75
Troublemakers '94
Undead or Alive '07
The Villain '79
Wackiest Wagon Train in the West '77
Wagons East '94
Waterhole Number 3 '67
Way Out West '37▶
Wild Rovers '71
Wild, Wild West Revisited '79
The Wistful Widow of Wagon Gap '47
Zachariah '70

Westerns

See also Sci-Fi Westerns; Spaghetti Western; Supernatural Westerns; Western Comedy; Westrogens

Abilene Town '46▶
Aces 'n Eights '08
Across the Line '00
The Adventures of Gallant Bess '48
Adventures of Red Ryder '40
After Sundown '06
Against a Crooked Sky '75
The Alamo '60▶
The Alamo '04
All Hell Broke Loose '09
All the Pretty Horses '00
Allegheny Uprising '39
Along the Great Divide '51
Along the Rio Grande '41
Alvarez Kelly '66
Ambush at Tomahawk Gap '53
American Bandits: Frank and Jesse James '10
American Empire '42
American Outlaws '01
Americano '55
Angel and the Badman '47▶
Angel and the Badman '09
Another Man, Another Chance '77
Another Pair of Aces: Three of a Kind '91▶
Apache '54
Apache Blood '75
Apache Rifles '64
Apache Rose '47
Apache Territory '58
The Appaloosa '66
Appaloosa '08▶
Arizona '40
Arizona Bushwackers '67
Arizona Raiders '65
Arrowhead '53
The Assassination of Jesse James by the Coward Robert Ford '07▶
The Avenging Angel '95
Avenging Angel '07
The Back Trail '24
Backlash '56
Bacurau '20
Bad Company '72▶
Bad Day at Black Rock '54▶
Bad Jim '89

▶ = rated three bones or higher

The Bad Man of Brimstone '38
Bad Men of Tombstone '49
The Badlanders '58
Badman's Territory '46 ▶
The Ballad of Buster Scruggs '18 ▶
The Ballad of Lefty Brown '17
Bandolero! '68
Banjo Hackett '76
Barbarosa '82 ▶
Baron of Arizona '51 ▶
Barricade '49
Battle of Rogue River '54
Battles of Chief Pontiac '52
Battling with Buffalo Bill '31
Bells of Coronado '50
Bells of San Fernando '47
Bend of the River '52 ▶
Best of the Badmen '50
Between God, the Devil & a Winchester '72
The Big Cat '49
The Big Country '58
A Big Hand for the Little Lady '66
Big Jake '71
The Big Sombrero '49
The Big Trail '30 ▶
Billy the Kid '30
Billy the Kid '41
Billy Two Hats '74
Bisbee '17 '18
Bite the Bullet '75 ▶
The Black Dakotas '54
Black Fox: Good Men and Bad '94
Black Fox: The Price of Peace '94
Black Patch '57
Blackthorn '11
Blind Justice '94
Blue '68
Boiling Point '32
Bone Tomahawk '15
Border River '47
Border Shootout '90
Borderland '37
Bounty '09
The Boy From Oklahoma '54
Branded '50
The Brass Legend '56
The Bravados '58 ▶
The Bravos '72
Breakheart Pass '76
Brimstone '17
Brokeback Mountain '05 ▶
Broken Arrow '50
Broken Lance '54 ▶
The Broken Star '56
Broken Trail '06 ▶
Buchanan Rides Alone '58
Buck and the Preacher '72
Buckskin '68
Buckskin Frontier '43
Buffalo Bill '44
Buffalo Bill & the Indians '76 ▶
Buffalo Bill Rides Again '47
Buffalo Soldiers '97 ▶
The Burning Hills '56
The Bushwackers '52
Butch and Sundance: The Early Days '79
Butch Cassidy and the Sundance Kid '69 ▶
Cahill: United States Marshal '73
Cain's Cutthroats '71
The California Trail '33
Call of the Canyon '42
Call of the Coyote '34
Call of the Forest '49
Cannon for Cordoba '70
Can't Help Singing '45
Canyon Passage '46 ▶
Canyon River '56
Captain Apache '71
The Capture '50 ▶
Carson City '52
Cast a Long Shadow '59
Cattle King '63
Cattle Queen of Montana '54
Cattle Town '52
Cavalcade of the West '36
Cavalier of the West '31
Cavalry Scout '51
Charro! '69
Chato's Land '71
Cheyenne '47
Cheyenne Autumn '64
Cheyenne Warrior '94
Chisum '70
Chuka '67
Cimarron '31
Cimarron '60
Cinderella '12
The Cisco Kid and the Lady '39
City of Bad Men '53
The Claim '00
A Cold Day in Hell '11
Cole Younger, Gunfighter '58
Colorado Serenade '46
Colorado Sundown '52
Colorado Territory '49
Colt Comrades '43
Comanche Moon '08
Comanche Station '60
The Comancheros '61 ▶
Come Hell or High Water '08
Conagher '91
Conquest of Cochise '53
Convict Cowboy '95
Copper Canyon '50
Cotter '72
Cow Town '50
Cowboy '58 ▶
Cowboy Millionaire '35
The Cowboys '72 ▶
Cowboys & Aliens '11
Crazy Horse and Custer: 'The Untold Story' '90
Crossfire Trail '01 ▶
Cry Blood, Apache '70
Culpepper Cattle Co. '72
Custer's Last Stand '36
The Cyclone Ranger '35
Dakota '45
Dakota Incident '56
Damsel '18
Dan Candy's Law '73
Daniel Boone '34
Daniel Boone: Trail Blazer '56
Dark Command '40 ▶
The Dark Tower '17
Davy Crockett, Indian Scout '50
Dawn at Socorro '54
Dawn Rider '12
Day of the Evil Gun '68
Dead for a Dollar '70
Dead Man '95
Dead Man's Burden '12 ▶
Dead Man's Revenge '93
Deadly Companions '61
The Deadly Trackers '73
Deadwood '65
Death of a Gunfighter '69
Decision at Sundown '57
Denver and the Rio Grande '52
Deputy Marshal '50
Desert Guns '36
The Desperadoes '43
The Desperados '70
The Desperate Mission '69 ▶
The Desperate Trail '94
Devil & Leroy Basset '73
The Devil Horse '26
Devil Horse '32
The Devil's Doorway '50
Diablo '16
Dirty Little Billy '72
Distant Drums '51
Django '68
Dodge City '39 ▶
Don't Fence Me In '45
Down in the Valley '05
Down Mexico Way '41
Dream West '86
Drum Beat '54
Drums Across the River '54
Drums Along the Mohawk '39 ▶
The Dude Bandit '33
The Duel '16
Duel at Diablo '66 ▶
Duel at Silver Creek '52
Duel in the Sun '46 ▶
Eagle's Wing '79
Edge of Eternity '59
El Condor '70
El Diablo '90
El Dorado '67 ▶
El Paso '49
El Topo '71
The Electric Horseman '79
Empty Saddles '36
Extreme Prejudice '87
Far Country '55 ▶
Fastest Guitar Alive '68
Fastest Gun Alive '56 ▶
The Fiend Who Walked the West '58
Fighting Fists of Shanghai Joe '65
The Fighting Kentuckian '49
The Fighting Lawman '53
Fighting with Kit Carson '33
Firecreek '68
First Cow '20 ▶
Five Card Stud '68
Five Guns to Tombstone '60
Flame of the Barbary Coast '45
Flame of the West '45
Flaming Frontiers '38
Flaming Star '60 ▶
Flesh and the Spur '57
Forbidden Trail '32
Forbidden Valley '38
Foresaken '16
Forsaken '15
Fort Apache '48 ▶
Fort Defiance '51
Fort Dobbs '58
Fort Osage '51
Fort Yuma '55
Forty Guns '57
Four Faces West '48
Four Fast Guns '59
Four Rode Out '69
Frank and Jesse '94
Frontier Marshal '39
Frontier Uprising '61
The Frontiersmen '38
The Furies '50
The Gambler from Natchez '54
The Gambler Returns: The Luck of the Draw '93
The Gambler, the Girl and the Gunslinger '09
Garden of Evil '54
The Gatling Gun '72
The Gay Buckaroo '32
The Gentleman from Arizona '39
The Gentleman Killer '69
Geronimo: An American Legend '93
Ghost City '32
Ghost Town '56
Girl of the Golden West '38
Go West '25 ▶
God's Gun '75
Gold of the Seven Saints '61
The Golden Stallion '49
Gone with the West '72
Good Day for a Hanging '58
A Good Day to Die '95
The Good Old Boys '95
The Good, the Bad, the Weird '08
Goodnight for Justice '11
Goodnight for Justice: Queen of Hearts '13
Goodnight for Justice: The Measure of a Man '12
Grand Canyon Trail '48
Grayeagle '77
Great Jesse James Raid '49
The Great Northfield Minnesota Raid '72
Gun Brothers '56
Gun Duel In Durango '57
Gun for a Coward '57
Gun Fury '53
Gun Glory '57
The Gun Hawk '63
Gun Riders '69
The Gun That Won the West '55
Gun the Man Down '56
A Gunfight '71
Gunfight at Comanche Creek '64
The Gunfight at Dodge City '59
Gunfight at the O.K. Corral '57 ▶
Gunfight in Abilene '67
The Gunfighter '50 ▶
Gunfighter '98
Gunfighters '47
The Gunfighters '87
Gunfighter's Moon '96
Guns of Diablo '64
Guns of the Magnificent Seven '69
Gunslinger's Revenge '98
Gunsmoke: Return to Dodge '87
The Half-Breed '51
The Halliday Brand '57
Hands Across the Border '43
The Hanged Man '74
The Hanging Tree '59 ▶
The Hangman '59
Hannie Caulder '72
Hard Bounty '94
Hard Ground '03
Harry Tracy '83
The Harvey Girls '46 ▶
The Hateful Eight '15 ▶
Hatfields & McCoys '12 ▶
Headin' for Trouble '31
Heart of the Rio Grande '42
Heaven With a Gun '69
Heaven's Gate '81
Hell or High Water '16 ▶
Heller in Pink Tights '60
Hell's Heroes '30
Hell's Hinges '16
Heroes of the Alamo '37
Hidden Guns '56 ▶
High Lonesome '50
High Noon '52 ▶
High Noon '00
High Plains Drifter '73
Hired Hand '71
Hole in the Sky '95
Hombre '67 ▶
Home in Oklahoma '47
The Homesman '14
Hopalong Cassidy Returns '36
Hopalong Cassidy: Riders of the Deadline '43
Hopalong Cassidy: The Devil's Playground '46
Hoppy Serves a Writ '43
Horizons West '52
Hostile Guns '67
Hostiles '17
Hour of the Gun '67
How the West Was Won '63 ▶
Hurricane Express '32
I Shot Jesse James '49 ▶
I Will Fight No More Forever '75 ▶
Idaho '43
In a Valley of Violence '16
In Old California '42
In the Days of the Thundering Herd & the Law & the Outlaw '14
The Indian Fighter '55 ▶
Indian Paint '64
The Invasion of Johnson County '76
Invitation to a Gunfighter '64
The Iron Horse '24 ▶
The Iron Sheriff '57
The Ivory Handled Gun '35
The Jack Bull '99
Jane Got a Gun '16
The Jayhawkers '59
Jeremiah Johnson '72 ▶
Jericho '01
Jesse James '39 ▶
Jesse James Rides Again '47
Jesse James' Women '54
Joe Kidd '72
Johnny Reno '66
Johnson County War '02
Jory '72
Joshua '76
Jubal '56
Junior Bonner '72 ▶
The Kansan '43
Kansas Pacific '53
Kansas Raiders '50
Kenny Rogers as the Gambler '80
Kenny Rogers as the Gambler, Part 2: The Adventure Continues '83
Kenny Rogers as the Gambler, Part 3: The Legend Continues '87
The Kentuckian '55
Kentucky Rifle '55
The Kid '19
Kid Vengeance '75
Kill or Be Killed '15
The King and Four Queens '56
King of Texas '02 ▶
King of the Grizzlies '69
Kit Carson '40
Land Raiders '69
Larry McMurtry's Dead Man's Walk '96
Larry McMurtry's Streets of Laredo '95 ▶
The Last Challenge '67
Last Days of Frank & Jesse James '86
Last Frontier '32
Last Gun '64
The Last Hard Men '76
The Last Hunt '56
The Last of the Dogmen '95
Last Outlaw '36
The Last Outlaw '93
The Last Posse '53
The Last Ride of the Dalton Gang '79
The Last Rites of Ransom Pride '09
Last Stand at Saber River '96
The Last Sunset '61
Last Train from Gun Hill '59 ▶
The Law and Jake Wade '58
Law and Order '53
Law of the Pampas '39
The Lawless Breed '52 ▶
A Lawless Street '55
Lawman '71 ▶
Leather Burners '43
The Left-Handed Gun '58 ▶
Legend of Alfred Packer '80
The Legend of Butch & Sundance '04
The Legend of Frank Woods '77
Legend of the Lone Ranger '81
The Legend of Zorro '05
The Light of Western Stars '30
Lightnin' Bill Carson '36
Lightning Warrior '31
Lights of Old Santa Fe '47
Little Big Horn '51
Little Big Man '70 ▶
Little Moon & Jud McGraw '78
Loaded Pistols '48
The Lone Defender '32
Lone Justice 2 '93
Lone Justice 3: Showdown at Plum Creek '96
The Lone Ranger '38
Lone Ranger '56
The Lone Ranger '13
Lone Rider '08
Lone Star '52
Lone Star '95 ▶
Lone Wolf McQuade '83
Lonely Are the Brave '62 ▶
The Lonely Man '57
Lonesome Dove '89 ▶
Lonesome Dove Church '14
Lonesome Trail '55
The Long Ride Home '01
The Long Riders '80 ▶
The Longest Drive '76
Love Comes Softly '03
Love's Abiding Joy '06
Love's Enduring Promise '04
Love's Long Journey '05
Lust for Gold '49
The Lusty Men '52 ▶
MacKenna's Gold '69
Madron '70
The Magnificent Seven '60 ▶
The Magnificent Seven '16
Mail Order Bride '08
Major Dundee '65
Man & Boy '71
A Man Called Horse '70 ▶
A Man Called Sledge '71
Man from Button Willow '65
Man from Colorado '49
Man from Del Rio '56
Man From God's Country '58
The Man from Laramie '55 ▶
The Man from Snowy River '82
Man from the Alamo '53 ▶
Man in the Saddle '51
Man in the Shadow '57
Man of the West '58
Man or Gun '58
The Man Who Came Back '08
Man Who Loved Cat Dancing '73
The Man Who Shook the Hand of Vicente Fernandez '12 ▶
The Man Who Shot Liberty Valance '62 ▶
Man Without a Star '55 ▶
The Manhunt '86
The Marshal's Daughter '53
Massacre '56
Massacre River '49
McCabe & Mrs. Miller '71 ▶
The McMasters '70
The Meanest Men in the West '67
Meek's Cutoff '10 ▶
Melody Ranch '40
Miracle at Sage Creek '05
Miracle in the Wilderness '91
The Miracle Rider '35
The Missing '03 ▶
Missouri Breaks '76
Mohawk '56
Molly & Lawless John '72
Montana '50
Monte Walsh '70 ▶
Monte Walsh '03
The Moonlighter '53
More Dead Than Alive '68
The Mountain Men '80
My Darling Clementine '46 ▶
My Outlaw Brother '51
My Pal Trigger '46
Mystery Mountain '34
Naked Hills '56
The Naked Spur '53 ▶
Ned Kelly '70
Nevada Smith '66
The Nevadan '50
Never Grow Old '19
Night of the Grizzly '66
Night Passage '57
No Man's Law '27
No Name on the Bullet '59 ▶
Noose for a Gunman '60
Nothing Too Good for a Cowboy '98
Oklahoma! '99 ▶
Oklahoma Annie '51
The Oklahoman '56
One-Eyed Jacks '61 ▶
One Foot in Hell '60
100 Rifles '69
One Little Indian '73
Only the Valiant '50
Open Range '03 ▶
The Outlaw '43
The Outlaw Josey Wales '76 ▶
Outlaw Justice '98
Outlaw Women '52
Outlaws and Angels '16
Outlaw's Son '57
The Outrage '64
The Outriders '50
The Outsider '02
The Outsider '19
The Over-the-Hill Gang '69
Overland Mail '42
The Ox-Bow Incident '43 ▶
The Painted Desert '31
Pale Rider '85 ▶
Pancho Villa '72
Panhandle '48 ▶
Passion '54
Pat Garrett & Billy the Kid '73 ▶
Peter Lundy and the Medicine Hat Stallion '77
The Phantom of Santa Fe '36
Phantom of the West '31
Pillars of the Sky '56
Pioneer Woman '73
A Place Called Glory '66
The Plainsman '37
The Pledge '08
Pony Express '53 ▶

▶ = rated three bones or higher

▶ = rated three bones or higher

I'll See You in My Dreams '15
Illegal Tender '07
In a Better World '10
In Secret '13
Incendiary '08
Innocence '00 ▸
The Intended '02
The Intern '15
It Happened to Jane '59
Jackie '16 ▸
Jackie Bouvier Kennedy Onassis '00
Jada '08
Jirga '19
John Wick '14
Joyful Noise '12
The Juggler '53
Kathleen '41
Kill Me Tomorrow '57
The King of Staten Island '20
King of the Wild Stallions '59
Kings and Queen '04 ▸
La Mission '09
La Petite Jerusalem '05
La Roue '23 ▸
The Lady Is a Square '58
Last Love '13
The Laundromat '19
The Legend of Lylah Clare '68
Lemon Tree '08
Lethal Weapon '87 ▸
Light from Light '19 ▸
Local Boys '02
The Long Way Home '98
The Lost & Found Family '09
The Lost Valentine '11
Love and Rage '99
Love at First Kill '08
Love Comes Softly '03
Love Happens '09
Love Liza '02
Love Me Tonight '32 ▸
Love's Christmas Journey '11
Love's Kitchen '11
Love's Unending Legacy '07
Loving Leah '09
Lucky Grandma '20
Lucky Star '29
Luxury Liner '48
Macabre '58
Madeo '09
Mail Order Bride '63
A Man Apart '03
The Man From Yesterday '32
Manderlay '05
Marilyn Hotchkiss' Ballroom Dancing & Charm School '06
Married Life '07 ▸
Meddling Mom '13
Menashe '17
The Merchant of Venice '04 ▸
The Merry Widow '25 ▸
Message in a Bottle '98
The Messenger '09 ▸
A Mighty Heart '07 ▸
Mrs. Henderson Presents '05
Mrs. Miracle '09
Monster's Ball '01 ▸
The Mother '03 ▸
Mother Is a Freshman '49
Mothers Cry '30
The Mothman Prophecies '02
Move Over, Darling '63
The Mudge Boy '03
My Brother Jonathan '85
My Brother Talks to Horses '47
My Cousin Rachel '52
My Life in Ruins '09
My Neighbor's Secret '09
My Reputation '46
Nancy Drew and the Hidden Staircase '19
The Nanny Express '08
Nanny McPhee '06
The National Tree '09
Night Unto Night '49
Nightmare Alley '47
Nightwaves '03
No Turning Back '01
Nobody Lives Forever '46 ▸
The Note '07
Nothing Personal '09
An Old-Fashioned Thanksgiving '08
Olive Kitteridge '14 ▸
On Thin Ice '03
One Last Thing '05
1000 Rupee Note '16 ▸
Opa! '05
Operation Heartbeat '69
Our Life '10
The Outriders '50
Pampered Youth '25
The Passion of Anna '70 ▸
Passionada '02
Past Tense '06
The People Against O'Hara '51
Pepe El Toro '53
The Pilot's Wife '01
A Place Called Home '04
Play the Game '09
The Pledge '08
Politics '31
Private Benjamin '80
The Proud and Profane '56
P.S. I Love You '07
The Psychopath '66
Pulling Strings '13
Pure '02 ▸
Quiet Chaos '08
The Quitter '34
Race to Space '01
The Reading Room '05
Red Roses and Petrol '03
Relative Strangers '99
Return to Me '00
Rick '03
The Road Home '01 ▸
Rocky Balboa '06
The Roman Spring of Mrs. Stone '03
Ruby Blue '07
The Sacrifice '05
Safe Harbour '07
Safe Haven '13
St. Patrick's Day '99
The Salton Sea '02
Sam Whiskey '69
Satin Rouge '02
Schizo '04
The Second Time Around '61
The Secret '07
A Secret Affair '99
7 Faces of Dr. Lao '63 ▸
She Drives Me Crazy '07
The Shipping News '01
A Short Stay in Switzerland '09
Signs '02 ▸
Silent Waters '03
Silver Linings Playbook '12 ▸
Sixty Glorious Years '38
Skinwalkers '07
Sleepless in Seattle '93 ▸
Smart People '08
Smooch '11
Song of Love '47 ▸
Starman '84 ▸
Steve Martini's Undue Influence '96
Stoker '13
Storm Center '56
Straight from the Heart '03
Strayed '03 ▸
A Summer in Genoa '08
The Tall Man '12
That Evening Sun '09 ▸
That's What I Am '11
Things We Lost in the Fire '07
35 Shots of Rum '08
This Revolution '05
A Thousand Years of Good Prayers '07
Time of the Wolf '03 ▸
To Gillian on Her 37th Birthday '96
Together Again '43
The Treatment '06
The Tree '10
The Trial Begins '07
The Trial of Old Drum '00
Trouble in Paradise '32 ▸
The Truth About Charlie '02
Truth Be Told '11
Tumbledown '16
21 Grams '03 ▸
The Twilight Samurai '02 ▸
Tyrannosaur '11
Uncle Boonmee Who Can Recall His Past Lives '10
Unconditional '12
Under the Flag of the Rising Sun '72 ▸
Under the Mistletoe '06
Undertow '04
Unfinished Song '12
Untamed '55
Up '09 ▸
Upgrade '18
Used People '92
Victoria the Great '37
The Visit '64
The Visitor '07 ▸
Volver '06 ▸
Water '05
The Way '10
The Well-Digger's Daughter '11
We'll Meet Again '02
What Katy Did '99
What Time Is It There? '01
Where the Sidewalk Ends '50
White Night Wedding '08
White Noise '05
The Whole Shebang '01
Widow on the Hill '05
The Widowing of Mrs. Holroyd '95
Widows '02
Widows '18 ▸
Wild Oats '16
Wild Oranges '24
Wild River '60
Winner Take All '32
Winter Solstice '04 ▸
Wisegal '08
Witness '85 ▸
The Woman in the Fifth '11
Woman Obsessed '59
Worth: The Testimony of Johnny St. James '12
Young Ideas '43
Yours, Mine & Ours '68
Yours, Mine & Ours '05

Wild Kingdom

***See also** Bears; Birds; Cats; Dinosaurs; Elephants; Killer Apes and Monkeys; Killer Beasts; Killer Bugs and Slugs; Killer Dogs; Killer Kats; Killer Pigs; Killer Sea Critters; King of Beasts (Dogs); Monkeyshines; Nice Mice; Pigs; Rabbits; Talking Animals; Whales; Wilderness*

Ace Ventura: When Nature Calls '95
The Adventures of Ford Fairlane '90
The Adventures of Tarzan '21
Africa Texas Style '67
Alaska '96
All Creatures Great and Small '74 ▸
All Dogs Go to Heaven 2 '95
All Roads Lead Home '08
Alpha and Omega '10
The Amazing Panda Adventure '95
An American Tail '86
Andre '94
The Animal '01
Animal Farm '55 ▸
Appointment With Venus '51
Arctic Tale '07
Attack of the Sabretooth '05
Au Hasard Balthazar '66
Ava's Magical Adventure '94
Bambi '42 ▸
Bambi II '06
The Barefoot Executive '71
The Bear '89 ▸
The Bears & I '74
Beastmaster '82
The Beasts Are On the Streets '78
Bedtime for Bonzo '51
Black Cobra '83
Bless the Beasts and Children '71
Body at Brighton Rock '19
Born Free '66 ▸
Born to Be Wild '95
The Brave One '56 ▸
Bringing Up Baby '38 ▸
Brother Bear 2 '06
Brotherhood of the Wolf '01
Buddy '97
Call of the Wild '72
The Call of the Wild '20
Carnage '02
Cheetah '89
Chimpanzee '12
Christian the Lion '76
The Chronicles of Narnia '89 ▸
Clarence, the Cross-eyed Lion '65 ▸
The Crocodile Hunter: Collision Course '02
A Cry in the Dark '88 ▸
A Cry in the Wild '90 ▸
Day of the Animals '77
The Day of the Dolphin '73
Dr. Dolittle '98
Dr. Dolittle 2 '01
Doctor Dolittle '67
Duma '05 ▸
Dunston Checks In '95
Eaten Alive '76
Ed '96
The Edge '97
Ele, My Friend '93
The Electric Horseman '79
Elephant Boy '37 ▸
An Elephant Called Slowly '69
The Emperor's New Groove '00 ▸
Every Which Way But Loose '78
Fantastic Mr. Fox '09 ▸
Far from Home: The Adventures of Yellow Dog '94
Fearless Fagan '52
Fierce Creatures '96
50 First Dates '04
Flight of the Grey Wolf '76
Flipper '63 ▸
Flipper '96 ▸
Fly Away Home '96 ▸
The Fox and the Hound '81 ▸
Francis Covers the Big Town '53
Francis Goes to the Races '51
Francis Goes to West Point '52
Francis in the Haunted House '56
Francis in the Navy '55
Francis Joins the WACs '54
Francis the Talking Mule '49 ▸
Frasier the Sensuous Lion '73
Furry Vengeance '10
Gates of Heaven '78 ▸
Gentle Giant '67
George of the Jungle '97 ▸
The Ghost and the Darkness '96
Gladiator '00 ▸
The Golden Seal '83
Gordy '95
Gorilla '56
Gorillas in the Mist '88 ▸
The Great Rupert '50 ▸
Grizzly Man '05 ▸
Groundhog Day '93 ▸
Gus '76
Harry and the Hendersons '87
Hatari! '62 ▸
Hawmps! '76
Holiday in the Wild '19
Hollywood Safari '96
Homeward Bound 2: Lost in San Francisco '96
Hoot '06
I Dreamed of Africa '00
Ice Age '02 ▸
Ice Age: Continental Drift '12
I'm for the Hippopotamus '79
The Island of Dr. Moreau '96
Island of Lost Souls '32 ▸
Jane '17 ▸
Joey '98
Jumanji '95
Jungle '52
The Jungle Book 2 '03
The Jungle Book '67 ▸
Jungle Boy '96
Jungle Drums of Africa '53
King Kung Fu '87
King of the Grizzlies '69
Kong: Skull Island '17
Lassie, Come Home '43
The Legend of Tarzan '16
Leonard Part 6 '87
The Lion King '94 ▸
The Lion King '19
The Lion King 1 1/2 '04 ▸
The Lion King: Simba's Pride '98
Living Free '72
Madagascar: Escape 2 Africa '08
The Many Adventures of Winnie the Pooh '77
March of the Penguins '05 ▸
Max, Mon Amour '86
The Mighty Peking Man '77
The Misadventures of Merlin Jones '63
Mr. Toad's Wild Ride '96
Monkey Trouble '94
Monkeys, Go Home! '66
Monkey's Uncle '65
Mountain Family Robinson '79
My Sister, My Love '78
Napoleon '96
Napoleon and Samantha '72 ▸
Never Cry Wolf '83 ▸
Night of the Grizzly '66
Nikki, the Wild Dog of the North '61
Noah's Ark '99
Odongo '56
Once Upon a Forest '93
Operation Dumbo Drop '95
Operation Haylift '50
Pandas '18 ▸
Passion in the Desert '97
Paulie '98
Pet Sematary 2 '92
Piglet's Big Movie '03
Pippi Longstocking '69
Planet of the Apes '68 ▸
Project X '87
Razorback '84
The Rescuers '77 ▸
The Rescuers Down Under '90
Ring of Bright Water '69 ▸
Rock-a-Doodle '92
Rudyard Kipling's The Jungle Book '94
Rudyard Kipling's the Second Jungle Book: Mowgli and Baloo '97
Running Free '94
Running Wild '99
Sabretooth '01
The Secret of NIMH '82 ▸
Shakma '89
Silver Streak '76 ▸
Slappy and the Stinkers '97
Soul of the Beast '23
The Story of the Weeping Camel '03 ▸
A Summer to Remember '84
Sweetgrass '09
Those Calloways '65
A Tiger Walks '64
To Walk with Lions '99
Two Brothers '04
Vampire Circus '71
The Wagons Roll at Night '41
Walk Like a Man '87
Waltz with Bashir '08 ▸
Watership Down '78
Whispers: An Elephant's Tale '00
The White Buffalo '77
White Pongo '45
White Wolves 2: Legend of the Wild '94
The Wild '06
Wild America '97 ▸
Wild Horses '82
The Wild Thornberrys Movie '02 ▸
The Yearling '46 ▸
The Yearling '94
Zebra in the Kitchen '65
Zeus and Roxanne '96

Wilderness

***See also** Trees & Forests*

Across the Great Divide '76
The Adventures of the Wilderness Family '76
Alaska '96
All Mine to Give '56
Almost Heroes '97
Alone Yet Not Alone '13
Arctic Blue '93
Backwoods '87
The Bear '89 ▸
Beyond Fear '93
Big Game '15
Black Mountain Side '16
Black Robe '91 ▸
Blood Money '17
Body at Brighton Rock '19
Brother Bear '03
Bullies '86
Bushwhacked '95
The Call of the Wild '35 ▸
Call of the Wild '04
The Call of the Wild '20
Call of the Yukon '38
Cannibal! The Musical '96
The Canyon '09
Captain Fantastic '16
Charlie the Lonesome Cougar '67
The Cold Lands '13
Cold River '81
Continental Divide '81
The Cowboys '72 ▸
Cross Creek '83
Davy Crockett and the River Pirates '56
Davy Crockett, King of the Wild Frontier '55 ▸
Death Do Us Part '14
Death Hunt '81
Desperate Search '52
A Dog's Way Home '19
Duma '05 ▸
The Edge '97
Edge of Honor '91
Edge of Madness '02
Enemies Closer '14
Far from Home: The Adventures of Yellow Dog '94
Father and Scout '94
Ferngully: The Last Rain Forest '92
Finding Mr. Wright '11
Flight from Glory '37
Further Adventures of the Wilderness Family, Part 2 '77
Gerry '02
Gone, But Not Forgotten '03
Great Adventure '75
The Great Divide '29
The Great Outdoors '88
Grizzly '76
Grizzly Falls '99
Grizzly Man '05 ▸
Grizzly Mountain '97
Happy People: A Year in the Taiga '13 ▸
Hunt to Kill '10
Ice Palace '60
Into the Wild '07 ▸
Jane '17 ▸
Jeremiah Johnson '72 ▸
Just Before Dawn '80
Kid Colter '85
The Kill Hole '12
Lamb '16
The Last of the Dogmen '95
Leave No Trace '18 ▸
Legend of the Northwest '78
The Legend of Wolf Mountain '92
The Levenger Tapes '16
Little Bigfoot '96
Lost in the Barrens '91
Lost Stallions:The Journey Home '08
Lure of the Wilderness '52
Man in the Wilderness '71
Man of the House '95
The Many Adventures of Winnie the Pooh '77
March of the Penguins '05 ▸
Mr. Jones '14

▸ = rated three bones or higher

▶ = rated three bones or higher

Colossal '17
Colossus and the Amazon Queen '60
Crouching Tiger, Hidden Dragon '00 ►
Cutthroat Island '95
Deadly Weapons '70
Death Proof '07
The Demolitionist '95
Do or Die '91
DOA: Dead or Alive '06
Doomsday '08
Elektra '05
Evita '96
The Executioners '93
Fugitive Rage '96
Get Christie Love! '74
Ghost in the Shell '17
G.I. Jane '97
God Said 'Ha!' '99 ►
The Great Texas Dynamite Chase '76
Harriet '19
Heartland '81 ►
Heavy Metal 2000 '00
Hercules the Legendary Journeys, Vol. 1: And the Amazon Women '94
Hidden Figures '17 ►
Hot Box '72
I Spit on Your Grave '77
Incredibles 2 '18 ►
Kidnap '17
Kill Bill Vol. 1 '03 ►
Kill Bill Vol. 2 '04 ►
Kilma, Queen of the Amazons '75
Kisses for My President '64
La Femme Nikita '91 ►
Lara Croft: Tomb Raider '01
Lara Croft Tomb Raider: The Cradle of Life '03
The Long Kiss Goodnight '96
Lucy '14
Mame '74
Marie '85 ►
The Messenger: The Story of Joan of Arc '99
My Name is Modesty: A Modesty Blaise Adventure '04
My Super Ex-Girlfriend '06
Nancy Drew, Reporter '39
Not Without My Daughter '90
On the Basis of Sex '18
One Million Years B.C. '66
The Perils of Pauline '34
Phoenix the Warrior '88
Pocahontas '95 ►
Point of No Return '93
Prehistoric Women '50
RBG '18 ►
Resident Evil: Retribution '12
Resurrection '80 ►
The River Wild '94
Savage Beach '89
Savage Streets '83
Sheena '84
She'll Be Wearing Pink Pajamas '84
The Silence of the Lambs '91 ►
Silver Hawk '04
Skyscraper '95
Speed 2: Cruise Control '97
Spice World: The Movie '97
Street Fighter: The Legend of Chun-Li '09
Sunstorm '01
Superchick '71
Supergirl '84
Sweet Revenge '87
Tarzan and the Amazons '45
Terminal Velocity '94
Thor and the Amazon Women '60
Tulsa '49 ►
The 24 Hour Woman '99
Untamed Women '52
Velvet Smooth '76
Waiting to Exhale '95 ►
Wanted '08 ►
Welcome to Marwen '18
The Wind and the Lion '75 ►
A Woman Rebels '36
Wonder Woman '74
Wonder Woman '17 ►
The World Is Not Enough '99
Zorro's Black Whip '44

Words Come to Life

***See also** Parallel Universe; Writers*

Adaptation '02 ►
Alex & Emma '03
American Dreamer '84
Cashback '06
The Crow Road '96
Final Draft '07
Gemma Bovery '15
Giulia Doesn't Date at Night '09
The Little Prince '16 ►
Lost in Austen '08
Love Comes Lately '07
Lovely by Surprise '07
Mysteria '11
Nim's Island '08
Not Another B Movie '10
The Number 23 '07
P.S. I Love You '07
Ruby Sparks '12
Sex and Lucia '01
Snow Flower and the Secret Fan '11
Something's Gotta Give '03 ►
Stranger Than Fiction '06
Winnie the Pooh '11 ►
The Words '12
You and Me '06

Workin' for a Livin'

About Sunny '12 ►
Adventureland '09 ►
All or Nothing '02
All We Had '16
Amateur Night '16
American Factory '19 ►
An American Romance '44
Annie Claus is Coming to Town '11
Armed Response '13
Assassin in Love '07
Astoria '00
Atlantics '19 ►
The Ballad of Josie '67
Bartleby '01
A Beautiful Life '08
Beauty and the Boss '33
Beauty & the Briefcase '10
Bee Movie '07
Belles on Their Toes '52
The Best Exotic Marigold Hotel '12 ►
Birds Do It '66
Birdsong '12
Bitter/Sweet '09
The Black House '00
Black Limousine '10
Blonde Ambition '07
Blue Valentine '10
Bluebird '13
Bob Funk '09
The Bouquet '13
The Boy With the Sun in His Eyes '09
The Bride Comes Home '35
Brief Moment '33
Brightest Star '14
Brown Sugar '02
Bubble '06
Caffeine '06
Can You Keep a Secret? '19
Car Babes '06
Carry On Regardless '61
Cesar Chavez '14
The Chambermaid '19
Chance at Heaven '33
Christmas Angel '09
The Church Mouse '34
City Island '09
City Streets '38
Clancy in Wall Street '30
Clerks 2 '06 ►
Clockwatchers '97
Close My Eyes '91
The Cobbler '14
C.O.G. '13
Colleen '36
Come Early Morning '06
Comfort and Joy '03
The Company Men '10
Conductor 1492 '24
Confessions of a Shopaholic '09
Congo Maisie '40
The Congressman '16
Cougar Hunting '11
Cow Belles '06
Dancehall Queen '97
Dark Horse '16
Day-Time Wife '39
Days and Clouds '07
Dear Me: A Blogger's Tale '08
Deepwater Horizon '16
Demoted '11
Departures '08
Diary of a Chambermaid '16
Diggers '06
The Dilemma '11
Dirty Lies '16
Dirty Pretty Things '03 ►
The Double '13 ►
Drinking Buddies '13
The Early Bird '25
Edge of the City '57
8.5 Hours '08
Elysium '13
Employee of the Month '06
Entry Level '07
Everyday Black Man '10
Everything Strange and New '09
Everything's Gone Green '06
The Ex '07
Exam '09
Expired '07
Extract '09
Factotum '06 ►
Falling Up '08
The Family Plan '05
Far from Heaven '02 ►
Fast Workers '33
Fatal Trust '06
Father of Invention '11
Flakes '07
Flame in the Streets '61
Flawless '07
Float '08
The Foot Fist Way '08
For a Good Time, Call... '12
Friday After Next '02
Friends & Crocodiles '05
Friends With Benefits '11
Frozen River '08 ►
The Gay Deception '35
Get a Job '16
Gidget Gets Married '72
The Gilded Lily '35
The Girl Said No '30
The Girlfriend Experience '09
Give Us the Moon '44
Going the Distance '10
The Good Girl '02 ►
The Good Guy '10
Happiness Ahead '34
Happy Times '00
Hard to Get '38
Her Secret '33
High School Musical 2 '07
Hit Parade of 1937 '37
Hoax for the Holidays '10
The Human Stain '03
Humble Pie '07
I Do (But I Don't) '04
I Don't Know How She Does It '11
I Hate Valentine's Day '09
I Really Hate My Job '07
Imagine That '09
In My Dreams '14
The Insurance Man '86
The Internship '13
Irina Palm '07
It Happened to Jane '59
I've Got Your Number '34
Janice Beard '99
The Janky Promoters '09
Jimmy the Gent '34
The Job '09
Joe '13 ►
Juke Girl '42
Just Add Water '07
Just My Luck '35
Killer of Sheep '77 ►
King of the Newsboys '38
Kinky Boots '06
The Last Brickmaker in America '01
Last Day of Summer '10
Letting Go '12
The Lightkeepers '09
Little '19
Living In a Big Way '47
A Lobster Tale '06
The Long Shot '04
The Long Summer of George Adams '82
Loose Cannons '10
Love Me Tonight '32 ►
Lucky in Love '14
Mad Money '08
Made in Dagenham '10 ►
Maid in Manhattan '02
Maisie Gets Her Man '42
The Man On the Flying Trapeze '35
The Man Without a Past '02 ►
Manpower '41
Me Before You '16
Meet the People '44
Memron '04
The Method '05 ►
Mildred Pierce '11
Miss London Ltd. '43
Miss Nobody '10
Mondays in the Sun '02
Moonlight & Mistletoe '08
More Than A Secretary '36
Morning Glory '10
Moscow, Belgium '08
My Boss's Daughter '03
The Mystic Masseur '01
The Nanny Diaries '07
A Nanny for Christmas '10
The Navigators '01
Netherbeast Incorporated '07
New in Town '09
Night Owls '15
Nightcrawler '14 ►
9 to 5 '80
No Time For Love '43 ►
North Country '05
Not So Dusty '56
Nothing Personal '09
Office Space '98
The Oklahoma City Dolls '81
On Body and Soul '17 ►
One Day '11
One Hour Photo '02 ►
101 Ways (The Things a Girl Will Do to Keep Her Volvo) '00
The One I Wrote For You '14
Order of Chaos '10
Our Blushing Brides '30
Our Life '10
Outsourced '06
Paddington 2 '17 ►
Parachute Jumper '32
The Passionate Plumber '32
Patti Cake$ '17
Pillars of the Earth '10
The Pool Boys '10
Post Grad '09
Potiche '10 ►
Pretty Baby '50
Prince Avalanche '13
A Promise '13
Punch-Drunk Love '02 ►
The Pursuit of Happyness '06
Read My Lips '01
Real Women Have Curves '02 ►
The Rebound '09
Repo Chick '09
Revolution #9 '01
Rock Jocks '12
Romantics Anonymous '10
Santa Baby 2: Santa Maybe '09
Saturday Night at the Baths '75
Saturday's Children '40
The Search for John Gissing '01
The Search for Santa Paws '10
Second Act '18
The Shape of Water '17 ►
She's Got Everything '37
The Shocking Miss Pilgrim '47
Shorts: The Adventures of the Wishing Rock '09
A Simple Curve '05
Skateland '10
Skyway '33
Sleeping Beauty '11
A Slight Case of Larceny '53
Slim '37
Slow as Lightning '23
Some Days Are Better Than Others '10
The Song of Sparrows '08
Sorry We Missed You '20 ►
Spiral '07
Spring Forward '99
Stiffs '06
Stranded '35
Sunlight Jr. '13
Sunshine Cleaning '09 ►
Support the Girls '18
Sweepings '33
Sweetgrass '09
Swing Shift Maisie '43
Take Me Home Tonight '11
Ten Inch Hero '07
10 Items or Less '06
They Came Together '14
Three and Out '08
Three-Cornered Moon '33
Time Out '01
Too Young to Marry '07
Tower Heist '11
Trainwreck '15 ►
Traveling Companion '96
Two Days, One Night '14 ►
Unbeatable Harold '06
Under Eighteen '32
An Unexpected Love '03
Up Goes Maisie '46
Up in the Air '09 ►
Up the Junction '68
Vacuuming Completely Nude in Paradise '01
Vagabond Lady '35
Very Annie Mary '00
The Way Way Back '13 ►
The Wedding Bros. '08
Wendy and Lucy '08 ►
Where Is Kyra? '17
Wonderful World '09
Working Girl '88 ►
Wrecking Crew '42
You Kill Me '07 ►

World War I

Ace of Aces '33
The African Queen '51 ►
All Quiet on the Western Front '30 ►
All Quiet on the Western Front '79
All the King's Men '99
Anne of Green Gables: The Continuing Story '99
Arsenal '29 ►
The Awakening '11
Behind the Lines '97
Beneath Hill 60 '10
The Better 'Ole '26
Beyond Victory '31
The Big Parade '25 ►
Biggles '85
Birdsong '12
The Blue Max '66
Capitaine Conan '96 ►
Catherine Cookson's The Cinder Path '94
Catherine Cookson's The Wingless Bird '97
The Chaplin Revue '58
Charge of the Model T's '76
Crimson Romance '34
Dark Journey '37 ►
Darling Lili '70
The Dawn Patrol '30 ►
Dawn Patrol '38 ►
Deathwatch '02
Devil in the Flesh '46 ►
Dishonored '31
Dr. Mabuse, The Gambler '22 ►
Doctor Zhivago '65 ►
Doctor Zhivago '03
Doughboys '30
The Eagle and the Hawk '33 ►
The End of St. Petersburg '27 ►
FairyTale: A True Story '97
A Farewell to Arms '32 ►
A Farewell to Arms '57
Fifth Day of Peace '72
The Fighting 69th '40 ►
Finding Rin Tin Tin '07
Flambards '78
Flyboys '06
For Me and My Gal '42
Fort Saganne '84
The Four Horsemen of the Apocalypse '21 ►
Four Sons '28
Frantz '17 ►
Gallipoli '81 ►
Gods and Monsters '98 ►
Golden Dawn '30
Grand Illusion '37 ►
Half-Shot at Sunrise '30
Hell's Angels '30 ►
Hotel Imperial '27
How Many Miles to Babylon? '82
In Love and War '96
Inside the Lines '30
J'accuse! '19 ►
Jericho '38
Journey's End '18
Joyeux Noel '05 ►
King and Country '64 ►
The King of Hearts '66 ►
La France '07
Lafayette Escadrille '58
The Land That Time Forgot '75
The Last Outpost '35
Lawrence of Arabia '62 ►
The Legend of Bagger Vance '00
Legends of the Fall '94
Les Destinees '00
The Life and Death of Colonel Blimp '43 ►
Life and Nothing But '89 ►
The Little American '17
Lost Battalion '01
The Lost Patrol '34 ►
The Love Light '21
The Man From Yesterday '32
Man of Legend '71
The Man Who Knew Infinity '16
Mata Hari '32 ►
Mata Hari '85
Miracle of Our Lady of Fatima '52
My Boy Jack '07
Nicholas and Alexandra '71
1917 '19 ►
1915 '82
1918 '85
Noah's Ark '28
Nurse Edith Cavell '39 ►
Oh! What a Lovely War '69
Once an Eagle '76
Passchendaele '10
Paths of Glory '57 ►
The Patriots '33 ►
Photographing Fairies '97
Pilgrimage '33
Private Peaceful '12
The Red Baron '08
Rendezvous '35
Return of the Soldier '82 ►
Revolt of the Zombies '36
The Road to Glory '36
Sergeant Klems '71
7th Heaven '27
Sgt. Stubby: An American Hero '18
Shopworn Angel '38 ►
Spy in Black '39 ►
Suicide Fleet '31
Suzy '36
Testament of Youth '79
Testament of Youth '15 ►
Theeb '15 ►
They Gave Him a Gun '37
They Shall Not Grow Old '19 ►
Today We Live '33
Tolkien '19
Tomorrow Is Forever '46
The Trench '99
The Unknown Soldier '98
A Very Long Engagement '04 ►
Vincere '09
War Horse '11
Waterloo Bridge '40 ►
What Price Glory? '52 ►

► = rated three bones or higher

The White Cliffs of Dover '44 ▶
The White Sister '33
Wilson '44 ▶
Wings '27
Wings of Eagles '57
Wonder Woman '17 ▶
Zeppelin '71

World War I Spies

***See also** Spies & World War One*

Charge of the Model T's '76
Dark Journey '37 ▶
Darling Lili '70
Dishonored '31
Hotel Imperial '27
Inside the Lines '30
The Love Light '21
Mata Hari '32 ▶
Mata Hari '85
Savages '12
Seas Beneath '31
Spy in Black '39▶
The 39 Steps '09
Three Faces East '30
Zeppelin '71

World War II

***See also** Biopics: Military; The Holocaust; The Homefront: England; The Homefront: U.S./Canada; Nazis & Postwar; POW/MIA; The Resistance; World War Two Spies*

Above and Beyond '53▶
Above and Beyond '06
Above Suspicion '43▶
Above Us the Waves '55▶
Action in the North Atlantic '43
Adolf Hitler: My Part in His Downfall '74
Adventures of Smilin' Jack '43
The Affair '95
After the Deluge '03▶
The Aftermath '19
Against the Sun '15
Air Force '43▶
Alexandria. . . Why? '78
All the Queen's Men '02
Ambush '99▶
American Guerrilla in the Philippines '50
The Americanization of Emily '64▶
And While We Were Here '13
Angels One Five '54
Angry Harvest '85▶
Anne Frank: The Whole Story '01▶
Another Time, Another Place '58
Anzio '68
Appointment in London '53
Appointment With Venus '51
Arch of Triumph '48▶
Arch of Triumph '85
The Army of Crime '10
Army of Shadows '69▶
The Ascent '76▶
Ashes and Diamonds '58▶
The Assisi Underground '84
Atonement '07▶
Attack! '56▶
Attack Force Z '84
Attack on Leningrad '09
The Attic: The Hiding of Anne Frank '88
Au Revoir les Enfants '87▶
The Audrey Hepburn Story '00
Away All Boats '56
Baaria '09
Back Home '90
Back to Bataan '45
Back to 1942 '12
The Bamboo Blonde '46
Band of Brothers '01▶
Bataan '43
Battle at Bloody Beach '61
Battle Cry '55▶
Battle of Britain '69
The Battle of El Alamein '68
Battle of Neretva '69
Battle of the Bulge '65
Battle of the Coral Sea '59
Battle of the Eagles '79
Battle of the Rails '46 ▶
Battleforce '78
Battleground '49 ▶
Beach Red '67 ▶
Beanpole '20 ▶
The Beasts of Marseilles '57
Bedknobs and Broomsticks '71
Behind Enemy Lines '85
Below '02
The Best Years of Our Lives '46 ▶
Between Heaven and Hell '56 ▶
Beyond Valkyrie: Dawn of the Fourth Reich '16
The Big Lift '50
The Big Red One '80 ▶
Bitter Victory '58
Black Brigade '69
Black Rain '88▶
Bless Me, Ultima '13
Blockhouse '73
Blood on the Sun '45
Bloodrayne: The Third Reich '11
The Boat Is Full '81▶
Bombardier '43
Bon Voyage '03▶
The Book Thief '13
The Boy in the Striped Pajamas '08▶
Brass Target '78
Breakthrough '50
Brideshead Revisited '08
The Bridge '59
The Bridge at Remagen '69
The Bridge on the River Kwai '57▶
Bridge to Hell '87
Bridge to the Sun '61
A Bridge Too Far '77
Brief Encounter '46▶
The Brylcreem Boys '96
The Burmese Harp '56▶
The Caine Mutiny '54▶
The Camomile Lawn '92
Canal Zone '42
A Canterbury Tale '44▶
The Canterville Ghost '44
Captain America: The First Avenger '11
Captain Corelli's Mandolin '01
Captain Newman, M.D. '63
Captains of the Clouds '42
Captive Heart '47▶
Captive Hearts '87
Carolina Blues '44
Carrie's War '04
Carry Me Home '04
Carry On England '76
Casablanca '42▶
Casablanca Express '89
Castle Keep '69▶
Catch-22 '70▶
The Catcher Was a Spy '18
Caught in the Draft '41▶
Chain Lightning '50
Charlotte Gray '01
Chicago Joe & the Showgirl '90
China '43
China Girl '42
Chosen '16
Christ Stopped at Eboli '79▶
Christabel '89
The Chronicles of Narnia: The Lion, the Witch and the Wardrobe '05
Churchill '17
Class of '44 '73
The Clock '45▶
Closely Watched Trains '66▶
Closing the Ring '07
Colditz: Escape of the Birdmen '71
The Colditz Story '55
Come and See '85▶
Come See the Paradise '90▶
Coming Home '98
Command Decision '48
Commando Attack '67
Commandos '73
Commandos Strike at Dawn '43
Company of Heroes '13
Confirm or Deny '41
Conspiracy '01
Conspiracy of Hearts '60 ▶
Contraband '40
Convoy '40
Cornered '45 ▶
Corregidor '43
Cottage to Let '41
Counter-Attack '45
Counterpoint '67
The Cranes Are Flying '57 ▶
Crash Dive '43
Cross of Iron '76
The Cross of Lorraine '43
The Cruel Sea '53 ▶
Cry Havoc '43
Cry of Battle '63
The Cuckoo '02
D-Day, the Sixth of June '56 ▶
Dam Busters '55 ▶
Danger UXB '81
Darby's Rangers '58
Dark Blue World '01
Darkest Hour '17▶
Das Boot '81▶
A Day in October '92
Day One '89▶
Days of Glory '43
Days of Glory '06
Deadly Mission '78
The Death of Adolf Hitler '84
December '91
December 7th: The Movie '91
Deep Six '58
Defiance '08
Desert Commandos '67
The Desert Fox '51▶
The Desert Rats '53▶
Despair '78▶
Desperate Journey '42
Destination Gobi '53
Destination Tokyo '43
Destroyer '43▶
The Devil's Brigade '68
Devils on the Doorstep '00
The Diary of Anne Frank '59▶
The Dirty Dozen '67▶
The Dirty Dozen: The Deadly Mission '87
The Dirty Dozen: The Fatal Mission '88
The Dirty Dozen: The Next Mission '85
Distant Voices, Still Lives '88▶
Dive Bomber '41▶
Divided We Fall '00
Dr. Akagi '98
Dominion: Prequel to the Exorcist '05
Dondi '61
Downfall '04▶
Dresden '06
The Dresser '83▶
The Dresser '15▶
Dunkirk '17▶
The Eagle Has Landed '77▶
Eagles Over London '69
Edge of Darkness '43▶
Eight Iron Men '52
Eighteen '04
The Elusive Corporal '62▶
Emperor '12
Empire of the Sun '87▶
The Empty Mirror '99
End of the Affair '55
The End of the Affair '99▶
Enemy at the Gates '00
Enemy Below '57▶
Enemy of Women '44
The English Patient '96▶
Enigma '01
Enigma Secret '79
Ensign Pulver '64
Era Notte a Roma '60▶
Escape from Sobibor '87▶
Escape to Athena '79
Europa, Europa '91▶
Every Time We Say Goodbye '86
Everyman's War '09
Everything is Illuminated '05▶
The Exception '17
The Execution '85
Eyes in the Night '42
The Fallen '05▶
Farewell to the King '89
Fat Man and Little Boy '89
Fateless '05 ▶
Father '67 ▶
Father Goose '64
Fighter Squadron '48
The Fighting Rats of Tobruk '44
Fighting Seabees '44
The Fighting Sullivans '42 ▶
The Final Countdown '80 ▶
Fires on the Plain '59 ▶
First Light '10
First to Fight '67
Fist of Legend '94
Five Came Back '17 ▶
Five Fingers '52 ▶
Five for Hell '67
Flags of Our Fathers '06 ▶
Flat Top '52
The Flemish Farm '43
Flying Leathernecks '51 ▶
Flying Tigers '42
For the Boys '91
For the Moment '94
Forbidden Games '52▶
Force of Arms '51
Force 10 from Navarone '78
Foreign Correspondent '40▶
A Foreign Field '93
Fortunes of War '87▶
The Forty-Ninth Parallel '41▶
Forty Thousand Horsemen '41
Four Bags Full '56
The Four Horsemen of the Apocalypse '62
Four in a Jeep '51
Four Jills in a Jeep '44
Four Sons '40
Fraulein '58
Free Men '12
From Hell to Victory '79
From Here to Eternity '53▶
Fury '14
G-Men *vs.* the Black Dragon '43
The Gallant Hours '60▶
The Gang's All Here '43
The Garden of the Finzi-Continis '71▶
Generale Della Rovere '09▶
A Generation '54▶
Generation War '13
Germany, Pale Mother '80
The Girl of Your Dreams '99
The Gleiwitz Case '61
Gloomy Sunday '02▶
Go for Broke! '51
God is My Co-Pilot '45
The Goebbels Experiment '05
Golden Earrings '47
The Great Escape '63▶
The Great Raid '05
The Great Water '04
Green for Danger '47
The Green Glove '52
Guadalcanal Diary '43
Guerillas in Pink Lace '64
The Guernsey Literary & Potato Peel Pie Society '18
Gung Ho! '43
The Guns of Navarone '61▶
The Gypsy Warriors '78
Hacksaw Ridge '16
The Halls of Montezuma '50
Hamsun '96
Hannibal Brooks '69
Hanover Street '79
Hart's War '02
Head in the Clouds '04
The Heat of the Day '91
Heaven Knows, Mr. Allison '57▶
Hell Boats '70
Hell Commandos '69
Hell Is for Heroes '62▶
Hell to Eternity '60
Hellcats of the Navy '57
The Heroes of Telemark '65
Hidden in Silence '96
A Hidden Life '19
The Hiding Place '75
High Barbaree '47
The Hill '65
Hiroshima '95▶
Hitler '62
Hitler: The Last Ten Days '73
Hold Back the Dawn '41
Hollywood Canteen '44 ▶
Holocaust '78 ▶
The Home Front '02
Homecoming '48
Hope and Glory '87 ▶
The Horizontal Lieutenant '62
Hornets' Nest '70
The Human Comedy '43 ▶
The Human Condition: A Soldier's Prayer '61 ▶
The Human Condition: No Greater Love '58 ▶
The Human Condition: Road to Eternity '59 ▶
Hustler Squad '76
I Was a Male War Bride '49 ▶
Identity Unknown '45
Ike: Countdown to D-Day '04
Ill Met By Moonlight '57
I'll Remember April '99
Mission of Honor '19
The Imitation Game '14▶
Imitation General '58
Immortal Battalion '44▶
Immortal Sergeant '43
In Darkness '11
In Enemy Hands '04
In Harm's Way '65
In Love and War '58
In Love and War '01
In Tranzit '07
In Which We Serve '43▶
The Incident '89▶
The Incredible Mr. Limpet '64
Infinity '96
The Inglorious Bastards '78
Inglourious Basterds '09▶
The Inheritors '82
The Innocents '16▶
Into the Storm '09
Into the White '12
Invasion Quartet '61
Is Paris Burning? '66▶
The Island on Bird Street '97
Ithaca '16
Jacob the Liar '74
Joan of Paris '42▶
Joe Maddison's War '10
Johnny Doesn't Live Here Any More '44
Jojo Rabbit '19▶
Journey for Margaret '42▶
Judgment at Nuremberg '61▶
Julia '77▶
Jungle Patrol '48
Kanal '56▶
Kapo '59▶
Katyn '07
The Keeper '18
Kelly's Heroes '70
The Key '58
King Rat '65▶
Kings Go Forth '58
La Grande Vadrouille '66▶
Land of Mine '15
Landscape After Battle '70
Lassiter '84
The Last Butterfly '92
The Last Chance '45▶
The Last Days of Patton '86
The Last Drop '05
The Last Lieutenant '94
The Last Metro '80▶
The Last of the Blonde Bombshells '00
The Last Sentence '12
The Last Train '74
The Last Warrior '89
A League of Their Own '92▶
Leon Morin, Priest '61
Letters from Iwo Jima '06▶
The Life and Death of Colonel Blimp '43▶
Life Is Beautiful '98▶
Lifeboat '44▶
Lilli Marlene '50
The Longest Day '62▶
Lore '13▶
The Lost Valentine '11
Lotna '64
Love Letters '45
MacArthur '77
Malaya '49
Malta Story '53
A Man Called Sarge '90
A Man Escaped '57 ▶
The Man Who Lies '68
The Man Who Lived at the Ritz '91
Map of the Human Heart '93
Maria's Lovers '84
Massacre in Rome '73
The Master Race '44
Max Manus: Man of War '08
The McConnell Story '55
McHale's Navy '64
McKenzie Break '70 ▶
Memoirs of a Geisha '05
Memorial Day '12
Memphis Belle '90 ▶
The Men '50 ▶
Mephisto '81 ▶
Merrill's Marauders '62
Merry Christmas, Mr. Lawrence '83 ▶
A Midnight Clear '92▶
Midway '76
Midway '19
Military Intelligence and You! '06
Miracle at Midnight '98
Miracle at St. Anna '08
The Miracle of the White Stallions '63
The Mirror '75▶
Missiles from Hell '58
Mission of the Shark '91▶
Mission to Death '66
Mrs. Henderson Presents '05
Mrs. Miniver '42▶
Mr. Klein '76▶
Mister Roberts '55▶
Mr. Skeffington '44▶
Mr. Winkle Goes to War '44
The Monuments Men '13
The Moon is Down '43
The More the Merrier '43▶
The Mortal Storm '40▶
Mosquito Squadron '70
Mother of Mine '05▶
Murphy's War '71
Music Box '89
Mussolini & I '85
The Nasty Girl '90▶
Navy Way '44
Never So Few '59
Never Wave at a WAC '52
Night Ambush '57
Night of the Fox '90
The Night of the Shooting Stars '82▶
1945 '17▶
1941 '79
The Ninth Day '04▶
No Man Is an Island '62
No Regrets for Our Youth '46▶
None But the Brave '65
The North Star '43▶
The Notebook '04
The Notebook '13
The Nun's Story '59▶
Objective, Burma! '45▶
The Ogre '96
Okinawa: The Afterburn '15
Once an Eagle '76
Once Before I Die '65
One Day You'll Understand '08
One of Our Aircraft Is Missing '41▶
One That Got Away '57▶
1,000 Plane Raid '69
Onionhead '58
Only the Brave '06
The Only Way '70
Open City '45▶
Operation Bikini '63
Operation Daybreak '75
Operation Eichmann '61
Operation Valkyrie '04
Outpost: Rise of the Spetsnaz '13
Overlanders '46▶
Overlord '18
The Pacific '10▶
Pacific Inferno '85
Paisan '46▶
Paradise Road '97
Paris After Dark '43
The Passage '79
Passage to Marseilles '44▶

The Password Is Courage '62
Patton '70 ▶
The Pawnbroker '65 ▶
Pearl '78
Pearl Harbor '01
The Philadelphia Experiment '84
Piece of Cake '88
Pilot No. 5 '43
Pin-Up Girl '44
Playing for Time '80 ▶
The Plot to Kill Hitler '90
Pride of the Marines '45 ▶
Prisoners of the Sun '91 ▶
Private Buckaroo '42
Private Navy of Sgt. O'Farrell '68
The Proud and Profane '56
PT 109 '63
The Purple Heart '44
The Purple Plain '54
Pursuit of the Graf Spee '57
Raggedy Man '81 ▶
Raid on Rommel '71
Raiders of Leyte Gulf '63
The Railway Man '13
The Ravagers '65
Reach for the Sky '56
Rebel '85
Rebel in the Rye '17
Red Tails '12
The Reflecting Skin '91
Remember '15
Resistance '03
Resistance '20
Return to Never Land '02
Reunion in France '42
Rodgers & Hammerstein's South Pacific '01
Rosenstrasse '03 ▶
Run Silent, Run Deep '58 ▶
Safe Conduct '01 ▶
Sahara '43 ▶
Sahara '95
Saigon '47
Sailor of the King '53
Saints and Soldiers '03
Saints and Soldiers: Airborne Creed '12
Salo, or the 120 Days of Sodom '75
Salute to the Marines '43
Sands of Iwo Jima '49 ▶
Saving Private Ryan '98 ▶
The Scarlet & the Black '83
Schindler's List '93 ▶
Screaming Eagles '56
Sea Chase '55
Sea of Sand '58
Sea Wife '57
Sea Wolves '81
The Search '48 ▶
The Secret Invasion '64
The Secret of Santa Vittoria '69
The Secret War of Harry Frigg '68
Seven Beauties '76 ▶
Seven Years in Tibet '97
Sherlock Holmes and the Secret Weapon '42 ▶
Sherlock Holmes and the Voice of Terror '42
Ship of Fools '65 ▶
Shoah '85 ▶
The Shop on Main Street '65 ▶
Signs of Life '68
The Silent Enemy '58
Silent Night '02
The Silver Fleet '43
Simon and the Oaks '12
Since You Went Away '44 ▶
Sink the Bismarck '60 ▶
The Sinking of the Laconia '10
Sisters of War '10
633 Squadron '64
The Skin '81
The Sky Is Falling '00
Slaughterhouse Five '72
The Small Back Room '49 ▶
So Proudly We Hail '43 ▶
So This Is Washington '43
Soldier of Orange '78 ▶
A Soldier's Story '84 ▶
A Soldier's Tale '91
Somewhere I'll Find You '42 ▶
Son of Lassie '45
The Song of Names '19
Sophie Scholl: The Final Days '05 ▶
The Sorrow and the Pity '71 ▶
The Sound of Music '65 ▶
South Pacific '58 ▶
South Sea Woman '53
Special Forces '68
Spitfire '42 ▶
The Square Peg '58
Stage Door Canteen '43
Stairway to Heaven '46 ▶
Stalag Luft '93
Stalingrad '94
Stand by for Action '42
Star Spangled Rhythm '42 ▶
The Steel Claw '61
The Story of G.I. Joe '45 ▶
Straight into Darkness '04
Strayed '03 ▶
Submarine Attack '54
The Sun '05
Sundown '41
Surviving Picasso '96
Sword of Honour '01
Taking Sides '01 ▶
The Tanks Are Coming '51
Tarawa Beachhead '58
Tarzan Triumphs '43
Task Force '49
Taxi for Tobruk '60 ▶
Tea with Mussolini '99
The Teahouse of the August Moon '56
The Tenth Man '88
Thank Your Lucky Stars '43 ▶
Their Finest '17 ▶
They Were Expendable '45 ▶
The Thin Red Line '64
The Thin Red Line '98 ▶
13 Minutes '17
Thirty Seconds Over Tokyo '44 ▶
36 Hours '64 ▶
This Is the Army '43
This Land Is Mine '43 ▶
Those People Next Door '52
Thousands Cheer '43
Three Came Home '50 ▶
Thunder Birds '42
The Tin Drum '79 ▶
To Be or Not to Be '42 ▶
To Be or Not to Be '83
To End All Wars '01
To Have & Have Not '44 ▶
To Hell and Back '55
To the Shores of Tripoli '42
Tobruk '66
Tomorrow Is Forever '46
Tonight and Every Night '45
Tonight We Raid Calais '43
Too Late the Hero '70 ▶
Tora! Tora! Tora! '70
Torpedo Run '58
A Town Like Alice '56
The Train '65 ▶
Transit '18
Treasure Island '99
Triumph of the Spirit '89 ▶
Triumph of the Will '34 ▶
The Truce '96 ▶
The Tuskegee Airmen '95 ▶
Twelve o'Clock High '49 ▶
The 25th Hour '67
25 Fireman's Street '73 ▶
Two Girls and a Sailor '44 ▶
Two Men Went to War '02
The Two of Us '68 ▶
Two Thousand Women '44
Two Women '61 ▶
U-571 '00
Unbroken '14
Uncertain Glory '44
Under the Flag of the Rising Sun '72 ▶
The Underdog '43
Underground '41
Underground '70
Underground '95 ▶
Until They Sail '57
Up in Arms '44
Uprising '01 ▶
USS Indianapolis: Men of Courage '16
Vacation from Marriage '45
Valiant '05
Valkyrie '08
Varian's War '01
Very Important Person '61
Victory '81
The Voice of the Turtle '47
Von Ryan's Express '65 ▶
The Von Trapp Family: A Life of Music '15
Voyage of the Damned '76 ▶
Wackiest Ship in the Army '61
Waiting for Dublin '07
Wake Island '42 ▶
Wake Up and Dream '46
A Walk in the Sun '46 ▶
Walking with the Enemy '13
Wallenberg: A Hero's Story '85 ▶
The Walls of Hell '64
The Wannsee Conference '84 ▶
War & Remembrance '88
War & Remembrance: The Final Chapter '89
War Lover '62
War of the Buttons '12
Warbirds '08
Waterloo Road '45
The Way Ahead '44
The Way to the Stars '45
We Dive at Dawn '43 ▶
We Were One Man '80
Wedding in White '72
Well-Digger's Daughter '46 ▶
We'll Meet Again '82
What Did You Do in the War, Daddy? '66
When Hell Broke Loose '58
When Trumpets Fade '98
When Willie Comes Marching Home '50 ▶
The White Cliffs of Dover '44 ▶
The Wind Cannot Read '58
The Winds of War '83
Windtalkers '02
A Wing and a Prayer '44 ▶
Winter in Wartime '10
Women in Bondage '43
Women of Valor '86
World War II: When Lions Roared '94
A Yank in the R.A.F. '41
Yanks '79
Yesterday's Enemy '59
You'll Never Get Rich '41 ▶
The Young Lions '58 ▶
Zelary '03 ▶
Zone Troopers '84
The Zookeeper's Wife '17

World War II Spies

***See also** Nazis & Spies & World War Two*

Above Suspicion '43 ▶
Across the Pacific '42 ▶
Action in Arabia '44
Against the Wind '48
Air Raid Wardens '43
All the Queen's Men '02
All Through the Night '42 ▶
Allied '16
Anthropoid '16
Any Human Heart '11
Background to Danger '43 ▶
Berlin Correspondent '42
Berlin Express '48 ▶
Betrayed '54 ▶
Black Book '06 ▶
Bon Voyage '03 ▶
Cairo '42
Carve Her Name with Pride '58
Charlotte Gray '01
Cloak and Dagger '46
Code Name: Emerald '85
Confessions of a Nazi Spy '39
Counterblast '48
The Counterfeit Traitor '62 ▶
Dad's Army '16
Dangerously We Live '41
David Harding, Counterspy '50
Decision Before Dawn '51
Enigma '01
Eva '09
The Exception '17
Eye of the Needle '81
The Fallen Sparrow '43 ▶
Five Fingers '52 ▶
Five for Hell '67
Five Graves to Cairo '43 ▶
Foreign Correspondent '40 ▶
Head in the Clouds '04
The Heat of the Day '91
Holt of the Secret Service '42
I See a Dark Stranger '46 ▶
I Was an American Spy '51
Invisible Agent '42
The Lady From Lisbon '42
Lust, Caution '07
The Man Who Never Was '55 ▶
The Master Race '44
The Mediterranean in Flames '72
Ministry of Fear '44 ▶
Monte Carlo '86
Morituri '65 ▶
Mother Night '96 ▶
My Favorite Blonde '42 ▶
My Favorite Spy '51
My Name Is Ivan '62 ▶
The Next of Kin '42
Night Train to Munich '40 ▶
Notorious '46 ▶
On the Double '61
Once Upon a Honeymoon '42
Operation Amsterdam '60
Operation Cross Eagles '69
Operation Crossbow '65 ▶
Operation Secret '52
Panama Hattie '42
Rio Rita '42
Robot Pilot '41
The Rocketeer '91 ▶
Saboteur '42 ▶
The Second Front '05
Shining Through '92
Ship Ahoy '42
Stalag 17 '53 ▶
The Stranger '46 ▶
Tampico '44
13 Rue Madeleine '46 ▶
36 Hours '64 ▶
Triple Cross '67 ▶
Two Thousand Women '44
Under the Rainbow '81
Up Periscope '59
Watch on the Rhine '43 ▶
Waterfront '44
Where Eagles Dare '68 ▶

Wrestling

. . .All the Marbles '81
Below the Belt '80
Black Mask 2: City of Masks '02
Body Slam '87
The Calamari Wrestler '04
Fighting with My Family '19
Flesh '32
The Foul King '00
Foxcatcher '14 ▶
The Hammer '07
The Jesse Ventura Story '99
Legendary '10
Lone Tiger '94
Lowlife '18
Mad Bull '77
Man on the Moon '99
The Masked Saint '16
Nacho Libre '06
No Holds Barred '89
On Again-Off Again '37
The One and Only '78
Paradise Alley '78
The Peanut Butter Falcon '19
Pin Down Girls '51
Queens of the Ring '13
Ready to Rumble '00
Samson in the Wax Museum '63
Secret Society '00
Sit Tight '31
Spider-Man '02 ▶
Superargo '67
Swing Your Lady '38
Vision Quest '85
Waves '19 ▶
Win Win '11
Women in Love '70 ▶
The World According to Garp '82 ▶
The Wrestler '73
The Wrestler '08 ▶

Writers

***See also** This Is Your Life*

Adaptation '02 ▶
The Adderall Diaries '16
The Adventures of Mark Twain '44 ▶
Agatha '79
Agatha Christie: A Life in Pictures '04
Albatross '11
Alex & Emma '03
Alias Betty '01
All Is True '18
All the Wrong Places '00
American Dreamer '84
American Splendor '03 ▶
Amuck! '71
Amy's O '02
And While We Were Here '13
Angel '07
An Angel at My Table '89 ▶
Ann Rule Presents: The Stranger Beside Me '03
Anne of Green Gables: The Continuing Story '99
Anonymous '11
Another Man's Poison '52
The Answer Man '09
Any Human Heart '11
Anything Else '03
The Ape '05
As Good As It Gets '97 ▶
Ask the Dust '06
The Assistants '09
Atonement '07 ▶
Author! Author! '82
Author: The JT LeRoy Story '16
Authors Anonymous '14
The Awakening '11
Bag of Bones '11
Balzac: A Life of Passion '99 ▶
Bamboozled '00
Barton Fink '91 ▶
Basic Instinct 2 '06
The Basketball Diaries '95
Beat '00
Beau Brummell: This Charming Man '06
A Beautiful Day in the Neighborhood '19 ▶
Beautiful Dreamers '92
This Beautiful Fantastic '17
Becoming Jane '07
Before Night Falls '00 ▶
Before Sunset '04 ▶
Behind the Lines '97
Being Flynn '12
Beloved Infidel '59
Beloved Sisters '14 ▶
The Best Man '99 ▶
Best Seller '87 ▶
Big Bad Love '02
The Big Slice '90
Big Sur '13
Black Butterfly '17
The Blue Tooth Virgin '09
Bone Daddy '97
Borstal Boy '00
The Bounce Back '16
The Brand New Testament '15 ▶
Breakfast at Tiffany's '61 ▶
Breakfast of Champions '98
Breakin' All The Rules '04
Bridal Fever '08
The Bride Goes Wild '48
Bright Young Things '03
The Bronte Sisters '79
The Brontes of Haworth '73
Burial of the Rats '95
A Business Affair '93
Bye Bye Braverman '67
Cabin by the Lake '00
Can You Ever Forgive Me? '18 ▶
Capote '05 ▶
Casanova '05 ▶
A Case of You '13
Celebrity '98 ▶
Chaos Theory '08
Chapter Two '79
Cheaper by the Dozen '03
Chelsea Walls '01
Chicklit '16
Chinese Puzzle '13
City of Gold '16 ▶
The City of Your Final Destination '09
Closed Curtain '13 ▶
Closer '04 ▶
Closer and Closer '96
Colombiana '11
Come Live With Me '40
Coming Through '85
Crashing '07
Cross Creek '83
Croupier '97 ▶
Dark Crimes '16
The Dark Half '91
The Dark Side of the Heart '92
Dead Cool '04
Dean Koontz's Mr. Murder '98
Deathtrap '82
Deconstructing Harry '97
Dedication '07
Delirious '91
Derrida '02
Devotion '46
Dinner and Driving '97
The Dinner Party '20
The Disappearance of Garcia Lorca '96
Divine Secrets of the Ya-Ya Sisterhood '02
Doctor Zhivago '65 ▶
Doctor Zhivago '03
The Dog Problem '06
A Dog Year '09
The Door in the Floor '04 ▶
Double Whammy '01
Down With Love '03
Duplex '03
Easier With Practice '10
Eat, Pray, Love '10
Echoes '15
The Eclipse '09
11-11-11 '11
The End of the Affair '99 ▶
Enemies of Laughter '00
Eternity and a Day '97
Eva '62
Every Day '10
Every Thing Will Be Fine '15
Evidence of Blood '97
Evil Eyes '04
Evil Lives '92
Factotum '06 ▶
Faithless '00 ▶
Fall '97
A Fantastic Fear of Everything '14
Far Out Isn't Enough: The Tomi Ungerer '13
Fathers and Daughters '16
Father's Day '96
The Fault In Our Stars '14
Fear and Loathing in Las Vegas '98
Feed the Fish '09
Final Draft '07
Finding Forrester '00
A Fine Madness '66 ▶
Fireflies in the Garden '08
The Flower of My Secret '95 ▶
Footsteps '03
For Hire '98
For the Love of Grace '08
1408 '07
Freedom Writers '07
Fresh Cut Grass '04
From Noon Till Three '76
Full Speed '96
The Fundamentals of Caring '16
The Gambler '97
Game 6 '05
Genius '16
Gentlemen Broncos '09
Ghost Writer '07
The Ghost Writer '10
Ghosts Never Sleep '05
A Girl Cut in Two '07
The Girl in the Book '15
Girl Meets Boy '13
Girl Most Likely '12
Giulia Doesn't Date at Night '09
Glam '97
Goosebumps '15 ▶
Gothic '87 ▶
The Great Sinner '49
Guernica '16

▶ *= rated three bones or higher*

The Guernsey Literary & Potato Peel Pie Society '18
Half a Hero '53
Hamsun '96
Hangman '17
Happy Hour '03
Harriet the Spy '96
Harriet the Spy: Blog Wars '10
Haunted Summer '88
Hav Plenty '97 ▸
Heart Beat '80
Heartburn '86 ▸
Hell Is Sold Out '51
The Help '11 ▸
Hemingway & Gelhorn '12
Hemingway's Garden of Eden '08
Henry & June '90 ▸
Her Alibi '88
Hit and Runway '01
The Hoax '06
Horrors of the Black Museum '59
Hot Type: 150 Years of The Nation '15
The Hours '02 ▸
How to Be '08
How to Build a Girl '20
How to Kill Your Neighbor's Dog '01
How to Lose Your Lover '04
The Human Stain '03
Humor Me '17
Hustler White '96
I Am Not Your Negro '17 ▸
I Capture the Castle '02
Ice Twisters '09
Impromptu '90 ▸
In Praise of Love '01
In the Cut '03
In the Deep Woods '91
In the Mouth of Madness '95
In the Realms of the Unreal '04 ▸
Infamous '06
The Infinite Worlds of H.G. Wells '01
The Invisible Woman '13 ▸
Iris '01 ▸
Isn't She Great '00
Jack London '44
James Joyce: A Portrait of the Artist as a Young Man '77 ▸
Jane Doe '96
Jexi '19
Jim Hanvey, Detective '37
Joe Gould's Secret '00
Just Write '97
The Keeper: The Legend of Omar Khayyam '05
Kill Your Darlings '13
Kissing a Fool '98
Knight of Cups '15
The Kovak Box '06
Lady in the Water '06
Lady on a Train '45 ▸
The Last International Playboy '08
The Last Station '09
The Last Word '08
Late August, Early September '98
Letters from a Killer '98
Lies and Whispers '98
The Life of Emile Zola '37 ▸
Limitless '11
Listen Up Philip '14
Little Women '18
Little Women '19 ▸
Look at Me '04 ▸
The Lost Boys '78 ▸
Love and Death on Long Island '97
Love Between the Covers '15
Love by the 10th Date '17
Love Comes Lately '07
A Love Song for Bobby Long '04
Lovely by Surprise '07
Lovers Courageous '32
Lovers of Hate '10
A Loving Father '02
Lucia, Lucia '03
Magic Beyond Words: The JK Rowling Story '11
The Magic of Belle Isle '12
The Majestic '01
Maladies '13
Mambo Italiano '03
The Man from Elysian Fields '01 ▸
The Man Who Invented Christmas '17
Margot at the Wedding '07
Mark Felt: The Man Who Brought Down the White House '17
Martian Child '07
The Mask of Dimitrios '44 ▸
Maya Dardel '17
Maybe Baby '99
Melissa '97
Mercy '09
Merrily We Live '38 ▸
A Merry War '97 ▸
Miles Ahead '16 ▸
Misery '90 ▸
Miss Monday '98
Mission '00
Mrs. Palfrey at the Claremont '05
Mrs. Parker and the Vicious Circle '94
Mr. Belvedere Rings the Bell '51
Mr. Jealousy '98
Mr. Woodcock '07
Mitch Albom's Have a Little Faith '11
Mixing Nia '98
Moliere '07
The Moon's Our Home '36
Mother '96
mother! '17
Motherhood '09
The Motive '18
Moulin Rouge '01 ▸
A Murder of Crows '99
The Muse '99
My Afternoons with Marguerite '10 ▸
My Boy Jack '07
My Brilliant Career '79 ▸
My Childhood '38 ▸
My Effortless Brilliance '08
My Future Boyfriend '11
My Girlfriend's Boyfriend '10
My House in Umbria '03 ▸
My Left Foot '89 ▸
My Sister Eileen '42
Mysteria '11
The Mystery of Rampo '94 ▸
Mystery Woman: Mystery Weekend '05
The Mystic Masseur '01
Naked Lunch '91 ▸
Nelson Algren: The End Is Nothing, the Road Is All '15
Nerolio '96
The Night and the Moment '94
Night Train to Lisbon '13
Nim's Island '08
No Time For Comedy '40
Nobody Else But You '11
Non-Fiction '18
Not Another Happy Ending '13
Novel Romance '06
Old Acquaintance '43
101 Ways (The Things a Girl Will Do to Keep Her Volvo) '00
Our Idiot Brother '11
Our Lady of the Assassins '01
Out of Africa '85 ▸
Out of Order '03
Pandaemonium '00
Paper Man '09
Paperback Romance '96
The Paranoids '08
The Passion of Ayn Rand '99
A Perfect Day '06
Personal Velocity: Three Portraits '02 ▸
Personals '00
Petrified Forest '36 ▸
The Pillow Book '95
Playing House '06
Pornography: A Thriller '10
Portraits Chinois '96
Possession '02
Postmortem '98
Presumed Dead '06
The Prize '63 ▸
Psychosis '10
Pulp '72
Purple Violets '07
Pussycat, Pussycat, I Love You '70
Quills '00
The Raven '12
Re-Cycle '06
Reach Me '14
The Real Howard Spitz '98
The Reaper '97
Recipe for a Perfect Christmas '05
Redeemer '02
Reds '81 ▸
Reprise '06
Restaurant '98
The Rewrite '15
The Riddle '07
The Road to Coronation Street '10
Roman de Gare '07
Romancing the Stone '84 ▸
Romantic Comedy '83
Route 30 '08
Rowing with the Wind '88
The Royal Tenenbaums '01 ▸
Ruby Sparks '12
Ruslan '09
Russian Dolls '05
Salem's Lot '04
Salinger '13
The Savages '07 ▸
The Sculptress '97
The Sea Gull '68
Second Best '05
The Secret in Their Eyes '09 ▸
The Secret Life of Walter Mitty '13
Secret Window '04
Seven Keys to Baldpate '29
Seven Keys to Baldpate '35
Seven Psychopaths '12 ▸
Sex and Lucia '01
Sex and the City: The Movie '08
Shadowlands '93 ▸
The Shadows '07
Shakespeare in Love '98 ▸
She's Funny That Way '15
The Shining '80
A Short History of Decay '13
The Singing Detective '03
Sinister '12
Sink or Swim '97
Sitting Pretty '48 ▸
Sixth and Main '77
The Skin '81
Slam '98
Slash '16
The Sleepy Time Gal '01
Sleuth '07
Slipstream '07
The Snows of Kilimanjaro '52 ▸
Something's Gotta Give '03 ▸
Spotlight '15 ▸
The Squid and the Whale '05 ▸
Stand by Me '86 ▸
Starting Out in the Evening '07
Stay Cool '09
The Sticky Fingers of Time '97
Stone Reader '02 ▸
Storytelling '01 ▸
Stranger Than Fiction '06
Street Smart '87
Sweet and Lowdown '99
Swimming Pool '03 ▸
Sylvia '03
A Taxi Driver '17 ▸
Teach Me '97
The Tenants '06
Thanks for the Memory '38
Theodora Goes Wild '36 ▸
There Be Dragons '11
The Third Man '49 ▸
Third Person '13
Thrill of the Kill '06
Tickled '16 ▸
Time Regained '99
Tom & Viv '94 ▸
Toni Morrison: The Pieces I Am '19 ▸
Touched With Fire '16
The Town That Banned Christmas '06
Trainwreck '15 ▸
The Trials of Oscar Wilde '60 ▸
The Trip '02
The Trip to Italy '14
True Confession '37
Tumbledown '16
The TV Set '06
2046 '04
Twixt '12
Two Ninas '00
Two Shades of Blue '98
Under the Tuscan Sun '03
Undercover Angel '99
United States of Leland '03
Unsane '82
Untogether '19
The Vanishing of Sidney Hall '17
Venom '18
The Voice of Merrill '52
A Walk in the Woods '15
The Weather Man '05
The Wedding Night '35
The Whole Wide World '96 ▸
Wiener-Dog '16
The Wife '17
The Wild Pear Tree '18 ▸
Wilde '97
Winter Passing '05
The Witches of Oz '11
The Witnesses '07
The Woman in the Fifth '11
The Women '68
Wonder Boys '00 ▸
The Words '12
Words and Pictures '13
The World According to Garp '82 ▸
World's Greatest Dad '09 ▸
Yalom's Cure '14
You and Me '06
You Stupid Man '02
Young Adult '11
Young Ideas '43
Youngblood Hawke '64
Your Vice is a Closed Room and Only I Have the Key '72
Zeder '83
Zora Is My Name! '90
Zorba the Greek '64 ▸

The Wrong Man

***See** Frame-Ups; Mistaken Identity*

Wrong Side of the Tracks

***See also** Rags to Riches*

Aaron Loves Angela '75
Algiers '38 ▸
Alice Adams '35
All Good Things '10
Amarilly of Clothesline Alley '18
Angel and the Badman '47 ▸
Angels with Dirty Faces '38 ▸
Anna Christie '30
Arthur '11
Bachelor Party '84
Back Door to Heaven '39 ▸
Battle of the Year '13
Beastly '11
Breaking Away '79 ▸
The Bride of Frank '96
The Bride Wore Red '37
Camille '36 ▸
Cannery Row '82
Captains Courageous '37 ▸
Captives '94
Carbon Copy '81
Cardboard Boxer '16
Careful, He Might Hear You '84 ▸
Carrie '52 ▸
Cat Ballou '65 ▸
Chance at Heaven '33
Cherry Crush '07
Climbing High '38
Cool and the Crazy '94
Cool As Ice '91
Courtship '87 ▸
crazy/beautiful '01
Cruise '18
Cry-Baby '90 ▸
Desierto '16
Diary of a Chambermaid '46 ▸
Dirty Dancing '87 ▸
Dragstrip Girl '94
The Earl of Chicago '40
Eegah! '62
Endless Love '14
Far and Away '92
Federal Hill '94
The Fence '94
Fire with Fire '86
The Flamingo Kid '84 ▸
The Florida Project '17 ▸
Foxfire Light '82
Fresh Horses '88
Future Kill '85
Gandu '10
Gimme Shelter '14
Grease '78 ▸
Great Expectations '97
The Great Gatsby '74
The Great Gatsby '13
The Hairy Ape '44
Havoc '05
Here on Earth '00
Hindle Wakes '27
The Hireling '73
Huddle '32
Hush '98
Iron Maze '91
It '27
It Happened One Night '34 ▸
Jailbait! '00
Jersey Girl '92
Jungle Fever '91 ▸
King Ralph '91
Last Exit to Brooklyn '90 ▸
Liar's Moon '82
Listen to Your Heart '10
Little Minister '34 ▸
The Loves of Carmen '48
The Man from Snowy River '82
Manhattan Melodrama '34 ▸
Masquerade '88 ▸
Meskada '10
Min & Bill '30
My Forbidden Past '51
My Man Godfrey '36 ▸
Naked Youth '59
Nobody's Children '52
Outpost in Morocco '49
The Phantom of the Opera '25 ▸
A Place in the Sun '51 ▸
The Pope of Greenwich Village '84
Port of New York '49
Pretty in Pink '86
Primrose Path '40
Princess Tam Tam '35 ▸
Private Number '36
Pygmalion '38 ▸
The Rage: Carrie 2 '99
Reckless '84
The Restless Years '58
Return to Snowy River '88 ▸
Riff Raff '92 ▸
Rocky '76 ▸
Romance of the Limberlost '38
Room at the Top '59 ▸
Rosewood '96 ▸
Ruby Gentry '52
Rumble Fish '83 ▸
San Francisco '36 ▸
The Second Chance '06
The Servant '63 ▸
Set It Off '96
sex, lies and videotape '89 ▸
She's All That '99
Show People '28 ▸
Some Kind of Wonderful '87
Somebody Up There Likes Me '56 ▸
Starter for 10 '06
Stay Hungry '76 ▸
Step Up '06
Step Up 2 the Streets '08
Stomp the Yard '07
Suburbia '83
The Swan '56 ▸
The Tamarind Seed '74
That Night '93
This Sporting Life '63 ▸
Those People Next Door '52
Tortilla Flat '42 ▸
A Tree Grows in Brooklyn '45 ▸
Under the Boardwalk '89
Valley Girl '83
The Valley of Decision '45 ▸
Vivacious Lady '38 ▸
Waterloo Bridge '40 ▸
White Palace '90
The White Sin '24
The World of Suzie Wong '60
Wuthering Heights '12
The Young Philadelphians '59 ▸

Yakuza

***See also** Crime & Japan; Organized Crime*

Adrenaline Drive '99
American Yakuza '94
Another Lonely Hitman '95
Bad Guys '08
Beautiful Beast '95
Black Rain '89
Blind Woman's Curse '70
The Bodyguard '76
Boiling Point '90
Brother '00
Cops *vs.* Thugs '75
Dead or Alive 2 '00
Dolls '02 ▸
Everly '14
Fudoh: The New Generation '96
Girls of the White Orchid '85
Gonin 2 '96
Gozu '03
Graveyard of Honor '02
Hard As Nails '01
Ichi the Killer '01
Johnny Mnemonic '95
Kill! '68
Kill Bill Vol. 1 '03 ▸
No Way Back '96
Organ '96
Organized Crime & Triad Bureau '93
Outrage '10
Pale Flower '64
Rain Fall '09
Showdown in Little Tokyo '91
Sonatine '96 ▸
The Street Fighter's Last Revenge '74
War '07
Wasabi '01
Wicked City '92
The Wolves '82 ▸
The Yakuza '75
Yakuza Apocalypse '15
Zatoichi: The Life and Opinion of Masseur Ichi '62
Zatoichi: Zatoichi's Flashing Sword '64

Yoga

Bleeding Heart '15
The Crippled Masters '82
Hollywood Homicide '03
The Next Best Thing '00
The Strike '16
What Women Want '00
Yoga Hosers '16

You are Getting Sleepy!

The Angry Red Planet '59
Belladonna '08
Blood of Dracula '57
Brainscan '94
Carefree '38 ▸
Cowboy from Brooklyn '38
The Curse of the Jade Scorpion '01
Dead Again '91 ▸
Devil Doll '36 ▸
Devour '05
Echoes '15
The Exorcist 2: The Heretic '77
The Fourth Kind '09
Frankie and Alice '10
The Great Buck Howard '09 ▸
The Guilt of Janet Ames '47
Haunting Fear '91

Horrors of the Black Museum '59
The Hypnotic Eye '60
Killer by Nature '10
A Killing in a Small Town '90 ▶
The Magician '26
The Mask of Diijon '46
The Matrimonial Bed '30
The Misadventures of Merlin Jones '63
Molly Moon and The Incredible Book of Hypnotism '15
On a Clear Day You Can See Forever '70
Parasomnia '08
The Pit and the Pendulum '09
Shallow Hal '01
The She-Creature '56
She Creature '01
Somewhere in Time '80
The Sorcerers '67
Stir of Echoes '99
Swing Fever '43
Telefon '77
Threat of Exposure '02
The Three Faces of Eve '57
Thumbsucker '05 ▶
Trance '13
A Wind from Wyoming '94

You Big Dummy!

***See also** Killer Toys*

Dead Silence '07
Devil Doll '64
Dummy '02
The Great Gabbo '29
Knock on Wood '54
Magic '78
1941 '79
The Ten '07
The Unholy Three '25 ▶

You Lose, You Die

***See also** Game Shows; Post-Apocalypse*

Alien *vs.* Predator '04
Arcade '93
Are You Scared? '06
The Arena '73
Arena '11
Battle Creek Brawl '80
Battle Royale '00
Blade Boxer '97
Bloodsport 4: The Dark Kumite '98
The Condemned '07
Cruel World '05
Death Race '08
Death Race 2 '10
Death Race 2000 '75
Deathrow Gameshow '88
DOA: Dead or Alive '06
Freerunner '10
Futuresport '98
The Game '97 ▶
Gamebox 1.0 '04
Gamer '09
Hostel: Part 2 '07
The Human Race '14
The Hunger Games '12 ▶
The Hunger Games: Catching Fire '13 ▶
Last Resort '09
Mad Max: Beyond Thunderdome '85
Mean Guns '97
Mortal Challenge '97
Nemesis Game '03
Nerve '16
Never Surrender '09
Nine Dead '10
Open Graves '09
Prayer of the Rollerboys '91
Predators '10
Robot Jox '90
Rollerball '75
Rollerball '02
The Running Man '87
Sci-Fighter '04
Smokin' Aces 2: Assassins' Ball '10
Solarbabies '86
Star Hunter '95
Stay Alive '06
10th Victim '65 ▶
Terror Trap '10
13 '10
31 '16
Thr3e '07
The Tournament '09
Tron '82
Vacancy '07
Wrong Turn 2: Dead End '07

Yuppie Nightmares

***See also** Strained Suburbia*

Addams Family Values '93
Alice '90 ▶
Almost You '85
Amos and Andrew '93
Baby Boom '87
Bad Influence '90
Barbarians at the Gate '93 ▶
Bedroom Eyes '86
Beetlejuice '88 ▶
The Big Chill '83 ▶
Blind Date '87
Blind Side '93
Boiler Room '00 ▶
The Bonfire of the Vanities '90
The Boost '88
Bright Lights, Big City '88
Cape Fear '91 ▶
City of Hope '91 ▶
Clara's Heart '88
Clean and Sober '88 ▶
Cold Creek Manor '03
Coma '78 ▶
Consenting Adults '92
Curly Sue '91
Dead Calm '89 ▶
Desperately Seeking Susan '85
Down and Out in Beverly Hills '86
Drop Dead Fred '91
Edge of Honor '91
The End of Innocence '90
Eye of the Demon '87
Fatal Attraction '87 ▶
The First Wives Club '96
The Fisher King '91 ▶
Folks! '92
Fun with Dick and Jane '77
The Further Adventures of Tennessee Buck '88
The Game '97 ▶
The Guardian '90
The Hand that Rocks the Cradle '92
Happiness '98 ▶
The Hard Way '91 ▶
He Said, She Said '91
Heartburn '86 ▶
Hiding Out '87
In the Company of Men '96
Indian Summer '93
Jungle Fever '91 ▶
L.A. Story '91 ▶
Limit Up '89
Lost in America '85 ▶
Maid to Order '87
The Malibu Beach Vampires '91
Maniac '77
Micki & Maude '84
Mifune '99
The Mighty Ducks '92
The Money Pit '86
Mother's Boys '94
Moving '88
My New Gun '92
Neighbors '81
New Year's Day '89 ▶
Nothing But Trouble '91
Nothing in Common '86
Oasis of the Zombies '82
The Object of Beauty '91 ▶
Pacific Heights '90 ▶
Preppies '82
Private Benjamin '80
Quicksilver '86
The Quiet '05
Reversal of Fortune '90 ▶
Roadhouse 66 '84
Ruthless People '86 ▶
The Safety of Objects '01
St. Elmo's Fire '85
The Secret of My Success '87
September '88
sex, lies and videotape '89 ▶
Shattered '91
A Shock to the System '90 ▶
Six Degrees of Separation '93
A Smile Like Yours '96
Something Wild '86
Stay Tuned '92
Straw Dogs '72 ▶
Summer Rental '85
Taking Care of Business '90
The Temp '93
Three Men and a Little Lady '90
The Tie That Binds '95
The Toxic Avenger, Part 3: The Last Temptation of Toxie '89
Trading Places '83
The Trigger Effect '96
Truth or Consequences, N.M. '97
Under Pressure '98
Unlawful Entry '92
The Vagrant '92
Voodoo Dawn '89
Wall Street '87 ▶
The War of the Roses '89 ▶
Westworld '73 ▶
What about Bob? '91 ▶
When a Man Loves a Woman '94
Wolf '94
Your Friends & Neighbors '98 ▶

Ziegfeld Follies

***See also** Stagestruck*

Deep in My Heart '54
Easter Parade '48 ▶
The Eddie Cantor Story '53
Funny Girl '68 ▶
Glorifying the American Girl '30
The Great Ziegfeld '36 ▶
The Helen Morgan Story '57
I'll See You in My Dreams '51
The Jolson Story '46 ▶
Love Me or Leave Me '55 ▶
Singin' in the Rain '52 ▶
The Story of Will Rogers '52
Ziegfeld Follies '46
Ziegfeld Girl '41 ▶

Zombie Soldiers

***See also** Zombies*

Akira Kurosawa's Dreams '90
Army of Darkness '92 ▶
The Dark Power '85
Dead Snow '09
Dead Snow: Red *vs.* Dead '14 ▶
Deathdream '72
Hard Rock Zombies '85
The Haunted World of El Superbeasto '09
House '86 ▶
Jonah Hex '10
Oasis of the Zombies '82
Osombie '12
Outpost '07
Outpost: Black Sun '12
Revolt of the Zombies '36
Scream and Scream Again '70
She Demons '58
Shock Waves '77
They Saved Hitler's Brain '64
Zombie Lake '80

Zombies

***See also** Death & Ghosts, Ghouls, & Zombie Soldiers*

Abraham Lincoln *vs.* Zombies '12
After Sundown '06
Aftermath '12
The Alchemist '81
Alice '09
Alien Dead '79
Alien Massacre '67
All Souls Day '05
Almost Dead '94
American Zombie '07
Amigo Undead '15
The Astro-Zombies '67
Astro-Zombies M3: Cloned '10
Astro-Zombies M4: Invaders from Cyberspace '12
Attack of the Herbals '11
Attack of the Moon Zombies '11
Automaton Transfusion '06
Bad Meat '11
The Basement '89
Battle of the Damned '14
Beast of Blood '71
Beast Within '08
The Beyond '82
Beyond Re-Animator '03
Bikini Bloodbath Carwash '08
Bikini Bloodbath Christmas '09
Biozombie '98
Black Demons '91
Boo! A Madea Halloween '16
Bride of Re-Animator '89
Burying the Ex '15
Cabin Fever '03
The Cabin in the Woods '12 ▶
Carnival of Souls '62 ▶
Cell '16
Cemetery Man '95
Children of the Living Dead '00
Children Shouldn't Play with Dead Things '72
The Chilling '89
Chopper Chicks in Zombietown '91
City of the Walking Dead '80
Creatures from the Pink Lagoon '07
The Cured '18
Dance of the Dead '08
Dawn of the Dead '78 ▶
Dawn of the Dead '04 ▶
Dawn of the Mummy '82
Day of the Dead '85
The Dead 2 '13
Dead Air '08
Dead Alive '93
Dead Creatures '01
The Dead Don't Die '19
The Dead Hate the Living '99
Dead Heat '88
Dead Heist '07
Dead in the Water '06
Dead Men Don't Die '91
The Dead Next Door '89
The Dead One '07
Dead Pit '89
Dead Rising: End Game '16
Dead Snow '09
Deadgirl '08
Deadlands 2: Trapped '08
Death Becomes Her '92 ▶
The Death Curse of Tartu '66
Death Valley: The Revenge of Bloody Bill '04
Deathdream '72
Diary of the Dead '07
Dylan Dog: Dead of Night '11
Ed and His Dead Mother '93
Fido '06
Flesh Eaters from Outer Space '05
Flick '07
Flight of the Living Dead: Outbreak on a Plane '07
The Four '12
Freaks of Nature '15
George A. Romero's Land of the Dead '05 ▶
The Ghost Brigade '93
The Ghoul '75
The Girl with All the Gifts '17
The Grapes of Death '78
The Hanging Woman '72
Haunting Fear '91
Hellgate '89
Hell's Ground '08
Horror Rises from the Tomb '72
The House of Seven Corpses '73
House of the Dead 2: Dead Aim '05
House of the Dead '78
House of the Dead '03
I Am Legend '07 ▶
I Eat Your Skin '64
I Sell the Dead '09
I Walked with a Zombie '43 ▶
I Was a Teenage Zombie '87
Infected '13
Infested: Invasion of the Killer Bugs '02
Invisible Invaders '59
Isle of the Dead '45
John Carpenter's Ghosts of Mars '01
King of the Zombies '41
Kiss Daddy Goodbye '81
The Last Days on Mars '13
The Legend of the 7 Golden Vampires '73
Let Sleeping Corpses Lie '74
Life After Beth '14
Little Monsters '19
The Lost Future '10
Maggie '15
Mark of the Astro-Zombies '02
Maze Runner: The Death Cure '18
Messiah of Evil '74
Mortuary '05
Mulberry Street '06
The Mummy '32 ▶
The Mummy '59 ▶
The Mummy '99
Mutant Chronicles '08
Mutants '09
My Boyfriend's Back '93
Navy Seals *vs.* Zombies '15
Neon Maniacs '86
Night of the Comet '84
Night of the Creeps '86
Night of the Death Cult '75
Night of the Ghouls '59
Night of the Living Dead '68 ▶
Night of the Living Dead '90
Night of the Living Deb '14
Nightmare Weekend '86
Oasis of the Zombies '82
Orgy of the Dead '65
Otto: Or, Up with Dead People '08
Overlord '18
Overtime '11
ParaNorman '12 ▶
Patient Zero '18
Pet Sematary 2 '92
Phantasm 3: Lord of the Dead '94
Plague of the Zombies '66
Plan 9 from Outer Space '56
Planet Terror '07
Pontypool '09
Pride and Prejudice and Zombies '16
Quatermass 2 '57 ▶
Raw Meat '72
Re-Animator '84 ▶
[Rec] '07
[REC] 3: Genesis '12
[REC] 4: Apocalyse '14
Redneck Zombies '88
Resident Evil '02
Resident Evil: Afterlife '10
Resident Evil: Apocalypse '04
Resident Evil: Extinction '07
Resident Evil: Retribution '12
Resident Evil: The Final Chapter '16
Return of the Evil Dead '75
Return of the Living Dead '85
Return of the Living Dead 2 '88
Return of the Living Dead 3 '93
Return of the Living Dead: Rave to the Grave '05
The Returned '14
Revenge of the Dead '84
Revenge of the Living Zombies '88
Revolt of the Zombies '36
Ring of Darkness '04
Scout's Guide to the Zombie Apocalypse '15
Seeding of a Ghost '86
Seedpeople '92
Shanks '74
Shaun of the Dead '04 ▶
Shock Waves '77
Skeleton Key 2: 667, the Neighbor of the Beast '08
Slither '06 ▶
Sole Survivor '84
The Stuff '85
Sugar Hill '74
Survival of the Dead '09
Svengali '31 ▶
Tamara '05
Teenage Zombies '58
They Came Back '04
Torture Chamber of Baron Blood '72
28 Days Later '02
28 Weeks Later '07
Undead '05
Undead or Alive '07
The Vanguard '08
Vengeance of the Zombies '72
Venom '05
Versus '00
Virgin among the Living Dead '71
Voodoo Dawn '89
Walking Deceased '15
War of the Satellites '58
Warm Bodies '13
The White Zombie '32 ▶
Wild Zero '00
Winterbeast '92
Woke Up Dead '09
World War Z '13
Zombi Child '20
Zombie '80
Zombie High '87
Zombie Honeymoon '04
Zombie Island Massacre '84
Zombie Lake '80
Zombie Nightmare '86
Zombie Strippers '08
Zombieland '09 ▶
Zombieland: Double Tap '19 ▶
Zombies of Mass Destruction '10
Zombies of Moratau '57
Zombies of the Stratosphere '52
Zombies on Broadway '44
Zombieworld '15

Zoos

Fierce Creatures '96
The Reformer and the Redhead '50
We Bought a Zoo '11
The Zookeeper's Wife '17

▶ = rated three bones or higher

Kibbles and Series List

The **Kibbles** and **Series** indexes have been combined into one index. This is where you'll find info on where your favorite movies came from—literary, theatrical, cartoon, and television adaptations to name a few, as well as the behind the scenes talents that make movies possible, such as producers and special effects wizards. Another important feature of this index is the quality check it provides, with categories like **Woofs!**, **4 Bones**, and **Top Grossing Films** by year. This index also provides information on recurring characters like James Bond, Jack Ryan, or Mike Hammer, as well as notable screen partnerships. Some examples include Abbott & Costello, Hope & Crosby, and De Niro & Scorsese. **A tipped triangle denotes a three-bone or higher rating** The categories are as follows, with an asterisk (*) denoting a new category:

** = new to this edition*

Edith Wharton
William Wharton
E.B. White
Oscar Wilde
Thornton Wilder
Ben Ames Williams
Virginia Woolf
Cornell Woolrich
Herman Wouk
Emile Zola
Boston Blackie
The Bowery Boys
Broken Lizard
Buffalo Bill Cody
Bulldog Drummond
Captain Nemo
Carry On
Charlie Brown and the Peanuts Gang
Charlie Chan
Cisco Kid
Corman's Mama
Dead End Kids
Director/Star Teams:
Allen & Johansson
Almodovar & Banderas
Almodovar & Cruz
Altman & Gould
Altman & Murphy
Anderson & Hoffman
Anderson & Murray
Bergman & Ullmann
Bergman & von Sydow
Boetticher & Scott
Brooks & Wilder
Bunuel & F. Rey
Burton & Bonham Carter
Burton & Depp
Capra & Stewart
Carpenter & Russell
Chabrol & Audran
Chabrol & Huppert
Coraci & Sandler
Cukor & Hepburn
Donen & Kelly
Donner & Gibson
Dugan & Sandler
Fellini & Mastroianni
Fincher & Pitt
Ford & Wayne
Frankeneheimer & Lancaster
Greengrass & Damon
Hathaway & Cooper
Hawks & Wayne
Herzog & Kinski
Hill & Newman
Hitchcock & Grant
Hitchcock & Stewart
Holofcener & Keener
Howard & Hanks
Howard & Keaton
Huston & Bogart
Jarman & Swinton
Jordan & Rea
Kasdan & Kline
Kazan & Brando
King & Peck
Kurosawa & Mifune
LaBute & Eckart
Lean & Guinness
Lee & J. Turturro
Lee & Washington
Leone & Eastwood
Linklater & Hawke
Lynch & L. Dern
Lynch & Nance
Mann & Stewart
McKay & Ferrell
McLaglen & Stewart
McLaglen & Wayne
Needham & Reynolds
Newman & Woodward
Nolan & Bale
Nolan & Caine
Poitier & Cosby
Pollack & Redford
Rafelson & Nicholson
Raimi & Campbell
Raimi & 1973 Oldsmobile Delta 88
Reiner & Martin
Ritt & Newman
Rodriguez & Banderas
Sayles & Clapp
Sayles & Cooper
Sayles & Strathairn
Scorsese & De Niro
Scorsese & Keitel
Scott (Ridley) & Crowe
Scott (Tony) & Washington
Shadyac & Carrey
Sheridan & Day-Lewis
Siegel & Eastwood
Sirk & Hudson
Soderburgh & Clooney
Soderburgh & Roberts
Spielberg & Dreyfuss
Spielberg & Hanks
Sturges & McCrea
Tashin & Lewis
Techine & Deneuve
Thorpe & R. Taylor
Truffault & Leaud
Verbinski & Depp
Verhoeven & R. Hauer
von Sternberg & Dietrich
Walsh & Bogart
Wilder & Lemmon
Woo & Fat
Zemeckis & Hanks
Dirty Harry
Disney Animated Movies
Disney Family Movies
Doc Holliday
Dr. Christian
Dr. Kildare
Dr. Mabuse
Dr. Seuss
Dracula
Dreamworks Animated Movies
87th Precinct
Elvisfilm
The Falcon
4 Bones
Francis the Talking Mule
Frankenstein
Fu Manchu
Godzilla and Friends
Hallmark Hall of Fame
Hammer Films: Horror
Hammer Films: Sci Fi & Fantasy
Hannibal Lecter
Hercule Poirot
Hercules
Highest Grossing Films of All Time
Hopalong Cassidy
Indiana Jones
Inspector Clouseau
Jack Ryan
Jack the Ripper
James Bond
James Bond Spoofs
Jason Bourne
Jesse James
John McClane
Jungle Jim
King, Martin Luther, Jr.
Lassie
Live Action/Animation Combos
The Lone Rider
Ma & Pa Kettle
Maisie
The Marx Brothers
Mexican Spitfire
MGM Musicals
Mike Hammer
Miss Marple
Mister Moto
Mr. Wong
Modern Shakespeare
Monty Python
The Muppets
Perry Mason
Peter Pan
Philip Marlowe
Pixar Animated Movies
The Planet of the Apes
Plays to Film:
Maxwell Anderson
James M. Barrie
Anton Chekov
Noel Coward
Horton Foote
Beth Henley
David Mamet
Arthur Miller
Ferenc Molnar
Eugene O'Neill
Rodgers & Hammerstein
Arthur Schnitzler
William Shakespeare
George Bernard Shaw
Sam Shepard
Robert E. Sherwood
Neil Simon
Tom Stoppard
John Van Druten
Tennessee Williams
Producers:
Irwin Allen
Robert Altman
Judd Apatow
Bruckheimer/Simpson
William Castle
Coppola/American Zoetrope
Roger Corman/New World
Val Lewton
George Lucas
Merchant Ivory
George Pal
Shaw Brothers
Steven Spielberg
Andy Warhol
Rambo
The Rangebusters
Recycled Footage/Redubbed Dialogue
Renfrew of the Mounties
Restored Footage
Rin Tin Tin
The Ritz Brothers
Robin Hood
Rusty the Dog
The Saint
Sam Spade
Sinbad
Screen Teams:
Abbott & Costello
Allen & Farrow
Allen & Keaton
Astaire & Rogers
Avalon & Funicello
Ball & Arnaz
Belushi & Aykroyd
Bogart & Bacall
Bronson & Ireland
Burton & Taylor
Cagney & O'Brien
Cheech & Chong
Colbert & MacMurray
Cronyn & Tandy
Cusack & Piven
Cusack & Robbins
Damon & B. Affleck
Davis & Brent
De Niro & Keitel
De Niro & Pesci
Depardieu & Deneuve
Douglas & Lancaster
Eastwood & Locke
Eddy & McDonald
Farley & Spade
Favreau & Vaughn
Flynn & de Havilland
Francis & Brent
Gable & Crawford
Gable & Loy
Gable & Turner
Garland & Rooney
Garson & Pidgeon
Gaynor & Farrell
Gibson & Glover
Hawn & Russell
Hepburn & Grant
Hepburn & Tracy
Hope & Crosby
Ladd & Lake
Laurel & Hardy
Lee & Cushing
Lemmon & Matthau
Loy & Powell
MacMurray & Goddard
MacMurray & Stanwyck
Martin & Lewis
Mastroianni & Loren
Newman & Woodward
Powell & Keeler
Power & Tierney
Power & L. Young
Redford & Newman
Reynolds & DeLuise
Reynolds & Field
Reynolds & Reed
Rogers & Evans
Snipes & Harrelson
Stewart & Sullavan
Stiller & O. Wilson
Turner & Douglas
Wayne & O'Hara
Wheeler & Woolsey
Wilder & Pryor
Scrooge
Sexton Blake
Sherlock Holmes
Special FX Wizards:
Rick Baker
Rob Bottin
Anton Furst
Ray Harryhausen
Herschell Gordon Lewis
Tom Savini
Dick Smith
Douglas Trumball
Star Wars
Superman
Tarzan
The Texas Rangers
The Thin Man
The Three Mesquiteers
The Three Musketeers
Three Stooges
Tom Ripley
Top Grossing Films: 1939-2018
The Trail Blazers
Troma Films
Wild Bill Hickok
The Wolfman
Wyatt Earp
Zorro
Zucker/Abrahams/Zucker

* = new to this edition

Kibbles and Series Index

Recurrent characters, cinematic collaborations, various adaptations, and important behind-the-scenes personnel information is the focus of the **Kibbles and Series Index.** These categories are listed alphabetically. **A tipped triangle indicates a video rated three bones or higher.**

Adapted from a Cartoon

The Addams Family *'91*
Addams Family Values *'93*
Adventures of Red Ryder *'40*
Adventures of Smilin' Jack *'43*
Aeon Flux *'05*
Alvin and the Chipmunks *'07*
Barbarella *'68*
The Belles of St. Trinian's *'53* ▶
Blondie *'38*
Blondie Brings Up Baby *'39*
Blondie Goes Latin *'42*
Blondie Goes to College *'42*
Blondie Has Trouble *'40*
Blondie in Society *'41*
Blondie Meets the Boss *'39*
Blondie On a Budget *'40*
Blondie Plays Cupid *'40*
Blondie Takes a Vacation *'39*
Bratz *'07*
Casper *'95* ▶
Casshern *'04*
Cool World *'92*
Death Note 2: The Last Name *'07*
Death Note 3: L Change the World *'08*
Death Note *'06* ▶
Dennis the Menace *'93*
Dennis the Menace Strikes Again *'98*
Dick Tracy *'37*
Disney's Teacher's Pet *'04* ▶
Doogal *'05*
Dudley Do-Right *'99*
Edward Scissorhands *'90* ▶
Elvira, Mistress of the Dark *'88*
Fat Albert *'04*
The Flash *'90*
Flash Gordon *'80*
Flesh Gordon 2: Flesh Gordon Meets the Cosmic Cheerleaders *'90*
The Flintstones *'94*
The Flintstones in Viva Rock Vegas *'00*
Friday Foster *'75*
Frostbiter: Wrath of the Wendigo *'94*
George of the Jungle *'97* ▶
The Great St. Trinian's Train Robbery *'66*
The Guyver *'91*
Guyver 2: Dark Hero *'94*
Heavy Metal *'81* ▶
Inspector Gadget *'99*
Jane & the Lost City *'87*
Josie and the Pussycats *'01*
The Last Airbender *'10*
Li'l Abner *'40*
Little Nemo: Adventures in Slumberland *'92*
The Mask *'94* ▶
Masters of the Universe *'87*
Mighty Morphin Power Rangers: The Movie *'95*
Mr. Magoo *'97*
Office Space *'98*
The Perils of Gwendoline *'84*
Phantom 2040 Movie: The Ghost Who Walks *'95*
The Pink Panther *'64* ▶
The Pink Panther Strikes Again *'76* ▶
Prince Valiant *'54*
The Pure Hell of St. Trinian's *'61*
Queer Duck: The Movie *'06*
The Return of Swamp Thing *'89*
Richie Rich *'94*
The Sad Sack *'57*
Scooby-Doo *'02*
Scooby-Doo 2: Monsters Unleashed *'04*
The SpongeBob SquarePants Movie *'04*
Supergirl *'84*
Superman 2 *'80* ▶
Tank Girl *'94*
Teenage Mutant Ninja Turtles: The Movie *'90*
Teenage Mutant Ninja Turtles 2: The Secret of the Ooze *'91*
Teenage Mutant Ninja Turtles 3 *'93*
Teenage Mutant Ninja Turtles *'14*
Timecop *'94*
Tom and Jerry: The Movie *'93*
Transformers *'07*
Turbo: A Power Rangers Movie *'96*
The Villain *'79*
Wild Palms *'93*
Yu-Gi-Oh! The Movie: Pyramid of Light *'04*

Adapted from a Disney Amusement Park Ride

The Country Bears *'02*
The Haunted Mansion *'03*
Pirates of the Caribbean: Dead Man's Chest *'06*
Pirates of the Caribbean: The Curse of the Black Pearl *'03* ▶

Adapted from a Fairy Tale

The Adventures of Pinocchio *'96*
Aladdin *'92* ▶
Alice in Wonderland *'50*
Beauty and the Beast *'46* ▶
Beauty and the Beast *'91* ▶
Beauty and the Beast: A Dark Tale *'10*
The Blue Light *'32* ▶
The Brothers Grimm *'05*
Butterfly Ball *'76*
Chicken Little *'05*
Cinderella *'50* ▶
Cinderella *'64*
Cinderella *'97*
Cinderella *'15*
A Cinderella Story *'04*
Cinderella 2000 *'78*
Cinderfella *'60*
The Company of Wolves *'85* ▶
Deadtime Stories *'86*
Donkey Skin *'70* ▶
Ella Enchanted *'04* ▶
Enchanted *'07*
Ever After: A Cinderella Story *'98* ▶
Fairy Tales *'76*
Freeway *'95*
Fun & Fancy Free *'47* ▶
George Balanchine's The Nutcracker *'93*
The Glass Slipper *'55*
Green Snake *'93*
Grimm's Snow White *'12*
Hans Christian Andersen *'52*
Hansel & Gretel *'13*
Happily Ever After *'93*
Happily N'Ever After *'07*
Hoodwinked *'05* ▶
Hoodwinked Too! Hood *vs.* Evil *'11*
Into the Woods *'14*
Jack & the Beanstalk *'52*
Jack and the Beanstalk *'09*
Jack and the Beanstalk: The Real Story *'01*
Jack the Giant Slayer *'13*
Lady in the Water *'06*
The Little Mermaid *'75*
The Little Mermaid *'89* ▶
The Magic Sword *'62*
Maleficent *'14*
March of the Wooden Soldiers *'34* ▶
Mirror Mirror *'12*
The Muppets' Wizard of Oz *'05*
The NeverEnding Story *'84* ▶
The NeverEnding Story 3: Escape from Fantasia *'94*
The Nutcracker Prince *'91*
Once Upon a Brothers Grimm *'77*
Peau D'Ane *'71* ▶
Peter Pan *'53* ▶
Peter Pan *'60* ▶
The Pied Piper of Hamelin *'57*
Pin. . . *'88*
Pinocchio's Revenge *'96*
The Princess Bride *'87* ▶
Puss in Boots *'11* ▶
Red Riding Hood *'88*
The Red Shoes *'05*
Rumpelstiltskin *'86*
Shrek 2 *'04* ▶
The Singing Princess *'49*
Sleeping Beauty *'59* ▶
Sleeping Beauty *'89*
The Sleeping Beauty *'10*
The Slipper and the Rose *'76*
The Snow Queen *'02*
Snow White *'89*
Snow White: A Tale of Terror *'97*
Snow White and the Huntsman *'12*
Snow White and the Three Stooges *'61*
Snow White: The Fairest of Them All *'02*
The Swan *'56* ▶
The Swan Princess *'94*
Sydney White *'07*
Tangled *'10* ▶
Thumbelina *'94*
Tom Thumb *'58* ▶
Who Slew Auntie Roo? *'71*
The Witches *'90* ▶

Adapted from a Game

Alien *vs.* Predator *'04*
Aliens *vs.* Predator: Requiem *'07*
Alone in the Dark 2 *'08*
Alone in the Dark *'05*
BloodRayne 2: Deliverance *'07*
BloodRayne *'06*
Bloodrayne: The Third Reich *'11*
Clue *'85*
DOA: Dead or Alive *'06*
Doom *'05*
Double Dragon *'94*
Dungeons and Dragons *'00*
Far Cry *'08*
Final Encounter *'00*
Final Fantasy: The Spirits Within *'01*
Hitman *'07*
House of the Dead *'03*
In the Name of the King: A Dungeon Siege Tale *'08*
The King of Kong: A Fistful of Quarters *'07* ▶
Lara Croft: Tomb Raider *'01*
Lara Croft Tomb Raider: The Cradle of Life *'03*
Mass Effect: Paragon Lost *'12*
Max Payne *'08*
Mortal Kombat 1: The Movie *'95*
Mortal Kombat 2: Annihilation *'97*
Need for Speed *'14*
Ouija *'14*
Postal *'07*
Prince of Persia: The Sands of Time *'10*
Red Faction: Origins *'11*
Resident Evil *'02*
Resident Evil: Afterlife *'10*
Resident Evil: Apocalypse *'04*
Resident Evil: Extinction *'07*
Silent Hill *'06*
Street Fighter *'94*
Street Fighter: The Legend of Chun-Li *'09*
Super Mario Bros. *'93*
Ultramarines: A Warhammer 40,000 Movie *'10*
Wing Commander *'99*
Yu-Gi-Oh! The Movie: Pyramid of Light *'04*

Adapted from a Musical

Annie *'82*
Annie *'99* ▶
Annie *'14*

Adapted

Babes in Arms '39
Babes in Toyland '61
Bells Are Ringing '60 ▶
Best Foot Forward '43
The Best Little Whorehouse in Texas '82
Black Nativity '13
The Boys From Syracuse '40
Brand New Day '10
Brigadoon '54 ▶
Bye, Bye, Birdie '63 ▶
Bye Bye Birdie '95
Cabaret '72 ▶
Can-Can '60
Chicago '02 ▶
A Chorus Line '85
Damn Yankees '58 ▶
Dark Streets '08
The Desert Song '53
Dreamgirls '06 ▶
Evita '96
The Fantasticks '95
Fiddler on the Roof '71 ▶
Finian's Rainbow '68 ▶
Flower Drum Song '61
Flying High '31
A Funny Thing Happened on the Way to the Forum '66 ▶
The Gay Divorcee '34 ▶
Gentlemen Prefer Blondes '53 ▶
Girl Crazy '32
Godspell '73
Grease 2 '82
Grease '78 ▶
Gypsy '62 ▶
Gypsy '93
Hair '79 ▶
Hairspray '07 ▶
Hello, Dolly! '69
Into the Woods '14
Irma La Douce '63
Jersey Boys '14
The King and I '56 ▶
Kiss Me Kate '53 ▶
Lady Be Good '41
The Last Five Years '14 ▶
Les Miserables '12 ▶
A Little Night Music '77
Mame '74
Maytime '37 ▶
The Merry Widow '34 ▶
The Music Man '62 ▶
My Fair Lady '64 ▶
Nine '09
Oh! Calcutta! '72
On a Clear Day You Can See Forever '70
Paint Your Wagon '69
The Pajama Game '57 ▶
The Phantom of the Opera '04
The Producers '05
Rain or Shine '30
Rock of Ages '12
Sally '29
1776 '72 ▶
Show Boat '36 ▶
Show Boat '51
Sunny '30
Sweeney Todd: The Demon Barber of Fleet Street '84
Sweeney Todd: The Demon Barber of Fleet Street '07
Sweet Charity '69 ▶
The Threepenny Opera '31
Top Banana '54
West Side Story '61 ▶
The Wiz '78

Adapted from a Play
Adapted from a Movie

The Abdication '74
For Colored Girls '10
Hairspray '07 ▶
Little Shop of Horrors '86 ▶
Nine '09
The Producers '05

Adapted from a Poem

The Bells '26 ▶
Beowulf '98
Beowulf '07 ▶
Beowulf & Grendel '06
Braveheart '95 ▶
The Castilian '63
The Charge of the Light Brigade '36 ▶
The Charge of the Light Brigade '68
Evangeline '29
Gunga Din '39 ▶
Hiawatha '52
Howl '10
The Man from Snowy River '82
The Odyssey '97
Perceval '78
The Set-Up '49 ▶
The Song of Hiawatha '97
Troy '04
Ulysses '55
The White Cliffs of Dover '44 ▶
Wild Party '74

Adapted from a Radio Show

Buck Benny Rides Again '40
Check & Double Check '30
Counterspy Meets Scotland Yard '50
Dead Man's Eyes '44
Dreaming Out Loud '40
Gang Busters '42
Gang Busters '55
Gildersleeve on Broadway '43
Goon Movie '52
The Green Hornet '11
Heavenly Days '44
Here We Go Again! '42
Hyde Park on Hudson '12
The Lone Ranger '13
Mr. Arkadin '55 ▶
Mr. District Attorney '41
My Friend Irma '49
My Friend Irma Goes West '50
Nick Carter, Master Detective '39
Night Editor '46
The Phantom of Crestwood '32
Phantom Raiders '40
A Prairie Home Companion '06
Queen for a Day '51
The Shadow '94
Sky Murder '40
Sorry, Wrong Number '48 ▶
The War of the Worlds '53 ▶

Adapted from a Song

Alice's Restaurant '69
The Baron and the Kid '84
Beer for My Horses '08
Beyond the Wall of Sleep '06
Born in East L.A. '87
Convoy '78
Coward of the County '81
Frankie and Johnny '65
The Gambler Returns: The Luck of the Draw '93
Girls Just Want to Have Fun '85
The Indian Runner '91
Is There Life Out There? '94
Kenny Rogers as the Gambler '80
Kenny Rogers as the Gambler, Part 2: The Adventure Continues '83
Kenny Rogers as the Gambler, Part 3: The Legend Continues '87
Lilli Marlene '50
Love Potion #9 '92
My Boyfriend's Back '93
The Night the Lights Went Out in Georgia '81
Ode to Billy Joe '76
Take This Job & Shove It '81
Unanswered Prayers '10
Yellow Submarine '68 ▶
You Light Up My Life '77

Adapted from a Toy

Battleship '12
G.I. Joe: The Rise of Cobra '09
G.I. Joe: Retaliation '13
Kit Kittredge: An American Girl '08
Masters of the Universe '87
Transformers '07
Transformers: Age of Extinction '14
Transformers: Dark of the Moon '11
Transformers: Revenge of the Fallen '09

Adapted from an Article

All Mine to Give '56
American Gangster '07 ▶
Biker Boyz '03
Black Market Babies '45
Blue Crush '02 ▶
Christiane F. '82 ▶
City by the Sea '02
Coyote Ugly '00
Fearless Fagan '52
Gangster Squad '13
The Hunting Party '07
I Was a Communist for the FBI '51
The Insider '99 ▶
Isn't She Great '00
Joe Gould's Secret '00
The Last American Hero '73 ▶
The Last Shot '04
Money for Nothing '93
My Sister Eileen '42
New Jersey Drive '95
Pushing Tin '99 ▶
Resurrecting the Champ '07
The Sessions '12 ▶
Shattered Glass '03 ▶
Trade '07
Two or Three Things I Know about Her '66
Witness Protection '99 ▶

Adapted from an Opera

Aria '88
Balalaika '39
Beggar's Opera '54
Carmen '83 ▶
Carmen: A Hip Hopera '01
Carmen, Baby '66
Carmen Jones '54 ▶
The Chocolate Soldier '41
The Desert Song '43
Don Giovanni '79
Farewell My Concubine '93
Fitzcarraldo '82 ▶
The Great Caruso '51
The Great Waltz '38 ▶
Gypsy Blood '18
Jesus Christ, Superstar '73 ▶
La Grande Vadrouille '66 ▶
The Magic Flute '73 ▶
The Medium '51
Meeting Venus '91
Midnight Girl '25
Otello '86 ▶
The Panther's Claw '42
The Phantom of the Opera '25 ▶
The Phantom of the Opera '43 ▶
The Red Mill '27
Rick '03
Rose Marie '36 ▶
Ruddigore '82
The Tales of Hoffmann '51
The Toast of New Orleans '50
Wagner: The Complete Epic '85

Adapted from Children's Literature

Bridge to Terabithia '07
The Chronicles of Narnia '89 ▶
The Chronicles of Narnia: Prince Caspian '08
The Chronicles of Narnia: The Lion, the Witch and the Wardrobe '05
The Chronicles of Narnia: The Voyage of the Dawn Treader '10
Coraline '09 ▶
Diary of a Wimpy Kid 2: Rodrick Rules '11
Diary of a Wimpy Kid '10
Diary of a Wimpy Kid: Dog Days '12
Ella Enchanted '04 ▶
Ernest & Celestine '13
Harry Potter and the Chamber of Secrets '02 ▶
Harry Potter and the Deathly Hallows, Part 1 '10 ▶
Harry Potter and the Deathly Hallows, Part 2 '11 ▶
Harry Potter and the Goblet of Fire '05 ▶
Harry Potter and the Half-Blood Prince '09
Harry Potter and the Order of the Phoenix '07
Harry Potter and the Prisoner of Azkaban '04
Harry Potter and the Sorcerer's Stone '01 ▶
Holes '03 ▶
Hugo '11 ▶
Lemony Snicket's A Series of Unfortunate Events '04
Percy Jackson & The Olympians: The Lightning Thief '10
Percy Jackson: Sea of Monsters '13
The Spiderwick Chronicles '08 ▶
Tuck Everlasting '02

Adapted from Comics

The Adventures of Tintin '11
Alive '02
American Splendor '03 ▶
Annie '82
Art School Confidential '06
Astro Boy '09
Azumi 2 '05
Azumi '03 ▶
Baba Yaga '73
Barb Wire '96
Batman '66
Batman '89 ▶
Batman and Robin '97
Batman Begins '05 ▶
Batman Forever '95 ▶
Batman Returns '92
Battle of the Warriors '06
Black Mask '96
Blade 2 '02
Blade '98
Blade: Trinity '04
Blue Spring '01
Brenda Starr '86
Bulletproof Monk '03
Captain America '44
Captain America '79
Captain America '89
Captain America 2: Death Too Soon '79
Casper '95 ▶
Catwoman '04
Constantine '05
Corky of Gasoline Alley '51
Creepshow '82
The Crow '93
The Crow 2: City of Angels '96
The Crow: Salvation '00
The Crow: Wicked Prayer '05
Crows Zero '07
Daredevil '03
The Dark Myth '90
Dark Water '02
The Dead One '07
Death Note 2: The Last Name '07
Death Note 3: L Change the World '08
Death Note '06 ▶
Dennis the Menace '93
Dennis the Menace Strikes Again '98
Dick Tracy '90 ▶
Doing Time '02
Dondi '61
Dororo '07
Dragon Tiger Gate '07
Dredd '12 ▶
Elektra '05
Fantastic Four '05
Fantastic Four: Rise of the Silver Surfer '07
Faust: Love of the Damned '00
Fist of the North Star '95
The French Minister '13
Fudoh: The New Generation '96
Fury of the Congo '51
Garfield: A Tail of Two Kitties '06
Garfield: The Movie '04
Gasoline Alley '51
Ghost in the Shell '95 ▶
Ghost Rider '07
Ghost World '01 ▶
Hellboy '04
Hercules '14
A History of Violence '05 ▶
Holy Flame of the Martial World '83
Howard the Duck '86
Hulk '03
Ichi the Killer '01
Immortal '04
The Incredible Hulk '77
The Incredible Hulk Returns '88
Josie and the Pussycats '01
Judge Dredd '95
Jungle Manhunt '51
Jungle Moon Men '55
Kick-Ass '10 ▶
Kick-Ass 2 '13
Kingsman: The Secret Service '15
Kull the Conqueror '97
Lady Snowblood '73 ▶
The League of Extraordinary Gentlemen '03
Marmaduke '10
The Mask '94 ▶
Masked Rider-The First '05
Men in Black '97 ▶
Modesty Blaise '66
Monkeybone '01
Moonlight Whispers '99
My Name is Modesty: A Modesty Blaise Adventure '04
Mystery Men '99
Negative Happy Chainsaw Edge '08
Over the Hedge '06 ▶
Persepolis '07 ▶
The Phantom '96
The Phantom '09
Ping Pong '02 ▶
The Princess Blade '02
The Punisher '90
The Punisher '04
Pygmy Island '50
The Rabbi's Cat '11
Red Shadow '01
The Return of the Swamp Thing '89
Richie Rich '94
Ringu 0 '01
Ringu 2 '99
Ringu '98 ▶
R.I.P.D. '13
Sabrina the Teenage Witch '96
St. Trinian's '07
Scott Pilgrim *vs.* the World '10
The Scribbler '14
Shogun Assassin 2: Lightning Swords of Death '73 ▶
Sin City '05
Sin City: A Dame to Kill For '14
The Smurfs '11
The Smurfs 2 '13
Snowpiercer '14 ▶
Spawn '97 ▶
Spider-Man '02 ▶
Spider-Man 2 '04 ▶
Spider-Man 3 '07
The Spirit '87
The Spirit '08
Spriggan '98
Steel '97
Stray Dog '91
Superman: The Movie '78 ▶
Superman 2 '80 ▶
Superman 3 '83
Superman 4: The Quest for Peace '87
Superman Returns '06
Surrogates '09
Swamp Thing '82
Tales from the Crypt '72 ▶
Tales from the Crypt Presents Bordello of Blood '96
Tales from the Crypt Presents Demon Knight '94
Tales from the Crypt Presents Ritual '02
Tamara Drewe '10
XIII '08
30 Days of Night '07
30 Days of Night: Dark Days '10
300 '07
300: Rise of an Empire '13
TMNT: Teenage Mutant Ninja Turtles '07
Todd McFarlane's Spawn '97 ▶
Tomie '99
Uzumaki '00
V for Vendetta '06
Vampirella '96
Vault of Horror '73
Virus '98
Wanted '08 ▶
Wicked City '92
X-Men '00
X2: X-Men United '03 ▶
Yu-Gi-Oh! The Movie: Pyramid of Light '04
Zoom '06

Adapted from DC/Vertigo Comics

Batman '89 ▶
Batman and Robin '97
Batman Begins '05 ▶
Batman Forever '95 ▶
Batman Returns '92
Catwoman '04
The Dark Knight '08 ▶
The Dark Knight Rises '12 ▶
The Flash '90
Green Lantern '11
Jonah Hex '10
The League of Extraordinary Gentlemen '03
Man of Steel '13
RED '10
The Return of the Swamp Thing '89
Superman: The Movie '78 ▶
Superman 2 '80 ▶
Superman 3 '83
Superman 4: The Quest for Peace '87
Superman Returns '06
Swamp Thing '82
V for Vendetta '06
Watchmen '09
Wonder Woman '74

Adapted from Marvel Comics

The Amazing Spider-Man 2 '14
The Amazing Spider-Man '12 ▶
The Avengers '12 ▶
Big Hero 6 '14
Blade 2 '02
Blade: Trinity '04
Captain America '44
Captain America '79
Captain America '89
Captain America: The First Avenger '11
Captain America: The Winter Soldier '14 ▶
Captain America 2: Death Too Soon '79
Daredevil '03
Fantastic Four '05
Fantastic Four: Rise of the Silver Surfer '07
Guardians of the Galaxy '14 ▶
Hellboy II: The Golden Army '08 ▶
Hulk '03
The Incredible Hulk '08
The Invincible Iron Man '07
Iron Man '08 ▶

▶ = rated three bones or higher

Iron Man 2 '10 ►
Iron Man 3 '13 ►
Men in Black 2 '02
Men in Black '97 ►
The Punisher '04
Punisher: War Zone '08
Spider-Man '02 ►
Spider-Man 2 '04 ►
Spider-Man 3 '07
Thor '11 ►
Thor: The Dark World '13
The Wolverine '13
X-Men '00
X-Men: Days of Future Past '14 ►
X-Men: First Class '11 ►
X-Men Origins: Wolverine '09
X-Men: The Last Stand '06
X2: X-Men United '03 ►

Adapted from Memoirs or Diaries

Adolf Hitler: My Part in His Downfall '74
American Loser '07
American Sniper '14
Angela's Ashes '99
Anna and the King '99
Anne Frank: The Whole Story '01 ►
At First Sight '98
Bandit Queen '94
The Basketball Diaries '95
Belles on Their Toes '52
Beyond the Blackboard '11
The Big Year '11
The Boys Are Back '09
A Business Affair '93
Caro Diario '93 ►
Chicken Every Sunday '48
Christopher and His Kind '11 ►
The Color of Freedom '07
Control '07
The Counterfeiters '07 ►
Cowboy '58 ►
Danger UXB '81
Daphne '07
Deserter '02
The Diary of Anne Frank '59 ►
The Diary of Anne Frank '08
The Diving Bell and the Butterfly '07 ►
A Dog Year '09
Doing Time '02
Downfall '04 ►
Duffy of San Quentin '54
Eat, Pray, Love '10
An Education '09 ►
Edvard Munch '74
First Light '10
The Flame Trees of Thika '81 ►
A Free Soul '31
Girl, Interrupted '99
God is My Co-Pilot '45
Gypsy '62 ►
The Happy Hooker '75
The Happy Hooker Goes Hollywood '80
The Happy Hooker Goes to Washington '77
Haywire '80
Heart Beat '80
Heartland '81 ►
Henry & June '90 ►
Higher Ground '11 ►
How to Lose Friends & Alienate People '08
I Remember Mama '48 ►
I'll Cry Tomorrow '55 ►
Ill Met By Moonlight '57
I'm Dancing as Fast as I Can '82
In Love and War '96
In Love and War '01
In the Name of the Father '93 ►
Iris '01 ►
John Rabe '09
Julia '77 ►
Julie & Julia '09 ►
The Kid Stays in the Picture '02 ►
Killing Bono '11
Kings in Grass Castles '97
The Lady and the Duke '01
Last Call: The Final Chapter of F. Scott Fitzgerald '02
The Lawless Breed '52 ►
Lay the Favorite '12
Life Itself '14 ►
Maids of Wilko '79
Man on Wire '08
Marley & Me '08
Mesrine: Part 1-Killer Instinct '08
Mesrine: Part 2-Public Enemy Number 1 '08
A Mighty Heart '07 ►
Mommie Dearest '81
The Motorcycle Diaries '04 ►
My Dog Tulip '09 ►
My Gal Sal '42
My Life and Times with Antonin Artaud '93 ►
My Own Country '98
My Sister's Keeper '02
My Week With Marilyn '11
October Sky '99 ►
Opium: Diary of a Madwoman '07
The Other Side of Heaven '02
Our Lady of the Assassins '01
Papa's Delicate Condition '63 ►
The Passion of Ayn Rand '99
The Pianist '02 ►
The Pillow Book '95
The Pregnancy Project '12
The Railway Man '13
The Road from Coorain '02
Romulus, My Father '07 ►
Rosewater '14
The Secret Diaries of Miss Anne Lister '10
See Here, Private Hargrove '44
Seven Years in Tibet '97
Shake Hands With the Devil '07
Shot in the Heart '01 ►
So Goes My Love '46
Stars and Stripes Forever '52 ►
Stella Days '12
The Summer of Aviya '88
Taking Woodstock '09
The Theory of Everything '14
This Boy's Life '93 ►
Toast '10
Touch the Top of the World '06
True Story '15
Under the Domim Tree '95
The Vanishing Virginian '41
Village of Dreams '97
We Bought a Zoo '11
What's Love Got to Do with It? '93
When Did You Last See Your Father? '07
The Whole Wide World '96 ►
Why I Wore Lipstick to My Mastectomy '06
Wild '14 ►
Wish You Were Here '87 ►
Yes Man '08
Young Cassidy '65

Adapted from Saturday Night Live

The Blues Brothers '80 ►
Blues Brothers 2000 '98
Coneheads '93
It's Pat: The Movie '94
The Ladies Man '00
MacGruber '10
A Night at the Roxbury '98
Stuart Saves His Family '94
Superstar '99
Wayne's World 2 '93
Wayne's World '92 ►

Adapted from Television

The A-Team '10 ►
Absolutely Fabulous: The Movie '16
The Addams Family '91
Addams Family Values '93
The Adventures of Rocky & Bullwinkle '00
Aeon Flux '05
Alien Nation: Dark Horizon '94
Aqua Teen Hunger Force Colon Movie Film for Theaters '07
Astro Boy '09
The Avengers '98
Batman '66
Batman: Mask of the Phantasm '93
Bean '97 ►
Beavis and Butt-Head Do America '96
The Beverly Hillbillies '93
Bewitched '05
Big Top Pee-wee '88
The Brady Bunch Movie '95 ►
Car 54, Where Are You? '94
Charlie's Angels '00
Charlie's Angels: Full Throttle '03
Clifford's Really Big Movie '04
Coneheads '93
The Crawling Eye '58
Dark Shadows '12
Days of Wine and Roses '62 ►
Dennis the Menace '93
Dennis the Menace Strikes Again '98
Doctor Who '96
Doogal '05
Dragnet '87
Dragonball: Evolution '09
Dudley Do-Right '99
The Dukes of Hazzard '05
The Dukes of Hazzard: The Beginning '06
The Equalizer '14
The Extreme Adventures of Super Dave '98
Fat Albert '04
The Flintstones '94
The Flintstones in Viva Rock Vegas '00
Flipper '96 ►
The Fugitive '93 ►
Gargoyles, The Movie: The Heroes Awaken '94
George of the Jungle '97 ►
Get Smart, Again! '89
Good Burger '97
Hannah Montana: The Movie '09
The Honeymooners '05
I Spy '02
Jackass: The Movie '02
Jetsons: The Movie '90
Jiminy Glick in LaLa Wood '05
Joe's Apartment '96
Kevin & Perry Go Large '00
Kids in the Hall: Brain Candy '96
Land of the Lost '09
Lassie '94
The Last Airbender '10
Leave It to Beaver '97
The Left-Handed Gun '58 ►
The Lizzie McGuire Movie '03
Lost in Space '98
Maverick '94
McHale's Navy '64
McHale's Navy '97
Miami Vice '06
Mission: Impossible 2 '00 ►
Mission: Impossible '96 ►
Mr. Peabody & Sherman '14
The Mod Squad '99
Munster, Go Home! '66
My Favorite Martian '98
Mystery Science Theater 3000: The Movie '96
The Naked Gun: From the Files of Police Squad '88 ►
Naked Gun 33 1/3: The Final Insult '94
Naked Gun 2 1/2: The Smell of Fear '91
No Escape '53
Noah's Arc: Jumping the Broom '08
The Nude Bomb '80
Our Miss Brooks '56
Pee-wee's Big Adventure '85 ►
Pennies from Heaven '81 ►
Phantom 2040 Movie: The Ghost Who Walks '95
Pokemon: The First Movie '99
Pootie Tang '01
Postman Pat: The Movie '14
Pufnstuf '70
Queen for a Day '51
Reno 911! Miami '07
Requiem for a Heavyweight '62 ►
Rescue from Gilligan's Island '78
The Return of the Beverly Hillbillies '81
Ringmaster '98
Rugrats Go Wild! '03
Rugrats in Paris: The Movie '00 ►
The Rugrats Movie '98 ►
Serenity '05 ►
Sgt. Bilko '95
Sex and the City: The Movie '08
The Simpsons Movie '07 ►
The Singing Detective '03
The Smurfs '11
The Smurfs 2 '13
South Park: Bigger, Longer and Uncut '99
Speed Racer '08
The SpongeBob Movie: Sponge Out of Water '15
Star Trek: The Motion Picture '79
Star Trek 2: The Wrath of Khan '82 ►
Star Trek 3: The Search for Spock '84
Star Trek 4: The Voyage Home '86 ►
Star Trek 5: The Final Frontier '89
Star Trek 6: The Undiscovered Country '91
Star Trek: First Contact '96 ►
Star Trek: Generations '94 ►
Star Trek: Insurrection '98
Star Trek: Into Darkness '13 ►
Star Trek: Nemesis '02
Stargate: Continuum '08
Starsky & Hutch '04
State of Play '09 ►
Strange Frequency 2 '01
Strangers with Candy '06
S.W.A.T. '03
The Sweeney '12
Tales from the Crypt Presents Bordello of Blood '96
Tales from the Crypt Presents Demon Knight '94
Thomas and the Magic Railroad '00
Thunder in Paradise 2 '94
Thunder in Paradise 3 '94
21 Jump Street '12 ►
Twin Peaks: Fire Walk with Me '92
Underdog '07
The Untouchables '87 ►
Veronica Mars '14
A Very Brady Sequel '96
Wackiest Wagon Train in the West '77
The Wild Thornberrys Movie '02 ►
Wild Wild West '99
The X-Files '98
The X Files: I Want to Believe '08
Yogi Bear '10

Adapted from the Bible

Abraham '94
A.D. '85
The Bible '66
David '97
David and Bathsheba '51 ►
The Decalogue '88 ►
Esther '98
Exodus: Gods and Kings '14
Godspell '73
The Gospel According to St. Matthew '64 ►
The Gospel of John '03
Jacob '94
Jeremiah '98
Jesus '00
Jesus Christ, Superstar '73 ►
Jesus Christ Superstar '00
Joseph '95
Joseph and the Amazing Technicolor Dreamcoat '00 ►
King David '85
King of Kings '27
The King of Kings '61 ►
The Last Supper '76 ►
Mary, Mother of Jesus '99
The Miracle Maker: The Story of Jesus '00
Moses '76
Moses '96
Noah '14
Noah's Ark '99
One Night with the King '06
The Passion of the Christ '04 ►
Peter and Paul '81
Prince of Egypt '98 ►
Salome '53
Samson and Delilah '49 ►
Samson and Delilah '84
Samson and Delilah '96
Saul and David '64
Sins of Jezebel '54
Solomon '98
Son of God '14
The Story of Jacob & Joseph '74 ►
The Ten Commandments '23
The Ten Commandments '56 ►

Adapted from Young Adult Literature

The Adventurer: The Curse of the Midas Box '13
Beautiful Creatures '13
Blood & Chocolate '07
The Book Thief '13
The Boy in the Striped Pajamas '08 ►
Cirque du Freak: The Vampire's Assistant '09
City of Ember '08
Divergent '14
The DUFF '15
Ender's Game '13
Eragon '06
Fat Kid Rules the World '12
The Fault In Our Stars '14
The Giver '14
The Golden Compass '07
How I Live Now '13
How to Train Your Dragon 2 '14
The Hunger Games '12 ►
The Hunger Games: Catching Fire '13 ►
The Hunger Games: Mockingjay--Part 1 '14
I Am Number Four '11
If I Stay '14
Inkheart '09
Insurgent '15
Little Women '33 ►
Little Women '49 ►
Little Women '78
Little Women '94 ►
The Maze Runner '14
The Mortal Instruments: City of Bones '13
Nick & Norah's Infinite Playlist '08 ►
The Outsiders '83
The Perks of Being a Wallflower '12 ►
Seventh Son '15
The Sisterhood of the Traveling Pants '05
The Sisterhood of the Traveling Pants 2 '08
The Spectacular Now '13 ►
Tiger Eyes '13
Twilight '08
The Twilight Saga: Breaking Dawn, Part 1 '11
The Twilight Saga: Breaking Dawn, Part 2 '12
The Twilight Saga: Eclipse '10
The Twilight Saga: New Moon '09
Vampire Academy '14
Warm Bodies '13

Andy Hardy

Andy Hardy Comes Home '58
Andy Hardy Gets Spring Fever '39
Andy Hardy Meets Debutante '40
Andy Hardy's Blonde Trouble '44
Andy Hardy's Double Life '42
Andy Hardy's Private Secretary '41
The Courtship of Andy Hardy '42
A Family Affair '37
The Hardys Ride High '39
Judge Hardy and Son '39
Judge Hardy's Children '38
Life Begins for Andy Hardy '41 ►
Love Finds Andy Hardy '38 ►
Love Laughs at Andy Hardy '46
Out West With the Hardys '38
You're Only Young Once '37

Batman

Batman '66
Batman '89 ►
Batman and Robin '97
Batman Begins '05 ►
Batman Forever '95 ►
Batman: Mask of the Phantasm '93
Batman Returns '92
The Dark Knight '08 ►
The Dark Knight Rises '12 ►
The Lego Batman Movie '17 ►
The Lego Movie '14 ►

BBC TV Productions

The Whale '13

Beach Party

Back to the Beach '87
Beach Blanket Bingo '65 ►
Beach Party '63
Bikini Beach '64
Ghost in the Invisible Bikini '66
How to Stuff a Wild Bikini '65
Muscle Beach Party '64
Pajama Party '64

Beatlesfilm

Across the Universe '07
All You Need Is Cash '78 ►
Backbeat '94 ►
George Harrison: Living in the Material World '11
A Hard Day's Night '64 ►
Help! '65 ►
I Wanna Hold Your Hand '78
Lennon Naked '10
Let It Be '70
Nowhere Boy '09
Yellow Submarine '68 ►
Yesterday '19

Billy the Kid

Billy the Kid '30
Billy the Kid '41
Billy the Kid Versus Dracula '66
BloodRayne 2: Deliverance '07
Chisum '70
Deadwood '65
Dirty Little Billy '72
The Left-Handed Gun '58 ►
The Outlaw '43
Pat Garrett & Billy the Kid '73 ►
Thundering Gunslingers '44
Young Guns 2 '90
Young Guns '88

► = *rated three bones or higher*

Blondie
Blondie '38
Blondie Brings Up Baby '39
Blondie Goes Latin '42
Blondie Goes to College '42
Blondie Has Trouble '40
Blondie in Society '41
Blondie Meets the Boss '39
Blondie On a Budget '40
Blondie Plays Cupid '40
Blondie Takes a Vacation '39

Bomba, the Jungle Boy
African Treasure '52
Bomba and the Hidden City '50
Bomba and the Jungle Girl '52
Bomba on Panther Island '49
Bomba, the Jungle Boy '49
Elephant Stampede '51
The Golden Idol '54
Killer Leopard '54
The Lion Hunters '51
Lord of the Jungle '55
The Lost Volcano '50
Safari Drums '53

Books to Film: Adams, Richard
The Girl in a Swing '89
The Plague Dogs '82
Watership Down '78

Books to Film: Alcott, Louisa May
The Inheritance '97
Little Men '34
Little Men '40
Little Men '98
Little Women '33 ►
Little Women '49 ►
Little Women '78
Little Women '94 ►
Little Women '19
The March Sisters at Christmas '12
An Old-Fashioned Thanksgiving '08

Books to Film: Algren, Nelson
The Man with the Golden Arm '55 ►
Walk on the Wild Side '62

Books to Film: Ambler, Eric
Background to Danger '43 ►
The Mask of Dimitrios '44 ►

Books to Film: Amis, Kingsley
Lucky Jim '58
Take a Girl Like You '70
That Uncertain Feeling '41

Books to Film: Amis, Martin
The Rachel Papers '89 ►

Books to Film: Andersen, Hans Christian
The Red Shoes '48 ►
The Sleeping Beauty '10
The Snow Queen '02

Books to Film: Angelou, Maya
Georgia, Georgia '72

Books to Film: Asimov, Isaac
Bicentennial Man '99
I, Robot '04
Isaac Asimov's Nightfall '00
Nightfall '88

Books to Film: Asinof, Eliot
Breakout '75
Eight Men Out '88 ►

Books to Film: Austen, Jane
Bride & Prejudice '04
Emma '72
Emma '96 ►
Emma '97 ►
Emma '09
Emma '20
From Prada to Nada '11
Lost in Austen '08
Mansfield Park '85
Mansfield Park '99
Mansfield Park '07
Northanger Abbey '87
Northanger Abbey '07
Persuasion '71
Persuasion '95 ►
Persuasion '07
Pride and Prejudice '40 ►
Pride and Prejudice '85
Pride and Prejudice '95 ►
Pride and Prejudice '05 ►
Sense & Sensibility '85
Sense and Sensibility '95 ►
Sense & Sensibility '07

Books to Film: Balzac, Honore de
Cousin Bette '97
The Duchess of Langeais '07 ►
Passion in the Desert '97

Books to Film: Banks, Russell
Affliction '97 ►
Sunshine '07
The Sweet Hereafter '96 ►

Books to Film: Barker, Clive
Candyman 2: Farewell to the Flesh '94
Candyman '92
Clive Barker's Book of Blood '08
Dread '09
Hellbound: Hellraiser 2 '88
Hellraiser '87
Hellraiser 3: Hell on Earth '92
Hellraiser 4: Bloodline '95
Lord of Illusions '95
The Midnight Meat Train '08
Nightbreed '90
Rawhead Rex '87

Books to Film: Benchley, Peter
The Beast '96
The Deep '77
Jaws '75 ►

Books to Film: Berger, Thomas
Little Big Man '70 ►
Neighbors '81

Books to Film: Binchy, Maeve
Circle of Friends '94
How About You '07
Tara Road '05

Books to Film: Bloch, Robert
The Skull '65
Torture Garden '67

Books to Film: Block, Lawrence
Burglar '87
Nightmare Honeymoon '73
A Walk Among the Tombstones '14

Books to Film: Blume, Judy
Tiger Eyes '13

Books to Film: Boileau, Pierre
Body Parts '91
Diabolique '55 ►
Diabolique '96
The Horror Chamber of Dr. Faustus '59 ►
Vertigo '58 ►

Books to Film: Boulle, Pierre
The Bridge on the River Kwai '57 ►
Dawn of the Planet of the Apes '14 ►
Planet of the Apes '68 ►
Planet of the Apes '01 ►
Rise of the Planet of the Apes '11 ►

Books to Film: Bowden, Mark
Black Hawk Down '01 ►
Money for Nothing '93

Books to Film: Bradbury, Ray
The Beast from 20,000 Fathoms '53
Fahrenheit 451 '66 ►
The Illustrated Man '69 ►
It Came from Outer Space '53 ►
The Martian Chronicles: Part 1 '79
The Martian Chronicles: Part 2 '79
The Martian Chronicles: Part 3 '79
The Picasso Summer '69
Something Wicked This Way Comes '83
A Sound of Thunder '05

Books to Film: Bradford, Barbara Taylor
Hold the Dream '86
A Secret Affair '99
A Woman of Substance '84

Books to Film: Brand, Max
Branded '50
The Desperadoes '43
Destry Rides Again '39 ►
My Outlaw Brother '51

Books to Film: Bronte Sisters
Devotion '46
Emily Bronte's Wuthering Heights '92
Jane Eyre '34
Jane Eyre '44 ►
Jane Eyre '83 ►
Jane Eyre '96 ►
Jane Eyre '97
Jane Eyre '06
Jane Eyre '11
MTV's Wuthering Heights '03
The Tenant of Wildfell Hall '96
Wuthering Heights '39 ►
Wuthering Heights '70
Wuthering Heights '98
Wuthering Heights '09

Books to Film: Brothers Grimm
Grimm's Snow White '12
Maleficent '14
Mirror Mirror '12
The Princess and the Frog '09 ►
Rumpelstiltskin '86
Snow White: A Tale of Terror '97
Snow White and the Seven Dwarfs '37 ►
Tangled '10 ►
Tom Thumb '58 ►

Books to Film: Buck, Pearl S.
Dragon Seed '44
The Good Earth '37 ►
Pavilion of Women '01

Books to Film: Bukowski, Charles
Factotum '06 ►
My Old Man '79

Books to Film: Burnett, Frances Hodgson
Little Lord Fauntleroy '36 ►
Little Lord Fauntleroy '95
The Little Princess '39 ►
The Little Princess '87
A Little Princess '95 ►
The Making of a Lady '12
The Secret Garden '49 ►
The Secret Garden '84
The Secret Garden '87 ►
The Secret Garden '93

Books to Film: Burnett, W.R.
Arrowhead '53
The Badlanders '58
Dance Hall '41
Dark Command '40 ►
High Sierra '41 ►
I Died a Thousand Times '55
Law and Order '53
Little Caesar '30 ►
The Whole Town's Talking '35 ►

Books to Film: Burroughs, Edgar Rice
At the Earth's Core '76
Greystoke: The Legend of Tarzan, Lord of the Apes '84
John Carter '12
The Land That Time Forgot '75
The Land That Time Forgot '09
The People That Time Forgot '77
Princess of Mars '09
Tarzan '99 ►
Tarzan and His Mate '34 ►
Tarzan and the Green Goddess '38
Tarzan and the Lost Safari '57
Tarzan and the She-Devil '53
Tarzan and the Slave Girl '50
Tarzan and the Trappers '58
Tarzan Escapes '36 ►
Tarzan Finds a Son '39 ►
Tarzan, the Ape Man '32 ►
Tarzan, the Ape Man '81
Tarzan the Fearless '33
Tarzan the Magnificent '60
Tarzan's Fight for Life '58
Tarzan's Greatest Adventure '59
Tarzan's Hidden Jungle '55
Tarzan's Magic Fountain '48
Tarzan's New York Adventure '42
Tarzan's Peril '51
Tarzan's Revenge '38
Tarzan's Savage Fury '52
Tarzan's Secret Treasure '41

Books to Film: Burroughs, William
Naked Lunch '91 ►

Books to Film: Cain, James M.
Butterfly '82
Double Indemnity '44 ►
Mildred Pierce '45 ►
Mildred Pierce '11
The Postman Always Rings Twice '46 ►
The Postman Always Rings Twice '81
Serenade '56
Slightly Scarlet '56
Wife, Husband and Friend '39

Books to Film: Capote, Truman
Breakfast at Tiffany's '61 ►
Children On Their Birthdays '02
The Glass House '72 ►
The Grass Harp '95
In Cold Blood '67 ►
In Cold Blood '96
Other Voices, Other Rooms '95

Books to Film: Carter, Forrest
The Education of Little Tree '97 ►
The Outlaw Josey Wales '76 ►

Books to Film: Cartland, Barbara
Duel of Hearts '92
The Lady and the Highwayman '89
Love Comes Lately '07

Books to Film: Cather, Willa
O Pioneers! '91
The Song of the Lark '01

Books to Film: Cervantes, Miguel de
Don Quixote '35 ►
Man of La Mancha '72

Books to Film: Chandler, Raymond
The Big Sleep '46 ►
The Big Sleep '78
The Falcon Takes Over '42
Farewell, My Lovely '75 ►
Lady in the Lake '46
The Long Goodbye '73 ►
Marlowe '69
Murder, My Sweet '44 ►

Books to Film: Chase, James Hadley
The Catamount Killing '74
Crime & Passion '75
Eva '62
The Grissom Gang '71 ►
Man Bait '52
Mission to Venice '63
Night of the Generals '67 ►
No Orchids for Miss Blandish '48
Palmetto '98
Rough Magic '95
The Set Up '95

Books to Film: Chayefsky, Paddy
Altered States '80 ►
As Young As You Feel '51 ►
The Catered Affair '56 ►

Books to Film: Cheever, John
The Swimmer '68 ►

Books to Film: Christie, Agatha
Agatha Christie's A Caribbean Mystery '83
Agatha Christie's Murder is Easy '82
Agatha Christie's Murder with Mirrors '85
Agatha Christie's Sparkling Cyanide '83
Agatha Christie's The Pale Horse '96
Agatha Christie's Thirteen at Dinner '85
The Alphabet Murders '65
And Then There Were None '45 ►
Appointment With Death '10
The Body in the Library '84
Death on the Nile '78
Endless Night '71
Evil under the Sun '82
Love from a Stranger '37
The Mirror Crack'd '80
Murder Ahoy '64
Murder at the Gallop '63 ►
Murder Most Foul '65 ►
Murder on the Orient Express '74 ►
Murder on the Orient Express '01
Murder on the Orient Express '10 ►
Murder She Said '61
Ten Little Indians '75
Towards Zero '07
Witness for the Prosecution '57 ►

Books to Film: Clancy, Tom
Clear and Present Danger '94
The Hunt for Red October '90 ►
Patriot Games '92 ►
The Sum of All Fears '02

Books to Film: Clark, Mary Higgins
Before I Say Goodbye '03
He Sees You When You're Sleeping '02
Mary Higgins Clark: Lucky Day '02
My Gal Sunday '14
We'll Meet Again '02

Books to Film: Clarke, Arthur C.
2001: A Space Odyssey '68 ►
2010: The Year We Make Contact '84 ►

Books to Film: Clavell, James
King Rat '65 ►
Noble House '88
Shogun '80 ►
Tai-Pan '86

Books to Film: Collins, Jackie
The Bitch '78
Hollywood Wives: The New Generation '03

Books to Film: Collins, Suzanne
The Hunger Games '12 ►
The Hunger Games: Catching Fire '13 ►
The Hunger Games: Mockingjay—Part 1 '14

Books to Film: Collins, Wilkie
Basil '98
The Moonstone '72
The Moonstone '97 ►
The Woman in White '97

Books to Film: Condon, Richard
The Happy Thieves '61
The Manchurian Candidate '62 ►
The Manchurian Candidate '04 ►
Prizzi's Honor '85 ►
Winter Kills '79 ►

Books to Film: Conrad, Joseph
Apocalypse Now '79 ►
The Duellists '77 ►
Gabrielle '05
Lord Jim '65 ►
Sabotage '36 ►
The Secret Agent '96
Swept from the Sea '97
Victory '95

Books to Film: Conroy, Pat
The Great Santini '80 ►
The Lords of Discipline '83
The Prince of Tides '91 ►

Books to Film: Cook, Robin
Coma '78 ►
Robin Cook's Invasion '97
Robin Cook's Terminal '96
Sphinx '81

► = rated three bones or higher

Books to Film: Cookson, Catherine
Catherine Cookson's Colour Blind '98
Catherine Cookson's The Black Candle '92
Catherine Cookson's The Black Velvet Gown '92
Catherine Cookson's The Cinder Path '94
Catherine Cookson's The Dwelling Place '94
Catherine Cookson's The Fifteen Streets '90
Catherine Cookson's The Gambling Man '98
Catherine Cookson's The Girl '96
Catherine Cookson's The Glass Virgin '95
Catherine Cookson's The Man Who Cried '93
Catherine Cookson's The Moth '96
Catherine Cookson's The Rag Nymph '96
Catherine Cookson's The Secret '00 ▸
Catherine Cookson's The Tide of Life '96
Catherine Cookson's The Wingless Bird '97
Catherine Cookson's Tilly Trotter '99

Books to Film: Cooper, James Fenimore
The Last of the Mohicans '20 ▸
The Last of the Mohicans '32
The Last of the Mohicans '36
The Last of the Mohicans '92 ▸
The Pathfinder '96

Books to Film: Crane, Stephen
Face of Fire '59
The Red Badge of Courage '51 ▸

Books to Film: Crichton, Michael
The Andromeda Strain '71
The Andromeda Strain '08
The Carey Treatment '72
Congo '95
The Great Train Robbery '79 ▸
Jurassic Park '93 ▸
The Lost World: Jurassic Park 2 '97
Rising Sun '93 ▸
Sphere '97
The Terminal Man '74
The 13th Warrior '99
Timeline '03
Westworld '73 ▸

Books to Film: Cunningham, Michael
A Home at the End of the World '04
The Hours '02 ▸

Books to Film: Cussler, Clive
Raise the Titanic '80
Sahara '05

Books to Film: Dahl, Roald
Charlie and the Chocolate Factory '05 ▸
Fantastic Mr. Fox '09 ▸
James and the Giant Peach '96 ▸
Matilda '96 ▸
Willy Wonka & the Chocolate Factory '71 ▸
The Witches '90 ▸

Books to Film: de Maupassant, Guy
Bel Ami '12
Diary of a Madman '63
Le Plaisir '52
The Private Affairs of Bel Ami '47 ▸
A Woman Without Love '51 ▸

Books to Film: Defoe, Daniel
The Amorous Adventures of Moll Flanders '65
Crusoe '89
Man Friday '75
Moll Flanders '96
Robinson Crusoe '54
Robinson Crusoe '96
Robinson Crusoe on Mars '64

Books to Film: Deighton, Len
Billion Dollar Brain '67
Funeral in Berlin '66 ▸
The Ipcress File '65 ▸
Oh! What a Lovely War '69

Books to Film: Dexter, Pete
God's Pocket '14
Michael '96
Mulholland Falls '95
The Paperboy '12
Wild Bill '95

Books to Film: Dick, Phillip K.
The Adjustment Bureau '11
Blade Runner '82 ▸
Impostor '02
Minority Report '02 ▸
Next '07
Paycheck '03
A Scanner Darkly '06
Screamers '96
Screamers: The Hunting '09
Total Recall '90 ▸
Total Recall '12
Total Recall 2070: Machine Dreams '99

Books to Film: Dickens, Charles
An American Carol '08
An American Christmas Carol '79
Bleak House '85
Bleak House '05
A Christmas Carol '38 ▸
A Christmas Carol '51 ▸
A Christmas Carol '84 ▸
A Christmas Carol '99
A Christmas Carol '09
David Copperfield '35 ▸
David Copperfield '70
David Copperfield '99
Great Expectations '34
Great Expectations '46 ▸
Great Expectations '81
Great Expectations '97
Great Expectations '99
Great Expectations '11
Great Expectations '12
The Life and Adventures of Nicholas Nickleby '81 ▸
Little Dorrit '08
Martin Chuzzlewit '94
The Muppet Christmas Carol '92
The Mystery of Edwin Drood '35
The Mystery of Edwin Drood '12
Nicholas Nickleby '46 ▸
Nicholas Nickleby '02 ▸
The Old Curiosity Shop '94
The Old Curiosity Shop '07
Oliver! '68 ▸
Oliver & Company '88
Oliver Twist '22 ▸
Oliver Twist '33
Oliver Twist '48 ▸
Oliver Twist '82 ▸
Oliver Twist '85 ▸
Oliver Twist '97
Oliver Twist '00 ▸
Oliver Twist '05 ▸
Oliver Twist '07
Our Mutual Friend '98
The Pickwick Papers '54
Scrooge '70
A Tale of Two Cities '36 ▸
A Tale of Two Cities '58 ▸
A Tale of Two Cities '80
A Tale of Two Cities '89 ▸
Twist '03 ▸
Twisted '96

Books to Film: Diehl, William
Primal Fear '96
Sharky's Machine '81

Books to Film: Doctorow, E.L.
Billy Bathgate '91
Daniel '83
Jolene '08
Ragtime '81 ▸
Welcome to Hard Times '67

Books to Film: Dostoyevski, Fyodor
The Brothers Karamazov '58 ▸
Crime and Punishment '70
Crime and Punishment in Suburbia '00
Crime and Punishment, USA '59
The Double '13 ▸
The Gambler '97
The Great Sinner '49
Notes from Underground '95
White Nights '57 ▸

Books to Film: Doyle, Sir Arthur Conan
The Adventures of Sherlock Holmes '39
The Crucifer of Blood '91
Dressed to Kill '46
The Fighting Eagle '27
The Hound of the Baskervilles '39 ▸
The Hound of the Baskervilles '59
The Hound of the Baskervilles '77
The Hound of the Baskervilles '83
The Hound of the Baskervilles '00
The Hound of the Baskervilles '02 ▸
House of Fear '45
King of the Lost World '06
The Lost World '25
The Lost World '60
The Lost World '92
The Lost World '02
Murder at the Baskervilles '37
The Pearl of Death '44
Return to the Lost World '93
Scarlet Claw '44 ▸
Sherlock Holmes '22
Sherlock Holmes '09
Sherlock Holmes '10
Sherlock Holmes and the Deadly Necklace '62
Sherlock Holmes and the Secret Weapon '42 ▸
Sherlock Holmes and the Voice of Terror '42
The Sign of Four '83
The Sign of Four '01
Tales from the Darkside: The Movie '90
The Triumph of Sherlock Holmes '35
The Woman in Green '49

Books to Film: Du Maurier, Daphne
The Birds '63 ▸
Don't Look Now '73 ▸
Frenchman's Creek '44
Frenchman's Creek '98
Jamaica Inn '39
Jamaica Inn '82
My Cousin Rachel '52
Rebecca '40 ▸
Rebecca '97 ▸
The Scapegoat '59
The Scapegoat '12

Books to Film: Dumas, Alexandre
At Sword's Point '51
Black Magic '49
The Black Tulip '64
Camille '36 ▸
Camille '84
Camille 2000 '69
The Corsican Brothers '42
The Count of Monte Cristo '12
The Count of Monte Cristo '34 ▸
The Count of Monte Cristo '99
The Count of Monte Cristo '02 ▸
The Four Musketeers '75 ▸
The 4 Musketeers '05
The Iron Mask '29
The Man in the Iron Mask '39 ▸
The Man in the Iron Mask '77 ▸
The Man in the Iron Mask '97
The Man in the Iron Mask '98 ▸
Monte Cristo '22
The Musketeer '01
The Prince of Thieves '48
Queen Margot '94 ▸
Robin Hood '22 ▸
The Three Musketeers '21 ▸
The Three Musketeers '33
The Three Musketeers '39
The Three Musketeers '48
The Three Musketeers '74 ▸
The Three Musketeers '11

Books to Film: Duncan, Lois
I Know What You Did Last Summer '97 ▸
I've Been Waiting for You '98
Killing Mr. Griffin '97
Summer of Fear '78

Books to Film: Duras, Marguerite
Hiroshima, Mon Amour '59 ▸
The Lover '92
Nathalie Granger '72

Books to Film: Eliot, George
Daniel Deronda '02
Middlemarch '93 ▸
The Mill on the Floss '39
The Mill on the Floss '97
Silas Marner '85 ▸
A Simple Twist of Fate '94

Books to Film: Ellis, Bret Easton
American Psycho '99
The Informers '09
Less Than Zero '87
The Rules of Attraction '02

Books to Film: Ellroy, James
The Black Dahlia '06
Brown's Requiem '98
Cop '88
Dark Blue '03 ▸
L.A. Confidential '97 ▸
Street Kings '08

Books to Film: Fast, Howard
April Morning '88
The Crossing '00
Freedom Road '79

Books to Film: Faulkner, William
Intruder in the Dust '49 ▸
Land of the Pharaohs '55
The Long, Hot Summer '58 ▸
The Long, Hot Summer '86 ▸
The Reivers '69 ▸
Tarnished Angels '57 ▸
Today We Live '33
Tomorrow '72 ▸

Books to Film: Ferber, Edna
Cimarron '31
Cimarron '60
Come and Get It '36 ▸
Dinner at Eight '33 ▸
Dinner at Eight '89
Giant '56 ▸
Saratoga Trunk '45
Show Boat '36 ▸
Show Boat '51 ▸
Stage Door '37 ▸

Books to Film: Fielding, Henry
Joseph Andrews '77
Tom Jones '63 ▸
Tom Jones '98 ▸

Books to Film: Fitzgerald, F. Scott
The Curious Case of Benjamin Button '08 ▸
G '02
The Great Gatsby '74
The Great Gatsby '01
The Great Gatsby '13
The Last Time I Saw Paris '54
The Last Tycoon '76 ▸
Tender Is the Night '62

Books to Film: Flaubert, Gustov
Madame Bovary '49 ▸
Madame Bovary '91 ▸

Books to Film: Fleming, Ian
Casino Royale '67
Casino Royale '06 ▸
Chitty Chitty Bang Bang '68
Diamonds Are Forever '71 ▸
Dr. No '62 ▸
For Your Eyes Only '81 ▸
From Russia with Love '63 ▸
Goldfinger '64 ▸
License to Kill '89 ▸
Live and Let Die '73
The Living Daylights '87 ▸
The Man with the Golden Gun '74
Moonraker '79
Never Say Never Again '83
Octopussy '83
On Her Majesty's Secret Service '69 ▸
The Poppy Is Also a Flower '66
The Spy Who Loved Me '77
Thunderball '65
A View to a Kill '85
You Only Live Twice '67

Books to Film: Flynn, Gillian
Gone Girl '14 ▸

Books to Film: Follett, Ken
Capricorn One '78 ▸
Eye of the Needle '81
Pillars of the Earth '10

Books to Film: Forster, E.M.
Howard's End '92 ▸
Maurice '87 ▸
A Passage to India '84 ▸
A Room with a View '86 ▸
A Room With a View '08
Where Angels Fear to Tread '91 ▸

Books to Film: Forsyth, Frederick
The Day of the Jackal '73 ▸
Death Has a Bad Reputation '90
The Dogs of War '81
The Fourth Protocol '87 ▸
Just Another Secret '89
A Little Piece of Sunshine '90
The Odessa File '74
The Price of the Bride '90
Pride and Extreme Prejudice '90
Wolverine '96

Books to Film: Fowles, John
The Collector '65 ▸
Ebony Tower '86
The French Lieutenant's Woman '81 ▸

Books to Film: Galsworthy, John
Old English '30
Skin Game '31
A Summer Story '88 ▸
That Forsyte Woman '50
21 Days '40

Books to Film: Gary, Romain
Lady L '65
White Dog '82

Books to Film: Godden, Rumer
Black Narcissus '47 ▸
In This House of Brede '75 ▸
The River '51 ▸

Books to Film: Gogol, Nikolai
Taras Bulba '62

Books to Film: Goldman, William
Heat '87
Magic '78
Marathon Man '76 ▸
The Princess Bride '87 ▸
Wild Card '15

Books to Film: Goodis, David
Dark Passage '47
Moon in the Gutter '83
Murder C.O.D. '90
Nightfall '56 ▸
Shoot the Piano Player '62 ▸

Books to Film: Goudge, Elizabeth
Green Dolphin Street '47
The Secret of Moonacre '08

Books to Film: Grahame, Kenneth
The Adventures of Ichabod and Mr. Toad '49 ▸
Mr. Toad's Wild Ride '96

Books to Film: Greene, Grahame
Across the Bridge '57
Brighton Rock '47 ▸
The Comedians '67
Confidential Agent '45
End of the Affair '55
The End of the Affair '99 ▸
The Fallen Idol '49 ▸
The Fugitive '48 ▸
The Green Cockatoo '37
The Human Factor '79
Ministry of Fear '44 ▸
Our Man in Havana '59 ▸
The Quiet American '02 ▸
Strike It Rich '90
The Tenth Man '88
The Third Man '49 ▸
This Gun for Hire '42 ▸
This Gun for Hire '90
Travels with My Aunt '72

Books to Film: Grey, Zane
Fighting Caravans '31
Gunfighters '47
The Light of Western Stars '30
Riders of the Purple Sage '96
Robbers' Roost '55
To the Last Man '33
The Vanishing American '25
West of the Pecos '45

▸ = rated three bones or higher

Books to Film: Grisham, John

The Chamber '96
Christmas With the Kranks '04
The Client '94
The Firm '93 ►
John Grisham's The Rainmaker '97
A Painted House '03
The Pelican Brief '93
Runaway Jury '03 ►
A Time to Kill '96 ►

Books to Film: Haggard, H. Rider

Allan Quartermain and the Temple of Skulls '08
Allan Quatermain and the Lost City of Gold '86
King Solomon's Mines '37 ►
King Solomon's Mines '50 ►
King Solomon's Mines '85
She '25
She '35
She '65

Books to Film: Hailey, Arthur

Airport '70 ►
Arthur Hailey's The Moneychangers '76
Hotel '67
Time Lock '57
Zero Hour! '57

Books to Film: Haley, Alex

Malcolm X '92 ►
Mama Flora's Family '98
Queen '93 ►
Roots '77 ►
Roots: The Gift '88
Roots: The Next Generation '79 ►

Books to Film: Hammett, Dashiell

After the Thin Man '36 ►
Another Thin Man '39
The Dain Curse '78
The Glass Key '42 ►
Hammett '82
The Maltese Falcon '31 ►
The Maltese Falcon '41 ►
No Good Deed '02
Satan Met a Lady '36
Shadow of the Thin Man '41 ►
Song of the Thin Man '47
The Thin Man '34 ►
The Thin Man Goes Home '44
Woman in the Shadows '34

Books to Film: Hardy, Thomas

The Claim '00
Far from the Madding Crowd '67 ►
Far from the Madding Crowd '97 ►
Jude '96 ►
Jude the Obscure '71
The Mayor of Casterbridge '03
The Return of the Native '94
The Scarlet Tunic '97
Tamara Drewe '10
Tess '79 ►
Tess of the D'Urbervilles '98
Tess of the D'Urbervilles '08
Trishna '11
Under the Greenwood Tree '05

Books to Film: Harlequin Romances

Another Woman '94
At the Midnight Hour '95
The Awakening '95
Broken Lullaby '94
A Change of Place '94
Diamond Girl '98
Dreams Lost, Dreams Found '87
Hard to Forget '98
Loving Evangeline '98
Recipe for Revenge '98
This Matter of Marriage '98
Treacherous Beauties '94
The Waiting Game '98

Books to Film: Harris, Robert

Archangel '05
Enigma '01
The Ghost Writer '10

Books to Film: Harris, Thomas

Black Sunday '77
Hannibal '01
Manhunter '86 ►
Red Dragon '02
The Silence of the Lambs '91 ►

Books to Film: Harrison, Jim

Carried Away '95
Dalva '95
Legends of the Fall '94
Revenge '90
Wolf '94

Books to Film: Hawthorne, Nathaniel

The House of the Seven Gables '40
The Scarlet Letter '34
The Scarlet Letter '73 ►
The Scarlet Letter '79 ►
The Scarlet Letter '95
Twice-Told Tales '63 ►

Books to Film: Hemingway, Ernest

After the Storm '01
The Breaking Point '50 ►
A Farewell to Arms '32 ►
A Farewell to Arms '57
For Whom the Bell Tolls '43 ►
The Gun Runners '58
Hemingway's Garden of Eden '08
Islands in the Stream '77
The Killers '46 ►
The Killers '64
My Old Man '79
The Old Man and the Sea '58 ►
The Old Man and the Sea '90
The Snows of Kilimanjaro '52 ►
The Sun Also Rises '57
To Have & Have Not '44 ►
Women & Men: Stories of Seduction '90

Books to Film: Henry, O.

The Cisco Kid '94
The Gift of Love '90
Ruthless People '86 ►

Books to Film: Higgins, Jack

The Eagle Has Landed '77 ►
Night of the Fox '90
Prayer for the Dying '87
The Wrath of God '72

Books to Film: Highsmith, Patricia

The American Friend '77 ►
Carol '15 ►
The Cry of the Owl '09
Once You Kiss a Stranger '69
Purple Noon '60 ►
Ripley's Game '02 ►
Strangers on a Train '51 ►
The Talented Mr. Ripley '99
The Two Faces of January '14

Books to Film: Hillerman, Tony

Coyote Waits '03
The Dark Wind '91
Skinwalker '02
A Thief of Time '04

Books to Film: Hilton, James

Goodbye, Mr. Chips '02
Lost Horizon '37 ►
Lost Horizon '73
Rage in Heaven '41
Random Harvest '42 ►
So Well Remembered '47

Books to Film: Hinton, S.E.

The Outsiders '83
Rumble Fish '83 ►
Tex '82
That Was Then. . . This Is Now '85

Books to Film: Hornby, Nick

About a Boy '02 ►
An Education '09 ►
Fever Pitch '96
Fever Pitch '05
High Fidelity '00 ►
A Long Way Down '14

Books to Film: Hugo, Victor

Delusions of Grandeur '76
The Hunchback '97
The Hunchback of Notre Dame '23 ►
The Hunchback of Notre Dame '39 ►
The Hunchback of Notre Dame '57
The Hunchback of Notre Dame '82 ►
The Hunchback of Notre Dame '96 ►
Les Miserables '35 ►
Les Miserables '52 ►
Les Miserables '57 ►
Les Miserables '78 ►
Les Miserables '97 ►
Les Miserables '12 ►

Books to Film: Hunter, Evan (aka Ed McBain)

Blackboard Jungle '55 ►
Cop Hater '58
Ed McBain's 87th Precinct: Heatwave '97
Ed McBain's 87th Precinct: Lightning '95
Fuzz '72
High & Low '62 ►
Mister Buddwing '66
The Mugger '58
Strangers When We Meet '60
Stray Dog '49 ►
The Young Savages '61

Books to Film: Hurst, Fanny

Back Street '41
Back Street '61
Five and Ten '31
Four Daughters '38 ►
Imitation of Life '34
Imitation of Life '59 ►
Symphony of Six Million '32
Young at Heart '54

Books to Film: Irving, John

The Cider House Rules '99 ►
The Door in the Floor '04 ►
The Hotel New Hampshire '84
The World According to Garp '82 ►

Books to Film: Irving, Washington

The Adventures of Ichabod and Mr. Toad '49 ►
Sleepy Hollow '99 ►

Books to Film: Isaacs, Susan

Shining Through '92

Books to Film: Jaffe, Rona

Mazes and Monsters '82

Books to Film: Jakes, John

The Bastard '78
North and South Book 1 '85 ►
North and South Book 2 '86 ►

Books to Film: James, Henry

The American '01
The Bostonians '84
Daisy Miller '74
The Europeans '79 ►
The Golden Bowl '72 ►
The Golden Bowl '00
The Green Room '78
The Haunting of Hell House '99
The Heiress '49 ►
In the Shadows '98
The Innocents '61 ►
The Lost Moment '47
The Nightcomers '72
P.D. James: The Murder Room '04
Portrait of a Lady '67
Portrait of a Lady '96 ►
The Turn of the Screw '74
The Turn of the Screw '92
The Turn of the Screw '99
Washington Square '97 ►
What Maisie Knew '12 ►
The Wings of the Dove '97 ►

Books to Film: James, P.D.

A Certain Justice '99
Children of Men '06 ►
Death Comes to Pemberley '13
Devices and Desires '91 ►
A Mind to Murder '96
P.D. James: Death in Holy Orders '03

Books to Film: Jones, James

From Here to Eternity '53 ►
Some Came Running '58 ►
The Thin Red Line '64
The Thin Red Line '98 ►

Books to Film: Joyce, James

Bloom '03
The Dead '87 ►
James Joyce: A Portrait of the Artist as a Young Man '77 ►
Ulysses '67

Books to Film: Kafka, Franz

The Trial '63 ►
The Trial '93

Books to Film: Kennedy, Douglas

The Big Picture '10
Welcome to Woop Woop '97
The Woman in the Fifth '11

Books to Film: King, Stephen

Apt Pupil '97
Bag of Bones '11
Carrie '76 ►
Carrie '02
Carrie '13
Cat's Eye '85
Children of the Corn '84
Children of the Corn '09
Christine '84
Creepshow '82
Creepshow 2 '87
Cujo '83
The Dark Half '91
Dead Zone '83 ►
The Dead Zone '02
Dolan's Cadillac '09
Dolores Claiborne '94 ►
Dreamcatcher '03
Firestarter '84
1408 '07
A Good Marriage '14
Graveyard Shift '90
The Green Mile '99
Hearts in Atlantis '01
The Lawnmower Man '92
The Mangler '94
Maximum Overdrive '86
Misery '90 ►
The Mist '07 ►
Needful Things '93
Pet Sematary '89
Return to Salem's Lot '87
Riding the Bullet '04
The Running Man '87
Salem's Lot '79
Salem's Lot '04
Secret Window '04
The Shawshank Redemption '94 ►
The Shining '80
Silver Bullet '85
Sleepwalkers '92
Sometimes They Come Back '91
Sometimes They Come Back. . . Again '96
Stand by Me '86 ►
Stephen King's Golden Years '91
Stephen King's It '90
Stephen King's Rose Red '02
Stephen King's The Langoliers '95
Stephen King's The Night Flier '96
Stephen King's The Stand '94
Stephen King's The Storm of the Century '99
Stephen King's The Tommyknockers '93
Stephen King's Thinner '96
Tales from the Darkside: The Movie '90
Trucks '97

Books to Film: Kinsella, W.P.

Dance Me Outside '95
Field of Dreams '89 ►

Books to Film: Kipling, Rudyard

Captains Courageous '37 ►
Captains Courageous '95
A Fool There Was '14
Gunga Din '39 ►
The Jungle Book '42
Kim '50 ►
Kim '84
The Man Who Would Be King '75 ►
Rudyard Kipling's The Jungle Book '94
Rudyard Kipling's the Second Jungle Book: Mowgli and Baloo '97
Wee Willie Winkie '37 ►

Books to Film: Klavan, Andrew

Don't Say a Word '01
True Crime '99

Books to Film: Koontz, Dean R.

Dean Koontz's Black River '01
Dean Koontz's Intensity '97
Dean Koontz's Mr. Murder '98
Demon Seed '77 ►
Hideaway '94
Odd Thomas '13
Phantoms '97
Servants of Twilight '91
Watchers '88
Watchers Reborn '98
Whispers '89

Books to Film: Krantz, Judith

Mistral's Daughter '84
Princess Daisy '83
Scruples '80

Books to Film: L'Amour, Louis

Apache Territory '58
The Burning Hills '56
Cancel My Reservation '72
Conagher '91
Crossfire Trail '01 ►
The Diamond of Jeru '01
Heller in Pink Tights '60
Hondo '53 ►
The Quick and the Dead '87
The Sacketts '79
The Shadow Riders '82
Shalako '68
Stranger on Horseback '55

Books to Film: Lardner, Ring

Alibi Ike '35
Champion '49 ►
So This Is New York '48

Books to Film: Lawrence, D.H.

Lady Chatterley '92
Lady Chatterley '10 ►
Lady Chatterley's Lover '55
Lady Chatterley's Lover '81
The Rainbow '89 ►
The Rocking Horse Winner '49
Sons and Lovers '60 ►
The Virgin and the Gypsy '70
The Widowing of Mrs. Holroyd '95
Women in Love '70 ►
Women in Love '11
Young Lady Chatterly 2 '85

Books to Film: Le Carre, John

The Constant Gardener '05 ►
The Little Drummer Girl '84 ►
The Looking Glass War '69
A Most Wanted Man '14
A Murder of Quality '90
A Perfect Spy '88
The Russia House '90
Smiley's People '82
The Spy Who Came in from the Cold '65 ►
The Tailor of Panama '00 ►
Tinker, Tailor, Soldier, Spy '80 ►
Tinker Tailor Soldier Spy '11 ►

Books to Film: Lee, Harper

To Kill a Mockingbird '62 ►

Books to Film: Lehane, Dennis

The Drop '14 ►
Gone Baby Gone '07 ►
Mystic River '03 ►
Shutter Island '09 ►

Books to Film: Leonard, Elmore

The Ambassador '84
Be Cool '05
The Big Bounce '69
The Big Bounce '04
Cat Chaser '90
Elmore Leonard's Gold Coast '97
52 Pick-Up '86
Freaky Deaky '12
Get Shorty '95 ►
Hombre '67 ►
Jackie Brown '97 ►
Killshot '09
Last Stand at Saber River '96
Life of Crime '13
Mr. Majestyk '74
The Moonshine War '70
Out of Sight '98 ►
Stick '85
3:10 to Yuma '57 ►
3:10 to Yuma '07 ►
Touch '96
Valdez Is Coming '71

► = rated three bones or higher

Books to Film: Levin, Ira
The Boys from Brazil '78
A Kiss Before Dying '91
Rosemary's Baby '68 ▸
Rosemary's Baby '14
Sliver '93
The Stepford Wives '75 ▸
The Stepford Wives '04

Books to Film: Lewis, C.S.
The Chronicles of Narnia '89 ▸
The Chronicles of Narnia: Prince Caspian '08
The Chronicles of Narnia: The Lion, the Witch and the Wardrobe '05
The Chronicles of Narnia: The Voyage of the Dawn Treader '10

Books to Film: Lewis, Michael
The Big Short '15 ▸
The Blind Side '09
Moneyball '11 ▸

Books to Film: Lewis, Sinclair
Arrowsmith '31
Dodsworth '36 ▸
Elmer Gantry '60 ▸
There Will Be Blood '07 ▸

Books to Film: Lindgren, Astrid
The Land of Faraway '87
The New Adventures of Pippi Longstocking '88
Pippi Goes on Board '69
Pippi in the South Seas '70
Pippi Longstocking '69
Pippi on the Run '70

Books to Film: London, Jack
The Assassination Bureau '69 ▸
Barricade '49
Burning Daylight '28
Burning Daylight '10
Call of the Wild 3D '09
The Call of the Wild '35 ▸
Call of the Wild '72
Call of the Wild '93
The Fighter '52 ▸
Great Adventure '75
Jack London's The Call of the Wild '97
The Legend of Sea Wolf '75
The Mutiny of the Elsinore '39
White Fang '36
White Fang '91 ▸
White Fang and the Hunter '85

Books to Film: Lovecraft, H.P.
Beyond the Wall of Sleep '06
Blood Island '68
Bride of Re-Animator '89
Chill '06
Cthulhu '08
The Curse '87
Die, Monster, Die! '65
The Dunwich Horror '70
From Beyond '86 ▸
The Haunted Palace '63
H.P. Lovecraft's The Color Out of Space '10
Lurking Fear '94
Re-Animator '84 ▸
The Resurrected '91
The Unnamable 2: The Statement of Randolph Carter '92
The Unnamable '88

Books to Film: Ludlum, Robert
The Apocalypse Watch '97
The Bourne Identity '88 ▸
The Bourne Identity '02 ▸
The Bourne Supremacy '04 ▸
The Bourne Ultimatum '07 ▸
The Hades Factor '06
The Holcroft Covenant '85
The Osterman Weekend '83

Books to Film: Maas, Peter
King of the Gypsies '78
Marie '85 ▸
Serpico '73 ▸

Books to Film: MacLean, Alistair
Breakheart Pass '76
Detonator 2: Night Watch '95
Detonator '93
Force 10 from Navarone '78
The Guns of Navarone '61 ▸
Ice Station Zebra '68
Puppet on a Chain '72
River of Death '90
The Satan Bug '65
When Eight Bells Toll '71
Where Eagles Dare '68 ▸

Books to Film: Mailer, Norman
An American Dream '66
The Executioner's Song '82
Pursuit '72 ▸
Tough Guys Don't Dance '87

Books to Film: Malamud, Bernard
The Angel Levine '70
The Natural '84 ▸
The Tenants '06

Books to Film: Matheson, Richard
The Box '09
Cold Sweat '71
Duel '71 ▸
I Am Legend '07 ▸
I Am Omega '07
Icy Breasts '75 ▸
The Incredible Shrinking Man '57 ▸
The Incredible Shrinking Woman '81
The Last Man on Earth '64
The Legend of Hell House '73 ▸
Omega Man '71
Real Steel '11
Somewhere in Time '80
Stir of Echoes '99
Trilogy of Terror '75
Trilogy of Terror 2 '96
What Dreams May Come '98

Books to Film: Maugham, W. Somerset
Beachcomber '38 ▸
Being Julia '04 ▸
Encore '52 ▸
The Letter '29
The Letter '40 ▸
The Magician '26
Miss Sadie Thompson '53 ▸
The Moon and Sixpence '43 ▸
Of Human Bondage '34 ▸
Of Human Bondage '64
The Painted Veil '34
The Painted Veil '06
Rain '32
The Razor's Edge '46 ▸
The Razor's Edge '84
The Right to Live '35
Sadie Thompson '28 ▸
Up at the Villa '00

Books to Film: McCarthy, Cormac
All the Pretty Horses '00
Child of God '14
No Country for Old Men '07 ▸
The Road '09
The Sunset Limited '11

Books to Film: McCullough, Colleen
The Thorn Birds '83 ▸
Tim '79

Books to Film: McEwan, Ian
Atonement '07 ▸
The Cement Garden '93
The Comfort of Strangers '91 ▸
The Innocent '93

Books to Film: McMillan, Terry
A Day Late and a Dollar Short '14
Disappearing Acts '00
How Stella Got Her Groove Back '98
Waiting to Exhale '95 ▸

Books to Film: McMurtry, Larry
The Best Little Whorehouse in Texas '82
Comanche Moon '08
Hud '63 ▸
Larry McMurtry's Dead Man's Walk '96
The Last Picture Show '71 ▸
Lonesome Dove '89 ▸
Terms of Endearment '83 ▸
Texasville '90

Books to Film: Melville, Herman
Age of the Dragons '11
Bartleby '70
Bartleby '01
Enchanted Island '58
Moby Dick '56 ▸
Moby Dick '98
Moby Dick '11
Pola X '99
2010: Moby Dick '10

Books to Film: Meyer, Stephenie
The Host '13
Twilight '08
The Twilight Saga: Breaking Dawn, Part 1 '11
The Twilight Saga: Breaking Dawn, Part 2 '12
The Twilight Saga: Eclipse '10
The Twilight Saga: New Moon '09

Books to Film: Michener, James
The Bridges at Toko-Ri '55 ▸
Centennial '78 ▸
Dynasty '76
Hawaii '66 ▸
Return to Paradise '53
Sayonara '57 ▸
Texas '94
Until They Sail '57

Books to Film: Miller, Sue
Family Pictures '93 ▸
The Good Mother '88
Inventing the Abbotts '97

Books to Film: Montgomery, L.M.
Anne of Avonlea '87 ▸
Anne of Green Gables '34 ▸
Anne of Green Gables '85 ▸

Books to Film: Moore, Brian
Black Robe '91 ▸
Catholics '73 ▸
Cold Heaven '92
The Lonely Passion of Judith Hearne '87 ▸

Books to Film: Morpugo, Michael
Private Peaceful '12
War Horse '11

Books to Film: Nabokov, Vladimir
Despair '78 ▸
Lolita '62 ▸
Lolita '97
The Luzhin Defence '00

Books to Film: Nathan, Robert
The Bishop's Wife '47 ▸
Pagan Love Song '50
Portrait of Jennie '48 ▸
The Preacher's Wife '96
Wake Up and Dream '46

Books to Film: Nichols, John
The Milagro Beanfield War '88 ▸
The Sterile Cuckoo '69 ▸

Books to Film: Nordhoff, Charles
High Barbaree '47
The Hurricane '37 ▸
Hurricane '79
Mutiny on the Bounty '35 ▸
Mutiny on the Bounty '62
Passage to Marseilles '44 ▸

Books to Film: Oates, Joyce Carol
Blonde '01
Foxfire '96
Smooth Talk '85 ▸

Books to Film: O'Hara, John
Butterfield 8 '60 ▸
From the Terrace '60
Pal Joey '57 ▸
A Rage to Live '65

Books to Film: Oke, Janette
Love Begins '11
Love Comes Softly '03
Love Finds a Home '09
Love Takes Wing '09
Love's Abiding Joy '06
Love's Christmas Journey '11
Love's Enduring Promise '04
Love's Everlasting Courage '11
Love's Long Journey '05
Love's Unending Legacy '07
Love's Unfolding Dream '07
When Calls the Heart '13

Books to Film: O'Connor, Flannery
Wise Blood '79 ▸

Books to Film: Orwell, George
Animal Farm '99
A Merry War '97 ▸
1984 '56 ▸
1984 '84 ▸

Books to Film: Pagnol, Marcel
Fanny '32 ▸
Jean de Florette '87 ▸
Manon of the Spring '87 ▸
Marius '31 ▸
My Father's Glory '91 ▸
My Mother's Castle '91 ▸

Books to Film: Palahniuk, Chuck
Choke '08
Fight Club '99 ▸

Books to Film: Parker, Robert B.
Appaloosa '08 ▸
Jesse Stone: Death in Paradise '06
Jesse Stone: Innocents Lost '11
Jesse Stone: Night Passage '06
Jesse Stone: No Remorse '10
Jesse Stone: Sea Change '07
Jesse Stone: Stone Cold '05
Jesse Stone: Thin Ice '09
Monte Walsh '03
Poodle Springs '98
Spenser: A Savage Place '94
Spenser: Ceremony '93
Spenser: Pale Kings & Princes '94
Spenser: The Judas Goat '94
Thin Air '00

Books to Film: Parrott, Ursula
The Divorcee '30
Love Affair '32
Next Time We Love '36
Strangers May Kiss '31
There's Always Tomorrow '56

Books to Film: Patterson, James
Alex Cross '12
Along Came a Spider '01
Kiss the Girls '97

Books to Film: Perrault, Charles
Bluebeard '09
Cinderella '50 ▸
Ever After: A Cinderella Story '98 ▸
Maleficent '14
Puss in Boots '11 ▸
Red Riding Hood '88
Red Riding Hood '11
Sleeping Beauty '59 ▸
The Sleeping Beauty '10
The Slipper and the Rose '76

Books to Film: Picoult, Jodi
Jodi Picoult's Salem Falls '11
My Sister's Keeper '09
Plain Truth '04
The Tenth Circle '08

Books to Film: Pileggi, Nicholas
Casino '95 ▸
Goodfellas '90 ▸

Books to Film: Poe, Edgar Allan
The Bells '26 ▸
The Black Cat '34 ▸
The Black Cat '81
Dr. Tarr's Torture Dungeon '75
The Fall of the House of Usher '49
The Fall of the House of Usher '60 ▸
The Fall of the House of Usher '80
The Haunted Palace '63
Haunting Fear '91
The Haunting of Morella '91
The House of Usher '06
Manfish '56
Masque of the Red Death '65 ▸
Murders in the Rue Morgue '71
The Murders in the Rue Morgue '86 ▸
The Mystery of Marie Roget '42
The Oblong Box '69
The Pit and the Pendulum '61 ▸
The Pit & the Pendulum '91
Premature Burial '62
The Raven '15
The Raven '63 ▸
The Raven '07
Spirits of the Dead '68 ▸
Stonehearst Asylum '13
Tales of Terror '62
The Tell-Tale Heart '60
The Tomb '09
Tomb of Ligeia '64 ▸
The Torture Chamber of Dr. Sadism '69
Two Evil Eyes '90
Web of the Spider '70

Books to Film: Porter, Katherine Anne
Ship of Fools '65 ▸

Books to Film: Price, Richard
Bloodbrothers '78
Clockers '95 ▸
Freedomland '06
Wanderers '79 ▸

Books to Film: Puzo, Mario
The Godfather '72 ▸
The Godfather, Part 2 '74 ▸
The Godfather, Part 3 '90 ▸
The Last Don '97
The Sicilian '87

Books to Film: Remarque, Erich Maria
All Quiet on the Western Front '30 ▸
All Quiet on the Western Front '79
Arch of Triumph '48 ▸
Arch of Triumph '85
Bobby Deerfield '77
The Other Love '47
So Ends Our Night '41 ▸
Three Comrades '38 ▸

Books to Film: Rendell, Ruth
Alias Betty '01
The Bridesmaid '04
A Demon in My View '92
La Ceremonie '95 ▸
Live Flesh '97 ▸

Books to Film: Rice, Anne
Anne Rice's The Feast of All Saints '01
Exit to Eden '94
Interview with the Vampire '94
Queen of the Damned '02

Books to Film: Richler, Mordecai
The Apprenticeship of Duddy Kravitz '74 ▸
Barney's Version '10
Jacob Two Two Meets the Hooded Fang '99
St. Urbain's Horseman '07

Books to Film: Robbins, Harold
The Adventurers '70
The Betsy '78
The Carpetbaggers '64
King Creole '58
Nevada Smith '66
Never Love a Stranger '58
Where Love Has Gone '64

Books to Film: Robbins, Tom
Made in Heaven '87

Books to Film: Roberts, Nora
Angels Fall '07
Blue Smoke '07
Carnal Innocence '11
Carolina Moon '07
High Noon '09
Midnight Bayou '09
Montana Sky '07
Northern Lights '09
Tribute '09

Books to Film: Rohmer, Sax
Brides of Fu Manchu '66
The Castle of Fu Manchu '68
The Face of Fu Manchu '65
The Fiendish Plot of Dr. Fu Manchu '80

▸ = *rated three bones or higher*

Kiss and Kill '68
The Mask of Fu Manchu '32
The Vengeance of Fu Manchu '67

Books to Film: Roth, Philip
Elegy '08
Goodbye, Columbus '69 ▶
The Human Stain '03

Books to Film: Rowling, J.K.
Harry Potter and the Chamber of Secrets '02 ▶
Harry Potter and the Deathly Hallows, Part 1 '10 ▶
Harry Potter and the Deathly Hallows, Part 2 '11 ▶
Harry Potter and the Goblet of Fire '05 ▶
Harry Potter and the Half-Blood Prince '09
Harry Potter and the Order of the Phoenix '07
Harry Potter and the Prisoner of Azkaban '04
Harry Potter and the Sorcerer's Stone '01 ▶

Books to Film: Rule, Ann
And Never Let Her Go '01
Ann Rule Presents: The Stranger Beside Me '03
Dead by Sunset '95
The Hunt for the I-5 Killer '11

Books to Film: Runyon, Damon
Big Street '42
Bloodhounds of Broadway '52
Bloodhounds of Broadway '89
40 Pounds of Trouble '62
Guys and Dolls '55 ▶
It Ain't Hay '43
Lady for a Day '33 ▶
The Lemon Drop Kid '51
Little Miss Marker '34 ▶
Little Miss Marker '80
Money from Home '53
Pocketful of Miracles '61 ▶
Professional Soldier '35
Sorrowful Jones '49

Books to Film: Sabatini, Rafael
Bardelys the Magnificent '26
The Black Swan '42 ▶
Captain Blood '35 ▶
Christopher Columbus '49
Scaramouche '23
Scaramouche '52 ▶

Books to Film: Scott, Sir Walter
Ivanhoe '52 ▶
Ivanhoe '82
Ivanhoe '97 ▶
King Richard and the Crusaders '54
Quentin Durward '55

Books to Film: Segal, Erich
Love Story '70 ▶
Man, Woman & Child '83
Oliver's Story '78
Only Love '98

Books to Film: Selby, Hubert Jr.
Last Exit to Brooklyn '90 ▶
Requiem for a Dream '00 ▶

Books to Film: Shaw, Irwin
Easy Living '49
In the French Style '63
Tip On a Dead Jockey '57
Two Weeks in Another Town '62
The Young Lions '58 ▶

Books to Film: Sheldon, Sidney
If Tomorrow Comes '86
The Naked Face '84
The Other Side of Midnight '77

Books to Film: Shelley, Mary
The Bride of Frankenstein '35 ▶
Frankenstein '31 ▶
Frankenstein '73
Frankenstein '93
Frankenstein Unbound '90 ▶
Mary Shelley's Frankenstein '94

Books to Film: Shepherd, Jean
A Christmas Story '83 ▶
My Summer Story '94

Books to Film: Simenon, Georges
All Good Things '10
Betty '92
The Brothers Rico '57
Man on the Eiffel Tower '48 ▶
Midnight Episode '50
Monsieur Hire '89 ▶
Red Lights '04 ▶

Books to Film: Sinclair, Upton
The Gnome-Mobile '67
There Will Be Blood '07 ▶
The Wet Parade '32

Books to Film: Sparks, Nicholas
The Best of Me '14
Dear John '10
The Last Song '10
The Longest Ride '15
The Lucky One '12
Message in a Bottle '98
The Notebook '04
Safe Haven '13
A Walk to Remember '02

Books to Film: Spillane, Mickey
The Girl Hunters '63
I, the Jury '82
My Gun Is Quick '57

Books to Film: Steel, Danielle
Danielle Steel's Changes '91
Danielle Steel's Daddy '91
Danielle Steel's Fine Things '90
Danielle Steel's Heartbeat '93
Danielle Steel's Kaleidoscope '90
Danielle Steel's Palomino '91
Danielle Steel's Star '93
Now and Forever '82
The Promise '79
Safe Harbour '07

Books to Film: Steinbeck, John
Cannery Row '82
East of Eden '54 ▶
East of Eden '80
The Grapes of Wrath '40 ▶
Lifeboat '44 ▶
The Moon is Down '43
Of Mice and Men '39 ▶
Of Mice and Men '81 ▶
Of Mice and Men '92 ▶
The Red Pony '49 ▶
Tortilla Flat '42 ▶
The Wayward Bus '57

Books to Film: Stendhal
La Chartreuse de Parme '48
Vanina Vanini '61 ▶

Books to Film: Stevenson, Richard
Ice Blues: A Donald Strachey Mystery '08
Shock to the System '06
Third Man Out: A Donald Strachey Mystery '05

Books to Film: Stevenson, Robert Louis
Abbott and Costello Meet Dr. Jekyll and Mr. Hyde '52
Black Arrow '48 ▶
The Body Snatcher '45 ▶
Dr. Jekyll and Mr. Hyde '20 ▶
Dr. Jekyll and Mr. Hyde '32 ▶
Dr. Jekyll and Mr. Hyde '41 ▶
Dr. Jekyll and Mr. Hyde '68
Dr. Jekyll and Mr. Hyde '73
Dr. Jekyll and Mr. Hyde '08
Dr. Jekyll and Sister Hyde '71
The Ebb-Tide '97
I, Monster '71 ▶
Jekyll '07
Jekyll and Hyde '90
Jekyll & Hyde. . . Together Again '82
Kidnapped '38
Kidnapped '48
Kidnapped '60
Kidnapped '95
Kidnapped '05 ▶
The Master of Ballantrae '53
Muppet Treasure Island '96
Robert Louis Stevenson's The Game of Death '99
St. Ives '98
Strange Case of Dr. Jekyll & Mr. Hyde '68
The Strange Case of Dr. Jekyll and Mr. Hyde '06
The Strange Door '51
Treasure Island '34 ▶
Treasure Island '50 ▶
Treasure Island '72
Treasure Island '89
Treasure Island '99
Treasure Island '12
Treasure Planet '02
The Wrong Box '66 ▶

Books to Film: Stoker, Bram
Alucard '08
Argento's Dracula 3D '13
Blood from the Mummy's Tomb '71
Bram Stoker's Dracula '92
Bram Stoker's Shadowbuilder '98
Bram Stoker's The Mummy '97
Burial of the Rats '95
Count Dracula '71
Count Dracula '77
Dracula '06
Dracula '31 ▶
Dracula Spanish Version '31
Dracula '73
Dracula '79
The Horror of Dracula '58 ▶
The Lair of the White Worm '88 ▶
Nosferatu the Vampyre '79
Van Helsing '04 ▶

Books to Film: Stowe, Harriet Beecher
Uncle Tom's Cabin '27

Books to Film: Susann, Jacqueline
The Love Machine '71
Once Is Not Enough '75

Books to Film: Swarthout, Glendon
Bless the Beasts and Children '71
The Homesman '14
Seventh Cavalry '56
The Shootist '76 ▶
They Came to Cordura '59
Where the Boys Are '84 '84
Where the Boys Are '60

Books to Film: Swift, Jonathan
Gulliver's Travels '39
Gulliver's Travels '77
Gulliver's Travels '95
Gulliver's Travels '10
The Three Worlds of Gulliver '59
The 3 Worlds of Gulliver '60

Books to Film: Tarkington, Booth
Alice Adams '35
By the Light of the Silvery Moon '53
The Magnificent Ambersons '42 ▶
The Magnificent Ambersons '02
Monsieur Beaucaire '24
Monsieur Beaucaire '46 ▶
Monte Carlo '30
On Moonlight Bay '51
Penrod and Sam '31
Presenting Lily Mars '43

Books to Film: Thackeray, William Makepeace
Barry Lyndon '75 ▶
Becky Sharp '35
Vanity Fair '32
Vanity Fair '99
Vanity Fair '04

Books to Film: Theroux, Paul
Half Moon Street '86
The Mosquito Coast '86
Saint Jack '79 ▶

Books to Film: Thompson, Jim
After Dark, My Sweet '90 ▶
Coup de Torchon '81 ▶
The Getaway '72
The Getaway '93
The Grifters '90 ▶
Hit Me '96
The Kill-Off '89
The Killer Inside Me '10

Books to Film: Thorp, Roderick
The Detective '68 ▶
Die Hard '88 ▶

Books to Film: Thurber, James
Billy Liar '63 ▶
The Secret Life of Walter Mitty '47 ▶

Books to Film: Tolkien, J.R.R.
The Hobbit '78 ▶
The Hobbit: An Unexpected Journey '12
The Hobbit: The Battle of the Five Armies '14
The Hobbit: The Desolation of Smaug '13 ▶
Lord of the Rings: The Fellowship of the Ring '01 ▶
Lord of the Rings: The Two Towers '02 ▶
The Lord of the Rings '78
Lord of the Rings: The Return of the King '03 ▶
The Return of the King '80

Books to Film: Tolstoy, Leo
Anna Karenina '35 ▶
Anna Karenina '48
Anna Karenina '96
Anna Karenina '00
Anna Karenina '12
The Kreutzer Sonata '08
The Last Gangster '37
Night Sun '90
Prisoner of the Mountains '96 ▶
War and Peace '56
War and Peace '68 ▶
War and Peace '73
We Live Again '34

Books to Film: Turow, Scott
Presumed Innocent '90 ▶

Books to Film: Twain, Mark
The Adventures of Huck Finn '93 ▶
The Adventures of Huckleberry Finn '39 ▶
The Adventures of Huckleberry Finn '60
The Adventures of Huckleberry Finn '85
The Adventures of Tom Sawyer '38 ▶
Arthur's Quest '99
Ava's Magical Adventure '94
A Connecticut Yankee in King Arthur's Court '49
Huck and the King of Hearts '93
Huckleberry Finn '74
A Kid in King Arthur's Court '95
A Knight in Camelot '98
A Million to Juan '94
The Modern Adventures of Tom Sawyer '99
The Prince and the Pauper '37 ▶
The Prince and the Pauper '62
The Prince and the Pauper '78
The Prince and the Pauper '01
The Prince and the Pauper '07
The Prince and the Surfer '99
Tom and Huck '95 ▶
Tom Sawyer '73
Unidentified Flying Oddball '79

Books to Film: Tyler, Anne
The Accidental Tourist '88 ▶
Earthly Possessions '99

Books to Film: Updike, John
Rabbit, Run '70
Roommate '84
Too Far to Go '79 ▶
The Witches of Eastwick '87

Books to Film: Uris, Leon
Battle Cry '55 ▶
Exodus '60 ▶
QB VII '74 ▶
Topaz '69 ▶

Books to Film: Verne, Jules
Around the World in 80 Days '56 ▶
Around the World in 80 Days '89
Around the World in 80 Days '04
Around the World in a Daze '63
Captain Nemo and the Underwater City '69
800 Leagues Down the Amazon '93
Five Weeks in a Balloon '62
In Search of the Castaways '62 ▶
Journey to the Center of the Earth '59 ▶
Journey to the Center of the Earth '88
Journey to the Center of the Earth '93
Journey to the Center of the Earth '99
Journey to the Center of the Earth '08
Jules Verne's Mysterious Island '10
Light at the Edge of the World '71
Master of the World '61
Mysterious Island '61 ▶
Mysterious Island '05
The Southern Star '69
Those Fantastic Flying Fools '67
20,000 Leagues under the Sea '16 ▶
20,000 Leagues under the Sea '54 ▶
20,000 Leagues Under the Sea '97
Valley of the Dragons '61
Where Time Began '77

Books to Film: Vonnegut, Kurt
Breakfast of Champions '98
Mother Night '96 ▶
Slaughterhouse Five '72

Books to Film: Walker, Alice
The Color Purple '85 ▶

Books to Film: Wallace, Edgar
Again, the Ringer '64
Chamber of Horrors '40
Creature with the Blue Hand '70
Dead Eyes of London '61
Door with the Seven Locks '62
The Human Monster '39
The Indian Scarf '63
The Mysterious Magician '65
The Secret Four '39
Secret of the Black Trunk '62
The Squeaker '65

Books to Film: Wambaugh, Joseph
The Black Marble '79 ▶
The Choirboys '77
The New Centurions '72
The Onion Field '79 ▶

Books to Film: Waugh, Evelyn
The Bandit of Sherwood Forest '46
Brideshead Revisited '81 ▶
Brideshead Revisited '08
Bright Young Things '03
Decline and Fall...of a Birdwatcher '68
A Handful of Dust '88
The Loved One '65
Rogues of Sherwood Forest '50
Sword of Honour '01

Books to Film: Wells, H.G.
Empire of the Ants '77
First Men in the Moon '64
Food of the Gods '76
Food of the Gods: Part 2 '88
Half a Sixpence '67
H.G. Wells' War of the Worlds '05
The History of Mr. Polly '07
The Invisible Man '33 ▶
The Invisible Man's Revenge '44
The Island of Dr. Moreau '77
The Island of Dr. Moreau '96
Island of Lost Souls '32 ▶
The Man Who Could Work Miracles '37 ▶
Terror Is a Man '59
Things to Come '36 ▶
The Time Machine '60 ▶
The Time Machine '02
Village of the Giants '65
War of the Worlds 2: The Next Wave '08
The War of the Worlds '53 ▶
War of the Worlds '05 ▶

▸ = rated three bones or higher

How the West Was Won '63 ▶
The Long Voyage Home '40 ▶
The Man Who Shot Liberty Valance '62 ▶
The Quiet Man '52 ▶
Rio Grande '50 ▶
The Searchers '56 ▶
She Wore a Yellow Ribbon '49 ▶
Stagecoach '39 ▶
They Were Expendable '45 ▶
Three Godfathers '48 ▶
Wings of Eagles '57

Director/Star Teams: Frank Tashlin & Jerry Lewis
Artists and Models '55
Cinderfella '60
Disorderly Orderly '64
The Geisha Boy '58
Hollywood or Bust '56
It's Only Money '62
Rock-A-Bye Baby '57
Who's Minding the Store? '63

Director/Star Teams: Frankenheimer & Lancaster
Birdman of Alcatraz '62 ▶
The Gypsy Moths '69
Seven Days in May '64 ▶
Terror Out of the Sky '78
The Train '65 ▶
The Young Savages '61

Director/Star Teams: Greengrass & Damon
The Bourne Supremacy '04 ▶
The Bourne Ultimatum '07 ▶
Green Zone '10 ▶

Director/Star Teams: Hawks & Wayne
El Dorado '67 ▶
Hatari! '62 ▶
Red River '48 ▶
Rio Bravo '59 ▶
Rio Lobo '70

Director/Star Teams: Henry Hathaway & Gary Cooper
Garden of Evil '54
The Lives of a Bengal Lancer '35 ▶
Now and Forever '34
Peter Ibbetson '35
The Real Glory '39 ▶
Souls at Sea '37
You're In the Navy Now '51

Director/Star Teams: Herzog & Kinski
Aguirre, the Wrath of God '72 ▶
Cobra Verde '88
Fitzcarraldo '82 ▶
Nosferatu the Vampyre '79 ▶
Woyzeck '78 ▶

Director/Star Teams: Hill & Newman
Butch Cassidy and the Sundance Kid '69 ▶
Daydream Nation '10
Slap Shot '77 ▶
The Sting '73 ▶

Director/Star Teams: Hitchcock & Grant
North by Northwest '59 ▶
Notorious '46 ▶
Suspicion '41 ▶
To Catch a Thief '55 ▶

Director/Star Teams: Hitchcock & Stewart
The Man Who Knew Too Much '56
Rear Window '54 ▶
Rope '48 ▶
Vertigo '58 ▶

Director/Star Teams: Holofcener & Keener
Friends with Money '06
Lovely & Amazing '02 ▶
Please Give '10
Walking and Talking '96

Director/Star Teams: Howard & Hanks
Angels & Demons '09
Apollo 13 '95 ▶
The Da Vinci Code '06 ▶

Director/Star Teams: Howard & Keaton
Gung Ho '86
Night Shift '82

Director/Star Teams: Huston & Bogart
Across the Pacific '42 ▶
The African Queen '51 ▶
Beat the Devil '53 ▶
Key Largo '48 ▶
The Maltese Falcon '41 ▶
Treasure of the Sierra Madre '48 ▶

Director/Star Teams: Jarman & Swinton
Aria '88
Caravaggio '86 ▶
Edward II '92
The Last of England '87 ▶
Trois Couleurs: Bleu '93 ▶
Wittgenstein '93

Director/Star Teams: Jordan & Rea
The Butcher Boy '97 ▶
The Company of Wolves '85 ▶
The Crying Game '92 ▶
Danny Boy '82 ▶
The End of the Affair '99 ▶
In Dreams '98
Interview with the Vampire '94
Michael Collins '96 ▶

Director/Star Teams: Kasdan & Kline
The Big Chill '83 ▶
Darling Companion '12
French Kiss '95
Grand Canyon '91 ▶
I Love You to Death '90
Silverado '85 ▶

Director/Star Teams: Kazan & Brando
On the Waterfront '54 ▶
A Streetcar Named Desire '51 ▶
Viva Zapata! '52 ▶

Director/Star Teams: King & Peck
Beloved Infidel '59
The Bravados '58 ▶
The Gunfighter '50 ▶
The Snows of Kilimanjaro '52 ▶
Twelve o'Clock High '49 ▶

Director/Star Teams: Kurosawa & Mifune
The Bad Sleep Well '60 ▶
Drunken Angel '48 ▶
The Hidden Fortress '58 ▶
High & Low '62 ▶
A Quiet Duel '49
Rashomon '51 ▶
Red Beard '65 ▶
Sanjuro '62 ▶
Scandal '50
Seven Samurai '54 ▶
Stray Dog '49 ▶
Throne of Blood '57 ▶
Yojimbo '61 ▶

Director/Star Teams: LaBute & Eckhart
In the Company of Men '96
Nurse Betty '00 ▶
Possession '02
Your Friends & Neighbors '98 ▶

Director/Star Teams: Lean & Guinness
The Bridge on the River Kwai '57 ▶
Doctor Zhivago '65 ▶
Great Expectations '46 ▶
Lawrence of Arabia '62 ▶
Oliver Twist '48 ▶
A Passage to India '84 ▶

Director/Star Teams: Lee & Turturro
Clockers '95 ▶
Do the Right Thing '89 ▶
Girl 6 '96
He Got Game '98
Jungle Fever '91 ▶
Miracle at St. Anna '08
Mo' Better Blues '90
She Hate Me '04
Summer of Sam '99

Director/Star Teams: Lee & Washington
He Got Game '98
Inside Man '06 ▶
Malcolm X '92 ▶
Mo' Better Blues '90

Director/Star Teams: Leone & Eastwood
A Fistful of Dollars '64 ▶
For a Few Dollars More '65
The Good, the Bad and the Ugly '67 ▶

Director/Star Teams: Linklater & Hawke
Before Sunrise '94
Before Sunset '04 ▶
Boyhood '14 ▶
The Newton Boys '97
Tape '01 ▶
Waking Life '01

Director/Star Teams: Lynch & Dern
Blue Velvet '86 ▶
Inland Empire '06
Wild at Heart '90 ▶

Director/Star Teams: Lynch & Nance
Blue Velvet '86 ▶
Dune '84
Eraserhead '78 ▶
Lost Highway '96
Twin Peaks: Fire Walk with Me '92
Wild at Heart '90 ▶

Director/Star Teams: Mann & Stewart
Bend of the River '52 ▶
Far Country '55 ▶
The Man from Laramie '55 ▶
The Naked Spur '53 ▶
Winchester '73 '50 ▶

Director/Star Teams: McKay & Ferrell
Anchorman: The Legend of Ron Burgundy '04
The Other Guys '10
Step Brothers '08
Talladega Nights: The Ballad of Ricky Bobby '06

Director/Star Teams: McLaglen & Stewart
Bandolero! '68
The Rare Breed '66
Shenandoah '65 ▶

Director/Star Teams: McLaglen & Wayne
Cahill: United States Marshal '73
Chisum '70
Hellfighters '68
McLintock! '63 ▶
The Undefeated '69

Director/Star Teams: Needham & Reynolds
Cannonball Run 2 '84
Cannonball Run '81
Hooper '78
Smokey and the Bandit '77
Smokey and the Bandit 2 '80
Stroker Ace '83

Director/Star Teams: Newman & Woodward
The Glass Menagerie '87 ▶
Harry & Son '84
Rachel, Rachel '68 ▶

Director/Star Teams: Nolan & Bale
Batman Begins '05 ▶
The Dark Knight '08 ▶
The Prestige '06 ▶

Director/Star Teams: Nolan & Caine
Batman Begins '05 ▶
The Dark Knight '08 ▶
The Prestige '06 ▶

Director/Star Teams: Poitier & Cosby
Ghost Dad '90
Let's Do It Again '75
Piece of the Action '77
Uptown Saturday Night '74

Director/Star Teams: Pollack & Redford
The Electric Horseman '79
Havana '90
Jeremiah Johnson '72 ▶
Out of Africa '85 ▶
This Property Is Condemned '66
Three Days of the Condor '75 ▶
The Way We Were '73 ▶

Director/Star Teams: R. Rodriguez & Banderas
Desperado '95 ▶
Four Rooms '95
Machete Kills '13
Spy Kids 2: The Island of Lost Dreams '02 ▶
Spy Kids '01 ▶

Director/Star Teams: Rafelson & Nicholson
Blood & Wine '96
Five Easy Pieces '70 ▶
Head '68 ▶
The King of Marvin Gardens '72
Man Trouble '92
The Postman Always Rings Twice '81

Director/Star Teams: Raimi & 1973 Oldsmobile Delta 88
Army of Darkness '92 ▶
Darkman '90 ▶
Evil Dead '83
Evil Dead 2: Dead by Dawn '87
For Love of the Game '99
The Gift '00
A Simple Plan '98 ▶
Spider-Man '02 ▶
Spider-Man 2 '04 ▶
Spider-Man 3 '07

Director/Star Teams: Raimi & Campbell
Army of Darkness '92 ▶
Darkman '90 ▶
Evil Dead '83
Evil Dead 2: Dead by Dawn '87
Spider-Man '02 ▶
Spider-Man 2 '04 ▶
Spider-Man 3 '07

Director/Star Teams: Reiner & Martin
All of Me '84
Dead Men Don't Wear Plaid '82
The Jerk '79
The Man with Two Brains '83 ▶

Director/Star Teams: Ritt & Newman
Hombre '67 ▶
Hud '63 ▶
The Long, Hot Summer '58 ▶
Paris Blues '61

Director/Star Teams: Sayles & Clapp
Eight Men Out '88 ▶
Matewan '87 ▶
Return of the Secaucus 7 '80 ▶
Sunshine State '02 ▶

Director/Star Teams: Sayles & Cooper
City of Hope '91 ▶
Lone Star '95 ▶
Matewan '87 ▶
Silver City '04

Director/Star Teams: Sayles & Strathairn
The Brother from Another Planet '84 ▶
City of Hope '91 ▶
Eight Men Out '88 ▶
Limbo '99
Matewan '87 ▶
Passion Fish '92 ▶
Return of the Secaucus 7 '80 ▶

Director/Star Teams: Scorsese & De Niro
Cape Fear '91 ▶
Casino '95 ▶
Goodfellas '90 ▶
King of Comedy '82 ▶
Mean Streets '73 ▶
New York, New York '77 ▶
Raging Bull '80 ▶
Taxi Driver '76 ▶

Director/Star Teams: Scorsese & DiCaprio
The Aviator '85
The Departed '06 ▶
Gangs of New York '02 ▶
Shutter Island '09 ▶
The Wolf of Wall Street '13 ▶

Director/Star Teams: Scorsese & Keitel
Alice Doesn't Live Here Anymore '74
The Last Temptation of Christ '88 ▶
Mean Streets '73 ▶
Taxi Driver '76 ▶
Who's That Knocking at My Door? '68 ▶

Director/Star Teams: Scott & Crowe
American Gangster '07 ▶
Body of Lies '08
Gladiator '00 ▶
A Good Year '06
Robin Hood '10

Director/Star Teams: Scott & Washington
Crimson Tide '95 ▶
Deja Vu '06
Man on Fire '04
The Taking of Pelham 123 '09
Unstoppable '10 ▶

Director/Star Teams: Shadyac & Carrey
Ace Ventura: Pet Detective '93
Bruce Almighty '03
Liar Liar '97

Director/Star Teams: Sheridan & Day-Lewis
The Boxer '97
In the Name of the Father '93 ▶
My Left Foot '89 ▶

Director/Star Teams: Siegel & Eastwood
The Beguiled '70 ▶
Coogan's Bluff '68 ▶
Dirty Harry '71 ▶
Escape from Alcatraz '79 ▶
Two Mules for Sister Sara '70 ▶

Director/Star Teams: Sirk & Hudson
All That Heaven Allows '55 ▶
Battle Hymn '57
Captain Lightfoot '55
Has Anybody Seen My Gal? '52
Tarnished Angels '57 ▶
Taza, Son of Cochise '54
Written on the Wind '56 ▶

Director/Star Teams: Smith & Affleck
Chasing Amy '97
Clerks 2 '06 ▶
Dogma '99
Jay and Silent Bob Strike Back '01
Jersey Girl '04
Mallrats '95

Director/Star Teams: Soderbergh & Clooney
The Good German '06
The Limey '99 ▶
Ocean's Eleven '01 ▶
Ocean's Thirteen '07 ▶
Ocean's Twelve '04
Out of Sight '98 ▶
Solaris '02

Director/Star Teams: Soderburgh & Roberts
Erin Brockovich '00 ▶
Full Frontal '02
Ocean's Eleven '01 ▶
Ocean's Twelve '04

Director/Star Teams: Spielberg & Dreyfuss
Always '89
Close Encounters of the Third Kind '77 ▶
Grimm Love '06
Jaws '75 ▶

Director/Star Teams: Spielberg & Hanks
Catch Me If You Can '02
Saving Private Ryan '98 ▶
The Terminal '04

Director/Star Teams: Sturges & McCrea
The Great Moment '44
The Palm Beach Story '42 ▶
Sullivan's Travels '41 ▶

Director/Star Teams: Techine & Deneuve
Ma Saison Preferee '93 ▶

Director/Star Teams: Thorpe & R. Taylor
All the Brothers Were Valiant '53
The Crowd Roars '38
Ivanhoe '52 ▶
Knights of the Round Table '53
Quentin Durward '55
Tip On a Dead Jockey '57

Director/Star Teams: Truffaut & Leaud
Bed and Board '70 ▶
Day for Night '73 ▶
The 400 Blows '59 ▶
Hotel America '81
Stolen Kisses '68 ▶

▶ = rated three bones or higher

Two English Girls '72 ▸

Director/Star Teams: Verbinski & Depp

The Lone Ranger '13
Pirates of the Caribbean: At World's End '07
Pirates of the Caribbean: Dead Man's Chest '06
Pirates of the Caribbean: The Curse of the Black Pearl '03 ▸
Rango '11 ▸

Director/Star Teams: Verhoeven & Hauer

Flesh and Blood '85
Katie Tippel '75
Soldier of Orange '78 ▸
Spetters '80
Turkish Delight '73

Director/Star Teams: von Sternberg & Dietrich

Blonde Venus '32 ▸
The Blue Angel '30 ▸
The Devil Is a Woman '35 ▸
Dishonored '31
Morocco '30 ▸
Scarlet Empress '34 ▸
Shanghai Express '32 ▸

Director/Star Teams: Walsh & Bogart

The Enforcer '51
High Sierra '41 ▸
The Roaring Twenties '39 ▸
They Drive by Night '40 ▸

Director/Star Teams: Wilder & Lemmon

The Apartment '60 ▸
Avanti! '72
The Fortune Cookie '66 ▸
The Front Page '74
Irma La Douce '63
Some Like It Hot '59 ▸

Director/Star Teams: Woo & Fat

A Better Tomorrow, Part 1 '86
A Better Tomorrow, Part 2 '88
A Bullet in the Head '90 ▸
Hard-Boiled '92
The Killer '90 ▸

Director/Star Teams: Zemeckis & Hanks

Cast Away '00 ▸
Forrest Gump '94 ▸
The Polar Express '04

Dirty Harry

The Dead Pool '88
Dirty Harry '71 ▸
The Enforcer '76
Magnum Force '73
Sudden Impact '83

Disney Animated Movies

Aladdin '92 ▸
Aladdin and the King of Thieves '96
Alice in Wonderland '51 ▸
The Aristocats '70 ▸
Bambi '42 ▸
Bambi II '06
Beauty and the Beast '91 ▸
Bionicle 3: Web of Shadows '05
The Black Cauldron '85
Bolt '08 ▸
Brave '12
Brother Bear 2 '06
Brother Bear '03
Cars '06 ▸
Chicken Little '05
A Christmas Carol '09
Cinderella '50 ▸
Dinosaur '00
Doug's 1st Movie '99 ▸
DuckTales the Movie: Treasure of the Lost Lamp '90
The Emperor's New Groove '00 ▸
Fantasia '40 ▸
Fantasia/2000 '00
The Fox and the Hound 2 '06
The Fox and the Hound '81 ▸
Frankenweenie '12 ▸
Frozen '13 ▸
Gnomeo & Juliet '11
A Goofy Movie '94
The Great Mouse Detective '86 ▸
Hercules '97 ▸
The Hunchback of Notre Dame '96 ▸
The Incredibles '04 ▸
The Jungle Book 2 '03
The Jungle Book '67 ▸
Lady and the Tramp '55 ▸
Leroy and Stitch '06
Lilo & Stitch '02 ▸
The Lion King '94 ▸
The Lion King 1 1/2 '04 ▸
The Lion King: Simba's Pride '98
The Little Mermaid '89 ▸
The Many Adventures of Winnie the Pooh '77
Meet the Robinsons '07
Melody Time '48 ▸
Monsters University '13
Mulan 2 '04
Mulan '98
The Nightmare Before Christmas '93 ▸
Oliver & Company '88
101 Dalmatians '61 ▸
Peter Pan '53 ▸
Piglet's Big Movie '03
Pinocchio '40 ▸
Planes '13
Planes: Fire & Rescue '14
Pocahontas '95 ▸
The Princess and the Frog '09 ▸
The Rescuers '77 ▸
The Rescuers Down Under '90
The Return of Jafar '94
Return to Never Land '02
Robin Hood '73 ▸
Sleeping Beauty '59 ▸
Snow White and the Seven Dwarfs '37 ▸
Strange Magic '15
The Sword in the Stone '63 ▸
Tangled '10 ▸
Tarzan 2 '05
Tarzan '99 ▸
The Three Caballeros '45
Treasure Planet '02
Up '09 ▸
Valiant '05
The Wild '06
Winnie the Pooh '11 ▸
Wreck-It Ralph '12

Disney Family Movies

The Absent-Minded Professor '61 ▸
The Adventures of Bullwhip Griffin '66
The Adventures of Huck Finn '93 ▸
The Adventures of Ichabod and Mr. Toad '49 ▸
The Air Up There '94
Alexander and the Terrible, Horrible, No Good, Very Bad Day '14
Almost Angels '62
Amy '81
Angels in the Endzone '98
Angels in the Outfield '94
The Apple Dumpling Gang '75
The Apple Dumpling Gang Rides Again '79
Babes in Toyland '61
The Barefoot Executive '71
Bears '14
The Bears & I '74
Bedknobs and Broomsticks '71
Bedtime Stories '08
Benji the Hunted '87
Beverly Hills Chihuahua 3: Viva La Fiesta! '12
Beverly Hills Chihuahua '08
Big Red '62
Black Arrow '48 ▸
The Black Hole '79
Blackbeard's Ghost '67
Blank Check '93
Bon Voyage! '62
Bridge to Terabithia '07
Candleshoe '78
The Castaway Cowboy '74
The Cat from Outer Space '78
Charley and the Angel '73
Charlie the Lonesome Cougar '67
Cheetah '89
The Cheetah Girls: One World '08
Child of Glass '78
Chimpanzee '12
The Chronicles of Narnia: Prince Caspian '08
The Chronicles of Narnia: The Lion, the Witch and the Wardrobe '05
Cinderella '15
College Road Trip '08
The Computer Wore Tennis Shoes '69
Condorman '81
The Country Bears '02
D3: The Mighty Ducks '96
Darby O'Gill & the Little People '59 ▸
Davy Crockett and the River Pirates '56
Davy Crockett, King of the Wild Frontier '55 ▸
The Devil & Max Devlin '81
Dr. Syn, Alias the Scarecrow '64
Emil and the Detectives '64
Enchanted '07
Escape to Witch Mountain '75 ▸
A Far Off Place '93
The Fighting Prince of Donegal '66
Flight of the Grey Wolf '76
Flight of the Navigator '86
Flubber '97
Freaky Friday '76
Freaky Friday '03 ▸
Fun & Fancy Free '47 ▸
Geek Charming '11
The Gnome-Mobile '67
Goal! The Dream Begins '06
Gone Are the Days '84
A Goofy Movie '94
The Great Locomotive Chase '56
Greyfriars Bobby '61
Gus '76
Halloweentown 2: Kalabar's Revenge '01
Halloweentown '98
Halloweentown High '04
Heavyweights '94
Herbie: Fully Loaded '05
Herbie Goes Bananas '80
Herbie Goes to Monte Carlo '77
Herbie Rides Again '74
High School Musical '06
Homeward Bound: The Incredible Journey '93 ▸
Honey, I Blew Up the Kid '92
Honey, I Shrunk the Kids '89
Honey, We Shrunk Ourselves '97
The Horse in the Gray Flannel Suit '68
The Horse Without a Head '63
Hot Lead & Cold Feet '78
The Hunchback of Notre Dame '96 ▸
In Search of the Castaways '62 ▸
The Incredible Journey '63
The Incredibles '04 ▸
Invincible '06 ▸
Iron Will '93
The Island at the Top of the World '74
Johnny Shiloh '63
Johnny Tremain & the Sons of Liberty '58
The Journey of Natty Gann '85 ▸
Jump In! '07
Justin Morgan Had a Horse '81
King of the Grizzlies '69
The Last Flight of Noah's Ark '80
The Last Song '10
Lemonade Mouth '11
Lt. Robin Crusoe, U.S.N. '66
The Littlest Horse Thieves '76
The Littlest Outlaw '54
The Love Bug '68
Maleficent '14
Mary Poppins '64 ▸
McFarland USA '15
Menace on the Mountain '70
Million Dollar Arm '14
Million Dollar Duck '71
The Miracle of the White Stallions '63
The Misadventures of Merlin Jones '63
Monkeys, Go Home! '66
Monkey's Uncle '65
Moon Pilot '62
The Moon-Spinners '64
The Muppets '11 ▸
Muppets Most Wanted '14
My Dog, the Thief '69
My Favorite Martian '98
Napoleon and Samantha '72 ▸
Never a Dull Moment '68
Newsies '92
Night Crossing '81
Nikki, the Wild Dog of the North '61
No Deposit, No Return '76
The North Avenue Irregulars '79
Now You See Him, Now You Don't '72
The Odd Life of Timothy Green '12
Old Dogs '09
Old Yeller '57 ▸
The One and Only, Genuine, Original Family Band '68 ▸
101 Dalmatians '96
102 Dalmatians '00
One Little Indian '73
One Magic Christmas '85
One of Our Dinosaurs Is Missing '75
Oz the Great and Powerful '13
The Parent Trap '61
Pete's Dragon '77
Pocahontas '95 ▸
Pollyanna '60 ▸
Princess Protection Program '09
Race to Witch Mountain '09
Real Steel '11
Return from Witch Mountain '78
Return to Halloweentown '06
Return to Oz '85
Ride a Wild Pony '75 ▸
Rob Roy-The Highland Rogue '53
The Rocketeer '91 ▸
Savage Sam '63
Scandalous John '71
The Shaggy D.A. '76
The Shaggy Dog '59
The Shaggy Dog '06
The Sign of Zorro '60
Sky High '05 ▸
Smith! '69
Snow Dogs '02
Snowball Express '72
So Dear to My Heart '49 ▸
Son of Flubber '63
The Sorcerer's Apprentice '10
StarStruck '10
The Story of Robin Hood & His Merrie Men '52 ▸
The Strongest Man in the World '75
Summer Magic '63
Summer of the Monkeys '98
Superdad '73
The Swiss Family Robinson '60 ▸
The Sword & the Rose '53
Tall Tale: The Unbelievable Adventures of Pecos Bill '95
Teen Beach Movie '13
Ten Who Dared '60
That Darn Cat '65
That Darn Cat '96
Third Man on the Mountain '59
Those Calloways '65
The Three Lives of Thomasina '63 ▸
3 Ninjas '92
3 Ninjas Kick Back '94
A Tiger Walks '64
Toby Tyler '59 ▸
Tom and Huck '95 ▸
Tonka '58
Toothless '97
Toy Story '95 ▸
Treasure Island '50 ▸
The Treasure of Matecumbe '76
Tron: Legacy '10
20,000 Leagues under the Sea '54 ▸
The Ugly Dachshund '65
Underdog '07
Unidentified Flying Oddball '79
Waltz King '63
The Watcher in the Woods '81
Westward Ho, the Wagons! '56
White Fang 2: The Myth of the White Wolf '94
White Fang '91 ▸
The Wild Country '71
Wild Hearts Can't Be Broken '91 ▸
The World's Greatest Athlete '73

Doc Holliday

Cheyenne Autumn '64
Gunfight at the O.K. Corral '57 ▸
Hour of the Gun '67
My Darling Clementine '46 ▸
Tombstone '93 ▸
Wyatt Earp '94
Wyatt Earp's Revenge '12

Doctor Christian

Courageous Dr. Christian '40
Meet Dr. Christian '39
Melody for Three '41
Remedy for Riches '40

Doctor Kildare

Calling Dr. Kildare '39
Dr. Kildare Goes Home '40
Dr. Kildare's Crisis '40
Dr. Kildare's Strange Case '40
Dr. Kildare's Victory '42
Dr. Kildare's Wedding Day '41
The People vs. Dr. Kildare '41
The Secret of Dr. Kildare '39
Young Dr. Kildare '38

Doctor Mabuse

Dr. Mabuse, The Gambler '22 ▸
Dr. Mabuse vs. Scotland Yard '64
The Invisible Dr. Mabuse '62 ▸
The Return of Dr. Mabuse '61
The Thousand Eyes of Dr. Mabuse '60

Doctor Seuss

Dr. Seuss' Horton Hears a Who! '08 ▸
Dr. Seuss' How the Grinch Stole Christmas '00
Dr. Seuss' The Cat in the Hat '03
Dr. Seuss' The Lorax '12
The 5000 Fingers of Dr. T '53 ▸

Dracula

Abbott and Costello Meet Frankenstein '48 ▸
Alucard '08
Argento's Dracula 3D '13
Blood of Dracula '57
Blood of Dracula's Castle '69
Bonnie and Clyde vs. Dracula '08
Bram Stoker's Dracula '92
Bram Stoker's Way of the Vampire '05
The Brides of Dracula '60
Count Dracula '71
Count Dracula '77
The Creeps '97
Dracula '06
Dracula 2: Ascension '03
Dracula 3: Legacy '05
Dracula '31 ▸
Dracula Spanish Version '31
Dracula '73
Dracula '79
Dracula A.D. 1972 '72
Dracula: Dead and Loving It '95
Dracula Has Risen from the Grave '68
Dracula, Prince of Darkness '66
Dracula Rising '93
Dracula: The Dark Prince '01
Dracula 2000 '00
Dracula Untold '14
Dracula vs. Frankenstein '69
Dracula vs. Frankenstein '71
Dracula's Daughter '36 ▸
Dracula's Great Love '72
Dracula's Last Rites '79
Dracula's Widow '88
Gallery of Horrors '67
The Horror of Dracula '58 ▸
House of Dracula '45
House of Frankenstein '44
Hysterical '83
The Legend of the 7 Golden Vampires '73
Love at First Bite '79
Lust for Dracula '04
Mad Monster Party '68
The Monster Squad '87
Return of Dracula '58
Return of the Vampire '43
The Satanic Rites of Dracula '73
The Scars of Dracula '70
The Screaming Dead '72
Son of Dracula '43 ▸
Taste the Blood of Dracula '70
To Die For '89
Transylvania 6-5000 '85
Vampire Circus '71
Van Helsing '04 ▸
Waxwork '88
Zoltan. . . Hound of Dracula '78

Dreamworks Animated Movies

Antz '98 ▸
Bee Movie '07
Chicken Run '00 ▸
The Croods '13
How to Train Your Dragon 2 '14
Kung Fu Panda '08 ▸
Kung Fu Panda 2 '11 ▸
Madagascar: Escape 2 Africa '08
Madagascar 3: Europe's Most Wanted '12
Madagascar '05
Megamind '10 ▸
Mr. Peabody & Sherman '14
Monsters vs. Aliens '09
Over the Hedge '06 ▸
Penguins of Madagascar '14
Prince of Egypt '98 ▸
Puss in Boots '11 ▸
Rise of the Guardians '12
The Road to El Dorado '00
Shark Tale '04

▸ = rated three bones or higher

Shrek 2 *'04* ▸
Shrek *'01* ▸
Sinbad: Legend of the Seven Seas *'03*
Spirit: Stallion of the Cimarron *'02*
Turbo *'13*
Wallace & Gromit in The Curse of the Were-Rabbit *'05* ▸

East End Kids

Kid Dynamite *'43*
Mr. Wise Guy *'42*
Smart Alecks *'42*

Eighty Seventh Precinct

Cop Hater *'58*
Ed McBain's 87th Precinct: Heatwave *'97*
Ed McBain's 87th Precinct: Lightning *'95*
Fuzz *'72*
The Mugger *'58*

Elvisfilm

Blue Hawaii *'62*
Bubba Ho-Tep *'03* ▸
Change of Habit *'69*
Charro! *'69*
Clambake *'67*
Double Trouble *'67*
Easy Come, Easy Go *'67*
Eddie Presley *'92*
Elvis Has Left the Building *'04*
Elvis in Hollywood *'93* ▸
Elvis: The Movie *'79*
Finding Graceland *'98*
Flaming Star *'60* ▸
Follow That Dream *'61*
Frankie and Johnny *'65*
Fun in Acapulco *'63*
G.I. Blues *'60*
Girl Happy *'65*
Girls! Girls! Girls! *'62*
Guns, Girls and Gambling *'11*
Harum Scarum *'65*
Heartbreak Hotel *'88*
Honeymoon in Vegas *'92*
Hounddog *'08*
The Identical *'14*
It Happened at the World's Fair *'63*
Jailhouse Rock *'57* ▸
Kid Galahad *'62*
King Creole *'58*
Kissin' Cousins *'64*
Live a Little, Love a Little *'68*
Love Me Tender *'56*
Loving You *'57*
Paradise, Hawaiian Style *'66*
Protecting the King *'07*
Rock-a-Doodle *'92*
Roustabout *'64*
Six-String Samurai *'98*
Speedway *'68*
Spinout *'66*
Stay Away, Joe *'68*
This Is Elvis *'81*
3000 Miles to Graceland *'01*
Tickle Me *'65*
Top Secret! *'84* ▸
The Trouble with Girls (and How to Get into It) *'69* ▸
True Romance *'93*
Viva Las Vegas *'63*
Wild in the Country *'61*
The Woman Who Loved Elvis *'93*

The Falcon

A Date With the Falcon *'42*
The Falcon and the Co-Eds *'43*
The Falcon in Danger *'43*
The Falcon in Mexico *'44*
The Falcon Strikes Back *'43*
The Falcon Takes Over *'42*
The Gay Falcon *'41*

Four Bones

A Nous la Liberte *'31* ▸
Abe Lincoln in Illinois *'40* ▸
Adam's Rib *'50* ▸
The Adventures of Robin Hood *'38* ▸
The African Queen *'51* ▸
All About Eve *'50* ▸
All Quiet on the Western Front *'30* ▸
All the King's Men *'49* ▸
An American in Paris *'51* ▸
Anatomy of a Murder *'59* ▸
Andrei Rublev *'66* ▸
An Angel at My Table *'89* ▸
Angels with Dirty Faces *'38* ▸
Annie Hall *'77* ▸
Apocalypse Now *'79* ▸
Argo *'12* ▸
The Artist *'11* ▸
The Asphalt Jungle *'50* ▸
Au Revoir les Enfants *'87* ▸
Avengers: Endgame *'19*
The Awful Truth *'37* ▸
The Ballad of Narayama *'83* ▸
Bambi *'42* ▸
The Bank Dick *'40* ▸
The Battleship Potemkin *'25* ▸
Beauty and the Beast *'46* ▸
Beauty and the Beast *'91* ▸
Ben-Hur *'26* ▸
Ben-Hur *'59* ▸
Best of Youth *'03* ▸
The Best Years of Our Lives *'46* ▸
The Bicycle Thief *'48* ▸
The Big Parade *'25* ▸
The Big Sleep *'46* ▸
The Birth of a Nation *'15* ▸
Black Girl *'66*
The Blue Angel *'30* ▸
The Boys of St. Vincent *'93* ▸
Breathless *'59* ▸
Brian's Song *'71* ▸
The Bride of Frankenstein *'35* ▸
The Bridge on the River Kwai *'57* ▸
Brief Encounter *'46* ▸
Bringing Up Baby *'38* ▸
The Burmese Harp *'56* ▸
Butch Cassidy and the Sundance Kid *'69* ▸
The Cabinet of Dr. Caligari *'19* ▸
The Caine Mutiny *'54* ▸
The Cameraman *'28* ▸
Casablanca *'42* ▸
Cesar *'36* ▸
Children of Paradise *'44* ▸
Chimes at Midnight *'67* ▸
Chinatown *'74* ▸
Christ Stopped at Eboli *'79* ▸
A Christmas Carol *'51* ▸
A Christmas Story *'83* ▸
Citizen Kane *'41* ▸
City Lights *'31* ▸
A Clockwork Orange *'71* ▸
Close Encounters of the Third Kind *'77* ▸
Cobain: Montage of Heck *'15*
Colonel Redl *'84* ▸
Come and See *'85* ▸
Commissar *'68* ▸
The Conformist *'71* ▸
Cyrano de Bergerac *'50* ▸
Cyrano de Bergerac *'90* ▸
Danton *'82* ▸
The Dark Knight *'08* ▸
Das Boot *'81* ▸
David Copperfield *'35* ▸
Day for Night *'73* ▸
Day of Wrath *'43* ▸
Dead of Night *'45* ▸
The Deer Hunter *'78* ▸
Deliverance *'72* ▸
Destry Rides Again *'39* ▸
Dinner at Eight *'33* ▸
The Discreet Charm of the Bourgeoisie *'72* ▸
Dr. Strangelove, or: How I Learned to Stop Worrying and Love the Bomb *'64* ▸
Don Quixote *'35* ▸
Double Indemnity *'44* ▸
Duck Soup *'33* ▸
The Earrings of Madame De. . . *'54* ▸
Earth *'30* ▸
East of Eden *'54* ▸
8 1/2 *'63* ▸
Eight Men Out *'88*
El Norte *'83* ▸
The Elephant Man *'80* ▸
The Empire Strikes Back *'80* ▸
Encounters at the End of the World *'79*
The English Patient *'96* ▸
E.T.: The Extra-Terrestrial *'82* ▸
Every Man for Himself *'79*
Every Man for Himself & God Against All *'75* ▸
Fanny *'32* ▸
Fanny and Alexander *'83* ▸
Fantasia *'40* ▸
Festival Express *'03* ▸
Finding Nemo *'03* ▸
Fitzcarraldo *'82* ▸
Five Easy Pieces *'70* ▸
Flight *'12*
Forbidden Games *'52* ▸
Foreign Correspondent *'40* ▸
Forever and a Day *'43* ▸
42nd Street *'33* ▸
The Four Feathers *'39* ▸
The 400 Blows *'59* ▸
Frankenstein *'31* ▸
The Freshman *'25* ▸
From Here to Eternity *'53* ▸
Frozen River *'08*
The Fugitive *'48* ▸
Gallipoli *'81* ▸
The Garden of the Finzi-Continis *'71* ▸
The General *'26* ▸
Gigi *'58* ▸
The Godfather *'72* ▸
The Godfather, Part 2 *'74* ▸
The Gold Rush *'25* ▸
Gone with the Wind *'39* ▸
Goodfellas *'90* ▸
The Gospel According to St. Matthew *'64* ▸
The Graduate *'67* ▸
Grand Illusion *'37* ▸
The Great Dictator *'40* ▸
Great Expectations *'46* ▸
Gunga Din *'39* ▸
Hamlet *'48* ▸
Hamlet *'96* ▸
Harlan County, U.S.A. *'76* ▸
Harold and Maude *'71* ▸
Hearts of Darkness: A Filmmaker's Apocalypse *'91* ▸
Henry V *'44* ▸
Henry V *'89* ▸
Henry: Portrait of a Serial Killer *'90* ▸
Here Comes Mr. Jordan *'41* ▸
High Noon *'52* ▸
Hiroshima, Mon Amour *'59* ▸
His Girl Friday *'40* ▸
Hollywood Canteen *'44* ▸
Hoop Dreams *'94* ▸
How Green Was My Valley *'41* ▸
Howard's End *'92* ▸
Hud *'63* ▸
The Hunchback of Notre Dame *'39* ▸
The Hustler *'61* ▸
I Am a Fugitive from a Chain Gang *'32* ▸
The Idiot *'51* ▸
If. . . *'69* ▸
Ikiru *'52* ▸
The Informer *'35* ▸
Inherit the Wind *'60* ▸
Intolerance *'16* ▸
The Invisible Man *'33* ▸
It Happened One Night *'34* ▸
It's a Wonderful Life *'46* ▸
Ivan the Terrible, Part 1 *'44* ▸
James Joyce: A Portrait of the Artist as a Young Man *'77* ▸
Ju Dou *'90* ▸
Judgment at Nuremberg *'61* ▸
Jules and Jim *'62* ▸
Killer of Sheep *'77*
The Killers *'46* ▸
The King and I *'56* ▸
King Kong *'33* ▸
The King's Speech *'10* ▸
Knife in the Water *'62* ▸
Koyaanisqatsi *'83* ▸
Kriemhilde's Revenge *'24* ▸
Kwaidan *'64* ▸
L.A. Confidential *'97* ▸
La Dolce Vita *'60* ▸
La Notte *'60* ▸
La Strada *'54* ▸
Lady and the Tramp *'55* ▸
The Lady Eve *'41* ▸
The Lady Vanishes *'38* ▸
The Last Command *'28* ▸
The Last Detail *'73* ▸
The Last Emperor *'87* ▸
The Last Picture Show *'71* ▸
The Last Seduction *'94* ▸
Late Spring *'49* ▸
Laura *'44* ▸
Lawrence of Arabia *'62* ▸
Le Trou *'59* ▸
Les Miserables *'35* ▸
The Letter *'40* ▸
A Letter to Three Wives *'49* ▸
Letters from Iwo Jima *'06* ▸
The Life and Death of Colonel Blimp *'43* ▸
The Life and Times of Hank Greenberg *'99* ▸
Life Is Beautiful *'98* ▸
Lincoln *'12* ▸
The Lion in Winter *'68* ▸
The Lion King *'94* ▸
Little Women *'33* ▸
Little Women *'94* ▸
The Lives of a Bengal Lancer *'35* ▸
Local Hero *'83* ▸
Lola Montes *'55* ▸
Long Day's Journey into Night *'62* ▸
Lord of the Rings: The Two Towers *'02* ▸
Lord of the Rings: The Return of the King *'03* ▸
Lost Horizon *'37* ▸
The Lost Weekend *'45* ▸
M *'31* ▸
The Magnificent Ambersons *'42* ▸
The Magnificent Seven *'60* ▸
Male and Female *'19* ▸
The Maltese Falcon *'41* ▸
A Man for All Seasons *'66* ▸
The Man Who Would Be King *'75* ▸
The Manchurian Candidate *'62* ▸
Manhattan *'79* ▸
Marius *'31* ▸
The Marriage of Maria Braun *'79* ▸
M*A*S*H *'70* ▸
Master and Commander: The Far Side of the World *'03* ▸
McCabe & Mrs. Miller *'71* ▸
Mean Streets *'73* ▸
Metropolis *'26* ▸
Miracle of Morgan's Creek *'44* ▸
Miracle on 34th Street *'47* ▸
Mrs. Miniver *'42* ▸
Mr. & Mrs. Bridge *'90* ▸
Mister Roberts *'55* ▸
Mr. Smith Goes to Washington *'39* ▸
Modern Times *'36* ▸
Mon Oncle *'58* ▸
Monster's Ball *'01* ▸
Murderball *'05* ▸
The Music Man *'62* ▸
Mutiny on the Bounty *'35* ▸
My Left Foot *'89* ▸
My Life As a Dog *'85* ▸
My Life to Live *'62* ▸
My Man Godfrey *'36* ▸
Nashville *'75* ▸
National Velvet *'44* ▸
The New World *'05* ▸
A Night at the Opera *'35* ▸
The Night of the Hunter *'55* ▸
The Night of the Shooting Stars *'82* ▸
No Country for Old Men *'07* ▸
North by Northwest *'59* ▸
Notorious *'46* ▸
O Lucky Man! *'73* ▸
Objective, Burma! *'45* ▸
Of Mice and Men *'39* ▸
Oldboy *'03* ▸
Oliver Twist *'48* ▸
On the Waterfront *'54* ▸
One Flew Over the Cuckoo's Nest *'75* ▸
Only Angels Have Wings *'39* ▸
Open City *'45* ▸
Osama *'03* ▸
Our Hospitality *'23* ▸
The Outlaw Josey Wales *'76* ▸
The Ox-Bow Incident *'43* ▸
Pandora's Box *'28* ▸
Pan's Labyrinth *'06* ▸
Passion of Joan of Arc *'28* ▸
Pather Panchali *'54* ▸
Paths of Glory *'57* ▸
Pelle the Conqueror *'88* ▸
Persona *'66* ▸
Petulia *'68* ▸
The Philadelphia Story *'40* ▸
Pinocchio *'40* ▸
Pixote *'81* ▸
Poltergeist *'82* ▸
The Private Life of Henry VIII *'33* ▸
Psycho *'60* ▸
Pulp Fiction *'94* ▸
The Quiet Man *'52* ▸
Quiz Show *'94* ▸
Raging Bull *'80* ▸
Raiders of the Lost Ark *'81* ▸
A Raisin in the Sun *'61* ▸
Ran *'85* ▸
Rashomon *'51* ▸
Ratatouille *'07*
Rear Window *'54* ▸
Rebecca *'40* ▸
Rebel without a Cause *'55* ▸
Red River *'48* ▸
The Red Shoes *'48* ▸
Ride the High Country *'62* ▸
The River *'51* ▸
Road to Perdition *'02* ▸
Rocketman *'19*
A Room with a View *'86* ▸
Roots *'77* ▸
Rosemary's Baby *'68* ▸
Ruggles of Red Gap *'35* ▸
The Rules of the Game *'39* ▸
S21: The Khmer Rouge Killing Machine *'03* ▸
Sansho the Bailiff *'54* ▸
Saving Private Ryan *'98* ▸
Scenes from a Marriage *'73* ▸
Schindler's List *'93* ▸
The Searchers *'56* ▸
Sergeant York *'41* ▸
Seven Beauties *'76* ▸
Seven Samurai *'54* ▸
The Seventh Seal *'56* ▸
Shakespeare in Love *'98* ▸
Shane *'53* ▸
Shin Heike Monogatari *'55* ▸
Shoah *'95*
Shoeshine *'47* ▸
Shoot the Piano Player *'62* ▸
The Shop on Main Street *'65* ▸
Show Boat *'36* ▸
Siegfried *'24* ▸
The Simpsons Movie *'07*
Singin' in the Rain *'52* ▸
Small Change *'76* ▸
Snow White and the Seven Dwarfs *'37* ▸
Some Like It Hot *'59* ▸
The Sound of Music *'65* ▸
Sounder *'72* ▸
The Southerner *'45* ▸
Spartacus *'60* ▸
Spider *'02* ▸
Stagecoach *'39* ▸
Stalag 17 *'53* ▸
Star Wars *'77* ▸
Storm over Asia *'28* ▸
Strangers on a Train *'51* ▸
A Streetcar Named Desire *'51* ▸
The Stunt Man *'80* ▸
Sullivan's Travels *'41* ▸
Sunrise *'27* ▸
A Tale of Two Cities *'36* ▸
The Third Man *'49* ▸
The 39 Steps *'35* ▸
The Three Burials of Melquiades Estrada *'05* ▸
Throne of Blood *'57* ▸
The Tin Drum *'79* ▸
To Kill a Mockingbird *'62* ▸
To Live *'94* ▸
Tokyo Story *'53* ▸
Tom Jones *'63* ▸
Tootsie *'82* ▸
Top Hat *'35* ▸
Touch of Evil *'58* ▸
Toy Story *'95* ▸
Toy Story 2 *'99* ▸
Toy Story 3 *'10*
The Train *'65* ▸
Treasure of the Sierra Madre *'48* ▸
The Triplets of Belleville *'02* ▸
The Truman Show *'98* ▸
Twelve Angry Men *'57* ▸
Twentieth Century *'34* ▸
2001: A Space Odyssey *'68* ▸
Two Women *'61* ▸
Umberto D *'55* ▸
Under the Flag of the Rising Sun *'72* ▸
Vampyr *'31* ▸
Variety *'25* ▸
Vertigo *'58* ▸
Viridiana *'61* ▸
Viva Zapata! *'52* ▸
Wages of Fear *'55* ▸
Warrior *'11*
Who's Afraid of Virginia Woolf? *'66* ▸
The Wild Bunch *'69* ▸
Wild Strawberries *'57* ▸
The Wizard of Oz *'39* ▸
Woman in the Dunes *'64* ▸
Woman of the Year *'42* ▸
Woodstock *'70* ▸
The World of Apu *'59* ▸
The Wrestler *'08*
Wuthering Heights *'39* ▸
Xala *'75*
Yankee Doodle Dandy *'42* ▸
Yojimbo *'61* ▸
Young Frankenstein *'74* ▸
Z *'69* ▸
Zero Dark Thirty *'12*
Zvenigora *'28* ▸

Francis the Talking Mule

Francis Covers the Big Town *'53*
Francis Goes to the Races *'51*
Francis Goes to West Point *'52*
Francis in the Haunted House *'56*
Francis in the Navy *'55*
Francis Joins the WACs *'54*
Francis the Talking Mule *'49* ▸

Frankenstein

Abbott and Costello Meet Frankenstein *'48* ▸
Andy Warhol's Frankenstein *'74*
Blackenstein *'73*
Boltneck *'98*
The Bride *'85*
The Bride of Frankenstein *'35* ▸
The Creeps *'97*
The Curse of Frankenstein *'57*
Dr. Frankenstein's Castle of Freaks *'74*
Dracula *vs.* Frankenstein *'69*
Dracula *vs.* Frankenstein *'71*
The Evil of Frankenstein *'64*
Frankenstein *'31* ▸
Frankenstein 1970 *'58*
Frankenstein *'73*
Frankenstein *'93*
Frankenstein and the Monster from Hell *'74*
Frankenstein Conquers the World *'64*
Frankenstein Created Woman *'66* ▸
Frankenstein '80 *'79*
Frankenstein Island *'81*

Frankenstein Meets the Space Monster '65
Frankenstein Meets the Wolfman '42 ▶
Frankenstein Must Be Destroyed '69
Frankenstein Reborn '98
The Frankenstein Syndrome '10
The Frankenstein Theory '13
Frankenstein Unbound '90 ▶
Frankenstein's Daughter '58
Frankenstein's Great Aunt Tillie '83
The Ghost of Frankenstein '42
Gothic '87 ▶
The Horror of Frankenstein '70
Hotel Transylvania '12
House of Dracula '45
House of Frankenstein '44
Jesse James Meets Frankenstein's Daughter '65
Lady Frankenstein '72
Mad Monster Party '68
Mary Shelley's Frankenstein '94
The Munsters' Revenge '81
Prototype '83 ▶
The Revenge of Frankenstein '58
Rites of Frankenstein '72
The Screaming Dead '72
Son of Frankenstein '39 ▶
Subject Two '06
Van Helsing '04 ▶
Young Frankenstein '74 ▶

Fu Manchu

Brides of Fu Manchu '66
The Castle of Fu Manchu '68
The Face of Fu Manchu '65
The Fiendish Plot of Dr. Fu Manchu '80
Kiss and Kill '68
The Mask of Fu Manchu '32
The Vengeance of Fu Manchu '67

Godzilla and Friends

Dagora, the Space Monster '65
Destroy All Monsters '68
Destroy All Planets '68
Frankenstein Conquers the World '64
Gamera vs. Barugon '66
Gamera vs. Gaos '67
Gamera vs. Guiron '69
Gamera vs. Zigra '71
Gappa the Trifibian Monster '67
Ghidrah the Three Headed Monster '65
Godzilla '54
Godzilla '98
Godzilla '14 ▶
Godzilla Against Mechagodzilla '02
Godzilla: Final Wars '04
Godzilla, King of the Monsters '56
Godzilla, Mothra, and King Ghidorah: Giant Monsters All-Out Attack '01
Godzilla on Monster Island '72
Godzilla Raids Again '55
Godzilla-Tokyo S.O.S. '03
Godzilla 2000 '99 ▶
Godzilla vs. Destroyah '95
Godzilla vs. King Ghidora '91
Godzilla vs. Mechagodzilla II '93
Godzilla vs. Megaguirus '00
Godzilla vs. Megalon '76
Godzilla vs. Monster Zero '68
Godzilla vs. Mothra '64
Godzilla vs. Mothra '92
Godzilla vs. SpaceGodzilla '94
Godzilla vs. the Cosmic Monster '74
Godzilla vs. the Sea Monster '66
Godzilla vs. the Smog Monster '72
Godzilla's Revenge '69
King Kong Escapes '67
King Kong vs. Godzilla '63
Mothra '62 ▶
Rebirth of Mothra 2 '97
Rebirth of Mothra '96
Rodan '56
Son of Godzilla '66
Terror of Mechagodzilla '78
War of the Gargantuas '70
Yog, Monster from Space '71

Hallmark Hall of Fame

April Morning '88
The Boys Next Door '96
Camille '84
Christmas In Conway '13
Christmas with Holly '12
Cupid & Cate '00
Decoration Day '90 ▶
A Dog Named Christmas '09
Ellen Foster '97
Fallen Angel '03
Firelight '12
Follow the Stars Home '01
Foxfire '87 ▶
Harvest of Fire '95
In Love and War '01
In My Dreams '14
Lisa, Bright and Dark '73
Little John '02
The Locket '02
The Lost Child '00
The Love Letter '98
The Makeover '13
Mitch Albom's Have a Little Faith '11
My Sister's Keeper '02
November Christmas '10
O Pioneers! '91
A Painted House '03
The Piano Lesson '94 ▶
Pictures of Hollis Woods '07
Promise '86 ▶
Remember Sunday '13
Resting Place '86
The Return of the Native '94
Rose Hill '97
The Runaway '00
Sarah, Plain and Tall '91 ▶
Sarah, Plain and Tall: Skylark '93
Sarah, Plain and Tall: Winter's End '99 ▶
A Season for Miracles '99
The Secret Garden '87 ▶
The Seventh Stream '01
The Shell Seekers '89
A Smile as Big as the Moon '12
Sweet Nothing in My Ear '08
That Russell Girl '08
To Dance with the White Dog '93 ▶
20,000 Leagues Under the Sea '97
What the Deaf Man Heard '98 ▶
When Love Is Not Enough: The Lois Wilson Story '10

Hammer Films: Horror

The Abominable Snowman '57
Asylum '72
Blood of the Vampire '58
The Brides of Dracula '60
Captain Kronos: Vampire Hunter '74 ▶
The Creeping Flesh '72
Crescendo '69
The Curse of Frankenstein '57
The Curse of the Werewolf '61
The Devil Rides Out '68 ▶
Die Screaming, Marianne '73
Dr. Jekyll and Sister Hyde '71
Dracula A.D. 1972 '72
Dracula Has Risen from the Grave '68
Dracula, Prince of Darkness '66
Dynasty of Fear '72
The Evil of Frankenstein '64
Frankenstein and the Monster from Hell '74
Frankenstein Created Woman '66 ▶
Frankenstein Must Be Destroyed '69
The Ghoul '75
The Gorgon '64
Hands of the Ripper '71
The Horror of Dracula '58 ▶
The Horror of Frankenstein '70
The Hound of the Baskervilles '59
Hysteria '64
Kiss of the Vampire '62 ▶
The Legend of the 7 Golden Vampires '73
Lust for a Vampire '71
The Man Who Could Cheat Death '59
Maniac '63
The Mummy '59 ▶
The Mummy's Shroud '67
The Nanny '65
Nightmare '63
Paranoiac '62
The Phantom of the Opera '62
Plague of the Zombies '66
The Quiet Ones '14
Rasputin the Mad Monk '66
The Reptile '66
The Revenge of Frankenstein '58
The Satanic Rites of Dracula '73
The Scars of Dracula '70
Tales from the Crypt '72 ▶
Tales That Witness Madness '73
Taste the Blood of Dracula '70
Theatre of Blood '73 ▶
To the Devil, a Daughter '76
Twins of Evil '71
The Two Faces of Dr. Jekyll '60
Vampire Circus '71
The Vampire Lovers '70
Vault of Horror '73
Wake Wood '10
The Witches '66

Hammer Films: Sci Fi & Fantasy

Creatures the World Forgot '70
Four Sided Triangle '53
Moon Zero Two '70
One Million Years B.C. '66
Prehistoric Women '67
Quatermass 2 '57 ▶
The Quatermass Experiment '56 ▶
She '65
Spaceways '53
These Are the Damned '63
The Vengeance of She '68
The Viking Queen '67
X The Unknown '56

Hannibal Lecter

Hannibal '01
Hannibal Rising '07
Manhunter '86 ▶
Red Dragon '02
The Silence of the Lambs '91 ▶

Hercule Poirot

Agatha Christie's Thirteen at Dinner '85
The Alphabet Murders '65
Appointment With Death '10
Death on the Nile '78
Murder on the Orient Express '74 ▶
Murder on the Orient Express '01
Murder on the Orient Express '10 ▶

Hercules

Conquest of Mycene '63
The Fury of Hercules '61
Hercules 2 '85
Hercules '58
Hercules '97 ▶
Hercules '14
Hercules Against the Mongols '63
Hercules against the Moon Men '64
Hercules and the Captive Women '63
Hercules and the Tyrants of Babylon '64
Hercules in New York '70
Hercules in the Haunted World '64
Hercules, Prisoner of Evil '64
Hercules the Legendary Journeys, Vol. 1: And the Amazon Women '94
Hercules the Legendary Journeys, Vol. 2: The Lost Kingdom '94
Hercules the Legendary Journeys, Vol. 3: The Circle of Fire '94
Hercules the Legendary Journeys, Vol. 4: In the Underworld '94
Hercules Unchained '59
Hercules vs. the Sons of the Sun '64
Jason and the Argonauts '63 ▶
The Loves of Hercules '60
Samson and His Mighty Challenge '64
The Three Stooges Meet Hercules '61
The Triumph of Hercules '66
Young Hercules '97

Highest Grossing Films of All Time

Avatar '09 ▶
Avengers: Endgame '19 ▶
Avengers: Infinity War '18 ▶
Star Wars: The Force Awakens '15 ▶
Titanic '97 ▶

Hopalong Cassidy

Borderland '37
Colt Comrades '43
The Frontiersmen '38
Hell's Ground '08
Hopalong Cassidy Returns '36
Hopalong Cassidy: Riders of the Deadline '43
Hopalong Cassidy: The Devil's Playground '46
Hoppy Serves a Writ '43
Law of the Pampas '39
Leather Burners '43
Seance '06
The Showdown '40

Indiana Jones

Indiana Jones and the Kingdom of the Crystal Skull '08
Indiana Jones and the Last Crusade '89 ▶
Indiana Jones and the Temple of Doom '84 ▶
Raiders of the Lost Ark '81 ▶

Inspector Clouseau

Curse of the Pink Panther '83
Inspector Clouseau '68
The Pink Panther '64 ▶
The Pink Panther '06
The Pink Panther Strikes Again '76 ▶
Return of the Pink Panther '74
Revenge of the Pink Panther '78
A Shot in the Dark '64 ▶
Son of the Pink Panther '93
Trail of the Pink Panther '82

Jack Ryan

Clear and Present Danger '94
The Hunt for Red October '90 ▶
Patriot Games '92 ▶
The Sum of All Fears '02

Jack the Ripper

Cosh Boy '52
Deadly Advice '93
From Hell '01 ▶
Hands of the Ripper '71
Hell's Gate '01
Jack the Ripper '60
Jack the Ripper '76
Jack the Ripper '88 ▶
The Lodger '26 ▶
Man in the Attic '53
A Man with a Maid '73
Murder by Decree '79 ▶
Phantom Fiend '35
The Ripper '86
Ripper: Letter from Hell '01
Shanghai Knights '03
A Study in Terror '66 ▶
Time After Time '79 ▶

James Bond

Casino Royale '06 ▶
Diamonds Are Forever '71 ▶
Die Another Day '02
Dr. No '62 ▶
For Your Eyes Only '81 ▶
From Russia with Love '63 ▶
Goldeneye '95 ▶
Goldfinger '64 ▶
License to Kill '89 ▶
Live and Let Die '73
The Living Daylights '87 ▶
The Man with the Golden Gun '74
Moonraker '79
Never Say Never Again '83
Octopussy '83
On Her Majesty's Secret Service '69 ▶
Quantum of Solace '08
Skyfall '12 ▶
Spectre '15
The Spy Who Loved Me '77
Thunderball '65
Tomorrow Never Dies '97
A View to a Kill '85
The World Is Not Enough '99
You Only Live Twice '67

James Bond Spoofs

The Ambushers '67
Austin Powers: International Man of Mystery '97 ▶
Austin Powers 2: The Spy Who Shagged Me '99 ▶
Austin Powers In Goldmember '02
Casino Royale '67
Deadlier Than the Male '67
Espionage in Tangiers '65
If Looks Could Kill '91
In Like Flint '67
Murderers' Row '66
Our Man Flint '66
The Silencers '66

Jason Bourne

The Bourne Identity '88 ▶
The Bourne Identity '02 ▶
The Bourne Legacy '12 ▶
The Bourne Supremacy '04 ▶
The Bourne Ultimatum '07 ▶

Jesse James

American Bandits: Frank and Jesse James '10
American Outlaws '01
The Assassination of Jesse James by the Coward Robert Ford '07 ▶
Frank and Jesse '94
I Shot Jesse James '49 ▶
Jesse James '39 ▶
Jesse James Meets Frankenstein's Daughter '65
Jesse James Rides Again '47
Jesse James' Women '54
Kansas Raiders '50
Last Days of Frank & Jesse James '86
The Long Riders '80 ▶
Return of Jesse James '50
The True Story of Jesse James '57
Woman They Almost Lynched '53

John McClane

Die Hard '88 ▶
Die Hard 2: Die Harder '90 ▶
Die Hard: With a Vengeance '95
A Good Day to Die Hard '13
Live Free or Die Hard '07

Jungle Jim

Fury of the Congo '51
Jungle Manhunt '51
Jungle Moon Men '55
Pygmy Island '50

King, Martin Luther Jr.

Betty & Coretta '13
Boycott '02 ▶
King '78 ▶
Lee Daniels' The Butler '13
The Rosa Parks Story '02
Selma '14 ▶
Selma, Lord, Selma '99

Lassie

Courage of Lassie '46
The Hills of Home '48 ▶
Lassie, Come Home '43
Lassie's Great Adventure '62
The Painted Hills '51
Son of Lassie '45
The Sun Comes Up '49

Live Action/Animation Combos

The Adventures of Rocky & Bullwinkle '00
Alice '88 ▶
Alice in Wonderland '50
Aliens in the Attic '09
Alvin and the Chipmunks '07
Alvin and the Chipmunks: Chipwrecked '11
Alvin and the Chipmunks: The Squeakuel '09
Anchors Aweigh '45 ▶
Arthur and the Invisibles '06
Bedknobs and Broomsticks '71
Butterfly Ball '76
Cats & Dogs '01
Cats & Dogs: The Revenge of Kitty Galore '10
The Congress '13
Cool World '92
Dangerous When Wet '53
Diary of a Wimpy Kid '10
Enchanted '07
Fun & Fancy Free '47 ▶
G-Force '09
Garfield: A Tail of Two Kitties '06
Garfield: The Movie '04
Hollywood Party '34
Hop '11
The Incredible Mr. Limpet '64
James and the Giant Peach '96 ▶
Looney Tunes: Back in Action '03
Mary Poppins '64 ▶
MirrorMask '05
Monkeybone '01
Osmosis Jones '01
The Pagemaster '94
Pete's Dragon '77
The Picasso Summer '69
The Polar Express '04
Racing Stripes '05
A Scanner Darkly '06
Scooby-Doo 2: Monsters Unleashed '04
Small Soldiers '98
The Smurfs '11
The Smurfs 2 '13
So Dear to My Heart '49 ▶
Space Jam '96
The Spiderwick Chronicles '08 ▶
The SpongeBob Movie: Sponge Out of Water '15
The SpongeBob SquarePants Movie '04

Stuart Little '99
Tank Girl '94
Ted '12 ▶
That's My Baby! '44
Thomas and the Magic Railroad '00
The Three Caballeros '45
Thunderbirds '04
The Toe Tactic '08
Tron '82
Tron: Legacy '10
Underdog '07
What the #$*! Do We Know? '04
Who Framed Roger Rabbit '88 ▶
Xanadu '80

Ma and Pa Kettle
Egg and I '47 ▶
The Kettles in the Ozarks '56
The Kettles on Old MacDonald's Farm '57
Ma and Pa Kettle '49
Ma and Pa Kettle at Home '54
Ma and Pa Kettle at the Fair '52
Ma and Pa Kettle at Waikiki '55
Ma and Pa Kettle Back On the Farm '51
Ma and Pa Kettle Go to Town '50
Ma and Pa Kettle on Vacation '53

Maisie
Congo Maisie '40
Gold Rush Maisie '40
Maisie '39
Maisie Gets Her Man '42
Maisie Goes to Reno '44
Maisie Was a Lady '41
Ringside Maisie '41
Swing Shift Maisie '43
Undercover Maisie '47
Up Goes Maisie '46

Mandela, Nelson
The Color of Freedom '07
Endgame '09
Invictus '09 ▶
Mandela '87 ▶
Mandela and de Klerk '97
Mandela: Long Walk to Freedom '13
Winnie Mandela '13

The Marx Brothers
Animal Crackers '30 ▶
At the Circus '39
Big Store '41
The Cocoanuts '29
A Day at the Races '37 ▶
Duck Soup '33 ▶
Go West '40
Horse Feathers '32 ▶
Love Happy '50
Monkey Business '31 ▶
A Night at the Opera '35 ▶
A Night in Casablanca '46 ▶
Room Service '38

Mexican Spitfire
The Girl From Mexico '39
Mexican Spitfire '40
Mexican Spitfire at Sea '42
The Mexican Spitfire Out West '40
The Mexican Spitfire Sees a Ghost '42

MGM Musicals
An American in Paris '51 ▶
Anchors Aweigh '45 ▶
Annie Get Your Gun '50 ▶
Athena '54
The Band Wagon '53 ▶
The Barkleys of Broadway '49 ▶
Because You're Mine '52
Bells Are Ringing '60 ▶
Big Store '41
Born to Dance '36
Broadway Melody '29
Broadway Melody of 1936 '35 ▶
Broadway Melody of 1938 '37
Broadway Melody of 1940 '40
Broadway Rhythm '44
Broadway Serenade '39
Chasing Rainbows '30
The Chocolate Soldier '41
Dancing Co-Ed '39
Dancing Lady '33
Deep in My Heart '54
Double Trouble '67
The Duchess of Idaho '50
Easter Parade '48 ▶
Easy to Love '53
Everybody Sing '38
Everything I Have is Yours '52
Excuse My Dust '51
The Firefly '37
Flying High '31
For Me and My Gal '42
Gigi '58 ▶
Girl of the Golden West '38
Give a Girl a Break '53
Going Hollywood '33 ▶
Good News '47
Goodbye, Mr. Chips '69
The Great Ziegfeld '36 ▶
Harum Scarum '65
Holiday in Mexico '46
Hollywood Revue of 1929 '29
Honolulu '39
Hullabaloo '40
I Love Melvin '53
I Married an Angel '42
In the Good Old Summertime '49 ▶
It Happened at the World's Fair '63
It Happened in Brooklyn '47
Jupiter's Darling '55
The Kissing Bandit '48
Lady Be Good '41
Les Girls '57
Little Nellie Kelly '40
Live a Little, Love a Little '68
Living In a Big Way '47
Lord Byron of Broadway '30
Love Me or Leave Me '55 ▶
Lovely to Look At '52 ▶
Luxury Liner '48
Madam Satan '30
Maytime '37 ▶
Meet Me in St. Louis '44 ▶
The Merry Widow '34 ▶
Million Dollar Mermaid '52
Mrs. Brown, You've Got a Lovely Daughter '68
Music For Millions '44
On an Island with You '48
On the Town '49 ▶
Pagan Love Song '50
Painting the Clouds With Sunshine '51
Rich, Young and Pretty '51
Rosalie '38
Rose Marie '36 ▶
Rose Marie '54 ▶
Royal Wedding '51 ▶
Seven Brides for Seven Brothers '54 ▶
Seven Sweethearts '42
Ship Ahoy '42
Show Boat '51
Singin' in the Rain '52 ▶
Skirts Ahoy! '52
Small Town Girl '53
Spinout '66
Stay Away, Joe '68
Strike Up the Band '40
The Student Prince '54
Summer Stock '50 ▶
Sweethearts '38 ▶
Swing Fever '43
Take Me Out to the Ball Game '49
Ten Thousand Bedrooms '57
Texas Carnival '51
That Midnight Kiss '49
That's Dancing! '85 ▶
That's Entertainment '74 ▶
That's Entertainment, Part 2 '76
That's Entertainment, Part 3 '93
This Time for Keeps '47
Three Little Words '50
Thrill of a Romance '45
Till the Clouds Roll By '46
The Toast of New Orleans '50
The Trouble with Girls (and How to Get into It) '69 ▶
Two Girls on Broadway '40
Two Sisters From Boston '46
The Unsinkable Molly Brown '64 ▶
Viva Las Vegas '63
The Wizard of Oz '39 ▶
Words and Music '48
Yankee Doodle Dandy '42 ▶
Yolanda and the Thief '45
Ziegfeld Follies '46
Ziegfeld Girl '41 ▶

Mike Hammer
The Girl Hunters '63
I, the Jury '82
Kiss Me Deadly '55 ▶
My Gun Is Quick '57

Miss Marple
Agatha Christie's A Caribbean Mystery '83
Agatha Christie's Murder with Mirrors '85
The Body in the Library '84
Murder Ahoy '64
Murder at the Gallop '63 ▶
Murder She Said '61

Mister Moto
Mr. Moto in Danger Island '39
Mr. Moto's Gamble '38
Thank you, Mr. Moto '37
Think Fast, Mr. Moto '37

Mister Wong
Doomed to Die '40
The Fatal Hour '40
Mr. Wong, Detective '38
Mr. Wong in Chinatown '39
Mystery of Mr. Wong '39

Monty Python
The Adventures of Baron Munchausen '89 ▶
All You Need Is Cash '78 ▶
And Now for Something Completely Different '72 ▶
Brazil '85 ▶
Clockwise '86
Consuming Passions '88
Down Among the Z Men '52
Erik the Viking '89
A Fish Called Wanda '88 ▶
The Fisher King '91 ▶
Jabberwocky '77
The Missionary '82
Monty Python and the Holy Grail '75 ▶
Monty Python's Life of Brian '79 ▶
Monty Python's The Meaning of Life '83 ▶
Nuns on the Run '90
Personal Services '87
A Private Function '84
Privates on Parade '84
Rentadick '72
The Secret Policeman's Other Ball '82 ▶
Time Bandits '81
Yellowbeard '83

The Muppets
Being Elmo: A Puppeteer's Journey '11
The Great Muppet Caper '81 ▶
Labyrinth '86 ▶
The Muppet Christmas Carol '92
The Muppet Movie '79 ▶
Muppet Treasure Island '96
The Muppets '11 ▶
Muppets from Space '99
Muppets Most Wanted '14
The Muppets Take Manhattan '84 ▶
Sesame Street Presents: Follow That Bird '85

Perry Mason
The Case of the Black Cat '36
The Case of the Curious Bride '35
The Case of the Howling Dog '34
The Case of the Stuttering Bishop '37

Peter Pan
FairyTale: A True Story '97
Finding Neverland '04 ▶
Hook '91
Neverland '11
Peter Pan '24
Peter Pan '53 ▶
Peter Pan '60 ▶
Peter Pan '03
Peter Pan Live! '14
Return to Never Land '02

Philip Marlowe
The Big Sleep '46 ▶
Farewell, My Lovely '75 ▶
Lady in the Lake '46
The Long Goodbye '73 ▶
Marlowe '69
Murder, My Sweet '44 ▶
Poodle Springs '98

Pixar Animated Movies
Brave '12
A Bug's Life '98 ▶
Cars 2 '11
Cars 3 '17
Cars '06 ▶
Coco '17
Finding Dory '16 ▶
Finding Nemo '03 ▶
The Good Dinosaur '15
The Incredibles '04 ▶
Incredibles 2 '18 ▶
Inside Out '15 ▶
Monsters, Inc. '01 ▶
Monsters University '13
Onward '20
Ratatouille '07 ▶
Toy Story '95 ▶
Toy Story 2 '99 ▶
Toy Story 3 '10 ▶
Toy Story 4 '19 ▶
Up '09 ▶
WALL-E '08 ▶

Planet of the Apes
Battle for the Planet of the Apes '73
Beneath the Planet of the Apes '70
Conquest of the Planet of the Apes '72
Dawn of the Planet of the Apes '14 ▶
Escape from the Planet of the Apes '71 ▶
Planet of the Apes '68 ▶
Rise of the Planet of the Apes '11 ▶

Plays to Film: Anderson, Maxwell
Anne of the Thousand Days '69 ▶
The Bad Seed '56
The Bad Seed '85
Joan of Arc '48
Key Largo '48 ▶
Mary of Scotland '36 ▶
Meet Joe Black '98
The Private Lives of Elizabeth & Essex '39 ▶
Saturday's Children '40
What Price Glory? '52 ▶
Winterset '36

Plays to Film: Barrie, James M.
The Admirable Crichton '57
Hook '91
Little Minister '34 ▶
Peter Pan '24
Peter Pan '53 ▶
Peter Pan '60 ▶
Peter Pan '03
Quality Street '37

Plays to Film: Chekhov, Anton
Anton Chekhov's The Duel '09
August '95
The Cherry Orchard '99
Country Life '95
Days and Nights '14
La Petite Lili '03
The Lady with the Dog '59 ▶
The Sea Gull '68
The Seagull '75
The Shooting Party '77
An Unfinished Piece for a Player Piano '77 ▶
Vanya on 42nd Street '94 ▶
Ward No. 6 '09

Plays to Film: Coward, Noel
Bitter Sweet '33
Bitter Sweet '40
Blithe Spirit '45 ▶
Brief Encounter '46 ▶
Cavalcade '33 ▶
Design for Living '33
Easy Virtue '08
Private Lives '31 ▶
Relative Values '99
This Happy Breed '47 ▶
We Were Dancing '42

Plays to Film: Foote, Horton
Baby, the Rain Must Fall '64
The Chase '66
Courtship '87 ▶
Lily Dale '96
1918 '85
The Trip to Bountiful '85 ▶
The Trip to Bountiful '14 ▶

Plays to Film: Henley, Beth
Crimes of the Heart '86
Miss Firecracker '89 ▶
Nobody's Fool '86
True Stories '86 ▶

Plays to Film: Mamet, David
About Last Night. . . '86 ▶
About Last Night '14
American Buffalo '95
Edmond '05
Glengarry Glen Ross '92 ▶
Lakeboat '00
Oleanna '94

Plays to Film: Miller, Arthur
The Crucible '96 ▶
Death of a Salesman '86 ▶
Everybody Wins '90
Focus '01

Plays to Film: Molnar, Ferenc
Breath of Scandal '60
The Bride Wore Red '37
Carousel '56 ▶
The Chocolate Soldier '41
Double Wedding '37 ▶
The Good Fairy '35 ▶
Liliom '30
Liliom '35 ▶
No Greater Glory '34
One Romantic Night '30
One, Two, Three '61 ▶
The Swan '56 ▶

Plays to Film: O'Neill, Eugene
Ah, Wilderness! '35 ▶
Anna Christie '23 ▶
Anna Christie '30
Desire Under the Elms '58
Emperor Jones '33
The Hairy Ape '44
The Iceman Cometh '60 ▶
The Iceman Cometh '73
Long Day's Journey into Night '62 ▶
Long Day's Journey into Night '88
The Long Voyage Home '40 ▶
On Borrowed Time '39 ▶
Strange Interlude '32 ▶
Summer Holiday '48

Plays to Film: Rodgers & Hammerstein
Carousel '56 ▶
Cinderella '64
Flower Drum Song '61
The King and I '56 ▶
Oklahoma! '55 ▶
Rodgers & Hammerstein's South Pacific '01
The Sound of Music '65 ▶
South Pacific '58 ▶

Plays to Film: Schnitzler, Arthur
Affairs of Anatol '21
Circle of Love '64
Eyes Wide Shut '99
La Ronde '51 ▶

Plays to Film: Shakespeare
All Night Long '62
Antony and Cleopatra '73
As You Like It '36
As You Like It '06
The Boys From Syracuse '40
Carry On Cleo '65
Coriolanus '11 ▶
Cymbeline '15
Gnomeo & Juliet '11
Hamlet '48 ▶
Hamlet '90 ▶
Hamlet '96 ▶
Hamlet '00 ▶
Hamlet '01
Henry V '44 ▶
Henry V '89 ▶
Julius Caesar '53 ▶
Julius Caesar '70
King Lear '98 ▶
King of Texas '02 ▶
Looking for Richard '96 ▶
Love's Labour's Lost '00
Macbeth '48 ▶
Macbeth '70 ▶
Macbeth '71 ▶
Macbeth '06
The Merchant of Venice '73 ▶
The Merchant of Venice '04 ▶
A Midsummer Night's Dream '35 ▶
A Midsummer Night's Dream '68
A Midsummer Night's Dream '96
Much Ado about Nothing '93 ▶
Much Ado About Nothing '05
Much Ado About Nothing '13 ▶
NOW: In the Wings on a World Stage '14
Othello '22
Othello '52 ▶
Othello '65 ▶
Othello '95 ▶
Othello '01 ▶
Private Romeo '11
Prospero's Books '91 ▶
Ran '85 ▶
Richard III '55 ▶
Richard III '95 ▶
Romeo and Juliet '36 ▶
Romeo and Juliet '54
Romeo and Juliet '68 ▶
Romeo & Juliet '13
Shakespeare in Love '98 ▶
The Taming of the Shrew '29
The Taming of the Shrew '67 ▶
The Tempest '82 ▶
The Tempest '10
Ten Things I Hate about You '99 ▶
Titus '99
Tromeo & Juliet '95
Twelfth Night '96
Were the World Mine '08
William Shakespeare's A Midsummer Night's Dream '99

▶ = rated three bones or higher

William Shakespeare's Romeo and Juliet '96 ▸

Plays to Film: Shaw, George Bernard

Androcles and the Lion '52
Caesar and Cleopatra '46
The Doctor's Dilemma '58
Major Barbara '41 ▸
The Millionairess '60
Pygmalion '38 ▸
Saint Joan '57

Plays to Film: Shepard, Sam

Curse of the Starving Class '94
Fool for Love '86
Simpatico '99

Plays to Film: Sherwood, Robert E.

Abe Lincoln in Illinois '40 ▸
Idiot's Delight '39 ▸
Jupiter's Darling '55
Petrified Forest '36 ▸
Rebecca '40 ▸
The Royal Bed '31
Waterloo Bridge '40 ▸

Plays to Film: Simon, Neil

Barefoot in the Park '67 ▸
Biloxi Blues '88
Brighton Beach Memoirs '86
California Suite '78 ▸
Chapter Two '79
The Cheap Detective '78 ▸
Come Blow Your Horn '63 ▸
The Goodbye Girl '77 ▸
The Heartbreak Kid '72 ▸
Last of the Red Hot Lovers '72
Lost in Yonkers '93
The Marrying Man '91
Max Dugan Returns '83
Murder by Death '76
The Odd Couple '68 ▸
One Trick Pony '80
Only When I Laugh '81 ▸
The Out-of-Towners '70 ▸
Plaza Suite '71 ▸
Prisoner of Second Avenue '74
Seems Like Old Times '80
The Slugger's Wife '85
Star Spangled Girl '71
The Sunshine Boys '75 ▸
Sweet Charity '69 ▸

Plays to Film: Stoppard, Tom

Rosencrantz & Guildenstern Are Dead '90 ▸

Plays to Film: Van Druten, John

Bell, Book and Candle '58
Cabaret '72 ▸
I Remember Mama '48 ▸
If I Were Free '33
New Morals for Old '32
Old Acquaintance '43
The Voice of the Turtle '47

Plays to Film: Williams, Tenessee

Baby Doll '56 ▸
Cat on a Hot Tin Roof '58 ▸
Cat on a Hot Tin Roof '84
The Fugitive Kind '60
The Glass Menagerie '87 ▸
The Last of the Mobile Hot-shots '69
The Loss of a Teardrop Diamond '08
The Night of the Iguana '64 ▸
Period of Adjustment '62 ▸
Roman Spring of Mrs. Stone '61 ▸
The Rose Tattoo '55 ▸
A Streetcar Named Desire '51 ▸
A Streetcar Named Desire '95
Suddenly, Last Summer '59 ▸
Summer and Smoke '61
Sweet Bird of Youth '62 ▸
Sweet Bird of Youth '89
This Property Is Condemned '66

Producers: Allen, Irwin

The Amazing Captain Nemo '78
Beyond the Poseidon Adventure '79
The Big Circus '59
Cave-In! '79
City Beneath the Sea '71
Fire '77
Five Weeks in a Balloon '62
Flood! '76
Genghis Khan '65
Hanging By a Thread '79
The Night the Bridge Fell Down '83
The Poseidon Adventure '72
Story of Mankind '57
The Swarm '78
The Towering Inferno '74
Voyage to the Bottom of the Sea '61 ▸
When Time Ran Out '80

Producers: Altman, Robert

Buffalo Bill & the Indians '76 ▸
Kansas City '95 ▸
The Late Show '77 ▸
Nashville '75 ▸
Quintet '79
A Wedding '78

Producers: Apatow, Judd

Anchorman: The Legend of Ron Burgundy '04
Bridesmaids '11 ▸
The Cable Guy '96
Celtic Pride '96
Drillbit Taylor '08
Forgetting Sarah Marshall '08
The 40 Year Old Virgin '05 ▸
Funny People '09
Get Him to the Greek '10
Heavyweights '94
Kicking & Screaming '05
Knocked Up '07
Pineapple Express '08 ▸
Step Brothers '08
Superbad '07 ▸
Talladega Nights: The Ballad of Ricky Bobby '06
This Is 40 '12
The TV Set '06
Walk Hard: The Dewey Cox Story '07
Year One '09

Producers: Bruckheimer/Simpson

Bad Boys '95
Beverly Hills Cop '84
Beverly Hills Cop 2 '87
Crimson Tide '95 ▸
Dangerous Minds '95
Days of Thunder '90
Flashdance '83
The Ref '93 ▸
The Rock '96 ▸
Thief of Hearts '84
Top Gun '86

Producers: Castle, William

Bug '75
House on Haunted Hill '58
Riot '69
Rosemary's Baby '68 ▸
Strait-Jacket '64
13 Ghosts '60
Zotz! '62

Producers: Coppola/ American Zoetrope

American Graffiti '73 ▸
The Black Stallion '79 ▸
The Conversation '74 ▸
The Escape Artist '82 ▸
The Godfather, Part 2 '74 ▸
Hammett '82

Producers: Corman/ New World

The Arousers '70
Atlas '60
Avalanche '78
Battle Beyond the Stars '80
Battle Beyond the Sun '63
The Beast With a Million Eyes '56
Beyond the Call of Duty '92
Big Bad Mama 2 '87
Big Bad Mama '74
The Big Bird Cage '72
The Big Doll House '71
Bloodfist '89
Bloodfist 2 '90
Bloody Mama '70
Boxcar Bertha '72
A Bucket of Blood '59 ▸
Caged Heat '74
Candy Stripe Nurses '74
Carnival Rock '57
Cockfighter '74 ▸
Crazy Mama '75
Day the World Ended '55
Death Race 2000 '75
Death Sport '78
Dementia 13 '63
Dinocroc Vs. Supergator '10
The Dunwich Horror '70
Eat My Dust '76
Eye of the Eagle 3 '91
The Fall of the House of Usher '60 ▸
Fighting Mad '76
Forbidden World '82
Futurekick '91
Galaxy of Terror '81
Gas-s-s-s! '70
Grand Theft Auto '77
The Gunslinger '56
The Haunted Palace '63
Humanoids from the Deep '80
I, Mobster '58
I Never Promised You a Rose Garden '77 ▸
Jackson County Jail '76
Lady in Red '79
The Last Woman on Earth '61
Little Shop of Horrors '60 ▸
Masque of the Red Death '65 ▸
Monster from the Ocean Floor '54
Munchies '87
Nam Angels '88
Not of This Earth '57
Not of This Earth '96
Piranha '78
The Pit and the Pendulum '61 ▸
Premature Burial '62
Private Duty Nurses '71
Raiders of the Sun '92
The Raven '63 ▸
Rock 'n' Roll High School Forever '91
The St. Valentine's Day Massacre '67
Small Change '76 ▸
Smokey Bites the Dust '81
Stripped to Kill '87
The Student Nurses '70
T-Bird Gang '59
Tales of Terror '62
Targets '68 ▸
Teenage Caveman '58
The Terror '63
Thunder and Lightning '77
Tomb of Ligeia '64 ▸
The Trip '67
The Undead '57
Unholy Rollers '72
The Viking Women and the Sea Serpent '57
Voyage to the Planet of Prehistoric Women '68
War of the Satellites '58
The Wasp Woman '59
The Wasp Woman '96
The Wild Angels '66
X: The Man with X-Ray Eyes '63 ▸
The Young Nurses '73

Producers: Lewton, Val

Bedlam '45 ▸
The Body Snatcher '45 ▸
Cat People '42 ▸
Isle of the Dead '45
The Leopard Man '43

Producers: Lucas, George

The Empire Strikes Back '80 ▸
The Ewok Adventure '84
More American Graffiti '79
Raiders of the Lost Ark '81 ▸
Return of the Jedi '83 ▸

Producers: Merchant Ivory

The Ballad of the Sad Cafe '91
Bombay Talkie '70
The Courtesans of Bombay '85 ▸
The Europeans '79 ▸
Feast of July '95
The Golden Bowl '00
Howard's End '92 ▸
Hullabaloo over Georgie & Bonnie's Pictures '78
Jane Austen in Manhattan '80
Jefferson in Paris '94
Maurice '87 ▸
Mr. & Mrs. Bridge '90 ▸
The Remains of the Day '93 ▸
A Room with a View '86 ▸
Roseland '77 ▸
Shakespeare Wallah '65 ▸
A Soldier's Daughter Never Cries '98
Surviving Picasso '96
The White Countess '05 ▸

Producers: Pal, George

Atlantis, the Lost Continent '61
Conquest of Space '55
Destination Moon '50
Doc Savage '75
The Great Rupert '50 ▸
Naked Jungle '54 ▸
7 Faces of Dr. Lao '63 ▸
The War of the Worlds '53 ▸
When Worlds Collide '51

Producers: Shaw Brothers

Black Magic '06
The Brave Archer '77
The Brave Archer and His Mate '82
The Cave of the Silken Web '67
Come Drink with Me '65 ▸
Corpse Mania '81
The Delightful Forest '72
The Duel of the Century '81
Five Deadly Venoms '78 ▸
Five Element Ninjas '82
Golden Swallow '68 ▸
Have Sword, Will Travel '69
Heaven & Hell '78
Heroes of the East '08 ▸
Heroes Shed No Tears '86
The Heroic Ones '70
The Heroic Trio '93
Holy Flame of the Martial World '83
House of Traps '81
Infra-Man '76
Intimate Confessions of a Chinese Courtesan '72
Journey of the Doomed '85
King Boxer '72
The Legend of the 7 Golden Vampires '73
Legendary Weapons of China '82
The Magic Blade '08
The Magnificent Trio '66
The One-Armed Swordsman '67 ▸
Opium and Kung-Fu Master '84 ▸
Seeding of a Ghost '86
Sword Masters: Brothers Five '70
Sword Masters: The Battle Wizard '77
Sword Masters: Two Champions of Shaolin '80
Sword Masters: Web of Death '76
The 36th Chamber of Shaolin '78 ▸

Producers: Spielberg, Steven

An American Tail '86
An American Tail: Fievel Goes West '91
Back to the Future '85 ▸
The Color Purple '85 ▸
Empire of the Sun '87 ▸
The Goonies '85
Gremlins '84 ▸
Honey, I Shrunk the Kids '89
Innerspace '87
Jurassic Park '93 ▸
Poltergeist '82 ▸
The Terminal '04
Twilight Zone: The Movie '83
Who Framed Roger Rabbit '88 ▸
Young Sherlock Holmes '85

Producers: Warhol, Andy

Andy Warhol's Bad '77 ▸
Cocaine Cowboys '79
Flesh '68 ▸
Heat '72 ▸
Trash '70

Rambo

First Blood '82
Rambo: First Blood, Part 2 '85
Rambo 3 '88

Recycled Footage/ Redubbed Dialogue

Battle Beyond the Sun '63
Contact '97
Dead Men Don't Wear Plaid '82
Fast, Cheap & Out of Control '97 ▸
Ferocious Female Freedom Fighters '88
Forrest Gump '94 ▸
Good Night, and Good Luck '05 ▸
J-Men Forever! '79 ▸
Last Action Hero '93
The Legend of Drunken Master '94 ▸
Mystery Science Theater 3000: The Movie '96
Planet of Blood '66
Twin Dragons '92
Voyage to the Planet of Prehistoric Women '68
Voyage to the Prehistoric Planet '65
What's Up, Tiger Lily? '66 ▸
Zelig '83 ▸

Restored Footage

Army of Shadows '69 ▸
Ashes of Time Redux '08
Crimes of Passion '84 ▸
Dr. Jekyll and Mr. Hyde '32 ▸
Foolish Wives '22 ▸
Frankenstein '31 ▸
Lawrence of Arabia '62 ▸
The Leopard '63 ▸
Lost Horizon '37 ▸
The Lost World '25
New York, New York '77 ▸
Othello '52 ▸
Que Viva Mexico '32 ▸
Red River '48 ▸
The Rules of the Game '39 ▸
Sadie Thompson '28 ▸
Spartacus '60 ▸
Spiders '18 ▸
A Star Is Born '54 ▸
Star Trek: The Motion Picture '79
Tarzan and His Mate '34 ▸
Twelve o'Clock High '49 ▸
Two English Girls '72 ▸
Wages of Fear '55 ▸
When Time Ran Out '80

Rin Tin Tin

Caryl of the Mountains '36
Lightning Warrior '31
The Lone Defender '32
Pride of the Legion '32
Where the North Begins '23

The Ritz Brothers

Blazing Stewardesses '75
The Goldwyn Follies '38
The Gorilla '39
Kentucky Moonshine '38
You Can't Have Everything '37

Robin Hood

The Adventures of Robin Hood '38 ▸
The Bandit of Sherwood Forest '46
Beyond Sherwood Forest '09
The Prince of Thieves '48
Princess of Thieves '01
Robin and Marian '76
Robin Hood '22 ▸
Robin Hood '73 ▸
Robin Hood '91 ▸
Robin Hood '10
Robin Hood: Men in Tights '93
Robin Hood: Prince of Thieves '91
Robin Hood. . . The Legend: Robin Hood and the Sorcerer '83
Robin of Locksley '95
Rogues of Sherwood Forest '50
The Story of Robin Hood & His Merrie Men '52 ▸
Sword of Sherwood Forest '60
Time Bandits '81
Young Ivanhoe '95

The Saint

The Saint '97
The Saint in London '39
The Saint in Palm Springs '41
The Saint Meets the Tiger '43
The Saint Strikes Back '39
The Saint Takes Over '40
The Saint's Double Trouble '40

Sam Spade

The Maltese Falcon '31 ▸
The Maltese Falcon '41 ▸

Screen Teams: Abbott & Costello

Abbott and Costello Go to Mars '53
Abbott and Costello in Hollywood '45
Abbott and Costello in the Foreign Legion '50
Abbott and Costello Meet Captain Kidd '52
Abbott and Costello Meet Dr. Jekyll and Mr. Hyde '52
Abbott and Costello Meet Frankenstein '48 ▸
Abbott and Costello Meet the Invisible Man '51 ▸
Abbott and Costello Meet the Keystone Kops '54
Abbott and Costello Meet the Killer, Boris Karloff '49
Abbott and Costello Meet the Mummy '55
Africa Screams '49
Buck Privates '41
Buck Privates Come Home '47 ▸
Comin' Round the Mountain '51
Dance with Me, Henry '56
Here Come the Co-Eds '45
Hit the Ice '43

▸ = rated three bones or higher

Hold That Ghost '41 ▶
In Society '44
In the Navy '41
It Ain't Hay '43
Jack & the Beanstalk '52
Keep 'Em Flying '41
Little Giant '46
Lost in a Harem '44
Lost in Alaska '52
Mexican Hayride '48
The Naughty Nineties '45
The Noose Hangs High '48 ▶
One Night in the Tropics '40
Pardon My Sarong '42
Ride 'Em Cowboy '42
Rio Rita '42
The 30-Foot Bride of Candy Rock '59
The Time of Their Lives '46
Who Done It? '42
The Wistful Widow of Wagon Gap '47

Screen Teams: Allen & Farrow

Alice '90 ▶
Another Woman '88 ▶
Broadway Danny Rose '84 ▶
Crimes & Misdemeanors '89 ▶
Hannah and Her Sisters '86 ▶
Husbands and Wives '92 ▶
A Midsummer Night's Sex Comedy '82 ▶
New York Stories '89 ▶
The Purple Rose of Cairo '85 ▶
Radio Days '87 ▶
September '88
Shadows and Fog '92
Zelig '83 ▶

Screen Teams: Allen & Keaton

Annie Hall '77 ▶
Interiors '78 ▶
Love and Death '75 ▶
Manhattan '79 ▶
Manhattan Murder Mystery '93 ▶
Play It Again, Sam '72 ▶
Sleeper '73 ▶

Screen Teams: Astaire & Rogers

The Barkleys of Broadway '49 ▶
Carefree '38 ▶
Flying Down to Rio '33
Follow the Fleet '36 ▶
The Gay Divorcee '34 ▶
Roberta '35 ▶
Shall We Dance '37 ▶
The Story of Vernon and Irene Castle '39 ▶
Swing Time '36 ▶
Top Hat '35 ▶

Screen Teams: Avalon and Funicello

Back to the Beach '87
Beach Blanket Bingo '65 ▶
Beach Party '63
Bikini Beach '64
Dr. Goldfoot and the Bikini Machine '66
Fireball 500 '66
How to Stuff a Wild Bikini '65
Muscle Beach Party '64
Pajama Party '64
Ski Party '65
Troop Beverly Hills '89

Screen Teams: Ball & Arnaz

The Long, Long Trailer '54

Screen Teams: Belushi & Aykroyd

The Blues Brothers '80 ▶
Neighbors '81
1941 '79

Screen Teams: Bogart & Bacall

The Big Sleep '46 ▶
Dark Passage '47
Key Largo '48 ▶
To Have & Have Not '44 ▶

Screen Teams: Bronson & Ireland

Breakheart Pass '76
Breakout '75
Chino '75
Cold Sweat '71
Death Wish 2 '82
The Family '70
From Noon Till Three '76
Hard Times '75 ▶
Love and Bullets '79
The Mechanic '72
Rider on the Rain '70 ▶
Someone Behind the Door '71
The Valachi Papers '72
Villa Rides '68

Screen Teams: Burton & Taylor

Cleopatra '63
The Comedians '67
Divorce His, Divorce Hers '72
Doctor Faustus '68
The Sandpiper '65
The Taming of the Shrew '67 ▶
Under Milk Wood '73
The V.I.P.'s '63 ▶
Who's Afraid of Virginia Woolf? '66 ▶

Screen Teams: Cagney & O'Brien

Angels with Dirty Faces '38 ▶
Boy Meets Girl '38 ▶
The Fighting 69th '40 ▶
Here Comes the Navy '34
The Irish in Us '35
Ragtime '81 ▶
Torrid Zone '40

Screen Teams: Cheech & Chong

After Hours '85 ▶
Cheech and Chong: Still Smokin' '83
Cheech and Chong: Things Are Tough All Over '82
Cheech & Chong's Animated Movie! '13
Cheech and Chong's Next Movie '80
Cheech and Chong's Nice Dreams '81
Cheech and Chong's The Corsican Brothers '84
Cheech and Chong's Up in Smoke '79

Screen Teams: Colbert & MacMurray

The Bride Comes Home '35
Egg and I '47 ▶
Family Honeymoon '49
The Gilded Lily '35
Maid of Salem '37
No Time For Love '43 ▶

Screen Teams: Cronyn & Tandy

*batteries not included '87
Camilla '94
Cocoon '85 ▶
Cocoon: The Return '88
Foxfire '87 ▶
Gin Game '84 ▶
The Green Years '46
Honky Tonk Freeway '81
The Moon and Sixpence '43 ▶
To Dance with the White Dog '93 ▶

Screen Teams: Cusack & Piven

Bob Roberts '92 ▶
Floundering '94
The Grifters '90 ▶
Grosse Pointe Blank '97 ▶
One Crazy Summer '86
The Player '92 ▶
Runaway Jury '03 ▶
Say Anything '89 ▶
Serendipity '01

Screen Teams: Cusack & Robbins

Bob Roberts '92 ▶
The Cradle Will Rock '99
High Fidelity '00 ▶
The Player '92 ▶
The Sure Thing '85 ▶
Tapeheads '89

Screen Teams: Damon & Affleck

Chasing Amy '97
Dogma '99
Good Will Hunting '97
Jay and Silent Bob Strike Back '01
Jersey Girl '04
School Ties '92 ▶

Screen Teams: Davis & Brent

Dark Victory '39 ▶
Front Page Woman '35
The Golden Arrow '36
The Great Lie '41 ▶
Housewife '34
In This Our Life '42
Jezebel '38 ▶
The Old Maid '39 ▶
The Rich Are Always With Us '32

Screen Teams: De Niro & Keitel

The Bridge of San Luis Rey '05
Cop Land '97 ▶
Falling in Love '84
Mean Streets '73 ▶
Taxi Driver '76 ▶

Screen Teams: De Niro & Pesci

A Bronx Tale '93 ▶
Casino '95 ▶
Goodfellas '90 ▶
Once Upon a Time in America '84 ▶
Raging Bull '80 ▶

Screen Teams: Depardieu & Deneuve

Changing Times '04
Fort Saganne '84
The Last Metro '80 ▶
Potiche '10 ▶

Screen Teams: Eastwood & Locke

Any Which Way You Can '80
Bronco Billy '80
Every Which Way But Loose '78
The Gauntlet '77
The Outlaw Josey Wales '76 ▶
Sudden Impact '83

Screen Teams: Eddy & McDonald

Bitter Sweet '40
Girl of the Golden West '38
I Married an Angel '42
Maytime '37 ▶
Naughty Marietta '35
New Moon '40
Rose Marie '36 ▶
Sweethearts '38 ▶

Screen Teams: Farley & Spade

Black Sheep '96
Coneheads '93
Tommy Boy '95

Screen Teams: Favreau & Vaughn

The Break Up '98
Four Christmases '08
Made '01
Rudy '93
Swingers '96 ▶

Screen Teams: Flynn & de Havilland

Captain Blood '35 ▶
The Charge of the Light Brigade '36 ▶
Dodge City '39 ▶
Four's a Crowd '38
The Private Lives of Elizabeth & Essex '39 ▶
Santa Fe Trail '40
They Died with Their Boots On '41 ▶

Screen Teams: Francis & Brent

Give Me Your Heart '36
The Goose and the Gander '35
Living on Velvet '35
Stranded '35

Screen Teams: Gable & Crawford

Chained '34
Dance Fools Dance '31 ▶
Dancing Lady '33
Forsaking All Others '35
Laughing Sinners '31
Love on the Run '36
Possessed '31
Strange Cargo '40

Screen Teams: Gable & Loy

Manhattan Melodrama '34 ▶
Men in White '34
Test Pilot '38 ▶
Too Hot to Handle '38 ▶
Wife Versus Secretary '36 ▶

Screen Teams: Gable & Turner

Betrayed '54 ▶
Homecoming '48
Honky Tonk '41 ▶
Somewhere I'll Find You '42 ▶

Screen Teams: Garland & Rooney

Andy Hardy Meets Debutante '40
Babes in Arms '39
Babes on Broadway '41
Girl Crazy '43 ▶
Life Begins for Andy Hardy '41 ▶
Love Finds Andy Hardy '38 ▶
Strike Up the Band '40
Thoroughbreds Don't Cry '37
Thousands Cheer '43
Words and Music '48

Screen Teams: Garson & Pidgeon

Blossoms in the Dust '41
Julia Misbehaves '48 ▶
Madame Curie '43 ▶
The Miniver Story '50
Mrs. Miniver '42 ▶
Mrs. Parkington '44
Scandal at Scourie '53
That Forsyte Woman '50

Screen Teams: Gaynor & Farrell

Lucky Star '29
The Man Who Came Back '08
7th Heaven '27
Street Angel '28
Tess of the Storm Country '22

Screen Teams: Gibson & Glover

Lethal Weapon '87 ▶
Lethal Weapon 2 '89 ▶
Lethal Weapon 3 '92
Lethal Weapon 4 '98
Maverick '94

Screen Teams: Hepburn & Grant

Bringing Up Baby '38 ▶
Holiday '38 ▶
The Philadelphia Story '40 ▶
Sylvia Scarlett '35

Screen Teams: Hepburn & Tracy

Adam's Rib '50 ▶
Desk Set '57 ▶
Guess Who's Coming to Dinner '67 ▶
Pat and Mike '52 ▶
The Sea of Grass '47
State of the Union '48 ▶
Without Love '45
Woman of the Year '42 ▶

Screen Teams: Hope & Crosby

Cancel My Reservation '72
My Favorite Blonde '42 ▶
My Favorite Brunette '47
The Princess and the Pirate '44 ▶
The Road to Bali '53 ▶
The Road to Hong Kong '62
The Road to Morocco '42 ▶
The Road to Rio '47 ▶
The Road to Singapore '40
The Road to Utopia '46 ▶
The Road to Zanzibar '41 ▶
Scared Stiff '53 ▶
Star Spangled Rhythm '42 ▶

Screen Teams: Ladd & Lake

The Blue Dahlia '46 ▶
The Glass Key '42 ▶
This Gun for Hire '42 ▶

Screen Teams: Lancaster & Douglas

Gunfight at the O.K. Corral '57 ▶
The List of Adrian Messenger '63 ▶
Seven Days in May '64 ▶
Tough Guys '86
Victory at Entebbe '76

Screen Teams: Laurel & Hardy

Air Raid Wardens '43
Beyond the Blackboard '11
Block-heads '38 ▶
Bohemian Girl '36 ▶
Bonnie Scotland '35
The Devil's Brother '33
The Flying Deuces '39 ▶
Great Guns '41
Hollywood Party '34
Nothing But Trouble '44
Our Relations '36 ▶
Pack Up Your Troubles '32
Pardon Us '31
Pick a Star '37
Sons of the Desert '33 ▶
Swiss Miss '38
Utopia '51
Way Out West '37 ▶
The Young Victoria '09 ▶

Screen Teams: Lee & Cushing

The Creeping Flesh '72
The Curse of Frankenstein '57
Dracula A.D. 1972 '72
The Gorgon '64
Hamlet '48 ▶
Horror Express '72
The Horror of Dracula '58 ▶
The Hound of the Baskervilles '59
The House that Dripped Blood '71
Island of the Burning Doomed '67
Lost Souls '98
Miracle Run '04
Moulin Rouge '52 ▶
The Mummy '59 ▶
Nothing But the Night '72
The Satanic Rites of Dracula '73
Scream and Scream Again '70
The Skull '65

Screen Teams: Lemmon & Matthau

The Fortune Cookie '66 ▶
The Front Page '74
The Grass Harp '95
Grumpier Old Men '95
Grumpy Old Men '93 ▶
JFK '91 ▶
The Odd Couple 2 '98
The Odd Couple '68 ▶
Out to Sea '97

Screen Teams: Loy & Powell

After the Thin Man '36 ▶
Another Thin Man '39
Double Wedding '37 ▶
Evelyn Prentice '34
The Great Ziegfeld '36 ▶
I Love You Again '40 ▶
Libeled Lady '36 ▶
Love Crazy '41 ▶
Manhattan Melodrama '34 ▶
Shadow of the Thin Man '41 ▶
Song of the Thin Man '47
The Thin Man '34 ▶
The Thin Man Goes Home '44

Screen Teams: MacMurray & Goddard

On Our Merry Way '48
Star Spangled Rhythm '42 ▶

Screen Teams: MacMurray & Stanwyck

Double Indemnity '44 ▶
The Moonlighter '53
Remember the Night '40 ▶
There's Always Tomorrow '56

Screen Teams: Martin & Lewis

Artists and Models '55
At War with the Army '50
The Caddy '53
Hollywood or Bust '56
Jumping Jacks '52
Living It Up '54
Money from Home '53
My Friend Irma '49
My Friend Irma Goes West '50
Pardners '56
The Road to Bali '53 ▶
Sailor Beware '52
Scared Stiff '53 ▶
The Stooge '51
That's My Boy '51
You're Never Too Young '55

Screen Teams: Mastroianni & Loren

Blood Feud '79
Marriage Italian Style '64 ▶
The Priest's Wife '71
Ready to Wear '94
A Special Day '77 ▶
Too Bad She's Bad '54
Yesterday, Today and Tomorrow '64 ▶

Screen Teams: Newman & Woodward

The Drowning Pool '75
From the Terrace '60
The Long, Hot Summer '58 ▶
Mr. & Mrs. Bridge '90 ▶
A New Kind of Love '63
Paris Blues '61
Rally 'Round the Flag, Boys! '58

Screen Teams: Powell & Keeler

Colleen '36
Dames '34 ▶
Flirtation Walk '34
Footlight Parade '33 ▶
42nd Street '33 ▶

▶ = rated three bones or higher

Gold Diggers of 1933 '33 ►
Shipmates Forever '35

Screen Teams: Power & Tierney

The Razor's Edge '46 ►
Return of Frank James '40 ►
Son of Fury '42 ►
That Wonderful Urge '48

Screen Teams: Power & Young

Cafe Metropole '37
Love Is News '37 ►
Second Honeymoon '37

Screen Teams: Redford & Newman

Butch Cassidy and the Sundance Kid '69 ►
The Sting '73 ►

Screen Teams: Reynolds & DeLuise

The Best Little Whorehouse in Texas '82
Cannonball Run 2 '84
Cannonball Run '81
The End '78 ►
Smokey and the Bandit 2 '80

Screen Teams: Reynolds & Field

The End '78 ►
Hooper '78
Smokey and the Bandit '77
Smokey and the Bandit 2 '80

Screen Teams: Reynolds & Reed

Gator '76
Smokey and the Bandit '77
Smokey and the Bandit 2 '80
Smokey and the Bandit, Part 3 '83
W.W. and the Dixie Dancekings '75

Screen Teams: Rogers & Evans

Apache Rose '47
Bells of Coronado '50
Don't Fence Me In '45
The Golden Stallion '49
Home in Oklahoma '47
My Pal Trigger '46
Susanna Pass '49
Trigger, Jr. '50
Under Nevada Skies '46

Screen Teams: Snipes & Harrelson

Money Train '95
White Men Can't Jump '92
Wildcats '86

Screen Teams: Stewart & Sullavan

The Mortal Storm '40 ►
The Shop Around the Corner '40 ►
Shopworn Angel '38 ►

Screen Teams: Stiller & O. Wilson

Meet the Fockers '04
Meet the Parents '00 ►
Permanent Midnight '98
The Royal Tenenbaums '01 ►
Starsky & Hutch '04
Zoolander '01

Screen Teams: Turner & Douglas

The Jewel of the Nile '85
Romancing the Stone '84 ►
The War of the Roses '89 ►

Screen Teams: Wayne & O'Hara

Big Jake '71
McLintock! '63 ►
The Quiet Man '52 ►
Rio Grande '50 ►

Wings of Eagles '57

Screen Teams: Wheeler & Woolsey

Caught Plastered '31
Cracked Nuts '31
Dixiana '30
Girl Crazy '32
Half-Shot at Sunrise '30
High Flyers '37
Hold 'Em Jail '32
Hook, Line and Sinker '30
Kentucky Kernels '34
Mummy's Boys '36
The Nitwits '35
On Again-Off Again '37
The Rainmakers '35
Rio Rita '29

Screen Teams: Wilder & Pryor

Another You '91
See No Evil, Hear No Evil '89
Silver Streak '76 ►
Stir Crazy '80

Scrooge

An American Christmas Carol '79
A Christmas Carol '38 ►
A Christmas Carol '51 ►
A Christmas Carol '84 ►
A Christmas Carol '99
Scrooged '88

Sexton Blake

Echo Murders '45
Sexton Blake and the Hooded Terror '38

Sherlock Holmes

The Adventures of Sherlock Holmes '39
The Adventures of Sherlock Holmes' Smarter Brother '78 ►
The Crucifer of Blood '91
Dr. Bell and Mr. Doyle: The Dark Beginnings of Sherlock Holmes '00
Dressed to Kill '46
Hands of a Murderer '90
The Hound of the Baskervilles '39 ►
The Hound of the Baskervilles '59
The Hound of the Baskervilles '77
The Hound of the Baskervilles '83
The Hound of the Baskervilles '00
The Hound of the Baskervilles '02 ►
House of Fear '45
Murder at the Baskervilles '37
Murder by Decree '79 ►
The Pearl of Death '44
The Private Life of Sherlock Holmes '70 ►
Pursuit to Algiers '45
Scarlet Claw '44 ►
The Seven-Per-Cent Solution '76 ►
Sherlock: Case of Evil '02
Sherlock Holmes '22
Sherlock Holmes '09
Sherlock Holmes '10
Sherlock Holmes: A Game of Shadows '11
Sherlock Holmes and the Deadly Necklace '62
Sherlock Holmes and the Incident at Victoria Falls '91
Sherlock Holmes and the Secret Weapon '42 ►
Sherlock Holmes and the Voice of Terror '42
Sherlock Holmes Faces Death '43 ►
Sherlock Holmes in Washington '43
The Sign of Four '83
The Sign of Four '01
The Speckled Band '31 ►

A Study in Scarlet '33
A Study in Terror '66 ►
They Might Be Giants '71 ►
The Triumph of Sherlock Holmes '35
Without a Clue '88
The Woman in Green '49
Young Sherlock Holmes '85

Sinbad

Captain Sinbad '63
Golden Voyage of Sinbad '73
Invitation to the Dance '56
The Magic Voyage of Sinbad '52
The Seventh Voyage of Sinbad '58 ►
Sinbad and the Eye of the Tiger '77
Sinbad and the Minotaur '11
Sinbad: Legend of the Seven Seas '03

Special FX Extravaganzas

The Abyss '89 ►
Alice in Wonderland '85
Alien: Resurrection '97 ►
Aliens '86 ►
An American Werewolf in Paris '97
Anaconda '96
The Arrival '96
Baby Geniuses '98
Batman '89 ►
Batman and Robin '97
Batman Forever '95 ►
Beetlejuice '88 ►
Big Trouble in Little China '86
The Black Hole '79
Blithe Spirit '45 ►
The Borrowers '97
Captain Sinbad '63
The Chronicles of Riddick '04
Crash Dive '43
Dante's Peak '97
Daylight '96
Dragonheart '96
Event Horizon '97
The Ewok Adventure '84
The Exorcist '73 ►
The Exorcist 2: The Heretic '77
FairyTale: A True Story '97
Fantastic Voyage '66 ►
The Fifth Element '97
Forbidden Planet '56 ►
Hideaway '94
Highlander: The Final Dimension '94
Independence Day '96 ►
Innerspace '87
Judge Dredd '95
Jumanji '95
Jurassic Park '93 ►
Lifeforce '85
The Lost World: Jurassic Park 2 '97
Mars Attacks! '96
Mary Shelley's Frankenstein '94
The Mask '94 ►
My Favorite Martian '98
Poltergeist '82 ►
The Rains Came '39
Return of the Jedi '83 ►
The Shadow '94
Small Soldiers '98
Solar Crisis '92
Spawn '97 ►
Species '95
Species 2 '98
Star Trek 2: The Wrath of Khan '82 ►
Star Trek 4: The Voyage Home '86 ►
Star Trek: Generations '94 ►
Superman 2 '80 ►
Terminator 2: Judgment Day '91 ►
The Terminator '84 ►
The Thing '82
Total Recall '90 ►
Twister '96

2001: A Space Odyssey '68 ►
2010: The Year We Make Contact '84 ►
Virtuosity '95
Virus '98
Volcano '97
Who Framed Roger Rabbit '88 ►
Wolfen '81 ►

Special FX Extravaganzas: Make-Up

An American Werewolf in London '81 ►
The Associate '96
Bad Moon '96
Batman and Robin '97
Battle for the Planet of the Apes '73
Beetlejuice '88 ►
Beneath the Planet of the Apes '70
Body Melt '93
Conquest of the Planet of the Apes '72
Darkman 2: The Return of Durant '94
Darkman 3: Die Darkman Die '95
Dawn of the Dead '78 ►
Dawn of the Planet of the Apes '14 ►
Day of the Dead '85
Escape from the Planet of the Apes '71 ►
The Exorcist '73 ►
The Fly '86 ►
The Fly 2 '89
Freaked '93
Hocus Pocus '93
The Howling '81 ►
The Island of Dr. Moreau '96
The Man Without a Face '93
Mary Shelley's Frankenstein '94
Nutty Professor 2: The Klumps '00
The Nutty Professor '96 ►
Planet of the Apes '68 ►
Planet of the Apes '01 ►
Scanners '81
Sssssss '73
The Thing '82
Vampire in Brooklyn '95
Warriors of Virtue '97
Wolf '94

Special FX Wizards: Baker, Rick

An American Werewolf in London '81 ►
Food of the Gods '76
The Funhouse '81
The Fury '78
Greystoke: The Legend of Tarzan, Lord of the Apes '84
Harry and the Hendersons '87
Incredible Melting Man '77
The Incredible Shrinking Woman '81
It's Alive '74 ►
King Kong '76
Maleficent '14
Men in Black '97 ►
Mighty Joe Young '98
The Nutty Professor '96 ►
Octaman '71
Planet of the Apes '01 ►
Schlock '73
Squirm '76
Star Wars '77 ►
Tanya's Island '81
Track of the Moonbeast '76
Videodrome '83
Wolf '94

Special FX Wizards: Bottin, Rob

Bugsy '91 ►
Explorers '85
Fear and Loathing in Las Vegas '98
The Fog '78
The Howling '81 ►

Humanoids from the Deep '80
Innerspace '87
Legend '86
Mission: Impossible '96 ►
RoboCop '87 ►
Tanya's Island '81
The Thing '82
Total Recall '90 ►
Twilight Zone: The Movie '83
The Witches of Eastwick '87

Special FX Wizards: Furst, Anton

Alien '79 ►
Batman '89 ►
The Company of Wolves '85 ►
Full Metal Jacket '87 ►
Moonraker '79
Star Wars '77 ►

Special FX Wizards: Harryhausen, Ray

The Beast from 20,000 Fathoms '53
Clash of the Titans '81
Earth *vs.* the Flying Saucers '56
First Men in the Moon '64
Golden Voyage of Sinbad '73
It Came from Beneath the Sea '55 ►
Jason and the Argonauts '63 ►
Mighty Joe Young '49
Mysterious Island '61 ►
One Million Years B.C. '66
The Seventh Voyage of Sinbad '58 ►
Sinbad and the Eye of the Tiger '77
The Three Worlds of Gulliver '59
20 Million Miles to Earth '57
The Valley of Gwangi '69 ►

Special FX Wizards: Lewis, Herschell Gordon

Blood Feast '63
Color Me Blood Red '64
Gruesome Twosome '67
Just for the Hell of It '68
Moonshine Mountain '64
The Psychic '68
She-Devils on Wheels '68
Suburban Roulette '67
This Stuff'll Kill Ya! '71
2000 Maniacs '64
The Wizard of Gore '70

Special FX Wizards: Savini, Tom

Creepshow '82
Dawn of the Dead '78 ►
Day of the Dead '85
Deathdream '72
Deranged '74 ►
Friday the 13th '80
Friday the 13th, Part 4: The Final Chapter '84
Knightriders '81
Maniac '80
Martin '77 ►
Midnight '81
Monkey Shines '88
The Prowler '81
The Ripper '86
The Texas Chainsaw Massacre 2 '86

Special FX Wizards: Smith, Dick

Altered States '80 ►
Amadeus '84 ►
The Exorcist '73 ►
Ghost Story '81
The Godfather '72 ►
House of Dark Shadows '70 ►
Little Big Man '70 ►
Marathon Man '76 ►
Midnight Cowboy '69 ►
Scanners '81
The Sentinel '76
The Stepford Wives '75 ►

The Sunshine Boys '75 ►
Taxi Driver '76 ►
The World of Henry Orient '64 ►

Special FX Wizards: Trumball, Douglas

The Andromeda Strain '71
Blade Runner '82 ►
Brainstorm '83
Close Encounters of the Third Kind '77 ►
Silent Running '71 ►
Star Trek: The Motion Picture '79
2001: A Space Odyssey '68 ►

Star Wars

The Empire Strikes Back '80 ►
The Ewok Adventure '84
The Ewoks: Battle for Endor '85
Fanboys '09
Return of the Jedi '83 ►
Rogue One: A Star Wars Story '16 ►
Solo: A Star Wars Story '18
Star Wars '77 ►
Star Wars: Episode 1-The Phantom Menace '99 ►
Star Wars: Episode 2-Attack of the Clones '02 ►
Star Wars: Episode 3-Revenge of the Sith '05 ►
Star Wars: The Clone Wars '08
Star Wars: The Force Awakens '15 ►
Star Wars: The Last Jedi '17 ►
Star Wars: The Rise of Skywalker '19

Superman

Batman v Superman: Dawn of Justice '16
Justice League '17
Man of Steel '13
Superman: The Movie '78 ►
Superman 2 '80 ►
Superman 3 '83
Superman 4: The Quest for Peace '87
Superman Returns '06
Superman: Unbound '13

Tarzan

Greystoke: The Legend of Tarzan, Lord of the Apes '84
The New Adventures of Tarzan '35
Tarzan 2 '05
Tarzan '99 ►
Tarzan and His Mate '34 ►
Tarzan and the Amazons '45
Tarzan and the Great River '67
Tarzan and the Green Goddess '38
Tarzan and the Huntress '47
Tarzan and the Jungle Boy '68
Tarzan and the Leopard Woman '46
Tarzan and the Lost City '98
Tarzan and the Lost Safari '57
Tarzan and the Mermaids '48
Tarzan and the She-Devil '53
Tarzan and the Slave Girl '50
Tarzan and the Trappers '58
Tarzan and the Valley of Gold '65
Tarzan Escapes '36 ►
Tarzan Finds a Son '39 ►
Tarzan Goes to India '62
Tarzan, the Ape Man '32 ►
Tarzan, the Ape Man '81
Tarzan the Fearless '33
Tarzan the Magnificent '60
Tarzan the Tiger '29

► = rated three bones or higher

Tarzan Triumphs '43
Tarzan's Desert Mystery '43
Tarzan's Fight for Life '58
Tarzan's Greatest Adventure '59
Tarzan's Hidden Jungle '55
Tarzan's Magic Fountain '48
Tarzan's New York Adventure '42
Tarzan's Peril '51
Tarzan's Revenge '38
Tarzan's Savage Fury '52
Tarzan's Secret Treasure '41
Tarzan's Three Challenges '63
Walk Like a Man '87

The Texas Rangers

Comanche Moon '08
The Lone Ranger '13
Man of the House '05
The Over-the-Hill Gang '69
The Over-the-Hill Gang Rides Again '70
Rio Rita '29
Trade '07
True Grit '10 ▸
The Wonderful Country '59

The Thin Man

After the Thin Man '36 ▸
Another Thin Man '39
Shadow of the Thin Man '41 ▸
Song of the Thin Man '47
The Thin Man '34 ▸
The Thin Man Goes Home '44

The Three Musketeers

The Four Musketeers '75 ▸
The 4 Musketeers '05
The Man in the Iron Mask '98 ▸
The Musketeer '01
Revenge of the Musketeers '63
Ring of the Musketeers '93
The Three Musketeers '21 ▸
The Three Musketeers '33
The Three Musketeers '39 ▸
The Three Musketeers '48
The Three Musketeers '74 ▸
The Three Musketeers '93
The Three Musketeers '11
The Yellow Rolls Royce '64

Three Stooges

Around the World in a Daze '63
Dancing Lady '33
Have Rocket Will Travel '59
Hollywood Party '34
It's a Mad, Mad, Mad, Mad World '63
The Outlaws Is Coming! '65
Snow White and the Three Stooges '61
Tempo '03
Three Stooges in Orbit '62
The Three Stooges Meet Hercules '61
Time Out for Rhythm '41

Tom Ripley

The American Friend '77 ▸
Purple Noon '60 ▸
Ripley's Game '02 ▸
The Talented Mr. Ripley '99

Top Grossing Films of 1939

Gone with the Wind '39 ▸
The Hunchback of Notre Dame '39 ▸
Jesse James '39 ▸
Mr. Smith Goes to Washington '39 ▸
The Wizard of Oz '39 ▸

Top Grossing Films of 1940

Boom Town '40
Fantasia '40 ▸
Pinocchio '40 ▸
Rebecca '40 ▸
Santa Fe Trail '40

Top Grossing Films of 1941

Honky Tonk '41 ▸
The Philadelphia Story '40 ▸
Sergeant York '41 ▸
A Yank in the R.A.F. '41

Top Grossing Films of 1942

Bambi '42 ▸
Casablanca '42 ▸
Mrs. Miniver '42 ▸
Random Harvest '42 ▸
Yankee Doodle Dandy '42 ▸

Top Grossing Films of 1943

The Outlaw '43
The Song of Bernadette '43 ▸
Stage Door Canteen '43
This Is the Army '43

Top Grossing Films of 1944

Going My Way '44 ▸
Meet Me in St. Louis '44 ▸
Since You Went Away '44 ▸
Thirty Seconds Over Tokyo '44 ▸

Top Grossing Films of 1945

Anchors Aweigh '45 ▸
The Bells of St. Mary's '45 ▸
Spellbound '45 ▸
Weekend at the Waldorf '45 ▸

Top Grossing Films of 1946

The Best Years of Our Lives '46 ▸
Duel in the Sun '46 ▸
The Jolson Story '46 ▸

Top Grossing Films of 1947

Egg and I '47 ▸
Life with Father '47 ▸

Top Grossing Films of 1948

Johnny Belinda '48 ▸
On an Island with You '48
The Paleface '48 ▸
Red River '48 ▸
The Red Shoes '48 ▸
The Three Musketeers '48

Top Grossing Films of 1949

Battleground '49 ▸
Jolson Sings Again '49
Samson and Delilah '49 ▸
Sands of Iwo Jima '49 ▸

Top Grossing Films of 1950

Annie Get Your Gun '50 ▸
Cinderella '50 ▸
Father of the Bride '50 ▸
King Solomon's Mines '50 ▸

Top Grossing Films of 1951

Alice in Wonderland '51 ▸
David and Bathsheba '51 ▸
The Great Caruso '51
Quo Vadis '51 ▸
Show Boat '51

Top Grossing Films of 1952

The Greatest Show on Earth '52 ▸
Hans Christian Andersen '52
Ivanhoe '52 ▸
The Snows of Kilimanjaro '52 ▸

Top Grossing Films of 1953

From Here to Eternity '53 ▸
How to Marry a Millionaire '53
Peter Pan '53 ▸
The Robe '53
Shane '53 ▸

Top Grossing Films of 1954

The Caine Mutiny '54 ▸
The Glenn Miller Story '54 ▸
Rear Window '54 ▸
20,000 Leagues under the Sea '54 ▸
White Christmas '54 ▸

Top Grossing Films of 1955

Battle Cry '55 ▸
Lady and the Tramp '55 ▸
Mister Roberts '55 ▸
Oklahoma! '55 ▸

Top Grossing Films of 1956

Around the World in 80 Days '56 ▸
Giant '56 ▸
The King and I '56 ▸
The Ten Commandments '56 ▸

Top Grossing Films of 1957

The Bridge on the River Kwai '57 ▸
Old Yeller '57 ▸
Peyton Place '57 ▸
Raintree County '57
Sayonara '57 ▸

Top Grossing Films of 1958

Auntie Mame '58 ▸
Cat on a Hot Tin Roof '58 ▸
Gigi '58 ▸
No Time for Sergeants '58 ▸
South Pacific '58 ▸

Top Grossing Films of 1959

Ben-Hur '59 ▸
Darby O'Gill & the Little People '59 ▸
Operation Petticoat '59 ▸
The Shaggy Dog '59
Sleeping Beauty '59 ▸

Top Grossing Films of 1960

The Alamo '60 ▸
Exodus '60 ▸
Psycho '60 ▸
Spartacus '60 ▸
The Swiss Family Robinson '60 ▸

Top Grossing Films of 1961

The Absent-Minded Professor '61 ▸
El Cid '61 ▸
The Guns of Navarone '61 ▸
West Side Story '61 ▸

Top Grossing Films of 1962

How the West Was Won '63 ▸
In Search of the Castaways '62 ▸
Lawrence of Arabia '62 ▸
The Longest Day '62 ▸
The Music Man '62 ▸

Top Grossing Films of 1963

Cleopatra '63
Irma La Douce '63
It's a Mad, Mad, Mad, Mad World '63
The Sword in the Stone '63 ▸
Tom Jones '63 ▸

Top Grossing Films of 1964

The Carpetbaggers '64
From Russia with Love '63 ▸
Goldfinger '64 ▸
Mary Poppins '64 ▸
My Fair Lady '64 ▸

Top Grossing Films of 1965

Doctor Zhivago '65 ▸
The Sound of Music '65 ▸
That Darn Cat '65
Those Magnificent Men in Their Flying Machines '65 ▸
Thunderball '65

Top Grossing Films of 1966

Hawaii '66 ▸
Lt. Robin Crusoe, U.S.N. '66
A Man for All Seasons '66 ▸
Who's Afraid of Virginia Woolf? '66 ▸

Top Grossing Films of 1967

Bonnie & Clyde '67 ▸
The Dirty Dozen '67 ▸
The Graduate '67 ▸
Guess Who's Coming to Dinner '67 ▸
The Jungle Book '67 ▸

Top Grossing Films of 1968

Bullitt '68 ▸
Funny Girl '68 ▸
The Odd Couple '68 ▸
Romeo and Juliet '68 ▸
2001: A Space Odyssey '68 ▸

Top Grossing Films of 1969

Butch Cassidy and the Sundance Kid '69 ▸
Easy Rider '69 ▸
Hello, Dolly! '69
The Love Bug '68
Midnight Cowboy '69 ▸

Top Grossing Films of 1970

Airport '70 ▸
Love Story '70 ▸
M*A*S*H '70 ▸
Patton '70 ▸

Top Grossing Films of 1971

Billy Jack '71
Diamonds Are Forever '71 ▸
Fiddler on the Roof '71 ▸
The French Connection '71 ▸
Summer of '42 '71 ▸

Top Grossing Films of 1972

Deliverance '72 ▸
The Godfather '72 ▸
Jeremiah Johnson '72 ▸
The Poseidon Adventure '72
What's Up, Doc? '72 ▸

Top Grossing Films of 1973

American Graffiti '73 ▸
The Exorcist '73 ▸
Papillon '73 ▸
The Sting '73 ▸
The Way We Were '73 ▸

Top Grossing Films of 1974

Blazing Saddles '74 ▸
Earthquake '74
The Towering Inferno '74
The Trial of Billy Jack '74
Young Frankenstein '74 ▸

Top Grossing Films of 1975

Dog Day Afternoon '75 ▸
Jaws '75 ▸
One Flew Over the Cuckoo's Nest '75 ▸

Top Grossing Films of 1976

All the President's Men '76 ▸
King Kong '76
Rocky '76 ▸
Silver Streak '76 ▸
A Star Is Born '76

Top Grossing Films of 1977

Close Encounters of the Third Kind '77 ▸
The Goodbye Girl '77 ▸
Saturday Night Fever '77
Smokey and the Bandit '77
Star Wars '77 ▸

Top Grossing Films of 1978

Every Which Way But Loose '78
Grease '78 ▸
Jaws 2 '78
National Lampoon's Animal House '78 ▸
Superman: The Movie '78 ▸

Top Grossing Films of 1979

Alien '79 ▸
The Jerk '79
Kramer vs. Kramer '79 ▸
Rocky 2 '79
Star Trek: The Motion Picture '79

Top Grossing Films of 1980

Airplane! '80 ▸
Any Which Way You Can '80
The Empire Strikes Back '80 ▸
9 to 5 '80
Stir Crazy '80

Top Grossing Films of 1981

Arthur '81 ▸
Cannonball Run '81
On Golden Pond '81 ▸
Raiders of the Lost Ark '81 ▸
Stripes '81
Superman 2 '80 ▸

Top Grossing Films of 1982

E.T.: The Extra-Terrestrial '82 ▸
An Officer and a Gentleman '82 ▸
Porky's '82
Rocky 3 '82

Top Grossing Films of 1983

Return of the Jedi '83 ▸
Superman 3 '83
Terms of Endearment '83 ▸
Trading Places '83
WarGames '83 ▸

Top Grossing Films of 1984

Beverly Hills Cop '84
Ghostbusters '84 ▸
Gremlins '84 ▸
Indiana Jones and the Temple of Doom '84 ▸
The Karate Kid '84 ▸

Top Grossing Films of 1985

Back to the Future '85 ▸
The Color Purple '85 ▸
Out of Africa '85 ▸
Rambo: First Blood, Part 2 '85
Rocky 4 '85

Top Grossing Films of 1986

Crocodile Dundee '86 ▸
The Karate Kid: Part 2 '86
Platoon '86 ▸
Star Trek 4: The Voyage Home '86 ▸
Top Gun '86

Top Grossing Films of 1987

Beverly Hills Cop 2 '87
Fatal Attraction '87 ▸
Platoon '86
Three Men and a Baby '87
The Untouchables '87 ▸

Top Grossing Films of 1988

Big '88
Coming to America '88 ▸
Crocodile Dundee 2 '88
Good Morning, Vietnam '87
Who Framed Roger Rabbit '88 ▸

Top Grossing Films of 1989

Batman '89 ▸
Honey, I Shrunk the Kids '89
Indiana Jones and the Last Crusade '89 ▸
Lethal Weapon 2 '89 ▸
Rain Man '88

Top Grossing Films of 1990

Ghost '90 ▸
Home Alone '90 ▸
The Hunt for Red October '90 ▸
Pretty Woman '90 ▸
Teenage Mutant Ninja Turtles: The Movie '90

Top Grossing Films of 1991

City Slickers '91 ▸
Home Alone '90
Robin Hood: Prince of Thieves '91
The Silence of the Lambs '91 ▸
Terminator 2: Judgment Day '91 ▸

Top Grossing Films of 1992

Batman Returns '92
Home Alone 2: Lost in New York '92
Lethal Weapon 3 '92
Sister Act '92
Wayne's World '92 ▸

Top Grossing Films of 1993

The Firm '93 ▸
The Fugitive '93 ▸
Jurassic Park '93 ▸
Mrs. Doubtfire '93
Sleepless in Seattle '93 ▸

Top Grossing Films of 1994

The Flintstones '94
Forrest Gump '94 ▸
The Lion King '94 ▸
The Santa Clause '94
True Lies '94

Top Grossing Films of 1995

Ace Ventura: When Nature Calls '95
Apollo 13 '95 ▸
Batman Forever '95 ▸
Pocahontas '95 ▸
Toy Story '95 ▸

Top Grossing Films of 1996

Independence Day '96 ▸
Mission: Impossible '96 ▸
The Nutty Professor '96 ▸
The Rock '96 ▸
Twister '96

Top Grossing Films of 1997

Air Force One '97 ▸
Liar Liar '97
The Lost World: Jurassic Park 2 '97
Men in Black '97 ▸
Star Wars '77 ▸

▸ = rated three bones or higher

▸ *= rated three bones or higher*

The Demon Lover '77
Demon of Paradise '87
Demonia '90
Deuce Bigalow: European Gigolo '05
The Devil's Rejects '05
Devil's Son-in-Law '77
Devil's Wedding Night '73
Die Laughing '80
Dirty Love '05
Dirty Mind of Young Sally '72
Doctor Butcher M.D. '80
Dr. Orloff's Monster '64
Dr. Tarr's Torture Dungeon '75
Don't Go in the Woods '81
Don't Look in the Attic '81
Don't Open the Door! '74
Don't Open Till Christmas '84
Doom Asylum '88
Doomsday Prophecy '11
Dorm That Dripped Blood '82
Dracula: Dead and Loving It '95
Dracula vs. Frankenstein '71
Dracula's Great Love '72
Dracula's Last Rites '79
Drifter '09
Driller Killer '79
Drive-In '76
Drive-In Massacre '74
Driver's Seat '73
Drop Dead Fred '91
Drum '76
Drums O'Voodoo '34
Dutch Girls '87
Eating Out 3: All You Can Eat '09
Ed '96
Eegah! '62
8mm 2 '05
Empire of Assassins '11
End Game '09
End of the World '76
Equilibrium '02
Escape from Hell '79
Escape 2000 '81
Eve of Destruction '90
Everything's Ducky '61
Evil Laugh '86
The Evil Within '89
Evilspeak '82
Exploding Sun '13
Expose '97
Eyes of a Stranger '81
Fade to Black '80
Fair Game '86
Fair Game '89
Fanatic '82
Fantasies '73
Far Cry '08
Far Out Man '89
Farmhouse '08
Fascination '04
The Fat Spy '66
The Fear Chamber '68
Feed '05
Feeders '96
Fiend '83
The Fiendish Plot of Dr. Fu Manchu '80
Final Exam '81
Final Payback '99
The Final Storm '09
Fire From Below '09
Fire Serpent '07
The First 9 1/2 Weeks '98
Flesh Feast '69
Flight to Nowhere '46
Flu Birds '08
Food of the Gods '76
Food of the Gods: Part 2 '88
Foolish '99
The Forbidden Dance '90
Forbidden World '82
Foreplay '75
Frankenstein '80 '79
Frankenstein Island '81
Frankenstein Meets the Space Monster '65
Frankenstein's Great Aunt Tillie '83
Freddy Got Fingered '01
Friday the 13th, Part 2 '81
Friday the 13th, Part 3 '82
Friday the 13th, Part 4: The Final Chapter '84
Friday the 13th, Part 5: A New Beginning '85
Friday the 13th, Part 6: Jason Lives '86
Friday the 13th, Part 7: The New Blood '88
From Hell It Came '57
From Justin to Kelly '03
Fun Down There '88
Furry Vengeance '10
Galactic Gigolo '87
The Garbage Pail Kids Movie '87
Gates of Hell '80
Getaway '13
Getting Away With Murder '96
The Ghastly Ones '68
Ghost Fever '87
Ghoulies 3: Ghoulies Go to College '91
Giant from the Unknown '58
Giants of Rome '63
The Girl in Room 2A '76
Girl on a Chain Gang '65
The Girl Who Knew Too Much '69
Glen or Glenda? '53
Glitter '01
The Glory Stompers '67
Goblin '93
Godzilla vs. the Sea Monster '66
Goliath and the Dragon '61
Gone Fishin' '97
The Green Berets '68
The Green Slime '68
Grotesque '87
Guess What We Learned in School Today? '70
Gummo '97
H-Man '59
Hallowed '05
Hands of Steel '86
Hangmen '87
Hardbodies 2 '86
A Haunted House '13
Hawmps! '76
The Hearse '80
Heart of America '03
Hell Night '81
Hell of the Living Dead '83
Hell Up in Harlem '73
Hellcats '68
Hellgate '89
Helter Skelter Murders '71
Hick '11
High Tension '03
Hillbillies in a Haunted House '67
The Hills Have Eyes '77
His Name Was King '71
The Hollywood Strangler Meets the Skid Row Slasher '79
Hometown U.S.A. '79
Horror House on Highway 5 '86
Horror of Party Beach '64
Horror of the Blood Monsters '70
Hostel: Part 3 '11
Hot Box '72
Hot Rods to Hell '67
The Hound of the Baskervilles '77
House of 1000 Corpses '03
House of the Dead '03
House of Whipcord '75
Housebroken '09
The Human Centipede: First Sequence '10
The Human Centipede 2: Full Sequence '11
The Human Centipede 3: The Final Sequence '15
Humanoids from the Deep '80
Humongous '82
Hurricane '79
Hyenas '10
I Dismember Mama '74
I Eat Your Skin '64
I, Frankenstein '13
I Spit on Your Corpse '74
I Spit on Your Grave '77
I Was a Communist for the FBI '51
I Was a Teenage TV Terrorist '87
Idaho Transfer '73
If I Die Before I Wake '98
Ilsa, Harem Keeper of the Oil Sheiks '76
Ilsa, the Wicked Warden '78
Impulse '74
In the Mix '05
Incredible Melting Man '77
The Incredible Petrified World '58
The Incredible Two-Headed Transplant '71
Incredibly Strange Creatures Who Stopped Living and Became Mixed-Up Zombies '63
Incubus '82
Infra-Man '76
Inner Sanctum '91
Inseminoid '80
Invasion of the Animal People '62
Invasion of the Blood Farmers '72
Invasion of the Girl Snatchers '73
Invasion of the Star Creatures '63
Invitation to Hell '82
The Island '80
It Waits '05
It's Alive 2: It Lives Again '78
It's All Gone, Pete Tong '04
It's Pat: The Movie '94
Jack Frost 2: Revenge of the Mutant Killer Snowman '00
Jarhead 2: Field of Fire '14
Jason Goes to Hell: The Final Friday '93
Jaws of Satan '81
The Jazz Singer '80
Jennifer On My Mind '71
The Jerky Boys '95
Jewtopia '12
Journey to the Center of the Earth '93
Joy Sticks '83
Just for the Hell of It '68
The Kate Logan Affair '10
Keepin' It Real '01
Kill Factor '78
Killer Party '86
Killers from Space '54
Killing Moon '00
Kilma, Queen of the Amazons '75
King Kong Escapes '67
King of Kong Island '78
King of the Zombies '41
LA Apocalypse '14
Lake Placid 2 '07
Lap Dancing '95
Larry the Cable Guy: Health Inspector '06
Las Vegas Serial Killer '86
Laserblast '78
Last Hour '08
Last House on Dead End Street '77
The Last Slumber Party '87
The Last Woman on Earth '61
Lauderdale '89
Legacy of Horror '78
The Legend of Bloody Jack '07
The Legend of Hercules '14
Legend of the Dinosaurs and Monster Birds '77
Legend of the Liquid Sword '93
Leprechaun '93
Leprechaun 4: In Space '96
Leprechaun 5: In the Hood '99
Leprechaun 6: Back 2 Tha Hood '03
Lethal '04
The Life of Lucky Cucumber '08
Link '86
Lipstick '76
Lisa and the Devil '75
Lisztomania '75
A Little Bit of Heaven '11
Loaded Guns '75
The Lone Runner '88
The Long Weekend '05
The Longshot '86
Lost Boys: The Tribe '08
The Loves of Hercules '60
Lurkers '88
Lust for Dracula '04
Luther the Geek '90
Machined '06
The Mad Bomber '72
Mad Doctor of Blood Island '68
Mad Dog '84
Madigan's Millions '67
The Malibu Beach Vampires '91
Malibu Shark Attack '09
Mama Dracula '80
Maniac '34
Maniac '80
Maniac Nurses Find Ecstasy '94
Mannequin 2: On the Move '91
Manos, the Hands of Fate '66
Mardi Gras Massacre '78
Mardi Gras: Spring Break '11
Mask Maker '10
Maslin Beach '97
A Matter of Time '76
Maximum Thrust '88
Megafault '09
Memron '04
Mesa of Lost Women '52
Meteor '79
Miami Connection '87
The Mighty Peking Man '77
Mindhunters '05
Mirror Wars: Reflection One '05
Miss March '09
Mr. Jingles '06
Mom '89
Monsignor '82
Monster '08
Monster a Go-Go! '65
Monster Dog '82
Moonshine Mountain '64
Mortuary '05
Moscow Zero '06
Moses '76
Motor Psycho '65
Mountain of the Cannibal God '79
Mountaintop Motel Massacre '86
Movie 43 '13
Murderer's Keep '70
Mutant Hunt '87
Mutants '08
My First Wedding '04
Myra Breckinridge '70
Nail Gun Massacre '86
The Naked Flame '68
Naked Youth '59
The Narcotics Story '58
National Lampoon Presents Cattle Call '06
National Lampoon's Class Reunion '82
National Lampoon's Dirty Movie '11
National Lampoon's Gold Diggers '04
National Lampoon's The Legend of Awesomest Maximus '11
National Lampoon's The Stoned Aged '07
National Lampoon's Van Wilder 2: The Rise of Taj '06
Navy vs. the Night Monsters '66
Neon Maniacs '86
The New Gladiators '83
New Year's Eve '11
New York Ripper '82
A Night in Heaven '83
Night of Terror '87
Night of the Bloody Apes '68
Night of the Demon '80
Night of the Demons 3 '97
Night of the Ghouls '59
Night of the Sharks '87
Night of the Sorcerers '70
Night Patrol '85
Night Stalker '09
Night Train Murders '75
Night Train to Terror '84
Night Watcher '08
Nightmare Sisters '87
Nightstalker '81
Nine Deaths of the Ninja '85
1990: The Bronx Warriors '83
No One Cries Forever '85
No Way Back '90
Nobody's Perfekt '79
Nude on the Moon '61
#1 Cheerleader Camp '10
Nun of That '09
A Nymphoid Barbarian in Dinosaur Hell '94
The Obsession '06
The Occultist '89
Oddballs '84
On Deadly Ground '94
One Down, Two to Go! '82
One of Them '03
The Oogieloves in the Big Balloon Adventure '12
Orca '77
Orgy of the Dead '65
The Other Side of Midnight '77
Parasite '82
Percentage '13
Phobia '80
The Phynx '70
Pieces '83
Piranha 3DD '11
Plan 9 from Outer Space '56
Please Don't Eat My Mother '72
Police Academy 5: Assignment Miami Beach '88
Prehistoric Bimbos in Armageddon City '93
Prehistoric Women '50
The Prime Time '60
The Psychic '68
Psychic Experiment '10
Psychos in Love '87
Puff, Puff, Pass '06
Python 2 '02
Queen of Outer Space '58
Quick, Let's Get Married '71
Rabid Grannies '89
Raise the Titanic '80
The Rape of the Sabines '61
Rat Pfink a Boo-Boo '66
Razorteeth '05
Rebel Vixens '69
Recon 2023: The Gauda Prime Conspiracy '08
The Red Menace '49
Return to Frogtown '92
Revenge '86
Ring of Darkness '04
Ringmaster '98
The Ripper '86
River: The Legend of La Llorona '06
Rocket Attack U.S.A. '58
Roller Boogie '79
The Rookie '59
The Room '03
The Roommate '11
Rumpelstiltskin '96
Sabretooth '01
Safehouse '08
Samurai Cop '89
Sanctimony '01
Sasquatch '76
Satan's Cheerleaders '77
Savage Is Loose '74
Savage Weekend '80
Saving Christmas '14
Scar '07
The Scarlet Letter '95
Scary Movie 5 '13
Score '95
Scout's Honor: Badge to the Bone '09
Scream Bloody Murder '72
Scream of the Demon Lover '71
Screwed '00
See Spot Run '01
Sgt. Kabukiman N.Y.P.D. '94
Sgt. Pepper's Lonely Hearts Club Band '78
The Serpent and the Rainbow '87
The 7 Adventures of Sinbad '10
The Severed Arm '73
Sex on the Run '78
Sextette '78
She Demons '58
She-Devils on Wheels '68
Sheena '84
Showgirls '95
Shriek of the Mutilated '74
The Sidehackers '69
Silent Hill: Revelation 3D '12
Sincerely Yours '55
Single White Female 2: The Psycho '05
The Sinister Urge '60
Skidoo '68
Skinned Alive '89
Slashdance '89
Slaughterhouse '87
The Slayer '82
Sledgehammer '83
Sleepaway Camp 3: Teenage Wasteland '89
The Slime People '63
Slugs '87
Slumber Party Massacre 2 '87
Slumber Party Massacre 3 '90
Smashing Time '67
The Snow Creature '54
Snow White: A Deadly Summer '12
Social Intercourse '01
Something Weird '68
Sorority House Massacre '86
Sorority House Massacre 2: Nighty Nightmare '92
Soul Hustler '76
Soul Survivors '01
Spaced Out '80
Spare Parts '79
Sphinx '81
Splatter University '84
Splitz '84
The Squeeze '87
Squeeze Play '79
Stalked '99
Starship Troopers 2: Hero of the Federation '04
State Property 2 '05
Stepsisters '74
Stone Cold '91
Stranger from Venus '54
Street People '76
Street Trash '87
Strike '07
Stroker Ace '83
The Stud '78
Student Bodies '81
Sugar Cookies '77
Summer School Teachers '75
Sunset Strip '91
Super Capers '09
Super Eruption '11
Super Storm '12
Superbabies: Baby Geniuses 2 '04
Superchick '71
Supernova '09
Supersonic Man '78
Sweet Insanity '06
Sweet Spirits '71
Sword Masters: Web of Death '76
Tales of an Ancient Empire '11
The Tartars '61
Tarzan, the Ape Man '81
Tarzeena: Queen of Kong Island '08
Teenage Mother '67
Teenage Zombies '58
Teenagers from Outer Space '59
The Temp '93
10 Rules for Sleeping Around '13
10 Violent Women '79
Tender Flesh '97
Tentacles '77
The Terror '79
Terror House '97
Terror Inside '08

Wyatt Earp

Zorro

Zucker/Abrahams/Zucker

▸ = *rated three bones or higher*

Awards Index

The Awards Index lists films honored (or dishonored, in some cases) by nine national and international award bodies, representing over 100 categories of recognition. This information can also be found in the reviews, following the credits. **Only features available on video and reviewed in the main section are listed in this index; movies not yet released on video are not covered here.** As award-winning and nominated films find their way to video, they will be added to the review section and covered in this index. **Nominations are once again covered in this index; they are not covered in the individual reviews.** The awards covered include:

Academy Awards
British Academy of Film and Television Arts
Directors Guild of America
Golden Globes
Golden Raspberries
Independent Spirit Awards
National Film Registry
Screen Actors Guild Awards
Writers Guild of America

ACADEMY AWARDS

ACTOR

1928
★Emil Jannings/*The Last Command*
Charlie Chaplin/*The Circus*

1929
Chester Morris/*Alibi*

1930
Wallace Beery/*The Big House*
Maurice Chevalier/*The Love Parade*

1931
★Lionel Barrymore/*A Free Soul*
Richard Dix/*Cimarron*
Adolphe Menjou/*The Front Page*

1932
★Wallace Beery/*The Champ*
★Fredric March/*Dr. Jekyll and Mr. Hyde*

1933
★Charles Laughton/*The Private Life of Henry VIII*
Paul Muni/*I Am a Fugitive from a Chain Gang*

1934
★Clark Gable/*It Happened One Night*
William Powell/*The Thin Man*

1935
★Victor McLaglen/*The Informer*
Clark Gable/*Mutiny on the Bounty*
Charles Laughton/*Mutiny on the Bounty*
Paul Muni/*Black Fury*
Franchot Tone/*Mutiny on the Bounty*

1936
Gary Cooper/*Mr. Deeds Goes to Town*
Walter Huston/*Dodsworth*
William Powell/*My Man Godfrey*
Spencer Tracy/*San Francisco*

1937
★Spencer Tracy/*Captains Courageous*
Charles Boyer/*Conquest*
Fredric March/*A Star Is Born*
Robert Montgomery/*Night Must Fall*
Paul Muni/*The Life of Emile Zola*

1938
★Spencer Tracy/*Boys Town*
Charles Boyer/*Algiers*
James Cagney/*Angels with Dirty Faces*
Robert Donat/*The Citadel*
Leslie Howard/*Pygmalion*

1939
★Robert Donat/*Goodbye, Mr. Chips*
Clark Gable/*Gone with the Wind*
Laurence Olivier/*Wuthering Heights*
Mickey Rooney/*Babes in Arms*
James Stewart/*Mr. Smith Goes to Washington*

1940
★James Stewart/*The Philadelphia Story*
Charlie Chaplin/*The Great Dictator*
Henry Fonda/*The Grapes of Wrath*
Raymond Massey/*Abe Lincoln in Illinois*
Laurence Olivier/*Rebecca*

1941
★Gary Cooper/*Sergeant York*
Cary Grant/*Penny Serenade*
Walter Huston/*The Devil & Daniel Webster*
Robert Montgomery/*Here Comes Mr. Jordan*
Orson Welles/*Citizen Kane*

1942
★James Cagney/*Yankee Doodle Dandy*
Ronald Colman/*Random Harvest*
Gary Cooper/*The Pride of the Yankees*
Walter Pidgeon/*Mrs. Miniver*

1943
★Paul Lukas/*Watch on the Rhine*
Humphrey Bogart/*Casablanca*
Gary Cooper/*For Whom the Bell Tolls*
Walter Pidgeon/*Madame Curie*
Mickey Rooney/*The Human Comedy*

1944
★Bing Crosby/*Going My Way*
Charles Boyer/*Gaslight*
Barry Fitzgerald/*Going My Way*
Cary Grant/*None But the Lonely Heart*
Alexander Knox/*Wilson*

1945
★Ray Milland/*The Lost Weekend*
Bing Crosby/*The Bells of St. Mary's*
Gene Kelly/*Anchors Aweigh*
Gregory Peck/*The Keys of the Kingdom*
Cornel Wilde/*A Song to Remember*

1946
★Fredric March/*The Best Years of Our Lives*
Laurence Olivier/*Henry V*
Larry Parks/*The Jolson Story*
Gregory Peck/*The Yearling*
James Stewart/*It's a Wonderful Life*

1947
★Ronald Colman/*A Double Life*
John Garfield/*Body and Soul*
Gregory Peck/*Gentleman's Agreement*
William Powell/*Life with Father*

1948
★Laurence Olivier/*Hamlet*
Lew Ayres/*Johnny Belinda*
Montgomery Clift/*The Search*
Clifton Webb/*Sitting Pretty*

1949
★Broderick Crawford/*All the King's Men*
Kirk Douglas/*Champion*
Gregory Peck/*Twelve o'Clock High*
John Wayne/*Sands of Iwo Jima*

1950
★Jose Ferrer/*Cyrano de Bergerac*
Louis Calhern/*The Magnificent Yankee*
William Holden/*Sunset Boulevard*
James Stewart/*Harvey*
Spencer Tracy/*Father of the Bride*

1951
★Humphrey Bogart/*The African Queen*
Marlon Brando/*A Streetcar Named Desire*
Montgomery Clift/*A Place in the Sun*
Fredric March/*Death of a Salesman*

1952
★Gary Cooper/*High Noon*
Marlon Brando/*Viva Zapata!*
Kirk Douglas/*The Bad and the Beautiful*
Jose Ferrer/*Moulin Rouge*
Alec Guinness/*The Lavender Hill Mob*

1953
★William Holden/*Stalag 17*
Marlon Brando/*Julius Caesar*
Richard Burton/*The Robe*
Montgomery Clift/*From Here to Eternity*
Burt Lancaster/*From Here to Eternity*

1954
★Marlon Brando/*On the Waterfront*
Humphrey Bogart/*The Caine Mutiny*
Bing Crosby/*Country Girl*
James Mason/*A Star Is Born*
Dan O'Herlihy/*Robinson Crusoe*

1955
★Ernest Borgnine/*Marty*
James Cagney/*Love Me or Leave Me*
James Dean/*East of Eden*
Frank Sinatra/*The Man with the Golden Arm*
Spencer Tracy/*Bad Day at Black Rock*

1956
★Yul Brynner/*The King and I*
James Dean/*Giant*
Kirk Douglas/*Lust for Life*
Rock Hudson/*Giant*
Laurence Olivier/*Richard III*

1957
★Alec Guinness/*The Bridge on the River Kwai*
Marlon Brando/*Sayonara*
Charles Laughton/*Witness for the Prosecution*
Anthony Quinn/*Wild Is the Wind*

1958
★David Niven/*Separate Tables*
Tony Curtis/*The Defiant Ones*
Paul Newman/*Cat on a Hot Tin Roof*
Sidney Poitier/*The Defiant Ones*
Spencer Tracy/*The Old Man and the Sea*

1959
★Charlton Heston/*Ben-Hur*
Anthony (Tony) Franciosa/*A Hatful of Rain*
Laurence Harvey/*Room at the Top*
Jack Lemmon/*Some Like It Hot*
James Stewart/*Anatomy of a Murder*

1960
★Burt Lancaster/*Elmer Gantry*
Jack Lemmon/*The Apartment*
Laurence Olivier/*The Entertainer*
Spencer Tracy/*Inherit the Wind*

★ = winner

Academy Awards

1961

★Maximilian Schell/*Judgment at Nuremberg*

Charles Boyer/*Fanny*

Paul Newman/*The Hustler*

Spencer Tracy/*Judgment at Nuremberg*

Stuart Whitman/*The Mark*

1962

★Gregory Peck/*To Kill a Mockingbird*

Burt Lancaster/*Birdman of Alcatraz*

Jack Lemmon/*Days of Wine and Roses*

Marcello Mastroianni/*Divorce-Italian Style*

Peter O'Toole/*Lawrence of Arabia*

1963

★Sidney Poitier/*Lilies of the Field*

Albert Finney/*Tom Jones*

Richard Harris/*This Sporting Life*

Rex Harrison/*Cleopatra*

Paul Newman/*Hud*

1964

★Rex Harrison/*My Fair Lady*

Richard Burton/*Becket*

Peter O'Toole/*Becket*

Anthony Quinn/*Zorba the Greek*

Peter Sellers/*Dr. Strangelove, or: How I Learned to Stop Worrying and Love the Bomb*

1965

★Lee Marvin/*Cat Ballou*

Richard Burton/*The Spy Who Came in from the Cold*

Laurence Olivier/*Othello*

Rod Steiger/*The Pawnbroker*

Oskar Werner/*Ship of Fools*

1966

★Paul Scofield/*A Man for All Seasons*

Alan Arkin/*The Russians Are Coming, the Russians Are Coming*

Richard Burton/*Who's Afraid of Virginia Woolf?*

Michael Caine/*Alfie*

Steve McQueen/*The Sand Pebbles*

1967

★Rod Steiger/*In the Heat of the Night*

Warren Beatty/*Bonnie & Clyde*

Dustin Hoffman/*The Graduate*

Paul Newman/*Cool Hand Luke*

Spencer Tracy/*Guess Who's Coming to Dinner*

1968

★Cliff Robertson/*Charly*

Alan Arkin/*The Heart Is a Lonely Hunter*

Ron Moody/*Oliver!*

Peter O'Toole/*The Lion in Winter*

1969

★John Wayne/*True Grit*

Richard Burton/*Anne of the Thousand Days*

Dustin Hoffman/*Midnight Cowboy*

Peter O'Toole/*Goodbye, Mr. Chips*

Jon Voight/*Midnight Cowboy*

1970

★George C. Scott/*Patton*

Melvyn Douglas/*I Never Sang for My Father*

James Earl Jones/*The Great White Hope*

Jack Nicholson/*Five Easy Pieces*

Ryan O'Neal/*Love Story*

1971

★Gene Hackman/*The French Connection*

Peter Finch/*Sunday, Bloody Sunday*

Walter Matthau/*Kotch*

George C. Scott/*The Hospital*

Topol/*Fiddler on the Roof*

1972

★Marlon Brando/*The Godfather*

Michael Caine/*Sleuth*

Laurence Olivier/*Sleuth*

Peter O'Toole/*The Ruling Class*

Paul Winfield/*Sounder*

1973

★Jack Lemmon/*Save the Tiger*

Marlon Brando/*Last Tango in Paris*

Jack Nicholson/*The Last Detail*

Al Pacino/*Serpico*

Robert Redford/*The Sting*

1974

★Art Carney/*Harry and Tonto*

Albert Finney/*Murder on the Orient Express*

Dustin Hoffman/*Lenny*

Jack Nicholson/*Chinatown*

Al Pacino/*The Godfather, Part 2*

1975

★Jack Nicholson/*One Flew Over the Cuckoo's Nest*

Walter Matthau/*The Sunshine Boys*

Al Pacino/*Dog Day Afternoon*

Maximilian Schell/*The Man in the Glass Booth*

James Whitmore/*Give 'Em Hell, Harry!*

1976

★Peter Finch/*Network*

Robert De Niro/*Taxi Driver*

Giancarlo Giannini/*Seven Beauties*

William Holden/*Network*

Sylvester Stallone/*Rocky*

1977

★Richard Dreyfuss/*The Goodbye Girl*

Woody Allen/*Annie Hall*

Richard Burton/*Equus*

Marcello Mastroianni/*A Special Day*

John Travolta/*Saturday Night Fever*

1978

★Jon Voight/*Coming Home*

Warren Beatty/*Heaven Can Wait*

Gary Busey/*The Buddy Holly Story*

Robert De Niro/*The Deer Hunter*

Laurence Olivier/*The Boys from Brazil*

1979

★Dustin Hoffman/*Kramer vs. Kramer*

Jack Lemmon/*The China Syndrome*

Al Pacino/*And Justice for All*

Roy Scheider/*All That Jazz*

Peter Sellers/*Being There*

1980

★Robert De Niro/*Raging Bull*

Robert Duvall/*The Great Santini*

John Hurt/*The Elephant Man*

Peter O'Toole/*The Stunt Man*

1981

★Henry Fonda/*On Golden Pond*

Warren Beatty/*Reds*

Burt Lancaster/*Atlantic City*

Dudley Moore/*Arthur*

Paul Newman/*Absence of Malice*

1982

★Ben Kingsley/*Gandhi*

Dustin Hoffman/*Tootsie*

Jack Lemmon/*Missing*

Paul Newman/*The Verdict*

Peter O'Toole/*My Favorite Year*

1983

★Robert Duvall/*Tender Mercies*

Michael Caine/*Educating Rita*

Tom Courtenay/*The Dresser*

Albert Finney/*The Dresser*

1984

★F. Murray Abraham/*Amadeus*

Jeff Bridges/*Starman*

Albert Finney/*Under the Volcano*

Tom Hulce/*Amadeus*

Sam Waterston/*The Killing Fields*

1985

★William Hurt/*Kiss of the Spider Woman*

Harrison Ford/*Witness*

James Garner/*Murphy's Romance*

Jack Nicholson/*Prizzi's Honor*

Jon Voight/*Runaway Train*

1986

★Paul Newman/*The Color of Money*

Dexter Gordon/*Round Midnight*

Bob Hoskins/*Mona Lisa*

William Hurt/*Children of a Lesser God*

James Woods/*Salvador*

1987

★Michael Douglas/*Wall Street*

William Hurt/*Broadcast News*

Jack Nicholson/*Ironweed*

Robin Williams/*Good Morning, Vietnam*

1988

★Dustin Hoffman/*Rain Man*

Gene Hackman/*Mississippi Burning*

Tom Hanks/*Big*

Edward James Olmos/*Stand and Deliver*

Max von Sydow/*Pelle the Conqueror*

1989

★Daniel Day-Lewis/*My Left Foot*

Kenneth Branagh/*Henry V*

Tom Cruise/*Born on the Fourth of July*

Morgan Freeman/*Driving Miss Daisy*

Robin Williams/*Dead Poets Society*

1990

★Jeremy Irons/*Reversal of Fortune*

Kevin Costner/*Dances with Wolves*

Robert De Niro/*Awakenings*

Gerard Depardieu/*Cyrano de Bergerac*

Richard Harris/*The Field*

1991

★Anthony Hopkins/*The Silence of the Lambs*

Warren Beatty/*Bugsy*

Robert De Niro/*Cape Fear*

Nick Nolte/*The Prince of Tides*

Robin Williams/*The Fisher King*

1992

★Al Pacino/*Scent of a Woman*

Robert Downey, Jr./*Chaplin*

Clint Eastwood/*Unforgiven*

Stephen Rea/*The Crying Game*

Denzel Washington/*Malcolm X*

1993

★Tom Hanks/*Philadelphia*

Daniel Day-Lewis/*In the Name of the Father*

Laurence Fishburne/*What's Love Got to Do with It?*

Anthony Hopkins/*The Remains of the Day*

Liam Neeson/*Schindler's List*

1994

★Tom Hanks/*Forrest Gump*

Morgan Freeman/*The Shawshank Redemption*

Nigel Hawthorne/*The Madness of King George*

Paul Newman/*Nobody's Fool*

John Travolta/*Pulp Fiction*

1995

★Nicolas Cage/*Leaving Las Vegas*

Richard Dreyfuss/*Mr. Holland's Opus*

Anthony Hopkins/*Nixon*

Sean Penn/*Dead Man Walking*

Massimo Troisi/*The Postman*

1996

★Geoffrey Rush/*Shine*

Tom Cruise/*Jerry Maguire*

Ralph Fiennes/*The English Patient*

Woody Harrelson/*The People vs. Larry Flynt*

Billy Bob Thornton/*Sling Blade*

1997

★Jack Nicholson/*As Good As It Gets*

Matt Damon/*Good Will Hunting*

Robert Duvall/*The Apostle*

Peter Fonda/*Ulee's Gold*

Dustin Hoffman/*Wag the Dog*

1998

★Roberto Benigni/*Life Is Beautiful*

Tom Hanks/*Saving Private Ryan*

Ian McKellen/*Gods and Monsters*

Nick Nolte/*Affliction*

Edward Norton/*American History X*

1999

★Kevin Spacey/*American Beauty*

Russell Crowe/*The Insider*

Richard Farnsworth/*The Straight Story*

Sean Penn/*Sweet and Lowdown*

Denzel Washington/*The Hurricane*

2000

★Russell Crowe/*Gladiator*

Javier Bardem/*Before Night Falls*

Tom Hanks/*Cast Away*

Ed Harris/*Pollock*

Geoffrey Rush/*Quills*

2001

★Denzel Washington/*Training Day*

Russell Crowe/*A Beautiful Mind*

Sean Penn/*I Am Sam*

Will Smith/*Ali*

Tom Wilkinson/*In the Bedroom*

2002

★Adrien Brody/*The Pianist*

Nicolas Cage/*Adaptation*

Michael Caine/*The Quiet American*

Daniel Day-Lewis/*Gangs of New York*

Jack Nicholson/*About Schmidt*

2003

★Sean Penn/*Mystic River*

Johnny Depp/*Pirates of the Caribbean: The Curse of the Black Pearl*

Ben Kingsley/*House of Sand and Fog*

Jude Law/*Cold Mountain*

Bill Murray/*Lost in Translation*

2004

★Jamie Foxx/*Ray*

Don Cheadle/*Hotel Rwanda*

Johnny Depp/*Finding Neverland*

Leonardo DiCaprio/*The Aviator*

Clint Eastwood/*Million Dollar Baby*

2005

★Philip Seymour Hoffman/*Capote*

Terrence Howard/*Hustle & Flow*

Heath Ledger/*Brokeback Mountain*

Joaquin Rafael (Leaf) Phoenix/*Walk the Line*

David Strathairn/*Good Night, and Good Luck*

2006

★Forest Whitaker/*The Last King of Scotland*

Leonardo DiCaprio/*Blood Diamond*

Ryan Gosling/*Half Nelson*

Peter O'Toole/*Venus*

Will Smith/*The Pursuit of Happyness*

2007

★Daniel Day-Lewis/*There Will Be Blood*

George Clooney/*Michael Clayton*

Johnny Depp/*Sweeney Todd: The Demon Barber of Fleet Street*

Tommy Lee Jones/*In the Valley of Elah*

Viggo Mortensen/*Eastern Promises*

2008

★Sean Penn/*Milk*

Richard Jenkins/*The Visitor*

Frank Langella/*Frost/Nixon*

Brad Pitt/*The Curious Case of Benjamin Button*

Mickey Rourke/*The Wrestler*

2009

★Jeff Bridges/*Crazy Heart*

George Clooney/*Up in the Air*

Colin Firth/*A Single Man*

Morgan Freeman/*Invictus*

Jeremy Renner/*The Hurt Locker*

2010

★Colin Firth/*The King's Speech*

Javier Bardem/*Biutiful*

Jeff Bridges/*True Grit*

Jesse Eisenberg/*The Social Network*

James Franco/*127 Hours*

2011

★Jean Dujardin/*The Artist*

Demian Bechir/*A Better Life*

George Clooney/*The Descendants*

Gary Oldman/*Tinker Tailor Soldier Spy*

Brad Pitt/*Moneyball*

2012

★Daniel Day-Lewis/*Lincoln*

Bradley Cooper/*Silver Linings Playbook*

Hugh Jackman/*Les Miserables*

Joaquin Rafael (Leaf) Phoenix/*The Master*

Denzel Washington/*Flight*

2013

★Matthew McConaughey/*Dallas Buyers Club*

Christian Bale/*American Hustle*

Bruce Dern/*Nebraska*

Leonardo DiCaprio/*The Wolf of Wall Street*

Chiwetel Ejiofor/*12 Years a Slave*

2014

★Eddie Redmayne/*The Theory of Everything*

Steve Carell/*Foxcatcher*

Bradley Cooper/*American Sniper*

Benedict Cumberbatch/*The Imitation Game*

Michael Keaton/*Birdman, or (The Unexpected Virtue of Ignorance)*

2015

★Leonardo DiCaprio/*The Revenant*

Bryan Cranston/*Trumbo*

Matt Damon/*The Martian*

Michael Fassbender/*Steve Jobs*

Eddie Redmayne/*The Danish Girl*

2016

★Casey Affleck/*Manchester by the Sea*

Andrew Garfield/*Hacksaw Ridge*

Ryan Gosling/*La La Land*

Viggo Mortensen/*Captain Fantastic*

Denzel Washington/*Fences*

2017

★Gary Oldman/*Darkest Hour*

Timothée Chalamet/*Call Me by Your Name*

Daniel Day-Lewis/*Phantom Thread*

Daniel Kaluuya/*Get Out*

Denzel Washington/*Roman J. Israel, Esq.*

★ = winner

2018
- ★Rami Malek/*Bohemian Rhapsody*
- Christian Bale/*Vice*
- Bradley Cooper/*A Star Is Born*
- Willem Dafoe/*At Eternity's Gate*
- Viggo Mortensen/*Green Book*

2019
- ★Joaquin Rafael (Leaf) Phoenix/*Joker*
- Antonio Banderas/*Pain and Glory*
- Leonardo DiCaprio/*Once Upon A Time... In Hollywood*
- Adam Driver/*Marriage Story*
- Jonathan Pryce/*The Two Popes*

ACTOR—SUPPORTING

1936
- ★Walter Brennan/*Come and Get It*
- Mischa Auer/*My Man Godfrey*
- Stuart Erwin/*Pigskin Parade*
- Basil Rathbone/*Romeo and Juliet*
- Akim Tamiroff/*The General Died at Dawn*

1937
- ★Joseph Schildkraut/*The Life of Emile Zola*
- Ralph Bellamy/*The Awful Truth*
- Thomas Mitchell/*The Hurricane*
- H.B. Warner/*Lost Horizon*
- Roland Young/*Topper*

1938
- ★Walter Brennan/*Kentucky*
- John Garfield/*Four Daughters*
- Gene Lockhart/*Algiers*
- Robert Morley/*Marie Antoinette*

1939
- ★Thomas Mitchell/*Stagecoach*
- Brian Aherne/*Juarez*
- Harry Carey, Sr./*Mr. Smith Goes to Washington*
- Brian Donlevy/*Beau Geste*
- Claude Rains/*Mr. Smith Goes to Washington*

1940
- ★Walter Brennan/*The Westerner*
- Albert Bassermann/*Foreign Correspondent*
- Jack Oakie/*The Great Dictator*
- James Stephenson/*The Letter*

1941
- ★Donald Crisp/*How Green Was My Valley*
- Walter Brennan/*Sergeant York*
- Charles Coburn/*The Devil & Miss Jones*
- James Gleason/*Here Comes Mr. Jordan*
- Sydney Greenstreet/*The Maltese Falcon*

1942
- ★Van Heflin/*Johnny Eager*
- William Bendix/*Wake Island*
- Walter Huston/*Yankee Doodle Dandy*
- Frank Morgan/*Tortilla Flat*
- Henry Travers/*Mrs. Miniver*

1943
- ★Charles Coburn/*The More the Merrier*
- Charles Bickford/*The Song of Bernadette*
- J. Carrol Naish/*Sahara*
- Claude Rains/*Casablanca*
- Akim Tamiroff/*For Whom the Bell Tolls*

1944
- ★Barry Fitzgerald/*Going My Way*
- Claude Rains/*Mr. Skeffington*
- Clifton Webb/*Laura*
- Monty Woolley/*Since You Went Away*

1945
- ★James Dunn/*A Tree Grows in Brooklyn*
- Michael Chekhov/*Spellbound*
- John Dall/*The Corn Is Green*
- Robert Mitchum/*The Story of G.I. Joe*

1946
- ★Harold Russell/*The Best Years of Our Lives*
- Charles Coburn/*The Green Years*
- William Demarest/*The Jolson Story*
- Claude Rains/*Notorious*
- Clifton Webb/*The Razor's Edge*

1947
- ★Edmund Gwenn/*Miracle on 34th Street*
- Thomas Gomez/*Ride the Pink Horse*
- *Ride the Pink Horse*
- Robert Ryan/*Crossfire*
- Richard Widmark/*Kiss of Death*

1948
- ★Walter Huston/*Treasure of the Sierra Madre*
- Charles Bickford/*Johnny Belinda*
- Jose Ferrer/*Joan of Arc*
- Oscar Homolka/*I Remember Mama*

1949
- ★Dean Jagger/*Twelve o'Clock High*
- John Ireland/*All the King's Men*
- Cecil Kellaway/*The Luck of the Irish*
- Arthur Kennedy/*Champion*
- Ralph Richardson/*The Heiress*
- James Whitmore/*Battleground*

1950
- ★George Sanders/*All About Eve*
- Jeff Chandler/*Broken Arrow*
- Edmund Gwenn/*Mister 880*
- Sam Jaffe/*The Asphalt Jungle*
- Erich von Stroheim/*Sunset Boulevard*

1951
- ★Karl Malden/*A Streetcar Named Desire*
- Leo Genn/*Quo Vadis*
- Kevin McCarthy/*Death of a Salesman*
- Peter Ustinov/*Quo Vadis*

1952
- ★Anthony Quinn/*Viva Zapata!*
- Richard Burton/*My Cousin Rachel*
- Victor McLaglen/*The Quiet Man*
- Jack Palance/*Sudden Fear*

1953
- ★Frank Sinatra/*From Here to Eternity*
- Eddie Albert/*Roman Holiday*
- Brandon de Wilde/*Shane*
- Jack Palance/*Shane*
- Robert Strauss/*Stalag 17*

1954
- ★Edmond O'Brien/*The Barefoot Contessa*
- Lee J. Cobb/*On the Waterfront*
- Karl Malden/*On the Waterfront*
- Rod Steiger/*On the Waterfront*
- Tom Tully/*The Caine Mutiny*

1955
- ★Jack Lemmon/*Mister Roberts*
- Arthur Kennedy/*Trial*
- Joe Mantell/*Marty*
- Sal Mineo/*Rebel without a Cause*
- Arthur O'Connell/*Picnic*
- *Trial*

1956
- ★Anthony Quinn/*Lust for Life*
- Don Murray/*Bus Stop*
- Anthony Perkins/*Friendly Persuasion*
- Robert Stack/*Written on the Wind*

1957
- ★Red Buttons/*Sayonara*
- Vittorio De Sica/*A Farewell to Arms*
- Sessue Hayakawa/*The Bridge on the River Kwai*
- Arthur Kennedy/*Peyton Place*
- Russ Tamblyn/*Peyton Place*

1958
- ★Burl Ives/*The Big Country*
- Theodore Bikel/*The Defiant Ones*
- Lee J. Cobb/*The Brothers Karamazov*
- Arthur Kennedy/*Some Came Running*
- Gig Young/*Teacher's Pet*

1959
- ★Hugh Griffith/*Ben-Hur*
- Arthur O'Connell/*Anatomy of a Murder*
- George C. Scott/*Anatomy of a Murder*
- Robert Vaughn/*The Young Philadelphians*
- Ed Wynn/*The Diary of Anne Frank*

1960
- ★Peter Ustinov/*Spartacus*
- Peter Falk/*Murder, Inc.*
- Trevor Howard/*Sons and Lovers*
- Jack Kruschen/*The Apartment*
- Sal Mineo/*Exodus*
- Chill Wills/*The Alamo*

1961
- ★George Chakiris/*West Side Story*
- Montgomery Clift/*Judgment at Nuremberg*
- Peter Falk/*Pocketful of Miracles*
- Jackie Gleason/*The Hustler*
- George C. Scott/*The Hustler*

1962
- ★Ed Begley, Sr./*Sweet Bird of Youth*
- Victor Buono/*What Ever Happened to Baby Jane?*
- Telly Savalas/*Birdman of Alcatraz*
- Omar Sharif/*Lawrence of Arabia*
- Terence Stamp/*Billy Budd*

1963
- ★Melvyn Douglas/*Hud*
- Nick Adams/*Twilight of Honor*
- Bobby Darin/*Captain Newman, M.D.*
- Hugh Griffith/*Tom Jones*
- John Huston/*The Cardinal*

1964
- ★Peter Ustinov/*Topkapi*
- John Gielgud/*Becket*
- Stanley Holloway/*My Fair Lady*
- Edmond O'Brien/*Seven Days in May*
- Lee Tracy/*The Best Man*

1965
- ★Martin Balsam/*A Thousand Clowns*
- Ian Bannen/*The Flight of the Phoenix*
- Tom Courtenay/*Doctor Zhivago*
- Michael Dunn/*Ship of Fools*
- Frank Finlay/*Othello*

1966
- ★Walter Matthau/*The Fortune Cookie*
- Mako/*The Sand Pebbles*
- James Mason/*Georgy Girl*
- George Segal/*Who's Afraid of Virginia Woolf?*
- Robert Shaw/*A Man for All Seasons*

1967
- ★George Kennedy/*Cool Hand Luke*
- John Cassavetes/*The Dirty Dozen*
- Gene Hackman/*Bonnie & Clyde*
- Cecil Kellaway/*Guess Who's Coming to Dinner*
- Michael J. Pollard/*Bonnie & Clyde*

1968
- ★Jack Albertson/*The Subject Was Roses*
- Seymour Cassel/*Faces*
- Daniel Massey/*Star!*
- Jack Wild/*Oliver!*
- Gene Wilder/*The Producers*

1969
- ★Gig Young/*They Shoot Horses, Don't They?*
- Rupert Crosse/*The Reivers*
- Elliott Gould/*Bob & Carol & Ted & Alice*
- Jack Nicholson/*Easy Rider*
- Anthony Quayle/*Anne of the Thousand Days*

1970
- ★John Mills/*Ryan's Daughter*
- Richard S. Castellano/*Lovers and Other Strangers*
- Chief Dan George/*Little Big Man*
- Gene Hackman/*I Never Sang for My Father*
- John Marley/*Love Story*

1971
- ★Ben Johnson/*The Last Picture Show*
- Jeff Bridges/*The Last Picture Show*
- Leonard Frey/*Fiddler on the Roof*
- Richard Jaeckel/*Sometimes a Great Notion*
- Roy Scheider/*The French Connection*

1972
- ★Joel Grey/*Cabaret*
- Eddie Albert/*The Heartbreak Kid*
- James Caan/*The Godfather*
- Robert Duvall/*The Godfather*
- Al Pacino/*The Godfather*

1973
- ★John Houseman/*The Paper Chase*
- Vincent Gardenia/*Bang the Drum Slowly*
- Jack Gilford/*Save the Tiger*
- Jason Miller/*The Exorcist*
- Randy Quaid/*The Last Detail*

1974
- ★Robert De Niro/*The Godfather, Part 2*
- Fred Astaire/*The Towering Inferno*
- Jeff Bridges/*Thunderbolt & Lightfoot*
- Michael V. Gazzo/*The Godfather, Part 2*
- Lee Strasberg/*The Godfather, Part 2*

1975
- ★George Burns/*The Sunshine Boys*
- Brad Dourif/*One Flew Over the Cuckoo's Nest*
- Burgess Meredith/*The Day of the Locust*
- Chris Sarandon/*Dog Day Afternoon*
- Jack Warden/*Shampoo*

1976
- ★Jason Robards, Jr./*All the President's Men*
- Ned Beatty/*Network*
- Burgess Meredith/*Rocky*
- Laurence Olivier/*Marathon Man*
- Burt Young/*Rocky*

1977
- ★Jason Robards, Jr./*Julia*
- Mikhail Baryshnikov/*The Turning Point*
- Peter Firth/*Equus*
- Alec Guinness/*Star Wars*
- Maximilian Schell/*Julia*

1978
- ★Christopher Walken/*The Deer Hunter*
- Bruce Dern/*Coming Home*
- Richard Farnsworth/*Comes a Horseman*
- John Hurt/*Midnight Express*
- Jack Warden/*Heaven Can Wait*

1979
- ★Melvyn Douglas/*Being There*
- Robert Duvall/*Apocalypse Now*
- Frederic Forrest/*The Rose*
- Justin Henry/*Kramer vs. Kramer*
- Mickey Rooney/*The Black Stallion*

1980
- ★Timothy Hutton/*Ordinary People*
- Judd Hirsch/*Ordinary People*
- Michael O'Keefe/*The Great Santini*
- Joe Pesci/*Raging Bull*
- Jason Robards, Jr./*Melvin and Howard*

1981
- ★John Gielgud/*Arthur*
- James Coco/*Only When I Laugh*
- Ian Holm/*Chariots of Fire*
- Jack Nicholson/*Reds*
- Howard E. Rollins, Jr./*Ragtime*

1982
- ★Louis Gossett, Jr./*An Officer and a Gentleman*
- Charles Durning/*The Best Little Whorehouse in Texas*
- John Lithgow/*The World According to Garp*
- James Mason/*The Verdict*
- Robert Preston/*Victor/Victoria*

1983
- ★Jack Nicholson/*Terms of Endearment*
- Charles Durning/*To Be or Not to Be*
- John Lithgow/*Terms of Endearment*
- Sam Shepard/*The Right Stuff*
- Rip Torn/*Cross Creek*

1984
- ★Haing S. Ngor/*The Killing Fields*
- Adolph Caesar/*A Soldier's Story*
- John Malkovich/*Places in the Heart*
- Noriyuki 'Pat' Morita/*The Karate Kid*
- Ralph Richardson/*Greystoke: The Legend of Tarzan, Lord of the Apes*

1985
- ★Don Ameche/*Cocoon*
- Klaus Maria Brandauer/*Out of Africa*
- William Hickey/*Prizzi's Honor*
- Robert Loggia/*The Jagged Edge*
- Eric Roberts/*Runaway Train*

1986
- ★Michael Caine/*Hannah and Her Sisters*
- Tom Berenger/*Platoon*
- Willem Dafoe/*Platoon*
- Denholm Elliott/*A Room with a View*
- Dennis Hopper/*Hoosiers*

1987
- ★Sean Connery/*The Untouchables*
- Albert Brooks/*Broadcast News*
- Morgan Freeman/*Street Smart*
- Vincent Gardenia/*Moonstruck*
- Denzel Washington/*Cry Freedom*

1988
- ★Kevin Kline/*A Fish Called Wanda*
- Martin Landau/*Tucker: The Man and His Dream*
- River Phoenix/*Running on Empty*
- Dean Stockwell/*Married to the Mob*

1989
- ★Denzel Washington/*Glory*
- Danny Aiello/*Do the Right Thing*
- Dan Aykroyd/*Driving Miss Daisy*
- Marlon Brando/*A Dry White Season*
- Martin Landau/*Crimes & Misdemeanors*

1990
- ★Joe Pesci/*Goodfellas*
- Bruce Davison/*Longtime Companion*
- Andy Garcia/*The Godfather, Part 3*
- Graham Greene/*Dances with Wolves*
- Al Pacino/*Dick Tracy*

1991
- ★Jack Palance/*City Slickers*
- Tommy Lee Jones/*JFK*
- Harvey Keitel/*Bugsy*
- Ben Kingsley/*Bugsy*
- Michael Lerner/*Barton Fink*

★ = winner

1992

★Gene Hackman/*Unforgiven*

Jaye Davidson/*The Crying Game*

Jack Nicholson/*A Few Good Men*

Al Pacino/*Glengarry Glen Ross*

David Paymer/*Mr. Saturday Night*

1993

★Tommy Lee Jones/*The Fugitive*

Leonardo DiCaprio/*What's Eating Gilbert Grape*

Ralph Fiennes/*Schindler's List*

John Malkovich/*In the Line of Fire*

Pete Postlethwaite/*In the Name of the Father*

1994

★Martin Landau/*Ed Wood*

Samuel L. Jackson/*Pulp Fiction*

Chazz Palminteri/*Bullets over Broadway*

Paul Scofield/*Quiz Show*

Gary Sinise/*Forrest Gump*

1995

★Kevin Spacey/*The Usual Suspects*

James Cromwell/*Babe*

Ed Harris/*Apollo 13*

Brad Pitt/*12 Monkeys*

Tim Roth/*Rob Roy*

1996

★Cuba Gooding, Jr./*Jerry Maguire*

William H. Macy/*Fargo*

Armin Mueller-Stahl/*Shine*

Edward Norton/*Primal Fear*

James Woods/*Ghosts of Mississippi*

1997

★Robin Williams/*Good Will Hunting*

Robert Forster/*Jackie Brown*

Anthony Hopkins/*Amistad*

Greg Kinnear/*As Good As It Gets*

Burt Reynolds/*Boogie Nights*

1998

★James Coburn/*Affliction*

Robert Duvall/*A Civil Action*

Ed Harris/*The Truman Show*

Geoffrey Rush/*Shakespeare in Love*

Billy Bob Thornton/*A Simple Plan*

1999

★Michael Caine/*The Cider House Rules*

Tom Cruise/*Magnolia*

Michael Clarke Duncan/*The Green Mile*

Jude Law/*The Talented Mr. Ripley*

Haley Joel Osment/*The Sixth Sense*

2000

★Benicio Del Toro/*Traffic*

Jeff Bridges/*The Contender*

Willem Dafoe/*Shadow of the Vampire*

Albert Finney/*Erin Brockovich*

Joaquin Rafael (Leaf) Phoenix/*Gladiator*

2001

★Jim Broadbent/*Iris*

Ethan Hawke/*Training Day*

Ben Kingsley/*Sexy Beast*

Ian McKellen/*Lord of the Rings: The Fellowship of the Ring*

Jon Voight/*Ali*

2002

★Chris Cooper/*Adaptation*

Ed Harris/*The Hours*

Paul Newman/*Road to Perdition*

John C. Reilly/*Chicago*

Christopher Walken/*Catch Me If You Can*

2003

★Tim Robbins/*Mystic River*

Alec Baldwin/*The Cooler*

Benicio Del Toro/*21 Grams*

Djimon Hounsou/*In America*

Ken(saku) Watanabe/*The Last Samurai*

2004

★Morgan Freeman/*Million Dollar Baby*

Alan Alda/*The Aviator*

Thomas Haden Church/*Sideways*

Jamie Foxx/*Collateral*

Clive Owen/*Closer*

2005

★George Clooney/*Syriana*

Matt Dillon/*Crash*

Paul Giamatti/*Cinderella Man*

Jake Gyllenhaal/*Brokeback Mountain*

William Hurt/*A History of Violence*

2006

★Alan Arkin/*Little Miss Sunshine*

Jackie Earle Haley/*Little Children*

Djimon Hounsou/*Blood Diamond*

Eddie Murphy/*Dreamgirls*

Mark Wahlberg/*The Departed*

2007

★Javier Bardem/*No Country for Old Men*

Casey Affleck/*The Assassination of Jesse James by the Coward Robert Ford*

Philip Seymour Hoffman/*Charlie Wilson's War*

Hal Holbrook/*Into the Wild*

Tom Wilkinson/*Michael Clayton*

2008

★Heath Ledger/*The Dark Knight*

Josh Brolin/*Milk*

Robert Downey, Jr./*Tropic Thunder*

Philip Seymour Hoffman/*Doubt*

Michael Shannon/*Revolutionary Road*

2009

★Christoph Waltz/*Inglourious Basterds*

Matt Damon/*Invictus*

Woody Harrelson/*The Messenger*

Christopher Plummer/*The Last Station*

Stanley Tucci/*The Lovely Bones*

2010

★Christian Bale/*The Fighter*

John Hawkes/*Winter's Bone*

Jeremy Renner/*The Town*

Mark Ruffalo/*The Kids Are All Right*

Geoffrey Rush/*The King's Speech*

2011

★Christopher Plummer/*Beginners*

Kenneth Branagh/*My Week With Marilyn*

Jonah Hill/*Moneyball*

Nick Nolte/*Warrior*

Max von Sydow/*Extremely Loud and Incredibly Close*

2012

★Christoph Waltz/*Django Unchained*

Alan Arkin/*Argo*

Robert De Niro/*Silver Linings Playbook*

Philip Seymour Hoffman/*The Master*

Tommy Lee Jones/*Lincoln*

2013

★Jared Leto/*Dallas Buyers Club*

Barkhad Adbi/*Captain Phillips*

Bradley Cooper/*American Hustle*

Michael Fassbender/*12 Years a Slave*

Jonah Hill/*The Wolf of Wall Street*

2014

★J.K. Simmons/*Whiplash*

Robert Duvall/*The Judge*

Ethan Hawke/*Boyhood*

Edward Norton/*Birdman, or (The Unexpected Virtue of Ignorance)*

Mark Ruffalo/*Foxcatcher*

2015

★Mark Rylance/*Bridge of Spies*

Christian Bale/*The Big Short*

Tom (Thomas) Hardy/*The Revenant*

Mark Ruffalo/*Spotlight*

Sylvester Stallone/*Creed*

2016

★Mahershala Ali/*Moonlight*

Jeff Bridges/*Hell or High Water*

Lucas Hedges/*Manchester by the Sea*

Dev Patel/*Lion*

Michael Shannon/*Nocturnal Animals*

2017

★Sam Rockwell/*Three Billboards Outside Ebbing, Missouri*

Willem Dafoe/*The Florida Project*

Woody Harrelson/*Three Billboards Outside Ebbing, Missouri*

Richard Jenkins/*The Shape of Water*

Christopher Plummer/*All the Money in the World*

2018

★Mahershala Ali/*Green Book*

Adam Driver/*BlacKkKlansman*

Sam Elliott/*A Star Is Born*

Richard E. Grant/*Can You Ever Forgive Me?*

Sam Rockwell/*Vice*

2019

★Brad Pitt/*Once Upon A Time... In Hollywood*

Tom Hanks/*A Beautiful Day in the Neighborhood*

Anthony Hopkins/*The Two Popes*

Al Pacino/*The Irishman*

Joe Pesci/*The Irishman*

ACTRESS

1928

★Janet Gaynor/*7th Heaven*

★Janet Gaynor/*Street Angel*

★Janet Gaynor/*Sunrise*

Gloria Swanson/*Sadie Thompson*

1929

Ruth Chatterton/*Madame X*

Corinne Griffith/*The Divine Lady*

Bessie Love/*Broadway Melody*

Norma Shearer/*Their Own Desire*

1930

★Norma Shearer/*The Divorcee*

Greta Garbo/*Anna Christie*

Greta Garbo/*Romance*

1931

★Marie Dressler/*Min & Bill*

Marlene Dietrich/*Morocco*

Irene Dunne/*Cimarron*

Norma Shearer/*A Free Soul*

1932

★Helen Hayes/*The Sin of Madelon Claudet*

Marie Dressler/*Emma*

1933

★Katharine Hepburn/*Morning Glory*

May Robson/*Lady for a Day*

Diana Wynyard/*Cavalcade*

1934

★Claudette Colbert/*It Happened One Night*

Bette Davis/*Of Human Bondage*

Norma Shearer/*The Barretts of Wimpole Street*

1935

★Bette Davis/*Dangerous*

Katharine Hepburn/*Alice Adams*

Miriam Hopkins/*Becky Sharp*

1936

★Luise Rainer/*The Great Ziegfeld*

Irene Dunne/*Theodora Goes Wild*

Carole Lombard/*My Man Godfrey*

Norma Shearer/*Romeo and Juliet*

1937

★Luise Rainer/*The Good Earth*

Irene Dunne/*The Awful Truth*

Greta Garbo/*Camille*

Janet Gaynor/*A Star Is Born*

Barbara Stanwyck/*Stella Dallas*

1938

★Bette Davis/*Jezebel*

Wendy Hiller/*Pygmalion*

Norma Shearer/*Marie Antoinette*

Margaret Sullavan/*Three Comrades*

1939

★Vivien Leigh/*Gone with the Wind*

Bette Davis/*Dark Victory*

Irene Dunne/*Love Affair*

Greta Garbo/*Ninotchka*

Greer Garson/*Goodbye, Mr. Chips*

1940

★Ginger Rogers/*Kitty Foyle*

Bette Davis/*The Letter*

Joan Fontaine/*Rebecca*

Katharine Hepburn/*The Philadelphia Story*

Martha Scott/*Our Town*

1941

★Joan Fontaine/*Suspicion*

Bette Davis/*The Little Foxes*

Greer Garson/*Blossoms in the Dust*

Barbara Stanwyck/*Ball of Fire*

1942

★Greer Garson/*Mrs. Miniver*

Bette Davis/*Now, Voyager*

Olivia de Havilland/*Hold Back the Dawn*

Katharine Hepburn/*Woman of the Year*

Rosalind Russell/*My Sister Eileen*

Teresa Wright/*The Pride of the Yankees*

1943

★Jennifer Jones/*The Song of Bernadette*

Jean Arthur/*The More the Merrier*

Ingrid Bergman/*For Whom the Bell Tolls*

Joan Fontaine/*The Constant Nymph*

Greer Garson/*Madame Curie*

1944

★Ingrid Bergman/*Gaslight*

Claudette Colbert/*Since You Went Away*

Bette Davis/*Mr. Skeffington*

Greer Garson/*Mrs. Parkington*

Barbara Stanwyck/*Double Indemnity*

1945

★Joan Crawford/*Mildred Pierce*

Ingrid Bergman/*The Bells of St. Mary's*

Greer Garson/*The Valley of Decision*

Jennifer Jones/*Love Letters*

Gene Tierney/*Leave Her to Heaven*

1946

Celia Johnson/*Brief Encounter*

Jennifer Jones/*Duel in the Sun*

Jane Wyman/*The Yearling*

1947

Joan Crawford/*The Possessed*

Susan Hayward/*Smash-Up: The Story of a Woman*

Dorothy McGuire/*Gentleman's Agreement*

1948

★Jane Wyman/*Johnny Belinda*

Ingrid Bergman/*Joan of Arc*

Olivia de Havilland/*The Snake Pit*

Irene Dunne/*I Remember Mama*

Barbara Stanwyck/*Sorry, Wrong Number*

1949

★Olivia de Havilland/*The Heiress*

Jeanne Crain/*Pinky*

Deborah Kerr/*Edward, My Son*

Loretta Young/*Come to the Stable*

1950

★Judy Holliday/*Born Yesterday*

Anne Baxter/*All About Eve*

Bette Davis/*All About Eve*

Eleanor Parker/*Caged*

Gloria Swanson/*Sunset Boulevard*

1951

★Vivien Leigh/*A Streetcar Named Desire*

Katharine Hepburn/*The African Queen*

Eleanor Parker/*Detective Story*

Shelley Winters/*A Place in the Sun*

1952

★Shirley Booth/*Come Back, Little Sheba*

Joan Crawford/*Sudden Fear*

Bette Davis/*The Star*

Julie Harris/*The Member of the Wedding*

Susan Hayward/*With a Song in My Heart*

1953

★Audrey Hepburn/*Roman Holiday*

Leslie Caron/*Lili*

Ava Gardner/*Mogambo*

Deborah Kerr/*From Here to Eternity*

Maggie McNamara/*The Moon Is Blue*

1954

★Grace Kelly/*Country Girl*

Dorothy Dandridge/*Carmen Jones*

Judy Garland/*A Star Is Born*

Audrey Hepburn/*Sabrina*

Jane Wyman/*Magnificent Obsession*

1955

★Anna Magnani/*The Rose Tattoo*

Susan Hayward/*I'll Cry Tomorrow*

Katharine Hepburn/*Summertime*

Jennifer Jones/*Love Is a Many-Splendored Thing*

Eleanor Parker/*Interrupted Melody*

1956

★Ingrid Bergman/*Anastasia*

Carroll Baker/*Baby Doll*

Katharine Hepburn/*The Rainmaker*

Nancy Kelly/*The Bad Seed*

Deborah Kerr/*The King and I*

1957

★Joanne Woodward/*The Three Faces of Eve*

Deborah Kerr/*Heaven Knows, Mr. Allison*

Anna Magnani/*Wild Is the Wind*

Elizabeth Taylor/*Raintree County*

Lana Turner/*Peyton Place*

1958

★Susan Hayward/*I Want to Live!*

Deborah Kerr/*Separate Tables*

Shirley MacLaine/*Some Came Running*

Rosalind Russell/*Auntie Mame*

Elizabeth Taylor/*Cat on a Hot Tin Roof*

1959

★Simone Signoret/*Room at the Top*

Doris Day/*Pillow Talk*

Audrey Hepburn/*The Nun's Story*

Katharine Hepburn/*Suddenly, Last Summer*

Elizabeth Taylor/*Suddenly, Last Summer*

1960

★Elizabeth Taylor/*Butterfield 8*

Greer Garson/*Sunrise at Campobello*

Deborah Kerr/*The Sundowners*

Shirley MacLaine/*The Apartment*

Melina Mercouri/*Never on Sunday*

★ = *winner*

1961

★Sophia Loren/*Two Women*

Audrey Hepburn/*Breakfast at Tiffany's*

Piper Laurie/*The Hustler*

Geraldine Page/*Summer and Smoke*

Natalie Wood/*Splendor in the Grass*

1962

★Anne Bancroft/*The Miracle Worker*

Bette Davis/*What Ever Happened to Baby Jane?*

Katharine Hepburn/*Long Day's Journey into Night*

Geraldine Page/*Sweet Bird of Youth*

Lee Remick/*Days of Wine and Roses*

1963

★Patricia Neal/*Hud*

Shirley MacLaine/*Irma La Douce*

Rachel Roberts/*This Sporting Life*

1964

★Julie Andrews/*Mary Poppins*

Anne Bancroft/*The Pumpkin Eater*

Sophia Loren/*Marriage Italian Style*

Debbie Reynolds/*The Unsinkable Molly Brown*

Kim Stanley/*Seance on a Wet Afternoon*

1965

★Julie Christie/*Darling*

Julie Andrews/*The Sound of Music*

Samantha Eggar/*The Collector*

Elizabeth Hartman/*A Patch of Blue*

Simone Signoret/*Ship of Fools*

1966

★Elizabeth Taylor/*Who's Afraid of Virginia Woolf?*

Anouk Aimee/*A Man and a Woman*

Edith Evans/*The Whisperers*

Ida Kaminska/*The Shop on Main Street*

Lynn Redgrave/*Georgy Girl*

Vanessa Redgrave/*Morgan: A Suitable Case for Treatment*

1967

★Katharine Hepburn/*Guess Who's Coming to Dinner*

Anne Bancroft/*The Graduate*

Faye Dunaway/*Bonnie & Clyde*

Audrey Hepburn/*Wait until Dark*

1968

★Katharine Hepburn/*The Lion in Winter*

★Barbra Streisand/*Funny Girl*

Patricia Neal/*The Subject Was Roses*

Joanne Woodward/*Rachel, Rachel*

1969

★Maggie Smith/*The Prime of Miss Jean Brodie*

Genevieve Bujold/*Anne of the Thousand Days*

Jane Fonda/*They Shoot Horses, Don't They?*

Liza Minnelli/*The Sterile Cuckoo*

Jean Simmons/*The Happy Ending*

1970

★Glenda Jackson/*Women in Love*

Jane Alexander/*The Great White Hope*

Ali MacGraw/*Love Story*

Sarah Miles/*Ryan's Daughter*

1971

★Jane Fonda/*Klute*

Julie Christie/*McCabe & Mrs. Miller*

Glenda Jackson/*Sunday, Bloody Sunday*

Vanessa Redgrave/*Mary, Queen of Scots*

Janet Suzman/*Nicholas and Alexandra*

1972

★Liza Minnelli/*Cabaret*

Diana Ross/*Lady Sings the Blues*

Maggie Smith/*Travels with My Aunt*

Cicely Tyson/*Sounder*

1973

★Glenda Jackson/*A Touch of Class*

Ellen Burstyn/*The Exorcist*

Marsha Mason/*Cinderella Liberty*

Barbra Streisand/*The Way We Were*

Joanne Woodward/*Summer Wishes, Winter Dreams*

1974

★Ellen Burstyn/*Alice Doesn't Live Here Anymore*

Faye Dunaway/*Chinatown*

Valerie Perrine/*Lenny*

Gena Rowlands/*A Woman under the Influence*

1975

★Louise Fletcher/*One Flew Over the Cuckoo's Nest*

Isabelle Adjani/*The Story of Adele H.*

Ann-Margret/*Tommy*

Carol Kane/*Hester Street*

1976

★Faye Dunaway/*Network*

Marie-Christine Barrault/*Cousin, Cousine*

Talia Shire/*Rocky*

Sissy Spacek/*Carrie*

Liv Ullmann/*Face to Face*

1977

★Diane Keaton/*Annie Hall*

Anne Bancroft/*The Turning Point*

Jane Fonda/*Julia*

Shirley MacLaine/*The Turning Point*

Marsha Mason/*The Goodbye Girl*

1978

★Jane Fonda/*Coming Home*

Ingrid Bergman/*Autumn Sonata*

Ellen Burstyn/*Same Time, Next Year*

Jill Clayburgh/*An Unmarried Woman*

Geraldine Page/*Interiors*

1979

★Sally Field/*Norma Rae*

Jill Clayburgh/*Starting Over*

Jane Fonda/*The China Syndrome*

Marsha Mason/*Chapter Two*

Bette Midler/*The Rose*

1980

★Sissy Spacek/*Coal Miner's Daughter*

Ellen Burstyn/*Resurrection*

Goldie Hawn/*Private Benjamin*

Mary Tyler Moore/*Ordinary People*

Gena Rowlands/*Gloria*

1981

★Katharine Hepburn/*On Golden Pond*

Diane Keaton/*Reds*

Marsha Mason/*Only When I Laugh*

Susan Sarandon/*Atlantic City*

Meryl Streep/*The French Lieutenant's Woman*

1982

★Meryl Streep/*Sophie's Choice*

Julie Andrews/*Victor/Victoria*

Jessica Lange/*Frances*

Sissy Spacek/*Missing*

Debra Winger/*An Officer and a Gentleman*

1983

★Shirley MacLaine/*Terms of Endearment*

Jane Alexander/*Testament*

Meryl Streep/*Silkwood*

Julie Walters/*Educating Rita*

Debra Winger/*Terms of Endearment*

1984

★Sally Field/*Places in the Heart*

Judy Davis/*A Passage to India*

Jessica Lange/*Country*

Vanessa Redgrave/*The Bostonians*

Sissy Spacek/*The River*

1985

★Geraldine Page/*The Trip to Bountiful*

Anne Bancroft/*Agnes of God*

Whoopi Goldberg/*The Color Purple*

Jessica Lange/*Sweet Dreams*

Meryl Streep/*Out of Africa*

1986

★Marlee Matlin/*Children of a Lesser God*

Jane Fonda/*The Morning After*

Sissy Spacek/*Crimes of the Heart*

Kathleen Turner/*Peggy Sue Got Married*

Sigourney Weaver/*Aliens*

1987

★Cher/*Moonstruck*

Glenn Close/*Fatal Attraction*

Holly Hunter/*Broadcast News*

Sally Kirkland/*Anna*

Meryl Streep/*Ironweed*

1988

★Jodie Foster/*The Accused*

Glenn Close/*Dangerous Liaisons*

Melanie Griffith/*Working Girl*

Meryl Streep/*A Cry in the Dark*

Sigourney Weaver/*Gorillas in the Mist*

1989

★Jessica Tandy/*Driving Miss Daisy*

Isabelle Adjani/*Camille Claudel*

Pauline Collins/*Shirley Valentine*

Jessica Lange/*Music Box*

Michelle Pfeiffer/*The Fabulous Baker Boys*

1990

★Kathy Bates/*Misery*

Anjelica Huston/*The Grifters*

Julia Roberts/*Pretty Woman*

Meryl Streep/*Postcards from the Edge*

Joanne Woodward/*Mr. & Mrs. Bridge*

1991

★Jodie Foster/*The Silence of the Lambs*

Geena Davis/*Thelma & Louise*

Laura Dern/*Rambling Rose*

Bette Midler/*For the Boys*

Susan Sarandon/*Thelma & Louise*

1992

★Emma Thompson/*Howard's End*

Catherine Deneuve/*Indochine*

Mary McDonnell/*Passion Fish*

Michelle Pfeiffer/*Love Field*

Susan Sarandon/*Lorenzo's Oil*

1993

★Holly Hunter/*The Piano*

Angela Bassett/*What's Love Got to Do with It?*

Stockard Channing/*Six Degrees of Separation*

Emma Thompson/*The Remains of the Day*

Debra Winger/*Shadowlands*

1994

★Jessica Lange/*Blue Sky*

Jodie Foster/*Nell*

Miranda Richardson/*Tom & Viv*

Winona Ryder/*Little Women*

Susan Sarandon/*The Client*

1995

★Susan Sarandon/*Dead Man Walking*

Elisabeth Shue/*Leaving Las Vegas*

Sharon Stone/*Casino*

Meryl Streep/*The Bridges of Madison County*

Emma Thompson/*Sense and Sensibility*

1996

★Frances McDormand/*Fargo*

Brenda Blethyn/*Secrets and Lies*

Diane Keaton/*Marvin's Room*

Kristin Scott Thomas/*The English Patient*

Emily Watson/*Breaking the Waves*

1997

★Helen Hunt/*As Good As It Gets*

Helena Bonham Carter/*The Wings of the Dove*

Julie Christie/*Afterglow*

Dame Judi Dench/*Mrs. Brown*

Kate Winslet/*Titanic*

1998

★Gwyneth Paltrow/*Shakespeare in Love*

Cate Blanchett/*Elizabeth*

Fernanda Montenegro/*Central Station*

Meryl Streep/*One True Thing*

Emily Watson/*Hilary and Jackie*

1999

★Hilary Swank/*Boys Don't Cry*

Annette Bening/*American Beauty*

Janet McTeer/*Tumbleweeds*

Julianne Moore/*The End of the Affair*

Meryl Streep/*Music of the Heart*

2000

★Julia Roberts/*Erin Brockovich*

Joan Allen/*The Contender*

Juliette Binoche/*Chocolat*

Ellen Burstyn/*Requiem for a Dream*

Laura Linney/*You Can Count On Me*

2001

★Halle Berry/*Monster's Ball*

Dame Judi Dench/*Iris*

Nicole Kidman/*Moulin Rouge*

Sissy Spacek/*In the Bedroom*

Renée Zellweger/*Bridget Jones's Diary*

2002

★Nicole Kidman/*The Hours*

Salma Hayek/*Frida*

Diane Lane/*Unfaithful*

Julianne Moore/*Far from Heaven*

Renée Zellweger/*Chicago*

2003

★Charlize Theron/*Monster*

Keisha Castle-Hughes/*Whale Rider*

Diane Keaton/*Something's Gotta Give*

Naomi Watts/*21 Grams*

2004

★Hilary Swank/*Million Dollar Baby*

Annette Bening/*Being Julia*

Catalina Sandino Moreno/*Maria Full of Grace*

Imelda Staunton/*Vera Drake*

Kate Winslet/*Eternal Sunshine of the Spotless Mind*

2005

★Reese Witherspoon/*Walk the Line*

Dame Judi Dench/*Mrs. Henderson Presents*

Felicity Huffman/*Transamerica*

Keira Knightley/*Pride and Prejudice*

Charlize Theron/*North Country*

2006

★Dame Helen Mirren/*The Queen*

Penelope Cruz/*Volver*

Dame Judi Dench/*Notes on a Scandal*

Meryl Streep/*The Devil Wears Prada*

Kate Winslet/*Little Children*

2007

★Marion Cotillard/*La Vie en Rose*

Cate Blanchett/*Elizabeth: The Golden Age*

Julie Christie/*Away From Her*

Laura Linney/*The Savages*

Ellen Page/*Juno*

2008

★Kate Winslet/*The Reader*

Anne Hathaway/*Rachel Getting Married*

Angelina Jolie/*Changeling*

Melissa Leo/*Frozen River*

Meryl Streep/*Doubt*

2009

★Sandra Bullock/*The Blind Side*

Dame Helen Mirren/*The Last Station*

Carey Mulligan/*An Education*

Gabourney 'Gabby' Sidibe/*Precious: Based on the Novel 'Push' by Sapphire*

Meryl Streep/*Julie & Julia*

2010

★Natalie Portman/*Black Swan*

Annette Bening/*The Kids Are All Right*

Nicole Kidman/*Rabbit Hole*

Jennifer Lawrence/*Winter's Bone*

Michelle Williams/*Blue Valentine*

2011

★Meryl Streep/*The Iron Lady*

Glenn Close/*Albert Nobbs*

Viola Davis/*The Help*

Rooney Mara/*The Girl With the Dragon Tattoo*

Michelle Williams/*My Week With Marilyn*

2012

★Jennifer Lawrence/*Silver Linings Playbook*

Jessica Chastain/*Zero Dark Thirty*

Emmanuelle Riva/*Amour*

Quvenzhane Wallis/*Beasts of the Southern Wild*

Naomi Watts/*The Impossible*

2013

★Cate Blanchett/*Blue Jasmine*

★Sandra Bullock/*Gravity*

Amy Adams/*American Hustle*

Dame Judi Dench/*Philomena*

Meryl Streep/*August: Osage County*

2014

★Julianne Moore/*Still Alice*

Marion Cotillard/*Two Days, One Night*

Felicity Jones/*The Theory of Everything*

Rosamund Pike/*Gone Girl*

Reese Witherspoon/*Wild*

2015

★Brie Larson/*Room*

Cate Blanchett/*Carol*

Jennifer Lawrence/*Joy*

Charlotte Rampling/*45 Years*

Saoirse Ronan/*Brooklyn*

2016

★Emma Stone/*La La Land*

Isabelle Huppert/*Elle*

Ruth Negga/*Loving*

Natalie Portman/*Jackie*

Meryl Streep/*Florence Foster Jenkins*

2017

★Frances McDormand/*Three Billboards Outside Ebbing, Missouri*

Sally Hawkins/*The Shape of Water*

Margot Robbie/*I, Tonya*

Saoirse Ronan/*Lady Bird*

Meryl Streep/*The Post*

2018

★Olivia Colman/*The Favourite*

Yalitza Aparicio/*Roma*

Glenn Close/*The Wife*

Lady Gaga/*A Star Is Born*

Melissa McCarthy/*Can You Ever Forgive Me?*

2019

★Renée Zellweger/*Judy*

Cynthia Erivo/*Harriet*

Scarlett Johansson/*Marriage Story*

Saoirse Ronan/*Little Women*

Charlize Theron/*Bombshell*

★ = winner

ACTRESS—SUPPORTING

1936
★Gale Sondergaard/*Anthony Adverse*
Beulah Bondi/*The Gorgeous Hussy*
Alice Brady/*My Man Godfrey*
Maria Ouspenskaya/*Dodsworth*

1937
★Alice Brady/*In Old Chicago*
Andrea Leeds/*Stage Door*
Anne Shirley/*Stella Dallas*
Claire Trevor/*Dead End*
May Whitty/*Night Must Fall*

1938
★Fay Bainter/*Jezebel*
Beulah Bondi/*Of Human Hearts*
Billie Burke/*Merrily We Live*
Spring Byington/*You Can't Take It with You*
Milza Korjus/*The Great Waltz*

1939
★Hattie McDaniel/*Gone with the Wind*
Olivia de Havilland/*Gone with the Wind*
Geraldine Fitzgerald/*Wuthering Heights*
Edna May Oliver/*Drums Along the Mohawk*
Maria Ouspenskaya/*Love Affair*

1940
★Jane Darwell/*The Grapes of Wrath*
Judith Anderson/*Rebecca*
Ruth Hussey/*The Philadelphia Story*
Barbara O'Neil/*All This and Heaven Too*
Marjorie Rambeau/*Primrose Path*

1941
★Mary Astor/*The Great Lie*
Sara Allgood/*How Green Was My Valley*
Patricia Collinge/*The Little Foxes*
Teresa Wright/*The Little Foxes*
Margaret Wycherly/*Sergeant York*

1942
★Teresa Wright/*Mrs. Miniver*
Gladys Cooper/*Now, Voyager*
Agnes Moorehead/*The Magnificent Ambersons*
Susan Peters/*Random Harvest*
May Whitty/*Mrs. Miniver*

1943
★Katina Paxinou/*For Whom the Bell Tolls*
Gladys Cooper/*The Song of Bernadette*
Paulette Goddard/*So Proudly We Hail*
Anne Revere/*The Song of Bernadette*
Lucile Watson/*Watch on the Rhine*

1944
★Ethel Barrymore/*None But the Lonely Heart*
Jennifer Jones/*Since You Went Away*
Angela Lansbury/*Gaslight*
Aline MacMahon/*Dragon Seed*
Agnes Moorehead/*Mrs. Parkington*

1945
★Anne Revere/*National Velvet*
Eve Arden/*Mildred Pierce*
Ann Blyth/*Mildred Pierce*
Angela Lansbury/*Picture of Dorian Gray*
Joan Lorring/*The Corn Is Green*

1946
★Anne Baxter/*The Razor's Edge*
Ethel Barrymore/*The Spiral Staircase*
Lillian Gish/*Duel in the Sun*
Flora Robson/*Saratoga Trunk*
Gale Sondergaard/*Anna and the King of Siam*

1947
★Celeste Holm/*Gentleman's Agreement*
Ethel Barrymore/*The Paradine Case*
Gloria Grahame/*Crossfire*
Marjorie Main/*Egg and I*
Anne Revere/*Gentleman's Agreement*

1948
★Claire Trevor/*Key Largo*
Barbara Bel Geddes/*I Remember Mama*
Ellen Corby/*I Remember Mama*
Agnes Moorehead/*Johnny Belinda*
Jean Simmons/*Hamlet*

1949
★Mercedes McCambridge/*All the King's Men*
Ethel Barrymore/*Pinky*
Celeste Holm/*Come to the Stable*
Elsa Lanchester/*Come to the Stable*
Ethel Waters/*Pinky*

1950
★Josephine Hull/*Harvey*
Hope Emerson/*Caged*
Celeste Holm/*All About Eve*
Nancy Olson/*Sunset Boulevard*
Thelma Ritter/*All About Eve*

1951
★Kim Hunter/*A Streetcar Named Desire*
Mildred Dunnock/*Death of a Salesman*
Lee Grant/*Detective Story*

1952
★Gloria Grahame/*The Bad and the Beautiful*
Jean Hagen/*Singin' in the Rain*
Colette Marchand/*Moulin Rouge*
Terry Moore/*Come Back, Little Sheba*
Thelma Ritter/*With a Song in My Heart*

1953
★Donna Reed/*From Here to Eternity*
Grace Kelly/*Mogambo*
Geraldine Page/*Hondo*
Marjorie Rambeau/*Torch Song*
Thelma Ritter/*Pickup on South Street*

1954
★Eva Marie Saint/*On the Waterfront*
Nina Foch/*Executive Suite*
Katy Jurado/*Broken Lance*
Jan Sterling/*The High and the Mighty*
Claire Trevor/*The High and the Mighty*

1955
★Jo Van Fleet/*East of Eden*
Betsy Blair/*Marty*
Peggy Lee/*Pete Kelly's Blues*
Marisa Pavan/*The Rose Tattoo*
Natalie Wood/*Rebel without a Cause*

1956
★Dorothy Malone/*Written on the Wind*
Mildred Dunnock/*Baby Doll*
Eileen Heckart/*The Bad Seed*
Mercedes McCambridge/*Giant*
Patty McCormack/*The Bad Seed*

1957
★Miyoshi Umeki/*Sayonara*
Elsa Lanchester/*Witness for the Prosecution*
Hope Lange/*Peyton Place*
Diane Varsi/*Peyton Place*

1958
★Wendy Hiller/*Separate Tables*
Peggy Cass/*Auntie Mame*
Martha Hyer/*Some Came Running*
Cara Williams/*The Defiant Ones*

1959
★Shelley Winters/*The Diary of Anne Frank*
Hermione Baddeley/*Room at the Top*
Susan Kohner/*Imitation of Life*
Juanita Moore/*Imitation of Life*
Thelma Ritter/*Pillow Talk*

1960
★Shirley Jones/*Elmer Gantry*
Glynis Johns/*The Sundowners*
Janet Leigh/*Psycho*
Mary Ure/*Sons and Lovers*

1961
★Rita Moreno/*West Side Story*
Fay Bainter/*The Children's Hour*
Judy Garland/*Judgment at Nuremberg*
Lotte Lenya/*Roman Spring of Mrs. Stone*
Una Merkel/*Summer and Smoke*

1962
★Patty Duke/*The Miracle Worker*
Mary Badham/*To Kill a Mockingbird*
Shirley Knight/*Sweet Bird of Youth*
Angela Lansbury/*The Manchurian Candidate*
Thelma Ritter/*Birdman of Alcatraz*

1963
★Margaret Rutherford/*The V.I.P.'s*
Diane Cilento/*Tom Jones*
Edith Evans/*Tom Jones*
Joyce Redman/*Tom Jones*
Lilia Skala/*Lilies of the Field*

1964
★Lila Kedrova/*Zorba the Greek*
Gladys Cooper/*My Fair Lady*
Edith Evans/*The Chalk Garden*
Grayson Hall/*The Night of the Iguana*
Agnes Moorehead/*Hush, Hush, Sweet Charlotte*

1965
★Shelley Winters/*A Patch of Blue*
Ruth Gordon/*Inside Daisy Clover*
Joyce Redman/*Othello*
Maggie Smith/*Othello*
Peggy Wood/*The Sound of Music*

1966
★Sandy Dennis/*Who's Afraid of Virginia Woolf?*
Wendy Hiller/*A Man for All Seasons*
Jocelyn Lagarde/*Hawaii*
Vivien Merchant/*Alfie*
Geraldine Page/*You're a Big Boy Now*

1967
★Estelle Parsons/*Bonnie & Clyde*
Carol Channing/*Thoroughly Modern Millie*
Mildred Natwick/*Barefoot in the Park*
Beah Richards/*Guess Who's Coming to Dinner*
Katharine Ross/*The Graduate*

1968
★Ruth Gordon/*Rosemary's Baby*
Lynn Carlin/*Faces*
Sondra Locke/*The Heart Is a Lonely Hunter*
Kay Medford/*Funny Girl*
Estelle Parsons/*Rachel, Rachel*

1969
★Goldie Hawn/*Cactus Flower*
Dyan Cannon/*Bob & Carol & Ted & Alice*
Sylvia Miles/*Midnight Cowboy*
Susannah York/*They Shoot Horses, Don't They?*

1970
★Helen Hayes/*Airport*
Karen Black/*Five Easy Pieces*
Sally Kellerman/*M*A*S*H*
Maureen Stapleton/*Airport*

1971
★Cloris Leachman/*The Last Picture Show*
Ann-Margret/*Carnal Knowledge*
Ellen Burstyn/*The Last Picture Show*
Margaret Leighton/*The Go-Between*

1972
★Eileen Heckart/*Butterflies Are Free*
Jeannie Berlin/*The Heartbreak Kid*
Geraldine Page/*Pete 'n' Tillie*
Susan Tyrrell/*Fat City*
Shelley Winters/*The Poseidon Adventure*

1973
★Tatum O'Neal/*Paper Moon*
Linda Blair/*The Exorcist*
Candy Clark/*American Graffiti*
Madeline Kahn/*Paper Moon*
Sylvia Sidney/*Summer Wishes, Winter Dreams*

1974
★Ingrid Bergman/*Murder on the Orient Express*
Valentina Cortese/*Day for Night*
Madeline Kahn/*Blazing Saddles*
Diane Ladd/*Alice Doesn't Live Here Anymore*
Talia Shire/*The Godfather, Part 2*

1975
★Lee Grant/*Shampoo*
Ronee Blakley/*Nashville*
Sylvia Miles/*Farewell, My Lovely*
Lily Tomlin/*Nashville*
Brenda Vaccaro/*Once Is Not Enough*

1976
★Beatrice Straight/*Network*
Jane Alexander/*All the President's Men*
Jodie Foster/*Taxi Driver*
Lee Grant/*Voyage of the Damned*
Piper Laurie/*Carrie*

1977
★Vanessa Redgrave/*Julia*
Leslie Browne/*The Turning Point*
Quinn Cummings/*The Goodbye Girl*
Melinda Dillon/*Close Encounters of the Third Kind*

1978
★Maggie Smith/*California Suite*
Dyan Cannon/*Heaven Can Wait*
Penelope Milford/*Coming Home*
Maureen Stapleton/*Interiors*
Meryl Streep/*The Deer Hunter*

1979
★Meryl Streep/*Kramer vs. Kramer*
Jane Alexander/*Kramer vs. Kramer*
Barbara Barrie/*Breaking Away*
Candice Bergen/*Starting Over*
Mariel Hemingway/*Manhattan*

1980
★Mary Steenburgen/*Melvin and Howard*
Eileen Brennan/*Private Benjamin*
Eva LeGallienne/*Resurrection*
Cathy Moriarty/*Raging Bull*
Diana Scarwid/*Inside Moves*

1981
★Maureen Stapleton/*Reds*
Melinda Dillon/*Absence of Malice*
Jane Fonda/*On Golden Pond*
Joan Hackett/*Only When I Laugh*
Elizabeth McGovern/*Ragtime*

1982
★Jessica Lange/*Tootsie*
Glenn Close/*The World According to Garp*
Teri Garr/*Tootsie*
Kim Stanley/*Frances*
Lesley Ann Warren/*Victor/Victoria*

1983
★Linda Hunt/*The Year of Living Dangerously*
Cher/*Silkwood*
Glenn Close/*The Big Chill*
Amy Irving/*Yentl*
Alfre Woodard/*Cross Creek*

1984
★Peggy Ashcroft/*A Passage to India*
Glenn Close/*The Natural*
Lindsay Crouse/*Places in the Heart*
Christine Lahti/*Swing Shift*
Geraldine Page/*The Pope of Greenwich Village*

1985
★Anjelica Huston/*Prizzi's Honor*
Margaret Avery/*The Color Purple*
Amy Madigan/*Twice in a Lifetime*
Meg Tilly/*Agnes of God*
Oprah Winfrey/*The Color Purple*

1986
★Dianne Wiest/*Hannah and Her Sisters*
Tess Harper/*Crimes of the Heart*
Piper Laurie/*Children of a Lesser God*
Mary Elizabeth Mastrantonio/*The Color of Money*
Maggie Smith/*A Room with a View*

1987
★Olympia Dukakis/*Moonstruck*
Anne Archer/*Fatal Attraction*
Anne Ramsey/*Throw Momma from the Train*
Ann Sothern/*The Whales of August*

1988
★Geena Davis/*The Accidental Tourist*
Joan Cusack/*Working Girl*
Frances McDormand/*Mississippi Burning*
Michelle Pfeiffer/*Dangerous Liaisons*
Sigourney Weaver/*Working Girl*

1989
★Brenda Fricker/*My Left Foot*
Anjelica Huston/*Enemies, a Love Story*
Lena Olin/*Enemies, a Love Story*
Julia Roberts/*Steel Magnolias*
Dianne Wiest/*Parenthood*

1990
★Whoopi Goldberg/*Ghost*
Annette Bening/*The Grifters*
Lorraine Bracco/*Goodfellas*
Diane Ladd/*Wild at Heart*
Mary McDonnell/*Dances with Wolves*

1991
★Mercedes Ruehl/*The Fisher King*
Diane Ladd/*Rambling Rose*
Juliette Lewis/*Cape Fear*
Kate Nelligan/*The Prince of Tides*
Jessica Tandy/*Fried Green Tomatoes*

1992
★Marisa Tomei/*My Cousin Vinny*
Judy Davis/*Husbands and Wives*
Joan Plowright/*Enchanted April*
Vanessa Redgrave/*Howard's End*
Miranda Richardson/*Damage*

1993
★Anna Paquin/*The Piano*
Holly Hunter/*The Firm*
Rosie Perez/*Fearless*
Winona Ryder/*The Age of Innocence*
Emma Thompson/*In the Name of the Father*

★ = winner

1994

★Dianne Wiest/*Bullets over Broadway*

Rosemary Harris/*Tom & Viv*

Dame Helen Mirren/*The Madness of King George*

Uma Thurman/*Pulp Fiction*

Jennifer Tilly/*Bullets over Broadway*

1995

★Mira Sorvino/*Mighty Aphrodite*

Joan Allen/*Nixon*

Kathleen Quinlan/*Apollo 13*

Mare Winningham/*Georgia*

Kate Winslet/*Sense and Sensibility*

1996

★Juliette Binoche/*The English Patient*

Joan Allen/*The Crucible*

Lauren Bacall/*The Mirror Has Two Faces*

Barbara Hershey/*Portrait of a Lady*

Marianne Jean-Baptiste/*Secrets and Lies*

1997

★Kim Basinger/*L.A. Confidential*

Joan Cusack/*In and Out*

Minnie Driver/*Good Will Hunting*

Julianne Moore/*Boogie Nights*

Gloria Stuart/*Titanic*

1998

★Dame Judi Dench/*Shakespeare in Love*

Kathy Bates/*Primary Colors*

Brenda Blethyn/*Little Voice*

Rachel Griffiths/*Hilary and Jackie*

Lynn Redgrave/*Gods and Monsters*

1999

★Angelina Jolie/*Girl, Interrupted*

Toni Collette/*The Sixth Sense*

Catherine Keener/*Being John Malkovich*

Samantha Morton/*Sweet and Lowdown*

Chloë Sevigny/*Boys Don't Cry*

2000

★Marcia Gay Harden/*Pollock*

Dame Judi Dench/*Chocolat*

Kate Hudson/*Almost Famous*

Frances McDormand/*Almost Famous*

Julie Walters/*Billy Elliot*

2001

★Jennifer Connelly/*A Beautiful Mind*

Dame Helen Mirren/*Gosford Park*

Maggie Smith/*Gosford Park*

Marisa Tomei/*In the Bedroom*

Kate Winslet/*Iris*

2002

★Catherine Zeta-Jones/*Chicago*

Kathy Bates/*About Schmidt*

Julianne Moore/*The Hours*

Queen Latifah/*Chicago*

Meryl Streep/*Adaptation*

2003

★Renée Zellweger/*Cold Mountain*

Shohreh Aghdashloo/*House of Sand and Fog*

Patricia Clarkson/*Pieces of April*

Marcia Gay Harden/*Mystic River*

Holly Hunter/*Thirteen*

Samantha Morton/*In America*

2004

★Cate Blanchett/*The Aviator*

Laura Linney/*Kinsey*

Virginia Madsen/*Sideways*

Sophie Okonedo/*Hotel Rwanda*

Natalie Portman/*Closer*

2005

★Rachel Weisz/*The Constant Gardener*

Amy Adams/*Junebug*

Catherine Keener/*Capote*

Frances McDormand/*North Country*

Michelle Williams/*Brokeback Mountain*

2006

★Jennifer Hudson/*Dreamgirls*

Adriana Barraza/*Babel*

Cate Blanchett/*Notes on a Scandal*

Abigail Breslin/*Little Miss Sunshine*

Rinko Kikuchi/*Babel*

2007

★Tilda Swinton/*Michael Clayton*

Cate Blanchett/*I'm Not There*

Ruby Dee/*American Gangster*

Saoirse Ronan/*Atonement*

Amy Ryan/*Gone Baby Gone*

2008

★Penelope Cruz/*Vicky Cristina Barcelona*

Amy Adams/*Doubt*

Viola Davis/*Doubt*

Taraji P. Henson/*The Curious Case of Benjamin Button*

Marisa Tomei/*The Wrestler*

2009

★Mo'Nique/*Precious: Based on the Novel 'Push' by Sapphire*

Penelope Cruz/*Nine*

Vera Farmiga/*Up in the Air*

Maggie Gyllenhaal/*Crazy Heart*

Anna Kendrick/*Up in the Air*

2010

★Melissa Leo/*The Fighter*

Amy Adams/*The Fighter*

Helena Bonham Carter/*The King's Speech*

Hailee Steinfeld/*True Grit*

Jacki Weaver/*Animal Kingdom*

2011

★Octavia Spencer/*The Help*

Berenice Bejo/*The Artist*

Jessica Chastain/*The Help*

Melissa McCarthy/*Bridesmaids*

Janet McTeer/*Albert Nobbs*

2012

★Anne Hathaway/*Les Miserables*

Amy Adams/*The Master*

Sally Field/*Lincoln*

Helen Hunt/*The Sessions*

Jacki Weaver/*Silver Linings Playbook*

2013

★Lupita Nyong'o/*12 Years a Slave*

Sally Hawkins/*Blue Jasmine*

Jennifer Lawrence/*American Hustle*

Julia Roberts/*August: Osage County*

June Squibb/*Nebraska*

2014

★Patricia Arquette/*Boyhood*

Laura Dern/*Wild*

Keira Knightley/*The Imitation Game*

Emma Stone/*Birdman, or (The Unexpected Virtue of Ignorance)*

Meryl Streep/*Into the Woods*

2015

★Alicia Vikander/*The Danish Girl*

Jennifer Jason Leigh/*The Hateful Eight*

Rooney Mara/*Carol*

Rachel McAdams/*Spotlight*

Kate Winslet/*Steve Jobs*

2016

★Viola Davis/*Fences*

Naomie Harris/*Moonlight*

Hidden Figures

Nicole Kidman/*Lion*

Octavia Spencer/*Hidden Figures*

Michelle Williams/*Manchester by the Sea*

2017

★Allison Janney/*I, Tonya*

Mary J. Blige/*Mudbound*

Lesley Manville/*Phantom Thread*

Laurie Metcalf/*Lady Bird*

Octavia Spencer/*The Shape of Water*

2018

★Regina King/*If Beale Street Could Talk*

Amy Adams/*Vice*

Emma Stone/*The Favourite*

Marina de Tavira/*Roma*

Rachel Weisz/*The Favourite*

2019

★Laura Dern/*Marriage Story*

Kathy Bates/*Richard Jewell*

Scarlett Johansson/*Jojo Rabbit*

Florence Pugh/*Little Women*

Margot Robbie/*Bombshell*

ART DIRECTION

1928

★*Tempest*

7th Heaven

Street Angel

Sunrise

1931

★*Cimarron*

★Max Ree/*Cimarron*

Anton Grot/*Svengali*

Morocco

Svengali

1938

Merrily We Live

1957

★*Sayonara*

Funny Face

Les Girls

Pal Joey

Raintree County

1958

★*Gigi*

Auntie Mame

Bell, Book and Candle

Vertigo

1967

★*Camelot*

Doctor Dolittle

Guess Who's Coming to Dinner

The Taming of the Shrew

Thoroughly Modern Millie

1968

★*Oliver!*

The Shoes of the Fisherman

Star!

2001: A Space Odyssey

War and Peace

1969

★*Hello, Dolly!*

Anne of the Thousand Days

Sweet Charity

They Shoot Horses, Don't They?

1970

★*Patton*

Airport

The Molly Maguires

Scrooge

Tora! Tora! Tora!

1971

★*Nicholas and Alexandra*

The Andromeda Strain

Bedknobs and Broomsticks

Fiddler on the Roof

Mary, Queen of Scots

1972

★*Cabaret*

Lady Sings the Blues

The Poseidon Adventure

Travels with My Aunt

Young Winston

1973

★*The Sting*

Brother Sun, Sister Moon

The Exorcist

Tom Sawyer

The Way We Were

1974

★*The Godfather, Part 2*

Chinatown

Earthquake

The Island at the Top of the World

The Towering Inferno

1975

★*Barry Lyndon*

The Hindenburg

The Man Who Would Be King

Shampoo

The Sunshine Boys

1976

★*All the President's Men*

The Last Tycoon

Logan's Run

The Shootist

1977

★*Star Wars*

Airport '77

Close Encounters of the Third Kind

The Spy Who Loved Me

The Turning Point

1978

★*Heaven Can Wait*

Brink's Job

California Suite

Interiors

The Wiz

1979

★*All That Jazz*

Alien

Apocalypse Now

The China Syndrome

Star Trek: The Motion Picture

1980

★*Tess*

Altered States

Coal Miner's Daughter

The Elephant Man

The Empire Strikes Back

Kagemusha

1981

★*Raiders of the Lost Ark*

The French Lieutenant's Woman

Heaven's Gate

Ragtime

Reds

1982

★*Gandhi*

Annie

Blade Runner

Victor/Victoria

1983

★*Fanny and Alexander*

Return of the Jedi

The Right Stuff

Terms of Endearment

Yentl

1984

★*Amadeus*

The Cotton Club

The Natural

A Passage to India

2010: The Year We Make Contact

1985

★*Out of Africa*

Brazil

The Color Purple

Ran

Witness

1986

★*A Room with a View*

Aliens

The Color of Money

Hannah and Her Sisters

The Mission

1987

★*The Last Emperor*

Empire of the Sun

Hope and Glory

Radio Days

The Untouchables

1988

★*Dangerous Liaisons*

Beaches

Rain Man

Tucker: The Man and His Dream

Who Framed Roger Rabbit

1989

★*Batman*

The Abyss

The Adventures of Baron Munchausen

Driving Miss Daisy

Glory

1990

★*Dick Tracy*

Cyrano de Bergerac

Dances with Wolves

The Godfather, Part 3

Hamlet

1991

★*Bugsy*

Barton Fink

The Fisher King

Hook

The Prince of Tides

1992

★*Howard's End*

Bram Stoker's Dracula

Chaplin

Toys

Unforgiven

1993

★*Schindler's List*

Addams Family Values

The Age of Innocence

Orlando

The Remains of the Day

1994

★*The Madness of King George*

Bullets over Broadway

Forrest Gump

Interview with the Vampire

Legends of the Fall

1995

★*Restoration*

Apollo 13

Babe

A Little Princess

Richard III

1996

★*The English Patient*

The Birdcage

Evita

Hamlet

William Shakespeare's Romeo and Juliet

1997

★*Titanic*

Gattaca

Kundun

L.A. Confidential

Men in Black

1998

★*Shakespeare in Love*

Elizabeth

Pleasantville

Saving Private Ryan

What Dreams May Come

1999

★*Sleepy Hollow*

Anna and the King

The Cider House Rules

The Talented Mr. Ripley

Topsy Turvy

2000

★*Crouching Tiger, Hidden Dragon*

Dr. Seuss' How the Grinch Stole Christmas

Gladiator

Quills

2001

★*Moulin Rouge*

Amelie

Gosford Park

Harry Potter and the Sorcerer's Stone

Lord of the Rings: The Fellowship of the Ring

2002

★*Chicago*

Frida

Gangs of New York

Lord of the Rings: The Two Towers

Road to Perdition

2003

★*Lord of the Rings: The Return of the King*

Girl with a Pearl Earring

The Last Samurai

Lord of the Rings: The Return of the King

Master and Commander: The Far Side of the World

Seabiscuit

2004

★*The Aviator*

Finding Neverland

Lemony Snicket's A Series of Unfortunate Events

The Phantom of the Opera

A Very Long Engagement

2005

★*Memoirs of a Geisha*

Good Night, and Good Luck

Harry Potter and the Goblet of Fire

King Kong

Pride and Prejudice

★ = winner

2006
★Pan's Labyrinth
Dreamgirls
The Good Shepherd
Pirates of the Caribbean: Dead Man's Chest
The Prestige
2007
★Sweeney Todd: The Demon Barber of Fleet Street
American Gangster
Atonement
The Golden Compass
There Will Be Blood
2008
★The Curious Case of Benjamin Button
Changeling
The Dark Knight
The Duchess
Revolutionary Road
2009
★Avatar
The Imaginarium of Doctor Parnassus
Nine
Sherlock Holmes
The Young Victoria
2010
★Alice in Wonderland
Harry Potter and the Deathly Hallows, Part 1
Inception
The King's Speech
True Grit
2011
★Hugo
The Artist
Harry Potter and the Deathly Hallows, Part 2
Midnight in Paris
War Horse

ART DIRECTION (B&W)

1930
The Love Parade
1942
Sam Comer/Hold Back the Dawn
Hans Dreier/Hold Back the Dawn
Robert Usher/Hold Back the Dawn
1943
★This Above All
No Time For Love
1946
★Anna and the King of Siam
1947
★Great Expectations
Maurice Ransford/The Foxes of Harrow
Lyle Wheeler/The Foxes of Harrow
1948
★Hamlet
Johnny Belinda
1949
★The Heiress
Come to the Stable
Madame Bovary
1950
★Sunset Boulevard
All About Eve
1951
★A Streetcar Named Desire
La Ronde
Too Young to Kiss
1952
★The Bad and the Beautiful
Carrie
My Cousin Rachel
Rashomon
Viva Zapata!
1953
★Julius Caesar
Martin Luther
Roman Holiday
Titanic
1954
★On the Waterfront
Country Girl
Executive Suite
Le Plaisir
Sabrina
1955
★The Rose Tattoo
Blackboard Jungle
I'll Cry Tomorrow
The Man with the Golden Arm
Marty
1956
★Somebody Up There Likes Me
The Proud and Profane
Seven Samurai
Solid Gold Cadillac
1959
★The Diary of Anne Frank
Career
Some Like It Hot
Suddenly, Last Summer
1960
★The Apartment
The Facts of Life
Psycho
Sons and Lovers
1961
★The Hustler
The Absent-Minded Professor
The Children's Hour
Judgment at Nuremberg
La Dolce Vita
1962
★To Kill a Mockingbird
Days of Wine and Roses
The Longest Day
Period of Adjustment
1963
★America America
8 1/2
Hud
Twilight of Honor
1964
★Zorba the Greek
The Americanization of Emily
Hush, Hush, Sweet Charlotte
The Night of the Iguana
Seven Days in May
1965
★Ship of Fools
King Rat
A Patch of Blue
Hal Pereira/The Slender Thread
Jack Poplin/The Slender Thread
The Slender Thread
The Spy Who Came in from the Cold
1966
★Who's Afraid of Virginia Woolf?
The Fortune Cookie
The Gospel According to St. Matthew
Is Paris Burning?

ART DIRECTION (COLOR)

1942
★My Gal Sal
1947
★Black Narcissus
Life with Father
1948
★The Red Shoes
Joan of Arc
1949
★Little Women
Adventures of Don Juan
1950
★Samson and Delilah
Annie Get Your Gun
Destination Moon
1951
★An American in Paris
David and Bathsheba
Quo Vadis
The Tales of Hoffmann
1952
★Moulin Rouge
Hans Christian Andersen
The Quiet Man
The Snows of Kilimanjaro
1953
★The Robe
Knights of the Round Table
Lili
Young Bess
1954
★20,000 Leagues under the Sea
Brigadoon
Desiree
Red Garters
A Star Is Born
1955
★Picnic
Daddy Long Legs
Guys and Dolls
Love Is a Many-Splendored Thing
To Catch a Thief
1956
★The King and I
Around the World in 80 Days
Giant
Lust for Life
The Ten Commandments
1959
★Ben-Hur
Journey to the Center of the Earth
North by Northwest
Pillow Talk
1960
★Spartacus
Cimarron
It Started in Naples
Sunrise at Campobello
1961
★West Side Story
Breakfast at Tiffany's
El Cid
Flower Drum Song
Summer and Smoke
1962
★Lawrence of Arabia
The Music Man
Mutiny on the Bounty
That Touch of Mink
1963
★Cleopatra
The Cardinal
Come Blow Your Horn
How the West Was Won
Tom Jones
1964
★My Fair Lady
Becket
Mary Poppins
The Unsinkable Molly Brown
1965
★Doctor Zhivago
The Agony and the Ecstasy
The Greatest Story Ever Told
Inside Daisy Clover
The Sound of Music
1966
★Fantastic Voyage
Gambit
Juliet of the Spirits
The Sand Pebbles

CINEMATOGRAPHY

1928
★Sunrise
My Best Girl
Sadie Thompson
Street Angel
Tempest
1929
★White Shadows in the South Seas
The Divine Lady
Our Dancing Daughters
1930
All Quiet on the Western Front
Anna Christie
Hell's Angels
1931
★Tabu: A Story of the South Seas
Cimarron
Lee Garmes/Morocco
Morocco
Svengali
1932
★Shanghai Express
Arrowsmith
Dr. Jekyll and Mr. Hyde
1933
★A Farewell to Arms
The Sign of the Cross
1934
★Cleopatra
1935
★A Midsummer Night's Dream
Barbary Coast
The Crusades
Les Miserables
1936
★Anthony Adverse
The General Died at Dawn
The Gorgeous Hussy
1937
★The Good Earth
Dead End
1938
★The Great Waltz
Algiers
Jezebel
Mad About Music
Merrily We Live
Suez
Vivacious Lady
You Can't Take It with You
The Young in Heart
1942
Leo Tover/Hold Back the Dawn
1957
★The Bridge on the River Kwai
An Affair to Remember
Funny Face
Peyton Place
Sayonara
1960
★Freddie Francis/Sons and Lovers
1967
★Bonnie & Clyde
Camelot
Doctor Dolittle
The Graduate
In Cold Blood
1968
★Romeo and Juliet
Funny Girl
Ice Station Zebra
Oliver!
Star!
1969
★Butch Cassidy and the Sundance Kid
Anne of the Thousand Days
Bob & Carol & Ted & Alice
Hello, Dolly!
Marooned
1970
★Ryan's Daughter
Airport
Patton
Tora! Tora! Tora!
Women in Love
1971
★Fiddler on the Roof
The French Connection
The Last Picture Show
Nicholas and Alexandra
Summer of '42
1972
★Cabaret
Butterflies Are Free
The Poseidon Adventure
1776
Travels with My Aunt
1973
★Cries and Whispers
The Exorcist
Jonathan Livingston Seagull
The Sting
The Way We Were
1974
★The Towering Inferno
Chinatown
Earthquake
Lenny
Murder on the Orient Express
1975
★Barry Lyndon
The Day of the Locust
Funny Lady
The Hindenburg
One Flew Over the Cuckoo's Nest
1976
★Bound for Glory
King Kong
Logan's Run
Network
A Star Is Born
1977
★Close Encounters of the Third Kind
Islands in the Stream
Julia
The Turning Point
1978
★Days of Heaven
The Deer Hunter
Heaven Can Wait
Same Time, Next Year
The Wiz
1979
★Apocalypse Now
All That Jazz
The Black Hole
Kramer vs. Kramer
1941
1980
★Tess
The Blue Lagoon
Coal Miner's Daughter
The Formula
Raging Bull
1981
★Reds
Excalibur
On Golden Pond
Ragtime
Raiders of the Lost Ark
1982
★Gandhi
Das Boot
E.T.: The Extra-Terrestrial
Sophie's Choice
Tootsie
1983
★Fanny and Alexander
Flashdance
The Right Stuff
WarGames
Zelig
1984
★The Killing Fields
Amadeus
The Natural
A Passage to India
The River
1985
★Out of Africa
The Color Purple
Murphy's Romance
Ran
Witness
1986
★The Mission
Peggy Sue Got Married
Platoon
A Room with a View
Star Trek 4: The Voyage Home
1987
★The Last Emperor
Broadcast News
Empire of the Sun
Hope and Glory
Matewan
1988
★Mississippi Burning
Rain Man
Tequila Sunrise
The Unbearable Lightness of Being
Who Framed Roger Rabbit
1989
★Glory
The Abyss
Blaze
Born on the Fourth of July
The Fabulous Baker Boys
1990
★Dances with Wolves
Avalon
Dick Tracy
The Godfather, Part 3
Henry & June
1991
★JFK
Bugsy
The Prince of Tides
Terminator 2: Judgment Day
Thelma & Louise

1992
★A River Runs Through It
Hoffa
Howard's End
The Lover
Unforgiven
1993
★Schindler's List
Farewell My Concubine
The Fugitive
The Piano
Searching for Bobby Fischer
1994
★Legends of the Fall
Forrest Gump
The Shawshank Redemption
Trois Couleurs: Rouge
Wyatt Earp
1995
★Braveheart
Batman Forever
A Little Princess
Sense and Sensibility
Shanghai Triad
1996
★The English Patient
Evita
Fargo
Fly Away Home
Michael Collins
1997
★Titanic
Amistad
Kundun
L.A. Confidential
The Wings of the Dove
1998
★Saving Private Ryan
A Civil Action
Elizabeth
The Thin Red Line
1999
★American Beauty
The End of the Affair
The Insider
Sleepy Hollow
Snow Falling on Cedars
2000
★Crouching Tiger, Hidden Dragon
Gladiator
O Brother Where Art Thou?
The Patriot
2001
★Lord of the Rings: The Fellowship of the Ring
Amelie
Black Hawk Down
The Man Who Wasn't There
Moulin Rouge
2002
★Road to Perdition
Chicago
Far from Heaven
Gangs of New York
The Pianist
2003
★Master and Commander: The Far Side of the World
City of God
Cold Mountain
Girl with a Pearl Earring
Seabiscuit
2004
★The Aviator
House of Flying Daggers
The Passion of the Christ
The Phantom of the Opera
A Very Long Engagement
2005
★Memoirs of a Geisha
Batman Begins
Brokeback Mountain
Good Night, and Good Luck
The New World
2006
★Pan's Labyrinth
The Black Dahlia
Children of Men
The Illusionist
The Prestige
2007
★There Will Be Blood
The Assassination of Jesse James by the Coward Robert Ford
Atonement
The Diving Bell and the Butterfly
No Country for Old Men
2008
★Slumdog Millionaire
Changeling
The Curious Case of Benjamin Button
The Dark Knight
The Reader
2009
★Avatar
Harry Potter and the Half-Blood Prince
The Hurt Locker
Inglourious Basterds
The White Ribbon
2010
★Inception
Black Swan
The King's Speech
The Social Network
True Grit
2011
★Hugo
The Artist
The Girl With the Dragon Tattoo
The Tree of Life
War Horse
2012
★Life of Pi
Anna Karenina
Django Unchained
Lincoln
Skyfall
2013
★Gravity
The Grandmaster
Inside Llewyn Davis
Nebraska
Prisoners
2014
★Birdman, or (The Unexpected Virtue of Ignorance)
The Grand Budapest Hotel
Ida
Mr. Turner
Unbroken
2015
★The Revenant
Carol
The Hateful Eight
Mad Max: Fury Road
Sicario
2016
★La La Land
Arrival
Lion
Moonlight
Silence
2017
★Blade Runner 2049
Darkest Hour
Dunkirk
Mudbound
The Shape of Water
2018
★Roma
Cold War
The Favourite
Never Look Away
A Star Is Born
2019
★1917
The Irishman
Joker
The Lighthouse
Once Upon A Time... In Hollywood

CINEMATOGRAPHY (B&W)

1930
The Love Parade
1939
★Wuthering Heights
First Love
Gunga Din
Intermezzo
Juarez
Of Mice and Men
Only Angels Have Wings
The Rains Came
Stagecoach
1940
★Rebecca
Abe Lincoln in Illinois
All This and Heaven Too
Boom Town
Foreign Correspondent
The Letter
The Long Voyage Home
Spring Parade
Waterloo Bridge
1941
★How Green Was My Valley
The Chocolate Soldier
Citizen Kane
Dr. Jekyll and Mr. Hyde
Here Comes Mr. Jordan
Sergeant York
Sundown
That Hamilton Woman
1942
★Mrs. Miniver
Kings Row
The Magnificent Ambersons
Moontide
The Pride of the Yankees
Talk of the Town
1943
★The Song of Bernadette
Air Force
Casablanca
Five Graves to Cairo
The Human Comedy
Madame Curie
The North Star
Sahara
So Proudly We Hail
This Above All
1944
★Laura
Double Indemnity
Dragon Seed
Gaslight
Going My Way
Lifeboat
Since You Went Away
Thirty Seconds Over Tokyo
The Uninvited
The White Cliffs of Dover
1945
★Picture of Dorian Gray
The Keys of the Kingdom
The Lost Weekend
Mildred Pierce
Spellbound
1946
★Anna and the King of Siam
The Green Years
1947
★Great Expectations
The Ghost and Mrs. Muir
Green Dolphin Street
1948
★The Naked City
I Remember Mama
Johnny Belinda
Portrait of Jennie
1949
★Battleground
Champion
Come to the Stable
The Heiress
1950
★The Third Man
All About Eve
The Asphalt Jungle
Prince of Foxes
Sunset Boulevard
1951
★A Place in the Sun
Death of a Salesman
The Furies
Strangers on a Train
A Streetcar Named Desire
1952
★The Bad and the Beautiful
My Cousin Rachel
Sudden Fear
1953
★From Here to Eternity
Julius Caesar
Martin Luther
Roman Holiday
1954
★On the Waterfront
Country Girl
Executive Suite
Sabrina
1955
★The Rose Tattoo
Blackboard Jungle
I'll Cry Tomorrow
Marty
Queen Bee
1956
★Somebody Up There Likes Me
Baby Doll
The Bad Seed
The Harder They Fall
1958
★The Defiant Ones
Desire Under the Elms
I Want to Live!
Separate Tables
The Young Lions
1959
★The Diary of Anne Frank
Anatomy of a Murder
Career
The Gazebo
Some Like It Hot
The Young Philadelphians
1960
The Apartment
The Facts of Life
Inherit the Wind
Psycho
1961
★The Hustler
The Absent-Minded Professor
The Children's Hour
Judgment at Nuremberg
One, Two, Three
1962
★The Longest Day
Birdman of Alcatraz
To Kill a Mockingbird
Two for the Seesaw
What Ever Happened to Baby Jane?
1963
★Hud
The Balcony
The Caretakers
Lilies of the Field
1964
★Zorba the Greek
The Americanization of Emily
Hush, Hush, Sweet Charlotte
The Night of the Iguana
1965
★Ship of Fools
In Harm's Way
King Rat
Morituri
A Patch of Blue
1966
★Who's Afraid of Virginia Woolf?
The Fortune Cookie
Georgy Girl
Is Paris Burning?
Seconds

CINEMATOGRAPHY (COLOR)

1936
★The Garden of Allah
1937
★A Star Is Born
1938
★Sweethearts
1939
★Gone with the Wind
Drums Along the Mohawk
The Four Feathers
The Private Lives of Elizabeth & Essex
The Wizard of Oz
1940
★The Thief of Bagdad
Bitter Sweet
The Blue Bird
Down Argentine Way
Northwest Passage
1941
★Blood and Sand
Billy the Kid
Blossoms in the Dust
Dive Bomber
Louisiana Purchase
1942
★The Black Swan
Arabian Nights
Captains of the Clouds
The Jungle Book
Reap the Wild Wind
To the Shores of Tripoli
1943
★The Phantom of the Opera
For Whom the Bell Tolls
Heaven Can Wait
Hello, Frisco, Hello
Lassie, Come Home
Thousands Cheer
1944
★Wilson
Cover Girl
Edward Cronjager/Home In Indiana
Home In Indiana
Kismet
Meet Me in St. Louis
1945
★Leave Her to Heaven
Anchors Aweigh
National Velvet
A Song to Remember
The Spanish Main
1946
★The Yearling
The Jolson Story
1947
★Black Narcissus
Life with Father
Mother Wore Tights
1948
★Joan of Arc
The Loves of Carmen
The Three Musketeers
1949
★She Wore a Yellow Ribbon
The Barkleys of Broadway
Jolson Sings Again
Little Women
1950
★King Solomon's Mines
Annie Get Your Gun
Broken Arrow
The Flame & the Arrow
Samson and Delilah
1951
★An American in Paris
David and Bathsheba
Quo Vadis
Show Boat
When Worlds Collide
1952
★The Quiet Man
Hans Christian Andersen
Ivanhoe
Million Dollar Mermaid
The Snows of Kilimanjaro
1953
★Shane
All the Brothers Were Valiant
Beneath the 12-Mile Reef
Lili
The Robe
1954
★Three Coins in the Fountain
The Egyptian
Rear Window
Seven Brides for Seven Brothers
The Silver Chalice
1955
★To Catch a Thief
Guys and Dolls
Love Is a Many-Splendored Thing
A Man Called Peter
Oklahoma!
1956
★Around the World in 80 Days
The Eddy Duchin Story
The King and I
The Ten Commandments
War and Peace

★ = winner

1958
★*Gigi*
Auntie Mame
Cat on a Hot Tin Roof
The Old Man and the Sea
South Pacific
1959
★*Ben-Hur*
The Five Pennies
The Nun's Story
1960
★*Spartacus*
The Alamo
Butterfield 8
Exodus
1961
★*West Side Story*
Fanny
Flower Drum Song
A Majority of One
One-Eyed Jacks
1962
★*Lawrence of Arabia*
Gypsy
Hatari!
Mutiny on the Bounty
1963
★*Cleopatra*
The Cardinal
How the West Was Won
Irma La Douce
It's a Mad, Mad, Mad, Mad World
1964
★*My Fair Lady*
Becket
Cheyenne Autumn
Mary Poppins
The Unsinkable Molly Brown
1965
★*Doctor Zhivago*
The Agony and the Ecstasy
The Great Race
The Greatest Story Ever Told
The Sound of Music
1966
★*A Man for All Seasons*
Fantastic Voyage
Hawaii
The Professionals
The Sand Pebbles

COSTUME DESIGN

1951
The Black Rose
1957
★*Les Girls*
An Affair to Remember
Funny Face
Pal Joey
Raintree County
1958
★*Gigi*
Bell, Book and Candle
The Buccaneer
Some Came Running
1967
★*Camelot*
Bonnie & Clyde
The Happiest Millionaire
The Taming of the Shrew
Thoroughly Modern Millie
1968
★*Romeo and Juliet*
The Lion in Winter
Oliver!
Planet of the Apes
Star!
1969
★*Anne of the Thousand Days*
Hello, Dolly!
Sweet Charity
They Shoot Horses, Don't They?
1970
★*Cromwell*
Airport
Darling Lili
Scrooge
1971
★*Nicholas and Alexandra*
Bedknobs and Broomsticks
Death in Venice
Mary, Queen of Scots
What's the Matter with Helen?
1972
★*Travels with My Aunt*
The Godfather
Lady Sings the Blues
The Poseidon Adventure
Young Winston
1973
★*The Sting*
Cries and Whispers
Tom Sawyer
The Way We Were
1974
★*The Great Gatsby*
Chinatown
Daisy Miller
The Godfather, Part 2
Murder on the Orient Express
1975
★*Barry Lyndon*
The Four Musketeers
Funny Lady
The Magic Flute
The Man Who Would Be King
1976
Bound for Glory
The Seven-Per-Cent Solution
1977
★*Star Wars*
Airport '77
Julia
A Little Night Music
The Other Side of Midnight
1978
★*Death on the Nile*
Days of Heaven
The Swarm
The Wiz
1979
★*All That Jazz*
Agatha
Butch and Sundance: The Early Days
The Europeans
La Cage aux Folles
1980
★*Tess*
The Elephant Man
My Brilliant Career
Somewhere in Time
When Time Ran Out
1981
★*Chariots of Fire*
The French Lieutenant's Woman
Pennies from Heaven
Ragtime
Reds
1982
★*Gandhi*
Sophie's Choice
Tron
Victor/Victoria
1983
★*Fanny and Alexander*
Cross Creek
Heart Like a Wheel
The Return of Martin Guerre
Zelig
1984
★*Amadeus*
The Bostonians
A Passage to India
Places in the Heart
2010: The Year We Make Contact
1985
★*Ran*
The Color Purple
The Journey of Natty Gann
Out of Africa
Prizzi's Honor
1986
★*A Room with a View*
The Mission
Otello
Peggy Sue Got Married
1987
★*The Last Emperor*
The Dead
Empire of the Sun
Maurice
The Untouchables
1988
★*Dangerous Liaisons*
Coming to America
A Handful of Dust
Sunset
Tucker: The Man and His Dream
1989
★*Henry V*
The Adventures of Baron Munchausen
Driving Miss Daisy
Harlem Nights
Valmont
1990
★*Cyrano de Bergerac*
Avalon
Dances with Wolves
Dick Tracy
Hamlet
1991
★*Bugsy*
The Addams Family
Barton Fink
Hook
Madame Bovary
1992
★*Bram Stoker's Dracula*
Enchanted April
Howard's End
Malcolm X
Toys
1993
★*The Age of Innocence*
Orlando
The Piano
The Remains of the Day
Schindler's List
1994
★*The Adventures of Priscilla, Queen of the Desert*
Bullets over Broadway
Little Women
Maverick
Queen Margot
1995
★*Restoration*
Braveheart
Richard III
Sense and Sensibility
12 Monkeys
1996
★*The English Patient*
Angels and Insects
Emma
Hamlet
Portrait of a Lady
1997
★*Titanic*
Amistad
Kundun
Oscar and Lucinda
The Wings of the Dove
1998
★*Shakespeare in Love*
Beloved
Elizabeth
Pleasantville
Velvet Goldmine
1999
★*Topsy Turvy*
Anna and the King
The Talented Mr. Ripley
Titus
2000
★*Gladiator*
Crouching Tiger, Hidden Dragon
Dr. Seuss' How the Grinch Stole Christmas
102 Dalmatians
Quills
2001
★*Moulin Rouge*
The Affair of the Necklace
Gosford Park
Harry Potter and the Sorcerer's Stone
Lord of the Rings: The Fellowship of the Ring
2002
★*Chicago*
Frida
Gangs of New York
The Pianist
2003
★*Lord of the Rings: The Return of the King*
Girl with a Pearl Earring
The Last Samurai
Master and Commander: The Far Side of the World
Seabiscuit
2004
★*The Aviator*
Finding Neverland
Lemony Snicket's A Series of Unfortunate Events
Ray
2005
★*Memoirs of a Geisha*
Charlie and the Chocolate Factory
Mrs. Henderson Presents
Pride and Prejudice
Walk the Line
2006
★*Marie Antoinette*
Curse of the Golden Flower
The Devil Wears Prada
Dreamgirls
The Queen
2007
★*Elizabeth: The Golden Age*
Across the Universe
Atonement
La Vie en Rose
Sweeney Todd: The Demon Barber of Fleet Street
2008
★*The Duchess*
Australia
The Curious Case of Benjamin Button
Milk
Revolutionary Road
2009
★*The Young Victoria*
Bright Star
Coco Before Chanel
The Imaginarium of Doctor Parnassus
Nine
2010
★*Alice in Wonderland*
I Am Love
The King's Speech
The Tempest
True Grit
2011
★*The Artist*
Anonymous
Hugo
Jane Eyre
W.E.
2012
★*Anna Karenina*
Les Miserables
Lincoln
Mirror Mirror
Snow White and the Huntsman
2013
★*The Great Gatsby*
American Hustle
The Grandmaster
The Invisible Woman
12 Years a Slave
2014
★*The Grand Budapest Hotel*
Inherent Vice
Into the Woods
Maleficent
Mr. Turner
2015
★*Mad Max: Fury Road*
Carol
Cinderella
The Danish Girl
The Revenant
2016
★*Fantastic Beasts and Where to Find Them*
Allied
Florence Foster Jenkins
Jackie
La La Land
2017
★*Phantom Thread*
Beauty and the Beast
Darkest Hour
The Shape of Water
Victoria & Abdul
2018
★*Black Panther*
The Ballad of Buster Scruggs
The Favourite
Mary Poppins Returns
Mary Queen of Scots
2019
★*Little Women*
The Irishman
Jojo Rabbit
Joker
Once Upon A Time... In Hollywood

COSTUME DESIGN (B&W)

1948
★*Hamlet*
B.F.'s Daughter
1949
★*The Heiress*
1950
★*All About Eve*
Born Yesterday
The Magnificent Yankee
The Mudlark
Prince of Foxes
1951
★*A Place in the Sun*
The Model and the Marriage Broker
A Streetcar Named Desire
1952
★*The Bad and the Beautiful*
Affair in Trinidad
Carrie
My Cousin Rachel
Sudden Fear
1953
★*Roman Holiday*
From Here to Eternity
1954
★*Sabrina*
The Earrings of Madame De. . .
Executive Suite
It Should Happen to You
1955
★*I'll Cry Tomorrow*
The Pickwick Papers
Queen Bee
The Rose Tattoo
Ugetsu
1956
★*Solid Gold Cadillac*
The Power and the Prize
The Proud and Profane
Helen Rose/The Power and the Prize
Seven Samurai
1959
★*Some Like It Hot*
Career
The Diary of Anne Frank
The Young Philadelphians
1960
★*The Facts of Life*
Never on Sunday
The Rise and Fall of Legs Diamond
Seven Thieves
The Virgin Spring
1961
★*La Dolce Vita*
The Children's Hour
Claudelle Inglish
Judgment at Nuremberg
Yojimbo
1962
Days of Wine and Roses
The Man Who Shot Liberty Valance
The Miracle Worker
Phaedra
What Ever Happened to Baby Jane?
1963
★*8 1/2*
Toys in the Attic
1964
★*The Night of the Iguana*
Hush, Hush, Sweet Charlotte
Kisses for My President
The Visit

★ = winner

1965

★*Darling*

Edith Head/*The Slender Thread*

Morituri

A Rage to Live

Ship of Fools

The Slender Thread

1966

★*Who's Afraid of Virginia Woolf?*

The Gospel According to St. Matthew

Morgan: A Suitable Case for Treatment

COSTUME DESIGN (COLOR)

1948

★*Joan of Arc*

1949

★*Adventures of Don Juan*

Mother Is a Freshman

1950

★*Samson and Delilah*

That Forsyte Woman

1951

★*An American in Paris*

David and Bathsheba

The Great Caruso

Quo Vadis

The Tales of Hoffmann

1952

★*Moulin Rouge*

The Greatest Show on Earth

Hans Christian Andersen

With a Song in My Heart

1953

★*The Robe*

The Band Wagon

How to Marry a Millionaire

Young Bess

1954

★*Gate of Hell*

Brigadoon

Desiree

A Star Is Born

There's No Business Like Show Business

1955

★*Love Is a Many-Splendored Thing*

Guys and Dolls

Interrupted Melody

To Catch a Thief

The Virgin Queen

1956

★*The King and I*

Around the World in 80 Days

Giant

The Ten Commandments

War and Peace

1959

★*Ben-Hur*

The Best of Everything

The Five Pennies

1960

★*Spartacus*

Can-Can

Sunrise at Campobello

1961

★*West Side Story*

Babes in Toyland

Back Street

Flower Drum Song

Pocketful of Miracles

1962

Bon Voyage!

Gypsy

The Music Man

My Geisha

1963

★*Cleopatra*

The Cardinal

How the West Was Won

A New Kind of Love

1964

★*My Fair Lady*

Becket

Mary Poppins

The Unsinkable Molly Brown

1965

★*Doctor Zhivago*

The Agony and the Ecstasy

The Greatest Story Ever Told

Inside Daisy Clover

The Sound of Music

1966

★*A Man for All Seasons*

Gambit

Hawaii

Juliet of the Spirits

DIRECTOR

1928

★Frank Borzage/*7th Heaven*

Charlie Chaplin/*The Circus*

Ted Wilde/*Speedy*

1929

★Frank Lloyd/*The Divine Lady*

Lionel Barrymore/*Madame X*

Harry Beaumont/*Broadway Melody*

1930

★Lewis Milestone/*All Quiet on the Western Front*

Clarence Brown/*Anna Christie*

Clarence Brown/*Romance*

Robert Z. Leonard/*The Divorcee*

Ernst Lubitsch/*The Love Parade*

King Vidor/*Hallelujah!*

1931

Clarence Brown/*A Free Soul*

Lewis Milestone/*The Front Page*

Wesley Ruggles/*Cimarron*

Josef von Sternberg/*Morocco*

1932

King Vidor/*The Champ*

Josef von Sternberg/*Shanghai Express*

1933

★Frank Lloyd/*Cavalcade*

Frank Capra/*Lady for a Day*

George Cukor/*Little Women*

1934

★Frank Capra/*It Happened One Night*

W.S. Van Dyke/*The Thin Man*

1935

★John Ford/*The Informer*

Michael Curtiz/*Captain Blood*

Henry Hathaway/*The Lives of a Bengal Lancer*

Frank Lloyd/*Mutiny on the Bounty*

1936

★Frank Capra/*Mr. Deeds Goes to Town*

Gregory La Cava/*My Man Godfrey*

Robert Z. Leonard/*The Great Ziegfeld*

W.S. Van Dyke/*San Francisco*

William Wyler/*Dodsworth*

1937

★Leo McCarey/*The Awful Truth*

William Dieterle/*The Life of Emile Zola*

Sidney Franklin/*The Good Earth*

Gregory La Cava/*Stage Door*

William A. Wellman/*A Star Is Born*

1938

★Frank Capra/*You Can't Take It with You*

Michael Curtiz/*Angels with Dirty Faces*

Michael Curtiz/*Four Daughters*

Norman Taurog/*Boys Town*

King Vidor/*The Citadel*

1939

★Victor Fleming/*Gone with the Wind*

Frank Capra/*Mr. Smith Goes to Washington*

John Ford/*Stagecoach*

Sam Wood/*Goodbye, Mr. Chips*

William Wyler/*Wuthering Heights*

1940

★John Ford/*The Grapes of Wrath*

George Cukor/*The Philadelphia Story*

Alfred Hitchcock/*Rebecca*

Sam Wood/*Kitty Foyle*

William Wyler/*The Letter*

1941

★John Ford/*How Green Was My Valley*

Alexander Hall/*Here Comes Mr. Jordan*

Howard Hawks/*Sergeant York*

Orson Welles/*Citizen Kane*

William Wyler/*The Little Foxes*

1942

★William Wyler/*Mrs. Miniver*

Michael Curtiz/*Yankee Doodle Dandy*

John Farrow/*Wake Island*

Mervyn LeRoy/*Random Harvest*

Sam Wood/*Kings Row*

1943

★Michael Curtiz/*Casablanca*

Clarence Brown/*The Human Comedy*

Henry King/*The Song of Bernadette*

Ernst Lubitsch/*Heaven Can Wait*

George Stevens/*The More the Merrier*

1944

★Leo McCarey/*Going My Way*

Alfred Hitchcock/*Lifeboat*

Henry King/*Wilson*

Otto Preminger/*Laura*

Billy Wilder/*Double Indemnity*

1945

★Billy Wilder/*The Lost Weekend*

Clarence Brown/*National Velvet*

Alfred Hitchcock/*Spellbound*

Leo McCarey/*The Bells of St. Mary's*

Jean Renoir/*The Southerner*

1946

★William Wyler/*The Best Years of Our Lives*

Clarence Brown/*The Yearling*

Frank Capra/*It's a Wonderful Life*

David Lean/*Brief Encounter*

Robert Siodmak/*The Killers*

1947

★Elia Kazan/*Gentleman's Agreement*

George Cukor/*A Double Life*

Edward Dmytryk/*Crossfire*

Henry Koster/*The Bishop's Wife*

David Lean/*Great Expectations*

1948

★John Huston/*Treasure of the Sierra Madre*

Anatole Litvak/*The Snake Pit*

Jean Negulesco/*Johnny Belinda*

Laurence Olivier/*Hamlet*

Fred Zinnemann/*The Search*

1949

★Joseph L. Mankiewicz/*A Letter to Three Wives*

Carol Reed/*The Fallen Idol*

Robert Rossen/*All the King's Men*

William A. Wellman/*Battleground*

William Wyler/*The Heiress*

1950

★Joseph L. Mankiewicz/*All About Eve*

George Cukor/*Born Yesterday*

John Huston/*The Asphalt Jungle*

Carol Reed/*The Third Man*

Billy Wilder/*Sunset Boulevard*

1951

★George Stevens/*A Place in the Sun*

John Huston/*The African Queen*

Elia Kazan/*A Streetcar Named Desire*

Vincente Minnelli/*An American in Paris*

William Wyler/*Detective Story*

1952

★John Ford/*The Quiet Man*

Cecil B. DeMille/*The Greatest Show on Earth*

John Huston/*Moulin Rouge*

Joseph L. Mankiewicz/*Five Fingers*

Fred Zinnemann/*High Noon*

1953

★Fred Zinnemann/*From Here to Eternity*

George Stevens/*Shane*

Charles Walters/*Lili*

Billy Wilder/*Stalag 17*

William Wyler/*Roman Holiday*

1954

★Elia Kazan/*On the Waterfront*

Alfred Hitchcock/*Rear Window*

George Seaton/*Country Girl*

William A. Wellman/*The High and the Mighty*

Billy Wilder/*Sabrina*

1955

★Delbert Mann/*Marty*

Elia Kazan/*East of Eden*

David Lean/*Summertime*

Joshua Logan/*Picnic*

John Sturges/*Bad Day at Black Rock*

1956

★George Stevens/*Giant*

Michael Anderson, Sr./*Around the World in 80 Days*

Walter Lang/*The King and I*

King Vidor/*War and Peace*

William Wyler/*Friendly Persuasion*

1957

★David Lean/*The Bridge on the River Kwai*

Joshua Logan/*Sayonara*

Sidney Lumet/*Twelve Angry Men*

Mark Robson/*Peyton Place*

Billy Wilder/*Witness for the Prosecution*

1958

★Vincente Minnelli/*Gigi*

Richard Brooks/*Cat on a Hot Tin Roof*

Stanley Kramer/*The Defiant Ones*

Mark Robson/*The Inn of the Sixth Happiness*

Robert Wise/*I Want to Live!*

1959

★William Wyler/*Ben-Hur*

Jack Clayton/*Room at the Top*

George Stevens/*The Diary of Anne Frank*

Billy Wilder/*Some Like It Hot*

Fred Zinnemann/*The Nun's Story*

1960

★Billy Wilder/*The Apartment*

Jack Cardiff/*Sons and Lovers*

Jules Dassin/*Never on Sunday*

Alfred Hitchcock/*Psycho*

Fred Zinnemann/*The Sundowners*

1961

★Robert Wise/*West Side Story*

Federico Fellini/*La Dolce Vita*

Stanley Kramer/*Judgment at Nuremberg*

Robert Rossen/*The Hustler*

J. Lee Thompson/*The Guns of Navarone*

1962

★David Lean/*Lawrence of Arabia*

Pietro Germi/*Divorce-Italian Style*

Robert Mulligan/*To Kill a Mockingbird*

Arthur Penn/*The Miracle Worker*

Frank Perry/*David and Lisa*

1963

★Tony Richardson/*Tom Jones*

Federico Fellini/*8 1/2*

Elia Kazan/*America America*

Otto Preminger/*The Cardinal*

Martin Ritt/*Hud*

1964

★George Cukor/*My Fair Lady*

Michael Cacoyannis/*Zorba the Greek*

Peter Glenville/*Becket*

Stanley Kubrick/*Dr. Strangelove, or: How I Learned to Stop Worrying and Love the Bomb*

Robert Stevenson/*Mary Poppins*

Hiroshi Teshigahara/*Woman in the Dunes*

1965

★Robert Wise/*The Sound of Music*

David Lean/*Doctor Zhivago*

John Schlesinger/*Darling*

William Wyler/*The Collector*

1966

★Fred Zinnemann/*A Man for All Seasons*

Michelangelo Antonioni/*Blow-Up*

Richard Brooks/*The Professionals*

Claude Lelouch/*A Man and a Woman*

Mike Nichols/*Who's Afraid of Virginia Woolf?*

1967

★Mike Nichols/*The Graduate*

Richard Brooks/*In Cold Blood*

Norman Jewison/*In the Heat of the Night*

Stanley Kramer/*Guess Who's Coming to Dinner*

Arthur Penn/*Bonnie & Clyde*

1968

★Carol Reed/*Oliver!*

Anthony Harvey/*The Lion in Winter*

Stanley Kubrick/*2001: A Space Odyssey*

Gillo Pontecorvo/*The Battle of Algiers*

Franco Zeffirelli/*Romeo and Juliet*

1969

★John Schlesinger/*Midnight Cowboy*

Constantin Costa-Gavras/*Z*

George Roy Hill/*Butch Cassidy and the Sundance Kid*

Arthur Penn/*Alice's Restaurant*

Sydney Pollack/*They Shoot Horses, Don't They?*

1970

★Franklin J. Schaffner/*Patton*

Robert Altman/*M*A*S*H*

Federico Fellini/*Fellini Satyricon*

Arthur Hiller/*Love Story*

Ken Russell/*Women in Love*

1971

★William Friedkin/*The French Connection*

Peter Bogdanovich/*The Last Picture Show*

Norman Jewison/*Fiddler on the Roof*

Stanley Kubrick/*A Clockwork Orange*

John Schlesinger/*Sunday, Bloody Sunday*

1972

★Bob Fosse/*Cabaret*

John Boorman/*Deliverance*

Francis Ford Coppola/*The Godfather*

Joseph L. Mankiewicz/*Sleuth*

1973

★George Roy Hill/*The Sting*

Ingmar Bergman/*Cries and Whispers*

Bernardo Bertolucci/*Last Tango in Paris*

William Friedkin/*The Exorcist*

George Lucas/*American Graffiti*

1974

★Francis Ford Coppola/*The Godfather, Part 2*

John Cassavetes/*A Woman under the Influence*

Bob Fosse/*Lenny*

Roman Polanski/*Chinatown*

Francois Truffaut/*Day for Night*

1975

★Milos Forman/*One Flew Over the Cuckoo's Nest*

Robert Altman/*Nashville*

Federico Fellini/*Amarcord*

Stanley Kubrick/*Barry Lyndon*

Sidney Lumet/*Dog Day Afternoon*

★ = winner

1976
★John G. Avildsen/*Rocky*
Ingmar Bergman/*Face to Face*
Sidney Lumet/*Network*
Alan J. Pakula/*All the President's Men*
Lina Wertmuller/*Seven Beauties*

1977
★Woody Allen/*Annie Hall*
George Lucas/*Star Wars*
Herbert Ross/*The Turning Point*
Steven Spielberg/*Close Encounters of the Third Kind*
Fred Zinnemann/*Julia*

1978
★Michael Cimino/*The Deer Hunter*
Woody Allen/*Interiors*
Hal Ashby/*Coming Home*
Warren Beatty/*Heaven Can Wait*
Buck Henry/*Heaven Can Wait*
Alan Parker/*Midnight Express*

1979
★Robert Benton/*Kramer vs. Kramer*
Francis Ford Coppola/*Apocalypse Now*
Bob Fosse/*All That Jazz*
Edouard Molinaro/*La Cage aux Folles*
Peter Yates/*Breaking Away*

1980
★Robert Redford/*Ordinary People*
David Lynch/*The Elephant Man*
Roman Polanski/*Tess*
Richard Rush/*The Stunt Man*
Martin Scorsese/*Raging Bull*

1981
★Warren Beatty/*Reds*
Hugh Hudson/*Chariots of Fire*
Louis Malle/*Atlantic City*
Mark Rydell/*On Golden Pond*
Steven Spielberg/*Raiders of the Lost Ark*

1982
★Richard Attenborough/*Gandhi*
Sidney Lumet/*The Verdict*
Wolfgang Petersen/*Das Boot*
Sydney Pollack/*Tootsie*
Steven Spielberg/*E.T.: The Extra-Terrestrial*

1983
★James L. Brooks/*Terms of Endearment*
Bruce Beresford/*Tender Mercies*
Ingmar Bergman/*Fanny and Alexander*
Mike Nichols/*Silkwood*
Peter Yates/*The Dresser*

1984
★Milos Forman/*Amadeus*
Woody Allen/*Broadway Danny Rose*
Robert Benton/*Places in the Heart*
Roland Joffé/*The Killing Fields*
David Lean/*A Passage to India*

1985
★Sydney Pollack/*Out of Africa*
Hector Babenco/*Kiss of the Spider Woman*
John Huston/*Prizzi's Honor*
Akira Kurosawa/*Ran*
Peter Weir/*Witness*

1986
★Oliver Stone/*Platoon*
Woody Allen/*Hannah and Her Sisters*
James Ivory/*A Room with a View*
Roland Joffé/*The Mission*
David Lynch/*Blue Velvet*

1987
★Bernardo Bertolucci/*The Last Emperor*
John Boorman/*Hope and Glory*
Lasse Hallstrom/*My Life As a Dog*
Norman Jewison/*Moonstruck*
Adrian Lyne/*Fatal Attraction*

1988
★Barry Levinson/*Rain Man*
Charles Crichton/*A Fish Called Wanda*
Mike Nichols/*Working Girl*
Alan Parker/*Mississippi Burning*
Martin Scorsese/*The Last Temptation of Christ*

1989
★Oliver Stone/*Born on the Fourth of July*
Woody Allen/*Crimes & Misdemeanors*
Kenneth Branagh/*Henry V*
Jim Sheridan/*My Left Foot*
Peter Weir/*Dead Poets Society*

1990
★Kevin Costner/*Dances with Wolves*
Francis Ford Coppola/*The Godfather, Part 3*
Stephen Frears/*The Grifters*
Barbet Schroeder/*Reversal of Fortune*
Martin Scorsese/*Goodfellas*

1991
★Jonathan Demme/*The Silence of the Lambs*
Barry Levinson/*Bugsy*
Ridley Scott/*Thelma & Louise*
John Singleton/*Boyz N the Hood*
Oliver Stone/*JFK*

1992
★Clint Eastwood/*Unforgiven*
Robert Altman/*The Player*
Martin Brest/*Scent of a Woman*
James Ivory/*Howard's End*
Neil Jordan/*The Crying Game*

1993
★Steven Spielberg/*Schindler's List*
Robert Altman/*Short Cuts*
Jane Campion/*The Piano*
James Ivory/*The Remains of the Day*
Jim Sheridan/*In the Name of the Father*

1994
★Robert Zemeckis/*Forrest Gump*
Woody Allen/*Bullets over Broadway*
Krzysztof Kieslowski/*Trois Couleurs: Rouge*
Robert Redford/*Quiz Show*
Quentin Tarantino/*Pulp Fiction*

1995
★Mel Gibson/*Braveheart*
Mike Figgis/*Leaving Las Vegas*
Chris Noonan/*Babe*
Michael Radford/*The Postman*
Tim Robbins/*Dead Man Walking*

1996
★Anthony Minghella/*The English Patient*
Joel Coen/*Fargo*
Milos Forman/*The People vs. Larry Flynt*
Scott Hicks/*Shine*
Mike Leigh/*Secrets and Lies*

1997
★James Cameron/*Titanic*
Peter Cattaneo/*The Full Monty*
Atom Egoyan/*The Sweet Hereafter*
Curtis Hanson/*L.A. Confidential*
Gus Van Sant/*Good Will Hunting*

1998
★Steven Spielberg/*Saving Private Ryan*
Roberto Benigni/*Life Is Beautiful*
John Madden/*Shakespeare in Love*
Terrence Malick/*The Thin Red Line*
Peter Weir/*The Truman Show*

1999
★Sam Mendes/*American Beauty*
Lasse Hallstrom/*The Cider House Rules*
Spike Jonze/*Being John Malkovich*
Michael Mann/*The Insider*
M. Night Shyamalan/*The Sixth Sense*

2000
★Steven Soderbergh/*Traffic*
Stephen Daldry/*Billy Elliot*
Ang Lee/*Crouching Tiger, Hidden Dragon*
Ridley Scott/*Gladiator*
Steven Soderbergh/*Erin Brockovich*

2001
★Ron Howard/*A Beautiful Mind*
Robert Altman/*Gosford Park*
Peter Jackson/*Lord of the Rings: The Fellowship of the Ring*
David Lynch/*Mulholland Drive*
Ridley Scott/*Black Hawk Down*

2002
★Roman Polanski/*The Pianist*
Pedro Almodóvar/*Talk to Her*
Stephen Daldry/*The Hours*
Rob Marshall/*Chicago*
Martin Scorsese/*Gangs of New York*

2003
★Peter Jackson/*Lord of the Rings: The Return of the King*
Sofia Coppola/*Lost in Translation*
Clint Eastwood/*Mystic River*
Fernando Meirelles/*City of God*
Peter Weir/*Master and Commander: The Far Side of the World*

2004
★Clint Eastwood/*Million Dollar Baby*
Taylor Hackford/*Ray*
Mike Leigh/*Vera Drake*
Alexander Payne/*Sideways*
Martin Scorsese/*The Aviator*

2005
★Ang Lee/*Brokeback Mountain*
George Clooney/*Good Night, and Good Luck*
Paul Haggis/*Crash*
Bennett Miller/*Capote*
Steven Spielberg/*Munich*

2006
★Martin Scorsese/*The Departed*
Clint Eastwood/*Letters from Iwo Jima*
Stephen Frears/*The Queen*
Paul Greengrass/*United 93*
Alejandro Gonzalez Inarritu/*Babel*

2007
★Ethan Coen/*No Country for Old Men*
★Joel Coen/*No Country for Old Men*
Paul Thomas Anderson/*There Will Be Blood*
Tony Gilroy/*Michael Clayton*
Jason Reitman/*Juno*
Julian Schnabel/*The Diving Bell and the Butterfly*

2008
★Danny Boyle/*Slumdog Millionaire*
Stephen Daldry/*The Reader*
David Fincher/*The Curious Case of Benjamin Button*
Ron Howard/*Frost/Nixon*
Gus Van Sant/*Milk*

2009
★Kathryn Bigelow/*The Hurt Locker*
James Cameron/*Avatar*
Lee Daniels/*Precious: Based on the Novel 'Push' by Sapphire*
Jason Reitman/*Up in the Air*
Quentin Tarantino/*Inglourious Basterds*

2010
★Tom Hooper/*The King's Speech*
Darren Aronofsky/*Black Swan*
Ethan Coen/*True Grit*
Joel Coen/*True Grit*
David Fincher/*The Social Network*
David O. Russell/*The Fighter*

2011
★Michel Hazanavicius/*The Artist*
Woody Allen/*Midnight in Paris*
Terrence Malick/*The Tree of Life*
Alexander Payne/*The Descendants*
Martin Scorsese/*Hugo*

2012
★Ang Lee/*Life of Pi*
Michael Haneke/*Amour*
David O. Russell/*Silver Linings Playbook*
Steven Spielberg/*Lincoln*
Benh Zeitlin/*Beasts of the Southern Wild*

2013
★Alfonso Cuarón/*Gravity*
Steve McQueen/*12 Years a Slave*
Alexander Payne/*Nebraska*
David O. Russell/*American Hustle*
Martin Scorsese/*The Wolf of Wall Street*

2014
★Alejandro Gonzalez Inarritu/*Birdman, or (The Unexpected Virtue of Ignorance)*
Wes Anderson/*The Grand Budapest Hotel*
Richard Linklater/*Boyhood*
Bennett Miller/*Foxcatcher*
Morten Tyldum/*The Imitation Game*

2015
★Alejandro Gonzalez Inarritu/*The Revenant*
Lenny Abrahamson/*Room*
Tom McCarthy/*Spotlight*
Adam McKay/*The Big Short*
George Miller/*Mad Max: Fury Road*

2016
★Damien Chazelle/*La La Land*
Mel Gibson/*Hacksaw Ridge*
Barry Jenkins/*Moonlight*
Kenneth Lonergan/*Manchester by the Sea*
Denis Villeneuve/*Arrival*

2017
★Guillermo del Toro/*The Shape of Water*
Paul Thomas Anderson/*Phantom Thread*
Greta Gerwig/*Lady Bird*
Christopher Nolan/*Dunkirk*
Jordan Peele/*Get Out*

2018
★Alfonso Cuarón/*Roma*
Yorgos Lanthimos/*The Favourite*
Spike Lee/*BlacKkKlansman*
Adam McKay/*Vice*
Pawel Pawlikowski/*Cold War*

2019
★Joon-ho Bong/*Parasite*
Sam Mendes/*1917*
Todd Phillips/*Joker*
Martin Scorsese/*The Irishman*
Quentin Tarantino/*Once Upon A Time... In Hollywood*

FILM

1928
★*Sunrise*
★*Wings*
Chang: A Drama of the Wilderness
The Last Command

1929
★*Broadway Melody*
Alibi
Hollywood Revue of 1929

1930
★*All Quiet on the Western Front*
The Big House
The Divorcee
The Love Parade

1931
★*Cimarron*
Five Star Final
The Front Page

1932
★*Grand Hotel*
Arrowsmith
The Champ
One Hour with You
Shanghai Express
The Smiling Lieutenant

1933
★*Cavalcade*
A Farewell to Arms
42nd Street
I Am a Fugitive from a Chain Gang
Lady for a Day
Little Women
The Private Life of Henry VIII
She Done Him Wrong
Smilin' Through

1934
★*It Happened One Night*
The Barretts of Wimpole Street
Cleopatra
Flirtation Walk
The Gay Divorcee
Here Comes the Navy
Imitation of Life
The Thin Man

1935
★*Mutiny on the Bounty*
Alice Adams
Broadway Melody of 1936
Captain Blood
David Copperfield
The Informer
Les Miserables
The Lives of a Bengal Lancer
A Midsummer Night's Dream
Naughty Marietta
Ruggles of Red Gap
Top Hat

1936
★*The Great Ziegfeld*
Anthony Adverse
Dodsworth
Libeled Lady
Mr. Deeds Goes to Town
Romeo and Juliet
San Francisco
A Tale of Two Cities
Three Smart Girls

1937
★*The Life of Emile Zola*
The Awful Truth
Captains Courageous
Dead End
The Good Earth
In Old Chicago
Lost Horizon
100 Men and a Girl
Stage Door
A Star Is Born

1938
★*You Can't Take It with You*
The Adventures of Robin Hood
Alexander's Ragtime Band
Boys Town
The Citadel
Four Daughters
Grand Illusion
Jezebel
Pygmalion
Test Pilot

1939
★*Gone with the Wind*
Dark Victory
Goodbye, Mr. Chips
Love Affair
Mr. Smith Goes to Washington
Ninotchka
Of Mice and Men
Stagecoach
The Wizard of Oz
Wuthering Heights

1940
★*Rebecca*
All This and Heaven Too
Foreign Correspondent
The Grapes of Wrath
The Great Dictator
Kitty Foyle
The Letter
The Long Voyage Home
Our Town
The Philadelphia Story

★ = winner

1941
★How Green Was My Valley
Blossoms in the Dust
Citizen Kane
Here Comes Mr. Jordan
The Little Foxes
The Maltese Falcon
One Foot in Heaven
Sergeant York
Suspicion

1942
★Mrs. Miniver
Hold Back the Dawn
Kings Row
The Magnificent Ambersons
The Pride of the Yankees
Random Harvest
Talk of the Town
Wake Island
Yankee Doodle Dandy

1943
★Casablanca
For Whom the Bell Tolls
Heaven Can Wait
The Human Comedy
In Which We Serve
Madame Curie
The More the Merrier
The Ox-Bow Incident
The Song of Bernadette
Watch on the Rhine

1944
★Going My Way
Double Indemnity
Gaslight
Since You Went Away
Wilson

1945
★The Lost Weekend
Anchors Aweigh
The Bells of St. Mary's
Mildred Pierce
Spellbound

1946
★The Best Years of Our Lives
Henry V
It's a Wonderful Life
The Razor's Edge
The Yearling

1947
★Gentleman's Agreement
The Bishop's Wife
Crossfire
Great Expectations
Miracle on 34th Street

1948
★Hamlet
Johnny Belinda
The Red Shoes
The Snake Pit
Treasure of the Sierra Madre

1949
★All the King's Men
Battleground
The Heiress
A Letter to Three Wives
Twelve o'Clock High

1950
★All About Eve
Born Yesterday
Father of the Bride
King Solomon's Mines
Sunset Boulevard

1951
★An American in Paris
Decision Before Dawn
A Place in the Sun
Quo Vadis
A Streetcar Named Desire

1952
★The Greatest Show on Earth
High Noon
Ivanhoe
Moulin Rouge
The Quiet Man

1953
★From Here to Eternity
Julius Caesar
The Robe
Roman Holiday
Shane

1954
★On the Waterfront
The Caine Mutiny
Country Girl
Seven Brides for Seven Brothers
Three Coins in the Fountain

1955
★Marty
Love Is a Many-Splendored Thing
Mister Roberts
Picnic
The Rose Tattoo

1956
★Around the World in 80 Days
Friendly Persuasion
Giant
The King and I
The Ten Commandments

1957
★The Bridge on the River Kwai
Peyton Place
Sayonara
Twelve Angry Men
Witness for the Prosecution

1958
★Gigi
Auntie Mame
Cat on a Hot Tin Roof
The Defiant Ones
Separate Tables

1959
★Ben-Hur
Anatomy of a Murder
The Diary of Anne Frank
The Nun's Story
Room at the Top

1960
★The Apartment
The Alamo
Elmer Gantry
Sons and Lovers
The Sundowners

1961
★West Side Story
Fanny
The Guns of Navarone
The Hustler
Judgment at Nuremberg

1962
★Lawrence of Arabia
The Longest Day
The Music Man
Mutiny on the Bounty
To Kill a Mockingbird

1963
★Tom Jones
America America
Cleopatra
How the West Was Won
Lilies of the Field

1964
★My Fair Lady
Becket
Dr. Strangelove, or: How I Learned to Stop Worrying and Love the Bomb
Mary Poppins
Zorba the Greek

1965
★The Sound of Music
Darling
Doctor Zhivago
Ship of Fools
A Thousand Clowns

1966
★A Man for All Seasons
Alfie
The Russians Are Coming, the Russians Are Coming
The Sand Pebbles
Who's Afraid of Virginia Woolf?

1967
★In the Heat of the Night
Bonnie & Clyde
Doctor Dolittle
The Graduate
Guess Who's Coming to Dinner

1968
★Oliver!
Funny Girl
The Lion in Winter
Rachel, Rachel
Romeo and Juliet

1969
★Midnight Cowboy
Anne of the Thousand Days
Butch Cassidy and the Sundance Kid
Hello, Dolly!
Z

1970
★Patton
Airport
Five Easy Pieces
Love Story
M*A*S*H

1971
★The French Connection
A Clockwork Orange
Fiddler on the Roof
The Last Picture Show
Nicholas and Alexandra

1972
★The Godfather
Cabaret
Deliverance
Sounder

1973
★The Sting
American Graffiti
Cries and Whispers
The Exorcist
A Touch of Class

1974
★The Godfather, Part 2
Chinatown
The Conversation
Lenny
The Towering Inferno

1975
★One Flew Over the Cuckoo's Nest
Barry Lyndon
Dog Day Afternoon
Jaws
Nashville

1976
★Rocky
All the President's Men
Bound for Glory
Network
Taxi Driver

1977
★Annie Hall
The Goodbye Girl
Julia
Star Wars
The Turning Point

1978
★The Deer Hunter
Coming Home
Heaven Can Wait
Midnight Express
An Unmarried Woman

1979
★Kramer vs. Kramer
All That Jazz
Apocalypse Now
Breaking Away
Norma Rae

1980
★Ordinary People
Coal Miner's Daughter
The Elephant Man
Raging Bull
Tess

1981
★Chariots of Fire
Atlantic City
On Golden Pond
Raiders of the Lost Ark
Reds

1982
★Gandhi
E.T.: The Extra-Terrestrial
Missing
Tootsie
The Verdict

1983
★Terms of Endearment
The Big Chill
The Dresser
The Right Stuff
Tender Mercies

1984
★Amadeus
The Killing Fields
A Passage to India
Places in the Heart
A Soldier's Story

1985
★Out of Africa
The Color Purple
Kiss of the Spider Woman
Prizzi's Honor
Witness

1986
★Platoon
Children of a Lesser God
Hannah and Her Sisters
The Mission
A Room with a View

1987
★The Last Emperor
Broadcast News
Fatal Attraction
Hope and Glory
Moonstruck

1988
★Rain Man
The Accidental Tourist
Dangerous Liaisons
Mississippi Burning
Working Girl

1989
★Driving Miss Daisy
Born on the Fourth of July
Dead Poets Society
Field of Dreams
My Left Foot

1990
★Dances with Wolves
Awakenings
Ghost
The Godfather, Part 3
Goodfellas

1991
★The Silence of the Lambs
Beauty and the Beast
Bugsy
JFK
The Prince of Tides

1992
★Unforgiven
The Crying Game
A Few Good Men
Howard's End
Scent of a Woman

1993
★Schindler's List
The Fugitive
In the Name of the Father
The Piano
The Remains of the Day

1994
★Forrest Gump
Four Weddings and a Funeral
Pulp Fiction
Quiz Show
The Shawshank Redemption

1995
★Braveheart
Apollo 13
Babe
The Postman
Sense and Sensibility

1996
★The English Patient
Fargo
Jerry Maguire
Secrets and Lies
Shine

1997
★Titanic
As Good As It Gets
The Full Monty
Good Will Hunting
L.A. Confidential

1998
★Shakespeare in Love
Elizabeth
Life Is Beautiful
Saving Private Ryan
The Thin Red Line

1999
★American Beauty
The Cider House Rules
The Green Mile
The Insider
The Sixth Sense

2000
★Gladiator
Chocolat
Crouching Tiger, Hidden Dragon
Erin Brockovich
Traffic

2001
★A Beautiful Mind
Gosford Park
In the Bedroom
Lord of the Rings: The Fellowship of the Ring
Moulin Rouge

2002
★Chicago
Gangs of New York
The Hours
Lord of the Rings: The Two Towers
The Pianist

2003
★Lord of the Rings: The Return of the King
Lost in Translation
Master and Commander: The Far Side of the World
Mystic River
Seabiscuit

2004
★Million Dollar Baby
The Aviator
Finding Neverland
Ray
Sideways

2005
★Crash
Brokeback Mountain
Capote
Good Night, and Good Luck
Munich

2006
★The Departed
Babel
Letters from Iwo Jima
Little Miss Sunshine
The Queen

2007
★No Country for Old Men
Atonement
Juno
Michael Clayton
There Will Be Blood

2008
★Slumdog Millionaire
The Curious Case of Benjamin Button
Frost/Nixon
Milk
The Reader

2009
★The Hurt Locker
Avatar
The Blind Side
District 9
An Education
Inglourious Basterds
Precious: Based on the Novel 'Push' by Sapphire
A Serious Man
Up
Up in the Air

2010
★The King's Speech
Black Swan
The Fighter
Inception
The Kids Are All Right
127 Hours
The Social Network
Toy Story 3
True Grit
Winter's Bone

2011
★The Artist
The Descendants
Extremely Loud and Incredibly Close
The Help
Hugo
Midnight in Paris
Moneyball
The Tree of Life
War Horse

★ = winner

2012
★Argo
Amour
Beasts of the Southern Wild
Django Unchained
Les Miserables
Life of Pi
Lincoln
Silver Linings Playbook
Zero Dark Thirty

2013
★12 Years a Slave
American Hustle
Captain Phillips
Dallas Buyers Club
Gravity
Her
Nebraska
Philomena
The Wolf of Wall Street

2014
★Birdman, or (The Unexpected Virtue of Ignorance)
American Sniper
Boyhood
The Grand Budapest Hotel
The Imitation Game
Selma
The Theory of Everything
Whiplash

2015
★Spotlight
The Big Short
Bridge of Spies
Brooklyn
Mad Max: Fury Road
The Martian
The Revenant
Room

2016
★Moonlight
Arrival
Fences
Hacksaw Ridge
Hell or High Water
Hidden Figures
La La Land
Lion
Manchester by the Sea

2017
★The Shape of Water
Call Me by Your Name
Darkest Hour
Dunkirk
Get Out
Lady Bird
Phantom Thread
The Post
Three Billboards Outside Ebbing, Missouri

2018
★Green Book
Black Panther
BlacKkKlansman
Bohemian Rhapsody
The Favourite
Roma
A Star Is Born
Vice

2019
★Parasite
Ford v Ferrari
The Irishman
Jojo Rabbit
Joker
Little Women
Marriage Story
1917
Once Upon A Time... In Hollywood

FEATURE DOCUMENTARY

1970
★Woodstock

1971
★The Hellstrom Chronicle
The Sorrow and the Pity

1972
★Marjoe

1974
★Hearts & Minds

1976
★Harlan County, U.S.A.

1977
The Children of Theatre Street

1980
★From Mao to Mozart: Isaac Stern in China

1984
★Times of Harvey Milk

1988
Let's Get Lost

1989
★Common Threads: Stories from the Quilt

1990
★American Dream

1993
The War Room

1996
★When We Were Kings

1998
★The Last Days

1999
Buena Vista Social Club

2000
★Into the Arms of Strangers: Stories of the Kindertransport

2002
★Bowling for Columbine
Prisoner of Paradise
Spellbound
Winged Migration

2003
★The Fog of War: Eleven Lessons from the Life of Robert S. McNamara
Capturing the Friedmans
My Architect: A Son's Journey
The Weather Underground

2004
★Born Into Brothels: Calcutta's Red Light Kids
The Story of the Weeping Camel
Super Size Me

2005
★March of the Penguins
Darwin's Nightmare
Enron: The Smartest Guys in the Room
Murderball

2006
★An Inconvenient Truth
Jesus Camp

2007
No End in Sight
Sicko

2008
★Man on Wire
Encounters at the End of the World

2009
★The Cove
Food, Inc.
Which Way Home

2010
★Inside Job
Exit Through the Gift Shop
GasLand
Restrepo
Waste Land

2011
★Undefeated
Hell and Back Again
If a Tree Falls: A Story of the Earth Liberation Front
Paradise Lost 3: Purgatory
Pina

2012
★Searching For Sugar Man
5 Broken Cameras
The Gatekeepers
How to Survive a Plague

2013
★20 Feet from Stardom
The Act of Killing
Cutie and the Boxer
Dirty Wars
The Square

2014
★Citizenfour
Finding Vivian Maier
Last Days in Vietnam
The Salt of the Earth
Virunga

2015
★Amy
What Happened, Miss Simone?
Winter on Fire: Ukraine's Fight for Freedom

2016
Fire at Sea
I Am Not Your Negro
Life, Animated

2017
★Icarus
Faces Places
Last Men In Aleppo
Strong Island

2018
★Free Solo
Hale County This Morning, This Evening
Minding the Gap
Of Fathers and Sons
RBG

2019
★American Factory
The Cave
The Edge of Democracy
For Sama
Honeyland

FILM EDITING

1934
Cleopatra

1935
★A Midsummer Night's Dream
David Copperfield
The Informer
Les Miserables
The Lives of a Bengal Lancer
Mutiny on the Bounty

1936
★Anthony Adverse
Come and Get It
The Great Ziegfeld
Lloyds of London
A Tale of Two Cities
Theodora Goes Wild

1937
★Lost Horizon
The Awful Truth
Captains Courageous
The Good Earth
100 Men and a Girl

1938
★The Adventures of Robin Hood
Alexander's Ragtime Band
The Great Waltz
Test Pilot
You Can't Take It with You

1939
★Gone with the Wind
Goodbye, Mr. Chips
Mr. Smith Goes to Washington
The Rains Came
Stagecoach

1940
The Grapes of Wrath
The Letter
The Long Voyage Home
Rebecca

1941
★Sergeant York
Citizen Kane
Dr. Jekyll and Mr. Hyde
How Green Was My Valley
The Little Foxes

1942
★The Pride of the Yankees
Mrs. Miniver
Talk of the Town
Yankee Doodle Dandy

1943
★Air Force
Casablanca
Five Graves to Cairo
For Whom the Bell Tolls
The Song of Bernadette
This Above All

1944
★Wilson
Going My Way
None But the Lonely Heart
Since You Went Away

1945
★National Velvet
The Bells of St. Mary's
The Lost Weekend
Objective, Burma!
A Song to Remember

1946
★The Best Years of Our Lives
It's a Wonderful Life
The Jolson Story
The Killers
The Yearling

1947
★Body and Soul
The Bishop's Wife
Gentleman's Agreement
Green Dolphin Street
Odd Man Out

1948
★The Naked City
Joan of Arc
Johnny Belinda
Red River
The Red Shoes

1949
★Champion
All the King's Men
Battleground
Sands of Iwo Jima
The Window

1950
★King Solomon's Mines
Annie Get Your Gun
Sunset Boulevard
The Third Man

1951
★A Place in the Sun
An American in Paris
Decision Before Dawn
Quo Vadis
The Well

1952
★High Noon
Come Back, Little Sheba
Flat Top
The Greatest Show on Earth
Moulin Rouge

1953
★From Here to Eternity
The Moon Is Blue
Roman Holiday
The War of the Worlds

1954
★On the Waterfront
The Caine Mutiny
Seven Brides for Seven Brothers
20,000 Leagues under the Sea

1955
★Picnic
Blackboard Jungle
The Bridges at Toko-Ri
Oklahoma!
The Rose Tattoo

1956
★Around the World in 80 Days
The Brave One
Giant
Somebody Up There Likes Me
The Ten Commandments

1957
★The Bridge on the River Kwai
Gunfight at the O.K. Corral
Pal Joey
Sayonara
Witness for the Prosecution

1958
★Gigi
Auntie Mame
Cowboy
The Defiant Ones
I Want to Live!

1959
★Ben-Hur
Anatomy of a Murder
North by Northwest
The Nun's Story
On the Beach

1960
★The Apartment
The Alamo
Inherit the Wind
Spartacus

1961
★West Side Story
Fanny
The Guns of Navarone
Judgment at Nuremberg
The Parent Trap

1962
★Lawrence of Arabia
The Longest Day
The Manchurian Candidate
The Music Man
Mutiny on the Bounty

1963
★How the West Was Won
The Cardinal
Cleopatra
The Great Escape
It's a Mad, Mad, Mad, Mad World

1964
★Mary Poppins
Becket
Father Goose
Hush, Hush, Sweet Charlotte
My Fair Lady

1965
★The Sound of Music
Cat Ballou
Doctor Zhivago
The Flight of the Phoenix
The Great Race

1966
★Grand Prix
Fantastic Voyage
The Russians Are Coming, the Russians Are Coming
The Sand Pebbles
Who's Afraid of Virginia Woolf?

1967
★In the Heat of the Night
The Dirty Dozen
Doctor Dolittle
Guess Who's Coming to Dinner

1968
★Bullitt
Funny Girl
The Odd Couple
Oliver!
Wild in the Streets

1969
★Z
Hello, Dolly!
Midnight Cowboy
They Shoot Horses, Don't They?

1970
★Patton
Airport
M*A*S*H
Tora! Tora! Tora!
Woodstock

1971
★The French Connection
The Andromeda Strain
A Clockwork Orange
Kotch
Summer of '42

1972
★Cabaret
Deliverance
The Godfather
The Hot Rock
The Poseidon Adventure

1973
★The Sting
American Graffiti
The Day of the Jackal
The Exorcist
Jonathan Livingston Seagull

1974
★The Towering Inferno
Blazing Saddles
Chinatown
Earthquake
The Longest Yard

1975
★Jaws
Dog Day Afternoon
The Man Who Would Be King
One Flew Over the Cuckoo's Nest
Three Days of the Condor

★ = winner

1976
★Rocky
All the President's Men
Bound for Glory
Network
Two Minute Warning
1977
★Star Wars
Close Encounters of the Third Kind
Julia
Smokey and the Bandit
The Turning Point
1978
★The Deer Hunter
The Boys from Brazil
Coming Home
Midnight Express
Superman: The Movie
1979
★All That Jazz
Apocalypse Now
The Black Stallion
Kramer vs. Kramer
The Rose
1980
★Raging Bull
Coal Miner's Daughter
The Competition
The Elephant Man
Fame
1981
★Raiders of the Lost Ark
Chariots of Fire
The French Lieutenant's Woman
On Golden Pond
Reds
1982
★Gandhi
Das Boot
E.T.: The Extra-Terrestrial
An Officer and a Gentleman
Tootsie
1983
★The Right Stuff
Blue Thunder
Flashdance
Silkwood
Terms of Endearment
1984
★The Killing Fields
Amadeus
The Cotton Club
A Passage to India
Romancing the Stone
1985
★Witness
A Chorus Line
Out of Africa
Prizzi's Honor
Runaway Train
1986
★Platoon
Aliens
Hannah and Her Sisters
The Mission
Top Gun
1987
★The Last Emperor
Broadcast News
Empire of the Sun
Fatal Attraction
RoboCop
1988
★Who Framed Roger Rabbit
Die Hard
Gorillas in the Mist
Mississippi Burning
Rain Man
1989
★Born on the Fourth of July
The Bear
Driving Miss Daisy
The Fabulous Baker Boys
Glory
1990
★Dances with Wolves
Ghost
The Godfather, Part 3
Goodfellas
The Hunt for Red October
1991
★JFK
The Commitments
The Silence of the Lambs
Terminator 2: Judgment Day
Thelma & Louise
1992
★Unforgiven
Basic Instinct
The Crying Game
A Few Good Men
The Player
1993
★Schindler's List
The Fugitive
In the Line of Fire
In the Name of the Father
The Piano
1994
★Forrest Gump
Hoop Dreams
Pulp Fiction
The Shawshank Redemption
Speed
1995
★Apollo 13
Babe
Braveheart
Crimson Tide
Seven
1996
★The English Patient
Evita
Fargo
Jerry Maguire
Shine
1997
★Titanic
Air Force One
As Good As It Gets
Good Will Hunting
L.A. Confidential
1998
★Saving Private Ryan
Life Is Beautiful
Out of Sight
Shakespeare in Love
The Thin Red Line
1999
★The Matrix
American Beauty
The Cider House Rules
The Insider
The Sixth Sense
2000
★Traffic
Almost Famous
Crouching Tiger, Hidden Dragon
Gladiator
Wonder Boys
2001
★Black Hawk Down
A Beautiful Mind
Lord of the Rings: The Fellowship of the Ring
Memento
Moulin Rouge
2002
★Chicago
Gangs of New York
The Hours
Lord of the Rings: The Two Towers
The Pianist
2003
★Lord of the Rings: The Return of the King
City of God
Cold Mountain
Master and Commander: The Far Side of the World
Seabiscuit
2004
★The Aviator
Collateral
Finding Neverland
Million Dollar Baby
Ray
2005
★Crash
Cinderella Man
The Constant Gardener
Munich
Walk the Line
2006
★The Departed
Babel
Blood Diamond
Children of Men
United 93
2007
★The Bourne Ultimatum
The Diving Bell and the Butterfly
Into the Wild
No Country for Old Men
There Will Be Blood
2008
★Slumdog Millionaire
The Curious Case of Benjamin Button
The Dark Knight
Frost/Nixon
Milk
2009
★The Hurt Locker
Avatar
District 9
Inglourious Basterds
Precious: Based on the Novel 'Push' by Sapphire
2010
★The Social Network
Black Swan
The Fighter
The King's Speech
127 Hours
2011
★The Girl With the Dragon Tattoo
The Artist
The Descendants
Hugo
Moneyball
2012
★Argo
Life of Pi
Lincoln
Silver Linings Playbook
Zero Dark Thirty
2013
★Gravity
American Hustle
Captain Phillips
Dallas Buyers Club
12 Years a Slave
2014
★Whiplash
American Sniper
Boyhood
The Grand Budapest Hotel
The Imitation Game
2015
★Mad Max: Fury Road
The Big Short
The Revenant
Spotlight
Star Wars: The Force Awakens
2016
★Hacksaw Ridge
Arrival
Hell or High Water
La La Land
Moonlight
2017
★Dunkirk
Baby Driver
I, Tonya
The Shape of Water
Three Billboards Outside Ebbing, Missouri
2018
★Bohemian Rhapsody
BlacKkKlansman
The Favourite
Green Book
Vice
2019
★Ford v Ferrari
The Irishman
Jojo Rabbit
Joker
Parasite

MAKEUP

1981
★An American Werewolf in London
1982
★Quest for Fire
Gandhi
1984
★Amadeus
Greystoke: The Legend of Tarzan, Lord of the Apes
2010: The Year We Make Contact
1985
★Mask
The Color Purple
Remo Williams: The Adventure Begins
1986
★The Fly
The Clan of the Cave Bear
Legend
1987
★Harry and the Hendersons
Happy New Year
1988
★Beetlejuice
1989
★Driving Miss Daisy
The Adventures of Baron Munchausen
Dad
1990
★Dick Tracy
Cyrano de Bergerac
Edward Scissorhands
1991
★Terminator 2: Judgment Day
Hook
Star Trek 6: The Undiscovered Country
1992
★Bram Stoker's Dracula
Batman Returns
Hoffa
1993
★Mrs. Doubtfire
Philadelphia
Schindler's List
1994
★Ed Wood
Forrest Gump
Mary Shelley's Frankenstein
1995
★Braveheart
My Family
Roommates
1996
★The Nutty Professor
Ghosts of Mississippi
Star Trek: First Contact
1997
★Men in Black
Mrs. Brown
Titanic
1998
★Elizabeth
Saving Private Ryan
Shakespeare in Love
1999
★Topsy Turvy
Austin Powers 2: The Spy Who Shagged Me
Bicentennial Man
Life
2000
The Cell
Dr. Seuss' How the Grinch Stole Christmas
Shadow of the Vampire
2001
A Beautiful Mind
Lord of the Rings: The Fellowship of the Ring
Moulin Rouge
2002
★Frida
The Time Machine
2003
★Lord of the Rings: The Return of the King
Master and Commander: The Far Side of the World
Pirates of the Caribbean: The Curse of the Black Pearl
2004
★Lemony Snicket's A Series of Unfortunate Events
The Passion of the Christ
The Sea Inside
2005
★The Chronicles of Narnia: The Lion, the Witch and the Wardrobe
Cinderella Man
Star Wars: Episode 3-Revenge of the Sith
2006
★Pan's Labyrinth
Apocalypto
Click
2007
★La Vie en Rose
Norbit
Pirates of the Caribbean: At World's End
2008
★The Curious Case of Benjamin Button
The Dark Knight
Hellboy II: The Golden Army
2009
★Star Trek
Il Divo
Star Trek
The Young Victoria
2010
★The Wolfman
Barney's Version
The Way Back
2011
★The Iron Lady
Albert Nobbs
Harry Potter and the Deathly Hallows, Part 2
2012
★Les Miserables
Hitchcock
The Hobbit: An Unexpected Journey
2013
★Dallas Buyers Club
Jackass Presents: Bad Grandpa
2014
★The Grand Budapest Hotel
Foxcatcher
Guardians of the Galaxy
2015
★Mad Max: Fury Road
The 100-Year-Old Man Who Climbed Out the Window and Disappeared
The Revenant
2016
★Suicide Squad
A Man Called Ove
Star Trek: Beyond
2017
★Darkest Hour
Victoria & Abdul
Wonder
2018
★Vice
Mary Queen of Scots
2019
★Bombshell
Joker
Judy
Maleficent: Mistress of Evil
1917

ADAPTED SCORE

1962
★The Music Man
Billy Rose's Jumbo
Gypsy
1963
★Irma La Douce
Bye, Bye, Birdie
A New Kind of Love
The Sword in the Stone
1964
★My Fair Lady
A Hard Day's Night
Robin and the 7 Hoods
The Unsinkable Molly Brown
1965
★The Sound of Music
Cat Ballou
A Thousand Clowns
1966
★A Funny Thing Happened on the Way to the Forum
The Gospel According to St. Matthew
Return of the Magnificent Seven
The Singing Nun

★ = winner

1967
★Camelot
Guess Who's Coming to Dinner
Valley of the Dolls
1968
★Oliver!
Star!

ORIGINAL DRAMATIC SCORE

1941
★The Devil & Daniel Webster
Ball of Fire
Cheers for Miss Bishop
Citizen Kane
Dr. Jekyll and Mr. Hyde
How Green Was My Valley
King of the Zombies
The Little Foxes
Sergeant York
So Ends Our Night
Sundown
Suspicion
That Uncertain Feeling
1942
★Now, Voyager
Arabian Nights
Bambi
The Black Swan
The Corsican Brothers
Flying Tigers
Joan of Paris
The Jungle Book
The Pride of the Yankees
Random Harvest
The Shanghai Gesture
Silver Queen
Talk of the Town
To Be or Not to Be
1943
★The Song of Bernadette
The Amazing Mrs. Holiday
Casablanca
Commandos Strike at Dawn
The Fallen Sparrow
For Whom the Bell Tolls
Hangmen Also Die
Hi Diddle Diddle
Johnny Come Lately
The Kansan
Lady of Burlesque
Madame Curie
The Moon and Sixpence
The North Star
War of the Wildcats
1944
★Cover Girl
★Since You Went Away
The Adventures of Mark Twain
The Bridge of San Luis Rey
Casanova Brown
Double Indemnity
Fighting Seabees
The Hairy Ape
Higher and Higher
Jack London
None But the Lonely Heart
The Princess and the Pirate
Wilson
The Woman of the Town
1945
★Spellbound
The Bells of St. Mary's
Brewster's Millions
Captain Kidd
The Enchanted Cottage
Flame of the Barbary Coast
Guest in the House
Guest Wife
The Keys of the Kingdom
The Lost Weekend
Objective, Burma!
A Song to Remember
The Southerner
The Valley of Decision
Woman in the Window

1946
★The Best Years of Our Lives
Anna and the King of Siam
Henry V
Humoresque
The Killers
1947
★A Double Life
The Bishop's Wife
Captain from Castile
Forever Amber
Life with Father
The Road to Rio
1948
★The Red Shoes
Hamlet
Joan of Arc
Johnny Belinda
The Snake Pit
1949
★The Heiress
Champion
1950
★Sunset Boulevard
All About Eve
The Flame & the Arrow
Samson and Delilah
1951
★A Place in the Sun
David and Bathsheba
Quo Vadis
A Streetcar Named Desire
1952
★High Noon
Ivanhoe
Miracle of Our Lady of Fatima
The Thief
Viva Zapata!
1953
★Lili
Above and Beyond
From Here to Eternity
Julius Caesar
1954
★The High and the Mighty
The Caine Mutiny
Genevieve
On the Waterfront
The Silver Chalice
1955
★Love Is a Many-Splendored Thing
Battle Cry
The Man with the Golden Arm
Picnic
The Rose Tattoo
1956
★Around the World in 80 Days
Anastasia
Between Heaven and Hell
Giant
The Rainmaker
1958
★The Old Man and the Sea
The Big Country
Separate Tables
The Young Lions
1959
★Ben-Hur
The Diary of Anne Frank
The Nun's Story
On the Beach
Pillow Talk

1960
★Exodus
The Alamo
Elmer Gantry
The Magnificent Seven
Spartacus
1961
★Breakfast at Tiffany's
El Cid
Fanny
The Guns of Navarone
Summer and Smoke
1971
★Summer of '42
Mary, Queen of Scots
Nicholas and Alexandra
Shaft
Straw Dogs
1972
Napoleon and Samantha
The Poseidon Adventure
Sleuth
1973
★The Way We Were
Cinderella Liberty
The Day of the Dolphin
Papillon
A Touch of Class
1974
★The Godfather, Part 2
Chinatown
Murder on the Orient Express
The Towering Inferno
1995
★The Postman
Apollo 13
Braveheart
Nixon
Sense and Sensibility
1996
★The English Patient
Hamlet
Michael Collins
Shine
Sleepers
1998
★Life Is Beautiful
Elizabeth
Pleasantville
Saving Private Ryan

ORIGINAL MUSICAL/ COMEDY SCORE

1997
★The Full Monty
Anastasia
As Good As It Gets
Men in Black
My Best Friend's Wedding
1998
★Shakespeare in Love
A Bug's Life
Mulan
Patch Adams
Prince of Egypt

ORIGINAL SONG SCORE AND/OR ADAPTATION

1957
★The Bridge on the River Kwai
1970
★Let It Be
The Baby Maker
Darling Lili
Scrooge

1971
★Fiddler on the Roof
Bedknobs and Broomsticks
The Boy Friend
Willy Wonka & the Chocolate Factory
1972
★Cabaret
Lady Sings the Blues
Man of La Mancha
1973
★The Sting
Jesus Christ, Superstar
Tom Sawyer
1974
★The Great Gatsby
The Little Prince
Phantom of the Paradise
1975
★Barry Lyndon
Funny Lady
1976
★Bound for Glory
A Star Is Born
1977
★A Little Night Music
Pete's Dragon
1978
★The Buddy Holly Story
Pretty Baby
The Wiz
1979
★All That Jazz
Breaking Away
The Muppet Movie
1982
★Victor/Victoria
Annie
One from the Heart
1983
★Yentl
The Sting 2
Trading Places
1984
★Purple Rain
The Muppets Take Manhattan
Songwriter
2016
★"City of Stars"/La La Land
"Audition (The Fools Who Dream)"/La La Land
"Can't Stop the Feeling"/ Trolls
"How Far I'll Go"/Moana
2017
★"Remember Me"/Coco
"Mighty River"/Mudbound
"Mystery of Love"/Call Me by Your Name
"Stand Up for Something"/ Marshall
"This Is Me"/The Greatest Showman

SCORE

1934
The Gay Divorcee
The Lost Patrol
1935
★The Informer
Mutiny on the Bounty
1936
★Anthony Adverse
The Charge of the Light Brigade
The Garden of Allah
The General Died at Dawn
Winterset

1937
★100 Men and a Girl
The Hurricane
In Old Chicago
The Life of Emile Zola
Lost Horizon
Make a Wish
Maytime
Prisoner of Zenda
Quality Street
Snow White and the Seven Dwarfs
Something to Sing About
Souls at Sea
Way Out West
1938
★Alexander's Ragtime Band
Carefree
The Goldwyn Follies
Jezebel
Mad About Music
Sweethearts
1939
★Stagecoach
Babes in Arms
First Love
The Hunchback of Notre Dame
Intermezzo
Mr. Smith Goes to Washington
The Private Lives of Elizabeth & Essex
Swanee River
They Shall Have Music
1940
Irene
Our Town
The Sea Hawk
Second Chorus
Strike Up the Band
1942
My Gal Sal
Alfred Newman/My Gal Sal
Victor Young/Hold Back the Dawn
1943
Coney Island
1957
An Affair to Remember
Raintree County
1959
Say One for Me
2001
A. I.: Artificial Intelligence
A Beautiful Mind
Harry Potter and the Sorcerer's Stone
Lord of the Rings: The Fellowship of the Ring
Monsters, Inc.
2002
Catch Me If You Can
Far from Heaven
The Hours
Road to Perdition

SCORING OF A MUSICAL

1941
Birth of the Blues
Buck Privates
The Chocolate Soldier
Strawberry Blonde
Sunny
You'll Never Get Rich
1942
★Yankee Doodle Dandy
For Me and My Gal
Holiday Inn
It Started with Eve
You Were Never Lovelier

1943
★This Is the Army
The Phantom of the Opera
The Sky's the Limit
Stage Door Canteen
Star Spangled Rhythm
Thousands Cheer
1944
Hollywood Canteen
Irish Eyes Are Smiling
Meet Me in St. Louis
Alfred Newman/Irish Eyes Are Smiling
Sensations of 1945
Up in Arms
1945
★Anchors Aweigh
Can't Help Singing
Rhapsody in Blue
State Fair
The Three Caballeros
Tonight and Every Night
Wonder Man
1946
★The Jolson Story
Blue Skies
The Harvey Girls
Night and Day
1947
★Mother Wore Tights
1948
★Easter Parade
Emperor Waltz
The Pirate
Romance on the High Seas
1949
★On the Town
Jolson Sings Again
Look for the Silver Lining
1950
★Annie Get Your Gun
Cinderella
Three Little Words
The West Point Story
1951
★An American in Paris
Alice in Wonderland
The Great Caruso
Show Boat
1952
Hans Christian Andersen
The Medium
Singin' in the Rain
1953
The Band Wagon
Calamity Jane
The 5000 Fingers of Dr. T
Kiss Me Kate
1954
★Seven Brides for Seven Brothers
Carmen Jones
The Glenn Miller Story
A Star Is Born
There's No Business Like Show Business
1955
★Oklahoma!
Daddy Long Legs
Guys and Dolls
It's Always Fair Weather
Love Me or Leave Me
1956
★The King and I
The Eddy Duchin Story
High Society
1958
★Gigi
Damn Yankees
South Pacific

★ = winner

1959
The Five Pennies
Li'l Abner
Sleeping Beauty

1960
★Song Without End
Bells Are Ringing
Can-Can
Let's Make Love

1961
★West Side Story
Babes in Toyland
Flower Drum Song
Paris Blues

1968
Finian's Rainbow
Funny Girl

1969
★Hello, Dolly!
Goodbye, Mr. Chips
Paint Your Wagon
Sweet Charity
They Shoot Horses, Don't They?

ORIGINAL SCORE

1935
Peter Ibbetson

1938
★The Adventures of Robin Hood
The Cowboy and the Lady
Marie Antoinette
Louis Silvers/Suez
Suez
The Young in Heart

1939
★The Wizard of Oz
Dark Victory
Eternally Yours
Golden Boy
Gone with the Wind
Gulliver's Travels
The Man in the Iron Mask
Nurse Edith Cavell
Of Mice and Men
The Rains Came
Wuthering Heights

1940
★Pinocchio
Arizona
Dark Command
The Grapes of Wrath
The Great Dictator
The Howards of Virginia
The Letter
The Long Voyage Home
The Mark of Zorro
My Favorite Wife
One Million B.C.
Rebecca
Spring Parade
The Thief of Bagdad
Waterloo Bridge

1952
★With a Song in My Heart

1962
★Lawrence of Arabia
Mutiny on the Bounty
Taras Bulba
To Kill a Mockingbird

1963
★Tom Jones
Cleopatra
55 Days at Peking
How the West Was Won
It's a Mad, Mad, Mad, Mad World

1964
★Mary Poppins
Becket
The Fall of the Roman Empire
Hush, Hush, Sweet Charlotte
Mary Poppins
The Pink Panther
Umbrellas of Cherbourg

1965
★Doctor Zhivago
The Agony and the Ecstasy
The Greatest Story Ever Told
A Patch of Blue

1966
★Born Free
The Bible
Cool Hand Luke
Hawaii
The Sand Pebbles
Who's Afraid of Virginia Woolf?

1967
★Thoroughly Modern Millie
Doctor Dolittle
Far from the Madding Crowd
In Cold Blood
Thoroughly Modern Millie

1968
★The Lion in Winter
Planet of the Apes
The Shoes of the Fisherman
The Thomas Crown Affair

1969
★Butch Cassidy and the Sundance Kid
Anne of the Thousand Days
The Reivers
The Wild Bunch

1970
★Love Story
Airport
Cromwell
Patton

1975
★Jaws
Bite the Bullet
One Flew Over the Cuckoo's Nest
Tommy
The Wind and the Lion

1976
★The Omen
Bugsy Malone
Obsession
The Outlaw Josey Wales
Taxi Driver
Voyage of the Damned

1977
★Star Wars
Close Encounters of the Third Kind
Julia
The Message
The Spy Who Loved Me

1978
★Midnight Express
The Boys from Brazil
Days of Heaven
Heaven Can Wait
Superman: The Movie

1979
★A Little Romance
The Amityville Horror
The Champ
Star Trek: The Motion Picture
10

1980
★Fame
Altered States
The Elephant Man
The Empire Strikes Back
Tess

1981
★Chariots of Fire
Dragonslayer
On Golden Pond
Ragtime
Raiders of the Lost Ark

1982
★E.T.: The Extra-Terrestrial
Gandhi
An Officer and a Gentleman
Poltergeist
Sophie's Choice

1983
★The Right Stuff
Cross Creek
Return of the Jedi
Terms of Endearment
Under Fire

1984
★A Passage to India
Indiana Jones and the Temple of Doom
The Natural
The River
Under the Volcano

1985
★Out of Africa
Agnes of God
The Color Purple
Silverado
Witness

1986
★Round Midnight
Aliens
Hoosiers
The Mission
Star Trek 4: The Voyage Home

1987
★The Last Emperor
Cry Freedom
Empire of the Sun
The Untouchables
The Witches of Eastwick

1988
★The Milagro Beanfield War
The Accidental Tourist
Dangerous Liaisons
Gorillas in the Mist
Rain Man

1989
★The Little Mermaid
Born on the Fourth of July
The Fabulous Baker Boys
Field of Dreams
Indiana Jones and the Last Crusade

1990
★Dances with Wolves
Avalon
Ghost
Havana
Home Alone

1991
★Beauty and the Beast
Bugsy
The Fisher King
JFK
The Prince of Tides

1992
★Aladdin
Basic Instinct
Chaplin
Howard's End
A River Runs Through It

1993
★Schindler's List
The Age of Innocence
The Firm
The Fugitive
The Remains of the Day

1994
★The Lion King
Forrest Gump
Interview with the Vampire
Little Women
The Shawshank Redemption

1995
★Pocahontas
The American President
Sabrina
Toy Story
Unstrung Heroes

1996
★Emma
The First Wives Club
The Hunchback of Notre Dame
James and the Giant Peach
The Preacher's Wife

1997
★Titanic
Amistad
Good Will Hunting
Kundun
L.A. Confidential

1999
★The Red Violin
American Beauty
Angela's Ashes
The Cider House Rules
The Talented Mr. Ripley

2000
★Crouching Tiger, Hidden Dragon
Chocolat
The Patriot

2002
★Frida

2003
★Lord of the Rings: The Return of the King
Big Fish
Cold Mountain
Finding Nemo
House of Sand and Fog

2004
★Finding Neverland
Harry Potter and the Prisoner of Azkaban
Lemony Snicket's A Series of Unfortunate Events
The Passion of the Christ
The Village

2005
★Brokeback Mountain
The Constant Gardener
Memoirs of a Geisha
Munich
Pride and Prejudice

2006
★Babel
The Good German
Notes on a Scandal
Pan's Labyrinth
The Queen

2007
★Atonement
The Kite Runner
Michael Clayton
Ratatouille
3:10 to Yuma

2008
★Slumdog Millionaire
The Curious Case of Benjamin Button
Defiance
Milk
WALL-E

2009
★Up
Avatar
Fantastic Mr. Fox
The Hurt Locker
Sherlock Holmes

2010
★The Social Network
How to Train Your Dragon
Inception
The King's Speech
127 Hours

2011
★The Artist
The Adventures of Tintin
Hugo
Tinker Tailor Soldier Spy
War Horse

2012
★Life of Pi
Anna Karenina
Argo
Lincoln
Skyfall

2013
★Gravity
The Book Thief
Her
Philomena
Saving Mr. Banks

2014
★The Grand Budapest Hotel
The Imitation Game
Interstellar
Mr. Turner
The Theory of Everything

2015
★The Hateful Eight
Bridge of Spies
Carol
Sicario
Star Wars: The Force Awakens

2016
★La La Land
Jackie
Lion
Moonlight
Passengers

2017
★The Shape of Water
Dunkirk
Phantom Thread
Star Wars: The Last Jedi
Three Billboards Outside Ebbing, Missouri

2018
★Black Panther
BlacKkKlansman
If Beale Street Could Talk
Isle of Dogs
Mary Poppins Returns

2019
★Joker
Little Women
Marriage Story
1917
Star Wars: The Rise of Skywalker

SONG

1934
★"The Continental"/The Gay Divorcee
"Carioca"/Flying Down to Rio

1935
★"Lullaby of Broadway"/Gold Diggers of 1935
"Cheek to Cheek"/Top Hat
"Lovely to Look At"/Roberta

1936
★"Pennies from Heaven"/Pennies from Heaven
★"The Way You Look Tonight"/Swing Time
"A Melody from the Sky"/The Trail of the Lonesome Pine
"Did I Remember"/Suzy
"I've Got You Under My Skin"/Born to Dance
When Did You Leave Heaven/Sing, Baby, Sing

1937
★"Sweet Leilani"/Waikiki Wedding
"They Can't Take That Away From Me"/Shall We Dance
Whispers in the Dark/Artists and Models

1938
★"Thanks for the Memories"/The Big Broadcast of 1938
"Always and Always"/Mannequin
"Change Partners and Dance with Me"/Carefree
"Merrily We Live"/Merrily We Live
"My Own"/That Certain Age
"Now It Can Be Told"/Alexander's Ragtime Band
"The Cowboy and the Lady"/The Cowboy and the Lady

1939
★"Over the Rainbow"/The Wizard of Oz
"Faithful Forever"/Gulliver's Travels
"Wishing"/Love Affair

1940
★"When You Wish Upon a Star"/Pinocchio
"Down Argentine Way"/Down Argentine Way
"I'd Know You Anywhere"/You'll Find Out
"It's a Blue World"/Music in My Heart
"Love of My Life"/Second Chorus
"Only Forever"/Rhythm on the River
"Our Love Affair"/Strike Up the Band
"Waltzing in the Clouds"/Spring Parade

1941
★"The Last Time I Saw Paris"/Lady Be Good
"Be Honest With Me"/Ridin' on a Rainbow
"Blues In the Night"/Blues in the Night
"Boogie Woogie Bugle Boy of Company B"/Buck Privates
"Since I Kissed My Baby Goodbye"/You'll Never Get Rich

1942
★"White Christmas"/Holiday Inn
"Dearly Beloved"/You Were Never Lovelier
"How About You?"/Babes on Broadway
"I've Got a Gal in Kalamazoo"/Orchestra Wives
"Love Is a Song"/Bambi
"There's a Breeze on Lake Louise"/The Mayor of 44th Street

★ = winner

1943

★"You'll Never Know"/*Hello, Frisco, Hello*

"Happiness Is a Thing Called Joe"/*Cabin in the Sky*

"My Shining Hour"/*The Sky's the Limit*

"That Old Black Magic"/*Star Spangled Rhythm*

"They're Either Too Young or Too Old"/*Thank Your Lucky Stars*

"We Mustn't Say Goodbye"/*Stage Door Canteen*

1944

★"Swinging on a Star"/*Going My Way*

"I Couldn't Sleep A Wink Last Night"/*Higher and Higher*

"I'm Making Believe"/*Sweet and Low-Down*

"Long Ago and Far Away"/*Cover Girl*

"Now I Know"/*Up in Arms*

"Sweet Dreams Sweetheart"/*Hollywood Canteen*

"The Trolley Song"/*Meet Me in St. Louis*

1945

★"It Might as Well Be Spring"/*State Fair*

"Accentuate the Positive"/*Here Come the Waves*

"Anywhere"/*Tonight and Every Night*

"Aren't You Glad You're You"/*The Bells of St. Mary's*

"I Fall in Love Too Easily"/*Anchors Aweigh*

"More and More"/*Can't Help Singing*

"So in Love"/*Wonder Man*

"Some Sunday Morning"/*San Antonio*

1946

★"On the Atchison, Topeka and Santa Fe"/*The Harvey Girls*

"I Can't Begin to Tell You"/*The Dolly Sisters*

"You Keep Coming Back Like a Song"/*Blue Skies*

1947

"I Wish I Didn't Love You So"/*The Perils of Pauline*

"Pass That Peace Pipe"/*Good News*

"You Do"/*Mother Wore Tights*

1948

★"Buttons and Bows"/*The Paleface*

"It's Magic"/*Romance on the High Seas*

1949

★"Baby It's Cold Outside"/*Neptune's Daughter*

"It's a Great Feeling"/*It's a Great Feeling*

"Lavender Blue"/*So Dear to My Heart*

"Through a Long and Sleepless Night"/*Come to the Stable*

1950

★"Mona Lisa"/*Captain Carey, U.S.A.*

"Be My Love"/*The Toast of New Orleans*

"Bibbidy-Bobbidi-Boo"/*Cinderella*

"Wilhelmina"/*Wabash Avenue*

1951

★"In the Cool, Cool, Cool of the Evening"/*Here Comes the Groom*

"Never"/*Golden Girl*

"Too Late Now"/*Royal Wedding*

"Wonder Why"/*Rich, Young and Pretty*

1952

★"High Noon (Do Not Forsake Me, Oh My Darlin')"/*High Noon*

"Am I in Love"/*Son of Paleface*

"Because You're Mine"/*Because You're Mine*

"Thumbelina"/*Hans Christian Andersen*

"Zing a Little Zong"/*Just for You*

1953

★"Secret Love"/*Calamity Jane*

"My Flaming Heart"/*Small Town Girl*

"Sadie Thompson's Song (Blue Pacific Blues)"/*Miss Sadie Thompson*

"That's Amore"/*The Caddy*

"The Moon is Blue"/*The Moon Is Blue*

1954

★"Three Coins in the Fountain"/*Three Coins in the Fountain*

"Count Your Blessings Instead of Sheep"/*White Christmas*

"Hold My Hand"/*Susan Slept Here*

"The High and the Mighty"/*The High and the Mighty*

"The Man That Got Away"/*A Star Is Born*

1955

★"Love Is a Many-Splendored Thing"/*Love Is a Many-Splendored Thing*

"I'll Never Stop Loving You"/*Love Me or Leave Me*

"(Love Is) The Tender Trap"/*The Tender Trap*

"Something's Gotta Give"/*Daddy Long Legs*

1956

★"Que Sera, Sera"/*The Man Who Knew Too Much*

"Friendly Persuasion (Thee I Love)"/*Friendly Persuasion*

"Julie"/*Julie*

"True Love"/*High Society*

"Written on the Wind"/*Written on the Wind*

1957

"An Affair to Remember"/*An Affair to Remember*

"Tammy"/*Tammy and the Bachelor*

"Wild Is the Wind"/*Wild Is the Wind*

1958

★"Gigi"/*Gigi*

"A Very Precious Love"/*Marjorie Morningstar*

"Almost in Your Arms (Love Song from Houseboat)"/*Houseboat*

"To Love and Be Loved"/*Some Came Running*

1959

★"High Hopes"/*A Hole in the Head*

"Strange Are the Ways of Love"/*The Young Land*

"The Best of Everything"/*The Best of Everything*

"The Five Pennies"/*The Five Pennies*

"The Hanging Tree"/*The Hanging Tree*

1960

★"Never on Sunday"/*Never on Sunday*

"The Facts of Life"/*The Facts of Life*

"The Green Leaves of Summer"/*The Alamo*

1961

★"Moon River"/*Breakfast at Tiffany's*

"Bachelor in Paradise"/*Bachelor in Paradise*

"Love Theme (The Falcon and the Dove)"/*El Cid*

"Pocketful of Miracles"/*Pocketful of Miracles*

"Town without Pity"/*Town without Pity*

1962

★"Days of Wine and Roses"/*Days of Wine and Roses*

"Love Song (Follow Me)"/*Mutiny on the Bounty*

"Song fromm Two for the Seesaw (Second Chance)"/*Two for the Seesaw*

"Tender Is the Night"/*Tender Is the Night*

"Walk on the Wild Side"/*Walk on the Wild Side*

1963

★"Call Me Irresponsible"/*Papa's Delicate Condition*

"Charade"/*Charade*

"It's a Mad, Mad, Mad, Mad World"/*It's a Mad, Mad, Mad, Mad World*

"More"/*Mondo Cane*

"So Little Time"/*55 Days at Peking*

1964

★"Chim Chim Cher-ee"/*Mary Poppins*

Dear Heart/*Dear Heart*

"Hush, Hush, Sweet Charlotte"/*Hush, Hush, Sweet Charlotte*

"I Will Wait for You"/*Umbrellas of Cherbourg*

"My Kind of Town"/*Robin and the 7 Hoods*

"Where Love Has Gone"/*Where Love Has Gone*

1965

★"The Shadow of Your Smile"/*The Sandpiper*

"The Ballad of Cat Ballou"/*Cat Ballou*

"The Sweetheart Tree"/*The Great Race*

"What's New Pussycat?"/*What's New Pussycat?*

1966

★"Born Free"/*Born Free*

"A Time for Love"/*An American Dream*

"Alfie"/*Alfie*

"Georgy Girl"/*Georgy Girl*

"My Wishing Doll"/*Hawaii*

1967

★"Talk to the Animals"/*Doctor Dolittle*

"The Bare Necessities"/*The Jungle Book*

"The Look of Love"/*Casino Royale*

"Thoroughly Modern Millie"/*Thoroughly Modern Millie*

1968

★"The Windmills of Your Mind"/*The Thomas Crown Affair*

"Chitty Chitty Bang Bang"/*Chitty Chitty Bang Bang*

"For Love of Ivy"/*For Love of Ivy*

"Funny Girl"/*Funny Girl*

"Star!"/*Star!*

1969

★"Raindrops Keep Fallin' on My Head"/*Butch Cassidy and the Sundance Kid*

"Come Saturday Morning"/*The Sterile Cuckoo*

"Jean"/*The Prime of Miss Jean Brodie*

"True Grit"/*True Grit*

"What Are You Doing the Rest of Your Life?"/*The Happy Ending*

1970

★"For All We Know"/*Lovers and Other Strangers*

"Pieces of Dreams"/*Pieces of Dreams*

"Thank You Very Much"/*Scrooge*

"Till Love Touches Your Life"/*Madron*

"Whistling Away the Dark"/*Darling Lili*

1971

★"Theme from Shaft"/*Shaft*

"All His Children"/*Sometimes a Great Notion*

"Bless the Beasts and the Children"/*Bless the Beasts and Children*

"Life Is What You Make It"/*Kotch*

"The Age of Not Believing"/*Bedknobs and Broomsticks*

1972

★"The Morning After"/*The Poseidon Adventure*

"Marmalade, Molasses & Honey"/*Life & Times of Judge Roy Bean*

"Strange Are the Ways of Love"/*The Stepmother*

1973

★"The Way We Were"/*The Way We Were*

"All That Love Went to Waste"/*A Touch of Class*

"Live and Let Die"/*Live and Let Die*

"Love"/*Robin Hood*

"You're So Nice to Be Around"/*Cinderella Liberty*

1974

★"We May Never Love Like This Again"/*The Towering Inferno*

"Benji's Theme (I Feel Love)"/*Benji*

"Blazing Saddles"/*Blazing Saddles*

"Little Prince"/*The Little Prince*

1975

★"I'm Easy"/*Nashville*

"How Lucky Can You Get"/*Funny Lady*

"Now That We're in Love"/*Whiffs*

"Richard's Window"/*The Other Side of the Mountain*

"Theme from Mahogany"/*Mahogany*

1976

★"Evergreen"/*A Star Is Born*

"Ave Satani"/*The Omen*

"Come to Me"/*The Pink Panther Strikes Again*

"Gonna Fly Now"/*Rocky*

1977

★"You Light Up My Life"/*You Light Up My Life*

"Candle on the Water"/*Pete's Dragon*

"Nobody Does It Better"/*The Spy Who Loved Me*

"Someone's Waiting for You"/*The Rescuers*

1978

★"Last Dance"/*Thank God It's Friday*

"Hopelessly Devoted to You"/*Grease*

"Ready to Take a Chance Again"/*Foul Play*

"The Last Time I Felt Like This"/*Same Time, Next Year*

1979

★"It Goes Like It Goes"/*Norma Rae*

"Song from 10 (It's Easy to Say)"/*10*

"The Rainbow Connection"/*The Muppet Movie*

"Theme from Ice Castles-Through the Eyes of Love"/*Ice Castles*

"Theme from The Promise: I'll Never Say Goodbye"/*The Promise*

1980

★"Fame"/*Fame*

"Nine to Five"/*9 to 5*

"On the Road Again"/*Honeysuckle Rose*

"Out Here on My Own"/*Fame*

"People Alone"/*The Competition*

1981

★"Arthur's Theme"/*Arthur*

"Endless Love"/*Endless Love*

"For Your Eyes Only"/*For Your Eyes Only*

"One More Hour"/*Ragtime*

"The First Time It Happens"/*The Great Muppet Caper*

1982

★"Up Where We Belong"/*An Officer and a Gentleman*

"Eye of the Tiger"/*Rocky 3*

"How Do You Keep the Music Playing?"/*Best Friends*

"If We Were in Love"/*Yes, Giorgio*

"It Might Be You"/*Tootsie*

1983

★"Flashdance. . .What a Feeling"/*Flashdance*

"Maniac"/*Flashdance*

"Over You"/*Tender Mercies*

"Papa, Can You Hear Me?"/*Yentl*

"The Way He Makes Me Feel"/*Yentl*

1984

★"I Just Called to Say I Love You"/*The Woman in Red*

"Against All Odds (Take a Look at Me Now)"/*Against All Odds*

"Footloose"/*Footloose*

"Ghostbusters"/*Ghostbusters*

"Let's Hear It for the Boy"/*Footloose*

1985

★"Say You, Say Me"/*White Nights*

"Miss Celie's Blues (Sister)"/*The Color Purple*

"Separate Lives (Love Theme from White Nights)"/*White Nights*

"Surprise, Surprise"/*A Chorus Line*

"The Power of Love"/*Back to the Future*

1986

★"Take My Breath Away"/*Top Gun*

"Glory of Love"/*The Karate Kid: Part 2*

"Life in a Looking Glass"/*That's Life!*

"Mean Green Mother from Outer Space"/*Little Shop of Horrors*

"Somewhere Out There"/*An American Tail*

1987

★"(I've Had) the Time of My Life"/*Dirty Dancing*

"Cry Freedom"/*Cry Freedom*

"Nothing's Gonna Stop Us Now"/*Mannequin*

"Shakedown"/*Beverly Hills Cop 2*

"Storybook Love"/*The Princess Bride*

1988

★"Let the River Run"/*Working Girl*

"Calling You"/*Bagdad Cafe*

"Two Hearts"/*Buster*

1989

★"Under the Sea"/*The Little Mermaid*

"After All"/*Chances Are*

"I Love to See You Smile"/*Parenthood*

"Kiss the Girl"/*The Little Mermaid*

"The Girl Who Used to Be Me"/*Shirley Valentine*

1990

★"Sooner or Later"/*Dick Tracy*

"Blaze of Glory"/*Young Guns 2*

"I'm Checkin' Out"/*Postcards from the Edge*

"Promise Me You'll Remember"/*The Godfather, Part 3*

"Somewhere in My Memory"/*Home Alone*

1991

★"Beauty and the Beast"/*Beauty and the Beast*

"Be Our Guest"/*Beauty and the Beast*

"Belle"/*Beauty and the Beast*

"(Everything I Do) I Do It for You"/*Robin Hood: Prince of Thieves*

"When You're Alone"/*Hook*

1992

★"A Whole New World"/*Aladdin*

"Beautiful Maria of My Soul"/*The Mambo Kings*

"Friend Like Me"/*Aladdin*

"I Have Nothing"/*The Bodyguard*

"Run to You"/*The Bodyguard*

1993

★"Streets of Philadelphia"/*Philadelphia*

"A Wink and a Smile"/*Sleepless in Seattle*

"Again"/*Poetic Justice*

"Philadelphia"/*Philadelphia*

"The Day I Fall in Love"/*Beethoven's 2nd*

1994

★"Can You Feel the Love Tonight"/*The Lion King*

"Circle of Life"/*The Lion King*

"Hakuna Matata"/*The Lion King*

"Look What Love Has Done"/*Junior*

"Make Up Your Mind"/*The Paper*

1995

★"Colors of the Wind"/*Pocahontas*

"Dead Man Walking"/*Dead Man Walking*

"Have You Ever Really Loved a Woman?"/*Don Juan DeMarco*

"Moonlight"/*Sabrina*

"You've Got a Friend"/*Toy Story*

1996

★"You Must Love Me"/*Evita*

"Because You Loved Me"/*Up Close and Personal*

"For the First Time"/*One Fine Day*

"I've Finally Found Someone"/*The Mirror Has Two Faces*

"That Thing You Do!"/*That Thing You Do!*

★ = winner

1997
★"My Heart Will Go On"/Titanic
"Go the Distance"/Hercules
"How Do I Live"/Con Air
"Journey to the Past"/Anastasia
"Miss Misery"/Good Will Hunting
1998
★"When You Believe"/Prince of Egypt
"A Soft Place to Fall"/The Horse Whisperer
"I Don't Want to Miss a Thing"/Armageddon
"That'll Do"/Babe: Pig in the City
"The Prayer"/Quest for Camelot
1999
★"You'll Be In My Heart"/Tarzan
"Blame Canada"/South Park: Bigger, Longer and Uncut
"Music of My Heart"/Music of the Heart
"Save Me"/Magnolia
"When She Loved Me"/Toy Story 2
2000
★"Things Have Changed"/Wonder Boys
"A Fool in Love"/Meet the Parents
"A Love Before Time"/Crouching Tiger, Hidden Dragon
"I've Seen It All"/Dancer in the Dark
"My Funny Friend and Me"/The Emperor's New Groove
2001
★"If I Didn't Have You"/Monsters, Inc.
"May It Be"/Lord of the Rings: The Fellowship of the Ring
"There You'll Be"/Pearl Harbor
"Until"/Kate & Leopold
"Vanilla Sky"/Vanilla Sky
2002
★"Lose Yourself"/8 Mile
"Burn It Blue"/Frida
"Father and Daughter"/The Wild Thornberrys Movie
"I Move On"/Chicago
"The Hands That Built America"/Gangs of New York
2003
★"Into the West"/Lord of the Rings: The Return of the King
"A Kiss at the End of the Rainbow"/A Mighty Wind
"Belleville Rendez-Vous"/The Triplets of Belleville
"Scarlet Tide"/Cold Mountain
2004
★"Al Otro Lado Del Rio"/The Motorcycle Diaries
"Accidently in Love"/Shrek 2
"Believe"/The Polar Express
"Learn to be Lonely"/The Phantom of the Opera
2005
★"It's Hard Out Here for a Pimp"/Hustle & Flow
"In the Deep"/Crash
"Travelin' Thru"/Transamerica
2006
★"I Need to Wake Up"/An Inconvenient Truth
"Listen"/Dreamgirls
"Love You I Do"/Dreamgirls
"Our Town"/Cars
"Patience"/Dreamgirls

2007
★"Falling Slowly"/Once
"Happy Working Song"/Enchanted
"Raise It Up"/August Rush
"So Close"/Enchanted
"That's How You Know"/Enchanted
2008
★"Jai Ho"/Slumdog Millionaire
"Down to Earth"/WALL-E
"O Saya"/Slumdog Millionaire
2009
★"The Weary Kind"/Crazy Heart
"Almost There"/The Princess and the Frog
"Down in New Orleans"/The Princess and the Frog
"Loin de Paname"/Paris 36
"Take It All"/Nine
2010
★"We Belong Together"/Toy Story 3
"Coming Home"/Country Strong
"I See the Light"/Tangled
"If I Rise"/127 Hours
2011
★"Man or Muppet"/The Muppets
"Real in Rio"/Rio
2012
★"Skyfall"/Skyfall
Before My Time/Chasing Ice
"Everybody Needs a Best Friend"/Ted
"Pi's Lullaby"/Life of Pi
"Suddenly"/Les Miserables
2013
★"Let It Go"/Frozen
"Happy"/Despicable Me 2
"Ordinary Love"/Mandela: Long Walk to Freedom
"The Moon Song"/Her
2014
★"Glory"/Selma
"Everything is Awesome"/The Lego Movie
"Grateful"/Beyond the Lights
"Lost Stars"/Begin Again
2015
★"Writing's on the Wall"/Spectre
"Earned It"/Fifty Shades of Grey
"Simple Song #3"/Youth
"Til It Happens to You"/The Hunting Ground
2018
★"Shallow"/A Star Is Born
"All the Stars"/Black Panther
"I'll Fight"/RBG
"The Place Where Lost Things Go"/Mary Poppins Returns
"When a Cowboy Trades His Spurs for Wings"/The Ballad of Buster Scruggs
2019
★"I'm Gonna Love Me Again"/Rocketman
"I Can't Let You Throw Yourself Away"/Toy Story 4
"I'm Standing With You"/Breakthrough
"Into The Unknown"/Frozen II
"Stand Up"/Harriet

SOUND

1930
The Love Parade

1933
★A Farewell to Arms
42nd Street
Gold Diggers of 1933
I Am a Fugitive from a Chain Gang
1934
Cleopatra
The Gay Divorcee
Imitation of Life
1935
★Naughty Marietta
The Bride of Frankenstein
Captain Blood
The Lives of a Bengal Lancer
1936
★San Francisco
The Charge of the Light Brigade
Dodsworth
Mr. Deeds Goes to Town
The Texas Rangers
Three Smart Girls
1937
★The Hurricane
In Old Chicago
The Life of Emile Zola
Lost Horizon
Maytime
100 Men and a Girl
Topper
1938
★The Cowboy and the Lady
Four Daughters
Merrily We Live
Suez
Sweethearts
That Certain Age
Vivacious Lady
You Can't Take It with You
1939
Balalaika
Gone with the Wind
Goodbye, Mr. Chips
The Hunchback of Notre Dame
Mr. Smith Goes to Washington
Of Mice and Men
The Private Lives of Elizabeth & Essex
The Rains Came
1940
★Strike Up the Band
The Grapes of Wrath
The Howards of Virginia
Kitty Foyle
Our Town
The Sea Hawk
Spring Parade
1941
★That Hamilton Woman
Ball of Fire
The Chocolate Soldier
Citizen Kane
How Green Was My Valley
Sergeant York
Too Many Husbands
Topper Returns
1942
★Yankee Doodle Dandy
Arabian Nights
Bambi
Flying Tigers
Mrs. Miniver
Once Upon a Honeymoon
The Pride of the Yankees
The Road to Morocco
You Were Never Lovelier

1943
★This Land Is Mine
Madame Curie
The North Star
The Phantom of the Opera
Sahara
So This Is Washington
The Song of Bernadette
This Above All
This Is the Army
War of the Wildcats
1944
★Wilson
Casanova Brown
Cover Girl
Double Indemnity
His Butler's Sister
Hollywood Canteen
1945
★The Bells of St. Mary's
Flame of the Barbary Coast
Lady on a Train
Leave Her to Heaven
Rhapsody in Blue
A Song to Remember
The Southerner
They Were Expendable
The Three Caballeros
Wonder Man
1946
★The Jolson Story
The Best Years of Our Lives
It's a Wonderful Life
1947
★The Bishop's Wife
Green Dolphin Street
T-Men
1948
★The Snake Pit
Johnny Belinda
The Smallest Show on Earth
1949
★Twelve o'Clock High
Sands of Iwo Jima
1950
★All About Eve
Cinderella
1951
★The Great Caruso
A Streetcar Named Desire
Two Tickets to Broadway
1952
Hans Christian Andersen
The Promoter
The Quiet Man
With a Song in My Heart
1953
★From Here to Eternity
Calamity Jane
Knights of the Round Table
The War of the Worlds
1954
★The Glenn Miller Story
Brigadoon
The Caine Mutiny
Rear Window
Susan Slept Here
1955
★Oklahoma!
Love Is a Many-Splendored Thing
Love Me or Leave Me
Mister Roberts
Not as a Stranger
1956
★The King and I
The Brave One
The Eddy Duchin Story
Friendly Persuasion
The Ten Commandments

1957
★Sayonara
Gunfight at the O.K. Corral
Les Girls
Pal Joey
Witness for the Prosecution
1958
★South Pacific
I Want to Live!
Vertigo
The Young Lions
1959
★Ben-Hur
Journey to the Center of the Earth
The Nun's Story
1960
★The Alamo
The Apartment
Cimarron
Sunrise at Campobello
1961
★West Side Story
The Children's Hour
Flower Drum Song
The Guns of Navarone
The Parent Trap
1962
★Lawrence of Arabia
Bon Voyage!
The Music Man
That Touch of Mink
What Ever Happened to Baby Jane?
1963
★How the West Was Won
Bye, Bye, Birdie
Captain Newman, M.D.
Cleopatra
It's a Mad, Mad, Mad, Mad World
1964
★My Fair Lady
Becket
Father Goose
Mary Poppins
The Unsinkable Molly Brown
1965
★The Sound of Music
The Agony and the Ecstasy
Doctor Zhivago
The Great Race
Shenandoah
1966
★Grand Prix
Gambit
Hawaii
The Sand Pebbles
Who's Afraid of Virginia Woolf?
1967
★In the Heat of the Night
Camelot
The Dirty Dozen
Doctor Dolittle
Thoroughly Modern Millie
1968
★Oliver!
Bullitt
Finian's Rainbow
Funny Girl
Star!
1969
★Hello, Dolly!
Anne of the Thousand Days
Butch Cassidy and the Sundance Kid
Marooned

1970
★Patton
Airport
Ryan's Daughter
Tora! Tora! Tora!
Woodstock
1971
★Fiddler on the Roof
Diamonds Are Forever
The French Connection
Kotch
Mary, Queen of Scots
1972
★Cabaret
Butterflies Are Free
The Candidate
The Godfather
The Poseidon Adventure
1973
★The Exorcist
The Day of the Dolphin
The Paper Chase
Paper Moon
The Sting
1974
★Earthquake
Chinatown
The Conversation
The Towering Inferno
Young Frankenstein
1975
★Jaws
Bite the Bullet
Funny Lady
The Hindenburg
The Wind and the Lion
1976
★All the President's Men
King Kong
Rocky
Silver Streak
A Star Is Born
1977
★Star Wars
Close Encounters of the Third Kind
The Deep
Sorcerer
The Turning Point
1978
★The Deer Hunter
The Buddy Holly Story
Days of Heaven
Hooper
Superman: The Movie
1979
★Apocalypse Now
The Electric Horseman
Meteor
1941
The Rose
1980
★The Empire Strikes Back
Coal Miner's Daughter
Fame
Raging Bull
1981
★Raiders of the Lost Ark
On Golden Pond
Outland
Pennies from Heaven
Reds
1982
★Gandhi
Das Boot
E.T.: The Extra-Terrestrial
Tootsie
Tron

1983
★The Right Stuff
Never Cry Wolf
Return of the Jedi
Terms of Endearment
WarGames
1984
★Amadeus
Dune
A Passage to India
The River
2010: The Year We Make Contact
1985
★Out of Africa
Back to the Future
A Chorus Line
Ladyhawke
Silverado
1986
★Platoon
Aliens
Heartbreak Ridge
Star Trek 4: The Voyage Home
Top Gun
1987
★The Last Emperor
Empire of the Sun
Lethal Weapon
RoboCop
The Witches of Eastwick
1988
★Bird
Die Hard
Gorillas in the Mist
Mississippi Burning
Who Framed Roger Rabbit
1989
★Glory
The Abyss
Black Rain
Born on the Fourth of July
Indiana Jones and the Last Crusade
1990
★Dances with Wolves
Days of Thunder
Dick Tracy
The Hunt for Red October
Total Recall
1991
★Terminator 2: Judgment Day
Backdraft
Beauty and the Beast
JFK
The Silence of the Lambs
1992
★The Last of the Mohicans
Aladdin
A Few Good Men
Under Siege
Unforgiven
1993
★Jurassic Park
Cliffhanger
The Fugitive
Geronimo: An American Legend
Schindler's List
1994
★Speed
Clear and Present Danger
Forrest Gump
Legends of the Fall
The Shawshank Redemption
1995
★Apollo 13
Batman Forever
Braveheart
Crimson Tide
Waterworld
1996
★The English Patient
Evita
Independence Day
The Rock
Twister
1997
★Titanic
Air Force One
Con Air
Contact
L.A. Confidential
1998
★Saving Private Ryan
Armageddon
The Mask of Zorro
Shakespeare in Love
The Thin Red Line
1999
★The Matrix
The Green Mile
The Insider
The Mummy
Star Wars: Episode 1-The Phantom Menace
2000
★Gladiator
The Patriot
The Perfect Storm
U-571
2001
★Black Hawk Down
Amelie
Lord of the Rings: The Fellowship of the Ring
Moulin Rouge
Pearl Harbor
2002
★Chicago
Gangs of New York
Lord of the Rings: The Two Towers
Road to Perdition
Spider-Man
2003
★Lord of the Rings: The Return of the King
The Last Samurai
Lord of the Rings: The Return of the King
Master and Commander: The Far Side of the World
Pirates of the Caribbean: The Curse of the Black Pearl
Seabiscuit
2004
★Ray
The Aviator
The Incredibles
The Polar Express
Spider-Man 2
2005
★King Kong
The Chronicles of Narnia: The Lion, the Witch and the Wardrobe
Memoirs of a Geisha
Walk the Line
War of the Worlds
2006
★Dreamgirls
Apocalypto
Blood Diamond
Flags of Our Fathers
Pirates of the Caribbean: Dead Man's Chest
2007
★The Bourne Ultimatum
No Country for Old Men
Ratatouille
3:10 to Yuma
Transformers
2008
★Slumdog Millionaire
The Curious Case of Benjamin Button
The Dark Knight
WALL-E
Wanted
2009
★The Hurt Locker
Avatar
Inglourious Basterds
Star Trek
Transformers: Revenge of the Fallen
2010
★Inception
The King's Speech
Salt
The Social Network
True Grit
2011
★Hugo
The Girl With the Dragon Tattoo
Moneyball
Transformers: Dark of the Moon
War Horse
2012
★Les Miserables
Argo
Life of Pi
Lincoln
Skyfall
2013
★Gravity
Captain Phillips
The Hobbit: The Desolation of Smaug
Inside Llewyn Davis
Lone Survivor
2014
★Whiplash
American Sniper
Birdman, or (The Unexpected Virtue of Ignorance)
Interstellar
Unbroken
2015
★Mad Max: Fury Road
Bridge of Spies
The Martian
The Revenant
Sicario
Star Wars: The Force Awakens
2017
★Dunkirk
Baby Driver
Blade Runner 2049
The Shape of Water
Star Wars: The Last Jedi
2018
★Bohemian Rhapsody
Black Panther
First Man
A Quiet Place
Roma
A Star Is Born
2019
★1917
Ad Astra
Ford v Ferrari
Joker
Once Upon A Time... In Hollywood

SOUND EFFECTS EDITING

1963
★It's a Mad, Mad, Mad, Mad World
1964
★Goldfinger
1965
★The Great Race
1966
★Grand Prix
1967
★The Dirty Dozen
1975
★The Hindenburg
1977
★Close Encounters of the Third Kind
1979
★The Black Stallion
1986
★Aliens
1990
★The Hunt for Red October
1991
★Terminator 2: Judgment Day
1992
★Bram Stoker's Dracula
Aladdin
Under Siege
1993
★Jurassic Park
Cliffhanger
The Fugitive
1996
★The Ghost and the Darkness
Daylight
The English Patient
1997
★Titanic
Face/Off
The Fifth Element
1998
★Saving Private Ryan
Armageddon
The Mask of Zorro
2000
★U-571
Space Cowboys
2003
★Master and Commander: The Far Side of the World
Finding Nemo
Master and Commander: The Far Side of the World
2004
★The Incredibles
The Polar Express
Spider-Man 2
2006
★Letters from Iwo Jima
Apocalypto
Blood Diamond
Flags of Our Fathers
Pirates of the Caribbean: Dead Man's Chest
2007
★The Bourne Ultimatum
No Country for Old Men
Ratatouille
There Will Be Blood
Transformers
2008
★The Dark Knight
Iron Man
Slumdog Millionaire
WALL-E
Wanted
2009
★The Hurt Locker
Avatar
Inglourious Basterds
Star Trek
Up
2010
★Inception
Toy Story 3
Tron: Legacy
True Grit
Unstoppable
2011
★Hugo
Drive
The Girl With the Dragon Tattoo
Transformers: Dark of the Moon
War Horse
2012
★Skyfall
★Zero Dark Thirty
Argo
Django Unchained
Life of Pi
2013
★Gravity
Captain Phillips
The Hobbit: The Desolation of Smaug
Lone Survivor
2014
★American Sniper
Birdman, or (The Unexpected Virtue of Ignorance)
The Hobbit: The Battle of the Five Armies
Interstellar
Unbroken
2015
★Mad Max: Fury Road
The Martian
The Revenant
Star Wars: The Force Awakens
2016
★Arrival
Deepwater Horizon
Hacksaw Ridge
La La Land
Sully
2017
Baby Driver
Blade Runner 2049
The Shape of Water
Star Wars: The Last Jedi
2018
★Bohemian Rhapsody
Black Panther
First Man
Roma
2019
★Ford v Ferrari
Joker
1917
Once Upon A Time... In Hollywood
Star Wars: The Rise of Skywalker

ADAPTED SCREENPLAY

1928
★7th Heaven
The Jazz Singer
1931
★Cimarron
The Criminal Code
Little Caesar
1932
Arrowsmith
Dr. Jekyll and Mr. Hyde
1933
★Little Women
Lady for a Day
1934
★It Happened One Night
The Thin Man
1956
★Around the World in 80 Days
Baby Doll
Friendly Persuasion
Giant
Lust for Life
1957
★The Bridge on the River Kwai
Heaven Knows, Mr. Allison
Peyton Place
Sayonara
Twelve Angry Men
1958
★Gigi
Cat on a Hot Tin Roof
The Horse's Mouth
I Want to Live!
Separate Tables
1959
★Room at the Top
Anatomy of a Murder
Ben-Hur
The Nun's Story
Some Like It Hot
1960
★Elmer Gantry
T.E.B. Clarke/Sons and Lovers
Inherit the Wind
Gavin Lambert/Sons and Lovers
The Sundowners
Tunes of Glory
1961
★Judgment at Nuremberg
Breakfast at Tiffany's
The Guns of Navarone
The Hustler
West Side Story
1962
★To Kill a Mockingbird
David and Lisa
Lawrence of Arabia
Lolita
The Miracle Worker
1963
★Tom Jones
Captain Newman, M.D.
Hud
Lilies of the Field
1964
★Becket
Dr. Strangelove, or: How I Learned to Stop Worrying and Love the Bomb
Mary Poppins
My Fair Lady
Zorba the Greek
1965
★Doctor Zhivago
Cat Ballou
The Collector
Ship of Fools
A Thousand Clowns
1966
★A Man for All Seasons
Alfie
Cool Hand Luke
The Professionals
The Russians Are Coming, the Russians Are Coming
Who's Afraid of Virginia Woolf?

★ = winner

1967
★*In the Heat of the Night*
The Graduate
In Cold Blood
Ulysses
1968
★*The Lion in Winter*
The Odd Couple
Oliver!
Rachel, Rachel
Rosemary's Baby
1969
★*Midnight Cowboy*
Anne of the Thousand Days
Goodbye, Columbus
They Shoot Horses, Don't They?
Z
1970
★*M*A*S*H*
Airport
I Never Sang for My Father
Lovers and Other Strangers
Women in Love
1971
★*The French Connection*
A Clockwork Orange
The Conformist
The Garden of the Finzi-Continis
The Last Picture Show
1972
★*The Godfather*
Cabaret
Pete 'n' Tillie
Sounder
1973
★*The Exorcist*
The Last Detail
The Paper Chase
Paper Moon
Serpico
1974
★*The Godfather, Part 2*
The Apprenticeship of Duddy Kravitz
Lenny
Murder on the Orient Express
Young Frankenstein
1975
★*One Flew Over the Cuckoo's Nest*
Barry Lyndon
The Man Who Would Be King
The Scent of a Woman
The Sunshine Boys
1976
★*All the President's Men*
Bound for Glory
The Seven-Per-Cent Solution
Voyage of the Damned
1977
★*Julia*
Equus
I Never Promised You a Rose Garden
Oh, God!
That Obscure Object of Desire
1978
★*Midnight Express*
Bloodbrothers
California Suite
Heaven Can Wait
Same Time, Next Year
1979
★*Kramer vs. Kramer*
Apocalypse Now
La Cage aux Folles
A Little Romance
Norma Rae
1980
★*Ordinary People*
Breaker Morant
Coal Miner's Daughter
The Elephant Man
The Stunt Man
1981
★*On Golden Pond*
The French Lieutenant's Woman
Pennies from Heaven
Prince of the City
Ragtime
1982
★*Missing*
Das Boot
Sophie's Choice
The Verdict
Victor/Victoria
1983
★*Terms of Endearment*
The Dresser
Educating Rita
1984
★*Amadeus*
Greystoke: The Legend of Tarzan, Lord of the Apes
The Killing Fields
A Passage to India
A Soldier's Story
1985
★*Out of Africa*
The Color Purple
Kiss of the Spider Woman
Prizzi's Honor
The Trip to Bountiful
1986
★*A Room with a View*
Children of a Lesser God
The Color of Money
Crimes of the Heart
Stand by Me
1987
★*The Last Emperor*
The Dead
Fatal Attraction
Full Metal Jacket
My Life As a Dog
1988
★*Dangerous Liaisons*
The Accidental Tourist
Gorillas in the Mist
The Unbearable Lightness of Being
1989
★*Driving Miss Daisy*
Born on the Fourth of July
Enemies, a Love Story
Field of Dreams
My Left Foot
1990
★*Dances with Wolves*
Awakenings
Goodfellas
The Grifters
Reversal of Fortune
1991
★*The Silence of the Lambs*
Europa, Europa
Fried Green Tomatoes
JFK
The Prince of Tides
1992
★*Howard's End*
Enchanted April
The Player
A River Runs Through It
Scent of a Woman
1993
★*Schindler's List*
The Age of Innocence
In the Name of the Father
The Remains of the Day
Shadowlands
1994
★*Forrest Gump*
The Madness of King George
Nobody's Fool
Quiz Show
The Shawshank Redemption
1995
★*Sense and Sensibility*
Apollo 13
Babe
Leaving Las Vegas
The Postman
1996
★*Sling Blade*
The Crucible
The English Patient
Hamlet
Trainspotting
1997
★*L.A. Confidential*
Donnie Brasco
The Sweet Hereafter
Wag the Dog
The Wings of the Dove
1998
★*Gods and Monsters*
Out of Sight
Primary Colors
A Simple Plan
The Thin Red Line
1999
★*The Cider House Rules*
Election
The Green Mile
The Insider
The Talented Mr. Ripley
2000
★*Traffic*
Chocolat
Crouching Tiger, Hidden Dragon
O Brother Where Art Thou?
Wonder Boys
2001
★*A Beautiful Mind*
Ghost World
In the Bedroom
Lord of the Rings: The Fellowship of the Ring
Shrek
2002
★*The Pianist*
About a Boy
Adaptation
Chicago
The Hours
2003
★*Lord of the Rings: The Return of the King*
American Splendor
City of God
Mystic River
Seabiscuit
2004
★*Sideways*
Before Sunset
Finding Neverland
Million Dollar Baby
The Motorcycle Diaries
2005
★*Brokeback Mountain*
Capote
The Constant Gardener
A History of Violence
Munich
2006
★*The Departed*
Borat: Cultural Learnings of America for Make Benefit Glorious Nation of Kazakhstan
Children of Men
Little Children
Notes on a Scandal
2007
★*No Country for Old Men*
Atonement
Away From Her
The Diving Bell and the Butterfly
There Will Be Blood
2008
★*Slumdog Millionaire*
The Curious Case of Benjamin Button
Doubt
Frost/Nixon
The Reader
2009
★*Precious: Based on the Novel 'Push' by Sapphire*
District 9
An Education
In the Loop
Up in the Air
2010
★*The Social Network*
127 Hours
Toy Story 3
True Grit
Winter's Bone
2011
★*The Descendants*
Hugo
The Ides of March
Moneyball
Tinker Tailor Soldier Spy
2012
★*Argo*
Beasts of the Southern Wild
Life of Pi
Lincoln
Silver Linings Playbook
2013
★*12 Years a Slave*
Before Midnight
Captain Phillips
Philomena
The Wolf of Wall Street
2014
★*The Imitation Game*
American Sniper
Inherent Vice
The Theory of Everything
Whiplash
2015
★*The Big Short*
Brooklyn
Carol
The Martian
Room
2016
★*Moonlight*
Arrival
Fences
Hidden Figures
Lion
2017
★*Call Me by Your Name*
The Disaster Artist
Logan
Molly's Game
Mudbound
2018
★*BlacKkKlansman*
The Ballad of Buster Scruggs
Can You Ever Forgive Me?
If Beale Street Could Talk
A Star Is Born
2019
★*Jojo Rabbit*
The Irishman
Joker
Little Women
The Two Popes

ORIGINAL SCREENPLAY

1940
★*The Great McGinty*
Angels Over Broadway
Foreign Correspondent
The Great Dictator
1941
★*Citizen Kane*
The Devil & Miss Jones
Sergeant York
Tall, Dark and Handsome
Karl Tunberg/*Tall, Dark and Handsome*
Darrell Ware/*Tall, Dark and Handsome*
1942
★*Woman of the Year*
One of Our Aircraft Is Missing
The Road to Morocco
Wake Island
1943
Air Force
In Which We Serve
The North Star
So Proudly We Hail
1944
★*Wilson*
Hail the Conquering Hero
Miracle of Morgan's Creek
Music For Millions
Two Girls and a Sailor
A Wing and a Prayer
1945
Dillinger
1946
The Blue Dahlia
Children of Paradise
Notorious
The Road to Utopia
1947
★*The Bachelor and the Bobby-Soxer*
Body and Soul
A Double Life
Monsieur Verdoux
Shoeshine
1956
Julie
La Strada
The Ladykillers
1963
America America
1968
The Battle of Algiers
1974
★*Chinatown*
Alice Doesn't Live Here Anymore
The Conversation
Day for Night
Harry and Tonto
1975
★*Dog Day Afternoon*
Amarcord
And Now My Love
Shampoo
1976
★*Network*
Cousin, Cousine
The Front
Rocky
Seven Beauties
1977
★*Annie Hall*
The Goodbye Girl
The Late Show
Star Wars
The Turning Point
1978
★*Coming Home*
Autumn Sonata
The Deer Hunter
Interiors
An Unmarried Woman
1979
★*Breaking Away*
All That Jazz
And Justice for All
The China Syndrome
Manhattan
1980
★*Melvin and Howard*
Brubaker
Fame
Mon Oncle d'Amerique
Private Benjamin
1981
★*Chariots of Fire*
Absence of Malice
Arthur
Atlantic City
Reds
1982
★*Gandhi*
Diner
E.T.: The Extra-Terrestrial
An Officer and a Gentleman
Tootsie
1983
★*Tender Mercies*
The Big Chill
Fanny and Alexander
Silkwood
WarGames
1984
★*Places in the Heart*
Beverly Hills Cop
Broadway Danny Rose
El Norte
Splash
1985
★*Witness*
Back to the Future
Brazil
The Official Story
The Purple Rose of Cairo
1986
★*Hannah and Her Sisters*
Crocodile Dundee
My Beautiful Laundrette
Platoon
Salvador
1987
★*Moonstruck*
Au Revoir les Enfants
Broadcast News
Hope and Glory
Radio Days

★ = winner

1988
★*Rain Man*
Big
Bull Durham
A Fish Called Wanda
Running on Empty
1989
★*Dead Poets Society*
Crimes & Misdemeanors
Do the Right Thing
sex, lies and videotape
When Harry Met Sally. . .
1990
★*Ghost*
Alice
Avalon
Green Card
Metropolitan
1991
★*Thelma & Louise*
Boyz N the Hood
Bugsy
The Fisher King
Grand Canyon
1992
★*The Crying Game*
Husbands and Wives
Lorenzo's Oil
Passion Fish
Unforgiven
1993
★*The Piano*
Dave
In the Line of Fire
Philadelphia
Sleepless in Seattle
1994
★*Pulp Fiction*
Bullets over Broadway
Four Weddings and a Funeral
Heavenly Creatures
Trois Couleurs: Rouge
1995
★*The Usual Suspects*
Braveheart
Mighty Aphrodite
Nixon
Toy Story
1996
★*Fargo*
Jerry Maguire
Lone Star
Secrets and Lies
Shine
1997
★*Good Will Hunting*
As Good As It Gets
Boogie Nights
Deconstructing Harry
The Full Monty
1998
★*Shakespeare in Love*
Bulworth
Life Is Beautiful
Saving Private Ryan
The Truman Show
1999
★*American Beauty*
Being John Malkovich
Magnolia
The Sixth Sense
Topsy Turvy
2000
★*Almost Famous*
Billy Elliot
Erin Brockovich
Gladiator
You Can Count On Me
2001
★*Gosford Park*
Amelie
Memento
Monster's Ball
The Royal Tenenbaums
2002
★*Talk to Her*
Far from Heaven
Gangs of New York
My Big Fat Greek Wedding
Y Tu Mama Tambien
2003
★*Lost in Translation*
The Barbarian Invasions
Dirty Pretty Things
Finding Nemo
In America
2004
★*Eternal Sunshine of the Spotless Mind*
The Aviator
Hotel Rwanda
The Incredibles
Vera Drake
2005
★*Crash*
Good Night, and Good Luck
Match Point
The Squid and the Whale
Syriana
2006
★*Little Miss Sunshine*
Babel
Letters from Iwo Jima
Pan's Labyrinth
The Queen
2007
★*Juno*
Lars and the Real Girl
Michael Clayton
Ratatouille
The Savages
2008
★*Milk*
Frozen River
Happy-Go-Lucky
In Bruges
WALL-E
2009
★*The Hurt Locker*
Inglourious Basterds
The Messenger
A Serious Man
Up
2010
★*The King's Speech*
Another Year
The Fighter
Inception
The Kids Are All Right
2011
★*Midnight in Paris*
The Artist
Bridesmaids
Margin Call
A Separation
2012
★*Django Unchained*
Amour
Flight
Moonrise Kingdom
Zero Dark Thirty
2013
★*Her*
American Hustle
Blue Jasmine
Dallas Buyers Club
Nebraska
2014
★*Birdman, or (The Unexpected Virtue of Ignorance)*
Boyhood
Foxcatcher
The Grand Budapest Hotel
Nightcrawler
2015
★*Spotlight*
Bridge of Spies
Ex Machina
Inside Out
Straight Outta Compton
2016
★*Manchester by the Sea*
Hell or High Water
La La Land
The Lobster
20th Century Women
2017
★*Get Out*
The Big Sick
Lady Bird
The Shape of Water
Three Billboards Outside Ebbing, Missouri
2018
★*Green Book*
The Favourite
First Reformed
Roma
Vice
2019
★*Parasite*
Knives Out
Marriage Story
1917
Once Upon A Time... In Hollywood

SCREENPLAY

1935
★*The Informer*
The Lives of a Bengal Lancer
Mutiny on the Bounty
1936
After the Thin Man
Dodsworth
Mr. Deeds Goes to Town
My Man Godfrey
1937
★*The Life of Emile Zola*
The Awful Truth
Captains Courageous
Stage Door
1938
★*Pygmalion*
The Citadel
Four Daughters
You Can't Take It with You
1939
★*Gone with the Wind*
Goodbye, Mr. Chips
Wuthering Heights
1940
★*The Philadelphia Story*
The Grapes of Wrath
Kitty Foyle
The Long Voyage Home
Rebecca
1941
★*Here Comes Mr. Jordan*
How Green Was My Valley
The Little Foxes
The Maltese Falcon
1942
★*Mrs. Miniver*
Charles Brackett/*Hold Back the Dawn*
The Forty-Ninth Parallel
The Pride of the Yankees
Random Harvest
Talk of the Town
Billy Wilder/*Hold Back the Dawn*
1943
★*Casablanca*
The More the Merrier
The Song of Bernadette
Watch on the Rhine
1944
★*Going My Way*
Double Indemnity
Gaslight
Laura
Meet Me in St. Louis
1945
★*The Lost Weekend*
Mildred Pierce
A Tree Grows in Brooklyn
1946
★*The Best Years of Our Lives*
Anna and the King of Siam
Brief Encounter
The Killers
Open City
1947
★*Miracle on 34th Street*
Boomerang
Crossfire
Gentleman's Agreement
Great Expectations
1948
★*Treasure of the Sierra Madre*
Johnny Belinda
The Search
The Snake Pit
1949
★*A Letter to Three Wives*
All the King's Men
The Bicycle Thief
Champion
The Fallen Idol
1950
★*All About Eve*
The Asphalt Jungle
Born Yesterday
Broken Arrow
Father of the Bride
1951
★*A Place in the Sun*
The African Queen
Detective Story
La Ronde
A Streetcar Named Desire
1952
★*The Bad and the Beautiful*
Five Fingers
High Noon
The Man in the White Suit
The Quiet Man
1953
★*From Here to Eternity*
The Cruel Sea
Lili
Roman Holiday
Shane
Titanic
1954
★*Country Girl*
The Caine Mutiny
Rear Window
Sabrina
Seven Brides for Seven Brothers
1955
★*Marty*
Bad Day at Black Rock
Blackboard Jungle
East of Eden
Interrupted Melody
Love Me or Leave Me

STORY

1928
The Last Command
1931
Public Enemy
Smart Money
1932
★*The Champ*
What Price Hollywood?
1933
The Prizefighter and the Lady
Rasputin and the Empress
1934
★*Manhattan Melodrama*
1935
Broadway Melody of 1936
The Gay Deception
1936
Fury
The Great Ziegfeld
San Francisco
Three Smart Girls
1937
★*A Star Is Born*
In Old Chicago
100 Men and a Girl
1938
★*Boys Town*
Alexander's Ragtime Band
Angels with Dirty Faces
The Black Legion
Mad About Music
Test Pilot
1939
★*Mr. Smith Goes to Washington*
Bachelor Mother
Love Affair
Ninotchka
Young Mr. Lincoln
1940
Comrade X
Edison the Man
My Favorite Wife
The Westerner
1941
★*Here Comes Mr. Jordan*
Ball of Fire
The Lady Eve
Meet John Doe
Tom, Dick, and Harry
1942
★*The Forty-Ninth Parallel*
Holiday Inn
The Pride of the Yankees
Talk of the Town
Yankee Doodle Dandy
1943
★*The Human Comedy*
Action in the North Atlantic
Destination Tokyo
The More the Merrier
Shadow of a Doubt
1944
★*Going My Way*
Lifeboat
1945
★*House on 92nd Street*
Objective, Burma!
A Song to Remember
1946
★Clemence Dane/*Vacation from Marriage*
★*Vacation from Marriage*
Dark Mirror
The Strange Love of Martha Ivers
The Stranger
1947
★*Miracle on 34th Street*
Kiss of Death
Smash-Up: The Story of a Woman
1948
★*The Search*
Louisiana Story
The Naked City
Red River
The Red Shoes
1949
★*The Stratton Story*
Come to the Stable
Sands of Iwo Jima
White Heat
1950
★*Panic in the Streets*
Bitter Rice
The Gunfighter
1951
Bullfighter & the Lady
Here Comes the Groom
When Willie Comes Marching Home
1952
★*The Greatest Show on Earth*
Leo McCarey/*My Son John*
My Son John
The Narrow Margin
Pride of St. Louis
1953
★*Roman Holiday*
Above and Beyond
Captain's Paradise
Hondo
Titanic
1954
★*Broken Lance*
Forbidden Games
Night People
There's No Business Like Show Business
1955
★*Love Me or Leave Me*
Rebel without a Cause
The Sheep Has Five Legs
Strategic Air Command
1956
★*The Brave One*
The Eddy Duchin Story
High Society
Umberto D

STORY & SCREENPLAY

1949
★*Battleground*
Jolson Sings Again
Paisan
Passport to Pimlico
1950
★*Sunset Boulevard*
Adam's Rib
Caged
The Men
No Way Out
1951
★*An American in Paris*
David and Bathsheba
Go for Broke!
The Well
1952
★*The Lavender Hill Mob*
The Atomic City
Pat and Mike
Viva Zapata!

★ = winner

1953
★*Titanic*
The Band Wagon
The Desert Rats
The Naked Spur
1954
★*On the Waterfront*
The Barefoot Contessa
Genevieve
The Glenn Miller Story
1955
★*Interrupted Melody*
The Court Martial of Billy Mitchell
It's Always Fair Weather
Mr. Hulot's Holiday
The Seven Little Foys
1957
★*Designing Woman*
Funny Face
I Vitelloni
Man of a Thousand Faces
The Tin Star
1958
★*The Defiant Ones*
The Goddess
Houseboat
Teacher's Pet
1959
★*Pillow Talk*
The 400 Blows
North by Northwest
Operation Petticoat
Wild Strawberries
1960
★*The Apartment*
The Facts of Life
Hiroshima, Mon Amour
Never on Sunday
1961
★*Splendor in the Grass*
Ballad of a Soldier
La Dolce Vita
Lover Come Back
1962
★*Divorce-Italian Style*
Last Year at Marienbad
That Touch of Mink
Through a Glass Darkly
1963
★*How the West Was Won*
8 1/2
1964
★*Father Goose*
Alun Owen/A Hard Day's Night
Umbrellas of Cherbourg
1965
★*Darling*
Casanova '70
Those Magnificent Men in Their Flying Machines
The Train
1966
★*A Man and a Woman*
Blow-Up
The Fortune Cookie
Khartoum
The Naked Prey
1967
★*Guess Who's Coming to Dinner*
Bonnie & Clyde
Divorce American Style
Two for the Road
1968
★*The Producers*
Faces
Hot Millions
2001: A Space Odyssey

1969
★*Butch Cassidy and the Sundance Kid*
Bob & Carol & Ted & Alice
The Damned
Easy Rider
My Night at Maud's
The Wild Bunch
1970
★*Patton*
Five Easy Pieces
Joe
Love Story
1971
★*The Hospital*
Klute
Summer of '42
Sunday, Bloody Sunday
1972
★*The Candidate*
The Discreet Charm of the Bourgeoisie
Lady Sings the Blues
Murmur of the Heart
Young Winston
1973
★*The Sting*
American Graffiti
Cries and Whispers
Save the Tiger
A Touch of Class

WRITING
1929
Our Dancing Daughters
1930
★*The Dawn Patrol*
All Quiet on the Western Front
The Divorcee
1931
Smart Money
1938
The Black Legion
1943
Nunnally Johnson/*Holy Matrimony*

FILM—FOREIGN LANGUAGE
1947
★*Shoeshine*
1948
★*Monsieur Vincent*
1949
★*The Bicycle Thief*
1951
★*Rashomon*
1952
★*Forbidden Games*
1954
★*Gate of Hell*
1955
★*Samurai 1: Musashi Miyamoto*
1956
★*La Strada*
The Burmese Harp
Gervaise
1957
★*Nights of Cabiria*
1958
★*Mon Oncle*
Big Deal on Madonna Street
1959
★*Black Orpheus*
The Bridge
1960
★*The Virgin Spring*
Kapo
1961
★*Through a Glass Darkly*

1963
★*8 1/2*
Knife in the Water
1964
★*Yesterday, Today and Tomorrow*
Sallah
Umbrellas of Cherbourg
Woman in the Dunes
1965
★*The Shop on Main Street*
Kwaidan
Marriage Italian Style
1966
★*A Man and a Woman*
The Battle of Algiers
Loves of a Blonde
1967
★*Closely Watched Trains*
1968
★*War and Peace*
The Firemen's Ball
Stolen Kisses
1969
★*Z*
Battle of Neretva
My Night at Maud's
1970
First Love
1971
★*The Garden of the Finzi-Continis*
Dodes 'ka-den
1972
★*The Discreet Charm of the Bourgeoisie*
I Love You Rosa
The New Land
1973
★*Day for Night*
Turkish Delight
1974
★*Amarcord*
Cat's Play
The Deluge
1975
★*Dersu Uzala*
Land of Promise
The Scent of a Woman
1976
★*Black and White in Color*
Cousin, Cousine
Jacob the Liar
Nights and Days
Seven Beauties
1977
Iphigenia
Operation Thunderbolt
A Special Day
That Obscure Object of Desire
1978
★*Get Out Your Handkerchiefs*
1979
★*The Tin Drum*
Maids of Wilko
1980
★*Moscow Does Not Believe in Tears*
Kagemusha
The Last Metro
1981
★*Mephisto*
The Boat Is Full
Man of Iron
Three Brothers
1982
Coup de Torchon

1983
★*Fanny and Alexander*
Carmen
Entre-Nous
1984
★*Dangerous Moves*
Camila
1985
★*The Official Story*
Angry Harvest
Colonel Redl
Three Men and a Cradle
When Father Was Away on Business
1986
Betty Blue
The Decline of the American Empire
1987
★*Babette's Feast*
Au Revoir les Enfants
1988
★*Pelle the Conqueror*
The Music Teacher
Salaam Bombay!
Women on the Verge of a Nervous Breakdown
1989
★*Cinema Paradiso*
Camille Claudel
Jesus of Montreal
1990
★*Journey of Hope*
Cyrano de Bergerac
Ju Dou
The Nasty Girl
1991
The Ox
Raise the Red Lantern
Sweetie
1992
★*Indochine*
A Place in the World
Schtonk
1993
★*Belle Epoque*
Farewell My Concubine
The Scent of Green Papaya
The Wedding Banquet
1994
★*Burnt by the Sun*
Before the Rain
Eat Drink Man Woman
Farinelli
Strawberry and Chocolate
1995
★*Antonia's Line*
All Things Fair
The Star Maker
1996
★*Kolya*
A Chef in Love
The Other Side of Sunday
Prisoner of the Mountains
Ridicule
1997
★*Character*
Beyond Silence
Four Days in September
The Thief
1998
★*Life Is Beautiful*
Central Station
Children of Heaven
The Grandfather
Tango

1999
★*All About My Mother*
East-West
Himalaya
Solomon and Gaenor
Under the Sun
2000
★*Crouching Tiger, Hidden Dragon*
Amores Perros
Divided We Fall
Everybody's Famous!
The Taste of Others
2001
★*No Man's Land*
Amelie
Lagaan: Once upon a Time in India
The Son of the Bride
2002
★*Nowhere in Africa*
The Crime of Father Amaro
Elling
Hero
The Man Without a Past
The Twilight Samurai
Zus & Zo
2003
★*The Barbarian Invasions*
Evil
Zelary
2004
★*The Sea Inside*
As It Is In Heaven
The Chorus
Downfall
2005
★*Tsotsi*
Don't Tell
Joyeux Noel
Paradise Now
Sophie Scholl: The Final Days
2006
★*The Lives of Others*
After the Wedding
Days of Glory
Pan's Labyrinth
Water
2007
★*The Counterfeiters*
Beaufort
Katyn
Mongol
12
2008
★*Departures*
The Baader Meinhof Complex
The Class
Waltz with Bashir
2009
★*The Secret in Their Eyes*
Ajami
The Milk of Sorrow
A Prophet
The White Ribbon
2010
★*In a Better World*
Biutiful
Dogtooth
Incendies
Outside the Law
2011
★*A Separation*
Bullhead
Footnote
In Darkness
Monsieur Lazhar

2012
★*Amour*
Kon-Tiki
No
A Royal Affair
War Witch
2013
★*The Great Beauty*
The Hunt
2014
★*Ida*
Leviathan
2015
★*Son of Saul*
Embrace of the Serpent
Mustang
Theeb
A War
2016
★*The Salesman*
Land of Mine
A Man Called Ove
Toni Erdmann
2017
★*A Fantastic Woman*
The Insult
Loveless
On Body and Soul
The Square
2018
★*Roma*
Capernaum
Cold War
Never Look Away
Shoplifters
2019
★*Parasite*
Corpus Christi
Honeyland
Les misérables
Pain and Glory

VISUAL EFFECTS
1963
★*Cleopatra*
1964
★*Mary Poppins*
1965
★*Thunderball*
1966
★*Fantastic Voyage*
1967
★*Doctor Dolittle*
1968
★*2001: A Space Odyssey*
1969
★*Marooned*
1970
★*Tora! Tora! Tora!*
1971
★*Bedknobs and Broomsticks*
1972
★*The Poseidon Adventure*
1974
★*Earthquake*
1975
★*The Hindenburg*
1976
★*King Kong*
★*Logan's Run*
1977
★*Star Wars*
1978
★*Superman: The Movie*
1979
★*Alien*
1980
★*The Empire Strikes Back*

★ = *winner*

1981
★*Raiders of the Lost Ark*
1982
★*E.T.: The Extra-Terrestrial*
1983
★*Return of the Jedi*
1984
★*Indiana Jones and the Temple of Doom*
1985
★*Cocoon*
1986
★*Aliens*
1987
★*Innerspace*
1988
★*Who Framed Roger Rabbit*
1989
★*The Abyss*
1990
★*Total Recall*
1991
★*Terminator 2: Judgment Day*
Backdraft
Hook
1992
★*Death Becomes Her*
Alien 3
Batman Returns
1993
★*Jurassic Park*
Cliffhanger
The Nightmare Before Christmas
1994
★*Forrest Gump*
The Mask
True Lies
1995
★*Babe*
1996
★*Independence Day*
Dragonheart
Twister
1997
★*Titanic*
The Lost World: Jurassic Park 2
Starship Troopers
1998
★*What Dreams May Come*
Armageddon
Mighty Joe Young
1999
★*The Matrix*
Star Wars: Episode 1-The Phantom Menace
Stuart Little
2000
★*Gladiator*
Hollow Man
The Perfect Storm
2001
A. I.: Artificial Intelligence
Lord of the Rings: The Fellowship of the Ring
Pearl Harbor
2002
★*Lord of the Rings: The Two Towers*
Spider-Man
Star Wars: Episode 2-Attack of the Clones
2003
★*Lord of the Rings: The Return of the King*
Master and Commander: The Far Side of the World
Pirates of the Caribbean: The Curse of the Black Pearl
2004
★*Spider-Man 2*
Harry Potter and the Prisoner of Azkaban
I, Robot
2005
★*King Kong*
The Chronicles of Narnia: The Lion, the Witch and the Wardrobe
War of the Worlds
2006
★*Pirates of the Caribbean: Dead Man's Chest*
Poseidon
Superman Returns
2007
★*The Golden Compass*
Pirates of the Caribbean: At World's End
Transformers
2008
★*The Curious Case of Benjamin Button*
The Dark Knight
Iron Man
2009
★*Avatar*
District 9
Star Trek
2010
★*Inception*
Alice in Wonderland
Harry Potter and the Deathly Hallows, Part 1
Hereafter
Iron Man 2
2011
★*Hugo*
Harry Potter and the Deathly Hallows, Part 2
Real Steel
Rise of the Planet of the Apes
Transformers: Dark of the Moon
2012
★*Life of Pi*
The Avengers
The Hobbit: An Unexpected Journey
Prometheus
Snow White and the Huntsman
2013
★*Gravity*
The Hobbit: The Desolation of Smaug
Iron Man 3
The Lone Ranger
Star Trek: Into Darkness
2014
★*Interstellar*
Captain America: The Winter Soldier
Dawn of the Planet of the Apes
Guardians of the Galaxy
X-Men: Days of Future Past
2015
★*Ex Machina*
Mad Max: Fury Road
The Martian
The Revenant
Star Wars: The Force Awakens
2016
★*The Jungle Book*
Deepwater Horizon
Doctor Strange
Kubo and the Two Strings
Rogue One: A Star Wars Story
2017
★*Blade Runner 2049*
Guardians of the Galaxy Vol. 2
Kong: Skull Island
Star Wars: The Last Jedi
War for the Planet of the Apes
2018
★*First Man*
Avengers: Infinity War
Christopher Robin
Ready Player One
Solo: A Star Wars Story
2019
★*1917*
Avengers: Endgame
The Irishman
The Lion King
Star Wars: The Rise of Skywalker

ANIMATED FILM

2001
★*Shrek*
Jimmy Neutron: Boy Genius
Monsters, Inc.
2002
★*Spirited Away*
Ice Age
Lilo & Stitch
Spirit: Stallion of the Cimarron
Treasure Planet
2003
★*Finding Nemo*
Brother Bear
The Triplets of Belleville
2004
★*The Incredibles*
Shark Tale
Shrek 2
2005
★*Wallace & Gromit in The Curse of the Were-Rabbit*
Howl's Moving Castle
2006
★*Happy Feet*
Cars
Monster House
2007
★*Ratatouille*
Persepolis
Surf's Up
2008
★*WALL-E*
Bolt
Kung Fu Panda
2009
★*Up*
Coraline
Fantastic Mr. Fox
The Princess and the Frog
The Secret of Kells
2010
★*Toy Story 3*
How to Train Your Dragon
The Illusionist
2011
★*Rango*
A Cat in Paris
Chico & Rita
Kung Fu Panda 2
Puss in Boots
2012
★*Brave*
Frankenweenie
ParaNorman
The Pirates! Band of Misfits
Wreck-It Ralph
2013
★*Frozen*
The Croods
Despicable Me 2
2014
★*Big Hero 6*
The Boxtrolls
How to Train Your Dragon 2
The Tale of the Princess Kaguya
2015
★*Inside Out*
Anomalisa
Boy & the World
Shaun the Sheep Movie
2016
★*Zootopia*
Kubo and the Two Strings
Moana
My Life as a Zucchini
The Red Turtle
2017
★*Coco*
The Boss Baby
The Breadwinner
Ferdinand
Loving Vincent
2018
★*Spider-Man: Into the Spider-Verse*
Incredibles 2
Isle of Dogs
Mirai
Ralph Breaks the Internet
2019
★*Toy Story 4*
How to Train Your Dragon: The Hidden World
I Lost My Body
Klaus
Missing Link

PRODUCTION DESIGN

2012
★*Lincoln*
Anna Karenina
The Hobbit: An Unexpected Journey
Les Miserables
Life of Pi
2013
★*The Great Gatsby*
American Hustle
Gravity
Her
12 Years a Slave
2014
★*The Grand Budapest Hotel*
The Imitation Game
Interstellar
Into the Woods
Mr. Turner
2015
★*Mad Max: Fury Road*
Bridge of Spies
The Danish Girl
The Martian
The Revenant
2016
★*La La Land*
Arrival
Fantastic Beasts and Where to Find Them
Hail, Caesar!
Passengers
2017
★*The Shape of Water*
Beauty and the Beast
Blade Runner 2049
Darkest Hour
Dunkirk
2018
★*Black Panther*
The Favourite
First Man
Mary Poppins Returns
Roma
2019
★*Once Upon A Time... In Hollywood*
The Irishman
Jojo Rabbit
1917
Parasite

BRITISH ACADEMY OF FILM AND TELEVISION ARTS

ACTOR

1952
★Marlon Brando/*Viva Zapata!*
1953
★Marlon Brando/*Julius Caesar*
★John Gielgud/*Julius Caesar*
1954
★Marlon Brando/*On the Waterfront*
★Kenneth More/*Doctor in the House*
1955
★Ernest Borgnine/*Marty*
★Laurence Olivier/*Richard III*
1956
★Francois Perier/*Gervaise*
1957
★Henry Fonda/*Twelve Angry Men*
★Alec Guinness/*The Bridge on the River Kwai*
1958
★Trevor Howard/*The Key*
★Sidney Poitier/*The Defiant Ones*
1959
★Jack Lemmon/*Some Like It Hot*
★Peter Sellers/*I'm All Right Jack*
1960
★Jack Lemmon/*The Apartment*
1961
★Paul Newman/*The Hustler*
1962
★Burt Lancaster/*Birdman of Alcatraz*
★Peter O'Toole/*Lawrence of Arabia*
1963
★Dirk Bogarde/*The Servant*
★Marcello Mastroianni/*Divorce-Italian Style*
1964
★Richard Attenborough/*Seance on a Wet Afternoon*
★Marcello Mastroianni/*Yesterday, Today and Tomorrow*
1965
★Dirk Bogarde/*Darling*
★Lee Marvin/*Cat Ballou*
1966
★Richard Burton/*Who's Afraid of Virginia Woolf?*
★Rod Steiger/*The Pawnbroker*
1967
★Paul Scofield/*A Man for All Seasons*
★Rod Steiger/*In the Heat of the Night*
1968
★Spencer Tracy/*Guess Who's Coming to Dinner*
1969
★Dustin Hoffman/*Midnight Cowboy*
1970
★Robert Redford/*Butch Cassidy and the Sundance Kid*
1971
★Peter Finch/*Sunday, Bloody Sunday*
1972
★Gene Hackman/*The French Connection*
1973
★Walter Matthau/*Pete 'n' Tillie*
1974
★Jack Nicholson/*Chinatown*
★Jack Nicholson/*The Last Detail*
1975
★Al Pacino/*Dog Day Afternoon*
1976
★Jack Nicholson/*One Flew Over the Cuckoo's Nest*
1977
★Peter Finch/*Network*
1978
★Richard Dreyfuss/*The Goodbye Girl*
1979
★Jack Lemmon/*The China Syndrome*
1980
★John Hurt/*The Elephant Man*
1981
★Burt Lancaster/*Atlantic City*
1982
★Ben Kingsley/*Gandhi*
1983
★Michael Caine/*Educating Rita*
★Dustin Hoffman/*Tootsie*
1984
★Haing S. Ngor/*The Killing Fields*
1985
★William Hurt/*Kiss of the Spider Woman*
1986
★Bob Hoskins/*Mona Lisa*
1987
★Sean Connery/*The Name of the Rose*
1988
★John Cleese/*A Fish Called Wanda*
1989
★Daniel Day-Lewis/*My Left Foot*
1990
★Philippe Noiret/*Cinema Paradiso*
1991
★Anthony Hopkins/*The Silence of the Lambs*
1992
★Robert Downey, Jr./*Chaplin*
1993
★Anthony Hopkins/*The Remains of the Day*
Daniel Day-Lewis/*In the Name of the Father*
Anthony Hopkins/*Shadowlands*
Liam Neeson/*Schindler's List*

★ = winner

1994

★Hugh Grant/*Four Weddings and a Funeral*

1995

★Nigel Hawthorne/*The Madness of King George*

Nicolas Cage/*Leaving Las Vegas*

Jonathan Pryce/*Carrington*

Massimo Troisi/*The Postman*

1996

★Geoffrey Rush/*Shine*

Ralph Fiennes/*The English Patient*

Ian McKellen/*Richard III*

Timothy Spall/*Secrets and Lies*

1997

★Robert Carlyle/*The Full Monty*

Billy Connolly/*Mrs. Brown*

Kevin Spacey/*L.A. Confidential*

Ray Winstone/*Nil by Mouth*

1998

★Roberto Benigni/*Life Is Beautiful*

Michael Caine/*Little Voice*

Joseph Fiennes/*Shakespeare in Love*

Tom Hanks/*Saving Private Ryan*

1999

★Kevin Spacey/*American Beauty*

Jim Broadbent/*Topsy Turvy*

Russell Crowe/*The Insider*

Ralph Fiennes/*The End of the Affair*

Om Puri/*East Is East*

2000

★Jamie Bell/*Billy Elliot*

2001

★Russell Crowe/*A Beautiful Mind*

Jim Broadbent/*Iris*

Ian McKellen/*Lord of the Rings: The Fellowship of the Ring*

Kevin Spacey/*The Shipping News*

Tom Wilkinson/*In the Bedroom*

2002

★Daniel Day-Lewis/*Gangs of New York*

Adrien Brody/*The Pianist*

Nicolas Cage/*Adaptation*

Michael Caine/*The Quiet American*

Jack Nicholson/*About Schmidt*

2003

★Johnny Depp/*Pirates of the Caribbean: The Curse of the Black Pearl*

★Bill Murray/*Lost in Translation*

Benicio Del Toro/*21 Grams*

Jude Law/*Cold Mountain*

Sean Penn/*Mystic River*

Sean Penn/*21 Grams*

2004

★Jamie Foxx/*Ray*

Gael Garcia Bernal/*The Motorcycle Diaries*

Jim Carrey/*Eternal Sunshine of the Spotless Mind*

Johnny Depp/*Finding Neverland*

Leonardo DiCaprio/*The Aviator*

2005

★Philip Seymour Hoffman/*Capote*

Ralph Fiennes/*The Constant Gardener*

Terrence Howard/*Hustle & Flow*

Heath Ledger/*Brokeback Mountain*

Joaquin Rafael (Leaf) Phoenix/*Walk the Line*

David Strathairn/*Good Night, and Good Luck*

2006

★Forest Whitaker/*The Last King of Scotland*

Daniel Craig/*Casino Royale*

Leonardo DiCaprio/*The Departed*

Richard Griffiths/*The History Boys*

Peter O'Toole/*Venus*

2007

★Daniel Day-Lewis/*There Will Be Blood*

George Clooney/*Michael Clayton*

James McAvoy/*Atonement*

Viggo Mortensen/*Eastern Promises*

Ulrich Muehe/*The Lives of Others*

2008

★Mickey Rourke/*The Wrestler*

Frank Langella/*Frost/Nixon*

Dev Patel/*Slumdog Millionaire*

Sean Penn/*Milk*

Brad Pitt/*The Curious Case of Benjamin Button*

2009

★Colin Firth/*A Single Man*

Jeff Bridges/*Crazy Heart*

George Clooney/*Up in the Air*

Jeremy Renner/*The Hurt Locker*

Andy Serkis/*Sex & Drugs & Rock & Roll*

2010

★Colin Firth/*The King's Speech*

Javier Bardem/*Biutiful*

Jeff Bridges/*True Grit*

Jesse Eisenberg/*The Social Network*

James Franco/*127 Hours*

2011

★Jean Dujardin/*The Artist*

George Clooney/*The Descendants*

Michael Fassbender/*Shame*

Gary Oldman/*Tinker Tailor Soldier Spy*

Brad Pitt/*Moneyball*

2012

★Daniel Day-Lewis/*Lincoln*

Ben Affleck/*Argo*

Bradley Cooper/*Silver Linings Playbook*

Hugh Jackman/*Les Miserables*

Joaquin Rafael (Leaf) Phoenix/*The Master*

2013

★Chiwetel Ejiofor/*12 Years a Slave*

Christian Bale/*American Hustle*

Bruce Dern/*Nebraska*

Leonardo DiCaprio/*The Wolf of Wall Street*

Tom Hanks/*Captain Phillips*

2014

★Eddie Redmayne/*The Theory of Everything*

Benedict Cumberbatch/*The Imitation Game*

Ralph Fiennes/*The Grand Budapest Hotel*

Jake Gyllenhaal/*Nightcrawler*

Michael Keaton/*Birdman, or (The Unexpected Virtue of Ignorance)*

2015

★Leonardo DiCaprio/*The Revenant*

Bryan Cranston/*Trumbo*

Matt Damon/*The Martian*

Michael Fassbender/*Steve Jobs*

Eddie Redmayne/*The Danish Girl*

2016

★Casey Affleck/*Manchester by the Sea*

Andrew Garfield/*Hacksaw Ridge*

Ryan Gosling/*La La Land*

Jake Gyllenhaal/*Nocturnal Animals*

Viggo Mortensen/*Captain Fantastic*

2017

★Gary Oldman/*Darkest Hour*

Jamie Bell/*Film Stars Don't Die in Liverpool*

Timothée Chalamet/*Call Me by Your Name*

Daniel Day-Lewis/*Phantom Thread*

Daniel Kaluuya/*Get Out*

2018

★Rami Malek/*Bohemian Rhapsody*

Christian Bale/*Vice*

Steve Coogan/*Stan & Ollie*

Bradley Cooper/*A Star Is Born*

Viggo Mortensen/*Green Book*

2019

★Joaquin Rafael (Leaf) Phoenix/*Joker*

Leonardo DiCaprio/*Once Upon A Time... In Hollywood*

Adam Driver/*Marriage Story*

Taron Egerton/*Rocketman*

Jonathan Pryce/*The Two Popes*

ACTOR—SUPPORTING

1969

★Laurence Olivier/*Oh! What a Lovely War*

1971

★Edward Fox/*The Go-Between*

1972

★Ben Johnson/*The Last Picture Show*

1973

★Arthur Lowe/*O Lucky Man!*

1974

★John Gielgud/*Murder on the Orient Express*

1975

★Fred Astaire/*The Towering Inferno*

1976

★Brad Dourif/*One Flew Over the Cuckoo's Nest*

1977

★Edward Fox/*A Bridge Too Far*

1978

★John Hurt/*Midnight Express*

1979

★Robert Duvall/*Apocalypse Now*

1981

★Ian Holm/*Chariots of Fire*

1982

★Jack Nicholson/*Reds*

1983

★Denholm Elliott/*Trading Places*

1984

★Denholm Elliott/*A Private Function*

1985

★Denholm Elliott/*Defense of the Realm*

1986

★Ray McAnally/*The Mission*

1987

★Daniel Auteuil/*Jean de Florette*

1988

★Michael Palin/*A Fish Called Wanda*

1989

★Ray McAnally/*My Left Foot*

1990

★Salvatore Cascio/*Cinema Paradiso*

1991

★Alan Rickman/*Robin Hood: Prince of Thieves*

1992

★Gene Hackman/*Unforgiven*

1993

★Ralph Fiennes/*Schindler's List*

Tommy Lee Jones/*The Fugitive*

Ben Kingsley/*Schindler's List*

John Malkovich/*In the Line of Fire*

1994

★Samuel L. Jackson/*Pulp Fiction*

1995

★Tim Roth/*Rob Roy*

Ian Holm/*The Madness of King George*

Martin Landau/*Ed Wood*

Alan Rickman/*Sense and Sensibility*

1996

★Paul Scofield/*The Crucible*

John Gielgud/*Shine*

Edward Norton/*Primal Fear*

Alan Rickman/*Michael Collins*

1997

★Tom Wilkinson/*The Full Monty*

Mark Addy/*The Full Monty*

Rupert Everett/*My Best Friend's Wedding*

Burt Reynolds/*Boogie Nights*

1998

★Geoffrey Rush/*Shakespeare in Love*

Ed Harris/*The Truman Show*

Geoffrey Rush/*Elizabeth*

Tom Wilkinson/*Shakespeare in Love*

1999

★Jude Law/*The Talented Mr. Ripley*

Wes Bentley/*American Beauty*

Michael Caine/*The Cider House Rules*

Rhys Ifans/*Notting Hill*

Timothy Spall/*Topsy Turvy*

2000

★Benicio Del Toro/*Traffic*

2001

★Jim Broadbent/*Moulin Rouge*

Hugh Bonneville/*Iris*

Robbie Coltrane/*Harry Potter and the Sorcerer's Stone*

Colin Firth/*Bridget Jones's Diary*

Eddie Murphy/*Shrek*

2002

★Christopher Walken/*Catch Me If You Can*

Chris Cooper/*Adaptation*

Ed Harris/*The Hours*

Alfred Molina/*Frida*

Paul Newman/*Road to Perdition*

2003

★Bill Nighy/*Love Actually*

Paul Bettany/*Master and Commander: The Far Side of the World*

Albert Finney/*Big Fish*

Ian McKellen/*Lord of the Rings: The Return of the King*

Tim Robbins/*Mystic River*

2004

★Clive Owen/*Closer*

Alan Alda/*The Aviator*

Philip Davis/*Vera Drake*

Rodrigo de la Serna/*The Motorcycle Diaries*

Jamie Foxx/*Collateral*

2005

★Jake Gyllenhaal/*Brokeback Mountain*

Don Cheadle/*Crash*

George Clooney/*Good Night, and Good Luck*

George Clooney/*Syriana*

Matt Dillon/*Crash*

2006

★Alan Arkin/*Little Miss Sunshine*

James McAvoy/*The Last King of Scotland*

Jack Nicholson/*The Departed*

Leslie Phillips/*Venus*

Brad Pitt/*Burn After Reading*

Michael Sheen/*The Queen*

2007

★Javier Bardem/*No Country for Old Men*

Paul Dano/*There Will Be Blood*

Philip Seymour Hoffman/*Charlie Wilson's War*

Tommy Lee Jones/*No Country for Old Men*

Tom Wilkinson/*Michael Clayton*

2008

★Heath Ledger/*The Dark Knight*

Robert Downey, Jr./*Tropic Thunder*

Brendan Gleeson/*In Bruges*

Philip Seymour Hoffman/*Doubt*

2009

★Christoph Waltz/*Inglourious Basterds*

Alec Baldwin/*It's Complicated*

Christian McKay/*Me and Orson Welles*

Alfred Molina/*An Education*

Stanley Tucci/*The Lovely Bones*

2010

★Geoffrey Rush/*The King's Speech*

Christian Bale/*The Fighter*

Andrew Garfield/*The Social Network*

Pete Postlethwaite/*The Town*

Mark Ruffalo/*The Kids Are All Right*

2011

★Kenneth Branagh/*My Week With Marilyn*

★Christopher Plummer/*Beginners*

Jim Broadbent/*The Iron Lady*

Jonah Hill/*Moneyball*

Philip Seymour Hoffman/*The Ides of March*

2012

★Christoph Waltz/*Django Unchained*

Alan Arkin/*Argo*

Javier Bardem/*Skyfall*

Philip Seymour Hoffman/*The Master*

Tommy Lee Jones/*Lincoln*

2013

★Barkhad Adbi/*Captain Phillips*

Daniel Brühl/*Rush*

Bradley Cooper/*American Hustle*

Matt Damon/*Behind the Candelabra*

Michael Fassbender/*12 Years a Slave*

2014

★J.K. Simmons/*Whiplash*

Steve Carell/*Foxcatcher*

Ethan Hawke/*Boyhood*

Edward Norton/*Birdman, or (The Unexpected Virtue of Ignorance)*

Mark Ruffalo/*Foxcatcher*

2015

★Mark Rylance/*Bridge of Spies*

Christian Bale/*The Big Short*

Benicio Del Toro/*Sicario*

Idris Elba/*Beasts of No Nation*

Mark Ruffalo/*Spotlight*

2016

★Dev Patel/*Lion*

Jeff Bridges/*Hell or High Water*

Hugh Grant/*Florence Foster Jenkins*

Aaron Taylor-Johnson/*Nocturnal Animals*

2017

★Sam Rockwell/*Three Billboards Outside Ebbing, Missouri*

Willem Dafoe/*The Florida Project*

Hugh Grant/*Paddington 2*

Woody Harrelson/*Three Billboards Outside Ebbing, Missouri*

Christopher Plummer/*All the Money in the World*

2018

★Mahershala Ali/*Green Book*

Timothée Chalamet/*Beautiful Boy*

Adam Driver/*BlacKkKlansman*

Richard E. Grant/*Can You Ever Forgive Me?*

Sam Rockwell/*Vice*

★ = winner

2019

★Brad Pitt/*Once Upon A Time... In Hollywood*

Tom Hanks/*A Beautiful Day in the Neighborhood*

Anthony Hopkins/*The Two Popes*

Al Pacino/*The Irishman*

Joe Pesci/*The Irishman*

ACTRESS

1952

★Vivien Leigh/*A Streetcar Named Desire*

1953

★Leslie Caron/*Lili*

★Audrey Hepburn/*Roman Holiday*

1955

★Betsy Blair/*Marty*

★Katie Johnson/*The Ladykillers*

1956

★Anna Magnani/*The Rose Tattoo*

1958

★Simone Signoret/*Room at the Top*

1959

★Audrey Hepburn/*The Nun's Story*

1960

★Shirley MacLaine/*The Apartment*

★Rachel Roberts/*Saturday Night and Sunday Morning*

1961

★Sophia Loren/*Two Women*

1962

★Anne Bancroft/*The Miracle Worker*

1963

★Patricia Neal/*Hud*

★Rachel Roberts/*This Sporting Life*

1964

★Audrey Hepburn/*Charade*

1965

★Julie Christie/*Darling*

★Patricia Neal/*In Harm's Way*

1966

★Elizabeth Taylor/*Who's Afraid of Virginia Woolf?*

1967

★Anouk Aimee/*A Man and a Woman*

1968

★Katharine Hepburn/*Guess Who's Coming to Dinner*

1969

★Maggie Smith/*The Prime of Miss Jean Brodie*

1970

★Katharine Ross/*Butch Cassidy and the Sundance Kid*

1971

★Glenda Jackson/*Sunday, Bloody Sunday*

1972

★Liza Minnelli/*Cabaret*

1973

★Delphine Seyrig/*The Discreet Charm of the Bourgeoisie*

1974

★Joanne Woodward/*Summer Wishes, Winter Dreams*

1975

★Ellen Burstyn/*Alice Doesn't Live Here Anymore*

1976

★Louise Fletcher/*One Flew Over the Cuckoo's Nest*

1977

★Diane Keaton/*Annie Hall*

1978

★Jane Fonda/*Julia*

1979

★Jane Fonda/*The China Syndrome*

1980

★Judy Davis/*My Brilliant Career*

1981

★Meryl Streep/*The French Lieutenant's Woman*

1982

★Katharine Hepburn/*On Golden Pond*

1983

★Julie Walters/*Educating Rita*

1984

★Maggie Smith/*A Private Function*

1985

★Peggy Ashcroft/*A Passage to India*

1986

★Maggie Smith/*A Room with a View*

1987

★Anne Bancroft/*84 Charing Cross Road*

1988

★Maggie Smith/*The Lonely Passion of Judith Hearne*

1989

★Pauline Collins/*Shirley Valentine*

1990

★Jessica Tandy/*Driving Miss Daisy*

1991

★Jodie Foster/*The Silence of the Lambs*

1992

★Emma Thompson/*Howard's End*

1993

★Holly Hunter/*The Piano*

Miranda Richardson/*Tom & Viv*

Debra Winger/*Shadowlands*

1994

★Susan Sarandon/*The Client*

Emma Thompson/*The Remains of the Day*

1995

★Emma Thompson/*Sense and Sensibility*

Nicole Kidman/*To Die For*

Dame Helen Mirren/*The Madness of King George*

Elisabeth Shue/*Leaving Las Vegas*

1996

★Brenda Blethyn/*Secrets and Lies*

Frances McDormand/*Fargo*

Kristin Scott Thomas/*The English Patient*

Emily Watson/*Breaking the Waves*

1997

★Dame Judi Dench/*Mrs. Brown*

Kim Basinger/*L.A. Confidential*

Helena Bonham Carter/*The Wings of the Dove*

Kathy Burke/*Nil by Mouth*

1998

★Cate Blanchett/*Elizabeth*

Jane Horrocks/*Little Voice*

Gwyneth Paltrow/*Shakespeare in Love*

Emily Watson/*Hilary and Jackie*

1999

★Annette Bening/*American Beauty*

Linda Bassett/*East Is East*

Julianne Moore/*The End of the Affair*

Emily Watson/*Angela's Ashes*

2000

★Julia Roberts/*Erin Brockovich*

2001

★Dame Judi Dench/*Iris*

Nicole Kidman/*The Others*

Sissy Spacek/*In the Bedroom*

Audrey Tautou/*Amelie*

Renée Zellweger/*Bridget Jones's Diary*

2002

★Nicole Kidman/*The Hours*

Halle Berry/*Monster's Ball*

Salma Hayek/*Frida*

Meryl Streep/*The Hours*

Renée Zellweger/*Chicago*

2003

★Scarlett Johansson/*Lost in Translation*

Scarlett Johansson/*Girl with a Pearl Earring*

Uma Thurman/*Kill Bill Vol. 1*

Naomi Watts/*21 Grams*

2004

★Imelda Staunton/*Vera Drake*

Charlize Theron/*Monster*

Kate Winslet/*Eternal Sunshine of the Spotless Mind*

Kate Winslet/*Finding Neverland*

2005

★Reese Witherspoon/*Walk the Line*

Dame Judi Dench/*Mrs. Henderson Presents*

Keira Knightley/*Pride and Prejudice*

Charlize Theron/*North Country*

Rachel Weisz/*The Constant Gardener*

2006

★Dame Helen Mirren/*The Queen*

Penelope Cruz/*Volver*

Dame Judi Dench/*Notes on a Scandal*

Meryl Streep/*The Devil Wears Prada*

Kate Winslet/*Little Children*

2007

★Marion Cotillard/*La Vie en Rose*

Cate Blanchett/*Elizabeth: The Golden Age*

Julie Christie/*Away From Her*

Keira Knightley/*Atonement*

Ellen Page/*Juno*

2008

★Kate Winslet/*The Reader*

Angelina Jolie/*Changeling*

Kristin Scott Thomas/*I've Loved You So Long*

Meryl Streep/*Doubt*

Kate Winslet/*Revolutionary Road*

2009

★Carey Mulligan/*An Education*

Saoirse Ronan/*The Lovely Bones*

Gabourney 'Gabby' Sidibe/*Precious: Based on the Novel 'Push' by Sapphire*

Meryl Streep/*Julie & Julia*

Audrey Tautou/*Coco Before Chanel*

2010

★Natalie Portman/*Black Swan*

Annette Bening/*The Kids Are All Right*

Julianne Moore/*The Kids Are All Right*

Noomi Rapace/*The Girl With the Dragon Tattoo*

Hailee Steinfeld/*True Grit*

2011

★Meryl Streep/*The Iron Lady*

★Michelle Williams/*My Week With Marilyn*

Berenice Bejo/*The Artist*

Viola Davis/*The Help*

Tilda Swinton/*We Need to Talk About Kevin*

2012

★Emmanuelle Riva/*Amour*

Jessica Chastain/*Zero Dark Thirty*

Marion Cotillard/*Rust and Bone*

Jennifer Lawrence/*Silver Linings Playbook*

2013

★Cate Blanchett/*Blue Jasmine*

Amy Adams/*American Hustle*

Sandra Bullock/*Gravity*

Dame Judi Dench/*Philomena*

Emma Thompson/*Saving Mr. Banks*

2014

★Julianne Moore/*Still Alice*

Amy Adams/*Big Eyes*

Felicity Jones/*The Theory of Everything*

Rosamund Pike/*Gone Girl*

Reese Witherspoon/*Wild*

2015

Cate Blanchett/*Carol*

Saoirse Ronan/*Brooklyn*

Maggie Smith/*The Lady in the Van*

Alicia Vikander/*The Danish Girl*

2016

★Emma Stone/*La La Land*

Amy Adams/*Arrival*

Emily Blunt/*The Girl on the Train*

Natalie Portman/*Jackie*

Meryl Streep/*Florence Foster Jenkins*

2017

★Frances McDormand/*Three Billboards Outside Ebbing, Missouri*

Annette Bening/*Film Stars Don't Die in Liverpool*

Glenn Close/*The Wife*

Sally Hawkins/*The Shape of Water*

Margot Robbie/*I, Tonya*

Saoirse Ronan/*Lady Bird*

2018

★Olivia Colman/*The Favourite*

Viola Davis/*Widows*

Lady Gaga/*A Star Is Born*

Melissa McCarthy/*Can You Ever Forgive Me?*

2019

★Renée Zellweger/*Judy*

Jessie Buckley/*Wild Rose*

Scarlett Johansson/*Marriage Story*

Saoirse Ronan/*Little Women*

Charlize Theron/*Bombshell*

ACTRESS—SUPPORTING

1969

★Celia Johnson/*The Prime of Miss Jean Brodie*

Mary Wimbush/*Oh! What a Lovely War*

1970

★Susannah York/*They Shoot Horses, Don't They?*

1971

★Margaret Leighton/*The Go-Between*

1972

★Cloris Leachman/*The Last Picture Show*

1973

★Valentina Cortese/*Day for Night*

1974

★Ingrid Bergman/*Murder on the Orient Express*

1975

★Diane Ladd/*Alice Doesn't Live Here Anymore*

1976

★Jodie Foster/*Taxi Driver*

1977

★Jenny Agutter/*Equus*

Vivien Merchant/*The Homecoming*

1978

★Geraldine Page/*Interiors*

★Vanessa Redgrave/*Julia*

1979

★Rachel Roberts/*Yanks*

1982

★Rohini Hattangadi/*Gandhi*

★Maureen Stapleton/*Reds*

1983

★Jamie Lee Curtis/*Trading Places*

1984

★Liz Smith/*A Private Function*

Tuesday Weld/*Once Upon a Time in America*

1985

★Rosanna Arquette/*Desperately Seeking Susan*

1986

★Dame Judi Dench/*A Room with a View*

1987

★Susan Wooldridge/*Hope and Glory*

1988

★Dame Judi Dench/*A Handful of Dust*

1989

★Michelle Pfeiffer/*Dangerous Liaisons*

1990

★Whoopi Goldberg/*Ghost*

1991

★Kate Nelligan/*Frankie and Johnny*

1992

★Miranda Richardson/*Damage*

1993

★Miriam Margolyes/*The Age of Innocence*

Holly Hunter/*The Firm*

Maggie Smith/*The Secret Garden*

1994

★Kristin Scott Thomas/*Four Weddings and a Funeral*

Winona Ryder/*The Age of Innocence*

1995

★Kate Winslet/*Sense and Sensibility*

Joan Allen/*Nixon*

Mira Sorvino/*Mighty Aphrodite*

Elizabeth Spriggs/*Sense and Sensibility*

1996

★Juliette Binoche/*The English Patient*

Lauren Bacall/*The Mirror Has Two Faces*

Marianne Jean-Baptiste/*Secrets and Lies*

Lynn Redgrave/*Shine*

1997

★Sigourney Weaver/*The Ice Storm*

Jennifer Ehle/*Wilde*

Lesley Sharp/*The Full Monty*

Zoe Wanamaker/*Wilde*

1998

★Dame Judi Dench/*Shakespeare in Love*

Kathy Bates/*Primary Colors*

Brenda Blethyn/*Little Voice*

Lynn Redgrave/*Gods and Monsters*

1999

★Maggie Smith/*Tea with Mussolini*

Thora Birch/*American Beauty*

Cate Blanchett/*The Talented Mr. Ripley*

Cameron Diaz/*Being John Malkovich*

Mena Suvari/*American Beauty*

2000

★Julie Walters/*Billy Elliot*

2001

★Jennifer Connelly/*A Beautiful Mind*

Dame Judi Dench/*The Shipping News*

Dame Helen Mirren/*Gosford Park*

Maggie Smith/*Gosford Park*

Kate Winslet/*Iris*

2002

★Catherine Zeta-Jones/*Chicago*

Toni Collette/*About a Boy*

Julianne Moore/*The Hours*

Queen Latifah/*Chicago*

Meryl Streep/*Adaptation*

2003

★Renée Zellweger/*Cold Mountain*

Holly Hunter/*Thirteen*

Laura Linney/*Mystic River*

Judy Parfitt/*Girl with a Pearl Earring*

Emma Thompson/*Love Actually*

2004

★Cate Blanchett/*The Aviator*

Julie Christie/*Finding Neverland*

Heather Craney/*Vera Drake*

Natalie Portman/*Closer*

Meryl Streep/*The Manchurian Candidate*

2005

★Thandie Newton/*Crash*

Brenda Blethyn/*Pride and Prejudice*

Catherine Keener/*Capote*

Frances McDormand/*North Country*

Michelle Williams/*Brokeback Mountain*

★ = *winner*

2006
★Jennifer Hudson/*Dreamgirls*
Emily Blunt/*The Devil Wears Prada*
Abigail Breslin/*Little Miss Sunshine*
Toni Collette/*Little Miss Sunshine*
Frances de la Tour/*The History Boys*
Tilda Swinton/*Burn After Reading*
2007
★Tilda Swinton/*Michael Clayton*
Cate Blanchett/*I'm Not There*
Kelly Macdonald/*No Country for Old Men*
Samantha Morton/*Control*
Saoirse Ronan/*Atonement*
2008
★Penelope Cruz/*Vicky Cristina Barcelona*
Amy Adams/*Doubt*
Penelope Cruz/*Vicky Cristina Barcelona*
Freida Pinto/*Slumdog Millionaire*
Marisa Tomei/*The Wrestler*
2009
★Mo'Nique/*Precious: Based on the Novel 'Push' by Sapphire*
Anne-Marie Duff/*Nowhere Boy*
Vera Farmiga/*Up in the Air*
Anna Kendrick/*Up in the Air*
Kristin Scott Thomas/*Nowhere Boy*
2010
★Helena Bonham Carter/*The King's Speech*
Amy Adams/*The Fighter*
Barbara Hershey/*Black Swan*
Lesley Manville/*Another Year*
Miranda Richardson/*Made in Dagenham*
2011
★Octavia Spencer/*The Help*
Jessica Chastain/*The Help*
Dame Judi Dench/*My Week With Marilyn*
Melissa McCarthy/*Bridesmaids*
Carey Mulligan/*Drive*
2012
★Anne Hathaway/*Les Miserables*
Amy Adams/*The Master*
Dame Judi Dench/*Skyfall*
Helen Hunt/*The Sessions*
2013
★Jennifer Lawrence/*American Hustle*
Sally Hawkins/*Blue Jasmine*
Lupita Nyong'o/*12 Years a Slave*
Julia Roberts/*August: Osage County*
Oprah Winfrey/*Lee Daniels' The Butler*
2014
★Patricia Arquette/*Boyhood*
Keira Knightley/*The Imitation Game*
Rene Russo/*Nightcrawler*
Imelda Staunton/*Pride*
Emma Stone/*Birdman, or (The Unexpected Virtue of Ignorance)*
2015
★Kate Winslet/*Steve Jobs*
Jennifer Jason Leigh/*The Hateful Eight*
Rooney Mara/*Carol*
Alicia Vikander/*Ex Machina*
Julie Walters/*Brooklyn*
2016
★Viola Davis/*Fences*
Naomie Harris/*Moonlight*
Nicole Kidman/*Lion*
Hayley Squires/*I, Daniel Blake*
Michelle Williams/*Manchester by the Sea*
2017
★Allison Janney/*I, Tonya*
Lesley Manville/*Phantom Thread*
Laurie Metcalf/*Lady Bird*
Kristin Scott Thomas/*Darkest Hour*
Octavia Spencer/*The Shape of Water*
2018
★Rachel Weisz/*The Favourite*
Amy Adams/*Vice*
Claire Foy/*First Man*
Margot Robbie/*Mary Queen of Scots*
Emma Stone/*The Favourite*
2019
★Laura Dern/*Marriage Story*
Scarlett Johansson/*Jojo Rabbit*
Florence Pugh/*Little Women*
Margot Robbie/*Bombshell*
Margot Robbie/*Once Upon A Time... In Hollywood*

ART DIRECTION

1969
★*Oh! What a Lovely War*
1997
★*William Shakespeare's Romeo and Juliet*
1999
★*Sleepy Hollow*
American Beauty
Angela's Ashes
The End of the Affair
The Matrix

CINEMATOGRAPHY

1969
★*Oh! What a Lovely War*
1984
Once Upon a Time in America
1995
★*Braveheart*
Apollo 13
The Madness of King George
Sense and Sensibility
1996
★*The English Patient*
1997
★*The Wings of the Dove*
L.A. Confidential
Titanic
William Shakespeare's Romeo and Juliet
1998
★*Elizabeth*
Saving Private Ryan
Shakespeare in Love
The Truman Show
1999
★*American Beauty*
Angela's Ashes
The End of the Affair
The Matrix
The Talented Mr. Ripley
2000
★*Gladiator*
2001
Black Hawk Down
Lord of the Rings: The Fellowship of the Ring
Moulin Rouge
2002
★*Road to Perdition*
Chicago
Gangs of New York
Lord of the Rings: The Two Towers
The Pianist
2003
★*Lord of the Rings: The Return of the King*
Cold Mountain
Girl with a Pearl Earring
Lost in Translation
Master and Commander: The Far Side of the World
2004
★*Collateral*
The Aviator
Finding Neverland
House of Flying Daggers
The Motorcycle Diaries
2005
★*Memoirs of a Geisha*
Brokeback Mountain
The Constant Gardener
Crash
March of the Penguins
2006
★*Children of Men*
Babel
Casino Royale
Pan's Labyrinth
United 93
2007
★*No Country for Old Men*
American Gangster
Atonement
The Bourne Ultimatum
There Will Be Blood
2008
★*Slumdog Millionaire*
Changeling
The Curious Case of Benjamin Button
The Dark Knight
The Reader
2009
★*The Hurt Locker*
Avatar
District 9
Inglourious Basterds
The Road
2010
★*True Grit*
Black Swan
Inception
The King's Speech
127 Hours
2011
★*The Artist*
The Girl With the Dragon Tattoo
Hugo
War Horse
2012
★*Life of Pi*
Anna Karenina
Les Miserables
Lincoln
Skyfall
2013
★*Gravity*
Captain Phillips
Inside Llewyn Davis
Nebraska
12 Years a Slave
2014
★*Birdman, or (The Unexpected Virtue of Ignorance)*
The Grand Budapest Hotel
Ida
Interstellar
Mr. Turner
2015
★*The Revenant*
Bridge of Spies
Carol
Mad Max: Fury Road
Sicario
2016
★*La La Land*
Arrival
Hell or High Water
Lion
Nocturnal Animals
2017
★*Blade Runner 2049*
Darkest Hour
Dunkirk
The Shape of Water
Three Billboards Outside Ebbing, Missouri
2018
★*Roma*
Bohemian Rhapsody
Cold War
The Favourite
First Man
2019
★*1917*
Ford v Ferrari
The Irishman
Joker
The Lighthouse

COSTUME DESIGN

1969
★*Oh! What a Lovely War*
1984
★*Once Upon a Time in America*
1997
★*Mrs. Brown*
L.A. Confidential
Titanic
The Wings of the Dove
1998
★*Velvet Goldmine*
Elizabeth
The Mask of Zorro
Shakespeare in Love
1999
★*Sleepy Hollow*
The End of the Affair
An Ideal Husband
Tea with Mussolini
2001
★*Gosford Park*
Harry Potter and the Sorcerer's Stone
Lord of the Rings: The Fellowship of the Ring
Moulin Rouge
Planet of the Apes
2002
★*Lord of the Rings: The Two Towers*
Catch Me If You Can
Chicago
Gangs of New York
2003
★*Master and Commander: The Far Side of the World*
Cold Mountain
Girl with a Pearl Earring
Lord of the Rings: The Return of the King
Pirates of the Caribbean: The Curse of the Black Pearl
2004
★*Vera Drake*
The Aviator
Finding Neverland
House of Flying Daggers
2005
★*Memoirs of a Geisha*
Charlie and the Chocolate Factory
The Chronicles of Narnia: The Lion, the Witch and the Wardrobe
Mrs. Henderson Presents
Pride and Prejudice
2006
★*Pan's Labyrinth*
The Devil Wears Prada
Marie Antoinette
Pirates of the Caribbean: Dead Man's Chest
The Queen
2007
★*La Vie en Rose*
Elizabeth: The Golden Age
Lust, Caution
Sweeney Todd: The Demon Barber of Fleet Street
2008
★*The Duchess*
Changeling
The Curious Case of Benjamin Button
The Dark Knight
Revolutionary Road
2009
★*The Young Victoria*
Bright Star
Coco Before Chanel
An Education
A Single Man
2010
★*Alice in Wonderland*
Black Swan
The King's Speech
Made in Dagenham
True Grit
2011
★*The Artist*
Hugo
Jane Eyre
My Week With Marilyn
Tinker Tailor Soldier Spy
2012
★*Anna Karenina*
Great Expectations
Les Miserables
Lincoln
Snow White and the Huntsman
2013
★*The Great Gatsby*
American Hustle
Behind the Candelabra
The Invisible Woman
Saving Mr. Banks
2014
★*The Grand Budapest Hotel*
The Imitation Game
Into the Woods
Mr. Turner
The Theory of Everything
2015
★*Mad Max: Fury Road*
Brooklyn
Carol
Cinderella
The Danish Girl
2016
★*Jackie*
Fantastic Beasts and Where to Find Them
Florence Foster Jenkins
La La Land
2017
★*Phantom Thread*
Allied
Beauty and the Beast
Darkest Hour
I, Tonya
The Shape of Water
2018
★*The Favourite*
The Ballad of Buster Scruggs
Bohemian Rhapsody
Mary Poppins Returns
Mary Queen of Scots
2019
★*Little Women*
The Irishman
Jojo Rabbit
Judy
Once Upon A Time... In Hollywood

DIRECTOR

1955
★Laurence Olivier/*Richard III*
1968
★Mike Nichols/*The Graduate*
1969
★John Schlesinger/*Midnight Cowboy*
Richard Attenborough/*Oh! What a Lovely War*
1970
★George Roy Hill/*Butch Cassidy and the Sundance Kid*
1971
★John Schlesinger/*Sunday, Bloody Sunday*
1972
★Bob Fosse/*Cabaret*
1973
★Francois Truffaut/*Day for Night*
1974
★Roman Polanski/*Chinatown*
1975
★Stanley Kubrick/*Barry Lyndon*
1976
★Milos Forman/*One Flew Over the Cuckoo's Nest*
1977
★Woody Allen/*Annie Hall*
1978
★Alan Parker/*Midnight Express*
1979
★Francis Ford Coppola/*Apocalypse Now*
1980
★Akira Kurosawa/*Kagemusha*
1981
★Louis Malle/*Atlantic City*
1982
★Richard Attenborough/*Gandhi*

★ = winner

1983
★Bill Forsyth/*Local Hero*
1984
★Wim Wenders/*Paris, Texas*
Sergio Leone/*Once Upon a Time in America*
1986
★Woody Allen/*Hannah and Her Sisters*
1987
★Oliver Stone/*Platoon*
1988
★Louis Malle/*Au Revoir les Enfants*
1989
★Kenneth Branagh/*Henry V*
1990
★Martin Scorsese/*Goodfellas*
1991
★Alan Parker/*The Commitments*
1992
★Clint Eastwood/*Unforgiven*
1993
★Steven Spielberg/*Schindler's List*
Richard Attenborough/*Shadowlands*
1994
★Mike Newell/*Four Weddings and a Funeral*
Jane Campion/*The Piano*
James Ivory/*The Remains of the Day*
1995
★Michael Radford/*The Postman*
Mel Gibson/*Braveheart*
Nicholas Hytner/*The Madness of King George*
Ang Lee/*Sense and Sensibility*
1996
★Joel Coen/*Fargo*
Scott Hicks/*Shine*
Mike Leigh/*Secrets and Lies*
Anthony Minghella/*The English Patient*
1997
★Baz Luhrmann/*William Shakespeare's Romeo and Juliet*
James Cameron/*Titanic*
Peter Cattaneo/*The Full Monty*
Curtis Hanson/*L.A. Confidential*
1998
★Peter Weir/*The Truman Show*
Shekhar Kapur/*Elizabeth*
John Madden/*Shakespeare in Love*
Steven Spielberg/*Saving Private Ryan*
1999
★Pedro Almodóvar/*All About My Mother*
Neil Jordan/*The End of the Affair*
Sam Mendes/*American Beauty*
Anthony Minghella/*The Talented Mr. Ripley*
M. Night Shyamalan/*The Sixth Sense*
2000
★Ang Lee/*Crouching Tiger, Hidden Dragon*
2001
★Peter Jackson/*Lord of the Rings: The Fellowship of the Ring*
Robert Altman/*Gosford Park*
Ron Howard/*A Beautiful Mind*
Jean-Pierre Jeunet/*Amelie*
Baz Luhrmann/*Moulin Rouge*
2002
★Roman Polanski/*The Pianist*
Stephen Daldry/*The Hours*
Peter Jackson/*Lord of the Rings: The Two Towers*
Rob Marshall/*Chicago*
Martin Scorsese/*Gangs of New York*
2003
★Peter Weir/*Master and Commander: The Far Side of the World*
Tim Burton/*Big Fish*
Sofia Coppola/*Lost in Translation*
Peter Jackson/*Lord of the Rings: The Return of the King*
Anthony Minghella/*Cold Mountain*
2004
★Mike Leigh/*Vera Drake*
Marc Forster/*Finding Neverland*
Michel Gondry/*Eternal Sunshine of the Spotless Mind*
Michael Mann/*Collateral*
Martin Scorsese/*The Aviator*
2005
George Clooney/*Good Night, and Good Luck*
Fernando Meirelles/*The Constant Gardener*
Bennett Miller/*Capote*
2006
★Paul Greengrass/*United 93*
Jonathan Dayton/*Little Miss Sunshine*
Valerie Faris/*Little Miss Sunshine*
Stephen Frears/*The Queen*
Alejandro Gonzalez Inarritu/*Babel*
Martin Scorsese/*The Departed*
2007
★Ethan Coen/*No Country for Old Men*
★Joel Coen/*No Country for Old Men*
Paul Thomas Anderson/*There Will Be Blood*
Paul Greengrass/*The Bourne Ultimatum*
Florian Henskel von Donnersmarck/*The Lives of Others*
Joe Wright/*Atonement*
2008
★Danny Boyle/*Slumdog Millionaire*
Stephen Daldry/*The Reader*
Clint Eastwood/*Changeling*
David Fincher/*The Curious Case of Benjamin Button*
Ron Howard/*Frost/Nixon*
2009
★Kathryn Bigelow/*The Hurt Locker*
Neill Blomkamp/*District 9*
James Cameron/*Avatar*
Lone Scherfig/*An Education*
Quentin Tarantino/*Inglourious Basterds*
2010
★David Fincher/*The Social Network*
Darren Aronofsky/*Black Swan*
Danny Boyle/*127 Hours*
Tom Hooper/*The King's Speech*
Christopher Nolan/*Inception*
2011
★Michel Hazanavicius/*The Artist*
Tomas Alfredson/*Tinker Tailor Soldier Spy*
Lynne Ramsey/*We Need to Talk About Kevin*
Nicolas Winding Refn/*Drive*
Martin Scorsese/*Hugo*
2012
★Ben Affleck/*Argo*
Kathryn Bigelow/*Zero Dark Thirty*
Michael Haneke/*Amour*
Ang Lee/*Life of Pi*
Quentin Tarantino/*Django Unchained*
2013
★Alfonso Cuarón/*Gravity*
Paul Greengrass/*Captain Phillips*
Steve McQueen/*12 Years a Slave*
David O. Russell/*American Hustle*
Martin Scorsese/*The Wolf of Wall Street*
2014
★Richard Linklater/*Boyhood*
Wes Anderson/*The Grand Budapest Hotel*
Damien Chazelle/*Whiplash*
Alejandro Gonzalez Inarritu/*Birdman, or (The Unexpected Virtue of Ignorance)*
James Marsh/*The Theory of Everything*
2015
★Alejandro Gonzalez Inarritu/*The Revenant*
Todd Haynes/*Carol*
Adam McKay/*The Big Short*
Ridley Scott/*The Martian*
Steven Spielberg/*Bridge of Spies*
2016
★Damien Chazelle/*La La Land*
Tom Ford/*Nocturnal Animals*
Ken Loach/*I, Daniel Blake*
Kenneth Lonergan/*Manchester by the Sea*
Denis Villeneuve/*Arrival*
2017
★Guillermo del Toro/*The Shape of Water*
★*The Shape of Water*
Luca Guadagnino/*Call Me by Your Name*
Martin McDonagh/*Three Billboards Outside Ebbing, Missouri*
Christopher Nolan/*Dunkirk*
Denis Villeneuve/*Blade Runner 2049*
2018
★Alfonso Cuarón/*Roma*
Bradley Cooper/*A Star Is Born*
Yorgos Lanthimos/*The Favourite*
Spike Lee/*BlacKkKlansman*
Pawel Pawlikowski/*Cold War*
2019
★Sam Mendes/*1917*
Joon-ho Bong/*Parasite*
Todd Phillips/*Joker*
Martin Scorsese/*The Irishman*
Quentin Tarantino/*Once Upon A Time... In Hollywood*

FILM

1947
★*The Best Years of Our Lives*
★*Odd Man Out*
1948
★*The Fallen Idol*
★*Hamlet*
1949
★*The Bicycle Thief*
★*The Third Man*
1950
★*All About Eve*
★*The Blue Lamp*
1951
★*La Ronde*
★*The Lavender Hill Mob*
1953
★*Forbidden Games*
★*Genevieve*
1954
★*Hobson's Choice*
★*Wages of Fear*
1955
★*Richard III*
1956
★*Gervaise*
★*Reach for the Sky*
1957
★*The Bridge on the River Kwai*
1958
★*Room at the Top*
1959
★*Ben-Hur*
★*Sapphire*
1960
★*The Apartment*
★*Saturday Night and Sunday Morning*
1961
★*Ballad of a Soldier*
★*The Hustler*
1962
★*Lawrence of Arabia*
1963
★*Tom Jones*
1964
★*Dr. Strangelove, or: How I Learned to Stop Worrying and Love the Bomb*
★*King and Country*
1965
★*The Ipcress File*
★*My Fair Lady*
1966
★*The Spy Who Came in from the Cold*
★*Who's Afraid of Virginia Woolf?*
1967
★*A Man for All Seasons*
1968
★*The Graduate*
1969
★*Midnight Cowboy*
Oh! What a Lovely War
1970
★*Butch Cassidy and the Sundance Kid*
1971
★*Sunday, Bloody Sunday*
1972
★*Cabaret*
1973
★*Day for Night*
1975
★*Alice Doesn't Live Here Anymore*
1976
★*One Flew Over the Cuckoo's Nest*
1977
★*Annie Hall*
1978
★*Julia*
1979
★*Manhattan*
1980
★*The Elephant Man*
1981
★*Chariots of Fire*
1982
★*Gandhi*
1983
★*Educating Rita*
1984
★*The Killing Fields*
1985
★*The Purple Rose of Cairo*
1986
★*A Room with a View*
1987
★*Hope and Glory*
★*Jean de Florette*
1988
★*The Last Emperor*
1989
★*Dead Poets Society*
1990
★*Goodfellas*
1991
★*The Commitments*
1992
★*Unforgiven*
1993
★*Schindler's List*
★*Shadowlands*
Naked
Raining Stones
Tom & Viv
1994
★*Four Weddings and a Funeral*
The Piano
The Remains of the Day
1995
★*Sense and Sensibility*
Babe
Carrington
The Madness of King George
Trainspotting
The Usual Suspects
1996
★*The English Patient*
Fargo
Secrets and Lies
Shine
1997
★*The Full Monty*
★*Nil by Mouth*
Behind the Lines
The Borrowers
L.A. Confidential
Mrs. Brown
Titanic
1998
★*Elizabeth*
★*Shakespeare in Love*
Hilary and Jackie
Little Voice
Lock, Stock and 2 Smoking Barrels
My Name Is Joe
Saving Private Ryan
Sliding Doors
The Truman Show
1999
★*American Beauty*
★*East Is East*
The End of the Affair
Notting Hill
Onegin
Ratcatcher
The Sixth Sense
The Talented Mr. Ripley
Topsy Turvy
Wonderland
2000
★*Billy Elliot*
★*Gladiator*
2001
★*Gosford Park*
★*Lord of the Rings: The Fellowship of the Ring*
Amelie
A Beautiful Mind
Bridget Jones's Diary
Harry Potter and the Sorcerer's Stone
Iris
Moulin Rouge
Shrek
2002
★*The Pianist*
Chicago
Gangs of New York
The Hours
Lord of the Rings: The Two Towers
2003
★*Lord of the Rings: The Return of the King*
Big Fish
Cold Mountain
Lost in Translation
The Magdalene Sisters
Master and Commander: The Far Side of the World
2004
★*The Aviator*
Eternal Sunshine of the Spotless Mind
The Motorcycle Diaries
Vera Drake
2005
★*Brokeback Mountain*
Capote
The Constant Gardener
Crash
Good Night, and Good Luck
2006
★*The Queen*
Babel
The Departed
The Last King of Scotland
Little Miss Sunshine
2007
★*Atonement*
American Gangster
The Lives of Others
No Country for Old Men
There Will Be Blood
2008
★*Slumdog Millionaire*
The Curious Case of Benjamin Button
Frost/Nixon
Milk
The Reader
2009
★*The Hurt Locker*
Avatar
An Education
Precious: Based on the Novel 'Push' by Sapphire
Up in the Air

★ = winner

2010
★The King's Speech
Black Swan
Inception
The Social Network
True Grit
2011
★The Artist
The Descendants
Drive
The Help
Tinker Tailor Soldier Spy
2012
★Argo
Les Miserables
Life of Pi
Lincoln
Zero Dark Thirty
2013
★12 Years a Slave
American Hustle
Captain Phillips
Gravity
Philomena
2014
★Boyhood
Birdman, or (The Unexpected Virtue of Ignorance)
The Grand Budapest Hotel
The Theory of Everything
2015
★The Revenant
The Big Short
Bridge of Spies
Carol
Spotlight
2016
★La La Land
Arrival
I, Daniel Blake
Manchester by the Sea
Moonlight
2017
★Three Billboards Outside Ebbing, Missouri
Call Me by Your Name
Darkest Hour
Dunkirk
The Shape of Water
2018
★Roma
BlacKkKlansman
The Favourite
Green Book
A Star Is Born
2019
★1917
The Irishman
Joker
Once Upon A Time... In Hollywood
Parasite

FEATURE DOCUMENTARY

1987
★Shoah
2011
★Senna
George Harrison: Living in the Material World
Project Nim
2012
★Searching For Sugar Man
The Imposter
West of Memphis
2013
★The Act of Killing
The Armstrong Lie
Blackfish
Tim's Vermeer
We Steal Secrets: The Story of WikiLeaks
2014
★Citizenfour
Finding Vivian Maier
20 Feet from Stardom
20,000 Days on Earth
Virunga
2015
★Amy
He Named Me Malala
2016
The Eagle Huntress
2017
★I Am Not Your Negro
City of Ghosts
Icarus
An Inconvenient Sequel: Truth to Power
Jane
2018
★Free Solo
McQueen
RBG
They Shall Not Grow Old
Three Identical Strangers
2019
★For Sama
American Factory
Apollo 11
Diego Maradona
The Great Hack

FILM EDITING

1969
Oh! What a Lovely War
1997
★L.A. Confidential
The Full Monty
Titanic
William Shakespeare's Romeo and Juliet
1998
★Shakespeare in Love
Elizabeth
Lock, Stock and 2 Smoking Barrels
Saving Private Ryan
1999
★American Beauty
Being John Malkovich
The Matrix
The Sixth Sense
2001
Amelie
Black Hawk Down
Lord of the Rings: The Fellowship of the Ring
Moulin Rouge
2002
Chicago
Gangs of New York
The Hours
Lord of the Rings: The Two Towers
2003
★Lost in Translation
Cold Mountain
Kill Bill Vol. 1
Lord of the Rings: The Return of the King
21 Grams
2004
★Eternal Sunshine of the Spotless Mind
The Aviator
Collateral
House of Flying Daggers
Vera Drake
2005
★The Constant Gardener
Brokeback Mountain
Crash
Good Night, and Good Luck
March of the Penguins
2006
★United 93
Babel
Casino Royale
The Departed
The Queen
2007
★The Bourne Ultimatum
American Gangster
Atonement
Michael Clayton
No Country for Old Men
2008
★Slumdog Millionaire
Changeling
The Curious Case of Benjamin Button
The Dark Knight
Frost/Nixon
In Bruges
2009
Avatar
District 9
Inglourious Basterds
Up in the Air
2010
★The Social Network
Black Swan
Inception
The King's Speech
127 Hours
The Social Network
2011
★Senna
The Artist
Drive
Hugo
Tinker Tailor Soldier Spy
2012
★Argo
Django Unchained
Life of Pi
Skyfall
Zero Dark Thirty
2013
★Rush
Captain Phillips
Gravity
12 Years a Slave
The Wolf of Wall Street
2014
★Whiplash
Birdman, or (The Unexpected Virtue of Ignorance)
The Imitation Game
Interstellar
Nightcrawler
2015
★Mad Max: Fury Road
The Big Short
Bridge of Spies
The Martian
The Revenant
2016
★Hacksaw Ridge
Arrival
La La Land
Manchester by the Sea
Nocturnal Animals
2017
★Baby Driver
Blade Runner 2049
Dunkirk
The Shape of Water
Three Billboards Outside Ebbing, Missouri
2018
★Vice
Bohemian Rhapsody
The Favourite
First Man
Roma
2019
★Ford v Ferrari
The Irishman
Jojo Rabbit
Joker
Once Upon A Time... In Hollywood

MAKEUP

1997
★The Wings of the Dove
1999
★Topsy Turvy
American Beauty
The End of the Affair
An Ideal Husband
2002
★Frida
Chicago
The Hours
Lord of the Rings: The Two Towers
2003
★Pirates of the Caribbean: The Curse of the Black Pearl
Big Fish
Cold Mountain
Girl with a Pearl Earring
Lord of the Rings: The Return of the King
2004
★The Aviator
Finding Neverland
Harry Potter and the Prisoner of Azkaban
House of Flying Daggers
Vera Drake
2005
★The Chronicles of Narnia: The Lion, the Witch and the Wardrobe
Charlie and the Chocolate Factory
Harry Potter and the Goblet of Fire
Memoirs of a Geisha
Pride and Prejudice
2006
★Pan's Labyrinth
The Devil Wears Prada
Marie Antoinette
Pirates of the Caribbean: Dead Man's Chest
The Queen
2007
★La Vie en Rose
Atonement
Elizabeth: The Golden Age
Hairspray
Sweeney Todd: The Demon Barber of Fleet Street
2008
★The Curious Case of Benjamin Button
The Dark Knight
The Duchess
Frost/Nixon
Milk
2009
★The Young Victoria
Coco Before Chanel
An Education
The Imaginarium of Doctor Parnassus
Nine
2010
★Alice in Wonderland
Black Swan
Harry Potter and the Deathly Hallows, Part 1
The King's Speech
Made in Dagenham
2011
★The Iron Lady
The Artist
Harry Potter and the Deathly Hallows, Part 2
Hugo
My Week With Marilyn
2012
★Les Miserables
Anna Karenina
Hitchcock
The Hobbit: An Unexpected Journey
Lincoln
2013
★American Hustle
Behind the Candelabra
The Great Gatsby
The Hobbit: The Desolation of Smaug
Lee Daniels' The Butler
2014
★The Grand Budapest Hotel
Guardians of the Galaxy
Into the Woods
Mr. Turner
The Theory of Everything
2015
★Mad Max: Fury Road
Brooklyn
Carol
The Danish Girl
The Revenant
2016
★Florence Foster Jenkins
Doctor Strange
Hacksaw Ridge
Nocturnal Animals
Rogue One: A Star Wars Story
2017
★Darkest Hour
Blade Runner 2049
I, Tonya
Victoria & Abdul
Wonder
2018
★The Favourite
Bohemian Rhapsody
Mary Queen of Scots
Stan & Ollie
Vice
2019
★Bombshell
Joker
Judy
1917
Rocketman

SCORE

1993
Schindler's List
Sleepless in Seattle
1994
The Piano
1995
★The Postman
Braveheart
The Madness of King George
Sense and Sensibility
1996
★The English Patient
1997
★William Shakespeare's Romeo and Juliet
The Full Monty
L.A. Confidential
Titanic
1998
★Elizabeth
Hilary and Jackie
Saving Private Ryan
Shakespeare in Love
1999
★American Beauty
2000
★Crouching Tiger, Hidden Dragon
2001
★Moulin Rouge
Amelie
Lord of the Rings: The Fellowship of the Ring
Mulholland Drive
Shrek
2002
★The Hours
Catch Me If You Can
Chicago
Gangs of New York
The Pianist
2003
★Cold Mountain

ORIGINAL SCORE

1984
★Once Upon a Time in America
1999
Buena Vista Social Club
The End of the Affair
The Talented Mr. Ripley
2003
Girl with a Pearl Earring
Kill Bill Vol. 1
Lord of the Rings: The Return of the King
Lost in Translation
2004
★The Motorcycle Diaries
The Aviator
Finding Neverland
Ray
2005
★Memoirs of a Geisha
The Constant Gardener
Mrs. Henderson Presents
2006
★Babel
Casino Royale
Dreamgirls
Happy Feet
The Queen
2007
★La Vie en Rose
American Gangster
Atonement
The Kite Runner
There Will Be Blood
2008
★Slumdog Millionaire
The Curious Case of Benjamin Button
The Dark Knight
Mamma Mia!
WALL-E
2009
★Up
Avatar
Crazy Heart
Fantastic Mr. Fox
Sex & Drugs & Rock & Roll

★ = winner

2010
★The King's Speech
Alice in Wonderland
How to Train Your Dragon
Inception
127 Hours
2011
★The Artist
The Girl With the Dragon Tattoo
Hugo
Tinker Tailor Soldier Spy
War Horse
2012
★Skyfall
Anna Karenina
Argo
Life of Pi
Lincoln
2013
★Gravity
The Book Thief
Captain Phillips
Saving Mr. Banks
12 Years a Slave
2014
★The Grand Budapest Hotel
Birdman, or (The Unexpected Virtue of Ignorance)
Interstellar
The Theory of Everything
Under the Skin
2015
★The Hateful Eight
Bridge of Spies
The Revenant
Sicario
Star Wars: The Force Awakens
2016
★La La Land
Arrival
Jackie
Lion
Nocturnal Animals
2017
★The Shape of Water
Blade Runner 2049
Darkest Hour
Dunkirk
Phantom Thread
2018
★A Star Is Born
BlacKkKlansman
If Beale Street Could Talk
Isle of Dogs
Mary Poppins Returns
2019
★Joker
Jojo Rabbit
Little Women
1917
Star Wars: The Rise of Skywalker

SOUND

1997
★L.A. Confidential
The Full Monty
Titanic
William Shakespeare's Romeo and Juliet
1998
★Saving Private Ryan
Hilary and Jackie
Little Voice
Shakespeare in Love
1999
★The Matrix
American Beauty
Buena Vista Social Club
2001
★Moulin Rouge
Black Hawk Down
Harry Potter and the Sorcerer's Stone
Lord of the Rings: The Fellowship of the Ring
Shrek
2002
★Chicago
Gangs of New York
Harry Potter and the Chamber of Secrets
Lord of the Rings: The Two Towers
The Pianist
2003
★Master and Commander: The Far Side of the World
Cold Mountain
Kill Bill Vol. 1
Lord of the Rings: The Return of the King
Pirates of the Caribbean: The Curse of the Black Pearl
2004
★Ray
The Aviator
Collateral
House of Flying Daggers
Spider-Man 2
2005
★Walk the Line
Batman Begins
The Constant Gardener
Crash
King Kong
2006
★Casino Royale
Babel
Pan's Labyrinth
Pirates of the Caribbean: Dead Man's Chest
United 93
2007
★The Bourne Ultimatum
La Vie en Rose
No Country for Old Men
There Will Be Blood
2008
★Slumdog Millionaire
Changeling
The Dark Knight
Quantum of Solace
WALL-E
2009
★The Hurt Locker
Avatar
District 9
Star Trek
Up
2010
★Inception
Black Swan
The King's Speech
127 Hours
True Grit
2011
★The Artist
Harry Potter and the Deathly Hallows, Part 2
Hugo
Tinker Tailor Soldier Spy
War Horse
2012
★Les Miserables
Django Unchained
The Hobbit: An Unexpected Journey
Life of Pi
Skyfall
2013
★Gravity
All is Lost
Captain Phillips
Inside Llewyn Davis
Rush
2014
★Whiplash
American Sniper
Birdman, or (The Unexpected Virtue of Ignorance)
The Grand Budapest Hotel
The Imitation Game
2015
★The Revenant
Bridge of Spies
Mad Max: Fury Road
The Martian
Star Wars: The Force Awakens
2016
★Arrival
Deepwater Horizon
Fantastic Beasts and Where to Find Them
Hacksaw Ridge
La La Land
2017
★Dunkirk
Baby Driver
Blade Runner 2049
The Shape of Water
Star Wars: The Last Jedi
2018
★Bohemian Rhapsody
First Man
Mission: Impossible-Fallout
A Quiet Place
A Star Is Born
2019
★1917
Ford v Ferrari
Joker
Rocketman
Star Wars: The Rise of Skywalker

ADAPTED SCREENPLAY

1983
★Heat and Dust
1984
★The Killing Fields
1985
★Prizzi's Honor
1986
★Out of Africa
1987
★Jean de Florette
1988
★The Unbearable Lightness of Being
1989
★Dangerous Liaisons
1990
★Goodfellas
1991
★The Commitments
1992
★The Player
1993
★Schindler's List
In the Name of the Father
Scent of a Woman
Schindler's List
Shadowlands
1994
★Quiz Show
The Remains of the Day
1995
★Trainspotting
Babe
Leaving Las Vegas
The Madness of King George
The Postman
Sense and Sensibility
1996
★The English Patient
The Crucible
Evita
Richard III
1997
★William Shakespeare's Romeo and Juliet
The Ice Storm
L.A. Confidential
The Wings of the Dove
1998
★Primary Colors
Hilary and Jackie
Little Voice
Wag the Dog
1999
★The End of the Affair
East Is East
An Ideal Husband
The Talented Mr. Ripley
2000
★Traffic
2001
★Shrek
A Beautiful Mind
Bridget Jones's Diary
Iris
Lord of the Rings: The Fellowship of the Ring
2002
★Adaptation
About a Boy
Catch Me If You Can
The Hours
The Pianist
2003
★Lord of the Rings: The Return of the King
Big Fish
Cold Mountain
Girl with a Pearl Earring
Mystic River
2004
★Sideways
Closer
Finding Neverland
The Motorcycle Diaries
2005
★Brokeback Mountain
Capote
The Constant Gardener
A History of Violence
Pride and Prejudice
2006
★The Last King of Scotland
Casino Royale
The Departed
The Devil Wears Prada
Notes on a Scandal
2007
★The Diving Bell and the Butterfly
Atonement
The Kite Runner
No Country for Old Men
There Will Be Blood
2008
★Slumdog Millionaire
The Curious Case of Benjamin Button
Frost/Nixon
The Reader
Revolutionary Road
2009
★Up in the Air
District 9
An Education
In the Loop
Precious: Based on the Novel 'Push' by Sapphire
2010
★The Social Network
The Girl With the Dragon Tattoo
127 Hours
Toy Story 3
True Grit
2011
★Tinker Tailor Soldier Spy
The Descendants
The Help
The Ides of March
Moneyball
2012
★Silver Linings Playbook
Argo
Beasts of the Southern Wild
Life of Pi
Lincoln
2013
★Philomena
Behind the Candelabra
Captain Phillips
12 Years a Slave
The Wolf of Wall Street
2014
★The Theory of Everything
American Sniper
Gone Girl
The Imitation Game
Paddington
2015
★The Big Short
Brooklyn
Carol
Room
Steve Jobs
2016
★Lion
Arrival
Hacksaw Ridge
Hidden Figures
Nocturnal Animals
2017
★Call Me by Your Name
The Death of Stalin
Film Stars Don't Die in Liverpool
Molly's Game
Paddington 2
2018
★BlacKkKlansman
Can You Ever Forgive Me?
First Man
If Beale Street Could Talk
A Star Is Born
2019
★Jojo Rabbit
The Irishman
Joker
Little Women
The Two Popes

ORIGINAL SCREENPLAY

1983
★King of Comedy
1984
★Broadway Danny Rose
1985
★The Purple Rose of Cairo
1986
★Hannah and Her Sisters
1987
★Wish You Were Here
1988
★A World Apart
1989
★When Harry Met Sally. . .
1990
★Cinema Paradiso
1991
★Truly, Madly, Deeply
1992
★Husbands and Wives
1993
★Groundhog Day
In the Line of Fire
Sleepless in Seattle
1994
★Pulp Fiction
The Piano
1995
★The Usual Suspects
Bullets over Broadway
Muriel's Wedding
Seven
1996
★Secrets and Lies
Brassed Off
Fargo
Lone Star
Shine
1997
★Nil by Mouth
Boogie Nights
The Full Monty
Mrs. Brown
1998
★The Truman Show
Elizabeth
Life Is Beautiful
Shakespeare in Love
1999
★Being John Malkovich
All About My Mother
American Beauty
The Sixth Sense
Topsy Turvy
2001
★Amelie
Gosford Park
Moulin Rouge
The Others
The Royal Tenenbaums
2002
★Talk to Her
Gangs of New York
Y Tu Mama Tambien
2003
★The Barbarian Invasions
★The Station Agent
Finding Nemo
Lost in Translation
21 Grams
2004
★Eternal Sunshine of the Spotless Mind
The Aviator
Collateral
Ray
Vera Drake
2005
★Crash
Cinderella Man
Good Night, and Good Luck
Mrs. Henderson Presents
2006
★Little Miss Sunshine
Babel
Pan's Labyrinth
The Queen
United 93

★ = winner

2007
★Juno
American Gangster
The Lives of Others
Michael Clayton
This Is England
2008
★In Bruges
Burn After Reading
Changeling
I've Loved You So Long
Milk
2009
★The Hurt Locker
The Hangover
Inglourious Basterds
A Serious Man
Up
2010
★The King's Speech
Black Swan
The Fighter
Inception
The Kids Are All Right
2011
★The Artist
Bridesmaids
The Guard
The Iron Lady
Midnight in Paris
2012
★Django Unchained
Amour
The Master
Moonrise Kingdom
Zero Dark Thirty
2013
★American Hustle
Blue Jasmine
Inside Llewyn Davis
Nebraska
2014
★The Grand Budapest Hotel
Birdman, or (The Unexpected Virtue of Ignorance)
Boyhood
Nightcrawler
Whiplash
2015
★Spotlight
Bridge of Spies
Ex Machina
The Hateful Eight
Inside Out
2016
★Manchester by the Sea
Hell or High Water
I, Daniel Blake
La La Land
Moonlight
2017
★Three Billboards Outside Ebbing, Missouri
Get Out
I, Tonya
Lady Bird
The Shape of Water
2018
★The Favourite
Cold War
Green Book
Roma
Vice
2019
★Parasite
Booksmart
Knives Out
Marriage Story
Once Upon A Time... In Hollywood

SCREENPLAY

1955
★The Ladykillers
1956
★The Man Who Never Was
1957
★The Bridge on the River Kwai
1959
★I'm All Right Jack
1961
★The Day the Earth Caught Fire
1962
★Lawrence of Arabia
1963
★Tom Jones
1964
★The Pumpkin Eater
1965
★Darling
1966
★Morgan: A Suitable Case for Treatment
1967
★A Man for All Seasons
1968
★The Graduate
1969
★Midnight Cowboy
1970
★Butch Cassidy and the Sundance Kid
1971
★The Go-Between
1972
★The Hospital
★The Last Picture Show
1973
★The Discreet Charm of the Bourgeoisie
1974
★Chinatown
★The Last Detail
1975
★Alice Doesn't Live Here Anymore
1976
★Bugsy Malone
1977
★Annie Hall
1978
★Julia
1979
★Manhattan
1981
★Gregory's Girl
1982
★Missing
2003
The Magdalene Sisters

FILM—FOREIGN LANGUAGE

1982
★Christ Stopped at Eboli
1983
★Danton
1984
★Carmen
1985
★Colonel Redl
1986
★Ran
1987
★The Sacrifice
1988
★Babette's Feast
1989
★Life and Nothing But
1990
★Cinema Paradiso
1991
★The Nasty Girl
1992
★Raise the Red Lantern
1993
★Farewell My Concubine
Indochine
Like Water for Chocolate
Un Coeur en Hiver
1994
★To Live
1995
★The Postman
Burnt by the Sun
Queen Margot
1996
Antonia's Line
Kolya
Nelly et Monsieur Arnaud
1997
Ma Vie en Rose
The Tango Lesson
1998
★Central Station
Life Is Beautiful
Live Flesh
1999
★All About My Mother
Buena Vista Social Club
The Celebration
Run Lola Run
2000
★Crouching Tiger, Hidden Dragon
2001
★Amores Perros
★Behind the Sun
Amelie
Monsoon Wedding
2002
★Talk to Her
Y Tu Mama Tambien
2003
★In This World
The Barbarian Invasions
Good Bye, Lenin!
Spirited Away
The Triplets of Belleville
2004
★The Motorcycle Diaries
Bad Education
House of Flying Daggers
A Very Long Engagement
2005
★The Beat My Heart Skipped
Tsotsi
2006
★Pan's Labyrinth
Apocalypto
Volver
2007
★The Lives of Others
The Diving Bell and the Butterfly
The Kite Runner
La Vie en Rose
Lust, Caution
2008
★I've Loved You So Long
Persepolis
Waltz with Bashir
2009
★A Prophet
Broken Embraces
Coco Before Chanel
Let the Right One In
The White Ribbon
2010
★The Girl With the Dragon Tattoo
Biutiful
I Am Love
Of Gods and Men
The Secret in Their Eyes
2011
★The Skin I Live In
Incendies
Pina
Potiche
A Separation
2012
★Amour
Headhunters
The Intouchables
Rust and Bone
2013
★The Great Beauty
The Act of Killing
Blue is the Warmest Color
Wadjda
2014
★Ida
Leviathan
The Lunchbox
Two Days, One Night
2015
★Son of Saul
★Wild Tales
The Assassin
Force Majeure
Mustang
Timbuktu
Trash
2016
Dheepan
Julieta
Moana
Toni Erdmann
2017
★The Handmaiden
Elle
First They Killed My Father
Loveless
The Salesman
2018
★Roma
Capernaum
Cold War
Shoplifters
2019
★Parasite
The Farewell
For Sama
Pain and Glory
Portrait of a Lady on Fire

VISUAL EFFECTS

1997
★The Fifth Element
1999
★The Matrix
Sleepy Hollow
2001
★Lord of the Rings: The Fellowship of the Ring
A. I.: Artificial Intelligence
Harry Potter and the Sorcerer's Stone
Moulin Rouge
Shrek
2002
★Lord of the Rings: The Two Towers
Gangs of New York
Harry Potter and the Chamber of Secrets
Minority Report
Spider-Man
2003
★Lord of the Rings: The Return of the King
Big Fish
Kill Bill Vol. 1
Master and Commander: The Far Side of the World
Pirates of the Caribbean: The Curse of the Black Pearl
2004
★The Day After Tomorrow
The Aviator
Harry Potter and the Prisoner of Azkaban
House of Flying Daggers
Spider-Man 2
2005
★King Kong
Batman Begins
Charlie and the Chocolate Factory
The Chronicles of Narnia: The Lion, the Witch and the Wardrobe
Harry Potter and the Goblet of Fire
2006
★Pirates of the Caribbean: Dead Man's Chest
Casino Royale
Children of Men
Pan's Labyrinth
Superman Returns
2007
★The Golden Compass
The Bourne Ultimatum
Harry Potter and the Order of the Phoenix
Pirates of the Caribbean: At World's End
Spider-Man 3
2008
★The Curious Case of Benjamin Button
The Dark Knight
Indiana Jones and the Kingdom of the Crystal Skull
Iron Man
Quantum of Solace
2009
★Avatar
District 9
Harry Potter and the Half-Blood Prince
The Hurt Locker
Star Trek
2010
★Inception
Alice in Wonderland
Black Swan
Harry Potter and the Deathly Hallows, Part 1
Toy Story 3
2011
★Harry Potter and the Deathly Hallows, Part 2
The Adventures of Tintin
Hugo
Rise of the Planet of the Apes
War Horse
2012
★Life of Pi
The Avengers
The Dark Knight Rises
The Hobbit: An Unexpected Journey
Prometheus
2013
★Gravity
The Hobbit: The Desolation of Smaug
Iron Man 3
Pacific Rim
Star Trek: Into Darkness
2014
★Interstellar
Dawn of the Planet of the Apes
Guardians of the Galaxy
The Hobbit: The Battle of the Five Armies
X-Men: Days of Future Past
2015
★Star Wars: The Force Awakens
Ant-Man
Ex Machina
Mad Max: Fury Road
The Martian
2016
★The Jungle Book
Arrival
Doctor Strange
Fantastic Beasts and Where to Find Them
Rogue One: A Star Wars Story
2017
★Blade Runner 2049
Dunkirk
The Shape of Water
Star Wars: The Last Jedi
War for the Planet of the Apes
2018
★Black Panther
Avengers: Infinity War
Fantastic Beasts: The Crimes of Grindelwald
First Man
Ready Player One
2019
★1917
Avengers: Endgame
The Irishman
The Lion King
Star Wars: The Rise of Skywalker

ANIMATED FILM

2006
★Happy Feet
Cars
Flushed Away
2007
★Ratatouille
Shrek the Third
The Simpsons Movie
2008
★WALL-E
Persepolis
Waltz with Bashir
2009
★Up
Coraline
Fantastic Mr. Fox
2010
★Toy Story 3
Despicable Me
How to Train Your Dragon
2011
★Rango
The Adventures of Tintin
Arthur Christmas
2012
★Brave
Frankenweenie
ParaNorman
2013
★Frozen
Despicable Me 2
Monsters University
2014
★The Lego Movie
Big Hero 6
The Boxtrolls

★ = winner

2015
★*Inside Out*
Minions
Shaun the Sheep Movie
2016
★*Kubo and the Two Strings*
Finding Dory
Zootopia
2017
★*Coco*
Loving Vincent
My Life as a Zucchini
2018
★*Spider-Man: Into the Spider-Verse*
Incredibles 2
Isle of Dogs
2019
★*Klaus*
Frozen II
A Shaun the Sheep Movie: Farmageddon
Toy Story 4

PRODUCTION DESIGN

2012
★*Les Miserables*
Anna Karenina
Life of Pi
Lincoln
Skyfall
2013
★*The Great Gatsby*
American Hustle
Behind the Candelabra
Gravity
12 Years a Slave
2014
★*The Grand Budapest Hotel*
Big Eyes
The Imitation Game
Interstellar
Mr. Turner
2015
★*Mad Max: Fury Road*
Bridge of Spies
Carol
The Martian
Star Wars: The Force Awakens
2016
★*Fantastic Beasts and Where to Find Them*
Doctor Strange
Hail, Caesar!
La La Land
Nocturnal Animals
2017
★*The Shape of Water*
Beauty and the Beast
Blade Runner 2049
Darkest Hour
Dunkirk
2018
★*The Favourite*
Fantastic Beasts: The Crimes of Grindelwald
First Man
Mary Poppins Returns
Roma
2019
★*1917*
The Irishman
Jojo Rabbit
Joker
Once Upon A Time... In Hollywood

DIRECTORS GUILD OF AMERICA

DIRECTOR

1948
★Joseph L. Mankiewicz/*A Letter to Three Wives*
1949
★Carol Reed/*The Third Man*
1950
★Joseph L. Mankiewicz/*All About Eve*
1951
★George Stevens/*A Place in the Sun*
1952
★John Ford/*The Quiet Man*
1953
★Fred Zinnemann/*From Here to Eternity*
1954
★Elia Kazan/*On the Waterfront*
1955
★Delbert Mann/*Marty*
1956
★George Stevens/*Giant*
1957
★David Lean/*The Bridge on the River Kwai*
1958
★Vincente Minnelli/*Gigi*
1959
★William Wyler/*Ben-Hur*
1960
★Billy Wilder/*The Apartment*
1961
★Jerome Robbins/*West Side Story*
★Robert Wise/*West Side Story*
1962
★David Lean/*Lawrence of Arabia*
1963
★Tony Richardson/*Tom Jones*
1964
★George Cukor/*My Fair Lady*
1965
★Robert Wise/*The Sound of Music*
1966
★Fred Zinnemann/*A Man for All Seasons*
1967
★Mike Nichols/*The Graduate*
1968
★Anthony Harvey/*The Lion in Winter*
1969
★John Schlesinger/*Midnight Cowboy*
1970
★Franklin J. Schaffner/*Patton*
1971
★William Friedkin/*The French Connection*
1972
★Francis Ford Coppola/*The Godfather*
1973
★George Roy Hill/*The Sting*
1974
★Francis Ford Coppola/*The Godfather, Part 2*
1975
★Milos Forman/*One Flew Over the Cuckoo's Nest*
1976
★John G. Avildsen/*Rocky*
1977
★Woody Allen/*Annie Hall*
1978
★Michael Cimino/*The Deer Hunter*
1979
★Robert Benton/*Kramer vs. Kramer*
1980
★Robert Redford/*Ordinary People*
1981
★Warren Beatty/*Reds*
1982
★Richard Attenborough/*Gandhi*
1983
★James L. Brooks/*Terms of Endearment*
1984
★Milos Forman/*Amadeus*
1985
★Steven Spielberg/*The Color Purple*
1986
★Oliver Stone/*Platoon*
1987
★Bernardo Bertolucci/*The Last Emperor*
1988
★Barry Levinson/*Rain Man*
1989
★Oliver Stone/*Born on the Fourth of July*
1990
★Kevin Costner/*Dances with Wolves*
1991
★Jonathan Demme/*The Silence of the Lambs*
1992
★Clint Eastwood/*Unforgiven*
1993
★Steven Spielberg/*Schindler's List*
Jane Campion/*The Piano*
Andrew Davis/*The Fugitive*
James Ivory/*The Remains of the Day*
Martin Scorsese/*The Age of Innocence*
1994
★Robert Zemeckis/*Forrest Gump*
Frank Darabont/*The Shawshank Redemption*
Mike Newell/*Four Weddings and a Funeral*
Robert Redford/*Quiz Show*
Quentin Tarantino/*Pulp Fiction*
1995
★Ron Howard/*Apollo 13*
Mike Figgis/*Leaving Las Vegas*
Mel Gibson/*Braveheart*
Ang Lee/*Sense and Sensibility*
Michael Radford/*The Postman*
1996
★Anthony Minghella/*The English Patient*
Joel Coen/*Fargo*
Cameron Crowe/*Jerry Maguire*
Scott Hicks/*Shine*
Mike Leigh/*Secrets and Lies*
1997
★James Cameron/*Titanic*
James L. Brooks/*As Good As It Gets*
Curtis Hanson/*L.A. Confidential*
Steven Spielberg/*Amistad*
Gus Van Sant/*Good Will Hunting*
1998
★Steven Spielberg/*Saving Private Ryan*
Roberto Benigni/*Life Is Beautiful*
John Madden/*Shakespeare in Love*
Terrence Malick/*The Thin Red Line*
Peter Weir/*The Truman Show*
1999
★Sam Mendes/*American Beauty*
Frank Darabont/*The Green Mile*
Spike Jonze/*Being John Malkovich*
Michael Mann/*The Insider*
M. Night Shyamalan/*The Sixth Sense*
2000
★Ang Lee/*Crouching Tiger, Hidden Dragon*
Cameron Crowe/*Almost Famous*
Ridley Scott/*Gladiator*
Steven Soderbergh/*Erin Brockovich*
Steven Soderbergh/*Traffic*
2001
★Ron Howard/*A Beautiful Mind*
Peter Jackson/*Lord of the Rings: The Fellowship of the Ring*
Baz Luhrmann/*Moulin Rouge*
Christopher Nolan/*Memento*
Ridley Scott/*Black Hawk Down*
2002
★Rob Marshall/*Chicago*
Stephen Daldry/*The Hours*
Peter Jackson/*Lord of the Rings: The Two Towers*
Roman Polanski/*The Pianist*
Martin Scorsese/*Gangs of New York*
2003
★Peter Jackson/*Lord of the Rings: The Return of the King*
Sofia Coppola/*Lost in Translation*
Clint Eastwood/*Mystic River*
Gary Ross/*Seabiscuit*
Peter Weir/*Master and Commander: The Far Side of the World*
2004
★Clint Eastwood/*Million Dollar Baby*
Marc Forster/*Finding Neverland*
Taylor Hackford/*Ray*
Alexander Payne/*Sideways*
Martin Scorsese/*The Aviator*
2005
★Ang Lee/*Brokeback Mountain*
George Clooney/*Good Night, and Good Luck*
Paul Haggis/*Crash*
Bennett Miller/*Capote*
Steven Spielberg/*Munich*
2006
★Martin Scorsese/*The Departed*
Bill Condon/*Dreamgirls*
Jonathan Dayton/*Little Miss Sunshine*
Valerie Faris/*Little Miss Sunshine*
Stephen Frears/*The Queen*
Alejandro Gonzalez Inarritu/*Babel*
2007
★Ethan Coen/*No Country for Old Men*
★Joel Coen/*No Country for Old Men*
Paul Thomas Anderson/*There Will Be Blood*
Tony Gilroy/*Michael Clayton*
Sean Penn/*Into the Wild*
Julian Schnabel/*The Diving Bell and the Butterfly*
2008
★Danny Boyle/*Slumdog Millionaire*
David Fincher/*The Curious Case of Benjamin Button*
Ron Howard/*Frost/Nixon*
Christopher Nolan/*The Dark Knight*
Gus Van Sant/*Milk*
2009
★Kathryn Bigelow/*The Hurt Locker*
James Cameron/*Avatar*
Lee Daniels/*Precious: Based on the Novel 'Push' by Sapphire*
Jason Reitman/*Up in the Air*
Quentin Tarantino/*Inglourious Basterds*
2010
★Tom Hooper/*The King's Speech*
Darren Aronofsky/*Black Swan*
David Fincher/*The Social Network*
Christopher Nolan/*Inception*
David O. Russell/*The Fighter*
2011
★Michel Hazanavicius/*The Artist*
Woody Allen/*Midnight in Paris*
David Fincher/*The Girl With the Dragon Tattoo*
Alexander Payne/*The Descendants*
Martin Scorsese/*Hugo*
2012
★Ben Affleck/*Argo*
★Ang Lee/*Life of Pi*
Kathryn Bigelow/*Zero Dark Thirty*
Tom Hooper/*Les Miserables*
Steven Spielberg/*Lincoln*
2013
★Alfonso Cuarón/*Gravity*
Paul Greengrass/*Captain Phillips*
Steve McQueen/*12 Years a Slave*
David O. Russell/*American Hustle*
Martin Scorsese/*The Wolf of Wall Street*
2014
★Alejandro Gonzalez Inarritu/*Birdman, or (The Unexpected Virtue of Ignorance)*
Wes Anderson/*The Grand Budapest Hotel*
Clint Eastwood/*American Sniper*
Richard Linklater/*Boyhood*
Morten Tyldum/*The Imitation Game*
2015
★Alejandro Gonzalez Inarritu/*The Revenant*
Tom McCarthy/*Spotlight*
Adam McKay/*The Big Short*
George Miller/*Mad Max: Fury Road*
Ridley Scott/*The Martian*
2016
★Damien Chazelle/*La La Land*
Garth Davis/*Lion*
Barry Jenkins/*Moonlight*
Kenneth Lonergan/*Manchester by the Sea*
Denis Villeneuve/*Arrival*
2017
★Guillermo del Toro/*The Shape of Water*
Greta Gerwig/*Lady Bird*
Martin McDonagh/*Three Billboards Outside Ebbing, Missouri*
Christopher Nolan/*Dunkirk*
Jordan Peele/*Get Out*
2018
★Alfonso Cuarón/*Roma*
Bradley Cooper/*A Star Is Born*
Peter Farrelly/*Green Book*
Spike Lee/*BlacKkKlansman*
Adam McKay/*Vice*
2019
★Sam Mendes/*1917*
Joon-ho Bong/*Parasite*
Martin Scorsese/*The Irishman*
Quentin Tarantino/*Once Upon A Time... In Hollywood*
Taika Waititi/*Jojo Rabbit*

DOCUMENTARY DIRECTOR

1992
★Joe Berlinger/*Brother's Keeper*
★Bruce Sinofsky/*Brother's Keeper*
1995
★Terry Zwigoff/*Crumb*
1996
★Al Pacino/*Looking for Richard*
2003
★Nathaniel Kahn/*My Architect: A Son's Journey*
Sam Green/*The Weather Underground*
Andrew Jarecki/*Capturing the Friedmans*
Errol Morris/*The Fog of War: Eleven Lessons from the Life of Robert S. McNamara*
Bill Siegel/*The Weather Underground*
2004
★Luigi Falorni/*The Story of the Weeping Camel*
Zana Briski/*Born Into Brothels: Calcutta's Red Light Kids*
Ross Kauffman/*Born Into Brothels: Calcutta's Red Light Kids*
Michael Moore/*Fahrenheit 9/11*
Jehane Noujaim/*Control Room*
2005
★Werner Herzog/*Grizzly Man*
2008
★Ari Folman/*Waltz with Bashir*
2010
★Charles Ferguson/*Inside Job*
2011
★James Marsh/*Project Nim*
Joe Berlinger/*Paradise Lost 3: Purgatory*
Richard Press/*Bill Cunningham New York*
Martin Scorsese/*George Harrison: Living in the Material World*

★ = *winner*

2012

★Malik Bendjelloul/*Searching For Sugar Man*

David France/*How to Survive a Plague*

Lauren Greenfield/*The Queen of Versailles*

Alison Klayman/*Ai Weiwei: Never Sorry*

2013

★Jehane Noujaim/*The Square*

Zachary Heinzerling/*Cutie and the Boxer*

Joshua Oppenheimer/*The Act of Killing*

2014

★*Citizenfour*

★Laura Poitras/*Citizenfour*

John Maloof/*Finding Vivian Maier*

The Overnighters

Charlie Siskel/*Finding Vivian Maier*

Orlando Von Einsiedel/*Virunga*

2015

Asif Kapadia/*Amy*

2016

Otto Bell/*The Eagle Huntress*

Raoul Peck/*I Am Not Your Negro*

Roger Ross Williams/*Life, Animated*

2017

★Matthew Heineman/*City of Ghosts*

Ken Burns/*The Vietnam War*

Bryan Fogel/*Icarus*

Lynn Novick/*The Vietnam War*

2018

★Tim Wardle/*Three Identical Strangers*

Elizabeth Chai Vasarhelyi/*Free Solo*

Jimmy Chin/*Free Solo*

Julie Cohen/*RBG*

Morgan Neville/*Won't You Be My Neighbor?*

RaMell Ross/*Hale County This Morning, This Evening*

Betsy West/*RBG*

2019

★Steven Bognar/*American Factory*

★Julia Reichert/*American Factory*

Feras Fayyad/*The Cave*

Alex Holmes/*Maiden*

Tamara Kotevska/*Honeyland*

Ljubomir Stefanov/*Honeyland*

Nanfu Wang/*One Child Nation*

Jialing Zhang/*One Child Nation*

GOLDEN GLOBE AWARDS

ACTOR—DRAMA

1944

★Paul Lukas/*Watch on the Rhine*

1945

★Alexander Knox/*Wilson*

1946

★Ray Milland/*The Lost Weekend*

1947

★Gregory Peck/*The Yearling*

1948

★Ronald Colman/*A Double Life*

1949

★Laurence Olivier/*Hamlet*

1950

★Broderick Crawford/*All the King's Men*

1951

★Jose Ferrer/*Cyrano de Bergerac*

1953

★Gary Cooper/*High Noon*

1955

★Marlon Brando/*On the Waterfront*

1956

★Ernest Borgnine/*Marty*

1957

★Kirk Douglas/*Lust for Life*

1958

★Alec Guinness/*The Bridge on the River Kwai*

1959

★David Niven/*Separate Tables*

1960

★Anthony (Tony) Franciosa/*Career*

1961

★Burt Lancaster/*Elmer Gantry*

1962

★Maximilian Schell/*Judgment at Nuremberg*

1963

★Gregory Peck/*To Kill a Mockingbird*

1964

★Sidney Poitier/*Lilies of the Field*

1965

★Peter O'Toole/*Becket*

1966

★Omar Sharif/*Doctor Zhivago*

1967

★Paul Scofield/*A Man for All Seasons*

1968

★Rod Steiger/*In the Heat of the Night*

1969

★Peter O'Toole/*The Lion in Winter*

1970

★John Wayne/*True Grit*

1971

★George C. Scott/*Patton*

1972

★Gene Hackman/*The French Connection*

1973

★Marlon Brando/*The Godfather*

1974

★Al Pacino/*Serpico*

1975

★Jack Nicholson/*Chinatown*

1976

★Jack Nicholson/*One Flew Over the Cuckoo's Nest*

1977

★Peter Finch/*Network*

1978

★Richard Burton/*Equus*

1979

★Jon Voight/*Coming Home*

1980

★Dustin Hoffman/*Kramer vs. Kramer*

1981

★Robert De Niro/*Raging Bull*

1982

★Henry Fonda/*On Golden Pond*

1983

★Robert Duvall/*Tender Mercies*

★Ben Kingsley/*Gandhi*

1984

★Tom Courtenay/*The Dresser*

1985

★F. Murray Abraham/*Amadeus*

1986

★Jon Voight/*Runaway Train*

1987

★Bob Hoskins/*Mona Lisa*

1988

★Michael Douglas/*Wall Street*

1989

★Dustin Hoffman/*Rain Man*

1990

★Tom Cruise/*Born on the Fourth of July*

1991

★Jeremy Irons/*Reversal of Fortune*

1992

★Nick Nolte/*The Prince of Tides*

1993

★Al Pacino/*Scent of a Woman*

1994

★Tom Hanks/*Philadelphia*

Daniel Day-Lewis/*In the Name of the Father*

Harrison Ford/*The Fugitive*

Anthony Hopkins/*The Remains of the Day*

Liam Neeson/*Schindler's List*

1995

★Tom Hanks/*Forrest Gump*

Richard Dreyfuss/*Mr. Holland's Opus*

Morgan Freeman/*The Shawshank Redemption*

Paul Newman/*Nobody's Fool*

Brad Pitt/*Legends of the Fall*

John Travolta/*Pulp Fiction*

1996

★Nicolas Cage/*Leaving Las Vegas*

Anthony Hopkins/*Nixon*

Ian McKellen/*Richard III*

Sean Penn/*Dead Man Walking*

1997

★Geoffrey Rush/*Shine*

Ralph Fiennes/*The English Patient*

Mel Gibson/*Ransom*

Woody Harrelson/*The People vs. Larry Flynt*

Liam Neeson/*Michael Collins*

1998

★Peter Fonda/*Ulee's Gold*

Matt Damon/*Good Will Hunting*

Daniel Day-Lewis/*The Boxer*

Leonardo DiCaprio/*Titanic*

Djimon Hounsou/*Amistad*

Ian McKellen/*Gods and Monsters*

1999

★Jim Carrey/*The Truman Show*

Stephen Fry/*Wilde*

Tom Hanks/*Saving Private Ryan*

Nick Nolte/*Affliction*

2000

★Denzel Washington/*The Hurricane*

Russell Crowe/*The Insider*

Matt Damon/*The Talented Mr. Ripley*

Richard Farnsworth/*The Straight Story*

Kevin Spacey/*American Beauty*

2001

★Tom Hanks/*Cast Away*

Javier Bardem/*Before Night Falls*

Ellen Burstyn/*Requiem for a Dream*

Russell Crowe/*Gladiator*

Michael Douglas/*Wonder Boys*

Geoffrey Rush/*Quills*

2002

★Russell Crowe/*A Beautiful Mind*

Will Smith/*Ali*

Kevin Spacey/*The Shipping News*

Billy Bob Thornton/*The Man Who Wasn't There*

Denzel Washington/*Training Day*

2003

★Jack Nicholson/*About Schmidt*

Adrien Brody/*The Pianist*

Michael Caine/*The Quiet American*

Daniel Day-Lewis/*Gangs of New York*

Leonardo DiCaprio/*Catch Me If You Can*

2004

★Sean Penn/*Mystic River*

Russell Crowe/*Master and Commander: The Far Side of the World*

Tom Cruise/*The Last Samurai*

Ben Kingsley/*House of Sand and Fog*

Jude Law/*Cold Mountain*

2005

★Leonardo DiCaprio/*The Aviator*

Javier Bardem/*The Sea Inside*

Don Cheadle/*Hotel Rwanda*

Liam Neeson/*Kinsey*

2006

★Philip Seymour Hoffman/*Capote*

Russell Crowe/*Cinderella Man*

Terrence Howard/*Hustle & Flow*

Heath Ledger/*Brokeback Mountain*

David Strathairn/*Good Night, and Good Luck*

2007

★Forest Whitaker/*The Last King of Scotland*

Leonardo DiCaprio/*Blood Diamond*

Leonardo DiCaprio/*The Departed*

Peter O'Toole/*Venus*

Will Smith/*The Pursuit of Happyness*

2008

★Daniel Day-Lewis/*There Will Be Blood*

George Clooney/*Michael Clayton*

James McAvoy/*Atonement*

Viggo Mortensen/*Eastern Promises*

Denzel Washington/*American Gangster*

2009

★Mickey Rourke/*The Wrestler*

Leonardo DiCaprio/*Revolutionary Road*

Frank Langella/*Frost/Nixon*

Sean Penn/*Milk*

Brad Pitt/*The Curious Case of Benjamin Button*

2010

★Jeff Bridges/*Crazy Heart*

George Clooney/*Up in the Air*

Colin Firth/*A Single Man*

Morgan Freeman/*Invictus*

Tobey Maguire/*Brothers*

2011

★Colin Firth/*The King's Speech*

Jesse Eisenberg/*The Social Network*

James Franco/*127 Hours*

Ryan Gosling/*Blue Valentine*

Mark Wahlberg/*The Fighter*

2012

★George Clooney/*The Descendants*

Leonardo DiCaprio/*J. Edgar*

Michael Fassbender/*Shame*

Ryan Gosling/*The Ides of March*

Brad Pitt/*Moneyball*

2013

★Daniel Day-Lewis/*Lincoln*

Richard Gere/*Arbitrage*

John Hawkes/*The Sessions*

Joaquin Rafael (Leaf) Phoenix/*The Master*

Denzel Washington/*Flight*

2014

★Matthew McConaughey/*Dallas Buyers Club*

Chiwetel Ejiofor/*12 Years a Slave*

Idris Elba/*Mandela: Long Walk to Freedom*

Tom Hanks/*Captain Phillips*

Robert Redford/*All is Lost*

2015

★Eddie Redmayne/*The Theory of Everything*

Steve Carell/*Foxcatcher*

Benedict Cumberbatch/*The Imitation Game*

Jake Gyllenhaal/*Nightcrawler*

David Oyelowo/*Selma*

2016

★Leonardo DiCaprio/*The Revenant*

Bryan Cranston/*Trumbo*

Michael Fassbender/*Steve Jobs*

Eddie Redmayne/*The Danish Girl*

Will Smith/*Concussion*

Alicia Vikander/*The Danish Girl*

2017

★Casey Affleck/*Manchester by the Sea*

Joel Edgerton/*Loving*

Andrew Garfield/*Hacksaw Ridge*

Viggo Mortensen/*Captain Fantastic*

Denzel Washington/*Fences*

2018

★Gary Oldman/*Darkest Hour*

Timothée Chalamet/*Call Me by Your Name*

Daniel Day-Lewis/*Phantom Thread*

Tom Hanks/*The Post*

Denzel Washington/*Roman J. Israel, Esq.*

2019

★Rami Malek/*Bohemian Rhapsody*

Bradley Cooper/*A Star Is Born*

Willem Dafoe/*At Eternity's Gate*

Lucas Hedges/*Boy Erased*

John David Washington/*BlacKkKlansman*

2020

★Joaquin Rafael (Leaf) Phoenix/*Joker*

Christian Bale/*Ford v Ferrari*

Antonio Banderas/*Pain and Glory*

Adam Driver/*Marriage Story*

Jonathan Pryce/*The Two Popes*

ACTOR—MUSICAL/COMEDY

1951

★Fred Astaire/*Three Little Words*

1953

★Donald O'Connor/*Singin' in the Rain*

1954

★David Niven/*The Moon Is Blue*

1955

★James Mason/*A Star Is Born*

1956

★Tom Ewell/*The Seven Year Itch*

1957

★Cantinflas/*Around the World in 80 Days*

1958

★Frank Sinatra/*Pal Joey*

1960

★Jack Lemmon/*Some Like It Hot*

1961

★Jack Lemmon/*The Apartment*

1962

★Glenn Ford/*Pocketful of Miracles*

1963

★Marcello Mastroianni/*Divorce-Italian Style*

1965

★Rex Harrison/*My Fair Lady*

1966

★Lee Marvin/*Cat Ballou*

1967

★Alan Arkin/*The Russians Are Coming, the Russians Are Coming*

1968

★Richard Harris/*Camelot*

1969

★Ron Moody/*Oliver!*

1970

★Peter O'Toole/*Goodbye, Mr. Chips*

1971

★Albert Finney/*Scrooge*

1972

★Topol/*Fiddler on the Roof*

1974

★George Segal/*A Touch of Class*

1975

★Art Carney/*Harry and Tonto*

1976

★Walter Matthau/*The Sunshine Boys*

1977

★Kris Kristofferson/*A Star Is Born*

★ = winner

1978

★Richard Dreyfuss/*The Goodbye Girl*

1979

★Warren Beatty/*Heaven Can Wait*

1980

★Peter Sellers/*Being There*

1981

★Ray Sharkey/*Idolmaker*

1982

★Dudley Moore/*Arthur*

1983

★Dustin Hoffman/*Tootsie*

1984

★Michael Caine/*Educating Rita*

1985

★Dudley Moore/*Micki & Maude*

1986

★Jack Nicholson/*Prizzi's Honor*

1987

★Paul Hogan/*Crocodile Dundee*

1988

★Robin Williams/*Good Morning, Vietnam*

1989

★Tom Hanks/*Big*

1990

★Morgan Freeman/*Driving Miss Daisy*

1991

★Gerard Depardieu/*Green Card*

1992

★Robin Williams/*The Fisher King*

1993

★Tim Robbins/*The Player*

1994

★Robin Williams/*Mrs. Doubtfire*

Johnny Depp/*Benny & Joon*

Tom Hanks/*Sleepless in Seattle*

Kevin Kline/*Dave*

Colm Meaney/*The Snapper*

1995

★Hugh Grant/*Four Weddings and a Funeral*

Jim Carrey/*The Mask*

Johnny Depp/*Ed Wood*

Arnold Schwarzenegger/*Junior*

Terence Stamp/*The Adventures of Priscilla, Queen of the Desert*

1996

★John Travolta/*Get Shorty*

Michael Douglas/*The American President*

Harrison Ford/*Sabrina*

Steve Martin/*Father of the Bride Part 2*

Patrick Swayze/*To Wong Foo, Thanks for Everything, Julie Newmar*

1997

★Tom Cruise/*Jerry Maguire*

Antonio Banderas/*Evita*

Kevin Costner/*Tin Cup*

Tom Cruise/*Jerry Maguire*

Nathan Lane/*The Birdcage*

Eddie Murphy/*The Nutty Professor*

1998

★Jack Nicholson/*As Good As It Gets*

Antonio Banderas/*The Mask of Zorro*

Jim Carrey/*Liar Liar*

Dustin Hoffman/*Wag the Dog*

Samuel L. Jackson/*Jackie Brown*

Kevin Kline/*In and Out*

1999

★Michael Caine/*Little Voice*

John Travolta/*Primary Colors*

Robin Williams/*Patch Adams*

2000

★Jim Carrey/*Man on the Moon*

Robert De Niro/*Analyze This*

Rupert Everett/*An Ideal Husband*

Hugh Grant/*Notting Hill*

Sean Penn/*Sweet and Lowdown*

2001

★George Clooney/*O Brother Where Art Thou?*

Jim Carrey/*Dr. Seuss' How the Grinch Stole Christmas*

Joan Cusack/*High Fidelity*

Robert De Niro/*Meet the Parents*

Mel Gibson/*What Women Want*

2002

★Gene Hackman/*The Royal Tenenbaums*

★*Moulin Rouge*

Hugh Jackman/*Kate & Leopold*

Ewan McGregor/*Moulin Rouge*

John Cameron Mitchell/*Hedwig and the Angry Inch*

Billy Bob Thornton/*Bandits*

2003

★Richard Gere/*Chicago*

Nicolas Cage/*Adaptation*

Kieran Culkin/*Igby Goes Down*

Hugh Grant/*About a Boy*

Adam Sandler/*Punch-Drunk Love*

2004

★Bill Murray/*Lost in Translation*

Jack Black/*School of Rock*

Johnny Depp/*Pirates of the Caribbean: The Curse of the Black Pearl*

Jack Nicholson/*Something's Gotta Give*

Billy Bob Thornton/*Bad Santa*

2005

★Jamie Foxx/*Ray*

Jim Carrey/*Eternal Sunshine of the Spotless Mind*

Paul Giamatti/*Sideways*

Kevin Kline/*De-Lovely*

Kevin Spacey/*Beyond the Sea*

2006

★Joaquin Rafael (Leaf) Phoenix/*Walk the Line*

Jeff Daniels/*The Squid and the Whale*

Johnny Depp/*Charlie and the Chocolate Factory*

Nathan Lane/*The Producers*

2007

★Sacha Baron Cohen/*Borat: Cultural Learnings of America for Make Benefit Glorious Nation of Kazakhstan*

Johnny Depp/*Pirates of the Caribbean: Dead Man's Chest*

Aaron Eckhart/*Thank You for Smoking*

Chiwetel Ejiofor/*Kinky Boots*

Will Ferrell/*Stranger Than Fiction*

2008

★Johnny Depp/*Sweeney Todd: The Demon Barber of Fleet Street*

Ryan Gosling/*Lars and the Real Girl*

Tom Hanks/*Charlie Wilson's War*

Philip Seymour Hoffman/*The Savages*

John C. Reilly/*Walk Hard: The Dewey Cox Story*

2009

★Colin Farrell/*In Bruges*

Javier Bardem/*Vicky Cristina Barcelona*

James Franco/*Pineapple Express*

Brendan Gleeson/*In Bruges*

Dustin Hoffman/*Last Chance Harvey*

Mamma Mia!

2010

★Robert Downey, Jr./*Sherlock Holmes*

Matt Damon/*The Informant!*

Daniel Day-Lewis/*Nine*

Joseph Gordon-Levitt/*(500) Days of Summer*

Michael Stuhlbarg/*A Serious Man*

2011

★Paul Giamatti/*Barney's Version*

Johnny Depp/*Alice in Wonderland*

Johnny Depp/*The Tourist*

Jake Gyllenhaal/*Love and Other Drugs*

Kevin Spacey/*Casino Jack*

2012

★Jean Dujardin/*The Artist*

Brendan Gleeson/*The Guard*

Joseph Gordon-Levitt/*50/50*

Ryan Gosling/*Crazy, Stupid, Love.*

Owen Wilson/*Midnight in Paris*

2013

★Hugh Jackman/*Les Miserables*

Jack Black/*Bernie*

Bradley Cooper/*Silver Linings Playbook*

Ewan McGregor/*Salmon Fishing in the Yemen*

Bill Murray/*Hyde Park on Hudson*

2014

★Leonardo DiCaprio/*The Wolf of Wall Street*

Christian Bale/*American Hustle*

Bruce Dern/*Nebraska*

Oscar Isaac/*Inside Llewyn Davis*

Joaquin Rafael (Leaf) Phoenix/*Her*

2015

★Michael Keaton/*Birdman, or (The Unexpected Virtue of Ignorance)*

Ralph Fiennes/*The Grand Budapest Hotel*

Bill Murray/*St. Vincent*

Joaquin Rafael (Leaf) Phoenix/*Inherent Vice*

Christoph Waltz/*Big Eyes*

2016

★Matt Damon/*The Martian*

Christian Bale/*The Big Short*

Steve Carell/*The Big Short*

Al Pacino/*Danny Collins*

2017

★Ryan Gosling/*La La Land*

Colin Farrell/*The Lobster*

Hugh Grant/*Florence Foster Jenkins*

Jonah Hill/*War Dogs*

Ryan Reynolds/*Deadpool*

2018

★James Franco/*The Disaster Artist*

Steve Carell/*Battle of the Sexes*

Ansel Elgort/*Baby Driver*

Hugh Jackman/*The Greatest Showman*

Daniel Kaluuya/*Get Out*

2019

★Christian Bale/*Vice*

Lin-Manuel Miranda/*Mary Poppins Returns*

Viggo Mortensen/*Green Book*

Robert Redford/*The Old Man & the Gun*

John C. Reilly/*Stan & Ollie*

Stan & Ollie

2020

★Taron Egerton/*Rocketman*

Daniel Craig/*Knives Out*

Roman Griffin Davis/*Jojo Rabbit*

Leonardo DiCaprio/*Once Upon A Time... In Hollywood*

Eddie Murphy/*Dolemite Is My Name*

ACTOR—SUPPORTING

1945

★Barry Fitzgerald/*Going My Way*

1947

★Clifton Webb/*The Razor's Edge*

1948

★Edmund Gwenn/*Miracle on 34th Street*

1949

★Walter Huston/*Treasure of the Sierra Madre*

1950

★James Whitmore/*Battleground*

1952

★Peter Ustinov/*Quo Vadis*

1954

★Frank Sinatra/*From Here to Eternity*

1955

★Edmond O'Brien/*The Barefoot Contessa*

1957

★Earl Holliman/*The Rainmaker*

1958

★Red Buttons/*Sayonara*

1959

★Burl Ives/*The Big Country*

1960

★Stephen Boyd/*Ben-Hur*

1961

★Sal Mineo/*Exodus*

1962

★George Chakiris/*West Side Story*

1963

★Omar Sharif/*Lawrence of Arabia*

1964

★John Huston/*The Cardinal*

1965

★Edmond O'Brien/*Seven Days in May*

1966

★Oskar Werner/*The Spy Who Came in from the Cold*

1967

★Richard Attenborough/*The Sand Pebbles*

1968

★Richard Attenborough/*Doctor Dolittle*

1970

★Gig Young/*They Shoot Horses, Don't They?*

1971

★John Mills/*Ryan's Daughter*

1972

★Ben Johnson/*The Last Picture Show*

1973

★Joel Grey/*Cabaret*

1974

★John Houseman/*The Paper Chase*

1975

★Fred Astaire/*The Towering Inferno*

1976

★Richard Benjamin/*The Sunshine Boys*

1977

★Laurence Olivier/*Marathon Man*

1978

★Peter Firth/*Equus*

1979

★John Hurt/*Midnight Express*

1980

★Melvyn Douglas/*Being There*

★Robert Duvall/*Apocalypse Now*

1981

★Timothy Hutton/*Ordinary People*

1982

★John Gielgud/*Arthur*

1983

★Louis Gossett, Jr./*An Officer and a Gentleman*

1984

★Jack Nicholson/*Terms of Endearment*

1985

★Haing S. Ngor/*The Killing Fields*

1986

★Klaus Maria Brandauer/*Out of Africa*

1987

★Tom Berenger/*Platoon*

1988

★Sean Connery/*The Untouchables*

1989

★Martin Landau/*Tucker: The Man and His Dream*

1990

★Denzel Washington/*Glory*

Joe Pesci/*Goodfellas*

1991

★Bruce Davison/*Longtime Companion*

1992

★Jack Palance/*City Slickers*

1993

★Gene Hackman/*Unforgiven*

1994

★Tommy Lee Jones/*The Fugitive*

Leonardo DiCaprio/*What's Eating Gilbert Grape*

Ralph Fiennes/*Schindler's List*

John Malkovich/*In the Line of Fire*

Sean Penn/*Carlito's Way*

1995

★Martin Landau/*Ed Wood*

Kevin Bacon/*The River Wild*

Samuel L. Jackson/*Pulp Fiction*

Gary Sinise/*Forrest Gump*

John Turturro/*Quiz Show*

1996

★Brad Pitt/*12 Monkeys*

Ed Harris/*Apollo 13*

John Leguizamo/*To Wong Foo, Thanks for Everything, Julie Newmar*

Tim Roth/*Rob Roy*

Kevin Spacey/*The Usual Suspects*

1997

★Edward Norton/*Primal Fear*

Cuba Gooding, Jr./*Jerry Maguire*

Samuel L. Jackson/*A Time to Kill*

Paul Scofield/*The Crucible*

James Woods/*Ghosts of Mississippi*

1998

★Burt Reynolds/*Boogie Nights*

Rupert Everett/*My Best Friend's Wedding*

Anthony Hopkins/*Amistad*

Burt Reynolds/*Boogie Nights*

Jon Voight/*John Grisham's The Rainmaker*

Robin Williams/*Good Will Hunting*

1999

★Ed Harris/*The Truman Show*

Robert Duvall/*A Civil Action*

Bill Murray/*Rushmore*

Geoffrey Rush/*Shakespeare in Love*

Donald Sutherland/*Without Limits*

Billy Bob Thornton/*A Simple Plan*

2000

★Tom Cruise/*Magnolia*

Michael Caine/*The Cider House Rules*

Michael Clarke Duncan/*The Green Mile*

Jude Law/*The Talented Mr. Ripley*

Haley Joel Osment/*The Sixth Sense*

2001

★Benicio Del Toro/*Traffic*

Jeff Bridges/*The Contender*

Willem Dafoe/*Shadow of the Vampire*

Albert Finney/*Erin Brockovich*

Joaquin Rafael (Leaf) Phoenix/*Gladiator*

2002

★Jim Broadbent/*Iris*

Steve Buscemi/*Ghost World*

Hayden Christensen/*Life as a House*

Ben Kingsley/*Sexy Beast*

Jude Law/*A. I.: Artificial Intelligence*

Jon Voight/*Ali*

2003

★Chris Cooper/*Adaptation*

Ed Harris/*The Hours*

Paul Newman/*Road to Perdition*

Dennis Quaid/*Far from Heaven*

John C. Reilly/*Chicago*

★ = winner

2004
★Tim Robbins/*Mystic River*
Alec Baldwin/*The Cooler*
Albert Finney/*Big Fish*
William H. Macy/*Seabiscuit*
Peter Sarsgaard/*Shattered Glass*
Ken(saku) Watanabe/*The Last Samurai*

2005
★Clive Owen/*Closer*
David Carradine/*Kill Bill Vol. 2*
Thomas Haden Church/*Sideways*
Jamie Foxx/*Collateral*
Morgan Freeman/*Million Dollar Baby*

2006
★George Clooney/*Syriana*
Matt Dillon/*Crash*
Bob Hoskins/*Mrs. Henderson Presents*

2007
★Eddie Murphy/*Dreamgirls*
Ben Affleck/*Hollywoodland*
Jack Nicholson/*The Departed*
Brad Pitt/*Babel*
Mark Wahlberg/*The Departed*

2008
★Javier Bardem/*No Country for Old Men*
Casey Affleck/*The Assassination of Jesse James by the Coward Robert Ford*
Philip Seymour Hoffman/*Charlie Wilson's War*
John Travolta/*Hairspray*
Tom Wilkinson/*Michael Clayton*

2009
Tom Cruise/*Tropic Thunder*
Robert Downey, Jr./*Tropic Thunder*
Ralph Fiennes/*The Duchess*
Philip Seymour Hoffman/*Doubt*

2010
★Christoph Waltz/*Inglourious Basterds*
Matt Damon/*Invictus*
Woody Harrelson/*The Messenger*
Stanley Tucci/*The Lovely Bones*

2011
★Christian Bale/*The Fighter*
Michael Douglas/*Wall Street 2: Money Never Sleeps*
Andrew Garfield/*The Social Network*
Jeremy Renner/*The Town*
Geoffrey Rush/*The King's Speech*

2012
★Christopher Plummer/*Beginners*
Kenneth Branagh/*My Week With Marilyn*
Albert Brooks/*Drive*
Jonah Hill/*Moneyball*
Viggo Mortensen/*A Dangerous Method*

2013
★Christoph Waltz/*Django Unchained*
Alan Arkin/*Argo*
Leonardo DiCaprio/*Django Unchained*
Philip Seymour Hoffman/*The Master*
Tommy Lee Jones/*Lincoln*

2014
★Jared Leto/*Dallas Buyers Club*
Barkhad Adbi/*Captain Phillips*
Daniel Brühl/*Rush*
Bradley Cooper/*American Hustle*
Michael Fassbender/*12 Years a Slave*

2015
★J.K. Simmons/*Whiplash*
Robert Duvall/*The Judge*
Ethan Hawke/*Boyhood*
Edward Norton/*Birdman, or (The Unexpected Virtue of Ignorance)*
Mark Ruffalo/*Foxcatcher*

2016
★Sylvester Stallone/*Creed*
★Kate Winslet/*Steve Jobs*
Paul Dano/*Love & Mercy*
Idris Elba/*Beasts of No Nation*
Mark Rylance/*Bridge of Spies*
Michael Shannon/*99 Homes*

2017
★Aaron Taylor-Johnson/*Nocturnal Animals*
Mahershala Ali/*Moonlight*
Jeff Bridges/*Hell or High Water*
Simon Helberg/*Florence Foster Jenkins*
Dev Patel/*Lion*

2018
★Sam Rockwell/*Three Billboards Outside Ebbing, Missouri*
Willem Dafoe/*The Florida Project*
Armie Hammer/*Call Me by Your Name*
Richard Jenkins/*The Shape of Water*
Christopher Plummer/*All the Money in the World*

2019
★Mahershala Ali/*Green Book*
Timothée Chalamet/*Beautiful Boy*
Adam Driver/*BlacKkKlansman*
Richard E. Grant/*Can You Ever Forgive Me?*
Sam Rockwell/*Vice*

2020
★Brad Pitt/*Once Upon A Time... In Hollywood*
Tom Hanks/*A Beautiful Day in the Neighborhood*
Anthony Hopkins/*The Two Popes*
Al Pacino/*The Irishman*
Joe Pesci/*The Irishman*

ACTRESS—DRAMA

1944
★Jennifer Jones/*The Song of Bernadette*

1945
★Ingrid Bergman/*Gaslight*

1946
★Ingrid Bergman/*The Bells of St. Mary's*

1949
★Jane Wyman/*Johnny Belinda*

1950
★Olivia de Havilland/*The Heiress*

1951
★Gloria Swanson/*Sunset Boulevard*

1953
★Shirley Booth/*Come Back, Little Sheba*

1954
★Audrey Hepburn/*Roman Holiday*

1955
★Grace Kelly/*Country Girl*

1956
★Anna Magnani/*The Rose Tattoo*

1957
★Ingrid Bergman/*Anastasia*

1958
★Joanne Woodward/*The Three Faces of Eve*

1959
★Susan Hayward/*I Want to Live!*

1960
★Elizabeth Taylor/*Suddenly, Last Summer*

1961
★Greer Garson/*Sunrise at Campobello*

1962
★Geraldine Page/*Summer and Smoke*

1963
★Geraldine Page/*Sweet Bird of Youth*

1966
★Samantha Eggar/*The Collector*

1967
★Anouk Aimee/*A Man and a Woman*

1969
★Joanne Woodward/*Rachel, Rachel*

1970
★Genevieve Bujold/*Anne of the Thousand Days*

1971
★Ali MacGraw/*Love Story*

1972
★Jane Fonda/*Klute*

1974
★Marsha Mason/*Cinderella Liberty*

1975
★Gena Rowlands/*A Woman under the Influence*

1976
★Louise Fletcher/*One Flew Over the Cuckoo's Nest*

1977
★Faye Dunaway/*Network*

1978
★Jane Fonda/*Julia*

1979
★Jane Fonda/*Coming Home*

1980
★Sally Field/*Norma Rae*

1981
★Mary Tyler Moore/*Ordinary People*

1982
★Meryl Streep/*The French Lieutenant's Woman*

1983
★Meryl Streep/*Sophie's Choice*

1984
★Shirley MacLaine/*Terms of Endearment*

1985
★Sally Field/*Places in the Heart*

1986
★Whoopi Goldberg/*The Color Purple*

1987
★Marlee Matlin/*Children of a Lesser God*

1988
★Sally Kirkland/*Anna*
★Sigourney Weaver/*Gorillas in the Mist*

1989
★Jodie Foster/*The Accused*
★Shirley MacLaine/*Madame Sousatzka*

1990
★Michelle Pfeiffer/*The Fabulous Baker Boys*

1991
★Kathy Bates/*Misery*

1992
★Jodie Foster/*The Silence of the Lambs*

1993
★Emma Thompson/*Howard's End*

1994
★Holly Hunter/*The Piano*
Juliette Binoche/*Trois Couleurs: Bleu*
Michelle Pfeiffer/*The Age of Innocence*
Emma Thompson/*The Remains of the Day*

1995
★Jessica Lange/*Blue Sky*
Jodie Foster/*Nell*
Jennifer Jason Leigh/*Mrs. Parker and the Vicious Circle*
Miranda Richardson/*Tom & Viv*
Meryl Streep/*The River Wild*

1996
★Sharon Stone/*Casino*
Susan Sarandon/*Dead Man Walking*
Elisabeth Shue/*Leaving Las Vegas*
Meryl Streep/*The Bridges of Madison County*
Emma Thompson/*Sense and Sensibility*

1997
★Brenda Blethyn/*Secrets and Lies*
Courtney Love/*The People vs. Larry Flynt*
Kristin Scott Thomas/*The English Patient*
Meryl Streep/*Marvin's Room*
Emily Watson/*Breaking the Waves*

1998
★Dame Judi Dench/*Mrs. Brown*
Helena Bonham Carter/*The Wings of the Dove*
Jodie Foster/*Contact*
Jessica Lange/*A Thousand Acres*
Emily Watson/*Hilary and Jackie*
Kate Winslet/*Titanic*

1999
★Cate Blanchett/*Elizabeth*
Fernanda Montenegro/*Central Station*
Susan Sarandon/*Stepmom*
Meryl Streep/*One True Thing*

2000
★Hilary Swank/*Boys Don't Cry*
Annette Bening/*American Beauty*
Julianne Moore/*The End of the Affair*
Meryl Streep/*Music of the Heart*
Sigourney Weaver/*A Map of the World*

2001
★Julia Roberts/*Erin Brockovich*
Joan Allen/*The Contender*
Bjork/*Dancer in the Dark*
Laura Linney/*You Can Count On Me*

2002
★Sissy Spacek/*In the Bedroom*
Halle Berry/*Monster's Ball*
Dame Judi Dench/*Iris*
Nicole Kidman/*The Others*
Tilda Swinton/*The Deep End*

2003
★Nicole Kidman/*The Hours*
Salma Hayek/*Frida*
Diane Lane/*Unfaithful*
Julianne Moore/*Far from Heaven*
Meryl Streep/*The Hours*

2004
★Charlize Theron/*Monster*
Cate Blanchett/*Veronica Guerin*
Scarlett Johansson/*Girl with a Pearl Earring*
Nicole Kidman/*Cold Mountain*
Imelda Staunton/*Vera Drake*
Uma Thurman/*Kill Bill Vol. 1*
Evan Rachel Wood/*Thirteen*

2005
★Hilary Swank/*Million Dollar Baby*
Nicole Kidman/*Birth*
Uma Thurman/*Kill Bill Vol. 2*

2006
★Felicity Huffman/*Transamerica*
Maria Bello/*A History of Violence*
Gwyneth Paltrow/*Proof*
Charlize Theron/*North Country*

2007
★Dame Helen Mirren/*The Queen*
Penelope Cruz/*Volver*
Dame Judi Dench/*Notes on a Scandal*
Maggie Gyllenhaal/*Sherrybaby*
Kate Winslet/*Little Children*

2008
★Julie Christie/*Away From Her*
Cate Blanchett/*Elizabeth: The Golden Age*
Jodie Foster/*The Brave One*
Angelina Jolie/*A Mighty Heart*
Keira Knightley/*Atonement*

2009
★Kate Winslet/*Revolutionary Road*
Anne Hathaway/*Rachel Getting Married*
Angelina Jolie/*Changeling*
Kristin Scott Thomas/*I've Loved You So Long*
Meryl Streep/*Doubt*

2010
★Sandra Bullock/*The Blind Side*
Emily Blunt/*The Young Victoria*
Dame Helen Mirren/*The Last Station*
Carey Mulligan/*An Education*
Gabourney 'Gabby' Sidibe/*Precious: Based on the Novel 'Push' by Sapphire*

2011
★Natalie Portman/*Black Swan*
Halle Berry/*Frankie and Alice*
Nicole Kidman/*Rabbit Hole*
Jennifer Lawrence/*Winter's Bone*
Michelle Williams/*Blue Valentine*

2012
★Meryl Streep/*The Iron Lady*
Glenn Close/*Albert Nobbs*
Viola Davis/*The Help*
Rooney Mara/*The Girl With the Dragon Tattoo*
Tilda Swinton/*We Need to Talk About Kevin*

2013
★Jessica Chastain/*Zero Dark Thirty*
Marion Cotillard/*Rust and Bone*
Dame Helen Mirren/*Hitchcock*
Naomi Watts/*The Impossible*
Rachel Weisz/*The Deep Blue Sea*

2014
★Cate Blanchett/*Blue Jasmine*
Sandra Bullock/*Gravity*
Dame Judi Dench/*Philomena*

2015
★Julianne Moore/*Still Alice*
Jennifer Aniston/*Cake*
Felicity Jones/*The Theory of Everything*
Dame Helen Mirren/*The Hundred-Foot Journey*
Rosamund Pike/*Gone Girl*
Still Alice
Reese Witherspoon/*Wild*

2016
★Brie Larson/*Room*
Cate Blanchett/*Carol*
Rooney Mara/*Carol*
Saoirse Ronan/*Brooklyn*

2017
★Isabelle Huppert/*Elle*
Amy Adams/*Arrival*
Jessica Chastain/*Miss Sloane*
Ruth Negga/*Loving*
Natalie Portman/*Jackie*

2018
★Frances McDormand/*Three Billboards Outside Ebbing, Missouri*
Jessica Chastain/*Molly's Game*
Sally Hawkins/*The Shape of Water*
Meryl Streep/*The Post*
Michelle Williams/*All the Money in the World*

2019
★Glenn Close/*The Wife*
Lady Gaga/*A Star Is Born*
Nicole Kidman/*Destroyer*
Melissa McCarthy/*Can You Ever Forgive Me?*
Rosamund Pike/*A Private War*

2020
★Renée Zellweger/*Judy*
Cynthia Erivo/*Harriet*
Scarlett Johansson/*Marriage Story*
Saoirse Ronan/*Little Women*
Charlize Theron/*Bombshell*

★ = winner

ACTRESS—MUSICAL/COMEDY

1951
★Judy Holliday/*Born Yesterday*
1955
★Judy Garland/*A Star Is Born*
1956
★Jean Simmons/*Guys and Dolls*
1957
★Deborah Kerr/*The King and I*
1958
★Kay Kendall/*Les Girls*
1959
★Rosalind Russell/*Auntie Mame*
1960
★Marilyn Monroe/*Some Like It Hot*
1961
★Shirley MacLaine/*The Apartment*
1963
★Doris Day/*Move Over, Darling*
★Rosalind Russell/*Gypsy*
1964
★Shirley MacLaine/*Irma La Douce*
1965
★Julie Andrews/*Mary Poppins*
1966
★Julie Andrews/*The Sound of Music*
1967
★Lynn Redgrave/*Georgy Girl*
1968
★Anne Bancroft/*The Graduate*
1969
★Barbra Streisand/*Funny Girl*
1972
★Twiggy/*The Boy Friend*
1973
★Liza Minnelli/*Cabaret*
1974
★Glenda Jackson/*A Touch of Class*
1975
★Raquel Welch/*The Three Musketeers*
1976
★Ann-Margret/*Tommy*
1977
★Barbra Streisand/*A Star Is Born*
1978
★Diane Keaton/*Annie Hall*
★Marsha Mason/*The Goodbye Girl*
1979
★Ellen Burstyn/*Same Time, Next Year*
★Maggie Smith/*California Suite*
1980
★Bette Midler/*The Rose*
1981
★Sissy Spacek/*Coal Miner's Daughter*
1982
★Bernadette Peters/*Pennies from Heaven*
1983
★Julie Andrews/*Victor/Victoria*
1984
★Julie Walters/*Educating Rita*
1985
★Kathleen Turner/*Romancing the Stone*
1986
★Kathleen Turner/*Prizzi's Honor*
1987
★Sissy Spacek/*Crimes of the Heart*
1988
★Cher/*Moonstruck*
1989
★Melanie Griffith/*Working Girl*
1990
★Jessica Tandy/*Driving Miss Daisy*
1991
★Julia Roberts/*Pretty Woman*
Andie MacDowell/*Green Card*
1992
★Bette Midler/*For the Boys*
1993
★Miranda Richardson/*Enchanted April*
1994
★Angela Bassett/*What's Love Got to Do with It?*
Stockard Channing/*Six Degrees of Separation*
Anjelica Huston/*Addams Family Values*
Diane Keaton/*Manhattan Murder Mystery*
Meg Ryan/*Sleepless in Seattle*
1995
★Jamie Lee Curtis/*True Lies*
Geena Davis/*Speechless*
Andie MacDowell/*Four Weddings and a Funeral*
Shirley MacLaine/*Guarding Tess*
Emma Thompson/*Junior*
1996
★Nicole Kidman/*To Die For*
Annette Bening/*The American President*
Sandra Bullock/*While You Were Sleeping*
Toni Collette/*Muriel's Wedding*
Vanessa Redgrave/*A Month by the Lake*
1997
★Madonna/*Evita*
Glenn Close/*101 Dalmatians*
Frances McDormand/*Fargo*
Debbie Reynolds/*Mother*
Barbra Streisand/*The Mirror Has Two Faces*
1998
★Helen Hunt/*As Good As It Gets*
Joey Lauren Adams/*Chasing Amy*
Pam Grier/*Jackie Brown*
Jennifer Lopez/*Selena*
Julia Roberts/*My Best Friend's Wedding*
1999
★Gwyneth Paltrow/*Shakespeare in Love*
Cameron Diaz/*There's Something about Mary*
Jane Horrocks/*Little Voice*
Christina Ricci/*The Opposite of Sex*
Meg Ryan/*You've Got Mail*
2000
★Janet McTeer/*Tumbleweeds*
Julianne Moore/*An Ideal Husband*
Julia Roberts/*Notting Hill*
Sharon Stone/*The Muse*
Reese Witherspoon/*Election*
2001
★Renée Zellweger/*Nurse Betty*
Juliette Binoche/*Chocolat*
Brenda Blethyn/*Saving Grace*
Sandra Bullock/*Miss Congeniality*
Tracey Ullman/*Small Time Crooks*
2002
★Nicole Kidman/*Moulin Rouge*
Thora Birch/*Ghost World*
Cate Blanchett/*Bandits*
Reese Witherspoon/*Legally Blonde*
Renée Zellweger/*Bridget Jones's Diary*
2003
★Renée Zellweger/*Chicago*
Maggie Gyllenhaal/*Secretary*
Goldie Hawn/*The Banger Sisters*
Nia Vardalos/*My Big Fat Greek Wedding*
Catherine Zeta-Jones/*Chicago*
2004
★Diane Keaton/*Something's Gotta Give*
Jamie Lee Curtis/*Freaky Friday*
Scarlett Johansson/*Lost in Translation*
Diane Lane/*Under the Tuscan Sun*
Dame Helen Mirren/*Calendar Girls*
2005
★Annette Bening/*Being Julia*
Ashley Judd/*De-Lovely*
Emmy Rossum/*The Phantom of the Opera*
Kate Winslet/*Eternal Sunshine of the Spotless Mind*
Renée Zellweger/*Bridget Jones: The Edge of Reason*
2006
★Reese Witherspoon/*Walk the Line*
Dame Judi Dench/*Mrs. Henderson Presents*
Keira Knightley/*Pride and Prejudice*
Laura Linney/*The Squid and the Whale*
Sarah Jessica Parker/*The Family Stone*
2007
★Meryl Streep/*The Devil Wears Prada*
Annette Bening/*Running with Scissors*
Toni Collette/*Little Miss Sunshine*
Beyonce Knowles/*Dreamgirls*
Renée Zellweger/*Miss Potter*
2008
★Marion Cotillard/*La Vie en Rose*
Amy Adams/*Enchanted*
Nicole Blonsky/*Hairspray*
Helena Bonham Carter/*Sweeney Todd: The Demon Barber of Fleet Street*
Ellen Page/*Juno*
2009
★Sally Hawkins/*Happy-Go-Lucky*
Rebecca Hall/*Vicky Cristina Barcelona*
Frances McDormand/*Burn After Reading*
Meryl Streep/*Mamma Mia!*
Emma Thompson/*Last Chance Harvey*
2010
★Meryl Streep/*Julie & Julia*
Sandra Bullock/*The Proposal*
Marion Cotillard/*Nine*
Julia Roberts/*Duplicity*
Meryl Streep/*It's Complicated*
2011
★Annette Bening/*The Kids Are All Right*
Anne Hathaway/*Love and Other Drugs*
Angelina Jolie/*The Tourist*
Julianne Moore/*The Kids Are All Right*
Emma Stone/*Easy A*
2012
★Michelle Williams/*My Week With Marilyn*
Jodie Foster/*Carnage*
Charlize Theron/*Young Adult*
Kristen Wiig/*Bridesmaids*
Kate Winslet/*Carnage*
2013
★Jennifer Lawrence/*Silver Linings Playbook*
Emily Blunt/*Salmon Fishing in the Yemen*
Dame Judi Dench/*The Best Exotic Marigold Hotel*
Maggie Smith/*Quartet*
Meryl Streep/*Hope Springs*
2014
★Amy Adams/*American Hustle*
Julie Delpy/*Before Midnight*
Greta Gerwig/*Frances Ha*
Julia Louis-Dreyfus/*Enough Said*
Meryl Streep/*August: Osage County*
Emma Thompson/*Saving Mr. Banks*
2015
★Amy Adams/*Big Eyes*
Emily Blunt/*Into the Woods*
Maps to the Stars
Julianne Moore/*Maps to the Stars*
Quvenzhane Wallis/*Annie*
2016
★Jennifer Lawerence/*Joy*
Melissa McCarthy/*Spy*
Mark Ruffalo/*Infinitely Polar Bear*
Amy Schumer/*Trainwreck*
Maggie Smith/*The Lady in the Van*
Lily Tomlin/*Grandma*
2017
★Emma Stone/*La La Land*
Annette Bening/*20th Century Women*
Lily Collins/*Rules Don't Apply*
Hailee Steinfeld/*The Edge of Seventeen*
Meryl Streep/*Florence Foster Jenkins*
2018
★Saoirse Ronan/*Lady Bird*
Dame Judi Dench/*Victoria & Abdul*
Dame Helen Mirren/*The Leisure Seeker*
Margot Robbie/*I, Tonya*
Emma Stone/*Battle of the Sexes*
2019
★Olivia Colman/*The Favourite*
Emily Blunt/*Mary Poppins Returns*
Elsie Fisher/*Eighth Grade*
Charlize Theron/*Tully*
Constance Wu/*Crazy Rich Asians*
2020
★Nora Lum/*The Farewell*
Ana de Armas/*Knives Out*
Cate Blanchett/*Where'd You Go, Bernadette*
Beanie Feldstein/*Booksmart*
Emma Thompson/*Late Night*

ACTRESS—SUPPORTING

1945
★Agnes Moorehead/*Mrs. Parkington*
1946
★Angela Lansbury/*Picture of Dorian Gray*
1947
★Anne Baxter/*The Razor's Edge*
1948
★Celeste Holm/*Gentleman's Agreement*
1949
★Ellen Corby/*I Remember Mama*
1950
★Mercedes McCambridge/*All the King's Men*
1951
★Josephine Hull/*Harvey*
1952
★Kim Hunter/*A Streetcar Named Desire*
1953
★Katy Jurado/*High Noon*
1954
★Grace Kelly/*Mogambo*
1955
★Jan Sterling/*The High and the Mighty*
1956
★Marisa Pavan/*The Rose Tattoo*
1957
★Eileen Heckart/*The Bad Seed*
1958
★Elsa Lanchester/*Witness for the Prosecution*
1959
★Hermione Gingold/*Gigi*
1960
★Susan Kohner/*Imitation of Life*
1961
★Janet Leigh/*Psycho*
1962
★Rita Moreno/*West Side Story*
1963
★Angela Lansbury/*The Manchurian Candidate*
1964
★Margaret Rutherford/*The V.I.P.'s*
1965
★Agnes Moorehead/*Hush, Hush, Sweet Charlotte*
1966
★Ruth Gordon/*Inside Daisy Clover*
1967
★Jocelyn Lagarde/*Hawaii*
1968
★Carol Channing/*Thoroughly Modern Millie*
1969
★Ruth Gordon/*Rosemary's Baby*
1970
★Goldie Hawn/*Cactus Flower*
1971
★Karen Black/*Five Easy Pieces*
★Maureen Stapleton/*Airport*
1972
★Ann-Margret/*Carnal Knowledge*
1973
★Shelley Winters/*The Poseidon Adventure*
1974
★Linda Blair/*The Exorcist*
1975
★Karen Black/*The Great Gatsby*
1976
★Brenda Vaccaro/*Once Is Not Enough*
1977
★Katharine Ross/*Voyage of the Damned*
1978
★Vanessa Redgrave/*Julia*
1979
★Dyan Cannon/*Heaven Can Wait*
1980
★Meryl Streep/*Kramer vs. Kramer*
1981
★Mary Steenburgen/*Melvin and Howard*
1982
★Joan Hackett/*Only When I Laugh*
1983
★Jessica Lange/*Tootsie*
1984
★Cher/*Silkwood*
1985
★Peggy Ashcroft/*A Passage to India*
1986
★Meg Tilly/*Agnes of God*
1987
★Maggie Smith/*A Room with a View*
1988
★Olympia Dukakis/*Moonstruck*
1989
★Sigourney Weaver/*Working Girl*
1990
★Julia Roberts/*Steel Magnolias*
Lorraine Bracco/*Goodfellas*
1991
★Whoopi Goldberg/*Ghost*
Nicole Kidman/*Billy Bathgate*
1992
★Mercedes Ruehl/*The Fisher King*
1993
★Joan Plowright/*Enchanted April*
1994
★Winona Ryder/*The Age of Innocence*
Penelope Ann Miller/*Carlito's Way*
Anna Paquin/*The Piano*
Rosie Perez/*Fearless*
Emma Thompson/*In the Name of the Father*

★ = winner

1995
★Dianne Wiest/*Bullets over Broadway*
Kirsten Dunst/*Interview with the Vampire*
Sophia Loren/*Ready to Wear*
Uma Thurman/*Pulp Fiction*
Robin Wright/*Forrest Gump*
1996
★Mira Sorvino/*Mighty Aphrodite*
Anjelica Huston/*The Crossing Guard*
Kathleen Quinlan/*Apollo 13*
Kyra Sedgwick/*Something to Talk About*
Kate Winslet/*Sense and Sensibility*
1997
★Lauren Bacall/*The Mirror Has Two Faces*
Joan Allen/*The Crucible*
Juliette Binoche/*The English Patient*
Barbara Hershey/*Portrait of a Lady*
Marianne Jean-Baptiste/*Secrets and Lies*
Marion Ross/*The Evening Star*
1998
★Kim Basinger/*L.A. Confidential*
Joan Cusack/*In and Out*
Julianne Moore/*Boogie Nights*
Gloria Stuart/*Titanic*
Sigourney Weaver/*The Ice Storm*
1999
★Lynn Redgrave/*Gods and Monsters*
Kathy Bates/*Primary Colors*
Brenda Blethyn/*Little Voice*
Dame Judi Dench/*Shakespeare in Love*
Sharon Stone/*The Mighty*
2000
★Angelina Jolie/*Girl, Interrupted*
Cameron Diaz/*Being John Malkovich*
Catherine Keener/*Being John Malkovich*
Samantha Morton/*Sweet and Lowdown*
Natalie Portman/*Anywhere But Here*
Chloë Sevigny/*Boys Don't Cry*
2001
★Kate Hudson/*Almost Famous*
Dame Judi Dench/*Chocolat*
Frances McDormand/*Almost Famous*
Julie Walters/*Billy Elliot*
2002
★Jennifer Connelly/*A Beautiful Mind*
Cameron Diaz/*Vanilla Sky*
Dame Helen Mirren/*Gosford Park*
Maggie Smith/*Gosford Park*
Marisa Tomei/*In the Bedroom*
Kate Winslet/*Iris*
2003
★Meryl Streep/*Adaptation*
Kathy Bates/*About Schmidt*
Cameron Diaz/*Gangs of New York*
Queen Latifah/*Chicago*
Susan Sarandon/*Igby Goes Down*

2004
★Renée Zellweger/*Cold Mountain*
Maria Bello/*The Cooler*
Patricia Clarkson/*Pieces of April*
Hope Davis/*American Splendor*
Holly Hunter/*Thirteen*
2005
★Natalie Portman/*Closer*
Cate Blanchett/*The Aviator*
Laura Linney/*Kinsey*
Virginia Madsen/*Sideways*
Meryl Streep/*The Manchurian Candidate*
2006
★Rachel Weisz/*The Constant Gardener*
Will Ferrell/*The Producers*
Scarlett Johansson/*Match Point*
Shirley MacLaine/*In Her Shoes*
Frances McDormand/*North Country*
Michelle Williams/*Brokeback Mountain*
2007
★Jennifer Hudson/*Dreamgirls*
Adriana Barraza/*Babel*
Cate Blanchett/*Notes on a Scandal*
Emily Blunt/*The Devil Wears Prada*
Rinko Kikuchi/*Babel*
2008
★Cate Blanchett/*I'm Not There*
Julia Roberts/*Charlie Wilson's War*
Saoirse Ronan/*Atonement*
Amy Ryan/*Gone Baby Gone*
Tilda Swinton/*Michael Clayton*
2009
★Kate Winslet/*The Reader*
Amy Adams/*Doubt*
Penelope Cruz/*Vicky Cristina Barcelona*
Viola Davis/*Doubt*
Marisa Tomei/*The Wrestler*
2010
★Mo'Nique/*Precious: Based on the Novel 'Push' by Sapphire*
Penelope Cruz/*Nine*
Vera Farmiga/*Up in the Air*
Anna Kendrick/*Up in the Air*
Julianne Moore/*A Single Man*
Christopher Plummer/*The Last Station*
2011
★Melissa Leo/*The Fighter*
Amy Adams/*The Fighter*
Helena Bonham Carter/*The King's Speech*
Mila Kunis/*Black Swan*
Jacki Weaver/*Animal Kingdom*
2012
★Octavia Spencer/*The Help*
Berenice Bejo/*The Artist*
Jessica Chastain/*The Help*
Janet McTeer/*Albert Nobbs*
Shailene Woodley/*The Descendants*
2013
★Anne Hathaway/*Les Miserables*
Amy Adams/*The Master*
Sally Field/*Lincoln*
Helen Hunt/*The Sessions*
Nicole Kidman/*The Paperboy*

2014
★Jennifer Lawrence/*American Hustle*
Sally Hawkins/*Blue Jasmine*
Lupita Nyong'o/*12 Years a Slave*
Julia Roberts/*August: Osage County*
June Squibb/*Nebraska*
2015
★Patricia Arquette/*Boyhood*
Jessica Chastain/*A Most Violent Year*
Keira Knightley/*The Imitation Game*
Emma Stone/*Birdman, or (The Unexpected Virtue of Ignorance)*
Meryl Streep/*Into the Woods*
2016
Jane Fonda/*Youth*
Jennifer Jason Leigh/*The Hateful Eight*
Dame Helen Mirren/*Trumbo*
Alicia Vikander/*Ex Machina*
2017
★Viola Davis/*Fences*
Naomie Harris/*Moonlight*
Nicole Kidman/*Lion*
Octavia Spencer/*Hidden Figures*
Michelle Williams/*Manchester by the Sea*
2018
★Allison Janney/*I, Tonya*
Mary J. Blige/*Mudbound*
Hong Chau/*Downsizing*
Laurie Metcalf/*Lady Bird*
Octavia Spencer/*The Shape of Water*
2019
★Regina King/*If Beale Street Could Talk*
Amy Adams/*Vice*
Claire Foy/*First Man*
Emma Stone/*The Favourite*
Rachel Weisz/*The Favourite*
2020
★Laura Dern/*Marriage Story*
Kathy Bates/*Richard Jewell*
Annette Bening/*The Report*
Jennifer Lopez/*Hustlers*
Margot Robbie/*Bombshell*

BEST FILM—DRAMA

1944
★*The Song of Bernadette*
1945
★*Going My Way*
1946
★*The Lost Weekend*
1947
★*The Best Years of Our Lives*
1948
★*Gentleman's Agreement*
1949
★*Johnny Belinda*
★*Treasure of the Sierra Madre*
1950
★*All the King's Men*
1951
★*Sunset Boulevard*
1952
★*A Place in the Sun*
1953
★*The Greatest Show on Earth*
1954
★*The Robe*
1955
★*On the Waterfront*

1956
★*East of Eden*
1957
★*Around the World in 80 Days*
1958
★*The Bridge on the River Kwai*
1959
★*The Defiant Ones*
1960
★*Ben-Hur*
1961
★*Spartacus*
1962
★*The Guns of Navarone*
1963
★*Lawrence of Arabia*
1964
★*The Cardinal*
1965
★*Becket*
1966
★*Doctor Zhivago*
1967
★*A Man for All Seasons*
1968
★*In the Heat of the Night*
1969
★*The Lion in Winter*
1970
★*Anne of the Thousand Days*
1971
★*Love Story*
1972
★*The French Connection*
1973
★*The Godfather*
1974
★*The Exorcist*
1975
★*Chinatown*
1976
★*One Flew Over the Cuckoo's Nest*
1977
★*Rocky*
1978
★*The Turning Point*
1979
★*Midnight Express*
1980
★*Kramer vs. Kramer*
1981
★*Ordinary People*
1982
★*On Golden Pond*
1983
★*E.T.: The Extra-Terrestrial*
1984
★*Terms of Endearment*
1985
★*Amadeus*
1986
★*Out of Africa*
1987
★*Platoon*
1988
★*The Last Emperor*
1989
★*Rain Man*
1990
★*Born on the Fourth of July*
Goodfellas
1991
★*Dances with Wolves*
1992
★*Bugsy*

1993
★*Scent of a Woman*
1994
★*Schindler's List*
The Age of Innocence
In the Name of the Father
The Piano
The Remains of the Day
1995
★*Forrest Gump*
Legends of the Fall
Nell
Pulp Fiction
Quiz Show
1996
★*Sense and Sensibility*
Apollo 13
Braveheart
The Bridges of Madison County
Leaving Las Vegas
1997
★*The English Patient*
Breaking the Waves
The People vs. Larry Flynt
Secrets and Lies
Shine
1998
★*Titanic*
Amistad
The Boxer
Good Will Hunting
The Horse Whisperer
L.A. Confidential
1999
★*Saving Private Ryan*
Elizabeth
Gods and Monsters
The Truman Show
2000
★*American Beauty*
The End of the Affair
The Hurricane
The Insider
The Talented Mr. Ripley
2001
★*Gladiator*
2002
★*A Beautiful Mind*
In the Bedroom
Lord of the Rings: The Fellowship of the Ring
The Man Who Wasn't There
Mulholland Drive
2003
★*The Hours*
About Schmidt
Gangs of New York
Lord of the Rings: The Two Towers
The Pianist
2004
★*Lord of the Rings: The Return of the King*
Cold Mountain
Master and Commander: The Far Side of the World
Mystic River
Seabiscuit
2005
★*The Aviator*
Closer
Finding Neverland
Hotel Rwanda
Kinsey
Million Dollar Baby
2006
★*Brokeback Mountain*
The Constant Gardener
Good Night, and Good Luck
A History of Violence
Match Point

2007
★*Babel*
Bobby
The Departed
Little Children
The Queen
2008
★*Atonement*
American Gangster
Eastern Promises
The Great Debaters
Michael Clayton
No Country for Old Men
There Will Be Blood
2009
★*Slumdog Millionaire*
The Curious Case of Benjamin Button
Frost/Nixon
The Reader
Revolutionary Road
2010
★*Avatar*
The Hurt Locker
Inglourious Basterds
Precious: Based on the Novel 'Push' by Sapphire
Up in the Air
2011
★*The Social Network*
Black Swan
The Fighter
Inception
The King's Speech
2012
★*The Descendants*
The Descendants
The Help
Hugo
The Ides of March
Moneyball
War Horse
2013
★*Argo*
Django Unchained
Life of Pi
Lincoln
Zero Dark Thirty
2014
★*12 Years a Slave*
Captain Phillips
Gravity
Philomena
Rush
2015
★*Boyhood*
Foxcatcher
The Imitation Game
Selma
The Theory of Everything
2016
★*The Revenant*
Carol
Mad Max: Fury Road
Room
Spotlight
2017
★*Moonlight*
Hacksaw Ridge
Hell or High Water
Lion
Manchester by the Sea
2018
★*Three Billboards Outside Ebbing, Missouri*
Call Me by Your Name
Dunkirk
The Post
The Shape of Water

★ = winner

2019
★Bohemian Rhapsody
Black Panther
BlacKkKlansman
If Beale Street Could Talk
A Star Is Born
2020
★1917
The Irishman
Joker
Marriage Story
The Two Popes

BEST FILM—MUSICAL/COMEDY

201
Chocolat
1952
★An American in Paris
1955
★Carmen Jones
1956
★Guys and Dolls
1957
★The King and I
1958
★Les Girls
1959
★Gigi
1960
★Some Like It Hot
1961
★The Apartment
★Song Without End
1962
★West Side Story
1963
★The Music Man
★That Touch of Mink
1964
★Tom Jones
1965
★My Fair Lady
1966
★The Sound of Music
1967
★The Russians Are Coming, the Russians Are Coming
1968
★The Graduate
1969
★Oliver!
1971
★M*A*S*H
1972
★Fiddler on the Roof
1973
★Cabaret
1974
★American Graffiti
1975
★The Longest Yard
1976
★The Sunshine Boys
1977
★A Star Is Born
1978
★The Goodbye Girl
1979
★Heaven Can Wait
1980
★Breaking Away
1981
★Coal Miner's Daughter
1982
★Arthur
1983
★Tootsie
1984
★Yentl
1985
★Romancing the Stone
1986
★Prizzi's Honor
1987
★Hannah and Her Sisters
1988
★Hope and Glory
1989
★Working Girl
1990
★Driving Miss Daisy
1991
★Green Card
1992
★Beauty and the Beast
1993
★The Player
1994
★Mrs. Doubtfire
Dave
Much Ado about Nothing
Sleepless in Seattle
Strictly Ballroom
1995
★The Lion King
The Adventures of Priscilla, Queen of the Desert
Ed Wood
Four Weddings and a Funeral
Ready to Wear
1996
★Babe
The American President
Get Shorty
Sabrina
Toy Story
1997
★Evita
The Birdcage
Everyone Says I Love You
Fargo
Jerry Maguire
1998
★As Good As It Gets
The Full Monty
The Mask of Zorro
Men in Black
My Best Friend's Wedding
Wag the Dog
1999
★Shakespeare in Love
Warren Beatty/Bulworth
Bulworth
Patch Adams
Still Crazy
There's Something about Mary
2000
★Toy Story 2
Analyze This
Being John Malkovich
Man on the Moon
Notting Hill
2001
★Almost Famous
2002
★Moulin Rouge
Bridget Jones's Diary
Gosford Park
Legally Blonde
Shrek
2003
★Chicago
About a Boy
Adaptation
My Big Fat Greek Wedding
Nicholas Nickleby
2004
★Lost in Translation
Bend It Like Beckham
Big Fish
Finding Nemo
Love Actually
2005
★Sideways
Eternal Sunshine of the Spotless Mind
The Incredibles
The Phantom of the Opera
Ray
2006
★Walk the Line
Mrs. Henderson Presents
Pride and Prejudice
The Producers
The Squid and the Whale
2007
★Dreamgirls
Borat: Cultural Learnings of America for Make Benefit Glorious Nation of Kazakhstan
The Devil Wears Prada
Little Miss Sunshine
Thank You for Smoking
2008
★Sweeney Todd: The Demon Barber of Fleet Street
Across the Universe
Charlie Wilson's War
Hairspray
Juno
2009
★Vicky Cristina Barcelona
Burn After Reading
Happy-Go-Lucky
In Bruges
2010
★The Hangover
(500) Days of Summer
It's Complicated
Julie & Julia
Nine
2011
★The Kids Are All Right
Alice in Wonderland
Burlesque
RED
The Tourist
2012
★The Artist
Bridesmaids
50/50
Midnight in Paris
My Week With Marilyn
2013
★Les Miserables
The Best Exotic Marigold Hotel
Moonrise Kingdom
Salmon Fishing in the Yemen
Silver Linings Playbook
2014
★American Hustle
Her
Inside Llewyn Davis
The Wolf of Wall Street
2015
★The Grand Budapest Hotel
★The Martian
Birdman, or (The Unexpected Virtue of Ignorance)
Into the Woods
Pride
St. Vincent
2016
The Big Short
Joy
Spy
Trainwreck
2017
★La La Land
Deadpool
Florence Foster Jenkins
Sing Street
20th Century Women
2018
★Lady Bird
The Disaster Artist
Get Out
The Greatest Showman
I, Tonya
2019
★Green Book
Crazy Rich Asians
The Favourite
Mary Poppins Returns
Vice
2020
★Once Upon A Time... In Hollywood
Dolemite Is My Name
Jojo Rabbit
Knives Out
Rocketman

DIRECTOR

1944
★Henry King/The Song of Bernadette
1945
★Leo McCarey/Going My Way
1946
★Billy Wilder/The Lost Weekend
1947
★Frank Capra/It's a Wonderful Life
1948
★Elia Kazan/Gentleman's Agreement
1949
★John Huston/Treasure of the Sierra Madre
1950
★Robert Rossen/All the King's Men
1951
★Billy Wilder/Sunset Boulevard
1953
★Cecil B. DeMille/The Greatest Show on Earth
1954
Fred Zinnemann/From Here to Eternity
1955
★Elia Kazan/On the Waterfront
1956
★Joshua Logan/Picnic
1957
★Elia Kazan/Baby Doll
1958
★David Lean/The Bridge on the River Kwai
1959
★Vincente Minnelli/Gigi
1960
★William Wyler/Ben-Hur
1962
★Stanley Kramer/Judgment at Nuremberg
1963
★David Lean/Lawrence of Arabia
1965
★George Cukor/My Fair Lady
1966
★David Lean/Doctor Zhivago
1967
★Fred Zinnemann/A Man for All Seasons
1968
★Mike Nichols/The Graduate
1969
★Paul Newman/Rachel, Rachel
1970
★Charles Jarrott/Anne of the Thousand Days
1971
★Arthur Hiller/Love Story
1972
★William Friedkin/The French Connection
1973
★Francis Ford Coppola/The Godfather
1974
★William Friedkin/The Exorcist
1975
★Roman Polanski/Chinatown
1976
★Milos Forman/One Flew Over the Cuckoo's Nest
1977
★Sidney Lumet/Network
1978
★Herbert Ross/The Turning Point
1979
★Michael Cimino/The Deer Hunter
1980
★Francis Ford Coppola/Apocalypse Now
1981
★Robert Redford/Ordinary People
1982
★Warren Beatty/Reds
1983
★Richard Attenborough/Gandhi
1984
★Barbra Streisand/Yentl
1985
★Milos Forman/Amadeus
Sergio Leone/Once Upon a Time in America
1986
★John Huston/Prizzi's Honor
1987
★Oliver Stone/Platoon
1988
★Bernardo Bertolucci/The Last Emperor
1989
★Clint Eastwood/Bird
1990
★Oliver Stone/Born on the Fourth of July
Martin Scorsese/Goodfellas
1991
★Kevin Costner/Dances with Wolves
1992
★Oliver Stone/JFK
1993
★Clint Eastwood/Unforgiven
1994
★Steven Spielberg/Schindler's List
Jane Campion/The Piano
Andrew Davis/The Fugitive
James Ivory/The Remains of the Day
Martin Scorsese/The Age of Innocence
1995
★Robert Zemeckis/Forrest Gump
Robert Redford/Quiz Show
Oliver Stone/Natural Born Killers
Quentin Tarantino/Pulp Fiction
Edward Zwick/Legends of the Fall
1996
★Mel Gibson/Braveheart
Mike Figgis/Leaving Las Vegas
Ron Howard/Apollo 13
Ang Lee/Sense and Sensibility
Rob Reiner/The American President
Martin Scorsese/Casino
1997
★Milos Forman/The People vs. Larry Flynt
Joel Coen/Fargo
Scott Hicks/Shine
Anthony Minghella/The English Patient
Alan Parker/Evita
1998
★James Cameron/Titanic
James L. Brooks/As Good As It Gets
Curtis Hanson/L.A. Confidential
Jim Sheridan/The Boxer
Steven Spielberg/Amistad
1999
★Steven Spielberg/Saving Private Ryan
Shekhar Kapur/Elizabeth
John Madden/Shakespeare in Love
Robert Redford/The Horse Whisperer
Peter Weir/The Truman Show
2000
★Sam Mendes/American Beauty
Norman Jewison/The Hurricane
Neil Jordan/The End of the Affair
Michael Mann/The Insider
Anthony Minghella/The Talented Mr. Ripley
2001
★Ang Lee/Crouching Tiger, Hidden Dragon
2002
★Robert Altman/Gosford Park
Ron Howard/A Beautiful Mind
Peter Jackson/Lord of the Rings: The Fellowship of the Ring
Baz Luhrmann/Moulin Rouge
David Lynch/Mulholland Drive
Steven Spielberg/A. I.: Artificial Intelligence
2003
★Martin Scorsese/Gangs of New York
Stephen Daldry/The Hours
Peter Jackson/Lord of the Rings: The Two Towers
Spike Jonze/Adaptation
Rob Marshall/Chicago
Alexander Payne/About Schmidt

★ = winner

2004
★Peter Jackson/*Lord of the Rings: The Return of the King*
Sofia Coppola/*Lost in Translation*
Clint Eastwood/*Mystic River*
Anthony Minghella/*Cold Mountain*
Peter Weir/*Master and Commander: The Far Side of the World*

2005
★Clint Eastwood/*Million Dollar Baby*
Woody Allen/*Match Point*
Marc Forster/*Finding Neverland*
Mike Nichols/*Closer*
Alexander Payne/*Sideways*
Martin Scorsese/*The Aviator*

2006
★Ang Lee/*Brokeback Mountain*
George Clooney/*Good Night, and Good Luck*
Peter Jackson/*King Kong*
Fernando Meirelles/*The Constant Gardener*
Steven Spielberg/*Munich*

2007
★Martin Scorsese/*The Departed*
Clint Eastwood/*Flags of Our Fathers*
Clint Eastwood/*Letters from Iwo Jima*
Stephen Frears/*The Queen*
Alejandro Gonzalez Inarritu/*Babel*

2008
★Julian Schnabel/*The Diving Bell and the Butterfly*
Tim Burton/*Sweeney Todd: The Demon Barber of Fleet Street*
Ethan Coen/*No Country for Old Men*
Joel Coen/*No Country for Old Men*
Ridley Scott/*American Gangster*
Joe Wright/*Atonement*

2009
★Danny Boyle/*Slumdog Millionaire*
Stephen Daldry/*The Reader*
David Fincher/*The Curious Case of Benjamin Button*
Ron Howard/*Frost/Nixon*
Sam Mendes/*Revolutionary Road*

2010
★James Cameron/*Avatar*
Kathryn Bigelow/*The Hurt Locker*
Clint Eastwood/*Invictus*
Jason Reitman/*Up in the Air*
Quentin Tarantino/*Inglourious Basterds*

2011
★David Fincher/*The Social Network*
Darren Aronofsky/*Black Swan*
Tom Hooper/*The King's Speech*
Christopher Nolan/*Inception*
David O. Russell/*The Fighter*

2012
★Martin Scorsese/*Hugo*
Woody Allen/*Midnight in Paris*
George Clooney/*The Ides of March*
Michel Hazanavicius/*The Artist*
Alexander Payne/*The Descendants*

2013
★Ben Affleck/*Argo*
Kathryn Bigelow/*Zero Dark Thirty*
Steven Spielberg/*Lincoln*
Quentin Tarantino/*Django Unchained*

2014
★Alfonso Cuarón/*Gravity*
Paul Greengrass/*Captain Phillips*
Steve McQueen/*12 Years a Slave*
Alexander Payne/*Nebraska*
David O. Russell/*American Hustle*

2015
★Richard Linklater/*Boyhood*
Wes Anderson/*The Grand Budapest Hotel*
Ava DuVernay/*Selma*
David Fincher/*Gone Girl*
Alejandro Gonzalez Inarritu/*Birdman, or (The Unexpected Virtue of Ignorance)*

2016
★Alejandro Gonzalez Inarritu/*The Revenant*
Todd Haynes/*Carol*
Tom McCarthy/*Spotlight*
George Miller/*Mad Max: Fury Road*
Ridley Scott/*The Martian*

2017
★Damien Chazelle/*La La Land*
Tom Ford/*Nocturnal Animals*
Mel Gibson/*Hacksaw Ridge*
Barry Jenkins/*Moonlight*
Kenneth Lonergan/*Manchester by the Sea*

2018
★Alfonso Cuarón/*Roma*
★Guillermo del Toro/*The Shape of Water*
Martin McDonagh/*Three Billboards Outside Ebbing, Missouri*
Christopher Nolan/*Dunkirk*
Ridley Scott/*All the Money in the World*
Steven Spielberg/*The Post*

2019
Bradley Cooper/*A Star Is Born*
Peter Farrelly/*Green Book*
Spike Lee/*BlacKkKlansman*
Adam McKay/*Vice*

2020
★Sam Mendes/*1917*
Joon-ho Bong/*Parasite*
Todd Phillips/*Joker*
Martin Scorsese/*The Irishman*
Quentin Tarantino/*Once Upon A Time... In Hollywood*

SCORE

1948
★*Life with Father*

1949
★*The Red Shoes*

1950
★*The Inspector General*

1951
★*Sunset Boulevard*

1952
★*September Affair*

1953
★*High Noon*

1960
★*On the Beach*

1961
★*The Alamo*

1962
★*The Guns of Navarone*

1963
★*To Kill a Mockingbird*

1965
★*The Fall of the Roman Empire*

1966
★*Doctor Zhivago*

1967
★*Hawaii*

1968
★*Camelot*

1969
★*The Shoes of the Fisherman*

1970
★*Butch Cassidy and the Sundance Kid*

1971
★*Love Story*

1972
★*Shaft*

1973
★*The Godfather*

1974
★*Jonathan Livingston Seagull*

1975
★*The Little Prince*

1976
★*Jaws*

1977
★*A Star Is Born*

1978
★*Star Wars*

1979
★*Midnight Express*

1980
★*Apocalypse Now*

1981
★*The Stunt Man*

1983
★*E.T.: The Extra-Terrestrial*

1984
★*Flashdance*

1985
★*A Passage to India*

1986
★*Out of Africa*

1987
★*The Mission*

1988
★*The Last Emperor*

1989
★*Gorillas in the Mist*

1990
★*The Little Mermaid*

1991
★*The Sheltering Sky*

1993
★*Aladdin*

1994
★*Heaven and Earth*
The Nightmare Before Christmas
The Piano
Schindler's List
Trois Couleurs: Bleu

1995
★*The Lion King*
Forrest Gump
Interview with the Vampire
Legends of the Fall
Nell

1996
★*A Walk in the Clouds*
Braveheart
Don Juan DeMarco
Pocahontas
Sense and Sensibility

1997
★*The English Patient*
The Hunchback of Notre Dame
Michael Collins
The Mirror Has Two Faces
Shine

1998
★*Titanic*
Gattaca
Kundun
L.A. Confidential
Seven Years in Tibet

1999
★*The Truman Show*
A Bug's Life
Mulan
Prince of Egypt
Saving Private Ryan

2000
★*The Legend of 1900*

2001
★*Gladiator*

2002
★*Moulin Rouge*
A. I.: Artificial Intelligence
Ali
A Beautiful Mind
Lord of the Rings: The Fellowship of the Ring
Mulholland Drive
Pearl Harbor
The Shipping News

2003
★*Frida*
★*25th Hour*
Far from Heaven
The Hours
Rabbit-Proof Fence

2017
★*La La Land*
Arrival
Hidden Figures
Lion
Moonlight

ORIGINAL SCORE

1985
Once Upon a Time in America

2000
American Beauty
Angela's Ashes
Anna and the King
The End of the Affair
Eyes Wide Shut
The Insider
The Straight Story
The Talented Mr. Ripley

2004
★*Lord of the Rings: The Return of the King*
Big Fish
Cold Mountain
Girl with a Pearl Earring
The Last Samurai

2005
★*The Aviator*
Finding Neverland
Million Dollar Baby
Sideways
Spanglish

2006
★*Memoirs of a Geisha*
Brokeback Mountain
The Chronicles of Narnia: The Lion, the Witch and the Wardrobe
King Kong
Syriana

2007
★*The Painted Veil*
Babel
The Da Vinci Code
The Fountain

2008
★*Atonement*
Eastern Promises
Grace Is Gone
Into the Wild
The Kite Runner

2009
★*Slumdog Millionaire*
Changeling
The Curious Case of Benjamin Button
Defiance
Frost/Nixon

2010
★*Up*
Avatar
The Informant!
A Single Man
Where the Wild Things Are

2011
★*The Social Network*
Alice in Wonderland
Inception
The King's Speech
127 Hours

2012
★*The Artist*
The Girl With the Dragon Tattoo
Hugo
War Horse
W.E.

2013
★*Life of Pi*
Anna Karenina
Argo
Cloud Atlas

2014
★*All is Lost*
The Book Thief
Gravity
Mandela: Long Walk to Freedom
12 Years a Slave

2015
★*The Theory of Everything*
Birdman, or (The Unexpected Virtue of Ignorance)
Gone Girl
The Imitation Game
Interstellar

2016
★*The Hateful Eight*
Carol
The Danish Girl
The Revenant
Steve Jobs

2018
★*The Shape of Water*
Dunkirk
Phantom Thread
The Post
Three Billboards Outside Ebbing, Missouri

2019
★*First Man*
Black Panther
Isle of Dogs
Mary Poppins Returns
A Quiet Place

2020
★*Joker*
Little Women
Marriage Story
Motherless Brooklyn
1917

SONG

1961
★"Town without Pity"/*Town without Pity*

1965
★"Circus World"/*Circus World*

1968
★"If Ever I Should Leave You"/*Camelot*

1969
★"The Windmills of Your Mind"/*The Thomas Crown Affair*

1970
★"Jean"/*The Prime of Miss Jean Brodie*

1971
★"Whistling Away the Dark"/*Darling Lili*

1972
★"Life Is What You Make It"/*Kotch*

1974
★"The Way We Were"/*The Way We Were*

1975
★"I Feel Love"/*Benji*

1976
★"I'm Easy"/*Nashville*

1977
★"Evergreen"/*A Star Is Born*

1978
★"You Light Up My Life"/*You Light Up My Life*

1980
★"The Rose"/*The Rose*

1981
★"Fame"/*Fame*

1982
★"Arthur's Theme"/*Arthur*

1983
★"Up Where We Belong"/*An Officer and a Gentleman*

1984
★"Flashdance. . .What a Feeling"/*Flashdance*

1985
★"I Just Called to Say I Love You"/*The Woman in Red*

1986
★"Say You, Say Me"/*White Nights*

1987
★"Take My Breath Away"/*Top Gun*

1988
★"(I've Had) the Time of My Life"/*Dirty Dancing*

1989
★"Let the River Run"/*Working Girl*

1990
★"Under the Sea"/*The Little Mermaid*

1991
★"Blaze of Glory"/*Young Guns 2*

1993
★"A Whole New World"/*Aladdin*

★ = winner

Golden Globe Awards

1994
★"Streets of Philadelphia"/*Philadelphia*
"Again"/*Poetic Justice*
"Stay"/*Faraway, So Close!*
"The Day I Fall in Love"/*Beethoven's 2nd*
"(You Made Me the) Thief of Your Heart"/*In the Name of the Father*
1995
★"Can You Feel the Love Tonight?"/*The Lion King*
"Circle of Life"/*The Lion King*
"Far Longer than Forever"/*The Swan Princess*
"I'll Remember"/*With Honors*
"Look What Love Has Done"/*Junior*
"The Color of the Night"/*Color of Night*
1996
★"Colors of the Wind"/*Pocahontas*
"Have You Ever Really Loved a Woman?"/*Don Juan DeMarco*
"Hold Me, Thrill Me, Kiss Me, Kill Me"/*Batman Forever*
"Moonlight"/*Sabrina*
"You Got a Friend in Me"/*Toy Story*
1997
★"You Must Love Me"/*Evita*
"Because You Loved Me"/*Up Close and Personal*
"For the First Time"/*One Fine Day*
"I've Finally Found Someone"/*The Mirror Has Two Faces*
"That Thing You Do!"/*That Thing You Do!*
1998
★"My Heart Will Go On"/*Titanic*
"Go the Distance"/*Hercules*
"Journey to the Past"/*Anastasia*
"Once Upon a December"/*Anastasia*
"Tomorrow Never Dies"/*Tomorrow Never Dies*
1999
★"The Prayer"/*Quest for Camelot*
"Reflection"/*Mulan*
"The Flame Still Burns"/*Still Crazy*
"The Magic Sword"/*Quest for Camelot*
"The Mighty"/*The Mighty*
"Uninvited"/*City of Angels*
"When You Believe"/*Prince of Egypt*
2000
★"You'll Be In My Heart"/*Tarzan*
"Beautiful Stranger"/*Austin Powers 2: The Spy Who Shagged Me*
"How Can I Not Love You"/*Anna and the King*
"Save Me"/*Magnolia*
"When She Loved Me"/*Toy Story 2*
2001
★"Things Have Changed"/*Wonder Boys*
2002
★"Until"/*Kate & Leopold*
"Come What May"/*Moulin Rouge*
"May It Be"/*Lord of the Rings: The Fellowship of the Ring*
"There You'll Be"/*Pearl Harbor*
"Vanilla Sky"/*Vanilla Sky*
2003
★"The Hands That Built America"/*Gangs of New York*
"Die Another Day"/*Die Another Day*
"Father and Daughter"/*The Wild Thornberrys Movie*
"Here I Am"/*Spirit: Stallion of the Cimarron*
"Lose Yourself"/*8 Mile*
2004
★"Into the West"/*Lord of the Rings: The Return of the King*
"Man of the Hour"/*Big Fish*
"The Heart of Every Girl"/*Mona Lisa Smile*
"Time Enough for Tears"/*In America*
"You Will Be My Ain True Love"/*Cold Mountain*
2005
★"Old Habits Die Hard"/*Alfie*
"Accidently in Love"/*Shrek 2*
"Believe"/*The Polar Express*
"Learn to be Lonely"/*The Phantom of the Opera*
"Million Voices"/*Hotel Rwanda*
2006
★"A Love That Will Never Grow Old"/*Brokeback Mountain*
"There's Nothing Like a Show on Broadway"/*The Producers*
"Travelin' Thru"/*Transamerica*
"Wunderkind"/*The Chronicles of Narnia: The Lion, the Witch and the Wardrobe*
2007
★"The Song of the Heart"/*Happy Feet*
"A Father's Way"/*The Pursuit of Happyness*
"Listen"/*Dreamgirls*
"Never Gonna Break My Faith"/*Bobby*
2008
★"Guaranteed"/*Into the Wild*
"Grace is Gone"/*Grace Is Gone*
"That's How You Know"/*Enchanted*
"Walk Hard"/*Walk Hard: The Dewey Cox Story*
2009
★"The Wrestler"/*The Wrestler*
"Down to Earth"/*WALL-E*
"Gran Torino"/*Gran Torino*
"I Thought I Lost You"/*Bolt*
"Once in a Lifetime"/*Cadillac Records*
2010
★"The Weary Kind"/*Crazy Heart*
"Cinema Italiano"/*Nine*
"I See You"/*Avatar*
"(I Want to) Come Home"/*Everybody's Fine*
"Winter"/*Brothers*
2011
★"You Haven't Seen the Last of Me"/*Burlesque*
"Bound to You"/*Burlesque*
"Coming Home"/*Country Strong*
"I See the Light"/*Tangled*
"There's a Place For Us"/*The Chronicles of Narnia: The Voyage of the Dawn Treader*
2012
★"Masterpiece"/*W.E.*
"Hello Hello"/*Gnomeo & Juliet*
"Lay Your Heart Down"/*Albert Nobbs*
"The Keeper"/*Machine Gun Preacher*
"The Living Proof"/*The Help*
2013
★"Skyfall"/*Skyfall*
"For You"/*Act of Valor*
"Not Running Anymore"/*Stand Up Guys*
"Safe and Sound"/*The Hunger Games*
"Suddenly"/*Les Miserables*
2014
★"Ordinary Love"/*Mandela: Long Walk to Freedom*
"Atlas"/*The Hunger Games: Catching Fire*
"Let It Go"/*Frozen*
"Please Mr. Kennedy"/*Inside Llewyn Davis*
2015
★"Glory"/*Selma*
"Big Eyes"/*Big Eyes*
"Mercy Is"/*Noah*
"Opportunity"/*Annie*
2016
★"Writing's on the Wall"/*Spectre*
"Love Me Like You Do"/*Fifty Shades of Grey*
"One Kind of Love"/*Love & Mercy*
"See You Again"/*Furious 7*
"Simple Song #3"/*Youth*
2017
★"City of Stars"/*La La Land*
"Can't Stop the Feeling"/*Trolls*
"Faith"/*Sing*
"Gold"/*Gold*
"How Far I'll Go"/*Moana*
2018
★"This Is Me"/*The Greatest Showman*
"Home"/*Ferdinand*
"Mighty River"/*Mudbound*
"Remember Me"/*Coco*
"The Star"/*The Star*
2019
★"Shallow"/*A Star Is Born*
"All the Stars"/*Black Panther*
"Requiem for A Private War"/*A Private War*
"Revelation"/*Boy Erased*
2020
★"I'm Gonna Love Me Again"/*Rocketman*
"Beautiful Ghosts"/*Cats*
"Into the Unknown"/*Frozen II*
"Spirit"/*The Lion King*
"Stand Up"/*Harriet*

SCREENPLAY

1948
★*Miracle on 34th Street*
1949
★*The Search*
1950
★*Battleground*
1951
★*All About Eve*
1953
★*Five Fingers*
1954
★*Lili*
1955
★*Sabrina*
1966
★*Doctor Zhivago*
1967
★*A Man for All Seasons*
1968
★*In the Heat of the Night*
1969
★*Charly*
1970
★*Anne of the Thousand Days*
1971
★*Love Story*
1972
★*The Hospital*
1973
★*The Godfather*
1974
★*The Exorcist*
1975
★*Chinatown*
1976
★*One Flew Over the Cuckoo's Nest*
1977
★*Network*
1978
★*The Goodbye Girl*
1979
★*Midnight Express*
1980
★*Kramer vs. Kramer*
1981
★*The Ninth Configuration*
1982
★*On Golden Pond*
1983
★*Gandhi*
1984
★*Terms of Endearment*
1985
★*Amadeus*
1986
★*The Purple Rose of Cairo*
1987
★*The Mission*
1988
★*The Last Emperor*
1989
★*Running on Empty*
1990
★*Born on the Fourth of July*
Goodfellas
1991
★*Dances with Wolves*
1993
★*Scent of a Woman*
1994
★*Schindler's List*
Philadelphia
The Piano
The Remains of the Day
Short Cuts
1995
★*Pulp Fiction*
Forrest Gump
Four Weddings and a Funeral
Mr. Holland's Opus
Quiz Show
The Shawshank Redemption
1996
★*Sense and Sensibility*
The American President
Braveheart
Dead Man Walking
Get Shorty
1997
★*The People vs. Larry Flynt*
The English Patient
Fargo
Lone Star
Shine
1998
★*Good Will Hunting*
As Good As It Gets
L.A. Confidential
Titanic
Wag the Dog
1999
★*Shakespeare in Love*
Bulworth
Happiness
Saving Private Ryan
The Truman Show
2000
★*American Beauty*
Being John Malkovich
The Cider House Rules
The Insider
The Sixth Sense
2001
★*Traffic*
2002
★*A Beautiful Mind*
Gosford Park
The Man Who Wasn't There
Memento
Mulholland Drive
2003
★*About Schmidt*
Adaptation
Chicago
Far from Heaven
The Hours
2004
★*Lost in Translation*
Cold Mountain
In America
Love Actually
Mystic River
2005
★*Sideways*
The Aviator
Closer
Eternal Sunshine of the Spotless Mind
Finding Neverland
2006
★*Brokeback Mountain*
Crash
Good Night, and Good Luck
Match Point
Munich
2007
★*The Queen*
Babel
The Departed
Little Children
Notes on a Scandal
2008
★*No Country for Old Men*
Atonement
Charlie Wilson's War
The Diving Bell and the Butterfly
Juno
2009
★*Slumdog Millionaire*
The Curious Case of Benjamin Button
Doubt
Frost/Nixon
The Reader
2010
★*Up in the Air*
District 9
The Hurt Locker
Inglourious Basterds
It's Complicated
2011
★*The Social Network*
Inception
The Kids Are All Right
The King's Speech
127 Hours
2012
★*Midnight in Paris*
The Artist
The Descendants
The Ides of March
Moneyball
2013
★*Django Unchained*
Argo
Lincoln
Silver Linings Playbook
Zero Dark Thirty
2014
★*Her*
American Hustle
Nebraska
Philomena
12 Years a Slave
2015
★*Birdman, or (The Unexpected Virtue of Ignorance)*
Boyhood
Gone Girl
The Grand Budapest Hotel
The Imitation Game
2016
★*Steve Jobs*
The Big Short
The Hateful Eight
Room
Spotlight
2017
★*La La Land*
Hell or High Water
Manchester by the Sea
Moonlight
Nocturnal Animals
2018
★*Three Billboards Outside Ebbing, Missouri*
Lady Bird
Molly's Game
The Post
The Shape of Water
Aaron Sorkin/*Molly's Game*
2019
★*Green Book*
The Favourite
If Beale Street Could Talk
Roma
Vice
2020
★*Once Upon A Time... In Hollywood*
The Irishman
Marriage Story
Parasite
The Two Popes

FILM—FOREIGN LANGUAGE

1950
★*The Bicycle Thief*
1955
★*Genevieve*
1956
★*Ordet*

★ = winner

1957
★Richard III
★War and Peace
1959
★A Night to Remember
1960
★Black Orpheus
★Wild Strawberries
1961
★The Virgin Spring
1962
★Two Women
1963
★Divorce-Italian Style
1964
★Tom Jones
1965
★Marriage Italian Style
★Sallah
1966
★Darling
1967
★Alfie
★A Man and a Woman
1969
★Romeo and Juliet
★War and Peace
1970
★Oh! What a Lovely War
★Z
1971
★Rider on the Rain
★Women in Love
1972
★Sunday, Bloody Sunday
1973
★Young Winston
1975
★Scenes from a Marriage
1977
★Face to Face
1978
★A Special Day
1979
★Autumn Sonata
1980
★La Cage aux Folles
1981
★Tess
1982
★Chariots of Fire
1983
★Gandhi
1984
★Fanny and Alexander
1985
★A Passage to India
1986
★The Official Story
1988
★My Life As a Dog
1989
★Pelle the Conqueror
1990
★Cinema Paradiso
1991
★Cyrano de Bergerac
1992
★Europa, Europa
1993
★Indochine
1994
★Farewell My Concubine
Flight of the Innocent
Trois Couleurs: Bleu
The Wedding Banquet

1995
★Farinelli
Eat Drink Man Woman
Queen Margot
To Live
Trois Couleurs: Rouge
1996
Brother of Sleep
French Twist
Shanghai Triad
1997
★Kolya
Prisoner of the Mountains
Ridicule
1998
★Ma Vie en Rose
Artemisia
The Best Man
Lea
The Thief
1999
★Central Station
The Celebration
Hombres Armados
2000
★All About My Mother
The Red Violin
2001
★Crouching Tiger, Hidden Dragon
Amores Perros
The Widow of Saint-Pierre
2002
Amelie
Monsoon Wedding
2003
★Talk to Her
City of God
The Crime of Father Amaro
2004
The Barbarian Invasions
2005
★The Sea Inside
House of Flying Daggers
The Motorcycle Diaries
A Very Long Engagement
2006
★Paradise Now
Tsotsi
2007
★Letters from Iwo Jima
Apocalypto
Pan's Labyrinth
Volver
2008
★The Diving Bell and the Butterfly
The Kite Runner
Lust, Caution
2009
★Waltz with Bashir
I've Loved You So Long
2010
★The White Ribbon
Baaria
Broken Embraces
The Maid
A Prophet
2011
★In a Better World
Biutiful
The Concert
The Edge
I Am Love
2012
★A Separation
The Flowers of War
In the Land of Blood and Honey
The Kid with a Bike
Kon-Tiki
The Skin I Live In

2013
★Amour
The Intouchables
A Royal Affair
Rust and Bone
2014
★The Great Beauty
Blue is the Warmest Color
The Hunt
The Past
2015
★Leviathan
Force Majeure
Ida
2016
★Son of Saul
The Brand New Testament
The Club
The Fencer
Mustang
2017
★Elle
Neruda
The Salesman
Toni Erdmann
2018
★In the Fade
A Fantastic Woman
First They Killed My Father
Loveless
The Square
2019
★Roma
Capernaum
Girl
Never Look Away
Shoplifters
2020
★Parasite
The Farewell
Les Misérables
Pain and Glory
Portrait of a Lady on Fire

ANIMATED FILM

2007
★Cars
Happy Feet
Monster House
2008
★Ratatouille
Bee Movie
The Simpsons Movie
2009
★WALL-E
Bolt
Kung Fu Panda
2010
★Up
Cloudy with a Chance of Meatballs
Coraline
Fantastic Mr. Fox
The Princess and the Frog
2011
★Toy Story 3
Despicable Me
How to Train Your Dragon
The Illusionist
Tangled
2012
★The Adventures of Tintin
Arthur Christmas
Cars 2
Puss in Boots
Rango

2013
★Brave
Frankenweenie
Hotel Transylvania
Rise of the Guardians
Wreck-It Ralph
2014
★Frozen
The Croods
Despicable Me 2
2015
★How to Train Your Dragon 2
Big Hero 6
The Book of Life
The Boxtrolls
The Lego Movie
2016
★Inside Out
Anomalisa
The Good Dinosaur
The Peanuts Movie
Shaun the Sheep Movie
2017
★Zootopia
Kubo and the Two Strings
Moana
My Life as a Zucchini
Sing
2018
★Coco
The Boss Baby
The Breadwinner
Ferdinand
Loving Vincent
2019
★Spider-Man: Into the Spider-Verse
Incredibles 2
Isle of Dogs
Mirai
Ralph Breaks the Internet
2020
★Missing Link
Frozen II
How to Train Your Dragon: The Hidden World
The Lion King
Toy Story 4

GOLDEN RASPBERRY AWARDS

WORST PICTURE

1980
★Can't Stop the Music
1981
★Mommie Dearest
1984
★Bolero
1985
★Rambo: First Blood, Part 2
1986
★Howard the Duck
★Under the Cherry Moon
1987
★Leonard Part 6
1988
★Cocktail
1989
★Star Trek 5: The Final Frontier
1990
★The Adventures of Ford Fairlane
1991
★Hudson Hawk
1992
★Shining Through
1993
★Indecent Proposal

1994
★Color of Night
On Deadly Ground
The Specialist
Wyatt Earp
1995
★Showgirls
Congo
It's Pat: The Movie
Waterworld
1996
★Striptease
Barb Wire
Ed
The Island of Dr. Moreau
The Stupids
1997
★The Postman
Anaconda
Batman and Robin
Fire Down Below
Speed 2: Cruise Control
1998
★An Alan Smithee Film: Burn, Hollywood, Burn
Armageddon
The Avengers
Godzilla
Spice World: The Movie
1999
★Wild Wild West
Big Daddy
The Blair Witch Project
The Haunting
Star Wars: Episode 1-The Phantom Menace
2000
★Battlefield Earth
Book of Shadows: Blair Witch 2
The Flintstones in Viva Rock Vegas
Little Nicky
The Next Best Thing
2001
★Freddy Got Fingered
2002
★Swept Away
2003
★Gigli
Charlie's Angels: Full Throttle
Dr. Seuss' The Cat in the Hat
From Justin to Kelly
2004
★Catwoman
Alexander
Superbabies: Baby Geniuses 2
Surviving Christmas
White Chicks
2005
★Dirty Love
Deuce Bigalow: European Gigolo
The Dukes of Hazzard
House of Wax
Son of the Mask
2006
★Basic Instinct 2
BloodRayne
Lady in the Water
Little Man
The Wicker Man
2007
★I Know Who Killed Me
Bratz
Daddy Day Camp
I Now Pronounce You Chuck and Larry
Norbit

2008
★The Love Guru
Disaster Movie
The Happening
The Hottie and the Nottie
In the Name of the King: A Dungeon Siege Tale
Meet the Spartans
2009
★Transformers: Revenge of the Fallen
All About Steve
G.I. Joe: The Rise of Cobra
Land of the Lost
Old Dogs
2010
★The Last Airbender
The Bounty Hunter
Sex and the City 2
The Twilight Saga: Eclipse
Vampires Suck
2011
★Jack and Jill
Bucky Larson: Born to Be a Star
New Year's Eve
Transformers: Dark of the Moon
The Twilight Saga: Breaking Dawn, Part 1
2012
★The Twilight Saga: Breaking Dawn, Part 2
Battleship
The Oogieloves in the Big Balloon Adventure
That's My Boy
A Thousand Words
2013
★Movie 43
After Earth
Grown Ups 2
The Lone Ranger
Tyler Perry's A Madea Christmas
2014
★Saving Christmas
Left Behind
The Legend of Hercules
Teenage Mutant Ninja Turtles
Transformers: Age of Extinction
2015
★Fantastic Four
★Fifty Shades of Grey
Jupiter Ascending
Paul Blart: Mall Cop 2
Pixels
2016
★Hillary's America: The Secret History of the Democratic Party
Batman v Superman: Dawn of Justice
Dirty Grandpa
Gods of Egypt
Independence Day: Resurgence
Zoolander 2
2017
★The Emoji Movie
Baywatch
Fifty Shades Darker
The Mummy
Transformers: The Last Knight
2018
★Holmes & Watson
Gotti
The Happytime Murders
Robin Hood
Winchester

★ = winner

2019
★*Cats*
The Fanatic
The Haunting of Sharon Tate
A Madea Family Funeral
Rambo: Last Blood

WORST REMAKE

2006
★*Little Man*
The Pink Panther
Poseidon
The Shaggy Dog
The Wicker Man

2007
★*I Know Who Killed Me*
Are We Done Yet?
Bratz
Epic Movie
Who's Your Caddy?

2009
★*Land of the Lost*
G.I. Joe: The Rise of Cobra
The Pink Panther 2

WORST REMAKE/ SEQUEL

1994
★*Wyatt Earp*
The Flintstones

1995
★*The Scarlet Letter*

1997
★*Speed 2: Cruise Control*
Batman and Robin
Home Alone 3
The Lost World: Jurassic Park 2
McHale's Navy

1998
★*The Avengers*
★*Godzilla*
★*Psycho*
Godzilla
Lost in Space
Meet Joe Black
Psycho

2000
★*Book of Shadows: Blair Witch 2*
Dr. Seuss' How the Grinch Stole Christmas
The Flintstones in Viva Rock Vegas
Get Carter
Mission: Impossible 2

2001
★*Planet of the Apes*

2003
★*Charlie's Angels: Full Throttle*
Dumb and Dumberer: When Harry Met Lloyd
From Justin to Kelly
The Texas Chainsaw Massacre
2 Fast 2 Furious

2004
★*Scooby-Doo 2: Monsters Unleashed*
Alien vs. Predator
Anacondas: The Hunt for the Blood Orchid
Around the World in 80 Days
Exorcist: The Beginning

2005
★*Son of the Mask*
Bewitched
Deuce Bigalow: European Gigolo
The Dukes of Hazzard
House of Wax

2011
★*Ripoff of 'Glen or Glenda'/ Jack and Jill*
Arthur
The Hangover, Part 2
Rip-off of 'Boogie Nights' and 'A Star is Born'/Bucky Larson: Born to Be a Star
The Twilight Saga: Breaking Dawn, Part 1

2012
★*The Twilight Saga: Breaking Dawn, Part 2*
Ghost Rider: Spirit of Vengeance
Madea's Witness Protection
Piranha 3DD

2013
★*The Lone Ranger*
Grown Ups 2
The Hangover, Part III
Scary Movie 5
The Smurfs 2

2014
★*Annie*
Atlas Shrugged 3: Who Is John Galt?
The Legend of Hercules
Teenage Mutant Ninja Turtles
Transformers: Age of Extinction

2015
★*Fantastic Four*
Alvin and the Chipmunks: Road Chip
Hot Tub Time Machine 2
The Human Centipede 3: The Final Sequence
Paul Blart: Mall Cop 2

2016
Alice Through the Looking Glass
Fifty Shades of Black

2017
★*Fifty Shades Darker*
Baywatch
Boo 2! A Madea Halloween
The Mummy
Transformers: The Last Knight

2018
★*Holmes & Watson*
Death of a Nation
Death Wish
The Meg
Robin Hood

2019
★*Rambo: Last Blood*
Dark Phoenix
Godzilla: King of the Monsters
Hellboy
A Madea Family Funeral

WORST SEQUEL/ PREQUEL

2006
★*Basic Instinct 2*
Big Momma's House 2
Garfield: A Tail of Two Kitties
The Santa Clause 3: The Escape Clause
The Texas Chainsaw Massacre: The Beginning

2007
★*Daddy Day Camp*
Aliens vs. Predator: Requiem
Evan Almighty
Hannibal Rising
Hostel: Part 2

2008
★*Indiana Jones and the Kingdom of the Crystal Skull*
The Day the Earth Stood Still
Disaster Movie
Meet the Spartans
Speed Racer
Star Wars: The Clone Wars

2009
The Pink Panther 2
Transformers: Revenge of the Fallen
The Twilight Saga: New Moon

2010
★*Sex and the City 2*
Clash of the Titans
The Last Airbender
The Twilight Saga: Eclipse

2016
★*Batman v Superman: Dawn of Justice*
Independence Day: Resurgence
Teenage Mutant Ninja Turtles: Out of the Shadows
Zoolander 2

WORST ENSEMBLE CAST

2011
★*Jack and Jill*
Bucky Larson: Born to Be a Star
New Year's Eve
Transformers: Dark of the Moon
The Twilight Saga: Breaking Dawn, Part 1

2012
★*The Twilight Saga: Breaking Dawn, Part 2*
Battleship
Madea's Witness Protection
The Oogieloves in the Big Balloon Adventure
That's My Boy

2013
★*After Earth*
Grown Ups 2
Movie 43
Scary Movie 5
Tyler Perry's A Madea Christmas

WORST ACTOR

1980
★Neil Diamond/*The Jazz Singer*

1981
★Klinton Spilsbury/*Legend of the Lone Ranger*

1983
★Christopher Atkins/*A Night in Heaven*

1984
★Sylvester Stallone/ *Rhinestone*

1985
★Sylvester Stallone/*Rambo: First Blood, Part 2*
★Sylvester Stallone/*Rocky 4*

1986
★Prince/*Under the Cherry Moon*

1987
★Bill Cosby/*Leonard Part 6*

1988
★Sylvester Stallone/*Rambo 3*

1989
★William Shatner/*Star Trek 5: The Final Frontier*

1990
★Andrew Silverstein/*The Adventures of Ford Fairlane*

1991
★Kevin Costner/*Robin Hood: Prince of Thieves*

1992
★Sylvester Stallone/*Stop! or My Mom Will Shoot*

1993
★Burt Reynolds/*Cop and a Half*

1994
★Kevin Costner/*Wyatt Earp*
Macaulay Culkin/*Getting Even with Dad*
Macaulay Culkin/*The Pagemaster*
Macaulay Culkin/*Richie Rich*
Bruce Willis/*Color of Night*

1995
★Pauly Shore/*Jury Duty*
Kevin Costner/*Waterworld*
Kyle MacLachlan/*Showgirls*
Sylvester Stallone/*Assassins*
Sylvester Stallone/*Judge Dredd*

1996
★Tom Arnold/*Big Bully*
★Tom Arnold/*Carpool*
★Tom Arnold/*The Stupids*
★Pauly Shore/*Bio-Dome*
Keanu Reeves/*Chain Reaction*
Adam Sandler/*Bulletproof*
Adam Sandler/*Happy Gilmore*
Sylvester Stallone/*Daylight*

1997
★Kevin Costner/*The Postman*
Val Kilmer/*The Saint*
Shaquille O'Neal/*Steel*
Steven Seagal/*Fire Down Below*
Jon Voight/*Anaconda*

1998
★Bruce Willis/*Armageddon*
★Bruce Willis/*Mercury Rising*
★Bruce Willis/*The Siege*
Ralph Fiennes/*The Avengers*
Ryan O'Neal/*An Alan Smithee Film: Burn, Hollywood, Burn*
Ryan Phillippe/*54*
Adam Sandler/*The Waterboy*

1999
★Adam Sandler/*Big Daddy*
Kevin Costner/*For Love of the Game*
Kevin Costner/*Message in a Bottle*
Kevin Kline/*Wild Wild West*
Arnold Schwarzenegger/*End of Days*
Robin Williams/*Bicentennial Man*
Robin Williams/*Jakob the Liar*

2000
★John Travolta/*Battlefield Earth*
Leonardo DiCaprio/*The Beach*
Adam Sandler/*Little Nicky*
Arnold Schwarzenegger/*The 6th Day*
Sylvester Stallone/*Get Carter*

2001
★Tom Green/*Freddy Got Fingered*

2002
★Roberto Benigni/*Pinocchio*

2003
★Ben Affleck/*Daredevil*
★Ben Affleck/*Gigli*
★Ben Affleck/*Paycheck*
Cuba Gooding, Jr./*Boat Trip*
Cuba Gooding, Jr./*The Fighting Temptations*
Cuba Gooding, Jr./*Radio*
Justin Guarini/*From Justin to Kelly*
Ashton Kutcher/*Cheaper by the Dozen*
Ashton Kutcher/*Just Married*
Ashton Kutcher/*My Boss's Daughter*
Mike Myers/*Dr. Seuss' The Cat in the Hat*

2004
★George W. Bush/ *Fahrenheit 9/11*
Ben Affleck/*Jersey Girl*
Ben Affleck/*Surviving Christmas*
Vin Diesel/*The Chronicles of Riddick*
Colin Farrell/*Alexander*
Ben Stiller/*Along Came Polly*
Ben Stiller/*Anchorman: The Legend of Ron Burgundy*
Ben Stiller/*Dodgeball: A True Underdog Story*
Ben Stiller/*Envy*
Ben Stiller/*Starsky & Hutch*

2005
★Rob Schneider/*Deuce Bigalow: European Gigolo*
Tom Cruise/*War of the Worlds*
Will Ferrell/*Bewitched*
Dwayne 'The Rock' Johnson/*Doom*
Jamie Kennedy/*Son of the Mask*

2006
★M. Night Shyamalan/*Lady in the Water*
★Marlon Wayans/*Little Man*
★Shawn Wayans/*Little Man*
Tim Allen/*The Santa Clause 3: The Escape Clause*
Tim Allen/*The Shaggy Dog*
Tim Allen/*Zoom*
Nicolas Cage/*The Wicker Man*
Larry the Cable Guy/*Larry the Cable Guy: Health Inspector*
Rob Schneider/*The Benchwarmers*
David Thewlis/*Basic Instinct 2*

2007
★Eddie Murphy/*Norbit*
Nicolas Cage/*Ghost Rider*
Jim Carrey/*The Number 23*
Cuba Gooding, Jr./*Daddy Day Camp*
Adam Sandler/*I Now Pronounce You Chuck and Larry*

2008
★Mike Myers/*The Love Guru*
Larry the Cable Guy/*Witless Protection*
Eddie Murphy/*Meet Dave*
Al Pacino/*88 Minutes*
Al Pacino/*Righteous Kill*
Mark Wahlberg/*The Happening*
Mark Wahlberg/*Max Payne*

2009
★Joe Jonas/*Jonas Brothers: The 3D Concert Experience*
★Kevin Jonas/*Jonas Brothers: The 3D Concert Experience*
★Nick Jonas/*Jonas Brothers: The 3D Concert Experience*
Will Ferrell/*Land of the Lost*
Steve Martin/*The Pink Panther 2*
Eddie Murphy/*Imagine That*
John Travolta/*Old Dogs*

2010
★Ashton Kutcher/*Killers*
★Ashton Kutcher/*Valentine's Day*
Jennifer Aniston/*The Switch*
Jack Black/*Gulliver's Travels*
Gerard Butler/*The Bounty Hunter*
Taylor Lautner/*The Twilight Saga: Eclipse*
Taylor Lautner/*Valentine's Day*
Robert Pattinson/*Remember Me*
Robert Pattinson/*The Twilight Saga: Eclipse*

2011
★Adam Sandler/*Jack and Jill*
★Adam Sandler/*Just Go With It*
Russell Brand/*Arthur*
Nicolas Cage/*Drive Angry*
Nicolas Cage/*Season of the Witch*
Nicolas Cage/*Trespass*
Taylor Lautner/*Abduction*
Taylor Lautner/*The Twilight Saga: Breaking Dawn, Part 1*
Nick Swardson/*Bucky Larson: Born to Be a Star*

2012
★Adam Sandler/*That's My Boy*
Nicolas Cage/*Ghost Rider: Spirit of Vengeance*
Nicolas Cage/*Seeking Justice*
Eddie Murphy/*A Thousand Words*
Robert Pattinson/*The Twilight Saga: Breaking Dawn, Part 2*
Tyler Perry/*Alex Cross*
Tyler Perry/*Tyler Perry's Good Deeds*

2013
★Jaden Smith/*After Earth*
Johnny Depp/*The Lone Ranger*
Ashton Kutcher/*Jobs*
Adam Sandler/*Grown Ups 2*
Sylvester Stallone/*Bullet to the Head*
Sylvester Stallone/*Grudge Match*

2014
★Kirk Cameron/*Saving Christmas*
Nicolas Cage/*Left Behind*
Kellan Lutz/*The Legend of Hercules*
Seth MacFarlane/*A Million Ways to Die In the West*
Adam Sandler/*Blended*

2015
★Jamie Dornan/*Fifty Shades of Grey*
Johnny Depp/*Mortdecai*
Kevin James/*Paul Blart: Mall Cop 2*
Adam Sandler/*The Cobbler*
Adam Sandler/*Pixels*
Channing Tatum/*Jupiter Ascending*

★ = *winner*

2016

★Dinesh D'Souza/*Hillary's America: The Secret History of the Democratic Party*

Ben Affleck/*Batman v Superman: Dawn of Justice*

Gerard Butler/*London Has Fallen*

Robert De Niro/*Dirty Grandpa*

Ben Stiller/*Zoolander 2*

2017

★Tom Cruise/*The Mummy*

Johnny Depp/*Pirates of the Caribbean: Dead Men Tell No Tales*

Jamie Dornan/*Fifty Shades Darker*

Zac Efron/*Baywatch*

Mark Wahlberg/*Daddy's Home 2*

Mark Wahlberg/*Transformers: The Last Knight*

2018

★Donald J. Trump/*Fahrenheit 11/9*

Johnny Depp/*Sherlock Gnomes*

Will Ferrell/*Holmes & Watson*

John Travolta/*Gotti*

Bruce Willis/*Death Wish*

2019

★John Travolta/*The Fanatic*

★John Travolta/*Trading Paint*

James Franco/*Zeroville*

David Harbour/*Hellboy*

Matthew McConaughey/*Serenity*

Sylvester Stallone/*Rambo: Last Blood*

Bruce Willis/*Glass*

WORST ACTRESS

1980

★Brooke Shields/*The Blue Lagoon*

1981

★Bo Derek/*Tarzan, the Ape Man*

★Faye Dunaway/*Mommie Dearest*

1982

★Pia Zadora/*Butterfly*

1984

★Bo Derek/*Bolero*

1985

★Linda Blair/*Night Patrol*

★Linda Blair/*Savage Island*

★Linda Blair/*Savage Streets*

1986

★Madonna/*Shanghai Surprise*

1987

★Madonna/*Who's That Girl?*

★Liza Minnelli/*Arthur 2: On the Rocks*

1988

★Liza Minnelli/*Rent-A-Cop*

1989

★Heather Locklear/*The Return of the Swamp Thing*

1991

★Sean Young/*A Kiss Before Dying*

1992

★Melanie Griffith/*Shining Through*

★Melanie Griffith/*A Stranger Among Us*

1993

★Madonna/*Body of Evidence*

1994

★Sharon Stone/*Intersection*

★Sharon Stone/*The Specialist*

Uma Thurman/*Even Cowgirls Get the Blues*

1995

★Elizabeth Berkley/*Showgirls*

1996

★Demi Moore/*Striptease*

Whoopi Goldberg/*Bogus*

Whoopi Goldberg/*Eddie*

Whoopi Goldberg/*Theodore Rex*

Melanie Griffith/*Two Much*

Demi Moore/*The Juror*

Julia Roberts/*Mary Reilly*

1997

★Demi Moore/*G.I. Jane*

Sandra Bullock/*Speed 2: Cruise Control*

Fran Drescher/*The Beautician and the Beast*

Lauren Holly/*A Smile Like Yours*

Lauren Holly/*Turbulence*

Alicia Silverstone/*Excess Baggage*

1998

★Victoria (Posh Spice) Beckham/*Spice World: The Movie*

★Melanie (Scary Spice) Brown/*Spice World: The Movie*

★Emma (Baby Spice) Bunton/*Spice World: The Movie*

★Melanie (Sporty Spice) Chisholm/*Spice World: The Movie*

★Geri (Ginger Spice) Halliwell/*Spice World: The Movie*

Yasmine Bleeth/*BASEketball*

Anne Heche/*Psycho*

Jessica Lange/*Hush*

Uma Thurman/*The Avengers*

1999

★Heather Donahue/*The Blair Witch Project*

Melanie Griffith/*Crazy in Alabama*

Milla Jovovich/*The Messenger: The Story of Joan of Arc*

Sharon Stone/*Gloria*

Catherine Zeta-Jones/*Entrapment*

Catherine Zeta-Jones/*The Haunting*

2000

★Madonna/*The Next Best Thing*

Kim Basinger/*Bless the Child*

Kim Basinger/*I Dreamed of Africa*

Melanie Griffith/*Cecil B. Demented*

Bette Midler/*Isn't She Great*

Demi Moore/*Passion of Mind*

2001

★Mariah Carey/*Glitter*

2002

★Madonna/*Swept Away*

★Britney Spears/*Crossroads*

2003

★Jennifer Lopez/*Gigli*

Drew Barrymore/*Charlie's Angels: Full Throttle*

Kelly Clarkson/*From Justin to Kelly*

Cameron Diaz/*Charlie's Angels: Full Throttle*

Angelina Jolie/*Beyond Borders*

Angelina Jolie/*Lara Croft Tomb Raider: The Cradle of Life*

2004

★Halle Berry/*Catwoman*

Hilary Duff/*A Cinderella Story*

Hilary Duff/*Raise Your Voice*

Angelina Jolie/*Alexander*

Angelina Jolie/*Taking Lives*

Ashley (Fuller) Olsen/*New York Minute*

Mary-Kate Olsen/*New York Minute*

Marlon Wayans/*White Chicks*

Shawn Wayans/*White Chicks*

2005

★Jenny McCarthy/*Dirty Love*

Jessica Alba/*Fantastic Four*

Jessica Alba/*Into the Blue*

Hilary Duff/*Cheaper by the Dozen 2*

Hilary Duff/*The Perfect Man*

Jennifer Lopez/*Monster-in-Law*

Tara Reid/*Alone in the Dark*

2006

★Sharon Stone/*Basic Instinct 2*

Haylie Duff/*Material Girls*

Hilary Duff/*Material Girls*

Lindsay Lohan/*Just My Luck*

Kristanna Loken/*BloodRayne*

Jessica Simpson/*Employee of the Month*

2007

★Lindsay Lohan/*I Know Who Killed Me*

Jessica Alba/*Awake*

Logan Browning/*Bratz*

Elisha Cuthbert/*Captivity*

Diane Keaton/*Because I Said So*

Janel Parrish/*Bratz*

Nathalia Ramos/*Bratz*

Skyler Shaye/*Bratz*

2008

★Paris Hilton/*The Hottie and the Nottie*

Jessica Alba/*The Eye*

Jessica Alba/*The Love Guru*

Annette Bening/*The Women*

Cameron Diaz/*What Happens in Vegas*

Kate Hudson/*Fool's Gold*

Kate Hudson/*My Best Friend's Girl*

Eva Mendes/*The Women*

Debra Messing/*The Women*

Jada Pinkett Smith/*The Women*

Meg Ryan/*The Women*

2009

★Sandra Bullock/*All About Steve*

Miley Cyrus/*Hannah Montana: The Movie*

Megan Fox/*Jennifer's Body*

Megan Fox/*Transformers: Revenge of the Fallen*

Beyonce Knowles/*Obsessed*

Sarah Jessica Parker/*Did You Hear About the Morgans?*

Kelly Preston/*Old Dogs*

2010

★Kim Cattrall/*Sex and the City 2*

★Kristin Davis/*Sex and the City 2*

★Cynthia Nixon/*Sex and the City 2*

★Sarah Jessica Parker/*Sex and the City 2*

Jennifer Aniston/*The Bounty Hunter*

Miley Cyrus/*The Last Song*

Megan Fox/*Jonah Hex*

Kristen Stewart/*The Twilight Saga: Eclipse*

2011

★Adam Sandler/*Jack and Jill*

Martin Lawrence/*Big Mommas: Like Father, Like Son*

Sarah Palin/*The Undefeated*

Sarah Jessica Parker/*I Don't Know How She Does It*

Sarah Jessica Parker/*New Year's Eve*

Kristen Stewart/*The Twilight Saga: Breaking Dawn, Part 1*

2012

★Kristen Stewart/*Snow White and the Huntsman*

★Kristen Stewart/*The Twilight Saga: Breaking Dawn, Part 2*

Katherine Heigl/*One for the Money*

Milla Jovovich/*Resident Evil: Retribution*

Tyler Perry/*Madea's Witness Protection*

Barbra Streisand/*The Guilt Trip*

2013

★Tyler Perry/*Tyler Perry's A Madea Christmas*

Halle Berry/*The Call*

Halle Berry/*Movie 43*

Selena Gomez/*Getaway*

Lindsay Lohan/*The Canyons*

Naomi Watts/*Diana*

Naomi Watts/*Movie 43*

2014

★Cameron Diaz/*The Other Woman*

★Cameron Diaz/*Sex Tape*

Drew Barrymore/*Blended*

Melissa McCarthy/*Tammy*

Charlize Theron/*A Million Ways to Die In the West*

Gaia Weiss/*The Legend of Hercules*

2015

★Dakota Johnson/*Fifty Shades of Grey*

Mila Kunis/*Jupiter Ascending*

Jennifer Lopez/*The Boy Next Door*

Gwyneth Paltrow/*Mortdecai*

2016

★Rebekah Turner/*Hillary's America: The Secret History of the Democratic Party*

★*Zoolander 2*

Megan Fox/*Teenage Mutant Ninja Turtles: Out of the Shadows*

Tyler Perry/*Boo! A Madea Halloween*

Julia Roberts/*Mother's Day*

Naomi Watts/*Allegiant*

Naomi Watts/*Shut In*

2017

★Tyler Perry/*Boo 2! A Madea Halloween*

Katherine Heigl/*Unforgettable*

Dakota Johnson/*Fifty Shades Darker*

Jennifer Lawrence/*mother!*

Amanda Seyfried/*The Clapper*

Emma Watson/*The Circle*

2018

★Melissa McCarthy/*The Happytime Murders*

★Melissa McCarthy/*Life of the Party*

Jennifer Garner/*Peppermint*

Amber Heard/*London Fields*

Dame Helen Mirren/*Winchester*

2019

★Hilary Duff/*The Haunting of Sharon Tate*

Anne Hathaway/*The Hustle*

Anne Hathaway/*Serenity*

Francesca Hayward/*Cats*

Tyler Perry/*A Madea Family Funeral*

Rebel Wilson/*The Hustle*

WORST SUPPORTING ACTOR

1980

★John Adams/*Gloria*

★Laurence Olivier/*The Jazz Singer*

1981

★Steve Forrest/*Mommie Dearest*

1982

★Ed McMahon/*Butterfly*

1983

★Jim Nabors/*Stroker Ace*

1985

★Rob Lowe/*St. Elmo's Fire*

1986

★Jerome Benton/*Under the Cherry Moon*

1987

★David Mendenhall/*Over the Top*

1988

★Dan Aykroyd/*Caddyshack 2*

1991

★Dan Aykroyd/*Nothing But Trouble*

1993

★Woody Harrelson/*Indecent Proposal*

1994

★O.J. Simpson/*Naked Gun 33 1/3: The Final Insult*

1995

★Dennis Hopper/*Waterworld*

Robert Davi/*Showgirls*

1996

Marlon Brando/*The Island of Dr. Moreau*

Val Kilmer/*The Ghost and the Darkness*

Val Kilmer/*The Island of Dr. Moreau*

Burt Reynolds/*Striptease*

Steven Seagal/*Executive Decision*

Quentin Tarantino/*From Dusk Till Dawn*

1997

★Dennis Rodman/*Double Team*

Willem Dafoe/*Speed 2: Cruise Control*

Chris O'Donnell/*Batman and Robin*

Arnold Schwarzenegger/*Batman and Robin*

Jon Voight/*Most Wanted*

Jon Voight/*U-Turn*

1998

★Joe Eszterhas/*An Alan Smithee Film: Burn, Hollywood, Burn*

Sean Connery/*The Avengers*

Joe Pesci/*Lethal Weapon 4*

Sylvester Stallone/*An Alan Smithee Film: Burn, Hollywood, Burn*

1999

Kenneth Branagh/*Wild Wild West*

Gabriel Byrne/*End of Days*

Gabriel Byrne/*Stigmata*

Jake Lloyd/*Star Wars: Episode 1-The Phantom Menace*

Rob Schneider/*Big Daddy*

2000

★Barry Pepper/*Battlefield Earth*

Stephen Baldwin/*The Flintstones in Viva Rock Vegas*

Keanu Reeves/*The Watcher*

Forest Whitaker/*Battlefield Earth*

2001

★Charlton Heston/*Planet of the Apes*

2002

★Hayden Christensen/*Star Wars: Episode 2-Attack of the Clones*

2003

★Sylvester Stallone/*Spy Kids 3-D: Game Over*

Anthony Anderson/*Kangaroo Jack*

Alec Baldwin/*Dr. Seuss' The Cat in the Hat*

Al Pacino/*Gigli*

Christopher Walken/*Gigli*

Christopher Walken/*Kangaroo Jack*

2004

★Donald Rumsfeld/*Fahrenheit 9/11*

Val Kilmer/*Alexander*

Arnold Schwarzenegger/*Around the World in 80 Days*

Jon Voight/*Superbabies: Baby Geniuses 2*

Lambert Wilson/*Catwoman*

2005

★Hayden Christensen/*Star Wars: Episode 3-Revenge of the Sith*

Alan Cumming/*Son of the Mask*

Will Ferrell/*Kicking & Screaming*

Bob Hoskins/*Son of the Mask*

Eugene Levy/*Cheaper by the Dozen 2*

Burt Reynolds/*The Dukes of Hazzard*

Burt Reynolds/*The Longest Yard*

2006

Danny DeVito/*Deck the Halls*

Ben Kingsley/*BloodRayne*

Martin Short/*The Santa Clause 3: The Escape Clause*

2007

★Eddie Murphy/*Norbit*

Orlando Bloom/*Pirates of the Caribbean: At World's End*

Kevin James/*I Now Pronounce You Chuck and Larry*

Rob Schneider/*I Now Pronounce You Chuck and Larry*

Jon Voight/*Bratz*

2008

★Pierce Brosnan/*Mamma Mia!*

Uwe Boll/*Postal*

Ben Kingsley/*The Love Guru*

Ben Kingsley/*The Wackness*

Ben Kingsley/*War, Inc.*

Burt Reynolds/*Deal*

Burt Reynolds/*In the Name of the King: A Dungeon Siege Tale*

Verne Troyer/*The Love Guru*

Verne Troyer/*Postal*

★ = winner

2009

★Billy Ray Cyrus/*Hannah Montana: The Movie*

Hugh Hefner/*Miss March*

Robert Pattinson/*The Twilight Saga: New Moon*

Jorma Taccone/*Land of the Lost*

Marlon Wayans/*G.I. Joe: The Rise of Cobra*

2010

★Jackson Rathbone/*The Last Airbender*

★Jackson Rathbone/*The Twilight Saga: Eclipse*

Billy Ray Cyrus/*The Spy Next Door*

George Lopez/*Marmaduke*

George Lopez/*The Spy Next Door*

George Lopez/*Valentine's Day*

Dev Patel/*The Last Airbender*

Rob Schneider/*Grown Ups*

2011

★Al Pacino/*Jack and Jill*

Patrick Dempsey/*Transformers: Dark of the Moon*

James Franco/*Your Highness*

Ken Jeong/*Big Mommas: Like Father, Like Son*

Ken Jeong/*The Hangover, Part 2*

Ken Jeong/*Transformers: Dark of the Moon*

Ken Jeong/*Zookeeper*

Nick Swardson/*Jack and Jill*

Nick Swardson/*Just Go With It*

2012

★Taylor Lautner/*The Twilight Saga: Breaking Dawn, Part 2*

David Hasselhoff/*Piranha 3DD*

Liam Neeson/*Battleship*

Liam Neeson/*Wrath of the Titans*

Vanilla Ice/*That's My Boy*

2013

★Will Smith/*After Earth*

Chris Brown/*Battle of the Year*

Larry the Cable Guy/*Tyler Perry's A Madea Christmas*

Taylor Lautner/*Grown Ups 2*

Nick Swardson/*Grown Ups 2*

Nick Swardson/*A Haunted House*

2014

★Kelsey Grammer/*The Expendables 3*

★Kelsey Grammer/*Legends of Oz: Dorothy's Return*

★Kelsey Grammer/*Transformers: Age of Extinction*

Mel Gibson/*The Expendables 3*

Shaquille O'Neal/*Blended*

Arnold Schwarzenegger/*The Expendables 3*

Kiefer Sutherland/*Pompeii*

2015

★Eddie Redmayne/*Jupiter Ascending*

Chevy Chase/*Hot Tub Time Machine 2*

Chevy Chase/*Vacation*

Josh Gad/*Pixels*

Josh Gad/*The Wedding Ringer*

Kevin James/*Pixels*

Jason Lee/*Alvin and the Chipmunks: Road Chip*

2016

★Jesse Eisenberg/*Batman v Superman: Dawn of Justice*

Nicolas Cage/*Snowden*

Henry Cavill/*Batman v Superman: Dawn of Justice*

Johnny Depp/*Alice Through the Looking Glass*

Will Ferrell/*Zoolander 2*

Jared Leto/*Suicide Squad*

Owen Wilson/*Zoolander 2*

2017

★Mel Gibson/*Daddy's Home 2*

Javier Bardem/*mother!*

Javier Bardem/*Pirates of the Caribbean: Dead Men Tell No Tales*

Russell Crowe/*The Mummy*

Josh Duhamel/*Transformers: The Last Knight*

Anthony Hopkins/*Collide*

Anthony Hopkins/*Transformers: The Last Knight*

2018

★John C. Reilly/*Holmes & Watson*

Jamie Foxx/*Robin Hood*

Joel McHale/*The Happytime Murders*

Justice Smith/*Jurassic World: Fallen Kingdom*

2019

★James Corden/*Cats*

Tyler Perry/*A Madea Family Funeral*

Seth Rogen/*Zeroville*

WORST SUPPORTING ACTRESS

1980

★Amy Irving/*Honeysuckle Rose*

1981

★Diana Scarwid/*Mommie Dearest*

1982

★Aileen Quinn/*Annie*

1983

★Sybil Danning/*Chained Heat*

★Sybil Danning/*Hercules*

1984

★Lynn-Holly Johnson/*Where the Boys Are '84*

1985

★Brigitte Nielsen/*Rocky 4*

1987

★Daryl Hannah/*Wall Street*

1988

★Kristy McNichol/*Two Moon Junction*

1990

★Sofia Coppola/*The Godfather, Part 3*

1991

★Sean Young/*A Kiss Before Dying*

1992

★Estelle Getty/*Stop! or My Mom Will Shoot*

1993

★Faye Dunaway/*The Temp*

1994

★Rosie O'Donnell/*Car 54, Where Are You?*

★Rosie O'Donnell/*Exit to Eden*

★Rosie O'Donnell/*The Flintstones*

Elizabeth Taylor/*The Flintstones*

1995

★Madonna/*Four Rooms*

Gina Gershon/*Showgirls*

1996

★Melanie Griffith/*Mulholland Falls*

Faye Dunaway/*The Chamber*

Faye Dunaway/*Dunston Checks In*

Jami Gertz/*Twister*

Daryl Hannah/*Two Much*

Teri Hatcher/*Heaven's Prisoners*

Teri Hatcher/*Two Days in the Valley*

1997

★Alicia Silverstone/*Batman and Robin*

Faye Dunaway/*Albino Alligator*

Milla Jovovich/*The Fifth Element*

Julia Louis-Dreyfus/*Father's Day*

Demi Moore/*G.I. Jane*

Uma Thurman/*Batman and Robin*

1998

★Maria Pitillo/*Godzilla*

Ellen A. Dow/*54*

Jenny McCarthy/*BASEketball*

Roger Moore/*Spice World: The Movie*

Liv Tyler/*Armageddon*

Raquel Welch/*Chairman of the Board*

1999

★Denise Richards/*The World Is Not Enough*

Sofia Coppola/*Star Wars: Episode 1-The Phantom Menace*

Salma Hayek/*Dogma*

Salma Hayek/*Wild Wild West*

Juliette Lewis/*The Other Sister*

2000

★Kelly Preston/*Battlefield Earth*

Patricia Arquette/*Little Nicky*

Joan Collins/*The Flintstones in Viva Rock Vegas*

Thandie Newton/*Mission: Impossible 2*

Rene Russo/*The Adventures of Rocky & Bullwinkle*

2001

★Estella Warren/*Planet of the Apes*

2002

★Madonna/*Die Another Day*

2003

★Demi Moore/*Charlie's Angels: Full Throttle*

Lainie Kazan/*Gigli*

Brittany Murphy/*Just Married*

Kelly Preston/*Dr. Seuss' The Cat in the Hat*

Tara Reid/*My Boss's Daughter*

2004

★Britney Spears/*Fahrenheit 9/11*

Carmen Electra/*Starsky & Hutch*

Jennifer Lopez/*Jersey Girl*

Condoleeza Rice/*Fahrenheit 9/11*

Sharon Stone/*Catwoman*

2005

★Paris Hilton/*House of Wax*

Carmen Electra/*Dirty Love*

Katie Holmes/*Batman Begins*

Jessica Simpson/*The Dukes of Hazzard*

2006

★Carmen Electra/*Date Movie*

Kate (Catherine) Bosworth/*Superman Returns*

Kristin Chenoweth/*Deck the Halls*

Kristin Chenoweth/*The Pink Panther*

Kristin Chenoweth/*RV*

Jenny McCarthy/*John Tucker Must Die*

Michelle Rodriguez/*BloodRayne*

2007

★Eddie Murphy/*Norbit*

Jessica Biel/*I Now Pronounce You Chuck and Larry*

Carmen Electra/*Epic Movie*

Julia Ormond/*I Know Who Killed Me*

Nicolette Sheridan/*Code Name: The Cleaner*

2008

★Paris Hilton/*Repo! The Genetic Opera*

Carmen Electra/*Disaster Movie*

Carmen Electra/*Meet the Spartans*

Kim Kardashian/*Disaster Movie*

Jenny McCarthy/*Witless Protection*

Leelee Sobieski/*88 Minutes*

Leelee Sobieski/*In the Name of the King: A Dungeon Siege Tale*

2009

★Sienna Miller/*G.I. Joe: The Rise of Cobra*

Candice Bergen/*Bride Wars*

Ali Larter/*Obsessed*

2010

★Jessica Alba/*The Killer Inside Me*

★Jessica Alba/*Little Fockers*

★Jessica Alba/*Machete*

★Jessica Alba/*Valentine's Day*

Cher/*Burlesque*

Liza Minnelli/*Sex and the City 2*

Nicola Peltz/*The Last Airbender*

Barbra Streisand/*Little Fockers*

2011

★David Spade/*Jack and Jill*

Katie Holmes/*Jack and Jill*

Rosie Huntington-Whiteley/*Transformers: Dark of the Moon*

Brandon T. Jackson/*Big Mommas: Like Father, Like Son*

Nicole Kidman/*Just Go With It*

2012

★Rhianna/*Battleship*

Jessica Biel/*Playing for Keeps*

Jessica Biel/*Total Recall*

Brooklyn Decker/*Battleship*

Brooklyn Decker/*What to Expect When You're Expecting*

Ashley Greene/*The Twilight Saga: Breaking Dawn, Part 2*

Jennifer Lopez/*What to Expect When You're Expecting*

2013

★Kim Kardashian/*Tyler Perry's Temptation: Confessions of a Marriage Counselor*

Lady Gaga/*Machete Kills*

Salma Hayek/*Grown Ups 2*

Katherine Heigl/*The Big Wedding*

Lindsay Lohan/*Scary Movie 5*

2014

★Megan Fox/*Teenage Mutant Ninja Turtles*

Cameron Diaz/*Annie*

Nicola Peltz/*Transformers: Age of Extinction*

Brigette Ridenour/*Saving Christmas*

Susan Sarandon/*Tammy*

2015

Kaley Cuoco/*Alvin and the Chipmunks: Road Chip*

Kaley Cuoco/*The Wedding Ringer*

Rooney Mara/*Pan*

Michelle Monaghan/*Pixels*

Julianne Moore/*Seventh Son*

Amanda Seyfried/*Love the Coopers*

Amanda Seyfried/*Pan*

2016

★Kristen Wiig/*Zoolander 2*

Julianne Hough/*Dirty Grandpa*

Kate Hudson/*Mother's Day*

Aubrey Plaza/*Dirty Grandpa*

Jane Seymour/*Fifty Shades of Black*

2017

★Kim Basinger/*Fifty Shades Darker*

Sofia Boutella/*The Mummy*

Laura Haddock/*Transformers: The Last Knight*

Goldie Hawn/*Snatched*

Susan Sarandon/*A Bad Moms Christmas*

2018

Marcia Gay Harden/*Fifty Shades Freed*

Kelly Preston/*Gotti*

Jaz Sinclair/*Slender Man*

2019

★Rebel Wilson/*Cats*

Jessica Chastain/*Dark Phoenix*

Cassi Davis/*A Madea Family Funeral*

Dame Judi Dench/*Cats*

Fenessa Pineda/*Rambo: Last Blood*

WORST DIRECTOR

1980

★Robert Greenwald/*Xanadu*

1981

★Michael Cimino/*Heaven's Gate*

1982

★Ken Annakin/*Pirate Movie*

1984

★John Derek/*Bolero*

1985

★Sylvester Stallone/*Rocky 4*

1986

★Prince/*Under the Cherry Moon*

1987

★Norman Mailer/*Tough Guys Don't Dance*

★Elaine May/*Ishtar*

1988

★Blake Edwards/*Sunset*

★Stewart Raffill/*Mac and Me*

1989

★William Shatner/*Star Trek 5: The Final Frontier*

1991

★Michael Lehmann/*Hudson Hawk*

1992

★David Seltzer/*Shining Through*

1993

★Jennifer Lynch/*Boxing Helena*

1994

★Steven Seagal/*On Deadly Ground*

1995

★Paul Verhoeven/*Showgirls*

1996

★Andrew Bergman/*Striptease*

John Frankenheimer/*The Island of Dr. Moreau*

Stephen Frears/*Mary Reilly*

John Landis/*The Stupids*

Brian Levant/*Jingle All the Way*

1997

★Kevin Costner/*The Postman*

Jan De Bont/*Speed 2: Cruise Control*

Luis Llosa/*Anaconda*

Joel Schumacher/*Batman and Robin*

Oliver Stone/*U-Turn*

1998

★Gus Van Sant/*Psycho*

Michael Bay/*Armageddon*

Jeremiah S. Chechik/*The Avengers*

Roland Emmerich/*Godzilla*

Arthur Hiller/*An Alan Smithee Film: Burn, Hollywood, Burn*

1999

★Barry Sonnenfeld/*Wild Wild West*

Jan De Bont/*The Haunting*

Dennis Dugan/*Big Daddy*

Peter Hyams/*End of Days*

George Lucas/*Star Wars: Episode 1-The Phantom Menace*

2000

★Roger Christian/*Battlefield Earth*

Brian De Palma/*Mission to Mars*

John Schlesinger/*The Next Best Thing*

2001

★Tom Green/*Freddy Got Fingered*

2002

★Guy Ritchie/*Swept Away*

2003

★Martin Brest/*Gigli*

Robert Iscove/*From Justin to Kelly*

Mort Nathan/*Boat Trip*

Lana Wachowski/*The Matrix Reloaded*

Lana Wachowski/*The Matrix Revolutions*

Lilly Wachowski/*The Matrix Reloaded*

Lilly Wachowski/*The Matrix Revolutions*

Bo Welch/*Dr. Seuss' The Cat in the Hat*

2004

★Pitof/*Catwoman*

Bob (Benjamin) Clark/*Superbabies: Baby Geniuses 2*

Renny Harlin/*Exorcist: The Beginning*

Oliver Stone/*Alexander*

Keenen Ivory Wayans/*White Chicks*

2005

★John Mallory Asher/*Dirty Love*

Uwe Boll/*Alone in the Dark*

Jay Chandrasekhar/*The Dukes of Hazzard*

Nora Ephron/*Bewitched*

Lawrence (Larry) Guterman/*Son of the Mask*

★ = winner

2006

★M. Night Shyamalan/*Lady in the Water*

Uwe Boll/*BloodRayne*

Michael Caton-Jones/*Basic Instinct 2*

Ron Howard/*The Da Vinci Code*

Keenen Ivory Wayans/*Little Man*

2007

★Chris Siverston/*I Know Who Killed Me*

Dennis Dugan/*I Now Pronounce You Chuck and Larry*

Roland Joffé/*Captivity*

Brian Robbins/*Norbit*

Fred Savage/*Daddy Day Camp*

2008

★Uwe Boll/*In the Name of the King: A Dungeon Siege Tale*

★Uwe Boll/*Postal*

Jason Friedberg/*Disaster Movie*

Jason Friedberg/*Meet the Spartans*

Tom Putnam/*The Hottie and the Nottie*

Marco Schnabel/*The Love Guru*

Aaron Seltzer/*Disaster Movie*

Aaron Seltzer/*Meet the Spartans*

M. Night Shyamalan/*The Happening*

2009

★Michael Bay/*Transformers: Revenge of the Fallen*

Walt Becker/*Old Dogs*

Brad Silberling/*Land of the Lost*

Stephen Sommers/*G.I. Joe: The Rise of Cobra*

Phil Traill/*All About Steve*

2010

★M. Night Shyamalan/*The Last Airbender*

Jason Friedberg/*Vampires Suck*

Michael Patrick King/*Sex and the City 2*

Aaron Seltzer/*Vampires Suck*

David Slade/*The Twilight Saga: Eclipse*

Sylvester Stallone/*The Expendables*

2011

★Dennis Dugan/*Jack and Jill*

★Dennis Dugan/*Just Go With It*

Michael Bay/*Transformers: Dark of the Moon*

Tom Brady/*Bucky Larson: Born to Be a Star*

Bill Condon/*The Twilight Saga: Breaking Dawn, Part 1*

Garry Marshall/*New Year's Eve*

2012

★Bill Condon/*The Twilight Saga: Breaking Dawn, Part 2*

Sean Anders/*That's My Boy*

Peter Berg/*Battleship*

Tyler Perry/*Madea's Witness Protection*

Tyler Perry/*Tyler Perry's Good Deeds*

John Putch/*Atlas Shrugged 2: The Strike*

2013

★Steven Brill/*Movie 43*

★Steve Carr/*Movie 43*

★Rusty Cundieff/*Movie 43*

★James Duffy/*Movie 43*

★James Dunn/*Movie 43*

★Griffin Dunne/*Movie 43*

★Patrik Forsberg/*Movie 43*

★Will Graham/*Movie 43*

★Bob Odenkirk/*Movie 43*

★Brett Ratner/*Movie 43*

★Jonathan Van Tulleken/*Movie 43*

Elizabeth Banks/*Movie 43*

Dennis Dugan/*Grown Ups 2*

Peter Farrelly/*Movie 43*

Tyler Perry/*Tyler Perry's A Madea Christmas*

M. Night Shyamalan/*After Earth*

Gore Verbinski/*The Lone Ranger*

2014

★Michael Bay/*Transformers: Age of Extinction*

Darren Doane/*Saving Christmas*

Renny Harlin/*The Legend of Hercules*

Jonathan Liebesman/*Teenage Mutant Ninja Turtles*

Seth MacFarlane/*A Million Ways to Die In the West*

2015

★Josh Trank/*Fantastic Four*

Andy Fickman/*Paul Blart: Mall Cop 2*

Tom Six/*The Human Centipede 3: The Final Sequence*

Sam Taylor-Johnson/*Fifty Shades of Grey*

Lana Wachowski/*Jupiter Ascending*

Lilly Wachowski/*Jupiter Ascending*

2016

★Dinesh D'Souza/*Hillary's America: The Secret History of the Democratic Party*

★Deborah Snyder/*Batman v Superman: Dawn of Justice*

Roland Emmerich/*Independence Day: Resurgence*

Alex Proyas/*Gods of Egypt*

Ben Stiller/*Zoolander 2*

2017

★Tony Leondis/*The Emoji Movie*

Darren Aronofsky/*mother!*

Michael Bay/*Transformers: The Last Knight*

James Foley/*Fifty Shades Darker*

Alex Kurtzman/*The Mummy*

2018

★Etan Cohen/*Holmes & Watson*

Kevin Connolly/*Gotti*

James Foley/*Fifty Shades Freed*

Brian Henson/*The Happytime Murders*

Michael Spierig/*Winchester*

Peter Spierig/*Winchester*

2019

★Tom Hooper/*Cats*

Fred Durst/*The Fanatic*

James Franco/*Zeroville*

Adrian Grunberg/*Rambo: Last Blood*

Neil Marshall/*Hellboy*

WORST SCREENPLAY

1980

★*Can't Stop the Music*

1981

★*Mommie Dearest*

1984

★*Bolero*

1985

★*Rambo: First Blood, Part 2*

★*Rocky 4*

1986

★*Howard the Duck*

1987

★*Leonard Part 6*

1988

★*Cocktail*

1989

★*Harlem Nights*

1990

★*The Adventures of Ford Fairlane*

1991

★*Hudson Hawk*

1992

★*Stop! or My Mom Will Shoot*

1993

★*Indecent Proposal*

1994

★*The Flintstones*

1995

★*Showgirls*

1996

★*Striptease*

Barb Wire

Ed

The Island of Dr. Moreau

The Stupids

1997

★*The Postman*

Anaconda

Batman and Robin

The Lost World: Jurassic Park 2

Speed 2: Cruise Control

1998

★*An Alan Smithee Film: Burn, Hollywood, Burn*

Armageddon

The Avengers

Godzilla

Spice World: The Movie

1999

★*Wild Wild West*

Big Daddy

The Haunting

The Mod Squad

Star Wars: Episode 1-The Phantom Menace

2000

★*Battlefield Earth*

Book of Shadows: Blair Witch 2

Dr. Seuss' How the Grinch Stole Christmas

Little Nicky

The Next Best Thing

2001

★*Freddy Got Fingered*

2003

★*Gigli*

Charlie's Angels: Full Throttle

Dr. Seuss' The Cat in the Hat

Dumb and Dumberer: When Harry Met Lloyd

From Justin to Kelly

2004

★*Catwoman*

Alexander

Superbabies: Baby Geniuses 2

Surviving Christmas

White Chicks

2005

★*Dirty Love*

Bewitched

Deuce Bigalow: European Gigolo

The Dukes of Hazzard

Son of the Mask

2006

★*Basic Instinct 2*

BloodRayne

Lady in the Water

Little Man

The Wicker Man

2007

★*I Know Who Killed Me*

Daddy Day Camp

Epic Movie

I Now Pronounce You Chuck and Larry

Norbit

2008

★*The Love Guru*

The Happening

The Hottie and the Nottie

In the Name of the King: A Dungeon Siege Tale

Meet the Spartans

2009

★*Transformers: Revenge of the Fallen*

All About Steve

G.I. Joe: The Rise of Cobra

Land of the Lost

The Twilight Saga: New Moon

2010

★*The Last Airbender*

The Last Airbender

Little Fockers

Sex and the City 2

The Twilight Saga: Eclipse

Vampires Suck

2011

★*Jack and Jill*

Bucky Larson: Born to Be a Star

New Year's Eve

Transformers: Dark of the Moon

The Twilight Saga: Breaking Dawn, Part 1

2012

★*That's My Boy*

Atlas Shrugged 2: The Strike

Battleship

A Thousand Words

The Twilight Saga: Breaking Dawn, Part 2

2013

★*Movie 43*

Grown Ups 2

The Lone Ranger

Tyler Perry's A Madea Christmas

2014

★*Saving Christmas*

Left Behind

Sex Tape

Teenage Mutant Ninja Turtles

Transformers: Age of Extinction

2015

★*Fifty Shades of Grey*

Fantastic Four

Jupiter Ascending

Paul Blart: Mall Cop 2

Pixels

2016

★*Batman v Superman: Dawn of Justice*

Gods of Egypt

Hillary's America: The Secret History of the Democratic Party

Independence Day: Resurgence

Suicide Squad

2017

★*The Emoji Movie*

Baywatch

Fifty Shades Darker

The Mummy

Transformers: The Last Knight

2018

★*Fifty Shades Freed*

Death of a Nation

Gotti

The Happytime Murders

Winchester

2019

★*Cats*

The Haunting of Sharon Tate

Hellboy

A Madea Family Funeral

Rambo: Last Blood

WORST SONG

1980

★"The Man with Bogart's Face"/*The Man with Bogart's Face*

1982

★"Pumpin' and Blowin'"/*Pirate Movie*

1984

★"Drinkenstein"/*Rhinestone*

1985

★"Peace In Our Life"/*Rambo: First Blood, Part 2*

1986

★"Love or Money"/*Under the Cherry Moon*

1987

★"I Want Your Sex"/*Beverly Hills Cop 2*

1988

★"Jack Fresh"/*Caddyshack 2*

1989

★"Bring Your Daughter to the Slaughter"/*A Nightmare on Elm Street 5: Dream Child*

1990

★"He's Comin' Back (The Devil!)"/*Repossessed*

1991

★"Addams Groove"/*The Addams Family*

1992

★"High Times, Hard Times"/*Newsies*

1993

★"WHOOMP! There It Is"/*Addams Family Values*

1994

★"Marry the Mole"/*Thumbelina*

1995

★"Walk into the Wind"/*Showgirls*

1996

★"Pussy, Pussy, Pussy (Whose Kitty Cat Are You?)"/*Striptease*

"Welcome to Planet Boom!"/*Barb Wire*

"Whenever There is Love"/*Daylight*

1997

★Entire Song Score/*The Postman*

"Fire Down Below"/*Fire Down Below*

"How Do I Live"/*Con Air*

"My Dream"/*Speed 2: Cruise Control*

"The End is The Beginning is The End"/*Batman and Robin*

1998

★"I Wanna Be Mike Ovitz!"/*An Alan Smithee Film: Burn, Hollywood, Burn*

"Barney, The Song"/*Barney's Great Adventure*

"I Don't Want to Miss a Thing"/*Armageddon*

"Storm"/*The Avengers*

"Too Much"/*Spice World: The Movie*

1999

★"Wild Wild West"/*Wild Wild West*

2002

★"I'm Not a Girl, Not Yet a Woman"/*Crossroads*

WORST NEW STAR

1981

★Klinton Spilsbury/*Legend of the Lone Ranger*

1982

★Pia Zadora/*Butterfly*

1983

★Lou Ferrigno/*Hercules*

1984

★Olivia D'Abo/*Bolero*

★Olivia D'Abo/*Conan the Destroyer*

1985

★Brigitte Nielsen/*Red Sonja*

★Brigitte Nielsen/*Rocky 4*

1987

★David Mendenhall/*Over the Top*

1990

★Sofia Coppola/*The Godfather, Part 3*

1991

★Vanilla Ice/*Cool As Ice*

1992

★Pauly Shore/*Encino Man*

1993

★Janet Jackson/*Poetic Justice*

1994

★Anna Nicole Smith/*Naked Gun 33 1/3: The Final Insult*

1995

★Elizabeth Berkley/*Showgirls*

David Caruso/*Kiss of Death*

Cindy Crawford/*Fair Game*

Julia Sweeney/*It's Pat: The Movie*

1996

★Pamela Anderson/*Barb Wire*

Ellen DeGeneres/*Mr. Wrong*

1997

★Dennis Rodman/*Double Team*

Tori Spelling/*The House of Yes*

Howard Stern/*Private Parts*

Chris Tucker/*The Fifth Element*

Chris Tucker/*Money Talks*

★ = winner

1998
★Joe Eszterhas/*An Alan Smithee Film: Burn, Hollywood, Burn*
★Jerry Springer/*Ringmaster*
Barney/*Barney's Great Adventure*
Carrot Top/*Chairman of the Board*
The Spice Girls/*Spice World: The Movie*

INDEPENDENT SPIRIT AWARDS

ACTOR

1986
★M. Emmet Walsh/*Blood Simple*
1987
★James Woods/*Salvador*
1988
★Dennis Quaid/*The Big Easy*
1989
★Edward James Olmos/*Stand and Deliver*
1990
★Matt Dillon/*Drugstore Cowboy*
1991
★Danny Glover/*To Sleep with Anger*
1992
★River Phoenix/*My Own Private Idaho*
1993
★Harvey Keitel/*Bad Lieutenant*
1994
★Jeff Bridges/*American Heart*
Mitchell Lichtenstein/*The Wedding Banquet*
Tyrin Turner/*Menace II Society*
1995
★Samuel L. Jackson/*Pulp Fiction*
Sihung Lung/*Eat Drink Man Woman*
William H. Macy/*Oleanna*
Campbell Scott/*Mrs. Parker and the Vicious Circle*
Jon Seda/*I Like It Like That*
1996
★Sean Penn/*Dead Man Walking*
Nicolas Cage/*Leaving Las Vegas*
Tim Roth/*Little Odessa*
Jimmy Smits/*My Family*
Kevin Spacey/*Swimming with Sharks*
1997
★William H. Macy/*Fargo*
Chris Cooper/*Lone Star*
Christopher Penn/*The Funeral*
1998
★Robert Duvall/*The Apostle*
Peter Fonda/*Ulee's Gold*
Christopher Guest/*Waiting for Guffman*
Philip Baker Hall/*Hard Eight*
John Turturro/*Box of Moonlight*
1999
★Ian McKellen/*Gods and Monsters*
Dylan Baker/*Happiness*
Nick Nolte/*Affliction*
Sean Penn/*Hurlyburly*
Courtney B. Vance/*Blind Faith*
2000
★Richard Farnsworth/*The Straight Story*
John Cusack/*Being John Malkovich*
Terence Stamp/*The Limey*
David Strathairn/*Limbo*
2001
★Javier Bardem/*Before Night Falls*
Adrien Brody/*Restaurant*
Billy Crudup/*Jesus' Son*
Mark Ruffalo/*You Can Count On Me*
2002
★Tom Wilkinson/*In the Bedroom*
Brian Cox/*L.I.E.*
Jake Gyllenhaal/*Donnie Darko*
John Cameron Mitchell/*Hedwig and the Angry Inch*
2003
★Derek Luke/*Antwone Fisher*
Graham Greene/*Skins*
Jeremy Renner/*Dahmer*
Campbell Scott/*Roger Dodger*
2004
★Bill Murray/*Lost in Translation*
Peter Dinklage/*The Station Agent*
Paul Giamatti/*American Splendor*
Ben Kingsley/*House of Sand and Fog*
Lee Pace/*Soldier's Girl*
2005
★Paul Giamatti/*Sideways*
Kevin Bacon/*The Woodsman*
Jeff Bridges/*The Door in the Floor*
Liam Neeson/*Kinsey*
2006
★Philip Seymour Hoffman/*Capote*
Jeff Daniels/*The Squid and the Whale*
Terrence Howard/*Hustle & Flow*
Heath Ledger/*Brokeback Mountain*
David Strathairn/*Good Night, and Good Luck*
2007
★Ryan Gosling/*Half Nelson*
Aaron Eckhart/*Thank You for Smoking*
Edward Norton/*The Painted Veil*
Forest Whitaker/*American Gun*
2008
★Philip Seymour Hoffman/*The Savages*
Don Cheadle/*Talk to Me*
Tony Leung Chiu-Wai/*Lust, Caution*
2009
★Mickey Rourke/*The Wrestler*
Javier Bardem/*Vicky Cristina Barcelona*
Richard Jenkins/*The Visitor*
Sean Penn/*Milk*
Jeremy Renner/*The Hurt Locker*
JimMyron Ross/*Ballast*
2010
★Jeff Bridges/*Crazy Heart*
Colin Firth/*A Single Man*
Joseph Gordon-Levitt/*(500) Days of Summer*
Souleymane Sy Savane/*Goodbye Solo*
Adam Scott/*The Vicious Kind*
2011
★James Franco/*127 Hours*
Aaron Eckhart/*Rabbit Hole*
John C. Reilly/*Cyrus*
Ben Stiller/*Greenberg*
2012
★Jean Dujardin/*The Artist*
Demian Bechir/*A Better Life*
Ryan Gosling/*Drive*
Woody Harrelson/*Rampart*
Michael Shannon/*Take Shelter*
2013
★John Hawkes/*The Sessions*
Jack Black/*Bernie*
Bradley Cooper/*Silver Linings Playbook*
Thure Lindhardt/*Keep the Lights On*
Matthew McConaughey/*Killer Joe*
Wendell Pierce/*Four*
2014
★Matthew McConaughey/*Dallas Buyers Club*
Bruce Dern/*Nebraska*
Chiwetel Ejiofor/*12 Years a Slave*
Oscar Isaac/*Inside Llewyn Davis*
Michael B. Jordan/*Fruitvale Station*
Robert Redford/*All is Lost*
2015
★Michael Keaton/*Birdman, or (The Unexpected Virtue of Ignorance)*
Andre Benjamin/*Jimi: All Is by My Side*
Jake Gyllenhaal/*Nightcrawler*
Ethan Hawke/*Boyhood*
John Lithgow/*Love Is Strange*
David Oyelowo/*Selma*
2016
★Abraham Attah/*Beasts of No Nation*
Christopher Abbott/*James White*
Ben Mendelsohn/*Mississippi Grind*
Jason Segel/*The End of the Tour*
2017
★Casey Affleck/*Manchester by the Sea*
Viggo Mortensen/*Captain Fantastic*
Jesse Plemons/*Other People*
Tim Roth/*Chronic*
2018
★Timothée Chalamet/*Call Me by Your Name*
Harris Dickinson/*Beach Rats*
James Franco/*The Disaster Artist*
Daniel Kaluuya/*Get Out*
Robert Pattinson/*Good Time*
2019
★Ethan Hawke/*First Reformed*
John Cho/*Searching*
Leonardo DiCaprio/*Once Upon A Time... In Hollywood*
Daveed Diggs/*Blindspotting*
Christian Malheiros/*Socrates*
Joaquin Rafael (Leaf) Phoenix/*You Were Never Really Here*
2020
★Adam Sandler/*Uncut Gems*
Chris Galust/*Give Me Liberty*
Kelvin Harrison, Jr./*Luce*
Robert Pattinson/*The Lighthouse*
Matthias Schoenaerts/*THE MUSTANG*

ACTOR—SUPPORTING

1988
★Morgan Freeman/*Street Smart*
1989
★Lou Diamond Phillips/*Stand and Deliver*
1990
★Max Perlich/*Drugstore Cowboy*
1991
★Bruce Davison/*Longtime Companion*
1992
★David Strathairn/*City of Hope*
1993
★Steve Buscemi/*Reservoir Dogs*
1994
★Christopher Lloyd/*Twenty Bucks*
David Chung/*Combination Platter*
Tate Donovan/*Inside Monkey Zetterland*
Edward Furlong/*American Heart*
1995
★Chazz Palminteri/*Bullets over Broadway*
Giancarlo Esposito/*Fresh*
Larry Pine/*Vanya on 42nd Street*
Eric Stoltz/*Pulp Fiction*
Nicholas Turturro/*Federal Hill*
1996
★Benicio Del Toro/*The Usual Suspects*
James LeGros/*Living in Oblivion*
David Morse/*The Crossing Guard*
Max Perlich/*Georgia*
Harold Perrineau, Jr./*Smoke*
1997
★Benicio Del Toro/*Basquiat*
Kevin Corrigan/*Walking and Talking*
Matthew Faber/*Welcome to the Dollhouse*
Gary Farmer/*Dead Man*
Richard Jenkins/*Flirting with Disaster*
1998
★Jason Lee/*Chasing Amy*
Efrain Figueroa/*Star Maps*
Samuel L. Jackson/*Hard Eight*
Roy Scheider/*The Myth of Fingerprints*
1999
★Bill Murray/*Rushmore*
James Coburn/*Affliction*
Charles S. Dutton/*Blind Faith*
Gary Farmer/*Smoke Signals*
Philip Seymour Hoffman/*Happiness*
2000
★Steve Zahn/*Happy, Texas*
Charles S. Dutton/*Cookie's Fortune*
Clark Gregg/*The Adventures of Sebastian Cole*
Luis Guzman/*The Limey*
Terrence Howard/*The Best Man*
2001
Cole Hauser/*Tigerland*
Gary Oldman/*The Contender*
Giovanni Ribisi/*The Gift*
2002
★Steve Buscemi/*Ghost World*
Billy Kay/*L.I.E.*
Garrett Morris/*Jackpot*
John C. Reilly/*The Anniversary Party*
2003
★Dennis Quaid/*Far from Heaven*
Alan Arkin/*Thirteen Conversations About One Thing*
Ray Liotta/*Narc*
John C. Reilly/*The Good Girl*
2004
★Djimon Hounsou/*In America*
Judah Friedlander/*American Splendor*
Troy Garity/*Soldier's Girl*
Alessandro Nivola/*Laurel Canyon*
Peter Sarsgaard/*Shattered Glass*
2005
★Thomas Haden Church/*Sideways*
Jon(athan) Gries/*Napoleon Dynamite*
Roger Robinson/*Brother to Brother*
Peter Sarsgaard/*Kinsey*
2006
★Matt Dillon/*Crash*
Jesse Eisenberg/*The Squid and the Whale*
2007
★Alan Arkin/*Little Miss Sunshine*
Daniel Craig/*Infamous*
Paul Dano/*Little Miss Sunshine*
Channing Tatum/*A Guide to Recognizing Your Saints*
2008
★Chiwetel Ejiofor/*Talk to Me*
Marcus Carl Franklin/*I'm Not There*
Kene Holliday/*Great World of Sound*
Irfan Khan/*The Namesake*
Steve Zahn/*Rescue Dawn*
2009
★James Franco/*Milk*
Anthony Mackie/*The Hurt Locker*
Charlie McDermott/*Frozen River*
Haaz Sleiman/*The Visitor*
2010
★Woody Harrelson/*The Messenger*
Jemaine Clement/*Gentlemen Broncos*
Christian McKay/*Me and Orson Welles*
Ray McKinnon/*That Evening Sun*
Christopher Plummer/*The Last Station*
2011
★John Hawkes/*Winter's Bone*
Samuel L. Jackson/*Mother and Child*
Bill Murray/*Get Low*
Mark Ruffalo/*The Kids Are All Right*
2012
★Christopher Plummer/*Beginners*
Albert Brooks/*Drive*
John Hawkes/*Martha Marcy May Marlene*
John C. Reilly/*Cedar Rapids*
Corey Stoll/*Midnight in Paris*
2013
★Matthew McConaughey/*Magic Mike*
David Oyelowo/*Middle of Nowhere*
Michael Peña/*End of Watch*
Sam Rockwell/*Seven Psychopaths*
Bruce Willis/*Moonrise Kingdom*
2014
★Jared Leto/*Dallas Buyers Club*
Michael Fassbender/*12 Years a Slave*
Will Forte/*Nebraska*
James Gandolfini/*Enough Said*
Lakeith Stanfield/*Short Term 12*
2015
★J.K. Simmons/*Whiplash*
Riz Ahmed/*Nightcrawler*
Alfred Molina/*Love Is Strange*
Edward Norton/*Birdman, or (The Unexpected Virtue of Ignorance)*
2016
★Idris Elba/*Beasts of No Nation*
Kevin Corrigan/*Results*
Paul Dano/*Love & Mercy*
Richard Jenkins/*Bone Tomahawk*
Michael Shannon/*99 Homes*
2017
★Ben Foster/*Hell or High Water*
Ralph Fiennes/*A Bigger Splash*
Lucas Hedges/*Manchester by the Sea*
Shia LaBeouf/*American Honey*
Craig Robinson/*Morris from America*
2018
★Sam Rockwell/*Three Billboards Outside Ebbing, Missouri*
Nnamdi Asomugha/*Crown Heights*
Armie Hammer/*Call Me by Your Name*
Barry Keoghan/*The Killing of a Sacred Deer*
Benny Safdie/*Good Time*
2019
★Richard E. Grant/*Can You Ever Forgive Me?*
Raúl Castillo/*We the Animals*
Adam Driver/*BlacKkKlansman*
Josh Hamilton/*Eighth Grade*
John David Washington/*Monsters and Men*
2020
★Willem Dafoe/*The Lighthouse*
Noah Jupe/*Honey Boy*
Shia LaBeouf/*Honey Boy*
Jonathan Majors/*The Last Black Man in San Francisco*
Wendell Pierce/*Burning Cane*

★ = winner

ACTRESS

1986

★Geraldine Page/*The Trip to Bountiful*

1987

★Isabella Rossellini/*Blue Velvet*

1988

★Sally Kirkland/*Anna*

1989

★Jodie Foster/*Five Corners*

1990

★Andie MacDowell/*sex, lies and videotape*

1991

★Anjelica Huston/*The Grifters*

1992

★Judy Davis/*Impromptu*

1993

★Fairuza Balk/*Gas Food Lodging*

1994

Suzy Amis/*The Ballad of Little Jo*

May Chin/*The Wedding Banquet*

Ariyan Johnson/*Just Another Girl on the I.R.T.*

Emma Thompson/*Much Ado about Nothing*

1995

★Linda Fiorentino/*The Last Seduction*

Jennifer Jason Leigh/*Mrs. Parker and the Vicious Circle*

Karen Sillas/*What Happened Was. . .*

Lauren Velez/*I Like It Like That*

Chien-Lien Wu/*Eat Drink Man Woman*

1996

★Elisabeth Shue/*Leaving Las Vegas*

Jennifer Jason Leigh/*Georgia*

Elina Lowensohn/*Nadja*

Julianne Moore/*Safe*

1997

★Frances McDormand/*Fargo*

Maria Conchita Alonso/*Caught*

Scarlett Johansson/*Manny & Lo*

Catherine Keener/*Walking and Talking*

Renée Zellweger/*The Whole Wide World*

1998

★Julie Christie/*Afterglow*

Stacy Edwards/*In the Company of Men*

Alison Folland/*All Over Me*

Lisa Harrow/*Sunday*

1999

★Ally Sheedy/*High Art*

Katrin Cartlidge/*Claire Dolan*

Christina Ricci/*The Opposite of Sex*

Robin Tunney/*Niagara, Niagara*

Alfre Woodard/*Down in the Delta*

2000

★Hilary Swank/*Boys Don't Cry*

Diane Lane/*A Walk on the Moon*

Janet McTeer/*Tumbleweeds*

Reese Witherspoon/*Election*

2001

★Ellen Burstyn/*Requiem for a Dream*

Joan Allen/*The Contender*

Sanaa Lathan/*Love and Basketball*

Laura Linney/*You Can Count On Me*

Kelly Macdonald/*Two Family House*

2002

★Sissy Spacek/*In the Bedroom*

Molly Parker/*The Center of the World*

Tilda Swinton/*The Deep End*

Kerry Washington/*Lift*

2003

★Julianne Moore/*Far from Heaven*

Jennifer Aniston/*The Good Girl*

Maggie Gyllenhaal/*Secretary*

Catherine Keener/*Lovely & Amazing*

Parker Posey/*Personal Velocity: Three Portraits*

2004

★Charlize Theron/*Monster*

Agnes Bruckner/*Blue Car*

Zooey Deschanel/*All the Real Girls*

Samantha Morton/*In America*

2005

★Catalina Sandino Moreno/*Maria Full of Grace*

Kimberly Elise/*Woman, Thou Art Loosed*

2006

★Felicity Huffman/*Transamerica*

Vera Farmiga/*Down to the Bone*

Angelina Jolie/*A Mighty Heart*

Laura Linney/*The Squid and the Whale*

Sienna Miller/*Interview*

2007

★Shareeka Epps/*Half Nelson*

Catherine O'Hara/*For Your Consideration*

Michelle Williams/*Land of Plenty*

Robin Wright/*Sorry, Haters*

2008

★*Juno*

Parker Posey/*Broken English*

Tang Wei/*Lust, Caution*

2009

★Melissa Leo/*Frozen River*

Summer Bishil/*Towelhead*

Anne Hathaway/*Rachel Getting Married*

Melissa Leo/*Frozen River*

Tarra Riggs/*Ballast*

Michelle Williams/*Wendy and Lucy*

2010

★Gabourney 'Gabby' Sidibe/*Precious: Based on the Novel 'Push' by Sapphire*

Maria Bello/*Downloading Nancy*

Nisreen Faour/*Amreeka*

Dame Helen Mirren/*The Last Station*

Gwyneth Paltrow/*Two Lovers*

2011

★Natalie Portman/*Black Swan*

Annette Bening/*The Kids Are All Right*

Greta Gerwig/*Greenberg*

Nicole Kidman/*Rabbit Hole*

Jennifer Lawrence/*Winter's Bone*

Michelle Williams/*Blue Valentine*

2012

★Michelle Williams/*My Week With Marilyn*

Lauren Ambrose/*Think of Me*

Rachael Harris/*Natural Selection*

Adepero Oduye/*Pariah*

Elizabeth Olsen/*Martha Marcy May Marlene*

2013

★Jennifer Lawrence/*Silver Linings Playbook*

Linda Cardellini/*Return*

Emayatzy Corinealdi/*Middle of Nowhere*

Quvenzhane Wallis/*Beasts of the Southern Wild*

Mary Elizabeth Winstead/*Smashed*

2014

★Cate Blanchett/*Blue Jasmine*

Julie Delpy/*Before Midnight*

Gaby Hoffman/*Crystal Fairy & the Magical Cactus*

Brie Larson/*Short Term 12*

Shailene Woodley/*The Spectacular Now*

2015

★Julianne Moore/*Still Alice*

Marion Cotillard/*The Immigrant*

Rinko Kikuchi/*Kumiko the Treasure Hunter*

Jenny Slate/*Obvious Child*

Still Alice

Tilda Swinton/*Only Lovers Left Alive*

2016

★Brie Larson/*Room*

Cate Blanchett/*Carol*

Rooney Mara/*Carol*

Bel Powley/*The Diary of a Teenage Girl*

Kitana Kiki Rodriquez/*Tangerine*

2017

★Isabelle Huppert/*Elle*

Annette Bening/*20th Century Women*

Sasha Lane/*American Honey*

Ruth Negga/*Loving*

Natalie Portman/*Jackie*

2018

★Frances McDormand/*Three Billboards Outside Ebbing, Missouri*

Salma Hayek/*Beatriz at Dinner*

Margot Robbie/*I, Tonya*

Saoirse Ronan/*Lady Bird*

Shinobu Terajima/*Oh Lucy!*

Regina Williams/*Life & Nothing More*

2019

★Glenn Close/*The Wife*

Toni Collette/*Hereditary*

Elsie Fisher/*Eighth Grade*

Regina Hall/*Support the Girls*

Helena Howard/*Madeline's Madeline*

Carey Mulligan/*Wildlife*

2020

★Renée Zellweger/*Judy*

Karen Allen/*Colewell*

Hong Chau/*Driveways*

Elisabeth Moss/*Her Smell*

Mary Kay Place/*Diane*

Alfre Woodard/*Clemency*

ACTRESS—SUPPORTING

1988

★Anjelica Huston/*The Dead*

1989

★Rosanna Desoto/*Stand and Deliver*

1990

★Laura San Giacomo/*sex, lies and videotape*

1991

★Sheryl Lee Ralph/*To Sleep with Anger*

1992

★Diane Ladd/*Rambling Rose*

1993

★Alfre Woodard/*Passion Fish*

1994

Ah-Leh Gua/*The Wedding Banquet*

Lucinda Jenney/*American Heart*

Julianne Moore/*Short Cuts*

1995

★Dianne Wiest/*Bullets over Broadway*

V.S. Brodie/*Go Fish*

Carla Gallo/*Spanking the Monkey*

Brooke Smith/*Vanya on 42nd Street*

1996

★Mare Winningham/*Georgia*

Jennifer Lopez/*My Family*

Vanessa Redgrave/*Little Odessa*

Chloë Sevigny/*Kids*

Celia Weston/*Dead Man Walking*

1997

★Elizabeth Pena/*Lone Star*

Mary Kay Place/*Manny & Lo*

Queen Latifah/*Set It Off*

Lili Taylor/*Girls Town*

Lily Tomlin/*Flirting with Disaster*

1998

★Debbi (Deborah) Morgan/*Eve's Bayou*

Farrah Fawcett/*The Apostle*

Miranda Richardson/*The Apostle*

Patricia Richardson/*Ulee's Gold*

1999

★Lynn Redgrave/*Gods and Monsters*

Stockard Channing/*The Baby Dance*

Patricia Clarkson/*High Art*

Lisa Kudrow/*The Opposite of Sex*

Joely Richardson/*In the Shadows*

2000

★Chloë Sevigny/*Boys Don't Cry*

Barbara Barrie/*Judy Berlin*

Vanessa Martinez/*Limbo*

Julianne Nicholson/*Tully*

Sarah Polley/*Go*

Jean Smart/*Guinevere*

2001

Pat Carroll/*Songcatcher*

Jennifer Connelly/*Requiem for a Dream*

Marcia Gay Harden/*Pollock*

Lupe Ontiveros/*Chuck & Buck*

2002

★Carrie-Anne Moss/*Memento*

Uma Thurman/*Tape*

Tamara Tunie/*The Caveman's Valentine*

2003

★Emily Mortimer/*Lovely & Amazing*

Viola Davis/*Antwone Fisher*

2004

★Shohreh Aghdashloo/*House of Sand and Fog*

★Hope Davis/*The Secret Lives of Dentists*

Sarah Bolger/*In America*

Patricia Clarkson/*Pieces of April*

Frances McDormand/*Laurel Canyon*

2005

★Virginia Madsen/*Sideways*

Cate Blanchett/*Coffee and Cigarettes*

Loretta Devine/*Woman, Thou Art Loosed*

Yenny Paola Vega/*Maria Full of Grace*

2006

★Amy Adams/*Junebug*

Maggie Gyllenhaal/*Happy Endings*

Michelle Williams/*Brokeback Mountain*

2007

★Frances McDormand/*Friends with Money*

Melonie Diaz/*A Guide to Recognizing Your Saints*

Marcia Gay Harden/*American Gun*

2008

★Cate Blanchett/*I'm Not There*

Anna Kendrick/*Rocket Science*

Jennifer Jason Leigh/*Margot at the Wedding*

Tamara Podemski/*Four Sheets to the Wind*

Marisa Tomei/*Before the Devil Knows You're Dead*

2009

★Penelope Cruz/*Vicky Cristina Barcelona*

Rosemarie DeWitt/*Rachel Getting Married*

Misty Upham/*Frozen River*

Debra Winger/*Rachel Getting Married*

2010

★Mo'Nique/*Precious: Based on the Novel 'Push' by Sapphire*

Dina Korzun/*Cold Souls*

Samantha Morton/*The Messenger*

Nathalie Press/*Fifty Dead Men Walking*

Mia Wasikowska/*That Evening Sun*

2011

★Dale Dickey/*Winter's Bone*

Ashley Bell/*The Last Exorcism*

Allison Janney/*Life During Wartime*

Daphne Rubin-Vega/*Jack Goes Boating*

Naomi Watts/*Mother and Child*

2012

★Shailene Woodley/*The Descendants*

Jessica Chastain/*Take Shelter*

Anjelica Houston/*50/50*

Janet McTeer/*Albert Nobbs*

Harmony Santana/*Gun Hill Road*

2013

★Helen Hunt/*The Sessions*

Rosemarie DeWitt/*Your Sister's Sister*

Ann Dowd/*Compliance*

Brit Marling/*Sound of My Voice*

Lorraine Toussaint/*Middle of Nowhere*

2014

★Lupita Nyong'o/*12 Years a Slave*

Melonie Diaz/*Fruitvale Station*

Sally Hawkins/*Blue Jasmine*

June Squibb/*Nebraska*

Stand Clear of the Closing Doors

2015

★Patricia Arquette/*Boyhood*

Jessica Chastain/*A Most Violent Year*

Carmen Ejogo/*Selma*

Emma Stone/*Birdman, or (The Unexpected Virtue of Ignorance)*

Andrea Suarez Paz/*Stand Clear of the Closing Doors*

2016

★Mya Taylor/*Tangerine*

Marin Ireland/*Glass Chin*

Jennifer Jason Leigh/*Anomalisa*

Cynthia Nixon/*James White*

Robin Bartlett/*H.*

2017

★Molly Shannon/*Other People*

Paulina Garcia/*Little Men*

Lily Gladstone/*Certain Women*

Riley Keough/*American Honey*

2018

★Allison Janney/*I, Tonya*

Holly Hunter/*The Big Sick*

Laurie Metcalf/*Lady Bird*

Lois Smith/*Marjorie Prime*

Taliah Webster/*Good Time*

2019

★Regina King/*If Beale Street Could Talk*

Tyne Daly/*A Bread Factory, Part One*

Thomasin McKenzie/*Leave No Trace*

J. Smith-Cameron/*Nancy*

2020

★Shuzhen Zhao/*The Farewell*

Jennifer Lopez/*Hustlers*

Taylor Russell/*Waves*

Lauren Spencer/*Give Me Liberty*

Octavia Spencer/*Luce*

CINEMATOGRAPHY

1986

★*Trouble in Mind*

1987

★*Platoon*

1988

★*Matewan*

1989

★*The Unbearable Lightness of Being*

1990

★*Drugstore Cowboy*

1991

★*Wild at Heart*

1993

★*Night on Earth*

1994

★*Menace II Society*

American Heart

1995

★*Barcelona*

Eat Drink Man Woman

I Like It Like That

Suture

★ = winner

1996
★Leaving Las Vegas
Little Odessa
Nadja
The Underneath
The Usual Suspects
1997
★Fargo
Bound
Color of a Brisk and Leaping Day
Dead Man
The Funeral
1998
★Kama Sutra: A Tale of Love
Habit
Hard Eight
Sunday
1999
★Velvet Goldmine
Affliction
Belly
High Art
2000
Judy Berlin
Julien Donkey-boy
Twin Falls Idaho
2001
★Requiem for a Dream
Before Night Falls
Hamlet
Shadow of the Vampire
2002
★Mulholland Drive
The Deep End
Hedwig and the Angry Inch
Memento
2003
★Far from Heaven
Narc
Personal Velocity: Three Portraits
2004
★In America
Elephant
Northfork
Shattered Glass
2005
★The Motorcycle Diaries
Saints and Soldiers
We Don't Live Here Anymore
2006
★Good Night, and Good Luck
Capote
Youth Without Youth
2007
★Pan's Labyrinth
Brothers of the Head
2008
★The Diving Bell and the Butterfly
Lust, Caution
The Savages
2009
★The Wrestler
Ballast
Milk
2010
★A Serious Man
Bad Lieutenant: Port of Call New Orleans
Cold Souls
Sin Nombre
2011
★Black Swan
Greenberg
Never Let Me Go
Tiny Furniture
Winter's Bone

2012
★The Artist
Bellflower
The Dynamiter
Midnight in Paris
The Off Hours
2013
★Beasts of the Southern Wild
End of Watch
Here
Moonrise Kingdom
Seven Psychopaths
Valley of Saints
2014
★12 Years a Slave
All is Lost
Computer Chess
Inside Llewyn Davis
Spring Breakers
2015
★Birdman, or (The Unexpected Virtue of Ignorance)
A Girl Walks Home Alone at Night
The Immigrant
It Felt Like Love
Selma
2016
★Carol
Beasts of No Nation
It Follows
Meadowland
2017
★Moonlight
American Honey
Lol Crawley/The Childhood of a Leader
The Eyes of My Mother
Robbie Ryan/American Honey
2018
★Call Me by Your Name
Beach Rats
Columbus
The Killing of a Sacred Deer
The Rider
Wildlife
2019
★Suspiria
Madeline's Madeline
Mandy
Zak Mulligan/We the Animals
We the Animals
2020
★Jarin Blaschke/The Lighthouse
Todd Banhazl/Hustlers
Natasha Braier/Honey Boy
Chananun Chotrungro/The Third Wife
Pawel Pogorzelski/Midsommar

DIRECTOR

1986
★Joel Coen/Blood Simple
★Martin Scorsese/After Hours
1987
★Oliver Stone/Platoon
1988
★John Huston/The Dead
1989
★Ramon Menendez/Stand and Deliver
1990
★Steven Soderbergh/sex, lies and videotape
1991
★Charles Burnett/To Sleep with Anger
1992
★Martha Coolidge/Rambling Rose
1993
★Carl Franklin/One False Move
1994
★Robert Altman/Short Cuts
Ang Lee/The Wedding Banquet
Robert Rodriguez/El Mariachi
John Turturro/Mac
1995
★Quentin Tarantino/Pulp Fiction
John Dahl/Red Rock West
Ang Lee/Eat Drink Man Woman
Roman Polanski/Death and the Maiden
Alan Rudolph/Mrs. Parker and the Vicious Circle
1996
★Mike Figgis/Leaving Las Vegas
Michael Almereyda/Nadja
Ulu Grosbard/Georgia
Todd Haynes/Safe
John Sayles/The Secret of Roan Inish
1997
★Joel Coen/Fargo
Abel Ferrara/The Funeral
David O. Russell/Flirting with Disaster
Todd Solondz/Welcome to the Dollhouse
Robert M. Young/Caught
1998
★Robert Duvall/The Apostle
Larry Fessenden/Habit
Victor Nunez/Ulee's Gold
Paul Schrader/Touch
Wim Wenders/The End of Violence
1999
★Wes Anderson/Rushmore
Todd Haynes/Velvet Goldmine
Lodge Kerrigan/Claire Dolan
Paul Schrader/Affliction
Todd Solondz/Happiness
2000
★Alexander Payne/Election
Harmony Korine/Julien Donkey-boy
Doug Liman/Go
David Lynch/The Straight Story
Steven Soderbergh/The Limey
2001
★Ang Lee/Crouching Tiger, Hidden Dragon
Darren Aronofsky/Requiem for a Dream
Miguel Arteta/Chuck & Buck
Christopher Guest/Best in Show
Julian Schnabel/Before Night Falls
2002
★Christopher Nolan/Memento
Michael Cuesta/L.I.E.
Richard Linklater/Waking Life
John Cameron Mitchell/Hedwig and the Angry Inch

2003
★Todd Haynes/Far from Heaven
Joe Carnahan/Narc
Nicole Holofcener/Lovely & Amazing
2004
★Sofia Coppola/Lost in Translation
Shari Springer Berman/American Splendor
Robert Pulcini/American Splendor
Jim Sheridan/In America
Peter Sollett/Raising Victor Vargas
Gus Van Sant/Elephant
2005
★Alexander Payne/Sideways
Shane Carruth/Primer
Joshua Marston/Maria Full of Grace
Walter Salles/The Motorcycle Diaries
Mario Van Peebles/Baadasssss!
2006
★Ang Lee/Brokeback Mountain
Noah Baumbach/The Squid and the Whale
George Clooney/Good Night, and Good Luck
2007
★Jonathan Dayton/Little Miss Sunshine
★Valerie Faris/Little Miss Sunshine
Robert Altman/A Prairie Home Companion
Ryan Fleck/Half Nelson
Steven Soderbergh/Bubble
2008
★Julian Schnabel/The Diving Bell and the Butterfly
Todd Haynes/I'm Not There
Tamara Jenkins/The Savages
Jason Reitman/Juno
2009
★Thomas (Tom) McCarthy/The Visitor
Jonathan Demme/Rachel Getting Married
Lance Hammer/Ballast
Courtney Hunt/Frozen River
2010
★Lee Daniels/Precious: Based on the Novel 'Push' by Sapphire
Ethan Coen/A Serious Man
Joel Coen/A Serious Man
Cary Fukunaga/Sin Nombre
James Gray/Two Lovers
Michael Hoffman/The Last Station
2011
★Darren Aronofsky/Black Swan
Danny Boyle/127 Hours
Lisa Cholodenko/The Kids Are All Right
Debra Granik/Winter's Bone
John Cameron Mitchell/Rabbit Hole
2012
★Michel Hazanavicius/The Artist
Mike Mills/Beginners
Alexander Payne/The Descendants
Nicolas Winding Refn/Drive

2013
★David O. Russell/Silver Linings Playbook
Wes Anderson/Moonrise Kingdom
Julia Loktev/The Loneliest Planet
Ira Sachs/Keep the Lights On
Benh Zeitlin/Beasts of the Southern Wild
2014
★Steve McQueen/12 Years a Slave
Shane Carruth/Upstream Color
J.C. Chandor/All is Lost
Jeff Nichols/Mud
Alexander Payne/Nebraska
2015
★Richard Linklater/Boyhood
★Someone to Watch, Rania Attieh and Daniel Garcia/H.
Damien Chazelle/Whiplash
Ava DuVernay/Selma
Alejandro Gonzalez Inarritu/Birdman, or (The Unexpected Virtue of Ignorance)
David Zellner/Kumiko the Treasure Hunter
2016
★Tom McCarthy/Spotlight
Sean Baker/Tangerine
Cary Fukunaga/Beasts of No Nation
Todd Haynes/Carol
Duke Johnson/Anomalisa
Charlie Kaufman/Anomalisa
David Robert Mitchell/It Follows
2017
★Barry Jenkins/Moonlight
Andrea Arnold/American Honey
Pablo Larrain/Jackie
Jeff Nichols/Loving
Kelly Reichardt/Certain Women
2018
★Jordan Peele/Get Out
Sean Baker/The Florida Project
Jonas Carpignano/A Ciambra
Luca Guadagnino/Call Me by Your Name
Benny Safdie/Good Time
Josh Safdie/Good Time
Chloé Zhao/The Rider
2019
★Barry Jenkins/If Beale Street Could Talk
Debra Granik/Leave No Trace
Lynne Ramsay/You Were Never Really Here
Paul Schrader/First Reformed
2020
★Benny Safdie/Uncut Gems
★Josh Safdie/Uncut Gems
Robert Eggers/The Lighthouse
Alma Har'el/Honey Boy
Julius Onah/Luce
Lorene Scafaria/Hustlers

FILM

1986
★After Hours
1987
★Platoon
1988
★River's Edge

1989
★Stand and Deliver
1990
★sex, lies and videotape
1991
★The Grifters
1992
★Rambling Rose
1993
★The Player
1994
★Short Cuts
Much Ado about Nothing
The Wedding Banquet
1995
★Pulp Fiction
Bullets over Broadway
Eat Drink Man Woman
Mrs. Parker and the Vicious Circle
Wes Craven's New Nightmare
1996
★Leaving Las Vegas
Living in Oblivion
Safe
The Secret of Roan Inish
1997
★Fargo
Dead Man
The Funeral
Lone Star
Welcome to the Dollhouse
1998
★The Apostle
Chasing Amy
Ulee's Gold
Waiting for Guffman
1999
★Gods and Monsters
Affliction
Claire Dolan
A Soldier's Daughter Never Cries
Velvet Goldmine
2000
★Election
Cookie's Fortune
The Limey
The Straight Story
Sugar Town
Tully
2001
★Crouching Tiger, Hidden Dragon
Before Night Falls
Ghost Dog: The Way of the Samurai
Requiem for a Dream
2002
★Memento
Hedwig and the Angry Inch
L.I.E.
Waking Life
2003
★Far from Heaven
The Good Girl
Lovely & Amazing
Secretary
2004
★Lost in Translation
American Splendor
In America
Raising Victor Vargas
Shattered Glass
2005
★Sideways
Baadasssss!
Kinsey
Maria Full of Grace
Primer

★ = winner

2006
★Brokeback Mountain
Capote
Good Night, and Good Luck
The Squid and the Whale
2007
★Little Miss Sunshine
American Gun
Half Nelson
Pan's Labyrinth
2008
★Juno
The Diving Bell and the Butterfly
I'm Not There
A Mighty Heart
2009
★The Wrestler
Ballast
Frozen River
Rachel Getting Married
Wendy and Lucy
2010
★Precious: Based on the Novel 'Push' by Sapphire
Amreeka
(500) Days of Summer
The Last Station
Sin Nombre
2011
★Black Swan
Greenberg
The Kids Are All Right
127 Hours
Winter's Bone
2012
★The Artist
Beginners
The Descendants
Drive
50/50
Take Shelter
2013
★Silver Linings Playbook
Beasts of the Southern Wild
Bernie
Keep the Lights On
Moonrise Kingdom
2014
★12 Years a Slave
All is Lost
Frances Ha
Inside Llewyn Davis
Nebraska
2015
★Birdman, or (The Unexpected Virtue of Ignorance)
Boyhood
Love Is Strange
Selma
Whiplash
2016
★Spotlight
Anomalisa
Beasts of No Nation
Best Documentary/The Russian Woodpecker
Best First Feature; Best Cinematography/Songs My Brother Taught Me
Carol
Tangerine
2017
★Moonlight
American Honey
Chronic
Jackie
Manchester by the Sea
2018
★Get Out
Call Me by Your Name
The Florida Project
Lady Bird
The Rider
2019
★If Beale Street Could Talk
Eighth Grade
First Reformed
Leave No Trace
You Were Never Really Here
2020
★The Farewell
Clemency
A Hidden Life
Marriage Story
Uncut Gems

FEATURE DOCUMENTARY

2003
★Bowling for Columbine
2004
★The Fog of War: Eleven Lessons from the Life of Robert S. McNamara
My Architect: A Son's Journey
2005
★Metallica: Some Kind of Monster
Tarnation
2006
★Enron: The Smartest Guys in the Room
Grizzly Man
2007
★The Road to Guantanamo
2008
★Crazy Love
2010
★Anvil! The Story of Anvil
Food, Inc.
More Than a Game
2011
★Exit Through the Gift Shop
Marwencol
Restrepo
Sweetgrass
2012
★The Interrupters
An African Election
Bill Cunningham New York
The Redemption of General Butt Naked
We Were Here
2013
The Central Park Five
How to Survive a Plague
Marina Abramovic the Artist Is Present
The Waiting Room
2014
★20 Feet from Stardom
The Act of Killing
After Tiller
Gideon's Army
Gloria
The Square
2015
★Citizenfour
The Salt of the Earth
20,000 Days on Earth
Virunga
2016
Best of Enemies
2017
Cameraperson
I Am Not Your Negro
2018
★Faces Places
The Departure
Last Men In Aleppo
Minding the Gap
Motherland
Of Fathers and Sons
Quest
2019
★Won't You Be My Neighbor?
Hale County This Morning, This Evening
2020
★American Factory
Apollo 11
For Sama
Honeyland
Island of the Hungry Ghosts

FILM EDITING

2014
★Short Term 12
Frances Ha
Museum Hours
Una Noche
Upstream Color
2015
Boyhood
The Guest
A Most Violent Year
Nightcrawler
Ron Patane/A Most Violent Year
Whiplash
2016
★Spotlight
Heaven Knows What
It Follows
Room
2017
★Moonlight
Hell or High Water
Jackie
Manchester by the Sea
Swiss Army Man
2018
★I, Tonya
Call Me by Your Name
Get Out
Good Time
The Rider
2019
★You Were Never Really Here
American Animals
Mid90s
The Tale
We the Animals
2020
★Uncut Gems
Give Me Liberty
Sword of Trust
The Lighthouse
The Third Wife

FIRST FEATURE

1987
★She's Gotta Have It
1988
★Dirty Dancing
1989
★Mystic Pizza
1990
★Heathers
1991
★Metropolitan
1992
★Straight out of Brooklyn
1993
★The Waterdance
1994
★El Mariachi
American Heart
Combination Platter
Mac
Menace II Society
1995
★Spanking the Monkey
Clean, Shaven
Clerks
I Like It Like That
Suture
1996
★The Brothers McMullen
Kids
Little Odessa
Picture Bride
River of Grass
1997
★Sling Blade
Big Night
I Shot Andy Warhol
Manny & Lo
Tony Shalhoub/Big Night
Tree's Lounge
Stanley Tucci/Big Night
1998
★Eve's Bayou
Hard Eight
In the Company of Men
Star Maps
1999
★The Opposite of Sex
Buffalo 66
High Art
Pi
Slums of Beverly Hills
2000
★Being John Malkovich
The Blair Witch Project
Boys Don't Cry
Judy Berlin
Twin Falls Idaho
Xiu Xiu: The Sent Down Girl
2001
★You Can Count On Me
Boiler Room
Girlfight
Love and Basketball
2002
★In the Bedroom
The Anniversary Party
Donnie Darko
Ghost World
2003
★The Dangerous Lives of Altar Boys
Paid in Full
Roger Dodger
2004
★Monster
House of Sand and Fog
Pieces of April
2005
★Garden State
Brother to Brother
Napoleon Dynamite
Saints and Soldiers
The Woodsman
2006
★Crash
Transamerica
2008
★The Lookout
Rocket Science
2 Days in Paris
2009
★Synecdoche, New York
2010
★Crazy Heart
The Messenger
Paranormal Activity
A Single Man
2011
★Tiny Furniture
Get Low
The Last Exorcism
2012
★Margin Call
Another Earth
In the Family
Martha Marcy May Marlene
Natural Selection
2013
★The Perks of Being a Wallflower
Fill the Void
Gimme the Loot
Safety Not Guaranteed
Sound of My Voice
2014
★Fruitvale Station
Concussion
Una Noche
Wadjda
2015
★Nightcrawler
Dear White People
A Girl Walks Home Alone at Night
Obvious Child
2016
★The Diary of a Teenage Girl
★Alex Garland/Ex Machina
James White
2017
★The Witch
The Childhood of a Leader
The Fits
Other People
Swiss Army Man
2020
★Booksmart
Diane
The Last Black Man in San Francisco
The Mustang
See You Yesterday
The Climb

SCREENPLAY

1986
★The Trip to Bountiful
1987
★Platoon
1988
★River's Edge
1989
★Stand and Deliver
1990
★Drugstore Cowboy
1991
★To Sleep with Anger
1992
★My Own Private Idaho
1993
★The Waterdance
1994
★Short Cuts
Combination Platter
The Wedding Banquet
1995
★Pulp Fiction
Bullets over Broadway
Eat Drink Man Woman
Mrs. Parker and the Vicious Circle
Red Rock West
1996
★The Usual Suspects
Leaving Las Vegas
Living in Oblivion
Safe
The Secret of Roan Inish
1997
★Fargo
Dead Man
Flirting with Disaster
The Funeral
Lone Star
1998
★Chasing Amy
The Apostle
Touch
Ulee's Gold
Waiting for Guffman
1999
★The Opposite of Sex
Affliction
Blind Faith
Gods and Monsters
The Spanish Prisoner
2000
★Election
Dogma
Guinevere
The Limey
SLC Punk!
Tully
2001
★You Can Count On Me
Chuck & Buck
Love & Sex
Two Family House
Waking the Dead
2002
★Memento
In the Bedroom
Monster's Ball
Waking Life
2003
★The Good Girl
Roger Dodger
Thirteen Conversations About One Thing
2004
★Lost in Translation
American Splendor
A Mighty Wind
Pieces of April
Shattered Glass
2005
★Sideways
Baadasssss!
Before Sunset
The Door in the Floor
Kinsey
2006
★Capote
The Squid and the Whale
2007
★Thank You for Smoking
Friends with Money
The Illusionist
Sorry, Haters
2008
★The Savages
The Diving Bell and the Butterfly
Waitress
Year of the Dog
2009
★Vicky Cristina Barcelona
Savage Grace
Synecdoche, New York

★ = winner

2010
★(500) Days of Summer
Adventureland
The Last Station
The Messenger
The Vicious Kind
2011
★The Kids Are All Right
Life During Wartime
Please Give
Rabbit Hole
Winter's Bone
2012
★The Descendants
The Artist
Beginners
Footnote
Win Win
2013
★Silver Linings Playbook
Keep the Lights On
Moonrise Kingdom
Ruby Sparks
2014
★12 Years a Slave
Before Midnight
Blue Jasmine
Enough Said
The Spectacular Now
2015
★Nightcrawler
Big Eyes
Love Is Strange
A Most Violent Year
Only Lovers Left Alive
2016
★Spotlight
Anomalisa
Best First Screenplay/The Mend
Bone Tomahawk
Carol
The End of the Tour
2017
★Moonlight
Hell or High Water
Little Men
Manchester by the Sea
20th Century Women
2018
★Lady Bird
Beatriz at Dinner
Get Out
The Lovers
Three Billboards Outside Ebbing, Missouri
2019
★Can You Ever Forgive Me?
First Reformed
Sorry to Bother You
2020
★Marriage Story
Clemency
High Flying Bird
To Dust
Uncut Gems

DEBUT PERFORMANCE

1995
★Sean Nelson/Fresh
Jeff Anderson/Clerks
Jeremy Davies/Spanking the Monkey
Alicia Witt/Fun
Renée Zellweger/Love and a .45
1996
★Justin Pierce/Kids
Jason Andrews/Rhythm Thief
Lisa Bowman/River of Grass
Gabriel Casseus/New Jersey Drive
Rose McGowan/The Doom Generation
1997
★Heather Matarazzo/Welcome to the Dollhouse
Jena Malone/Bastard out of Carolina
Brendan Sexton, III/Welcome to the Dollhouse
Arie Verveen/Caught
Jeffrey Wright/Basquiat
1998
★Aaron Eckhart/In the Company of Men
Tyrone Burton/Squeeze
Eddie Cutanda/Squeeze
Phuong Duong/Squeeze
Lysa Flores/Star Maps
Darling Narita/Bang
Douglas Spain/Star Maps
1999
★Evan Adams/Smoke Signals
Anthony Roth Costanzo/A Soldier's Daughter Never Cries
Andrea Hart/Miss Monday
Sonja Sohn/Slam
Saul Williams/Slam
2000
★Kimberly J. Brown/Tumbleweeds
Bob Burrus/Tully
Jessica Campbell/Election
Chris Stafford/Edge of Seventeen
2001
★Michelle Rodriguez/Girlfight
Rory Culkin/You Can Count On Me
Emmy Rossum/Songcatcher
Mike White/Chuck & Buck
2002
★Paul Dano/L.I.E.
2003
★Nia Vardalos/My Big Fat Greek Wedding
America Ferrera/Real Women Have Curves
Raven Goodwin/Lovely & Amazing
Artel Kayaru/Dahmer
2004
★Nikki Reed/Thirteen
Anna Kendrick/Camp
Judy Marte/Raising Victor Vargas
Victor Rasuk/Raising Victor Vargas
2005
★Rodrigo de la Serna/The Motorcycle Diaries
Anthony Mackie/Brother to Brother
David Sullivan/Primer
The Woodsman

FIRST SCREENPLAY

1995
★Spanking the Monkey
Clerks
Fun
What Happened Was. . .
1996
Kids
Little Odessa
Postcards from America
River of Grass
Smoke
1997
★Big Night
Girl 6
Manny & Lo
Tree's Lounge
The Whole Wide World
1998
★In the Company of Men
Critical Care
Hard Eight
Star Maps
1999
★Pi
High Art
Niagara, Niagara
Slums of Beverly Hills
Smoke Signals
2000
★Being John Malkovich
The Adventures of Sebastian Cole
Boys Don't Cry
Cookie's Fortune
The Straight Story
2004
★The Station Agent
Blue Car
Monster
Raising Victor Vargas
Thirteen
2005
★Maria Full of Grace
Brother to Brother
Garden State
Primer
2006
★Transamerica
Junebug
2007
★Little Miss Sunshine
Conversations with Other Women
A Guide to Recognizing Your Saints
Half Nelson
The Painted Veil
2008
★Juno
Before the Devil Knows You're Dead
Broken English
A Mighty Heart
Rocket Science
2009
★Milk
Ballast
Frozen River
Rachel Getting Married
The Wackness
2010
★Precious: Based on the Novel 'Push' by Sapphire
Amreeka
Cold Souls
Crazy Heart
A Single Man
2011
★Tiny Furniture
Jack Goes Boating
Lovely, Still
2012
★50/50
Another Earth
Cedar Rapids
Margin Call
Terri
2013
★Safety Not Guaranteed
Celeste & Jesse Forever
Fill the Void
Gayby
Robot & Frank
2014
★Nebraska
Afternoon Delight
In a World...
The Inevitable Defeat of Mister & Pete
2015
★Dear White People
Appropriate Behavior
Sara Colangelo/Little Accidents
Little Accidents
The One I Love
2016
★Room
The Diary of a Teenage Girl
Me and Earl and the Dying Girl
2017
★The Witch
Christine
Other People
2018
★The Big Sick
Blame
Columbus
Donald Cried
Ingrid Goes West
Women Who Kill
2019
★Eighth Grade
Nancy
The Tale
Thoroughbreds
2020
★See You Yesterday
Blow The Man Down
Driveways
Greener Grass
The Vast of Night

CAST

2012
★Margin Call
2014
★Mud
2015
★Inherent Vice

FILM—FOREIGN LANGUAGE

1986
★Kiss of the Spider Woman
1987
★A Room with a View
1988
★My Life As a Dog
1989
★Wings of Desire
1990
★My Left Foot
1992
★An Angel at My Table
1993
★The Crying Game
1994
★The Piano
Like Water for Chocolate
Naked
Orlando
The Story of Qiu Ju
1995
★Trois Couleurs: Rouge
The Blue Kite
The Boys of St. Vincent
Ladybird, Ladybird
32 Short Films about Glenn Gould
1996
★Before the Rain
The City of Lost Children
Exotica
I Am Cuba
1997
Breaking the Waves
Chungking Express
Lamerica
Secrets and Lies
Trainspotting
1998
★The Sweet Hereafter
Happy Together
Mouth to Mouth
Nenette and Boni
Underground
1999
★The Celebration
Central Station
The Eel
Fireworks
The General
2000
★Run Lola Run
All About My Mother
My Son the Fanatic
Rosetta
Topsy Turvy
2001
★Dancer in the Dark
In the Mood for Love
The Terrorist
The War Zone
2002
Amelie
Amores Perros
Lumumba
Sexy Beast
2003
★Y Tu Mama Tambien
Bloody Sunday
The Fast Runner
The Piano Teacher
Time Out
2004
★Whale Rider
City of God
The Magdalene Sisters
The Triplets of Belleville
2005
★The Sea Inside
Bad Education
Red Lights
2006
★Paradise Now
2008
★Once
Persepolis
2009
★The Class
2010
★An Education
Everlasting Moments
Madeo
The Maid
A Prophet
2011
★The King's Speech
Kisses
Of Gods and Men
Uncle Boonmee Who Can Recall His Past Lives
2012
★A Separation
The Kid with a Bike
Melancholia
Shame
Tyrannosaur
2013
★Amour
Once Upon a Time in Anatolia
Rust and Bone
Sister
War Witch
2014
★Blue is the Warmest Color
The Great Beauty
The Hunt
A Touch of Sin
2015
★Ida
Force Majeure
Leviathan
Mommy
Under the Skin
2016
★Son of Saul
Best First Feature; Best Editing/Manos sucias
Best First Feature; Best First Screenplay; Best Male Lead/Mediterranea
Embrace of the Serpent
Girlhood
Mustang
A Pigeon Sat on a Branch Reflecting on Existence
2017
★Toni Erdmann
Aquarius
Chevalier
My Golden Days
Under the Shadow
2018
★A Fantastic Woman
BPM (Beats Per Minute)
Happy as Lazzaro
I Am Not a Witch
Lady Macbeth
Loveless
2019
★Roma
Burning
The Favourite
Shoplifters
2020
★Parasite
Invisible Life
Les Misérables
Portrait of a Lady on Fire
Retablo
The Souvenir

NATIONAL FILM REGISTRY

1955
The Phenix City Story
1989
The Best Years of Our Lives
Casablanca
Citizen Kane
Dr. Strangelove, or: How I Learned to Stop Worrying and Love the Bomb
The General
Gone with the Wind
The Grapes of Wrath
High Noon
Intolerance
The Learning Tree
The Maltese Falcon
Mr. Smith Goes to Washington
Modern Times
Nanook of the North
On the Waterfront
The Searchers
Singin' in the Rain
Snow White and the Seven Dwarfs
Some Like It Hot
Star Wars
Sunrise
Sunset Boulevard
Vertigo
The Wizard of Oz

★ = winner

1990
All About Eve
All Quiet on the Western Front
Bringing Up Baby
Dodsworth
Duck Soup
Fantasia
The Freshman
The Godfather
Harlan County, U.S.A.
How Green Was My Valley
It's a Wonderful Life
Killer of Sheep
Ninotchka
Raging Bull
Rebel without a Cause
Red River
Sullivan's Travels
Top Hat
Treasure of the Sierra Madre
A Woman under the Influence

1991
Chinatown
City Lights
David Holzman's Diary
Frankenstein
Gigi
I Am a Fugitive from a Chain Gang
The Italian
King Kong
Lawrence of Arabia
The Magnificent Ambersons
My Darling Clementine
Out of the Past
A Place in the Sun
Prisoner of Zenda
Shadow of a Doubt
2001: A Space Odyssey

1992
Adam's Rib
Annie Hall
The Bank Dick
The Big Parade
The Birth of a Nation
Bonnie & Clyde
Carmen Jones
Detour
Dog Star Man
Double Indemnity
Footlight Parade
The Gold Rush
Letter from an Unknown Woman
Morocco
Nashville
The Night of the Hunter
Paths of Glory
Psycho
Ride the High Country
Salt of the Earth

1993
An American in Paris
Badlands
The Black Pirate
Blade Runner
Cat People
The Godfather, Part 2
His Girl Friday
It Happened One Night
Lassie, Come Home
A Night at the Opera
Nothing but a Man
One Flew Over the Cuckoo's Nest
Shadows
Shane
Sweet Smell of Success
Touch of Evil
Yankee Doodle Dandy

1994
The African Queen
The Apartment
E.T.: The Extra-Terrestrial
Force of Evil
Freaks
Hell's Hinges
Invasion of the Body Snatchers
The Lady Eve
Louisiana Story
The Manchurian Candidate
Marty
Meet Me in St. Louis
Midnight Cowboy
Pinocchio
Safety Last
Scarface
Tabu: A Story of the South Seas
Taxi Driver

1995
The Adventures of Robin Hood
All That Heaven Allows
American Graffiti
The Band Wagon
Cabaret
Chan Is Missing
The Conversation
The Day the Earth Stood Still
El Norte
The Four Horsemen of the Apocalypse
Fury
The Hospital
The Last of the Mohicans
North by Northwest
The Philadelphia Story
Stagecoach
To Kill a Mockingbird

1996
The Awful Truth
Broken Blossoms
The Deer Hunter
Destry Rides Again
The Graduate
The Heiress
The Jazz Singer
*M*A*S*H*
Mildred Pierce
The Outlaw Josey Wales
The Producers
The Road to Morocco
She Done Him Wrong
Shock Corridor
Show Boat
The Thief of Baghdad
To Be or Not to Be
Woodstock

1997
Ben-Hur
The Big Sleep
The Bridge on the River Kwai
The Great Dictator
Harold and Maude
How the West Was Won
The Hustler
Knute Rockne: All American
Little Fugitive
Mean Streets
The Naked Spur
Rear Window
Return of the Secaucus 7
The Thin Man
West Side Story
Wings

1998
The Bride of Frankenstein
Don't Look Back
Easy Rider
42nd Street
From the Manger to the Cross
Gun Crazy
The Hitch-Hiker
The Last Picture Show
Little Miss Marker
The Lost World
The Ox-Bow Incident
The Phantom of the Opera
Public Enemy
Tootsie
Twelve o'Clock High

1999
Civilization
Do the Right Thing
Emperor Jones
Gunga Din
Jazz on a Summer's Day
Kiss Me Deadly
Laura
My Man Godfrey
Night of the Living Dead
Raiders of the Lost Ark
Roman Holiday
The Shop Around the Corner
A Streetcar Named Desire
The Ten Commandments
The Wild Bunch
Woman of the Year

2000
Apocalypse Now
Dracula
Five Easy Pieces
Goodfellas
Koyaanisqatsi
The Life of Emile Zola
Little Caesar
Love Finds Andy Hardy
Network
Peter Pan
Regeneration
Shaft
A Star Is Born
The Tall T
Will Success Spoil Rock Hunter?

2001
Abbott and Costello Meet Frankenstein
All That Jazz
All the King's Men
Hoosiers
It
Jaws
Manhattan
Miracle of Morgan's Creek
National Lampoon's Animal House
Planet of the Apes
The Sound of Music
Stormy Weather
The Thin Blue Line
The Thing

2002
Alien
The Bad and the Beautiful
Beauty and the Beast
The Black Stallion
Boyz N the Hood
The Endless Summer
From Here to Eternity
In the Heat of the Night
Lady Windermere's Fan
Melody Ranch
Sabrina
Stranger than Paradise
This Is Spinal Tap

2003
Atlantic City
Butch Cassidy and the Sundance Kid
Gold Diggers of 1933
The Hunters
Medium Cool
National Velvet
Naughty Marietta
Patton
Show People
Tarzan and His Mate
White Heat
Young Frankenstein
Young Mr. Lincoln

2004
Ben-Hur
The Court Jester
Daughters of the Dust
D.O.A.
Enter the Dragon
Eraserhead
Going My Way
Jailhouse Rock
The Nutty Professor
Schindler's List
Seven Brides for Seven Brothers
Swing Time

2005
Baby Face
The Cameraman
Cool Hand Luke
The Fall of the House of Usher
Fast Times at Ridgemont High
The French Connection
Giant
Hoop Dreams
Imitation of Life
Miracle on 34th Street
The Music Man
A Raisin in the Sun
The Rocky Horror Picture Show
The Sting
Toy Story

2006
Applause
The Big Trail
Blazing Saddles
Fargo
The Flesh and the Devil
Groundhog Day
Halloween
The Last Command
Notorious
Red Dust
Rocky
sex, lies and videotape
The T.A.M.I. Show
Traffic in Souls

2007
Back to the Future
Bullitt
Close Encounters of the Third Kind
Dance, Girl, Dance
Dances with Wolves
Days of Heaven
Grand Hotel
In a Lonely Place
The Man Who Shot Liberty Valance
The Naked City
Now, Voyager
Oklahoma!
Strong Man
Tol'able David
Twelve Angry Men
The Women
Wuthering Heights

2008
The Asphalt Jungle
Deliverance
A Face in the Crowd
Flower Drum Song
Foolish Wives
Hallelujah!
In Cold Blood
The Invisible Man
Johnny Guitar
The Killers
The Pawnbroker
Sergeant York
The Seventh Voyage of Sinbad
The Terminator

2009
Dog Day Afternoon
The Exiles
The Incredible Shrinking Man
Jezebel
The Mark of Zorro
Mrs. Miniver
The Muppet Movie
Once Upon a Time in the West
Pillow Talk
The Story of G.I. Joe
Under Western Stars

2010
Airplane!
All the President's Men
The Empire Strikes Back
The Exorcist
The Front Page
Grey Gardens
It's a Gift
Make Way for Tomorrow
Malcolm X
McCabe & Mrs. Miller
The Pink Panther
Saturday Night Fever
A Tree Grows in Brooklyn

2011
Bambi
The Big Heat
El Mariachi
Faces
Forrest Gump
Hester Street
The Iron Horse
The Lost Weekend
Norma Rae
The Silence of the Lambs
Stand and Deliver
Twentieth Century
The War of the Worlds

2012
Anatomy of a Murder
Born Yesterday
Breakfast at Tiffany's
A Christmas Story
Dirty Harry
A League of Their Own
The Matrix
Slacker
Sons of the Desert
The Spook Who Sat by the Door
3:10 to Yuma
Times of Harvey Milk
Two Lane Blacktop

2013
Forbidden Planet
Gilda
Judgment at Nuremberg
The Magnificent Seven
Mary Poppins
Midnight
Pulp Fiction
The Quiet Man
The Right Stuff
Roger & Me
Who's Afraid of Virginia Woolf?
Wild Boys of the Road

2014
The Big Lebowski
Down Argentine Way
Ferris Bueller's Day Off
The Gang's All Here
House of Wax
Little Big Man
The Power and the Glory
Rio Bravo
Rosemary's Baby
Ruggles of Red Gap
Saving Private Ryan
Willy Wonka & the Chocolate Factory

2015
Being There
Dracula Spanish Version
A Fool There Was
Ghostbusters
Hail the Conquering Hero
Humoresque
Imitation of Life
L.A. Confidential
Mark of Zorro
Our Daily Bread
Seconds
The Shawshank Redemption
Top Gun
Winchester '73

2016
The Atomic Cafe
Ball of Fire
The Birds
Blackboard Jungle
The Breakfast Club
East of Eden
Funny Girl
The Lion King
Lost Horizon
Paris Is Burning
Point Blank
The Princess Bride
Putney Swope
Rushmore
Steamboat Bill, Jr.
Thelma & Louise
20,000 Leagues under the Sea
A Walk in the Sun
Who Framed Roger Rabbit

2017
Ace in the Hole
Boulevard Nights
Die Hard
Field of Dreams
Gentleman's Agreement
The Goonies
Guess Who's Coming to Dinner
He Who Gets Slapped
La Bamba
Lives of Performers
Memento
Only Angels Have Wings
Spartacus
Superman: The Movie
Titanic
To Sleep with Anger
Wanda

2018
Bad Day at Black Rock
Broadcast News
Brokeback Mountain
Cinderella
Days of Wine and Roses
Eve's Bayou
Hearts & Minds
Hud
The Informer
Jurassic Park
The Lady from Shanghai
Leave Her to Heaven
Monterey Pop
My Fair Lady
On the Town
One-Eyed Jacks
Pickup on South Street
Rebecca
The Shining
Smoke Signals

★ = winner

2019

Amadeus
Becky Sharp
Before Stonewall
Body and Soul
Boys Don't Cry
Clerks
Coal Miner's Daughter
Emigrants Landing at Ellis Island
Employees' Entrance
The Fog of War: Eleven Lessons from the Life of Robert S. McNamara
Gaslight
George Washington Carver at Tuskegee Institute
Girlfriends
I am Somebody
The Last Waltz
My Name Is Oona
A New Leaf
Old Yeller
The Phenix City Story
Platoon
Purple Rain
Real Women Have Curves
She's Gotta Have It
Sleeping Beauty
Zoot Suit

SCREEN ACTORS GUILD AWARDS

ACTOR

1994

★Tom Hanks/*Forrest Gump*
Morgan Freeman/*The Shawshank Redemption*
Paul Newman/*Nobody's Fool*
Tim Robbins/*The Shawshank Redemption*
John Travolta/*Pulp Fiction*

1995

★Nicolas Cage/*Leaving Las Vegas*
Anthony Hopkins/*Nixon*
James Earl Jones/*Cry, the Beloved Country*
Sean Penn/*Dead Man Walking*
Massimo Troisi/*The Postman*

1996

★Geoffrey Rush/*Shine*
Tom Cruise/*Jerry Maguire*
Ralph Fiennes/*The English Patient*
Woody Harrelson/*The People vs. Larry Flynt*
Billy Bob Thornton/*Sling Blade*

1997

★Jack Nicholson/*As Good As It Gets*
Matt Damon/*Good Will Hunting*
Robert Duvall/*The Apostle*
Peter Fonda/*Ulee's Gold*
Dustin Hoffman/*Wag the Dog*

1998

★Roberto Benigni/*Life Is Beautiful*
Joseph Fiennes/*Shakespeare in Love*
Tom Hanks/*Saving Private Ryan*
Ian McKellen/*Gods and Monsters*
Nick Nolte/*Affliction*

1999

★Kevin Spacey/*American Beauty*
Jim Carrey/*Man on the Moon*
Russell Crowe/*The Insider*
Philip Seymour Hoffman/*Flawless*
Denzel Washington/*The Hurricane*

2000

★Benicio Del Toro/*Traffic*
Jamie Bell/*Billy Elliot*
Russell Crowe/*Gladiator*
Geoffrey Rush/*Quills*

2001

★Russell Crowe/*A Beautiful Mind*
Kevin Kline/*Life as a House*
Sean Penn/*I Am Sam*
Denzel Washington/*Training Day*
Tom Wilkinson/*In the Bedroom*

2002

★Daniel Day-Lewis/*Gangs of New York*
Adrien Brody/*The Pianist*
Nicolas Cage/*Adaptation*
Richard Gere/*Chicago*
Jack Nicholson/*About Schmidt*

2003

★Johnny Depp/*Pirates of the Caribbean: The Curse of the Black Pearl*
Peter Dinklage/*The Station Agent*
Ben Kingsley/*House of Sand and Fog*
Bill Murray/*Lost in Translation*
Sean Penn/*Mystic River*

2004

★Jamie Foxx/*Ray*
Don Cheadle/*Hotel Rwanda*
Johnny Depp/*Finding Neverland*
Leonardo DiCaprio/*The Aviator*
Paul Giamatti/*Sideways*

2005

★Philip Seymour Hoffman/*Capote*
Russell Crowe/*Cinderella Man*
Heath Ledger/*Brokeback Mountain*
Joaquin Rafael (Leaf) Phoenix/*Walk the Line*
David Strathairn/*Good Night, and Good Luck*

2006

★Forest Whitaker/*The Last King of Scotland*
Leonardo DiCaprio/*Blood Diamond*
Ryan Gosling/*Half Nelson*
Peter O'Toole/*Venus*
Will Smith/*The Pursuit of Happyness*

2007

★Daniel Day-Lewis/*There Will Be Blood*
George Clooney/*Michael Clayton*
Ryan Gosling/*Lars and the Real Girl*
Emile Hirsch/*Into the Wild*
Viggo Mortensen/*Eastern Promises*

2008

★Sean Penn/*Milk*
Richard Jenkins/*The Visitor*
Frank Langella/*Frost/Nixon*
Brad Pitt/*The Curious Case of Benjamin Button*
Mickey Rourke/*The Wrestler*

2009

★Jeff Bridges/*Crazy Heart*
George Clooney/*Up in the Air*
Colin Firth/*A Single Man*
Morgan Freeman/*Invictus*
Jeremy Renner/*The Hurt Locker*

2010

★Colin Firth/*The King's Speech*
Jeff Bridges/*True Grit*
Robert Duvall/*Get Low*
Jesse Eisenberg/*The Social Network*
James Franco/*127 Hours*

2011

★Jean Dujardin/*The Artist*
Demian Bechir/*A Better Life*
George Clooney/*The Descendants*
Leonardo DiCaprio/*J. Edgar*
Brad Pitt/*Moneyball*

2012

★Daniel Day-Lewis/*Lincoln*
Bradley Cooper/*Silver Linings Playbook*
John Hawkes/*The Sessions*
Hugh Jackman/*Les Miserables*
Denzel Washington/*Flight*

2013

★Matthew McConaughey/*Dallas Buyers Club*
Bruce Dern/*Nebraska*
Chiwetel Ejiofor/*12 Years a Slave*
Tom Hanks/*Captain Phillips*
Forest Whitaker/*Lee Daniels' The Butler*

2014

★Eddie Redmayne/*The Theory of Everything*
Steve Carell/*Foxcatcher*
Benedict Cumberbatch/*The Imitation Game*
Jake Gyllenhaal/*Nightcrawler*
Michael Keaton/*Birdman, or (The Unexpected Virtue of Ignorance)*

2015

★Leonardo DiCaprio/*The Revenant*
Bryan Cranston/*Trumbo*
Johnny Depp/*Black Mass*
Michael Fassbender/*Steve Jobs*
Eddie Redmayne/*The Danish Girl*

2016

★Denzel Washington/*Fences*
Casey Affleck/*Manchester by the Sea*
Andrew Garfield/*Hacksaw Ridge*
Ryan Gosling/*La La Land*
Viggo Mortensen/*Captain Fantastic*

2017

★Gary Oldman/*Darkest Hour*
Timothée Chalamet/*Call Me by Your Name*
James Franco/*The Disaster Artist*
Daniel Kaluuya/*Get Out*
Denzel Washington/*Roman J. Israel, Esq.*

2018

★Rami Malek/*Bohemian Rhapsody*
Christian Bale/*Vice*
Bradley Cooper/*A Star Is Born*
Viggo Mortensen/*Green Book*
John David Washington/*BlacKkKlansman*

2019

★Joaquin Rafael (Leaf) Phoenix/*Joker*
Christian Bale/*Ford v Ferrari*
Leonardo DiCaprio/*Once Upon A Time... In Hollywood*
Adam Driver/*Marriage Story*
Taron Egerton/*Rocketman*

ACTOR—SUPPORTING

1994

★Martin Landau/*Ed Wood*
Gary Sinise/*Forrest Gump*

1995

★Ed Harris/*Apollo 13*
Kevin Bacon/*Murder in the First*
Kenneth Branagh/*Othello*
Don Cheadle/*Devil in a Blue Dress*
Kevin Spacey/*The Usual Suspects*

1996

★Cuba Gooding, Jr./*Jerry Maguire*
Hank Azaria/*The Birdcage*
Nathan Lane/*The Birdcage*
William H. Macy/*Fargo*
Noah Taylor/*Shine*

1997

★Robin Williams/*Good Will Hunting*
Billy Connolly/*Mrs. Brown*
Anthony Hopkins/*Amistad*
Greg Kinnear/*As Good As It Gets*
Burt Reynolds/*Boogie Nights*

1998

★Robert Duvall/*A Civil Action*
James Coburn/*Affliction*
David Kelly/*Waking Ned Devine*
Geoffrey Rush/*Shakespeare in Love*
Billy Bob Thornton/*A Simple Plan*

1999

★Michael Caine/*The Cider House Rules*
Chris Cooper/*American Beauty*
Tom Cruise/*Magnolia*
Michael Clarke Duncan/*The Green Mile*
Haley Joel Osment/*The Sixth Sense*

2000

★Albert Finney/*Erin Brockovich*
Jeff Bridges/*The Contender*
Willem Dafoe/*Shadow of the Vampire*
Gary Oldman/*The Contender*
Joaquin Rafael (Leaf) Phoenix/*Gladiator*

2001

★Ian McKellen/*Lord of the Rings: The Fellowship of the Ring*
Jim Broadbent/*Iris*
Hayden Christensen/*Life as a House*
Ethan Hawke/*Training Day*
Ben Kingsley/*Sexy Beast*

2002

★Christopher Walken/*Catch Me If You Can*
Chris Cooper/*Adaptation*
Ed Harris/*The Hours*
Alfred Molina/*Frida*
Dennis Quaid/*Far from Heaven*

2003

★Tim Robbins/*Mystic River*
Alec Baldwin/*The Cooler*
Chris Cooper/*Seabiscuit*
Benicio Del Toro/*21 Grams*

2004

★Morgan Freeman/*Million Dollar Baby*
Thomas Haden Church/*Sideways*
Jamie Foxx/*Collateral*
James Garner/*The Notebook*
Freddie Highmore/*Finding Neverland*

2005

★Paul Giamatti/*Cinderella Man*
Don Cheadle/*Crash*
George Clooney/*Syriana*
Matt Dillon/*Crash*
Jake Gyllenhaal/*Brokeback Mountain*

2006

★Eddie Murphy/*Dreamgirls*
Alan Arkin/*Little Miss Sunshine*
Leonardo DiCaprio/*The Departed*
Jackie Earle Haley/*Little Children*
Djimon Hounsou/*Blood Diamond*

2007

★Javier Bardem/*No Country for Old Men*
Casey Affleck/*The Assassination of Jesse James by the Coward Robert Ford*
Hal Holbrook/*Into the Wild*
Tommy Lee Jones/*No Country for Old Men*
Tom Wilkinson/*Michael Clayton*

2008

★Heath Ledger/*The Dark Knight*
Josh Brolin/*Milk*
Robert Downey, Jr./*Tropic Thunder*
Philip Seymour Hoffman/*Doubt*
Dev Patel/*Slumdog Millionaire*

2009

★Christoph Waltz/*Inglourious Basterds*
Matt Damon/*Invictus*
Woody Harrelson/*The Messenger*
Christopher Plummer/*The Last Station*
Stanley Tucci/*The Lovely Bones*

2010

★Christian Bale/*The Fighter*
John Hawkes/*Winter's Bone*
Jeremy Renner/*The Town*
Mark Ruffalo/*The Kids Are All Right*
Geoffrey Rush/*The King's Speech*

2011

★Christopher Plummer/*Beginners*
Kenneth Branagh/*My Week With Marilyn*
Armie Hammer/*J. Edgar*
Jonah Hill/*Moneyball*
Nick Nolte/*Warrior*

2012

★Tommy Lee Jones/*Lincoln*
Alan Arkin/*Argo*
Javier Bardem/*Skyfall*
Robert De Niro/*Silver Linings Playbook*
Philip Seymour Hoffman/*The Master*

2013

★Jared Leto/*Dallas Buyers Club*
Barkhad Adbi/*Captain Phillips*
Daniel Brühl/*Rush*
Michael Fassbender/*12 Years a Slave*
James Gandolfini/*Enough Said*

2014

★J.K. Simmons/*Whiplash*
Robert Duvall/*The Judge*
Ethan Hawke/*Boyhood*
Mark Ruffalo/*Foxcatcher*

2015

★Idris Elba/*Beasts of No Nation*
Christian Bale/*The Big Short*
Mark Rylance/*Bridge of Spies*
Michael Shannon/*99 Homes*
Jacob Tremblay/*Room*

2016

★Mahershala Ali/*Moonlight*
Jeff Bridges/*Hell or High Water*
Hugh Grant/*Florence Foster Jenkins*
Lucas Hedges/*Manchester by the Sea*
Dev Patel/*Lion*

2017

★Sam Rockwell/*Three Billboards Outside Ebbing, Missouri*
Steve Carell/*Battle of the Sexes*
Willem Dafoe/*The Florida Project*
Woody Harrelson/*Three Billboards Outside Ebbing, Missouri*
Richard Jenkins/*The Shape of Water*

2018

★Mahershala Ali/*Green Book*
Timothée Chalamet/*Beautiful Boy*
Adam Driver/*BlacKkKlansman*
Sam Elliott/*A Star Is Born*
Richard E. Grant/*Can You Ever Forgive Me?*

2019

★Brad Pitt/*Once Upon A Time... In Hollywood*
Jamie Foxx/*Just Mercy*
Tom Hanks/*A Beautiful Day in the Neighborhood*
Al Pacino/*The Irishman*
Joe Pesci/*The Irishman*

ACTRESS

1994

★Jodie Foster/*Nell*
Jessica Lange/*Blue Sky*
Meg Ryan/*When a Man Loves a Woman*
Susan Sarandon/*The Client*
Meryl Streep/*The River Wild*

1995

★Susan Sarandon/*Dead Man Walking*
Joan Allen/*Nixon*
Elisabeth Shue/*Leaving Las Vegas*
Meryl Streep/*The Bridges of Madison County*
Emma Thompson/*Sense and Sensibility*

1996

★Frances McDormand/*Fargo*
Brenda Blethyn/*Secrets and Lies*
Diane Keaton/*Marvin's Room*
Gena Rowlands/*Unhook the Stars*
Kristin Scott Thomas/*The English Patient*

1997

★Helen Hunt/*As Good As It Gets*
Helena Bonham Carter/*The Wings of the Dove*
Dame Judi Dench/*Mrs. Brown*
Pam Grier/*Jackie Brown*
Kate Winslet/*Titanic*
Robin Wright/*She's So Lovely*

★ = winner

1998

★Gwyneth Paltrow/*Shakespeare in Love*

Cate Blanchett/*Elizabeth*

Jane Horrocks/*Little Voice*

Meryl Streep/*One True Thing*

Emily Watson/*Hilary and Jackie*

1999

★Annette Bening/*American Beauty*

Janet McTeer/*Tumbleweeds*

Julianne Moore/*The End of the Affair*

Meryl Streep/*Music of the Heart*

Hilary Swank/*Boys Don't Cry*

2000

★Julia Roberts/*Erin Brockovich*

Joan Allen/*The Contender*

Juliette Binoche/*Chocolat*

Ellen Burstyn/*Requiem for a Dream*

Laura Linney/*You Can Count On Me*

2001

★Halle Berry/*Monster's Ball*

Jennifer Connelly/*A Beautiful Mind*

Dame Judi Dench/*Iris*

Sissy Spacek/*In the Bedroom*

Renée Zellweger/*Bridget Jones's Diary*

2002

★Renée Zellweger/*Chicago*

Salma Hayek/*Frida*

Nicole Kidman/*The Hours*

Diane Lane/*Unfaithful*

Julianne Moore/*Far from Heaven*

2003

★Charlize Theron/*Monster*

Patricia Clarkson/*The Station Agent*

Diane Keaton/*Something's Gotta Give*

Naomi Watts/*21 Grams*

Evan Rachel Wood/*Thirteen*

2004

★Hilary Swank/*Million Dollar Baby*

Annette Bening/*Being Julia*

Cloris Leachman/*Spanglish*

Catalina Sandino Moreno/*Maria Full of Grace*

Imelda Staunton/*Vera Drake*

Kate Winslet/*Eternal Sunshine of the Spotless Mind*

2005

★Reese Witherspoon/*Walk the Line*

Dame Judi Dench/*Mrs. Henderson Presents*

Felicity Huffman/*Transamerica*

Charlize Theron/*North Country*

2006

★Dame Helen Mirren/*The Queen*

Penelope Cruz/*Volver*

Dame Judi Dench/*Notes on a Scandal*

Meryl Streep/*The Devil Wears Prada*

Kate Winslet/*Little Children*

2007

★Julie Christie/*Away From Her*

Cate Blanchett/*Elizabeth: The Golden Age*

Marion Cotillard/*La Vie en Rose*

Angelina Jolie/*A Mighty Heart*

Ellen Page/*Juno*

2008

★Meryl Streep/*Doubt*

Anne Hathaway/*Rachel Getting Married*

Angelina Jolie/*Changeling*

Melissa Leo/*Frozen River*

2009

★Sandra Bullock/*The Blind Side*

Vera Farmiga/*Up in the Air*

Anna Kendrick/*Up in the Air*

Dame Helen Mirren/*The Last Station*

Carey Mulligan/*An Education*

Gabourney 'Gabby' Sidibe/*Precious: Based on the Novel 'Push' by Sapphire*

Meryl Streep/*Julie & Julia*

2010

★Natalie Portman/*Black Swan*

Annette Bening/*The Kids Are All Right*

Nicole Kidman/*Rabbit Hole*

Jennifer Lawrence/*Winter's Bone*

Hilary Swank/*Conviction*

2011

★Viola Davis/*The Help*

Glenn Close/*Albert Nobbs*

Meryl Streep/*The Iron Lady*

Tilda Swinton/*We Need to Talk About Kevin*

Michelle Williams/*My Week With Marilyn*

2012

★Jennifer Lawrence/*Silver Linings Playbook*

Jessica Chastain/*Zero Dark Thirty*

Marion Cotillard/*Rust and Bone*

Dame Helen Mirren/*Hitchcock*

Naomi Watts/*The Impossible*

2013

★Cate Blanchett/*Blue Jasmine*

Sandra Bullock/*Gravity*

Dame Judi Dench/*Philomena*

Meryl Streep/*August: Osage County*

Emma Thompson/*Saving Mr. Banks*

2014

★Julianne Moore/*Still Alice*

Jennifer Aniston/*Cake*

Felicity Jones/*The Theory of Everything*

Rosamund Pike/*Gone Girl*

Still Alice

Reese Witherspoon/*Wild*

2015

★Brie Larson/*Room*

Cate Blanchett/*Carol*

Dame Helen Mirren/*Woman in Gold*

Saoirse Ronan/*Brooklyn*

Sarah Silverman/*I Smile Back*

2016

★Viola Davis/*Fences*

★Emma Stone/*La La Land*

Amy Adams/*Arrival*

Emily Blunt/*The Girl on the Train*

Natalie Portman/*Jackie*

2017

★Glenn Close/*The Wife*

★Frances McDormand/*Three Billboards Outside Ebbing, Missouri*

Dame Judi Dench/*Victoria & Abdul*

Sally Hawkins/*The Shape of Water*

Margot Robbie/*I, Tonya*

Saoirse Ronan/*Lady Bird*

2018

Emily Blunt/*Mary Poppins Returns*

Olivia Colman/*The Favourite*

Lady Gaga/*A Star Is Born*

Melissa McCarthy/*Can You Ever Forgive Me?*

2019

★Renée Zellweger/*Judy*

Cynthia Erivo/*Harriet*

Scarlett Johansson/*Marriage Story*

Lupita Nyong'o/*Us*

Charlize Theron/*Bombshell*

ACTRESS—SUPPORTING

1994

★Dianne Wiest/*Bullets over Broadway*

Sally Field/*Forrest Gump*

Robin Wright/*Forrest Gump*

1995

★Kate Winslet/*Sense and Sensibility*

Stockard Channing/*Smoke*

Anjelica Huston/*The Crossing Guard*

Mira Sorvino/*Mighty Aphrodite*

Mare Winningham/*Georgia*

1996

★Lauren Bacall/*The Mirror Has Two Faces*

Juliette Binoche/*The English Patient*

Marisa Tomei/*Unhook the Stars*

Gwen Verdon/*Marvin's Room*

Renée Zellweger/*Jerry Maguire*

1997

★Kim Basinger/*L.A. Confidential*

★Gloria Stuart/*Titanic*

Minnie Driver/*Good Will Hunting*

Alison Elliott/*The Wings of the Dove*

Julianne Moore/*Boogie Nights*

1998

★Kathy Bates/*Primary Colors*

Brenda Blethyn/*Little Voice*

Dame Judi Dench/*Shakespeare in Love*

Rachel Griffiths/*Hilary and Jackie*

Lynn Redgrave/*Gods and Monsters*

1999

★Angelina Jolie/*Girl, Interrupted*

Cameron Diaz/*Being John Malkovich*

Angelina Jolie/*Girl, Interrupted*

Catherine Keener/*Being John Malkovich*

Julianne Moore/*Magnolia*

Chloë Sevigny/*Boys Don't Cry*

2000

★Dame Judi Dench/*Chocolat*

Kate Hudson/*Almost Famous*

Frances McDormand/*Almost Famous*

Julie Walters/*Billy Elliot*

Kate Winslet/*Quills*

2001

★Dame Helen Mirren/*Gosford Park*

Cate Blanchett/*Bandits*

Dame Judi Dench/*The Shipping News*

Cameron Diaz/*Vanilla Sky*

Dakota Fanning/*I Am Sam*

2002

★Catherine Zeta-Jones/*Chicago*

Kathy Bates/*About Schmidt*

Julianne Moore/*The Hours*

Michelle Pfeiffer/*White Oleander*

Queen Latifah/*Chicago*

2003

★Renée Zellweger/*Cold Mountain*

Maria Bello/*The Cooler*

Keisha Castle-Hughes/*Whale Rider*

Patricia Clarkson/*Pieces of April*

Holly Hunter/*Thirteen*

Ken(saku) Watanabe/*The Last Samurai*

2004

★Cate Blanchett/*The Aviator*

Laura Linney/*Kinsey*

Virginia Madsen/*Sideways*

Sophie Okonedo/*Hotel Rwanda*

2005

★Rachel Weisz/*The Constant Gardener*

Amy Adams/*Junebug*

Catherine Keener/*Capote*

Frances McDormand/*North Country*

Michelle Williams/*Brokeback Mountain*

2006

★Jennifer Hudson/*Dreamgirls*

Adriana Barraza/*Babel*

Cate Blanchett/*Notes on a Scandal*

Abigail Breslin/*Little Miss Sunshine*

Rinko Kikuchi/*Babel*

2007

★Ruby Dee/*American Gangster*

Cate Blanchett/*I'm Not There*

Catherine Keener/*Into the Wild*

Amy Ryan/*Gone Baby Gone*

Tilda Swinton/*Michael Clayton*

2008

★Kate Winslet/*The Reader*

Amy Adams/*Doubt*

Penelope Cruz/*Vicky Cristina Barcelona*

Viola Davis/*Doubt*

Taraji P. Henson/*The Curious Case of Benjamin Button*

2009

★Mo'Nique/*Precious: Based on the Novel 'Push' by Sapphire*

Penelope Cruz/*Nine*

Diane Kruger/*Inglourious Basterds*

2010

★Melissa Leo/*The Fighter*

Amy Adams/*The Fighter*

Helena Bonham Carter/*The King's Speech*

Mila Kunis/*Black Swan*

Hailee Steinfeld/*True Grit*

2011

★Octavia Spencer/*The Help*

Berenice Bejo/*The Artist*

Jessica Chastain/*The Help*

Melissa McCarthy/*Bridesmaids*

Janet McTeer/*Albert Nobbs*

2012

★Anne Hathaway/*Les Miserables*

Sally Field/*Lincoln*

Helen Hunt/*The Sessions*

Nicole Kidman/*The Paperboy*

Maggie Smith/*The Best Exotic Marigold Hotel*

2013

★Lupita Nyong'o/*12 Years a Slave*

Jennifer Lawrence/*American Hustle*

Julia Roberts/*August: Osage County*

Oprah Winfrey/*Lee Daniels' The Butler*

2014

★Patricia Arquette/*Boyhood*

Keira Knightley/*The Imitation Game*

Edward Norton/*Birdman, or (The Unexpected Virtue of Ignorance)*

June Squibb/*Nebraska*

Emma Stone/*Birdman, or (The Unexpected Virtue of Ignorance)*

Meryl Streep/*Into the Woods*

Naomi Watts/*St. Vincent*

2015

★Alicia Vikander/*The Danish Girl*

Rooney Mara/*Carol*

Rachel McAdams/*Spotlight*

Dame Helen Mirren/*Trumbo*

Kate Winslet/*Steve Jobs*

2016

Naomie Harris/*Moonlight*

Nicole Kidman/*Lion*

Octavia Spencer/*Hidden Figures*

Michelle Williams/*Manchester by the Sea*

2017

★Allison Janney/*I, Tonya*

Mary J. Blige/*Mudbound*

Hong Chau/*Downsizing*

Holly Hunter/*The Big Sick*

Laurie Metcalf/*Lady Bird*

2018

★Emily Blunt/*A Quiet Place*

Amy Adams/*Vice*

Margot Robbie/*Mary Queen of Scots*

Emma Stone/*The Favourite*

Rachel Weisz/*The Favourite*

2019

★Laura Dern/*Marriage Story*

Scarlett Johansson/*Jojo Rabbit*

Nicole Kidman/*Bombshell*

Jennifer Lopez/*Hustlers*

Margot Robbie/*Bombshell*

ORIGINAL SCREENPLAY

2015

Bridge of Spies

CAST

1995

★*Apollo 13*

Get Shorty

How to Make an American Quilt

Nixon

Sense and Sensibility

1996

★*The Birdcage*

The English Patient

Marvin's Room

Shine

Sling Blade

1997

★*The Full Monty*

Boogie Nights

Good Will Hunting

L.A. Confidential

Titanic

1998

★*Shakespeare in Love*

Life Is Beautiful

Little Voice

Saving Private Ryan

Waking Ned Devine

1999

★*American Beauty*

Being John Malkovich

The Cider House Rules

The Green Mile

Magnolia

2000

★*Traffic*

Almost Famous

Billy Elliot

Chocolat

Gladiator

2001

★*Gosford Park*

A Beautiful Mind

In the Bedroom

Lord of the Rings: The Fellowship of the Ring

Moulin Rouge

2002

★*Chicago*

Adaptation

The Hours

Lord of the Rings: The Two Towers

My Big Fat Greek Wedding

2003

★*Lord of the Rings: The Return of the King*

In America

Mystic River

Seabiscuit

The Station Agent

2004

★*Sideways*

The Aviator

Finding Neverland

Hotel Rwanda

Million Dollar Baby

Ray

2005

★*Crash*

Brokeback Mountain

Capote

Good Night, and Good Luck

Hustle & Flow

2006

★*Little Miss Sunshine*

Babel

Bobby

The Departed

Dreamgirls

2007

★*No Country for Old Men*

American Gangster

Hairspray

Into the Wild

3:10 to Yuma

2008

★*Slumdog Millionaire*

The Curious Case of Benjamin Button

Doubt

Frost/Nixon

Milk

★ = *winner*

2009
★Inglourious Basterds
An Education
The Hurt Locker
Nine
Precious: Based on the Novel 'Push' by Sapphire
2010
★The King's Speech
Black Swan
The Fighter
The Kids Are All Right
The Social Network
2011
★The Help
The Artist
Bridesmaids
The Descendants
Midnight in Paris
2012
★Argo
The Best Exotic Marigold Hotel
Les Miserables
Lincoln
Silver Linings Playbook
2013
★American Hustle
August: Osage County
Dallas Buyers Club
12 Years a Slave
2014
★Birdman, or (The Unexpected Virtue of Ignorance)
Boyhood
The Grand Budapest Hotel
Lee Daniels' The Butler
The Theory of Everything
2015
★Spotlight
Beasts of No Nation
The Big Short
The Imitation Game
Straight Outta Compton
Trumbo
2016
★Hidden Figures
Captain Fantastic
Fences
Manchester by the Sea
Moonlight
2017
★Three Billboards Outside Ebbing, Missouri
The Big Sick
Get Out
Lady Bird
Mudbound
2018
★Black Panther
BlacKkKlansman
Bohemian Rhapsody
Crazy Rich Asians
A Star Is Born
2019
★Parasite
Bombshell
The Irishman
Jojo Rabbit
Once Upon A Time... In Hollywood

WRITERS GUILD OF AMERICA

ADAPTED SCREENPLAY

1968
★Goodbye, Columbus
1969
★Butch Cassidy and the Sundance Kid
★Midnight Cowboy
1970
★I Never Sang for My Father
★M*A*S*H
1971
★The French Connection
★Kotch
1972
★Cabaret
★The Godfather
1973
★Paper Moon
★Serpico
1974
★The Apprenticeship of Duddy Kravitz
★The Godfather, Part 2
1975
★One Flew Over the Cuckoo's Nest
★The Sunshine Boys
1976
★All the President's Men
★The Pink Panther Strikes Again
1977
★Julia
★Oh, God!
1978
★Heaven Can Wait
★Midnight Express
1979
★Being There
★Kramer vs. Kramer
1980
★Airplane!
★Ordinary People
1981
★On Golden Pond
★Rich and Famous
1982
★Missing
★Victor/Victoria
1983
★Terms of Endearment
1984
★The Killing Fields
1985
★Prizzi's Honor
1986
★A Room with a View
1987
★Roxanne
1988
★Dangerous Liaisons
1989
★Driving Miss Daisy
1990
★Dances with Wolves
1991
★The Silence of the Lambs
1992
★The Player
1993
★Schindler's List
The Fugitive
In the Name of the Father
The Joy Luck Club
The Remains of the Day
1994
★Forrest Gump
Little Women
The Madness of King George
Quiz Show
The Shawshank Redemption
1995
★Sense and Sensibility
Apollo 13
Babe
Get Shorty
Leaving Las Vegas
1996
★Sling Blade
The Birdcage
Emma
The English Patient
Trainspotting
1997
★L.A. Confidential
Donnie Brasco
The Ice Storm
Wag the Dog
The Wings of the Dove
1998
★Out of Sight
A Civil Action
Gods and Monsters
Primary Colors
A Simple Plan
1999
★Election
The Cider House Rules
The Insider
October Sky
The Talented Mr. Ripley
2000
★Traffic
Chocolat
Crouching Tiger, Hidden Dragon
High Fidelity
Wonder Boys
2001
★A Beautiful Mind
Black Hawk Down
Bridget Jones's Diary
Ghost World
Lord of the Rings: The Fellowship of the Ring
2002
★The Hours
About a Boy
About Schmidt
Adaptation
Chicago
2003
★American Splendor
Cold Mountain
Lord of the Rings: The Return of the King
Mystic River
Seabiscuit
2004
★Sideways
Before Sunset
Mean Girls
Million Dollar Baby
The Motorcycle Diaries
2005
★Brokeback Mountain
Capote
The Constant Gardener
A History of Violence
Syriana
2006
★The Departed
The Devil Wears Prada
Little Children
Thank You for Smoking
2007
★No Country for Old Men
The Diving Bell and the Butterfly
Into the Wild
There Will Be Blood
Zodiac
2008
★Slumdog Millionaire
The Curious Case of Benjamin Button
The Dark Knight
Doubt
Frost/Nixon
2009
★Up in the Air
Crazy Heart
Julie & Julia
Precious: Based on the Novel 'Push' by Sapphire
Star Trek
2010
★The Social Network
I Love You Phillip Morris
127 Hours
The Town
True Grit
2011
★The Descendants
The Girl With the Dragon Tattoo
The Help
Hugo
Moneyball
2012
★Argo
Life of Pi
Lincoln
The Perks of Being a Wallflower
Silver Linings Playbook
2013
★Captain Phillips
August: Osage County
Before Midnight
Lone Survivor
The Wolf of Wall Street
2014
★The Imitation Game
American Sniper
Gone Girl
Guardians of the Galaxy
2015
★The Big Short
Carol
The Martian
Steve Jobs
Trumbo
Wild
2016
★Arrival
Deadpool
Fences
Hidden Figures
Nocturnal Animals
2017
★Call Me by Your Name
The Disaster Artist
Logan
Molly's Game
Mudbound
2018
★Can You Ever Forgive Me?
Black Panther
BlacKkKlansman
If Beale Street Could Talk
A Star Is Born
2019
★Jojo Rabbit
A Beautiful Day in the Neighborhood
The Irishman
Joker
Little Women

ORIGINAL SCREENPLAY

1967
★Bonnie & Clyde
1968
★The Producers
1969
★Bob & Carol & Ted & Alice
1970
★The Out-of-Towners
★Patton
1971
★The Hospital
★Sunday, Bloody Sunday
1972
★The Candidate
★What's Up, Doc?
1973
★Save the Tiger
★A Touch of Class
1974
★Blazing Saddles
★Chinatown
1975
★Dog Day Afternoon
★Shampoo
1976
★The Bad News Bears
★Network
1977
★Annie Hall
★The Turning Point
1978
★Coming Home
★Movie, Movie
1979
★Breaking Away
★The China Syndrome
1980
★Melvin and Howard
★Private Benjamin
1981
★Arthur
★Reds
1982
★E.T.: The Extra-Terrestrial
★Tootsie
1983
★The Big Chill
★Tender Mercies
1984
★Broadway Danny Rose
1985
★Witness
1986
★Hannah and Her Sisters
1987
★Moonstruck
1988
★Bull Durham
1989
★Crimes & Misdemeanors
1990
★Avalon
1991
★Thelma & Louise
1992
★The Crying Game
1993
★The Piano
Dave
In the Line of Fire
Philadelphia
Sleepless in Seattle
1994
★Four Weddings and a Funeral
The Adventures of Priscilla, Queen of the Desert
Bullets over Broadway
Ed Wood
Heavenly Creatures
1995
★Braveheart
The American President
Clueless
Mighty Aphrodite
Muriel's Wedding
1996
★Fargo
Jerry Maguire
Lone Star
Secrets and Lies
Shine
1997
★As Good As It Gets
Boogie Nights
The Full Monty
Good Will Hunting
Titanic
1998
★Shakespeare in Love
Bulworth
The Opposite of Sex
Saving Private Ryan
The Truman Show
1999
★American Beauty
Being John Malkovich
Magnolia
The Sixth Sense
Three Kings
2000
★You Can Count On Me
Almost Famous
Best in Show
Billy Elliot
Erin Brockovich
2001
★Gosford Park
The Man Who Wasn't There
Monster's Ball
Moulin Rouge
The Royal Tenenbaums
2002
★Bowling for Columbine
Antwone Fisher
Far from Heaven
Gangs of New York
My Big Fat Greek Wedding
2003
★Lost in Translation
Bend It Like Beckham
Dirty Pretty Things
In America
The Station Agent
2004
★Eternal Sunshine of the Spotless Mind
The Aviator
Garden State
Hotel Rwanda
Kinsey
2005
★Crash
Cinderella Man
The 40 Year Old Virgin
Good Night, and Good Luck
The Squid and the Whale
2006
★Little Miss Sunshine
Babel
The Queen
Stranger Than Fiction
United 93

★ = winner

2007
★*Juno*
Knocked Up
Lars and the Real Girl
Michael Clayton
The Savages
2008
★*Milk*
Burn After Reading
Vicky Cristina Barcelona
The Wrestler
2009
★*The Hurt Locker*
Avatar
(500) Days of Summer
The Hangover
A Serious Man
2010
★*Inception*
Black Swan
The Fighter
The Kids Are All Right
Please Give
2011
★*Midnight in Paris*
Bridesmaids
50/50
Win Win
Young Adult
2012
★*Zero Dark Thirty*
Flight
Looper
The Master
Moonrise Kingdom
2013
★*Her*
American Hustle
Blue Jasmine
Dallas Buyers Club
Nebraska
2015
★*The Grand Budapest Hotel*
★*Spotlight*
Boyhood
Foxcatcher
Nightcrawler
Sicario
Straight Outta Compton
Trainwreck
Whiplash
2016
★*Moonlight*
Hell or High Water
La La Land
Loving
Manchester by the Sea
2017
★*Get Out*
The Big Sick
I, Tonya
Lady Bird
The Shape of Water
2018
★*Eighth Grade*
Green Book
A Quiet Place
Roma
Vice
2019
★*Parasite*
Booksmart
Knives Out
Marriage Story
1917

DOCUMENTARY SCREENPLAY

2005
★*Enron: The Smartest Guys in the Room*
2009
★*The Cove*
2010
★*Inside Job*
2012
★*Searching For Sugar Man*
The Central Park Five
Mea Maxima Culpa: Silence in the House of God
We Are Legion: The Story of the Hacktivists
West of Memphis
2013
Dirty Wars
2014
★*The Internet's Own Boy: The Story of Aaron Swartz*
Finding Vivian Maier
Last Days in Vietnam
2016
★*Going Clear: Scientology and the Prison of Belief*
Author: The JT LeRoy Story
Being Canadian
Cobain: Montage of Heck
Zero Days
2017
★*Jane*
Betting on Zero
No Stone Unturned
Oklahoma City
2018
★*Bathtubs Over Broadway*
Fahrenheit 11/9
Generation Wealth
In Search of Greatness
2019
★*The Inventor: Out For Blood In Silicon Valley*
Citizen K
Foster
Joseph Pulitzer: Voice of the People
The Kingmaker

★ = *winner*

Cast Index

The Cast Index provides a complete videography for cast members with more than two appearances on video. The listings for the actor names follow an alphabetical sort by last name (although the names appear in a first name-last name format). The videographies are listed chronologically, from earliest appearance to most recent film, making it easier to trace the development of your favorite actor's career. When a cast member appears in more than one film in the same year, these movies are listed alphabetically within the year. A (V) beside a movie title indicates voice-only work, while an (N) indicates narrator duties. A (C) indicates a cameo appearance.

Lee Aaker (1943-)
The Atomic City *'52*
Desperate Search *'52*
Hondo *'53*
Jeopardy *'53*

Aaliyah (1979-2001)
Romeo Must Die *'00*
Queen of the Damned *'02*

Angela Aames (1956-88)
Bachelor Party *'84*
Basic Training *'86*

Willie Aames (1960-)
Frankenstein *'73*
Paradise *'82*
Zapped! *'82*
Cut and Run *'85*

Caroline Aaron (1952-)
Heartburn *'86*
Crimes & Misdemeanors *'89*
Alice *'90*
Edward Scissorhands *'90*
A Modern Affair *'94*
House Arrest *'96*
Deconstructing Harry *'97*
Weapons of Mass Distraction *'97*
Primary Colors *'98*
Anywhere But Here *'99*
Tuesdays with Morrie *'99*
Running Mates *'00*
What Planet Are You From? *'00*
Joe Dirt *'01*
Never Again *'01*
Amy's O *'02*
Pumpkin *'02*
The Secret of Zoey *'02*
Two Days *'03*
Beyond the Sea *'04*
Cellular *'04*
A Day Without a Mexican *'04*
Grilled *'06*
Love Comes Lately *'07*
Nancy Drew *'07*
Meeting Spencer *'11*

Bonnie Aarons
I Know Who Killed Me *'07*
The Nun *'18*

William Abadie
My Sassy Girl *'08*
Give 'Em Hell Malone *'09*

Diego Abatantuono (1955-)
The Best Man *'97*
Nirvana *'97*
Children of Hannibal *'98*
I'm Not Scared *'03*

Sean Abbananto
Bikini House Calls *'96*
Bikini Med School *'98*

Hiam Abbass (1960-)
Satin Rouge *'02*
Free Zone *'05*
Munich *'05*
Paradise Now *'05*
The Nativity Story *'06*
Disengagement *'07*
The Visitor *'07*
Lemon Tree *'08*
Amreeka *'09*
Miral *'10*
May in Summer *'13*
May in the Summer *'13*
Exodus: Gods and Kings *'14*

Graham Abbey
Secrets of Eden *'12*
Milton's Secret *'16*

Bruce Abbott (1954-)
Re-Animator *'84*
Summer Heat *'87*
Bad Dreams *'88*
Bride of Re-Animator *'89*
The Demolitionist *'95*
The Prophecy 2: Ashtown *'97*

Bud Abbott (1895-1974)
One Night in the Tropics *'40*
Buck Privates *'41*
Hold That Ghost *'41*
In the Navy *'41*
Keep 'Em Flying *'41*
Pardon My Sarong *'42*
Ride 'Em Cowboy *'42*
Rio Rita *'42*
Who Done It? *'42*
Hit the Ice *'43*
It Ain't Hay *'43*
In Society *'44*
Lost in a Harem *'44*
Abbott and Costello in Hollywood *'45*
Here Come the Co-Eds *'45*
The Naughty Nineties *'45*
Little Giant *'46*
The Time of Their Lives *'46*
Buck Privates Come Home *'47*
The Wistful Widow of Wagon Gap *'47*
Abbott and Costello Meet Frankenstein *'48*
Mexican Hayride *'48*
The Noose Hangs High *'48*
Abbott and Costello Meet the Killer, Boris Karloff *'49*
Africa Screams *'49*
Abbott and Costello in the Foreign Legion *'50*
Abbott and Costello Meet the Invisible Man *'51*
Comin' Round the Mountain *'51*
Abbott and Costello Meet Captain Kidd *'52*
Abbott and Costello Meet Dr. Jekyll and Mr. Hyde *'52*
Jack & the Beanstalk *'52*
Lost in Alaska *'52*
Abbott and Costello Go to Mars *'53*
Abbott and Costello Meet the Keystone Kops *'54*
Abbott and Costello Meet the Mummy *'55*
Dance with Me, Henry *'56*

Christopher Abbott (1986-)
Hello I Must Be Going *'12*
Criminal Activities *'15*
James White *'15*
Whiskey Tango Foxtrot *'16*
It Comes at Night *'17*
Sweet Virginia *'17*
Piercing *'18*

Diahnne Abbott (1945-)
New York, New York *'77*
King of Comedy *'82*
Jo Jo Dancer, Your Life Is Calling *'86*

John Abbott (1905-96)
Mrs. Miniver *'42*
Pursuit to Algiers *'45*
Anna and the King of Siam *'46*
The Bandit of Sherwood Forest *'46*
Deception *'46*
Humoresque *'46*
The Steel Lady *'53*

Michael Abbott, Jr.
Shotgun Stories *'07*
The Death of Dick Long *'19*

Khalid Abdalla
United 93 *'06*
The Kite Runner *'07*

Barkhad Abdi
Eye in the Sky *'15*
Good Time *'17*
The Pirates of Somalia *'17*

Paula Abdul (1962-)
The Waiting Game *'98*
Mr. Rock 'n' Roll: The Alan Freed Story *'99*

Kareem Abdul-Jabbar (1947-)
The Fish that Saved Pittsburgh *'79*
Game of Death *'79*
Airplane! *'80*
Fletch *'85*
Chuck Berry: Hail! Hail! Rock 'n' Roll *'87*
D2: The Mighty Ducks *'94* (C)
Stephen King's The Stand *'94*
Slam Dunk Ernest *'95*
Rebound: The Legend of Earl 'The Goat' Manigault *'96* (C)
BASEketball *'98*

Hiroshi Abe (1964-)
Moon over Tao *'97*
Godzilla 2000 *'99*
Tokyo Raiders *'00*
After the Storm *'17*

Sadao Abe (1970-)
Uzumaki *'00*
Kamikaze Girls *'04*
The Great Yokai War *'05*

Toru Abe (1917-93)
The Human Condition: No Greater Love *'58*
Blind Woman's Curse *'70*
Lady Snowblood: Love Song of Vengeance *'74*

Danny A. Abeckaser
Holy Rollers *'10*
A Stand Up Guy *'16*

Alfred Abel (1879-1937)
Dr. Mabuse, The Gambler *'22*
Phantom *'22*
The Finances of the Grand Duke *'24*
Metropolis *'26*

Dominique Abel
L'Iceberg *'05*
Lost in Paris *'17*

Jake Abel (1987-)
Flash of Genius *'08*
Angel of Death *'09*
The Host *'13*
Percy Jackson: Sea of Monsters *'13*
Against the Sun *'15*
Good Kill *'15*
Almost Friends *'17*

Walter Abel (1898-1987)
Fury *'36*
The Green Light *'37*
Dance, Girl, Dance *'40*
Michael Shayne: Private Detective *'40*
Hold Back the Dawn *'41*
Beyond the Blue Horizon *'42*
Holiday Inn *'42*
Wake Island *'42*
So Proudly We Hail *'43*
An American Romance *'44*
Mr. Skeffington *'44*
The Kid from Brooklyn *'46*
13 Rue Madeleine *'46*
Island in the Sky *'53*
So This Is Love *'53*
Night People *'54*
The Indian Fighter *'55*
Raintree County *'57*
Mirage *'66*
Quick, Let's Get Married *'71*
Silent Night, Bloody Night *'73*

Lionel Abelanski (1964-)
My Wife is an Actress *'01*
The Grand Role *'04*
The Concert *'09*

Alan Abelew
The First Nudie Musical *'75*
Invasion *'07*

Alistair Abell (1970-)
How It All Went Down *'03*
His and Her Christmas *'05*
Stranger in My Bed *'05*

Tim Abell (1958-)
Attack of the 60-Foot Centerfold *'95*
Masseuse *'95*
Over the Wire *'95*
Sexual Roulette *'96*
Death and Desire *'97*
Hybrid *'97*
Steel Sharks *'97*
The Base *'99*
Rapid Assault *'99*
The Substitute 4: Failure is Not an Option *'00*
Dead Simple *'01*
Instinct to Kill *'01*

Special Forces *'03*
Miracle at Sage Creek *'05*
American Bandits: Frank and Jesse James *'10*
Collision Course *'12*
Snow White: A Deadly Summer *'12*
Sniper: Special Ops *'16*

Ian Abercrombie (1934-2012)
Backstairs at the White House *'79*
Puppet Master 3: Toulon's Revenge *'90*
Zandalee *'91*
Army of Darkness *'92*
Test Tube Teens from the Year 2000 *'93*
Scooby-Doo 2: Monsters Unleashed *'04 (V)*
Garfield: A Tail of Two Kitties *'06*
Inland Empire *'06*
Marilyn Hotchkiss' Ballroom Dancing & Charm School *'06*
Star Wars: The Clone Wars *'08 (V)*

Keith Aberdein (1943-)
Smash Palace *'82*
Wild Horses *'82*

Sivi Aberg (1944-)
The Killing of Sister George *'69*
Dr. Death, Seeker of Souls *'73*

Simon Abkarian (1962-)
Almost Peaceful *'02*
Ararat *'02*
Yes *'04*
Casino Royale *'06*
Persepolis *'07 (V)*
The Wedding Song *'09*
The Army of Crime *'10*
Overdrive *'17*

Whitney Able (1982-)
All the Boys Love Mandy Lane *'06*
Dead Lenny *'06*
Love and Mary *'07*
Remarkable Power *'08*
Mercy *'09*
The Kane Files *'10*
Monsters *'10*
Pound of Flesh *'10*
Bad Actress *'11*
Tales of an Ancient Empire *'11*

Alon Aboutboul (1965-)
Body of Lies *'08*
The Dark Knight Rises *'12*
Septembers of Shiraz *'16*

F. Murray Abraham (1939-)
They Might Be Giants *'71*
Serpico *'73*
Prisoner of Second Avenue *'74*
The Sunshine Boys *'75*
All the President's Men *'76*
The Ritz *'76*
Madman *'79*
Scarface *'83*
Amadeus *'84*
Dream West *'86*
The Name of the Rose *'86*
Beyond the Stars *'89*
An Innocent Man *'89*
Intimate Power *'89*
Slipstream *'89*
The Bonfire of the Vanities *'90 (C)*
Mobsters *'91*
Journey to the Center of the Earth *'93*
Last Action Hero *'93*
National Lampoon's Loaded Weapon 1 *'93*
Sweet Killing *'93*
Surviving the Game *'94*
Children of the Revolution *'95*
Dillinger and Capone *'95*
Mighty Aphrodite *'95*
Larry McMurtry's Dead Man's Walk *'96*
Looking for Richard *'96*
Mimic *'97*
All New Adventures of Laurel and Hardy: For Love or Mummy *'98*
Esther *'98*
Star Trek: Insurrection *'98*
Excellent Cadavers *'99*
Muppets from Space *'99*
Noah's Ark *'99*
Finding Forrester *'00*
13 Ghosts *'01*
Joshua *'02*
The Bridge of San Luis Rey *'05*
The Stone Merchant *'06*
Blood Monkey *'07*
Language of the Enemy *'07*
Carnera: The Walking Mountain *'08*
Shark Swarm *'08*
Perestroika *'09*
Sword of War *'09*
Dead Man Down *'13*
The Grand Budapest Hotel *'14*
How to Train Your Dragon: The Hidden World *'19*

Ken Abraham
Creepozoids *'87*
Vice Academy *'88*

Doug Abrahams
Killer Bees *'02*
Double Cross *'06*
The Christmas Clause *'08*

Jim Abrahams (1944-)
Kentucky Fried Movie *'77*
Airplane! *'80*

Jon Abrahams (1977-)
Dead Man Walking *'95*
Kids *'95*
The Faculty *'98*
Bringing Out the Dead *'99*
Outside Providence *'99*
Boiler Room *'00*
Meet the Parents *'00*
Scary Movie *'00*
Scenes of the Crime *'01*
Texas Rangers *'01*
Wes Craven Presents: They *'02*
My Boss's Daughter *'03*
House of Wax *'05*
Prime *'05*
Standing Still *'05*
Bottoms Up *'06*
Deceit *'06*
Who Do You Love *'08*
Not Since You *'09*
Condemned *'15*

Jared Abrahamson
Finding a Family *'10*
Seattle Superstorm *'12*
Detour *'17*
Sweet Virginia *'17*
American Animals *'18*

Aaron Abrams
Cyborg Soldier *'08*
Closet Monster *'16*

Austin Abrams (1996-)
Ticking Clock *'10*
Paper Towns *'15*
Brad's Status *'17*
Puzzle *'18*

Michele Abrams
Buffy the Vampire Slayer *'92*
Cool World *'92*

Roy Abramsohn
Escape From Tomorrow *'13*
Area 51 *'15*

Josef Abrham (1939-)
All My Loved Ones *'00*
I Served the King of England *'07*

Victoria Abril (1959-)
Moon in the Gutter *'83*
On the Line *'84*
Max, Mon Amour *'86*
If They Tell You I Fell *'89*
Tie Me Up! Tie Me Down! *'90*
High Heels *'91*
Intruso *'93*
Jimmy Hollywood *'94*
Kika *'94*
French Twist *'95*
Between Your Legs *'99*
My Father, My Mother, My Brothers and My Sisters *'99*
101 Reykjavik *'00*
No News from God *'01*
Swindled *'04*

Susie Abromeit (1982-)
Beatdown *'10*
Mothman *'10*

Joe Absolom
Extreme Ops *'02*
Hatfields & McCoys *'12*
I Spit on Your Grave 2 *'13*

Omid Abtahi (1979-)
The Mysteries of Pittsburgh *'08*
Space Chimps *'08 (V)*
You Don't Mess with the Zohan *'08*
Boys of Abu Ghraib *'14*

Yussef Abu-Warda
Kadosh *'99*
Amreeka *'09*

Candice Accola (1987-)
On the Doll *'07*
Deadgirl *'08*

Stefano Accorsi (1971-)
The Son's Room *'00*
His Secret Life *'01*
The Last Kiss *'01*
Blame It on Fidel *'06*
Saturn in Opposition *'07*
Shall We Kiss? *'07*

Kirk Acevedo (1971-)
The Sunshine Boys *'95*
The Thin Red Line *'98*
Witness to the Mob *'98*
Bait *'00*
Boiler Room *'00*
Dinner Rush *'00*
In the Weeds *'00*
Band of Brothers *'01*
Getting High *'06*
Invincible *'06*
Collision Earth *'11*
Dawn of the Planet of the Apes *'14*
Insidious: The Last Key *'18*

Amy Acker (1976-)
Groom Lake *'02*
A Near-Death Experience *'08*
Dear Santa *'11*
The Cabin in the Woods *'12*
Much Ado About Nothing *'13*
Let's Kill Ward's Wife *'14*

Sharon Acker (1935-)
Lucky Jim *'58*
The Hanged Man *'74*
Happy Birthday to Me *'81*

Ed Ackerman (1977-)
Frozen *'10*
Hatchet 2 *'10*

Forrest J Ackerman (1916-2008)
Planet of Blood *'66*
Dracula *vs.* Frankenstein *'71*
Schlock *'73 (C)*
Kentucky Fried Movie *'77*
The Howling *'81 (C)*
Aftermath *'85*
Amazon Women on the Moon *'87*
Curse of the Queerwolf *'87*
Evil Spawn *'87*
Innocent Blood *'92*
Dead Alive *'93*
Attack of the 60-Foot Centerfold *'95*

Leslie Ackerman (1956-)
Law and Disorder *'74*
The First Nudie Musical *'75*
Blame It on the Night *'84*

Joss Ackland (1928-)
Crescendo *'69*
Cry of the Penguins *'71*
The House that Dripped Blood *'71*
Villain *'71*
Mind Snatchers *'72*
Hitler: The Last Ten Days *'73*
The Little Prince *'74*
S*P*Y*S *'74*
Operation Daybreak *'75*
Royal Flash *'75*
Watership Down *'78 (V)*
Who Is Killing the Great Chefs of Europe? *'78*
The Big Scam *'79*
Saint Jack *'79*
The Apple *'80*
Tinker, Tailor, Soldier, Spy *'80*
Lady Jane *'85*
Queenie *'87*
The Sicilian *'87*
White Mischief *'88*
A Zed & Two Noughts *'88*
Lethal Weapon 2 *'89*
To Kill a Priest *'89*
The Hunt for Red October *'90*
Jekyll and Hyde *'90*
A Murder of Quality *'90*
Bill & Ted's Bogus Journey *'91*
The Man Who Lived at the Ritz *'91*
The Object of Beauty *'91*
The Mighty Ducks *'92*
Once Upon a Crime *'92*
Nowhere to Run *'93*
Jacob *'94*
Miracle on 34th Street *'94*
Mother's Boys *'94*
Shameless *'94*
Citizen X *'95*
A Kid in King Arthur's Court *'95*
D3: The Mighty Ducks *'96*
Deadly Voyage *'96*
Surviving Picasso *'96*
Firelight *'97*
Swept from the Sea *'97*
Heat of the Sun *'99*
Passion of Mind *'00*
K-19: The Widowmaker *'02*
No Good Deed *'02*
I'll Be There *'03*
A Different Loyalty *'04*
Asylum *'05*
Frederick Forsyth's Icon *'05*
Above and Beyond *'06*
Hogfather *'06*
Moscow Zero *'06*
These Foolish Things *'06*
Flawless *'07*
How About You *'07*

Oliver Ackland (1979-)
Wasted on the Young *'10*
The Mystery of a Hansom Cab *'12*
100 Bloody Acres *'12*

Danneel Ackles (1979-)
See Danneel Harris

Jensen Ackles (1978-)
Blonde *'01*
Devour *'05*
Ten Inch Hero *'07*
My Bloody Valentine 3D *'09*

David Ackroyd (1940-)
A Gun in the House *'81*
Cocaine: One Man's Seduction *'83*
The Sky's No Limit *'84*
The Children of Times Square *'86*
Poor Little Rich Girl: The Barbara Hutton Story *'87*
Memories of Me *'88*
Love, Cheat & Steal *'93*
Against the Wall *'94*
Raven *'97*

Rodolfo Acosta (1920-74)
Yankee Buccaneer *'52*
Hondo *'53*
Drum Beat *'54*
Trooper Hook *'57*
Flaming Star *'60*
Impasse *'69*
Savage Run *'70*

Jay Acovone (1955-)
Doctor Mordrid: Master of the Unknown *'90*
Quicksand: No Escape *'91*
The Magician *'93*
Showdown *'94*
Crash Dive *'96*
Rancid *'04*
InAlienable *'08*

Acquanetta (1921-2004)
Dead Man's Eyes *'44*
Tarzan and the Leopard Woman *'46*
The Lost Continent *'51*

Ava Acres
Free Ride *'13*
The Face of an Angel *'14*

Eddie Acuff (1908-56)
Shipmates Forever *'35*
The Black Legion *'37*
They Died with Their Boots On *'41*
Guadalcanal Diary *'43*
It Happened Tomorrow *'44*

Jason 'Wee Man' Acuna (1973-)
Jackass: The Movie *'02*
Jackass 3D *'10*

Michelle Acuna
Parasite *'03*
Bounty *'09*

Jean Adair
Arsenic and Old Lace *'44*
Living In a Big Way *'47*

Robert Adair (1900-54)
Ticket of Leave Man *'37*
The Face at the Window *'39*
Norman Conquest *'53*

Amy Adams (1974-)
Cruel Intentions 2 *'99*
Drop Dead Gorgeous *'99*
Psycho Beach Party *'00*
The Slaughter Rule *'01*
Catch Me If You Can *'02*
Pumpkin *'02*
Serving Sara *'02*
Junebug *'05*
Standing Still *'05*
The Wedding Date *'05*
Talladega Nights: The Ballad of Ricky Bobby *'06*
Tenacious D in the Pick of Destiny *'06*
Charlie Wilson's War *'07*
Enchanted *'07*
The Ex *'07*
Underdog *'07 (V)*
Doubt *'08*
Miss Pettigrew Lives for a Day *'08*
Julie & Julia *'09*
Moonlight Serenade *'09*
Night at the Museum: Battle of the Smithsonian *'09*
Sunshine Cleaning *'09*
The Fighter *'10*
Leap Year *'10*
The Muppets *'11*
The Master *'12*
On the Road *'12*
Trouble with the Curve *'12*
American Hustle *'13*
Her *'13*
Man of Steel *'13*
Big Eyes *'14*
Lullaby *'14*
Arrival *'16*
Batman v Superman: Dawn of Justice *'16*
Nocturnal Animals *'16*
Justice League *'17*
Vice *'18*

Beverly Adams (1940-)
Roustabout *'64*
How to Stuff a Wild Bikini *'65*
Winter a Go-Go *'65*
Birds Do It *'66*
Murderers' Row *'66*
The Silencers *'66*
The Ambushers *'67*
Devil's Angels *'67*
Torture Garden *'67*
Hammerhead *'68*

Brandon Adams (1979-)
The People under the Stairs *'91*
Ghost in the Machine *'93*
The Sandlot *'93*
MacArthur Park *'01*

Brooke Adams (1949-)
James Dean *'76*
Shock Waves *'77*
Days of Heaven *'78*
Invasion of the Body Snatchers *'78*
Cuba *'79*
A Man, a Woman, and a Bank *'79*
Tell Me a Riddle *'80*
Dead Zone *'83*
Lace *'84*
Almost You *'85*
Lace 2 *'85*
The Stuff *'85*
Sometimes They Come Back *'91*
The Unborn *'91*
Gas Food Lodging *'92*
The Sandlot *'93*
The Baby-Sitters' Club *'95*
The Legend of Lucy Keyes *'06*

Catlin Adams (1950-)
Panic in Echo Park *'77*
The Jerk *'79*
The Jazz Singer *'80*

Christine Adams
Submerged *'05*
Eye of the Dolphin *'06*

CJ Adams
The Odd Life of Timothy Green *'12*
Against the Wild *'14*

Claire Adams (1898-1978)
The Penalty *'20*
Where the North Begins *'23*
The Big Parade *'25*

Don Adams (1923-2005)
The Nude Bomb *'80*
Back to the Beach *'87*
Get Smart, Again! *'89*
Inspector Gadget *'99 (V)*

Donald Adams
The Betrayed *'08*
Merlin and the Book of Beasts *'09*

Dorothy Adams (1899-1988)
So Proudly We Hail *'43*
Laura *'44*
The Best Years of Our Lives *'46*
Streets of Sin *'49*
The Prodigal *'55*

Edie Adams (1929-2008)
The Apartment *'60*
Lover Come Back *'61*
Call Me Bwana *'63*
It's a Mad, Mad, Mad, Mad World *'63*
Under the Yum-Yum Tree *'63*
The Best Man *'64*
Made in Paris *'65*
The Honey Pot *'67*
Evil Roy Slade *'71*
Cheech and Chong's Up in Smoke *'79*
Portrait of an Escort *'80*
Armistead Maupin's Tales of the City *'93*

Evan Adams (1966-)
Lost in the Barrens *'91*
Smoke Signals *'98*
The Business of Fancydancing *'02*

Jane Adams (1921-)
House of Dracula *'45*
Lost City of the Jungle *'45*

Jane Adams (1965-)
Vital Signs *'90*
I Love Trouble *'94*
Father of the Bride Part 2 *'95*
Kansas City *'95*

Music from Another Room '97
Day at the Beach '98
Happiness '98
A Fish in the Bathtub '99
Mumford '99
Songcatcher '99
A Texas Funeral '99
Wonder Boys '00
The Anniversary Party '01
Orange County '02
Eternal Sunshine of the Spotless Mind '04
Jesse Stone: Stone Cold '05
Last Holiday '06
The Sensation of Sight '06
The Wackness '08
Alexander the Last '09
Calvin Marshall '09
Restless '11
All the Light in the Sky '13

Joey Lauren Adams (1968-)
Dazed and Confused '93
The Program '93
S.F.W. '94
Sleep with Me '94
Mallrats '95
Bio-Dome '96
Chasing Amy '97
A Cool, Dry Place '98
Big Daddy '99
The Dress Code '99
Beautiful '00
Dr. Dolittle 2 '01 (V)
Harvard Man '01
In the Shadows '01
Jay and Silent Bob Strike Back '01
The Gunman '03
The Big Empty '04
The Break-Up '06
Bunny Whipped '06
Trucker '08
ExTerminators '09
Endure '10
Art Machine '12
Making the Rules '14
Valley Inn '14

Julie Adams (1926-)
Hollywood Story '51
Horizons West '52
The Lawless Breed '52
Man from the Alamo '53
The Mississippi Gambler '53
Creature from the Black Lagoon '54
Francis Joins the WACs '54
One Desire '55
Away All Boats '56
Tarawa Beachhead '58
The Gunfight at Dodge City '59
Tickle Me '65
McQ '74
The McCullochs '75
Psychic Killer '75
The Killer Inside Me '76
Black Roses '88
Backtrack '89

Kathryn Adams (1920-)
Blonde for a Day '46
One Missed Call 2 '05

Kristin Adams (1982-)
Falling Angels '03
Where the Truth Lies '05

Lynne Adams (1946-)
Blood Relations '87
The Carpenter '89
Silent Hunter '94
Psychopath '97
The Ultimate Weapon '97
Requiem for Murder '99
Dangerous Liaisons '03

Marla Adams (1938-)
Gotcha! '85
The President's Man '00

Mason Adams (1919-2005)
The Final Conflict '81
Adam '83
Half Slave, Half Free '85
F/X '86
Who Is Julia? '86
Son-in-Law '93
Houseguest '94
Touch '96
From the Earth to the Moon '98

Maud Adams (1945-)
The Girl in Blue '74
The Man with the Golden Gun '74
Rollerball '75
Playing for Time '80
Octopussy '83
Jane & the Lost City '87
Angel 3: The Final Chapter '88
Deadly Intent '88
A Man of Passion '88
Intimate Power '89
Silent Night, Deadly Night 4: Initiation '90

Nick Adams (1931-68)
Mister Roberts '55
Picnic '55
Rebel without a Cause '55
Our Miss Brooks '56
No Time for Sergeants '58
Teacher's Pet '58
The FBI Story '59
Pillow Talk '59
Hell Is for Heroes '62
The Interns '62
The Hook '63
Twilight of Honor '63
Frankenstein Conquers the World '64
Die, Monster, Die! '65
Godzilla vs. Monster Zero '68

Patrick J. Adams (1981-)
Christmas in Boston '05
3 Days Gone '08
Weather Girl '09
Rosemary's Baby '14
Clara '19

Polly Adams (1939-)
Element of Doubt '96
The Juror '96
Celebrity '98
People I Know '02
Uptown Girls '03
United 93 '06
David & Layla '07

Stanley Adams (1915-77)
Hell Bound '57
Hell Ship Mutiny '57
High School Big Shot '59
Requiem for a Heavyweight '62
Lilies of the Field '63
Thunder Alley '67
The Passing of Evil '70

Steve Adams (1939-)
Strange Fits of Passion '99
The Blue Butterfly '04

Tom Adams (1938-)
The Great Escape '63
The Fighting Prince of Donegal '66
Fathom '67
The House that Dripped Blood '71
License to Kill '89

Chris(topher) Adamson
Shameless '94
Razor Blade Smile '98
Dead of Night '99
Freakshow '07
Allan Quartermain and the Temple of Skulls '08

George Adamson (1906-89)
An Elephant Called Slowly '69
Christian the Lion '76

Robert Adamson (1985-)
Princess Protection Program '09
The Prankster '10

Meat Loaf Aday (1947-)
The Rocky Horror Picture Show '75
Americathon '79
Roadie '80
The Squeeze '87
Motorama '91
Leap of Faith '92
Wayne's World '92
Spice World: The Movie '97
Black Dog '98
Gunshy '98
The Mighty '98
Crazy in Alabama '99
Fight Club '99
Focus '01
Formula 51 '01
Rustin '01
Extreme Dating '04
A Hole in One '04
Chasing Ghosts '05
Crazylove '05
The Pleasure Drivers '05
BloodRayne '06
Tenacious D in the Pick of Destiny '06
Citizen Jane '09
The Moment '13
Stage Fright '14

Anthony Addabbo (1960-)
The Gunfighters '87
Red Shoe Diaries 5: Weekend Pass '95

Dawn Addams (1930-85)
The Hour of 13 '52
The Robe '53
Return to Treasure Island '54
A King in New York '57
The Silent Enemy '58
Voulez-Vous Danser avec Moi? '59
The Thousand Eyes of Dr. Mabuse '60
The Two Faces of Dr. Jekyll '60
The Black Tulip '64
Ballad in Blue '66
Zeta One '69
The Vampire Lovers '70
Vault of Horror '73

Milo Addica (1963-)
Monster's Ball '01
Birth '04
The King '05

Robert Addie (1960-2003)
Excalibur '81
Another Country '84
Captain Jack '98
A Knight in Camelot '98

Chris Addison
In the Loop '09
The Look of Love '13

Nancy Addison (1948-2002)
The Dain Curse '78
Somewhere Tomorrow '85

Mark Addy (1964-)
The Full Monty '96
Jack Frost '98
The Flintstones in Viva Rock Vegas '00
Down to Earth '01
A Knight's Tale '01
The Time Machine '02
The Order '03
Around the World in 80 Days '04
Red Riding, Part 3: 1983 '09
Barney's Version '10
Robin Hood '10
Great Expectations '11

Wesley Addy (1913-96)
The Big Knife '55
Kiss Me Deadly '55
Seconds '66
Tora! Tora! Tora! '70
The Grissom Gang '71
Network '76
The Europeans '79
The Verdict '82
The Bostonians '84
A Modern Affair '94
Hiroshima '95

Tunde Adebimpe
Rachel Getting Married '08
Nasty Baby '15

Paul Adelstein (1969-)
Intolerable Cruelty '03
Be Cool '05
Frenemy '09
Return to Zero '14
The Phenom '16

Jovan Adepo
Fences '16
Overlord '18

Patrick Adiarte
The King and I '56
High Time '60

Isabelle Adjani (1955-)
The Story of Adele H. '75
Barocco '76
The Tenant '76
The Driver '78
The Bronte Sisters '79
Nosferatu the Vampyre '79
Possession '81
Quartet '81
One Deadly Summer '83
Subway '85
Ishtar '87
Camille Claudel '89
Queen Margot '94
Diabolique '96
Bon Voyage '03
Monsieur Ibrahim '03
Mammuth '10

Scott Adkins (1976-)
Black Mask 2: City of Masks '02
Special Forces '03
Undisputed 2: Last Man Standing '06
The Shepherd: Border Patrol '08
Stag Night '08
The Tournament '09
El Gringo '12
Universal Soldier: Day of Reckoning '12
The Legend of Hercules '14
Close Range '15
Zero Tolerance '15
Eliminators '16
Hard Target 2 '16
Home Invasion '16
Jarhead 3: The Siege '16
Avengement '19
Ip Man 4: The Finale '19
Triple Threat '19

Seth Adkins (1989-)
First Do No Harm '97
Gepetto '00
Taming Andrew '00

Trace Adkins (1962-)
An American Carol '08
Lifted '10
The Lincoln Lawyer '11
Wyatt Earp's Revenge '12
Moms' Night Out '14
Stagecoach: The Texas Jack Story '16
Traded '16
I Can Only Imagine '18
Bennett's War '19
The Outsider '19

Bill Adler (1952-)
Pom Pom Girls '76
Blue Sunshine '78
Van Nuys Blvd. '79

Jay Adler (1896-1978)
99 River Street '53
The Killing '56
Crime of Passion '57
Grave of the Vampire '72

Jerry Adler (1929-)
The Public Eye '92
Manhattan Murder Mystery '93
Six Ways to Sunday '99
In Her Shoes '05
Find Me Guilty '06
Goodbye Baby '07
Remember Sunday '13
A Most Violent Year '14

Joanna Adler (1964-)
The Event '03
Book of Love '04
The Big Bad Swim '06

Luther Adler (1903-84)
Cornered '45
Saigon '47
The Loves of Carmen '48
D.O.A. '49
House of Strangers '49
Wake of the Red Witch '49
Kiss Tomorrow Goodbye '50
The Desert Fox '51
Hoodlum Empire '52
The Miami Story '54
The Girl in the Red Velvet Swing '55
Hot Blood '56
The Brotherhood '68
The Man in the Glass Booth '75
Mean Johnny Barrows '75
Murph the Surf '75
Voyage of the Damned '76
Absence of Malice '81

Matt Adler (1966-)
Flight of the Navigator '86
North Shore '87
White Water Summer '87

Sarah Adler
Our Music '04
Foxtrot '18

Gideon Adlon
Blockers '18
The Mustang '19

Renee Adoree (1898-1933)
The Big Parade '25
The Black Bird '26
La Boheme '26
Mr. Wu '27
The Show '27
The Pagan '29
Tide of Empire '29

Mario Adorf (1930-)
The Bird with the Crystal Plumage '70
Short Night of Glass Dolls '71
Caliber 9 '72
Hired to Kill '73
The Italian Connection '73
Manhunt '73
The Lost Honor of Katharina Blum '75
The Tin Drum '79
Lola '81
The Holcroft Covenant '85
Smilla's Sense of Snow '96

Raz Adoti (1973-)
Haven '04
Resident Evil: Apocalypse '04
Doom '05
Cover '08

Iris Adrian (1912-94)
The Road to Zanzibar '41
I Killed That Man '42
Action in the North Atlantic '43
Submarine Base '43
Career Girl '44
I'm from Arkansas '44
Swing Hostess '44
The Stork Club '45
The Bamboo Blonde '46
The Paleface '48
Hi-Jacked '50
The Fast and the Furious '54
Carnival Rock '57
Blue Hawaii '62

Max Adrian (1903-73)
Henry V '44
The Boy Friend '71
The Devils '71

Scott Adsit (1965-)
Last Night '10
The Music Never Stopped '11
Appropriate Behavior '14
Big Hero 6 '14 (V)
Uncle Nick '15

Sean Michael Afable (1988-)
Akeelah and the Bee '06
To Save a Life '10

Ben Affleck (1972-)
Buffy the Vampire Slayer '92
School Ties '92
Dazed and Confused '93
Mallrats '95
Glory Daze '96
Chasing Amy '97
Going All the Way '97
Good Will Hunting '97
Phantoms '97
Armageddon '98
Shakespeare in Love '98
200 Cigarettes '98
Daddy & Them '99
Dogma '99
Forces of Nature '99
Boiler Room '00
Bounce '00
Reindeer Games '00
Jay and Silent Bob Strike Back '01
Pearl Harbor '01
Changing Lanes '02
The Sum of All Fears '02
The Third Wheel '02
Daredevil '03
Gigli '03
Paycheck '03
Jersey Girl '04
Surviving Christmas '04
Clerks 2 '06 (C)
Hollywoodland '06
Smokin' Aces '07
Extract '09
He's Just Not That Into You '09
State of Play '09
The Company Men '10
The Town '10
Argo '12
To the Wonder '12
Runner Runner '13
Gone Girl '14
The Accountant '16
Batman v Superman: Dawn of Justice '16
Live by Night '16
Justice League '17
Triple Frontier '19
The Way Back '20

Casey Affleck (1975-)
To Die For '95
Race the Sun '96
Good Will Hunting '97
Desert Blue '98
200 Cigarettes '98
American Pie '99
Attention Shoppers '99
Committed '99
Drowning Mona '00
Hamlet '00
American Pie 2 '01
Ocean's Eleven '01
Soul Survivors '01
Gerry '02
Ocean's Twelve '04
The Last Kiss '06
Lonesome Jim '06
The Assassination of Jesse James by the Coward Robert Ford '07
Gone Baby Gone '07
Ocean's Thirteen '07
I'm Still Here '10
The Killer Inside Me '10
Tower Heist '11
ParaNorman '12 (V)
Ain't Them Bodies Saints '13
Out of the Furnace '13
Interstellar '14
Triple 9 '15
The Finest Hours '16
Manchester by the Sea '16
A Ghost Story '17
The Old Man & the Gun '18

John Agar (1921-2002)
Fort Apache '48
Adventure in Baltimore '49
Sands of Iwo Jima '49
She Wore a Yellow Ribbon '49
Breakthrough '50
The Woman on Pier 13 '50
Along the Great Divide '51
The Magic Carpet '51
Bait '54
The Rocket Man '54
Lonesome Trail '55
Revenge of the Creature '55
Tarantula '55
The Mole People '56

The Brain from Planet Arous '57
The Daughter of Dr. Jekyll '57
Flesh and the Spur '57
Attack of the Puppet People '58
Invisible Invaders '59
Journey to the Seventh Planet '62
Cavalry Command '63
Curse of the Swamp Creature '66
Johnny Reno '66
Zontar, the Thing from Venus '66
Night Fright '67
The St. Valentine's Day Massacre '67
The Undefeated '69
Chisum '70
Big Jake '71
King Kong '76
Miracle Mile '89
Fear '90
Body Bags '93

Tetchie Agbayani (1961-)
Gymkata '85
Mission Manila '87
Rikky and Pete '88

Suzanne Ager
Evil Toons '90
Fatal Justice '93

Shohreh Aghdashloo (1952-)
Maryam '00
America So Beautiful '01
House of Sand and Fog '03
The Exorcism of Emily Rose '05
American Dreamz '06
The Lake House '06
The Nativity Story '06
X-Men: The Last Stand '06
House of Saddam '08
The Sisterhood of the Traveling Pants 2 '08
The Stoning of Soraya M. '08
On the Inside '11
Rosewater '14
Septembers of Shiraz '16
The Promise '17

Pierre Agostino
The Hollywood Strangler Meets the Skid Row Slasher '79
Las Vegas Serial Killer '86

Janet Agren (1949-)
The Uranium Conspiracy '78
Emerald Jungle '80
Gates of Hell '80
Hands of Steel '86
Night of the Sharks '87

Dianna Agron (1986-)
The Romantics '10
Glee: The 3D Concert Movie '11
The Hunters '11
I Am Number Four '11
The Family '13
Novitiate '17

George Aguilar
The Trial of Billy Jack '74
A French Gigolo '08

Kris Aguilar
Bloodfist '89
Bloodfist 2 '90

Jenny Agutter (1952-)
East of Sudan '64
Star! '68
The Railway Children '70
Walkabout '71
Logan's Run '76
The Eagle Has Landed '77
Equus '77
The Man in the Iron Mask '77
Gunfire '78
Dominique '79
The Riddle of the Sands '79
Sweet William '79
Survivor '80
An American Werewolf in London '81
Amy '81
Silas Marner '85
Child's Play 2 '90
Darkman '90
The Buccaneers '95
September '96
The Railway Children '00
Irina Palm '07
Glorious 39 '09
Outside Bet '12
Sometimes Always Never '19

Brian Aherne (1902-86)
The Song of Songs '33
I Live My Life '35
Sylvia Scarlett '35
The Great Garrick '37
Merrily We Live '38
Juarez '39
The Lady in Question '40
Vigil in the Night '40
Smilin' Through '41
My Sister Eileen '42
A Night to Remember '42
Forever and a Day '43
The Locket '46
Smart Woman '48
I Confess '53
Titanic '53
A Bullet Is Waiting '54
Prince Valiant '54
The Swan '56
The Best of Everything '59
Susan Slade '61
Sword of Lancelot '63
Waltz King '63

Borje Ahlstedt (1939-)
I Am Curious (Yellow) '67
Saraband '03

Jassa Ahluwalia (1990-)
The Whale '13
Dragonheart 3: The Sorcerer's Curse '15

Waris Ahluwalia
Inside Man '06
I Am Love '09

Ahmed Ahmed
Vince Vaughn's Wild West Comedy Show '06 (C)
Iron Man '08

Riz Ahmed (1982-)
Shifty '08
Wired '08
Day of the Falcon '11
Trishna '11
Closed Circuit '13
Nightcrawler '14
Jason Bourne '16
Una '17
The Sisters Brothers '18
Venom '18

Rizwan Ahmed (1982-)
The Road to Guantanamo '06
Centurion '10
Four Lions '10

Philip Ahn (1911-78)
The General Died at Dawn '36
Thank you, Mr. Moto '37
Hawaii Calls '38
Drums of Fu Manchu '40
Across the Pacific '42
China '43
Back to Bataan '45
They Were Expendable '45
The Chinese Ring '47
Impact '49
I Was an American Spy '51
Japanese War Bride '52
Battle Circus '53
His Majesty O'Keefe '53
Hell's Half Acre '54
Battle Hymn '57
Yesterday's Enemy '59
Confessions of an Opium Eater '62
Shock Corridor '63
Paradise, Hawaiian Style '66

Sung-kee Ahn (1952-)
The Soul Guardians '98
Musa: The Warrior '01
Chihwaseon: Painted Fire '02
Battle of the Warriors '06

Charles Aidman (1925-93)
Pork Chop Hill '59
War Hunt '62
Hour of the Gun '67
Countdown '68
Adam at 6 a.m. '70
Menace on the Mountain '70
Dirty Little Billy '72
Deliver Us From Evil '73
The Invasion of Carol Enders '74
Picture of Dorian Gray '74
House of the Dead '78
Zone of the Dead '78
Zoot Suit '81
Prime Suspect '82

Danny Aiello (1933-2019)
Bang the Drum Slowly '73
The Godfather, Part 2 '74
The Front '76
Bloodbrothers '78
Fingers '78
Defiance '79
Hide in Plain Sight '80
Fort Apache, the Bronx '81
Old Enough '84
Once Upon a Time in America '84
Protector '85
The Purple Rose of Cairo '85
The Stuff '85
Alone in the Neon Jungle '87
Moonstruck '87
The Pick-Up Artist '87
Radio Days '87
Do the Right Thing '89
Harlem Nights '89
The January Man '89
Jacob's Ladder '90
Hudson Hawk '91
Mistress '91
Once Around '91
29th Street '91
Ruby '92
The Cemetery Club '93
Me and the Kid '93
The Pickle '93
Power of Attorney '94
The Professional '94
Ready to Wear '94
City Hall '95
Mojave Moon '96
Two Days in the Valley '96
Two Much '96
A Brooklyn State of Mind '97
The Last Don '97
Dead Silence '98
The Last Don 2 '98 (C)
Hitman's Journal '99
Dinner Rush '00
Mambo Cafe '00
Prince of Central Park '00
Brooklyn Lobster '05
The Last Request '06
Lucky Number Slevin '06
Stiffs '06
Reach Me '14

Rick Aiello (1958-)
Jungle Fever '91
29th Street '91
Hollywood Confidential '97
Brooklyn Lobster '05

Sho Aikawa (1961-)
Dead or Alive 2 '00
Dead or Alive '00
Dead or Alive: Final '02
Gozu '03
Zebraman '04

Elaine Aiken (1927-98)
The Lonely Man '57
Caddyshack '80

Liam Aiken (1990-)
Stepmom '98
I Dreamed of Africa '00
Sweet November '01
Road to Perdition '02
Good Boy! '03
Lemony Snicket's A Series of Unfortunate Events '04
Fay Grim '06
The Killer Inside Me '10
Girls Against Boys '12

Laura Aikman
Blood Monkey '07
The Hatching '16

Anouk Aimee (1932-)
The Golden Salamander '51
The Journey '59
La Dolce Vita '60
Lola '61
Sodom and Gomorrah '62
8 1/2 '63
A Man and a Woman '66
Justine '69
Model Shop '69
Success Is the Best Revenge '84
A Man and a Woman: 20 Years Later '86
Ready to Wear '94
Solomon '98
Festival at Cannes '02
Napoleon '03
Happily Ever After '04

Anthony Ainley (1932-2004)
Naked Evil '66
Inspector Clouseau '68
The Land That Time Forgot '75

Richard Ainley (1910-67)
Above Suspicion '43
I Dood It '43

Holly Aird (1969-)
The Flame Trees of Thika '81
Fever Pitch '96
Dreaming of Joseph Lees '99
The Criminal '00
Possession '02
Scenes of a Sexual Nature '06
Page Eight '11

Andrew Airlie (1961-)
A Decent Proposal '06
Normal '07
The Christmas Clause '08
Storm Cell '08
Collision Earth '11

Spottiswoode Aitken (1868-1933)
The Birth of a Nation '15
Monte Cristo '22

Franklin Ajaye (1949-)
Car Wash '76
Sweet Revenge '76
Convoy '78
The Jazz Singer '80
Get Crazy '83
Fraternity Vacation '85
The Wrong Guys '88
American Yakuza '94

Denis Akayama
Johnny Mnemonic '95
Killing Moon '00
My Baby's Daddy '04

Demet Akbag
The Net 2.0 '06
Winter Sleep '14

Chantal Akerman (1950-2015)
Je Tu Il Elle '74
News from Home '76 (N)
No Home Movie '15

Jeremy Akerman
November Christmas '10
Jesse Stone: Benefit of the Doubt '12

Malin Akerman (1978-)
The Utopian Society '03
The Brothers Solomon '07
The Heartbreak Kid '07
Heavy Petting '07
The Invasion '07
27 Dresses '08
Couples Retreat '09
The Proposal '09
Watchmen '09
The Bang Bang Club '10
Elektra Luxx '10
Happythankyoumoreplease '10
The Romantics '10
Catch.44 '11
The Giant Mechanical Man '12
Stolen '12
Wanderlust '12
CBGB '13
Cottage Country '13
The Numbers Station '13
The Final Girls '15
Misconduct '16
The Ticket '17
Rampage '18

Karen Akers (1945-)
The Purple Rose of Cairo '85
Heartburn '86

Adeel Akhtar
Four Lions '10
Victoria & Abdul '17

Hano Aki
Rebirth of Mothra '96
Rebirth of Mothra 2 '97

Gbenga Akinnagbe
The Lottery Ticket '10
Knucklehead '15
The Sun Is Also a Star '19

Adewale Akinnuoye-Agbaje (1967-)
Legionnaire '98
Lip Service '00
The Mummy Returns '01
The Bourne Identity '02
Get Rich or Die Tryin' '05
The Mistress of Spices '05
Preaching to the Choir '05
G.I. Joe: The Rise of Cobra '09
Faster '10
The Thing '11
Bullet to the Head '12
The Inevitable Defeat of Mister & Pete '13
Pompeii '14
Concussion '15
Trumbo '15
Farming '19

Claude Akins (1918-94)
From Here to Eternity '53
The Caine Mutiny '54
Down Three Dark Streets '54
Sea Chase '55
The Burning Hills '56
The Kettles on Old MacDonald's Farm '57
Onionhead '58
Rio Bravo '59
Comanche Station '60
Inherit the Wind '60
Claudelle Inglish '61
Black Gold '62
Merrill's Marauders '62
A Distant Trumpet '64
The Killers '64
Return of the Magnificent Seven '66
First to Fight '67
Waterhole Number 3 '67
The Devil's Brigade '68
Flap '70
A Man Called Sledge '71
The Night Stalker '71
Skyjacked '72
Battle for the Planet of the Apes '73
The Norliss Tapes '73
The Big Push '75
Kiss Me...Kill Me '76
Tarantulas: The Deadly Cargo '77
Tentacles '77
Concrete Cowboys '79
Dream West '86
Monster in the Closet '86
The Curse '87
Falling from Grace '92
The Gambler Returns: The Luck of the Draw '93

Carl Alacchi
The Pianist '91
Taken '99

Marc Alaimo (1942-)
Tango and Cash '89
Quicksand: No Escape '91
The Fence '94

Steve Alaimo (1939-)
The Hooked Generation '69
Wild Rebels '71
Alligator Alley '72

Rico Alaniz (1919-)
Siege at Red River '54
War of the Colossal Beast '58

Nelly Alard
Eating '90
Venice, Venice '92

Joe Alaskey (1949-2016)
Lucky Stiff '88
Casper '95 (V)
The Rugrats Movie '98 (V)
Looney Tunes: Back in Action '03 (V)

Carlos Alazraqui (1962-)
I Downloaded a Ghost '04
Reno 911! Miami '07
Delhi Safari '12 (V)
Planes '13 (V)

Jessica Alba (1981-)
Camp Nowhere '94
Idle Hands '99
Never Been Kissed '99
The Sleeping Dictionary '02
Honey '03
Fantastic Four '05
Into the Blue '05
Sin City '05
Awake '07
Fantastic Four: Rise of the Silver Surfer '07
Good Luck Chuck '07
Meet Bill '07
The Ten '07
The Eye '08
The Love Guru '08
The Killer Inside Me '10
Little Fockers '10
Machete '10
Valentine's Day '10
An Invisible Sign '11
Spy Kids 4: All the Time in the World '11
A.C.O.D. '13
Escape From Planet Earth '13 (V)
Machete Kills '13
Sin City: A Dame to Kill For '14
Barely Lethal '15
Some Kind of Beautiful '15
Dear Eleanor '16
Mechanic: Resurrection '16
Killers Anonymous '19

Maria Alba (1910-99)
Hell's Heroes '30
Mr. Robinson Crusoe '32
Chandu on the Magic Island '34
Return of Chandu '34
Flirting With Danger '35

Javier Albala (1969-)
Between Your Legs '99
Second Skin '99

Carlo Alban (1979-)
The Tavern '00
Strangers with Candy '06

Antonio Albanese (1964-)
Days and Clouds '07
To Rome with Love '12

Capt. Lou Albano (1933-)
Wise Guys '86
Body Slam '87

Kevin Alber (1963-)
Alien Terminator '95
Burial of the Rats '95
The Showgirl Murders '95

Anna Maria Alberghetti (1936-)
Here Comes the Groom '51
The Medium '51
Ten Thousand Bedrooms '57
Cinderfella '60
Friends and Family '01
The Whole Shebang '01

Luis Alberni (1887-1962)
The California Trail *'33*
Goodbye Love *'34*
Dancing Pirate *'36*
Follow Your Heart *'36*
The Great Garrick *'37*
Hats Off *'37*
Submarine Base *'43*
Men On Her Mind *'44*

Hans Albers (1892-1960)
The Blue Angel *'30*
F.P. 1 Doesn't Answer *'33*
Baron Munchausen *'43*

Eddie Albert (1906-2005)
Brother Rat *'38*
Four Wives *'39*
Brother Rat and a Baby *'40*
My Love Came Back *'40*
Four Mothers *'41*
Out of the Fog *'41*
The Wagons Roll at Night *'41*
Bombardier *'43*
Smash-Up: The Story of a Woman *'47*
The Dude Goes West *'48*
You Gotta Stay Happy *'48*
The Fuller Brush Girl *'50*
Meet Me After the Show *'51*
You're In the Navy Now *'51*
Actors and Sin *'52*
Carrie *'52*
Roman Holiday *'53*
I'll Cry Tomorrow *'55*
Oklahoma! *'55*
Attack! *'56*
The Teahouse of the August Moon *'56*
The Sun Also Rises *'57*
The Gun Runners *'58*
Beloved Infidel *'59*
Two Little Bears *'61*
The Longest Day *'62*
Captain Newman, M.D. *'63*
The Miracle of the White Stallions *'63*
Who's Got the Action? *'63*
The Heartbreak Kid *'72*
The Longest Yard *'74*
McQ *'74*
The Take *'74*
Devil's Rain *'75*
Escape to Witch Mountain *'75*
Whiffs *'75*
Moving Violation *'76*
The Concorde: Airport '79 *'79*
Beulah Land *'80*
How to Beat the High Cost of Living *'80*
The Oklahoma City Dolls *'81*
Peter and Paul *'81*
Take This Job & Shove It *'81*
The Victory *'81*
Yes, Giorgio *'82*
Burning Rage *'84*
Dreamscape *'84*
Brenda Starr *'86*
Dress Gray *'86*
Head Office *'86*
The Big Picture *'89*

Edward Albert (1951-2006)
Butterflies Are Free *'72*
Forty Carats *'73*
The Domino Principle *'77*
The Greek Tycoon *'78*
The Rip Off *'78*
The Squeeze *'80*
When Time Ran Out *'80*
Galaxy of Terror *'81*
Butterfly *'82*
House Where Evil Dwells *'82*
Time to Die *'83*
Ellie *'84*
The Rescue *'88*
Accidents *'89*
The Ice Runner *'93*
Sexual Malice *'93*
Guarding Tess *'94*
Hard Drive *'94*
Sorceress *'94*
The Secret Agent Club *'96*
The Man in the Iron Mask *'97*
Ablaze *'00*
Extreme Honor *'01*
Mimic 2 *'01*

Laura Albert
Death by Dialogue *'88*
The Unnamable *'88*
Author: The JT LeRoy Story *'16*

Marv Albert (1941-)
Remo Williams: The Adventure Begins *'85*
The Cookout *'04 (C)*

Shari Albert (1971-)
The Brothers McMullen *'94*
The Groomsmen *'06*

Giorgio Albertazzi (1923-)
Last Year at Marienbad *'61*
Eva *'62*

Guido Alberti (1909-96)
Casanova '70 *'65*
Ten Days Wonder *'72*
Contraband *'80*

Micah Alberti (1984-)
Forget Me Not *'09*
Triggerman *'09*

Giampiero Albertini (1927-91)
Burn! *'70*
Return of Sabata *'71*
The Case of the Bloody Iris *'72*
Commandos *'73*
Zorro *'74*

Frank Albertson (1909-64)
Son of the Gods *'30*
Huddle *'32*
Ah, Wilderness! *'35*
Alice Adams *'35*
Fury *'36*
Navy Blue and Gold *'37*
Room Service *'38*
Louisiana Purchase *'41*
Junior G-Men of the Air *'42*
Wake Island *'42*
It's a Wonderful Life *'46*
Killer Dill *'47*
Shed No Tears *'48*
Girl On the Run *'53*
Nightfall *'56*
Psycho *'60*

Jack Albertson (1907-81)
Miracle on 34th Street *'47*
Top Banana *'54*
Teacher's Pet *'58*
Lover Come Back *'61*
Days of Wine and Roses *'62*
Period of Adjustment *'62*
Who's Got the Action? *'63*
How to Murder Your Wife *'64*
Kissin' Cousins *'64*
The Patsy *'64*
Roustabout *'64*
Flim-Flam Man *'67*
The Subject Was Roses *'68*
Justine *'69*
Rabbit, Run *'70*
Willy Wonka & the Chocolate Factory *'71*
The Poseidon Adventure *'72*
Marriage Is Alive and Well *'80*
Dead and Buried *'81*
The Fox and the Hound *'81 (V)*

Mabel Albertson (1901-82)
Ma and Pa Kettle at Waikiki *'55*
Home Before Dark *'58*
Barefoot in the Park *'67*

Karl Otto Alberty (1933-)
The Great Escape *'63*
Battle of the Bulge *'65*

Jens Albinus
The Idiots *'99*
The Boss of It All *'06*

Ariauna Albright (1969-)
Witchouse *'99*
Ancient Evil: Scream of the Mummy *'00*
Witchouse 2: Blood Coven *'00*
Mom's Outta Sight *'01*

Dan Albright
To Dance with the White Dog *'93*
I Know What You Did Last Summer *'97*
Bobby Jones: Stroke of Genius *'04*

Hardie Albright (1903-75)
Jewel Robbery *'32*
The Purchase Price *'32*
A Successful Calamity *'32*
The House on 56th Street *'33*
The Song of Songs *'33*
Three-Cornered Moon *'33*
The Working Man *'33*
The Scarlet Letter *'34*
Bambi *'42 (V)*
The Jade Mask *'45*
Mom & Dad *'47*

Lola Albright (1924-2017)
The Killer That Stalked New York *'47*
Champion *'49*
The Tender Trap *'55*
The Monolith Monsters *'57*
Kid Galahad *'62*
Joy House *'64*
Lord Love a Duck *'66*
The Way West *'67*
The Impossible Years *'68*

Tucker Albrizzi
Spooky Buddies *'11*
Treasure Buddies *'12 (V)*

Damian Alcazar (1953-)
Hombres Armados *'97*
The Crime of Father Amaro *'02*
And Starring Pancho Villa as Himself *'03*
Cronicas *'04*

Alan Alda (1936-)
Gone Are the Days *'63*
Purlie Victorious *'63*
Paper Lion *'68*
The Moonshine War *'70*
The Mephisto Waltz *'71*
The Glass House *'72*
California Suite *'78*
Same Time, Next Year *'78*
The Seduction of Joe Tynan *'79*
The Four Seasons *'81*
M*A*S*H: Goodbye, Farewell & Amen *'83*
Sweet Liberty *'86*
Crimes & Misdemeanors *'89*
Betsy's Wedding *'90*
Whispers in the Dark *'92*
And the Band Played On *'93*
Manhattan Murder Mystery *'93*
Canadian Bacon *'94*
White Mile *'94*
Flirting with Disaster *'95*
Everyone Says I Love You *'96*
Mad City *'97*
Murder at 1600 *'97*
The Object of My Affection *'98*
What Women Want *'00*
The Aviator *'04*
Resurrecting the Champ *'07*
Diminished Capacity *'08*
Flash of Genius *'08*
Nothing But the Truth *'08*
Tower Heist *'11*
Wanderlust *'12*
Bridge of Spies *'15*
The Longest Ride *'15*

Antony Alda (1956-2009)
Homeboy *'88*
The Killing Device *'92*

Robert Alda (1914-86)
Rhapsody in Blue *'45*
The Beast with Five Fingers *'46*
Cloak and Dagger *'46*
The Man I Love *'46*
Nora Prentiss *'47*
Homicide *'49*
Tarzan and the Slave Girl *'50*
Force of Impulse *'60*
Revenge of the Barbarians *'60*
The Devil's Hand *'61*
The Girl Who Knew Too Much *'69*
Night Flight from Moscow *'73*
Lisa and the Devil *'75*
I Will, I Will...for Now *'76*
Love by Appointment *'76*
Every Girl Should Have One *'78*
The Rip Off *'78*
The Squeeze *'80*

Rutanya Alda (1942-)
Scarecrow *'73*
The Deer Hunter *'78*
The Fury *'78*
When a Stranger Calls *'79*
Christmas Evil *'80*
Mommie Dearest *'81*
Amityville 2: The Possession *'82*
Girls Night Out *'83*
Vigilante *'83*
Racing with the Moon *'84*
Black Widow *'87*
Prancer *'89*
Last Exit to Brooklyn *'90*
The Dark Half *'91*
Article 99 *'92*
Leaving Normal *'92*
The Souler Opposite *'97*
Murder Without Conviction *'04*

Jennifer (Jenny) Alden
Wedding Crashers *'05*
Fall Down Dead *'07*

Mary Alden (1883-1946)
The Birth of a Nation *'15*
The Plastic Age *'25*
Strange Interlude *'32*

Norman Alden (1924-2012)
The Nutty Professor *'63*
The Sword in the Stone *'63 (V)*
The Patsy *'64*
Good Times *'67*
The Devil's Brigade *'68*
Tora! Tora! Tora! *'70*
Kansas City Bomber *'72*

Eddie Alderson
Reservation Road *'07*
Changeling *'08*

Erville Alderson (1882-1957)
America *'24*
Sally of the Sawdust *'25*
Sergeant York *'41*
Objective, Burma! *'45*

John Alderton (1940-)
The Girl Getters *'66*
Duffy *'68*
Hannibal Brooks *'69*
Macbeth *'70*
Zardoz *'73*
Speedy Death *'99*
Calendar Girls *'03*

Mari Aldon (1925-2004)
Distant Drums *'51*
The Tanks Are Coming *'51*
This Woman Is Dangerous *'52*
Race for Life *'55*
Summertime *'55*

Tom Aldredge (1928-2011)
The Rain People *'69*
O Pioneers! *'91*
Other People's Money *'91*
What about Bob? *'91*
The Adventures of Huck Finn *'93*
Andersonville *'95*
Harvest of Fire *'95*
Commandments *'96*
Lawn Dogs *'96*
Message in a Bottle *'98*
Rounders *'98*
A Stranger in the Kingdom *'98*
Cold Mountain *'03*
Intolerable Cruelty *'03*
Game 6 *'05*
The Assassination of Jesse James by the Coward Robert Ford *'07*

Sarah Aldrich
Miracle at Sage Creek *'05*
Big Bad Wolf *'06*

Ben Aldridge (1985-)
Compulsion *'08*
First Light *'10*

Kitty Aldridge (1962-)
Slipstream *'89*
To Play the King *'93*
The Ice House *'97*

Michael Aldridge (1920-94)
Love for Lydia *'79*
Tinker, Tailor, Soldier, Spy *'80*
Bullshot *'83*

Sabrina Aldridge
Deck the Halls *'06*
April Fool's Day *'08*

Virginia Aldridge (1938-)
High School Big Shot *'59*
Riot in Juvenile Prison *'59*

Buzz Aldrin (1930-)
See Edwin E. Aldrin, Jr.

Edwin E. Aldrin, Jr. (1930-)
Fly Me to the Moon *'08 (V)*
Apollo 11 *'19*

Norma Aleandro (1936-)
The Official Story *'85*
Cousins *'89*
One Man's War *'90*
Vital Signs *'90*
Autumn Sun *'98*
The Son of the Bride *'01*
Live-In Maid *'04*
The City of Your Final Destination *'09*

Kevin Alejandro
Wake *'09*
Safelight *'15*

Aki Aleong (1934-)
Hanoi Hilton *'87*
Braddock: Missing in Action 3 *'88*
Farewell to the King *'89*
The Quest *'96*
Lewis and Clark and George *'97*
Missing Brendan *'03*
Sci-Fighter *'04*

Yassmin Alers
The American Mall *'08*
Chain Link *'08*

John Ales (1969-)
Ride with the Devil *'99*
Nutty Professor 2: The Klumps *'00*
Burning Down the House *'01*
Uprising *'01*
Life of the Party *'05*
Dragon Wars *'07*

Fausto Russo Alesi
The Double Hour *'09*
Vincere *'09*

Raquel Alessi
Ghost Rider *'07*
Miss March *'09*

Barbara Lee Alexander (1953-)
See Barbara Niven

Ben Alexander (1911-69)
The Little American *'17*
All Quiet on the Western Front *'30*
This Day and Age *'33*
Criminals Within *'41*
Dragnet *'54*
Man in the Shadow *'57*

Elizabeth (Liz) Alexander (1952-)
The Chant of Jimmie Blacksmith *'78*
Salem's Lot *'04*

Erika Alexander (1969-)
30 Years to Life *'01*
Love Liza *'02*
Deja Vu *'06*
La Mission *'09*
Elsa & Fred *'14*

Flex Alexander (1970-)
Santa and Pete *'99*
She's All That *'99*
Man in the Mirror: The Michael Jackson Story *'04*
Poor Man's Game *'06*
Snakes on a Plane *'06*
The Hills Have Eyes 2 *'07*
Love and Other Four Letter Words *'07*

Jace Alexander (1964-)
Matewan *'87*
Crocodile Dundee 2 *'88*
Eight Men Out *'88*
City of Hope *'91*
Mistress *'91*
Love and a .45 *'94*

Jaimie Alexander (1984-)
Evil Dead Trap 2: Hideki *'91*
Rest Stop *'06*
Loosies *'11*
Collision *'13*
The Last Stand *'13*
Savannah *'14*
Broken Vows *'16*

Jane Alexander (1939-)
The Great White Hope *'70*
A Gunfight *'71*
The New Centurions *'72*
All the President's Men *'76*
Eleanor & Franklin *'76*
The Betsy *'78*
Kramer vs. Kramer *'79*
Brubaker *'80*
Playing for Time *'80*
Night Crossing *'81*
In the Custody of Strangers *'82*
Testament *'83*
City Heat *'84*
Blood and Orchids *'86*
The Rumor Mill *'86*
Square Dance *'87*
Glory *'89*
In Love and War *'91*
The Cider House Rules *'99*
The Ring *'02*
Sunshine State *'02*
Carry Me Home *'04*
Fur: An Imaginary Portrait of Diane Arbus *'06*
Feast of Love *'07*
Gigantic *'08*
Terminator Salvation *'09*
The Unborn *'09*
Dream House *'11*
William & Catherine: A Royal Romance *'11*
Last Love *'13*

Jason Alexander (1959-)
The Burning *'82*
Brighton Beach Memoirs *'86*
The Mosquito Coast *'86*
Jacob's Ladder *'90*
Pretty Woman *'90*
White Palace *'90*
I Don't Buy Kisses Anymore *'92*
Coneheads *'93*
Blankman *'94*
The Paper *'94*
The Return of Jafar *'94 (V)*
Bye Bye Birdie *'95*
Dunston Checks In *'95*
For Better or Worse *'95*
The Hunchback of Notre Dame *'96 (V)*
The Last Supper *'96*
Love! Valour! Compassion! *'96*
Cinderella *'97*
Something About Sex *'98*
Love and Action in Chicago *'99*
The Adventures of Rocky & Bullwinkle *'00*
Shallow Hal *'01*
The Trumpet of the Swan *'01 (V)*
On Edge *'03*
How to Go Out on a Date in Queens *'06*
Ira & Abby *'06*
Hachiko: A Dog's Tale *'09*

Meteor '09
Rock Slyde: Private Eye '09
Wild Card '15

Jeff Alexander (1910-89)
Curse of the Swamp Creature '66
Twisted Brain '74

John Alexander (1897-1982)
Arsenic and Old Lace '44
Mr. Skeffington '44
The Horn Blows at Midnight '45
Junior Miss '45
A Tree Grows in Brooklyn '45
The Jolson Story '46
Where There's Life '47
Fancy Pants '50
The Marrying Kind '52

Katherine Alexander (1898-1981)
The Barretts of Wimpole Street '34
Death Takes a Holiday '34
Operator 13 '34
After Office Hours '35
The Girl from 10th Ave. '35
The Devil Is a Sissy '36
That Certain Woman '37
Dance, Girl, Dance '40
John Loves Mary '48

Khandi Alexander (1957-)
Streetwalkin' '85
CB4: The Movie '93
What's Love Got to Do with It? '93
Greedy '94
Sugar Hill '94
Robin Cook's Terminal '96
There's Something about Mary '98
Thick as Thieves '99
The Corner '00
Killing Emmett Young '02
Dark Blue '03
Rain '06
A Woman, A Part '17

Olivia Alexander
Attack of the 50 Foot Cheerleader '12
30 Nights of Paranormal Activity with the Devil Inside the Girl with the Dragon Tattoo '12

Olly Alexander (1990-)
Enter the Void '09
Tormented '09
The Dish & the Spoon '11
God Help the Girl '14
Le Week-End '14

Peter Alexander
Color of a Brisk and Leaping Day '95
Seamless '00

Richard Alexander (1902-89)
The Mysterious Lady '28
All Quiet on the Western Front '30
S.O.S. Coast Guard '37

Robert Alexander (1952-)
See Michael Gross

Ross Alexander (1907-37)
Flirtation Walk '34
Captain Blood '35
A Midsummer Night's Dream '35
Shipmates Forever '35
China Clipper '36

Sarah Alexander (1971-)
I Could Never Be Your Woman '06
Stardust '07

Sasha Alexander (1973-)
All Over the Guy '01
Mission: Impossible 3 '06
The Last Lullaby '08
Yes Man '08
Tenure '09

Tad Alexander (1922-)
Ambassador Bill '31
Rasputin and the Empress '33

Terence Alexander (1923-2009)
The Runaway Bus '54
The Square Peg '58
The Mind Benders '63
What's Good for the Goose '69

Terry Alexander (1947-)
Flashpoint '84
Day of the Dead '85
The Horror Show '89
Amateur '94
Hurricane Streets '96
Conspiracy Theory '97

Charlotta Alexandra
A Real Young Girl '75
Good-bye, Emmanuelle '77

Tiana Alexandra
Pearl '78
Catch the Heat '87

Manuel Alexandre (1917-2010)
Two Tough Guys '03
Swindled '04

Victor Alfieri
The Roman Spring of Mrs. Stone '03
I-See-You.Com '06

Lidia Alfonsi (1928-)
The Trojan Horse '62
Black Sabbath '64
Life Is Beautiful '98

David Alford
A Death in the Family '02
The Second Chance '06

Phillip Alford (1948-)
To Kill a Mockingbird '62
Shenandoah '65

Hans Alfredson (1931-)
The Shame '68
Pippi on the Run '70
The New Land '72

Mahershala Ali (1974-)
The Curious Case of Benjamin Button '08
Predators '10
The Wronged Man '10
The Place Beyond the Pines '13
Free State of Jones '16
Moonlight '16
Green Book '18
Spider-Man: Into the Spider-Verse '18 (V)
Alita: Battle Angel '19

Muhammad Ali (1942-2016)
Requiem for a Heavyweight '62
The Greatest '77
Freedom Road '79
Body & Soul '81
Doin' Time '85
Soul Power '08

Tatyana Ali (1979-)
The Brothers '01
Nora's Hair Salon '04
Back in the Day '05
Nora's Hair Salon 2: A Cut Above '08
Mother and Child '09
Home Again '13

Mary Alice (1941-)
Sparkle '76
The Women of Brewster Place '89
To Sleep with Anger '90
Down in the Delta '98
Catfish in Black Bean Sauce '00
Sunshine State '02
The Matrix Revolutions '03

Ana Alicia (1956-)
Coward of the County '81
Romero '89

Taraneh Alidoosti
Shirin '09
The Salesman '16

Dean Alioto
L.A. Dicks '05
Shadowheart '09

Roger Allam (1953-)
The Roman Spring of Mrs. Stone '03
V for Vendetta '06
Speed Racer '08
Tamara Drewe '10
The Iron Lady '11
The Woman in Black '12
The Book Thief '13
The Lady in the Van '15

Elizabeth Allan (1908-90)
Ace of Aces '33
Men in White '34
Phantom Fiend '35
Camille '36
A Tale of Two Cities '36
A Woman Rebels '36
Slave Ship '37
No Highway in the Sky '51
The Haunted Strangler '58

Hugh Allan (1903-)
Dress Parade '27
Wild Beauty '27

Louise Allbritton (1920-79)
Pittsburgh '42
Who Done It? '42
Son of Dracula '43
Egg and I '47
Sitting Pretty '48
Walk a Crooked Mile '48

Michael Alldredge (1941-)
Hostage Flight '85
About Last Night. . . '86
Robot Jox '90

Catherine Allegret (1946-)
Last Tango in Paris '73
La Vie en Rose '07

Aleisha Allen (1991-)
School of Rock '03
Are We There Yet? '05
Are We Done Yet? '07

Alfie Allen (1986-)
John Wick '14
Plastic '14

Andrew James Allen (1987-)
Recipe for Disaster '03
Smiley '12
Hansel & Gretel Get Baked '13

Barbara Jo Allen (1905-74)
Design for Scandal '41
Sleeping Beauty '59 (V)
The Sword in the Stone '63 (V)

Bill Allen (1962-)
Maniac '77
Streamers '83
Born on the Fourth of July '89
Sioux City '94

Chad Allen (1974-)
The Bad Seed '85
Camp Cucamonga: How I Spent My Summer Vacation '90
Murder in New Hampshire: The Pamela Smart Story '91
What Matters Most '01
Third Man Out: A Donald Strachey Mystery '05
End of the Spear '06
Shock to the System '06
Save Me '07
Ice Blues: A Donald Strachey Mystery '08
On the Other Hand, Death '08
Hollywood, Je T'Aime '09
Fright Flick '10
Spork '10

Christa B. Allen (1991-)
13 Going on 30 '04
The Town That Banned Christmas '06

Corey Allen (1934-2010)
The Night of the Hunter '55
Rebel without a Cause '55
The Big Caper '57
Shadow on the Window '57
Darby's Rangers '58
Party Girl '58

Crystal Allen (1978-)
Anaconda 3: The Offspring '08
Anacondas: Trail of Blood '09
Crooked Arrows '12

Debbie Allen (1950-)
The Fish that Saved Pittsburgh '79
Roots: The Next Generation '79
Ragtime '81
Jo Jo Dancer, Your Life Is Calling '86
All About You '01
The Old Settler '01
Fame '09
Next Day Air '09

Elizabeth Allen (1929-2006)
Donovan's Reef '63
Star Spangled Girl '71
The Carey Treatment '72

Fred Allen (1894-1956)
Thanks a Million '35
Sally, Irene and Mary '38
It's in the Bag! '45
We're Not Married '52
Into the Abyss '11

Ginger Lynn Allen (1962-)
Vice Academy '88
Buried Alive '89
Leather Jackets '90
Vice Academy 2 '90
Young Guns 2 '90
Vice Academy 3 '91
Mind, Body & Soul '92
Bound and Gagged: A Love Story '93
The Independent '00

Gracie Allen (1902-64)
International House '33
We're Not Dressing '34
Here Comes Cookie '35
Love in Bloom '35
A Damsel in Distress '37
College Swing '38
The Gracie Allen Murder Case '39
Honolulu '39
Two Girls and a Sailor '44

Jack Allen (1908-95)
The Four Feathers '39
Radio Cab Murder '54

Jeffrey Allen (1910-79)
Moonshine Mountain '64
2000 Maniacs '64
Something Weird '68
This Stuff'll Kill Ya! '71

Jo Harvey Allen (1942-)
True Stories '86
Checking Out '89
Tapeheads '89
The Wendell Baker Story '05

Joan Allen (1956-)
Manhunter '86
Peggy Sue Got Married '86
Tucker: The Man and His Dream '88
In Country '89
Ethan Frome '92
Josh and S.A.M. '93
Searching for Bobby Fischer '93
Mad Love '95
Nixon '95
The Crucible '96
Face/Off '97
The Ice Storm '97
Pleasantville '98
It's the Rage '99
When the Sky Falls '99
The Contender '00

Mists of Avalon '01
Off the Map '03
The Bourne Supremacy '04
The Notebook '04
Yes '04
The Upside of Anger '05
Bonneville '06
The Bourne Ultimatum '07
Death Race '08
Georgia O'Keefe '09
Hachiko: A Dog's Tale '09
The Bourne Legacy '12
A Good Marriage '14
Room '15

Jonelle Allen (1944-)
The River Niger '76
The Midnight Hour '86
Grave Secrets: The Legacy of Hilltop Drive '92
Next Time '99
Mr. Barrington '03

Joshua Michael Allen
Shark Island '12
Age of Dinosaurs '13

Judith Allen (1911-96)
This Day and Age '33
Bright Eyes '34
Night Alarm '34
The Old-Fashioned Way '34
Behind the Green Lights '35
Healer '36

Karen Allen (1951-)
National Lampoon's Animal House '78
Manhattan '79
Wanderers '79
Cruising '80
East of Eden '80
A Small Circle of Friends '80
Raiders of the Lost Ark '81
Shoot the Moon '82
Starman '84
Until September '84
The Glass Menagerie '87
Backfire '88
Scrooged '88
Sweet Talker '91
Malcolm X '92 (C)
The Turning '92
Ghost in the Machine '93
The Sandlot '93
Til There Was You '96
Wind River '98
The Basket '99
The Perfect Storm '00
In the Bedroom '01
Shaka Zulu: The Last Great Warrior '01
World Traveler '01
Plain Dirty '04
Poster Boy '04
When Will I Be Loved '04
Indiana Jones and the Kingdom of the Crystal Skull '08
A Dog Year '09 (V)
November Christmas '10
White Irish Drinkers '10
Colewell '19

Keith Allen (1953-)
A Very British Coup '88
Chicago Joe & the Showgirl '90
Nightscare '93
The Young Americans '93
Captives '94
Second Best '94
Shallow Grave '94
Loch Ness '95
Prince of Poisoners: The Life and Crimes of William Palmer '98
Rancid Aluminium '00
My Wife is an Actress '01
24 Hour Party People '01
Agent Cody Banks 2: Destination London '04
De-Lovely '04
Eddie the Eagle '16
I Am Vengeance '18

Krista Allen (1971-)
The Haunted Sea '97
Raven '97
Sunset Strip '99
Totally Blonde '01

Anger Management '03
Shut Up and Kiss Me '05
Feast '06
Tony n' Tina's Wedding '07
Meet Market '08
Silent Venom '08
The Final Destination '09
Jesse Stone: No Remorse '10

Laura Allen (1974-)
How You Look to Me '05
Sucker Free City '05
Old Dogs '09
Clown '16

Marty Allen (1922-2018)
Jailbreakin' '72
Harrad Summer '74

Nancy Allen (1950-)
The Last Detail '73
Carrie '76
I Wanna Hold Your Hand '78
Home Movies '79
1941 '79
Dressed to Kill '80
Blow Out '81
Strange Invaders '83
Not for Publication '84
The Philadelphia Experiment '84
The Gladiator '86
RoboCop '87
Sweet Revenge '87
Poltergeist 3 '88
Limit Up '89
RoboCop 2 '90
RoboCop 3 '91
The Last Assassins '96
Against the Law '98
Highway Hitcher '98
Out of Sight '98
Secre of the Andes '98
Children of the Corn 666: Isaac's Return '99
Kiss Toledo Goodbye '00

Parry Allen (1973-)
See Parry Shen

Patrick Allen (1927-2006)
The Long Haul '57
Tread Softly Stranger '58
Never Take Candy From a Stranger '60
Island of the Burning Doomed '67
Puppet on a Chain '72
Sea Wolves '81
Agatha Christie's Murder is Easy '82
Body & Soul '93

Penelope Allen (1943-)
Scarecrow '73
Looking for Richard '96
The Thin Red Line '98

Ray Allen (1975-)
He Got Game '98
Harvard Man '01

Rex Allen (1921-99)
Trail of Robin Hood '50
Colorado Sundown '52
I Dream of Jeannie '52
Charlie the Lonesome Cougar '67 (N)
The Secret of Navajo Cave '76 (N)
Me, Myself, and Irene '00 (V)

Robert 'Tex' Allen (1906-98)
The Perils of Pauline '34
Air Hawks '35
The Black Room '35
The Awful Truth '37

Ronald Allen (1930-91)
Hell Boats '70
Eat the Rich '87

Rosalind Allen (1957-)
Children of the Corn 2: The Final Sacrifice '92
Ticks '93
Pinocchio's Revenge '96

Sage Allen
Mr. Saturday Night '92
Suspended Animation '02

Sheila Allen (1932-2011)
Children of the Damned *'63*
The Alphabet Murders *'65*
Steve Allen (1921-2000)
The Benny Goodman Story *'55*
Heart Beat *'80*
Ratings Game *'84*
Alice in Wonderland *'85*
Amazon Women on the Moon *'87*
Great Balls of Fire *'89*
The Player *'92*
The St. Tammany Miracle *'94 (C)*
Casino *'95*
Tanya Allen (1975-)
Spenser: Ceremony *'93*
The Morrison Murders *'96*
Behind the Lines *'97*
White Lies *'98*
Tail Lights Fade *'99*
Lone Hero *'02*
Silent Hill *'06*
Tim Allen (1953-)
The Santa Clause *'94*
Toy Story *'95 (V)*
Jungle 2 Jungle *'96*
For Richer or Poorer *'97*
Galaxy Quest *'99*
Toy Story 2 *'99 (V)*
Joe Somebody *'01*
Big Trouble *'02*
The Santa Clause 2 *'02*
Who is Cletis Tout? *'02*
Christmas With the Kranks *'04*
The Santa Clause 3: The Escape Clause *'06*
The Shaggy Dog *'06*
Zoom *'06*
Wild Hogs *'07*
Redbelt *'08*
The Six Wives of Henry Lefay *'09*
Crazy on the Outside *'10*
Toy Story 3 *'10 (V)*
Chimpanzee *'12 (N)*
Toy Story 4 *'19*
Todd Allen (1960-)
Witchboard *'87*
Storm and Sorrow *'90*
Wyatt Earp *'94*
Pinocchio's Revenge *'96*
The Apostle *'97*
The Postman *'97*
Woody Allen (1935-)
What's New Pussycat? *'65*
What's Up, Tiger Lily? *'66 (N)*
Casino Royale *'67*
Take the Money and Run *'69*
Bananas *'71*
Everything You Always Wanted to Know about Sex (But Were Afraid to Ask) *'72*
Play It Again, Sam *'72*
Sleeper *'73*
Love and Death *'75*
The Front *'76*
Annie Hall *'77*
Manhattan *'79*
Stardust Memories *'80*
A Midsummer Night's Sex Comedy *'82*
Zelig *'83*
Broadway Danny Rose *'84*
Hannah and Her Sisters *'86*
Radio Days *'87 (N)*
Crimes & Misdemeanors *'89*
New York Stories *'89*
Scenes from a Mall *'91*
Husbands and Wives *'92*
Shadows and Fog *'92*
Manhattan Murder Mystery *'93*
Mighty Aphrodite *'95*
The Sunshine Boys *'95*
Everyone Says I Love You *'96*
Deconstructing Harry *'97*
Antz *'98 (V)*
The Imposters *'98*
Picking Up the Pieces *'99*
Sweet and Lowdown *'99*
Company Man *'00*
Small Time Crooks *'00*
The Curse of the Jade Scorpion *'01*
Hollywood Ending *'02*
Anything Else *'03*
Scoop *'06*
To Rome with Love *'12*
Fading Gigolo *'13*
Fernando Allende (1954-)
Heartbreaker *'83*
Naked Lies *'98*
Kirstie Alley (1951-)
Star Trek 2: The Wrath of Khan *'82*
Blind Date *'84*
Champions *'84*
Runaway *'84*
North and South Book 1 *'85*
North and South Book 2 *'86*
Prince of Bel Air *'87*
Summer School *'87*
Shoot to Kill *'88*
Look Who's Talking *'89*
Loverboy *'89*
Look Who's Talking, Too *'90*
Sibling Rivalry *'90*
Look Who's Talking Now *'93*
It Takes Two *'95*
Village of the Damned *'95*
Deconstructing Harry *'97*
For Richer or Poorer *'97*
The Last Don *'97*
Toothless *'97*
The Last Don 2 *'98*
Drop Dead Gorgeous *'99*
Blonde *'01*
The Salem Witch Trials *'02*
Sara Allgood (1883-1950)
Blackmail *'29*
Juno and the Paycock *'30*
It's Love Again *'36*
Storm in a Teacup *'37*
Dr. Jekyll and Mr. Hyde *'41*
How Green Was My Valley *'41*
That Hamilton Woman *'41*
Life Begins at Eight-Thirty *'42*
Roxie Hart *'42*
City Without Men *'43*
Between Two Worlds *'44*
Jane Eyre *'44*
The Keys of the Kingdom *'44*
The Strange Affair of Uncle Harry *'45*
The Spiral Staircase *'46*
The Fabulous Dorseys *'47*
Mother Wore Tights *'47*
My Wild Irish Rose *'47*
Cheaper by the Dozen *'50*
Don Allison
The Haunting of Lisa *'96*
Snap Decision *'01*
Hoax for the Holidays *'10*
Dorothy Allison (1925-92)
The Scamp *'57*
See No Evil *'71*
Rikky and Pete *'88*
Thom Allison
Leaving Metropolis *'02*
I Me Wed *'07*
Claud Allister (1888-1970)
Monte Carlo *'30*
The Sea Ghost *'31*
The Private Life of Henry VIII *'33*
Lillian Russell *'40*
Gregg Allman (1947-2017)
Rush Week *'88*
Rush *'91*
Jamie Anne Allman
Farmhouse *'08*
Prairie Fever *'08*
The Last Rites of Joe May *'11*
Any Day Now *'12*
Marshall Allman (1984-)
Dishdogz *'05*
Hostage *'05*
Blue Like Jazz *'12*
James Allodi (1967-)
Invasion! *'99*
Men with Brooms *'02*
Snow Cake *'06*
Christopher Allport (1947-2008)
Savage Weekend *'80*
Special Bulletin *'83*
News at Eleven *'86*
Jack Frost *'97*
Jack Frost 2: Revenge of the Mutant Killer Snowman *'00*
Though None Go With Me *'06*
Garden Party *'08*
Corbin Allred (1979-)
Josh Kirby. . .Time Warrior: Chapter 1, Planet of the Dino-Knights *'95*
Josh Kirby. . . Time Warrior: Chapter 2, The Human Pets *'95*
Josh Kirby. . . Time Warrior: Chapter 3, Trapped on Toyworld *'95*
Josh Kirby. . . Time Warrior: Chapter 4, Eggs from 70 Million B.C. *'95*
Address Unknown *'96*
Josh Kirby. . . Time Warrior: Chapter 5, Journey to the Magic Cavern *'96*
Josh Kirby. . . Time Warrior: Chapter 6, Last Battle for the Universe *'96*
Diamonds *'99*
Saints and Soldiers *'03*
Saints and Soldiers: Airborne Creed *'12*
Astrid Allwyn (1905-78)
Love Affair *'32*
Beggars in Ermine *'34*
Charlie Chan's Secret *'35*
Hands Across the Table *'35*
Stowaway *'36*
Love Affair *'39*
Miracles for Sale *'39*
No Hands on the Clock *'41*
June Allyson (1917-2006)
Best Foot Forward *'43*
Girl Crazy *'43*
Thousands Cheer *'43*
Meet the People *'44*
Music For Millions *'44*
Two Girls and a Sailor *'44*
Her Highness and the Bellboy *'45*
The Secret Heart *'46*
Till the Clouds Roll By *'46*
Two Sisters From Boston *'46*
Good News *'47*
High Barbaree *'47*
The Bride Goes Wild *'48*
The Three Musketeers *'48*
Words and Music *'48*
Little Women *'49*
The Stratton Story *'49*
The Reformer and the Redhead *'50*
Right Cross *'50*
Too Young to Kiss *'51*
The Girl in White *'52*
Battle Circus *'53*
Executive Suite *'54*
The Glenn Miller Story *'54*
The McConnell Story *'55*
Strategic Air Command *'55*
The Opposite Sex *'56*
My Man Godfrey *'57*
They Only Kill Their Masters *'72*
Blackout *'78*
Vegas *'78*
Gila Almagor (1939-)
Sallah *'63*
Death Merchants *'73*
Every Time We Say Goodbye *'86*
The Summer of Aviya *'88*
Under the Domim Tree *'95*
Munich *'05*
The Debt *'07*
Joaquim Almeida (1957-)
The Celestine Prophecy *'06*
Bobby Z *'07*
Fast Five *'11*
Susan Almgren
Twin Sisters *'91*
The Witness *'99*
Adrian Alonso
The Legend of Zorro *'05*
Under the Same Moon *'07*
Chelo Alonso (1933-)
Son of Samson *'62*
The Good, the Bad and the Ugly *'67*
Daniella Alonso
The Hills Have Eyes 2 *'07*
Wrong Turn 2: Dead End *'07*
Paul Blart: Mall Cop 2 *'15*
Darkness Falls *'20*
Johnny Alonso (1970-)
Safehouse *'08*
Coffin *'11*
Laz Alonso (1974-)
G *'02*
All Souls Day *'05*
Jarhead *'05*
Bunny Whipped *'06*
The Tenants *'06*
Captivity *'07*
Divine Intervention *'07*
Stomp the Yard *'07*
This Christmas *'07*
Miracle at St. Anna *'08*
Avatar *'09*
Fast & Furious *'09*
Jumping the Broom *'11*
Straw Dogs *'11*
Battle of the Year *'13*
Maria Conchita Alonso (1957-)
Moscow on the Hudson *'84*
Fear City *'85*
A Fine Mess *'86*
Touch and Go *'86*
Extreme Prejudice *'87*
The Running Man *'87*
Colors *'88*
Vampire's Kiss *'88*
Predator 2 *'90*
Teamster Boss: The Jackie Presser Story *'92*
The House of the Spirits *'93*
Texas *'94*
Roosters *'95*
Caught *'96*
Blackheart *'98*
Footsteps *'98*
Blind Heat *'00*
Chain of Command *'00*
High Noon *'00*
The Code Conspiracy *'01*
Chasing Papi *'03*
Heart of America *'03*
ESL: English as a Second Language *'05*
Material Girls *'06*
The Dead One *'07*
The Art of Travel *'08*
Maneater *'09*
Spread *'09*
Wolf Moon *'09*
Without Men *'11*
The Lords of Salem *'13*
Ryan Alosio (1973-)
Something About Sex *'98*
Darkwolf *'03*
David Alpay (1980-)
Ararat *'02*
All Hat *'07*
Closing the Ring *'07*
They're Watching *'16*
Murray Alper
Seven Keys to Baldpate *'35*
They Were Expendable *'45*
Carol Alt (1960-)
Bye Bye Baby *'88*
Millions *'90*
Beyond Justice *'92*
Thunder in Paradise *'93*
Thunder in Paradise 2 *'94*
Thunder in Paradise 3 *'94*
Body Armor *'96*
Deadly Game *'98*
Storm Trooper *'98*
Revelation *'00*
Snakehead Terror *'04*
Fatal Trust *'06*
The Town That Banned Christmas *'06*
The Man Who Came Back *'08*
John Altamura
The Toxic Avenger, Part 2 *'89*
The Toxic Avenger, Part 3: The Last Temptation of Toxie *'89*
Bikini Bistro *'94*
Ernesto Alterio (1970-)
Swindled *'04*
The Method *'05*
Hector Alterio (1929-)
Cria Cuervos *'76*
Camila *'84*
The Official Story *'85*
I, the Worst of All *'90*
The Son of the Bride *'01*
Allen Altman
Dead Silent *'99*
Incendies *'10*
Bruce Altman (1955-)
The Favor, the Watch, & the Very Big Fish *'92*
Glengarry Glen Ross *'92*
My New Gun *'92*
Mr. Jones *'93*
Mr. Wonderful *'93*
Vibrations *'94*
White Mile *'94*
To Gillian on Her 37th Birthday *'96*
L.I.E. *'01*
Matchstick Men *'03*
Running Scared *'06*
Recount *'08*
Bride Wars *'09*
Peter and Vandy *'09*
The Skeptic *'09*
The American *'10*
The Sitter *'11*
Game Change *'12*
Kilimanjaro *'13*
The Odd Way Home *'13*
Shelter *'15*
Touched With Fire *'16*
The Sound of Silence *'19*
Carlen Altman
You Wont Miss Me *'09*
The Color Wheel *'11*
Jeff Altman (1951-)
Doin' Time *'85*
Russian Roulette *'93*
Marnie Alton
In Hell *'03*
Shadowheart *'09*
Aviv Alush (1982-)
See Avraham Aviv Alush
Avraham Aviv Alush (1982-)
The Women's Balcony *'16*
The Shack *'17*
Angela Alvarado (1964-)
Hollywood Confidential *'97*
Boss of Bosses *'99*
Lone Rider *'08*
Don Alvarado (1904-67)
Battle of the Sexes *'28*
Rio Rita *'29*
Beau Ideal *'31*
Nobody's Baby *'37*
Big Steal *'49*
Magali Alvarado
Salsa *'88*
Mi Vida Loca *'94*
Trini Alvarado (1967-)
Times Square *'80*
Mrs. Soffel *'84*
Sweet Lorraine *'87*
Nitti: The Enforcer *'88*
Satisfaction *'88*
Stella *'89*
American Friends *'91*
The Babe *'92*
Little Women *'94*
The Perez Family *'94*
The Frighteners *'96*
Paulie *'98*
John Alvin (1917-2009)
The Fighting Sullivans *'42*
Objective, Burma! *'45*
Shanghai Chest *'48*
This Side of the Law *'50*
Joe Alwyn (1991-)
Billy Lynn's Long Halftime Walk *'16*
The Favourite *'18*
Mary Queen of Scots *'18*
Harriet *'19*
Kirk Alyn (1910-99)
The Trap *'46*
Atom Man *vs.* Superman *'50*
Lyle Alzado (1949-92)
Oceans of Fire *'86*
Ernest Goes to Camp *'87*
Tapeheads *'89*
Who's Harry Crumb? *'89*
Zapped Again *'89*
Club Fed *'90*
Hangfire *'91*
Shigeru Amachi (1931-85)
Zatoichi: The Life and Opinion of Masseur Ichi *'62*
Zatoichi: The Blind Swordsman's Vengeance *'66*
Magali Amadei
House of D *'04*
Taxi *'04*
Said Amadia
A Few Days in September *'06*
The Situation *'06*
Chisco Amado (1962-)
Nico and Dani *'00*
My Mother Likes Women *'02*
Mathieu Amalric (1965-)
My Sex Life. . . Or How I Got into an Argument *'96*
Late August, Early September *'98*
Kings and Queen *'04*
La Moustache *'05*
Munich *'05*
The Diving Bell and the Butterfly *'07*
Heartbeat Detector *'07*
A Secret *'07*
A Christmas Tale *'08*
Mesrine: Part 2-Public Enemy Number 1 *'08*
Quantum of Solace *'08*
Wild Grass *'09*
On Tour *'10*
Chicken With Plums *'11*
The Rabbi's Cat *'11 (V)*
Cosmopolis *'12*
You Ain't Seen Nothin' Yet *'12*
Jimmy P. *'13*
Venus in Fur *'13*
Bird People *'14 (N)*
The Grand Budapest Hotel *'14*
Hitchcock/Truffaut *'15*
My Golden Days *'15*
At Eternity's Gate *'18*
Yuki Amami
Serial Bomber *'96*
Inugami *'01*
Eisei Amamoto (1926-2003)
Matango *'63*
What's Up, Tiger Lily? *'66*
King Kong Escapes *'67*
Godzilla's Revenge *'69*
Masked Rider-The First *'05*
Tom Amandes (1959-)
The Long Kiss Goodnight *'96*
Billboard Dad *'98*
From the Earth to the Moon *'98*
Second Chances *'98*
Brokedown Palace *'99*
When Good Ghouls Go Bad *'01*
Live from Baghdad *'03*

Bonneville *'06*
Lucky *'11*

Betty Amann (1906-90)
Rich and Strange *'32*
Nancy Drew, Reporter *'39*

Pio Amato
Mediterranea *'15*
A Ciambra *'17*

Vincenzo Amato (1966-)
Respiro *'02*
Did You Hear About the Morgans? *'09*
War Story *'14*
Unbroken: Path to Redemption *'18*

Robert Amaya
Courageous *'11*
Moms' Night Out *'14*

Audrey Amber
See Andriana Ambesi

Andriana Ambesi
Secret Agent Super Dragon *'66*
Fangs of the Living Dead *'68*

Joss Ambler (1900-59)
The Silver Fleet *'43*
Spin a Dark Web *'56*

Lauren Ambrose (1978-)
In and Out *'97*
Can't Hardly Wait *'98*
Psycho Beach Party *'00*
Swimming *'00*
Diggers *'06*
Starting Out in the Evening *'07*
Cold Souls *'09*
A Dog Year *'09*
Loving Leah *'09*
Where the Wild Things Are *'09 (V)*
Think of Me *'11*
About Sunny *'12*
Coma *'12*
Sleepwalk with Me *'12*
Wanderlust *'12*

Tangie Ambrose
Ringmaster *'98*
Jackie's Back *'99*

Don Ameche (1908-93)
One in a Million *'36*
Ramona *'36*
In Old Chicago *'37*
Love Is News *'37*
You Can't Have Everything *'37*
Alexander's Ragtime Band *'38*
Gateway *'38*
Happy Landing *'38*
Josette *'38*
Hollywood Cavalcade *'39*
Midnight *'39*
The Story of Alexander Graham Bell *'39*
Swanee River *'39*
The Three Musketeers *'39*
Down Argentine Way *'40*
Four Sons *'40*
Lillian Russell *'40*
Confirm or Deny *'41*
Moon over Miami *'41*
That Night in Rio *'41*
Heaven Can Wait *'43*
Greenwich Village *'44*
A Wing and a Prayer *'44*
Guest Wife *'45*
It's in the Bag! *'45*
So Goes My Love *'46*
That's My Man *'47*
Sleep, My Love *'48*
Slightly French *'49*
A Fever In the Blood *'61*
Picture Mommy Dead *'66*
The Boatniks *'70*
Suppose They Gave a War and Nobody Came? *'70*
Gidget Gets Married *'72*
Trading Places *'83*
Cocoon *'85*
Harry and the Hendersons *'87*
Pals *'87*
Cocoon: The Return *'88*
Coming to America *'88*
Things Change *'88*
Oscar *'91*
Folks! *'92*
Homeward Bound: The Incredible Journey *'93 (V)*
Corrina, Corrina *'94*

John Patrick Amedori (1987-)
The Butterfly Effect *'04*
Little Athens *'05*
Addicted to Her Love *'06*
Stick It *'06*
Timer *'09*

Robbie Amell (1988-)
Picture This! *'08*
The Hunters *'13*
The DUFF *'15*
Max *'15*
Nine Lives *'16*
The Babysitter *'17*

Stephen Amell (1981-)
Closing the Ring *'07*
The Cutting Edge: Fire and Ice *'10*
Justice for Natalee *'11*
When Calls the Heart *'13*
Teenage Mutant Ninja Turtles: Out of the Shadows *'16*

Claudio Amendola (1963-)
La Scorta *'94*
Queen Margot *'94*
The Horseman on the Roof *'95*
Jesus *'00*
Caterina in the Big City *'03*

Tony Amendola (1951-)
Three of Hearts *'93*
The Mask of Zorro *'98*
Dragon Storm *'04*
Crimson Force *'05*
The Dead One *'07*
The Perfect Sleep *'08*
Annabelle *'14*
The Devil's Candy *'17*

Adrienne Ames (1907-47)
The Death Kiss *'33*
Harmony Lane *'35*

Heather Ames
Blood of Dracula *'57*
How to Make a Monster *'58*

Leon Ames (1902-93)
State's Attorney *'31*
Uptown New York *'32*
Alimony Madness *'33*
Mutiny Ahead *'35*
Charlie Chan on Broadway *'37*
Pilot X *'37*
International Settlement *'38*
Suez *'38*
Mr. Moto in Danger Island *'39*
Thirty Seconds Over Tokyo *'44*
Anchors Aweigh *'45*
Son of Lassie *'45*
They Were Expendable *'45*
Weekend at the Waldorf *'45*
Yolanda and the Thief *'45*
Lady in the Lake *'46*
The Postman Always Rings Twice *'46*
Merton of the Movies *'47*
Song of the Thin Man *'47*
Undercover Maisie *'47*
A Date with Judy *'48*
On an Island with You *'48*
Battleground *'49*
Scene of the Crime *'49*
Ambush *'50*
The Big Hangover *'50*
Crisis *'50*
Dial 1119 *'50*
The Happy Years *'50*
Watch the Birdie *'50*
On Moonlight Bay *'51*
Angel Face *'52*
By the Light of the Silvery Moon *'53*
Let's Do It Again *'53*
Peyton Place *'57*
From the Terrace *'60*
The Absent-Minded Professor *'61*
The Misadventures of Merlin Jones *'63*
Son of Flubber *'63*
Monkey's Uncle *'65*
Tora! Tora! Tora! *'70*
The Big Push *'75*
Peggy Sue Got Married *'86*

Robert Ames (1889-1931)
The Voice of the City *'29*
Behind Office Doors *'31*
Millie *'31*

Madchen Amick (1970-)
Don't Tell Her It's Me *'90*
Sleepwalkers *'92*
Twin Peaks: Fire Walk with Me *'92*
Dream Lover *'93*
Love, Cheat & Steal *'93*
The Great American Sex Scandal *'94*
Trapped in Paradise *'94*
Bombshell *'97*
Psychopath *'97*
The List *'99*
Mr. Rock 'n' Roll: The Alan Freed Story *'99*
Hangman *'00*
The Rats *'01*
Scenes of the Crime *'01*
Four Corners of Suburbia *'05*
Unanswered Prayers *'10*
Priest *'11*

Suzy Amis (1962-)
Fandango *'85*
Big Town *'87*
Rocket Gibraltar *'88*
Twister *'89*
Where the Heart Is *'90*
The Ballad of Little Jo *'93*
Rich in Love *'93*
Blown Away *'94*
Nadja *'95*
One Good Turn *'95*
The Usual Suspects *'95*
Cadillac Ranch *'96*
Last Stand at Saber River *'96*
Firestorm *'97*
Titanic *'97*
Judgment Day *'99*

Jessica Amlee (1994-)
Absolute Zero *'05*
Last Chance Cafe *'06*
Beneath *'07*

Luigi Amodeo (1969-)
Red Shoe Diaries 6: How I Met My Husband *'95*
B.A.P.'s *'97*
Art House *'98*

Christine Amor (1952-)
Now and Forever *'82*
Bloodmoon *'90*

John Amos (1939-)
Sweet Sweetback's Baadasssss Song *'71*
The World's Greatest Athlete *'73*
Let's Do It Again *'75*
Roots *'77*
Beastmaster *'82*
American Flyers *'85*
Coming to America *'88*
Lock Up *'89*
Die Hard 2: Die Harder *'90*
Two Evil Eyes *'90*
Ricochet *'91*
Mac *'93*
Mardi Gras for the Devil *'93*
For Better or Worse *'95*
Hologram Man *'95*
The Players Club *'98*
Disappearing Acts *'00*
My Baby's Daddy *'04*
Voodoo Moon *'05*
Dr. Dolittle 3 *'06*
Madea's Witness Protection *'12*

John Amplas (1949-)
Martin *'77*
Midnight *'81*
Creepshow *'82*

Morey Amsterdam (1908-96)
Murder, Inc. *'60*
Beach Party *'63*
Muscle Beach Party *'64*
Don't Worry, We'll Think of a Title *'66*
Sooner or Later *'78*

Nikki Amuka-Bird (1976-)
Five Days *'07*
The Disappeared *'08*
Small Island *'09*
Jupiter Ascending *'15*

Eva Amurri (1985-)
The Banger Sisters *'02*
Saved! *'04*
The Life Before Her Eyes *'07*
Animals *'08*

Susie Amy (1981-)
La Femme Musketeer *'03*
Modigliani *'04*
House of 9 *'05*

Kristina Anapau (1979-)
Madison *'01*
Cruel Intentions 3 *'04*
Cursed *'04*

Elena Anaya (1975-)
Sex and Lucia *'01*
Two Tough Guys *'03*
Dead Fish *'04*
Van Helsing *'04*
Fragile *'05*
In the Land of Women *'06*
Savage Grace *'07*
Mesrine: Part 1-Killer Instinct *'08*
Cairo Time *'09*
Point Blank *'10*
The Skin I Live In *'11*

Leo Anchoriz (1932-87)
The Invincible Gladiator *'62*
The Blancheville Monster *'63*
Sandokan the Great *'63*

Dominic Anciano (1959-)
Final Cut *'98*
Love, Honour & Obey *'00*

Richard Anconina (1953-)
Love Songs *'84*
Police *'85*

Mini Anden (1978-)
My Best Friend's Girl *'08*
The Mechanic *'11*

Avalon Anders
Bikini Summer 2 *'92*
The Portrait *'99*

David Anders (1981-)
Circadian Rhythm *'05*
Left in Darkness *'06*
Children of the Corn *'09*
Into the Blue 2: The Reef *'09*

Glenn Anders (1889-1981)
Nothing But the Truth *'41*
The Lady from Shanghai *'48*
Nancy Goes to Rio *'50*
Tarzan's Peril *'51*

Luana Anders (1938-96)
Night Tide *'61*
The Pit and the Pendulum *'61*
Dementia 13 *'63*
Games *'67 (C)*
The Trip *'67*
Easy Rider *'69*
Manipulator *'71*
Greaser's Palace *'72*
The Killing Kind *'73*
Goin' South *'78*
Irreconcilable Differences *'84*
Movers and Shakers *'85*
Border Radio *'88*
Limit Up *'89*

Merry Anders (1934-2012)
Phffft! *'54*
The Dalton Girls *'57*
Death in Small Doses *'57*
Desk Set *'57*
No Time to Be Young *'57*
Violent Road *'58*
The Hypnotic Eye *'60*
The Quick Gun *'64*
Raiders from Beneath the Sea *'64*
Blood Legacy *'73*

Rudolph Anders (1895-1987)
Counter-Attack *'45*
Under Nevada Skies *'46*
Actors and Sin *'52*
Phantom from Space *'53*
She Demons *'58*
36 Hours *'64*

Bridgette Andersen (1975-97)
Savannah Smiles *'82*
A Summer to Remember *'84*
The Parent Trap II *'86*

Elga Andersen (1939-94)
The Twilight Girls *'57*
Coast of Skeletons *'63*
Your Turn Darling *'63*
Le Mans *'71*
Night Flight from Moscow *'73*

Susy Andersen
Thor and the Amazon Women *'60*
Black Sabbath *'64*

Andy Anderson (1947-)
The Junction Boys *'02*
Garage Days *'03*
Salem's Lot *'04*

Anthony Anderson (1970-)
Liberty Heights *'99*
Life *'99*
Big Momma's House *'00*
Me, Myself, and Irene *'00*
Romeo Must Die *'00*
Urban Legends 2: Final Cut *'00*
Exit Wounds *'01*
Kingdom Come *'01*
See Spot Run *'01*
Two Can Play That Game *'01*
Barbershop *'02*
Kangaroo Jack *'02*
Cradle 2 the Grave *'03*
Malibu's Most Wanted *'03*
Scary Movie 3 *'03*
Agent Cody Banks 2: Destination London *'04*
Harold and Kumar Go to White Castle *'04*
My Baby's Daddy *'04*
Hoodwinked *'05 (V)*
Hustle & Flow *'05*
King's Ransom *'05*
Arthur and the Invisibles *'06 (V)*
The Departed *'06*
Scary Movie 4 *'06*
Transformers *'07*
The Back-Up Plan *'10*
Scream 4 *'11*
The Power of Few *'13*
The Town That Dreaded Sundown *'14*

Benjamin Anderson
Jack Squad *'08*
The Final Project *'16*

Donna Anderson (1925-)
On the Beach *'59*
Inherit the Wind *'60*

Eddie Anderson (1905-77)
False Faces *'32*
The Green Pastures *'36*
Jezebel *'38*
Thanks for the Memory *'38*
You Can't Take It with You *'38*
Gone with the Wind *'39*
Honolulu *'39*
You Can't Cheat an Honest Man *'39*
Buck Benny Rides Again *'40*
Birth of the Blues *'41*
Topper Returns *'41*
Star Spangled Rhythm *'42*
Tales of Manhattan *'42*
Cabin in the Sky *'43*
Broadway Rhythm *'44*
Brewster's Millions *'45*
It's a Mad, Mad, Mad, Mad World *'63*

Ella Anderson
The Possession of Michael King *'14*
The Boss *'16*
The Glass Castle *'17*

Erich Anderson
Friday the 13th, Part 4: The Final Chapter *'84*
Bat 21 *'88*
Due East *'02*

Erika Anderson (1963-)
A Nightmare on Elm Street 5: Dream Child *'89*
Zandalee *'91*
Object of Obsession *'95*
Red Shoe Diaries 8: Night of Abandon *'97*

Gillian Anderson (1968-)
The Turning *'92*
Chicago Cab *'98*
The Mighty *'98*
Playing by Heart *'98*
Princess Mononoke *'98 (V)*
The X-Files *'98*
House of Mirth *'00*
Bleak House *'05*
The Mighty Celt *'05*
Tristram Shandy: A Cock and Bull Story *'05*
The Last King of Scotland *'06*
Closure *'07*
How to Lose Friends & Alienate People *'08*
The X Files: I Want to Believe *'08*
Boogie Woogie *'09*
Any Human Heart *'11*
Great Expectations *'11*
Johnny English Reborn *'11*
Moby Dick *'11*
The Crimson Petal and the White *'12*
Shadow Dancer *'12*
Sister *'12*
I'll Follow You Down *'13*
Last Love *'13*
Viceroy's House *'17*

Harry Anderson (1952-2018)
Stephen King's It *'90*
Spies, Lies and Naked Thighs *'91*

Herbert Anderson (1917-94)
Dive Bomber *'41*
The Male Animal *'42*
Battleground *'49*
Night Passage *'57*
I Bury the Living *'58*
Hold On! *'66*

James Anderson (1872-1953)
The Freshman *'25*
Sergeant York *'41*
Five *'51*

James Anderson (1921-69)
Hellgate *'52*
Running Target *'56*
The Connection *'61*
Take the Money and Run *'69*

Jean Anderson (1907-2001)
A Town Like Alice *'56*
Lucky Jim *'58*
The Night Digger *'71*
Back Home *'90*
Prince Brat and the Whipping Boy *'95*

Jeff Anderson (1970-)
Clerks *'94*
Dogma *'99*
Now You Know *'02*
Clerks 2 *'06*
Zack and Miri Make a Porno *'08*

A Tiger Walks '64
Youngblood Hawke '64
Birds Do It '66
The Glass Bottom Boat '66
The Over-the-Hill Gang '69
The Trouble with Girls (and How to Get into It) '69
Tora! Tora! Tora! '70
How to Frame a Figg '71
Avanti! '72
Undercover With the KKK '78
Sixteen Candles '84

Giuseppe Andrews (1979-)
Independence Day '96
American History X '98
Detroit Rock City '99
Local Boys '02
Cabin Fever '03
Tweek City '05
2001 Maniacs '05
Cabin Fever 2: Spring Fever '08

Harry Andrews (1911-89)
Alexander the Great '55
Helen of Troy '56
Moby Dick '56
Saint Joan '57
633 Squadron '64
The System '64
The Agony and the Ecstasy '65
The Hill '65
Sands of the Kalahari '65
The Girl Getters '66
Modesty Blaise '66
The Charge of the Light Brigade '68
Dandy in Aspic '68
The Sea Gull '68
Battle of Britain '69
The Southern Star '69
Too Late the Hero '70
Wuthering Heights '70
Horrors of Burke & Hare '71
Nicholas and Alexandra '71
I Want What I Want '72
Man of La Mancha '72
The Nightcomers '72
The Ruling Class '72
What the Peeper Saw '72
The Final Programme '73
Internecine Project '73
Mackintosh Man '73
Theatre of Blood '73
The Story of Jacob & Joseph '74
Sky Riders '76
Equus '77
The Big Sleep '78
Death on the Nile '78
The Four Feathers '78
The Medusa Touch '78
Watership Down '78 (V)
S.O.S. Titanic '79
Hawk the Slayer '81
Mesmerized '84
All Passion Spent '86
Cause Celebre '87

Jason Andrews
Last Exit to Brooklyn '90
Federal Hill '94
Rhythm Thief '94

Julie Andrews (1935-)
The Singing Princess '49
The Americanization of Emily '64
Mary Poppins '64
The Sound of Music '65
Hawaii '66
Torn Curtain '66
Thoroughly Modern Millie '67
Star! '68
Darling Lili '70
The Tamarind Seed '74
10 '79
Little Miss Marker '80
S.O.B. '81
Victor/Victoria '82
The Man Who Loved Women '83
That's Life! '86
Our Sons '91
A Fine Romance '92
One Special Night '99
Relative Values '99
The Princess Diaries '01
Eloise at the Plaza '03
The Princess Diaries 2: Royal Engagement '04
Shrek 2 '04 (V)
Enchanted '07 (N)
Shrek the Third '07 (V)
Despicable Me '10 (V)
Shrek Forever After '10 (V)
Tooth Fairy '10

Naveen Andrews (1969-)
The Buddha of Suburbia '92
The English Patient '96
Kama Sutra: A Tale of Love '96
My Own Country '98
Drowning on Dry Land '00
Rollerball '02
Bride & Prejudice '04
The Brave One '07
Planet Terror '07
Animals '08
Diana '13

Peter Andrews (1963-)
See Steven Soderbergh

Real Andrews (1963-)
Showdown '94
Expect No Mercy '95
Family of Cops 2: Breach of Faith '97

Russell Andrews
The In-Laws '03
The Punisher '04

Shawn Andrews
City of Ghosts '03
Fix '08

Stanley Andrews (1891-1969)
Blondie '38
Beau Geste '39
Brigham Young: Frontiersman '40
Crash Dive '43
Short Grass '50

Tige Andrews (1920-2007)
Mister Roberts '55
Imitation General '58

Tod Andrews (1914-72)
They Died with Their Boots On '41
Between Heaven and Hell '56
She Demons '58
In Harm's Way '65

Andrews Sisters
Buck Privates '41
Hold That Ghost '41
In the Navy '41
Private Buckaroo '42
The Road to Rio '47
Melody Time '48 (V)

Anemone (1950-)
Twisted Obsession '90
Son of Gascogne '95
A Song of Innocence '05

Michael Angarano (1987-)
Little Secrets '02
Speak '04
Dear Wendy '05
Lords of Dogtown '05
One Last Thing '05
Sky High '05
Black Irish '07
The Final Season '07
Snow Angels '07
The Forbidden Kingdom '08
Gentlemen Broncos '09
Ceremony '10
The Art of Getting By '11
Red State '11
Haywire '12
The English Teacher '13
The Stanford Prison Experiment '15
Wild Card '15

Julie Ange (1940-)
Girl on a Chain Gang '65
Teenage Mother '67

Heather Angel (1909-86)
Pilgrimage '33
Daniel Boone '34
Headline Woman '35
The Informer '35
The Mystery of Edwin Drood '35
The Bold Caballero '36
The Last of the Mohicans '36
Bulldog Drummond Escapes '37
Bulldog Drummond's Bride '39
Suspicion '41
Lifeboat '44
Peter Pan '53 (V)
Premature Burial '62
Backstairs at the White House '79

Mikel Angel (1917-2005)
The Black Six '74
Grotesque '87
Evil Spirits '91

Vanessa Angel (1966-)
Kingpin '96
Kissing a Fool '98
Made Men '99
Partners '99
Camouflage '00
Enemies of Laughter '00
Firetrap '01
Sabretooth '01
The Perfect Score '04
Superbabies: Baby Geniuses 2 '04
Criminal Intent '05
Cougar Hunting '11

Pier Angeli (1932-71)
The Devil Makes Three '52
The Story of Three Loves '53
The Silver Chalice '54
Somebody Up There Likes Me '56
Merry Andrew '58
S.O.S. Pacific '60
Sodom and Gomorrah '62
Battle of the Bulge '65
Octaman '71

Michael Angelis (1944-2020)
No Surrender '86
G.B.H. '91

Chris Angelo
I Got Five on It '05
The Damned '06
Illegal Business '06
San Franpsycho '06

Maya Angelou (1928-2014)
Roots '77
How to Make an American Quilt '95
The Runaway '00
Madea's Family Reunion '06

Muriel Angelus (1909-2004)
Night Birds '31
The Great McGinty '40

Angelyne (1958-)
Earth Girls Are Easy '89
The Malibu Beach Vampires '91

Luciana Angiolillo (1925-)
The Girl with a Suitcase '60
The Trojan Horse '62

Jean-Hugues Anglade (1955-)
L'Homme Blesse '83
Subway '85
Betty Blue '86
La Femme Nikita '91
Killing Zoe '94
Queen Margot '94
Nelly et Monsieur Arnaud '95
Maximum Risk '96
Innocents '00
Mortal Transfer '01
Taking Lives '04
Shake Hands With the Devil '07

Philip Anglim (1953-)
Testament '83
Haunted Summer '88

Chriss Anglin
King of the Lost World '06
An American Carol '08

Alex Angulo (1953-2014)
Live Flesh '97
My Mother Likes Women '02
Pan's Labyrinth '06

Christien Anholt (1971-)
The Blackheath Poisonings '92
Preaching to the Perverted '97
Appetite '98
The Waiting Time '99
Dark Corners '06
Flyboys '06

Jennifer Aniston (1969-)
Leprechaun '93
Dream for an Insomniac '96
Picture Perfect '96
She's the One '96
Til There Was You '96
The Object of My Affection '98
Office Space '98
The Iron Giant '99 (V)
Rock Star '01
The Good Girl '02
Bruce Almighty '03
Along Came Polly '04
Derailed '05
Rumor Has It. . . '05
The Break-Up '06
Friends with Money '06
Marley & Me '08
He's Just Not That Into You '09
Love Happens '09
Management '09
The Bounty Hunter '10
The Switch '10
Horrible Bosses '11
Just Go With It '11
Wanderlust '12
Life of Crime '13
We're the Millers '13
Cake '14
Horrible Bosses 2 '14
Mother's Day '16
Office Christmas Party '16
Storks '16

Paul Anka (1941-)
Look in Any Window '61
The Longest Day '62
The Return of Spinal Tap '92 (C)
Shake, Rattle & Rock! '94

Evelyn Ankers (1918-85)
Hold That Ghost '41
The Wolf Man '41
The Ghost of Frankenstein '42
Sherlock Holmes and the Voice of Terror '42
Son of Dracula '43
His Butler's Sister '44
The Invisible Man's Revenge '44
The Pearl of Death '44
Flight to Nowhere '46
Spoilers of the North '47
Tarzan's Magic Fountain '48
Parole, Inc. '49

Morris Ankrum (1898-1964)
Hopalong Cassidy Returns '36
Borderland '37
The Showdown '40
I Wake Up Screaming '41
Swing Fever '43
Desire Me '47
High Wall '47
Colorado Territory '49
Borderline '50
The Damned Don't Cry '50
Short Grass '50
Southside 1-1000 '50
Fort Osage '51
The Lion Hunters '51
My Favorite Spy '51
Tomorrow Is Another Day '51
Fort Vengeance '53
Invaders from Mars '53
Drums Across the River '54
Southwest Passage '54
Taza, Son of Cochise '54
Silver Star '55
Earth *vs.* the Flying Saucers '56
Quincannon, Frontier Scout '56
Beginning of the End '57
The Giant Claw '57
Giant from the Unknown '58
How to Make a Monster '58
Most Dangerous Man Alive '61
X: The Man with X-Ray Eyes '63

Ann-Margret (1941-)
Pocketful of Miracles '61
State Fair '62
Bye, Bye, Birdie '63
Viva Las Vegas '63
Kitten with a Whip '64
The Cincinnati Kid '65
Made in Paris '65
Murderers' Row '66
Stagecoach '66
Tiger and the Pussycat '67
C.C. & Company '70
R.P.M.* (*Revolutions Per Minute) '70
Carnal Knowledge '71
Train Robbers '73
Tommy '75
The Twist '76
Joseph Andrews '77
The Last Remake of Beau Geste '77
The Cheap Detective '78
Magic '78
The Villain '79
Lookin' to Get Out '82
Return of the Soldier '82
Twice in a Lifetime '85
52 Pick-Up '86
Our Sons '91
Newsies '92
Grumpy Old Men '93
Queen '93
Following Her Heart '94
Scarlett '94
Grumpier Old Men '95
Any Given Sunday '99
Perfect Murder, Perfect Town '00
The 10th Kingdom '00
Blonde '01
A Woman's a Helluva Thing '01
Interstate 60 '02
A Place Called Home '04
Taxi '04
The Break-Up '06
Memory '06
The Loss of a Teardrop Diamond '08
All's Faire in Love '09
Old Dogs '09
Lucky '11
Going in Style '17

Anna-Lisa
Have Rocket Will Travel '59
12 to the Moon '60

Annabella (1909-96)
Le Million '31
Under the Red Robe '36
Dinner at the Ritz '37
Wings of the Morning '37
The Baroness and the Butler '38
Suez '38
Tonight We Raid Calais '43
13 Rue Madeleine '46

Amina Annabi (1962-)
The Sheltering Sky '90
The Advocate '93
Mr. Average '06

Dave (David) Annable (1979-)
What's Your Number? '11
You May Not Kiss the Bride '12

Odette Annable (1985-)
Cloverfield '08
The Unborn '09
And Soon the Darkness '10
Group Sex '10
Operation: Endgame '10
You Again '10
Beverly Hills Chihuahua 3: Viva La Fiesta! '12 (V)

Odette Yustman Annable
Beverly Hills Chihuahua 2 '10 (V)
The Double '11

Jim Annan
Cyborg Soldier '08
Cottage Country '13

Glory Annen
Alien Prey '78
Spaced Out '80

Francesca Annis (1945-)
Flipper's New Adventure '64
Murder Most Foul '65
The Walking Stick '70
Macbeth '71
Edward the King '75
Lillie '79
Krull '83
Dune '84
Under the Cherry Moon '86
Onassis '88
Doomsday Gun '94
Reckless '97
Reckless: The Sequel '98
Onegin '99
Wives and Daughters '01
The Libertine '05
Revolver '05
Jane Eyre '06
Cranford '08
Shifty '08
Return to Cranford '09

Hideaki Anno
Death Kappa '10
The Wind Rises '13 (V)

Nonso Anozie
The Grey '12
7 Days in Entebbe '18

Michael Ansara (1922-2013)
Action in Arabia '44
The Golden Hawk '52
The Lawless Breed '52
The Egyptian '54
Princess of the Nile '54
Abbott and Costello Meet the Mummy '55
Diane '55
Jupiter's Darling '55
New Orleans Uncensored '55
Gun Brothers '56
Pillars of the Sky '56
Quantez '57
Voyage to the Bottom of the Sea '61
Harum Scarum '65
Texas Across the River '66
Guns of the Magnificent Seven '69
The Phynx '70
Quick, Let's Get Married '71
Dear Dead Delilah '72
The Doll Squad '73
The Bears & I '74
It's Alive '74
Day of the Animals '77
The Message '77
Centennial '78
The Manitou '78
Mission to Glory '80
Assassination '87
Border Shootout '90

Aziz Ansari (1983-)
30 Minutes or Less '11
Epic '13 (V)

Zachary Ansley (1972-)
Christmas Comes to Willow Creek '87
This Boy's Life '93
The Spring '00

Susan Anspach (1942-2018)
Five Easy Pieces '70
The Landlord '70
Deadly Encounter '72
Play It Again, Sam '72
Blume in Love '73
Mad Bull '77

Portrait of an Escort '80
The Devil & Max Devlin '81
Montenegro '81
Gone Are the Days '84
Blood Red '88
Into the Fire '88

Adam Ant (1954-)
Nomads '86
Cold Steel '87
Slamdance '87
Last Action Hero '93 (C)
Cyber Bandits '94
Desert Winds '95

Carl Anthony
Plan 9 from Outer Space '56
The Sinister Urge '60

Emjay Anthony
Chef '14
Replicas '18

Lysette Anthony (1963-)
Ivanhoe '82
Oliver Twist '82
Krull '83
The Bretts '88
Without a Clue '88
The Lady and the Highwayman '89
Husbands and Wives '92
The Advocate '93
Look Who's Talking Now '93
Dr. Jekyll and Ms. Hyde '95
Dracula: Dead and Loving It '95
The Fiance '96
Robinson Crusoe '96
Trilogy of Terror 2 '96
Misbegotten '98
Russell Mulcahy's Tale of the Mummy '99
Beneath Loch Ness '01

Marc Anthony (1968-)
Big Night '95
The Substitute '96
Bringing Out the Dead '99
In the Time of the Butterflies '01
Man on Fire '04
El Cantante '06

Michael Anthony
Night of Bloody Horror '69
Mosquito Squadron '70

Paul Anthony (1975-)
House Party '90
Blade: Trinity '04
Eighteen '04
Time and Again '07
Suck '09

Ray Anthony (1922-)
The Girl Can't Help It '56
High School Confidential '58

Tony Anthony (1937-)
Force of Impulse '60
1931: Once Upon a Time in New York '72

Steve Antin (1958-)
Last American Virgin '82
The Accused '88
Survival Quest '89
Inside Monkey Zetterland '93

Benz Antoine
Cyber Seduction: His Secret Life '05
Ice Soldiers '13

Susan Anton (1950-)
Cannonball Run 2 '84
Making Mr. Right '86
Lena's Holiday '90

Laura Antonelli (1941-2015)
A Man Called Sledge '71
The Innocent '76
Collector's Item '89

Gabriele Antonini
Samson and the 7 Miracles of the World '62
Hero of Rome '63

Jose Antonio (1939-)
See Anthony (Jose, J. Antonio, J.A.) Mayans

Lou Antonio (1934-)
America America '63
Cool Hand Luke '67
The Phynx '70

Alexander Antonov
Strike '24
The Battleship Potemkin '25

Omero Antonutti (1935-2019)
Padre Padrone '77
The Night of the Shooting Stars '82
Kaos '85
Farinelli '94

Scott Antony (1950-)
Savage Messiah '72
The Freakmaker '73

Cas Anvar
Psychopath '97
Seducing Maarya '99
Shattered Glass '03
Dr. Jekyll and Mr. Hyde '08
The Phantom '09
Neverland '11
The Operative '19

Gabrielle Anwar (1970-)
If Looks Could Kill '91
Wild Hearts Can't Be Broken '91
Scent of a Woman '92
Body Snatchers '93
For Love or Money '93
The Three Musketeers '93
In Pursuit of Honor '95
Innocent Lies '95
Things to Do in Denver When You're Dead '95
Sub Down '97
The Guilty '99
My Little Assassin '99
If You Only Knew '00
Turbulence 3: Heavy Metal '00
Sherlock: Case of Evil '02
Mysterious Island '05
Crazy Eights '06
The Librarian: Return to King Solomon's Mines '06
Long Lost Son '06
iMurders '08
Carnal Innocence '11
A Warrior's Heart '11

Anya
Naked Weapon '03
Kung Fu Killer '08

Perry Anzilotti
Air Bud 2: Golden Receiver '98
Kiss of Fire '98
Down and Derby '05

Yu Aoi (1985-)
All About Lily Chou-Chou '01
Hana & Alice '04
Hula Girls '06
Tokyo! '09

Devon Aoki (1982-)
2 Fast 2 Furious '03
D.E.B.S. '04
Sin City '05
DOA: Dead or Alive '06
War '07
Mutant Chronicles '08
Rosencrantz & Guildenstern Are Undead '10

Rika Aoki
Rica '72
Rica 2: Lonely Wanderer '73
Rica 3: Juvenile's Lullaby '73

Magda Apanowicz
Every Second Counts '08
Caprica '09
12 Disasters '12

Iris Apatow
Funny People '09
This Is 40 '12

Judd Apatow (1967-)
Zookeeper '11 (V)
Hal '18

Maude Apatow (1997-)
Funny People '09
This Is 40 '12
Other People '16
The House of Tomorrow '18

Andreas Apergis
Deadly Isolation '05
Secrets of the Mountain '10

Oscar Apfel (1878-1939)
Five Star Final '31
Alias the Doctor '32
It's Tough to Be Famous '32
Shopworn '32

Jacqueline Apitananon
The Bodyguard 2 '07
The Vanquisher '10

Apollonia (1959-)
Heartbreaker '83
Purple Rain '84
Tricks of the Trade '88
Ministry of Vengeance '89

Anna Appel (1888-1963)
Faithless '32
Symphony of Six Million '32

Peter Appel (1959-)
Man of the House '95
Extreme Measures '96
Six Ways to Sunday '99
Tadpole '02

Shiri Appleby (1978-)
Deal of a Lifetime '99
A Time for Dancing '00
Swimfan '02
The Battle of Shaker Heights '03
Darklight '04
Undertow '04
Everything You Want '05
Havoc '05
When Do We Eat? '05
I-See-You.Com '06
I'm Reed Fish '06
The Killing Floor '06
Thrill of the Kill '06
What Love Is '07
The Devil's Candy '17
Lemon '17

Christina Applegate (1971-)
Jaws of Satan '81
Grace Kelly '83
Streets '90
Don't Tell Mom the Babysitter's Dead '91
Across the Moon '94
Vibrations '94
Wild Bill '95
The Big Hit '98
Kiss of Fire '98
Mafia! '98
The Brutal Truth '99
Out in Fifty '99
Just Visiting '01
The Sweetest Thing '02
Grand Theft Parsons '03
View from the Top '03
Wonderland '03
Anchorman: The Legend of Ron Burgundy '04
Surviving Christmas '04
The Rocker '08
Alvin and the Chipmunks: The Squeakuel '09 (V)
Cats & Dogs: The Revenge of Kitty Galore '10
Going the Distance '10
Alvin and the Chipmunks: Chipwrecked '11 (V)
Hall Pass '11
Anchorman 2: The Legend Continues '13
The Book of Life '14 (V)
Alvin and the Chipmunks: Road Chip '15 (V)
Vacation '15
Bad Moms '16
Crash Pad '17

Royce D. Applegate (1939-2003)
Gettysburg '93
Inherit the Wind '99
O Brother Where Art Thou? '00
The Rookie '02

Gods and Generals '03
Intolerable Cruelty '03
Seabiscuit '03

Hale Appleman (1986-)
Beautiful Ohio '06
Private Romeo '11

Pierluigi Apra (1943-81)
Machine Gun McCain '69
How to Kill a Judge '75

John Aprea (1941-)
Caged Heat '74
The Godfather, Part 2 '74
Idolmaker '80
Picasso Trigger '89
Savage Beach '89
Cyber-Tracker '93
Direct Hit '93
To the Limit '95
Dead Man on Campus '97

Onata Aprile
What Maisie Knew '12
About Scout '15

Annabelle Apsion (1960-)
Framed '93
The War Zone '98
From Hell '01
My Uncle Silas '01

Amy Aquino (1957-)
Descending Angel '90
My Brother's Keeper '95
Undisputed '02
White Oleander '02
In Good Company '04
A Lot Like Love '05
The Lazarus Effect '15

Angelica Aragon (1953-)
Like A Bride '94
A Walk in the Clouds '95
The Crime of Father Amaro '02
Bella '06
Looking for Palladin '08

Julian (Sonny) Arahanga (1972-)
Once Were Warriors '94
The Matrix '99

Hirofumi Arai (1979-)
Captive '87
Blue Spring '01
Blood and Bones '04
Sway '06

Robert Aramayo
The Standoff at Sparrow Creek '19
Exit Plan '20

Tomas Arana (1955-)
The Last Temptation of Christ '88
The Devil's Daughter '91
The Bodyguard '92
The Church '98
Wildflowers '99
Gladiator '00
Derailed '02
This Girl's Life '03
The Bourne Supremacy '04
Frankenfish '04
Rampage: The Hillside Strangler Murders '04
Bats: Human Harvest '07
Defiance '08
The Roommate '11
The Dark Knight Rises '12
Romeo & Juliet '13

Manuel Aranguiz (1945-)
A Paper Wedding '89
Levity '03

Ray Aranha (1939-)
City of Hope '91
The Kid '97

Yoshisaburo Arashi
47 Ronin, Part 1 '42
47 Ronin, Part 2 '42

Arata
After Life '98
Ping Pong '02

Michiyo Aratama (1930-2001)
The Human Condition: No Greater Love '58
The Human Condition: Road to Eternity '59
The Human Condition: A Soldier's Prayer '61
Kwaidan '64

Alfonso Arau (1932-)
El Topo '71
Scandalous John '71
Posse '75
Romancing the Stone '84
Three Amigos '86
Committed '99
Picking Up the Pieces '99

Pascale Arbillot
Let It Rain '08
Little White Lies '10

Allan Arbus (1918-2013)
Greaser's Palace '72
Cinderella Liberty '73
Coffy '73
The Young Nurses '73
Damien: Omen 2 '78
Americathon '79
M*A*S*H: Goodbye, Farewell & Amen '83

Nathaniel Arcand (1971-)
Grey Owl '99
American Outlaws '01
Skins '02
Wildfire 7: The Inferno '02
Black Cloud '04
Ginger Snaps Back: The Beginning '04
Clawed: The Legend of Sasquatch '05
Montana Sky '07

Bernard Archard (1916-2008)
Village of the Damned '60
The Horror of Frankenstein '70

Anne Archer (1947-)
Cancel My Reservation '72
The All-American Boy '73
Lifeguard '76
Good Guys Wear Black '78
Paradise Alley '78
Hero at Large '80
Raise the Titanic '80
Green Ice '81
Waltz across Texas '83
The Naked Face '84
The Sky's No Limit '84
Fatal Attraction '87
Love at Large '89
Narrow Margin '90
Body of Evidence '92
The Last of His Tribe '92
Patriot Games '92
Short Cuts '93
Clear and Present Danger '94
Mojave Moon '96
Nico the Unicorn '98
The Art of War '00
Innocents '00
Rules of Engagement '00
Whispers: An Elephant's Tale '00 (V)
Uncle Nino '03
The Iris Effect '04
Man of the House '05
November '05
Cut Off '06
End Game '06
Judicial Indiscretion '07
Felon '08
Ghosts of Girlfriends Past '09
Lullaby '14

Jesse Archer
A Four Letter Word '07
Violet Tendencies '10

John Archer (1915-99)
Gangs, Inc. '41
King of the Zombies '41
Paper Bullets '41
Crash Dive '43
Guadalcanal Diary '43
Hello, Frisco, Hello '43
Sherlock Holmes in Washington '43
Colorado Territory '49
White Heat '49

Best of the Badmen '50
High Lonesome '50
My Favorite Spy '51
Santa Fe '51
Decision at Sundown '57
She Devil '57
City of Fear '59
Blue Hawaii '62

Leila Arcieri (1973-)
Wild Things 2 '04
King's Ransom '05
Mammoth '06
Death Toll '07
Love N' Dancing '09

Fanny Ardant (1949-)
The Woman Next Door '81
Confidentially Yours '83
Life Is a Bed of Roses '83
Love Unto Death '84
Swann in Love '84
Melo '86
Afraid of the Dark '92
Beyond the Clouds '95
Sabrina '95
Ridicule '96
Elizabeth '98
Balzac: A Life of Passion '99
Change My Life '01
No News from God '01
Callas Forever '02
8 Women '02
Nathalie '03
Paris, je t'aime '06
Roman de Gare '07
The Secrets '07
The Trial Begins '07
Hello Goodbye '08
Bright Days Ahead '14

Eve Arden (1907-90)
Dancing Lady '33
Stage Door '37
Having a Wonderful Time '38
Letter of Introduction '38
At the Circus '39
Eternally Yours '39
Comrade X '40
No, No Nanette '40
Slightly Honorable '40
Manpower '41
That Uncertain Feeling '41
Whistling in the Dark '41
Ziegfeld Girl '41
Cover Girl '44
Mildred Pierce '45
The Kid from Brooklyn '46
My Reputation '46
Night and Day '46
The Voice of the Turtle '47
One Touch of Venus '48
Whiplash '48
My Dream Is Yours '49
Tea for Two '50
Three Husbands '50
Goodbye My Fancy '51
Phone Call from a Stranger '52
We're Not Married '52
Our Miss Brooks '56
Anatomy of a Murder '59
Sergeant Deadhead '65
The Strongest Man in the World '75
Grease '78
A Guide for the Married Woman '78
Under the Rainbow '81
Grease 2 '82

Michael Arden
Bride Wars '09
Source Code '11

Robert Arden (1922-2004)
Mr. Arkadin '55
Never Take Candy From a Stranger '60
The Final Conflict '81

George Ardisson (1931-)
The Invaders '63
Hercules in the Haunted World '64

Pierre Arditti (1944-)
Blaise Pascal '71
Life Is a Bed of Roses '83
Love Unto Death '84
Melo '86

The Horseman on the Roof '95
The Count of Monte Cristo '99
Private Fears in Public Places '06
Change of Plans '09
You Ain't Seen Nothin' Yet '12

Carlos Areces
The Last Circus '10
I'm So Excited '13

Rosita (Rosa) Arenas (1933-)
El Bruto '52
The Witch's Mirror '60

Lee Arenberg (1962-)
Brain Dead '89
Tapeheads '89
Bob Roberts '92
Waterworld '95
The Cradle Will Rock '99
Dungeons and Dragons '00
Pirates of the Caribbean: The Curse of the Black Pearl '03
Pirates of the Caribbean: Dead Man's Chest '06
Pirates of the Caribbean: At World's End '07

Geoffrey Arend (1978-)
It Runs in the Family '03
The Ringer '05
Loveless in Los Angeles '07
(500) Days of Summer '09
Devil '10
Save the Date '12

Eddi Arent (1925-2013)
Dead Eyes of London '61
Door with the Seven Locks '62
The Mysterious Magician '65
The Squeaker '65
Circus of Fear '67

Niels Arestrup (1949-)
Je Tu Il Elle '74
Meeting Venus '91
The Beat My Heart Skipped '05
The Diving Bell and the Butterfly '07
A Prophet '09
Sarah's Key '10
War Horse '11
Our Children '12
The French Minister '13
By the Sea '15

Raul Arevalo (1979-)
Dark Blue Almost Black '06
Even the Rain '10
I'm So Excited '13

Robert Arevalo (1938-)
The Ravagers '65
The Siege of Firebase Gloria '89
Lords of the Barrio '02
Hood Vengeance '09

Luca Argentero
Saturn in Opposition '07
Eat, Pray, Love '10

Asia Argento (1975-)
Demons 2 '87
Dario Argento's Trauma '93
Queen Margot '94
The Stendahl Syndrome '95
Traveling Companion '96
B. Monkey '97
The Church '98
New Rose Hotel '98
The Phantom of the Opera '98
Scarlet Diva '00
Red Siren '02
XXX '02
The Heart Is Deceitful Above All Things '04
George A. Romero's Land of the Dead '05
Last Days '05
Marie Antoinette '06
Boarding Gate '07
Mother of Tears '08
Argento's Dracula 3D '13

Dario Argento (1940-)
The Bird with the Crystal Plumage '70
Innocent Blood '92

Fiore Argento (1970-)
Creepers '85
Demons '86

Carmen Argenziano (1943-)
Death Force '78
When a Stranger Calls '79
Starchaser: The Legend of Orin '85 (V)
The Accused '88
Red Scorpion '89
Unlawful Entry '92
Final Combination '93
Andersonville '95
Warm Blooded Killers '01
Identity '03
Street Boss '09

Victor Argo (1934-2004)
Boxcar Bertha '72
Mean Streets '73
After Hours '85
The Pick-Up Artist '87
King of New York '90
Quick Change '90
Bad Lieutenant '92
True Romance '93
Blue in the Face '95
Smoke '95
Lulu on the Bridge '98
Next Stop, Wonderland '98
Ghost Dog: The Way of the Samurai '99
Blue Moon '00
The Yards '00
Angel Eyes '01
Don't Say a Word '01
Double Whammy '01
'R Xmas '01
Anything But Love '02

David Argue (1959-)
Gallipoli '81
BMX Bandits '83
Razorback '84
Napoleon '96 (V)

Nina Arianda (1984-)
Higher Ground '11
Midnight in Paris '11
Lucky Them '13
Rob the Mob '14
Florence Foster Jenkins '16
Stan & Ollie '18

Imanol Arias (1956-)
Camila '84
Intruso '93
The Flower of My Secret '95
The Liberator '13

Moises Arias (1994-)
Nacho Libre '06
Beethoven's Big Break '08
Hannah Montana: The Movie '09
The Perfect Game '09
The Secret World of Arrietty '10 (V)
Despicable Me 2 '13 (V)
The Kings of Summer '13
The Land '16
Five Feet Apart '19
Monos '19
The King of Staten Island '20

Yancey Arias (1971-)
The Time Machine '02
Live Free or Die Hard '07
Behind Enemy Lines 3: Colombia '08
Ticking Clock '10
Cesar Chavez '14

Anna Aries
Omega Man '71
Invasion of the Bee Girls '73

Ineko Arima (1932-)
Equinox Flower '58
The Human Condition: No Greater Love '58
Bushido: The Cruel Code of the Samurai '63

Ben Aris (1937-2003)
The Charge of the Light Brigade '68
If. . . '69
Tommy '75

Yareli Arizmendi (1970-)
Like Water for Chocolate '93
The Big Green '95
Bloody Proof '99
A Day Without a Mexican '04

Yoshiki Arizono
The Happiness of the Katakuris '01
Sabu '04

Adria Arjona
The Belko Experiment '17
6 Underground '19

Adam Arkin (1956-)
Pearl '78
Fourth Wise Man '85
Necessary Parties '88
Heat Wave '90
The Doctor '91
Halloween: H20 '98
Hanging Up '99
A Slight Case of Murder '99
Mission '00
Off Season '01
Stark Raving Mad '02
Hitch '05
Kids in America '05
Marilyn Hotchkiss' Ballroom Dancing & Charm School '06
Murder on Pleasant Drive '06
Graduation '07
Just Peck '09
A Serious Man '09
Summer Eleven '10
Armed Response '13

Alan Arkin (1934-)
The Russians Are Coming, the Russians Are Coming '66
Wait until Dark '67
Woman Times Seven '67
The Heart Is a Lonely Hunter '68
Inspector Clouseau '68
Popi '69
Catch-22 '70
Little Murders '71
Last of the Red Hot Lovers '72
Freebie & the Bean '74
Hearts of the West '75
The Seven-Per-Cent Solution '76
The In-Laws '79
Simon '80
The Last Unicorn '82 (V)
Return of Captain Invincible '83
Bad Medicine '85
Fourth Wise Man '85
Big Trouble '86
Escape from Sobibor '87
Necessary Parties '88
Coupe de Ville '90
Edward Scissorhands '90
Havana '90
The Rocketeer '91
Glengarry Glen Ross '92
Indian Summer '93
So I Married an Axe Murderer '93 (C)
Doomsday Gun '94
Heck's Way Home '95
The Jerky Boys '95
Steal Big, Steal Little '95
Mother Night '96
Four Days in September '97
Gattaca '97
Grosse Pointe Blank '97
Slums of Beverly Hills '98
Blood Money '99
Jakob the Liar '99
Thirteen Conversations About One Thing '01
Varian's War '01
And Starring Pancho Villa as Himself '03
Eros '04
Noel '04

Firewall '06
Little Miss Sunshine '06
Raising Flagg '06
The Santa Clause 3: The Escape Clause '06
Rendition '07
Get Smart '08
Marley & Me '08
City Island '09
The Private Lives of Pippa Lee '09
Sunshine Cleaning '09
Argo '12
Stand Up Guys '12
Thin Ice '12
Armed Response '13
Grudge Match '13
The Incredible Burt Wonderstone '13
Million Dollar Arm '14
Love the Coopers '15
Going in Style '17
Dumbo '19
Spenser Confidential '20

David Arkin (1941-90)
I Love You, Alice B. Toklas! '68
M*A*S*H '70
The Long Goodbye '73
Nashville '75
All the President's Men '76

Matthew Arkin
Second Best '05
Raising Flagg '06

John Arledge (1907-47)
Huddle '32
Shipmates Forever '35
Murder On a Bridle Path '36

Elizabeth Arlen (1964-)
The Whoopee Boys '86
Lucky Stiff '88
The First Power '89
Separate Lives '94

Richard Arlen (1898-1976)
Wings '27
Beggars of Life '28
Feel My Pulse '28
The Light of Western Stars '30
Island of Lost Souls '32
Tiger Shark '32
Alice in Wonderland '33
College Humor '33
Three-Cornered Moon '33
Let 'Em Have It '35
Artists and Models '37
Call of the Yukon '38
Flying Blind '41
Power Dive '41
Wildcat '42
Wrecking Crew '42
That's My Baby! '44
Identity Unknown '45
Buffalo Bill Rides Again '47
Hidden Guns '56
The Mountain '56
Warlock '59
Cavalry Command '63
The Crawling Hand '63
The Human Duplicators '64
Johnny Reno '66
Hostile Guns '67 (C)
Road to Nashville '67

Arletty (1898-1992)
Le Jour Se Leve '39
Children of Paradise '44
Portrait of an Assassin '49
The Longest Day '62

George Arliss (1868-1946)
Old English '30
The Man Who Played God '32
A Successful Calamity '32
The Working Man '33
Cardinal Richelieu '35
Transatlantic Tunnel '35
East Meets West '36
Dr. Syn '37

Andrei Arlovski
Universal Soldier: Regeneration '09
Universal Soldier: Day of Reckoning '12

Ana de Armas (1988-)
Knock Knock '15
Exposed '16
Hands of Stone '16
Blade Runner 2049 '17
Knives Out '19

Jillian Armenante (1968-)
Delivered '98
North Country '05
Prairie Fever '08

Pedro Armendariz, Jr. (1940-2011)
The Deadly Trackers '73
Don't Be Afraid of the Dark '73
A Home of Our Own '75
Spree '79
La Chevre '81
The Treasure of the Amazon '85
Old Gringo '89
Tombstone '93
Like A Bride '94
Esmeralda Comes by Night '98
The Mask of Zorro '98
Original Sin '01
The Crime of Father Amaro '02
And Starring Pancho Villa as Himself '03
Once Upon a Time in Mexico '03
Looking for Palladin '08
Casa de mi Padre '12

Pedro Armendariz, Sr. (1912-63)
Border River '47
Fort Apache '48
The Fugitive '48
Three Godfathers '48
Tulsa '49
The Torch '50
El Bruto '52
The Littlest Outlaw '54
Diane '55
The Conqueror '56
The Big Boodle '57
Beyond All Limits '59
The Wonderful Country '59
Captain Sinbad '63
From Russia with Love '63

Sebastian Armesto
Blood Monkey '07
Anonymous '11

Henry Armetta (1888-1945)
Street Angel '28
Speak Easily '32
The Black Cat '34
The Cat and the Fiddle '34
The Merry Widow '34
Let's Sing Again '36
Fisherman's Wharf '39
Big Store '41
Colonel Effingham's Raid '45

Fred Armisen (1966-)
Anchorman: The Legend of Ron Burgundy '04
Eurotrip '04
Deuce Bigalow: European Gigolo '05
Tenacious D in the Pick of Destiny '06
The Ex '07
The Promotion '08
The Rocker '08
Confessions of a Shopaholic '09
Post Grad '09
Easy A '10
The Smurfs '11 (V)
Addicted to Fresno '15
Phantom Boy '16
Band Aid '17
The LEGO Ninjago Movie '17 (V)

Richard Armitage (1971-)
Captain America: The First Avenger '11
The Hobbit: An Unexpected Journey '12
The Hobbit: The Desolation of Smaug '13
The Hobbit: The Battle of the Five Armies '14

Into the Storm '14
The Lodge '19

Russell Arms (1920-2012)
Captains of the Clouds '42
Cover Up '49
By the Light of the Silvery Moon '53

Alun Armstrong (1946-)
Get Carter '71
White Hunter, Black Heart '90
Split Second '92
An Awfully Big Adventure '94
Black Beauty '94
Braveheart '95
The Saint '97
Aristocrats '99
The Aristocrats '99
David Copperfield '99
Onegin '99
Sleepy Hollow '99
Proof of Life '00
The Mummy Returns '01
Strictly Sinatra '01
Harrison's Flowers '02
It's All About Love '03
Carrie's War '04
Van Helsing '04
Millions '05
Oliver Twist '05
Eragon '06
Filth '08
Little Dorrit '08
The Mystery of Edwin Drood '12

Bess Armstrong (1953-)
The Four Seasons '81
Jekyll & Hyde. . . Together Again '82
High Road to China '83
Jaws 3 '83
Lace '84
Nothing in Common '86
Second Sight '89
Dream Lover '93
The Skateboard Kid '93
That Darn Cat '96
Forever Love '98
Pecker '98
Diamond Men '01
Corporate Affairs '07

Curtis Armstrong (1953-)
Risky Business '83
Revenge of the Nerds '84
Bad Medicine '85
Better Off Dead '85
One Crazy Summer '86
Revenge of the Nerds 2: Nerds in Paradise '87
Revenge of the Nerds 3: The Next Generation '92
The Adventures of Huck Finn '93
Revenge of the Nerds 4: Nerds in Love '94
Big Bully '95
Gale Force '01
National Lampoon's Van Wilder '02
Project Viper '02
Quigley '03
Ray '04
Man of the House '05
Akeelah and the Bee '06
Southland Tales '06
Moola '07
Shredderman Rules '07
Foreign Exchange '08
Route 30 '08
Legally Blondes '09
National Lampoon's Ratko: The Dictator's Son '09
The Gold Retrievers '10
Beethoven's Christmas Adventure '11
Planes: Fire & Rescue '14 (V)

Jonas Armstrong (1981-)
Clive Barker's Book of Blood '08
Twenty8k '12
Walking with the Enemy '13
The Whale '13

Lance Armstrong (1971-)
Dodgeball: A True Underdog Story '04 (C)
The Armstrong Lie '13

Louis Armstrong (1900-71)
Pennies from Heaven '36
Cabin in the Sky '43
New Orleans '47
Here Comes the Groom '51 (C)
The Glenn Miller Story '54
High Society '56
The Five Pennies '59
Paris Blues '61
A Man Called Adam '66
Hello, Dolly! '69

Melinda Armstrong
Bikini Summer '91
Bikini Summer 2 '92

Neil Alden Armstrong (1930-2012)
Apollo 11 '19
Armstrong '19

R.G. Armstrong (1917-2012)
No Name on the Bullet '59
The Fugitive Kind '60
Ride the High Country '62
El Dorado '67
Angels Die Hard '70
The Great White Hope '70
Final Comedown '72
The Great Northfield Minnesota Raid '72
Boss '74
My Name Is Nobody '74
Race with the Devil '75
Dixie Dynamite '76
The Car '77
The Pack '77
Devil Dog: The Hound of Hell '78
Where the Buffalo Roam '80
The Beast Within '82
Evilspeak '82
The Shadow Riders '82
Children of the Corn '84
Predator '87
Bulletproof '88
Dick Tracy '90
Warlock: The Armageddon '93

R.L. Armstrong (1924-78)
The Hard Ride '71
Slumber Party '57 '76

Robert Armstrong (1890-1973)
Big News '29
The Racketeer '29
Be Yourself '30
Danger Lights '30
Paid '30
Suicide Fleet '31
The Most Dangerous Game '32
Penguin Pool Murder '32
Fast Workers '33
King Kong '33
Son of Kong '33
Manhattan Love Song '34
Palooka '34
Search for Beauty '34
Flirting With Danger '35
'G' Men '35
Ex-Mrs. Bradford '36
Nobody's Baby '37
Dive Bomber '41
Gang Busters '42
The Kansan '43
Action in Arabia '44
Mr. Winkle Goes to War '44
Navy Way '44
Blood on the Sun '45
Decoy '46
The Fugitive '48
The Paleface '48
Mighty Joe Young '49

Samaire Armstrong (1980-)
Darkwolf '03
It's a Boy Girl Thing '06
Just My Luck '06
Stay Alive '06
Around June '08

Todd Armstrong (1939-93)
Jason and the Argonauts '63
King Rat '65
Dead Heat on a Merry-Go-Round '66
Thunder at the Border '66

François Arnaud (1985-)
I Killed My Mother '09
Copperhead '13
Permission '18

Desi Arnaz, Jr. (1953-)
The Voyage of the Yes '72
Marco '73
Billy Two Hats '74
Joyride '77
A Wedding '78
Fake Out '82
The Night the Bridge Fell Down '83
The Mambo Kings '92

Desi Arnaz, Sr. (1917-86)
Too Many Girls '40
Bataan '43
The Long, Long Trailer '54
Forever Darling '56
The Escape Artist '82

Lucie Arnaz (1951-)
The Jazz Singer '80
Second Thoughts '83
Down to You '00

Denis Arndt (1939-)
Basic Instinct '92
Amelia Earhart: The Final Flight '94
The Beast '96
Metro '96
Asteroid '97
Undisputed '02
Anacondas: The Hunt for the Blood Orchid '04
Sniper 3 '04
Bandidas '06
Behind Enemy Lines 2: Axis of Evil '06

Peter Arne (1920-83)
Tarzan's Hidden Jungle '55
The Atomic Man '56
Tarzan and the Lost Safari '57
The Secret of Monte Cristo '61
Pirates of Blood River '62
Black Torment '64
Battle Beneath the Earth '68
The Oblong Box '69
Straw Dogs '72
Victor/Victoria '82

James Arness (1923-2011)
Battleground '49
Stars in My Crown '50
Wagon Master '50
Cavalry Scout '51
The People Against O'Hara '51
The Thing '51
Big Jim McLain '52
Carbine Williams '52
Hellgate '52
Horizons West '52
Hondo '53
Island in the Sky '53
Them! '54
Flame of the Islands '55
Many Rivers to Cross '55
Sea Chase '55
Gun the Man Down '56
Alias Jesse James '59 (C)
The Alamo: Thirteen Days to Glory '87
Gunsmoke: Return to Dodge '87

Will Arnett (1970-)
The Waiting Game '99
Series 7: The Contenders '01 (N)
Monster-in-Law '05
The Great New Wonderful '06
Ice Age: The Meltdown '06 (V)
Let's Go to Prison '06
RV '06
Wristcutters: A Love Story '06
Blades of Glory '07
The Brothers Solomon '07
The Comebacks '07
Hot Rod '07
Ratatouille '07 (V)
Dr. Seuss' Horton Hears a Who! '08 (V)
The Rocker '08
Semi-Pro '08
Brief Interviews With Hideous Men '09
G-Force '09
Monsters vs. Aliens '09 (V)
When in Rome '09
Despicable Me '10 (V)
Jonah Hex '10
The Secret World of Arrietty '10 (V)
The Lego Movie '14 (V)
The Nut Job '14 (V)
Teenage Mutant Ninja Turtles '14
Teenage Mutant Ninja Turtles: Out of the Shadows '16
The LEGO Batman Movie '17
The Nut Job 2: Nutty by Nature '17
Show Dogs '18
The LEGO Movie 2: The Second Part '19

Jeanetta Arnette (1954-)
Class Reunion Massacre '77
The Shadow Riders '82
Ladybugs '92
Boys Don't Cry '99
The '70s '00
The Shipping News '01
Sniper 3 '04
Snow Angels '07

Nora Arnezeder
Paris 36 '08
Maniac '12
Safe House '12

Stefan Arngrim (1955-)
Fear No Evil '80
Getting Wasted '80
Class of 1984 '82
Misbegotten '98
Whispers and Lies '08

Alice Arno (1946-)
Female Vampire '73
The Perverse Countess '73

Edward Arnold (1890-1956)
The Barbarian '33
I'm No Angel '33
Rasputin and the Empress '33
The White Sister '33
Sadie McKee '34
Thirty Day Princess '34
Cardinal Richelieu '35
Come and Get It '36
Meet Nero Wolfe '36
Easy Living '37
Toast of New York '37
The Crowd Roars '38
You Can't Take It with You '38
Idiot's Delight '39
Let Freedom Ring '39
Mr. Smith Goes to Washington '39
The Earl of Chicago '40
Johnny Apollo '40
Lillian Russell '40
Slightly Honorable '40
Design for Scandal '41
The Devil & Daniel Webster '41
Meet John Doe '41
Nothing But the Truth '41
Eyes in the Night '42
Johnny Eager '42
The Youngest Profession '43
Kismet '44
Mrs. Parkington '44
Weekend at the Waldorf '45
Ziegfeld Follies '46
The Hucksters '47
My Brother Talks to Horses '47
John Loves Mary '48
Three Daring Daughters '48
Take Me Out to the Ball Game '49
Annie Get Your Gun '50
Belles on Their Toes '52
Living It Up '54
The Ambassador's Daughter '56

Jack Arnold (1916-92)
The Mummy's Tomb '42
Into the Night '85 (C)
The Favor, the Watch, & the Very Big Fish '92

Justin Arnold
The Final '10
5 Time Champion '11
Mercury Plains '16

Mal Arnold
Blood Feast '63
Scum of the Earth '63

Mark Arnold (1957-)
Trancers 4: Jack of Swords '93
Threesome '94
Trancers 5: Sudden Deth '94
WWJD: What Would Jesus Do? '10

Tichina Arnold (1969-)
Little Shop of Horrors '86
Civil Brand '02
Preaching to the Choir '05
Wild Hogs '07
The Lena Baker Story '08
A Day Late and a Dollar Short '14
The Last Black Man in San Francisco '19

Tom Arnold (1959-)
Backfield in Motion '91
Freddy's Dead: The Final Nightmare '91
Hero '92
Undercover Blues '93
The Woman Who Loved Elvis '93
True Lies '94
Big Bully '95
Nine Months '95
The Stupids '95
Carpool '96
Touch '96
Austin Powers: International Man of Mystery '97 (C)
McHale's Navy '97
Sink or Swim '97
Blue Ridge Fall '99
Jackie's Back '99
Malicious Intent '99
National Lampoon's Golf Punks '99
Ablaze '00
Animal Factory '00
Bar Hopping '00
Lloyd '00
Shriek If You Know What I Did Last Friday the 13th '00
Exit Wounds '01
Children On Their Birthdays '02
Cradle 2 the Grave '03
Mr. 3000 '04 (C)
Soul Plane '04
Chasing Christmas '05
Happy Endings '05
The Kid and I '05
The Final Season '07
Palo Alto '07
Pride '07
A Christmas Proposal '08
Gardens of the Night '08
Good Dick '08
Moonlight & Mistletoe '08
Remarkable Power '08
The Year of Getting to Know Us '08
The Great Buck Howard '09
The Skeptic '09
Endure '10
Group Sex '10
The Pool Boys '10
Beethoven's Christmas Adventure '11 (V)
Brother's Justice '11
A Christmas Wedding Tail '11
Knockdown '11
Hit and Run '12
Madea's Witness Protection '12
Pulling Strings '13
Any Day '15
Maximum Impact '18

Victor Arnold (1936-2012)
Shaft '71
The Yards '00

David Arnott (1976-)
Crisscross '92
The Last Man '00

Francoise Arnoul (1931-)
The Vanquished '52
French Can-Can '55
After Sex '97

Charles Arnt (1908-90)
It Happened in Hollywood '37
Gambler's Choice '44
Strange Illusion '45
That Brennan Girl '46

Gaetano Aronica
Malena '00
Baaria '09

Judie Aronson (1964-)
Friday the 13th, Part 4: The Final Chapter '84
American Ninja '85
After Midnight '89

Alexis Arquette (1969-2016)
Down and Out in Beverly Hills '86
Last Exit to Brooklyn '90
Jumpin' at the Boneyard '92
Miracle Beach '92
The Ghost Brigade '93
Don't Do It '94
Frank and Jesse '94
Grief '94
Jack Be Nimble '94
Pulp Fiction '94
Threesome '94
Frisk '95
Wigstock: The Movie '95
Never Met Picasso '96
Sometimes They Come Back. . . Again '96
Things I Never Told You '96
I Think I Do '97
The Wedding Singer '97
Bride of Chucky '98
Children of the Corn 5: Fields of Terror '98
Love Kills '98
She's All That '99
Cleopatra's Second Husband '00
Spun '02
The Trip '02

David Arquette (1971-)
Buffy the Vampire Slayer '92
Where the Day Takes You '92
The Ghost Brigade '93
Airheads '94
Fall Time '94
Roadracers '94
Wild Bill '95
Beautiful Girls '96
johns '96
Larry McMurtry's Dead Man's Walk '96
Scream '96
Dream with the Fishes '97
R.P.M. '97
Scream 2 '97
The Alarmist '98
Free Money '99
Muppets from Space '99
Never Been Kissed '99
Ravenous '99
Ready to Rumble '00
Scream 3 '00
The Grey Zone '01
See Spot Run '01
3000 Miles to Graceland '01
Eight Legged Freaks '02
2 Brothers & a Bride '03
Never Die Alone '04
Riding the Bullet '04
Stealing Sinatra '04
The Adventures of Sharkboy and Lavagirl in 3-D '05
The Darwin Awards '06
The Tripper '06
Hamlet 2 '08
Black Limousine '10
Scream 4 '11
Bone Tomahawk '15
Casual Encounters '16
Mope '19

Lewis Arquette (1935-2001)
Nobody's Fool '86
Tango and Cash '89
Syngenor '90
Book of Love '91
Rock 'n' Roll High School Forever '91
The Linguini Incident '92
Attack of the 50 Ft. Woman '93
Sleep with Me '94
Waiting for Guffman '96
Almost Heroes '97
A River Made to Drown In '97
Scream 2 '97
Get a Clue! '98
Kiki's Delivery Service '98 (V)
Little Nicky '00
Ready to Rumble '00

Patricia Arquette (1968-)
A Nightmare on Elm Street 3: Dream Warriors '87
Far North '88
The Indian Runner '91
Prayer of the Rollerboys '91
Wildflower '91
Ethan Frome '92
Trouble Bound '92
Inside Monkey Zetterland '93
True Romance '93
Ed Wood '94
Holy Matrimony '94
Beyond Rangoon '95
Flirting with Disaster '95
Infinity '96
Lost Highway '96
Nightwatch '96
The Secret Agent '96
The Hi-Lo Country '98
Bringing Out the Dead '99
Goodbye, Lover '99
Stigmata '99
Little Nicky '00
The Badge '02
Human Nature '02
Holes '03
Tiptoes '03
Fast Food Nation '06
Girl in Progress '12
A Glimpse Inside the Mind of Charles Swan III '12
Boyhood '14
Permanent '17
Otherhood '19

Richmond Arquette (1963-)
Girls in Prison '94
Love to Kill '97
The Treat '98
Sugar Town '99
Spent '00
The Tripper '06
Made of Honor '08
National Lampoon Presents: Endless Bummer '09
This is Martin Bonner '13

Rosanna Arquette (1959-)
Zuma Beach '78
More American Graffiti '79
S.O.B. '81
Baby It's You '82
The Executioner's Song '82
After Hours '85
The Aviator '85
Desperately Seeking Susan '85
Silverado '85
Nobody's Fool '86
Amazon Women on the Moon '87
The Big Blue '88
New York Stories '89
. . .Almost '90
Flight of the Intruder '90

Sweet Revenge '90
Black Rainbow '91
In the Deep Woods '91
The Linguini Incident '92
Nowhere to Run '93
Pulp Fiction '94
Search and Destroy '94
Crash '95
Buffalo 66 '97
Deceiver '97
Gone Fishin' '97
Hell's Kitchen NYC '97
Hope Floats '98
I'm Losing You '98
The '60s '99
Sugar Town '99
Voodoo Dawn '99
The Whole Nine Yards '00
Good Advice '01
Things Behind the Sun '01
Big Bad Love '02
Dead Cool '04
Iowa '05
Kids in America '05
I-See-You.Com '06
American Pie Presents: Book of Love '09
Northern Lights '09
Repo Chick '09
Inhale '10
Frank & Lola '16
Lovesong '17
Maya Dardel '17
The Etruscan Smile '19

Jeri Arredondo (1955-)
Spirit of the Eagle '90
Silent Tongue '92
Color of a Brisk and Leaping Day '95
The Doe Boy '01
Four Sheets to the Wind '07

Enrique Arreola
Duck Season '04
Nora's Will '09

Lisa Arrindell (1969-)
See Lisa Arrindell Anderson

Gemma Arterton (1986-)
St. Trinian's '07
Lost in Austen '08
Quantum of Solace '08
Tess of the D'Urbervilles '08
Three and Out '08
The Disappearance of Alice Creed '09
Clash of the Titans '10
Prince of Persia: The Sands of Time '10
Tamara Drewe '10
Byzantium '12
Hansel & Gretel: Witch Hunters '12
Unfinished Song '12
Runner Runner '13
Gemma Bovery '15
The Voices '15
The Girl with All the Gifts '17
100 Streets '17
Their Finest '17
The Escape '18
Vita & Virginia '19

Bea Arthur (1923-2009)
How to Commit Marriage '69
Lovers and Other Strangers '70
Mame '74
History of the World: Part 1 '81
For Better or Worse '95
Enemies of Laughter '00

George K. Arthur (1899-1985)
Her Sister from Paris '25
Lady of the Night '25
Kiki '26
Spring Fever '27
Chasing Rainbows '30

Indus Arthur (1941-84)
Alvarez Kelly '66
M*A*S*H '70

Jean Arthur (1900-91)
Danger Lights '30
The Silver Horde '30
The Defense Rests '34
Whirlpool '34
Public Menace '35
The Whole Town's Talking '35
Adventure in Manhattan '36
Ex-Mrs. Bradford '36
If You Could Only Cook '36
Mr. Deeds Goes to Town '36
More Than A Secretary '36
Easy Living '37
History Is Made at Night '37
The Plainsman '37
You Can't Take It with You '38
Mr. Smith Goes to Washington '39
Only Angels Have Wings '39
Arizona '40
Too Many Husbands '40
The Devil & Miss Jones '41
Talk of the Town '42
Lady Takes a Chance '43
The More the Merrier '43
The Impatient Years '44
Shane '53

Johnny Arthur (1883-1951)
The Monster '25
The Ghost Walks '34
Danger on the Air '38
The Road to Singapore '40

Maureen Arthur (1934-)
How to Succeed in Business without Really Trying '67
The Love God? '70
The Love Machine '71

Robert Arthur (1925-2008)
Mother Wore Tights '47
Yellow Sky '48
Mother Is a Freshman '49
Twelve o'Clock High '49
September Affair '50
Ace in the Hole '51
Belles on Their Toes '52
Just for You '52
The Ring '52
The System '53
Hellcats of the Navy '57
Naked Youth '59

Michael Artura
Amongst Friends '93
Kiss of Death '94
Money Train '95
Apt Pupil '97

Lisa Arturo
18 Fingers of Death '05
Insanitarium '08

Jan Arvan (1913-79)
20 Million Miles to Earth '57
Curse of the Faceless Man '58

Tadanobu Asano (1973-)
Maborosi '95
Taboo '99
Ichi the Killer '01
Bright Future '03
Zatoichi '03
Hana: The Tale of a Reluctant Samurai '07
Mongol '07
Kabei: Our Mother '08
Battleship '12
47 Ronin '13
Silence '16

Pilou Asbaek (1982-)
A Hijacking '13
A War '15
Ghost in the Shell '17
Woodshock '17
Overlord '18

Ariane Ascaride (1954-)
Marius and Jeannette '97
The Town Is Quiet '00
Lulu '02
My Life on Ice '02
The Army of Crime '10

Katie (Kathryn) Asselton (1978-)
Feed the Fish '09
Easier With Practice '10
The Freebie '10
Black Rock '12
Deep Murder '19
The Tomorrow Man '19

Neus Asensi (1965-)
The Girl of Your Dreams '99
Arachnid '01

Leslie Ash (1960-)
Quadrophenia '79
Curse of the Pink Panther '83

Ashanti (1980-)
Coach Carter '05
The Muppets' Wizard of Oz '05
John Tucker Must Die '06
Resident Evil: Extinction '07

Jayne Ashbourne (1969-)
Sharpe's Gold '94
Prince of Poisoners: The Life and Crimes of William Palmer '98

Lorraine Ashbourne (1961-)
Distant Voices, Still Lives '88
Fever Pitch '96
Murderland '09
Oranges and Sunshine '10

Dana Ashbrook (1967-)
Return of the Living Dead 2 '88
Waxwork '88
She's Out of Control '89
Ghost Dad '90
Twin Peaks: Fire Walk with Me '92
Kisses in the Dark '97
Angels Don't Sleep Here '00
Python 2 '02
Sundown: The Vampire in Retreat '08
The Aggression Scale '12

Daphne Ashbrook (1963-)
Quiet Cool '86
Doctor Who '96
The Love Letter '98

Linden Ashby (1960-)
Wyatt Earp '94
Cadillac Ranch '96
Shelter '98
Where the Truth Lies '99
Facing the Enemy '00
Tick Tock '00
Sniper 2 '02
A Woman Hunted '03
Wild Things 2 '04
Wild Things 3: Diamonds in the Rough '05
My Neighbor's Keeper '07
Resident Evil: Extinction '07
Against the Dark '08
Impact Point '08
Accused at 17 '09
Anacondas: Trail of Blood '09
Mean Girls 2 '11

Peggy Ashcroft (1907-91)
The 39 Steps '35
The Nun's Story '59
Sunday, Bloody Sunday '71
Hullabaloo over Georgie & Bonnie's Pictures '78
The Jewel in the Crown '84
A Passage to India '84
When the Wind Blows '86 (V)
Madame Sousatzka '88
The Heat of the Day '91

Eve Brent Ashe (1930-2011)
See Eve Brent

Jane Asher (1946-)
The Prince and the Pauper '62
Masque of the Red Death '65
Alfie '66
The Buttercup Chain '70
Dreamchild '85
A Voyage 'Round My Father '89
Death at a Funeral '07

Renee Asherson (1915-2014)
Henry V '44
Immortal Battalion '44
The Way to the Stars '45
Rasputin the Mad Monk '66
Edwin '84
Grey Owl '99
The Others '01

Ron Asheton (1948-)
Frostbiter: Wrath of the Wendigo '94
Mosquito '95

Kate Ashfield (1972-)
The War Zone '98
Do or Die '01
The Last Minute '01
Pure '02
Beyond Borders '03
Fakers '04
Shaun of the Dead '04
Secret Smile '05
Assassin in Love '07
The Diary of Anne Frank '08
Collision '09
My Brothers '10
Late Bloomers '11
Exit Plan '20

Makoto Ashikawa
Violent Cop '89
Ju-On 2 '00

Clare-Hope Ashitey
Children of Men '06
Jimi: All Is by My Side '14

Lior Ashkenazi (1969-)
Late Marriage '01
Hello Goodbye '08
Rabies '10
Footnote '11
Yossi '12
Norman '17
Foxtrot '18

Edward Ashley (1904-2000)
Bitter Sweet '40
Sky Murder '40
Maisie Was a Lady '41
The Black Swan '42
Nocturne '46
Dick Tracy Meets Gruesome '47
Tarzan and the Mermaids '48
Beyond the Next Mountain '87

Elizabeth Ashley (1939-)
The Carpetbaggers '64
Ship of Fools '65
The Third Day '65
Shattered Silence '71
Golden Needles '74
Rancho Deluxe '75
Great Scout & Cathouse Thursday '76
One of My Wives Is Missing '76
Coma '78
Windows '80
Svengali '83
Stagecoach '86
Dragnet '87
Dangerous Curves '88
A Man of Passion '88
Vampire's Kiss '88
The Buccaneers '95
Happiness '98
Just the Ticket '98
The Cake Eaters '07

Jennifer Ashley
Hell on Wheels '67
Barn of the Naked Dead '73
Pom Pom Girls '76
Inseminoid '80

Joel Ashley (1919-2000)
Ghost Town '56
Zombies of Moratau '57

John Ashley (1934-97)
Dragstrip Girl '57
Frankenstein's Daughter '58
How to Make a Monster '58
High School Caesar '60
Beach Party '63
Hud '63
Bikini Beach '64
Muscle Beach Party '64
Beach Blanket Bingo '65
The Eye Creatures '65
How to Stuff a Wild Bikini '65
Hell on Wheels '67
Brides of the Beast '68
Mad Doctor of Blood Island '68
Beast of the Yellow Night '70
Beast of Blood '71
Twilight People '72
Beyond Atlantis '73
Savage Sisters '74

Aaron Ashmore (1979-)
My Husband's Double Life '01
Treed Murray '01
The Skulls 2 '02
Brave New Girl '04
Prom Queen '04
A Separate Peace '04
Palo Alto '07
The Stone Angel '07
The Christmas Cottage '08
The Thaw '09
The Shrine '10
Regression '16

Frank Ashmore
The Clonus Horror '79
Bigfoot: The Lost Coast Tapes '12

Shawn Ashmore (1979-)
X-Men '00
X2: X-Men United '03
The Quiet '05
Underclassman '05
X-Men: The Last Stand '06
The Ruins '08
Frozen '10
Mother's Day '10
The Day '11
The Barrens '12
Acts of Violence '18
Darkness Falls '20

John Ashton (1948-)
Honky Tonk Freeway '81
The Adventures of Buckaroo Banzai Across the Eighth Dimension '84
Beverly Hills Cop '84
The Deliberate Stranger '86
King Kong Lives '86
Beverly Hills Cop 2 '87
Some Kind of Wonderful '87
Midnight Run '88
She's Having a Baby '88
I Know My First Name Is Steven '89
Stephen King's The Tommyknockers '93
Hidden Assassin '94
Little Big League '94
Trapped in Paradise '94
Meet the Deedles '98
Avalanche '99
Instinct '99
Gone Baby Gone '07

Joseph Ashton (1986-)
The Education of Little Tree '97
Slappy and the Stinkers '97

Roger Ashton-Griffiths (1957-)
Haunted Honeymoon '86
Vanity Fair '99
Princess of Thieves '01
Gangs of New York '02
You Will Meet a Tall Dark Stranger '10

Tom Ashworth
Killer Tomatoes Strike Back '90
Killer Tomatoes Eat France '91

Desmond Askew (1972-)
Go '99
Repli-Kate '01
Fabled '02
The Hills Have Eyes '06
Turistas '06

Luke Askew (1937-2012)
Cool Hand Luke '67
Hurry Sundown '67
The Devil's Brigade '68
The Green Berets '68
Easy Rider '69
Angel Unchained '70
The Great Northfield Minnesota Raid '72
Posse '75
The Longest Drive '76
Wanda Nevada '79
The Warrior & the Sorceress '84
Kung Fu: The Movie '86
Traveller '96
Frailty '02
The Greatest Game Ever Played '05

Arthur Askey (1900-82)
The Ghost Train '41
Miss London Ltd. '43
Bees in Paradise '44

Leon Askin (1907-2005)
South Sea Woman '53
Knock on Wood '54
Sherlock Holmes and the Deadly Necklace '62
Dr. Death, Seeker of Souls '73
Savage Island '85

Robin Askwith (1950-)
Hans Brinker '69
Flesh and Blood Show '73
Horror Hospital '73
Confessions of a Window Cleaner '74
Confessions of a Driving Instructor '76

Gregoire Aslan (1908-82)
The Red Inn '51
The Snorkel '58
Our Man in Havana '59
The 3 Worlds of Gulliver '60
The Happy Thieves '61
Invasion Quartet '61
Paris When It Sizzles '64
The High Bright Sun '65
The 25th Hour '67
Golden Voyage of Sinbad '73

Ed Asner (1929-)
Kid Galahad '62
The Satan Bug '65
The Slender Thread '65
El Dorado '67
The Venetian Affair '67
Change of Habit '69
Halls of Anger '70
They Call Me Mr. Tibbs! '70
Skin Game '71
The Todd Killings '71
The Girl Most Likely to. . . '73
The Wrestler '73
Gus '76
Rich Man, Poor Man '76
The Gathering '77
Roots '77
Fort Apache, the Bronx '81
O'Hara's Wife '82
Daniel '83
Kate's Secret '86
Moon over Parador '88
JFK '91
Gypsy '93
Happily Ever After '93 (V)
Gargoyles, The Movie: The Heroes Awaken '94 (V)
Armistead Maupin's More Tales of the City '97 (C)
Hard Rain '97
The Bachelor '99
Love and Action in Chicago '99
Above Suspicion '00
Perfect Game '00
The Animal '01
Elf '03
Missing Brendan '03
National Lampoon's Christmas Vacation 2: Cousin Eddie's Big Island Adventure '03
Out of the Woods '05
Sheeba '05
The Christmas Card '06
The Heart Specialist '06
Hard Four '07
Gigantic '08
Up '09 (V)
Not Another B Movie '10
Hopelessly in June '11

Let Go *'11*
Too Big to Fail *'11*
Home Alone: The Holiday Heist *'12*

Kumiko Aso (1978-)
Dr. Akagi *'98*
Pulse *'01*
Red Shadow *'01*
Ringu 0 *'01*
Casshern *'04*
Black House *'07*

Fred Asparagus (1947-98)
Colors *'88*
Just the Ticket *'98*

Jennifer Aspen
L.A. Twister *'04*
Unanswered Prayers *'10*

Armand Assante (1949-)
The Lords of Flatbush *'74*
Paradise Alley *'78*
Prophecy *'79*
Love and Money *'80*
Private Benjamin *'80*
I, the Jury *'82*
Unfaithfully Yours *'84*
Belizaire the Cajun *'86*
Napoleon and Josephine: A Love Story *'87*
Jack the Ripper *'88*
Q & A *'90*
Fever *'91*
The Marrying Man *'91*
1492: Conquest of Paradise *'92*
Hoffa *'92*
The Mambo Kings *'92*
Fatal Instinct *'93*
Blind Justice *'94*
Trial by Jury *'94*
Judge Dredd *'95*
Kidnapped *'95*
Gotti *'96*
Striptease *'96*
The Odyssey *'97*
The Hunley *'99*
Looking for an Echo *'99*
On the Beach *'00*
The Road to El Dorado *'00* (V)
After the Storm *'01*
Last Run *'01*
Federal Protection *'02*
Confessions of a Pit Fighter *'05*
Dot.Kill *'05*
Mirror Wars: Reflection One *'05*
Two for the Money *'05*
Dead Lenny *'06*
Soul's Midnight *'06*
American Gangster *'07*
California Dreamin' *'07*
The Line *'08*
The Man Who Came Back *'08*
Shark Swarm *'08*
The Bleeding *'09*
Breaking Point *'09*
The Chaos Experiment *'09*
Chicago Overcoat *'09*
Killer by Nature *'10*
Magic Man *'10*
Jesse *'11*
The Return of Joe Rich *'11*
Dead Man Down *'13*
Once Upon a Time in Brooklyn *'13*

Pat Ast (1942-2001)
Heat *'72*
Reform School Girls *'86*

Fred Astaire (1899-1987)
Dancing Lady *'33*
Flying Down to Rio *'33*
The Gay Divorcee *'34*
Roberta *'35*
Top Hat *'35*
Follow the Fleet *'36*
Swing Time *'36*
A Damsel in Distress *'37*
Shall We Dance *'37*
Carefree *'38*
The Story of Vernon and Irene Castle *'39*
Broadway Melody of 1940 *'40*
Second Chorus *'40*
You'll Never Get Rich *'41*
Holiday Inn *'42*
You Were Never Lovelier *'42*
The Sky's the Limit *'43*
Yolanda and the Thief *'45*
Blue Skies *'46*
Ziegfeld Follies *'46*
Easter Parade *'48*
The Barkleys of Broadway *'49*
Let's Dance *'50*
Three Little Words *'50*
Royal Wedding *'51*
The Belle of New York *'52*
The Band Wagon *'53*
Daddy Long Legs *'55*
Funny Face *'57*
Silk Stockings *'57*
On the Beach *'59*
The Notorious Landlady *'62*
Paris When It Sizzles *'64*
Finian's Rainbow *'68*
The Over-the-Hill Gang Rides Again *'70*
That's Entertainment *'74*
The Towering Inferno *'74*
That's Entertainment, Part 2 *'76 (N)*
Ghost Story *'81*
That's Dancing! *'85*

Nils Asther (1897-1981)
Laugh, Clown, Laugh *'28*
Our Dancing Daughters *'28*
Wild Orchids *'28*
The Single Standard *'29*
But the Flesh Is Weak *'32*
The Bitter Tea of General Yen *'33*
If I Were Free *'33*
Dr. Kildare's Wedding Day *'41*
Flying Blind *'41*
Night Monster *'42*
Bluebeard *'44*
Son of Lassie *'45*

Adriana Asti (1933-)
Accatone! *'61*
Phantom of Liberty *'74*
Zorro *'74*
Caligula *'80*
Best of Youth *'03*
Unforgivable *'11*

John Astin (1930-)
That Touch of Mink *'62*
Move Over, Darling *'63*
The Wheeler Dealers *'63*
Candy *'68*
Viva Max *'69*
Evil Roy Slade *'71*
Get to Know Your Rabbit *'72*
Pepper and His Wacky Taxi *'72*
Brothers O'Toole *'73*
Only with Married Men *'74*
Freaky Friday *'76*
National Lampoon's European Vacation *'85*
Body Slam *'87*
Teen Wolf Too *'87*
Return of the Killer Tomatoes! *'88*
Gremlins 2: The New Batch *'90*
Killer Tomatoes Strike Back *'90*
Killer Tomatoes Eat France *'91*
Stepmonster *'92*
Huck and the King of Hearts *'93*
The Frighteners *'96*
School of Life *'06*

MacKenzie Astin (1973-)
The Garbage Pail Kids Movie *'87*
Iron Will *'93*
Wyatt Earp *'94*
Dream for an Insomniac *'96*
The Evening Star *'96*
In Love and War *'96*
The Last Days of Disco *'98*
The Mating Habits of the Earthbound Human *'99*
Stranger than Fiction *'99*
How to Deal *'03*
Two Days *'03*
Love's Enduring Promise *'04*
Off the Lip *'04*
Military Intelligence and You! *'06*

Sean Astin (1971-)
The Goonies *'85*
Like Father, Like Son *'87*
White Water Summer *'87*
Staying Together *'89*
The War of the Roses *'89*
Memphis Belle *'90*
The Willies *'90*
Toy Soldiers *'91*
Encino Man *'92*
Where the Day Takes You *'92*
Rudy *'93*
Safe Passage *'94*
The Low Life *'95*
Courage Under Fire *'96*
Bulworth *'98*
Dish Dogs *'98*
Deterrence *'00*
Lord of the Rings: The Fellowship of the Ring *'01*
The Final Hit *'02*
Lord of the Rings: The Two Towers *'02*
Lord of the Rings: The Return of the King *'03*
Elvis Has Left the Building *'04*
50 First Dates *'04*
Bigger Than the Sky *'05*
Smile *'05*
Click *'06*
Love and Debate *'06*
Marilyn Hotchkiss' Ballroom Dancing & Charm School *'06*
Borderland *'07*
The Final Season *'07*
What Love Is *'07*
The Color of Magic *'08*
Forever Strong *'08*
Stay Cool *'09*
And They're Off *'11*
Demoted *'11*
Love's Christmas Journey *'11*
The Witches of Oz *'11*
Boys of Abu Ghraib *'14*
Moms' Night Out *'14*
Do You Believe? *'15*
Gloria Bell *'18*

Skylar Astin (1987-)
Hamlet 2 *'08*
21 & Over *'13*
Pitch Perfect 2 *'15*

John Aston
A Death in California *'85*
Last Resort *'86*
I Want to Go Home *'89*

Gertrude Astor (1887-1977)
Through the Back Door *'21*
Beyond the Rocks *'22*
Kiki *'26*
Strong Man *'26*
The Cat and the Canary *'27*
Be Yourself *'30*
Empty Saddles *'36*

Mary Astor (1906-87)
Mark of Zorro *'20*
Beau Brummel *'24*
Don Q., Son of Zorro *'25*
Don Juan *'26*
Behind Office Doors *'31*
Other Men's Women *'31*
The Royal Bed *'31*
Red Dust *'32*
A Successful Calamity *'32*
Those We Love *'32*
The Kennel Murder Case *'33*
The Little Giant *'33*
The Case of the Howling Dog *'34*
The Man with Two Faces *'34*
Upperworld *'34*
And So They Were Married *'36*
Dodsworth *'36*
The Hurricane *'37*
Prisoner of Zenda *'37*
Listen, Darling *'38*
Paradise for Three *'38*
Midnight *'39*
Brigham Young: Frontiersman *'40*
The Great Lie *'41*
The Maltese Falcon *'41*
Across the Pacific *'42*
The Palm Beach Story *'42*
Thousands Cheer *'43*
Young Ideas *'43*
Meet Me in St. Louis *'44*
Claudia and David *'46*
Cass Timberlane *'47*
Cynthia *'47*
Act of Violence *'48*
Any Number Can Play *'49*
Little Women *'49*
The Power and the Prize *'56*
Return to Peyton Place *'61*
Youngblood Hawke *'64*
Hush, Hush, Sweet Charlotte *'65*

Patti Astor
The Foreigner *'78*
Assault of the Killer Bimbos *'88*

Astro
See Brian 'Astro' Bradley

Emily Atack (1989-)
Outside Bet *'12*
Get Lucky *'13*

Roscoe Ates (1892-1962)
Cimarron *'31*
Politics *'31*
The Champ *'32*
Freaks *'32*
Woman in the Shadows *'34*
Colorado Serenade *'46*

Ted Atherton (1962-)
Nothing Too Good for a Cowboy *'98*
The Company *'07*
Everest *'07*
The Stone Angel *'07*
Max Payne *'08*
An Old-Fashioned Thanksgiving *'08*
XIII *'08*
The Santa Suit *'10*

William Atherton (1947-)
Class of '44 *'73*
The Sugarland Express *'74*
The Day of the Locust *'75*
The Hindenburg *'75*
Centennial *'78*
Ghostbusters *'84*
Real Genius *'85*
No Mercy *'86*
Die Hard *'88*
Buried Alive *'90*
Die Hard 2: Die Harder *'90*
The Pelican Brief *'93*
Frank and Jesse *'94*
Broken Trust *'95*
Saints and Sinners *'95*
Bio-Dome *'96*
Hoodlum *'96*
Mad City *'97*
Executive Power *'98*
Introducing Dorothy Dandridge *'99*
The Crow: Salvation *'00*
Burning Down the House *'01*
Race to Space *'01*
Headspace *'02*
The Last Samurai *'03*
Ghouls *'07*
Towards Darkness *'07*
Aces 'n Eights *'08*
The Kane Files *'10*
Jersey Shore Shark Attack *'12*
Tim and Eric's Billion Dollar Movie *'12*
Jinn *'14*

Mamoudou Athie
Patti Cake$ *'17*
Underwater *'20*

Moran Atias (1981-)
Mother of Tears *'08*
The Next Three Days *'10*
Third Person *'13*

Aure Atika
OSS 117: Cairo, Nest of Spies *'06*
Mademoiselle Chambon *'09*

Harvey Atkin (1942-)
Meatballs *'79*
Critical Care *'97*
Why I Wore Lipstick to My Mastectomy *'06*

Feodor Atkine (1948-)
Le Beau Mariage *'82*
Le Choc *'82*
Pauline at the Beach *'83*
Sorceress *'88*
High Heels *'91*
Sharpe's Siege *'96*
Doctor Chance *'97*
Sharpe's Revenge *'97*
Ronin *'98*
Spy Games *'99*
Vatel *'00*
Angel of Death *'02*
Carnage *'02*
Alexander *'04*

Christopher Atkins (1961-)
The Blue Lagoon *'80*
Child Bride of Short Creek *'81*
Pirate Movie *'82*
A Night in Heaven *'83*
Secret Weapons *'85*
Beaks: The Movie *'87*
Shakma *'89*
Mortuary Academy *'91*
Fatal Charm *'92*
Die Watching *'93*
Dracula Rising *'93*
Bullet Down Under *'94*
It's My Party *'95*
Project Shadowchaser 3000 *'95*
Red Shoe Diaries: Four on the Floor *'96*
Malicious Intent *'99*
13th Child: Legend of the Jersey Devil *'02*
Quigley *'03*
100 Million BC *'08*
Blue Lagoon: The Awakening *'12*

Dave Atkins (1940-2008)
Bury Me an Angel *'71*
Britannia Hospital *'82*
Hellraiser *'87*
Personal Services *'87*
Prick Up Your Ears *'87*
The Advocate *'93*
The Last Seduction 2 *'98*
Plunkett & Macleane *'98*

Eileen Atkins (1934-)
I Don't Want to Be Born *'75*
She Fell Among Thieves *'78*
Oliver Twist *'82*
Smiley's People *'82*
The Dresser *'83*
Let Him Have It *'91*
The Lost Language of Cranes *'92*
Cold Comfort Farm *'94*
Wolf *'94*
Jack and Sarah *'95*
A Dance to the Music of Time *'97*
The Avengers *'98*
Gosford Park *'01*
Wit *'01*
The Hours *'02*
Cold Mountain *'03*
What a Girl Wants *'03*
Vanity Fair *'04*
Ask the Dust *'06*
Scenes of a Sexual Nature *'06*
Ballet Shoes *'07*
Evening *'07*
Cranford *'08*
Last Chance Harvey *'08*
Murder on the Orient Express *'10*
Robin Hood *'10*
Wild Target *'10*
Upstairs Downstairs *'11*
The Scapegoat *'12*
Beautiful Creatures *'13*
Magic in the Moonlight *'14*
Tea with the Dames *'18*

Essence Atkins (1972-)
How High *'01*
Deliver Us from Eva *'03*
Love and Other Four Letter Words *'07*
Dance Flick *'09*
Preacher's Kid *'10*
A Haunted House *'13*
A Haunted House 2 *'14*

Tom Atkins (1935-)
The Detective *'68*
Tarantulas: The Deadly Cargo *'77*
The Fog *'78*
Escape from New York *'81*
Desperate Lives *'82*
Halloween 3: Season of the Witch *'82*
Night of the Creeps *'86*
Lethal Weapon *'87*
Maniac Cop *'88*
The Heist *'89*
Two Evil Eyes *'90*
Bob Roberts *'92*
Bruiser *'00*
Out of the Black *'01*
My Bloody Valentine 3D *'09*

Frank Atkinson (1893-1963)
The Green Cockatoo *'37*
Young and Innocent *'37*
Pygmalion *'38*

Jayne Atkinson (1959-)
Capone *'89*
Free Willy *'93*
Free Willy 2: The Adventure Home *'95*
Our Town *'03*
The Village *'04*
12 and Holding *'05*

Rowan Atkinson (1955-)
Never Say Never Again *'83*
The Tall Guy *'89*
The Witches *'90*
Bernard and the Genie *'91*
Hot Shots! Part Deux *'93*
Four Weddings and a Funeral *'94*
The Lion King *'94 (V)*
Bean *'97*
Maybe Baby *'99*
Rat Race *'01*
Scooby-Doo *'02*
Johnny English *'03*
Love Actually *'03*
Keeping Mum *'05*
Mr. Bean's Holiday *'07*
Johnny English Reborn *'11*
Johnny English Strikes Again *'18*

Yvan Attal (1965-)
Love, etc. *'96*
Portraits Chinois *'96*
The Criminal *'00*
My Wife is an Actress *'01*
And Now Ladies and Gentlemen *'02*
Bon Voyage *'03*
Happily Ever After *'04*
The Interpreter *'05*
Munich *'05*
Rush Hour 3 *'07*
Rapt *'09*
The Last Diamond *'14*
Seberg *'19*

Dave Attell (1965-)
Pootie Tang *'01*
Scary Movie 4 *'06*

Richard Attenborough (1923-2014)
In Which We Serve *'43*
Stairway to Heaven *'46*
Brighton Rock *'47*
Boys in Brown *'49*
Morning Departure *'50*
Hell Is Sold Out *'51*
The Scamp *'57*
Sea of Sand *'58*
The League of Gentlemen *'60*
S.O.S. Pacific *'60*
All Night Long *'62*
Trial & Error *'62*
The Great Escape *'63*
Guns at Batasi *'64*

Seance on a Wet Afternoon '64
The Flight of the Phoenix '65
The Sand Pebbles '66
Doctor Dolittle '67
The Bliss of Mrs. Blossom '68
The Magic Christian '69
David Copperfield '70
The Last Grenade '70
A Severed Head '70
10 Rillington Place '71
Brannigan '75
Conduct Unbecoming '75
Ten Little Indians '75
The Human Factor '79
Jurassic Park '93
Miracle on 34th Street '94
Hamlet '96
The Lost World: Jurassic Park 2 '97
Elizabeth '98
Joseph and the Amazing Technicolor Dreamcoat '00
The Railway Children '00
Jack and the Beanstalk: The Real Story '01

Malcolm Atterbury (1907-92)
Crime in the Streets '56
Blood of Dracula '57
Crime of Passion '57
How to Make a Monster '58
High School Big Shot '59
Emperor of the North Pole '73

Edward Atterton (1962-)
Catherine Cookson's The Wingless Bird '97
The Hunchback '97
The Man in the Iron Mask '98
Relative Values '99
Britannic '00
Mists of Avalon '01
Carolina '03
Children of Dune '03

Michael Attwell (1943-2006)
Joseph '95
Poldark '96

Barry Atwater (1918-78)
Pork Chop Hill '59
Vice Raid '60
Night Gallery '69
The Night Stalker '71

Edith Atwater (1911-86)
The Body Snatcher '45
It Happened at the World's Fair '63
Strait-Jacket '64
True Grit '69
Pieces of Dreams '70
The Love Machine '71
Die Sister, Die! '74
Our Time '74
Family Plot '76

Hayley Atwell (1982-)
The Line of Beauty '06
Ruby in the Smoke '06
How About You '07
Mansfield Park '07
The Shadow in the North '07
Brideshead Revisited '08
The Duchess '08
The Prisoner '09
Pillars of the Earth '10
Any Human Heart '11
Captain America: The First Avenger '11
The Sweeney '12
Jimi: All Is by My Side '14
Ant-Man '15
Christopher Robin '18

Lionel Atwill (1885-1946)
Doctor X '32
The Vampire Bat '32
Mystery of the Wax Museum '33
The Song of Songs '33
The Age of Innocence '34
Beggars in Ermine '34
Captain Blood '35
The Devil Is a Woman '35
The Murder Man '35
Rendezvous '35
The Great Garrick '37
High Command '37
The Great Waltz '38
Three Comrades '38
Balalaika '39
The Gorilla '39
The Hound of the Baskervilles '39
The Secret of Dr. Kildare '39
Son of Frankenstein '39
The Three Musketeers '39
Boom Town '40
Charlie Chan in Panama '40
Charlie Chan's Murder Cruise '40
Johnny Apollo '40
Cairo '42
Frankenstein Meets the Wolfman '42
The Ghost of Frankenstein '42
Junior G-Men of the Air '42
Night Monster '42
Pardon My Sarong '42
Sherlock Holmes and the Secret Weapon '42
The Strange Case of Dr. Rx '42
To Be or Not to Be '42
Captain America '44
House of Frankenstein '44
Raiders of Ghost City '44
Fog Island '45
House of Dracula '45
Lost City of the Jungle '45

Anat Atzmon (1958-)
Dead End Street '83
Every Time We Say Goodbye '86

Robert Atzorn (1945-)
From the Life of the Marionettes '80
The Wannsee Conference '84

Rene Auberjonois (1940-2019)
Lilith '64
Petulia '68
Brewster McCloud '70
M*A*S*H '70
Colditz: Escape of the Birdmen '71
McCabe & Mrs. Miller '71
Images '72
Pete 'n' Tillie '72
King Kong '76
Eyes of Laura Mars '78
Wild, Wild West Revisited '79
Where the Buffalo Roam '80
3:15: The Moment of Truth '86
Walker '87
My Best Friend Is a Vampire '88
Police Academy 5: Assignment Miami Beach '88
The Little Mermaid '89 (V)
Little Nemo: Adventures in Slumberland '92 (V)
The Lost Language of Cranes '92 (C)
The Player '92
The Ballad of Little Jo '93
Batman Forever '95
Cats Don't Dance '97 (V)
Inspector Gadget '99
Gepetto '00
The Patriot '00
Sally Hemings: An American Scandal '00
We All Fall Down '00
Burning Down the House '01
Eulogy '04
First Cow '20

K.D. Aubert (1978-)
Friday After Next '02
Frankenfish '04
Soul Plane '04
In the Mix '05

Lenore Aubert (1913-93)
Action in Arabia '44
Abbott and Costello Meet Frankenstein '48
Abbott and Costello Meet the Killer, Boris Karloff '49

James Aubrey (1947-2010)
Lord of the Flies '63
The Terror '79
The Hunger '83
Home Before Midnight '84
Forever Young '85
Riders of the Storm '88

Jimmy Aubrey (1887-1983)
Night Cargo '36
Ghost of Hidden Valley '46

Juliet Aubrey (1966-)
Middlemarch '93
Jacob '94
Catherine Cookson's The Moth '96
Welcome to Sarajevo '97
Still Crazy '98
The Unknown Soldier '98
Extremely Dangerous '99
Iris '01
The Mayor of Casterbridge '03
The Constant Gardener '05
Super Eruption '11

Skye Aubrey (1945-)
The Carey Treatment '72
The Phantom of Hollywood '74

Danielle Aubry
Bikini Beach '64
Operation C.I.A. '65

Jacques Aubuchon (1924-91)
The Big Boodle '57
Gun Glory '57
Thunder Road '58
Twenty Plus Two '61

Michel Auclair (1922-88)
Beauty and the Beast '46
Murder at 45 R.P.M. '65

Kentucker Audley
Sun Don't Shine '12
The Sacrament '13
Christmas, Again '15
Felt '15
Queen of Earth '15

Maxine Audley (1923-92)
A King in New York '57
Peeping Tom '60
The Trials of Oscar Wilde '60
Frankenstein Must Be Destroyed '69

Stephane Audran (1932-)
The Cousins '59
Les Cousins '59
Les Bonnes Femmes '60
Les Biches '68
Six in Paris '68
La Femme Infidele '69
Le Boucher '69
La Rupture '70
Just Before Nightfall '71
The Discreet Charm of the Bourgeoisie '72
Wedding in Blood '74
Ten Little Indians '75
The Twist '76
Violette '78
Eagle's Wing '79
The Big Red One '80
Brideshead Revisited '81
Coup de Torchon '81
Le Choc '82
Cop Au Vin '85
La Cage aux Folles 3: The Wedding '86
Babette's Feast '87
Poor Little Rich Girl: The Barbara Hutton Story '87
Faceless '88
Quiet Days in Clichy '90
Betty '92
The Turn of the Screw '92
Son of Gascogne '95
Maximum Risk '96
Madeline '98
The Girl From Monaco '08

Mischa Auer (1905-67)
Inside the Lines '30
Drums of Jeopardy '31
Sinister Hands '32
Corruption '33
Condemned to Live '35
The Crusades '35
The Lives of a Bengal Lancer '35
The Gay Desperado '36
My Man Godfrey '36
The Princess Comes Across '36
Three Smart Girls '36
100 Men and a Girl '37
Pick a Star '37
The Rage of Paris '38
Sweethearts '38
You Can't Take It with You '38
Destry Rides Again '39
East Side of Heaven '39
Seven Sinners '40
Spring Parade '40
The Flame of New Orleans '41
Hold That Ghost '41
And Then There Were None '45
Brewster's Millions '45
For You I Die '47
Mr. Arkadin '55
The Christmas That Almost Wasn't '66

Claudine Auger (1941-2019)
Thunderball '65
The Killing Game '67
Triple Cross '67
The Cats '68
The Black Belly of the Tarantula '71
Twitch of the Death Nerve '71
Ricco '74
The Associate '79

Pernilla August (1958-)
The Best Intentions '92
Mary, Mother of Jesus '99
Star Wars: Episode 1-The Phantom Menace '99
Gossip '00
Star Wars: Episode 2-Attack of the Clones '02
The Last Sentence '12

Robert August (1945-)
The Endless Summer '66
The Endless Summer 2 '94

Sherman Augustus (1959-)
Colors '88
Virus '98
ZigZag '02
The Foreigner '03
Bad Guys '08

Ewa Aulin (1949-)
Candy '68
Start the Revolution without Me '70

Marie Ault
The Lodger '26
Hindle Wakes '27

Jean-Pierre Aumont (1913-2001)
Bizarre Bizarre '39
The Cross of Lorraine '43
Heartbeat '46
Lili '53
Charge of the Lancers '54
Napoleon '55
The Devil at 4 O'Clock '61
Carnival of Crime '62
The Horse Without a Head '63
Castle Keep '69
Day for Night '73
The Happy Hooker '75
Mahogany '75
Blackout '78
The French Atlantic Affair '79
Something Short of Paradise '79
A Time for Miracles '80
Don't Look in the Attic '81
A Tale of Two Cities '89
Jefferson in Paris '94

Michel Aumont (1936-)
Les Comperes '83
A Sunday in the Country '84
The Closet '00

Tina Aumont (1946-2006)
The Game Is Over '66
Texas Across the River '66
Man, Pride and Vengeance '67
Partner '68
Man of Legend '71
Sergeant Klems '71
Torso '73
Lifespan '75
A Matter of Time '76

Alana Austin (1982-)
A Simple Twist of Fate '94
Miracle Dogs '03
Miracle Dogs Too '06

Charlotte Austin (1933-)
Les Miserables '52
Monkey Business '52
How to Marry a Millionaire '53
Desiree '54
There's No Business Like Show Business '54
Daddy Long Legs '55
The Man Who Turned to Stone '57
The Bride & the Beast '58
Frankenstein 1970 '58

Jake T. Austin (1994-)
The Ant Bully '06 (V)
Everyone's Hero '06 (V)
Hotel for Dogs '09
The Perfect Game '09
The Wizards of Waverly Place: The Movie '09
Rio '11 (V)

Julie Austin
Urban Ghost Story '98
The Flying Scotsman '06

Karen Austin (1950-)
The Jagged Edge '85
Summer Rental '85
Assassin '86
Far from Home '89
When a Stranger Calls Back '93
Confined '10

Pam(ela) Austin (1941-)
Blue Hawaii '62
Rome Adventure '62
Kissin' Cousins '64
Evil Roy Slade '71
Agatha '79

Steve Austin (1964-)
The Longest Yard '05
The Condemned '07
The Expendables '10
Hunt to Kill '10
The Stranger '10
Knockout '11
Recoil '11
Tactical Force '11
Maximum Conviction '12
The Package '12
Chain of Command '15

William Austin (1884-1975)
Suds '20
It '27
The Private Life of Henry VIII '33

Shaun Austin-Olsen
Extreme Measures '96
Battlefield Earth '00

Daniel Auteuil (1950-)
Jean de Florette '87
Manon of the Spring '87
Ma Saison Preferee '93
Un Coeur en Hiver '93
Queen Margot '94
The Separation '94
Les Voleurs '96
The Girl on the Bridge '98
La Separation '98
The Lost Son '98
The Closet '00
Sade '00
The Widow of Saint-Pierre '00
Apres-Vous '03
On Guard! '03
The 36th Precinct '04
Hidden '05
My Best Friend '06
The Valet '06
The Well-Digger's Daughter '11

Alan Autry (1952-)
Southern Comfort '81
At Close Range '86
Proud Men '87

Gene Autry (1907-98)
Mystery Mountain '34
The Phantom Empire '35
Manhattan Merry-Go-Round '37
South of the Border '39
Melody Ranch '40
Down Mexico Way '41
Ridin' on a Rainbow '41
Call of the Canyon '42
Heart of the Rio Grande '42
Sioux City Sue '46
Robin Hood of Texas '47
Loaded Pistols '48
The Big Sombrero '49
Cow Town '50
Alias Jesse James '59 (C)

Frankie Avalon (1940-)
The Alamo '60
Sail a Crooked Ship '61
Voyage to the Bottom of the Sea '61
Panic in Year Zero! '62
Beach Party '63
The Castilian '63
Drums of Africa '63
Operation Bikini '63
Bikini Beach '64
Muscle Beach Party '64
Pajama Party '64
Beach Blanket Bingo '65
How to Stuff a Wild Bikini '65
I'll Take Sweden '65
Sergeant Deadhead '65
Ski Party '65
Dr. Goldfoot and the Bikini Machine '66
Fireball 500 '66
Skidoo '68
The Take '74
Grease '78
Blood Song '82
Back to the Beach '87
Casino '95

Luis Avalos (1946-2014)
Ghost Fever '87
Lone Justice 2 '93
Jungle 2 Jungle '96
Lone Justice 3: Showdown at Plum Creek '96

Erik Avari (1952-)
The Beast '88
Encino Man '92
Stargate '94
The Mummy '99
Planet of the Apes '01
Mr. Deeds '02
Three Days of Rain '02
Daredevil '03
Dancing in Twilight '05
The Librarian: Return to King Solomon's Mines '06
American East '07
Choose Connor '07
Dark Matter '07
Flight of the Living Dead: Outbreak on a Plane '07
InAlienable '08
Hachiko: A Dog's Tale '09
Paul Blart: Mall Cop '09

Electra Avellan (1986-)
Scout's Honor: Badge to the Bone '09
The Black Waters of Echo's Pond '10

Joe Mari Avellana (1941-2011)
Bloodfist '89
Bloodfist 2 '90

Brian Avenet-Bradley
Ghost of the Needle '03
Jack O'Lantern '04

Brian Avery (1940-)
The Graduate '67
Forced to Kill '93

James Avery (1948-2013)
Fletch '85
License to Drive '88
Home for Christmas '93
Spirit Lost '96
The Colony '98
Prince of Egypt '98 (V)
Dancing in September '00
Divine Intervention '07
Transformers: Dark of the Moon '11 (V)

Margaret Avery (1944-)
Cool Breeze '72
Terror at Red Wolf Inn '72
Hell Up in Harlem '73
Magnum Force '73
Scott Joplin '77
Which Way Is Up? '77
The Fish that Saved Pittsburgh '79
The Lathe of Heaven '80
The Color Purple '85
Blueberry Hill '88
Heat Wave '90
The Jacksons: An American Dream '92
Mardi Gras for the Devil '93
White Man's Burden '95
Tyler Perry's Meet the Browns '08
Welcome Home Roscoe Jenkins '08
Proud Mary '18

Shondrella Avery (1971-)
Napoleon Dynamite '04
Domino '05

Tol Avery
Buchanan Rides Alone '58
The Case Against Brooklyn '58

Val Avery (1924-2009)
Nevada Smith '66
Faces '68
A Dream of Kings '69
The Anderson Tapes '71
Minnie and Moskowitz '71
Firehouse '72
Black Caesar '73
The Amityville Horror '79
Wanderers '79
Choices '81
The Chosen '81
Continental Divide '81
The Pope of Greenwich Village '84
Courage '86

Marie Avgeropoulos (1986-)
Hunt to Kill '10
Fugitive at 17 '12
Walking the Halls '12
Tracers '15
Dead Rising: End Game '16

Angel Aviles
Mi Vida Loca '94
Somebody to Love '94 (C)
Scorpion Spring '96

Rick Aviles (1953-95)
Mystery Train '89
Ghost '90
The Saint of Fort Washington '93
Stephen King's The Stand '94

Mili Avital (1972-)
Stargate '94
Dead Man '95
Polish Wedding '97
Kissing a Fool '98
The Young Girl and the Monsoon '99
Arabian Nights '00
Bad Seed '00
After the Storm '01
Uprising '01
The Human Stain '03
Colombian Love '04
When Do We Eat? '05

Natalie Avital
Shallow Ground '04
Attack of the Sabretooth '05

Aviva (1984-)
Down in the Valley '05
Superbad '07

Aki Avni (1967-)
Time of Favor '00
Free Zone '05

Chris Avram (1931-89)
Twitch of the Death Nerve '71
California '77

Alejandro Awada (1961-)
The Road '00
The Aura '05

Keiko Awaji
The Bridges at Toko-Ri '55
Inugami '01

Chikage Awashima (1924-2012)
Early Summer '51
The Human Condition: No Greater Love '58

Awkwafina (1989-)
See Nora Lum

Nina Axelrod
Motel Hell '80
Time Walker '82

Robert Axelrod (1949-2019)
The Big Turnaround '88
Repo Jake '90

Hannelore Axman
The Red Menace '49
Five Fingers '52

Hoyt Axton (1938-99)
The Black Stallion '79
Endangered Species '82
The Junkman '82
Heart Like a Wheel '83
Gremlins '84
Christmas Comes to Willow Creek '87
Dixie Lanes '88
Retribution '88
Disorganized Crime '89
We're No Angels '89
Buried Alive '90
The Rousters '90
Number One Fan '94
Season of Change '94
King Cobra '98

Yano Ayana (1972-)
A Christmas Story '83
Better Off Dead '85

Charlotte Ayanna (1976-)
Dancing at the Blue Iguana '00
Love the Hard Way '01
Training Day '01
Once Upon a Wedding '05
The Insatiable '06
Push '06
The Thirst '06

Ann Ayars (1920-95)
Dr. Kildare's Victory '42
Reunion in France '42

Haruka Ayase (1985-)
Ichi '08
Our Little Sister '16

Nicki Aycox (1975-)
Slap Her, She's French '02
Jeepers Creepers 2 '03
Momentum '03
Dead Birds '04
Perfect Stranger '07
Animals '08
Joy Ride 2: Dead Ahead '08
Christina '10
Lifted '10
Beyond the Blackboard '11
The Girl On the Train '13

Debbon Ayer
The Waiting Game '99
Death and Cremation '10

Dan Aykroyd (1952-)
All You Need Is Cash '78
Mr. Mike's Mondo Video '79
1941 '79
The Blues Brothers '80
Neighbors '81
Doctor Detroit '83
Trading Places '83
Twilight Zone: The Movie '83
Ghostbusters '84
Into the Night '85
Spies Like Us '85
The Couch Trip '87
Dragnet '87
Caddyshack 2 '88
The Great Outdoors '88
My Stepmother Is an Alien '88
Driving Miss Daisy '89
Ghostbusters 2 '89
Loose Cannons '90
My Girl '91
Nothing But Trouble '91
Chaplin '92
Sneakers '92
This Is My Life '92
Coneheads '93
Canadian Bacon '94
Exit to Eden '94
My Girl 2 '94
Casper '95 (C)
Sgt. Bilko '95
Tommy Boy '95
Celtic Pride '96
Feeling Minnesota '96
Getting Away With Murder '96
My Fellow Americans '96
Grosse Pointe Blank '97
Antz '98 (V)
Blues Brothers 2000 '98
Dying to Get Rich '98
Diamonds '99
House of Mirth '00
Loser '00
Stardom '00
The Curse of the Jade Scorpion '01
Earth *vs.* the Spider '01
Evolution '01
Pearl Harbor '01
Crossroads '02
Bright Young Things '03
Unconditional Love '03
Christmas With the Kranks '04
50 First Dates '04
White Coats '04
I Now Pronounce You Chuck and Larry '07
War, Inc. '08
Yogi Bear '10 (V)
The Campaign '12
Behind the Candelabra '13
Get On Up '14
Legends of Oz: Dorothy's Return '14 (V)
Tammy '14

Arthur Aylesworth (1883-1946)
The Plot Thickens '36
Beau Geste '39
King of the Underworld '39
Treasure of Fear '45

Reiko Aylesworth (1972-)
Crazylove '05
The Killing Floor '06
Magma: Volcanic Disaster '06
Aliens *vs.* Predator: Requiem '07
Mr. Brooks '07
The Assistants '09
Bad Parents '12

Felix Aylmer (1889-1979)
The Evil Mind '34
As You Like It '36
Nine Days a Queen '36
Victoria the Great '37
Sixty Glorious Years '38
The Case of the Frightened Lady '39
Night Train to Munich '40
The Girl in the News '41
Spellbound '41
Thursday's Child '43
Henry V '44
The Way to the Stars '45
The Wicked Lady '45
Ghosts of Berkeley Square '47
The Magic Bow '47
A Man About the House '47
Hamlet '48
Eye Witness '49
Prince of Foxes '49
Alice in Wonderland '50
The Lady With the Lamp '51
Quo Vadis '51
Ivanhoe '52
Knights of the Round Table '53
The Master of Ballantrae '53
Anastasia '56
Saint Joan '57
The Doctor's Dilemma '58
Separate Tables '58
The Mummy '59
Exodus '60
From the Terrace '60
The Hands of Orlac '60
Never Take Candy From a Stranger '60
The Chalk Garden '64
Hostile Witness '68

John Aylward (1946-)
Three Fugitives '89
From the Earth to the Moon '98
Instinct '99
Swing Vote '99
Just Visiting '01
Path to War '02
Down With Love '03
Crimes of the Past '09

Richard Ayoade
The Watch '12
Early Man '18

Rakie Ayola
Shades of Fear '93
The I Inside '04

Agnes Ayres (1898-1940)
Affairs of Anatol '21
The Sheik '21

Fraser Ayres
Intimacy '00
Wide Sargasso Sea '06

Leah Ayres (1957-)
The Burning '82
Eddie Macon's Run '83
Bloodsport '88

Lew Ayres (1908-96)
Big News '29
The Kiss '29
All Quiet on the Western Front '30
Doorway to Hell '30
Murder With Pictures '36
Holiday '38
King of the Newsboys '38
Young Dr. Kildare '38
Broadway Serenade '39
Calling Dr. Kildare '39
Ice Follies of 1939 '39
The Secret of Dr. Kildare '39
Those Glamour Girls '39
Dr. Kildare Goes Home '40
Dr. Kildare's Crisis '40
Dr. Kildare's Strange Case '40
Dr. Kildare's Wedding Day '41
Maisie Was a Lady '41
The People *vs.* Dr. Kildare '41
Dr. Kildare's Victory '42
Dark Mirror '46
Johnny Belinda '48
The Capture '50
Donovan's Brain '53
No Escape '53
Advise and Consent '62
The Carpetbaggers '64
Earth II '71
Battle for the Planet of the Apes '73
The Questor Tapes '74
End of the World '76
Damien: Omen 2 '78
Salem's Lot '79
Of Mice and Men '81

Robert Ayres (1914-68)
Time Lock '57
Battle Beneath the Earth '68

Rosalind Ayres (1946-)
That'll Be the Day '73
The Slipper and the Rose '76
Gods and Monsters '98
Beautiful People '99
Christmas in the Clouds '01

Rochelle Aytes (1976-)
White Chicks '04
Madea's Family Reunion '06
The Inheritance '10

Lubna Azabal (1973-)
Almost Peaceful '02
Changing Times '04
Paradise Now '05
Incendies '10
Free Men '12
Here '12

Kévin Azaïs
Neither Heaven Nor Earth '16
Summertime '16

Hank Azaria (1964-)
Cool Blue '88
Quiz Show '94
The Birdcage '95
Heat '95
Anastasia '97 (V)
Great Expectations '97
Grosse Pointe Blank '97
Homegrown '97
Celebrity '98
Godzilla '98
The Cradle Will Rock '99
Mystery, Alaska '99
Mystery Men '99
Tuesdays with Morrie '99
Fail Safe '00
America's Sweethearts '01
Uprising '01
Bark! '02
Shattered Glass '03
Along Came Polly '04
Dodgeball: A True Underdog Story '04
Eulogy '04
Chicago 10 '07 (V)
Run, Fatboy, Run '07
The Simpsons Movie '07 (V)
Night at the Museum: Battle of the Smithsonian '09
Year One '09
Love and Other Drugs '10
Happy Feet Two '11 (V)
Hop '11 (V)
The Smurfs '11 (V)
Lovelace '13
The Smurfs 2 '13 (V)

Sabine Azema (1949-)
Life Is a Bed of Roses '83
Love Unto Death '84
A Sunday in the Country '84
Melo '86
Life and Nothing But '89
La Buche '00
Wild Grass '09
The Well-Digger's Daughter '11
You Ain't Seen Nothin' Yet '12
Cosmos '16

Tony Azito (1949-95)
Union City '81
Private Resort '84
Bloodhounds of Broadway '89

Anthony Azizi (1969-)
Phobic '02
American East '07
Eagle Eye '08

Shabana Azmi (1950-)
The Bengali Night '88
Madame Sousatzka '88
City of Joy '92
Son of the Pink Panther '93
In Custody '94
Fire '96

Charles Aznavour (1924-)
The Testament of Orpheus '59
Taxi for Tobruk '60
Shoot the Piano Player '62
Candy '68
Carbon Copy '69
The Adventurers '70
Blockhouse '73
Ten Little Indians '75
Sky Riders '76
The Twist '76
The Tin Drum '79
Ararat '02
The Truth About Charlie '02 (C)

Eloy Azorin (1977-)
All About My Mother '99
Mad Love '01

Candice Azzara (1945-)
House Calls '78
Fatso '80
Divorce Wars: A Love Story '82
Easy Money '83
In Her Shoes '05
The Christmas Pageant '11

Lisa B (1971-)
See Lisa Barbuscia

Michael B.
Brave '07
The Sanctuary '09

B-Real (1970-)
See Louis Freese

Karin Baal (1940-)
Dead Eyes of London '61
Lola '81

Obba Babatunde (1951-)
God Bless the Child '88
Miami Blues '90
The Silence of the Lambs '91
Philadelphia '93
Undercover Blues '93
A Reason to Believe '95
Multiplicity '96
Soul of the Game '96
That Thing You Do! '96
Miss Evers' Boys '97
The Temptations '98
Introducing Dorothy Dandridge '99
Life '99
The Visit '00
How High '01
John Q '02
Redeemer '02
The Wild Thornberrys Movie '02 (V)
After the Sunset '04
The Celestine Prophecy '06
Material Girls '06
Cover '08
The Eye '08
Black Dynamite '09
Why Am I Doing This? '09
Santa Paws 2: The Santa Pups '12

Barbara Babcock (1937-)
Day of the Evil Gun '68
The Black Marble '79
The Lords of Discipline '83
That Was Then. . . This Is Now '85
News at Eleven '86
Happy Together '89
The Heart of Dixie '89
Far and Away '92
Space Cowboys '00

Todd Babcock
Single White Female 2: The Psycho '05
Break-In '06

Fabienne Babe (1962-)
Les Voleurs '96
La Vie Promise '02

Lauren Bacall (1924-2014)
To Have & Have Not '44
Confidential Agent '45
The Big Sleep '46
Dark Passage '47
Key Largo '48
Bright Leaf '50
Young Man with a Horn '50
How to Marry a Millionaire '53

Blood Alley '55
The Cobweb '55
Written on the Wind '56
Designing Woman '57
Flame Over India '59
North West Frontier '59
Sex and the Single Girl '64
Harper '66
Murder on the Orient Express '74
The Shootist '76
The Fan '81
Mr. North '88
Dinner at Eight '89
A Little Piece of Sunshine '90
Misery '90
All I Want for Christmas '91
A Foreign Field '93
Ready to Wear '94
From the Mixed-Up Files of Mrs. Basil E. Frankweiler '95
The Mirror Has Two Faces '96
My Fellow Americans '96
Diamonds '99
Dogville '03
Gone Dark '03
Birth '04
Howl's Moving Castle '04 (V)
Manderlay '05
These Foolish Things '06
The Walker '07
Ernest & Celestine '13 (V)

Michael Bacall (1973-)
Urban Legends 2: Final Cut '00
Manic '01
Death Proof '07
Inglourious Basterds '09

Salvatore Baccaloni (1900-69)
Full of Life '56
Rock-A-Bye Baby '57
Merry Andrew '58

Morena Baccarin (1979-)
Serenity '05
Stargate: The Ark of Truth '08
Stolen '09
Back in the Day '14
The Red Tent '14
Deadpool 2 '18
Ode to Joy '19

Barbara Bach (1947-)
The Black Belly of the Tarantula '71
Short Night of Glass Dolls '71
Street Law '74
The Legend of Sea Wolf '75
Stateline Motel '75
The Spy Who Loved Me '77
Force 10 from Navarone '78
The Big Alligator River '79
Jaguar Lives '79
Screamers '80
Up the Academy '80
Caveman '81
The Great Alligator '81
Princess Daisy '83
Give My Regards to Broad Street '84

Catherine Bach (1954-)
Nicole '72
Strange New World '75
Cannonball Run 2 '84
Criminal Act '88
Rage and Honor '92
The Nutt House '95 (C)
You Again '10

John Bach (1946-)
Wild Horses '82
Crimebroker '93
Ike: Countdown to D-Day '04
Kidnapped '05

Dian Bachar (1970-)
BASEketball '98
Orgazmo '98
The Adventures of Rocky & Bullwinkle '00

The Life of Lucky Cucumber '08

Burt Bacharach (1928-)
Austin Powers 2: The Spy Who Shagged Me '99 (C)
Austin Powers In Goldmember '02 (C)

Alicja Bachleda-Curus
Trade '07
Ondine '09
The American Side '16

Hans Bachmann
Outerworld '87
Invader '91

Steve Bacic (1965-)
Bounty Hunters 2: Hardball '97
The 6th Day '00
Ballistic: Ecks vs. Sever '02
Encrypt '03
Firefight '03
Threshold '03
Safe Harbor '06
The Tooth Fairy '06
Afghan Knights '07
The Final Storm '09
Tactical Force '11
Nearlyweds '13

George Back
Sam & Janet '02
The Comebacks '07

Brian Backer (1956-)
The Burning '82
Fast Times at Ridgemont High '82
Moving Violations '85
The Money Pit '86

Chris Backus
All In '06
3 Days Gone '08

Jim Backus (1913-89)
A Dangerous Profession '49
The Great Lover '49
His Kind of Woman '51
Hollywood Story '51
I'll See You in My Dreams '51
The Man With a Cloak '51
Don't Bother to Knock '52
Pat and Mike '52
Above and Beyond '53
I Love Melvin '53
Francis in the Navy '55
Rebel without a Cause '55
The Girl He Left Behind '56
Naked Hills '56
Man of a Thousand Faces '57
The Pied Piper of Hamelin '57
Top Secret Affair '57
Macabre '58
1001 Arabian Nights '59 (V)
Ice Palace '60
The Horizontal Lieutenant '62
Zotz! '62
Critic's Choice '63
It's a Mad, Mad, Mad, Mad World '63
Johnny Cool '63
Operation Bikini '63
Sunday in New York '63
The Wheeler Dealers '63
Advance to the Rear '64
Billie '65
Hurry Sundown '67
Hello Down There '69
Myra Breckinridge '70
Now You See Him, Now You Don't '72
The Girl Most Likely to. . . '73
Crazy Mama '75
Pete's Dragon '77
Rescue from Gilligan's Island '78
C.H.O.M.P.S. '79

Olga Baclanova (1899-1974)
The Man Who Laughs '27
Downstairs '32
Freaks '32
Claudia '43

Irving Bacon (1893-1965)
This Is the Night '32
Internes Can't Take Money '37
Blondie Brings Up Baby '39
Blondie Meets the Boss '39
Blondie Takes a Vacation '39
Blondie Has Trouble '40
Blondie On a Budget '40
Blondie Plays Cupid '40
Dreaming Out Loud '40
Gold Rush Maisie '40
The Howards of Virginia '40
Caught in the Draft '41
Western Union '41
The Bashful Bachelor '42
Blondie Goes Latin '42
Monsieur Verdoux '47
Dynamite '49
The Green Promise '49
Cause for Alarm '51
Ma and Pa Kettle at Home '54

Kevin Bacon (1958-)
National Lampoon's Animal House '78
Starting Over '79
Friday the 13th '80
Hero at Large '80
Only When I Laugh '81
Diner '82
Footloose '84
Quicksilver '86
Planes, Trains & Automobiles '87
White Water Summer '87
End of the Line '88
She's Having a Baby '88
The Big Picture '89
Criminal Law '89
Tremors '89
Flatliners '90
He Said, She Said '91
JFK '91
Queens Logic '91
A Few Good Men '92
The Air Up There '94
The River Wild '94
Apollo 13 '95
Balto '95 (V)
Murder in the First '95
Picture Perfect '96
Sleepers '96
Telling Lies in America '96
Digging to China '98
Wild Things '98
My Dog Skip '99
Stir of Echoes '99
Hollow Man '00
Novocaine '01
Trapped '02
In the Cut '03
Mystic River '03
The Woodsman '04
Beauty Shop '05
Loverboy '05
Where the Truth Lies '05
The Air I Breathe '07
Death Sentence '07
Rails & Ties '07
Frost/Nixon '08
My One and Only '09
Taking Chance '09
Super '10
Crazy, Stupid, Love. '11
Elephant White '11
X-Men: First Class '11
Jayne Mansfield's Car '13
R.I.P.D. '13
Cop Car '15
The Darkness '16
Patriots Day '17
You Should Have Left '20

Max Bacon (1906-69)
Miss London Ltd. '43
Bees in Paradise '44
Give Us the Moon '44
Privilege '67

Jean-Pierre Bacri (1951-)
Entre-Nous '83
Un Air de Famille '96
Place Vendome '98
The Taste of Others '00
The Housekeeper '02
Look at Me '04
Let It Rain '08

Marco Bacuzzi
Borderland '07
Species 4: The Awakening '07

Angelo Badalamenti (1937-)
Blue Velvet '86
Mulholland Drive '01

Michael Badalucco (1954-)
Jungle Fever '91
Night and the City '92
Mac '93
The Professional '94
The Search for One-Eye Jimmy '94
Blue in the Face '95
The Sunshine Boys '95
Two If by Sea '95
Love Walked In '97
You've Got Mail '98
Summer of Sam '99
O Brother Where Art Thou? '00
The Man Who Wasn't There '01
13 Moons '02
2B Perfectly Honest '04
Bewitched '05

Dan Badarau
Ghouls '07
Born to Raise Hell '10

Hermione Baddeley (1906-86)
Brighton Rock '47
Dear Mr. Prohack '49
Passport to Pimlico '49
A Christmas Carol '51
Hell Is Sold Out '51
Cosh Boy '52
The Belles of St. Trinian's '53
The Pickwick Papers '54
Room at the Top '59
Mary Poppins '64
The Unsinkable Molly Brown '64
Do Not Disturb '65
Marriage on the Rocks '65
The Aristocats '70 (V)

Alan Badel (1923-82)
Children of the Damned '63
This Sporting Life '63
Arabesque '66
Otley '68
The Adventurers '70
The Day of the Jackal '73
Luther '74
The Medusa Touch '78
The Riddle of the Sands '79
Nijinsky '80

Sarah Badel (1943-)
She Fell Among Thieves '78
Dangerous Corner '83
Not Without My Daughter '90
Mrs. Dalloway '97
Cotton Mary '99
Just Visiting '01

Diedrich Bader (1966-)
The Beverly Hillbillies '93
Office Space '98
Jay and Silent Bob Strike Back '01
The Country Bears '02 (V)
Evil Alien Conquerors '02
Ice Age '02 (V)
Eurotrip '04
Napoleon Dynamite '04
Miss Congeniality 2: Armed and Fabulous '05
National Lampoon Presents Cattle Call '06
Balls of Fury '07
Surf's Up '07 (V)
Meet the Spartans '08
Open Season 2 '08 (V)
Space Buddies '08
Calvin Marshall '09
Vampires Suck '10
Spooky Buddies '11 (V)
Atlas Shrugged 2: The Strike '12
The Starving Games '13
Superman: Unbound '13

Russ Badger
The Gore-Gore Girls '72
Shanghai Noon '00

Penn Badgley (1986-)
John Tucker Must Die '06
Forever Strong '08
The Stepfather '09
Easy A '10
Margin Call '11
Greetings from Tim Buckley '12
Parts Per Billion '14
Cymbeline '15

Mary Badham (1952-)
To Kill a Mockingbird '62
This Property Is Condemned '66

Mina Badie (1970-)
Mrs. Parker and the Vicious Circle '94
Georgia '95
The Anniversary Party '01
Road to Perdition '02
Roger Dodger '02
Laws of Attraction '04
Mind the Gap '04
Touched '05

Mini Badiyi (1970-)
See Mina Badie

Annette Badland (1950-)
Jabberwocky '77
Captives '94
Angels and Insects '95
Little Voice '98
Secret Society '00
The Kovak Box '06

Jane Badler (1953-)
Terror Among Us '81
V '83
Easy Kill '89
Under the Gun '95
Needle '10

Sayed Badreya (1957-)
American East '07
Iron Man '08
W. '08
The Dictator '12

Erykah Badu (1971-)
Deep Red: Hatchet Murders '75
Blues Brothers 2000 '98
The Cider House Rules '99
House of D '04

Du-na Bae (1979-)
The Ring Virus '99
Barking Dogs Never Bite '00
Take Care of My Cat '01
Sympathy for Mr. Vengeance '02
Tube '03
Linda Linda Linda '05
The Host '06

Buddy Baer (1915-86)
Quo Vadis '51
Jack & the Beanstalk '52
Dream Wife '53
Giant from the Unknown '58

Edouard Baer (1966-)
Alias Betty '01
Moliere '07
Wild Grass '09 (N)
Chicken With Plums '11
Phantom Boy '16

Harry Baer (1947-)
Whity '70
Fox and His Friends '75
Rulers of the City '76
Rulers of the City '77

John Baer (1923-2006)
Above and Beyond '53
The Mississippi Gambler '53
The Miami Story '54
We're No Angels '55
Tarawa Beachhead '58

Marcelle Baer
Journey to Promethea '10
Scream of the Banshee '11

Max Baer, Jr. (1937-)
Colditz: Escape of the Birdmen '71
Macon County Line '74
The McCullochs '75

Max Baer, Sr. (1909-59)
The Prizefighter and the Lady '33
Buckskin Frontier '43
Africa Screams '49
The Harder They Fall '56

Parley Baer (1914-2002)
The Young Lions '58
The FBI Story '59
The Adventures of Huckleberry Finn '60
Cash McCall '60
Wake Me When It's Over '60
Gypsy '62
The Brass Bottle '63
Two On a Guillotine '65
The Ugly Dachshund '65
Sixteen '72
Rodeo Girl '80
License to Drive '88
Almost an Angel '90
Dave '93

Nathan Baesel
Behind the Mask: The Rise of Leslie Vernon '06
20 Years After '08

Veerle Baetens
The Broken Circle Breakdown '12
The Ardennes '17

Joan Baez (1941-)
Don't Look Back '67
Dynamite Chicken '70
Hugh Hefner: Playboy, Activist and Rebel '09
Rolling Thunder Revue: A Bob Dylan Story by Martin Scorsese '19

Rafael Baez
Went to Coney Island on a Mission from God. . . Be Back by Five '98
Shanghai Noon '00

Paloma Baeza (1975-)
A Kid in King Arthur's Court '95
Far from the Madding Crowd '97
The Odyssey '97
A Knight in Camelot '98
Anna Karenina '00
The Way We Live Now '02

Regina Baff
Road Movie '72
Below the Belt '80

Larry Bagby (1974-)
Saints and Soldiers '03
Walk the Line '05
Believe '07
Forever Strong '08
The Trial '10
Age of the Dragons '11

William Bagdad (1920-75)
The Astro-Zombies '67
The Doll Squad '73
Blood Orgy of the She-Devils '74

Carol Bagdasarian
Charge of the Model T's '76
The Aurora Encounter '85

Vladas Bagdonas
Come and See '85
House of Fools '02

Lorri Bagley (1973-)
Trick '99
Ice Age '02 (V)

Tim Bagley (1957-)
The Fluffer '01
Memron '04
Employee of the Month '06
Knocked Up '07
Operation: Endgame '10

Vernel Bagneris (1949-)
Pennies from Heaven '81
Down by Law '86

Marcus Bagwell (1970-)
Day of the Warrior '96
Terror Tract '00

Madhur Bahadur (1933-)
See Madhur Jaffrey

Zahary Baharov
Command Performance '09
Double Identity '10

Blake Bahner (1959-)
Thrilled to Death '88
Deadly Breed '89
Blackbelt 2: Fatal Force '93
Wizards of the Demon Sword '94
Cyberstalker '96

Maxine Bahns (1971-)
The Brothers McMullen '94
She's the One '96
Dangerous Curves '99
Cutaway '00
Conjurer '08
The Hitman Diaries '09
WWJD: What Would Jesus Do? '10

Iris Bahr
Larry the Cable Guy: Health Inspector '06
The Last Exorcism '10

Wu Bai (1968-)
The Personals '98
Time and Tide '00

Bill Bailey (1964-)
On the Edge '86
Heat and Sunlight '87
Chalet Girls '11

Blake Bailey
Lurking Fear '94
Head of the Family '96

Eion Bailey (1976-)
Fight Club '99
Almost Famous '00
Center Stage '00
Band of Brothers '01
The Home Front '02
And Starring Pancho Villa as Himself '03
Life of the Party '05
Mindhunters '05
Language of the Enemy '07
The Canyon '09
(Untitled) '09

G.W. Bailey (1944-)
M*A*S*H: Goodbye, Farewell & Amen '83
Rustler's Rhapsody '85
Burglar '87
Mannequin '87
Police Academy 6: City under Siege '89
Held Hostage '91
Police Academy 7: Mission to Moscow '94
Jesus '00
The Thin Blue Lie '00
Scorcher '02
Home on the Range '04 (V)
Cake: A Wedding Story '07

Jack Bailey
Queen for a Day '51
The Vanguard '08

Laura Bailey
Four Sheets to the Wind '07
Mass Effect: Paragon Lost '12 (V)

Marion Bailey
All or Nothing '02
Mr. Turner '14

Mark Bailey
The Unbelievable Truth '90
Simple Men '92

Miranda Bailey (1977-)
The Oh in Ohio '06
Body at Brighton Rock '19

Pearl Bailey (1918-90)
Carmen Jones '54
The Landlord '70
Norman, Is That You? '76
The Fox and the Hound '81 (V)
Peter Gunn '89

Preston Bailey (2000-)
Children of the Corn '09
Judy Moody and the Not Bummer Summer '11

Raymond Bailey (1904-80)
Picnic '55
The Incredible Shrinking Man '57
Vertigo '58
The Gallant Hours '60

Robert Bailey, Jr. (1990-)
Dragonfly '02
Little John '02
What the #$*! Do We Know? '04
The Happening '08
Coraline '09 (V)
To Save a Life '10

Scott Bailey
Just Ask My Children '01
Prayers for Bobby '09

David Bailie (1937-)
Pirates of the Caribbean: The Curse of the Black Pearl '03
Pirates of the Caribbean: Dead Man's Chest '06

Nick Baillie
Eternal '04
All the Good Ones Are Married '07
My Neighbor's Secret '09

Adrienne Bailon (1983-)
The Cheetah Girls '03
The Cheetah Girls 2 '06
The Cheetah Girls: One World '08
The Coalition '13

Kirk Baily (1952-)
Voodoo Dawn '89
The Sixth Man '97
3 Ninjas: High Noon at Mega Mountain '97

Barbara Bain (1931-)
Murder Once Removed '71
Destination Moonbase Alpha '75
Spirit of '76 '91
Panic '00
American Gun '02
Trapped '06
Haunted Echoes '08

Conrad Bain (1923-2013)
The Anderson Tapes '71
Bananas '71
C.H.O.M.P.S. '79
Child Bride of Short Creek '81
Postcards from the Edge '90

Cynthia Bain (1963-)
Pumpkinhead '88
Spontaneous Combustion '89
Danielle Steel's Changes '91

Sherry Bain (1947-)
The Hard Ride '71
Wild Riders '71
Jailbreakin' '72

Fay Bainter (1892-1968)
Make Way for Tomorrow '37
Quality Street '37
Jezebel '38
The Shining Hour '38
Daughters Courageous '39
Our Town '40
Young Tom Edison '40
Babes on Broadway '41
Journey for Margaret '42
Woman of the Year '42
Cry Havoc '43
The Human Comedy '43
Presenting Lily Mars '43
Salute to the Marines '43
Dark Waters '44
The Heavenly Body '44
State Fair '45
The Kid from Brooklyn '46
The Virginian '46
Deep Valley '47
The Secret Life of Walter Mitty '47

Close to My Heart '51
The Children's Hour '61

Jimmy Baio (1962-)
The Bad News Bears in Breaking Training '77
Brass '85
Playing for Keeps '86

Scott Baio (1960-)
Bugsy Malone '76
Foxes '80
Senior Trip '81
Zapped! '82
Alice in Wonderland '85
I Love N.Y. '87
Bar Hopping '00
The Bread, My Sweet '01
Cursed '04 (C)
Superbabies: Baby Geniuses 2 '04
Finish Line '08

Diora Baird (1983-)
Bachelor Party Vegas '05
Wedding Crashers '05
Accepted '06
Hot Tamale '06
The Texas Chainsaw Massacre: The Beginning '06
My Best Friend's Girl '08
Night of the Demons '09
Stan Helsing '09
30 Days of Night: Dark Days '10
Transit '12
Riddle '13

Harry Baird (1931-2005)
Thor and the Amazon Women '60
The Story of a Three Day Pass '68
Castle Keep '69
The Oblong Box '69

Jenni Baird (1976-)
Alien Trespass '09
Backtrack '16

Jimmy Baird (1948-)
Return of Dracula '58
Black Orchid '59

Scott Bairstow (1970-)
White Fang 2: The Myth of the White Wolf '94
Black Circle Boys '97
Killing Mr. Griffin '97
The Postman '97
Two for Texas '97
Wild America '97
Delivered '98
Dead in the Water '01
New Best Friend '02
Tuck Everlasting '02

Mitsuko Baisho (1946-)
Vengeance Is Mine '79
Akira Kurosawa's Dreams '90
The Eel '96

Jon Robin Baitz (1961-)
Last Summer In the Hamptons '96
One Fine Day '96

Helmut Bakaitis (1944-)
The Matrix Reloaded '03
The Matrix Revolutions '03

Richard Bakalyan (1931-2015)
Up Periscope '59
Panic in Year Zero! '62
Von Ryan's Express '65
The St. Valentine's Day Massacre '67
The Computer Wore Tennis Shoes '69
The Strongest Man in the World '75
The Fox and the Hound '81 (V)

Ariyon Bakare (1971-)
A Respectable Trade '98
After the Rain '99
Happy Ever Afters '09
Life '17
Frankie '19

Art Baker (1898-1966)
Homecoming '48
A Southern Yankee '48
Cover Up '49
Impact '49
Massacre River '49
Night Unto Night '49
Task Force '49
The Underworld Story '50

Benny Baker (1907-94)
Murder With Pictures '36
Loan Shark '52

Blanche Baker (1956-)
French Postcards '79
Sixteen Candles '84
Shakedown '88
The Handmaid's Tale '90
Livin' Large '91
Fake '10

Carlee Baker
Wicked Lake '08
The Woman '11

Carroll Baker (1931-)
Easy to Love '53
Baby Doll '56
Giant '56
The Big Country '58
Bridge to the Sun '61
Something Wild '61
How the West Was Won '63
The Carpetbaggers '64
Cheyenne Autumn '64
The Greatest Story Ever Told '65
Harlow '65
Paranoia '69
Captain Apache '71
Baba Yaga '73
Kiss Me, Kill Me '73
Bloodbath '76
Andy Warhol's Bad '77
The Watcher in the Woods '81
Star 80 '83
Ironweed '87
Kindergarten Cop '90
Dalva '95
The Game '97

Christopher Baker
Ike: Countdown to D-Day '04
The Condemned '07

Colin Baker (1943-)
The Moonstone '72
War and Peace '73
The Waiting Time '99

David Aaron Baker (1963-)
The Tao of Steve '00
Kate & Leopold '01
Kissing Jessica Stein '02
Boarding School '18

Diane Baker (1938-)
The Best of Everything '59
The Diary of Anne Frank '59
Journey to the Center of the Earth '59
The 300 Spartans '62
The Prize '63
Stolen Hours '63
Marnie '64
Strait-Jacket '64
Mirage '66
The Horse in the Gray Flannel Suit '68
Krakatoa East of Java '69
Killer by Night '72
Baker's Hawk '76
A Woman of Substance '84
The Silence of the Lambs '91
The Joy Luck Club '93
Twenty Bucks '93
Imaginary Crimes '94
The Net '95
The Cable Guy '96
Murder at 1600 '97
Jackie Bouvier Kennedy Onassis '00
Harrison's Flowers '02
The Keeper: The Legend of Omar Khayyam '05
The Surrogate '13

Dylan Baker (1959-)
Planes, Trains & Automobiles '87
The Long Walk Home '89
Delirious '91
The Last of the Mohicans '92
Love Potion #9 '92
Disclosure '94
Celebrity '98
From the Earth to the Moon '98
Happiness '98
Oxygen '99
Random Hearts '99
Simply Irresistible '99
The Cell '00
Thirteen Days '00
Along Came a Spider '01
A Gentleman's Game '01
Changing Lanes '02
Road to Perdition '02
Head of State '03
How to Deal '03
Rick '03
Kinsey '04
Spider-Man 2 '04
Hide and Seek '05
Fido '06
Let's Go to Prison '06
The Matador '06
Chicago 10 '07 (V)
The Hunting Party '07
Spider-Man 3 '07
The Stone Angel '07
When a Man Falls in the Forest '07
Diminished Capacity '08
Revolutionary Road '08
Trick 'r Treat '08
Secretariat '10
Think of Me '11
About Sunny '12
Selma '14
The Benefactor '16

Fay Baker (1917-87)
The Star '52
She Devil '57

Frank Baker (1892-1980)
The New Adventures of Tarzan '35
Tarzan and the Green Goddess '38

George Baker (1931-2011)
Tread Softly Stranger '58
Sword of Lancelot '63
Goodbye, Mr. Chips '69
A Woman of Substance '84
The Charmer '87
Little Lord Fauntleroy '95

Jay Baker (1961-)
April Fool's Day '86
Storm and Sorrow '90
Naked Lies '98

Jill Baker (1951-)
Hope and Glory '87
Catherine Cookson's The Girl '96
Secret Smile '05

Joby Baker (1934-)
Gidget '59
Looking for Love '64
Blackbeard's Ghost '67

Joe Don Baker (1936-)
Cool Hand Luke '67
Guns of the Magnificent Seven '69
Adam at 6 a.m. '70
Mongo's Back In Town '71
Wild Rovers '71
Junior Bonner '72
Welcome Home, Soldier Boys '72
Charley Varrick '73
The Outfit '73
Walking Tall '73
Golden Needles '74
Framed '75
Mitchell '75
The Pack '77
Shadow of Chikara '77
Joy Sticks '83
Final Justice '84
The Natural '84
Fletch '85

Edge of Darkness '86
The Killing Time '87
Leonard Part 6 '87
The Living Daylights '87
Criminal Law '89
Cape Fear '91
Citizen Cohn '92
The Distinguished Gentleman '92
Reality Bites '94
Congo '95
Felony '95
Goldeneye '95
The Grass Harp '95
Panther '95
The Underneath '95
Mars Attacks! '96
George Wallace '97
Tomorrow Never Dies '97
Poodle Springs '98
The Dukes of Hazzard '05
Strange Wilderness '08

Jolyon Baker
Duel of Hearts '92
Final Analysis '92
Attila '01
Out of the Ashes '03

Jonathan Baker
Savage Harvest 2: October Blood '06
Great World of Sound '07

Jordan Baker
Paparazzi '04
Another Earth '11

Josephine Baker (1906-75)
Siren of the Tropics '27
Zou Zou '34
Princess Tam Tam '35

Kathy Baker (1950-)
The Right Stuff '83
A Killing Affair '85
Street Smart '87
Clean and Sober '88
Permanent Record '88
Dad '89
The Image '89
Jacknife '89
Edward Scissorhands '90
Article 99 '92
Jennifer 8 '92
Mad Dog and Glory '93
To Gillian on Her 37th Birthday '96
Inventing the Abbotts '97
Weapons of Mass Distraction '97
The Cider House Rules '99
Ratz '99
A Season for Miracles '99
Things You Can Tell Just by Looking at Her '00
The Glass House '01
A Little Inside '01
Too Young to Be a Dad '02
Assassination Tango '03
Cold Mountain '03
13 Going on 30 '04
Nine Lives '05
Sucker Free City '05
All the King's Men '06
The Jane Austen Book Club '07
Jesse Stone: Sea Change '07
Last Chance Harvey '08
Jesse Stone: Thin Ice '09
Jesse Stone: No Remorse '10
Miss Nobody '10
Good Day for It '11
Jesse Stone: Innocents Lost '11
Machine Gun Preacher '11
Take Shelter '11
Big Miracle '12
Jesse Stone: Benefit of the Doubt '12
Saving Mr. Banks '13
Return to Zero '14
The Age of Adaline '15
Boulevard '15
The Ballad of Lefty Brown '17

Kenny Baker (1934-)
Star Wars *'77*
The Elephant Man *'80*
The Empire Strikes Back *'80*
Time Bandits *'81*
Return of the Jedi *'83*
Amadeus *'84*
Sleeping Beauty *'89*
Star Wars: Episode 2-Attack of the Clones *'02*
Star Wars: Episode 3-Revenge of the Sith *'05*

Kenny L. Baker (1912-85)
At the Circus *'39*
Silver Skates *'43*
The Harvey Girls *'46*

Kirsten Baker (1962-)
Gas Pump Girls *'79*
Friday the 13th, Part 2 *'81*

Max Baker
Looking for Kitty *'04*
Bailey's Billion$ *'05*
Constantine *'05*
The Island *'05*
Newlyweds *'11*

Phil Baker (1896-1963)
The Goldwyn Follies *'38*
The Gang's All Here *'43*

Ray Baker (1948-)
Places in the Heart *'84*
Everybody's All American *'88*
Heart Condition *'90*
Camp Nowhere *'94*
Speechless *'94*
Anywhere But Here *'99*
The Trip *'02*
44 Minutes: The North Hollywood Shootout *'03*
Without a Paddle *'04*

Rick Baker (1950-)
The Thing with Two Heads *'72*
King Kong *'76*
Kentucky Fried Movie *'77*

Robert Baker (1979-)
Chinese Connection *'73*
Out of Time *'03*
Seraphim Falls *'06*
Special *'06*
Save Me *'07*

Sarah Baker
The Campaign *'12*
The Death of Dick Long *'19*

Simon Baker (1969-)
L.A. Confidential *'97*
Most Wanted *'97*
Restaurant *'98*
Smoke Signals *'98*
Ride with the Devil *'99*
Sunset Strip *'99*
Red Planet *'00*
The Affair of the Necklace *'01*
The Missing *'03*
Book of Love *'04*
George A. Romero's Land of the Dead *'05*
The Ring 2 *'05*
The Devil Wears Prada *'06*
Something New *'06*
Sex and Death 101 *'07*
The Lodger *'09*
Not Forgotten *'09*
Women in Trouble *'09*
The Killer Inside Me *'10*
Margin Call *'11*
I Give It a Year *'13*

Stanley Baker (1928-76)
The Hidden Room *'49*
Lilli Marlene *'50*
The Cruel Sea *'53*
Knights of the Round Table *'53*
Richard III *'55*
Child in the House *'56*
Helen of Troy *'56*
Campbell's Kingdom *'57*
Yesterday's Enemy *'59*
The Guns of Navarone *'61*
Very Important Person *'61*
Eva *'62*
Sodom and Gomorrah *'62*
In the French Style *'63*
Zulu *'64*
Sands of the Kalahari *'65*
Accident *'67*
The Last Grenade *'70*
Butterfly Affair *'71*
A Lizard in a Woman's Skin *'71*
Innocent Bystanders *'72*
Zorro *'74*

Stephen Baker
Little Marines *'90*
Dead Lenny *'06*

Timothy Baker
Bloodfist 2 *'90*
Out for Blood *'93*

Tom Baker (1934-)
Angels Die Hard *'70*
Nicholas and Alexandra *'71*
The Freakmaker *'73*
Golden Voyage of Sinbad *'73*
Vault of Horror *'73*
Candy Stripe Nurses *'74*
The Chronicles of Narnia *'89*
Selling Hitler *'91*
Dungeons and Dragons *'00*
Doogal *'05 (V)*

Edward Baker-Duly (1977-)
De-Lovely *'04*
Botched *'07*
Upstairs Downstairs *'11*

Gary Bakewell
Backbeat *'94*
Neil Gaiman's NeverWhere *'96*

William 'Billy' Bakewell (1908-93)
West Point *'27*
Battle of the Sexes *'28*
The Iron Mask *'29*
On with the Show *'29*
All Quiet on the Western Front *'30*
Dance Fools Dance *'31*
Politics *'31*
Reducing *'31*
Three-Cornered Moon *'33*
The Quitter *'34*
Exiled to Shanghai *'37*
Mile a Minute Love *'37*
Gone with the Wind *'39*
Romance on the High Seas *'48*
You Gotta Stay Happy *'48*
The Capture *'50*
Radar Men from the Moon *'52*
Lucky Me *'54*
Davy Crockett, King of the Wild Frontier *'55*

Dato Bakhtadze
Wanted *'08*
The Darkest Hour *'11*

Brenda Bakke (1963-)
Hardbodies 2 *'86*
Hot Shots! Part Deux *'93*
Lone Justice 2 *'93*
Star Quest *'94*
Tales from the Crypt Presents Demon Knight *'94*
Under Siege 2: Dark Territory *'95*
Lone Justice 3: Showdown at Plum Creek *'96*
The Fixer *'97*
Trucks *'97*
Shelter *'98*
The Quickie *'01*

Brigitte Bako (1967-)
Red Shoe Diaries *'92*
A Man in Uniform *'93*
Replikator: Cloned to Kill *'94*
Strange Days *'95*
Dinner and Driving *'97*
Paranoia *'98*

Adam Bakri
Omar *'13*
Official Secrets *'19*

Muhamad (Mohammed) Bakri (1953-)
Cup Final *'92*
The Mummy Lives *'93*
The Lark Farm *'07*

Saleh Bakri
The Band's Visit *'07*
Salt of the Sea *'08*

Scott Bakula (1954-)
Sibling Rivalry *'90*
Necessary Roughness *'91*
Mercy Mission *'93*
Color of Night *'94*
My Family *'94*
Lord of Illusions *'95*
Cats Don't Dance *'97 (V)*
Major League 3: Back to the Minors *'98*
Tom Clancy's Netforce *'98*
American Beauty *'99*
Luminarias *'99*
Above Suspicion *'00*
The Trial of Old Drum *'00*
A Girl Thing *'01*
Life as a House *'01*
Blue Smoke *'07*
The Informant! *'09*
Behind the Candelabra *'13*
Elsa & Fred *'14*

Bob Balaban (1945-)
Midnight Cowboy *'69*
Catch-22 *'70*
The Strawberry Statement *'70*
Bank Shot *'74*
Report to the Commissioner *'75*
Close Encounters of the Third Kind *'77*
Girlfriends *'78*
Altered States *'80*
Absence of Malice *'81*
Whose Life Is It Anyway? *'81*
2010: The Year We Make Contact *'84*
End of the Line *'88*
Dead Bang *'89*
Alice *'90*
Bob Roberts *'92*
Amos and Andrew *'93*
For Love or Money *'93*
Greedy *'94*
Pie in the Sky *'95*
The Late Shift *'96*
Waiting for Guffman *'96*
Clockwatchers *'97*
Deconstructing Harry *'97*
No Money Down *'97*
The Cradle Will Rock *'99*
Jakob the Liar *'99*
Swing Vote *'99*
Three to Tango *'99*
Best in Show *'00*
Ghost World *'01*
Gosford Park *'01*
The Majestic *'01*
The Mexican *'01*
A Mighty Wind *'03*
Marie and Bruce *'04*
Capote *'05*
For Your Consideration *'06*
Lady in the Water *'06*
Dedication *'07*
No Reservations *'07*
Recount *'08*
Howl *'10*
Girl Most Likely *'12*
Thin Ice *'12*
The Monuments Men *'13*
The Grand Budapest Hotel *'14 (C)*
Isle of Dogs *'18 (V)*
An L.A. Minute *'18*

Liane Balaban (1980-)
New Waterford Girl *'99*
World Traveler *'01*
Spliced *'03*
Eternal *'04*
Above and Beyond *'06*
St. Urbain's Horseman *'07*
Definitely, Maybe *'08*
Last Chance Harvey *'08*
One Week *'08*
Coach *'10*
The Grand Seduction *'13*

Belinda Balaski (1947-)
Cannonball *'76*
The Howling *'81*
Proud Men *'87*
Gremlins 2: The New Batch *'90*
Runaway Daughters *'94*

Josiane Balasko (1950-)
French Fried Vacation *'79*
Hotel America *'81*
Too Beautiful for You *'88*
Grosse Fatigue *'94*
French Twist *'95*
Ruby Blue *'07*
A French Gigolo *'08*
The Hedgehog *'09*
Retour Chez Ma Mere *'16*
Let the Sunshine In *'17*

Leonor Baldaque
I'm Going Home *'00*
Belle Toujours *'06*

Raf Baldassarre
Gun for 100 Graves *'68*
Thor the Conqueror *'83*

Rebecca Balding
Deadly Game *'77*
Silent Scream *'80*

Renato Baldini (1921-95)
Submarine Attack *'54*
The Snow Devils *'67*

A. Michael Baldwin (1963-)
Phantasm *'79*
Phantasm 3: Lord of the Dead *'94*
Vice Girls *'96*
Phantasm 4: Oblivion *'98*
Phantasm: Ravager *'16*

Adam Baldwin (1962-)
My Bodyguard *'80*
Ordinary People *'80*
D.C. Cab *'84*
Reckless *'84*
3:15: The Moment of Truth *'86*
Full Metal Jacket *'87*
The Chocolate War *'88*
Cohen and Tate *'88*
Next of Kin *'89*
Predator 2 *'90*
Guilty by Suspicion *'91*
Deadbolt *'92*
Radio Flyer *'92*
Where the Day Takes You *'92*
Cold Sweat *'93*
800 Leagues Down the Amazon *'93*
Blind Justice *'94*
Digital Man *'94*
Wyatt Earp *'94*
Independence Day *'96*
From the Earth to the Moon *'98*
Dr. Jekyll & Mr. Hyde *'99*
The Patriot *'00*
The Right Temptation *'00*
Double Bang *'01*
Jackpot *'01*
Hypersonic *'02*
Lady Jayne Killer *'03*
Evil Eyes *'04*
The Poseidon Adventure *'05*
Serenity *'05*
The Thirst *'06*
Gospel Hill *'08*
Frenemy *'09*
InSight *'11*

Alec Baldwin (1958-)
Code of Honor *'84*
Dress Gray *'86*
The Alamo: Thirteen Days to Glory *'87*
Forever, Lulu *'87*
Beetlejuice *'88*
Married to the Mob *'88*
She's Having a Baby *'88*
Talk Radio *'88*
Working Girl *'88*
Great Balls of Fire *'89*
Alice *'90*
The Hunt for Red October *'90*
Miami Blues *'90*
The Marrying Man *'91*
Glengarry Glen Ross *'92*
Prelude to a Kiss *'92*
The Getaway *'93*
Malice *'93*
The Shadow *'94*
Heaven's Prisoners *'95*
A Streetcar Named Desire *'95*
Ghosts of Mississippi *'96*
The Juror *'96*
Looking for Richard *'96*
Two Bits *'96 (V)*
The Edge *'97*
The Confession *'98*
Mercury Rising *'98*
Outside Providence *'99*
Thick as Thieves *'99*
Nuremberg *'00*
State and Main *'00*
Thomas and the Magic Railroad *'00*
Cats & Dogs *'01 (V)*
Final Fantasy: The Spirits Within *'01 (V)*
Pearl Harbor *'01*
The Royal Tenenbaums *'01 (N)*
Path to War *'02*
The Cooler *'03*
Dr. Seuss' The Cat in the Hat *'03*
Along Came Polly *'04*
The Aviator *'04*
The Last Shot *'04*
The SpongeBob SquarePants Movie *'04 (V)*
Elizabethtown *'05*
Fun With Dick and Jane *'05*
The Departed *'06*
The Good Shepherd *'06*
Running with Scissors *'06*
Brooklyn Rules *'07*
Suburban Girl *'07*
Lymelife *'08*
Madagascar: Escape 2 Africa *'08 (V)*
My Best Friend's Girl *'08*
It's Complicated *'09*
My Sister's Keeper *'09*
Cats & Dogs: The Revenge of Kitty Galore *'10 (V)*
Hick *'11*
Rise of the Guardians *'12 (V)*
Rock of Ages *'12*
To Rome with Love *'12*
Blue Jasmine *'13*
Still Alice *'14*
Concussion *'15*
Andron: The Black Labyrinth *'16*
Rules Don't Apply *'16*
The Boss Baby *'17*
Paris Can Wait *'17*
The Public *'18*
Drunk Parents *'19*
Motherless Brooklyn *'19*

Daniel Baldwin (1960-)
Born on the Fourth of July *'89*
Harley Davidson and the Marlboro Man *'91*
Attack of the 50 Ft. Woman *'93*
Knight Moves *'93*
Car 54, Where Are You? *'94*
Family of Cops *'95*
Mulholland Falls *'95*
The Invader *'96*
Tree's Lounge *'96*
John Carpenter's Vampires *'97*
Love Kills *'98*
On the Border *'98*
Phoenix *'98*
The Treat *'98*
Active Stealth *'99*
Desert Thunder *'99*
Silicon Towers *'99*
Wild Grizzly *'99*
Homicide: The Movie *'00*
In Pursuit *'00*
Killing Moon *'00*
King of the Ants *'03*
Water's Edge *'03*
Anonymous Rex *'04*
Paparazzi *'04*
Stealing Candy *'04*
Sidekick *'05*
Final Move *'06*
The Devil's Dominoes *'07*
Moola *'07*
Born of Earth *'08*
Grey Gardens *'09*
Death and Cremation *'10*
Nine Dead *'10*
The Truth *'10*

Dick Baldwin (1911-96)
International Settlement *'38*
Mr. Moto's Gamble *'38*

Janit Baldwin (1953-)
Born Innocent *'74*
The California Kid *'74*
Ruby *'77*
Humongous *'82*

Peter Baldwin (1929-)
Era Notte a Roma *'60*
The Ghost *'63*

Robert Baldwin (1904-96)
Meet Dr. Christian *'39*
Courageous Dr. Christian *'40*
Gambling Daughters *'41*

Stephen Baldwin (1966-)
The Beast *'88*
Born on the Fourth of July *'89*
Last Exit to Brooklyn *'90*
Crossing the Bridge *'92*
Posse *'93*
8 Seconds *'94*
Fall Time *'94*
The Great American Sex Scandal *'94*
A Simple Twist of Fate *'94*
Threesome *'94*
The Usual Suspects *'95*
Bio-Dome *'96*
Crimetime *'96*
Fled *'96*
Half-Baked *'97*
Sub Down *'97*
Dean Koontz's Mr. Murder *'98*
One Tough Cop *'98*
Scarred City *'98*
Absence of the Good *'99*
Friends & Lovers *'99*
The Sex Monster *'99*
Cutaway *'00*
The Flintstones in Viva Rock Vegas *'00*
Mercy *'00*
Table One *'00*
Xchange *'00*
Dead Awake *'01*
Greenmail *'01*
Protection *'01*
Spider's Web *'01*
Zebra Lounge *'01*
Slap Shot 2: Breaking the Ice *'02*
Firefight *'03*
Lost Treasure *'03*
Shelter Island *'03*
Six: The Mark Unleashed *'04*
Bound by Lies *'05*
Snakeman *'05*
Earthstorm *'06*
Jesse Stone: Night Passage *'06*
Midnight Clear *'06*
Death Squad *'14*

Walter Baldwin (1889-1977)
Mr. Winkle Goes to War *'44*
The Best Years of Our Lives *'46*
Winter Meeting *'48*
The Long, Long Trailer *'54*
Interrupted Melody *'55*

William Baldwin (1963-)
Born on the Fourth of July *'89*
Flatliners *'90*
Internal Affairs *'90*
Backdraft *'91*
Sliver *'93*
Three of Hearts *'93*
Curdled *'95*
Fair Game *'95*

A Pyromaniac's Love Story '95
Shattered Image '98
Virus '98
Brotherhood of Murder '99
Relative Values '99
Double Bang '01
Say Nothing '01
You Stupid Man '02
Art Heist '05
The Squid and the Whale '05
Full Count '06
Adrift in Manhattan '07
Humble Pie '07
Noise '07
Forgetting Sarah Marshall '08
A Plumm Summer '08
The Craigslist Killer '11
Be My Valentine '13
Sexy Evil Genius '13
The Stranger Within '13
Welcome to Acapulco '19

Christian Bale (1974-)
Empire of the Sun '87
The Land of Faraway '87
Henry V '89
Treasure Island '89
A Murder of Quality '90
Newsies '92
Swing Kids '93
Little Women '94
Royal Deceit '94
Pocahontas '95 (V)
Portrait of a Lady '96
The Secret Agent '96
Metroland '97
All the Little Animals '98
Velvet Goldmine '98
American Psycho '99
Mary, Mother of Jesus '99
William Shakespeare's A Midsummer Night's Dream '99
Shaft '00
Captain Corelli's Mandolin '01
Equilibrium '02
Laurel Canyon '02
Reign of Fire '02
Howl's Moving Castle '04 (V)
The Machinist '04
Batman Begins '05
Harsh Times '05
The New World '05
The Prestige '06
Rescue Dawn '06
I'm Not There '07
3:10 to Yuma '07
The Dark Knight '08
Public Enemies '09
Terminator Salvation '09
The Fighter '10
The Flowers of War '11
The Dark Knight Rises '12
American Hustle '13
Out of the Furnace '13
Exodus: Gods and Kings '14
The Big Short '15
Knight of Cups '15
Hostiles '17
The Promise '17
Mowgli: Legend of the Jungle '18
Vice '18
Ford v Ferrari '19

Caitriona Balfe (1979-)
Money Monster '16
Ford v Ferrari '19

Eric Balfour (1977-)
What Women Want '00
The Texas Chainsaw Massacre '03
Face of Terror '04
The Elder Son '06
Rx '06
Hell Ride '08
The Spirit '08
Horsemen '09
Rise of the Gargoyles '09
Dinoshark '10
Skyline '10
Cell 213 '11

Michael Balfour (1918-97)
Moulin Rouge '52
Genevieve '53
Murder on Approval '56
Quatermass 2 '57
Fiend without a Face '58
The Flesh and the Fiends '60
The Private Life of Sherlock Holmes '70
The Canterbury Tales '71

Jennifer Balgobin
Repo Man '83
City Limits '85
Roadside Prophets '92

Jeanne Balibar (1968-)
My Sex Life. . . Or How I Got into an Argument '96
Late August, Early September '98
Comedy of Innocence '00
Sade '00
Va Savoir '01
Code 46 '03
Clean '04
The Duchess of Langeais '07
The Girl From Monaco '08

Ina Balin (1937-90)
Black Orchid '59
From the Terrace '60
The Comancheros '61
The Patsy '64
Charro! '69
The Projectionist '71
The Don Is Dead '73
Hostage Flight '85

Andras Balint (1943-)
Father '67
Love Film '70
25 Fireman's Street '73
Colonel Redl '84
Citizen X '95
The Moon & the Stars '07

Eszter Balint (1966-)
Stranger than Paradise '84
The Linguini Incident '92
Tree's Lounge '96

Fairuza Balk (1974-)
Return to Oz '85
The Worst Witch '86
Valmont '89
Gas Food Lodging '92
Imaginary Crimes '94
Things to Do in Denver When You're Dead '95
The Craft '96
The Island of Dr. Moreau '96
American History X '98
The Maker '98
The Waterboy '98
Almost Famous '00
Life in the Fast Lane '00
Red Letters '00
Deuces Wild '02
Personal Velocity: Three Portraits '02
Don't Come Knocking '05
Wild Tigers I Have Known '06
Grindstone Road '07
Humboldt County '08
Bad Lieutenant: Port of Call New Orleans '09
Dose of Reality '12
Beyond Clueless '14

Angeline Ball (1969-)
The Commitments '91
Trojan Eddie '96
The Gambler '97
The General '98
Terror in the Mall '98
Kitchen Privileges '00
Bait '02
Bloom '03

Lucille Ball (1911-89)
Murder at the Vanities '34
Roberta '35
Top Hat '35
Follow the Fleet '36
Stage Door '37
Having a Wonderful Time '38
Joy of Living '38
Next Time I Marry '38
Room Service '38
Dance, Girl, Dance '40
Too Many Girls '40
Look Who's Laughing '41
Big Street '42
Seven Days' Leave '42
Best Foot Forward '43
Du Barry Was a Lady '43
Thousands Cheer '43
Meet the People '44
Without Love '45
Dark Corner '46
Easy to Wed '46
Two Smart People '46
Ziegfeld Follies '46
Her Husband's Affairs '47
Lured '47
Easy Living '49
Miss Grant Takes Richmond '49
Sorrowful Jones '49
Fancy Pants '50
The Fuller Brush Girl '50
The Magic Carpet '51
The Long, Long Trailer '54
Forever Darling '56
The Facts of Life '60
Critic's Choice '63
A Guide for the Married Man '67 (C)
Yours, Mine & Ours '68
Mame '74

Nicholas Ball (1946-)
Lifeforce '85
Croupier '97

Sam Ball
The Absent '11
The Pact '12

Samuel Ball (1973-)
Urbania '00
The Last Castle '01
Pumpkin '02
Net Games '03
Misconceptions '08

Suzan Ball
Yankee Buccaneer '52
War Arrow '53

Vincent Ball (1923-)
Terror Ship '54
Blood of the Vampire '58
Sea of Sand '58
A Matter of WHO '62
Where Eagles Dare '68
Oh! What a Lovely War '69
Not Tonight Darling '72
Breaker Morant '80
Sirens '94

Carl Ballantine (1917-2009)
Speedway '68
The Girl Most Likely to. . . '73
Revenge of the Cheerleaders '76
World's Greatest Lover '77
Mr. Saturday Night '92
Dying to Get Rich '98

Jeff(rey) Ballard (1987-)
Children of the Corn: Revelation '01
Dead in a Heartbeat '02
National Lampoon's Ratko: The Dictator's Son '09
The Marine 3: Homefront '11
Pressed '11
Perfect Sisters '14

Kaye Ballard (1925-)
Freaky Friday '76
The Ritz '76
Tiger Warsaw '87
Modern Love '90
Ava's Magical Adventure '94

Ella Ballentine
Against the Wild II: Survive the Seregenti '16
Milton's Secret '16
The Monster '16
Standoff '16

Edoardo Ballerini (1970-)
I Shot Andy Warhol '96
The Pest '96
Looking for an Echo '99
Dinner Rush '00
Romeo Must Die '00
No God, No Master '12

Timothy Balme (1967-)
Dead Alive '93
Jack Brown, Genius '94
The Vector File '03

Jean-Francois Balmer (1946-)
Madame Bovary '91
Beaumarchais the Scoundrel '96
The Swindle '97
Time Regained '99
Belphegor: Phantom of the Louvre '01
Comedy of Power '06
Tokyo! '09
Cosmos '16

Martin Balsam (1919-96)
Time Limit '57
Twelve Angry Men '57
Marjorie Morningstar '58
Al Capone '59
Middle of the Night '59
Psycho '60
Ada '61
Breakfast at Tiffany's '61
Cape Fear '61
The Carpetbaggers '64
Seven Days in May '64
Bedford Incident '65
Harlow '65
A Thousand Clowns '65
After the Fox '66
Hombre '67
The Good Guys and the Bad Guys '69
Catch-22 '70
Little Big Man '70
Tora! Tora! Tora! '70
The Anderson Tapes '71
Brand New Life '72
Confessions of a Police Captain '72
Eyes Behind the Stars '72
The Stone Killer '73
Summer Wishes, Winter Dreams '73
Murder on the Orient Express '74
The Taking of Pelham One Two Three '74
Death Among Friends '75
Mitchell '75
All the President's Men '76
The Lindbergh Kidnapping Case '76
Meet Him and Die '76
Two Minute Warning '76
Contract on Cherry Street '77
Death Rage '77
Raid on Entebbe '77
The House on Garibaldi Street '79
The People *vs.* Jean Harris '81
The Salamander '82
Death Wish 3 '85
St. Elmo's Fire '85
Delta Force '86
Queenie '87
Two Evil Eyes '90
Cape Fear '91

Talia Balsam (1959-)
Mass Appeal '84
Nadia '84
Crawlspace '86
In the Mood '87
Coldblooded '94 (C)
Into the Fire '05
All the King's Men '06
The Cake Eaters '07
The Wackness '08
No Strings Attached '11
Return '11
The Girl in the Book '15

Kirk Baltz (1959-)
Reservoir Dogs '92
Following Her Heart '94
Probable Cause '95
Forfeit '07

Alexander Baluyev (1958-)
The Peacemaker '97
Deep Impact '98

David Bamber (1954-)
High Hopes '88
The Buddha of Suburbia '92
Stalag Luft '93
Pride and Prejudice '95
The Railway Children '00
Daniel Deronda '02
Miss Potter '06
Valkyrie '08
Collision '09

Jamie Bamber (1973-)
Lady Audley's Secret '00
Band of Brothers '01
Horatio Hornblower: The Adventure Continues '01
Daniel Deronda '02
Pulse 2: Afterlife '08
John Doe: Vigilante '14

Judy Bamber (1936-)
A Bucket of Blood '59
The Atomic Brain '64

Gerry Bamman (1941-)
The Chase '91
Home Alone 2: Lost in New York '92
Lorenzo's Oil '92
Runaway Jury '03

Eric Bana (1968-)
The Castle '97
Chopper '00
Black Hawk Down '01
The Nugget '02
Finding Nemo '03 (V)
Hulk '03
Troy '04
Munich '05
Lucky You '07
Romulus, My Father '07
The Other Boleyn Girl '08
Funny People '09
Mary and Max '09
Star Trek '09
The Time Traveler's Wife '09
Hanna '11
Deadfall '12
Closed Circuit '13
Lone Survivor '13
Deliver Us From Evil '14
The Finest Hours '16
King Arthur: Legend of the Sword '17
The Forgiven '18

Orly Silbersatz Banai
Broken Wings '02
Yossi '12

Anne Bancroft (1931-2005)
Don't Bother to Knock '52
Demetrius and the Gladiators '54
Savage Wilderness '55
Nightfall '56
Girl in Black Stockings '57
The Miracle Worker '62
The Pumpkin Eater '64
The Slender Thread '65
The Graduate '67
Young Winston '72
Prisoner of Second Avenue '74
The Hindenburg '75
Arthur Hailey's The Moneychangers '76
Lipstick '76
Silent Movie '76
Jesus of Nazareth '77
The Turning Point '77
The Bell Jar '79
The Elephant Man '80
Fatso '80
To Be or Not to Be '83
Garbo Talks '84
Agnes of God '85
84 Charing Cross Road '86
'night, Mother '86
Torch Song Trilogy '88
Bert Rigby, You're a Fool '89
Honeymoon in Vegas '92
Love Potion #9 '92
Malice '93
Mr. Jones '93
Point of No Return '93
Dracula: Dead and Loving It '95
Home for the Holidays '95
How to Make an American Quilt '95
Oldest Confederate Widow Tells All '95
Homecoming '96
Sunchaser '96
Critical Care '97
G.I. Jane '97
Great Expectations '97
Antz '98 (V)
Keeping the Faith '00
Up at the Villa '00
Heartbreakers '01
The Roman Spring of Mrs. Stone '03
Delgo '08 (V)

Bradford Bancroft
Bachelor Party '84
Damned River '89
A Time to Die '91

Cameron Bancroft (1967-)
Anything for Love '93
Just One of the Girls '93
Love and Human Remains '93
MVP2: Most Vertical Primate '01
Anything But Love '02
He Sees You When You're Sleeping '02
Don't Cry Now '07
Mail Order Bride '08
Flirting with Forty '09
Tornado Valley '09
Garage Sale Mystery '13

George Bancroft (1882-1956)
White Gold '28
Mr. Deeds Goes to Town '36
Angels with Dirty Faces '38
Each Dawn I Die '39
Stagecoach '39
Little Men '40
Young Tom Edison '40
Texas '41
Syncopation '42
Whistling in Dixie '42

Antonio Banderas (1960-)
Law of Desire '86
Matador '86
Women on the Verge of a Nervous Breakdown '88
If They Tell You I Fell '89
Against the Wind '90
Tie Me Up! Tie Me Down! '90
Terranova '91
The Mambo Kings '92
The House of the Spirits '93
Outrage '93
Philadelphia '93
Interview with the Vampire '94
Of Love and Shadows '94
Assassins '95
Desperado '95
Four Rooms '95
Miami Rhapsody '95
Never Talk to Strangers '95
Evita '96
Two Much '96
The Mask of Zorro '98
Play It to the Bone '99
The 13th Warrior '99
White River '99
The Body '01
Original Sin '01
Spy Kids '01
Ballistic: Ecks *vs.* Sever '02
Femme Fatale '02
Frida '02
Spy Kids 2: The Island of Lost Dreams '02
And Starring Pancho Villa as Himself '03
Once Upon a Time in Mexico '03
Spy Kids 3-D: Game Over '03
Imagining Argentina '04
Shrek 2 '04 (V)
The Legend of Zorro '05
Bordertown '06
Take the Lead '06
Shrek the Third '07 (V)
My Mom's New Boyfriend '08

The Other Man '08
The Code '09
Shrek Forever After '10 (V)
You Will Meet a Tall Dark Stranger '10
The Big Bang '11
Day of the Falcon '11
Puss in Boots '11 (V)
The Skin I Live In '11
Spy Kids 4: All the Time in the World '11
Haywire '12
Ruby Sparks '12
Machete Kills '13
The Expendables 3 '14
The SpongeBob Movie: Sponge Out of Water '15
The 33 '15
Finding Altamira '16
Acts of Vengeance '17
Black Butterfly '17
Bullet Head '17
Gun Shy '17
The Laundromat '19
Pain and Glory '19
Dolittle '20

Richard Banel (1988-)
Edges of the Lord '01
The Interrogation of Michael Crowe '02

Victor Banerjee (1946-)
Hullabaloo over Georgie & Bonnie's Pictures '78
A Passage to India '84
Foreign Body '86
Bitter Moon '92

Lisa Banes (1955-)
The Hotel New Hampshire '84
Marie '85
Cocktail '88
Dragonfly '02
Pumpkin '02
Legally Blondes '09
Gone Girl '14

Claes Bang
The Square '17
The Burnt Orange Heresy '20

Joy Bang (1947-)
Play It Again, Sam '72
Messiah of Evil '74

Tallulah Bankhead (1902-68)
The Cheat '31
The Devil and the Deep '32
Faithless '32
Stage Door Canteen '43
Lifeboat '44
A Royal Scandal '45
Die! Die! My Darling! '65

Aaron Banks
The Bodyguard '76
Fist of Fear, Touch of Death '80

Boyd Banks (1964-)
Dawn of the Dead '04
George A. Romero's Land of the Dead '05

Dennis Banks (1937-)
The Last of the Mohicans '92
Thunderheart '92

Elizabeth Banks (1974-)
Wet Hot American Summer '01
Ordinary Sinner '02
Swept Away '02
Seabiscuit '03
The Trade '03
Heights '04
Spider-Man 2 '04
The Baxter '05
Daltry Calhoun '05
The 40 Year Old Virgin '05
The Sisters '05
Invincible '06
Slither '06
Fred Claus '07
Meet Bill '07
Spider-Man 3 '07
Comanche Moon '08
Definitely, Maybe '08
Lovely, Still '08
Meet Dave '08
Role Models '08
W. '08
Zack and Miri Make a Porno '08
The Uninvited '09
The Next Three Days '10
The Details '11
Our Idiot Brother '11
The Hunger Games '12
Man on a Ledge '12
People Like Us '12
Pitch Perfect '12
What to Expect When You're Expecting '12
The Hunger Games: Catching Fire '13
Movie 43 '13
The Hunger Games: Mockingjay--Part 1 '14
The Lego Movie '14 (V)
Little Accidents '14
Walk of Shame '14
Every Secret Thing '15
The Hunger Games: Mockingjay-Part 2 '15
Love & Mercy '15
Power Rangers '17
The Happytime Murders '18
Brightburn '19
Charlie's Angels '19
The LEGO Movie 2: The Second Part '19

Emily Banks
Gunfight in Abilene '67
Hell's Bloody Devils '70

Ernie Banks (1931-2015)
King '78
Pastime '91 (C)
Finding Buck McHenry '00
Red Shoe Diaries: Luscious Lola '00

Jonathan Banks (1947-)
The Girl in the Empty Grave '77
The Adventures of Buckaroo Banzai Across the Eighth Dimension '84
Beverly Hills Cop '84
Nadia '84
Armed and Dangerous '86
Assassin '86
Who Is Julia? '86
Cold Steel '87
Nightmare '91
Freejack '92
There Goes the Neighborhood '92
Body Shot '93
Boiling Point '93
Last Man Standing '95
Dark Breed '96
Flipper '96
Dollar for the Dead '98
Foolish '99
Let the Devil Wear Black '99
Crocodile Dundee in Los Angeles '01
R.S.V.P. '02
Reign Over Me '07
Authors Anonymous '14
Horrible Bosses 2 '14
Mudbound '17
The Commuter '18

Leslie Banks (1890-1952)
The Most Dangerous Game '32
The Man Who Knew Too Much '34
Red Ensign '34
Sanders of the River '35
Transatlantic Tunnel '35
Fire Over England '37
Wings of the Morning '37
The Arsenal Stadium Mystery '39
Jamaica Inn '39
Chamber of Horrors '40
21 Days '40
Cottage to Let '41
Henry V '44
Eye Witness '49
Madeleine '50

Tyra Banks (1973-)
Higher Learning '94
Love Stinks '99
Coyote Ugly '00
Life-Size '00
Halloween: Resurrection '02
Tropic Thunder '08 (C)

Vilma Banky (1903-91)
The Eagle '25
The Winning of Barbara Worth '26

Ian Bannen (1928-99)
A Tale of Two Cities '58
Carlton Browne of the F.O. '59
Psyche 59 '64
The Flight of the Phoenix '65
The Hill '65
Too Late the Hero '70
Fright '71
Ride to Glory '71
Doomwatch '72
Driver's Seat '73
From Beyond the Grave '73
Mackintosh Man '73
The Offence '73
Bite the Bullet '75
The Inglorious Bastards '78
Tinker, Tailor, Soldier, Spy '80
Eye of the Needle '81
The Watcher in the Woods '81
Gandhi '82
Defense of the Realm '85
Lamb '85
Hope and Glory '87
Catherine Cookson's The Fifteen Streets '90
Ghost Dad '90
The Big Man: Crossing the Line '91
Blue Ice '92
Damage '92
Braveheart '95
Waking Ned Devine '98
To Walk with Lions '99

David Banner (1974-)
Black Snake Moan '07
The Confidant '10
The Experiment '10
Stomp the Yard 2: Homecoming '10
Lee Daniels' The Butler '13
Carter High '15

Jill Banner (1946-82)
Spider Baby '64
The President's Analyst '67

John Banner (1910-73)
The Fallen Sparrow '43
Immortal Sergeant '43
Guilty of Treason '50
Operation Eichmann '61
36 Hours '64

Kanu Bannerjee (1905-85)
Pather Panchali '54
Aparajito '58

Karuna Bannerjee (1919-2001)
Pather Panchali '54
Aparajito '58

Reggie Bannister (1945-)
Phantasm '79
Phantasm 2 '88
Survival Quest '89
Silent Night, Deadly Night 4: Initiation '90
Phantasm 3: Lord of the Dead '94
Phantasm 4: Oblivion '98
Bubba Ho-Tep '03
Acts of Death '07
The Rage '07
Psychic Experiment '10
Abolition '11
The Ghastly Love of Johnny X '12
Phantasm: Ravager '16

Jack Bannon (1940-)
Miracle of the Heart: A Boys Town Story '86
DaVinci's War '92

Jim Bannon (1911-86)
Johnny O'Clock '47
Miraculous Journey '48
Man from Colorado '49
Unknown World '51

Ildiko Bansagi (1947-)
Mephisto '81
Meeting Venus '91

Chen Baoguo
Women from the Lake of Scented Souls '94
Robin-B-Hood '06

Ivana Baquero
Pan's Labyrinth '06
Feedback '20

Theda Bara (1890-1955)
A Fool There Was '14
The Love Goddesses '65

John Baragrey (1918-75)
Shockproof '49
Pardners '56
Colossus of New York '58
Gamera, the Invincible '66

Angelika Baran
My 5 Wives '00
The Art of Travel '08

Christine Baranski (1952-)
Crackers '84
9 1/2 Weeks '86
The Pick-Up Artist '87
Reversal of Fortune '90
Addams Family Values '93
The Night We Never Met '93
The Ref '93
To Dance with the White Dog '93
The War '94
The Birdcage '95
Jeffrey '95 (C)
New Jersey Drive '95
Bulworth '98
Cruel Intentions '98
The Odd Couple 2 '98
Bowfinger '99
Dr. Seuss' How the Grinch Stole Christmas '00
Chicago '02
The Guru '02
Eloise at the Plaza '03
Marci X '03
Welcome to Mooseport '04
Recipe for a Perfect Christmas '05
Bonneville '06
Falling for Grace '06
Relative Strangers '06
Mamma Mia! '08
The Bounty Hunter '10
Who Is Simon Miller? '11
Into the Woods '14
Trolls '16
A Bad Moms Christmas '17

Olivia Barash (1965-)
Child of Glass '78
Repo Man '83
Tuff Turf '85
Dr. Alien '88

Richie Barathy
Caged Fury '90
Body Trouble '92

Luca Barbareschi (1956-)
Cannibal Holocaust '80
Bye Bye Baby '88

Marc Barbe
My Life and Times with Antonin Artaud '93
Mozart's Sister '10
Almayer's Folly '12

Adrienne Barbeau (1945-)
Return to Fantasy Island '77
The Fog '78
Cannonball Run '81
Escape from New York '81
Creepshow '82
Swamp Thing '82
Next One '84
Seduced '85
Back to School '86
Open House '86
Cannibal Women in the Avocado Jungle of Death '89
Two Evil Eyes '90
Jailbreakers '94
Burial of the Rats '95
Across the Line '00
The Convent '00
Jack Frost 2: Revenge of the Mutant Killer Snowman '00
Ring of Darkness '04
Christmas Do-Over '06
Unholy '07
Reach for Me '08
Tales of Halloween '15

Ellen Barber
Dealing: Or the Berkeley-to-Boston Forty-Brick Lost-Bag Blues '72
The Premonition '75

Frances Barber (1957-)
Home Sweet Home '82
Castaway '87
Prick Up Your Ears '87
A Zed & Two Noughts '88
Behaving Badly '89
The Ice House '97
Photographing Fairies '97
Still Crazy '98
Esther Kahn '00
Shiner '00
Red Siren '02
Goal! The Dream Begins '06
Goal 2: Living the Dream '07
The Escape '18

Gillian Barber (1958-)
In Cold Blood '96
Double Jeopardy '99
Suspicious River '00
Stealing Sinatra '04

Glynis Barber (1955-)
The Terror '79
Edge of Sanity '89
Deja Vu '98

Jay Barber
Alucard '08
Skeleton Key 2: 667, the Neighbor of the Beast '08

Paul Barber (1952-)
The Long Good Friday '80
The Full Monty '96

Urbano Barberini (1961-)
Demons '86
Gor '88
Opera '88
Torrents of Spring '90

Vincent Barbi (1912-98)
The Blob '58
The Astro-Zombies '67
Lady Godiva Rides '68
Runaways '75

George Barbier (1864-1945)
The Smiling Lieutenant '31
No Man of Her Own '32
One Hour with You '32
Turn Back the Clock '33
The Merry Widow '34
The Crusades '35
Here Comes Cookie '35
Life Begins at Forty '35
Old Man Rhythm '35
The Princess Comes Across '36
Wife Versus Secretary '36
It's Love I'm After '37
On the Avenue '37
Waikiki Wedding '37
The Adventures of Marco Polo '38
Little Miss Broadway '38
My Lucky Star '38
The Man Who Came to Dinner '41
Week-End in Havana '41
Thunder Birds '42

Lisa Barbuscia (1971-)
Almost Heroes '97
Highlander: Endgame '00
Bridget Jones's Diary '01

Artur Barcis (1956-)
No End '84
The Decalogue '88

Caroline Barclay
American Gothic '88
Within the Rock '96

Emily Barclay (1984-)
Terror Peak '03
The Silence '06
Legend of the Guardians: The Owls of Ga'Hoole '10 (V)

Joan Barclay (1914-2002)
Finishing School '33
Blake of Scotland Yard '36
Prison Shadows '36
Shadow of Chinatown '36
The Gentleman from Arizona '39

Roy Barcroft (1902-69)
The Frontiersmen '38
The Showdown '40
Hoppy Serves a Writ '43
The Purple Monster Strikes '45
Jesse James Rides Again '47
Lights of Old Santa Fe '47
Spoilers of the North '47
Hoodlum Empire '52
Radar Men from the Moon '52
The WAC From Walla Walla '52
The Last Hunt '56
The Kettles on Old MacDonald's Farm '57
Billy the Kid Versus Dracula '66

Ben Bard (1893-1974)
7th Heaven '27
The Ghost Ship '43

Carlos Bardem (1963-)
Dance with the Devil '97
Che '08
Cell 211 '09
Americano '11
Escobar: Paradise Lost '15

Javier Bardem (1969-)
Running Out of Time '94
Mouth to Mouth '95
Extasis '96
Dance with the Devil '97
Live Flesh '97
Between Your Legs '99
Second Skin '99
Before Night Falls '00
The Dancer Upstairs '02
Mondays in the Sun '02
Collateral '04
The Sea Inside '04
Goya's Ghosts '06
No Country for Old Men '07
Vicky Cristina Barcelona '08
Biutiful '10
Eat, Pray, Love '10
Skyfall '12
To the Wonder '12
The Counselor '13
The Gunman '15
The Last Face '17
mother! '17
Pirates of the Caribbean: Dead Men Tell No Tales '17
Everybody Knows '18

Pilar Bardem (1939-)
Vacas '91
Live Flesh '97

Trevor Bardette (1902-77)
Gun Crazy '49
The Monolith Monsters '57
Thunder Road '58
Papa's Delicate Condition '63

Aleksander Bardini (1913-95)
No End '84
The Decalogue '88
The Double Life of Veronique '91
Trois Couleurs: Blanc '94

Brick Bardo (1940-77)
See Ron Haydock

Brigitte Bardot (1934-)
Doctor at Sea *'56*
Helen of Troy *'56*
Plucking the Daisy *'56*
And God Created Woman *'57*
The Night Heaven Fell *'57*
That Naughty Girl *'58*
Voulez-Vous Danser avec Moi? *'59*
Please Not Now! *'61*
Le Repos du Guerrier *'62*
Love on a Pillow *'62*
Contempt *'64*
Ravishing Idiot *'64*
Dear Brigitte *'65*
Viva Maria! *'65*
A Coeur Joie *'67*
Head Over Heels *'67*
Shalako *'68*
Spirits of the Dead *'68*
The Women *'68*
Don Juan (Or If Don Juan Were a Woman) *'73*

Sonny Barger (1938-)
Hell's Angels on Wheels *'67*
Hell's Angels '69 *'69*

Tawfeek Barhom
The Idol *'15*
Worlds Apart *'17*

Ashraf Barhoum (1979-)
Paradise Now *'05*
The Kingdom *'07*
Agora *'09*

Lynn Bari (1913-89)
Always Goodbye *'38*
Mr. Moto's Gamble *'38*
Charlie Chan in City of Darkness *'39*
The Return of the Cisco Kid *'39*
Kit Carson *'40*
Lillian Russell *'40*
Sleepers West *'41*
China Girl *'42*
The Falcon Takes Over *'42*
Orchestra Wives *'42*
Secret Agent of Japan *'42*
Hello, Frisco, Hello *'43*
The Bridge of San Luis Rey *'44*
Sweet and Low-Down *'44*
Tampico *'44*
Nocturne *'46*
Shock! *'46*
The Amazing Mr. X *'48*
The Kid From Cleveland *'49*
I'd Climb the Highest Mountain *'51*
Has Anybody Seen My Gal? *'52*
I Dream of Jeannie *'52*
Abbott and Costello Meet the Keystone Kops *'54*
Francis Joins the WACs *'54*
Trauma *'62*

Ike Barinholtz (1977-)
Disaster Movie *'08*
Sisters *'15*
Neighbors 2: Sorority Rising *'16*
Mark Felt: The Man Who Brought Down the White House *'17*
Snatched *'17*
Blockers *'18*
The Oath *'18*
The Hunt *'20*

Clive Barker (1952-)
Sleepwalkers *'92*
Quicksilver Highway *'98 (C)*

Eric Barker (1912-90)
Carry On Sergeant *'58*
Carry On Constable *'60*
Dentist In the Chair *'60*
Carry On Spying *'64*

Jess Barker (1912-2000)
Dragonfly Squadron *'54*
Kentucky Rifle *'55*
Shack Out on 101 *'55*
Three Bad Sisters *'56*

Josh Barker
Lethal Target *'99*
Last Stand *'00*
Northfork *'03*

Lex Barker (1919-73)
Mr. Blandings Builds His Dream House *'48*
Tarzan's Magic Fountain *'48*
Tarzan and the Slave Girl *'50*
Tarzan's Peril *'51*
Battles of Chief Pontiac *'52*
Tarzan's Savage Fury *'52*
Tarzan and the She-Devil *'53*
The Black Devils of Kali *'55*
Away All Boats *'56*
The Price of Fear *'56*
Girl in Black Stockings *'57*
Strange Awakening *'58*
La Dolce Vita *'60*
Pirates of the Coast *'61*
The Return of Dr. Mabuse *'61*
The Invisible Dr. Mabuse *'62*
Executioner of Venice *'63*
Apache's Last Battle *'64*
24 Hours to Kill *'65*
A Place Called Glory *'66*
Woman Times Seven *'67*
The Torture Chamber of Dr. Sadism *'69*

Ronnie Barker (1929-2005)
Kill or Cure *'62*
The Man Outside *'68*
Robin and Marian *'76*
Porridge *'91*
The Gathering Storm *'02*
My House in Umbria *'03*

Steve Barkett (1950-)
Aftermath *'85*
Dark Universe *'93*
Bikini Drive-In *'94*

Ellen Barkin (1954-)
Diner *'82*
Daniel *'83*
Eddie and the Cruisers *'83*
Tender Mercies *'83*
The Adventures of Buckaroo Banzai Across the Eighth Dimension *'84*
Harry & Son *'84*
Desert Bloom *'86*
Down by Law *'86*
The Big Easy *'87*
Made in Heaven *'87 (C)*
Blood Money: The Story of Clinton and Nadine *'88*
Johnny Handsome *'89*
Sea of Love *'89*
Switch *'91*
Into the West *'92*
Man Trouble *'92*
Mac *'93*
This Boy's Life *'93*
Bad Company *'94*
Wild Bill *'95*
The Fan *'96*
Trigger Happy *'96*
Fear and Loathing in Las Vegas *'98*
Drop Dead Gorgeous *'99*
White River *'99*
Crime and Punishment in Suburbia *'00*
Mercy *'00*
Someone Like You *'01*
Palindromes *'04*
She Hate Me *'04*
Trust the Man *'06*
Ocean's Thirteen *'07*
Brooklyn's Finest *'09*
Happy Tears *'09*
Operation: Endgame *'10*
Another Happy Day *'11*
Very Good Girls *'13*
The Cobbler *'14*

Marcie Barkin
Chesty Anderson USN *'76*
Fade to Black *'80*

Samantha Barks
Bitter Harvest *'17*
For Love or Money *'19*

Peter Barkworth (1929-2006)
Where Eagles Dare *'68*
The Littlest Horse Thieves *'76*
Champions *'84*

Pat Barlow
April Fool's Day *'86*
Nanny McPhee *'06*

Reginald Barlow
His Private Secretary *'33*
Mutiny Ahead *'35*

Aneurin Barnard (1987-)
Citadel *'12*
The Adventurer: The Curse of the Midas Box *'13*
Trap for Cinderella *'13*
The Truth About Emanuel *'13*
Bitter Harvest *'17*
Dunkirk *'17*

Ivor Barnard (1887-1953)
Esther Waters *'48*
Madeleine *'50*
Beat the Devil *'53*

Barry Barnes
The Girl in the News *'41*
Veronica Guerin *'03*
Kings *'07*

Ben Barnes (1981-)
The Chronicles of Narnia: Prince Caspian *'08*
Easy Virtue *'08*
Dorian Gray *'09*
The Chronicles of Narnia: The Voyage of the Dawn Treader *'10*
Killing Bono *'11*
The Big Wedding *'13*
By the Gun *'14*
Seventh Son *'15*

Binnie Barnes (1903-98)
The Private Life of Henry VIII *'33*
Private Life of Don Juan *'34*
Rendezvous *'35*
The Last of the Mohicans *'36*
Three Smart Girls *'36*
Broadway Melody of 1938 *'37*
The Adventures of Marco Polo *'38*
Always Goodbye *'38*
The Divorce of Lady X *'38*
Gateway *'38*
Holiday *'38*
Three Blind Mice *'38*
Day-Time Wife *'39*
Frontier Marshal *'39*
The Three Musketeers *'39*
Wife, Husband and Friend *'39*
If Winter Comes *'41*
Melody Master *'41*
I Married an Angel *'42*
In Old California *'42*
Getting Gertie's Garter *'45*
It's in the Bag! *'45*
The Spanish Main *'45*
The Time of Their Lives *'46*
The Dude Goes West *'48*
The Pirates of Capri *'49*
Decameron Nights *'53*
The Trouble with Angels *'66*
Where Angels Go, Trouble Follows *'68*
Forty Carats *'73*

Chris Barnes (1965-)
The Bad News Bears *'76*
The Bad News Bears in Breaking Training *'77*

Christopher Daniel Barnes (1972-)
The Little Mermaid *'89 (V)*
Murder Without Motive *'92*
The Brady Bunch Movie *'95*
A Very Brady Sequel *'96*
Shut Up and Kiss Me *'05*
Cinderella III: A Twist in Time *'07 (V)*

Joanna Barnes (1934-)
Spartacus *'60*
The Parent Trap *'61*
Don't Make Waves *'67*
The War Wagon *'67*
I Wonder Who's Killing Her Now? *'76*
The Parent Trap *'98*

Priscilla Barnes (1955-)
The Seniors *'78*
The Last Married Couple in America *'80*
License to Kill *'89*
Body Trouble *'92*
Stepfather 3: Father's Day *'92*
Talons of the Eagle *'92*
Ava's Magical Adventure *'94*
The Crossing Guard *'94*
Erotique *'94*
Mallrats *'95*
The Killing Grounds *'97*
Implicated *'98*
Alone with a Stranger *'99*
Final Payback *'99*
Alien 3000 *'04*
The Devil's Rejects *'05*
Thr3e *'07*
American Cowslip *'09*
First Dog *'10*

Rayford Barnes (1920-2000)
Sunday in New York *'63*
Jesse James Meets Frankenstein's Daughter *'65*

Susan Barnes
Freeway *'95*
Serving in Silence: The Margarethe Cammermeyer Story *'95*
Nothing to Lose *'96*
Nurse Betty *'00*
Where the Money Is *'00*

T. Roy Barnes (1880-1937)
Chicago *'27*
Sally *'29*

Walter Barnes (1918-98)
Revenge of the Musketeers *'63*
Challenge of the Gladiator *'65*
The Big Gundown *'66*
Hallelujah for Django *'67*
Cahill: United States Marshal *'73*
High Plains Drifter *'73*
Escape to Witch Mountain *'75*
Every Which Way But Loose *'78*
Bronco Billy *'80*

Charlie Barnett (1954-)
D.C. Cab *'84*
Nobody's Fool *'86*

Griff Barnett (1884-1958)
Gunfighters *'47*
The Millerson Case *'47*
Holiday Affair *'49*
Two of a Kind *'51*

Tom Barnett
Ghost Cat *'03*
The Reagans *'04*
Niagara Motel *'06*

Vince Barnett (1902-77)
The Death Kiss *'33*
The Prizefighter and the Lady *'33*
Crimson Romance *'34*
Thirty Day Princess *'34*
I Live My Life *'35*
Captain Calamity *'36*
Yellow Cargo *'36*
Blonde Comet *'41*
Gangs, Inc. *'41*
I Killed That Man *'42*
High Wall *'47*
Kentucky Jubilee *'51*
Red Planet Mars *'52*
Charade *'53*

Kacey Barnfield (1988-)
Lake Placid 3 *'10*
Roadkill *'11*

Jean Marie Barnwell
Blue River *'95*
Born to Be Wild *'95*

From the Mixed-Up Files of Mrs. Basil E. Frankweiler *'95*

David Baron (1930-2008)
See Harold Pinter

Joanne Baron
Crazy in Love *'92*
Allie & Me *'97*
St. Patrick's Day *'99*
Burning Down the House *'01*
Hard Luck *'01*
The Prince & Me *'04*
The Perfect Witness *'07*
iMurders *'08*
Bare Knuckles *'10*
Frankie and Alice *'10*

Lita Baron (1929-)
Savage Drums *'51*
Jesse James' Women *'54*
The Broken Star *'56*

Lynda Baron (1942-)
Hot Millions *'68*
The Road to Coronation Street *'10*

Sandy Baron (1937-2001)
Sweet November *'68*
Targets *'68*
If It's Tuesday, This Must Be Belgium *'69*
The Out-of-Towners *'70*
Birdy *'84*
Broadway Danny Rose *'84*
Vamp *'86*
Motorama *'91*
Leprechaun 2 *'94*

Sacha Baron Cohen (1971-)
The Jolly Boys' Last Stand *'00*
Madagascar *'05 (V)*
Borat: Cultural Learnings of America for Make Benefit Glorious Nation of Kazakhstan *'06*
Talladega Nights: The Ballad of Ricky Bobby *'06*
Sweeney Todd: The Demon Barber of Fleet Street *'07*
Madagascar: Escape 2 Africa *'08 (V)*
Bruno *'09*
Hugo *'11*
The Dictator *'12*
Les Miserables *'12*
Madagascar 3: Europe's Most Wanted *'12 (V)*
Alice Through the Looking Glass *'16*
The Brothers Grimsby *'16*

Elizabeth Barondes (1964-)
Night of the Scarecrow *'95*
Adrenalin: Fear the Rush *'96*
Not of This Earth *'96*
Love to Kill *'97*

Byron Barr (1917-66)
Double Indemnity *'44*
Love Letters *'45*

Douglas Barr (1949-)
Deadly Blessing *'81*
Spaced Invaders *'90*

Jean-Marc Barr (1960-)
Hope and Glory *'87*
The Big Blue *'88*
Zentropa *'92*
Breaking the Waves *'95*
The Scarlet Tunic *'97*
Don't Let Me Die on a Sunday *'98*
St. Ives *'98*
Dancer in the Dark *'99*
Red Siren *'02*
Dogville *'03*
Le Divorce *'03*
Cote d'Azur *'05*
Manderlay *'05*
Tara Road *'05*
Making Plans for Lena *'09*
Big Sur *'13*

Matt Barr (1984-)
Protecting the King *'07*
7 Below *'11*
Hatfields & McCoys *'12*
The Layover *'17*

Patrick Barr (1908-85)
The Case of the Frightened Lady *'39*
The Vanquished *'52*
Flesh and Blood Show *'73*
The Satanic Rites of Dracula *'73*
House of Whipcord *'75*

Gianfranco Barra (1940-)
Avanti! *'72*
Screw Loose *'99*

Maria Barranco (1961-)
Women on the Verge of a Nervous Breakdown *'88*
Tie Me Up! Tie Me Down! *'90*
Mouth to Mouth *'95*
The Girl of Your Dreams *'99*
Gaudi Afternoon *'01*

Robert Barrat (1889-1970)
Heroes for Sale *'33*
Wild Boys of the Road *'33*
Dark Hazard *'34*
Fog Over Frisco *'34*
Here Comes the Navy *'34*
Hi, Nellie! *'34*
Housewife *'34*
Massacre *'34*
Upperworld *'34*
The Murder Man *'35*
Stranded *'35*
The Charge of the Light Brigade *'36*
Exclusive Story *'36*
Mary of Scotland *'36*
The Trail of the Lonesome Pine *'36*
The Black Legion *'37*
Charlie Chan in Honolulu *'38*
The Texans *'38*
The Cisco Kid and the Lady *'39*
The Return of the Cisco Kid *'39*
Union Pacific *'39*
Go West *'40*
Northwest Passage *'40*
They Came to Blow Up America *'43*
The Adventures of Mark Twain *'44*
They Were Expendable *'45*
Magnificent Doll *'46*
The Road to Utopia *'46*
American Guerrilla in the Philippines *'50*
Davy Crockett, Indian Scout *'50*
Distant Drums *'51*

Julian Barratt
Lucky Break *'01*
Bunny and the Bull *'09*
In Fabric *'18*

George Barraud (1888-1970)
Little Old New York *'23*
The Last of Mrs. Cheyney *'29*
Road to Paradise *'30*

Jean-Louis Barrault (1910-94)
Beethoven *'36*
Children of Paradise *'44*
La Ronde *'51*
The Testament of Dr. Cordelier *'59*
The Longest Day *'62*

Marie-Christine Barrault (1944-)
My Night at Maud's *'69*
The Daydreamer *'70*
Chloe in the Afternoon *'72*
Cousin, Cousine *'76*
The Medusa Touch *'78*
Perceval *'78*
Stardust Memories *'80*
Table for Five *'83*
Swann in Love *'84*
Le Jupon Rouge *'87*
Jesus of Montreal *'89*
Obsession *'97*
Making Plans for Lena *'09*

Adriana Barraza (1956-)
Amores Perros '00
Babel '06
Henry Poole Is Here '08
Drag Me to Hell '09
From Prada to Nada '11
Cake '14
Night Has Settled '14
Rambo: Last Blood '19

Sasha Barrese
The Hangover '09
Let Me In '10

Amy Barrett
Caged Heat '74
House Where Evil Dwells '82

Brendon Ryan Barrett
Logan's War: Bound by Honor '98
Lloyd '00

Claudia Barrett (1929-)
The Happy Years '50
Robot Monster '53

Edith Barrett (1907-77)
Ladies in Retirement '41
Lady for a Night '42
You Can't Escape Forever '42
The Ghost Ship '43
I Walked with a Zombie '43
Jane Eyre '44
The Lady Gambles '49

Jacinda Barrett (1972-)
The Human Stain '03
Bridget Jones: The Edge of Reason '04
Ladder 49 '04
The Last Kiss '06
The Namesake '06
Poseidon '06
School for Scoundrels '06
Middle Men '10
So B. It '17

Jane Barrett (1923-69)
The Sword & the Rose '53
Bond of Fear '56

Majel Barrett (1932-2008)
Westworld '73
The Questor Tapes '74
Star Trek: The Motion Picture '79
Star Trek 4: The Voyage Home '86
Star Trek: Generations '94 (V)
Mommy '95
Star Trek: Nemesis '02 (V)
Star Trek '09 (V)

Nancy Barrett (1943-)
House of Dark Shadows '70
Night of Dark Shadows '71
Belizaire the Cajun '86

Nitchie Barrett
Preppies '82
A Time to Die '91

Ray Barrett (1927-2009)
The Reptile '66
Revenge '71
Don's Party '76
The Chant of Jimmie Blacksmith '78
Where the Green Ants Dream '84
Rebel '85
Hotel de Love '96
Heaven's Burning '97
In the Winter Dark '98
After the Deluge '03
Visitors '03

Sean Barrett (1940-)
War and Peace '56
Sink the Bismarck '60

Tony Barrett (1916-74)
Dick Tracy Meets Gruesome '47
Impact '49

Bill Barretta
The Muppets' Wizard of Oz '05 (V)
The Muppets '11 (V)

The Happytime Murders '18 (V)

Barbara Barrie (1931-)
The Caretakers '63
Child of Glass '78
Backstairs at the White House '79
The Bell Jar '79
Breaking Away '79
Private Benjamin '80
The Children Nobody Wanted '81
The Execution '85
Real Men '87
End of the Line '88
Scarlett '94
Hercules '97 (V)
Judy Berlin '99
Spent '00
Second Best '05
The Six Wives of Henry Lefay '09
Harvest '10

Chris (Christopher) Barrie (1960-)
Lara Croft: Tomb Raider '01
Back in Business '06
When Evil Calls '06

John Barrie
Victim '61
The File of the Golden Goose '69

Mona Barrie (1909-64)
Charlie Chan in London '34
I Met Him in Paris '37
I Take This Woman '40
The Strange Case of Dr. Rx '42
Cass Timberlane '47

Wendy Barrie (1912-78)
The Private Life of Henry VIII '33
Love on a Bet '36
Speed '36
Dead End '37
Day-Time Wife '39
The Hound of the Baskervilles '39
The Saint Strikes Back '39
The Witness Vanishes '39
Men Against the Sky '40
The Saint Takes Over '40
The Gay Falcon '41
The Saint in Palm Springs '41
A Date With the Falcon '42
Follies Girl '43

Edgar Barrier (1907-64)
Arabian Nights '42
The Phantom of the Opera '43
Cobra Woman '44
Nob Hill '45
Tarzan and the Leopard Woman '46
Rumble on the Docks '56
The Giant Claw '57

Pat Barrington (1941-2014)
Orgy of the Dead '65
Agony of Love '66
Mantis in Lace '68

Chuck Barris (1929-2017)
Hugo Pool '97
Confessions of a Dangerous Mind '02 (C)

Desmond Barrit (1944-)
A Midsummer Night's Dream '96
A Christmas Carol '99
Northanger Abbey '07

Dana Barron (1966-)
National Lampoon's Vacation '83
City of Industry '96
The Man in the Iron Mask '97
The Perfect Nanny '00
National Lampoon's Christmas Vacation 2: Cousin Eddie's Big Island Adventure '03

John Barron (1920-2004)
Hitler: The Last Ten Days '73
Agatha Christie's Thirteen at Dinner '85

Keith Barron (1934-)
Nothing But the Night '72
At the Earth's Core '76
Take Me '01
Plain Jane '02

Robert V. Barron (1932-2000)
The Big Turnaround '88
Bill & Ted's Excellent Adventure '89

George Barrows (1913-94)
Robot Monster '53
Hillbillies in a Haunted House '67

Barta Barry (1911-)
Gladiators 7 '62
Dr. Jekyll and the Wolfman '71

Cian Barry
In the Spider's Web '07
Hard Times '09

Donald (Don 'Red') Barry (1912-80)
Adventures of Red Ryder '40
The Purple Heart '44
Square Dance Jubilee '51
Jesse James' Women '54
7 Men From Now '56
Gun Duel In Durango '57
Frankenstein 1970 '58
Born Reckless '59
The Last Mile '59
Iron Angel '64
Hostile Guns '67 (C)
The Shakiest Gun in the West '68
Johnny Got His Gun '71
Blazing Stewardesses '75

Gene Barry (1921-2009)
The Atomic City '52
The War of the Worlds '53
Red Garters '54
Soldier of Fortune '55
China Gate '57
Forty Guns '57
The 27th Day '57
Thunder Road '58
Columbo: Prescription Murder '67
Maroc 7 '67
Second Coming of Suzanne '80
The Gambler Returns: The Luck of the Draw '93
These Old Broads '01
War of the Worlds '05

Jason Barry (1972-)
The Last of the High Kings '96
Monument Ave. '98
When the Sky Falls '99
Death Games '02
Beyond Re-Animator '03
Conspiracy of Silence '03
MirrorMask '05
Honor '06
The Still Life '07
Legend of the Bog '08

Joan Barry
Rich and Strange '32
Rome Express '32

Neill Barry (1965-)
Old Enough '84
Joey '85
O.C. and Stiggs '87
Friends & Lovers '99
Atlas Shrugged: Part 1 '11

Patricia Barry (1921-)
Cry Wolf '47
Dear Heart '64
Kitten with a Whip '64
Twilight Zone: The Movie '83

Raymond J. Barry (1939-)
Christmas Evil '80
Year of the Dragon '85
Cop '88

Born on the Fourth of July '89
Drug Wars: The Camarena Story '90
K2: The Ultimate High '92
Rapid Fire '92
The Turning '92
Cool Runnings '93
Falling Down '93
The Ref '93
Dead Man Walking '95
Sudden Death '95
The Chamber '96
Headless Body in Topless Bar '96
Flubber '97
Best Men '98
The Deep End '01
Training Day '01
Interview with the Assassin '02
Just Married '03
Steel City '06
American Crude '07
Flight of the Living Dead: Outbreak on a Plane '07
Walk Hard: The Dewey Cox Story '07
The Hitman Diaries '09
The Shortcut '09
Across the Line: The Exodus of Charlie Wright '10
The Hammer '11
The River Murders '11
The Devil's in the Details '13
LA Apocalypse '14

Thom Barry (1950-)
Steel '97
The Fast and the Furious '01
2 Fast 2 Furious '03

Toni Barry
Proteus '95
Endgame '01

Tony Barry (1941-)
Little Boy Lost '78
The Odd Angry Shot '79
Goodbye Pork Pie '81
We of the Never Never '82
Initiation '87
Doing Time for Patsy Cline '97
Solo '06

Deborah Barrymore (1963-)
See Deborah Maria Moore

Drew Barrymore (1975-)
Altered States '80
E.T.: The Extra-Terrestrial '82
Firestarter '84
Irreconcilable Differences '84
Cat's Eye '85
Far from Home '89
See You in the Morning '89
Doppelganger: The Evil Within '90
Motorama '91
Waxwork 2: Lost in Time '91
Guncrazy '92
Poison Ivy '92
Sketch Artist '92
The Amy Fisher Story '93
Wayne's World 2 '93
Bad Girls '94
Boys on the Side '94
Batman Forever '95
Mad Love '95
Everyone Says I Love You '96
Scream '96
Wishful Thinking '96
The Wedding Singer '97
Best Men '98
Ever After: A Cinderella Story '98
Home Fries '98
Never Been Kissed '99
Charlie's Angels '00
Skipped Parts '00
Titan A.E. '00 (V)
Donnie Darko '01
Riding in Cars with Boys '01
Confessions of a Dangerous Mind '02

Charlie's Angels: Full Throttle '03
Duplex '03
50 First Dates '04
Fever Pitch '05
Curious George '06 (V)
Lucky You '07
Music & Lyrics '07
Beverly Hills Chihuahua '08 (V)
Everybody's Fine '09
Grey Gardens '09
He's Just Not That Into You '09
Whip It '09
Going the Distance '10
Big Miracle '12
Blended '14
Miss You Already '15

Ethel Barrymore (1879-1959)
Rasputin and the Empress '33
None But the Lonely Heart '44
The Spiral Staircase '46
Night Song '47
The Paradine Case '47
Portrait of Jennie '48
The Smallest Show on Earth '48
The Great Sinner '49
Pinky '49
That Midnight Kiss '49
The Red Danube '50
It's a Big Country '51
Just for You '52
The Story of Three Loves '53
Young at Heart '54

John Barrymore (1882-1942)
Dr. Jekyll and Mr. Hyde '20
Sherlock Holmes '22
Beau Brummel '24
Don Juan '26
The Beloved Rogue '27
When a Man Loves '27
Tempest '28
State's Attorney '31
Svengali '31
Grand Hotel '32
Counsellor-at-Law '33
Dinner at Eight '33
Night Flight '33
Rasputin and the Empress '33
Twentieth Century '34
Romeo and Juliet '36
Bulldog Drummond Comes Back '37
Maytime '37
True Confession '37
Bulldog Drummond's Peril '38
Marie Antoinette '38
Spawn of the North '38
Midnight '39
The Invisible Woman '40
Playmates '41
Shadow on the Window '57

John Drew (Blythe) Barrymore, Jr. (1932-2004)
High Lonesome '50
The Big Night '51
High School Confidential '58
Never Love a Stranger '58
The Trojan Horse '62
Americana '81
Smokey Bites the Dust '81

Lionel Barrymore (1878-1954)
America '24
The Bells '26
The Temptress '26
The Show '27
Sadie Thompson '28
Free and Easy '30 (C)
A Free Soul '31
Grand Hotel '32
Mata Hari '32
Dinner at Eight '33
Night Flight '33
One Man's Journey '33
Rasputin and the Empress '33

Sweepings '33
The Girl from Missouri '34
Treasure Island '34
Ah, Wilderness! '35
David Copperfield '35
The Little Colonel '35
Camille '36
Devil Doll '36
The Gorgeous Hussy '36
The Road to Glory '36
Captains Courageous '37
A Family Affair '37
Navy Blue and Gold '37
Saratoga '37
Test Pilot '38
You Can't Take It with You '38
Young Dr. Kildare '38
Calling Dr. Kildare '39
Let Freedom Ring '39
On Borrowed Time '39
The Secret of Dr. Kildare '39
Dr. Kildare Goes Home '40
Dr. Kildare's Crisis '40
Dr. Kildare's Strange Case '40
The Bad Man '41
Dr. Kildare's Wedding Day '41
Lady Be Good '41
The People *vs.* Dr. Kildare '41
Calling Dr. Gillespie '42
Dr. Gillespie's New Assistant '42
Dr. Kildare's Victory '42
Dr. Gillespie's Criminal Case '43
Thousands Cheer '43
Since You Went Away '44
Three Men in White '44
Between Two Women '45
The Valley of Decision '45
Duel in the Sun '46
It's a Wonderful Life '46
The Secret Heart '46
Dark Delusion '47
Key Largo '48
Malaya '49
Right Cross '50
Lone Star '52

Judith Barsi (1977-88)
Eye of the Tiger '86
Jaws: The Revenge '87
The Land Before Time '88 (V)
All Dogs Go to Heaven '89 (V)

Roger Bart (1962-)
The Stepford Wives '04
The Producers '05
American Gangster '07
Hostel: Part 2 '07
Harold & Kumar Escape from Guantanamo Bay '08
The Midnight Meat Train '08
Spy School '08
Excision '12
Smiley '12

Paul Bartel (1938-2000)
Cannonball '76
Eat My Dust '76
Hollywood Boulevard '76
Grand Theft Auto '77
Piranha '78
Rock 'n' Roll High School '79
Heartbeeps '81
Eating Raoul '82
Get Crazy '83
Into the Night '85 (C)
Chopping Mall '86
Killer Party '86
Amazon Women on the Moon '87
Munchies '87
Out of the Dark '88
Far Out Man '89
Gremlins 2: The New Batch '90
Mortuary Academy '91
Desire and Hell at Sunset Motel '92
Evil Lives '92
Liquid Dreams '92
Armistead Maupin's Tales of the City '93

Posse '93 (C)
Grief '94
Number One Fan '94
The Jerky Boys '95
The Usual Suspects '95
Basquiat '96
Armistead Maupin's More Tales of the City '97 (C)
Lewis and Clark and George '97
Billy's Hollywood Screen Kiss '98
Hamlet '00

Eddie Barth (1931-2010)
Thunder and Lightning '77
Boardwalk '79
Mr. Write '92

Isolde Barth
Quiet Days in Clichy '90
Rosenstrasse '03

Jessica Barth
Ted 2 '15
Along Came the Devil '18

Justin Bartha (1978-)
Gigli '03
National Treasure '04
Failure to Launch '06
Trust the Man '06
National Treasure: Book of Secrets '07
The Hangover '09
The Rebound '09
Holy Rollers '10
Dark Horse '11
The Hangover, Part 2 '11
CBGB '13
The Hangover, Part III '13
White Girl '16

Richard Barthelmess (1895-1963)
Broken Blossoms '19
The Idol Dancer '20
The Love Flower '20
Way Down East '20
Tol'able David '21
Shore Leave '25
Ranson's Folly '26
Weary River '29
The Dawn Patrol '30
Son of the Gods '30
The Last Flight '31
Alias the Doctor '32
Central Airport '33
Heroes for Sale '33
Massacre '34
Only Angels Have Wings '39
The Mayor of 44th Street '42
The Spoilers '42

Freddie Bartholomew (1924-92)
Anna Karenina '35
David Copperfield '35
Professional Soldier '35
The Devil Is a Sissy '36
Little Lord Fauntleroy '36
Lloyds of London '36
Captains Courageous '37
Kidnapped '38
Listen, Darling '38
Tom Brown's School Days '40
A Yank at Eton '42
Sepia Cinderella '47
St. Benny the Dip '51

Logan Bartholomew (1984-)
Love's Enduring Promise '04
Love's Long Journey '05
Nearing Grace '05
Love's Abiding Joy '06
The Ultimate Life '13

Bonnie Bartlett (1929-)
The Legend of Lizzie Borden '75
Dempsey '83
Love Letters '83
The Deliberate Stranger '86
Twins '88
Dave '93
Ghosts of Mississippi '96
Shiloh '97
Primary Colors '98
Shiloh 2: Shiloh Season '99
Tuesdays with Morrie '99
Of Two Minds '12

Jamie Bartlett
Ernest Goes to Africa '97
Beyond Borders '03

Martine Bartlett (1925-2006)
Lord Love a Duck '66
Sybil '76

Richard Bartlett (1922-94)
Lonesome Trail '55
Silver Star '55

Robin Bartlett (1951-)
Baby Boom '87
Lean on Me '89
Alice '90
Postcards from the Edge '90
Deceived '91
If Looks Could Kill '91
Regarding Henry '91
Dangerous Minds '95
Honey, We Shrunk Ourselves '97
City of Angels '98
H. '15

Eva Bartok (1926-98)
Crimson Pirate '52
Norman Conquest '53
Spaceways '53
Ten Thousand Bedrooms '57
Operation Amsterdam '60
S.O.S. Pacific '60
Blood and Black Lace '64

Jayce Bartok (1974-)
Murder at Devil's Glen '99
The Tollbooth '04
Red Doors '05
The Cake Eaters '07

Luciano Bartoli
Henry IV '85
Bizarre '87

Diana Barton (1966-)
Body of Influence '93
Sexual Malice '93

J Barton
Legally Blonde 2: Red White & Blonde '03
A Separate Peace '04

James Barton (1890-1962)
The Shepherd of the Hills '41
The Time of Your Life '48
The Daughter of Rosie O'Grady '50
Golden Girl '51
Here Comes the Groom '51
Naked Hills '56
The Misfits '61

Margaret Barton
Brief Encounter '46
The Gay Dog '54

Mischa Barton (1986-)
Lawn Dogs '96
Pups '99
The Sixth Sense '99
Skipped Parts '00
Lost and Delirious '01
Tart '01
Pulse '03
The Oh in Ohio '06
Closing the Ring '07
St. Trinian's '07
Virgin Territory '07
Assassination of a High School President '08
Homecoming '09
You and I '11
SWAT: Unit 887 '15
The ToyBox '18

Peter Barton (1956-)
Hell Night '81
Friday the 13th, Part 4: The Final Chapter '84

Skye McCole Bartusiak (1992-2014)
Blonde '01
Don't Say a Word '01
Riding in Cars with Boys '01
Firestarter 2: Rekindled '02
Love Comes Softly '03
Boogeyman '05
Kill Your Darlings '06

Billy Barty (1924-2000)
The Bride of Frankenstein '35
A Midsummer Night's Dream '35
Mickey the Great '39
Pygmy Island '50
The Undead '57
Roustabout '64
Harum Scarum '65
Pufnstuf '70
The Day of the Locust '75
Foul Play '78
Under the Rainbow '81
Night Patrol '85
Legend '86
Rumpelstiltskin '86
Tough Guys '86
Body Slam '87
Masters of the Universe '87
Willow '88
Lobster Man from Mars '89
Snow White '89
UHF '89
Life Stinks '91
Wishful Thinking '92

Siri Baruc (1978-)
The Glass Trap '04
Blood Angels '05
The Foursome '06
Megasnake '07
Unholy '07
Tommy and the Cool Mule '09

Jay Baruchel (1982-)
Nemesis Game '03
Million Dollar Baby '04
I'm Reed Fish '06
Just Buried '07
Knocked Up '07
Nick & Norah's Infinite Playlist '08
Real Time '08
Tropic Thunder '08
Fanboys '09
The Trotsky '09
Good Neighbors '10
How to Train Your Dragon '10 (V)
She's Out of My League '10
The Sorcerer's Apprentice '10
Cosmopolis '12
Goon '12
The Art of the Steal '13
This Is the End '13
Don Peyote '14
How to Train Your Dragon 2 '14 (V)
RoboCop '14
How to Train Your Dragon: The Hidden World '19

Mikhail Baryshnikov (1948-)
The Turning Point '77
That's Dancing! '85
White Nights '85
Dancers '87
Company Business '91

Gary Basaraba (1959-)
One Magic Christmas '85
Sweet Dreams '85
Fried Green Tomatoes '91
The War '94
A Horse for Danny '95
Dead Silence '96
K-9 3: P.I. '01
Unfaithful '02
Charlotte's Web '06
Jesse Stone: Death in Paradise '06
The Smurfs '11

David Alan Basche (1968-)
Carry Me Home '04
Crazylove '05
War of the Worlds '05
United 93 '06
I'll Believe You '07

Dante Basco (1975-)
Hook '91
Riot in the Streets '96
Extremedays '01
Take the Lead '06
Blood and Bone '09
Jarhead 3: The Siege '16

Dion Basco
Race the Sun '96
Why Am I Doing This? '09

Richard Basehart (1914-84)
Cry Wolf '47
He Walked by Night '48
Reign of Terror '49
Tension '50
Decision Before Dawn '51
Fixed Bayonets! '51
Titanic '53
La Strada '54
Il Bidone '55
Moby Dick '56
Time Limit '57
The Brothers Karamazov '58
Portrait in Black '60
Hitler '62
Kings of the Sun '63
The Satan Bug '65
Hans Brinker '69
The Andersonville Trial '70
Chato's Land '71
City Beneath the Sea '71
Colditz: Escape of the Birdmen '71
Rage '72
Flood! '76
Mansion of the Doomed '76
The Island of Dr. Moreau '77
Great Bank Hoax '78
Being There '79

Blake Bashoff (1981-)
Big Bully '95
Together Again for the First Time '08

Alain Bashung (1947-)
My Father, My Mother, My Brothers and My Sisters '99
Confusion of Genders '00

Count Basie (1904-84)
Stage Door Canteen '43
Cinderfella '60
Sex and the Single Girl '64
Blazing Saddles '74

Toni Basil (1943-)
Pajama Party '64
Village of the Giants '65
Easy Rider '69
Mother, Jugs and Speed '76
Angel 3: The Final Chapter '88
Eating '90
Rockula '90

Salvatore Basile
Cannibal Holocaust '80
Cobra Verde '88

Kim Basinger (1953-)
Hard Country '81
Killjoy '81
Mother Lode '82
The Man Who Loved Women '83
Never Say Never Again '83
The Natural '84
Fool for Love '86
9 1/2 Weeks '86
No Mercy '86
Blind Date '87
Nadine '87
My Stepmother Is an Alien '88
Batman '89
The Marrying Man '91
Cool World '92
Final Analysis '92
The Getaway '93
The Real McCoy '93
Wayne's World 2 '93
Ready to Wear '94
L.A. Confidential '97
Bless the Child '00
I Dreamed of Africa '00
8 Mile '02
People I Know '02
Cellular '04
The Door in the Floor '04
Elvis Has Left the Building '04
Even Money '06
The Mermaid Chair '06
The Sentinel '06
The Burning Plain '08

While She Was Out '08
The Informers '09
Charlie St. Cloud '10
Third Person '13
The 11th Hour '14
Fifty Shades Darker '17

Austin Basis (1976-)
American Zombie '07
Boxboarders! '07
My Sassy Girl '08
The Other End of the Line '08

Elya Baskin (1950-)
Moscow on the Hudson '84
The Name of the Rose '86
Deepstar Six '89
Enemies, a Love Story '89
Air Force One '97
Running Red '99
Thirteen Days '00
The Dukes '07

Antoine Basler
Irma Vep '96
A Prophet '09
The Last Diamond '14

Marianne Basler (1964-)
A Soldier's Tale '91
Va Savoir '01

Lena Basquette (1907-94)
The Midnight Lady '32
Heroes of the Heart '94

Alfie Bass (1921-87)
It Always Rains on Sunday '47
The Lavender Hill Mob '51
Made in Heaven '52
Blackout '54
Help! '65
Alfie '66
The Fearless Vampire Killers '67

Tamara La Seon Bass (1978-)
Bellyfruit '99
Baby Boy '01

Albert Bassermann (1862-1952)
Dr. Ehrlich's Magic Bullet '40
Escape '40
Foreign Correspondent '40
Melody Master '41
A Woman's Face '41
Invisible Agent '42
Reunion in France '42
The Shanghai Gesture '42
Madame Curie '43
The Moon and Sixpence '43
Since You Went Away '44
Rhapsody in Blue '45
The Private Affairs of Bel Ami '47
The Red Shoes '48

Gaby Basset (1902-2001)
Grisbi '53
Hijack Highway '55

Angela Bassett (1958-)
F/X '86
Boyz N the Hood '91
City of Hope '91
Critters 4 '91
Innocent Blood '92
The Jacksons: An American Dream '92
Malcolm X '92
Passion Fish '92
What's Love Got to Do with It? '93
Strange Days '95
Vampire in Brooklyn '95
Waiting to Exhale '95
Contact '97
How Stella Got Her Groove Back '98
Music of the Heart '99
Supernova '99
Boesman & Lena '00
Whispers: An Elephant's Tale '00 (V)
Ruby's Bucket of Blood '01
The Score '01
The Rosa Parks Story '02
Sunshine State '02
Masked and Anonymous '03

Mr. 3000 '04
Mr. & Mrs. Smith '05 (V)
Akeelah and the Bee '06
Meet the Robinsons '07 (V)
Gospel Hill '08
Nothing But the Truth '08
Of Boys and Men '08
Tyler Perry's Meet the Browns '08
Notorious '09
Green Lantern '11
Jumping the Broom '11
This Means War '12
Betty & Coretta '13
Black Nativity '13
Olympus Has Fallen '13
White Bird in a Blizzard '14
Chi-raq '15
Otherhood '19

Linda Bassett (1950-)
Waiting for the Moon '87
Mary Reilly '95
Oscar and Lucinda '97
Beautiful People '99
East Is East '99
The Hours '02
Calendar Girls '03
Separate Lies '05
Kinky Boots '06

Steve Bassett (1955-)
Spring Break '83
The Jackal '97

Annalise Basso (1998-)
Love Takes Wing '09
Standing Up '13
Ouija: Origin of Evil '16
Slender Man '18

Gabriel Basso
The Kings of Summer '13
The Whole Truth '16

Claudia Bassols (1979-)
One In the Chamber '12
The Returned '14

Alexandra Bastedo (1946-2014)
The Blood Spattered Bride '72
The Ghoul '75

Tabitha Bastien
Run Hide Die '15
ECCO '19

Steve Bastoni (1966-)
15 Amore '98
Dr. Jekyll & Mr. Hyde '99
Rodgers & Hammerstein's South Pacific '01
The Crocodile Hunter: Collision Course '02
Pros and Ex-cons '05
Macbeth '06

Othon Bastos (1933-)
Central Station '98
Behind the Sun '01

Michal Bat-Adam (1945-)
I Love You Rosa '72
Rachel's Man '75
The Impossible Spy '87

Alexei Batalov (1928-)
The Cranes Are Flying '57
The Lady with the Dog '59
Moscow Does Not Believe in Tears '80

Nikolai Batalov (1899-1937)
Aelita: Queen of Mars '24
Mother '26
Bed and Sofa '27

Pierre Batcheff (1901-32)
Feu Mathias Pascal '26
The Chess Player '27
Siren of the Tropics '27

Anthony Bate (1927-2012)
Tinker, Tailor, Soldier, Spy '80
Smiley's People '82
Philby, Burgess and MacLean: Spy Scandal of the Century '84

Gabriel Bateman
Lights Out '16
Child's Play '19

Playmobil: The Movie '19
Think Like a Dog '20

Geoffrey Bateman
Another Country '84
Manderlay '05

Jason Bateman (1969-)
Teen Wolf Too '87
Necessary Roughness '91
A Taste for Killing '92
Love Stinks '99
Sol Goode '01
One Way Out '02
The Sweetest Thing '02
Dodgeball: A True Underdog Story '04
Starsky & Hutch '04
Arthur and the Invisibles '06 (V)
The Break-Up '06
The Ex '07
Juno '07
The Kingdom '07
Mr. Magorium's Wonder Emporium '07
Smokin' Aces '07
Forgetting Sarah Marshall '08
Hancock '08
Couples Retreat '09
Extract '09
The Invention of Lying '09
State of Play '09
Up in the Air '09
The Switch '10
The Change-Up '11
Horrible Bosses '11
Paul '11
Bad Words '13
Identity Thief '13
Horrible Bosses 2 '14
The Longest Week '14
This Is Where I Leave You '14
The Gift '15
A Lego Brickumentary '15
Central Intelligence '16
The Family Fang '16
Office Christmas Party '16
Zootopia '16 (V)
Game Night '18

Justine Bateman (1966-)
Satisfaction '88
The Fatal Image '90
Deadbolt '92
The Night We Never Met '93
Another Woman '94
God's Lonely Man '96
Highball '97
Out of Order '03
To Have and to Hold '06
The TV Set '06
Hybrid '07

Nick Bateman
Hobo With a Shotgun '11
Hidden in the Woods '16

Alan Bates (1934-2003)
The Entertainer '60
Zorba the Greek '64
Georgy Girl '66
The King of Hearts '66
Far from the Madding Crowd '67
Women in Love '70
A Day in the Death of Joe Egg '71
The Go-Between '71
The Story of Jacob & Joseph '74 (N)
In Celebration '75
Royal Flash '75
An Unmarried Woman '78
The Rose '79
Nijinsky '80
Quartet '81
Britannia Hospital '82
Return of the Soldier '82
Pack of Lies '87
Prayer for the Dying '87
A Voyage 'Round My Father '89
Hamlet '90
Silent Tongue '92
The Cherry Orchard '99
Arabian Nights '00
St. Patrick: The Irish Legend '00
Gosford Park '01
The Prince and the Pauper '01
Evelyn '02
The Mothman Prophecies '02
The Sum of All Fears '02
Hollywood North '03
The Statement '03

Barbara Bates (1925-69)
The Inspector General '49
Cheaper by the Dozen '50
I'd Climb the Highest Mountain '51
Let's Make It Legal '51
Belles on Their Toes '52
All Ashore '53
The Caddy '53
Rhapsody '54
Apache Territory '58

Florence Bates (1888-1954)
Rebecca '40
The Son of Monte Cristo '40
The Chocolate Soldier '41
Love Crazy '41
Road Show '41
Mexican Spitfire at Sea '42
We Were Dancing '42
Heaven Can Wait '43
Mr. Lucky '43
The Moon and Sixpence '43
Slightly Dangerous '43
His Butler's Sister '44
Kismet '44
The Mask of Dimitrios '44
Since You Went Away '44
San Antonio '45
Saratoga Trunk '45
Diary of a Chambermaid '46
The Secret Life of Walter Mitty '47
I Remember Mama '48
Portrait of Jennie '48
Winter Meeting '48
The Judge Steps Out '49
A Letter to Three Wives '49
My Dear Secretary '49
Lullaby of Broadway '51
The Tall Target '51
The San Francisco Story '52

Granville Bates (1882-1940)
It Happened in Hollywood '37
Nancy Steele Is Missing '37
Waikiki Wedding '37
A Man to Remember '38
Next Time I Marry '38
Blackwell's Island '39
Flowing Gold '40
My Favorite Wife '40

Jeanne Bates (1918-2007)
The Mask of Diijon '46
Sabaka '55
The Strangler '64
Eraserhead '78
Mom '89

Kathy Bates (1948-)
Straight Time '78
The Morning After '86
Summer Heat '87
My Best Friend Is a Vampire '88
Men Don't Leave '89
Signs of Life '89
Dick Tracy '90
Misery '90
White Palace '90
Fried Green Tomatoes '91
Prelude to a Kiss '92
Shadows and Fog '92
Used People '92
A Home of Our Own '93
Curse of the Starving Class '94
Dolores Claiborne '94
Stephen King's The Stand '94
Angus '95
Diabolique '96
The Late Shift '96
The War at Home '96
Swept from the Sea '97
Titanic '97
Primary Colors '98
The Waterboy '98
Annie '99
The Dress Code '99
American Outlaws '01
About Schmidt '02
Dragonfly '02
Love Liza '02
My Sister's Keeper '02
Unconditional Love '03
Around the World in 80 Days '04
Little Black Book '04
The Bridge of San Luis Rey '05
Bonneville '06
Charlotte's Web '06 (V)
Failure to Launch '06
Relative Strangers '06
Bee Movie '07 (V)
Fred Claus '07
The Golden Compass '07
P.S. I Love You '07
The Day the Earth Stood Still '08
The Family That Preys '08
Revolutionary Road '08
Alice '09
The Blind Side '09
Cheri '09
Personal Effects '09
Valentine's Day '10
A Little Bit of Heaven '11
Midnight in Paris '11
You May Not Kiss the Bride '12
Tammy '14
Bad Santa 2 '16
Complete Unknown '16
The Great Gilly Hopkins '16
On the Basis of Sex '18
The Highwaymen '19
Richard Jewell '19

Michael Bates (1920-78)
Bedazzled '68
Hammerhead '68
Salt & Pepper '68
Patton '70
A Clockwork Orange '71
Frenzy '72
No Sex Please-We're British '73

Paul Bates
Coming to America '88
Crazy People '90
Mr. Wonderful '93
True Romance '93
The Preacher's Wife '96
Instinct '99
8 Mile '02

Ralph Bates (1940-91)
The Horror of Frankenstein '70
Taste the Blood of Dracula '70
Dr. Jekyll and Sister Hyde '71
Lust for a Vampire '71
Dynasty of Fear '72
I Don't Want to Be Born '75
Poldark 2 '75
Poldark '75

R(ichard) C(arlos) Bates (1946-)
. . .And God Spoke '94
Werewolf '95

Timothy Bateson (1926-2009)
The Mouse That Roared '59
Our Man in Havana '59
Ring-a-Ding Rhythm '62
Joseph '95
The 10th Kingdom '00

Randall Batinkoff (1968-)
Streetwalkin' '85
For Keeps '88
Buffy the Vampire Slayer '92
The Player '92
School Ties '92
Christy '94
Walking and Talking '96
As Good As It Gets '97
The Curve '97
The Peacemaker '97
Heartwood '98
The Last Marshal '99
Let the Devil Wear Black '99
April's Shower '03
Touched '05
Venice Underground '05
The Last Lullaby '08
Kick-Ass '10

Stiv Bators (1949-90)
Polyester '81
Tapeheads '89

Susan Batson (1944-)
Girl 6 '96
Bamboozled '00

Bryan Batt
Jeffrey '95
The Last of Robin Hood '13
12 Years a Slave '13

Matt Battaglia (1965-)
Raven '97
Half Past Dead '02

Rick (Rik) Battaglia (1930-)
Caesar the Conqueror '63
Apache's Last Battle '64
'Tis a Pity She's a Whore '73

Cyia Batten (1975-)
Red Shoe Diaries: Swimming Naked '00
Killer Movie '08

Guiseppe Battiston (1968-)
Bread and Tulips '01
Don't Tell '05
Days and Clouds '07

Hinton Battle (1956-)
Foreign Student '94
Child Star: The Shirley Temple Story '01

Texas Battle (1980-)
Coach Carter '05
Final Destination 3 '06
Wrong Turn 2: Dead End '07
Dragonball: Evolution '09
Hydra '09
10 Minutes Gone '19

Patrick Bauchau (1938-)
La Collectionneuse '67
Entre-Nous '83
Choose Me '84
Emmanuelle 4 '84
Creepers '85
Love Among Thieves '86
The Music Teacher '88
The Rapture '91
Terranova '91
Blood Ties '92
And the Band Played On '93
Lisbon Story '94
The New Age '94
Twin Falls Idaho '99
The Beatnicks '00
The Cell '00
Jackpot '01 (V)
Panic Room '02
Secretary '02
Shade '03
Ray '04
Boy Culture '06
Karla '06
Chrysalis '07
The Perfect Sleep '08
Extraordinary Measures '10

Vanessa Bauche (1973-)
Highway Patrolman '91
Amores Perros '00
The Three Burials of Melquiades Estrada '05

Amanda Bauer
The Myth of the American Sleepover '10
Betrayed at 17 '11

Belinda Bauer (1950-)
Winter Kills '79
Flashdance '83
Timerider '83
Samson and Delilah '84
RoboCop 2 '90
Servants of Twilight '91
Poison Ivy 2: Lily '95

Chris Bauer (1966-)
The Devil's Advocate '97
8mm '98
Flawless '99
The Hunley '99
61* '01
Broken Flowers '05
Flags of Our Fathers '06
The Notorious Bettie Page '06
A Dog's Way Home '19

David Bauer (1917-73)
Inspector Clouseau '68
Tropic of Cancer '70

Michelle (McClellan) Bauer (1958-)
Nightmare Sisters '87
Phantom Empire '87
Sorority Babes in the Slimeball Bowl-A-Rama '87
Beverly Hills Vamp '88
Hollywood Chainsaw Hookers '88
Assault of the Party Nerds '89
Evil Toons '90
Vampire Vixens from Venus '94
Assault of the Party Nerds 2: Heavy Petting Detective '95
Attack of the 60-Foot Centerfold '95

Steven Bauer (1956-)
Scarface '83
Thief of Hearts '84
Running Scared '86
Sword of Gideon '86
The Beast '88
Wildfire '88
Gleaming the Cube '89
Drug Wars: The Camarena Story '90
False Arrest '92
Raising Cain '92
Red Shoe Diaries 2: Double Dare '92
Snapdragon '93
Woman of Desire '93
Star Quest '94
Stranger by Night '94
Body Count '95
Wild Side '95
Plato's Run '96
Primal Fear '96
Navajo Blues '97
Naked Lies '98
Bloody Proof '99
Boss of Bosses '99
Along for the Ride '00
For Love or Country: The Arturo Sandoval Story '00
Hooded Angels '00
Traffic '00
The Learning Curve '01
King of Texas '02
Raptor Island '04
How the Garcia Girls Spent Their Summer '05
The Lost City '05
Pit Fighter '05
Dead Lenny '06
Kings of South Beach '07
Behind Enemy Lines 3: Colombia '08
Dark World '08
Fast Lane '08
Mutants '08
From Mexico With Love '09
The Hitman Diaries '09
Enemies Among Us '10
Werewolf: The Beast Among Us '12
The Lookalike '14

Kathrine Baumann (1949-)
Chrome and Hot Leather '71
The Thing with Two Heads '72
Slashed Dreams '74

Marie Baumer
Dresden '06
The Counterfeiters '07

Harry Baur (1880-1943)
Poil de Carotte '31
Beethoven '36

Dave Bautista (1969-)
House of the Rising Sun '11
The Scorpion King 3: Battle for Redemption '11
The Man with the Iron Fists '12
Riddick '13
Guardians of the Galaxy '14
Spectre '15
Kickboxer: Vengeance '16
Marauders '16
Bushwick '17
Enter the Warriors Gate '17
Guardians of the Galaxy Vol. 2 '17
Escape Plan 2: Hades '18
Final Score '18
My Spy '19
Stuber '19

Frances Bavier (1902-89)
The Day the Earth Stood Still '51
The Lady Says No '51
The Stooge '51
Horizons West '52
My Wife's Best Friend '52
Man in the Attic '53
It Started with a Kiss '59

Barbara Baxley (1923-90)
All Fall Down '62
Countdown '68
Nashville '75
A Shock to the System '90

George L. Baxt (1923-2003)
Last Days of Pompeii '35
Which Way to the Front? '70

Alan Baxter (1908-76)
Big Brown Eyes '36
The Last Gangster '37
Wide Open Faces '38
Each Dawn I Die '39
Let Us Live '39
Abe Lincoln in Illinois '40
Shadow of the Thin Man '41
Saboteur '42
Pilot No. 5 '43
Submarine Base '43
Close-Up '48
The Set-Up '49
She Shoulda Said No '49
Judgment at Nuremberg '61

Amy Lynn Baxter (1967-)
Bikini Bistro '94
Broadcast Bombshells '95

Anne Baxter (1923-85)
Charley's Aunt '41
The Fighting Sullivans '42
The Magnificent Ambersons '42
Crash Dive '43
Five Graves to Cairo '43
The North Star '43
Guest in the House '44
Sunday Dinner for a Soldier '44
A Royal Scandal '45
Angel on My Shoulder '46
The Razor's Edge '46
Homecoming '48
The Luck of the Irish '48
Yellow Sky '48
All About Eve '50
My Wife's Best Friend '52
The Blue Gardenia '53
I Confess '53
Carnival Story '54
Bedevilled '55
One Desire '55
The Ten Commandments '56
Three Violent People '57
Chase a Crooked Shadow '58
Cimarron '60
Walk on the Wild Side '62
The Busy Body '67
Lisa, Bright and Dark '73
East of Eden '80
Jane Austen in Manhattan '80

Jane Baxter (1909-96)
The Evil Mind '34
We Live Again '34
The Flemish Farm '43

Jennifer Baxter
Dark Water '02
George A. Romero's Land of the Dead '05

Keith Baxter (1933-)
Chimes at Midnight '67
Ash Wednesday '73
Berlin Blues '89
Lynsey Baxter (1965-)
The Prime of Miss Jean Brodie '78
The French Lieutenant's Woman '81
To the Lighthouse '83
The Girl in a Swing '89
Clarissa '91
The Gospel of John '03
Meredith Baxter (1947-)
The Invasion of Carol Enders '74
All the President's Men '76
Little Women '78
Beulah Land '80
Broken Badge '85
Kate's Secret '86
Jezebel's Kiss '90
Till Murder Do Us Part '92
Betrayed: A Story of Three Women '95
The Inheritance '97
Crash Course '00
A Long Way Home '01
Murder on the Orient Express '01
Devil's Pond '03
Paradise, Texas '05
Bound by a Secret '09
Airline Disaster '10
Shadow on the Mesa '13
Warner Baxter (1889-1951)
Behind That Curtain '29
The Squaw Man '31
42nd Street '33
Penthouse '33
Broadway Bill '34
Stand Up and Cheer '34
The Prisoner of Shark Island '36
The Road to Glory '36
Slave Ship '37
Kidnapped '38
The Return of the Cisco Kid '39
Wife, Husband and Friend '39
Adam Had Four Sons '41
The Millerson Case '47
Frances Bay (1919-2011)
Foul Play '78
The Attic '80
Honky Tonk Freeway '81
The Karate Kid '84
The Karate Kid: Part 3 '89
Critters 3 '91
The Pit & the Pendulum '91
Single White Female '92
Inside Monkey Zetterland '93
The Neighbor '93
In the Mouth of Madness '95
Changing Habits '96
Happy Gilmore '96
Goodbye, Lover '99
Inspector Gadget '99
Finder's Fee '01
The Operator '01
Edmond '05
Sara Bay (1939-)
See Rosalba Neri
Nathalie Baye (1948-)
Day for Night '73
The Man Who Loved Women '77
The Green Room '78
Every Man for Himself '79
Beau Pere '81
La Balance '82
The Return of Martin Guerre '83
Notre Histoire '84
Detective '85
And the Band Played On '93
Venus Beauty Institute '98
An Affair of Love '99
Catch Me If You Can '02
Le Petit Lieutenant '05
Tell No One '06
A French Gigolo '08
Laurence Anyways '12
Queens of the Ring '13
Geoffrey Bayldon (1924-)
King Rat '65
Casino Royale '67
Asylum '72
Cause Celebre '87
Madame Sousatzka '88
Porridge '91
Hal Baylor (1918-98)
Sands of Iwo Jima '49
Island in the Sky '53
The Young Lions '58
Emperor of the North Pole '73
A Boy and His Dog '75
Jordan Bayne
Poltergeist: The Legacy '96
A Stranger in the Kingdom '98
Under Hellgate Bridge '99
Lawrence Bayne
Black Robe '91
Getting Gotti '94
Ario Bayu
Dead Mine '12
Java Heat '13
Adam Beach (1972-)
Spirit Rider '93
Squanto: A Warrior's Tale '94
Dance Me Outside '95
The Song of Hiawatha '97
Smoke Signals '98
The Last Stop '99
Joe Dirt '01
Now & Forever '02
Posers '02
Skinwalker '02
Windtalkers '02
Coyote Waits '03
The Big Empty '04
A Thief of Time '04
Flags of Our Fathers '06
Bury My Heart at Wounded Knee '07
Luna: Spirit of the Whale '07
Comanche Moon '08
Older Than America '08
The Stranger '10
Cowboys & Aliens '11
A Warrior's Heart '11
Ice Soldiers '13
A Fighting Man '14
Diablo '16
Michael Beach (1963-)
Cadence '89
Lean on Me '89
Internal Affairs '90
One False Move '91
True Romance '93
Bad Company '94
Waiting to Exhale '95
A Family Thing '96
Rebound: The Legend of Earl 'The Goat' Manigault '96
Casualties '97
Soul Food '97
Ruby Bridges '98
Asunder '99
Made Men '99
Crazy as Hell '02
Full Count '06
First Sunday '08
Stargate: The Ark of Truth '08
Play Dead '09
Relative Stranger '09
Justice for Natalee '11
Sparkle '12
500 MPH Storm '13
Stephanie Beacham (1947-)
Dracula A.D. 1972 '72
The Nightcomers '72
And Now the Screaming Starts '73
Super Bitch '73
The Confessional '75
Schizo '77
Inseminoid '80
Riders '88
Troop Beverly Hills '89
A Change of Place '94
Wedding Bell Blues '96
Unconditional Love '03
Love and Other Disasters '06
Seven Days of Grace '06
The Witches Hammer '06
Kate Beahan (1974-)
Chopper '00
The Crocodile Hunter: Collision Course '02
After the Deluge '03
Flightplan '05
The Return '06
The Wicker Man '06
John Beal (1909-97)
Little Minister '34
Break of Hearts '35
Les Miserables '35
Double Wedding '37
Madame X '37
The Cat and the Canary '39
The Great Commandment '41
Edge of Darkness '43
Key Witness '47
Ten Who Dared '60
Amityville 3: The Demon '83
The Firm '93
Simon Russell Beale (1961-)
Persuasion '95
Hamlet '96
A Dance to the Music of Time '97
The Gathering '02
Deep Water '06 (V)
The Deep Blue Sea '12
The Death of Stalin '17
My Cousin Rachel '17
Jennifer Beals (1963-)
My Bodyguard '80
Flashdance '83
The Bride '85
That's Dancing! '85
The Gamble '88
Split Decisions '88
Vampire's Kiss '88
Blood & Concrete: A Love Story '91
In the Soup '92
Mrs. Parker and the Vicious Circle '94
The Search for One-Eye Jimmy '94
Devil in a Blue Dress '95
Four Rooms '95
The Thief and the Cobbler '96 (V)
Wishful Thinking '96
The Prophecy 2: Ashtown '97
The Twilight of the Golds '97
Body and Soul '98
The Last Days of Disco '98
Militia '99
Something More '99
Turbulence 2: Fear of Flying '99
Out of Line '00
Anne Rice's The Feast of All Saints '01
The Anniversary Party '01
Roger Dodger '02
13 Moons '02
Break a Leg '03
Runaway Jury '03
Catch That Kid '04
The Grudge 2 '06
My Name Is Sarah '07
Queen to Play '09
The Book of Eli '10
The Night Before the Night Before Christmas '10
A Night for Dying Tigers '10
Full Out '15
After '19
Lee Ann Beaman
Tropical Heat '93
Starved '97
Orson Bean (1928-2020)
Anatomy of a Murder '59
Lola '69
The Hobbit '78 (V)
The Return of the King '80 (V)
Innerspace '87
Instant Karma '90
Being John Malkovich '99
Burning Down the House '01
Frank McKlusky, C.I. '02
Safe Harbor '09
Sean Bean (1959-)
Caravaggio '86
Stormy Monday '88
Troubles '88
Catherine Cookson's The Fifteen Streets '90
The Field '90
Lorna Doone '90
Clarissa '91
Fool's Gold: The Story of the Brink's-Mat Robbery '92
Lady Chatterley '92
Patriot Games '92
Sharpe's Eagle '93
Sharpe's Rifles '93
Shopping '93
A Woman's Guide to Adultery '93
Black Beauty '94
Jacob '94
Scarlett '94
Sharpe's Battle '94
Sharpe's Company '94
Sharpe's Enemy '94
Sharpe's Gold '94
Sharpe's Honour '94
Sharpe's Sword '94
Goldeneye '95
Anna Karenina '96
Sharpe's Mission '96
Sharpe's Regiment '96
Sharpe's Siege '96
Sharpe's Justice '97
Sharpe's Legend '97
Sharpe's Revenge '97
Sharpe's Waterloo '97
Airborne '98
Ronin '98
Essex Boys '99
Extremely Dangerous '99
Don't Say a Word '01
Lord of the Rings: The Fellowship of the Ring '01
Equilibrium '02
Tom & Thomas '02
Lord of the Rings: The Return of the King '03
The Big Empty '04
National Treasure '04
Troy '04
Flightplan '05
The Island '05
North Country '05
Sharpe's Challenge '06
Silent Hill '06
Far North '07
The Hitcher '07
Outlaw '07
Sharpe's Peril '08
Red Riding, Part 1: 1974 '09
Red Riding, Part 2: 1980 '09
Red Riding, Part 3: 1983 '09
Black Death '10
Death Race 2 '10
The Lost Future '10
Percy Jackson & The Olympians: The Lightning Thief '10
Cleanskin '12
Mirror Mirror '12
Silent Hill: Revelation 3D '12
Wicked Blood '13
Any Day '15
Jupiter Ascending '15
The Young Messiah '16
Drone '17
Dark River '18
Matthew Beard (1989-)
An Education '09
Chatroom '10
The Look of Love '13
Matthew 'Stymie' Beard (1925-81)
Dead Reckoning '47
Backstairs at the White House '79
East of Eden '80
When Did You Last See Your Father? '07
Amanda Bearse (1958-)
Protocol '84
Fraternity Vacation '85
Fright Night '85
Emmanuelle Beart (1965-)
Date with an Angel '87
Manon of the Spring '87
La Belle Noiseuse '90
I Don't Kiss '91
L'Enfer '93
Un Coeur en Hiver '93
Nelly et Monsieur Arnaud '95
Mission: Impossible '96
Time Regained '99
La Buche '00
Les Destinees '00
8 Women '02
Nathalie '03
The Story of Marie and Julien '03
Strayed '03
The 4 Musketeers '05
A Crime '06
The Witnesses '07
Allyce Beasley (1954-)
Ratings Game '84
Moonlighting '85
Silent Night, Deadly Night 4: Initiation '90
Motorama '91
National Lampoon's Loaded Weapon 1 '93
Stephen King's The Tommyknockers '93
Entertaining Angels: The Dorothy Day Story '96
Rumpelstiltskin '96
Dream with the Fishes '97
2 Brothers & a Bride '03
John Beasley (1943-)
Lucky Day '91
The Apostle '97
Crazy in Alabama '99
The General's Daughter '99
Freedom Song '00
The Gift '00
Lost Souls '00
The Sum of All Fears '02
Walking Tall '04
Stephanie Beaton (1972-)
Witchcraft 9: Bitter Flesh '96
Witchcraft 10: Mistress of the Craft '98
Witchcraft 11: Sisters in Blood '00
The Bagman '02
Blood Gnome '02
Stephanie Beatriz
Short Term 12 '13
The Light of the Moon '17
The LEGO Movie 2: The Second Part '19
Maureen Beattie
The Last Musketeer '00
The Decoy Bride '11
Clyde Beatty (1903-65)
The Lost Jungle '34
Africa Screams '49
May (Mae) Beatty (1880-1945)
Mad Love '35
I Wake Up Screaming '41
Nancy Beatty
Henry & Verlin '94
Eye '96
The Confessor '04
Lars and the Real Girl '07
Ned Beatty (1937-)
Deliverance '72
Dying Room Only '73
The Last American Hero '73
White Lightning '73
Nashville '75
Sniper '75
W.W. and the Dixie Dancekings '75
All the President's Men '76
The Big Bus '76
Mikey & Nicky '76
Network '76
Silver Streak '76
The Exorcist 2: The Heretic '77
Gray Lady Down '77
Our Town '77
Great Bank Hoax '78
Superman: The Movie '78
Friendly Fire '79
1941 '79
Promises in the Dark '79
Wise Blood '79
The Guyana Tragedy: The Story of Jim Jones '80
Hopscotch '80
Superman 2 '80
The Incredible Shrinking Woman '81
The Toy '82
A Woman Called Golda '82
Stroker Ace '83
The Last Days of Pompeii '84
Hostage Flight '85
Konrad '85
Back to School '86
The Big Easy '87
The Fourth Protocol '87
Midnight Crossing '87
Switching Channels '88
The Unholy '88
Captain America '89
Chattahoochee '89
Ministry of Vengeance '89
Physical Evidence '89
Back to Hannibal: The Return of Tom Sawyer and Huckleberry Finn '90
Big Bad John '90
A Cry in the Wild '90
Repossessed '90
Robert Kennedy and His Times '90
Going Under '91
Prelude to a Kiss '92
Ed and His Dead Mother '93
Rudy '93
Just Cause '94
Radioland Murders '94
Replikator: Cloned to Kill '94
The Affair '95
Gulliver's Travels '95
Larry McMurtry's Streets of Laredo '95
He Got Game '98
Cookie's Fortune '99
Life '99
Spring Forward '99
Homicide: The Movie '00
Sweet Land '05
Charlie Wilson's War '07
Shooter '07
The Walker '07
In the Electric Mist '08
The Killer Inside Me '10
Toy Story 3 '10 (V)
Rampart '11
Rango '11 (V)
Robert Beatty (1909-92)
Appointment with Crime '45
Against the Wind '48
Counterblast '48
The Twenty Questions Murder Mystery '50
Captain Horatio Hornblower '51
Wings of Danger '52
Man on a Tightrope '53
Loves of Three Queens '54
Tarzan's Hidden Jungle '55
Postmark for Danger '56
Tarzan and the Lost Safari '57
Time Lock '57
2001: A Space Odyssey '68
Where Eagles Dare '68
Warren Beatty (1937-)
Roman Spring of Mrs. Stone '61
Splendor in the Grass '61
All Fall Down '62
Lilith '64
Mickey One '65
Kaleidoscope '66
Bonnie & Clyde '67
Dollars '71
McCabe & Mrs. Miller '71
The Parallax View '74
Shampoo '75

Heaven Can Wait *'78*
Reds *'81*
Ishtar *'87*
Dick Tracy *'90*
Bugsy *'91*
Love Affair *'94*
Bulworth *'98*
Town and Country *'01*
Rules Don't Apply *'16*

Madisen Beaty (1995-)
Bedtime Stories *'08*
The Curious Case of Benjamin Button *'08*
The Five *'10*
The Pregnancy Pact *'10*
Jamie Marks is Dead *'13*
Other People *'16*
Outlaws and Angels *'16*

Michelle Beaudoin (1975-)
Sabrina the Teenage Witch *'96*
Escape Velocity *'99*

Hugh Beaumont (1909-82)
South of Panama *'41*
To the Shores of Tripoli *'42*
Wake Island *'42*
The Fallen Sparrow *'43*
The Seventh Victim *'43*
Mr. Winkle Goes to War *'44*
The Lady Confesses *'45*
Objective, Burma! *'45*
Blonde for a Day *'46*
The Blue Dahlia *'46*
Larceny in her Heart *'46*
Money Madness *'47*
Railroaded *'47*
Cavalry Charge *'51*
The Lost Continent *'51*
Savage Drums *'51*
Phone Call from a Stranger *'52*
Wild Stallion *'52*
The Mole People *'56*
Night Passage *'57*
The Human Duplicators *'64*

Kathryn Beaumont (1937-)
Alice in Wonderland *'51 (V)*
Peter Pan *'53 (V)*

Lucy Beaumont (1873-1937)
The Family Secret *'24*
Torrent *'26*
Caught Plastered *'31*
A Free Soul *'31*
Condemned to Live *'35*
Devil Doll *'36*

Gabrielle Beauvais (1972-)
See Gabrielle Union

Garcelle Beauvais (1966-)
Manhunter *'86*
Wild Wild West *'99*
Double Take *'01*
Bad Company *'02*
Barbershop 2: Back in Business *'04*
American Gun *'05*
I Know Who Killed Me *'07*
Maneater *'09*
And Then There Was You *'13*
Small Time *'14*

Xavier Beauvois (1967-)
Ponette *'95*
Farewell, My Queen *'12*
Let the Sunshine In *'17*

Nicolas Beauvy (1958-)
Shoot Out *'71*
The Cowboys *'72*
Rage *'72*
The Toolbox Murders *'78*

Jim Beaver (1950-)
In Country *'89*
Bad Girls *'94*
The Life of David Gale *'03*
Next *'07*
Dark and Stormy Night *'09*
The Frontier *'16*

Louise Beavers (1902-62)
Too Busy to Work *'32*
Girl Missing *'33*
She Done Him Wrong *'33*
Imitation of Life *'34*
The Merry Frinks *'34*
It Happened in New Orleans *'36*
Bullets or Ballots *'38*
No Time For Comedy *'40*
Big Street *'42*
Reap the Wild Wind *'42*
Du Barry Was a Lady *'43*
Dixie Jamboree *'44*
Delightfully Dangerous *'45*
Mr. Blandings Builds His Dream House *'48*
Tell It to the Judge *'49*
The Jackie Robinson Story *'50*
My Blue Heaven *'50*
Goodbye, My Lady *'56*
Tammy and the Bachelor *'57*

Demian Bechir (1963-)
Solo *'96*
No News from God *'01*
A Better Life *'11*
Dom Hemingway *'13*

Jennifer Beck (1974-)
Tightrope *'84*
Troll *'86*
Gypsy *'93*

John Beck (1943-)
Lawman *'71*
Nightmare Honeymoon *'73*
Sleeper *'73*
Sidekicks *'74*
Rollerball *'75*
The Big Bus *'76*
Sky Riders *'76*
Audrey Rose *'77*
The Other Side of Midnight *'77*
In the Cold of the Night *'89*
Black Day Blue Night *'95*
Agent of Death *'99*
Militia *'99*
Extreme Limits *'01*
Timecop 2: The Berlin Decision *'03*

Julian Beck (1925-85)
Oedipus Rex *'67*
Poltergeist 2: The Other Side *'86*

Kimberly Beck (1956-)
Massacre at Central High *'76*
Zuma Beach *'78*
Roller Boogie *'79*
Friday the 13th, Part 4: The Final Chapter *'84*
Nightmare at Noon *'87*
In the Deep Woods *'91*

Michael Beck (1949-)
Holocaust *'78*
Madman *'79*
The Warriors *'79*
Xanadu *'80*
Warlords of the 21st Century *'82*
The Golden Seal *'83*

Thomas Beck (1909-95)
Charlie Chan in Egypt *'35*
Charlie Chan in Paris *'35*
Life Begins at Forty *'35*
Charlie Chan at the Opera *'36*
Charlie Chan at the Race Track *'36*
White Fang *'36*
Thank you, Mr. Moto *'37*
Think Fast, Mr. Moto *'37*

Graham Beckel (1949-)
The Paper Chase *'73*
The Money *'75*
Lost Angels *'89*
A Family of Spies *'90*
O Pioneers! *'91*
Separate but Equal *'91*
Jennifer 8 *'92*
The Disappearance of Vonnie *'94*
L.A. Confidential *'97*
Black Dog *'98*
Bulworth *'98*
Blue Streak *'99*
No Vacancy *'99*
True Crime *'99*
The '70s *'00*
Hardball *'01*
Just Ask My Children *'01*
Northfork *'03*
Two Days *'03*
Bachelor Party Vegas *'05*
Brokeback Mountain *'05*
Peacock *'09*
Atlas Shrugged: Part 1 *'11*
Killing Lincoln *'13*

Ben Becker (1964-)
Brother of Sleep *'95*
Samson and Delilah *'96*
The Harmonists *'99*
Gloomy Sunday *'02*

Gerry Becker (1951-)
The Public Eye *'92*
Donnie Brasco *'96*
Eraser *'96*
Mickey Blue Eyes *'99*
Blood Work *'02*
Spider-Man *'02*

Gretchen Becker
Firehead *'90*
Huck and the King of Hearts *'93*
Maniac Cop 3: Badge of Silence *'93*

Hartmut Becker (1948-)
Escape from Sobibor *'87*
The Waiting Time *'99*

Jacques Becker (1906-60)
Boudu Saved from Drowning *'32*
Grand Illusion *'37*

Josh Becker (1958-)
Evil Dead 2: Dead by Dawn *'87*
Army of Darkness *'92*

Kuno Becker (1978-)
Lucia, Lucia *'03*
ESL: English as a Second Language *'05*
Once Upon a Wedding *'05*
Goal! The Dream Begins *'06*
Goal 2: Living the Dream *'07*
Sex and Breakfast *'07*
From Mexico With Love *'09*

Meret Becker (1969-)
The Wicked, Wicked West *'97*
The Harmonists *'99*
Munich *'05*
Wetlands *'13*

Natalie Becker
The World Unseen *'07*
The Scorpion King 2: Rise of a Warrior *'08*
Tremors 5: Bloodlines *'15*

Randy Becker (1970-)
Lie Down with Dogs *'95*
Love! Valour! Compassion! *'96*
American Adobo *'02*

Tony Becker (1963-)
Agent Red *'00*
The Hunters *'11*

Scotty Beckett (1929-68)
Stand Up and Cheer *'34*
The Charge of the Light Brigade *'36*
Conquest *'37*
Devil's Party *'38*
Listen, Darling *'38*
Marie Antoinette *'38*
Love Affair *'39*
Gold Rush Maisie *'40*
My Favorite Wife *'40*
The Vanishing Virginian *'41*
Ali Baba and the Forty Thieves *'43*
Heaven Can Wait *'43*
The Climax *'44*
The Jolson Story *'46*
Battleground *'49*
The Happy Years *'50*
Nancy Goes to Rio *'50*
Corky of Gasoline Alley *'51*
Gasoline Alley *'51*
The Oklahoman *'56*

Tyson Beckford (1970-)
Biker Boyz *'03*
Into the Blue *'05*
Searching for Bobby D *'05*
Kings of the Evening *'08*
Addicted *'14*

David Beckham (1975-)
Goal! The Dream Begins *'06 (C)*
Goal 2: Living the Dream *'07 (C)*

Kate Beckinsale (1973-)
Much Ado about Nothing *'93*
Cold Comfort Farm *'94*
Royal Deceit *'94*
Uncovered *'94*
Haunted *'95*
Emma *'97*
The Last Days of Disco *'98*
Shooting Fish *'98*
Brokedown Palace *'99*
The Golden Bowl *'00*
Pearl Harbor *'01*
Serendipity *'01*
Laurel Canyon *'02*
Tiptoes *'03*
Underworld *'03*
The Aviator *'04*
Van Helsing *'04*
Underworld: Evolution *'05*
Click *'06*
Snow Angels *'07*
Vacancy *'07*
Fragments *'08*
Nothing But the Truth *'08*
Everybody's Fine *'09*
Underworld: Rise of the Lycans *'09*
Whiteout *'09*
Contraband *'12*
Total Recall *'12*
Underworld: Awakening *'12*
Stonehearst Asylum *'13*
The Trials of Cate McCall *'13*
The Face of an Angel *'14*
The Disappointments Room *'16*
Love & Friendship *'16*
Underworld: Blood Wars *'16*
Absolutely Anything *'17*
The Only Living Boy in New York *'17*
Farming *'19*

Tony Beckley (1927-80)
The Italian Job *'69*
The Fiend *'71*
Get Carter *'71*
When a Stranger Calls *'79*

William Beckley (1930-)
The Killing of Sister George *'69*
Too Late the Hero *'70*

Claire Beckman (1961-)
Fallout *'01*
The Thing About My Folks *'05*

Owen Beckman
Crash and Burn *'07*
Dream Boy *'08*

Reginald Beckwith (1908-65)
Another Man's Poison *'52*
Penny Princess *'52*
Genevieve *'53*
The Runaway Bus *'54*
Curse of the Demon *'57*
Lucky Jim *'58*
Doctor in Love *'60*
Burn, Witch, Burn! *'62*
Just for Fun *'63*

Irene Bedard (1967-)
Squanto: A Warrior's Tale *'94*
Pocahontas *'95 (V)*
Navajo Blues *'97*
The Song of Hiawatha *'97*
True Women *'97*
Two for Texas *'97*
Smoke Signals *'98*
Wildflowers *'99*
The Lost Child *'00*
Love's Long Journey *'05*
Miracle at Sage Creek *'05*
The New World *'05*
Tortilla Heaven *'07*
Songs My Brother Taught Me *'15*

Don Beddoe (1891-1991)
Blondie Meets the Boss *'39*
Golden Boy *'39*
Blondie On a Budget *'40*
Charlie Chan's Murder Cruise *'40*
The Big Boss *'41*
The Best Years of Our Lives *'46*
Buck Privates Come Home *'47*
Welcome Stranger *'47*
Gun Crazy *'49*
Caged *'50*
Corky of Gasoline Alley *'51*
The Enforcer *'51*
Gasoline Alley *'51*
Carson City *'52*
The Narrow Margin *'52*
The System *'53*
Loophole *'54*
The Night of the Hunter *'55*
Boy Who Caught a Crook *'61*
Jack the Giant Killer *'62*
Saintly Sinners *'62*
Papa's Delicate Condition *'63*

Bonnie Bedelia (1948-)
Then Came Bronson *'68*
The Gypsy Moths *'69*
They Shoot Horses, Don't They? *'69*
Lovers and Other Strangers *'70*
Salem's Lot *'79*
Heart Like a Wheel *'83*
The Boy Who Could Fly *'86*
Violets Are Blue *'86*
The Stranger *'87*
Die Hard *'88*
Prince of Pennsylvania *'88*
Fat Man and Little Boy *'89*
Die Hard 2: Die Harder *'90*
Presumed Innocent *'90*
Somebody Has to Shoot the Picture *'90*
The Fire Next Time *'93*
Needful Things *'93*
Speechless *'94*
Homecoming *'96*
Bad Manners *'98*
Gloria *'98*
Anywhere But Here *'99*
Flowers for Algernon *'00*
Sordid Lives *'00*
Berkeley *'05*

Rodney Bedell
Gruesome Twosome *'67*
Just for the Hell of It *'68*

Barbara Bedford (1903-81)
The Last of the Mohicans *'20*
Tumbleweeds *'25*
Mockery *'27*
The Notorious Lady *'27*
Sunny *'30*

Brian Bedford (1935-)
Grand Prix *'66*
Robin Hood *'73 (V)*
The Last Best Year *'90*
Scarlett *'94*
Nixon *'95*
Armistead Maupin's More Tales of the City *'97 (C)*
Mr. St. Nick *'02*

Kabir Bedi (1946-)
Demon Rage *'82*
Octopussy *'83*
The Beast *'88*
Beyond Justice *'92*
The Lost Empire *'01*

Gerry Bednob (1950-)
Brutal Massacre: A Comedy *'07*
Zack and Miri Make a Porno *'08*
Why Am I Doing This? *'09*
Rock Jocks *'12*
Honey 2 *'14*
All Out Dysfunktion! *'16*

Alfonso Bedoya (1904-57)
Border River *'47*
Treasure of the Sierra Madre *'48*
Border Incident *'49*
The Stranger Wore a Gun *'53*

Bruce Beeby
Radio Cab Murder *'54*
Pit of Darkness *'61*

Janet Beecher (1884-1955)
Gallant Lady *'33*
I'd Give My Life *'36*
Love Before Breakfast *'36*
Big City *'37*
The Mark of Zorro *'40*

David Beecroft (1955-)
Shadowzone *'89*
The Awakening *'95*
Octopus *'00*

Daniel Beer
Creepshow 2 *'87*
Point Break *'91*
The Last Best Sunday *'98*

Paula Beer (1995-)
Frantz *'17*
Never Look Away *'18*
Transit *'18*

Noah Beery, Jr. (1913-94)
Mark of Zorro *'20*
Fighting with Kit Carson *'33*
The Three Musketeers *'33*
Tailspin Tommy *'34*
Savage Fury *'35*
Ace Drummond *'36*
Forbidden Valley *'38*
Of Mice and Men *'39*
Only Angels Have Wings *'39*
Sergeant York *'41*
Overland Mail *'42*
Gung Ho! *'43*
Red River *'48*
Davy Crockett, Indian Scout *'50*
Rocketship X-M *'50*
Cavalry Charge *'51*
The Story of Will Rogers *'52*
Wagons West *'52*
War Arrow *'53*
The Black Dakotas *'54*
Fastest Gun Alive *'56*
Jubal *'56*
Decision at Sundown *'57*
Inherit the Wind *'60*
7 Faces of Dr. Lao *'63*
Heaven With a Gun *'69*
Richard Petty Story *'72*
Walking Tall *'73*
Sidekicks *'74*
The Spikes Gang *'74*
Savages *'75*
Walking Tall: Part 2 *'75*
The Bastard *'78*
Mysterious Two *'82*

Noah Beery, Sr. (1884-1945)
A Mormon Maid *'17*
Mark of Zorro *'20*
Soul of the Beast *'23*
The Vanishing American *'25*
Noah's Ark *'28*
Bright Lights *'30*
Golden Dawn *'30*
Devil Horse *'32*
Kid from Spain *'32*
Fighting with Kit Carson *'33*
She Done Him Wrong *'33*
To the Last Man *'33*
David Harum *'34*
Kentucky Kernels *'34*
Zorro Rides Again *'37*
The Bad Man of Brimstone *'38*
Adventures of Red Ryder *'40*
Overland Mail *'42*
Clancy Street Boys *'43*

Wallace Beery (1885-1949)
The Last of the Mohicans *'20*
The Four Horsemen of the Apocalypse *'21*
Robin Hood *'22*
White Tiger *'23*
The Red Lily *'24*
The Sea Hawk *'24*
The Lost World *'25*
Beggars of Life *'28*

Tom Bell (1933-2006)
Ballad in Blue '66
Quest for Love '71
Dressed for Death '74
Royal Flash '75
Wish You Were Here '87
Let Him Have It '91
Prospero's Books '91
Prime Suspect '92
Catherine Cookson's The Cinder Path '94
Feast of July '95
The Boxer '97 (C)
Preaching to the Perverted '97
Swept from the Sea '97
The Last Minute '01

Zoe Bell (1978-)
Death Proof '07
Angel of Death '09
Gamer '09
Whip It '09
Game of Death '10
The Big Take '18

Rachael Bella (1984-)
The Blood Oranges '97
The Ring '02
Jimmy & Judy '06

Bill Bellamy (1965-)
Who's the Man? '93
Love Jones '96
Def Jam's How to Be a Player '97
Any Given Sunday '99
Love Stinks '99
The Brothers '01
Buying the Cow '02
Getting Played '05
The Lottery Ticket '10
The Bounce Back '16
Kindergarten Cop 2 '16

Diana Bellamy (1944-2001)
Stripped to Kill '87
The Nest '88
Amelia Earhart: The Final Flight '94

Madge Bellamy (1899-1990)
Lorna Doone '22
Soul of the Beast '23
The Iron Horse '24
The White Sin '24
Lazybones '25
The White Zombie '32
The Ivory Handled Gun '35
Northwest Trail '46

Ned Bellamy (1957-)
Bob Roberts '92
Carnosaur '93
Ed Wood '94
Angel's Dance '99
Saw '04
Tenacious D in the Pick of Destiny '06
Two Tickets to Paradise '06
The Contract '07
Wind Chill '07
War, Inc. '08
Blood Money '17

Ralph Bellamy (1904-91)
The Secret Six '31
West of Broadway '31
Forbidden '32
Young America '32
Ace of Aces '33
Picture Snatcher '33
Spitfire '34
Woman in the Shadows '34
Air Hawks '35
Hands Across the Table '35
The Wedding Night '35
Healer '36
The Awful Truth '37
Boy Meets Girl '38
Carefree '38
Let Us Live '39
Brother Orchid '40
Dance, Girl, Dance '40
Flight Angels '40
His Girl Friday '40
Dive Bomber '41
Footsteps in the Dark '41
The Wolf Man '41
The Ghost of Frankenstein '42
Lady in a Jam '42
Guest in the House '44
Delightfully Dangerous '45
Lady on a Train '45
The Court Martial of Billy Mitchell '55
Sunrise at Campobello '60
The Professionals '66
Rosemary's Baby '68
Doctors' Wives '70
Cancel My Reservation '72
Missiles of October '74
Murder on Flight 502 '75
Search for the Gods '75
Arthur Hailey's The Moneychangers '76
The Boy in the Plastic Bubble '76
Once an Eagle '76
Oh, God! '77
Testimony of Two Men '77
Trading Places '83
The Winds of War '83
Fourth Wise Man '85
Amazon Women on the Moon '87
Disorderlies '87
The Good Mother '88
War & Remembrance '88
War & Remembrance: The Final Chapter '89
Pretty Woman '90

Jana Bellan
Six-Pack Annie '75
Black Heat '76

Clara Bellar (1972-)
Romance and Rejection '96
David '97
The First 9 1/2 Weeks '98
A. I.: Artificial Intelligence '01
Kill the Poor '03
Dominion: Prequel to the Exorcist '05

Harry Bellaver (1905-93)
House on 92nd Street '45
No Way Out '50
The Lemon Drop Kid '51
The Tanks Are Coming '51
From Here to Eternity '53
The Great Diamond Robbery '53
The Old Man and the Sea '58

Annie Belle (1956-)
Forever Emmanuelle '75
Lips of Blood '75

Camilla Belle (1986-)
Annie: A Royal Adventure '95
Secre of the Andes '98
Back to the Secret Garden '01
The Ballad of Jack and Rose '05
The Chumscrubber '05
The Quiet '05
When a Stranger Calls '06
10,000 B.C. '08
Push '09
Father of Invention '11
From Prada to Nada '11
Open Road '13
The American Side '16
Diablo '16
Sundown '16

David Belle (1973-)
District B13 '04
District 13: Ultimatum '09
Brick Mansions '14

Kathleen Beller (1956-)
The Godfather, Part 2 '74
Mary White '77
The Betsy '78
Promises in the Dark '79
Fort Apache, the Bronx '81
The Manions of America '81
Sword & the Sorcerer '82

Ryan Belleville
Finn on the Fly '09
Step Dogs '13

Agostina Belli (1947-)
The Night of the Devils '72
Seduction of Mimi '72
Revolver '75
The Scent of a Woman '75
The Chosen '77

Jimmy Bellinger
Geek Charming '11
A Smile as Big as the Moon '12
I Am Potential '15

Troian Bellisario (1985-)
C.O.G. '13
Martyrs '16
Clara '19

Gina Bellman (1966-)
Leon the Pig Farmer '93
David '97
Silent Trigger '97
7 Days to Live '00
Jekyll '07

Maria Bello (1967-)
Payback '98
Permanent Midnight '98
Coyote Ugly '00
Duets '00
Auto Focus '02
100 Mile Rule '02
The Cooler '03
Secret Window '04
Silver City '04
Assault on Precinct 13 '05
A History of Violence '05
The Sisters '05
Flicka '06
Thank You for Smoking '06
World Trade Center '06
The Jane Austen Book Club '07
Shattered '07
Towelhead '07
Downloading Nancy '08
The Mummy: Tomb of the Dragon Emperor '08
The Yellow Handkerchief '08
The Private Lives of Pippa Lee '09
Beautiful Boy '10
The Company Men '10
Grown Ups '10
Abduction '11
Carjacked '11
Grown Ups 2 '13
Prisoners '13
Third Person '13
McFarland USA '15
The Confirmation '16
Lights Out '16
Max Steel '16
In Search of Fellini '17
Giant Little Ones '19

Sara Bellomo (1974-)
Bikini Drive-In '94
Beach Babes 2: Cave Girl Island '95

Gil Bellows (1967-)
Love and a .45 '94
The Shawshank Redemption '94
Black Day Blue Night '95
Miami Rhapsody '95
The Substance of Fire '96
Snow White: A Tale of Terror '97
Beautiful Joe '00
Chasing Sleep '00
The Courage to Love '00
She Creature '01
Blind Horizon '04
The Weather Man '05
Final Days of Planet Earth '06
Infected '08
The Promotion '08
24: Redemption '08
Goblin '10
Hunt to Kill '10
A Night for Dying Tigers '10
Passchendaele '10
Unthinkable '10
Debbie Macomber's Trading Christmas '11
The Year Dolly Parton Was My Mom '11
House at the End of the Street '12
The Calling '14
Extraterrestrial '14
Life on the Line '16
Scary Stories to Tell in the Dark '19

Monica Bellucci (1964-)
Bram Stoker's Dracula '92
Like a Fish Out of Water '99
Malena '00
Under Suspicion '00
Brotherhood of the Wolf '01
Irreversible '02
The Matrix Reloaded '03
The Matrix Revolutions '03
Tears of the Sun '03
The Passion of the Christ '04
She Hate Me '04
The Brothers Grimm '05
How Much Do You Love Me? '05
Shoot 'Em Up '07
The Private Lives of Pippa Lee '09
The Sorcerer's Apprentice '10
A Burning Hot Summer '11
The Whistleblower '11
Spectre '15
The Wonders '15

Pamela Bellwood (1951-)
Hangar 18 '80
Agatha Christie's Sparkling Cyanide '83
Cocaine: One Man's Seduction '83
Going Shopping '05

Jean-Paul Belmondo (1933-)
Breathless '59
Classe Tous Risque '60
Love and the Frenchwoman '60
A Woman Is a Woman '60
Le Doulos '61
Leon Morin, Priest '61
A Man Named Rocca '61
Two Women '61
Cartouche '62
Greed In the Sun '64
Pierrot le Fou '65
Is Paris Burning? '66
Casino Royale '67
The Thief of Paris '67
The Brain '69
Mississippi Mermaid '69
Borsalino '70
Stavisky '74
Le Magnifique '76
Le Professionnel '81
Stuntwoman '81

Daisy Belmore (1874-1954)
Alias French Gertie '30
Sylvia Scarlett '35

Lionel Belmore (1867-1953)
The Man Who Had Everything '20
Oliver Twist '22
Bardelys the Magnificent '26
The Love Parade '29
Monte Carlo '30
Frankenstein '31
Son of Frankenstein '39

Robert Beltran (1953-)
Eating Raoul '82
Night of the Comet '84
Latino '85
El Diablo '90
Bugsy '91
The Chase '91
Luminarias '99
Manticore '05
Fire Serpent '07
Repo Chick '09
Taking Chances '09

Mark Beltzman (1960-)
Mo' Money '92
Billy Madison '94

James Belushi (1954-)
The Fury '78
Thief '81
Trading Places '83
The Man with One Red Shoe '85
About Last Night. . . '86
Jumpin' Jack Flash '86
Little Shop of Horrors '86
Salvador '86
The Principal '87
Real Men '87
Red Heat '88
Homer and Eddie '89
K-9 '89
Who's Harry Crumb? '89
Abraxas: Guardian of the Universe '90
Mr. Destiny '90
Taking Care of Business '90
Curly Sue '91
Diary of a Hitman '91
Only the Lonely '91
Once Upon a Crime '92
Traces of Red '92
Last Action Hero '93 (C)
Wild Palms '93
Canadian Bacon '94
The Pebble and the Penguin '94 (V)
Separate Lives '94
Sahara '95
Gang Related '96
Jingle All the Way '96
Race the Sun '96
Living in Peril '97
Retroactive '97
The Florentine '98
Angel's Dance '99
Backlash '99
K-911 '99
Made Men '99
Echo of Murder '00
Return to Me '00
Joe Somebody '01
K-9 3: P.I. '01
One Way Out '02
Hoodwinked '05 (V)
The Wild '06 (V)
Underdog '07
Snow Buddies '08 (V)
Cougars, Inc. '10
The Ghost Writer '10
Thunderstruck '12
Legends of Oz: Dorothy's Return '14 (V)
The Whole Truth '16

Jim Belushi
The Hollow Point '16
Wonder Wheel '17

John Belushi (1949-82)
All You Need Is Cash '78
Goin' South '78
National Lampoon's Animal House '78
1941 '79
Old Boyfriends '79
The Blues Brothers '80
Continental Divide '81
Neighbors '81

Lucas Belvaux
Cop Au Vin '85
Joyeux Noel '05

Richard Belzer (1944-)
The Groove Tube '72
Fame '80
Student Bodies '81
Night Shift '82
Scarface '83
Freeway '88
The Wrong Guys '88
The Big Picture '89
Fletch Lives '89
Mad Dog and Glory '93
The Puppet Masters '94
Get On the Bus '96
Girl 6 '96
Not of This Earth '96
A Very Brady Sequel '96
Homicide: The Movie '00

Cliff Bemis
Modern Love '90
Au Pair 2: The Fairy Tale Continues '01

Paul Ben-Victor (1965-)
Body Parts '91
True Romance '93
Houseguest '94
Maximum Risk '96
Metro '96
Ed McBain's 87th Precinct: Heatwave '97
The Corruptor '99
Crazy in Alabama '99
Drowning Mona '00
Gun Shy '00
Kiss Toledo Goodbye '00
Daredevil '03
On the Doll '07
Venus and Vegas '10
Mighty Fine '12
By the Gun '14

Jordy Benattar (1993-)
Comfort and Joy '03
Fallen Angel '03
Charlie & Me '08

Brian Benben (1956-)
Clean and Sober '88
I Come in Peace '90
Radioland Murders '94
Surf's Up '07 (V)

Adel Bencherif
A Prophet '09
Of Gods and Men '10

Robert Benchley (1889-1945)
Dancing Lady '33
Rafter Romance '33
China Seas '35
The Robert Benchley Miniatures Collection '35
Live, Love and Learn '37
Foreign Correspondent '40
You'll Never Get Rich '41
The Major and the Minor '42
Syncopation '42
The Sky's the Limit '43
See Here, Private Hargrove '44
It's in the Bag! '45
The Stork Club '45
Weekend at the Waldorf '45
The Bride Wore Boots '46
The Road to Utopia '46

Russ Bender (1910-69)
I Bury the Living '58
War of the Colossal Beast '58
The Ghost of Dragstrip Hollow '59
Anatomy of a Psycho '61
Raiders from Beneath the Sea '64
Wild On the Beach '65
Navy *vs.* the Night Monsters '66

Michael C. Bendetti (1967-)
Netherworld '90
Red Shoe Diaries: Luscious Lola '00

William Bendix (1906-64)
The Glass Key '42
Star Spangled Rhythm '42
Wake Island '42
Who Done It? '42
Woman of the Year '42
China '43
Guadalcanal Diary '43
Greenwich Village '44
The Hairy Ape '44
Lifeboat '44
Don Juan Quilligan '45
It's in the Bag! '45
The Blue Dahlia '46
Dark Corner '46
Calcutta '47
Where There's Life '47
Babe Ruth Story '48
Race Street '48
The Time of Your Life '48
Big Steal '49
A Connecticut Yankee in King Arthur's Court '49
Cover Up '49
Kill the Umpire '50
Detective Story '51
Blackbeard the Pirate '52
Macao '52
Deep Six '58
Idol on Parade '59
The Rough and the Smooth '59
For Love or Money '63

Nelly Benedetti
The Soft Skin '64
Make Your Bets Ladies '65

The Great Lover '49
It's a Mad, Mad, Mad, Mad World '63
A Guide for the Married Man '67 (C)

Melissa Benoist
Whiplash '14
Danny Collins '15
Lowriders '17
Jay and Silent Bob Reboot '19

Abraham Benrubi (1969-)
Crossing the Bridge '92
The Program '93
The Shadow '94
Twister '96
George of the Jungle '97
U-Turn '97
Under Oath '97
Open Range '03
Without a Paddle '04
Miss Congeniality 2: Armed and Fabulous '05
Charlotte's Web '06 (V)
Wristcutters: A Love Story '06
Calvin Marshall '09
Venus and Vegas '10
Deep Dark Canyon '12
Bounty Killer '13
Ava & Lala '14

Tyrone Benskin
The Christmas Choir '08
My Nanny's Secret '09

Amber Benson (1977-)
The Crush '93
Bye Bye, Love '94
Taboo '02
Latter Days '04
Holiday Wishes '06
Kiss the Bride '07
7 Things to Do Before I'm 30 '08
Strictly Sexual '08
The Blue Tooth Virgin '09
The Killing Jar '10

Amber Nicole Benson (1977-)
See Amber Benson

Ashley Benson (1989-)
Bring It On: In It to Win It '07
Bart Got a Room '08
Christmas Cupid '10
Spring Breakers '13
Ratter '16

Deborah Benson
September 30, 1955 '77
Just Before Dawn '80

George Benson (1911-83)
Convoy '40
The Creeping Flesh '72

Jodi Benson (1961-)
The Little Mermaid '89 (V)
Thumbelina '94 (V)
Toy Story 2 '99 (V)
Toy Story 3 '10 (V)

Julia Benson (1979-)
The Unquiet '08
Earth's Final Hours '12
Chupacabra vs. the Alamo '13
Death Do Us Part '14
Interrogation '16

Lucille Benson (1914-84)
Duel '71
Private Parts '72
Huckleberry Finn '74
Mame '74

Martin Benson (1918-2010)
Recoil '53
The King and I '56
Spin a Dark Web '56
Exodus '60
A Matter of WHO '62
The Omen '76

Peter Benson
Trophy Wife '06
Christmas Lodge '11
The Pregnancy Project '12
Death Do Us Part '14

Robby Benson (1956-)
Jory '72
All the Kind Strangers '74
The Death of Richie '76
The Last of Mrs. Lincoln '76
Ode to Billy Joe '76
The Virginia Hill Story '76
One on One '77
Our Town '77
The End '78
Ice Castles '79
Die Laughing '80
The Chosen '81
National Lampoon Goes to the Movies '81
Running Brave '83
Harry & Son '84
City Limits '85
Rent-A-Cop '88
Modern Love '90
Beauty and the Beast '91 (V)
Dragonheart: A New Beginning '00 (V)
MXP: Most Xtreme Primate '03

Wendy Benson (1971-)
Wishmaster '97
Luck of the Draw '00

Lyriq Bent
Saw 3 '06
Saw 4 '07
Guns '08
Home Again '13
Aaliyah: The Princess of R&B '14
A Day Late and a Dollar Short '14
Pay the Ghost '15
Acrimony '18

Timothy Bentinck (1953-)
Year of the Comet '92
Sharpe's Rifles '93

Michael Bentine (1922-96)
Down Among the Z Men '52
Goon Movie '52
Rentadick '72

Fabrizio Bentivoglio (1957-)
Apartment Zero '88
Eternity and a Day '97
Loro '19

Dana Bentley
Bad Girls from Mars '90
Karate Cop '91
Sorority House Massacre 2: Nighty Nightmare '92

John Bentley (1916-2009)
The Way Out '56
White Huntress '57

Lamont Bentley (1973-2005)
Tales from the Hood '95
The Wash '01

Wes Bentley (1978-)
American Beauty '99
White River '99
The Claim '00
Soul Survivors '01
The Four Feathers '02
The Game of Their Lives '05
Ghost Rider '07
P2 '07
The Perfect Witness '07
Weirdsville '07
The Last Word '08
Dolan's Cadillac '09
The Tomb '09
There Be Dragons '11
Gone '12
The Hunger Games '12
Rites of Passage '12
The Time Being '12
Pioneer '13
The Better Angels '14
Cesar Chavez '14
Interstellar '14
Amnesiac '15
Knight of Cups '15
We Are Your Friends '15
Welcome to Me '15
Broken Vows '16
Pete's Dragon '16
The Best of Enemies '19

Barbi Benton (1950-)
The Third Girl from the Left '73
For the Love of It '80
Deathstalker '83

Jerome Benton
Under the Cherry Moon '86
Graffiti Bridge '90

Mark Benton (1965-)
Catherine Cookson's The Girl '96
Career Girls '97
Topsy Turvy '99
Flick '07
Land Girls '09

Susanne Benton (1948-)
That Cold Day in the Park '69
Catch-22 '70
Best Friends '75
A Boy and His Dog '75

Michael Bentt (1965-)
Ali '01
State Property 2 '05

Femi Benussi (1945-)
The Hawks & the Sparrows '67
Hatchet for the Honeymoon '70
The Italian Connection '73

Luke Benward (1995-)
Because of Winn-Dixie '05
How to Eat Fried Worms '06
Dog Gone '08
Minutemen '08
Girl vs. Monster '12
Field of Lost Shoes '14

Michael Benyaer
Postal '07
Deadpool '16

Julie Benz (1972-)
Darkdrive '98
Jawbreaker '98
Shriek If You Know What I Did Last Friday the 13th '00
The Brothers '01
Taken '02
The Long Shot '04
8mm 2 '05
Locusts: The 8th Plague '05
Circle of Friends '06
Kill Your Darlings '06
Punisher: War Zone '08
Rambo '08
Saw 5 '08
The Boondock Saints II: All Saints Day '09
Held Hostage '09
Answers to Nothing '11
Life on the Line '16

A.J. Benza (1962-)
P.S. Your Cat is Dead! '02
Rocky Balboa '06

Daniel Benzali (1950-)
Pack of Lies '87
Messenger of Death '88
A Day in October '92
The Last of His Tribe '92
The End of Violence '97
Murder at 1600 '97
All the Little Animals '98
Boss of Bosses '99
Screwed '00
Dead Heat '01
The Grey Zone '01
Believers '07
How Do You Know '10

John Beradino (1917-96)
7 Men From Now '56
The World Was His Jury '58
Seven Thieves '60
Moon of the Wolf '72

Ady Berber (1913-66)
Dead Eyes of London '61
Door with the Seven Locks '62

Marcel Berbert
Mississippi Mermaid '69
The Green Room '78

Emmanuelle Bercot
It All Starts Today '99
Polisse '11

Luca Bercovici (1957-)
Frightmare '81
Parasite '82
American Flyers '85
Clean and Sober '88
Pacific Heights '90
K2: The Ultimate High '92
Inside Monkey Zetterland '93
Drop Zone '94
The Big Squeeze '96
Burning Down the House '01
Dirt Boy '01
Hard Luck '01
Letting Go '12

Blaze Berdahl (1980-)
Pet Sematary '89
We're Back! A Dinosaur's Story '93 (V)

Ingrid Bolso Berdal (1980-)
Cold Prey II '08
The ABCs of Death '12 (V)
Chernobyl Diaries '12
Escape '12
Hercules '14

Omar Berdouni
The Hamburg Cell '04
Extraordinary Rendition '07

Oscar Beregi
36 Hours '64
The Christine Jorgensen Story '70

Tom Berenger (1949-)
The Sentinel '76
In Praise of Older Women '78
Butch and Sundance: The Early Days '79
The Dogs of War '81
Beyond Obsession '82
The Big Chill '83
Eddie and the Cruisers '83
Fear City '85
Rustler's Rhapsody '85
If Tomorrow Comes '86
Platoon '86
Someone to Watch Over Me '87
Betrayed '88
Last Rites '88
Shoot to Kill '88
Born on the Fourth of July '89
Love at Large '89
Major League '89
The Field '90
Shattered '91
Sniper '92
Gettysburg '93
Sliver '93
Chasers '94
Major League 2 '94
The Avenging Angel '95
Body Language '95
The Last of the Dogmen '95
An Occasional Hell '96
The Substitute '96
The Gingerbread Man '97
Rough Riders '97
One Man's Hero '98
Shadow of Doubt '98
Diplomatic Siege '99
A Murder of Crows '99
Turbulence 2: Fear of Flying '99
Cutaway '00
Cruel and Unusual '01
Eye See You '01
The Hollywood Sign '01
Training Day '01
True Blue '01
Johnson County War '02
The Junction Boys '02
Sniper 2 '02
Sniper 3 '04
The Christmas Miracle of Jonathan Toomey '07
Silent Venom '08
Stiletto '08
Breaking Point '09
The Hitman Diaries '09
Faster '10
Inception '10
Sinners and Saints '10
Smokin' Aces 2: Assassins' Ball '10
Brake '12
Hatfields & McCoys '12
War Flowers '12
Bad Country '14
Lonesome Dove Church '14
Sniper: Legacy '14

Marisa Berenson (1947-)
Death in Venice '71
Cabaret '72
Barry Lyndon '75
Sex on the Run '78
S.O.B. '81
White Hunter, Black Heart '90
Women '97
People '04
I Am Love '09

Harry Beresford (1864-1944)
The Sign of the Cross '33
Klondike Annie '36

Justin Berfield (1986-)
Invisible Mom '96
Mom, Can I Keep Her? '98
Invisible Mom 2 '99
The Kid with the X-Ray Eyes '99
Max Keeble's Big Move '01

Peter Berg (1964-)
Never on Tuesday '88
Going Overboard '89
Shocker '89
Tale of Two Sisters '89
Crooked Hearts '91
Late for Dinner '91
A Midnight Clear '92
Aspen Extreme '93
Fire in the Sky '93
Across the Moon '94
The Last Ride '94
The Last Seduction '94
Girl 6 '96
The Great White Hype '96
Cop Land '97
Corky Romano '01
Collateral '04
Lions for Lambs '07
Smokin' Aces '07

Sonia Bergamasco (1966-)
Best of Youth '03
Giulia Doesn't Date at Night '09
Me and You '12

Francine Berge (1940-)
Circle of Love '64
Judex '64

Candice Bergen (1946-)
The Group '66
The Sand Pebbles '66
The Adventurers '70
Getting Straight '70
Soldier Blue '70
Carnal Knowledge '71
11 Harrowhouse '74
Bite the Bullet '75
The Wind and the Lion '75
The Domino Principle '77
A Night Full of Rain '78
Oliver's Story '78
Starting Over '79
Rich and Famous '81
Gandhi '82
2010: The Year We Make Contact '84 (V)
Stick '85
Mayflower Madam '87
Miss Congeniality '00
Sweet Home Alabama '02
Footsteps '03
The In-Laws '03
View from the Top '03
Sex and the City: The Movie '08
The Women '08
Bride Wars '09
The Romantics '10
Home Again '17
Book Club '18

Edgar Bergen (1903-78)
The Goldwyn Follies '38
Letter of Introduction '38
You Can't Cheat an Honest Man '39
Look Who's Laughing '41
Here We Go Again! '42
Stage Door Canteen '43
Fun & Fancy Free '47 (N)
I Remember Mama '48
Don't Make Waves '67
Homecoming: A Christmas Story '71
The Muppet Movie '79 (C)

Frances Bergen (1922-2006)
The Morning After '86
Eating '90

Polly Bergen (1930-2014)
At War with the Army '50
The Stooge '51
That's My Boy '51
Escape from Fort Bravo '53
Cape Fear '61
The Caretakers '63
Move Over, Darling '63
Kisses for My President '64
A Guide for the Married Man '67 (C)
Murder on Flight 502 '75
The Winds of War '83
Making Mr. Right '86
War & Remembrance '88
My Brother's Wife '89
War & Remembrance: The Final Chapter '89
Cry-Baby '90
Dr. Jekyll and Ms. Hyde '95
Once Upon a Time . . . When We Were Colored '95
Paradise, Texas '05
A Very Serious Person '06

Tushka Bergen (1969-)
Wrangler '88
Swing Kids '93
Barcelona '94
Lovelife '97
The Cherry Orchard '99
Invisible Child '99
Journey to the Center of the Earth '99

Helmut Berger (1944-)
The Damned '69
Dorian Gray '70
The Garden of the Finzi-Continis '71
Ludwig '72
Ash Wednesday '73
Order to Kill '73
Conversation Piece '75
Romantic Englishwoman '75
Victory at Entebbe '76
Mad Dog Killer '77
Battleforce '78
Mad Dog '84
Code Name: Emerald '85
Faceless '88
The Godfather, Part 3 '90

Nicole Berger (1935-67)
The Siege of Sidney Street '60
Shoot the Piano Player '62
The Story of a Three Day Pass '68

Senta Berger (1941-)
Secret of the Black Trunk '62
Sherlock Holmes and the Deadly Necklace '62
Testament of Dr. Mabuse '62
Waltz King '63
Bang! Bang! You're Dead! '66
Cast a Giant Shadow '66
The Quiller Memorandum '66
The Ambushers '67
Diabolically Yours '67
To Commit a Murder '67
When Women Had Tails '70
The Scarlet Letter '73
Smugglers '75
When Women Lost Their Tails '75

Cross of Iron '76
Swiss Conspiracy '77
Blitz '85
Sidney Berger (1936-)
Carnival of Souls '62
Carnival of Souls '98
William Berger (1928-93)
Ringo's Big Night '66
Sabata '69
Five Dolls for an August Moon '70
Today We Kill, Tomorrow We Die '71
California '77
Oil '78
Hercules '83
Day of the Cobra '84
Hercules 2 '85
Django Strikes Again '87
Jacques Bergerac (1927-2014)
Gigi '58
The Hypnotic Eye '60
Fury of Achilles '62
Astrid Berges-Frisbey (1986-)
The Well-Digger's Daughter '11
I Origins '14
King Arthur: Legend of the Sword '17
Thommy Berggren (1937-)
Elvira Madigan '67
The Adventurers '70
Herbert Berghof (1909-90)
Assignment: Paris '52
Five Fingers '52
Red Planet Mars '52
Fraulein '58
Harry and Tonto '74
Patrick Bergin (1951-)
Taffin '88
Mountains of the Moon '90
The Real Charlotte '91
Robin Hood '91
Sleeping with the Enemy '91
Patriot Games '92
Frankenstein '93
Map of the Human Heart '93
Lawnmower Man 2: Beyond Cyberspace '95
Triplecross '95
The Proposition '96
Suspicious Minds '96
The Apocalypse Watch '97
The Island on Bird Street '97
Stolen Women, Captured Hearts '97
One Man's Hero '98
Escape Velocity '99
Eye of the Beholder '99
Treasure Island '99
When the Sky Falls '99
Cause of Death '00
Deadline '00
Invisible Circus '00
St. Patrick: The Irish Legend '00
Amazons and Gladiators '01
Beneath Loch Ness '01
The Devil's Prey '01
King of Texas '02
The Boys and Girl From County Clare '03
Brush with Fate '03
Ella Enchanted '04
Frederick Forsyth's Icon '05
Johnny Was '05
False Prophets '06
The Far Side of Jericho '06
Played '06
Secret of the Cave '06
Eva '09
Shark Island '12
Emily Bergl (1975-)
The Rage: Carrie 2 '99
Chasing Sleep '00
Happy Campers '01
Taken '02
Henry Bergman (1868-1946)
City Lights '31
Modern Times '36
Ingrid Bergman (1915-82)
Intermezzo '36
A Woman's Face '38
Intermezzo '39
June Night '40
Adam Had Four Sons '41
Dr. Jekyll and Mr. Hyde '41
Rage in Heaven '41
Casablanca '42
For Whom the Bell Tolls '43
Gaslight '44
The Bells of St. Mary's '45
Saratoga Trunk '45
Spellbound '45
Notorious '46
Arch of Triumph '48
Joan of Arc '48
Under Capricorn '49
Voyage in Italy '53
Anastasia '56
Elena and Her Men '56
Indiscreet '58
The Inn of the Sixth Happiness '58
The Visit '64
The Yellow Rolls Royce '64
Cactus Flower '69
Walk in the Spring Rain '70
The Hideaways '73
Murder on the Orient Express '74
A Matter of Time '76
Autumn Sonata '78
A Woman Called Golda '82
Jaime Bergman (1975-)
Daybreak '01
Darkwolf '03
Boa *vs.* Python '04
Sandahl Bergman (1951-)
Xanadu '80
Airplane 2: The Sequel '82
Conan the Barbarian '82
She '83
Red Sonja '85
Hell Comes to Frogtown '88
Raw Nerve '91
Body of Influence '93
Lipstick Camera '93
Ice Cream Man '95
Tim Bergmann
Regular Guys '96
Sasha '10
Elisabeth Bergner (1900-86)
Catherine the Great '34
As You Like It '36
Cry of the Banshee '70
Helena Bergstrom (1964-)
Still Crazy '98
Under the Sun '98
Gossip '00
Christian Berkel (1957-)
The Experiment '01
Safe Conduct '01
Downfall '04
Guys and Balls '04
Black Book '06
Valkyrie '08
Ballard Berkeley
East Meets West '36
They Made Me a Fugitive '47
Busby Berkeley (1895-1976)
42nd Street '33
Dames '34
Fashions of 1934 '34
Babes on Broadway '41
Million Dollar Mermaid '52
Xander Berkeley (1955-)
Sid & Nancy '86
Straight to Hell '87
Tapeheads '89
Internal Affairs '90
Candyman '92
A Few Good Men '92
The Gun in Betty Lou's Handbag '92
Attack of the 50 Ft. Woman '93
Roswell: The U.F.O. Cover-Up '94
Apollo 13 '95
Heat '95
Poison Ivy 2: Lily '95
Safe '95
Barb Wire '96
Bulletproof '96
If These Walls Could Talk '96
The Killing Jar '96
Persons Unknown '96
The Rock '96
Within the Rock '96
Air Force One '97
Phoenix '98
Winchell '98
The Cherry Orchard '99
Universal Soldier: The Return '99
Shanghai Noon '00
Time Code '00
Quicksand '01
In Enemy Hands '04
Deepwater '05
Drop Dead Sexy '05
Standing Still '05
Magma: Volcanic Disaster '06
Fracture '07
Taken '08
The Toe Tactic '08
Repo Chick '09
Faster '10
Kick-Ass '10
Seeking Justice '12
Small Time '14
Elizabeth Berkley (1972-)
Point Break '91
White Wolves 2: Legend of the Wild '94
Showgirls '95
The First Wives Club '96
The Real Blonde '97
Random Encounter '98
The Taxman '98
Any Given Sunday '99
Tail Lights Fade '99
The Curse of the Jade Scorpion '01
Roger Dodger '02
Moving Malcolm '03
Student Seduction '03
Meet Market '08
S. Darko: A Donnie Darko Tale '09
Lucky Christmas '11
Steven Berkoff (1937-)
A Clockwork Orange '71
The Passenger '75
Outland '81
Octopussy '83
Beverly Hills Cop '84
Rambo: First Blood, Part 2 '85
Revolution '85
War & Remembrance '88
War & Remembrance: The Final Chapter '89
Fair Game '95
Another 9 1/2 Weeks '96
Flynn '96
Legionnaire '98
Rancid Aluminium '00
Attila '01
Children of Dune '03
Charlie '04
Head in the Clouds '04
The Flying Scotsman '06
The Big I Am '10
Dead Cert '10
Drop Dead Gorgeous '10
The Road to Coronation Street '10
The Tourist '10
The Girl With the Dragon Tattoo '11
Milton Berle (1908-2002)
Mark of Zorro '20
New Faces of 1937 '37
Tall, Dark and Handsome '41
Whispering Ghosts '42
Margin for Error '43
The Bellboy '60 (C)
Let's Make Love '60
It's a Mad, Mad, Mad, Mad World '63
The Loved One '65
Who's Minding the Mint? '67
Where Angels Go, Trouble Follows '68 (C)
Evil Roy Slade '71
Journey Back to Oz '71 (V)
Legend of Valentino '75
Lepke '75
The Muppet Movie '79 (C)
Cracking Up '83
Broadway Danny Rose '84
Storybook '95
Francois Berleand (1952-)
Au Revoir les Enfants '87
Capitaine Conan '96
Place Vendome '98
Seventh Heaven '98
Romance '99
A Model Employee '02
The Transporter '02
Whatever You Say '02
The Chorus '04
The Grand Role '04
Transporter 2 '05
Comedy of Power '06
Tell No One '06
A Girl Cut in Two '07
Cash '08
Transporter 3 '08
The Concert '09
Jeannie Berlin (1949-)
The Baby Maker '70
Getting Straight '70
The Strawberry Statement '70
The Heartbreak Kid '72
Housewife '72
Margaret '11
Café Society '16
Charles Berling (1958-)
Nelly et Monsieur Arnaud '95
Love, etc. '96
Ridicule '96
Dry Cleaning '97
Obsession '97
L'Ennui '98
Those Who Love Me Can Take the Train '98
The Bridge '00
Comedy of Innocence '00
Les Destinees '00
Stardom '00
Demonlover '02
How I Killed My Father '03
The Man of My Life '06
Summer Hours '08
The Clearstream Affair '15
Elle '16
Peter Berling (1934-)
Aguirre, the Wrath of God '72
Revolver '75
Cobra Verde '88
Francesco '93
Warren Berlinger (1937-)
Teenage Rebel '56
Because They're Young '60
All Hands on Deck '61
Billie '65
Spinout '66
Thunder Alley '67
The Girl Most Likely to. . . '73
The Long Goodbye '73
Four Deuces '75
The World According to Garp '82
Hero '92
Backlash '99
Shelley Berman (1925-)
The Wheeler Dealers '63
The Best Man '64
Divorce American Style '67
Beware! The Blob '72
Motorama '91
Meet the Fockers '04
The Holiday '06
You Don't Mess with the Zohan '08
Susan Berman
Smithereens '82
Curtain Call '97
Jamie Bernadette
Son of Sam '08
Night Stalker '09
Gael Garcia Bernal (1978-)
Amores Perros '00
No News from God '01
Y Tu Mama Tambien '01
The Crime of Father Amaro '02
Fidel '02
I'm with Lucy '02
Cuban Blood '03
Dot the I '03
Bad Education '04
The Motorcycle Diaries '04
The King '05
Babel '06
The Science of Sleep '06
Blindness '08
The Limits of Control '09
Mammoth '09
Rudo y Cursi '09
Even the Rain '10
Letters to Juliet '10
A Little Bit of Heaven '11
Casa de mi Padre '12
The Loneliest Planet '12
No '12
Rosewater '14
Desierto '16
Neruda '16
Coco '17
Andre Bernard
The Crying Game '92
The Sea Change '98
Crystal Bernard (1961-)
Slumber Party Massacre 2 '87
Jackpot '01
Welcome to Paradise '07
Jason Bernard (1938-96)
Wilma '77
Uncle Joe Shannon '78
All of Me '84
The Children of Times Square '86
No Way Out '87
While You Were Sleeping '95
Liar Liar '97
Susan Bernard (1948-2019)
Faster, Pussycat! Kill! Kill! '65
Teenager '74
Herschel Bernardi (1923-86)
Green Fields '37
Murder by Contract '58
1001 Arabian Nights '59 (V)
The George Raft Story '61
Irma La Douce '63
Journey Back to Oz '71 (V)
The Story of Jacob & Joseph '74
The Front '76
Nerio Bernardi
Hercules and the Black Pirate '60
Caesar the Conqueror '63
Lynn Bernay (1931-2008)
I Bury the Living '58
The Pit and the Pendulum '61
Sandra Bernhard (1955-)
Cheech and Chong's Nice Dreams '81
King of Comedy '82
Sesame Street Presents: Follow That Bird '85
Track 29 '88
Heavy Petting '89
Hudson Hawk '91
Inside Monkey Zetterland '93
The Apocalypse '96
The Late Shift '96
An Alan Smithee Film: Burn, Hollywood, Burn '97
Plump Fiction '97
Somewhere in the City '97
Footsteps '98
Wrongfully Accused '98
Dinner Rush '00
Playing Mona Lisa '00
Dare '09
Daniel Bernhardt (1965-)
Bloodsport 4: The Dark Kumite '98
Perfect Target '98
G2: Mortal Conquest '99
The Matrix Reloaded '03
The Cutter '05
Precious Cargo '16
Kevin Bernhardt (1961-)
Midnight Warrior '89
Hellraiser 3: Hell on Earth '92
The Immortals '95
Mara Berni (1934-)
The Fury of Hercules '61
Samson '61
Collin Bernsen
Puppet Master 2 '90
Hangfire '91
Corbin Bernsen (1954-)
Eat My Dust '76
King Kong '76
Hello Again '87
Bert Rigby, You're a Fool '89
Disorganized Crime '89
Major League '89
Shattered '91
Final Mission '93
The Ghost Brigade '93
Ring of the Musketeers '93
Major League 2 '94
The New Age '94
Radioland Murders '94
Savage Land '94
The Soft Kill '94
Where Are My Children? '94
Baja '95
Tales from the Hood '95
The Dentist '96
The Great White Hype '96
Kounterfeit '96
Menno's Mind '96
The Dentist 2: Brace Yourself '98
Major League 3: Back to the Minors '98
Recipe for Revenge '98
Riddler's Moon '98
Spacejacked '98
An American Affair '99
Final Payback '99
Killer Instinct '00
Rangers '00
The Tomorrow Man '01
The Santa Trap '02
Love Comes Softly '03
Call Me: The Rise and Fall of Heidi Fleiss '04
They Are Among Us '04
Carpool Guy '05
Kiss Kiss Bang Bang '05
Paid '06
Dead Air '08
Depth Charge '08
For the Love of Grace '08
Vipers '08
Donna on Demand '09
Rust '09
Across the Line: The Exodus of Charlie Wright '10
First Lady '20
Jon Bernthal (1976-)
Day Zero '07
Night at the Museum: Battle of the Smithsonian '09
The Ghost Writer '10
Snitch '13
The Wolf of Wall Street '13
Fury '14
Sicario '15
The Accountant '16
Sweet Virginia '17
Wind River '17
Widows '18
Ford v Ferrari '19
Claude Berri (1934-2009)
Please Not Now! '61
Va Savoir '01
Happily Ever After '04
Elizabeth Berridge (1962-)
The Funhouse '81
Amadeus '84
Silence of the Heart '84
Five Corners '88

When the Party's Over *'91*
Hidalgo *'04*

Elizabeth Berrington (1970-)
Urban Ghost Story *'98*
Tristram Shandy: A Cock and Bull Story *'05*
Fred Claus *'07*

Chuck Berry (1926-2017)
Rock, Rock, Rock *'56*
Go, Johnny Go! *'59*
Chuck Berry: Hail! Hail! Rock 'n' Roll *'87*

Halle Berry (1968-)
Jungle Fever *'91*
The Last Boy Scout *'91*
Strictly Business *'91*
Boomerang *'92*
Father Hood *'93*
The Program *'93*
Queen *'93*
The Flintstones *'94*
Losing Isaiah *'94*
Executive Decision *'96*
Girl 6 *'96*
Race the Sun *'96*
The Rich Man's Wife *'96*
B.A.P.'s *'97*
Bulworth *'98*
Why Do Fools Fall in Love? *'98*
Introducing Dorothy Dandridge *'99*
X-Men *'00*
Monster's Ball *'01*
Swordfish *'01*
Die Another Day *'02*
Gothika *'03*
X2: X-Men United *'03*
Catwoman *'04*
Robots *'05 (V)*
X-Men: The Last Stand *'06*
Perfect Stranger *'07*
Things We Lost in the Fire *'07*
Frankie and Alice *'10*
New Year's Eve *'11*
Cloud Atlas *'12*
Dark Tide *'12*
The Call *'13*
Movie 43 *'13*
X-Men: Days of Future Past *'14*
Kevin Hart: What Now? *'16*
Kidnap *'17*
Kings *'17*
Kingsman: The Golden Circle *'17*
John Wick: Chapter 3-Parabellum *'19*

Jules Berry (1883-1951)
The Crime of Monsieur Lange *'36*
Le Jour Se Leve *'39*

Ken Berry (1933-)
Hello Down There *'69*
Herbie Rides Again *'74*
The Cat from Outer Space *'78*

Marilou Berry
Look at Me *'04*
A French Gigolo *'08*
Queens of the Ring *'13*

Mark Berry
Delivered *'98*
Blade: Trinity *'04*

Michael Berry
The Touch of Satan *'70*
Beyond the Law *'92*

Richard Berry (1950-)
A Man and a Woman: 20 Years Later *'86*
L'Appat *'94*
The Valet *'06*
22 Bullets *'10*

Veronica Berry (1986-)
Father of Lies *'07*
Lords of the Street *'08*
Ticking Clock *'10*

Vincent Berry (1987-)
Amnesia *'96*
Free Willy 3: The Rescue *'97*

Sugar Town *'99*
Baby *'00*

Dorothee Berryman (1948-)
The Decline of the American Empire *'86*
A Paper Wedding *'89*
The Pianist *'91*
Winter Lily *'98*
Taken *'99*
The Barbarian Invasions *'03*

Michael Berryman (1948-)
Gator King *'70*
One Flew Over the Cuckoo's Nest *'75*
The Hills Have Eyes *'77*
Deadly Blessing *'81*
The Hills Have Eyes, Part 2 *'84*
Cut and Run *'85*
Star Trek 4: The Voyage Home *'86*
Voyage of the Rock Aliens *'87*
Aftershock *'88*
Saturday the 14th Strikes Back *'88*
Evil Spirits *'91*
The Guyver *'91*
Haunting Fear *'91*
Teenage Exorcist *'93*
Wizards of the Demon Sword *'94*
The Devil's Rejects *'05*
Outrage Born in Terror *'09*
Mask Maker *'10*
The Lords of Salem *'13*

Julien Bertheau (1910-95)
Madame Sans-Gene *'62*
Phantom of Liberty *'74*
That Obscure Object of Desire *'77*

Anders W. Berthelsen (1969-)
Mifune *'99*
The Weight of Water *'00*
Italian for Beginners *'01*
Just Another Love Story *'08*

Jacques Berthier (1923-94)
The Master of Ballantrae *'53*
Ladies' Man *'62*
The Old Testament *'62*

Aldo Berti
An Angel for Satan *'66*
Go With God Gringo *'66*

Dehl Berti (1921-91)
Sweet Hostage *'75*
Wolfen *'81*
Bullies *'86*

Marina Berti (1925-2002)
Prince of Foxes *'49*
Quo Vadis *'51*
Madame Sans-Gene *'62*
Night Train Murders *'75*

Francoise Bertin (1925-2014)
Dad On the Run *'00*
Happenstance *'00*
A Christmas Tale *'08*

Roland Bertin (1930-)
Diva *'82*
L'Homme Blesse *'83*
Cyrano de Bergerac *'90*
The Hairdresser's Husband *'92*

Valerie Bertinelli (1960-)
C.H.O.M.P.S. *'79*
Silent Witness *'85*
Number One with a Bullet *'87*
Wilderness Love *'02*
Saved! *'04 (C)*
True Confessions of a Hollywood Starlet *'08*

Jane Bertish
Dance with a Stranger *'85*
The Roman Spring of Mrs. Stone *'03*

Suzanne Bertish (1951-)
The Hunger *'83*
To the Lighthouse *'83*
Venice, Venice *'92*

The Scarlet Pimpernel 3: The Kidnapped King *'99*
The Roman Spring of Mrs. Stone *'03*

Juliet Berto (1947-90)
The Joy of Knowledge *'65*
La Chinoise *'67*
Mr. Klein *'76*

Paul Bertoya
Hot Rods to Hell *'67*
Angels from Hell *'68*

Gene Bervoets (1956-)
The Vanishing *'88*
The Memory of a Killer *'03*

Bibi Besch (1940-96)
Peter Lundy and the Medicine Hat Stallion *'77*
Backstairs at the White House *'79*
Death of a Centerfold *'81*
The Beast Within *'82*
Star Trek 2: The Wrath of Khan *'82*
Date with an Angel *'87*
Kill Me Again *'89*
Tremors *'89*
Betsy's Wedding *'90*
Crazy from the Heart *'91*
Doing Time on Maple Drive *'92*
Abandoned and Deceived *'95*

Melchior Beslon
The Princess and the Warrior *'00*
Paris, je t'aime *'06*

Dominique Besnehard (1954-)
A Nos Amours *'84*
Beaumarchais the Scoundrel *'96*

Ardon Bess
Spenser: The Judas Goat *'94*
Moving Target *'96*

Ted Bessell (1935-96)
Billie *'65*
Don't Drink the Water *'69*
Breaking Up Is Hard to Do *'79*

Joe Besser (1907-88)
Feudin', Fussin', and A-Fightin' *'48*
Africa Screams *'49*
Sins of Jezebel *'54*

Matt Besser
Undead or Alive *'07*
Walk Hard: The Dewey Cox Story *'07*

Eugenie Besserer (1868-1934)
The Greatest Question *'19*
Anna Christie *'23*
The Flesh and the Devil *'27*
The Jazz Singer *'27*
A Lady of Chance *'28*
Madame X *'29*
Speedway *'29*

Claudia Besso
The Reagans *'04*
The Tipping Point *'07*

Ahmed Best (1973-)
Star Wars: Episode 1-The Phantom Menace *'99 (V)*
Star Wars: Episode 2-Attack of the Clones *'02 (V)*
Star Wars: Episode 3-Revenge of the Sith *'05*
Mother and Child *'09*
2001 Maniacs: Field of Screams *'10*

Edna Best (1900-74)
The Man Who Knew Too Much *'34*
Intermezzo *'39*
The Ghost and Mrs. Muir *'47*

James Best (1926-2015)
Kansas Raiders *'50*
Ma and Pa Kettle at the Fair *'52*
Cole Younger, Gunfighter *'58*

Cast a Long Shadow *'59*
The Killer Shrews *'59*
Ride Lonesome *'59*
Verboten! *'59*
Black Gold *'62*
Shock Corridor *'63*
The Quick Gun *'64*
Shenandoah *'65*
First to Fight *'67*
Savage Run *'70*
Mind Warp *'72*
Sounder *'72*
Ode to Billy Joe *'76*
Death Mask *'98*
Moondance Alexander *'07*
The Sweeter Side of Life *'13*

Willie Best (1913-62)
Kentucky Kernels *'34*
The Littlest Rebel *'35*
The Bride Walks Out *'36*
The Ghost Breakers *'40*
High Sierra *'41*
Nothing But the Truth *'41*
The Smiling Ghost *'41*
The Hidden Hand *'42*
Whispering Ghosts *'42*
The Kansan *'43*
The Bride Wore Boots *'46*
Dangerous Money *'46*

Barbara Bestar (1929-)
Safari Drums *'53*
Killers from Space *'54*

Martine Beswick (1941-)
From Russia with Love *'63*
Thunderball *'65*
One Million Years B.C. *'66*
Prehistoric Women *'67*
A Bullet for the General *'68*
Dr. Jekyll and Sister Hyde *'71*
Seizure *'74*
Strange New World *'75*
Devil Dog: The Hound of Hell *'78*
The Happy Hooker Goes Hollywood *'80*
Balboa *'82*
Cyclone *'87*
The Offspring *'87*
Miami Blues *'90*
Trancers 2: The Return of Jack Deth *'90*
Evil Spirits *'91*
Wide Sargasso Sea *'92*
Night of the Scarecrow *'95*

Anne Betancourt
Seedpeople *'92*
Fools Rush In *'97*
Bless the Child *'00*

Erin Bethea
Fireproof *'08*
Texas Rein *'16*

Wilson Bethel (1984-)
Generation Kill *'08*
Tunnel Rats *'08*
Wyatt Earp's Revenge *'12*

Sabine Bethmann (1931-)
Journey to the Lost City *'58*
Dr. Mabuse *vs.* Scotland Yard *'64*

Zena Bethune (1945-2012)
Sunrise at Campobello *'60*
Who's That Knocking at My Door? *'68*

Paul Bettany (1971-)
Bent *'97*
Sharpe's Waterloo *'97*
Coming Home *'98*
After the Rain *'99*
Every Woman Knows a Secret *'99*
Robert Louis Stevenson's The Game of Death *'99*
Gangster No. 1 *'00*
A Beautiful Mind *'01*
A Knight's Tale *'01*
The Heart of Me *'02*
Dogville *'03*
Master and Commander: The Far Side of the World *'03*
The Reckoning *'03*
Wimbledon *'04*
The Da Vinci Code *'06*

Firewall *'06*
Iron Man *'08 (V)*
The Secret Life of Bees *'08*
Creation *'09*
Inkheart *'09*
The Young Victoria *'09*
Iron Man 2 *'10 (V)*
Legion *'10*
The Tourist *'10*
Margin Call *'11*
Priest *'11*
The Avengers *'12 (V)*
Iron Man 3 *'13 (V)*
Transcendence *'14*
Mortdecai *'15*
Journey's End *'18*

Francoise Bette
It All Starts Today *'99*
The Girl from Paris *'02*

Dominique Bettenfeld
A Very Long Engagement *'04*
Sleepless Night *'11*

Lyle Bettger (1915-2003)
Union Station *'50*
Denver and the Rio Grande *'52*
All I Desire *'53*
Carnival Story *'54*
Drums Across the River *'54*
Sea Chase *'55*
Lone Ranger *'56*
Johnny Reno *'66*
Nevada Smith *'66*
Return of the Gunfighter *'67*
Impasse *'69*

Laura Betti (1927-2004)
Teorema *'68*
Hatchet for the Honeymoon *'70*
The Canterbury Tales *'71*
Twitch of the Death Nerve *'71*
Sonny and Jed *'73*
1900 *'76*
Lovers and Liars *'81*
Courage Mountain *'89*

Val Bettin (1916-)
The Great Mouse Detective *'86 (V)*
The Return of Jafar *'94 (V)*

Angela Bettis (1973-)
The Last Best Sunday *'98*
Bless the Child *'00*
Carrie *'02*
Coastlines *'02*
May *'02*
Scar *'07*
The Woman *'11*

Valerie Bettis
Affair in Trinidad *'52*
Let's Do It Again *'53*

Daniel Betts (1970-)
The Canterville Ghost *'96*
Heat of the Sun *'99*
The Magical Legend of the Leprechauns *'99*

Jack Betts (1929-)
The Bloody Brood *'59*
Hallelujah for Django *'67*
Django and Sartana; It's the End *'70*
One Fine Day, When Django Met Sartana *'70*
Dead Men Don't Die *'91*
Gods and Monsters *'98*
Southern Man *'99*
Spider-Man *'02*

Carl Betz (1921-78)
City of Bad Men *'53*
Dangerous Crossing *'53*
Powder River *'53*
Spinout *'66*

Matthew Betz (1881-1938)
The Unholy Three *'25*
Tarzan the Fearless *'33*
Mutiny Ahead *'35*

Billy Bevan (1887-1957)
The White Sin *'24*
Vanity Fair *'32*
Cavalcade *'33*
The Lost Patrol *'34*

The Last Outpost *'35*
Girl of the Golden West *'38*
Dr. Jekyll and Mr. Hyde *'41*
Mrs. Miniver *'42*
The Woman in Green *'49*
Rogues of Sherwood Forest *'50*

Clem Bevans (1879-1963)
Abe Lincoln in Illinois *'40*
Sergeant York *'41*
The Kansan *'43*
Wake Up and Dream *'46*
The Millerson Case *'47*

Ken Bevel
Fireproof *'08*
Courageous *'11*

Helen Beverly (1916-2011)
Green Fields *'37*
The Light Ahead *'39*
The Master Race *'44*
Meeting at Midnight *'44*

Charlie Bewley
Like Crazy *'11*
Collision *'13*
Bachelor Games *'16*
Renegades *'17*

Nathan Bexton (1977-)
Go *'99*
The In Crowd *'00*
Psycho Beach Party *'00*

Marki Bey (1946-)
The Landlord *'70*
Sugar Hill *'74*

Turhan Bey (1920-2012)
Footsteps in the Dark *'41*
The Gay Falcon *'41*
Arabian Nights *'42*
Junior G-Men of the Air *'42*
The Mummy's Tomb *'42*
Ali Baba and the Forty Thieves *'43*
Background to Danger *'43*
The Climax *'44*
Dragon Seed *'44*
Out of the Blue *'47*
The Amazing Mr. X *'48*
Parole, Inc. *'49*
Virtual Combat *'95*

Alexander Beyer (1973-)
The Legend of Rita *'99*
Good Bye, Lenin! *'03*

Brad Beyer (1973-)
Crazy in Alabama *'99*
The General's Daughter *'99*
Trick *'99*
Monday Night Mayhem *'02*
Sorority Boys *'02*

Troy Beyer (1964-)
Rooftops *'89*
Weekend at Bernie's 2 *'93*
B.A.P.'s *'97*
John Q *'02*
A Light in the Darkness *'02*

Richard Beymer (1938-)
Johnny Tremain & the Sons of Liberty *'58*
The Diary of Anne Frank *'59*
High Time *'60*
West Side Story *'61*
Bachelor Flat *'62*
Five Finger Exercise *'62*
The Longest Day *'62*
Silent Night, Deadly Night 3: Better Watch Out! *'89*
Black Belt *'92*
Foxfire *'96*

Didier Bezace (1946-2020)
Les Voleurs *'96*
The Chambermaid on the Titanic *'97*

Dante Beze (1973-)
See Mos Def

Aletta Bezuidenhout
Dark Kingdom: The Dragon King *'04*
In My Country *'04*

Raoul Bhaneja
Touch of Pink *'04*
Weirdsville *'07*

Mayim Bialik (1975-)
Beaches *'88*
The Dog Who Saved Halloween *'11 (V)*

Viva Bianca
Bad Bush *'09*
The Reckoning *'14*

Eleanora Bianchi
Fury of Achilles *'62*
Goliath and the Sins of Babylon *'64*

Rosa Maria Bianchi
Amores Perros *'00*
Nicotina *'03*

Yuen Biao (1957-)
The Prodigal Son *'82*
Project A *'83*
Zu: Warriors from the Magic Mountain *'83*
The Millionaire's Express *'86*
Eastern Condors *'87*
Dragons Forever *'88*
Miracles *'89*
Once Upon a Time in China *'91*
Robin-B-Hood *'06*

Leslie Bibb (1974-)
The Skulls *'00*
See Spot Run *'01*
Talladega Nights: The Ballad of Ricky Bobby *'06*
Wristcutters: A Love Story *'06*
Sex and Death 101 *'07*
Iron Man *'08*
The Midnight Meat Train *'08*
Trick 'r Treat *'08*
Confessions of a Shopaholic *'09*
Law Abiding Citizen *'09*
Iron Man 2 *'10*
Miss Nobody *'10*
A Good Old Fashioned Orgy *'11*
Zookeeper *'11*
Meeting Evil *'12*
7500 *'12*
No Good Deed *'14*
Flight 7500 *'16*
Awakening the Zodiac *'17*
Running with the Devil *'19*

Abner Biberman (1909-77)
Gunga Din *'39*
The Rains Came *'39*
His Girl Friday *'40*
The Leopard Man *'43*
The Keys of the Kingdom *'44*
Elephant Walk *'54*
Knock on Wood *'54*

Robert Bice (1914-68)
Invasion U.S.A. *'52*
Loan Shark *'52*
1,000 Years From Now *'52*
The Gun That Won the West *'55*

Bruno Bichir (1967-)
Highway Patrolman *'91*
Midaq Alley *'95*
No News from God *'01*
Julia *'08*

Demian Bichir (1963-)
In the Time of the Butterflies *'01*
Che *'08*
Savages *'12*
The Heat *'13*
Machete Kills *'13*
The Hateful Eight *'15*
Alien: Covenant *'17*
Lowriders *'17*
The Nun *'18*

Stewart Bick
Captive *'98*
One Special Night *'99*
Lip Service *'00*
Mercy *'00*
Sex & Mrs. X *'00*
Life with Judy Garland-Me and My Shadows *'01*
Danger Beneath the Sea *'02*
Hollywood Wives: The New Generation *'03*
False Pretenses *'04*
The Reagans *'04*
My Nanny's Secret *'09*

Charles Bickford (1889-1967)
Anna Christie *'30*
Hell's Heroes *'30*
East of Borneo *'31*
The Squaw Man *'31*
This Day and Age *'33*
White Woman *'33*
Little Miss Marker *'34*
The Farmer Takes a Wife *'35*
High, Wide and Handsome *'37*
The Plainsman *'37*
Mutiny in the Big House *'39*
Of Mice and Men *'39*
Stand Up and Fight *'39*
Reap the Wild Wind *'42*
Tarzan's New York Adventure *'42*
Mr. Lucky *'43*
The Song of Bernadette *'43*
A Wing and a Prayer *'44*
Fallen Angel *'45*
Duel in the Sun *'46*
Brute Force *'47*
The Woman on the Beach *'47*
Babe Ruth Story *'48*
Command Decision *'48*
Four Faces West *'48*
Johnny Belinda *'48*
Whirlpool *'49*
Branded *'50*
Guilty of Treason *'50*
Riding High *'50*
Elopement *'51*
Jim Thorpe: All American *'51*
The Last Posse *'53*
A Star Is Born *'54*
The Court Martial of Billy Mitchell *'55*
Not as a Stranger *'55*
The Big Country *'58*
The Unforgiven *'60*
Days of Wine and Roses *'62*
A Big Hand for the Little Lady *'66*

Andrew Bicknell
Heidi *'93*
Buffalo Girls *'95*
Prince Brat and the Whipping Boy *'95*
A Dog of Flanders *'99*
Attack Force *'06*

Jean-Luc Bideau (1940-)
Revenge of the Musketeers *'94*
The Red Violin *'98*
Let My People Go! *'11*

Michael Biehn (1956-)
Coach *'78*
Grease *'78*
Zuma Beach *'78*
The Fan *'81*
The Lords of Discipline *'83*
The Terminator *'84*
Aliens *'86*
Rampage *'87*
The Seventh Sign *'88*
The Abyss *'89*
Navy SEALS *'90*
Timebomb *'91*
K2: The Ultimate High *'92*
A Taste for Killing *'92*
Deadfall *'93*
Strapped *'93*
Tombstone *'93*
Deep Red *'94*
Jade *'95*
Mojave Moon *'96*
The Rock *'96*
Asteroid *'97*
Dead Men Can't Dance *'97*
Dying to Get Rich *'98*
The Magnificent Seven *'98*
Silver Wolf *'98*
The Art of War *'00*
Chain of Command *'00*
Cherry Falls *'00*
Borderline *'02*
Clockstoppers *'02*
The Legend of Butch & Sundance *'04*
Havoc *'05*
The Insatiable *'06*
Planet Terror *'07*
Spin *'07*
Stiletto *'08*
Saving Grace B. Jones *'09*
Streets of Blood *'09*
Psych: 9 *'10*
Puncture *'11*
Take Me Home Tonight *'11*
The Scorpion King 4: Quest for Power *'15*
Hidden in the Woods *'16*

Dick Biel
Splatter University *'84*
Slime City *'89*

Jessica Biel (1982-)
Ulee's Gold *'97*
I'll Be Home for Christmas *'98*
Summer Catch *'01*
The Rules of Attraction *'02*
The Texas Chainsaw Massacre *'03*
Blade: Trinity *'04*
Cellular *'04*
Elizabethtown *'05*
London *'05*
Stealth *'05*
Home of the Brave *'06*
The Illusionist *'06*
I Now Pronounce You Chuck and Larry *'07*
Next *'07*
Easy Virtue *'08*
Planet 51 *'09 (V)*
Powder Blue *'09*
The A-Team *'10*
Valentine's Day *'10*
New Year's Eve *'11*
Hitchcock *'12*
Playing for Keeps *'12*
The Tall Man *'12*
Total Recall *'12*
The Truth About Emanuel *'13*
Accidental Love *'15*
Bleeding Heart *'15*
The Book of Love *'16*
A Kind of Murder *'16*
Spark: A Space Tail *'17 (V)*
Shock and Awe *'18*

Josef Bierbichler (1948-)
Heart of Glass *'74*
Woyzeck *'78*
Winter Sleepers *'97*
The White Ribbon *'09*

Ramon Bieri (1929-2001)
The Grasshopper *'69*
The Passing of Evil *'70*
The Andromeda Strain *'71*
Nicole *'72*
Badlands *'74*
It's Good to Be Alive *'74*
Love Affair: The Eleanor & Lou Gehrig Story *'77*
Panic in Echo Park *'77*
Sorcerer *'77*
The Frisco Kid *'79*
A Christmas Without Snow *'80*
Grandview U.S.A. *'84*

Craig Bierko (1964-)
Danielle Steel's Star *'93*
The Long Kiss Goodnight *'96*
Til There Was You *'96*
Fear and Loathing in Las Vegas *'98*
Sour Grapes *'98*
The Suburbans *'99*
The Thirteenth Floor *'99*
Dickie Roberts: Former Child Star *'03*
Cinderella Man *'05*
Scary Movie 4 *'06*
Equity *'16*

Big Boi (1975-)
See Antwan Andre Patton

Big Pun (1971-2000)
Thicker than Water *'99*
Urban Menace *'99*

The Big Show
See Paul Wight

Chief John Big Tree
The Primitive Lover *'22*
She Wore a Yellow Ribbon *'49*

Claudio Bigagli (1955-)
The Night of the Shooting Stars *'82*
Kaos *'85*
Fiorile *'93*

Dan Biggers (1931-2011)
Basket Case 3: The Progeny *'92*
Flash *'98*
Elizabethtown *'05*

Sean Biggerstaff (1983-)
The Winter Guest *'97*
Harry Potter and the Sorcerer's Stone *'01*
Cashback *'06*

Jason Biggs (1978-)
American Pie *'99*
Boys and Girls *'00*
Loser *'00*
American Pie 2 *'01*
Jay and Silent Bob Strike Back *'01 (C)*
Prozac Nation *'01*
Saving Silverman *'01*
American Wedding *'03*
Anything Else *'03*
Jersey Girl *'04*
Eight Below *'06*
Wedding Daze *'06*
Lower Learning *'08*
My Best Friend's Girl *'08*
Over Her Dead Body *'08*
American Reunion *'12*
Amateur Night *'16*
Dear Dictator *'18*

Richard Biggs (1960-2004)
Forever Love *'98*
Ablaze *'00*

Roxann Biggs-Dawson (1964-)
Broken Angel *'88*
Guilty by Suspicion *'91*
Midnight's Child *'93*
Darkman 3: Die Darkman Die *'95*

Jan Bijvoet
Borgman *'13*
Embrace of the Serpent *'15*
The Ardennes *'17*
Exit Plan *'20*

Theodore Bikel (1924-2015)
The African Queen *'51*
Moulin Rouge *'52*
Never Let Me Go *'53*
Above Us the Waves *'55*
Enemy Below *'57*
The Pride and the Passion *'57*
The Defiant Ones *'58*
Fraulein *'58*
I Bury the Living *'58*
I Want to Live! *'58*
A Dog of Flanders *'59*
Woman Obsessed *'59*
My Fair Lady *'64*
Sands of the Kalahari *'65*
The Russians Are Coming, the Russians Are Coming *'66*
Sweet November *'68*
My Side of the Mountain *'69*
200 Motels *'71*
Killer by Night *'72*
Murder on Flight 502 *'75*
Victory at Entebbe *'76*
Testimony of Two Men *'77*
The Return of the King *'80 (V)*
See You in the Morning *'89*
Shattered *'91*
Benefit of the Doubt *'93*
The Shadow Conspiracy *'96*
Second Chances *'98*

Fernando Bilbao
Fangs of the Living Dead *'68*
The Screaming Dead *'72*

Lydia Bilbrook (1888-1990)
The Mexican Spitfire Out West *'40*
The Mexican Spitfire's Baby *'41*

Nicole Bilderback (1975-)
Paper Bullets *'99*
Bring It On *'00*
The New Twenty *'08*

Leo Bill (1980-)
Two Men Went to War *'02*
Lethal Dose *'03*
The Fall *'06*
Becoming Jane *'07*
Me and Orson Welles *'09*
The Girl With the Dragon Tattoo *'11*

Tony Bill (1940-)
Come Blow Your Horn *'63*
Soldier in the Rain *'63*
Marriage on the Rocks *'65*
None But the Brave *'65*
You're a Big Boy Now *'66*
Ice Station Zebra *'68*
Never a Dull Moment *'68*
Castle Keep *'69*
Flap *'70*
Shampoo *'75*
Washington: Behind Closed Doors *'77*
Initiation of Sarah *'78*
Heart Beat *'80*
Little Dragons *'80*
Portrait of an Escort *'80*
Pee-wee's Big Adventure *'85*
The Killing Mind *'90*
Barb Wire *'96*

Raoul Billerey (1920-)
Sorceress *'88*
Revenge of the Musketeers *'94*

Don Billett
Prince of the City *'81*
Gloria *'98*

Roy Billing (1947-)
Siam Sunset *'99*
Strange Bedfellows *'04*
Aquamarine *'06*

Dawn Ann Billings
Trancers 3: Deth Lives *'92*
Warlock: The Armageddon *'93*
Human Desires *'97*

Earl Billings (1945-)
Stakeout *'87*
One False Move *'91*
Antwone Fisher *'02*
American Splendor *'03*
Christmas at Water's Edge *'04*
Mr. 3000 *'04*
Something New *'06*

Beau Billingslea (1953-)
Final Justice *'94*
Silent Predators *'99*
Vacancy 2: The First Cut *'08*

Barbara Billingsley (1915-2010)
The Careless Years *'57*
Airplane! *'80*
Back to the Beach *'87*
Eye of the Demon *'87*
Leave It to Beaver *'97*

Jennifer Billingsley (1942-)
Lady in a Cage *'64*
C.C. & Company *'70*
White Lightning *'73*
The Thirsty Dead *'74*
Hollywood Man *'76*

John Billingsley (1960-)
Just Ask My Children *'01*
Out of Time *'03*
The Nickel Children *'05*
The Twelve Dogs of Christmas *'05*
The Man from Earth *'07*
Ripple Effect *'07*
The Least of These *'08*
Trade of Innocents *'12*
Red Line *'13*

Peter Billingsley (1971-)
Death Valley *'81*
Honky Tonk Freeway *'81*
A Christmas Story *'83*
Dirt Bike Kid *'86*
Russkies *'87*
Beverly Hills Brats *'89*
Arcade *'93*
The Break-Up *'06*
Iron Man *'08*
A Case of You *'13*

Stephen Billington (1969-)
Braveheart *'95*
Resident Evil *'02*
Dracula 2: Ascension *'03*

Jean-Luc Bilodeau (1990-)
16 Wishes *'10*
Piranha 3DD *'11*
Love Me *'12*

Bruno Bilotta (1959-)
The Black Cobra *'87*
Double Team *'97*
Excellent Cadavers *'99*
Titus *'99*

Rachel Bilson (1981-)
The Last Kiss *'06*
Jumper *'08*
New York, I Love You *'09*
Life Happens *'11*
Waiting for Forever *'11*
The To Do List *'13*

Mike Binder (1958-)
The Hollywood Knights *'80*
The Sex Monster *'99*
The Search for John Gissing *'01*
Minority Report *'02*
The Upside of Anger *'05*
Reign Over Me *'07*

Sybilla Binder (1898-1962)
Blanche Fury *'48*
Counterblast *'48*
The Golden Salamander *'51*

John Bindon (1943-93)
Inspector Clouseau *'68*
Performance *'70*

Herman Bing (1889-1947)
Crimson Romance *'34*
The Merry Widow *'34*
Maytime *'37*
Bluebeard's Eighth Wife *'38*
Every Day's a Holiday *'38*
The Great Waltz *'38*
Paradise for Three *'38*
Bitter Sweet *'40*

Geoffrey Binney
Hot Potato *'76*
Raw Force *'81*

Edward Binns (1916-90)
Vice Squad *'53*
Beyond a Reasonable Doubt *'56*
Portland Expose *'57*
Twelve Angry Men *'57*
Compulsion *'59*
Judgment at Nuremberg *'61*
The Americanization of Emily *'64*
Chubasco *'67*
Patton *'70*
Night Moves *'75*
Oliver's Story *'78*
The Verdict *'82*

Juliette Binoche (1964-)
Hail Mary *'85*
Rendez-vous *'85*
Mauvais Sang *'86*
The Unbearable Lightness of Being *'88*
The Lovers on the Bridge *'91*
Women & Men: In Love There Are No Rules *'91*
Damage *'92*
Emily Bronte's Wuthering Heights *'92*
Trois Couleurs: Bleu *'93*
Trois Couleurs: Blanc *'94 (C)*
Trois Couleurs: Rouge *'94 (C)*
A Couch in New York *'95*

The Horseman on the Roof '95
The English Patient '96
Children of the Century '99
Chocolat '00
Code Unknown '00
The Widow of Saint-Pierre '00
Jet Lag '02
In My Country '04
Bee Season '05
Hidden '05
Breaking and Entering '06
A Few Days in September '06
Paris, je t'aime '06
Dan in Real Life '07
Disengagement '07
Flight of the Red Balloon '08
Paris '08
Summer Hours '08
Shirin '09
Certified Copy '10
Elles '11
The Son of No One '11
Cosmopolis '12
Words and Pictures '13
Godzilla '14
Clouds of Sils Maria '15
The 33 '15
Ghost in the Shell '17
Let the Sunshine In '17
High Life '18
Non-Fiction '18

Maurice Biraud (1922-82)
Taxi for Tobruk '60
Any Number Can Win '63
The Last Train '74
A Slightly Pregnant Man '79

Mike Birbiglia (1978-)
Your Sister's Sister '11
Sleepwalk with Me '12
The Fault In Our Stars '14
Digging for Fire '15
Trainwreck '15
Don't Think Twice '16

Paul Birch (1913-69)
Ride Clear of Diablo '54
Day the World Ended '55
The Beast With a Million Eyes '56
The White Squaw '56
Not of This Earth '57
Queen of Outer Space '58

Thora Birch (1982-)
All I Want for Christmas '91
Paradise '91
Patriot Games '92
Hocus Pocus '93
Clear and Present Danger '94
Monkey Trouble '94
Now and Then '95
Alaska '96
American Beauty '99
Dungeons and Dragons '00
The Smokers '00
Ghost World '01
The Hole '01
Homeless to Harvard: The Liz Murray Story '03
Silver City '04
Dark Corners '06
Train '08
Winter of Frozen Dreams '08
Deadline '09
The Pregnancy Pact '10
Petunia '13
The Etruscan Smile '19

Billie Bird (1908-2002)
Rhubarb '51
Unwed Mother '58
Sixteen Candles '84
Ernest Saves Christmas '88
The End of Innocence '90
Home Alone '90
Dennis the Menace '93

Brad Bird (1957-)
The Incredibles '04 (V)
Ratatouille '07 (V)

John Bird (1936-)
The Best House in London '69
High Tide '80

Larry Bird (1956-)
Blue Chips '94 (C)
Celtic Pride '96 (C)

Norman Bird (1924-2005)
Cash on Demand '61
Very Important Person '61
Victim '61
Burn, Witch, Burn! '62
The Mind Benders '63
Term of Trial '63
Black Torment '64
The Hill '65
Hands of the Ripper '71
The Slipper and the Rose '76

Jesse Birdsall (1963-)
Wish You Were Here '87
Getting It Right '89
Nightscare '93
September '96

Mary Birdsong (1968-)
Pizza '05
Reno 911! Miami '07
Halloween II '09

Tala Birell (1907-58)
Air Hawks '35
The White Legion '36
Josette '38
The Purple Heart '44
Song of Love '47

David Birkin (1977-)
Charlotte Gray '01
All the Queen's Men '02
Sylvia '03

Jane Birkin (1946-)
Blow-Up '66
La Piscine '69
Slogan '69
Wonderwall: The Movie '69
Swimming Pool '70
Romance of a Horsethief '71
Seven Deaths in the Cat's Eye '72
Don Juan (Or If Don Juan Were a Woman) '73
Death on the Nile '78
Evil under the Sun '82
Daddy Nostalgia '90
La Belle Noiseuse '90
A Soldier's Daughter Never Cries '98
The Last September '99
Merci Docteur Rey '04
Around a Small Mountain '09
Twice Born '12

Len Birman (1932-)
Captain America '79
Captain America 2: Death Too Soon '79

Matt Birman
Back in Action '94
Family of Cops 2: Breach of Faith '97

Serafina Birman (1890-1976)
Ivan the Terrible, Part 1 '44
Ivan the Terrible, Part 2 '46

Gil Birmingham (1953-)
Twilight '08
Love Ranch '10
The Twilight Saga: Eclipse '10
Crooked Arrows '12
Hell or High Water '16

David Birney (1939-)
Only with Married Men '74
Choice of Weapons '76
Testimony of Two Men '77
Oh, God! Book 2 '80
Nightfall '88

Reed Birney (1954-)
Four Friends '81
From the Earth to the Moon '98

Christopher Birt
The Bodyguard '92
To Sir, With Love 2 '96

Eva Birthistle (1974-)
Borstal Boy '00
The American '01
A Fond Kiss '04
Breakfast on Pluto '05
Imagine Me & You '06
Middletown '06
The State Within '06
Nightwatching '07
The Children '08
The Last Enemy '08
Wake Wood '10
Life's a Breeze '14

Donna Biscoe
Frankenfish '04
Blood Done Sign My Name '10
The Fundamentals of Caring '16

Kerry Bishe (1984-)
Virtuality '09
Nice Guy Johnny '10
Newlyweds '11
The Fitzgerald Family Christmas '12
Grand Piano '13
Goodbye World '14
The Ticket '17

Summer Bishil (1988-)
Return to Halloweentown '06
Towelhead '07
Crossing Over '09
Mooz-Lum '10

Anthony Bishop
Operation Delta Force 5: Random Fire '00
Styx '00

Debbie Bishop
Scrubbers '82
Sid & Nancy '86

Ed Bishop (1932-2005)
Journey to the Far Side of the Sun '69
Brass Target '78
S.O.S. Titanic '79
Saturn 3 '80

Jennifer Bishop (1942-)
Horror of the Blood Monsters '70
Impulse '74
Jaws of Death '76
We Don't Live Here Anymore '04

Joey Bishop (1918-2007)
Deep Six '58
Onionhead '58
Ocean's 11 '60
Sergeants 3 '62
Johnny Cool '63
Texas Across the River '66
Valley of the Dolls '67
Who's Minding the Mint? '67
Delta Force '86
Betsy's Wedding '90
Trigger Happy '96 (C)

Julie Bishop (1914-2001)
Tarzan the Fearless '33
The Black Cat '34
Bohemian Girl '36
Night Cargo '36
The Hidden Hand '42
Action in the North Atlantic '43
Northern Pursuit '43
Rhapsody in Blue '45
Sands of Iwo Jima '49
Westward the Women '51
The High and the Mighty '54

Kelly Bishop (1944-)
Dirty Dancing '87
Queens Logic '91
Miami Rhapsody '95
Private Parts '96
A Novel Romance '11

Kevin Bishop (1980-)
Muppet Treasure Island '96
Food of Love '02
L'Auberge Espagnole '02
Russian Dolls '05
Irina Palm '07
Moonwalkers '16

Kirsten Bishop
The Little Mermaid '75 (V)
Rudy: The Rudy Giulani Story '03

Larry Bishop (1948-)
Angel Unchained '70
Shanks '74
Soul Hustler '76
Trigger Happy '96
Underworld '96
Kill Bill Vol. 1 '03
Hell Ride '08

Nicholas Bishop (1973-)
Walking on Water '02
Black Limousine '10

Pat Bishop
Don's Party '76
Women of Valor '86

Stephen Bishop (1951-)
National Lampoon's Animal House '78
The Blues Brothers '80
Twilight Zone: The Movie '83
Someone to Love '87
Moneyball '11

Wes Bishop (1933-93)
Rebel Vixens '69
Chrome and Hot Leather '71
Chain Gang Women '72
The Thing with Two Heads '72
Black Gestapo '75
Dixie Dynamite '76

William Bishop (1918-59)
The Killer That Stalked New York '47
Thunderhoof '48
Breakdown '53
The Redhead from Wyoming '53
Top Gun '55
Wyoming Renegades '55
The Boss '56
The White Squaw '56

Steve Bisley (1950-)
Chain Reaction '80
Mad Max '80
Red Hill '10

Whit Bissell (1909-96)
Brute Force '47
Chicken Every Sunday '48
He Walked by Night '48
Raw Deal '48
The Family Secret '51
The Lost Continent '51
The Atomic Kid '54
The Caine Mutiny '54
Creature from the Black Lagoon '54
Shack Out on 101 '55
Invasion of the Body Snatchers '56
Man from Del Rio '56
The Young Stranger '57
No Name on the Bullet '59
The Time Machine '60
Spencer's Mountain '63
Advance to the Rear '64
Seven Days in May '64
A Covenant With Death '67
Once You Kiss a Stranger '69
City Beneath the Sea '71
Cry Rape! '73
Soylent Green '73

Jacqueline Bisset (1944-)
Cul de Sac '66
Casino Royale '67
Two for the Road '67
Bullitt '68
The Detective '68
The Sweet Ride '68
The First Time '69
The Grasshopper '69
Airport '70
The Passing of Evil '70
The Mephisto Waltz '71
Secrets '71
Life & Times of Judge Roy Bean '72
Day for Night '73
Murder on the Orient Express '74
Spiral Staircase '75
Le Magnifique '76
St. Ives '76
The Deep '77
The Greek Tycoon '78
Who Is Killing the Great Chefs of Europe? '78
When Time Ran Out '80
Rich and Famous '81
Class '83
Under the Volcano '84
Choices '86
Napoleon and Josephine: A Love Story '87
High Season '88
Wild Orchid '90
Crimebroker '93
Crime Broker '94
La Ceremonie '95
September '96
Dangerous Beauty '98
Joan of Arc '99
Let the Devil Wear Black '99
Britannic '00
Jesus '00
Sex & Mrs. X '00
The Sleepy Time Gal '01
Fascination '04
Latter Days '04
Domino '05
Save the Last Dance 2 '06
Carolina Moon '07
Death in Love '08
An Old-Fashioned Thanksgiving '08
2 Jacks '12
Welcome to New York '15
Backstabbing for Beginners '18

Josie Bissett (1970-)
All-American Murder '91
Book of Love '91
Mikey '92
Obituary '06
The Other Woman '08

Chris Bisson
East Is East '99
Chicken Tikka Masala '05

Yannick Bisson (1969-)
I Do (But I Don't) '04
Crazy for Christmas '05
The Secrets of Comfort House '06
Casino Jack '10

Joel Bissonnette
A Nightmare Come True '97
Suspicious River '00
Passenger Side '09

Danielle Bisutti
Tropix '02
Curse of Chucky '13

Chhabi Biswas (1900-62)
Jalsaghar '58
Devi '60

Seema Biswas
Bandit Queen '94
Water '05

Bill Bixby (1934-93)
Lonely Are the Brave '62
Under the Yum-Yum Tree '63
Clambake '67
Speedway '68
The Apple Dumpling Gang '75
Fantasy Island '76
The Invasion of Johnson County '76
Rich Man, Poor Man '76
The Incredible Hulk '77
Kentucky Fried Movie '77
Agatha Christie's Murder is Easy '82
The Incredible Hulk Returns '88
The Trial of the Incredible Hulk '89
Death of the Incredible Hulk '90

Dragan Bjelogric (1963-)
Hey, Babu Riba '88
Pretty Village, Pretty Flame '96

Bjork (1965-)
The Juniper Tree '87
Dancer in the Dark '99

Anita Bjork (1923-2012)
Miss Julie '50
Secrets of Women '52
Night People '54

Halvar Bjork (1928-)
The New Land '72
Autumn Sonata '78

Irina Bjorklund
Ambush '99
Lost '05

Anna Bjorn
More American Graffiti '79
Sword & the Sorcerer '82

Gunnar Bjornstrand (1909-86)
Torment '44
Smiles of a Summer Night '55
The Seventh Seal '56
Wild Strawberries '57
The Magician '58
Through a Glass Darkly '61
The Winter Light '62
Persona '66
The Shame '68
The Rite '69
Face to Face '76
Autumn Sonata '78

Claudia Black (1973-)
Pitch Black '00
Queen of the Damned '02
Stargate: Continuum '08
Stargate: The Ark of Truth '08

Clint Black
Maverick '94 (C)
Flicka: Country Pride '12

Denise Black
The Scarlet Pimpernel 2: Mademoiselle Guillotine '99
The Last Tree '19

Gerry Black
Backstairs at the White House '79
Re-Animator '84
The Majestic '01

Isobel Black (1943-)
Kiss of the Vampire '62
10 Rillington Place '71

Jack Black (1969-)
Bob Roberts '92
Airborne '93
Demolition Man '93
Blind Justice '94
Bye Bye, Love '94
The NeverEnding Story 3: Escape from Fantasia '94
Dead Man Walking '95
Waterworld '95
Bio-Dome '96
The Cable Guy '96
Crossworlds '96
The Fan '96
Mars Attacks! '96
The Jackal '97
Johnny Skidmarks '97
Bongwater '98
Enemy of the State '98
I Still Know What You Did Last Summer '98
The Cradle Will Rock '99
Jesus' Son '99
The Love Letter '99
High Fidelity '00
Saving Silverman '01
Shallow Hal '01
Ice Age '02 (V)
Orange County '02
School of Rock '03
Anchorman: The Legend of Ron Burgundy '04
Envy '04
Shark Tale '04 (V)
King Kong '05
Danny Roane: First Time Director '06
The Holiday '06
Nacho Libre '06
Tenacious D in the Pick of Destiny '06
Margot at the Wedding '07

Walk Hard: The Dewey Cox Story *'07*
Be Kind Rewind *'08*
Kung Fu Panda *'08 (V)*
Tropic Thunder *'08*
Year One *'09*
Gulliver's Travels *'10*
The Big Year *'11*
Kung Fu Panda 2 *'11 (V)*
Bernie *'12*
The D Train *'15*
Goosebumps *'15*
Kung Fu Panda 3 *'16*
Jumanji: Welcome to the Jungle *'17*
Don't Worry, He Won't Get Far on Foot *'18*
The House with a Clock in Its Walls *'18*
The Polka King *'18*
Jumanji: The Next Level *'19*

James Black (1962-)
The First 9 1/2 Weeks *'98*
Standing on Fishes *'99*
The Substitute 3: Winner Takes All *'99*
Unshackled *'00*

Johanna Black (1971-)
The Contract *'98*
Hide and Seek *'00*
Hush Little Baby *'07*

Karen Black (1942-2013)
The Prime Time *'60*
You're a Big Boy Now *'66*
Easy Rider *'69*
Hard Contract *'69*
Five Easy Pieces *'70*
Born to Win *'71*
A Gunfight *'71*
Little Laura & Big John *'73*
The Outfit *'73*
The Pyx *'73*
The Great Gatsby *'74*
Law and Disorder *'74*
Airport '75 *'75*
Crime & Passion *'75*
The Day of the Locust *'75*
Nashville *'75*
Trilogy of Terror *'75*
Burnt Offerings *'76*
Family Plot *'76*
Capricorn One *'78*
In Praise of Older Women *'78*
The Rip Off *'78*
The Squeeze *'80*
Miss Right *'81*
Separate Ways *'82*
Can She Bake a Cherry Pie? *'83*
Killing Heat *'84*
Savage Dawn *'84*
Cut and Run *'85*
Invaders from Mars *'86*
Eternal Evil *'87*
It's Alive 3: Island of the Alive *'87*
Dixie Lanes *'88*
Out of the Dark *'88*
Homer and Eddie *'89*
Twisted Justice *'89*
Zapped Again *'89*
Club Fed *'90*
The Killer's Edge *'90*
Mirror, Mirror *'90*
Evil Spirits *'91*
Haunting Fear *'91*
Quiet Fire *'91*
Children of the Night *'92*
The Player *'92*
Armistead Maupin's Tales of the City *'93*
Bound and Gagged: A Love Story *'93*
Children of the Corn 4: The Gathering *'96*
Crimetime *'96*
Dinosaur Valley Girls *'96*
Angel Blue *'97*
Conceiving Ada *'97*
Dogtown *'97*
Invisible Dad *'97*
Men *'97*
First Degree *'98*
Red Dirt *'99*
The Independent *'00 (C)*
Gypsy 83 *'01*
Hard Luck *'01*
A Light in the Darkness *'02*
House of 1000 Corpses *'03*
Ghost Writer *'07*
One Long Night *'07*
The Blue Tooth Virgin *'09*
Irene in Time *'09*
Repo Chick *'09*

Lewis Black (1948-)
Hannah and Her Sisters *'86*
Jacob's Ladder *'90*
Accepted *'06*
Falling for Grace *'06*
Man of the Year *'06*
Unaccompanied Minors *'06*
Peep World *'10 (N)*
Inside Out *'15 (V)*
Rock Dog *'17*

Lucas Black (1982-)
The War *'94*
Ghosts of Mississippi *'96*
Sling Blade *'96*
Flash *'98*
The X-Files *'98*
Crazy in Alabama *'99*
All the Pretty Horses *'00*
The Miracle Worker *'00*
Cold Mountain *'03*
Friday Night Lights *'04*
Killer Diller *'04*
Deepwater *'05*
Jarhead *'05*
The Fast and the Furious: Tokyo Drift *'06*
Get Low *'09*
Legion *'10*
Seven Days in Utopia *'11*
42 *'13*
Furious 7 *'15*

Marina Black
Vampire Clan *'02*
Dog Gone Love *'03*
The Trail to Hope Rose *'04*

Michael Ian Black (1971-)
The Bogus Witch Project *'00*
Wet Hot American Summer *'01*
The Baxter *'05*
Take Me Home Tonight *'11*

Ryan Black (1973-)
Geronimo *'93*
Dance Me Outside *'95*
Stryker *'04*
Eye of the Beast *'07*

Shane Black (1961-)
Predator *'87*
An Alan Smithee Film: Burn, Hollywood, Burn *'97 (C)*
As Good As It Gets *'97*
Any Day *'15*

Sofia Black-D'Elia
Project Almanac *'15*
Viral *'16*

Richard Blackburn
A Man in Uniform *'93*
Sugartime *'95*
Under the Piano *'95*
In Love and War *'96*
Murder at 1600 *'97*
Down in the Delta *'98*
Stephen King's The Storm of the Century *'99*
A Christmas Wedding *'06*
Blue State *'07*

Stephen Blackehart (1967-)
Retro Puppet Master *'99*
666: The Beast *'07*
100 Million BC *'08*
The Land That Time Forgot *'09*
The Terminators *'09*

Jamie Blackley (1991-)
Prowl *'10*
And While We Were Here *'13*
If I Stay *'14*

Honor Blackman (1925-2020)
Conspirator *'49*
Green Grow the Rushes *'51*
A Night to Remember *'58*
The Square Peg *'58*
A Matter of WHO *'62*
Jason and the Argonauts *'63*
Goldfinger *'64*
Shalako *'68*
Lola *'69*
The Last Grenade *'70*
The Virgin and the Gypsy *'70*
Fright *'71*
To the Devil, a Daughter *'76*
The Cat and the Canary *'79*
The First Olympics: Athens 1896 *'84*
Lace *'84*
Russell Mulcahy's Tale of the Mummy *'99*
To Walk with Lions *'99*

Jeremy Blackman
Magnolia *'99*
Crown Heights *'02*

Joan Blackman (1938-)
Good Day for a Hanging *'58*
Career *'59*
Blue Hawaii *'62*
Kid Galahad *'62*
Twilight of Honor *'63*
Macon County Line *'74*

Sidney Blackmer (1895-1973)
Little Caesar *'30*
Mothers Cry *'30*
The Count of Monte Cristo *'34*
Goodbye Love *'34*
Behind the Green Lights *'35*
The Little Colonel *'35*
Missing Girls *'36*
The President's Mystery *'36*
Charlie Chan at Monte Carlo *'37*
Heidi *'37*
The House of Secrets *'37*
In Old Chicago *'37*
Thank you, Mr. Moto *'37*
Law of the Pampas *'39*
Third Finger, Left Hand *'40*
Love Crazy *'41*
The Panther's Claw *'42*
I Escaped from the Gestapo *'43*
War of the Wildcats *'43*
Buffalo Bill *'44*
Wilson *'44*
People Will Talk *'51*
The San Francisco Story *'52*
The High and the Mighty *'54*
Beyond a Reasonable Doubt *'56*
High Society *'56*
Tammy and the Bachelor *'57*
How to Murder Your Wife *'64*
A Covenant With Death *'67*
Rosemary's Baby *'68*
Revenge Is My Destiny *'71*

Paul Blackthorne (1969-)
Lagaan: Once upon a Time in India *'01*
Four Corners of Suburbia *'05*
Special *'06*

David Blackwell
China O'Brien *'88*
The Rookie *'02*

Vas Blackwood
Mean Machine *'01*
Mercenaries *'11*

Taurean Blacque (1941-)
Oliver & Company *'88 (V)*
Deepstar Six *'89*

Ruben Blades (1948-)
Crossover Dreams *'85*
Critical Condition *'86*
Fatal Beauty *'87*
Homeboy *'88*
The Milagro Beanfield War *'88*
Disorganized Crime *'89*
The Josephine Baker Story *'90*
The Lemon Sisters *'90*
Mo' Better Blues *'90*
One Man's War *'90*
Predator 2 *'90*
The Two Jakes *'90*
Crazy from the Heart *'91*
The Super *'91*
Life with Mikey *'93 (C)*
Color of Night *'94*
A Million to Juan *'94 (C)*
The Devil's Own *'96*
Scorpion Spring *'96*
Chinese Box *'97*
The Cradle Will Rock *'99*
All the Pretty Horses *'00*
Assassination Tango *'03*
The Maldonado Miracle *'03*
Once Upon a Time in Mexico *'03*
Imagining Argentina *'04*
Spin *'04*
For Greater Glory *'12*
Safe House *'12*
Hands of Stone *'16*

Estella Blain (1936-81)
The Twilight Girls *'57*
Pirates of the Coast *'61*
The Diabolical Dr. Z *'65*
Angelique and the King *'66*

Gerard Blain (1930-2000)
Le Beau Serge *'58*
The Cousins *'59*
Les Cousins *'59*
Hatari! *'62*
The American Friend *'77*

Charlene Blaine
Fugitive Champion *'99*
Hard Four *'07*

Vivian Blaine (1921-95)
Greenwich Village *'44*
Something for the Boys *'44*
Nob Hill *'45*
State Fair *'45*
Doll Face *'46*
If I'm Lucky *'46*
Three Little Girls In Blue *'46*
Skirts Ahoy! *'52*
Guys and Dolls *'55*
The Dark *'79*
Parasite *'82*

Betsy Blair (1923-2009)
The Guilt of Janet Ames *'47*
Marty *'55*
The Halliday Brand *'57*
Il Grido *'57*
All Night Long *'62*
Scarlett *'94*

Bre Blair
The Baby-Sitters' Club *'95*
Small Town Saturday Night *'10*

Isla Blair (1944-)
Taste the Blood of Dracula *'70*
The Final Cut *'95*

Jacob Blair (1984-)
Christmas in Canaan *'09*
Wrecked *'10*
Christmas Comes Home to Canaan *'11*

Janet Blair (1921-2007)
Blondie Goes to College *'42*
Broadway *'42*
My Sister Eileen *'42*
Tonight and Every Night *'45*
The Fabulous Dorseys *'47*
Black Arrow *'48*
The Fuller Brush Man *'48*
Boys' Night Out *'62*
Burn, Witch, Burn! *'62*
The One and Only, Genuine, Original Family Band *'68*

Joan Blair
Mr. District Attorney *'41*
The Constant Nymph *'43*

June Blair
Hell Bound *'57*
Island of Lost Women *'59*

Kimberly Blair
Mulberry Street *'06*
The Mighty Macs *'09*

Linda Blair (1959-)
The Exorcist *'73*
Born Innocent *'74*
Airport '75 *'75*
Sweet Hostage *'75*
Victory at Entebbe *'76*
The Exorcist 2: The Heretic *'77*
Summer of Fear *'78*
Roller Boogie *'79*
Wild Horse Hank *'79*
Hell Night *'81*
Ruckus *'81*
Chained Heat *'83*
Savage Streets *'83*
Night Patrol *'85*
Red Heat *'85*
Savage Island *'85*
Grotesque *'87*
Witchery *'88*
The Chilling *'89*
Moving Target *'89*
Zapped Again *'89*
Bail Out *'90*
Repossessed *'90*
Dead Sleep *'91*
Sorceress *'94*
Prey of the Jaguar *'96*
Scream *'96 (C)*
Gang Boys *'97*

Macon Blair
Blue Ruin *'13*
Green Room *'15*
Gold *'16*

Nicky Blair (1926-98)
Viva Las Vegas *'63*
The Crossing Guard *'94*

Pamela Blair (1949-)
Svengali *'83*
Beavis and Butt-Head Do America *'96 (V)*

Patricia Blair (1933-2013)
Jump Into Hell *'55*
City of Fear *'59*
Cage of Evil *'60*

Paul Blair
Outpost *'07*
Clive Barker's Book of Blood *'08*

Selma Blair (1972-)
Brown's Requiem *'98*
Cruel Intentions *'98*
Girl *'98*
Down to You *'00*
Highway *'01*
Kill Me Later *'01*
Legally Blonde *'01*
Storytelling *'01*
The Sweetest Thing *'02*
Dallas 362 *'03*
A Guy Thing *'03*
Coast to Coast *'04*
A Dirty Shame *'04*
Hellboy *'04*
In Good Company *'04*
The Deal *'05*
The Fog *'05*
Pretty Persuasion *'05*
Lies & Alibis *'06*
The Night of the White Pants *'06*
Feast of Love *'07*
The Killing Gene *'07*
Purple Violets *'07*
Hellboy II: The Golden Army *'08*
My Mom's New Boyfriend *'08*
The Poker House *'09*
Columbus Circle *'10*
Dark Horse *'11*
In Their Skin *'12*
After *'19*

Tom Blair
Sure Fire *'90*
The Bed You Sleep In *'93*

Jennifer Blaire
The Lost Skeleton of Cadavra *'01*
Dark and Stormy Night *'09*

Isabelle Blais (1975-)
Savage Messiah *'02*
Human Trafficking *'05*
The High Cost of Living *'10*

Nesbitt Blaisdell (1928-)
Kennedy *'83*
Addicted to Love *'96*
The Mothman Prophecies *'02*

Paul Blaisdell (1929-83)
Day the World Ended *'55*
Dragstrip Girl *'57*
The Undead *'57*

Amanda Blake (1929-89)
Counterspy Meets Scotland Yard *'50*
The Duchess of Idaho *'50*
Stars in My Crown *'50*
Cattle Town *'52*
The Glass Slipper *'55*
Betrayal *'74*
Gunsmoke: Return to Dodge *'87*
The Boost *'88*

Andre B. Blake
Who's the Man? *'93*
Just the Ticket *'98*
The Other Brother *'02*
Hair Show *'04*

Ellen Blake
Last Resort *'86*
Suspect Zero *'04*

Geoffrey Blake (1962-)
Philadelphia Experiment 2 *'93*
Forrest Gump *'94*
Entertaining Angels: The Dorothy Day Story *'96*
The War at Home *'96*
Contact *'97*
Cast Away *'00*
Life Without Dick *'01*

Julia Blake (1936-)
My Brilliant Career *'79*
Lonely Hearts *'82*
Man of Flowers *'84*
Hotel de Love *'96*
The Thorn Birds: The Missing Years *'96*
Passion *'99*
Innocence *'00*
Salem's Lot *'04*
Aquamarine *'06*
The Boys Are Back *'09*

Larry J. Blake (1914-82)
The Trap *'46*
Holiday Affair *'49*
Beginning of the End *'57*
Demon Seed *'77*

Madge Blake (1899-1969)
The Prowler *'51*
Singin' in the Rain *'52*
The Long, Long Trailer *'54*
Batman *'66*

Marie Blake (1896-1978)
Love Finds Andy Hardy *'38*
Sensations of 1945 *'44*
Between Two Women *'45*
She Devil *'57*

Marsha Stephanie Blake
Stand Clear of the Closing Doors *'13*
Crown Heights *'17*
See You Yesterday *'19*

Megan Blake
Lost Stallions:The Journey Home *'08*
Eyeborgs *'09*

Mia Blake
Visitor Q *'01*
The Tattooist *'07*

Noah Blake (1964-)
Trapper County War *'89*
The Base *'99*

Oliver Blake (1905-92)
Casablanca *'42*
Ma and Pa Kettle at Waikiki *'55*

Pamela Blake (1915-2009)
Kid Dynamite *'43*
Rolling Home *'48*

Rachael Blake (1971-)
Lantana *'01*
Perfect Strangers *'03*
Clapham Junction *'07*
The Diplomat *'08*
The Prisoner *'09*
Sleeping Beauty *'11*
Gods of Egypt *'16*

Robert (Bobby) Blake (1933-)
Andy Hardy's Double Life *'42*
China Girl *'42*
Mokey *'42*
Woman in the Window *'44*
Humoresque *'46*
Treasure of the Sierra Madre *'48*
The Black Rose *'50*
Rumble on the Docks *'56*
Screaming Eagles *'56*
Revolt in the Big House *'58*
Pork Chop Hill *'59*
The Purple Gang *'59*
Town without Pity *'61*
PT 109 *'63*
This Property Is Condemned *'66*
In Cold Blood *'67*
Tell Them Willie Boy Is Here *'69*
Counter Punch *'71*
Corky *'72*
Electra Glide in Blue *'73*
Busting *'74*
Of Mice and Men *'81*
Second-Hand Hearts *'81*
Money Train *'95*
Lost Highway *'96*

Sondra Blake
The Prize Pulitzer *'89*
The Caretaker *'16*

Whitney Blake (1923-2002)
My Gun Is Quick *'57*
30 *'59*

Aaron Blakely
Frayed *'07*
Outside In *'17*

Colin Blakely (1930-87)
This Sporting Life *'63*
Decline and Fall...of a Birdwatcher *'68*
The Vengeance of She *'68*
The Private Life of Sherlock Holmes *'70*
The National Health *'73*
Murder on the Orient Express *'74*
The Pink Panther Strikes Again *'76*
Equus *'77*
The Big Sleep *'78*
Nijinsky *'80*
The Dogs of War *'81*
Evil under the Sun *'82*
Loophole *'83*

Donald Blakely (?-2004)
Strike Force *'75*
Short Eyes *'79*
Vigilante *'83*

Gene Blakely
Battle of the Coral Sea *'59*
Beach Red *'67*

Susan Blakely (1950-)
Savages *'72*
The Way We Were *'73*
The Lords of Flatbush *'74*
The Towering Inferno *'74*
Report to the Commissioner *'75*
Rich Man, Poor Man *'76*
The Concorde: Airport '79 *'79*
The Oklahoma City Dolls *'81*
Blood and Orchids *'86*
Over the Top *'86*
April Morning *'88*
Broken Angel *'88*
The Incident *'89*
My Mom's a Werewolf *'89*
Wildflower *'91*
Russian Roulette *'93*
The Perfect Nanny *'00*
Extreme Limits *'01*
L.A. Twister *'04*
Hate Crime *'05*
Mating Dance *'08*
Beverly Hills Chihuahua 2 *'10*

Sean Blakemore (1967-)
Keepin' It Real *'01*
Motives *'03*
Woman, Thou Art Loosed *'04*
Motives 2-Retribution *'07*

Olive Blakeney (1903-59)
Gangway *'37*
Billy the Kid *'41*

Claudie Blakley (1974-)
Gosford Park *'01*
Pride and Prejudice *'05*
Severance *'06*
Return to Cranford *'09*

Ronee Blakley (1945-)
Nashville *'75*
The Private Files of J. Edgar Hoover *'77*
She Came to the Valley *'77*
The Driver *'78*
The Oklahoma City Dolls *'81*
A Nightmare on Elm Street *'84*
Return to Salem's Lot *'87*
Someone to Love *'87*
Student Confidential *'87*

Roba Blal
The Bubble *'06*
Miral *'10*

Jolene Blalock (1975-)
Jason and the Argonauts *'00*
Slow Burn *'05*
I Dream of Murder *'06*
Shadow Puppets *'07*
Starship Troopers 3: Marauder *'08*

Larry Blamire
The Lost Skeleton of Cadavra *'01*
Dark and Stormy Night *'09*

Dominique Blanc (1956-)
Indochine *'92*
Queen Margot *'94*
Total Eclipse *'95*
A Soldier's Daughter Never Cries *'98*
Those Who Love Me Can Take the Train *'98*
One Day You'll Understand *'08*
A Cat in Paris *'11 (V)*

Erika Blanc (1942-)
Kill, Baby, Kill *'66*
Hallelujah for Django *'67*
Special Forces *'68*
Fistful of Lead *'70*
Sartana's Here. . . Trade Your Pistol for a Coffin *'70*
The Devil's Nightmare *'71*
The Night Evelyn Came Out of the Grave *'71*
Sweet Spirits *'71*
Mark of the Devil 2 *'72*
His Secret Life *'01*

Jennifer Blanc (1974-)
Cool and the Crazy *'94*
Kiss Tomorrow Goodbye *'00*
Fish Without a Bicycle *'03*
The Absent *'11*
Hidden in the Woods *'16*

Manuel Blanc
I Don't Kiss *'91*
Beaumarchais the Scoundrel *'96*

Mel Blanc (1908-89)
Neptune's Daughter *'49*
Gay Purr-ee *'62 (V)*
Hey There, It's Yogi Bear *'64 (V)*
Kiss Me, Stupid! *'64*
Phantom Tollbooth *'69 (V)*
Buck Rogers in the 25th Century *'79 (V)*
Looney Looney Looney Bugs Bunny Movie *'81 (V)*
Strange Brew *'83 (V)*
Who Framed Roger Rabbit *'88 (V)*
Jetsons: The Movie *'90 (V)*

Michel Blanc (1952-)
The Tenant *'76*
French Fried Vacation *'79*
Menage *'86*
Monsieur Hire *'89*
Prospero's Books *'91*
The Favor, the Watch, & the Very Big Fish *'92*
Grosse Fatigue *'94*
Ready to Wear *'94*
The Monster *'96*
The Witnesses *'07*
The Girl on the Train *'09*
The Hundred-Foot Journey *'14*

Bernard Blancan (1958-)
A Song of Innocence *'05*
Days of Glory *'06*
Outside the Law *'10*

Jewel Blanch
Baffled *'72*
Against a Crooked Sky *'75*

Dominique Blanchar (1892-1963)
Decision Before Dawn *'51*
L'Avventura *'60*

Jarred Blanchard
The Yearling *'94*
The Boys Club *'96*

Mari Blanchard (1927-70)
Abbott and Costello Go to Mars *'53*
The Crooked Web *'55*
She Devil *'57*

Rachel Blanchard (1976-)
Iron Eagle 4 *'95*
Young Ivanhoe *'95*
The Rage: Carrie 2 *'99*
Road Trip *'00*
Chasing Holden *'01*
Sugar & Spice *'01*
Without a Paddle *'04*
Where the Truth Lies *'05*
Snakes on a Plane *'06*
Careless *'07*
Adoration *'08*
Spread *'09*
Daydream Nation *'10*
Open House *'10*
The Case for Christmas *'11*
Dark Hearts *'12*
My Gal Sunday *'14*

Tammy Blanchard (1976-)
Life with Judy Garland-Me and My Shadows *'01*
Stealing Harvard *'02*
Bella *'06*
The Good Shepherd *'06*
Cadillac Records *'08*
Living Proof *'08*
The Ramen Girl *'08*
Deadline *'09*
Amish Grace *'10*
Rabbit Hole *'10*
Moneyball *'11*
The Music Never Stopped *'11*
Of Two Minds *'12*
Blue Jasmine *'13*
Burning Blue *'14*
The Invitation *'16*

Francis Blanche (1919-74)
Monsieur Gangster *'63*
The Great Spy Chase *'64*

Cate Blanchett (1969-)
Oscar and Lucinda *'97*
Paradise Road *'97*
The Wedding Party *'97*
Elizabeth *'98*
An Ideal Husband *'99*
Pushing Tin *'99*
The Talented Mr. Ripley *'99*
The Gift *'00*
The Man Who Cried *'00*
Bandits *'01*
Charlotte Gray *'01*
Heaven *'01*
Lord of the Rings: The Fellowship of the Ring *'01*
The Shipping News *'01*
Lord of the Rings: The Two Towers *'02*
Coffee and Cigarettes *'03*
Lord of the Rings: The Return of the King *'03*
The Missing *'03*
Veronica Guerin *'03*
The Aviator *'04*
The Life Aquatic with Steve Zissou *'04*
Little Fish *'05*
Babel *'06*
The Good German *'06*
Notes on a Scandal *'06*
Elizabeth: The Golden Age *'07*
Hot Fuzz *'07*
I'm Not There *'07*
The Curious Case of Benjamin Button *'08*
Indiana Jones and the Kingdom of the Crystal Skull *'08*
Ponyo *'08 (V)*
Robin Hood *'10*
Hanna *'11*
The Hobbit: An Unexpected Journey *'12*
Blue Jasmine *'13*
Girl Rising *'13 (N)*
The Monuments Men *'13*
The Hobbit: The Battle of the Five Armies *'14*
How to Train Your Dragon 2 *'14 (V)*
Carol *'15*
Cinderella *'15*
Knight of Cups *'15*
Truth *'15*
Song to Song *'17*
Thor: Ragnarok *'17*
The House with a Clock in Its Walls *'18*
Mowgli: Legend of the Jungle *'18*
Ocean's 8 *'18*
How to Train Your Dragon: The Hidden World *'19*
Where'd You Go, Bernadette *'19*

Dorothee Blanck (1934-)
Cleo from 5 to 7 *'61*
Umbrellas of Cherbourg *'64*

Clara Blandick (1880-1962)
The Girl Said No *'30*
Romance *'30*
The Easiest Way *'31*
Murder at Midnight *'31*
Shopworn *'32*
The Bitter Tea of General Yen *'33*
The Girl from Missouri *'34*
The Gorgeous Hussy *'36*
The Wizard of Oz *'39*
Dreaming Out Loud *'40*
Tomboy *'40*
It Started with Eve *'41*
Dead Man's Eyes *'44*

Sally Blane (1910-97)
Vagabond Lover *'29*
Ten Cents a Dance *'31*
Pride of the Legion *'32*
City Park *'34*
The Silver Streak *'34*
Charlie Chan at Treasure Island *'39*
The Story of Alexander Graham Bell *'39*

Mark Blankfield (1950-)
Jekyll & Hyde. . . Together Again *'82*
The Midnight Hour *'86*
Angel 3: The Final Chapter *'88*
Robin Hood: Men in Tights *'93*
The Great American Sex Scandal *'94*
Dracula: Dead and Loving It *'95*

Billy Blanks (1955-)
Bloodfist *'89*
The Last Boy Scout *'91*
Timebomb *'91*
Talons of the Eagle *'92*
Back in Action *'94*
Expect No Mercy *'95*
Shadow Warriors *'97*

Arell Blanton
Wild Riders *'71*
Assault of the Killer Bimbos *'88*

Kirby Bliss Blanton (1990-)
Scar *'07*
Project X *'11*
The Green Inferno *'14*

Caio Blat
Carandiru *'03*
The Year My Parents Went on Vacation *'07*

Maddie (Maddeleine) Blaustein (1960-2008)
Pokemon 3: The Movie *'01 (V)*
Yu-Gi-Oh! The Movie: Pyramid of Light *'04 (V)*

Hans-Christian Blech (1915-93)
Decision Before Dawn *'51*
The Visit *'64*
Battle of the Bulge *'65*
The Scarlet Letter *'73*
Innocents with Dirty Hands *'76*
The Wrong Move *'78*
Colonel Redl *'84*

Jonah Blechman (1975-)
This Boy's Life *'93*
Fall Time *'94*
Treasure Island *'99*
Luster *'02*
Arc *'06*

Alexis Bledel (1981-)
Tuck Everlasting *'02*
Sin City *'05*
The Sisterhood of the Traveling Pants *'05*
I'm Reed Fish *'06*
The Sisterhood of the Traveling Pants 2 *'08*
Post Grad *'09*
The Good Guy *'10*
The Kate Logan Affair *'10*
Violet & Daisy *'11*
Remember Sunday *'13*
Parts Per Billion *'14*
Crypto *'19*

Tempestt Bledsoe (1973-)
Santa and Pete *'99*
Johnny B. *'00*
ParaNorman *'12 (V)*

Debra Blee (1961-)
Beach Girls *'82*
Savage Streets *'83*

Yasmine Bleeth (1968-)
BASEketball *'98*
It Came from the Sky *'98*
Coming Soon *'99*
Undercover Angel *'99*

Moritz Bleibtreu (1971-)
Run Lola Run *'98*
Invisible Circus *'00*
The Experiment *'01*
Taking Sides *'01*
The Keeper: The Legend of Omar Khayyam *'05*
Munich *'05*
The Lark Farm *'07*
The Walker *'07*
Adam Resurrected *'08*
The Baader Meinhof Complex *'08*
Young Goethe in Love *'11*

Claudiu Bleont (1959-)
Vlad *'03*
Born to Raise Hell *'10*

Brian Blessed (1936-)
Trojan Women *'71*
Man of La Mancha *'72*
King Arthur, the Young Warlord *'75*
Young Warlord *'75*
Flash Gordon *'80*
High Road to China *'83*
The Hound of the Baskervilles *'83*
The Last Days of Pompeii *'84*
Henry V *'89*
Prisoner of Honor *'91*
Robin Hood: Prince of Thieves *'91*
Much Ado about Nothing *'93*
Catherine the Great *'95*
Kidnapped *'95*
Hamlet *'96*
Tom Jones *'98*
Star Wars: Episode 1-The Phantom Menace *'99*
Tarzan *'99 (V)*
Alexander *'04*
As You Like It *'06*
Back in Business *'06*
Day of Wrath *'06*
The Pirates! Band of Misfits *'12 (V)*

Jack Blessing (1951-)
Galaxy of Terror *'81*
The Last of His Tribe *'92*
Above Suspicion *'00*

Billy Bletcher (1894-1979)
Boiling Point *'32*
Hollywood Party *'34 (V)*

Brenda Blethyn (1946-)
Grown Ups *'80*
The Witches *'90*
The Buddha of Suburbia *'92*
A River Runs Through It *'92*
Secrets and Lies *'95*
Music from Another Room *'97*
In the Winter Dark *'98*
Little Voice *'98*
Daddy & Them *'99*
RKO 281 *'99*
Saving Grace *'00*
Anne Frank: The Whole Story *'01*
Lovely & Amazing *'02*
Pumpkin *'02*
The Sleeping Dictionary *'02*
Sonny *'02*
Undertaking Betty *'02*
The Wild Thornberrys Movie *'02 (V)*
Beyond the Sea *'04*
A Way of Life *'04*
On a Clear Day *'05*
Pride and Prejudice *'05*
Atonement *'07*
Introducing the Dwights *'07*
Dead Man Running *'09*
London River *'09*
Christmas Angel *'11*
Mary and Martha *'13*

Corbin Bleu (1989-)
Catch That Kid *'04*
High School Musical *'06*
High School Musical 2 *'07*
Jump In! *'07*
High School Musical 3: Senior Year *'08*
Free Style *'09*
Nurse 3D *'13*

Ronnie Gene Blevins (1977-)
American Cowslip *'09*
Joe *'13*

Jason Blicker
Crown Heights *'02*
Owning Mahowny *'03*
Earthstorm *'06*
The Santa Suit *'10*

Bernard Blier (1916-89)
Jenny Lamour *'47*
Les Miserables *'57*
Monsieur Gangster *'63*
The Great Spy Chase *'64*
Greed in the Sun *'64*
The Organizer *'64*
Casanova '70 *'65*
To Commit a Murder *'67*
The Daydreamer *'70*
Catch Me a Spy *'71*
The Tall Blond Man with One Black Shoe *'72*
Buffet Froid *'79*

Mary J. Blige (1971-)
I Can Do Bad All By Myself *'09*
Betty & Coretta *'13*
Black Nativity *'13*
Mudbound *'17*
Sherlock Gnomes *'18*

Boti Ann Bliss (1975-)
Warlock 3: The End of Innocence *'98*
Pulse 2: Afterlife *'08*
The Perfect Teacher *'10*

Caroline Bliss (1961-)
My Brother Jonathan '85
The Living Daylights '87
License to Kill '89

Ian Bliss (1966-)
Siam Sunset '99
The Matrix Revolutions '03
Stealth '05

Hunt Block (1955-)
Secret Weapons '85
The Dirty Dozen: The Fatal Mission '88

Dan Blocker (1928-72)
The Errand Boy '61
Lady in Cement '68

Dirk Blocker (1957-)
Starman '84
Trouble in Mind '86
Prince of Darkness '87
Night of the Scarecrow '95
Inherit the Wind '99

Michael Blodgett (1940-2007)
40 Guns to Apache Pass '67
The Trip '67
Beyond the Valley of the Dolls '70
The Velvet Vampire '71

Anneke Blok
Zus & Zo '01
Winter in Wartime '10

Sebastian Blomberg (1972-)
Anatomy '00
What to Do in Case of Fire '02
Go for Zucker '05
The Countess '09
The Silence '10

Susan Blommaert (1947-)
Henry Hill '00
United 93 '06

Simone Blondel
See Simonetta Vitelli

Joan Blondell (1909-79)
Blonde Crazy '31
God's Gift to Women '31
Illicit '31
Millie '31
Night Nurse '31
Other Men's Women '31
Public Enemy '31
The Reckless Hour '31
The Crowd Roars '32
Lawyer Man '32
Make Me a Star '32
Miss Pinkerton '32
Three Broadway Girls '32
Union Depot '32
Blondie Johnson '33
Footlight Parade '33
Gold Diggers of 1933 '33
Dames '34
I've Got Your Number '34
Colleen '36
Gold Diggers of 1937 '36
Stand-In '37
Bullets or Ballots '38
East Side of Heaven '39
Two Girls on Broadway '40
Topper Returns '41
Lady for a Night '42
Cry Havoc '43
Don Juan Quilligan '45
A Tree Grows in Brooklyn '45
Nightmare Alley '47
For Heaven's Sake '50
The Opposite Sex '56
Desk Set '57
Will Success Spoil Rock Hunter? '57
Angel Baby '61
Advance to the Rear '64
The Cincinnati Kid '65
Waterhole Number 3 '67
Kona Coast '68
Stay Away, Joe '68
Support Your Local Gunfighter '71
Death at Love House '75
Opening Night '77
The Glove '78
Grease '78
The Champ '79
The Woman Inside '83
The Baron '88

Nicole Blonsky (1988-)
Hairspray '07
Harold '08
Queen Sized '08
Waiting for Forever '11

Moon Bloodgood (1975-)
Eight Below '06
Pathfinder '07
Moonlight Serenade '09
Street Fighter: The Legend of Chun-Li '09
Terminator Salvation '09
Beautiful Boy '10
Faster '10
The Sessions '12
The Power of Few '13

Brian Bloom (1970-)
Once Upon a Time in America '84
Walls of Glass '85
Confessions of Sorority Girls '94
Vampirella '96
Extramarital '98
The Sender '98
Blood Money '99
Knocking on Death's Door '99
Across the Line '00
The A-Team '10

Claire Bloom (1931-)
Limelight '52
Alexander the Great '55
Richard III '55
The Brothers Karamazov '58
The Buccaneer '58
Look Back in Anger '58
The Chapman Report '62
The Haunting '63
The Outrage '64
The Spy Who Came in from the Cold '65
Charly '68
The Illustrated Man '69
A Severed Head '70
A Doll's House '73
Islands in the Stream '77
Backstairs at the White House '79
Brideshead Revisited '81
Clash of the Titans '81
Deja Vu '84
Florence Nightingale '85
Promises to Keep '85
Anastasia: The Mystery of Anna '86
Hold the Dream '86
Queenie '87
Crimes & Misdemeanors '89
The Camomile Lawn '92
The Princess and the Goblin '94 (V)
Shameless '94
Mighty Aphrodite '95
A Village Affair '95
Daylight '96
What the Deaf Man Heard '98
Wrestling with Alligators '98
Imagining Argentina '04
The Chatterley Affair '06
And While We Were Here '13 (V)

John Bloom (1945-99)
Brain of Blood '71
Dracula *vs.* Frankenstein '71
The Incredible Two-Headed Transplant '71
The Dark '79
Bachelor Party '84
The Hills Have Eyes, Part 2 '84
Runaway Train '85
Harry and the Hendersons '87
The Great Outdoors '88

John (Joe Bob Briggs) Bloom (1953-)
The Texas Chainsaw Massacre 2 '86
Stephen King's The Stand '94
Casino '95

Lindsay Bloom (1950-)
Cover Girl Models '75
Six-Pack Annie '75
French Quarter '78

Orlando Bloom (1977-)
Black Hawk Down '01
Lord of the Rings: The Fellowship of the Ring '01
Lord of the Rings: The Two Towers '02
Lord of the Rings: The Return of the King '03
Ned Kelly '03
Pirates of the Caribbean: The Curse of the Black Pearl '03
Haven '04
Troy '04
Elizabethtown '05
Kingdom of Heaven '05
Pirates of the Caribbean: Dead Man's Chest '06
Pirates of the Caribbean: At World's End '07
New York, I Love You '09
Main Street '10
Sympathy for Delicious '10
The Good Doctor '11
The Three Musketeers '11
The Hobbit: The Desolation of Smaug '13
The Hobbit: The Battle of the Five Armies '14
Digging for Fire '15
Pirates of the Caribbean: Dead Men Tell No Tales '17
Unlocked '17
S.M.A.R.T. Chase '18

Rachel Bloom
The Angry Birds Movie 2 '19
Trolls World Tour '20

Verna Bloom (1939-)
Medium Cool '69
Hired Hand '71
Badge 373 '73
High Plains Drifter '73
Where Have All the People Gone? '74
Contract on Cherry Street '77
National Lampoon's Animal House '78
Playing for Time '80
Honkytonk Man '82
After Hours '85
The Journey of Natty Gann '85
The Last Temptation of Christ '88

Eric Blore (1887-1959)
Flying Down to Rio '33
The Gay Divorcee '34
Folies Bergere de Paris '35
I Live My Life '35
Old Man Rhythm '35
Seven Keys to Baldpate '35
To Beat the Band '35
Top Hat '35
Ex-Mrs. Bradford '36
Swing Time '36
Breakfast for Two '37
It's Love I'm After '37
Quality Street '37
Shall We Dance '37
Joy of Living '38
Swiss Miss '38
The Boys From Syracuse '40
The Lone Wolf Meets a Lady '40
Music in My Heart '40
Confirm or Deny '41
The Lady Eve '41
The Road to Zanzibar '41
Sullivan's Travels '41
Counter-Espionage '42
The Shanghai Gesture '42
Holy Matrimony '43
The Moon and Sixpence '43
Passport to Suez '43
Submarine Base '43
Romance on the High Seas '48
The Adventures of Ichabod and Mr. Toad '49 (V)
Fancy Pants '50
Love Happy '50

Roberts Blossom (1924-2011)
The Hospital '71
Slaughterhouse Five '72
Deranged '74
Citizens Band '77
Escape from Alcatraz '79
Resurrection '80
Family Reunion '81
Christine '84
Flashpoint '84
Vision Quest '85
The Last Temptation of Christ '88
Always '89
Home Alone '90
Doc Hollywood '91
The Quick and the Dead '95
Balloon Farm '97

Lisa Blount (1957-2010)
September 30, 1955 '77
Dead and Buried '81
An Officer and a Gentleman '82
Cut and Run '85
Prince of Darkness '87
Great Balls of Fire '89
Blind Fury '90
Box of Moonlight '96

Kurtis Blow (1959-)
Krush Groove '85
The Show '95

Marc Blucas (1972-)
Jay and Silent Bob Strike Back '01
Summer Catch '01
I Capture the Castle '02
Sunshine State '02
We Were Soldiers '02
Wes Craven Presents: They '02
Prey for Rock and Roll '03
The Alamo '04
First Daughter '04
The Killing Floor '06
The Jane Austen Book Club '07
Thr3e '07
Animals '08
Meet Dave '08
Deadline '09
Mother and Child '09
Stay Cool '09
Stuntmen '09
Knight and Day '10
Touchback '11
The Big Wedding '13
Brawl in Cell Block 99 '17

Ben Blue (1901-75)
Artists and Models '37
The Big Broadcast of 1938 '38
College Swing '38
For Me and My Gal '42
Panama Hattie '42
Broadway Rhythm '44
Two Girls and a Sailor '44
Easy to Wed '46
Two Sisters From Boston '46
My Wild Irish Rose '47
One Sunday Afternoon '48
The Russians Are Coming, the Russians Are Coming '66
The Busy Body '67

Callum Blue (1977-)
In Love and War '01
The Princess Diaries 2: Royal Engagement '04
Caffeine '06
Frenemy '09
Red Sands '09
Colombiana '11
And Now a Word From Our Sponsor '13

Monte Blue (1890-1963)
Affairs of Anatol '21
Orphans of the Storm '21
The Marriage Circle '24
White Shadows in the South Seas '29
Her Forgotten Past '33
The Lives of a Bengal Lancer '35
Prison Shadows '36
Undersea Kingdom '36
Across the Pacific '42
Casablanca '42
The Mask of Dimitrios '44
Homicide '49
Backfire '50
This Side of the Law '50

Brady Bluhm (1983-)
The Crazysitter '94
Alone in the Woods '95

Mark Blum (1950-2020)
Desperately Seeking Susan '85
Crocodile Dundee '86
Blind Date '87
The Presidio '88
Worth Winning '89
Indictment: The McMartin Trial '95
Steve Martini's The Judge '01
Shattered Glass '03
I Don't Know How She Does It '11

Trevor Blumas (1984-)
The Wall '99
The Unsaid '01
Ice Princess '05
Too Young to Marry '07

Alan Blumenfeld (1952-)
Worth Winning '89
Instant Karma '90
Problem Child 2 '91
Black Belt '92
Ed McBain's 87th Precinct: Lightning '95
Righteous Kill '08

Graeme Blundell (1945-)
Don's Party '76
The Odd Angry Shot '79
The Year My Voice Broke '87
Idiot Box '97
Marking Time '03

Emily Blunt (1983-)
Warrior Queen '03
Gideon's Daughter '05
My Summer of Love '05
The Devil Wears Prada '06
Irresistible '06
Charlie Wilson's War '07
Dan in Real Life '07
The Jane Austen Book Club '07
Wind Chill '07
The Great Buck Howard '09
Sunshine Cleaning '09
The Wolfman '09
The Young Victoria '09
Gulliver's Travels '10
Wild Target '10
The Adjustment Bureau '11
Gnomeo & Juliet '11 (V)
Salmon Fishing in the Yemen '11
Your Sister's Sister '11
The Five-Year Engagement '12
Looper '12
Edge of Tomorrow '14
Into the Woods '14
Sicario '15
The Girl on the Train '16
The Huntsman: Winter's War '16
Animal Crackers '17
My Little Pony: The Movie '17
Mary Poppins Returns '18
A Quiet Place '18
Sherlock Gnomes '18

Erin Blunt (1963-)
The Bad News Bears '76
The Bad News Bears in Breaking Training '77
The Bad News Bears Go to Japan '78

Lothaire Bluteau (1957-)
Jesus of Montreal '89
Black Robe '91
Orlando '92
Other Voices, Other Rooms '95
I Shot Andy Warhol '96
Bent '97
Shot Through the Heart '98
Restless Spirits '99
Urbania '00
Dead Heat '01
The Healer '02
On Thin Ice '03
Disappearances '06
Don't Look Up '08
Snow Buddies '08 (V)

John Bluthal (1928-)
Help! '65
Dark City '97
The Fifth Element '97

Margaret Blye (1942-)
Waterhole Number 3 '67
The Italian Job '69
Ash Wednesday '73
Melvin Purvis: G-Man '74
Undercover With the KKK '78
Mischief '85

Ann Blyth (1928-)
Mildred Pierce '45
Brute Force '47
Killer McCoy '47
The Great Caruso '51
I'll Never Forget You '51
Thunder on the Hill '51
One Minute to Zero '52
The World in His Arms '52
All the Brothers Were Valiant '53
Rose Marie '54
The Student Prince '54
The King's Thief '55
Kismet '55
The Helen Morgan Story '57
Slander '57

Betty Blythe (1893-1972)
Nomads of the North '20
She '25
The Scarlet Letter '34
Romance of the Limberlost '38
Honky Tonk '41
Girls in Chains '43
A Fig Leaf for Eve '44
They Were Expendable '45

Domini Blythe (1947-2010)
Vampire Circus '71
Afterglow '97
Savage Messiah '02
Affinity '08
The Trotsky '09

Janus Blythe
Eaten Alive '76
The Hills Have Eyes '77
The Hills Have Eyes, Part 2 '84

John Blythe (1921-93)
This Happy Breed '47
Lilli Marlene '50
The Frightened Man '52
The Gay Dog '54

Peter Blythe (1934-2004)
Frankenstein Created Woman '66
Carrington '95
The Luzhin Defence '00

Bruce Boa (1930-2004)
Full Metal Jacket '87
Murder Story '89
The Neighbor '93

Kwesi Boakye
I Can Do Bad All By Myself '09
Unconditional '12

Eleanor Boardman (1898-1991)
Souls for Sale '23
Bardelys the Magnificent '26
Tell It to the Marines '26
The Squaw Man '31

Michael Boatman (1964-)
Hamburger Hill '87
Urban Crossfire '94
The Glass Shield '95
The Peacemaker '97
Woman, Thou Art Loosed '04
And Then Came Love '07
Bad Parents '12

Anne Bobby (1967-)
Nightbreed '90
Baby of the Bride '91
Beautiful Girls '96
What the Deaf Man Heard '98

Jonah Bobo (1997-)
Around the Bend '04
Zathura '05
Crazy, Stupid, Love. '11

Barbara Bobulova (1974-)
In Love and War '01
The Spectator '04
Coco Chanel '08

Delia Boccardo (1948-)
Inspector Clouseau '68
Ring of Death '69
Shoot First, Die Later '74
Tentacles '77
Nostalghia '83

Hart Bochner (1956-)
East of Eden '80
Haywire '80
Terror Train '80
Rich and Famous '81
Supergirl '84
Making Mr. Right '86
Apartment Zero '88
Die Hard '88
War & Remembrance '88
War & Remembrance: The Final Chapter '89
Mr. Destiny '90
Batman: Mask of the Phantasm '93 (V)
The Innocent '93
A Good Day to Die '95
The Break Up '98
Anywhere But Here '99
Urban Legends 2: Final Cut '00
Say Nothing '01
Liberty Stands Still '02
Spread '09

Lloyd Bochner (1924-2005)
Drums of Africa '63
Point Blank '67
Tony Rome '67
The Detective '68
The Horse in the Gray Flannel Suit '68
The Dunwich Horror '70
They Call It Murder '71
Ulzana's Raid '72
Satan's School for Girls '73
It Seemed Like a Good Idea at the Time '75
Mazes and Monsters '82
Crystal Heart '87
Millennium '89
Naked Gun 2 1/2: The Smell of Fear '91
Morning Glory '93
Bram Stoker's The Mummy '97
Before I Say Goodbye '03

Rainer Bock (1954-)
The White Ribbon '09
Passion '13
A Most Wanted Man '14

Robert Bockstael (1923-)
All I Wanna Do '98
Invasion! '99
The Golden Spiders: A Nero Wolfe Mystery '00
Snap Decision '01
Homeless to Harvard: The Liz Murray Story '03
Plain Truth '04
Time Bomb '08

Jose Bodalo (1916-85)
Django '68
One After Another '68

Wolfgang Bodison (1966-)
A Few Good Men '92
Little Big League '94
Freeway '95
Most Wanted '97

Jenna Bodnar
Friend of the Family 2 '96
The Portrait '99

Kim Bodnia (1965-)
Pusher '96
In a Better World '10
Rosewater '14

Sergei Bodrov, Jr. (1971-2002)
Prisoner of the Mountains '96
Brother '97
East-West '99
The Quickie '01

Karl-Heinz Boehm (1928-2014)
Unnatural '52
Peeping Tom '60
The Four Horsemen of the Apocalypse '62
The Venetian Affair '67
Fox and His Friends '75
Mother Kusters Goes to Heaven '76

Earl Boen (1945-)
The Terminator '84
Terminator 2: Judgment Day '91
Norma Jean and Marilyn '95
Within the Rock '96
Nutty Professor 2: The Klumps '00
Clifford's Really Big Movie '04 (V)

Jim Boeven (1967-)
Torso '02
Sun Choke '16

Dirk Bogarde (1920-99)
Esther Waters '48
The Blue Lamp '49
Boys in Brown '49
Dear Mr. Prohack '49
Hunted '52
Penny Princess '52
Appointment in London '53
Doctor in the House '53
The Sleeping Tiger '54
Cast a Dark Shadow '55
Simba '55
Doctor at Sea '56
Campbell's Kingdom '57
Doctor at Large '57
Ill Met By Moonlight '57
Night Ambush '57
The Spanish Gardener '57
The Doctor's Dilemma '58
A Tale of Two Cities '58
The Wind Cannot Read '58
Libel '59
Song Without End '60
Victim '61
Damn the Defiant '62
The Password Is Courage '62
Doctor in Distress '63
I Could Go on Singing '63
The Mind Benders '63
The Servant '63
Hot Enough for June '64
King and Country '64
Darling '65
The High Bright Sun '65
Modesty Blaise '66
Accident '67
Our Mother's House '67
The Damned '69
Justine '69
Death in Venice '71
Night Flight from Moscow '73
The Night Porter '74
A Bridge Too Far '77
Despair '78
Daddy Nostalgia '90

Stephen Bogardus (1954-)
Love! Valour! Compassion! '96
States of Control '98

Humphrey Bogart (1899-1957)
Up the River '30
Love Affair '32
Midnight '34
China Clipper '36
The Great O'Malley '36
Petrified Forest '36
The Black Legion '37
Dead End '37
Kid Galahad '37
Marked Woman '37
San Quentin '37
Stand-In '37
Amazing Dr. Clitterhouse '38
Angels with Dirty Faces '38
Bullets or Ballots '38
Crime School '38
Swing Your Lady '38
Dark Victory '39
Invisible Stripes '39
King of the Underworld '39
Oklahoma Kid '39
The Roaring Twenties '39
You Can't Get Away With Murder '39
Brother Orchid '40
It All Came True '40
They Drive by Night '40
Virginia City '40
High Sierra '41
The Maltese Falcon '41
The Wagons Roll at Night '41
Across the Pacific '42
All Through the Night '42
The Big Shot '42
Casablanca '42
Action in the North Atlantic '43
Sahara '43
Thank Your Lucky Stars '43
Passage to Marseilles '44
To Have & Have Not '44
Conflict '45
The Big Sleep '46
Dark Passage '47
Dead Reckoning '47
The Two Mrs. Carrolls '47
Key Largo '48
Treasure of the Sierra Madre '48
Knock on Any Door '49
Tokyo Joe '49
Chain Lightning '50
In a Lonely Place '50
The African Queen '51
The Enforcer '51
Sirocco '51
Battle Circus '53
Beat the Devil '53
The Barefoot Contessa '54
The Caine Mutiny '54
Sabrina '54
Desperate Hours '55
The Left Hand of God '55
We're No Angels '55
The Harder They Fall '56

Peter Bogdanovich (1939-)
The Wild Angels '66
The Trip '67
Targets '68
Voyage to the Planet of Prehistoric Women '68 (N)
Saint Jack '79
Highball '97
Mr. Jealousy '98
Coming Soon '99
The Independent '00 (C)
Rated X '00
Festival at Cannes '02
Out of Order '03
Infamous '06
Dedication '07
The Dukes '07
Humboldt County '08
Abandoned '10
Are You Here '13
Cold Turkey '13
Hitchcock/Truffaut '15
78/52: Hitchcock's Shower Scene '17
The Other Side of the Wind '18

Eric Bogosian (1953-)
Special Effects '85
The Caine Mutiny Court Martial '88
Talk Radio '88
Naked in New York '93 (C)
Under Siege 2: Dark Territory '95
Beavis and Butt-Head Do America '96 (V)
The Thief and the Cobbler '96 (V)
Deconstructing Harry '97
Office Killer '97 (C)
A Bright Shining Lie '98
Gossip '99
In the Weeds '00
Blonde '01
Shot in the Heart '01
Ararat '02
Igby Goes Down '02
Charlie's Angels: Full Throttle '03
Wonderland '03
Blade: Trinity '04
Heights '04
King of the Corner '04
Cadillac Records '08
Listen Up Philip '14 (N)

Elizabeth Bogush (1977-)
Eastside '99
Tweek City '05
Jam '06
Believers '07

Ian Bohen (1976-)
Wyatt Earp '94
Young Hercules '97
Hometown Legend '02
Special '06
Marigold '07
Little Women '18

Hark Bohm (1939-)
Lola '81
Underground '95

Karlheinz Bohm (1928-2014)
See Karl-Heinz Boehm

Roman Bohnen (1894-1949)
The Hard Way '43
The Hairy Ape '44
Counter-Attack '45
The Best Years of Our Lives '46
Song of Love '47
Open Secret '48
Mr. Soft Touch '49

Corinne Bohrer (1958-)
Jekyll & Hyde. . . Together Again '82
Vice Versa '88
Revenge of the Nerds 4: Nerds in Love '94
Kisses in the Dark '97
Star Kid '97
Big Eden '00

Richard Bohringer (1942-)
Diva '82
Subway '85
The Cook, the Thief, His Wife & Her Lover '90
The Perfume of Yvonne '94
Transfixed '01
Crime Spree '03

Romane Bohringer (1973-)
Total Eclipse '95
Portraits Chinois '96
The Chambermaid on the Titanic '97
The King Is Alive '00
He Died With a Falafel in His Hand '01
Renoir '12

Samuel Boidin
The Life of Jesus '96
Flanders '06

Curt Bois (1901-91)
Amazing Dr. Clitterhouse '38
Gold Diggers in Paris '38
The Great Waltz '38
The Hunchback of Notre Dame '39
Bitter Sweet '40
Boom Town '40
The Lady in Question '40
That Night in Rio '41
Blue, White and Perfect '42
Casablanca '42
Princess O'Rourke '43
Swing Fever '43
Caught '49
The Boat Is Full '81
Wings of Desire '88

Julien Boisselier
A Loving Father '02
Sleepless Night '11

Christine Boisson (1956-)
Identification of a Woman '82
Sorceress '88
The Truth About Charlie '02

James Bolam (1935-)
The Loneliness of the Long Distance Runner '62
Crucible of Terror '72
Dressed for Death '74
In Celebration '75
Stella Does Tricks '96
Dirty Tricks '00
To Kill a King '03

Brian Boland
Pearl Diver '04
Paranormal Activity 2 '10

Joanne Boland (1975-)
Brave New Girl '04
George A. Romero's Land of the Dead '05

Katie Boland (1988-)
The Salem Witch Trials '02
The Note '07
The Note 2: Taking a Chance on Love '09

Mary Boland (1880-1965)
Three-Cornered Moon '33
Four Frightened People '34
Stingaree '34
Ruggles of Red Gap '35
Danger: Love at Work '37
Artists and Models Abroad '38
The Women '39
New Moon '40
One Night in the Tropics '40
Pride and Prejudice '40
Nothing But Trouble '44
Julia Misbehaves '48

Philip Daniel Bolden (1995-)
Johnson Family Vacation '04
Are We There Yet? '05
Are We Done Yet? '07
Fly Me to the Moon '08

John Boles (1895-1969)
Rio Rita '29
Frankenstein '31
The Age of Innocence '34
Stand Up and Cheer '34
Curly Top '35
The Littlest Rebel '35
Orchids to You '35
A Message to Garcia '36
Stella Dallas '37
Thousands Cheer '43

Steve Boles
Rockin' Road Trip '85
Accidental Love '15

Emma Bolger
In America '02
Intermission '03

John Bolger (1954-)
Parting Glances '86
Just Looking '99

Ray Bolger (1904-87)
The Great Ziegfeld '36
Rosalie '38
Sweethearts '38
The Wizard of Oz '39
Sunny '41
Stage Door Canteen '43
The Harvey Girls '46
Look for the Silver Lining '49
April in Paris '52
Babes in Toyland '61
That's Dancing! '85

Sarah Bolger (1991-)
A Secret Affair '99
A Love Divided '01
In America '02
Alex Rider: Operation Stormbreaker '06
The Spiderwick Chronicles '08
The Moth Diaries '11
As Cool As I Am '13
Crush '13
The Lazarus Effect '15
My All American '15

Florinda Bolkan (1941-)
Ring of Death '69
Black Lemons '70
The Last Valley '71
A Lizard in a Woman's Skin '71
Don't Torture a Duckling '72
Master Touch '74
Primal Impulse '74
Royal Flash '75
Some Girls '88
Collector's Item '89

Jean-Claude Bolle-Reddat (1949-)
Ricky '09
The New Girlfriend '14

Tiffany Bolling (1946-)
Bonnie's Kids '73
Wicked, Wicked '73
The Centerfold Girls '74
Wild Party '74
Kingdom of the Spiders '77

Ryan Bollman (1972-)
Children of the Corn 2: The Final Sacrifice '92
The NeverEnding Story 3: Escape from Fantasia '94
No Vacancy '99
Black Dawn '05

Joseph Bologna (1934-)
Cops and Robbers '73
Honor Thy Father '73
The Big Bus '76
Chapter Two '79
Torn Between Two Lovers '79
My Favorite Year '82
Blame It on Rio '84
The Woman in Red '84
Transylvania 6-5000 '85
Rags to Riches '87
Alligator 2: The Mutation '90
Coupe de Ville '90
Citizen Cohn '92
Jersey Girl '92
Revenge of the Nerds 4: Nerds in Love '94
Heaven Before I Die '96 (C)
Love Is All There Is '96
National Lampoon's The Don's Analyst '97
Big Daddy '99
Players '03
The Boynton Beach Club '05
Ice Age: The Meltdown '06 (V)

Melissa Bolona
Acts of Violence '18
The Hurricane Heist '18

Josh Bolt (1994-)
Nowhere Boy '09
Just Henry '11

Christopher Bolton (1970-)
City Boy '93
Ordeal in the Arctic '93
Killing Moon '00

Nathalie Boltt
Route 30 '08
24 Hours to Live '17

Matt Bomer (1977-)
The Texas Chainsaw Massacre: The Beginning '06
In Time '11
Magic Mike '12
Superman: Unbound '13 (V)
The Normal Heart '14
Space Station 76 '14
Magic Mike XXL '15
The Nice Guys '16

Walking Out *'17*
Jonathan *'19*

Jon Bon Jovi (1962-)
Young Guns 2 *'90*
Moonlight and Valentino *'95*
The Leading Man *'96*
Homegrown *'97*
Little City *'97*
No Looking Back *'98*
Row Your Boat *'98*
Pay It Forward *'00*
U-571 *'00*
John Carpenter Presents Vampires: Los Muertos *'02*
Cry Wolf *'05*
New Year's Eve *'11*

Ronaldo Bonacchi (1950-)
The Wide Blue Road *'57*
Orchestra Rehearsal *'78*

Paolo Bonacelli (1939-)
Salo, or the 120 Days of Sodom *'75*
Christ Stopped at Eboli *'79*
Caligula *'80*
Henry IV *'85*
Night on Earth *'91*
Francesco *'93*
The Stendahl Syndrome *'95*
The American *'10*

Danny Bonaduce (1959-)
Charlotte's Web *'73 (V)*
Baker's Hawk *'76*
H.O.T.S. *'79*

Olivia Bonamy
Read My Lips *'01*
Paris *'08*

Fortunio Bonanova (1895-1969)
The Black Swan *'42*
Ali Baba and the Forty Thieves *'43*
Five Graves to Cairo *'43*
For Whom the Bell Tolls *'43*
Double Indemnity *'44*
Bad Men of Tombstone *'49*
An Affair to Remember *'57*

Ivan Bonar (1924-88)
MacArthur *'77*
The Haunting Passion *'83*

Casey Bond
Ring the Bell *'13*
The Meanest Man in Texas *'19*

Derek Bond (1920-2006)
Nicholas Nickleby *'46*
Inheritance *'47*
Scott of the Antarctic *'48*
Tony Draws a Horse *'51*
The Hour of 13 *'52*
Stranger from Venus *'54*
Svengali *'55*
Gideon's Day *'58*
When Eight Bells Toll *'71*

Gary Bond (1940-95)
Zulu *'64*
Outback *'71*

Jackson Bond (1996-)
The Invasion *'07*
Memorial Day *'12*

James Bond, III
The Fish that Saved Pittsburgh *'79*
Go Tell It on the Mountain *'84*
School Daze *'88*
Def by Temptation *'90*

Lillian Bond (1908-91)
Hot Saturday *'32*
The Old Dark House *'32*
Double Harness *'33*
China Seas *'35*
The Westerner *'40*
Man in the Attic *'53*

Rudy Bond
Run Silent, Run Deep *'58*
Because They're Young *'60*

Samantha Bond (1961-)
Catherine Cookson's The Black Candle *'92*
Goldeneye *'95*
Emma *'97*
Tomorrow Never Dies *'97*
The World Is Not Enough *'99*
Die Another Day *'02*
P.D. James: The Murder Room *'04*
Yes *'04*
Clapham Junction *'07*
Fanny Hill *'07*

Steve Bond (1953-)
Tarzan and the Jungle Boy *'68*
Massacre at Central High *'76*
Gas Pump Girls *'79*
H.O.T.S. *'79*
Picasso Trigger *'89*
To Die For *'89*
Spacejacked *'98*

Sudie Bond (1928-84)
Tomorrow *'72*
I Am the Cheese *'83*

Tommy 'Butch' Bond
City Streets *'38*
Atom Man *vs.* Superman *'50*

Ward Bond (1903-60)
The Big Trail *'30*
Virtue *'32*
Heroes for Sale *'33*
Wild Boys of the Road *'33*
It Happened One Night *'34*
Whirlpool *'34*
You Only Live Once *'37*
Amazing Dr. Clitterhouse *'38*
Born to Be Wild *'38*
Bringing Up Baby *'38*
Hawaii Calls *'38*
Mr. Moto's Gamble *'38*
Prison Break *'38*
Drums Along the Mohawk *'39*
The Girl From Mexico *'39*
Gone with the Wind *'39*
Oklahoma Kid *'39*
Young Mr. Lincoln *'39*
Kit Carson *'40*
The Maltese Falcon *'41*
Manpower *'41*
Sergeant York *'41*
The Shepherd of the Hills *'41*
Tobacco Road *'41*
The Falcon Takes Over *'42*
The Fighting Sullivans *'42*
Gentleman Jim *'42*
Hello, Frisco, Hello *'43*
They Came to Blow Up America *'43*
Home In Indiana *'44*
Tall in the Saddle *'44*
Dakota *'45*
They Were Expendable *'45*
Canyon Passage *'46*
It's a Wonderful Life *'46*
My Darling Clementine *'46*
Unconquered *'47*
Fort Apache *'48*
The Fugitive *'48*
Three Godfathers *'48*
The Time of Your Life *'48*
Kiss Tomorrow Goodbye *'50*
Only the Valiant *'50*
Riding High *'50*
Wagon Master *'50*
On Dangerous Ground *'51*
Hellgate *'52*
The Quiet Man *'52*
Hondo *'53*
Johnny Guitar *'53*
The Moonlighter *'53*
The Long Gray Line *'55*
Mister Roberts *'55*
Dakota Incident *'56*
Pillars of the Sky *'56*
The Searchers *'56*
The Halliday Brand *'57*
Wings of Eagles *'57*
Alias Jesse James *'59 (C)*
Rio Bravo *'59*

Sergei Bondarchuk (1920-94)
Era Notte a Roma *'60*
A Summer to Remember *'61*
War and Peace *'68*
Battle of Neretva *'69*

Beulah Bondi (1888-1981)
Street Scene *'31*
Rain *'32*
Finishing School *'33*
The Good Fairy *'35*
The Gorgeous Hussy *'36*
The Invisible Ray *'36*
The Moon's Our Home *'36*
The Trail of the Lonesome Pine *'36*
Maid of Salem *'37*
Make Way for Tomorrow *'37*
Of Human Hearts *'38*
The Sisters *'38*
Vivacious Lady *'38*
Mr. Smith Goes to Washington *'39*
On Borrowed Time *'39*
Our Town *'40*
Remember the Night *'40*
One Foot in Heaven *'41*
Penny Serenade *'41*
The Shepherd of the Hills *'41*
Tonight We Raid Calais *'43*
Watch on the Rhine *'43*
Back to Bataan *'45*
The Southerner *'45*
Breakfast in Hollywood *'46*
It's a Wonderful Life *'46*
The Snake Pit *'48*
Mr. Soft Touch *'49*
So Dear to My Heart *'49*
The Furies *'50*
Baron of Arizona *'51*
Lone Star *'52*
Track of the Cat *'54*
A Summer Place *'59*
Tammy Tell Me True *'61*

De'Aundre Bonds (1976-)
Tales from the Hood *'95*
Get On the Bus *'96*
Sunset Park *'96*
The Wood *'99*
Lockdown *'00*
Three Strikes *'00*

Peter Bonerz (1938-)
A Session with The Committee *'68*
Medium Cool *'69*
Catch-22 *'70*
Jennifer On My Mind *'71*
The Bastard *'78*
Serial *'80*
Man on the Moon *'99*

Ken Bones
Bellman and True *'88*
Jack the Ripper *'88*
Perfect Hideout *'08*

Lisa Bonet (1967-)
Angel Heart *'87*
Final Combination *'93*
Enemy of the State *'98*
High Fidelity *'00*
The Lathe of Heaven *'02*
Biker Boyz *'03*
Road to Paloma *'14*

Nai Bonet (1945-)
Devil's Angels *'67*
Fairy Tales *'76*
Soul Hustler *'76*

Diego Boneta (1990-)
Mean Girls 2 *'11*
Rock of Ages *'12*
Summer Camp *'16*

Massimo Bonetti (1951-)
The Night of the Shooting Stars *'82*
Kaos *'85*
Night Sun *'90*
Terranova *'91*

Crispin Bonham Carter (1969-)
Pride and Prejudice *'95*
Catherine Cookson's The Rag Nymph *'96*
Wuthering Heights *'98*
Ghostboat *'06*

Helena Bonham Carter (1966-)
Lady Jane *'85*
A Room with a View *'86*
Maurice *'87*
Getting It Right *'89*
Hamlet *'90*
Where Angels Fear to Tread *'91*
Howard's End *'92*
Fatal Deception: Mrs. Lee Harvey Oswald *'93*
Francesco *'93*
Mary Shelley's Frankenstein *'94*
Margaret's Museum *'95*
Mighty Aphrodite *'95*
Portraits Chinois *'96*
Twelfth Night *'96*
A Merry War *'97*
The Wings of the Dove *'97*
Merlin *'98*
Sweet Revenge *'98*
Fight Club *'99*
Novocaine *'01*
Planet of the Apes *'01*
The Heart of Me *'02*
Till Human Voices Wake Us *'02*
Big Fish *'03*
Live from Baghdad *'03*
Charlie and the Chocolate Factory *'05*
Conversations with Other Women *'05*
Tim Burton's Corpse Bride *'05 (V)*
Wallace & Gromit in The Curse of the Were-Rabbit *'05 (V)*
Harry Potter and the Order of the Phoenix *'07*
Sweeney Todd: The Demon Barber of Fleet Street *'07*
Harry Potter and the Half-Blood Prince *'09*
Terminator Salvation *'09*
Alice in Wonderland *'10*
Harry Potter and the Deathly Hallows, Part 1 *'10*
The King's Speech *'10*
Toast *'10*
Harry Potter and the Deathly Hallows, Part 2 *'11*
Dark Shadows *'12*
Great Expectations *'12*
Les Miserables *'12*
Burton and Taylor *'13*
The Lone Ranger *'13*
Cinderella *'15*
Suffragette *'15*
The Young and Prodigious T.S. Spivet *'15*

Alessio Boni (1966-)
Best of Youth *'03*
Don't Tell *'05*
Caravaggio *'07*

Gabrielle Boni (1985-)
Daddy's Girl *'96*
Little Men *'98*

Luisella Boni (1935-)
The Fury of Hercules *'61*
Samson *'61*
The Invincible Gladiator *'62*

Nazanin Boniadi
The Next Three Days *'10*
Ben-Hur *'16*
Hotel Mumbai *'18*

Evan Bonifant (1985-)
3 Ninjas Kick Back *'94*
Blues Brothers 2000 *'98*
Breakout *'98*

Daniel Bonjour (1981-)
Dragonquest *'09*
Ambushed *'13*

Jacques Bonnaffe (1958-)
First Name: Carmen *'83*
Jeanne and the Perfect Guy *'98*
Venus Beauty Institute *'98*
Va Savoir *'01*
Cote d'Azur *'05*
Lemming *'05*
Around a Small Mountain *'09*

Sandrine Bonnaire (1967-)
A Nos Amours *'84*
Police *'85*
Vagabond *'85*
Monsieur Hire *'89*
Jeanne la Pucelle *'94*
La Ceremonie *'95*
Circle of Passion *'97*
The Color of Lies *'99*
East-West *'99*
Resistance *'03*
Intimate Strangers *'04*
Queen to Play *'09*

Damien Bonnard
Staying Vertical *'16*
Thirst Street *'17*
Les Misérables *'19*

Vivian Bonnell (1924-2003)
The Josephine Baker Story *'90*
Christmas in Connecticut *'92*

Beverly Bonner
Basket Case *'82*
Brain Damage *'88*
Basket Case 2 *'90*
Frankenhooker *'90*

Frank Bonner (1942-)
Equinox *'71*
You Can't Hurry Love *'88*
The Colony *'95*
Shut Up and Kiss Me *'05*

Mariah Bonner
Universal Soldier: Day of Reckoning *'12*
Shadow People *'13*

Tony Bonner (1943-)
Creatures the World Forgot *'70*
Eye Witness *'70*
Inn of the Damned *'74*
Quigley Down Under *'90*
Dead Sleep *'91*
Hurricane Smith *'92*

Valerie Bonneton (1970-)
Jeanne and the Perfect Guy *'98*
Summer Hours *'08*
Little White Lies *'10*

Maria Bonnevie (1973-)
The Polar Bear King *'94*
Insomnia *'97*
Reconstruction *'03*
I Am David *'04*

Hugh Bonneville (1963-)
Stalag Luft *'93*
Heat of the Sun *'99*
Mansfield Park *'99*
Notting Hill *'99*
Blow Dry *'00*
The Emperor's New Clothes *'01*
Iris *'01*
Daniel Deronda *'02*
The Gathering Storm *'02*
Tipping the Velvet *'02*
Conspiracy of Silence *'03*
Asylum *'05*
Underclassman *'05*
Beau Brummell: This Charming Man *'06*
Four Last Songs *'06*
Scenes of a Sexual Nature *'06*
Five Days *'07*
Miss Austen Regrets *'07*
Filth *'08*
French Film *'08*
Lost in Austen *'08*
Glorious 39 *'09*
Shanghai *'09*
Ben Hur *'10*
Burke & Hare *'10*
Murder on the Orient Express *'10*
The Monuments Men *'13*
Paddington *'14*
Paddington 2 *'17*
Viceroy's House *'17*

Celine Bonnier (1965-)
A Wind from Wyoming *'94*
The Assignment *'97*
Far Side of the Moon *'03*
Human Trafficking *'05*

Sonny Bono (1935-98)
Good Times *'67*
Murder on Flight 502 *'75*
Escape to Athena *'79*
Airplane 2: The Sequel *'82*
Balboa *'82*
Troll *'86*
Hairspray *'88*
Under the Boardwalk *'89*

Brian Bonsall (1981-)
Mikey *'92*
Blank Check *'93*
Father Hood *'93*
Father and Scout *'94*

Deanna (Dee) Booher (1951-)
Deathstalker 2: Duel of the Titans *'87*
Slashdance *'89*
Home for Christmas *'93*

Sorrell Booke (1930-94)
The Iceman Cometh *'60*
Gone Are the Days *'63*
Purlie Victorious *'63*
Joy House *'64*
A Fine Madness *'66*
Bye Bye Braverman *'67*
Up the Down Staircase *'67*
The Iceman Cometh *'73*
Bank Shot *'74*
Devil Times Five *'74*
The Other Side of Midnight *'77*
Rock-a-Doodle *'92 (V)*

Daniel Booko (1983-)
Foreign Exchange *'08*
Jersey Shore Shark Attack *'12*
Wyatt Earp's Revenge *'12*

Dany Boon (1966-)
Joyeux Noel *'05*
My Best Friend *'06*
The Valet *'06*
Change of Plans *'09*
Micmacs *'09*
Lolo *'15*

Charles Eugene Boone (1934-)
See Pat Boone

Debbie Boone (1956-)
Hollywood Safari *'96*
Treehouse Hostage *'99*

Mark Boone, Jr. (1955-)
Last Exit to Brooklyn *'90*
Fever *'91*
Rosewood *'96*
Tree's Lounge *'96*
John Carpenter's Vampires *'97*
The Treat *'98*
Buddy Boy *'99*
The General's Daughter *'99*
Animal Factory *'00*
The Beatnicks *'00*
Memento *'00*
2 Fast 2 Furious *'03*
Dead Birds *'04*
Frankenfish *'04*
Batman Begins *'05*
Venice Underground *'05*
Full Clip *'06*
The Legend of Lucy Keyes *'06*
Lonesome Jim *'06*
Wristcutters: A Love Story *'06*
30 Days of Night *'07*
Frozen River *'08*
Vice *'08*
The Donner Party *'09*
Happiness Runs *'10*
Pete Smalls Is Dead *'10*
Life of Crime *'13*
The Birth of a Nation *'16*
Casual Encounters *'16*

Megan Boone (1983-)
My Bloody Valentine 3D *'09*
Step Up Revolution *'12*
Welcome to the Jungle *'13*

Pat Boone (1934-)
April Love *'57*
Journey to the Center of the Earth *'59*
All Hands on Deck *'61*
State Fair *'62*
The Greatest Story Ever Told *'65*

The Cross & the Switchblade '72
Roger & Me '89
Hugh Hefner: Playboy, Activist and Rebel '09

Richard Boone (1916-81)
The Halls of Montezuma '50
Call Me Mister '51
The Australian Story '52
Red Skies of Montana '52
Way of a Gaucho '52
Beneath the 12-Mile Reef '53
City of Bad Men '53
Man on a Tightrope '53
The Robe '53
Dragnet '54
Siege at Red River '54
Ten Wanted Men '54
Robbers' Roost '55
Away All Boats '56
The Garment Jungle '57
The Tall T '57
I Bury the Living '58
The Alamo '60
A Thunder of Drums '61
Rio Conchos '64
The War Lord '65
Hombre '67
Kona Coast '68
The Arrangement '69
The Night of the Following Day '69
The Kremlin Letter '70
Madron '70
Big Jake '71
Against a Crooked Sky '75
God's Gun '75
The Shootist '76
The Last Dinosaur '77
The Big Sleep '78
The Hobbit '78 (V)
Winter Kills '79
The Bushido Blade '80

Mika Boorem (1987-)
Along Came a Spider '01
Hearts in Atlantis '01
Riding in Cars with Boys '01
Blue Crush '02
Carolina '03
Dirty Dancing: Havana Nights '04
Sleepover '04
Smile '05
The Initiation of Sarah '06
The Ward '10
Good Day for It '11

Charley Boorman (1966-)
Deliverance '72
Excalibur '81
The Emerald Forest '85
Hope and Glory '87
Picture Windows '95
The Serpent's Kiss '97
In My Country '04

Katrine Boorman (1958-)
Hope and Glory '87
Camille Claudel '89

Adrian Booth (1917-)
The Man They Could Not Hang '39
So Proudly We Hail '43
Captain America '44
Spoilers of the North '47

Anthony Booth (1931-)
Confessions of a Window Cleaner '74
Confessions of a Driving Instructor '76
Owd Bob '97
Extremely Dangerous '99

Connie Booth (1941-)
John Cleese on How to Irritate People '68
And Now for Something Completely Different '72
Monty Python and the Holy Grail '75
Hawks '89
American Friends '91
Leon the Pig Farmer '93
The Buccaneers '95

Douglas Booth (1992-)
Christopher and His Kind '11
Great Expectations '11
LOL '12
Romeo & Juliet '13
Noah '14
Jupiter Ascending '15
The Limehouse Golem '17
Loving Vincent '17
Mary Shelley '17

Emma Booth (1982-)
Introducing the Dwights '07
Blood Creek '09
The Boys Are Back '09
Cloudstreet '11

James Booth (1927-2005)
The Trials of Oscar Wilde '60
Zulu '64
The Bliss of Mrs. Blossom '68
Adam's Woman '70
Revenge '71
Rentadick '72
That'll Be the Day '73
Brannigan '75
Zorro, the Gay Blade '81
Pray for Death '85
American Ninja 4: The Annihilation '91
Keeping Mum '05

Karin (Karen, Katharine) Booth (1919-92)
The Unfinished Dance '47
Let's Do It Again '53
Charge of the Lancers '54
Jungle Man-Eaters '54
Tobor the Great '54
Seminole Uprising '55
Top Gun '55
The World Was His Jury '58
Beloved Infidel '59

Kristin Booth (1974-)
The Salem Witch Trials '02
Defendor '09
Harriet the Spy: Blog Wars '10
Cloudburst '11
The Kennedys '11
Signed, Sealed, Delivered for Christmas '14
At First Light '18

Lindy Booth (1979-)
Teenage Space Vampires '99
American Psycho 2: All American Girl '02
The Skulls 2 '02
Hollywood North '03
Wrong Turn '03
Dawn of the Dead '04
Christmas in Boston '05
Cry Wolf '05
Behind the Wall '08
Dark Honeymoon '08
Christmas Magic '11
Kick-Ass 2 '13

Shirley Booth (1907-92)
Come Back, Little Sheba '52
The Matchmaker '58

Zachary Booth (1983-)
Nick & Norah's Infinite Playlist '08
White Irish Drinkers '10
The Beaver '11
Keep the Lights On '12
Last Weekend '14

Powers Boothe (1948-2017)
Cruising '80
The Guyana Tragedy: The Story of Jim Jones '80
Southern Comfort '81
Red Dawn '84
The Emerald Forest '85
Extreme Prejudice '87
By Dawn's Early Light '89
A Family of Spies '90
Blue Sky '91
Rapid Fire '92
Tombstone '93
Dalva '95
Nixon '95
Sudden Death '95
True Women '97
U-Turn '97
Joan of Arc '99
Men of Honor '00
Attila '01
Frailty '02
Sin City '05
The Final Season '07
24: Redemption '08
Guns, Girls and Gambling '11
Hatfields & McCoys '12
Sin City: A Dame to Kill For '14

Nick Boraine
Operation Delta Force 5: Random Fire '00
Queen's Messenger II '01
Cape of Good Hope '04

Caterina Boratto (1915-2010)
8 1/2 '63
Juliet of the Spirits '65
Castle Keep '69
Salo, or the 120 Days of Sodom '75

Brad Borbridge
Daniel's Daughter '08
Gossip '08
Before You Say 'I Do' '09

Cesar Bordon
The Headless Woman '08
Wild Tales '14

David Boreanaz (1969-)
Valentine '01
I'm with Lucy '02
The Crow: Wicked Prayer '05
These Girls '05
Mr. Fix It '06
Ghost Writer '07
The Mighty Macs '09
Officer Down '13

Veda Ann Borg (1915-73)
False Faces '32
It's Love I'm After '37
Kid Galahad '37
San Quentin '37
Melody Ranch '40
Honky Tonk '41
The Corsican Brothers '42
I Married an Angel '42
Isle of Forgotten Sins '43
Irish Eyes Are Smiling '44
Don Juan Quilligan '45
Fog Island '45
Treasure of Fear '45
Wife Wanted '46
The Bachelor and the Bobby-Soxer '47
Chicken Every Sunday '48
Julia Misbehaves '48
Big Jim McLain '52
Mr. Scoutmaster '53
Three Sailors and a Girl '53
Guys and Dolls '55
I'll Cry Tomorrow '55
Love Me or Leave Me '55
Wings of Eagles '57
The Fearmakers '58
The Alamo '60

Nelly Borgeaud (1931-2004)
Mississippi Mermaid '69
The Man Who Loved Women '77

Alexandre Borges (1966-)
Foreign Land '95
Bossa Nova '99

Sal Borgese (1937-)
Adios, Sabata '71
Flight of the Innocent '93

Paul Borghese
61* '01
Find Me Guilty '06

Ernest Borgnine (1917-2012)
The Mob '51
From Here to Eternity '53
Johnny Guitar '53
The Stranger Wore a Gun '53
Vera Cruz '53
Bad Day at Black Rock '54
Demetrius and the Gladiators '54
Marty '55
Run for Cover '55
Violent Saturday '55
The Catered Affair '56
Jubal '56
Three Brave Men '57
The Badlanders '58
Torpedo Run '58
The Vikings '58
Man On a String '60
Barabbas '62
McHale's Navy '64
The Flight of the Phoenix '65
Chuka '67
The Dirty Dozen '67
Ice Station Zebra '68
The Legend of Lylah Clare '68
The Split '68
The Wild Bunch '69
The Adventurers '70
Bullet for Sandoval '70
Suppose They Gave a War and Nobody Came? '70
Counter Punch '71
Hannie Caulder '72
The Poseidon Adventure '72
The Revengers '72
Emperor of the North Pole '73
Neptune Factor '73
Law and Disorder '74
Vengeance Is Mine '74
Devil's Rain '75
Love by Appointment '76
Fire '77
The Greatest '77
Jesus of Nazareth '77
Convoy '78
The Prince and the Pauper '78
All Quiet on the Western Front '79
The Black Hole '79
The Double McGuffin '79
When Time Ran Out '80
Deadly Blessing '81
Escape from New York '81
High Risk '81
Super Fuzz '81
Code Name: Wild Geese '84
Codename: Wildgeese '84
The Last Days of Pompeii '84
Alice in Wonderland '85
The Dirty Dozen: The Next Mission '85
The Manhunt '86
The Dirty Dozen: The Deadly Mission '87
The Big Turnaround '88
The Dirty Dozen: The Fatal Mission '88
Moving Target '89
The Opponent '89
Skeleton Coast '89
Any Man's Death '90
Laser Mission '90
Mistress '91
All Dogs Go to Heaven 2 '95 (V)
Gattaca '97
McHale's Navy '97 (C)
BASEketball '98
Small Soldiers '98 (V)
The Lost Treasure of Sawtooth Island '99
The Long Ride Home '01
The Trail to Hope Rose '04
A Grandpa for Christmas '07
Aces 'n Eights '08
Strange Wilderness '08
RED '10
Love's Christmas Journey '11
The Man Who Shook the Hand of Vicente Fernandez '12

Hilda Borgstrom (1871-1953)
The Phantom Chariot '20
The Phantom Carriage '21
Night Is My Future '47

Bobby Boriello
Private Parts '96
Enemy of the State '98
A Walk on the Moon '99

Angel Boris (1974-)
Warlock 3: The End of Innocence '98
Interceptor Force '99
Epoch: Evolution '03
Dragon Storm '04

Gene Borkan
The All-American Boy '73
Bound '96

Christian Borle (1973-)
Peter Pan Live! '14
Blackhat '15

Matt Borlenghi (1967-)
Kate's Addiction '99
Blood Surf '00
The Crew '00

Kyle Bornheimer
You Again '10
Bachelorette '12
Timmy Failure: Mistakes Were Made '20

Katherine Borowitz (1954-)
Men of Respect '91
Mac '93
Illuminata '98
The Man Who Wasn't There '01

Jesse Borrego (1962-)
Blood In . . . Blood Out: Bound by Honor '93
I Like It Like That '94
Mi Vida Loca '94
Con Air '97
Retroactive '97
The Maker '98
The Maldonado Miracle '03
La Mission '09
Colombiana '11

Dieter Borsche (1909-82)
Dead Eyes of London '61
The Phantom of Soho '64
The Mad Executioners '65

Alex Borstein (1973-)
Dawg '02
The Lizzie McGuire Movie '03
Catwoman '04
Seeing Other People '04
Good Night, and Good Luck '05
The Lookout '07
Killers '10
Love the Coopers '15

Michelle Borth (1978-)
Komodo vs. Cobra '05
Timer '09
A Good Old Fashioned Orgy '11

Jason Bortz (1970-)
Slaves to the Underground '96
Take It to the Limit '00

Jean-Mark Bory (1934-2001)
The Lovers '59
Le Repos du Guerrier '62
Love on a Pillow '62

Frank Borzage (1893-1962)
The Wrath of the Gods '14
A Mormon Maid '17

John Yong Bosch (1976-)
Mighty Morphin Power Rangers: The Movie '95
Turbo: A Power Rangers Movie '96
Devon's Ghost: Legend of the Bloody Boy '05

Johnny Yong Bosch
Bleach the Movie 4: Hell Verse '10 (V)
Promare '19

Philip Bosco (1930-)
The Pope of Greenwich Village '84
Heaven Help Us '85
Walls of Glass '85
Children of a Lesser God '86
The Money Pit '86
Suspect '87
Three Men and a Baby '87
Another Woman '88
Working Girl '88
The Dream Team '89
Blue Steel '90
Quick Change '90
F/X 2: The Deadly Art of Illusion '91
The Return of Eliot Ness '91
True Colors '91
Shadows and Fog '92
Straight Talk '92
Against the Wall '94
Angie '94
Milk Money '94
Nobody's Fool '94
Safe Passage '94
It Takes Two '95
The First Wives Club '96
Critical Care '97
Deconstructing Harry '97
My Best Friend's Wedding '97
Borough of Kings '98
Moon over Broadway '98
Bonanno: A Godfather's Story '99
Cupid & Cate '00
Shaft '00
Wonder Boys '00
Kate & Leopold '01
Abandon '02
The Savages '07

Lucia Bose (1931-2020)
Story of a Love Affair '50
Nathalie Granger '72
Harem '99

Miguel Bose (1956-)
California '77
High Heels '91
Queen Margot '94

Rahul Bose
Everybody Says I'm Fine! '06
Before the Rains '07

Chadwick Boseman (1976-)
The Kill Hole '12
42 '13
Draft Day '14
Get On Up '14
Marshall '17
Black Panther '18
21 Bridges '19

Guilio Bosetti
Incantato '03
Il Divo '08

Andrea Bosic (1919-2012)
Maciste in Hell '60
Pirates of the Seven Seas '62
Sandokan the Great '63
Hornets' Nest '70

Todd Bosley (1984-)
Little Giants '94
Jack '96
Treehouse Hostage '99
Lloyd '00

Tom Bosley (1927-2010)
The World of Henry Orient '64
Bang Bang Kid '67
Divorce American Style '67
The Secret War of Harry Frigg '68
Yours, Mine & Ours '68
Night Gallery '69
A Step Out of Line '71
The Streets of San Francisco '72
Gus '76
Testimony of Two Men '77
The Bastard '78
The Triangle Factory Fire Scandal '79
For the Love of It '80
O'Hara's Wife '82
The Jesse Owens Story '84
Million Dollar Mystery '87
Wicked Stepmother '89

Little Bigfoot 2: The Journey Home '97
Christmas at Water's Edge '04
Hidden Places '06
Charlie & Me '08

Simon Bossell
Hotel de Love '96
Aberration '97
Better Than Sex '00
Cut '00

Barbara Bosson (1939-)
A Session with The Committee '68
Mame '74
The Last Starfighter '84
Hostage Flight '85
Little Sweetheart '90
The Great American Sex Scandal '94

Devon Bostick (1991-)
Citizen Duane '06
Adoration '08
Diary of a Wimpy Kid '10
Diary of a Wimpy Kid 2: Rodrick Rules '11
The Entitled '11
Sacrifice '11
Diary of a Wimpy Kid: Dog Days '12
Small Time '14
Being Charlie '16
Regression '16

Linda Boston
Street Kings 2: Motor City '11
A Girl Like Her '15

Rachel Boston (1982-)
(500) Days of Summer '09
It's a Disaster '12

Barry Bostwick (1945-)
Road Movie '72
Fantastic Planet '73 (V)
The Rocky Horror Picture Show '75
Movie, Movie '78
You Can't Take It With You '79
Scruples '80
A Woman of Substance '84
Jailbait: Betrayed By Innocence '86
War & Remembrance '88
800 Leagues Down the Amazon '93
Russian Roulette '93
Weekend at Bernie's 2 '93
The Secret Agent Club '96
Spy Hard '96
Evening '07
Nancy Drew '07
Depth Charge '08
Holiday Baggage '08
Home Run Showdown '10
Secrets of the Mountain '10
2010: Moby Dick '10
The Scorpion King 4: Quest for Power '15

Brian Bosworth (1965-)
Stone Cold '91
One Man's Justice '95
Back in Business '96
Virus '96
Mach 2 '00
The Longest Yard '05
Rock Slyde: Private Eye '09
Revelation Road: The Beginning of the End '13

Hobart Bosworth (1867-1943)
The Little American '17
A Mormon Maid '17
Little Church Around the Corner '23
The Big Parade '25
My Best Girl '27
Hangman's House '28
The Smart Set '28
Abraham Lincoln '30
Shipmates '31
Sit Tight '31
This Modern Age '31
The Last of the Mohicans '32
The Crusades '35
The Keeper of the Bees '35
Steamboat Round the Bend '35
The Dark Hour '36

Kate (Catherine) Bosworth (1983-)
The Horse Whisperer '97
Remember the Titans '00
Blue Crush '02
The Rules of Attraction '02
Wonderland '03
Beyond the Sea '04
Win a Date with Tad Hamilton! '04
Bee Season '05
Superman Returns '06
21 '08
Another Happy Day '11
Life Happens '11
Straw Dogs '11
Black Rock '12
And While We Were Here '13
Big Sur '13
Homefront '13
Movie 43 '13
Still Alice '14
Amnesiac '15
Before I Wake '15
90 Minutes in Heaven '15
Life on the Line '16

Wade Boteler (1888-1943)
Big News '29
Navy Blues '29
The Mandarin Mystery '37
You Only Live Once '37
The Green Hornet '39

Niki Botelho
The Ewoks: Battle for Endor '85
No Turning Back '01

Rodrigo Botero
Beach Babes 2: Cave Girl Island '95
True Friends '98

Sara Botsford (1951-)
Still of the Night '82
Jumpin' Jack Flash '86 (C)
Ricky Nelson: Original Teen Idol '99
Tremors 4: The Legend Begins '04
The Fog '05
Lizzie Borden Took an Ax '14

Juan Diego Botto (1975-)
If They Tell You I Fell '89
Martin (Hache) '97
Broken Silence '01
The Dancer Upstairs '02

Maria Botto (1974-)
If They Tell You I Fell '89
Jealousy '99
Broken Silence '01
My Life in Ruins '09
Risen '16

Christine Bottomley (1979-)
The Waiting Room '07
Land Girls '09
The Secret Diaries of Miss Anne Lister '10

Joseph Bottoms (1954-)
The Dove '74
Crime & Passion '75
High Rolling in a Hot Corvette '77
Holocaust '78
The Black Hole '79
Blind Date '84
Open House '86
Inner Sanctum '91

Sam Bottoms (1955-2008)
The Last Picture Show '71
Class of '44 '73
Zandy's Bride '74
Savages '75
The Outlaw Josey Wales '76
Apocalypse Now '79
Up from the Depths '79
Bronco Billy '80
East of Eden '80
Desperate Lives '82
Gardens of Stone '87
Ragin' Cajun '90
Hearts of Darkness: A Filmmaker's Apocalypse '91
Dolly Dearest '92
Project Shadowchaser 3000 '95
Angel Blue '97
The Unsaid '01
Shopgirl '05
Sherrybaby '06

Timothy Bottoms (1951-)
Johnny Got His Gun '71
The Last Picture Show '71
Love and Pain and the Whole Damn Thing '73
The Paper Chase '73
Operation Daybreak '75
The White Dawn '75
Arthur Hailey's The Moneychangers '76
A Small Town in Texas '76
The Story of David '76
Rollercoaster '77
The Other Side of the Mountain, Part 2 '78
Hurricane '79
East of Eden '80
Tin Man '83
Invaders from Mars '86
The Land of Faraway '87
The Drifter '88
The Gift of Love '90
Texasville '90
Ava's Magical Adventure '94
Lone Tiger '94
Hourglass '95
Top Dog '95
Personal Vendetta '96
Uncle Sam '96
The Man in the Iron Mask '97
Mortal Challenge '97
Diamondbacks '99
The Prince and the Surfer '99
Elephant '03
DC 9/11: Time of Crisis '04
The Girl Next Door '04
Ike: Countdown to D-Day '04
Paradise, Texas '05
Vampire Bats '05
Holiday in Handcuffs '07
Shanghai Kiss '07
Lone Rider '08
Parasomnia '08
American Girl: Chrissa Stands Strong '09
Bound by a Secret '09
Call of the Wild 3D '09
The Land That Time Forgot '09
Pound of Flesh '10
The Shed '19

Mathew Botuchis
3 Ninjas: High Noon at Mega Mountain '97
I-See-You.Com '06

Sami Bouajila (1966-)
Bye-Bye '96
The Siege '98
Change My Life '01
The Nest '02
Days of Glory '06
The Witnesses '07
London River '09
Ultimate Heist '09
Outside the Law '10

Raymond Bouchard
Seducing Doctor Lewis '03
Funkytown '11

Barbara Bouchet (1943-)
In Harm's Way '65
Casino Royale '67
Amuck! '71
The Black Belly of the Tarantula '71
Caliber 9 '72
Cry of a Prostitute: Love Kills '72
Don't Torture a Duckling '72
Mean Machine '73

Willis Bouchey (1907-77)
Dangerous Crossing '53
Suddenly '54
Battle Cry '55
The Bridges at Toko-Ri '55
Pillars of the Sky '56
Zero Hour! '57
The Sheepman '58
The Horse Soldiers '59
Incident in an Alley '62
The Man Who Shot Liberty Valance '62
Panic in Year Zero! '62

Elodie Bouchez (1973-)
Wild Reeds '94
Full Speed '96
Don't Let Me Die on a Sunday '98
The Dreamlife of Angels '98
The Beatnicks '00
CQ '01
Sorry, Haters '05
Apres Lui '07
Four Lovers '10

Chili Bouchier (1909-99)
The Ghost Goes West '36
Old Mother Riley's New Venture '49

Patrick Bouchitey (1946-)
The Best Way '76
My Afternoons with Marguerite '10

Jacques Boudet (1939-)
Waiting for the Moon '87
Farinelli '94
Marius and Jeannette '97
The Town Is Quiet '00
The Names of Love '10

Chafia Boudraa
Outside the Law '10
Just Like a Woman '13

Jean Bouise (1929-89)
I Am Cuba '64
Le Dernier Combat '84
La Femme Nikita '91

Michel Boujenah (1952-)
Three Men and a Cradle '85
Cinderella '12 (V)

Daniel Boulanger (1922-2014)
Breathless '59
The King of Hearts '66
The Bride Wore Black '68
Bed and Board '70

Pierre Boulanger (1987-)
Monsieur Ibrahim '03
Monte Carlo '11
God Help the Girl '14

Matthew Boulton (1883-1962)
Sabotage '36
Night Must Fall '37
Counter-Espionage '42

Carole Bouquet (1957-)
That Obscure Object of Desire '77
Buffet Froid '79
For Your Eyes Only '81
Too Beautiful for You '88
New York Stories '89
A Business Affair '93
Grosse Fatigue '94
The Bridge '00
Wasabi '01
Red Lights '04
Unforgivable '11
Rosemary's Baby '14

Michel Bouquet (1925-)
Monsieur Vincent '47
Who's Got the Black Box? '67
The Bride Wore Black '68
La Femme Infidele '69
Mississippi Mermaid '69
Borsalino '70
La Rupture '70
Just Before Nightfall '71
Cop Au Vin '85
Toto le Heros '91
Tous les Matins du Monde '92
How I Killed My Father '03
Renoir '12

Sacha Bourdo (1962-)
Western '96
The Science of Sleep '06

John Bourgeois (1956-)
Dead Silence '96
Ginger Snaps '01
The Interrogation of Michael Crowe '02
Rudy: The Rudy Giulani Story '03
A Different Loyalty '04
The Prince & Me '04
XIII '08
The 19th Wife '10
When Love Is Not Enough: The Lois Wilson Story '10

Stacie Bourgeois
See Stacie Randall

Louise Bourgoin (1981-)
The Girl From Monaco '08
Black Heaven '10
The Love Punch '13
Mojave '15

J.R. Bourne (1970-)
13 Ghosts '01
Ginger Snaps Back: The Beginning '04
The Exorcism of Emily Rose '05
The Butterfly Effect 2 '06
Everything's Gone Green '06
The Lost Treasure of the Grand Canyon '08
Brake '12

Whitney Bourne (1914-88)
Flight from Glory '37
Head Over Heels '37

Philip Bourneuf (1908-79)
The Big Night '51
Beyond a Reasonable Doubt '56

Andre Bourvil (1917-70)
Four Bags Full '56
Les Miserables '57
La Grande Vadrouille '66
The Brain '69
Le Cercle Rouge '70

Joy Boushel (1959-)
Humongous '82
The Fly '86

Nathalie Boutefeu (1968-)
Irma Vep '96
Kings and Queen '04

Sofia Boutella (1982-)
Kingsman: The Secret Service '15
The Mummy '17
Climax '18
Hotel Artemis '18

Dennis Boutsikaris (1952-)
*batteries not included '87
The Dream Team '89
Beyond Betrayal '94
The Yarn Princess '94
In Dreams '98
Taken '99
Perfect Murder, Perfect Town '00
They Crawl '01
Cherry Crush '07
My Soul to Take '10

Denise Boutte (1982-)
Death Valley: The Revenge of Bloody Bill '04
Bram Stoker's Way of the Vampire '05
Sister's Keeper '07
Tyler Perry's Why Did I Get Married? '07
The Bounce Back '16

Duane Boutte
Stonewall '95
Brother to Brother '04
You Belong to Me '07

Jean-Pierre Bouvier (1948-)
Good-bye, Emmanuelle '77
Subversion '79
Ma Saison Preferee '93

Raoul Bova (1971-)
Avenging Angelo '02
Facing Windows '03
Under the Tuscan Sun '03
Alien vs. Predator '04
The Company '07
Our Life '10
The Tourist '10
Treasure Guards '11
All Roads Lead to Rome '15

Julie Bovasso (1930-91)
The Iceman Cometh '60
The Verdict '82
Wise Guys '86
Moonstruck '87
Betsy's Wedding '90
Article 99 '92

Brunella Bovo (1932-)
Miracle in Milan '51
The White Sheik '52

Clara Bow (1905-65)
Down to the Sea in Ships '22
The Plastic Age '25
Dancing Mothers '26
It '27
Wings '27
Call Her Savage '32

Simmy Bow (1922-88)
The Doberman Gang '72
Zoltan. . . Hound of Dracula '78

Bow Wow (1987-)
Carmen: A Hip Hopera '01
All About the Benjamins '02
Like Mike '02
Johnson Family Vacation '04
Roll Bounce '05
The Fast and the Furious: Tokyo Drift '06
Hurricane Season '09
The Lottery Ticket '10
Madea's Big Happy Family '11
Allegiance '12

Katrina Bowden (1988-)
National Lampoon's Ratko: The Dictator's Son '09
The Shortcut '09
Tucker & Dale vs. Evil '10
Piranha 3DD '11
Hold Your Breath '12
Nurse 3D '13

Dorris Bowdon (1914-2005)
Drums Along the Mohawk '39
The Grapes of Wrath '40
The Moon is Down '43

David Bowe (1964-)
Back to the Beach '87
UHF '89
Dark Justice '00
Rubber '10

John Bowe (1950-)
Prime Suspect '92
Body & Soul '93
Poldark '96
Cleopatra '99
Split Second '99
Tipping the Velvet '02
Secret Smile '05
Cranford '08
Murder On the Home Front '13

AJ Bowen (1977-)
Creepshow III '06
The House of the Devil '09
Hatchet 2 '10
A Horrible Way to Die '10
The Sacrament '13
You're Next '13
Synchronicity '16
Satanic Panic '19

Andrea Bowen (1990-)
Highball '97
Girl, Positive '07
G.B.F. '13

Andrew Bowen (1972-)
The Haunting of Hell House '99

Conjurer '08
Rock Jocks '12

Christopher Bowen (1959-)
The Shell Seekers '89
Cold Comfort Farm '94
Gaudi Afternoon '01

Clare Bowen (1989-)
The Clinic '10
Dead Man's Burden '12

Dennis Bowen
Gas Pump Girls '79
Van Nuys Blvd. '79

Julie Bowen (1970-)
Runaway Daughters '94
Happy Gilmore '96
Multiplicity '96
An American Werewolf in Paris '97
Joe Somebody '01
The Killing Club '01
Kids in America '05
Sex and Death 101 '07
Crazy on the Outside '10
Horrible Bosses '11
Jumping the Broom '11
Knife Fight '13
Planes: Fire & Rescue '14 (V)
Life of the Party '18

Michael Bowen (1953-)
Forbidden World '82
Valley Girl '83
Night of the Comet '84
Echo Park '86
Iron Eagle '86
The Player '92
Love and a .45 '94
True Crime '95
Excess Baggage '96
Jackie Brown '97
Magnolia '99
Kill Bill Vol. 1 '03
Walking Tall '04
Autopsy '08
Cabin Fever 2: Spring Fever '08
Dear Me: A Blogger's Tale '08
Love at First Kill '08
The Hessen Conspiracy '09
The Last House on the Left '09
The Perfect Student '11
Soda Springs '11
Deep Dark Canyon '12

Roger Bowen (1932-96)
Petulia '68
M*A*S*H '70
Zapped! '82
What about Bob? '91

Malick Bowens
Out of Africa '85
The Believers '87
Bopha! '93
Ali '01
Tears of the Sun '03

Adrian Bower (1970-)
The Waiting Room '07
Lennon Naked '10

Antoinette Bower (1932-)
Die Sister, Die! '74
Prom Night '80
Blood Song '82
The Evil That Men Do '84

Jamie Campbell Bower (1988-)
Sweeney Todd: The Demon Barber of Fleet Street '07
Harry Potter and the Deathly Hallows, Part 1 '10
Winter in Wartime '10
Anonymous '11
The Mortal Instruments: City of Bones '13

Tom Bower (1938-)
Massive Retaliation '85
The Lightship '86
River's Edge '87
True Believer '89
Raising Cain '92
Relentless 3 '93
Against the Wall '94
Far from Home: The Adventures of Yellow Dog '94
The Avenging Angel '95
White Man's Burden '95
The Killing Jar '96
The Last Time I Committed Suicide '96
Buffalo Soldiers '97
The Million Dollar Hotel '99
A Slipping Down Life '99
Hearts in Atlantis '01
The Badge '02
High Crimes '02
Flannel Pajamas '06
The Hills Have Eyes '06
Thr3e '07
Valley of the Heart's Delight '07
Appaloosa '08
Familiar Strangers '08
Gospel Hill '08
Bad Lieutenant: Port of Call New Orleans '09
Crazy Heart '09
The Killer Inside Me '10
I Melt With You '11
13 Sins '13
Lamb '16

David Bowers
Star Wars: Episode 2-Attack of the Clones '02
Star Wars: Episode 3-Revenge of the Sith '05

John Bowers (1899-1936)
The Ace of Hearts '21
Lorna Doone '22
The White Sin '24
Say It With Songs '29

David Bowie (1947-2016)
The Man Who Fell to Earth '76
Christiane F. '82
The Hunger '83
Merry Christmas, Mr. Lawrence '83
Yellowbeard '83
Into the Night '85
Absolute Beginners '86
Labyrinth '86
The Last Temptation of Christ '88
The Linguini Incident '92
Twin Peaks: Fire Walk with Me '92
Basquiat '96
Gunslinger's Revenge '98
B.U.S.T.E.D. '99
Mr. Rice's Secret '00
Arthur and the Invisibles '06 (V)
The Prestige '06
August '08
Bandslam '09 (C)

Judi Bowker (1954-)
Brother Sun, Sister Moon '73
In This House of Brede '75
Count Dracula '77
Clash of the Titans '81
Dangerous Corner '83
The Shooting Party '85

Grant Bowler (1968-)
On the Beach '00
Atlas Shrugged: Part 1 '11
Liz & Dick '12
I Do '13
Swelter '14

Paul Bowles (1910-99)
The Sheltering Sky '90
Halfmoon '95 (N)

Peter Bowles (1936-)
Blow-Up '66
The Charge of the Light Brigade '68
A Day in the Death of Joe Egg '71
Endless Night '71
The Legend of Hell House '73
The Offence '73
In Love and War '01
Color Me Kubrick '05
Love's Kitchen '11
Lilting '14

Jessica Bowman (1980-)
Joy Ride '01
Derailed '02

Joshua Bowman (1988-)
Prowl '10
Love's Kitchen '11
So Undercover '13

Laura Bowman (1881-1957)
Drums O'Voodoo '34
Son of Ingagi '40

Lee Bowman (1914-79)
I Met Him in Paris '37
Internes Can't Take Money '37
Having a Wonderful Time '38
A Man to Remember '38
Next Time I Marry '38
Dancing Co-Ed '39
Fast and Furious '39
Love Affair '39
Miracles for Sale '39
Society Lawyer '39
Stronger Than Desire '39
Gold Rush Maisie '40
Third Finger, Left Hand '40
Buck Privates '41
Design for Scandal '41
Tish '42
We Were Dancing '42
Bataan '43
Cover Girl '44
The Impatient Years '44
She Wouldn't Say Yes '45
Tonight and Every Night '45
Smash-Up: The Story of a Woman '47
My Dream Is Yours '49
Youngblood Hawke '64

Lisa Bowman
River of Grass '94
Dead Dog '00

Paul Bown (1957-)
Anne of Green Gables '85
Morons from Outer Space '85
Butterfly Kiss '94

John Boxer (1909-82)
The Bridge on the River Kwai '57
Pros and Ex-cons '05

Bruce Boxleitner (1950-)
Six-Pack Annie '75
Kiss Me...Kill Me '76
East of Eden '80
Kenny Rogers as the Gambler '80
Tron '82
Kenny Rogers as the Gambler, Part 2: The Adventure Continues '83
Kenny Rogers as the Gambler, Part 3: The Legend Continues '87
From the Dead of Night '89
The Babe '92
Kuffs '92
The Secret '93
The Perfect Nanny '00
Hope Ranch '02
Gods and Generals '03
Snakehead Terror '04
They Are Among Us '04
Double Cross '06
King of the Lost World '06
Bone Eater '07
Pandemic '07
Sharpshooter '07
Aces 'n Eights '08
Transmorphers: Fall of Man '09
Tron: Legacy '10
Area 51 '11
Love's Everlasting Courage '11

Boy George (1961-)
The Wolves of Kromer '98 (N)
I Love You Baby '01

Sully Boyar (1923-2001)
Car Wash '76
The Manhattan Project '86
In the Soup '92

Alan Boyce (1961-)
Permanent Record '88
Totally F***ed Up '94

Brandon Boyce
Public Access '93
Milk '08

Cameron Boyce (1999-2019)
Eagle Eye '08
Mirrors '08

Todd Boyce
Jefferson in Paris '94
Spy Game '01

Alexandra Boyd
Dog Gone Love '03
Karla '06

Billy Boyd (1968-)
Lord of the Rings: The Fellowship of the Ring '01
Lord of the Rings: The Two Towers '02
Lord of the Rings: The Return of the King '03
Master and Commander: The Far Side of the World '03
Seed of Chucky '04 (V)
On a Clear Day '05
The Flying Scotsman '06
Moby Dick '11
The Witches of Oz '11

Blake Boyd
Raiders of the Sun '92
First Kid '96

Cameron Boyd (1984-)
Bye Bye, Love '94
Manny & Lo '96

Cayden Boyd
The Adventures of Sharkboy and Lavagirl in 3-D '05
Fireflies in the Garden '08

Darren Boyd (1971-)
High Heels and Low Lifes '01
Imagine Me & You '06

Guy Boyd (1943-)
Ticket to Heaven '81
Body Double '84
The Jagged Edge '85
Firefighter '86
The Dark Side of the Sun '88
Drug Wars: The Camarena Story '90
The Last of the Finest '90
Past Midnight '92
Retroactive '97
The Final Patient '05

Jenna Boyd (1993-)
Dickie Roberts: Former Child Star '03
The Missing '03
The Sisterhood of the Traveling Pants '05

Lynda Boyd (1965-)
Leaving Metropolis '02
Final Destination 2 '03
The Fast and the Furious: Tokyo Drift '06
True Confessions of a Hollywood Starlet '08
Rampage '09
The Client List '10

Patti Boyd
A Hard Day's Night '64
George Harrison: Living in the Material World '11

Stephen Boyd (1928-77)
The Man Who Never Was '55
The Beasts of Marseilles '57
The Night Heaven Fell '57
The Bravados '58
Ben-Hur '59
The Best of Everything '59
Woman Obsessed '59
Billy Rose's Jumbo '62
Lisa '62
Imperial Venus '63
The Fall of the Roman Empire '64
Genghis Khan '65
The Bible '66
Fantastic Voyage '66
Assignment K '68
Shalako '68
Black Brigade '69
The Big Game '72
Hannie Caulder '72
The Treasure of Jamaica Reef '74
The Squeeze '77

Tanya Boyd (1951-)
Black Heat '76
Black Shampoo '76
Ilsa, Harem Keeper of the Oil Sheiks '76
Roots '77

William Boyd (1898-1972)
The Road to Yesterday '25
Dress Parade '27
King of Kings '27
Yankee Clipper '27
The Flying Fool '29
Beyond Victory '31
The Painted Desert '31
Suicide Fleet '31
Hopalong Cassidy Returns '36
Borderland '37
The Frontiersmen '38
Law of the Pampas '39
The Showdown '40
Colt Comrades '43
Hopalong Cassidy: Riders of the Deadline '43
Hoppy Serves a Writ '43
Leather Burners '43
Hopalong Cassidy: The Devil's Playground '46

William 'Stage' Boyd (1889-1935)
State's Attorney '31
The House on 56th Street '33
Laughing at Life '33
Oliver Twist '33
The Lost City '34

John Boyega (1992-)
Attack the Block '11
Star Wars: The Force Awakens '15
The Circle '17
Detroit '17
Star Wars: The Last Jedi '17
Pacific Rim: Uprising '18
Star Wars: The Rise of Skywalker '19

Charles Boyer (1899-1978)
The Man From Yesterday '32
Red Headed Woman '32
Break of Hearts '35
Liliom '35
The Garden of Allah '36
Mayerling '36
Conquest '37
History Is Made at Night '37
Algiers '38
Love Affair '39
All This and Heaven Too '40
Back Street '41
Hold Back the Dawn '41
Tales of Manhattan '42
The Constant Nymph '43
Heart of a Nation '43 (N)
Together Again '43
Gaslight '44
Confidential Agent '45
Arch of Triumph '48
The Earrings of Madame De. . . '54
The Cobweb '55
Nana '55
Around the World in 80 Days '56
The Buccaneer '58
Fanny '61
The Four Horsemen of the Apocalypse '62
Love Is a Ball '63
A Very Special Favor '65
How to Steal a Million '66
Is Paris Burning? '66
Barefoot in the Park '67
Casino Royale '67
The Madwoman of Chaillot '69
Lost Horizon '73
Stavisky '74
A Matter of Time '76

Christopher Boyer (1960-)
Uninvited '93
Levitation '97

Katy Boyer
Tapeheads '89
A Nightmare Come True '97

Myriam Boyer (1948-)
Tous les Matins du Monde '92
Un Coeur en Hiver '93
Mesrine: Part 1-Killer Instinct '08

William Boyett (1927-2004)
Sam Whiskey '69
The Hidden '87
Girls in Prison '94

Eileen April Boylan
Sleepover '04
Jesse Stone: Innocents Lost '11

John Boylan
Before You Say 'I Do' '09
Land of the Lost '09

Sarain Boylan
Posers '02
Bon Cop Bad Cop '06
Freezer Burn: The Invasion of Laxdale '08
Witchslayer Gretl '12

Lara Flynn Boyle (1970-)
Poltergeist 3 '88
Dead Poets Society '89
How I Got into College '89
The Rookie '90
The Dark Backward '91
Eye of the Storm '91
Mobsters '91
Wayne's World '92
Where the Day Takes You '92
Red Rock West '93
The Temp '93
Baby's Day Out '94
Jacob '94
The Road to Wellville '94
Threesome '94
The Big Squeeze '96
Afterglow '97
Cafe Society '97
Since You've Been Gone '97
Dying to Get Rich '98
Happiness '98
Red Meat '98
Chain of Fools '00
Men in Black 2 '02
The House Next Door '06
Land of the Blind '06
Baby on Board '08
Life is Hot in Cracktown '08
Cougar Hunting '11
Hansel & Gretel Get Baked '13

Lisa Boyle (1964-)
Friend of the Family '95
I Like to Play Games '95
Lost Highway '96
The Last Marshal '99

Peter Boyle (1933-2006)
Medium Cool '69
Joe '70
The Candidate '72
Slither '73
Steelyard Blues '73
Young Frankenstein '74
Swashbuckler '76
Taxi Driver '76
Brink's Job '78
F.I.S.T. '78
Beyond the Poseidon Adventure '79
Hardcore '79
Where the Buffalo Roam '80
Outland '81
Hammett '82
Yellowbeard '83
Johnny Dangerously '84
Turk 182! '85

The Adventures of Huckleberry Finn '60
The George Raft Story '61
The Last Sunset '61
Birdman of Alcatraz '62
Hero's Island '62
That Darn Cat '65
Tora! Tora! Tora! '70
The Mad Bomber '72
Cahill: United States Marshal '73
The Deadly Trackers '73
Psychic Killer '75
Eaten Alive '76
The Longest Drive '76
Hi-Riders '77
The Ninth Configuration '79
Without Warning '80
Evils of the Night '85

Russell Brand (1975-)
St. Trinian's '07
Bedtime Stories '08
Forgetting Sarah Marshall '08
Despicable Me '10 (V)
Get Him to the Greek '10
The Tempest '10
Arthur '11
Hop '11 (V)
Rock of Ages '12
Despicable Me 2 '13 (V)
Army of One '16

Steven Brand (1969-)
The Scorpion King '02
The Diary of Ellen Rimbauer '03
The Human Contract '08
Hellraiser: Revelations '11
Echoes '15
Mayhem '17

Klaus Maria Brandauer (1943-)
Mephisto '81
Never Say Never Again '83
Colonel Redl '84
Out of Africa '85
The Lightship '86
The Russia House '90
White Fang '91
Jeremiah '98
Introducing Dorothy Dandridge '99
Druids '01
Between Strangers '02
The Crown Prince '06
Tetro '09

Larry Brandenburg (1948-)
Mo' Money '92
The Mod Squad '99
What the #$*! Do We Know? '04

Walter Brandi (?-1996)
The Bloody Pit of Horror '65
Terror Creatures from the Grave '66

Jonathan Brandis (1976-2003)
Stepfather 2: Make Room for Daddy '89
Stephen King's It '90
NeverEnding Story 2: The Next Chapter '91
Ladybugs '92
Two Came Back '97
Outside Providence '99
Ride with the Devil '99
Hart's War '02
Puerto Vallarta Squeeze '04

Thomas Brandise (1976-)
Gravesend '97
The Jesse Ventura Story '99
A Packing Suburbia '99

Jocelyn Brando (1919-2005)
The Big Heat '53
Ten Wanted Men '54
Nightfall '56
The Explosive Generation '61

Marlon Brando (1924-2004)
The Men '50
A Streetcar Named Desire '51
Viva Zapata! '52
Julius Caesar '53
Desiree '54
On the Waterfront '54
The Wild One '54
Guys and Dolls '55
The Teahouse of the August Moon '56
Sayonara '57
The Young Lions '58
The Fugitive Kind '60
One-Eyed Jacks '61
Mutiny on the Bounty '62
Bedtime Story '63
The Ugly American '63
Morituri '65
The Appaloosa '66
The Chase '66
A Countess from Hong Kong '67
Reflections in a Golden Eye '67
Candy '68
The Night of the Following Day '69
Burn! '70
The Godfather '72
The Nightcomers '72
Last Tango in Paris '73
Missouri Breaks '76
Superman: The Movie '78
Apocalypse Now '79
Roots: The Next Generation '79 (C)
The Formula '80
A Dry White Season '89
The Freshman '90
Don Juan DeMarco '94
The Island of Dr. Moreau '96
Free Money '99
The Score '01
Superman Returns '06

Rikki Brando
The Bikini Car Wash Company 2 '92
Zipperface '92

Clark Brandon (1958-)
My Tutor '82
Fast Food '89

Derek Brandon
Dark Fields '09
Small Town Santa '14

Henry (Kleinbach) Brandon (1912-90)
March of the Wooden Soldiers '34
Big Brown Eyes '36
The Garden of Allah '36
The Black Legion '37
Beau Geste '39
Drums of Fu Manchu '40
Wagons West '52
Raiders of the Seven Seas '53
War Arrow '53
The Searchers '56
The Land Unknown '57
Assault on Precinct 13 '76

Michael Brandon (1945-)
Lovers and Other Strangers '70
Jennifer On My Mind '71
Four Flies on Grey Velvet '72
Heavy Traffic '73
The Third Girl from the Left '73
James Dean '76
Promises in the Dark '79
A Change of Seasons '80
Rich and Famous '81
Deja Vu '98
Contaminated Man '00
The Detonator '06

Carlo Brandt
Indochine '92
Ridicule '96

Carolyn Brandt (1940-)
Eegah! '62
Wild Guitar '62
Incredibly Strange Creatures Who Stopped Living and Became Mixed-Up Zombies '63
The Thrill Killers '65
Rat Pfink a Boo-Boo '66
The Hollywood Strangler Meets the Skid Row Slasher '79

Brandy (1979-)
See Brandy Norwood

Brigid Brannagh (1972-)
The Day My Parents Ran Away '93
The Inheritance '97
The Man in the Iron Mask '97
Life Without Dick '01
Acceptance '09
They're Watching '16
Vanished-Left Behind: Next Generation '16

Paul Brannigan
Under the Skin '13
Edie '19

Marjorie Bransfield
Easy Wheels '89
Abraxas: Guardian of the Universe '90

Jennifer Bransford (1968-)
Amy's O '02
Love Thy Neighbor '02

Jeff Branson
The Big Bad Swim '06
I Spit on Your Grave '10

Betsy Brantley (1955-)
Five Days One Summer '82
Another Country '84
Dreams Lost, Dreams Found '87
The Fourth Protocol '87
Havana '90
I Come in Peace '90
Little Lord Fauntleroy '95
Schizopolis '97
Washington Square '97
Deep Impact '98
From the Earth to the Moon '98
Rogue Trader '98

Nicoletta Braschi (1960-)
Down by Law '86
Mystery Train '89
The Monster '96
Life Is Beautiful '98
Pinocchio '02
The Tiger and the Snow '05

Keefe Brasselle (1923-81)
Streets of Sin '49
Dial 1119 '50
It's a Big Country '51
A Place in the Sun '51
Skirts Ahoy! '52
The Eddie Cantor Story '53
Black Gunn '72

Claude Brasseur (1936-)
The Horror Chamber of Dr. Faustus '59
Please Not Now! '61
The Elusive Corporal '62
Band of Outsiders '64
La Boum '81
Detective '85
Avenue Montaigne '06

Pierre Brasseur (1905-72)
Children of Paradise '44
Portrait of an Assassin '49
Le Plaisir '52
The Horror Chamber of Dr. Faustus '59
Where the Hot Wind Blows '59
Carthage in Flames '60
The King of Hearts '66

Christian Brassington
Incubus '05
Fisherman's Friends '19

Benjamin Bratt (1963-)
Bright Angel '91
One Good Cop '91
Blood In . . . Blood Out: Bound by Honor '93
Demolition Man '93
The River Wild '94
Texas '94
Miss Congeniality '00
The Next Best Thing '00
Red Planet '00
Traffic '00
After the Storm '01
Pinero '01
Abandon '02
The Final Hit '02
Catwoman '04
The Woodsman '04
The Great Raid '05
Thumbsucker '05
The Andromeda Strain '08
Trucker '08
Cloudy with a Chance of Meatballs '09 (V)
La Mission '09
Despicable Me 2 '13 (V)
Snitch '13
The Infiltrator '16
Ride Along 2 '16
Coco '17
A Score to Settle '19

Creed Bratton (1943-)
Terri '11
The Ghastly Love of Johnny X '12

Andre Braugher (1962-)
Glory '89
Somebody Has to Shoot the Picture '90
Striking Distance '93
The Tuskegee Airmen '95
Get On the Bus '96
Primal Fear '96
City of Angels '98
It's the Rage '99
Love Songs '99
Passing Glory '99
Thick as Thieves '99
A Better Way to Die '00
Duets '00
Frequency '00
Homicide: The Movie '00
10,000 Black Men Named George '02
Soldier's Girl '03
Salem's Lot '04
Poseidon '06
Fantastic Four: Rise of the Silver Surfer '07
Live! '07
The Mist '07
The Andromeda Strain '08
Passengers '08
The Baytown Outlaws '12

Nicholas Braun (1988-)
Walter and Henry '01
Carry Me Home '04
Sky High '05
Minutemen '08
Princess Protection Program '09
Prom '11
Red State '11
Date and Switch '13
Freaks of Nature '15
Get a Job '16
Good Kids '16

Pinkas Braun (1923-2008)
The Man Outside '68
Mission Stardust '68
Samson and Delilah '96

Steve Braun
The Trip '02
Wrong Turn 2: Dead End '07

Asher Brauner (1946-)
American Eagle '90
Merchants of War '90
Living to Die '91

Arthur Brauss (1936-)
The Train '65
Cross of Iron '76

Bart Braverman (1946-)
The Great Texas Dynamite Chase '76
Alligator '80
From the Earth to the Moon '98
Running Red '99

Hilda Brawner
The Iceman Cometh '60
One Plus One '61

Toni Braxton (1968-)
Kingdom Come '01
The Oogieloves in the Big Balloon Adventure '12

Robert Bray (1917-83)
The Caine Mutiny '54
The Accursed '57
My Gun Is Quick '57
Never Love a Stranger '58

Thom Bray (1954-)
Deepstar Six '89
The Horror Show '89

Jay Brazeau (1953-)
Slam Dunk Ernest '95
Double Play '96
Kissed '96
Air Bud '97
Trucks '97
Air Bud 2: Golden Receiver '98
Better Than Chocolate '99
Double Jeopardy '99
Suspicious River '00
Chilly Dogs '01
Head Over Heels '01
Last Wedding '01
Wes Craven Presents: They '02
Ann Rule Presents: The Stranger Beside Me '03
Moving Malcolm '03
Presumed Dead '06
Trophy Wife '06
Far Cry '08
Polar Storm '09
The Possession '12
Seattle Superstorm '12

Rossano Brazzi (1916-94)
We the Living '42
The Barefoot Contessa '54
Barrier of the Law '54
Three Coins in the Fountain '54
Summertime '55
Legend of the Lost '57
South Pacific '58
Light in the Piazza '61
Rome Adventure '62
The Christmas That Almost Wasn't '66
The Bobo '67
Woman Times Seven '67
The Italian Job '69
Krakatoa East of Java '69
The Adventurers '70
Dr. Frankenstein's Castle of Freaks '74
A Time for Miracles '80
The Final Conflict '81
The Far Pavilions '84
Final Justice '84
Fear City '85

Sebastian Breaks (1940-)
The Heroes of Telemark '65
The Night Digger '71

George Breakston (1920-73)
Mrs. Wiggs of the Cabbage Patch '34
No Greater Glory '34

Egon Brecher (1880-1946)
The Black Cat '34
Judge Hardy and Son '39
So Dark the Night '46

Jonathan Breck (1965-)
Jeepers Creepers '01
Jeepers Creepers 2 '03
Jeepers Creepers 3 '17

Peter Breck (1929-2012)
Thunder Road '58
The Beatniks '60
The Crawling Hand '63
Shock Corridor '63
Benji '74
Highway 61 '91

Alexandra Breckenridge
Vampire Clan '02
The Bridge to Nowhere '09
Broken Vows '16

Laura Breckenridge
Southern Belles '05
Amusement '08

Leticia Bredice (1972-)
Burnt Money '00
Nine Queens '00

Bobby Breen (1927-)
It Happened in New Orleans '36
Let's Sing Again '36
Make a Wish '37
Hawaii Calls '38
Fisherman's Wharf '39

Patrick Breen (1960-)
Nobody's Perfect '90
Passed Away '92
For Love or Money '93
Just the Ticket '98
One True Thing '98
Just a Kiss '02
Stark Raving Mad '02
Radio '03
Christmas With the Kranks '04
Space Chimps '08 (V)

Thomas E. Breen (1924-2000)
Luxury Liner '48
Battleground '49
The River '51

Edmund Breese (1871-1936)
The Early Bird '25
All Quiet on the Western Front '30
Bright Lights '30

Mario Brega (1923-94)
An Angel for Satan '66
The Good, the Bad and the Ugly '67
Death Rides a Horse '69
Once Upon a Time in America '84

Tracy Bregman (1963-)
Happy Birthday to Me '81
Sex & Mrs. X '00

Catherine Breillat (1948-)
The Housekeeper '02
Anatomy of Hell '04

Zabou Breitman
Almost Peaceful '02
24 Days '14

Brian Bremer
Test Tube Teens from the Year 2000 '93
Permanent '17

Lucille Bremer (1917-96)
Meet Me in St. Louis '44
Yolanda and the Thief '45
Till the Clouds Roll By '46
Ziegfeld Follies '46
Dark Delusion '47
Ruthless '48

Richard Bremmer (1953-)
The 13th Warrior '99
Just Visiting '01
Half Past Dead '02

Ewen Bremner (1972-)
Naked '93
Trainspotting '95
The Acid House '98
Julien Donkey-boy '99
Snatch '00
Black Hawk Down '01
The Reckoning '03
The Rundown '03
16 Years of Alcohol '03
Alien vs. Predator '04
Around the World in 80 Days '04
Match Point '05
Death at a Funeral '07
Mister Foe '07
Fool's Gold '08
Page Eight '11
Perfect Sense '11
Great Expectations '12
Jack the Giant Slayer '13
Snowpiercer '14
Renegades '17
T2 Trainspotting '17
First Cow '20

El Brendel (1890-1964)
Wings '27
The Big Trail '30

West of Broadway *'31*
Happy Landing *'38*
If I Had My Way *'40*
I'm from Arkansas *'44*
The Beautiful Blonde from Bashful Bend *'49*

Julia Brendler (1975-)
Moondance *'95*
Deeply *'99*
Phantom Pain *'09*

Nicholas Brendon (1971-)
Psycho Beach Party *'00*
Survival Island *'02*
Fire Serpent *'07*
Unholy *'07*
A Golden Christmas *'09*
My Neighbor's Secret *'09*
Coherence *'13*

Josh Brener
Baked in Brooklyn *'16*
Max Steel *'16*
What Men Want *'19*

Shirly Brener (1974-)
Righteous Kill *'08*
War, Inc. *'08*
Streets of Blood *'09*
Letting Go *'12*

Brid Brennan (1955-)
Four Days in July *'85*
Guinevere *'94*
Cracker: Brotherly Love *'95*
Trojan Eddie *'96*
Dancing at Lughnasa *'98*
Felicia's Journey *'99*
Shadow Dancer *'12*

Eileen Brennan (1932-2013)
Divorce American Style *'67*
Scarecrow *'73*
The Sting *'73*
Daisy Miller *'74*
Come Die With Me *'75*
The Death of Richie *'76*
Great Smokey Roadblock *'76*
Murder by Death *'76*
The Cheap Detective *'78*
FM *'78*
My Old Man *'79*
Private Benjamin *'80*
Clue *'85*
Fourth Wise Man *'85*
Blood Vows: The Story of a Mafia Wife *'87*
The New Adventures of Pippi Longstocking *'88*
Sticky Fingers *'88*
Stella *'89*
Texasville *'90*
White Palace *'90*
I Don't Buy Kisses Anymore *'92*
Changing Habits *'96*
If These Walls Could Talk *'96*
Jeepers Creepers *'01*
The Hollow *'04*

Michael Brennan (1912-82)
No Trace *'50*
Fright *'71*

Stephen Brennan
St. Patrick: The Irish Legend *'00*
The Boys and Girl From County Clare *'03*

Walter Brennan (1894-1974)
The Invisible Man *'33*
Barbary Coast *'35*
The Bride of Frankenstein *'35*
The Man On the Flying Trapeze *'35*
The Wedding Night *'35*
Come and Get It *'36*
Fury *'36*
The Moon's Our Home *'36*
Three Godfathers *'36*
The Adventures of Tom Sawyer *'38*
The Cowboy and the Lady *'38*
Kentucky *'38*
The Texans *'38*
The Story of Vernon and Irene Castle *'39*
They Shall Have Music *'39*
Northwest Passage *'40*
The Westerner *'40*
Meet John Doe *'41*
Sergeant York *'41*
Hangmen Also Die *'42*
The Pride of the Yankees *'42*
Stand by for Action *'42*
The North Star *'43*
Slightly Dangerous *'43*
Home In Indiana *'44*
The Princess and the Pirate *'44*
To Have & Have Not *'44*
Dakota *'45*
My Darling Clementine *'46*
Nobody Lives Forever *'46*
A Stolen Life *'46*
Red River *'48*
The Green Promise *'49*
Task Force *'49*
Best of the Badmen *'50*
Along the Great Divide *'51*
Lure of the Wilderness *'52*
Bad Day at Black Rock *'54*
Drums Across the River *'54*
Far Country *'55*
Goodbye, My Lady *'56*
Tammy and the Bachelor *'57*
Rio Bravo *'59*
How the West Was Won *'63*
Those Calloways *'65*
The Gnome-Mobile *'67*
Who's Minding the Mint? *'67*
The One and Only, Genuine, Original Family Band *'68*
The Over-the-Hill Gang *'69*
Support Your Local Sheriff *'69*
The Over-the-Hill Gang Rides Again *'70*

Amy Brenneman (1964-)
Bye Bye, Love *'94*
Casper *'95*
Heat *'95*
Daylight *'96*
Fear *'96*
Your Friends & Neighbors *'98*
The Suburbans *'99*
Things You Can Tell Just by Looking at Her *'00*
Off the Map *'03*
Nine Lives *'05*
The Jane Austen Book Club *'07*
Downloading Nancy *'08*
88 Minutes *'08*
Mother and Child *'09*
The Face of Love *'13*
Words and Pictures *'13*

Dori Brenner (1946-2000)
Summer Wishes, Winter Dreams *'73*
Altered States *'80*
Baby Boom *'87*
For the Boys *'91*
Silent Victim *'92*
Infinity *'96*

Lisa Brenner (1974-)
The Diary of Ellen Rimbauer *'03*
Finding Home *'03*
The Pledge *'08*

Eve Brent (1930-2011)
Forty Guns *'57*
Tarzan and the Trappers *'58*
Tarzan's Fight for Life *'58*
Stakeout *'62*
Fade to Black *'80*
Brainwaves *'82*
The Green Mile *'99*

Evelyn Brent (1899-1975)
Trapped by the Mormons *'22*
The Last Command *'28*
Framed *'30*
The Silver Horde *'30*
The Crusader *'32*
The World Gone Mad *'33*
The Nitwits *'35*
Hopalong Cassidy Returns *'36*
The President's Mystery *'36*
Robot Pilot *'41*
Holt of the Secret Service *'42*
Wrecking Crew *'42*
The Payoff *'43*
The Seventh Victim *'43*

George Brent (1904-79)
Lightning Warrior *'31*
Miss Pinkerton *'32*
The Purchase Price *'32*
The Rich Are Always With Us *'32*
They Call It Sin *'32*
Baby Face *'33*
42nd Street *'33*
Housewife *'34*
The Painted Veil *'34*
Front Page Woman *'35*
The Goose and the Gander *'35*
Living on Velvet *'35*
The Right to Live *'35*
Stranded *'35*
Give Me Your Heart *'36*
The Golden Arrow *'36*
More Than A Secretary *'36*
Gold Is Where You Find It *'38*
Jezebel *'38*
Dark Victory *'39*
The Old Maid *'39*
The Rains Came *'39*
Wings of the Navy *'39*
The Fighting 69th *'40*
The Great Lie *'41*
In This Our Life *'42*
Silver Queen *'42*
You Can't Escape Forever *'42*
Experiment Perilous *'45*
My Reputation *'46*
The Spiral Staircase *'46*
Tomorrow Is Forever *'46*
Out of the Blue *'47*
Luxury Liner *'48*
The Kid From Cleveland *'49*
FBI Girl *'52*
Man Bait *'52*
Born Again *'78*

Romney Brent (1902-76)
East Meets West *'36*
Under the Red Robe *'36*
Head Over Heels *'37*
Adventures of Don Juan *'49*
The Virgin Queen *'55*
Screaming Mimi *'58*
The Sign of Zorro *'60*

Timothy Brent (1942-2001)
See Giancarlo Prete

Amy Brentano
Blood Sisters *'86*
Breeders *'86*

Edmund Breon (1882-1951)
The Scarlet Pimpernel *'34*
Crackerjack *'38*
Casanova Brown *'44*
Gaslight *'44*
The White Cliffs of Dover *'44*
Woman in the Window *'44*
Dressed to Kill *'46*
Forever Amber *'47*

Bobbie Bresee (1950-)
Mausoleum *'83*
Ghoulies *'84*
Evil Spawn *'87*
Surf Nazis Must Die *'87*

Abigail Breslin (1996-)
Signs *'02*
Keane *'04*
Raising Helen *'04*
The Family Plan *'05*
Air Bud 6: Air Buddies *'06 (V)*
Little Miss Sunshine *'06*
No Reservations *'07*
The Ultimate Gift *'07*
Definitely, Maybe *'08*
Kit Kittredge: An American Girl *'08*
Nim's Island *'08*
My Sister's Keeper *'09*
Zombieland *'09*
Janie Jones *'10*
New Year's Eve *'11*
Rango *'11 (V)*
Adventures in Zambezia *'12*
The Call *'13*
Ender's Game *'13*
Haunter *'13*
Wicked Blood *'13*
Perfect Sisters *'14*
Maggie *'15*
Freak Show *'18*
Zombieland: Double Tap *'19*

Patricia Breslin (1931-2011)
Andy Hardy Comes Home *'58*
Homicidal *'61*

Spencer Breslin (1992-)
Disney's The Kid *'00*
Return to Never Land *'02 (V)*
The Santa Clause 2 *'02*
Dr. Seuss' The Cat in the Hat *'03*
Raising Helen *'04*
Air Bud 6: Air Buddies *'06 (V)*
The Santa Clause 3: The Escape Clause *'06*
The Shaggy Dog *'06*
Zoom *'06*
The Happening *'08*
Harold *'08*
Born 2 Race *'11*
Some Kind of Hate *'15*

Felix Bressart (1895-1949)
Ninotchka *'39*
Swanee River *'39*
Bitter Sweet *'40*
Comrade X *'40*
Edison the Man *'40*
Escape *'40*
It All Came True *'40*
The Shop Around the Corner *'40*
Third Finger, Left Hand *'40*
Blossoms in the Dust *'41*
Kathleen *'41*
Ziegfeld Girl *'41*
Crossroads *'42*
Iceland *'42*
To Be or Not to Be *'42*
Greenwich Village *'44*
Without Love *'45*
Her Sister's Secret *'46*
I've Always Loved You *'46*
Portrait of Jennie *'48*
A Song Is Born *'48*

Bernard Bresslaw (1934-93)
Carry On Cowboy *'66*
Morgan: A Suitable Case for Treatment *'66*
Carry On Up the Khyber *'68*
Carry On Up the Jungle *'70*
Carry On Camping *'71*
Carry On Abroad *'72*
Carry On Matron *'72*

Martin Brest (1951-)
Fast Times at Ridgemont High *'82*
Spies Like Us *'85*

Geoff Breton
The Old Curiosity Shop *'07*
The Diary of Anne Frank *'08*

Jean Bretonniere (1924-2001)
The Green Glove *'52*
That Naughty Girl *'58*

Danielle Brett
Jill the Ripper *'00*
Rated X *'00*
Road Rage *'01*

Jeremy Brett (1935-95)
War and Peace *'56*
My Fair Lady *'64*
The Merchant of Venice *'73*
The Medusa Touch *'78*
Florence Nightingale *'85*
Shameless *'94*
Moll Flanders *'96*

Jim Breuer (1967-)
Half-Baked *'97*
Dick *'99*
Once in the Life *'00*
Titan A.E. *'00 (V)*

Marita Breuer (1953-)
Heimat 1 *'84*
The Princess and the Warrior *'00*

Jonathan Brewer
Apocalypto *'06*
Journey to the Center of the Earth *'08*

Juliette Brewer
The Little Rascals *'94*
Balto *'95 (V)*

Diane Brewster (1931-91)
Black Patch *'57*
The Pharaoh's Curse *'57*
Torpedo Run *'58*
King of the Wild Stallions *'59*
The Man in the Net *'59*

Jordana Brewster (1980-)
The Faculty *'98*
The '60s *'99*
Invisible Circus *'00*
The Fast and the Furious *'01*
D.E.B.S. *'04*
Nearing Grace *'05*
Annapolis *'06*
The Texas Chainsaw Massacre: The Beginning *'06*
Fast & Furious *'09*
Fast Five *'11*
Fast & Furious 6 *'13*
American Heist *'15*
Furious 7 *'15*

Paget Brewster (1969-)
The Adventures of Rocky & Bullwinkle *'00*
The Specials *'00*
Now You Know *'02*
Man of the House *'05*
The Big Bad Swim *'06*
Cyxork 7 *'06*
Lost Behind Bars *'06*
A Perfect Day *'06*
Unaccompanied Minors *'06*
Sublime *'07*
Uncle Nick *'15*

Maia Brewton (1977-)
Back to the Future *'85*
Adventures in Babysitting *'87*

Kevin Breznahan (1968-)
Alive *'93*
I Love Trouble *'94*
SLC Punk! *'99*
Winter's Bone *'10*

Tom Breznahan (1965-)
Twice Dead *'88*
Ski School *'91*
Terrified *'94*

Jean-Claude Brialy (1933-2007)
Le Beau Serge *'58*
The Cousins *'59*
The 400 Blows *'59*
Les Cousins *'59*
A Woman Is a Woman *'60*
Cleo from 5 to 7 *'61*
The Burning Court *'62*
Circle of Love *'64*
Tonio Kroger *'65*
The King of Hearts *'66*
The Bride Wore Black *'68*
Manon *'68*
Claire's Knee *'71*
Phantom of Liberty *'74*
Barocco *'76*
L'Annee Sainte *'76*
Queen Margot *'94*
Son of Gascogne *'95*
Beaumarchais the Scoundrel *'96*
The Monster *'96*
Portraits Chinois *'96*
The Count of Monte Cristo *'99*
People *'04*

David Brian (1914-93)
Flamingo Road *'49*
Intruder in the Dust *'49*
Breakthrough *'50*
The Damned Don't Cry *'50*
Inside the Walls of Folsom Prison *'51*
Million Dollar Mermaid *'52*
Springfield Rifle *'52*
This Woman Is Dangerous *'52*
Ambush at Tomahawk Gap *'53*
Dawn at Socorro *'54*
The High and the Mighty *'54*
The White Squaw *'56*
Pocketful of Miracles *'61*

Mary Brian (1908-2002)
Peter Pan *'24*
The Light of Western Stars *'30*
Blessed Event *'32*
It's Tough to Be Famous *'32*
Girl Missing *'33*
Hard to Handle *'33*
The World Gone Mad *'33*
Charlie Chan in Paris *'35*
The Man On the Flying Trapeze *'35*
Navy Blues *'37*
I Escaped from the Gestapo *'43*

Shane Briant (1946-)
Demons of the Mind *'72*
Captain Kronos: Vampire Hunter *'74*
Dressed for Death *'74*
Frankenstein and the Monster from Hell *'74*
Picture of Dorian Gray *'74*
Lady Chatterley's Lover *'81*
Agatha Christie's Murder is Easy *'82*
Moving Targets *'87*
Wrangler *'88*
Tunnel Vision *'95*
Twisted *'96*
The Diplomat *'08*

Fanny Brice (1891-1951)
Be Yourself *'30*
The Great Ziegfeld *'36 (C)*
Everybody Sing *'38*
Ziegfeld Follies *'46*

Pierre Brice (1929-2015)
Mill of the Stone Women *'60*
Murder By Two *'60*
Sweet Ecstasy *'62*
Apache's Last Battle *'64*
A Place Called Glory *'66*
Thunder at the Border *'66*
Lady of the Evening *'75*

Ron Brice
Fly by Night *'93*
Fresh *'94*
A Horse for Danny *'95*
Ripe *'97*
Tar *'97*
Mulberry Street *'06*

Alexander Brickel
Palindromes *'04*
Satan's Little Helper *'04*

Beth Brickell (1941-)
Death Game *'77*
Seducers *'77*

Alan Bridge (1891-1957)
Sullivan's Travels *'41*
Miracle of Morgan's Creek *'44*

Sean Bridgers
Jug Face *'13*
The Best of Me *'14*
The Man Who Killed Hitler and Then the Bigfoot *'19*

Beau Bridges (1941-)
The Red Pony *'49*
Village of the Giants *'65*
For Love of Ivy *'68*
Adam's Woman *'70*
The Landlord *'70*
Child's Play *'72*
The Other Side of the Mountain *'75*
Swashbuckler *'76*
Two Minute Warning *'76*
Greased Lightning *'77*
The Four Feathers *'78*
The Child Stealer *'79*
The Fifth Musketeer *'79*
Norma Rae *'79*
Honky Tonk Freeway *'81*

Night Crossing '81
Love Child '82
Heart Like a Wheel '83
Silver Dream Racer '83
The Hotel New Hampshire '84
Alice in Wonderland '85
The Killing Time '87
Seven Hours to Judgment '88
The Fabulous Baker Boys '89
The Iron Triangle '89
Just Another Secret '89
Signs of Life '89
The Wizard '89
Daddy's Dyin'. . . Who's Got the Will? '90
Women & Men: Stories of Seduction '90
Wildflower '91
Married to It '93
The Positively True Adventures of the Alleged Texas Cheerleader-Murdering Mom '93
Hidden in America '96
Losing Chase '96
Nightjohn '96
RocketMan '97
The Second Civil War '97
Meeting Daddy '98
Inherit the Wind '99
P.T. Barnum '99
White River '99
Sordid Lives '00
Voyage of the Unicorn '00
Out of the Ashes '03
The Ballad of Jack and Rose '05
Smile '05
Charlotte's Web '06
The Good German '06
I-See-You.Com '06
Max Payne '08
Stargate: Continuum '08
Stargate: The Ark of Truth '08
Columbus Circle '10
Free Willy: Escape from Pirate's Cove '10
My Girlfriend's Boyfriend '10
The Descendants '11
Game Time: Tackling the Past '11
Hit and Run '12
Rushlights '13
The Tale of the Princess Kaguya '13 (V)
The Mountain Between Us '17

Chloe Bridges (1991-)
Forget Me Not '09
Camp Rock 2: The Final Jam '10
Mother '13

Chris Bridges (1977-)
2 Fast 2 Furious '03
Crash '05
Hustle & Flow '05
Fred Claus '07
Max Payne '08
RocknRolla '08
Fast Five '11
Justin Bieber: Never Say Never '11
New Year's Eve '11
No Strings Attached '11
Fast & Furious 6 '13
Furious 7 '15
Show Dogs '18 (V)

Jeff Bridges (1949-)
Halls of Anger '70
The Last Picture Show '71
Bad Company '72
Fat City '72
The Iceman Cometh '73
The Last American Hero '73
Lolly-Madonna XXX '73
Thunderbolt & Lightfoot '74
Hearts of the West '75
Rancho Deluxe '75
King Kong '76
Stay Hungry '76
Winter Kills '79
Cutter's Way '81
Heaven's Gate '81
Kiss Me Goodbye '82
The Last Unicorn '82 (V)
Tron '82
Against All Odds '84
Starman '84
The Jagged Edge '85
The Morning After '86
Nadine '87
Tucker: The Man and His Dream '88
Cold Feet '89
The Fabulous Baker Boys '89
See You in the Morning '89
Texasville '90
The Fisher King '91
American Heart '92
Fearless '93
The Vanishing '93
Blown Away '94
Wild Bill '95
Hidden in America '96 (C)
The Mirror Has Two Faces '96
White Squall '96
The Big Lebowski '97
Arlington Road '99
The Muse '99
Simpatico '99
The Contender '00
K-PAX '01
Scenes of the Crime '01
Lost in La Mancha '03 (N)
Masked and Anonymous '03
Seabiscuit '03
The Door in the Floor '04
The Moguls '05
Tideland '05
Stick It '06
Surf's Up '07 (V)
How to Lose Friends & Alienate People '08
Iron Man '08
Crazy Heart '09
A Dog Year '09
The Men Who Stare at Goats '09
The Open Road '09
Tron: Legacy '10
True Grit '10
A Place at the Table '13
R.I.P.D. '13
The Giver '14
Seventh Son '15
Hell or High Water '16
The Little Prince '16
Kingsman: The Golden Circle '17
The Only Living Boy in New York '17
Only the Brave '17
Bad Times at the El Royale '18

Jordan Bridges (1973-)
P.T. Barnum '99
Frequency '00
Happy Campers '01
Mona Lisa Smile '03
The Family Plan '05
Love Finds a Home '09
Love Takes Wing '09
Holiday Engagement '11
Rushlights '13

Krista Bridges (1968-)
Narc '02
George A. Romero's Land of the Dead '05
Cheaters' Club '06
She Drives Me Crazy '07
Dr. Jekyll and Mr. Hyde '08

Lloyd Bridges (1913-98)
Blondie Goes to College '42
Canal Zone '42
Passport to Suez '43
Sahara '43
The Master Race '44
Abilene Town '46
Canyon Passage '46
A Walk in the Sun '46
Ramrod '47
The Smallest Show on Earth '48
Trapped '49
Rocketship X-M '50
The White Tower '50
Little Big Horn '51
Three Steps North '51
High Noon '52
City of Bad Men '53
The Limping Man '53
Tall Texan '53
The Rainmaker '56
Wetbacks '56
The Goddess '58
Around the World Under the Sea '65
The Happy Ending '69
The Tattered Web '71
Running Wild '73
Roots '77
Airplane! '80
East of Eden '80
Airplane 2: The Sequel '82
The Blue and the Gray '82
Grace Kelly '83
Alice in Wonderland '85
Dress Gray '86
North and South Book 2 '86
Tucker: The Man and His Dream '88
Cousins '89
Winter People '89
Joe Versus the Volcano '90
The Queen of Mean '90
Hot Shots! '91
Honey, I Blew Up the Kid '92
Hot Shots! Part Deux '93
Blown Away '94
Mafia! '98
Meeting Daddy '98

Sean Bridges
The Woman '11
Room '15

Spencir Bridges (1998-)
The Reading Room '05
Daddy Day Camp '07

Todd Bridges (1965-)
Roots '77
Twice Dead '88
She's Out of Control '89
Inhumanity '00
I Got Five on It '05
The Damned '06
San Franpsycho '06

Alison Brie (1982-)
The Five-Year Engagement '12
Save the Date '12
The Lego Movie '14 (V)
Get Hard '15
Sleeping with Other People '15
Get a Job '16
The Disaster Artist '17
The Little Hours '17
Horse Girl '20

Anita Briem (1982-)
Journey to the Center of the Earth '08
Dylan Dog: Dead of Night '11

Richard Briers (1934-2013)
A Matter of WHO '62
Fathom '67
Rentadick '72
The Norman Conquests, Part 1: Table Manners '78
The Norman Conquests, Part 2: Living Together '78
The Norman Conquests, Part 3: Round and Round the Garden '78
Watership Down '78 (V)
A Chorus of Disapproval '89
Henry V '89
Peter's Friends '92
Much Ado about Nothing '93
Mary Shelley's Frankenstein '94
A Midwinter's Tale '95
Hamlet '96
Spice World: The Movie '97
Love's Labour's Lost '00
Peter Pan '03
Unconditional Love '03

Johnny Briggs (1935-)
The Leather Boys '63
Au Pair Girls '72

Cameron Bright (1993-)
Birth '04
Godsend '04
Running Scared '06
Thank You for Smoking '06
Ultraviolet '06
X-Men: The Last Stand '06
Normal '07
An American Affair '09
The Twilight Saga: New Moon '09
The Twilight Saga: Eclipse '10
Earth's Final Hours '12
Goodnight for Justice: The Measure of a Man '12

Richard Bright (1937-2006)
Odds Against Tomorrow '59
Panic in Needle Park '71
The Godfather '72
Rancho Deluxe '75
Marathon Man '76
Idolmaker '80
Vigilante '83
Once Upon a Time in America '84
Red Heat '88
The Ambulance '90
The Godfather, Part 3 '90
The Ref '93
Who's the Man? '93
Beautiful Girls '96
Witness to the Mob '98

Susie Bright (1958-)
Virgin Machine '88
Bound '96

Paul Brightwell
Sliding Doors '97
Blackbeard '06

Paolo Briguglia
Caravaggio '07
The Sicilian Girl '09

Charlie Brill (1938-)
Bloodstone '88
Bail Out '90

Fran Brill (1946-)
Old Enough '84
What about Bob? '91

Steven Brill (1962-)
sex, lies and videotape '89
The Mighty Ducks '92

Will Brill
Not Fade Away '12
The Eyes of My Mother '16

Nick Brimble (1944-)
S.O.S. Titanic '79
Frankenstein Unbound '90
Robin Hood: Prince of Thieves '91
The Final Cut '95
Loch Ness '95
The One That Got Away '96
Gone Fishin' '97
Ivanhoe '97
Fortress 2: Re-Entry '99
7 Days to Live '00
Out of Reach '04
Submerged '05

Cynthia Brimhall (1964-)
Hard Ticket to Hawaii '87
Hard Hunted '92
Fit to Kill '93

Wilford Brimley (1934-)
True Grit '69
The China Syndrome '79
The Electric Horseman '79
Borderline '80
Rodeo Girl '80
Absence of Malice '81
Death Valley '81
The Thing '82
High Road to China '83
Ten to Midnight '83
Tender Mercies '83
Tough Enough '83
Country '84
Harry & Son '84
The Hotel New Hampshire '84
The Natural '84
The Stone Boy '84
Cocoon '85
The Ewoks: Battle for Endor '85
Remo Williams: The Adventure Begins '85
American Justice '86
Cocoon: The Return '88
End of the Line '88
Thompson's Last Run '90
Where the Red Fern Grows: Part 2 '92
The Firm '93
Hard Target '93
The Good Old Boys '95
The Last of the Dogmen '95 (N)
My Fellow Americans '96
In and Out '97
Progeny '98
Summer of the Monkeys '98
Brigham City '01
Crossfire Trail '01

Paul Brinegar (1918-95)
How to Make a Monster '58
Charro! '69
Spaceship '81

Mark Bringleson (1957-)
The Lawnmower Man '92
Dead Man '95
Soldier '98

Christie Brinkley (1954-)
National Lampoon's Vacation '83
Vegas Vacation '96 (C)

John Brinkley (1931-)
Teenage Doll '57
A Bucket of Blood '59
T-Bird Gang '59

Ritch Brinkley (1944-)
Cabin Boy '94
Breakdown '96

Bo Brinkman (1956-)
Gettysburg '93
Gods and Generals '03

Vera Briole
Pigalle '95
A Single Girl '96

Francoise Brion (1933-)
Ladies' Man '62
L'Immortelle '63
Nelly et Monsieur Arnaud '95
Dangerous Liaisons '03

Syd Brisbane
Alien Visitor '95
Dead Letter Office '98

David Brisbin (1952-)
Kiss Daddy Goodnight '87
Forrest Gump '94
Leaving Las Vegas '95
From the Earth to the Moon '98
Goodbye, Lover '99

Brent Briscoe (1961-)
Sling Blade '96
Another Day in Paradise '98
A Simple Plan '98
Beautiful '00
Double Take '01
Driven '01
Madison '01
The Majestic '01
Mulholland Drive '01
Say It Isn't So '01
Waking Up in Reno '02
The Big Empty '04
Home of the Giants '07
Small Town Saturday Night '10
Beneath '13

Danielle Brisebois (1969-)
The Premonition '75
Big Bad Mama 2 '87
As Good As It Gets '97

Virginia Brissac (1894-1979)
Black Friday '40
Phantom Lady '44
Two of a Kind '51

Carl Brisson (1893-1958)
The Ring '27
The Manxman '29
Murder at the Vanities '34

May Britt (1934-)
War and Peace '56
The Hunters '58
The Young Lions '58
Murder, Inc. '60
Haunts '77

Charlotte Brittain
Get Real '99
Secret Society '00

Will Brittain
Blow The Man Down '19
Haunt '19

Morgan Brittany (1951-)
The Birds '63
Yours, Mine & Ours '68
Initiation of Sarah '78
Sundown '91
Body Armor '96
The Biggest Fan '02
Sundown: The Vampire in Retreat '08

Aileen Britton (1916-86)
My Brilliant Career '79
Now and Forever '82

Barbara Britton (1919-80)
Louisiana Purchase '41
Reap the Wild Wind '42
Wake Island '42
So Proudly We Hail '43
Captain Kidd '45
The Virginian '46
Gunfighters '47
Loaded Pistols '48
Cover Up '49
I Shot Jesse James '49
Champagne for Caesar '50
Dragonfly Squadron '54

Connie Britton (1968-)
The Brothers McMullen '94
Escape Clause '96
No Looking Back '98
Child Star: The Shirley Temple Story '01
The Next Big Thing '02
Friday Night Lights '04
Looking for Kitty '04
The Last Winter '06
The Lather Effect '06
Women in Trouble '09
A Nightmare on Elm Street '10
The Fitzgerald Family Christmas '12
Seeking a Friend for the End of the World '12
Angels Sing '13
The To Do List '13
This Is Where I Leave You '14
American Ultra '15
Me and Earl and the Dying Girl '15
Beatriz at Dinner '17
Professor Marston and the Wonder Women '17
The Land of Steady Habits '18
The Mustang '19

Pamela Britton (1923-74)
Anchors Aweigh '45
D.O.A. '49
If It's Tuesday, This Must Be Belgium '69

Tony Britton (1924-2019)
The Rough and the Smooth '59
Operation Amsterdam '60
Dr. Syn, Alias the Scarecrow '64
Cry of the Penguins '71
Sunday, Bloody Sunday '71
The Day of the Jackal '73
Agatha '79

Ross Britz
Mask Maker '10
Wrong Side of Town '10

Herman Brix (1906-2007)
See Bruce Bennett

Nicolas Bro (1972-)
The Green Butchers '03
Adam's Apples '05
Antboy '14
Men & Chicken '15

Jim Broadbent (1949-)
The Insurance Man '86
The Good Father '87
Erik the Viking '89
Life Is Sweet '90
The Crying Game '92
Enchanted April '92
The Wedding Gift '93
Bullets over Broadway '94
Princess Caraboo '94
Widow's Peak '94
Richard III '95
Rough Magic '95
The Secret Agent '96
Smilla's Sense of Snow '96
The Borrowers '97
The Avengers '98
Little Voice '98
Topsy Turvy '99
Bridget Jones's Diary '01
Iris '01
Moulin Rouge '01
Gangs of New York '02
The Gathering Storm '02
Nicholas Nickleby '02
And Starring Pancho Villa as Himself '03
Bright Young Things '03
Around the World in 80 Days '04
Bridget Jones: The Edge of Reason '04
Vanity Fair '04
The Chronicles of Narnia: The Lion, the Witch and the Wardrobe '05
Doogal '05 (V)
Robots '05 (V)
Valiant '05 (V)
Art School Confidential '06
Longford '06
Hot Fuzz '07
When Did You Last See Your Father? '07
Indiana Jones and the Kingdom of the Crystal Skull '08
The Damned United '09
Harry Potter and the Half-Blood Prince '09
Inkheart '09
Perrier's Bounty '09
The Young Victoria '09
Another Year '10
Any Human Heart '11
Arthur Christmas '11 (V)
The Iron Lady '11
Cloud Atlas '12
Closed Circuit '13
Le Week-End '14
Big Game '15
Brooklyn '15
The Lady in the Van '15
Bridget Jones's Baby '16
The Sense of an Ending '17
Dolittle '20

Kent Broadhurst (1940-)
Silver Bullet '85
The Dark Half '91
A Couch in New York '95

Remi Broadway
Swimming Upstream '03
Malibu Shark Attack '09

Peter Brocco (1903-92)
Ma and Pa Kettle on Vacation '53
The Balcony '63
Johnny Got His Gun '71
One Flew Over the Cuckoo's Nest '75
Jekyll & Hyde. . . Together Again '82

Lizzie Brochere (1985-)
One to Another '06
The Wedding Song '09
After Fall, Winter '11

Anne Brochet (1966-)
The Bengali Night '88
Cyrano de Bergerac '90
Tous les Matins du Monde '92
Driftwood '97
Dust '01
The Story of Marie and Julien '03
Intimate Strangers '04
The Hedgehog '09

Bill Brochtrup
Betrayed: A Story of Three Women '95
Duck '05

Devin Brochu
In the Valley of Elah '07
Ghosts of Girlfriends Past '09
Hesher '10

Phil Brock (1953-)
Dollman vs Demonic Toys '93
Mercy '96

Stan Brock (1931-91)
Tin Men '87
Return to Africa '89
UHF '89

Tyler Brockington (1982-)
Fright Flick '10
Hold Your Peace '11

Roy Brocksmith (1945-2001)
King of the Gypsies '78
Tales of Ordinary Madness '83
Big Business '88
Arachnophobia '90
Total Recall '90
Bill & Ted's Bogus Journey '91
The Road to Wellville '94
Kull the Conqueror '97

Gladys Brockwell (1894-1929)
Oliver Twist '22
Twinkletoes '26
7th Heaven '27

Beth Broderick (1959-)
Psycho Beach Party '00
Mystery Woman: Mystery Weekend '05
Revenge of the Bridesmaids '10
Bad Actress '11

Helen Broderick (1891-1959)
To Beat the Band '35
Top Hat '35
The Bride Walks Out '36
Love on a Bet '36
Murder On a Bridle Path '36
Swing Time '36
She's Got Everything '37
The Rage of Paris '38
Stand Up and Fight '39
Because of Him '45

James Broderick (1927-82)
Girl of the Night '60
The Iceman Cometh '60
The Group '66
Alice's Restaurant '69
The Taking of Pelham One Two Three '74
Dog Day Afternoon '75

Matthew Broderick (1962-)
Max Dugan Returns '83
WarGames '83
Ladyhawke '85
1918 '85
Ferris Bueller's Day Off '86
On Valentine's Day '86
Project X '87
Biloxi Blues '88
Torch Song Trilogy '88
Family Business '89
Glory '89
The Freshman '90
A Life in the Theater '93
The Night We Never Met '93
The Lion King '94 (V)
Mrs. Parker and the Vicious Circle '94
The Road to Wellville '94
Addicted to Love '96
The Cable Guy '96
Infinity '96
The Thief and the Cobbler '96 (V)
Godzilla '98
The Lion King: Simba's Pride '98 (V)
Election '99
Inspector Gadget '99
You Can Count On Me '99
Good Boy! '03 (V)
The Last Shot '04
The Lion King 1 1/2 '04 (V)
Marie and Bruce '04
The Stepford Wives '04
The Producers '05
Deck the Halls '06
Strangers with Candy '06
All the Good Ones Are Married '07
Bee Movie '07 (V)
Then She Found Me '07
Diminished Capacity '08
Finding Amanda '08
The Tale of Despereaux '08 (V)
Wonderful World '09
Margaret '11
Tower Heist '11
The American Side '16
Rules Don't Apply '16
Love Is Blind '19
To Dust '19

Don Brodie (1899-2001)
Pinocchio '40 (V)
Detour '46
Eat My Dust '76

Helen Brodie
Monsoon '97
Tales of the Kama Sutra 2: Monsoon '98

Steve Brodie (1919-92)
Thirty Seconds Over Tokyo '44
Badman's Territory '46
A Walk in the Sun '46
Desperate '47
Out of the Past '47
The Admiral Was a Lady '50
Armored Car Robbery '50
It's a Small World '50
Kiss Tomorrow Goodbye '50
Treasure of Monte Cristo '50
The Steel Helmet '51
The Beast from 20,000 Fathoms '53
Donovan's Brain '53
The Caine Mutiny '54
Gun Duel In Durango '57
Spy in the Sky '58
Three Came to Kill '61
Blue Hawaii '62
Roustabout '64
The Giant Spider Invasion '75

V.S. Brodie
Go Fish '94
The Owls '09

Thomas Brodie-Sangster (1990-)
Station Jim '01
Bobbie's Girl '02
Love Actually '03
Nanny McPhee '06
Tristan & Isolde '06
The Last Legion '07
Bright Star '09
Nowhere Boy '09
Albatross '11
The Baytown Outlaws '12
The Maze Runner '14
Maze Runner: The Scorch Trials '15
Maze Runner: The Death Cure '18

Adam Brody (1980-)
Grind '03
Missing Brendan '03
Mr. & Mrs. Smith '05
In the Land of Women '06
Thank You for Smoking '06
Smiley Face '07
The Ten '07
Death in Love '08
Jennifer's Body '09
Cop Out '10
The Romantics '10
Damsels in Distress '11
Scream 4 '11
The Oranges '12
Seeking a Friend for the End of the World '12
Lovelace '13
Some Girl(s) '13
Welcome to the Jungle '13
Life Partners '14
Yoga Hosers '16
CHIPS '17
Isabelle '19
Ready or Not '19
Shazam! '19

Adrien Brody (1973-)
Bullet '94
Jailbreakers '94
The Last Time I Committed Suicide '96
Solo '96
The Undertaker's Wedding '97
Restaurant '98
Ten Benny '98
The Thin Red Line '98
Liberty Heights '99
Oxygen '99
Six Ways to Sunday '99
Summer of Sam '99
Bread and Roses '00
The Affair of the Necklace '01
Love the Hard Way '01
Dummy '02
Harrison's Flowers '02
The Pianist '02
The Singing Detective '03
The Village '04
The Jacket '05
King Kong '05
Hollywoodland '06
The Darjeeling Limited '07
Cadillac Records '08
A Matador's Mistress '08
The Brothers Bloom '09
Fantastic Mr. Fox '09 (V)
Giallo '09
The Experiment '10
High School '10
Predators '10
Splice '10
Wrecked '10
Midnight in Paris '11
Back to 1942 '12
Detachment '12
Third Person '13
The Grand Budapest Hotel '14
Houdini '14
American Heist '15
Dragon Blade '15
Backtrack '16
Septembers of Shiraz '16
Bullet Head '17

Estelle Brody
Hindle Wakes '27
Never Take Candy From a Stranger '60

James Brolin (1940-)
Von Ryan's Express '65
Fantastic Voyage '66
Our Man Flint '66
The Boston Strangler '68
Skyjacked '72
Westworld '73
The Car '77
Capricorn One '78
The Amityville Horror '79
High Risk '81
The Ambush Murders '82
Pee-wee's Big Adventure '85
Hold the Dream '86
Bad Jim '89
Twin Sisters '91
Gas Food Lodging '92
Cheatin' Hearts '93
City Boy '93
Ted & Venus '93
Visions of Murder '93
Final Justice '94
Indecent Behavior 2 '94
Relative Fear '95
The Haunted Sea '97
Lewis and Clark and George '97
My Brother's War '97
Traffic '00
Catch Me If You Can '02
Master of Disguise '02
A Guy Thing '03
The Reagans '04
Category 7: The End of the World '05
Widow on the Hill '05
Lies & Alibis '06
Wedding Wars '06
The Hunting Party '07
Last Chance Harvey '08
Lost City Raiders '08
Bitter/Sweet '09
The Goods: Live Hard, Sell Hard '09
Love, Wedding, Marriage '11
Elsa & Fred '14
The 33 '15

Josh Brolin (1968-)
The Goonies '85
Thrashin' '86
Bed of Roses '95
Flirting with Disaster '95
Gang in Blue '96
Nightwatch '96
Mimic '97
My Brother's War '97
Best Laid Plans '99
It's the Rage '99
The Mod Squad '99
Hollow Man '00
Slow Burn '00
Coastlines '02
Milwaukee, Minnesota '03
Into the Blue '05
The Dead Girl '06
American Gangster '07
In the Valley of Elah '07
No Country for Old Men '07
Planet Terror '07
Milk '08
W. '08
Women in Trouble '09
Jonah Hex '10
The Tillman Story '10 (N)
True Grit '10
Wall Street 2: Money Never Sleeps '10
You Will Meet a Tall Dark Stranger '10
Men in Black 3 '12
Gangster Squad '13
Labor Day '13
Oldboy '13
Guardians of the Galaxy '14
Inherent Vice '14
Sin City: A Dame to Kill For '14
Everest '15
Sicario '15
Hail, Caesar! '16
Only the Brave '17
Deadpool 2 '18
Sicario: Day of the Soldado '18

Shane Brolly (1970-)
Flypaper '97
Underworld '03
Underworld: Evolution '05
48 Angels '06
Underworld: Rise of the Lycans '09

J. Edward Bromberg (1903-51)
Girl's Dormitory '36
Charlie Chan on Broadway '37
Second Honeymoon '37
The Baroness and the Butler '38
Four Men and a Prayer '38
Suez '38
Hollywood Cavalcade '39
The Mark of Zorro '40
Return of Frank James '40
Strange Cargo '40
Invisible Agent '42
Life Begins at Eight-Thirty '42
Reunion in France '42
The Phantom of the Opera '43
Son of Dracula '43
Dead Man's Eyes '44
Cloak and Dagger '46
A Song Is Born '48

John Bromfield (1922-2005)
Rope of Sand '49
The Furies '50
Flat Top '52
Easy to Love '53
The Black Dakotas '54
Big Bluff '55
Revenge of the Creature '55
Hot Cars '56
Manfish '56
Quincannon, Frontier Scout '56
Three Bad Sisters '56

Valri Bromfield (1949-)
Mr. Mom '83
Who's Harry Crumb? '89
Nothing But Trouble '91

Elaine Bromka
Uncle Buck '89
In the Family '11

Sheila Bromley (1911-2003)
See Sheila Mannors

Sydney Bromley (1909-87)
Frankenstein and the Monster from Hell '74
The NeverEnding Story '84
Crystalstone '88

Eleanor Bron (1938-)
Help! '65
Alfie '66
Two for the Road '67
Bedazzled '68
Women in Love '70
The National Health '73
The Attic: The Hiding of Anne Frank '88
Black Beauty '94
A Little Princess '95
Vanity Fair '99
House of Mirth '00
Iris '01
The Heart of Me '02
Wimbledon '04

Brick Bronsky (1964-)
Class of Nuke 'Em High 2: Subhumanoid Meltdown '91
Class of Nuke 'Em High 3: The Good, the Bad and the Subhumanoid '94
Sgt. Kabukiman N.Y.P.D. '94

Betty Bronson (1906-71)
Peter Pan '24
Ben-Hur '26
The Singing Fool '28
Naked Kiss '64

Charles Bronson (1921-2003)
Pat and Mike '52
House of Wax '53
Miss Sadie Thompson '53
Vera Cruz '53
Apache '54
Crime Wave '54
Drum Beat '54
Big House, U.S.A. '55
Target Zero '55
Jubal '56
Showdown at Boot Hill '58
When Hell Broke Loose '58
Never So Few '59
The Magnificent Seven '60
Master of the World '61
A Thunder of Drums '61
Kid Galahad '62
Four for Texas '63
The Great Escape '63
Guns of Diablo '64
Battle of the Bulge '65
The Sandpiper '65
This Property Is Condemned '66
The Dirty Dozen '67
The Meanest Men in the West '67
Honor Among Thieves '68
Once Upon a Time in the West '68
Villa Rides '68
Lola '69
The Family '70
Rider on the Rain '70
Chato's Land '71
Cold Sweat '71
Red Sun '71
Someone Behind the Door '71
The Mechanic '72
The Valachi Papers '72
The Stone Killer '73

Death Wish '74
Mr. Majestyk '74
Breakout '75
Chino '75
Hard Times '75
Breakheart Pass '76
From Noon Till Three '76
St. Ives '76
Raid on Entebbe '77
Telefon '77
The White Buffalo '77
Love and Bullets '79
Borderline '80
Cabo Blanco '81
Death Hunt '81
Death Wish 2 '82
Ten to Midnight '83
The Evil That Men Do '84
Death Wish 3 '85
Murphy's Law '86
Assassination '87
Death Wish 4: The Crackdown '87
Messenger of Death '88
Kinjite: Forbidden Subjects '89
The Indian Runner '91
Death Wish 5: The Face of Death '94
Family of Cops '95
Family of Cops 2: Breach of Faith '97
Family of Cops 3 '98

Lillian Bronson (1903-95)
Family Honeymoon '49
The Next Voice You Hear '50
Excuse My Dust '51
No Room for the Groom '52
Spencer's Mountain '63

Claudio Brook (1929-95)
Daniel Boone: Trail Blazer '56
The Young One '61
The Exterminating Angel '62
Samson in the Wax Museum '63
Viva Maria! '65
The Peking Blond '68
Devil's Rain '75
Dr. Tarr's Torture Dungeon '75
Cronos '94

Clive Brook (1887-1974)
The Man From Yesterday '32
Shanghai Express '32
Cavalcade '33
Gallant Lady '33
If I Were Free '33
Convoy '40
The Flemish Farm '43
On Approval '44

Faith Brook (1922-2012)
To Sir, with Love '67
War and Peace '73
Bloodbath '76
Eye of the Needle '81

Isabel Brook
Faust: Love of the Damned '00
About a Boy '02

Jayne Brook (1960-)
Kindergarten Cop '90
Doing Time on Maple Drive '92
Bye Bye, Love '94
Clean Slate '94
Ed '96
Last Dance '96
Gattaca '97

Kelly Brook
House of 9 '05
Fishtales '07

Lyndon Brook (1926-2004)
The Purple Plain '54
Above Us the Waves '55
The Spanish Gardener '57

Hillary Brooke (1914-99)
The Philadelphia Story '40
Counter-Espionage '42
To the Shores of Tripoli '42
Wake Island '42
Sherlock Holmes Faces Death '43
Jane Eyre '44
Ministry of Fear '44
The Enchanted Cottage '45
The Road to Utopia '46
Strange Impersonation '46
The Strange Woman '46
Up Goes Maisie '46
Africa Screams '49
The Woman in Green '49
The Lost Continent '51
Abbott and Costello Meet Captain Kidd '52
Never Wave at a WAC '52
Invaders from Mars '53
The Man Who Knew Too Much '56

Paul Brooke (1944-)
The Lair of the White Worm '88
Dead of Night '99
The Affair of the Necklace '01

Tyler Brooke
The Divorcee '30
Monte Carlo '30

Walter Brooke (1914-86)
Conquest of Space '55
The Landlord '70
Tora! Tora! Tora! '70
ZigZag '70
The Return of Count Yorga '71

Richard Brooker (1954-)
Friday the 13th, Part 3 '82
Deathstalker '83
Friday the 13th, Part 4: The Final Chapter '84

Jacqueline Brookes (1930-2013)
The Gambler '74
Rodeo Girl '80
Silent Witness '85
Naked Gun 2 1/2: The Smell of Fear '91

Michelle Brookhurst
Can't Hardly Wait '98
Recipe for Disaster '03

Adam Brooks
Manborg '11
Father's Day '12

Aimee Brooks (1974-)
Say Anything '89
Critters 3 '91
Monster Man '03
The Hillside Stranglings '04

Albert Brooks (1947-)
Taxi Driver '76
Real Life '79
Private Benjamin '80
Modern Romance '81
Twilight Zone: The Movie '83
Unfaithfully Yours '84
Lost in America '85
Broadcast News '87
Defending Your Life '91
I'll Do Anything '93
The Scout '94
Mother '96
Critical Care '97
Dr. Dolittle '98 (V)
Out of Sight '98
The Muse '99
My First Mister '01
Finding Nemo '03 (V)
The In-Laws '03
Looking for Comedy in the Muslim World '06
The Simpsons Movie '07 (V)
Drive '11
A Most Violent Year '14
Concussion '15
Finding Dory '16
The Secret Life of Pets '16

Amanda Brooks (1981-)
River's End '05
Cut Off '06
Dragon Wars '07
My Best Friend's Girl '08
Stiletto '08
Hellhounds '09
The Canyons '13

Andrea Brooks
What Goes Up '09
Independence Daysaster '13
Zodiac: Signs of the Apocalypse '14
No Men Beyond This Point '15

Angelle Brooks
Blue Hill Avenue '01
The Brothers '01
The Accompanist '20

Avery Brooks (1948-)
Half Slave, Half Free '85
Roots: The Gift '88
Spenser: Ceremony '93
Spenser: A Savage Place '94
Spenser: Pale Kings & Princes '94
Spenser: The Judas Goat '94
American History X '98
The Big Hit '98
15 Minutes '01

Carroll Brooks
Boy Meets Girl '84
Mauvais Sang '86

Conrad Brooks (1931-)
Glen or Glenda? '53
Jail Bait '54
Bride of the Monster '55
Plan 9 from Outer Space '56
The Sinister Urge '60
Curse of the Queerwolf '87
Test Tube Teens from the Year 2000 '93
Bikini Drive-In '94
Ed Wood '94
Skeleton Key 2: 667, the Neighbor of the Beast '08

David Allan Brooks (1947-)
Cast Away '00
Jack Frost 2: Revenge of the Mutant Killer Snowman '00

Foster Brooks (1912-2001)
The Villain '79
Cracking Up '83
Oddballs '84

Geraldine Brooks (1925-77)
Cry Wolf '47
The Possessed '47
Reckless Moment '49
The Green Glove '52
Mr. Ricco '75

Golden Brooks (1970-)
Motives '03
Beauty Shop '05
Something New '06
The Inheritance '10

Hazel Brooks (1924-2002)
Body and Soul '47
Sleep, My Love '48

Hildy Brooks
The Iceman Cometh '73
The Chosen '81
Forbidden Love '82

Jason Brooks (1966-)
You've Got a Friend '07
Accused at 17 '09
Asteroid *vs.* Earth '14
Blood Lake '14

Jean Brooks (1916-63)
Klondike Fury '42
Boss of Big Town '43
The Falcon and the Co-Eds '43
The Falcon in Danger '43
The Leopard Man '43
The Seventh Victim '43

Jennifer Brooks (1948-)
See Laurie Rose

Joel Brooks (1949-)
Indecent Proposal '93
The Man Who Captured Eichmann '96
Bound by Lies '05

Leslie Brooks (1922-2011)
You Were Never Lovelier '42
City Without Men '43
Tonight and Every Night '45
Blonde Ice '48
Romance on the High Seas '48
The Scar '48

Louise Brooks (1906-85)
It's the Old Army Game '26
The Show Off '26
Beggars of Life '28
Pandora's Box '28
Diary of a Lost Girl '29
Prix de Beaute '30
God's Gift to Women '31
Empty Saddles '36

Mehcad Brooks (1980-)
Glory Road '06
Just Wright '10
Creature '11
Nobody's Fool '18

Mel Brooks (1926-)
The Producers '68
Putney Swope '69
The Twelve Chairs '70
Blazing Saddles '74
Silent Movie '76
High Anxiety '77
The Muppet Movie '79 (C)
History of the World: Part 1 '81
To Be or Not to Be '83
Spaceballs '87
Look Who's Talking, Too '90 (V)
Life Stinks '91
Robin Hood: Men in Tights '93
Dracula: Dead and Loving It '95
Screw Loose '99
The Producers '05
Robots '05 (V)
Mr. Peabody & Sherman '14 (V)
Hotel Transylvania 2 '15 (V)

Phyllis Brooks (1915-95)
To Beat the Band '35
In Old Chicago '37
Charlie Chan in Honolulu '38
Little Miss Broadway '38
Rebecca of Sunnybrook Farm '38
Slightly Honorable '40
The Shanghai Gesture '42

Rand Brooks (1918-2003)
Gone with the Wind '39
Hopalong Cassidy: The Devil's Playground '46
Kilroy Was Here '47
To Hell and Back '55
Comanche Station '60

Randi Brooks (1956-)
Forbidden Love '82
The Man with Two Brains '83
Ratings Game '84
Tightrope '84
Colors '88
Cop '88

Ray Brooks (1939-)
The Knack '65
Daleks-Invasion Earth 2150 A.D. '66
The Last Grenade '70
Flesh and Blood Show '73
House of Whipcord '75

Richard Brooks (1962-)
The Hidden '87
Shakedown '88
Shocker '89
To Sleep with Anger '90
The Crow 2: City of Angels '96
The Substitute '96
Wolverine '96
Johnny B. '00
The Sin Seer '15

Terron Brooks (1974-)
The Temptations '98
All About You '01

Edward Brophy (1895-1960)
The Cameraman '28
Doughboys '30
The Champ '32
Speak Easily '32
Evelyn Prentice '34
China Seas '35
Mad Love '35
Mister Cinderella '36
Hit Parade of 1937 '37
Jim Hanvey, Detective '37
The Last Gangster '37
Gold Diggers in Paris '38
A Slight Case of Murder '38
Dance, Girl, Dance '40
The Invisible Woman '40
The Gay Falcon '41
Sleepers West '41
Larceny, Inc. '42
Air Force '43
Destroyer '43
Cover Girl '44
It Happened Tomorrow '44
The Thin Man Goes Home '44
Renegade Girl '46
Swing Parade of 1946 '46
It Happened on 5th Avenue '47
The Last Hurrah '58

Kevin Brophy (1953-)
Hell Night '81
The Seduction '82
Time Walker '82
Delos Adventure '86

Pierce Brosnan (1953-)
The Long Good Friday '80
The Mirror Crack'd '80
The Manions of America '81
Nomads '86
The Fourth Protocol '87
The Deceivers '88
Noble House '88
Taffin '88
Around the World in 80 Days '89
The Heist '89
Mister Johnson '91
Murder 101 '91
Victim of Love '91
The Lawnmower Man '92
Live Wire '92
Detonator '93
Mrs. Doubtfire '93
Love Affair '94
Detonator 2: Night Watch '95
Goldeneye '95
Mars Attacks! '96
The Mirror Has Two Faces '96
Robinson Crusoe '96
Dante's Peak '97
The Nephew '97
Tomorrow Never Dies '97
Quest for Camelot '98 (V)
Grey Owl '99
The Thomas Crown Affair '99
The World Is Not Enough '99
The Tailor of Panama '00
Die Another Day '02
Evelyn '02
After the Sunset '04
Laws of Attraction '04
The Matador '06
Seraphim Falls '06
Married Life '07
Shattered '07
Mamma Mia! '08
The Greatest '09
The Ghost Writer '10
Percy Jackson & The Olympians: The Lightning Thief '10
Remember Me '10
Bag of Bones '11
I Don't Know How She Does It '11
Salvation Boulevard '11
The Love Punch '13
The World's End '13
A Long Way Down '14
The November Man '14
No Escape '15
Some Kind of Beautiful '15
I.T. '16
Urge '16
The Foreigner '17
The Only Living Boy in New York '17
Final Score '18
Mamma Mia! Here We Go Again '18
Spinning Man '18

Sean Brosnan (1983-)
When Evil Calls '06
Surveillance 24/7 '07
Alien Uprising '12

Dr. Joyce Brothers (1927-2013)
Embryo '76
Desperate Lives '82
The Lonely Guy '84
Love at Stake '87 (C)
The Naked Gun: From the Files of Police Squad '88 (C)
National Lampoon's Loaded Weapon 1 '93

John Brotherton
Surprise, Surprise '09
Gone '10
Precious Cargo '16

Alan Brough
Siam Sunset '99
The Nugget '02

Rebecca Broussand
The Two Jakes '90
Cannes Man '96

Israel Broussard (1994-)
The Bling Ring '13
Jack of the Red Hearts '15
Good Kids '16
Happy Death Day '17
Happy Death Day 2U '19

Liliane Brousse
Paranoiac '62
Maniac '63

Ben Browder (1962-)
A Kiss Before Dying '91
Boogie Boy '98
Stargate: Continuum '08
Stargate: The Ark of Truth '08
Outlaws and Angels '16

Barbara Brown (1902-75)
The Fighting Sullivans '42
Hollywood Canteen '44
Three Men in White '44
Born Yesterday '50
Ma and Pa Kettle Go to Town '50
Ma and Pa Kettle Back On the Farm '51
Jack & the Beanstalk '52
Ma and Pa Kettle on Vacation '53
My Sister Eileen '55
The Terror of the Tongs '61

Barry Brown (1951-78)
Flesh '68
Bad Company '72
The Bravos '72

Bille Brown (1952-2013)
Fierce Creatures '96
Oscar and Lucinda '97
The Dish '00
The Man Who Sued God '01

Billy Aaron Brown (1981-)
Jeepers Creepers 2 '03
Attack of the Sabretooth '05
Headless Horseman '07

Blair Brown (1946-)
The Choirboys '77
The Child Stealer '79
Altered States '80
One Trick Pony '80
Continental Divide '81
Kennedy '83
The Bad Seed '85
A Flash of Green '85
Stealing Home '88
Strapless '90
Passed Away '92
The Day My Parents Ran Away '93
The Astronaut's Wife '99
In His Life: The John Lennon Story '00
Space Cowboys '00

Follow the Stars Home '01
Hamlet '01
Dogville '03
Loverboy '05
Griffin & Phoenix '06
The Sentinel '06
The Treatment '06
Dark Matter '07
The Speed of Thought '11

Bobby Brown (1969-)
A Thin Line Between Love and Hate '96
Two Can Play That Game '01
Gang of Roses '03
Nora's Hair Salon '04
Nora's Hair Salon 2: A Cut Above '08
Whitney '18

Brianna Brown
Mysterious Museum '99
Conversations with Other Women '05

Bruce Brown (1937-)
The Endless Summer '66 (N)
Eddie and the Cruisers '83
Zipperface '92
The Endless Summer 2 '94 (N)

Bryan Brown (1947-)
The Chant of Jimmie Blacksmith '78
The Irishman '78
Newsfront '78
The Odd Angry Shot '79
Breaker Morant '80
The Winter of Our Dreams '82
The Thorn Birds '83
Give My Regards to Broad Street '84
Kim '84
Rebel '85
F/X '86
The Good Wife '86
Tai-Pan '86
Cocktail '88
Gorillas in the Mist '88
Dead in the Water '91
F/X 2: The Deadly Art of Illusion '91
Prisoners of the Sun '91
Sweet Talker '91
Blame It on the Bellboy '92
Dead Heart '96
Twisted '96 (N)
On the Border '98
Tracked '98
Two Hands '98
Grizzly Falls '99
Journey to the Center of the Earth '99
On the Beach '00
Risk '00
Styx '00
Dirty Deeds '02
Footsteps '03
Along Came Polly '04
The Poseidon Adventure '05
Australia '08
Dean Spanley '08
Beautiful Kate '09

Charles D. Brown (1887-1949)
Gold Diggers of 1937 '36
Shopworn Angel '38
Mr. Moto in Danger Island '39
Brother Orchid '40
Old Swimmin' Hole '40
Night Editor '46
Merton of the Movies '47
Undercover Maisie '47
I Wouldn't Be in Your Shoes '48

Chris Brown (1989-)
This Christmas '07
Takers '10
Battle of the Year '13

Clancy Brown (1959-)
Bad Boys '83
The Adventures of Buckaroo Banzai Across the Eighth Dimension '84
The Bride '85
Highlander '86
Extreme Prejudice '87
Shoot to Kill '88
Blue Steel '90
Past Midnight '92
Pet Sematary 2 '92
Last Light '93
Pom Poko '94 (V)
The Shawshank Redemption '94
Female Perversions '96
Flubber '97
Starship Troopers '97
Boss of Bosses '99
The Hurricane '99
Vendetta '99
Snow White: The Fairest of Them All '02
Normal '03
The SpongeBob SquarePants Movie '04 (V)
The Guardian '06
Pathfinder '07
The Express '08
A Nightmare on Elm Street '10
Cowboys & Aliens '11
Green Lantern '11 (V)
John Dies at the End '12
Sparks '13
The Trials of Cate McCall '13
The Trip to Bountiful '14
When the Game Stands Tall '14
The SpongeBob Movie: Sponge Out of Water '15 (V)
Stronger '17

David Brown
The Riverman '04
Freezer Burn: The Invasion of Laxdale '08

Drew 'Bundini' Brown (1928-87)
Shaft '71
Shaft's Big Score '72

D.W. Brown
Weekend Pass '84
Mischief '85

Dwier Brown (1959-)
Field of Dreams '89
The Guardian '90
The Cutting Edge '92
Mom and Dad Save the World '92
Gettysburg '93
Intimate Betrayal '96
Same River Twice '97
Fast Girl '07
Locked Down '10

Eric Brown (1964-)
Private Lessons '75
They're Playing with Fire '84

Erin Brown (1979-)
See Misty Mundae

Garrett M. Brown
Uncle Buck '89
Kick-Ass '10

Gary Brown
The Glory Boys '84
Invasion of the Space Preachers '90

Gaye Brown (1941-)
Masque of the Red Death '65
Mata Hari '85
An American Haunting '05

Georg Stanford Brown (1943-)
Colossus: The Forbin Project '70
Roots '77
Roots: The Next Generation '79
Stir Crazy '80
The Jesse Owens Story '84
North and South Book 1 '85
Alone in the Neon Jungle '87
House Party 2: The Pajama Jam '91
Murder Without Motive '92
Ava's Magical Adventure '94
The Reading Room '05

Georgia Brown (1933-92)
Nothing But the Night '72
Tales That Witness Madness '73
Love at Stake '87
Victim of Love '91

Henry Brown
The Man in the Glass Booth '75
Stepfather 2: Make Room for Daddy '89
Everyday Black Man '10

James Brown (1920-92)
Wake Island '42
Air Force '43
Objective, Burma! '45
Sands of Iwo Jima '49
Montana '50
Woman They Almost Lynched '53
Five Guns to Tombstone '60
Targets '68
Adios Amigo '75

James Brown (1933-2006)
The Blues Brothers '80
Doctor Detroit '83
Blues Brothers 2000 '98
Undercover Brother '02
Soul Power '08

Jefferson Brown
Pigs '07
Silent Hill: Revelation 3D '12
Witchslayer Gretl '12
Make Your Move '13
Dear Viola '14

Jim Brown (1936-)
Rio Conchos '64
The Dirty Dozen '67
Dark of the Sun '68
Ice Station Zebra '68
The Split '68
The Grasshopper '69
100 Rifles '69
Riot '69
El Condor '70
The Passing of Evil '70
Tick... Tick... Tick '70
Black Gunn '72
Slaughter '72
Kenner '73
The Slams '73
Slaughter's Big Ripoff '73
Three the Hard Way '74
Kid Vengeance '75
Take a Hard Ride '75
Fingers '78
One Down, Two to Go! '82
Pacific Inferno '85
The Running Man '87
I'm Gonna Git You Sucka '88
L.A. Heat '88
Crack House '89
L.A. Vice '89
Twisted Justice '89
Mars Attacks! '96
Original Gangstas '96
He Got Game '98
Small Soldiers '98 (V)
Any Given Sunday '99
On the Edge '02
She Hate Me '04
Animal '05
Hugh Hefner: Playboy, Activist and Rebel '09

Joe E. Brown (1892-1973)
On with the Show '29
Painted Faces '29
Sally '29
Eleven Men and a Girl '30
Going Wild '30
Lottery Bride '30
Sit Tight '31
The Tenderfoot '32
You Said a Mouthful '32
Elmer the Great '33
Alibi Ike '35
A Midsummer Night's Dream '35
Fit for a King '37
When's Your Birthday? '37
Wide Open Faces '38
Pin-Up Girl '44
Show Boat '51
Around the World in 80 Days '56
Some Like It Hot '59
It's a Mad, Mad, Mad, Mad World '63
The Comedy of Terrors '64

Johnny Mack Brown (1904-74)
A Lady of Chance '28
Our Dancing Daughters '28
The Single Standard '29
Billy the Kid '30
Montana Moon '30
The Last Flight '31
The Secret Six '31
Malay Nights '32
Fighting with Kit Carson '33
Belle of the Nineties '34
St. Louis Woman '34
Rustlers of Red Dog '35
Flaming Frontiers '38
Ride 'Em Cowboy '42
Flame of the West '45
Stampede '49
Short Grass '50

Jonathan Daniel Brown
Project X '11
Kid Cannabis '14

Juanita Brown
Caged Heat '74
Foxy Brown '74

Julie Brown (1958-)
Bloody Birthday '80
Earth Girls Are Easy '89
Spirit of '76 '91
Shakes the Clown '92
Nervous Ticks '93
The Opposite Sex and How to Live With Them '93
Raining Stones '93
Clueless '95
Fist of the North Star '95
Plump Fiction '97
Boxboarders! '07

Julie Brown (1963-)
Ride '98
Bug Buster '99

Kimberly J. Brown (1984-)
Halloweentown '98
Tumbleweeds '98
Halloweentown 2: Kalabar's Revenge '01
My Sister's Keeper '02
Stephen King's Rose Red '02
Bringing Down the House '03
Halloweentown High '04
Big Bad Wolf '06

Lou Brown (1952-)
The Irishman '78
Death Games '80

Lowell Brown
The Girl in Lover's Lane '60
High School Caesar '60

Marcus Lyle Brown (1970-)
Heart of the Storm '04
Venom '05
Mammoth '06
House of Bones '09
Seeking Justice '12

Melanie (Scary Spice) Brown (1975-)
Spice World: The Movie '97
Lethal Dose '03
Telling Lies '06

Murray Brown (1937-)
Dracula '73
Vampyres '74

Natalie Brown (1973-)
Descent '05
Cradle of Lies '06
Something Beneath '07
Cancel Christmas '11
Be My Valentine '13
Exploding Sun '13

Olivia Brown
Streets of Fire '84
Fast Lane '08

Orlando Brown
Max Keeble's Big Move '01
The Proud Family Movie '05 (V)

Pamela Brown (1917-75)
One of Our Aircraft Is Missing '41
I Know Where I'm Going '45
Alice in Wonderland '50
Lust for Life '56
The Scapegoat '59
Cleopatra '63
Wuthering Heights '70
The Night Digger '71
Dracula '73
In This House of Brede '75

Pat Crawford Brown (1929-)
Elvira, Mistress of the Dark '88
Stuck On You '03

Peter Brown (1935-)
Darby's Rangers '58
Merrill's Marauders '62
Kitten with a Whip '64
Ride the Wild Surf '64
A Tiger Walks '64
Eagles Attack at Dawn '70
Chrome and Hot Leather '71
Foxy Brown '74
Slashed Dreams '74
The Aurora Encounter '85
Three Bad Men '05

Pfeifer Brown
The Gallows '15
The Gallows Act II '19

Phil Brown (1916-2006)
Calling Dr. Gillespie '42
The Impatient Years '44
Over 21 '45
Without Reservations '46
The Hidden Room '49
Obsession '49
Operation Cross Eagles '69
Tropic of Cancer '70

P.J. Brown (1956-)
Double Parked '00
Rick '03

Ralph Brown (1913-90)
Withnail and I '87
Buster '88
Christabel '89
Impromptu '90
Alien 3 '92
The Crying Game '92
Wayne's World 2 '93
Ivanhoe '97
Star Wars: Episode 1-The Phantom Menace '99

Ralph Brown (1957-)
Extremely Dangerous '99
Mean Machine '01
I'll Be There '03
Closure '07
The Contractor '07
Dark Tide '12

Reb Brown (1948-)
Captain America '79
Captain America 2: Death Too Soon '79
Uncommon Valor '83
Yor, the Hunter from the Future '83
Howling 2: Your Sister Is a Werewolf '85
Space Mutiny '88
The Cage '89
The Firing Line '91

Rob Brown (1984-)
Finding Forrester '00
Coach Carter '05
Take the Lead '06
Live! '07
The Express '08
Stop-Loss '08
Criminal Activities '15

Robert Brown (1918-2003)
The Abominable Snowman '57
Campbell's Kingdom '57
It Takes a Thief '60
Tower of London '62
One Million Years B.C. '66
Octopussy '83
A View to a Kill '85
The Living Daylights '87
License to Kill '89

Robin Joi Brown
Test Tube Teens from the Year 2000 '93
Criminal Desire '98

Roger Aaron Brown (1949-)
Tall Tale: The Unbelievable Adventures of Pecos Bill '95
Miracle in Lane Two '00

Ron Brown
Charlie the Lonesome Cougar '67
The Legend of Black Thunder Mountain '79

Russ Brown
Damn Yankees '58
It Happened to Jane '59

Samantha Brown (1976-)
New Jersey Drive '95
Lift '01

Sara Suzanne Brown
The Bikini Car Wash Company '90
The Bikini Car Wash Company 2 '92
Test Tube Teens from the Year 2000 '93

Sarah Brown
Heart of the Beholder '05
It Was One of Us '07

Stanley Brown (1914-2001)
Blondie Meets the Boss '39
Atlantic City '44

Sterling K. Brown (1976-)
Frozen II '19
Waves '19

Sterling K. Brown
The Suspect '14
Marshall '17
Hotel Artemis '18
The Rhythm Section '19

Thomas Wilson Brown (1972-)
Honey, I Shrunk the Kids '89
Welcome Home '89
Diggstown '92

Timothy Brown (1937-2020)
M*A*S*H '70
Sweet Sugar '72
Girls Are for Loving '73
The Dynamite Brothers '74
Black Heat '76
Losin' It '82
Code Name: Zebra '84
Pacific Inferno '85

Tom Brown (1913-90)
Central Airport '33
Three-Cornered Moon '33
Anne of Green Gables '34
Sweepstake Annie '35
I'd Give My Life '36
In Old Chicago '37
Jim Hanvey, Detective '37
Maytime '37
Navy Blue and Gold '37
Merrily We Live '38
Adventures of Smilin' Jack '43
The Payoff '43
Buck Privates Come Home '47
Operation Haylift '50
The Choppers '61

Tyrone Brown
Gun Hill Road '11
Baked in Brooklyn '16

Vanessa Brown (1928-99)
The Foxes of Harrow '47
The Ghost and Mrs. Muir '47
Mother Wore Tights '47
The Heiress '49

Tarzan and the Slave Girl '50
Three Husbands '50
The Fighter '52
Witch Who Came from the Sea '76

W. Earl Brown (1963-)
Excessive Force '93
Scream '96
There's Something about Mary '98
Dancing at the Blue Iguana '00
Lost Souls '00
Killer Diller '04
The Big White '05
Bloodworth '10
The Sessions '12
Chasing Ghosts '14
Wild '14

Wally Brown (1904-61)
Zombies on Broadway '44
Radio Stars on Parade '45
The High and the Mighty '54
Westbound '58
The Absent-Minded Professor '61

Wes Brown (1982-)
Love Begins '11
Love's Everlasting Courage '11
Weather Wars '11
Shadow on the Mesa '13

Woody Brown (1956-)
Killer Party '86
The Accused '88
Alligator 2: The Mutation '90
Animal Instincts 2 '94
Secret Games 3 '94

Jessica Brown Findlay (1989-)
Labyrinth '12
Lullaby '14
Winter's Tale '14
Victor Frankenstein '15
This Beautiful Fantastic '17
The Guernsey Literary & Potato Peel Pie Society '18

Coral Browne (1913-91)
Auntie Mame '58
The Legend of Lylah Clare '68
The Killing of Sister George '69
The Ruling Class '72
Theatre of Blood '73
Eleanor: First Lady of the World '82
American Dreamer '84
Dreamchild '85

Edrick Browne
Jules Verne's Mysterious Island '10
Nine Dead '10
Wrong Side of Town '10
Dragon Eyes '12
Stolen '12

Irene Browne (1896-1965)
The Letter '29
All at Sea '57
Serious Charge '59

Leslie Browne (1957-)
The Turning Point '77
Nijinsky '80
Dancers '87

Lucille Browne (1907-76)
Battling with Buffalo Bill '31
The Devil's Brother '33
Double Harness '33
Mystery Squadron '33
Law of the Wild '34

Roscoe Lee Browne (1925-2007)
The Connection '61
Black Like Me '64
Uptight '68
The Liberation of L.B. Jones '70
The Cowboys '72
The World's Greatest Athlete '73
Logan's Run '76
King '78
Unknown Powers '80
Jumpin' Jack Flash '86 (C)
Legal Eagles '86
Oliver & Company '88 (V)
Moon 44 '90
Eddie Presley '92
The Mambo Kings '92
Naked in New York '93
Babe '95 (N)
Forest Warrior '95
The Pompatus of Love '95
Dear God '96
Last Summer In the Hamptons '96
Babe: Pig in the City '98 (N)
Morgan's Ferry '99
Hamlet '01
Treasure Planet '02 (V)
Garfield: A Tail of Two Kitties '06 (V)

Suzanne Browne
See Sara Suzanne Brown

Victor Browne
Love's Unending Legacy '07
Love's Unfolding Dream '07

Zachary Browne (1985-)
Man of the House '95
Shiloh 2: Shiloh Season '99

Alistair Browning (1954-2019)
Merry Christmas, Mr. Lawrence '83
Rain '01

Chris Browning (1964-)
Linewatch '08
Beneath the Dark '10
The Philly Kid '12

Emily Browning (1988-)
Ghost Ship '02
Ned Kelly '03
Lemony Snicket's A Series of Unfortunate Events '04
The Uninvited '09
Sleeping Beauty '11
Sucker Punch '11
Magic Magic '13
Plush '13
Summer in February '13
God Help the Girl '14
Pompeii '14
Legend '15
Golden Exits '17

Logan Browning
Bratz '07
The Perfection '19

Ricou Browning (1930-)
Creature from the Black Lagoon '54
The Creature Walks among Us '56
Flipper's New Adventure '64

Ryan Browning (1974-)
The Smokers '00
Extremedays '01
The Legend of Butch & Sundance '04
Stealing Sinatra '04

Carrie Brownstein (1974-)
Some Days Are Better Than Others '10
Don't Worry, He Won't Get Far on Foot '18
The Oath '18

Jeanette Brox
Devil in the Flesh 2 '00
Easier With Practice '10

Betty Bruce
Gypsy '62
Island of Love '63

Brenda Bruce (1919-96)
Peeping Tom '60
Nightmare '63
That'll Be the Day '73
The Tenth Man '88
Back Home '90
December Bride '91
Splitting Heirs '93
The Widowing of Mrs. Holroyd '95

Cheryl Lynn Bruce
Music Box '89
Daughters of the Dust '91
To Sir, With Love 2 '96

Colin Bruce
Gotham '88
Crusoe '89
Chicago Joe & the Showgirl '90

David Bruce (1916-76)
Sergeant York '41
The Smiling Ghost '41
Can't Help Singing '45
Lady on a Train '45
Hi-Jacked '50
Pygmy Island '50
Jungle Hell '55

Dylan Bruce (1980-)
Love's Christmas Journey '11
Flowers in the Attic '14
Petals on the Wind '14

Kate Bruce (1858-1946)
Judith of Bethulia '14
The Idol Dancer '20
Way Down East '20
Struggle '31

Nigel Bruce (1895-1953)
The Scarlet Pimpernel '34
Stand Up and Cheer '34
Treasure Island '34
Becky Sharp '35
She '35
The Charge of the Light Brigade '36
Follow Your Heart '36
The Trail of the Lonesome Pine '36
The Last of Mrs. Cheyney '37
Thunder in the City '37
The Baroness and the Butler '38
Kidnapped '38
The Adventures of Sherlock Holmes '39
The Hound of the Baskervilles '39
The Rains Came '39
The Blue Bird '40
Hudson's Bay '40
Lillian Russell '40
Rebecca '40
Susan and God '40
The Chocolate Soldier '41
Play Girl '41
Suspicion '41
Journey for Margaret '42
Roxie Hart '42
Sherlock Holmes and the Secret Weapon '42
Sherlock Holmes and the Voice of Terror '42
This Above All '42
Lassie, Come Home '43
Sherlock Holmes Faces Death '43
Sherlock Holmes in Washington '43
Frenchman's Creek '44
The Pearl of Death '44
Scarlet Claw '44
The Corn Is Green '45
House of Fear '45
Pursuit to Algiers '45
Son of Lassie '45
Dressed to Kill '46
The Two Mrs. Carrolls '47
Julia Misbehaves '48
The Woman in Green '49
Limelight '52
World for Ransom '54

Virginia Bruce (1910-82)
Downstairs '32
Kongo '32
Winner Take All '32
Jane Eyre '34
Let 'Em Have It '35
The Murder Man '35
Shadow of Doubt '35
Born to Dance '36
The Great Ziegfeld '36
Arsene Lupin Returns '38
The Bad Man of Brimstone '38
Let Freedom Ring '39
Society Lawyer '39
Stronger Than Desire '39
Flight Angels '40
The Invisible Woman '40
Adventure in Washington '41
Pardon My Sarong '42
Action in Arabia '44
State Department File 649 '49
Strangers When We Meet '60

Volker Bruch (1980-)
The Red Baron '08
Treasure Guards '11
Young Goethe in Love '11
Generation War '13

Agnes Bruckner (1985-)
Home Room '02
Murder by Numbers '02
Blue Car '03
Rick '03
The Woods '03
Haven '04
The Iris Effect '04
Stateside '04
Venom '05
Dreamland '06
Peaceful Warrior '06
Blood & Chocolate '07
Vacancy 2: The First Cut '08
Last Resort '09
The Craigslist Killer '11
Anna Nicole '13

Amy Bruckner (1991-)
They Are Among Us '04
Nancy Drew '07

Maximilian Bruckner
Guys and Balls '04
Cherry Blossoms '08

Patrick Bruel (1959-)
Secret Obsession '88
Sabrina '95
Lost and Found '99
Comedy of Power '06
O Jerusalem '07
A Secret '07
Change of Plans '09

Justin Bruening (1979-)
Blue-Eyed Butcher '12
The March Sisters at Christmas '12

Amanda Brugel (1978-)
What If God Were the Sun? '07
Room '15

Mads Brügger
The Ambassador '11
Cold Case Hammarskjöld '19

Alex Bruhanski
Showdown at Williams Creek '91
Black Point '01

Daniel Brühl (1978-)
Good Bye, Lenin! '03
The Edukators '04
Ladies in Lavender '04
Joyeux Noel '05
The Bourne Ultimatum '07
In Tranzit '07
The Countess '09
Inglourious Basterds '09
John Rabe '09
Intruders '11
The Fifth Estate '13
Rush '13
The Face of an Angel '14
Burnt '15
Woman in Gold '15
The Zookeeper's Wife '17
7 Days in Entebbe '18

Robin Brule
Killer Instinct: From the Files of Agent Candice DeLong '03
Why I Wore Lipstick to My Mastectomy '06

Argentina Brunetti
The Lawless '50
The Brothers Rico '57

Valeria Bruni-Tedeschi (1964-)
Nenette and Boni '96
Those Who Love Me Can Take the Train '98
The Color of Lies '99
5x2 '04
Cote d'Azur '05
Munich '05
Time to Leave '05
40 Love '15

Chris Bruno (1966-)
The Dead Zone '02
The Cell 2 '09
Prison Break: The Final Break '09

Dylan Bruno (1972-)
When Trumpets Fade '98
The Simian Line '99
Where the Heart Is '00
Going Greek '01
The One '01
Fresh Cut Grass '04
Quid Pro Quo '08

Nando (Fernando) Bruno (1895-1963)
Open City '45
Two Nights with Cleopatra '54

Philip Bruns (1931-2012)
Harry and Tonto '74
The Stunt Man '80
Return of the Living Dead 2 '88
Dead Men Don't Die '91
The Opposite Sex and How to Live With Them '93

Keith Brunsmann
Sticks '98
Tropix '02
Tweek City '05

Eric Bruskotter (1966-)
Can't Buy Me Love '87
In the Line of Fire '93
Major League 2 '94
The Fan '96
Starship Troopers '97
Major League 3: Back to the Minors '98

Dora Bryan (1923-2014)
The Fallen Idol '49
No Trace '50
Made in Heaven '52
My Son, the Vampire '52
Twilight Women '52
Mad About Men '54
Child in the House '56
The Great St. Trinian's Train Robbery '66
Hands of the Ripper '71
Apartment Zero '88
MirrorMask '05

Jane Bryan (1918-2009)
The Case of the Black Cat '36
Kid Galahad '37
Marked Woman '37
Brother Rat '38
The Sisters '38
A Slight Case of Murder '38
Each Dawn I Die '39
Invisible Stripes '39
The Old Maid '39
Those Glamour Girls '39
Brother Rat and a Baby '40

Sabrina Bryan (1984-)
The Cheetah Girls '03
The Cheetah Girls 2 '06
The Cheetah Girls: One World '08

Zachery Ty Bryan (1981-)
Bigfoot: The Unforgettable Encounter '94
First Kid '96
True Heart '97
The Rage: Carrie 2 '99
Rustin '01
A Killing Spring '02
The Game of Their Lives '05
Annapolis '06
The Fast and the Furious: Tokyo Drift '06

Aidy Bryant
The Star '17
I Feel Pretty '18

Clara Bryant
Due East '02
Bone Eater '07

John Bryant (1916-89)
From Here to Eternity '53
Run Silent, Run Deep '58

Joy Bryant (1974-)
Antwone Fisher '02
Baadasssss! '03
Honey '03
3-Way '04
Get Rich or Die Tryin' '05
London '05
The Skeleton Key '05
Bobby '06
Welcome Home Roscoe Jenkins '08
Virtuality '09
Hit and Run '12
About Last Night '14

Lee Bryant (1945-)
Half Slave, Half Free '85
Alien Nation: Dark Horizon '94

Lucas Bryant (1978-)
More Sex and the Single Mom '05
Playing House '06
A Very Merry Daughter of the Bride '08
Merry In-Laws '12

Michael Bryant (1928-2002)
The Mind Benders '63
Goodbye, Mr. Chips '69
Girly '70
The Ruling Class '72
Hamlet '96
King Lear '98
The Miracle Maker: The Story of Jesus '00 (V)

Nana Bryant (1888-1955)
Meet Nero Wolfe '36
Pennies from Heaven '36
Give Me a Sailor '38
Out West With the Hardys '38
If I Had My Way '40
The Possessed '47
Harvey '50

Pablo Bryant
The Big Empty '98
Out of Line '00

William (Bill) Bryant (1924-2001)
The Hanged Man '74
Corvette Summer '78
Mountain Family Robinson '79

Paul Bryar (1910-85)
The Night of the Hunter '55
Saintly Sinners '62

Scott Bryce (1958-)
Stalking Laura '93
Visions of Murder '93
Up Close and Personal '96

Rob Brydon (1965-)
MirrorMask '05
Tristram Shandy: A Cock and Bull Story '05
The Trip '10
The Best of Men '12
The Trip to Italy '14
The Trip to Spain '17
Holmes & Watson '18

Larry Bryggman (1938-)
Die Hard: With a Vengeance '95
Spy Game '01

Greg Bryk (1972-)
Poor Man's Game '06
Grindstone Road '07
Weirdsville '07
XIII '08
Dolan's Cadillac '09
Screamers: The Hunting '09
Red: Werewolf Hunter '10
Mistletoe Over Manhattan '11

Andrew Bryniarski (1969-)
Batman Returns '92
The Program '93
Cyborg 3: The Recycler '95
Black Mask 2: City of Masks '02
44 Minutes: The North Hollywood Shootout '03
The Texas Chainsaw Massacre '03
7 Mummies '06
The Texas Chainsaw Massacre: The Beginning '06
Some Kind of Hate '15

Yul Brynner (1915-85)
Port of New York '49
Anastasia '56
The King and I '56
The Ten Commandments '56
The Brothers Karamazov '58
The Buccaneer '58
The Journey '59
Solomon and Sheba '59
The Testament of Orpheus '59
The Magnificent Seven '60
Once More, With Feeling '60
Escape From Zahrain '62
Taras Bulba '62
Kings of the Sun '63
Flight From Ashiya '64
Invitation to a Gunfighter '64
Morituri '65
Cast a Giant Shadow '66
The Poppy Is Also a Flower '66
Return of the Magnificent Seven '66
The Double Man '67
Triple Cross '67
Villa Rides '68
Battle of Neretva '69
The File of the Golden Goose '69
The Madwoman of Chaillot '69
The Magic Christian '69
Adios, Sabata '71
Catlow '71
Light at the Edge of the World '71
Romance of a Horsethief '71
Fuzz '72
Night Flight from Moscow '73
Westworld '73
The Ultimate Warrior '75
Futureworld '76
Death Rage '77

Reine Brynolfsson (1953-)
Les Miserables '97
A Song for Martin '01
Kitchen Stories '03

Crystal Buble
Call of the Wild '04
Dress to Kill '07
My Name Is Sarah '07

Michael Buble (1975-)
Totally Blonde '01
The Snow Walker '03

Flavio Bucci (1947-2020)
Night Train Murders '75
Suspiria '77
Il Divo '08

Andrew Buchan (1979-)
Jane Eyre '06
The Sinking of the Laconia '10

Judith Buchan
I Dream of Murder '06
Lost Holiday: The Jim & Suzanne Shemwell Story '07
The Other Woman '08

Colin Buchanan (1967-)
Moll Flanders '96
Catherine Cookson's The Secret '00

Edgar Buchanan (1903-79)
Arizona '40
Too Many Husbands '40
Penny Serenade '41
Texas '41
Talk of the Town '42
City Without Men '43
The Desperadoes '43
Destroyer '43
Bride by Mistake '44
Buffalo Bill '44
The Impatient Years '44
Strange Affair '44
Abilene Town '46
The Bandit of Sherwood Forest '46
If I'm Lucky '46
Framed '47
The Sea of Grass '47
The Swordsman '47
Black Arrow '48
Lust for Gold '49
Man from Colorado '49
The Big Hangover '50
Cheaper by the Dozen '50
The Devil's Doorway '50
Rawhide '50
Big Trees '52
Wild Stallion '52
Shane '53
Dawn at Socorro '54
Human Desire '54
Lonesome Trail '55
Rage at Dawn '55
Silver Star '55
The Devil's Partner '58
The Sheepman '58
Edge of Eternity '59
Four Fast Guns '59
It Started with a Kiss '59
King of the Wild Stallions '59
Tammy Tell Me True '61
Ride the High Country '62
McLintock! '63
Move Over, Darling '63
Man from Button Willow '65 (V)
The Rounders '65
The Over-the-Hill Gang '69
The Over-the-Hill Gang Rides Again '70
Yuma '70

Ian Buchanan (1957-)
The Cool Surface '92
Blue Flame '93
Ivory Tower '97
Panic Room '02
American Loser '07
Make the Yuletide Gay '09

Jack Buchanan (1891-1957)
Monte Carlo '30
The Band Wagon '53

Lachlan Buchanan
Newcastle '08
Muck '15

Robert Buchanan
The Girl Who Knew Too Much '63
That Sinking Feeling '79

Sherry Buchanan
Eyes Behind the Stars '72
Doctor Butcher M.D. '80

Christopher Buchholz (1962-)
Covert Assassin '94
Eros '04
Operation Valkyrie '04
Free Men '12

Horst Buchholz (1932-2003)
Tiger Bay '59
The Magnificent Seven '60
Fanny '61
One, Two, Three '61
The Catamount Killing '74
Raid on Entebbe '77
Return to Fantasy Island '77
The Amazing Captain Nemo '78
Avalanche Express '79
From Hell to Victory '79
Berlin Tunnel 21 '81
Code Name: Emerald '85
Aces: Iron Eagle 3 '92
Faraway, So Close! '93
Life Is Beautiful '98
The Enemy '01

David Buck (1936-89)
The Mummy's Shroud '67
Mosquito Squadron '70

Samantha Buck (1974-)
The Sticky Fingers of Time '97
Wirey Spindell '99

John Buckler (1906-36)
The Black Room '35
Tarzan Escapes '36

A. J. Buckley (1978-)
Jimmy & Judy '06
The Box '07

A.J. Buckley (1978-)
Extremedays '01
Blue Car '03
In Enemy Hands '04
Manticore '05
Jimmy & Judy '06
Walking Tall: The Payback '07
Christmas Mail '10
Skateland '10
Doomsday Prophecy '11

Andrew Buckley (1965-)
The Big Day '99
Skeletons '10
Jimi: All Is by My Side '14

Betty Buckley (1947-)
Carrie '76
Tender Mercies '83
Roses Are for the Rich '87
Another Woman '88
Frantic '88
Babycakes '89
Rain Without Thunder '93
Wyatt Earp '94
Simply Irresistible '99
The Happening '08
5 Time Champion '11
Split '16

Jessie Buckley
Beast '17
Wild Rose '18
Judy '19
Dolittle '20

Keith Buckley (1941-)
The Virgin Witch '70
Excalibur '81
Half Moon Street '86

Susan Buckner (1951-)
Grease '78
Deadly Blessing '81

Dragos Bucur (1977-)
Police, Adjective '09
The Way Back '10

Jan Budar
Up and Down '04
Dark Spirits '08

Helen Buday (1963-)
Mad Max: Beyond Thunderdome '85
Dingo '90

Rebecca Budig (1973-)
Bad Parents '12
Getaway '13

Genevieve Buechner (1991-)
Bob the Butler '05
Vipers '08
Courage '09

Jack Buetel (1915-89)
The Outlaw '43
Best of the Badmen '50
The Half-Breed '51
Jesse James' Women '54

Jimmy Buffett (1946-)
Rancho Deluxe '75
FM '78
From the Earth to the Moon '98
Hoot '06

Celso Bugallo (1947-)
Mondays in the Sun '02
The Sea Inside '04

Niall Buggy (1948-)
Zardoz '73
The Playboys '92
Anton Chekhov's The Duel '09

Valerie Buhagiar (1963-)
Roadkill '89
Highway 61 '91

Gerard Buhr (1928-88)
Bob le Flambeur '55
The Night of the Following Day '69

Julia Buisel
Belle Toujours '06
Eccentricities of a Blonde-Haired Girl '10

Genevieve Bujold (1942-)
The King of Hearts '66
La Guerre Est Finie '66
The Thief of Paris '67
Anne of the Thousand Days '69
Trojan Women '71
Earthquake '74
Obsession '76
Swashbuckler '76
Another Man, Another Chance '77
Coma '78
Murder by Decree '79
Final Assignment '80
The Last Flight of Noah's Ark '80
Monsignor '82
Choose Me '84
Tightrope '84
Trouble in Mind '86
Dead Ringers '88
The Moderns '88
A Paper Wedding '89
Eye '96
The House of Yes '97
Last Night '98
Eye of the Beholder '99
Finding Home '03
Jericho Mansions '03
Disappearances '06
The Trotsky '09
Still Mine '13

Donald Buka (1920-2009)
Watch on the Rhine '43
The Street with No Name '48
Between Midnight and Dawn '50
Operation Eichmann '61

Raymond Buktenica (1943-)
The Jayne Mansfield Story '80
My Girl '91

Joyce Bulifant
Hanging By a Thread '79
Airplane! '80

Peter Bull (1912-84)
Sabotage '36
Marie Antoinette '38
The African Queen '51
A Christmas Carol '51
The Scapegoat '59
Tom Jones '63
Dr. Strangelove, or: How I Learned to Stop Worrying and Love the Bomb '64
Doctor Dolittle '67

Richard Bull (1924-2014)
Lawman '71
Different Story '78
Normal '03
Sugar '09

Amelia Bullmore (1964-)
Mrs. Dalloway '97
Catherine Cookson's Tilly Trotter '99
State of Play '03

Jeremy Bulloch (1945-)
Hoffman '70
The Empire Strikes Back '80
Return of the Jedi '83

Donna Bullock (1955-)
Air Force One '97
The Girl Next Door '04

Sandra Bullock (1964-)
Hangmen '87
A Fool and His Money '88
When the Party's Over '91
Love Potion #9 '92
Who Shot Pat? '92
Demolition Man '93
Fire on the Amazon '93
The Thing Called Love '93
The Vanishing '93
Wrestling Ernest Hemingway '93
Me and the Mob '94
Speed '94
The Net '95
Two If by Sea '95
While You Were Sleeping '95
In Love and War '96
A Time to Kill '96
Speed 2: Cruise Control '97
Hope Floats '98
Practical Magic '98
Prince of Egypt '98 (V)
Forces of Nature '99
Gun Shy '00
Miss Congeniality '00
28 Days '00
Lisa Picard Is Famous '01 (C)
Divine Secrets of the Ya-Ya Sisterhood '02
Murder by Numbers '02
Two Weeks Notice '02
Crash '05
Loverboy '05
Miss Congeniality 2: Armed and Fabulous '05
Infamous '06
The Lake House '06
Premonition '07
All About Steve '09
The Blind Side '09
The Proposal '09
Extremely Loud and Incredibly Close '11
Gravity '13
The Heat '13
Minions '15 (V)
Our Brand is Crisis '15
Ocean's 8 '18

Rodger Bumpass (1951-)
Heavy Metal '81 (V)
The SpongeBob SquarePants Movie '04 (V)
The SpongeBob Movie: Sponge Out of Water '15 (V)

Alan Bunce
The Last Mile '59
Homicidal '61

Stuart Bunce (1971-)
Behind the Lines '97
All the King's Men '99
The Gospel of John '03
Clapham Junction '07

Brooke Bundy (1944-)
The Gay Deceivers '69
Explorers '85
Two Fathers' Justice '85
A Nightmare on Elm Street 3: Dream Warriors '87
A Nightmare on Elm Street 4: Dream Master '88
Twice Dead '88
The Hunger Games '12

Marie Bunel (1961-)
Ma Vie en Rose '97
Close to Leo '02
The Chorus '04
A Girl Cut in Two '07
Inspector Bellamy '09

Edward (Eddie) Bunker (1933-2005)
Straight Time '78
Runaway Train '85
The Running Man '87
Fear '88
Best of the Best '89
Miracle Mile '89
Relentless '89
Tango and Cash '89
Reservoir Dogs '92
Best of the Best 2 '93
Somebody to Love '94
Shadrach '98
Animal Factory '00
The Longest Yard '05

Avis Bunnage (1923-90)
The Loneliness of the Long Distance Runner '62
The Whisperers '66
No Surrender '86

Herbert Bunston (1874-1935)
The Last of Mrs. Cheyney '29
Dracula '31

Cara Buono (1974-)
Gladiator '92
Waterland '92
The Cowboy Way '94
Kicking and Screaming '95
Killer: A Journal of Murder '95
Next Stop, Wonderland '98
River Red '98
Attention Shoppers '99
Chutney Popcorn '99
In a Class of His Own '99
Man of the Century '99
Happy Accidents '00
Two Ninas '00
Hulk '03
From Other Worlds '04
Cthulhu '08
The Unquiet '08
Let Me In '10
Drew Peterson: Untouchable '12
A Good Marriage '14
All Saints '17

Victor Buono (1938-82)
What Ever Happened to Baby Jane? '62
Four for Texas '63
Robin and the 7 Hoods '64
The Strangler '64
Hush, Hush, Sweet Charlotte '65
The Silencers '66
Boot Hill '69
Beneath the Planet of the Apes '70
The Mad Butcher '72
The Wrath of God '72
The Evil '78
Backstairs at the White House '79
The Man with Bogart's Face '80
More Wild, Wild West '80
Flight of Dragons '82 (V)

Sonny Bupp (1928-2007)
Three Faces West '40
Citizen Kane '41

Tommy Bupp (1924-83)
It's a Gift '34
Hey! Hey! USA! '38

Hugh Burden (1913-85)
Immortal Battalion '44
The Way Ahead '44
Ghost Ship '53
Funeral in Berlin '66
Blood from the Mummy's Tomb '71

Suzanne Burden (1958-)
Strapless '90
A Mind to Murder '96

Ray Burdis (1958-)
Final Cut '98
Love, Honour & Obey '00

Dora Madison Burge
Cowgirls 'n Angels '12
My Dog the Champion '14

Gregg Burge (1957-98)
A Chorus Line '85
School Daze '88

Dorothy Burgess (1907-61)
Malay Nights '32
Taxi! '32
Hold Your Man '33
Girls in Chains '43

John Burgess
Christabel '89
Rosencrantz & Guildenstern Are Dead '90

Richard Burgi (1958-)
Cellular '04
Darklight '04

Starship Troopers 2: Hero of the Federation '04
Torn Apart '04
Fun With Dick and Jane '05
In Her Shoes '05
Hostel: Part 2 '07
In God's Country '07
The Christmas Cottage '08
Super Eruption '11
F6 Twister '12

Zlatko Buric (1953-)
Pusher '96
Dirty Pretty Things '03
Teen Spirit '18
Killerman '19

MyAnna Buring (1979-)
The Descent '05
Doomsday '08
Vampire Killers '09
Witchville '10
Super Eruption '11
Kill List '12
Hyena '15

Alfred Burke (1918-2011)
Bitter Victory '58
Children of the Damned '63
The Nanny '65
Night Caller from Outer Space '66
The Brontes of Haworth '73
The House on Garibaldi Street '79

Billie Burke (1885-1970)
Christopher Strong '33
Dinner at Eight '33
Finishing School '33
After Office Hours '35
Becky Sharp '35
Doubting Thomas '35
Forsaking All Others '35
The Bride Wore Red '37
Navy Blue and Gold '37
Parnell '37
Topper '37
Everybody Sing '38
Merrily We Live '38
The Young in Heart '38
Eternally Yours '39
The Wizard of Oz '39
Hullabaloo '40
Irene '40
The Man Who Came to Dinner '41
Topper Returns '41
In This Our Life '42
Gildersleeve on Broadway '43
Breakfast in Hollywood '46
The Barkleys of Broadway '49
Father of the Bride '50
Father's Little Dividend '51
Small Town Girl '53
The Young Philadelphians '59
Sergeant Rutledge '60

Billy Burke (1966-)
To Cross the Rubicon '91
Without Limits '97
Don't Look Down '98
Mafia! '98
Komodo '99
The Independent '00
Along Came a Spider '01
Lost Junction '03
Ladder 49 '04
Feast of Love '07
Forfeit '07
Fracture '07
Three Days to Vegas '07
Twilight '08
Untraceable '08
The Twilight Saga: New Moon '09
The Twilight Saga: Eclipse '10
Drive Angry '11
Red Riding Hood '11
The Twilight Saga: Breaking Dawn, Part 1 '11
Freaky Deaky '12
Highland Park '13
Angels in Stardust '14
Lights Out '16
Breaking In '18

Brooke Burke
The Hazing '04
Knuckle Sandwich '04

David Burke
Vibrations '94
King Lear '98

Delta Burke (1956-)
Sordid Lives '00
What Women Want '00
Dangerous Child '01
Good Boy! '03 (V)
Bridal Fever '08

James Burke (1886-1968)
Lady by Choice '34
Make a Million '35
Ruggles of Red Gap '35
Dead End '37
Dawn Patrol '38
At the Circus '39
Beau Geste '39
Down to Earth '47
Cavalry Charge '51
Lucky Me '54
In Enemy Hands '04

Joe Michael Burke (1973-)
The Last Warrior '99
Wild Things 2 '04

Kathleen Burke (1913-80)
Island of Lost Souls '32
The Last Outpost '35
The Lives of a Bengal Lancer '35
Mutiny Ahead '35

Kathy Burke (1964-)
Nil by Mouth '96
Dancing at Lughnasa '98
Elizabeth '98
Kevin & Perry Go Large '00
Love, Honour & Obey '00
Once Upon a Time in the Midlands '02
Flushed Away '06 (V)
Tinker Tailor Soldier Spy '11

Marie Burke
Bad Blonde '53
The Terror of the Tongs '61

Marylouise Burke (1941-)
Series 7: The Contenders '01
Sideways '04
Pizza '05
A Prairie Home Companion '06
An Invisible Sign '11

Michael Reilly Burke (1969-)
Red Shoe Diaries: Luscious Lola '00
Octopus 2: River of Fear '02
The Collector '09

Michelle Burke (1970-)
See Michelle Rene Thomas

Paul Burke (1926-2009)
Francis Goes to West Point '52
Francis in the Navy '55
Screaming Eagles '56
Valley of the Dolls '67
Daddy's Gone A-Hunting '69
Once You Kiss a Stranger '69
Psychic Killer '75
Beach Patrol '79

Robert John Burke (1960-)
The Unbelievable Truth '90
Rambling Rose '91
RoboCop 3 '91
Simple Men '92
Dust Devil '93
A Far Off Place '93
Tombstone '93
Killer: A Journal of Murder '95
Fled '96
Stephen King's Thinner '96
Somewhere in the City '97
A Bright Shining Lie '98
From the Earth to the Moon '98
No Such Thing '01
Connie and Carla '04
Speak '04
Good Night, and Good Luck '05
Hide and Seek '05
Miracle at St. Anna '08
Endgame '09
Limitless '11
2 Guns '13
BlacKkKlansman '18

Robert Karl Burke
Big and Hairy '98
The Basket '99

Simon Burke (1961-)
The Devil's Playground '76
The Irishman '78
The One That Got Away '96
Passion '99
Pitch Black '00
Rodgers & Hammerstein's South Pacific '01
After the Deluge '03
The Alice '04

Tom Burke (1981-)
All the King's Men '99
Dracula '06
I Want Candy '07
Donkey Punch '08
Telstar: The Joe Meek Story '08
Cleanskin '12
The Invisible Woman '13
Only God Forgives '13
The Souvenir '19

Gedeon Burkhard
We'll Meet Again '02
Inglourious Basterds '09

Max Burkholder (1997-)
Love for Rent '05
The Rainbow Tribe '11
The Purge '13

Dennis Burkley (1945-)
Bummer '73
Murphy's Romance '85
Lambada '89
The Doors '91
Stop! or My Mom Will Shoot '92
Son-in-Law '93
Father's Day '96
Tin Cup '96
The First 9 1/2 Weeks '98
Possums '99

Nichola Burley
Donkey Punch '08
Wuthering Heights '12

Tom Burlinson (1956-)
The Man from Snowy River '82
Flesh and Blood '85
Piece of Cake '88
Return to Snowy River '88
Showdown at Williams Creek '91
The Cup '11

Leo Burmester (1944-2007)
The Abyss '89
Passion Fish '92
Fly by Night '93
A Perfect World '93
The Neon Bible '95
Truman '95
Mistrial '96
Switchback '97
Eye of the Storm '98
River Red '98
Limbo '99
Speed of Life '99
City by the Sea '02
Carry Me Home '04

Tam Dean Burn
The Acid House '98
Longford '06

Carol Burnett (1933-)
Pete 'n' Tillie '72
The Front Page '74
A Wedding '78
Friendly Fire '79
The Four Seasons '81
Annie '82
Noises Off '92
Moon over Broadway '98
The Trumpet of the Swan '01 (V)
Dr. Seuss' Horton Hears a Who! '08 (V)
Post Grad '09
The Secret World of Arrietty '10 (V)

Don Burnett (1929-)
Untamed Youth '57
Damon and Pythias '62

Olivia Burnette (1977-)
Final Verdict '91
The Thorn Birds: The Missing Years '96
Flourish '06

Smiley Burnette (1911-67)
Mystery Mountain '34
Harmony Lane '35
The Phantom Empire '35
Undersea Kingdom '36
Dick Tracy '37
Under Western Stars '38
South of the Border '39
Down Mexico Way '41
Ridin' on a Rainbow '41
Call of the Canyon '42
Heart of the Rio Grande '42
Idaho '43

Mark Burnham
Wrong Cops '13
Lowlife '18

Aaron Burns
The Green Inferno '14
Knock Knock '15
The Stranger '15

Alex Burns (1977-)
Thirteen Conversations About One Thing '01
National Lampoon's Van Wilder '02
Brother to Brother '04

Bob Burns (1890-1956)
Rhythm on the Range '36
Waikiki Wedding '37

Brooke Burns (1978-)
Shallow Hal '01
The Salon '05
Single White Female 2: The Psycho '05
Trophy Wife '06
Time and Again '07
The Art of Travel '08
The Most Wonderful Time of the Year '08
Smoke Jumpers '08
Titanic 2 '10
A Star for Christmas '12
Undercover Bridesmaid '12

Catherine Lloyd Burns (1961-)
Everything Put Together '00
The Baxter '05

Edward Burns (1968-)
The Brothers McMullen '94
She's the One '96
No Looking Back '98
Saving Private Ryan '98
15 Minutes '01
Sidewalks of New York '01
Ash Wednesday '02
Life or Something Like It '02
Confidence '03
The Breakup Artist '04 (C)
Looking for Kitty '04
The River King '05
A Sound of Thunder '05
The Groomsmen '06
The Holiday '06
Purple Violets '07
One Missed Call '08
27 Dresses '08
Echelon Conspiracy '09
Nice Guy Johnny '10
Newlyweds '11
Alex Cross '12
The Fitzgerald Family Christmas '12
Friends with Kids '12

George Burns (1896-1996)
College Humor '33
International House '33
We're Not Dressing '34
Here Comes Cookie '35
Love in Bloom '35
A Damsel in Distress '37
College Swing '38
Honolulu '39
Solid Gold Cadillac '56 (N)
The Sunshine Boys '75
Oh, God! '77
Sgt. Pepper's Lonely Hearts Club Band '78
Going in Style '79
Oh, God! Book 2 '80
Oh, God! You Devil '84
18 Again! '88
Radioland Murders '94

Heather Burns (1975-)
You've Got Mail '98
Miss Congeniality '00
You Are Here * '00
Two Weeks Notice '02
Kill the Poor '03
Bewitched '05
Brooklyn Lobster '05
Miss Congeniality 2: Armed and Fabulous '05
The Groomsmen '06
Perception '06
Valley of the Sun '11
What's Your Number? '11
The Fitzgerald Family Christmas '12

James C. Burns
Lake Dead '07
Coldwater '14

Jennifer Burns
Josh Kirby. . .Time Warrior: Chapter 1, Planet of the Dino-Knights '95
Josh Kirby. . . Time Warrior: Chapter 2, The Human Pets '95
Josh Kirby. . . Time Warrior: Chapter 3, Trapped on Toyworld '95
Josh Kirby. . . Time Warrior: Chapter 4, Eggs from 70 Million B.C. '95
Josh Kirby. . . Time Warrior: Chapter 5, Journey to the Magic Cavern '96
Josh Kirby. . . Time Warrior: Chapter 6, Last Battle for the Universe '96
Isaac Asimov's Nightfall '00

Jere Burns (1954-)
The Gambler Returns: The Luck of the Draw '93
Greedy '94
Santa Fe '97
Life-Size '00
Crocodile Dundee in Los Angeles '01
What's Up, Scarlet? '05
2:13 '09
Love Begins '11
Prom '11

Marilyn Burns (1950-2014)
The Texas Chainsaw Massacre '74
Eaten Alive '76
Helter Skelter '76
Kiss Daddy Goodbye '81
Future Kill '85
The Texas Chainsaw Massacre 4: The Next Generation '95

Marion Burns (1907-93)
Me and My Gal '32
Flirting With Danger '35

Mark Burns (1936-2007)
The Charge of the Light Brigade '68
The Virgin and the Gypsy '70
Death in Venice '71
House of the Living Dead '73
Count Dracula '77
Bullseye! '90

Martha Burns (1958-)
The Life Before This '99
What Katy Did '99
Siblings '04
The Trojan Horse '08
The Good Samaritan '12

Megan Burns (1986-)
Liam '00
28 Days Later '02

Michael Burns (1947-)
40 Guns to Apache Pass '67
That Cold Day in the Park '69
Gidget Gets Married '72
Thumb Tripping '72
Santee '73

Tim Burns (1953-)
Mad Max '80
Freaked '93 (C)

Raymond Burr (1917-93)
Abandoned '47
Desperate '47
Raw Deal '48
Ruthless '48
Sleep, My Love '48
Walk a Crooked Mile '48
Adventures of Don Juan '49
Black Magic '49
Red Light '49
Borderline '50
Key to the City '50
Love Happy '50
Bride of the Gorilla '51
His Kind of Woman '51
The Magic Carpet '51
A Place in the Sun '51
FBI Girl '52
Horizons West '52
Mara Maru '52
The Bandits of Corsica '53
The Blue Gardenia '53
Tarzan and the She-Devil '53
Casanova's Big Night '54
Party Girls for Sale '54
Passion '54
Rear Window '54
They Were So Young '55
You're Never Too Young '55
The Brass Legend '56
Godzilla, King of the Monsters '56
Crime of Passion '57
Tomorrow Never Comes '77
The Bastard '78 (N)
Centennial '78
Out of the Blue '80
Peter and Paul '81
Airplane 2: The Sequel '82
Perry Mason Returns '85
Delirious '91
Showdown at Williams Creek '91

Robert Burr (1926-2000)
The Possession of Joel Delaney '72
Netherworld '90

Sheila Burrell (1922-2011)
Cloudburst '51
Paranoiac '62
Cold Comfort Farm '94

Ty Burrell (1967-)
Black Hawk Down '01
Evolution '01
Dawn of the Dead '04
In Good Company '04
The Darwin Awards '06
Friends with Money '06
Fur: An Imaginary Portrait of Diane Arbus '06
The Incredible Hulk '08
Fair Game '10
Morning Glory '10
Butter '12
Goats '12
Mr. Peabody & Sherman '14 (V)
Muppets Most Wanted '14
The Skeleton Twins '14
Storks '16

Hedy Burress (1973-)
Foxfire '96
Cabin by the Lake '00
Valentine '01

Bonnie Burroughs
Hard to Kill '89
One Small Hero '99

Jackie Burroughs (1939-2010)
Heavy Metal '81 (V)
Anne of Green Gables '85
Careful '92
Armistead Maupin's More Tales of the City '97
Bleeders '97
Last Night '98
Lost and Delirious '01
A Guy Thing '03
The Republic of Love '03
Willard '03
Re-Generation '04
Snow '04
King's Ransom '05
Small Town Murder Songs '10

William S. Burroughs (1914-97)
Haxan: Witchcraft through the Ages '22 (N)
Bloodhounds of Broadway '89
Drugstore Cowboy '89
Twister '89

Darren E. Burrows (1966-)
Class of 1999 '90
Cry-Baby '90
The Hi-Lo Country '98
Sunset Strip '99
Forty Shades of Blue '05
NoNames '10
Love Is Strange '14

Saffron Burrows (1972-)
Circle of Friends '94
Welcome II the Terrordome '95
Hotel de Love '96
Lovelife '97
The Matchmaker '97
The Loss of Sexual Innocence '98
Deep Blue Sea '99
Miss Julie '99
Wing Commander '99
Gangster No. 1 '00
Time Code '00
Enigma '01
Hotel '01
The Seventh Stream '01
Tempted '01
Frida '02
Peter Pan '03 (N)
Troy '04
Fay Grim '06
Klimt '06
Reign Over Me '07
The Bank Job '08
The Guitar '08
Shrink '09
Knife Fight '13

Ellen Burstyn (1932-)
Pit Stop '67
Alex in Wonderland '70
Tropic of Cancer '70
The Last Picture Show '71
The King of Marvin Gardens '72
The Exorcist '73
Alice Doesn't Live Here Anymore '74
Harry and Tonto '74
Same Time, Next Year '78
Resurrection '80
The People vs. Jean Harris '81
The Ambassador '84
Into Thin Air '85
Twice in a Lifetime '85
Pack of Lies '87
Dying Young '91
The Cemetery Club '93
Getting Gotti '94
Getting Out '94
Primal Secrets '94
When a Man Loves a Woman '94
The Baby-Sitters' Club '95
Follow the River '95
How to Make an American Quilt '95
My Brother's Keeper '95
Roommates '95
The Spitfire Grill '95
Deceiver '97
Flash '98
Playing by Heart '98
Mermaid '00
Requiem for a Dream '00
The Yards '00
Dodson's Journey '01
Divine Secrets of the Ya-Ya Sisterhood '02
Red Dragon '02 (V)
Brush with Fate '03
Mrs. Harris '05 (C)
The Elephant King '06
The Fountain '06
The Wicker Man '06
For One More Day '07
The Stone Angel '07
According to Greta '08
The Loss of a Teardrop Diamond '08
Lovely, Still '08
W. '08
The Mighty Macs '09
Main Street '10
Another Happy Day '11
Someday This Pain Will Be Useful to You '11
Coma '12
The Calling '14
Draft Day '14
Flowers in the Attic '14
Interstellar '14
Petals on the Wind '14
The Age of Adaline '15
Wiener-Dog '16
The House of Tomorrow '18
Nostalgia '18
The Tale '18

Corey Burton (1955-)
Dudley Do-Right '99 (N)
Atlantis: The Lost Empire '01 (V)
Return to Never Land '02 (V)
Treasure Planet '02 (V)
Star Wars: The Clone Wars '08 (V)

Frederick Burton (1871-1957)
An American Tragedy '31
One Way Passage '32
Too Busy to Work '32

Harry Burton (1961-)
Fortunes of War '87
Devices and Desires '91

Hilarie Burton (1982-)
Havoc 2: Normal Adolescent Behavior '07
The List '07
The Secret Life of Bees '08
Bloodworth '10
Growing Up Smith '17

Jennifer Burton
Truck Stop Women '74
Play Time '94
Watch Me '96
Death and Desire '97

John Burton (1904-87)
Lloyds of London '36
Mrs. Miniver '42

Julian Burton (1932-2006)
A Bucket of Blood '59
Masque of the Red Death '65

Kate Burton (1957-)
Big Trouble in Little China '86
August '95
Mistrial '96
Ellen Foster '97
The Ice Storm '97
Celebrity '98
Obsessed '02
Swimfan '02
Unfaithful '02
The Diary of Ellen Rimbauer '03
Empire Falls '05
Stay '05
Lovely by Surprise '07
Max Payne '08
Quid Pro Quo '08
Spooner '08
The City of Your Final Destination '09
127 Hours '10
Puncture '11
Liberal Arts '12
Barefoot '14
Bleeding Heart '15
Martyrs '16

LeVar Burton (1957-)
Roots '77
Dummy '79
The Guyana Tragedy: The Story of Jim Jones '80
The Hunter '80
Grambling's White Tiger '81
The Jesse Owens Story '84
The Midnight Hour '86
Roots: The Gift '88
Star Trek: Generations '94
Star Trek: First Contact '96
Star Trek: Insurrection '98
Dancing in September '00
Ali '01
Star Trek: Nemesis '02
Reach for Me '08
Taken in Broad Daylight '09
The Jensen Project '10
Rise of the Zombies '12

Norman Burton (1923-2003)
Fright '56
Diamonds Are Forever '71
Simon, King of the Witches '71
Save the Tiger '73
The Terminal Man '74
Fade to Black '80
Mausoleum '83
Crimes of Passion '84
Bloodsport '88

Richard Burton (1925-84)
Green Grow the Rushes '51
My Cousin Rachel '52
The Desert Rats '53
The Robe '53
Alexander the Great '55
The Rains of Ranchipur '55
Sea Wife '57
Bitter Victory '58
Look Back in Anger '58
Ice Palace '60
The Longest Day '62
Cleopatra '63
The V.I.P.'s '63
Becket '64
The Night of the Iguana '64
Zulu '64 (N)
The Sandpiper '65
The Spy Who Came in from the Cold '65
Who's Afraid of Virginia Woolf? '66
The Comedians '67
The Taming of the Shrew '67
Candy '68
Doctor Faustus '68
Where Eagles Dare '68
Anne of the Thousand Days '69
Raid on Rommel '71
Villain '71
Assassination of Trotsky '72
Bluebeard '72
Divorce His, Divorce Hers '72
Massacre in Rome '73
Under Milk Wood '73
The Klansman '74
Equus '77
The Exorcist 2: The Heretic '77
The Medusa Touch '78
Wild Geese '78
Lovespell '79
Circle of Two '80
Absolution '81
1984 '84
Wagner: The Complete Epic '85

Robert Burton (1895-1962)
My Man and I '52
Above and Beyond '53
All the Brothers Were Valiant '53
The Girl Who Had Everything '53
A Man Called Peter '55
The Tall T '57
Compulsion '59
The Gallant Hours '60
Invasion of the Animal People '62
The Slime People '63

Robert (Skip) Burton
Bucktown '75
Trilogy of Terror '75

Steve (Stephen) Burton (1970-)
Cyber-Tracker 2 '95
The Last Castle '01
Taken '02

Tony Burton (1937-2016)
Assault on Precinct 13 '76
Rocky '76
The Shining '80
Armed and Dangerous '86
Oceans of Fire '86
House Party 2: The Pajama Jam '91
The Magnificent Seven '98
Rocky Balboa '06
Hack! '07

Tyrone Burton
Squeeze '97
Auto Recovery '08

Warren Burton (1944-)
Gettysburg '93
Bloodfist 8: Hard Way Out '96
Humanoids from the Deep '96

Wendell Burton (1947-)
The Sterile Cuckoo '69
East of Eden '80

Clemency Burton-Hill (1981-)
La Femme Musketeer '03
Supernova '05
The Prince & Me 2: Royal Wedding '06

Sean Bury (1954-)
If. . . '69
The Abominable Dr. Phibes '71
Friends '71

Cindy Busby (1983-)
A Life Interrupted '07
Picture This! '08
American Pie Presents: Book of Love '09
Behemoth '11

Steve Buscemi (1957-)
Parting Glances '86
Heart '87
Mystery Train '89
New York Stories '89
Slaves of New York '89
King of New York '90
Tales from the Darkside: The Movie '90
Barton Fink '91
Billy Bathgate '91
Crisscross '92
In the Soup '92
Reservoir Dogs '92
Ed and His Dead Mother '93
The Hudsucker Proxy '93
The Last Outlaw '93
Rising Sun '93
Twenty Bucks '93
Airheads '94
Billy Madison '94
Floundering '94
Living in Oblivion '94
Me and the Mob '94 (C)
Pulp Fiction '94
The Search for One-Eye Jimmy '94
Somebody to Love '94
Desperado '95
Kansas City '95
Things to Do in Denver When You're Dead '95
Escape from L.A. '96
Fargo '96
Tree's Lounge '96
The Big Lebowski '97
Con Air '97
The Real Blonde '97
The Wedding Singer '97
Armageddon '98
The Imposters '98
The Impostors '98
Big Daddy '99
Animal Factory '00
28 Days '00
Domestic Disturbance '01
Double Whammy '01
Final Fantasy: The Spirits Within '01 (V)
Ghost World '01
The Grey Zone '01
Monsters, Inc. '01 (V)
The Laramie Project '02
Love in the Time of Money '02
Mr. Deeds '02
Spy Kids 2: The Island of Lost Dreams '02
13 Moons '02
Big Fish '03
Coffee and Cigarettes '03
Spy Kids 3-D: Game Over '03
Home on the Range '04 (V)
Tanner on Tanner '04 (C)
The Island '05
Romance & Cigarettes '05
Art School Confidential '06
Charlotte's Web '06 (V)
Delirious '06
Monster House '06 (V)
Paris, je t'aime '06
I Now Pronounce You Chuck and Larry '07
I Think I Love My Wife '07
Interview '07
Igor '08 (V)
G-Force '09
Handsome Harry '09
John Rabe '09
The Messenger '09
Saint John of Las Vegas '09
Grown Ups '10 (C)
Pete Smalls Is Dead '10
Youth in Revolt '10
Rampart '11
Hotel Transylvania '12 (V)
Grown Ups 2 '13
The Incredible Burt Wonderstone '13
Monsters University '13 (V)
The Cobbler '14
Time Out of Mind '14
Hotel Transylvania 2 '15 (V)
The Boss Baby '17
The Death of Stalin '17
Lean on Pete '17
Norman '17
Nancy '18
The Dead Don't Die '19

Charles Busch (1954-)
Psycho Beach Party '00
Die Mommie Die! '03
A Very Serious Person '06

Mae Busch (1897-1946)
Foolish Wives '22
Souls for Sale '23
The Unholy Three '25
Alibi '29
Doctor X '32
The Rider of Death Valley '32
Blondie Johnson '33
Sons of the Desert '33
Bohemian Girl '36
The Clutching Hand '36
Marie Antoinette '38
Ziegfeld Girl '41
The Mad Monster '42

Gary Busey (1944-)
Angels Hard As They Come '71
Dirty Little Billy '72
Charms '73
The Last American Hero '73
Lolly-Madonna XXX '73
Thunderbolt & Lightfoot '74
Gumball Rally '76
A Star Is Born '76
Big Wednesday '78
The Buddy Holly Story '78
Straight Time '78
Carny '80
Barbarosa '82
D.C. Cab '84
Insignificance '85
Silver Bullet '85
Eye of the Tiger '86
Lethal Weapon '87
Let's Get Harry '87
Bulletproof '88
Predator 2 '90
Point Break '91
The Player '92
South Beach '92
Under Siege '92
The Firm '93
Rookie of the Year '93
Chasers '94
Drop Zone '94
Surviving the Game '94
Carried Away '95
Man with a Gun '95
Black Sheep '96
Lost Highway '96
Plato's Run '96
The Rage '96
Suspicious Minds '96
Diary of a Serial Killer '97
Rough Riders '97
Steel Sharks '97
Fear and Loathing in Las Vegas '98
The Girl Next Door '98
Soldier '98
Two Shades of Blue '98
Jacob Two Two Meets the Hooded Fang '99
No Tomorrow '99
A Crack in the Floor '00
Hooded Angels '00
Tribulation '00
On the Edge '02
Sam & Janet '02
Slap Shot 2: Breaking the Ice '02
Border Blues '03
Latin Dragon '03
Quigley '03
El Padrino '04
Chasing Ghosts '05
Crooked '05
Maneater '07
Piranha 3DD '11
Sharknado: The 4th Awakens '16

Jake Busey (1971-)
P.C.U. '94
S.F.W. '94
Windrunner '94
The Frighteners '96
Twister '96
Contact '97
Starship Troopers '97
Black Cat Run '98
Enemy of the State '98
Home Fries '98
Tail Lights Fade '99
Held Up '00
Fast Sofa '01
Tomcats '01
The First $20 Million is Always the Hardest '02
The Hitcher 2: I've Been Waiting '03
Identity '03
Lost Junction '03
Christmas With the Kranks '04
H.G. Wells' War of the Worlds '05
Road House 2: Last Call '06
Wristcutters: A Love Story '06
Comanche Moon '08
Time Bomb '08
Play Dead '09
The Killing Jar '10
Cross '11
Beverly Hills Chihuahua 3: Viva La Fiesta! '12 (V)
Crazy Eyes '12
Girl Meets Boy '13
Sparks '13
Wicked Blood '13
Reaper '15

Timothy Busfield (1957-)
Revenge of the Nerds '84
Revenge of the Nerds 2: Nerds in Paradise '87
Field of Dreams '89
Sneakers '92
The Skateboard Kid '93
Striking Distance '93
Little Big League '94
First Kid '96

Buffalo Soldiers *'97*
The Souler Opposite *'97*
Trucks *'97*
Wanted *'98*
Dead in a Heartbeat *'02*
Terminal Error *'02*
National Security *'03*
Beyond the Blackboard *'11*
Save the Date *'12*

Billy Green Bush (1935-)
Five Easy Pieces *'70*
Culpepper Cattle Co. *'72*
Welcome Home, Soldier Boys *'72*
Electra Glide in Blue *'73*
Alice Doesn't Live Here Anymore *'74*
The Invasion of Johnson County *'76*
The Beasts Are On the Streets *'78*
Tom Horn *'80*
The River *'84*
Critters *'86*
The Deliberate Stranger *'86*
The Hitcher *'86*
Conagher *'91*
Jason Goes to Hell: The Final Friday *'93*

George W. Bush (1946-)
Fahrenheit 9/11 *'04*
An Inconvenient Sequel: Truth to Power *'17*
Fahrenheit 11/9 *'18*

Grand L. Bush (1955-)
Stir Crazy *'80*
Streets of Fire *'84*
Brewster's Millions *'85*
Colors *'88*
Die Hard *'88*
Lethal Weapon 2 *'89*
Freejack *'92*
Demolition Man *'93*
Extreme Honor *'01*
Boa *'02*

James Bush (1907-87)
Beggars in Ermine *'34*
Crimson Romance *'34*
A Shot in the Dark *'35*
Children of the Wild *'37*

Matthew Bush (1986-)
One Last Thing *'05*
High School *'10*
Nice Guy Johnny *'10*
Piranha 3DD *'11*
The Kitchen *'12*

Shoshana Bush
Fling *'08*
Dance Flick *'09*

Sophia Bush (1982-)
John Tucker Must Die *'06*
Stay Alive *'06*
The Hitcher *'07*
The Narrows *'08*
Table for Three *'09*
Chalet Girls *'11*

Anthony Bushell (1904-97)
The Royal Bed *'31*
Vanity Fair *'32*
The Ghoul *'34*
The Scarlet Pimpernel *'34*
Dark Journey *'37*
The Arsenal Stadium Mystery *'39*
The Small Back Room *'49*
Angel with the Trumpet *'50*
The Miniver Story *'50*
A Night to Remember *'58*

Francis X. Bushman (1883-1966)
Ben-Hur *'26*
Midnight Faces *'26*
The Girl Said No *'30*
Last Frontier *'32*
The Three Musketeers *'33*
Honky Tonk *'41*
David and Bathsheba *'51*
Sabrina *'54*
12 to the Moon *'60 (N)*
The Phantom Planet *'61*

Ralph Bushman
Four Sons *'28*
Caryl of the Mountains *'36*

Anthony Bushnell (1904-97)
Three Faces East *'30*
Five Star Final *'31*
The Return of the Scarlet Pimpernel *'37*
Bitter Victory *'58*

Akosua Busia (1966-)
The Final Terror *'83*
The Color Purple *'85*
Hard Lessons *'86*
The Seventh Sign *'88*
Larry McMurtry's Dead Man's Walk *'96*
Rosewood *'96*
Tears of the Sun *'03*

Pascale Bussieres (1968-)
When Night Is Falling *'95*
The Twilight of the Ice Nymphs *'97*
The Five Senses *'99*
Girls Can't Swim *'99*
Xchange *'00*
The Blue Butterfly *'04*
Afterwards *'08*

Raymond Bussieres (1907-82)
Beauties of the Night *'52*
Casque d'Or *'52*
Paris When It Sizzles *'64*

Budd Buster (1891-1965)
Desert Guns *'36*
Zorro's Fighting Legion *'39*

Humberto Busto
Amores Perros *'00*
Dinoshark *'10*

Adam Butcher
Saint Ralph *'04*
Hellhounds *'09*

Paul Butcher
My Neighbor Totoro *'88 (V)*
Landspeed *'01*

Michelle Buteau
Always Be My Maybe *'19*
Someone Great *'19*

Mitchell Butel (1970-)
Dark City *'97*
Strange Fits of Passion *'99*
The Bank *'01*

Dick Butkus (1942-)
Mother, Jugs and Speed *'76*
Cracking Up *'83*
Johnny Dangerously *'84*
Spontaneous Combustion *'89*

Austin Butler (1991-)
Aliens in the Attic *'09*
The Bling Ring *'11*
Sharpay's Fabulous Adventure *'11*

Brett Butler (1958-)
The Dress Code *'99*
Militia *'99*
Vampire Bats *'05*
Age Out *'19*

Cindy Butler
Grayeagle *'77*
Boggy Creek II *'83*

Dan E. Butler (1954-)
The Manhattan Project *'86*
Manhunter *'86*
The Long Walk Home *'89*
Longtime Companion *'90*
The Silence of the Lambs *'91*
Captain Ron *'92*
Dave *'93*
Rising Sun *'93*
I Love Trouble *'94*
The Fan *'96*
Armistead Maupin's More Tales of the City *'97*
Enemy of the State *'98*
From the Earth to the Moon *'98*
The First $20 Million is Always the Hardest *'02*
Sniper 2 *'02*
Prayers for Bobby *'09*

Dean Butler (1956-)
Desert Hearts *'86*
The Final Goal *'94*

Gerard Butler (1969-)
Mrs. Brown *'97*
The Cherry Orchard *'99*
One More Kiss *'99*
Dracula 2000 *'00*
Shooters *'00*
Attila *'01*
Harrison's Flowers *'02*
Reign of Fire *'02*
Lara Croft Tomb Raider: The Cradle of Life *'03*
Timeline *'03*
Dear Frankie *'04*
The Phantom of the Opera *'04*
The Game of Their Lives *'05*
Beowulf & Grendel *'06*
P.S. I Love You *'07*
Shattered *'07*
300 *'07*
Nim's Island *'08*
RocknRolla *'08*
Gamer *'09*
Law Abiding Citizen *'09*
The Ugly Truth *'09*
The Bounty Hunter *'10*
How to Train Your Dragon *'10 (V)*
Coriolanus *'11*
Machine Gun Preacher *'11*
Chasing Mavericks *'12*
Playing for Keeps *'12*
Movie 43 *'13*
Olympus Has Fallen *'13*
How to Train Your Dragon 2 *'14 (V)*
Gods of Egypt *'16*
London Has Fallen *'16*
Geostorm *'17*
Den of Thieves *'18*
Hunter Killer *'18*
Angel Has Fallen *'19*
How to Train Your Dragon: The Hidden World *'19*
The Vanishing *'19*

Jimmy Butler (1921-45)
Manhattan Melodrama *'34*
Mrs. Wiggs of the Cabbage Patch *'34*
No Greater Glory *'34*

Kerry Butler
Borough of Kings *'98*
The Miseducation of Cameron Post *'18*

Lois Butler (1931-89)
Mickey *'48*
High Lonesome *'50*

Paul Butler
To Sleep with Anger *'90*
Zebrahead *'92*
Romeo Is Bleeding *'93*
A Single Man *'09*

Sarah Butler (1985-)
Flu Birds *'08*
I Spit on Your Grave *'10*
The Philly Kid *'12*
The Stranger Within *'13*
Free Fall *'14*
I Spit on Your Grave: Vengeance Is Mine *'15*

Tom Butler (1951-)
Ronnie and Julie *'97*
The Long Way Home *'98*
Deadlocked *'00*
Life-Size *'00*
Josie and the Pussycats *'01*
Freddy *vs.* Jason *'03*
Everything's Gone Green *'06*
Making Mr. Right *'08*
Call Me Mrs. Miracle *'10*

William Butler (1968-)
Leatherface: The Texas Chainsaw Massacre 3 *'89*
Night of the Living Dead *'90*
Inner Sanctum *'91*
Blue Hill Avenue *'01*

Yancy Butler (1970-)
Hard Target *'93*
Drop Zone *'94*
The Treat *'98*

Thin Air *'00*
The Witness Files *'00*
The Last Letter *'04*
Double Cross *'06*
Wolvesbayne *'09*
Kick-Ass *'10*
Lake Placid 3 *'10*
Lake Placid: The Final Chapter *'12*
Shark Island *'12*
Hansel & Gretel Get Baked *'13*
Kick-Ass 2 *'13*

Merritt Butrick (1959-89)
Star Trek 2: The Wrath of Khan *'82*
Zapped! *'82*
Code of Honor *'84*
Star Trek 3: The Search for Spock *'84*
Promises to Keep *'85*
When the Bough Breaks *'86*
From the Dead of Night *'89*

Asa Butterfield (1997-)
The Wolfman *'09*
Nanny McPhee Returns *'10*
Hugo *'11*
Ender's Game *'13*
A Brilliant Young Mind *'14*
Ten Thousand Saints *'15*
Miss Peregrine's Home for Peculiar Children *'16*
The Space Between Us *'17*
The House of Tomorrow *'18*
Journey's End *'18*
Time Freak *'18*

Charles Butterworth (1896-1946)
Illicit *'31*
Love Me Tonight *'32*
Beauty and the Boss *'33*
The Nuisance *'33*
Penthouse *'33*
The Cat and the Fiddle *'34*
Hollywood Party *'34*
Forsaking All Others *'35*
Magnificent Obsession *'35*
Orchids to You *'35*
It Happened in New Orleans *'36*
The Moon's Our Home *'36*
Swing High, Swing Low *'37*
Every Day's a Holiday *'38*
Thanks for the Memory *'38*
Let Freedom Ring *'39*
The Boys From Syracuse *'40*
Second Chorus *'40*
Road Show *'41*
Dixie Jamboree *'44*

Donna Butterworth (1956-)
The Family Jewels *'65*
Paradise, Hawaiian Style *'66*

Peter Butterworth (1919-79)
Carry On Cowboy *'66*
Don't Lose Your Head *'66*
Carry On Up the Khyber *'68*
Carry On Abroad *'72*

Stephanie Buttle
A Couch in New York *'95*
Urban Ghost Story *'98*

Red Buttons (1919-2006)
13 Rue Madeleine *'46*
Sayonara *'57*
Imitation General *'58*
The Big Circus *'59*
Five Weeks in a Balloon *'62*
Gay Purr-ee *'62 (V)*
Hatari! *'62*
The Longest Day *'62*
Your Cheatin' Heart *'64*
Harlow *'65*
Stagecoach *'66*
They Shoot Horses, Don't They? *'69*
The Poseidon Adventure *'72*
Pete's Dragon *'77*
Viva Knievel *'77*
Movie, Movie *'78*
C.H.O.M.P.S. *'79*
When Time Ran Out *'80*
Leave 'Em Laughing *'81*
Alice in Wonderland *'85*
Reunion at Fairborough *'85*

18 Again! *'88*
The Ambulance *'90*
It Could Happen to You *'94*
The Story of Us *'99*

Pat Buttram (1917-94)
Twilight of Honor *'63*
Roustabout *'64*
The Aristocats *'70 (V)*
Evil Roy Slade *'71 (N)*
The Gatling Gun *'72*
Robin Hood *'73 (V)*
The Rescuers *'77 (V)*
The Fox and the Hound *'81 (V)*
Back to the Future, Part 3 *'90*

Norbert Lee Butz (1967-)
West of Here *'02*
Dan in Real Life *'07*
Higher Ground *'11*
Greetings from Tim Buckley *'12*
The English Teacher *'13*
Better Living Through Chemistry *'14*

Sarah Buxton (1965-)
Welcome to Spring Break *'88*
Rock 'n' Roll High School Forever *'91*
The Climb *'97*
Today You Die *'05*

Margherita Buy (1962-)
Not of This World *'99*
His Secret Life *'01*
Caterina in the Big City *'03*
Days and Clouds *'07*
Saturn in Opposition *'07*
Me, Myself and Her *'16*
Mia Madre *'16*

George Buza (1949-)
Still Small Voices *'07*
The Case for Christmas *'11*
The Way of the West *'11*
A Christmas Horror Story *'15*

Agata Buzek (1976-)
Zemsta *'02*
Redemption *'13*
The Innocents *'16*
High Life *'18*

Ruth Buzzi (1936-)
Freaky Friday *'76*
Once Upon a Brothers Grimm *'77*
The North Avenue Irregulars *'79*
The Villain *'79*
The Being *'83*
Dixie Lanes *'88*
My Mom's a Werewolf *'89*
Wishful Thinking *'92*
Troublemakers *'94*
Boys Will Be Boys *'97*

Ezra Buzzington
The Haunting of Marsten Manor *'07*
Trash Fire *'16*

Dave Buzzotta
Gang Boys *'97*
Children of the Corn 5: Fields of Terror *'98*
The Prophecy 3: The Ascent *'99*
She's All That *'99*

Bobbie Byers
Savages from Hell *'68*
Wild Rebels *'71*

Christin Byers
December Boys *'07*
Hey Hey It's Esther Blueberger *'08*

Max Bygraves (1922-)
A Cry from the Streets *'57*
Bobbikins *'59*

Spring Byington (1893-1971)
Little Women *'33*
Ah, Wilderness! *'35*
Mutiny on the Bounty *'35*
Orchids to You *'35*
Werewolf of London *'35*

The Charge of the Light Brigade *'36*
Theodora Goes Wild *'36*
A Family Affair *'37*
The Green Light *'37*
It's Love I'm After *'37*
Jezebel *'38*
You Can't Take It with You *'38*
The Story of Alexander Graham Bell *'39*
The Blue Bird *'40*
Lucky Partners *'40*
My Love Came Back *'40*
The Devil & Miss Jones *'41*
Meet John Doe *'41*
The Vanishing Virginian *'41*
When Ladies Meet *'41*
Rings on Her Fingers *'42*
Roxie Hart *'42*
Heaven Can Wait *'43*
The Heavenly Body *'44*
I'll Be Seeing You *'44*
The Enchanted Cottage *'45*
Salty O'Rourke *'45*
Thrill of a Romance *'45*
Dragonwyck *'46*
Cynthia *'47*
Living In a Big Way *'47*
My Brother Talks to Horses *'47*
B.F.'s Daughter *'48*
The Big Wheel *'49*
In the Good Old Summertime *'49*
Angels in the Outfield *'51*
Because You're Mine *'52*
No Room for the Groom *'52*
The Rocket Man *'54*
Please Don't Eat the Daisies *'60*

John Byner (1938-)
Great Smokey Roadblock *'76*
The Black Cauldron *'85 (V)*
Transylvania 6-5000 *'85*
My 5 Wives *'00*

Amanda Bynes (1986-)
Big Fat Liar *'02*
What a Girl Wants *'03*
Robots *'05 (V)*
She's the Man *'06*
Hairspray *'07*
Sydney White *'07*
Living Proof *'08*
Easy A *'10*

Dan Byrd (1985-)
A Cinderella Story *'04*
Salem's Lot *'04*
Mortuary *'05*
The Hills Have Eyes *'06*
Jam *'06*
Easy A *'10*
Norman *'10*

David Byrd (1933-2001)
The Proposition *'97*
Thick as Thieves *'99*

Eugene Byrd (1975-)
Lift *'01*
8 Mile *'02*
Survival Island *'02*
Anacondas: The Hunt for the Blood Orchid *'04*
Paranoia 1.0 *'04*
Confess *'05*
Rails & Ties *'07*
How to Make Love to a Woman *'09*

Ralph Byrd (1909-52)
Blake of Scotland Yard *'36*
Dick Tracy *'37*
S.O.S. Coast Guard *'37*
Born to Be Wild *'38*
Dick Tracy Returns *'38*
The Howards of Virginia *'40*
The Son of Monte Cristo *'40*
Desperate Cargo *'41*
Dick Tracy *vs.* Crime Inc. *'41*
Life Begins for Andy Hardy *'41*
The Jungle Book *'42*
Moontide *'42*
Guadalcanal Diary *'43*

Dick Tracy Meets Gruesome *'47*
Stage Struck *'48*

Thomas Jefferson Byrd (1941-)
Girls of the White Orchid *'85*
Get On the Bus *'96*
Set It Off *'96*
He Got Game *'98*
Bamboozled *'00*
MacArthur Park *'01*
Ray *'04*
Red Hook Summer *'12*

Anne Byrne (1943-)
A Night Full of Rain *'78*
Manhattan *'79*

Antony Byrne (1969-)
Catherine Cookson's The Cinder Path *'94*
Touching Evil *'97*
High Plains Invaders *'09*

Barbara Byrne
Svengali *'83*
Sunday in the Park with George *'86*

David Byrne (1952-)
True Stories *'86*
Heavy Petting *'89*
This Must Be the Place *'12*

Gabriel Byrne (1950-)
Excalibur *'81*
Defense of the Realm *'85*
Gothic *'87*
Hello Again *'87*
Lionheart *'87*
Dark Obsession *'90*
Miller's Crossing *'90*
Shipwrecked *'90*
A Soldier's Tale *'91*
Cool World *'92*
Into the West *'92*
Point of No Return *'93*
Little Women *'94*
Royal Deceit *'94*
A Simple Twist of Fate *'94*
Trial by Jury *'94*
Buffalo Girls *'95*
Dead Man *'95*
The Usual Suspects *'95*
The Brylcreem Boys *'96*
The Last of the High Kings *'96*
Smilla's Sense of Snow *'96*
Trigger Happy *'96*
The End of Violence *'97*
Polish Wedding *'97*
Weapons of Mass Distraction *'97*
Enemy of the State *'98*
The Man in the Iron Mask *'98*
Quest for Camelot *'98 (V)*
End of Days *'99*
Stigmata *'99*
Ghost Ship *'02*
Killing Emmett Young *'02*
Spider *'02*
Shade *'03*
P.S. *'04*
Vanity Fair *'04*
Assault on Precinct 13 *'05*
The Bridge of San Luis Rey *'05*
Wah-Wah *'05*
Jindabyne *'06*
Played *'06*
Autumn Hearts: A New Beginning *'07*
Attack on Leningrad *'09*
Perrier's Bounty *'09 (V)*
Capital *'12*
Secret State *'12*
All Things to All Men *'13*
Vampire Academy *'14*
Louder Than Bombs *'16*
Carrie Pilby *'17*
Hereditary *'18*
An L.A. Minute *'18*

Michael Byrne (1943-)
Vampyres *'74*
Smiley's People *'82*
The Good Father *'87*
Indiana Jones and the Last Crusade *'89*
Sharpe's Enemy *'94*
Sharpe's Honour *'94*
The Infiltrator *'95*
Agatha Christie's The Pale Horse *'96*
Apt Pupil *'97*
The Saint *'97*
Gunshy *'98*
Heat of the Sun *'99*
Battlefield Earth *'00*
Mists of Avalon *'01*
The Musketeer *'01*
The Sum of All Fears *'02*
Outpost: Black Sun *'12*

P.J. Byrne (1974-)
29 Palms *'03*
Finding Bliss *'09*
Final Destination 5 *'11*
The Wolf of Wall Street *'13*

Rose Byrne (1979-)
Two Hands *'98*
The Goddess of 1967 *'00*
I Capture the Castle *'02*
Star Wars: Episode 2-Attack of the Clones *'02*
City of Ghosts *'03*
The Night We Called It a Day *'03*
The Rage In Placid Lake *'03*
Troy *'04*
Wicker Park *'04*
Casanova *'05*
The Dead Girl *'06*
Marie Antoinette *'06*
The Tenants *'06*
Just Buried *'07*
Sunshine *'07*
28 Weeks Later *'07*
The Boxer and the Bombshell *'08*
Adam *'09*
Knowing *'09*
Get Him to the Greek *'10*
Insidious *'10*
Bridesmaids *'11*
X-Men: First Class *'11*
I Give It a Year *'13*
Insidious: Chapter 2 *'13*
The Internship *'13*
The Place Beyond the Pines *'13*
Annie *'14*
Neighbors *'14*
This Is Where I Leave You *'14*
The Meddler *'15*
Spy *'15*
Neighbors 2: Sorority Rising *'16*
Instant Family *'18*
Juliet, Naked *'18*
Peter Rabbit *'18*
Jexi *'19*
Irresistible *'20*
Like a Boss *'20*

David Byrnes (1952-)
Witchcraft 7: Judgement Hour *'95*
Witchcraft 9: Bitter Flesh *'96*

Edd Byrnes (1932-2020)
Darby's Rangers *'58*
The Secret Invasion *'64*
Any Gun Can Play *'67*
Go Kill and Come Back *'68*
Wicked, Wicked *'73*
Grease *'78*
Back to the Beach *'87*
Troop Beverly Hills *'89*

Jim Byrnes (1948-)
Highlander: Endgame *'00*
Don't Cry Now *'07*
Highlander: The Source *'07*

Josephine Byrnes (1966-)
Brides of Christ *'91*
Oscar and Lucinda *'97*

Arthur Byron (1872-1943)
The Mummy *'32*
Gabriel Over the White House *'33*
Fog Over Frisco *'34*
The Casino Murder Case *'35*
The Whole Town's Talking *'35*

A.S. Byron (1876-)
Fast Life *'32*
The Secret Bride *'35*

David Byron
My Brother's Wife *'89*
Doing Time on Maple Drive *'92*

Jean Byron (1925-2006)
The Magnetic Monster *'53*
Jungle Moon Men *'55*
Invisible Invaders *'59*

Jeffrey Byron (1955-)
Hot Rods to Hell *'67*
Legend of the Northwest *'78*
The Seniors *'78*
Dungeonmaster *'83*
Metalstorm: The Destruction of Jared Syn *'83*

Kathleen Byron (1921-2009)
Stairway to Heaven *'46*
Black Narcissus *'47*
The Small Back Room *'49*
Hell Is Sold Out *'51*
I'll Never Forget You *'51*
The Gambler & the Lady *'52*
Young Bess *'53*
Burn, Witch, Burn! *'62*
Twins of Evil *'71*
The Golden Bowl *'72*
The Moonstone *'72*
The Abdication *'74*
From a Far Country: Pope John Paul II *'81*

Walter Byron (1899-1972)
Queen Kelly *'29*
The Last Flight *'31*
The Reckless Hour *'31*
The Crusader *'32*
Three Wise Girls *'32*
Vanity Fair *'32*
East of Fifth Avenue *'33*
Folies Bergere de Paris *'35*

Susan Byun
Final Combination *'93*
Deadly Target *'94*
Sgt. Kabukiman N.Y.P.D. *'94*

James Caan (1939-)
Lady in a Cage *'64*
Red Line 7000 *'65*
El Dorado *'67*
Games *'67*
Countdown *'68*
The Rain People *'69*
Rabbit, Run *'70*
Brian's Song *'71*
The Godfather *'72*
Gone with the West *'72*
Cinderella Liberty *'73*
Slither *'73*
Freebie & the Bean *'74*
The Gambler *'74*
The Godfather, Part 2 *'74*
Funny Lady *'75*
The Killer Elite *'75*
Rollerball *'75*
Harry & Walter Go to New York *'76*
Silent Movie *'76*
Another Man, Another Chance *'77*
A Bridge Too Far *'77*
Comes a Horseman *'78*
Little Moon & Jud McGraw *'78*
Chapter Two *'79*
Hide in Plain Sight *'80*
Thief *'81*
Bolero *'82*
Kiss Me Goodbye *'82*
Gardens of Stone *'87*
Alien Nation *'88*
Dick Tracy *'90*
Misery *'90*
The Dark Backward *'91*
For the Boys *'91*
Honeymoon in Vegas *'92*
Flesh and Bone *'93*
The Program *'93*
Bottle Rocket *'95*
Bulletproof *'96*
Eraser *'96*
North Star *'96*
Poodle Springs *'98*
Mickey Blue Eyes *'99*
This Is My Father *'99*
Luckytown *'00*
Way of the Gun *'00*
The Yards *'00*
Dead Simple *'01*
A Glimpse of Hell *'01*
In the Shadows *'01*
Blood Crime *'02*
The Lathe of Heaven *'02*
Night at the Golden Eagle *'02 (C)*
City of Ghosts *'03*
Dallas 362 *'03*
Dogville *'03*
Elf *'03*
The Incredible Mrs. Ritchie *'03*
Jericho Mansions *'03*
This Thing of Ours *'03*
Get Smart *'08*
Wisegal *'08*
Cloudy with a Chance of Meatballs *'09 (V)*
Hugh Hefner: Playboy, Activist and Rebel *'09*
Mercy *'09*
New York, I Love You *'09*
Henry's Crime *'10*
Middle Men *'10*
Detachment *'12*
Small Apartments *'12*
That's My Boy *'12*
Blood Ties *'13*
Cloudy with a Chance of Meatballs 2 *'13 (V)*
The Tale of the Princess Kaguya *'13 (V)*
A Fighting Man *'14*
The Outsider *'14*
The Good Neighbor *'16*
Out of Blue *'19*

Scott Caan (1976-)
Bongwater *'98*
Enemy of the State *'98*
Varsity Blues *'98*
Black and White *'99*
Speed of Life *'99*
Boiler Room *'00*
Gone in 60 Seconds *'00*
Ready to Rumble *'00*
American Outlaws *'01*
Novocaine *'01*
Ocean's Eleven *'01*
Sonny *'02*
Dallas 362 *'03*
In Enemy Hands *'04*
Ocean's Twelve *'04*
Into the Blue *'05*
The Dog Problem *'06*
Friends with Money *'06*
Lonely Hearts *'06*
Brooklyn Rules *'07*
Ocean's Thirteen *'07*
Meet Dave *'08*
Mercy *'09*
A Beginner's Guide to Endings *'10*
Rock the Kasbah *'15*

Katia Caballero
Sharpe's Eagle *'93*
Madeline *'98*

Bruce Cabot (1904-72)
Finishing School *'33*
King Kong *'33*
His Greatest Gamble *'34*
Murder On the Blackboard *'34*
Night Alarm *'34*
Let 'Em Have It *'35*
Fury *'36*
The Last of the Mohicans *'36*
The Bad Man of Brimstone *'38*
Smashing the Rackets *'38*
Dodge City *'39*
Susan and God *'40*
The Flame of New Orleans *'41*
Sundown *'41*
Silver Queen *'42*
The Desert Song *'43*
Fallen Angel *'45*
Salty O'Rourke *'45*
Angel and the Badman *'47*
Gunfighters *'47*
Sorrowful Jones *'49*
Best of the Badmen *'50*
Fancy Pants *'50*
Kid Monk Baroni *'52*
Lost in Alaska *'52*
Goliath and the Barbarians *'60*
The Comancheros *'61*
Goliath and the Dragon *'61*
Hatari! *'62*
McLintock! *'63*
In Harm's Way *'65*
The War Wagon *'67*
The Green Berets *'68*
Hellfighters *'68*
The Undefeated *'69*
Chisum *'70*
Diamonds Are Forever *'71*

Christina Cabot (1969-)
The Italian Job *'03*
The Maldonado Miracle *'03*
The Incredible Hulk *'08*

Sebastian Cabot (1918-77)
Old Mother Riley's New Venture *'49*
Midnight Episode *'50*
Old Mother Riley's Jungle Treasure *'51*
Captain's Paradise *'53*
Romeo and Juliet *'54*
Westward Ho, the Wagons! *'56*
Black Patch *'57*
Omar Khayyam *'57*
Johnny Tremain & the Sons of Liberty *'58*
Terror in a Texas Town *'58*
Seven Thieves *'60*
The Time Machine *'60*
The Sword in the Stone *'63 (V)*
Twice-Told Tales *'63*
The Family Jewels *'65*
The Jungle Book *'67 (V)*
The Many Adventures of Winnie the Pooh *'77 (N)*

Susan Cabot (1927-86)
Duel at Silver Creek *'52*
Son of Ali Baba *'52*
Ride Clear of Diablo *'54*
Carnival Rock *'57*
The Viking Women and the Sea Serpent *'57*
Fort Massacre *'58*
War of the Satellites *'58*
The Wasp Woman *'59*

Manuel Cabral
Manito *'03*
Apartment 12 *'06*

Richard Cabral
Paranormal Activity: The Marked Ones *'14*
Breaking In *'18*

Santiago Cabrera (1978-)
Love and Other Disasters *'06*
Che *'08*
Transformers: The Last Knight *'17*

Jesus Cabrero (1965-)
Yerma *'99*
Km. 0 *'00*

Daniel Gimenez Cacho (1961-)
Cabeza de Vaca *'90*
Midaq Alley *'95*
Deep Crimson *'96*
Jealousy *'99*
Nicotina *'03*
Bad Education *'04*
Innocent Voices *'04*
Get the Gringo *'12*
The Promise *'17*
Zama *'17*

Jean Cadell (1884-1967)
Love from a Stranger *'37*
Pygmalion *'38*
Madeleine *'50*

Anne-Marie Cadieux (1963-)
Far Side of the Moon *'03*
The Trotsky *'09*
Good Neighbors *'10*

Jason Cadieux
Iron Eagle 4 *'95*
Lilies *'96*

Michael Cadman (1942-)
If. . . *'69*
Poldark 2 *'75*

Frank Cady (1915-2012)
Ace in the Hole *'51*
Let's Make It Legal *'51*
Half a Hero *'53*
The Bad Seed *'56*
Zandy's Bride *'74*

Adolph Caesar (1933-86)
Fist of Fear, Touch of Death *'80*
A Soldier's Story *'84*
The Color Purple *'85*
Club Paradise *'86*

Harry Caesar (1928-94)
Emperor of the North Pole *'73*
The Longest Yard *'74*
The Offspring *'87*
Bird on a Wire *'90*

Sid Caesar (1922-2014)
The Guilt of Janet Ames *'47*
It's a Mad, Mad, Mad, Mad World *'63*
The Busy Body *'67*
A Guide for the Married Man *'67 (C)*
Airport '75 *'75*
Silent Movie *'76*
The Cheap Detective *'78*
Grease *'78*
The Fiendish Plot of Dr. Fu Manchu *'80*
History of the World: Part 1 *'81*
The Munsters' Revenge *'81*
Grease 2 *'82*
Cannonball Run 2 *'84*
Alice in Wonderland *'85*
Vegas Vacation *'96 (C)*
The Wonderful Ice Cream Suit *'98*
Comic Book: The Movie *'04*

Takeshi Caesar
Fudoh: The New Generation *'96*
The Way To Fight *'96*

Cheri Caffaro (1945-)
The Abductors *'72*
Ginger *'72*
Girls Are for Loving *'73*
Savage Sisters *'74*

Peter Caffrey (1949-2008)
Danny Boy *'82*
A Love Divided *'01*

Stephen Caffrey (1959-)
Tour of Duty *'87*
Longtime Companion *'90*
The Babe *'92*
Blowback *'99*

Andrea Cagan
Hot Box *'72*
Teenager *'74*

Nicolas Cage (1964-)
Fast Times at Ridgemont High *'82*
Rumble Fish *'83*
Valley Girl *'83*
Birdy *'84*
The Cotton Club *'84*
Racing with the Moon *'84*
Boy in Blue *'86*
Peggy Sue Got Married *'86*
Moonstruck *'87*
Raising Arizona *'87*
Vampire's Kiss *'88*
Time to Kill *'89*
Fire Birds *'90*
Wild at Heart *'90*
Zandalee *'91*
Honeymoon in Vegas *'92*
Amos and Andrew *'93*
Deadfall *'93*
Red Rock West *'93*
Guarding Tess *'94*
It Could Happen to You *'94*
Kiss of Death *'94*
Trapped in Paradise *'94*
Leaving Las Vegas *'95*

The Rock '96
Con Air '97
Face/Off '97
City of Angels '98
8mm '98
Snake Eyes '98
Bringing Out the Dead '99
Family Man '00
Gone in 60 Seconds '00
Captain Corelli's Mandolin '01
Adaptation '02
Sonny '02
Windtalkers '02
Matchstick Men '03
National Treasure '04
Lord of War '05
The Weather Man '05
The Ant Bully '06 (V)
The Wicker Man '06
World Trade Center '06
Ghost Rider '07
National Treasure: Book of Secrets '07
Next '07
Bangkok Dangerous '08
Astro Boy '09 (V)
Bad Lieutenant: Port of Call New Orleans '09
G-Force '09 (V)
Knowing '09
Kick-Ass '10
Season of the Witch '10
The Sorcerer's Apprentice '10
Drive Angry '11
Trespass '11
Ghost Rider: Spirit of Vengeance '12
Seeking Justice '12
Stolen '12
The Croods '13 (V)
The Frozen Ground '13
Joe '13
Dying of the Light '14
Left Behind '14
Rage '14
Pay the Ghost '15
The Runner '15
Army of One '16
Dog Eat Dog '16
Snowden '16
The Trust '16
USS Indianapolis: Men of Courage '16
Arsenal '17
Inconceivable '17
Mandy '18
211 '18
Color Out of Space '19
Primal '19
Running with the Devil '19
A Score to Settle '19

James Cagney (1899-1986)
Doorway to Hell '30
Blonde Crazy '31
Other Men's Women '31
Public Enemy '31
Smart Money '31
The Crowd Roars '32
Taxi! '32
Winner Take All '32
Footlight Parade '33
Hard to Handle '33
Lady Killer '33
The Mayor of Hell '33
Picture Snatcher '33
Here Comes the Navy '34
Jimmy the Gent '34
Frisco Kid '35
'G' Men '35
The Irish in Us '35
A Midsummer Night's Dream '35
Something to Sing About '36
Angels with Dirty Faces '38
Boy Meets Girl '38
Each Dawn I Die '39
Oklahoma Kid '39
The Roaring Twenties '39
City for Conquest '40
The Fighting 69th '40
Torrid Zone '40
The Bride Came C.O.D. '41
Strawberry Blonde '41
Captains of the Clouds '42
Yankee Doodle Dandy '42
Johnny Come Lately '43
Blood on the Sun '45
13 Rue Madeleine '46
The Time of Your Life '48
White Heat '49
Kiss Tomorrow Goodbye '50
The West Point Story '50
What Price Glory? '52
A Lion Is in the Streets '53
Love Me or Leave Me '55
Mister Roberts '55
Run for Cover '55
The Seven Little Foys '55
These Wilder Years '56
Tribute to a Bad Man '56
Man of a Thousand Faces '57
The Gallant Hours '60
One, Two, Three '61
Ragtime '81

Jeanne Cagney (1908-84)
Yankee Doodle Dandy '42
The Time of Your Life '48
Quicksand '50
Don't Bother to Knock '52
A Lion Is in the Streets '53
Kentucky Rifle '55

William Cagney (1902-88)
Ace of Aces '33
Palooka '34
Flirting With Danger '35

Eddie Cahill (1978-)
Miracle '04
The Narrows '08

Erin Cahill (1980-)
Boogeyman 3 '08
Beverly Hills Chihuahua 2 '10
Weather Wars '11
Beverly Hills Chihuahua 3: Viva La Fiesta! '12
Resident Evil: Vendetta '17

Stan Cahill (1964-)
JFK: Reckless Youth '93
Goldrush: A Real Life Alaskan Adventure '98

Dean Cain (1966-)
Best Men '98
Futuresport '98
Tracked '98
Militia '99
The Broken Hearts Club '00
Final Encounter '00
No Alibi '00
The Runaway '00
Firetrap '01
Rat Race '01
Boa '02
Breakaway '02
Out of Time '03
I Do (But I Don't) '04
Post Impact '04
Bailey's Billion$ '05
Lost '05
A Christmas Wedding '06
September Dawn '07
Ace of Hearts '08
Final Approach '08
Making Mr. Right '08
Aussie and Ted's Great Adventure '09
The Dog Who Saved Christmas '09
The Gambler, the Girl and the Gunslinger '09
Abandoned '10
Bed & Breakfast '10
The Dog Who Saved Christmas Vacation '10
Home Run Showdown '10
Kill Katie Malone '10
A Nanny for Christmas '10
The Case for Christmas '11
The Dog Who Saved Halloween '11
The Dog Who Saved the Holidays '12
Heaven's Door '12
Meant to Be '12
The Tale of the Princess Kaguya '13 (V)
Airplane vs. Volcano '14
A Belle for Christmas '14
God's Not Dead '14
Horse Camp '14
Small Town Santa '14
The Dog Who Saved Easter '15
The Dog Who Saved Summer '15
Vendetta '15

Howard Caine (1926-93)
Pressure Point '62
Watermelon Man '70

Michael Caine (1933-)
Zulu '64
The Ipcress File '65
Alfie '66
Funeral in Berlin '66
Gambit '66
The Wrong Box '66
Billion Dollar Brain '67
Hurry Sundown '67
Woman Times Seven '67
Battle of Britain '69
The Italian Job '69
Too Late the Hero '70
Get Carter '71
The Last Valley '71
Pulp '72
Sleuth '72
X, Y & Zee '72
The Destructors '74
The Man Who Would Be King '75
Romantic Englishwoman '75
The Wilby Conspiracy '75
Harry & Walter Go to New York '76
A Bridge Too Far '77
The Eagle Has Landed '77
California Suite '78
The Swarm '78
Ashanti, Land of No Mercy '79
Beyond the Poseidon Adventure '79
Dressed to Kill '80
The Island '80
The Hand '81
Victory '81
Deathtrap '82
Educating Rita '83
Blame It on Rio '84
The Holcroft Covenant '85
Water '85
Half Moon Street '86
Hannah and Her Sisters '86
Mona Lisa '86
Sweet Liberty '86
The Fourth Protocol '87
Jaws: The Revenge '87
The Whistle Blower '87
Dirty Rotten Scoundrels '88
Jack the Ripper '88
Without a Clue '88
Bullseye! '90
Jekyll and Hyde '90
Mr. Destiny '90
A Shock to the System '90
Blue Ice '92
Death Becomes Her '92
The Muppet Christmas Carol '92
Noises Off '92
On Deadly Ground '94
World War II: When Lions Roared '94
Blood & Wine '96
Curtain Call '97
Mandela and de Klerk '97
Little Voice '98
The Cider House Rules '99
Get Carter '00
Miss Congeniality '00
Quills '00
Shiner '00
Last Orders '01
Quicksand '01
Austin Powers In Goldmember '02
The Quiet American '02
Secondhand Lions '03
The Statement '03
Around the Bend '04
Batman Begins '05
Bewitched '05
The Weather Man '05
Children of Men '06
The Prestige '06
Flawless '07
Sleuth '07
The Dark Knight '08
Is Anybody There? '08
Harry Brown '09
Inception '10
Cars 2 '11 (V)
Gnomeo & Juliet '11 (V)
The Dark Knight Rises '12
Journey 2: The Mysterious Island '12
Last Love '13
Now You See Me '13
Stonehearst Asylum '13
Interstellar '14
Kingsman: The Secret Service '15
Youth '15
Now You See Me 2 '16
Going in Style '17
Dear Dictator '18

John Cairney (1930-)
A Night to Remember '58
The Flesh and the Fiends '60
The Devil-Ship Pirates '64

Leah Cairns (1974-)
Blood Angels '05
Helen '09
Super Storm '12

Jonathan Cake (1967-)
Catherine Cookson's The Girl '96
The Tenant of Wildfell Hall '96
A Dance to the Music of Time '97
Rebecca '97
Diamond Girl '98
Noah's Ark '99
Out of the Ashes '03
Brideshead Revisited '08
Krews '10

Tony Calabretta
Federal Protection '02
Banshee '06

Thomas Calabro (1959-)
Chill '06
Cake: A Wedding Story '07
Ice Spiders '07
Safehouse '08
Hidden Away '13

Clara Calamai (1915-98)
Ossessione '42
White Nights '57
Deep Red: Hatchet Murders '75

Todd Caldecott
Fear '96
Mother, May I Sleep With Danger? '96

David Calder (1946-)
A Question of Attribution '91
Cracker: Brotherly Love '95
The World Is Not Enough '99
The King Is Alive '00
Love or Money '01
Titanic '12

Anna Calder-Marshall (1947-)
Pussycat, Pussycat, I Love You '70
Wuthering Heights '70

Paul Calderon (1959-)
Q & A '90
Bad Lieutenant '92
Crisscross '92
Condition Red '95
Four Rooms '95
Lotto Land '95
Girlfight '99
Once in the Life '00
The Last Castle '01
3 A.M. '01
Kill the Poor '03
21 Grams '03
The Sentinel '06
Pistol Whipped '08
The Hungry Ghosts '09
Burning Daylight '10
Gun '10
Why Stop Now '12
Welcome to New York '15
The Strike '16

Sergio Calderon (1945-)
Old Gringo '89
Border Shootout '90
Men in Black '97
The Missing '03
Little Fockers '10

Andrew Caldwell
Shredderman Rules '07
College '08
Haunt '19

L. Scott Caldwell (1944-)
God Bless the Child '88
Like Dandelion Dust '09
Division 19 '19

Sandra Caldwell
Love Songs '99
The Cheetah Girls '03
Double Wedding '10

Zoe Caldwell (1933-2020)
The Purple Rose of Cairo '85
Just a Kiss '02
Lilo & Stitch '02 (V)
Birth '04
Leroy and Stitch '06 (V)
Extremely Loud and Incredibly Close '11

David Cale
The Slaughter Rule '01
Light from Light '19

Paula Cale (1970-)
Milo '98
Brian's Song '01

Anthony Calf (1959-)
Sirens '02
Dead Cool '04
Beau Brummell: This Charming Man '06
Upstairs Downstairs '11

Don Calfa (1939-)
Cinderella Liberty '73
Foul Play '78
Return of the Living Dead '85
Weekend at Bernie's '89
Chopper Chicks in Zombietown '91
Terrified '94

Nicole Calfan
The Four Musketeers '75
A Model Employee '02

Louis Calhern (1895-1956)
Blonde Crazy '31
Frisco Jenny '32
Night After Night '32
They Call It Sin '32
Duck Soup '33
20,000 Years in Sing Sing '33
The World Gone Mad '33
The Count of Monte Cristo '34
The Man with Two Faces '34
Last Days of Pompeii '35
The Gorgeous Hussy '36
Fast Company '38
Juarez '39
I Take This Woman '40
Heaven Can Wait '43
The Bridge of San Luis Rey '44
Up in Arms '44
Notorious '46
Arch of Triumph '48
The Red Pony '49
Annie Get Your Gun '50
The Asphalt Jungle '50
The Devil's Doorway '50
A Life of Her Own '50
The Magnificent Yankee '50
Nancy Goes to Rio '50
The Red Danube '50
Two Weeks with Love '50
Invitation '51
The Man With a Cloak '51
Prisoner of Zenda '52
We're Not Married '52
Confidentially Connie '53
Julius Caesar '53
Athena '54
Betrayed '54
Executive Suite '54
Men of the Fighting Lady '54
Rhapsody '54
The Student Prince '54
Blackboard Jungle '55
The Prodigal '55
Forever Darling '56
High Society '56

Monica Calhoun (1971-)
Bagdad Cafe '88
The Players Club '98
The Best Man '99
Civil Brand '02
Gang of Roses '03
The Salon '05
The Best Man Holiday '13

Rory Calhoun (1922-99)
The Red House '47
That Hagen Girl '47
Miraculous Journey '48
Massacre River '49
I'd Climb the Highest Mountain '51
Meet Me After the Show '51
Way of a Gaucho '52
With a Song in My Heart '52
Powder River '53
The Silver Whip '53
A Bullet Is Waiting '54
Dawn at Socorro '54
River of No Return '54
The Big Caper '57
Apache Territory '58
Hard Drivin' '60
Thunder in Carolina '60
The Colossus of Rhodes '61
The Secret of Monte Cristo '61
The Gun Hawk '63
Operation Cross Eagles '69
Night of the Lepus '72
Mission to Glory '80
Motel Hell '80
Smokey & the Judge '80
Angel '84
Avenging Angel '85
Hell Comes to Frogtown '88
Bad Jim '89
Pure Country '92

Joseph Cali (1950-)
Saturday Night Fever '77
The Competition '80

George Calil
Pterodactyl '05
Lost Colony: The Legend of Roanoke '07

Natasha Calis (1999-)
Christmas Caper '07
Held Hostage '09
Daydream Nation '10
Donovan's Echo '11
The Possession '12

Brandon Call (1976-)
The Adventures of Ford Fairlane '90
Blind Fury '90
For the Boys '91

David Call (1982-)
Beautiful Ohio '06
Tiny Furniture '10
Dead Man's Burden '12

R.D. Call (1950-)
The Children of Times Square '86
Colors '88
Young Guns 2 '90
Other People's Money '91
Stephen King's Golden Years '91
Waterworld '95
Last Man Standing '96
Logan's War: Bound by Honor '98
Murder by Numbers '02
Dark Heart '06

James Callahan (1930-2007)
Tropic of Cancer '70
Lady Sings the Blues '72
Missiles of October '74
Outlaw Blues '77
Freddy vs. Jason '03

Mars Callahan (1971-)
Kalifornia *'93*
Poolhall Junkies *'02*
What Love Is *'07*
Steve Callahan
East Side Story *'07*
Role/Play *'10*
K. Callan (1942-)
A Touch of Class *'73*
American Gigolo *'79*
Frankie and Johnny *'91*
The Unborn *'91*
Crazylove *'05*
Midnight Clear *'06*
Michael Callan (1935-)
Because They're Young *'60*
Gidget Goes Hawaiian *'61*
Mysterious Island *'61*
Bon Voyage! *'62*
The Interns *'62*
13 West Street *'62*
Cat Ballou *'65*
You Must Be Joking! *'65*
Frasier the Sensuous Lion *'73*
Lepke *'75*
The Cat and the Canary *'79*
Double Exposure *'82*
Freeway *'88*
Leprechaun 3 *'95*
Charlie Callas (1927-2011)
Pete's Dragon *'77 (V)*
History of the World: Part 1 *'81*
Amazon Women on the Moon *'87*
Vampire Vixens from Venus *'94*
Joseph Calleia (1897-1975)
Riff Raff *'35*
After the Thin Man *'36*
Exclusive Story *'36*
Algiers *'38*
The Bad Man of Brimstone *'38*
Marie Antoinette *'38*
Golden Boy *'39*
Juarez *'39*
My Little Chickadee *'40*
Sundown *'41*
The Glass Key *'42*
The Jungle Book *'42*
The Cross of Lorraine *'43*
For Whom the Bell Tolls *'43*
The Conspirators *'44*
Deadline at Dawn *'46*
Gilda *'46*
Lured *'47*
The Noose Hangs High *'48*
Branded *'50*
Captain Carey, U.S.A. *'50*
The Iron Mistress *'52*
Yankee Buccaneer *'52*
The Caddy *'53*
The Littlest Outlaw *'54*
Hot Blood *'56*
Serenade *'56*
Wild Is the Wind *'57*
Touch of Evil *'58*
The Alamo *'60*
Bryan Callen (1967-)
Fish Without a Bicycle *'03*
Scary Movie 4 *'06*
I Do & I Don't *'07*
10 Rules for Sleeping Around *'13*
My Man Is a Loser *'14*
Ride Along *'14*
Dayton Callie (1946-)
The Last Days of Frankie the Fly *'96*
Executive Target *'97*
Undisputed *'02*
The Motel Life *'12*
Abattoir *'17*
Sarah Wayne Callies (1977-)
The Celestine Prophecy *'06*
Whisper *'07*
Prison Break: The Final Break *'09*
Faces in the Crowd *'11*
Into the Storm *'14*
Pay the Ghost *'15*
The Other Side of the Door *'16*
James Callis (1971-)
Heat of the Sun *'99*
The Scarlet Pimpernel 2: Mademoiselle Guillotine *'99*
Bridget Jones's Diary *'01*
Helen of Troy *'03*
Bridget Jones: The Edge of Reason *'04*
Dead Cool *'04*
Merlin and the Book of Beasts *'09*
Austenland *'13*
Simon Callow (1949-)
Amadeus *'84*
A Room with a View *'86*
The Good Father *'87*
Maurice *'87*
Mr. & Mrs. Bridge *'90*
The Crucifer of Blood *'91*
Howard's End *'92 (C)*
Four Weddings and a Funeral *'94*
Street Fighter *'94*
Ace Ventura: When Nature Calls *'95*
Victory *'95*
James and the Giant Peach *'96 (V)*
The Scarlet Tunic *'97*
The Woman in White *'97*
Bedrooms and Hallways *'98*
Shakespeare in Love *'98*
No Man's Land *'01*
Angels in America *'03*
Bright Young Things *'03*
George and the Dragon *'04*
Merci Docteur Rey *'04*
The Phantom of the Opera *'04*
Bob the Butler *'05*
The Curse of King Tut's Tomb *'06*
Arn: The Knight Templar *'07*
Surveillance 24/7 *'07*
Love's Kitchen *'11*
The Man Who Invented Christmas *'17*
Blue Iguana *'18*
Cab Calloway (1907-94)
International House *'33*
Manhattan Merry-Go-Round *'37*
Stormy Weather *'43*
Sensations of 1945 *'44*
The Cincinnati Kid *'65*
The Littlest Angel *'69*
The Blues Brothers *'80*
Kirk Calloway (1960-)
Summertree *'71*
Cinderella Liberty *'73*
Vanessa Bell Calloway (1957-)
Number One with a Bullet *'87*
Coming to America *'88*
Bebe's Kids *'92 (V)*
What's Love Got to Do with It? *'93*
America's Dream *'95*
Crimson Tide *'95*
Daylight *'96*
The Temptations *'98*
All About You *'01*
The Red Sneakers *'01*
Dawg *'02*
Biker Boyz *'03*
Cheaper by the Dozen *'03*
Love Don't Cost a Thing *'03*
Aussie and Ted's Great Adventure *'09*
Southside with You *'16*
Carla Calo (1926-2019)
Caesar the Conqueror *'63*
Ali Baba and the Seven Saracens *'64*
Michael Caloz (1985-)
Screamers *'96*
Little Men *'98*
Escape from Wildcat Canyon *'99*
Daniel Caltagirone (1972-)
The Fall *'06*
The Reeds *'09*
Outpost: Black Sun *'12*
Eliminators *'16*
Donald Calthrop (1888-1940)
Blackmail *'29*
Red Ensign *'34*
The Phantom Light *'35*
Phyllis Calvert (1915-2002)
The Man in Grey *'43*
Two Thousand Women *'44*
Madonna of the Seven Moons *'45*
The Magic Bow *'47*
Man of Evil *'48*
Appointment With Danger *'51*
Child in the House *'56*
Indiscreet *'58*
The Walking Stick *'70*
Corinne Calvet (1925-2001)
Rope of Sand *'49*
My Friend Irma Goes West *'50*
What Price Glory? *'52*
Powder River *'53*
Far Country *'55*
Henry Calvin (1918-75)
The Broken Star *'56*
Toby Tyler *'59*
The Sign of Zorro *'60*
John Calvin (1947-)
Winter Kill *'74*
California Dreaming *'79*
Ghostwarrior *'86*
Back to the Beach *'87*
The Siege of Firebase Gloria *'89*
The Magic Bubble *'93*
Armando Calvo (1919-96)
The Witch's Mirror *'60*
Ringo's Mark of Vengeance *'67*
Ringo, the Lone Rider *'68*
Jose Calvo
Fort Yuma Gold *'66*
Twice a Judas *'69*
Mark Camacho (1964-)
The Kid *'97*
Codename: Jaguar *'98*
Stalker *'98*
Dead Silent *'99*
Killing Moon *'00*
Nowhere in Sight *'01*
Stiletto Dance *'01*
Obsessed *'02*
Jericho Mansions *'03*
My Neighbor's Secret *'09*
Javier Camara (1967-)
Sex and Lucia *'01*
Talk to Her *'02*
Torremolinos 73 *'03*
Bad Education *'04*
Chef's Special *'08*
I'm So Excited *'13*
Christian Camargo (1971-)
Harlem Aria *'99*
Lip Service *'00*
K-19: The Widowmaker *'02*
The Hurt Locker *'08*
Happy Tears *'09*
Europa Report *'13*
Days and Nights *'14*
Danielle Camastra
Price of Glory *'00*
ESL: English as a Second Language *'05*
Godfrey Cambridge (1933-76)
Gone Are the Days *'63*
Purlie Victorious *'63*
The Busy Body *'67*
Bye Bye Braverman *'67*
The President's Analyst *'67*
The Biggest Bundle of Them All *'68*
Cotton Comes to Harlem *'70*
Watermelon Man *'70*
Beware! The Blob *'72*
Friday Foster *'75*
Whiffs *'75*
Scott Joplin *'77*
Joan Camden (1929-2000)
The Captive City *'52*
Gunfight at the O.K. Corral *'57*
Cody Cameron (1970-)
Shrek the Third *'07 (V)*
Open Season 2 *'08 (V)*
Open Season 3 *'10 (V)*
Dean Cameron (1962-)
Summer School *'87*
Bad Dreams *'88*
Rockula *'90*
Ski School *'91*
Miracle Beach *'92*
The Ghost Brigade *'93*
Ski School 2 *'94*
Sleep with Me *'94*
Highball *'97*
Earl Cameron (1917-2020)
Submarine Attack *'54*
Flame in the Streets *'61*
Tarzan's Three Challenges *'63*
The Interpreter *'05*
James Cameron (1954-)
Last Action Hero *'93 (C)*
The Muse *'99 (C)*
Kirk Cameron (1970-)
The Best of Times *'86*
Like Father, Like Son *'87*
The Growing Pains Movie *'00*
Left Behind: The Movie *'00*
Growing Pains: Return of the Seavers *'04*
Fireproof *'08*
Saving Christmas *'14*
Rod Cameron (1910-83)
No Hands on the Clock *'41*
Wake Island *'42*
G-Men *vs.* the Black Dragon *'43*
Panhandle *'48*
Stampede *'49*
Short Grass *'50*
Cavalry Scout *'51*
Fort Osage *'51*
Jungle *'52*
Wagons West *'52*
The Steel Lady *'53*
Southwest Passage *'54*
The Electronic Monster *'57*
The Gun Hawk *'63*
Thunder at the Border *'66*
Evel Knievel *'72*
Psychic Killer *'75*
Trent Cameron (1979-)
The Wood *'99*
Shot *'01*
Fighting the Odds: The Marilyn Gambrell Story *'05*
Candace Cameron Bure (1976-)
NightScreams *'97*
Moonlight & Mistletoe *'08*
Truth Be Told *'11*
Finding Normal *'13*
Jesse Cameron-Glickenhaus
Slaughter of the Innocents *'93*
Timemaster *'95*
Jaime Camil
Pulling Strings *'13*
Madness in the Method *'19*
Terry Camillieri (1949-)
The Cars That Ate Paris *'74*
Bill & Ted's Excellent Adventure *'89*
The Invisibles *'99*
Anna Camp (1982-)
Pitch Perfect *'12*
Goodbye to All That *'14*
Pitch Perfect 3 *'17*
The Wedding Year *'19*
The Lovebirds *'20*
Bill Camp
Tamara Drewe *'10*
Compliance *'12*
12 Years a Slave *'13*
Woman Walks Ahead *'17*
Skin *'18*
Wildlife *'18*
Native Son *'19*
Colleen Camp (1953-)
Cat in the Cage *'68*
The Last Porno Flick *'74*
The Swinging Cheerleaders *'74*
Smile *'75*
She Devils in Chains *'76*
Death Game *'77*
Seducers *'77*
Apocalypse Now *'79*
Game of Death *'79*
They All Laughed *'81*
The Seduction *'82*
Smokey and the Bandit, Part 3 *'83*
Valley Girl *'83*
Clue *'85*
D.A.R.Y.L. *'85*
Doin' Time *'85*
Police Academy 2: Their First Assignment *'85*
Rosebud Beach Hotel *'85*
Illegally Yours *'87*
Police Academy 4: Citizens on Patrol *'87*
Walk Like a Man *'87*
Track 29 *'88*
Wicked Stepmother *'89*
Backfield in Motion *'91*
Wayne's World *'92*
The Magic Bubble *'93*
Sliver *'93*
Greedy *'94*
Die Hard: With a Vengeance *'95*
Plump Fiction *'97*
Speed 2: Cruise Control *'97*
Election *'99*
Loser *'00*
Joshua *'02*
Trapped *'02*
In Good Company *'04*
Mystery Woman: Mystery Weekend *'05*
Four Christmases *'08*
Psych: 9 *'10*
Knock Knock *'15*
Hamilton Camp (1934-2005)
Eating Raoul *'82*
Under Fire *'83*
Meatballs 2 *'84*
Rosebud Beach Hotel *'85*
Attack of the 50 Ft. Woman *'93*
All Dogs Go to Heaven 2 *'95 (V)*
Almost Heroes *'97*
Hard Four *'07*
Bernard Campan
How Much Do You Love Me? *'05*
The Man of My Life *'06*
Frank Campanella (1919-2006)
The Producers *'68*
Chesty Anderson USN *'76*
Blood Red *'88*
Joseph Campanella (1924-)
The St. Valentine's Day Massacre *'67*
Murder Once Removed *'71*
Terror on the 40th Floor *'74*
Return to Fantasy Island *'77*
Pearl *'78 (N)*
Meteor *'79*
Hangar 18 *'80*
Steele Justice *'87*
Down the Drain *'89*
Body Chemistry *'90*
Club Fed *'90*
Last Call *'90*
Original Intent *'91*
Magic Kid *'92*
James Dean: Live Fast, Die Young *'97*
The Dukes *'07*
Adam Campbell (1980-)
Date Movie *'06*
Epic Movie *'07*
Spin *'07*
Alex Campbell (1984-)
Verdict in Blood *'02*
Siblings *'04*
Beatrice Campbell (1922-79)
Last Holiday *'50*
The Mudlark *'50*
I'll Never Forget You *'51*
Grand National Night *'53*
The Master of Ballantrae *'53*
Billy Campbell (1959-)
The Rocketeer *'91*
Bram Stoker's Dracula *'92*
Armistead Maupin's Tales of the City *'93*
Gettysburg *'93*
The Brylcreem Boys *'96*
The Cold Equations *'96*
Menno's Mind *'96*
Armistead Maupin's More Tales of the City *'97*
Rudyard Kipling's the Second Jungle Book: Mowgli and Baloo *'97*
Enough *'02*
The Rising Place *'02*
Ann Rule Presents: The Stranger Beside Me *'03*
Gods and Generals *'03*
The Circuit *'08*
Ghost Town *'08*
Meteor *'09*
Fat Kid Rules the World *'12*
Copperhead *'13*
Killing Lincoln *'13*
Lizzie Borden Took an Ax *'14*
The Scribbler *'14*
Bruce Campbell (1958-)
Evil Dead *'83*
Going Back *'83*
Evil Dead 2: Dead by Dawn *'87*
Thou Shalt Not Kill. . .Except *'87*
Maniac Cop *'88*
Darkman *'90*
Maniac Cop 2 *'90*
Mindwarp *'91*
Sundown *'91*
Waxwork 2: Lost in Time *'91*
Army of Darkness *'92*
Eddie Presley *'92 (C)*
The Hudsucker Proxy *'93*
Escape from L.A. *'96*
Menno's Mind *'96*
Tornado! *'96*
McHale's Navy *'97*
From Dusk Till Dawn 2: Texas Blood Money *'98*
Goldrush: A Real Life Alaskan Adventure *'98*
The Ice Rink *'99*
The Majestic *'01*
Serving Sara *'02*
Spider-Man *'02 (C)*
Terminal Invasion *'02*
Bubba Ho-Tep *'03*
The Woods *'03*
Comic Book: The Movie *'04 (C)*
Spider-Man 2 *'04*
Alien Apocalypse *'05*
Sky High *'05*
The Ant Bully *'06 (V)*
Touch the Top of the World *'06*
Aqua Teen Hunger Force Colon Movie Film for Theaters *'07 (V)*
Spider-Man 3 *'07*
My Name Is Bruce *'08*
Sundown: The Vampire in Retreat *'08*
Cloudy with a Chance of Meatballs *'09 (V)*
Oz the Great and Powerful *'13 (C)*
Cheryl Campbell (1949-)
Lillie *'79*
Testament of Youth *'79*
Chariots of Fire *'81*
Greystoke: The Legend of Tarzan, Lord of the Apes *'84*
The Shooting Party *'85*

The Mill on the Floss '97
The Way We Live Now '02
Appointment With Death '10

Christa Campbell (1972-)
Showdown at Area 51 '07
Hero Wanted '08
Lies and Illusions '09
Hyenas '10
2001 Maniacs: Field of Screams '10
The Mechanic '11
Spiders '13
Straight A's '13

Christian Campbell (1972-)
City Boy '93
I've Been Waiting for You '98
Too Smooth '98
Next Time '99
Trick '99
Banshee '06
The Betrayed '08
Casino Jack '10
Banner 4th of July '13

Colin Campbell (1859-1928)
Big Boy '30
The Leather Boys '63

Danielle Campbell (1995-)
StarStruck '10
Prom '11
Madea's Witness Protection '12
Being Frank '19

Emma Campbell (1971-)
The Hound of the Baskervilles '00
Nightwaves '03
The House Next Door '06

Glen Campbell (1936-)
True Grit '69
Rock-a-Doodle '92 (V)

J. Kenneth Campbell (1947-)
Operation Delta Force 2: Mayday '97
Ulee's Gold '97
U.S. Seals '98

Jessica Campbell (1982-)
Election '99
The Safety of Objects '01

Judy Campbell (1916-2004)
Convoy '40
Cry of the Penguins '71

Julia Campbell (1962-)
Opportunity Knocks '90
Livin' Large '91
Diary of a Serial Killer '97
Romy and Michele's High School Reunion '97
Poodle Springs '98
A Slight Case of Murder '99
Bounce '00
Stephen King's Rose Red '02
The Craigslist Killer '11

Ken Campbell (1941-)
The Big Red One '80
Smart Money '88

Ken H. Campbell (1963-)
Down Periscope '96
Breakfast of Champions '98

Larry Joe Campbell (1970-)
Jiminy Glick in LaLa Wood '05
Wedding Crashers '05

Louise Campbell (1911-97)
Bulldog Drummond Comes Back '37
Bulldog Drummond's Peril '38
Men with Wings '38

Maia Campbell (1976-)
Parental Guidance '98
Trippin' '99

Michael Leydon Campbell
Sidewalks of New York '01
Knots '05
Bob Funk '09

Naomi Campbell (1970-)
Cool As Ice '91
Miami Rhapsody '95
Girl 6 '96
Prisoner of Love '99

Nell Campbell (1953-)
Lisztomania '75
The Rocky Horror Picture Show '75
Shock Treatment '81
Pink Floyd: The Wall '82
Great Expectations '97

Neve Campbell (1973-)
The Canterville Ghost '96
The Craft '96
Scream '96
Scream 2 '97
54 '98
The Lion King: Simba's Pride '98 (V)
Too Smooth '98
Wild Things '98
Three to Tango '99
Drowning Mona '00
Panic '00
Scream 3 '00
Intimate Affairs '01
Last Call: The Final Chapter of F. Scott Fitzgerald '02
The Company '03
Lost Junction '03
When Will I Be Loved '04
Relative Strangers '06
Closing the Ring '07
I Really Hate My Job '07
Partition '07
Scream 4 '11
Skyscraper '18

Nicholas (Nick) Campbell (1952-)
A Bridge Too Far '77
Fast Company '78
The Victory '81
Children of the Night '85
Rampage '87
The Big Slice '90
Naked Lunch '91
No Contest '94
The Boys Club '96
Hard to Forget '98
New Waterford Girl '99
Full Disclosure '00
We All Fall Down '00
Prozac Nation '01
Turning Paige '01
Siblings '04
Cinderella Man '05
Antiviral '12
Goon '12
Awakening the Zodiac '17

Owen Campbell
Conviction '10
Super Dark Times '17

Paul Campbell (1979-)
The Lunatic '92
Dancehall Queen '97
Third World Cop '99
We'll Meet Again '02
The Long Weekend '05
Play the Game '09

Rob Campbell
Unforgiven '92
Lone Justice 2 '93
The Crucible '96
Hostile Waters '97
Boys Don't Cry '99
Hedwig and the Angry Inch '00

Scott Michael Campbell (1971-)
Radioland Murders '94
Hart's War '02
The Maldonado Miracle '03
Flight of the Phoenix '04
Brokeback Mountain '05
Brothers Three '07
Who's Your Monkey '07
Crazy '08

Sean Campbell
Blackwoods '02
He Sees You When You're Sleeping '02

Tisha Campbell (1968-)
Little Shop of Horrors '86
Rags to Riches '87
School Daze '88
Rooftops '89
Another 48 Hrs. '90
House Party '90
House Party 2: The Pajama Jam '91
Boomerang '92
House Party 3 '94
Sprung '96
Lemonade Mouth '11

William Campbell (1923-2011)
Breakthrough '50
Battle Circus '53
Escape from Fort Bravo '53
The High and the Mighty '54
Battle Cry '55
Cell 2455, Death Row '55
Man Without a Star '55
Backlash '56
Love Me Tender '56
Man in the Vault '56
The Sheriff of Fractured Jaw '59
Night of Evil '62
Dementia 13 '63
The Secret Invasion '64
Portrait in Terror '66
Track of the Vampire '66

Antonia Campbell-Hughes (1982-)
Bright Star '09
Storage 24 '12
The Canal '14
Never Grow Old '19

Frank Campeau (1864-1943)
His Majesty, the American '19
When the Clouds Roll By '19
The First Auto '27
Abraham Lincoln '30
Empty Saddles '36

Bobby Campo (1983-)
The Final Destination '09
Legally Blondes '09
Love's Christmas Journey '11
Unbroken: Path to Redemption '18

Bruno Campos (1973-)
Mimic 2 '01
Dopamine '03
Crazylove '05
The Princess and the Frog '09 (V)

Rafael Campos (1936-85)
Trial '55
Lady in a Cage '64
The Astro-Zombies '67
The Doll Squad '73
The Hanged Man '74
Slumber Party '57 '76
Centennial '78
Where the Buffalo Roam '80
V '83

Cam'ron (1976-)
Paid in Full '02
Killa Season '06
Percentage '13

Ron Canada (1949-)
Play Nice '92
The American President '95
Lone Star '95
Man of the House '95
Pinocchio's Revenge '96
Dean Koontz's Black River '01
The Human Stain '03
The Hunted '03
United States of Leland '03
Cinderella Man '05
Just like Heaven '05
Wedding Crashers '05
Islander '06
Snowglobe '07
The Haunting of Molly Hartley '08
Noble Things '08

Gianna Maria Canale (1927-2009)
Go for Broke! '51
Man from Cairo '54
Sins of Rome '54
I, Vampiri '56
Hercules '58
Colossus and the Amazon Queen '60
The Secret of Monte Cristo '61
The Slave '62
Tiger of the Seven Seas '62

Maria Canals (1966-)
My Family '94
Master of Disguise '02
Imagining Argentina '04

Maria Canals-Barrera
Camp Rock '08
The Wizards of Waverly Place: The Movie '09
God's Not Dead 2 '16

David Canary (1938-)
Melvin Purvis: G-Man '74
Johnny Firecloud '75
Posse '75

Bobby Canavale
Fast Food Nation '06
Ant-Man and the Wasp '18

Urbain Cancellier
Amelie '01
Intimate Strangers '04

Isabelle Candelier
A Good Year '06
Gemma Bovery '15

Candy Candido (1913-99)
Rhythm Parade '43
Peter Pan '53 (V)
The Great Mouse Detective '86 (V)

John Candy (1950-94)
Class of '44 '73
It Seemed Like a Good Idea at the Time '75
Tunnelvision '76
The Silent Partner '78
Lost and Found '79
1941 '79
The Blues Brothers '80
Heavy Metal '81 (V)
Stripes '81
Clown Murders '83
Going Berserk '83
National Lampoon's Vacation '83
Splash '84
Brewster's Millions '85
Sesame Street Presents: Follow That Bird '85
Summer Rental '85
Volunteers '85
Armed and Dangerous '86
Little Shop of Horrors '86
Planes, Trains & Automobiles '87
Spaceballs '87
The Great Outdoors '88
Hot to Trot! '88 (V)
Uncle Buck '89
Who's Harry Crumb? '89
Home Alone '90
The Rescuers Down Under '90 (V)
Career Opportunities '91
Delirious '91
JFK '91
Nothing But Trouble '91
Only the Lonely '91
Once Upon a Crime '92
Cool Runnings '93
Canadian Bacon '94
Wagons East '94

Charles Cane (1899-1973)
Dead Reckoning '47
Revenge of the Creature '55

Natalie Canerday (1962-)
One False Move '91
Sling Blade '96
Gunshy '98
October Sky '99
Tully '00
Shotgun Stories '07
Valley Inn '14

Guillaume Canet (1973-)
The Beach '00
Whatever You Say '02
Love Me if You Dare '03
Joyeux Noel '05
Tell No One '06
Farewell '09
Last Night '10
The Program '15
Non-Fiction '18

Ridge Canipe
The Bad News Bears '05
Pictures of Hollis Woods '07

Bobby Cannavale (1970-)
The Bone Collector '99
3 A.M. '01
Washington Heights '02
The Station Agent '03
The Breakup Artist '04 (C)
Fresh Cut Grass '04
Haven '04
Shall We Dance? '04
Happy Endings '05
Recipe for a Perfect Christmas '05
Romance & Cigarettes '05
The Night Listener '06
Snakes on a Plane '06
10 Items or Less '06
Dedication '07
The Ten '07
Diminished Capacity '08
The Merry Gentleman '08
100 Feet '08
The Promotion '08
Brief Interviews With Hideous Men '09
Paul Blart: Mall Cop '09
Marry Me '10
The Other Guys '10
Weakness '10
Roadie '11
Win Win '11
Blue Jasmine '13
Lovelace '13
Annie '14
Ant-Man '15
Danny Collins '15
Spy '15
Ferdinand '17
I, Tonya '17
The Nut Job 2: Nutty by Nature '17
The Irishman '19
Motherless Brooklyn '19

Stephen J. Cannell (1942-2010)
Posse '93 (C)
Half Past Dead '02
Threshold '03
Ice Spiders '07

Sara Canning (1987-)
Taken in Broad Daylight '09
The Hunt for the I-5 Killer '11
Hannah's Law '12
Garage Sale Mystery '13
The Right Kind Of Wrong '13

Dyan Cannon (1937-)
The Rise and Fall of Legs Diamond '60
Bob & Carol & Ted & Alice '69
Doctors' Wives '70
The Anderson Tapes '71
The Love Machine '71
Such Good Friends '71
The Last of Sheila '73
Shamus '73
The Virginia Hill Story '76
Heaven Can Wait '78
Revenge of the Pink Panther '78
Honeysuckle Rose '80
Author! Author! '82
Deathtrap '82
Caddyshack 2 '88
The End of Innocence '90
Christmas in Connecticut '92
The Pickle '93
8 Heads in a Duffel Bag '96
That Darn Cat '96
Allie & Me '97
Out to Sea '97
Diamond Girl '98

The Sender '98
The Boynton Beach Club '05

Esma Cannon (1896-1972)
Carry On Regardless '61
Carry On Cabby '63

J.D. Cannon (1922-2005)
An American Dream '66
Cool Hand Luke '67
Heaven With a Gun '69
Krakatoa East of Java '69
1,000 Plane Raid '69
Operation Heartbeat '69
Cotton Comes to Harlem '70
Lawman '71
Scorpio '73
Raise the Titanic '80
Death Wish 2 '82

Katherine (Kathy) Cannon (1953-)
Private Duty Nurses '71
The Red Fury '84

Nick Cannon (1980-)
Drumline '02
Love Don't Cost a Thing '03
Garfield: The Movie '04 (V)
Shall We Dance? '04
Roll Bounce '05
Underclassman '05
Bobby '06
Even Money '06
Monster House '06 (V)
American Son '08
The Killing Room '09
Chi-raq '15

Wanda Cannon (1960-)
For the Moment '94
The 6th Day '00
The Christmas Blessing '05
A Trick of the Mind '06

Sibylle Canonica (1957-)
Beyond Silence '96
Mostly Martha '01

Judy Canova (1913-83)
Oklahoma Annie '51
The WAC From Walla Walla '52
The Adventures of Huckleberry Finn '60
Cannonball '76

Anne Canovos
Zeder '83
Ready to Wear '94

Antonio Cantafora (1944-)
And God Said to Cain '69
Torture Chamber of Baron Blood '72
Gabriela '84
Intervista '87

Chandler Canterbury (1998-)
Knowing '09
After.life '10
A Bag of Hammers '11
Angels Sing '13
Standing Up '13

Aldo Canti (1941-90)
Five for Hell '67
Sabata '69
Reactor '78

Jose Pablo Cantillo (1979-)
Crank '06
Cleaner '07
Disturbia '07
Redbelt '08
Streets of Blood '09
Virtuality '09
Chappie '15
El Chicano '19

Marilyne Canto (1963-)
Apres-Vous '03
Comedy of Power '06

Eric Cantona (1966-)
Elizabeth '98
French Film '08
Looking for Eric '09

Mario Cantone (1959-)
The Last Request '06
Surf's Up '07 (V)
Three Days to Vegas '07
Sex and the City: The Movie '08

Hostile Makeover '09
Killer Hair '09
Sex and the City 2 '10
National Lampoon's Dirty Movie '11

Eddie Cantor (1892-1964)
Glorifying the American Girl '30
Whoopee! '30
Kid from Spain '32
Kid Millions '34
Thank Your Lucky Stars '43
Hollywood Canteen '44
Show Business '44
If You Knew Susie '48

Yakima Canutt (1895-1986)
Wild Horse Canyon '25
The Devil Horse '26
Westward Bound '30
Battling with Buffalo Bill '31
Last Frontier '32
Ten Laps to Go '36
Gone with the Wind '39
For Whom the Bell Tolls '43

Peter Capaldi (1958-)
Local Hero '83
Dangerous Liaisons '88
The Lair of the White Worm '88
Selling Hitler '91
Captives '94
The Crow Road '96
Neil Gaiman's NeverWhere '96
Smilla's Sense of Snow '96
Bean '97
Shooting Fish '98
Max '02
Modigliani '04
House of 9 '05
Wild Country '05
Pinochet's Last Stand '06
In the Loop '09
The Fifth Estate '13
Paddington '14

Peter Capell (1912-86)
Walk East on Beacon '52
The Burglar '57
Paths of Glory '57

Robert Capelli, Jr.
Waltzing Anna '06
Breaking Point '09

Laurent Capelluto
A Christmas Tale '08
The Clearstream Affair '15

Virginia Capers (1925-2004)
The North Avenue Irregulars '79
Ferris Bueller's Day Off '86
Jo Jo Dancer, Your Life Is Calling '86

Lizzy Caplan (1982-)
Mean Girls '04
Addicted to Her Love '06
Crashing '07
Cloverfield '08
My Best Friend's Girl '08
The Last Rites of Ransom Pride '09
Hot Tub Time Machine '10
127 Hours '10
Bachelorette '12
Save the Date '12
3, 2, 1...Frankie Go Boom '12
The Interview '14
The Night Before '15
Allied '16
Now You See Me 2 '16

Carissa Capobianco
Dance of the Dead '08
Secretariat '10

Carmine Capobianco (1958-)
Galactic Gigolo '87
Psychos in Love '87

John Capodice (1941-)
The Children of Times Square '86
Family Business '89
Internal Affairs '90
Fever '91
The Hard Way '91
Honeymoon in Vegas '92
Trial by Jury '94
Independence Day '96
Wedding Bell Blues '96
Enemy of the State '98
Executive Power '98
Ringmaster '98
True Friends '98
Double Bang '01
Out of the Black '01
Shut Up and Kiss Me '05

Lino Capolicchio (1943-)
The Garden of the Finzi-Continis '71
The Bloodstained Shadow '78
Fiorile '93
Traveling Companion '96

Joolia Cappleman
Bleak Moments '71
Who's Who '78

Pier Paolo Capponi (1938-)
The King of Hearts '66
Man of Legend '71
Seven Blood-Stained Orchids '72
The Boss '73

Francis Capra (1983-)
A Bronx Tale '93
Kazaam '96
A Simple Wish '97
Venice Underground '05
Black Irish '07
Veronica Mars '14

Ahna Capri (1944-2010)
The Brotherhood of Satan '71
Enter the Dragon '73
Payday '73
The Specialist '75

Vittorio Caprioli (1921-89)
L'Automobile '71
Kidnap Syndicate '76
Le Magnifique '76
Rulers of the City '76

Robert Capron (1998-)
Diary of a Wimpy Kid 2: Rodrick Rules '11
Diary of a Wimpy Kid: Dog Days '12
Frankenweenie '12 (V)

Jessica Capshaw (1976-)
The Locusts '97
Something About Sex '98
Valentine '01
Minority Report '02
Blind Trust '06
The Groomsmen '06
One Angry Juror '10

Kate Capshaw (1953-)
A Little Sex '82
Best Defense '84
Dreamscape '84
Indiana Jones and the Temple of Doom '84
Power '86
SpaceCamp '86
Code Name: Dancer '87
The Quick and the Dead '87
Black Rain '89
Love at Large '89
Just Cause '94
Love Affair '94
How to Make an American Quilt '95
The Locusts '97
The Alarmist '98
The Love Letter '99
A Girl Thing '01
Due East '02

Capucine (1933-90)
North to Alaska '60
Song Without End '60
Walk on the Wild Side '62
The Pink Panther '64
The Seventh Dawn '64
What's New Pussycat? '65
The Queens '66
The Honey Pot '67
Fellini Satyricon '69
The Switch '76
From Hell to Victory '79
Jaguar Lives '79
The Con Artists '80
Trail of the Pink Panther '82
Curse of the Pink Panther '83

Irene Cara (1959-)
Aaron Loves Angela '75
Sparkle '76
Roots: The Next Generation '79
Fame '80
City Heat '84
D.C. Cab '84
Happily Ever After '93 (V)
The Magic Voyage '93 (V)

Paul Carafotes (1963-)
Choices '81
All the Right Moves '83
Journey to the Center of the Earth '88

Ion Caramitru (1942-)
Two Deaths '94
Citizen X '95
Amen '02

Gina Carano (1982-)
Haywire '12
Fast & Furious 6 '13
In the Blood '13
Extraction '15
Madness in the Method '19

Antony Carbone (1927-)
A Bucket of Blood '59
Creature from the Haunted Sea '60
The Last Woman on Earth '61
The Pit and the Pendulum '61
Sex Through a Window '72
The Last Porno Flick '74
Skateboard '77

Nestor Carbonell (1967-)
Attention Shoppers '99
The Laramie Project '02
The Lost City '05
Smokin' Aces '07
The Dark Knight '08
Killer Movie '08
The Dark Knight Rises '12
For Greater Glory '12
Dead Drop '13
Imperium '16

Linda Cardellini (1975-)
Dead Man on Campus '97
Dee Snider's Strangeland '98
The Prince and the Surfer '99
The Unsaid '01
Scooby-Doo '02
Scooby-Doo 2: Monsters Unleashed '04
American Gun '05
Brokeback Mountain '05
Jiminy Glick in LaLa Wood '05
Grandma's Boy '06
Comanche Moon '08
The Lazarus Project '08
Kill the Irishman '11
Return '11
Daddy's Home '15
Welcome to Me '15
Daddy's Home 2 '17
The Founder '17
Green Book '18
Hunter Killer '18
The Curse of La Llorona '19
Capone '20

Stephen Antonio Cardenas (1974-)
Mighty Morphin Power Rangers: The Movie '95
Turbo: A Power Rangers Movie '96

Bill 'Chilly Billy' Cardille (1928-)
Night of the Living Dead '68
Night of the Living Dead '90

Ben Cardinal
By Dawn's Early Light '00
Deepwater '05
Megasnake '07

Tantoo Cardinal (1950-)
Dances with Wolves '90
Black Robe '91
By Way of the Stars '92
Silent Tongue '92
Spirit Rider '93
Legends of the Fall '94
Where the Rivers Flow North '94
The Education of Little Tree '97
Big Bear '98
Smoke Signals '98
The Lost Child '00
Dodson's Journey '01
Edge of Madness '02
Luna: Spirit of the Whale '07
Mom, Dad and Her '08
Older Than America '08
From Above '13

Claudia Cardinale (1938-)
Big Deal on Madonna Street '58
Upstairs and Downstairs '59
The Girl with a Suitcase '60
Rocco and His Brothers '60
Cartouche '62
8 1/2 '63
The Leopard '63
Circus World '64
The Pink Panther '64
The Lost Command '66
The Professionals '66
The Queens '66
Don't Make Waves '67
Once Upon a Time in the West '68
Red Tent '69
Butterfly Affair '71
Conversation Piece '75
Jesus of Nazareth '77
Escape to Athena '79
The Skin '81
Fitzcarraldo '82
The Salamander '82
Princess Daisy '83
Henry IV '85
A Man in Love '87
Son of the Pink Panther '93
And Now Ladies and Gentlemen '02
The String '09
All Roads Lead to Rome '15
Effie Gray '15

Vivien Cardone
A Beautiful Mind '01
All Roads Lead Home '08

John Cardos (1928-)
Blood of Dracula's Castle '69
Satan's Sadists '69

Pedro Cardoso (1962-)
Four Days in September '97
Bossa Nova '99

James B. Cardwell (1920-54)
The Fighting Sullivans '42
Sweet and Low-Down '44
A Walk in the Sun '46
The Devil on Wheels '47

David Cardy
Xtro '83
Fool's Gold: The Story of the Brink's-Mat Robbery '92

Steve Carell (1962-)
Bruce Almighty '03
Anchorman: The Legend of Ron Burgundy '04
Bewitched '05
The 40 Year Old Virgin '05
Little Miss Sunshine '06
Over the Hedge '06 (V)
Dan in Real Life '07
Evan Almighty '07
Dr. Seuss' Horton Hears a Who! '08 (V)
Get Smart '08
Date Night '10
Despicable Me '10 (V)
Dinner for Schmucks '10
Crazy, Stupid, Love. '11
Hope Springs '12
Seeking a Friend for the End of the World '12
Anchorman 2: The Legend Continues '13
Despicable Me 2 '13 (V)
The Incredible Burt Wonderstone '13
The Way Way Back '13
Alexander and the Terrible, Horrible, No Good, Very Bad Day '14
Foxcatcher '14
The Big Short '15
Freeheld '15
Café Society '16
Battle of the Sexes '17
Despicable Me 3 '17 (V)
Last Flag Flying '17
Beautiful Boy '18
Vice '18
Welcome to Marwen '18
Irresistible '20

Julien Carette (1897-1966)
Grand Illusion '37
La Bete Humaine '38
The Rules of the Game '39
The Red Inn '51

Arthur Edmund Carewe (1884-1937)
The Phantom of the Opera '25
The Cat and the Canary '27
The Matrimonial Bed '30
Doctor X '32

Clare Carey (1967-)
Zombie High '87
Betrayed: A Story of Three Women '95
La Cucina '07
Shredderman Rules '07
Flu Birds '08
Doc West '09
The Trial '10

Drew Carey (1958-)
Gepetto '00
Robots '05 (V)

Harry Carey, Jr. (1921-2012)
Pursued '47
Red River '48
The Smallest Show on Earth '48
Three Godfathers '48
She Wore a Yellow Ribbon '49
Copper Canyon '50
Rio Grande '50
Wagon Master '50
Niagara '52
Island in the Sky '53
House of Bamboo '55
Mister Roberts '55
Gun the Man Down '56
The Searchers '56
Seventh Cavalry '56
Rio Bravo '59
Noose for a Gunman '60
Shenandoah '65
Alvarez Kelly '66
Billy the Kid Versus Dracula '66
Bandolero! '68
The Devil's Brigade '68
Death of a Gunfighter '69
The Undefeated '69
The Moonshine War '70
Big Jake '71
Cahill: United States Marshal '73
Trinity Is Still My Name '75
Nickelodeon '76
The Long Riders '80
Endangered Species '82
Mask '85
Challenge to White Fang '86
Crossroads '86
The Whales of August '87
Bad Jim '89
Breaking In '89
Back to the Future, Part 3 '90
Tombstone '93
Last Stand at Saber River '96
Sunchaser '96

Harry Carey, Sr. (1878-1947)
Judith of Bethulia '14
The Trail of '98 '28
Cavalier of the West '31
Vanishing Legion '31
Devil Horse '32
The Last of the Mohicans '32
Last Outlaw '36
Little Miss Nobody '36
The Prisoner of Shark Island '36
Kid Galahad '37
Souls at Sea '37
You and Me '38
Mr. Smith Goes to Washington '39
Beyond Tomorrow '40
The Shepherd of the Hills '41
Sundown '41
The Spoilers '42
Air Force '43
The Great Moment '44
Duel in the Sun '46
Angel and the Badman '47
The Sea of Grass '47
Red River '48
So Dear to My Heart '49

Helen Carey (1944-)
Black Knight '01
21 '08
Julie & Julia '09
The Next Three Days '10

Joyce Carey (1898-1993)
Blithe Spirit '45
Brief Encounter '46

Leonard Carey (1887-1977)
His Greatest Gamble '34
The Snows of Kilimanjaro '52

MacDonald Carey (1913-94)
Wake Island '42
Shadow of a Doubt '43
Copper Canyon '50
The Lawless '50
Excuse My Dust '51
Let's Make It Legal '51
Meet Me After the Show '51
My Wife's Best Friend '52
Odongo '56
Man or Gun '58
Tammy and the Doctor '63
These Are the Damned '63
Gidget Gets Married '72
End of the World '76
Roots '77
Summer of Fear '78
It's Alive 3: Island of the Alive '87

Mariah Carey (1969-)
The Bachelor '99
Glitter '01
Wisegirls '02
Tennessee '08
You Don't Mess with the Zohan '08 (C)
Precious: Based on the Novel 'Push' by Sapphire '09
Lee Daniels' The Butler '13

Matthew Carey (1980-)
The Banger Sisters '02
Old School '03
November '05

Michele Carey (1943-)
El Dorado '67
Live a Little, Love a Little '68
The Desperados '70
Scandalous John '71

Olive Carey (1896-1988)
The Searchers '56
Gunfight at the O.K. Corral '57
Night Passage '57
The Alamo '60
Billy the Kid Versus Dracula '66

Phil Carey (1925-2009)
I Was a Communist for the FBI '51
The Tanks Are Coming '51

Cattle Town '52
Springfield Rifle '52
This Woman Is Dangerous '52
Gun Fury '53
Pushover '54
The Long Gray Line '55
Mister Roberts '55
Three Stripes in the Sun '55
Wyoming Renegades '55
Shadow on the Window '57
Tonka '58
Black Gold '62
FBI Code 98 '63
Dead Ringer '64
Once You Kiss a Stranger '69
Scream of the Wolf '74
Fighting Mad '76
Monster '78

Philip Carey (1925-2009)
Inside the Walls of Folsom Prison '51
Screaming Mimi '58

Ron Carey (1935-2007)
High Anxiety '77
Fatso '80
History of the World: Part 1 '81
Lucky Luke '94
Troublemakers '94
Into the Arms of Strangers '07

Timothy Carey (1925-94)
White Witch Doctor '53
Crime Wave '54
The Killing '56
Rumble on the Docks '56
Paths of Glory '57
Revolt in the Big House '58
One-Eyed Jacks '61
The Mermaids of Tiburon '62
Bikini Beach '64
Beach Blanket Bingo '65
Head '68
Minnie and Moskowitz '71
The Outfit '73
The Killing of a Chinese Bookie '76
Fast Walking '82
Echo Park '86

Tom Carey
Hush Little Baby '07
Held Hostage '09

Patrick Cargill (1918-96)
Help! '65
A Countess from Hong Kong '67
Hammerhead '68
Inspector Clouseau '68

Timothy Carhart (1953-)
Party Animal '83
Ghostbusters '84
The Manhattan Project '86
Pink Cadillac '89
Quicksand: No Escape '91
Thelma & Louise '91
Red Rock West '93
Beverly Hills Cop 3 '94
Candyman 2: Farewell to the Flesh '94
America's Dream '95
Black Sheep '96
Black Dawn '05

Gia Carides (1964-)
Strictly Ballroom '92
Bad Company '94
Last Breath '96
Paperback Romance '96
The Extreme Adventures of Super Dave '98
Letters from a Killer '98
Primary Colors '98
Austin Powers 2: The Spy Who Shagged Me '99
A Secret Affair '99
Maze '01
My Big Fat Greek Wedding '02
Exposed '03
Stick It '06

Carmine Caridi (1934-2019)
KISS Meets the Phantom of the Park '78

The Money Pit '86
Split Decisions '88
Life Stinks '91
Top Dog '95

Bruno Cariello
The Wedding Director '06
Vincere '09

Leo Carillo
City Streets '38
Society Lawyer '39

Len Cariou (1939-)
A Little Night Music '77
The Four Seasons '81
The Lady in White '88
Never Talk to Strangers '95
Executive Decision '96
Nuremberg '00
Thirteen Days '00
About Schmidt '02
Secret Window '04
The Boynton Beach Club '05
The Greatest Game Ever Played '05
Flags of Our Fathers '06
Into the Storm '09

Richard Carle (1871-1941)
Sin Takes a Holiday '30
One Hour with You '32
The Ghost Walks '34
Love in Bloom '35
Love Before Breakfast '36
Mistaken Identity '36
Maisie '39

Claire Carleton (1913-79)
Gildersleeve on Broadway '43
The Fighter '52
The Devil's Partner '58

George Carlin (1937-2008)
Car Wash '76
Americathon '79 (N)
Outrageous Fortune '87
Bill & Ted's Excellent Adventure '89
Bill & Ted's Bogus Journey '91
The Prince of Tides '91
Larry McMurtry's Streets of Laredo '95
Dogma '99
Jay and Silent Bob Strike Back '01
Scary Movie 3 '03
Jersey Girl '04
Tarzan 2 '05 (V)
Cars '06 (V)
Happily N'Ever After '07 (V)

Gloria Carlin
Hanoi Hilton '87
Varian's War '01

Lynn Carlin (1938-)
Faces '68
Tick... Tick... Tick '70
A Step Out of Line '71
Wild Rovers '71
Deathdream '72
Forbidden Love '82
Superstition '82
A Killer in the Family '83

Anne Carlisle (1956-)
Liquid Sky '83
Perfect Strangers '84

Jodi Carlisle (1960-)
The Wild Thornberrys Movie '02 (V)
Rugrats Go Wild! '03 (V)

Mary Carlisle (1912-)
Held for Murder '32
College Humor '33
East of Fifth Avenue '33
Kentucky Kernels '34
The Old Homestead '35
One Frightened Night '35
Double or Nothing '37
Dance, Girl, Dance '40
Dead Men Walk '43

Kitty Carlisle Hart (1910-2007)
Here is My Heart '34
Murder at the Vanities '34
A Night at the Opera '35
Radio Days '87

Six Degrees of Separation '93

Christine Carlo
Nora's Hair Salon '04
Nora's Hair Salon 2: A Cut Above '08

Ismael Carlo (1942-)
El Padrino '04
Bandidas '06

Johann Carlo (1957-)
Nadia '84
Quiz Show '94
Fair Game '95

Margit Carlquist (1932-)
To Joy '50
Smiles of a Summer Night '55

Amy Carlson (1968-)
If These Walls Could Talk 2 '00
Anamorph '07
Green Lantern '11

Jeff Carlson (1953-)
Slap Shot '77
Slap Shot 2: Breaking the Ice '02
The Killing Floor '06

June Carlson (1924-96)
Delinquent Daughters '44
Mom & Dad '47

Karen Carlson (1945-)
The Student Nurses '70
The Candidate '72
Octagon '80
Fleshburn '84
Wild Horses '84
Brotherly Love '85
A Horse for Danny '95

Kelly Carlson (1976-)
Starship Troopers 2: Hero of the Federation '04
Break-In '06
The Marine '06
Made of Honor '08
Player 5150 '08

Leslie (Les) Carlson (1933-2014)
Deranged '74
A Christmas Story '83

Richard Carlson (1912-77)
The Young in Heart '38
Dancing Co-Ed '39
Those Glamour Girls '39
Beyond Tomorrow '40
The Ghost Breakers '40
The Howards of Virginia '40
No, No Nanette '40
Too Many Girls '40
Back Street '41
Hold That Ghost '41
The Little Foxes '41
Presenting Lily Mars '43
Young Ideas '43
So Well Remembered '47
The Amazing Mr. X '48
King Solomon's Mines '50
Flat Top '52
All I Desire '53
It Came from Outer Space '53
The Magnetic Monster '53
Seminole '53
Creature from the Black Lagoon '54
The Helen Morgan Story '57
Tormented '60
Change of Habit '69
The Valley of Gwangi '69

Steve Carlson (1943-)
Deadlier Than the Male '67
Brothers O'Toole '73

Steve Carlson (1955-)
Slap Shot '77
Slap Shot 2: Breaking the Ice '02

Veronica Carlson (1944-)
Dracula Has Risen from the Grave '68
Frankenstein Must Be Destroyed '69

The Horror of Frankenstein '70
Freakshow '95

Hope Marie Carlton (1966-)
Hard Ticket to Hawaii '87
Picasso Trigger '89
Savage Beach '89
Slumber Party Massacre 3 '90

Robert Carlyle (1961-)
Riff Raff '92
Being Human '94
Cracker: To Be a Somebody '94
Priest '94
Trainspotting '95
The Full Monty '96
Carla's Song '97
Face '97
Plunkett & Macleane '98
Angela's Ashes '99
Ravenous '99
The World Is Not Enough '99
The Beach '00
Formula 51 '01
To End All Wars '01
Once Upon a Time in the Midlands '02
Hitler: The Rise of Evil '03
Dead Fish '04
Human Trafficking '05
The Mighty Celt '05
Eragon '06
Marilyn Hotchkiss' Ballroom Dancing & Charm School '06
Flood '07
28 Weeks Later '07
The Last Enemy '08
24: Redemption '08
The Tournament '09
The Unloved '09
California Solo '12
T2 Trainspotting '17

Chris Carmack (1980-)
Suburban Girl '07
The Butterfly Effect 3: Revelation '09
Into the Blue 2: The Reef '09
Alpha and Omega '10 (V)
Beauty & the Briefcase '10
Deadly Honeymoon '10
Shark Night 3D '11

Roger C. Carmel (1932-86)
Alvarez Kelly '66
Gambit '66
The Silencers '66
The Venetian Affair '67
My Dog, the Thief '69
Thunder and Lightning '77

Julie Carmen (1954-)
Gloria '80
Blue City '86
Fright Night 2 '88
The Milagro Beanfield War '88
In the Mouth of Madness '95
True Women '97
King of the Jungle '01

Jean Carmet (1920-94)
Monsieur Vincent '47
Any Number Can Win '63
La Rupture '70
Just Before Nightfall '71
The Tall Blond Man with One Black Shoe '72
Black and White in Color '76
Violette '78
Buffet Froid '79
Secret Obsession '88
Sorceress '88

Caitlin Carmichael
Bag of Bones '11
Martyrs '16
Wheelman '17

Hoagy Carmichael (1899-1981)
Topper '37
To Have & Have Not '44
The Best Years of Our Lives '46
Canyon Passage '46

Night Song '47
Young Man with a Horn '50
Belles on Their Toes '52

Ian Carmichael (1920-2010)
Betrayed '54
The Colditz Story '55
Simon and Laura '55
Storm Over the Nile '55
Lucky Jim '58
I'm All Right Jack '59
School for Scoundrels '60
Heavens Above '63
Smashing Time '67
Dark Obsession '90
Wives and Daughters '01

Laura Carmichael
Madame Bovary '15
A United Kingdom '17

Tullio Carminati (1894-1971)
The Duchess of Buffalo '26
Roman Holiday '53
War and Peace '56

Michael Carmine (1959-89)
Band of the Hand '86
*batteries not included '87
Leviathan '89

Francesco Carnelutti
The Order '03
Spring '15

Primo Carnera (1906-67)
The Prizefighter and the Lady '33
A Kid for Two Farthings '55
Hercules Unchained '59

Ryan Carnes
Leaving Barstow '08
The Phantom '09

Alan Carney (1911-73)
Zombies on Broadway '44
Radio Stars on Parade '45
The Pretender '47

Art Carney (1918-2003)
Pot o' Gold '41
The Yellow Rolls Royce '64
Harry and Tonto '74
Katherine '75
W.W. and the Dixie Dancekings '75
The Late Show '77
Scott Joplin '77
House Calls '78
Movie, Movie '78
Defiance '79
Going in Style '79
You Can't Take It With You '79
Roadie '80
Bitter Harvest '81
Take This Job & Shove It '81
St. Helen's, Killer Volcano '82
Firestarter '84
The Muppets Take Manhattan '84 (C)
The Naked Face '84
Izzy & Moe '85
Miracle of the Heart: A Boys Town Story '86
Last Action Hero '93

George Carney (1887-1942)
Love on the Dole '41
In Which We Serve '43
I Know Where I'm Going '45
Waterloo Road '45
Brighton Rock '47

Morris Carnovsky (1897-1992)
Address Unknown '44
Our Vines Have Tender Grapes '45
Rhapsody in Blue '45
Dead Reckoning '47
Saigon '47
Gun Crazy '49
Cyrano de Bergerac '50

Cindy Carol (1944-)
Gidget Goes to Rome '63
Dear Brigitte '65

Linda Carol (1970-)
Reform School Girls '86
Carnal Crimes '91

Martine Carol (1920-67)
Beauties of the Night '52
Lola Montes '55
Nana '55
Around the World in 80 Days '56

Adam Carolla (1964-)
Art House '98
Too Smooth '98
The Hammer '07
Road Hard '15

Leslie Caron (1931-)
An American in Paris '51
The Man With a Cloak '51
Lili '53
The Story of Three Loves '53
Daddy Long Legs '55
The Glass Slipper '55
The Doctor's Dilemma '58
Gigi '58
Fanny '61
Guns of Darkness '62
Father Goose '64
A Very Special Favor '65
Is Paris Burning? '66
Madron '70
Chandler '71
Nicole '72
QB VII '74
The Man Who Loved Women '77
Valentino '77
Dangerous Moves '84
Courage Mountain '89
The Man Who Lived at the Ritz '91
Damage '92
Funny Bones '94
Chocolat '00
The Last of the Blonde Bombshells '00
Murder on the Orient Express '01
Le Divorce '03

Memmo Carotenuto (1908-80)
Too Bad She's Bad '54
Big Deal on Madonna Street '58

Todd Carpent
Feeders '96
Razorteeth '05

Carleton Carpenter (1926-)
Lost Boundaries '49
Summer Stock '50
Two Weeks with Love '50
Fearless Fagan '52
Sky Full of Moon '52
Up Periscope '59

Charisma Carpenter (1970-)
Voodoo Moon '05
Cheaters' Club '06
House of Bones '09
The Expendables '10
Psychosis '10
The Expendables 2 '12
Heaven's Door '12
A Horse Tale '15

David Carpenter (1951-2006)
Warlock '91
Gettysburg '93
Amelia Earhart: The Final Flight '94
Spiders '00

Horace Carpenter (1875-1945)
The Dude Bandit '33
Maniac '34

Jack Carpenter (1984-)
Sydney White '07
I Love You, Beth Cooper '09
Harvest '10

Jennifer Carpenter (1979-)
White Chicks '04
The Exorcism of Emily Rose '05
Battle in Seattle '07

Quarantine '08
The Factory '10
Faster '10
Gone '12
Seeking Justice '12
Brawl in Cell Block 99 '17

John Carpenter (1948-)
Body Bags '93
The Cradle Will Rock '99

Paul Carpenter (1921-64)
Black Glove '54
Paid to Kill '54
Unholy Four '54
Fire Maidens from Outer Space '56
Call Me Bwana '63

Peter Carpenter
Blood Mania '70
Point of Terror '71

James Carpinello (1975-)
The Great Raid '05
Let's Kill Ward's Wife '14

Camilla Carr (1942-)
Don't Look in the Basement '73
Logan's Run '76
Keep My Grave Open '80
Making Love '82

Carole Carr (1928-97)
Down Among the Z Men '52
Goon Movie '52

Darleen Carr (1950-)
The Jungle Book '67 (V)
Death of a Gunfighter '69
The Horror at 37,000 Feet '73
Once an Eagle '76
Piranha '95

Jane Carr (1950-)
The Church Mouse '34
The Lady From Lisbon '42
The Prime of Miss Jean Brodie '69

Katie Carr (1973-)
Dinotopia '02
Four Corners of Suburbia '05
Game Time: Tackling the Past '11
A Perfect Man '13

Marian Carr (1926-)
World for Ransom '54
Cell 2455, Death Row '55
Ghost Town '56
The Indestructible Man '56

Mary Carr (1874-1973)
Red Kimono '25
Kept Husbands '31
Forbidden Trail '32

Paul Carr (1934-2006)
The Severed Arm '73
The Bat People '74
Truck Stop Women '74
Sniper '75
Sisters of Death '76

Thomas Carr (1907-97)
The Idol Dancer '20
S.O.S. Coast Guard '37

Raffaella Carra (1943-)
Mole Men Against the Son of Hercules '61
Caesar the Conqueror '63
Von Ryan's Express '65

David Carradine (1936-2009)
Violent Ones '68
The Good Guys and the Bad Guys '69
Heaven With a Gun '69
The McMasters '70
Maybe I'll Come Home in the Spring '71
Boxcar Bertha '72
Kung Fu '72
The Long Goodbye '73 (C)
Mean Streets '73
Death Race 2000 '75
Bound for Glory '76
Cannonball '76
Gray Lady Down '77
Thunder and Lightning '77
Circle of Iron '78
Death Sport '78
The Serpent's Egg '78
The Long Riders '80
Americana '81
Q (The Winged Serpent) '82
Lone Wolf McQuade '83
On the Line '84
The Warrior & the Sorceress '84
The Bad Seed '85
North and South Book 1 '85
Armed Response '86
Kung Fu: The Movie '86
Oceans of Fire '86
Warlords '88
Future Force '89
Bird on a Wire '90
Evil Toons '90
Future Zone '90
Double Trouble '91
Karate Cop '91
Project: Eliminator '91
Sundown '91
Waxwork 2: Lost in Time '91
Animal Instincts '92
Roadside Prophets '92
The Gambler Returns: The Luck of the Draw '93
Capital Punishment '96
Last Stand at Saber River '96
The Rage '96
Children of the Corn 5: Fields of Terror '98
Codename: Jaguar '98
Criminal Desire '98
Cybercity '99
Dangerous Curves '99
Knocking on Death's Door '99
By Dawn's Early Light '00
Isaac Asimov's Nightfall '00
The Outsider '02
Kill Bill Vol. 1 '03 (V)
Kill Bill Vol. 2 '04
Miracle at Sage Creek '05
Final Move '06
Big Stan '07
Camille '07
Epic Movie '07
Fall Down Dead '07
How to Rob a Bank '07
National Lampoon's The Stoned Aged '07
Treasure Raiders '07
The Golden Boys '08
Hell Ride '08
Kung Fu Killer '08
Last Hour '08
Sundown: The Vampire in Retreat '08
All Hell Broke Loose '09
Break '09
Dark Fields '09
Road of No Return '09
Dinocroc Vs. Supergator '10

Ever Carradine
Life Without Dick '01
Cleaverville '07
Guns for Hire '15

John Carradine (1906-88)
The Invisible Man '33
To the Last Man '33
The Black Cat '34
Daniel Boone '34
The Bride of Frankenstein '35
Les Miserables '35
Dimples '36
The Garden of Allah '36
Mary of Scotland '36
The Prisoner of Shark Island '36
Ramona '36
White Fang '36
Winterset '36
Captains Courageous '37
Danger: Love at Work '37
The Hurricane '37
The Last Gangster '37
Nancy Steele Is Missing '37
Thank you, Mr. Moto '37
Alexander's Ragtime Band '38
Four Men and a Prayer '38
International Settlement '38
Kentucky Moonshine '38
Kidnapped '38
Of Human Hearts '38
Drums Along the Mohawk '39
Frontier Marshal '39
The Hound of the Baskervilles '39
Jesse James '39
Mr. Moto's Last Warning '39
Stagecoach '39
The Three Musketeers '39
Brigham Young: Frontiersman '40
Chad Hanna '40
The Grapes of Wrath '40
Return of Frank James '40
Blood and Sand '41
Man Hunt '41
Western Union '41
Reunion in France '42
Son of Fury '42
Whispering Ghosts '42
I Escaped from the Gestapo '43
Isle of Forgotten Sins '43
The Adventures of Mark Twain '44
Bluebeard '44
House of Frankenstein '44
The Invisible Man's Revenge '44
Waterfront '44
Captain Kidd '45
Fallen Angel '45
House of Dracula '45
The Private Affairs of Bel Ami '47
The C-Man '49
Johnny Guitar '53
Casanova's Big Night '54
The Egyptian '54
The Kentuckian '55
Stranger on Horseback '55
Around the World in 80 Days '56
The Black Sleep '56
The Court Jester '56
Hidden Guns '56
The Ten Commandments '56
Hell Ship Mutiny '57
The True Story of Jesse James '57
The Unearthly '57
The Incredible Petrified World '58
The Last Hurrah '58
Showdown at Boot Hill '58
The Cosmic Man '59
Invisible Invaders '59
The Adventures of Huckleberry Finn '60
Sex Kittens Go to College '60
Tarzan the Magnificent '60
Invasion of the Animal People '62
The Man Who Shot Liberty Valance '62
Cheyenne Autumn '64
Horrors of the Red Planet '64
The Patsy '64
House of the Black Death '65
Billy the Kid Versus Dracula '66
Munster, Go Home! '66
Alien Massacre '67
The Astro-Zombies '67
Gallery of Horrors '67
Hillbillies in a Haunted House '67
The Hostage '67
Blood of Dracula's Castle '69
The Good Guys and the Bad Guys '69
Gun Riders '69
The Trouble with Girls (and How to Get into It) '69
Bigfoot '70
Horror of the Blood Monsters '70
The McMasters '70
Myra Breckinridge '70
Shinbone Alley '70 (V)
Cain's Cutthroats '71
Blood of Ghastly Horror '72
Boxcar Bertha '72
Everything You Always Wanted to Know about Sex (But Were Afraid to Ask) '72
The Gatling Gun '72
The Night Strangler '72
Blood Legacy '73
The House of Seven Corpses '73
Silent Night, Bloody Night '73
Death at Love House '75
The Killer Inside Me '76
The Last Tycoon '76
Mary, Mary, Bloody Mary '76
The Sentinel '76
The Shootist '76
Satan's Cheerleaders '77
Shock Waves '77
The White Buffalo '77
Monster '78
The Vampire Hookers '78
The Boogey Man '80
The Nesting '80
Frankenstein Island '81
The Howling '81
Demon Rage '82
The Secret of NIMH '82 (V)
Boogey Man 2 '83
Ice Pirates '84
Evils of the Night '85
The Monster Club '85
Monster in the Closet '86
Peggy Sue Got Married '86
Revenge '86
Evil Spawn '87
Star Slammer '87
Buried Alive '89
Jack-O '95

Keith Carradine (1949-)
A Gunfight '71
McCabe & Mrs. Miller '71
Kung Fu '72
Charms '73
Emperor of the North Pole '73
Idaho Transfer '73
Thieves Like Us '74
Nashville '75
The Duellists '77
Pretty Baby '78
An Almost Perfect Affair '79
Old Boyfriends '79
The Long Riders '80
Southern Comfort '81
Choose Me '84
Maria's Lovers '84
Trouble in Mind '86
Backfire '88
The Moderns '88
Capone '89
Cold Feet '89
Daddy's Dyin'. . . Who's Got the Will? '90
Judgment '90
The Ballad of the Sad Cafe '91
Crisscross '92
Andre '94
Is There Life Out There? '94
The Tie That Binds '95
Wild Bill '95
Larry McMurtry's Dead Man's Walk '96
Last Stand at Saber River '96
Two Days in the Valley '96
Hunter's Moon '97
A Thousand Acres '97
Out of the Cold '99
A Song From the Heart '99
Baby '00
Hostage Hotel '00
The Diamond of Jeru '01
The Outsider '02
Coyote Waits '03
Monte Walsh '03
All Hat '07
Bobby Z '07
Elvis and Annabelle '07
Lake City '08
Winter of Frozen Dreams '08
Peacock '09
The Family Tree '10
Cowboys & Aliens '11
Ain't Them Bodies Saints '13
A Quiet Passion '17

Robert Carradine (1954-)
The Cowboys '72
Mean Streets '73
Aloha, Bobby and Rose '74
Cannonball '76
Jackson County Jail '76
Massacre at Central High '76
Pom Pom Girls '76
Joyride '77
Orca '77
Blackout '78
Coming Home '78
The Big Red One '80
The Long Riders '80
Just the Way You Are '84
Revenge of the Nerds '84
Monte Carlo '86
Conspiracy: The Trial of the Chicago Eight '87
Number One with a Bullet '87
Revenge of the Nerds 2: Nerds in Paradise '87
The Incident '89
Somebody Has to Shoot the Picture '90
The Player '92
Revenge of the Nerds 3: The Next Generation '92
Body Bags '93
Stephen King's The Tommyknockers '93
Revenge of the Nerds 4: Nerds in Love '94
Bird of Prey '95
Humanoids from the Deep '96
Scorpio One '97
Breakout '98
Gunfighter '98
Dangerous Curves '99
The Kid with the X-Ray Eyes '99
Shepherd '99
Max Keeble's Big Move '01
The Lizzie McGuire Movie '03
Attack of the Sabretooth '05
Supercross: The Movie '05
Tooth and Nail '07
Deep Winter '08
Cross '11
Jesse Stone: Benefit of the Doubt '12

Carlos Carrasco (1948-)
Speed '94
One Man's Hero '98
Double Take '01

Isabelle Carre (1971-)
The Horseman on the Roof '95
Children of the Century '99
He Loves Me . . . He Loves Me Not '02
Private Fears in Public Places '06
A French Gigolo '08
Hideaway '09
Romantics Anonymous '10
Meet the Guilbys '15

Dany Carrel (1935-)
The Hands of Orlac '60
Mill of the Stone Women '60

Barbara Carrera (1944-)
Embryo '76
The Island of Dr. Moreau '77
Centennial '78
When Time Ran Out '80
Condorman '81
Masada '81
I, the Jury '82
Lone Wolf McQuade '83
Never Say Never Again '83
Love at Stake '87
Loverboy '89
Wicked Stepmother '89
Point of Impact '93
Love Is All There Is '96

Tia Carrere (1967-)
Zombie Nightmare '86
Noble House '88
Fatal Mission '89
Showdown in Little Tokyo '91
Wayne's World '92
Quick '93
Rising Sun '93
Wayne's World 2 '93
True Lies '94
Hollow Point '95
The Immortals '95
Jury Duty '95
My Teacher's Wife '95
High School High '96
Natural Enemy '96
Kull the Conqueror '97
Top of the World '97
Scarred City '98
Tracked '98
Lilo & Stitch '02 (V)
Torn Apart '04
Back in the Day '05
Lilo & Stitch 2: Stitch Has a Glitch '05 (V)
Supernova '05
Leroy and Stitch '06 (V)
Dark Honeymoon '08
Wild Cherry '09
Collision Course '12
You May Not Kiss the Bride '12
Taken for Ransom '13
Asteroid vs. Earth '14
Gutshot Straight '14

Jim Carrey (1962-)
Once Bitten '85
Peggy Sue Got Married '86
The Dead Pool '88
Earth Girls Are Easy '89
Pink Cadillac '89
Doing Time on Maple Drive '92
Ace Ventura: Pet Detective '93
Dumb & Dumber '94
The Mask '94
Ace Ventura: When Nature Calls '95
Batman Forever '95
The Cable Guy '96
Liar Liar '97
Simon Birch '98 (N)
The Truman Show '98
Man on the Moon '99
Dr. Seuss' How the Grinch Stole Christmas '00
Me, Myself, and Irene '00
The Majestic '01
Bruce Almighty '03
Eternal Sunshine of the Spotless Mind '04
Lemony Snicket's A Series of Unfortunate Events '04
Fun With Dick and Jane '05
The Number 23 '07
Dr. Seuss' Horton Hears a Who! '08 (V)
Yes Man '08
A Christmas Carol '09 (V)
I Love You Phillip Morris '10
Mr. Popper's Penguins '11
The Incredible Burt Wonderstone '13
Kick-Ass 2 '13
Dumb and Dumber To '14
Dark Crimes '16
The Bad Batch '17
Sonic the Hedgehog '20

Corey Carrier (1980-)
Men Don't Leave '89
After Dark, My Sweet '90
Savage Land '94

Matthieu Carriere (1950-)
Don Juan (Or If Don Juan Were a Woman) '73
Born for Hell '76
Coup de Grace '78
The Associate '79
The Aviator's Wife '80
Luther '03

Elpidia Carrillo (1961-)
The Border '82
Salvador '86
Let's Get Harry '87
Predator '87
My Family '94
Dangerous Passion '95
Bread and Roses '00

Nine Lives '05
Seven Pounds '08

Leo Carrillo (1881-1961)
The Guilty Generation '31
Parachute Jumper '32
Four Frightened People '34
Manhattan Melodrama '34
In Caliente '35
The Gay Desperado '36
If You Could Only Cook '36
Fit for a King '37
History Is Made at Night '37
Girl of the Golden West '38
Too Hot to Handle '38
Fisherman's Wharf '39
Lillian Russell '40
One Night in the Tropics '40
Riders of Death Valley '41
American Empire '42
The Phantom of the Opera '43
The Fugitive '48

Debbie Lee Carrington (1959-)
Club Fed '90
Spaced Invaders '90
Tiptoes '03

Luciana Carro
Dr. Dolittle 3 '06
Phantom Racer '09

Regina Carrol (1943-92)
Satan's Sadists '69
Brain of Blood '71
Dracula *vs.* Frankenstein '71
Angels' Wild Women '72
Blood of Ghastly Horror '72
Blazing Stewardesses '75
Black Heat '76

Barbara Carroll
The Last Days of Pompeii '60
Goliath Against the Giants '63

Beeson Carroll
Werewolf of Washington '73
Coming Home '78

Brandon Carroll
Home Sick '08
A Horrible Way to Die '10

Diahann Carroll (1935-2019)
Carmen Jones '54
Paris Blues '61
Hurry Sundown '67
The Split '68
From the Dead of Night '89
The Five Heartbeats '91
Eve's Bayou '97
Having Our Say: The Delany Sisters' First 100 Years '99
The Courage to Love '00
Sally Hemings: An American Scandal '00
Patricia Cornwell's At Risk '10
Patricia Cornwell's The Front '10
Peeples '13
The Masked Saint '16

Erica Carroll
Confined '10
Interrogation '16

Helen Carroll
Backstairs at the White House '79
The Dead '87

James Carroll
He Knows You're Alone '80
Senior Trip '81
Girls Night Out '83
Police Academy 4: Citizens on Patrol '87
Under the Piano '95
DC 9/11: Time of Crisis '04

James Dennis (Jim) Carroll (1950-2009)
The Unholy '88
The Basketball Diaries '95

Janet Carroll (1940-2012)
Risky Business '83
Memories of Me '88
Family Business '89
Forces of Nature '99
The Omega Code '99
Enough '02
(Untitled) '09

Joan Carroll (1932-)
Primrose Path '40
Tomorrow the World '44
The Jack of Diamonds '49

John Carroll (1905-79)
Pilot X '37
Zorro Rides Again '37
Only Angels Have Wings '39
Congo Maisie '40
Go West '40
Susan and God '40
Lady Be Good '41
Sunny '41
Flying Tigers '42
Rio Rita '42
The Youngest Profession '43
Decision at Sundown '57
Rock, Baby, Rock It '57

Justin Carroll
Dark Secrets '95
Stormswept '95

Kevin Carroll
Paid in Full '02
Pipe Dream '02
The Secret Lives of Dentists '02
The Notorious Bettie Page '06

Leo G. Carroll (1892-1972)
Murder On a Honeymoon '35
The Right to Live '35
A Christmas Carol '38
Charlie Chan in City of Darkness '39
The Private Lives of Elizabeth & Essex '39
The Tower of London '39
Wuthering Heights '39
Charlie Chan's Murder Cruise '40
Rebecca '40
Suspicion '41
House on 92nd Street '45
Spellbound '45
Forever Amber '47
The Paradine Case '47
Song of Love '47
Enchantment '48
Father of the Bride '50
The Happy Years '50
Strangers on a Train '51
The Bad and the Beautiful '52
The Snows of Kilimanjaro '52
Tarantula '55
We're No Angels '55
North by Northwest '59
One Plus One '61
The Parent Trap '61
The Prize '63
That Funny Feeling '65

Luke Carroll
The Alice '04
Stoned Bros. '09

Madeleine Carroll (1906-87)
The World Moves On '34
The 39 Steps '35
The General Died at Dawn '36
Lloyds of London '36
The Secret Agent '36
On the Avenue '37
Prisoner of Zenda '37
My Love For Yours '39
My Favorite Blonde '42
The Fan '49

Madeline Carroll (1996-)
When a Stranger Calls '06
Swing Vote '08
Cafe '10
Flipped '10
The Spy Next Door '10
Machine Gun Preacher '11
Mr. Popper's Penguins '11
The Magic of Belle Isle '12
I Can Only Imagine '18

Nancy Carroll (1904-65)
Hot Saturday '32
That Certain Age '38

Pat Carroll (1927-)
With Six You Get Eggroll '68
Brothers O'Toole '73
My Neighbor Totoro '88 *(V)*
The Little Mermaid '89 *(V)*
Songcatcher '99
Freedom Writers '07
Redacted '07

Peter Carroll (1944-)
The Last Wave '77
The Chant of Jimmie Blacksmith '78
Sleeping Beauty '11

Rocky Carroll (1963-)
Crimson Tide '95
The Great White Hype '96
Best Laid Plans '99

Carrot Top (1967-)
Chairman of the Board '97
Dennis the Menace Strikes Again '98

Shane Carruth (1972-)
Primer '04
Upstream Color '13

Ben Carruthers (1936-83)
Shadows '60
Riot '69

Julius J. Carry, III (1952-2008)
Avenging Disco Godfather '76
The Last Dragon '85

Charles Carson (1886-1977)
There Goes the Bride '32
The Secret Agent '36
Victoria the Great '37
Sixty Glorious Years '38
Beau Brummell '54

Crystal Carson (1967-)
Cartel '90
Killer Tomatoes Strike Back '90

Hunter Carson (1975-)
Paris, Texas '83
Invaders from Mars '86
Mr. North '88

Jack Carson (1910-63)
High Flyers '37
Stage Door '37
Stand-In '37
Carefree '38
Having a Wonderful Time '38
Vivacious Lady '38
Destry Rides Again '39
Mr. Smith Goes to Washington '39
I Take This Woman '40
Lucky Partners '40
Blues in the Night '41
The Bride Came C.O.D. '41
Love Crazy '41
Mr. & Mrs. Smith '41
Strawberry Blonde '41
Gentleman Jim '42
Larceny, Inc. '42
The Male Animal '42
The Hard Way '43
Princess O'Rourke '43
Thank Your Lucky Stars '43
Arsenic and Old Lace '44
Hollywood Canteen '44
Mildred Pierce '45
Roughly Speaking '45
John Loves Mary '48
Romance on the High Seas '48
It's a Great Feeling '49
My Dream Is Yours '49
Bright Leaf '50
The Groom Wore Spurs '51
Dangerous When Wet '53
Phffft! '54
Red Garters '54
A Star Is Born '54
Tarnished Angels '57
Cat on a Hot Tin Roof '58
Rally 'Round the Flag, Boys! '58
The King of the Roaring '20s: The Story of Arnold Rothstein '61

Jeannie Carson
Love in Pawn '53
An Alligator Named Daisy '55

John Carson (1927-)
Plague of the Zombies '66
Taste the Blood of Dracula '70
Emma '72
Captain Kronos: Vampire Hunter '74

John David Carson (1952-2009)
Pretty Maids All In a Row '71
Savage Is Loose '74
Charge of the Model T's '76
Creature from Black Lake '76
Empire of the Ants '77

Lisa Nicole Carson (1969-)
Devil in a Blue Dress '95
Love Jones '96
Eve's Bayou '97
Aftershock: Earthquake in New York '99
Life '99

L.M. Kit Carson (1941-2014)
David Holzman's Diary '67
Running on Empty '88
Hurricane Streets '96

Shawn Carson
The Funhouse '81
Something Wicked This Way Comes '83

Silas Carson (1965-)
Hidalgo '04
Star Wars: Episode 3-Revenge of the Sith '05

Sunset Carson (1922-90)
Stage Door Canteen '43
Alien Outlaw '85

Terrence 'T.C.' Carson (1958-)
Livin' Large '91
Gang Related '96
Relax. . . It's Just Sex! '98
U-571 '00
Final Destination 2 '03

Peter Carsten (1928-2012)
Secret of the Black Trunk '62
Dark of the Sun '68
And God Said to Cain '69
Black Lemons '70
Web of the Spider '70
Zeppelin '71

Margit Carstensen (1940-)
The Bitter Tears of Petra von Kant '72
Tenderness of the Wolves '73
Fear of Fear '75
Mother Kusters Goes to Heaven '76
Satan's Brew '76
Possession '81
Angry Harvest '85
Chinese Roulette '86

Alex Carter (1964-)
The Morrison Murders '96
Recipe for Revenge '98
Hitched '01
Out of Time '03
The Mermaid Chair '06
40 Days and Nights '12
House of Versace '13

Ann Carter (1936-2014)
Curse of the Cat People '44
Song of Love '47
The Two Mrs. Carrolls '47

Ben Carter (1907-46)
Sleepers West '41
Crash Dive '43

Dixie Carter (1939-2010)
Going Berserk '83
The Big Day '99
Comfort and Joy '03
That Evening Sun '09

Finn Carter (1960-)
How I Got into College '89
Tremors '89
Sweet Justice '92

Helena Carter (1923-2000)
Something in the Wind '47
Kiss Tomorrow Goodbye '50
Double Crossbones '51
The Golden Hawk '52
Invaders from Mars '53

Helena Bonham Carter (1966-)
Alice Through the Looking Glass '16
Ocean's 8 '18
Sgt. Stubby: An American Hero '18

Jack Carter (1923-2015)
The Horizontal Lieutenant '62
Viva Las Vegas '63
Resurrection of Zachary Wheeler '71
The Happy Hooker Goes to Washington '77
The Glove '78
Alligator '80
Octagon '80
History of the World: Part 1 '81
Death Blow '87
Lethal Victims '87
Play It to the Bone '99
One Last Ride '03

Janis Carter (1913-94)
I Married an Angel '42
Just Off Broadway '42
Lady of Burlesque '43
Night Editor '46
Framed '47
Miss Grant Takes Richmond '49
Slightly French '49
The Woman on Pier 13 '50
Flying Leathernecks '51
The Half-Breed '51
My Forbidden Past '51
Santa Fe '51

Jason Carter (1960-)
Behind the Red Door '02
Acts of Death '07

Jim Carter (1948-)
Haunted Honeymoon '86
A Month in the Country '87
A Very British Coup '88
The Advocate '93
Black Beauty '94
Cracker: The Big Crunch '94
The Madness of King George '94
Brassed Off '96
A Merry War '97
Legionnaire '98
Shakespeare in Love '98
The Little Vampire '00
102 Dalmatians '00
Dinotopia '02
The Way We Live Now '02
Bright Young Things '03
The Secret Life of Mrs. Beeton '06
The Thief Lord '06
Cranford '08
The Oxford Murders '08
Creation '09
Return to Cranford '09
The Good Liar '19

Joelle Carter (1972-)
High Fidelity '00
It Had to Be You '00
Just One Time '00
Swimming '00
When Will I Be Loved '04
Room 314 '07
A Perfect Man '13

Lauren Ashley Carter
The Woman '11
Jug Face '13
The Mind's Eye '16

Louise Carter (1875-1957)
East of Fifth Avenue '33
Paddy O'Day '35

Lynda Carter (1951-)
Bobbie Jo and the Outlaw '76
Last Song '80
Baby Broker '81
Danielle Steel's Daddy '91
Super Troopers '01
Terror Peak '03
The Dukes of Hazzard '05
Sky High '05
Slayer '06

Nell Carter (1948-2003)
Hair '79
Modern Problems '81
Bebe's Kids '92 *(V)*
Final Shot: The Hank Gathers Story '92
The Crazysitter '94
The Grass Harp '95

Nick Carter
Class Reunion Massacre '77
The Hollow '04

Pip Carter
Christopher and His Kind '11
1917 '19

Sarah Carter (1980-)
A Date With Darkness '03
Final Destination 2 '03
Berkeley '05
DOA: Dead or Alive '06
Misconceptions '08
Jodi Picoult's Salem Falls '11

Terry Carter (1929-)
Foxy Brown '74
Battlestar Galactica '78

Thomas Carter (1953-)
Monkey Hustle '77
Whose Life Is It Anyway? '81

T.K. Carter (1956-)
The Hollywood Knights '80
Seems Like Old Times '80
Southern Comfort '81
The Thing '82
Doctor Detroit '83
Runaway Train '85
Amazon Women on the Moon '87
He's My Girl '87
Ski Patrol '89
A Rage in Harlem '91
The Corner '00
Baadasssss! '03
Domino '05

Anna Carteret (1942-)
The Shell Seekers '89
The Heat of the Day '91
Mrs. Palfrey at the Claremont '05

Gabrielle Carteris (1961-)
Raising Cain '92
Trapped: Buried Alive '02
12 Christmas Wishes For My Dog '11

Katrin Cartlidge (1961-2002)
Naked '93
Before the Rain '94
Breaking the Waves '95
Career Girls '97
Claire Dolan '97
Hi-Life '98
The Lost Son '98
The Cherry Orchard '99
The Weight of Water '00
From Hell '01
No Man's Land '01
Sword of Honour '01

Angela Cartwright (1952-)
The Sound of Music '65
High School USA '84
Lost in Space '98 *(C)*

Lynn Cartwright (1928-2004)
Queen of Outer Space '58
The Wasp Woman '59

Nancy Cartwright (1957-)
Twilight Zone: The Movie '83
The Little Mermaid '89 (V)
The Land Before Time 6: The Secret of Saurus Rock '98 (V)
Rugrats Go Wild! '03 (V)
The Simpsons Movie '07 (V)

Veronica Cartwright (1949-)
The Children's Hour '61
The Birds '63
One Man's Way '63
Spencer's Mountain '63
Inserts '76
Goin' South '78
Invasion of the Body Snatchers '78
Alien '79
Prime Suspect '82
Nightmares '83
The Right Stuff '83
Flight of the Navigator '86
Wisdom '87
The Witches of Eastwick '87
Robert Kennedy and His Times '90
Dead in the Water '91
Man Trouble '92
Candyman 2: Farewell to the Flesh '94
Mirror, Mirror 2: Raven Dance '94
My Brother's Keeper '95
Money Talks '97
Quicksilver Highway '98
A Slipping Down Life '99
Sparkler '99
Scary Movie 2 '01
Just Married '03
Kinsey '04
The Invasion '07
Call of the Wild 3D '09
InSight '11
The Odd Way Home '13
The Town That Dreaded Sundown '14

Lisa Marie Caruk (1971-)
Call Me: The Rise and Fall of Heidi Fleiss '04
Blood Angels '05
Destination: Infestation '07
The Other Woman '08

Anthony Caruso (1913-2003)
Watch on the Rhine '43
Objective, Burma! '45
Pride of the Marines '45
Tarzan and the Leopard Woman '46
The Asphalt Jungle '50
The Iron Mistress '52
Raiders of the Seven Seas '53
The Steel Lady '53
The Boy From Oklahoma '54
Cattle Queen of Montana '54
Drum Beat '54
Fort Massacre '58
Most Dangerous Man Alive '61
Escape From Zahrain '62
Zebra Force '76

David Caruso (1956-)
Getting Wasted '80
Without Warning '80
First Blood '82
An Officer and a Gentleman '82
Blue City '86
King of New York '90
Mad Dog and Glory '93
Kiss of Death '94
Jade '95
Body Count '97
Cold Around the Heart '97
Elmore Leonard's Gold Coast '97
Deadlocked '00
Proof of Life '00
Black Point '01
Session 9 '01

Brigitte Carva
Orloff and the Invisible Man '70
Dr. Orloff and the Invisible Man '72

Alfonso Carvajal
Mad Doctor of Blood Island '68
Beast of Blood '71

Betty Carvalho
Halloween 5: The Revenge of Michael Myers '89
Best of the Best 2 '93

Brent Carver (1951-)
Crossbar '79
Millennium '89
Lilies '96
Deeply '99
Ararat '02
The Event '03

Lynne Carver (1909-55)
The Bride Wore Red '37
Madame X '37
Maytime '37
A Christmas Carol '38
Everybody Sing '38
Young Dr. Kildare '38
The Adventures of Huckleberry Finn '39
Calling Dr. Kildare '39
Bataan '43
Flame of the West '45

Dana Carvey (1955-)
Racing with the Moon '84
This Is Spinal Tap '84
Tough Guys '86
Moving '88
Opportunity Knocks '90
Wayne's World '92
Wayne's World 2 '93
Clean Slate '94
The Road to Wellville '94
Trapped in Paradise '94
Little Nicky '00
Master of Disguise '02
The Secret Life of Pets '16

James Carville
The People *vs.* Larry Flynt '96
The Assassination of Jesse James by the Coward Robert Ford '07

Katarina Cas
The Guard '11
The Wolf of Wall Street '13

Gisele Casadesus
My Afternoons with Marguerite '10
Sarah's Key '10

Anabella Casanova (1986-)
Mask Maker '10
Stealing Las Vegas '12

Alex Casanovas
Kika '94
What It's All About '95

Amira Casar (1971-)
Murder on the Orient Express '01
How I Killed My Father '03
Sylvia '03
Anatomy of Hell '04
Piano Tuner of Earthquakes '05
Call Me by Your Name '17

Maria Casares (1922-96)
Children of Paradise '44
The Ladies of the Bois de Bologne '44
La Chartreuse de Parme '48
Orpheus '49
The Testament of Orpheus '59

Antonio Casas (1911-82)
Four Dollars of Revenge '66
The Texican '66

Regina Case
Me You Them '00
The Second Mother '15

Max Casella (1967-)
Newsies '92
Ed Wood '94
Windrunner '94
Sgt. Bilko '95
Trial and Error '96
Analyze This '98
Dinosaur '00 (V)
Revolutionary Road '08
Blue Jasmine '13
The Last of Robin Hood '13
Wild Card '15
Wonder Wheel '17
Night Comes On '18
The Rhythm Section '19

Chiara Caselli (1967-)
My Own Private Idaho '91
Fiorile '93
Beyond the Clouds '95
Forgotten City '98
Sleepless '01
Ripley's Game '02
Father of My Children '09

Bernie Casey (1939-)
Guns of the Magnificent Seven '69
Tick... Tick... Tick '70
Brian's Song '71
Black Gunn '72
Boxcar Bertha '72
Hit Man '72
Cleopatra Jones '73
Cornbread, Earl & Me '75
Dr. Black, Mr. Hyde '76
The Man Who Fell to Earth '76
Ants '77
The Martian Chronicles: Part 1 '79
The Martian Chronicles: Part 2 '79
The Martian Chronicles: Part 3 '79
Sharky's Machine '81
Never Say Never Again '83
Revenge of the Nerds '84
Spies Like Us '85
Steele Justice '87
Backfire '88
I'm Gonna Git You Sucka '88
Rent-A-Cop '88
Bill & Ted's Excellent Adventure '89
Another 48 Hrs. '90
Chains of Gold '92
The Cemetery Club '93
In the Mouth of Madness '95
The Last Brickmaker in America '01
Tomcats '01
On the Edge '02
When I Find the Ocean '06

Dillon Casey (1983-)
Too Young to Marry '07
My Nanny's Secret '09
Creature '11

Lawrence Casey (1940-)
The Gay Deceivers '69
The Student Nurses '70
Acapulco Gold '78

Neil Casey
Fort Tilden '14
Greener Grass '19

Johnny Cash (1932-2003)
Door to Door Maniac '61
Road to Nashville '67
A Gunfight '71
Pride of Jesse Hallum '81
Murder in Coweta County '83
The Baron and the Kid '84
North and South Book 1 '85
Last Days of Frank & Jesse James '86
Stagecoach '86

June Carter Cash (1929-2003)
Murder in Coweta County '83
The Baron and the Kid '84
Last Days of Frank & Jesse James '86
The Apostle '97

Rosalind Cash (1938-95)
Omega Man '71
Hickey & Boggs '72
The All-American Boy '73
Amazing Grace '74
Cornbread, Earl & Me '75
Dr. Black, Mr. Hyde '76
Monkey Hustle '77
Wrong Is Right '82
The Adventures of Buckaroo Banzai Across the Eighth Dimension '84
Go Tell It on the Mountain '84
The Offspring '87
Tales from the Hood '95

Stefania Casini (1948-)
Andy Warhol's Dracula '74
Andy Warhol's Bad '77
Suspiria '77
The Bloodstained Shadow '78

Francesco Casisa
Respiro '02
The Sicilian Girl '09

Philip Casnoff (1949-)
Message from Space '78
North and South Book 2 '86
Sinatra '92
Kiss Tomorrow Goodbye '00
The President's Man 2: A Line in the Sand '02
Field of Vision '11

John Cason (1918-61)
Rimfire '49
From Here to Eternity '53
Jungle Drums of Africa '53

Katrina Caspary (1970-)
Can't Buy Me Love '87
Mac and Me '88
My Mom's a Werewolf '89

Christopher Cass
The Family Plan '05
The One '11

Peggy Cass (1924-99)
The Marrying Kind '52
Auntie Mame '58
Gidget Goes Hawaiian '61
If It's Tuesday, This Must Be Belgium '69
Cheaters '84

John Cassavetes (1929-89)
The Night Holds Terror '55
Crime in the Streets '56
Edge of the City '57
Saddle the Wind '58
The Killers '64
Devil's Angels '67
The Dirty Dozen '67
Rosemary's Baby '68
Machine Gun McCain '69
Husbands '70
Minnie and Moskowitz '71
Mikey & Nicky '76
Two Minute Warning '76
Opening Night '77
Brass Target '78
The Fury '78
Whose Life Is It Anyway? '81
Incubus '82
The Tempest '82

Nick Cassavetes (1959-)
The Wraith '87
Assault of the Killer Bimbos '88
Backstreet Dreams '90
Blind Fury '90
Delta Force 3: The Killing Game '91
Body of Influence '93
Class of 1999 2: The Substitute '93
Mrs. Parker and the Vicious Circle '94
Face/Off '97
The Astronaut's Wife '99
Life '99
The Independent '00 (C)

Cecile Cassel
The Romance of Astrea and Celadon '07
Sword of War '09

Jean-Pierre Cassel (1932-2007)
The Elusive Corporal '62
Those Magnificent Men in Their Flying Machines '65
Is Paris Burning? '66
The Killing Game '67
Army of Shadows '69
La Rupture '70
The Discreet Charm of the Bourgeoisie '72
Murder on the Orient Express '74
The Three Musketeers '74
The Four Musketeers '75
The Killing of a Chinese Bookie '76
The Twist '76
Les Rendez-vous D'Anna '78
Who Is Killing the Great Chefs of Europe? '78
From Hell to Victory '79
La Truite '83
Alice '86
The Fatal Image '90
The Phantom of the Opera '90
The Favor, the Watch, & the Very Big Fish '92
Ready to Wear '94
La Ceremonie '95
The Ice Rink '99
Sade '00
The Crimson Rivers '01
Stuck On You '03

Seymour Cassel (1935-)
Too Late Blues '61
The Killers '64
Faces '68
Minnie and Moskowitz '71
Death Game '77
Scott Joplin '77
Seducers '77
Valentino '77
California Dreaming '79
The Mountain Men '80
Double Exposure '82
Eye of the Tiger '86
Best Seller '87
Tin Men '87
Colors '88
Johnny Be Good '88
Track 29 '88
Cold Dog Soup '89
Sweet Bird of Youth '89
Wicked Stepmother '89
Dick Tracy '90
Diary of a Hitman '91
White Fang '91
Honeymoon in Vegas '92
In the Soup '92
There Goes My Baby '92
Trouble Bound '92
Boiling Point '93
Hand Gun '93
Indecent Proposal '93
Chasers '94
Imaginary Crimes '94
It Could Happen to You '94
Bad Love '95
Cannes Man '96
Dream for an Insomniac '96
Things I Never Told You '96
Tree's Lounge '96
Obsession '97
Emma's Wish '98
Motel Blue '98
Relax. . . It's Just Sex! '98
Rushmore '98
The Treat '98
Me & Will '99
Animal Factory '00
The Crew '00
Just One Night '00
Bartleby '01
The Royal Tenenbaums '01
61* '01
The Sleepy Time Gal '01
Manna from Heaven '02
Passionada '02
Sonny '02
Stealing Harvard '02
The Life Aquatic with Steve Zissou '04
The Black Widow '05
Circadian Rhythm '05
The Wendell Baker Story '05
Beer League '06
Lonesome Jim '06
The Tenants '06
Chasing 3000 '07
Reach for Me '08
Staten Island '09
Freerunner '10
Pete Smalls Is Dead '10
Fort McCoy '11

Vincent Cassel (1966-)
Cafe au Lait '94
Hate '95
Elizabeth '98
The Messenger: The Story of Joan of Arc '99
Brotherhood of the Wolf '01
The Crimson Rivers '01
Read My Lips '01
Shrek '01 (V)
Birthday Girl '02
Irreversible '02
The Reckoning '03
Ocean's Twelve '04
Derailed '05
Sheitan '06
Eastern Promises '07
Ocean's Thirteen '07
Mesrine: Part 1-Killer Instinct '08
Mesrine: Part 2-Public Enemy Number 1 '08
Black Swan '10
A Dangerous Method '11
Trance '13
Beauty and the Beast '14
Child 44 '15
Tale of Tales '15
Jason Bourne '16
Underwater '20

Alan Cassell (1932-)
Breaker Morant '80
The Club '81
Strange Bedfellows '04

Seth Cassell
#1 Cheerleader Camp '10
Hold Your Breath '12

Wally Cassell (1912-2015)
The Story of G.I. Joe '45
Saigon '47
Sands of Iwo Jima '49
White Heat '49
Highway 301 '50
Breakdown '53
Island in the Sky '53
Law and Order '53
Until They Sail '57

Andrew Cassese (1972-)
Revenge of the Nerds '84
Revenge of the Nerds 2: Nerds in Paradise '87

Gabriel Casseus (1972-)
Lone Star '95
New Jersey Drive '95
Get On the Bus '96
Nightjohn '96
Buffalo Soldiers '97
Don King: Only in America '97
Fallen '97
Black Dog '98
Modern Vampires '98
Harlem Aria '99
Bedazzled '00
Lockdown '00
Black Hawk Down '01
Tales from the Crypt Presents Ritual '02

David Cassidy (1950-2017)
Instant Karma '90
Spirit of '76 '91

Edward Cassidy (1893-1968)
A Face in the Fog '36
Buffalo Bill Rides Again '47

Elaine Cassidy (1979-)
Felicia's Journey '99
Disco Pigs '01
The Others '01
The Lost World '02
When Did You Last See Your Father? '07
A Room With a View '08
Just Henry '11

Jack Cassidy (1927-76)
Look in Any Window '61
FBI Code 98 '63
The Andersonville Trial '70
Columbo: Murder by the Book '71
The Phantom of Hollywood '74
Death Among Friends '75
The Eiger Sanction '75

Joanna Cassidy (1945-)
The Outfit '73
Bank Shot '74
The Late Show '77
Prime Time '77
Stunts '77
The Glove '78
Blade Runner '82
Under Fire '83
Invitation to Hell '84
The Children of Times Square '86
Club Paradise '86
The Fourth Protocol '87
A Father's Revenge '88
Who Framed Roger Rabbit '88
1969 '89
The Package '89
A Girl of the Limberlost '90
Where the Heart Is '90
All-American Murder '91
Don't Tell Mom the Babysitter's Dead '91
Lonely Hearts '91
Nightmare at Bittercreek '91
Barbarians at the Gate '93
Stephen King's The Tommyknockers '93
Chain Reaction '96
The Second Civil War '97
Dangerous Beauty '98
Executive Power '98
John Carpenter's Ghosts of Mars '01
Wildfire 7: The Inferno '02
The Reading Room '05
Witches of the Caribbean '05
Larry the Cable Guy: Health Inspector '06
Kiss the Bride '07
The Human Contract '08
For Sale by Owner '09
Stolen '09
Carjacked '11
Heaven's Door '12
Visions '16

Katie Cassidy (1986-)
Black Christmas '06
Click '06
When a Stranger Calls '06
Live! '07
Spin '07
Taken '08
A Nightmare on Elm Street '10
Monte Carlo '11
Kill for Me '12
The Scribbler '14

Michael Cassidy (1983-)
Zoom '06
Night of the Living Deb '14
The Stray '17

Patrick Cassidy (1962-)
Angel Dusted '81
Just the Way You Are '84
Dress Gray '86
Love at Stake '87
Napoleon and Josephine: A Love Story '87
Longtime Companion '90
How the West Was Fun '95
The Fiance '96

Raffey Cassidy (2002-)
Molly Moon and The Incredible Book of Hypnotism '15
Tomorrowland '15
The Killing of a Sacred Deer '17
Vox Lux '18

Raquel Cassidy
Do I Love You? '02
Tick Tock Lullaby '07

Shaun Cassidy (1958-)
Roots: The Gift '88
Texas Guns '90

Ted Cassidy (1932-79)
Butch Cassidy and the Sundance Kid '69
MacKenna's Gold '69
Genesis II '73
Poor Pretty Eddie '73
The Slams '73
Convict Women '74
Planet Earth '74
Thunder County '74
Women's Prison Escape '74
Goin' Coconuts '78

Kyle Cassie (1976-)
Children of the Corn: Revelation '01
His and Her Christmas '05
Trophy Wife '06
Death Do Us Part '14
Deadpool '16

Claudio Cassinelli (1938-85)
The Big Alligator River '79
Mountain of the Cannibal God '79
The Great Alligator '81
Scorpion with Two Tails '82
The New Gladiators '83
Hercules 2 '85
Hands of Steel '86

John Cassini
Man's Best Friend '93
Chain of Fools '00
Get Carter '00
Break a Leg '03
Catwoman '04
Window Theory '04
Vice '08
The Traveler '10

Nadia Cassini (1949-)
Pulp '72
Star Crash '78

Carla Cassola (1947-)
Death Rides a Horse '69
Demonia '90
The Devil's Daughter '91

Laetitia Casta (1978-)
Born in 68 '08
Gainsbourg: A Heroic Life '10
Arbitrage '12
War of the Buttons '12

Jean-Pierre Castaldi (1944-)
A Fine Romance '92
The Musketeer '01
Extreme Ops '02
George and the Dragon '04

David Castaneda
El Chicano '19
We Die Young '19

Lou Castel (1943-)
A Bullet for the General '68
Paranoia '69
Beware of a Holy Whore '70
The Scarlet Letter '73
The American Friend '77
Irma Vep '96
Heartbeat Detector '07

Dan Castellaneta (1958-)
Nothing in Common '86
The War of the Roses '89
The Return of Jafar '94 (V)
Plump Fiction '97
The Settlement '99
Hey Arnold! The Movie '02 (V)
I-See-You.Com '06
The Pursuit of Happyness '06
The Simpsons Movie '07 (V)
Relative Stranger '09

Richard S. Castellano (1933-88)
A Fine Madness '66
Lovers and Other Strangers '70
The Godfather '72
Honor Thy Father '73

Vincent Castellanos (1962-)
Anaconda '96
The Crow 2: City of Angels '96
K-911 '99
The Last Marshal '99
Mulholland Drive '01

Sergio Castellitto (1953-)
The Big Blue '88
The Star Maker '95
Portraits Chinois '96
For Sale '98
Mostly Martha '01
Va Savoir '01
My Mother's Smile '02
Caterina in the Big City '03
Paris, je t'aime '06
The Wedding Director '06
The Chronicles of Narnia: Prince Caspian '08
Around a Small Mountain '09

Willy Castello (1910-53)
Cocaine Fiends '36
Confessions of a Vice Baron '42

Federico Castelluccio (1964-)
El Cantante '06
Lucky Days '08
The Decoy Bride '11

Nino Castelnuovo (1936-)
Umbrellas of Cherbourg '64
Camille 2000 '69
The Five Man Army '69
The English Patient '96

Movita Castenada (1915-2015)
See Movita

Movita Castendada (1915-2015)
See Movita

Movita Casteneda (1915-2015)
See Movita

Christopher Castile (1980-)
Beethoven '92
Beethoven's 2nd '93

Alexandra Castillo
Eye of the Beast '07
Taken in Broad Daylight '09

Elias Castillo
The Damned '06
San Franpsycho '06

Enrique Castillo (1949-)
Blood In . . . Blood Out: Bound by Honor '93
My Family '94
The End of Violence '97
The Hi-Lo Country '98

Raúl Castillo (1977-)
We the Animals '18
El Chicano '19

Don Castle (1917-66)
Out West With the Hardys '38
Power Dive '41
Wake Island '42
Seven Were Saved '47
I Wouldn't Be in Your Shoes '48
Stampede '49

John Castle (1940-)
Blow-Up '66
The Lion in Winter '68
Man of La Mancha '72
Antony and Cleopatra '73
The Prime of Miss Jean Brodie '78
Lillie '79
The Bretts '88
The Crucifer of Blood '91
RoboCop 3 '91
A Harlot's Progress '06

Maggie Castle (1983-)
The Other Side of the Law '95
Between Truth and Lies '06
Weirdsville '07

Hank and Mike '08
StarStruck '10

Mary Castle (1931-98)
Criminal Lawyer '51
White Fire '53

Nick Castle (1947-)
Artists and Models '55
Halloween '78
Halloween '18

Peggie Castle (1927-73)
Harem Girl '52
Jesse James' Women '54
Target Zero '55
Quincannon, Frontier Scout '56
The Counterfeit Plan '57

Peggy Castle (1927-73)
Payment on Demand '51
Invasion U.S.A. '52
99 River Street '53
The White Orchid '54
Beginning of the End '57
The Seven Hills of Rome '58

Roy Castle (1932-94)
Alice Through the Looking Glass '66
Carry On Up the Khyber '68

William Castle (1914-77)
Rosemary's Baby '68
Bug '75
Shampoo '75

Keisha Castle-Hughes (1990-)
Whale Rider '02
Star Wars: Episode 3-Revenge of the Sith '05
The Nativity Story '06
Hey Hey It's Esther Blueberger '08
A Heavenly Vintage '09
Thank You for Your Service '17

Alfredo Castro
No '12
The Club '16

David Castro
Little Fugitive '06
Where God Left His Shoes '07

Raquel Castro (1996-)
Jersey Girl '04
America '09

Shanley Caswell
Detention '11
Snow White: A Deadly Summer '12

Coralina Cataldi-Tassoni (1971-)
Demons 2 '87
Opera '88
Evil Clutch '89
The Phantom of the Opera '98
Ghost Son '06
Mother of Tears '08

Diego Catano
Duck Season '04
Desierto '16

Field Cate
Space Buddies '08 (V)
Santa Buddies '09 (V)

Luciano Catenacci (1933-90)
How to Kill a Judge '75
Crime Busters '78
Initiation '87

John Cater (1932-2009)
Captain Kronos: Vampire Hunter '74
The Duchess of Duke Street '78

Georgina Cates (1975-)
An Awfully Big Adventure '94
Stiff Upper Lips '96
Clay Pigeons '98
Illuminata '98
The Treat '98
Big City Blues '99
Sinner '07

Jackass Presents: Bad Grandpa '13

Helen Cates
A Taste for Killing '92
The Underneath '95
The Whole Wide World '96

Phoebe Cates (1963-)
Fast Times at Ridgemont High '82
Paradise '82
Private School '83
Gremlins '84
Lace '84
Lace 2 '85
Date with an Angel '87
Bright Lights, Big City '88
The Heart of Dixie '89
Shag: The Movie '89
Gremlins 2: The New Batch '90
I Love You to Death '90 (C)
Drop Dead Fred '91
Bodies, Rest & Motion '93
My Life's in Turnaround '94 (C)
Princess Caraboo '94
The Anniversary Party '01

Anna Cathcart (2003-)
To All the Boys I've Loved Before '18
To All the Boys: P.S. I Still Love You '20

Emma Catherwood (1981-)
In the Spider's Web '07
Against the Dark '08
The Reeds '09

Reg E. Cathey (1958-2018)
Quick Change '90
Airheads '94
Tank Girl '94
Seven '95
Pootie Tang '01
Boycott '02
S.W.A.T. '03
The Machinist '04
20 Years After '08
Nasty Baby '15

Brigitte Catillon (1951-)
Un Coeur en Hiver '93
Artemisia '97
Merci pour le Chocolat '00
The Taste of Others '00
The Housekeeper '02
The Spectator '04
Love is in the Air '13

Kyle Catlett
Poltergeist '15
The Young and Prodigious T.S. Spivet '15
A Vigilante '19

Mary Jo Catlett (1938-)
Battling for Baby '92
Serial Mom '94
Bram Stoker's The Mummy '97
Ablaze '00
The SpongeBob SquarePants Movie '04 (V)
The Benchwarmers '06
Surprise, Surprise '09

Walter Catlett (1889-1960)
The Front Page '31
It's Tough to Be Famous '32
Rain '32
The Captain Hates the Sea '34
Cain and Mabel '36
Follow Your Heart '36
Mr. Deeds Goes to Town '36
A Tale of Two Cities '36
Love Is News '37
On the Avenue '37
Varsity Show '37
Wake Up and Live '37
Bringing Up Baby '38
Every Day's a Holiday '38
Exile Express '39
Pinocchio '40 (V)
Remedy for Riches '40
It Started with Eve '41
Manpower '41
My Gal Sal '42
Syncopation '42

Yankee Doodle Dandy '42
They Got Me Covered '43
His Butler's Sister '44
The Inspector General '49

Juliette Caton (1975-)
The Last Temptation of Christ '88
Courage Mountain '89
Lady Audley's Secret '00

Michael Caton (1943-)
The Thorn Birds: The Missing Years '96
The Castle '97
The Interview '98
The Animal '01
Strange Bedfellows '04
Last Cab to Darwin '16

Kim Cattrall (1956-)
Deadly Harvest '72
The Bastard '78
Scruples '80
Ticket to Heaven '81
Porky's '82
Police Academy '84
City Limits '85
Turk 182! '85
Big Trouble in Little China '86
Mannequin '87
Midnight Crossing '87
Masquerade '88
The Bonfire of the Vanities '90
Miracle in the Wilderness '91
Star Trek 6: The Undiscovered Country '91
Split Second '92
Wild Palms '93
Above Suspicion '95
The Heidi Chronicles '95
Live Nude Girls '95
Unforgettable '96
Where Truth Lies '96
Robin Cook's Invasion '97
Baby Geniuses '98
Modern Vampires '98
15 Minutes '01
Crossroads '02
Ice Princess '05
The Tiger's Tale '06
My Boy Jack '07
Sex and the City: The Movie '08
The Ghost Writer '10
Meet Monica Velour '10
Sex and the City 2 '10
Any Human Heart '11

Caroline Catz (1970-)
The Guilty '92
Chicklit '16

Philippe Caubere (1950-)
My Father's Glory '91
My Mother's Castle '91

Daniel Cauchy (1930-)
Grisbi '53
Bob le Flambeur '55

Jessica Cauffiel (1976-)
Urban Legends 2: Final Cut '00
Legally Blonde '01
Valentine '01
You Stupid Man '02
Legally Blonde 2: Red White & Blonde '03
D.E.B.S. '04
White Chicks '04
Guess Who '05
Hoot '06

Emma Caulfield (1973-)
Darkness Falls '03
In Her Mother's Footsteps '06
A Valentine Carol '07
Timer '09
Why Am I Doing This? '09
Confined '10
Back in the Day '14

Joan Caulfield (1922-91)
Blue Skies '46
Monsieur Beaucaire '46
The Unsuspected '47
Welcome Stranger '47
The Lady Says No '51

The Rains of Ranchipur *'55*
Cattle King *'63*
Buckskin *'68*
Daring Dobermans *'73*
Pony Express Rider *'76*

Maxwell Caulfield (1959-)
Grease 2 *'82*
The Boys Next Door *'85*
Dance with Death *'91*
Sundown *'91*
Animal Instincts *'92*
Alien Intruder *'93*
Gettysburg *'93*
Midnight Witness *'93*
No Escape, No Return *'93*
Backlash: Oblivion 2 *'95*
Empire Records *'95*
Prey of the Jaguar *'96*
The Real Blonde *'97*
Perfect Tenant *'99*
Facing the Enemy *'00*
Submerged *'00*
The Hit *'01*
Dragon Storm *'04*
Sundown: The Vampire in Retreat *'08*

Tony Caunter (1937-)
The Hill *'65*
S.O.S. Titanic *'79*

Catherine Cavadini (1967-)
An American Tail: Fievel Goes West *'91 (V)*
The Powerpuff Girls Movie *'02 (V)*

Gary Cavagnaro (1963-)
The Bad News Bears *'76*
Drive-In *'76*

Gianni Cavalieri
Two Nights with Cleopatra *'54*
The Priest's Wife *'71*

Michael Cavalieri
Seduced: Pretty When You Cry *'01*
Crooked *'05*

Kristin Cavallari (1987-)
Beach Kings *'08*
Van Wilder: Freshman Year *'08*
Wild Cherry *'09*

Valeria Cavalli (1959-)
A Blade in the Dark *'83*
Joseph *'95*
Double Team *'97*
A Girl Cut in Two *'07*
Mother of Tears *'08*

Megan Cavanagh (1960-)
A League of Their Own *'92*
Robin Hood: Men in Tights *'93*
I Love Trouble *'94*
Dracula: Dead and Loving It *'95*
For Richer or Poorer *'97*
Meet the Deedles *'98*
Jimmy Neutron: Boy Genius *'01 (V)*

Paul Cavanagh (1895-1959)
The Squaw Man *'31*
Curtain at Eight *'33*
Tarzan and His Mate *'34*
Goin' to Town *'35*
Reno *'39*
I Take This Woman *'40*
Maisie Was a Lady *'41*
Captains of the Clouds *'42*
The Strange Case of Dr. Rx *'42*
The Hard Way *'43*
Maisie Goes to Reno *'44*
House of Fear *'45*
Humoresque *'46*
Wife Wanted *'46*
Black Arrow *'48*
The Woman in Green *'49*
Hi-Jacked *'50*
Rogues of Sherwood Forest *'50*
Bride of the Gorilla *'51*
The Strange Door *'51*
The Golden Hawk *'52*
Charade *'53*
House of Wax *'53*
The Mississippi Gambler *'53*
The Prodigal *'55*
Francis in the Haunted House *'56*
The Man Who Turned to Stone *'57*
Four Skulls of Jonathan Drake *'59*
The Most Wonderful Time of the Year *'08*

Tom Cavanagh (1963-)
Something More *'99*
Heart of the Storm *'04*
Snow *'04*
Gray Matters *'06*
How to Eat Fried Worms *'06*
Breakfast With Scot *'07*
Sublime *'07*
The Capture of the Green River Killer *'08*
Snow 2: Brain Freeze *'08*
Yogi Bear *'10 (V)*
Debbie Macomber's Trading Christmas *'11*
The Bird Men *'13*

Christine Cavanaugh (1963-2014)
Babe *'95 (V)*
The Rugrats Movie *'98 (V)*
Rugrats in Paris: The Movie *'00 (V)*

Hobart Cavanaugh (1886-1950)
I Cover the Waterfront *'33*
Hi, Nellie! *'34*
Housewife *'34*
Wings in the Dark *'35*
Cain and Mabel *'36*
Wife Versus Secretary *'36*
Rose of Washington Square *'39*
Gildersleeve on Broadway *'43*
The Kansan *'43*
Black Angel *'46*
Up in Central Park *'48*

Michael Cavanaugh (1942-)
Black Thunder *'98*
Dancing in September *'00*
Poison *'01*

Patrick Cavanaugh
Bloody Murder *'99*
Gamebox 1.0 *'04*
Transylmania *'09*

Lumi Cavazos (1968-)
Like Water for Chocolate *'93*
Bottle Rocket *'95*
Manhattan Merenque! *'95*
Last Stand at Saber River *'96*
Sugar Town *'99*
Bless the Child *'00*
In the Time of the Butterflies *'01*
Exposed *'03*

Nick Cave (1957-)
Johnny Suede *'92*
20,000 Days on Earth *'14*

Marc Cavell
The Purple Gang *'59*
Cool Hand Luke *'67*

Ingrid Caven (1938-)
The American Soldier *'70*
Beware of a Holy Whore *'70*
Tenderness of the Wolves *'73*
Mother Kusters Goes to Heaven *'76*
Satan's Brew *'76*
In a Year of 13 Moons *'78*

Nicola Cavendish
Air Bud *'97*
The Bouquet *'13*

Dick Cavett (1936-)
Annie Hall *'77*
A Nightmare on Elm Street 3: Dream Warriors *'87*
Beetlejuice *'88*
Moon over Parador *'88*
Duane Hopwood *'05*
Hugh Hefner: Playboy, Activist and Rebel *'09*
Deceptive Practice: The Mysteries and Mentors of Ricky Jay *'13*
I Am Not Your Negro *'17*

James (Jim) Caviezel (1968-)
Diggstown *'92*
Wyatt Earp *'94*
Ed *'96*
The Rock *'96*
G.I. Jane *'97*
The Thin Red Line *'98*
Ride with the Devil *'99*
Frequency *'00*
Pay It Forward *'00*
Angel Eyes *'01*
Madison *'01*
The Count of Monte Cristo *'02*
High Crimes *'02*
Highwaymen *'03*
Bobby Jones: Stroke of Genius *'04*
The Final Cut *'04*
I Am David *'04*
The Passion of the Christ *'04*
Deja Vu *'06*
Nature's Grave *'08*
Outlander *'08*
The Stoning of Soraya M. *'08*
The Prisoner *'09*
Transit *'12*

Jim Caviezel (1968-)
Escape Plan *'13*
Savannah *'14*
When the Game Stands Tall *'14*
Paul, Apostle of Christ *'18*
Running for Grace *'18*

Henry Cavill (1983-)
The Count of Monte Cristo *'02*
I Capture the Castle *'02*
Hellraiser: Hellworld *'05*
Tristan & Isolde *'06*
Stardust *'07*
Blood Creek *'09*
Whatever Works *'09*
Immortals *'11*
The Cold Light of Day *'12*
Man of Steel *'13*
The Man from U.N.C.L.E. *'15*
Batman v Superman: Dawn of Justice *'16*
Justice League *'17*
Mission: Impossible-Fallout *'18*
Night Hunter *'19*

Joseph Cawthorn (1869-1949)
The Taming of the Shrew *'29*
They Call It Sin *'32*
The White Zombie *'32*
The Cat and the Fiddle *'34*
Harmony Lane *'35*

Fernando Cayo
The Orphanage *'07*
Kidnapped *'10*

Laura Cayouette (1964-)
Deranged *'01*
Pulse 2: Afterlife *'08*
Django Unchained *'12*

Elizabeth Cayton (1960-)
See Elizabeth Kaitan

John Cazale (1936-78)
The Godfather *'72*
The Conversation *'74*
The Godfather, Part 2 *'74*
Dog Day Afternoon *'75*
The Deer Hunter *'78*

Christopher Cazenove (1943-2010)
Royal Flash *'75*
The Duchess of Duke Street *'78*
Eye of the Needle *'81*
From a Far Country: Pope John Paul II *'81*
Heat and Dust *'82*
Until September *'84*
Lace 2 *'85*
Mata Hari *'85*
Souvenir *'88*
Tears in the Rain *'88*
Three Men and a Little Lady *'90*
Aces: Iron Eagle 3 *'92*
A Knight's Tale *'01*
Johnson County War *'02*

Daniel Ceccaldi (1927-2003)
The Soft Skin *'64*
Make Your Bets Ladies *'65*
Bed and Board *'70*
Chloe in the Afternoon *'72*
Twisted Obsession *'90*

Sandra Ceccarelli
Light of My Eyes *'01*
The Crown Prince *'06*

Carlo Cecchi (1939-)
La Scorta *'94*
Stealing Beauty *'96*
Steam: A Turkish Bath *'96*
The Red Violin *'98*

Fulvio Cecere (1960-)
Valentine *'01*
Dead in a Heartbeat *'02*
The Perfect Score *'04*
Assault on Precinct 13 *'05*
Her Fatal Flaw *'06*
John Tucker Must Die *'06*
Second Sight *'07*
Resident Evil: Afterlife *'10*

Jonathan Cecil (1939-)
Agatha Christie's Thirteen at Dinner *'85*
The Rector's Wife *'94*

Jon Cedar (1931-2011)
Day of the Animals *'77*
The Manitou *'78*
Kiss Daddy Goodbye *'81*

Larry Cedar (1955-)
Feds *'88*
Constantine *'05*

Julio Cesar Cedillo
The Three Burials of Melquiades Estrada *'05*
Killing Down *'06*
Hostile Border *'16*

Cedric the Entertainer (1964-)
Ride *'98*
Big Momma's House *'00*
Kingdom Come *'01*
Barbershop *'02*
Ice Age *'02 (V)*
Serving Sara *'02*
Intolerable Cruelty *'03*
Barbershop 2: Back in Business *'04*
Johnson Family Vacation *'04*
Be Cool *'05*
The Honeymooners *'05*
Madagascar *'05 (V)*
Man of the House *'05*
Charlotte's Web *'06 (V)*
Code Name: The Cleaner *'07*
Talk to Me *'07*
Cadillac Records *'08*
Madagascar: Escape 2 Africa *'08 (V)*
Street Kings *'08*
Welcome Home Roscoe Jenkins *'08*
All's Faire in Love *'09*
Larry Crowne *'11*
Madagascar 3: Europe's Most Wanted *'12 (V)*
A Haunted House *'13*
Planes *'13 (V)*
A Haunted House 2 *'14*
Planes: Fire & Rescue *'14 (V)*
Top Five *'14*
Barbershop: The Next Cut *'16*
Why Him? *'16*
First Reformed *'17*

Pablo Cedron (1958-)
Felicidades *'00*
The Aura *'05*

Babou Ceesay
Severance *'06*
The Best of Enemies *'19*

Elisa Cegani (1911-96)
Nana *'55*
Medusa Against the Son of Hercules *'62*
Saul and David *'64*

Clementine Celarie (1957-)
Betty Blue *'86*
Lawless Heart *'01*
Love is in the Air *'13*

Henry Cele (1949-2007)
Shaka Zulu *'83*
The Ghost and the Darkness *'96*
Shaka Zulu: The Last Great Warrior *'01*

Maria Celedonio
How to Make an American Quilt *'95*
Freeway 2: Confessions of a Trickbaby *'99*

Adriano Celentano (1938-)
The Switch *'76*
The Con Artists *'80*

Adolfo Celi (1922-86)
The Agony and the Ecstasy *'65*
Thunderball *'65*
Von Ryan's Express *'65*
The King of Hearts *'66*
Target for Killing *'66*
The Bobo *'67*
Grand Slam *'67*
The Honey Pot *'67*
Danger: Diabolik *'68*
Ring of Death *'69*
Fragment of Fear *'70*
Night of the Assassin *'70*
Murders in the Rue Morgue *'71*
1931: Once Upon a Time in New York *'72*
Who Saw Her Die? *'72*
Hired to Kill *'73*
Hitler: The Last Ten Days *'73*
The Italian Connection *'73*
Phantom of Liberty *'74*
Ten Little Indians *'75*
The Arab Conspiracy *'76*
Live Like a Cop, Die Like a Man *'76*
Cafe Express *'83*

Stanislawa Celinska (1947-)
Landscape After Battle *'70*
Maids of Wilko *'79*

Teco Celio
Trois Couleurs: Rouge *'94*
The Truce *'96*

Teresa Celli (1924-)
Border Incident *'49*
The Asphalt Jungle *'50*
Right Cross *'50*

Caroline Cellier (1945-)
This Man Must Die *'70*
Cop Au Vin *'85*
Farinelli *'94*

Frank Cellier (1884-1948)
The Passing of the Third Floor Back *'35*
The 39 Steps *'35*
Nine Days a Queen *'36*
Non-Stop New York *'37*
Cottage to Let *'41*
The Magic Bow *'47*

Peter Cellier (1928-)
Luther *'74*
Man Friday *'75*
And the Ship Sails On *'83*

John Cena (1977-)
The Marine *'06*
12 Rounds *'09*
Fred: The Movie *'10*
Legendary *'10*
The Reunion *'11*
Ferdinand *'17*
The Wall *'17*
Blockers *'18*
Bumblebee *'18*
Playing with Fire *'19*

Noah Centineo (1996-)
To All the Boys I've Loved Before *'18*
The Perfect Date *'19*
To All the Boys: P.S. I Still Love You *'20*

Angie Cepeda (1974-)
Love for Rent *'05*
The Dead One *'07*
A Night in Old Mexico *'14*
Wild Horses *'15*

Michael Cera (1988-)
What Katy Did *'99*
Confessions of a Dangerous Mind *'02*
My Louisiana Sky *'02*
Juno *'07*
Superbad *'07*
Extreme Movie *'08*
Nick & Norah's Infinite Playlist *'08*
Paper Heart *'09*
Year One *'09*
Scott Pilgrim *vs.* the World *'10*
Youth in Revolt *'10*
Crystal Fairy & the Magical Cactus *'13*
Magic Magic *'13*
This Is the End *'13*
Sausage Party *'16*
The LEGO Batman Movie *'17*
Lemon *'17*
Molly's Game *'17*

Ivan Cermak
Stranger in My Bed *'05*
Destination: Infestation *'07*

Daniel Cerny (1981-)
Demonic Toys *'90*
Children of the Corn 3: Urban Harvest *'95*

Erica Cerra (1979-)
The Stranger *'10*
Super Storm *'12*

Mike Cerrone (1957-)
Kingpin *'96*
Outside Providence *'99*
Me, Myself, and Irene *'00*

Enzo Cerusico
Hercules, Samson and Ulysses *'64*
Zorro *'74*

Claude Cerval (1921-72)
The Cousins *'59*
Les Cousins *'59*
Classe Tous Risque *'60*
Any Number Can Win *'63*

Carlos Cervantes
Fugitive Champion *'99*
Coronado *'03*

Gary Cervantes (1953-)
The Base 2: Guilty as Charged *'00*
Bandidas *'06*

Gino Cervi (1901-74)
Fabiola *'48*
Les Miserables *'52*

Valentina Cervi (1976-)
Artemisia *'97*
Children of Hannibal *'98*
James Dean *'01*
Miracle at St. Anna *'08*
Jane Eyre *'11*

Michela Cescon
David's Birthday *'09*
Vincere *'09*

Richard Cetrone
John Carpenter's Ghosts of Mars *'01*
Underworld: Evolution *'05*

Michael Ceveris (1990-)
Rock 'n' Roll High School Forever *'91*
A Woman, Her Men and Her Futon *'92*
The Mexican *'01*
Stake Land *'10*

Alain Chabat (1958-)
French Twist '95
The Taste of Others '00
Happily Ever After '04
I Do '06
The Science of Sleep '06
Night at the Museum: Battle of the Smithsonian '09

Lacey Chabert (1982-)
Lost in Space '98
Not Another Teen Movie '01
Tart '01
The Home Front '02
Hometown Legend '02
The Wild Thornberrys Movie '02 (V)
Daddy Day Care '03
Rugrats Go Wild! '03 (V)
Mean Girls '04
The Pleasure Drivers '05
Black Christmas '06
Fatwa '06
A New Wave '07
What If God Were the Sun? '07
Reach for Me '08
Sherman's Way '08
Ghosts of Girlfriends Past '09
A Holiday Heist '11
A Royal Christmas '14

Claude Chabrol (1930-2010)
Who's Got the Black Box? '67
Six in Paris '68

Thomas Chabrol (1963-)
Comedy of Power '06
The French Minister '13

Tom Chadbon (1946-)
The Beast Must Die '75
Dance with a Stranger '85
Devices and Desires '91

Alexsei Chadov
Night Watch '04
Day Watch '06

Cyril Chadwick
The Iron Horse '24
Peter Pan '24

June Chadwick (1951-)
Forbidden World '82
Agatha Christie's Sparkling Cyanide '83
This Is Spinal Tap '84
The Return of Spinal Tap '92

Sarah Chadwick (1960-)
The Adventures of Priscilla, Queen of the Desert '94
Journey to the Center of the Earth '99

Suzy Chaffee (1946-)
Snowblind '78
Fire and Ice '87

George Chakiris (1934-)
West Side Story '61
Diamond Head '62
Kings of the Sun '63
Flight From Ashiya '64
633 Squadron '64
The High Bright Sun '65
Is Paris Burning? '66
The Young Girls of Rochefort '68
Return to Fantasy Island '77

Samrat Chakrabarti (1975-)
Kissing Cousins '08
The Waiting City '09

Timothée Chalamet
Love the Coopers '15
Miss Stevens '16
Call Me by Your Name '17
Lady Bird '17
Beautiful Boy '18
The King '19

Kathleen Chalfant (1945-)
Bob Roberts '92
Jumpin' at the Boneyard '92
David Searching '97
A Price Above Rubies '97
A Death in the Family '02
Kinsey '04
2B Perfectly Honest '04
The Last New Yorker '07
Perfect Stranger '07
Duplicity '09
Georgia O'Keefe '09

Feodor Chaliapin, Jr. (1907-92)
The Name of the Rose '86
Moonstruck '87
The King's Whore '90
Stanley and Iris '90
The Inner Circle '91
The Church '98

Chris Chalk
Lila & Eve '15
Come and Find Me '16

Garry Chalk (1952-)
Take Me Home: The John Denver Story '00
Lone Hero '02
Video Voyeur: The Susan Wilson Story '02
His and Her Christmas '05
A Little Thing Called Murder '06
Unthinkable '07
Christmas Town '08
Tornado Valley '09
Behemoth '11
The Hunt for the I-5 Killer '11

James Chalke
The Defender '04
Missionary Man '07
Command Performance '09
Direct Contact '09

Sarah Chalke (1977-)
City Boy '93
Robin of Locksley '95
I've Been Waiting for You '98
Nothing Too Good for a Cowboy '98
Alchemy '05
Cake '05
Why I Wore Lipstick to My Mastectomy '06
Mama's Boy '07
Chaos Theory '08
Maneater '09

William Challee (1904-89)
Desperate '47
Billy the Kid Versus Dracula '66
Zachariah '70

Rudy Challenger
Cool Breeze '72
Sheba, Baby '75

Andrew Chalmers (1992-)
Comfort and Joy '03
A Home at the End of the World '04
Siblings '04

Georges Chamarat (1901-82)
The French Touch '54
Diabolique '55

Howland Chamberlain (1911-84)
The Best Years of Our Lives '46
Francis the Talking Mule '49

Richard Chamberlain (1934-)
The Secret of the Purple Reef '60
A Thunder of Drums '61
Twilight of Honor '63
Portrait of a Lady '67
Petulia '68
The Madwoman of Chaillot '69
Julius Caesar '70
The Three Musketeers '74
The Towering Inferno '74
The Four Musketeers '75
The Slipper and the Rose '76
The Last Wave '77
The Man in the Iron Mask '77
Centennial '78
The Swarm '78
Shogun '80
The Thorn Birds '83
King Solomon's Mines '85
Wallenberg: A Hero's Story '85
Allan Quatermain and the Lost City of Gold '86
Dream West '86
The Bourne Identity '88
Ordeal in the Arctic '93
Bird of Prey '95
The Thorn Birds: The Missing Years '96
A River Made to Drown In '97
Blackbeard '06
I Now Pronounce You Chuck and Larry '07
The Perfect Family '11
We Are the Hartmans '11
Nightmare Cinema '19

Kevin Chamberlin (1963-)
Suspect Zero '04
Bound by Lies '05
Lucky Number Slevin '06

Faune A. Chambers (1976-)
Bring It On Again '03
White Chicks '04
Epic Movie '07
Krews '10

Justin Chambers (1970-)
Rose Hill '97
Liberty Heights '99
The Musketeer '01
The Wedding Planner '01
Hysterical Blindness '02
Leo '02
Southern Belles '05
The Zodiac '05

Marilyn Chambers (1952-2009)
Rabid '77
Angel of H.E.A.T. '82
Bikini Bistro '94

Michael 'Boogaloo Shrimp' Chambers (1967-)
Breakin' 2: Electric Boogaloo '84
Breakin' '84

Munro Chambers
Beethoven's Christmas Adventure '11
Turbo Kid '15

Jo Champa (1969-)
Direct Hit '93
The Whole Shebang '01

Gower Champion (1921-80)
Show Boat '51
Everything I Have is Yours '52
Lovely to Look At '52
Give a Girl a Break '53
Jupiter's Darling '55
Three for the Show '55

Marge Champion (1919-)
Everything I Have is Yours '52
Lovely to Look At '52
Give a Girl a Break '53
Jupiter's Darling '55
Three for the Show '55
The Party '68
The Swimmer '68

Michael Champion
The Swordsman '92
Private Wars '93

Dennis Chan
Kickboxer '89
Kickboxer 3: The Art of War '92
Naked Weapon '03
Seventh Moon '08

Jackie Chan (1954-)
Come Drink with Me '65
Master with Cracked Fingers '71
Enter the Dragon '73
Young Tiger '74
New Fist of Fury '76
Half a Loaf of Kung Fu '78
Battle Creek Brawl '80
The Big Brawl '80
Young Master '80
Dragon Lord '82
Project A '83
Cannonball Run 2 '84
Eagle's Shadow '84
Fantasy Mission Force '84
Heart of Dragon '85
Police Story '85
Protector '85
Operation Condor 2: The Armour of the Gods '86
Project A: Part 2 '87
Dragons Forever '88
Miracles '89
The Prisoner '90
Operation Condor '91
Supercop '92
Twin Dragons '92
Crime Story '93
Supercop 2 '93
The Legend of Drunken Master '94
Jackie Chan's First Strike '96
Rumble in the Bronx '96
An Alan Smithee Film: Burn, Hollywood, Burn '97 (C)
Jackie Chan's Who Am I '98
Mr. Nice Guy '98
Rush Hour '98
Gen-X Cops '99
Gorgeous '99
Shanghai Noon '00
The Accidental Spy '01
Rush Hour 2 '01
The Tuxedo '02
The Medallion '03
Shanghai Knights '03
Vampire Effect '03
Around the World in 80 Days '04
New Police Story '04
Jackie Chan's The Myth '05
Robin-B-Hood '06
Rush Hour 3 '07
The Forbidden Kingdom '08
Kung Fu Panda '08 (V)
The Karate Kid '10
The Spy Next Door '10
Kung Fu Panda 2 '11 (V)
1911 '11
Dragon Blade '15
Earth: One Amazing Day '17
The Foreigner '17
The LEGO Ninjago Movie '17 (V)
The Nut Job 2: Nutty by Nature '17
Railroad Tigers '17
The Climbers '19

Jacqueline 'Jackie' Chan
The World of Suzie Wong '60
Krakatoa East of Java '69

Kim Chan (1917-2008)
Who's the Man? '93
The Corruptor '99
Shanghai Knights '03
The Honeymooners '05

Kwok-Kwan Chan
Kung Fu Hustle '04
Ip Man 4: The Finale '19

Michael Paul Chan (1950-)
Rapid Fire '92
Falling Down '93
The Joy Luck Club '93
U.S. Marshals '98
The Insider '99
Molly '99
Once in the Life '00
Spy Game '01

Philip Chan (1945-)
Hard-Boiled '92
Twin Dragons '92

Shen Chan (1940-84)
Intimate Confessions of a Chinese Courtesan '72
King Boxer '72
Bat Without Wings '80
Shaolin & Wu Tang '81
Opium and Kung-Fu Master '84

Larry Chance
Battles of Chief Pontiac '52
War Drums '57
Fort Bowie '58

Naomi Chance (1930-2003)
The Gambler & the Lady '52
Wings of Danger '52
Terror Ship '54

Anna Chancellor (1965-)
Pride and Prejudice '95
The Man Who Knew Too Little '97
Heart '99
Longitude '00
Crush '02
Tipping the Velvet '02
The Dreamers '03
What a Girl Wants '03
Agent Cody Banks 2: Destination London '04
The Hitchhiker's Guide to the Galaxy '05
A Waste of Shame '05
The Secret Life of Mrs. Beeton '06
St. Trinian's '07
Hidden '11
How I Live Now '13
This Beautiful Fantastic '17

Norman Chancer
Victor/Victoria '82
Local Hero '83

Rohan Chand
Jack and Jill '11
Bad Words '13

Chick Chandler (1905-88)
Circumstantial Evidence '35
Murder On a Honeymoon '35
Mistaken Identity '36
Swanee River '39
Blondie in Society '41
I Wake Up Screaming '41
Action in the North Atlantic '43
Rhythm Parade '43
Maisie Goes to Reno '44
Seven Doors to Death '44
The Lost Continent '51
The Girl Who Knew Too Much '69

David Chandler (1950-)
Warp Speed '81
The Grey Zone '01
Hide and Seek '05

George Chandler (1898-1985)
The Light of Western Stars '30
Me and My Gal '32
Lady Killer '33
Beau Geste '39
Arizona '40
Roxie Hart '42
Strange Impersonation '46
The Next Voice You Hear '50
Westward the Women '51
Island in the Sky '53
The High and the Mighty '54
Dead Ringer '64

Helen Chandler (1906-65)
Mothers Cry '30
Dracula '31
The Last Flight '31
Alimony Madness '33
Christopher Strong '33

Jeff Chandler (1918-61)
Abandoned '47
Broken Arrow '50
Bird of Paradise '51
Yankee Buccaneer '52
War Arrow '53
Taza, Son of Cochise '54
Female On the Beach '55
Away All Boats '56
Pillars of the Sky '56
Jeanne Eagels '57
Man in the Shadow '57
The Jayhawkers '59
The Plunderers '60
Return to Peyton Place '61
Merrill's Marauders '62

John Davis Chandler (1935-2010)
Mad Dog Coll '61
The Young Savages '61
Ride the High Country '62
Shoot Out '71
Alligator Alley '72

Kyle Chandler (1965-)
Pure Country '92
Convict Cowboy '95
Angel's Dance '99
And Starring Pancho Villa as Himself '03
King Kong '05
The Day the Earth Stood Still '08
Morning '10
Super 8 '11
Argo '12
Zero Dark Thirty '12
Broken City '13
The Spectacular Now '13
The Wolf of Wall Street '13
Carol '15
Manchester by the Sea '16
The Vanishing of Sidney Hall '17
First Man '18
Game Night '18
Godzilla: King of the Monsters '19

Lane Chandler (1899-1972)
The Single Standard '29
Heroes of the Alamo '37
Sergeant York '41
Laura '44
Border River '47
Money Madness '47
Noose for a Gunman '60

Simon Chandler (1953-)
Who's Who '78
Lace '84
Middlemarch '93
Incognito '97
The Man Who Knew Too Little '97

Tanis Chandler (1924-)
Shadows Over Chinatown '46
The Trap '46
Lured '47

John Chandos (1917-87)
The Next of Kin '42
The Long Memory '53

Jay Chandrasekhar (1968-)
Super Troopers '01
Club Dread '04
Beerfest '06
The Slammin' Salmon '09
The Babymakers '12
Super Troopers 2 '18

Helene Chanel (1941-)
Maciste in Hell '60
Samson and the 7 Miracles of the World '62
Cjamango '67

Lon Chaney, Jr. (1906-73)
Bird of Paradise '32
Last Frontier '32
The Three Musketeers '33
Undersea Kingdom '36
Mr. Moto's Gamble '38
Charlie Chan in City of Darkness '39
Of Mice and Men '39
One Million B.C. '40
Billy the Kid '41
Riders of Death Valley '41
The Wolf Man '41
Frankenstein Meets the Wolfman '42
The Ghost of Frankenstein '42
The Mummy's Tomb '42
Overland Mail '42
Son of Dracula '43
Cobra Woman '44
Dead Man's Eyes '44
House of Frankenstein '44
Here Come the Co-Eds '45
House of Dracula '45
My Favorite Brunette '47
Abbott and Costello Meet Frankenstein '48

Only the Valiant '50
Bride of the Gorilla '51
Battles of Chief Pontiac '52
Behave Yourself! '52
The Black Castle '52
The Bushwackers '52
High Noon '52
Springfield Rifle '52
A Lion Is in the Streets '53
Raiders of the Seven Seas '53
The Boy From Oklahoma '54
Passion '54
Big House, U.S.A. '55
I Died a Thousand Times '55
The Indian Fighter '55
Not as a Stranger '55
Silver Star '55
The Black Sleep '56
Cyclops '56
Daniel Boone: Trail Blazer '56
The Indestructible Man '56
Manfish '56
Pardners '56
The Defiant Ones '58
The Haunted Palace '63
Spider Baby '64
House of the Black Death '65
Johnny Reno '66
Alien Massacre '67
Gallery of Horrors '67
Hillbillies in a Haunted House '67
Welcome to Hard Times '67
Buckskin '68
Dracula *vs.* Frankenstein '71

Lon Chaney, Sr. (1883-1930)
Nomads of the North '20
The Penalty '20
The Ace of Hearts '21
Outside the Law '21
Flesh and Blood '22
Oliver Twist '22
Shadows '22
The Trap '22
The Hunchback of Notre Dame '23
The Shock '23
He Who Gets Slapped '24
The Monster '25
The Phantom of the Opera '25
The Unholy Three '25
The Black Bird '26
Tell It to the Marines '26
Mr. Wu '27
Mockery '27
Laugh, Clown, Laugh '28
The Unholy Three '30

Chen 'Chang Chen' Chang (1976-)
Happy Together '96
Crouching Tiger, Hidden Dragon '00
Chinese Odyssey 2002 '02
Eros '04
2046 '04
Red Cliff '08
The Grandmaster '13
The Assassin '15

King Hou Chang
Piccadilly '29
Son of the Gods '30

Jason Chang
Formula 17 '04
The Heirloom '05

Katie Chang
The Bling Ring '13
A Birder's Guide to Everything '14

Sylvia Chang (1953-)
Mad Mission 3 '84
Twin Dragons '92
Eat Drink Man Woman '94
The Red Violin '98
American Fusion '05
Mountains May Depart '16

Yi Chang
The Bells of Death '68
Sword Masters: Brothers Five '70

Yin Chang
The Bling Ring '11
Prom '11

Louis Ozawa Changchien
Robot Stories '03
Predators '10

Carol Channing (1921-)
Thoroughly Modern Millie '67
Skidoo '68
Shinbone Alley '70 (V)
Alice in Wonderland '85
Happily Ever After '93 (V)
Thumbelina '94 (V)

Stockard Channing (1944-)
The Hospital '71
The Girl Most Likely to. . . '73
The Big Bus '76
Sweet Revenge '76
The Cheap Detective '78
Grease '78
The Fish that Saved Pittsburgh '79
Without a Trace '83
Heartburn '86
The Men's Club '86
Perfect Witness '89
Staying Together '89
Bitter Moon '92
Married to It '93
Six Degrees of Separation '93
Edie & Pen '95
Smoke '95
To Wong Foo, Thanks for Everything, Julie Newmar '95
The First Wives Club '96
Lily Dale '96
Moll Flanders '96
Up Close and Personal '96
The Baby Dance '98
Practical Magic '98
Twilight '98
Isn't She Great '00
The Truth About Jane '00
Where the Heart Is '00
The Business of Strangers '01
A Girl Thing '01
Behind the Red Door '02
Life or Something Like It '02
Anything Else '03
Bright Young Things '03
Hitler: The Rise of Evil '03
Le Divorce '03
Must Love Dogs '05
Red Mercury '05
Sparkle '07
Multiple Sarcasms '10
Sundays at Tiffany's '10
Pulling Strings '13

Hsin Yen Chao
The Bells of Death '68
Golden Swallow '68

Rosalind Chao (1957-)
Battle Creek Brawl '80
The Big Brawl '80
M*A*S*H: Goodbye, Farewell & Amen '83
Drug Wars: The Camarena Story '90
Memoirs of an Invisible Man '92
The Joy Luck Club '93
The End of Violence '97
What Dreams May Come '98
Enemies of Laughter '00
Freaky Friday '03
Just like Heaven '05
Life of the Party '05
Plus One '19

Vic Chao
Mad Cowgirl '06
Mega Shark Vs. Giant Octopus '09

Winston Chao (1960-)
The Wedding Banquet '93
Eat Drink Man Woman '94
1911 '11
The Meg '18

Damian Chapa (1963-)
Blood In . . . Blood Out: Bound by Honor '93
Final Combination '93
Street Fighter '94
Saints and Sinners '95
Footsteps '98
Cypress Edge '99
Hitman's Run '99
Sometimes They Come Back. . . For More '99
Hell's Gate '01
U.S. Seals 2 '01
Lady Jayne Killer '03
El Padrino '04
Mexican Gangster '08

Omar Chaparro
Pulling Strings '13
Compadres '16
Tod@s Caen '19

Billy Chapin (1943-)
Tobor the Great '54
The Night of the Hunter '55
Violent Saturday '55

Miles Chapin (1954-)
Bless the Beasts and Children '71
French Postcards '79
The Funhouse '81
Get Crazy '83
The People *vs.* Larry Flynt '96
Lightning: Fire from the Sky '00

Ben Chaplin (1969-)
Feast of July '95
The Truth about Cats and Dogs '96
Washington Square '97
The Thin Red Line '98
Lost Souls '00
Birthday Girl '02
Murder by Numbers '02
Stage Beauty '04
Two Weeks '06
The Water Horse: Legend of the Deep '07
Dorian Gray '09
Me and Orson Welles '09
London Boulevard '10
Twixt '12
The Children Act '18

Carmen Chaplin (1977-)
Ma Saison Preferee '93
The Serpent's Kiss '97
All About the Benjamins '02
Snapshots '02
Don't Look Up '08

Charles Chaplin, Jr. (1925-68)
Fangs of the Wild '54
High School Confidential '58

Charlie Chaplin (1889-1977)
Tillie's Punctured Romance '14
The Gold Rush '25
The Circus '28
City Lights '31
Modern Times '36
The Great Dictator '40
Monsieur Verdoux '47
Limelight '52
A King in New York '57
The Chaplin Revue '58

Dolores Chaplin
The Ice Rink '99
The Counterfeiters '07

Geraldine Chaplin (1944-)
Doctor Zhivago '65
Innocent Bystanders '72
Zero Population Growth '72
The Three Musketeers '74
The Four Musketeers '75
Nashville '75
Buffalo Bill & the Indians '76
Roseland '77
A Wedding '78
The Mirror Crack'd '80
Bolero '82
Life Is a Bed of Roses '83
The Moderns '88
White Mischief '88
I Want to Go Home '89
Chaplin '92
Duel of Hearts '92
The Age of Innocence '93
A Foreign Field '93
Gulliver's Travels '95
Home for the Holidays '95
Crimetime '96
Jane Eyre '96
Cousin Bette '97
Mother Teresa: In the Name of God's Poor '97
The Odyssey '97
Mary, Mother of Jesus '99
To Walk with Lions '99
Talk to Her '02
The Bridge of San Luis Rey '05
BloodRayne '06
The Orphanage '07
The Wolfman '09
Americano '11
There Be Dragons '11
Panzer '13

Josephine Chaplin (1949-)
The Canterbury Tales '71
Jack the Ripper '76

Syd Chaplin (1885-1965)
The Better 'Ole '26
The Chaplin Revue '58
Cria Cuervos '76

Syd Chaplin (1926-2009)
Limelight '52
Land of the Pharaohs '55
Abdulla the Great '56
Quantez '57
A Countess from Hong Kong '67
Double Face '70
The Sibling '72
The Woman Hunter '72
Satan's Cheerleaders '77

Alexander Chapman (1976-)
Lilies '96
Cop Dog '08

Daniel Chapman (1952-94)
Death Collector '89
Philadelphia '93

Dean-Charles Chapman
Breathe '17
Blinded by the Light '19
1917 '19

Edward Chapman (1901-77)
Juno and the Paycock '30
The Church Mouse '34
Convoy '40
It Always Rains on Sunday '47
Madeleine '50
Bhowani Junction '56
X The Unknown '56
The Square Peg '58

Edythe Chapman (1863-1948)
Beyond the Rocks '22
The Ten Commandments '23
Lazybones '25
The Idle Rich '29
Navy Blues '29

Georgina Chapman (1976-)
The Business '05
Derailed '05
Awake '07

Graham Chapman (1941-89)
John Cleese on How to Irritate People '68
The Magic Christian '69
And Now for Something Completely Different '72
Monty Python and the Holy Grail '75
Monty Python's Life of Brian '79
The Secret Policeman's Other Ball '82
Monty Python's The Meaning of Life '83
Yellowbeard '83

Judith Chapman (1951-)
And God Created Woman '88
Dead Space '90
Fire on the Amazon '93
Scorpio One '97

Kevin Chapman (1962-)
Mystic River '03
In Good Company '04
Two for the Money '05
Black Dynamite '09
Sunshine Cleaning '09
Unstoppable '10
Street Kings 2: Motor City '11

Lonny (Lonnie) Chapman (1920-2007)
The Birds '63
Take the Money and Run '69
I Walk the Line '70
Where the Red Fern Grows '74
Moving Violation '76
Witch Who Came from the Sea '76
Alexander: The Other Side of Dawn '77
Terror Out of the Sky '78
Cave-In! '79
Hanging By a Thread '79
52 Pick-Up '86
Nightwatch '96
The Hunted '03

Marguerite Chapman (1918-99)
Destroyer '43
Strange Affair '44
Counter-Attack '45
The Green Promise '49
Kansas Raiders '50
Bloodhounds of Broadway '52
Flight to Mars '52
Man Bait '52

Mark Lindsay Chapman (1954-)
American Gothic '88
Separate Lives '94
Stephen King's The Langoliers '95
Bram Stoker's The Mummy '97
Beethoven's 4th '01
Trapped: Buried Alive '02

Sean Chapman (1961-)
Hellraiser '87
Hellbound: Hellraiser 2 '88
The Sea Change '98
7 Days to Live '00

Dave Chappelle (1973-)
Robin Hood: Men in Tights '93
The Nutty Professor '96
Con Air '97
Half-Baked '97
Woo '97
200 Cigarettes '98
You've Got Mail '98
Blue Streak '99
Screwed '00
Undercover Brother '02
Dave Chappelle's Block Party '06
A Star Is Born '18

Antoine Chappey (1960-)
I'm Going Home '00
5x2 '04
Le Petit Lieutenant '05

Patricia Charbonneau (1959-)
Desert Hearts '86
Manhunter '86
Stalking Danger '86
Shakedown '88
Brain Dead '89
RoboCop 2 '90
K2: The Ultimate High '92
Portraits of a Killer '95
Kiss the Sky '98
One Special Night '99
100 Feet '08

Tara Charendoff (1973-)
See Tara Strong

Cyd Charisse (1921-2008)
The Harvey Girls '46
The Unfinished Dance '47
On an Island with You '48
Words and Music '48
Tension '50
Singin' in the Rain '52
The Wild North '52
The Band Wagon '53
Brigadoon '54
Deep in My Heart '54
It's Always Fair Weather '55
Silk Stockings '57
Party Girl '58
Black Tights '60
Two Weeks in Another Town '62
Assassination in Rome '65
The Silencers '66
Maroc 7 '67
Portrait of an Escort '80
That's Dancing! '85
Swimsuit '89

Andre Charles (1960-)
See RuPaul Charles

Josh Charles (1971-)
Dead Poets Society '89
Don't Tell Mom the Babysitter's Dead '91
Crossing the Bridge '92
Coldblooded '94
Threesome '94
Norma Jean and Marilyn '95
Pie in the Sky '95
Things to Do in Denver When You're Dead '95
Crossworlds '96
Little City '97
Meeting Daddy '98
Muppets from Space '99
Our America '02
S.W.A.T. '03
Seeing Other People '04
Four Brothers '05
The Ex '07
Brief Interviews With Hideous Men '09
After.life '10
Weakness '10
Bird People '14
Northpole '14
Freeheld '15
I Smile Back '15
Norman '17

Max Charles (2003-)
November Christmas '10
Mr. Peabody & Sherman '14 (V)
Northpole '14

Ray Charles (1930-2004)
Ballad in Blue '66
The Blues Brothers '80
Limit Up '89

RuPaul Charles (1960-)
Crooklyn '94
Blue in the Face '95
The Brady Bunch Movie '95
Smoke '95
To Wong Foo, Thanks for Everything, Julie Newmar '95
Wigstock: The Movie '95
A Very Brady Sequel '96
But I'm a Cheerleader '99
EDtv '99
The Eyes of Tammy Faye '00 (N)
The Truth About Jane '00
Skinwalker '02
Who is Cletis Tout? '02

Ian Charleson (1949-90)
Chariots of Fire '81
Gandhi '82
Greystoke: The Legend of Tarzan, Lord of the Apes '84
Opera '88
Troubles '88

Ray Charleson
Out For a Kill '03
Dark Corners '06
United 93 '06

Kim Charney
Suddenly '54
Man From God's Country '58

Charo (1945-)
The Concorde: Airport '79 *'79*
Moon over Parador *'88*
Thumbelina *'94 (V)*

Charpin (1887-1944)
Marius *'31*
Fanny *'32*
Cesar *'36*
Well-Digger's Daughter *'46*

Spencer Charters (1875-1943)
The Bat Whispers *'30*
Movie Crazy *'32*
The Ghost Walks *'34*
The Moon's Our Home *'36*
Three Comrades *'38*
High Sierra *'41*

Melanie Chartoff (1948-)
Doin' Time *'85*
Kenny Rogers as the Gambler, Part 3: The Legend Continues *'87*
The Rugrats Movie *'98 (V)*
Rugrats in Paris: The Movie *'00 (V)*
Rugrats Go Wild! *'03 (V)*

David Charvet (1972-)
Beach Kings *'08*
The Perfect Teacher *'10*

Alden 'Steve' Chase (1902-82)
Cowboy Millionaire *'35*
Buried Alive *'39*
The Blob *'58*

Annazette Chase
Truck Turner *'74*
Fist *'76*

Charley Chase (1893-1940)
Sons of the Desert *'33*
Block-heads *'38*

Cheryl Chase
Rugrats in Paris: The Movie *'00 (V)*
Rugrats Go Wild! *'03 (V)*

Chevy Chase (1943-)
The Groove Tube *'72*
Tunnelvision *'76*
Foul Play *'78*
Caddyshack *'80*
Oh, Heavenly Dog! *'80*
Seems Like Old Times *'80*
Modern Problems *'81*
Under the Rainbow *'81*
Deal of the Century *'83*
National Lampoon's Vacation *'83*
Fletch *'85*
National Lampoon's European Vacation *'85*
Sesame Street Presents: Follow That Bird *'85*
Spies Like Us *'85*
Three Amigos *'86*
Caddyshack 2 *'88*
Funny Farm *'88*
Fletch Lives *'89*
National Lampoon's Christmas Vacation *'89*
Nothing But Trouble *'91*
Hero *'92*
Memoirs of an Invisible Man *'92*
Last Action Hero *'93 (C)*
Cops and Robbersons *'94*
Man of the House *'95*
Vegas Vacation *'96*
Dirty Work *'97*
Snow Day *'00*
Orange County *'02*
Karate Dog *'04 (V)*
Our Italian Husband *'04*
Ellie Parker *'05*
Zoom *'06*
Jack and the Beanstalk *'09*
Stay Cool *'09*
Hot Tub Time Machine *'10*
Hot Tub Time Machine 2 *'15*
Vacation *'15*
The Last Movie Star *'17*

Courtney Chase (1988-)
Nick of Time *'95*
Mean Girls *'04*
13 Going on 30 *'04*

Daveigh Chase (1990-)
The Rats *'01*
Spirited Away *'01 (V)*
Lilo & Stitch *'02 (V)*
The Ring *'02*
Beethoven's 5th *'03*
The Ring 2 *'05*
Leroy and Stitch *'06 (V)*
S. Darko: A Donnie Darko Tale *'09*

Frank Chase (1923-2004)
The Creature Walks among Us *'56*
Attack of the 50 Foot Woman *'58*

Ilka Chase (1905-78)
The Animal Kingdom *'32*
Stronger Than Desire *'39*
Now, Voyager *'42*
No Time For Love *'43*
Miss Tatlock's Millions *'48*
The Big Knife *'55*

Jeffrey Chase (1968-)
Scream of the Demon Lover *'71*
In the Shadows *'01*
Kids in America *'05*
Transporter 2 *'05*
The Mechanic *'11*
Swamp Shark *'11*

Jonathan Chase (1979-)
Dead Tone *'07*
Dorfman in Love *'11*

Stephan Chase (1900-78)
My Favorite Spy *'51*
Macbeth *'71*
Florence Nightingale *'85*

Will Chase (1970-)
4 Single Fathers *'09*
The Lost Valentine *'11*
After the Wedding *'19*

Jessica Chastain (1981-)
Blackbeard *'06*
Jolene *'08*
Stolen *'09*
The Debt *'10*
Murder on the Orient Express *'10*
Coriolanus *'11*
The Help *'11*
Take Shelter *'11*
Texas Killing Fields *'11*
The Tree of Life *'11*
Lawless *'12*
Zero Dark Thirty *'12*
Mama *'13*
The Disappearance of Eleanor Rigby *'14*
Interstellar *'14*
Miss Julie *'14*
A Most Violent Year *'14*
Crimson Peak *'15*
The Martian *'15*
The Huntsman: Winter's War *'16*
Miss Sloane *'16*
Molly's Game *'17*
Woman Walks Ahead *'17*
The Zookeeper's Wife *'17*
Dark Phoenix *'19*
It Chapter Two *'19*

Peter Chatel (1943-86)
Who Saw Her Die? *'72*
Fox and His Friends *'75*

Christine Chatelain
Dr. Dolittle 4: Tail to the Chief *'08*
Death Do Us Part *'14*

Wes Chatham
In the Valley of Elah *'07*
The Philly Kid *'12*
All I See Is You *'17*

Anucha Chatkaew
The Iron Ladies *'00*
The Iron Ladies 2 *'03*

Sorapong Chatree
The Legend of Suriyothai *'02*
Ong Bak 2 *'08*

Soumitra Chatterjee (1935-)
The World of Apu *'59*
Devi *'60*
Charulata *'64*
The Bengali Night *'88*

Ruth Chatterton (1893-1961)
Madame X *'29*
Frisco Jenny *'32*
The Rich Are Always With Us *'32*
Dodsworth *'36*
Girl's Dormitory *'36*

Tom Chatterton (1881-1952)
Drums of Fu Manchu *'40*
Flash Gordon Conquers the Universe *'40*
Overland Mail *'42*

Charlotte Chatton
Hellraiser 4: Bloodline *'95*
Stand-Ins *'97*

Justin Chatwin (1982-)
The Incredible Mrs. Ritchie *'03*
Superbabies: Baby Geniuses 2 *'04*
Taking Lives *'04*
The Chumscrubber *'05*
War of the Worlds *'05*
The Invisible *'07*
Dragonball: Evolution *'09*
Funkytown *'11*
Urge *'16*

Francois Chau (1959-)
Teenage Mutant Ninja Turtles 2: The Secret of the Ooze *'91*
Beverly Hills Ninja *'96*
21 & Over *'13*

Hong Chau
Downsizing *'17*
Driveways *'19*

Osric Chau
Kung Fu Killer *'08*
Fun Size *'12*

Anthony Wong Chau-Sang (1961-)
Infernal Affairs 2 *'03*
Infernal Affairs 3 *'03*
House of Fury *'05*
Exiled *'06*

Emmanuelle Chaulet
Boyfriends & Girlfriends *'88*
All the Vermeers in New York *'91*

Lilyan Chauvin (1925-2008)
Bloodlust *'59*
Lost, Lonely, and Vicious *'59*
Silent Night, Deadly Night *'84*

Ricardo Chavira (1971-)
Chasing 3000 *'07*
Kings of South Beach *'07*
Saving God *'08*

Maury Chaykin (1949-2010)
Curtains *'83*
Mrs. Soffel *'84*
Def-Con 4 *'85*
Iron Eagle 2 *'88*
Breaking In *'89*
Millennium *'89*
Dances with Wolves *'90*
Mr. Destiny *'90*
Where the Heart Is *'90*
The Adjuster *'91*
The Pianist *'91*
Hero *'92*
Leaving Normal *'92*
Money for Nothing *'93*
Northern Extremes *'93*
Sommersby *'93*
Camilla *'94*
Cutthroat Island *'95*
Devil in a Blue Dress *'95*
Sugartime *'95*
Unstrung Heroes *'95*
The Sweet Hereafter *'96*
A Life Less Ordinary *'97*
Love and Death on Long Island *'97*
Mouse Hunt *'97*
Pale Saints *'97*
Strip Search *'97*
Jerry and Tom *'98*
The Mask of Zorro *'98*
Entrapment *'99*
Jacob Two Two Meets the Hooded Fang *'99*
Joan of Arc *'99*
Let the Devil Wear Black *'99*
Mystery, Alaska *'99*
The Art of War *'00*
The Golden Spiders: A Nero Wolfe Mystery *'00*
What's Cooking? *'00*
Bartleby *'01*
The Doorbell Rang: A Nero Wolfe Mystery *'01*
Varian's War *'01*
Owning Mahowny *'03*
Being Julia *'04*
White Coats *'04*
Where the Truth Lies *'05*
Heavens Fall *'06*
It's a Boy Girl Thing *'06*
Blindness *'08*

Mariann (Marie-Anne) Chazel (1951-)
French Fried Vacation *'79*
The Visitors *'95*

Suzanne Chazelle (1935-)
See Dany Carrel

Don Cheadle (1964-)
Hamburger Hill *'87*
Colors *'88*
Devil in a Blue Dress *'95*
Things to Do in Denver When You're Dead *'95*
Rebound: The Legend of Earl 'The Goat' Manigault *'96*
Rosewood *'96*
Boogie Nights *'97*
Volcano *'97*
Bulworth *'98*
Out of Sight *'98*
The Rat Pack *'98*
A Lesson Before Dying *'99*
Fail Safe *'00*
Family Man *'00*
Mission to Mars *'00*
Traffic *'00*
Manic *'01*
Ocean's Eleven *'01*
Rush Hour 2 *'01*
Swordfish *'01*
Things Behind the Sun *'01*
United States of Leland *'03*
After the Sunset *'04*
Hotel Rwanda *'04*
Ocean's Twelve *'04*
The Assassination of Richard Nixon *'05*
Crash *'05*
The Dog Problem *'06*
Ocean's Thirteen *'07*
Reign Over Me *'07*
Talk to Me *'07*
Traitor *'08*
Brooklyn's Finest *'09*
Hotel for Dogs *'09*
Iron Man 2 *'10*
The Guard *'11*
Flight *'12*
Iron Man 3 *'13*
Kevin Hart: What Now? *'16*
Miles Ahead *'16*

Amari Cheatom
Night Catches Us *'10*
Knucklehead *'15*
Crown Heights *'17*

Andrea Checchi (1916-74)
Black Sunday *'60*
The Invaders *'63*
Diary of a Rebel *'68*

Molly Cheek (1950-)
Smoke Signals *'98*
American Pie *'99*
American Pie 2 *'01*
American Wedding *'03*
April's Shower *'03*
A Lot Like Love *'05*

Derk Cheetwood (1973-)
U-571 *'00*
Frailty *'02*

Micheline Cheirel (1917-2002)
Cornered *'45*
So Dark the Night *'46*

Michael Chekhov (1891-1955)
Spellbound *'45*
Invitation *'51*
Rhapsody *'54*

Daoming Chen (1955-)
Hero *'02*
Infernal Affairs 3 *'03*
Silver Hawk *'04*
Coming Home *'14*

Edison Chen (1980-)
Infernal Affairs 2 *'03*
Vampire Effect *'03*
Dog Bite Dog *'06*
The Grudge 2 *'06*

Joan Chen (1961-)
Dim Sum: A Little Bit of Heart *'85*
Tai-Pan *'86*
The Last Emperor *'87*
Night Stalker *'87*
The Blood of Heroes *'89*
Deadlock *'91*
Golden Gate *'93*
Heaven and Earth *'93*
The Hunted *'94*
On Deadly Ground *'94*
Temptation of a Monk *'94*
Judge Dredd *'95*
Wild Side *'95*
In a Class of His Own *'99*
What's Cooking? *'00*
Saving Face *'04*
Lust, Caution *'07*
Mao's Last Dancer *'09*
1911 *'11*
Hemingway & Gelhorn *'12*
White Frog *'12*

Kelly Chen (1973-)
Tokyo Raiders *'00*
Infernal Affairs 3 *'03*
Breaking News *'04*
An Empress and the Warriors *'08*

Kuan Tai Chen (1945-)
Heroes Two *'73*
The Master *'80*
Opium and Kung-Fu Master *'84*
Dragon Tiger Gate *'07*

Lynn Chen (1976-)
Saving Face *'04*
The People I've Slept With *'09*
Why Am I Doing This? *'09*

Michael Chen
Children of Invention *'09*
A Birder's Guide to Everything *'14*

Moira Chen (1950-)
See Laura Gemser

Terry Chen (1975-)
Crash & Byrnes *'99*
Almost Famous *'00*
Ballistic: Ecks *vs.* Sever *'02*
Stark Raving Mad *'02*
Memory *'06*
Snakes on a Plane *'06*
Storm Seekers *'08*

Tina Chen (1945-)
Alice's Restaurant *'69*
Paper Man *'71*
Almost Perfect *'11*

Adam Cheng (1947-)
Shaolin & Wu Tang *'81*
Zu: Warriors from the Magic Mountain *'83*
Fantasy Mission Force *'84*
Painted Skin *'93*

Ekin Cheng (1967-)
The Cave of the Silken Web *'67*
Tokyo Raiders *'00*
Zu Warriors *'01*
Vampire Effect *'03*
Six Strong Guys *'04*
Running Out of Time 2 *'06*

Kent Cheng (1951-)
Once Upon a Time in China *'91*
Crime Story *'93*
The Bodyguard from Beijing *'94*
Flash Point *'07*
Ip Man 2 *'10*

Lei Cheng
The Magnificent Trio *'66*
The One-Armed Swordsman *'67*

Pei Pei Cheng (1946-)
Golden Swallow *'68*
Sword Masters: Brothers Five *'70*
Naked Weapon *'03*
Kung Fu Killer *'08*
Lilting *'14*
The Guardsman *'15*

Sammi Cheng
Infernal Affairs *'02*
Infernal Affairs 3 *'03*

Taisheng ('Cheng Tai Shen') Cheng
Jade Warrior *'06*
Biutiful *'10*

Kristin Chenoweth (1968-)
Annie *'99*
Bewitched *'05*
Deck the Halls *'06*
The Pink Panther *'06*
Running with Scissors *'06*
RV *'06*
Four Christmases *'08*
Space Chimps *'08 (V)*
Into Temptation *'09*
12 Men of Christmas *'09*
You Again *'10*
Hit and Run *'12*
Family Weekend *'13*
A Bet's a Bet *'14*
Rio 2 *'14 (V)*
The Boy Next Door *'15*
Strange Magic *'15 (V)*
My Little Pony: The Movie *'17*

Cher (1946-)
Good Times *'67*
Silkwood *'83*
Mask *'85*
Moonstruck *'87*
Suspect *'87*
The Witches of Eastwick *'87*
Mermaids *'90*
The Player *'92 (C)*
Ready to Wear *'94*
Faithful *'95*
If These Walls Could Talk *'96*
Tea with Mussolini *'99*
Stuck On You *'03*
Burlesque *'10*
Zookeeper *'11 (V)*

Patrice Chereau (1944-2013)
Danton *'82*
The Last of the Mohicans *'92*
Time Regained *'99 (V)*
Time of the Wolf *'03*

Nikolai Cherkassov (1903-66)
Happiness *'32*
Baltic Deputy *'37*
Alexander Nevsky *'38*
Ivan the Terrible, Part 1 *'44*
Ivan the Terrible, Part 2 *'46*
Don Quixote *'57*

Jonas Chernick (1973-)
A Woman's a Helluva Thing *'01*
Edge of Madness *'02*
Eloise at the Plaza *'03*
Intimate Stranger *'06*

Michael Chernus (1977-)
Lovely by Surprise *'07*
Feed the Fish *'09*

Captain Phillips *'13*
Glass Chin *'14*
Mistress America *'15*
People Places Things *'15*
The Dinner *'17*

Jake Cherry (1996-)
Miracle Run *'04*
Night at the Museum *'06*
Night at the Museum: Battle of the Smithsonian *'09*
The Son of No One *'11*
Transit *'12*

Jonathan Cherry (1978-)
Final Destination 2 *'03*
House of the Dead *'03*
Christmas in Boston *'05*
Marker *'05*

George Chesebro (1888-1959)
Wolf Blood *'25*
The Miracle Rider *'35*
S.O.S. Coast Guard *'37*
Holt of the Secret Service *'42*

Patrick Chesnais (1947-)
After Sex *'97*
The Diving Bell and the Butterfly *'07*
Change of Plans *'09*
Bright Days Ahead *'14*

Arthur Chesney
The Lodger *'26*
Hindle Wakes *'27*

Craig Chester (1965-)
Swoon *'91*
Grief *'94*
Frisk *'95*
I Shot Andy Warhol *'96*
Kiss Me, Guido *'97*
Adam & Steve *'05*

Elijah Chester
American Warships *'01*
American Warship *'12*

Hal E. Chester (1921-)
Dead End Kids: Little Tough Guy *'38*
Junior G-Men *'40*

Vanessa Lee Chester (1984-)
A Little Princess *'95*
Harriet the Spy *'96*
The Lost World: Jurassic Park 2 *'97*

Morris Chestnut (1969-)
Boyz N the Hood *'91*
The Last Boy Scout *'91*
Under Siege 2: Dark Territory *'95*
G.I. Jane *'97*
The Best Man *'99*
The Brothers *'01*
Scenes of the Crime *'01*
Two Can Play That Game *'01*
Half Past Dead *'02*
Like Mike *'02*
Confidence *'03*
Anacondas: The Hunt for the Blood Orchid *'04*
Breakin' All The Rules *'04*
Ladder 49 *'04*
The Cave *'05*
The Game Plan *'07*
The Perfect Holiday *'07*
Not Easily Broken *'09*
The Best Man Holiday *'13*
The Call *'13*
Identity Thief *'13*
Kick-Ass 2 *'13*
The Perfect Guy *'15*
When the Bough Breaks *'16*

Cecilia Cheung (1980-)
Tokyo Raiders *'00*
Shaolin Soccer *'01*
Zu Warriors *'01*
Running on Karma *'03*
The Promise *'05*
Dangerous Liaisons *'12*

Cindy Cheung
Robot Stories *'03*
Children of Invention *'09*
The Light of the Moon *'17*

George Kee Cheung (1949-)
Opposing Force *'87*
High Voltage *'98*
Starsky & Hutch *'04*
Mongolian Death Worm *'10*

Jacky Cheung (1961-)
As Tears Go By *'88*
A Bullet in the Head *'90*
Days of Being Wild *'91*
Once Upon a Time in China *'91*
Wicked City *'92*
Ashes of Time *'94*
Meltdown *'95*
Perhaps Love *'05*
Ashes of Time Redux *'08*

Karin Anna Cheung (1974-)
Better Luck Tomorrow *'02*
The People I've Slept With *'09*

Leslie Cheung (1956-2003)
A Better Tomorrow, Part 1 *'86*
A Better Tomorrow, Part 2 *'88*
Once a Thief *'90*
Days of Being Wild *'91*
The Bride with White Hair *'93*
The Bride with White Hair 2 *'93*
Farewell My Concubine *'93*
Ashes of Time *'94*
The Phantom Lover *'95*
Happy Together *'96*
Temptress Moon *'96*
Ashes of Time Redux *'08*

Maggie Cheung (1964-)
Police Story *'85*
Project A: Part 2 *'87*
As Tears Go By *'88*
Days of Being Wild *'91*
Supercop *'92*
Twin Dragons *'92*
The Executioners *'93*
Green Snake *'93*
The Heroic Trio *'93*
Ashes of Time *'94*
Irma Vep *'96*
Chinese Box *'97*
In the Mood for Love *'00*
Hero *'02*
Clean *'04*
2046 *'04*
Ashes of Time Redux *'08*
Inglourious Basterds *'09*

Nick Cheung
Breaking News *'04*
Exiled *'06*
The White Storm *'13*

Roy Cheung (1963-)
City on Fire *'87*
Wicked City *'92*
Organized Crime & Triad Bureau *'93*
Beast Cops *'98*
The Mission *'99*
Infernal Affairs 2 *'03*
Exiled *'06*

Siu-fai Cheung
Running on Karma *'03*
Dog Bite Dog *'06*

Kevin Timothy Chevalia (1986-)
Folks! *'92*
Homeward Bound: The Incredible Journey *'93*
Homeward Bound 2: Lost in San Francisco *'96*

Maurice Chevalier (1888-1972)
The Love Parade *'29*
The Smiling Lieutenant *'31*
Love Me Tonight *'32*
One Hour with You *'32*
The Merry Widow *'34*
Folies Bergere de Paris *'35*
Love in the Afternoon *'57*
Gigi *'58*
Black Tights *'60 (N)*
Breath of Scandal *'60*
Can-Can *'60*
Fanny *'61*
In Search of the Castaways *'62*
Panic Button *'62*
A New Kind of Love *'63*
Monkeys, Go Home! *'66*
The Sorrow and the Pity *'71*

Richard Chevolleau (1966-)
Blood Brothers *'93*
Indian Summer *'93*
Rude *'96*
Tracked *'98*
The Wall *'99*
Flowers for Algernon *'00*
No Alibi *'00*
True Blue *'01*
Narc *'02*
Who is Cletis Tout? *'02*

Arno Chevrier
Agnes Browne *'99*
The Red Dwarf *'99*

Laureen Chew
Chan Is Missing *'82*
Dim Sum: A Little Bit of Heart *'85*

Chao-Li Chi
Battle Creek Brawl *'80*
Warriors of Virtue *'97*

Minoru Chiaki (1917-99)
Rashomon *'51*
Seven Samurai *'54*
Godzilla Raids Again *'55*
Throne of Blood *'57*
The Hidden Fortress *'58*
The Human Condition: Road to Eternity *'59*
Face of Another *'66*

Dominic Chianese (1931-)
The Godfather, Part 2 *'74*
Dog Day Afternoon *'75*
All the President's Men *'76*
And Justice for All *'79*
Firepower *'79*
On the Yard *'79*
Second Sight *'89*
Q & A *'90*
Out for Justice *'91*
The Public Eye *'92*
The Night We Never Met *'93*
If Lucy Fell *'95*
Gotti *'96*
Looking for Richard *'96*
Love Is All There Is *'96*
Night Falls on Manhattan *'96*
Went to Coney Island on a Mission from God. . . Be Back by Five *'98*
The Cradle Will Rock *'99*
Under Hellgate Bridge *'99*
Once in the Life *'00*
Unfaithful *'02*
Crimes of Fashion *'04*
King of the Corner *'04*
When Will I Be Loved *'04*
Adrift in Manhattan *'07*
The Last New Yorker *'07*

David Chiang (1947-)
Have Sword, Will Travel *'69*
The Heroic Ones *'70*
Duel of Fists *'71*
Heaven & Hell *'78*
The Kumite *'03*

Sheng Chiang
Five Deadly Venoms *'78*
House of Traps *'81*

Marco Chiappi
After the Deluge *'03*
The Mystery of a Hansom Cab *'12*

Walter Chiari (1924-91)
Bellissima *'51*
Nana *'55*
Bonjour Tristesse *'57*
The Inveterate Bachelor *'58*
The Valachi Papers *'72*

Stephen Chiau (1962-)
See Stephen (Chiau) Chow

Sofiko Chiaureli (1937-)
The Color of Pomegranates *'69*
Ashik Kerib *'88*

Sonny Chiba (1939-)
Invasion of the Neptune Men *'61*
Terror Beneath the Sea *'66*
Return of the Street Fighter *'74*
The Street Fighter *'74*
The Street Fighter's Last Revenge *'74*
The Bodyguard *'76*
Sister Street Fighter *'76*
Message from Space *'78*
Hunter in the Dark *'80*
Samurai Reincarnation *'81*
Fall Guy *'82*
Virus *'82*
Aces: Iron Eagle 3 *'92*
Immortal Combat *'94*
Body Count *'95*
Kill Bill Vol. 1 *'03*
Kill Bill Vol. 2 *'04*
Wind and Cloud: The Storm Riders *'04*
The Fast and the Furious: Tokyo Drift *'06*
Sushi Girl *'12*

Etienne Chicot (1949-)
Hotel America *'81*
Le Choc *'82*
36 Fillete *'88*
The Da Vinci Code *'06*

Takeo Chii
Kill! *'68*
Lady Snowblood *'73*

Caroline Chikezie (1979-)
Aeon Flux *'05*
Eragon *'06*
Mayhem *'17*

Michael Chiklis (1963-)
Body and Soul *'98*
Soldier *'98*
The Taxman *'98*
Silent Witness *'99*
Spirited Away *'01 (V)*
Fantastic Four *'05*
Fantastic Four: Rise of the Silver Surfer *'07*
Rise: Blood Hunter *'07*
Eagle Eye *'08*
High School *'10*
Parker *'13*
Pawn *'13*
When the Game Stands Tall *'14*
10 Minutes Gone *'19*

Jeremy Child (1944-)
Privilege *'67*
Florence Nightingale *'85*
Fool's Gold: The Story of the Brink's-Mat Robbery *'92*
Sharpe's Enemy *'94*
Behind the Lines *'97*
Frenchman's Creek *'98*

Samuel Child (1976-)
Marked *'07*
April Fool's Day *'08*
The Thompsons *'12*

Ambyr Childers (1988-)
Playback *'12*
We Are What We Are *'13*
Vice *'15*

Patricia Childress (1971-)
Shake, Rattle & Rock! *'94*
Larry McMurtry's Dead Man's Walk *'96*

Linden Chiles (1933-2013)
A Rage to Live *'65*
Texas Across the River *'66*
Counterpoint *'67*
Forbidden World *'82*
Abandoned and Deceived *'95*

Lois Chiles (1947-)
The Way We Were *'73*
Coma *'78*
Death on the Nile *'78*
Moonraker *'79*
Broadcast News *'87*
Creepshow 2 *'87*
Twister *'89*
Diary of a Hitman *'91*
The Babysitter *'95*
Curdled *'95*
Bliss *'96*
Wish upon a Star *'96*
Speed 2: Cruise Control *'97*

Han Chin
The Heroic Ones *'70*
Sword Masters: Brothers Five *'70*

Ping Chin
The Magnificent Trio *'66*
The Bells of Death *'68*

Siu-hou Chin (1963-)
Sword Masters: Two Champions of Shaolin *'80*
House of Traps *'81*
The Brave Archer and His Mate *'82*

Tsai Chin (1936-)
The Face of Fu Manchu *'65*
Brides of Fu Manchu *'66*
The Vengeance of Fu Manchu *'67*
You Only Live Twice *'67*
The Castle of Fu Manchu *'68*
Kiss and Kill *'68*
The Virgin Soldiers *'69*
Rentadick *'72*
The Joy Luck Club *'93*
Red Corner *'97*
Long Life, Happiness and Prosperity *'02*
The Diary of Ellen Rimbauer *'03*
The Interpreter *'05*
Memoirs of a Geisha *'05*
Lucky Grandma *'20*

Li Ching
Sword Masters: Web of Death *'76*
The Magic Blade *'08*

William Ching (1913-89)
The Wistful Widow of Wagon Gap *'47*
D.O.A. *'49*
Never Wave at a WAC *'52*
Pat and Mike *'52*
Give a Girl a Break *'53*
The Moonlighter *'53*
Terror in the Haunted House *'58*

Kieu Chinh (1937-)
Operation C.I.A. *'65*
Hamburger Hill *'87*
The Joy Luck Club *'93*
Riot in the Streets *'96*
Catfish in Black Bean Sauce *'00*
Green Dragon *'01*
Tempted *'03*

Nick (Nicholas) Chinlund (1961-)
The Ambulance *'90*
Lethal Weapon 3 *'92*
Red Shoe Diaries 4: Auto Erotica *'93*
Bad Girls *'94*
Eraser *'96*
A Brother's Kiss *'97*
Con Air *'97*
Mr. Magoo *'97*
Rough Riders *'97*
Frogs for Snakes *'98*
Chutney Popcorn *'99*
Beyond Suspicion *'00*
Disney's The Kid *'00*
Once in the Life *'00*
Training Day *'01*
Amy's O *'02*
Below *'02*
100 Mile Rule *'02*
Tears of the Sun *'03*
The Chronicles of Riddick *'04*
The Legend of Zorro *'05*
Ultraviolet *'06*
Avenging Angel *'07*
Sinner *'07*
Felon *'08*
Wyvern *'09*
5 Star Day *'10*
Speed-Dating *'10*
Close Range *'15*
Mercury Plains *'16*

Jimmy Chisholm (1956-)
Ivanhoe *'97*
Strictly Sinatra *'01*

David Chisum
Dark Mirror *'07*
Flight of the Living Dead: Outbreak on a Plane *'07*

Khan Chittenden (1983-)
Introducing the Dwights *'07*
In Her Skin *'09*
National Lampoon Presents: Endless Bummer *'09*
Sisters of War *'10*

Erik Chitty (1907-77)
First Men in the Moon *'64*
Doctor Zhivago *'65*

Tony Leung Chiu-wai (1962-)
Days of Being Wild *'91*
Chinese Odyssey 2002 *'02*
Infernal Affairs *'02*
Seoul Raiders *'05*

Anna Chlumsky (1980-)
My Girl *'91*
My Girl 2 *'94*
Trading Mom *'94*
Gold Diggers: The Secret of Bear Mountain *'95*
In the Loop *'09*
12 Men of Christmas *'09*
The Good Guy *'10*
The End of the Tour *'15*

Arden Cho (1985-)
Hoodrats 2 *'08*
Walking the Halls *'12*

John Cho (1972-)
Yellow *'98*
American Pie *'99*
Earth *vs.* the Spider *'01*
Pavilion of Women *'01*
Better Luck Tomorrow *'02*
Harold and Kumar Go to White Castle *'04*
Bam Bam & Celeste *'05*
American Dreamz *'06*
Bickford Shmeckler's Cool Ideas *'06*
Harold & Kumar Escape from Guantanamo Bay *'08*
Saint John of Las Vegas *'09*
Star Trek *'09*
A Very Harold & Kumar Christmas *'11*
Total Recall *'12*
Identity Thief *'13*
Star Trek: Into Darkness *'13*
Zipper *'15*
Star Trek: Beyond *'16*
Columbus *'17*
Gemini *'17*
Mirai *'18*
The Oath *'18*
Searching *'18*

Margaret Cho (1969-)
The Doom Generation *'95*
It's My Party *'95*
Face/Off *'97*
Sweethearts *'97*
Ground Control *'98*
Spent *'00*
The Tavern *'00*
Bam Bam & Celeste *'05*
Falling for Grace *'06*
One Missed Call *'08*
Call Me Lucky *'15*

Tim Choate (1954-2004)
Def-Con 4 *'85*
Blind Witness *'89*
Live Nude Girls *'95*

Charlene (Cheuk-Yin) Choi (1982-)
Vampire Effect *'03*
New Police Story *'04*
House of Fury *'05*
The Assassin's Blade *'08*
The Sorcerer and the White Snake *'13*

Min-Sik Choi (1962-)
No. 3 *'97*
The Quiet Family *'98*
Chihwaseon: Painted Fire *'02*
Oldboy *'03*

I Saw the Devil '10
Lucy '14

Si Won Choi
Battle of the Warriors '06
Dragon Blade '15

David Chokachi (1968-)
Crimson Force '05
Bats: Human Harvest '07
Murder.com '08
Born Bad '11
Collision Course '12
Abner the Invisible Dog '13

Monia Chokri
Heartbeats '11
Laurence Anyways '12

Justin Chon (1981-)
Twilight '08
Balls Out: Gary the Tennis Coach '09
Crossing Over '09
The Twilight Saga: New Moon '09
Rock Jocks '12
21 & Over '13
Revenge of the Green Dragons '14
Satanic '15

Marcus Chong (1967-)
Panther '95
The Matrix '99
The Crow: Wicked Prayer '05

Rae Dawn Chong (1961-)
Stony Island '77
Quest for Fire '82
Beat Street '84
Cheech and Chong's The Corsican Brothers '84
Choose Me '84
American Flyers '85
City Limits '85
The Color Purple '85
Commando '85
Fear City '85
Soul Man '86
The Principal '87
The Squeeze '87
Far Out Man '89
Tales from the Darkside: The Movie '90
When the Party's Over '91
Time Runner '92
Dangerous Relations '93
Hideaway '94
Power of Attorney '94
The Break '95
Smalltime '96
Highball '97
Mask of Death '97
Protector '97
The Visit '00
Jeff, Who Lives at Home '12

Thomas Chong (1938-)
Cheech and Chong's Up in Smoke '79
Cheech and Chong's Next Movie '80
Cheech and Chong's Nice Dreams '81
Cheech and Chong: Things Are Tough All Over '82
Cheech and Chong: Still Smokin' '83
Yellowbeard '83
Cheech and Chong's The Corsican Brothers '84
After Hours '85 (C)
Far Out Man '89
Spirit of '76 '91
Ferngully: The Last Rain Forest '92 (V)
National Lampoon's Senior Trip '95
Half-Baked '97
McHale's Navy '97
The Wash '01
Hoodwinked Too! Hood *vs.* Evil '11 (V)

Priyanka Chopra (1982-)
Planes '13 (V)
Baywatch '17
A Kid Like Jake '18
Isn't It Romantic '19

Lara Jean Chorostecki (1984-)
The 19th Wife '10
The Masked Saint '16

Collin Chou (1967-)
The Bodyguard from Beijing '94
Jet Li's The Enforcer '95
The Matrix Revolutions '03
American Fusion '05
DOA: Dead or Alive '06
Jet Li's Fearless '06
Flash Point '07
The Forbidden Kingdom '08
Kingdom of Blood: The Final Battle '16

Jay Chou
Curse of the Golden Flower '06
The Green Hornet '11
Now You See Me 2 '16

Lawrence Chou
The Eye '02
Re-Cycle '06

Sarita Choudhury (1966-)
Mississippi Masala '92
The House of the Spirits '93
Kama Sutra: A Tale of Love '96
Subway Stories '97
A Perfect Murder '98
3 A.M. '01
Just a Kiss '02
It Runs in the Family '03
The Breakup Artist '04
The War Within '05
Lady in the Water '06
Admission '13
Generation Um... '13
Learning to Drive '15
A Hologram for the King '16

Etchika Choureau (1929-)
The Vanquished '52
Darby's Rangers '58
Lafayette Escadrille '58

China Chow (1974-)
The Big Hit '98
Head Over Heels '01
Sol Goode '01
Frankenfish '04

Stephen (Chiau) Chow (1962-)
Shaolin Soccer '01
Kung Fu Hustle '04

Valerie Chow (1970-)
Chungking Express '95
Meltdown '95

Yun-Fat Chow (1955-)
See Chow Yun-Fat

Navin Chowdhry (1971-)
Madame Sousatzka '88
The Seventh Coin '92
Red Mercury '05

Ranjit (Chaudry) Chowdhry (1955-2020)
Mississippi Masala '92
Bleeding Hearts '94
Fire '96
Last Holiday '06

Emma Choy
Speed Dating '07
The Vanguard '08

Joseph Chrest
The Underneath '95
Welcome to the Rileys '10
Seeking Justice '12

Emmanuelle Chriqui (1977-)
100 Girls '00
Snow Day '00
A. I.: Artificial Intelligence '01
On the Line '01
Rick '03
Wrong Turn '03
The Crow: Wicked Prayer '05
In the Mix '05
National Lampoon's Adam & Eve '05
Waiting '05
Deceit '06

Waltzing Anna '06
August '08
Cadillac Records '08
Tortured '08
You Don't Mess with the Zohan '08
Saint John of Las Vegas '09
Taking Chances '09
Women in Trouble '09
Elektra Luxx '10
13 '10
5 Days of War '11
A Short History of Decay '13
The Knight Before Christmas '19

Marilyn Chris (1938-)
Honeymoon Killers '70
Backstairs at the White House '79
Waltzing Anna '06

David Christensen
Over the Wire '95
Turn of the Blade '97

Erika Christensen (1982-)
Traffic '00
The Banger Sisters '02
Home Room '02
Swimfan '02
MTV's Wuthering Heights '03
The Perfect Score '04
Riding the Bullet '04
Flightplan '05
The Sisters '05
The Upside of Anger '05
How to Rob a Bank '07
Mercy '09
Veronika Decides to Die '15
The Case for Christ '17

Hayden Christensen (1981-)
Life as a House '01
Star Wars: Episode 2-Attack of the Clones '02
Shattered Glass '03
Star Wars: Episode 3-Revenge of the Sith '05
Factory Girl '06
Awake '07
Virgin Territory '07
Jumper '08
New York, I Love You '09
Takers '10
Vanishing on 7th Street '10
American Heist '15
90 Minutes in Heaven '15
First Kill '17
The Last Man '19

Jesper Christensen (1948-)
Sofie '92
The White Lioness '96
Uprising '01
The Interpreter '05
Casino Royale '06
Everlasting Moments '08
Quantum of Solace '08
The Young Victoria '09
The Debt '10
Melancholia '11
The Last Sentence '12
The Lady Vanishes '13

Cheri Christian
Dark Remains '05
Curveball '15

Claudia Christian (1965-)
The Hidden '87
Clean and Sober '88
Never on Tuesday '88
Mom '89
Tale of Two Sisters '89
Maniac Cop 2 '90
The Dark Backward '91
Hexed '93
Final Voyage '99
The Haunting of Hell House '99
The Substitute 3: Winner Takes All '99
Atlantis: The Lost Empire '01 (V)
Half Past Dead '02
Meteor Apocalypse '10

John Christian (1957-)
Mob War '88
Airboss '97
Blood Relic '05

Linda Christian (1923-2011)
Tarzan and the Mermaids '48
Battle Zone '52
Athena '54
The House of the Seven Hawks '59
The Devil's Hand '61
The V.I.P.'s '63

Michael Christian (1943-)
Poor Pretty Eddie '73
The Legend of Frank Woods '77
Private Obsession '94

Shawn Christian (1965-)
Tremors 3: Back to Perfection '01
Murder in the Hamptons '05
Mating Dance '08
Meet Dave '08
Secrets of the Mountain '10
Small Town Saturday Night '10

Mady Christians (1900-51)
The Finances of the Grand Duke '24
Address Unknown '44
Letter from an Unknown Woman '48

Benjamin Christiansen (1879-1959)
Haxan: Witchcraft through the Ages '22
The Only Way '70

Audrey Christie (1912-89)
Keeper of the Flame '42
Splendor in the Grass '61
Frankie and Johnny '65
Mame '74
Harper Valley P.T.A. '78

Julie Christie (1940-)
Billy Liar '63
Darling '65
Doctor Zhivago '65
Young Cassidy '65
Fahrenheit 451 '66
Far from the Madding Crowd '67
Petulia '68
The Go-Between '71
McCabe & Mrs. Miller '71
Don't Look Now '73
Nashville '75
Shampoo '75
Demon Seed '77
Heaven Can Wait '78
Heat and Dust '82
Return of the Soldier '82
Power '86
Secret Obsession '88
Dragonheart '96
Hamlet '96
Afterglow '97
The Miracle Maker: The Story of Jesus '00 (V)
Belphegor: Phantom of the Louvre '01
No Such Thing '01
I'm with Lucy '02
Snapshots '02
Finding Neverland '04
Harry Potter and the Prisoner of Azkaban '04
Troy '04
Away From Her '06
Glorious 39 '09
New York, I Love You '09
Red Riding Hood '11
The Company You Keep '12

Morven Christie (1979-)
House of 9 '05
The Flying Scotsman '06
Oliver Twist '07
Lilting '14

Warren Christie (1975-)
My Baby Is Missing '07
Bachelor Party 2: The Last Temptation '08

The Most Wonderful Time of the Year '08
Apollo 18 '11

Katia Christine (1946-)
Spirits of the Dead '68
Cosmos: War of the Planets '80

Virginia Christine (1920-96)
Raiders of Ghost City '44
The Killers '46
Cover Up '49
The Cobweb '55
The Killer Is Loose '56
The Careless Years '57
Three Brave Men '57
Incident in an Alley '62
One Man's Way '63
Billy the Kid Versus Dracula '66

Eric Christmas (1916-2000)
Harold and Maude '71
Johnny Got His Gun '71
Attack of the Killer Tomatoes '77
An Enemy of the People '77
Porky's '82
Porky's 2: The Next Day '83
All of Me '84
The Philadelphia Experiment '84
Porky's Revenge '85
Air Bud '97
Mouse Hunt '97

Debra Christofferson (1963-)
Mouse Hunt '97
The Day the World Ended '01
Jesse Stone: Death in Paradise '06

Francoise Christophe (1923-2012)
The Invaders '63
The King of Hearts '66
Borsalino '70

Bojesse Christopher
Point Break '91
Meatballs 4 '92
Out in Fifty '99

Bostin Christopher
Otis '08
The Scorpion King 3: Battle for Redemption '11

Dennis Christopher (1955-)
The Young Graduates '71
September 30, 1955 '77
3 Women '77
A Wedding '78
Breaking Away '79
California Dreaming '79
Elvis: The Movie '79
Fade to Black '80
Chariots of Fire '81
Jake Speed '86
A Sinful Life '89
Circuitry Man '90
Doppelganger: The Evil Within '90
Stephen King's It '90
False Arrest '92
Boys Life '94
Plughead Rewired: Circuitry Man 2 '94
It's My Party '95
The Silencers '96
Trapped '06
Django Unchained '12

Scott Christopher (1967-)
The Robin Hood Gang '98
The Stray '17

Thom Christopher (1940-)
Peril '00
Jackie, Ethel, Joan: The Kennedy Women '01

Tyler Christopher (1972-)
Catfish in Black Bean Sauce '00
Face the Music '00
Out of the Black '01
U.S. SEALs: Dead or Alive '02
Beyond the Lights '14

William (Bill) Christopher (1932-)
With Six You Get Eggroll '68
For the Love of It '80
M*A*S*H: Goodbye, Farewell & Amen '83

Kathy Christopherson
Guyver 2: Dark Hero '94
Executive Target '97

Emily Chu (1960-)
Heart of Dragon '85
A Better Tomorrow, Part 1 '86

Ke Chu
House of Traps '81
Five Element Ninjas '82

Norman Chu (1955-)
The 36th Chamber of Shaolin '78
Seeding of a Ghost '86
Legend of the Liquid Sword '93
Heroes of the East '08

Paul Chubb (1949-2002)
Sweet Talker '91
Cosi '95
The Well '97

Danielle Chuchran (1993-)
The Wild Stallion '09
A Christmas Wish '11
Osombie '12
12 Dogs of Christmas: Great Puppy Rescue '12
Storm Rider '13
Riot '15

Delphine Chuillot
Pola X '99
Heartbeat Detector '07
Mozart's Sister '10
The Woman in the Fifth '11

Brett Chukerman
The Curiosity of Chance '06
Eating Out 2: Sloppy Seconds '06

Babz Chula (1946-2010)
Last Wedding '01
Moving Malcolm '03
Connie and Carla '04

Christy Chung (1970-)
The Bride with White Hair 2 '93
The Bodyguard from Beijing '94
The Medallion '03

David Chung (1946-2006)
The Ballad of Little Jo '93
Combination Platter '93
Color of a Brisk and Leaping Day '95

Gillian (Yan-Tung) Chung (1981-)
Vampire Effect '03
House of Fury '05

Jamie Chung (1983-)
Princess Protection Program '09
Sorority Row '09
The Hangover, Part 2 '11
Sucker Punch '11
The Man with the Iron Fists '12
Premium Rush '12
The Hangover, Part III '13
Knife Fight '13
Big Hero 6 '14 (V)
Flight 7500 '16

Mok Siu Chung (1960-)
Once Upon a Time in China II '92
Once Upon a Time in China III '93

Dan Chupong
Born to Fight '07
Ong Bak 2 '08

Thomas Haden Church (1960-)
Tombstone '93
Tales from the Crypt Presents Demon Knight '94
George of the Jungle '97

One Night Stand '97
Dean Koontz's Mr. Murder '98
Dying to Get Rich '98
Free Money '99
The Specials '00
3000 Miles to Graceland '01
Lone Star State of Mind '02
Serial Killing 101 '04
Sideways '04
Spanglish '04
Broken Trail '06
Charlotte's Web '06 (V)
Idiocracy '06
Over the Hedge '06 (V)
Spider-Man 3 '07
Smart People '08
Aliens in the Attic '09 (V)
All About Steve '09
Don McKay '09
Imagine That '09
Easy A '10
Another Happy Day '11
Killer Joe '11
We Bought a Zoo '11
John Carter '12
Lucky Them '13
Heaven Is for Real '14
Daddy's Home '15
Max '15
Cardboard Boxer '16
Crash Pad '17
The Peanut Butter Falcon '19

Berton Churchill (1876-1940)
Air Eagles '31
False Faces '32
Frisco Jenny '32
Two Seconds '32
Doctor Bull '33
The Little Giant '33
Strictly Dynamite '34
The Rainmakers '35
Steamboat Round the Bend '35
Vagabond Lady '35
The Dark Hour '36
Dimples '36
Mistaken Identity '36
In Old Chicago '37
Danger on the Air '38
Four Men and a Prayer '38
Wide Open Faces '38
Stagecoach '39

Donald Churchill (1930-91)
Victim '61
The Hound of the Baskervilles '83

Marguerite Churchill (1909-2000)
They Had to See Paris '29
The Big Trail '30
Ambassador Bill '31
Dracula's Daughter '36
Bunco Squad '50

Sarah Churchill (1914-82)
He Found a Star '41
Royal Wedding '51
Serious Charge '59

Chyna (1969-2016)
See Joan Laurer

Julien Ciamaca (1978-)
My Father's Glory '91
My Mother's Castle '91

Sergio Ciani (1935-)
Hercules and the Black Pirate '60
Three Avengers '64

Eduardo Ciannelli (1889-1969)
Marked Woman '37
Angels Wash Their Faces '39
Bulldog Drummond's Bride '39
Gunga Din '39
Society Lawyer '39
Foreign Correspondent '40
Kitty Foyle '40
The Mummy's Hand '40
Strange Cargo '40
They Met in Bombay '41
Cairo '42
You Can't Escape Forever '42
They Got Me Covered '43
The Mask of Dimitrios '44
Passage to Marseilles '44
Heartbeat '46
Mambo '55
Houseboat '58
Monster from Green Hell '58
MacKenna's Gold '69

Eddie Cibrian (1973-)
Logan's War: Bound by Honor '98
But I'm a Cheerleader '99
Say It Isn't So '01
The Cave '05
Northern Lights '09
Not Easily Broken '09
Working Miracles '10
Tyler Perry's Good Deeds '12
The Best Man Holiday '13
Tyler Perry's The Single Moms' Club '14

Jude Ciccolella (1947-)
Shakedown '88
Glengarry Glen Ross '92
Mad Love '95
Beloved '98
High Crimes '02
Star Trek: Nemesis '02
Washington Heights '02
Head of State '03
The Terminal '04
Sin City '05
A Perfect Day '06
Julia '08
Alpha Alert '13

Phyllis Cicero
Steele's Law '91
America's Dream '95

Jennifer Ciesar (1968-)
Red Shoe Diaries 7: Burning Up '96
Red Shoe Diaries: Strip Poker '96

Enzo Cilenti (1974-)
Millions '05
The Fourth Kind '09
Free Fire '17

Diane Cilento (1933-2011)
The Admirable Crichton '57
Stop Me Before I Kill! '60
I Thank a Fool '62
Tom Jones '63
The Agony and the Ecstasy '65
Hombre '67
Zero Population Growth '72
Hitler: The Last Ten Days '73
The Wicker Man '75
Winner Takes All '84

Maria Cina
Suspended Animation '02
April's Shower '03

Kelly Cinnante
True Love '89
Christmas in Connecticut '92

Luis Miguel Cintra (1949-)
Abraham's Valley '93
The Convent '95
The Dancer Upstairs '02

Charles Cioffi (1935-)
Klute '71
Mongo's Back In Town '71
Shaft '71
The Don Is Dead '73
The Arab Conspiracy '76
Time After Time '79
Missing '82
All the Right Moves '83
Remo Williams: The Adventure Begins '85
Peter Gunn '89
Newsies '92
Used People '92
The Shadow Conspiracy '96
Amy's O '02

Greg Cipes (1980-)
Ring of Darkness '04
The Wild '06 (V)
Simon Says '07
Teen Titans Go! To the Movies '18 (V)

Roberto Citran (1955-)
The Truce '96
Nora '00

Franco Citti (1935-)
Accatone! '61
Mamma Roma '62
Oedipus Rex '67
Porcile '69
The Decameron '70
Arabian Nights '74
Live Like a Cop, Die Like a Man '76

Francois Civil
As Above, So Below '14
Frank '14

Louis CK (1967-)
Diminished Capacity '08
The Invention of Lying '09
American Hustle '13
Blue Jasmine '13

Sam Claflin (1986-)
The Lost Future '10
Pillars of the Earth '10
Any Human Heart '11
Pirates of the Caribbean: On Stranger Tides '11
United '11
Snow White and the Huntsman '12
The Hunger Games: Catching Fire '13
Mary and Martha '13
The Hunger Games: Mockingjay--Part 1 '14
The Quiet Ones '14
Me Before You '16
My Cousin Rachel '17
Their Finest '17
Adrift '18
Journey's End '18
The Nightingale '18

Jany Clair (1938-)
Conquest of Mycene '63
Hercules against the Moon Men '64

Cyrielle Claire (1955-)
Le Professionnel '81
Sword of the Valiant '83
Code Name: Emerald '85

Gertrude Claire (1852-1928)
The Cradle of Courage '20
Her Sister from Paris '25

Ina Claire (1892-1985)
Three Broadway Girls '32
Ninotchka '39
Claudia '43

Ralph Clanton
Hot Cars '56
The 27th Day '57

Rony Clanton
The Education of Sonny Carson '74
Def by Temptation '90

Gordon Clapp (1948-)
Return of the Secaucus 7 '80
Matewan '87
Eight Men Out '88
A Family of Spies '90
Fever '91
Family of Strangers '93
Abandoned and Deceived '95
The Morrison Murders '96
The Rage: Carrie 2 '99
Skeletons in the Closet '00
Sunshine State '02
The Game Plan '07
Falling Up '08

Eric Clapton (1945-)
Tommy '75
Water '85 (C)
Chuck Berry: Hail! Hail! Rock 'n' Roll '87
George Harrison: Living in the Material World '11

Diane Clare (1938-2013)
The Reluctant Debutante '58
The Haunting '63
Beast of Morocco '66
Plague of the Zombies '66

Mary Clare (1894-1970)
Lorna Doone '34
Power '34
Young and Innocent '37
The Challenge '38
The Mill on the Floss '39
The Night Has Eyes '42
The Three Weird Sisters '48
Moulin Rouge '52
Penny Princess '52
Beggar's Opera '54
Mambo '55

O.B. Clarence (1870-1955)
The Scarlet Pimpernel '34
Pygmalion '38
On Approval '44
Great Expectations '46

Hans Clarin
Pippi Goes on Board '69
Pippi Longstocking '69

Aime Clariond (1894-1960)
La Marseillaise '37
Monsieur Vincent '47

Anthony Clark (1964-)
Dogfight '91
The Thing Called Love '93
Hourglass '95
The Rock '96
Paid in Full '02
Say Uncle '05
Big Bag of $ '09

Blake Clark (1946-)
Johnny Handsome '89
Grave Secrets: The Legacy of Hilltop Drive '92
Ladybugs '92
Shakes the Clown '92
The Waterboy '98
Critical Mass '00
Little Nicky '00
Mr. Deeds '02
50 First Dates '04
The Ladykillers '04
The Benchwarmers '06
I Now Pronounce You Chuck and Larry '07
Grown Ups '10
Toy Story 3 '10 (V)
That's My Boy '12

Bob (Benjamin) Clark (1941-2007)
Porky's '82
A Christmas Story '83

Bobby Clark
Satan's Sadists '69
Wild Wheels '69

Bobby Clark (1944-)
Invasion of the Body Snatchers '56
Gun Duel In Durango '57
The Happy Road '57

Brett (Baxter) Clark
Eye of the Eagle '87
Inner Sanctum '91
Deathstalker 4: Match of Titans '92

Candy Clark (1947-)
Fat City '72
American Graffiti '73
James Dean '76
The Man Who Fell to Earth '76
Citizens Band '77
The Big Sleep '78
More American Graffiti '79
Rodeo Girl '80
National Lampoon Goes to the Movies '81
Q (The Winged Serpent) '82
Amityville 3: The Demon '83
Blue Thunder '83
Cocaine and Blue Eyes '83
Cat's Eye '85
At Close Range '86
The Blob '88
Cool As Ice '91
Original Intent '91
Buffy the Vampire Slayer '92
Cherry Falls '00
Zodiac '07

Cliff Clark (1889-1953)
Miracles for Sale '39
The Wagons Roll at Night '41
The Falcon and the Co-Eds '43
The Falcon in Danger '43
The Falcon Strikes Back '43

Dane Clark (1913-98)
The Glass Key '42
Action in the North Atlantic '43
Destination Tokyo '43
Hollywood Canteen '44
God is My Co-Pilot '45
Pride of the Marines '45
A Stolen Life '46
Deep Valley '47
The Smallest Show on Earth '48
Whiplash '48
Barricade '49
Backfire '50
Highly Dangerous '50
Fort Defiance '51
The Gambler & the Lady '52
Blackout '54
Paid to Kill '54
Massacre '56
Outlaw's Son '57
The McMasters '70
Murder on Flight 502 '75
James Dean '76
Once an Eagle '76
Blood Song '82
Last Rites '88

Daniel Clark (1985-)
Grizzly Falls '99
That Russell Girl '08

Dick Clark (1929-2012)
Because They're Young '60
Wild in the Streets '68

Ernest Clark (1912-94)
1984 '56
Sink the Bismarck '60
The Devil-Ship Pirates '64
Salt & Pepper '68
Castle Keep '69

Eugene Clark (1955-)
TekWar '94
Turn It Up '00
Wilder '00
Jasper, Texas '03
Man in the Mirror: The Michael Jackson Story '04
Fighting the Odds: The Marilyn Gambrell Story '05
George A. Romero's Land of the Dead '05
Still Small Voices '07
Home Again '13

Fred Clark (1914-68)
Ride the Pink Horse '47
The Unsuspected '47
Cry of the City '48
Flamingo Road '49
The Jackpot '50
Sunset Boulevard '50
Hollywood Story '51
The Lemon Drop Kid '51
Meet Me After the Show '51
The Caddy '53
Here Come the Girls '53
Abbott and Costello Meet the Keystone Kops '54
Living It Up '54
The Court Martial of Billy Mitchell '55
Daddy Long Legs '55
Solid Gold Cadillac '56
Don't Go Near the Water '57
It Started with a Kiss '59
The Mating Game '59
Bells Are Ringing '60
Zotz! '62
Move Over, Darling '63
Sergeant Deadhead '65
Dr. Goldfoot and the Bikini Machine '66
The Horse in the Gray Flannel Suit '68

Greydon Clark (1943-)
Satan's Sadists '69
Bad Bunch '76

Harvey Clark (1885-1938)
Red Headed Woman '32
Peck's Bad Boy '34
Empty Saddles '36

Ken Clark (1927-2009)
Between Heaven and Hell '56
12 to the Moon '60
Hercules Against the Mongols '63
Desert Commandos '67

Marlene Clark (1949-)
Slaughter '72
Ganja and Hess '73
The Beast Must Die '75
The Baron '88

Matt Clark (1936-)
The Great Northfield Minnesota Raid '72
Emperor of the North Pole '73
Melvin Purvis: G-Man '74
The Outlaw Josey Wales '76
The Driver '78
Brubaker '80
The Children Nobody Wanted '81
An Eye for an Eye '81
Legend of the Lone Ranger '81
Ruckus '81
In the Custody of Strangers '82
Love Letters '83
The Adventures of Buckaroo Banzai Across the Eighth Dimension '84
Country '84
Return to Oz '85
Tuff Turf '85
Kenny Rogers as the Gambler, Part 3: The Legend Continues '87
Let's Get Harry '87
The Quick and the Dead '87
Blind Witness '89
The Horror Show '89
Back to the Future, Part 3 '90
Class Action '91
The Harvest '92
Barbarians at the Gate '93
Trilogy of Terror 2 '96
Homegrown '97
Kiss of Fire '98

Morfydd Clark
Love & Friendship '16
Crawl '19

Mystro Clark (1966-)
Chairman of the Board '97
Storm Catcher '99
Out at the Wedding '07

Oliver Clark (1939-)
Mikey & Nicky '76
A Star Is Born '76
Hanging By a Thread '79
Ernest Saves Christmas '88

Petula Clark (1932-)
London Town '46
Made in Heaven '52
The Promoter '52
The Gay Dog '54
The Runaway Bus '54
Track the Man Down '55
Finian's Rainbow '68
Goodbye, Mr. Chips '69

Roger Clark (1909-78)
Girls in Chains '43
Lost Lagoon '58
Monster '78

Spencer Treat Clark (1987-)
Arlington Road '99
Double Jeopardy '99
Gladiator '00
Unbreakable '00
Minority Report '02
Mystic River '03
Superheroes '07

The Last House on the Left '09
Camp Hell '10
Deep Dark Canyon '12
The Last Exorcism Part II '13

Susan Clark (1940-)
Coogan's Bluff '68
Madigan '68
Tell Them Willie Boy Is Here '69
Colossus: The Forbin Project '70
Skin Game '71
Valdez Is Coming '71
Showdown '73
Airport '75 '75
The Apple Dumpling Gang '75
Babe! '75
Night Moves '75
Murder by Decree '79
Nobody's Perfekt '79
The North Avenue Irregulars '79
Promises in the Dark '79
Porky's '82
Snowbound: The Jim and Jennifer Stolpa Story '94

Ted Clark
Happy Hell Night '92
Wrong Turn '03

Wallis (Clarke) Clark (1886-1961)
Forbidden Trail '32
Missing Girls '36
Murder by Invitation '41
Penny Serenade '41

Angela (Clark) Clarke (1909-2010)
The Gunfighter '50
The Great Caruso '51
Miracle of Our Lady of Fatima '52
Beneath the 12-Mile Reef '53
Houdini '53
House of Wax '53
The Egyptian '54
The Seven Little Foys '55
The Interns '62
Harrad Summer '74

Brian Patrick Clarke (1952-)
Sleepaway Camp 2: Unhappy Campers '88
Private Wars '93
Ace Ventura Jr.: Pet Detective '08

Caitlin Clarke (1952-2004)
Dragonslayer '81
Penn and Teller Get Killed '90

Cam(eron) Clarke (1957-)
Clifford's Really Big Movie '04 (V)
The Pirates Who Don't Do Anything: A VeggieTales Movie '08 (V)

Emilia Clarke (1987-)
Dom Hemingway '13
Terminator Genisys '15
Me Before You '16
Voice from the Stone '17
Solo: A Star Wars Story '18
Last Christmas '19

Gary Clarke (1933-)
How to Make a Monster '58
Missile to the Moon '59
Date Bait '60

Hope Clarke (1943-)
Piece of the Action '77
Seventeen Again '00

Jason Clarke (1969-)
Risk '00
The Outsider '02
Rabbit-Proof Fence '02
Death Race '08
The Human Contract '08
Under Still Waters '08
Trust '10
Texas Killing Fields '11
Yelling to the Sky '11
Lawless '12
Zero Dark Thirty '12
The Great Gatsby '13
White House Down '13
The Better Angels '14
Dawn of the Planet of the Apes '14
Terminator Genisys '15
All I See Is You '17
Chappaquiddick '17
Mudbound '17
First Man '18
Winchester '18
The Aftermath '19
Pet Sematary '19
Serenity '19

Justine Clarke (1971-)
Danny Deckchair '03
Japanese Story '03
Look Both Ways '05

Lenny Clarke (1953-)
Two If by Sea '95
Rounders '98
There's Something about Mary '98
Me, Myself, and Irene '00
What's the Worst That Could Happen? '01
Fever Pitch '05
What Doesn't Kill You '08

Mae Clarke (1907-92)
Frankenstein '31
The Front Page '31
Public Enemy '31
Penguin Pool Murder '32
Three Wise Girls '32
Fast Workers '33
Lady Killer '33
Penthouse '33
Turn Back the Clock '33
The Man with Two Faces '34
The Daring Young Man '35
Hats Off '37
Flying Tigers '42
Here Come the Waves '45
King of the Rocketmen '49
Pat and Mike '52
Women's Prison '55

Melinda (Mindy) Clarke (1969-)
Return of the Living Dead 3 '93
Killer Tongue '96
Spawn '97
She Drives Me Crazy '07

Noel Clarke (1975-)
Centurion '10
4.3.2.1 '10
Heartless '10
Storage 24 '12
The Anomaly '15

Richard Clarke (1930-2005)
Charlie Chan in City of Darkness '39
A Night to Remember '58
Identity Crisis '90

Robert Clarke (1920-2005)
Bedlam '45
The Enchanted Cottage '45
Hard, Fast and Beautiful '51
The Man from Planet X '51
1,000 Years From Now '52
Sword of Venus '53
Hideous Sun Demon '59
Beyond the Time Barrier '60
Secret File of Hollywood '62
Attack from Mars '88
Alienator '89

Robin Clarke
Inseminoid '80
White Wolves 3: Cry of the White Wolf '98

Sarah Clarke (1972-)
Thirteen '03
Happy Endings '05
The Lather Effect '06
Women in Trouble '09
The Twilight Saga: Eclipse '10

Warren Clarke (1947-2014)
A Clockwork Orange '71
Antony and Cleopatra '73
O Lucky Man! '73
S.O.S. Titanic '79
Tinker, Tailor, Soldier, Spy '80
From a Far Country: Pope John Paul II '81
Enigma '82
Firefox '82
Cold Room '84
Lassiter '84
Mandela '87
Hands of a Murderer '90
Joseph '95
A Respectable Trade '98
Blow Dry '00
Greenfingers '00
The Debt '03
Red Riding, Part 1: 1974 '09
Red Riding, Part 2: 1980 '09
Red Riding, Part 3: 1983 '09

D. A. Clarke-Smith (1888-1959)
The Ghoul '34
The Man Who Knew Too Much '34

Kelly Clarkson (1982-)
From Justin to Kelly '03
UglyDolls '19 (V)

Lana Clarkson (1962-2003)
Deathstalker '83
Blind Date '84
Barbarian Queen '85
Barbarian Queen 2: The Empress Strikes Back '89
The Haunting of Morella '91
Vice Girls '96

Patricia Clarkson (1959-)
The Dead Pool '88
Rocket Gibraltar '88
The Old Man and the Sea '90
Tune in Tomorrow '90
Pharoah's Army '95
High Art '98
Playing by Heart '98
The Green Mile '99
Simply Irresistible '99
Joe Gould's Secret '00
The Pledge '00
The Safety of Objects '01
Wendigo '01
Carrie '02
Far from Heaven '02
Welcome to Collinwood '02
All the Real Girls '03
Dogville '03
Pieces of April '03
The Station Agent '03
The Woods '03
Miracle '04
The Dying Gaul '05
Good Night, and Good Luck '05
All the King's Men '06
Lars and the Real Girl '07
Married Life '07
No Reservations '07
Blind Date '08
Elegy '08
Phoebe in Wonderland '08
Vicky Cristina Barcelona '08
Cairo Time '09
Shutter Island '09
Whatever Works '09
Easy A '10
Legendary '10
Main Street '10
Five '11
Friends With Benefits '11
One Day '11
The East '13
Last Weekend '14
The Maze Runner '14
Learning to Drive '15
The Party '17
Jonathan '19
Out of Blue '19

Robert Clary (1926-)
New Faces of 1952 '54
Holocaust Survivors. . . Remembrance of Love '83

Kevin Clash (1960-)
Teenage Mutant Ninja Turtles: The Movie '90 (V)
Being Elmo: A Puppeteer's Journey '11

Kira Clavell
House of the Dead '03
It Was One of Us '07
Kickin' It Old Skool '07

Christian Clavier (1952-)
French Fried Vacation '79
The Visitors '95
Just Visiting '01
Napoleon '03
The Crown Prince '06

Andrew Dice Clay (1957-)
See Andrew Silverstein

Nicholas Clay (1946-2000)
The Night Digger '71
Lovespell '79
Excalibur '81
Lady Chatterley's Lover '81
Evil under the Sun '82
The Hound of the Baskervilles '83
The Last Days of Pompeii '84
Lionheart '87
Sleeping Beauty '89
The Odyssey '97
Merlin '98

Jill Clayburgh (1944-2010)
The Wedding Party '69
The Telephone Book '71
The Terminal Man '74
Hustling '75
Griffin and Phoenix: A Love Story '76
Silver Streak '76
Semi-Tough '77
An Unmarried Woman '78
Starting Over '79
It's My Turn '80
First Monday in October '81
I'm Dancing as Fast as I Can '82
Where Are the Children? '85
Miles to Go '86
Whispers in the Dark '92
Naked in New York '93
Rich in Love '93
Fools Rush In '97
Going All the Way '97
My Little Assassin '99
Never Again '01
Running with Scissors '06
Bridesmaids '11

Garrett Clayton
Holiday Spin '12
Teen Beach Movie '13
King Cobra '16
Don't Hang Up '17

June Clayworth (1912-93)
Dick Tracy Meets Gruesome '47
At Sword's Point '51

John Cleese (1939-)
The Bliss of Mrs. Blossom '68
John Cleese on How to Irritate People '68
The Magic Christian '69
The Rise and Rise of Michael Rimmer '70
And Now for Something Completely Different '72
Monty Python and the Holy Grail '75
Monty Python's Life of Brian '79
The Great Muppet Caper '81
Time Bandits '81
The Secret Policeman's Other Ball '82
Monty Python's The Meaning of Life '83
Yellowbeard '83
Privates on Parade '84
Silverado '85
Clockwise '86
A Fish Called Wanda '88
The Big Picture '89
Erik the Viking '89
Bullseye! '90
An American Tail: Fievel Goes West '91 (V)
Splitting Heirs '93
Mary Shelley's Frankenstein '94
Rudyard Kipling's The Jungle Book '94
The Swan Princess '94 (V)
Fierce Creatures '96
Mr. Toad's Wild Ride '96
George of the Jungle '97 (V)
Parting Shots '98
The Out-of-Towners '99
The World Is Not Enough '99
Isn't She Great '00
Harry Potter and the Sorcerer's Stone '01
Rat Race '01
The Adventures of Pluto Nash '02
Die Another Day '02
Harry Potter and the Chamber of Secrets '02
Scorched '02
Charlie's Angels: Full Throttle '03
Around the World in 80 Days '04
Shrek 2 '04 (V)
Valiant '05 (V)
Charlotte's Web '06 (V)
Shrek the Third '07 (V)
The Day the Earth Stood Still '08
Igor '08 (V)
The Pink Panther 2 '09
Planet 51 '09 (V)
Beethoven's Christmas Adventure '11 (N)
Winnie the Pooh '11 (N)
Planes '13 (V)
Arctic Dogs '19 (V)

Ellen Cleghorne (1965-)
Mr. Wrong '95
Coyote Ugly '00
MacArthur Park '01

Adelaide Clemens (1989-)
Wasted on the Young '10
Silent Hill: Revelation 3D '12
Generation Um... '13
The Great Gatsby '13
The World Made Straight '15

Paul Clemens (1958-)
The Passage '79
Promises in the Dark '79
The Beast Within '82
They're Playing with Fire '84

Christian Clemenson (1958-)
Bad Influence '90
Hero '92
And the Band Played On '93
Lost and Found '99
United 93 '06

Aurore Clement (1945-)
Les Rendez-vous D'Anna '78
Paris, Texas '83
For Sale '98
Bon Voyage '03
The Bridesmaid '04
The New Girlfriend '14
A Bigger Splash '15

Jemaine Clement (1974-)
Eagle vs. Shark '07
Diagnosis: Death '09
Gentlemen Broncos '09
Despicable Me '10 (V)
Dinner for Schmucks '10
Men in Black 3 '12
Rio 2 '14 (V)
What We Do in the Shadows '14
Don Verdean '15
People Places Things '15
The BFG '16
Moana '16
Brad's Status '17
Humor Me '17

Suzanne Clément (1969-)
I Killed My Mother '09
Laurence Anyways '12
Mommy '14
The Other Half '17

Pierre Clementi (1942-99)
The Leopard '63
Belle de Jour '67
Partner '68
Porcile '69
The Conformist '71
Steppenwolf '74
Sweet Movie '75
Hideous Kinky '99

John Clements (1910-88)
The Four Feathers '39
Convoy '40
The Silent Enemy '58
The Mind Benders '63
I Remember Nelson '82

Kennedi Clements (2007-)
A Family Thanksgiving '10
Jingle All the Way 2 '14
Poltergeist '15

Stanley Clements (1926-81)
Salty O'Rourke '45
Destination Murder '50
The Rocket Man '54
Wiretapper '55
Saintly Sinners '62

Kiersey Clemons
Dope '15
Neighbors 2: Sorority Rising '16
Flatliners '17
Hearts Beat Loud '18
An L.A. Minute '18

David Clennon (1943-)
Go Tell the Spartans '78
Ladies and Gentlemen, the Fabulous Stains '82
Missing '82
The Thing '82
The Right Stuff '83
Star 80 '83
Falling in Love '84
Sweet Dreams '85
Blood and Orchids '86
Legal Eagles '86
Conspiracy: The Trial of the Chicago Eight '87
The Couch Trip '87
Light Sleeper '92
Man Trouble '92
Matinee '92
And the Band Played On '93 (C)
Black Widow Murders: The Blanche Taylor Moore Story '93
Acts of Contrition '95
From the Earth to the Moon '98
The Visit '00
Silver City '04
Life of the Party '05
Syriana '05
Saving Sarah Cain '07
Gone Girl '14
Amigo Undead '15

Corinne Clery (1950-)
The Story of O '75
Insanity '76
Love by Appointment '76
The Switch '76
Moonraker '79
The Con Artists '80
Yor, the Hunter from the Future '83

Carol Cleveland (1942-)
And Now for Something Completely Different '72
Monty Python and the Holy Grail '75
Monty Python's Life of Brian '79
Monty Python's The Meaning of Life '83

Chris Cleveland
Relax. . . It's Just Sex! '98
Babysitters Beware '08
Border Lost '08

George Cleveland (1886-1957)
Revolt of the Zombies '36
Mutiny in the Big House '39
Drums of Fu Manchu '40
Tomboy '40
Playmates '41
Texas Legionnaires '43
Dead Man's Eyes '44
It Happened Tomorrow '44

Has Anybody Seen My Gal? *'52*
Monkey Business *'52*
Gentlemen Prefer Blondes *'53*
Trouble along the Way *'53*
The Rocket Man *'54*
Around the World in 80 Days *'56*
The Power and the Prize *'56*
The Remarkable Mr. Pennypacker *'59*

James Coburn (1928-2002)
Ride Lonesome *'59*
The Magnificent Seven *'60*
Hell Is for Heroes *'62*
Charade *'63*
The Great Escape *'63*
The Americanization of Emily *'64*
The Loved One *'65*
Major Dundee *'65*
Dead Heat on a Merry-Go-Round *'66*
Our Man Flint *'66*
What Did You Do in the War, Daddy? *'66*
In Like Flint *'67*
The President's Analyst *'67*
Waterhole Number 3 *'67*
Candy *'68*
Duffy *'68*
Hard Contract *'69*
The Last of the Mobile Hotshots *'69*
The Carey Treatment *'72*
A Fistful of Dynamite *'72*
Harry in Your Pocket *'73*
Internecine Project *'73*
The Last of Sheila *'73*
Pat Garrett & Billy the Kid *'73*
A Reason to Live, a Reason to Die *'73*
Bite the Bullet *'75*
Hard Times *'75*
Cross of Iron *'76*
The Last Hard Men *'76*
Midway *'76*
Sky Riders *'76*
The Dain Curse *'78*
Firepower *'79*
The Muppet Movie *'79 (C)*
Loving Couples *'80*
High Risk *'81*
Looker *'81*
Young Guns 2 *'90*
Hudson Hawk *'91*
Hugh Hefner: Once Upon a Time *'92 (N)*
The Player *'92*
Deadfall *'93*
Sister Act 2: Back in the Habit *'93*
Maverick *'94*
The Avenging Angel *'95*
The Set Up *'95*
The Cherokee Kid *'96*
Eraser *'96*
Keys to Tulsa *'96*
The Nutty Professor *'96*
Affliction *'97*
The Second Civil War *'97*
Dean Koontz's Mr. Murder *'98*
Payback *'98*
Noah's Ark *'99*
Proximity *'00*
The Man from Elysian Fields *'01*
Monsters, Inc. *'01 (V)*
Walter and Henry *'01*
American Gun *'02*
Snow Dogs *'02*

Michael Coby (1943-)
The Bitch *'78*
Supersonic Man *'78*

Imogene Coca (1908-2001)
Under the Yum-Yum Tree *'63*
The Return of the Beverly Hillbillies *'81*
National Lampoon's Vacation *'83*
Alice in Wonderland *'85*

Dean Cochran (1969-)
Target of Opportunity *'04*
The Cutter *'05*

Eddie Cochran (1938-60)
The Girl Can't Help It *'56*
Untamed Youth *'57*
Go, Johnny Go! *'59*

Robert Cochran (1908-)
The Third Clue *'34*
Sanders of the River *'35*
I Stand Condemned *'36*

Shannon Cochran (1958-)
The Ring *'02*
Star Trek: Nemesis *'02*

Steve Cochran (1917-65)
Wonder Man *'45*
The Best Years of Our Lives *'46*
The Chase *'46*
Copacabana *'47*
A Song Is Born *'48*
White Heat *'49*
The Damned Don't Cry *'50*
Highway 301 *'50*
Inside the Walls of Folsom Prison *'51*
Jim Thorpe: All American *'51*
Raton Pass *'51*
Storm Warning *'51*
The Tanks Are Coming *'51*
Tomorrow Is Another Day *'51*
Operation Secret *'52*
Back to God's Country *'53*
The Desert Song *'53*
She's Back on Broadway *'53*
Carnival Story *'54*
Private Hell 36 *'54*
The Weapon *'56*
Il Grido *'57*
Slander *'57*
I, Mobster *'58*
Deadly Companions *'61*

Michael Cochrane (1947-)
Sharpe's Eagle *'93*
Sharpe's Regiment *'96*
Incognito *'97*
A Different Loyalty *'04*
Sharpe's Challenge *'06*
Sharpe's Peril *'08*

Rory Cochrane (1972-)
Dazed and Confused *'93*
Love and a .45 *'94*
Empire Records *'95*
The Low Life *'95*
Dogtown *'97*
The Last Don *'97*
Black & White *'99*
Flawless *'99*
Sunset Strip *'99*
The Prime Gig *'00*
Hart's War *'02*
Right at Your Door *'06*
A Scanner Darkly *'06*
The Company *'07*
Public Enemies *'09*
Bringing Up Bobby *'11*
Argo *'12*
Oculus *'14*
Hostiles *'17*

Arlene Cockburn
The Winter Guest *'97*
The Acid House *'98*
The Governess *'98*

Gary Cockrell
Lolita *'62*
War Lover *'62*

James Coco (1929-87)
Ensign Pulver *'64*
End of the Road *'70*
The Strawberry Statement *'70*
A New Leaf *'71*
Such Good Friends *'71*
Man of La Mancha *'72*
Wild Party *'74*
Murder by Death *'76*
The Cheap Detective *'78*
Wholly Moses! *'80*
Only When I Laugh *'81*
The Muppets Take Manhattan *'84 (C)*
Hunk *'87*

Camille Coduri (1965-)
Hawks *'89*
Nuns on the Run *'90*
Strapless *'90*
King Ralph *'91*

Bill Cody (1891-1948)
Ghost City *'32*
The Cyclone Ranger *'35*

Iron Eyes Cody (1904-99)
The Road to Yesterday *'25*
Under Nevada Skies *'46*
Massacre River *'49*
Fort Defiance *'51*
Son of Paleface *'52*
Sitting Bull *'54*
Black Gold *'62*
El Condor *'70*
The Longest Drive *'76*
Grayeagle *'77*
Ernest Goes to Camp *'87*
Spirit of '76 *'91*

Kathleen (Kathy) Cody (1954-)
Charley and the Angel *'73*
Girls on the Road *'73*
Superdad *'73*

Lew Cody (1884-1934)
Mickey *'17*
Souls for Sale *'23*
Within the Law *'23*
Beyond Victory *'31*
Dishonored *'31*
Sporting Blood *'31*
The Crusader *'32*
A Parisian Romance *'32*
The Tenderfoot *'32*

Barry Coe (1934-2019)
House of Bamboo *'55*
Love Me Tender *'56*
Peyton Place *'57*
The Bravados *'58*
One Foot in Hell *'60*
The 300 Spartans *'62*
Fantastic Voyage *'66*
Dr. Death, Seeker of Souls *'73*

George Coe (1929-2015)
Bustin' Loose *'81*
A Flash of Green *'85*
Remo Williams: The Adventure Begins *'85*
Blood and Orchids *'86*
Best Seller *'87*
Blind Date *'87*
The End of Innocence *'90*
The Omega Code *'99*
Big Eden *'00*
Diamond Men *'01*
Corporate Affairs *'07*

Peter Coe (1918-93)
House of Frankenstein *'44*
Hellgate *'52*

Noell Coet
5 Time Champion *'11*
Mischief Night *'13*
Revelation Road: The Beginning of the End *'13*

Paul Coeur
Cool Runnings *'93*
White Fang 2: The Myth of the White Wolf *'94*

Denise Coffey (1936-)
Georgy Girl *'66*
Start the Revolution without Me *'70*

Elizabeth Coffey
Pink Flamingos *'72*
Female Trouble *'74*

Scott Coffey (1967-)
Zombie High *'87*
Satisfaction *'88*
Shag: The Movie *'89*
Shout *'91*
Dream Lover *'93*
The Temp *'93*
Tank Girl *'94*
Lost Highway *'96*
Route 9 *'98*
Mulholland Drive *'01*
Ellie Parker *'05*
Inland Empire *'06 (V)*

Peter Coffield (1945-83)
Cry Rape! *'73*
Times Square *'80*

Frederick Coffin (1943-2003)
The Bedroom Window *'87*
Shoot to Kill *'88*
Hard to Kill *'89*
There Goes My Baby *'92*
Andersonville *'95*
A Streetcar Named Desire *'95*
The Base *'99*
Identity *'03*

Pierre Coffin
Despicable Me *'10 (V)*
Minions *'15 (V)*

Tristram Coffin (1909-90)
Holt of the Secret Service *'42*
Under Nevada Skies *'46*
Jesse James Rides Again *'47*
King of the Rocketmen *'49*
Queen for a Day *'51*
Ma Barker's Killer Brood *'60*
Good Neighbor Sam *'64*

Frank 'Junior' Coghlan (1916-2009)
Yankee Clipper *'27*
Penrod and Sam *'31*
Hell's House *'32*
The Last of the Mohicans *'32*

Lauren Cohan (1982-)
National Lampoon's Van Wilder 2: The Rise of Taj *'06*
Float *'08*
Death Race 2 *'10*
The Boy *'16*
Mile 22 *'18*

Alain Cohen (1958-)
The Two of Us *'68*
Happily Ever After *'04*

Ari Cohen
Category 6: Day of Destruction *'04*
A Job to Kill For *'06*
A Little Thing Called Murder *'06*
Not My Life *'06*
Hush Little Baby *'07*
The Tracey Fragments *'07*
Small Town Murder Songs *'10*

Assi Cohen (1974-)
Yossi & Jagger *'02*
Bonjour Monsieur Shlomi *'03*
Colombian Love *'04*

Bern Cohen
Project Nim *'11*
To Dust *'19*

Emma Cohen (1946-)
Cannibal Man *'71*
Horror Rises from the Tomb *'72*

Emory Cohen (1990-)
Afterschool *'08*
The Hungry Ghosts *'09*
Four *'12*
The Place Beyond the Pines *'13*
Beneath the Harvest Sky *'14*
Brooklyn *'15*
The Duel *'16*
Stealing Cars *'16*
Detour *'17*
Vincent N Roxxy *'17*
War Machine *'17*
Killerman *'19*
The Wolf Hour *'19*

Gilles Cohen (1963-)
The Beat My Heart Skipped *'05*
The Girl From Monaco *'08*
A Prophet *'09*

J.J. (Jeffrey Jay) Cohen (1965-)
Back to the Future *'85*
The Principal *'87*
976-EVIL *'88*
Back to the Future, Part 2 *'89*
Back to the Future, Part 3 *'90*

Kaipo Cohen (1978-)
The Summer of Aviya *'88*
Under the Domim Tree *'95*

Lynn Cohen (1933-2020)
Manhattan Murder Mystery *'93*
Vanya on 42nd Street *'94*
Hurricane Streets *'96*
I Shot Andy Warhol *'96*
Walking and Talking *'96*
The Jimmy Show *'01*
Munich *'05*
Then She Found Me *'07*
Eagle Eye *'08*
Sex and the City: The Movie *'08*
The Extra Man *'10*

Matt Cohen (1982-)
Boogeyman 2 *'07*
Dark House *'09*
Chain Letter *'10*

Michael Cohen (1970-)
La Petite Jerusalem *'05*
Shall We Kiss? *'07*

Oshri Cohen (1984-)
Bonjour Monsieur Shlomi *'03*
Beaufort *'07*
Lebanon *'09*

Scott Cohen (1961-)
Vibrations *'94*
Sweet Evil *'95*
Gotti *'96*
Gia *'98*
Perfect Murder, Perfect Town *'00*
The 10th Kingdom *'00*
Kissing Jessica Stein *'02*
Knots *'05*
Fatal Contact: Bird Flu in America *'06*
For One More Day *'07*
Winter of Frozen Dreams *'08*
Moonlight Serenade *'09*
Love and Other Drugs *'10*
Justice for Natalee *'11*
3 Weeks to Daytona *'11*

Ethan Cohn (1979-)
The Experiment *'10*
Rubber *'10*

Mindy Cohn (1966-)
Alone with a Stranger *'99*
Sex and Death 101 *'07*
Violet Tendencies *'10*

Lucy Cohu (1968-)
The Queen's Sister *'05*
Ballet Shoes *'07*
Murderland *'09*

Rhys Coiro (1979-)
Order of Chaos *'10*
30 Days of Night: Dark Days *'10*
Chlorine *'13*

Helen Coker
All or Nothing *'02*
Vera Drake *'04*

Giorgio Colangeli
Il Divo *'08*
Our Life *'10*

Enrico Colantoni (1963-)
Money Train *'95*
The Wrong Guy *'96*
Galaxy Quest *'99*
Stigmata *'99*
A. I.: Artificial Intelligence *'01*
James Dean *'01*
The First $20 Million is Always the Hardest *'02*
Full Frontal *'02*
Celine *'08*
My Mom's New Boyfriend *'08*
Sherman's Way *'08*
The Chaperone *'11*
Contagion *'11*
The Kennedys *'11*
House of Versace *'13*
Veronica Mars *'14*

Nicholas Colasanto (1924-85)
Fat City *'72*
Family Plot *'76*
Mad Bull *'77*
Raging Bull *'80*

Catero Colbert
Sweet Perfection *'90*
Zombie Strippers *'08*

Claudette Colbert (1903-96)
The Smiling Lieutenant *'31*
The Man From Yesterday *'32*
I Cover the Waterfront *'33*
The Sign of the Cross *'33*
Three-Cornered Moon *'33*
Torch Singer *'33*
Cleopatra *'34*
Four Frightened People *'34*
Imitation of Life *'34*
It Happened One Night *'34*
The Bride Comes Home *'35*
The Gilded Lily *'35*
I Met Him in Paris *'37*
Bluebeard's Eighth Wife *'38*
Drums Along the Mohawk *'39*
It's a Wonderful World *'39*
Midnight *'39*
Boom Town *'40*
Remember the Day *'41*
The Palm Beach Story *'42*
No Time For Love *'43*
So Proudly We Hail *'43*
Since You Went Away *'44*
Guest Wife *'45*
The Secret Heart *'46*
Tomorrow Is Forever *'46*
Without Reservations *'46*
Egg and I *'47*
Sleep, My Love *'48*
Family Honeymoon *'49*
Three Came Home *'50*
Let's Make It Legal *'51*
Thunder on the Hill *'51*
Texas Lady *'56*
Parrish *'61*
The Love Goddesses *'65*

Stephen Colbert (1964-)
Bewitched *'05*
The Great New Wonderful *'06*
Strangers with Candy *'06*
The Love Guru *'08*
Monsters *vs.* Aliens *'09 (V)*
Mr. Peabody & Sherman *'14 (V)*

Tim Colceri (1951-)
Full Metal Jacket *'87*
Leprechaun 4: In Space *'96*

Ben Cole
Edge of Sanity *'89*
Howling 5: The Rebirth *'89*
A Trick of the Mind *'06*

Carol Cole
The Mad Room *'69*
Model Shop *'69*

Christina Cole (1982-)
What a Girl Wants *'03*
He Knew He Was Right *'04*
Jane Eyre *'06*
The Deaths of Ian Stone *'07*
Miss Pettigrew Lives for a Day *'08*
Emma *'09*
Appointment With Death *'10*
Rosemary's Baby *'14*

Dennis Cole (1940-2009)
Cave-In! *'79*
Death House *'88*

Eric Michael Cole (1976-)
Steve Martini's Undue Influence *'96*
White Squall *'96*
Outrage *'98*
New Best Friend *'02*
Snapshots *'02*

Gary Cole (1956-)
The Old Man and the Sea *'90*
In the Line of Fire *'93*
The Brady Bunch Movie *'95*

Greg Collins
Operation Delta Force 3: Clear Target '98
U.S. Seals '98

Jessica Collins (1971-)
Best of the Best: Without Warning '98
Dirty Love '05
The Loss of a Teardrop Diamond '08
Open House '10
So B. It '17

Joan Collins (1933-)
Cosh Boy '52
Decameron Nights '53
Tough Guy '53
The Adventures of Sadie '55
The Girl in the Red Velvet Swing '55
Land of the Pharaohs '55
The Virgin Queen '55
The Opposite Sex '56
Sea Wife '57
Stopover Tokyo '57
The Wayward Bus '57
The Bravados '58
Rally 'Round the Flag, Boys! '58
Esther and the King '60
Seven Thieves '60
The Road to Hong Kong '62
The Executioner '70
Quest for Love '71
Revenge '71
Dynasty of Fear '72
Tales from the Crypt '72
Tales That Witness Madness '73
Great Adventure '75
I Don't Want to Be Born '75
Oh, Alfie '75
Arthur Hailey's The Moneychangers '76
Empire of the Ants '77
Fearless '77
The Big Sleep '78
The Bitch '78
The Stud '78
Homework '82
Making of a Male Model '83
Cartier Affair '84
Sins '85
Monte Carlo '86
Annie: A Royal Adventure '95
A Midwinter's Tale '95
The Flintstones in Viva Rock Vegas '00
Joseph and the Amazing Technicolor Dreamcoat '00
These Old Broads '01
Molly Moon and The Incredible Book of Hypnotism '15

Joely Collins
Diamond Girl '98
Almost Heaven '06

Judy Collins (1939-)
Junior '94
A Town Has Turned to Dust '98

Karley Scott Collins (1999-)
Pulse 2: Afterlife '08
The Collector '09
Open Season 3 '10 (V)

K.C. Collins
Poor Man's Game '06
Animal 2 '07

Lauren Collins
Take the Lead '06
Picture This! '08

Lewis Collins (1946-2013)
Code Name: Wild Geese '84
Codename: Wildgeese '84
Jack the Ripper '88

Lily Collins (1989-)
The Blind Side '09
Abduction '11
Priest '11
Mirror Mirror '12
Stuck in Love '12
The English Teacher '13
The Mortal Instruments: City of Bones '13
Rules Don't Apply '16

Lynn Collins (1977-)
The Merchant of Venice '04
Bug '06
The Dog Problem '06
The Lake House '06
Numb '07
The Number 23 '07
Towelhead '07
Uncertainty '08
X-Men Origins: Wolverine '09
Angels Crest '11
John Carter '12
10 Years '12
Unconditional '12
The Hollow Point '16
Beneath Us '20

Misha Collins (1974-)
Finding Home '03
Karla '06
Stonehenge Apocalypse '10

Mo Collins (1965-)
Jiminy Glick in LaLa Wood '05
Danny Roane: First Time Director '06
And They're Off '11

Monte (Monty) Collins (1856-1929)
Our Hospitality '23
King of Kings '27

Patricia Collins
Pin. . . '88
Speaking Parts '89

Patrick Collins (1951-)
Dirt Bike Kid '86
Friends and Family '01
A Crime '06

Pauline Collins (1940-)
Shirley Valentine '89
City of Joy '92
My Mother's Courage '95
Paradise Road '97
You Will Meet a Tall Dark Stranger '10
Albert Nobbs '11
Quartet '12

Phil Collins (1951-)
Buster '88
Hook '91
And the Band Played On '93 (C)
Balto '95 (V)
The Jungle Book 2 '03 (V)

Ray Collins (1889-1965)
Citizen Kane '41
The Magnificent Ambersons '42
Commandos Strike at Dawn '43
The Human Comedy '43
Salute to the Marines '43
Whistling in Brooklyn '43
Can't Help Singing '45
Leave Her to Heaven '45
The Best Years of Our Lives '46
Crack-Up '46
Up Goes Maisie '46
The Bachelor and the Bobby-Soxer '47
A Double Life '47
The Swordsman '47
Command Decision '48
For the Love of Mary '48
Good Sam '48
Homecoming '48
The Fountainhead '49
Francis the Talking Mule '49
The Heiress '49
Man from Colorado '49
Kill the Umpire '50
Ma and Pa Kettle Go to Town '50
The Reformer and the Redhead '50
Summer Stock '50
Invitation '51
Ma and Pa Kettle Back On the Farm '51
The Racket '51
You're In the Navy Now '51
Bad for Each Other '53
The Desert Song '53
Ma and Pa Kettle on Vacation '53
Desperate Hours '55
Solid Gold Cadillac '56
Touch of Evil '58

Rick Collins
The Toxic Avenger, Part 2 '89
The Toxic Avenger, Part 3: The Last Temptation of Toxie '89

Roberta Collins (1944-2008)
The Big Doll House '71
Unholy Rollers '72
Caged Heat '74
Death Race 2000 '75
Eaten Alive '76
Hardbodies '84

Russell Collins (1897-1965)
Shockproof '49
Niagara '52
Miss Sadie Thompson '53
Savage Wilderness '55
Soldier of Fortune '55
Enemy Below '57
The Matchmaker '58

Ruth (Coreen) Collins
Galactic Gigolo '87
Doom Asylum '88
Cemetery High '89
Death Collector '89

Shanna Collins (1983-)
On the Doll '07
Sublime '07
The Haunting of Molly Hartley '08
Cinema Verite '11

Stephen Collins (1947-)
All the President's Men '76
Between the Lines '77
The Promise '79
Star Trek: The Motion Picture '79
The Henderson Monster '80
Loving Couples '80
Summer Solstice '81
Brewster's Millions '85
Hold the Dream '86
Jumpin' Jack Flash '86
The Big Picture '89
Stella '89
My New Gun '92
Till Murder Do Us Part '92
High Stakes '93
Scarlett '94
The First Wives Club '96
Drive Me Crazy '99
Blood Diamond '06
Because I Said So '07
Every Second Counts '08
The Three Stooges '12

Wayne Collins
Bebe's Kids '92 (V)
Way Past Cool '00

Madeleine Collinson (1952-)
The Love Machine '71
Twins of Evil '71

Mary Collinson (1952-)
The Love Machine '71
Twins of Evil '71

Frank Collison (1950-)
Dollman '90
O Brother Where Art Thou? '00
Hidalgo '04
The Village '04
The Whole Ten Yards '04
The Happening '08

Silvia Colloca (1977-)
Van Helsing '04
The Detonator '06
Vampire Killers '09

Roy Collodi
She-Devils on Wheels '68
Something Weird '68

June Collyer (1907-68)
Four Sons '28
Hangman's House '28
Drums of Jeopardy '31
The Ghost Walks '34
A Face in the Fog '36

Pamela Collyer
Evil Judgment '85
The Kiss '88

Booth Colman (1923-2014)
World Without End '56
My Gun Is Quick '57
Raiders from Beneath the Sea '64
Wild On the Beach '65

Olivia Colman (1974-)
Much Ado About Nothing '05
Confetti '06
Hot Fuzz '07
Le Donk & Scor-Zay-Zee '09
The Iron Lady '11
Tyrannosaur '11
Hyde Park on Hudson '12
I Give It a Year '13
Locke '13
Cuban Fury '14
The Lobster '16
The Favourite '18
Them That Follow '19

Ronald Colman (1891-1958)
The White Sister '23
Her Night of Romance '24
Her Sister from Paris '25
Lady Windermere's Fan '25
Romola '25
Kiki '26
The Winning of Barbara Worth '26
Raffles '30
Arrowsmith '31
Clive of India '35
A Tale of Two Cities '36
Lost Horizon '37
Prisoner of Zenda '37
Lucky Partners '40
Random Harvest '42
Talk of the Town '42
Kismet '44
A Double Life '47
Champagne for Caesar '50
Around the World in 80 Days '56
Story of Mankind '57

Marcus Coloma (1978-)
Material Girls '06
Beverly Hills Chihuahua 2 '10
Beverly Hills Chihuahua 3: Viva La Fiesta! '12

Scott Colomby (1952-)
Caddyshack '80
Porky's '82
Porky's 2: The Next Day '83
Porky's Revenge '85

Hector Colome
Dark Blue Almost Black '06
[REC] 4: Apocalypse '14

Miriam Colon (1936-)
The House of the Spirits '93
Lone Star '95
Sabrina '95
All the Pretty Horses '00
Goal! The Dream Begins '06
The Cry: La Llorona '07
Goal 2: Living the Dream '07
Bless Me, Ultima '13

Jerry Colonna (1904-86)
Rosalie '38
The Road to Singapore '40
Atlantic City '44
Alice in Wonderland '51 (V)
Kentucky Jubilee '51

Clara Colosimo (1922-94)
Alfredo, Alfredo '72
Orchestra Rehearsal '78

Vince Colosimo (1966-)
Moving Out '83
Chopper '00
Lantana '01
The Hard Word '02
Walking on Water '02
After the Deluge '03
Solo '06
Body of Lies '08
Daybreakers '09

Mike Colter (1976-)
The Dreamers '03
Million Dollar Baby '04
Black and Blue '19

Jacque Lynn Colton (1939-)
Big Bad Mama 2 '87
Heartbreak Hotel '88

John Colton
Lethal '04
A Christmas Wedding Tail '11

Randy Colton
Blackwater Valley Exorcism '06
In the Eyes of a Killer '09

Ellar Coltrane (1994-)
Boyhood '14
Blood Money '17
The Circle '17
The Last Movie Star '17

Robbie Coltrane (1950-)
Defense of the Realm '85
National Lampoon's European Vacation '85
Caravaggio '86
Mona Lisa '86
Bert Rigby, You're a Fool '89
Henry V '89
Let It Ride '89
Slipstream '89
Nuns on the Run '90
Where the Heart Is '90
The Adventures of Huck Finn '93
Cracker: Men Should Weep '94
Cracker: The Big Crunch '94
Cracker: To Be a Somebody '94
Cracker: Brotherly Love '95
Goldeneye '95
Buddy '97
The Ebb-Tide '97
Frogs for Snakes '98
Message in a Bottle '98
Alice in Wonderland '99
The World Is Not Enough '99
From Hell '01
Harry Potter and the Sorcerer's Stone '01
Harry Potter and the Chamber of Secrets '02
Harry Potter and the Prisoner of Azkaban '04
Ocean's Twelve '04
Van Helsing '04
Harry Potter and the Goblet of Fire '05
Alex Rider: Operation Stormbreaker '06
Harry Potter and the Order of the Phoenix '07
The Tale of Despereaux '08 (V)
The Brothers Bloom '09
Gooby '09 (V)
Harry Potter and the Half-Blood Prince '09
Murderland '09
Harry Potter and the Deathly Hallows, Part 1 '10
Harry Potter and the Deathly Hallows, Part 2 '11
Brave '12 (V)
Great Expectations '12

Catherine Colvey (1951-2011)
Captive '98
Levity '03
A Deadly Encounter '04

Peter Colvey
April Morning '88
Silent Hunter '94
Dead Silent '99

Pinto Colvig (1892-1967)
Snow White and the Seven Dwarfs '37 (V)
Sleeping Beauty '59 (V)

Jack Colvin (1934-2005)
The Incredible Hulk '77
Child's Play '88
The Incredible Hulk Returns '88

Michael Colyar
Hot Shots! Part Deux '93
House Party 3 '94

Roger Coma (1976-)
Caresses '97
To Die, Or Not '99

Holly Marie Combs (1973-)
Sweet Hearts Dance '88
Born on the Fourth of July '89
Dr. Giggles '92
Simple Men '92
Ocean's Eleven '01 (C)

Jeffrey Combs (1954-)
Re-Animator '84
From Beyond '86
Cyclone '87
Phantom Empire '87
Bride of Re-Animator '89
Doctor Mordrid: Master of the Unknown '90
Trancers 2: The Return of Jack Deth '90
The Guyver '91
The Pit & the Pendulum '91
Love and a .45 '94
Lurking Fear '94
Castle Freak '95
Cyberstalker '96
The Frighteners '96
Caught Up '98
I Still Know What You Did Last Summer '98
Spoiler '98
House on Haunted Hill '99
Faust: Love of the Damned '00
The Attic Expeditions '01
Feardotcom '02
Beyond Re-Animator '03
All Souls Day '05
Edmond '05
Voodoo Moon '05
Abominable '06
Blackwater Valley Exorcism '06
Return to House on Haunted Hill '07
The Wizard of Gore '07
Parasomnia '08
Dark House '09
American Bandits: Frank and Jesse James '10

Ryan Combs (1974-)
Straight out of Compton '99
I Accidentally Domed Your Son '04

Sean (Puffy, Puff Daddy, P. Diddy) Combs (1969-)
Made '01
Monster's Ball '01
Carlito's Way: Rise to Power '05
A Raisin in the Sun '08
Get Him to the Greek '10

Danny Comden (1969-)
Sol Goode '01
Pretty Persuasion '05

Andy Comeau (1970-)
8 Heads in a Duffel Bag '96
Virtual Obsession '98
One Hour Photo '02
The Babysitters '07
Animals '08

Anjanette Comer (1939-)
The Loved One '65
The Appaloosa '66
Rabbit, Run '70
The Baby '72
Night of a Thousand Cats '72
Terror on the 40th Floor '74
Dead of Night '77
The Long Summer of George Adams '82
Netherworld '90
Larry McMurtry's Streets of Laredo '95
The Underneath '95

Dorothy Comingore (1913-71)
Prison Train *'38*
Citizen Kane *'41*
The Hairy Ape *'44*
The Big Night *'51*

Common (1972-)
American Gangster *'07*
Smokin' Aces *'07*
Street Kings *'08*
Wanted *'08*
Terminator Salvation *'09*
Date Night *'10*
Just Wright *'10*
LUV *'13*
Pawn *'13*
Selma *'14*
Being Charlie *'16*
John Wick: Chapter 2 *'17*
All About Nina *'18*
Hunter Killer *'18*
Smallfoot *'18*
The Tale *'18*
Saint Judy *'19*

Perry Como (1912-2001)
Something for the Boys *'44*
Doll Face *'46*
If I'm Lucky *'46*
Words and Music *'48*

Betty Compson (1897-1974)
Paths to Paradise *'25*
The Great Gabbo *'29*
On with the Show *'29*
Weary River *'29*
Inside the Lines *'30*
The Lady Refuses *'31*
Notorious But Nice *'33*
The Drag-Net *'36*
Two Minutes to Play *'37*
A Slight Case of Murder *'38*
Mystic Circle Murder *'39*
The Invisible Ghost *'41*

Martin Compston (1984-)
Sweet Sixteen *'02*
Wild Country *'05*
A Guide to Recognizing Your Saints *'06*
Red Road *'06*
The Disappearance of Alice Creed *'09*
Sister *'12*

Maurice Compte
The Dream Catcher *'99*
Fidel *'02*
All the Real Girls *'03*
I Do *'13*

Fay Compton (1894-1978)
The Mill on the Floss *'39*
Esther Waters *'48*
The Forbidden Street *'49*
Othello *'52*
The Vanquished *'52*
The Haunting *'63*

Joyce Compton (1907-97)
False Faces *'32*
A Parisian Romance *'32*
Under Eighteen *'32*
Let 'Em Have It *'35*
Rustlers of Red Dog *'35*
Love Before Breakfast *'36*
Murder With Pictures *'36*
Sitting On the Moon *'36*
The Awful Truth *'37*
Artists and Models Abroad *'38*
Balalaika *'39*
Rose of Washington Square *'39*
Sky Murder *'40*
Manpower *'41*
Silver Skates *'43*
Christmas in Connecticut *'45*
A Southern Yankee *'48*

O'Neal Compton (1951-)
Attack of the 50 Ft. Woman *'93*
Roadracers *'94*
Deep Impact *'98*
Life *'99*
Big Eden *'00*
Kill Me Later *'01*

Oliver Conant (1955-)
Summer of '42 *'71*
Class of '44 *'73*

Cristi Conaway (1964-)
Batman Returns *'92*
Attack of the 50 Ft. Woman *'93*
Nina Takes a Lover *'94*
Intimate Betrayal *'96*
My Brother's War *'97*
The Colony *'98*

Jeff Conaway (1950-2011)
I Never Promised You a Rose Garden *'77*
Pete's Dragon *'77*
Grease *'78*
Breaking Up Is Hard to Do *'79*
For the Love of It *'80*
Making of a Male Model *'83*
The Patriot *'86*
The Dirty Dozen: The Fatal Mission *'88*
Elvira, Mistress of the Dark *'88*
Tale of Two Sisters *'89*
Mirror Images *'91*
Sunset Strip *'91*
A Time to Die *'91*
Bikini Summer 2 *'92*
Jawbreaker *'98*

Kerry Condon (1983-)
How Harry Became a Tree *'01*
Intermission *'03*
The Last Station *'09*
This Must Be the Place *'12*
Dom Hemingway *'13*
Bad Samaritan *'18*

Lana Condor (1997-)
To All the Boys I've Loved Before *'18*
To All the Boys: P.S. I Still Love You *'20*

Chester Conklin (1888-1971)
Tillie's Punctured Romance *'14*
Anna Christie *'23*
A Woman of the World *'25*
The Duchess of Buffalo *'26*
Hallelujah, I'm a Bum *'33*
Modern Times *'36*
The Great Dictator *'40*
Sullivan's Travels *'41*
Miracle of Morgan's Creek *'44*
The Beast With a Million Eyes *'56*

Peggy Conklin (1906-2003)
The Devil Is a Sissy *'36*
Having a Wonderful Time *'38*

Corinne Conley
Breakaway *'02*
Legacy of Fear *'06*
Wolfcop *'15*

Jack Conley (1958-)
Brown's Requiem *'98*
Payback *'98*
Out of the Black *'01*
Johnson County War *'02*
Shade *'03*
Clawed: The Legend of Sasquatch *'05*
Harold & Kumar Escape from Guantanamo Bay *'08*
A Taste of Romance *'12*

Joe Conley (1928-2013)
Crime of Passion *'57*
A Day for Thanks on Walton's Mountain *'82*

Brigid Conley Walsh (1972-)
See Brigid Brannagh

Jimmy Conlin (1884-1962)
Sullivan's Travels *'41*
Miracle of Morgan's Creek *'44*
Operation Haylift *'50*

Tim Conlon
Prom Night 3: The Last Kiss *'89*
My Silent Partner *'06*

Tommy Conlon
Those We Love *'32*
Young America *'32*

Didi Conn (1951-)
You Light Up My Life *'77*
Grease *'78*
Grease 2 *'82*
Thomas and the Magic Railroad *'00*

Chad Connell (1983-)
Posers *'02*
Prom Wars *'08*
Double Wedding *'10*

Maureen Connell (1931-)
The Abominable Snowman *'57*
Lucky Jim *'58*
Skyjacked *'72*

Christopher Connelly (1941-88)
Corky *'72*
They Only Kill Their Masters *'72*
Benji *'74*
The Invasion of Carol Enders *'74*
Hawmps! *'76*
The Martian Chronicles: Part 3 *'79*
Return of the Rebels *'81*
Liar's Moon *'82*
Manhattan Baby *'82*
1990: The Bronx Warriors *'83*
Django Strikes Again *'87*
Night of the Sharks *'87*

Edward Connelly (1859-1928)
The Saphead *'21*
The Merry Widow *'25*
Torrent *'26*
Across to Singapore *'28*
The Mysterious Lady *'28*

Jennifer Connelly (1970-)
Once Upon a Time in America *'84*
Creepers *'85*
Labyrinth *'86*
Seven Minutes in Heaven *'86*
Some Girls *'88*
The Hot Spot *'90*
Career Opportunities *'91*
The Rocketeer *'91*
Higher Learning *'94*
Of Love and Shadows *'94*
Mulholland Falls *'95*
Dark City *'97*
Inventing the Abbotts *'97*
Pollock *'00*
Requiem for a Dream *'00*
Waking the Dead *'00*
A Beautiful Mind *'01*
Dark Water *'02*
House of Sand and Fog *'03*
Hulk *'03*
Blood Diamond *'06*
Little Children *'06*
Reservation Road *'07*
The Day the Earth Stood Still *'08*
Creation *'09*
He's Just Not That Into You *'09*
9 *'09 (V)*
Virginia *'10*
The Dilemma *'11*
Salvation Boulevard *'11*
Stuck in Love *'12*
Noah *'14*
Winter's Tale *'14*
Shelter *'15*
American Pastoral *'16*
Only the Brave *'17*
Alita: Battle Angel *'19*

Marc Connelly (1890-1980)
Spirit of St. Louis *'57*
Tall Story *'60*

Jason Connery (1963-)
The First Olympics: Athens 1896 *'84*
Winner Takes All *'84*
Bye Bye Baby *'88*
Casablanca Express *'89*
Urban Ghost Story *'98*
Shanghai Noon *'00*
Wishmaster 3: Beyond the Gates of Hell *'01*
The Far Side of Jericho *'06*
Night Skies *'07*
Alone in the Dark 2 *'08*
Brotherhood of Blood *'08*
Dragonquest *'09*

Sean Connery (1930-)
Time Lock *'57*
Another Time, Another Place *'58*
Darby O'Gill & the Little People *'59*
Tarzan's Greatest Adventure *'59*
The Frightened City *'61*
Dr. No *'62*
The Longest Day *'62*
From Russia with Love *'63*
Goldfinger *'64*
Marnie *'64*
The Hill *'65*
Thunderball *'65*
A Fine Madness *'66*
You Only Live Twice *'67*
Shalako *'68*
Red Tent *'69*
The Molly Maguires *'70*
The Anderson Tapes *'71*
Diamonds Are Forever *'71*
The Offence *'73*
Zardoz *'73*
Murder on the Orient Express *'74*
The Terrorists *'74*
The Man Who Would Be King *'75*
The Wind and the Lion *'75*
The Arab Conspiracy *'76*
Robin and Marian *'76*
A Bridge Too Far *'77*
Cuba *'79*
The Great Train Robbery *'79*
Meteor *'79*
Outland *'81*
Time Bandits *'81*
Five Days One Summer *'82*
Wrong Is Right *'82*
Never Say Never Again *'83*
Sword of the Valiant *'83*
Highlander *'86*
The Name of the Rose *'86*
The Untouchables *'87*
Memories of Me *'88*
The Presidio *'88*
Family Business *'89*
Indiana Jones and the Last Crusade *'89*
The Hunt for Red October *'90*
The Russia House *'90*
Highlander 2: The Quickening *'91*
Robin Hood: Prince of Thieves *'91 (C)*
Medicine Man *'92*
Rising Sun *'93*
A Good Man in Africa *'94*
Just Cause *'94*
First Knight *'95*
Dragonheart *'96 (V)*
The Rock *'96*
The Avengers *'98*
Playing by Heart *'98*
Entrapment *'99*
Finding Forrester *'00*
The League of Extraordinary Gentlemen *'03*

Harry Connick, Jr. (1967-)
Memphis Belle *'90*
Little Man Tate *'91*
Copycat *'95*
Excess Baggage *'96*
Independence Day *'96*
Hope Floats *'98*
The Iron Giant *'99 (V)*
My Dog Skip *'99 (N)*
The Simian Line *'99*
Life Without Dick *'01*
Rodgers & Hammerstein's South Pacific *'01*
Basic *'03*
Bug *'06*
P.S. I Love You *'07*
Living Proof *'08*
New in Town *'09*
Dolphin Tale *'11*
Angels Sing *'13*
Dolphin Tale 2 *'14*

Billy Connolly (1942-)
Absolution *'81*
The Secret Policeman's Other Ball *'82*
The Big Man: Crossing the Line *'91*
Indecent Proposal *'93*
Pocahontas *'95 (V)*
Muppet Treasure Island *'96*
Mrs. Brown *'97*
Deacon Brodie *'98*
The Imposters *'98*
Still Crazy *'98*
Boondock Saints *'99*
Beautiful Joe *'00*
An Everlasting Piece *'00*
Gabriel & Me *'01*
Gentlemen's Relish *'01*
The Man Who Sued God *'01*
White Oleander *'02*
Who is Cletis Tout? *'02*
The Last Samurai *'03*
Timeline *'03*
Lemony Snicket's A Series of Unfortunate Events *'04*
Fido *'06*
Garfield: A Tail of Two Kitties *'06*
Open Season *'06 (V)*
Open Season 2 *'08 (V)*
The X Files: I Want to Believe *'08*
The Boondock Saints II: All Saints Day *'09*
Gulliver's Travels *'10*
Brave *'12 (V)*
Quartet *'12*
The Hobbit: The Battle of the Five Armies *'14*

Kevin Connolly (1974-)
The Beverly Hillbillies *'93*
Antwone Fisher *'02*
John Q *'02*
The Notebook *'04*
He's Just Not That Into You *'09*
The Ugly Truth *'09*
Secretariat *'10*
Reach Me *'14*
Entourage *'15*

Kristen Connolly (1980-)
The Bay *'12*
The Cabin in the Woods *'12*
A Good Marriage *'14*
Houdini *'14*

Walter Connolly (1887-1940)
No More Orchids *'32*
The Bitter Tea of General Yen *'33*
East of Fifth Avenue *'33*
Lady for a Day *'33*
Broadway Bill *'34*
The Captain Hates the Sea *'34*
It Happened One Night *'34*
Lady by Choice *'34*
Twentieth Century *'34*
Libeled Lady *'36*
The Good Earth *'37*
Nancy Steele Is Missing *'37*
Nothing Sacred *'37*
Four's a Crowd *'38*
Too Hot to Handle *'38*
The Adventures of Huckleberry Finn *'39*
Fifth Avenue Girl *'39*

Kate Connor
You've Got a Friend *'07*
Fort McCoy *'11*

Kenneth Connor (1915-92)
The Ladykillers *'55*
Carry On Sergeant *'58*
Carry On Nurse *'59*
Carry On Constable *'60*
Dentist In the Chair *'60*
Carry On Regardless *'61*
What a Carve-Up! *'62*
Carry On Cabby *'63*
Carry On Cleo *'65*
Captain Nemo and the Underwater City *'69*
Carry On Up the Jungle *'70*
Carry On Henry VIII *'71*
Carry On Abroad *'72*
Carry On Matron *'72*
Carry On England *'76*

Kevin Connor (1940-)
Phantasm 3: Lord of the Dead *'94*
Blackbeard *'06*

Krystle Connor
Death Racers *'08*
Sunday School Musical *'08*
The Terminators *'09*

Chuck Connors (1921-92)
Pat and Mike *'52*
South Sea Woman *'53*
Dragonfly Squadron *'54*
Good Morning, Miss Dove *'55*
Target Zero *'55*
Three Stripes in the Sun *'55*
Hot Rod Girl *'56*
Walk the Dark Street *'56*
Death in Small Doses *'57*
Designing Woman *'57*
Old Yeller *'57*
The Big Country *'58*
Flipper *'63*
Move Over, Darling *'63*
Synanon *'65*
Captain Nemo and the Underwater City *'69*
Colditz: Escape of the Birdmen *'71*
Ride to Glory *'71*
Embassy *'72*
The Mad Bomber *'72*
Pancho Villa *'72*
The Proud and the Damned *'72*
The Horror at 37,000 Feet *'73*
Soylent Green *'73*
99 & 44/100 Dead *'74*
The Legend of Sea Wolf *'75*
Roots *'77*
Tourist Trap *'79*
Airplane 2: The Sequel *'82*
Balboa *'82*
Virus *'82*
Texas Guns *'90*
Salmonberries *'91*
The Gambler Returns: The Luck of the Draw *'93*

Mike Connors (1925-)
Sudden Fear *'52*
Island in the Sky *'53*
Day the World Ended *'55*
Swamp Women *'55*
Flesh and the Spur *'57*
Shake, Rattle and Rock *'57*
Panic Button *'62*
Good Neighbor Sam *'64*
Harlow *'65*
Stagecoach *'66*
Avalanche Express *'79*
James Dean: Live Fast, Die Young *'97*

Chris Conrad (1970-)
Airborne *'93*
Young Hercules *'97*
Criminal Desire *'98*
The Promotion *'08*

David Conrad (1967-)
Return to Paradise *'98*
A Season for Miracles *'99*
Men of Honor *'00*
The Weekend *'00*
Anything Else *'03*
Wedding Crashers *'05*
Crazy *'08*
Think of Me *'11*
About Sunny *'12*

Michael Conrad (1925-83)
The War Lord *'65*
Blackbeard's Ghost *'67*
Castle Keep *'69*
Gone with the West *'72*

Thumb Tripping *'72*
Scream Blacula Scream *'73*
The Longest Yard *'74*

Mikel Conrad (1919-82)
Abbott and Costello Meet the Killer, Boris Karloff *'49*
The Flying Saucer *'50*
Untamed Women *'52*

Robert Conrad (1935-2020)
Palm Springs Weekend *'63*
Murph the Surf *'75*
Sudden Death *'77*
Centennial *'78*
Breaking Up Is Hard to Do *'79*
Lady in Red *'79*
Wild, Wild West Revisited *'79*
More Wild, Wild West *'80*
Wrong Is Right *'82*
Hard Knox *'83*
Two Fathers' Justice *'85*
Assassin *'86*
Two Fathers: Justice for the Innocent *'94*
Jingle All the Way *'96*

William Conrad (1920-94)
The Killers *'46*
Body and Soul *'47*
Dial 1119 *'50*
Tension *'50*
Cry Danger *'51*
The Racket *'51*
The Desert Song *'53*
Naked Jungle *'54*
5 Against the House *'55*
The Conqueror *'56*
The Ride Back *'57*
Zero Hour! *'57 (N)*
30 *'59*
The Return of the King *'80 (V)*
Blitz *'85*

Hans Conried (1917-82)
His Butler's Sister *'44*
Passage to Marseilles *'44*
My Friend Irma *'49*
Nancy Goes to Rio *'50*
Summer Stock *'50*
Rich, Young and Pretty *'51*
Too Young to Kiss *'51*
Behave Yourself! *'52*
The World in His Arms *'52*
The Affairs of Dobie Gillis *'53*
The 5000 Fingers of Dr. T *'53*
Peter Pan *'53 (V)*
Davy Crockett, King of the Wild Frontier *'55*
Birds & the Bees *'56*
Bus Stop *'56*
Jet Pilot *'57*
The Monster That Challenged the World *'57*
Rock-A-Bye Baby *'57*
1001 Arabian Nights *'59 (V)*
The Patsy *'64*
Robin and the 7 Hoods *'64*
Phantom Tollbooth *'69 (V)*
Brothers O'Toole *'73*
The Hobbit *'78 (V)*
Oh, God! Book 2 *'80*

Frances Conroy (1953-)
Another Woman *'88*
Rocket Gibraltar *'88*
Scent of a Woman *'92*
The Adventures of Huck Finn *'93*
The Neon Bible *'95*
The Crucible *'96*
Murder in a Small Town *'99*
Maid in Manhattan *'02*
Die Mommie Die! *'03*
The Aviator *'04*
Catwoman *'04*
Broken Flowers *'05*
Shopgirl *'05*
Ira & Abby *'06*
A Perfect Day *'06*
The Wicker Man *'06*
The Seeker: The Dark Is Rising *'07*
Humboldt County *'08*
The Tale of Despereaux *'08 (V)*
Love Happens *'09*
New in Town *'09*
The Smell of Success *'09*
Bloodworth *'10*
Stone *'10*
Waking Madison *'10*
Ring of Fire *'13*
6 Souls *'13*
Chasing Ghosts *'14*
Making the Rules *'14*
Joker *'19*

Frank Conroy (1890-1964)
Ace of Aces *'33*
Midnight Mary *'33*
The Cat and the Fiddle *'34*
Manhattan Melodrama *'34*
The Call of the Wild *'35*
I Live My Life *'35*
The Gorgeous Hussy *'36*
Crash Dive *'43*
The Ox-Bow Incident *'43*
The Day the Earth Stood Still *'51*
Lightning Strikes Twice *'51*
The Last Mile *'59*

Kevin Conroy (1955-)
Kennedy *'83*
Batman: Mask of the Phantasm *'93 (V)*

Neill Conroy
The Van *'95*
Bloom *'03*
Intermission *'03*
Kisses *'08*

Ruaidhri Conroy (1978-)
Into the West *'92*
Moondance *'95*
The Van *'95*
When the Sky Falls *'99*
Deathwatch *'02*

Charlotte Considine (1941-)
See Charlotte Stewart

John Considine (1935-)
Reunion in France *'42*
Dr. Death, Seeker of Souls *'73*
The Thirsty Dead *'74*
The Late Show *'77*
A Wedding *'78*
Endangered Species *'82*
Forbidden Love *'82*
Choose Me *'84*
Dixie: Changing Habits *'85*
Trouble in Mind *'86*
Opposing Force *'87*
Gia *'98*

Paddy Considine (1974-)
Born Romantic *'00*
24 Hour Party People *'01*
Close Your Eyes *'02*
In America *'02*
Dead Man's Shoes *'04*
Cinderella Man *'05*
My Summer of Love *'05*
Stoned *'05*
The Backwoods *'06*
PU-239 *'06*
The Bourne Ultimatum *'07*
Hot Fuzz *'07*
My Zinc Bed *'08*
The Cry of the Owl *'09*
Le Donk & Scor-Zay-Zee *'09*
Red Riding, Part 2: 1980 *'09*
Submarine *'10*
Blitz *'11*
Now Is Good *'12*
The World's End *'13*
Pride *'14*
Child 44 *'15*
Macbeth *'15*
Miss You Already *'15*
The Death of Stalin *'17*
The Girl with All the Gifts *'17*
How to Build a Girl *'20*

Tim Considine (1940-)
The Clown *'53*
The Shaggy Dog *'59*
Sunrise at Campobello *'60*
Patton *'70*
Daring Dobermans *'73*

Anne Consigny (1963-)
The 36th Precinct *'04*
The Diving Bell and the Butterfly *'07*
A Christmas Tale *'08*
Mesrine: Part 2-Public Enemy Number 1 *'08*
John Rabe *'09*
Rapt *'09*
Wild Grass *'09*
You Ain't Seen Nothin' Yet *'12*
Elle *'16*

Michel Constantin (1924-2003)
Le Trou *'59*
Le Deuxieme Souffle *'66*
The Family *'70*

Eddie Constantine (1917-93)
S.O.S. Pacific *'60*
Cleo from 5 to 7 *'61*
Ladies' Man *'62*
Your Turn Darling *'63*
License to Kill *'64*
Alphaville *'65*
Hail Mafia *'65*
Make Your Bets Ladies *'65*
Attack of the Robots *'66*
Beware of a Holy Whore *'70*
It's Alive 2: It Lives Again *'78*
The Long Good Friday *'80*
Zentropa *'92*

Michael Constantine (1927-)
The Last Mile *'59*
The Hustler *'61*
Island of Love *'63*
Skidoo *'68*
Don't Drink the Water *'69*
If It's Tuesday, This Must Be Belgium *'69*
Justine *'69*
The Reivers *'69*
Voyage of the Damned *'76*
The North Avenue Irregulars *'79*
In the Mood *'87*
Prancer *'89*
My Life *'93*
The Juror *'96*
Stephen King's Thinner *'96*
Winds of Terror *'01*
My Big Fat Greek Wedding *'02*

Sarah Constible
Maneater *'07*
High Life *'09*

Mark Consuelos (1971-)
My Super Ex-Girlfriend *'06*
Wedding Daze *'06*
For the Love of Grace *'08*
Hostile Makeover *'09*
Killer Hair *'09*
Cop Out *'10*
Nine Lives *'16*

John Conte (1915-2006)
Lost in a Harem *'44*
The Man with the Golden Arm *'55*
Trauma *'62*

Richard Conte (1914-75)
Guadalcanal Diary *'43*
The Purple Heart *'44*
Somewhere in the Night *'46*
13 Rue Madeleine *'46*
A Walk in the Sun *'46*
The Other Love *'47*
Call Northside 777 *'48*
Cry of the City *'48*
House of Strangers *'49*
Whirlpool *'49*
Hollywood Story *'51*
The Fighter *'52*
The Blue Gardenia *'53*
Big Combo *'55*
I'll Cry Tomorrow *'55*
Race for Life *'55*
Target Zero *'55*
Full of Life *'56*
The Brothers Rico *'57*
They Came to Cordura *'59*
Ocean's 11 *'60*
Circus World *'64*
Synanon *'65*
Assault on a Queen *'66*
Hotel *'67*
Tony Rome *'67*
Lady in Cement *'68*
Operation Cross Eagles *'69*
The Godfather *'72*
1931: Once Upon a Time in New York *'72*
The Boss *'73*
Shoot First, Die Later *'74*

Albert Conti (1887-1967)
One Romantic Night *'30*
State's Attorney *'31*
This Modern Age *'31*
The Black Cat *'34*

Tom Conti (1941-)
The Duellists *'77*
The Norman Conquests, Part 1: Table Manners *'78*
The Norman Conquests, Part 2: Living Together *'78*
The Norman Conquests, Part 3: Round and Round the Garden *'78*
Merry Christmas, Mr. Lawrence *'83*
American Dreamer *'84*
Beyond Therapy *'86*
The Quick and the Dead *'87*
Deep Cover *'88*
Shirley Valentine *'89*
The Inheritance *'97*
Sub Down *'97*
The Enemy *'01*
Derailed *'05*
Almost Heaven *'06*
Paid *'06*
O Jerusalem *'07*
Blind Revenge *'10*
The Tempest *'10*
The Dark Knight Rises *'12*

Chantal Contouri (1949-)
The Night After Halloween *'79*
Thirst *'79*

Patricio Contreras (1947-)
The Official Story *'85*
Old Gringo *'89*
Of Love and Shadows *'94*

Frank Converse (1938-)
Hurry Sundown *'67*
The Tattered Web *'71*
The Bushido Blade *'80*
Alone in the Neon Jungle *'87*
Anne of Avonlea *'87*
Everybody Wins *'90*
Brother Future *'91*
Tales of the Unexpected *'91*
Our Town *'03*

William Converse-Roberts
1918 *'85*
On Valentine's Day *'86*
Courtship *'87*
Serving in Silence: The Margarethe Cammermeyer Story *'95*
Kiss the Girls *'97*
Crazy in Alabama *'99*
Drive Me Crazy *'99*
Bandits *'01*

Bert Convy (1933-91)
A Bucket of Blood *'59*
Susan Slade *'61*
The Love Bug *'68*
Semi-Tough *'77*
Hanging By a Thread *'79*
Hero at Large *'80*
Cannonball Run *'81*

Dan Conway
Blast-Off Girls *'67*
Things Change *'88*

Gary Conway (1936-)
How to Make a Monster *'58*
Young Guns of Texas *'62*
Black Gunn *'72*
American Ninja 2: The Confrontation *'87*

Kevin Conway (1942-2020)
F.I.S.T. *'78*
Paradise Alley *'78*
The Scarlet Letter *'79*
The Lathe of Heaven *'80*
The Funhouse *'81*
Homeboy *'88*
One Good Cop *'91*
Rambling Rose *'91*
Jennifer 8 *'92*
Gettysburg *'93*
Larry McMurtry's Streets of Laredo *'95*
Lawnmower Man 2: Beyond Cyberspace *'95*
Prince Brat and the Whipping Boy *'95*
The Quick and the Dead *'95*
Looking for Richard *'96*
The Confession *'98*
Mercury Rising *'98*
Two Family House *'99*
Thirteen Days *'00*
Black Knight *'01*
Gods and Generals *'03*
Invincible *'06*
American Loser *'07*
The Bronx Is Burning *'07*

Morgan Conway (1903-81)
The Saint Takes Over *'40*
Tornado *'43*

Pat Conway (1931-81)
The Deadly Mantis *'57*
Brighty of the Grand Canyon *'67*

Russ Conway (1913-2009)
Twelve o'Clock High *'49*
Love Me Tender *'56*
Fort Dobbs *'58*
Twelve Hours to Kill *'60*

Tim Conway (1933-2019)
McHale's Navy *'64*
The World's Greatest Athlete *'73*
The Apple Dumpling Gang *'75*
Gus *'76*
The Shaggy D.A. *'76*
The Billion Dollar Hobo *'78*
They Went That-a-Way & That-a-Way *'78*
The Apple Dumpling Gang Rides Again *'79*
Prize Fighter *'79*
The Private Eyes *'80*
Cannonball Run 2 *'84*
The Longshot *'86*
Dear God *'96*
Speed 2: Cruise Control *'97 (C)*
Air Bud 2: Golden Receiver *'98*
Spooky Buddies *'11 (V)*
Treasure Buddies *'12 (V)*
Super Buddies *'13 (V)*

Tom Conway (1904-67)
The Bad Man *'41*
Lady Be Good *'41*
The People *vs.* Dr. Kildare *'41*
Tarzan's Secret Treasure *'41*
Cat People *'42*
Mrs. Miniver *'42*
Rio Rita *'42*
The Falcon and the Co-Eds *'43*
The Falcon in Danger *'43*
The Falcon Strikes Back *'43*
I Walked with a Zombie *'43*
The Seventh Victim *'43*
The Falcon in Mexico *'44*
One Touch of Venus *'48*
Bride of the Gorilla *'51*
Painting the Clouds With Sunshine *'51*
Norman Conquest *'53*
Peter Pan *'53 (N)*
Tarzan and the She-Devil *'53*
Murder on Approval *'56*
The She-Creature *'56*
Atomic Submarine *'59*
12 to the Moon *'60*

Angell Conwell (1983-)
Baby Boy *'01*
The Wash *'01*
What About Your Friends: Weekend Getaway *'02*

Jackie Coogan (1914-84)
Oliver Twist *'22*
Free and Easy *'30 (C)*
College Swing *'38*
Kilroy Was Here *'47*
Mesa of Lost Women *'52*
Outlaw Women *'52*
High School Confidential *'58*
The Space Children *'58*
Sex Kittens Go to College *'60*
Girl Happy *'65*
A Fine Madness *'66*
The Shakiest Gun in the West *'68*
The Phantom of Hollywood *'74*
The Escape Artist *'82*

Keith Coogan (1970-)
The Fox and the Hound *'81 (V)*
Adventures in Babysitting *'87*
Hiding Out *'87*
Cheetah *'89*
Cousins *'89*
Under the Boardwalk *'89*
Book of Love *'91*
Don't Tell Mom the Babysitter's Dead *'91*
Toy Soldiers *'91*
The Power Within *'95*
Downhill Willie *'96*
Ivory Tower *'97*

Richard Coogan (1914-2014)
Girl On the Run *'53*
Three Hours to Kill *'54*
Vice Raid *'60*

Steve Coogan (1965-)
Mr. Toad's Wild Ride *'96*
Sweet Revenge *'98*
24 Hour Party People *'01*
Coffee and Cigarettes *'03*
Around the World in 80 Days *'04*
Ella Enchanted *'04 (V)*
Happy Endings *'05*
Tristram Shandy: A Cock and Bull Story *'05*
Lies & Alibis *'06*
Marie Antoinette *'06*
Night at the Museum *'06*
Hot Fuzz *'07*
Finding Amanda *'08*
Hamlet 2 *'08*
Tropic Thunder *'08*
In the Loop *'09*
Night at the Museum: Battle of the Smithsonian *'09*
What Goes Up *'09*
Marmaduke *'10 (V)*
The Other Guys *'10*
Percy Jackson & The Olympians: The Lightning Thief *'10*
The Trip *'10*
Our Idiot Brother *'11*
Ruby Sparks *'12*
What Maisie Knew *'12*
Alan Partridge *'13*
Despicable Me 2 *'13 (V)*
The Look of Love *'13*
Philomena *'13*
Night at the Museum: Secret of the Tomb *'14*
The Trip to Italy *'14*
The Dinner *'17*
The Trip to Spain *'17*
Irreplaceable You *'18*
Stan & Ollie *'18*

A.J. Cook (1978-)
The Virgin Suicides *'99*
The House Next Door *'01*
Out Cold *'01*
Ripper: Letter from Hell *'01*
Wishmaster 3: Beyond the Gates of Hell *'01*
Final Destination 2 *'03*
I'm Reed Fish *'06*
Vanished *'06*
Night Skies *'07*
Misconceptions *'08*
Bringing Ashley Home *'11*

Ben Cook
Little Men '98
Restless Spirits '99

Carole Cook (1924-)
The Incredible Mr. Limpet '64
Sixteen Candles '84
Lost and Found '99
Home on the Range '04 (V)

Clyde Cook (1891-1984)
White Gold '28
The White Cliffs of Dover '44

Dale 'Apollo' Cook (1958-)
American Kickboxer 2: To the Death '93
Raw Target '95

Dane Cook (1972-)
Simon Sez '99
London '05
Waiting '05
Employee of the Month '06
Dan in Real Life '07
Good Luck Chuck '07
Mr. Brooks '07
My Best Friend's Girl '08
Answers to Nothing '11
Detention '11
Guns, Girls and Gambling '11
Planes '13 (V)
Planes: Fire & Rescue '14 (V)

Donald Cook (1901-61)
Party Husband '31
Public Enemy '31
Safe in Hell '31
The Conquerors '32
Frisco Jenny '32
The Man Who Played God '32
Penguin Pool Murder '32
Baby Face '33
Brief Moment '33
Whirlpool '34
The Casino Murder Case '35
Show Boat '36
Here Come the Co-Eds '45

Elisha Cook, Jr. (1906-95)
Pigskin Parade '36
Love Is News '37
They Won't Forget '37
I Wake Up Screaming '41
The Maltese Falcon '41
Sergeant York '41
Wildcat '42
Dark Waters '44
Phantom Lady '44
Dillinger '45
The Big Sleep '46
Two Smart People '46
Born to Kill '47
The Long Night '47
Behave Yourself! '52
Don't Bother to Knock '52
Shane '53
Drum Beat '54
The Indian Fighter '55
The Killing '56
Chicago Confidential '57
Plunder Road '57
House on Haunted Hill '58
The Day of the Outlaw '59
One-Eyed Jacks '61
Black Zoo '63
The Haunted Palace '63
Papa's Delicate Condition '63
Welcome to Hard Times '67
Rosemary's Baby '68
El Condor '70
Blacula '72
The Great Northfield Minnesota Raid '72
Electra Glide in Blue '73
Emperor of the North Pole '73
The Outfit '73
Messiah of Evil '74
St. Ives '76
The Champ '79
1941 '79
Salem's Lot '79
Carny '80
Leave 'Em Laughing '81
Hammett '82

Marianne Cook (1931-)
See Marianne Koch

Michael Cook (1954-)
Signs & Wonders '00
The Monster of Phantom Lake '06
It Came From Another World '07
Attack of the Moon Zombies '11

Peter Cook (1937-95)
Alice in Wonderland '66
The Wrong Box '66
Bedazzled '68
Dandy in Aspic '68
The Bed Sitting Room '69
Those Daring Young Men in Their Jaunty Jalopies '69
The Rise and Rise of Michael Rimmer '70
The Hound of the Baskervilles '77
Yellowbeard '83
The Princess Bride '87
Without a Clue '88
Getting It Right '89
Great Balls of Fire '89
Black Beauty '94

Rachael Leigh Cook (1979-)
The Baby-Sitters' Club '95
Tom and Huck '95
Carpool '96
The Eighteenth Angel '97
The House of Yes '97
True Women '97
All I Wanna Do '98
The Bumblebee Flies Anyway '98
She's All That '99
Antitrust '00
Blow Dry '00
Get Carter '00
Josie and the Pussycats '01
Tangled '01
Texas Rangers '01
Scorched '02
Bookies '03
11:14 '03
Tempo '03
29 Palms '03
American Crime '04
The Big Empty '04
My First Wedding '04
Stateside '04
All Hat '07
Blonde Ambition '07
The Final Season '07
Nancy Drew '07
Falling Up '08
Bob Funk '09
The Lodger '09
Left to Die: The Sandra and Tammi Chase Story '12
Red Sky '14

Roderick Cook (1932-90)
Our Time '74
9 1/2 Weeks '86

Ron Cook (1948-)
Sharpe's Honour '94
Secrets and Lies '95
The Odyssey '97
Topsy Turvy '99
102 Dalmatians '00
Charlotte Gray '01
Lucky Break '01
Dead Gorgeous '02
The Hound of the Baskervilles '02
The Other Boleyn Girl '03
The Merchant of Venice '04
Thunderbirds '04
On a Clear Day '05
The Diary of Anne Frank '08
Filth '08

Tommy Cook (1930-)
Adventures of Red Ryder '40
Tarzan and the Leopard Woman '46
The Kid From Cleveland '49
American Guerrilla in the Philippines '50
Battle Cry '55
Night Passage '57
Missile to the Moon '59

Vera Cook
Never Take Candy From a Stranger '60
Cash on Demand '61
Kiss of the Vampire '62

Amelia Cooke
Species 3 '04
Alien Agent '07

Christian Cooke
Cemetery Junction '10
Romeo & Juliet '13

Christopher Cooke
The Unbelievable Truth '90
Rhythm Thief '94

Josh Cooke (1979-)
Wasted '06
Snowglobe '07
Bachelor Party 2: The Last Temptation '08
Group Sex '10

Keaton Nigel Cooke
Wiener-Dog '16
A Bread Factory, Part Two '18

Keith Cooke (1959-)
China O'Brien '88
Heatseeker '95

Olivia Cooke (1993-)
Ouija '14
The Quiet Ones '14
The Signal '14
Me and Earl and the Dying Girl '15
The Limehouse Golem '17
Thoroughbreds '17
Ready Player One '18

Scott Cooke
Street Gun '96
Thugs '96

Sophie Cookson (1990-)
Kingsman: The Secret Service '15
Red Joan '19

Hallam Cooley (1895-1971)
The Monster '25
Sporting Blood '31
Frisco Jenny '32

Jennifer Coolidge (1963-)
Trial and Error '96
Slappy and the Stinkers '97
American Pie '99
Best in Show '00
American Pie 2 '01
Down to Earth '01
Legally Blonde '01
Pootie Tang '01
Women vs. Men '02
American Wedding '03
Carolina '03
Legally Blonde 2: Red White & Blonde '03
A Mighty Wind '03
Testosterone '03
A Cinderella Story '04
Robots '05 (V)
American Dreamz '06
Click '06
Date Movie '06
For Your Consideration '06
Epic Movie '07
Foreign Exchange '08
Igor '08 (V)
Living Proof '08
Soul Men '08
Bad Lieutenant: Port of Call New Orleans '09
ExTerminators '09
Gentlemen Broncos '09
Beauty & the Briefcase '10
American Reunion '12
Austenland '13
Alexander and the Terrible, Horrible, No Good, Very Bad Day '14
Alvin and the Chipmunks: Road Chip '15

Philip Coolidge (1908-67)
The Tingler '59
Inherit the Wind '60

Coolio (1963-)
Phat Beach '96
An Alan Smithee Film: Burn, Hollywood, Burn '97
Judgment Day '99
Leprechaun 5: In the Hood '99
The Convent '00
Dope Case Pending '00
Gangland '00
In Pursuit '00
Shriek If You Know What I Did Last Friday the 13th '00
Submerged '00
Get Over It! '01 (C)
Red Water '01
Code Hunter '02
Exposed '03
Tapped Out '03
Stealing Candy '04
Pterodactyl '05
Three Days to Vegas '07

James Coombes
Agatha Christie's Murder with Mirrors '85
A Knight in Camelot '98

Brenda Cooney
Automatons '06
I Sell the Dead '09

Kevin Cooney (1945-)
Full Moon in Blue Water '88
If These Walls Could Talk '96
Clockwatchers '97
Bring It On Again '03
Fragments '08
The Haunting of Molly Hartley '08

Alice Cooper (1948-)
Sextette '78
Roadie '80
Monster Dog '82
Prince of Darkness '87
Freddy's Dead: The Final Nightmare '91
Wayne's World '92
Suck '09

Ben Cooper (1933-2020)
Johnny Guitar '53
Woman They Almost Lynched '53
The Rose Tattoo '55
Rebel in Town '56
Outlaw's Son '57
Gunfight at Comanche Creek '64

Bradley Cooper (1975-)
Wet Hot American Summer '01
Bending All the Rules '02
The Last Cowboy '03
Wedding Crashers '05
Failure to Launch '06
The Comebacks '07
The Midnight Meat Train '08
Older Than America '08
The Rocker '08
Yes Man '08
All About Steve '09
The Hangover '09
He's Just Not That Into You '09
New York, I Love You '09
The A-Team '10
Case 39 '10
Valentine's Day '10
Brother's Justice '11
The Hangover, Part 2 '11
Limitless '11
Hit and Run '12
Silver Linings Playbook '12
The Words '12
American Hustle '13
The Hangover, Part III '13
The Place Beyond the Pines '13
American Sniper '14
Guardians of the Galaxy '14 (V)
Serena '14
Aloha '15
Burnt '15
Joy '15
10 Cloverfield Lane '16 (V)
War Dogs '16
Guardians of the Galaxy Vol. 2 '17
The Mule '18
A Star Is Born '18

Camille (Cami) Cooper
Shocker '89
Lawnmower Man 2: Beyond Cyberspace '95

Chris Cooper (1951-)
Matewan '87
A Little Piece of Sunshine '90
City of Hope '91
Guilty by Suspicion '91
Return to Lonesome Dove '93
This Boy's Life '93
Lone Star '95
Money Train '95
Pharoah's Army '95
A Time to Kill '96
Breast Men '97
Great Expectations '97
The Horse Whisperer '97
Horton Foote's Alone '97
American Beauty '99
October Sky '99
Me, Myself, and Irene '00
The Patriot '00
Adaptation '02
The Bourne Identity '02
Interstate 60 '02
My House in Umbria '03
Seabiscuit '03
Silver City '04
Capote '05
Jarhead '05
Syriana '05
Breach '07
The Kingdom '07
Married Life '07
New York, I Love You '09
Where the Wild Things Are '09 (V)
The Company Men '10
Remember Me '10
The Tempest '10
The Town '10
The Muppets '11
August: Osage County '13
Demolition '15
Cars 3 '17 (V)
A Beautiful Day in the Neighborhood '19
Irresistible '20

Clancy Cooper (1906-75)
Girls in Chains '43
Naked Youth '59

Dominic Cooper (1978-)
The History Boys '06
Starter for 10 '06
Sense & Sensibility '07
The Duchess '08
The Escapist '08
God on Trial '08
Mamma Mia! '08
Brief Interviews With Hideous Men '09
An Education '09
Tamara Drewe '10
Captain America: The First Avenger '11
The Devil's Double '11
My Week With Marilyn '11
Abraham Lincoln: Vampire Hunter '12
Dead Man Down '13
Summer in February '13
Dracula Untold '14
Need for Speed '14
Reasonable Doubt '14
The Lady in the Van '15
Miss You Already '15
Warcraft '16
The Escape '18

Garry Cooper (1955-)
Quadrophenia '79
Universal Soldier: Regeneration '09

Gary Cooper (1901-61)
The Winning of Barbara Worth '26
It '27
Wings '27
Morocco '30
Fighting Caravans '31
The Devil and the Deep '32
A Farewell to Arms '32
If I Had a Million '32
Alice in Wonderland '33
Design for Living '33
One Sunday Afternoon '33
Today We Live '33
Now and Forever '34
Operator 13 '34
The Lives of a Bengal Lancer '35
Peter Ibbetson '35
The Wedding Night '35
The General Died at Dawn '36
Mr. Deeds Goes to Town '36
The Plainsman '37
Souls at Sea '37
The Adventures of Marco Polo '38
Bluebeard's Eighth Wife '38
The Cowboy and the Lady '38
Beau Geste '39
The Real Glory '39
The Westerner '40
Ball of Fire '41
Meet John Doe '41
Sergeant York '41
The Pride of the Yankees '42
For Whom the Bell Tolls '43
Casanova Brown '44
Along Came Jones '45
Saratoga Trunk '45
Cloak and Dagger '46
Unconquered '47
Good Sam '48
The Fountainhead '49
It's a Great Feeling '49
Task Force '49
Bright Leaf '50
Distant Drums '51
It's a Big Country '51
You're In the Navy Now '51
High Noon '52
Springfield Rifle '52
Return to Paradise '53
Vera Cruz '53
Garden of Evil '54
The Court Martial of Billy Mitchell '55
Friendly Persuasion '56
Love in the Afternoon '57
Man of the West '58
Alias Jesse James '59 (C)
The Hanging Tree '59
They Came to Cordura '59
The Wreck of the Mary Deare '59

George Cooper (1892-1943)
Little Church Around the Corner '23
Smouldering Fires '25
The Trail of '98 '28
Forbidden Trail '32
Uptown New York '32
Eight Iron Men '52

Gladys Cooper (1888-1971)
Kitty Foyle '40
Rebecca '40
The Black Cat '41
The Gay Falcon '41
That Hamilton Woman '41
Now, Voyager '42
This Above All '42
Mr. Lucky '43
Princess O'Rourke '43
The Song of Bernadette '43
Mrs. Parkington '44
The White Cliffs of Dover '44
Love Letters '45
The Valley of Decision '45
The Green Years '46
The Bishop's Wife '47
Homecoming '48
The Pirate '48
Madame Bovary '49
The Secret Garden '49
At Sword's Point '51
Thunder on the Hill '51
Separate Tables '58
My Fair Lady '64

Jackie Cooper (1922-2011)
The Champ '32
Peck's Bad Boy '34
Treasure Island '34
The Devil Is a Sissy '36
Gangster's Boy '38
That Certain Age '38
What a Life '39
Gallant Sons '40
Return of Frank James '40
Ziegfeld Girl '41
Syncopation '42
Where Are Your Children? '44
Kilroy Was Here '47
Everything's Ducky '61
The Love Machine '71
Maybe I'll Come Home in the Spring '71
Superman: The Movie '78
Superman 2 '80
Superman 3 '83

Jeanne Cooper (1928-2013)
The Redhead from Wyoming '53
Over-Exposed '56
Plunder Road '57
Unwed Mother '58
Shame '61
House of Women '62
13 West Street '62
Black Zoo '63
Kansas City Bomber '72
The All-American Boy '73
Sweet Hostage '75
Carpool Guy '05
Donna on Demand '09

Jeff Cooper
Born Losers '67
The Impossible Years '68
Circle of Iron '78

Justin Cooper (1988-)
Liar Liar '97
Dennis the Menace Strikes Again '98

Maggie Cooper (1965-)
And Baby Makes Six '79
Death Ray 2000 '81
An Eye for an Eye '81
Divorce Wars: A Love Story '82

Melville Cooper (1896-1973)
Private Life of Don Juan '34
The Scarlet Pimpernel '34
The Gorgeous Hussy '36
The Great Garrick '37
Thin Ice '37
The Adventures of Robin Hood '38
Dawn Patrol '38
Four's a Crowd '38
Garden of the Moon '38
Gold Diggers in Paris '38
Murder over New York '40
Rebecca '40
Too Many Husbands '40
The Lady Eve '41
Life Begins at Eight-Thirty '42
Immortal Sergeant '43
Heartbeat '46
13 Rue Madeleine '46
Let's Dance '50
The Underworld Story '50
The King's Thief '55
Around the World in 80 Days '56 (C)

Oliver Cooper
Project X '11
Burying the Ex '15

Pat Cooper (1929-)
Analyze This '98
Analyze That '02

Scott Cooper (1970-)
Broken Trail '06
For Sale by Owner '09
Get Low '09

Stan Cooper (1938-)
See Stelvio Rosi

Ted Cooper
Phantom from Space '53
The Caine Mutiny '54

Terence Cooper (1928-97)
Casino Royale '67
Heart of the Stag '84

Trevor Cooper (1953-)
Framed '93
Ivanhoe '97
The History of Mr. Polly '07

Wendy Cooper
Witchcraft 10: Mistress of the Craft '98
24 Hours in London '00

Robert Coote (1909-82)
Gunga Din '39
Mr. Moto's Last Warning '39
Nurse Edith Cavell '39
Vigil in the Night '40
Commandos Strike at Dawn '43
Stairway to Heaven '46
Forever Amber '47
The Ghost and Mrs. Muir '47
Lured '47
Macbeth '48
The Three Musketeers '48
Othello '52
Scaramouche '52
The Horse's Mouth '58
Merry Andrew '58
My Fair Lady '64
Alice Through the Looking Glass '66
The Cool Ones '67
Kenner '73
Theatre of Blood '73

Kenneth Cope (1931-)
Carry On at Your Convenience '71
Carry On Matron '72
Rentadick '72

Adam Copeland
Bending the Rules '12
Interrogation '16

Joan Copeland (1922-)
The Goddess '58
Middle of the Night '59
The Iceman Cometh '60
Roseland '77
Happy New Year '87
Her Alibi '88
The Peacemaker '97
The Adventures of Sebastian Cole '99
Brother Bear '03 (V)

Kristina Copeland (1973-)
How It All Went Down '03
Savage Island '03

Zane R. (Lil' Zane) Copeland, Jr. (1982-)
Finding Forrester '00
Dr. Dolittle 2 '01

Michael Copeman
Another Woman '94
Focus '01

Geoffrey Copleston
The Black Cat '81
The Belly of an Architect '91

Peter Copley (1915-2008)
The Golden Salamander '51
King and Country '64
Help! '65
Mosquito Squadron '70
A Dangerous Man: Lawrence after Arabia '91
Oliver Twist '05

Sharlto Copley (1973-)
District 9 '09
The A-Team '10
Elysium '13
Europa Report '13
Oldboy '13
Maleficent '14
Chappie '15
Hardcore Henry '15
The Hollars '16
Gringo '18

Teri Copley (1961-)
I Married a Centerfold '84
In the Line of Duty: The FBI Murders '88
Down the Drain '89
Transylvania Twist '89
Brain Donors '92

Michael Copon (1982-)
Bring It On: In It to Win It '07
The Scorpion King 2: Rise of a Warrior '08
Night of the Demons '09

Alicia Coppola (1968-)
Blood Money '99
Velocity Trap '99
Double Down '01
Sin '02
Fresh Cut Grass '04
National Treasure: Book of Secrets '07

Christopher Coppola (1962-)
Dog Gone Love '03
BloodRayne 2: Deliverance '07
Loveless in Los Angeles '07
Postal '07
Undead or Alive '07

Francis Ford Coppola (1939-)
Apocalypse Now '79
Hearts of Darkness: A Filmmaker's Apocalypse '91
Five Came Back '17

Sofia Coppola (1971-)
The Godfather '72
Peggy Sue Got Married '86
The Godfather, Part 3 '90
Inside Monkey Zetterland '93
Star Wars: Episode 1-The Phantom Menace '99

Vincent Corazza (1972-)
Hangman '00
Leaving Metropolis '02
The Cheetah Girls '03
I Downloaded a Ghost '04

Bruno Corazzari
Taste of Death '68
Seven Blood-Stained Orchids '72

Brady Corbet (1988-)
Thirteen '03
Mysterious Skin '04
Thunderbirds '04
Funny Games '07
Martha Marcy May Marlene '11
Melancholia '11
Escobar: Paradise Lost '15

Glenn Corbett (1934-93)
The Crimson Kimono '59
Man On a String '60
Homicidal '61
Pirates of Blood River '62
Shenandoah '65
Chisum '70
Dead Pigeon on Beethoven Street '72
Midway '76
Shadow Force '92

Gretchen Corbett (1947-)
Let's Scare Jessica to Death '71
Jaws of Satan '81
Time Warp '81
A Change of Heart '98

Harry H. Corbett (1925-82)
Ladies Who Do '63
Carry On Screaming '66
Jabberwocky '77
Silver Dream Racer '83

John Corbett (1961-)
Tombstone '93
Don't Look Back '96
The Morrison Murders '96
Wedding Bell Blues '96
Volcano '97
Dinner Rush '00
Prancer Returns '01
Serendipity '01
My Big Fat Greek Wedding '02
Elvis Has Left the Building '04
Raise Your Voice '04
Raising Helen '04
Bigger Than the Sky '05
Dreamland '06
The Messengers '07
Montana Sky '07
Baby on Board '08
The Burning Plain '08
Street Kings '08
I Hate Valentine's Day '09
November Christmas '10
Ramona and Beezus '10
The Hunt for the I-5 Killer '11
A Smile as Big as the Moon '12
The Lookalike '14
The Boy Next Door '15
All Saints '17
God's Not Dead: A Light in Darkness '18

Ronnie Corbett (1930-)
No Sex Please-We're British '73
Fierce Creatures '96
Burke & Hare '10

Barry Corbin (1940-)
Any Which Way You Can '80
Stir Crazy '80
Urban Cowboy '80
Bitter Harvest '81
Dead and Buried '81
Prime Suspect '82
Six Pack '82
Ratings Game '84
A Death in California '85
My Science Project '85
What Comes Around '85
Firefighter '86
Nothing in Common '86
Critters 2: The Main Course '88
Permanent Record '88
Secret Witness '88
Who's Harry Crumb? '89
The Hot Spot '90
Career Opportunities '91
The Chase '91
Conagher '91
Curdled '95
Solo '96
Held Up '00
Crossfire Trail '01
Race to Space '01
Hope Ranch '02
Monte Walsh '03
River's End '05
Hidden Places '06
In the Valley of Elah '07
No Country for Old Men '07
Beer for My Horses '08
Lake City '08
Feed the Fish '09
Not Since You '09
That Evening Sun '09
Wyvern '09
Bloodworth '10
NoNames '10
Universal Squadrons '11
Valley of the Sun '11
The Man Who Shook the Hand of Vicente Fernandez '12
Shadow on the Mesa '13
All Saints '17
Trading Paint '19

Ed Corbin
In the Flesh '97
True Grit '10

Ellen Corby (1913-99)
Bedlam '45
It's a Wonderful Life '46
I Remember Mama '48
Caged '50
Ma and Pa Kettle Go to Town '50
Angels in the Outfield '51
Goodbye My Fancy '51
On Moonlight Bay '51
Illegal '55
All Mine to Give '56
Night Passage '57
Vertigo '58
Saintly Sinners '62
The Caretakers '63
The Strangler '64
The Glass Bottom Boat '66
Homecoming: A Christmas Story '71
Support Your Local Gunfighter '71
A Day for Thanks on Walton's Mountain '82

Donna Corcoran (1942-)
Angels in the Outfield '51
Don't Bother to Knock '52
Young Man With Ideas '52
Scandal at Scourie '53

Kevin Corcoran (1949-)
Old Yeller '57
The Shaggy Dog '59
Toby Tyler '59
Pollyanna '60
The Swiss Family Robinson '60
Johnny Shiloh '63
Savage Sam '63
A Tiger Walks '64

Alex Cord (1933-)
Synanon '65
Stagecoach '66
A Minute to Pray, a Second to Die '67
The Brotherhood '68
The Last Grenade '70
Dead Are Alive '72
Genesis II '73
Inn of the Damned '74
Fire '77
Grayeagle '77
Sidewinder One '77
Jungle Warriors '84
The Dirty Dozen: The Fatal Mission '88
The Uninvited '88
C.I.A.: Code Name Alexa '92
To Be the Best '93
Air Rage '01
Fire From Below '09

Mara Corday (1930-)
Drums Across the River '54
Francis Joins the WACs '54
Tarantula '55
The Black Scorpion '57
The Giant Claw '57

Rita (Paula) Corday (1920-92)
The Falcon and the Co-Eds '43
The Falcon Strikes Back '43
The Leopard Man '43
The Body Snatcher '45
West of the Pecos '45
Too Young to Kiss '51
Because You're Mine '52
The Black Castle '52

Nathan (Nate) Corddry (1977-)
The Nanny Diaries '07
The Invention of Lying '09
The Ugly Truth '09
6 Souls '13

Rob Corddry (1971-)
Unaccompanied Minors '06
Wedding Daze '06
The Heartbreak Kid '07
I Now Pronounce You Chuck and Larry '07
The Ten '07
Harold & Kumar Escape from Guantanamo Bay '08
Lower Learning '08
Semi-Pro '08
W. '08
What Happens in Vegas '08
Taking Chances '09
The Winning Season '09
Hot Tub Time Machine '10
Operation: Endgame '10
Cedar Rapids '11
Butter '12
Seeking a Friend for the End of the World '12
Escape From Planet Earth '13 (V)
In a World... '13
Pain & Gain '13
Warm Bodies '13
The Way Way Back '13
Sex Tape '14
Hot Tub Time Machine 2 '15

Ricky Cordell
The Singing Nun '66
Kenner '73

James Corden (1978-)
All or Nothing '02
The History Boys '06
Telstar: The Joe Meek Story '08
Vampire Killers '09
Begin Again '13
One Chance '13
Into the Woods '14
Kill Your Friends '16
The Emoji Movie '17 (V)
Peter Rabbit '18 (V)
Smallfoot '18
Cats '19
Trolls World Tour '20

Harry Cording (1891-1954)
The Squall '29
The Black Cat '34
Man in the Attic '53

Pancho Cordova
The Exterminating Angel '62
A Home of Our Own '75

Allan Corduner (1950-)
Yentl '83
Mandela '87
The Imposters '98
Topsy Turvy '99
Joe Gould's Secret '00
The Grey Zone '01
Me Without You '01
The Search for John Gissing '01
Daniel Deronda '02
Food of Love '02
Moonlight Mile '02
The Way We Live Now '02
La Femme Musketeer '03
De-Lovely '04
The Merchant of Venice '04
Bigger Than the Sky '05
Friends & Crocodiles '05
The White Countess '05
Defiance '08
Lennon Naked '10
A Thousand Kisses Deep '11
Disobedience '17

Raymond Cordy (1898-1956)
A Nous la Liberte '31
Beauties of the Night '52

Nick(y) Corello
Colors '88
Blankman '94
Sugar Hill '94
Devil in a Blue Dress '95
Lansky '99

Brigitte Corey (1935-)
See Luisella Boni

Prof. Irwin Corey (1914-)
How to Commit Marriage '69
Fairy Tales '76
Stuck on You '84
The Curse of the Jade Scorpion '01

Isabel Corey (1939-)
Bob le Flambeur '55
The Invincible Gladiator '62

Jeff Corey (1914-2002)
My Friend Flicka '43
Brute Force '47
Kidnapped '48
A Southern Yankee '48
Bright Leaf '50
The Nevadan '50
The Next Voice You Hear '50
The Outriders '50
Rawhide '50
The Balcony '63
Lady in a Cage '64
Mickey One '65
Seconds '66
In Cold Blood '67
The Boston Strangler '68
Butch Cassidy and the Sundance Kid '69

Impasse '69
True Grit '69
Beneath the Planet of the Apes '70
Getting Straight '70
Little Big Man '70
They Call Me Mr. Tibbs! '70
Catlow '71
Shoot Out '71
The Premonition '75
Banjo Hackett '76
Oh, God! '77
Wild Geese '78
Butch and Sundance: The Early Days '79
Battle Beyond the Stars '80
Sword & the Sorcerer '82
Conan the Destroyer '84
Creator '85
Messenger of Death '88
Bird on a Wire '90
Deception '92
Sinatra '92
Color of Night '94
Surviving the Game '94

Wendell Corey (1914-68)
I Walk Alone '48
The Search '48
Sorry, Wrong Number '48
Any Number Can Play '49
Holiday Affair '49
The File on Thelma Jordon '50
The Furies '50
No Sad Songs For Me '50
Rich, Young and Pretty '51
Carbine Williams '52
My Man and I '52
The Wild North '52
Hell's Half Acre '54
Rear Window '54
The Big Knife '55
The Killer Is Loose '56
The Rack '56
The Rainmaker '56
Loving You '57
Alias Jesse James '59
The Astro-Zombies '67
Buckskin '68

Hermione Corfield
Fallen '17
Rust Creek '19

Emayatzy Corinealdi
Middle of Nowhere '12
Addicted '14
Miles Ahead '16

Michael Coristine (1980-)
The Secret of Zoey '02
Stealing Sinatra '04

Danny Corkill (1974-)
Mrs. Soffel '84
D.A.R.Y.L. '85

Al Corley (1956-)
Squeeze Play '79
Torchlight '85
Cowboy Up '00

Annie Corley
Beyond Betrayal '94
The Bridges of Madison County '95
Box of Moonlight '96
Free Willy 3: The Rescue '97
The '60s '99
Along for the Ride '00
Here on Earth '00
If You Only Knew '00
Juwanna Mann '02
Monster '03
Seabiscuit '03
The Lucky Ones '08

Pat Corley (1930-2006)
Coming Home '78
Nightwing '79
The Two Worlds of Jenny Logan '79
Of Mice and Men '81
Night Shift '82
Silent Witness '85
Poker Alice '87
Mr. Destiny '90
Come Early Morning '06

Sharron Corley (1971-)
New Jersey Drive '95
The Substitute '96

Danielle Cormack (1970-)
Siam Sunset '99
The Price of Milk '00
Maiden Voyage: Ocean Hijack '04

Maddie Corman (1970-)
Seven Minutes in Heaven '86
The Adventures of Ford Fairlane '90
My New Gun '92
I Think I Do '97

Roger Corman (1926-)
Atlas '60
Creature from the Haunted Sea '60 (C)
The Godfather, Part 2 '74
Cannonball '76
The Howling '81 (C)
Swing Shift '84
The Silence of the Lambs '91
Body Bags '93 (C)
Philadelphia '93
The Independent '00 (C)
Scream 3 '00
Dinoshark '10

Lee Cormie
Darkness Falls '03
December Boys '07

Michael Cornelison (1952-2011)
Mommy '95
Mommy 2: Mommy's Day '96
Real Time: Siege at Lucas Street Market '00

Don Cornelius (1936-2012)
No Way Back '74
Tapeheads '89

Ellie Cornell (1963-)
Halloween 4: The Return of Michael Myers '88
Halloween 5: The Revenge of Michael Myers '89
House of the Dead '03
All Souls Day '05

Christelle Cornil (1977-)
Illegal '10
The Unknown Girl '17

Clovis Cornillac (1967-)
The Unbearable Lightness of Being '88
Carnage '02
Gilles' Wife '04
A Very Long Engagement '04
Cash '08
Paris 36 '08
Inspector Bellamy '09

Abbie Cornish (1982-)
Marking Time '03
One Perfect Day '04
Somersault '04
Candy '06
A Good Year '06
Elizabeth: The Golden Age '07
Stop-Loss '08
Bright Star '09
Legend of the Guardians: The Owls of Ga'Hoole '10 (V)
Limitless '11
Sucker Punch '11
W.E. '11
Seven Psychopaths '12
RoboCop '14
Solace '16
Geostorm '17
Three Billboards Outside Ebbing, Missouri '17

Nick Cornish (1976-)
Code Hunter '02
Hometown Legend '02
Dark Honeymoon '08

Robert Cornthwaite (1917-2006)
The Thing '51
The War of the Worlds '53
Matinee '92

Charlotte Cornwell
White Hunter, Black Heart '90
Couples Retreat '09

Judy Cornwell (1940-)
Two for the Road '67
Wuthering Heights '70
Santa Claus: The Movie '85
Persuasion '95
Prince of Poisoners: The Life and Crimes of William Palmer '98

Jose Coronado (1957-)
The Disappearance of Garcia Lorca '96
Goya in Bordeaux '99

Antoni Corone
Raging Hormones '99
Reservation Road '07
We Own the Night '07

Ryan Corr (1989-)
Not Suitable for Children '12
6 Plots '12
Wolf Creek 2 '13

Teodoro Corra (1934-96)
Five Dolls for an August Moon '70
Roy Colt and Winchester Jack '70
Crime Boss '72

Gino Corrado (1893-1982)
La Boheme '26
Flirting With Danger '35
Two Sisters From Boston '46

Georges Corraface (1952-)
Impromptu '90
Not Without My Daughter '90
Escape from L.A. '96
Red Shoe Diaries: Four on the Floor '96
Only Love '98
Km. 0 '00
The Prankster '10

Adrienne Corri (1931-)
The River '51
Devil Girl from Mars '54
Meet Mr. Callaghan '54
Three Men in a Boat '56
Corridors of Blood '58
The Rough and the Smooth '59
The Tell-Tale Heart '60
Doctor Zhivago '65
Africa Texas Style '67
The Viking Queen '67
The File of the Golden Goose '69
Moon Zero Two '70
A Clockwork Orange '71
Vampire Circus '71
Madhouse '74

Nick Corri (1963-)
See Jsu Garcia

Emmett Corrigan
An American Tragedy '31
The Beast of the City '32

Kevin Corrigan (1969-)
Zebrahead '92
True Romance '93
Kiss of Death '94
Living in Oblivion '94
Rhythm Thief '94
Bandwagon '95
Tree's Lounge '96
Walking and Talking '96
Buffalo 66 '97
Kicked in the Head '97
Brown's Requiem '98
Henry Fool '98
Lulu on the Bridge '98
Slums of Beverly Hills '98
Chain of Fools '00
Steal This Movie! '00
Chelsea Walls '01
Scotland, PA '02

Break a Leg '03
Anchorman: The Legend of Ron Burgundy '04
Delirious '06
The Departed '06
The Dog Problem '06
The Last Winter '06
Lonesome Jim '06
American Gangster '07
Goodbye Baby '07
Superbad '07
Definitely, Maybe '08
Don't Look Up '08
Pineapple Express '08
The Toe Tactic '08
Big Fan '09
Today's Special '09
Unstoppable '10
The Chaperone '11
Supporting Characters '13
Results '15

Lloyd Corrigan (1900-69)
High School '40
The Lady in Question '40
Young Tom Edison '40
The Mexican Spitfire's Baby '41
Maisie Gets Her Man '42
The Mystery of Marie Roget '42
Tarzan's Desert Mystery '43
Gambler's Choice '44
Since You Went Away '44
The Thin Man Goes Home '44
The Bandit of Sherwood Forest '46
The Chase '46
Two Smart People '46
Lights of Old Santa Fe '47
Stallion Road '47
Father Is a Bachelor '50
When Willie Comes Marching Home '50
Cavalry Charge '51

Ray Corrigan (1907-76)
Undersea Kingdom '36
Join the Marines '37
Renegade Girl '46
Trail of Robin Hood '50
It! The Terror from Beyond Space '58

Shirley Corrigan
The Devil's Nightmare '71
Dr. Jekyll and the Wolfman '71

Aneta Corsaut (1933-95)
The Blob '58
The Toolbox Murders '78
Return to Mayberry '85

Silvana Corsini
Accatone! '61
Mamma Roma '62

Bill Cort (1936-93)
See William Cort

Bud Cort (1948-)
Sweet Charity '69
Brewster McCloud '70
Gas-s-s-s! '70
M*A*S*H '70
The Strawberry Statement '70
The Traveling Executioner '70
Harold and Maude '71
Why Shoot the Teacher '79
Die Laughing '80
Hysterical '83
Love Letters '83
Maria's Lovers '84
Invaders from Mars '86
Love at Stake '87
The Chocolate War '88
Out of the Dark '88
Brain Dead '89
Going Under '91
Ted & Venus '93
Heat '95
Sweet Jane '98
But I'm a Cheerleader '99
Dogma '99
The Million Dollar Hotel '99
Coyote Ugly '00
Pollock '00

South of Heaven, West of Hell '00
The Big Empty '04
The Life Aquatic with Steve Zissou '04

William Cort (1936-93)
Wackiest Wagon Train in the West '77
Elvira, Mistress of the Dark '88

Dan Cortese (1967-)
Demolition Man '93
The Triangle '01
Locusts: The 8th Plague '05
Everybody Wants to Be Italian '08
Soccer Mom '08

Joe Cortese (1948-)
Family Enforcer '76
Windows '80
Evilspeak '82
Letting Go '85
Stalking Danger '86
Ruby '92
To Protect and Serve '92
American History X '98
Against the Ropes '04

Valentina Cortese (1923-2019)
The Glass Mountain '49
Malaya '49
Les Miserables '52
The Barefoot Contessa '54
The Girl Who Knew Too Much '63
The Visit '64
Juliet of the Spirits '65
The Legend of Lylah Clare '68
The Secret of Santa Vittoria '69
First Love '70
Assassination of Trotsky '72
Brother Sun, Sister Moon '73
Day for Night '73
Kidnap Syndicate '76
When Time Ran Out '80
The Adventures of Baron Munchausen '89

Bella Cortez (1944-)
The Giant of Metropolis '61
The Tartars '61
Ali Baba and the Seven Saracens '64

Ricardo Cortez (1899-1977)
Torrent '26
Mockery '27
The Lost Zeppelin '29
Montana Moon '30
Behind Office Doors '31
Illicit '31
The Maltese Falcon '31
Ten Cents a Dance '31
Flesh '32
The Phantom of Crestwood '32
Symphony of Six Million '32
The House on 56th Street '33
Midnight Mary '33
Torch Singer '33
The Man with Two Faces '34
Wonder Bar '34
Frisco Kid '35
Shadow of Doubt '35
The White Cockatoo '35
The Case of the Black Cat '36
Mr. Moto's Last Warning '39
Murder over New York '40
I Killed That Man '42
Tomorrow We Live '42
The Locket '46
Bunco Squad '50
The Last Hurrah '58

Connor Corum
Heaven Is for Real '14
The Stray '17

Bill Cosby (1937-)
Man & Boy '71
To All My Friends on Shore '71
Hickey & Boggs '72

Uptown Saturday Night '74
Let's Do It Again '75
Mother, Jugs and Speed '76
Piece of the Action '77
California Suite '78
The Devil & Max Devlin '81
Leonard Part 6 '87
Ghost Dad '90
The Meteor Man '93
Jack '96
Fat Albert '04 (C)

Howard Cosell (1920-95)
Bananas '71
The World's Greatest Athlete '73 (C)
Broadway Danny Rose '84

Daniel Cosgrove (1970-)
Too Busy to Work '32
The Object of My Affection '98
They Crawl '01
Valentine '01
National Lampoon's Van Wilder '02

Miranda Cosgrove (1993-)
School of Rock '03
Yours, Mine & Ours '05
Keeping Up with the Steins '06
The Wild Stallion '09
Despicable Me '10 (V)
Despicable Me 2 '13 (V)
Despicable Me 3 '17 (V)
3022 '19

Robert Cosgrove, Jr.
Bikini Bloodbath '06
Bikini Bloodbath Carwash '08

Joaquin Cosio
Quantum of Solace '08
A Night in Old Mexico '14

James Cosmo (1948-)
Orde Wingate '76
Stormy Monday '88
Braveheart '95
Emma '96
Ivanhoe '97
Babe: Pig in the City '98 (V)
Urban Ghost Story '98
One More Kiss '99
Split Second '99
To End All Wars '01
All the Queen's Men '02
Troy '04
The Chronicles of Narnia: The Lion, the Witch and the Wardrobe '05
The Last Legion '07
The Seeker: The Dark Is Rising '07
The Color of Magic '08
The Santa Incident '10
Citadel '12
Get Lucky '13
Eliminators '16

Ernest Cossart (1876-1951)
The Great Ziegfeld '36
Murder With Pictures '36
Three Smart Girls Grow Up '39
Kitty Foyle '40

James Cossins (1933-97)
The Anniversary '68
Wuthering Heights '70
Dynasty of Fear '72

James Costa
Joe the King '99
L.I.E. '01

Laia Costa (1985-)
Victoria '15
Piercing '18

Mary Costa (1930-)
The Big Caper '57
Sleeping Beauty '59 (V)

Constantin Costa-Gavras (1933-)
Spies Like Us '85
The Stupids '95 (C)

Suzanne Costallos
True Love '89
Lotto Land '95

Paulo Costanzo (1978-)
Road Trip *'00*
Gypsy 83 *'01*
Josie and the Pussycats *'01*
40 Days and 40 Nights *'02*
Scorched *'02*
Everything's Gone Green *'06*
A Beginner's Guide to Endings *'10*

Robert Costanzo (1942-)
Ratings Game *'84*
The Vegas Strip Wars *'84*
Die Hard 2: Die Harder *'90*
Honeymoon in Vegas *'92*
The Cemetery Club *'93*
Man's Best Friend *'93*
Relentless 3 *'93*
Ring of Fire 3: Lion Strike *'94*
For Better or Worse *'95*
Storybook *'95*
Underworld *'96*
Plump Fiction *'97*
Air Bud 2: Golden Receiver *'98*
61* *'01*
In the Mix *'05*

Bob Costas (1952-)
The Scout *'94*
BASEketball *'98*
Pootie Tang *'01 (C)*
Head Games *'12*

Dolores Costello (1903-79)
Old San Francisco *'27*
When a Man Loves *'27*
Noah's Ark *'28*
Little Lord Fauntleroy *'36*
The Magnificent Ambersons *'42*

Don Costello (1901-45)
Sleepers West *'41*
Whistling in the Dark *'41*
The Blue Dahlia *'46*

Elvis Costello (1954-)
Americathon *'79*
No Surrender *'86*
Straight to Hell *'87*
Spice World: The Movie *'97 (C)*
200 Cigarettes *'98*
Austin Powers 2: The Spy Who Shagged Me *'99 (C)*
I Love Your Work *'03 (C)*
De-Lovely *'04*

Lou Costello (1906-59)
One Night in the Tropics *'40*
Buck Privates *'41*
Hold That Ghost *'41*
In the Navy *'41*
Keep 'Em Flying *'41*
Pardon My Sarong *'42*
Ride 'Em Cowboy *'42*
Rio Rita *'42*
Who Done It? *'42*
Hit the Ice *'43*
It Ain't Hay *'43*
In Society *'44*
Lost in a Harem *'44*
Abbott and Costello in Hollywood *'45*
Here Come the Co-Eds *'45*
The Naughty Nineties *'45*
Little Giant *'46*
The Time of Their Lives *'46*
Buck Privates Come Home *'47*
The Wistful Widow of Wagon Gap *'47*
Abbott and Costello Meet Frankenstein *'48*
Mexican Hayride *'48*
The Noose Hangs High *'48*
Abbott and Costello Meet the Killer, Boris Karloff *'49*
Africa Screams *'49*
Abbott and Costello in the Foreign Legion *'50*
Abbott and Costello Meet the Invisible Man *'51*
Comin' Round the Mountain *'51*
Abbott and Costello Meet Captain Kidd *'52*
Abbott and Costello Meet Dr. Jekyll and Mr. Hyde *'52*
Jack & the Beanstalk *'52*
Lost in Alaska *'52*
Abbott and Costello Go to Mars *'53*
Abbott and Costello Meet the Keystone Kops *'54*
Abbott and Costello Meet the Mummy *'55*
Dance with Me, Henry *'56*
The 30-Foot Bride of Candy Rock *'59*

Ward (Edward) Costello (1919-2009)
The Gallant Hours *'60*
MacArthur *'77*

John A. Costelloe (1961-2008)
Billy Bathgate *'91*
Me and the Mob *'94*
Kazaam *'96*
Doubt *'08*

Nicolas Coster (1934-)
My Blood Runs Cold *'65*
MacArthur *'77*
The Electric Horseman *'79*
Stir Crazy *'80*
Betsy's Wedding *'90*

Ritchie Coster (1967-)
The Tuxedo *'02*
The Sentinel *'06*
The Dark Knight *'08*
Virtuality *'09*
Pete Smalls Is Dead *'10*
By the Gun *'14*
Blackhat *'15*

Nikolaj Coster-Waldau (1970-)
Bent *'97*
Black Hawk Down *'01*
My Name Is Modesty: A Modesty Blaise Adventure *'04*
Wimbledon *'04*
Kingdom of Heaven *'05*
Firewall *'06*
Assassin in Love *'07*
Virtuality *'09*
Blackthorn *'11*
Headhunters *'11*
Mama *'13*
Oblivion *'13*
The Other Woman *'14*
Gods of Egypt *'16*
Domino *'19*
Exit Plan *'20*

George Costigan (1947-)
Rita, Sue & Bob Too *'87*
The Hawk *'93*
Love or Money *'01*
Calendar Girls *'03*
See No Evil: The Moors Murders *'06*

Kevin Costner (1955-)
Sizzle Beach U.S.A. *'74*
Night Shift *'82*
Stacy's Knights *'83*
Table for Five *'83*
Testament *'83*
Shadows Run Black *'84*
American Flyers *'85*
Fandango *'85*
Silverado *'85*
No Way Out *'87*
The Untouchables *'87*
Bull Durham *'88*
Field of Dreams *'89*
Dances with Wolves *'90*
Revenge *'90*
JFK *'91*
Robin Hood: Prince of Thieves *'91*
The Bodyguard *'92*
A Perfect World *'93*
The War *'94*
Wyatt Earp *'94*
Waterworld *'95*
Tin Cup *'96*
The Postman *'97*
Message in a Bottle *'98*
For Love of the Game *'99*
Thirteen Days *'00*
3000 Miles to Graceland *'01*
Dragonfly *'02*
Open Range *'03*
Rumor Has It. . . *'05*
The Upside of Anger *'05*
The Guardian *'06*
Mr. Brooks *'07*
Swing Vote *'08*
The Company Men *'10*
The New Daughter *'10*
Hatfields & McCoys *'12*
Man of Steel *'13*
Black or White *'14*
Draft Day *'14*
Jack Ryan: Shadow Recruit *'14*
3 Days to Kill *'14*
McFarland USA *'15*
Criminal *'16*
Hidden Figures *'17*
The Art of Racing in the Rain *'19*
The Highwaymen *'19*

Tina Cote
Omega Doom *'96*
Mean Guns *'97*

John Cothran, Jr. (1947-)
Ricochet *'91*
Black Snake Moan *'07*

Marion Cotillard (1975-)
Big Fish *'03*
Love Me if You Dare *'03*
A Very Long Engagement *'04*
A Good Year *'06*
You and Me *'06*
La Vie en Rose *'07*
Nine *'09*
Public Enemies *'09*
Inception *'10*
Little White Lies *'10*
Contagion *'11*
Midnight in Paris *'11*
The Dark Knight Rises *'12*
Rust and Bone *'12*
Blood Ties *'13*
The Immigrant *'13*
Mademoiselle C *'13*
Two Days, One Night *'14*
Macbeth *'15*
Allied *'16*
Assassin's Creed *'16*
The Little Prince *'16*

D.J. Cotrona (1980-)
Venom *'05*
Addicted to Her Love *'06*
Dear John *'10*

Jonathon Cott
Above and Beyond *'53*
Battle Circus *'53*

Joseph Cotten (1905-94)
Citizen Kane *'41*
The Magnificent Ambersons *'42*
Shadow of a Doubt *'43*
Gaslight *'44*
I'll Be Seeing You *'44*
Since You Went Away *'44*
Love Letters *'45*
Duel in the Sun *'46*
Portrait of Jennie *'48*
The Third Man *'49*
Under Capricorn *'49*
September Affair *'50*
The Man With a Cloak *'51*
Niagara *'52*
Othello *'52*
The Steel Trap *'52*
A Blueprint for Murder *'53*
The Killer Is Loose *'56*
The Halliday Brand *'57*
Touch of Evil *'58 (C)*
The Last Sunset *'61*
Hush, Hush, Sweet Charlotte *'65*
The Money Trap *'65*
Brighty of the Grand Canyon *'67*
Hellbenders *'67*
Petulia *'68*
White Comanche *'68*
The Grasshopper *'69*
The Passing of Evil *'70*
Tora! Tora! Tora! *'70*
The Abominable Dr. Phibes *'71*
City Beneath the Sea *'71*
Lady Frankenstein *'72*
Torture Chamber of Baron Blood *'72*
Soylent Green *'73*
The Big Push *'75*
The Lindbergh Kidnapping Case *'76*
Airport '77 *'77*
Return to Fantasy Island *'77*
The Hearse *'80*
Screamers *'80*
Survivor *'80*
Heaven's Gate *'81*

Chrissie Cotterill (1955-)
Scrubbers *'82*
Nil by Mouth *'96*

Ralph Cotterill (1932-)
Howling 3: The Marsupials *'87*
Bad Boy Bubby *'93*
Crimebroker *'93*

Mia Cottet (1968-)
Nine Months *'95*
Dawg *'02*
The Tuxedo *'02*

Jason Cottle
Cthulhu *'08*
Act of Valor *'12*
6 Below: Miracle on the Mountain *'17*

Ben Cotton (1975-)
The Bad Son *'07*
Scar *'07*
30 Days of Night: Dark Days *'10*
Love at the Thanksgiving Day Parade *'12*
Zodiac: Signs of the Apocalypse *'14*
No Men Beyond This Point *'15*

Maxwell Perry Cotton (2000-)
A Dennis the Menace Christmas *'07*
Like Dandelion Dust *'09*
Game Time: Tackling the Past *'11*
Mr. Popper's Penguins *'11*

Oliver Cotton (1944-)
The Camomile Lawn *'92*
Beowulf *'98*
The Dancer Upstairs *'02*
Shanghai Knights *'03*

Erin Cottrell (1975-)
Love's Long Journey *'05*
Love's Abiding Joy *'06*
Love's Unending Legacy *'07*
Love's Unfolding Dream *'07*
Love Takes Wing *'09*
The Identical *'14*

Marisa Coughlan (1974-)
Gossip *'99*
Teaching Mrs. Tingle *'99*
Freddy Got Fingered *'01*
Super Troopers *'01*
Pumpkin *'02*
I Love Your Work *'03*
Wasted *'06*
Already Dead *'07*
Space Station 76 *'14*
Infamous *'20*

Kevin Coughlin (1945-76)
Storm Center *'56*
The Gay Deceivers *'69*
Prom Wars *'08*

Dave Coulier (1959-)
The Family Holiday *'07*
Shredderman Rules *'07*

Sonia Couling
The Mark *'12*
The Mark 2: Redemption *'13*

Jean-Louis Coulloc'h
Lady Chatterley *'10*
Fidelio: Alice's Odyssey *'14*

George Coulouris (1903-89)
The Lady in Question *'40*
Citizen Kane *'41*
For Whom the Bell Tolls *'43*
This Land Is Mine *'43*
Watch on the Rhine *'43*
Between Two Worlds *'44*
The Master Race *'44*
Mr. Skeffington *'44*
None But the Lonely Heart *'44*
Confidential Agent *'45*
Lady on a Train *'45*
A Song to Remember *'45*
Nobody Lives Forever *'46*
The Verdict *'46*
Where There's Life *'47*
Sleep, My Love *'48*
A Southern Yankee *'48*
Appointment With Venus *'51*
Doctor in the House *'53*
The Runaway Bus *'54*
Race for Life *'55*
Tarzan's Hidden Jungle *'55*
Kill Me Tomorrow *'57*
Tarzan and the Lost Safari *'57*
Spy in the Sky *'58*
The Womaneater *'59*
The Skull *'65*
Arabesque *'66*
Blood from the Mummy's Tomb *'71*
Tower of Evil *'72*
Papillon *'73*
Murder on the Orient Express *'74*
The Long Good Friday *'80*

Keith Coulouris (1967-)
Take Down *'92*
Dead Man's Revenge *'93*

Bernie Coulson (1965-)
The Accused *'88*
Eddie and the Cruisers 2: Eddie Lives! *'89*
Hard Core Logo *'96*
The Highway Man *'99*
Cabin by the Lake *'00*

Grover Coulson
Friday Night Lights *'04*
A Ghost Story *'17*

Clare Coulter (1942-)
Hollywood North *'03*
Coast to Coast *'04*

Claudia Coulter
Jane Eyre *'06*
The Witches Hammer *'06*

Raymond Coulthard (1968-)
Emma *'97*
Agatha Christie: A Life in Pictures *'04*

Clotilde Courau (1969-)
The Pickle *'93*
Deterrence *'00*
Almost Peaceful *'02*
Whatever You Say *'02*
La Vie en Rose *'07*

Katie Couric (1957-)
Shark Tale *'04 (V)*
Fed Up *'14 (N)*

Hazel Court (1926-2008)
Ghost Ship *'53*
Devil Girl from Mars *'54*
The Curse of Frankenstein *'57*
The Man Who Could Cheat Death *'59*
Doctor Blood's Coffin *'62*
Premature Burial *'62*
The Raven *'63*
Masque of the Red Death *'65*

Jason Court
Grandview U.S.A. *'84*
A Night in the Life of Jimmy Reardon *'88*

Margaret Courtenay (1923-96)
Hot Millions *'68*
The Mirror Crack'd *'80*

Tom Courtenay (1937-)
The Loneliness of the Long Distance Runner *'62*
Billy Liar *'63*
King and Country *'64*
Doctor Zhivago *'65*
King Rat *'65*
Operation Crossbow *'65*
Night of the Generals *'67*
Dandy in Aspic *'68*
Otley *'68*
Catch Me a Spy *'71*
The Dresser *'83*
Happy New Year *'87*
Leonard Part 6 *'87*
Let Him Have It *'91*
The Last Butterfly *'92*
The Old Curiosity Shop *'94*
A Rather English Marriage *'98*
Last Orders *'01*
Nicholas Nickleby *'02*
Flood *'07*
The Golden Compass *'07*
Little Dorrit *'08*
Gambit *'12*
Quartet *'12*
Night Train to Lisbon *'13*
45 Years *'15*
Dad's Army *'16*
The Guernsey Literary & Potato Peel Pie Society *'18*

Jerome Courtland (1926-2012)
Together Again *'43*
Battleground *'49*
Man from Colorado *'49*
Tokyo Joe *'49*
Santa Fe *'51*
Tonka *'58*

Alex Courtney (1940-)
Enter the Ninja *'81*
And the Band Played On *'93 (C)*

Inez Courtney (1908-75)
Bright Lights *'30*
Sunny *'30*
Sweepstake Annie *'35*
Let's Sing Again *'36*
The Reckless Way *'36*
Suzy *'36*
Wedding Present *'36*

Jai Courtney (1986-)
Storm Boy
Felony *'13*
A Good Day to Die Hard *'13*
I, Frankenstein *'13*
Divergent *'14*
Unbroken *'14*
Insurgent *'15*
Terminator Genisys *'15*
The Water Diviner *'15*
Man Down *'16*
The Exception *'17*
Semper Fi *'19*
Buffaloed *'20*

Joel Courtney
Super 8 *'11*
Sins of Our Youth *'16*

Brian Cousins (1959-)
Longtime Companion *'90*
Invisible: The Chronicles of Benjamin Knight *'93*
Mandroid *'93*

Christian Cousins (1983-)
Danielle Steel's Heartbeat *'93*
Twinsitters *'95*

Christopher Cousins (1960-)
Hell High *'86*
Dead Dog *'00*
Earth *vs.* the Spider *'01*
The Long Shot *'04*
Wicker Park *'04*
The Grudge 2 *'06*
Final Approach *'08*
Legally Blondes *'09*
William & Kate *'11*

Randy Couture (1963-)
The Scorpion King 2: Rise of a Warrior *'08*
The Expendables *'10*
Setup *'11*
The Expendables 2 *'12*
Hijacked *'12*
Ambushed *'13*
The Expendables 3 *'14*

Allen Covert (1964-)
Airheads *'94*
Bulletproof *'96*
Happy Gilmore *'96*
The Wedding Singer *'97*
Little Nicky *'00*
Mr. Deeds *'02*
Anger Management *'03*
50 First Dates *'04*
Grandma's Boy *'06*
I Now Pronounce You Chuck and Larry *'07*
Strange Wilderness *'08*

Elliot Cowan (1976-)
Alexander *'04*
Love and Other Disasters *'06*
Lost in Austen *'08*

Jerome Cowan (1897-1972)
New Faces of 1937 *'37*
You Only Live Once *'37*
East Side of Heaven *'39*
Exile Express *'39*
The Gracie Allen Murder Case *'39*
The Saint Strikes Back *'39*
Castle on the Hudson *'40*
Torrid Zone *'40*
The Great Lie *'41*
High Sierra *'41*
The Maltese Falcon *'41*
Moontide *'42*
Who Done It? *'42*
Guest in the House *'44*
Fog Island *'45*
Getting Gertie's Garter *'45*
My Reputation *'46*
Cry Wolf *'47*
The West Point Story *'50*
Criminal Lawyer *'51*
The System *'53*
Have Rocket Will Travel *'59*
Black Zoo *'63*
Critic's Choice *'63*

Noel Coward (1899-1973)
In Which We Serve *'43*
Around the World in 80 Days *'56 (C)*
Our Man in Havana *'59*
Paris When It Sizzles *'64*
Bunny Lake Is Missing *'65*
The Italian Job *'69*

Brendan Cowell
To End All Wars *'01*
Beneath Hill 60 *'10*

Bruce Cowling (1919-86)
Battleground *'49*
The Stratton Story *'49*
Ambush *'50*
A Lady Without Passport *'50*
Cause for Alarm *'51*
The Painted Hills *'51*
To Hell and Back *'55*

Nicola Cowper (1967-)
Dreamchild *'85*
Lionheart *'87*
Journey to the Center of the Earth *'88*
Devices and Desires *'91*

Alan Cox (1970-)
Young Sherlock Holmes *'85*
An Awfully Big Adventure *'94*
Mrs. Dalloway *'97*
The Odyssey *'97*

Alex Cox (1954-)
Dead Beat *'94*
Dance with the Devil *'97*
The Oxford Murders *'08*

Brian Cox (1946-)
In Celebration *'75*
Therese Raquin *'80*
Florence Nightingale *'85*
Manhunter *'86*
Hidden Agenda *'90*
The Lost Language of Cranes *'92*
Sharpe's Eagle *'93*
Sharpe's Rifles *'93*
Royal Deceit *'94*
Braveheart *'95*
Rob Roy *'95*
Chain Reaction *'96*
The Glimmer Man *'96*
The Long Kiss Goodnight *'96*
The Boxer *'97*
Kiss the Girls *'97*
Desperate Measures *'98*
Poodle Springs *'98*
Retribution *'98*
Rushmore *'98*
The Corruptor *'99*
For Love of the Game *'99*
The Minus Man *'99*
Longitude *'00*
Nuremberg *'00*
A Shot at Glory *'00*
The Affair of the Necklace *'01*
L.I.E. *'01*
Strictly Sinatra *'01*
Super Troopers *'01*
Adaptation *'02*
The Bourne Identity *'02*
The Ring *'02*
The Rookie *'02*
Sin *'02*
25th Hour *'02*
X2: X-Men United *'03*
The Bourne Supremacy *'04*
Troy *'04*
Match Point *'05*
Red Eye *'05*
The Ringer *'05*
The Flying Scotsman *'06*
Running with Scissors *'06*
The Water Horse: Legend of the Deep *'07*
Zodiac *'07*
The Color of Magic *'08 (N)*
The Escapist *'08*
Trick 'r Treat *'08*
Battle for Terra *'09 (V)*
Fantastic Mr. Fox *'09 (V)*
The Good Heart *'09*
The Take *'09*
As Good As Dead *'10*
RED *'10*
The Sinking of the Laconia *'10*
Citizen Gangster *'11*
Coriolanus *'11*
Ironclad *'11*
Rise of the Planet of the Apes *'11*
The Campaign *'12*
An Adventure in Space and Time *'13*
RED 2 *'13*
The Anomaly *'15*
Forsaken *'15*
The Autopsy of Jane Doe *'16*
Foresaken *'16*
Churchill *'17*
The Etruscan Smile *'19*
Pretenders *'19*
Strange But True *'19*

Charlie Cox (1982-)
Dot the I *'03*
The Merchant of Venice *'04*
Casanova *'05*
Stardust *'07*
Glorious 39 *'09*
Moby Dick *'11*
There Be Dragons *'11*
The Theory of Everything *'14*

Christina Cox (1971-)
Street Law *'95*
Better Than Chocolate *'99*
Making Mr. Right *'08*
S.I.S. *'08*
Fugitive at 17 *'12*
Eve of Destruction *'13*

Claire Cox (1975-)
Shooting Fish *'98*
Luther *'03*

Courteney Cox (1964-)
Masters of the Universe *'87*
Cocoon: The Return *'88*
The Prize Pulitzer *'89*
Mr. Destiny *'90*
Blue Desert *'91*
Battling for Baby *'92*
Shaking the Tree *'92*
Ace Ventura: Pet Detective *'93*
The Opposite Sex and How to Live With Them *'93*
Commandments *'96*
Scream *'96*
Scream 2 *'97*
The Runner *'99*
Scream 3 *'00*
Get Well Soon *'01*
3000 Miles to Graceland *'01*
The Longest Yard *'05*
November *'05*
Barnyard *'06 (V)*
Zoom *'06*
Bedtime Stories *'08*
Scream 4 *'11*
Talhotblond *'12*

Jennifer Elise Cox (1969-)
The Brady Bunch Movie *'95*
Sometimes They Come Back. . . Again *'96*
A Very Brady Sequel *'96*
EDtv *'99*
Hard Pill *'05*

Joshua Cox (1965-)
Shockwave *'06*
The Last House on the Left *'09*
Drop Dead Gorgeous *'10*

Julie Cox (1973-)
20,000 Leagues Under the Sea *'97*
The Scarlet Pimpernel 2: Mademoiselle Guillotine *'99*
Dune *'00*
The War Bride *'01*
King of Texas *'02*
Byron *'03*
Children of Dune *'03*
Second in Command *'05*
The Riddle *'07*
The Oxford Murders *'08*

Laverne Cox
Grandma *'15*
Freak Show *'18*
Can You Keep a Secret? *'19*

Mitchell Cox
Strait-Jacket *'64*
Red Snow *'91*

Nikki Cox (1978-)
The Glimmer Man *'96*
Nutty Professor 2: The Klumps *'00*
A Christmas Wedding Tail *'11 (V)*

Richard Cox (1948-)
Cruising *'80*
Shattered Innocence *'87*
Zombie High *'87*
Snowbound: The Jim and Jennifer Stolpa Story *'94*
American Tragedy *'00*
Missing Brendan *'03*
The Toe Tactic *'08*

Ronny Cox (1938-)
Deliverance *'72*
Mind Snatchers *'72*
Bound for Glory *'76*
The Car *'77*
Gray Lady Down *'77*
Our Town *'77*
Harper Valley P.T.A. *'78*
The Onion Field *'79*
Kavik the Wolf Dog *'80*
Last Song *'80*
Taps *'81*
The Beast Within *'82*
Some Kind of Hero *'82*
Beverly Hills Cop *'84*
Vision Quest *'85*
Hollywood Vice Sqaud *'86*
Beverly Hills Cop 2 *'87*
RoboCop *'87*
Steele Justice *'87*
In the Line of Duty: The FBI Murders *'88*
Captain America *'89*
One Man Force *'89*
Loose Cannons *'90*
Total Recall *'90*
Scissors *'91*
Rebound: The Legend of Earl 'The Goat' Manigault *'96*
Murder at 1600 *'97*
Todd McFarlane's Spawn *'97 (V)*
From the Earth to the Moon *'98*
Forces of Nature *'99*
Perfect Murder, Perfect Town *'00*
American Outlaws *'01*
Crazy as Hell *'02*
Point of Origin *'02*
Imagine That *'09*
Truth Be Told *'11*
Age of Dinosaurs *'13*

Tony Cox (1958-)
Jekyll & Hyde. . . Together Again *'82*
Spaced Invaders *'90*
Me, Myself, and Irene *'00*
Bad Santa *'03*
I Accidentally Domed Your Son *'04*
Date Movie *'06*
Oz the Great and Powerful *'13*
Bad Santa 2 *'16*

Veanne Cox (1963-)
Big Eden *'00*
Erin Brockovich *'00*
Beethoven's 4th *'01*
Marci X *'03*

Wally Cox (1924-73)
State Fair *'62*
Spencer's Mountain *'63*
Fate Is the Hunter *'64*
Bedford Incident *'65*
Morituri *'65*
A Guide for the Married Man *'67 (C)*
The One and Only, Genuine, Original Family Band *'68*
The Boatniks *'70*
The Barefoot Executive *'71*
The Night Strangler *'72*

Chris Coy (1986-)
Hostel: Part 3 *'11*
Deliver Us From Evil *'14*

Jonathan Coy (1953-)
The Rector's Wife *'94*
The Scarlet Pimpernel *'99*
The Scarlet Pimpernel 2: Mademoiselle Guillotine *'99*
The Scarlet Pimpernel 3: The Kidnapped King *'99*
Conspiracy *'01*

Brendan Coyle (1963-)
Catherine Cookson's The Glass Virgin *'95*
Conspiracy *'01*
The Mapmaker *'01*
Perfect Parents *'06*
Me Before You *'16*

Richard Coyle (1972-)
Prince of Poisoners: The Life and Crimes of William Palmer *'98*
Lorna Doone *'01*
Othello *'01*
The Libertine *'05*
The History of Mr. Polly *'07*
Franklyn *'08*
Going Postal *'10*
5 Days of War *'11*
W.E. *'11*
Outpost: Black Sun *'12*

Peter Coyote (1941-)
Die Laughing *'80*
Tell Me a Riddle *'80*
The People *vs.* Jean Harris *'81*
Southern Comfort *'81*
Endangered Species *'82*
E.T.: The Extra-Terrestrial *'82*
Out *'82*
Cross Creek *'83*
Timerider *'83*
Slayground *'84*
The Jagged Edge *'85*
Legend of Billie Jean *'85*
A Man in Love *'87*
Outrageous Fortune *'87*
Crooked Hearts *'91*
Bitter Moon *'92*
Kika *'94*
Buffalo Girls *'95*
Dalva *'95*
Moonlight and Valentino *'95*
Terminal Justice: Cybertech P.D. *'95*
Unforgettable *'96*
Sphere *'97*
Top of the World *'97*
Two for Texas *'97*
Patch Adams *'98*
Road Ends *'98*
Route 9 *'98*
The Basket *'99*
Random Hearts *'99*
Erin Brockovich *'00*
More Dogs Than Bones *'00*
Red Letters *'00*
A Time for Dancing *'00*
Femme Fatale *'02*
Purpose *'02*
A Walk to Remember *'02*
Bon Voyage *'03*
Northfork *'03*
The Grand Role *'04*
Deepwater *'05*
A Little Trip to Heaven *'05*
Return of the Living Dead: Rave to the Grave *'05*
Behind Enemy Lines 2: Axis of Evil *'06*
Resurrecting the Champ *'07*
Adopt a Sailor *'08*
All Roads Lead Home *'08*
Dr. Dolittle 4: Tail to the Chief *'08*
$5 a Day *'08*
The Lena Baker Story *'08*
Hemingway & Gelhorn *'12*
The Etruscan Smile *'19*

Cylk Cozart (1957-)
White Men Can't Jump *'92*
Conspiracy Theory *'97*
Play It to the Bone *'99*
Three to Tango *'99*
16 Blocks *'06*

Buster Crabbe (1907-83)
Island of Lost Souls *'32 (C)*
Tarzan the Fearless *'33*
To the Last Man *'33*
The Oil Raider *'34*
Search for Beauty *'34*
Rocketship *'36*
Buck Rogers Conquers the Universe *'39*
Destination Saturn *'39*
Flash Gordon: Mars Attacks the World *'39*
Flash Gordon Conquers the Universe *'40*
Flash Gordon: Rocketship *'40*
Wildcat *'42*
Nabonga *'44*
Thundering Gunslingers *'44*
Ghost of Hidden Valley *'46*
Swamp Fire *'46*
Gun Brothers *'56*
Arizona Raiders *'65*
Alien Dead *'79*

Ruth Cracknell (1925-2002)
The Chant of Jimmie Blacksmith *'78*
Lilian's Story *'95*
Joey *'98*

Carolyn Craig (1934-70)
Portland Expose *'57*
Apache Territory *'58*
House on Haunted Hill *'58*
Studs Lonigan *'60*

Catherine Craig (1915-2004)
Here Come the Waves *'45*
The Pretender *'47*
Seven Were Saved *'47*

Daniel Craig (1968-)
Anglo-Saxon Attitudes *'92*
The Power of One *'92*
A Kid in King Arthur's Court *'95*
Kiss and Tell *'96*
Moll Flanders *'96*
The Ice House *'97*
Obsession *'97*
Elizabeth *'98*
Love Is the Devil *'98*
Love and Rage *'99*
The Trench *'99*
I Dreamed of Africa *'00*
Lara Croft: Tomb Raider *'01*
Sword of Honour *'01*
Road to Perdition *'02*
The Mother *'03*
Sylvia *'03*
Enduring Love *'04*
Archangel *'05*
Fateless *'05*
The Jacket *'05*
Layer Cake *'05*
Munich *'05*
Casino Royale *'06*
Infamous *'06*
Renaissance *'06 (V)*
The Golden Compass *'07*
The Invasion *'07*
Defiance *'08*
Flashbacks of a Fool *'08*
Quantum of Solace *'08*
The Adventures of Tintin *'11 (V)*
Cowboys & Aliens *'11*
Dream House *'11*
The Girl With the Dragon Tattoo *'11*
Skyfall *'12*
Spectre *'15*
Kings *'17*
Knives Out *'19*

Georgia Craig (1979-)
A Job to Kill For *'06*
Case 39 *'10*

Helen Craig (1912-86)
The Snake Pit *'48*
They Live by Night *'49*
The Legend of Lizzie Borden *'75*

James Craig (1912-85)
Black Friday *'40*
Kitty Foyle *'40*
Winners of the West *'40*
The Devil & Daniel Webster *'41*
The Human Comedy *'43*
Lost Angel *'43*
Swing Shift Maisie *'43*
The Heavenly Body *'44*
Kismet *'44*
Our Vines Have Tender Grapes *'45*
Dark Delusion *'47*
A Lady Without Passport *'50*
Side Street *'50*
Drums in the Deep South *'51*
Code Two *'53*
Fort Vengeance *'53*
Cyclops *'56*
Massacre *'56*
Shoot-out at Medicine Bend *'57*
Man or Gun *'58*
Four Fast Guns *'59*
The Devil's Brigade *'68*
The Tormentors *'71*

Josh Craig
The Monster of Phantom Lake *'06*
It Came From Another World *'07*
Cave Women on Mars *'08*
Destination: Outer Space *'10*

Michael Craig (1928-)
Campbell's Kingdom *'57*
Sea of Sand *'58*
The Silent Enemy *'58*
Sapphire *'59*
Upstairs and Downstairs *'59*
Doctor in Love *'60*
Trouble in the Sky *'60*
Mysterious Island *'61*
Stolen Hours *'63*
Modesty Blaise *'66*
Star! *'68*
Lola *'69*
Night of the Assassin *'70*
Vault of Horror *'73*
Inn of the Damned *'74*
Ride a Wild Pony *'75*
The Irishman *'78*
Escape 2000 *'81*

Philip Craig (1950-)
Behind the Red Door '02
Spider '02
Cradle of Lies '06

Wendy Craig (1934-)
Room at the Top '59
The Mind Benders '63
The Servant '63
The Nanny '65

Yvonne Craig (1937-2015)
The Young Land '59
High Time '60
It Happened at the World's Fair '63
Kissin' Cousins '64
Ski Party '65
Mars Needs Women '66
How to Frame a Figg '71

Jeanne Crain (1925-2003)
Home In Indiana '44
In the Meantime, Darling '44
Leave Her to Heaven '45
State Fair '45
Apartment for Peggy '48
The Fan '49
A Letter to Three Wives '49
Pinky '49
Cheaper by the Dozen '50
The Model and the Marriage Broker '51
People Will Talk '51
Belles on Their Toes '52
City of Bad Men '53
Dangerous Crossing '53
Man Without a Star '55
Fastest Gun Alive '56
Twenty Plus Two '61
Nefertiti, Queen of the Nile '64
Hot Rods to Hell '67
Skyjacked '72

Grant Cramer (1961-)
Hardbodies '84
Killer Klowns from Outer Space '88
Addicted to Murder 3: Bloodlust '99

Barbara Crampton (1958-)
Body Double '84
Re-Animator '84
Fraternity Vacation '85
Chopping Mall '86
From Beyond '86
Puppet Master '89
Trancers 2: The Return of Jack Deth '90
Robot Wars '93
Castle Freak '95
Space Truckers '97
Cold Harvest '98
The Godson '98
Lightning: Fire from the Sky '00
Poison '01
The Lords of Salem '13
You're Next '13
We are Still Here '15
Beyond the Gates '16
Little Sister '16
Sun Choke '16

Bob Crane (1928-78)
Return to Peyton Place '61
The Delphi Bureau: The Merchant of Death Assignment '72
Superdad '73
Gus '76

Chilton Crane
Big and Hairy '98
What Color Is Love? '08

Norma Crane (1928-73)
Tea and Sympathy '56
Night Gallery '69
They Call Me Mr. Tibbs! '70
Fiddler on the Roof '71

Richard Crane (1918-69)
Dynamite '49
Cavalry Charge '51
Guns Don't Argue '57
The Devil's Partner '58
Boy Who Caught a Crook '61

Tony Crane (1972-)
The War of the Roses '89
An American Summer '90
Wishmaster '97

Kenneth Cranham (1944-)
Brother Sun, Sister Moon '73
Therese Raquin '80
Danger UXB '81
Chocolat '88
Hellbound: Hellraiser 2 '88
Just Another Secret '89
Oranges Are Not the Only Fruit '89
Prospero's Books '91
Tale of a Vampire '92
Under Suspicion '92
The Tenant of Wildfell Hall '96
The Boxer '97
Deep in the Heart (of Texas) '98
Our Mutual Friend '98
Born Romantic '00
Gangster No. 1 '00
Lady Audley's Secret '00
Shiner '00
Two Men Went to War '02
Trauma '04
Layer Cake '05
The Chatterley Affair '06
A Good Year '06
Tess of the D'Urbervilles '08
Valkyrie '08
Closed Circuit '13

Lorcan Cranitch (1959-)
Cracker: Men Should Weep '94
Cracker: To Be a Somebody '94
Cracker: Brotherly Love '95
Dancing at Lughnasa '98
Deacon Brodie '98
Shackleton '02

Alex Cranmer
The Bronx Is Burning '07
Ratter '16

Patrick Cranshaw (1919-2005)
Nothing to Lose '96
Broken Vessels '98
Best in Show '00
Bubble Boy '01
Air Bud 5: Buddy Spikes Back '03

Bryan Cranston (1956-)
The Big Turnaround '88
Dead Space '90
High Stakes '93
Erotique '94
That Thing You Do! '96
From the Earth to the Moon '98
Saving Private Ryan '98
Terror Tract '00
National Lampoon's Holiday Reunion '03
Seeing Other People '04
Little Miss Sunshine '06
Hard Four '07
Contagion '11
Drive '11
Larry Crowne '11
The Lincoln Lawyer '11
Argo '12
John Carter '12
Red Tails '12
Rock of Ages '12
Total Recall '12
Cold Comes the Night '14
Godzilla '14
Trumbo '15
Get a Job '16
The Infiltrator '16
Kung Fu Panda 3 '16
Why Him? '16
In Dubious Battle '17
Last Flag Flying '17
The Upside '17
Wakefield '17
Isle of Dogs '18 (V)

Nick Cravat (1911-94)
The Flame & the Arrow '50
Crimson Pirate '52
Run Silent, Run Deep '58
The Scalphunters '68
The Island of Dr. Moreau '77

Noel Cravat (1910-60)
G-Men *vs.* the Black Dragon '43
The Razor's Edge '46
The 5000 Fingers of Dr. T '53

Frank Craven (1875-1945)
Vagabond Lady '35
You're Only Young Once '37
Miracles for Sale '39
City for Conquest '40
Dreaming Out Loud '40
Our Town '40
In This Our Life '42
Keeper of the Flame '42
Pittsburgh '42
Son of Dracula '43
Jack London '44
Colonel Effingham's Raid '45

James Craven (1892-1955)
Green Archer '40
Sherlock Holmes and the Secret Weapon '42
Immortal Sergeant '43

Matt Craven (1956-)
Till Death Do Us Part '72
Happy Birthday to Me '81
Chattahoochee '89
Jacob's Ladder '90
A Few Good Men '92
K2: The Ultimate High '92
Indian Summer '93
Bulletproof Heart '95
Crimson Tide '95
White Tiger '95
The Juror '96
From the Earth to the Moon '98
Paulie '98
Nuremberg '00
Things You Can Tell Just by Looking at Her '00
Varian's War '01
Dragonfly '02
Scared Silent '02
The Life of David Gale '03
The Statement '03
Timeline '03
The Clearing '04
Assault on Precinct 13 '05
A Simple Curve '05
American Venus '07
The Longshots '08
Devil '10
Awakening the Zodiac '17

Mimi (Meyer) Craven
Mikey '92
Midnight Heat '95
Daddy's Girl '96
Dogwatch '97

Wes Craven (1939-2015)
Body Bags '93 (C)
The Fear '94
Wes Craven's New Nightmare '94
Scream '96 (C)
ShadowZone: The Undead Express '96 (C)
Jay and Silent Bob Strike Back '01 (C)
Red Eye '05 (C)

Anne Crawford (1920-56)
Caravan '46
Thunder on the Hill '51
Tony Draws a Horse '51
Knights of the Round Table '53
Mad About Men '54

Broderick Crawford (1911-86)
Beau Geste '39
Eternally Yours '39
The Real Glory '39
Seven Sinners '40
Slightly Honorable '40
The Black Cat '41
Broadway '42
Larceny, Inc. '42
Black Angel '46
The Time of Your Life '48
All the King's Men '49
Bad Men of Tombstone '49
A Kiss in the Dark '49
Night Unto Night '49
Born Yesterday '50
Convicted '50
The Mob '51
Lone Star '52
Scandal Sheet '52
The Last Posse '53
Down Three Dark Streets '54
Human Desire '54
Night People '54
Big House, U.S.A. '55
Il Bidone '55
Not as a Stranger '55
Between Heaven and Hell '56
Fastest Gun Alive '56
The Decks Ran Red '58
Goliath and the Dragon '61
The Castilian '63
The Texican '66
Hell's Bloody Devils '70
The Tattered Web '71
Embassy '72
The Phantom of Hollywood '74
The Private Files of J. Edgar Hoover '77
A Little Romance '79
Dark Forces '83

Chace Crawford (1985-)
The Covenant '06
Long Lost Son '06
The Haunting of Molly Hartley '08
Loaded '08
Twelve '10
Peace, Love & Misunderstanding '11
What to Expect When You're Expecting '12
Undrafted '16
All About Nina '18

Cindy Crawford (1966-)
Fair Game '95
54 '98
The Simian Line '99

Clayne Crawford (1978-)
Swimfan '02
A Walk to Remember '02
Evil Remains '04
False Prophets '06
Steel City '06
Wristcutters: A Love Story '06
On the Doll '07
Strike '07
The Donner Party '09
The Perfect Host '10
Smokin' Aces 2: Assassins' Ball '10
The Baytown Outlaws '12
NYC Underground '13

Daz Crawford (1968-)
Blade 2 '02
Caffeine '06
TKO '06

H. Marion Crawford (1914-69)
See Howard Marion-Crawford

Howard Crawford (1914-69)
See Howard Marion-Crawford

Joan Crawford (1904-77)
Tramp, Tramp, Tramp '26
Spring Fever '27
West Point '27
Across to Singapore '28
Our Dancing Daughters '28
Our Modern Maidens '29
Untamed '29
Montana Moon '30
Our Blushing Brides '30
Paid '30
Dance Fools Dance '31
Laughing Sinners '31
Possessed '31
This Modern Age '31
Grand Hotel '32
Rain '32
Dancing Lady '33
Today We Live '33
Chained '34
Sadie McKee '34
Forsaking All Others '35
I Live My Life '35
No More Ladies '35
The Gorgeous Hussy '36
Love on the Run '36
The Bride Wore Red '37
The Last of Mrs. Cheyney '37
Mannequin '37
The Shining Hour '38
Ice Follies of 1939 '39
The Women '39
Strange Cargo '40
Susan and God '40
When Ladies Meet '41
A Woman's Face '41
Reunion in France '42
Above Suspicion '43
Hollywood Canteen '44
Mildred Pierce '45
Humoresque '46
Daisy Kenyon '47
The Possessed '47
Flamingo Road '49
It's a Great Feeling '49
The Damned Don't Cry '50
Goodbye My Fancy '51
Sudden Fear '52
This Woman Is Dangerous '52
Johnny Guitar '53
Torch Song '53
Female On the Beach '55
Queen Bee '55
The Best of Everything '59
What Ever Happened to Baby Jane? '62
The Caretakers '63
Strait-Jacket '64
Berserk! '67
Night Gallery '69
Trog '70

John Crawford (1920-2010)
The Invisible Monster '50
Actors and Sin '52
Zombies of the Stratosphere '52
Battle of Rogue River '54
The Severed Arm '73
The Enforcer '76

Johnny Crawford (1946-)
The Space Children '58
Indian Paint '64
Village of the Giants '65
El Dorado '67
The Great Texas Dynamite Chase '76
Outlaw Blues '77
Kenny Rogers as the Gambler, Part 2: The Adventure Continues '83
The Gambler Returns: The Luck of the Draw '93

Kathryn Crawford (1908-80)
Flying High '31
Emma '32
Skyway '33

Michael Crawford (1942-)
The Knack '65
A Funny Thing Happened on the Way to the Forum '66
How I Won the War '67
Hello, Dolly! '69
Condorman '81
Once Upon a Forest '93 (V)

Rachael Crawford (1969-)
When Night Is Falling '95
Rude '96
In His Father's Shoes '97
Pale Saints '97
Love Songs '99
The Man '05
Aaliyah: The Princess of R&B '14

Sophia Crawford (1966-)
Sword of Honor '94
U.S. Seals 2 '01

Wayne Crawford
Barracuda '78
Jake Speed '86

Charlie Creed-Miles (1972-)
The Young Poisoner's Handbook '94
Nil by Mouth '96
Essex Boys '99
Station Jim '01
King Arthur '04
Harry Brown '09
You and I '11
100 Streets '17

Esme Creed-Miles
Mister Lonely '07
Dark River '18

Laird Cregar (1916-44)
Hudson's Bay '40
Charley's Aunt '41
I Wake Up Screaming '41
The Black Swan '42
Joan of Paris '42
Rings on Her Fingers '42
This Gun for Hire '42
Heaven Can Wait '43
Hello, Frisco, Hello '43
Holy Matrimony '43
Hangover Square '45

Zach Cregger (1981-)
Miss March '09
Date and Switch '13
Love & Air Sex '14

Joseph Crehan (1886-1966)
Front Page Woman '35
The Case of the Stuttering Bishop '37
Smart Blonde '37
You Can't Get Away With Murder '39
Music in My Heart '40
They Died with Their Boots On '41
Hands Across the Border '43
Meeting at Midnight '44
Phantom Lady '44
Dangerous Money '46

Francis Creighton (1955-2003)
The Malibu Beach Vampires '91
Barcelona '94

Jack Creley (1926-2004)
Dr. Strangelove, or: How I Learned to Stop Worrying and Love the Bomb '64
The Reincarnate '71

Bruno Cremer (1929-2010)
Is Paris Burning? '66
Sorcerer '77
Menage '86
Under the Sand '00

Richard Crenna (1926-2003)
Pride of St. Louis '52
Our Miss Brooks '56
Over-Exposed '56
Made in Paris '65
The Sand Pebbles '66
Wait until Dark '67
Star! '68
Marooned '69
Doctors' Wives '70
Catlow '71
Ride to Glory '71
Jonathan Livingston Seagull '73 (V)
Breakheart Pass '76
Centennial '78
Devil Dog: The Hound of Hell '78
The Evil '78
Wild Horse Hank '79
Body Heat '81
First Blood '82
Table for Five '83
The Flamingo Kid '84
Broken Badge '85
Rambo: First Blood, Part 2 '85
Summer Rental '85
Rambo 3 '88
Leviathan '89
Hot Shots! Part Deux '93
Jade '95
A Pyromaniac's Love Story '95

Sabrina '95
20,000 Leagues Under the Sea '97
Wrongfully Accused '98
By Dawn's Early Light '00
The Day Reagan Was Shot '01
Out of the Ashes '03

Rebecca Creskoff (1971-)
Friends and Family '01
Knucklehead '10

Sevier Crespo (1976-)
Barrio Wars '02
Fast Lane '08

Pierre Cressoy (1924-80)
David and Goliath '61
The Lion of Thebes '64
The Triumph of Hercules '66

Lola Creton (1993-)
Bluebeard '09
Something in the Air '13

Amanda Crew (1986-)
Final Destination 3 '06
Meltdown '06
Sex Drive '08
The Haunting in Connecticut '09
Charlie St. Cloud '10
Crazy Kind of Love '12
The Identical '14
Weepah Way for Now '15
A Crooked Somebody '18
Isabelle '19
Tone-Deaf '19

Laura Hope Crews (1879-1942)
New Morals for Old '32
If I Were Free '33
Rafter Romance '33
The Age of Innocence '34
Camille '36
Angel '37
Thanks for the Memory '38
Gone with the Wind '39
The Rains Came '39
Reno '39
The Flame of New Orleans '41
The Rain People '69

Terry Crews (1968-)
The 6th Day '00
Friday After Next '02
Serving Sara '02
Baadasssss! '03
White Chicks '04
Harsh Times '05
The Longest Yard '05
The Benchwarmers '06
Idiocracy '06
Balls of Fury '07
How to Rob a Bank '07
Norbit '07
Get Smart '08
Street Kings '08
Gamer '09
The Expendables '10
The Lottery Ticket '10
Middle Men '10
The Expendables 2 '12
Blended '14
Draft Day '14
The Expendables 3 '14
Tyler Perry's The Single Moms' Club '14
Sorry to Bother You '18
The Willoughbys '20

Wendy Crewson (1956-)
Mazes and Monsters '82
Hobo's Christmas '87
Buffalo Jump '90
The Doctor '91
Spies, Lies and Naked Thighs '91
Folks! '92
The Good Son '93
Corrina, Corrina '94
The Santa Clause '94
Spenser: A Savage Place '94
Spenser: The Judas Goat '94
Gang Related '96
To Gillian on Her 37th Birthday '96
Air Force One '97
The Eighteenth Angel '97
From the Earth to the Moon '98
Better Than Chocolate '99
Bicentennial Man '99
Escape Velocity '99
Summer's End '99
Mercy '00
The 6th Day '00
The Last Brickmaker in America '01
Between Strangers '02
A Killing Spring '02
The Santa Clause 2 '02
Verdict in Blood '02
An Unexpected Love '03
The Clearing '04
Away From Her '06
The Covenant '06
Eight Below '06
Niagara Motel '06
The Santa Clause 3: The Escape Clause '06
Who Loves the Sun '06
The Seeker: The Dark Is Rising '07
The Summit '08
Formosa Betrayed '09
A Beginner's Guide to Endings '10
Antiviral '12
Winnie Mandela '13
Into the Forest '16

Bernard Cribbins (1928-)
The Mouse on the Moon '62
Carry On Jack '63
The Wrong Arm of the Law '63
Carry On Spying '64
She '65
You Must Be Joking! '65
Don't Raise the Bridge, Lower the River '68
The Railway Children '70
Frenzy '72
Carry On Columbus '92

Brenda Crichlow
Civic Duty '06
Home By Christmas '06
The Note 3: Notes from the Heart Healer '12

Lenora Crichlow (1985-)
Collision '09
Burton and Taylor '13
The Late Bloomer '16

Missy (Melissa) Crider (1974-)
Girls in Prison '94
Powder '95
The Beast '96
Stand-Ins '97
Quicksilver Highway '98
The Sex Monster '99
Instinct to Kill '01
Mulholland Drive '01
Frailty '02
Gigli '03
Out of the Woods '05

Lawrence Criner (1898-1965)
The Duke Is Tops '38
Miracle in Harlem '48

Erno Crisa (1924-68)
Lady Chatterley's Lover '55
Purple Noon '60
Death is Nimble, Death is Quick '67

Walter Crisham (1906-85)
No Orchids for Miss Blandish '48
Moulin Rouge '52
Love in Pawn '53

Donald Crisp (1880-1974)
The Birth of a Nation '15
Broken Blossoms '19
Don Q., Son of Zorro '25
The Black Pirate '26
The Viking '28
The Pagan '29
Svengali '31
Red Dust '32
Little Minister '34
Mutiny on the Bounty '35
Oil for the Lamps of China '35
The Charge of the Light Brigade '36
The Great O'Malley '36
A Woman Rebels '36
Parnell '37
That Certain Woman '37
Amazing Dr. Clitterhouse '38
Dawn Patrol '38
Jezebel '38
The Sisters '38
Daughters Courageous '39
Juarez '39
Oklahoma Kid '39
The Old Maid '39
The Private Lives of Elizabeth & Essex '39
Wuthering Heights '39
Brother Orchid '40
City for Conquest '40
Dr. Ehrlich's Magic Bullet '40
Knute Rockne: All American '40
The Sea Hawk '40
Dr. Jekyll and Mr. Hyde '41
How Green Was My Valley '41
Lassie, Come Home '43
The Adventures of Mark Twain '44
National Velvet '44
The Uninvited '44
Son of Lassie '45
The Valley of Decision '45
Ramrod '47
The Hills of Home '48
Whispering Smith '48
Bright Leaf '50
Prince Valiant '54
The Long Gray Line '55
The Man from Laramie '55
The Last Hurrah '58
Saddle the Wind '58
A Dog of Flanders '59
Pollyanna '60
Greyfriars Bobby '61
Spencer's Mountain '63

Quentin Crisp (1908-99)
The Bride '85
Orlando '92
Naked in New York '93 (C)

Anthony Criss (1970-)
See Treach

Darren Criss (1987-)
Glee: The 3D Concert Movie '11
Girl Most Likely '12
The Tale of the Princess Kaguya '13 (V)

Peter Criss (1945-)
KISS Meets the Phantom of the Park '78
Detroit Rock City '99

Linda Cristal (1931-2020)
The Fiend Who Walked the West '58
The Perfect Furlough '59
The Alamo '60
Two Rode Together '61
Panic in the City '68
Mr. Majestyk '74

Perla Cristal (1937-)
The Awful Dr. Orloff '62
Espionage in Tangiers '65
White Comanche '68
The Fury of the Wolfman '70

Michael Cristofer (1945-)
An Enemy of the People '77
The Little Drummer Girl '84
Chronic '16

Criswell (1907-82)
Plan 9 from Outer Space '56
Night of the Ghouls '59
Orgy of the Dead '65

Roark Critchlow (1963-)
18 Fingers of Death '05
Bone Eater '07
Shark Swarm '08
Hydra '09
Cupid '12
Earth's Final Hours '12
12 Disasters '12

Anthony Crivello (1955-)
The Lost Capone '90
Twisted '96
Running Woman '98

Adam Croasdell
The Prince & Me 3: A Royal Honeymoon '08
Werewolf: The Beast Among Us '12

Olivia Crocicchia
Terri '11
Men, Women & Children '14

Affion Crockett
Soul Men '08
Fifty Shades of Black '16

Jamie Croft (1981-)
Napoleon '96 (V)
Joey '98

Dona Croll (1959-)
Manderlay '05
The Shadow in the North '07

Jonathan Crombie (1966-2015)
Anne of Green Gables '85
Bullies '86
Anne of Avonlea '87
The Good Fight '92
The Waiting Game '98
Anne of Green Gables: The Continuing Story '99

Ben Crompton (1974-)
All the King's Men '99
102 Dalmatians '00
All or Nothing '02

James Cromwell (1940-)
Deadly Game '77
The Girl in the Empty Grave '77
A Christmas Without Snow '80
The Man with Two Brains '83
The Babe '92
Romeo Is Bleeding '93
Babe '95
Eraser '96
The People vs. Larry Flynt '96
Star Trek: First Contact '96
The Education of Little Tree '97
L.A. Confidential '97
Owd Bob '97
Babe: Pig in the City '98
Deep Impact '98
Species 2 '98
The Bachelor '99
The General's Daughter '99
The Green Mile '99
RKO 281 '99
A Slight Case of Murder '99
Snow Falling on Cedars '99
Space Cowboys '00
A Death in the Family '02
The Magnificent Ambersons '02
RFK '02
Spirit: Stallion of the Cimarron '02 (V)
The Sum of All Fears '02
Angels in America '03
The Snow Walker '03
I, Robot '04
Salem's Lot '04
The Longest Yard '05
The Queen '06
Becoming Jane '07
Spider-Man 3 '07
Tortured '08
W. '08
Impact '09
Surrogates '09
Secretariat '10
The Artist '11
Hide Away '11
Cowgirls 'n Angels '12
Memorial Day '12
Still Mine '13
The Trials of Cate McCall '13
Big Hero 6 '14 (V)
Marshall '17
The Laundromat '19

John Cromwell (1888-1979)
Top Secret Affair '57
3 Women '77

Richard Cromwell (1910-60)
Emma '32
The Strange Love of Molly Louvain '32
This Day and Age '33
Life Begins at Forty '35
The Lives of a Bengal Lancer '35
Young Mr. Lincoln '39

Gail Cronauer (1948-)
Carried Away '95
The Newton Boys '97
Walking Tall: The Payback '07
The Vast of Night '20

Neil Crone (1960-)
Cube 2: Hypercube '02
Verdict in Blood '02

David Cronenberg (1943-)
Into the Night '85 (C)
Nightbreed '90
Henry & Verlin '94 (C)
Blood & Donuts '95 (C)
The Stupids '95 (C)
Extreme Measures '96
Last Night '98
Resurrection '99
Jason X '01

Jeanette Cronin
Mr. Accident '99
Danny Deckchair '03

Laurel Cronin (1939-92)
Beethoven '92
Housesitter '92

Walter Cronkite (1916-2009)
We're Back! A Dinosaur's Story '93 (V)
Apollo 11 '19

Hume Cronyn (1911-2003)
The Cross of Lorraine '43
The Phantom of the Opera '43
Shadow of a Doubt '43
Lifeboat '44
The Green Years '46
The Postman Always Rings Twice '46
Ziegfeld Follies '46
Brute Force '47
The Bride Goes Wild '48
People Will Talk '51
Sunrise at Campobello '60
Cleopatra '63
The Arrangement '69
There Was a Crooked Man '70
The Parallax View '74
Honky Tonk Freeway '81
Rollover '81
The World According to Garp '82
Gin Game '84
Impulse '84
Brewster's Millions '85
Cocoon '85
*batteries not included '87
Foxfire '87
Cocoon: The Return '88
Age Old Friends '89
Day One '89
The Pelican Brief '93
To Dance with the White Dog '93
Camilla '94
Marvin's Room '96
Horton Foote's Alone '97
Santa and Pete '99
Sea People '00
Off Season '01
A Separate Peace '04

Tandy Cronyn (1945-)
Once Upon a Time in America '84
Age Old Friends '89
Getting Out '94

Mackenzie Crook (1971-)
Pirates of the Caribbean: The Curse of the Black Pearl '03
The Merchant of Venice '04
Land of the Blind '06
Pirates of the Caribbean: Dead Man's Chest '06
I Want Candy '07
Pirates of the Caribbean: At World's End '07
City of Ember '08
Three and Out '08
Sex & Drugs & Rock & Roll '10
The Adventures of Tintin '11 (V)
One Chance '13

Peter Crook (1958-)
Bird '88
Chaplin '92
Clean Slate '94
The Yarn Princess '94

Anna Cropper (1938-2007)
All Neat in Black Stockings '69
The Moonstone '72
The Lost Boys '78

Linda Cropper (1949-)
The Seventh Floor '93
Blackrock '97
Passion '99

Annette Crosbie (1934-)
Six Wives of Henry VIII '71
Edward the King '75
The Slipper and the Rose '76
Shooting Fish '98
Oliver Twist '00
Calendar Girls '03

Bing Crosby (1903-77)
College Humor '33
Going Hollywood '33
Here is My Heart '34
We're Not Dressing '34
Mississippi '35
Pennies from Heaven '36
Rhythm on the Range '36
Double or Nothing '37
Waikiki Wedding '37
Sing You Sinners '38
East Side of Heaven '39
If I Had My Way '40
Rhythm on the River '40
The Road to Singapore '40
Birth of the Blues '41
The Road to Zanzibar '41
Holiday Inn '42
My Favorite Blonde '42
The Road to Morocco '42
Star Spangled Rhythm '42
They Got Me Covered '43 (V)
Going My Way '44
The Princess and the Pirate '44
The Bells of St. Mary's '45
Here Come the Waves '45
Blue Skies '46
The Road to Utopia '46
My Favorite Brunette '47
The Road to Rio '47
Welcome Stranger '47
Emperor Waltz '48
The Adventures of Ichabod and Mr. Toad '49 (V)
A Connecticut Yankee in King Arthur's Court '49
Riding High '50
Here Comes the Groom '51
Just for You '52
The Road to Bali '53
Scared Stiff '53 (C)
Country Girl '54
White Christmas '54
Anything Goes '56
High Society '56
Alias Jesse James '59 (C)
Say One for Me '59
High Time '60
Let's Make Love '60
The Road to Hong Kong '62
Robin and the 7 Hoods '64
Stagecoach '66

Cancel My Reservation '72 (C)
That's Entertainment '74

Bob Crosby (1913-93)
Thousands Cheer '43
See Here, Private Hargrove '44

Cathy Lee Crosby (1944-)
Wonder Woman '74
Coach '78
The Dark '79
World War III '86
The Player '92
Untamed Love '94
The Real Howard Spitz '98
The Big Tease '99
A Memory In My Heart '99
Ablaze '00

David Crosby (1941-)
Gimme Shelter '70
Backdraft '91
Hook '91
Thunderheart '92
David Crosby: Remember My Name '19

Denise Crosby (1957-)
48 Hrs. '82
Curse of the Pink Panther '83
Desert Hearts '86
Miracle Mile '89
Pet Sematary '89
Skin Deep '89
Dolly Dearest '92
Red Shoe Diaries 2: Double Dare '92
Desperate Crimes '93
Relative Fear '95
Red Shoe Diaries: Four on the Floor '96
Deep Impact '98
Executive Power '98
Mortuary '05

Gary Crosby (1933-95)
Holiday for Lovers '59
Battle at Bloody Beach '61
The Right Approach '61
Operation Bikini '63
Girl Happy '65
Justin Morgan Had a Horse '81
Night Stalker '87
Chill Factor '90

Lindsay Crosby (1938-89)
Sergeants 3 '62
The Glory Stompers '67

Mary Crosby (1959-)
Pearl '78
Ice Pirates '84
Stagecoach '86
Tapeheads '89
Body Chemistry '90
Corporate Affairs '90
Eating '90
The Night Caller '97
The M Word '14

Henrietta Crosman (1861-1944)
Pilgrimage '33
Charlie Chan's Secret '35
The Right to Live '35
Follow Your Heart '36
The Moon's Our Home '36
Personal Property '37

Ben Cross (1947-)
Chariots of Fire '81
The Flame Trees of Thika '81
The Assisi Underground '84
The Far Pavilions '84
Steal the Sky '88
The Unholy '88
The Jeweller's Shop '90
Live Wire '92
Cold Sweat '93
First Knight '95
The Invader '96
Turbulence '96
20,000 Leagues Under the Sea '97
Solomon '98
Tower of the Firstborn '98
Anti-Terrorist Cell: Manhunt '01
Exorcist: The Beginning '04
Frederick Forsyth's Icon '05
The Russian Specialist '05
Behind Enemy Lines 2: Axis of Evil '06
Undisputed 2: Last Man Standing '06
Finding Rin Tin Tin '07
Species 4: The Awakening '07
Wicked Little Things '07
Hero Wanted '08
Lost City Raiders '08
War, Inc. '08
Hellhounds '09
Star Trek '09
Ben Hur '10
William & Kate '11
A Common Man '12
Jack the Giant Killer '13

David Cross (1964-)
The Cable Guy '96
Small Soldiers '98
Chain of Fools '00
Scary Movie 2 '01
Men in Black 2 '02
Eternal Sunshine of the Spotless Mind '04
Curious George '06 (V)
School for Scoundrels '06
She's the Man '06
Alvin and the Chipmunks '07
I'm Not There '07
Kung Fu Panda '08 (V)
Alvin and the Chipmunks: The Squeakuel '09
Battle for Terra '09 (V)
Year One '09
Megamind '10 (V)
Alvin and the Chipmunks: Chipwrecked '11
Demoted '11
Kung Fu Panda 2 '11 (V)
It's a Disaster '12
Kill Your Darlings '13
Call Me Lucky '15

Dennis Cross (1924-91)
Crime of Passion '57
How to Make a Monster '58

Flora Cross (1993-)
Bee Season '05
Margot at the Wedding '07
Chlorine '13

Harley Cross (1978-)
Where Are the Children? '85
The Believers '87
Cohen and Tate '88
The Fly 2 '89
Stanley and Iris '90
To Dance with the White Dog '93
Dance with the Devil '97
Shriek If You Know What I Did Last Friday the 13th '00

Joseph Cross (1986-)
Wide Awake '97
Desperate Measures '98
Jack Frost '98
The Spring '00
Flags of Our Fathers '06
Running with Scissors '06
Strangers with Candy '06
Falling Up '08
Milk '08
Untraceable '08
Born 2 Race '11
Citizen Gangster '11
Son of Morning '11
Art Machine '12
Lincoln '12
Jimmy P. '13
Last Weekend '14

Kendall Cross
16 Wishes '10
Takedown '10
Duke '12

Larry Cross (1913-76)
Time Lock '57
The Wind and the Lion '75

Marcia Cross (1962-)
Just Peck '09
Bringing Up Bobby '11

Peter Cross (1924-80)
See Pierre Cressoy

Rebecca Cross
Leprechaun 4: In Space '96
The Bachelor '99
The Last Warrior '99

Roger R. Cross (1969-)
A Father's Choice '00
Ballistic: Ecks vs. Sever '02
Interceptor Force 2 '02
What Color Is Love? '08
Polar Storm '09
Abducted: The Carlina White Story '12
12 Rounds 3: Lockdown '15

TJ Cross
Gone in 60 Seconds '00
Showtime '02

Rupert Crosse (1927-73)
Shadows '60
Ride in the Whirlwind '66
The Reivers '69

Syd Crossley (1885-1960)
That Certain Thing '28
Young and Innocent '37

Scatman Crothers (1910-86)
Between Heaven and Hell '56
The Sins of Rachel Cade '61
Lady in a Cage '64
The Patsy '64
Bloody Mama '70
The Great White Hope '70
Chandler '71
The King of Marvin Gardens '72
Detroit 9000 '73
Black Belt Jones '74
Truck Turner '74
One Flew Over the Cuckoo's Nest '75
Streetfight '75
Chesty Anderson USN '76
The Shootist '76
Silver Streak '76
Stay Hungry '76
Bronco Billy '80
The Shining '80
Zapped! '82
Twilight Zone: The Movie '83
Two of a Kind '83
The Journey of Natty Gann '85

Brian Croucher
Fool's Gold: The Story of the Brink's-Mat Robbery '92
I'll Sleep When I'm Dead '03

Lindsay Crouse (1948-)
All the President's Men '76
Eleanor & Franklin '76
Between the Lines '77
Slap Shot '77
Prince of the City '81
Summer Solstice '81
The Verdict '82
Daniel '83
Iceman '84
Places in the Heart '84
House of Games '87
Communion '89
Desperate Hours '90
Being Human '94
Bye Bye, Love '94
The Indian in the Cupboard '95
Norma Jean and Marilyn '95
The Arrival '96
If These Walls Could Talk '96
The Juror '96
Prefontaine '96
Progeny '98
The Insider '99
Cherish '02
Impostor '02
Mr. Brooks '07
Somewhere Slow '14

Roger Crouzet (1927-2000)
Double Agents '59
The Thief of Paris '67

Ashley Crow (1960-)
Final Verdict '91
Little Big League '94
Minority Report '02

Graham Crowden (1922-2010)
Morgan: A Suitable Case for Treatment '66
The File of the Golden Goose '69
If. . . '69
The Night Digger '71
The Abdication '74
The Little Prince '74
Britannia Hospital '82
Code Name: Emerald '85
The Company of Wolves '85
Out of Africa '85
The Innocent Sleep '95
Possession '02
Calendar Girls '03

Russell Crowe (1964-)
Hammers over the Anvil '91
Proof '91
The Efficiency Expert '92
Romper Stomper '92
The Silver Stallion: King of the Wild Brumbies '93
For the Moment '94
The Sum of Us '94
The Quick and the Dead '95
Rough Magic '95
Virtuosity '95
No Way Back '96
Breaking Up '97
Heaven's Burning '97
L.A. Confidential '97
The Insider '99
Mystery, Alaska '99
Gladiator '00
Proof of Life '00
A Beautiful Mind '01
Master and Commander: The Far Side of the World '03
Cinderella Man '05
A Good Year '06
American Gangster '07
Bra Boys '07 (V)
3:10 to Yuma '07
Body of Lies '08
Tenderness '08
State of Play '09
The Next Three Days '10
Robin Hood '10
Les Miserables '12
The Man with the Iron Fists '12
Broken City '13
Man of Steel '13
Noah '14
Winter's Tale '14
The Water Diviner '15
Fathers and Daughters '16
The Nice Guys '16
The Mummy '17
Boy Erased '18

Josephine Crowell (1849-1932)
The Birth of a Nation '15
The Greatest Question '19
The Merry Widow '25
The Man Who Laughs '27

Ben Crowley (1980-)
Sucker Free City '05
The Bridge to Nowhere '09
Beyond '11

Dermot Crowley (1947-)
Echoes '88
The Sculptress '97
Falling for a Dancer '98
Dead Gorgeous '02

Donncha Crowley
Death Games '02
Bloom '03
Kings '07

Jeananne Crowley (1946-)
Reilly: Ace of Spies '87
The Real Charlotte '91

Kathleen Crowley (1931-)
Westward Ho, the Wagons! '56
The Rebel Set '59

Kevin Crowley (1958-)
The Package '89
Donnybrook '18

Matt Crowley
The Mob '51
April Love '57

Pat Crowley
Money from Home '53
There's Always Tomorrow '56
Wild Women of Wongo '59

Pat(ricia) Crowley (1933-)
Forever Female '53
Red Garters '54
Hollywood or Bust '56
Menace on the Mountain '70
Return to Fantasy Island '77
61* '01

Suzan Crowley (1953-)
Christabel '89
Devices and Desires '91
The Devil Inside '12

Marie Josee Croze (1970-)
Battlefield Earth '00
Maelstrom '00
Ararat '02
Wolves in the Snow '02
The Barbarian Invasions '03
Munich '05
Tell No One '06
The Diving Bell and the Butterfly '07
Murder on the Orient Express '10
Birdsong '12
Collision '13
Calvary '14
Every Thing Will Be Fine '15

Billy Crudup (1968-)
Grind '96
Sleepers '96
Inventing the Abbotts '97
Without Limits '97
The Hi-Lo Country '98
Monument Ave. '98
Princess Mononoke '98 (V)
Jesus' Son '99
Almost Famous '00
Waking the Dead '00
Charlotte Gray '01
World Traveler '01
Big Fish '03
Stage Beauty '04
The Good Shepherd '06
Mission: Impossible 3 '06
Trust the Man '06
Dedication '07
Pretty Bird '08
Public Enemies '09
Watchmen '09
Eat, Pray, Love '10
Too Big to Fail '11
Thin Ice '12
Blood Ties '13
Glass Chin '14
The Longest Week '14
Rudderless '14
The Stanford Prison Experiment '15
Jackie '16
Alien: Covenant '17
20th Century Women '17
After the Wedding '19
Where'd You Go, Bernadette '19

Tom Cruise (1962-)
Endless Love '81
Taps '81
Losin' It '82
All the Right Moves '83
The Outsiders '83
Risky Business '83
The Color of Money '86
Legend '86
Top Gun '86
Cocktail '88
Rain Man '88
Born on the Fourth of July '89
Days of Thunder '90
Far and Away '92
A Few Good Men '92
The Firm '93
Interview with the Vampire '94
Jerry Maguire '96
Mission: Impossible '96
Eyes Wide Shut '99
Magnolia '99
Mission: Impossible 2 '00
Vanilla Sky '01
Austin Powers In Goldmember '02 (C)
Minority Report '02
The Last Samurai '03
Collateral '04
War of the Worlds '05
Mission: Impossible 3 '06
Lions for Lambs '07
Tropic Thunder '08
Valkyrie '08
Knight and Day '10
Mission: Impossible-Ghost Protocol '11
Jack Reacher '12
Rock of Ages '12
Oblivion '13
Edge of Tomorrow '14
Mission: Impossible Rogue Nation '15
Jack Reacher: Never Go Back '16
American Made '17
The Mummy '17
Mission: Impossible-Fallout '18

Jeremy Crutchley
Pride of Africa '97
Ask the Dust '06
Lost City Raiders '08

Rosalie Crutchley (1920-97)
The Lady With the Lamp '51
The Haunting '63
Creatures the World Forgot '70
Wuthering Heights '70
Six Wives of Henry VIII '71
Elizabeth R '72
And Now the Screaming Starts '73
Testament of Youth '79
The Hunchback of Notre Dame '82
Smiley's People '82
Four Weddings and a Funeral '94
A Village Affair '95

Abigail Cruttenden (1968-)
Sharpe's Mission '96
Sharpe's Regiment '96
Sharpe's Siege '96
Into the Blue '97
Jane Eyre '97
Sharpe's Justice '97
Sharpe's Revenge '97
Hideous Kinky '99
Charlotte Gray '01

Greg Cruttwell (1962-)
Naked '93
Two Days in the Valley '96
George of the Jungle '97

Alexis Cruz (1974-)
The Old Man and the Sea '90
Stargate '94
Larry McMurtry's Streets of Laredo '95
Riot in the Streets '96
Hostage High '97
Why Do Fools Fall in Love? '98
Darkwolf '03
Slayer '06
Tortilla Heaven '07

Brandon Cruz (1962-)
The Bad News Bears '76
Safe '95
The Lords of Salem '13

Celia Cruz (1924-2003)
The Mambo Kings '92
The Perez Family '94
Soul Power '08

Ernesto Cruz
El Norte '83
Midaq Alley '95

Penelope Cruz (1974-)
Belle Epoque '92
Framed '93

Blithe Spirit '45
In the Cool of the Day '63

Irving Cummings (1888-1959)
Sex '20
The Saphead '21
Hollywood Cavalcade '39

Jim (Jonah) Cummings (1952-)
A Goofy Movie '94 (V)
The Lion King '94 (V)
Balto '95 (V)
Piglet's Big Movie '03 (V)
Comic Book: The Movie '04 (C)
The Lion King 1 1/2 '04 (V)
The Princess and the Frog '09 (V)
Gnomeo & Juliet '11 (V)
Winnie the Pooh '11 (V)

Robert Cummings (1908-90)
Souls at Sea '37
The Texans '38
You and Me '38
Three Smart Girls Grow Up '39
One Night in the Tropics '40
Spring Parade '40
The Devil & Miss Jones '41
It Started with Eve '41
Kings Row '41
Moon over Miami '41
Saboteur '42
Forever and a Day '43
Princess O'Rourke '43
The Bride Wore Boots '46
The Chase '46
The Lost Moment '47
Sleep, My Love '48
Reign of Terror '49
Tell It to the Judge '49
For Heaven's Sake '50
The First Time '52
Dial 'M' for Murder '54
Lucky Me '54
My Geisha '62
Beach Party '63
The Carpetbaggers '64
Stagecoach '66
Five Golden Dragons '67

Susan Cummings (1930-)
Swamp Women '55
Man From God's Country '58
Verboten! '59

Whitney Cummings (1982-)
Made of Honor '08
3, 2, 1...Frankie Go Boom '12
Unforgettable '17
The Female Brain '18

Gregory Scott Cummins (1956-)
Lone Justice 2 '93
Watchers 3 '94
The Last of the Dogmen '95
Gang Related '96

Juliette Cummins (1964-)
Running Hot '83
Friday the 13th, Part 5: A New Beginning '85
Slumber Party Massacre 2 '87

Martin Cummins (1969-)
Friday the 13th, Part 8: Jason Takes Manhattan '89
Poltergeist: The Legacy '96
Love Come Down '00
We All Fall Down '00
Liberty Stands Still '02
Ice Men '04
Devour '05
I Dream of Murder '06
Smoke Screen '10
The Pastor's Wife '11
Duke '12
Radio Rebel '12
Seattle Superstorm '12
Mr. Hockey: The Gordie Howe Story '13

Peggy Cummins (1925-)
Gun Crazy '49
Carry On Admiral '57
Curse of the Demon '57
The Captain's Table '60
Dentist In the Chair '60

Rusty Cundieff (1965-)
Fear of a Black Hat '94
Tales from the Hood '95
Sprung '96

Emma Cunniffe (1973-)
All the King's Men '99
Great Expectations '99
Love or Money '01
Plain Jane '02
Place of Execution '09
Appointment With Death '10

Cecil Cunningham (1888-1959)
The Awful Truth '37
The Hidden Hand '42
Above Suspicion '43

Colin Cunningham (1966-)
The 6th Day '00
Stealing Sinatra '04
Lesser Evil '06
Breakfast With Scot '07
Fireball '09
Impact '09
Goblin '10
The Eleventh Victim '12

Danny Cunningham (1969-)
Loaded '94
24 Hour Party People '01

Jack Cunningham (1912-67)
Time Lock '57
The Quare Fellow '62

John Cunningham (1932-)
Lost and Found '79
The Jackal '97
States of Control '98
DC 9/11: Time of Crisis '04

June Cunningham
The Smallest Show on Earth '57
Horrors of the Black Museum '59

Liam Cunningham (1961-)
First Knight '95
A Little Princess '95
War of the Buttons '95
Jude '96
Falling for a Dancer '98
RKO 281 '99
Shooting the Past '99
When the Sky Falls '99
Attila '01
Dog Soldiers '01
A Love Divided '01
Breakfast on Pluto '05
The Wind That Shakes the Barley '06
Northanger Abbey '07
The Escapist '08
Hunger '08
The Mummy: Tomb of the Dragon Emperor '08
Harry Brown '09
Perrier's Bounty '09
The Tournament '09
Centurion '10
The Guard '11
The Whistleblower '11
Safe House '12
The Numbers Station '13
The Childhood of a Leader '16
24 Hours to Live '17

Alain Cuny (1908-94)
The Hunchback of Notre Dame '57
The Lovers '59
La Dolce Vita '60
The Milky Way '68
Fellini Satyricon '69
Emmanuelle '74
Christ Stopped at Eboli '79
Detective '85
Camille Claudel '89

Kaley Cuoco (1985-)
Crimes of Fashion '04
The Hollow '04
Wasted '06
Cougar Club '07
To Be Fat Like Me '07
Killer Movie '08
The Penthouse '10
Hop '11
Drew Peterson: Untouchable '12
The Last Ride '12
Authors Anonymous '14
Alvin and the Chipmunks: Road Chip '15 (V)
The Wedding Ringer '15

Barbara Cupisti (1962-)
Stagefright '87
Opera '88
The Church '98

Antonio Cupo (1978-)
Lost Behind Bars '06
Love Notes '07
Carnera: The Walking Mountain '08
Sword of War '09
Magic Beyond Words: The JK Rowling Story '11
Love at the Thanksgiving Day Parade '12
In My Dreams '14

Ben Cura (1988-)
Gun Shy '17
15 Minutes of War '19

Monique Gabriela Curnen (1970-)
Half Nelson '06
The Dark Knight '08
Legacy '10
Contagion '11

Roland Curram (1932-)
Darling '65
Parting Shots '98

Brittany Curran (1990-)
R.L. Stine's The Haunting Hour: Don't Even Think About It '07
Dog Gone '08
Legally Blondes '09

Jake Curran
Blackbeard '06
Dragonheart 3: The Sorcerer's Curse '15

Lynette Curran (1945-)
The Year My Voice Broke '87
Japanese Story '03
Somersault '04

Paul Curran (1913-86)
Poldark '75
Merlin '98

Tony Curran (1969-)
Being Human '94
Split Second '99
The 13th Warrior '99
Blade 2 '02
The League of Extraordinary Gentlemen '03
Flight of the Phoenix '04
Underworld: Evolution '05
Beowulf & Grendel '06
The Good German '06
Red Road '06
The Lazarus Project '08
The Midnight Meat Train '08
Ondine '09
Shuttle '09
Golf in the Kingdom '10
Pillars of the Earth '10
Labyrinth '12

Cherie Currie (1959-)
Foxes '80
Parasite '82
Twilight Zone: The Movie '83
Rosebud Beach Hotel '85

Finlay Currie (1878-1968)
The Good Companions '33
Edge of the World '37
The Forty-Ninth Parallel '41
I Know Where I'm Going '45
Great Expectations '46
The Black Rose '50
The Mudlark '50
Treasure Island '50
People Will Talk '51
Quo Vadis '51
The Australian Story '52
Ivanhoe '52
Stars and Stripes Forever '52
Walk East on Beacon '52
Captain Lightfoot '55
Footsteps in the Fog '55
Corridors of Blood '58
Ben-Hur '59
The Adventures of Huckleberry Finn '60
Billy Liar '63
Bunny Lake Is Missing '65

Gordon Currie (1965-)
Puppet Master 4 '93
Puppet Master 5: The Final Chapter '94
Blood & Donuts '95
Ripe '97
Dog Park '98
The Fear: Halloween Night '99
Laserhawk '99
Left Behind: The Movie '00
The Fraternity '01
Highwaymen '03
Possessed '05

Louise Currie (1913-)
The Bashful Bachelor '42
The Chinese Ring '47

Michael Currie (1928-2009)
Halloween 3: Season of the Witch '82
Sudden Impact '83
The Dead Pool '88

Sondra Currie (1952-)
Policewomen '73
Runaways '75

Frank Currier (1857-1928)
The Family Secret '24
The Red Lily '24
The Sea Hawk '24
Across to Singapore '28

Bernard Curry
The Junction Boys '02
The Road from Coorain '02

Christopher Curry (1948-)
C.H.U.D. '84
Home Alone 3 '97
City of Ghosts '03
The Details '11 (N)

Don 'DC' Curry
Next Friday '00
Friday After Next '02

Stephen Curry (1976-)
The Castle '97
Cut '00
Rogue '07
The Diplomat '08
Cloudstreet '11
The Cup '11

Tim Curry (1946-)
The Rocky Horror Picture Show '75
Times Square '80
Annie '82
Oliver Twist '82
The Ploughman's Lunch '83
Clue '85
Legend '86
The Worst Witch '86
The Hunt for Red October '90
Stephen King's It '90
Oscar '91
Ferngully: The Last Rain Forest '92 (V)
Home Alone 2: Lost in New York '92
Passed Away '92
National Lampoon's Loaded Weapon 1 '93
The Three Musketeers '93
The Pebble and the Penguin '94 (V)
The Shadow '94
Congo '95
Muppet Treasure Island '96
Titanic '96
McHale's Navy '97
Jackie's Back '99
Charlie's Angels '00
Four Dogs Playing Poker '00
Attila '01
Scary Movie 2 '01
The Home Front '02
The Wild Thornberrys Movie '02 (V)
Rugrats Go Wild! '03 (V)
Kinsey '04
Sorted '04
Bailey's Billion$ '05
Valiant '05 (V)
Garfield: A Tail of Two Kitties '06 (V)
Queer Duck: The Movie '06 (V)
Christmas in Wonderland '07
The Color of Magic '08
Fly Me to the Moon '08 (V)
The Secret of Moonacre '08
Alice '09
Return to Cranford '09
Appointment With Death '10
Burke & Hare '10

Catherine Curtin
Gold Star '17
The Light of the Moon '17

Jane Curtin (1947-)
Mr. Mike's Mondo Video '79
How to Beat the High Cost of Living '80
Divorce Wars: A Love Story '82
O.C. and Stiggs '87
Coneheads '93
Antz '98 (V)
Our Town '03
The Librarian: Quest for the Spear '04
Brooklyn Lobster '05
The Librarian: Return to King Solomon's Mines '06
The Shaggy Dog '06
The Librarian: Curse of the Judas Chalice '08
I Love You, Man '09
I Don't Know How She Does It '11
The Heat '13
Can You Ever Forgive Me? '18

Peter Curtin
Till Human Voices Wake Us '02
Darkness Falls '03

Valerie Curtin (1945-)
Great Smokey Roadblock '76
Different Story '78
A Christmas Without Snow '80
Maxie '85
Big Trouble '86
Down and Out in Beverly Hills '86

Alan Curtis (1909-53)
Last Outlaw '36
Mannequin '37
Shopworn Angel '38
Hollywood Cavalcade '39
Four Sons '40
Buck Privates '41
High Sierra '41
Melody Master '41
Gung Ho! '43
The Invisible Man's Revenge '44
Phantom Lady '44
The Naughty Nineties '45
Flight to Nowhere '46
Renegade Girl '46
The Pirates of Capri '49

Billy Curtis (1909-88)
Pygmy Island '50
Jungle Moon Men '55
The Incredible Shrinking Man '57
Little Cigars '73
Eating Raoul '82

Clifford Curtis (1968-)
Virus '98
Bringing Out the Dead '99
Three Kings '99
Blow '01
The Majestic '01
Training Day '01
Collateral Damage '02
Point of Origin '02
Whale Rider '02
Runaway Jury '03
River Queen '05
The Fountain '06
Fracture '07
Live Free or Die Hard '07
Sunshine '07
10,000 B.C. '08
Crossing Over '09
Push '09
The Last Airbender '10
Colombiana '11
A Thousand Words '12
The Dark Horse '14
Last Knights '15
Risen '16
The Meg '18
Doctor Sleep '19

Dick Curtis (1902-52)
Mutiny Ahead '35
Billy the Kid '41
Government Agents *vs.* Phantom Legion '51

Donald Curtis (1915-97)
Criminals Within '41
Bataan '43
Thirty Seconds Over Tokyo '44
Son of Lassie '45
They Were Expendable '45
The Amazing Mr. X '48
Stampede '49
It Came from Beneath the Sea '55
Earth *vs.* the Flying Saucers '56
Seventh Cavalry '56
Night Passage '57

Jackie Curtis (1947-85)
Flesh '68
WR: Mysteries of the Organism '71

Jamie Lee Curtis (1958-)
The Fog '78
Halloween '78
Prom Night '80
Terror Train '80
Death of a Centerfold '81
Escape from New York '81 (V)
Halloween 2: The Nightmare Isn't Over! '81
Road Games '81
Love Letters '83
Trading Places '83
The Adventures of Buckaroo Banzai Across the Eighth Dimension '84
Grandview U.S.A. '84
Perfect '85
Amazing Grace & Chuck '87
A Man in Love '87
Dominick & Eugene '88
A Fish Called Wanda '88
Blue Steel '90
My Girl '91
Queens Logic '91
Forever Young '92
The Return of Spinal Tap '92 (C)
Mother's Boys '94
My Girl 2 '94
True Lies '94
The Heidi Chronicles '95
Fierce Creatures '96
House Arrest '96
Homegrown '97 (C)
Halloween: H20 '98
Virus '98
Daddy & Them '99
Drowning Mona '00
The Tailor of Panama '00
Halloween: Resurrection '02
Freaky Friday '03
Christmas With the Kranks '04
Beverly Hills Chihuahua '08 (V)
You Again '10
Veronica Mars '14
Spare Parts '15
78/52: Hitchcock's Shower Scene '17
Halloween '18
Knives Out '19

Miley Cyrus (1992-)
Bolt '08 (V)
Hannah Montana: The Movie '09
The Last Song '10
Justin Bieber: Never Say Never '11
LOL '12
So Undercover '13

Henry Czerny (1959-)
The Boys of St. Vincent '93
Northern Extremes '93
Clear and Present Danger '94
Choices of the Heart: The Margaret Sanger Story '95
Notes from Underground '95
When Night Is Falling '95
Mission: Impossible '96
The Ice Storm '97
The Girl Next Door '98
Cement '99
Eye of the Killer '99
P.T. Barnum '99
Possessed '00
Range of Motion '00
The Salem Witch Trials '02
Gone Dark '03
Klepto '03
The Exorcism of Emily Rose '05
Fido '06
The Pink Panther '06
That Russell Girl '08
Prayers for Bobby '09
The A-Team '10
Ice Castles '10
Remember '15
The Other Half '17
Ready or Not '19

Matt Czuchry (1977-)
I Hope They Serve Beer in Hell '09
The 19th Wife '10

Chris D (1950-)
No Way Out '87
Border Radio '88

Deezer D
CB4: The Movie '93
Fear of a Black Hat '94

Da Brat (1974-)
Carmen: A Hip Hopera '01 (N)
Glitter '01
Civil Brand '02

Rebecca Da Costa (1984-)
Freerunner '10
7 Below '11
The Bag Man '14

Eric (DaRe) Da Re (1965-)
Silent Night, Deadly Night 3: Better Watch Out! '89
Twin Peaks: Fire Walk with Me '92
Number One Fan '94

Howard da Silva (1909-86)
Abe Lincoln in Illinois '40
Sergeant York '41
Keeper of the Flame '42
Reunion in France '42
Tonight We Raid Calais '43
The Lost Weekend '45
The Blue Dahlia '46
Unconquered '47
Border Incident '49
They Live by Night '49
Three Husbands '50
The Underworld Story '50
David and Lisa '62
The Outrage '64
Nevada Smith '66
1776 '72
The Great Gatsby '74
Missiles of October '74
Smile Jenny, You're Dead '74
Mommie Dearest '81
Garbo Talks '84

Parvin Dabas (1974-)
Monsoon Wedding '01
The Curse of King Tut's Tomb '06
The World Unseen '07

Cherien Dabis
May in Summer '13
May in the Summer '13

Augusta Dabney (1918-2008)
Cold River '81
Violets Are Blue '86
Running on Empty '88

Maryam D'Abo (1960-)
Xtro '83
The Living Daylights '87
Leon the Pig Farmer '93
Red Shoe Diaries 3: Another Woman's Lipstick '93
Tropical Heat '93
The Browning Version '94
Romance and Rejection '96
The Sea Change '98
An American Affair '99
Timelock '99
Doctor Zhivago '03
Helen of Troy '03
Evil Remains '04
The Prince & Me 2: Royal Wedding '06
Dorian Gray '09

Olivia D'Abo (1969-)
Bolero '84
Conan the Destroyer '84
Dream to Believe '85
Mission. . . Kill '85
Bullies '86
Into the Fire '88
Beyond the Stars '89
Spirit of '76 '91
Midnight's Child '93
Point of No Return '93
Wayne's World 2 '93
Clean Slate '94
Greedy '94
Pom Poko '94 (V)
The Big Green '95
Kicking and Screaming '95
Live Nude Girls '95
National Lampoon's Dad's Week Off '97
Sink or Swim '97
Soccer Dog: The Movie '98
The Velocity of Gary '98
A Texas Funeral '99
It Had to Be You '00
Seven Girlfriends '00
The Enemy '01
The Triangle '01
We Have Your Husband '11
Robo-Dog '15

Mark Dacascos (1964-)
American Samurai '92
Only the Strong '93
Double Dragon '94
Dragstrip Girl '94
Redemption: Kickboxer 5 '95
Drive '96
Sabotage '96
DNA '97
Redline '97
Boogie Boy '98
No Code of Conduct '98
Sanctuary '98
The Base '99
Brotherhood of the Wolf '01
Instinct to Kill '01
Scorcher '02
Cradle 2 the Grave '03
Final Approach '04
The Hunt for Eagle One: Crash Point '06
Only the Brave '06
Solar Attack '06
Alien Agent '07
Code Name: The Cleaner '07
I Am Omega '07
Wolvesbayne '09
Maximum Impact '18
John Wick: Chapter 3-Parabellum '19

Yaya DaCosta (1982-)
Take the Lead '06
Honeydripper '07
Racing for Time '08
The Kids Are All Right '10
Mother of George '13
Whitney '15

Jacques Dacqmine (1923-2010)
Phedre '68
Melo '86

Peter DaCunha
The Barrens '12
Haunter '13
Hellions '15
XX '17

Alexandra Daddario (1986-)
Bereavement '10
Percy Jackson: Sea of Monsters '13
Texas Chainsaw 3D '13
Burying the Ex '15
San Andreas '15
Baked in Brooklyn '16
The Choice '16
Baywatch '17
The Layover '17
Can You Keep a Secret? '19
Night Hunter '19

Matthew Daddario
Breathe In '13
When the Game Stands Tall '14

Cameron Daddo (1965-)
Anne of Green Gables: The Continuing Story '99
Zebra Lounge '01
Category 7: The End of the World '05
Pterodactyl '05
Blackwater Valley Exorcism '06
Towards Darkness '07
The Perfect Sleep '08
Wild Things: Foursome '10

Frances Dade (1910-68)
Raffles '30
Dracula '31

Werner Daehn (1967-)
XXX '02
Shadow Man '06
The 39 Steps '09

Willem Dafoe (1955-)
The Hunger '83
Loveless '83
Roadhouse 66 '84
Streets of Fire '84
To Live & Die in L.A. '85
Platoon '86
Off Limits '87
The Last Temptation of Christ '88
Mississippi Burning '88
Born on the Fourth of July '89
Triumph of the Spirit '89
Cry-Baby '90
Flight of the Intruder '90
Wild at Heart '90
Body of Evidence '92
Light Sleeper '92
White Sands '92
Faraway, So Close! '93
Clear and Present Danger '94
The Night and the Moment '94
Tom & Viv '94
Victory '95
Basquiat '96
The English Patient '96
Affliction '97
Speed 2: Cruise Control '97
Lulu on the Bridge '98
New Rose Hotel '98
American Psycho '99
Boondock Saints '99
eXistenZ '99
Animal Factory '00
Shadow of the Vampire '00
Edges of the Lord '01
Pavilion of Women '01
Auto Focus '02
Spider-Man '02
Finding Nemo '03 (V)
Once Upon a Time in Mexico '03
The Reckoning '03
The Aviator '04
The Clearing '04
The Life Aquatic with Steve Zissou '04
Spider-Man 2 '04
The Black Widow '05
Manderlay '05
XXX: State of the Union '05
American Dreamz '06
Inside Man '06
Paris, je t'aime '06
Anamorph '07
Mr. Bean's Holiday '07
The Walker '07
Adam Resurrected '08
Fireflies in the Garden '08
Antichrist '09
Cirque du Freak: The Vampire's Assistant '09
Daybreakers '09
Fantastic Mr. Fox '09 (V)
Farewell '09
My Son, My Son, What Have Ye Done '09
Miral '10
4:44 Last Day on Earth '11
The Hunter '12
John Carter '12
Tomorrow You're Gone '12
Odd Thomas '13
Out of the Furnace '13
Bad Country '14
The Fault In Our Stars '14
The Grand Budapest Hotel '14
John Wick '14
A Most Wanted Man '14
Dog Eat Dog '16
The Florida Project '17
The Great Wall '17
Aquaman '18
At Eternity's Gate '18
The Lighthouse '19
Motherless Brooklyn '19
Togo '19

Ifan Huw Dafydd
The Proposition '96
Cravings '06
Rise of the Gargoyles '09

Jensen (Jennifer) Daggett (1969-)
Friday the 13th, Part 8: Jason Takes Manhattan '89
Asteroid '97
Major League 3: Back to the Minors '98

Veronica D'Agostino
Respiro '02
The Sicilian Girl '09

Nicholas D'Agosto (1980-)
Inside '06
Rocket Science '07
Fired Up! '09
Dirty Girl '10
Final Destination 5 '11
From Prada to Nada '11
Mardi Gras: Spring Break '11

Lil Dagover (1897-1980)
Spiders '18
The Cabinet of Dr. Caligari '19
Destiny '21
Dr. Mabuse, The Gambler '22
Phantom '22
Tartuffe '25
Hungarian Rhapsody '28
The Woman From Monte Carlo '31

Arlene Dahl (1925-)
My Wild Irish Rose '47
The Bride Goes Wild '48
A Southern Yankee '48
Reign of Terror '49
Scene of the Crime '49
Ambush '50
The Outriders '50
Three Little Words '50
Watch the Birdie '50
Here Come the Girls '53
Slightly Scarlet '56
She Played With Fire '57
Journey to the Center of the Earth '59
Kisses for My President '64
Land Raiders '69
Night of the Warrior '91

Eva Dahlbeck (1920-2008)
Secrets of Women '52
Smiles of a Summer Night '55
Brink of Life '57
The Counterfeit Traitor '62

Yuko Daike (1971-)
Ju-On 2 '00
Zatoichi '03

Dan Dailey (1913-78)
Hullabaloo '40
Lady Be Good '41
Ziegfeld Girl '41
Mokey '42
Panama Hattie '42
Mother Wore Tights '47
Chicken Every Sunday '48
My Blue Heaven '50
When Willie Comes Marching Home '50
Call Me Mister '51
I Can Get It For You Wholesale '51
Pride of St. Louis '52
What Price Glory? '52
The Girl Next Door '53
There's No Business Like Show Business '54
It's Always Fair Weather '55
Oh, Men! Oh, Women! '57
The Wayward Bus '57
Wings of Eagles '57
The Private Files of J. Edgar Hoover '77

E.G. Dailey (1961-)
See Elizabeth Daily

Elizabeth Daily (1961-)
The Escape Artist '82
One Dark Night '82
Valley Girl '83
No Small Affair '84
Streets of Fire '84
Better Off Dead '85
Fandango '85
Pee-wee's Big Adventure '85
Bad Dreams '88
Loverboy '89
Dogfight '91
Dutch '91
Lorenzo's Oil '92
Babe: Pig in the City '98 (V)
The Rugrats Movie '98 (V)
Rugrats in Paris: The Movie '00 (V)
The Powerpuff Girls Movie '02 (V)
Rugrats Go Wild! '03 (V)
The Devil's Rejects '05
Happy Feet '06 (V)
Happy Feet Two '11 (V)

Masaki Daimon
Lady Snowblood '73
Godzilla *vs.* the Cosmic Monster '74

Nadia Dajani (1965-)
Happy Accidents '00
Sidewalks of New York '01
Alchemy '05
Game 6 '05

David Daker (1937-)
The Optimists '73
Woman in Black '89

Nino Dal Fabbro (1980-)
Too Bad She's Bad '54
Crime Boss '72

Robert Dalban (1903-87)
Diabolique '55
Hijack Highway '55

Alberto Dalbes (1922-83)
Rites of Frankenstein '72
The Screaming Dead '72

Alan Dale (1947-)
Don't Be Afraid of the Dark '11
Doomsday Prophecy '11
A Little Bit of Heaven '11

Cynthia Dale (1960-)
My Bloody Valentine '81
Boy in Blue '86
Spenser: A Savage Place '94
At the Midnight Hour '95
P.T. Barnum '99
A Broken Life '07

Dick Dale (1937-)
Beach Party '63
Muscle Beach Party '64
Back to the Beach '87

Esther Dale (1885-1961)
Curly Top '35
In Old Kentucky '35
The Wedding Night '35
The Awful Truth '37
Blondie Has Trouble '40
Back Street '41
Dangerously We Live '41
Wrecking Crew '42
A Stolen Life '46
The Unfinished Dance '47
Holiday Affair '49
Ma and Pa Kettle '49
Ma and Pa Kettle Go to Town '50
On Moonlight Bay '51
Ma and Pa Kettle at the Fair '52

Grover Dale (1935-)
Half a Sixpence '67
The Young Girls of Rochefort '68

Ian Anthony Dale (1978-)
Mr. 3000 '04
Wakefield '17

James Dale
Victoria the Great '37
The Departed '06

James Badge Dale (1978-)
The Departed '06
NoNames '10
The Pacific '10
Shame '11
The Grey '12
Iron Man 3 '13
The Lone Ranger '13
Parkland '13
World War Z '13
Miss Meadows '14
The Walk '15
13 Hours: The Secret Soldiers of Benghazi '16
Only the Brave '17
Donnybrook '18
Hold the Dark '18
The Kitchen '19
The Standoff at Sparrow Creek '19

Janet Dale
Prick Up Your Ears '87
The Buddha of Suburbia '92
The Tenant of Wildfell Hall '96

Jennifer Dale (1956-)
Ticket to Heaven '81
Of Unknown Origin '83
The Adjuster '91
Broken Lullaby '94
Once a Thief '96
Trail of a Serial Killer '98
The Life Before This '99
Love Come Down '00

Jim Dale (1935-)
Carry On Cabby '63
Carry On Jack '63
Carry On Spying '64
Carry On Cleo '65
Carry On Cowboy '66
Carry On Screaming '66
Don't Lose Your Head '66
Follow That Camel '67
Carry On Doctor '68
Carry On Again Doctor '69
The National Health '73
Adolf Hitler: My Part in His Downfall '74
Joseph Andrews '77
Pete's Dragon '77
Hot Lead & Cold Feet '78
Unidentified Flying Oddball '79
The Adventures of Huckleberry Finn '85
Carry On Columbus '92
The Hunchback '97

Virginia Dale (1917-94)
Buck Benny Rides Again '40
Las Vegas Nights '41
Holiday Inn '42
Docks of New Orleans '48

John Francis Daley (1985-)
Waiting '05
Horrible Bosses '11

Fabienne Dali (1941-)
Kill, Baby, Kill '66
Mayerling '68

Tracy Dali (1966-)
Virgin High '90
American Streetfighter '96

Marcel Dalio (1900-83)
Beethoven '36
Grand Illusion '37
The Rules of the Game '39
Casablanca '42
Paris After Dark '43
Tonight We Raid Calais '43
To Have & Have Not '44
Rich, Young and Pretty '51
Lovely to Look At '52
The Snows of Kilimanjaro '52
Lucky Me '54
Sabrina '54
Jump Into Hell '55
China Gate '57
Tip On a Dead Jockey '57
Lafayette Escadrille '58
The Perfect Furlough '59
Can-Can '60
Classe Tous Risque '60
The Monocle '64
Lady L '65
How to Steal a Million '66
The 25th Hour '67
How Sweet It Is! '68
The Mad Adventures of Rabbi Jacob '73

Evelyn Dall
He Found a Star '41
Miss London Ltd. '43

John Dall (1918-71)
The Corn Is Green '45
Something in the Wind '47
Rope '48
Gun Crazy '49
The Man Who Cheated Himself '50
Atlantis, the Lost Continent '61

Charlene Dallas
Rancho Deluxe '75
Criminal Act '88

Josh Dallas (1981-)
The Descent 2 '09
Ghost Machine '09

Matt Dallas (1982-)
The Indian '07
Babysitter Wanted '08
As Good As Dead '10
Beauty & the Briefcase '10
Wyatt Earp's Revenge '12
Along Came the Devil '18

Beatrice Dalle (1964-)
Betty Blue '86
Night on Earth '91
I Can't Sleep '93
Six Days, Six Nights '94
The Blackout '97
Time of the Wolf '03
Clean '04
The Intruder '04
Domain '09
Our Paradise '11

Jemma Dallender
I Spit on Your Grave 2 '13
Contract to Kill '16

Joe Dallesandro (1948-)
Flesh '68
Trash '70
Heat '72
Andy Warhol's Dracula '74
Andy Warhol's Frankenstein '74
Black Moon '75
Seeds of Evil '76
The Cotton Club '84
Sunset '88
Cry-Baby '90
Guncrazy '92
Wild Orchid 2: Two Shades of Blue '92
Sugar Hill '94
Bad Love '95
The Limey '99

Maurice Dallimore (1912-73)
The Collector '65
Johnny Got His Gun '71

Francesca D'Aloja (1963-)
Apartment Zero '88
Steam: A Turkish Bath '96
Scarlet Diva '00

Abby Dalton (1935-)
The Viking Women and the Sea Serpent '57
Cole Younger, Gunfighter '58
Cyber-Tracker '93

Audrey Dalton (1934-)
My Cousin Rachel '52
Titanic '53
Casanova's Big Night '54
The Prodigal '55
The Monster That Challenged the World '57
Separate Tables '58
Mr. Sardonicus '61
Kitten with a Whip '64

Darren Dalton (1965-)
Brotherhood of Justice '86
The Day the Earth Stopped '08
War of the Worlds 2: The Next Wave '08
The Land That Time Forgot '09

Kristen Dalton (1966-)
Digital Man '94
The Departed '06
The Perfect Family '11

Timothy Dalton (1944-)
The Lion in Winter '68
Cromwell '70
Wuthering Heights '70
Mary, Queen of Scots '71
Centennial '78
Sextette '78
Agatha '79
Flash Gordon '80
Jane Eyre '83
Mistral's Daughter '84
The Doctor and the Devils '85
Florence Nightingale '85
Sins '85
Brenda Starr '86
The Living Daylights '87
Hawks '89
License to Kill '89
The King's Whore '90
The Rocketeer '91
Framed '93
Last Action Hero '93 (C)
Naked in New York '93
Scarlett '94
The Beautician and the Beast '97
Cleopatra '99
Made Men '99
Possessed '00
American Outlaws '01
Looney Tunes: Back in Action '03
Hot Fuzz '07
The Tourist '10
Toy Story 3 '10 (V)

Roger Daltrey (1945-)
Lisztomania '75
Tommy '75
The Kids Are Alright '79
The Legacy '79
If Looks Could Kill '91
Lightning Jack '94
Vampirella '96
Like It Is '98
The Magical Legend of the Leprechauns '99
Chasing Destiny '00
Dracula: The Dark Prince '01
Strange Frequency 2 '01
Johnny Was '05

Andrew Daly
Semi-Pro '08
Post Grad '09
Middle School: The Worst Years of My Life '16

Candice Daly (1963-2004)
Liquid Dreams '92
Where Truth Lies '96

Eileen Daly (1963-)
Razor Blade Smile '98
Witchcraft 10: Mistress of the Craft '98

James Daly (1918-78)
The Court Martial of Billy Mitchell '55
The Young Stranger '57
Planet of the Apes '68
The Big Bounce '69
The Five Man Army '69
Operation Heartbeat '69
Resurrection of Zachary Wheeler '71

Mark Daly (1887-1957)
The Ghost Goes West '36
Good Morning, Boys '37

Timothy Daly (1956-)
Diner '82
I Married a Centerfold '84
Just the Way You Are '84
Made in Heaven '87
My Neighbor Totoro '88 (V)
Spellbinder '88
Year of the Comet '92
In the Line of Duty: Ambush in Waco '93
Queen '93
Dr. Jekyll and Ms. Hyde '95
The Associate '96
From the Earth to the Moon '98
The Object of My Affection '98
Stephen King's The Storm of the Century '99
Seven Girlfriends '00
The Outsider '02
Basic '03
Against the Ropes '04
Convicted '04
The Good Student '08
The Skeptic '09

Tyne Daly (1946-)
Angel Unchained '70
The Enforcer '76
Telefon '77
Zoot Suit '81
The Aviator '85
Movers and Shakers '85
Christy '94
Bye Bye Birdie '95
Money Kings '98
Absence of the Good '99
The Simian Line '99
Georgia O'Keefe '09
A Bread Factory, Part One '18
A Bread Factory, Part Two '18

Susan Damante-Shaw (1950-)
The Student Teachers '73
The Adventures of the Wilderness Family '76
Further Adventures of the Wilderness Family, Part 2 '77
Mountain Family Robinson '79

Bertila Damas
Nothing But Trouble '91
Mi Vida Loca '94
True Friends '98

Paul D'Amato
Slap Shot '77
The Deer Hunter '78

Nick Damici
In the Cut '03
Mulberry Street '06
Stake Land '10
Cold in July '14

Marcus D'Amico (1965-)
Full Metal Jacket '87
Armistead Maupin's Tales of the City '93

Francois Damiens (1973-)
Heartbreaker '10
The Rabbi's Cat '11 (V)
Delicacy '12
The Brand New Testament '15

Lili Damita (1901-94)
Fighting Caravans '31
The Woman Between '31
This Is the Night '32
Frisco Kid '35
The Devil on Horseback '36

Cathryn Damon (1933-87)
Friendship, Secrets and Lies '79
How to Beat the High Cost of Living '80
She's Having a Baby '88

Gabriel Damon (1976-)
The Land Before Time '88 (V)
RoboCop 2 '90
Iron Maze '91
Little Nemo: Adventures in Slumberland '92 (V)
Social Misfits '00

Mark Damon (1933-)
Between Heaven and Hell '56
Screaming Eagles '56
The Fall of the House of Usher '60
Black Sabbath '64
Johnny Yuma '66
Anzio '68
Byleth: The Demon of Incest '72
Crypt of the Living Dead '73
Devil's Wedding Night '73

Matt Damon (1970-)
The Good Mother '88
Mystic Pizza '88
School Ties '92
Geronimo: An American Legend '93
The Good Old Boys '95
Courage Under Fire '96
Glory Daze '96 (C)
Chasing Amy '97
Good Will Hunting '97
John Grisham's The Rainmaker '97
Rounders '98
Saving Private Ryan '98
Dogma '99
The Talented Mr. Ripley '99
All the Pretty Horses '00
The Legend of Bagger Vance '00
Titan A.E. '00 (V)
Jay and Silent Bob Strike Back '01 (C)
Ocean's Eleven '01
The Bourne Identity '02
Confessions of a Dangerous Mind '02 (C)
Gerry '02
Spirit: Stallion of the Cimarron '02 (V)
The Third Wheel '02
Stuck On You '03
The Bourne Supremacy '04
Eurotrip '04
Jersey Girl '04
Ocean's Twelve '04
The Brothers Grimm '05
Syriana '05
The Departed '06
The Good Shepherd '06
The Bourne Ultimatum '07
Ocean's Thirteen '07
Che '08 (C)
Ponyo '08 (V)
The Informant! '09
Invictus '09
Green Zone '10
Hereafter '10
Inside Job '10 (N)
True Grit '10
The Adjustment Bureau '11
Contagion '11
Happy Feet Two '11 (V)
Margaret '11
We Bought a Zoo '11
Promised Land '12
Behind the Candelabra '13
Elysium '13
The Monuments Men '13
The Zero Theorem '13
Interstellar '14
The Martian '15
Jason Bourne '16
Downsizing '17
The Great Wall '17
Suburbicon '17
Ford v Ferrari '19

Vic Damone (1928-2018)
Rich, Young and Pretty '51
Athena '54
Hit the Deck '55
Kismet '55
Hell to Eternity '60

JoJo D'Amore (1931-2005)
The Doberman Gang '72
Zoltan. . . Hound of Dracula '78

Barbara Dana (1940-)
Inspector Clouseau '68
Necessary Parties '88
Raising Flagg '06

Bill Dana (1924-)
The Busy Body '67
Harrad Summer '74
I Wonder Who's Killing Her Now? '76
Lena's Holiday '90

Leora Dana (1923-83)
3:10 to Yuma '57
Kings Go Forth '58
Change of Habit '69
Tora! Tora! Tora! '70
Baby It's You '82
Amityville 3: The Demon '83

Mark Dana (1920-2015)
Hot Cars '56
The Pharaoh's Curse '57
Tarzan Goes to India '62

Malcolm Danare (1962-)
Heaven Help Us '85
The Curse '87
Popcorn '89
Godzilla '98

Charles Dance (1946-)
For Your Eyes Only '81
The Jewel in the Crown '84
Plenty '85
The Golden Child '86
Hidden City '87
White Mischief '88
The Phantom of the Opera '90
China Moon '91
Tales of the Unexpected '91
Alien 3 '92
Last Action Hero '93
The Surgeon '94
Michael Collins '96
The Blood Oranges '97
In the Presence of Mine Enemies '97
Rebecca '97
Space Truckers '97
Hilary and Jackie '98
Dr. Bell and Mr. Doyle: The Dark Beginnings of Sherlock Holmes '00
Dark Blue World '01
Gosford Park '01
Swimming Pool '03
Bleak House '05
Scoop '06
Starter for 10 '06
The Contractor '07
Going Postal '10
Ironclad '11
Neverland '11
There Be Dragons '11
Your Highness '11
Berlin Job '12
Secret State '12
Underworld: Awakening '12
Patrick '13
Dracula Untold '14
The Imitation Game '14
Child 44 '15
Underworld: Blood Wars '16
Euphoria '19

Hugh Dancy (1975-)
Black Hawk Down '01
Daniel Deronda '02
The Sleeping Dictionary '02
Tempo '03
Ella Enchanted '04
King Arthur '04
Elizabeth I '05
Shooting Dogs '05
Basic Instinct 2 '06
Blood & Chocolate '07
Evening '07
The Jane Austen Book Club '07
Savage Grace '07
Adam '09
Confessions of a Shopaholic '09
Coach '10
The Wildest Dream: The Conquest of Everest '10 (V)
Hysteria '11
Martha Marcy May Marlene '11
Our Idiot Brother '11
Legends of Oz: Dorothy's Return '14 (V)
Late Night '19

Tom D'Andrea (1909-98)
Humoresque '46
Never Say Goodbye '46
Dark Passage '47
Fighter Squadron '48
Kill the Umpire '50
The Next Voice You Hear '50

Dorothy Dandridge (1922-65)
Sundown '41
Lady from Louisiana '42
Since You Went Away '44
Tarzan's Peril '51
Bright Road '53
Carmen Jones '54
Island in the Sun '57
The Decks Ran Red '58

Evelyne Dandry (1939-)
Sitcom '97
Potiche '10

Eric Dane (1972-)
The Basket '99
Feast '06
Wedding Wars '06
X-Men: The Last Stand '06
Marley & Me '08
Burlesque '10
Valentine's Day '10

Karl (Daen) Dane (1886-1934)
The Big Parade '25
The Red Mill '27
The Trail of '98 '28
Navy Blues '29
Speedway '29
The Big House '30
Billy the Kid '30

Lawrence Dane (1937-)
It Seemed Like a Good Idea at the Time '75
Rituals '79
Happy Birthday to Me '81
Scanners '81
Clown Murders '83
Of Unknown Origin '83
The Good Fight '92
Lethal Lolita-Amy Fisher: My Story '92
It Takes Two '95
National Lampoon's Senior Trip '95
Bride of Chucky '98
Thrill Seekers '99
Waking the Dead '00
Still Small Voices '07
Behind the Wall '08
You Lucky Dog '10
A Very Merry Mix-Up '13

Patricia Dane (1918-95)
Grand Central Murder '42
Johnny Eager '42
Rio Rita '42

Somewhere I'll Find You *'42*
I Dood It *'43*

Paul Daneman (1925-2001)
Time Without Pity *'57*
Zulu *'64*
Oh! What a Lovely War *'69*
Tears in the Rain *'88*
G.B.H. *'91*

Claire Danes (1979-)
Little Women *'94*
Home for the Holidays *'95*
How to Make an American Quilt *'95*
To Gillian on Her 37th Birthday *'96*
William Shakespeare's Romeo and Juliet *'96*
I Love You, I Love You Not *'97*
John Grisham's The Rainmaker *'97*
Les Miserables *'97*
Polish Wedding *'97*
U-Turn *'97*
Princess Mononoke *'98 (V)*
Brokedown Palace *'99*
The Mod Squad *'99*
The Hours *'02*
Igby Goes Down *'02*
It's All About Love *'03*
Terminator 3: Rise of the Machines *'03*
Stage Beauty *'04*
The Family Stone *'05*
Shopgirl *'05*
Evening *'07*
The Flock *'07*
Stardust *'07*
Me and Orson Welles *'09*
Temple Grandin *'10*
As Cool As I Am *'13*
Brigsby Bear *'17*
A Kid Like Jake *'18*

Beverly D'Angelo (1951-)
The Sentinel *'76*
Annie Hall *'77*
Every Which Way But Loose *'78*
Hair *'79*
Coal Miner's Daughter *'80*
Honky Tonk Freeway *'81*
National Lampoon's Vacation *'83*
National Lampoon's European Vacation *'85*
Big Trouble *'86*
In the Mood *'87*
Maid to Order *'87*
Aria *'88*
High Spirits *'88*
National Lampoon's Christmas Vacation *'89*
Daddy's Dyin'. . . Who's Got the Will? *'90*
Pacific Heights *'90*
Lonely Hearts *'91*
Man Trouble *'92*
The Crazysitter *'94*
Lightning Jack *'94*
Edie & Pen *'95 (C)*
An Eye for an Eye *'95*
Vegas Vacation *'96*
Pterodactyl Woman from Beverly Hills *'97*
American History X *'98*
Illuminata *'98*
Lansky *'99*
Sugar Town *'99*
King of the Corner *'04*
Gamers *'06*
Relative Strangers *'06*
Harold & Kumar Escape from Guantanamo Bay *'08*
The House Bunny *'08*
Aussie and Ted's Great Adventure *'09*
Accidental Love *'15*
Vacation *'15*
Wakefield *'17*

Carlo D'Angelo (1919-73)
I, Vampiri *'56*
Secret Agent Super Dragon *'66*

Mirella D'Angelo (1956-)
Unsane *'82*
Apartment Zero *'88*

Rodney Dangerfield (1921-2004)
The Projectionist *'71*
Caddyshack *'80*
Easy Money *'83*
Back to School *'86*
Moving *'88*
Rover Dangerfield *'91 (V)*
Ladybugs *'92*
Natural Born Killers *'94*
Casper *'95 (C)*
Meet Wally Sparks *'97*
The Godson *'98*
Little Nicky *'00*
My 5 Wives *'00*
The 4th Tenor *'02*

Dani (1947-)
Day for Night *'73*
Avenue Montaigne *'06*

Brittany Daniel (1976-)
Joe Dirt *'01*
Club Dread *'04*
Rampage: The Hillside Strangler Murders *'04*
White Chicks *'04*
Loveless in Los Angeles *'07*
Skyline *'10*

Floriane Daniel (1971-)
Winter Sleepers *'97*
Cherry Blossoms *'08*

Gregg Daniel
Gun Shy *'00*
A Marine Story *'10*

Jennifer Daniel (1939-)
Kiss of the Vampire *'62*
The Reptile *'66*

Marek Daniel (1971-)
Up and Down *'04*
Something Like Happiness *'05*
The Country Teacher *'08*

Robert Pike Daniel
Half-Caste *'04*
Death Racers *'08*

Isa Danieli (1937-)
Macaroni *'85*
Ciao, Professore! *'94*

Henry Daniell (1894-1963)
Camille *'36*
The Unguarded Hour *'36*
The Firefly *'37*
Madame X *'37*
All This and Heaven Too *'40*
The Great Dictator *'40*
The Philadelphia Story *'40*
The Sea Hawk *'40*
A Woman's Face *'41*
Reunion in France *'42*
Sherlock Holmes and the Voice of Terror *'42*
Mission to Moscow *'43*
Sherlock Holmes in Washington *'43*
Watch on the Rhine *'43*
Jane Eyre *'44*
The Body Snatcher *'45*
The Bandit of Sherwood Forest *'46*
Song of Love *'47*
Wake of the Red Witch *'49*
The Woman in Green *'49*
The Egyptian *'54*
Diane *'55*
The Prodigal *'55*
Lust for Life *'56*
The Man in the Gray Flannel Suit *'56*
Les Girls *'57*
Witness for the Prosecution *'57*
Four Skulls of Jonathan Drake *'59*

Alex Daniels (1956-)
Cyborg *'89*
Star Kid *'97*
The Guardian *'06*

Anthony Daniels (1946-)
Star Wars *'77*
The Empire Strikes Back *'80*
Return of the Jedi *'83*
Star Wars: Episode 2-Attack of the Clones *'02*
Star Wars: Episode 3-Revenge of the Sith *'05*
Star Wars: The Clone Wars *'08 (V)*

Bebe Daniels (1901-71)
Male and Female *'19*
Why Change Your Wife? *'20*
Affairs of Anatol *'21*
Monsieur Beaucaire *'24*
Feel My Pulse *'28*
Rio Rita *'29*
Alias French Gertie *'30*
Dixiana *'30*
The Maltese Falcon *'31*
Counsellor-at-Law *'33*
42nd Street *'33*

Ben Daniels (1964-)
Beautiful Thing *'95*
David *'97*
Passion in the Desert *'97*
Madeline *'98*
Aristocrats *'99*
The Aristocrats *'99*
Britannic *'00*
Conspiracy *'01*
Doom *'05*
The State Within *'06*
Locke *'13*

Erin Daniels (1973-)
One Hour Photo *'02*
House of 1000 Corpses *'03*
Few Options *'11*
A Portrait of James Dean: Joshua Tree, 1951 *'12*

Gary Daniels (1963-)
Firepower *'93*
Deadly Target *'94*
Fist of the North Star *'95*
Heatseeker *'95*
Rage *'95*
White Tiger *'95*
American Streetfighter *'96*
Capital Punishment *'96*
Hawk's Vengeance *'96*
Riot *'96*
American Streetfighter 2: The Full Impact *'97*
Bloodmoon *'97*
Recoil *'97*
Cold Harvest *'98*
Spoiler *'98*
Delta Force One-The Lost Patrol *'99*
No Tomorrow *'99*
Queen's Messenger II *'01*
Retrograde *'03*
Across the Line: The Exodus of Charlie Wright *'10*
The Expendables *'10*
Game of Death *'10*
Hunt to Kill *'10*
Forced to Fight *'11*
The Mark *'12*
The Mark 2: Redemption *'13*
Misfire *'14*
Zero Tolerance *'15*
I Am Vengeance *'18*

J.D. Daniels (1980-)
Man's Best Friend *'93*
Roswell: The U.F.O. Cover-Up *'94*

Jeff Daniels (1955-)
Ragtime *'81*
Terms of Endearment *'83*
Marie *'85*
The Purple Rose of Cairo *'85*
Heartburn *'86*
Something Wild *'86*
Radio Days *'87*
The Caine Mutiny Court Martial *'88*
The House on Carroll Street *'88*
Sweet Hearts Dance *'88*
Checking Out *'89*
Arachnophobia *'90*
Welcome Home, Roxy Carmichael *'90*
The Butcher's Wife *'91*
Love Hurts *'91*
Grand Tour: Disaster in Time *'92*
Teamster Boss: The Jackie Presser Story *'92*
There Goes the Neighborhood *'92*
Gettysburg *'93*
Rain Without Thunder *'93*
Dumb & Dumber *'94*
Speed *'94*
Fly Away Home *'96*
101 Dalmatians *'96*
Trial and Error *'96*
Two Days in the Valley *'96*
My Favorite Martian *'98*
Pleasantville *'98*
It's the Rage *'99*
Chasing Sleep *'00*
Cheaters *'00*
The Crossing *'00*
Escanaba in da Moonlight *'01*
Blood Work *'02*
The Hours *'02*
Gods and Generals *'03*
I Witness *'03*
Super Sucker *'03*
Because of Winn-Dixie *'05*
Good Night, and Good Luck *'05*
Imaginary Heroes *'05*
The Squid and the Whale *'05*
Infamous *'06*
RV *'06*
The Lookout *'07*
Mama's Boy *'07*
Space Chimps *'08 (V)*
Sweet Nothing in My Ear *'08*
Traitor *'08*
The Answer Man *'09*
Away We Go *'09*
Paper Man *'09*
State of Play *'09*
Howl *'10*
Dumb and Dumber To *'14*
Steve Jobs *'15*
Allegiant *'16*
The Catcher Was a Spy *'18*

John Daniels
Candy Tangerine Man *'75*
Black Shampoo *'76*
Bare Knuckles *'77*

Mark Daniels (1916-90)
The Vanishing Virginian *'41*
Undercover Maisie *'47*

Phil Daniels (1958-)
Quadrophenia *'79*
Scum *'79*
Breaking Glass *'80*
Meantime *'81*
The Bride *'85*
Bad Behavior *'92*
Still Crazy *'98*
Chicken Run *'00 (V)*

William Daniels (1927-)
A Thousand Clowns *'65*
The Graduate *'67*
The President's Analyst *'67*
Two for the Road *'67*
Marlowe *'69*
1776 *'72*
The Parallax View *'74*
Black Sunday *'77*
Oh, God! *'77*
The Bastard *'78*
The One and Only *'78*
The Blue Lagoon *'80*
All Night Long *'81*
Reds *'81*
Rehearsal for Murder *'82*
Blind Date *'87*
Her Alibi *'88*

Lynn Danielson-Rosenthal
Out of the Dark *'88*
Mortuary Academy *'91*

Eli Danker (1948-)
Impulse *'90*
Special Forces *'03*
The Cutter *'05*
Undisputed 2: Last Man Standing *'06*
My Mom's New Boyfriend *'08*

Ran Danker
Eyes Wide Open *'09*
Rabies *'10*

Rick Danko (1943-99)
The Kids Are Alright *'79*
Man Outside *'88*

Roger Dann (1910-)
I Confess *'53*
Two for the Road *'67*

Blythe Danner (1944-)
1776 *'72*
Sidekicks *'74*
Hearts of the West *'75*
The Seagull *'75*
Futureworld *'76*
Love Affair: The Eleanor & Lou Gehrig Story *'77*
Too Far to Go *'79*
You Can't Take It With You *'79*
The Great Santini *'80*
Man, Woman & Child *'83*
Guilty Conscience *'85*
Brighton Beach Memoirs *'86*
Another Woman *'88*
Alice *'90*
Judgment *'90*
Mr. & Mrs. Bridge *'90*
Never Forget *'91*
The Prince of Tides *'91*
Husbands and Wives *'92*
Homage *'95*
Oldest Confederate Widow Tells All *'95*
To Wong Foo, Thanks for Everything, Julie Newmar *'95*
Mad City *'97*
The Myth of Fingerprints *'97*
The Proposition *'97*
Eye of the Storm *'98*
From the Earth to the Moon *'98*
No Looking Back *'98*
The X-Files *'98*
Forces of Nature *'99*
The Love Letter *'99*
Invisible Circus *'00*
Meet the Parents *'00*
Sylvia *'03*
Howl's Moving Castle *'04 (V)*
Meet the Fockers *'04*
The Last Kiss *'06*
The Sisterhood of the Traveling Pants 2 *'08*
The Lightkeepers *'09*
Little Fockers *'10*
Paul *'11*
Waiting for Forever *'11*
What's Your Number? *'11*
Detachment *'12*
Hello I Must Be Going *'12*
The Lucky One *'12*
Murder of a Cat *'14*
I'll See You in My Dreams *'15*
Tumbledown *'16*
What They Had *'18*
The Tomorrow Man *'19*

Sybil Danning (1952-)
Cat in the Cage *'68*
Bluebeard *'72*
God's Gun *'75*
The Prince and the Pauper *'78*
The Concorde: Airport '79 *'79*
Battle Beyond the Stars *'80*
Kill Castro *'80*
The Man with Bogart's Face *'80*
The Mercenaries *'80*
Daughter of Death *'82*
The Salamander *'82*
Separate Ways *'82*
Chained Heat *'83*
Hercules *'83*
Day of the Cobra *'84*
Jungle Warriors *'84*
They're Playing with Fire *'84*
Howling 2: Your Sister Is a Werewolf *'85*
Malibu Express *'85*
Private Passions *'85*
Young Lady Chatterly 2 *'85*
Reform School Girls *'86*
Amazon Women on the Moon *'87*
Phantom Empire *'87*
Virus X *'10*

Paul Dano (1984-)
L.I.E. *'01*
The Emperor's Club *'02*
Too Young to Be a Dad *'02*
The Girl Next Door *'04*
Taking Lives *'04*
The Ballad of Jack and Rose *'05*
The King *'05*
Fast Food Nation *'06*
Little Miss Sunshine *'06*
There Will Be Blood *'07*
Explicit Ills *'08*
Gigantic *'08*
The Good Heart *'09*
Taking Woodstock *'09*
Where the Wild Things Are *'09 (V)*
The Extra Man *'10*
Knight and Day *'10*
Meek's Cutoff *'10*
Cowboys & Aliens *'11*
Being Flynn *'12*
Looper *'12*
Ruby Sparks *'12*
Prisoners *'13*
12 Years a Slave *'13*
Love & Mercy *'15*
Youth *'15*
Swiss Army Man *'16*
Okja *'17*

Royal Dano (1922-94)
The Red Badge of Courage *'51*
Bend of the River *'52*
Johnny Guitar *'53*
The Trouble with Harry *'55*
All Mine to Give *'56*
Santiago *'56*
Tribute to a Bad Man *'56*
Crime of Passion *'57*
Man in the Shadow *'57*
Man of the West *'58*
Saddle the Wind *'58*
Face of Fire *'59*
The Adventures of Huckleberry Finn *'60*
7 Faces of Dr. Lao *'63*
The Last Challenge *'67*
Welcome to Hard Times *'67*
Death of a Gunfighter *'69*
Moon of the Wolf *'72*
Electra Glide in Blue *'73*
Big Bad Mama *'74*
Messiah of Evil *'74*
Wild Party *'74*
The Killer Inside Me *'76*
The Outlaw Josey Wales *'76*
The Right Stuff *'83*
Something Wicked This Way Comes *'83*
Teachers *'84*
Ghoulies 2 *'87*
House 2: The Second Story *'87*
Killer Klowns from Outer Space *'88*
Spaced Invaders *'90*
Texas Guns *'90*
The Dark Half *'91*

Cesare Danova (1926-92)
Loves of Three Queens *'54*
Valley of the Dragons *'61*
Tender Is the Night *'62*
Gidget Goes to Rome *'63*
Viva Las Vegas *'63*
Boy, Did I Get a Wrong Number! *'66*
Mean Streets *'73*
Tentacles *'77*
National Lampoon's Animal House *'78*
St. Helen's, Killer Volcano *'82*

Ted Danson (1947-)
The Onion Field *'79*
Once Upon a Spy *'80*
Body Heat *'81*
Creepshow *'82*
A Fine Mess *'86*
Just Between Friends *'86*
When the Bough Breaks *'86*
Three Men and a Baby *'87*
Cousins *'89*

Dad '89
Three Men and a Little Lady '90
Made in America '93
Getting Even with Dad '94
Pontiac Moon '94
Gulliver's Travels '95
Loch Ness '95
Homegrown '97 (C)
Jerry and Tom '98
Saving Private Ryan '98
Mumford '99
Talking to Heaven '02
Knights of the South Bronx '05
The Moguls '05
The Human Contract '08
Mad Money '08
Nobel Son '08
The Open Road '09 (C)
Big Miracle '12
The One I Love '14
Hearts Beat Loud '18

Joe Dante (1946-)
Cannonball '76
Code Name: Zebra '84
Sleepwalkers '92

Michael Dante (1931-)
Fort Dobbs '58
Westbound '58
Seven Thieves '60
Operation Bikini '63
Apache Rifles '64
Naked Kiss '64
Beyond Evil '80
Big Score '83
The Cage '89
Crazy Horse and Custer: 'The Untold Story' '90

Peter Dante (1968-)
Mr. Deeds '02
Grandma's Boy '06
Strange Wilderness '08

Helmut Dantine (1917-82)
Casablanca '42
Desperate Journey '42
Mrs. Miniver '42
To Be or Not to Be '42
Edge of Darkness '43
Mission to Moscow '43
Northern Pursuit '43
Watch on the Rhine '43
Hollywood Canteen '44
Passage to Marseilles '44
Whispering City '47
Stranger from Venus '54
Alexander the Great '55
War and Peace '56
Fraulein '58
Operation Crossbow '65
Bring Me the Head of Alfredo Garcia '74
The Killer Elite '75
The Wilby Conspiracy '75
The Fifth Musketeer '79

Niki Dantine (1934-)
The Power and the Prize '56
Malibu Express '85

Ray Danton (1931-92)
I'll Cry Tomorrow '55
A Majority of One '56
Onionhead '58
Tarawa Beachhead '58
Too Much, Too Soon '58
The Rise and Fall of Legs Diamond '60
A Fever In the Blood '61
The George Raft Story '61
The Chapman Report '62
The Longest Day '62
FBI Code 98 '63
Secret Agent Super Dragon '66
Jailbreakin' '72
The Centerfold Girls '74
Apache Blood '75
Six-Pack Annie '75

Mark Danvers
Third World Cop '99
Rude Boy: The Jamaican Don '03

Tony Danza (1951-)
The Hollywood Knights '80
Truth or Die '86
She's Out of Control '89
Last Action Hero '93 (C)
Angels in the Outfield '94
A Brooklyn State of Mind '97
Glam '97
Love to Kill '97
Don Jon '13

Maia Danziger (1950-)
Last Exit to Brooklyn '90
The Ice Storm '97

Ho Chung Dao (1950-)
See Bruce Li

Ingeborga Dapkounaite (1963-)
Burnt by the Sun '94
Seven Years in Tibet '97
In Tranzit '07
Farewell '09

Patti D'Arbanville (1951-)
Flesh '68
Bilitis '77
Big Wednesday '78
Time After Time '79
Modern Problems '81
The Boys Next Door '85
Real Genius '85
Fresh Horses '88
The Fan '96
Father's Day '96
Celebrity '98
Personal Velocity: Three Portraits '02
A Tale of Two Pizzas '03
You Belong to Me '07
The Wedding Bros. '08
Happy Tears '09
The Extra Man '10
Morning Glory '10

Patrika Darbo (1948-)
Daddy's Dyin'. . . Who's Got the Will? '90
Leaving Normal '92
Speed 2: Cruise Control '97
Madhouse '04
Hatchet '07

Kim Darby (1947-)
True Grit '69
The Strawberry Statement '70
The Grissom Gang '71
The People '71
The Streets of San Francisco '72
Don't Be Afraid of the Dark '73
Rich Man, Poor Man '76
The One and Only '78
Better Off Dead '85
Teen Wolf Too '87
Halloween 6: The Curse of Michael Myers '95
The Last Best Sunday '98
Newsbreak '00

Rhys Darby (1974-)
Yes Man '08
Diagnosis: Death '09
Pirate Radio '09
Jumanji: Welcome to the Jungle '17

Mireille Darc (1938-)
Please Not Now! '61
The Great Spy Chase '64
Weekend '67
The Peking Blond '68
The Tall Blond Man with One Black Shoe '72
Icy Breasts '75

Denise Darcel (1925-2011)
Battleground '49
Tarzan and the Slave Girl '50
Westward the Women '51
Young Man With Ideas '52
Vera Cruz '53

Alexander D'Arcy (1908-96)
The Awful Truth '37
Prisoner of Zenda '37
Stolen Holiday '37
Man on a Tightrope '53
Soldier of Fortune '55
Abdulla the Great '56
Blood of Dracula's Castle '69
Dead Pigeon on Beethoven Street '72

James D'Arcy (1975-)
A Dance to the Music of Time '97
The Trench '99
Sherlock: Case of Evil '02
Dot the I '03
Master and Commander: The Far Side of the World '03
Exorcist: The Beginning '04
An American Haunting '05
Mansfield Park '07
Rise: Blood Hunter '07
Flashbacks of a Fool '08
Into the Storm '09
Virtuality '09
W.E. '11
Hitchcock '12
In Their Skin '12
The Making of a Lady '12
Let's Be Cops '14
Guernica '16

Roy D'Arcy (1894-1969)
The Merry Widow '25
Bardelys the Magnificent '26
La Boheme '26
The Temptress '26
The Gay Buckaroo '32
Captain Calamity '36
Revolt of the Zombies '36

Kieran Darcy-Smith (1965-)
The Cave '05
The Square '08
The Reef '10

Dexter Darden (1991-)
Joyful Noise '12
Maze Runner: The Death Cure '18

Severn Darden (1929-95)
Goldstein '64
Dead Heat on a Merry-Go-Round '66
The President's Analyst '67
The Mad Room '69
They Shoot Horses, Don't They? '69
Pussycat, Pussycat, I Love You '70
Hired Hand '71
Vanishing Point '71
Werewolves on Wheels '71
Conquest of the Planet of the Apes '72
Battle for the Planet of the Apes '73
The Day of the Dolphin '73
I Wonder Who's Killing Her Now? '76
Jackson County Jail '76
Wanda Nevada '79
Saturday the 14th '81
Real Genius '85
Back to School '86

Irene Dare (1931-)
Frolics on Ice '39
Silver Skates '43

Florence Darel (1968-)
A Tale of Springtime '89
The Stolen Children '92
Don't Let Me Die on a Sunday '98
The Count of Monte Cristo '99

Bobby Darin (1936-73)
Come September '61
Too Late Blues '61
Hell Is for Heroes '62
If a Man Answers '62
Pressure Point '62
State Fair '62
Captain Newman, M.D. '63
That Funny Feeling '65
Gunfight in Abilene '67
The Happy Ending '69

Ricardo Darin (1957-)
Nine Queens '00
The Son of the Bride '01
The Aura '05
The Secret in Their Eyes '09
Carancho '10
Wild Tales '14
Everybody Knows '18

Christopher Dark (1920-71)
Suddenly '54
World Without End '56
The Halliday Brand '57

Samantha Dark
Ultrachrist! '03
Malevolence '04

Candy Darling (1944-74)
Flesh '68
Silent Night, Bloody Night '73

David Darlow
Road to Perdition '02
Were the World Mine '08

Linda Darlow
Immediate Family '89
The Amy Fisher Story '93
Connie and Carla '04
Cries in the Dark '06
The Secret of Hidden Lake '06
Angels Fall '07

Gerard Darmon (1948-)
Diva '82
Betty Blue '86
The Good Thief '03

Linda Darnell (1921-65)
Day-Time Wife '39
Brigham Young: Frontiersman '40
Chad Hanna '40
The Mark of Zorro '40
Star Dust '40
Blood and Sand '41
City Without Men '43
Buffalo Bill '44
It Happened Tomorrow '44
Summer Storm '44
Sweet and Low-Down '44
Fallen Angel '45
Hangover Square '45
Anna and the King of Siam '46
My Darling Clementine '46
Forever Amber '47
Unfaithfully Yours '48
A Letter to Three Wives '49
Slattery's Hurricane '49
No Way Out '50
Blackbeard the Pirate '52
Island of Desire '52
Dakota Incident '56
Zero Hour! '57

James Darren (1936-)
Rumble on the Docks '56
The Brothers Rico '57
Operation Mad Ball '57
The Gene Krupa Story '59
Gidget '59
Gidget Goes Hawaiian '61
The Guns of Navarone '61
Diamond Head '62
Gidget Goes to Rome '63
Hey There, It's Yogi Bear '64 (V)
The Lively Set '64
Venus in Furs '70
City Beneath the Sea '71

Danielle Darrieux (1917-)
Mauvaise Graine '33
Mayerling '36
The Rage of Paris '38
La Ronde '51
Rich, Young and Pretty '51
Five Fingers '52
Le Plaisir '52
The Earrings of Madame De. . . '54
Alexander the Great '55
Lady Chatterley's Lover '55
Murder By Two '60
Murder at 45 R.P.M. '65
The Young Girls of Rochefort '68
L'Annee Sainte '76
Scene of the Crime '87
8 Women '02
Dangerous Liaisons '03
Persepolis '07 (V)
Towards Zero '07

Frankie Darro (1917-76)
Kiki '26
Lightning Warrior '31
Vanishing Legion '31
Devil Horse '32
The Mayor of Hell '33
Tugboat Annie '33
Wild Boys of the Road '33
Broadway Bill '34
Little Men '34
The Merry Frinks '34
No Greater Glory '34
The Phantom Empire '35
Pinocchio '40 (V)
Junior G-Men of the Air '42
Westward the Women '51
Forbidden Planet '56
Runaways '75

Jean-Pierre Darroussin (1953-)
Un Air de Famille '96
Marius and Jeannette '97
La Buche '00
The Town Is Quiet '00
Red Lights '04
How Much Do You Love Me? '05
The Army of Crime '10
22 Bullets '10
The Well-Digger's Daughter '11

Barbara Darrow (1931-)
Queen of Outer Space '58
Tall Story '60

Henry Darrow (1933-)
Computer Wizard '77
Where's Willie? '77
Death Blow '87
The Last of the Finest '90
Mom, Can I Keep Her? '98
Tequila Body Shots '99
A Girl Like Me: The Gwen Araujo Story '06
Soda Springs '11

John Darrow (1907-80)
Hell's Angels '30
The Lady Refuses '31
The Midnight Lady '32

Tony Darrow (1946-)
Goodfellas '90
Me and the Mob '94
Analyze This '98
Small Time Crooks '00
Searching for Bobby D '05
Kill the Irishman '11

Agam Darshi
Civic Duty '06
American Venus '07

Kammy Darweish
The Hamburg Cell '04
31 North 62 East '09

Jane Darwell (1879-1967)
Hot Saturday '32
Design for Living '33
Finishing School '33
One Sunday Afternoon '33
Bright Eyes '34
Curly Top '35
Life Begins at Forty '35
Paddy O'Day '35
Captain January '36
Little Miss Nobody '36
Private Number '36
Ramona '36
White Fang '36
Love Is News '37
Nancy Steele Is Missing '37
Slave Ship '37
Little Miss Broadway '38
Three Blind Mice '38
Gone with the Wind '39
Jesse James '39
The Rains Came '39
Brigham Young: Frontiersman '40
Chad Hanna '40
The Grapes of Wrath '40
The Devil & Daniel Webster '41
All Through the Night '42
The Ox-Bow Incident '43
Sunday Dinner for a Soldier '44
I Live in Grosvenor Square '46
My Darling Clementine '46
Three Godfathers '48
Caged '50
The Daughter of Rosie O'Grady '50
Three Husbands '50
Wagon Master '50
Excuse My Dust '51
The Lemon Drop Kid '51
We're Not Married '52
The Bigamist '53
There's Always Tomorrow '56
The Last Hurrah '58

Deepti Daryanani
The Cheetah Girls: One World '08
Acceptance '09

Nandita Das (1969-)
Fire '96
Earth '98
Before the Rains '07

Stacey Dash (1967-)
Moving '88
Mo' Money '92
Renaissance Man '94
Clueless '95
Cold Around the Heart '97
Personals '00
Paper Soldiers '02
Gang of Roses '03
Getting Played '05
I Could Never Be Your Woman '06
Soldiers of Change '06
Ghost Image '07
Nora's Hair Salon 2: A Cut Above '08
Cyborg Conquest '09
Phantom Punch '09
First Lady '20

Jules Dassin (1911-2008)
Rififi '54
Never on Sunday '60
Phaedra '61 (C)

Patrick D'Assumcao
Stranger by the Lake '13
I Lost My Body '19

Jean Daste (1904-94)
Boudu Saved from Drowning '32
L'Atalante '34
The Crime of Monsieur Lange '36
Grand Illusion '37
La Guerre Est Finie '66
The Wild Child '70
The Green Room '78
Love Unto Death '84

Alex Datcher (1962-)
Passenger 57 '92
Rage and Honor '92
Body Bags '93

Kristin Dattilo-Hayward (1970-)
Mirror, Mirror '90
Coronado '03

Brigitta Dau
The Inheritance '97
Retro Puppet Master '99

James Daughton (1950-)
Malibu Beach '78
Blind Date '84

Claude Dauphin (1903-78)
April in Paris '52
Casque d'Or '52
Le Plaisir '52
Stop Me Before I Kill! '60
Tiara Tahiti '62
Lady L '65
Is Paris Burning? '66
Two for the Road '67
Hard Contract '69
The Madwoman of Chaillot '69
The Tenant '76
Les Miserables '78

Jareb Dauplaise (1979-)
Meet the Spartans '08
Frat Party '09

The Prankster '10
Cougar Hunting '11

Alexa Davalos (1982-)
And Starring Pancho Villa as Himself '03
The Chronicles of Riddick '04
Feast of Love '07
The Mist '07
Defiance '08
Clash of the Titans '10

Richard (Dick) Davalos (1930-)
East of Eden '54
Sea Chase '55
Cool Hand Luke '67
Pit Stop '67
Kelly's Heroes '70
Blood Legacy '73
Something Wicked This Way Comes '83

Harry Davenport (1866-1949)
The Case of the Black Cat '36
Fit for a King '37
The Cowboy and the Lady '38
Marie Antoinette '38
You Can't Take It with You '38
Exile Express '39
Gone with the Wind '39
The Hunchback of Notre Dame '39
Juarez '39
The Story of Alexander Graham Bell '39
All This and Heaven Too '40
Foreign Correspondent '40
Lucky Partners '40
Too Many Husbands '40
The Bride Came C.O.D. '41
One Foot in Heaven '41
That Uncertain Feeling '41
Larceny, Inc. '42
Son of Fury '42
The Amazing Mrs. Holiday '43
Government Girl '43
The Ox-Bow Incident '43
Princess O'Rourke '43
Jack London '44
Kismet '44
Meet Me in St. Louis '44
The Thin Man Goes Home '44
The Enchanted Forest '45
She Wouldn't Say Yes '45
Courage of Lassie '46
The Bachelor and the Bobby-Soxer '47
Stallion Road '47
For the Love of Mary '48
Three Daring Daughters '48
Tell It to the Judge '49
Riding High '50
That Forsyte Woman '50
December 7th: The Movie '91

Jack Davenport (1973-)
Catherine Cookson's The Moth '96
Immortality '98
Ultraviolet '98
Russell Mulcahy's Tale of the Mummy '99
The Talented Mr. Ripley '99
The Wyvern Mystery '00
Pirates of the Caribbean: The Curse of the Black Pearl '03
The Incredible Journey of Mary Bryant '05
The Libertine '05
The Wedding Date '05
Pirates of the Caribbean: Dead Man's Chest '06
Pirates of the Caribbean: At World's End '07
Pirate Radio '09
Kingsman: The Secret Service '15
Guernica '16
A United Kingdom '17

Lucy Davenport
Soho Square '00
Sylvia '03
If Only '04

Madison Davenport (1996-)
Humboldt County '08
Kit Kittredge: An American Girl '08
Jack and the Beanstalk '09
The Possession '12

Mary Davenport
Sisters '73
Home Movies '79

Nigel Davenport (1928-2013)
Peeping Tom '60
Ladies Who Do '63
Sands of the Kalahari '65
Where the Spies Are '65
A Man for All Seasons '66
Sinful Davey '69
The Virgin Soldiers '69
The Mind of Mr. Soames '70
No Blade of Grass '70
The Last Valley '71
Mary, Queen of Scots '71
Villain '71
Living Free '72
Dracula '73
Phase 4 '74
Picture of Dorian Gray '74
The Island of Dr. Moreau '77
Zulu Dawn '79
Cry of the Innocent '80
The Ordeal of Dr. Mudd '80
Soul Patrol '80
Chariots of Fire '81
Nighthawks '81
A Christmas Carol '84
Greystoke: The Legend of Tarzan, Lord of the Apes '84
Caravaggio '86
Mountbatten: The Last Viceroy '86
Without a Clue '88

Brett Davern
Beautiful Ohio '06
The Pool Boys '10
Born to Race: Fast Track '14
Love & Mercy '15

Seamus Davey-Fitzpatrick (1998-)
The Omen '06
The Dinner '17

Robert Davi (1953-)
The Goonies '85
Die Hard '88
License to Kill '89
Maniac Cop 2 '90
Peacemaker '90
Predator 2 '90
White Hot: The Mysterious Murder of Thelma Todd '91
Center of the Web '92
Wild Orchid 2: Two Shades of Blue '92
Maniac Cop 3: Badge of Silence '93
Mardi Gras for the Devil '93
Quick '93
Son of the Pink Panther '93
Blind Justice '94
Cops and Robbersons '94
No Contest '94
Body Count '95
Showgirls '95
An Occasional Hell '96
The Bad Pack '98
My Little Assassin '99
The 4th Tenor '02
The Hot Chick '02
Verdict in Blood '02
One Last Ride '03
Call Me: The Rise and Fall of Heidi Fleiss '04
In the Mix '05
The Butcher '07
The Dukes '07
An American Carol '08
Ballistica '10
Game of Death '10
Magic Man '10
Kill the Irishman '11
Swamp Shark '11
The Iceman '12
Asteroid vs. Earth '14

Jacob Davich (1990-)
The Adventures of Sharkboy and Lavagirl in 3-D '05
The Virginity Hit '10

Alki David
Opa! '05
Fishtales '07

Angel David
Mixed Blood '84
The Crow '93
The Substitute 2: School's Out '97
Two Girls and a Guy '98

Charlie David (1980-)
A Four Letter Word '07
Mulligans '08
Judas Kiss '11

Clifford David (1932-)
The Last Mile '59
Resurrection '80

DeRay David
Code Name: The Cleaner '07
21 Jump Street '12

Eleanor David (1956-)
Pink Floyd: The Wall '82
The Scarlet Pimpernel '82
84 Charing Cross Road '86
Slipstream '89
The Guilty '92
Topsy Turvy '99

Ellen David
Random Encounter '98
Dr. Jekyll and Mr. Hyde '08

Joanna David (1947-)
Cotton Mary '99
The Way We Live Now '02

Karen Shenaz David
The Color of Magic '08
The Scorpion King 2: Rise of a Warrior '08

Keith David (1954-)
The Thing '82
Platoon '86
Off Limits '87
Bird '88
They Live '88
Always '89
Marked for Death '90
Men at Work '90
Article 99 '92
Final Analysis '92
The Last Outlaw '93
Gargoyles, The Movie: The Heroes Awaken '94 (V)
The Puppet Masters '94
Blue in the Face '95
Clockers '95
Dead Presidents '95
An Eye for an Eye '95
The Quick and the Dead '95
johns '96
Larger Than Life '96
Don King: Only in America '97
Executive Target '97
Todd McFarlane's Spawn '97 (V)
Volcano '97
Armageddon '98
There's Something about Mary '98
The Tiger Woods Story '98
Innocents '00
Pitch Black '00
The Replacements '00
Requiem for a Dream '00
Where the Heart Is '00
Final Fantasy: The Spirits Within '01 (V)
Novocaine '01
Seduced: Pretty When You Cry '01
Barbershop '02
Agent Cody Banks '03
Head of State '03
Hollywood Homicide '03
Kaena: The Prophecy '03 (V)
29 Palms '03
Agent Cody Banks 2: Destination London '04
The Chronicles of Riddick '04
Crash '05
Mr. & Mrs. Smith '05
Transporter 2 '05
ATL '06
Behind Enemy Lines 2: Axis of Evil '06
The Oh in Ohio '06
The Butcher '07
Chasing 3000 '07
Delta Farce '07
The Last Sentinel '07
Transformers '07 (V)
Against the Dark '08
Behind Enemy Lines 3: Colombia '08
The Fifth Commandment '08
First Sunday '08
Lost Treasure of the Maya '08
S.I.S. '08
Coraline '09 (V)
Don McKay '09
Endgame '09
The Hitman Diaries '09
The Princess and the Frog '09 (V)
Chain Letter '10
Death at a Funeral '10
The Inheritance '10
The Lottery Ticket '10
Meet Monica Velour '10
Stomp the Yard 2: Homecoming '10
Hopelessly in June '11
Christmas in Compton '12
Cloud Atlas '12
Field of Lost Shoes '14
The North Star '16
Night School '18
The Wedding Year '19

Larry David (1947-)
Whatever Works '09
The Three Stooges '12

Lolita David (1961-)
See Lolita Davidovich

Mark David (1974-)
Five Minutes of Heaven '09
Small Island '09

Thayer David (1927-78)
Journey to the Center of the Earth '59
The Story of Ruth '60
House of Dark Shadows '70
Night of Dark Shadows '71
Savages '72
Save the Tiger '73
The Eiger Sanction '75
The Duchess and the Dirtwater Fox '76
Rocky '76

Lolita Davidovich (1961-)
Adventures in Babysitting '87
Big Town '87
Blaze '89
The Inner Circle '91
JFK '91 (C)
The Object of Beauty '91
Leap of Faith '92
Raising Cain '92
Boiling Point '93
Intersection '93
Cobb '94
For Better or Worse '95
Harvest of Fire '95
Indictment: The McMartin Trial '95
Now and Then '95
Dead Silence '96
Jungle 2 Jungle '96
Touch '96
Santa Fe '97
Gods and Monsters '98
Mystery, Alaska '99
No Vacancy '99
Play It to the Bone '99
Snow in August '01
Steve Martini's The Judge '01
Dark Blue '03
Hollywood Homicide '03
Kill Your Darlings '06
September Dawn '07
Cinema Verite '11

Amy Davidson (1979-)
Annie's Point '05
Netherbeast Incorporated '07
The Capture of the Green River Killer '08

Ben Davidson (1940-)
The Black Six '74
Conan the Barbarian '82

Bruce Davidson
Touched '05
The Librarian: Curse of the Judas Chalice '08

Eileen Davidson (1959-)
The House on Sorority Row '83
Easy Wheels '89

Jack Davidson (1936-)
Shock Waves '77
Baby It's You '82
You Tell Me '06

Jaye Davidson (1968-)
The Crying Game '92
Stargate '94

John Davidson (1886-1968)
Monsieur Beaucaire '24
Bombay Mail '34
Tailspin Tommy '34

John Davidson (1941-)
The Happiest Millionaire '67
The Concorde: Airport '79 '79
The Squeeze '87
Edward Scissorhands '90

Pete Davidson
Big Time Adolescence '20
The King of Staten Island '20

Tommy Davidson (1965-)
Strictly Business '91
Ace Ventura: When Nature Calls '95
Booty Call '96
Plump Fiction '97
Woo '97
Pros & Cons '99
Bamboozled '00
Juwanna Mann '02
The Proud Family Movie '05 (V)
Black Dynamite '09

William B. Davidson (1888-1947)
Painted Faces '29
The Silver Horde '30
Held for Murder '32
I'm No Angel '33
The Singing Kid '36
They Were Expendable '45

Embeth Davidtz (1965-)
Army of Darkness '92
Schindler's List '93
Feast of July '95
Murder in the First '95
Matilda '96
Fallen '97
The Gingerbread Man '97
Bicentennial Man '99
Mansfield Park '99
Bridget Jones's Diary '01
The Hole '01
13 Ghosts '01
The Emperor's Club '02
Junebug '05
Fracture '07
Fragments '08
3 Backyards '10
The Girl With the Dragon Tattoo '11
The Amazing Spider-Man '12
Europa Report '13
Paranoia '13

Ben Davies
Courageous '11
I'm Not Ashamed '16
Texas Rein '16
Overcomer '19

Betty Ann Davies (1910-55)
It Always Rains on Sunday '47
The Blue Lamp '49
The Belles of St. Trinian's '53
Grand National Night '53
Blackout '54
Alias John Preston '56

Gwen Ffrangcon Davies (1891-)
The Witches '66
The Devil Rides Out '68

Jakob Davies
The Tall Man '12
If I Stay '14

Jeremy Davies (1969-)
Spanking the Monkey '94
Twister '96
Going All the Way '97
The Locusts '97
Saving Private Ryan '98
The Million Dollar Hotel '99
Ravenous '99
Up at the Villa '00
CQ '01
Intimate Affairs '01
The Laramie Project '02
Searching for Paradise '02
Secretary '02
Solaris '02
Dogville '03
29 Palms '03
Manderlay '05
Rescue Dawn '06

John Howard Davies (1939-2011)
Oliver Twist '48
The Rocking Horse Winner '49
Tom Brown's School Days '51

Kimberly Davies (1973-)
Twisted '96
Psycho Beach Party '00

Marion Davies (1897-1961)
Little Old New York '23
The Red Mill '27
The Patsy '28
Show People '28
The Bachelor Father '31
Five and Ten '31
Polly of the Circus '32
Going Hollywood '33
Operator 13 '34
Cain and Mabel '36

Morgana Davies
The Tree '10
The Hunter '12

Oliver Ford Davies (1939-)
Cause Celebre '87
Star Wars: Episode 1-The Phantom Menace '99
Star Wars: Episode 2-Attack of the Clones '02
The Way We Live Now '02
Johnny English '03
The Mother '03
Star Wars: Episode 3-Revenge of the Sith '05
Christopher Robin '18

Ray Davies (1944-)
Return to Waterloo '85
Absolute Beginners '86

Rudi Davies (1967-)
The Lonely Passion of Judith Hearne '87
The Object of Beauty '91

Rupert Davies (1916-76)
The Spy Who Came in from the Cold '65
Target for Killing '66
The Conqueror Worm '68
The Crimson Cult '68
Dracula Has Risen from the Grave '68
Zeppelin '71
Frightmare '74

Stephen Davies
The Long Good Friday '80
The Whoopee Boys '86
Hanoi Hilton '87

The Nest '88
Bloodfist 7: Manhunt '95
Dillinger and Capone '95
Tattoo, a Love Story '02
Tamara Davies (1972-)
Project Viper '02
Scorcher '02
Black Dawn '05
Luis Davila (1927-98)
Carnival of Crime '62
Espionage in Tangiers '65
Make Your Bets Ladies '65
Pancho Villa '72
Alex Davion (1929-)
Paranoiac '62
Blind Corner '63
Plague of the Zombies '66
Valley of the Dolls '67
The Bloodsuckers '70
Ann B. Davis (1926-2014)
Lover Come Back '61
Naked Gun 33 1/3: The Final Insult '94 (C)
The Brady Bunch Movie '95 (C)
Bette Davis (1908-89)
Hell's House '32
The Man Who Played God '32
Parachute Jumper '32
The Rich Are Always With Us '32
Bureau of Missing Persons '33
20,000 Years in Sing Sing '33
The Working Man '33
Fashions of 1934 '34
Fog Over Frisco '34
Housewife '34
Jimmy the Gent '34
Of Human Bondage '34
Bordertown '35
Dangerous '35
Front Page Woman '35
The Girl from 10th Ave. '35
The Golden Arrow '36
Petrified Forest '36
Satan Met a Lady '36
It's Love I'm After '37
Kid Galahad '37
Marked Woman '37
That Certain Woman '37
Jezebel '38
The Sisters '38
Dark Victory '39
Juarez '39
The Old Maid '39
The Private Lives of Elizabeth & Essex '39
All This and Heaven Too '40
The Letter '40
The Bride Came C.O.D. '41
The Great Lie '41
The Little Foxes '41
The Man Who Came to Dinner '41
In This Our Life '42
Now, Voyager '42
Old Acquaintance '43
Thank Your Lucky Stars '43
Watch on the Rhine '43
Hollywood Canteen '44
Mr. Skeffington '44
The Corn Is Green '45
Deception '46
A Stolen Life '46
Winter Meeting '48
All About Eve '50
Payment on Demand '51
Another Man's Poison '52
Phone Call from a Stranger '52
The Star '52
The Virgin Queen '55
The Catered Affair '56
Storm Center '56
The Scapegoat '59
Pocketful of Miracles '61
What Ever Happened to Baby Jane? '62
Dead Ringer '64
Where Love Has Gone '64
Hush, Hush, Sweet Charlotte '65
The Nanny '65
The Anniversary '68
Madame Sin '71
Burnt Offerings '76
Death on the Nile '78
Return from Witch Mountain '78
Family Reunion '81
The Watcher in the Woods '81
Agatha Christie's Murder with Mirrors '85
The Whales of August '87
Wicked Stepmother '89
Brad Davis (1949-91)
Sybil '76
The Campus Corpse '77
Midnight Express '78
A Small Circle of Friends '80
Chariots of Fire '81
Querelle '83
Cold Steel '87
Heart '87
The Caine Mutiny Court Martial '88
Rosalie Goes Shopping '89
The Plot to Kill Hitler '90
Robert Kennedy and His Times '90
Hangfire '91
The Player '92
Brianne Davis (1982-)
Swedish Auto '06
The Haunting of Marsten Manor '07
American Virgin '09
Synchronicity '16
Dead Water '19
Carole (Raphaelle) Davis (1958-)
The Flamingo Kid '84
Mannequin '87
The Shrimp on the Barbie '90
If Looks Could Kill '91
Cassi Davis (1964-)
Madea's Big Happy Family '11
Boo! A Madea Halloween '16
Boo 2! A Madea Halloween '17
A Madea Family Funeral '19
Clifton Davis (1945-)
Little Ladies of the Night '77
Scott Joplin '77
Kingdom Come '01
Max Keeble's Big Move '01
Halloweentown High '04
Soldiers of Change '06
Cover '08
Dana Davis (1978-)
Raise Your Voice '04
Prom Night '08
Relative Stranger '09
DeRay Davis
The Fog '05
Jiminy Glick in LaLa Wood '05
Who Made the Potatoe Salad? '05
The Hit '06
License to Wed '07
My Girlfriend's Back '10
Don S. Davis (1942-2008)
Suspicious River '00
Savage Island '03
Beneath '07
Loch Ness Terror '07
The Still Life '07
Far Cry '08
The Unquiet '08
Vipers '08
Wyvern '09
Dorothy Davis
Night Fright '67
The Little Girl Who Lives down the Lane '76
Drew Davis
Taken From Me: The Tiffany Rubin Story '10
All Hallow's Eve 2 '15
Duane Davis
Diggstown '92
Final Shot: The Hank Gathers Story '92
The Program '93
Rocky Marciano '99
Angels in the Infield '00
The Base 2: Guilty as Charged '00
Paparazzi '04
Essie Davis (1970-)
Lilian's Story '95
River Street '95
Kings in Grass Castles '97
After the Deluge '03
Code 46 '03
Girl with a Pearl Earring '03
The Matrix Revolutions '03
Charlotte's Web '06
The Silence '06
Hey Hey It's Esther Blueberger '08
Legend of the Guardians: The Owls of Ga'Hoole '10 (V)
Burning Man '11
Cloudstreet '11
The Babadook '14
True History of the Kelly Gang '20
Frank Davis
Return of the Killer Tomatoes! '88
Killer Tomatoes Strike Back '90
G. Paul Davis (1969-)
See Litefoot
Gail Davis (1925-97)
Cow Town '50
Flying Leathernecks '51
Alias Jesse James '59 (C)
Geena Davis (1957-)
Tootsie '82
Fletch '85
Secret Weapons '85
Transylvania 6-5000 '85
The Fly '86
The Accidental Tourist '88
Beetlejuice '88
Earth Girls Are Easy '89
Quick Change '90
Thelma & Louise '91
Hero '92
A League of Their Own '92
Angie '94
Speechless '94
Cutthroat Island '95
The Long Kiss Goodnight '96
Stuart Little '99
Stuart Little 2 '02
Stuart Little 3: Call of the Wild '06 (V)
Accidents Happen '09
Coma '12
In a World... '13
Marjorie Prime '17
Hope Davis (1964-)
Kiss of Death '94
The Daytrippers '96
The Myth of Fingerprints '97
The Imposters '98
Next Stop, Wonderland '98
Arlington Road '99
Mumford '99
Joe Gould's Secret '00
Final '01
Hearts in Atlantis '01
About Schmidt '02
The Secret Lives of Dentists '02
American Splendor '03
Duma '05
Proof '05
The Weather Man '05
The Hoax '06
Infamous '06
The Matador '06
Charlie Bartlett '07
The Nines '07
A Summer in Genoa '08
Synecdoche, New York '08
The Lodger '09
The Family Tree '10
The Special Relationship '10
Mildred Pierce '11
Real Steel '11
Louder Than Words '14
Wild Card '15
Jason Davis
A Little Bit of Heaven '11
Seeking Justice '12
Jeff Bryan Davis (1973-)
Evil Remains '04
Amigo Undead '15
Jim Davis (1915-81)
The Romance of Rosy Ridge '47
Hi-Jacked '50
Three Desperate Men '50
Cavalry Scout '51
Little Big Horn '51
Woman They Almost Lynched '53
Guns Don't Argue '57
Monster from Green Hell '58
Alias Jesse James '59
Noose for a Gunman '60
Frontier Uprising '61
Iron Angel '64
Jesse James Meets Frankenstein's Daughter '65
Zebra in the Kitchen '65
El Dorado '67
Gun Riders '69
Monte Walsh '70
Dracula *vs.* Frankenstein '71
Bad Company '72
Deliver Us From Evil '73
The Choirboys '77
Comes a Horseman '78
Day Time Ended '80
Joan Davis (1907-61)
On the Avenue '37
Thin Ice '37
Just Around the Corner '38
My Lucky Star '38
Sally, Irene and Mary '38
Day-Time Wife '39
Tail Spin '39
Hold That Ghost '41
Show Business '44
George White's Scandals '45
If You Knew Susie '48
Love That Brute '50
The Groom Wore Spurs '51
Harem Girl '52
Johnnie Davis
Cowboy from Brooklyn '38
Garden of the Moon '38
Josie Davis (1973-)
Carolina Moon '07
The Trouble with Romance '09
The Perfect Student '11
Judy Davis (1955-)
High Rolling in a Hot Corvette '77
My Brilliant Career '79
The Winter of Our Dreams '82
A Woman Called Golda '82
A Passage to India '84
High Tide '87
Alice '90
Impromptu '90
Barton Fink '91
Naked Lunch '91
Where Angels Fear to Tread '91
Husbands and Wives '92
The Ref '93
The New Age '94
Children of the Revolution '95
Serving in Silence: The Margarethe Cammermeyer Story '95
Blood & Wine '96
Absolute Power '97
Deconstructing Harry '97
Celebrity '98
Gaudi Afternoon '01
Life with Judy Garland-Me and My Shadows '01
The Man Who Sued God '01
Swimming Upstream '03
Coast to Coast '04
The Break-Up '06
A Little Thing Called Murder '06
Marie Antoinette '06
The Starter Wife '07
Page Eight '11
To Rome with Love '12
The Young and Prodigious T.S. Spivet '15
The Dressmaker '16
Julia Davis (1966-)
Power Play '02
Wilbur Wants to Kill Himself '02
Persuasion '07
Kristin Davis (1965-)
Doom Asylum '88
Alien Nation: Body and Soul '95
Nine Months '95
Atomic Train '99
Take Me Home: The John Denver Story '00
The Adventures of Sharkboy and Lavagirl in 3-D '05
Deck the Halls '06
The Shaggy Dog '06
Sex and the City: The Movie '08
Couples Retreat '09
Sex and the City 2 '10
Journey 2: The Mysterious Island '12
Of Two Minds '12
Holiday in the Wild '19
Kyle Davis (1978-)
The Last Lovecraft: Relic of Cthulhu '09
Into the Storm '14
Lex Scott Davis (1991-)
The First Purge '18
SuperFly '18
Lisa Davis (1936-)
The Dalton Girls '57
Queen of Outer Space '58
101 Dalmatians '61 (V)
Edge of Sanity '89
Lucy Davis (1973-)
Shaun of the Dead '04
Garfield: A Tail of Two Kitties '06
The TV Set '06
Bob Funk '09
Mac Davis (1942-)
North Dallas Forty '79
The Sting 2 '83
Angel's Dance '99
Possums '99
Jackpot '01
Mackenzie Davis (1987-)
Breathe In '13
What If '13
Bad Turn Worse '14
That Awkward Moment '14
Freaks of Nature '15
Always Shine '16
Tully '18
Terminator: Dark Fate '19
Marvin Davis (1931-2005)
The Fighting Sullivans '42
Tomorrow the World '44
Matthew Davis (1978-)
Tigerland '00
Urban Legends 2: Final Cut '00
Legally Blonde '01
Below '02
Blue Crush '02
Lone Star State of Mind '02
Heights '04
Seeing Other People '04
BloodRayne '06
Finding Bliss '09
S. Darko: A Donnie Darko Tale '09
Waiting for Forever '11
Michael Cory Davis (1977-)
The Vault '00
Raptor Island '04
Alien Apocalypse '05
Nancy Davis (1921-2016)
The Doctor and the Girl '49
East Side, West Side '49
The Next Voice You Hear '50
It's a Big Country '51
Donovan's Brain '53
Hellcats of the Navy '57
Crash Landing '58
Nathan Davis (1917-2008)
Code of Silence '85
Shaking the Tree '92
Dunston Checks In '95
Holes '03
Ossie Davis (1917-2005)
No Way Out '50
Gone Are the Days '63
Purlie Victorious '63
The Hill '65
A Man Called Adam '66
The Scalphunters '68
Night Gallery '69
Sam Whiskey '69
Let's Do It Again '75
Roots '77
King '78
Hot Stuff '80
Harry & Son '84
Avenging Angel '85
School Daze '88
Do the Right Thing '89
Joe Versus the Volcano '90
Jungle Fever '91
Gladiator '92
Grumpy Old Men '93
Queen '93
The Client '94
Stephen King's The Stand '94
The Android Affair '95
Get On the Bus '96
I'm Not Rappaport '96
Miss Evers' Boys '97
Dr. Dolittle '98
Dinosaur '00 (V)
Finding Buck McHenry '00
Anne Rice's The Feast of All Saints '01
Baadasssss! '03
Bubba Ho-Tep '03
She Hate Me '04
Owen Davis, Jr. (1907-49)
They Had to See Paris '29
All Quiet on the Western Front '30
Murder On a Bridle Path '36
The Plot Thickens '36
Philip Davis (1953-)
Who's Who '78
Quadrophenia '79
Grown Ups '80
The Bounty '84
High Hopes '88
Howling 5: The Rebirth '89
Face '97
Photographing Fairies '97
Still Crazy '98
Vera Drake '04
Like Father Like Son '05
Beau Brummell: This Charming Man '06
Five Days '07
Collision '09
Dead Man Running '09
Another Year '10
The Big I Am '10
Brighton Rock '10
Outside Bet '12
Phyllis E. Davis (1940-2013)
Beyond the Valley of the Dolls '70
Sweet Sugar '72
Terminal Island '73
Roger Davis (1939-)
House of Dark Shadows '70
Ruby '77
Sammi Davis (1964-)
Mona Lisa '86
Hope and Glory '87
Pack of Lies '87
Prayer for the Dying '87
Consuming Passions '88
The Lair of the White Worm '88
The Rainbow '89
Four Rooms '95
Stand-Ins '97

Sammy Davis, Jr. (1925-90)
Ocean's 11 *'60*
Sergeants 3 *'62*
Johnny Cool *'63*
Robin and the 7 Hoods *'64*
A Man Called Adam *'66*
Salt & Pepper *'68*
Sweet Charity *'69*
One More Time *'70*
Gone with the West *'72*
Little Moon & Jud McGraw *'78*
Cannonball Run *'81*
Cracking Up *'83*
Cannonball Run 2 *'84*
Alice in Wonderland *'85*
That's Dancing! *'85*
Moon over Parador *'88*
Tap *'89*

Sonny Carl Davis
Bad Channels *'92*
Seedpeople *'92*

Stringer Davis (1896-1973)
The Runaway Bus *'54*
The Smallest Show on Earth *'57*
Murder at the Gallop *'63*

Tom Davis (1952-2012)
Tunnelvision *'76*
All You Need Is Cash *'78*
Trading Places *'83*

Viola Davis (1952-)
Antwone Fisher *'02*
Far from Heaven *'02*
Solaris *'02*
Get Rich or Die Tryin' *'05*
Jesse Stone: Stone Cold *'05*
The Architect *'06*
Jesse Stone: Death in Paradise *'06*
Jesse Stone: Night Passage *'06*
Jesse Stone: Sea Change *'07*
The Andromeda Strain *'08*
Doubt *'08*
Nights in Rodanthe *'08*
Law Abiding Citizen *'09*
Madea Goes to Jail *'09*
State of Play *'09*
Eat, Pray, Love *'10*
It's Kind of a Funny Story *'10*
Knight and Day *'10*
Trust *'10*
Extremely Loud and Incredibly Close *'11*
The Help *'11*
Won't Back Down *'12*
Beautiful Creatures *'13*
Ender's Game *'13*
Prisoners *'13*
The Disappearance of Eleanor Rigby *'14*
Get On Up *'14*
Blackhat *'15*
Lila & Eve *'15*
Fences *'16*
Suicide Squad *'16*
Widows *'18*

Viveka Davis (1969-)
Shoot the Moon *'82*
Morgan Stewart's Coming Home *'87*
The End of Innocence *'90*
Man Trouble *'92*
Stalking Laura *'93*
Message in a Bottle *'98*
EDtv *'99*
Cast Away *'00*
Time Code *'00*

Warwick Davis (1970-)
The Ewok Adventure *'84*
The Ewoks: Battle for Endor *'85*
Willow *'88*
Leprechaun *'93*
Leprechaun 2 *'94*
Gulliver's Travels *'95*
Leprechaun 3 *'95*
Leprechaun 4: In Space *'96*
Leprechaun 5: In the Hood *'99*
The 10th Kingdom *'00*
Harry Potter and the Sorcerer's Stone *'01*
Harry Potter and the Chamber of Secrets *'02*
Snow White: The Fairest of Them All *'02*
Leprechaun 6: Back 2 Tha Hood *'03*
Ray *'04*
Harry Potter and the Goblet of Fire *'05*
The Hitchhiker's Guide to the Galaxy *'05*
Harry Potter and the Order of the Phoenix *'07*
The Chronicles of Narnia: Prince Caspian *'08*
Harry Potter and the Half-Blood Prince *'09*
Harry Potter and the Deathly Hallows, Part 1 *'10*
Harry Potter and the Deathly Hallows, Part 2 *'11*

William B. Davis (1938-)
Perpetrators of the Crime *'98*
The X-Files *'98*
Out of Line *'00*
The Proposal *'00*
Mindstorm *'01*
Snakehead Terror *'04*
Max Rules *'05*
Her Fatal Flaw *'06*
The Secret of Hidden Lake *'06*
Judicial Indiscretion *'07*
Numb *'07*
Possession *'08*
The Thaw *'09*
Medium Raw: Night of the Wolf *'10*
Behemoth *'11*
The Tall Man *'12*
Stonados *'13*

Bruce Davison (1946-)
The Strawberry Statement *'70*
Ulzana's Raid *'72*
The Affair *'73*
Mame *'74*
Mother, Jugs and Speed *'76*
The Gathering *'77*
Brass Target *'78*
French Quarter *'78*
The Gathering: Part 2 *'79*
Short Eyes *'79*
The Lathe of Heaven *'80*
High Risk *'81*
Crimes of Passion *'84*
Spies Like Us *'85*
Poor Little Rich Girl: The Barbara Hutton Story *'87*
Longtime Companion *'90*
Short Cuts *'93*
Six Degrees of Separation *'93*
Far from Home: The Adventures of Yellow Dog *'94*
The Skateboard Kid 2 *'94*
The Baby-Sitters' Club *'95*
The Cure *'95*
Homage *'95*
It's My Party *'95*
The Crucible *'96*
Grace of My Heart *'96*
Hidden in America *'96*
Apt Pupil *'97*
Lovelife *'97*
At First Sight *'98*
Paulie *'98*
A Memory In My Heart *'99*
Vendetta *'99*
The King Is Alive *'00*
X-Men *'00*
crazy/beautiful *'01*
Off Season *'01*
Summer Catch *'01*
Dahmer *'02*
High Crimes *'02*
Too Young to Be a Dad *'02*
Out of the Ashes *'03*
Runaway Jury *'03*
X2: X-Men United *'03*
Evergreen *'04*
8mm 2 *'05*
Going Shopping *'05*
Hate Crime *'05*
The Triangle *'05*
The Dead Girl *'06*
Breach *'07*
The Line *'08*
Christmas Angel *'09*
A Golden Christmas *'09*
Megafault *'09*
Camp Hell *'10*
Titanic 2 *'10*
Coffin *'11*
A Golden Christmas 2: The Second Tail *'11*
Earth's Final Hours *'12*
The Lords of Salem *'13*
Words and Pictures *'13*
Last Rampage *'17*
Along Came the Devil *'18*
Along Came the Devil 2 *'19*

Peter Davison (1951-)
Love for Lydia *'79*
Black Beauty *'94*
Parting Shots *'98*
Wuthering Heights *'98*

Ken Davitian (1953-)
Borat: Cultural Learnings of America for Make Benefit Glorious Nation of Kazakhstan *'06*
Float *'08*
Get Smart *'08*
Meet the Spartans *'08*
Not Forgotten *'09*
The Prankster *'10*
The Artist *'11*
You May Not Kiss the Bride *'12*

Andrew Davoli (1973-)
The Yards *'00*
Knockaround Guys *'01*
Welcome to Collinwood *'02*
Spartan *'04*

Ninetto Davoli (1948-)
The Hawks & the Sparrows *'67*
The Decameron *'70*
The Canterbury Tales *'71*
Arabian Nights *'74*

Marjorie Daw (1902-79)
Rebecca of Sunnybrook Farm *'17*
His Majesty, the American *'19*

Pam Dawber (1951-)
A Wedding *'78*
Holocaust Survivors. . . Remembrance of Love *'83*
Wild Horses *'84*
Through Naked Eyes *'87*
Stay Tuned *'92*
I'll Remember April *'99*

Marpessa Dawn (1934-2008)
Black Orpheus *'58*
The Womaneater *'59*

Anthony Dawson (1916-92)
The Queen of Spades *'49*
The Long Dark Hall *'51*
Dial 'M' for Murder *'54*
The Haunted Strangler *'58*
Libel *'59*
Tiger Bay *'59*
The Curse of the Werewolf *'61*
Dr. No *'62*
Seven Seas to Calais *'62*
Death Rides a Horse *'69*

Kim (Kimberly Dawn) Dawson (1963-)
The Voyeur *'94*
Bikini House Calls *'96*
Bikini Med School *'98*
Lethal Target *'99*
Jimmy Zip *'00*

Richard Dawson (1932-2012)
War and Peace *'56*
King Rat *'65*
Munster, Go Home! *'66*
The Devil's Brigade *'68*
The Running Man *'87*

Rosario Dawson (1979-)
Kids *'95*
He Got Game *'98*
Light It Up *'99*
Down to You *'00*
Chelsea Walls *'01*
Josie and the Pussycats *'01*
King of the Jungle *'01*
Sidewalks of New York *'01*
The Adventures of Pluto Nash *'02*
Ash Wednesday *'02*
The First $20 Million is Always the Hardest *'02*
Love in the Time of Money *'02*
Men in Black 2 *'02*
25th Hour *'02*
The Rundown *'03*
Shattered Glass *'03*
This Girl's Life *'03*
Alexander *'04*
The Devil's Rejects *'05*
Rent *'05*
Sin City *'05*
This Revolution *'05*
Clerks 2 *'06*
A Guide to Recognizing Your Saints *'06*
Death Proof *'07*
Descent *'07*
Eagle Eye *'08*
Explicit Ills *'08*
Seven Pounds *'08*
Killshot *'09*
Unstoppable *'10*
Five *'11*
Zookeeper *'11*
Fire With Fire *'12*
10 Years *'12*
Trance *'13*
The Captive *'14*
Cesar Chavez *'14*
Gimme Shelter *'14*
Parts Per Billion *'14*
Sin City: A Dame to Kill For *'14*
Top Five *'14*
Puerto Ricans in Paris *'16*
Ratchet & Clank *'16*
The LEGO Batman Movie *'17*
Unforgettable *'17*

Vicky Dawson
Carbon Copy *'81*
The Prowler *'81*

Micheline Dax (1924-)
Six in Paris *'68*
A Slightly Pregnant Man *'79*

Charlie Day (1976-)
Going the Distance *'10*
Horrible Bosses *'11*
Pacific Rim *'13*
Horrible Bosses 2 *'14*
The Lego Movie *'14 (V)*
Fist Fight *'17*
Pacific Rim: Uprising *'18*

Dennis Day (1916-88)
Buck Benny Rides Again *'40*
Melody Time *'48 (V)*
Golden Girl *'51*
The Girl Next Door *'53*

Doris Day (1910-98)
Lady Be Good *'41*
They Got Me Covered *'43*

Doris Day (1922-2019)
Romance on the High Seas *'48*
It's a Great Feeling *'49*
My Dream Is Yours *'49*
Tea for Two *'50*
The West Point Story *'50*
Young Man with a Horn *'50*
I'll See You in My Dreams *'51*
Lullaby of Broadway *'51*
On Moonlight Bay *'51*
Starlift *'51*
Storm Warning *'51*
April in Paris *'52*
The Winning Team *'52*
By the Light of the Silvery Moon *'53*
Calamity Jane *'53*
Lucky Me *'54*
Young at Heart *'54*
Love Me or Leave Me *'55*
Julie *'56*
The Man Who Knew Too Much *'56*
The Pajama Game *'57*
Teacher's Pet *'58*
The Tunnel of Love *'58*
It Happened to Jane *'59*
Pillow Talk *'59*
Please Don't Eat the Daisies *'60*
Lover Come Back *'61*
Billy Rose's Jumbo *'62*
That Touch of Mink *'62*
Move Over, Darling *'63*
The Thrill of It All! *'63*
Send Me No Flowers *'64*
Do Not Disturb *'65*
The Glass Bottom Boat *'66*
The Ballad of Josie *'67*
Caprice *'67*
With Six You Get Eggroll *'68*

Felecia Day
Dear Me: A Blogger's Tale *'08*
Prairie Fever *'08*

Felicia Day (1979-)
Red: Werewolf Hunter *'10*
Rock Jocks *'12*

Gary Day (1941-)
Night Nurse *'77*
Crime Broker *'94*

Josette Day (1914-78)
Beauty and the Beast *'46*
Well-Digger's Daughter *'46*

Laraine Day (1920-2007)
Calling Dr. Kildare *'39*
The Secret of Dr. Kildare *'39*
Dr. Kildare Goes Home *'40*
Dr. Kildare's Crisis *'40*
Dr. Kildare's Strange Case *'40*
Foreign Correspondent *'40*
I Take This Woman *'40*
The Bad Man *'41*
Dr. Kildare's Wedding Day *'41*
Kathleen *'41*
The People *vs.* Dr. Kildare *'41*
Journey for Margaret *'42*
Mr. Lucky *'43*
Bride by Mistake *'44*
Keep Your Powder Dry *'45*
The Locket *'46*
Tycoon *'47*
My Dear Secretary *'49*
The Woman on Pier 13 *'50*
The High and the Mighty *'54*
Murder on Flight 502 *'75*
Return to Fantasy Island *'77*

Larry Day (1963-)
Dead Silent *'99*
Cause of Death *'00*
Detention *'03*
A Deadly Encounter *'04*
Snakeman *'05*

Marceline Day (1907-2000)
The Beloved Rogue *'27*
Captain Salvation *'27*
The Cameraman *'28*
Paradise Island *'30*
Sunny Skies *'30*
The Crusader *'32*

Matt(hew) Day (1971-)
Muriel's Wedding *'94*
Doing Time for Patsy Cline *'97*
The Hound of the Baskervilles *'02*
Shackleton *'02*
And Starring Pancho Villa as Himself *'03*
My Year Without Sex *'09*

Morris Day (1957-)
Purple Rain *'84*
The Adventures of Ford Fairlane *'90*
Graffiti Bridge *'90*

Rosie Day
Ironclad: Battle for Blood *'14*
All Roads Lead to Rome *'15*

Vera Day (1935-)
Quatermass 2 *'57*
The Haunted Strangler *'58*
The Womaneater *'59*
The Riddle *'07*

Daniel Day-Lewis (1957-)
Sunday, Bloody Sunday *'71*
Gandhi *'82*
How Many Miles to Babylon? *'82*
Dangerous Corner *'83*
The Bounty *'84*
My Beautiful Laundrette *'85*
My Brother Jonathan *'85*
The Insurance Man *'86*
A Room with a View *'86*
The Unbearable Lightness of Being *'88*
My Left Foot *'89*
The Last of the Mohicans *'92*
The Age of Innocence *'93*
In the Name of the Father *'93*
The Crucible *'96*
The Boxer *'97*
Gangs of New York *'02*
The Ballad of Jack and Rose *'05*
There Will Be Blood *'07*
Nine *'09*
Lincoln *'12*
Phantom Thread *'17*

Manish Dayal
The Hundred-Foot Journey *'14*
Viceroy's House *'17*

Assaf Dayan (1945-2014)
See Assi Dayan

Assi Dayan (1945-2014)
The Sellout *'76*
Operation Thunderbolt *'77*
The Uranium Conspiracy *'78*
Time of Favor *'00*

Rebecca Dayan
Celeste & Jesse Forever *'12*
A Short History of Decay *'13*
H. *'15*

Gabrielle Daye (1911-2005)
10 Rillington Place *'71*
In Celebration *'75*

Joaquim de Almeida (1957-)
Clear and Present Danger *'94*
Only You *'94*
Desperado *'95*
Larry McMurtry's Dead Man's Walk *'96*
Women *'97*
Dollar for the Dead *'98*
One Man's Hero *'98*
La Cucaracha *'99*
No Vacancy *'99*
Vendetta *'99*
Behind Enemy Lines *'01*
Love and Debate *'06*
Moscow Zero *'06*
La Cucina *'07*
The Burning Plain *'08*
Che *'08*
Atlas Shrugged 3: Who Is John Galt? *'14*
Breaking & Exiting *'18*

Valentina de Angelis
Off the Map *'03*
Camp Hell *'10*

Maria de Aragon (1942-)
Blood Mania *'70*
The Cremators *'72*

Ana de Armas
War Dogs *'16*
Overdrive *'17*

Jean De Baer
84 Charing Cross Road *'86*
Broken Vows *'87*

Isaach de Bankole (1957-)
Chocolat *'88*
Night on Earth *'91*
The Keeper *'96*
A Soldier's Daughter Never Cries *'98*
Ghost Dog: The Way of the Samurai *'99*
3 A.M. *'01*

Marvin's Room '96
Sleepers '96
Cop Land '97
Great Expectations '97
Jackie Brown '97
Wag the Dog '97
Analyze This '98
Ronin '98
Flawless '99
The Adventures of Rocky & Bullwinkle '00
Meet the Parents '00
Men of Honor '00
15 Minutes '01
The Score '01
Analyze That '02
City by the Sea '02
Showtime '02
Godsend '04
Meet the Fockers '04
Shark Tale '04 (V)
The Bridge of San Luis Rey '05
Hide and Seek '05
Arthur and the Invisibles '06 (V)
The Good Shepherd '06
Stardust '07
Righteous Kill '08
What Just Happened '08
Everybody's Fine '09
Little Fockers '10
Machete '10
Stone '10
Killer Elite '11
Limitless '11
New Year's Eve '11
Being Flynn '12
Freelancers '12
Red Lights '12
Silver Linings Playbook '12
The Big Wedding '13
The Family '13
Grudge Match '13
Killing Season '13
Last Vegas '13
The Bag Man '14
The Intern '15
Joy '15
The Comedian '16
Dirty Grandpa '16
Hands of Stone '16
The Irishman '19
Joker '19

Ana Christine de Oliveira (1973-)
Taxi '04
Two Drifters '05

Rossy de Palma (1964-)
Women on the Verge of a Nervous Breakdown '88
Tie Me Up! Tie Me Down! '90
Kika '94
Ready to Wear '94
The Flower of My Secret '95
Talk of Angels '96
People '04

Miranda de Pencier (1968-)
Anne of Green Gables '85
Anne of Green Gables: The Continuing Story '99

Teresa De Priest (1970-)
The Doorway '00
Hit and Runway '01

Lya de Putti (1897-1931)
The Indian Tomb '21
Othello '22
Phantom '22
Variety '25
The Informer '29

Emilie de Ravin (1981-)
Carrie '02
Brick '06
The Hills Have Eyes '06
The Perfect Game '09
Public Enemies '09
Operation: Endgame '10
Remember Me '10

Portia de Rossi (1973-)
Sirens '94
Scream 2 '97
Girl '98
The Invisibles '99
Stigmata '99
Who is Cletis Tout? '02
I Witness '03
The Night We Called It a Day '03
Cursed '04

Anthony De Sando (1965-)
The Return of Eliot Ness '91
Federal Hill '94
Party Girl '94
Kiss Me, Guido '97
Cement '99
Double Parked '00
Hysterical Blindness '02
Beer League '06

Joe De Santis (1909-89)
The Man With a Cloak '51
Full of Life '56
The Case Against Brooklyn '58
Al Capone '59
The George Raft Story '61
Blue '68
Little Cigars '73
It's Good to Be Alive '74
Contract on Cherry Street '77

Silvia De Santis
Retrograde '03
I Am David '04

Andre De Shields (1946-)
Extreme Measures '96
Chloe & Theo '15

Christian de Sica (1951-)
Blaise Pascal '71
An Almost Perfect Affair '79
Detective School Dropouts '85
Men Men Men '95
The Tourist '10

Vittorio De Sica (1902-74)
The Earrings of Madame De. . . '54
The Gold of Naples '54
Too Bad She's Bad '54
A Farewell to Arms '57
The Inveterate Bachelor '58
It Started in Naples '60
The Millionairess '60
The Amorous Adventures of Moll Flanders '65
The Biggest Bundle of Them All '68
The Shoes of the Fisherman '68
Andy Warhol's Dracula '74
We All Loved Each Other So Much '77
Generale Della Rovere '09

Werner De Smedt (1970-)
Everybody's Famous! '00
The Memory of a Killer '03

Melissa De Sousa (1967-)
Ride '98
The Best Man '99
Lockdown '00
Miss Congeniality '00
30 Years to Life '01
Bats: Human Harvest '07
The Best Man Holiday '13

Edward De Souza (1932-)
Kiss of the Vampire '62
The Phantom of the Opera '62
A Question of Attribution '91

Jose-Luis De Villalonga (1920-2007)
The Lovers '59
Any Number Can Win '63
Darling '65
Blood and Sand '89

Brandon de Wilde (1942-72)
The Member of the Wedding '52
Shane '53
Goodbye, My Lady '56
Night Passage '57
Missouri Traveler '58
All Fall Down '62
Hud '63
In Harm's Way '65
Those Calloways '65

Jacqueline De Witt (1912-98)
See Jacqueline DeWit

Francis De Wolff (1913-84)
Geordie '55
The Smallest Show on Earth '57
The Man Who Could Cheat Death '59
The Two Faces of Dr. Jekyll '60
Devil Doll '64

Luke De Woolfson (1976-)
Stoned '05
Mr. Right '06

Cliff De Young (1945-)
The Secret of Zoey '02
Love's Enduring Promise '04
2012: Doomsday '08

Adam Deacon (1983-)
Bonded by Blood '09
Outside Bet '12

Brian Deacon (1949-)
Vampyres '74
A Zed & Two Noughts '88

Max Deacon
Flashbacks of a Fool '08
Into the Storm '14
Tommy's Honour '17

Richard Deacon (1921-84)
Them! '54
Abbott and Costello Meet the Mummy '55
Blackboard Jungle '55
Carousel '56
Francis in the Haunted House '56
Invasion of the Body Snatchers '56
The Kettles in the Ozarks '56
Everything's Ducky '61
Critic's Choice '63
Dear Heart '64
The Patsy '64
Billie '65
Don't Worry, We'll Think of a Title '66
Blackbeard's Ghost '67
The Gnome-Mobile '67
The One and Only, Genuine, Original Family Band '68
Piranha '78

Julia Deakin (1952-)
Liam '00
Down Terrace '10

Lucy Deakins (1971-)
The Boy Who Could Fly '86
The Great Outdoors '88
Little Nikita '88
Cheetah '89
There Goes My Baby '92
A Mother's Gift '95

Sarah Deakins
Criminal Intent '05
Possessed '05
Hollow Man 2 '06
The Sandlot 3: Heading Home '07
Mom, Dad and Her '08

Allison Dean
Coming to America '88
Where's Marlowe? '98
Incognito '99

Eddie Dean (1907-99)
Law of the Pampas '39
Colorado Serenade '46

Eric Dean (1971-)
Arizona Sky '08
The Men Next Door '12

Felicity Dean (1959-)
The Whistle Blower '87
Persuasion '95
The Last of the Blonde Bombshells '00

Isabel Dean (1918-97)
Light in the Piazza '61
Oh! What a Lovely War '69
Weather in the Streets '84

James Dean (1931-55)
Fixed Bayonets! '51
East of Eden '54
Rebel without a Cause '55
Giant '56

Jimmy Dean (1928-2010)
The Ballad of Andy Crocker '69
Diamonds Are Forever '71
Big Bad John '90

Loren Dean (1969-)
Say Anything '89
Billy Bathgate '91
1492: Conquest of Paradise '92
JFK: Reckless Youth '93
Apollo 13 '95
How to Make an American Quilt '95
The Passion of Darkly Noon '95
Mrs. Winterbourne '96
Rosewood '96
The End of Violence '97
Gattaca '97
Enemy of the State '98
Mumford '99
Space Cowboys '00
The War Bride '01
The Bronx Is Burning '07
The Poker Club '08
Conviction '10
Who Is Simon Miller? '11

Margia Dean (1922-)
Rimfire '49
Kentucky Jubilee '51
Savage Drums '51
Loan Shark '52
Fangs of the Wild '54
Sins of Jezebel '54
Lonesome Trail '55
The Quatermass Experiment '56
The Secret of the Purple Reef '60

Nathaniel Dean
Walking on Water '02
Somersault '04

Priscilla Dean (1896-1987)
Outside the Law '21
White Tiger '23

Rick Dean (1953-2006)
Nam Angels '88
Bloodfist 3: Forced to Fight '92
Raiders of the Sun '92
Saturday Night Special '92
Cheyenne Warrior '94
Stripteaser '95
Carnosaur 3: Primal Species '96

Ron Dean
Big Score '83
Above the Law '88
Cocktail '88
Rudy '93
The Client '94
The Wild Card '03
Wild Things 2 '04
The Dark Knight '08

Lezlie (Dean) Deane (1964-)
976-EVIL '88
Freddy's Dead: The Final Nightmare '91
To Protect and Serve '92

Edgar Dearing (1893-1974)
They Gave Him a Gun '37
Seven Doors to Death '44

Justin Deas (1948-)
Dream Lover '85
iMurders '08

Jamel Debbouze (1975-)
Amelie '01
She Hate Me '04
Angel-A '05
Days of Glory '06
Let It Rain '08
360 '12

Kristine DeBell (1954-)
Battle Creek Brawl '80
Cheerleaders' Wild Weekend '85

James DeBello (1980-)
Detroit Rock City '99
Crime and Punishment in Suburbia '00
100 Girls '00
Swimfan '02
Cabin Fever '03
Players '03
Ghouls '07
Transylmania '09
The Penthouse '10

John DeBello (1952-)
Attack of the Killer Tomatoes '77
Out of the Dark '88
Killer Tomatoes Strike Back '90
Killer Tomatoes Eat France '91

Burr DeBenning (1936-2003)
Beach Red '67
The Amazing Captain Nemo '78
Hanging By a Thread '79

Elizabeth Debicki (1990-)
The Tale '18
Vita & Virginia '19
The Burnt Orange Heresy '20

David Deblinger
Frogs for Snakes '98
Intern '00

Alycia Debnam-Carey (1993-)
Into the Storm '14
Friend Request '16

Jocelyn DeBoer
Dead Snow: Red vs. Dead '14
Greener Grass '19

Marcia DeBonis (1960-)
L.I.E. '01
12 and Holding '05
That's What She Said '12
Blame '17

Lee DeBroux (1941-)
Sweet Hostage '75
Hangfire '91
Mars '96
The Day the World Ended '01

Jean Debucourt (1894-1958)
Monsieur Vincent '47
The Earrings of Madame De. . . '54
Nana '55

Cathy DeBuono
Out at the Wedding '07
And Then Came Lola '09

Amanda DeCadenet (1972-)
Four Rooms '95
Fall '97

Rosemary DeCamp (1910-2001)
Cheers for Miss Bishop '41
The Jungle Book '42
Yankee Doodle Dandy '42
Commandos Strike at Dawn '43
Pride of the Marines '45
Rhapsody in Blue '45
Nora Prentiss '47
Look for the Silver Lining '49
Night Unto Night '49
The Story of Seabiscuit '49
On Moonlight Bay '51
Scandal Sheet '52
By the Light of the Silvery Moon '53
So This Is Love '53
Many Rivers to Cross '55
13 Ghosts '60
Saturday the 14th '81

Mark DeCarlo (1962-)
Buffy the Vampire Slayer '92
Jimmy Neutron: Boy Genius '01 (V)
The Ant Bully '06 (V)

Antonio Dechent (1960-)
Intacto '01
Carmen '03

Brooklyn Decker (1987-)
Just Go With It '11
Battleship '12
What to Expect When You're Expecting '12
Results '15
Casual Encounters '16
Lovesong '17

Eugene Deckers (1917-77)
Madeleine '50
The Golden Salamander '51
Flame Over India '59
North West Frontier '59
Lady L '65

Edward 'Blue' Deckert (1951-)
A Taste for Killing '92
Home Fries '98
The Rookie '02
The Alamo '04
Envy '04

Jan Decleir (1946-)
Antonia's Line '95
Character '97
Molokai: The Story of Father Damien '99
Running Free '00
The Memory of a Killer '03
Rosenstrasse '03

Xavier DeClie
Adrenalin: Fear the Rush '96
Gangster World '98

Guy Decomble (1910-64)
Bob le Flambeur '55
The 400 Blows '59

Joey Dedio (1963-)
Bomb the System '05
Lullaby '08

Frances Dee (1907-2004)
An American Tragedy '31
Finishing School '33
Little Women '33
One Man's Journey '33
Of Human Bondage '34
Becky Sharp '35
The Gay Deception '35
Souls at Sea '37
So Ends Our Night '41
Meet the Stewarts '42
I Walked with a Zombie '43
The Private Affairs of Bel Ami '47
Four Faces West '48
Payment on Demand '51
Mr. Scoutmaster '53

Janie Dee (1966-)
P.D. James: Death in Holy Orders '03
P.D. James: The Murder Room '04

Ruby Dee (1924-2014)
The Jackie Robinson Story '50
No Way Out '50
The Tall Target '51
Edge of the City '57
Take a Giant Step '59
A Raisin in the Sun '61
The Balcony '63
Gone Are the Days '63
Purlie Victorious '63
Uptight '68
Buck and the Preacher '72
It's Good to Be Alive '74
Roots: The Next Generation '79
Cat People '82
Go Tell It on the Mountain '84
Gore Vidal's Lincoln '88
Do the Right Thing '89
Love at Large '89
Decoration Day '90
Zora Is My Name! '90
Jungle Fever '91

Cop and a Half '93
Just Cause '94
Stephen King's The Stand '94
Mr. & Mrs. Loving '96
A Simple Wish '97
Baby Geniuses '98
Having Our Say: The Delany Sisters' First 100 Years '99
Passing Glory '99
The Wall '99
Finding Buck McHenry '00
Anne Rice's The Feast of All Saints '01
American Gangster '07
America '09
The Perfect Age of Rock 'n' Roll '10
A Thousand Words '12
Betty & Coretta '13 (N)

Sandra Dee (1942-2005)
Until They Sail '57
The Reluctant Debutante '58
The Restless Years '58
Gidget '59
Imitation of Life '59
A Summer Place '59
Portrait in Black '60
Come September '61
Tammy Tell Me True '61
If a Man Answers '62
Take Her, She's Mine '63
Tammy and the Doctor '63
That Funny Feeling '65
The Dunwich Horror '70
Fantasy Island '76

Kaie Deei (1910-91)
See Khigh Deigh

Olive Deering (1918-86)
Samson and Delilah '49
Caged '50

Rick Dees (1950-)
La Bamba '87
Jetsons: The Movie '90 (V)

Eddie Deezen (1957-)
Grease '78
I Wanna Hold Your Hand '78
Midnight Madness '80
A Polish Vampire in Burbank '80
Rosebud Beach Hotel '85
The Whoopee Boys '86
Million Dollar Mystery '87
Assault of the Killer Bimbos '88
Beverly Hills Vamp '88
Rock-a-Doodle '92 (V)
Teenage Exorcist '93
The Polar Express '04

Kaylee DeFer (1986-)
Underclassman '05
In My Pocket '11

Don DeFore (1917-93)
The Male Animal '42
Thirty Seconds Over Tokyo '44
The Stork Club '45
Without Reservations '46
It Happened on 5th Avenue '47
Ramrod '47
One Sunday Afternoon '48
Romance on the High Seas '48
My Friend Irma '49
Too Late for Tears '49
Dark City '50
Southside 1-1000 '50
Jumping Jacks '52
No Room for the Groom '52
She's Working Her Way Through College '52
Battle Hymn '57
The Facts of Life '60

Calvert Deforest (1921-2007)
Heaven Help Us '85
Mr. Write '92

Isabelle DeFunes (1944-)
Baba Yaga '73
Kiss Me, Kill Me '73

Raz Degan (1968-)
Alexander '04
Sword of War '09

Ellen DeGeneres (1958-)
Mr. Wrong '95
EDtv '99
Goodbye, Lover '99
The Love Letter '99
If These Walls Could Talk 2 '00
Finding Nemo '03 (V)
Finding Dory '16

Pia Degermark (1949-)
Elvira Madigan '67
The Looking Glass War '69
The Vampire Happening '71

Sam DeGrasse (1875-1953)
See Sam De Grasse

Raffaello Degruttola
Pulse '03
Dot.Kill '05
House of 9 '05

Dane DeHaan (1986-)
Patricia Cornwell's The Front '10
Chronicle '12
Jack and Diane '12
Kill Your Darlings '13
Metallica Through the Never '13
The Place Beyond the Pines '13
The Amazing Spider-Man 2 '14
Life After Beth '14
Life '15
A Cure for Wellness '17
Tulip Fever '17
Valerian and the City of a Thousand Planets '17
The Kid '19

Gloria DeHaven
Step Lively '44
Scene of the Crime '49

John Dehner (1915-92)
Counterspy Meets Scotland Yard '50
Destination Murder '50
Powder River '53
The Steel Lady '53
Apache '54
Southwest Passage '54
The King's Thief '55
The Prodigal '55
The Scarlet Coat '55
Top Gun '55
Fastest Gun Alive '56
Girl in Black Stockings '57
The Iron Sheriff '57
Trooper Hook '57
Apache Territory '58
The Left-Handed Gun '58
Man of the West '58
Cast a Long Shadow '59
Timbuktu '59
Critic's Choice '63
Youngblood Hawke '64
The Hallelujah Trail '65 (N)
The Cheyenne Social Club '70
Support Your Local Gunfighter '71
The Day of the Dolphin '73
Missiles of October '74
The Killer Inside Me '76
Airplane 2: The Sequel '82
Creator '85
The Jagged Edge '85

Nicole DeHuff (1974-2005)
Meet the Parents '00
Unbeatable Harold '06

Khigh Deigh (1910-91)
The Manchurian Candidate '62
Seconds '66
Noble House '88

Melinda Deines
Widow on the Hill '05
Bridal Fever '08

Olivia DeJonge
The Visit '15
Better Watch Out '17

Tim DeKay (1963-)
Big Eden '00
The Chumscrubber '05
Peaceful Warrior '06
That Russell Girl '08

David DeKeyser (1927-)
See David de Keyser

Albert Dekker (1904-68)
Marie Antoinette '38
Beau Geste '39
Dr. Cyclops '40
Seven Sinners '40
Strange Cargo '40
The Great Commandment '41
Honky Tonk '41
In Old California '42
Once Upon a Honeymoon '42
Wake Island '42
Buckskin Frontier '43
The Kansan '43
War of the Wildcats '43
The Woman of the Town '44
Experiment Perilous '45
The Killers '46
Suspense '46
Cass Timberlane '47
Gentleman's Agreement '47
The Pretender '47
Lulu Belle '48
Tarzan's Magic Fountain '48
Destination Murder '50
The Furies '50
As Young As You Feel '51
East of Eden '54
Illegal '55
Kiss Me Deadly '55
She Devil '57
Middle of the Night '59
Suddenly, Last Summer '59
The Wonderful Country '59
Gamera, the Invincible '66
The Wild Bunch '69

Thomas Dekker (1987-)
The Land Before Time 5: The Mysterious Island '97 (V)
The Land Before Time 6: The Secret of Saurus Rock '98 (V)
Land Before Time 7: The Stone of Cold Fire '00 (V)
Laid to Rest '09
My Sister's Keeper '09
A Nightmare on Elm Street '10
ChromeSkull: Laid to Rest 2 '11
Cinema Verite '11
Kaboom '11
Plush '13

Mark Deklin (1967-)
Never Say Macbeth '07
Riverworld '10
The Wedding Chapel '13

Frank DeKova (1910-81)
See Frank De Kova

Kate del Castillo (1972-)
Lime Salted Love '06
Under the Same Moon '07
Bad Guys '08
Julia '08
K-11 '11
Without Men '11
The Book of Life '14 (V)
No Good Deed '14

Louis Del Grande (1943-)
Of Unknown Origin '83
Northern Extremes '93
Sugartime '95

Maria Del Mar (1964-)
Price of Glory '00
The Christmas Shoes '02

Matthew Del Negro (1972-)
Ghost Image '07
Room 314 '07
A Novel Romance '11
Hot Pursuit '15

Angel Del Pozo (1934-)
Fort Yuma Gold '66
Horror Express '72
Pancho Villa '72

Dulio Del Prete (1938-98)
Alfredo, Alfredo '72
The Sensuous Nurse '76
Voices from Beyond '90

Dolores Del Rio (1905-83)
The Trail of '98 '28
Evangeline '29
Bird of Paradise '32
Flying Down to Rio '33
Wonder Bar '34
In Caliente '35
Accused '36
International Settlement '38
The Fugitive '48
Flaming Star '60
Cheyenne Autumn '64
More Than a Miracle '67
Children of Sanchez '79

Laura Del Sol (1961-)
Carmen '83
The Hit '85
El Amor Brujo '86
The Crew '95

Benicio Del Toro (1967-)
License to Kill '89
Drug Wars: The Camarena Story '90
China Moon '91
The Indian Runner '91
Fearless '93
Money for Nothing '93
Swimming with Sharks '94
The Usual Suspects '95
Basquiat '96
Excess Baggage '96
The Fan '96
The Funeral '96
Joyride '97
Fear and Loathing in Las Vegas '98
The Pledge '00
Snatch '00
Traffic '00
Way of the Gun '00
The Hunted '03
21 Grams '03
Sin City '05
Things We Lost in the Fire '07
Che '08
The Wolfman '09
Savages '12
Jimmy P. '13
Guardians of the Galaxy '14
Inherent Vice '14
Escobar: Paradise Lost '15
Sicario '15
A Perfect Day '16
Sicario: Day of the Soldado '18

Guillermo del Toro (1964-)
Five Came Back '17
78/52: Hitchcock's Shower Scene '17

Suzy Delair (1917-2020)
The Murderer Lives at Number 21 '42
Jenny Lamour '47
Utopia '51
Gervaise '56
Is Paris Burning? '66
The Mad Adventures of Rabbi Jacob '73

Lisa (Lise) Delamare (1913-2006)
La Marseillaise '37
Monsieur Vincent '47
Baxter '89

Louise Delamere (1969-)
Shameless '94
The Chatterley Affair '06
Cravings '06

Cassandra Delaney (1961-)
Fair Game '86
Hurricane Smith '92

Charles Delaney (1892-1959)
Barbara Frietchie '24
Corruption '33
Ten Laps to Go '36
The Gold Racket '37
Running Target '56

Dana Delaney (1956-)
Choices of the Heart: The Margaret Sanger Story '95
A Time to Remember '03
A Beautiful Life '08
Multiple Sarcasms '10

Joan Delaney
The President's Analyst '67
Don't Drink the Water '69

Kim Delaney (1961-)
That Was Then. . . This Is Now '85
Delta Force '86
Campus Man '87
Christmas Comes to Willow Creek '87
The Drifter '88
Body Parts '91
Hangfire '91
Darkman 2: The Return of Durant '94
Serial Killer '95
Closer and Closer '96
Mission to Mars '00
Finding a Family '10

Padraic Delaney (1977-)
The Wind That Shakes the Barley '06
Blackthorn '11

Pat Delaney
Zontar, the Thing from Venus '66
Creature of Destruction '67

Simon Delaney
This Must Be the Place '12
Delivery Man '13

Diane Delano (1957-)
A Painted House '03
The Ladykillers '04
The Wicker Man '06
Choose Connor '07

Michael Delano (1940-)
Catlow '71
Not of This Earth '88
Ring of Fire '91
Ring of Fire 2: Blood and Steel '92
Out for Blood '93
Private Wars '93

Dana Delany (1956-)
Almost You '85
Masquerade '88
Moon over Parador '88
Patty Hearst '88
Housesitter '92
Light Sleeper '92
Batman: Mask of the Phantasm '93 (V)
Tombstone '93
Wild Palms '93
The Enemy Within '94
Exit to Eden '94
Live Nude Girls '95
Fly Away Home '96
The Curve '97
True Women '97
Wide Awake '97
The Right Temptation '00
Conviction '02
Spin '04
Route 30 '08
Camp Hell '10

Yvonne Delarosa
Benny Bliss & the Disciples of Greatness '07
A Sierra Nevada Gunfight '13

Brian Delate (1949-)
The Truman Show '98
Buffalo Soldiers '01

Cyril Delevanti (1889-1975)
I Bury the Living '58
Dead Ringer '64
The Night of the Iguana '64
The Killing of Sister George '69
Black Eye '74

Cara Delevingne
The Face of an Angel '14
Pan '15
Paper Towns '15
Valerian and the City of a Thousand Planets '17
London Fields '18
Her Smell '19

Majandra Delfino (1981-)
Zeus and Roxanne '96
The Secret Life of Girls '99
Shriek If You Know What I Did Last Friday the 13th '00
The Learning Curve '01
R.S.V.P. '02

Roger Delgado (1918-73)
The Mind Benders '63
Hot Enough for June '64

Jorge d'Elia (1938-)
Lost Embrace '04
The Aura '05

Claudia Dell (1910-77)
Big Boy '30
Sit Tight '31
The Midnight Lady '32
The Lost City '34
Yellow Cargo '36

Gabriel Dell (1919-88)
Dead End '37
Angels with Dirty Faces '38
Crime School '38
Little Tough Guy '38
Angels Wash Their Faces '39
Hell's Kitchen '39
They Made Me a Criminal '39
Junior G-Men '40
Junior G-Men of the Air '42
Smart Alecks '42
Kid Dynamite '43
Framed '75
The Escape Artist '82
Mars '96

Gabriel Dell, Jr.
Dead End Kids: Little Tough Guy '38
Gangster World '98

Myrna Dell (1924-2011)
Nocturne '46
The Judge Steps Out '49
Destination Murder '50
The Bushwackers '52
Naked Hills '56
Ma Barker's Killer Brood '60

Michael DellaFemina (1965-)
Bloodlust: Subspecies 3 '93
Invisible: The Chronicles of Benjamin Knight '93
Italian Movie '93
Mandroid '93

Erik Todd Dellums (1964-)
She's Gotta Have It '86
Blackmale '99
Boycott '02

Nikki Deloach (1979-)
Gunfighter's Moon '96
Traveller '96
The Net 2.0 '06
Mask Maker '10
The Trial '10

Alain Delon (1935-)
Purple Noon '60
Rocco and His Brothers '60
The Eclipse '62
Any Number Can Win '63
The Leopard '63
The Black Tulip '64
Joy House '64
The Yellow Rolls Royce '64
Is Paris Burning? '66
The Lost Command '66
Texas Across the River '66
Diabolically Yours '67
The Last Adventure '67
Le Samourai '67
The Girl on a Motorcycle '68
Honor Among Thieves '68
Spirits of the Dead '68
La Piscine '69
Borsalino '70
Le Cercle Rouge '70
Swimming Pool '70
Red Sun '71
Assassination of Trotsky '72

Scorpio '73
Widow Couderc '74
Zorro '74
Gypsy '75
Icy Breasts '75
Le Gitan '75
Mr. Klein '76
The Concorde: Airport '79 '79
Le Choc '82
Notre Histoire '84
Swann in Love '84

Nathalie Delon (1941-)
Le Samourai '67
When Eight Bells Toll '71
Bluebeard '72
Eyes Behind the Stars '72
Game of Seduction '76

Michael Delorenzo (1959-)
My Family '94
Somebody to Love '94
The Wall '99
Gun Shy '00
Not Forgotten '09

Julie Delpy (1969-)
Mauvais Sang '86
Europa, Europa '91
The Three Musketeers '93
Before Sunrise '94
Killing Zoe '94
Trois Couleurs: Blanc '94
Trois Couleurs: Rouge '94 (C)
An American Werewolf in Paris '97
The Treat '98
But I'm a Cheerleader '99
The Passion of Ayn Rand '99
Sand '00
Intimate Affairs '01
MacArthur Park '01
Waking Life '01
Before Sunset '04
Broken Flowers '05
The Hoax '06
The Legend of Lucy Keyes '06
The Air I Breathe '07
2 Days in Paris '07
The Countess '09
Before Midnight '13
Lolo '15
Wiener-Dog '16

Rene Deltgen (1909-79)
Journey to the Lost City '58
Again, the Ringer '64

Xavier DeLuc (1958-)
Captive '87
The Other Side of the Law '95

Rudy DeLuca
The Return of Count Yorga '71
Life Stinks '91

Anne Marie Deluise (1969-)
Shock to the System '06
Ace of Hearts '08
The Thaw '09

David DeLuise (1971-)
Too Smooth '98
Terror Tract '00
BachelorMan '03
Jam '06
Who's Your Monkey '07
Bundy: A Legacy of Evil '08
A Christmas Proposal '08
Dear Me: A Blogger's Tale '08
National Lampoon Presents RoboDoc '08
Route 30 '08
The Wizards of Waverly Place: The Movie '09
Vampires Suck '10
Abner the Invisible Dog '13
Golden Shoes '15
Believe '16

Dom DeLuise (1933-2009)
Fail-Safe '64
The Glass Bottom Boat '66
The Busy Body '67
The Twelve Chairs '70
Evil Roy Slade '71
Blazing Saddles '74
Only with Married Men '74
Silent Movie '76
World's Greatest Lover '77
The Adventures of Sherlock Holmes' Smarter Brother '78
The Cheap Detective '78
The End '78
Sextette '78
The Muppet Movie '79 (C)
Fatso '80
Hot Stuff '80
The Last Married Couple in America '80
Smokey and the Bandit 2 '80
Wholly Moses! '80
Cannonball Run '81
History of the World: Part 1 '81
The Best Little Whorehouse in Texas '82
The Secret of NIMH '82 (V)
Cannonball Run 2 '84
Johnny Dangerously '84
An American Tail '86 (V)
Haunted Honeymoon '86
Spaceballs '87
Oliver & Company '88 (V)
All Dogs Go to Heaven '89 (V)
Loose Cannons '90
An American Tail: Fievel Goes West '91 (V)
Munchie '92 (V)
Happily Ever After '93 (V)
The Magic Voyage '93 (V)
Robin Hood: Men in Tights '93
The Skateboard Kid '93 (V)
A Troll in Central Park '94 (V)
All Dogs Go to Heaven 2 '95 (V)
Red Line '96
Boys Will Be Boys '97
Baby Geniuses '98
The Godson '98
The Secret of NIMH 2 '98 (V)
Girl Play '04

Michael DeLuise (1969-)
Encino Man '92
Boys Will Be Boys '97
Circle '10

Peter DeLuise (1966-)
The Midnight Hour '86
Children of the Night '92
Before I Say Goodbye '03
Yeti '08
21 Jump Street '12 (C)

Marya Delver (1974-)
Better Than Chocolate '99
Last Wedding '01

Gordon DeMain (1886-1954)
The Dude Bandit '33
The Mad Monster '42

William Demarest (1892-1983)
The First Auto '27
The Jazz Singer '27
Hands Across the Table '35
Charlie Chan at the Opera '36
The Great Ziegfeld '36
Love on the Run '36
Wedding Present '36
Big City '37
Rebecca of Sunnybrook Farm '38
Miracles for Sale '39
Christmas in July '40
The Great McGinty '40
The Devil & Miss Jones '41
The Lady Eve '41
Sullivan's Travels '41
All Through the Night '42
The Palm Beach Story '42
Pardon My Sarong '42
The Great Moment '44
Hail the Conquering Hero '44
Miracle of Morgan's Creek '44
Along Came Jones '45
Salty O'Rourke '45
The Jolson Story '46
The Perils of Pauline '47
On Our Merry Way '48
Whispering Smith '48
Jolson Sings Again '49
Sorrowful Jones '49
Riding High '50
Excuse My Dust '51
Behave Yourself! '52
What Price Glory? '52
Dangerous When Wet '53
Escape from Fort Bravo '53
Here Come the Girls '53
The Far Horizons '55
Jupiter's Darling '55
Sincerely Yours '55
The Mountain '56
Twenty Plus Two '61
It's a Mad, Mad, Mad, Mad World '63
Viva Las Vegas '63
Don't Be Afraid of the Dark '73
The McCullochs '75

Donna DeMario (1927-)
See Donna Martell

Derrick DeMarney (1906-78)
Things to Come '36
Young and Innocent '37
Frenzy '46
Inheritance '47
Meet Mr. Callaghan '54

Orane Demazis (1904-91)
Marius '31
Fanny '32
Cesar '36

William DeMeo (1971-)
Wannabes '01
Searching for Bobby D '05
Once Upon a Time in Brooklyn '13
Gotti '18

William Demerest (1892-1983)
Easy Living '37
When Willie Comes Marching Home '50

Irina Demick (1936-2004)
The Visit '64
Those Magnificent Men in Their Flying Machines '65

Cecil B. DeMille (1881-1959)
Free and Easy '30 (C)
Star Spangled Rhythm '42
Sunset Boulevard '50

Katherine DeMille (1911-95)
Belle of the Nineties '34
The Black Room '35
The Call of the Wild '35
The Crusades '35
Ramona '36
Charlie Chan at the Olympics '37
Unconquered '47
The Judge '49

Jonathan Demme (1944-2017)
Incredible Melting Man '77 (C)
Into the Night '85 (C)
Married to the Mob '88
That Thing You Do! '96

Mylene Demongeot (1935-)
Bonjour Tristesse '57
Upstairs and Downstairs '59
The Giant of Marathon '60
The Rape of the Sabines '61
Gold for the Caesars '63
The Man Who Lived at the Ritz '91
The Midwife '17

Darcy Demoss (1963-)
Friday the 13th, Part 6: Jason Lives '86
Can't Buy Me Love '87
Living to Die '91
Eden '93
Forbidden Zone: Alien Abduction '96

Anais Demoustier (1987-)
Time of the Wolf '03
The Beautiful Person '08
Give Me Your Hand '09
Elles '11
Therese '12
The French Minister '13
Bird People '14
The New Girlfriend '14

Brendan F. Dempsey
Waking Ned Devine '98
About Adam '00

Patrick Dempsey (1966-)
Heaven Help Us '85
Can't Buy Me Love '87
In the Mood '87
Some Girls '88
Happy Together '89
Loverboy '89
Coupe de Ville '90
Mobsters '91
JFK: Reckless Youth '93
Ava's Magical Adventure '94
With Honors '94
Hugo Pool '97
Jeremiah '98
Something About Sex '98
The Treat '98
Me & Will '99
Life in the Fast Lane '00
Scream 3 '00
Blonde '01
The Emperor's Club '02
Sweet Home Alabama '02
Lucky Seven '03
Brother Bear 2 '06 (V)
Enchanted '07
Freedom Writers '07
Made of Honor '08
Valentine's Day '10
Flypaper '11
Transformers: Dark of the Moon '11
Bridget Jones's Baby '16

Richard Dempsey (1973-)
The Chronicles of Narnia '89
The Aristocrats '99
Catherine Cookson's Tilly Trotter '99

Tanya Dempsey (1975-)
Shrieker '97
Witchouse 3: Demon Fire '01

Carol Dempster (1901-91)
The Love Flower '20
Dream Street '21
Sherlock Holmes '22
America '24
Sally of the Sawdust '25

Jeffrey DeMunn (1947-)
Christmas Evil '80
Ragtime '81
Frances '82
The Hitcher '86
Who Is Julia? '86
Betrayed '88
The Blob '88
Gore Vidal's Lincoln '88
Blaze '89
Eyes of an Angel '91
Barbarians at the Gate '93
Citizen X '95
Hiroshima '95
Phenomenon '96
Turbulence '96
RocketMan '97
Cash Crop '98
The X-Files '98
The Green Mile '99
Stephen King's The Storm of the Century '99
The Majestic '01
Our Town '03
Empire Falls '05
The Hades Factor '06
Hollywoodland '06
The Mist '07
Burn After Reading '08
Another Happy Day '11
6 Souls '13

Mathieu Demy (1972-)
One Hundred and One Nights '95
Jeanne and the Perfect Guy '98
The New Yorker '98
A Few Days in September '06
The Girl on the Train '09
Americano '11

Maggie Dence (1942-)
Outback '71
Danny Deckchair '03
Look Both Ways '05

Dame Judi Dench (1934-)
Four in the Morning '65
A Study in Terror '66
A Midsummer Night's Dream '68
Luther '74
Wetherby '85
84 Charing Cross Road '86
A Room with a View '86
Saigon: Year of the Cat '87
A Handful of Dust '88
Behaving Badly '89
Henry V '89
Goldeneye '95
Jack and Sarah '95
Hamlet '96
Mrs. Brown '97
Tomorrow Never Dies '97
Shakespeare in Love '98
Tea with Mussolini '99
The World Is Not Enough '99
Chocolat '00
Into the Arms of Strangers: Stories of the Kindertransport '00 (N)
The Last of the Blonde Bombshells '00
Iris '01
The Shipping News '01
Die Another Day '02
The Importance of Being Earnest '02
The Chronicles of Riddick '04
Home on the Range '04 (V)
Ladies in Lavender '04
Mrs. Henderson Presents '05
Pride and Prejudice '05
Casino Royale '06
Notes on a Scandal '06
Cranford '08
Quantum of Solace '08
Nine '09
Return to Cranford '09
J. Edgar '11
Jane Eyre '11
My Week With Marilyn '11
Pirates of the Caribbean: On Stranger Tides '11
The Best Exotic Marigold Hotel '12
Skyfall '12
Philomena '13
The Second Best Exotic Marigold Hotel '15
Victoria & Abdul '17
All Is True '18
Tea with the Dames '18
Cats '19
Red Joan '19

David Dencik (1974-)
The Girl With the Dragon Tattoo '11
Tinker Tailor Soldier Spy '11
A Royal Affair '12
Serena '14
Men & Chicken '15

Denden (1950-)
Cure '97
Ju-On 2 '00
Uzumaki '00
Red Shadow '01

Catherine Deneuve (1943-)
The Twilight Girls '57
Murder By Two '60
Umbrellas of Cherbourg '64
Repulsion '65
Belle de Jour '67
Manon '68
Mayerling '68
The Young Girls of Rochefort '68
April Fools '69
Mississippi Mermaid '69
Donkey Skin '70
Peau D'Ane '71
The Hustle '75
Lovers Like Us '75
The Savage '75
March or Die '77
A Slightly Pregnant Man '79
The Last Metro '80
Hotel America '81
Le Choc '82
The Hunger '83
Fort Saganne '84
Love Songs '84
Scene of the Crime '87
Indochine '92
Ma Saison Preferee '93
The Convent '95
Les Voleurs '96
Genealogies of a Crime '97
Place Vendome '98
Dancer in the Dark '99
East-West '99
Pola X '99
Time Regained '99
I'm Going Home '00
The Musketeer '01
8 Women '02
Dangerous Liaisons '03
Changing Times '04
Kings and Queen '04
Apres Lui '07
Persepolis '07 (V)
A Christmas Tale '08
The Girl on the Train '09
The Big Picture '10
Potiche '10
Beloved '11
On My Way '14
The Brand New Testament '15
The Midwife '17

Chao Deng
The Four '12
Kingdom of Blood: The Final Battle '16
The Mermaid '16
Shadow '18

Jake Dengel (1933-94)
Ironweed '87
Bloodsucking Pharoahs of Pittsburgh '90
Prayer of the Rollerboys '91

Christopher Denham (1985-)
Headspace '02
El Camino '08
Camp Hell '10
Sound of My Voice '11
The Bay '12
Fast Color '18

Maurice Denham (1909-2002)
Captain Boycott '47
Blanche Fury '48
Terror on a Train '53
The Purple Plain '54
Animal Farm '55 (V)
Simon and Laura '55
23 Paces to Baker Street '56
All at Sea '57
Curse of the Demon '57
Our Man in Havana '59
Sink the Bismarck '60
Invasion Quartet '61
The Mark '61
Damn the Defiant '62
Paranoiac '62
Hysteria '64
The Seventh Dawn '64
The Alphabet Murders '65
The Nanny '65
Night Caller from Outer Space '66
Sunday, Bloody Sunday '71
Luther '74
From a Far Country: Pope John Paul II '81
All Passion Spent '86
84 Charing Cross Road '86

Marianne (Cuau) Denicourt (1966-)
La Belle Noiseuse *'90*
La Sentinelle *'92*
Doomsday Gun *'94*
My Sex Life. . . Or How I Got into an Argument *'96*
The Lost Son *'98*
Sade *'00*
Me Without You *'01*

Lydie Denier (1964-)
Blood Relations *'87*
Mardi Gras for the Devil *'93*
Red Shoe Diaries 3: Another Woman's Lipstick *'93*
Guardian Angel *'94*

Alexis Denisof (1966-)
Sharpe's Justice *'97*
Sharpe's Revenge *'97*
Sharpe's Waterloo *'97*
Noah's Ark *'99*
Rip It Off *'02*
Much Ado About Nothing *'13*

Anthony John (Tony) Denison (1949-)
Full Exposure: The Sex Tape Scandals *'89*
City of Hope *'91*
The Harvest *'92*
The Amy Fisher Story *'93*
Full Eclipse *'93*
Getting Gotti *'94*
Men of War *'94*
Looking for an Echo *'99*
Now You Know *'02*
Wild Things 2 *'04*
Crash and Burn *'07*

Leslie Denison (1905-92)
Sherlock Holmes and the Secret Weapon *'42*
To Be or Not to Be *'42*
Five Graves to Cairo *'43*
The Bandit of Sherwood Forest *'46*
The Snow Creature *'54*

Michael Denison (1915-98)
The Glass Mountain *'49*
The Importance of Being Earnest *'52*
Angels One Five *'54*
Shadowlands *'93*

David Denman (1973-)
The Replacements *'00*
Big Fish *'03*
When a Stranger Calls *'06*
Shutter *'08*
Fair Game *'10*
Let Go *'11*
The Gift *'15*
13 Hours: The Secret Soldiers of Benghazi *'16*
Puzzle *'18*
Brightburn *'19*

Tony Denman (1979-)
Poor White Trash *'00*
Sorority Boys *'02*
Transylmania *'09*

Marie Denn
Wild Guitar *'62*
Bury Me an Angel *'71*

Brian Dennehy (1938-2020)
Ants *'77*
Semi-Tough *'77*
F.I.S.T. *'78*
Foul Play *'78*
Pearl *'78*
A Real American Hero *'78*
Butch and Sundance: The Early Days *'79*
Dummy *'79*
10 *'79*
Little Miss Marker *'80*
First Blood *'82*
Gorky Park *'83*
Never Cry Wolf *'83*
Cocoon *'85*
Silverado *'85*
Twice in a Lifetime *'85*
F/X *'86*
Legal Eagles *'86*
Best Seller *'87*
Cocoon: The Return *'88*
A Father's Revenge *'88*
Return to Snowy River *'88*
Day One *'89*
Perfect Witness *'89*
A Killing in a Small Town *'90*
The Last of the Finest *'90*
Presumed Innocent *'90*
Pride and Extreme Prejudice *'90*
The Belly of an Architect *'91*
F/X 2: The Deadly Art of Illusion *'91*
Gladiator *'92*
Teamster Boss: The Jackie Presser Story *'92*
To Catch a Killer *'92*
The Stars Fell on Henrietta *'94*
Tommy Boy *'95*
Larry McMurtry's Dead Man's Walk *'96*
Steve Martini's Undue Influence *'96*
William Shakespeare's Romeo and Juliet *'96*
Dish Dogs *'98*
Tom Clancy's Netforce *'98*
Out of the Cold *'99*
Silicon Towers *'99*
Fail Safe *'00*
Summer Catch *'01*
A Season on the Brink *'02*
Stolen Summer *'02*
The Roman Spring of Mrs. Stone *'03*
Category 6: Day of Destruction *'04*
She Hate Me *'04*
Assault on Precinct 13 *'05*
Everyone's Hero *'06 (V)*
10th & Wolf *'06*
Marco Polo *'07*
Ratatouille *'07 (V)*
The Ultimate Gift *'07*
War Eagle, Arkansas *'07*
Welcome to Paradise *'07*
Cat City *'08*
Righteous Kill *'08*
Alleged *'10*
Every Day *'10*
Meet Monica Velour *'10*
The Next Three Days *'10*
The Big Year *'11*
Knight of Cups *'15*

Ned Dennehy (1965-)
Death Games *'02*
Reign of Fire *'02*
Roadkill *'11*
Tyrannosaur *'11*
The Keeping Room *'15*
Mandy *'18*

Barry Dennen (1938-)
Jesus Christ, Superstar *'73*
The Shining *'80*
Liquid Dreams *'92*

Charles Denner (1926-95)
The Thief of Paris *'67*
The Bride Wore Black *'68*
The Two of Us *'68*
Z *'69*
The Holes *'72*
Mado *'76*
The Man Who Loved Women *'77*

Richard Denning (1914-98)
Golden Gloves *'40*
Adam Had Four Sons *'41*
Beyond the Blue Horizon *'42*
The Glass Key *'42*
Seven Were Saved *'47*
Unknown Island *'48*
Hangman's Knot *'52*
Battle of Rogue River *'54*
Creature from the Black Lagoon *'54*
The Crooked Web *'55*
Day the World Ended *'55*
The Gun That Won the West *'55*
An Affair to Remember *'57*
The Black Scorpion *'57*
Twice-Told Tales *'63*
Alice Through the Looking Glass *'66*

Kat Dennings (1986-)
Raise Your Voice *'04*
Down in the Valley *'05*
The 40 Year Old Virgin *'05*
Big Momma's House 2 *'06*
Charlie Bartlett *'07*
The House Bunny *'08*
Nick & Norah's Infinite Playlist *'08*
The Answer Man *'09*
Defendor *'09*
Shorts: The Adventures of the Wishing Rock *'09*
Daydream Nation *'10*
Thor *'11*
Thor: The Dark World *'13*
To Write Love On Her Arms *'14*

Gabrielle Dennis
Bring It On: Fight to the Finish *'09*
The Marc Pease Experience *'09*
Holly's Holiday *'12*
Black Coffee *'14*

Mark Dennis (1932-)
The Millerson Case *'47*
Time Trap *'17 (V)*

Nick Dennis (1904-80)
Eight Iron Men *'52*
The Glory Brigade *'53*
Kiss Me Deadly *'55*
Too Late Blues *'61*

Sandy Dennis (1937-92)
Splendor in the Grass *'61*
Who's Afraid of Virginia Woolf? *'66*
Up the Down Staircase *'67*
Sweet November *'68*
That Cold Day in the Park *'69*
The Out-of-Towners *'70*
God Told Me To *'76*
Nasty Habits *'77*
The Four Seasons *'81*
The Execution *'85*
Another Woman *'88*
976-EVIL *'88*
Parents *'89*
The Indian Runner *'91*

Julian Dennison
Hunt for the Wilderpeople *'16*
Deadpool 2 *'18*

Reginald Denny (1891-1967)
California Straight Ahead *'25*
Skinner's Dress Suit *'26*
Madam Satan *'30*
Parlor, Bedroom and Bath *'31*
Private Lives *'31*
Stepping Out *'31*
The Barbarian *'33*
The Lost Patrol *'34*
Of Human Bondage *'34*
The World Moves On *'34*
Anna Karenina *'35*
No More Ladies *'35*
Vagabond Lady *'35*
More Than A Secretary *'36*
Bulldog Drummond Comes Back *'37*
Bulldog Drummond Escapes *'37*
Join the Marines *'37*
Bulldog Drummond's Peril *'38*
Four Men and a Prayer *'38*
Bulldog Drummond's Bride *'39*
Rebecca *'40*
Spring Parade *'40*
Captains of the Clouds *'42*
Eyes in the Night *'42*
Sherlock Holmes and the Voice of Terror *'42*
Thunder Birds *'42*
Love Letters *'45*
Escape Me Never *'47*
My Favorite Brunette *'47*
Mr. Blandings Builds His Dream House *'48*
Abbott and Costello Meet Dr. Jekyll and Mr. Hyde *'52*
Fort Vengeance *'53*
World for Ransom *'54*
Escape to Burma *'55*
Sabaka *'55*
Around the World in 80 Days *'56 (C)*
Cat Ballou *'65*
Assault on a Queen *'66*
Batman *'66*

Catherine Dent (1965-)
The Majestic *'01*
Replicant *'01*
Someone Like You *'01*
Venomous *'01*
Taken *'02*
The Unseen *'05*
The Bad Son *'07*
The Natalee Holloway Story *'09*
Drew Peterson: Untouchable *'12*

Rhonda Dent (1978-)
Insecticidal *'05*
Presumed Dead *'06*

Vernon Dent (1895-1963)
Extra Girl *'23*
The Cameraman *'28*
Hitler: Beast of Berlin *'39*

Christa Denton (1972-)
The Bad Seed *'85*
The Gate *'87*

Donna Denton
Death Blow *'87*
Glory Years *'87*
Lethal Victims *'87*

Graham Denton (1914-66)
The Great St. Louis Bank Robbery *'59*
The Young One *'61*

James Denton (1963-)
Undead or Alive *'07*
Tortured *'08*
Grace Unplugged *'13*

Jamie Denton (1963-)
See James Denton

J.J. Denton
The Strangers *'98*
King of the Lost World *'06*

Will Denton
Palindromes *'04*
Camp Hell *'10*

Bob Denver (1935-2005)
Take Her, She's Mine *'63*
Who's Minding the Mint? *'67*
The Sweet Ride *'68*
Wackiest Wagon Train in the West *'77*
Rescue from Gilligan's Island *'78*
High School USA *'84*
Back to the Beach *'87*

John Denver (1943-97)
Oh, God! *'77*
Fire and Ice *'87 (N)*
Foxfire *'87*
Higher Ground *'88*
Walking Thunder *'94*

Elisabeth Depardieu (1941-)
Jean de Florette *'87*
Manon of the Spring *'87*

Gerard Depardieu (1948-)
The Holes *'72*
Nathalie Granger *'72*
Going Places *'74*
Stavisky *'74*
Barocco *'76*
Maitresse *'76*
1900 *'76*
Get Out Your Handkerchiefs *'78*
Buffet Froid *'79*
The Last Metro *'80*
Loulou *'80*
Mon Oncle d'Amerique *'80*
La Chevre *'81*
The Woman Next Door *'81*
Danton *'82*
Les Comperes *'83*
Moon in the Gutter *'83*
The Return of Martin Guerre *'83*
Fort Saganne *'84*
Police *'85*
Menage *'86*
Jean de Florette *'87*
Too Beautiful for You *'88*
Camille Claudel *'89*
I Want to Go Home *'89*
Cyrano de Bergerac *'90*
Green Card *'90*
1492: Conquest of Paradise *'92*
Tous les Matins du Monde *'92*
My Father the Hero *'93*
Helas pour Moi *'94*
A Pure Formality *'94*
The Horseman on the Roof *'95 (C)*
Bogus *'96*
Hamlet *'96*
The Secret Agent *'96*
Unhook the Stars *'96*
The Man in the Iron Mask *'98*
Balzac: A Life of Passion *'99*
The Count of Monte Cristo *'99*
The Bridge *'00*
The Closet *'00*
102 Dalmatians *'00*
Vatel *'00*
CQ *'01*
Between Strangers *'02*
A Loving Father *'02*
Bon Voyage *'03*
City of Ghosts *'03*
Crime Spree *'03*
La Femme Musketeer *'03*
Napoleon *'03*
Nathalie *'03*
Changing Times *'04*
The 36th Precinct *'04*
How Much Do You Love Me? *'05*
Last Holiday *'06*
Paris, je t'aime *'06*
La Vie en Rose *'07*
Babylon A.D. *'08*
Hello Goodbye *'08*
Mesrine: Part 1-Killer Instinct *'08*
Inspector Bellamy *'09*
Mammuth *'10*
My Afternoons with Marguerite *'10*
Potiche *'10*
Welcome to New York *'15*
Sgt. Stubby: An American Hero *'18*

Guillaume Depardieu (1971-2008)
Tous les Matins du Monde *'92*
The Count of Monte Cristo *'99*
Pola X *'99*
A Loving Father *'02*
Napoleon *'03*
The Duchess of Langeais *'07*
La France *'07*

Julie Depardieu (1973-)
The Count of Monte Cristo *'99*
Les Destinees *'00*
La Petite Lili *'03*
Blame It on Fidel *'06*
You and Me *'06*
Rush Hour 3 *'07*
A Secret *'07*
The Witnesses *'07*

Johnny Depp (1963-)
A Nightmare on Elm Street *'84*
Private Resort *'84*
Platoon *'86*
Cry-Baby *'90*
Edward Scissorhands *'90*
Freddy's Dead: The Final Nightmare *'91*
Benny & Joon *'93*
What's Eating Gilbert Grape *'93*
Arizona Dream *'94*
Don Juan DeMarco *'94*
Ed Wood *'94*
Dead Man *'95*
Nick of Time *'95*
Donnie Brasco *'96*
Fear and Loathing in Las Vegas *'98*
The Astronaut's Wife *'99*
The Ninth Gate *'99*
Sleepy Hollow *'99*
Before Night Falls *'00*
Chocolat *'00*
The Man Who Cried *'00*
Blow *'01*
From Hell *'01*
Once Upon a Time in Mexico *'03*
Pirates of the Caribbean: The Curse of the Black Pearl *'03*
Finding Neverland *'04*
Happily Ever After *'04*
Secret Window *'04*
Charlie and the Chocolate Factory *'05*
The Libertine *'05*
Tim Burton's Corpse Bride *'05 (V)*
Pirates of the Caribbean: Dead Man's Chest *'06*
Pirates of the Caribbean: At World's End *'07*
Sweeney Todd: The Demon Barber of Fleet Street *'07*
The Imaginarium of Doctor Parnassus *'09*
Public Enemies *'09*
Alice in Wonderland *'10*
The Tourist *'10*
Pirates of the Caribbean: On Stranger Tides *'11*
Rango *'11 (V)*
The Rum Diary *'11*
Dark Shadows *'12*
21 Jump Street *'12 (C)*
For No Good Reason *'13*
The Lone Ranger *'13*
Lucky Them *'13 (C)*
Into the Woods *'14*
Transcendence *'14*
Tusk *'14*
Black Mass *'15*
Mortdecai *'15*
Alice Through the Looking Glass *'16*
Yoga Hosers *'16*
Pirates of the Caribbean: Dead Men Tell No Tales *'17*
Fantastic Beasts: The Crimes of Grindelwald *'18*
Sherlock Gnomes *'18*
The Professor *'19*

Timothy Lee DePriest
Vampire Clan *'02*
Dishdogz *'05*

Emilie Dequenne (1981-)
Rosetta *'99*
Brotherhood of the Wolf *'01*
The Housekeeper *'02*
The Bridge of San Luis Rey *'05*
A Song of Innocence *'05*
The Girl on the Train *'09*
Our Children *'12*
Mobius *'13*

Gregori Derangere (1971-)
Bon Voyage *'03*
The 4 Musketeers *'05*

Eugenio Derbez (1962-)
Under the Same Moon *'07*
Jack and Jill *'11*
How to Be a Latin Lover *'17*
Overboard *'18*

Bo Derek (1956-)
Fantasies *'73*
Orca *'77*
10 *'79*
A Change of Seasons *'80*
Tarzan, the Ape Man *'81*
Bolero *'84*
Shattered Image *'93*
Woman of Desire *'93*
Tommy Boy *'95*
Sunstorm *'01*
Malibu's Most Wanted *'03*
The Hunt for the I-5 Killer *'11*
Sharknado 3: Oh Hell No! *'15*

John Derek (1926-98)
I'll Be Seeing You *'44*
All the King's Men *'49*
Knock on Any Door *'49*
Rogues of Sherwood Forest *'50*
The Family Secret *'51*
Scandal Sheet *'52*
Ambush at Tomahawk Gap *'53*
The Last Posse *'53*
Run for Cover *'55*
The Ten Commandments *'56*
Omar Khayyam *'57*
Exodus *'60*
Once Before I Die *'65*

Joe DeRita (1909-93)
Have Rocket Will Travel *'59*
Snow White and the Three Stooges *'61*
The Three Stooges Meet Hercules *'61*
Three Stooges in Orbit *'62*
Around the World in a Daze *'63*
Four for Texas *'63*
It's a Mad, Mad, Mad, Mad World *'63*
The Outlaws Is Coming! *'65*

Edouard Dermithe (1915-95)
Orpheus *'49*
Les Enfants Terrible *'50*
The Testament of Orpheus *'59*

Maeve Dermody (1985-)
Black Water *'07*
Beautiful Kate *'09*
Griff the Invisible *'10*

Bruce Dern (1936-)
Wild River *'60*
Marnie *'64*
Hush, Hush, Sweet Charlotte *'65*
The Wild Angels *'66*
The St. Valentine's Day Massacre *'67*
The Trip *'67*
The War Wagon *'67*
Waterhole Number 3 *'67*
Will Penny *'67*
Psych-Out *'68*
Castle Keep *'69*
Rebel Rousers *'69*
Support Your Local Sheriff *'69*
They Shoot Horses, Don't They? *'69*
Bloody Mama *'70*
The Incredible Two-Headed Transplant *'71*
Silent Running *'71*
The Cowboys *'72*
The King of Marvin Gardens *'72*
Thumb Tripping *'72*
The Great Gatsby *'74*
The Laughing Policeman *'74*
Posse *'75*
Smile *'75*
Family Plot *'76*
The Twist *'76*
Black Sunday *'77*
Coming Home *'78*
The Driver *'78*
That Championship Season *'82*
Harry Tracy *'83*
On the Edge *'86*
Big Town *'87*
Roses Are for the Rich *'87*
The 'Burbs *'89*
1969 *'89*
After Dark, My Sweet *'90*
Carolina Skeletons *'92*
Diggstown *'92*
Into the Badlands *'92*
Dead Man's Revenge *'93*
Amelia Earhart: The Final Flight *'94*
Mulholland Falls *'95*
Wild Bill *'95*
Down Periscope *'96*
Last Man Standing *'96*
Small Soldiers *'98 (V)*
The Haunting *'99*
All the Pretty Horses *'00*
The Glass House *'01*
Madison *'01*
Hard Ground *'03*
Masked and Anonymous *'03*
Milwaukee, Minnesota *'03*
Monster *'03*
Down in the Valley *'05*
Believe in Me *'06*
Walker Payne *'06*
The Astronaut Farmer *'07*
The Cake Eaters *'07*
The Golden Boys *'08*
Swamp Devil *'08*
American Cowslip *'09*
The Lightkeepers *'09*
Inside Out *'11*
Django Unchained *'12*
Twixt *'12*
Nebraska *'13*
American Violence *'17*
Chappaquiddick *'17*
Nostalgia *'18*
The Mustang *'19*

Laura Dern (1966-)
Alice Doesn't Live Here Anymore *'74*
Foxes *'80*
Ladies and Gentlemen, the Fabulous Stains *'82*
Teachers *'84*
Mask *'85*
Smooth Talk *'85*
Blue Velvet *'86*
Haunted Summer *'88*
Fat Man and Little Boy *'89*
Wild at Heart *'90*
Rambling Rose *'91*
Afterburn *'92*
Jurassic Park *'93*
A Perfect World *'93*
Citizen Ruth *'96*
The Baby Dance *'98*
Daddy & Them *'99*
October Sky *'99*
A Season for Miracles *'99*
Dr. T & the Women *'00*
Focus *'01*
I Am Sam *'01*
Jurassic Park 3 *'01*
Novocaine *'01*
We Don't Live Here Anymore *'04*
Happy Endings *'05*
The Prize Winner of Defiance, Ohio *'05*
Inland Empire *'06*
Lonely Hearts *'06*
Year of the Dog *'07*
Recount *'08*
Tenderness *'08*
Everything Must Go *'10*
The Master *'12*
The Fault In Our Stars *'14*
99 Homes *'14*
When the Game Stands Tall *'14*
Wild *'14*
Certain Women *'16*
The Founder *'17*
Wilson *'17*
The Tale *'18*
Trial by Fire *'18*
Cold Pursuit *'19*
Little Women *'19*
Marriage Story *'19*

Warren DeRosa
Black Dawn *'05*
The Art of War 3: Retribution *'08*

Richard Derr (1918-92)
Just Off Broadway *'42*
The Secret Heart *'46*
The Bride Goes Wild *'48*
Guilty of Treason *'50*
When Worlds Collide *'51*
Something to Live For *'52*
Terror Is a Man *'59*
Adam at 6 a.m. *'70*

Cleavant Derricks (1953-)
Moscow on the Hudson *'84*
The Slugger's Wife *'85*
Carnival of Souls *'98*
World Traveler *'01*
Miami Magma *'11*

Donna D'Errico (1968-)
Candyman 3: Day of the Dead *'98*
Austin Powers In Goldmember *'02 (C)*
Comic Book: The Movie *'04*

Sean Derry
The Bridge to Nowhere *'09*
Mafia *'11*

Debi Derryberry (1967-)
Kiki's Delivery Service *'98 (V)*
Whispers: An Elephant's Tale *'00 (V)*
Jimmy Neutron: Boy Genius *'01 (V)*
Comic Book: The Movie *'04*
Dr. Seuss' Horton Hears a Who! *'08 (V)*

Michael Des Barres (1948-)
I, Monster *'71*
Pink Cadillac *'89*
Waxwork 2: Lost in Time *'91*
The High Crusade *'92*
A Simple Twist of Fate *'94*
Poison Ivy 3: The New Seduction *'97*
Sugar Town *'99*
The Man from Elysian Fields *'01*
Mulholland Drive *'01*
Catch That Kid *'04*
California Solo *'12*

Jean Desailly (1920-2008)
The Soft Skin *'64*
Assassination of Trotsky *'72*
Le Professionnel *'81*

Anne DeSalvo (1949-)
My Favorite Year *'82*
D.C. Cab *'84*
Perfect *'85*
Burglar *'87*
Taking Care of Business *'90*
Dead in the Water *'91*
Hi-Life *'98*

Jaclyn DeSantis
Bomb the System *'05*
Carlito's Way: Rise to Power *'05*

Stanley DeSantis (1953-2005)
Candyman *'92*
Armistead Maupin's Tales of the City *'93*
Broken Trust *'95*
The Truth about Cats and Dogs *'96*
Clockwatchers *'97*
Fools Rush In *'97*
Heartwood *'98*
Lansky *'99*
Head Over Heels *'01*
I Am Sam *'01*
The Aviator *'04*

Alex Descas (1958-)
I Can't Sleep *'93*
Irma Vep *'96*
Nenette and Boni *'96*
Late August, Early September *'98*
Harem *'99*
Lumumba *'01*
Coffee and Cigarettes *'03*
Boarding Gate *'07*
35 Shots of Rum *'08*
The Limits of Control *'09*
Rapt *'09*

Jerome Deschamps
The Separation *'94*
La Separation *'98*

Emily Deschanel (1976-)
The Alamo *'04*
Spider-Man 2 *'04*
Boogeyman *'05*
Glory Road *'06*
The Perfect Family *'11*

Mary Jo Deschanel (1945-)
The Right Stuff *'83*
2010: The Year We Make Contact *'84*
Bark! *'02*

Zooey Deschanel (1980-)
Mumford *'99*
Almost Famous *'00*
Manic *'01*
Abandon *'02*
Big Trouble *'02*
The Good Girl *'02*
The New Guy *'02*
All the Real Girls *'03*
Elf *'03*
Eulogy *'04*
The Hitchhiker's Guide to the Galaxy *'05*
Winter Passing *'05*
Failure to Launch *'06*
The Assassination of Jesse James by the Coward Robert Ford *'07*
Bridge to Terabithia *'07*
Flakes *'07*
The Go-Getter *'07*
The Good Life *'07*
Surf's Up *'07 (V)*
Tin Man *'07*
Gigantic *'08*
The Happening *'08*
Yes Man *'08*
(500) Days of Summer *'09*
Our Idiot Brother *'11*
Your Highness *'11*
Rock the Kasbah *'15*
The Driftless Area *'16*
Trolls *'16*

Sandy Descher (1945-)
Them! *'54*
The Cobweb *'55*
The Prodigal *'55*
The Space Children *'58*

Alex Desert (1968-)
P.C.U. *'94*
Swingers *'96*
Pretty Persuasion *'05*

Marie Desgranges
Dad On the Run *'00*
Safe Conduct *'01*

Robert Desiderio (1951-)
Oh, God! You Devil *'84*
Maximum Security *'87*
Gross Anatomy *'89*
Take My Advice: The Ann & Abby Story *'99*
Liberal Arts *'12*

Cleo Desmond (1880-1958)
The Spirit of Youth *'37*
Mokey *'42*

Florence Desmond (1905-93)
Accused *'36*
Three Came Home *'50*

William Desmond (1878-1949)
Battling with Buffalo Bill *'31*
Phantom of the West *'31*
Tailspin Tommy *'34*
Rustlers of Red Dog *'35*

Ivan Desny (1928-2002)
Madeleine *'50*
Lola Montes *'55*
Anastasia *'56*
Song Without End *'60*
Daniella by Night *'61*
Sherlock Holmes and the Deadly Necklace *'62*
Mayerling *'68*
Little Mother *'71*
World on a Wire *'73*
Touch Me Not *'74*
The Marriage of Maria Braun *'79*
Lola *'81*
The Future of Emily *'85*
The Disenchanted *'90*
I Don't Kiss *'91*
Les Voleurs *'96*

Melissa Desormeaux-Poulin
Incendies *'10*
Gabrielle *'13*

Rosanna Desoto (1950-)
The In-Laws *'79*
La Bamba *'87*
Stand and Deliver *'88*
Family Business *'89*
Star Trek 6: The Undiscovered Country *'91*
The 24 Hour Woman *'99*
Mambo Cafe *'00*

Nada Despotovich (1967-)
Babycakes *'89*
Series 7: The Contenders *'01*

Natalie Desselle (1967-)
B.A.P.'s *'97*
Def Jam's How to Be a Player *'97*
Madea's Big Happy Family *'11*

Amanda Detmer (1971-)
Drop Dead Gorgeous *'99*
Boys and Girls *'00*
Final Destination *'00*
A Little Inside *'01*
The Majestic *'01*
Saving Silverman *'01*
Big Fat Liar *'02*
Extreme Dating *'04*
Final Move *'06*
Jam *'06*
Proof of Lies *'06*
You, Me and Dupree *'06*
American Crude *'07*
American East *'07*

Maruschka Detmers (1962-)
First Name: Carmen *'83*
Devil in the Flesh *'87*
The Mambo Kings *'92*
Hidden Assassin *'94*

Tamara DeTreaux (1959-90)
Don't Be Afraid of the Dark *'73*
Ghoulies *'84*

Madelyn Deutch
Mayor Cupcake *'11*
50 to 1 *'14*

Zoey Deutch (1994-)
Mayor Cupcake *'11*
Vampire Academy *'14*
Dirty Grandpa *'16*
Good Kids *'16*
Why Him? *'16*
Before I Fall *'17*
Rebel in the Rye *'17*
Vincent N Roxxy *'17*
Flower *'18*
The Professor *'19*
Zombieland: Double Tap *'19*
Buffaloed *'20*

Ernst Deutsch (1890-1969)
The Golem *'20*
The Third Man *'49*

Patti Deutsch (1945-)
Jetsons: The Movie *'90 (V)*
The Emperor's New Groove *'00 (V)*

William Devane (1937-)
McCabe & Mrs. Miller *'71*
Missiles of October *'74*
Report to the Commissioner *'75*
Family Plot *'76*
Marathon Man *'76*
The Bad News Bears in Breaking Training *'77*
Rolling Thunder *'77*
The Dark *'79*
Yanks *'79*
Honky Tonk Freeway *'81*
Jane Doe *'83*
Testament *'83*
Timestalkers *'87*
Murder C.O.D. *'90*
Vital Signs *'90*
Detonator 2: Night Watch *'95*
Payback *'98*
Hollow Man *'00*
Poor White Trash *'00*
Space Cowboys *'00*
Race to Space *'01*
The Badge *'02*
Threat of Exposure *'02*
Monte Walsh *'03*
Deceit *'04*
Jesse Stone: Death in Paradise *'06*
Jesse Stone: Sea Change *'07*
Stargate: Continuum *'08*
Chasing the Green *'09*
Jesse Stone: Thin Ice *'09*
The Least Among You *'09*
Jesse Stone: No Remorse *'10*
The Kane Files *'10*
The River Why *'10*
Jesse Stone: Innocents Lost *'11*
The Dark Knight Rises *'12*
Jesse Stone: Benefit of the Doubt *'12*
Red Clover *'12*
Bad Turn Worse *'14*
50 to 1 *'14*
Interstellar *'14*

Joanna DeVarona (1953-)
See Joanna Kerns

Devin Devasquez (1963-)
Can't Buy Me Love *'87*
House 2: The Second Story *'87*
Society *'92*

Nathaniel DeVeaux
Bad Attitude *'93*
Outrage *'98*
In a Class of His Own *'99*
My Neighbor's Keeper *'07*

Stuart Devenie
Dead Alive *'93*
Jack Brown, Genius *'94*

Kaitlyn Dever (1996-)
Cinema Verite *'11*
Short Term 12 *'13*
Men, Women & Children *'14*
Outside In *'17*
We Don't Belong Here *'17*
Booksmart *'19*
Them That Follow *'19*

Marie Devereux (1941-)
The Mark *'61*
Naked Kiss *'64*

Paula DeVicq (1965-)
Dinner and Driving *'97*
The Breakup Artist *'04*
His and Her Christmas *'05*
First Dog *'10*

Renee Devillers (1902-2000)
Heart of a Nation *'43*
The French Touch *'54*

Adam Devine (1983-)
Pitch Perfect *'12*
The Intern *'15*
Ice Age: Collision Course *'16*
Mike and Dave Need Wedding Dates *'16*
Isn't It Romantic *'19*
Jexi *'19*

Aidan Devine
Brian's Song *'01*
Life with Judy Garland-Me and My Shadows *'01*
Everything's Gone Green *'06*
Dolan's Cadillac *'09*

Andy Devine (1905-77)
The Man From Yesterday *'32*
Three Wise Girls *'32*
Chance at Heaven *'33*
Doctor Bull *'33*
Midnight Mary *'33*
Stingaree *'34*
Upperworld *'34*
Double or Nothing *'37*
In Old Chicago *'37*
A Star Is Born *'37*
Men with Wings *'38*
Never Say Die *'39*
Stagecoach *'39*
Buck Benny Rides Again *'40*
Torrid Zone *'40*
The Flame of New Orleans *'41*
Ali Baba and the Forty Thieves *'43*
Canyon Passage *'46*
Grand Canyon Trail *'48*

Under California Stars *'48*
The Red Badge of Courage *'51*
Island in the Sky *'53*
Around the World in 80 Days *'56 (C)*
The Adventures of Huckleberry Finn *'60*
Two Rode Together *'61*
The Man Who Shot Liberty Valance *'62*
How the West Was Won *'63*
Zebra in the Kitchen *'65*
The Ballad of Josie *'67*
The Over-the-Hill Gang *'69*
Myra Breckinridge *'70*
The Over-the-Hill Gang Rides Again *'70*
Robin Hood *'73 (V)*

George Devine (1910-66)
Beggar's Opera *'54*
Time Without Pity *'57*
Look Back in Anger *'58*
Tom Jones *'63*

Loretta Devine (1949-)
Stanley and Iris *'90*
Waiting to Exhale *'95*
Hoodlum *'96*
The Preacher's Wife *'96*
Rebound: The Legend of Earl 'The Goat' Manigault *'96*
Don King: Only in America *'97*
Down in the Delta *'98*
Love Kills *'98*
Urban Legend *'98*
The Breaks *'99*
Introducing Dorothy Dandridge *'99*
Freedom Song *'00*
Urban Legends 2: Final Cut *'00*
What Women Want *'00*
I Am Sam *'01*
Kingdom Come *'01*
Woman, Thou Art Loosed *'04*
Crash *'05*
King's Ransom *'05*
Dreamgirls *'06*
Cougar Club *'07*
Dirty Laundry *'07*
This Christmas *'07*
Beverly Hills Chihuahua *'08 (V)*
First Sunday *'08*
My Son, My Son, What Have Ye Done *'09*
Death at a Funeral *'10*
For Colored Girls *'10*
The Lottery Ticket *'10*
Jumping the Broom *'11*
Madea's Big Happy Family *'11*
Welcome to Me *'15*

Sean Devine (1970-)
Perpetrators of the Crime *'98*
Dead Silent *'99*
The Rendering *'02*

Danny DeVito (1944-)
Hurry Up or I'll Be Thirty *'73*
The Money *'75*
One Flew Over the Cuckoo's Nest *'75*
The Van *'77*
Goin' South *'78*
Terms of Endearment *'83*
Johnny Dangerously *'84*
Ratings Game *'84*
Romancing the Stone *'84*
The Jewel of the Nile *'85*
Head Office *'86*
Ruthless People *'86*
Wise Guys *'86*
Throw Momma from the Train *'87*
Tin Men *'87*
Twins *'88*
The War of the Roses *'89*
Other People's Money *'91*
Batman Returns *'92*
Hoffa *'92*
Jack the Bear *'93*
Look Who's Talking Now *'93 (V)*
Junior *'94*
Renaissance Man *'94*
Get Shorty *'95*
Mars Attacks! *'96*
Matilda *'96*
Space Jam *'96 (V)*
Hercules *'97 (V)*
John Grisham's The Rainmaker *'97*
L.A. Confidential *'97*
Living Out Loud *'98*
Man on the Moon *'99*
The Virgin Suicides *'99*
The Big Kahuna *'00*
Drowning Mona *'00*
Screwed *'00*
Heist *'01*
What's the Worst That Could Happen? *'01*
Austin Powers In Goldmember *'02 (C)*
Death to Smoochy *'02*
Anything Else *'03*
Big Fish *'03*
Be Cool *'05*
Deck the Halls *'06*
Even Money *'06*
Marilyn Hotchkiss' Ballroom Dancing & Charm School *'06*
The Oh in Ohio *'06*
Relative Strangers *'06*
10 Items or Less *'06*
The Good Night *'07*
Just Add Water *'07*
Reno 911! Miami *'07 (C)*
Nobel Son *'08*
Housebroken *'09*
Solitary Man *'10*
Dr. Seuss' The Lorax *'12 (V)*
The Comedian *'16*
Wiener-Dog *'16*
Dumbo *'19*

Matthew Devitt
Funnyman *'94*
Waking Ned Devine *'98*

Alan Devlin (1947-2011)
Danny Boy *'82*
The Lonely Passion of Judith Hearne *'87*
The Playboys *'92*
Bloom *'03*

Dean Devlin (1962-)
Real Genius *'85*
Moon 44 *'90*

D. G. Devon (1952-)
See Michael Gross

Laura Devon (1931-2007)
Red Line 7000 *'65*
A Covenant With Death *'67*

Richard Devon (1926-2010)
The Prodigal *'55*
Blood of Dracula *'57*
Teenage Doll *'57*
The Undead *'57*
The Viking Women and the Sea Serpent *'57*
War of the Satellites *'58*
The Silencers *'66*

Emmanuelle Devos (1964-)
My Sex Life. . . Or How I Got into an Argument *'96*
Dad On the Run *'00*
Esther Kahn *'00*
Read My Lips *'01*
Gilles' Wife *'04*
Kings and Queen *'04*
The Beat My Heart Skipped *'05*
La Moustache *'05*
A Christmas Tale *'08*
One Day You'll Understand *'08*
Coco Before Chanel *'09*
Wild Grass *'09*
The Other Son *'12*

Jon (John) DeVries (1947-)
The 4th Man *'79*
Lianna *'83*
Truth or Die *'86*
Sarah, Plain and Tall *'91*
Sarah, Plain and Tall: Skylark *'93*

Elaine Devry (1930-)
Man-Trap *'61*
Diary of a Madman *'63*
A Guide for the Married Man *'67*
The Cheyenne Social Club *'70*

Patrick Dewaere (1947-82)
Going Places *'74*
The Best Way *'76*
Get Out Your Handkerchiefs *'78*
Beau Pere *'81*
Hotel America *'81*

Jenna Dewan (1980-)
Tamara *'05*
Step Up *'06*
Take the Lead *'06*
Love Lies Bleeding *'07*
American Virgin *'09*
The Six Wives of Henry Lefay *'09*
The Jerk Theory *'11*
Setup *'11*

Colleen Dewhurst (1924-93)
The Nun's Story *'59*
Man On a String *'60*
A Fine Madness *'66*
The Last Run *'71*
The Cowboys *'72*
McQ *'74*
The Story of Jacob & Joseph *'74*
Annie Hall *'77*
And Baby Makes Six *'79*
Ice Castles *'79*
When a Stranger Calls *'79*
Final Assignment *'80*
The Guyana Tragedy: The Story of Jim Jones *'80*
The Blue and the Gray *'82*
Dead Zone *'83*
A.D. *'85*
Anne of Green Gables *'85*
The Boy Who Could Fly *'86*
Sword of Gideon *'86*
Anne of Avonlea *'87*
Danielle Steel's Kaleidoscope *'90*
Dying Young *'91*

William Dewhurst (1888-1937)
Sabotage *'36*
Non-Stop New York *'37*

Jacqueline DeWit (1912-98)
Lady on a Train *'45*
Little Giant *'46*
The Damned Don't Cry *'50*

Rosemarie DeWitt (1971-)
Cinderella Man *'05*
The Great New Wonderful *'06*
Rachel Getting Married *'08*
How I Got Lost *'09*
Tenure *'09*
The Company Men *'10*
A Little Bit of Heaven *'11*
Your Sister's Sister *'11*
Nobody Walks *'12*
The Odd Life of Timothy Green *'12*
The Watch *'12*
Kill the Messenger *'14*
Men, Women & Children *'14*
Poltergeist *'15*
La La Land *'16*
Sweet Virginia *'17*
Arizona *'18*
The Professor *'19*

Billy DeWolfe (1907-74)
Blue Skies *'46*
The Perils of Pauline *'47*
Tea for Two *'50*
Lullaby of Broadway *'51*
Billie *'65*

Noureen DeWulf (1984-)
American Dreamz *'06*
The Comebacks *'07*
Ocean's Thirteen *'07*
Pulse 2: Afterlife *'08*

Anthony Dexter (1913-2001)
Captain Kidd and the Slave Girl *'54*
Fire Maidens from Outer Space *'56*
12 to the Moon *'60*
Three Blondes in His Life *'61*

Brad Dexter (1917-2002)
The Asphalt Jungle *'50*
99 River Street *'53*
House of Bamboo *'55*
Violent Saturday *'55*
Between Heaven and Hell *'56*
The Oklahoman *'56*
Run Silent, Run Deep *'58*
Last Train from Gun Hill *'59*
The Magnificent Seven *'60*
Vice Raid *'60*
The George Raft Story *'61*
Twenty Plus Two *'61*
Johnny Cool *'63*
Kings of the Sun *'63*
None But the Brave *'65*
Von Ryan's Express *'65*
Vigilante Force *'76*
Winter Kills *'79*

Susan Dey (1952-)
Skyjacked *'72*
Little Women *'78*
Looker *'81*
Sunset Limousine *'83*
Echo Park *'86*
Beyond Betrayal *'94*
Blue River *'95*
Disappearance *'02*

Agyness Deyn
Sunset Song *'16*
Patient Zero *'18*

Cliff DeYoung (1945-)
Harry and Tonto *'74*
The Lindbergh Kidnapping Case *'76*
Blue Collar *'78*
Centennial *'78*
King *'78*
Shock Treatment *'81*
The Hunger *'83*
Protocol *'84*
Reckless *'84*
Secret Admirer *'85*
F/X *'86*
Flight of the Navigator *'86*
Code Name: Dancer *'87*
Bulldance *'88*
Fear *'88*
Pulse *'88*
Flashback *'89*
Forbidden Sun *'89*
Glory *'89*
Robert Kennedy and His Times *'90*
Dr. Giggles *'92*
Revenge of the Red Baron *'93*
Stephen King's The Tommyknockers *'93*
Carnosaur 2 *'94*
Star Quest *'94*
Andersonville *'95*
JAG *'95*
The Craft *'96*
The Substitute *'96*
George Wallace *'97*
The Last Don *'97*
Suicide Kings *'97*
Get a Clue! *'98*
The Runaway *'00*
Deliberate Intent *'01*
Gale Force *'01*
Path to War *'02*

Ayesha Dharker (1978-)
City of Joy *'92*
The Terrorist *'98*
The Mystic Masseur *'01*
The Mistress of Spices *'05*
Outsourced *'06*

Dharmendra
Deadly Thief *'78*
Hell's Ground *'08*

Caroline Dhavernas (1978-)
Out Cold *'01*
Edge of Madness *'02*
These Girls *'05*
Mr. Average *'06*
Niagara Motel *'06*
Breach *'07*
The Cry of the Owl *'09*
Devil *'10*
Passchendaele *'10*
Wrecked *'10*
Goodbye World *'14*

Sacha Dhawan (1984-)
The History Boys *'06*
The Mystery of Edwin Drood *'12*
An Adventure in Space and Time *'13*

Bernard Dheran (1926-)
Bernadette *'90*
Ridicule *'96*

Dalia di Lazzaro (1953-)
Andy Warhol's Frankenstein *'74*
Lady of the Evening *'75*
Creepers *'85*

Melissa Di Marco (1969-)
No Alibi *'00*
Hustle *'04*

Sophia Di Martino
Draw on Sweet Night *'15*
Yesterday *'19*

Andrea Di Stefano (1972-)
The Phantom of the Opera *'98*
Before Night Falls *'00*
Angela *'02*

Sergio Di Zio (1972-)
Just Buried *'07*
The Lookout *'07*

David Diaan (1959-)
America So Beautiful *'01*
The Stoning of Soraya M. *'08*
Cuck *'19*

Rick Dial (1955-2011)
Sling Blade *'96*
The Apostle *'97*
The General's Daughter *'99*
Beyond the Wall of Sleep *'06*
Bernie *'12*

Chris Diamantopoulos (1975-)
Wedding Daze *'06*
The Starter Wife *'07*
Three Days to Vegas *'07*
The Kennedys *'11*
The Three Stooges *'12*
The Art of the Steal *'13*

Don Diamond (1921-2011)
Borderline *'50*
The Old Man and the Sea *'58*
Hit Man *'72*

Harold Diamond
Hard Ticket to Hawaii *'87*
Picasso Trigger *'89*

Marcia Diamond (1942-)
Deranged *'74*
Love Letters *'99*

Neil Diamond (1941-)
The Jazz Singer *'80*
Saving Silverman *'01*
Keeping Up with the Steins *'06 (C)*

Reed Edward Diamond (1967-)
Memphis Belle *'90*
O Pioneers! *'91*
High Noon *'00*
Homicide: The Movie *'00*
Madison *'01*
Scared Silent *'02*
S.W.A.T. *'03*
Spider-Man 2 *'04*
Good Night, and Good Luck *'05*
Much Ado About Nothing *'13*

Selma Diamond (1920-85)
Bang the Drum Slowly *'73*
Twilight Zone: The Movie *'83*
All of Me *'84*
Ratings Game *'84*

Sheryl Lee Diamond (1967-)
See Sheryl Lee

Dimitri Diatchenko (1968-2020)
Chernobyl Diaries *'12*
Company of Heroes *'13*
They're Watching *'16*

Alyssa Diaz
The Jensen Project *'10*
Shark Night 3D *'11*

Cameron Diaz (1972-)
The Mask *'94*
Feeling Minnesota *'96*
Head Above Water *'96*
Keys to Tulsa *'96*
The Last Supper *'96*
She's the One *'96*
A Life Less Ordinary *'97*
My Best Friend's Wedding *'97*
Fear and Loathing in Las Vegas *'98*
There's Something about Mary *'98*
Very Bad Things *'98*
Any Given Sunday *'99*
Being John Malkovich *'99*
Charlie's Angels *'00*
Invisible Circus *'00*
Things You Can Tell Just by Looking at Her *'00*
Shrek *'01 (V)*
Vanilla Sky *'01*
Gangs of New York *'02*
Slackers *'02*
The Sweetest Thing *'02*
Charlie's Angels: Full Throttle *'03*
Shrek 2 *'04 (V)*
In Her Shoes *'05*
The Holiday *'06*
Shrek the Third *'07 (V)*
What Happens in Vegas *'08*
The Box *'09*
My Sister's Keeper *'09*
Knight and Day *'10*
Shrek Forever After *'10 (V)*
Bad Teacher *'11*
The Green Hornet *'11*
Gambit *'12*
What to Expect When You're Expecting *'12*
The Counselor *'13*
Annie *'14*
The Other Woman *'14*
Sex Tape *'14*

Guillermo Diaz (1975-)
Party Girl *'94*
Freeway *'95*
Girls Town *'95*
Stonewall *'95*
I'm Not Rappaport *'96*
Half-Baked *'97*
I Think I Do *'97*
200 Cigarettes *'98*
Just One Time *'00*
Fidel *'02*
West of Here *'02*
Undefeated *'03*
The Terminal *'04*
Tony n' Tina's Wedding *'07*
Across the Hall *'09*
Without Men *'11*

Joey Diaz (1963-)
The Dog Who Saved Christmas *'09*
The Dog Who Saved Christmas Vacation *'10*
The Dog Who Saved Halloween *'11*
The Dog Who Saved the Holidays *'12*

Jorge Diaz
Filly Brown *'12*
Paranormal Activity: The Marked Ones *'14*
An Encounter with the Messiah *'15*

Maria Isabel Diaz (1964-)
Extramarital *'98*
Volver *'06*

Melonie Diaz (1984-)
Raising Victor Vargas *'03*
A Guide to Recognizing Your Saints *'06*
Feel the Noise *'07*
Itty Bitty Titty Committee *'07*
Remember the Daze *'07*
American Son *'08*
Assassination of a High School President *'08*
Be Kind Rewind *'08*
Hamlet 2 *'08*
Nothing Like the Holidays *'08*
Fruitvale Station *'13*
Supporting Characters *'13*
Ghost Team *'16*
The Belko Experiment *'17*

Vic Diaz (1932-)
Blood Thirst *'65*
Beast of the Yellow Night *'70*
The Big Bird Cage *'72*
Project: Kill! *'77*

Tony DiBenedetto (1944-)
Exterminator *'80*
The Pope of Greenwich Village *'84*
Someone to Watch Over Me *'87*
Family Business *'89*
Dangerous Passion *'95*
Gloria *'98*

Luigi Diberti (1939-)
All Screwed Up *'74*
The Stendahl Syndrome *'95*
For Roseanna *'96*
Saturn in Opposition *'07*

Leonardo DiCaprio (1974-)
Critters 3 *'91*
This Boy's Life *'93*
What's Eating Gilbert Grape *'93*
The Basketball Diaries *'95*
The Quick and the Dead *'95*
Total Eclipse *'95*
Marvin's Room *'96*
William Shakespeare's Romeo and Juliet *'96*
Titanic *'97*
Celebrity *'98*
The Man in the Iron Mask *'98*
The Beach *'00*
Catch Me If You Can *'02*
Gangs of New York *'02*
The Aviator *'04*
Blood Diamond *'06*
The Departed *'06*
The 11th Hour *'07 (N)*
Body of Lies *'08*
Revolutionary Road *'08*
Shutter Island *'09*
Inception *'10*
J. Edgar *'11*
Django Unchained *'12*
The Great Gatsby *'13*
The Wolf of Wall Street *'13*
The Revenant *'15*
Before the Flood *'16*
Once Upon A Time... In Hollywood *'19*

George DiCenzo (1940-2010)
Helter Skelter *'76*
Las Vegas Lady *'76*
The Frisco Kid *'79*
The Ninth Configuration *'79*
Back to the Future *'85*
About Last Night. . . *'86*
Walk Like a Man *'87*
18 Again! *'88*
The New Adventures of Pippi Longstocking *'88*
Exorcist 3: Legion *'90*
Tempted *'01*
Hustle *'04*

Bobby DiCicco (1955-)
I Wanna Hold Your Hand *'78*
The Big Red One *'80*
National Lampoon Goes to the Movies *'81*
Night Shift *'82*
The Philadelphia Experiment *'84*
Splash *'84*
Number One with a Bullet *'87*
Tiger Warsaw *'87*
A Man Called Sarge *'90*
Ghoulies 4 *'93*
Maniac Cop 3: Badge of Silence *'93*
Killing Obsession *'94*
All Dogs Go to Heaven 2 *'95 (V)*

Andy Dick (1965-)
. . .And God Spoke *'94*
In the Army Now *'94*
The Cable Guy *'96*
Best Men *'98*
Bongwater *'98*
The Lion King: Simba's Pride *'98 (V)*
Inspector Gadget *'99*
Picking Up the Pieces *'99*
The Independent *'00*
Loser *'00*
Road Trip *'00*
Dr. Dolittle 2 *'01 (V)*
Scotland, PA *'02*
Old School *'03 (C)*
Hoodwinked *'05 (V)*
Danny Roane: First Time Director *'06*
Employee of the Month *'06*
Blonde Ambition *'07*
The Comebacks *'07*
Happily N'Ever After *'07 (V)*
Rock Slyde: Private Eye *'09*
Hoodwinked Too! Hood *vs.* Evil *'11 (V)*
Freaky Deaky *'12*

Bryan Dick (1978-)
Brothers of the Head *'06*
Blood & Chocolate *'07*
The Old Curiosity Shop *'07*

Douglas Dick (1920-)
Saigon *'47*
The Red Badge of Courage *'51*
The Iron Mistress *'52*
The Gambler from Natchez *'54*
The Oklahoman *'56*
Flaming Star *'60*

William Dick
The Company *'03*
The Merry Gentleman *'08*

Kim Dickens (1965-)
Palookaville *'95*
Great Expectations *'97*
Truth or Consequences, N.M. *'97*
Zero Effect *'97*
Mercury Rising *'98*
Committed *'99*
White River *'99*
The Gift *'00*
Hollow Man *'00*
Things Behind the Sun *'01*
House of Sand and Fog *'03*
Out of Order *'03*
Thank You for Smoking *'06*
Wild Tigers I Have Known *'06*
Red *'08*
One Way to Valhalla *'09*
Reviving Ophelia *'10*
Gone Girl *'14*
Lizzie *'18*

Bonnie Dickenson
Little Shots of Happiness *'97*
Bellyfruit *'99*

Beach Dickerson (1924-2005)
Teenage Caveman *'58*
T-Bird Gang *'59*
Creature from the Haunted Sea *'60*
The Trip *'67*
The Dunwich Horror *'70*

Edwina Findley Dickerson
Get Hard *'15*
Where Children Play *'15*

George Dickerson (1933-2015)
Cutter's Way *'81*
Blue Velvet *'86*
After Dark, My Sweet *'90*
Death Warrant *'90*

Dale Dickey
Winter's Bone *'10*
What Lola Wants *'15*
Bloodline *'19*

Lucinda Dickey (1960-)
Breakin' 2: Electric Boogaloo *'84*
Breakin' *'84*
Cheerleader Camp *'88*

Kate Dickie
Red Road *'06*
The Witch *'16*

Angie Dickinson (1931-)
Gun the Man Down *'56*
Hidden Guns *'56*
China Gate *'57*
Shoot-out at Medicine Bend *'57*
Cry Terror! *'58*
Rio Bravo *'59*
Ocean's 11 *'60*
A Fever In the Blood *'61*
The Sins of Rachel Cade *'61*
Rome Adventure *'62*
Captain Newman, M.D. *'63*
The Killers *'64*
Cast a Giant Shadow *'66*
The Chase *'66*
The Poppy Is Also a Flower *'66*
The Last Challenge *'67*
Point Blank *'67*
Sam Whiskey *'69*
Pretty Maids All In a Row *'71*
Resurrection of Zachary Wheeler *'71*
The Norliss Tapes *'73*
Big Bad Mama *'74*
Pearl *'78*
Klondike Fever *'79*
Dressed to Kill *'80*
Charlie Chan and the Curse of the Dragon Queen *'81*
Death Hunt *'81*
One Shoe Makes It Murder *'82*
Big Bad Mama 2 *'87*
Texas Guns *'90*
Wild Palms *'93*
Even Cowgirls Get the Blues *'94*
Sabrina *'95*
National Lampoon's The Don's Analyst *'97*
Duets *'00*
Pay It Forward *'00*
Ocean's Eleven *'01 (C)*
Big Bad Love *'02*
Elvis Has Left the Building *'04*

Elizabeth Anne Dickinson (1959-2014)
See Elizabeth Pena

Harris Dickinson (1996-)
Beach Rats *'17*
The Darkest Minds *'18*
Maleficent: Mistress of Evil *'19*

Gloria Dickson (1917-45)
They Won't Forget *'37*
Gold Diggers in Paris *'38*
The Big Boss *'41*

Michael Dickson
Wrecker *'15*
Black Mountain Side *'16*

Neil Dickson
Biggles *'85*
The Murders in the Rue Morgue *'86*

Bo Diddley (1928-2008)
Chuck Berry: Hail! Hail! Rock 'n' Roll *'87*
Eddie and the Cruisers 2: Eddie Lives! *'89 (C)*
Rockula *'90*

Gabino Diego (1966-)
Belle Epoque *'92*
Love Can Seriously Damage Your Health *'96*

Juan Diego (1942-)
Cabeza de Vaca *'90*
Between Your Legs *'99*
Yerma *'99*
Torremolinos 73 *'03*

August Diehl (1976-)
Love the Hard Way *'01*
Anatomy 2 *'03*
The Ninth Day *'04*
The Counterfeiters *'07*
Inglourious Basterds *'09*
Salt *'10*
Night Train to Lisbon *'13*
Dark Diamond *'16*
A Hidden Life *'19*

Hans Diehl
The Boat Is Full *'81*
Ancient Relic *'02*

John Diehl (1950-)
National Lampoon's Vacation *'83*
Angel *'84*
Miami Vice *'84*
Cool Blue *'88*
Kickboxer 2: The Road Back *'90*
Motorama *'91*
Mikey *'92*
Mo' Money *'92*
Falling Down *'93*
Gettysburg *'93*
Almost Dead *'94*
Stargate *'94*
Buffalo Girls *'95*
Color of a Brisk and Leaping Day *'95*
Three Wishes *'95*
Wes Craven Presents Mind Ripper *'95*
Foxfire *'96*
A Time to Kill *'96*
Casualties *'97*
The End of Violence *'97*
The Hi-Lo Country *'98*
Monument Ave. *'98*
Anywhere But Here *'99*
Fail Safe *'00*
Lost Souls *'00*
Tully *'00*
Jurassic Park 3 *'01*
Bookies *'03*
Land of Plenty *'04*
Down in the Valley *'05*
The Far Side of Jericho *'06*
Hidden Places *'06*
Jesse Stone: Death in Paradise *'06*
The Lucky Ones *'08*
Drifter *'09*
Natural Selection *'11*
Natural Selection *'12*
The North Star *'16*

Brett Dier (1990-)
Family in Hiding *'06*
Every Second Counts *'08*
Meteor Storm *'10*
Super Storm *'12*
The New Romantic *'18*

John Dierkes (1905-75)
The Red Badge of Courage *'51*
The Thing *'51*
Abbott and Costello Meet Dr. Jekyll and Mr. Hyde *'52*
The Moonlighter *'53*
The Daughter of Dr. Jekyll *'57*
The Alamo *'60*
Premature Burial *'62*
The Haunted Palace *'63*
Omega Man *'71*

Charles Dierkop (1936-)
The Sweet Ride *'68*
Angels Hard As They Come *'71*
Banzai Runner *'86*
Invisible Dad *'97*
SuperGuy: Behind the Cape *'02*

Vin Diesel (1967-)
Awakenings *'90*
Saving Private Ryan *'98*
The Iron Giant *'99 (V)*
Boiler Room *'00*
Pitch Black *'00*
The Fast and the Furious *'01*
Knockaround Guys *'01*
XXX *'02*
A Man Apart *'03*
The Chronicles of Riddick *'04*
The Pacifier *'05*
The Fast and the Furious: Tokyo Drift *'06*
Find Me Guilty *'06*
Babylon A.D. *'08*
Fast & Furious *'09*
Fast Five *'11*
Fast & Furious 6 *'13*
Riddick *'13*
Guardians of the Galaxy *'14 (V)*
Furious 7 *'15*
The Last Witch Hunter *'15*
Billy Lynn's Long Halftime Walk *'16*
The Fate of the Furious *'17*
Guardians of the Galaxy Vol. 2 *'17*
xXx: Return of Xander Cage *'17*
Bloodshot *'20*

Gustav Diesl (1899-1948)
Pandora's Box *'28*
Crimes of Dr. Mabuse *'32*
The Mistress of Atlantis *'32*

Marsha Dietlein (1965-)
Return of the Living Dead 2 *'88*
Newlyweds *'11*
The Fitzgerald Family Christmas *'12*

Marlene Dietrich (1901-92)
The Blue Angel *'30*
Morocco *'30*
Dishonored *'31*
Blonde Venus *'32*
Shanghai Express *'32*
The Song of Songs *'33*
Scarlet Empress *'34*
The Devil Is a Woman *'35*
The Garden of Allah *'36*
Angel *'37*
Knight Without Armour *'37*
Destry Rides Again *'39*
Seven Sinners *'40*
The Flame of New Orleans *'41*
Manpower *'41*
Pittsburgh *'42*
The Spoilers *'42*
Kismet *'44*
Golden Earrings *'47*
Jigsaw *'49 (C)*
Stage Fright *'50*
No Highway in the Sky *'51*
Rancho Notorious *'52*
Around the World in 80 Days *'56 (C)*
Witness for the Prosecution *'57*
Touch of Evil *'58*
Judgment at Nuremberg *'61*
Paris When It Sizzles *'64*
The Love Goddesses *'65*

Frank Dietz
Rock 'n' Roll Nightmare *'85*
Zombie Nightmare *'86*

Brian Dietzen (1977-)
From Justin to Kelly *'03*
Congratulations *'13*

Anton Diffring (1918-89)
The Colditz Story *'55*
The Accursed *'57*
The Beasts of Marseilles *'57*
The Man Who Could Cheat Death *'59*
Circus of Horrors *'60*
The Heroes of Telemark *'65*
The Blue Max *'66*
Fahrenheit 451 *'66*
Counterpoint *'67*
The Double Man *'67*
Where Eagles Dare *'68*
Little Mother *'71*
Zeppelin *'71*
Dead Pigeon on Beethoven Street *'72*
Mark of the Devil 2 *'72*
Seven Deaths in the Cat's Eye *'72*
Call Him Mr. Shatter *'74*
The Beast Must Die *'75*
Operation Daybreak *'75*
Valentino *'77*
The Winds of War *'83*
Faceless *'88*

Uschi Digart (1948-)
Superchick *'71*
Black Gestapo *'75*
Supervixens *'75*
Kentucky Fried Movie *'77*

Dudley Digges (1879-1947)
The Maltese Falcon *'31*
The Hatchet Man *'32*
Emperor Jones *'33*
The Invisible Man *'33*
The Mayor of Hell *'33*
Massacre *'34*
The World Moves On *'34*
China Seas *'35*
Mutiny on the Bounty *'35*
The General Died at Dawn *'36*
The Unguarded Hour *'36*
Love Is News *'37*
Raffles *'39*
Son of Fury *'42*

Daveed Diggs
Blindspotting *'18*
Velvet Buzzsaw *'19*

Robert Diggs (1966-)
See RZA

Taye Diggs (1971-)
How Stella Got Her Groove Back *'98*
The Best Man *'99*
Go *'99*
House on Haunted Hill *'99*
The Wood *'99*
Way of the Gun *'00*
Brown Sugar *'02*
Chicago *'02*
Equilibrium *'02*
Just a Kiss *'02*
New Best Friend *'02*
Basic *'03*
Malibu's Most Wanted *'03*
Cake *'05*
Rent *'05*
Slow Burn *'05*
Dylan Dog: Dead of Night *'11*
Between Us *'12*
Baggage Claim *'13*
The Best Man Holiday *'13*
The Trials of Cate McCall *'13*
My Little Pony: The Movie *'17*

Arthur Dignam (1939-)
The Devil's Playground *'76*
The Chant of Jimmie Blacksmith *'78*
Strange Behavior *'81*
We of the Never Never *'82*
The Wild Duck *'84*
The Right Hand Man *'87*
The Dreaming *'88*
The Everlasting Secret Family *'88*
The Nostradamus Kid *'92*
Gods and Monsters *'98*

Basil Dignam (1905-79)
Seven Seas to Calais *'62*
Naked Evil *'66*
Persuasion *'71*
The Moonstone *'72*

Mark Dignam (1909-89)
Sink the Bismarck *'60*
The Charge of the Light Brigade *'68*
Disraeli *'79*

Holly Dignard (1981-)
Kill Switch *'08*
Polar Storm *'09*
Ice Quake *'10*

12 Disasters '12
Bus Driver '16

Bogdan Diklic (1953-)
Cabaret Balkan '98
Fuse '03
Grbavica: The Land of My Dreams '06

Garret Dillahunt (1964-)
The Assassination of Jesse James by the Coward Robert Ford '07
No Country for Old Men '07
Pretty Bird '08
The Last House on the Left '09
The Road '09
Winter's Bone '10
Any Day Now '12
Looper '12
Talhotblond '12
12 Years a Slave '13
The Scribbler '14
Against the Sun '15
Just Before I Go '15
Come and Find Me '16
Wheelman '17
Benched '18

Richard Dillane (1964-)
Solomon '98
De-Lovely '04
Oranges and Sunshine '10

Stephen (Dillon) Dillane (1956-)
Christabel '89
The Rector's Wife '94
Two If by Sea '95
The Widowing of Mrs. Holroyd '95
Firelight '97
Kings in Grass Castles '97
Welcome to Sarajevo '97
Deja Vu '98
Love and Rage '99
Ordinary Decent Criminal '99
Anna Karenina '00
Spy Game '01
The Gathering '02
The Hours '02
The Truth About Charlie '02
Haven '04
King Arthur '04
The Greatest Game Ever Played '05
Nine Lives '05
Goal! The Dream Begins '06
Klimt '06
Goal 2: Living the Dream '07
Savage Grace '07
God on Trial '08
John Adams '08
44 Inch Chest '09
Perfect Sense '11
Secret State '12
Twenty8k '12
Darkest Hour '17
Mary Shelley '17

Richard Dillard
Walking Tall: The Payback '07
Abel's Field '12

Victoria Dillard (1969-)
Ricochet '91
Deep Cover '92
Out of Sync '95
The Best Man '99
Ali '01

Donald Dillaway
The Little Giant '33
Notorious But Nice '33

Phyllis Diller (1917-2012)
Splendor in the Grass '61
Boy, Did I Get a Wrong Number! '66
The Fat Spy '66
Eight on the Lam '67
Mad Monster Party '68 (V)
Private Navy of Sgt. O'Farrell '68
The Bone Yard '90
The Nutcracker Prince '91 (V)
Happily Ever After '93 (V)
A Bug's Life '98 (V)
Forget About It '06
Unbeatable Harold '06

Bradford Dillman (1930-2018)
In Love and War '58
Compulsion '59
A Rage to Live '65
Black Water Gold '69
The Bridge at Remagen '69
Brother John '70
Suppose They Gave a War and Nobody Came? '70
Escape from the Planet of the Apes '71
The Mephisto Waltz '71
Resurrection of Zachary Wheeler '71
The Delphi Bureau: The Merchant of Death Assignment '72
Moon of the Wolf '72
Deliver Us From Evil '73
The Iceman Cometh '73
The Way We Were '73
The Eyes of Charles Sand '74
99 & 44/100 Dead '74
Bug '75
The Enforcer '76
Piranha '78
The Swarm '78
Love and Bullets '79
Sudden Impact '83
The Treasure of the Amazon '85
Man Outside '88

Brendan Dillon
Hero's Island '62
The Killing of Sister George '69

Brendan Dillon, Jr.
Premature Burial '62
Bug '75

Hugh Dillon (1963-)
Hard Core Logo '96
Down to the Bone '04
Ginger Snaps Back: The Beginning '04
Assault on Precinct 13 '05
Surveillance '08

Kevin Dillon (1965-)
No Big Deal '83
Heaven Help Us '85
Platoon '86
The Blob '88
The Rescue '88
Immediate Family '89
When He's Not a Stranger '89
The Doors '91
A Midnight Clear '92
No Escape '94
True Crime '95
The Pathfinder '96
Stag '97
Misbegotten '98
Hidden Agenda '99
The Foursome '06
Poseidon '06
Hotel for Dogs '09
Compulsion '13
Entourage '15

Matt Dillon (1964-)
Over the Edge '79
My Bodyguard '80
Liar's Moon '82
Tex '82
The Outsiders '83
Rumble Fish '83
The Flamingo Kid '84
Rebel '85
Target '85
Big Town '87
Kansas '88
Bloodhounds of Broadway '89
Drugstore Cowboy '89
A Kiss Before Dying '91
Women & Men: In Love There Are No Rules '91
Singles '92
Golden Gate '93
Mr. Wonderful '93
The Saint of Fort Washington '93
To Die For '95
Albino Alligator '96
Beautiful Girls '96
Grace of My Heart '96
In and Out '97
There's Something about Mary '98
Wild Things '98
One Night at McCool's '01
Deuces Wild '02
City of Ghosts '03
Crash '05
Herbie: Fully Loaded '05
Loverboy '05
Factotum '06
You, Me and Dupree '06
Nothing But the Truth '08
Armored '09
Old Dogs '09
Takers '10
Girl Most Likely '12
The Art of the Steal '13
Sunlight Jr. '13
Bad Country '14
The House That Jack Built '18
Running for Grace '18
Capone '20

Melinda Dillon (1939-)
April Fools '69
Bound for Glory '76
Close Encounters of the Third Kind '77
Slap Shot '77
F.I.S.T. '78
Marriage Is Alive and Well '80
Absence of Malice '81
A Christmas Story '83
Songwriter '84
Shattered Spirits '86
Harry and the Hendersons '87
Shattered Innocence '87
Captain America '89
Spontaneous Combustion '89
Staying Together '89
The Prince of Tides '91
Sioux City '94
How to Make an American Quilt '95
To Wong Foo, Thanks for Everything, Julie Newmar '95
Entertaining Angels: The Dorothy Day Story '96
Magnolia '99
Cowboy Up '00
A Painted House '03
Reign Over Me '07

Mia Dillon (1955-)
Gods and Generals '03
Our Town '03
Never Rarely Sometimes Always '20

Paul Dillon
Kiss Daddy Goodnight '87
Blink '93
Austin Powers: International Man of Mystery '97
Chicago Cab '98

Tom Dillon (1895-1962)
Dressed to Kill '46
Night Tide '61

John DiMaggio (1968-)
The Pirates of Silicon Valley '99
Extreme Dating '04

Adam DiMarco
Kill for Me '12
Radio Rebel '12

Maisie Dimbelby
The Shell Seekers '06
Persuasion '07

Alex Dimitriades (1973-)
Head On '98
Subterano '01
Ghost Ship '02

Stephen Dimopoulos
Big Meat Eater '85
The Stranger '10

Oliver Dimsdale (1972-)
Byron '03
He Knew He Was Right '04

Alan Dinehart (1889-1944)
Lawyer Man '32
Street of Women '32
A Study in Scarlet '33
Supernatural '33
Sweepings '33
Baby, Take a Bow '34
Jimmy the Gent '34
Dante's Inferno '35
In Old Kentucky '35
Charlie Chan at the Race Track '36

Paul Dinello (1962-)
Plump Fiction '97
Strangers with Candy '06

Yi Ding
The Amazing Panda Adventure '95
Pavilion of Women '01
Smile '05

Charles Dingle (1887-1956)
The Little Foxes '41
Johnny Eager '42
Somewhere I'll Find You '42
Home In Indiana '44
Guest Wife '45
Here Come the Co-Eds '45
The Beast with Five Fingers '46
The Romance of Rosy Ridge '47
If You Knew Susie '48
A Southern Yankee '48
Half a Hero '53
The Court Martial of Billy Mitchell '55

Ernie Dingo (1956-)
Crocodile Dundee 2 '88
A Waltz Through the Hills '88
Until the End of the World '91
Dead Heart '96
Kings in Grass Castles '97
Brand New Day '10

Shaun Dingwall (1970-)
Touching Evil '97
On a Clear Day '05
Summer in February '13

Joe Dinicol (1983-)
Diary of the Dead '07
Weirdsville '07
Passchendaele '10

Peter Dinklage (1969-)
Living in Oblivion '94
Human Nature '02
13 Moons '02
Elf '03
The Station Agent '03
Tiptoes '03
The Baxter '05
Lassie '05
Find Me Guilty '06
Little Fugitive '06
Penelope '06
Death at a Funeral '07
Underdog '07
The Chronicles of Narnia: Prince Caspian '08
The Last Rites of Ransom Pride '09
Saint John of Las Vegas '09
Death at a Funeral '10
Pete Smalls Is Dead '10
A Little Bit of Heaven '11
Ice Age: Continental Drift '12 (V)
A Case of You '13
Knights of Badassdom '13
The Angriest Man in Brooklyn '14
X-Men: Days of Future Past '14
Pixels '15
The Boss '16
Rememory '17
I Think We're Alone Now '18

Reece Dinsdale (1959-)
Young Catherine '91
Hamlet '96
Romance and Rejection '96

Bruce Dinsmore (1965-)
Psychopath '97
Deadline '00
Nightwaves '03

Jake Dinwiddie (1987-)
Au Pair '99
Au Pair 2: The Fairy Tale Continues '01
Au Pair 3: Adventure in Paradise '09

Traci Dinwiddie (1973-)
Ball of Wax '03
Elena Undone '10

Madam Rose (Dion) Dione (1875-1936)
Suds '20
The Duchess of Buffalo '26
Freaks '32

Stefano Dionisi (1966-)
Farinelli '94
Joseph '95
The Truce '96
Kiss of Fire '98
The Loss of Sexual Innocence '98
Children of the Century '99
Sleepless '01
Ginostra '02
Gloomy Sunday '02

Silvia Dionisio (1951-)
Andy Warhol's Dracula '74
Live Like a Cop, Die Like a Man '76
Street War '76

Jo-Issa Diop (1985-)
See Issa Rae

Kim Director (1977-)
Book of Shadows: Blair Witch 2 '00
She Hate Me '04
A Crime '06
Inside Man '06
Tony n' Tina's Wedding '07

John DiResta
Miss Congeniality '00
15 Minutes '01

John Disanti (1938-)
Eyes of a Stranger '81
Man of the House '95

Warren Disbrow, Sr.
Invasion for Flesh and Blood '94
Flesh Eaters from Outer Space '05

Catherine Disher (1960-)
Coast to Coast '04
The Good Witch '08
The Good Witch's Garden '09

Bob (Robert) Dishy (1934-)
Lovers and Other Strangers '70
I Wonder Who's Killing Her Now? '76
Brighton Beach Memoirs '86
Used People '92
My Boyfriend's Back '93
Don Juan DeMarco '94
Jungle 2 Jungle '96
A Fish in the Bathtub '99
Judy Berlin '99
Along Came Polly '04
The Wackness '08

Walt Disney (1901-66)
Hollywood Party '34 (V)
Fantasia '40 (V)
Fun & Fancy Free '47 (V)

Divine (1945-88)
Pink Flamingos '72
Female Trouble '74
Polyester '81
Lust in the Dust '85
Trouble in Mind '86
Hairspray '88
Out of the Dark '88

Andrew Divoff (1955-)
Graveyard Shift '90
Toy Soldiers '91
Interceptor '92
A Low Down Dirty Shame '94
Oblivion '94
Backlash: Oblivion 2 '95
Xtro 3: Watch the Skies '95
Deadly Voyage '96
Nemesis 4: Cry of Angels '97
Wishmaster '97
Wishmaster 2: Evil Never Dies '98
Captured '99
Stealth Fighter '99
Faust: Love of the Damned '00
Blue Hill Avenue '01
Moscow Heat '04
The Rage '07
Treasure Raiders '07
The Boston Strangler: The Untold Story '08
Indiana Jones and the Kingdom of the Crystal Skull '08
Ballistica '10
Magic Man '10

Richard Dix (1894-1949)
Souls for Sale '23
The Ten Commandments '23
The Vanishing American '25
Seven Keys to Baldpate '29
Cimarron '31
The Public Defender '31
The Conquerors '32
Ace of Aces '33
Day of Reckoning '33
His Greatest Gamble '34
Stingaree '34
Transatlantic Tunnel '35
It Happened in Hollywood '37
Reno '39
Men Against the Sky '40
American Empire '42
Buckskin Frontier '43
The Ghost Ship '43
The Kansan '43

Robert Dix (1935-)
Forbidden Planet '56
Forty Guns '57
Deadwood '65
Blood of Dracula's Castle '69
Satan's Sadists '69
Wild Wheels '69
Hell's Bloody Devils '70
Horror of the Blood Monsters '70
Cain's Cutthroats '71
Killers '88

Madhuri Dixit (1967-)
Devdas '02
Total Dhamaal '19

Beth Dixon
The Ballad of the Sad Cafe '91
Infinitely Polar Bear '14

Donna Dixon (1957-)
Doctor Detroit '83
Spies Like Us '85
The Couch Trip '87
Lucky Stiff '88
Wayne's World '92

Ivan Dixon (1931-2008)
A Raisin in the Sun '61
Nothing but a Man '64
A Patch of Blue '65
Suppose They Gave a War and Nobody Came? '70
Fer-De-Lance '74
Car Wash '76

James Dixon
Black Caesar '73
Hell Up in Harlem '73
It's Alive '74
It's Alive 2: It Lives Again '78
Q (The Winged Serpent) '82
The Stuff '85
It's Alive 3: Island of the Alive '87
Return to Salem's Lot '87
Wicked Stepmother '89
The Ambulance '90
Maniac Cop 2 '90

Jean Dixon (1896-1981)
You Only Live Once *'37*
Joy of Living *'38*

Joan Dixon (1930-92)
Bunco Squad *'50*
Roadblock *'51*

Lee Dixon (1914-53)
Gold Diggers of 1937 *'36*
Hollywood Hotel *'37*
Varsity Show *'37*

MacIntyre Dixon (1931-)
Funny Farm *'88*
Gettysburg *'93*

Michael Dixon
Cashback *'06*
The Deaths of Ian Stone *'07*

Pamela Dixon (1944-)
Chance *'89*
C.I.A.: Code Name Alexa *'92*
Magic Kid *'92*
C.I.A. 2: Target Alexa *'94*

Reg Dixon
Love in Pawn *'53*
No Smoking *'55*

Russell Dixon
Liam *'00*
The Other Side of Heaven 2: Fire of Faith *'19*

Maria Dizzia
While We're Young *'14*
True Story *'15*
Christine *'16*
Humor Me *'17*

Omid Djalili (1965-)
The Mummy *'99*
Modigliani *'04*
Sky Captain and the World of Tomorrow *'04*
Casanova *'05*
The Love Guru *'08*
The Infidel *'10*
Mr. Nice *'10*
Shaun the Sheep Movie *'15*

Badja (Medu) Djola (1948-2005)
Penitentiary *'79*
The Serpent and the Rainbow *'87*
Mississippi Burning *'88*
An Innocent Man *'89*
A Rage in Harlem *'91*
Who's the Man? *'93*
Heaven's Prisoners *'95*
Rosewood *'96*
Gunshy *'98*
Deterrence *'00*

Branko Djuric (1949-)
No Man's Land *'01*
Triage *'09*

Serah D'Laine (1982-)
Wild Things 3: Diamonds in the Rough *'05*
The Rig *'10*

DMX (1970-)
Belly *'98*
Romeo Must Die *'00*
Exit Wounds *'01*
Cradle 2 the Grave *'03*
Never Die Alone *'04*
Death Toll *'07*
Father of Lies *'07*
Last Hour *'08*
Lords of the Street *'08*

Alan Dobie (1932-)
The Charge of the Light Brigade *'68*
The Chairman *'69*
War and Peace *'73*
White Mischief *'88*

Lawrence (Larry) Dobkin (1919-2002)
Twelve o'Clock High *'49*
Loan Shark *'52*
Above and Beyond *'53*
Jump Into Hell *'55*
Portland Expose *'57*
Johnny Yuma *'66*
Patton *'70*
Underground *'70*

Kata Dobo (1974-)
Detention *'03*
Out For a Kill *'03*

Alex Dobrenko
Bloody Homecoming *'12*
Krisha *'15*

Nina Dobrev (1989-)
Hearts of War *'07*
Too Young to Marry *'07*
The American Mall *'08*
Never Cry Werewolf *'08*
Chloe *'09*
Arena *'11*
The Perks of Being a Wallflower *'12*
Let's Be Cops *'14*
The Final Girls *'15*
Crash Pad *'17*
Flatliners *'17*
xXx: Return of Xander Cage *'17*
Dog Days *'18*
Run This Town *'20*

Karel Dobry (1969-)
The Girl of Your Dreams *'99*
The Ninth Day *'04*

Grigory Dobrygin (1986-)
How I Ended This Summer *'10*
A Most Wanted Man *'14*

James Dobson (1920-87)
Flying Leathernecks *'51*
The Tanks Are Coming *'51*
Impulse *'74*

Kevin Dobson (1943-)
Midway *'76*
All Night Long *'81*
Code of Honor *'84*
Mom, Can I Keep Her? *'98*

Peter Dobson (1964-)
Last Exit to Brooklyn *'90*
The Marrying Man *'91*
Where the Day Takes You *'92*
Forrest Gump *'94*
Norma Jean and Marilyn *'95*
The Big Squeeze *'96*
The Frighteners *'96*
Riot in the Streets *'96*
Quiet Days in Hollywood *'97*
Nowhere Land *'98*
Wicked Ways *'99*
Drowning Mona *'00*
Double Down *'01*
Lady Jayne Killer *'03*
Players *'03*
Protecting the King *'07*
A Stranger's Heart *'07*
The Nanny Express *'08*
2:22 *'08*

Tamara Dobson (1947-2006)
Cleopatra Jones *'73*
Cleopatra Jones & the Casino of Gold *'75*
Norman, Is That You? *'76*
Chained Heat *'83*

Vernon Dobtcheff (1934-)
The Assassination Bureau *'69*
Darling Lili *'70*
Murder on the Orient Express *'74*
The Savage *'75*
Nijinsky *'80*
M. Butterfly *'93*
Deja Vu *'98*
Hilary and Jackie *'98*
The Body *'01*
Red Siren *'02*
Empire of the Wolves *'05*
Priceless *'06*

Michelle Dockery (1981-)
Hogfather *'06*
Return to Cranford *'09*
Non-Stop *'14*
The Sense of an Ending *'17*
Downton Abbey *'19*
The Gentlemen *'20*

Gina Doctor
Dead Pet *'01*
Shopgirl *'05*

Claire Dodd (1908-73)
Alias the Doctor *'32*
Lawyer Man *'32*
Parachute Jumper *'32*
This Is the Night *'32*
Blondie Johnson *'33*
Elmer the Great *'33*
Hard to Handle *'33*
Massacre *'34*
The Case of the Curious Bride *'35*
The Goose and the Gander *'35*
The Singing Kid *'36*
Charlie Chan in Honolulu *'38*
Fast Company *'38*
Three Loves Has Nancy *'38*
If I Had My Way *'40*
The Black Cat *'41*

Jimmie Dodd (1910-64)
Snuffy Smith, Yard Bird *'42*
Too Late for Tears *'49*

K.K. Dodds (1965-)
A Life Less Ordinary *'97*
Soldier *'98*

Megan Dodds (1970-)
Ever After: A Cinderella Story *'98*
The Rat Pack *'98*
Bait *'00*
Urbania *'00*
Sword of Honour *'01*
Purpose *'02*
The Contract *'07*
Chatroom *'10*

Jack Dodson (1931-94)
The Getaway *'72*
Return to Mayberry *'85*

John Doe (1954-)
Slamdance *'87*
Great Balls of Fire *'89*
Liquid Dreams *'92*
Pure Country *'92*
Roadside Prophets *'92*
Shake, Rattle & Rock! *'94*
Wyatt Earp *'94*
Georgia *'95*
Scorpion Spring *'96*
Touch *'96*
Black Circle Boys *'97*
Boogie Nights *'97*
Highway Hitcher *'98*
Brokedown Palace *'99*
Forces of Nature *'99*
Knocking on Death's Door *'99*
The Rage: Carrie 2 *'99*
Sugar Town *'99*
Wildflowers *'99*
Drowning on Dry Land *'00*
Gypsy 83 *'01*
The Good Girl *'02*
MTV's Wuthering Heights *'03*
Players *'03*
Torque *'04*
Ten Inch Hero *'07*
Ring of Fire *'13*

Heather Doerksen
The Lost Treasure of the Grand Canyon *'08*
In the Name of the King 2: Two Worlds *'11*

Darrick Doerner
In God's Hands *'98*
Riding Giants *'04*

Meital Dohan (1976-)
Woke Up Dead *'09*
Monogamy *'10*

Matt Doherty (1978-)
The Mighty Ducks *'92*
So I Married an Axe Murderer *'93*
D3: The Mighty Ducks *'96*

Shannen Doherty (1971-)
Night Shift *'82*
Girls Just Want to Have Fun *'85*
Heathers *'89*
Almost Dead *'94*
Jailbreakers *'94*
Mallrats *'95*

Jay and Silent Bob Strike Back *'01 (C)*
The Rendering *'02*
Category 7: The End of the World *'05*
Christmas Caper *'07*
Kiss Me Deadly *'08*
The Lost Treasure of the Grand Canyon *'08*
Growing the Big One *'09*
Witchslayer Gretl *'12*
Blood Lake *'14*

Jason Dohring (1982-)
Black Cadillac *'03*
Veronica Mars *'14*
The Squeeze *'15*

Lexa Doig (1973-)
No Alibi *'00*
Jason X *'01*
Second Sight *'07*
Ba'al: The Storm God *'08*
Fireball *'09*
Tactical Force *'11*

Michael Dolan (1965-)
Hamburger Hill *'87*
Biloxi Blues *'88*
The Turning *'92*
The Hunley *'99*

Monica Dolan (1969-)
A Midsummer Night's Dream *'96*
Appropriate Adult *'11*
Sightseers *'12*
Alan Partridge *'13*

Xavier Dolan (1989-)
I Killed My Mother *'09*
Heartbeats *'11*

Thomas Dolby (1958-)
Howard the Duck *'86*
Rockula *'90*

Guy Doleman (1924-96)
The Ipcress File *'65*
Thunderball *'65*
Funeral in Berlin *'66*
Billion Dollar Brain *'67*

Ami Dolenz (1969-)
The Children of Times Square *'86*
Can't Buy Me Love *'87*
She's Out of Control *'89*
Children of the Night *'92*
Miracle Beach *'92*
Stepmonster *'92*
Ticks *'93*
Pumpkinhead 2: Blood Wings *'94*
2012: Doomsday *'08*

George Dolenz (1908-63)
My Cousin Rachel *'52*
A Bullet for Joey *'55*
Timbuktu *'59*
The Four Horsemen of the Apocalypse *'62*

Mickey Dolenz (1945-)
Head *'68*
Night of the Strangler *'73*
The Brady Bunch Movie *'95 (C)*
Invisible Mom *'96*
Invisible Mom 2 *'99*
Mega Python Vs. Gatoroid *'11 (C)*

Damon D'Oliveira
Back in Action *'94*
My Teacher Ate My Homework *'98*

Luisa D'Oliveira (1986-)
Ice Twisters *'09*
Seeds of Destruction *'11*
Super Storm *'12*

Dora Doll (1922-)
The Nude Set *'57*
The Young Lions *'58*
Black and White in Color *'76*

Patrick Dollaghan
Circle of Fear *'89*
The Bad Pack *'98*

Aubrey Dollar (1980-)
Other Voices, Other Rooms *'95*

Trapped: Buried Alive *'02*
Save the Last Dance 2 *'06*

Jason Dolley (1991-)
Saving Shiloh *'06*
Minutemen *'08*

Quentin Dolmaire
My Golden Days *'15*
The Midwife *'17*

Reilly Dolman
Goblin *'10*
Zodiac: Signs of the Apocalypse *'14*

John Doman (1945-)
The Opponent *'01*
City by the Sea *'02*
Killing Emmett Young *'02*
Sniper 3 *'04*
Rock the Paint *'05*
Fatwa *'06*
Gracie *'07*
Shoot First and Pray You Live *'08*
Blue Valentine *'10*
You Were Never Really Here *'17*

Arielle Dombasle (1958-)
Perceval *'78*
Le Beau Mariage *'82*
Pauline at the Beach *'83*
Lace *'84*
Lace 2 *'85*
The Boss' Wife *'86*
Around the World in 80 Days *'89*
Twisted Obsession *'90*
Celestial Clockwork *'94*
L'Ennui *'98*
Time Regained *'99*
Vatel *'00*
Gradiva *'06*

Andrea Domburg
Spy in the Sky *'58*
Katie Tippel *'75*

Faith Domergue (1925-99)
Where Danger Lives *'50*
Duel at Silver Creek *'52*
Cult of the Cobra *'55*
It Came from Beneath the Sea *'55*
This Island Earth *'55*
The Atomic Man *'56*
Spin a Dark Web *'56*
California *'63*
Voyage to the Prehistoric Planet *'65*
The Sibling *'72*
Blood Legacy *'73*
The House of Seven Corpses *'73*

Dagmara Dominczyk (1976-)
Rock Star *'01*
The Count of Monte Cristo *'02*
Wes Craven Presents: They *'02*
Kinsey *'04*
Trust the Man *'06*
Prisoner *'07*
Higher Ground *'11*
The Letter *'12*
The Immigrant *'13*
Phantom *'13*
Let's Kill Ward's Wife *'14*
A Woman, A Part *'17*
Abe *'20*

Marika Dominczyk
Who Do You Love *'08*
I Hope They Serve Beer in Hell *'09*

Colman Domingo
Beautiful Something *'16*
If Beale Street Could Talk *'18*

Placido Domingo (1941-)
Otello *'86*
Beverly Hills Chihuahua *'08 (V)*

Adriana Dominguez (1976-)
The Bridge of San Luis Rey *'05*
The Cry: La Llorona *'07*

Wade Dominguez (1966-98)
City of Industry *'96*
Shadow of Doubt *'98*
The Taxman *'98*

Arturo Dominici (1918-92)
Hercules *'58*
Black Sunday *'60*
The Trojan Horse *'62*

Fats Domino (1928-)
The Girl Can't Help It *'56*
Rock, Rock, Rock *'56*

Solveig Dommartin (1961-2007)
Wings of Desire *'88*
Until the End of the World *'91*
Faraway, So Close! *'93*

Angelica Domrose (1941-)
The Legend of Paul and Paula *'73*
The Mistake *'91*

Linda Dona
Futurekick *'91*
Delta Heat *'92*

Ron Donachie (1956-)
Extremely Dangerous *'99*
The Flying Scotsman *'06*
Sunset Song *'16*

Maurizio Donadoni (1958-)
My Mother's Smile *'02*
The Wedding Director *'06*

Elinor Donahue (1937-)
The Unfinished Dance *'47*
Three Daring Daughters *'48*
My Blue Heaven *'50*
Love Is Better Than Ever *'52*
Gidget Gets Married *'72*
Going Berserk *'83*
High School USA *'84*
Pretty Woman *'90*
Freddy's Dead: The Final Nightmare *'91*
The Princess Diaries 2: Royal Engagement *'04*

Heather Donahue (1974-)
The Blair Witch Project *'99*
Boys and Girls *'00*
Manticore *'05*
The Morgue *'07*

Jocelin Donahue
The House of the Devil *'09*
The Last Godfather *'10*
The Frontier *'16*
Holidays *'16*
Summer Camp *'16*

Troy Donahue (1936-2001)
Tarnished Angels *'57*
Imitation of Life *'59*
Monster on the Campus *'59*
A Summer Place *'59*
The Crowded Sky *'60*
Parrish *'61*
Susan Slade *'61*
Rome Adventure *'62*
Palm Springs Weekend *'63*
A Distant Trumpet *'64*
My Blood Runs Cold *'65*
Those Fantastic Flying Fools *'67*
Cockfighter *'74*
The Godfather, Part 2 *'74*
Seizure *'74*
The Legend of Frank Woods *'77*
Tin Man *'83*
Grandview U.S.A. *'84*
Cyclone *'87*
Hollywood Cop *'87*
Dr. Alien *'88*
Terminal Force *'88*
Assault of the Party Nerds *'89*
The Chilling *'89*
Cry-Baby *'90*
Omega Cop *'90*
Shock 'Em Dead *'90*

I'll Remember April *'99*
Runaway Bride *'99*
Madison *'01*
A Woman's a Helluva Thing *'01*
Crazy Little Thing *'02*
Insomnia *'02*
Comfort and Joy *'03*
Cars *'06 (V)*
Hairspray *'07*

Shaun Dooley (1974-)
Shackleton *'02*
The Road to Coronation Street *'10*
The Awakening *'11*
Great Expectations *'11*
South Riding *'11*
The Woman in Black *'12*

Lucinda Dooling
The Alchemist *'81*
Miracle on Ice *'81*

Omar Doom (1976-)
Death Proof *'07*
Inglourious Basterds *'09*

Patric Doonan (1927-58)
The Blue Lamp *'49*
Blackout *'50*

Mike Dopud (1968-)
White Noise *'05*
Ace of Hearts *'08*
In the Name of the King: A Dungeon Siege Tale *'08*
Journey to the Center of the Earth *'08*
Seed *'08*
Ruslan *'09*
Altitude *'10*
The Package *'12*

Robert DoQui (1934-2008)
Coffy *'73*
Nashville *'75*
RoboCop *'87*
Miracle Mile *'89*
Original Intent *'91*
Glam *'97*

Karin Dor (1938-)
The Invisible Dr. Mabuse *'62*
Strangler of Blackmoor Castle *'63*
The Face of Fu Manchu *'65*
You Only Live Twice *'67*
Dracula *vs.* Frankenstein *'69*
Topaz *'69*
The Torture Chamber of Dr. Sadism *'69*
Die Screaming, Marianne *'73*
Prisoner in the Middle *'74*

Ann Doran (1911-2000)
Missing Girls *'36*
Blondie *'38*
Criminals Within *'41*
Meet John Doe *'41*
Penny Serenade *'41*
Mr. Wise Guy *'42*
Air Force *'43*
Gildersleeve on Broadway *'43*
The More the Merrier *'43*
So Proudly We Hail *'43*
Here Come the Waves *'45*
Pride of the Marines *'45*
Roughly Speaking *'45*
Fear in the Night *'47*
Seven Were Saved *'47*
The Fountainhead *'49*
The Kid From Cleveland *'49*
No Sad Songs For Me *'50*
The Painted Hills *'51*
Tomahawk *'51*
Love Is Better Than Ever *'52*
Island in the Sky *'53*
The High and the Mighty *'54*
Rebel without a Cause *'55*
The Man Who Turned to Stone *'57*
It! The Terror from Beyond Space *'58*
Violent Road *'58*
Cast a Long Shadow *'59*
The FBI Story *'59*
The Brass Bottle *'63*
Kitten with a Whip *'64*
Backstairs at the White House *'79*

Mary Doran (1907-95)
Broadway Melody *'29*
The Divorcee *'30*
The Criminal Code *'31*
Party Husband *'31*
The Strange Love of Molly Louvain *'32*
Beauty and the Boss *'33*

Matt Doran (1976-)
The Matrix *'99*
Battle of the Damned *'14*

Richard Doran
Harrad Summer *'74*
Hollywood Boulevard *'76*

Adrienne Dore (1910-92)
Alias the Doctor *'32*
The Rich Are Always With Us *'32*
Street of Women *'32*

Edna Dore (1921-2014)
High Hopes *'88*
Nil by Mouth *'96*
Skellig: The Owl Man *'09*

Thomas Doret
The Kid with a Bike *'11*
Renoir *'12*

Stephen Dorff (1973-)
The Gate *'87*
The Power of One *'92*
Judgment Night *'93*
Backbeat *'94*
S.F.W. *'94*
Innocent Lies *'95*
Blood & Wine *'96*
City of Industry *'96*
I Shot Andy Warhol *'96*
Space Truckers *'97*
Blade *'98*
Earthly Possessions *'99*
Cecil B. Demented *'00*
The Last Minute *'01*
Deuces Wild *'02*
Feardotcom *'02*
Cold Creek Manor *'03*
Alone in the Dark *'05*
.45 *'06*
The Hades Factor *'06*
Shadowboxer *'06*
World Trade Center *'06*
Botched *'07*
Felon *'08*
XIII *'08*
Public Enemies *'09*
Somewhere *'10*
Bucky Larson: Born to Be a Star *'11*
Carjacked *'11*
Immortals *'11*
Brake *'12*
The Iceman *'12*
The Motel Life *'12*
Rites of Passage *'12*
Tomorrow You're Gone *'12*
Officer Down *'13*

David Dorfman (1993-)
Invisible Child *'99*
Bounce *'00*
Panic *'00*
100 Mile Rule *'02*
The Ring *'02*
The Texas Chainsaw Massacre *'03*
The Ring 2 *'05*
Drillbit Taylor *'08*

Diogo Doria (1953-)
Abraham's Valley *'93*
Voyage to the Beginning of the World *'96*
Eccentricities of a Blonde-Haired Girl *'10*

Cody Dorkin (1985-)
The Colony *'95*
Just Ask My Children *'01*

Francoise Dorleac (1942-67)
The Soft Skin *'64*
Genghis Khan *'65*
Where the Spies Are *'65*
Cul de Sac *'66*
Billion Dollar Brain *'67*
The Young Girls of Rochefort *'68*

Michael Dorman (1981-)
Acolytes *'08*
Daybreakers *'09*
Triangle *'09*
Needle *'10*

Natalie Dormer (1982-)
Casanova *'05*
W.E. *'11*
Rush *'13*
The Hunger Games: Mockingjay--Part 1 *'14*
The Hunger Games: Mockingjay-Part 2 *'15*
The Forest *'16*
Patient Zero *'18*
The Professor and the Madman *'19*

Richard Dormer (1969-)
Middletown *'06*
My Boy Jack *'07*
Five Minutes of Heaven *'09*
Ghost Machine *'09*
Hidden *'11*
'71 *'14*
Togo *'19*

Dolores Dorn (1934-)
Lucky Me *'54*
Underworld U.S.A. *'61*
13 West Street *'62*
Truck Stop Women *'74*

Kirstin Dorn
A Christmas Wish *'11*
Your Love Never Fails *'11*
Heaven's Door *'12*

Michael Dorn (1952-)
Rocky *'76*
The Jagged Edge *'85*
Star Trek 6: The Undiscovered Country *'91*
Star Trek: Generations *'94*
Timemaster *'95*
Menno's Mind *'96*
Star Trek: First Contact *'96*
Star Trek: Insurrection *'98*
The Prophet's Game *'99*
Mach 2 *'00*
Ali *'01*
The Santa Clause 2 *'02*
Star Trek: Nemesis *'02*
Shade *'03*
Descent *'05*
Heart of the Beholder *'05*
Night Skies *'07*

Philip Dorn (1901-75)
Escape *'40*
Tarzan's Secret Treasure *'41*
Underground *'41*
Ziegfeld Girl *'41*
Calling Dr. Gillespie *'42*
Random Harvest *'42*
Reunion in France *'42*
Paris After Dark *'43*
Passage to Marseilles *'44*
I've Always Loved You *'46*
The Fighting Kentuckian *'49*

Jamie Dornan (1982-)
Marie Antoinette *'06*
Turn the River *'07*
Fifty Shades of Grey *'15*
Anthropoid *'16*
The 9th Life of Louis Drax *'16*
Fifty Shades Darker *'17*
Fifty Shades Freed *'18*
A Private War *'18*
Robin Hood *'18*
Untogether *'19*
Endings, Beginnings *'20*

Sandra Dorne (1925-92)
Happy Go Lovely *'51*
Alias John Preston *'56*
Devil Doll *'64*
Eat the Rich *'87*

Diana Dors (1931-84)
Oliver Twist *'48*
Man Bait *'52*
An Alligator Named Daisy *'55*
A Kid for Two Farthings *'55*
Value for Money *'55*
The Long Haul *'57*
Tread Softly Stranger *'58*
The King of the Roaring '20s: The Story of Arnold Rothstein *'61*
On the Double *'61*
Berserk! *'67*
Hammerhead *'68*
There's a Girl in My Soup *'70*
Amazing Mr. Blunden *'72*
Hannie Caulder *'72*
Nothing But the Night *'72*
Pied Piper *'72*
From Beyond the Grave *'73*
A Man with a Maid *'73*
Theatre of Blood *'73*
Craze *'74*

Brooke D'Orsay (1982-)
Harold and Kumar Go to White Castle *'04*
King's Ransom *'05*
It's a Boy Girl Thing *'06*
The Boy Who Cried Werewolf *'10*
How to Fall in Love *'12*

Fifi d'Orsay (1904-83)
They Had to See Paris *'29*
Girl from Calgary *'32*
Going Hollywood *'33*
Submarine Base *'43*
Delinquent Daughters *'44*
Nabonga *'44*
The Gangster *'47*
Assignment to Kill *'69*

Jimmy Dorsey (1904-57)
Hollywood Canteen *'44*
The Fabulous Dorseys *'47*

Kerris Dorsey (1998-)
Moneyball *'11*
Girl *vs.* Monster *'12*
Alexander and the Terrible, Horrible, No Good, Very Bad Day *'14*

Omar J. Dorsey (1975-)
The Wronged Man *'10*
Dog Eat Dog *'16*

Tommy Dorsey (1905-56)
Presenting Lily Mars *'43*
The Fabulous Dorseys *'47*

Adrien Dorval (1963-)
Pressure *'02*
Ginger Snaps Back: The Beginning *'04*
In Her Mother's Footsteps *'06*
Super Hybrid *'10*

Anne Dorval (1960-)
I Killed My Mother *'09*
Heartbeats *'11*
Mommy *'14*

John Dossett
Longtime Companion *'90*
That Night *'93*

Angela Dotchin (1974-)
Dead Evidence *'00*
Beyond Justice *'01*
Maiden Voyage: Ocean Hijack *'04*

Karen Dotrice (1955-)
The Three Lives of Thomasina *'63*
Mary Poppins *'64*
The Gnome-Mobile *'67*
She Fell Among Thieves *'78*
The Thirty-Nine Steps *'79*

Michele Dotrice (1948-)
The Witches *'66*
And Soon the Darkness *'70*
Vanity Fair *'99*

Roy Dotrice (1923-)
The Heroes of Telemark *'65*
The Buttercup Chain *'70*
Family Reunion *'81*
Amadeus *'84*
Cheech and Chong's The Corsican Brothers *'84*
Suburban Commando *'91*
The Cutting Edge *'92*
The Scarlet Letter *'95*
Played *'06*
Hellboy II: The Golden Army *'08*

David Doty
Full Moon in Blue Water *'88*
Nancy Drew *'07*

Chris Doubek
Lovers of Hate *'10*
Tower *'16*

Kaitlin Doubleday (1984-)
Freshman Orientation *'04*
Waiting *'05*
The Tomb *'09*
The March Sisters at Christmas *'12*

Portia Doubleday (1988-)
Youth in Revolt *'10*
Big Mommas: Like Father, Like Son *'11*
K-11 *'11*
Carrie *'13*

Catherine Doucet (1875-1958)
Jim Hanvey, Detective *'37*
It Started with Eve *'41*

Paul Doucet (1970-)
America *'24*
Shattered City: The Halifax Explosion *'03*
The Terrorist Next Door *'08*
Funkytown *'11*

John Doucette (1921-94)
Cavalry Scout *'51*
Fixed Bayonets! *'51*
House of Bamboo *'55*
Seven Cities of Gold *'55*
Ghost Town *'56*
Quincannon, Frontier Scout *'56*
The Hunters *'58*
Nevada Smith *'66*
Paradise, Hawaiian Style *'66*
True Grit *'69*
Patton *'70*
Fighting Mad *'76*

Doug E. Doug (1970-)
Class Act *'91*
Hangin' with the Homeboys *'91*
Jungle Fever *'91*
Cool Runnings *'93*
Operation Dumbo Drop *'95*
That Darn Cat *'96*
Eight Legged Freaks *'02*
Shark Tale *'04 (V)*
Snowmen *'10*
A Novel Romance *'11*

Kenny Doughty (1975-)
Crush *'02*
My First Wedding *'04*
The Crew *'08*

Aaron Douglas (1971-)
One Angry Juror *'10*
Zodiac: Signs of the Apocalypse *'14*
The Monster *'16*

Angela Douglas (1940-)
Carry On Cowboy *'66*
Carry On Screaming *'66*
Carry On Up the Khyber *'68*

Brandon Douglas (1968-)
The Children of Times Square *'86*
The Growing Pains Movie *'00*

Burt Douglas (1930-2000)
High School Confidential *'58*
The Law and Jake Wade *'58*

Cameron Douglas (1978-)
It Runs in the Family *'03*
National Lampoon's Adam & Eve *'05*

Cullen Douglas
Ace Ventura Jr.: Pet Detective *'08*
Shuttle *'09*

Damon Douglas (1954-)
From Noon Till Three *'76*
Massacre at Central High *'76*

D.C. Douglas
Black Ops *'07*
Titanic 2 *'10*

Diana Douglas (1923-2015)
The Indian Fighter *'55*
Loving *'70*
It Runs in the Family *'03*

Donald Douglas
Diana: Her True Story *'93*
A Mind to Murder *'96*

Donald 'Don' Douglas (1905-45)
The Great Gabbo *'29*
The Spider's Web *'38*
Sergeant York *'41*
Sleepers West *'41*
Whistling in the Dark *'41*
Action in the North Atlantic *'43*
Murder, My Sweet *'44*
Tarzan and the Amazons *'45*

Donna Douglas (1933-2015)
Career *'59*
Frankie and Johnny *'65*
The Return of the Beverly Hillbillies *'81*

Earl Douglas
Mile a Minute Love *'37*
Tim Tyler's Luck *'37*

Eric Douglas (1958-2004)
Tomboy *'85*
Student Confidential *'87*
Delta Force 3: The Killing Game *'91*

Illeana Douglas (1965-)
The Last Temptation of Christ *'88*
Goodfellas *'90*
Cape Fear *'91*
Guilty by Suspicion *'91*
Alive *'93*
Grief *'94*
Search and Destroy *'94*
To Die For *'95*
Grace of My Heart *'96*
Picture Perfect *'96*
Wedding Bell Blues *'96*
Flypaper *'97*
Rough Riders *'97*
Sink or Swim *'97*
Weapons of Mass Distraction *'97*
Message in a Bottle *'98*
Happy, Texas *'99*
Lansky *'99*
Stir of Echoes *'99*
The Next Best Thing *'00*
Ghost World *'01*
The Adventures of Pluto Nash *'02*
Dummy *'02*
The New Guy *'02*
Point of Origin *'02*
Missing Brendan *'03*
Alchemy *'05*
Factory Girl *'06*
Not Like Everyone Else *'06*
Pittsburgh *'06*
Expired *'07*
Osso Bucco *'08*
Otis *'08*
The Year of Getting to Know Us *'08*
The Green *'11*
She's Funny That Way *'15*

James Douglas
G.I. Blues *'60*
A Thunder of Drums *'61*

James B. Douglas (1933-2009)
The Changeling *'80*
Boy in Blue *'86*
Men with Brooms *'02*

Jeff Douglas
The Showgirl Murders *'95*
Webs *'03*

Joanna Douglas
All the Good Ones Are Married *'07*
Standoff *'16*

Kirk Douglas (1916-2020)
The Strange Love of Martha Ivers *'46*
Out of the Past *'47*
I Walk Alone *'48*

Roma Downey (1960-)
Hercules the Legendary Journeys, Vol. 1: And the Amazon Women *'94*
Come Dance at My Wedding *'09*
Son of God *'14*

Penny Downie (1954-)
The Ice House *'97*
A Certain Justice *'99*
The Girl in the Cafe *'05*

David Downing (1943-)
Gordon's War *'73*
Backstairs at the White House *'79*

J. Downing
Ghoulies 2 *'87*
Robot Wars *'93*

Joe Downing
Invisible Stripes *'39*
You Can't Get Away With Murder *'39*

Rex Downing (1925-)
The Mayor of 44th Street *'42*
Gas House Kids *'46*

Cathy Downs (1924-76)
Dark Corner *'46*
My Darling Clementine *'46*
For You I Die *'47*
The Noose Hangs High *'48*
Panhandle *'48*
Massacre River *'49*
Short Grass *'50*
Kentucky Rifle *'55*
The Phantom from 10,000 Leagues *'56*
The She-Creature *'56*
The Curfew Breakers *'57*
Missile to the Moon *'59*

Elle Downs (1973-)
Godsend *'04*
Talk to Me *'07*

Frederic Downs (1998-16)
The California Kid *'74*
Bug *'75*

Johnny Downs (1913-94)
March of the Wooden Soldiers *'34*
Pigskin Parade *'36*
Adam Had Four Sons *'41*
The Mad Monster *'42*
Campus Rhythm *'43*
Rhapsody in Blue *'45*

Denise Dowse (1958-)
Bio-Dome *'96*
Killing Mr. Griffin *'97*
What About Your Friends: Weekend Getaway *'02*
Ray *'04*
Coach Carter *'05*
Guess Who *'05*

David Doyle (1925-97)
Paper Lion *'68*
Loving *'70*
Vigilante Force *'76*
The Comeback *'77*
My Boys Are Good Boys *'78*

Martin Doyle
Mail to the Chief *'00*
Daniel's Daughter *'08*

Maxine Doyle (1915-73)
Condemned to Live *'35*
S.O.S. Coast Guard *'37*

Mike Doyle (1972-)
29th & Gay *'05*
Getting High *'06*
Gayby *'12*
Jersey Boys *'14*

Shawn Doyle (1968-)
Frequency *'00*
Don't Say a Word *'01*
The Majestic *'01*
Stiletto Dance *'01*
A Killing Spring *'02*
Verdict in Blood *'02*
Do or Die *'03*
Eight Days to Live *'06*
Guns *'08*
Whiteout *'09*
Grown Up Movie Star *'10*
The Returned *'14*

Tony Doyle (1941-2000)
Amongst Women *'98*
A Love Divided *'01*

Maria Doyle Kennedy (1964-)
The Commitments *'91*
The Matchmaker *'97*
The General *'98*
Miss Julie *'99*
Titanic *'12*
Sing Street *'16*

Brian Doyle-Murray (1945-)
Caddyshack *'80*
Modern Problems *'81*
National Lampoon's Vacation *'83*
The Razor's Edge *'84*
Sixteen Candles *'84*
Club Paradise *'86*
Scrooged *'88*
Ghostbusters 2 *'89*
How I Got into College *'89*
National Lampoon's Christmas Vacation *'89*
JFK *'91*
Wayne's World *'92*
Groundhog Day *'93*
Cabin Boy *'94*
Jury Duty *'95*
My Brother's Keeper *'95*
Multiplicity *'96*
Waiting for Guffman *'96*
As Good As It Gets *'97*
Dennis the Menace Strikes Again *'98*
Stuart Little *'99*
Bedazzled *'00*
A Gentleman's Game *'01*
Snow Dogs *'02*
Daddy Day Camp *'07*

Heinz Drache (1923-2002)
The Avenger *'60*
Door with the Seven Locks *'62*
Coast of Skeletons *'63*
The Indian Scarf *'63*
Again, the Ringer *'64*
The Mysterious Magician *'65*
The Squeaker *'65*
Brides of Fu Manchu *'66*
Circus of Fear *'67*

Billy Drago (1945-2019)
Invasion U.S.A. *'85*
Vamp *'86*
The Untouchables *'87*
Freeway *'88*
Hero and the Terror *'88*
Prime Suspect *'88*
Delta Force 2: Operation Stranglehold *'90*
Guncrazy *'92*
Secret Games *'92*
Cyborg 2 *'93*
Death Ring *'93*
Never Say Die *'94*
Solar Force *'94*
Phoenix *'95*
Mirror, Mirror 3: The Voyeur *'96*
Sci-Fighters *'96*
Shadow Warriors *'97*
Convict 762 *'98*
Mysterious Skin *'04*
Tremors 4: The Legend Begins *'04*
Blood Relic *'05*
The Hills Have Eyes *'06*
Lime Salted Love *'06*
7 Mummies *'06*
The Dead One *'07*
Rounds *'08*
Wolf Moon *'09*
Children of the Corn: Genesis *'11*

BeBe Drake
Backstairs at the White House *'79*
Friday After Next *'02*

Betsy Drake (1923-)
Every Girl Should Be Married *'48*
Pretty Baby *'50*
Room for One More *'51*
The Second Woman *'51*
Will Success Spoil Rock Hunter? *'57*
Intent to Kill *'58*
Clarence, the Cross-eyed Lion *'65*

Charles Drake (1914-94)
Air Force *'43*
Conflict *'45*
A Night in Casablanca *'46*
The Pretender *'47*
Tarzan's Magic Fountain *'48*
Harvey *'50*
Winchester '73 *'50*
You Never Can Tell *'51*
It Came from Outer Space *'53*
Tobor the Great *'54*
Female On the Beach *'55*
To Hell and Back *'55*
The Price of Fear *'56*
Jeanne Eagels *'57*
Until They Sail *'57*
No Name on the Bullet *'59*
Back Street *'61*
The Lively Set *'64*
The Third Day *'65*
Valley of the Dolls *'67*

Claudia Drake (1918-97)
Campus Rhythm *'43*
Enemy of Women *'44*
The Lady Confesses *'45*
Detour *'46*
Renegade Girl *'46*

Dona Drake (1914-89)
Louisiana Purchase *'41*
The Road to Morocco *'42*
So This Is New York *'48*
The Girl from Jones Beach *'49*
The Bandits of Corsica *'53*
Princess of the Nile *'54*

Frances Drake (1908-2000)
Forsaking All Others *'35*
Les Miserables *'35*
Mad Love *'35*
I'd Give My Life *'36*
The Invisible Ray *'36*
It's a Wonderful World *'39*

Larry Drake (1950-2016)
This Stuff'll Kill Ya! *'71*
Dark Night of the Scarecrow *'81*
Darkman *'90*
Murder in New Hampshire: The Pamela Smart Story *'91*
Dr. Giggles *'92*
Darkman 2: The Return of Durant *'94*
The Journey of August King *'95*
The Beast *'96*
Overnight Delivery *'96*
Bean *'97*
Paranoia *'98*
The Treat *'98*
Desert Heat *'99*
Dark Asylum *'01*
Attack of the Gryphon *'07*
Dead Air *'08*

Penny Drake
Monarch of the Moon *'05*
Zombie Strippers *'08*

Tom Drake (1918-82)
The Howards of Virginia *'40*
Maisie Goes to Reno *'44*
Meet Me in St. Louis *'44*
Two Girls and a Sailor *'44*
The White Cliffs of Dover *'44*
Courage of Lassie *'46*
The Green Years *'46*
Cass Timberlane *'47*
The Hills of Home *'48*
Words and Music *'48*
Scene of the Crime *'49*
The Great Rupert *'50*
FBI Girl *'52*
Cyclops *'56*
House of the Black Death *'65*
Johnny Reno *'66*
The Singing Nun *'66*
Cycle Psycho *'72*
Savage Abduction *'73*

Franz Drameh
Attack the Block *'11*
100 Streets *'17*

Polly Draper (1955-)
Making Mr. Right *'86*
The Pick-Up Artist *'87*
Danielle Steel's Heartbeat *'93*
A Million to Juan *'94*
Gold Diggers: The Secret of Bear Mountain *'95*
Schemes *'95*
Hitman's Journal *'99*
The Tic Code *'99*
Dinner Rush *'00*
Second Best *'05*
Shooting Livien *'05*
Too Young to Marry *'07*
Obvious Child *'14*

Thomas Draper
Bikini House Calls *'96*
Bikini Med School *'98*

Rachel Dratch (1966-)
Down With Love *'03*
The Pleasure Drivers *'05*
Click *'06*
I Now Pronounce You Chuck and Larry *'07*
Harold *'08*
Spring Breakdown *'08*
I Hate Valentine's Day *'09*
Love N' Dancing *'09*
My Life in Ruins *'09*
Just Go With It *'11*

Jamie Draven
Butterfly Collectors *'99*
Badland *'07*

Milena Dravic (1940-)
Man Is Not a Bird *'65*
WR: Mysteries of the Organism *'71*

Tim Draxl (1981-)
Swimming Upstream *'03*
A Few Best Men *'11*

Alfred Drayton (1881-1949)
Red Ensign *'34*
First a Girl *'35*
Nicholas Nickleby *'46*
Things Happen at Night *'48*

Poppy Drayton (1991-)
When Calls the Heart *'13*
The Little Mermaid *'18*

Dr. Dre (1965-)
Gunmen *'93 (C)*
The Show *'95*
Training Day *'01*
The Wash *'01*

Alex Dreier (1916-2000)
Chandler *'71*
The Carey Treatment *'72*
Lady Cocoa *'75*

Fran Drescher (1957-)
Saturday Night Fever *'77*
Summer of Fear *'78*
The Hollywood Knights *'80*
Ragtime *'81*
Doctor Detroit *'83*
This Is Spinal Tap *'84*
Rosebud Beach Hotel *'85*
UHF *'89*
Cadillac Man *'90*
Car 54, Where Are You? *'94*
Jack *'96*
The Beautician and the Beast *'97*
Picking Up the Pieces *'99*
Hotel Transylvania *'12 (V)*

John Dresden
Raw Force *'81*
No Dead Heroes *'87*

Louise Dresser (1878-1965)
The Eagle *'25*
Mr. Wu *'27*
The Garden of Eden *'28*
Doctor Bull *'33*
David Harum *'34*
Scarlet Empress *'34*
The World Moves On *'34*
Maid of Salem *'37*

Lieux Dressler (1930-)
Grave of the Vampire *'72*
Truck Stop Women *'74*

Marie Dressler (1868-1934)
Tillie's Punctured Romance *'14*
The Patsy *'28*
The Divine Lady *'29*
Vagabond Lover *'29*
Anna Christie *'30*
Chasing Rainbows *'30*
The Girl Said No *'30*
Let Us Be Gay *'30*
Min & Bill *'30*
One Romantic Night *'30*
Politics *'31*
Reducing *'31*
Emma *'32*
Dinner at Eight *'33*
Tugboat Annie *'33*

Valerie Dreville
La Sentinelle *'92*
Heartbeat Detector *'07*

Ben Drew (1983-)
Harry Brown *'09*
The Sweeney *'12*

Ellen Drew (1913-2003)
Sing You Sinners *'38*
The Gracie Allen Murder Case *'39*
Buck Benny Rides Again *'40*
Christmas in July *'40*
That's My Baby! *'44*
Isle of the Dead *'45*
Johnny O'Clock *'47*
The Swordsman *'47*
Man from Colorado *'49*
Davy Crockett, Indian Scout *'50*
Stars in My Crown *'50*
Baron of Arizona *'51*
Man in the Saddle *'51*
Outlaw's Son *'57*

Gene Drew (1926-90)
Sweet Georgia *'72*
Truck Stop Women *'74*

Griffin (Griffen) Drew (1968-)
Friend of the Family *'95*
Masseuse *'95*
Sinful Intrigue *'95*
Dinosaur Valley Girls *'96*
The Kid with the X-Ray Eyes *'99*

Phelim Drew
Death Games *'02*
Bloom *'03*

Roland Drew (1900-88)
Fine Manners *'26*
Evangeline *'29*
Hitler: Beast of Berlin *'39*
The Smiling Ghost *'41*
Across the Pacific *'42*
The Hidden Hand *'42*

Sarah Drew (1980-)
Radio *'03*
Moms' Night Out *'14*

James Dreyfus (1968-)
Notting Hill *'99*
Color Me Kubrick *'05*

Jean-Claude Dreyfus (1946-)
Delicatessen *'92*
The City of Lost Children *'95*
Son of Gascogne *'95*
The Lady and the Duke *'01*
Two Brothers *'04*
A Very Long Engagement *'04*

Julie Dreyfus (1966-)
Kill Bill Vol. 1 *'03*
Kill Bill Vol. 2 *'04*
Inglourious Basterds *'09*

Richard Dreyfuss (1947-)
The Graduate *'67*
Valley of the Dolls *'67*
Hello Down There *'69*
American Graffiti *'73*
Dillinger *'73*
The Apprenticeship of Duddy Kravitz *'74*
Jaws *'75*
Inserts *'76*
Victory at Entebbe *'76*
Close Encounters of the Third Kind *'77*
The Goodbye Girl *'77*
The Competition *'80*
Second Coming of Suzanne *'80*
Whose Life Is It Anyway? *'81*
Down and Out in Beverly Hills *'86*
Stand by Me *'86*
Nuts *'87*
Stakeout *'87*
Tin Men *'87*
Moon over Parador *'88*
Always *'89*
Let It Ride *'89*
Postcards from the Edge *'90*
Rosencrantz & Guildenstern Are Dead *'90*
Once Around *'91*
Prisoner of Honor *'91*
What about Bob? *'91*
Another Stakeout *'93*
Lost in Yonkers *'93*
Silent Fall *'94*
The American President *'95*
The Last Word *'95*
Mr. Holland's Opus *'95*
James and the Giant Peach *'96 (V)*
Night Falls on Manhattan *'96*
Trigger Happy *'96*
Jack London's The Call of the Wild *'97 (N)*
Oliver Twist *'97*
Krippendorf's Tribe *'98*
Lansky *'99*
The Crew *'00*
Fail Safe *'00*
The Day Reagan Was Shot *'01*
Who is Cletis Tout? *'02*
Coast to Coast *'04*
Silver City *'04*
Poseidon *'06*
Tin Man *'07*
W. *'08*
Leaves of Grass *'09*
The Lightkeepers *'09*
My Life in Ruins *'09*
Piranha 3D *'10 (C)*
RED *'10*
Coma *'12*
Paranoia *'13*
Very Good Girls *'13*
Cas & Dylan *'15*
Zipper *'15*

Moosie Drier (1964-)
Ants *'77*
The Hollywood Knights *'80*

Brian Drillinger (1960-)
Brighton Beach Memoirs *'86*
How to Go Out on a Date in Queens *'06*

Bobby Driscoll (1937-68)
The Fighting Sullivans *'42*
Sunday Dinner for a Soldier *'44*
Identity Unknown *'45*
So Goes My Love *'46*
So Dear to My Heart *'49*
The Window *'49*
Treasure Island *'50*
Peter Pan *'53 (V)*

Robert Drivas (1938-86)
Cool Hand Luke *'67*
The Illustrated Man *'69*
Where It's At *'69*
Road Movie *'72*
God Told Me To *'76*

Adam Driver (1983-)
Bluebird *'13*
Frances Ha *'13*
Inside Llewyn Davis *'13*
What If *'13*
This Is Where I Leave You *'14*
Tracks *'14*
While We're Young *'14*
Hungry Hearts *'15*
Star Wars: The Force Awakens *'15*
Midnight Special *'16*

Paterson '16
Silence '16
Star Wars: The Last Jedi '17
BlacKkKlansman '18
The Man Who Killed Don Quixote '18
The Dead Don't Die '19
Marriage Story '19
The Report '19
Star Wars: The Rise of Skywalker '19

Minnie Driver (1970-)
Circle of Friends '94
Big Night '95
Goldeneye '95
Sleepers '96
Good Will Hunting '97
Grosse Pointe Blank '97
Hard Rain '97
The Governess '98
Princess Mononoke '98 (V)
Uncorked '98
An Ideal Husband '99
South Park: Bigger, Longer and Uncut '99 (V)
Tarzan '99 (V)
Beautiful '00
Return to Me '00
Slow Burn '00
High Heels and Low Lifes '01
Owning Mahowny '03
Ella Enchanted '04
The Phantom of the Opera '04
Ripple Effect '07
Motherhood '09
Barney's Version '10
Conviction '10
I Give It a Year '13
Beyond the Lights '14
Peter Pan Live! '14
The Red Tent '14
Return to Zero '14
Stage Fright '14
The Wilde Wedding '17
Spinning Man '18

Meredith Droeger
Extraordinary Measures '10
The Last Rites of Joe May '11

Samantha Droke (1987-)
Princess Protection Program '09
Seconds Apart '11

Jean-Claude Drouot (1938-)
Le Bonheur '65
La Rupture '70

Joanne Dru (1923-96)
Red River '48
All the King's Men '49
She Wore a Yellow Ribbon '49
711 Ocean Drive '50
Wagon Master '50
Mr. Belvedere Rings the Bell '51
Vengeance Valley '51
Pride of St. Louis '52
Thunder Bay '53
Duffy of San Quentin '54
Siege at Red River '54
Southwest Passage '54
Sincerely Yours '55
The Warriors '55
Super Fuzz '81

Dinara Drukarova (1976-)
Son of Gascogne '95
360 '12
My Golden Days '15

Alice Drummond (1928-)
Awakenings '90
Daybreak '93
Commandments '96
Til There Was You '96
Office Killer '97
I'll Take You There '99
The Love Letter '99
Joe Gould's Secret '00
The Rising Place '02
Pieces of April '03
House of D '04
For One More Day '07
Doubt '08

Brian Drummond (1969-)
Bionicle 3: Web of Shadows '05 (V)
Inspector Gadget's Biggest Caper Ever '05 (V)

James Drury (1934-2020)
The Tender Trap '55
Love Me Tender '56
Good Day for a Hanging '58
Ten Who Dared '60
Ride the High Country '62
The Meanest Men in the West '67
The Gambler Returns: The Luck of the Draw '93
Walker: Texas Ranger: One Riot, One Ranger '93
The Virginian '99

Fred (John F.) Dryer (1946-)
Prime Time '77
Death Before Dishonor '87
Wild Grizzly '99
The Independent '00
Shakedown '02

Robert Dryer
Heartbreaker '83
Savage Streets '83

Jeanie Drynan
Don's Party '76
Muriel's Wedding '94

Dinesh D'Souza (1961-)
2016: Obama's America '12
America: Imagine the World Without Her '14 (N)
Hillary's America: The Secret History of the Democratic Party '16
Death of a Nation '18

Dinesh Joseph D'souza (1961-)
See Dinesh D'Souza

Gerald du Maurier (1873-1934)
The Living Dead '33
Power '34

Michael Duane (1914-63)
City Without Men '43
Dr. Gillespie's Criminal Case '43
The Prince of Thieves '48

Don Dubbins (1928-91)
Tribute to a Bad Man '56
D.I. '57
The Illustrated Man '69
Savage Run '70

Conor Dubin (1976-)
Wannabes '01
A Tale of Two Pizzas '03

Ellen Dubin
Killer Deal '99
When Love Is Not Enough: The Lois Wilson Story '10

Jessica Dublin (1942-)
Troma's War '88
The Toxic Avenger, Part 3: The Last Temptation of Toxie '89

Casey Dubois (1993-)
The Final Cut '04
The Stranger Game '06

Ja'net DuBois (1945-2020)
Piece of the Action '77
I'm Gonna Git You Sucka '88
Heart Condition '90
Waterproof '99
Charlie's Angels: Full Throttle '03

Marie DuBois (1937-2014)
A Woman Is a Woman '60
Jules and Jim '62
Shoot the Piano Player '62
Circle of Love '64
The Thief of Paris '67
Night Flight from Moscow '73
Mon Oncle d'Amerique '80

Marta DuBois (1952-)
Boulevard Nights '79
Grace Kelly '83
The Trial of the Incredible Hulk '89
Fear '90
Luminarias '99

Paulette Dubost (1911-2011)
The Rules of the Game '39
The Sheep Has Five Legs '54
Viva Maria! '65
The Last Metro '80

Paul Dubov (1918-79)
Day the World Ended '55
China Gate '57
Guns Don't Argue '57
Atomic Submarine '59
The Crimson Kimono '59
The Purple Gang '59
Verboten! '59
Ma Barker's Killer Brood '60
Underworld U.S.A. '61
Shock Corridor '63

Kristie Ducati
The Bikini Car Wash Company '90
The Bikini Car Wash Company 2 '92

Michel Duchaussoy (1938-2012)
The Killing Game '67
La Femme Infidele '69
This Man Must Die '70
Fort Saganne '84
The Widow of Saint-Pierre '00
Amen '02
The Bridesmaid '04
Intimate Strangers '04
Mesrine: Part 1-Killer Instinct '08
Mesrine: Part 2-Public Enemy Number 1 '08
Sarah's Key '10

David Duchovny (1960-)
New Year's Day '89
Don't Tell Mom the Babysitter's Dead '91
The Rapture '91
Beethoven '92
Chaplin '92
Red Shoe Diaries '92
Red Shoe Diaries 2: Double Dare '92
Ruby '92
Venice, Venice '92
Kalifornia '93
Red Shoe Diaries 3: Another Woman's Lipstick '93
Red Shoe Diaries 4: Auto Erotica '93
Red Shoe Diaries 6: How I Met My Husband '95
Playing God '96
Red Shoe Diaries 7: Burning Up '96
Red Shoe Diaries: Four on the Floor '96
Red Shoe Diaries: Strip Poker '96
Red Shoe Diaries 8: Night of Abandon '97
The X-Files '98
Red Shoe Diaries: Luscious Lola '00
Red Shoe Diaries: Swimming Naked '00
Return to Me '00
Evolution '01
Zoolander '01
Full Frontal '02
Connie and Carla '04
House of D '04
Queer Duck: The Movie '06 (V)
Trust the Man '06
The TV Set '06
The Secret '07
Things We Lost in the Fire '07
The X Files: I Want to Believe '08
The Joneses '09
Goats '12

Phantom '13
Louder Than Words '14

Ric(k) Ducommun (1952-2015)
No Small Affair '84
Die Hard '88
The 'Burbs '89
Little Monsters '89
Class Act '91
Encino Man '92
Blank Check '93
Ghost in the Machine '93
Final Voyage '99
MVP: Most Valuable Primate '00

Louis Ducreux (1901-92)
A Sunday in the Country '84
The Story of Women '88
The Double Life of Veronique '91

Anne Dudek (1975-)
White Chicks '04
10 Items or Less '06
Shadow People '13

Neil Dudgeon (1961-)
Piece of Cake '88
Different for Girls '96
Speedy Death '99
Dirty Tricks '00
Son of Rambow '07

Michael Dudikoff (1954-)
The Black Marble '79
Bloody Birthday '80
Making Love '82
Bachelor Party '84
American Ninja '85
American Ninja 2: The Confrontation '87
River of Death '90
American Ninja 4: The Annihilation '91
Chain of Command '95
Virtual Assassin '95
Bounty Hunters '96
Crash Dive '96
Moving Target '96
Bounty Hunters 2: Hardball '97
The Shooter '97
Black Thunder '98
Freedom Strike '98
Ringmaster '98
Counter Measures '99
Fugitive Mind '99
The Silencer '99
Ablaze '00
Black Horizon '01
Gale Force '01
Quicksand '01
Navy Seals *vs.* Zombies '15

Lola Duenas (1971-)
The Sea Inside '04
Volver '06
Chef's Special '08
Broken Embraces '09
The Women on the Sixth Floor '10
I'm So Excited '13
Zama '17

Carl Duering (1923-)
Underground '70
A Clockwork Orange '71
Operation Daybreak '75

John Duerler
Mysterious Museum '99
Battle Planet '08

Anne-Marie Duff (1970-)
Amongst Women '98
Aristocrats '99
The Aristocrats '99
The Magdalene Sisters '02
The History of Mr. Polly '07
The Waiting Room '07
French Film '08
Is Anybody There? '08
The Last Station '09
Margot '09
Nowhere Boy '09
Closed Circuit '13
Before I Go to Sleep '14
Molly Moon and The Incredible Book of Hypnotism '15

Suffragette '15
On Chesil Beach '17

Denice Duff (1965-)
Bloodstone: Subspecies 2 '92
Return to Frogtown '92
Bloodfist 5: Human Target '93
Bloodlust: Subspecies 3 '93
Bloodstorm: Subspecies 4 '98

Haylie Duff (1985-)
Napoleon Dynamite '04
Dishdogz '05
Material Girls '06
Nightmare '07
Backwoods '08
Legacy '08
Love Finds a Home '09
Love Takes Wing '09
My Nanny's Secret '09
Holiday Engagement '11
A Belle for Christmas '14

Hilary Duff (1987-)
Agent Cody Banks '03
Cheaper by the Dozen '03
The Lizzie McGuire Movie '03
A Cinderella Story '04
Raise Your Voice '04
Cheaper by the Dozen 2 '05
The Perfect Man '05
Material Girls '06
According to Greta '08
War, Inc. '08
Stay Cool '09
What Goes Up '09
Beauty & the Briefcase '10
Bloodworth '10
The Haunting of Sharon Tate '19

Howard Duff (1917-90)
Brute Force '47
The Naked City '48
Woman in Hiding '49
Spaceways '53
Private Hell 36 '54
Flame of the Islands '55
Women's Prison '55
The Broken Star '56
While the City Sleeps '56
Boys' Night Out '62
Panic in the City '68
Snowblind '78
A Wedding '78
Kramer *vs.* Kramer '79
East of Eden '80
Oh, God! Book 2 '80
Monster in the Closet '86
No Way Out '87
Roses Are for the Rich '87

Julia Duffy (1951-)
Children in the Crossfire '84
Dumb and Dumberer: When Harry Met Lloyd '03
Intolerable Cruelty '03
7 Things to Do Before I'm 30 '08
Together Again for the First Time '08
Bed & Breakfast '10
On Strike for Christmas '10

Karen Duffy (1962-)
Blank Check '93
Dumb & Dumber '94
Reality Bites '94 (C)
Synapse '95
The 24 Hour Woman '99
Fantastic Mr. Fox '09 (V)

Patrick Duffy (1949-)
The Last of Mrs. Lincoln '76
Alice in Wonderland '85
Murder C.O.D. '90
Danielle Steel's Daddy '91
Texas '94
Perfect Game '00
Love Takes Wing '09
Working Miracles '10
You Again '10

Quinn Duffy
The Chaos Experiment '09
Game of Death '10

Thomas F. Duffy (1955-)
Eye of the Stranger '93
Wagons East '94
The Lost World: Jurassic Park 2 '97
Varsity Blues '98

Dennis Dugan (1946-)
Night Call Nurses '72
Night Moves '75
Norman, Is That You? '76
Unidentified Flying Oddball '79
The Howling '81
Can't Buy Me Love '87
The New Adventures of Pippi Longstocking '88
She's Having a Baby '88
Parenthood '89
Happy Gilmore '96
The Benchwarmers '06
I Now Pronounce You Chuck and Larry '07

John Dugan (1940-)
The Texas Chainsaw Massacre '74
The Texas Chainsaw Massacre 4: The Next Generation '95

Michael Dugan
She Wore a Yellow Ribbon '49
Gun Glory '57

Tom Dugan (1889-1955)
The Galloping Ghost '31
Blessed Event '32
Skyway '33
Mister Cinderella '36
Pennies from Heaven '36
Pick a Star '37
To Be or Not to Be '42
Bataan '43
Gambler's Choice '44
Take Me Out to the Ball Game '49
Nightwish '89
I've Been Waiting for You '98

Andrew Duggan (1923-88)
Decision at Sundown '57
Westbound '58
The Chapman Report '62
House of Women '62
Merrill's Marauders '62
FBI Code 98 '63
Palm Springs Weekend '63
The Incredible Mr. Limpet '64
Seven Days in May '64
In Like Flint '67
The Secret War of Harry Frigg '68
Skin Game '71
Firehouse '72
Housewife '72
The Streets of San Francisco '72
The Bears & I '74
It's Alive '74
Missiles of October '74
Once an Eagle '76
It's Alive 2: It Lives Again '78
Backstairs at the White House '79
The Long Days of Summer '80
Frankenstein Island '81
Doctor Detroit '83
The Winds of War '83
Return to Salem's Lot '87

Tommy Duggan (1909-98)
Frankenstein 1970 '58
The Final Conflict '81

Josh Duhamel (1972-)
Win a Date with Tad Hamilton! '04
Turistas '06
Transformers '07
Transformers: Revenge of the Fallen '09
When in Rome '09
Life As We Know It '10
Ramona and Beezus '10
The Romantics '10
New Year's Eve '11

Transformers: Dark of the Moon '11
Fire With Fire '12
Movie 43 '13
Safe Haven '13
Scenic Route '13
Don Peyote '14
Misconduct '16
Transformers: The Last Knight '17
Love, Simon '18
Think Like a Dog '20

Kevin Duhaney
Treed Murray '01
How She Move '08

Jean Dujardin (1972-)
OSS 117: Cairo, Nest of Spies '06
Cash '08
OSS 117: Lost in Rio '09
Little White Lies '10
The Artist '11
Mobius '13
The Monuments Men '13
The Wolf of Wall Street '13
The Connection '15

Davor Dujmovic (1969-99)
Time of the Gypsies '90
Underground '95

Olympia Dukakis (1931-)
Lilith '64
Death Wish '74
The Seagull '75
Wanderers '79
Idolmaker '80
Walls of Glass '85
Moonstruck '87
Working Girl '88
Dad '89
Look Who's Talking '89
Steel Magnolias '89
Look Who's Talking, Too '90
Lucky Day '91
Sinatra '92
Armistead Maupin's Tales of the City '93
The Cemetery Club '93
Look Who's Talking Now '93
Over the Hill '93
I Love Trouble '94
Mother '94
Jeffrey '95
Mighty Aphrodite '95
Mr. Holland's Opus '95
Picture Perfect '96
Armistead Maupin's More Tales of the City '97
Borough of Kings '98
Mafia! '98
The Pentagon Wars '98
Joan of Arc '99
The Last of the Blonde Bombshells '00
And Never Let Her Go '01
The Intended '02
Strange Relations '02
The Event '03
The Librarian: Quest for the Spear '04
The Thing About My Folks '05
Away From Her '06
The Great New Wonderful '06
In the Land of Women '06
The Librarian: Return to King Solomon's Mines '06
Cloudburst '11

Bill Duke (1943-)
American Gigolo '79
Commando '85
Predator '87
Bird on a Wire '90
Menace II Society '93
Dying to Get Rich '98
Payback '98
Fever '99
Foolish '99
The Limey '99
Exit Wounds '01
Never Again '01
Red Dragon '02
National Security '03
Get Rich or Die Tryin' '05
X-Men: The Last Stand '06
Yellow '06
The Go-Getter '07 (C)
Henry's Crime '10

Clark Duke (1985-)
Sex Drive '08
Hot Tub Time Machine '10
Kick-Ass '10
A Thousand Words '12
The Croods '13 (V)
Hot Tub Time Machine 2 '15
The Last Movie Star '17

Patty Duke (1946-2016)
The Goddess '58
The 4D Man '59
The Miracle Worker '62
Billie '65
Valley of the Dolls '67
Fire '77
The Swarm '78
Hanging By a Thread '79
The Miracle Worker '79
Amityville 4: The Evil Escapes '89
Grave Secrets: The Legacy of Hilltop Drive '92
A Killer Among Friends '92
Prelude to a Kiss '92
Family of Strangers '93
Harvest of Fire '95
A Season for Miracles '99
Little John '02
Murder Without Conviction '04
Bigger Than the Sky '05
Love Finds a Home '09
Unanswered Prayers '10

Robin Duke (1954-)
Club Paradise '86
Motorama '91
I Love Trouble '94

Winston Duke
Us '19
Spenser Confidential '20

Ken Duken (1979-)
Max Manus: Man of War '08
The Sinking of the Laconia '10
Chalet Girls '11
Northman: A Viking Saga '15

David Dukes (1945-2000)
The Strawberry Statement '70
Wild Party '74
The Triangle Factory Fire Scandal '79
The First Deadly Sin '80
Only When I Laugh '81
Miss All-American Beauty '82
The Winds of War '83
Without a Trace '83
Cat on a Hot Tin Roof '84
The Men's Club '86
Catch the Heat '87
Date with an Angel '87
Rawhead Rex '87
War & Remembrance '88
See You in the Morning '89
War & Remembrance: The Final Chapter '89
The Josephine Baker Story '90
Held Hostage '91
And the Band Played On '93 (C)
Me and the Kid '93
Norma Jean and Marilyn '95
Last Stand at Saber River '96
Gods and Monsters '98
The Love Letter '98
Supreme Sanction '99
Tick Tock '00
Stephen King's Rose Red '02

Caitlin Dulany
Class of 1999 2: The Substitute '93
Maniac Cop 3: Badge of Silence '93

Keir Dullea (1936-)
The Hoodlum Priest '61
David and Lisa '62
Mail Order Bride '63
The Thin Red Line '64
Bunny Lake Is Missing '65
Madame X '66
2001: A Space Odyssey '68
Black Water Gold '69
Black Christmas '75
Leopard in the Snow '78
Brainwaves '82
Blind Date '84
Next One '84
2010: The Year We Make Contact '84
The Audrey Hepburn Story '00
The Good Shepherd '06
The Accidental Husband '08
Infinitely Polar Bear '14

Sandrine Dumas (1963-)
The Double Life of Veronique '91
Father of My Children '09
Let the Sunshine In '17

Douglass Dumbrille (1890-1974)
Baby Face '33
Heroes for Sale '33
Fog Over Frisco '34
Hi, Nellie! '34
Operator 13 '34
Treasure Island '34
Air Hawks '35
Cardinal Richelieu '35
The Lives of a Bengal Lancer '35
Naughty Marietta '35
Peter Ibbetson '35
Public Menace '35
The Secret Bride '35
Mr. Deeds Goes to Town '36
The Princess Comes Across '36
A Day at the Races '37
The Emperor's Candlesticks '37
The Firefly '37
Charlie Chan at Treasure Island '39
Charlie Chan in City of Darkness '39
Mr. Moto in Danger Island '39
The Three Musketeers '39
Michael Shayne: Private Detective '40
Virginia City '40
Big Store '41
I Married an Angel '42
Ride 'Em Cowboy '42
Stand by for Action '42
Lost in a Harem '44
Uncertain Glory '44
Flame of the West '45
The Road to Utopia '46
Under Nevada Skies '46
Abbott and Costello in the Foreign Legion '50
Riding High '50
Son of Paleface '52
World for Ransom '54
Jupiter's Darling '55
The Ten Commandments '56
Shake, Rattle and Rock '57

Ralph Dumke (1899-1964)
The Breaking Point '50
The Fireball '50

Hayley DuMond
Raptor Island '04
All In '06

James DuMont (1965-)
Combination Platter '93
Fast Girl '07
Enemies Among Us '10
Journey to Promethea '10
The Banker '20

Margaret Dumont (1889-1965)
The Cocoanuts '29
Animal Crackers '30
Duck Soup '33
A Night at the Opera '35
A Day at the Races '37
High Flyers '37
At the Circus '39
The Women '39
Big Store '41
Never Give a Sucker an Even Break '41
Tales of Manhattan '42
Rhythm Parade '43
Up in Arms '44
The Horn Blows at Midnight '45
Shake, Rattle and Rock '57
Zotz! '62

Dennis Dun (1952-)
Big Trouble in Little China '86
The Last Emperor '87
Prince of Darkness '87

Steffi Duna (1910-92)
Dancing Pirate '36
Hitler: Beast of Berlin '39
Law of the Pampas '39

Deanna Dunagan (1940-)
Mitch Albom's Have a Little Faith '11
The Visit '15

Donnie Dunagan (1934-)
Son of Frankenstein '39
Bambi '42 (V)

Faye Dunaway (1941-)
Bonnie & Clyde '67
Hurry Sundown '67
The Thomas Crown Affair '68
The Arrangement '69
Little Big Man '70
Oklahoma Crude '73
Chinatown '74
The Three Musketeers '74
The Towering Inferno '74
The Four Musketeers '75
Three Days of the Condor '75
Network '76
Voyage of the Damned '76
Eyes of Laura Mars '78
The Champ '79
The First Deadly Sin '80
Mommie Dearest '81
Supergirl '84
Agatha Christie's Thirteen at Dinner '85
Barfly '87
Midnight Crossing '87
The Gamble '88
The Handmaid's Tale '90
Scorchers '92
The Temp '93
Arizona Dream '94
Don Juan DeMarco '94
Dunston Checks In '95
Albino Alligator '96
The Chamber '96
Drunks '96
Rebecca '97
The Twilight of the Golds '97
Gia '98
The Messenger: The Story of Joan of Arc '99
The Thomas Crown Affair '99
Running Mates '00
The Yards '00
The Rules of Attraction '02
Anonymous Rex '04
Blind Horizon '04
Chronicle of the Raven '04
El Padrino '04
Ghosts Never Sleep '05
Cut Off '06
Rain '06
Cougar Club '07 (C)
Flick '07
The Gene Generation '07
Pandemic '07
Midnight Bayou '09
A Family Thanksgiving '10
The Bye Bye Man '17
The Case for Christ '17
Inconceivable '17

Adrian Dunbar (1958-)
My Left Foot '89
The Crying Game '92
The Playboys '92
A Woman's Guide to Adultery '93
Widow's Peak '94
Innocent Lies '95
Melissa '97
The General '98
Relative Strangers '99
Shooters '00
How Harry Became a Tree '01
Triggermen '02
Suspicion '03
Kidnapped '05
Eye of the Dolphin '06

Helen Dunbar (1863-1933)
Beyond the Rocks '22
Fine Manners '26

Rockmond Dunbar (1973-)
Kiss Kiss Bang Bang '05
Dirty Laundry '07
Alien Raiders '08
The Family That Preys '08
Jada '08
A Taste of Romance '12
Highland Park '13
Curveball '15

Andrew Duncan
The Rain People '69
Loving '70
Slap Shot '77
Morgan Stewart's Coming Home '87

Archie Duncan
Postman's Knock '62
Ring of Bright Water '69

Arletta Duncan (1914-95)
Frankenstein '31
Mile a Minute Love '37

Carmen Duncan (1942-)
Now and Forever '82
Dark Forces '83
Moving Targets '87
Counterstrike '03

Kenne Duncan (1903-72)
The Spider's Web '38
The Spider Returns '41
Flesh and the Spur '57
Night of the Ghouls '59
The Sinister Urge '60

Lindsay Duncan (1950-)
Grown Ups '80
Prick Up Your Ears '87
A Year in Provence '89
Traffik '90
Body Parts '91
G.B.H. '91
The Reflecting Skin '91
The Rector's Wife '94
City Hall '95
A Midsummer Night's Dream '96
An Ideal Husband '99
Mansfield Park '99
Shooting the Past '99
Dirty Tricks '00
Oliver Twist '00
Almost Strangers '01
Under the Tuscan Sun '03
Longford '06
Starter for 10 '06
Margot '09
Alice in Wonderland '10
The Sinking of the Laconia '10
Christopher and His Kind '11
Last Passenger '14
Le Week-End '14
Gifted '17

Mary Duncan (1895-1993)
City Girl '30
Five and Ten '31
State's Attorney '31
Morning Glory '33

Michael Clarke Duncan (1957-2012)
Armageddon '98
The Green Mile '99
They Call Me Sirr '00
The Whole Nine Yards '00
Cats & Dogs '01 (V)
Planet of the Apes '01
See Spot Run '01
The Scorpion King '02
Brother Bear '03 (V)
Daredevil '03
D.E.B.S. '04
The Island '05
Racing Stripes '05 (V)
Sin City '05
Air Bud 6: Air Buddies '06 (V)
One Way '06
School for Scoundrels '06
Talladega Nights: The Ballad of Ricky Bobby '06
American Crude '07
The Last Mimzy '07
Slipstream '07
Delgo '08 (V)
Kung Fu Panda '08 (V)
Welcome Home Roscoe Jenkins '08
The Slammin' Salmon '09
Street Fighter: The Legend of Chun-Li '09
Cats & Dogs: The Revenge of Kitty Galore '10 (V)
Redemption Road '10
Cross '11
Green Lantern '11 (V)

Michaelle Duncan
Driving Lessons '06
The Broken '08

Pamela Duncan
My Gun Is Quick '57
The Undead '57

Rachel Duncan (1985-)
The Crazysitter '94
Amityville Dollhouse '96
Last Stand at Saber River '96

Sandy Duncan (1946-)
Million Dollar Duck '71
Star Spangled Girl '71
Roots '77
The Cat from Outer Space '78
The Fox and the Hound '81 (V)
Rock-a-Doodle '92 (V)
The Swan Princess '94 (V)
Never Again '01

Jennifer (Jennie) Dundas Lowe (1971-)
The Beniker Gang '83
The Hotel New Hampshire '84
Mrs. Soffel '84
Heaven Help Us '85
Legal Eagles '86
The First Wives Club '96
Swimming '00
Changing Lanes '02
Puccini for Beginners '06

Claude Duneton
The Double Life of Veronique '91
Trois Couleurs: Bleu '93

Christine Dunford
Reversal of Fortune '90
Ulee's Gold '97
How to Go Out on a Date in Queens '06

Lena Dunham (1986-)
Tiny Furniture '10
The Innkeepers '11
Supporting Characters '13
Happy Christmas '14
My Entire High School Sinking Into the Sea '17

Robert Dunham (1931-2001)
Face of Another '66
The Green Slime '68
Godzilla vs. Megalon '76

Stephen Dunham (1964-2012)
The Mummy '99
Monster-in-Law '05
Paranormal Activity 4 '12

Dawn Dunlap (1963-)
Forbidden World '82
Heartbreaker '83
Barbarian Queen '85

Lesley Dunlop (1956-)
Agatha Christie's Thirteen at Dinner '85
Tess of the D'Urbervilles '98

Conrad Dunn
Mask of Death '97
Silent Trigger '97

The Last Don 2 '98
Animal 2 '07

Eddie Dunn (1896-1951)
Billy the Kid '41
A Date With the Falcon '42
Mexican Spitfire at Sea '42
The Falcon in Danger '43
A Fig Leaf for Eve '44
Call Northside 777 '48

Emma Dunn (1875-1966)
The Guilty Generation '31
This Modern Age '31
Blessed Event '32
Hell's House '32
Under Eighteen '32
The Quitter '34
George White's Scandals of 1935 '35
The Keeper of the Bees '35
Ladies Crave Excitement '35
Madame X '37
Three Loves Has Nancy '38
The Secret of Dr. Kildare '39
Son of Frankenstein '39
Dr. Kildare Goes Home '40
The Great Dictator '40
Talk of the Town '42

Harvey B. Dunn (1894-1968)
Bride of the Monster '55
Teenagers from Outer Space '59
The Sinister Urge '60

James Dunn (1905-67)
Bad Girl '31
Baby, Take a Bow '34
Bright Eyes '34
Stand Up and Cheer '34
365 Nights in Hollywood '34
The Daring Young Man '35
George White's Scandals of 1935 '35
Government Girl '43
A Tree Grows in Brooklyn '45
That Brennan Girl '46
Killer McCoy '47

Josephine Dunn (1906-83)
The Singing Fool '28
Our Modern Maidens '29

Kevin Dunn (1956-)
Mississippi Burning '88
Hot Shots! '91
Only the Lonely '91
Chaplin '92
Dave '93
Little Big League '94
JAG '95
Mad Love '95
Nixon '95
Chain Reaction '96
Picture Perfect '96
Almost Heroes '97
The Second Civil War '97
The Sixth Man '97
Godzilla '98
Small Soldiers '98
Snake Eyes '98
Stir of Echoes '99
Ann Rule Presents: The Stranger Beside Me '03
All the King's Men '06
The Black Dahlia '06
Gridiron Gang '06
A Perfect Day '06
Lions for Lambs '07
Transformers '07
Vicky Cristina Barcelona '08
Transformers: Revenge of the Fallen '09
Unstoppable '10
Transformers: Dark of the Moon '11
Warrior '11
You May Not Kiss the Bride '12
The Frozen Ground '13
Prosecuting Casey Anthony '13
Captive State '19

Liam Dunn (1917-76)
Catch-22 '70
Emperor of the North Pole '73
Blazing Saddles '74
Young Frankenstein '74

Michael Dunn (1934-73)
Ship of Fools '65
You're a Big Boy Now '66
Madigan '68
Murders in the Rue Morgue '71
The Freakmaker '73
Werewolf of Washington '73
The Abdication '74
Dr. Frankenstein's Castle of Freaks '74

Nora Dunn (1952-)
Working Girl '88
How I Got into College '89
Miami Blues '90
Passion Fish '92
Born Yesterday '93
I Love Trouble '94
Shake, Rattle & Rock! '94
The Last Supper '96
Air Bud 2: Golden Receiver '98
Bulworth '98
Drop Dead Gorgeous '99
Three Kings '99
What Planet Are You From? '00
Heartbreakers '01
Max Keeble's Big Move '01
What's the Worst That Could Happen? '01
Cherish '02
Bruce Almighty '03
Die Mommie Die! '03
Runaway Jury '03
Laws of Attraction '04
Love for Rent '05
November '05
Southland Tales '06
Pineapple Express '08
The Answer Man '09
It's Complicated '09
3, 2, 1...Frankie Go Boom '12

Roger Dunn
The Sandy Bottom Orchestra '00
Ignition '01
Owning Mahowny '03
The Baby Formula '08
Before You Say 'I Do' '09

Ryan Dunn (1977-2011)
Jackass: The Movie '02
Jackass Number Two '06
Jackass 3D '10
Living Will '10

John Dunn-Hill
Bleeders '97
Wilder '00
Varian's War '01
Secret Window '04

Dominick Dunne (1925-2009)
Addicted to Love '96
An Alan Smithee Film: Burn, Hollywood, Burn '97 (C)

Dominique Dunne (1959-82)
Poltergeist '82
The Shadow Riders '82

Griffin Dunne (1955-)
The Other Side of the Mountain '75
An American Werewolf in London '81
The Fan '81
Johnny Dangerously '84
After Hours '85
Almost You '85
Amazon Women on the Moon '87
Who's That Girl? '87
The Big Blue '88
White Palace '90
My Girl '91
Once Around '91
Big Girls Don't Cry. . . They Get Even '92
Straight Talk '92
The Pickle '93 (C)
I Like It Like That '94
Quiz Show '94
Search and Destroy '94
The Android Affair '95
Blonde '01
Lisa Picard Is Famous '01
40 Days and 40 Nights '02
Game 6 '05
Snow Angels '07
The Great Buck Howard '09
Last Night '10
Dallas Buyers Club '13
Fugly! '14
Rob the Mob '14
Touched With Fire '16

Irene Dunne (1898-1990)
Cimarron '31
Symphony of Six Million '32
If I Were Free '33
The Age of Innocence '34
Stingaree '34
Magnificent Obsession '35
Roberta '35
Show Boat '36
Theodora Goes Wild '36
The Awful Truth '37
High, Wide and Handsome '37
Joy of Living '38
Love Affair '39
My Favorite Wife '40
Penny Serenade '41
Lady in a Jam '42
Together Again '43
The White Cliffs of Dover '44
Over 21 '45
Anna and the King of Siam '46
Life with Father '47
I Remember Mama '48
The Mudlark '50

Murphy Dunne (1942-)
The Blues Brothers '80
Going Berserk '83
Blues Brothers 2000 '98
Live from Baghdad '03

Robin Dunne (1976-)
Cruel Intentions 2 '99
Teenage Space Vampires '99
Au Pair 2: The Fairy Tale Continues '01
The Fraternity '01
American Psycho 2: All American Girl '02
The Skulls 2 '02
The Snow Walker '03
Species 3 '04
Jack and Jill vs. the World '08
Beyond Sherwood Forest '09

Steve (Stephen) Dunne (1918-77)
Colonel Effingham's Raid '45
The Big Sombrero '49
The Underworld Story '50
The WAC From Walla Walla '52
Above and Beyond '53
Home Before Dark '58
The Explosive Generation '61

Mildred Dunnock (1901-91)
The Corn Is Green '45
Death of a Salesman '51
The Girl in White '52
The Jazz Singer '52
Viva Zapata! '52
Bad for Each Other '53
The Trouble with Harry '55
Baby Doll '56
Love Me Tender '56
Peyton Place '57
The Nun's Story '59
Butterfield 8 '60
Something Wild '61
Sweet Bird of Youth '62
Behold a Pale Horse '64
Youngblood Hawke '64
Whatever Happened to Aunt Alice? '69
Brand New Life '72
Spiral Staircase '75
And Baby Makes Six '79
The Pick-Up Artist '87

Rosemary Dunsmore (1952-)
Dancing in the Dark '86
Anne of Avonlea '87
Breaking the Surface: The Greg Louganis Story '96
The Long Way Home '98
The Interrogation of Michael Crowe '02
Dreamcatcher '03
Citizen Duane '06
Playing House '06
Wedding Wars '06
They Come Back '07
The Baby Formula '08
Orphan '09
Red: Werewolf Hunter '10
The Santa Suit '10
When Love Is Not Enough: The Lois Wilson Story '10
Fugitive at 17 '12

Kirsten Dunst (1982-)
Interview with the Vampire '94
Little Women '94
Jumanji '95
Mother Night '96
Anastasia '97 (V)
Tower of Terror '97
True Heart '97
Wag the Dog '97
All I Wanna Do '98
Kiki's Delivery Service '98 (V)
Small Soldiers '98
Deeply '99
The Devil's Arithmetic '99
Dick '99
Drop Dead Gorgeous '99
Lover's Prayer '99
The Virgin Suicides '99
Bring It On '00
The Crow: Salvation '00
Luckytown '00
The Cat's Meow '01
crazy/beautiful '01
Get Over It! '01
Spider-Man '02
Kaena: The Prophecy '03 (V)
Levity '03
Mona Lisa Smile '03
Eternal Sunshine of the Spotless Mind '04
Spider-Man 2 '04
Wimbledon '04
Elizabethtown '05
Marie Antoinette '06
Spider-Man 3 '07
How to Lose Friends & Alienate People '08
All Good Things '10
Melancholia '11
Bachelorette '12
On the Road '12
Mademoiselle C '13
Upside Down '13
The Two Faces of January '14
Midnight Special '16
The Beguiled '17
Hidden Figures '17
Woodshock '17

Molly Dunsworth
Hobo With a Shotgun '11
Septic Man '14

Cheryl Dunye (1966-)
The Watermelon Woman '97
The Owls '09

Don Duong (1957-2011)
Green Dragon '01
We Were Soldiers '02

Anny (Annie Legras) Duperey (1947-)
Two or Three Things I Know about Her '66
The Women '68
Stavisky '74
Bobby Deerfield '77
From Hell to Victory '79
Les Comperes '83

Daphne Lynn Duplaix (1976-)
Foolish '99
Lost and Found '99
Survival Island '02

Jay Duplass (1973-)
Beatriz at Dinner '17
Landline '17
Outside In '17

Mark Duplass (1976-)
Hannah Takes the Stairs '07
Humpday '09
Greenberg '10
Your Sister's Sister '11
Darling Companion '12
People Like Us '12
Safety Not Guaranteed '12
The One I Love '14
Tammy '14
Creep '15
The Lazarus Effect '15
Blue Jay '16
Tully '18
Paddleton '19

Starletta DuPois (1941-)
Hollywood Shuffle '87
A Raisin in the Sun '89
Big Momma's House '00
Three Strikes '00
Friday After Next '02
The Least Among You '09

Elaine DuPont
The Ghost of Dragstrip Hollow '59
The Beach Girls and the Monster '65

Tiffany DuPont
One Night with the King '06
Hijacked '12

Albert Dupontel (1964-)
Irreversible '02
A Very Long Engagement '04
Avenue Montaigne '06
Chrysalis '07
Paris '08
The Prey '11

Monique Dupree
Bachelor Party in the Bungalow of the Damned '08
Skeleton Key 2: 667, the Neighbor of the Beast '08

June Duprez (1918-84)
The Four Feathers '39
Spy in Black '39
The Thief of Bagdad '40
None But the Lonely Heart '44
And Then There Were None '45
That Brennan Girl '46
Calcutta '47

Roy Dupuis (1963-)
Bleeders '97
The Rocket '05
That Beautiful Somewhere '06
Autumn Hearts: A New Beginning '07
Shake Hands With the Devil '07
Mesrine: Part 1-Killer Instinct '08

Michelle Duquet
Say Nothing '01
Widow on the Hill '05

Poldi Dur (1917-96)
Margin for Error '43
They Came to Blow Up America '43

Erica Durance (1978-)
Sasquatch '02
House of the Dead '03
The Butterfly Effect 2 '06
Stranded '06
I Me Wed '07
Beyond Sherwood Forest '09
Painkillers '15

Kevin Durand (1974-)
12 Hours to Live '06
Smokin' Aces '07
3:10 to Yuma '07
Who's Your Monkey '07
Wild Hogs '07
The Echo '08
X-Men Origins: Wolverine '09
Legion '10
Robin Hood '10
Citizen Gangster '11
I Am Number Four '11
Real Steel '11
Cosmopolis '12
Resident Evil: Retribution '12
Fruitvale Station '13
The Mortal Instruments: City of Bones '13
The Captive '14
Devil's Knot '14
Noah '14
Garm Wars: The Last Druid '15
Tragedy Girls '17
Primal '19

Christopher Durang (1949-)
Heaven Help Us '85
Mr. North '88
The Butcher's Wife '91
Housesitter '92
Simply Irresistible '99

Jimmy Durante (1893-1980)
The Passionate Plumber '32
Speak Easily '32
The Wet Parade '32
Hollywood Party '34
Palooka '34
Strictly Dynamite '34
Little Miss Broadway '38
Sally, Irene and Mary '38
Melody Ranch '40
The Man Who Came to Dinner '41
Music For Millions '44
Two Girls and a Sailor '44
Two Sisters From Boston '46
Ziegfeld Follies '46
It Happened in Brooklyn '47
This Time for Keeps '47
On an Island with You '48
The Great Rupert '50
Billy Rose's Jumbo '62
It's a Mad, Mad, Mad, Mad World '63
Alice Through the Looking Glass '66

Deanna Durbin (1921-2013)
Three Smart Girls '36
100 Men and a Girl '37
Mad About Music '38
That Certain Age '38
First Love '39
Three Smart Girls Grow Up '39
Spring Parade '40
It Started with Eve '41
The Amazing Mrs. Holiday '43
His Butler's Sister '44
Because of Him '45
Can't Help Singing '45
Lady on a Train '45
Something in the Wind '47
For the Love of Mary '48
Up in Central Park '48

John Durbin
Ain't No Way Back '89
Tapeheads '89
No Way Back '90

Richard Durden (1944-)
The First 9 1/2 Weeks '98
Pumpkinhead 4: Blood Feud '07
From Paris With Love '10
Churchill '17

Romain Duris (1974-)
The Crazy Stranger '98
L'Auberge Espagnole '02
Le Divorce '03
The Beat My Heart Skipped '05
Russian Dolls '05
Inside Paris '06
Moliere '07

Afterwards *'08*
Paris *'08*
The Big Picture *'10*
Heartbreaker *'10*
Chinese Puzzle *'13*
Mood Indigo *'13*
The New Girlfriend *'14*
All the Money in the World *'17*

Junior Durkin (1915-35)
Hell's House *'32*
Little Men *'34*

Charles Durning (1923-2012)
I Walk the Line *'70*
Sisters *'73*
The Sting *'73*
The Front Page *'74*
Dog Day Afternoon *'75*
The Hindenburg *'75*
Queen of the Stardust Ballroom *'75*
Breakheart Pass *'76*
Harry & Walter Go to New York *'76*
The Choirboys *'77*
An Enemy of the People *'77*
The Fury *'78*
The Muppet Movie *'79 (C)*
North Dallas Forty *'79*
When a Stranger Calls *'79*
Die Laughing *'80*
The Final Countdown *'80*
Dark Night of the Scarecrow *'81*
Sharky's Machine *'81*
True Confessions *'81*
The Best Little Whorehouse in Texas *'82*
Tootsie *'82*
To Be or Not to Be *'83*
Two of a Kind *'83*
Mass Appeal *'84*
The Man with One Red Shoe *'85*
Stick *'85*
Big Trouble *'86*
Brenda Starr *'86*
Death of a Salesman *'86*
Solarbabies *'86*
Tough Guys *'86*
Where the River Runs Black *'86*
Happy New Year *'87*
Kenny Rogers as the Gambler, Part 3: The Legend Continues *'87*
Cop *'88*
Far North *'88*
Dinner at Eight *'89*
Cat Chaser *'90*
Dick Tracy *'90*
The Return of Eliot Ness *'91*
V.I. Warshawski *'91*
The Hudsucker Proxy *'93*
The Music of Chance *'93*
The Story Lady *'93*
When a Stranger Calls Back *'93*
A Woman of Independent Means *'94*
The Grass Harp *'95*
Home for the Holidays *'95*
The Last Supper *'96*
Mrs. Santa Claus *'96*
One Fine Day *'96*
Spy Hard *'96*
Hi-Life *'98*
Jerry and Tom *'98*
Shelter *'98*
Backlash *'99*
Hostage Hotel *'00*
Lakeboat *'00*
O Brother Where Art Thou? *'00*
State and Main *'00*
L.A.P.D.: To Protect and Serve *'01*
Steve Martini's The Judge *'01*
Mr. St. Nick *'02*
One Last Ride *'03*
A Boyfriend for Christmas *'04*
River's End *'05*
Forget About It *'06*
Local Color *'06*
Miracle Dogs Too *'06*
Unbeatable Harold *'06*
Deal *'08*
The Golden Boys *'08*
iMurders *'08*
Break *'09*

Dick Durock (1937-2009)
The Enforcer *'76*
Swamp Thing *'82*
The Return of Swamp Thing *'89*
The Return of the Swamp Thing *'89*

Jason Durr (1967-)
Sharpe's Battle *'94*
Killer Tongue *'96*
Mysterious Island *'05*

Michael Durrell (1943-)
V *'83*
Magma: Volcanic Disaster *'06*

Fred Durst (1970-)
Sorry, Haters *'05*
Population 436 *'06*
Play Dead *'09*

Ian Dury (1942-2000)
The Raggedy Rawney *'90*
Split Second *'92*
The Crow 2: City of Angels *'96*

Dan Duryea (1907-68)
Ball of Fire *'41*
The Little Foxes *'41*
The Pride of the Yankees *'42*
Sahara *'43*
Ministry of Fear *'44*
None But the Lonely Heart *'44*
Woman in the Window *'44*
Along Came Jones *'45*
Great Flamarion *'45*
Lady on a Train *'45*
Scarlet Street *'45*
The Valley of Decision *'45*
Black Angel *'46*
Criss Cross *'48*
Too Late for Tears *'49*
The Underworld Story *'50*
Winchester '73 *'50*
Chicago Calling *'52*
Thunder Bay *'53*
Ride Clear of Diablo *'54*
Silver Lode *'54*
Terror Street *'54*
World for Ransom *'54*
Battle Hymn *'57*
The Burglar *'57*
Night Passage *'57*
The Flight of the Phoenix *'65*
Five Golden Dragons *'67*
The Hills Run Red *'67*
The Bamboo Saucer *'68*

George Duryea (1896-1963)
See Tom Keene

Marj Dusay (1936-2020)
Sweet November *'68*
The Child Stealer *'79*
Made in Heaven *'87*
Love Walked In *'97*

Vittorio Duse
Mad Dog Killer *'77*
Queen of Hearts *'89*

Jaroslav Dusek (1961-)
Divided We Fall *'00*
Up and Down *'04*

Ann Dusenberry (1952-)
The Possessed *'77*
Little Women *'78*
Heart Beat *'80*
Cutter's Way *'81*
Killjoy *'81*
Basic Training *'86*
The Men's Club *'86*

Eliza Dushku (1980-)
That Night *'93*
This Boy's Life *'93*
Bye Bye, Love *'94*
True Lies *'94*
Race the Sun *'96*
Bring It On *'00*
Jay and Silent Bob Strike Back *'01*
Soul Survivors *'01*
City by the Sea *'02*
The New Guy *'02*
Wrong Turn *'03*
Sex and Breakfast *'07*
The Alphabet Killer *'08*
Nobel Son *'08*
Open Graves *'09*
The Scribbler *'14*

Nate Dushku (1977-)
The Zodiac *'05*
Blood Night: The Legend of Mary Hatchet *'09*

Nancy Dussault (1936-)
The In-Laws *'79*
The Nurse *'97*

Marta Dusseldorp (1973-)
Innocence *'00*
After the Deluge *'03*

Andre Dussollier (1946-)
And Now My Love *'74*
Perceval *'78*
Le Beau Mariage *'82*
Life Is a Bed of Roses *'83*
Love Unto Death *'84*
Three Men and a Cradle *'85*
Melo *'86*
Un Coeur en Hiver *'93*
Amelie *'01 (N)*
The 36th Precinct *'04*
A Very Long Engagement *'04*
Lemming *'05*
Private Fears in Public Places *'06*
Tell No One *'06*
The Lark Farm *'07*
Micmacs *'09*
Wild Grass *'09*
My Worst Nightmare *'11*
Unforgivable *'11*
Queens of the Ring *'13*
Beauty and the Beast *'14*

Jacques Dutronc (1943-)
Every Man for Himself *'79*
Tricheurs *'84*
Van Gogh *'92*
Place Vendome *'98*
Merci pour le Chocolat *'00*

Charles S. Dutton (1951-)
Cat's Eye *'85*
The Murder of Mary Phagan *'87*
Crocodile Dundee 2 *'88*
Jacknife *'89*
An Unremarkable Life *'89*
Q & A *'90*
Alien 3 *'92*
The Distinguished Gentleman *'92*
Mississippi Masala *'92*
Menace II Society *'93*
Rudy *'93*
Foreign Student *'94*
A Low Down Dirty Shame *'94*
The Piano Lesson *'94*
Surviving the Game *'94*
Cry, the Beloved Country *'95*
Nick of Time *'95*
Get On the Bus *'96*
A Time to Kill *'96*
Mimic *'97*
True Women *'97*
Black Dog *'98*
Blind Faith *'98*
Aftershock: Earthquake in New York *'99*
Cookie's Fortune *'99*
Random Hearts *'99*
The '60s *'99*
Deadlocked *'00*
For Love or Country: The Arturo Sandoval Story *'00*
Eye See You *'01*
Conviction *'02*
10,000 Black Men Named George *'02*
Gothika *'03*
Against the Ropes *'04*
Secret Window *'04*
Something the Lord Made *'04*
The Bronx Is Burning *'07*
Honeydripper *'07*
The Express *'08*
Racing for Time *'08*
Fame *'09*
Legion *'10*
LUV *'13*
Android Cop *'14*
Carter High *'15*
The Perfect Guy *'15*
What Lola Wants *'15*

Tim Dutton (1964-)
Tom & Viv *'94*
Melissa *'97*
Darkness Falls *'98*
Frenchman's Creek *'98*
Hard to Forget *'98*
St. Ives *'98*
Oliver Twist *'00*
The Bourne Identity *'02*

Kenton Duty
Christmas in Paradise *'07*
Crazy on the Outside *'10*
Contest *'13*

Daniel Duval (1944-2013)
Time of the Wolf *'03*
The 36th Precinct *'04*
Time to Leave *'05*
District 13: Ultimatum *'09*

Diane Duval (1914-2001)
See Julie Bishop

James Duval (1972-)
Totally F***ed Up *'94*
The Doom Generation *'95*
Independence Day *'96*
A River Made to Drown In *'97*
Go *'99*
SLC Punk! *'99*
Gone in 60 Seconds *'00*
The Weekend *'00*
The Doe Boy *'01*
Donnie Darko *'01*
Comic Book Villains *'02*
May *'02*
Players *'03*
Window Theory *'04*
Chasing Ghosts *'05*
Venice Underground *'05*
Mad Cowgirl *'06*
Roman *'06*
The Pacific and Eddy *'07*
The Art of Travel *'08*
Cornered! *'09*
The Black Waters of Echo's Pond *'10*
Kaboom *'11*
Sushi Girl *'12*
Appetites *'15*

Clea DuVall (1977-)
The Faculty *'98*
The Astronaut's Wife *'99*
But I'm a Cheerleader *'99*
Committed *'99*
Girl, Interrupted *'99*
She's All That *'99*
Wildflowers *'99*
How to Make a Monster *'01*
John Carpenter's Ghosts of Mars *'01*
The Slaughter Rule *'01*
Thirteen Conversations About One Thing *'01*
Identity *'03*
21 Grams *'03*
The Grudge *'04*
Two Weeks *'06*
Anamorph *'07*
Ten Inch Hero *'07*
Passengers *'08*
The Watch *'08*
The Killing Room *'09*
Virtuality *'09*
Conviction *'10*
Argo *'12*
Armed Response *'13*
Lizzie Borden Took an Ax *'14*
The Intervention *'16*

Robert Duvall (1931-)
To Kill a Mockingbird *'62*
Captain Newman, M.D. *'63*
The Chase *'66*
Bullitt *'68*
Countdown *'68*
The Detective *'68*
The Rain People *'69*
True Grit *'69*
M*A*S*H *'70*
Lawman *'71*
THX 1138 *'71*
The Godfather *'72*
The Great Northfield Minnesota Raid *'72*
Joe Kidd *'72*
Tomorrow *'72*
Badge 373 *'73*
Lady Ice *'73*
The Outfit *'73*
The Conversation *'74*
The Godfather, Part 2 *'74*
Breakout *'75*
The Killer Elite *'75*
Network *'76*
The Seven-Per-Cent Solution *'76*
The Eagle Has Landed *'77*
The Greatest *'77*
The Betsy *'78*
Invasion of the Body Snatchers *'78*
Apocalypse Now *'79*
The Great Santini *'80*
True Confessions *'81*
Tender Mercies *'83*
The Natural *'84*
The Stone Boy *'84*
Belizaire the Cajun *'86*
The Lightship *'86*
Let's Get Harry *'87*
Colors *'88*
Lonesome Dove *'89*
Days of Thunder *'90*
The Handmaid's Tale *'90*
A Show of Force *'90*
Hearts of Darkness: A Filmmaker's Apocalypse *'91*
Rambling Rose *'91*
Newsies *'92*
Falling Down *'93*
Geronimo: An American Legend *'93*
Wrestling Ernest Hemingway *'93*
The Paper *'94*
The Stars Fell on Henrietta *'94*
The Scarlet Letter *'95*
Something to Talk About *'95*
A Family Thing *'96*
The Man Who Captured Eichmann *'96*
Phenomenon *'96*
Sling Blade *'96*
The Apostle *'97*
The Gingerbread Man *'97*
A Civil Action *'98*
Deep Impact *'98*
Gone in 60 Seconds *'00*
A Shot at Glory *'00*
The 6th Day *'00*
John Q *'02*
Assassination Tango *'03*
Gods and Generals *'03*
Open Range *'03*
Secondhand Lions *'03*
Kicking & Screaming *'05*
Broken Trail *'06*
Thank You for Smoking *'06*
Lucky You *'07*
We Own the Night *'07*
Four Christmases *'08*
Crazy Heart *'09*
Get Low *'09*
The Road *'09*
Seven Days in Utopia *'11*
Hemingway & Gelhorn *'12*
Jack Reacher *'12*
Jayne Mansfield's Car *'13*
The Judge *'14*
A Night in Old Mexico *'14*
Wild Horses *'15*
In Dubious Battle *'17*

Shelley Duvall (1949-)
Brewster McCloud *'70*
McCabe & Mrs. Miller *'71*
Thieves Like Us *'74*
Nashville *'75*
Annie Hall *'77*
3 Women *'77*
Popeye *'80*
The Shining *'80*
Time Bandits *'81*
Roxanne *'87*
Suburban Commando *'91*
The Underneath *'95*
Changing Habits *'96*
Portrait of a Lady *'96*
Horton Foote's Alone *'97*
The Twilight of the Ice Nymphs *'97*
Boltneck *'98*
Home Fries *'98*
My Teacher Ate My Homework *'98*
The 4th Floor *'99*
Russell Mulcahy's Tale of the Mummy *'99*

Steph Duvall
The Keeper *'09*
Woodshock *'17*

Wayne Duvall (1958-)
Hard Rain *'97*
A Better Way to Die *'00*
O Brother Where Art Thou? *'00*
Killing Emmett Young *'02*
Leatherheads *'08*
Pride and Glory *'08*
Duplicity *'09*
Breathless *'12*
The Hunt *'20*

Nicolas Duvauchelle (1980-)
The Girl on the Train *'09*
Wild Grass *'09*
Four Lovers *'10*
White Material *'10*
Polisse *'11*
The Well-Digger's Daughter *'11*

Janine Duvitsky (1952-)
Dracula *'79*
Grown Ups *'80*
Angel *'07*

Ann Dvorak (1912-79)
Scarface *'31*
The Crowd Roars *'32*
The Strange Love of Molly Louvain *'32*
Housewife *'34*
Massacre *'34*
'G' Men *'35*
Thanks a Million *'35*
The Case of the Stuttering Bishop *'37*
Manhattan Merry-Go-Round *'37*
Merrily We Live *'38*
Stronger Than Desire *'39*
Flame of the Barbary Coast *'45*
Abilene Town *'46*
The Long Night *'47*
Out of the Blue *'47*
The Private Affairs of Bel Ami *'47*
A Life of Her Own *'50*
Return of Jesse James *'50*
I Was an American Spy *'51*

Peter Dvorsky (1951-)
Videodrome *'83*
The Kiss *'88*
Mesmer *'94*
The Long Way Home *'98*

Earl Dwire (1883-1940)
Assassin of Youth *'35*
Caryl of the Mountains *'36*
Cavalcade of the West *'36*

Bill Dwyer
Ski School 2 *'94*
Little Shots of Happiness *'97*

David Dwyer
To Dance with the White Dog *'93*
Deadline *'12*

Hilary Dwyer (1945-2020)
The Conqueror Worm *'68*
The Oblong Box *'69*
Cry of the Banshee *'70*
Wuthering Heights *'70*

Leslie Dwyer (1906-86)
Immortal Battalion *'44*
The Way Ahead *'44*
Midnight Episode *'50*
The Hour of 13 *'52*

Where There's a Will '55
Not So Dusty '56
Die, Monster, Die! '65

Franklin Dyall (1874-1950)
Easy Virtue '27
The Private Life of Henry VIII '33

Valentine Dyall (1908-85)
Henry V '44
Brief Encounter '46
Frenzy '46
The Golden Salamander '51
Horror Hotel '60
The Haunting '63
The Body in the Library '84

Cameron Dye (1959-)
Valley Girl '83
Body Rock '84
The Last Starfighter '84
Fraternity Vacation '85
Scenes from the Goldmine '87
Out of the Dark '88
The Apocalypse '96
The Tavern '00

Dale Dye (1944-)
Invaders from Mars '86
Platoon '86
Billionaire Boys Club '87
Always '89
Born on the Fourth of July '89
Casualties of War '89
Spontaneous Combustion '89
Fire Birds '90
The Fourth War '90
Blue Sky '91
JFK '91
Relentless 2: Dead On '91
Servants of Twilight '91
Sniper '92
Under Siege '92
Heaven and Earth '93
Guarding Tess '94
Outbreak '94
The Puppet Masters '94
Sgt. Bilko '95
Under Siege 2: Dark Territory '95
Mission: Impossible '96
Trial and Error '96
Within the Rock '96
Operation Delta Force 2: Mayday '97
Rough Riders '97
Starship Troopers '97
Saving Private Ryan '98
Rules of Engagement '00
Band of Brothers '01
44 Minutes: The North Hollywood Shootout '03
Missing Brendan '03
The Great Raid '05
Knight and Day '10
Sniper: Special Ops '16

John Dye (1963-2011)
Campus Man '87
Best of the Best '89
Heart of the Beholder '05

Mason Dye
Flowers in the Attic '14
Vanished-Left Behind: Next Generation '16

Danny Dyer (1977-)
Human Traffic '99
The Trench '99
Borstal Boy '00
Greenfingers '00
High Heels and Low Lifes '01
Mean Machine '01
The Business '05
The Other Half '06
Severance '06
Closure '07
Outlaw '07
Dead Man Running '09
Malice in Wonderland '09
Dead Cert '10
Freerunner '10

Karen Dyer
Corrupt '99
Urban Menace '99

Russell Dykstra (1966-)
Criminal Ways '03
Garage Days '03
Ned Kelly '03
Introducing the Dwights '07
Romulus, My Father '07
Hey Hey It's Esther Blueberger '08

Matthew Dyktynski
Heaven's Burning '97
Japanese Story '03

Bob Dylan (1941-)
Don't Look Back '67
Pat Garrett & Billy the Kid '73
Backtrack '89
Masked and Anonymous '03
Rolling Thunder Revue: A Bob Dylan Story by Martin Scorsese '19

Louise Dylan
Emma '09
Vampire Killers '09

Peter Dyneley (1921-77)
Beau Brummell '54
Strange Awakening '58
The Manster '59
Soul Patrol '80

James Dyrenforth (1895-1973)
Never Take Candy From a Stranger '60
Lolita '62

Trine Dyrholm (1972-)
In a Better World '10
A Royal Affair '12
Queen of Hearts '19

Richard Dysart (1929-2015)
Petulia '68
The Hospital '71
The Autobiography of Miss Jane Pittman '74
The Terminal Man '74
The Day of the Locust '75
The Hindenburg '75
An Enemy of the People '77
Being There '79
Meteor '79
Prophecy '79
The Ordeal of Dr. Mudd '80
Bitter Harvest '81
The People vs. Jean Harris '81
The Thing '82
The Falcon and the Snowman '85
Mask '85
Pale Rider '85
Warning Sign '85
Blood and Orchids '86
The Last Days of Patton '86
The Rumor Mill '86
Wall Street '87
Day One '89
Back to the Future, Part 3 '90
Panther '95
Truman '95
Hard Rain '97
Todd McFarlane's Spawn '97 (V)

Richard Dyszel (1947-)
The Alien Factor '78
Night Beast '83

Alexis Dziena (1984-)
Mimic 3: Sentinel '03
She's Too Young '04
Broken Flowers '05
Pizza '05
Sex and Breakfast '07
Fool's Gold '08
Nick & Norah's Infinite Playlist '08
Tenderness '08
When in Rome '09

George Dzundza (1945-)
The Deer Hunter '78
Honky Tonk Freeway '81
Streamers '83
Best Defense '84
Broken Badge '85
Brotherly Love '85
No Mercy '86
Glory Years '87
No Way Out '87
The Beast '88
Impulse '90
White Hunter, Black Heart '90
The Butcher's Wife '91
Basic Instinct '92
The Enemy Within '94
Crimson Tide '95
Dangerous Minds '95
That Darn Cat '96
Species 2 '98
Instinct '99
Above Suspicion '00
City by the Sea '02
National Lampoon's Adam & Eve '05

Sheila E (1957-)
Krush Groove '85
The Adventures of Ford Fairlane '90

George Eads (1967-)
The Spring '00
Monte Walsh '03
Gutshot Straight '14
Battle of Jangsari '19

Mitch Eakins
Boxboarders! '07
Tunnel Rats '08

Michael Ealy (1973-)
Barbershop '02
2 Fast 2 Furious '03
Barbershop 2: Back in Business '04
Never Die Alone '04
November '05
Sleeper Cell '05
Miracle at St. Anna '08
Seven Pounds '08
For Colored Girls '10
Takers '10
Think Like a Man '12
Unconditional '12
Underworld: Awakening '12
About Last Night '14
Think Like a Man Too '14
The Perfect Guy '15
The Intruder '19

Edward Earle (1882-1972)
The Family Secret '24
Spite Marriage '29
Alimony Madness '33
Mutiny Ahead '35
I Accuse My Parents '45
Command Decision '48

Marilee Earle
The Fearmakers '58
The Lost Missile '58

Harry Earles (1902-85)
The Unholy Three '25
The Unholy Three '30
Freaks '32

Jason Earles (1977-)
American Pie Presents Band Camp '05
Gordon Glass '07
Space Buddies '08 (V)
Hannah Montana: The Movie '09
Super Buddies '13

Bo Eason
Miami Rhapsody '95
Tornado! '96

Carlos East (1942-94)
The Fear Chamber '68
The Snake People '68

Jeff East (1957-)
Tom Sawyer '73
Huckleberry Finn '74
Flight of the Grey Wolf '76
The Campus Corpse '77
Summer of Fear '78
Deadly Blessing '81
Pumpkinhead '88

Leslie Easterbrook (1949-)
Police Academy '84
Private Resort '84
Police Academy 3: Back in Training '86
Police Academy 5: Assignment Miami Beach '88
Police Academy 6: City under Siege '89
Police Academy 7: Mission to Moscow '94
The Biggest Fan '02
The Devil's Rejects '05
A Dead Calling '06
Retribution Road '07

Steve Eastin (1948-)
Last Man Standing '95
Little Bigfoot 2: The Journey Home '97
Stealth Fighter '99
Agent Red '00
Peril '00
Catch Me If You Can '02
A Man Apart '03
Matchstick Men '03
When a Stranger Calls '06

George Eastman (1854-1932)
Call of the Wild '72
Kiss Me, Kill Me '73
Kidnapped '74
Belle Starr '79
Anthropophagus: The Grim Reaper '80
Grim Reaper '81
After the Fall of New York '85
Detective School Dropouts '85
Hands of Steel '86

George Eastman (1942-)
Django: Last Killer '67
Baba Yaga '73
The Big Alligator River '79

Rodney Eastman (1967-)
A Nightmare on Elm Street 3: Dream Warriors '87
A Nightmare on Elm Street 4: Dream Master '88
Blue Ridge Fall '99
Sand '00
The Caveman's Valentine '01
I Spit on Your Grave '10
Spork '10

Michael Easton (1967-)
Murder at Devil's Glen '99
Total Recall 2070: Machine Dreams '99
The '70s '00

Richard Easton (1933-2019)
The Red Badge of Courage '51
Henry V '89
Dead Again '91
Pizza '05
Revolutionary Road '08

Robert Easton (1930-2011)
Belles on Their Toes '52
When Hell Broke Loose '58
The Nun and the Sergeant '62
Johnny Got His Gun '71
Heavy Traffic '73
The Giant Spider Invasion '75
Working Girl '88
Just One Night '00

Sam Easton (1979-)
Final Destination 3 '06
Decoys: The Second Seduction '07

Sheena Easton (1959-)
Body Bags '93
Indecent Proposal '93
All Dogs Go to Heaven 2 '95 (V)

Alison Eastwood (1972-)
Tightrope '84
Midnight in the Garden of Good and Evil '97
Breakfast of Champions '98
Black & White '99
Friends & Lovers '99
Just a Little Harmless Sex '99
If You Only Knew '00
The Spring '00
Poolhall Junkies '02
Power Play '02
The Lost Angel '04
They Are Among Us '04
Don't Tell '05
How to Go Out on a Date in Queens '06
Lesser Evil '06
One Long Night '07
Shadow People '13

Clint Eastwood (1930-)
Francis in the Navy '55
Revenge of the Creature '55
Tarantula '55
Away All Boats '56
Lafayette Escadrille '58
A Fistful of Dollars '64
For a Few Dollars More '65
The Good, the Bad and the Ugly '67
Hang 'Em High '67
Coogan's Bluff '68
Where Eagles Dare '68
Paint Your Wagon '69
The Beguiled '70
Kelly's Heroes '70
Two Mules for Sister Sara '70
Dirty Harry '71
Play Misty for Me '71
Joe Kidd '72
High Plains Drifter '73
Magnum Force '73
Thunderbolt & Lightfoot '74
The Eiger Sanction '75
The Enforcer '76
The Outlaw Josey Wales '76
The Gauntlet '77
Every Which Way But Loose '78
Escape from Alcatraz '79
Any Which Way You Can '80
Bronco Billy '80
Firefox '82
Honkytonk Man '82
Sudden Impact '83
City Heat '84
Tightrope '84
Pale Rider '85
Heartbreak Ridge '86
The Dead Pool '88
Pink Cadillac '89
The Rookie '90
White Hunter, Black Heart '90
Unforgiven '92
In the Line of Fire '93
A Perfect World '93
The Bridges of Madison County '95
Casper '95 (C)
Absolute Power '97
True Crime '99
Space Cowboys '00
Blood Work '02
Million Dollar Baby '04
Gran Torino '08
Trouble with the Curve '12
The Mule '18

Francesca Ruth Eastwood (1993-)
The Stars Fell on Henrietta '94
Outlaws and Angels '16
MDMA '18
Awake '19

Jayne (Jane) Eastwood (1946-)
That Old Feeling '96
Life with Judy Garland-Me and My Shadows '01
Dawn of the Dead '04
Wedding Wars '06
You Kill Me '07
Real Time '08
Northern Lights '09
Harriet the Spy: Blog Wars '10
Cas & Dylan '15

Kyle Eastwood (1968-)
The Outlaw Josey Wales '76
Honkytonk Man '82

Scott Eastwood (1986-)
Chasing Mavericks '12
Trouble with the Curve '12
Texas Chainsaw 3D '13
Fury '14
The Longest Ride '15
Diablo '16
Mercury Plains '16
Overdrive '17
Pacific Rim: Uprising '18

Brando Eaton (1986-)
Born 2 Race '11
Talhotblond '12

Marjorie Eaton (1901-86)
Night Tide '61
The Atomic Brain '64
The Attic '80

Mary Eaton (1901-48)
The Cocoanuts '29
Glorifying the American Girl '30

Shirley Eaton (1937-)
Doctor in the House '53
Three Men in a Boat '56
Doctor at Large '57
Carry On Sergeant '58
Further Up the Creek '58
The Naked Truth '58
Carry On Nurse '59
Carry On Constable '60
What a Carve-Up! '62
The Girl Hunters '63
Goldfinger '64
Around the World Under the Sea '65
Eight on the Lam '67
Kiss and Kill '68

Luke Eberl (1986-)
Planet of the Apes '01
A Painted House '03
Eyeborgs '09
Surprise, Surprise '09
Taken for Ransom '13

Christine Ebersole (1953-)
Tootsie '82
Amadeus '84
Thief of Hearts '84
Mac and Me '88
Ghost Dad '90
Dead Again '91
Folks! '92
Gypsy '93
My Girl 2 '94
Richie Rich '94
Pie in the Sky '95
Black Sheep '96
Til There Was You '96
My Favorite Martian '98
Double Platinum '99
True Crime '99
An Unexpected Love '03
Confessions of a Shopaholic '09
The Big Wedding '13
The Wolf of Wall Street '13
Driveways '19

Eriq Ebouaney (1967-)
Lumumba '01
Femme Fatale '02
Cape of Good Hope '04
The Front Line '06
The Nativity Story '06
Disgrace '08
3 Days to Kill '14

Buddy Ebsen (1908-2003)
Broadway Melody of 1936 '35
Born to Dance '36
Captain January '36
Broadway Melody of 1938 '37
Girl of the Golden West '38
My Lucky Star '38
Night People '54
Red Garters '54
Davy Crockett, King of the Wild Frontier '55
Attack! '56
Between Heaven and Hell '56
Davy Crockett and the River Pirates '56
Breakfast at Tiffany's '61
The Interns '62
Mail Order Bride '63
The One and Only, Genuine, Original Family Band '68
The Andersonville Trial '70

The Horror at 37,000 Feet '73
The Bastard '78
The Return of the Beverly Hillbillies '81
The Beverly Hillbillies '93 (C)

Maude Eburne (1875-1960)
The Passionate Plumber '32
The Vampire Bat '32
Ruggles of Red Gap '35
Courageous Dr. Christian '40
The Boogie Man Will Get You '42

Aimee (Amy) Eccles (1949-)
Little Big Man '70
Lovelines '84

Christopher Eccleston (1964-)
Let Him Have It '91
Cracker: To Be a Somebody '94
Shallow Grave '94
Jude '96
A Price Above Rubies '97
Elizabeth '98
eXistenZ '99
Heart '99
Gone in 60 Seconds '00
Invisible Circus '00
Othello '01
The Others '01
28 Days Later '02
Perfect Parents '06
The Seeker: The Dark Is Rising '07
Amelia '09
G.I. Joe: The Rise of Cobra '09
Lennon Naked '10
Unfinished Song '12
Thor: The Dark World '13
Legend '15

Juan Echanove (1961-)
The Flower of My Secret '95
No News from God '01
A Matador's Mistress '08

Pablo Echarri (1969-)
Burnt Money '00
Chronicle of an Escape '06

Hector Echavarria
Confessions of a Pit Fighter '05
Never Surrender '09

Emilio Echeverria (1944-)
Amores Perros '00
Die Another Day '02
The Alamo '04

Megalyn Echikunwoke (1983-)
Fix '08
Who Do You Love '08
Damsels in Distress '11

Aaron Eckhart (1968-)
In the Company of Men '96
Your Friends & Neighbors '98
Any Given Sunday '99
Molly '99
Erin Brockovich '00
Nurse Betty '00
The Pledge '00
Possession '02
The Core '03
The Missing '03
Paycheck '03
Suspect Zero '04
Conversations with Other Women '05
The Black Dahlia '06
Thank You for Smoking '06
The Wicker Man '06
Meet Bill '07
No Reservations '07
Towelhead '07
The Dark Knight '08
Love Happens '09
Rabbit Hole '10
Battle: Los Angeles '11
The Rum Diary '11
Erased '12
I, Frankenstein '13
Olympus Has Fallen '13
My All American '15
Bleed for This '16
Sully '16

Steven Eckholdt (1961-)
Message in a Bottle '98
And Never Let Her Go '01
Comfort and Joy '03

James Eckhouse (1955-)
The Christmas Wife '88
Leaving Normal '92
Junior '94
Robin Cook's Terminal '96
One True Thing '98
Jimmy & Judy '06
Love's Everlasting Courage '11

Billy Eckstine (1914-93)
Skirts Ahoy! '52
Jo Jo Dancer, Your Life Is Calling '86

Jean-Philippe Ecoffey (1959-)
Portraits Chinois '96
Ma Vie en Rose '97
Wolves in the Snow '02
Cold Showers '05

Paul Eddington (1927-95)
The Devil Rides Out '68
The Camomile Lawn '92

Duane Eddy
A Thunder of Drums '61
Kona Coast '68

Helen Jerome Eddy (1897-1990)
Rebecca of Sunnybrook Farm '17
The Divine Lady '29
Frisco Jenny '32
Make Me a Star '32
The Girl from 10th Ave. '35
A Shot in the Dark '35
Klondike Annie '36
City Streets '38

Nelson Eddy (1901-67)
Dancing Lady '33
Naughty Marietta '35
Rose Marie '36
Maytime '37
Girl of the Golden West '38
Rosalie '38
Sweethearts '38
Balalaika '39
Let Freedom Ring '39
Bitter Sweet '40
New Moon '40
The Chocolate Soldier '41
I Married an Angel '42
The Phantom of the Opera '43

Gregg Edelman (1958-)
Green Card '90
Little Children '06

Herb Edelman (1930-96)
Barefoot in the Park '67
I Love You, Alice B. Toklas! '68
The Odd Couple '68
The Way We Were '73
The Yakuza '75
Charge of the Model T's '76
Goin' Coconuts '78
Marathon '80
Cracking Up '83

Eric Edelstein (1977-)
The Hills Have Eyes 2 '07
Welcome to the Jungle '13
Flower '18

Lisa Edelstein (1966-)
Keeping the Faith '00
What Women Want '00
Dean Koontz's Black River '01
Obsessed '02
A Date With Darkness '03
Say Uncle '05
Grilled '06
Special Delivery '08
Blue-Eyed Butcher '12

Barbara Eden (1931-)
Flaming Star '60
From the Terrace '60
Twelve Hours to Kill '60
Voyage to the Bottom of the Sea '61
Five Weeks in a Balloon '62
The Brass Bottle '63
7 Faces of Dr. Lao '63
Ride the Wild Surf '64
Quick, Let's Get Married '71
The Woman Hunter '72
The Stranger Within '74
Harper Valley P.T.A. '78
Return of the Rebels '81
Visions of Murder '93
A Very Brady Sequel '96
Loco Love '03

Harry Eden (1990-)
Pure '02
Oliver Twist '05
Flashbacks of a Fool '08

Jerome Eden
Blood Feast '63
Color Me Blood Red '64
2000 Maniacs '64
The Defilers '65

Mark Eden (1928-)
Blind Corner '63
Seance on a Wet Afternoon '64
Doctor Zhivago '65
The Crimson Cult '68

Richard Eden (1956-)
Killer Deal '99
Undercover Angel '99
Disappearing in America '08

Robert Edeson (1868-1931)
The Prisoner of Zenda '22
Chicago '27
King of Kings '27

George Edgely
Free, White, and 21 '62
Common Law Wife '63

Joel Edgerton (1974-)
The Hard Word '02
Ned Kelly '03
The Night We Called It a Day '03
King Arthur '04
Kinky Boots '06
Open Window '06
Smokin' Aces '07
Whisper '07
Acolytes '08
$9.99 '08 (V)
The Square '08
Animal Kingdom '09
The Waiting City '09
Legend of the Guardians: The Owls of Ga'Hoole '10 (V)
The Thing '11
Warrior '11
The Odd Life of Timothy Green '12
Wish You Were Here '12
Zero Dark Thirty '12
Felony '13
The Great Gatsby '13
Exodus: Gods and Kings '14
Black Mass '15
The Gift '15
Jane Got a Gun '16
Loving '16
Midnight Special '16
Bright '17
It Comes at Night '17
Boy Erased '18
Gringo '18
Red Sparrow '18
The King '19

Gigi Edgley
Showdown at Area 51 '07
Newcastle '08

Walker Edmiston (1925-2007)
Everything's Ducky '61
The Beach Girls and the Monster '65

Linda Edmond
Georgia O'Keefe '09
The Missing Person '09

Valerie Edmond (1969-)
The Crow Road '96
Love and Rage '99
One More Kiss '99
Saving Grace '00

Dartanyan Edmonds (1972-)
Ride '98
Rangers '00
Deliver Us from Eva '03

Louis Edmonds (1923-2001)
House of Dark Shadows '70
Next Year in Jerusalem '98

Sarah Edmondson (1977-)
My Name Is Sarah '07
Hostile Makeover '09
Killer Hair '09

Bobby Edner (1988-)
The Trial of Old Drum '00
The Day the World Ended '01
Spy Kids 3-D: Game Over '03
Welcome to Paradise '07

Beatie Edney (1962-)
Highlander '86
Just Another Secret '89
Mister Johnson '91
In the Name of the Father '93
The Affair '95
The Tenant of Wildfell Hall '96
Highlander: Endgame '00
In Your Dreams '07

Richard Edson (1954-)
Stranger than Paradise '84
Desperately Seeking Susan '85
Ferris Bueller's Day Off '86
Howard the Duck '86
Platoon '86
Good Morning, Vietnam '87
Eight Men Out '88
Do the Right Thing '89
Let It Ride '89
Jungle Fever '91
Crossing the Bridge '92
Attack of the 50 Ft. Woman '93
Love, Cheat & Steal '93
Posse '93
Super Mario Bros. '93
Bad Love '95
Jury Duty '95
Strange Days '95
Intimate Betrayal '96
An Occasional Hell '96
Scorpion Spring '96
Things I Never Told You '96
Wedding Bell Blues '96
The Winner '96
Lulu on the Bridge '98
The Million Dollar Hotel '99
Thick as Thieves '99
Time Code '00
Sunshine State '02
Frankenfish '04
Land of Plenty '04
Starsky & Hutch '04
The Kid and I '05
Columbus Day '08
The Smell of Success '09

Allan Edwall (1924-97)
The New Land '72
Fanny and Alexander '83
The Sacrifice '86

Alan Edwards (1892-1954)
Clear All Wires! '33
The White Sister '33
If You Could Only Cook '36
Forty Naughty Girls '37
Men On Her Mind '44

Anthony Edwards (1962-)
Fast Times at Ridgemont High '82
Heart Like a Wheel '83
Revenge of the Nerds '84
Gotcha! '85
The Sure Thing '85
Top Gun '86
Revenge of the Nerds 2: Nerds in Paradise '87
Summer Heat '87
Mr. North '88
Downtown '89
Hawks '89
How I Got into College '89
Miracle Mile '89
El Diablo '90
Delta Heat '92
Pet Sematary 2 '92
Charlie's Ghost: The Secret of Coronado '94
The Client '94
In Cold Blood '96
Playing by Heart '98
Jackpot '01
Northfork '03
The Forgotten '04
Thunderbirds '04
Motherhood '09
Flipped '10
Big Sur '13

Barbara (Lee) Edwards (1960-)
Malibu Express '85
House Party 3 '94

Bill Edwards (1918-99)
First Man into Space '59
War Lover '62

Cliff Edwards (1895-1971)
So This Is College '29
Doughboys '30
Lord Byron of Broadway '30
Montana Moon '30
Dance Fools Dance '31
Laughing Sinners '31
Parlor, Bedroom and Bath '31
Shipmates '31
Sidewalks of New York '31
The Sin of Madelon Claudet '31
Stepping Out '31
Fast Life '32
George White's Scandals of 1935 '35
Saratoga '37
The Bad Man of Brimstone '38
Girl of the Golden West '38
Gone with the Wind '39
Maisie '39
Flowing Gold '40
His Girl Friday '40
Pinocchio '40 (V)
Power Dive '41
The Falcon Strikes Back '43
Fun & Fancy Free '47 (V)

Cory Edwards
Hoodwinked '05 (V)
Hoodwinked Too! Hood vs. Evil '11

Dean Edwards
A New Wave '07
Tony n' Tina's Wedding '07

Elaine Edwards
Curse of the Faceless Man '58
The Purple Gang '59
Three Blondes in His Life '61

Glynn Edwards (1931-)
Zulu '64
Get Carter '71

Gwendolyn Edwards
The Last Confederate: The Story of Robert Adams '05
In the Eyes of a Killer '09

Henry Edwards (1882-1952)
Madeleine '50
The Golden Salamander '51

Hilton Edwards (1903-82)
Othello '52
David and Goliath '61
Victim '61
The Quare Fellow '62

James Edwards (1918-70)
The Set-Up '49
The Steel Helmet '51
The Member of the Wedding '52
The Phenix City Story '55
The Killing '56
Men in War '57
Tarzan's Fight for Life '58
Pork Chop Hill '59
The Manchurian Candidate '62
Patton '70

Jennifer Edwards (1957-)
Heidi '67
S.O.B. '81
The Man Who Loved Women '83
That's Life! '86
Sunset '88
Peter Gunn '89

Lance Edwards
Peacemaker '90
A Woman, Her Men and Her Futon '92

Luke Edwards (1980-)
I Know My First Name Is Steven '89
The Wizard '89
Guilty by Suspicion '91
Newsies '92
Little Big League '94
Mother's Boys '94
Cheaters '00

Mark Edwards (1942-)
Blood from the Mummy's Tomb '71
Tower of Evil '72

Megan Edwards
Poison Ivy 3: The New Seduction '97
Tattoo, a Love Story '02

Meredith Edwards (1917-99)
The Magnet '50
Midnight Episode '50
The Gambler & the Lady '52
Race for Life '55
The Electronic Monster '57

Penny Edwards (1928-98)
Feudin', Fussin', and A-Fightin' '48
Trail of Robin Hood '50
Powder River '53
The Dalton Girls '57

Ralph Edwards
Radio Stars on Parade '45
The Bamboo Blonde '46

Ronnie Clair Edwards (1933-)
A Day for Thanks on Walton's Mountain '82
8 Seconds '94

Sam Edwards (1915-2004)
Bambi '42 (V)
Twelve o'Clock High '49
Gang Busters '55
Guns Don't Argue '57
The Beatniks '60

Snitz Edwards (1862-1937)
Souls for Sale '23
The Thief of Baghdad '24
The Phantom of the Opera '25
Battling Butler '26
The Red Mill '27
The Right of Way '31
Sit Tight '31

Stacy Edwards (1965-)
In the Company of Men '96
Houdini '98
Primary Colors '98
The Bachelor '99
Black and White '99
Four Dogs Playing Poker '00
Mexico City '00
The Next Best Thing '00
Driven '01
Prancer Returns '01
Joshua '02
Local Boys '02
Superbad '07

Vince Edwards (1926-96)
Hiawatha '52
Sailor Beware '52
Cell 2455, Death Row '55
The Night Holds Terror '55
The Killing '56
Serenade '56
The Three Faces of Eve '57
Murder by Contract '58
City of Fear '59

Too Late Blues '61
The Devil's Brigade '68
Hammerhead '68
Firehouse '72
The Mad Bomber '72
The Seduction '82
The Dirty Dozen: The Deadly Mission '87
Return to Horror High '87
Andy and the Airwave Rangers '89
Motorama '91
Original Intent '91
The Fear '94
Jailbreakers '94

Paul Eenhoorn
Max Rules '05
This is Martin Bonner '13
Land Ho! '14

Virginie Efira (1977-)
My Worst Nightmare '11
Elle '16

Svetlana Efremova
White Oleander '02
Stick It '06
Killer by Nature '10

Marshall Efron (1938-2019)
Is There Sex After Death? '71
Home on the Range '04 (V)

Zac Efron (1987-)
Miracle Run '04
The Derby Stallion '05
High School Musical '06
Hairspray '07
High School Musical 2 '07
High School Musical 3: Senior Year '08
Me and Orson Welles '09
17 Again '09
Charlie St. Cloud '10
New Year's Eve '11
Dr. Seuss' The Lorax '12 (V)
Liberal Arts '12
The Lucky One '12
The Paperboy '12
Parkland '13
Neighbors '14
That Awkward Moment '14
We Are Your Friends '15
Dirty Grandpa '16
Mike and Dave Need Wedding Dates '16
Neighbors 2: Sorority Rising '16
Baywatch '17
The Greatest Showman '17
The Beach Bum '19
Extremely Wicked, Shockingly Evil and Vile '19
Scoob! '20

Aeryk Egan
Flatliners '90
Book of Love '91
The Secret Life of Girls '99

Christopher Egan (1984-)
Alpha Male '06
Eragon '06
Resident Evil: Extinction '07
Smokin' Aces '07
Crush '09
Letters to Juliet '10

Eddie Egan (1930-95)
The French Connection '71
Badge 373 '73

Michael Egan
Street Gun '96
Thugs '96

Peter Egan (1946-)
The Hireling '73
Hennessy '75
Lillie '79
A Woman of Substance '84
A Perfect Spy '88
The Price of the Bride '90
Bean '97
2001: A Space Travesty '00
The I Inside '04
The Wedding Date '05
Death at a Funeral '07

Richard Egan (1921-87)
The Damned Don't Cry '50
Highway 301 '50
Hollywood Story '51
Blackbeard the Pirate '52
The Devil Makes Three '52
One Minute to Zero '52
The Glory Brigade '53
Split Second '53
Demetrius and the Gladiators '54
GOG '54
Seven Cities of Gold '55
Untamed '55
Violent Saturday '55
Love Me Tender '56
The Hunters '58
A Summer Place '59
Esther and the King '60
Pollyanna '60
The 300 Spartans '62
Chubasco '67
The Day of the Wolves '71
Mission to Glory '80

Susan Egan (1970-)
Hercules '97 (V)
Man of the Century '99
Spirited Away '01 (V)
Meet Market '08

Will Egan
Glitch! '88
Ninja Academy '90

Julie Ege (1943-2008)
On Her Majesty's Secret Service '69
Creatures the World Forgot '70
Rentadick '72
The Freakmaker '73
The Legend of the 7 Golden Vampires '73
Not Now Darling '73
Craze '74

Joe Egender
April Fool's Day '08
The Frankenstein Theory '13

Tamsin Egerton (1988-)
Keeping Mum '05
Driving Lessons '06
St. Trinian's '07
The Legend of Fritton's Gold '09
4.3.2.1 '10
Chalet Girls '11
Grand Piano '13
The Look of Love '13
Queen and Country '14

Taron Egerton (1989-)
Kingsman: The Secret Service '15
Testament of Youth '15
Eddie the Eagle '16
Sing '16
Kingsman: The Golden Circle '17
Billionaire Boys Club '18
Robin Hood '18
Rocketman '19

Samantha Eggar (1939-)
Doctor in Distress '63
Psyche 59 '64
The Collector '65
Walk, Don't Run '66
Doctor Dolittle '67
The Molly Maguires '70
A Name for Evil '70
The Walking Stick '70
Light at the Edge of the World '71
Dead Are Alive '72
All the Kind Strangers '74
The Seven-Per-Cent Solution '76
Battleforce '78
The Brood '79
Why Shoot the Teacher '79
Exterminator '80
Unknown Powers '80
Demonoid, Messenger of Death '81
Curtains '83
Love Among Thieves '86
Ragin' Cajun '90
Tales of the Unexpected '91
Dark Horse '92
The Magic Voyage '93 (V)
The Phantom '96
Hercules '97 (V)
The Astronaut's Wife '99

Nicole Eggert (1972-)
The Haunting of Morella '91
Anything for Love '93
Blown Away '93
Just One of the Girls '93
The Demolitionist '95
Submerged '00
Decoys '04
Dead Lenny '06
National Lampoon Presents Cattle Call '06
Holiday Switch '07
A Christmas Proposal '08
Phantom Racer '09
Turbulent Skies '10

Colin Egglesfield (1973-)
Carnal Innocence '11
Something Borrowed '11
Open Road '13

Ryan Eggold (1984-)
Lucky Them '13
Tyler Perry's The Single Moms' Club '14
Lovesong '17
Never Rarely Sometimes Always '20

Stan(ford) Egi (1969-)
Come See the Paradise '90
Golden Gate '93
Rising Sun '93
Escape Clause '96
Paradise Road '97
Special Delivery '08

Atom Egoyan (1960-)
Calendar '93
The Stupids '95 (C)

Jennifer Ehle (1969-)
The Camomile Lawn '92
Backbeat '94
Pride and Prejudice '95
Melissa '97
Paradise Road '97
Wilde '97
Bedrooms and Hallways '98
Sunshine '99
Possession '02
The River King '05
Alpha Male '06
Before the Rains '07
Pride and Glory '08
That Russell Girl '08
The Greatest '09
The King's Speech '10
Contagion '11
Black or White '14
A Little Chaos '14
RoboCop '14
Fifty Shades of Grey '15
The Fundamentals of Caring '16
Little Men '16
A Quiet Passion '17
The Miseducation of Cameron Post '18
Vox Lux '18
The Professor and the Madman '19
The Wolf Hour '19

Jerome Ehlers (1958-)
Quigley Down Under '90
Sahara '95
The Marine '06

Alden Ehrenreich (1989-)
Tetro '09
Beautiful Creatures '13
Stoker '13
Hail, Caesar! '16
Rules Don't Apply '16
The Yellow Birds '17
Solo: A Star Wars Story '18

Lisa Eichhorn (1952-)
The Europeans '79
Yanks '79
Cutter's Way '81
Weather in the Streets '84
Opposing Force '87
Moon 44 '90
Pride and Extreme Prejudice '90
The Vanishing '93
A Modern Affair '94
First Kid '96
Angel Blue '97
Goodbye, Lover '99
The Talented Mr. Ripley '99
Boys and Girls '00

Paul Eiding
The Personals '83
American Zombie '07

Lars Eidinger
Everyone Else '09
Clouds of Sils Maria '15
Personal Shopper '17

Gard B. Eidsvold (1966-)
The Last Lieutenant '94
Zero Degrees Kelvin '95
A Somewhat Gentle Man '10

Christopher Eigeman (1965-)
Metropolitan '90
Barcelona '94
Kicking and Screaming '95
Highball '97
The Last Days of Disco '98
Mr. Jealousy '98
Crazy Little Thing '02
Maid in Manhattan '02
The Next Big Thing '02
Path to War '02
The Treatment '06

David Eigenberg (1964-)
Daybreak '93
The Mothman Prophecies '02
Garfield: The Movie '04 (V)
Love, Ludlow '05
Sex and the City: The Movie '08
The Trouble with Romance '09
Sex and the City 2 '10
Liz & Dick '12

Jill Eikenberry (1947-)
Between the Lines '77
Butch and Sundance: The Early Days '79
Hide in Plain Sight '80
Arthur '81
The Manhattan Project '86
Manna from Heaven '02
Young Adult '11

Cindy Eilbacher (1958-)
The Big Bounce '69
Shanks '74

Lisa Eilbacher (1956-)
An Officer and a Gentleman '82
Ten to Midnight '83
Beverly Hills Cop '84
Monte Carlo '86
Deadly Intent '88
Leviathan '89
Live Wire '92

Sally Eilers (1908-78)
Doughboys '30
Let Us Be Gay '30
Bad Girl '31
The Black Camel '31
Reducing '31
Central Airport '33
Made On Broadway '33
Strange Illusion '45

Bob Einstein (1942-)
Modern Romance '81
The Extreme Adventures of Super Dave '98
Ocean's Thirteen '07

Hal Eisen
2103: Deadly Wake '97
The Baby Formula '08

Aron Eisenberg (1969-2019)
The Horror Show '89
Pterodactyl Woman from Beverly Hills '97

Hallie Kate Eisenberg (1992-)
Paulie '98
Bicentennial Man '99
The Insider '99
Beautiful '00
The Miracle Worker '00
A Little Inside '01
How to Eat Fried Worms '06

Jesse Eisenberg (1983-)
Lightning: Fire from the Sky '00
The Emperor's Club '02
Roger Dodger '02
Cursed '04
The Squid and the Whale '05
The Hunting Party '07
The Living Wake '07
Adventureland '09
Zombieland '09
Camp Hell '10
Holy Rollers '10
The Social Network '10
Solitary Man '10
Rio '11 (V)
30 Minutes or Less '11
Free Samples '12
To Rome with Love '12
Why Stop Now '12
The Double '13
Night Moves '13
Now You See Me '13
Rio 2 '14 (V)
American Ultra '15
The End of the Tour '15
Batman v Superman: Dawn of Justice '16
Café Society '16
Louder Than Bombs '16
Now You See Me 2 '16
The Hummingbird Project '18
The Art of Self-Defense '19
Zombieland: Double Tap '19
Resistance '20

Ned Eisenberg (1957-)
The Burning '82
Last Man Standing '96
Path to Paradise '97
Limitless '11

Ike Eisenmann (1962-)
Escape to Witch Mountain '75
Banjo Hackett '76
The Bastard '78
Devil Dog: The Hound of Hell '78
Return from Witch Mountain '78
Terror Out of the Sky '78

Debra Eisenstadt (1964-)
Oleanna '94
The Heidi Chronicles '95
Chicago 10 '07 (V)

Andre Eisermann (1967-)
Kaspar Hauser '93
Brother of Sleep '95

Anthony Eisley (1925-2003)
The Wasp Woman '59
Naked Kiss '64
Frankie and Johnny '65
Navy vs. the Night Monsters '66
Journey to the Center of Time '67
Lightning Bolt '67
Star! '68
The Witchmaker '69
Dracula vs. Frankenstein '71
The Tormentors '71
The Doll Squad '73
Monster '78

India Eisley (1993-)
Underworld: Awakening '12
Look Away '18

David Eisner
Happy Birthday to Me '81
Will You Merry Me? '08

Eita
Blue Spring '01
Hara-Kiri: Death of a Samurai '11

Felix Eitner (1967-)
The Trio '97
The Tunnel '01
Cherry Blossoms '08
13 Minutes '17

Chiwetel Ejiofor (1977-)
Three Blind Mice '02
Dirty Pretty Things '03
Love Actually '03
She Hate Me '04
Four Brothers '05
Melinda and Melinda '05
Serenity '05
Slow Burn '05
Children of Men '06
Inside Man '06
Kinky Boots '06
American Gangster '07
Talk to Me '07
Redbelt '08
Endgame '09
2012 '09
Salt '10
12 Years a Slave '13
Savannah '14
Secret in Their Eyes '15
Triple 9 '15
Z for Zachariah '15
Doctor Strange '16
Sherlock Gnomes '18
The Boy Who Harnessed the Wind '19
The Lion King '19
Mary Magdalene '19

Carmen Ejogo (1973-)
Metro '96
The Avengers '98
Catherine Cookson's Colour Blind '98
Love's Labour's Lost '00
Sally Hemings: An American Scandal '00
What's the Worst That Could Happen? '01
Boycott '02
The Brave One '07
Pride and Glory '08
Away We Go '09
Alex Cross '12
Sparkle '12
The Purge: Anarchy '14
Selma '14
Born to Be Blue '15
It Comes at Night '17
Roman J. Israel, Esq. '17
Rattlesnake '19

Anita Ekberg (1931-2015)
Abbott and Costello Go to Mars '53
Artists and Models '55
Blood Alley '55
Hollywood or Bust '56
Man in the Vault '56
War and Peace '56
Zarak '56
Paris Holiday '57
Pickup Alley '57
Valerie '57
Screaming Mimi '58
La Dolce Vita '60
The Mongols '60
Boccaccio '70 '62
Call Me Bwana '63
Four for Texas '63
The Alphabet Murders '65
Woman Times Seven '67
The Cobra '68
Fangs of the Living Dead '68
We All Loved Each Other So Much '77
Gold of the Amazon Women '79
Intervista '87
The Red Dwarf '99

Stina Ekblad (1954-)
Like It Never Was Before '95
Gossip '00

Lars Ekborg (1926-69)
Monika '52
Summer With Monica '53

Britt Ekland (1942-)
The Happy Thieves '61
Advance to the Rear '64
After the Fox '66
The Bobo '67
The Double Man '67
Machine Gun McCain '69
The Night They Raided Minsky's '69
Endless Night '71
Get Carter '71
Asylum '72
What the Peeper Saw '72

The Man with the Golden Gun '74
Royal Flash '75
The Wicker Man '75
King Solomon's Treasure '76
Slavers '77
Sex on the Run '78
Demon Rage '82
Fraternity Vacation '85
The Monster Club '85
Beverly Hills Vamp '88
Scandal '89

Michael Eklund (1962-)
We'll Meet Again '02
House of the Dead '03
Eight Days to Live '06
BloodRayne 2: Deliverance '07
Termination Point '07
The Gambler, the Girl and the Gunslinger '09
Hunt to Kill '10
The Day '11
The Marine 3: Homefront '11
Pressed '11
The Call '13
Vendetta '15
Into the Forest '16
Cold Pursuit '19

Gosta Ekman (1890-1938)
Faust '26
Intermezzo '36

Hasse (Hans) Ekman (1915-2004)
Intermezzo '36
Devil's Wanton '49

Kessarin Ektawatkul
Born to Fight '07
The Vanquisher '10

Nour (el-Sherif) el-Cherif (1946-)
An Egyptian Story '82
Destiny '97

Jack Elam (1916-2003)
She Shoulda Said No '49
High Lonesome '50
Rawhide '50
Bird of Paradise '51
The Bushwackers '52
Kansas City Confidential '52
Lure of the Wilderness '52
My Man and I '52
Rancho Notorious '52
The Ring '52
The Moonlighter '53
Ride, Vaquero! '53
Vera Cruz '53
Cattle Queen of Montana '54
Princess of the Nile '54
Ride Clear of Diablo '54
Artists and Models '55
Kiss Me Deadly '55
The Man from Laramie '55
Pardners '56
Gunfight at the O.K. Corral '57
Night Passage '57
The Gun Runners '58
Edge of Eternity '59
The Girl in Lover's Lane '60
The Last Sunset '61
Pocketful of Miracles '61
Four for Texas '63
The Rare Breed '66
The Last Challenge '67
The Way West '67
Firecreek '68
Never a Dull Moment '68
Once Upon a Time in the West '68
The Over-the-Hill Gang '69
Support Your Local Sheriff '69
Rio Lobo '70
Support Your Local Gunfighter '71
Hannie Caulder '72
Sidekicks '74
Creature from Black Lake '76
Pony Express Rider '76
Grayeagle '77
The Apple Dumpling Gang Rides Again '79
The Sacketts '79
The Villain '79
Cannonball Run '81
Sacred Ground '83
Cannonball Run 2 '84
The Aurora Encounter '85
Big Bad John '90
Suburban Commando '91
Shadow Force '92
Uninvited '93

Idris Elba (1972-)
Ultraviolet '98
The Gospel '05
Sometimes in April '05
American Gangster '07
Daddy's Little Girls '07
The Reaping '07
This Christmas '07
28 Weeks Later '07
The Human Contract '08
Prom Night '08
RocknRolla '08
Obsessed '09
The Unborn '09
Legacy '10
The Losers '10
Takers '10
Thor '11
Ghost Rider: Spirit of Vengeance '12
Prometheus '12
Mandela: Long Walk to Freedom '13
Pacific Rim '13
Thor: The Dark World '13
No Good Deed '14
Beasts of No Nation '15
The Jungle Book '16
Star Trek: Beyond '16
The Take '16
Zootopia '16 (V)
The Dark Tower '17
Molly's Game '17
The Mountain Between Us '17
100 Streets '17
Thor: Ragnarok '17
Fast & Furious Presents: Hobbs & Shaw '19

Vincent Elbaz (1971-)
Almost Peaceful '02
The 4 Musketeers '05

Pascal Elbe
The Other Son '12
24 Days '14

Dana Elcar (1927-2005)
A Lovely Way to Die '68
The Learning Tree '69
Adam at 6 a.m. '70
Soldier Blue '70
ZigZag '70
A Gunfight '71
The Bravos '72
Dying Room Only '73
The Sting '73
Missiles of October '74
The Nude Bomb '80
Condorman '81
Forbidden Love '82
All of Me '84
Code of Honor '84

Ron Eldard (1965-)
True Love '89
Drop Dead Fred '91
Scent of a Woman '92
Sex and the Other Man '95
Bastard out of Carolina '96
The Last Supper '96
Sleepers '96
Deep Impact '98
Delivered '98
When Trumpets Fade '98
Mystery, Alaska '99
The Runner '99
Black Hawk Down '01
Ghost Ship '02
Just a Kiss '02
House of Sand and Fog '03
Diggers '06
Freedomland '06
Already Dead '07
The Tenth Circle '08
Roadie '11
Super 8 '11
Jobs '13
Higher Power '18

Steven Elder
Cold and Dark '05
Blackbeard '06
The 39 Steps '09
The King '19

Kevin Eldon (1960-)
High Heels and Low Lifes '01
Hot Fuzz '07
Johnny English Strikes Again '18

George Eldredge (1914-92)
Sherlock Holmes and the Secret Weapon '42
Mom & Dad '47
Hi-Jacked '50
Fury of the Congo '51

John Eldredge (1904-61)
Dangerous '35
The Girl from 10th Ave. '35
The Goose and the Gander '35
Oil for the Lamps of China '35
The White Cockatoo '35
The Woman in Red '35
King of the Underworld '39
Dr. Kildare's Strange Case '40
Whispering Smith '48
Stampede '49
Loophole '54

Craig Eldridge
Taming Andrew '00
Solar Attack '06
12 Men of Christmas '09

Florence Eldridge (1901-88)
The Matrimonial Bed '30
Les Miserables '35
Mary of Scotland '36
Christopher Columbus '49
Inherit the Wind '60

John Eldridge (1917-60)
The Black Cat '41
Seven Were Saved '47
Square Dance Jubilee '51
I Married a Monster from Outer Space '58

Carmen Electra (1972-)
American Vampire '97
The Chosen One: Legend of the Raven '98
The Mating Habits of the Earthbound Human '99
Scary Movie '00
Get Over It! '01
Perfume '01
Sol Goode '01
Whacked! '02
My Boss's Daughter '03
Starsky & Hutch '04
Cheaper by the Dozen 2 '05
Dirty Love '05
Getting Played '05
Searching for Bobby D '05
Date Movie '06
Hot Tamale '06
Scary Movie 4 '06
Christmas in Wonderland '07
Epic Movie '07
Full of It '07 (C)
I Want Candy '07
Disaster Movie '08
Meet the Spartans '08
Oy Vey! My Son is Gay! '09
Mardi Gras: Spring Break '11
2-Headed Shark Attack '12

Karra Elejalde (1960-)
Running Out of Time '94
Tierra '95
The Nameless '99
Even the Rain '10

Erika Eleniak (1969-)
E.T.: The Extra-Terrestrial '82
Broken Angel '88
Under Siege '92
The Beverly Hillbillies '93
Chasers '94
A Pyromaniac's Love Story '95
Tales from the Crypt Presents Bordello of Blood '96
Ed McBain's 87th Precinct: Heatwave '97
Captive '98
First Degree '98
Aftershock: Earthquake in New York '99
Final Voyage '99
Stealth Fighter '99
The Opponent '01
Breakaway '02
He Sees You When You're Sleeping '02
Shakedown '02
Lady Jayne Killer '03
Absolute Zero '05
Holiday Spin '12
Meant to Be '12

Sandor Eles (1936-2002)
The Evil of Frankenstein '64
And Soon the Darkness '70

Bodhi (Pine) Elfman (1969-)
Enemy of the State '98
The Mod Squad '99
The Pirates of Silicon Valley '99
Gone in 60 Seconds '00
Keeping the Faith '00
Sand '00
Coyote Waits '03
Collateral '04
Fielder's Choice '05

Danny Elfman (1953-)
Forbidden Zone '80
The Nightmare Before Christmas '93 (V)
Tim Burton's Corpse Bride '05 (V)
78/52: Hitchcock's Shower Scene '17

Jenna Elfman (1971-)
Can't Hardly Wait '98
Krippendorf's Tribe '98
EDtv '99
Keeping the Faith '00
Town and Country '01
Obsessed '02
Looney Tunes: Back in Action '03
Clifford's Really Big Movie '04 (V)
Touched '05
Love Hurts '09
The Six Wives of Henry Lefay '09
Friends With Benefits '11

Taina Elg (1930-)
Diane '55
The Prodigal '55
Les Girls '57
Imitation General '58
Hercules in New York '70

Ansel Elgort (1994-)
Carrie '13
Divergent '14
The Fault In Our Stars '14
Men, Women & Children '14
Insurgent '15
Baby Driver '17
November Criminals '17
Billionaire Boys Club '18
The Goldfinch '19
Jonathan '19

Nicholas Elia (1997-)
White Noise '05
When a Man Falls in the Forest '07
The Shortcut '09

Alix Elias (1942-)
Citizens Band '77
Rock 'n' Roll High School '79
True Stories '86
Munchies '87

Arie Elias (1921-)
Bonjour Monsieur Shlomi '03
James' Journey to Jerusalem '03

Carmen Elias (1951-)
The Flower of My Secret '95
To Die, Or Not '99
A Love to Keep '07

Hector Elias (1941-)
Katherine '75
Buddy Boy '99
Envy '04

Christine Elise (1965-)
Child's Play 2 '90
Boiling Point '93
Nowhere to Land '00
The Hit '01
Route 30 '08
Prom '11

Kimberly Elise (1971-)
Set It Off '96
Beloved '98
Bait '00
Bojangles '01
John Q '02
The Manchurian Candidate '04
Woman, Thou Art Loosed '04
Diary of a Mad Black Woman '05
The Great Debaters '07
Pride '07
Gifted Hands: The Ben Carson Story '09
For Colored Girls '10
Hannah's Law '12
Alpha Alert '13
Highland Park '13
A Day Late and a Dollar Short '14
Almost Christmas '16
Ad Astra '19

Holly Elissa (1981-)
See Holly Dignard

Shannon Elizabeth (1973-)
Dish Dogs '98
American Pie '99
Scary Movie '00
Seamless '00
American Pie 2 '01
Jay and Silent Bob Strike Back '01
13 Ghosts '01
Tomcats '01
Love Actually '03
Cursed '04
Johnson Family Vacation '04
Confessions of an American Bride '05
The Kid and I '05
Deal '08
Night of the Demons '09
A Novel Romance '11
American Reunion '12
The Outsider '14

Hector Elizondo (1936-)
Born to Win '71
Valdez Is Coming '71
Pocket Money '72
The Taking of Pelham One Two Three '74
Report to the Commissioner '75
The Dain Curse '78
American Gigolo '79
Cuba '79
The Fan '81
Young Doctors in Love '82
The Flamingo Kid '84
Private Resort '84
Courage '86
Nothing in Common '86
Leviathan '89
Pretty Woman '90
Taking Care of Business '90
Frankie and Johnny '91
Necessary Roughness '91
Chains of Gold '92
Samantha '92
There Goes the Neighborhood '92
Being Human '94
Beverly Hills Cop 3 '94
Exit to Eden '94
Getting Even with Dad '94
Dear God '96
Turbulence '96
The Other Sister '98
Runaway Bride '99
Safe House '99
How High '01
The Princess Diaries '01
Tortilla Soup '01
The Princess Diaries 2: Royal Engagement '04
Raising Helen '04
The Celestine Prophecy '06
I-See-You.Com '06
Georgia Rule '07
Music Within '07
Valentine's Day '10
New Year's Eve '11
The Book of Life '14 (V)

Ronit Elkabetz (1964-)
Late Marriage '01
The Band's Visit '07
The Girl on the Train '09

Jeremie Elkaim (1978-)
Come Undone '00
You'll Get Over It '02
Declaration of War '11

Harry Ellerbe (1901-92)
Murder On a Honeymoon '35
The Magnetic Monster '53
Desk Set '57
The Fall of the House of Usher '60

Duke Ellington (1899-1974)
Check & Double Check '30
Murder at the Vanities '34
Cabin in the Sky '43
Anatomy of a Murder '59

Tate Ellington
The Elephant King '06
The Kitchen '12
Sinister 2 '15

Biff (Elliott) Elliot (1923-2012)
House of Bamboo '55
Pork Chop Hill '59
The Hard Ride '71
The Dark '79

David James Elliot (1960-)
Big Town '87
Confined '10
Exploding Sun '13

Ross Elliot (1917-99)
Chicago Calling '52
The Beast from 20,000 Fathoms '53
Skyjacked '72

Sam Elliot
Once an Eagle '76
The Big Bang '11

Shawn Elliot
Caught '96
Hurricane Streets '96

Alison Elliott (1970-)
Home Before Midnight '84
Wyatt Earp '94
The Buccaneers '95
Indictment: The McMartin Trial '95
The Spitfire Grill '95
The Underneath '95
The Wings of the Dove '97
The Eternal '99
The External '99
The Miracle Worker '00
The Song of the Lark '01
Griffin & Phoenix '06
The Assassination of Jesse James by the Coward Robert Ford '07

Bob Elliott (1923-)
Quick Change '90
Cabin Boy '94

Brennan Elliott (1975-)
The Silencer '99
The Nanny Express '08
Take Me Home '11
Curse of Chucky '13

Chris Elliott (1960-)
The Abyss '89
New York Stories '89
CB4: The Movie '93
Groundhog Day '93
Cabin Boy '94

Kingpin *'96*
There's Something about Mary *'98*
Nutty Professor 2: The Klumps *'00*
Snow Day *'00*
Osmosis Jones *'01*
Scary Movie 2 *'01*
Scary Movie 4 *'06*
I'll Believe You *'07*
Pigs *'07*
Dance Flick *'09*
Speed-Dating *'10*
The Rewrite *'15*
Better Off Single *'16*

David Elliott (1959-)
The Possession of Joel Delaney *'72*
Pearl *'78*
Ali *'01*

David James Elliott (1960-)
Degree of Guilt *'95*
JAG *'95*
Clockwatchers *'97*
Dodson's Journey *'01*
Gooby *'09*
Impact *'09*
The Storm *'09*
Terror Trap *'10*
The Rainbow Tribe *'11*
Truth Be Told *'11*

Denholm Elliott (1922-92)
Dear Mr. Prohack *'49*
The Sound Barrier *'52*
The Cruel Sea *'53*
The Leather Boys *'63*
The High Bright Sun *'65*
King Rat *'65*
You Must Be Joking! *'65*
Alfie *'66*
Dr. Jekyll and Mr. Hyde *'68*
The Sea Gull *'68*
Strange Case of Dr. Jekyll & Mr. Hyde *'68*
The Night They Raided Minsky's *'69*
The Rise and Rise of Michael Rimmer *'70*
Too Late the Hero *'70*
The House that Dripped Blood *'71*
Quest for Love *'71*
A Doll's House *'73*
Vault of Horror *'73*
The Apprenticeship of Duddy Kravitz *'74*
Russian Roulette *'75*
Orde Wingate *'76*
Robin and Marian *'76*
To the Devil, a Daughter *'76*
Voyage of the Damned *'76*
A Bridge Too Far *'77*
The Hound of the Baskervilles *'77*
The Boys from Brazil *'78*
Watership Down *'78 (V)*
Cuba *'79*
Saint Jack *'79*
Zulu Dawn *'79*
Bad Timing: A Sensual Obsession *'80*
Raiders of the Lost Ark *'81*
Brimstone & Treacle *'82*
The Missionary *'82*
The Hound of the Baskervilles *'83*
Trading Places *'83*
Camille *'84*
A Private Function *'84*
The Razor's Edge *'84*
Bleak House *'85*
Defense of the Realm *'85*
A Room with a View *'86*
The Whoopee Boys *'86*
Maurice *'87*
The Bourne Identity *'88*
Deep Cover *'88*
September *'88*
Indiana Jones and the Last Crusade *'89*
A Murder of Quality *'90*
Toy Soldiers *'91*
Catherine Cookson's The Black Candle *'92*
Noises Off *'92*
Scorchers *'92*

John Elliott (1876-1956)
A Face in the Fog *'36*
Rogue's Tavern *'36*
Pilot X *'37*
The Wizard of Gore *'70*

Robert Elliott (1879-1951)
Doorway to Hell *'30*
The Maltese Falcon *'31*
Murder at Midnight *'31*

Ross Elliott (1917-99)
Woman On the Run *'50*
Ma and Pa Kettle at Home *'54*
Tarantula *'55*
The Indestructible Man *'56*
The Lively Set *'64*
Paper Man *'71*

Sam Elliott (1944-)
Butch Cassidy and the Sundance Kid *'69*
Frogs *'72*
Molly & Lawless John *'72*
I Will Fight No More Forever *'75*
Lifeguard *'76*
The Legacy *'79*
The Sacketts *'79*
The Shadow Riders *'82*
A Death in California *'85*
Mask *'85*
Fatal Beauty *'87*
The Quick and the Dead *'87*
Shakedown *'88*
Prancer *'89*
Road House *'89*
Sibling Rivalry *'90*
Conagher *'91*
Rush *'91*
Gettysburg *'93*
Tombstone *'93*
The Desperate Trail *'94*
Blue River *'95*
Buffalo Girls *'95*
Hole in the Sky *'95*
The Big Lebowski *'97*
Dogwatch *'97*
Rough Riders *'97*
The Hi-Lo Country *'98*
You Know My Name *'99*
The Contender *'00*
Fail Safe *'00*
Seduced: Pretty When You Cry *'01*
We Were Soldiers *'02*
Hulk *'03*
Off the Map *'03*
Barnyard *'06 (V)*
Lies & Alibis *'06*
Thank You for Smoking *'06*
Ghost Rider *'07*
The Golden Compass *'07*
Did You Hear About the Morgans? *'09*
Up in the Air *'09*
November Christmas *'10*
The Company You Keep *'12*
Digging for Fire *'15*
The Hero *'17*
A Star Is Born *'18*
Lady and the Tramp *'19*
The Man Who Killed Hitler and Then the Bigfoot *'19*

Shawn Elliott
Short Eyes *'79*
Crossover Dreams *'85*
Bloodsucking Pharoahs of Pittsburgh *'90*
Impulse *'90*
The New Yorker *'98*
Double Take *'01*
Thirteen Conversations About One Thing *'01*

Stephen Elliott (1918-2005)
Three Hours to Kill *'54*
The Hospital *'71*
Report to the Commissioner *'75*
The Invasion of Johnson County *'76*
Betrayal *'78*
Arthur *'81*
Cutter's Way *'81*
Beverly Hills Cop *'84*
Roadhouse 66 *'84*
Assassination *'87*
Arthur 2: On the Rocks *'88*
Taking Care of Business *'90*

William (Bill) Elliott (1934-83)
Change of Habit *'69*
They Call It Murder *'71*
Night of the Lepus *'72*
Coffy *'73*

Aunjanue Ellis (1969-)
Girls Town *'95*
Disappearing Acts *'00*
Men of Honor *'00*
The Caveman's Valentine *'01*
The Opponent *'01*
Lovely & Amazing *'02*
Undercover Brother *'02*
Brother to Brother *'04*
Ray *'04*
Freedomland *'06*
Perception *'06*
Cover *'08*
Racing for Time *'08*
Gifted Hands: The Ben Carson Story *'09*
The Hungry Ghosts *'09*
The Resident *'10*
The Help *'11*
Abducted: The Carlina White Story *'12*
Pimp *'18*

Chris Ellis (1956-)
Apollo 13 *'95*
Home Fries *'98*
October Sky *'99*
The Watcher *'00*
Catch Me If You Can *'02*
In Enemy Hands *'04*
The Devil's Rejects *'05*
Transformers *'07*
Faults *'15*

Edward Ellis (1870-1952)
I Am a Fugitive from a Chain Gang *'32*
Girl Missing *'33*
The Thin Man *'34*
Fury *'36*
The Texas Rangers *'36*
Maid of Salem *'37*
A Man to Remember *'38*

Greg Ellis (1968-)
Crash & Byrnes *'99*
To End All Wars *'01*
Red Roses and Petrol *'03*

James Ellis (1931-2014)
No Surrender *'86*
Priest *'94*
Conspiracy of Silence *'03*

Jay Ellis
A Boy. A Girl. A Dream. *'18*
Escape Room *'19*

Mirko Ellis (1923-2014)
Two Gladiators *'64*
Django: Last Killer *'67*
Hate for Hate *'67*

Nelsan Ellis (1978-2017)
The Express *'08*
Secretariat *'10*
Get On Up *'14*

Patricia Ellis (1916-70)
Elmer the Great *'33*
Picture Snatcher *'33*
The Case of the Lucky Legs *'35*
Stranded *'35*
Block-heads *'38*
Back Door to Heaven *'39*

Robert Ellis (1892-1974)
The Love Trap *'29*
American Madness *'32*
Reform Girl *'33*
The Green Promise *'49*

Robin Ellis (1942-)
Elizabeth R *'72*
The Moonstone *'72*
Poldark 2 *'75*
Poldark *'75*
The Europeans *'79*

Tom Ellis (1979-)
Much Ado About Nothing *'05*
Miss Conception *'08*

Tracey Ellis
This Boy's Life *'93*
The NeverEnding Story 3: Escape from Fantasia *'94*
The Crow 2: City of Angels *'96*

Chase Ellison (1993-)
Mysterious Skin *'04*
End of the Spear *'06*
Towelhead *'07*
You've Got a Friend *'07*
The Year of Getting to Know Us *'08*
The Boy Who Cried Werewolf *'10*
Tooth Fairy *'10*
That's What I Am *'11*

James Ellison (1910-93)
Borderland *'37*
23 1/2 Hours Leave *'37*
Next Time I Marry *'38*
Vivacious Lady *'38*
Fifth Avenue Girl *'39*
Charley's Aunt *'41*
Play Girl *'41*
The Gang's All Here *'43*
I Walked with a Zombie *'43*
Johnny Doesn't Live Here Any More *'44*
Kentucky Jubilee *'51*

Gad Elmaleh (1971-)
Priceless *'06*
The Valet *'06*
The Adventures of Tintin *'11 (V)*
A Monster in Paris *'11*
Capital *'12*
Mood Indigo *'13*

Rebekah Elmaloglou (1974-)
The Sum of Us *'94*
Back of Beyond *'95*

Nicoletta Elmi (1964-)
Who Saw Her Die? *'72*
Andy Warhol's Frankenstein *'74*
Primal Impulse *'74*
Deep Red: Hatchet Murders *'75*
Demons *'86*

Eric Elmosnino
Father of My Children *'09*
Gainsbourg: A Heroic Life *'10*

Michael Elphick (1946-2002)
Cry of the Banshee *'70*
The Elephant Man *'80*
The Element of Crime *'84*
Withnail and I *'87*
Let Him Have It *'91*

Scott Elrod (1975-)
Tricks of a Woman *'08*
Hellhounds *'09*
Death and Cremation *'10*
The Switch *'10*
Home Run *'13*

Hannelore Elsner (1942-)
Go for Zucker *'05*
Cherry Blossoms *'08*

Isobel Elsom (1893-1981)
Ladies in Retirement *'41*
Casanova Brown *'44*
The White Cliffs of Dover *'44*
Two Sisters From Boston *'46*
Escape Me Never *'47*
The Ghost and Mrs. Muir *'47*
Monsieur Verdoux *'47*
Love Is a Many-Splendored Thing *'55*
Over-Exposed *'56*

Cary Elwes (1962-)
Another Country *'84*
Oxford Blues *'84*
The Bride *'85*
Lady Jane *'85*
The Princess Bride *'87*
Glory *'89*
Days of Thunder *'90*
Leather Jackets *'90*
Hot Shots! *'91*
Bram Stoker's Dracula *'92*
The Crush *'93*
Robin Hood: Men in Tights *'93*
Rudyard Kipling's The Jungle Book *'94*
Twister *'96*
Kiss the Girls *'97*
Liar Liar *'97*
From the Earth to the Moon *'98*
The Pentagon Wars *'98*
Quest for Camelot *'98 (V)*
The Cradle Will Rock *'99*
Race Against Time *'00*
Shadow of the Vampire *'00*
Wish You Were Dead *'00*
The Cat's Meow *'01*
Uprising *'01*
Comic Book Villains *'02*
American Crime *'04*
Ella Enchanted *'04*
The Riverman *'04*
Saw *'04*
Edison Force *'05*
Georgia Rule *'07*
The Alphabet Killer *'08*
As Good As Dead *'10*
Psych: 9 *'10*
Saw 3D: The Final Chapter *'10*
No Strings Attached *'11*
The Oogieloves in the Big Balloon Adventure *'12*
Anna Nicole *'13*
Armed Response *'13*
Reach Me *'14*
Being Charlie *'16*

Chris Elwood
How High *'01*
Dog Gone Love *'03*

Ron Ely (1938-)
The Fiend Who Walked the West *'58*
The Remarkable Mr. Pennypacker *'59*
Once Before I Die *'65*
Doc Savage *'75*
Slavers *'77*

Ouassini Embarek
Bye-Bye *'96*
The Good Thief *'03*

Ethan (Randall) Embry (1978-)
All I Want for Christmas *'91*
Dutch *'91*
A Far Off Place *'93*
Evolver *'94*
Season of Change *'94*
Empire Records *'95*
That Thing You Do! *'96*
Vegas Vacation *'96*
White Squall *'96*
Can't Hardly Wait *'98*
Dancer, Texas-Pop. 81 *'98*
Disturbing Behavior *'98*
The Independent *'00*
Sweet Home Alabama *'02*
Wes Craven Presents: They *'02*
Timeline *'03*
Harold and Kumar Go to White Castle *'04*
Pizza *'05*
Standing Still *'05*
Vacancy *'07*
Player 5150 *'08*
The Kane Files *'10*
The Reunion *'11*
The Witches of Oz *'11*
Armed Response *'13*
Cheap Thrills *'14*
The Devil's Candy *'17*
Blindspotting *'18*

Georgia Emelin (1969-)
Deadly Relations *'93*
A Reason to Believe *'95*

Faye Emerson (1917-83)
Juke Girl *'42*
Air Force *'43*
Destination Tokyo *'43*
Between Two Worlds *'44*
The Mask of Dimitrios *'44*
Uncertain Glory *'44*
Nobody Lives Forever *'46*

Hope Emerson (1891-1960)
Adam's Rib *'50*
Caged *'50*
Westward the Women *'51*
All Mine to Give *'56*

Karrie Emerson (1960-)
Evils of the Night *'85*
Chopping Mall *'86*

Michael Emerson (1954-)
The Legend of Zorro *'05*
29th & Gay *'05*
Ready? OK! *'08*

Roy Emerton (1892-1944)
Lorna Doone *'34*
Nine Days a Queen *'36*
Henry V *'44*

Gideon Emery (1972-)
Queen's Messenger II *'01*
Primeval *'07*
Train *'08*
Blue Crush 2 *'11*

Gilbert Emery (1875-1945)
Behind That Curtain *'29*
Let Us Be Gay *'30*
The Lady Refuses *'31*
The Royal Bed *'31*
Now and Forever *'34*
Goin' to Town *'35*
Ladies Crave Excitement *'35*
Wife Versus Secretary *'36*
Return of the Vampire *'43*

John Emery (1905-64)
Here Comes Mr. Jordan *'41*
Eyes in the Night *'42*
Ship Ahoy *'42*
The Spanish Main *'45*
Rocketship X-M *'50*
Double Crossbones *'51*
The Mad Magician *'54*
A Lawless Street *'55*
Forever Darling *'56*
The Girl Can't Help It *'56*
Kronos *'57*

Julie Ann Emery (1972-)
Hitch *'05*
Pictures of Hollis Woods *'07*
The Rainbow Tribe *'11*
The Letter *'12*

Katherine Emery (1907-80)
Isle of the Dead *'45*
The Locket *'46*
The Private Affairs of Bel Ami *'47*

David Emge (1946-)
Dawn of the Dead *'78*
Hellmaster *'92*

Robert Emhardt (1914-94)
3:10 to Yuma *'57*
Shame *'61*
Underworld U.S.A. *'61*
Change of Habit *'69*
Die Sister, Die! *'74*

Michael Emil (1937-)
Tracks *'76*
Sitting Ducks *'80*
Can She Bake a Cherry Pie? *'83*
Always *'85*
Insignificance *'85*
Someone to Love *'87*
New Year's Day *'89*

Daniel Emilfork (1924-2006)
Lady L *'65*
The Devil's Nightmare *'71*
Subversion *'79*
The City of Lost Children *'95*

Eminem (1972-)
Da Hip Hop Witch *'00*
8 Mile *'02*

Alphonsia Emmanuel (1961-)
Peter's Friends *'92*
Under Suspicion *'92*

Colette Emmanuelle
The Devil's Nightmare *'71*
Gilles' Wife *'04*

Noah Emmerich (1965-)
Beautiful Girls *'96*
Cop Land *'97*

Monument Ave. '98
The Truman Show '98
Tumbleweeds '98
Crazy in Alabama '99
Life '99
Frequency '00
Love & Sex '00
Windtalkers '02
Beyond Borders '03
Cellular '04
Miracle '04
Sometimes in April '05
Little Children '06
Pride and Glory '08
Fair Game '10
Sympathy for Delicious '10
Trust '10
Super 8 '11
Warrior '11
Blood Ties '13
Jane Got a Gun '16

Fern Emmett (1896-1946)
Westward Bound '30
Assassin of Youth '35
Dead Men Walk '43

Cliff Emmich (1936-)
Invasion of the Bee Girls '73
Jackson County Jail '76

Robert Emms
Broken '13
Kick-Ass 2 '13

Linda Emond (1959-)
North Country '05
A Dog Named Christmas '09
Julie & Julia '09
Indignation '16
3 Generations '17

Akira (Tsukamoto) Emoto (1948-)
Godzilla *vs.* SpaceGodzilla '94
The Eel '96
Shall We Dance? '96
Dr. Akagi '98
Onmyoji '01
Zebraman '04
Rain Fall '09
Shin Godzilla '16

Celia Emrie
St. Trinian's '07
Return to Cranford '09

Kyoko Enami (1942-)
Gamera *vs.* Barugon '66
The Wolves '82

Hannah Endicott-Douglas (1994-)
The Good Witch's Gift '10
The Good Witch's Family '11
The Good Witch's Charm '12

Kenichi Endo (1961-)
The Happiness of the Katakuris '01
Visitor Q '01
Azumi '03
Flower & Snake '04
Azumi 2 '05
Flower & Snake 2 '05
The Great Yokai War '05
Crows Zero '07

Lena Endre (1955-)
The Best Intentions '92
Faithless '00
Gossip '00
The Girl Who Kicked the Hornet's Nest '10
The Girl Who Played With Fire '10

Georgia Engel (1948-)
Signs of Life '89
Open Season '06 (V)
Open Season 2 '08 (V)
Open Season 3 '10 (V)
Grown Ups 2 '13

Tina Engel (1950-)
The Second Awakening of Christa Klages '78
The Boat Is Full '81

Constanze Engelbrecht (1955-2000)
Fiorile '93
The Count of Monte Cristo '99

Wera Engels (1909-88)
Fugitive Road '34
Sweepstake Annie '35

Audie England (1967-)
Delta of Venus '95
Miami Hustle '95
Venus Rising '95
Red Shoe Diaries 8: Night of Abandon '97
Free Enterprise '98
Legion '98

Dave England (1969-)
Jackass Number Two '06
Natural Born Pranksters '16

Sue England (1928-)
Kidnapped '48
Bomba and the Hidden City '50

Alice Englert (1994-)
Beautiful Creatures '13
Ginger & Rosa '13
In Fear '13

Bradford English (1943-)
Capone '89
Halloween 6: The Curse of Michael Myers '95
Sweet Nothing in My Ear '08

Ellia English
Good Luck Chuck '07
Cornered! '09

Marla English (1935-2012)
The She-Creature '56
Three Bad Sisters '56
Flesh and the Spur '57

Zach English (1983-)
The Real McCoy '93
The Thorn Birds: The Missing Years '96

Lina Englund (1975-)
Storm '05
Arn: The Knight Templar '07

Robert Englund (1947-)
Slashed Dreams '74
Eaten Alive '76
Great Smokey Roadblock '76
A Star Is Born '76
Stay Hungry '76
Dead and Buried '81
Galaxy of Terror '81
Mysterious Two '82
V '83
A Nightmare on Elm Street '84
V: The Final Battle '84
A Nightmare on Elm Street 2: Freddy's Revenge '85
A Nightmare on Elm Street 3: Dream Warriors '87
A Nightmare on Elm Street 4: Dream Master '88
A Nightmare on Elm Street 5: Dream Child '89
The Phantom of the Opera '89
The Adventures of Ford Fairlane '90
Freddy's Dead: The Final Nightmare '91
The Mangler '94
Wes Craven's New Nightmare '94
Killer Tongue '96
Wishmaster '97
Dee Snider's Strangeland '98
Meet the Deedles '98
Perfect Target '98
Urban Legend '98
The Prince and the Surfer '99
Python '00
Wish You Were Dead '00
Freddy *vs.* Jason '03
2001 Maniacs '05
Behind the Mask: The Rise of Leslie Vernon '06
Black Swarm '07
Hatchet '07
Red '08
Zombie Strippers '08
Good Day for It '11
Lake Placid: The Final Chapter '12
Sanitarium '13

Bill Engvall (1957-)
Delta Farce '07
Bait Shop '08
All's Faire in Love '09
Bed & Breakfast '10
Catching Faith '15

India Ennenga (1994-)
The Last International Playboy '08
The Women '08
Multiple Sarcasms '10
Nobody Walks '12
About Scout '15

Takaaki Enoki (1956-)
Heaven & Earth '90
Moon over Tao '97

John Enos (1962-)
Bullet '94
Miami Hustle '95
Red Shoe Diaries 6: How I Met My Husband '95
Stealth Fighter '99
Red Shoe Diaries: Luscious Lola '00
Brigham City '01
Dead Sexy '01
Love Thy Neighbor '02
Phone Booth '02
Missionary Man '07
Everybody Wants to Be Italian '08
Finish Line '08
San Saba '08
Shark Swarm '08

Mireille Enos (1975-)
Gangster Squad '13
World War Z '13
The Captive '14
Devil's Knot '14
If I Stay '14
Sabotage '14

Rene Enriquez (1933-90)
Harry and Tonto '74
Ants '77
The Evil That Men Do '84
Hostage Flight '85
Bulletproof '88

Michael Ensign (1944-)
Jekyll & Hyde. . . Together Again '82
House '86
Life Stinks '91
Born Yesterday '93
Confessions of a Dangerous Mind '02
The Drone Virus '04
Ladies of the House '08

John Entwhistle (1944-2002)
Tommy '75
The Kids Are Alright '79

Molly Ephraim (1986-)
Paranormal Activity 2 '10
Paranormal Activity: The Marked Ones '14
The Front Runner '18

Dieter Eppler (1927-2008)
Strangler of Blackmoor Castle '63
The Torture Chamber of Dr. Sadism '69

Mike Epps (1970-)
Bait '00
Next Friday '00
Dr. Dolittle 2 '01 (V)
How High '01
All About the Benjamins '02
Friday After Next '02
The Fighting Temptations '03
Resident Evil: Apocalypse '04
Guess Who '05
The Honeymooners '05
Roll Bounce '05
Something New '06
Resident Evil: Extinction '07
Talk to Me '07
Open Season 2 '08 (V)
Soul Men '08
Welcome Home Roscoe Jenkins '08
The Hangover '09
The Janky Promoters '09
Next Day Air '09
Faster '10
The Lottery Ticket '10
Jumping the Broom '11
Sparkle '12
The Hangover, Part III '13
Repentance '14
Fifty Shades of Black '16
Meet the Blacks '16
Dolemite Is My Name '19

Omar Epps (1973-)
Juice '92
Daybreak '93
The Program '93
Higher Learning '94
Major League 2 '94
Deadly Voyage '96
First Time Felon '97
Scream 2 '97
Breakfast of Champions '98
In Too Deep '99
The Mod Squad '99
The Wood '99
Brother '00
Dracula 2000 '00
Love and Basketball '00
Perfume '01
Big Trouble '02
Conviction '02
Against the Ropes '04
Alfie '04
A Day in the Life '09
Almost Christmas '16
3022 '19

Shareeka Epps (1989-)
Half Nelson '06
Mother and Child '09
The Winning Season '09
My Soul to Take '10

Yousef Erakat (1990-)
Boo! A Madea Halloween '16
Boo 2! A Madea Halloween '17

Kathryn Erbe (1966-)
What about Bob? '91
Rich in Love '93
D2: The Mighty Ducks '94
Kiss of Death '94
Dream with the Fishes '97
Stir of Echoes '99
The Runaway '00
3 Backyards '10

Stipe Erceg (1974-)
The Edukators '04
The Baader Meinhof Complex '08
Phantom Pain '09

Elizabeth Ercy (1944-)
Phaedra '61
The Sorcerers '67

Richard Erdman (1925-)
Objective, Burma! '45
Cry Danger '51
The Stooge '51
The San Francisco Story '52
The Blue Gardenia '53
Stalag 17 '53
The Steel Lady '53
Saddle the Wind '58
Face of Fire '59
Namu, the Killer Whale '66
Tomboy '85
The Learning Curve '01

Yilmaz Erdogan (1967-)
Once Upon a Time in Anatolia '12
The Water Diviner '15

Oris Erhuero (1968-)
Black Mask 2: City of Masks '02
Sometimes in April '05

Ethan Erickson (1973-)
Jawbreaker '98
Fear Runs Silent '99

Kandis Erickson (1985-)
Death Valley: The Revenge of Bloody Bill '04
Seance '06

Leif Erickson (1911-86)
Conquest '37
Waikiki Wedding '37
The Big Broadcast of 1938 '38
One Third of a Nation '39
H.M. Pulham Esquire '41
Nothing But the Truth '41
Arabian Nights '42
Night Monster '42
Pardon My Sarong '42
Joan of Arc '48
Miss Tatlock's Millions '48
The Snake Pit '48
The Lady Gambles '49
Mother Didn't Tell Me '50
Three Secrets '50
The Tall Target '51
Abbott and Costello Meet Captain Kidd '52
My Wife's Best Friend '52
Never Wave at a WAC '52
Sailor Beware '52
With a Song in My Heart '52
Invaders from Mars '53
Trouble along the Way '53
On the Waterfront '54
Fastest Gun Alive '56
Tea and Sympathy '56
Kiss Them for Me '57
The Carpetbaggers '64
Roustabout '64
Strait-Jacket '64
Penitentiary 2 '82
Rocky 3 '82
D.C. Cab '84

Jacob Ericksson (1967-)
The Girl Who Kicked the Hornet's Nest '10
The Girl Who Played With Fire '10

Eric Ericson (1974-)
Storm '05
Four More Years '10

John Ericson (1926-2020)
Bad Day at Black Rock '54
Rhapsody '54
The Student Prince '54
Green Fire '55
Forty Guns '57
7 Faces of Dr. Lao '63
The Bamboo Saucer '68
Hustler Squad '76
House of the Dead '78
Zone of the Dead '78

Kaj-Erik Eriksen (1979-)
Captains Courageous '95
Disaster Zone: Volcano in New York '06
Ice Twisters '09
12 Disasters '12

Cynthia Erivo (1987-)
Bad Times at the El Royale '18
Harriet '19

R. Lee Ermey (1944-2018)
The Boys in Company C '77
Apocalypse Now '79
Full Metal Jacket '87
Mississippi Burning '88
Demonstone '89
Fletch Lives '89
The Siege of Firebase Gloria '89
Body Snatchers '93
Hexed '93
Sommersby '93
French Silk '94
Love Is a Gun '94
Naked Gun 33 1/3: The Final Insult '94
On Deadly Ground '94
Chain of Command '95
Dead Man Walking '95
Leaving Las Vegas '95
Murder in the First '95
Seven '95
Toy Story '95 (V)
The Frighteners '96
Prefontaine '96
Soul of the Game '96
Dead Men Can't Dance '97
Rough Riders '97
Switchback '97
Weapons of Mass Distraction '97
Gunshy '98
The Sender '98
Avalanche '99
Life '99
Toy Story 2 '99 (V)
You Know My Name '99
Chaos Factor '00
Skipped Parts '00
Jericho '01
On the Borderline '01
Saving Silverman '01
Scenes of the Crime '01
Taking Sides '01
The Salton Sea '02
The Texas Chainsaw Massacre '03
Willard '03
Man of the House '05
The Texas Chainsaw Massacre: The Beginning '06
Toy Story 3 '10 (V)

Mario Erpichini
Escape from Death Row '73
The Best Man '97

Krista Errickson (1964-)
Jekyll & Hyde. . . Together Again '82
Killer Image '92
Martial Outlaw '93

Melissa Errico (1970-)
Frequency '00
Mockingbird Don't Sing '01
Life or Something Like It '02
Loverboy '05

Leon Errol (1881-1951)
The Captain Hates the Sea '34
We're Not Dressing '34
The Great Ziegfeld '36
Make a Wish '37
Dancing Co-Ed '39
The Girl From Mexico '39
Mexican Spitfire '40
The Mexican Spitfire Out West '40
The Mexican Spitfire's Baby '41
Never Give a Sucker an Even Break '41
Mexican Spitfire at Sea '42
The Mexican Spitfire Sees a Ghost '42
Higher and Higher '44
The Invisible Man's Revenge '44
The Noose Hangs High '48

Patrick Ersgard (1964-)
Mandroid '93
Living in Peril '97
Backlash '99
Rancid '04

Homayon Ershadi (1947-)
The Taste of Cherry '96
The Kite Runner '07
A Most Wanted Man '14

Eileen Erskine (1914-95)
Great Expectations '46
This Happy Breed '47

Marilyn Erskine (1926-)
Westward the Women '51
Above and Beyond '53
The Eddie Cantor Story '53
A Slight Case of Larceny '53

Victor Ertmanis
Brainscan '94
Paris, France '94

Bill Erwin (1914-2010)
Somewhere in Time '80
Hard Knox '83
Chairman of the Board '97

Mike Erwin (1978-)
Hulk '03
Freshman Orientation '04
She's Too Young '04
Chaos Theory '08

Hallelujah, I'm a Bum '33
Made On Broadway '33
The Mayor of Hell '33
The Nuisance '33
Stand Up and Cheer '34
David Copperfield '35
Transatlantic Tunnel '35
Exclusive Story '36
Pennies from Heaven '36

Mark Evans (1963-)
The Orphan '79
Lake Placid 3 '10

Maurice Evans (1901-89)
Androcles and the Lion '52
The War Lord '65
Planet of the Apes '68
Rosemary's Baby '68
Operation Heartbeat '69
Beneath the Planet of the Apes '70
The Jerk '79
Agatha Christie's A Caribbean Mystery '83

Mike Evans (1949-2006)
The Voyage of the Yes '72
The House on Skull Mountain '74

Mitch Evans
Alien Massacre '67
Gallery of Horrors '67

Monica Evans (1940-)
The Odd Couple '68
Robin Hood '73 (V)

Muriel Evans (1910-2000)
The Prizefighter and the Lady '33
Manhattan Melodrama '34
Missing Girls '36
Ten Laps to Go '36
The House of Secrets '37

Rex Evans (1903-69)
The Matchmaker '58
On the Double '61

Richard Evans (1935-)
Too Soon to Love '60
Dirty Little Billy '72

Robert Evans (1930-)
Man of a Thousand Faces '57
The Sun Also Rises '57
The Fiend Who Walked the West '58
The Best of Everything '59
An Alan Smithee Film: Burn, Hollywood, Burn '97 (C)
The Kid Stays in the Picture '02 (N)

Robin Evans
One Dark Night '82
Rage of Honor '87

Rupert Evans (1977-)
Hellboy '04
Guantanamero '07
Agora '09
Emma '09
The Canal '14
The Boy '16

Shaun Evans (1980-)
The Boys and Girl From County Clare '03
Being Julia '04
Cashback '06
Boy A '07
Sparkle '07
Dread '09
Princess Kaiulani '09
The Take '09

Terrence Evans (1944-2015)
Curse 2: The Bite '88
The Texas Chainsaw Massacre '03
Mr. Fix It '06

Troy Evans (1948-)
Article 99 '92
Kuffs '92
The Lawnmower Man '92
Ace Ventura: Pet Detective '93
Father and Scout '94
My Summer Story '94
The Frighteners '96
I'll Remember April '99
The Black Dahlia '06

Edith Evanson (1900-80)
The Jade Mask '45
Caged '50
The Damned Don't Cry '50
The Magnificent Yankee '50
The Day the Earth Stood Still '51
Elephant Stampede '51
The Girl in the Red Velvet Swing '55
Silver Star '55

Eve (1978-)
Barbershop '02
Barbershop 2: Back in Business '04
The Cookout '04
The Woodsman '04
Flashbacks of a Fool '08
Whip It '09
Barbershop: The Next Cut '16

Alice Eve (1982-)
Big Nothing '06
Starter for 10 '06
Crossing Over '09
She's Out of My League '10
The Decoy Bride '11
ATM '12
Men in Black 3 '12
The Raven '12
Decoding Annie Parker '13
Some Velvet Morning '13
Star Trek: Into Darkness '13
Before We Go '14
Cold Comes the Night '14
Misconduct '16
Please Stand By '17
Replicas '18

Trevor Eve (1951-)
Dracula '79
Lace '84
Appetite '98
David Copperfield '99
Heat of the Sun '99
Possession '02
Troy '04
Framed '10
Death Comes to Pemberley '13

Judith Evelyn (1913-67)
The Egyptian '54
Rear Window '54
The Tingler '59

Kimberly Evenson (1932-)
The Big Bet '85
Porky's Revenge '85

Barbara Everest (1890-1968)
There Goes the Bride '32
Phantom Fiend '35
Gaslight '44
Jane Eyre '44
The Valley of Decision '45
Madeleine '50
Tony Draws a Horse '51

Chad Everett (1936-2012)
Claudelle Inglish '61
Rome Adventure '62
Get Yourself a College Girl '64
Made in Paris '65
The Singing Nun '66
First to Fight '67
The Last Challenge '67
Return of the Gunfighter '67
The Impossible Years '68
Centennial '78
The French Atlantic Affair '79
Airplane 2: The Sequel '82
The Rousters '90
When Time Expires '97
Hard to Forget '98
Psycho '98
Mulholland Drive '01
Anchorman: The Legend of Ron Burgundy '04
The Pink Conspiracy '07
Break '09

Denton Blane Everett
The Lawless '07
Mad Bad '07
Psychic Experiment '10

Dylan Everett (1995-)
Breakfast With Scot '07
The Devil's Mercy '07
Booky's Crush '09

Rupert Everett (1959-)
Another Country '84
The Far Pavilions '84
Dance with a Stranger '85
The Right Hand Man '87
The Comfort of Strangers '91
Inside Monkey Zetterland '93
The Madness of King George '94
Ready to Wear '94
Cemetery Man '95
Dunston Checks In '95
B. Monkey '97
My Best Friend's Wedding '97
Shakespeare in Love '98
An Ideal Husband '99
Inspector Gadget '99
William Shakespeare's A Midsummer Night's Dream '99
The Next Best Thing '00
The Importance of Being Earnest '02
The Wild Thornberrys Movie '02 (V)
Dangerous Liaisons '03
To Kill a King '03
Unconditional Love '03
A Different Loyalty '04
People '04
Shrek 2 '04 (V)
Stage Beauty '04
The Chronicles of Narnia: The Lion, the Witch and the Wardrobe '05 (V)
Separate Lies '05
St. Trinian's '07
Shrek the Third '07 (V)
Stardust '07
The Legend of Fritton's Gold '09
Wild Target '10
Hysteria '11
A Royal Night Out '15
Finding Altamira '16
Miss Peregrine's Home for Peculiar Children '16

Tom Everett (1948-)
Friday the 13th, Part 4: The Final Chapter '84
Best of the Best '89
Leatherface: The Texas Chainsaw Massacre 3 '89
Eddie Presley '92
My Fellow Americans '96
Air Force One '97
XXX '02
The Alamo '04

Nancy Everhard (1957-)
Deepstar Six '89
Demonstone '89
The Trial of the Incredible Hulk '89
This Gun for Hire '90

Angie Everhart (1969-)
Jade '95
Another 9 1/2 Weeks '96
Tales from the Crypt Presents Bordello of Blood '96
Trigger Happy '96 (C)
Executive Target '97
Bitter Sweet '98
Something About Sex '98
D.R.E.A.M. Team '99
Running Red '99
The Stray '00
The Substitute 4: Failure is Not an Option '00
Welcome to Hollywood '00
Heart of Stone '01
Bugs '03
Take Me Home Tonight '11

Rex Everhart (1920-2000)
Family Business '89
Beauty and the Beast '91 (V)

J.D. Evermore (1968-)
Jules Verne's Mysterious Island '10
Stolen '12
Maggie '15

Jason Evers (1922-2005)
The Green Berets '68
Escape from the Planet of the Apes '71
Fer-De-Lance '74
Barracuda '78
Basket Case 2 '90

Nick Eversman (1986-)
Cinema Verite '11
Hellraiser: Revelations '11
Deep Dark Canyon '12
The DUFF '15

Cory (Corinna) Everson (1959-)
Double Impact '91
Felony '95

Steve Evets
Looking for Eric '09
Wuthering Heights '12

Deak Evgenikos
Itty Bitty Titty Committee '07
The Owls '09

Briana Evigan (1986-)
Spectre '96
Step Up 2 the Streets '08
S. Darko: A Donnie Darko Tale '09
Sorority Row '09
Rites of Passage '12
A Star for Christmas '12
Stash House '12
Step Up: All In '14

Greg Evigan (1953-)
Stripped to Kill '87
Deepstar Six '89
Lies Before Kisses '92
TekWar '94
Spectre '96
He Sees You When You're Sleeping '02
Arizona Summer '03
Straight from the Heart '03
Cerberus '05
River's End '05
My Silent Partner '06
Mail Order Bride '08
100 Million BC '08
Poison Ivy 4: The Secret Society '08
Phantom Racer '09
6 Guns '10
Metal Tornado '11
Shadow on the Mesa '13

Vanessa Lee Evigan (1981-)
Holiday in Handcuffs '07
Project Solitude: Buried Alive '09
Christmas Mail '10

Pat Evison (1924-2010)
Tim '79
Starstruck '82

Fred Ewanuick (1971-)
Absolute Zero '05
Just Friends '05
Dress to Kill '07

John Ewart (1928-94)
Blue Fire Lady '78
Newsfront '78

Dwight Ewell (1968-)
Chasing Amy '97
Man of the Century '99
Intern '00
Jay and Silent Bob Strike Back '01

Kayla Ewell
Senior Skip Day '08
Norman Rockwell's Shuffleton's Barbershop '13

Tom Ewell (1909-94)
Adam's Rib '50
American Guerrilla in the Philippines '50
A Life of Her Own '50
Lost in Alaska '52
The Seven Year Itch '55
The Girl Can't Help It '56
The Great American Pastime '56
State Fair '62
Tender Is the Night '62
They Only Kill Their Masters '72
Easy Money '83

Barbara Ewing (1944-)
Dracula Has Risen from the Grave '68
Brothers of the Head '06

Adele Exarchopoulos
Blue is the Warmest Color '13
The Last Face '17
The White Crow '18

Richard Eyer (1945-)
Desperate Hours '55
Canyon River '56
The Kettles in the Ozarks '56
Fort Dobbs '58
The Seventh Voyage of Sinbad '58

Peter Eyre (1942-)
Diamond's Edge '88
Orlando '92
Princess Caraboo '94
Scarlett '94
Sharpe's Gold '94
Joseph '95
Surviving Picasso '96
The Tango Lesson '97
Dangerous Beauty '98
The Golden Bowl '00
The Affair of the Necklace '01

William Eythe (1918-57)
The Ox-Bow Incident '43
Wilson '44
A Wing and a Prayer '44
Colonel Effingham's Raid '45
House on 92nd Street '45
A Royal Scandal '45

Maynard Eziashi (1965-)
Mister Johnson '91
Bopha! '93
Ace Ventura: When Nature Calls '95

Shelley Fabares (1944-)
Ride the Wild Surf '64
Girl Happy '65
Hold On! '66
Spinout '66
Clambake '67
Operation Heartbeat '69
Brian's Song '71
Friendship, Secrets and Lies '79
Hot Pursuit '87
Deadly Relations '93
A Nightmare Come True '97

Matthew Faber (1973-2020)
Bob Roberts '92
Welcome to the Dollhouse '95
Ride with the Devil '99
Hard Luck '01
Palindromes '04

Fabian (1943-)
High Time '60
North to Alaska '60
Five Weeks in a Balloon '62
The Longest Day '62
Mr. Hobbs Takes a Vacation '62
Ride the Wild Surf '64
Dear Brigitte '65
Fireball 500 '66
Thunder Alley '67
Little Laura & Big John '73
Soul Hustler '76
Kiss Daddy Goodbye '81
Get Crazy '83
Runaway Daughters '94

Mr. Rock 'n' Roll: The Alan Freed Story '99 (C)

Ava Fabian (1962-)
To Die For '89
Welcome Home, Roxy Carmichael '90
Ski School '91
Last Man Standing '95
Capital Punishment '96

Francoise Fabian (1933-)
That Naughty Girl '58
Belle de Jour '67
The Thief of Paris '67
My Night at Maud's '69
Happy New Year '73
How to Kill a Judge '75
Love by Appointment '76
Madame Claude '77
The French Woman '79
La Buche '00
5x2 '04

Patrick Fabian (1964-)
Snow '04
Twitches '05
Twitches Too '07
Snow 2: Brain Freeze '08
Black Limousine '10
The Last Exorcism '10
Atlas Shrugged 2: The Strike '12

Joel Fabiani (1936-)
One of My Wives Is Missing '76
Snake Eyes '98

Fabio (1961-)
Exorcist 3: Legion '90
Scenes from a Mall '91 (C)
Death Becomes Her '92 (C)
Bubble Boy '01

Nanette Fabray (1920-)
The Private Lives of Elizabeth & Essex '39
The Band Wagon '53
Alice Through the Looking Glass '66
The Happy Ending '69
Harper Valley P.T.A. '78
Amy '81

Aldo Fabrizi (1905-90)
Open City '45
The Flowers of St. Francis '50
Three Steps North '51

Franco Fabrizi (1916-95)
I Vitelloni '53
Il Bidone '55
The Italian Connection '73
Ginger & Fred '86

Peter Facinelli (1973-)
Foxfire '96
Can't Hardly Wait '98
Dancer, Texas-Pop. 81 '98
Telling You '98
Blue Ridge Fall '99
Supernova '99
The Big Kahuna '00
Riding in Cars with Boys '01
Tempted '01
The Scorpion King '02
Arc '06
Hollow Man 2 '06
The Lather Effect '06
Touch the Top of the World '06
All the Good Ones Are Married '07
Finding Amanda '08
Twilight '08
The Twilight Saga: New Moon '09
The Twilight Saga: Eclipse '10
Loosies '11
The Twilight Saga: Breaking Dawn, Part 1 '11
The Twilight Saga: Breaking Dawn, Part 2 '12
Freezer '14
Countdown '19
Running with the Devil '19

Robert Factor
Fear '88
Ninja Academy '90
Bad Channels '92

Bill Fagerbakke (1957-)
The Reluctant Agent '89
Gargoyles, The Movie: The Heroes Awaken '94 (V)
Stephen King's The Stand '94
Quigley '03
The SpongeBob SquarePants Movie '04 (V)
Space Buddies '08 (V)
The SpongeBob Movie: Sponge Out of Water '15 (V)

Jeff Fahey (1954-)
Execution of Raymond Graham '85
Silverado '85
Psycho 3 '86
Riot on 42nd Street '87
Backfire '88
Split Decisions '88
Wrangler '88
True Blood '89
Impulse '90
The Last of the Finest '90
White Hunter, Black Heart '90
Body Parts '91
Iron Maze '91
The Lawnmower Man '92
Sketch Artist '92
Quick '93
Woman of Desire '93
Firefall '94
Wyatt Earp '94
Darkman 3: Die Darkman Die '95
The Sweeper '95
Smalltime '96
The Underground '97
Extramarital '98
When Justice Fails '98
Johnny 2.0 '99
No Tomorrow '99
Blind Heat '00
Revelation '00
Inferno '01
No Witness '04
Absolute Zero '05
Frederick Forsyth's Icon '05
Locusts: The 8th Plague '05
Manticore '05
The Eden Formula '06
The Hunt for Eagle One: Crash Point '06
Planet Terror '07
Machete '10
Terror Trap '10
Guns, Girls and Gambling '11
Alien Storm '12
Lake Effects '12
Beneath '13

Megan Fahlenbock (1971-)
Snap Decision '01
The Baby Formula '08

Elinor Fair (1903-57)
Kismet '20
Through the Back Door '21
My Friend from India '27
Yankee Clipper '27

Jody Fair
High School Confidential '58
The Ghost of Dragstrip Hollow '59

Tracey Fairaway
Hellraiser: Revelations '11
A Hologram for the King '16

Bruce Fairbairn (1947-99)
The Vampire Hookers '78
Cyclone '87

Christopher Fairbank (1959-)
How Many Miles to Babylon? '82
The Scarlet Pimpernel '99
The Scarlet Pimpernel 2: Mademoiselle Guillotine '99
The Scarlet Pimpernel 3: The Kidnapped King '99
Below '02
Tess of the D'Urbervilles '08
Lennon Naked '10
Lady Macbeth '17

Douglas Fairbanks, Jr. (1909-2000)
Our Modern Maidens '29
The Dawn Patrol '30
Little Caesar '30
Loose Ankles '30
One Night at Susie's '30
Party Girl '30
It's Tough to Be Famous '32
Parachute Jumper '32
Union Depot '32
Morning Glory '33
Catherine the Great '34
Accused '36
Prisoner of Zenda '37
Having a Wonderful Time '38
Joy of Living '38
The Rage of Paris '38
The Young in Heart '38
Gunga Din '39
Angels Over Broadway '40
The Corsican Brothers '42
Sinbad, the Sailor '47
Ghost Story '81

Douglas Fairbanks, Sr. (1883-1939)
His Picture in the Papers '16
His Majesty, the American '19
When the Clouds Roll By '19
Mark of Zorro '20
The Three Musketeers '21
Robin Hood '22
The Thief of Baghdad '24
Don Q., Son of Zorro '25
The Black Pirate '26
The Gaucho '27
The Iron Mask '29
The Taming of the Shrew '29
Mr. Robinson Crusoe '32
Private Life of Don Juan '34

Craig Fairbrass (1964-)
Cliffhanger '93
Nightscare '93
Proteus '95
The Long Weekend '05
Rise of the Footsoldier '07
White Noise 2: The Light '07
Far Cry '08
31 North 62 East '09
Dead Cert '10
House of the Rising Sun '11
Berlin Job '12
Hijacked '12
Get Lucky '13
Vikingdom '13
The Outsider '14
Avengement '19

Morgan Fairchild (1950-)
Initiation of Sarah '78
Concrete Cowboys '79
The Seduction '82
Pee-wee's Big Adventure '85
North and South Book 2 '86
Campus Man '87
Midnight Cop '88
Phantom of the Mall: Eric's Revenge '89
Sleeping Beauty '89
Body Chemistry 3: Point of Seduction '93
Freaked '93
Test Tube Teens from the Year 2000 '93
Gospa '94
Venus Rising '95
Holy Man '98
Nice Guys Sleep Alone '99
Peril '00
Unshackled '00
Arizona Summer '03
Knuckle Sandwich '04
The Initiation of Sarah '06
Shock to the System '06
The Slammin' Salmon '09
A Perfect Ending '12

Virginia Brown Faire (1904-80)
Monte Cristo '22
Peter Pan '24

Heather Fairfield
The War of the Roses '89
A Girl of the Limberlost '90

Michelle Fairley
Anton Chekhov's The Duel '09
A Short Stay in Switzerland '09
Philomena '13
Ironclad: Battle for Blood '14

Michael Fairman (1934-)
The Nurse '97
Forces of Nature '99
Thirteen Days '00
Dead Silence '07
Dark Streets '08

Donald Adeosun Faison (1974-)
Sugar Hill '94
Clueless '95
New Jersey Drive '95
Waiting to Exhale '95
Never 2 Big '98
Supreme Sanction '99
Trippin' '99
Remember the Titans '00
Double Whammy '01
Josie and the Pussycats '01 (C)
Big Fat Liar '02
Good Boy! '03 (V)
Uptown Girls '03
Bachelor Party Vegas '05
King's Ransom '05
Something New '06
Next Day Air '09
Skyline '10
Venus and Vegas '10
Kick-Ass 2 '13
A Snow Globe Christmas '13
Let's Kill Ward's Wife '14

Frankie Faison (1949-)
Ragtime '81
Manhunter '86
The Money Pit '86
Coming to America '88
Mississippi Burning '88
Do the Right Thing '89
Betsy's Wedding '90
City of Hope '91
The Silence of the Lambs '91
Freejack '92
Sommersby '93
I Love Trouble '94
Stephen King's The Langoliers '95
The Stupids '95
Mother Night '96
The Rich Man's Wife '96
Julian Po '97
The Thomas Crown Affair '99
Down to Earth '01
Hannibal '01
A Little Inside '01
The Sleepy Time Gal '01
Thirteen Conversations About One Thing '01
Red Dragon '02
Showtime '02
Gods and Generals '03
Highwaymen '03
The Cookout '04
In Good Company '04
White Chicks '04
Tyler Perry's Meet the Browns '08
Adam '09
Breaking Point '09
Cirque du Freak: The Vampire's Assistant '09
For Sale by Owner '09
Splinterheads '09
Mayor Cupcake '11
The Case for Christ '17

Dolores Faith (1942-)
The Phantom Planet '61
The Human Duplicators '64

Marianne Faithfull (1946-)
I'll Never Forget What's 'Isname '67
The Girl on a Motorcycle '68
The Turn of the Screw '92
Shopping '93
Moondance '95
Crimetime '96 (C)
Intimacy '00
Marie Antoinette '06
Paris, je t'aime '06
Irina Palm '07
Faces in the Crowd '11

Eduardo Fajardo (1918-)
Ringo's Big Night '66
Ringo's Mark of Vengeance '67
Django '68
Gun for 100 Graves '68
Mean Machine '73
The Killer Must Kill Again '75
Lisa and the Devil '75

Lola Falana (1942-)
A Man Called Adam '66
Lola Colt '67
The Liberation of L.B. Jones '70
The Klansman '74
Lady Cocoa '75

Edie Falco (1963-)
Sweet Lorraine '87
Trust '90
Laws of Gravity '92
The Sunshine Boys '95
Hurricane Streets '96
Cop Land '97
A Price Above Rubies '97
Judy Berlin '99
Random Hearts '99
Sunshine State '02
The Quiet '05
Freedomland '06
The Great New Wonderful '06
3 Backyards '10
The Comedian '16
Landline '17
Megan Leavey '17
Outside In '17
The Land of Steady Habits '18

Andre Falcon (1924-2009)
Happy New Year '73
The Mad Adventures of Rabbi Jacob '73
A Slightly Pregnant Man '79

Ben Falcone
Smiley Face '07
What to Expect When You're Expecting '12
Bad Words '13
Enough Said '13
Tammy '14
Can You Ever Forgive Me? '18

Lisanne Falk
Heathers '89
Night on Earth '91
The First to Go '97
Suicide Kings '97
Shattered Image '98

Peter Falk (1927-2011)
The Bloody Brood '59
Murder, Inc. '60
The Secret of the Purple Reef '60
Pocketful of Miracles '61
Pressure Point '62
The Balcony '63
Beach Party '63
It's a Mad, Mad, Mad, Mad World '63
Robin and the 7 Hoods '64
The Great Race '65
Columbo: Prescription Murder '67
Luv '67
Anzio '68
Castle Keep '69
Machine Gun McCain '69
Husbands '70
Columbo: Murder by the Book '71
A Step Out of Line '71
A Woman under the Influence '74
Griffin and Phoenix: A Love Story '76
Mikey & Nicky '76
Murder by Death '76
Brink's Job '78
The Cheap Detective '78
The In-Laws '79
. . .All the Marbles '81
The Great Muppet Caper '81
Big Trouble '86
Happy New Year '87
The Princess Bride '87
Vibes '88
Wings of Desire '88
Cookie '89
Tune in Tomorrow '90
The Player '92
Faraway, So Close! '93
Roommates '95
The Sunshine Boys '95
Money Kings '98
Enemies of Laughter '00
Lakeboat '00
Corky Romano '01
Made '01
The Lost World '02
Three Days of Rain '02
Undisputed '02
Shark Tale '04 (V)
The Thing About My Folks '05
Next '07
Three Days to Vegas '07
American Cowslip '09

Rossella Falk (1926-)
8 1/2 '63
Modesty Blaise '66
The Legend of Lylah Clare '68
The Black Belly of the Tarantula '71
Seven Blood-Stained Orchids '72

Deborah Fallender
Jabberwocky '77
S.O.S. Titanic '79

Jimmy Fallon (1974-)
Almost Famous '00
Band of Brothers '01
Anything Else '03
Taxi '04
Fever Pitch '05
Arthur and the Invisibles '06 (V)
Factory Girl '06
The Year of Getting to Know Us '08
Whip It '09

John Fallon (1978-)
100 Feet '08
Recon 2023: The Gauda Prime Conspiracy '08

Mark Famiglietti (1979-)
Terminator 3: Rise of the Machines '03
The March Sisters at Christmas '12

Bingbing Fan (1981-)
Battle of the Warriors '06
Flash Point '07
Lost in Beijing '07
Iron Man 3 '13

Roger Fan
Corky Romano '01
Better Luck Tomorrow '02
Annapolis '06
The Trouble with Romance '09

Anthony Fanelli
The Black Water Vampire '13
Day of the Mummy '14

Mien Fang
Intimate Confessions of a Chinese Courtesan '72
King Boxer '72

Al Fann (1925-)
Parasite '82
Frankie and Johnny '91

Dakota Fanning (1994-)
I Am Sam '01
Sweet Home Alabama '02
Taken '02 (N)
Trapped '02
Dr. Seuss' The Cat in the Hat '03
Uptown Girls '03
Man on Fire '04
Dreamer: Inspired by a True Story '05
Hide and Seek '05
Lilo & Stitch 2: Stitch Has a Glitch '05 (V)
Nine Lives '05
War of the Worlds '05
Charlotte's Web '06
Fragments '08
Hounddog '08
The Secret Life of Bees '08
Coraline '09 (V)
Push '09
The Twilight Saga: New Moon '09
The Runaways '10
The Twilight Saga: Eclipse '10
The Twilight Saga: Breaking Dawn, Part 1 '11
The Motel Life '12
Now Is Good '12
The Last of Robin Hood '13
Night Moves '13
Very Good Girls '13
Effie Gray '15
Every Secret Thing '15
American Pastoral '16
The Benefactor '16
Brimstone '17
Please Stand By '17

Elle Fanning (1998-)
The Door in the Floor '04
Because of Winn-Dixie '05
Babel '06
Reservation Road '07
The Curious Case of Benjamin Button '08
Phoebe in Wonderland '08
Somewhere '10
Super 8 '11
We Bought a Zoo '11
Twixt '12
Ginger & Rosa '13
The Boxtrolls '14 (V)
Maleficent '14
Young Ones '14
Trumbo '15
Leap! '16
Live by Night '16
The Neon Demon '16
The Beguiled '17
How To Talk To Girls At Parties '17
Mary Shelley '17
3 Generations '17
20th Century Women '17
The Vanishing of Sidney Hall '17
I Think We're Alone Now '18
Teen Spirit '18
Maleficent: Mistress of Evil '19

Franco Fantasia (1928-)
Revenge of the Musketeers '63
Adios, Sabata '71
Mountain of the Cannibal God '79
Emerald Jungle '80

Ennio Fantastichini (1955-)
The Blonde '92
Napoleon '03
Saturn in Opposition '07
Loose Cannons '10

Sergio Fantoni (1930-2020)
Esther and the King '60
The Giant of Marathon '60
Atom Age Vampire '61
The Prize '63
Do Not Disturb '65
Von Ryan's Express '65
What Did You Do in the War, Daddy? '66
Hornets' Nest '70
The Belly of an Architect '91

Stephanie Faracy (1952-)
Blind Date '87
The Great Outdoors '88
Hocus Pocus '93
Flightplan '05

Golshifteh Farahani (1983-)
Boutique '04
Body of Lies '08
Shirin '09
Just Like a Woman '13
Exodus: Gods and Kings '14
Paterson '16

Violet Farebrother (1888-1969)
Easy Virtue '27
She Played With Fire '57

Debrah Farentino (1961-)
Capone '89
Bugsy '91
Son of the Pink Panther '93
Stephen King's The Storm of the Century '99

James Farentino (1938-2012)
Psychomania '63
Ensign Pulver '64
The War Lord '65
The Possessed '77
The Final Countdown '80
Dead and Buried '81
License to Kill '84
A Summer to Remember '84
Sins '85
Her Alibi '88
Naked Lie '89
Bulletproof '96
Termination Man '97

Debra Fares
Killer Tomatoes Strike Back '90
Killer Tomatoes Eat France '91

Fares Fares (1973-)
Kill Your Darlings '06
Easy Money: Hard to Kill '12
Child 44 '15

Nadia Fares (1962-)
The Crimson Rivers '01
The Nest '02

Antonio Fargas (1946-)
Gator King '70
Shaft '71
Across 110th Street '72
Busting '74
Foxy Brown '74
Cornbread, Earl & Me '75
Car Wash '76
Pretty Baby '78
Nurse '80
The Ambush Murders '82
Firestarter '84
Streetwalkin' '85
Night of the Sharks '87
I'm Gonna Git You Sucka '88
Shakedown '88
Howling 6: The Freaks '90
Milo '98
The Suburbans '99
Three Strikes '00
Extreme Honor '01
Bad Guys '08
Stealing Las Vegas '12

Carolyn Farina
The Mayor of Hell '33
Metropolitan '90

Dennis Farina (1944-2013)
Thief '81
Code of Silence '85
Jo Jo Dancer, Your Life Is Calling '86
Manhunter '86
Midnight Run '88
Men of Respect '91
Street Crimes '92
Another Stakeout '93
High Stakes '93
Mac '93
Striking Distance '93
Little Big League '94
Get Shorty '95
Eddie '96
That Old Feeling '96
Out of Sight '98
Saving Private Ryan '98
The Mod Squad '99
Bad Seed '00
Reindeer Games '00
Snatch '00
Sidewalks of New York '01
Big Trouble '02
Stealing Harvard '02
Paparazzi '04
Empire Falls '05
Purple Violets '07
You Kill Me '07
What Happens in Vegas '08
Knucklehead '10
The Last Rites of Joe May '11
Authors Anonymous '14

Daniela Farinacci
Lantana '01
Look Both Ways '05

Gabriella Farinon (1941-)
Assignment Outer Space '61
Blood and Roses '61

Anna Faris (1976-)
Scary Movie '00
Scary Movie 2 '01
The Hot Chick '02
May '02
Lost in Translation '03
Scary Movie 3 '03
Brokeback Mountain '05
Just Friends '05
Southern Belles '05
Waiting '05
My Super Ex-Girlfriend '06
Scary Movie 4 '06
Mama's Boy '07
Smiley Face '07
The House Bunny '08
Alvin and the Chipmunks: The Squeakuel '09 (V)
Cloudy with a Chance of Meatballs '09 (V)
Observe and Report '09
Yogi Bear '10 (V)
Alvin and the Chipmunks: Chipwrecked '11 (V)
Take Me Home Tonight '11
What's Your Number? '11
The Dictator '12
Cloudy with a Chance of Meatballs 2 '13 (V)
I Give It a Year '13
Movie 43 '13
Alvin and the Chipmunks: Road Chip '15 (V)
The Emoji Movie '17 (V)
Overboard '18

Sean Faris (1982-)
Brotherhood 2: The Young Warlocks '01
Sleepover '04
Yours, Mine & Ours '05
Forever Strong '08
Never Back Down '08
Ghost Machine '09
Freerunner '10
The Lost Valentine '11
Christmas with Holly '12
Stash House '12
NYC Underground '13
Pawn '13

Albert Farley (1926-96)
See Alberto Farnese

Chris Farley (1964-97)
Coneheads '93
Wayne's World 2 '93
Airheads '94
Billy Madison '94
Tommy Boy '95
Beverly Hills Ninja '96
Black Sheep '96
Almost Heroes '97
Dirty Work '97

Jim Farley (1882-1947)
The General '26
The Voice of the City '29

John Farley
Believers '07
Blonde and Blonder '07

Kevin Farley (1965-)
Frank McKlusky, C.I. '02
Danny Roane: First Time Director '06
Blonde and Blonder '07
An American Carol '08
Dog Gone '08
Cellmates '12
Paranormal Movie '13

Marianne Farley
No Brother of Mine '07
The Christmas Choir '08

Morgan Farley (1898-1988)
Open Secret '48
Abbott and Costello Meet the Killer, Boris Karloff '49
Barricade '49
Goodbye My Fancy '51
The Wild North '52

Teresa Farley
Bad Girls Dormitory '84
Breeders '86

Benjamin Farmer
The Falls: Testament of Love '13
The Falls: Covenant of Grace '16

Bill Farmer (1952-)
A Goofy Movie '94 (V)
Mickey, Donald, Goofy: The Three Musketeers '04 (V)

Frances Farmer (1913-70)
Come and Get It '36
Rhythm on the Range '36
Toast of New York '37
Flowing Gold '40
Son of Fury '42

Gary Farmer (1953-)
Big Town '87
Powwow Highway '89
Blown Away '93
Henry & Verlin '94
Sioux City '94
Tales from the Crypt Presents Demon Knight '94
Dead Man '95
Smoke Signals '98
Heater '99
The Virginian '99
Angels Don't Sleep Here '00
The Score '01
Adaptation '02
Skins '02
The Republic of Love '03
Twist '03
The Big Empty '04
Evergreen '04
A Thief of Time '04
Disappearances '06
All Hat '07
Good Neighbors '10
Jimmy P. '13

Mimsy Farmer (1945-)
Spencer's Mountain '63
Devil's Angels '67
Hot Rods to Hell '67
Riot on Sunset Strip '67
More '69
Four Flies on Grey Velvet '72
Autopsy '75
The Black Cat '81
Codename: Wildgeese '84

Suzan Farmer (1943-)
The Devil-Ship Pirates '64
Die, Monster, Die! '65
Dracula, Prince of Darkness '66
Rasputin the Mad Monk '66

Taissa Farmiga (1994-)
Higher Ground '11
At Middleton '13
The Bling Ring '13
Jamesy Boy '14
The Final Girls '15
In a Valley of Violence '16
The Mule '18
The Nun '18
What They Had '18

Vera Farmiga (1973-)
Return to Paradise '98
Autumn in New York '00
15 Minutes '01
Dummy '02
Love in the Time of Money '02
Snow White: The Fairest of Them All '02
Down to the Bone '04
The Manchurian Candidate '04
Breaking and Entering '06
The Departed '06
Running Scared '06
In Tranzit '07
Joshua '07
Never Forever '07
The Boy in the Striped Pajamas '08
Nothing But the Truth '08
Quid Pro Quo '08
A Heavenly Vintage '09
Orphan '09
Up in the Air '09
Henry's Crime '10
Higher Ground '11
Source Code '11
Goats '12
Safe House '12
At Middleton '13
The Conjuring '13
The Judge '14
The Conjuring 2 '16
Boundaries '18
The Commuter '18
The Front Runner '18
Annabelle Comes Home '19
Captive State '19
Godzilla: King of the Monsters '19

Alberto Farnese (1926-96)
The White Angel '55
The Giants of Thessaly '60
Gladiator of Rome '63
Two Gladiators '64
Scalps '83

Matt Farnsworth (1975-)
The Stepdaughter '00
Iowa '05

Richard Farnsworth (1920-2000)
Texas Across the River '66
Strange New World '75
Comes a Horseman '78
Resurrection '80
Tom Horn '80
Legend of the Lone Ranger '81
Ruckus '81
Waltz across Texas '83
The Natural '84
Rhinestone '84
Anne of Green Gables '85
Into the Night '85
Sylvester '85
Witchery '88
Havana '90
Misery '90
The Two Jakes '90
The Fire Next Time '93
Lassie '94
The Straight Story '99

Franklyn Farnum (1878-1961)
Battling with Buffalo Bill '31
Prison Train '38
Destination Murder '50

William Farnum (1876-1953)
The Painted Desert '31
Mr. Robinson Crusoe '32
Supernatural '33
The Silver Streak '34
The Crusades '35
The Clutching Hand '36
Custer's Last Stand '36
Undersea Kingdom '36
The Vigilantes Are Coming '36
South of the Border '39
Adventures of Red Ryder '40
My Dog Shep '46
Trail of Robin Hood '50
Jack & the Beanstalk '52
Lone Star '52

Derek Farr (1912-86)
Spellbound '41
Value for Money '55

Diane Farr (1969-)
SuperFire '02
Collision Earth '11
About Cherry '12

Felicia Farr (1932-)
The First Texan '56
Jubal '56
3:10 to Yuma '57
Onionhead '58
Kiss Me, Stupid! '64
The Venetian Affair '67
Kotch '71
Charley Varrick '73

Jamie Farr (1936-)
Blackboard Jungle '55
No Time for Sergeants '58
The Loved One '65
Who's Minding the Mint? '67
With Six You Get Eggroll '68
Heavy Traffic '73
Cannonball Run '81
Return of the Rebels '81
M*A*S*H: Goodbye, Farewell & Amen '83
Cannonball Run 2 '84
Happy Hour '87
Curse 2: The Bite '88
Scrooged '88
Fearless Tiger '94
A Grandpa for Christmas '07

Judi Farr
The Year My Voice Broke '87
Walking on Water '02

Patricia Farr (1915-48)
Tailspin Tommy '34
Mistaken Identity '36

David Farrar (1908-95)
The Hooded Terror '38
Echo Murders '45
Black Narcissus '47
The Small Back Room '49
The Black Shield of Falworth '54
Let's Make Up '55
Pearl of the South Pacific '55
Sea Chase '55
Beat Girl '60
The 300 Spartans '62

Charles Farrell (1900-90)
7th Heaven '27
Street Angel '28
Lucky Star '29
City Girl '30
Liliom '30
After Tomorrow '32
Just Around the Corner '38
Moonlight Sonata '38
Tail Spin '39

Charles Farrell (1901-88)
Boys Will Be Boys '35
They Made Me a Fugitive '47
Night and the City '50
Crimson Pirate '52
The Sheriff of Fractured Jaw '59
The Girl Hunters '63
The Vampire Lovers '70
The Abominable Dr. Phibes '71

Colin Farrell (1938-)
Oh! What a Lovely War '69
The Land That Time Forgot '75
A Bridge Too Far '77
The Imaginarium of Doctor Parnassus '09
Winter's Tale '14

Colin Farrell (1976-)
Falling for a Dancer '98
The War Zone '98
Ordinary Decent Criminal '99
Tigerland '00
American Outlaws '01
Hart's War '02
Minority Report '02
Phone Booth '02
Daredevil '03
Intermission '03
The Recruit '03
S.W.A.T. '03
Veronica Guerin '03
Alexander '04
A Home at the End of the World '04
The New World '05
Ask the Dust '06
Miami Vice '06
In Bruges '08
Pride and Glory '08
Crazy Heart '09
Ondine '09
Triage '09
London Boulevard '10
The Way Back '10
Fright Night '11
Horrible Bosses '11
Seven Psychopaths '12
Total Recall '12
Dead Man Down '13
Epic '13 (V)
Saving Mr. Banks '13
Miss Julie '14
Fantastic Beasts and Where to Find Them '16
The Lobster '16
Solace '16
The Beguiled '17
The Killing of a Sacred Deer '17
Roman J. Israel, Esq. '17
Dumbo '19
The Gentlemen '20

Frida Farrell
Cyborg Conquest '09
Behind Your Eyes '11

Glenda Farrell (1904-71)
Little Caesar '30
I Am a Fugitive from a Chain Gang '32
Bureau of Missing Persons '33
Girl Missing '33
Lady for a Day '33
Mystery of the Wax Museum '33
Dark Hazard '34
Hi, Nellie! '34
I've Got Your Number '34
Go Into Your Dance '35
Gold Diggers of 1935 '35
In Caliente '35
The Secret Bride '35
Gold Diggers of 1937 '36
Breakfast for Two '37
Hollywood Hotel '37
Smart Blonde '37
Prison Break '38
Johnny Eager '42
Talk of the Town '42
City Without Men '43
Heading for Heaven '47
Lulu Belle '48
The Girl in the Red Velvet Swing '55
Middle of the Night '59
Disorderly Orderly '64
Kissin' Cousins '64

Mike Farrell (1939-)
Escape from Planet Earth '67
The Graduate '67
The Questor Tapes '74
Prime Suspect '82
M*A*S*H: Goodbye, Farewell & Amen '83
Lockdown '90
The Price of the Bride '90
Out at the Wedding '07

Nicholas Farrell (1955-)
Hold the Dream '86
To Play the King '93
A Midwinter's Tale '95
Othello '95
Hamlet '96
Sharpe's Regiment '96
Twelfth Night '96
Legionnaire '98
Beautiful People '99
Bloody Sunday '01
Charlotte Gray '01
Bait '02
Amazing Grace '06
Blackbeard '06
Driving Lessons '06
The Diary of Anne Frank '08
Collision '09

The Iron Lady '11
Finding Altamira '16

Sharon Farrell (1946-)
40 Pounds of Trouble '62
A Lovely Way to Die '68
Marlowe '69
The Reivers '69
The Love Machine '71
The Eyes of Charles Sand '74
It's Alive '74
The Premonition '75
The Stunt Man '80
Baby Broker '81
Night of the Comet '84
Can't Buy Me Love '87
One Man Force '89
Arcade '93
Beyond Desire '94

Terry Farrell (1963-)
Back to School '86
Hellraiser 3: Hell on Earth '92
Danielle Steel's Star '93
Legion '98
Deep Core '00

Timothy Farrell (1923-89)
Test Tube Babies '48
The Devil's Sleep '51
Pin Down Girls '51
Glen or Glenda? '53
Jail Bait '54

Mia Farrow (1945-)
Guns at Batasi '64
Dandy in Aspic '68
Rosemary's Baby '68
Goodbye, Raggedy Ann '71
See No Evil '71
The Great Gatsby '74
Avalanche '78
Death on the Nile '78
A Wedding '78
Hurricane '79
The Last Unicorn '82 (V)
A Midsummer Night's Sex Comedy '82
Zelig '83
Broadway Danny Rose '84
Supergirl '84
The Purple Rose of Cairo '85
Hannah and Her Sisters '86
Radio Days '87
Another Woman '88
September '88
Crimes & Misdemeanors '89
New York Stories '89
Alice '90
Husbands and Wives '92
Shadows and Fog '92
Widow's Peak '94
Miami Rhapsody '95
Miracle at Midnight '98
Coming Soon '99
A Girl Thing '01
Purpose '02
The Secret of Zoey '02
Arthur and the Invisibles '06
The Omen '06
The Ex '07
Be Kind Rewind '08
Dark Horse '11

Tisa Farrow (1951-)
Fingers '78
Initiation of Sarah '78
Manhattan '79
Winter Kills '79
Anthropophagus: The Grim Reaper '80
The Last Hunter '80
Zombie '80
Grim Reaper '81
Search and Destroy '81

Michael Fassbender (1977-)
Angel '07
300 '07
Hunger '08
Blood Creek '09
Fish Tank '09
Inglourious Basterds '09
Centurion '10
Jonah Hex '10
A Dangerous Method '11
Jane Eyre '11
Shame '11
X-Men: First Class '11
Haywire '12
Prometheus '12
The Counselor '13
12 Years a Slave '13
Frank '14
X-Men: Days of Future Past '14
Macbeth '15
Slow West '15
Steve Jobs '15
Assassin's Creed '16
The Light Between Oceans '16
Trespass Against Us '16
X-Men: Apocalypse '16
Alien: Covenant '17
The Snowman '17
Song to Song '17
Dark Phoenix '19

Rainer Werner Fassbinder (1946-82)
The American Soldier '70
Beware of a Holy Whore '70
Whity '70
Tenderness of the Wolves '73
Fox and His Friends '75

Ron Fassler (1957-)
Alien Nation: Dark Horizon '94
Alien Nation: The Enemy Within '96

Alexia Fast
Past Tense '06
Kickin' It Old Skool '07
The Party Never Stops '07
Helen '09
Triple Dog '09
The 19th Wife '10
Jack Reacher '12
Last Kind Words '12
The Captive '14

Fat Joe (1970-)
Thicker than Water '99
Urban Menace '99
Empire '02

Daniel Fathers (1966-)
Crazy for Christmas '05
Camp Rock 2: The Final Jam '10
The Void '17

Joey Fatone (1977-)
On the Line '01
My Big Fat Greek Wedding '02
The Cooler '03
Beethoven's Big Break '08

Kent Faulcon (1971-)
Strange Fruit '04
Sister's Keeper '07

Andrew Faulds (1922-2000)
The Devils '71
Lisztomania '75

James Faulkner (1948-)
Conduct Unbecoming '75
Lace 2 '85
Just Another Secret '89
Devices and Desires '91
The Blackheath Poisonings '92
Crimetime '96
A Kid in Aladdin's Palace '97
All the Little Animals '98
I Capture the Castle '02
The Target '02
Agent Cody Banks 2: Destination London '04
Day of Wrath '06
The Bank Job '08
Franklyn '08
Paul, Apostle of Christ '18

Sally Faulkner (1944-)
Vampyres '74
Alien Prey '78

Stephanie Faulkner
Death Journey '76
Virus '82

Chad Faust (1980-)
Saved! '04
Nearing Grace '05
Tamara '05
Descent '07

David Faustino (1974-)
Perfect Harmony '91
Alien Nation: Millennium '96
Criminal Desire '98
Killer Bud '00
MacArthur Park '01
The Boston Strangler: The Untold Story '08
National Lampoon Presents RoboDoc '08
Not Another B Movie '10

Paul Fauteux
Hustle '04
The Prodigy '19

Pierfrancesco Favino (1969-)
The Last Kiss '01
Our Italian Husband '04
The Unknown Woman '06
Saturn in Opposition '07
The Chronicles of Narnia: Prince Caspian '08
Miracle at St. Anna '08

Jon Favreau (1966-)
Rudy '93
P.C.U. '94
Batman Forever '95
Notes from Underground '95
Persons Unknown '96
Swingers '96
Dogtown '97
Deep Impact '98
Very Bad Things '98
Rocky Marciano '99
Love & Sex '00
The Replacements '00
Made '01
Daredevil '03
Elf '03
Something's Gotta Give '03
The Big Empty '04
Wimbledon '04
The Break-Up '06
Open Season '06 (V)
Four Christmases '08
Iron Man '08
Couples Retreat '09
G-Force '09 (V)
I Love You, Man '09
Iron Man 2 '10
Brother's Justice '11
Zookeeper '11 (V)
Identity Thief '13
Iron Man 3 '13
The Wolf of Wall Street '13
Chef '14
Term Life '16
Spider-Man: Homecoming '17
Spider-Man: Far from Home '19

Farrah Fawcett (1946-2009)
Myra Breckinridge '70
Murder on Flight 502 '75
Logan's Run '76
Saturn 3 '80
Cannonball Run '81
The Burning Bed '85
Extremities '86
Poor Little Rich Girl: The Barbara Hutton Story '87
See You in the Morning '89
The Substitute Wife '94
Dalva '95
A Good Day to Die '95
Man of the House '95
The Apostle '97
Baby '00
Dr. T & the Women '00
Hollywood Wives: The New Generation '03
The Cookout '04

George Fawcett (1860-1939)
The Greatest Question '19
The Merry Widow '25
Up the Ladder '25
Captain Salvation '27
The Flesh and the Devil '27
Spring Fever '27
Tempest '28
Tide of Empire '29
Ladies of Leisure '30
Drums of Jeopardy '31

William 'Bill' Fawcett (1894-1974)
Seminole Uprising '55
Gun Glory '57
Storm Rider '57
Jesse James Meets Frankenstein's Daughter '65
King Rat '65

Nat Faxon (1975-)
Club Dread '04
Zookeeper '11
The Babymakers '12
The Way Way Back '13
Sex Tape '14
Tammy '14

Frank Fay (1891-1961)
Bright Lights '30
The Matrimonial Bed '30
God's Gift to Women '31
Spotlight Scandals '43
Love Nest '51

Meagen Fay (1957-)
Armistead Maupin's Tales of the City '93
The Country Bears '02
Working Miracles '10

Alice Faye (1915-98)
365 Nights in Hollywood '34
George White's Scandals of 1935 '35
Sing, Baby, Sing '36
Stowaway '36
In Old Chicago '37
On the Avenue '37
Wake Up and Live '37
You Can't Have Everything '37
Alexander's Ragtime Band '38
Sally, Irene and Mary '38
Hollywood Cavalcade '39
Rose of Washington Square '39
Tail Spin '39
Lillian Russell '40
The Great American Broadcast '41
That Night in Rio '41
Week-End in Havana '41
The Gang's All Here '43
Hello, Frisco, Hello '43
Fallen Angel '45
State Fair '62
Every Girl Should Have One '78

Denise Faye (1963-)
The Next Step '95
American Pie 2 '01

Janina Faye (1948-)
Never Take Candy From a Stranger '60
Day of the Triffids '63

Julia Faye
Chicago '27
The Fighting Eagle '27

Frank Faylen (1905-85)
They Won't Forget '37
Gone with the Wind '39
Sergeant York '41
Across the Pacific '42
Wake Island '42
Silver Skates '43
The Lost Weekend '45
Blue Skies '46
It's a Wonderful Life '46
The Road to Rio '47
Welcome Stranger '47
Race Street '48
Whispering Smith '48
Francis the Talking Mule '49
Convicted '50
Copper Canyon '50
The Nevadan '50
Detective Story '51
Hangman's Knot '52
The Sniper '52
99 River Street '53
Red Garters '54
Riot in Cell Block 11 '54
The McConnell Story '55
Seventh Cavalry '56
Gunfight at the O.K. Corral '57
When the Boys Meet the Girls '65

Ali Fazal (1986-)
Bollywood Hero '09
Victoria & Abdul '17

Louise Fazenda (1895-1962)
The Bat '26
On with the Show '29
Loose Ankles '30
Rain or Shine '30
Wonder Bar '34
Colleen '36
Swing Your Lady '38
The Old Maid '39

Ron Fazio
The Toxic Avenger, Part 2 '89
The Toxic Avenger, Part 3: The Last Temptation of Toxie '89
Basket Case 2 '90

Michael Feast (1946-)
Touching Evil '97
Velvet Goldmine '98
Penelope '06
The Deaths of Ian Stone '07

Katie Featherston (1982-)
Paranormal Activity '09
Paranormal Activity 2 '10
Psychic Experiment '10
Paranormal Activity 3 '11
Paranormal Activity 4 '12

Angela Featherstone (1965-)
Dark Angel: The Ascent '94
Family of Cops '95
Con Air '97
Family of Cops 2: Breach of Faith '97
The Wedding Singer '97
Zero Effect '97
Palmetto '98
200 Cigarettes '98
The Guilty '99
Skipped Parts '00
Federal Protection '02
One Way Out '02
Pressure '02
What Doesn't Kill You '08
Beneath the Dark '10

Birgitte Federspiel (1925-2005)
Ordet '55
Babette's Feast '87

Matreya Fedor
In Her Mother's Footsteps '06
Electra Woman & Dyna Girl '16

Melinda Fee (1942-2020)
Fade to Black '80
Doin' Time '85

Caroleen Feeney
Cadillac Ranch '96
Bad Manners '98
Avalanche '99
Happy Hour '03

Oakes Fegley
Pete's Dragon '16
Wonderstruck '17
The Goldfinch '19

Alexander Fehling
Young Goethe in Love '11
Three Peaks '19

Bekim Fehmiu (1936-2010)
The Adventurers '70
Ride to Glory '71
Battle of the Eagles '79

Brendan Fehr (1977-)
Christina's House '99
The Forsaken '01
Kill Me Later '01
Edge of Madness '02
Biker Boyz '03
Nemesis Game '03
The Long Weekend '05
The Cutting Edge: Fire and Ice '10
Ice Quake '10
Fort McCoy '11
Silent Night '12
Stranded '13

Oded Fehr (1970-)
Deuce Bigalow: Male Gigolo '99
The Mummy '99
The Mummy Returns '01
Texas Rangers '01
Resident Evil: Apocalypse '04
Deuce Bigalow: European Gigolo '05
Dreamer: Inspired by a True Story '05
Sleeper Cell '05
Resident Evil: Extinction '07
Super Hybrid '10
Resident Evil: Retribution '12

Trevor Fehrman (1981-)
Now You Know '02
Clerks 2 '06

Martin Feifel (1964-)
What to Do in Case of Fire '02
Rosenstrasse '03

Halley Feiffer (1984-)
The Squid and the Whale '05
Stephanie Daley '06
Margot at the Wedding '07
Gentlemen Broncos '09
Free Samples '12
Appropriate Behavior '14

J.J. Feild (1978-)
Last Orders '01
The Intended '02
Ruby in the Smoke '06
The Secret Life of Mrs. Beeton '06
Northanger Abbey '07
O Jerusalem '07
The Shadow in the North '07
Telstar: The Joe Meek Story '08
Centurion '10
Austenland '13
Professor Marston and the Wonder Women '17
The Etruscan Smile '19

Alan Feinstein (1941-)
Joe Panther '76
The Two Worlds of Jenny Logan '79

Fritz Feld (1900-93)
The Last Command '28
True Confession '37
Artists and Models Abroad '38
Bringing Up Baby '38
Gold Diggers in Paris '38
At the Circus '39
The Mexican Spitfire's Baby '41
Iceland '42
Maisie Gets Her Man '42
Mexican Hayride '48
The Noose Hangs High '48
Kentucky Jubilee '51
The Errand Boy '61
Promises! Promises! '63
The Strongest Man in the World '75
World's Greatest Lover '77
Herbie Goes Bananas '80
History of the World: Part 1 '81
Barfly '87
Get Smart, Again! '89

Andrea Feldman (1948-72)
Trash '70
Heat '72

Ben Feldman (1980-)
The Perfect Man '05
When Do We Eat? '05
As Above, So Below '14

Corey Feldman (1971-)
The Fox and the Hound '81 (V)

Friday the 13th, Part 4: The Final Chapter *'84*
Gremlins *'84*
Friday the 13th, Part 5: A New Beginning *'85*
The Goonies *'85*
Stand by Me *'86*
The Lost Boys *'87*
License to Drive *'88*
The 'Burbs *'89*
Dream a Little Dream *'89*
Teenage Mutant Ninja Turtles: The Movie *'90 (V)*
Edge of Honor *'91*
Rock 'n' Roll High School Forever *'91*
Meatballs 4 *'92*
Stepmonster *'92*
Blown Away *'93*
Lipstick Camera *'93*
The Magic Voyage *'93 (V)*
National Lampoon's Loaded Weapon 1 *'93*
A Dangerous Place *'94*
Dream a Little Dream 2 *'94*
National Lampoon's Last Resort *'94*
Voodoo *'95*
Red Line *'96*
South Beach Academy *'96*
Tales from the Crypt Presents Bordello of Blood *'96*
Born Bad *'97*
Legion *'98*
Storm Trooper *'98*
The Million Dollar Kid *'99*
No Witness *'04*
Lost Boys: The Tribe *'08*
Terror Inside *'08*
Lost Boys: The Thirst *'10*
6 Degrees of Hell *'12*
The M Word *'14*

Marty Feldman (1933-82)
Young Frankenstein *'74*
Silent Movie *'76*
The Last Remake of Beau Geste *'77*
The Adventures of Sherlock Holmes' Smarter Brother *'78*
Yellowbeard *'83*

Tibor Feldman (1947-)
River Red *'98*
David & Layla *'07*

Barbara Feldon (1933-)
Fitzwilly *'67*
Smile *'75*
No Deposit, No Return *'76*
A Guide for the Married Woman *'78*
Get Smart, Again! *'89*
The Last Request *'06*

Tovah Feldshuh (1953-)
The Amazing Howard Hughes *'77*
Holocaust *'78*
Terror Out of the Sky *'78*
The Triangle Factory Fire Scandal *'79*
Idolmaker *'80*
Brewster's Millions *'85*
Blue Iguana *'88*
A Day in October *'92*
The Corruptor *'99*
A Walk on the Moon *'99*
Happy Accidents *'00*
Friends and Family *'01*
Kissing Jessica Stein *'02*
The Tollbooth *'04*
Just My Luck *'06*
Lady in the Water *'06*
Language of the Enemy *'07*
Love Comes Lately *'07*
O Jerusalem *'07*

Beanie Feldstein
Neighbors 2: Sorority Rising *'16*
The Female Brain *'18*
Booksmart *'19*
How to Build a Girl *'20*

Jose Feliciano (1945-)
Aaron Loves Angela *'75 (C)*
Fargo *'96*

Maria Felix (1914-2002)
French Can-Can *'55*
Beyond All Limits *'59*

Norman Fell (1924-98)
Pork Chop Hill *'59*
Inherit the Wind *'60*
Ocean's 11 *'60*
It's a Mad, Mad, Mad, Mad World *'63*
The Killers *'64*
Fitzwilly *'67*
The Graduate *'67*
Bullitt *'68*
If It's Tuesday, This Must Be Belgium *'69*
The Boatniks *'70*
Catch-22 *'70*
Charley Varrick *'73*
The Stone Killer *'73*
Cleopatra Jones & the Casino of Gold *'75*
The End *'78*
For the Love of It *'80*
Transylvania 6-5000 *'85*
Stripped to Kill *'87*
The Bone Yard *'90*
For the Boys *'91*
Hexed *'93*

Tom Felleghi (1920-)
Revenge of the Barbarians *'60*
Hornets' Nest *'70*

Federico Fellini (1920-93)
Alex in Wonderland *'70 (C)*
Fellini's Roma *'72 (V)*
We All Loved Each Other So Much *'77*
Intervista *'87*
Fellini: I'm a Born Liar *'03*

Rosie Fellner (1978-)
The Crew *'08*
2 Jacks *'12*
The Trip to Italy *'14*

Julian Fellowes (1949-)
Baby. . . Secret of the Lost Legend *'85*
Damage *'92*
Sharpe's Rifles *'93*
The Final Cut *'95*
Behind the Lines *'97*
Aristocrats *'99*
The Aristocrats *'99*

Rockliffe Fellowes (1885-1950)
Regeneration *'15*
Monkey Business *'31*

Edith Fellows (1923-2011)
The Rider of Death Valley *'32*
The Keeper of the Bees *'35*
And So They Were Married *'36*
Pennies from Heaven *'36*
City Streets *'38*
Music in My Heart *'40*
Heart of the Rio Grande *'42*
In the Mood *'87*

Tom Felton (1987-)
The Borrowers *'97*
Anna and the King *'99*
Harry Potter and the Sorcerer's Stone *'01*
Harry Potter and the Chamber of Secrets *'02*
Harry Potter and the Prisoner of Azkaban *'04*
Harry Potter and the Goblet of Fire *'05*
Harry Potter and the Order of the Phoenix *'07*
The Disappeared *'08*
Harry Potter and the Half-Blood Prince *'09*
Harry Potter and the Deathly Hallows, Part 1 *'10*
Harry Potter and the Deathly Hallows, Part 2 *'11*
Rise of the Planet of the Apes *'11*
The Apparition *'12*
Labyrinth *'12*
Belle *'13*
In Secret *'13*
Against the Sun *'15*
Risen *'16*

Megan Leavey *'17*
A United Kingdom *'17*
Ophelia *'19*

Verna Felton (1890-1966)
Cinderella *'50 (V)*
Belles on Their Toes *'52*
Lady and the Tramp *'55 (V)*
Picnic *'55*
The Oklahoman *'56*
Sleeping Beauty *'59 (V)*
The Jungle Book *'67 (V)*

Freddy Fender (1937-2006)
She Came to the Valley *'77*
The Milagro Beanfield War *'88*

Edwige Fenech (1948-)
Five Dolls for an August Moon *'70*
The Case of the Bloody Iris *'72*
Your Vice is a Closed Room and Only I Have the Key *'72*
Escape from Death Row *'73*
Hostel: Part 2 *'07*

Shaofeng Feng
Painted Skin: The Resurrection *'12*
Wolf Totem *'15*

Sherilyn Fenn (1965-)
Silence of the Heart *'84*
Just One of the Guys *'85*
The Wraith *'87*
Zombie High *'87*
Two Moon Junction *'88*
True Blood *'89*
Backstreet Dreams *'90*
Wild at Heart *'90*
Diary of a Hitman *'91*
Desire and Hell at Sunset Motel *'92*
Of Mice and Men *'92*
Ruby *'92*
Boxing Helena *'93*
Fatal Instinct *'93*
Three of Hearts *'93*
Just Write *'97*
Lovelife *'97*
National Lampoon's The Don's Analyst *'97*
Darkness Falls *'98*
Cement *'99*
Off Season *'01*
Swindle *'02*
Nightwaves *'03*
United States of Leland *'03*
Deadly Isolation *'05*
The Dukes of Hazzard: The Beginning *'06*
Novel Romance *'06*
Presumed Dead *'06*
Treasure Raiders *'07*
The Scenesters *'09*
The Brittany Murphy Story *'14*

Emerald Fennell (1985-)
Any Human Heart *'11*
The Danish Girl *'15*

Parker Fennelly (1891-1988)
The Kettles on Old MacDonald's Farm *'57*
How to Frame a Figg *'71*

George Fenneman (1919-97)
The Thing *'51*
How to Succeed in Business without Really Trying *'67*

Shelby Fenner (1978-)
Local Boys *'02*
The Guardian *'06*

Frank Fenton (1906-57)
Isle of Forgotten Sins *'43*
Mexican Hayride *'48*
The Golden Stallion *'49*
Island in the Sky *'53*
Naked Hills *'56*
Hell Bound *'57*

Lance Fenton (1966-)
Night of the Demons *'88*
Heathers *'89*

Leslie Fenton (1902-78)
Lazybones *'25*
The Guilty Generation *'31*
Murder at Midnight *'31*
Public Enemy *'31*
The Hatchet Man *'32*
The Strange Love of Molly Louvain *'32*
F.P. 1 *'33*
Lady Killer *'33*
Fugitive Road *'34*
Marie Galante *'34*
Murder On a Bridle Path *'36*
The House of Secrets *'37*

Simon Fenton (1976-)
Matinee *'92*
The Rector's Wife *'94*
A Knight in Camelot *'98*

Robyn Rihanna Fenty (1988-)
See Rihanna

Perry Fenwick (1962-)
The Raggedy Rawney *'90*
The Winslow Boy *'98*

Colm Feore (1958-)
Beautiful Dreamers *'92*
32 Short Films about Glenn Gould *'93*
Truman *'95*
Night Falls on Manhattan *'96*
The Wrong Guy *'96*
Critical Care *'97*
Face/Off *'97*
Hostile Waters *'97*
Airborne *'98*
City of Angels *'98*
The Red Violin *'98*
The Insider *'99*
Stephen King's The Storm of the Century *'99*
Titus *'99*
The Virginian *'99*
The Perfect Son *'00*
The Caveman's Valentine *'01*
The Day Reagan Was Shot *'01*
Ignition *'01*
Pearl Harbor *'01*
Sins of the Father *'01*
Chicago *'02*
Point of Origin *'02*
The Sum of All Fears *'02*
Widows *'02*
And Starring Pancho Villa as Himself *'03*
Highwaymen *'03*
National Security *'03*
Paycheck *'03*
The Chronicles of Riddick *'04*
The Deal *'05*
The Exorcism of Emily Rose *'05*
Lies My Mother Told Me *'05*
Bon Cop Bad Cop *'06*
Bury My Heart at Wounded Knee *'07*
Hearts of War *'07*
Changeling *'08*
Guns *'08*
24: Redemption *'08*
WarGames: The Dead Code *'08*
The Trotsky *'09*
Thor *'11*
House of Versace *'13*
The Amazing Spider-Man 2 *'14*
Jack Ryan: Shadow Recruit *'14*
Painkillers *'15*
Higher Power *'18*
The Prodigy *'19*

Heino Ferch (1963-)
Winter Sleepers *'97*
Tower of the Firstborn *'98*
The Harmonists *'99*
Straight Shooter *'99*
The Tunnel *'01*
Extreme Ops *'02*
Napoleon *'03*
Downfall *'04*
The 4 Musketeers *'05*
The Trojan Horse *'08*
Vision *'09*

Pamelyn Ferdin (1959-)
Charlotte's Web *'73 (V)*
The Toolbox Murders *'78*

Peter Ferdinando
A Field in England *'14*
Hyena *'15*
Vita & Virginia *'19*

Tawny (Ellis) Fere
Angel 3: The Final Chapter *'88*
Rockula *'90*

Al Ferguson (1888-1971)
Tarzan the Tiger *'29*
The Three Musketeers *'33*
Rose Marie *'54*

Amy Ferguson
Garden State *'04*
Tanner Hall *'09*
Douchebag *'10*
Welcome to New York *'15*

Chloe Ferguson (1989-)
Alien Visitor *'95*
The Quiet Room *'96*

Colin Ferguson (1972-)
Rowing Through *'96*
Armistead Maupin's More Tales of the City *'97*
The Opposite of Sex *'98*
Confessions of a Sociopathic Social Climber *'05*
Mom at Sixteen *'05*
The House Next Door *'06*
Playing House *'06*
Because I Said So *'07*
Christmas in Paradise *'07*
Lake Placid 3 *'10*

Craig Ferguson (1962-)
The Big Tease *'99*
Born Romantic *'00*
Chain of Fools *'00*
Saving Grace *'00*
Life Without Dick *'01*
I'll Be There *'03*
Niagara Motel *'06*
How to Train Your Dragon *'10 (V)*
Winnie the Pooh *'11 (V)*
Brave *'12 (V)*
How to Train Your Dragon 2 *'14 (V)*

Frank Ferguson (1899-1978)
Abbott and Costello Meet Frankenstein *'48*
Slightly French *'49*
Wagons West *'52*
Johnny Guitar *'53*
Battle Cry *'55*
Gun Duel In Durango *'57*
Andy Hardy Comes Home *'58*

J. Don Ferguson (1933-2008)
Loveless *'83*
The Second Chance *'06*

Jay R. Ferguson (1974-)
Campfire Tales *'98*
Blue Ridge Fall *'99*
The Killer Inside Me *'10*
A Stand Up Guy *'16*

Jennifer Ferguson
Sam & Janet *'02*
Atom Nine Adventures *'07*

Keena Ferguson
Consinsual *'10*
Red Line *'13*

Kevin Ferguson
Locked Down *'10*
The Scorpion King 3: Battle for Redemption *'11*

Mark Ferguson (1961-)
Hercules the Legendary Journeys, Vol. 3: The Circle of Fire *'94*
Hercules the Legendary Journeys, Vol. 4: In the Underworld *'94*

Matthew Ferguson (1973-)
Love and Human Remains *'93*
Lilies *'96*

The Wall *'99*
Cube 2: Hypercube *'02*

Phoebe Ferguson (1993-)
Alien Visitor *'95*
The Quiet Room *'96*

Rebecca Ferguson (1983-)
Hercules *'14*
The Red Tent *'14*
Mission: Impossible Rogue Nation *'15*
Florence Foster Jenkins *'16*
The Girl on the Train *'16*
The Greatest Showman *'17*
Life *'17*
The Snowman *'17*
Mission: Impossible-Fallout *'18*
Doctor Sleep *'19*
Men in Black: International *'19*

Stacy 'Fergie' Ferguson (1975-)
Poseidon *'06*
Planet Terror *'07*
Nine *'09*
Marmaduke *'10 (V)*

Tom Ferguson (1946-)
Dark Universe *'93*
Biohazard: The Alien Force *'95*

Sabrina Ferilli
The Great Beauty *'13*
Me, Myself and Her *'16*

Jodelle Ferland (1994-)
Mermaid *'00*
Too Cool for Christmas *'04*
Tideland *'05*
The Secret of Hidden Lake *'06*
Silent Hill *'06*
Pictures of Hollis Woods *'07*
Celine *'08*
Seed *'08*
Wonderful World *'09*
Case 39 *'10*
Ice Quake *'10*
The Twilight Saga: Eclipse *'10*
Girl Fight *'11*
Home Alone: The Holiday Heist *'12*
Mighty Fine *'12*
The Tall Man *'12*

Vanessa Ferlito (1980-)
On_Line *'01*
Undefeated *'03*
Spider-Man 2 *'04*
Man of the House *'05*
Shadowboxer *'06*
Death Proof *'07*
Nothing Like the Holidays *'08*
Julie & Julia *'09*
Madea Goes to Jail *'09*
Wall Street 2: Money Never Sleeps *'10*
Stand Up Guys *'12*

Fernando Fernan-Gomez (1921-2007)
Spirit of the Beehive *'73*
Belle Epoque *'92*
Butterfly *'98*
The Grandfather *'98*

Fernandel (1903-71)
Well-Digger's Daughter *'46*
The Red Inn *'51*
The French Touch *'54*
The Sheep Has Five Legs *'54*
Around the World in 80 Days *'56 (C)*
Paris Holiday *'57*

Miguel Fernandes
The Kidnapping of the President *'80*
True Believer *'89*

Abel Fernandez (1930-)
Rose Marie *'54*
Fort Yuma *'55*
Target Zero *'55*
Pork Chop Hill *'59*

Adam Fidusiewicz (1985-)
In Desert and Wilderness *'01*
Lansdown *'01*

John Fiedler (1925-2005)
Twelve Angry Men *'57*
A Raisin in the Sun *'61*
Kiss Me, Stupid! *'64*
A Fine Madness *'66*
The Odd Couple *'68*
True Grit *'69*
Skyjacked *'72*
Bad Ronald *'74*
The Many Adventures of Winnie the Pooh *'77 (V)*
Harper Valley P.T.A. *'78*
The Fox and the Hound *'81 (V)*
Sharky's Machine *'81*
I Am the Cheese *'83*
The Emperor's New Groove *'00 (V)*
Piglet's Big Movie *'03 (V)*

Arabella Field (1965-)
Laws of Gravity *'92*
The Pompatus of Love *'95*
Dante's Peak *'97*
Godzilla *'98*
Blowin' Smoke *'99*
Paper Man *'09*

Betty Field (1913-73)
Of Mice and Men *'39*
What a Life *'39*
Blues in the Night *'41*
Kings Row *'41*
The Shepherd of the Hills *'41*
The Great Moment *'44*
Tomorrow the World *'44*
The Southerner *'45*
Picnic *'55*
Bus Stop *'56*
Peyton Place *'57*
Butterfield 8 *'60*
Birdman of Alcatraz *'62*
Coogan's Bluff *'68*

Chelsea Field (1957-)
Commando *'85*
Skin Deep *'89*
Murder C.O.D. *'90*
The Dark Half *'91*
Harley Davidson and the Marlboro Man *'91*
The Last Boy Scout *'91*
Dust Devil *'93*
Extreme Justice *'93*
Snapdragon *'93*
Andre *'94*
Texas *'94*
Indictment: The McMartin Trial *'95*
Flipper *'96*
Tom Clancy's Netforce *'98*
Wicked *'98*
The Unsaid *'01*

David Field
Blackrock *'97*
Two Hands *'98*
Mr. Accident *'99*
Chopper *'00*
Blood Crime *'02*
The Night We Called It a Day *'03*
Battle of the Damned *'14*

Karin (Karen) Field
Web of the Spider *'70*
The Mad Butcher *'72*

Margaret Field (1922-2011)
The Man from Planet X *'51*
1,000 Years From Now *'52*
Tall Lie *'53*

Mary Field (1896-1968)
Mrs. Miniver *'42*
Wake Island *'42*
To Hell and Back *'55*

Sally Field (1946-)
The Way West *'67*
Maybe I'll Come Home in the Spring *'71*
Mongo's Back In Town *'71*
Stay Hungry *'76*
Sybil *'76*
Heroes *'77*
Smokey and the Bandit *'77*
The End *'78*
Hooper *'78*
Beyond the Poseidon Adventure *'79*
Norma Rae *'79*
Smokey and the Bandit 2 *'80*
Absence of Malice *'81*
Back Roads *'81*
Kiss Me Goodbye *'82*
Places in the Heart *'84*
Murphy's Romance *'85*
Punchline *'88*
Steel Magnolias *'89*
Not Without My Daughter *'90*
Soapdish *'91*
Homeward Bound: The Incredible Journey *'93 (V)*
Mrs. Doubtfire *'93*
Forrest Gump *'94*
A Woman of Independent Means *'94*
An Eye for an Eye *'95*
Homeward Bound 2: Lost in San Francisco *'96 (V)*
Where the Heart Is *'00*
Say It Isn't So *'01*
Legally Blonde 2: Red White & Blonde *'03*
Two Weeks *'06*
The Amazing Spider-Man *'12*
Lincoln *'12*
The Amazing Spider-Man 2 *'14*

Shirley Anne Field (1938-)
Horrors of the Black Museum *'59*
Beat Girl *'60*
The Entertainer *'60*
Once More, With Feeling *'60*
Peeping Tom *'60*
Saturday Night and Sunday Morning *'60*
War Lover *'62*
Kings of the Sun *'63*
These Are the Damned *'63*
Alfie *'66*
Doctor in Clover *'66*
House of the Living Dead *'73*
My Beautiful Laundrette *'85*
Getting It Right *'89*
Shag: The Movie *'89*
Lady Chatterley *'92*

Todd Field (1964-)
Eye of the Eagle 2 *'89*
Gross Anatomy *'89*
Sleep with Me *'94*
Walking and Talking *'96*
Broken Vessels *'98*
Eyes Wide Shut *'99*
The Haunting *'99*
Stranger than Fiction *'99*
Rip It Off *'02*

Virginia Field (1917-92)
Career Woman *'36*
Lloyds of London *'36*
Charlie Chan at Monte Carlo *'37*
Think Fast, Mr. Moto *'37*
The Cisco Kid and the Lady *'39*
Mr. Moto's Last Warning *'39*
Dance, Girl, Dance *'40*
Hudson's Bay *'40*
Waterloo Bridge *'40*
John Loves Mary *'48*
A Connecticut Yankee in King Arthur's Court *'49*
Dial 1119 *'50*
The Explosive Generation *'61*

Emma Fielding (1966-)
The Scarlet Tunic *'97*
A Respectable Trade *'98*
Speedy Death *'99*
Pandaemonium *'00*
Cranford *'08*
Return to Cranford *'09*

Fenella Fielding (1930-)
Carry On Screaming *'66*
Doctor in Clover *'66*

Marjorie Fielding (1892-1956)
Spring in Park Lane *'48*
Conspirator *'49*
The Lavender Hill Mob *'51*

Alexis Fields (1979-)
Jacked Up *'01*
What About Your Friends: Weekend Getaway *'02*

Charlie (Charles) Fields (1971-)
Fish Hawk *'79*
The Beniker Gang *'83*

Christopher John Fields
Alien 3 *'92*
The Gun in Betty Lou's Handbag *'92*

Holly Fields (1976-)
Seedpeople *'92*
Runaway Daughters *'94*
Wishmaster 2: Evil Never Dies *'98*
Interceptor Force *'99*

Kim Fields (1969-)
Uninvited Guest *'99*
A Cross to Bear *'12*
A Question of Faith *'17*

Norman Fields
Octaman *'71*
Dirty Mind of Young Sally *'72*

Stanley Fields (1884-1941)
Cimarron *'31*
Cracked Nuts *'31*
Girl Crazy *'32*
Island of Lost Souls *'32*
The Gay Desperado *'36*
Wide Open Faces *'38*
Blackwell's Island *'39*
Hell's Kitchen *'39*

Tony Fields (1958-95)
Trick or Treat *'86*
Backstreet Dreams *'90*
Across the Moon *'94*

W.C. Fields (1879-1946)
Sally of the Sawdust *'25*
It's the Old Army Game *'26*
If I Had a Million *'32*
International House *'33*
It's a Gift *'34*
Mrs. Wiggs of the Cabbage Patch *'34*
The Old-Fashioned Way *'34*
David Copperfield *'35*
The Man On the Flying Trapeze *'35*
Mississippi *'35*
The Big Broadcast of 1938 *'38*
You Can't Cheat an Honest Man *'39*
The Bank Dick *'40*
My Little Chickadee *'40*
Never Give a Sucker an Even Break *'41*
Tales of Manhattan *'42*
Sensations of 1945 *'44 (C)*

Joseph Fiennes (1970-)
Stealing Beauty *'96*
Elizabeth *'98*
Shakespeare in Love *'98*
The Very Thought of You *'98*
Forever Mine *'99*
Enemy at the Gates *'00*
Rancid Aluminium *'00*
Dust *'01*
Killing Me Softly *'01*
Leo *'02*
Luther *'03*
Sinbad: Legend of the Seven Seas *'03 (V)*
The Merchant of Venice *'04*
The Great Raid *'05*
The Darwin Awards *'06*
Running with Scissors *'06*
The Color of Freedom *'07*
The Escapist *'08*
The Red Baron *'08*
Spring 1941 *'08*
Against the Current *'09*
Strangerland *'15*
Risen *'16*

Ralph Fiennes (1962-)
A Dangerous Man: Lawrence after Arabia *'91*
Emily Bronte's Wuthering Heights *'92*
Prime Suspect *'92*
Schindler's List *'93*
Quiz Show *'94*
Strange Days *'95*
The English Patient *'96*
Oscar and Lucinda *'97*
The Avengers *'98*
Prince of Egypt *'98 (V)*
The End of the Affair *'99*
Onegin *'99*
Sunshine *'99*
The Miracle Maker: The Story of Jesus *'00 (V)*
Maid in Manhattan *'02*
Red Dragon *'02*
Spider *'02*
The Good Thief *'03*
The Chumscrubber *'05*
The Constant Gardener *'05*
Harry Potter and the Goblet of Fire *'05*
Wallace & Gromit in The Curse of the Were-Rabbit *'05 (V)*
The White Countess *'05*
Land of the Blind *'06*
Harry Potter and the Order of the Phoenix *'07*
Bernard and Doris *'08*
The Duchess *'08*
The Hurt Locker *'08*
In Bruges *'08*
The Reader *'08*
Cemetery Junction *'10*
Clash of the Titans *'10*
Harry Potter and the Deathly Hallows, Part 1 *'10*
Nanny McPhee Returns *'10*
The Wildest Dream: The Conquest of Everest *'10 (V)*
Coriolanus *'11*
Harry Potter and the Deathly Hallows, Part 2 *'11*
Page Eight *'11*
Great Expectations *'12*
Skyfall *'12*
Wrath of the Titans *'12*
The Invisible Woman *'13*
The Grand Budapest Hotel *'14*
A Bigger Splash *'15*
Spectre *'15*
Hail, Caesar! *'16*
Kubo and the Two Strings *'16*
The LEGO Batman Movie *'17*
The White Crow *'18*

Enzo Fiermonte
The Secret Invasion *'64*
The War of the Planets *'65*

Harvey Fierstein (1954-)
Garbo Talks *'84*
Torch Song Trilogy *'88*
The Harvest *'92*
Mrs. Doubtfire *'93*
Bullets over Broadway *'94*
Dr. Jekyll and Ms. Hyde *'95*
Independence Day *'96*
Kull the Conqueror *'97*
Mulan *'98 (V)*
Safe Men *'98*
Double Platinum *'99*
Playing Mona Lisa *'00*
Death to Smoochy *'02*
Duplex *'03*
Mulan 2 *'04 (V)*

50 Cent (1975-)
Get Rich or Die Tryin' *'05*
Home of the Brave *'06*
Righteous Kill *'08*
Dead Man Running *'09*
Streets of Blood *'09*
Blood Out *'10*
Caught in the Crossfire *'10*
Gun *'10*
13 *'10*
Twelve *'10*
Setup *'11*
Freelancers *'12*
The Frozen Ground *'13*
Southpaw *'15*
Den of Thieves *'18*

George Figgs (1947-)
Pink Flamingos *'72*
Female Trouble *'74*
Polyester *'81*

Efrain Figueroa
Star Maps *'97*
The Apostate *'98*
Desperate Measures *'98*
Eastside *'99*
The Visit *'00*
ESL: English as a Second Language *'05*

Kasia (Katarzyna) Figura (1962-)
Ready to Wear *'94*
Zemsta *'02*
Dead Man's Bounty *'06*

Vera Filatova
The Pagan Queen *'09*
Vampire Killers *'09*

Nathan Fillion (1971-)
Blast from the Past *'98*
Water's Edge *'03*
Outing Riley *'04*
Serenity *'05*
Slither *'06*
Waitress *'07*
White Noise 2: The Light *'07*
Trucker *'08*
Super *'10*
Monsters University *'13 (V)*
Much Ado About Nothing *'13*
Percy Jackson: Sea of Monsters *'13*
Cars 3 *'17 (V)*

Clyde Fillmore (1875-1946)
My Sister Eileen *'42*
Watch on the Rhine *'43*
Laura *'44*

Travis Fimmel (1979-)
Restraint *'08*
The Experiment *'10*
Needle *'10*
Pure Country 2: The Gift *'10*
The Baytown Outlaws *'12*
Maggie's Plan *'16*
Warcraft *'16*
Lean on Pete *'17*
Danger Close *'19*
Finding Steve McQueen *'19*

Dennis Fimple (1940-2002)
Truck Stop Women *'74*
Creature from Black Lake *'76*
King Kong *'76*
Of Mice and Men *'81*
House of 1000 Corpses *'03*

Brittany Renee Finamore
Babysitters Beware *'08*
Forget Me Not *'09*

Jon Finch (1942-2012)
Macbeth *'71*
Frenzy *'72*
The Final Programme *'73*
Game of Seduction *'76*
Death on the Nile *'78*
Breaking Glass *'80*
Peter and Paul *'81*
Doktor Faustus *'82*
Unexplained Laughter *'89*
Lurking Fear *'94*
Kingdom of Heaven *'05*

Peter Finch (1916-77)
The Fighting Rats of Tobruk *'44*
The Story of Robin Hood & His Merrie Men *'52*
Elephant Walk *'54*
Simon and Laura *'55*
The Warriors *'55*
A Town Like Alice *'56*
Pursuit of the Graf Spee *'57*
Robbery under Arms *'57*
The Nun's Story *'59*
Kidnapped *'60*
Operation Amsterdam *'60*
The Trials of Oscar Wilde *'60*
The Sins of Rachel Cade *'61*
I Thank a Fool *'62*
In the Cool of the Day *'63*
First Men in the Moon *'64*
Girl with Green Eyes *'64*
The Pumpkin Eater *'64*
The Flight of the Phoenix *'65*
Far from the Madding Crowd *'67*
The Legend of Lylah Clare *'68*
Red Tent *'69*
Sunday, Bloody Sunday *'71*
Lost Horizon *'73*
The Abdication *'74*
Network *'76*
Raid on Entebbe *'77*

Deborah Findlay (1947-)
Heat of the Sun *'99*
Me Without You *'01*
Wives and Daughters *'01*
The Lady in the Van *'15*
The Ones Below *'16*

Larry Fine (1902-75)
Dancing Lady *'33*
Hollywood Party *'34*
Have Rocket Will Travel *'59*
Snow White and the Three Stooges *'61*
The Three Stooges Meet Hercules *'61*
Three Stooges in Orbit *'62*
Around the World in a Daze *'63*
Four for Texas *'63*
It's a Mad, Mad, Mad, Mad World *'63*
The Outlaws Is Coming! *'65*

Travis Fine (1968-)
Child's Play 3 *'91*
Tomcats *'01*

Sticky Fingaz (1973-)
See Kirk 'Sticky Fingaz' Jones

Fyvush Finkel (1922-)
Q & A *'90*
The Crew *'00*
A Serious Man *'09*

Carrie Finklea (1988-)
Elephant *'03*
Simon Says *'07*

Frank Finlay (1926-)
The Loneliness of the Long Distance Runner *'62*
Othello *'65*
A Study in Terror *'66*
I'll Never Forget What's 'Isname *'67*
Inspector Clouseau *'68*
Cromwell *'70*
The Molly Maguires *'70*
Gumshoe *'72*
Sitting Target *'72*
Neither the Sea Nor the Sand *'73*
Shaft in Africa *'73*
The Three Musketeers *'74*
The Four Musketeers *'75*
The Thief of Baghdad *'78*
Wild Geese *'78*
Murder by Decree *'79*
Enigma *'82*
Return of the Soldier *'82*
The Ploughman's Lunch *'83*
A Christmas Carol *'84*
The Death of Adolf Hitler *'84*
Arch of Triumph *'85*
Lifeforce *'85*
Gospa *'94*
A Mind to Murder *'96*
Romance and Rejection *'96*
Stiff Upper Lips *'96*
Dreaming of Joseph Lees *'99*
The Magical Legend of the Leprechauns *'99*
Longitude *'00*
Station Jim *'01*
The Pianist *'02*
The Statement *'03*
Lighthouse Hill *'04*
The Waiting Room *'07*

James Finlayson (1887-1953)
No Man's Law '27
Pardon Us '31
Pack Up Your Troubles '32
The Devil's Brother '33
Bonnie Scotland '35
Bohemian Girl '36
Our Relations '36
Pick a Star '37
Way Out West '37
Block-heads '38
The Flying Deuces '39
To Be or Not to Be '42
Cameron Finley (1987-)
Leave It to Beaver '97
Hope Floats '98
Perfect Game '00
Margot Finley (1980-)
In Cold Blood '96
Ronnie and Julie '97
William Finley (1942-2012)
The Wedding Party '69
Sisters '73
Phantom of the Paradise '74
Eaten Alive '76
The Fury '78
The Funhouse '81
The Black Dahlia '06
John Finn (1952-)
Glory '89
Cover-Up '91
Quicksand: No Escape '91
Turbulence '96
Atomic Train '99
True Crime '99
Deadlocked '00
Analyze That '02
Catch Me If You Can '02
The Hunted '03
Kate Finneran (1971-)
Night of the Living Dead '90
Baby on Board '08
Warren Finnerty (1925-74)
The Connection '61
Cool Hand Luke '67
Easy Rider '69
Panic in Needle Park '71
Cockfighter '74
Albert Finney (1936-)
The Entertainer '60
Saturday Night and Sunday Morning '60
Tom Jones '63
Night Must Fall '64
Two for the Road '67
The Picasso Summer '69
Scrooge '70
Gumshoe '72
Murder on the Orient Express '74
The Duellists '77
Looker '81
Wolfen '81
Annie '82
Shoot the Moon '82
The Dresser '83
Loophole '83
Under the Volcano '84
Orphans '87
The Image '89
Miller's Crossing '90
The Playboys '92
Rich in Love '93
The Browning Version '94
The Run of the Country '95
Washington Square '97
Breakfast of Champions '98
A Rather English Marriage '98
Simpatico '99
Erin Brockovich '00
Traffic '00
My Uncle Silas '01
The Gathering Storm '02
Big Fish '03
Tim Burton's Corpse Bride '05 (V)
Amazing Grace '06
A Good Year '06
Before the Devil Knows You're Dead '07
The Bourne Ultimatum '07
The Bourne Legacy '12
Shirley Jo Finney
Wilma '77
Echo Park '86
Jennifer Finnigan (1979-)
Beethoven's Big Break '08
What Color Is Love? '08
A Bet's a Bet '14
Angela Finocchiaro (1955-)
Don't Tell '05
My Brother Is an Only Child '07
Elena Fiore (1928-)
Seduction of Mimi '72
Seven Beauties '76
John Fiore
Hit and Runway '01
Tony n' Tina's Wedding '07
Maria Fiore
Neapolitan Carousel '54
Thor and the Amazon Women '60
Linda Fiorentino (1958-)
After Hours '85
Gotcha! '85
Vision Quest '85
The Moderns '88
Wildfire '88
Queens Logic '91
Shout '91
Beyond the Law '92
Charlie's Ghost: The Secret of Coronado '94
The Desperate Trail '94
The Last Seduction '94
Jade '95
Larger Than Life '96
Unforgettable '96
Body Count '97
Kicked in the Head '97
Men in Black '97
Dogma '99
Ordinary Decent Criminal '99
What Planet Are You From? '00
Where the Money Is '00
Liberty Stands Still '02
Once More With Feeling '08
Ann(e) Firbank (1933-)
A Severed Head '70
Persuasion '71
Asylum '72
Lillie '79
Eddie Firestone (1920-2007)
The Law and Jake Wade '58
Two for the Seesaw '62
Duel '71
MacKenzie Firgens (1975-)
Groove '00
Against the Wall '04
Sweet Insanity '06
The Pink Conspiracy '07
The Thompsons '12
Brandon Firla
Daniel's Daughter '08
Before You Say 'I Do' '09
Finn on the Fly '09
Fairfield Road '10
Colin Firth (1960-)
Another Country '84
Camille '84
Dutch Girls '87
A Month in the Country '87
The Secret Garden '87
Apartment Zero '88
Valmont '89
The Advocate '93
Circle of Friends '94
Pride and Prejudice '95
The Widowing of Mrs. Holroyd '95
The English Patient '96
Fever Pitch '96
A Thousand Acres '97
My Life So Far '98
Shakespeare in Love '98
Relative Values '99
The Turn of the Screw '99
Bridget Jones's Diary '01
Conspiracy '01
The Importance of Being Earnest '02
Girl with a Pearl Earring '03
Love Actually '03
What a Girl Wants '03
Bridget Jones: The Edge of Reason '04
Trauma '04
Where the Truth Lies '05
Nanny McPhee '06
The Last Legion '07
St. Trinian's '07
Then She Found Me '07
When Did You Last See Your Father? '07
The Accidental Husband '08
Easy Virtue '08
Mamma Mia! '08
A Summer in Genoa '08
A Christmas Carol '09 (V)
Dorian Gray '09
The Legend of Fritton's Gold '09
A Single Man '09
The King's Speech '10
Main Street '10
Tinker Tailor Soldier Spy '11
Gambit '12
The Railway Man '13
Before I Go to Sleep '14
Devil's Knot '14
Magic in the Moonlight '14
Kingsman: The Secret Service '15
Bridget Jones's Baby '16
Genius '16
Kingsman: The Golden Circle '17
Mamma Mia! Here We Go Again '18
The Mercy '19
1917 '19
Jonathan Firth (1967-)
Emily Bronte's Wuthering Heights '92
Middlemarch '93
Far from the Madding Crowd '97
Victoria & Albert '01
Bait '02
Luther '03
The Prince & Me 2: Royal Wedding '06
The Prince & Me 3: A Royal Honeymoon '08
The Prince & Me 4: The Elephant Adventure '10
Peter Firth (1953-)
King Arthur, the Young Warlord '75
Equus '77
Joseph Andrews '77
Tess '79
Lifeforce '85
Born of Fire '87
Northanger Abbey '87
The Incident '89
The Hunt for Red October '90
Prisoner of Honor '91
The Perfect Husband '92
Shadowlands '93
An Awfully Big Adventure '94
Mighty Joe Young '98
Chill Factor '99
Pearl Harbor '01
Me & Mrs. Jones '02
The Greatest Game Ever Played '05
South Riding '11
MI-5 '15
Risen '16
Jenna Fischer (1974-)
Slither '06
Blades of Glory '07
The Brothers Solomon '07
Walk Hard: The Dewey Cox Story '07
The Promotion '08
Solitary Man '10
Hall Pass '11
A Little Help '11
The Giant Mechanical Man '12
Brad's Status '17
Kate Fischer (1973-)
Sirens '94
Blood Surf '00
Andy Fischer-Price (1987-)
Killer Movie '08
National Lampoon Presents: Endless Bummer '09
Betrayed at 17 '11
Kaboom '11
Patrick Fischler (1969-)
The Black Dahlia '06
Garden Party '08
The Great Buck Howard '09
Big Sur '13
The Standoff at Sparrow Creek '19
Nancy Fish (1938-)
Exorcist 3: Legion '90
Death Becomes Her '92
Ghost in the Machine '93
Laurence Fishburne (1961-)
Cornbread, Earl & Me '75
Apocalypse Now '79
Death Wish 2 '82
Quicksilver '86
Gardens of Stone '87
A Nightmare on Elm Street 3: Dream Warriors '87
Red Heat '88
School Daze '88
Cadence '89
Decoration Day '90
King of New York '90
Boyz N the Hood '91
Class Action '91
Hearts of Darkness: A Filmmaker's Apocalypse '91
Deep Cover '92
Searching for Bobby Fischer '93
What's Love Got to Do with It? '93
Bad Company '94
Higher Learning '94
Just Cause '94
Othello '95
The Tuskegee Airmen '95
Fled '96
Hoodlum '96
Event Horizon '97
Miss Evers' Boys '97
Always Outnumbered Always Outgunned '98
The Matrix '99
Once in the Life '00
Osmosis Jones '01 (V)
Biker Boyz '03
The Matrix Reloaded '03
The Matrix Revolutions '03
Mystic River '03
Assault on Precinct 13 '05
Akeelah and the Bee '06
Bobby '06
Five Fingers '06
Mission: Impossible 3 '06
Bobby Z '07
Fantastic Four: Rise of the Silver Surfer '07 (V)
Tortured '08
21 '08
Armored '09
Predators '10
Contagion '11
Mitch Albom's Have a Little Faith '11
Thurgood '11
Man of Steel '13
Ride Along '14
Rudderless '14
The Signal '14
Passengers '16
Standoff '16
John Wick: Chapter 2 '17
Last Flag Flying '17
John Wick: Chapter 3-Parabellum '19
Running with the Devil '19
Carrie Fisher (1956-2016)
Shampoo '75
Star Wars '77
Mr. Mike's Mondo Video '79
The Blues Brothers '80
The Empire Strikes Back '80
Under the Rainbow '81
Return of the Jedi '83
Garbo Talks '84
The Man with One Red Shoe '85
Hannah and Her Sisters '86
Hollywood Vice Squad '86
Amazon Women on the Moon '87
The 'Burbs '89
Loverboy '89
When Harry Met Sally. . . '89
Sibling Rivalry '90
Sweet Revenge '90
Drop Dead Fred '91
Soapdish '91
This Is My Life '92
Austin Powers: International Man of Mystery '97 (C)
Scream 3 '00
Jay and Silent Bob Strike Back '01
Charlie's Angels: Full Throttle '03
Wonderland '03
Stateside '04
Undiscovered '05
Cougar Club '07 (C)
The Women '08
Sorority Row '09
Star Wars: The Force Awakens '15
Star Wars: The Last Jedi '17
Star Wars: The Rise of Skywalker '19
Cindy Fisher
Hometown U.S.A. '79
Liar's Moon '82
David Fisher (1948-)
Lethal Target '99
Last Stand '00
Eddie Fisher (1928-2010)
All About Eve '50
Bundle of Joy '56
Butterfield 8 '60
Elsie Fisher (2003-)
Despicable Me '10 (V)
Despicable Me 2 '13 (V)
Eighth Grade '18
Frances Fisher (1952-)
Can She Bake a Cherry Pie? '83
Heart '87
Tough Guys Don't Dance '87
Patty Hearst '88
Sudie & Simpson '90
Unforgiven '92
Attack of the 50 Ft. Woman '93
Babyfever '94
The Stars Fell on Henrietta '94
Female Perversions '96
Titanic '97
Wild America '97
The Big Tease '99
True Crime '99
The Audrey Hepburn Story '00
Gone in 60 Seconds '00
Jackie Bouvier Kennedy Onassis '00
The Rising Place '02
Blue Car '03
House of Sand and Fog '03
Laws of Attraction '04
Mrs. Harris '05
The Night of the White Pants '06
In the Valley of Elah '07
Sex and Death 101 '07
Jolene '08
The Perfect Game '09
Golf in the Kingdom '10
Janie Jones '10
The Lincoln Lawyer '11
The Roommate '11
Any Day Now '12
Beverly Hills Chihuahua 3: Viva La Fiesta! '12
The Seven Year Hitch '12
The Host '13
The Makeover '13
Plush '13
The M Word '14
Gregor Fisher (1953-)
1984 '84
The Railway Children '00
Love Actually '03
The Merchant of Venice '04
Kidnapped '05
Oliver Twist '07
Wild Target '10
Isla Fisher (1976-)
Scooby-Doo '02
Criminal Ways '03
Dallas 362 '03
London '05
Wedding Crashers '05
Wedding Daze '06
Hot Rod '07
The Lookout '07
Definitely, Maybe '08
Dr. Seuss' Horton Hears a Who! '08 (V)
Confessions of a Shopaholic '09
Burke & Hare '10
Rango '11 (V)
Bachelorette '12
Rise of the Guardians '12 (V)
The Great Gatsby '13
Life of Crime '13
Now You See Me '13
The Brothers Grimsby '16
Keeping Up with the Joneses '16
Nocturnal Animals '16
Visions '16
Tag '18
The Beach Bum '19
Isla Lang Fisher (1976-)
See Isla Fisher
Jaishon Fisher (1996-)
Lakeview Terrace '08
Christmas in Canaan '09
Gifted Hands: The Ben Carson Story '09
Jodie Fisher
Body of Influence 2 '96
Dead by Dawn '98
Joely Fisher (1967-)
Inspector Gadget '99
Cupid '12
Noel Fisher (1984-)
Max Keeble's Big Move '01
Killer Bees '02
National Lampoon's Holiday Reunion '03
Pope Dreams '06
Red '08
A Dog Named Christmas '09
Hatfields & McCoys '12
Teenage Mutant Ninja Turtles '14
Teenage Mutant Ninja Turtles: Out of the Shadows '16
Rashiya Fisher (1972-)
See Rah Digga
Stephen H. Fisher
Hellboy '04
Van Helsing '04
Thomas (Tom) Fisher (1968-)
Shanghai Knights '03
Van Helsing '04
Tricia Leigh Fisher (1969-)
Book of Love '91
Arizona Dream '94
Saving Grace B. Jones '09
Michael Fishman
Little Bigfoot 2: The Journey Home '97
Undrafted '16
Schuyler Fisk (1982-)
The Baby-Sitters' Club '95
Skeletons in the Closet '00
Snow Day '00
Orange County '02
I'm Reed Fish '06
Restless '11
Robert (Fisk) Fiske (1899-1944)
Mystic Circle Murder '39
Green Archer '40
Along the Rio Grande '41
The Big Boss '41
Mark Fite
Stuart Bliss '98
Off the Lip '04

Peter Fitz (1931-)
The Wannsee Conference '84
Au Revoir les Enfants '87

Lewis Fitz-Gerald (1958-)
Breaker Morant '80
Winner Takes All '84
A Cry in the Dark '88
The Four Minute Mile '88
Rikky and Pete '88
Dead Heart '96
Pitch Black '00
Not Suitable for Children '12

Parisa Fitz-Henley
The Jane Austen Book Club '07
My Spy '19

Barry Fitzgerald (1888-1961)
Juno and the Paycock '30 (N)
Bringing Up Baby '38
Dawn Patrol '38
Four Men and a Prayer '38
Marie Antoinette '38
The Saint Strikes Back '39
The Long Voyage Home '40
How Green Was My Valley '41
Tarzan's Secret Treasure '41
The Amazing Mrs. Holiday '43
Going My Way '44
None But the Lonely Heart '44
And Then There Were None '45
The Stork Club '45
Welcome Stranger '47
Miss Tatlock's Millions '48
The Naked City '48
The Story of Seabiscuit '49
Union Station '50
The Quiet Man '52
The Catered Affair '56

Caitlin FitzGerald (1983-)
It's Complicated '09
Damsels in Distress '11
Newlyweds '11
The Fitzgerald Family Christmas '12
Always Shine '16
The Man Who Killed Hitler and Then the Bigfoot '19

Ciaran Fitzgerald (1983-)
Into the West '92
The Canterville Ghost '96
The Last of the High Kings '96
The Boxer '97
The General '98

Ella Fitzgerald (1917-96)
Ride 'Em Cowboy '42
Pete Kelly's Blues '55

Geraldine Fitzgerald (1913-2005)
Dark Victory '39
The Mill on the Floss '39
Wuthering Heights '39
Watch on the Rhine '43
Wilson '44
The Strange Affair of Uncle Harry '45
Nobody Lives Forever '46
Three Strangers '46
The Pawnbroker '65
Rachel, Rachel '68
The Last American Hero '73
Harry and Tonto '74
Lovespell '79
Arthur '81
Easy Money '83
Kennedy '83
Dixie: Changing Habits '85
Poltergeist 2: The Other Side '86
Arthur 2: On the Rocks '88

Gerry Fitzgerald
Baby Geniuses '98
Superbabies: Baby Geniuses 2 '04

Glenn Fitzgerald (1971-)
Flirting with Disaster '95
Manny & Lo '96
A Price Above Rubies '97
The Sixth Sense '99
101 Ways (The Things a Girl Will Do to Keep Her Volvo) '00
Tully '00
The Believer '01
Buffalo Soldiers '01
Series 7: The Contenders '01
40 Days and 40 Nights '02
Confess '05

Leo Fitzgerald
Baby Geniuses '98
Superbabies: Baby Geniuses 2 '04

Myles Fitzgerald
Baby Geniuses '98
Superbabies: Baby Geniuses 2 '04

Patrick Fitzgerald (1962-)
Poltergeist: The Legacy '96
Day at the Beach '98

Sean Fitzgerald
The Power Within '95
Storybook '95

Tac Fitzgerald (1981-)
Here on Earth '00
Black Hawk Down '01

Tara Fitzgerald (1967-)
Anglo-Saxon Attitudes '92
The Camomile Lawn '92
Catherine Cookson's The Black Candle '92
Sirens '94
The Englishman Who Went up a Hill But Came down a Mountain '95
Brassed Off '96
The Tenant of Wildfell Hall '96
The Woman in White '97
Frenchman's Creek '98
New World Disorder '99
Rancid Aluminium '00
Dark Blue World '01
I Capture the Castle '02
Like Father Like Son '05
Jane Eyre '06
Una '17

Walter Fitzgerald (1896-1976)
Blanche Fury '48
Edward, My Son '49
The Fallen Idol '49
Treasure Island '50
Appointment in London '53
The Adventures of Sadie '55

Colleen (Ann) Fitzpatrick (1969-)
Hairspray '88
Higher Learning '94
St. Patrick's Day '99
Da Hip Hop Witch '00
Dracula 2000 '00
Get Over It! '01 (C)
Rock Star '01
Scary Movie 2 '01 (V)

Emma Fitzpatrick
The Collection '12
Before We Go '14
Bloodsucking Bastards '15

Gabrielle Fitzpatrick (1967-)
Mr. Nice Guy '98
Desert Heat '99

Jim (James) Fitzpatrick (1959-)
Operation Delta Force 3: Clear Target '98
U.S. Seals '98

Kate Fitzpatrick (1948-)
Night Nurse '77
Return of Captain Invincible '83

Leo Fitzpatrick (1978-)
Kids '95
Take It to the Limit '00
Bully '01
Storytelling '01
Personal Velocity: Three Portraits '02
Fay Grim '06
How to Rob a Bank '07
El Camino '08
Winter of Frozen Dreams '08
Jack and Diane '12
Cold Comes the Night '14

Richard Fitzpatrick
Trilogy of Terror 2 '96
New Blood '99
Verdict in Blood '02
Coast to Coast '04
Confessions of a Teenage Drama Queen '04
Lies and Crimes '07
Bridal Fever '08
Sticks and Stones '08
Survival of the Dead '09
November Christmas '10
A Very Merry Mix-Up '13

Emily Fitzroy (1860-1954)
Bardelys the Magnificent '26
The Bat '26
Mockery '27
The Trail of '98 '28
Don Quixote '35
The Frontiersmen '38

Maureen FitzSimmons (1920-2015)
See Maureen O'Hara

Paul Fix (1901-83)
Lucky Star '29
Mutiny Ahead '35
The Plot Thickens '36
The Prisoner of Shark Island '36
Mannequin '37
Black Friday '40
Dr. Cyclops '40
Sherlock Holmes and the Secret Weapon '42
Fighting Seabees '44
Tycoon '47
Red River '48
She Wore a Yellow Ribbon '49
Denver and the Rio Grande '52
Hondo '53
Island in the Sky '53
Johnny Guitar '53
The High and the Mighty '54
Blood Alley '55
The Bad Seed '56
Man in the Vault '56
Santiago '56
Toward the Unknown '56
Jet Pilot '57
Man in the Shadow '57
Night Passage '57
Lafayette Escadrille '58
To Kill a Mockingbird '62
Mail Order Bride '63
The Outrage '64
Shenandoah '65
Sons of Katie Elder '65
Nevada Smith '66
El Dorado '67
Welcome to Hard Times '67
Day of the Evil Gun '68
Zabriskie Point '70
Shoot Out '71
Night of the Lepus '72
Grayeagle '77
Wanda Nevada '79

Barbara Fixx
Come as You Are '05
Stranger in My Bed '05

Cash Flagg (1938-2009)
See Ray Dennis Steckler

Fannie Flagg (1944-)
Five Easy Pieces '70
Grease '78
My Best Friend Is a Vampire '88
Crazy in Alabama '99

Danny Flaherty
Contest '13
Goat '16
King Jack '16

Joe Flaherty (1941-)
Tunnelvision '76
Used Cars '80
Heavy Metal '81 (V)
Stripes '81
Going Berserk '83
Sesame Street Presents: Follow That Bird '85
One Crazy Summer '86
Back to the Future, Part 2 '89
Who's Harry Crumb? '89
Runaway Daughters '94
Stuart Saves His Family '94
Happy Gilmore '96
Snowboard Academy '96
The Wrong Guy '96
Slackers '02
National Security '03
Home on the Range '04 (V)

Lanny Flaherty (1942-)
The Ballad of the Sad Cafe '91
Sommersby '93
Tom and Huck '95
Home Fries '98

Pat Flaherty (1903-70)
Sergeant York '41
The Red House '47

Didier Flamand (1947-)
Women '97
The Chateau '01
The Crimson Rivers '01
The Chorus '04
Love '05
Factotum '06
Our Paradise '11
Retour Chez Ma Mere '16

Crista Flanagan
Disaster Movie '08
Best Night Ever '14

Fionnula Flanagan (1941-)
Picture of Dorian Gray '74
The Legend of Lizzie Borden '75
Mary White '77
The Ewok Adventure '84
Youngblood '86
Final Verdict '91
Money for Nothing '93
White Mile '94
Some Mother's Son '96
Kings in Grass Castles '97
Waking Ned Devine '98
A Secret Affair '99
For Love or Country: The Arturo Sandoval Story '00
The Others '01
Divine Secrets of the Ya-Ya Sisterhood '02
Tears of the Sun '03
Four Brothers '05
Transamerica '05
Slipstream '07
Yes Man '08
The Invention of Lying '09
The Guard '11
Kill the Irishman '11
Three Wise Women '11
Angels Sing '13
Life's a Breeze '14
Trash Fire '16

Tommy Flanagan (1965-)
Braveheart '95
Ratcatcher '99
Sunset Strip '99
Gladiator '00
Attila '01
Strictly Sinatra '01
All About the Benjamins '02
Alien *vs.* Predator '04
Trauma '04
The Last Drop '05
When a Stranger Calls '06
Smokin' Aces '07
Hero Wanted '08
Smokin' Aces 2: Assassins' Ball '10
Papillon '17

Ed Flanders (1934-95)
The Grasshopper '69
The Passing of Evil '70
Goodbye, Raggedy Ann '71
The Legend of Lizzie Borden '75
Eleanor & Franklin '76
The Amazing Howard Hughes '77
Mary White '77
Backstairs at the White House '79
The Ninth Configuration '79
Salem's Lot '79
True Confessions '81
Special Bulletin '83
Exorcist 3: Legion '90
Citizen Cohn '92
Bye Bye, Love '94

Sean Patrick Flanery (1965-)
Guinevere '94
The Grass Harp '95
Powder '95
Pale Saints '97
Suicide Kings '97
Best Men '98
Eden '98
Girl '98
Zack & Reba '98
Body Shots '99
Boondock Saints '99
Simply Irresistible '99
Ride the Wild Fields '00
Acceptable Risk '01
Eye See You '01
Borderline '02
Lone Hero '02
The Gunman '03
Into the Fire '05
The Insatiable '06
Ten Inch Hero '07
Veritas: Prince of Truth '07
Crystal River '08
The Boondock Saints II: All Saints Day '09
Citizen Jane '09
Deadly Impact '09
Mongolian Death Worm '10
Saw 3D: The Final Chapter '10
Sinners and Saints '10
InSight '11
Lake Effects '12
12 Dogs of Christmas: Great Puppy Rescue '12
Hidden Away '13
Phantom '13
Beyond Valkyrie: Dawn of the Fourth Reich '16

Joe Flanigan (1967-)
The Other Sister '98
Ferocious Planet '11
Good Day for It '11
6 Bullets '12

Susan Flannery (1939-)
Arthur Hailey's The Moneychangers '76
Gumball Rally '76
Anatomy of a Seduction '79

Barry Flatman (1950-)
Open Season '95
The Morrison Murders '96
Random Encounter '98
The Witness Files '00
Sea Wolf: The Pirate's Curse '05
Saw 3 '06
Daniel's Daughter '08
The Case for Christmas '11

James Flavin (1906-76)
King Kong '33
Air Force '43
So Proudly We Hail '43
Hollywood Canteen '44
Laura '44
Uncertain Glory '44
Cloak and Dagger '46
Easy to Wed '46
Abbott and Costello Meet the Killer, Boris Karloff '49
Homicide '49
Armored Car Robbery '50
Destination Murder '50
Abbott and Costello Go to Mars '53
Francis in the Haunted House '56
Night Passage '57
In Cold Blood '67

Flea (1962-)
Back to the Future, Part 2 '89
Motorama '91
My Own Private Idaho '91
The Chase '93
The Big Lebowski '97
Fear and Loathing in Las Vegas '98
Liar's Poker '99
The Wild Thornberrys Movie '02 (V)
Rugrats Go Wild! '03 (V)
Queen & Slim '19

John Fleck (1951-)
Tapeheads '89
Gunshy '98
On_Line '01

Rory Fleck-Byrne
The Quiet Ones '14
The Foreigner '17

Erick Fleeks (1948-)
Phat Beach '96
Campfire Tales '98

James Fleet (1954-)
Cracker: The Big Crunch '94
Four Weddings and a Funeral '94
Sense and Sensibility '95
Moll Flanders '96
Frenchman's Creek '98
Kevin & Perry Go Large '00
Charlotte Gray '01
Two Men Went to War '02
The Phantom of the Opera '04
Tristram Shandy: A Cock and Bull Story '05
Little Dorrit '08

Mick Fleetwood (1947-)
The Running Man '87
Zero Tolerance '93
Burning Down the House '01 (C)

Susan Fleetwood (1944-95)
Heat and Dust '82
Dangerous Corner '83
The Sacrifice '86
White Mischief '88
The Buddha of Suburbia '92
Persuasion '95

Charles Fleischer (1950-)
A Nightmare on Elm Street '84
Bad Dreams '88
Who Framed Roger Rabbit '88 (V)
Back to the Future, Part 2 '89
Honey, I Shrunk the Kids '89 (V)
Carry On Columbus '92
Straight Talk '92
We're Back! A Dinosaur's Story '93 (V)
Tales from the Crypt Presents Demon Knight '94
Gridlock'd '96
Boltneck '98
Ground Control '98
Permanent Midnight '98
The 4th Tenor '02
The Polar Express '04
Zodiac '07

Heidi Fleiss (1965-)
The Doom Generation '95
Alien 51 '04

Noah Fleiss (1984-)
Josh and S.A.M. '93
Joe the King '99
Double Parked '00
Things You Can Tell Just by Looking at Her '00
The Truth About Jane '00
Storytelling '01
Evergreen '04
Brick '06

Eric Fleming (1925-66)
Conquest of Space '55
Fright '56
Queen of Outer Space '58
The Glass Bottom Boat '66

Ian Fleming (1888-1969)
The Third Clue '34
The Triumph of Sherlock Holmes '35
Murder at the Baskervilles '37

Norman Conquest '53
Recoil '53
Land of Fury '55
The Trials of Oscar Wilde '60

Lone Fleming (1949-)
It Happened at Nightmare Inn '70
Return of the Evil Dead '75

Rhonda Fleming (1923-)
Since You Went Away '44
Spellbound '45
Abilene Town '46
The Spiral Staircase '46
Out of the Past '47
A Connecticut Yankee in King Arthur's Court '49
The Great Lover '49
Cavalry Charge '51
Cry Danger '51
The Golden Hawk '52
Pony Express '53
Tennessee's Partner '55
The Killer Is Loose '56
Odongo '56
Slightly Scarlet '56
While the City Sleeps '56
Gun Glory '57
Gunfight at the O.K. Corral '57
Home Before Dark '58
Alias Jesse James '59
The Big Circus '59
The Crowded Sky '60
The Nude Bomb '80

Jason Flemyng (1966-)
A Question of Attribution '91
Rob Roy '95
Alive and Kicking '96
Stealing Beauty '96
Spice World: The Movie '97
Deep Rising '98
Lock, Stock and 2 Smoking Barrels '98
The Red Violin '98
Tess of the D'Urbervilles '98
Bruiser '00
Snatch '00
The Body '01
From Hell '01
Mean Machine '01
Rock Star '01
Below '02
The League of Extraordinary Gentlemen '03
Lighthouse Hill '04
Seed of Chucky '04
Layer Cake '05
Transporter 2 '05
PU-239 '06
Telling Lies '06
Bobby Z '07
The Riddle '07
Stardust '07
The Curious Case of Benjamin Button '08
Shifty '08
Clash of the Titans '10
Dead Cert '10
Kick-Ass '10
Made in Romania '10
Ironclad '11
X-Men: First Class '11
Great Expectations '12
I Give It a Year '13
Stonehearst Asylum '13
Welcome to the Punch '13
Gemma Bovery '15
Revolt '17

Robert Flemyng (1912-95)
Head Over Heels '37
The Blue Lamp '49
Conspirator '49
Cast a Dark Shadow '55
The Man Who Never Was '55
The Horrible Dr. Hichcock '62
Blood Beast Terror '67
Oh! What a Lovely War '69
Travels with My Aunt '72

Diane Fleri
My Brother Is an Only Child '07
I Am Love '09

Bramwell Fletcher (1904-88)
Raffles '30
The Mummy '32
The Scarlet Pimpernel '34
Random Harvest '42

Brendan Fletcher (1981-)
Air Bud '97
Trucks '97
The Five Senses '99
Summer's End '99
Jimmy Zip '00
Turning Paige '01
The Unsaid '01
Freddy *vs.* Jason '03
Heart of America '03
Death Valley '04
Eighteen '04
The Final Cut '04
Ginger Snaps Back: The Beginning '04
Tideland '05
RV '06
BloodRayne 2: Deliverance '07
Rampage '09
Bloodrayne: The Third Reich '11
Blubberella '11
Citizen Gangster '11
Rampage: Capital Punishment '14
Rampage: President Down '16
Distorted '18
Night Hunter '19

Dexter Fletcher (1966-)
The Long Good Friday '80
Lionheart '87
The Rachel Papers '89
The Raggedy Rawney '90
Twisted Obsession '90
Lock, Stock and 2 Smoking Barrels '98
Below '02
Stander '03
Doom '05
In Your Dreams '07
Dead Cert '10
Terminal '18

Diane Fletcher (1944-)
House of Cards '90
To Play the King '93
The Final Cut '95
The Aristocrats '99

Dusty Fletcher (1897-1954)
Boardinghouse Blues '48
Killer Diller '48

Justin Fletcher
Shaun the Sheep Movie '15
A Shaun the Sheep Movie: Farmageddon '19

Louise Fletcher (1934-)
Thieves Like Us '74
One Flew Over the Cuckoo's Nest '75
Russian Roulette '75
The Exorcist 2: The Heretic '77
The Cheap Detective '78
Lady in Red '79
Mama Dracula '80
Strange Behavior '81
Brainstorm '83
Strange Invaders '83
Firestarter '84
A Summer to Remember '84
The Boy Who Could Fly '86
Invaders from Mars '86
Nobody's Fool '86
Flowers in the Attic '87
Two Moon Junction '88
Best of the Best '89
Shadowzone '89
Blue Steel '90
The Player '92
Edie & Pen '95 (C)
Virtuosity '95
High School High '96
Two Days in the Valley '96
Breast Men '97
Love to Kill '97
Cruel Intentions '98
Love Kills '98
The Devil's Arithmetic '99

A Map of the World '99
Big Eden '00
More Dogs Than Bones '00
Finding Home '03
A Time to Remember '03
Dancing in Twilight '05
Aurora Borealis '06
A Dad for Christmas '06
A Dennis the Menace Christmas '07
Of Two Minds '12
A Perfect Man '13

Neil Fletcher
Zontar, the Thing from Venus '66
Creature of Destruction '67

Page Fletcher
Humongous '82
Ordeal in the Arctic '93

Sara Fletcher
iCrime '11
Hansel & Gretel '13

Audrey Fleurot
The Intouchables '12
Queens of the Ring '13

Helen Flint (1898-1967)
Manhattan Love Song '34
The Black Legion '37

Jill Flint (1977-)
How I Got Lost '09
Fake '10
The Mule '18

Sam Flint (1882-1980)
Evelyn Prentice '34
A Face in the Fog '36
Two Minutes to Play '37
The Chinese Cat '44
Lights of Old Santa Fe '47
Command Decision '48
The Fireball '50

Jay C. Flippen (1900-71)
Marie Galante '34
They Live by Night '49
Buccaneer's Girl '50
Winchester '73 '50
Flying Leathernecks '51
The Lemon Drop Kid '51
The People Against O'Hara '51
Carnival Story '54
The Wild One '54
Far Country '55
Oklahoma! '55
The Killing '56
The King and Four Queens '56
Seventh Cavalry '56
The Halliday Brand '57
Jet Pilot '57
Night Passage '57
The Plunderers '60
Studs Lonigan '60
Wild River '60
Looking for Love '64
Firecreek '68
Hellfighters '68

Josh Flitter (1994-)
The Greatest Game Ever Played '05
Air Bud 6: Air Buddies '06 (V)
Big Momma's House 2 '06
License to Wed '07
Nancy Drew '07
Ace Ventura Jr.: Pet Detective '08
Dr. Seuss' Horton Hears a Who! '08 (V)
Snow Buddies '08 (V)
Santa Buddies '09 (V)
Snowmen '10

Bjorn Floberg (1947-)
Insomnia '97
Kitchen Stories '03
A Somewhat Gentle Man '10

Calista Flockhart (1964-)
The Birdcage '95
Drunks '96
Jane Doe '96
Telling Lies in America '96
William Shakespeare's A Midsummer Night's Dream '99

Things You Can Tell Just by Looking at Her '00
The Last Shot '04
Fragile '05

Suzanne Flon (1918-2005)
Moulin Rouge '52
The Train '65
Action Man '67
Zita '68
Mr. Klein '76
One Deadly Summer '83
Joyeux Noel '05
Avenue Montaigne '06

Dann Florek (1950-)
Angel Heart '87
The Flintstones '94
Getting Even with Dad '94
Hard Rain '97
A Nightmare Come True '97
From the Earth to the Moon '98
Beautiful Joe '00

Florelle (1901-74)
The Mistress of Atlantis '32
Liliom '35
The Crime of Monsieur Lange '36

Margaret Anne Florence (1978-)
The Mighty Macs '09
The One '11

Von Flores (1960-)
The Assignment '97
Tracked '98
The Confessor '04

Holly Floria (1966-)
Netherworld '90
Presumed Guilty '91
Private Wars '93

George 'Buck' Flower (1937-2004)
Dirty Mind of Young Sally '72
Devil & Leroy Basset '73
Candy Tangerine Man '75
Across the Great Divide '76
Further Adventures of the Wilderness Family, Part 2 '77
The Capture of Bigfoot '79
Mountain Family Robinson '79
Escape from New York '81
In Search of a Golden Sky '84
Lethal Victims '87
Sorority Babes in the Slimeball Bowl-A-Rama '87
Cheerleader Camp '88
Pumpkinhead '88
They Live '88
Relentless '89
Sundown: The Vampire in Retreat '08

Kim Flowers
Nobody's Perfect '90
Alien: Resurrection '97

James Floyd (1985-)
Compulsion '08
Tormented '09
My Brother the Devil '12

Robert Floyd (1957-)
Cold Hearts '99
The Song of the Lark '01
Soul's Midnight '06

Susan Floyd (1968-)
Random Hearts '99
Domestic Disturbance '01

Darlanne Fluegel (1958-)
Eyes of Laura Mars '78
Battle Beyond the Stars '80
Once Upon a Time in America '84
To Live & Die in L.A. '85
Running Scared '86
Tough Guys '86
Bulletproof '88
Deadly Stranger '88
Freeway '88
Lock Up '89
Pet Sematary 2 '92

Slaughter of the Innocents '93
Darkman 3: Die Darkman Die '95
Relative Fear '95

Patrick Flueger (1983-)
Spin '07
Brothers '09
Last Resort '09
Mother's Day '10
Footloose '11

Joel Fluellen (1907-90)
The Jackie Robinson Story '50
Sitting Bull '54
Run Silent, Run Deep '58
The Great White Hope '70
Man Friday '75

Barbara Flynn (1948-)
Cracker: To Be a Somebody '94
Cracker: Brotherly Love '95
King Lear '98
Lorna Doone '01
Wives and Daughters '01
Elizabeth I '05
Miss Potter '06
Cranford '08
Return to Cranford '09

Colleen Flynn (1962-)
The Temp '93
Serving in Silence: The Margarethe Cammermeyer Story '95

Errol Flynn (1909-59)
Captain Blood '35
The Case of the Curious Bride '35
The Charge of the Light Brigade '36
Another Dawn '37
The Green Light '37
The Prince and the Pauper '37
The Adventures of Robin Hood '38
Dawn Patrol '38
Four's a Crowd '38
The Sisters '38
Dodge City '39
The Private Lives of Elizabeth & Essex '39
Santa Fe Trail '40
The Sea Hawk '40
Virginia City '40
Dive Bomber '41
Footsteps in the Dark '41
They Died with Their Boots On '41
Desperate Journey '42
Gentleman Jim '42
Edge of Darkness '43
Northern Pursuit '43
Thank Your Lucky Stars '43
Uncertain Glory '44
Objective, Burma! '45
San Antonio '45
Never Say Goodbye '46
Cry Wolf '47
Escape Me Never '47
Adventures of Don Juan '49
It's a Great Feeling '49
Kim '50
Montana '50
Rocky Mountain '50
That Forsyte Woman '50
Against All Flags '52
Mara Maru '52
The Master of Ballantrae '53
Let's Make Up '55
The Warriors '55
The Big Boodle '57
The Sun Also Rises '57
Too Much, Too Soon '58
Assault of the Rebel Girls '59

Jerome Flynn (1963-)
A Summer Story '88
Edward II '92
A Mind to Murder '96

Joe Flynn (1924-74)
The Boss '56
30 '59
Lover Come Back '61
McHale's Navy '64

Divorce American Style '67
The Computer Wore Tennis Shoes '69
My Dog, the Thief '69
The Barefoot Executive '71
How to Frame a Figg '71
Million Dollar Duck '71
Now You See Him, Now You Don't '72
The Girl Most Likely to. . . '73
Superdad '73
The Strongest Man in the World '75
The Rescuers '77 (V)
Crusade: A March through Time '06

Johnny Flynn (1983-)
Clouds of Sils Maria '15
Beast '17
Emma '20

Kimberly Flynn
Boys Life '94
Rhythm Thief '94

Michael Flynn (1944-)
Address Unknown '96
Partners in Crime '99

Miriam Flynn (1951-)
National Lampoon's Vacation '83
18 Again! '88
National Lampoon's Christmas Vacation '89
Vegas Vacation '96
The Land Before Time 5: The Mysterious Island '97 (V)
The Land Before Time 6: The Secret of Saurus Rock '98 (V)
National Lampoon's Christmas Vacation 2: Cousin Eddie's Big Island Adventure '03
Bucky Larson: Born to Be a Star '11

Neil Flynn (1960-)
Mean Girls '04
Hoot '06
Indiana Jones and the Kingdom of the Crystal Skull '08
The Resurrection of Gavin Stone '17

Steve Flynn
Ed McBain's 87th Precinct: Lightning '95
Ulee's Gold '97
Scarred City '98
Jesse Stone: Death in Paradise '06

Arnoldo Foa (1916-)
The Tartars '61
Damon and Pythias '62

Brandon Fobbs
Pride '07
Tunnel Rats '08

Spiros Focas (1937-)
Rocco and His Brothers '60
The Jewel of the Nile '85
Rambo 3 '88
White Palace '90

Nina Foch (1924-2008)
Return of the Vampire '43
Strange Affair '44
A Song to Remember '45
The Guilt of Janet Ames '47
Johnny O'Clock '47
Johnny Allegro '49
The Undercover Man '49
An American in Paris '51
St. Benny the Dip '51
Scaramouche '52
Young Man With Ideas '52
Executive Suite '54
Illegal '55
You're Never Too Young '55
The Ten Commandments '56
Three Brave Men '57
Cash McCall '60
Spartacus '60
Columbo: Prescription Murder '67

Such Good Friends '71
Mahogany '75
Child of Glass '78
Dixie Lanes '88
Skin Deep '89
Armistead Maupin's Tales of the City '93
Morning Glory '93
Sliver '93
Til There Was You '96
Hush '98
Pumpkin '02
How to Deal '03

Brenda Fogarty
Deadly Fieldtrip '74
Fairy Tales '76

Adam Fogerty (1969-)
Greenfingers '00
Legend of the Bog '08

Dan Fogler (1976-)
Balls of Fury '07
Good Luck Chuck '07
Dr. Seuss' Horton Hears a Who! '08 (V)
Kung Fu Panda '08 (V)
The Wedding Bros. '08
Fanboys '09
Love Happens '09
Taking Woodstock '09
Mars Needs Moms '11 (V)
Take Me Home Tonight '11
Europa Report '13
Scenic Route '13
Don Peyote '14
Fantastic Beasts and Where to Find Them '16

Freda Foh Shen (1945-)
Mulan '98 (V)
The Tiger Woods Story '98
Red Doors '05

Marina Fois (1970-)
Change of Plans '09
Making Plans for Lena '09
The Big Picture '10
Four Lovers '10
22 Bullets '10
Polisse '11

Joe Folau
The Other Side of Heaven '02
The Legend of Johnny Lingo '03
The Other Side of Heaven 2: Fire of Faith '19

Dennis Folbigge
Zulu '64
Howling 4: The Original Nightmare '88

Dave Foley (1963-)
It's Pat: The Movie '94
Kids in the Hall: Brain Candy '96
The Wrong Guy '96
Sink or Swim '97
Blast from the Past '98
A Bug's Life '98 (V)
From the Earth to the Moon '98
Dick '99
Monkeybone '01
On the Line '01
Stark Raving Mad '02
Swindle '02
Prom Queen '04
White Coats '04
Sky High '05
California Dreaming '07
Netherbeast Incorporated '07
Postal '07
Suck '09
Vampires Suck '10
Monsters University '13 (V)

Ellen Foley (1951-)
Fatal Attraction '87
Married to the Mob '88
Lies I Told My Little Sister '14

Jeremy Foley (1983-)
Dante's Peak '97
Soccer Dog: The Movie '98

Scott Foley (1972-)
Forever Love '98
Scream 3 '00
Below '02
The Last Templar '09
Let's Kill Ward's Wife '14

Abel Folk (1959-)
Sharpe's Gold '94
The Dancer Upstairs '02
Face of Terror '04
Art Heist '05
The Cheetah Girls 2 '06

Alison Folland (1978-)
Before and After '95
To Die For '95
All Over Me '96
Boys Don't Cry '99
Things Behind the Sun '01
Milwaukee, Minnesota '03

Megan Follows (1968-)
Hockey Night '84
Anne of Green Gables '85
Silver Bullet '85
Anne of Avonlea '87
Back to Hannibal: The Return of Tom Sawyer and Huckleberry Finn '90
The Chase '91
The Nutcracker Prince '91 (V)
Under the Piano '95
Anne of Green Gables: The Continuing Story '99
What Katy Did '99
Christmas Child '03
2 Brothers & a Bride '03
Breakfast With Scot '07

Mikkel Boe Folsgaard
A Royal Affair '12
Land of Mine '15

Bridget Fonda (1964-)
Aria '88
You Can't Hurry Love '88
Scandal '89
Shag: The Movie '89
Frankenstein Unbound '90
The Godfather, Part 3 '90
Leather Jackets '90
Strapless '90
Doc Hollywood '91
Iron Maze '91
Army of Darkness '92
Single White Female '92
Singles '92
Bodies, Rest & Motion '93
Little Buddha '93
Point of No Return '93
Camilla '94
It Could Happen to You '94
The Road to Wellville '94
Balto '95 (V)
City Hall '95
Rough Magic '95
Grace of My Heart '96
Touch '96
Jackie Brown '97
The Break Up '98
Finding Graceland '98
Mr. Jealousy '98 (C)
A Simple Plan '98
Lake Placid '99
South of Heaven, West of Hell '00
Kiss of the Dragon '01
Monkeybone '01
The Whole Shebang '01
The Snow Queen '02

Henry Fonda (1905-82)
The Farmer Takes a Wife '35
The Moon's Our Home '36
The Trail of the Lonesome Pine '36
Slim '37
That Certain Woman '37
Wings of the Morning '37
You Only Live Once '37
Jezebel '38
Mad Miss Manton '38
Spawn of the North '38
Drums Along the Mohawk '39
Jesse James '39
Let Us Live '39
The Story of Alexander Graham Bell '39
Young Mr. Lincoln '39
Chad Hanna '40
The Grapes of Wrath '40
Lillian Russell '40
Return of Frank James '40
The Lady Eve '41
Big Street '42
The Male Animal '42
Rings on Her Fingers '42
Tales of Manhattan '42
Immortal Sergeant '43
The Ox-Bow Incident '43
My Darling Clementine '46
Daisy Kenyon '47
The Long Night '47
Fort Apache '48
The Fugitive '48
On Our Merry Way '48
Jigsaw '49 (C)
Mister Roberts '55
War and Peace '56
The Wrong Man '56
The Tin Star '57
Twelve Angry Men '57
Warlock '59
Advise and Consent '62
The Longest Day '62
How the West Was Won '63
Spencer's Mountain '63
The Best Man '64
Fail-Safe '64
Sex and the Single Girl '64
Battle of the Bulge '65
In Harm's Way '65
The Rounders '65
A Big Hand for the Little Lady '66
Welcome to Hard Times '67
The Boston Strangler '68
Firecreek '68
Madigan '68
Once Upon a Time in the West '68
Yours, Mine & Ours '68
The Cheyenne Social Club '70
There Was a Crooked Man '70
Too Late the Hero '70
Sometimes a Great Notion '71
Ash Wednesday '73
Night Flight from Moscow '73
My Name Is Nobody '74
Great Smokey Roadblock '76
Midway '76
Last Four Days '77
Rollercoaster '77
Tentacles '77
Battleforce '78
The Swarm '78
Meteor '79
Roots: The Next Generation '79
Wanda Nevada '79
Gideon's Trumpet '80
On Golden Pond '81
Summer Solstice '81

Jane Fonda (1937-)
Tall Story '60
The Chapman Report '62
Period of Adjustment '62
Walk on the Wild Side '62
In the Cool of the Day '63
Sunday in New York '63
Circle of Love '64
Joy House '64
Cat Ballou '65
Any Wednesday '66
The Chase '66
The Game Is Over '66
Barefoot in the Park '67
Hurry Sundown '67
Barbarella '68
Spirits of the Dead '68
They Shoot Horses, Don't They? '69
Klute '71
A Doll's House '73
Steelyard Blues '73
Fun with Dick and Jane '77
Julia '77
California Suite '78
Comes a Horseman '78
Coming Home '78
The China Syndrome '79
The Electric Horseman '79
9 to 5 '80
On Golden Pond '81
Rollover '81
Agnes of God '85
The Morning After '86
Old Gringo '89
Stanley and Iris '90
Monster-in-Law '05
Georgia Rule '07
Peace, Love & Misunderstanding '11
Lee Daniels' The Butler '13
Better Living Through Chemistry '14
This Is Where I Leave You '14
Youth '15
Book Club '18

Peter Fonda (1940-2019)
Tammy and the Doctor '63
Lilith '64
The Wild Angels '66
The Trip '67
Spirits of the Dead '68
Easy Rider '69
Hired Hand '71
Dirty Mary Crazy Larry '74
Race with the Devil '75
Fighting Mad '76
Futureworld '76
92 in the Shade '76
Outlaw Blues '77
Wanda Nevada '79
Cannonball Run '81
Fatal Mission '89
The Rose Garden '89
South Beach '92
Bodies, Rest & Motion '93
Deadfall '93
Love and a .45 '94
Nadja '95
Escape from L.A. '96
Grace of My Heart '96 (V)
Ulee's Gold '97
The Limey '99
The Passion of Ayn Rand '99
Second Skin '00
South of Heaven, West of Hell '00
Thomas and the Magic Railroad '00
The Laramie Project '02
The Maldonado Miracle '03
The Heart Is Deceitful Above All Things '04
A Thief of Time '04
Supernova '05
Ghost Rider '07
3:10 to Yuma '07
Journey to the Center of the Earth '08
The Boondock Saints II: All Saints Day '09
American Bandits: Frank and Jesse James '10
The Perfect Age of Rock 'n' Roll '10
The Trouble With Bliss '11
As Cool As I Am '13
Copperhead '13
House of Bodies '13
The Ultimate Life '13
The Runner '15
The Ballad of Lefty Brown '17
The Last Full Measure '19

Phil Fondacaro (1958-)
Troll '86
Ghoulies 2 '87
Dollman vs Demonic Toys '93
The Creeps '97
George A. Romero's Land of the Dead '05

Benson Fong (1916-87)
The Chinese Cat '44
The Purple Heart '44
The Scarlet Clue '45
Deception '46
His Majesty O'Keefe '53
Conquest of Space '55
Girls! Girls! Girls! '62
Our Man Flint '66
The Strongest Man in the World '75
Kung Fu: The Movie '86

Leo Fong (1928-)
The Last Reunion '80
Killpoint '84
Transformed '05

Lyndsy Fonseca (1987-)
Cyber Seduction: His Secret Life '05
Remember the Daze '07
Hot Tub Time Machine '10
Kick-Ass '10
The Ward '10
Five '11
Fort McCoy '11

Frank Fontaine (1920-78)
The Model and the Marriage Broker '51
Random Encounter '98
Nightwaves '03
Fatal Trust '06

Joan Fontaine (1917-2013)
No More Ladies '35
A Damsel in Distress '37
Gunga Din '39
The Women '39
Rebecca '40
Suspicion '41
This Above All '42
The Constant Nymph '43
Frenchman's Creek '44
Jane Eyre '44
Emperor Waltz '48
Letter from an Unknown Woman '48
You Gotta Stay Happy '48
September Affair '50
Ivanhoe '52
Othello '52
Something to Live For '52
The Bigamist '53
Decameron Nights '53
Casanova's Big Night '54
Beyond a Reasonable Doubt '56
Serenade '56
Island in the Sun '57
Until They Sail '57
Voyage to the Bottom of the Sea '61
Tender Is the Night '62
The Witches '66

Shawn Fonteno
Three Strikes '00
The Wash '01

Dolores Fonzi (1978-)
Burnt Money '00
The Bottom of the Sea '03
The Aura '05
The Film Critic '15

Jon Foo
House of Fury '05
Vikingdom '13
Weaponized '16
The Outsider '19

Hallie Foote (1950-)
1918 '85
On Valentine's Day '86
Courtship '87
Horton Foote's Alone '97

Horton Foote, Jr. (1954-)
1918 '85
On Valentine's Day '86
Blood Red '88

Dick Foran (1910-79)
Dangerous '35
Shipmates Forever '35
The Golden Arrow '36
Petrified Forest '36
The Black Legion '37
Boy Meets Girl '38
Cowboy from Brooklyn '38
Four Daughters '38
The Sisters '38
Daughters Courageous '39
Four Wives '39
The Fighting 69th '40
The House of the Seven Gables '40
The Mummy's Hand '40
My Little Chickadee '40
Winners of the West '40
Four Mothers '41
Riders of Death Valley '41
The Mummy's Tomb '42
Private Buckaroo '42
Ride 'Em Cowboy '42
Guest Wife '45
El Paso '49
Deputy Marshal '50
Chicago Confidential '57
The Fearmakers '58
Violent Road '58
Atomic Submarine '59
Studs Lonigan '60
Brighty of the Grand Canyon '67

June Foray (1917-2017)
Sabaka '55
Looney Looney Looney Bugs Bunny Movie '81 (V)
Who Framed Roger Rabbit '88 (V)
DuckTales the Movie: Treasure of the Lost Lamp '90 (V)
Thumbelina '94 (V)
Mulan '98 (V)
The Adventures of Rocky & Bullwinkle '00 (V)
Mulan 2 '04 (V)

Brenda Forbes (1909-96)
Vigil in the Night '40
Mrs. Miniver '42
The White Cliffs of Dover '44

Bryan Forbes (1926-2013)
Appointment in London '53
The Colditz Story '55
Satellite in the Sky '56
Quatermass 2 '57
Yesterday's Enemy '59
The League of Gentlemen '60
The Guns of Navarone '61
A Shot in the Dark '64
The Slipper and the Rose '76 (C)

Mary Forbes (1883-1974)
Vanity Fair '32
The Awful Truth '37
Outside of Paradise '38
You Can't Take It with You '38
You Can't Cheat an Honest Man '39
Klondike Fury '42
You Gotta Stay Happy '48

Michelle Forbes (1965-)
Kalifornia '93
Swimming with Sharks '94
Black Day Blue Night '95
Escape from L.A. '96
Homicide: The Movie '00
Perfume '01
Johnson County War '02
Unthinkable '07
Highland Park '13
The Hunters '13
Columbus '17

Ralph Forbes (1896-1951)
Mr. Wu '27
The Trail of '98 '28
Inside the Lines '30
The Bachelor Father '31
Beau Ideal '31
Smilin' Through '32
Bombay Mail '34
Riptide '34
Twentieth Century '34
The Goose and the Gander '35
I'll Name the Murderer '36
Make a Wish '37
Frenchman's Creek '44

Scott Forbes (1920-97)
Rocky Mountain '50
Inside the Walls of Folsom Prison '51
Raton Pass '51
Charade '53
The Mind of Mr. Soames '70

Anitra Ford (1942-)
The Big Bird Cage '72
Invasion of the Bee Girls '73
The Longest Yard '74

Ann Ford
The Love Machine *'71*
Logan's Run *'76*

Bette Ford (1937-)
Sudden Impact *'83*
The Landlady *'98*
Valley of the Sun *'11*

Colin Ford (1996-)
Lake City *'08*
Jack and the Beanstalk *'09*
We Bought a Zoo *'11*

Constance Ford (1923-93)
The Last Hunt *'56*
The Iron Sheriff *'57*
A Summer Place *'59*
Home from the Hill *'60*
Claudelle Inglish *'61*
All Fall Down *'62*
House of Women *'62*
Rome Adventure *'62*

Courtney Ford
Alien Raiders *'08*
Fling *'08*

Dawn Ford
Lost Junction *'03*
Garm Wars: The Last Druid *'15*

Dorothy Ford (1923-)
On Our Merry Way *'48*
Jack & the Beanstalk *'52*

Faith Ford (1964-)
You Talkin' to Me? *'87*
Sometimes They Come Back. . . For More *'99*
Beethoven's 5th *'03*
The Pacifier *'05*
Sorority Wars *'09*
Debbie Macomber's Trading Christmas *'11*
Field of Vision *'11*
Prom *'11*

Francis Ford (1881-1953)
Battling with Buffalo Bill *'31*
Steamboat Round the Bend *'35*
Charlie Chan at the Circus *'36*
The Texans *'38*
Stagecoach *'39*
Girls in Chains *'43*
She Wore a Yellow Ribbon *'49*
The Quiet Man *'52*

Glenn Ford (1916-2006)
Blondie Plays Cupid *'40*
The Lady in Question *'40*
So Ends Our Night *'41*
Texas *'41*
The Desperadoes *'43*
Destroyer *'43*
Gilda *'46*
A Stolen Life *'46*
Framed *'47*
The Loves of Carmen *'48*
The Doctor and the Girl *'49*
Lust for Gold *'49*
Man from Colorado *'49*
Mr. Soft Touch *'49*
The Undercover Man *'49*
Convicted *'50*
The White Tower *'50*
Affair in Trinidad *'52*
The Green Glove *'52*
Young Man With Ideas *'52*
Appointment in Honduras *'53*
The Big Heat *'53*
Man from the Alamo *'53*
Terror on a Train *'53*
Human Desire *'54*
Americano *'55*
Blackboard Jungle *'55*
Interrupted Melody *'55*
Trial *'55*
The Violent Men *'55*
Fastest Gun Alive *'56*
Jubal *'56*
Ransom! *'56*
The Teahouse of the August Moon *'56*
Don't Go Near the Water *'57*
3:10 to Yuma *'57*
Cowboy *'58*
Imitation General *'58*
The Sheepman *'58*
Torpedo Run *'58*
The Gazebo *'59*
It Started with a Kiss *'59*
Cimarron *'60*
Pocketful of Miracles *'61*
The Courtship of Eddie's Father *'62*
Experiment in Terror *'62*
The Four Horsemen of the Apocalypse *'62*
Love Is a Ball *'63*
Advance to the Rear *'64*
Dear Heart *'64*
Fate Is the Hunter *'64*
The Money Trap *'65*
The Rounders *'65*
Is Paris Burning? *'66*
The Last Challenge *'67*
Day of the Evil Gun *'68*
Heaven With a Gun *'69*
Smith! *'69*
Santee *'73*
Midway *'76*
Once an Eagle *'76*
Superman: The Movie *'78*
The Sacketts *'79*
The Visitor *'80*
Happy Birthday to Me *'81*
Virus *'82*
Casablanca Express *'89*
Border Shootout *'90*
Final Verdict *'91*
Raw Nerve *'91*

Harrison Ford (1884-1957)
Foolish Wives *'22*
The Primitive Lover *'22*
Shadows *'22*
Little Old New York *'23*
Blade Runner 2049 *'17*

Harrison Ford (1942-)
Dead Heat on a Merry-Go-Round *'66*
Getting Straight *'70*
Zabriskie Point *'70*
American Graffiti *'73*
The Conversation *'74*
Dynasty *'76*
Heroes *'77*
Star Wars *'77*
Force 10 from Navarone *'78*
Apocalypse Now *'79*
The Frisco Kid *'79*
Hanover Street *'79*
More American Graffiti *'79*
The Empire Strikes Back *'80*
Raiders of the Lost Ark *'81*
Blade Runner *'82*
Return of the Jedi *'83*
Indiana Jones and the Temple of Doom *'84*
Witness *'85*
The Mosquito Coast *'86*
Frantic *'88*
Working Girl *'88*
Indiana Jones and the Last Crusade *'89*
Presumed Innocent *'90*
Regarding Henry *'91*
Patriot Games *'92*
The Fugitive *'93*
Clear and Present Danger *'94*
Sabrina *'95*
The Devil's Own *'96*
Air Force One *'97*
Six Days, Seven Nights *'98*
Random Hearts *'99*
What Lies Beneath *'00*
K-19: The Widowmaker *'02*
Hollywood Homicide *'03*
Firewall *'06*
Indiana Jones and the Kingdom of the Crystal Skull *'08*
Crossing Over *'09*
Extraordinary Measures *'10*
Morning Glory *'10*
Cowboys & Aliens *'11*
Ender's Game *'13*
42 *'13*
Paranoia *'13*
The Expendables 3 *'14*
The Age of Adaline *'15*
Star Wars: The Force Awakens *'15*
Armstrong *'19 (N)*
The Secret Life of Pets 2 *'19*
The Call of the Wild *'20*

Luke Ford (1981-)
The Mummy: Tomb of the Dragon Emperor *'08*
Animal Kingdom *'09*
The Black Balloon *'09*
Ghost Machine *'09*
Red Dog *'11*

Maria Ford (1966-)
Stripped to Kill 2: Live Girls *'89*
Slumber Party Massacre 3 *'90*
Futurekick *'91*
The Haunting of Morella *'91*
Ring of Fire *'91*
Deathstalker 4: Match of Titans *'92*
Ring of Fire 2: Blood and Steel *'92*
Saturday Night Special *'92*
The Unnamable 2: The Statement of Randolph Carter *'92*
Angel of Destruction *'94*
Alien Terminator *'95*
Burial of the Rats *'95*
Night Hunter *'95*
The Showgirl Murders *'95*
Stripteaser *'95*
The Wasp Woman *'96*
Dark Planet *'97*
Future Fear *'97*

Mick Ford (1957-)
Scum *'79*
How to Get Ahead in Advertising *'89*

Paul Ford (1901-76)
Lust for Gold *'49*
Perfect Strangers *'50*
The Teahouse of the August Moon *'56*
The Matchmaker *'58*
Missouri Traveler *'58*
Advise and Consent *'62*
The Music Man *'62*
Who's Got the Action? *'63*
Never Too Late *'65*
The Russians Are Coming, the Russians Are Coming *'66*
The Comedians *'67*
Lola *'69*

Peter Ford
Fair Game *'86*
The Thorn Birds: The Missing Years *'96*

Ruth Ford (1911-2009)
The Hidden Hand *'42*
Wilson *'44*
The Woman Who Came Back *'45*
Strange Impersonation *'46*

Steven Ford (1956-)
Body Count *'87*
When Harry Met Sally. . . *'89*
Two Came Back *'97*
Against the Law *'98*
Black Hawk Down *'01*

Trent Ford (1979-)
Slap Her, She's French *'02*
How to Deal *'03*
September Dawn *'07*
Burning Blue *'14*

Wallace Ford (1898-1966)
Possessed *'31*
Are You Listening? *'32*
The Beast of the City *'32*
Freaks *'32*
Skyscraper Souls *'32*
East of Fifth Avenue *'33*
Employees' Entrance *'33*
Three-Cornered Moon *'33*
The Lost Patrol *'34*
The Informer *'35*
One Frightened Night *'35*
The Whole Town's Talking *'35*
Rogue's Tavern *'36*
Exiled to Shanghai *'37*
Mad About Money *'37*
Jericho *'38*
Back Door to Heaven *'39*
The Mummy's Hand *'40*
Two Girls on Broadway *'40*
Blues in the Night *'41*
Murder by Invitation *'41*
All Through the Night *'42*
The Mummy's Tomb *'42*
Shadow of a Doubt *'43*
Blood on the Sun *'45*
Spellbound *'45*
Black Angel *'46*
Crack-Up *'46*
The Green Years *'46*
Dead Reckoning *'47*
T-Men *'47*
Shed No Tears *'48*
Great Jesse James Raid *'49*
The Set-Up *'49*
The Breaking Point *'50*
The Furies *'50*
Harvey *'50*
Painting the Clouds With Sunshine *'51*
The Boy From Oklahoma *'54*
A Lawless Street *'55*
The Man from Laramie *'55*
The First Texan *'56*
The Rainmaker *'56*
The Last Hurrah *'58*
The Matchmaker *'58*
Warlock *'59*
A Patch of Blue *'65*

Willa Ford (1981-)
Impulse *'08*
Friday the 13th *'09*
Universal Squadrons *'11*

Ken Foree (1948-)
Dawn of the Dead *'78*
From Beyond *'86*
Leatherface: The Texas Chainsaw Massacre 3 *'89*
The Dentist *'96*
The Devil's Rejects *'05*
Devil's Den *'06*
Brutal Massacre: A Comedy *'07*
Brotherhood of Blood *'08*
The Lords of Salem *'13*

Amanda Foreman
Jam *'06*
All I Want for Christmas *'07*

Deborah Foreman (1962-)
Valley Girl *'83*
Real Genius *'85*
April Fool's Day *'86*
My Chauffeur *'86*
3:15: The Moment of Truth *'86*
Waxwork *'88*
Lobster Man from Mars *'89*
Sundown *'91*
Sundown: The Vampire in Retreat *'08*

Jamie Foreman (1958-)
Nil by Mouth *'96*
Gangster No. 1 *'00*
Saving Grace *'00*
I'll Sleep When I'm Dead *'03*
Layer Cake *'05*
Oliver Twist *'05*
Botched *'07*
Berlin Job *'12*

Michelle Foreman
Stripped to Kill *'87*
Sunset Strip *'91*

Mark Forest (1933-)
Goliath and the Dragon *'61*
Mole Men Against the Son of Hercules *'61*
Colossus of the Arena *'62*
Son of Samson *'62*
Hercules Against the Mongols *'63*
Goliath and the Sins of Babylon *'64*
Hercules *vs.* the Sons of the Sun *'64*
The Lion of Thebes *'64*

Michael Forest (1929-)
Atlas *'60*
The Message *'77*
Body of Evidence *'92*
Cast Away *'00*

Sara Forestier (1986-)
Games of Love and Chance *'03*
A Few Days in September *'06*
Wild Grass *'09*
Gainsbourg: A Heroic Life *'10*
The Names of Love *'10*

Sarah Foret (1984-)
American Crude *'07*
Lost Dream *'09*

Maud Forget (1982-)
Bad Company *'99*
La Vie Promise *'02*

Farrah Forke (1968-)
Journey to the Center of the Earth *'93*
Abandoned and Deceived *'95*
Ground Control *'98*
Kate's Addiction *'99*

Claire Forlani (1972-)
JFK: Reckless Youth *'93*
Mallrats *'95*
Basquiat *'96*
The Last Time I Committed Suicide *'96*
The Rock *'96*
Basil *'98*
Meet Joe Black *'98*
Mystery Men *'99*
Antitrust *'00*
Boys and Girls *'00*
Triggermen *'02*
Gone Dark *'03*
The Medallion *'03*
Northfork *'03*
Bobby Jones: Stroke of Genius *'04*
Memron *'04*
Green Street Hooligans *'05*
Carolina Moon *'07*
Mister Foe *'07*
Beer for My Horses *'08*
The Diplomat *'08*
Flashbacks of a Fool *'08*
In the Name of the King: A Dungeon Siege Tale *'08*
Not Forgotten *'09*
Shannon's Rainbow *'09*
Love's Kitchen *'11*
Precious Cargo *'16*

Milos Forman (1932-2018)
Heartburn *'86*
New Year's Day *'89*
Keeping the Faith *'00*
Beloved *'11*

Richard Foronjy (1937-)
Prince of the City *'81*
The Morning After *'86*
Midnight Run *'88*
DaVinci's War *'92*
The Public Eye *'92*
Man of the House *'95*

Veronica Forque (1955-)
Why Do They Call It Love When They Mean Sex? *'92*
Kika *'94*
I Love You Baby *'01*

Philippe Forquet (1940-2020)
In the French Style *'63*
Take Her, She's Mine *'63*

Christine Forrest
Martin *'77*
Monkey Shines *'88*

Frederic Forrest (1936-)
The Don Is Dead *'73*
The Conversation *'74*
Missouri Breaks *'76*
It's Alive 2: It Lives Again *'78*
Apocalypse Now *'79*
The Rose *'79*
Hammett *'82*
One from the Heart *'82*
Valley Girl *'83*
The Stone Boy *'84*
The Adventures of Huckleberry Finn *'85*
Where Are the Children? *'85*
The Deliberate Stranger *'86*
Saigon: Year of the Cat *'87*
Gotham *'88*
Tucker: The Man and His Dream *'88*
Lonesome Dove *'89*
Music Box *'89*
Cat Chaser *'90*
The Two Jakes *'90*
Hearts of Darkness: A Filmmaker's Apocalypse *'91*
Twin Sisters *'91*
Citizen Cohn *'92*
Dario Argento's Trauma *'93*
Falling Down *'93*
Rain Without Thunder *'93*
Against the Wall *'94*
Chasers *'94*
Lassie *'94*
Andersonville *'95*
One Night Stand *'95*
Crash Dive *'96*
The End of Violence *'97*
Horton Foote's Alone *'97*
Black Thunder *'98*
Boogie Boy *'98*
The First 9 1/2 Weeks *'98*
Implicated *'98*
Point Blank *'98*
Militia *'99*
The House Next Door *'01*
Path to War *'02*
All the King's Men *'06*

Irene Forrest (1944-2010)
Sitting Ducks *'80*
Bride of Re-Animator *'89*

Sally Forrest (1928-2015)
Streets of Sin *'49*
Mystery Street *'50*
Excuse My Dust *'51*
Hard, Fast and Beautiful *'51*
The Strange Door *'51*
Vengeance Valley *'51*
Code Two *'53*

Steve Forrest (1924-2013)
The Ghost Ship *'43*
Geisha Girl *'52*
Battle Circus *'53*
Bedevilled *'55*
It Happened to Jane *'59*
Flaming Star *'60*
Heller in Pink Tights *'60*
The Second Time Around *'61*
The Wild Country *'71*
The Hanged Man *'74*
Testimony of Two Men *'77*
Captain America *'79*
North Dallas Forty *'79*
Mommie Dearest *'81*
Spies Like Us *'85*
Amazon Women on the Moon *'87*
Gunsmoke: Return to Dodge *'87*
Killer: A Journal of Murder *'95*
S.W.A.T. *'03 (C)*

William Forrest (1902-89)
Wake Island *'42*
Air Force *'43*
Fighting Seabees *'44*
Dead Reckoning *'47*
I'll See You in My Dreams *'51*
The Story of Will Rogers *'52*
The Eddie Cantor Story *'53*
Jailhouse Rock *'57*
The Horse Soldiers *'59*
Good Neighbor Sam *'64*
Billy the Kid Versus Dracula *'66*

Cay Forrester (1921-2005)
D.O.A. *'49*
Door to Door Maniac *'61*

Constance Forslund (1950-)
River's Edge *'87*
Village of the Damned *'95*

Robert Forster (1941-2019)
Medium Cool *'69*
The Stalking Moon *'69*
Pieces of Dreams *'70*
The Don Is Dead *'73*
Stunts *'77*
Avalanche *'78*

The Black Hole '79
Alligator '80
Vigilante '83
Walking the Edge '83
Delta Force '86
Peacemaker '90
Committed '91
29th Street '91
Maniac Cop 3: Badge of Silence '93
Scanners: The Showdown '94
Uncle Sam '96
Jackie Brown '97
Night Vision '97
Psycho '98
It's the Rage '99
Supernova '99
Kiss Toledo Goodbye '00
Lakeboat '00
Me, Myself, and Irene '00
Diamond Men '01
Finder's Fee '01
Mulholland Drive '01
Road to Riches '01
Due East '02
Human Nature '02
Like Mike '02
Lone Hero '02
Murder in Greenwich '02
Charlie's Angels: Full Throttle '03
Confidence '03
Grand Theft Parsons '03
Undefeated '03
Firewall '06
Lucky Number Slevin '06
Cleaner '07
Dragon Wars '07
Rise: Blood Hunter '07
Jack and Jill *vs.* the World '08
Touching Home '08
Would Be Kings '08
The Code '09
Ghosts of Girlfriends Past '09
American Grindhouse '10
The Bannen Way '10
Kalamity '10
Middle Men '10
The Trial '10
The Descendants '11
Olympus Has Fallen '13
Somewhere Slow '14
The American Side '16
Bus Driver '16
The Case for Christ '17
The Big Take '18

Rudolph Forster (1884-1968)
The Threepenny Opera '31
The Return of Dr. Mabuse '61
The Mad Executioners '65

Bruce Forsyth (1928-)
Star! '68
Bedknobs and Broomsticks '71

Rosemary Forsyth (1943-)
Shenandoah '65
The War Lord '65
Texas Across the River '66
Whatever Happened to Aunt Alice? '69
Where It's At '69
City Beneath the Sea '71
Columbo: Murder by the Book '71
Black Eye '74
Gray Lady Down '77
The Gladiator '86
Disclosure '94
Daylight '96
Girl '98
John Carpenter's Ghosts of Mars '01
A Time to Remember '03
Sweet Nothing in My Ear '08

Drew Forsythe (1950-)
Wrangler '88
Billy's Holiday '95

Henderson Forsythe (1917-2006)
Carolina Skeletons '92
Teamster Boss: The Jackie Presser Story '92

John Forsythe (1918-2010)
Destination Tokyo '43
The Captive City '52
Escape from Fort Bravo '53
The Trouble with Harry '55
The Ambassador's Daughter '56
Kitten with a Whip '64
Madame X '66
In Cold Blood '67
The Happy Ending '69
Topaz '69
Murder Once Removed '71
Lisa, Bright and Dark '73
Cry Panic '74
Terror on the 40th Floor '74
Sniper '75
And Justice for All '79
A Time for Miracles '80
Mysterious Two '82
Scrooged '88
Charlie's Angels '00 (V)
Charlie's Angels: Full Throttle '03 (V)

William Forsythe (1955-)
Once Upon a Time in America '84
Savage Dawn '84
The Lightship '86
The Long, Hot Summer '86
Extreme Prejudice '87
Raising Arizona '87
Patty Hearst '88
Dead Bang '89
Dick Tracy '90
Torrents of Spring '90
Career Opportunities '91
Out for Justice '91
Stone Cold '91
The Waterdance '91
American Me '92
The Gun in Betty Lou's Handbag '92
Direct Hit '93
Relentless 3 '93
Beyond Desire '94
The Immortals '95
Palookaville '95
Things to Do in Denver When You're Dead '95
Virtuosity '95
Gotti '96
The Rock '96
The Substitute '96
Firestorm '97
First Time Felon '97
Hell's Kitchen NYC '97
Dollar for the Dead '98
Highway Hitcher '98
Row Your Boat '98
Big City Blues '99
Blue Streak '99
Deuce Bigalow: Male Gigolo '99
Hitman's Journal '99
The Last Marshal '99
Malicious Intent '99
Soundman '99
Camouflage '00
Luck of the Draw '00
Blue Hill Avenue '01
Hard Cash '01
City by the Sea '02
The Last Letter '04
The Devil's Rejects '05
Freedomland '06
Jam '06
Hack! '07
Halloween '07
88 Minutes '08
Final Approach '08
iMurders '08
Stiletto '08
The Rig '10
Born to Ride '11
Jesse '11
Loosies '11
Hidden in the Woods '16

Marlene Forte
The Bronx War '90
Our Song '01

Little Girl Lost: The Delimar Vera Story '08

Will Forte (1970-)
Around the World in 80 Days '04
Beerfest '06
The Brothers Solomon '07
MacGruber '10
A Good Old Fashioned Orgy '11
The Watch '12
Cloudy with a Chance of Meatballs 2 '13 (V)
Life of Crime '13
Nebraska '13
Run & Jump '13
Apartment Troubles '15
Don Verdean '15
My Life as a Zucchini '16 (V)
Extra Ordinary '20
Scoob! '20
The Willoughbys '20

Robert Fortier (1926-2005)
Incubus '65
3 Women '77

John Fortune (1939-)
The Tailor of Panama '00
Calendar Girls '03

Bob Fosse (1927-87)
The Affairs of Dobie Gillis '53
Give a Girl a Break '53
Kiss Me Kate '53
My Sister Eileen '55
The Little Prince '74

Nicole Fosse (1963-)
All That Jazz '79
A Chorus Line '85

Brigitte Fossey (1946-)
Forbidden Games '52
The Happy Road '57
Honor Among Thieves '68
Going Places '74
The Man Who Loved Women '77
Quintet '79
La Boum '81
Enigma '82
The Future of Emily '85
The Last Butterfly '92

Anthony Foster (1939-)
See Anthony (Jose, J. Antonio, J.A.) Mayans

Barry Foster (1931-2002)
King and Country '64
Inspector Clouseau '68
Frenzy '72
Orde Wingate '76
Heat and Dust '82
How Many Miles to Babylon? '82
Smiley's People '82
Beyond the Next Mountain '87
Maurice '87
The Whistle Blower '87

Ben Foster (1980-)
Liberty Heights '99
Get Over It! '01
Big Trouble '02
11:14 '03
Northfork '03
The Heart Is Deceitful Above All Things '04
The Punisher '04
Hostage '05
Alpha Dog '06
X-Men: The Last Stand '06
30 Days of Night '07
3:10 to Yuma '07
Birds of America '08
The Messenger '09
Pandorum '09
The Mechanic '11
Rampart '11
Contraband '12
Here '12
360 '12
Ain't Them Bodies Saints '13
Kill Your Darlings '13
Lone Survivor '13
The Program '15
The Finest Hours '16
Hell or High Water '16

Warcraft '16
Leave No Trace '18

Bren Foster
War Flowers '12
Force of Execution '13
Terminus '16

Dianne Foster (1928-)
Bad for Each Other '53
Drive a Crooked Road '54
Three Hours to Kill '54
The Kentuckian '55
The Violent Men '55
The Brothers Rico '57
Night Passage '57
The Last Hurrah '58
The King of the Roaring '20s: The Story of Arnold Rothstein '61
Iowa '05

Dudley Foster (1925-73)
Term of Trial '63
Moon Zero Two '70

George Foster
Killer Me '01
Centipede '05

Gloria Foster (1936-2001)
Nothing but a Man '64
The Angel Levine '70
Man & Boy '71
To All My Friends on Shore '71
Leonard Part 6 '87
The House of Dies Drear '88
City of Hope '91
The Matrix '99
The Matrix Reloaded '03

Helen Foster (1906-82)
Painted Faces '29
Boiling Point '32
Ghost City '32

Jodie Foster (1963-)
Menace on the Mountain '70
Kansas City Bomber '72
Napoleon and Samantha '72
One Little Indian '73
Tom Sawyer '73
Alice Doesn't Live Here Anymore '74
Smile Jenny, You're Dead '74
Bugsy Malone '76
Freaky Friday '76
The Little Girl Who Lives down the Lane '76
Taxi Driver '76
Candleshoe '78
Carny '80
Foxes '80
O'Hara's Wife '82
Svengali '83
The Hotel New Hampshire '84
Mesmerized '84
The Accused '88
Five Corners '88
Stealing Home '88
Backtrack '89
Little Man Tate '91
The Silence of the Lambs '91
Shadows and Fog '92
Sommersby '93
Maverick '94
Nell '94
Contact '97
Anna and the King '99
The Dangerous Lives of Altar Boys '02
Panic Room '02
A Very Long Engagement '04
Flightplan '05
Inside Man '06
The Brave One '07
Nim's Island '08
Motherhood '09 (C)
The Beaver '11
Carnage '11
Elysium '13
Hotel Artemis '18

Jon Foster (1984-)
Murder in Greenwich '02
The Door in the Floor '04
Stay Alive '06

The Mysteries of Pittsburgh '08
Tenderness '08
The Informers '09
The Last Rites of Ransom Pride '09
Brotherhood '10
Mr. Jones '14

Julia Foster (1943-)
The Loneliness of the Long Distance Runner '62
The System '64
Alfie '66
Half a Sixpence '67
Flick '07

Meg Foster (1948-)
Adam at 6 a.m. '70
Thumb Tripping '72
James Dean '76
Different Story '78
The Scarlet Letter '79
Carny '80
Ticket to Heaven '81
The Osterman Weekend '83
The Emerald Forest '85
Masters of the Universe '87
The Wind '87
They Live '88
Leviathan '89
Relentless '89
Stepfather 2: Make Room for Daddy '89
Blind Fury '90
Jezebel's Kiss '90
Futurekick '91
Relentless 2: Dead On '91
To Catch a Killer '92
Best of the Best 2 '93
Immortal Combat '94
Oblivion '94
Undercover '94
Backlash: Oblivion 2 '95
The Man in the Iron Mask '97
Spoiler '98
The Lords of Salem '13
31 '16
Jeepers Creepers 3 '17

Norman Foster (1900-76)
Alias the Doctor '32
Skyscraper Souls '32
Under Eighteen '32
Pilgrimage '33
Rafter Romance '33
Strictly Dynamite '34
Behind the Green Lights '35
Ladies Crave Excitement '35
The Other Side of the Wind '18

Phil Foster (1914-85)
Conquest of Space '55
Bang the Drum Slowly '73

Preston Foster (1902-70)
Doctor X '32
I Am a Fugitive from a Chain Gang '32
The Last Mile '32
Two Seconds '32
You Said a Mouthful '32
Corruption '33
Elmer the Great '33
Annie Oakley '35
The Informer '35
Last Days of Pompeii '35
Love Before Breakfast '36
American Empire '42
Secret Agent of Japan '42
Thunder Birds '42
Guadalcanal Diary '43
My Friend Flicka '43
The Valley of Decision '45
The Harvey Girls '46
Ramrod '47
The Hunted '48
Thunderhoof '48
The Big Cat '49
I Shot Jesse James '49
Three Desperate Men '50
The Big Night '51
Tomahawk '51
Kansas City Confidential '52
Law and Order '53
The Marshal's Daughter '53

Sara Foster (1981-)
The Big Bounce '04
D.E.B.S. '04
Bachelor Party 2: The Last Temptation '08
Psych: 9 '10

Stacie Foster
Steel Frontier '94
Cyber-Tracker 2 '95

Susanna Foster (1924-2009)
The Phantom of the Opera '43
The Climax '44

Robert Fotrer (1939-)
See Anthony (Jose, J. Antonio, J.A.) Mayans

Byron Foulger (1899-1968)
Prisoner of Zenda '37
Sullivan's Travels '41
The Panther's Claw '42
Hoppy Serves a Writ '43
Bells of San Fernando '47
The Chinese Ring '47
The Devil's Partner '58

Robert Foulk (1908-89)
Robin and the 7 Hoods '64
Emperor of the North Pole '73

Derek Fowlds (1937-2020)
East of Sudan '64
Frankenstein Created Woman '66
Over the Hill '93

Harry Fowler (1926-2012)
Fire Maidens from Outer Space '56
Lucky Jim '58

Douglas Fowley (1911-98)
Big Brown Eyes '36
Charlie Chan on Broadway '37
On the Avenue '37
Mr. Moto's Gamble '38
Charlie Chan at Treasure Island '39
Mr. Wise Guy '42
Colt Comrades '43
One Body Too Many '44
Larceny in her Heart '46
Desperate '47
Battleground '49
Susanna Pass '49
Armored Car Robbery '50
Bunco Squad '50
Tarzan's Peril '51
Singin' in the Rain '52
Cat Women of the Moon '53
A Slight Case of Larceny '53
The High and the Mighty '54
Lonesome Trail '55
The Broken Star '56
Man from Del Rio '56
The Good Guys and the Bad Guys '69
From Noon Till Three '76
The White Buffalo '77

Bernard Fox (1927-)
Strange Bedfellows '65
Hold On! '66
Munster, Go Home! '66
House of the Dead '78
Zone of the Dead '78
The Private Eyes '80
Titanic '97
The Mummy '99

Colin Fox (1938-)
Beautiful Dreamers '92
Daylight '96
Angels in the Infield '00
Left Behind: The Movie '00
The Doorbell Rang: A Nero Wolfe Mystery '01
Deathlands: Homeward Bound '03
Webs '03

David Fox (1941-)
Black Fox: Good Men and Bad '94
When Night Is Falling '95
Grey Owl '99
The Saddest Music in the World '03

Population 436 '06
That Beautiful Somewhere '06

Edward Fox (1937-)
The Mind Benders '63
Morgan: A Suitable Case for Treatment '66
Portrait of a Lady '67
Battle of Britain '69
The Go-Between '71
The Day of the Jackal '73
A Doll's House '73
A Bridge Too Far '77
The Duellists '77
The Squeeze '77
The Big Sleep '78
Force 10 from Navarone '78
Soldier of Orange '78
The Cat and the Canary '79
Edward and Mrs. Simpson '80
The Mirror Crack'd '80
Gandhi '82
The Dresser '83
Never Say Never Again '83
Shaka Zulu '83
The Bounty '84
The Shooting Party '85
Anastasia: The Mystery of Anna '86
The Crucifer of Blood '91
Robin Hood '91
Gulliver's Travels '95
A Month by the Lake '95
September '96
A Dance to the Music of Time '97
Lost in Space '98
All the Queen's Men '02
Daniel Deronda '02
The Importance of Being Earnest '02
Nicholas Nickleby '02
The Republic of Love '03
Stage Beauty '04
Lassie '05
Oliver Twist '07

Emilia Fox (1974-)
Rebecca '97
David Copperfield '99
The Scarlet Pimpernel '99
Shooting the Past '99
The Pianist '02
Three Blind Mice '02
Helen of Troy '03
The Republic of Love '03
Keeping Mum '05
The Tiger and the Snow '05
Cashback '06
Ballet Shoes '07
Dorian Gray '09
A Thousand Kisses Deep '11

Freddie Fox (1989-)
Any Human Heart '11
The Mystery of Edwin Drood '12
Black '47 '18

Huckleberry Fox (1975-)
Konrad '85
Pharoah's Army '95

James Fox (1939-)
The Magnet '50
Timbuktu '59
The Servant '63
King Rat '65
Those Magnificent Men in Their Flying Machines '65
The Chase '66
Thoroughly Modern Millie '67
Duffy '68
Performance '70
Greystoke: The Legend of Tarzan, Lord of the Apes '84
A Passage to India '84
Absolute Beginners '86
The Whistle Blower '87
High Season '88
Farewell to the King '89
The Mighty Quinn '89
The Russia House '90
A Question of Attribution '91
Afraid of the Dark '92
Patriot Games '92
The Remains of the Day '93
Catherine Cookson's The Dwelling Place '94
Doomsday Gun '94
The Old Curiosity Shop '94
Anna Karenina '96
Circle of Passion '97
Kings in Grass Castles '97
Lover's Prayer '99
Mickey Blue Eyes '99
The Golden Bowl '00
Sexy Beast '00
Up at the Villa '00
The Mystic Masseur '01
Shaka Zulu: The Last Great Warrior '01
The Lost World '02
Cambridge Spies '03
The Prince & Me '04
Charlie and the Chocolate Factory '05
Mister Lonely '07
Red Riding, Part 2: 1980 '09
Sherlock Holmes '09
W.E. '11
Cleanskin '12

Jerry Fox
Evil Spawn '87
Hollywood Chainsaw Hookers '88

Jorja Fox (1968-)
The Kill-Off '89
Happy Hell Night '92
Memento '00
3 Weeks to Daytona '11

Kerry Fox (1966-)
An Angel at My Table '89
Shallow Grave '94
The Affair '95
Country Life '95
A Village Affair '95
The Hanging Garden '97
Welcome to Sarajevo '97
Immortality '98
To Walk with Lions '99
Intimacy '00
The Gathering '02
P.D. James: The Murder Room '04
Bright Star '09
Burning Man '11
Cloudstreet '11
Intruders '11
Trap for Cinderella '13
Mayhem '17
Little Joe '19

Lauren Fox (1977-)
I Love You, I Love You Not '97
Standing on Fishes '99

Laurence Fox (1978-)
The Hole '01
Deathwatch '02
The Last Drop '05
Becoming Jane '07
A Room With a View '08
Wired '08
W.E. '11

Matthew Fox (1966-)
My Boyfriend's Back '93
Behind the Mask '99
We Are Marshall '06
Smokin' Aces '07
Speed Racer '08
Vantage Point '08
Alex Cross '12
Emperor '12
Bone Tomahawk '15

Megan Fox (1986-)
Confessions of a Teenage Drama Queen '04
Crimes of Fashion '04
Transformers '07
How to Lose Friends & Alienate People '08
Jennifer's Body '09
Transformers: Revenge of the Fallen '09
Jonah Hex '10
Passion Play '10
The Dictator '12
Friends with Kids '12
This Is 40 '12
Teenage Mutant Ninja Turtles '14
Teenage Mutant Ninja Turtles: Out of the Shadows '16
Battle of Jangsari '19
Zeroville '19
Think Like a Dog '20

Michael Fox (1921-96)
War of the Satellites '58
Bloody Mama '70
The Dunwich Horror '70
The Longest Yard '74

Michael J. Fox (1961-)
Midnight Madness '80
Class of 1984 '82
High School USA '84
Back to the Future '85
Teen Wolf '85
The Secret of My Success '87
Bright Lights, Big City '88
Back to the Future, Part 2 '89
Casualties of War '89
Back to the Future, Part 3 '90
Doc Hollywood '91
The Hard Way '91
For Love or Money '93
Homeward Bound: The Incredible Journey '93 (V)
Life with Mikey '93
Coldblooded '94 (C)
Greedy '94
Where the Rivers Flow North '94
The American President '95
Blue in the Face '95
The Frighteners '96
Homeward Bound 2: Lost in San Francisco '96 (V)
Mars Attacks! '96
Stuart Little '99 (V)
Atlantis: The Lost Empire '01 (V)
Interstate 60 '02 (C)
Stuart Little 2 '02 (V)
Stuart Little 3: Call of the Wild '06 (V)

Phoebe Fox
The Woman in Black 2: Angel of Death '15
Blue Iguana '18
The Aeronauts '19

Rick Fox (1969-)
The Collectors '99
Resurrection '99
Holes '03
Tyler Perry's Meet the Browns '08
Navy Seals vs. Zombies '15

Sidney (Sydney) Fox (1910-42)
Midnight '34
Don Quixote '35

Spencer Fox (1993-)
The Incredibles '04 (V)
Air Bud 6: Air Buddies '06 (V)
The Groomsmen '06

Vivica A. Fox (1964-)
Born on the Fourth of July '89
The Tuskegee Airmen '95
Booty Call '96
Independence Day '96
Set It Off '96
Batman and Robin '97
Soul Food '97
Solomon '98
Why Do Fools Fall in Love? '98
Idle Hands '99
A Saintly Switch '99
Teaching Mrs. Tingle '99
Hendrix '00
Kingdom Come '01
Two Can Play That Game '01
Juwanna Mann '02
Little Secrets '02
Boat Trip '03
Kill Bill Vol. 1 '03
Motives '03
Blast '04
Ella Enchanted '04
Kill Bill Vol. 2 '04
Getting Played '05
The Salon '05
Citizen Duane '06
Father of Lies '07
Kickin' It Old Skool '07
Motives 2-Retribution '07
Three Can Play That Game '07
Cover '08
Private Valentine: Blonde & Dangerous '08
San Saba '08
The Slammin' Salmon '09
Black Limousine '10
Miss Nobody '10
Annie Claus is Coming to Town '11
A Holiday Heist '11
Solid State '12
Home Run '13
Sharknado 2: The Second One '14
Carter High '15
Golden Shoes '15

Earle Foxe (1891-1973)
Four Sons '28
Hangman's House '28
Union Depot '32
Blondie Johnson '33
St. Louis Woman '34

Emily Foxler (1984-)
Deadly Honeymoon '10
Left to Die: The Sandra and Tammi Chase Story '12
Coherence '13

Robert Foxworth (1941-)
Frankenstein '73
The Questor Tapes '74
The Invisible Strangler '76
The Treasure of Matecumbe '76
Ants '77
Damien: Omen 2 '78
The Black Marble '79
Prophecy '79
Peter and Paul '81
Beyond the Stars '89
The Price of the Bride '90
Syriana '05
The Librarian: Return to King Solomon's Mines '06
Kiss the Bride '07
Transformers '07 (V)
Transformers: Revenge of the Fallen '09 (V)
Transformers: Dark of the Moon '11 (V)
Transformers: Age of Extinction '14 (V)

Jeff Foxworthy (1958-)
Racing Stripes '05 (V)
The Fox and the Hound 2 '06 (V)
The Smurfs '11 (V)

Jamie Foxx (1967-)
Booty Call '96
The Great White Hype '96
The Truth about Cats and Dogs '96
The Players Club '98
Any Given Sunday '99
Bait '00
Held Up '00
Ali '01
Shade '03
Breakin' All The Rules '04
Collateral '04
Ray '04
Jarhead '05
Stealth '05
Dreamgirls '06
Miami Vice '06
The Kingdom '07
Law Abiding Citizen '09
The Soloist '09
Due Date '10
Valentine's Day '10
Horrible Bosses '11
Rio '11 (V)
Django Unchained '12
White House Down '13
The Amazing Spider-Man 2 '14
Annie '14
Horrible Bosses 2 '14
Rio 2 '14 (V)
Baby Driver '17
Sleepless '17
Robin Hood '18
Just Mercy '19

Redd Foxx (1922-91)
Cotton Comes to Harlem '70
Norman, Is That You? '76
Harlem Nights '89

Charles Foy (1898-1984)
Mutiny in the Big House '39
The Wagons Roll at Night '41

Claire Foy (1984-)
Little Dorrit '08
Going Postal '10
Season of the Witch '10
Upstairs Downstairs '11
Rosewater '14
Breathe '17
First Man '18
The Girl in the Spider's Web '18
Unsane '18

Eddie Foy, Jr. (1905-83)
Yankee Doodle Dandy '42
Wilson '44
Lucky Me '54
The Pajama Game '57
Bells Are Ringing '60
Gidget Goes Hawaiian '61
Deadly Game '77

Mackenzie Foy (2000-)
The Twilight Saga: Breaking Dawn, Part 2 '12
Ernest & Celestine '13 (V)
Interstellar '14
The Little Prince '16
The Nutcracker and the Four Realms '18

Victoria Foyt (1958-)
Babyfever '94
Last Summer In the Hamptons '96
Deja Vu '98
Going Shopping '05

Tracy Fraim
Fear '96
Best Men '98

James Frain (1968-)
The Buccaneers '95
Loch Ness '95
The Mill on the Floss '97
Elizabeth '98
Hilary and Jackie '98
Red Meat '98
Sunshine '99
Titus '99
Arabian Nights '00
The Miracle Maker: The Story of Jesus '00 (V)
Reindeer Games '00
Where the Heart Is '00
The Count of Monte Cristo '02
Path to War '02
Into the Blue '05
The Front Line '06
Everybody's Fine '09
Tron: Legacy '10
Going for Gold: The '48 Games '12
Transit '12
Alpha Alert '13

Jonathan Frakes (1952-)
Beach Patrol '79
North and South Book 1 '85
Gargoyles, The Movie: The Heroes Awaken '94 (V)
Star Trek: Generations '94
Star Trek: First Contact '96
Star Trek: Insurrection '98
Star Trek: Nemesis '02

David 'Shark' Fralick (1962-)
Soultaker '90
The Legend of Wolf Mountain '92
Uncle Sam '96
Clawed: The Legend of Sasquatch '05
When I Find the Ocean '06

Peter Frampton (1950-)
Sgt. Pepper's Lonely Hearts Club Band '78
Almost Famous '00

C.V. France (1868-1949)
Skin Game '31
Night Train to Munich '40

Richard France (1930-)
The Crazies '73
Dawn of the Dead '78

Guillermo Francella
Rudo y Cursi '09
The Secret in Their Eyes '09

Victor Francen (1888-1977)
Hold Back the Dawn '41
The Desert Song '43
Madame Curie '43
The Conspirators '44
The Mask of Dimitrios '44
Passage to Marseilles '44
Confidential Agent '45
San Antonio '45
The Beast with Five Fingers '46
Devotion '46
Bedevilled '55

Teresa Franchini (1877-9720)
Chains '49
Nobody's Children '52

Anthony (Tony) Franciosa (1928-2006)
A Face in the Crowd '57
Wild Is the Wind '57
The Long, Hot Summer '58
Career '59
A Hatful of Rain '59
Period of Adjustment '62
Rio Conchos '64
Assault on a Queen '66
Fathom '67
The Sweet Ride '68
Web of the Spider '70
Earth II '71
Across 110th Street '72
The Drowning Pool '75
Daughter of Death '82
Death Wish 2 '82
Unsane '82
La Cicada '83
Stagecoach '86
Blood Vows: The Story of a Mafia Wife '87
Death House '88
Backstreet Dreams '90
City Hall '95

Alec B. Francis (1867-1934)
The Man Who Had Everything '20
Beyond the Rocks '22
Little Church Around the Corner '23
Beau Brummel '24
Tramp, Tramp, Tramp '26
Evangeline '29
The Bishop Murder Case '30
Mata Hari '32
His Private Secretary '33

Anne Francis (1930-2011)
Portrait of Jennie '48
Summer Holiday '48
Elopement '51
A Lion Is in the Streets '53
Bad Day at Black Rock '54
The Rocket Man '54
Susan Slept Here '54
Battle Cry '55
Blackboard Jungle '55
The Scarlet Coat '55
Forbidden Planet '56
The Great American Pastime '56
The Rack '56
Don't Go Near the Water '57
The Crowded Sky '60
Girl of the Night '60
The Satan Bug '65
Funny Girl '68
More Dead Than Alive '68
Impasse '69
The Love God? '70
Mongo's Back In Town '71
Pancho Villa '72

Cry Panic '74
Banjo Hackett '76
Born Again '78
Detour to Terror '80
Mazes and Monsters '82
Poor Little Rich Girl: The Barbara Hutton Story '87

Arlene Francis (1908-2001)
One, Two, Three '61
The Thrill of It All! '63

Clive Francis (1946-)
Poldark '75
The Bretts '88
Sharpe's Company '94
Longitude '00

Connie Francis (1938-)
Where the Boys Are '60
Follow the Boys '63
Looking for Love '64
When the Boys Meet the Girls '65

Derek Francis (1923-84)
Tomb of Ligeia '64
Rasputin the Mad Monk '66
What's Good for the Goose '69

Genie Francis (1962-)
North and South Book 1 '85
North and South Book 2 '86
Disney's Teacher's Pet '04 (V)
Thunderbirds '04
The Note '07
The Note 2: Taking a Chance on Love '09
The Note 3: Notes from the Heart Healer '12

Ivor Francis (1918-86)
Pieces of Dreams '70
Wackiest Wagon Train in the West '77
House of the Dead '78
Zone of the Dead '78

Jan Francis (1951-)
Champions '84
Bloodlines '05

Jon Francis (1957-)
See Jon(athan) Gries

Kay Francis (1899-1968)
The Cocoanuts '29
Raffles '30
Jewel Robbery '32
One Way Passage '32
Street of Women '32
Trouble in Paradise '32
The House on 56th Street '33
British Agent '34
Wonder Bar '34
The Goose and the Gander '35
Living on Velvet '35
Stranded '35
Give Me Your Heart '36
Another Dawn '37
Stolen Holiday '37
In Name Only '39
King of the Underworld '39
Little Men '40
Charley's Aunt '41
Play Girl '41
Four Jills in a Jeep '44
Wife Wanted '46

Noel Francis (1906-59)
Smart Money '31
Reform Girl '33
Mutiny Ahead '35

Paul Francis
Warlock 3: The End of Innocence '98
Tears of the Sun '03
Play Dead '09

Robert Francis (1930-55)
The Caine Mutiny '54
The Long Gray Line '55

Ryan Francis (1977-)
Social Misfits '00
Straight into Darkness '04

Sandra Francis
Time Lock '57
Spy in the Sky '58

James Franciscus (1934-91)
Four Boys and a Gun '57
The Mugger '58
Youngblood Hawke '64
Marooned '69
The Valley of Gwangi '69
Beneath the Planet of the Apes '70
Hell Boats '70
The Cat o' Nine Tails '71
Jonathan Livingston Seagull '73 (V)
One of My Wives Is Missing '76
Good Guys Wear Black '78
The Greek Tycoon '78
Butterfly '82
Secret Weapons '85

Don Francks (1932-)
Finian's Rainbow '68
Fast Company '78
Heavy Metal '81 (V)
My Bloody Valentine '81
Rock & Rule '83 (V)
Big Town '87
The Christmas Wife '88
Degree of Guilt '95
Bogus '96
Conspiracy of Fear '96
Summer of the Monkeys '98

Dave Franco (1985-)
The Shortcut '09
Greenberg '10
Bad Meat '11
Fright Night '11
21 Jump Street '12
Now You See Me '13
Warm Bodies '13
Neighbors '14
Unfinished Business '15
Nerve '16
Now You See Me 2 '16
The Disaster Artist '17
The LEGO Ninjago Movie '17 (V)
The Little Hours '17

David Franco
Time and Again '07
The Broken Tower '11

James Franco (1978-)
Whatever It Takes '00
James Dean '01
City by the Sea '02
Deuces Wild '02
Sonny '02
Spider-Man '02
The Company '03
Spider-Man 2 '04
The Ape '05
The Great Raid '05
Annapolis '06
The Dead Girl '06
Flyboys '06
Tristan & Isolde '06
The Wicker Man '06
An American Crime '07
Camille '07
In the Valley of Elah '07
Spider-Man 3 '07
Milk '08
Nights in Rodanthe '08
Pineapple Express '08
Date Night '10
Eat, Pray, Love '10
Howl '10
127 Hours '10
Shadows and Lies '10
The Broken Tower '11
Rise of the Planet of the Apes '11
Sal '11
Your Highness '11
The Iceman '12
The Letter '12
Lovelace '13
Mademoiselle C '13
Maladies '13
Oz the Great and Powerful '13
Spring Breakers '13
Third Person '13
This Is the End '13
Child of God '14
Good People '14
The Interview '14
Palo Alto '14
Veronica Mars '14 (C)
Every Thing Will Be Fine '15
True Story '15
Wild Horses '15
The Adderall Diaries '16
The Little Prince '16
Sausage Party '16
Why Him? '16
The Disaster Artist '17
The Heyday of the Insensitive Bastards '17
I Am Michael '17
In Dubious Battle '17
The Ballad of Buster Scruggs '18
Future World '18
Kin '18
Arctic Dogs '19 (V)
Pretenders '19
Zeroville '19

James Edward Franco (1978-)
See James Franco

Jess (Jesus) Franco (1930-2013)
The Diabolical Dr. Z '65
Venus in Furs '70
Rites of Frankenstein '72
Ilsa, the Wicked Warden '78

Margarita Franco
3 Ninjas '92
3 Ninjas: High Noon at Mega Mountain '97

Ramon Franco (1968-)
Heartbreak Ridge '86
Tour of Duty '87
Shattered Image '93

Diana Franco-Galindo
Behind the Wall '08
Goodbye Solo '08

Deborah Francois (1987-)
The Child '05
The Page Turner '06
Unmade Beds '09
Never Grow Old '19

Ben Frank (1934-90)
Don't Answer the Phone '80
Hollywood Vice Sqaud '86
Shattered Innocence '87

Billy Frank
Grotesque '87
Track 16 '02

Charles Frank (1947-)
Tarantulas: The Deadly Cargo '77
A Guide for the Married Woman '78
Snowblind '78
The Right Stuff '83
Lucky Stiff '88
Danielle Steel's Changes '91
CSA: The Confederate States of America '04

Diana Frank (1965-)
Monster High '89
Club Vampire '98

Gary Frank (1950-)
The Distinguished Gentleman '92
Take Down '92
Untamed Love '94
Prison of Secrets '97

Horst Frank (1929-99)
The Head '59
Desert Commandos '67
The Vengeance of Fu Manchu '67
Dead Are Alive '72
The Grand Duel '73
Cold Blood '75

Jason David Frank (1973-)
Mighty Morphin Power Rangers: The Movie '95
Turbo: A Power Rangers Movie '96

Jerry Frank
The Flaming Teen-Age '56
The Big Doll House '71

Joanna Frank (1941-)
Always '85
Say Anything '89

Marilyn Dodds Frank
Sweet Lies '88
The Company '03
The Game of Their Lives '05

Mark Frankel (1962-96)
Young Catherine '91
Leon the Pig Farmer '93
For Roseanna '96

Al Franken (1951-)
Tunnelvision '76
All You Need Is Cash '78
Trading Places '83
Stuart Saves His Family '94
From the Earth to the Moon '98
Harvard Man '01

Steve Franken (1932-2012)
Which Way to the Front? '70
Ants '77
Terror Out of the Sky '78
The Fiendish Plot of Dr. Fu Manchu '80
Freeway '88

Paul Frankeur (1905-75)
Nana '55
License to Kill '64
Le Deuxieme Souffle '66
The Milky Way '68
Phantom of Liberty '74

William Frankfather (1944-98)
Cool World '92
Born Yesterday '93

Aretha Franklin (1942-)
The Blues Brothers '80
Blues Brothers 2000 '98
Amazing Grace '19

Diane Franklin (1962-)
Amityville 2: The Possession '82
Last American Virgin '82
Second Time Lucky '84
Better Off Dead '85
Terrorvision '86

Don Franklin (1960-)
Fast Forward '84
Asteroid '97
Black Dawn '05
American Girl: Chrissa Stands Strong '09

Joe Franklin (1926-)
Ghoul School '90
29th Street '91

John Franklin (1959-)
Children of the Corn '84
The Addams Family '91
Children of the Corn 666: Isaac's Return '99

Nelson Franklin
Answer This '10
Puppet Master: The Littlest Reich '18

Pamela Franklin (1950-)
The Innocents '61
The Horse Without a Head '63
Flipper's New Adventure '64
A Tiger Walks '64
The Nanny '65
Our Mother's House '67
The Night of the Following Day '69
The Prime of Miss Jean Brodie '69
Sinful Davey '69
And Soon the Darkness '70
David Copperfield '70
The Witching '72
The Legend of Hell House '73
Satan's School for Girls '73
Eleanor & Franklin '76
Food of the Gods '76

Richard Franklin (1948-)
Into the Night '85 (C)
Cyborg Soldier '08

William Franklyn (1925-2006)
Quatermass 2 '57
The Snorkel '58
Pit of Darkness '61
The Satanic Rites of Dracula '73
Splitting Heirs '93

Chloe Franks (1959-)
The House that Dripped Blood '71
The Littlest Horse Thieves '76
Ivanhoe '82

Lily Franky
See Riri Furanki

Mary Frann (1943-98)
Portrait of an Escort '80
Fatal Charm '92

Adrienne Frantz (1978-)
Jimmy Zip '00
Hack! '07
Donna on Demand '09

Jacques Frantz (1947-)
The Housekeeper '02
Heartbreaker '10

Arthur Franz (1920-2006)
Jungle Patrol '48
Red Light '49
Sands of Iwo Jima '49
Abbott and Costello Meet the Invisible Man '51
Eight Iron Men '52
Flight to Mars '52
The Member of the Wedding '52
The Sniper '52
Bad for Each Other '53
The Eddie Cantor Story '53
Invaders from Mars '53
The Caine Mutiny '54
New Orleans Uncensored '55
Beyond a Reasonable Doubt '56
Running Target '56
Hellcats of the Navy '57
The Young Lions '58
Atomic Submarine '59
Monster on the Campus '59
Woman Obsessed '59
Dream No Evil '70
Missiles of October '74
The Human Factor '75
Sisters of Death '76

Dennis Franz (1944-)
The Fury '78
A Wedding '78
Dressed to Kill '80
Blow Out '81
Psycho 2 '83
Body Double '84
Kiss Shot '89
The Package '89
Die Hard 2: Die Harder '90
The Player '92
American Buffalo '95
City of Angels '98

Eduard Franz (1902-83)
The Scar '48
Francis the Talking Mule '49
Outpost in Morocco '49
Whirlpool '49
The Magnificent Yankee '50
The Great Caruso '51
The Thing '51
Everything I Have is Yours '52
The Jazz Singer '52
One Minute to Zero '52
Dream Wife '53
Sins of Jezebel '54
The Indian Fighter '55
Lady Godiva '55
The Burning Hills '56
Four Skulls of Jonathan Drake '59
The Story of Ruth '60
Johnny Got His Gun '71

Elizabeth Franz (1941-)
Sabrina '95
Stephen King's Thinner '96
The Substance of Fire '96
Christmas With the Kranks '04

Daniel Franzee (1978-)
Whirlygirl '04
Last Resort '09

Daniel Franzese (1978-)
Bully '01
Mean Girls '04
Stateside '04
Cruel World '05
Killer Pad '06
I Spit on Your Grave '10

Bill Fraser (1908-87)
Alias John Preston '56
Captain Nemo and the Underwater City '69
The Corn Is Green '79
Eye of the Needle '81

Brendan Fraser (1968-)
Dogfight '91
Encino Man '92
School Ties '92
Twenty Bucks '93
Airheads '94
The Scout '94
With Honors '94
Now and Then '95
The Passion of Darkly Noon '95
Glory Daze '96 (C)
Mrs. Winterbourne '96
George of the Jungle '97
Still Breathing '97
The Twilight of the Golds '97
Blast from the Past '98
Gods and Monsters '98
Dudley Do-Right '99
The Mummy '99
Bedazzled '00
Monkeybone '01
The Mummy Returns '01
The Quiet American '02
Dickie Roberts: Former Child Star '03 (C)
Looney Tunes: Back in Action '03
Crash '05
Journey to the End of the Night '06
The Last Time '06
The Air I Breathe '07
Journey to the Center of the Earth '08
The Mummy: Tomb of the Dragon Emperor '08
G.I. Joe: The Rise of Cobra '09
Inkheart '09
Extraordinary Measures '10
Furry Vengeance '10
Stand Off '11
A Case of You '13
Escape From Planet Earth '13 (V)
Gimme Shelter '14
The Nut Job '14 (V)
The Poison Rose '19

Duncan Fraser
Watchers '88
The Reflecting Skin '91
Call of the Wild '93
Timecop '94
Captains Courageous '95
Unforgettable '96
Octopus 2: River of Fear '02
The Exorcism of Emily Rose '05
Merlin's Apprentice '06
The Lost Treasure of the Grand Canyon '08
Tornado Valley '09

Elisabeth Fraser (1920-2005)
The Man Who Came to Dinner '41
The Hidden Hand '42
Young at Heart '54
The Tunnel of Love '58
Two for the Seesaw '62
A Patch of Blue '65

Helen Fraser (1942-)
Repulsion '65
Start the Revolution without Me '70

Four Skulls of Jonathan Drake '59

Victor French (1934-89)
Spencer's Mountain '63
Charro! '69
Death of a Gunfighter '69
Flap '70
Chato's Land '71
The Other '72
The House on Skull Mountain '74
Little House on the Prairie '74
The Nickel Ride '74
Choices '81

Pierre Fresnay (1897-1975)
Marius '31
Fanny '32
The Man Who Knew Too Much '34
Cesar '36
Grand Illusion '37
The Murderer Lives at Number 21 '42
Le Corbeau '43
Monsieur Vincent '47

Bernard Fresson (1931-2002)
Hiroshima, Mon Amour '59
Please Not Now! '61
Honor Among Thieves '68
French Connection 2 '75
The Tenant '76
Place Vendome '98
Brotherhood of the Wolf '01

Matt Frewer (1958-)
The Lords of Discipline '83
Monty Python's The Meaning of Life '83
Supergirl '84
The Fourth Protocol '87
Ishtar '87
Far from Home '89
Honey, I Shrunk the Kids '89
The Day My Parents Ran Away '93
The Positively True Adventures of the Alleged Texas Cheerleader-Murdering Mom '93
Twenty Bucks '93
Stephen King's The Stand '94
Lawnmower Man 2: Beyond Cyberspace '95
National Lampoon's Senior Trip '95
Breast Men '97
Hercules '97 (V)
Dead Fire '98
Quicksilver Highway '98
The Hound of the Baskervilles '00
Jailbait! '00
The Sign of Four '01
Taken '02
Dawn of the Dead '04
A Home at the End of the World '04
White Coats '04
Weirdsville '07
Alice '09
Attack on Darfur '09
Rampage '09
Watchmen '09
Battle of the Bulbs '10
Frankie and Alice '10
Bag of Bones '11

Glenn Frey (1948-)
Let's Get Harry '87
Jerry Maguire '96

Leonard Frey (1938-88)
The Magic Christian '69
The Boys in the Band '70
Fiddler on the Roof '71
Where the Buffalo Roam '80

Sami Frey (1937-)
Cleo from 5 to 7 '61
Band of Outsiders '64
Angelique and the King '66
Manon '68
Cesar & Rosalie '72
Diary of a Suicide '73
Sweet Movie '75
Nea '78

The Little Drummer Girl '84
Black Widow '87
War & Remembrance '88
War & Remembrance: The Final Chapter '89
My Life and Times with Antonin Artaud '93
Revenge of the Musketeers '94
The Wedding Director '06

Giovanni Frezza (1972-)
Manhattan Baby '82
The House by the Cemetery '83

Brenda Fricker (1945-)
My Left Foot '89
The Field '90
Brides of Christ '91
Home Alone 2: Lost in New York '92
Deadly Advice '93
So I Married an Axe Murderer '93
Angels in the Outfield '94
A Woman of Independent Means '94
Moll Flanders '96
A Time to Kill '96
The Wicked, Wicked West '97
Pete's Meteor '98
Relative Strangers '99
Cupid & Cate '00
The American '01
The War Bride '01
The Intended '02
Torso '02
Conspiracy of Silence '03
Veronica Guerin '03
Call Me: The Rise and Fall of Heidi Fleiss '04
Rory O'Shea Was Here '04
Trauma '04
Tara Road '05
Closing the Ring '07
How About You '07
Albert Nobbs '11
Cloudburst '11

Jonathan Frid (1924-2012)
House of Dark Shadows '70
Seizure '74

Gavin Friday (1959-)
Creepers '85
Breakfast on Pluto '05

Anthony Fridjhon
Mission of Death '97
Pride of Africa '97

Tom Fridley (1965-)
Friday the 13th, Part 6: Jason Lives '86
Vegas Vice '94
Navajo Blues '97

Christian Friedel
The White Ribbon '09
13 Minutes '17

Bonita Friedericy (1961-)
The Twelve Dogs of Christmas '05
Sleeping Dogs Lie '06
Alien Raiders '08

Joel Friedkin (1885-1954)
Money Madness '47
Impact '49
Fury of the Congo '51

Judah Friedlander (1969-)
Showtime '02
American Splendor '03
The Trade '03
Along Came Polly '04
Duane Hopwood '05
Pizza '05
The Unseen '05
Date Movie '06
Feast '06
Chapter 27 '07
Cabin Fever 2: Spring Fever '08
Meet Dave '08
I Hate Valentine's Day '09
Sharknado 2: The Second One '14

Will Friedle (1976-)
Trojan War '97
National Lampoon's Gold Diggers '04
Everything You Want '05

Peter Friedman (1949-)
Christmas Evil '80
The Seventh Sign '88
Single White Female '92
Blink '93
The Heidi Chronicles '95
Safe '95
I Shot Andy Warhol '96
Someone Like You '01
Power and Beauty '02
King of the Corner '04
The Savages '07
Breaking Upwards '09
Harvest '10

John Friedrich (1958-)
The Boy in the Plastic Bubble '76
Wanderers '79
The Final Terror '83

Anna Friel (1976-)
G.B.H. '91
Our Mutual Friend '98
Rogue Trader '98
St. Ives '98
Sunset Strip '99
William Shakespeare's A Midsummer Night's Dream '99
An Everlasting Piece '00
Me Without You '01
The War Bride '01
Timeline '03
Irish Jam '05
Goal! The Dream Begins '06
Niagara Motel '06
Goal 2: Living the Dream '07
Land of the Lost '09
London Boulevard '10
Limitless '11
Neverland '11
Treasure Guards '11
The Look of Love '13
Good People '14
I.T. '16

Colin Friels (1952-)
Malcolm '86
High Tide '87
Darkman '90
Dingo '90
Class Action '91
A Good Man in Africa '94
Back of Beyond '95
Cosi '95
Dark City '97
Child Star: The Shirley Temple Story '01
The Man Who Sued God '01
Solo '06

Philip Friend (1915-87)
The Flemish Farm '43
Enchantment '48
Buccaneer's Girl '50
Thunder on the Hill '51

Rupert Friend (1981-)
The Libertine '05
Mrs. Palfrey at the Claremont '05
Pride and Prejudice '05
The Last Legion '07
The Moon & the Stars '07
Outlaw '07
The Boy in the Striped Pajamas '08
Jolene '08
Cheri '09
The Young Victoria '09
5 Days of War '11
Starred Up '13
To Write Love On Her Arms '14
Hitman: Agent 47 '15
The Death of Stalin '17
At Eternity's Gate '18

Arno Frisch (1975-)
Benny's Video '92
Funny Games '97

Anne Frith
The Alien Factor '78
Alien Factor 2: The Alien Rampage '01

Willy Fritsch (1901-73)
Hungarian Rhapsody '28
Spies '28
Woman in the Moon '29

Lou Frizzell (1920-79)
Duel '71
The Other '72
The Nickel Ride '74
Devil Dog: The Hound of Hell '78

Gert Frobe (1912-88)
Party Girls for Sale '54
The Thousand Eyes of Dr. Mabuse '60
The Return of Dr. Mabuse '61
The Longest Day '62
Testament of Dr. Mabuse '62
Goldfinger '64
Greed In the Sun '64
Those Magnificent Men in Their Flying Machines '65
Tonio Kroger '65
Is Paris Burning? '66
Those Fantastic Flying Fools '67
Triple Cross '67
Chitty Chitty Bang Bang '68
Those Daring Young Men in Their Jaunty Jalopies '69
Dollars '71
Ludwig '72
Ten Little Indians '75
The Serpent's Egg '78

Joanne Froggatt
A Street Cat Named Bob '16
Mary Shelley '17
A Crooked Somebody '18

Samuel Froler (1957-)
The Best Intentions '92
Pulse '03

Ewa Froling (1952-)
Fanny and Alexander '83
The Ox '91
Gossip '00
The Girl With the Dragon Tattoo '09

Milton Frome (1908-89)
Pardners '56
The Nutty Professor '63
Batman '66
The St. Valentine's Day Massacre '67

Alex Frost (1987-)
Elephant '03
Drillbit Taylor '08
Calvin Marshall '09
The Vicious Kind '09

Enoch Frost
Outpost '07
Sniper: Ghost Shooter '16

Lee Frost (1935-2007)
The Thing with Two Heads '72
Black Gestapo '75

Lindsay Frost (1962-)
Dead Heat '88
Danielle Steel's Palomino '91
Dead by Sunset '95
Collateral Damage '02
The Ring '02

Nick Frost (1972-)
Shaun of the Dead '04
Kinky Boots '06
Hot Fuzz '07
Wild Child '08
Pirate Radio '09
Attack the Block '11
Paul '11
Snow White and the Huntsman '12
The World's End '13
The Boxtrolls '14 (V)
Cuban Fury '14
The Huntsman: Winter's War '16
Fighting with My Family '19

Sadie Frost (1965-)
Dark Obsession '90
Bram Stoker's Dracula '92
Shopping '93
Splitting Heirs '93
The Cisco Kid '94
A Pyromaniac's Love Story '95
Crimetime '96
Flypaper '97
Captain Jack '98
Final Cut '98
Love, Honour & Obey '00
Rancid Aluminium '00
Uprising '01
The Heavy '09

Terry Frost (1906-93)
The Monster Maker '44
Waterfront '44
Son of Billy the Kid '49

Catherine Frot (1956-)
Sorceress '88
Un Air de Famille '96
The Dinner Game '98
The New Eve '98
Chaos '01
The Page Turner '06
Marguerite '16
The Midwife '17

Dominique Frot (1962-)
La Ceremonie '95
Father of My Children '09
Sarah's Key '10

Jordan Fry (1993-)
Charlie and the Chocolate Factory '05
Meet the Robinsons '07 (V)

Lucy Fry
Vampire Academy '14
The Darkness '16
Mr. Church '16
Bright '17

Stephen Fry (1957-)
Peter's Friends '92
Stalag Luft '93
Cold Comfort Farm '94
I.Q. '94
Lone Justice 3: Showdown at Plum Creek '96
Mr. Toad's Wild Ride '96
Spice World: The Movie '97
Wilde '97
Relative Values '99
Longitude '00
Gosford Park '01
Le Divorce '03
The Hitchhiker's Guide to the Galaxy '05 (V)
MirrorMask '05
Tristram Shandy: A Cock and Bull Story '05
V for Vendetta '06
Eichmann '07
St. Trinian's '07
Alice in Wonderland '10
Sherlock Holmes: A Game of Shadows '11
The Man Who Knew Infinity '16
Missing Link '19

Taylor Fry (1981-)
Necessary Parties '88
A Little Princess '95

Brittain Frye
Hide and Go Shriek '87
Slumber Party Massacre 3 '90

Dwight Frye (1899-1943)
The Black Camel '31
Dracula '31
Frankenstein '31
The Maltese Falcon '31
The Vampire Bat '32
The Invisible Man '33
The Bride of Frankenstein '35
Drums of Fu Manchu '40
Frankenstein Meets the Wolfman '42
The Ghost of Frankenstein '42
Dead Men Walk '43

Soleil Moon Frye (1976-)
Invitation to Hell '84
Pumpkinhead 2: Blood Wings '94
The St. Tammany Miracle '94
Piranha '95
I've Been Waiting for You '98
Motel Blue '98
The Proud Family Movie '05 (V)

Virgil Frye (1930-2012)
Up from the Depths '79
Revenge of the Ninja '83
Running Hot '83
Hot Moves '84
Colors '88

Sheng Fu (1954-83)
Heroes Two '73
The Brave Archer '77
Heaven & Hell '78
Legendary Weapons of China '82
8 Diagram Pole Fighter '84

Gaby Fuchs
Mark of the Devil '69
The Werewolf vs. the Vampire Woman '70

Jason Fuchs (1986-)
Mafia! '98
Holy Rollers '10

Leo Fuchs (1910-94)
American Matchmaker '40
Avalon '90

Joachim Fuchsberger (1927-2014)
Dead Eyes of London '61
Inn on the River '62
Again, the Ringer '64
The Face of Fu Manchu '65
The Mysterious Magician '65

Robert Fucilla (1980-)
The Big I Am '10
Mercenaries '11

Alan Fudge (1934-2011)
Bug '75
Kiss Me...Kill Me '76
Too Young to Die '90

Carlos Fuentes
Km. 0 '00
Boystown '07

Athol Fugard (1932-)
Gandhi '82
The Killing Fields '84

Patrick Fugit (1982-)
Almost Famous '00
Spun '02
White Oleander '02
Dead Birds '04
Saved! '04
The Moguls '05
Bickford Shmeckler's Cool Ideas '06
Wristcutters: A Love Story '06
The Good Life '07
Cirque du Freak: The Vampire's Assistant '09
Horsemen '09
Cinema Verite '11
We Bought a Zoo '11
Thanks for Sharing '13
Gone Girl '14
Queen of Earth '15

Isabelle Fuhrman (1997-)
Orphan '09
Salvation Boulevard '11
The Hunger Games '12
Cell '16
Dear Eleanor '16
Down a Dark Hall '18

Emma Fuhrmann
The Magic of Belle Isle '12
Blended '14

Takako Fuji (1972-)
Ju-On 2 '00
Ju-On: The Grudge '03
The Grudge '04
The Grudge 2 '06

Band of Angels '57
Run Silent, Run Deep '58
Teacher's Pet '58
It Started in Naples '60
The Misfits '61

Eva Gabor (1924-95)
Captain Kidd and the Slave Girl '54
The Last Time I Saw Paris '54
The Mad Magician '54
Artists and Models '55
Don't Go Near the Water '57
My Man Godfrey '57
Gigi '58
It Started with a Kiss '59
A New Kind of Love '63
Youngblood Hawke '64
The Aristocats '70 (V)
The Rescuers '77 (V)
The Rescuers Down Under '90 (V)
Naked Gun 2 1/2: The Smell of Fear '91 (C)

Zsa Zsa Gabor (1917-2016)
Lovely to Look At '52
Moulin Rouge '52
We're Not Married '52
Lili '53
Death of a Scoundrel '56
Queen of Outer Space '58
Touch of Evil '58 (C)
Boys' Night Out '62
Picture Mommy Dead '66
Every Girl Should Have One '78
Frankenstein's Great Aunt Tillie '83
A Nightmare on Elm Street 3: Dream Warriors '87
The Beverly Hillbillies '93 (C)
Happily Ever After '93 (V)
A Very Brady Sequel '96 (C)

Betty Gabriel
Unfriended: Dark Web '18
Upgrade '18
Adopt a Highway '19

John Gabriel
The Hunters '58
Hell's Bloody Devils '70

Seychelle Gabriel (1991-)
The Last Airbender '10
Honey 2 '14
Sleight '17

Jenny Gabrielle
Festival at Cannes '02
Force of Execution '13

Monique Gabrielle (1963-)
Black Venus '83
Bachelor Party '84
Hard to Hold '84
Hot Moves '84
Amazon Women on the Moon '87
Deathstalker 2: Duel of the Titans '87
Emmanuelle 5 '87
Not of This Earth '88
The Return of the Swamp Thing '89
Evil Toons '90

Elisa Gabrielli
The Invincible Iron Man '07 (V)
Madagascar: Escape 2 Africa '08 (V)

Sebastian Gacki
Beastly Boyz '06
Nightmare at the End of the Hall '08

Josh Gad (1981-)
The Rocker '08
21 '08
Woke Up Dead '09
Love and Other Drugs '10
Mardi Gras: Spring Break '11
Frozen '13 (V)
The Internship '13
Jobs '13
Thanks for Sharing '13
Wish I Was Here '14
Pixels '15
The Wedding Ringer '15
The Angry Birds Movie '16
Beauty and the Beast '17
A Dog's Purpose '17 (V)
Marshall '17
The Angry Birds Movie 2 '19
A Dog's Journey '19
Frozen II '19
Little Monsters '19

Analia Gade
Madame Sans-Gene '62
Murder Mansion '70

Ariel Gade (1997-)
Dark Water '02
Envy '04
Aliens *vs.* Predator: Requiem '07
Call of the Wild 3D '09

John Gaden (1941-)
A Little Bit of Soul '97
The Wedding Party '97

Antonio Gades (1936-2004)
Blood Wedding '81
Carmen '83
El Amor Brujo '86

Sarah Gadon (1987-)
Siblings '04
A Dangerous Method '11
The Moth Diaries '11
Antiviral '12
Cosmopolis '12
Belle '13
Enemy '13
Dracula Untold '14
Maps to the Stars '14
A Royal Night Out '15
Indignation '16
The 9th Life of Louis Drax '16
The Death and Life of John F. Donovan '19

Gal Gadot (1985-)
Fast Five '11
Fast & Furious 6 '13
Triple 9 '15
Batman v Superman: Dawn of Justice '16
Keeping Up with the Joneses '16
Justice League '17
Wonder Woman '17
Ralph Breaks the Internet '18 (V)

Anna Gael (1943-)
Therese & Isabelle '67
Zeta One '69

Jim Gaffigan (1966-)
Final '01
Super Troopers '01
30 Years to Life '01
No Sleep 'Til Madison '02
13 Going on 30 '04
The Great New Wonderful '06
Stephanie Daley '06
The Living Wake '07
The Love Guru '08
Shoot First and Pray You Live '08
Away We Go '09
Going the Distance '10
It's Kind of a Funny Story '10
Salvation Boulevard '11
Love Sick Love '12
Kilimanjaro '13
Chappaquiddick '17
Chuck '17
Being Frank '19
The Day Shall Come '19
Drunk Parents '19
Light from Light '19
Playmobil: The Movie '19

Mo Gaffney (1958-)
Drop Dead Gorgeous '99
Jailbait! '00
12 Christmas Wishes For My Dog '11

Lady Gaga
Machete Kills '13
A Star Is Born '18

Kevin Gage (1959-)
Heat '95
Dee Snider's Strangeland '98
Gunshy '98
Point Blank '98
Blow '01
May '02
Lightning Bug '04
Paparazzi '04
Chaos '05
Big Stan '07
Chasing 3000 '07
Laid to Rest '09
Last Resort '09
The Killing Jar '10
7 Minutes '15

Patricia Gage (1940-2010)
Rabid '77
The Little Kidnappers '90
The Morrison Murders '96

Michael Gaglio
Tarzeena: Queen of Kong Island '08
American Bandits: Frank and Jesse James '10
8213: Gacy House '10

Holly Gagnier (1958-)
Girls Just Want to Have Fun '85
Alligator 2: The Mutation '90
The Undertaker's Wedding '97

Trevor Gagnon (1995-)
Fly Me to the Moon '08 (V)
Shorts: The Adventures of the Wishing Rock '09

Jenny Gago (1953-)
Old Gringo '89
Sweet 15 '90
My Family '94
Alien Nation: Millennium '96

Diane Gaidry (1964-)
America So Beautiful '01
Loving Annabelle '06

Dana Gaier
Despicable Me '10 (V)
Despicable Me 2 '13 (V)
Despicable Me 3 '17 (V)

David Gail
Two Came Back '97
Bending All the Rules '02

Max Gail (1943-)
Dirty Harry '71
Cardiac Arrest '74
Night Moves '75
Pearl '78
D.C. Cab '84
Where Are the Children? '85
Judgment in Berlin '88
Street Crimes '92
Deadly Target '94
Pontiac Moon '94
Forest Warrior '95
Good Luck '96
The Inheritance '97
Facing the Enemy '00
Underdog Kids '15

Peter Gail
Jarhead '05
Blues '08

Boyd Gaines (1953-)
Porky's '82
The Sure Thing '85
Heartbreak Ridge '86
Call Me '88
Piece of Cake '88
I'm Not Rappaport '96
The Confession '98
Second Best '05

Richard Gaines (1904-75)
The More the Merrier '43
Mr. Winkle Goes to War '44
The Enchanted Cottage '45
Do You Love Me? '46
Humoresque '46
Nobody Lives Forever '46
So Goes My Love '46
Ace in the Hole '51

M.C. Gainey (1948-)
Starman '84
Spellbinder '88
El Diablo '90
Leap of Faith '92
One Man's Justice '95
Breakdown '96
Citizen Ruth '96
The Fan '96
Con Air '97
Happy, Texas '99
The Country Bears '02
The Cooler '03
The Last Cowboy '03
Wonderland '03
Club Dread '04
Sideways '04
Are We There Yet? '05
The Dukes of Hazzard '05
Beerfest '06
Unearthed '07
Wild Hogs '07
Django Unchained '12
Stolen '12

Courtney Gains (1965-)
Children of the Corn '84
Hardbodies '84
Back to the Future '85
Lust in the Dust '85
The Children of Times Square '86
Can't Buy Me Love '87
Colors '88
The 'Burbs '89
Memphis Belle '90
Behind Enemy Lines '96
The Killing Grounds '97
King Cobra '98
No Code of Conduct '98
Sweet Home Alabama '02
Benny Bliss & the Disciples of Greatness '07
Faster '10
Mimesis '11

Charlotte Gainsbourg (1972-)
Love Songs '84
Night Sun '90
The Cement Garden '93
Grosse Fatigue '94 (C)
Jane Eyre '96
Love, etc. '96
La Buche '00
My Wife is an Actress '01
21 Grams '03
Happily Ever After '04
Lemming '05
I Do '06
The Science of Sleep '06
I'm Not There '07
Antichrist '09
The City of Your Final Destination '09
The Tree '10
Melancholia '11
Nymphomaniac, Volume 1 '13
Nymphomaniac: Volume II '14
Samba '14
Every Thing Will Be Fine '15
Dark Crimes '16
The Snowman '17
I Think We're Alone Now '18

Serge Gainsbourg (1928-91)
Voulez-Vous Danser avec Moi? '59
The Fury of Hercules '61
Samson '61
Slogan '69

Cristina Gaioni (1940-)
And the Wild, Wild Women '59
The Mighty Ursus '61
Fury of Achilles '62

Erika-Shaye Gair (1998-)
The Wicker Man '06
Time and Again '07

Paulina Gaitan (1992-)
Trade '07
Sin Nombre '09
We Are What We Are '11

Cristina Gajoni (1940-)
Ursus in the Valley of the Lions '62
Andy Warhol's Frankenstein '74

Janusz Gajos (1939-)
The Decalogue '88
Trois Couleurs: Blanc '94
Zemsta '02

Michel Galabru (1922-)
La Cage aux Folles '78
La Cage aux Folles 2 '81
Subway '85
La Cage aux Folles 3: The Wedding '86
Belle Epoque '92

David Gale (1936-91)
Savage Weekend '80
Re-Animator '84
Bride of Re-Animator '89
Syngenor '90
The Guyver '91

Ed Gale (1963-)
Chopper Chicks in Zombietown '91
O Brother Where Art Thou? '00

Eddra Gale (1921-2001)
8 1/2 '63
Revenge of the Cheerleaders '76

Lorena Gale (1958-2009)
Behind the Mask '99
The Mermaid Chair '06
Hush Little Baby '07
Love Notes '07

Vincent Gale
Brotherhood of Murder '99
Last Wedding '01
The Final Cut '04
The Twelve Days of Christmas Eve '04
Firewall '06
Meltdown '06
Murder on Pleasant Drive '06
Second Sight '07
Mail Order Bride '08

Johnny Galecki (1975-)
National Lampoon's Christmas Vacation '89
Backfield in Motion '91
Bean '97
I Know What You Did Last Summer '97
Suicide Kings '97
The Opposite of Sex '98
Morgan's Ferry '99
Bounce '00
Playing Mona Lisa '00
Vanilla Sky '01
Bookies '03
Happy Endings '05
Hancock '08
Table for Three '09
In Time '11
CBGB '13
Rings '17

Juan Luis Galiardo (1940-)
Tango '98
The Girl of Your Dreams '99

Anna Galiena (1954-)
The Hairdresser's Husband '92
Being Human '94
The Leading Man '96
Moses '96
Excellent Cadavers '99

Zach Galifianakis (1969-)
Out Cold '01
Below '02
Gigantic '08
What Happens in Vegas '08
Frenemy '09
G-Force '09
The Hangover '09
Up in the Air '09
Dinner for Schmucks '10
Due Date '10
It's Kind of a Funny Story '10
Operation: Endgame '10
Youth in Revolt '10
The Hangover, Part 2 '11
Puss in Boots '11 (V)
The Campaign '12
Are You Here '13
The Hangover, Part III '13
Birdman, or (The Unexpected Virtue of Ignorance) '14
Keeping Up with the Joneses '16
Masterminds '16
The LEGO Batman Movie '17
Between Two Ferns '19
Missing Link '19

Kelly Galindo
Angels of the City '89
The Malibu Beach Vampires '91

Nacho Galindo (1908-73)
Border River '47
Borderline '50
Green Fire '55
Wetbacks '56
Born Reckless '59

Annie Galipeau (1979-)
Map of the Human Heart '93
Grey Owl '99

Frank Gallacher (1943-2009)
Proof '91
Dark City '97
Till Human Voices Wake Us '02
December Boys '07

Bronagh Gallagher (1972-)
The Commitments '91
Mary Reilly '95
The Wicked, Wicked West '97
Tristan & Isolde '06
Botched '07
Malice in Wonderland '09
Tamara Drewe '10
Albert Nobbs '11

David Gallagher (1985-)
Phenomenon '96
Angels in the Endzone '98
Little Secrets '02

John Gallagher, Jr. (1984-)
Pieces of April '03
Short Term 12 '13
Olive Kitteridge '14
10 Cloverfield Lane '16
The Belko Experiment '17
The Miseducation of Cameron Post '18
Peppermint '18

Megan Gallagher (1960-)
The Ambulance '90
In a Stranger's Hand '92
A Time to Remember '03
Best Friends '05

Patrick Gallagher (1968-)
In Enemy Hands '04
Silent Partner '05
Night at the Museum '06

Peter Gallagher (1955-)
Idolmaker '80
Summer Lovers '82
Dreamchild '85
The Murder of Mary Phagan '87
The Caine Mutiny Court Martial '88
High Spirits '88
Long Day's Journey into Night '88
sex, lies and videotape '89
Tune in Tomorrow '90
Late for Dinner '91
Bob Roberts '92
The Player '92
The Hudsucker Proxy '93 (C)
Malice '93
Short Cuts '93
Mrs. Parker and the Vicious Circle '94
Mother's Boys '94
White Mile '94
The Underneath '95
While You Were Sleeping '95
Last Dance '96
Titanic '96
To Gillian on Her 37th Birthday '96

Cafe Society '97
Johnny Skidmarks '97
The Man Who Knew Too Little '97
Path to Paradise '97
Brave New World '98
Virtual Obsession '98
American Beauty '99
Brotherhood of Murder '99
House on Haunted Hill '99
Center Stage '00
Cupid & Cate '00
The Last Debate '00
Anne Rice's The Feast of All Saints '01
Perfume '01
Protection '01
Mr. Deeds '02
How to Deal '03
Center Stage: Turn It Up '08
Adam '09
Burlesque '10
Conviction '10
Someday This Pain Will Be Useful to You '11
Centerstage: On Pointe '16
After '19

Richard 'Skeets' Gallagher (1891-1955)
Possessed '31
Merrily We Go to Hell '32
The Phantom of Crestwood '32
Reform Girl '33
Riptide '34
Hats Off '37
Danger on the Air '38

Sean Gallagher
The Guilty '92
Extremely Dangerous '99

James Gallanders (1970-)
The Third Miracle '99
Shake Hands With the Devil '07
Charlie & Me '08

Camillo Gallardo
Singles '92
Of Love and Shadows '94

Carlos Gallardo (1966-)
El Mariachi '93
Desperado '95 (C)
Eastside '99
Planet Terror '07
Red 11 '19

Lucy Gallardo
The Exterminating Angel '62
How the Garcia Girls Spent Their Summer '05

Silvania Gallardo (1953-2012)
Silence of the Heart '84
Out of the Dark '88

John Gallaudet (1903-83)
Pennies from Heaven '36
Sing You Sinners '38
Shadows Over Chinatown '46
Wife Wanted '46
Docks of New Orleans '48
Stage Struck '48
Julie '56
The Decks Ran Red '58
In Cold Blood '67

Ely Galleani (1953-)
Five Dolls for an August Moon '70
Baba Yaga '73

Gina Gallego (1959-)
Lust in the Dust '85
My Demon Lover '87

Ida Galli (1942-)
Eagles Over London '69
The Case of the Scorpion's Tail '71

Zach Galligan (1964-)
Gremlins '84
Waxwork '88
Gremlins 2: The New Batch '90
Psychic '91
Waxwork 2: Lost in Time '91
Zandalee '91
All Tied Up '92
Ice '93
Warlock: The Armageddon '93
Cyborg 3: The Recycler '95
The First to Go '97
Storm Trooper '98
Arthur's Quest '99
Raw Nerve '99
Gabriela '01
The Tomorrow Man '01
Infested: Invasion of the Killer Bugs '02

Kyle Gallner (1986-)
Red Eye '05
Sublime '07
Gardens of the Night '08
Red '08
The Haunting in Connecticut '09
Jennifer's Body '09
Beautiful Boy '10
Cougars, Inc. '10
A Nightmare on Elm Street '10
Red State '11
Beautiful Creatures '13
CBGB '13
American Sniper '14
Dear White People '14
Just Before I Go '15

Carla Gallo (1975-)
Spanking the Monkey '94
Mission: Impossible 3 '06
Insanitarium '08

Michaela Gallo (1990-)
Beethoven's 3rd '00
Beethoven's 4th '01

Robert Gallo (1945-)
Sinners '89
Street Boss '09

Vincent Gallo (1961-)
The House of the Spirits '93
Angela '94
Arizona Dream '94
Palookaville '95
The Funeral '96
Nenette and Boni '96
Buffalo 66 '97
Truth or Consequences, N.M. '97
Freeway 2: Confessions of a Trickbaby '99
Hide and Seek '00
Get Well Soon '01
The Brown Bunny '03
Moscow Zero '06
Tetro '09
Loosies '11

Tom Gallop
The Bourne Supremacy '04
The Bourne Ultimatum '07

Don Galloway (1937-2009)
Gunfight in Abilene '67
Rough Night in Jericho '67
Snowblind '78
Demon Rage '82
Two Moon Junction '88

Jack Galloway
Codename: Icarus '85
A Different Loyalty '04

Rita Gam (1927-)
The Thief '52
Saadia '53
Night People '54
Mohawk '56
The King of Kings '61
Klute '71
Shoot Out '71
Seeds of Evil '76

Mason Gamble (1986-)
Dennis the Menace '93
Bad Moon '96
Rushmore '98
Arlington Road '99
A Gentleman's Game '01
Golf in the Kingdom '10

Nathan Gamble (1998-)
Babel '06
The Mist '07
The Dark Knight '08
Marley & Me '08
Dolphin Tale '11
Dolphin Tale 2 '14

Jacques Gamblin (1957-)
Dr. Akagi '98
The Color of Lies '99
Safe Conduct '01
Carnage '02
Inspector Bellamy '09
The Names of Love '10
24 Days '14

Michael Gambon (1940-)
The Beast Must Die '75
The Singing Detective '86
The Rachel Papers '89
The Cook, the Thief, His Wife & Her Lover '90
The Heat of the Day '91
Mobsters '91
Toys '92
The Browning Version '94
Clean Slate '94
Faith '94
Squanto: A Warrior's Tale '94
Two Deaths '94
The Innocent Sleep '95
Mary Reilly '95
Samson and Delilah '96
The Gambler '97
The Wings of the Dove '97
Dancing at Lughnasa '98
Plunkett & Macleane '98
The Insider '99
The Last September '99
Sleepy Hollow '99
Longitude '00
Almost Strangers '01
Charlotte Gray '01
Gosford Park '01
High Heels and Low Lifes '01
Wives and Daughters '01
Path to War '02
Angels in America '03
Deep Blue '03 (N)
Open Range '03
Sylvia '03
Being Julia '04
Harry Potter and the Prisoner of Azkaban '04
The Life Aquatic with Steve Zissou '04
Sky Captain and the World of Tomorrow '04
Harry Potter and the Goblet of Fire '05
Layer Cake '05
Amazing Grace '06
The Good Shepherd '06
The Omen '06
Assassin in Love '07
Harry Potter and the Order of the Phoenix '07
Brideshead Revisited '08
Cranford '08
Emma '09
Fantastic Mr. Fox '09 (V)
Harry Potter and the Half-Blood Prince '09
The Book of Eli '10
Harry Potter and the Deathly Hallows, Part 1 '10
The King's Speech '10
Harry Potter and the Deathly Hallows, Part 2 '11
Page Eight '11
Quartet '12
Dad's Army '16
Viceroy's House '17
Judy '19

The Game (1979-)
Waist Deep '06
Street Kings '08

Robin Gammell (1936-)
Panic in Echo Park '77
Between the Darkness and the Dawn '85
Project X '87
Gore Vidal's Lincoln '88
Guilty by Suspicion '91
Sinatra '92
If These Walls Could Talk '96
Bone Daddy '97
The Girl Next Door '98
Last Night '98

James Gammon (1940-2010)
Cool Hand Luke '67
1,000 Plane Raid '69
Deadly Encounter '72
The McCullochs '75
Vision Quest '85
Ironweed '87
Gore Vidal's Lincoln '88
The Milagro Beanfield War '88
Major League '89
Coupe de Ville '90
I Love You to Death '90
Revenge '90
Crisscross '92
Leaving Normal '92
The Adventures of Huck Finn '93
Cabin Boy '94
Hard Vice '94
Major League 2 '94
Vegas Vice '94
Wyatt Earp '94
Larry McMurtry's Streets of Laredo '95
Truman '95
Wild Bill '95
Traveller '96
The Man in the Iron Mask '97
The Hi-Lo Country '98
Logan's War: Bound by Honor '98
One Man's Hero '98
Point Blank '98
The Iron Giant '99 (V)
You Know My Name '99
The Cell '00
The Country Bears '02 (V)
Life or Something Like It '02
Cold Mountain '03
Monte Walsh '03
Silver City '04
Don't Come Knocking '05
Altered '06
The Far Side of Jericho '06
The Final Season '07
Appaloosa '08
In the Electric Mist '08
The New Daughter '10

Ken Gampu (1929-2003)
The Naked Prey '66
African Rage '78
Soul Patrol '80
Kill and Kill Again '81
American Ninja 4: The Annihilation '91

Orjan Gamst
Dead Snow '09
Dead Snow: Red vs. Dead '14

Chester Gan (1908-59)
Across the Pacific '42
Crash Dive '43

Nitin Ganatra (1967-)
Pure '02
The Mistress of Spices '05
Shifty '08

Michel Gand (1948-)
See Jean-Pierre Bouvier

James Gandolfini (1961-2013)
A Stranger Among Us '92
Italian Movie '93
Mr. Wonderful '93
Money for Nothing '93
True Romance '93
Angie '94
Terminal Velocity '94
Crimson Tide '95
Get Shorty '95
New World '95
The Juror '96
Night Falls on Manhattan '96
Dance with the Devil '97
Fallen '97
She's So Lovely '97
A Civil Action '98
8mm '98
The Mighty '98
Wildflowers '99
The Last Castle '01
The Man Who Wasn't There '01
The Mexican '01
Surviving Christmas '04
Romance & Cigarettes '05
All the King's Men '06
Lonely Hearts '06
Miracle at St. Anna '08
In the Loop '09
The Taking of Pelham 123 '09
Where the Wild Things Are '09 (V)
Welcome to the Rileys '10
Cinema Verite '11
Down the Shore '11
Violet & Daisy '11
Killing Them Softly '12
Not Fade Away '12
Enough Said '13
The Incredible Burt Wonderstone '13
The Drop '14

Tony Ganios (1959-)
Wanderers '79
Continental Divide '81
Porky's '82
Porky's 2: The Next Day '83
Porky's Revenge '85
Die Hard 2: Die Harder '90

Richard Ganoung
Parting Glances '86
Billy's Hollywood Screen Kiss '98

Richard Gant (1944-)
Krush Groove '85
The Freshman '90
Jason Goes to Hell: The Final Friday '93
The Glimmer Man '96
Bean '97
The Big Lebowski '97
Raven '97
Sour Grapes '98
Johnny B. '00
Nutty Professor 2: The Klumps '00
Kingdom Come '01
Daddy Day Camp '07

Robert Gant (1968-)
Save Me '07
Kiss Me Deadly '08
Special Delivery '08
A Portrait of James Dean: Joshua Tree, 1951 '12

Peter Gantzler (1958-)
Italian for Beginners '01
The Boss of It All '06

Paul Ganus (1961-)
Crash and Burn '90
The Silencer '92

Bruno Ganz (1941-)
The Marquise of O '76
The American Friend '77
Nosferatu the Vampyre '79
Wings of Desire '88
Strapless '90
Faraway, So Close! '93
Eternity and a Day '97
Bread and Tulips '01
Luther '03
Downfall '04
The Manchurian Candidate '04
Have No Fear: The Life of Pope John Paul II '05
Youth Without Youth '07
The Baader Meinhof Complex '08
The Reader '08
Unknown '11
Night Train to Lisbon '13
In Order of Disappearance '14
Remember '15
The Party '17
The House That Jack Built '18
A Hidden Life '19

Yehoram Gaon (1939-)
Eagles Attack at Dawn '70
Operation Thunderbolt '77
Dead End Street '83

Romola Garai (1982-)
Daniel Deronda '02
I Capture the Castle '02
Nicholas Nickleby '02
Dirty Dancing: Havana Nights '04
Rory O'Shea Was Here '04
Vanity Fair '04
The Incredible Journey of Mary Bryant '05
Amazing Grace '06
Renaissance '06
Scoop '06
Angel '07
Atonement '07
The Other Man '08
Emma '09
Glorious 39 '09
One Day '11
The Crimson Petal and the White '12
The Last Days on Mars '13

Kaz Garas (1940-)
Wonder Woman '74
Puppet Master 5: The Final Chapter '94
Humanoids from the Deep '96

Matthew Garber (1956-77)
The Three Lives of Thomasina '63
Mary Poppins '64
The Gnome-Mobile '67

Terri Garber (1960-)
North and South Book 1 '85
North and South Book 2 '86

Victor Garber (1949-)
Godspell '73
Life with Mikey '93
Queen '93
Sleepless in Seattle '93
Exotica '94
Jeffrey '95 (C)
The First Wives Club '96
Cinderella '97
Titanic '97
Annie '99
Invisible Child '99
Call Me Claus '01
Legally Blonde '01
Life with Judy Garland-Me and My Shadows '01
Home Room '02
Torso '02
Tuck Everlasting '02
Milk '08
The Last Templar '09
Ice Quake '10
You Again '10
The Entitled '11
Kung Fu Panda 2 '11 (V)
Take Me Home '11
William & Catherine: A Royal Romance '11
Argo '12
The Hunters '13
I'll Follow You Down '13

Greta Garbo (1905-90)
The Atonement of Gosta Berling '24
Joyless Street '25
The Temptress '26
Torrent '26
The Flesh and the Devil '27
The Mysterious Lady '28
Wild Orchids '28
The Kiss '29
The Single Standard '29
Anna Christie '30
Romance '30
Susan Lenox: Her Fall and Rise '31
Grand Hotel '32
Mata Hari '32
Queen Christina '33
The Painted Veil '34
Anna Karenina '35
Camille '36
Conquest '37
Ninotchka '39
The Love Goddesses '65

Ingrid Garbo
Dracula's Great Love '72
Touch Me Not '74

Paula Garces (1974-)
Cash Crop '98
Clockstoppers '02
Marci X '03

Harold and Kumar Go to White Castle '04
Spin '04
Man of the House '05
Harold & Kumar Escape from Guantanamo Bay '08
A Very Harold & Kumar Christmas '11

Adam Garcia (1973-)
Bootmen '00
Coyote Ugly '00
Riding in Cars with Boys '01
The First $20 Million is Always the Hardest '02
Confessions of a Teenage Drama Queen '04
Fascination '04
Standing Still '05

Aimee Garcia (1978-)
A Lot Like Love '05
Dirty '05
Dead Tone '07
Dragon Wars '07
Go For It! '10
El Chicano '19

Andy Garcia (1956-)
A Night in Heaven '83
Mean Season '85
The Untouchables '87
Blood Money: The Story of Clinton and Nadine '88
Stand and Deliver '88
Black Rain '89
The Godfather, Part 3 '90
Internal Affairs '90
A Show of Force '90
Dead Again '91
Hero '92
Jennifer 8 '92
When a Man Loves a Woman '94
Steal Big, Steal Little '95
Things to Do in Denver When You're Dead '95
The Disappearance of Garcia Lorca '96
Hoodlum '96
Night Falls on Manhattan '96
Desperate Measures '98
Just the Ticket '98
Swing Vote '99
For Love or Country: The Arturo Sandoval Story '00
Lakeboat '00
The Man from Elysian Fields '01
Ocean's Eleven '01
The Unsaid '01
Confidence '03
Modigliani '04
Ocean's Twelve '04
Twisted '04
The Lost City '05
The Air I Breathe '07
Ocean's Thirteen '07
Smokin' Aces '07
Beverly Hills Chihuahua '08 (V)
The Line '08
City Island '09
New York, I Love You '09
The Pink Panther 2 '09
Across the Line: The Exodus of Charlie Wright '10
5 Days of War '11
A Dark Truth '12
For Greater Glory '12
At Middleton '13
Christmas In Conway '13
Open Road '13
Kill the Messenger '14
Let's Be Cops '14
Rio 2 '14 (V)
Rob the Mob '14
Max Steel '16
Passengers '16

Carolina Garcia
Supercross: The Movie '05
Car Babes '06

Eddie Garcia (1929-2019)
Beast of the Yellow Night '70
Beast of Blood '71
Twilight People '72
Relax. . . It's Just Sex! '98

Jeff Garcia
Jimmy Neutron: Boy Genius '01 (V)
Barnyard '06 (V)

Jesse Garcia (1982-)
Quinceanera '06
The Comebacks '07
A Beautiful Life '08
Jarhead 2: Field of Fire '14
Hostile Border '16

Joanna Garcia (1979-)
Not Another Teen Movie '01
The Initiation of Sarah '06
A Very Merry Daughter of the Bride '08
Revenge of the Bridesmaids '10

Jorge Garcia (1973-)
The Good Humor Man '05
Little Athens '05
Deck the Halls '06

Jose Garcia
Apres-Vous '03
People '04
The Take '16

Jsu Garcia (1963-)
A Nightmare on Elm Street '84
Gotcha! '85
Wildcats '86
Slaves of New York '89
Predator 2 '90
Vampire in Brooklyn '95
Red Shoe Diaries: Four on the Floor '96
Woo '97
Candyman 3: Day of the Dead '98
Devil in the Flesh 2 '00
Traffic '00
The Quickie '01
Collateral Damage '02
We Were Soldiers '02
Klepto '03
Along Came Polly '04
The Lost City '05
Sueno '05
The Go-Getter '07
Atlas Shrugged: Part 1 '11

Juan Garcia
Bounce '00
Feast 2: Sloppy Seconds '08

Nicole Garcia (1946-)
Mon Oncle d'Amerique '80
Bolero '82
Corrupt '84
Alias Betty '01
La Petite Lili '03

Paulina Garcia
Gloria '13
Little Men '16

Dominik Garcia-Lorido (1983-)
Reflections '08
City Island '09
Wild Card '15

Manuel Garcia-Rulfo (1981-)
The Magnificent Seven '16
Murder on the Orient Express '17
Widows '18
Mary '19
6 Underground '19

Luce Garcia-Ville
Last Year at Marienbad '61
Nathalie Granger '72

Henri Garcin (1929-)
Someone Behind the Door '71
One Hundred and One Nights '95
The Dress '96
It's All So Quiet '13

Betty Garde
Call Northside 777 '48
Caged '50

Vincent Gardenia (1922-92)
Cop Hater '58
The Hustler '61
Mad Dog Coll '61
Parrish '61
Where's Poppa? '70
Cold Turkey '71
Little Murders '71
Bang the Drum Slowly '73
Death Wish '74
The Front Page '74
Lucky Luciano '74
Greased Lightning '77
Home Movies '79
The Last Flight of Noah's Ark '80
Death Wish 2 '82
Kennedy '83
Brass '85
Movers and Shakers '85
Little Shop of Horrors '86
Moonstruck '87
Age Old Friends '89
Skin Deep '89
The Super '91

Reginald Gardiner (1903-80)
Born to Dance '36
A Damsel in Distress '37
Everybody Sing '38
Marie Antoinette '38
The Flying Deuces '39
Doctor Takes a Wife '40
The Great Dictator '40
The Man Who Came to Dinner '41
Sundown '41
A Yank in the R.A.F. '41
Captains of the Clouds '42
Claudia '43
Immortal Sergeant '43
Christmas in Connecticut '45
The Horn Blows at Midnight '45
Do You Love Me? '46
The Dolly Sisters '46
The Halls of Montezuma '50
Wabash Avenue '50
Elopement '51
Black Widow '54
Birds & the Bees '56
Rock-A-Bye Baby '57
Back Street '61
Mr. Hobbs Takes a Vacation '62
Do Not Disturb '65

Arthur Gardner (1910-)
Assassin of Youth '35
Mystic Circle Murder '39

Ava Gardner (1922-90)
Reunion in France '42
Maisie Goes to Reno '44
Three Men in White '44
The Killers '46
Whistle Stop '46
The Hucksters '47
The Bribe '48
One Touch of Venus '48
East Side, West Side '49
The Great Sinner '49
My Forbidden Past '51
Pandora and the Flying Dutchman '51
Show Boat '51
Lone Star '52
The Snows of Kilimanjaro '52
Knights of the Round Table '53
Mogambo '53
Ride, Vaquero! '53
The Barefoot Contessa '54
Around the World in 80 Days '56 (C)
Bhowani Junction '56
The Sun Also Rises '57
On the Beach '59
55 Days at Peking '63
The Night of the Iguana '64
Seven Days in May '64
The Bible '66
Mayerling '68
Life & Times of Judge Roy Bean '72
Earthquake '74
The Cassandra Crossing '76
The Sentinel '76
The Kidnapping of the President '80
Regina '83
A.D. '85
The Long, Hot Summer '86

Joan Gardner (1915-99)
Private Life of Don Juan '34
The Scarlet Pimpernel '34
Dark Journey '37
The Man Who Could Work Miracles '37
The Challenge '38

Katya Gardner (1972-)
Careful '92
Cheaters' Club '06
Stir of Echoes 2: The Homecoming '07

Virginia Gardner
Project Almanac '15
Goat '16
Monster Party '18
Starfish '19

Jennifer Gareis (1970-)
Gangland '00
Luckytown '00
Miss Congeniality '00
The 6th Day '00
Boat Trip '03

Simi Garewal
Tarzan Goes to India '62
Siddhartha '72

Allen Garfield (1939-2020)
Greetings '68
Hi, Mom! '70
The Owl and the Pussycat '70
Bananas '71
Cry Uncle '71
The Candidate '72
Get to Know Your Rabbit '72
Slither '73
Busting '74
The Conversation '74
Nashville '75
Paco '75
The Million Dollar Rip-Off '76
Mother, Jugs and Speed '76
The Virginia Hill Story '76
Skateboard '77
Brink's Job '78
One Trick Pony '80
The Stunt Man '80
Continental Divide '81
Leave 'Em Laughing '81
Get Crazy '83
The Cotton Club '84
Irreconcilable Differences '84
Desert Bloom '86
Beverly Hills Cop 2 '87
Let It Ride '89
Night Visitor '89
Club Fed '90
Diabolique '96
Obsession '97
Absence of the Good '99
The Majestic '01

Andrew Garfield (1983-)
Boy A '07
Lions for Lambs '07
The Imaginarium of Doctor Parnassus '09
Red Riding, Part 1: 1974 '09
Red Riding, Part 2: 1980 '09
Red Riding, Part 3: 1983 '09
Never Let Me Go '10
The Social Network '10
The Amazing Spider-Man '12
The Amazing Spider-Man 2 '14
99 Homes '14
Hacksaw Ridge '16
Silence '16
Breathe '17
Under the Silver Lake '18

John Garfield (1913-52)
Four Daughters '38
Blackwell's Island '39
Daughters Courageous '39
Dust Be My Destiny '39
Four Wives '39 (C)
Juarez '39
They Made Me a Criminal '39
Castle on the Hudson '40
East of the River '40
Flowing Gold '40
Saturday's Children '40
Dangerously We Live '41
Out of the Fog '41
Tortilla Flat '42
Air Force '43
Destination Tokyo '43
The Fallen Sparrow '43
Thank Your Lucky Stars '43
Between Two Worlds '44
Hollywood Canteen '44
Pride of the Marines '45
Humoresque '46
Nobody Lives Forever '46
The Postman Always Rings Twice '46
Body and Soul '47
Gentleman's Agreement '47
Force of Evil '49
Jigsaw '49 (C)
The Breaking Point '50

John David Garfield (1943-94)
The Swimmer '68
MacKenna's Gold '69
That Cold Day in the Park '69
The Stepmother '71
Golden Voyage of Sinbad '73
The Other Side of the Mountain '75
White Line Fever '75

Art Garfunkel (1941-)
Catch-22 '70
Carnal Knowledge '71
Bad Timing: A Sensual Obsession '80
Boxing Helena '93
The Rebound '09

Edward (Ed) Gargan (1902-64)
Belle of the Nineties '34
Hands Across the Table '35
Jim Hanvey, Detective '37
The Saint Strikes Back '39
Spring Parade '40
A Date With the Falcon '42
The Falcon Takes Over '42
The Falcon and the Co-Eds '43
The Falcon in Danger '43
The Falcon Strikes Back '43

William Gargan (1905-79)
The Animal Kingdom '32
Rain '32
Night Flight '33
Sweepings '33
British Agent '34
Four Frightened People '34
Strictly Dynamite '34
Milky Way '36
You Only Live Once '37
The Crowd Roars '38
Devil's Party '38
Broadway Serenade '39
Star Dust '40
Cheers for Miss Bishop '41
I Wake Up Screaming '41
The Mayor of 44th Street '42
Who Done It? '42
Swing Fever '43
The Canterville Ghost '44
Night Editor '46
Strange Impersonation '46
Till the End of Time '46
Dynamite '49

William Dennis Gargan (1905-79)
See William Gargan

Troy Garity (1973-)
Steal This Movie! '00
Bandits '01
Barbershop '02
Milwaukee, Minnesota '03
Soldier's Girl '03
After the Sunset '04
Barbershop 2: Back in Business '04
Eichmann '07
Sunshine '07
Fragments '08
Lake City '08
Mercy '09
My One and Only '09
The Good Doctor '11
Gangster Squad '13
Red Sky '14

Gabriel Garko (1974-)
His Secret Life '01
Callas Forever '02

Gianni 'John' Garko (1935-)
Kapo '59
The Mongols '60
The Avenger '62
Saul and David '64
Five for Hell '67
Gunslinger '70
The Night of the Devils '72
The Boss '73

Beverly Garland (1926-2008)
D.O.A. '49
Killer Leopard '54
The Miami Story '54
Desperate Hours '55
New Orleans Uncensored '55
Swamp Women '55
The Gunslinger '56
Chicago Confidential '57
Not of This Earth '57
Twice-Told Tales '63
Pretty Poison '68
The Mad Room '69
The Voyage of the Yes '72
Where the Red Fern Grows '74
Sixth and Main '77
Roller Boogie '79
It's My Turn '80
National Lampoon's Christmas Vacation 2: Cousin Eddie's Big Island Adventure '03

Judy Garland (1922-69)
Pigskin Parade '36
Broadway Melody of 1938 '37
Thoroughbreds Don't Cry '37
Everybody Sing '38
Listen, Darling '38
Love Finds Andy Hardy '38
Babes in Arms '39
The Wizard of Oz '39
Andy Hardy Meets Debutante '40
Little Nellie Kelly '40
Strike Up the Band '40
Babes on Broadway '41
Life Begins for Andy Hardy '41
Ziegfeld Girl '41
For Me and My Gal '42
Girl Crazy '43
Presenting Lily Mars '43
Thousands Cheer '43
Meet Me in St. Louis '44
The Clock '45
The Harvey Girls '46
Till the Clouds Roll By '46
Ziegfeld Follies '46
Easter Parade '48
The Pirate '48
Words and Music '48
In the Good Old Summertime '49
Summer Stock '50
A Star Is Born '54
Judgment at Nuremberg '61
Gay Purr-ee '62 (V)
I Could Go on Singing '63
That's Entertainment '74

Richard Garland (1927-69)
The Undead '57
Panic in Year Zero! '62

Jeff Garlin (1962-)
Daddy Day Care '03
Sleepover '04
I Want Someone to Eat Cheese With '06
American Loser '07
The Rocker '08
Strange Wilderness '08
WALL-E '08 (V)
Toy Story 3 '10 (V)
ParaNorman '12 (V)
Laggies '13

Lee Garlington (1953-)
Psycho 3 *'86*
The Seventh Sign *'88*
Three Fugitives *'89*
A Killing in a Small Town *'90*
My Life *'93*
The Babysitter *'95*
Along for the Ride *'00*
The Hot Chick *'02*
The Sum of All Fears *'02*
Guarding Eddy *'04*
Johnson Family Vacation *'04*
A Lot Like Love *'05*
Mrs. Washington Goes to Smith *'09*

Ralph Garman (1964-)
Sharktopus *'10*
Yoga Hosers *'16*

Alice Garner (1969-)
Strange Planet *'99*
Jindabyne *'06*

James Garner (1928-2014)
The Girl He Left Behind *'56*
Toward the Unknown *'56*
Sayonara *'57*
Shoot-out at Medicine Bend *'57*
Darby's Rangers *'58*
Alias Jesse James *'59 (C)*
Up Periscope *'59*
Cash McCall *'60*
The Children's Hour *'61*
Boys' Night Out *'62*
The Great Escape *'63*
Move Over, Darling *'63*
The Thrill of It All! *'63*
The Wheeler Dealers *'63*
The Americanization of Emily *'64*
36 Hours *'64*
Duel at Diablo *'66*
Grand Prix *'66*
Mister Buddwing *'66*
Hour of the Gun *'67*
How Sweet It Is! *'68*
Marlowe *'69*
Support Your Local Sheriff *'69*
A Man Called Sledge *'71*
Skin Game *'71*
Support Your Local Gunfighter *'71*
They Only Kill Their Masters *'72*
One Little Indian *'73*
The Castaway Cowboy *'74*
The Fan *'81*
The Long Summer of George Adams *'82*
Victor/Victoria *'82*
Tank *'83*
Murphy's Romance *'85*
Promise *'86*
Sunset *'88*
My Name Is Bill W. *'89*
Decoration Day *'90*
The Distinguished Gentleman *'92*
Barbarians at the Gate *'93*
Fire in the Sky *'93*
Maverick *'94*
Larry McMurtry's Streets of Laredo *'95*
Dead Silence *'96*
My Fellow Americans *'96*
Legalese *'98*
Twilight *'98*
One Special Night *'99*
The Last Debate *'00*
Space Cowboys *'00*
Atlantis: The Lost Empire *'01 (V)*
Divine Secrets of the Ya-Ya Sisterhood *'02*
The Notebook *'04*
The Ultimate Gift *'07*
Battle for Terra *'09 (V)*

Jennifer Garner (1972-)
Larry McMurtry's Dead Man's Walk *'96*
Mr. Magoo *'97*
Rose Hill *'97*
Washington Square *'97*
1999 *'98*
Aftershock: Earthquake in New York *'99*
Dude, Where's My Car? *'00*
Pearl Harbor *'01*
Catch Me If You Can *'02*
Daredevil *'03*
13 Going on 30 *'04*
Elektra *'05*
Catch and Release *'07*
Juno *'07*
The Kingdom *'07*
Ghosts of Girlfriends Past *'09*
The Invention of Lying *'09*
Valentine's Day *'10*
Arthur *'11*
Butter *'12*
The Odd Life of Timothy Green *'12*
Dallas Buyers Club *'13*
Alexander and the Terrible, Horrible, No Good, Very Bad Day *'14*
Draft Day *'14*
Men, Women & Children *'14*
Danny Collins *'15*
Miracles From Heaven *'16*
Nine Lives *'16*
Wakefield *'17*
Love, Simon *'18*
Peppermint *'18*
Wonder Park *'19*

Julia Garner
We Are What We Are *'13*
Grandma *'15*

Kelli Garner (1984-)
Bully *'01*
The Aviator *'04*
Born Killers *'05*
London *'05*
Man of the House *'05*
Thumbsucker *'05*
Dreamland *'06*
Havoc 2: Normal Adolescent Behavior *'07*
Lars and the Real Girl *'07*
G-Force *'09*
Taking Woodstock *'09*
Going the Distance *'10*
Horns *'13*
One More Time *'15*

Peggy Ann Garner (1931-84)
Blondie Brings Up Baby *'39*
Jane Eyre *'44*
The Keys of the Kingdom *'44*
Junior Miss *'45*
Nob Hill *'45*
A Tree Grows in Brooklyn *'45*
Daisy Kenyon *'47*
Thunder in the Valley *'47*
The Big Cat *'49*
Bomba, the Jungle Boy *'49*
Black Widow *'54*
Eight Witnesses *'54*
Betrayal *'78*
A Wedding *'78*

Gale Garnett (1942-)
The Children *'80*
Mr. & Mrs. Bridge *'90*
32 Short Films about Glenn Gould *'93*

Tay Garnett (1898-1977)
Strong Man *'26*
Challenge To Be Free *'76 (C)*

Janeane Garofalo (1964-)
Armistead Maupin's Tales of the City *'93*
Bye Bye, Love *'94*
Coldblooded *'94*
Reality Bites *'94*
The Cable Guy *'96*
Kids in the Hall: Brain Candy *'96*
Larger Than Life *'96*
Touch *'96*
The Truth about Cats and Dogs *'96*
Cop Land *'97*
Half-Baked *'97*
The Matchmaker *'97*
Romy and Michele's High School Reunion *'97*
Sweethearts *'97*
The Bumblebee Flies Anyway *'98*
Clay Pigeons *'98*
Dog Park *'98*
Kiki's Delivery Service *'98 (V)*
Permanent Midnight *'98*
200 Cigarettes *'98*
Dogma *'99*
The Minus Man *'99*
Mystery Men *'99*
Thick as Thieves *'99*
The Adventures of Rocky & Bullwinkle *'00*
The Independent *'00*
Steal This Movie! *'00*
Titan A.E. *'00 (V)*
What Planet Are You From? *'00*
The Search for John Gissing *'01*
Wet Hot American Summer *'01*
Big Trouble *'02*
The Laramie Project *'02*
Wonderland *'03*
Duane Hopwood *'05*
Jiminy Glick in LaLa Wood *'05*
Stay *'05*
The Wild *'06 (V)*
Ratatouille *'07 (V)*
Girl's Best Friend *'08*
Labor Pains *'09*
Love Hurts *'09*
Bad Parents *'12*
A Bread Factory, Part One *'18*
Come As You Are *'20*

Teri Garr (1947-)
Pajama Party *'64*
Head *'68*
Speedway *'68 (C)*
The Conversation *'74*
Young Frankenstein *'74*
Close Encounters of the Third Kind *'77*
Oh, God! *'77*
Once Upon a Brothers Grimm *'77*
The Black Stallion *'79*
Mr. Mike's Mondo Video *'79*
Honky Tonk Freeway *'81*
The Escape Artist *'82*
One from the Heart *'82*
Prime Suspect *'82*
Tootsie *'82*
The Black Stallion Returns *'83*
Mr. Mom *'83*
The Sting 2 *'83*
To Catch a King *'84*
After Hours *'85*
Pack of Lies *'87*
Full Moon in Blue Water *'88*
Let It Ride *'89*
Out Cold *'89*
Waiting for the Light *'90*
Mom and Dad Save the World *'92*
The Player *'92*
Take Down *'92*
Dumb & Dumber *'94*
Ready to Wear *'94*
Changing Habits *'96*
Michael *'96*
NightScreams *'97*
Ronnie and Julie *'97*
A Simple Wish *'97*
Dick *'99*
Ghost World *'01*
Life Without Dick *'01*
Unaccompanied Minors *'06*
Expired *'07*

Martin Garralaga (1894-1981)
Casablanca *'42*
For Whom the Bell Tolls *'43*
Susanna Pass *'49*
Bela Lugosi Meets a Brooklyn Gorilla *'52*
The Fighter *'52*

Ivo Garrani (1924-2015)
The Day the Sky Exploded *'57*
Black Sunday *'60*
The Giant of Marathon *'60*
Atom Age Vampire *'61*
The Slave *'62*
Caliber 9 *'72*
Street People *'76*

Jean-Francoise Garreaud (1946-2020)
Violette *'78*
Betty *'92*

Esther Garrel (1991-)
Jealousy *'13*
Call Me by Your Name *'17*
Thirst Street *'17*

Louis Garrel (1983-)
The Dreamers *'03*
Inside Paris *'06*
Love Songs *'07*
The Beautiful Person *'08*
Frontier of Dawn *'08*
Making Plans for Lena *'09*
Beloved *'11*
A Burning Hot Summer *'11*
Jealousy *'13*

Maurice Garrel (1923-2011)
To Commit a Murder *'67*
Un Coeur en Hiver *'93*
Artemisia *'97*
Kings and Queen *'04*

Beau Garrett (1982-)
Turistas *'06*
Unearthed *'07*
Made of Honor *'08*
Kalamity *'10*
Tron: Legacy *'10*

Betty Garrett (1919-2011)
Words and Music *'48*
Neptune's Daughter *'49*
On the Town *'49*
Take Me Out to the Ball Game *'49*
My Sister Eileen *'55*
Shadow on the Window *'57*
The Long Way Home *'98*
Dark and Stormy Night *'09*

Brad Garrett (1960-)
Casper *'95 (V)*
Suicide Kings *'97*
A Bug's Life *'98 (V)*
Going Postal *'98*
The Country Bears *'02 (V)*
Stuart Little 2 *'02*
Finding Nemo *'03 (V)*
Garfield: The Movie *'04 (V)*
The Pacifier *'05*
Tarzan 2 *'05 (V)*
Music & Lyrics *'07*
Ratatouille *'07 (V)*
Underdog *'07*
Tangled *'10 (V)*
Hoodwinked Too! Hood vs. Evil *'11 (V)*
Delhi Safari *'12 (V)*
Not Fade Away *'12*
Planes *'13 (V)*
Planes: Fire & Rescue *'14 (V)*

Eliza (Simons) Garrett
Schlock *'73*
Love Is a Gun *'94*

Hank Garrett (1931-)
The Boys Next Door *'85*
Rosebud Beach Hotel *'85*

Jordan Garrett (1992-)
Final Approach *'04*
Saving Shiloh *'06*
Death Sentence *'07*
The Least of These *'08*

Leif Garrett (1961-)
Kid Vengeance *'75*
Peter Lundy and the Medicine Hat Stallion *'77*
Skateboard *'77*
Walking Tall: The Final Chapter *'77*
The Outsiders *'83*
Shaker Run *'85*
Cheerleader Camp *'88*
Party Line *'88*
Spirit of '76 *'91*
Dickie Roberts: Former Child Star *'03 (C)*

Patsy Garrett (1921-)
Benji *'74*
For the Love of Benji *'77*

Spencer Garrett (1963-)
Air Force One *'97*
I Know Who Killed Me *'07*
21 *'08*
Bitter/Sweet *'09*
No Escape *'15*

Barbara Garrick (1965-)
Eight Men Out *'88*
Armistead Maupin's Tales of the City *'93*
The Firm *'93*
Sleepless in Seattle *'93*
A Couch in New York *'95*
Miami Rhapsody *'95*
Armistead Maupin's More Tales of the City *'97*
Ellen Foster *'97*
Brooklyn Lobster *'05*

John Garrick (1902-66)
Lottery Bride *'30*
Song o' My Heart *'30*

Rian Garrick
Battle of the Coral Sea *'59*
Edge of Eternity *'59*

Joaquin Garrido
Solo *'96*
The Kids Are All Right *'10*

Lane Garrison (1980-)
Against the Wall *'04*
Crazy *'08*
Bonnie & Clyde *'13*
Camp X-Ray *'14*
The Iron Orchard *'19*

Robert Garrison (1960-2019)
The Worm Eaters *'77*
The Karate Kid *'84*

Julia Garro
Gracie *'07*
Havoc 2: Normal Adolescent Behavior *'07*

Riccardo Garrone (1926-)
Two Nights with Cleopatra *'54*
Eva *'62*
Swordsman of Siena *'62*
Terror Creatures from the Grave *'66*

Greer Garson (1908-96)
Goodbye, Mr. Chips *'39*
Pride and Prejudice *'40*
Blossoms in the Dust *'41*
When Ladies Meet *'41*
Mrs. Miniver *'42*
Random Harvest *'42*
Madame Curie *'43*
Mrs. Parkington *'44*
The Valley of Decision *'45*
Desire Me *'47*
Julia Misbehaves *'48*
The Miniver Story *'50*
That Forsyte Woman *'50*
The Law and the Lady *'51*
Julius Caesar *'53*
Scandal at Scourie *'53*
Strange Lady in Town *'55*
Sunrise at Campobello *'60*
The Singing Nun *'66*
The Happiest Millionaire *'67*
Little Women *'78*

Willie Garson (1964-)
Untamed Heart *'93*
The Rock *'96*
Play It to the Bone *'99*
What Planet Are You From? *'00*
Out Cold *'01*
Luster *'02*
Taken *'02*
Freaky Friday *'03*
Fever Pitch *'05*
Little Manhattan *'05*
Sex and the City: The Movie *'08*
Sex and the City 2 *'10*

Jennie Garth (1972-)
Danielle Steel's Star *'93*
My Brother's War *'97*
Telling You *'98*
The Last Cowboy *'03*
Girl, Positive *'07*
A Christmas Wedding Tail *'11*
The Eleventh Victim *'12*

Christopher Gartin (1968-)
No Big Deal *'83*
Danielle Steel's Changes *'91*
johns *'96*
Tremors 2: Aftershocks *'96*
Friends and Family *'01*
Tremors 3: Back to Perfection *'01*

Steve Garvey (1948-)
Bloodfist 6: Ground Zero *'94*
The Scout *'94*
Ice Cream Man *'95*
BASEketball *'98*

Elizabeth Garvie (1957-)
Pride and Prejudice *'85*
Diana: Her True Story *'93*

John Garwood
Hell's Angels on Wheels *'67*
The Losers *'70*

Linda Gary (1944-95)
The Land Before Time 2: The Great Valley Adventure *'94 (V)*
The Land Before Time 3: The Time of the Great Giving *'95 (V)*
The Land Before Time 4: Journey Through the Mists *'96 (V)*

Lorraine Gary (1937-)
Jaws *'75*
Jaws 2 *'78*
1941 *'79*
Jaws: The Revenge *'87*

Harold Gasnier
Hellbreeder *'04*
The Witches Hammer *'06*

Kyle Gass (1960-)
Bio-Dome *'96*
The Cradle Will Rock *'99*
Tenacious D in the Pick of Destiny *'06*

Alessandro Gassman (1965-)
A Month by the Lake *'95*
Samson and Delilah *'96*
Steam: A Turkish Bath *'96*
Transporter 2 *'05*
Quiet Chaos *'08*
David's Birthday *'09*
4 Single Fathers *'09*

Vittorio Gassman (1922-2000)
Bitter Rice *'49*
The Glass Wall *'53*
Rhapsody *'54*
Mambo *'55*
War and Peace *'56*
Big Deal on Madonna Street *'58*
Barabbas *'62*
Il Sorpasso *'63*
Tiger and the Pussycat *'67*
Woman Times Seven *'67*
The Scent of a Woman *'75*
The Desert of the Tartars *'76*
We All Loved Each Other So Much *'77*
A Wedding *'78*
Quintet *'79*
Sharky's Machine *'81*
The Tempest *'82*
Life Is a Bed of Roses *'83*
Abraham *'94*
Sleepers *'96*

Ana Gasteyer (1967-)
Meet the Deedles *'98*
Dick *'99*
Gepetto *'00*
What Women Want *'00*
What's the Worst That Could Happen? *'01*
Mean Girls *'04*
The Women *'08*
Dare *'09*
Finn on the Fly *'09*

Michael Gaston (1962-)
The Wedding Banquet *'93*
Ransom *'96*

Bless the Child '00
Cora Unashamed '00
High Crimes '02
Runaway '05
Stay '05
The Notorious Bettie Page '06
Body of Lies '08
Home '08
W. '08
Hurricane Season '09
Sugar '09
Big Miracle '12
First Reformed '17
Spenser Confidential '20

Lisa Gastoni (1935-)
The Runaway Bus '54
Three Men in a Boat '56
Intent to Kill '58
Three Avengers '64
The War of the Planets '65
Wild, Wild Planet '65
Voice from the Stone '17

Larry Gates (1915-96)
Has Anybody Seen My Gal? '52
Above and Beyond '53
Francis Covers the Big Town '53
Invasion of the Body Snatchers '56
The Brothers Rico '57
Jeanne Eagels '57
The Strange One '57
The Remarkable Mr. Pennypacker '59
One Foot in Hell '60
The Hoodlum Priest '61
Underworld U.S.A. '61
The Young Savages '61
Cattle King '63
Toys in the Attic '63
The Sand Pebbles '66
Death of a Gunfighter '69
Missiles of October '74
Funny Lady '75
Backstairs at the White House '79
The Henderson Monster '80

Nancy Gates (1926-)
The Master Race '44
At Sword's Point '51
The Atomic City '52
The Member of the Wedding '52
Torch Song '53
Hell's Half Acre '54
Suddenly '54
Stranger on Horseback '55
The Brass Legend '56
Death of a Scoundrel '56
The Search for Bridey Murphy '56
Wetbacks '56
World Without End '56
Some Came Running '58
The Gunfight at Dodge City '59
Comanche Station '60

Marjorie Gateson (1891-1977)
Street of Women '32
Happiness Ahead '34
Goin' to Town '35
Big Brown Eyes '36
Private Number '36
Meet the Stewarts '42
No Time For Love '43
The Youngest Profession '43

Edi Gathegi (1979-)
Gone Baby Gone '07
Twilight '08
My Bloody Valentine 3D '09
The Twilight Saga: New Moon '09
Atlas Shrugged: Part 1 '11
X-Men: First Class '11
Criminal Activities '15
Pimp '18

Mark Gatiss (1966-)
Starter for 10 '06
Sense & Sensibility '07
Appointment With Death '10
The Crimson Petal and the White '12

Victor Frankenstein '15
Dad's Army '16
Christopher Robin '18
The Mercy '19

Jill Gatsby
Return to Salem's Lot '87
The Ambulance '90

Daniele Gaubert (1943-87)
Flight From Ashiya '64
Camille 2000 '69
Underground '70

Stephane Gauger
Six-String Samurai '98
The Rebel '08

Jean-Paul Gaultier (1952-)
Ready to Wear '94
Mademoiselle C '13

Valerie Gaunt (1933-)
The Curse of Frankenstein '57
The Horror of Dracula '58

Chris Gauthier (1976-)
40 Days and 40 Nights '02
The Foursome '06
The Traveler '10
Metal Shifters '11

Dan Gauthier (1963-)
Teen Witch '89
Son-in-Law '93
Excessive Force 2: Force on Force '95
Groom Lake '02

Dick Gautier (1931-2017)
Divorce American Style '67
Marathon '80
Glitch! '88
Get Smart, Again! '89

Jean-Yves Gautier
A Chef in Love '96
Voyage to the Beginning of the World '96

Janina Gavankar (1980-)
Blindspotting '18
The Way Back '20

Erica Gavin (1947-)
Beyond the Valley of the Dolls '70
Caged Heat '74

John Gavin (1931-2018)
Quantez '57
Imitation of Life '59
Breath of Scandal '60
Psycho '60
Spartacus '60
Back Street '61
Tammy Tell Me True '61
Thoroughly Modern Millie '67
The Madwoman of Chaillot '69
Pussycat, Pussycat, I Love You '70
History of the World: Part 1 '81

Cassandra Gaviola (1959-)
The Black Room '82
Conan the Barbarian '82

Uri Gavriel (1955-)
Delta Force One-The Lost Patrol '99
House of Saddam '08
The Attack '13

Rafi Gavron (1989-)
Breaking and Entering '06
Nick & Norah's Infinite Playlist '08
Inkheart '09
Celeste & Jesse Forever '12
Snitch '13
Tracers '15
The Land '16

Peter Gawthorne (1884-1962)
Phantom Fiend '35
Good Morning, Boys '37
Ticket of Leave Man '37
Ask a Policeman '38
Paid to Kill '54

William Gaxton (1890-1963)
It's the Old Army Game '26
Best Foot Forward '43

Gregory Gay (1900-93)
Seven Doors to Death '44
The Magic Carpet '51
Jungle Man-Eaters '54

Lisa Gaye
The Toxic Avenger, Part 2 '89
The Toxic Avenger, Part 3: The Last Temptation of Toxie '89
Class of Nuke 'Em High 2: Subhumanoid Meltdown '91
Class of Nuke 'Em High 3: The Good, the Bad and the Subhumanoid '94

Lisa Gaye (1935-)
Drums Across the River '54
Shake, Rattle and Rock '57
Ten Thousand Bedrooms '57
The Sign of Zorro '60
Night of Evil '62

Marvin Gaye (1939-84)
The Ballad of Andy Crocker '69
Chrome and Hot Leather '71

Nona Gaye (1974-)
Harlem Nights '89
Ali '01
The Matrix Reloaded '03
The Matrix Revolutions '03
The Polar Express '04
Crash '05
The Gospel '05
XXX: State of the Union '05
Blood and Bone '09

Julie Gayet (1972-)
One Hundred and One Nights '95
Confusion of Genders '00
My Best Friend '06
Shall We Kiss? '07
The French Minister '13

Rebecca Gayheart (1971-)
Nothing to Lose '96
Robin Cook's Invasion '97
Scream 2 '97
Jawbreaker '98
Too Smooth '98
Urban Legend '98
From Dusk Till Dawn 3: The Hangman's Daughter '99
Harvard Man '01
Pipe Dream '02
The Christmas Blessing '05
Bunny Whipped '06

Jackie Gayle (1926-2002)
Pepper and His Wacky Taxi '72
Tin Men '87
Bert Rigby, You're a Fool '89
Mr. Saturday Night '92
Bulworth '98

Sami Gayle (1996-)
Stolen '12
Hateship Loveship '13

Anna Gaylor (1932-)
The Beasts of Marseilles '57
The Killing Game '67

Mitch Gaylord (1961-)
American Anthem '86
Animal Instincts '92

George Gaynes (1917-2016)
The Way We Were '73
Trilogy of Terror '75
The Girl in the Empty Grave '77
Breaking Up Is Hard to Do '79
Dead Men Don't Wear Plaid '82
Tootsie '82
It Came Upon a Midnight Clear '84
Micki & Maude '84
Police Academy '84

Police Academy 2: Their First Assignment '85
Police Academy 3: Back in Training '86
Police Academy 4: Citizens on Patrol '87
Police Academy 5: Assignment Miami Beach '88
Police Academy 6: City under Siege '89
Stepmonster '92
Police Academy 7: Mission to Moscow '94
Vanya on 42nd Street '94
The Crucible '96

Ari Gaynor (1983-)
An American Crime '07
What's Your Number? '11
Celeste & Jesse Forever '12

Janet Gaynor (1906-84)
7th Heaven '27
Sunrise '27
Street Angel '28
Lucky Star '29
The Farmer Takes a Wife '35
A Star Is Born '37
Three Loves Has Nancy '38
The Young in Heart '38

Mitzi Gaynor (1931-)
My Blue Heaven '50
Golden Girl '51
Bloodhounds of Broadway '52
We're Not Married '52
The I Don't Care Girl '53
There's No Business Like Show Business '54
Anything Goes '56
Birds & the Bees '56
Les Girls '57
South Pacific '58
For Love or Money '63

Eunice Gayson (1928-)
Carry On Admiral '57
The Revenge of Frankenstein '58
Dr. No '62
From Russia with Love '63

Wendy Gazelle
Hot Pursuit '87
Triumph of the Spirit '89
Crooked Hearts '91
The Net '95

Ben Gazzara (1930-2012)
The Strange One '57
Anatomy of a Murder '59
A Rage to Live '65
The Bridge at Remagen '69
Husbands '70
Shattered Silence '71
Pursuit '72
Neptune Factor '73
QB VII '74
The Death of Richie '76
The Killing of a Chinese Bookie '76
Voyage of the Damned '76
Opening Night '77
The Trial of Lee Harvey Oswald '77
Saint Jack '79
They All Laughed '81
Tales of Ordinary Madness '83
An Early Frost '85
Secret Obsession '88
Road House '89
Lies Before Kisses '92
Convict Cowboy '95
The Shadow Conspiracy '96
The Big Lebowski '97
Buffalo 66 '97
Lady Killer '97
Protector '97
The Spanish Prisoner '97
Stag '97
Happiness '98
Illuminata '98
Believe '99
The List '99
Summer of Sam '99
The Thomas Crown Affair '99
Blue Moon '00

Brian's Song '01
Hysterical Blindness '02
Dogville '03
Paris, je t'aime '06
Looking for Palladin '08
13 '10

Michael V. Gazzo (1923-95)
The Godfather, Part 2 '74
Black Sunday '77
Fingers '78
King of the Gypsies '78
Love and Bullets '79
Alligator '80
Kill Castro '80
The Mercenaries '80
Sudden Impact '83
Cookie '89

Devon Gearhart (1995-)
Bobby Jones: Stroke of Genius '04
Canvas '06
Funny Games '07
Shorts: The Adventures of the Wishing Rock '09
The Power of Few '13
The Wait '13

Anthony Geary (1947-)
Johnny Got His Gun '71
Disorderlies '87
You Can't Hurry Love '88
Crack House '89
UHF '89
Night of the Warrior '91
Scorchers '92
Disney's Teacher's Pet '04 (V)
Carpool Guy '05

Bud Geary (1898-1946)
Bataan '43
Immortal Sergeant '43

Cynthia Geary (1965-)
8 Seconds '94
To Grandmother's House We Go '94
The Awakening '95
The Heist '96
The Killing Grounds '97
When Time Expires '97
Smoke Signals '98
The Business of Fancydancing '02
Crimes of the Past '09

Karl Geary (1972-)
Nadja '95
The Book of Stars '99
The Eternal '99
The External '99
Hamlet '00
Mimic 3: Sentinel '03
Stag Night '08

Gordon Gebert (1941-)
Flying Leathernecks '51
The Narrow Margin '52
To Hell and Back '55

Nicholas Gecks (1952-)
Forever Young '85
The Mill on the Floss '97
Parting Shots '98
Sherlock: Case of Evil '02

Jeff Geddis (1975-)
Jesse Stone: Innocents Lost '11
Jesse Stone: Benefit of the Doubt '12

Martina Gedeck (1961-)
Mostly Martha '01
The Good Shepherd '06
The Lives of Others '06
Summer of '04 '06
The Baader Meinhof Complex '08
The Wall '13

Ruta Gedmintas (1983-)
The Lost Samaritan '08
Miss Conception '08
Prowl '10
Tonight You're Mine '11
A Street Cat Named Bob '16

Jason Gedrick (1965-)
The Heavenly Kid '85
Massive Retaliation '85
Iron Eagle '86

Promised Land '88
Rooftops '89
Backdraft '91
Crossing the Bridge '92
The Last Don '97
The Last Don 2 '98
Strange Frequency 2 '01
Summer Catch '01
A Date With Darkness '03
Hidden Places '06
Kings of South Beach '07
The Christmas Choir '08
Depth Charge '08
Wisegal '08
Sand Serpents '09
Shannon's Rainbow '09
War Flowers '12

Prunella Gee (1950-)
The Wilby Conspiracy '75
Never Say Never Again '83

Robbie Gee (1970-)
Snatch '00
Mean Machine '01
Underworld '03
Out of Reach '04

Ellen Geer (1941-)
Petulia '68
Harold and Maude '71
Silence '73
Babe! '75
Over the Edge '79
Bloody Birthday '80
The Odd Couple 2 '98

Kevin Geer
Sweet Bird of Youth '89
The Tavern '00
100 Feet '08

Will Geer (1902-78)
Spitfire '34
Johnny Allegro '49
Lust for Gold '49
Broken Arrow '50
Convicted '50
It's a Small World '50
To Please a Lady '50
Winchester '73 '50
Double Crossbones '51
The Tall Target '51
Salt of the Earth '54
Black Like Me '64
Seconds '66
In Cold Blood '67
The President's Analyst '67
Bandolero! '68
The Reivers '69
Brother John '70
The Moonshine War '70
Pieces of Dreams '70
Dear Dead Delilah '72
Jeremiah Johnson '72
Napoleon and Samantha '72
Executive Action '73
Silence '73
The Hanged Man '74
Hurricane '74
Moving Violation '76
The Billion Dollar Hobo '78
My Sister, My Love '78
A Woman Called Moses '78
Unknown Powers '80

Chris Geere
The Prince & Me 3: A Royal Honeymoon '08
The Prince & Me 4: The Elephant Adventure '10

Judy Geeson (1948-)
Berserk! '67
To Sir, with Love '67
Hammerhead '68
The Executioner '70
It Happened at Nightmare Inn '70
10 Rillington Place '71
Doomwatch '72
Dynasty of Fear '72
Murder on the Midnight Express '74
Poldark 2 '75
Poldark '75
Carry On England '76
Inseminoid '80
Danger UXB '81
The Plague Dogs '82 (V)
Houdini '98

The Duke *'99*
The Lords of Salem *'13*

Sally Geeson (1950-)
The Oblong Box *'69*
What's Good for the Goose *'69*
Cry of the Banshee *'70*

Deborah Geffner (1952-)
All That Jazz *'79*
Infestation *'09*

Martha Gehman
The Flamingo Kid *'84*
F/X *'86*
Father of the Bride *'91*
A Kiss Before Dying *'91*
Threesome *'94*
Going Shopping *'05*

Anna Geislerova (1976-)
Hidden in Silence *'96*
Zelary *'03*
Something Like Happiness *'05*
Anthropoid *'16*

Bob Geldof (1951-)
Pink Floyd: The Wall *'82*
The Secret Policeman's Other Ball *'82*
The Return of Spinal Tap *'92 (C)*
Spice World: The Movie *'97 (C)*

Alan Gelfant (1957-)
Forced to Kill *'93*
Next Stop, Wonderland *'98*
Apartment 12 *'06*

Daniel Gelin (1921-2002)
La Ronde *'51*
Le Plaisir *'52*
The Man Who Knew Too Much *'56*
Plucking the Daisy *'56*
The Testament of Orpheus *'59*
Is Paris Burning? *'66*
Slogan *'69*
Murmur of the Heart *'71*
Obsession *'97*

Sarah Michelle Gellar (1977-)
I Know What You Did Last Summer *'97*
Scream 2 *'97*
Cruel Intentions *'98*
Small Soldiers *'98 (V)*
She's All That *'99*
Simply Irresistible *'99*
Harvard Man *'01*
Scooby-Doo *'02*
The Grudge *'04*
Scooby-Doo 2: Monsters Unleashed *'04*
The Grudge 2 *'06*
The Return *'06*
Southland Tales *'06*
The Air I Breathe *'07*
Happily N'Ever After *'07 (V)*
Suburban Girl *'07*
TMNT: Teenage Mutant Ninja Turtles *'07 (V)*
Possession *'08*
Veronika Decides to Die *'15*

Yani Gellman (1985-)
The Lizzie McGuire Movie *'03*
47 Meters Down *'17*

Brett Gelman
Awful Nice *'14*
Joshy *'16*
Lemon *'17*

Larry Gelman (1930-)
Chatterbox *'76*
Slumber Party '57 *'76*
Prime Time *'77*

Dylan Gelula (1994-)
Flower *'18*
Support the Girls *'18*

Giuliano Gemma (1938-2013)
Angelique *'64*
Goliath and the Sins of Babylon *'64*
Hercules *vs.* the Sons of the Sun *'64*
Angelique: The Road to Versailles *'65*
Erik, the Viking *'65*
Fort Yuma Gold *'66*
Long Days of Revenge *'67*
The Cats *'68*
Sundance and the Kid *'69*
Master Touch *'74*
Smugglers *'75*
The Desert of the Tartars *'76*
California *'77*
Battleforce *'78*
Unsane *'82*
Mad Love *'01*

Ruth Gemmell (1967-)
Band of Gold *'95*
Fever Pitch *'96*
The Alchemists *'99*

Tristan Gemmill (1967-)
Speedy Death *'99*
The Adventurer: The Curse of the Midas Box *'13*

Laura Gemser (1950-)
Emmanuelle on Taboo Island *'76*
Emmanuelle, the Joys of a Woman *'76*
Crime Busters *'78*
Emmanuelle in the Country *'78*
Fury *'78*
Emmanuelle, the Queen *'79*
Emmanuelle's Daughter *'79*
Love Camp *'81*
Ator the Fighting Eagle *'83*
Black Cobra *'83*
Caged Women *'84*

Sophie Gendron
Demons from Her Past *'07*
Framed for Murder *'07*
My Nanny's Secret *'09*
Metal Tornado *'11*

Bryan Genesse (1964-)
Loose Screws *'85*
Night Siege Project: Shadowchaser 2 *'94*
Live Wire: Human Timebomb *'95*
Terminal Impact *'95*
Cold Harvest *'98*
Operation Delta Force 3: Clear Target *'98*
Spoiler *'98*
Agent of Death *'99*
We'll Meet Again *'02*

Leo Genn (1905-78)
Henry V *'44*
Immortal Battalion *'44*
Green for Danger *'47*
The Snake Pit *'48*
The Miniver Story *'50*
Quo Vadis *'51*
Lady Chatterley's Lover *'55*
Moby Dick *'56*
Era Notte a Roma *'60*
The Longest Day *'62*
Circus of Fear *'67*
Strange Case of Dr. Jekyll & Mr. Hyde *'68*
A Lizard in a Woman's Skin *'71*
Die Screaming, Marianne *'73*
Mackintosh Man *'73*

Maxim Gentchev
Dark Descent *'02*
Dragon Storm *'04*

Troy Gentile (1993-)
The Bad News Bears *'05*
Tenacious D in the Pick of Destiny *'06*
Drillbit Taylor *'08*
Hotel for Dogs *'09*

Minnie Gentry (1916-93)
Georgia, Georgia *'72*
Def by Temptation *'90*

Race Gentry (1934-)
Men in War *'57*
Thunder in Carolina *'60*

Roger Gentry (1934-2013)
Horrors of the Red Planet *'64*
Alien Massacre *'67*
Gallery of Horrors *'67*

Carrie Genzel (1971-)
Caged Hearts *'95*
Loch Ness Terror *'07*
They're Watching *'16*

Paul Geoffrey
Excalibur *'81*
Emily Bronte's Wuthering Heights *'92*

Stephen Geoffreys (1964-)
Fraternity Vacation *'85*
Fright Night *'85*
976-EVIL *'88*
Moon 44 *'90*

Bill George (1920-64)
See Jay Kirby

Brian George (1952-)
Pom Poko *'94 (V)*
Bubble Boy *'01*
Ghost World *'01*
Touch of Pink *'04*
Employee of the Month *'06*

Christopher George (1929-83)
El Dorado *'67*
Project X *'68*
1,000 Plane Raid *'69*
Chisum *'70*
Train Robbers *'73*
Dixie Dynamite *'76*
Grizzly *'76*
Mayday at 40,000 Feet *'76*
Midway *'76*
Day of the Animals *'77*
Exterminator *'80*
Gates of Hell *'80*
AngKor: Cambodia Express *'81*
Enter the Ninja *'81*
Graduation Day *'81*
Mortuary *'81*
Pieces *'83*

Chief Dan George (1899-1981)
Little Big Man *'70*
Cancel My Reservation *'72*
Dan Candy's Law *'73*
The Bears & I *'74*
Harry and Tonto *'74*
The Outlaw Josey Wales *'76*
Shadow of the Hawk *'76*
Americathon *'79*

Gladys George (1900-54)
Madame X *'37*
They Gave Him a Gun *'37*
Marie Antoinette *'38*
The Roaring Twenties *'39*
House Across the Bay *'40*
The Maltese Falcon *'41*
The Hard Way *'43*
The Best Years of Our Lives *'46*
Flamingo Road *'49*
Bright Leaf *'50*
Detective Story *'51*
Lullaby of Broadway *'51*

Goetz George (1938-)
Schtonk *'92*
The Trio *'97*

Heinrich George (1893-1946)
Metropolis *'26*
Jud Suess *'40*
Kolberg *'45*

Jason Winston George (1972-)
Three Can Play That Game *'07*
Kidnap *'17*

Chief Leonard George
Man of the House *'95*
Smoke Signals *'98*

Lynda Day George (1944-)
Death Among Friends *'75*
Mayday at 40,000 Feet *'76*
Once an Eagle *'76*
Aliens from Spaceship Earth *'77*
Ants *'77*
Day of the Animals *'77*
Roots *'77*
The Amazing Captain Nemo *'78*
Beyond Evil *'80*
Mortuary *'81*
The Junkman *'82*
Pieces *'83*

Maud(e) (Ford) George (1888-1963)
Blue Blazes Rawden *'18*
Foolish Wives *'22*

Melissa George (1976-)
Dark City *'97*
The Limey *'99*
Mulholland Drive *'01*
Sugar & Spice *'01*
Down With Love *'03*
The Amityville Horror *'05*
Derailed *'05*
Turistas *'06*
The Killing Gene *'07*
Music Within *'07*
30 Days of Night *'07*
The Betrayed *'08*
Triangle *'09*
Bag of Bones *'11*
A Lonely Place to Die *'11*
Swinging With the Finkels *'11*
Between Us *'12*
Felony *'13*

Rita George
On the Run *'73*
Hollywood Boulevard *'76*

Susan George (1950-)
The Sorcerers *'67*
All Neat in Black Stockings *'69*
Lola *'69*
The Looking Glass War *'69*
Eye Witness *'70*
Fright *'71*
Straw Dogs *'72*
Die Screaming, Marianne *'73*
Dr. Jekyll and Mr. Hyde *'73*
Sonny and Jed *'73*
Dirty Mary Crazy Larry *'74*
Mandingo *'75*
Out of Season *'75*
A Small Town in Texas *'76*
Tomorrow Never Comes *'77*
Enter the Ninja *'81*
House Where Evil Dwells *'82*
Venom *'82*
Lightning: The White Stallion *'86*
Jack the Ripper *'88*
In Your Dreams *'07*

Olga Georges-Picot (1944-97)
Honor Among Thieves *'68*
The Man Who Haunted Himself *'70*
The Day of the Jackal *'73*

Tom Georgeson (1937-)
No Surrender *'86*
A Fish Called Wanda *'88*
Devices and Desires *'91*
G.B.H. *'91*
Bleak House *'05*
Angel *'07*

Brian Geraghty (1975-)
Conversations with Other Women *'05*
Cruel World *'05*
Jarhead *'05*
Bobby *'06*
The Guardian *'06*
When a Stranger Calls *'06*
I Know Who Killed Me *'07*
Love Lies Bleeding *'07*
The Hurt Locker *'08*
Easier With Practice *'10*
Krews *'10*
Open House *'10*
Seven Days in Utopia *'11*
ATM *'12*
Flight *'12*
10 Years *'12*
Ass Backwards *'13*
Kilimanjaro *'13*
The Identical *'14*
The Standoff at Sparrow Creek *'19*

Carmelita Geraghty (1901-66)
The Pleasure Garden *'25*
My Best Girl *'27*
The Phantom of Santa Fe *'36*

K. Danor Gerald
Believe *'07*
The Eleventh Hour *'08*

Matt Gerald
In the Mix *'05*
Freelancers *'12*
Solace *'16*

Caitlin Gerard (1988-)
Smiley *'12*
The Assignment *'17*
Insidious: The Last Key *'18*
The Wind *'19*

Gil Gerard (1943-)
Buck Rogers in the 25th Century *'79*
Fury to Freedom: The Life Story of Raul Ries *'85*
Mom, Can I Keep Her? *'98*
The Stepdaughter *'00*
Air Rage *'01*
Bone Eater *'07*
Nuclear Hurricane *'07*
The Lost Valentine *'11*

Ivaylo Geraskov
Dragon Storm *'04*
Command Performance *'09*

Steven Geray (1904-73)
Inspector Hornleigh *'39*
Blue, White and Perfect *'42*
The Moon and Sixpence *'43*
Pilot No. 5 *'43*
The Conspirators *'44*
In Society *'44*
The Mask of Dimitrios *'44*
Meet the People *'44*
Tarzan and the Amazons *'45*
Gilda *'46*
So Dark the Night *'46*
A Lady Without Passport *'50*
Pygmy Island *'50*
Savage Drums *'51*
Affair in Trinidad *'52*
Knock on Wood *'54*
Tobor the Great *'54*
Jesse James Meets Frankenstein's Daughter *'65*

Joan Gerber (1935-)
Tobor the Great *'54*
DuckTales the Movie: Treasure of the Lost Lamp *'90 (V)*

Mark Gerber
Sirens *'94*
13 Gantry Row *'98*

George Gerdes
Iron Will *'93*
Jailbreakers *'94*

Richard Gere (1949-)
Report to the Commissioner *'75*
Strike Force *'75*
Bloodbrothers *'78*
Days of Heaven *'78*
American Gigolo *'79*
Yanks *'79*
An Officer and a Gentleman *'82*
Breathless *'83*
The Cotton Club *'84*
King David *'85*
No Mercy *'86*
Power *'86*
Internal Affairs *'90*
Pretty Woman *'90*
Rhapsody in August *'91*
Final Analysis *'92*
And the Band Played On *'93 (C)*
Intersection *'93*
Mr. Jones *'93*
Sommersby *'93*
First Knight *'95*
Primal Fear *'96*
The Jackal *'97*
Red Corner *'97*
Runaway Bride *'99*
Autumn in New York *'00*
Dr. T & the Women *'00*
Chicago *'02*
The Mothman Prophecies *'02*
Unfaithful *'02*
Shall We Dance? *'04*
Bee Season *'05*
The Hoax *'06*
The Flock *'07*
The Hunting Party *'07*
I'm Not There *'07*
Nights in Rodanthe *'08*
Amelia *'09*
Brooklyn's Finest *'09*
Hachiko: A Dog's Tale *'09*
The Double *'11*
Arbitrage *'12*
Movie 43 *'13*
Time Out of Mind *'14*
The Benefactor *'16*
Norman *'17*

Georges Geret (1924-96)
Diary of a Chambermaid *'64*
A Quiet Place in the Country *'69*
Z *'69*

Peter Gerety (1940-)
Went to Coney Island on a Mission from God. . . Be Back by Five *'98*
Homicide: The Movie *'00*
The Legend of Bagger Vance *'00*
The Curse of the Jade Scorpion *'01*
K-PAX *'01*
Hollywood Ending *'02*
Virgin *'03*
Runaway *'05*
Second Best *'05*
Inside Man *'06*
Charlie Wilson's War *'07*
Changeling *'08*
Leatherheads *'08*
The Loss of a Teardrop Diamond *'08*
Phoebe in Wonderland *'08*
My Dog Tulip *'09 (V)*
Paul Blart: Mall Cop *'09*
Muhammad Ali's Greatest Fight *'13*

Claudia Gerini (1971-)
Iris Blond *'98*
The Passion of the Christ *'04*
The Unknown Woman *'06*

Lauren German (1978-)
A Walk to Remember *'02*
Born Killers *'05*
Standing Still *'05*
Rx *'06*
Hostel: Part 2 *'07*
Love and Mary *'07*
Spin *'07*
Mating Dance *'08*
Dark Country *'09*

Gaia Germani (1942-)
Your Turn Darling *'63*
Castle of the Living Dead *'64*

Greg Germann (1958-)
Streetwalkin' *'85*
The Whoopee Boys *'86*
Once Around *'91*
The Night We Never Met *'93*
Jesus' Son *'99*
Down to Earth *'01*
Joe Somebody *'01*
Sweet November *'01*
Bigger Than the Sky *'05*
Crazylove *'05*
Down and Derby *'05*
The Family Plan *'05*
Heart of the Beholder *'05*
The Salon *'05*
The Sandlot 2 *'05*
Friends with Money *'06*
Kill Your Darlings *'06*
All I Want for Christmas *'07*
Bolt *'08*
Quarantine *'08*
Spectacular *'09*

Group Sex '10
The Santa Incident '10
Atlas Shrugged 3: Who Is John Galt? '14
Quitters '16

Elio Germano (1980-)
Respiro '02
My Brother Is an Only Child '07
Our Life '10
The Lady in the Car with Glasses and a Gun '16

Daniel Gerroll (1951-)
84 Charing Cross Road '86
Big Business '88
Drop Dead Fred '91
A Far Off Place '93

Alex Gerry (1904-93)
David Harding, Counterspy '50
The Jazz Singer '52
The Eddie Cantor Story '53
The Bellboy '60

Savina Gersak
Curse 2: The Bite '88
Beyond the Door 3 '91

Gina Gershon (1962-)
Pretty in Pink '86
Cocktail '88
Red Heat '88
Voodoo Dawn '89
City of Hope '91
Out for Justice '91
The Player '92
Sinatra '92
Best of the Best 3: No Turning Back '95
Showgirls '95
Bound '96
Touch '96
Face/Off '97
I'm Losing You '98
Legalese '98
Lies and Whispers '98
Lulu on the Bridge '98
One Tough Cop '98
Palmetto '98
Black & White '99
Guinevere '99
The Insider '99
Driven '01
Picture Claire '01
Borderline '02
Demonlover '02
Prey for Rock and Roll '03
3-Way '04
Category 7: The End of the World '05
One Last Thing '05
Delirious '06
Dreamland '06
I Want Someone to Eat Cheese With '06
Kettle of Fish '06
P.S. I Love You '07
What Love Is '07
Beer for My Horses '08
Just Business '08
Across the Line: The Exodus of Charlie Wright '10
Love Ranch '10
Killer Joe '11
Breathless '12
House of Versace '13
The Lookalike '14
The Scribbler '14
Inconceivable '17
9/11 '17
Permission '18

Betty Lou Gerson (1914-99)
The Red Menace '49
The Fly '58
101 Dalmatians '61 (V)

Jeanne Gerson (1905-92)
The Bride & the Beast '58
The Touch of Satan '70

Lisa Gerstein
My Life's in Turnaround '94
Border Blues '03

Frank Gerstle (1915-70)
Above and Beyond '53
Gang Busters '55
The Wasp Woman '59
Vice Raid '60
The Atomic Brain '64
Hell on Wheels '67

Valeska Gert (1892-1978)
Joyless Street '25
The Threepenny Opera '31
Juliet of the Spirits '65

Jami Gertz (1965-)
Endless Love '81
Alphabet City '84
Sixteen Candles '84
Mischief '85
Crossroads '86
Quicksilver '86
Solarbabies '86
Less Than Zero '87
The Lost Boys '87
Renegades '89
Don't Tell Her It's Me '90
Sibling Rivalry '90
Jersey Girl '92
Twister '96
Lip Service '00
Seven Girlfriends '00
Fighting the Odds: The Marilyn Gambrell Story '05
Keeping Up with the Steins '06
Lost Holiday: The Jim & Suzanne Shemwell Story '07

Ricky Gervais (1961-)
Valiant '05 (V)
For Your Consideration '06
Night at the Museum '06
Stardust '07
Ghost Town '08
The Invention of Lying '09
Night at the Museum: Battle of the Smithsonian '09
Cemetery Junction '10
Spy Kids 4: All the Time in the World '11 (V)
Escape From Planet Earth '13 (V)
Muppets Most Wanted '14

Greta Gerwig (1983-)
Hannah Takes the Stairs '07
Baghead '08
Nights and Weekends '08
The House of the Devil '09
Greenberg '10
Arthur '11
Damsels in Distress '11
The Dish & the Spoon '11
No Strings Attached '11
Lola Versus '12
To Rome with Love '12
Frances Ha '13
Mistress America '15
Jackie '16
Maggie's Plan '16
Wiener-Dog '16
20th Century Women '17

Erwin Geschonneck (1906-)
Carbide and Sorrel '63
Jacob the Liar '74

Zen Gesner (1970-)
Kingpin '96
There's Something about Mary '98
Me, Myself, and Irene '00
The Breed '01
Shallow Hal '01
Fever Pitch '05

Sumner Getchell (1906-90)
The Flying Fleet '29
Eleven Men and a Girl '30

Malcolm Gets (1964-)
Love in the Time of Money '02
Adam & Steve '05
Grey Gardens '09

Balthazar Getty (1975-)
Lord of the Flies '90
Young Guns 2 '90
December '91
Where the Day Takes You '92
Dead Beat '94
Don't Do It '94
Terrified '94
Lost Highway '96
White Squall '96
Habitat '97
Big City Blues '99
Out in Fifty '99
Voodoo Dawn '99
Four Dogs Playing Poker '00
The Center of the World '01
Hard Cash '01
MacArthur Park '01
Sol Goode '01
Deuces Wild '02
Ladder 49 '04
Feast '06
The Tripper '06
Big Sur '13

Estelle Getty (1923-2008)
Tootsie '82
Mask '85
Mannequin '87
Stop! or My Mom Will Shoot '92
Stuart Little '99

John Getz (1946-)
Thief of Hearts '84
Blood Simple '85
The Fly '86
Born on the Fourth of July '89
The Fly 2 '89
Curly Sue '91
Don't Tell Mom the Babysitter's Dead '91
Untamed Love '94
The Late Shift '96
Hunger Point '03
A Day Without a Mexican '04
Hard Four '07
Zodiac '07

Stan Getz (1927-91)
The Benny Goodman Story '55
Exterminator '80

Stephen Gevedon (1966-)
Blue in the Face '95
Smoke '95
Session 9 '01

Vida Ghahremani (1937-)
A Thousand Years of Good Prayers '07
The Stoning of Soraya M. '08

Luminita Gheorghiu (1949-)
Code Unknown '00
The Death of Mr. Lazarescu '05
Aurora '10

Dana Ghia (1932-)
Four Dollars of Revenge '66
Django: Last Killer '67
Burn! '70

Massimo Ghini (1954-)
Men Men Men '95
The Truce '96
Tea with Mussolini '99
Up at the Villa '00
CQ '01

Kulvinder Ghir
Rita, Sue & Bob Too '87
Blinded by the Light '19

Alice Ghostley (1926-2007)
New Faces of 1952 '54
To Kill a Mockingbird '62
The Graduate '67
With Six You Get Eggroll '68
Gator '76
Blue Sunshine '78
Grease '78
Not for Publication '84
The Odd Couple 2 '98
Whispers: An Elephant's Tale '00 (V)

Fosco Giachetti
We the Living '42
Fury of Achilles '62

Marcus Giamatti
The Business of Strangers '01
On the Doll '07

Paul Giamatti (1967-)
Private Parts '96
My Best Friend's Wedding '97
The Negotiator '98
Safe Men '98
Saving Private Ryan '98
The Truman Show '98
Winchell '98
The Cradle Will Rock '99
Man on the Moon '99
Big Momma's House '00
Duets '00
If These Walls Could Talk 2 '00
Planet of the Apes '01
Storytelling '01
Big Fat Liar '02
American Splendor '03
Confidence '03
Paycheck '03
Sideways '04
Cinderella Man '05
Robots '05 (V)
The Ant Bully '06 (V)
The Hawk Is Dying '06
The Illusionist '06
Lady in the Water '06
Fred Claus '07
The Nanny Diaries '07
Shoot 'Em Up '07
John Adams '08
Pretty Bird '08
Cold Souls '09
Duplicity '09
The Haunted World of El Superbeasto '09 (V)
The Last Station '09
Barney's Version '10
The Hangover, Part 2 '11
The Ides of March '11
Ironclad '11
Too Big to Fail '11
Win Win '11
Cosmopolis '12
John Dies at the End '12
Rock of Ages '12
The Congress '13
Ernest & Celestine '13 (V)
Parkland '13
Romeo & Juliet '13
Saving Mr. Banks '13
Turbo '13 (V)
12 Years a Slave '13
The Amazing Spider-Man 2 '14
Love & Mercy '15
Madame Bovary '15
The Phenom '16
Ratchet & Clank '16
I Think We're Alone Now '18

Louis Giambalvo (1945-)
The Ambush Murders '82
Ratings Game '84
The Jagged Edge '85
The Dead Pool '88
Weekend at Bernie's '89
Gia '98
Gun Shy '00

Rick Gianasi
Mutant Hunt '87
Maximum Thrust '88
The Occultist '89
Posed for Murder '89
Sgt. Kabukiman N.Y.P.D. '94

Adriano Giannini (1971-)
Swept Away '02
Sinbad: Legend of the Seven Seas '03 (V)

Giancarlo Giannini (1942-)
Anzio '68
The Secret of Santa Vittoria '69
The Black Belly of the Tarantula '71
Seduction of Mimi '72
Love and Anarchy '73
Swept Away. . . '75
The Innocent '76
Seven Beauties '76
A Night Full of Rain '78
Blood Feud '79
Lovers and Liars '81
American Dreamer '84
Blood Red '88
New York Stories '89
Time to Kill '89
Once Upon a Crime '92
Jacob '94
A Walk in the Clouds '95
The Disappearance of Garcia Lorca '96
Heaven Before I Die '96
Mimic '97
Dune '00
CQ '01
Hannibal '01
The Whole Shebang '01
Darkness '02
Joshua '02
Incantato '03
My House in Umbria '03
Man on Fire '04
Casino Royale '06
Quantum of Solace '08

Cynthia Gibb (1963-)
Stardust Memories '80
Modern Girls '86
Salvador '86
Youngblood '86
Malone '87
Short Circuit 2 '88
Death Warrant '90
Gypsy '93
The Woman Who Loved Elvis '93
Life with Judy Garland-Me and My Shadows '01 (N)
Christie's Revenge '07
Demons from Her Past '07
Accused at 17 '09
A Nanny for Christmas '10

Donald Gibb (1954-)
Bloodsport '88
Magic Kid 2 '94
Revenge of the Nerds 4: Nerds in Love '94

Blake Gibbons
The Legend of Butch & Sundance '04
Shockwave '06

Leeza Gibbons (1957-)
Soapdish '91
The Player '92

Marla Gibbs (1931-)
The Meteor Man '93
Foolish '99
Lost and Found '99
The Visit '00
The Brothers '01
The Heart Specialist '06
Madea's Witness Protection '12
Please Stand By '17

Alex Gibney (1953-)
The Armstrong Lie '13 (N)
Citizen K '19
The Inventor: Out For Blood In Silicon Valley '19

Rebecca Gibney (1964-)
Paperback Romance '96
Joey '98
13 Gantry Row '98
Introducing the Dwights '07
In Her Skin '09

Susan Gibney (1961-)
And You Thought Your Parents Were Weird! '91
Cabin by the Lake '00
Derailed '02

Deborah Gibson (1970-)
Coffee Date '06
Mega Shark Vs. Giant Octopus '09
Mega Python Vs. Gatoroid '11

Henry Gibson (1935-2009)
The Nutty Professor '63
Kiss Me, Stupid! '64
The Outlaws Is Coming! '65
Evil Roy Slade '71
Charlotte's Web '73 (V)
The Long Goodbye '73
Nashville '75
Kentucky Fried Movie '77
The Blues Brothers '80
For the Love of It '80
The Incredible Shrinking Woman '81
Brenda Starr '86
Monster in the Closet '86
Innerspace '87
Switching Channels '88
Around the World in 80 Days '89
Night Visitor '89
Gremlins 2: The New Batch '90
Tune in Tomorrow '90
Tom and Jerry: The Movie '93 (V)
Color of a Brisk and Leaping Day '95
Bio-Dome '96
Mother Night '96
A Stranger in the Kingdom '98
Wedding Crashers '05
Big Stan '07

Hoot Gibson (1892-1962)
The Texas Streak '26
Boiling Point '32
The Gay Buckaroo '32
The Dude Bandit '33
Cavalcade of the West '36
Last Outlaw '36
The Marshal's Daughter '53
The Horse Soldiers '59

Leah Gibson
A Night for Dying Tigers '10
The Twilight Saga: Eclipse '10

Martha Gibson
Outrageous! '77
Family of Strangers '93

Mel Gibson (1956-)
Summer City '77
Tim '79
Mad Max '80
Gallipoli '81
The Road Warrior '82
The Year of Living Dangerously '82
Attack Force Z '84
The Bounty '84
Mrs. Soffel '84
The River '84
Mad Max: Beyond Thunderdome '85
Lethal Weapon '87
Tequila Sunrise '88
Lethal Weapon 2 '89
Air America '90
Bird on a Wire '90
Hamlet '90
Forever Young '92
Lethal Weapon 3 '92
The Man Without a Face '93
Maverick '94
Braveheart '95
Casper '95 (C)
Pocahontas '95 (V)
Ransom '96
Conspiracy Theory '97
FairyTale: A True Story '97 (C)
Lethal Weapon 4 '98
Payback '98
The Million Dollar Hotel '99
Chicken Run '00 (V)
The Patriot '00
What Women Want '00
Signs '02
We Were Soldiers '02
The Singing Detective '03
Paparazzi '04 (C)
Edge of Darkness '10
The Beaver '11
Get the Gringo '12
Machete Kills '13
The Expendables 3 '14
Blood Father '16
Daddy's Home 2 '17
Dragged Across Concrete '18
The Professor and the Madman '19

Milo Gibson
Breaking & Exiting '18
Mission of Honor '19

Thomas Gibson (1962-)
Far and Away '92
Armistead Maupin's Tales of the City '93

Love and Human Remains '93
Barcelona '94
Sleep with Me '94
Armistead Maupin's More Tales of the City '97
The Inheritance '97
Eyes Wide Shut '99
The Flintstones in Viva Rock Vegas '00
Psycho Beach Party '00
Stardom '00
The Lost Empire '01
Brush with Fate '03
Category 6: Day of Destruction '04
I'll Believe You '07
Just Buried '07

Tyrese Gibson (1978-)
Baby Boy '01
2 Fast 2 Furious '03
Flight of the Phoenix '04
Four Brothers '05
Annapolis '06
Waist Deep '06
Transformers '07
Death Race '08
Transformers: Revenge of the Fallen '09
Legion '10
Fast Five '11
Transformers: Dark of the Moon '11
Black Nativity '13
Fast & Furious 6 '13
Furious 7 '15
The Fate of the Furious '17
Black and Blue '19

Virginia Gibson (1928-2013)
Tea for Two '50
Painting the Clouds With Sunshine '51
She's Back on Broadway '53
Athena '54
Seven Brides for Seven Brothers '54

Wynne Gibson (1899-1987)
Man of the World '31
If I Had a Million '32
Night After Night '32

Bond Gideon
Stepsisters '74
Gold of the Amazon Women '79

Pamela Gidley (1965-2018)
Thrashin' '86
Blue Iguana '88
Cherry 2000 '88
Permanent Record '88
Liebestraum '91
Cheatin' Hearts '93
Firefall '94
S.F.W. '94
Bad Love '95
The Crew '95
Aberration '97
Bombshell '97
Mafia! '98
The Treat '98
Liar's Poker '99
The Little Vampire '00
Landspeed '01
True Blue '01
Luster '02

John Gielgud (1904-2000)
The Good Companions '33
The Secret Agent '36
Hamlet '48 (V)
Julius Caesar '53
Romeo and Juliet '54
Richard III '55
Around the World in 80 Days '56 (C)
Saint Joan '57
Becket '64
The Loved One '65
Chimes at Midnight '67
The Charge of the Light Brigade '68
The Shoes of the Fisherman '68
Assignment to Kill '69
Oh! What a Lovely War '69
Julius Caesar '70
Probe '72
Lost Horizon '73
11 Harrowhouse '74
Murder on the Orient Express '74
QB VII '74
Edward the King '75
James Joyce: A Portrait of the Artist as a Young Man '77
Les Miserables '78
The Human Factor '79
Murder by Decree '79
Caligula '80
The Elephant Man '80
The Formula '80
Arthur '81
Brideshead Revisited '81
Chariots of Fire '81
Lion of the Desert '81
Priest of Love '81
Sphinx '81
Gandhi '82
The Hunchback of Notre Dame '82
The Scarlet & the Black '83
Camille '84
The Far Pavilions '84
Plenty '85
The Shooting Party '85
Wagner: The Complete Epic '85
The Canterville Ghost '86
The Whistle Blower '87
Arthur 2: On the Rocks '88
A Man for All Seasons '88
War & Remembrance '88
Getting It Right '89
War & Remembrance: The Final Chapter '89
Strike It Rich '90
Prospero's Books '91
The Power of One '92
Shining Through '92
Scarlett '94
First Knight '95
Gulliver's Travels '95
Haunted '95 (C)
Shine '95
Dragonheart '96 (V)
Hamlet '96
Looking for Richard '96
Portrait of a Lady '96
A Dance to the Music of Time '97
Elizabeth '98
Merlin '98 (C)
Quest for Camelot '98 (V)

Stefan Gierasch (1926-2014)
The Traveling Executioner '70
Jeremiah Johnson '72
High Plains Drifter '73
Carrie '76
Victory at Entebbe '76
Blue Sunshine '78
Dave '93
Murder in the First '95

Alan Gifford (1905-89)
Satellite in the Sky '56
Time Lock '57
Screaming Mimi '58
Town without Pity '61

Cassidy Gifford
The Gallows '15
Time Trap '17

Frances Gifford (1919-94)
American Empire '42
Cry Havoc '43
Tarzan Triumphs '43
Our Vines Have Tender Grapes '45
Thrill of a Romance '45
Luxury Liner '48
Riding High '50

Frank Gifford (1930-)
Up Periscope '59
Viva Knievel '77 (C)

Gloria Gifford
D.C. Cab '84
Vice Versa '88

Roland Gift (1963-)
Scandal '89
The Painted Lady '97

Elaine Giftos (1945-)
Gas-s-s-s! '70
The Student Nurses '70
The Wrestler '73
Angel '84

Fabrizio Gifuni (1966-)
Best of Youth '03
The Girl by the Lake '07

Cam Gigandet (1982-)
Never Back Down '08
Twilight '08
Pandorum '09
The Unborn '09
Burlesque '10
Easy A '10
The Experiment '10
5 Star Day '10
Priest '11
The Roommate '11
Trespass '11
Seal Team Six: The Raid on Osama Bin Laden '12
Free Ride '13
In the Blood '13
Plush '13
Red Sky '14
Broken Vows '16

Sandro Giglio (1900-79)
Assignment: Paris '52
The War of the Worlds '53
The Big Boodle '57

Ariadna Gil (1969-)
Belle Epoque '92
Celestial Clockwork '94
Talk of Angels '96
Second Skin '99
Pan's Labyrinth '06
Appaloosa '08

Vincent (Vince Gill) Gil (1939-)
Mad Max '80
Body Melt '93

Andrew S. Gilbert (1949-)
Idiot Box '97
Dirty Deeds '02
Look Both Ways '05

Billy Gilbert (1894-1971)
The Firefly '37
100 Men and a Girl '37
She's Got Everything '37
Snow White and the Seven Dwarfs '37 (V)
Toast of New York '37
Block-heads '38
Happy Landing '38
Joy of Living '38
Peck's Bad Boy with the Circus '38
Destry Rides Again '39
The Great Dictator '40
His Girl Friday '40
No, No Nanette '40
Seven Sinners '40
Melody Master '41
Week-End in Havana '41
Mr. Wise Guy '42
Spotlight Scandals '43
Fun & Fancy Free '47 (V)
The Kissing Bandit '48

Edmund Gilbert (1932-99)
36 Hours '64
Johnny Got His Gun '71
Tom and Jerry: The Movie '93 (V)

Helen Gilbert (1915-95)
Andy Hardy Gets Spring Fever '39
The Secret of Dr. Kildare '39
Beyond the Blue Horizon '42
The Falcon Takes Over '42

James Gilbert
The Cry of the Owl '09
Moby Dick '11

John Gilbert (1897-1936)
Heart o' the Hills '19
Monte Cristo '22
He Who Gets Slapped '24
The Big Parade '25
The Merry Widow '25
Bardelys the Magnificent '26
La Boheme '26
The Flesh and the Devil '27
The Show '27
The Phantom of Paris '31
West of Broadway '31
Downstairs '32
Fast Workers '33
Queen Christina '33
The Captain Hates the Sea '34

Lou Gilbert
Goldstein '64
The Great White Hope '70

Marcus Gilbert (1958-)
Riders '88
Army of Darkness '92

Maya Gilbert
The Perfect Man '11
Middle of Nowhere '12
Forgiveness '15

Melissa Gilbert (1964-)
Little House on the Prairie '74
The Miracle Worker '79
Sylvester '85
Choices '86
Blood Vows: The Story of a Mafia Wife '87
Family of Strangers '93
Hollywood Wives: The New Generation '03
Heart of the Storm '04
Safe Harbour '07
The Christmas Pageant '11

Sara Gilbert (1975-)
Sudie & Simpson '90
Poison Ivy '92
Dead Beat '94
Desert Blue '98
Light It Up '99
High Fidelity '00
Riding in Cars with Boys '01

Harrison Gilbertson (1993-)
Accidents Happen '09
Beneath Hill 60 '10
Virginia '10
Upgrade '18
In the Tall Grass '19

Connie Gilchrist (1901-85)
Hullabaloo '40
Tortilla Flat '42
Cry Havoc '43
Swing Shift Maisie '43
Nothing But Trouble '44
A Letter to Three Wives '49
Stars in My Crown '50
The Half-Breed '51
Here Comes the Groom '51
Thunder on the Hill '51
Houdini '53
Long John Silver '54
The Misadventures of Merlin Jones '63

Keir Gilchrist (1992-)
Just Peck '09
It's Kind of a Funny Story '10
It Follows '15
Tales of Halloween '15
The Good Neighbor '16
Len & Company '16

Lara Gilchrist
The Last Trimester '06
Goodnight for Justice '11

Richard Gilden
Lost, Lonely, and Vicious '59
The Black Klansman '66

Cameron Giles (1976-)
See Cam'ron

Nancy Giles (1960-)
States of Control '98
Loverboy '05
Superheroes '07

Rhett Giles (1973-)
Bram Stoker's Way of the Vampire '05
H.G. Wells' War of the Worlds '05
King of the Lost World '06
Pirates of Treasure Island '06
The Apocalypse '07
Lost Colony: The Legend of Roanoke '07
Contract Killers '08
Wolvesbayne '09
Beauty and the Beast: A Dark Tale '10

Gwynne Gilford (1946-)
Beware! The Blob '72
Satan's School for Girls '73
Fade to Black '80

Jack Gilford (1907-90)
A Funny Thing Happened on the Way to the Forum '66
Mister Buddwing '66
Catch-22 '70
They Might Be Giants '71
Save the Tiger '73
Harry & Walter Go to New York '76
Wholly Moses! '80
Caveman '81
Cocoon '85
Hostage Flight '85
Arthur 2: On the Rocks '88
Cocoon: The Return '88

Zach Gilford (1982-)
Dare '09
Post Grad '09
The River Why '10
Answers to Nothing '11
Crazy Kind of Love '12
Devil's Due '14
The Purge: Anarchy '14

Joe Gilgun
This Is England '06
Lockout '12

Dana Gilhooley
Outing Riley '04
Grace Is Gone '07

Thea Gill (1970-)
Eighteen '04
Lesser Evil '06
Mulligans '08
Seed '08
Stonados '13

Marie Gillain (1975-)
L'Appat '94
Harem '99
Safe Conduct '01
On Guard! '03
Coco Before Chanel '09

Karen Gillan (1987-)
Not Another Happy Ending '13
Guardians of the Galaxy '14
Oculus '14
In a Valley of Violence '16
The Circle '17
Jumanji: Welcome to the Jungle '17
Jumanji: The Next Level '19

Aidan Gillen (1968-)
Circle of Friends '94
Some Mother's Son '96
Buddy Boy '99
Lorna Doone '01
Shanghai Knights '03
Blackout '07
12 Rounds '09
Wake Wood '10
Blitz '11
Shadow Dancer '12
Beneath the Harvest Sky '14
Calvary '14
Maze Runner: The Scorch Trials '15
Sing Street '16
The Lovers '17

Dana Gillespie (1949-)
The People That Time Forgot '77
Scrubbers '82

Jay Gillespie
2001 Maniacs '05
#1 Cheerleader Camp '10

Aden (John) Gillett (1958-)
The Borrowers '97
Ivanhoe '97
Under the Lighthouse Dancing '97
The Winslow Boy '98
Shadow of the Vampire '00
The 10th Kingdom '00

Chris Gillett
Coast to Coast '04
Confessions of an American Bride '05
Come Dance With Me '12

Anita Gillette (1936-)
Ants '77
Marathon '80
Brass '85
Moonstruck '87
Bob Roberts '92
Boys on the Side '94
Larger Than Life '96
She's the One '96
Shall We Dance? '04
The Fitzgerald Family Christmas '12

Luciana Gilli (1944-)
Ursus in the Land of Fire '63
Sandok '65

Burton Gilliam (1938-)
Blazing Saddles '74
Killing Down '06

Seth Gilliam (1968-)
Jefferson in Paris '94
Courage Under Fire '96
Starship Troopers '97
Tar '97
Personal Velocity: Three Portraits '02
The Great New Wonderful '06
Did You Hear About the Morgans? '09
Still Alice '14

Terry Gilliam (1940-)
And Now for Something Completely Different '72
Monty Python and the Holy Grail '75
Monty Python's Life of Brian '79
Monty Python's The Meaning of Life '83
Spies Like Us '85

Larry (Lawrence) Gilliard, Jr. (1971-)
Straight out of Brooklyn '91
Fly by Night '93
Lotto Land '95
Money Train '95
The Substitute 2: School's Out '97
Next Stop, Wonderland '98
The Waterboy '98
Simply Irresistible '99
Cecil B. Demented '00
Gangs of New York '02
Kill the Poor '03
Brother to Brother '04
The Machinist '04
Walk of Shame '14

Jean Gillie
The Saint Meets the Tiger '43
Decoy '46

Andrew Gillies
Big Meat Eater '85
DC 9/11: Time of Crisis '04

Daniel Gillies (1976-)
Bride & Prejudice '04
Evil Remains '04
Spider-Man 2 '04
The Sensation of Sight '06
Captivity '07
Masters of Horror: Dream Cruise '07
Spider-Man 3 '07

Fiona Gillies
Frankenstein '93
A Woman's Guide to Adultery '93

Isabel Gillies (1970-)
Metropolitan '90
One Way Out '95
I Shot Andy Warhol '96
On_Line '01
Four and a Half Women '05

Richard Gilliland (1950-)
Bug '75
A Day for Thanks on Walton's Mountain '82

The Night the Bridge Fell Down '83
Happy Hour '87
A Killing in a Small Town '90
Dogwatch '97
Star Kid '97
Home Room '02
Vampire Clan '02
Audrey's Rain '03

Linda Gillin (1949-)
Terror at Red Wolf Inn '72
Alambrista! '77
Windows '80

Claude Gillingwater (1870-1939)
Illicit '31
Skyway '33
Green Eyes '34
Mississippi '35
The Prisoner of Shark Island '36

Ann Gillis (1927-2018)
The Adventures of Tom Sawyer '38
Peck's Bad Boy with the Circus '38
My Love Came Back '40
Bambi '42 (V)
Texas Legionnaires '43
In Society '44

James Gillis (1943-2010)
Night of the Zombies '81
Deranged '87

Margalo Gillmore (1897-1986)
The Happy Years '50
Perfect Strangers '50
Cause for Alarm '51
Elopement '51
The Law and the Lady '51

Kenneth Gilman
Bedroom Eyes '86
Take My Advice: The Ann & Abby Story '99

Alexie Gilmore (1976-)
I Do & I Don't '07
Surfer, Dude '08
Mercy '09
World's Greatest Dad '09
Willow Creek '13

Art Gilmore (1912-)
The Narcotics Story '58 (N)
The Gallant Hours '60

Danny Gilmore (1973-)
Lilies '96
Winter Lily '98

Lowell Gilmore (1906-60)
Days of Glory '43
Picture of Dorian Gray '45
Calcutta '47
King Solomon's Mines '50
Rogues of Sherwood Forest '50
Roadblock '51
Lone Star '52
Ma and Pa Kettle at Waikiki '55

Peter Gilmore (1931-2013)
Don't Lose Your Head '66
The Abominable Dr. Phibes '71

Virginia Gilmore (1919-86)
Tall, Dark and Handsome '41
Western Union '41
Berlin Correspondent '42
Orchestra Wives '42
Close-Up '48
Walk East on Beacon '52

Ian Gilmour (1955-)
The Chant of Jimmie Blacksmith '78
The Odd Angry Shot '79
Dangerous Summer '82

Betty Gilpin
A Dog's Journey '19
Isn't It Romantic '19
The Hunt '20

Jack Gilpin (1951-)
Something Wild '86
Funny Farm '88
Quick Change '90
Reversal of Fortune '90
Barcelona '94
White Mile '94
Commandments '96
Last Breath '96
From the Earth to the Moon '98
101 Ways (The Things a Girl Will Do to Keep Her Volvo) '00
The Life Before Her Eyes '07
21 '08

Marc Gilpin (1966-)
Computer Wizard '77
Where's Willie? '77

Peri Gilpin (1961-)
Spring Forward '99
Final Fantasy: The Spirits Within '01 (V)

Tom Gilroy
Harry and Max '04
Wild Tigers I Have Known '06
The Blue Tooth Virgin '09

Jessalyn Gilsig (1971-)
Quest for Camelot '98 (V)
Destination: Infestation '07
Flood '07
XIII '08
About Fifty '11
Smart Cookies '13
Somewhere Slow '14

Clarence Gilyard, Jr. (1955-)
Die Hard '88
Walker: Texas Ranger: One Riot, One Ranger '93
Left Behind: The Movie '00
From Above '13

Erica Gimpel (1964-)
The Fence '94
Smoke '95
Santa and Pete '99
Impostor '02
Blue Eyes '09

Teresa Gimpera (1936-)
The Night of the Devils '72
Crypt of the Living Dead '73
Spirit of the Beehive '73

Jack Ging (1931-)
Play Misty for Me '71
High Plains Drifter '73
Sssssss '73
That Man Bolt '73
Die Sister, Die! '74
Where the Red Fern Grows '74

Hermione Gingold (1897-1987)
Tough Guy '53
The Pickwick Papers '54
The Adventures of Sadie '55
Around the World in 80 Days '56 (C)
Bell, Book and Candle '58
Gigi '58
Gay Purr-ee '62 (V)
The Music Man '62
Munster, Go Home! '66
Those Fantastic Flying Fools '67
A Little Night Music '77
Garbo Talks '84

Bob Ginnaven (1937-2008)
Hootch Country Boys '75
The Day It Came to Earth '77

Robert Ginnaven
Visions of Evil '75
One False Move '91

Allen Ginsberg (1926-97)
Heavy Petting '89
Superstar: The Life and Times of Andy Warhol '90
Rolling Thunder Revue: A Bob Dylan Story by Martin Scorsese '19

Robert Ginty (1948-2009)
Coming Home '78
Exterminator '80
The Alchemist '81
Warrior of the Lost World '84
White Fire '84
Mission. . . Kill '85
Loverboy '89
Vietnam, Texas '90
Harley Davidson and the Marlboro Man '91
Lady Dragon '92
The Prophet's Game '99

Frank Gio (1929-)
Once Upon a Time in America '84
Backtrack '89
Analyze That '02
Assassination Tango '03

Vahina Giocante (1981-)
Lila Says '04
Inspector Bellamy '09
Ultimate Heist '09

Rocky Giordani
Tapeheads '89
After Dark, My Sweet '90
Cop and a Half '93

Daniela Giordano (1948-)
Four Times That Night '69
Gunslinger '70
The Girl in Room 2A '76
Inquisition '76

Domiziana Giordano (1960-)
Nostalghia '83
Interview with the Vampire '94

Maria Angela Giordano
Mad Dog Killer '77
The Devil's Daughter '91

Ty(rone) Giordano (1976-)
A Lot Like Love '05
The Family Stone '05
Untraceable '08
The Next Three Days '10

Elenora Giorgi (1953-)
Inferno '80
Beyond Obsession '82
Creepers '85

Tony Giorgio (1923-2012)
The Wrecking Crew '68
The Godfather '72
Foxy Brown '74
Escape to Witch Mountain '75
The Sting 2 '83
The Lonely Guy '84
American Me '92

Lexi Giovagnoli
Bloody Homecoming '12
Varsity Blood '14

Carmine D. Giovinazzo (1973-)
For Love of the Game '99
Terror Tract '00
Black Hawk Down '01
The Learning Curve '01
Big Shot: Confessions of a Campus Bookie '02
Players '03
In Enemy Hands '04

Hippolyte Giradot
The Perfume of Yvonne '94
One Day You'll Understand '08

Chaim Girafi
The Impossible Spy '87
More Dogs Than Bones '00

Joseph Girard (1871-1949)
Hurricane Express '32
The Ivory Handled Gun '35
The Drag-Net '36
Sergeant York '41
The Spider Returns '41

Remy Girard (1950-)
Jesus of Montreal '89
The Boys '97
Varian's War '01
The Barbarian Invasions '03
Human Trafficking '05
Incendies '10

Simone-Elise Girard
After the Storm '01
Shattered Glass '03
Carny '09

Michele Girardon (1938-75)
Death in the Garden '56
Devil of the Desert Against the Son of Hercules '62

Annie Girardot (1931-2011)
Love and the Frenchwoman '60
Rocco and His Brothers '60
The Organizer '64
It Rains In My Village '68
Dillinger Is Dead '69
Gypsy '75
Le Gitan '75
Mussolini & I '85
The Piano Teacher '01
Hidden '05

Etienne Girardot (1856-1939)
Twentieth Century '34
Breakfast for Two '37
The Great Garrick '37
Fast and Loose '39

Hippolyte Girardot (1955-)
Manon of the Spring '87
Love After Love '94
Kings and Queen '04
Modigliani '04
House of 9 '05
La Moustache '05
Paris, je t'aime '06
A Christmas Tale '08
Flight of the Red Balloon '08
Quiet Chaos '08
Lady Chatterley '10
Capital '12

Claude Giraud (1936-)
Angelique '64
Circle of Love '64
Angelique: The Road to Versailles '65
Phedre '68
The Mad Adventures of Rabbi Jacob '73

Joyce Giraud (1975-)
Latin Dragon '03
Miss Cast Away '04

Bernard Giraudeau (1947-2010)
Le Gitan '75
Bilitis '77
La Boum '81
Ridicule '96
Water Drops on Burning Rocks '99
La Petite Lili '03

Cindy Girling
Daughter of Death '82
Devotion '95

Francois Giroday (1952-)
Alex & Emma '03
Single White Female 2: The Psycho '05

Ennio Girolami (1934-)
Nights of Cabiria '57
Fury of Achilles '62

Remo Girone
Heaven '01
Voice from the Stone '17

Massimo Girotti (1918-2003)
Ossessione '42
Story of a Love Affair '50
Senso '54
Sins of Rome '54
The Giants of Thessaly '60
Gold for the Caesars '63
Teorema '68
Red Tent '69
Torture Chamber of Baron Blood '72
Last Tango in Paris '73
The Innocent '76
Mr. Klein '76
The Monster '96
Facing Windows '03

Annabeth Gish (1971-)
Desert Bloom '86
Hiding Out '87
Mystic Pizza '88
Shag: The Movie '89
When He's Not a Stranger '89
Coupe de Ville '90
Scarlett '94
Wyatt Earp '94
Nixon '95
Beautiful Girls '96
Don't Look Back '96
The Last Supper '96
Steel '97
True Women '97
Double Jeopardy '99
SLC Punk! '99
Pursuit of Happiness '01
Race to Space '01
Buying the Cow '02
A Death in the Family '02
Knots '05
The Celestine Prophecy '06
American Girl: Chrissa Stands Strong '09
Home Run Showdown '10
Patricia Cornwell's At Risk '10
Bag of Bones '11
The Chaperone '11
Texas Killing Fields '11
Before I Wake '15

Dorothy Gish (1898-1968)
Judith of Bethulia '14
Orphans of the Storm '21
Romola '25
The Cardinal '63

Lillian Gish (1896-1993)
Judith of Bethulia '14
The Birth of a Nation '15
Intolerance '16
Broken Blossoms '19
The Greatest Question '19
True Heart Susie '19
Way Down East '20
Orphans of the Storm '21
The White Sister '23
Romola '25
La Boheme '26
One Romantic Night '30
His Double Life '33
Commandos Strike at Dawn '43
Duel in the Sun '46
Portrait of Jennie '48
The Cobweb '55
The Night of the Hunter '55
The Unforgiven '60
The Love Goddesses '65
Follow Me, Boys! '66
The Comedians '67
Warning Shot '67
A Wedding '78
Hobson's Choice '83
The Adventures of Huckleberry Finn '85
Sweet Liberty '86
The Whales of August '87

Sheila Gish (1942-2005)
A Day in the Death of Joe Egg '71
Highlander '86
Jewels '92
Mansfield Park '99
Highlander: Endgame '00

Heinrich Giskes (1946-)
Under the Pavement Lies the Strand '75
Ancient Relic '02

Skyler Gisondo (1996-)
Snow Buddies '08 (V)
Spooky Buddies '11 (V)
Treasure Buddies '12 (V)
Night at the Museum: Secret of the Tomb '14
Vacation '15
Time Freak '18

Robert Gist (1924-98)
Jigsaw '49
One Minute to Zero '52
Jack the Giant Killer '62

Neil Giuntoli (1959-)
Capone '89
Memphis Belle '90
Henry: Portrait of a Serial Killer 2: Mask of Sanity '96

Paul(o) Giusti (1942-)
Emmanuelle on Taboo Island '76
Innocents with Dirty Hands '76
L'Annee Sainte '76

Carlo Giustini (1923-)
Intent to Kill '58
The War of the Planets '65

Adele Givens (1960-)
The Players Club '98
Queens of Comedy '01
Beauty Shop '05

Robin Givens (1964-)
The Penthouse '89
The Women of Brewster Place '89
A Rage in Harlem '91
Boomerang '92
Blankman '94
Foreign Student '94
Antibody '02
Head of State '03
Hollywood Wives: The New Generation '03
The Family That Preys '08
Enemies Among Us '10
Airplane *vs.* Volcano '14
God's Not Dead 2 '16
God Bless the Broken Road '18

Kathryn Givney (1896-1978)
Double Crossbones '51
Lightning Strikes Twice '51
The Wayward Bus '57
The Four Horsemen of the Apocalypse '62

George Givot (1903-84)
Hollywood Party '34
Thin Ice '37
Du Barry Was a Lady '43
The Falcon and the Co-Eds '43
Leather Burners '43
April in Paris '52
Three Sailors and a Girl '53
Lady and the Tramp '55 (V)
China Gate '57

Enver Gjokaj (1982-)
Stone '10
Come and Find Me '16
3022 '19

Liliana Glabczynska (1956-)
See Liliana Komorowska

Lily Gladstone
Certain Women '16
Walking Out '17

Kiara Glasco
Christmas Magic '11
The Devil's Candy '17

Paul Michael Glaser (1943-)
Fiddler on the Roof '71
Phobia '80
And Never Let Her Go '01
Something's Gotta Give '03
Starsky & Hutch '04 (C)
Live! '07

Vaughan Glaser (1872-1958)
What a Life '39
Adventure in Washington '41

Ned Glass (1906-84)
Fright '56
Requiem for a Heavyweight '56
The Rebel Set '59
West Side Story '61
Kid Galahad '62
Papa's Delicate Condition '63

Ron Glass (1945-)
Houseguest '94
It's My Party '95
Back in Business '96
Incognito '99
Serenity '05
Lakeview Terrace '08
Death at a Funeral '10

Isabel Glasser (1958-)
Forever Young *'92*
Pure Country *'92*
Death Ring *'93*
The Surgeon *'94*
Mother *'96*
Second Chances *'98*
Tactical Assault *'99*
Phillip Glasser (1978-)
An American Tail *'86 (V)*
An American Tail: Fievel Goes West *'91 (V)*
A Troll in Central Park *'94 (V)*
Voodoo Dawn *'99*
Summer Glau (1981-)
Serenity *'05*
The Initiation of Sarah *'06*
Mammoth *'06*
Deadly Honeymoon *'10*
Knights of Badassdom *'13*
Bob Glaudini
The Alchemist *'81*
Parasite *'82*
Coastlines *'02*
Lola Glaudini (1971-)
Groove *'00*
Invincible *'06*
Certain Prey *'11*
Karen Glave
Blind Faith *'98*
Last Night *'98*
Defending Our Kids: The Julie Posey Story *'03*
Matthew Glave (1963-)
Baby's Day Out *'94*
Plump Fiction *'97*
True Women *'97*
The Wedding Singer *'97*
Ricochet River *'98*
Corky Romano *'01*
Rock Star *'01*
Jimmy Vestvood: Amerikan Hero *'16*
Eugene Robert Glazer (1942-)
Vendetta *'85*
Hollywood Shuffle *'87*
No Way Out *'87*
I'm Gonna Git You Sucka *'88*
Stand and Deliver *'88*
Harlem Nights *'89*
Dollman *'90*
Eve of Destruction *'90*
The Five Heartbeats *'91*
The Substitute *'93*
It's My Party *'95*
Loving Evangeline *'98*
New Blood *'99*
Jackie Gleason (1916-87)
All Through the Night *'42*
Orchestra Wives *'42*
Springtime in the Rockies *'42*
The Hustler *'61*
Requiem for a Heavyweight *'62*
Papa's Delicate Condition *'63*
Soldier in the Rain *'63*
Skidoo *'68*
Don't Drink the Water *'69*
How to Commit Marriage *'69*
Mr. Billion *'77*
Smokey and the Bandit *'77*
Smokey and the Bandit 2 *'80*
The Toy *'82*
Smokey and the Bandit, Part 3 *'83*
The Sting 2 *'83*
Izzy & Moe *'85*
Nothing in Common *'86*
James Gleason (1886-1959)
The Matrimonial Bed *'30*
Beyond Victory *'31*
A Free Soul *'31*
Suicide Fleet *'31*
The Crooked Circle *'32*
Penguin Pool Murder *'32*
Clear All Wires! *'33*
Murder On the Blackboard *'34*
Search for Beauty *'34*
Murder On a Honeymoon *'35*
Ex-Mrs. Bradford *'36*
Murder On a Bridle Path *'36*
The Plot Thickens *'36*
Forty Naughty Girls *'37*
Here Comes Mr. Jordan *'41*
Meet John Doe *'41*
A Date With the Falcon *'42*
The Falcon Takes Over *'42*
My Gal Sal *'42*
Tales of Manhattan *'42*
Crash Dive *'43*
Arsenic and Old Lace *'44*
The Keys of the Kingdom *'44*
The Clock *'45*
A Tree Grows in Brooklyn *'45*
The Bishop's Wife *'47*
Down to Earth *'47*
Tycoon *'47*
The Dude Goes West *'48*
Smart Woman *'48*
Miss Grant Takes Richmond *'49*
The Jackpot *'50*
Key to the City *'50*
Riding High *'50*
I'll See You in My Dreams *'51*
The Story of Will Rogers *'52*
We're Not Married *'52*
What Price Glory? *'52*
Forever Female *'53*
Suddenly *'54*
The Night of the Hunter *'55*
Loving You *'57*
Man in the Shadow *'57*
Rock-A-Bye Baby *'57*
The Last Hurrah *'58*
Man or Gun *'58*
Joanna Gleason (1950-)
Heartburn *'86*
Crimes & Misdemeanors *'89*
F/X 2: The Deadly Art of Illusion *'91*
For Richer, for Poorer *'92*
Edie & Pen *'95 (C)*
If These Walls Could Talk *'96*
Boogie Nights *'97*
Road Ends *'98*
The Wedding Planner *'01*
Wedding Daze *'06*
My Sassy Girl *'08*
The Women *'08*
The Rebound *'09*
The Skeleton Twins *'14*
Mary Pat Gleason (1950-2020)
A Cinderella Story *'04*
Memron *'04*
Underclassman *'05*
Marilyn Hotchkiss' Ballroom Dancing & Charm School *'06*
Wristcutters: A Love Story *'06*
I Now Pronounce You Chuck and Larry *'07*
Killing Kennedy *'13*
Mike Gleason
The G-String Horror *'12*
Gleason *'16*
Pat Gleason
I Killed That Man *'42*
Detour *'46*
Paul Gleason (1939-2006)
Private Duty Nurses *'71*
Doc Savage *'75*
He Knows You're Alone *'80*
Trading Places *'83*
The Breakfast Club *'85*
The Ewoks: Battle for Endor *'85*
Forever, Lulu *'87*
Morgan Stewart's Coming Home *'87*
Die Hard *'88*
Ghost Chase *'88*
Johnny Be Good *'88*
She's Having a Baby *'88*
Miami Blues *'90*
There Goes My Baby *'92*
Boiling Point *'93*
Maniac Cop 3: Badge of Silence *'93*
National Lampoon's Loaded Weapon 1 *'93*
Digital Man *'94*
I Love Trouble *'94*
The Shadow Conspiracy *'96*
Money Talks *'97*
No Code of Conduct *'98*
The Thin Red Line *'98*
The Brutal Truth *'99*
Social Misfits *'00*
National Lampoon's Van Wilder *'02*
Abominable *'06*
Richard Gleason
The Chumscrubber *'05*
Amexico *'16*
Russell Gleason (1908-45)
The Flying Fool *'29*
All Quiet on the Western Front *'30*
Beyond Victory *'31*
Condemned to Live *'35*
Nicholas Gleaves (1969-)
Poldark *'96*
Half Light *'05*
A Congregation of Ghosts *'09*
Brendan Gleeson (1955-)
Braveheart *'95*
Michael Collins *'96*
Trojan Eddie *'96*
Turbulence *'96*
The Butcher Boy *'97*
The General *'98*
Lake Placid *'99*
This Is My Father *'99*
Mission: Impossible 2 *'00*
The Tailor of Panama *'00*
A. I.: Artificial Intelligence *'01*
Gangs of New York *'02*
Harrison's Flowers *'02*
28 Days Later *'02*
Cold Mountain *'03*
Dark Blue *'03*
In My Country *'04*
Troy *'04*
The Village *'04*
Breakfast on Pluto *'05*
Harry Potter and the Goblet of Fire *'05*
Kingdom of Heaven *'05*
The Tiger's Tale *'06*
Black Irish *'07*
Harry Potter and the Order of the Phoenix *'07*
In Bruges *'08*
Into the Storm *'09*
Perrier's Bounty *'09*
The Secret of Kells *'09 (V)*
Green Zone *'10*
Harry Potter and the Deathly Hallows, Part 1 *'10*
Albert Nobbs *'11*
The Cup *'11*
The Guard *'11*
The Company You Keep *'12*
The Pirates! Band of Misfits *'12 (V)*
The Raven *'12*
Safe House *'12*
The Grand Seduction *'13*
The Smurfs 2 *'13*
Stonehearst Asylum *'13*
Calvary *'14*
Edge of Tomorrow *'14*
In the Heart of the Sea *'15*
Suffragette *'15*
Assassin's Creed *'16*
Live by Night *'16*
Trespass Against Us *'16*
Paddington 2 *'17*
The Ballad of Buster Scruggs *'18*
Hampstead *'19*
Brian Gleeson
The Tiger's Tale *'06*
Wake Wood *'10*
The Bachelor Weekend *'13*
Hellboy *'19*
Domhnall Gleeson (1983-)
A Dog Year *'09*
True Grit *'10*
Anna Karenina *'12*
Shadow Dancer *'12*
About Time *'13*
Calvary *'14*
Frank *'14*
Unbroken *'14*
Brooklyn *'15*
Ex Machina *'15*
The Revenant *'15*
Star Wars: The Force Awakens *'15*
American Made *'17*
Crash Pad *'17*
Goodbye Christopher Robin *'17*
mother! *'17*
The Little Stranger *'18*
Peter Rabbit *'18*
The Kitchen *'19*
Paul Gleeson
Idiot Box *'97*
Komodo *'99*
Redmond M. Gleeson
St. Patrick's Day *'99*
2 Brothers & a Bride *'03*
Iain Glen (1961-)
Mountains of the Moon *'90*
Rosencrantz & Guildenstern Are Dead *'90*
The Young Americans *'93*
The Painted Lady *'97*
Mararia *'98*
Beautiful Creatures *'00*
The Wyvern Mystery *'00*
Gabriel & Me *'01*
Lara Croft: Tomb Raider *'01*
Wives and Daughters *'01*
Darkness *'02*
Resident Evil: Apocalypse *'04*
Kidnapped *'05*
Kingdom of Heaven *'05*
Tara Road *'05*
The Last Legion *'07*
Resident Evil: Extinction *'07*
The Diary of Anne Frank *'08*
Harry Brown *'09*
Into the Storm *'09*
The Iron Lady *'11*
The Red Tent *'14*
Resident Evil: The Final Chapter *'16*
My Cousin Rachel *'17*
Philip Glenister (1963-)
Sharpe's Justice *'97*
Vanity Fair *'99*
Horatio Hornblower: The Adventure Continues *'01*
Byron *'03*
Calendar Girls *'03*
The Other Boleyn Girl *'03*
State of Play *'03*
Cranford *'08*
Hidden *'11*
Bel Ami *'12*
Treasure Island *'12*
Robert Glenister (1960-)
Just Visiting *'01*
Sirens *'02*
Appropriate Adult *'11*
Kimiko Glenn
Like Father *'18*
Can You Keep a Secret? *'19*
Montgomery Glenn (1925-97)
See Silvano Tranquilli
Roy Glenn (1905-71)
Jungle Drums of Africa *'53*
Carmen Jones *'54*
Guess Who's Coming to Dinner *'67*
Scott Glenn (1941-)
The Baby Maker *'70*
Angels Hard As They Come *'71*
Charms *'73*
Nashville *'75*
Fighting Mad *'76*
She Came to the Valley *'77*
Apocalypse Now *'79*
More American Graffiti *'79*
Urban Cowboy *'80*
Personal Best *'82*
The Right Stuff *'83*
The River *'84*
Silverado *'85*
Off Limits *'87*
Miss Firecracker *'89*
The Hunt for Red October *'90*
Backdraft *'91*
The Silence of the Lambs *'91*
Women & Men: In Love There Are No Rules *'91*
The Player *'92*
Extreme Justice *'93*
Shadowhunter *'93*
Slaughter of the Innocents *'93*
Night of the Running Man *'94*
The Spy Within *'94*
Edie & Pen *'95*
Tall Tale: The Unbelievable Adventures of Pecos Bill *'95*
Courage Under Fire *'96*
Absolute Power *'97*
Carla's Song *'97*
Firestorm *'97*
The Last Marshal *'99*
The Virgin Suicides *'99*
Vertical Limit *'00*
Buffalo Soldiers *'01*
The Seventh Stream *'01*
The Shipping News *'01*
Training Day *'01*
A Painted House *'03*
Puerto Vallarta Squeeze *'04*
Journey to the End of the Night *'06*
The Bourne Ultimatum *'07*
Camille *'07*
Freedom Writers *'07*
Nights in Rodanthe *'08*
W. *'08*
Secretariat *'10*
Sucker Punch *'11*
The Bourne Legacy *'12*
Wendy Glenn
Mercy *'09*
11-11-11 *'11*
You're Next *'13*
Sharon Gless (1943-)
Centennial *'78*
Hobson's Choice *'83*
The Star Chamber *'83*
The Sky's No Limit *'84*
Letting Go *'85*
Tales of the Unexpected *'91*
The State Within *'06*
Hannah Free *'09*
Stacey Glick (1971-)
Brighton Beach Memoirs *'86*
Three O'Clock High *'87*
Brian Glover (1934-97)
Kes *'69*
An American Werewolf in London *'81*
The Company of Wolves *'85*
Alien 3 *'92*
Leon the Pig Farmer *'93*
Royal Deceit *'94*
Stiff Upper Lips *'96*
Bruce Glover (1932-)
C.C. & Company *'70*
Diamonds Are Forever *'71*
Black Gunn *'72*
Stunts *'77*
Big Bad Mama 2 *'87*
Warlock: The Armageddon *'93*
Night of the Scarecrow *'95*
Simon Says *'07*
Crispin Glover (1964-)
My Tutor *'82*
Friday the 13th, Part 4: The Final Chapter *'84*
Racing with the Moon *'84*
Teachers *'84*
Back to the Future *'85*
At Close Range *'86*
River's Edge *'87*
Back to the Future, Part 2 *'89*
Twister *'89*
Where the Heart Is *'90*
Wild at Heart *'90*
The Doors *'91*
What's Eating Gilbert Grape *'93*
Chasers *'94*
Even Cowgirls Get the Blues *'94 (C)*
Dead Man *'95*
The People *vs.* Larry Flynt *'96*
Charlie's Angels *'00*
Nurse Betty *'00*
Bartleby *'01*
Fast Sofa *'01*
Like Mike *'02*
Charlie's Angels: Full Throttle *'03*
Willard *'03*
Drop Dead Sexy *'05*
Beowulf *'07 (V)*
Epic Movie *'07*
Simon Says *'07*
The Wizard of Gore *'07*
Freezer Burn: The Invasion of Laxdale *'08*
Open Season 2 *'08 (V)*
The Donner Party *'09*
9 *'09 (V)*
Alice in Wonderland *'10*
Hot Tub Time Machine *'10*
Mr. Nice *'10*
Open Season 3 *'10 (V)*
Freaky Deaky *'12*
The Bag Man *'14*
Danny Glover (1946-)
Escape from Alcatraz *'79*
Out *'82*
Iceman *'84*
Places in the Heart *'84*
The Color Purple *'85*
Silverado *'85*
Stand-In *'85*
Witness *'85*
Lethal Weapon *'87*
Mandela *'87*
Bat 21 *'88*
Lethal Weapon 2 *'89*
Lonesome Dove *'89*
A Raisin in the Sun *'89*
Flight of the Intruder *'90*
Predator 2 *'90*
To Sleep with Anger *'90*
Grand Canyon *'91*
Pure Luck *'91*
A Rage in Harlem *'91*
Lethal Weapon 3 *'92*
Bopha! *'93*
Queen *'93*
The Saint of Fort Washington *'93*
Angels in the Outfield *'94*
Maverick *'94 (C)*
America's Dream *'95*
Operation Dumbo Drop *'95*
Buffalo Soldiers *'97*
Gone Fishin' *'97*
John Grisham's The Rainmaker *'97*
Switchback *'97*
Antz *'98 (V)*
Beloved *'98*
Lethal Weapon 4 *'98*
Prince of Egypt *'98 (V)*
Boesman & Lena *'00*
Freedom Song *'00*
The Royal Tenenbaums *'01*
3 A.M. *'01*
Good Fences *'03*
The Cookout *'04*
Saw *'04*
Manderlay *'05*
Barnyard *'06 (V)*
Dreamgirls *'06*
Poor Man's Game *'06*
The Shaggy Dog *'06*
Honeydripper *'07*
Shooter *'07*
Be Kind Rewind *'08*
Blindness *'08*
Gospel Hill *'08*
Battle for Terra *'09 (V)*
Night Train *'09*
2012 *'09*
Alpha and Omega *'10 (V)*
Death at a Funeral *'10*
Legendary *'10*

Mooz-Lum *'10*
Age of the Dragons *'11*
Donovan's Echo *'11*
Mysteria *'11*
Son of Morning *'11*
Hannah's Law *'12*
The Bouquet *'13*
From Above *'13*
Highland Park *'13*
LUV *'13*
Muhammad Ali's Greatest Fight *'13*
Norman Rockwell's Shuffleton's Barbershop *'13*
Space Warriors *'13*
Beyond the Lights *'14*
Day of the Mummy *'14*
Death Squad *'14*
Rage *'14*
Almost Christmas *'16*
Andron: The Black Labyrinth *'16*
Complete Unknown *'16*
The Good Catholic *'17*
The Old Man & the Gun *'18*
The Last Black Man in San Francisco *'19*

Donald Glover
The Lazarus Effect *'15*
Solo: A Star Wars Story *'18*

Jamie Glover (1969-)
Joseph *'95*
In His Life: The John Lennon Story *'00*

John Glover (1944-)
Annie Hall *'77*
Julia *'77*
Last Embrace *'79*
The Mountain Men *'80*
A Little Sex *'82*
Kennedy *'83*
The Evil That Men Do *'84*
An Early Frost *'85*
A Killing Affair *'85*
52 Pick-Up *'86*
Nutcracker: Money, Madness & Murder *'87*
The Chocolate War *'88*
Masquerade *'88*
Rocket Gibraltar *'88*
Scrooged *'88*
Meet the Hollowheads *'89*
Traveling Man *'89*
El Diablo *'90*
Gremlins 2: The New Batch *'90*
Ed and His Dead Mother *'93*
What Ever Happened To. . . *'93*
Night of the Running Man *'94*
In the Mouth of Madness *'95*
Schemes *'95*
Love! Valour! Compassion! *'96*
Batman and Robin *'97*
Payback *'98*
Dead Broke *'99*
On Edge *'03*
Sanitarium *'13*

Julian Glover (1935-)
Tom Jones *'63*
Girl with Green Eyes *'64*
The Alphabet Murders *'65*
I Was Happy Here *'66*
Theatre of Death *'67*
The Last Grenade *'70*
Antony and Cleopatra *'73*
Hitler: The Last Ten Days *'73*
Luther *'74*
The Story of Jacob & Joseph *'74*
The Empire Strikes Back *'80*
For Your Eyes Only *'81*
Heat and Dust *'82*
Ivanhoe *'82*
Kim *'84*
The Fourth Protocol *'87*
Mandela *'87*
The Secret Garden *'87*
Indiana Jones and the Last Crusade *'89*
Treasure Island *'89*
Tusks *'89*
The Infiltrator *'95*
Vatel *'00*
Harry Potter and the Chamber of Secrets *'02*
Two Men Went to War *'02*
Troy *'04*
Scoop *'06*
Mirrors *'08*
Princess Kaiulani *'09*
The Young Victoria *'09*
Spies of Warsaw *'13*

Richard Glover
Malevolence *'04*
A Field in England *'14*

Savion Glover (1973-)
Tap *'89*
The Wall *'99*
Bamboozled *'00*
Bojangles *'01*

Susan Glover
Eye *'96*
Random Encounter *'98*
Jericho Mansions *'03*

Griffin Gluck (2000-)
Just Go With It *'11*
Middle School: The Worst Years of My Life *'16*
Why Him? *'16*
Big Time Adolescence *'20*

Karl Glusman
Love *'15*
The Neon Demon *'16*

Carlin Glynn (1940-)
Continental Divide *'81*
Sixteen Candles *'84*
The Trip to Bountiful *'85*
Gardens of Stone *'87*
Blood Red *'88*
Judy Berlin *'99*

Tom Glynn-Carney
Dunkirk *'17*
The King *'19*

Mathias Gnaedinger (1941-)
The Boat Is Full *'81*
Journey of Hope *'90*

Luis Gnecco
No *'12*
The Stranger *'15*
Neruda *'16*
A Fantastic Woman *'18*
The Two Popes *'19*

George Gobel (1919-91)
Birds & the Bees *'56*
Ellie *'84*

Jean-Luc Godard (1930-)
Le Petit Soldat *'60*
Cleo from 5 to 7 *'61*
Contempt *'64*
First Name: Carmen *'83*

Beth Goddard (1969-)
The Last Seduction 2 *'98*
Take Me *'01*
Appointment With Death *'10*

John Goddard
Storm Rider *'57*
Naked Youth *'59*

Mark Goddard (1936-)
A Rage to Live *'65*
The Love-Ins *'67*
Blue Sunshine *'78*
Roller Boogie *'79*
Strange Invaders *'83*
Lost in Space *'98*

Paul Goddard
Holy Smoke *'99*
The Matrix *'99*

Paulette Goddard (1911-90)
Modern Times *'36*
The Young in Heart *'38*
The Cat and the Canary *'39*
The Women *'39*
The Ghost Breakers *'40*
The Great Dictator *'40*
Second Chorus *'40*
Hold Back the Dawn *'41*
Nothing But the Truth *'41*
Pot o' Gold *'41*
Reap the Wild Wind *'42*
Star Spangled Rhythm *'42*
So Proudly We Hail *'43*
Diary of a Chambermaid *'46*
An Ideal Husband *'47*
Unconquered *'47*
On Our Merry Way *'48*
The Torch *'50*
Vice Squad *'53*
Charge of the Lancers *'54*
Sins of Jezebel *'54*
Unholy Four *'54*

Trevor Goddard (1965-2003)
Men of War *'94*
Prey of the Jaguar *'96*
Shadow Warriors *'97*
Pirates of the Caribbean: The Curse of the Black Pearl *'03*
Flexing with Monty *'10*

Danielle Godet (1927-2009)
Operation Abduction *'58*
Kiss Kiss Kill Kill *'66*

Godfrey (1969-)
Soul Plane *'04*
Phat Girlz *'06*
What Up? *'08*

Arthur Godfrey (1903-83)
Four for Texas *'63*
The Glass Bottom Boat *'66*
Where Angels Go, Trouble Follows *'68 (C)*
Great Bank Hoax *'78*

Derek Godfrey (1924-83)
A Midsummer Night's Dream *'68*
The Vengeance of She *'68*
Hands of the Ripper *'71*

Patrick Godfrey (1933-)
Heat and Dust *'82*
Ever After: A Cinderella Story *'98*
The Importance of Being Earnest *'02*

Maurice Godin (1966-)
The Awakening *'95*
Vanished *'95*
Boat Trip *'03*

Adam Godley (1964-)
Charlie and the Chocolate Factory *'05*
The Old Curiosity Shop *'07*
The X Files: I Want to Believe *'08*
Nightmare Cinema *'19*

Judith Godreche (1972-)
The Disenchanted *'90*
Ridicule *'96*
The Man in the Iron Mask *'98*
Quicksand *'01*
L'Auberge Espagnole *'02*
Potiche *'10*
The Overnight *'15*
Under the Eiffel Tower *'18*

Alexander Godunov (1949-95)
Witness *'85*
The Money Pit *'86*
Die Hard *'88*
Waxwork 2: Lost in Time *'91*

Dave Goelz (1946-)
The Muppets' Wizard of Oz *'05 (V)*
The Muppets *'11 (V)*

Angela Goethals (1977-)
Heartbreak Hotel *'88*
Home Alone *'90*
V.I. Warshawski *'91*
Behind the Mask: The Rise of Leslie Vernon *'06*

Dave Goetz
The Muppet Movie *'79 (V)*
The Dark Crystal *'82 (V)*
Labyrinth *'86*
The Muppet Christmas Carol *'92 (V)*
Muppet Treasure Island *'96 (V)*
Muppets from Space *'99 (V)*

Peter Michael Goetz (1941-)
Wolfen *'81*
Beer *'85*
Jumpin' Jack Flash *'86 (C)*
King Kong Lives *'86*
Promise *'86*
Glory *'89*
Father of the Bride *'91*
My Girl *'91*
The Buccaneers *'95*
Father of the Bride Part 2 *'95*
Infinity *'96*
The Empty Mirror *'99*

Bernhard Goetzke (1884-1964)
Destiny *'21*
The Indian Tomb *'21*
Dr. Mabuse, The Gambler *'22*

John Goff
Devil & Leroy Basset *'73*
The Alpha Incident *'76*
The Capture of Bigfoot *'79*
Night Stalker *'87*

Norris Goff (1906-78)
Dreaming Out Loud *'40*
The Bashful Bachelor *'42*
So This Is Washington *'43*

Walton Goggins (1971-)
The Apostle *'97*
Major League 3: Back to the Minors *'98*
Daddy & Them *'99*
Red Dirt *'99*
Shanghai Noon *'00*
The Bourne Identity *'02*
House of 1000 Corpses *'03*
The Architect *'06*
Fragments *'08*
Miracle at St. Anna *'08*
That Evening Sun *'09*
Predators *'10*
Cowboys & Aliens *'11*
Straw Dogs *'11*
Django Unchained *'12*
Lincoln *'12*
G.I. Joe: Retaliation *'13*
Machete Kills *'13*
American Ultra *'15*
The Hateful Eight *'15*
Mojave *'15*
Diablo *'16*
Ant-Man and the Wasp *'18*
Tomb Raider *'18*
Them That Follow *'19*

Juliette Goglia
A Grandpa for Christmas *'07*
Fired Up! *'09*

Michelle Goh
Out For a Kill *'03*
Alien Lockdown *'04*

Alejandro Goic
The Maid *'09*
Gloria *'13*

Siena Goines (1969-)
Rancid *'04*
Jada *'08*
Creature of Darkness *'09*
The Least Among You *'09*

Joanna Going (1963-)
Wyatt Earp *'94*
A Good Day to Die *'95*
How to Make an American Quilt *'95*
Commandments *'96 (C)*
Keys to Tulsa *'96*
Inventing the Abbotts *'97*
Little City *'97*
Phantoms *'97*
Still Breathing *'97*
Eden *'98*
Tom Clancy's Netforce *'98*
Heaven *'99*
Cupid & Cate *'00*
Runaway Jury *'03*
My Silent Partner *'06*
Miles from Nowhere *'09*
The Tree of Life *'11*

Gila Golan (1940-)
Our Man Flint *'66*
The Valley of Gwangi *'69*

Natalie Gold (1976-)
Love and Other Drugs *'10*
The Land of Steady Habits *'18*

Tracey Gold (1969-)
The Child Stealer *'79*
Shoot the Moon *'82*
Wanted *'98*
The Growing Pains Movie *'00*
Wildfire 7: The Inferno *'02*
Growing Pains: Return of the Seavers *'04*
Safe Harbor *'06*
Final Approach *'08*

Adam Goldberg (1970-)
Dazed and Confused *'93*
Homeward Bound 2: Lost in San Francisco *'96 (V)*
Babe: Pig in the City *'98 (V)*
Saving Private Ryan *'98*
EDtv *'99*
Sunset Strip *'99*
All Over the Guy *'01*
A Beautiful Mind *'01*
Fast Sofa *'01*
Waking Life *'01*
The Salton Sea *'02*
How to Lose a Guy in 10 Days *'03*
Deja Vu *'06*
Keeping Up with the Steins *'06*
Stay Alive *'06*
2 Days in Paris *'07*
Zodiac *'07*
(Untitled) *'09*
Miss Nobody *'10*
Norman *'10*
Anna Nicole *'13*

Iddo Goldberg (1975-)
The Defender *'04*
Unmade Beds *'09*
And While We Were Here *'13*
Last Passenger *'14*
The Zookeeper's Wife *'17*

Whoopi Goldberg (1955-)
The Color Purple *'85*
Jumpin' Jack Flash *'86*
Burglar *'87*
Fatal Beauty *'87*
Clara's Heart *'88*
Homer and Eddie *'89*
Kiss Shot *'89*
The Long Walk Home *'89*
Ghost *'90*
Soapdish *'91*
The Player *'92*
Sarafina! *'92*
Sister Act *'92*
Made in America *'93*
Naked in New York *'93 (C)*
National Lampoon's Loaded Weapon 1 *'93*
Sister Act 2: Back in the Habit *'93*
Boys on the Side *'94*
Corrina, Corrina *'94*
The Lion King *'94 (V)*
The Little Rascals *'94 (C)*
The Pagemaster *'94 (V)*
Star Trek: Generations *'94*
Moonlight and Valentino *'95*
The Sunshine Boys *'95*
Theodore Rex *'95*
The Associate *'96*
Bogus *'96*
Eddie *'96*
Ghosts of Mississippi *'96*
An Alan Smithee Film: Burn, Hollywood, Burn *'97 (C)*
Cinderella *'97*
The Deep End of the Ocean *'98*
How Stella Got Her Groove Back *'98*
A Knight in Camelot *'98*
The Rugrats Movie *'98 (V)*
Alice in Wonderland *'99*
Girl, Interrupted *'99*
Jackie's Back *'99*
The Magical Legend of the Leprechauns *'99*
The Adventures of Rocky & Bullwinkle *'00*
More Dogs Than Bones *'00*
Call Me Claus *'01*
Kingdom Come *'01*
Monkeybone *'01*
Rat Race *'01*
Good Fences *'03*
The Lion King 1 1/2 *'04 (V)*
Jiminy Glick in LaLa Wood *'05 (C)*
Racing Stripes *'05 (V)*
Everyone's Hero *'06 (V)*
For Colored Girls *'10*
Toy Story 3 *'10 (V)*
Being Elmo: A Puppeteer's Journey *'11 (N)*
A Little Bit of Heaven *'11*
A Day Late and a Dollar Short *'14*
Teenage Mutant Ninja Turtles *'14*
Big Stone Gap *'15*
9/11 *'17*

Harold Goldblatt (1899-1982)
Children of the Damned *'63*
The Mind Benders *'63*

Jeff Goldblum (1952-)
Death Wish *'74*
Nashville *'75*
The Sentinel *'76*
Annie Hall *'77*
Between the Lines *'77*
Invasion of the Body Snatchers *'78*
Thank God It's Friday *'78*
Rehearsal for Murder *'82*
The Big Chill *'83*
The Right Stuff *'83*
The Adventures of Buckaroo Banzai Across the Eighth Dimension *'84*
Into the Night *'85*
Silverado *'85*
Transylvania 6-5000 *'85*
Beyond Therapy *'86*
The Fly *'86*
Vibes *'88*
Earth Girls Are Easy *'89*
The Tall Guy *'89*
Framed *'90*
Twisted Obsession *'90*
Deep Cover *'92*
The Favor, the Watch, & the Very Big Fish *'92*
The Player *'92*
Shooting Elizabeth *'92*
Jurassic Park *'93*
Hideaway *'94*
Nine Months *'95*
Powder *'95*
The Great White Hype *'96*
Independence Day *'96*
Trigger Happy *'96*
The Lost World: Jurassic Park 2 *'97*
Holy Man *'98*
Prince of Egypt *'98 (V)*
Beyond Suspicion *'00*
Chain of Fools *'00*
Cats & Dogs *'01*
Perfume *'01*
Igby Goes Down *'02*
Dallas 362 *'03*
The Life Aquatic with Steve Zissou *'04*
Fay Grim *'06*
Man of the Year *'06*
Pittsburgh *'06*
Adam Resurrected *'08*
Morning Glory *'10*
The Switch *'10*
Adventures in Zambezia *'12*
Tim and Eric's Billion Dollar Movie *'12*
The Grand Budapest Hotel *'14*
Le Week-End *'14*
Mortdecai *'15*
Independence Day: Resurgence *'16*
Thor: Ragnarok *'17*
Hotel Artemis *'18*
The Mountain *'19*

Annie Golden (1951-)
Hair *'79*
Desperately Seeking Susan *'85*
Streetwalkin' *'85*
Baby Boom *'87*
Forever, Lulu *'87*
Love at Stake *'87*

The Pebble and the Penguin '94 (V)
One Way Out '95
It Runs in the Family '03
Tom and Francie '05

Norman D. Golden, II (1984-)
Cop and a Half '93
America's Dream '95
Moby Dick '98

Olive Golden (1896-1988)
See Olive Carey

Devin Goldenberg (1949-)
Guess What We Learned in School Today? '70
Cry Uncle '71
Fanatic '82

Heather Goldenhersch (1973-)
Spin the Bottle '97
Kinsey '04
The Merchant of Venice '04
Southern Belles '05
Wedding Daze '06

Goldie (1965-)
B.U.S.T.E.D. '99
The World Is Not Enough '99

Ricky Paull Goldin (1965-)
The Blob '88
Lambada '89
Mirror, Mirror '90
Pastime '91

Henry Golding (1987-)
Crazy Rich Asians '18
A Simple Favor '18
Last Christmas '19

Meta Golding
Quiet Days in Hollywood '97
All Nighter '17

Diane Goldner (1956-)
Feast '06
Feast 2: Sloppy Seconds '08

Lelia Goldoni (1936-)
Shadows '60
Theatre of Death '67
The Spell '77
Bloodbrothers '78
Choices '81
Chain Link '08

Danny Goldring
Two Fathers: Justice for the Innocent '94
Chicago Overcoat '09

Renee Goldsberry (1971-)
All About You '01
Pistol Whipped '08
The House with a Clock in Its Walls '18
Waves '19
Hamilton '20

Jonathan Goldsmith
Go Tell the Spartans '78
Phantom of the Mall: Eric's Revenge '89

Jenette Goldstein (1960-)
Aliens '86
Near Dark '87
The Presidio '88
Lethal Weapon 2 '89
Fair Game '95
Home Room '02
Autopsy '08

Bobcat Goldthwait (1962-)
One Crazy Summer '86
Police Academy 3: Back in Training '86
Burglar '87
Police Academy 4: Citizens on Patrol '87
Hot to Trot! '88
Scrooged '88
Tapeheads '89
Shakes the Clown '92
Freaked '93 (V)
Radioland Murders '94 (C)
Back to Back '96
Hercules '97 (V)
Sweethearts '97
Blow '01

Tony Goldwyn (1960-)
Ghost '90
Kuffs '92
Traces of Red '92
The Pelican Brief '93
Doomsday Gun '94
A Woman of Independent Means '94
The Last Word '95
Nixon '95
Pocahontas: The Legend '95
Truman '95
The Boys Next Door '96
The Substance of Fire '96
Kiss the Girls '97
From the Earth to the Moon '98
Tarzan '99 (V)
Bounce '00
The 6th Day '00
An American Rhapsody '01
The Song of the Lark '01
Abandon '02
Joshua '02
The Last Samurai '03
American Gun '05
Ghosts Never Sleep '05
The Sisters '05
The Last House on the Left '09
The Mechanic '11
Divergent '14
Outlaw Prophet: Warren Jeffs '14
The Belko Experiment '17
Mark Felt: The Man Who Brought Down the White House '17

Valeria Golino (1965-)
Rain Man '88
The King's Whore '90
Torrents of Spring '90
Hot Shots! '91
The Indian Runner '91
Year of the Gun '91
Hot Shots! Part Deux '93
Clean Slate '94
Immortal Beloved '94
Four Rooms '95
Leaving Las Vegas '95
Escape from L.A. '96
An Occasional Hell '96
Harem '99
Spanish Judges '99
Things You Can Tell Just by Looking at Her '00
Frida '02
Respiro '02
The 36th Precinct '04
The Girl by the Lake '07
Cash '08
Quiet Chaos '08
Giulia Doesn't Date at Night '09
Portrait of a Lady on Fire '19

Ana Golja
Full Out '15
The Fanatic '19

Arlene Golonka (1936-)
Welcome to Hard Times '67
The In-Laws '79
My Tutor '82
Dr. Alien '88
A Family Affair '01

Yekaterina (Katia) Golubeva (1966-2011)
I Can't Sleep '93
Pola X '99
Twentynine Palms '03
The Intruder '04

Sam Golzari (1979-)
American Dreamz '06
21 '08

Minna Gombell (1892-1973)
Bad Girl '31
After Tomorrow '32
Wild Boys of the Road '33
The Merry Widow '34
Strictly Dynamite '34
The Thin Man '34
The White Cockatoo '35
Make Way for Tomorrow '37
The Great Waltz '38
High Sierra '41

The Mexican Spitfire Sees a Ghost '42
Johnny Doesn't Live Here Any More '44
The Best Years of Our Lives '46
Pagan Love Song '50
I'll See You in My Dreams '51

Carlos Gomez (1962-)
Desperado '95
Asteroid '97
Fools Rush In '97
The Peacemaker '97
The Negotiator '98
The Replacement Killers '98
House of Sand and Fog '03

Carmelo Gomez (1962-)
Vacas '91
Running Out of Time '94
Tierra '95
Mararia '98
Between Your Legs '99
The Method '05

Ian Gomez (1964-)
Get a Clue '02
My Big Fat Greek Wedding '02
Chasing Papi '03
Connie and Carla '04
The Last Shot '04
Underclassman '05
Wake '09
Larry Crowne '11
Free Fall '14

Jaime Gomez (1965-)
Solo '96
Gabriela '01
Training Day '01
Devil's Knight '03

Jose Luis Gomez (1940-)
Rowing with the Wind '88
Goya's Ghosts '06
Broken Embraces '09

Michelle Gomez (1966-)
The Acid House '98
Oliver Twist '07

Panchito Gomez (1963-)
Paco '75
Sweet 15 '90
Mi Vida Loca '94
Saints and Sinners '95

Rick Gomez (1972-)
Band of Brothers '01
11:14 '03
Ray '04
Sin City '05
Transformers '07
The Apparition '12

Selena Gomez (1992-)
Another Cinderella Story '08
Princess Protection Program '09
The Wizards of Waverly Place: The Movie '09
Ramona and Beezus '10
Monte Carlo '11
Hotel Transylvania '12 (V)
Getaway '13
Girl Rising '13 (N)
Spring Breakers '13
Rudderless '14
Hotel Transylvania 2 '15 (V)
In Dubious Battle '17
Hotel Transylvania 3: Summer Vacation '18 (V)

Thomas Gomez (1905-71)
Pittsburgh '42
Sherlock Holmes and the Voice of Terror '42
The Climax '44
In Society '44
Phantom Lady '44
Can't Help Singing '45
Captain from Castile '47
Johnny O'Clock '47
Ride the Pink Horse '47
Key Largo '48
Force of Evil '49
Sorrowful Jones '49
The Furies '50
The Woman on Pier 13 '50
The Sellout '51

The Gambler from Natchez '54
The Conqueror '56
Trapeze '56
Summer and Smoke '61
Stay Away, Joe '68
Beneath the Planet of the Apes '70

Milton Goncalves (1933-)
Kiss of the Spider Woman '85
Orfeu '99
Carandiru '03

Stella Gonet (1963-)
The Crow Road '96
Nicholas Nickleby '02

George Gonzales (1967-)
The Bad News Bears '76
The Bad News Bears in Breaking Training '77
The Bad News Bears Go to Japan '78

Augustin Gonzalez (1930-2005)
Caresses '97
The Grandfather '98

Eiza González (1990-)
Baby Driver '17
Bloodshot '20

Nicholas Gonzalez (1976-)
Anacondas: The Hunt for the Blood Orchid '04
Behind Enemy Lines 2: Axis of Evil '06
S.W.A.T.: Firefight '11
We Have Your Husband '11
Left to Die: The Sandra and Tammi Chase Story '12

Rick Gonzalez (1979-)
The Rookie '02
Biker Boyz '03
Old School '03
Coach Carter '05
Roll Bounce '05
War of the Worlds '05
Pulse '06
Illegal Tender '07
What We Do Is Secret '07
Pride and Glory '08
The Promotion '08

Pedro Gonzalez-Gonzalez (1925-2006)
Rio Bravo '59
The Young Land '59
Lust in the Dust '85

Julie Gonzalo (1981-)
Christmas With the Kranks '04
A Cinderella Story '04
Must Love Dogs '05
Cherry Crush '07
A Golden Christmas 2: The Second Tail '11

Christopher Good
A Bridge Too Far '77
Bullshot '83

Meagan Good (1981-)
Eve's Bayou '97
The Secret Life of Girls '99
Three Strikes '00
Biker Boyz '03
Deliver Us from Eva '03
The Cookout '04
D.E.B.S. '04
You Got Served '04
Roll Bounce '05
Venom '05
Brick '06
Waist Deep '06
Stomp the Yard '07
The Love Guru '08
One Missed Call '08
Saw 5 '08
The Unborn '09
35 and Ticking '10
Jumping the Broom '11
Think Like a Man '12
Anchorman 2: The Legend Continues '13
LUV '13
Think Like a Man Too '14
Love by the 10th Date '17

A Boy. A Girl. A Dream. '18
The Intruder '19

Jedidiah Goodacre
Way of the Wicked '14
The Recall '17

Caroline Goodall (1959-)
Hook '91
Cliffhanger '93
Schindler's List '93
The Silver Stallion: King of the Wild Brumbies '93
Disclosure '94
White Squall '96
Casualties '97
The Sculptress '97
Mists of Avalon '01
The Princess Diaries '01
Harrison's Flowers '02
Me & Mrs. Jones '02
Chasing Liberty '04
The Princess Diaries 2: Royal Engagement '04
The Chumscrubber '05
River's End '05
The Thief Lord '06
The Cold Light of Day '12
The Best of Me '14

Matthew Goode (1978-)
Chasing Liberty '04
Match Point '05
Imagine Me & You '06
The Lookout '07
Brideshead Revisited '08
A Single Man '09
Watchmen '09
Cemetery Junction '10
Leap Year '10
Burning Man '11
Birdsong '12
Death Comes to Pemberley '13
Stoker '13
The Imitation Game '14
Self/Less '15
Allied '16
The Sense of an Ending '17
Downton Abbey '19
Official Secrets '19

Donna Goodhand
Steve Martini's Undue Influence '96
Heart of a Stranger '02
Murder in the Hamptons '05

Cuba Gooding, Jr. (1968-)
Coming to America '88
Boyz N the Hood '91
A Few Good Men '92
Gladiator '92
Murder Without Motive '92
Daybreak '93
Judgment Night '93
Lightning Jack '94
Losing Isaiah '94
Outbreak '94
The Tuskegee Airmen '95
Jerry Maguire '96
As Good As It Gets '97
What Dreams May Come '98
Chill Factor '99
Instinct '99
A Murder of Crows '99
Men of Honor '00
In the Shadows '01
Pearl Harbor '01
Rat Race '01
Snow Dogs '02
Boat Trip '03
The Fighting Temptations '03
Radio '03
Home on the Range '04 (V)
Dirty '05
End Game '06
Shadowboxer '06
American Gangster '07
Daddy Day Camp '07
Norbit '07
What Love Is '07
Harold '08
Hero Wanted '08
Linewatch '08
The Way of War '08
The Devil's Tomb '09
Gifted Hands: The Ben Carson Story '09
Hardwired '09

Lies and Illusions '09
Wrong Turn at Tahoe '09
Ticking Clock '10
The Hit List '11
Sacrifice '11
Firelight '12
One In the Chamber '12
Red Tails '12
Absolute Deception '13
Lee Daniels' The Butler '13
Life of a King '13
Machete Kills '13
Freedom '14
Selma '14

Omar Gooding (1976-)
Baby Boy '01
The Gospel '05
Mysterious Island '05
Christmas in Compton '12
Percentage '13

Michael Goodliffe (1914-76)
The Way Out '56
A Night to Remember '58
Sink the Bismarck '60
The Gorgon '64
The Seventh Dawn '64
Von Ryan's Express '65
Macbeth '70
Hitler: The Last Ten Days '73
To the Devil, a Daughter '76

Benny Goodman (1909-86)
The Gang's All Here '43
Stage Door Canteen '43
Sweet and Low-Down '44
A Song Is Born '48

Brian Goodman (1963-)
The Last Castle '01
Annapolis '06
The Fast and the Furious: Tokyo Drift '06
What Doesn't Kill You '08

Cameron Goodman (1984-)
The Phantom '09
Shuttle '09
Sharpay's Fabulous Adventure '11

Dana Min Goodman
Deuce Bigalow: European Gigolo '05
The House Bunny '08

Dody Goodman (1914-2008)
Bedtime Story '63
Grease '78
Private Resort '84
Splash '84
Cool As Ice '91

Hazelle Goodman (1959-)
Deconstructing Harry '97
Hannibal '01

Henry Goodman (1950-)
Mary Reilly '95
Private Parts '96
The Saint '97
Green Street Hooligans '05
The Damned United '09
Taking Woodstock '09
The Road to Coronation Street '10

John Goodman (1952-)
Eddie Macon's Run '83
Survivors '83
C.H.U.D. '84
Maria's Lovers '84
Revenge of the Nerds '84
Sweet Dreams '85
True Stories '86
The Big Easy '87
Burglar '87
Raising Arizona '87
Everybody's All American '88
Punchline '88
The Wrong Guys '88
Always '89
Sea of Love '89
Stella '89
Arachnophobia '90
Barton Fink '91
King Ralph '91
The Babe '92

Matinee *'92*
Born Yesterday *'93*
We're Back! A Dinosaur's Story *'93 (V)*
The Flintstones *'94*
Pie in the Sky *'95*
A Streetcar Named Desire *'95*
Mother Night *'96*
The Big Lebowski *'97*
The Borrowers *'97*
Dirty Work *'97*
Fallen *'97*
Blues Brothers 2000 *'98*
Bringing Out the Dead *'99*
The Jack Bull *'99*
The Runner *'99*
The Adventures of Rocky & Bullwinkle *'00*
Coyote Ugly *'00*
The Emperor's New Groove *'00 (V)*
O Brother Where Art Thou? *'00*
What Planet Are You From? *'00*
Monsters, Inc. *'01 (V)*
My First Mister *'01*
One Night at McCool's *'01*
Storytelling *'01*
Dirty Deeds *'02*
The Jungle Book 2 *'03 (V)*
Masked and Anonymous *'03*
Beyond the Sea *'04*
Clifford's Really Big Movie *'04 (V)*
Freshman Orientation *'04*
Marilyn Hotchkiss' Ballroom Dancing & Charm School *'06*
Bee Movie *'07 (V)*
Death Sentence *'07*
Evan Almighty *'07*
Gigantic *'08*
In the Electric Mist *'08*
Speed Racer *'08*
Confessions of a Shopaholic *'09*
The Princess and the Frog *'09 (V)*
You Don't Know Jack *'10*
The Artist *'11*
Extremely Loud and Incredibly Close *'11*
Red State *'11*
Argo *'12*
Flight *'12*
ParaNorman *'12 (V)*
Trouble with the Curve *'12*
The Hangover, Part III *'13*
Inside Llewyn Davis *'13*
The Internship *'13 (C)*
Monsters University *'13 (V)*
The Monuments Men *'13*
The Gambler *'14*
Transformers: Age of Extinction *'14 (V)*
Love the Coopers *'15*
10 Cloverfield Lane *'16*
Atomic Blonde *'17*
Kong: Skull Island *'17*
Patriots Day *'17*
Captive State *'19*

Carol Goodner (1904-2001)
There Goes the Bride *'32*
Red Ensign *'34*

Joe Goodrich
Monster Man *'03*
Axe *'06*

Garry Goodrow (1933-2014)
The Connection *'61*
A Session with The Committee *'68*
Steelyard Blues *'73*
Cardiac Arrest *'74*
The Hollywood Knights *'80*

Liat Goodson
American Chinatown *'96*
Vice Girls *'96*

Alexander Goodwin (1987-)
Box of Moonlight *'96*
Mimic *'97*

Bill Goodwin (1910-58)
Wake Island *'42*
So Proudly We Hail *'43*
Bathing Beauty *'44*
The Stork Club *'45*
House of Horrors *'46*
The Jolson Story *'46*
Mickey *'48*
So This Is New York *'48*
It's a Great Feeling *'49*
Jolson Sings Again *'49*
Tea for Two *'50*
The First Time *'52*
The Atomic Kid *'54*
Lucky Me *'54*

Ginnifer Goodwin (1978-)
Mona Lisa Smile *'03*
Win a Date with Tad Hamilton! *'04*
Walk the Line *'05*
In the Land of Women *'06*
Day Zero *'07*
Birds of America *'08*
He's Just Not That Into You *'09*
A Single Man *'09*
Ramona and Beezus *'10*
Five *'11*
Something Borrowed *'11*
Killing Kennedy *'13*
Zootopia *'16 (V)*

Harold Goodwin (1902-87)
Suds *'20*
The Better 'Ole *'26*
The Cameraman *'28*
All Quiet on the Western Front *'30*
Abbott and Costello Meet the Keystone Kops *'54*
The Bridge on the River Kwai *'57*

Kia Joy Goodwin (1973-)
Strapped *'93*
Swimfan *'02*

Laurel Goodwin (1942-)
Girls! Girls! Girls! *'62*
Papa's Delicate Condition *'63*

Malcolm Goodwin (1982-)
The Lazarus Project *'08*
The Longshots *'08*
Miracle at St. Anna *'08*
Crazy on the Outside *'10*
Freelancers *'12*

Michael Goodwin
Between the Darkness and the Dawn *'85*
Date with an Angel *'87*
The Dead Pool *'88*

Raven Goodwin (1992-)
Lovely & Amazing *'02*
The Station Agent *'03*

Michael Goorjian (1971-)
Hard Rain *'97*
Deal of a Lifetime *'99*
The Invisibles *'99*
Silent Witness *'99*
SLC Punk! *'99*
Something More *'99*
Around June *'08*

Howard Goorney (1921-2007)
The Hill *'65*
Bedazzled *'68*

Allen Goorwitz (1939-2020)
See Allen Garfield

Claudio Gora (1913-98)
Adua and Her Friends *'60*
The Slave *'62*
An Angel for Satan *'66*
The Five Man Army *'69*
Seven Blood-Stained Orchids *'72*

Alicia (Lecy) Goranson (1974-)
How to Make an American Quilt *'95*
Boys Don't Cry *'99*
Love, Ludlow *'05*

David Gorcey (1921-84)
Dead End Kids: Little Tough Guy *'38*
Junior G-Men of the Air *'42*
Mr. Wise Guy *'42*
She Shoulda Said No *'49*

Leo Gorcey (1915-69)
Dead End *'37*
Mannequin *'37*
Angels with Dirty Faces *'38*
Crime School *'38*
Little Tough Guy *'38*
Angels Wash Their Faces *'39*
Hell's Kitchen *'39*
They Made Me a Criminal *'39*
Gallant Sons *'40*
Out of the Fog *'41*
Maisie Gets Her Man *'42*
Mr. Wise Guy *'42*
Smart Alecks *'42*
Clancy Street Boys *'43*
Destroyer *'43*
Kid Dynamite *'43*
So This Is New York *'48*
It's a Mad, Mad, Mad, Mad World *'63*

Barbara Gordon
Dead Ringers *'88*
Cube 2: Hypercube *'02*
Men with Brooms *'02*
Sex and the Single Mom *'03*
More Sex and the Single Mom *'05*
Skinwalkers *'07*
Still Small Voices *'07*

Barry J. Gordon (1948-)
The Girl Can't Help It *'56*
Pressure Point *'62*
A Thousand Clowns *'65*
Love at First Bite *'79*
Time Warp *'81*
Body Slam *'87*

C. Henry Gordon (1883-1940)
State's Attorney *'31*
The Crooked Circle *'32*
Kongo *'32*
Mata Hari *'32*
The Strange Love of Molly Louvain *'32*
Gabriel Over the White House *'33*
Made On Broadway *'33*
Penthouse *'33*
Rasputin and the Empress *'33*
Turn Back the Clock *'33*
Men in White *'34*
The Crusades *'35*
The Charge of the Light Brigade *'36*
Charlie Chan at the Olympics *'37*
Charlie Chan in City of Darkness *'39*
Kit Carson *'40*

Carl Gordon (1932-2010)
The Piano Lesson *'94*
Love Songs *'99*

Colin Gordon (1911-72)
Edward, My Son *'49*
The Hour of 13 *'52*
One That Got Away *'57*
Very Important Person *'61*
Burn, Witch, Burn! *'62*
The Body Beneath *'70*

Danso Gordon (1979-)
Dear Wendy *'05*
Dark House *'09*

Dexter Gordon (1923-90)
Round Midnight *'86*
Awakenings *'90*

Don Gordon (1926-)
Bullitt *'68*
Cannon for Cordoba *'70*
Slaughter *'72*
Zero Population Growth *'72*
The Mack *'73*
The Education of Sonny Carson *'74*
The Final Conflict *'81*
The Beast Within *'82*

Dorothy Gordon (1924-)
The Haunted Strangler *'58*
Where the Money Is *'00*

Eve Gordon (1960-)
Avalon *'90*
Paradise *'91*
Leaving Normal *'92*
The Heidi Chronicles *'95*
Honey, We Shrunk Ourselves *'97*
I'll Be Home for Christmas *'98*

Fiona Gordon
L'Iceberg *'05*
Lost in Paris *'17*

Gale Gordon (1906-95)
Here We Go Again! *'42*
Francis Covers the Big Town *'53*
Our Miss Brooks *'56*
Rally 'Round the Flag, Boys! *'58*
The 30-Foot Bride of Candy Rock *'59*
All Hands on Deck *'61*
Dondi *'61*
Sergeant Deadhead *'65*
Speedway *'68*
The 'Burbs *'89*

Gavin Gordon (1901-83)
Romance *'30*
The Silver Horde *'30*
American Madness *'32*
The Bitter Tea of General Yen *'33*
Bordertown *'35*
The Bride of Frankenstein *'35*
Gangs, Inc. *'41*
Murder by Invitation *'41*
Paper Bullets *'41*
I Killed That Man *'42*
Chicago Confidential *'57*
The Matchmaker *'58*
The Bat *'59*

Gerald Gordon (1934-2001)
Hell Up in Harlem *'73*
Ants *'77*

Hannah Taylor Gordon (1987-)
Jakob the Liar *'99*
Anne Frank: The Whole Story *'01*

Huntley Gordon
The Red-Haired Alibi *'32*
Corruption *'33*

Jack Gordon
Heartless *'10*
Bachelor Games *'16*

Julia Swayne Gordon (1879-1933)
Scaramouche *'23*
It *'27*
Wings *'27*
The Smart Set *'28*

Keith Gordon (1961-)
Jaws 2 *'78*
All That Jazz *'79*
Home Movies *'79*
Dressed to Kill *'80*
Christine *'84*
Legend of Billie Jean *'85*
Back to School *'86*
Static *'87*
I Love Trouble *'94*

Kim Gordon (1953-)
Last Days *'05*
Boarding Gate *'07*

Leo Gordon (1922-2000)
Hondo *'53*
The Egyptian *'54*
Riot in Cell Block 11 *'54*
Ten Wanted Men *'54*
Robbers' Roost *'55*
Seven Angry Men *'55*
Soldier of Fortune *'55*
Seventh Cavalry *'56*
Black Patch *'57*
Apache Territory *'58*
Ride a Crooked Trail *'58*
The Jayhawkers *'59*
Noose for a Gunman *'60*
Shame *'61*
The Nun and the Sergeant *'62*
Tarzan Goes to India *'62*
The Haunted Palace *'63*
Kings of the Sun *'63*
Kitten with a Whip *'64*
Devil's Angels *'67*
Bog *'84*
Alienator *'89*

Lucy Gordon (1980-2009)
Russian Dolls *'05*
Spider-Man 3 *'07*
The Last International Playboy *'08*
Gainsbourg: A Heroic Life *'10*

Mary Gordon (1882-1963)
The Irish in Us *'35*
Double Wedding *'37*
City Streets *'38*
The Adventures of Sherlock Holmes *'39*
Sherlock Holmes and the Secret Weapon *'42*
Sherlock Holmes and the Voice of Terror *'42*
Boss of Big Town *'43*
Little Giant *'46*
The Woman in Green *'49*

Molly Gordon
Life of the Party *'18*
Good Boys *'19*

Pamela Gordon (1937-2003)
Bloodstone: Subspecies 2 *'92*
Bloodlust: Subspecies 3 *'93*
Baadasssss! *'03*

Roy Gordon (1896-1978)
The Real Glory *'39*
Night Editor *'46*
The Gun That Won the West *'55*
Murder Is My Beat *'55*
Attack of the 50 Foot Woman *'58*
The Fearmakers *'58*
The Wasp Woman *'59*

Ruth Gordon (1896-1985)
Abe Lincoln in Illinois *'40*
Dr. Ehrlich's Magic Bullet *'40*
Action in the North Atlantic *'43*
Edge of Darkness *'43*
Inside Daisy Clover *'65*
Lord Love a Duck *'66*
Rosemary's Baby *'68*
Whatever Happened to Aunt Alice? *'69*
Where's Poppa? *'70*
Harold and Maude *'71*
The Big Bus *'76*
The Prince of Central Park *'77*
Every Which Way But Loose *'78*
Boardwalk *'79*
Any Which Way You Can *'80*
My Bodyguard *'80*
Maxie *'85*
Voyage of the Rock Aliens *'87*

Serena Gordon (1963-)
Riders *'88*
A Tale of Two Cities *'89*
Goldeneye *'95*
Aristocrats *'99*
The Aristocrats *'99*

Susan Gordon (1949-2011)
Attack of the Puppet People *'58*
Tormented *'60*
Picture Mommy Dead *'66*

Zachary Gordon (1998-)
Santa Buddies *'09 (V)*
Beverly Hills Chihuahua 2 *'10 (V)*
Diary of a Wimpy Kid *'10*
The Search for Santa Paws *'10 (V)*
Diary of a Wimpy Kid 2: Rodrick Rules *'11*
Diary of a Wimpy Kid: Dog Days *'12*

Joseph Gordon-Levitt (1981-)
Angels in the Outfield *'94*
Holy Matrimony *'94*
The Juror *'96*
Halloween: H20 *'98*
Sweet Jane *'98*
Picking Up the Pieces *'99*
Ten Things I Hate about You *'99*
Along for the Ride *'00*
Manic *'01*
Treasure Planet *'02 (V)*
Latter Days *'04*
Mysterious Skin *'04*
Havoc *'05*
Brick *'06*
Shadowboxer *'06*
The Lookout *'07*
Miracle at St. Anna *'08*
Stop-Loss *'08*
Uncertainty *'08*
(500) Days of Summer *'09*
G.I. Joe: The Rise of Cobra *'09*
Killshot *'09*
Women in Trouble *'09*
Elektra Luxx *'10*
Hesher *'10*
Inception *'10*
50/50 *'11*
The Dark Knight Rises *'12*
Lincoln *'12*
Looper *'12*
Premium Rush *'12*
Don Jon *'13*
Sin City: A Dame to Kill For *'14*
The Night Before *'15*
The Walk *'15*
Snowden *'16*

Charles Gordone (1925-95)
Streetfight *'75*
Angel Heart *'87*

Sandy Gore (1950-)
Wrangler *'88*
Brides of Christ *'91*

Christopher Gorham (1974-)
The Other Side of Heaven *'02*
Answer This *'10*
My Girlfriend's Boyfriend *'10*
The Ledge *'11*
The Other Side of Heaven 2: Fire of Faith *'19*

Mel Gorham (1959-)
Blue in the Face *'95*
Curdled *'95*
Smoke *'95*
Wishful Thinking *'96*
The Center of the World *'01*

Marius Goring (1912-98)
The Case of the Frightened Lady *'39*
Spy in Black *'39*
Stairway to Heaven *'46*
The Red Shoes *'48*
Highly Dangerous *'50*
The Barefoot Contessa *'54*
Quentin Durward *'55*
Ill Met By Moonlight *'57*
Night Ambush *'57*
Exodus *'60*
Lisa *'62*
The Crooked Road *'65*
The 25th Hour *'67*
Zeppelin *'71*
Holocaust *'78*

Esther Gorintin (1913-)
Carnage *'02*
Since Otar Left. . . *'03*

Burn Gorman (1974-)
Layer Cake *'05*
The Oxford Murders *'08*
Wuthering Heights *'09*
The Dark Knight Rises *'12*
Spies of Warsaw *'13*
Walking with the Enemy *'13*
Crimson Peak *'15*
Guernica *'16*
Pacific Rim: Uprising *'18*

Cliff Gorman (1936-2002)
The Boys in the Band *'70*
Cops and Robbers *'73*
Strike Force *'75*
An Unmarried Woman *'78*
All That Jazz *'79*
Cocaine and Blue Eyes *'83*
Angel *'84*
Hoffa *'92*
Night and the City *'92*
Ghost Dog: The Way of the Samurai *'99*
The '60s *'99*
King of the Jungle *'01*
Kill the Poor *'03*

Jonathan Gorman
Gang Justice *'94*
Bikini Bloodbath Christmas *'09*

Patrick Gorman
Gettysburg *'93*
Gods and Generals *'03*
The Land That Time Forgot *'09*

Robert Gorman (1980-)
Leprechaun *'93*
Mr. Nanny *'93*

Eydie Gorme (1931-2013)
Alice in Wonderland *'85*
Ocean's Eleven *'01 (C)*

Peggy Gormley
Bad Lieutenant *'92*
The Sleepy Time Gal *'01*

Karen (Lynn) Gorney (1945-)
Saturday Night Fever *'77*
The Hard Way *'91*
Ripe *'97*

Walt Gorney (1912-2004)
Friday the 13th *'80*
Friday the 13th, Part 2 *'81*

Lisa Gornick (1970-)
Do I Love You? *'02*
Tick Tock Lullaby *'07*
The Owls *'09*

Frederic Gorny (1973-)
Wild Reeds *'94*
Jeanne and the Perfect Guy *'98*

Irene Gorovaia (1989-)
It Runs in the Family *'03*
The Butterfly Effect *'04*

Ashley Gorrell
Thunder in Paradise 3 *'94*
Mail to the Chief *'00*

Frank Gorshin (1934-2005)
Between Heaven and Hell *'56*
Dragstrip Girl *'57*
Portland Expose *'57*
The True Story of Jesse James *'57*
Studs Lonigan *'60*
Where the Boys Are *'60*
The George Raft Story *'61*
Sail a Crooked Ship *'61*
That Darn Cat *'65*
Batman *'66*
Hollywood Vice Sqaud *'86*
Body Trouble *'92*
Sweet Justice *'92*
The Meteor Man *'93*
Hail Caesar *'94*
12 Monkeys *'95*
Bloodmoon *'97*
The Twilight of the Ice Nymphs *'97*
Man of the Century *'99*
Beethoven's 3rd *'00*
Luck of the Draw *'00*

Marjoe Gortner (1944-)
Marjoe *'72*
Earthquake *'74*
Bobbie Jo and the Outlaw *'76*
Food of the Gods *'76*
Mayday at 40,000 Feet *'76*
Sidewinder One *'77*
Viva Knievel *'77*
Acapulco Gold *'78*
Star Crash *'78*
Mausoleum *'83*
Jungle Warriors *'84*
American Ninja 3: Blood Hunt *'89*
Wild Bill *'95*

Ryan Gosling (1980-)
Nothing Too Good for a Cowboy *'98*
Remember the Titans *'00*
The Believer *'01*
The Slaughter Rule *'01*
Murder by Numbers *'02*
United States of Leland *'03*
The Notebook *'04*
Stay *'05*
Half Nelson *'06*
Fracture *'07*
Lars and the Real Girl *'07*
All Good Things *'10*
Blue Valentine *'10*
Crazy, Stupid, Love. *'11*
Drive *'11*
The Ides of March *'11*
Gangster Squad *'13*
Only God Forgives *'13*
The Place Beyond the Pines *'13*
The Big Short *'15*
La La Land *'16*
The Nice Guys *'16*
Blade Runner 2049 *'17*
Song to Song *'17*
First Man *'18*

David Goss
She *'83*
Hollywood Cop *'87*

Luke Goss (1968-)
Blade 2 *'02*
ZigZag *'02*
Charlie *'04*
Silver Hawk *'04*
Cold and Dark *'05*
The Man *'05*
One Night with the King *'06*
Bone Dry *'07*
Unearthed *'07*
Deep Winter *'08*
Hellboy II: The Golden Army *'08*
Across the Line: The Exodus of Charlie Wright *'10*
Blood Out *'10*
Death Race 2 *'10*
Witchville *'10*
Pressed *'11*
7 Below *'11*
Death Race 3: Inferno *'12*
Interview With a Hitman *'12*
Dead Drop *'13*

Walter Goss (1900-88)
See Roland Drew

Mark-Paul Gosselaar (1974-)
Necessary Parties *'88*
The St. Tammany Miracle *'94*
Kounterfeit *'96*
Dead Man on Campus *'97*
Specimen *'97*
Precious Cargo *'16*

Juliette Gosselin (1991-)
Familia *'05*
The Fall of the American Empire *'19*

Denise Gossett
Chain of Souls *'00*
River: The Legend of La Llorona *'06*

Louis Gossett, Jr. (1936-)
A Raisin in the Sun *'61*
The Landlord *'70*
Skin Game *'71*
Travels with My Aunt *'72*
It's Good to Be Alive *'74*
The Laughing Policeman *'74*
Sidekicks *'74*
The White Dawn *'75*
J.D.'s Revenge *'76*
The River Niger *'76*
The Choirboys *'77*
The Deep *'77*
Little Ladies of the Night *'77*
Backstairs at the White House *'79*
The Lazarus Syndrome *'79*
An Officer and a Gentleman *'82*
Jaws 3 *'83*
Enemy Mine *'85*
Firewalker *'86*
Iron Eagle *'86*
The Father Clements Story *'87*
The Principal *'87*
Iron Eagle 2 *'88*
Roots: The Gift *'88*
El Diablo *'90*
The Josephine Baker Story *'90*
The Punisher *'90*
Sudie & Simpson *'90*
Zora Is My Name! *'90*
Cover-Up *'91*
Murder on the Bayou *'91*
Toy Soldiers *'91*
Aces: Iron Eagle 3 *'92*
Carolina Skeletons *'92*
Diggstown *'92*
Dangerous Relations *'93*
Return to Lonesome Dove *'93*
Curse of the Starving Class *'94*
Flashfire *'94*
A Good Man in Africa *'94*
Iron Eagle 4 *'95*
Inside *'96*
Bram Stoker's The Mummy *'97*
In His Father's Shoes *'97*
The Inspectors *'98*
The Highway Man *'99*
Love Songs *'99*
The Inspectors 2: A Shred of Evidence *'00*
What About Your Friends: Weekend Getaway *'02*
Jasper, Texas *'03*
Momentum *'03*
All In *'06*
Daddy's Little Girls *'07*
Cover *'08*
Delgo *'08 (V)*
The Least Among You *'09*
The Perfect Game *'09*
Shannon's Rainbow *'09*
Tyler Perry's Why Did I Get Married Too *'10*
The Grace Card *'11*
A Fighting Man *'14*

Robert Gossett (1954-)
Arlington Road *'99*
Jimmy Zip *'00*

Roland Got (1916-48)
Across the Pacific *'42*
G-Men *vs.* the Black Dragon *'43*

Walter Gotell (1925-97)
The African Queen *'51*
The Guns of Navarone *'61*
From Russia with Love *'63*
These Are the Damned *'63*
Lord Jim *'65*
The File of the Golden Goose *'69*
The Spy Who Loved Me *'77*
Moonraker *'79*
For Your Eyes Only *'81*
Lace 2 *'85*
Basic Training *'86*
The Living Daylights *'87*
Sleepaway Camp 2: Unhappy Campers *'88*
Puppet Master 3: Toulon's Revenge *'90*

Mia Goth (1993-)
A Cure for Wellness *'17*
High Life *'18*
Suspiria *'18*
Emma *'20*

Michael Gothard (1939-93)
Up the Junction *'68*
The Valley Obscured by the Clouds *'70*
The Devils *'71*
King Arthur, the Young Warlord *'75*
Young Warlord *'75*
For Your Eyes Only *'81*
Lifeforce *'85*

Gilbert Gottfried (1955-)
Bad Medicine *'85*
Beverly Hills Cop 2 *'87*
The Adventures of Ford Fairlane *'90*
Problem Child *'90*
Problem Child 2 *'91*
Aladdin *'92 (V)*
The Return of Jafar *'94 (V)*
Thumbelina *'94 (V)*
Aladdin and the King of Thieves *'96 (V)*
Def Jam's How to Be a Player *'97*
Dr. Dolittle *'98 (V)*
Jack and the Beanstalk *'09*
Life, Animated *'16*

Carl Gottlieb (1938-)
A Session with The Committee *'68*
M*A*S*H *'70*
Jaws *'75*
Cannonball *'76*
The Jerk *'79*

Theodore Gottlieb (1906-2001)
See Brother Theodore

Thomas Gottschalk (1950-)
Ring of the Musketeers *'93*
Sister Act 2: Back in the Habit *'93*

Jenn Gotzon
Frost/Nixon *'08*
Alone Yet Not Alone *'13*

Jetta Goudal (1891-1985)
The Road to Yesterday *'25*
White Gold *'28*

Lloyd Gough (1907-84)
A Southern Yankee *'48*
That Wonderful Urge *'48*
Tension *'50*
Storm Warning *'51*

Michael Gough (1916-2011)
Anna Karenina *'48*
Blanche Fury *'48*
The Small Back Room *'49*
Rob Roy-The Highland Rogue *'53*
The Sword & the Rose *'53*
Richard III *'55*
Ill Met By Moonlight *'57*
The Horror of Dracula *'58*
The Horse's Mouth *'58*
Horrors of the Black Museum *'59*
The Phantom of the Opera *'62*
What a Carve-Up! *'62*
Black Zoo *'63*
The Skull *'65*
Alice in Wonderland *'66*
They Came from Beyond Space *'67*
The Crimson Cult *'68*
Crucible of Horror *'69*
Trog *'70*
Women in Love *'70*
The Go-Between *'71*
Savage Messiah *'72*
Horror Hospital *'73*
The Legend of Hell House *'73*
Smiley's People *'82*
Venom *'82*
The Dresser *'83*
To the Lighthouse *'83*
Oxford Blues *'84*
Top Secret! *'84*
Out of Africa *'85*
Caravaggio *'86*
The Fourth Protocol *'87*
The Serpent and the Rainbow *'87*
Batman *'89*
The Shell Seekers *'89*
Strapless *'90*
Let Him Have It *'91*
Batman Returns *'92*
The Advocate *'93*
The Age of Innocence *'93*
Wittgenstein *'93*
Uncovered *'94*
Batman Forever *'95*
A Village Affair *'95*
Batman and Robin *'97*
St. Ives *'98*
The Cherry Orchard *'99*
Sleepy Hollow *'99*
Tim Burton's Corpse Bride *'05 (V)*

Guillaume Gouix
Nobody Else But You *'11*
Beyond the Walls *'12*

Alexander Gould (1994-)
Mexico City *'00*
The Day the World Ended *'01*
Wes Craven Presents: They *'02*
Finding Nemo *'03 (V)*
Bambi II *'06 (V)*
How to Eat Fried Worms *'06*

Ben Gould (1980-)
Frankenstein Reborn *'98*
Home Room *'02*

Dominic Gould (1964-)
Close to Leo *'02*
Queen to Play *'09*

Elliott Gould (1938-)
Bob & Carol & Ted & Alice *'69*
The Night They Raided Minsky's *'69*
Getting Straight *'70*
M*A*S*H *'70*
Little Murders *'71*
Quick, Let's Get Married *'71*
The Long Goodbye *'73*
Busting *'74*
S*P*Y*S *'74*
Mean Johnny Barrows *'75*
Nashville *'75*
Whiffs *'75*
Harry & Walter Go to New York *'76*
I Will, I Will...for Now *'76*
A Bridge Too Far *'77*
Capricorn One *'78*
The Silent Partner *'78*
Escape to Athena *'79*
The Lady Vanishes *'79*
The Muppet Movie *'79 (C)*
Falling in Love Again *'80*
The Last Flight of Noah's Ark *'80*
The Devil & Max Devlin *'81*
The Naked Face *'84*
Conspiracy: The Trial of the Chicago Eight *'87*
Lethal Obsession *'87*
Night Visitor *'89*
The Lemon Sisters *'90*
Bugsy *'91*
Dead Men Don't Die *'91*
Beyond Justice *'92*
The Player *'92*
Bleeding Hearts *'94*
The Glass Shield *'95*
Kicking and Screaming *'95*
City of Industry *'96*
johns *'96*
American History X *'98*
The Big Hit *'98*
Picking Up the Pieces *'99*
Playing Mona Lisa *'00*
Ocean's Eleven *'01*
Ocean's Twelve *'04*
Open Window *'06*
Ocean's Thirteen *'07*
St. Urbain's Horseman *'07*
Saving Sarah Cain *'07*
The Caller *'08*
The Deal *'08*
Morning *'10*
A Very Mary Christmas *'10*
Contagion *'11*
Dorfman in Love *'11*
Ruby Sparks *'12*
Humor Me *'17*

Harold Gould (1923-2010)
Project X *'68*
The Sting *'73*
Love and Death *'75*
The Strongest Man in the World *'75*
Washington: Behind Closed Doors *'77*
The One and Only *'78*
Kenny Rogers as the Gambler *'80*
Seems Like Old Times *'80*
Baby Broker *'81*
Dream Chasers *'82*
Kenny Rogers as the Gambler, Part 2: The Adventure Continues *'83*
Fourth Wise Man *'85*
Playing for Keeps *'86*
Get Smart, Again! *'89*
Romero *'89*
Killer: A Journal of Murder *'95*
Brown's Requiem *'98*
My Giant *'98*
Patch Adams *'98*
Master of Disguise *'02*
Brother Bear *'03 (V)*
Freaky Friday *'03*
ESL: English as a Second Language *'05*

Jason Gould (1966-)
The Big Picture *'89*
Say Anything *'89*
The Prince of Tides *'91*
Subterfuge *'98*

Nolan Gould
Friends With Benefits *'11*
Field of Lost Shoes *'14*

Alain Goulem (1966-)
Silent Night *'02*
A Deadly Encounter *'04*
Eddie the Sleepwalking Cannibal *'12*
CAT. 8 *'13*

Robert Goulet (1933-2007)
Gay Purr-ee *'62 (V)*
Beetlejuice *'88*
Scrooged *'88*
Naked Gun 2 1/2: The Smell of Fear *'91*
Mr. Wrong *'95*
Toy Story 2 *'99 (V)*

Olivier Gourmet (1963-)
La Promesse *'96*
Rosetta *'99*
Read My Lips *'01*
Time of the Wolf *'03*
The Child *'05*
Lorna's Silence *'08*
Mesrine: Part 2-Public Enemy Number 1 *'08*
Home *'09*
40 Love *'15*
The Midwife *'17*

Gibson Gowland (1877-1951)
The Phantom of the Opera *'25*
Hell Harbor *'30*
S.O.S. Iceberg *'33*

Dakota Goyo (1999-)
Resurrecting the Champ *'07*
My Neighbor's Secret *'09*
Real Steel *'11*
Dark Skies *'13*
The Journey Home *'14*

Harry Goz (1932-2003)
Bill *'81*
Mommie Dearest *'81*
Bill: On His Own *'83*
Rappin' *'85*
The Underneath *'95*

GQ (1976-)
On the Line *'01*
What's the Worst That Could Happen? *'01*
Drumline *'02*

Lucas Grabeel (1984-)
Halloweentown High *'04*
High School Musical *'06*
Return to Halloweentown *'06*
Alice Upside Down *'07*
College Road Trip *'08*
High School Musical 3: Senior Year *'08*
Milk *'08*
Little Women *'18*

Betty Grable (1916-73)
Whoopee! *'30*
Hold 'Em Jail *'32*
The Gay Divorcee *'34*
The Nitwits *'35*
Old Man Rhythm *'35*

Follow the Fleet '36
Pigskin Parade '36
College Swing '38
Give Me a Sailor '38
Down Argentine Way '40
I Wake Up Screaming '41
Moon over Miami '41
A Yank in the R.A.F. '41
Springtime in the Rockies '42
Coney Island '43
Pin-Up Girl '44
The Dolly Sisters '46
Mother Wore Tights '47
The Shocking Miss Pilgrim '47
The Beautiful Blonde from Bashful Bend '49
My Blue Heaven '50
Wabash Avenue '50
Call Me Mister '51
Meet Me After the Show '51
How to Marry a Millionaire '53
Three for the Show '55
The Love Goddesses '65

Sofie Gråbol (1968-)
Mifune '99
Flickering Lights '01
The Boss of It All '06
The House That Jack Built '18

Anna Grace
Girls Town '95
Fiona '98

April Grace (1962-)
Headless Body in Topless Bar '96
Waterproof '99
Finding Forrester '00
The Assassination of Richard Nixon '05
American Son '08

Jeff Grace
The Scenesters '09
It's a Disaster '12

Maggie Grace (1983-)
Murder in Greenwich '02
The Fog '05
The Jane Austen Book Club '07
Suburban Girl '07
Taken '08
Malice in Wonderland '09
The Experiment '10
Faster '10
Knight and Day '10
Lockout '12
Taken 2 '12
The Twilight Saga: Breaking Dawn, Part 2 '12
Decoding Annie Parker '13
When Calls the Heart '13
About Alex '14
Taken 3 '15
The Choice '16
Aftermath '17
The Hurricane Heist '18

McKenna Grace (2006-)
Amityville: The Awakening '17
Gifted '17
Annabelle Comes Home '19

Nickolas Grace (1947-)
Heat and Dust '82
Robin Hood. . . The Legend: Robin Hood and the Sorcerer '83
Lace '84
Napolèon and Josephine: A Love Story '87
Diamond's Edge '88
Salome's Last Dance '88
Tom & Viv '94
Two Deaths '94
The Final Cut '95
Shooting Fish '98
Casanova '05

Topher Grace (1978-)
Traffic '00
Ocean's Eleven '01 (C)
Mona Lisa Smile '03
In Good Company '04
P.S. '04
Win a Date with Tad Hamilton! '04
Spider-Man 3 '07
Predators '10
Valentine's Day '10
The Double '11
Take Me Home Tonight '11
Too Big to Fail '11
The Giant Mechanical Man '12
The Big Wedding '13
The Calling '14
Playing It Cool '14
American Ultra '15
Truth '15
Opening Night '17
War Machine '17
BlacKkKlansman '18
Breakthrough '19

Elizabeth (Ward) Gracen (1961-)
Death of the Incredible Hulk '90
Lower Level '91
Discretion Assured '93
Final Mission '93
Interceptor Force 2 '02
Sundown: The Vampire in Retreat '08
Coherence '13

Sancho Gracia (1936-)
The Crime of Father Amaro '02
800 Bullets '02

Sally Gracie (1920-2001)
The Rain People '69
Opportunity Knocks '90

Genevieve Grad (1944-)
The Beast of Babylon Against the Son of Hercules '63
Sandokan the Great '63

David Graf (1950-2001)
Police Academy 2: Their First Assignment '85
Police Academy 3: Back in Training '86
Police Academy 4: Citizens on Patrol '87
Police Academy 5: Assignment Miami Beach '88
Shakedown on the Sunset Strip '88
Police Academy 6: City under Siege '89
Suture '93
Father and Scout '94
Police Academy 7: Mission to Moscow '94
The Brady Bunch Movie '95
Citizen Ruth '96
The Trial of Old Drum '00

David Alan Graf (1959-)
Auto Recovery '08
Heist '09

Ilene Graff (1949-)
Ladybugs '92
The Great American Sex Scandal '94
Rodgers & Hammerstein's South Pacific '01
Loving Annabelle '06

Todd Graff (1959-)
Sweet Lorraine '87
Dominick & Eugene '88
Five Corners '88
The Abyss '89
Framed '90
Opportunity Knocks '90
City of Hope '91
Fly by Night '93

Wilton Graff (1903-69)
Dead Man's Eyes '44
Key Witness '47
The West Point Story '50
Bloodlust '59
Compulsion '59

Aimee Graham (1971-)
Amos and Andrew '93
Dance with the Devil '97
Jackie Brown '97
Brokedown Palace '99
Shriek If You Know What I Did Last Friday the 13th '00
Time Code '00
Bark! '02

Allison Graham
Swamp Devil '08
My Nanny's Secret '09

Bill Graham (1931-91)
Gimme Shelter '70
Gardens of Stone '87
Bugsy '91
The Doors '91

Currie Graham (1967-)
Blood Money '98
Behind the Mask '99
Edge of Madness '02
Assault on Precinct 13 '05
The Capture of the Green River Killer '08
Stargate: The Ark of Truth '08
Would Be Kings '08
Smoke Screen '10
Total Recall '12

Fred Graham (1918-79)
The Fuller Brush Girl '50
Escape from Fort Bravo '53
The Last Hunt '56

Gary (Rand) Graham (1950-)
The Hollywood Knights '80
The Dirty Dozen: The Deadly Mission '87
The Last Warrior '89
Robot Jox '90
Alien Nation: Dark Horizon '94
Alien Nation: Body and Soul '95
Alien Nation: Millennium '96
Alien Nation: The Enemy Within '96
Running Woman '98
Amish Grace '10

Gerrit Graham (1949-)
Greetings '68
Hi, Mom! '70
Beware! The Blob '72
Phantom of the Paradise '74
Cannonball '76
Dynasty '76
Tunnelvision '76
Demon Seed '77
Pretty Baby '78
Home Movies '79
Used Cars '80
Spaceship '81
National Lampoon's Class Reunion '82
Ratings Game '84
The Man with One Red Shoe '85
Chopping Mall '86
Last Resort '86
Terrorvision '86
It's Alive 3: Island of the Alive '87
Child's Play 2 '90
Philadelphia Experiment 2 '93
This Boy's Life '93
Stuart Saves His Family '94
The Love Letter '98
One True Thing '98

Heather Graham (1970-)
License to Drive '88
Drugstore Cowboy '89
I Love You to Death '90
O Pioneers! '91
Shout '91
Diggstown '92
Guilty as Charged '92
Twin Peaks: Fire Walk with Me '92
The Ballad of Little Jo '93
Six Degrees of Separation '93
Don't Do It '94
Terrified '94
Desert Winds '95
Entertaining Angels: The Dorothy Day Story '96
Swingers '96
Boogie Nights '97
Scream 2 '97
Lost in Space '98
Two Girls and a Guy '98
Austin Powers 2: The Spy Who Shagged Me '99
Bowfinger '99
Committed '99
From Hell '01
Killing Me Softly '01
Say It Isn't So '01
Sidewalks of New York '01
The Guru '02
Anger Management '03
Cake '05
Bobby '06
Gray Matters '06
Adrift in Manhattan '07
Baby on Board '08
Miss Conception '08
Boogie Woogie '09
ExTerminators '09
The Hangover '09
Father of Invention '11
5 Days of War '11
Judy Moody and the Not Bummer Summer '11
Son of Morning '11
Compulsion '13
The Hangover, Part III '13
Horns '13
Flowers in the Attic '14
Goodbye to All That '14
Petals on the Wind '14
Norm of the North '16
Last Rampage '17

Jeff Dylan Graham (1983-)
Beyond the Dunwich Horror '08
Home Sick '08
Night Stalker '09

Jessica Graham
2 Minutes Later '07
And Then Came Lola '09

Julie Graham (1965-)
Preaching to the Perverted '97
Bedrooms and Hallways '98
Dirty Tricks '00
The History of Mr. Polly '07
The Bletchley Circle '13

Kat Graham (1989-)
Addicted '14
Honey 2 '14
All Eyez on Me '17

Lauren Graham (1967-)
Nightwatch '96
One True Thing '98
Chasing Destiny '00
Sweet November '01
The Third Wheel '02
Bad Santa '03
Seeing Other People '04
The Moguls '05
The Pacifier '05
Because I Said So '07
Evan Almighty '07
Birds of America '08
Flash of Genius '08
The Answer Man '09
Cloudy with a Chance of Meatballs '09 (V)
It's Kind of a Funny Story '10
Max '15
Middle School: The Worst Years of My Life '16

Marcus Graham (1963-)
Animal Instincts 3: The Seductress '95
Green Sails '00
Mulholland Drive '01

Morland Graham (1891-1949)
The Scarlet Pimpernel '34
Night Train to Munich '40
The Ghost Train '41
The Upturned Glass '47

Richard Graham
My Beautiful Laundrette '85
Le Donk & Scor-Zay-Zee '09

Ronny Graham (1919-99)
New Faces of 1952 '54
World's Greatest Lover '77
Gallipoli '81
Ratings Game '84
The Substance of Fire '96

Sasha Graham
Addicted to Murder '95
Addicted to Murder 2: Tainted Blood '97

Stephen Graham (1973-)
Snatch '00
Gangs of New York '02
The I Inside '04
Satan's Little Helper '04
Pit Fighter '05
This Is England '06
The Crew '08
Filth and Wisdom '08
The Damned United '09
Public Enemies '09
Season of the Witch '10
Texas Killing Fields '11
Tinker Tailor Soldier Spy '11
Hyena '15
Film Stars Don't Die in Liverpool '17
Journey's End '18

Stuart Graham (1967-)
Michael Collins '96
One Man's Hero '98
Hunger '08
Parked '10
Bad Day for the Cut '17
The Cured '18

Gloria Grahame (1925-81)
It's a Wonderful Life '46
Crossfire '47
It Happened in Brooklyn '47
Merton of the Movies '47
Song of the Thin Man '47
In a Lonely Place '50
The Bad and the Beautiful '52
The Greatest Show on Earth '52
Macao '52
Sudden Fear '52
The Big Heat '53
The Glass Wall '53
Man on a Tightrope '53
Human Desire '54
The Cobweb '55
The Man Who Never Was '55
Not as a Stranger '55
Oklahoma! '55
Odds Against Tomorrow '59
Chandler '71
The Todd Killings '71
Autopsy '73
Mansion of the Doomed '76
The Big Scam '79
The Nesting '80

Gawn Grainger (1940-)
August '95
Love and Death on Long Island '97

Holliday Grainger (1988-)
The Bad Mother's Handbook '07
Any Human Heart '11
Jane Eyre '11
Bel Ami '12
Great Expectations '12
Bonnie & Clyde '13
Cinderella '15
The Finest Hours '16
My Cousin Rachel '17
Tulip Fever '17
Tell It to the Bees '19

Greer Grammer (1992-)
Emma's Chance '16
Altitude '17

Kelsey Grammer (1954-)
Kennedy '83
Down Periscope '96
Anastasia '97 (V)
The Pentagon Wars '98
The Real Howard Spitz '98
Animal Farm '99 (V)
Standing on Fishes '99
Toy Story 2 '99 (V)
15 Minutes '01
Mr. St. Nick '02
Benedict Arnold: A Question of Honor '03
The Big Empty '04
Disney's Teacher's Pet '04 (V)
The Good Humor Man '05
Even Money '06
X-Men: The Last Stand '06
An American Carol '08
Swing Vote '08
Fame '09
Crazy on the Outside '10
I Don't Know How She Does It '11
Breaking the Bank '14
The Expendables 3 '14
Legends of Oz: Dorothy's Return '14 (V)
Transformers: Age of Extinction '14
Storks '16
Like Father '18

Albert Gran
Her Night of Romance '24
Four Sons '28

Alexander Granach (1893-1945)
Warning Shadows '23
Hangmen Also Die '42
Joan of Paris '42
Wrecking Crew '42
For Whom the Bell Tolls '43

Bjorn Granath (1946-)
Pelle the Conqueror '88
The Ox '91
The Last Sentence '12

Omari (Omarion) Grandberry (1984-)
Fat Albert '04
You Got Served '04
The Proud Family Movie '05 (V)
Feel the Noise '07

Dario Grandinetti (1959-)
The Dark Side of the Heart '92
Talk to Her '02
Wild Tales '14
Julieta '16

Pippa Grandison (1970-)
Over the Hill '93
Hotel de Love '96

Dorothy Granger (1912-95)
One Body Too Many '44
Killer Dill '47

Farley Granger (1925-2011)
The North Star '43
The Purple Heart '44
Enchantment '48
Rope '48
They Live by Night '49
Side Street '50
Strangers on a Train '51
Behave Yourself! '52
Hans Christian Andersen '52
Small Town Girl '53
The Story of Three Loves '53
Senso '54
The Girl in the Red Velvet Swing '55
Amuck! '71
Sweet Spirits '71
They Call Me Trinity '72
Night Flight from Moscow '73
Death Will Have Your Eyes '74
The Prowler '81
Imagemaker '86
The Next Big Thing '02

Michael Granger (1923-81)
Fort Vengeance '53
Tarzan and the She-Devil '53
Battle of Rogue River '54
Jungle Moon Men '55
Rumble on the Docks '56
Murder by Contract '58

Philip Granger
The Amy Fisher Story '93
Sasquatch '02
The Deal '05
Marker '05
Possessed '05
Long Lost Son '06

Past Sins *'06*
Unthinkable *'07*
Tucker & Dale *vs.* Evil *'10*

Stewart Granger (1913-93)
Convoy *'40*
The Man in Grey *'43*
Thursday's Child *'43*
Love Story *'44*
Madonna of the Seven Moons *'45*
Waterloo Road *'45*
Caesar and Cleopatra *'46*
Caravan *'46*
Captain Boycott *'47*
The Magic Bow *'47*
Blanche Fury *'48*
Man of Evil *'48*
Woman Hater *'49*
King Solomon's Mines *'50*
Prisoner of Zenda *'52*
Scaramouche *'52*
The Wild North *'52*
All the Brothers Were Valiant *'53*
Salome *'53*
Young Bess *'53*
Beau Brummell *'54*
Footsteps in the Fog *'55*
Green Fire *'55*
Moonfleet *'55*
Bhowani Junction *'56*
The Last Hunt *'56*
Gun Glory *'57*
North to Alaska *'60*
Sodom and Gomorrah *'62*
Swordsman of Siena *'62*
The Secret Invasion *'64*
The Crooked Road *'65*
Target for Killing *'66*
Wild Geese *'78*

William Grannel (1929-86)
The Abductors *'72*
Ginger *'72*
Girls Are for Loving *'73*

Greta Granstedt (1907-87)
Hitler: Beast of Berlin *'39*
The Eddie Cantor Story *'53*
Return of Dracula *'58*

Beth Grant (1949-)
Rain Man *'88*
The Dark Half *'91*
Love Field *'91*
White Sands *'92*
Speed *'94*
Lawn Dogs *'96*
Under Oath *'97*
Dance with Me *'98*
Blue Valley Songbird *'99*
Sordid Lives *'00*
Rock Star *'01*
Evil Alien Conquerors *'02*
The Rookie *'02*
Matchstick Men *'03*
Factory Girl *'06*
Hot Tamale *'06*
The House of Usher *'06*
Little Miss Sunshine *'06*
The Perfect Witness *'07*
Welcome to Paradise *'07*
Deadly Shift *'08*
Fragments *'08*
Henry Poole Is Here *'08*
Hide *'08*
Dear Lemon Lima *'09*
Stolen *'09*
The Artist *'11*
Life of Lemon *'11*
Valley of the Sun *'11*

Brea Grant (1981-)
Halloween II *'09*
The Perfect Student *'11*
Beyond the Gates *'16*

Cary Grant (1904-86)
Blonde Venus *'32*
The Devil and the Deep *'32*
Hot Saturday *'32*
Merrily We Go to Hell *'32*
This Is the Night *'32*
Alice in Wonderland *'33*
The Eagle and the Hawk *'33*
I'm No Angel *'33*
She Done Him Wrong *'33*
Kiss and Make Up *'34*
Thirty Day Princess *'34*
The Last Outpost *'35*
Sylvia Scarlett *'35*
Wings in the Dark *'35*
Big Brown Eyes *'36*
Suzy *'36*
Wedding Present *'36*
The Awful Truth *'37*
Toast of New York *'37*
Topper *'37*
Bringing Up Baby *'38*
Holiday *'38*
Gunga Din *'39*
In Name Only *'39*
Only Angels Have Wings *'39*
His Girl Friday *'40*
The Howards of Virginia *'40*
My Favorite Wife *'40*
The Philadelphia Story *'40*
Penny Serenade *'41*
Suspicion *'41*
Once Upon a Honeymoon *'42*
Talk of the Town *'42*
Destination Tokyo *'43*
Mr. Lucky *'43*
Arsenic and Old Lace *'44*
None But the Lonely Heart *'44*
Night and Day *'46*
Notorious *'46*
Without Reservations *'46 (C)*
The Bachelor and the Bobby-Soxer *'47*
The Bishop's Wife *'47*
Every Girl Should Be Married *'48*
Mr. Blandings Builds His Dream House *'48*
I Was a Male War Bride *'49*
Crisis *'50*
People Will Talk *'51*
Monkey Business *'52*
Dream Wife *'53*
To Catch a Thief *'55*
An Affair to Remember *'57*
Kiss Them for Me *'57*
The Pride and the Passion *'57*
Houseboat *'58*
Indiscreet *'58*
North by Northwest *'59*
Operation Petticoat *'59*
The Grass Is Greener *'61*
That Touch of Mink *'62*
Charade *'63*
Father Goose *'64*
Walk, Don't Run *'66*

Crystal Grant (1980-)
Teenage Caveman *'01*
Kids in America *'05*

Cy Grant (1919-2010)
Sea Wife *'57*
At the Earth's Core *'76*

David Marshall Grant (1955-)
American Flyers *'85*
Big Town *'87*
Bat 21 *'88*
Air America *'90*
Forever Young *'92*
And the Band Played On *'93 (C)*
Three Wishes *'95*
The Chamber *'96*
The Rock *'96*
The Stepford Wives *'04*
The Devil Wears Prada *'06*

Faye Grant (1957-)
Senior Trip *'81*
V *'83*
Internal Affairs *'90*
Omen 4: The Awakening *'91*
Vibrations *'94*
Drive Me Crazy *'99*
Manna from Heaven *'02*
My Best Friend's Girl *'08*

Hugh Grant (1960-)
Maurice *'87*
The Bengali Night *'88*
The Dawning *'88*
The Lair of the White Worm *'88*
Rowing with the Wind *'88*
White Mischief *'88*
The Lady and the Highwayman *'89*
Impromptu *'90*
The Big Man: Crossing the Line *'91*
Our Sons *'91*
Bitter Moon *'92*
Night Train to Venice *'93*
The Remains of the Day *'93*
An Awfully Big Adventure *'94*
Four Weddings and a Funeral *'94*
Restoration *'94*
Sirens *'94*
The Englishman Who Went up a Hill But Came down a Mountain *'95*
Nine Months *'95*
Sense and Sensibility *'95*
Extreme Measures *'96*
Mickey Blue Eyes *'99*
Notting Hill *'99*
Small Time Crooks *'00*
Bridget Jones's Diary *'01*
About a Boy *'02*
Two Weeks Notice *'02*
Love Actually *'03*
Bridget Jones: The Edge of Reason *'04*
American Dreamz *'06*
Music & Lyrics *'07*
Did You Hear About the Morgans? *'09*
Cloud Atlas *'12*
The Pirates! Band of Misfits *'12 (V)*
The Man from U.N.C.L.E. *'15*
The Rewrite *'15*
Florence Foster Jenkins *'16*
Paddington 2 *'17*

James Grant (1936-)
Prick Up Your Ears *'87*
The Innocent *'93*

Kathryn Grant (1933-)
Cell 2455, Death Row *'55*
The Phenix City Story *'55*
The Phenix City Story *'55*
The Brothers Rico *'57*
Operation Mad Ball *'57*
The Seventh Voyage of Sinbad *'58*
Anatomy of a Murder *'59*
The Big Circus *'59*
1001 Arabian Nights *'59 (V)*

Kirby Grant (1914-85)
In Society *'44*
Comin' Round the Mountain *'51*

Lawrence Grant (1870-1952)
The Mask of Fu Manchu *'32*
Shanghai Express *'32*
Speak Easily *'32*
Werewolf of London *'35*
S.O.S. Coast Guard *'37*
Son of Frankenstein *'39*

Lee Grant (1927-)
Detective Story *'51*
Middle of the Night *'59*
The Balcony *'63*
Divorce American Style *'67*
In the Heat of the Night *'67*
Valley of the Dolls *'67*
The Big Bounce *'69*
Marooned *'69*
The Landlord *'70*
There Was a Crooked Man *'70*
Plaza Suite *'71*
Internecine Project *'73*
The Seagull *'75*
Shampoo *'75*
Voyage of the Damned *'76*
Airport '77 *'77*
The Spell *'77*
Damien: Omen 2 *'78*
My Sister, My Love *'78*
The Swarm *'78*
Backstairs at the White House *'79*
Little Miss Marker *'80*
Charlie Chan and the Curse of the Dragon Queen *'81*
Visiting Hours *'82*
Teachers *'84*
Big Town *'87*
A Billion for Boris *'90*
Defending Your Life *'91*
Citizen Cohn *'92*
It's My Party *'95*
Dr. T & the Women *'00*
Mulholland Drive *'01*
Going Shopping *'05*

Leon Grant
Beat Street *'84*
Playing for Keeps *'86*

Rachel Grant (1977-)
The Purifiers *'04*
Brotherhood of Blood *'08*

Richard E. Grant (1957-)
Withnail and I *'87*
How to Get Ahead in Advertising *'89*
Henry & June *'90*
Mountains of the Moon *'90*
Hudson Hawk *'91*
L.A. Story *'91*
Warlock *'91*
Bram Stoker's Dracula *'92*
The Player *'92*
The Age of Innocence *'93*
Ready to Wear *'94*
Jack and Sarah *'95*
Portrait of a Lady *'96*
Twelfth Night *'96*
A Merry War *'97*
The Serpent's Kiss *'97*
Spice World: The Movie *'97*
St. Ives *'98*
A Christmas Carol *'99*
The Scarlet Pimpernel *'99*
The Scarlet Pimpernel 2: Mademoiselle Guillotine *'99*
The Scarlet Pimpernel 3: The Kidnapped King *'99*
The Little Vampire *'00*
The Miracle Maker: The Story of Jesus *'00 (V)*
Gosford Park *'01*
Strictly Sinatra *'01 (C)*
The Hound of the Baskervilles *'02*
Sherlock: Case of Evil *'02*
Bright Young Things *'03*
Monsieur N. *'03*
The Story of an African Farm *'04*
Color Me Kubrick *'05*
Tim Burton's Corpse Bride *'05 (V)*
Above and Beyond *'06*
Garfield: A Tail of Two Kitties *'06 (V)*
Penelope *'06*
Filth and Wisdom *'08*
Hemingway's Garden of Eden *'08*
Love Hurts *'09*
Angel in the House *'11*
The Iron Lady *'11*
The Crimson Petal and the White *'12*
Dom Hemingway *'13*
Queen and Country *'14*
The Hitman's Bodyguard *'17*

Rodney A. Grant (1959-)
Dances with Wolves *'90*
Geronimo: An American Legend *'93*
The Last Ride *'94*
Wagons East *'94*
The Substitute *'96*
The Killing Grounds *'97*
Two for Texas *'97*
White Wolves 3: Cry of the White Wolf *'98*
The Jack Bull *'99*
Wild Wild West *'99*
Don't Come Knocking *'05*

Salim Grant (1977-)
The Hitman *'91*
What About Your Friends: Weekend Getaway *'02*

Schuyler Grant (1970-)
Anne of Green Gables *'85*
Anne of Avonlea *'87*
Wrestling with Alligators *'98*
Anne of Green Gables: The Continuing Story *'99*

Shelby Grant (1936-2011)
Fantastic Voyage *'66*
Our Man Flint *'66*
The Witchmaker *'69*

Stacy Grant
The Fear: Halloween Night *'99*
One Special Night *'99*
Safe Harbor *'06*
A Trick of the Mind *'06*

Teach Grant (1973-)
Lost in the Dark *'07*
Nightmare *'07*
Goodnight for Justice: The Measure of a Man *'12*

Ryan Grantham (1998-)
Ice Quake *'10*
Marley & Me: The Puppy Years *'11 (V)*
Barricade *'12*

Gyton Grantley (1980-)
Beneath Hill 60 *'10*
The Reef *'10*

Bonita Granville (1923-88)
Call It a Day *'37*
It's Love I'm After *'37*
Maid of Salem *'37*
Quality Street *'37*
Hard to Get *'38*
Merrily We Live *'38*
Nancy Drew-Detective *'38*
Angels Wash Their Faces *'39*
Nancy Drew, Reporter *'39*
Nancy Drew-Trouble Shooter *'39*
Escape *'40*
Gallant Sons *'40*
The Mortal Storm *'40*
Third Finger, Left Hand *'40*
H.M. Pulham Esquire *'41*
The People *vs.* Dr. Kildare *'41*
The Glass Key *'42*
Now, Voyager *'42*
Syncopation *'42*
Andy Hardy's Blonde Trouble *'44*
Breakfast in Hollywood *'46*
Love Laughs at Andy Hardy *'46*
Suspense *'46*
Guilty of Treason *'50*
Lone Ranger *'56*

Charley Grapewin (1869-1956)
Hell's House *'32*
Heroes for Sale *'33*
Pilgrimage *'33*
Torch Singer *'33*
Anne of Green Gables *'34*
The Quitter *'34*
Ah, Wilderness! *'35*
Alice Adams *'35*
One Frightened Night *'35*
Rendezvous *'35*
Libeled Lady *'36*
Petrified Forest *'36*
Big City *'37*
Captains Courageous *'37*
A Family Affair *'37*
The Good Earth *'37*
Artists and Models Abroad *'38*
Of Human Hearts *'38*
Shopworn Angel *'38*
Three Comrades *'38*
Three Loves Has Nancy *'38*
The Wizard of Oz *'39*
The Grapes of Wrath *'40*
Johnny Apollo *'40*
Rhythm on the River *'40*
They Died with Their Boots On *'41*
Tobacco Road *'41*
Atlantic City *'44*
The Impatient Years *'44*

Karen Grassle (1942-)
Little House on the Prairie *'74*
Cocaine: One Man's Seduction *'83*
Harry's War *'84*
Between the Darkness and the Dawn *'85*
Wyatt Earp *'94*

Bill Gratton
Syngenor *'90*
Devil in the Flesh 2 *'00*

Ona Grauer (1975-)
House of the Dead *'03*
Deep Evil *'04*
Lost Behind Bars *'06*
Seattle Superstorm *'12*

Ernest Graves (1919-83)
One Plus One *'61*
Hercules in New York *'70*

Peter Graves (1911-94)
Miss London Ltd. *'43*
Bees in Paradise *'44*
Give Us the Moon *'44*
Spring in Park Lane *'48*
Derby Day *'52*
Encore *'52*
War Paint *'53*
Canyon River *'56*
The Admirable Crichton *'57*
Krakatoa East of Java *'69*
The Magic Christian *'69*
The Adventurers *'70*

Peter Graves (1925-2010)
Fort Defiance *'51*
Red Planet Mars *'52*
Beneath the 12-Mile Reef *'53*
Stalag 17 *'53*
Killers from Space *'54*
The Court Martial of Billy Mitchell *'55*
Fort Yuma *'55*
Let's Make Up *'55*
The Night of the Hunter *'55*
Robbers' Roost *'55*
Beginning of the End *'57*
Death in Small Doses *'57*
A Rage to Live *'65*
Texas Across the River *'66*
The Ballad of Josie *'67*
The Five Man Army *'69*
Scream of the Wolf *'74*
Where Have All the People Gone? *'74*
The Slipper and the Rose *'76*
The Clonus Horror *'79*
Spree *'79*
Airplane! *'80*
Airplane 2: The Sequel *'82*
Savannah Smiles *'82*
The Winds of War *'83*
Mad Mission 3 *'84*
Number One with a Bullet *'87*
These Old Broads *'01*
Men in Black 2 *'02 (C)*

Ralph Graves (1900-77)
The Greatest Question *'19*
Dream Street *'21*
Extra Girl *'23*
That Certain Thing *'28*
The Flying Fleet *'29*
Ladies of Leisure *'30*
Huddle *'32*

Rupert Graves (1963-)
A Room with a View *'86*
Fortunes of War *'87*
Maurice *'87*
A Handful of Dust *'88*
The Plot to Kill Hitler *'90*
Where Angels Fear to Tread *'91*
Damage *'92*
The Madness of King George *'94*
The Innocent Sleep *'95*
Different for Girls *'96*
The Tenant of Wildfell Hall *'96*
Bent *'97 (C)*
Mrs. Dalloway *'97*
Sweet Revenge *'98*
Cleopatra *'99*
Dreaming of Joseph Lees *'99*
All My Loved Ones *'00*
Extreme Ops *'02*
A Waste of Shame *'05*
V for Vendetta *'06*

Clapham Junction '07
Death at a Funeral '07
The Waiting Room '07
God on Trial '08
Secret State '12

Teresa Graves (1949-2002)
That Man Bolt '73
Black Eye '74
Get Christie Love! '74

Fernand Gravey (1905-70)
Bitter Sweet '33
The Great Waltz '38
The Fantastic Night '42
La Ronde '51
How to Steal a Million '66
The Madwoman of Chaillot '69

Carla Gravina (1941-)
Alfredo, Alfredo '72
And Now My Love '74

Cesare Gravina (1858-1954)
Foolish Wives '22
Merry-Go-Round '23
The Family Secret '24

Claudia Gravy
Byleth: The Demon of Incest '72
Kilma, Queen of the Amazons '75

Billy Gray (1938-)
Father Is a Bachelor '50
The Day the Earth Stood Still '51
On Moonlight Bay '51
By the Light of the Silvery Moon '53
The Girl Next Door '53
The Explosive Generation '61
Two for the Seesaw '62
Werewolves on Wheels '71

Bruce Gray (1936-)
Odd Birds '85
Dangerous Evidence: The Lori Jackson Story '99
The Last Debate '00
A Killing Spring '02
My Big Fat Greek Wedding '02
Dark Waters '03
Chasing Freedom '04

Charles Gray (1928-2000)
Night of the Generals '67
You Only Live Twice '67
The Devil Rides Out '68
The Man Outside '68
The File of the Golden Goose '69
Nine Ages of Nakedness '69 *(N)*
The Executioner '70
Mosquito Squadron '70
Diamonds Are Forever '71
Murder on the Midnight Express '74
The Beast Must Die '75
The Rocky Horror Picture Show '75
The Seven-Per-Cent Solution '76
The House on Garibaldi Street '79
The Mirror Crack'd '80
Shock Treatment '81
Dreams Lost, Dreams Found '87
Mr. & Mrs. Loving '96

Coleen Gray (1922-)
Kiss of Death '47
Nightmare Alley '47
Red River '48
Father Is a Bachelor '50
Riding High '50
Kansas City Confidential '52
Death of a Scoundrel '56
The Killing '56
The Leech Woman '59
The Phantom Planet '61

David Barry Gray
Cops and Robbersons '94
S.F.W. '94
Lawn Dogs '96

Dolores Gray (1924-2002)
Kismet '55
The Opposite Sex '56
Designing Woman '57

Donald Gray (1914-78)
The Four Feathers '39
Island of Desire '52
Satellite in the Sky '56

Dorian Gray (1936-2011)
Il Grido '57
Nights of Cabiria '57
Colossus and the Amazon Queen '60

Dulcie Gray (1919-2011)
A Man About the House '47
Mine Own Executioner '47
The Glass Mountain '49
Angels One Five '54

Elspet Gray (1929-)
The Girl in a Swing '89
Catherine Cookson's The Wingless Bird '97

Erin Gray (1950-)
Buck Rogers in the 25th Century '79
Six Pack '82
Jason Goes to Hell: The Final Friday '93
A Dangerous Place '94
T-Force '94
Ghouls '07
Nuclear Hurricane '07
Loaded '08

Eve Gray (1900-83)
Night Birds '31
Death on the Set '35

Gary Gray (1936-2006)
Father Is a Bachelor '50
The Next Voice You Hear '50
Two Weeks with Love '50
The Painted Hills '51

Gary LeRoi Gray (1985-)
Slappy and the Stinkers '97
Noah's Arc: Jumping the Broom '08

Gilda Gray (1901-59)
Piccadilly '29
The Great Ziegfeld '36

Jason S. Gray (1977-)
The Da Vinci Treasure '06
AVH: Alien vs. Hunter '07
Universal Soldiers '07

Lawrence Gray (1898-1970)
The Patsy '28
It's a Great Life '29
Going Wild '30
Sunny '30
Man of the World '31
The Old Homestead '35
A Face in the Fog '36

Linda Gray (1940-)
The Two Worlds of Jenny Logan '79
Haywire '80
Kenny Rogers as the Gambler, Part 3: The Legend Continues '87
A Very Mary Christmas '10

Lorna Gray (1917-)
See Adrian Booth

MacKenzie Gray (1957-)
Strip Search '97
My Teacher Ate My Homework '98
Voyage of the Unicorn '00
Storm Seekers '08

Macy Gray (1967-)
Training Day '01
Scary Movie 3 '03 *(C)*
Around the World in 80 Days '04
The Crow: Wicked Prayer '05
Domino '05
Idlewild '06
Shadowboxer '06
For Colored Girls '10
The Paperboy '12
Percentage '13

Where Children Play '15
Cardboard Boxer '16

Nadia Gray (1923-94)
The Captain's Table '60
La Dolce Vita '60
Maniac '63
The Crooked Road '65
Two for the Road '67

Pamela Gray
Commandments '96
Dogs: The Rise and Fall of an All-Girl Bookie Joint '96
The Devil's Advocate '97
Corn '04

Sally Gray (1916-2006)
The Saint in London '39
They Made Me a Fugitive '47
The Hidden Room '49
Obsession '49
I'll Get You '53
Keeper '76

Sam Gray (1923-)
Christmas Evil '80
Wolfen '81
Heart '87
Burnzy's Last Call '95

Spalding Gray (1941-2004)
Hard Choices '84
The Killing Fields '84
Almost You '85
True Stories '86
Swimming to Cambodia '87
Beaches '88
Clara's Heart '88
Heavy Petting '89
The Image '89
Our Town '89
Monster in a Box '92
Straight Talk '92
The Pickle '93 *(C)*
Twenty Bucks '93
Bad Company '94
The Paper '94
Beyond Rangoon '95
Bliss '96
Diabolique '96
Drunks '96
Glory Daze '96
Gray's Anatomy '96
Coming Soon '99
How High '01
Kate & Leopold '01
Revolution #9 '01
And Everything Is Going Fine '10

Vivean Gray (1924-)
Picnic at Hanging Rock '75
The Last Wave '77

Jason Gray-Stanford (1970-)
Lost in the Dark '07
Lucky Christmas '11
Earth to Echo '14

Sprague Grayden (1980-)
The Last Lullaby '08
Paranormal Activity 2 '10
Paranormal Activity 3 '11

Devon Graye (1987-)
Scar '07
Call of the Wild 3D '09
Legendary '10
Red Faction: Origins '11
13 Sins '13
Last Weekend '14
I Don't Feel at Home in This World Anymore '17

Steven Grayhm (1981-)
Unthinkable '07
The Boy Who Cried Werewolf '10
Wyatt Earp's Revenge '12

Ari Graynor (1983-)
Book of Love '04
Game 6 '05
The Great New Wonderful '06
Blues '08
Nick & Norah's Infinite Playlist '08
Whip It '09
Conviction '10
Holy Rollers '10

Youth in Revolt '10
Lucky '11
The Sitter '11
For a Good Time, Call... '12
10 Years '12
The Disaster Artist '17

Denise Grayson
Corn '04
Though None Go With Me '06

Kathryn Grayson (1922-2010)
Andy Hardy's Private Secretary '41
The Vanishing Virginian '41
Rio Rita '42
Seven Sweethearts '42
Thousands Cheer '43
Anchors Aweigh '45
Till the Clouds Roll By '46
Two Sisters From Boston '46
It Happened in Brooklyn '47
The Kissing Bandit '48
That Midnight Kiss '49
The Toast of New Orleans '50
Show Boat '51
Lovely to Look At '52
The Desert Song '53
Kiss Me Kate '53
So This Is Love '53

Agnese Graziani
The Wonders '15
Happy as Lazzaro '18

Nicholas Greaves
Incendiary '08
Murderland '09

Jose Greci (1941-)
Hercules Against the Mongols '63
Espionage in Tangiers '65

Jessica Greco
Treed Murray '01
Milton's Secret '16

Jose Greco (1918-2000)
Goliath and the Sins of Babylon '64
Ship of Fools '65

Juliette Greco (1927-)
Orpheus '49
The Green Glove '52
Elena and Her Men '56
The Sun Also Rises '57

Alice Greczyn (1986-)
The Dukes of Hazzard '05
Shrooms '07

Adolph Green (1915-2002)
Simon '80
My Favorite Year '82
Lily in Love '85
I Want to Go Home '89

Al Green (1946-)
Beverly Hills Cop 3 '94
On the Line '01

Anthony Green (1970-)
The Scarlet Pimpernel '99
The Scarlet Pimpernel 2: Mademoiselle Guillotine '99
The Scarlet Pimpernel 3: The Kidnapped King '99
Blackbeard '06
Anaconda 3: The Offspring '08

Brian Austin Green (1973-)
An American Summer '90
Cock & Bull Story '03
Fish Without a Bicycle '03
Domino '05
Impact Point '08
ChromeSkull: Laid to Rest 2 '11
Cross '11

Brian Lane Green (1962-)
Friends and Family '01
Circuit '02

Calvin Green
Exotica '94
Zombie Strippers '08

Danny Green (1903-73)
Non-Stop New York '37
The Ladykillers '55
The Seventh Voyage of Sinbad '58

Eva Green (1980-)
The Dreamers '03
Kingdom of Heaven '05
Casino Royale '06
The Golden Compass '07
Franklyn '08
Cracks '09
Womb '10
Perfect Sense '11
Dark Shadows '12
300: Rise of an Empire '13
The Salvation '14
Sin City: A Dame to Kill For '14
White Bird in a Blizzard '14
Miss Peregrine's Home for Peculiar Children '16
Dumbo '19
Euphoria '19

Harry Green (1892-1958)
Be Yourself '30
The Light of Western Stars '30
A King in New York '57

Janet-Laine Green (1951-)
Bullies '86
Cowboys Don't Cry '88
Anne of Green Gables: The Continuing Story '99
I Me Wed '07
My Gal Sunday '14
Born to Be Blue '15

Jordan-Claire Green (1991-)
School of Rock '03
The Twelve Dogs of Christmas '05

Kerri Green (1967-)
The Goonies '85
Summer Rental '85
Lucas '86
Blue Flame '93

Marika Green
Pickpocket '59
Emmanuelle '74

Martyn Green (1899-1975)
A Lovely Way to Die '68
The Iceman Cometh '73

Mitzie Green (1920-69)
Girl Crazy '32
Bloodhounds of Broadway '52
Lost in Alaska '52

Nigel Green (1924-72)
Reach for the Sky '56
Corridors of Blood '58
Beat Girl '60
Sword of Sherwood Forest '60
Mysterious Island '61
Pit of Darkness '61
Jason and the Argonauts '63
Zulu '64
The Face of Fu Manchu '65
The Ipcress File '65
Masque of the Red Death '65
The Skull '65
Khartoum '66
Tobruk '66
Africa Texas Style '67
Deadlier Than the Male '67
The Wrecking Crew '68
The Kremlin Letter '70
The Ruling Class '72

Robson Green (1964-)
Reckless '97
Touching Evil '97
Catherine Cookson's The Gambling Man '98
Reckless: The Sequel '98
The Last Musketeer '00
Take Me '01
Me & Mrs. Jones '02
Like Father Like Son '05
Little Devil '07
Joe Maddison's War '10

Scott Green
Last Days '05
Paranoid Park '07

Seth Green (1974-)
The Hotel New Hampshire '84
Can't Buy Me Love '87
Radio Days '87
My Stepmother Is an Alien '88
Airborne '93
Arcade '93
Austin Powers: International Man of Mystery '97
Can't Hardly Wait '98
Enemy of the State '98
Stonebrook '98
Austin Powers 2: The Spy Who Shagged Me '99
Idle Hands '99
America's Sweethearts '01
The Attic Expeditions '01
Josie and the Pussycats '01 *(C)*
Knockaround Guys '01
Rat Race '01
The Trumpet of the Swan '01 *(V)*
Austin Powers In Goldmember '02
The Italian Job '03
Party Monster '03
Scooby-Doo 2: Monsters Unleashed '04
Without a Paddle '04
Sex Drive '08
Old Dogs '09
Mars Needs Moms '11 *(V)*
Sexy Evil Genius '13
The Identical '14
Holidays '16
Dear Dictator '18

Tom Green (1971-)
Charlie's Angels '00
Road Trip '00
Freddy Got Fingered '01
Stealing Harvard '02
Bob the Butler '05
Freezer Burn: The Invasion of Laxdale '08
Legacy '08

Vince Green
Save the Last Dance '01
Of Boys and Men '08

Bryan Greenberg (1978-)
Prime '05
Love and Debate '06
Nobel Son '08
Bride Wars '09
The Good Guy '10
Friends With Benefits '11
The Kitchen '12
A Short History of Decay '13
Vice '15

Shon Greenblatt
Freddy's Dead: The Final Nightmare '91
There Goes My Baby '92

William Greenblatt (1987-)
The Abduction '96
Homecoming '96

Ashley Greene (1987-)
Twilight '08
Summer's Moon '09
The Twilight Saga: New Moon '09
Skateland '10
The Twilight Saga: Eclipse '10
The Twilight Saga: Breaking Dawn, Part 1 '11
A Warrior's Heart '11
The Apparition '12
Butter '12
LOL '12
The Twilight Saga: Breaking Dawn, Part 2 '12
CBGB '13
Burying the Ex '15
Urge '16

Billoah Greene
Levity '03
Preaching to the Choir '05

Mary Gregory
Sleeper *'73*
Coming Home *'78*
Michael Gregory (1944-)
Beach Patrol *'79*
Zero Tolerance *'93*
Spider's Web *'01*
Retribution Road *'07*
Natalie Gregory (1975-)
Alice in Wonderland *'85*
Oliver & Company *'88 (V)*
Nick Gregory
Happy Hell Night *'92*
Last Summer In the Hamptons *'96*
Paul Gregory (1904-42)
Whoopee! *'30*
Sit Tight *'31*
Sebastian Gregory
See Anthony (Tony) Vorno
Sebastian Gregory (1990-)
Acolytes *'08*
Return to Nim's Island *'13*
Joan Gregson
Sea People *'00*
Grindstone Road *'07*
John Gregson (1919-75)
The Lavender Hill Mob *'51*
Genevieve *'53*
Angels One Five *'54*
Above Us the Waves *'55*
Value for Money *'55*
Sea of Sand *'58*
The Captain's Table *'60*
S.O.S. Pacific *'60*
The Frightened City *'61*
The Secret of Monte Cristo *'61*
Night of the Generals *'67*
Hans Brinker *'69*
Fright *'71*
Stephen Greif (1944-)
Casanova *'05*
Eichmann *'07*
Robert Greig (1879-1958)
Animal Crackers *'30*
Tonight or Never *'31*
The Tenderfoot *'32*
Trouble in Paradise *'32*
Beauty and the Boss *'33*
Folies Bergere de Paris *'35*
Devil Doll *'36*
The Great Ziegfeld *'36*
Sullivan's Travels *'41*
Tamsin Greig (1966-)
The Diary of Anne Frank *'08*
Going Postal *'10*
Tamara Drewe *'10*
Breaking the Bank *'14*
Kim Greist (1958-)
C.H.U.D. *'84*
Brazil *'85*
Manhunter *'86*
Throw Momma from the Train *'87*
Punchline *'88*
Homeward Bound: The Incredible Journey *'93*
Houseguest *'94*
Roswell: The U.F.O. Cover-Up *'94*
Homeward Bound 2: Lost in San Francisco *'96*
Zoe *'01*
Joyce Grenfell (1910-79)
The Belles of St. Trinian's *'53*
Genevieve *'53*
Blue Murder at St. Trinian's *'56*
The Pure Hell of St. Trinian's *'61*
The Americanization of Emily *'64*
The Yellow Rolls Royce *'64*
Adrian Grenier (1976-)
The Adventures of Sebastian Cole *'99*
Drive Me Crazy *'99*
Cecil B. Demented *'00*
A. I.: Artificial Intelligence *'01*
Harvard Man *'01*
Hart's War *'02*
Love in the Time of Money *'02*
Anything Else *'03*
The Devil Wears Prada *'06*
Tony n' Tina's Wedding *'07*
Goodbye World *'14*
Entourage *'15*
Marauders *'16*
Trash Fire *'16*
Arsenal *'17*
Zach Grenier (1954-)
Donnie Brasco *'96*
Maximum Risk *'96*
Twister *'96*
Ride with the Devil *'99*
Chasing Sleep *'00*
Shaft *'00*
Swordfish *'01*
Pulse *'06*
Rescue Dawn *'06*
Zodiac *'07*
Macha Grenon (1968-)
The Pianist *'91*
Sworn Enemies *'96*
Dead Awake *'01*
Familia *'05*
The Secret *'07*
The Year Dolly Parton Was My Mom *'11*
Googy Gress
First Turn On *'83*
Promised Land *'88*
Vibes *'88*
Bloodhounds of Broadway *'89*
The Morgue *'07*
Joel Gretsch (1963-)
The Legend of Bagger Vance *'00*
The Emperor's Club *'02*
Taken *'02*
Glass House: The Good Mother *'06*
National Treasure: Book of Secrets *'07*
Saving Grace B. Jones *'09*
Of Two Minds *'12*
Zodiac: Signs of the Apocalypse *'14*
Laurent Grevill (1961-)
Camille Claudel *'89*
I Can't Sleep *'93*
Look at Me *'04*
I've Loved You So Long *'08*
Kevin Grevioux
Slayer *'06*
Underworld: Rise of the Lycans *'09*
Denise Grey (1896-1996)
Devil in the Flesh *'46*
Carve Her Name with Pride *'58*
La Boum *'81*
Jennifer Grey (1960-)
The Cotton Club *'84*
Reckless *'84*
Red Dawn *'84*
American Flyers *'85*
Ferris Bueller's Day Off *'86*
Dirty Dancing *'87*
Bloodhounds of Broadway *'89*
Wind *'92*
Portraits of a Killer *'95*
Since You've Been Gone *'97 (C)*
Outrage *'98*
Red Meat *'98*
Bounce *'00*
Tales from the Crypt Presents Ritual *'02*
Keith *'08*
The Bling Ring *'11*
In Your Eyes *'14*
Joel Grey (1932-)
Come September *'61*
Cabaret *'72*
Man on a Swing *'74*
Buffalo Bill & the Indians *'76*
The Seven-Per-Cent Solution *'76*
Remo Williams: The Adventure Begins *'85*
Queenie *'87*
The Player *'92*
The Music of Chance *'93*
The Fantasticks *'95*
A Christmas Carol *'99*
Dancer in the Dark *'99*
The Empty Mirror *'99*
Nan Grey (1918-93)
Dracula's Daughter *'36*
Three Smart Girls *'36*
The Black Doll *'38*
Danger on the Air *'38*
Three Smart Girls Grow Up *'39*
The Tower of London *'39*
The House of the Seven Gables *'40*
The Invisible Man Returns *'40*
Sasha Grey (1988-)
The Girlfriend Experience *'09*
I Melt With You *'11*
Open Windows *'14*
Shirley Grey (1902-81)
Air Eagles *'31*
The Public Defender *'31*
Hurricane Express *'32*
Uptown New York *'32*
Virtue *'32*
The Little Giant *'33*
Bombay Mail *'34*
Green Eyes *'34*
His Greatest Gamble *'34*
Circumstantial Evidence *'35*
Virginia Grey (1917-2004)
Uncle Tom's Cabin *'27*
Another Thin Man *'39*
Broadway Serenade *'39*
The Hardys Ride High *'39*
Hullabaloo *'40*
Big Store *'41*
Whistling in the Dark *'41*
Grand Central Murder *'42*
Tarzan's New York Adventure *'42*
Tish *'42*
Idaho *'43*
House of Horrors *'46*
Swamp Fire *'46*
Unconquered *'47*
Mexican Hayride *'48*
Miraculous Journey *'48*
So This Is New York *'48*
Unknown Island *'48*
Bullfighter & the Lady *'50*
Highway 301 *'50*
Three Desperate Men *'50*
The Fighting Lawman *'53*
All That Heaven Allows *'55*
The Rose Tattoo *'55*
Crime of Passion *'57*
Jeanne Eagels *'57*
Portrait in Black *'60*
Bachelor in Paradise *'61*
Back Street *'61*
Tammy Tell Me True *'61*
Black Zoo *'63*
Naked Kiss *'64*
Love Has Many Faces *'65*
Madame X *'66*
Zena Grey (1988-)
Max Keeble's Big Move *'01*
In Good Company *'04*
The Shaggy Dog *'06*
My Soul to Take *'10*
Michael Greyeyes (1967-)
Geronimo *'93*
Dance Me Outside *'95*
Firestorm *'97*
Stolen Women, Captured Hearts *'97*
True Women *'97*
The Magnificent Seven *'98*
The Minion *'98*
Smoke Signals *'98*
The Lost Child *'00*
Skipped Parts *'00*
Sunshine State *'02*
ZigZag *'02*
The New World *'05*
Passchendaele *'10*
Woman Walks Ahead *'17*
Togo *'19*
Clinton Greyn (1936-)
The Love Machine *'71*
Raid on Rommel *'71*
Eddie Gribbon (1890-1965)
Tell It to the Marines *'26*
The Cyclone Ranger *'35*
Harry Gribbon (1885-1961)
The Cameraman *'28*
You Said a Mouthful *'32*
Lara Grice (1971-)
Legendary *'10*
Wrong Side of Town *'10*
Richard Grieco (1965-)
If Looks Could Kill *'91*
Mobsters *'91*
Rebel Run *'94*
The Demolitionist *'95*
Absolution *'97*
When Time Expires *'97*
Against the Law *'98*
The Apostate *'98*
Blackheart *'98*
A Night at the Roxbury *'98*
Final Payback *'99*
Harold Robbins' Body Parts *'99*
Webs *'03*
Forget About It *'06*
Almighty Thor *'11*
21 Jump Street *'12 (C)*
AE: Apocalypse Earth *'13*
Helmut Griem (1932-2004)
The Damned *'69*
McKenzie Break *'70*
Cabaret *'72*
Ludwig *'72*
The Desert of the Tartars *'76*
Voyage of the Damned *'76*
Les Rendez-vous D'Anna *'78*
Escape *'90*
David Alan Grier (1956-)
A Soldier's Story *'84*
Beer *'85*
Off Limits *'87*
I'm Gonna Git You Sucka *'88*
Almost an Angel *'90*
Loose Cannons *'90*
Boomerang *'92*
The Player *'92*
Blankman *'94*
In the Army Now *'94*
Jumanji *'95*
Tales from the Hood *'95*
McHale's Navy *'97*
Top of the World *'97*
Freeway 2: Confessions of a Trickbaby *'99*
A Saintly Switch *'99*
The '60s *'99*
Stuart Little *'99 (V)*
The Adventures of Rocky & Bullwinkle *'00*
Angels in the Infield *'00*
Return to Me *'00*
Three Strikes *'00*
15 Minutes *'01*
King of Texas *'02*
Baadasssss! *'03*
The Woodsman *'04*
Bewitched *'05*
The Muppets' Wizard of Oz *'05*
Gym Teacher: The Movie *'08*
The Hustle *'08*
Kissing Cousins *'08*
Dance Flick *'09*
The Poker House *'09*
Peeples *'13*
Pam Grier (1949-)
Beyond the Valley of the Dolls *'70*
The Big Doll House *'71*
The Big Bird Cage *'72*
Cool Breeze *'72*
Hit Man *'72*
Twilight People *'72*
The Arena *'73*
Coffy *'73*
Scream Blacula Scream *'73*
Foxy Brown *'74*
Bucktown *'75*
Friday Foster *'75*
Sheba, Baby *'75*
Drum *'76*
Greased Lightning *'77*
Fort Apache, the Bronx *'81*
Something Wicked This Way Comes *'83*
Tough Enough *'83*
On the Edge *'86*
Above the Law *'88*
The Package *'89*
Class of 1999 *'90*
Bill & Ted's Bogus Journey *'91*
Posse *'93 (C)*
Serial Killer *'95*
Escape from L.A. *'96*
Mars Attacks! *'96*
Original Gangstas *'96*
Jackie Brown *'97*
Strip Search *'97*
Woo *'97*
Jawbreaker *'98*
Fortress 2: Re-Entry *'99*
Holy Smoke *'99*
In Too Deep *'99*
No Tomorrow *'99*
Snow Day *'00*
Wilder *'00*
Anne Rice's The Feast of All Saints *'01*
Bones *'01*
John Carpenter's Ghosts of Mars *'01*
Love the Hard Way *'01*
3 A.M. *'01*
The Adventures of Pluto Nash *'02*
Back in the Day *'05*
Ladies of the House *'08*
Just Wright *'10*
Larry Crowne *'11*
Mafia *'11*
Roosevelt 'Rosie' Grier (1932-)
Black Brigade *'69*
The Desperate Mission *'69*
Skyjacked *'72*
The Thing with Two Heads *'72*
The Treasure of Jamaica Reef *'74*
The Big Push *'75*
The Glove *'78*
Jon(athan) Gries (1957-)
Will Penny *'67*
More American Graffiti *'79*
Joy Sticks *'83*
Real Genius *'85*
Number One with a Bullet *'87*
Fright Night 2 *'88*
Kill Me Again *'89*
Fever *'91*
Casualties *'97*
Twin Falls Idaho *'99*
The Beatnicks *'00*
Jackpot *'01*
Northfork *'03*
The Rundown *'03*
The Snow Walker *'03*
The Big Empty *'04*
Napoleon Dynamite *'04*
Car Babes *'06*
The Sasquatch Gang *'06*
Stick It *'06*
The Astronaut Farmer *'07*
The Comebacks *'07*
Frank *'07*
September Dawn *'07*
Around June *'08*
Taken *'08*
Crazy on the Outside *'10*
Good Intentions *'10*
5 Time Champion *'11*
Natural Selection *'11*
Natural Selection *'12*
Taken 2 *'12*
Bad Turn Worse *'14*
Faults *'15*
Taken 3 *'15*
John Griesemer (1947-)
Where the Rivers Flow North *'94*
Henry Hill *'00*
Joe Grifasi (1944-)
The Deer Hunter *'78*
On the Yard *'79*
Honky Tonk Freeway *'81*
Still of the Night *'82*
The Pope of Greenwich Village *'84*
Bad Medicine *'85*
Brewster's Millions *'85*
F/X *'86*
Ironweed *'87*
Matewan *'87*
Chances Are *'89*
Perfect Witness *'89*
Presumed Innocent *'90*
City of Hope *'91*
Benny & Joon *'93*
Heavy *'94*
Naked Gun 33 1/3: The Final Insult *'94*
Batman Forever *'95*
Money Train *'95*
One Fine Day *'96*
Steve Martini's Undue Influence *'96*
Sunday *'96*
Two Bits *'96*
Looking for an Echo *'99*
61* *'01*
Bought and Sold *'03*
13 Going on 30 *'04*
A Crime *'06*
The Last New Yorker *'07*
Patricia Cornwell's The Front *'10*
Simone Griffeth (1950-)
Sixteen *'72*
Death Race 2000 *'75*
The Patriot *'86*
Ethel Griffies (1878-1975)
Old English *'30*
The Mystery of Edwin Drood *'35*
Devotion *'46*
The Birds *'63*
Eddie Griffin (1968-)
The Last Boy Scout *'91*
Deuce Bigalow: Male Gigolo *'99*
Foolish *'99*
The Mod Squad *'99*
Picking Up the Pieces *'99*
Double Take *'01*
John Q *'02*
The New Guy *'02*
Undercover Brother *'02*
Scary Movie 3 *'03*
Blast *'04*
My Baby's Daddy *'04*
Deuce Bigalow: European Gigolo *'05*
Irish Jam *'05*
The Wendell Baker Story *'05*
Who Made the Potatoe Salad? *'05*
Date Movie *'06*
Norbit *'07*
Redline *'07*
Urban Justice *'07*
Beethoven's Big Break *'08*
Going to America *'15*
Josephine Griffin (1928-2005)
The Man Who Never Was *'55*
Postmark for Danger *'56*
The Spanish Gardener *'57*
Kathy Griffin (1960-)
It's Pat: The Movie *'94*
The Cable Guy *'96*
Muppets from Space *'99*
Enemies of Laughter *'00*
Intern *'00*
Beethoven's 5th *'03*
On Edge *'03*
Bachelor Party Vegas *'05*
Dirty Love *'05*
Shrek Forever After *'10 (V)*
Luke Griffin
St. Patrick: The Irish Legend *'00*
Speed Dating *'07*
Lynne Griffin (1952-)
Curtains *'83*
Strange Brew *'83*

Santa Baby *'06*
She Drives Me Crazy *'07*

Merv Griffin (1925-2007)
So This Is Love *'53*
The Boy From Oklahoma *'54*
The Man with Two Brains *'83 (C)*
The Lonely Guy *'84*
Alice in Wonderland *'85*

Nikki Griffin (1978-)
The Dukes of Hazzard *'05*
The Fast and the Furious: Tokyo Drift *'06*

Rhonda Griffin
The Creeps *'97*
Hideous *'97*

Robert E. (Bob) Griffin (1902-60)
Crime of Passion *'57*
Monster from Green Hell *'58*

Tony Griffin (1959-)
Evil Laugh *'86*
Robin Hood: Men in Tights *'93*

Rhoda Griffis (1965-)
Girl, Positive *'07*
Mean Girls 2 *'11*
Teen Spirit *'11*

Andy Griffith (1926-2012)
A Face in the Crowd *'57*
No Time for Sergeants *'58*
Onionhead *'58*
The Second Time Around *'61*
Winter Kill *'74*
Hearts of the West *'75*
Savages *'75*
Deadly Game *'77*
The Girl in the Empty Grave *'77*
Washington: Behind Closed Doors *'77*
Centennial *'78*
Murder in Coweta County *'83*
Return to Mayberry *'85*
Rustler's Rhapsody *'85*
Spy Hard *'96*
Daddy & Them *'99*
Waitress *'07*

Anthony Griffith
Panther *'95*
Tales from the Hood *'95*

Charles B. Griffith (1930-2007)
Atlas *'60*
Hollywood Boulevard *'76*

Corinne Griffith (1894-1979)
The Garden of Eden *'28*
The Divine Lady *'29*

Ernesto Griffith
Breakaway *'02*
Tamara *'05*

Eva Griffith (1962-)
The Turn of the Screw *'74*
Ride a Wild Pony *'75*

Fred Griffith (1964-)
Miracle at Sage Creek *'05*
War of the Worlds 2: The Next Wave *'08*

Gattlin Griffith (1998-)
Changeling *'08*
Blood Done Sign My Name *'10*
The New Daughter *'10*
Labor Day *'13*

Hugh Griffith (1912-80)
Kind Hearts and Coronets *'49*
Beggar's Opera *'54*
The Sleeping Tiger *'54*
Lucky Jim *'58*
Ben-Hur *'59*
The Day They Robbed the Bank of England *'60*
Exodus *'60*
The Counterfeit Traitor *'62*
Lisa *'62*
Mutiny on the Bounty *'62*
Term of Trial *'63*
Tom Jones *'63*
How to Steal a Million *'66*
Oliver! *'68*
Cry of the Banshee *'70*
Start the Revolution without Me *'70*
Wuthering Heights *'70*
The Abominable Dr. Phibes *'71*
The Canterbury Tales *'71*
Who Slew Auntie Roo? *'71*
Doctor Phibes Rises Again *'72*
The Final Programme *'73*
Craze *'74*
Luther *'74*
The Big Scam *'79*

James J. Griffith (1916-93)
Eight Iron Men *'52*
No Escape *'53*
Rebel in Town *'56*
Tribute to a Bad Man *'56*
Man From God's Country *'58*
Advance to the Rear *'64*

Kenneth Griffith (1921-2006)
Track the Man Down *'55*
1984 *'56*
Lucky Jim *'58*
A Night to Remember *'58*
Tiger Bay *'59*
Circus of Horrors *'60*
The Frightened City *'61*
The Assassination Bureau *'69*
Revenge *'71*
Sea Wolves *'81*
Four Weddings and a Funeral *'94*
The Englishman Who Went up a Hill But Came down a Mountain *'95*

Kristin Griffith
Interiors *'78*
The Long Way Home *'98*

Melanie Griffith (1957-)
Harrad Experiment *'73*
The Drowning Pool *'75*
Night Moves *'75*
Smile *'75*
Once an Eagle *'76*
Joyride *'77*
One on One *'77*
Body Double *'84*
Fear City *'85*
Something Wild *'86*
Cherry 2000 *'88*
The Milagro Beanfield War *'88*
Stormy Monday *'88*
Working Girl *'88*
The Bonfire of the Vanities *'90*
Pacific Heights *'90*
Women & Men: Stories of Seduction *'90*
Paradise *'91*
Shining Through *'92*
A Stranger Among Us *'92*
Born Yesterday *'93*
Milk Money *'94*
Nobody's Fool *'94*
Buffalo Girls *'95*
Mulholland Falls *'95*
Now and Then *'95*
Two Much *'96*
Lolita *'97*
Another Day in Paradise *'98*
Celebrity *'98*
Shadow of Doubt *'98*
Crazy in Alabama *'99*
RKO 281 *'99*
Along for the Ride *'00*
Cecil B. Demented *'00*
Tart *'01*
Stuart Little 2 *'02 (V)*
The Night We Called It a Day *'03*
Shade *'03*
Tempo *'03*
The Pirates of Somalia *'17*

Raymond Griffith (1894-1937)
White Tiger *'23*
Paths to Paradise *'25*
All Quiet on the Western Front *'30*

Thomas Ian Griffith (1962-)
The Karate Kid: Part 3 *'89*
Excessive Force *'93*
Hollow Point *'95*
Behind Enemy Lines *'96*
John Carpenter's Vampires *'97*
Kull the Conqueror *'97*
Avalanche *'99*
Final Encounter *'00*
Black Point *'01*
Timecop 2: The Berlin Decision *'03*
Sea Wolf: The Pirate's Curse *'05*

Tom Griffith (1945-)
The Alien Factor *'78*
Night Beast *'83*

Tracy Griffith (1965-)
The Good Mother *'88*
Fast Food *'89*
The First Power *'89*
Sleepaway Camp 3: Teenage Wasteland *'89*
The Finest Hour *'91*
All Tied Up *'92*
Skeeter *'93*

Jane Griffiths (1929-75)
The Accursed *'57*
Tread Softly Stranger *'58*

Lucy Griffiths
Collision *'09*
Uncanny *'15*

Michael Griffiths
Living in Oblivion *'94*
Timeless *'96*

Rachel Griffiths (1968-)
Muriel's Wedding *'94*
Children of the Revolution *'95*
Cosi *'95*
Jude *'96*
My Best Friend's Wedding *'97*
My Son the Fanatic *'97*
Welcome to Woop Woop *'97*
Among Giants *'98*
Hilary and Jackie *'98*
Me Myself I *'99*
Blow Dry *'00*
Very Annie Mary *'00*
Blow *'01*
The Hard Word *'02*
The Rookie *'02*
After the Deluge *'03*
Ned Kelly *'03*
Angel Rodriguez *'05*
Step Up *'06*
Comanche Moon *'08*
Beautiful Kate *'09*
Burning Man *'11*
Underground: The Julian Assange Story *'12*
Patrick *'13*
Saving Mr. Banks *'13*

Richard Griffiths (1947-2013)
A Private Function *'84*
Shanghai Surprise *'86*
Withnail and I *'87*
Naked Gun 2 1/2: The Smell of Fear *'91*
Blame It on the Bellboy *'92*
Guarding Tess *'94*
Sleepy Hollow *'99*
Vatel *'00*
Harry Potter and the Sorcerer's Stone *'01*
Harry Potter and the Chamber of Secrets *'02*
The Hitchhiker's Guide to the Galaxy *'05 (V)*
Opa! *'05*
The History Boys *'06*
Venus *'06*
Ballet Shoes *'07*
Harry Potter and the Order of the Phoenix *'07*
Bedtime Stories *'08*
Harry Potter and the Half-Blood Prince *'09*
Harry Potter and the Deathly Hallows, Part 1 *'10*
Hugo *'11*
Pirates of the Caribbean: On Stranger Tides *'11*
Private Peaceful *'12*

Jeff Griggs (1963-)
Eden *'93*
Forbidden Games *'95*

Frank Grillo (1965-)
April's Shower *'03*
The Express *'08*
iMurders *'08*
Pride and Glory *'08*
Blue Eyes *'09*
Mother's Day *'10*
My Soul to Take *'10*
Warrior *'11*
End of Watch *'12*
The Grey *'12*
Lay the Favorite *'12*
Collision *'13*
Mary and Martha *'13*
Captain America: The Winter Soldier *'14*
The Purge: Anarchy *'14*
The Purge: Election Year *'16*
Wheelman *'17*
Donnybrook *'18*
Reprisal *'18*
Black and Blue *'19*

Dan Grimaldi (1950-)
Don't Go in the House *'80*
Joey *'85*
Chasing the Green *'09*

Eva Grimaldi
The Black Cobra *'87*
Quiet Days in Clichy *'90*

Frank Grimes (1947-)
Crystalstone *'88*
Catherine Cookson's The Wingless Bird *'97*

Gary Grimes (1955-)
Summer of '42 *'71*
Culpepper Cattle Co. *'72*
Cahill: United States Marshal *'73*
Class of '44 *'73*
The Spikes Gang *'74*

Kareem Grimes
Jarhead *'05*
Legendary *'10*

Luke Grimes (1984-)
All the Boys Love Mandy Lane *'06*
War Eagle, Arkansas *'07*
Assassination of a High School President *'08*
Taken 2 *'12*
The Wait *'13*
American Sniper *'14*
Fifty Shades of Grey *'15*
Freeheld *'15*

Scott Grimes (1971-)
It Came Upon a Midnight Clear *'84*
Critters *'86*
Critters 2: The Main Course *'88*
Mystery, Alaska *'99*
Band of Brothers *'01*
Who's Your Monkey *'07*
Robin Hood *'10*

Shenae Grimes (1989-)
Picture This! *'08*
True Confessions of a Hollywood Starlet *'08*

Tammy Grimes (1934-)
The Horror at 37,000 Feet *'73*
The Last Unicorn *'82 (V)*
No Big Deal *'83*
The Stuff *'85*
Mr. North *'88*
A Modern Affair *'94*
High Art *'98*

Jim Grimshaw
Basket Case 3: The Progeny *'92*
Chill Factor *'99*

Herbert Grimwood (1875-1929)
When the Clouds Roll By *'19*
Romola *'25*

Nikolai Grinko (1920-89)
Andrei Rublev *'66*
Solaris *'72*
Stalker *'79*

Rupert Grint (1988-)
Harry Potter and the Sorcerer's Stone *'01*
Harry Potter and the Chamber of Secrets *'02*
Harry Potter and the Prisoner of Azkaban *'04*
Harry Potter and the Goblet of Fire *'05*
Driving Lessons *'06*
Harry Potter and the Order of the Phoenix *'07*
Harry Potter and the Half-Blood Prince *'09*
Harry Potter and the Deathly Hallows, Part 1 *'10*
Wild Target *'10*
Harry Potter and the Deathly Hallows, Part 2 *'11*
Into the White *'12*
CBGB *'13*
Charlie Countryman *'13*
Postman Pat: The Movie *'14 (V)*
Moonwalkers *'16*

Stephen Grives (1951-)
Flambards *'78*
Inseminoid *'80*
Scooby-Doo *'02*

George Grizzard (1928-2007)
From the Terrace *'60*
Advise and Consent *'62*
Warning Shot *'67*
The Stranger Within *'74*
Comes a Horseman *'78*
Seems Like Old Times *'80*
Wrong Is Right *'82*
Bachelor Party *'84*
The Deliberate Stranger *'86*
Scarlett *'94*
Small Time Crooks *'00*
Flags of Our Fathers *'06*

Agnieszka Grochowska (1979-)
In Darkness *'11*
Teen Spirit *'18*

Charles Grodin (1935-)
The Meanest Men in the West *'67*
Rosemary's Baby *'68*
Catch-22 *'70*
The Heartbreak Kid *'72*
11 Harrowhouse *'74*
King Kong *'76*
Heaven Can Wait *'78*
Real Life *'79*
It's My Turn *'80*
Seems Like Old Times *'80*
The Great Muppet Caper *'81*
The Incredible Shrinking Woman *'81*
The Lonely Guy *'84*
The Woman in Red *'84*
Movers and Shakers *'85*
Last Resort *'86*
The Couch Trip *'87*
Ishtar *'87*
Midnight Run *'88*
You Can't Hurry Love *'88*
Taking Care of Business *'90*
Beethoven *'92*
Clifford *'92*
Beethoven's 2nd *'93*
Dave *'93*
Heart and Souls *'93*
So I Married an Axe Murderer *'93 (C)*
My Summer Story *'94*
The Ex *'07*

Jacob Grodnik
End of a Gun *'16*
The Fanatic *'19*

Kathryn Grody (1946-)
Parents *'89*
The Lemon Sisters *'90*
Quick Change *'90*
Hombres Armados *'97*
Limbo *'99*

Harry Groener (1951-)
Buddy Boy *'99*
Manna from Heaven *'02*

Jonathan Groff (1985-)
Taking Woodstock *'09*
C.O.G. *'13*
Frozen *'13 (V)*
The Normal Heart *'14*
Frozen II *'19*
Hamilton *'20*

David Groh (1939-2008)
Victory at Entebbe *'76*
A Hero Ain't Nothin' but a Sandwich *'78*
Hot Shot *'86*
Broken Vows *'87*
Spoiler *'98*
Blowback *'99*
Take My Advice: The Ann & Abby Story *'99*

Ake Gronberg (1914-69)
Monika *'52*
Sawdust & Tinsel *'53*

Marc-André Grondin (1984-)
Goon *'12*
Goon: Last of the Enforcers *'17*

Herbert Gronemeyer (1956-)
Das Boot *'81*
Spring Symphony *'86*

Sam Groom (1938-)
The Baby Maker *'70*
Betrayal *'74*
Beyond the Bermuda Triangle *'75*
Hanging By a Thread *'79*

Arye Gross (1960-)
Soul Man *'86*
The Couch Trip *'87*
House 2: The Second Story *'87*
Tequila Sunrise *'88*
Coupe de Ville *'90*
For the Boys *'91*
A Midnight Clear *'92*
Shaking the Tree *'92*
Hexed *'93*
The Opposite Sex and How to Live With Them *'93*
Mother Night *'96*
Chow Bella *'98*
Spoiler *'98*
Arthur's Quest *'99*
Big City Blues *'99*
The Prince and the Surfer *'99*
Timelock *'99*
Big Eden *'00*
Gone in 60 Seconds *'00*
Seven Girlfriends *'00*
Burning Down the House *'01*
Minority Report *'02*
Grey Gardens *'09*
Harvest *'10*

Edan Gross (1978-)
And You Thought Your Parents Were Weird! *'91*
Best of the Best 2 *'93*

Hannah Gross
Christmas, Again *'15*
Marjorie Prime *'17*
Colewell *'19*
The Mountain *'19*

Lance Gross (1981-)
Tyler Perry's Meet the Browns *'08*
Our Family Wedding *'10*
Tyler Perry's Temptation: Confessions of a Marriage Counselor *'13*

Mary Gross (1953-)
Club Paradise *'86*
Baby Boom *'87*
The Couch Trip *'87*
Big Business *'88*
Casual Sex? *'88*
Feds *'88*
Troop Beverly Hills *'89*
There Goes the Neighborhood *'92*
The Santa Clause *'94*
Jailbait! *'00*
40 Days and 40 Nights *'02*

Michael Gross (1947-)
Big Business *'88*
In the Line of Duty: The FBI Murders *'88*
Tremors *'89*
Cool As Ice *'91*
Snowbound: The Jim and Jennifer Stolpa Story *'94*
Kounterfeit *'96*
Sometimes They Come Back. . . Again *'96*
Tremors 2: Aftershocks *'96*
Ed McBain's 87th Precinct: Heatwave *'97*
True Heart *'97*
Ground Control *'98*
Tremors 3: Back to Perfection *'01*
Tremors 4: The Legend Begins *'04*
Mrs. Harris *'05*
100 Million BC *'08*
12 Christmas Wishes For My Dog *'11*
Blue-Eyed Butcher *'12*
Meant to Be *'12*

Michael Robert Gross (1952-)
See Michael Gross

Paul Gross (1959-)
Buffalo Jump *'90*
Armistead Maupin's Tales of the City *'93*
Aspen Extreme *'93*
Northern Extremes *'93*
20,000 Leagues Under the Sea *'97*
Men with Brooms *'02*
The Trojan Horse *'08*
Passchendaele *'10*
Hyena Road *'16*

Logan Grove
Arc *'06*
Christmas Do-Over *'06*

Deborah Grover
The Christmas Wife *'88*
Where the Truth Lies *'05*
Still Small Voices *'07*
Bag of Bones *'11*

Gulshan Grover (1955-)
Monsoon *'97*
Rudyard Kipling's the Second Jungle Book: Mowgli and Baloo *'97*
Tales of the Kama Sutra 2: Monsoon *'98*
Eastside *'99*
My Faraway Bride *'06*

Robin Groves
The Nesting *'80*
Silver Bullet *'85*

Robert Grubb (1950-)
My Brilliant Career *'79*
Gallipoli *'81*
Mad Max: Beyond Thunderdome *'85*
Salem's Lot *'04*

Gary Grubbs (1949-)
Foxfire *'87*
Gone Fishin' *'97*
Double Take *'01*
For One Night *'06*
Not Like Everyone Else *'06*
Deal *'08*
Good Intentions *'10*
Weather Wars *'11*
Let There Be Light *'17*

Franz Gruber
Deutschland im Jahre Null *'47*
Terror Beneath the Sea *'66*

Ioan Gruffudd (1973-)
Poldark *'96*
Solomon and Gaenor *'98*
Great Expectations *'99*
Horatio Hornblower *'99*
102 Dalmatians *'00*
Shooters *'00*
Very Annie Mary *'00*
Another Life *'01*
Black Hawk Down *'01*
Horatio Hornblower: The Adventure Continues *'01*
The Gathering *'02*
This Girl's Life *'03*
King Arthur *'04*
Fantastic Four *'05*
Amazing Grace *'06*
The TV Set *'06*
Fantastic Four: Rise of the Silver Surfer *'07*
Fireflies in the Garden *'08*
The Secret of Moonacre *'08*
W. *'08*
Angel in the House *'11*
Sanctum *'11*
The Adventurer: The Curse of the Midas Box *'13*
Playing It Cool *'14*
San Andreas *'15*
The Professor and the Madman *'19*

Greg Grunberg (1966-)
Dinner and Driving *'97*
Hollow Man *'00*
The Medicine Show *'01*
The Ladykillers *'04*
Mission: Impossible 3 *'06*
Star Trek *'09 (V)*
Bond of Silence *'10*
Group Sex *'10*
End of the World *'13*
Let's Kill Ward's Wife *'14*
Tales of Halloween *'15*

Olivier Gruner (1960-)
Angel Town *'89*
Nemesis *'93*
Mars *'96*
Mercenary *'96*
T.N.T. *'98*
Interceptor Force *'99*
Velocity Trap *'99*
Crackerjack 3 *'00*
Extreme Honor *'01*
The Circuit 2 *'02*
Interceptor Force 2 *'02*
Crooked *'05*
Assassin X *'16*

Ilka Gruning (1876-1964)
Joyless Street *'25*
Underground *'41*
Casablanca *'42*
Desperate *'47*

Ah-Leh Gua (1944-)
The Wedding Banquet *'93*
Eat Drink Man Woman *'94*

Nicky Guadagni
Cube *'98*
The Golden Spiders: A Nero Wolfe Mystery *'00*
Absolution *'05*

Christopher Guard (1953-)
The Lord of the Rings *'78 (V)*
A Woman of Substance *'84*

Dominic Guard (1956-)
The Go-Between *'71*
Picnic at Hanging Rock *'75*
Absolution *'81*

Pippa Guard (1952-)
All or Nothing at All *'93*
Scarlett *'94*

Harry Guardino (1925-95)
Houseboat *'58*
The Five Pennies *'59*
Pork Chop Hill *'59*
Hell Is for Heroes *'62*
The Adventures of Bullwhip Griffin *'66*
Madigan *'68*
Lovers and Other Strangers *'70*
Dirty Harry *'71*
Octaman *'71*
They Only Kill Their Masters *'72*
Get Christie Love! *'74*
Whiffs *'75*
The Enforcer *'76*
St. Ives *'76*
Contract on Cherry Street *'77*
Rollercoaster *'77*
Any Which Way You Can *'80*
Fist of Honor *'92*

Justin Guarini (1978-)
From Justin to Kelly *'03*
Fast Girl *'07*

Stephen Guarino
I Hate Valentine's Day *'09*
BearCity *'10*

Vincent Guastaferro (1950-)
Nitti: The Enforcer *'88*
Liberty Heights *'99*
Sweet and Lowdown *'99*

Matthew Gray Gubler (1980-)
Alvin and the Chipmunks *'07 (V)*
Alvin and the Chipmunks: The Squeakuel *'09 (V)*
(500) Days of Summer *'09*
Alvin and the Chipmunks: Chipwrecked *'11 (V)*
Life After Beth *'14*
Alvin and the Chipmunks: Road Chip *'15*
Endings, Beginnings *'20*

Hans Gudegast (1941-)
See Eric Braeden

Hilmir Snaer Gudnason (1969-)
The Sea *'02*
White Night Wedding *'08*

Sverrir Gudnason
Borg *vs.* McEnroe *'17*
The Girl in the Spider's Web *'18*

Roger Guenveur
Incognito *'99*
Mooz-Lum *'10*

Florence Guerin (1965-)
Black Venus *'83*
Bizarre *'87*

Michael Guerin (1967-)
Curse of the Puppet Master: The Human Experiment *'98*
Kraa! the Sea Monster *'98*

Castulo Guerra (1945-)
Where the River Runs Black *'86*
Beverly Hills Chihuahua 2 *'10*
Bless Me, Ultima *'13*

Evelyn Guerrero (1949-)
The Toolbox Murders *'78*
Cheech and Chong's Next Movie *'80*
Cheech and Chong's Nice Dreams *'81*
Cheech and Chong: Things Are Tough All Over *'82*

Franco Guerrero
One Armed Executioner *'80*
American Commandos *'84*

Oscar H. Guerrero
Vanished *'06*
Around June *'08*

Fausto Guerzoni (1904-67)
The Bicycle Thief *'48*
Black Orpheus *'58*

Samir Guesmi (1967-)
Halfmoon *'95*
Outside the Law *'10*
The Woman in the Fifth *'11*

Christopher Guest (1948-)
Girlfriends *'78*
The Long Riders *'80*
Heartbeeps *'81*
This Is Spinal Tap *'84*
Beyond Therapy *'86*
Little Shop of Horrors *'86*
The Princess Bride *'87*
Sticky Fingers *'88*
A Few Good Men *'92*
The Return of Spinal Tap *'92*
Waiting for Guffman *'96*
Small Soldiers *'98 (V)*
Best in Show *'00*
A Mighty Wind *'03*
Mrs. Henderson Presents *'05*
For Your Consideration *'06*
The Invention of Lying *'09*
Night at the Museum: Battle of the Smithsonian *'09*
Mascots *'16*

Cornelia Guest
Second Sight *'89*
Gardens of the Night *'08*

Lance Guest (1960-)
Halloween 2: The Nightmare Isn't Over! *'81*
Just the Way You Are *'84*
The Last Starfighter *'84*
Roommate *'84*
Jaws: The Revenge *'87*
Mach 2 *'00*
Flu Birds *'08*

Nicholas Guest (1951-)
The Long Riders *'80*
Trading Places *'83*
Criminal Act *'88*
National Lampoon's Christmas Vacation *'89*
Dollman *'90*
Grand Tour: Disaster in Time *'92*
Nemesis *'93*
Kickboxer 4: The Aggressor *'94*
Puppet Master 5: The Final Chapter *'94*
Night Hunter *'95*
Nemesis 4: Cry of Angels *'97*

Francois Guetary
Lace *'84*
Lace 2 *'85*

Makhouredia Gueye
Mandabi *'68*
Xala *'75*

Carla Gugino (1971-)
Murder Without Motive *'92*
Son-in-Law *'93*
This Boy's Life *'93*
The Buccaneers *'95*
Miami Rhapsody *'95*
Homeward Bound 2: Lost in San Francisco *'96 (V)*
Jaded *'96*
The War at Home *'96*
Wedding Bell Blues *'96*
Lovelife *'97*
Snake Eyes *'98*
A Season for Miracles *'99*
The Center of the World *'01*
The Jimmy Show *'01*
The One *'01*
She Creature *'01*
Spy Kids *'01*
Spy Kids 2: The Island of Lost Dreams *'02*
The Singing Detective *'03*
Spy Kids 3-D: Game Over *'03*
Sin City *'05*
Even Money *'06*
Night at the Museum *'06*
American Gangster *'07*
The Lookout *'07*
Rise: Blood Hunter *'07*
Righteous Kill *'08*
The Mighty Macs *'09*
Race to Witch Mountain *'09*
The Unborn *'09*
Watchmen *'09*
Women in Trouble *'09*
Elektra Luxx *'10*
Every Day *'10*
Faster *'10*
I Melt With You *'11*
Mr. Popper's Penguins *'11*
Sucker Punch *'11*
San Andreas *'15*
The Space Between Us *'17*

Marco Guglielmi (1926-2005)
Mill of the Stone Women *'60*
How to Kill a Judge *'75*

Noel Guglielmi (1970-)
Harsh Times *'05*
Splinter *'06*
Gordon Glass *'07*
Red Sands *'09*
Wrong Turn at Tahoe *'09*
Recoil *'11*

Noel Gugliemi
7 Mummies *'06*
The Devil's in the Details *'13*

Wandisa Guida (1937-)
I, Vampiri *'56*
Gladiator of Rome *'63*

Giovanni Guidelli (1966-)
Where Angels Fear to Tread *'91*
Fiorile *'93*

Anthony Guidera (1964-)
Undercover *'94*
Red Shoe Diaries 7: Burning Up *'96*
L.A. Dicks *'05*

Jeremy Guilbaut
The Snow Queen *'02*
The Bouquet *'13*

Ann Guilbert (1928-)
Grumpier Old Men *'95*
Sour Grapes *'98*
Please Give *'10*

Nancy Guild (1925-99)
Somewhere in the Night *'46*
Black Magic *'49*
Abbott and Costello Meet the Invisible Man *'51*
Francis Covers the Big Town *'53*

Paul Guilfoyle (1902-61)
The Saint Takes Over *'40*
The Saint in Palm Springs *'41*
It Happened Tomorrow *'44*
The Millerson Case *'47*
The Judge *'49*
Bomba and the Hidden City *'50*
Davy Crockett, Indian Scout *'50*
Actors and Sin *'52*
Apache *'54*
The Golden Idol *'54*
September *'96*

Paul Guilfoyle (1949-)
Billy Galvin *'86*
Howard the Duck *'86*
Beverly Hills Cop 2 *'87*
The Serpent and the Rainbow *'87*
Three Men and a Baby *'87*
Wall Street *'87*
Dealers *'89*
Cadillac Man *'90*
True Colors *'91*
Final Analysis *'92*
Hoffa *'92*
Mrs. Doubtfire *'93*
Amelia Earhart: The Final Flight *'94*
Gospa *'94*
Little Odessa *'94*
Mother's Boys *'94*
A Couch in New York *'95*
Heaven's Prisoners *'95*
Celtic Pride *'96*
Extreme Measures *'96*
Looking for Richard *'96*
Manny & Lo *'96*
Night Falls on Manhattan *'96*
Ransom *'96*
Striptease *'96*
Air Force One *'97*
Amistad *'97*
Cafe Society *'97*
L.A. Confidential *'97*
Path to Paradise *'97*
In Dreams *'98*
The Negotiator *'98*
One Tough Cop *'98*
Primary Colors *'98*
Anywhere But Here *'99*
Random Hearts *'99*
Session 9 *'01*
Live from Baghdad *'03*

Julianna Guill (1987-)
Road Trip: Beer Pong *'09*
Altitude *'10*
The Apparition *'12*

Marie Guillard
Chrysalis *'07*
Love Crime *'10*

Robert Guillaume (1927-)
Seems Like Old Times *'80*
North and South Book 1 *'85*
Wanted Dead or Alive *'86*
Lean on Me *'89*
The Penthouse *'89*
Death Warrant *'90*
You Must Remember This *'92*
The Meteor Man *'93*
The Lion King *'94 (V)*
A Good Day to Die *'95*
First Kid *'96*
Pandora's Clock *'96*
Panic in the Skies *'96*
The Lion King: Simba's Pride *'98 (V)*
Silicon Towers *'99*
13th Child: Legend of the Jersey Devil *'02*
Big Fish *'03*
The Lion King 1 1/2 *'04 (V)*
Columbus Circle *'10*
Satin *'10*

Sophie Guillemin (1977-)
L'Ennui *'98*
With a Friend Like Harry *'00*
He Loves Me . . . He Loves Me Not *'02*
My Afternoons with Marguerite *'10*

Fernando Guillen (1932-2013)
Women on the Verge of a Nervous Breakdown *'88*
Why Do They Call It Love When They Mean Sex? *'92*
Mouth to Mouth *'95*

Sienna Guillory (1975-)
The Time Machine *'02*
Helen of Troy *'03*
Love Actually *'03*
Resident Evil: Apocalypse *'04*
Sorted *'04*
Eragon *'06*
Perfect Victims *'08*
Inkheart *'09*
Virtuality *'09*
Resident Evil: Afterlife *'10*
The Big Bang *'11*
Resident Evil: Retribution *'12*
Don't Hang Up *'17*
Enter the Warriors Gate *'17*

Francis Guinan
Shining Through *'92*
Guinevere *'99*
Lansky *'99*
Hannibal *'01*
Killing Kennedy *'13*

Tim Guinee (1962-)
Tai-Pan *'86*
Once Around *'91*
The Night We Never Met *'93*
Men of War *'94*
Black Day Blue Night *'95*
Follow the River *'95*
How to Make an American Quilt *'95*
The Pompatus of Love *'95*
Beavis and Butt-Head Do America *'96 (V)*
Courage Under Fire *'96*
Lily Dale *'96*
Sudden Manhattan *'96*
John Carpenter's Vampires *'97*
Blade *'98*
Brave New World *'98*

It's a Dog's Life '55
The Trouble with Harry '55

David Gwillim (1948-)
The Island at the Top of the World '74
Peter and Paul '81
How Many Miles to Babylon? '82

Jack (Gwyllam) Gwillim (1909-2001)
One That Got Away '57
Flame Over India '59
North West Frontier '59
Sink the Bismarck '60
Sword of Sherwood Forest '60
Jason and the Argonauts '63

Michael Gwynn (1916-76)
The Revenge of Frankenstein '58
Never Take Candy From a Stranger '60
Village of the Damned '60
Jason and the Argonauts '63
The Scars of Dracula '70

Anne Gwynne (1918-2003)
Black Friday '40
Flash Gordon Conquers the Universe '40
Spring Parade '40
The Black Cat '41
Broadway '42
Ride 'Em Cowboy '42
The Strange Case of Dr. Rx '42
House of Frankenstein '44
Dick Tracy Meets Gruesome '47
Killer Dill '47
Panhandle '48
Breakdown '53
Adam at 6 a.m. '70

Fred Gwynne (1926-93)
Munster, Go Home! '66
The Littlest Angel '69
Simon '80
The Munsters' Revenge '81
The Cotton Club '84
Water '85 (C)
The Boy Who Could Fly '86
Fatal Attraction '87
Ironweed '87
The Secret of My Success '87
Disorganized Crime '89
Pet Sematary '89
My Cousin Vinny '92
Shadows and Fog '92

Michael C. Gwynne (1942-)
Payday '73
Harry Tracy '83
Seduced '85
Cherry 2000 '88
The Last of the Finest '90

Peter Gwynne
The Dove '74
Tim '79

Jake Gyllenhaal (1980-)
October Sky '99
Bubble Boy '01
Donnie Darko '01
Highway '01
The Good Girl '02
Lovely & Amazing '02
Moonlight Mile '02
The Day After Tomorrow '04
Brokeback Mountain '05
Jarhead '05
Proof '05
Rendition '07
Zodiac '07
Brothers '09
Love and Other Drugs '10
Prince of Persia: The Sands of Time '10
Source Code '11
End of Watch '12
Enemy '13
Prisoners '13
Nightcrawler '14
Demolition '15
Everest '15
Southpaw '15
Nocturnal Animals '16
Life '17
Stronger '17
The Sisters Brothers '18
Wildlife '18
Spider-Man: Far from Home '19
Velvet Buzzsaw '19

Maggie Gyllenhaal (1977-)
Cecil B. Demented '00
Donnie Darko '01
Riding in Cars with Boys '01
Adaptation '02
Confessions of a Dangerous Mind '02
40 Days and 40 Nights '02
Secretary '02
Casa de los Babys '03
Mona Lisa Smile '03
Criminal '04
Happy Endings '05
The Great New Wonderful '06
Monster House '06 (V)
Paris, je t'aime '06
Sherrybaby '06
Stranger Than Fiction '06
Trust the Man '06
World Trade Center '06
The Dark Knight '08
Away We Go '09
Crazy Heart '09
Nanny McPhee Returns '10
Hysteria '11
Won't Back Down '12
White House Down '13
Frank '14

Greta Gynt (1916-2000)
The Hooded Terror '38
Sexton Blake and the Hooded Terror '38
The Arsenal Stadium Mystery '39
The Human Monster '39
London Town '46

Jung-woo Ha (1978-)
Time '06
Never Forever '07
The Handmaiden '16

Emily Haack (1975-)
Absolution '03
Savage Harvest 2: October Blood '06

Johnathan Haagensen (1983-)
City of God '02
City of Men '07

Charles S. Haas (1952-)
Tex '82
Gremlins 2: The New Batch '90
Matinee '92

Hugo Haas (1902-68)
Days of Glory '43
Strange Affair '44
Summer Storm '44
Holiday in Mexico '46
Merton of the Movies '47
The Private Affairs of Bel Ami '47
For the Love of Mary '48
The Fighting Kentuckian '49
King Solomon's Mines '50
One Girl's Confession '53
Bait '54

Lukas Haas (1976-)
Testament '83
Witness '85
Shattered Spirits '86
Solarbabies '86
The Lady in White '88
Music Box '89
See You in the Morning '89
Rambling Rose '91
Leap of Faith '92
Boys '95
Everyone Says I Love You '96
johns '96
Mars Attacks! '96
Breakfast of Champions '98
Running Free '00
The Lathe of Heaven '02
Bookies '03
Last Days '05
Alpha Dog '06
Brick '06
The Cradle '06
Material Girls '06
Swedish Auto '06
The Tripper '06
Who Loves the Sun '06
Death in Love '08
While She Was Out '08
Inception '10
The Perfect Age of Rock 'n' Roll '10
Red Riding Hood '11
Contraband '12
Crazy Eyes '12
Jobs '13
The Revenant '15

Todd Haberkorn (1982-)
Summer Wars '09 (V)
Scream of the Banshee '11
Mass Effect: Paragon Lost '12 (V)

Matthias Habich (1940-)
Coup de Grace '78
Enemy at the Gates '00
Nowhere in Africa '02
Downfall '04
The Reader '08
Berlin Syndrome '17

Olivia Hack (1983-)
The Brady Bunch Movie '95
A Very Brady Sequel '96

Shelley Hack (1947-)
King of Comedy '82
Troll '86
The Stepfather '87
Blind Fear '89

George Hackathorne (1895-1940)
The Last of the Mohicans '20
Merry-Go-Round '23

Buddy Hackett (1924-2003)
God's Little Acre '58
All Hands on Deck '61
Everything's Ducky '61
The Music Man '62
It's a Mad, Mad, Mad, Mad World '63
Muscle Beach Party '64
Scrooged '88
The Little Mermaid '89 (V)
Paulie '98

Joan Hackett (1934-83)
The Group '66
Will Penny '67
Assignment to Kill '69
Support Your Local Sheriff '69
Rivals '72
The Last of Sheila '73
The Terminal Man '74
The Treasure of Matecumbe '76
Dead of Night '77
The Possessed '77
The Long Days of Summer '80
One Trick Pony '80
Only When I Laugh '81
The Escape Artist '82
The Long Summer of George Adams '82

Karl Hackett (1893-1948)
Lightnin' Bill Carson '36
The Gold Racket '37
Thundering Gunslingers '44

Raymond Hackett (1902-58)
Madame X '29
Let Us Be Gay '30
Our Blushing Brides '30

Gene Hackman (1930-)
Lilith '64
Hawaii '66
Bonnie & Clyde '67
A Covenant With Death '67
First to Fight '67
The Split '68
Downhill Racer '69
The Gypsy Moths '69
Marooned '69
Riot '69
Doctors' Wives '70
I Never Sang for My Father '70
The French Connection '71
The Poseidon Adventure '72
Prime Cut '72
Scarecrow '73
The Conversation '74
Young Frankenstein '74
Zandy's Bride '74
Bite the Bullet '75
French Connection 2 '75
Night Moves '75
A Bridge Too Far '77
The Domino Principle '77
March or Die '77
Superman: The Movie '78
Superman 2 '80
All Night Long '81
Eureka! '81
Reds '81
Uncommon Valor '83
Under Fire '83
Target '85
Twice in a Lifetime '85
Hoosiers '86
Power '86
No Way Out '87
Superman 4: The Quest for Peace '87
Another Woman '88
Bat 21 '88
Full Moon in Blue Water '88
Mississippi Burning '88
Split Decisions '88
The Package '89
Loose Cannons '90
Narrow Margin '90
Postcards from the Edge '90
Class Action '91
Company Business '91
Unforgiven '92
The Firm '93
Geronimo: An American Legend '93
Wyatt Earp '94
The Birdcage '95
Crimson Tide '95
Get Shorty '95
The Quick and the Dead '95
The Chamber '96
Extreme Measures '96
Absolute Power '97
Antz '98 (V)
Enemy of the State '98
Twilight '98
The Replacements '00
Under Suspicion '00
Behind Enemy Lines '01
Heartbreakers '01
Heist '01
The Mexican '01
The Royal Tenenbaums '01
Runaway Jury '03
Welcome to Mooseport '04

Michiko Hada (1968-)
The Mystery of Rampo '94
Rowing Through '96
Flowers of Shanghai '98

Jonathan Hadary (1948-)
The New Age '94
Private Parts '96
A Simple Wish '97
Intolerable Cruelty '03

Ellie Haddington
The Wyvern Mystery '00
Lawless Heart '01

Tiffany Haddish (1979-)
Racing for Time '08
Keanu '16
Girls Trip '17
Night School '18
Nobody's Fool '18
The Oath '18
The Kitchen '19
The LEGO Movie 2: The Second Part '19
Like a Boss '20

Laura Haddock (1985-)
Storage 24 '12
Transformers: The Last Knight '17

Dayle Haddon (1948-)
The World's Greatest Athlete '73
The Cheaters '76
Madame Claude '77
North Dallas Forty '79
Bedroom Eyes '86
Cyborg '89

Peter Haddon (1898-1962)
The Silent Passenger '35
Secret of Stamboul '36

Krystof Hadek (1982-)
Dark Blue World '01
Mission of Honor '19

Sara Haden (1897-1981)
Finishing School '33
Anne of Green Gables '34
Spitfire '34
Mad Love '35
Magnificent Obsession '35
Little Miss Nobody '36
A Family Affair '37
You're Only Young Once '37
Out West With the Hardys '38
Andy Hardy Gets Spring Fever '39
The Hardys Ride High '39
Judge Hardy and Son '39
Andy Hardy Meets Debutante '40
Hullabaloo '40
The Shop Around the Corner '40
Andy Hardy's Double Life '42
The Courtship of Andy Hardy '42
Somewhere I'll Find You '42
Our Vines Have Tender Grapes '45
She Wouldn't Say Yes '45
Love Laughs at Andy Hardy '46
Mr. Ace '46
The Great Rupert '50
A Life of Her Own '50
Andy Hardy Comes Home '58

Bill Hader (1978-)
Hot Rod '07
Superbad '07
Forgetting Sarah Marshall '08
Pineapple Express '08
Tropic Thunder '08
Adventureland '09
Cloudy with a Chance of Meatballs '09 (V)
Ice Age: Dawn of the Dinosaurs '09 (V)
Night at the Museum: Battle of the Smithsonian '09
Hoodwinked Too! Hood vs. Evil '11 (V)
Paul '11
Cloudy with a Chance of Meatballs 2 '13 (V)
The To Do List '13
Turbo '13 (V)
The Disappearance of Eleanor Rigby '14
The Skeleton Twins '14
They Came Together '14
Inside Out '15 (V)
Trainwreck '15
The Angry Birds Movie '16
Sausage Party '16
The Angry Birds Movie 2 '19
It Chapter Two '19
Noelle '19

Mark Hadfield
A Midwinter's Tale '95
A Royal Night Out '15

Reed Hadley (1911-74)
Zorro's Fighting Legion '39
The Bank Dick '40
I'll Wait for You '41
Whistling in the Dark '41
Ziegfeld Girl '41
Guadalcanal Diary '43
Dark Corner '46
Doll Face '46
If I'm Lucky '46
It Shouldn't Happen to a Dog '46
Panhandle '48
A Southern Yankee '48
I Shot Jesse James '49
Rimfire '49
Return of Jesse James '50
Baron of Arizona '51
The Half-Breed '51
Little Big Horn '51
Kansas Pacific '53
Big House, U.S.A. '55
Brain of Blood '71

Adèle Haenel
BPM (Beats Per Minute) '17
The Unknown Girl '17
Portrait of a Lady on Fire '19

Hendrick Haese
Contaminated Man '00
The Enemy '01

Marianne Hagan (1966-)
Halloween 6: The Curse of Michael Myers '95
I Think I Do '97
Rick '03

Molly Hagan (1961-)
Code of Silence '85
Some Kind of Wonderful '87
Ringmaster '98
Election '99
Miracle in Lane Two '00
Playing Mona Lisa '00
The Lucky Ones '08
Talhotblond '12
Navy Seals vs. Zombies '15

Richard Hageman (1882-1966)
New Orleans '47
The Great Caruso '51

Jean Hagen (1923-77)
Adam's Rib '50
Ambush '50
The Asphalt Jungle '50
A Life of Her Own '50
Side Street '50
Carbine Williams '52
Singin' in the Rain '52
Half a Hero '53
The Big Knife '55
The Shaggy Dog '59
Sunrise at Campobello '60
Panic in Year Zero! '62
Dead Ringer '64
Alexander: The Other Side of Dawn '77

Pal Sverre Hagen
Kon-Tiki '12
In Order of Disappearance '14

Ross Hagen (1938-2011)
Hellcats '68
Speedway '68
The Sidehackers '69
Angels' Wild Women '72
Night Creature '79
Angel '84
Avenging Angel '85
Armed Response '86
Phantom Empire '87
Star Slammer '87
Warlords '88
Alienator '89
Bikini Drive-In '94
Midnight Tease 2 '95

Uta Hagen (1919-2004)
The Other '72
The Boys from Brazil '78
Reversal of Fortune '90

Kristen Hager (1984-)
Recipe for a Perfect Christmas '05
Sorority Wars '09
Sexting '11
The Right Kind Of Wrong '13
Clara '19

Kristi Hager
Sure Fire '90
Wanted '08

Ron Hagerthy (1932-)
Starlift '51
Saintly Sinners '62

Julie Hagerty (1955-)
Airplane! '80
Airplane 2: The Sequel '82
A Midsummer Night's Sex Comedy '82

Bad Medicine '85
Lost in America '85
Beyond Therapy '86
Necessary Parties '88
Bloodhounds of Broadway '89
Reversal of Fortune '90
What about Bob? '91
Noises Off '92
The Wife '95
Boys Will Be Boys '97
U-Turn '97
Jackie's Back '99
The Story of Us '99
Held Up '00
Freddy Got Fingered '01
Storytelling '01
The Badge '02
A Guy Thing '03
Just Friends '05
Pizza '05
She's the Man '06
Confessions of a Shopaholic '09
Noelle '19

Michael G. (Mike) Hagerty (1954-)
Speed 2: Cruise Control '97
Best Laid Plans '99
Inspector Gadget '99
Rampage: The Hillside Strangler Murders '04

Dan Haggerty (1941-2016)
Angels Die Hard '70
Bury Me an Angel '71
Terror Out of the Sky '78
Chance '89
The Chilling '89
Repo Jake '90
Spirit of the Eagle '90
The Magic Voyage '93 (V)
Cheyenne Warrior '94
Grizzly Mountain '97
Big Stan '07

Don Haggerty (1914-88)
Command Decision '48
Loophole '54
The Gunfight at Dodge City '59
Hell Is for Heroes '62
The Killers '64

Dylan Haggerty (1984-)
Grizzly Mountain '97
Interview with the Assassin '02

Larry Hagman (1939-2012)
Ensign Pulver '64
Fail-Safe '64
In Harm's Way '65
The Group '66
Hired Hand '71 (C)
Beware! The Blob '72
Deadly Encounter '72
Antonio '73
Harry and Tonto '74
Hurricane '74
Sidekicks '74
The Big Bus '76
Mother, Jugs and Speed '76
The Eagle Has Landed '77
S.O.B. '81
Nixon '95
Primary Colors '98

Frank S. Hagney (1884-1973)
Sit Tight '31
Tomorrow We Live '42

Garrick Hagon
Shadow Man '06
Erased '12

Archie Hahn (1941-)
Phantom of the Paradise '74
Cannonball '76
Pray TV '80
Meatballs 2 '84
Protocol '84
This Is Spinal Tap '84
Amazon Women on the Moon '87
Glory Years '87

Gisela Hahn (1943-)
Rulers of the City '76
Rulers of the City '77
Devil Hunter '08

Jess Hahn (1922-98)
Topkapi '64
Secret Agent Super Dragon '66
Triple Cross '67
The Night of the Following Day '69
Escape from Death Row '73
The Grand Duel '73
Mean Frank and Crazy Tony '75
Mama Dracula '80
White Fire '84

Kathryn Hahn (1973-)
How to Lose a Guy in 10 Days '03
Win a Date with Tad Hamilton! '04
A Lot Like Love '05
The Holiday '06
The Last Mimzy '07
Revolutionary Road '08
Step Brothers '08
The Goods: Live Hard, Sell Hard '09
How Do You Know '10
Our Idiot Brother '11
Wanderlust '12
Afternoon Delight '13
Bad Words '13
We're the Millers '13
This Is Where I Leave You '14
The D Train '15
The Visit '15
Bad Moms '16
Captain Fantastic '16
Len & Company '16
A Bad Moms Christmas '17
Flower '18

Charles Haid (1943-)
The Choirboys '77
The Bastard '78
Oliver's Story '78
Who'll Stop the Rain? '78
Altered States '80
Divorce Wars: A Love Story '82
Children in the Crossfire '84
Cop '88
The Rescue '88
Capone '89
The Chinatown Murders: Man against the Mob '89
Nightbreed '90
Storyville '92
The Fire Next Time '93
Broken Trust '95
The Third Miracle '99
Home on the Range '04 (V)

Ion Haiduc (1947-)
Bloodstone: Subspecies 2 '92
Bloodlust: Subspecies 3 '93
Ghouls '07

Stacy Haiduk (1968-)
Luther the Geek '90
Desert Thunder '99
Gabriela '01
Attack of the Sabretooth '05
The Sitter '07

David Haig (1955-)
Four Weddings and a Funeral '94
Station Jim '01
Two Weeks Notice '02
My Boy Jack '07
The 39 Steps '09

Sid Haig (1939-2019)
Spider Baby '64
Track of the Vampire '66
Pit Stop '67
Point Blank '67
C.C. & Company '70
The Big Doll House '71
The Big Bird Cage '72
Coffy '73
Emperor of the North Pole '73
Busting '74
Foxy Brown '74
Savage Sisters '74
Galaxy of Terror '81
Aftermath '85
Warlords '88

The Forbidden Dance '90
Jackie Brown '97
House of 1000 Corpses '03
The Devil's Rejects '05
House of the Dead 2: Dead Aim '05
A Dead Calling '06
Brotherhood of Blood '08
Wolf Moon '09
Creature '11
Mimesis '11
The Lords of Salem '13
Bone Tomahawk '15
3 from Hell '19

Kenneth Haigh (1931-)
Teenage Bad Girl '59
Cleopatra '63
A Lovely Way to Die '68
The Bitch '78

Leisha Hailey (1971-)
All Over Me '96
La Cucina '07
Fertile Ground '10

Corey Haim (1972-2010)
Murphy's Romance '85
Secret Admirer '85
Silver Bullet '85
Lucas '86
The Lost Boys '87
License to Drive '88
Watchers '88
Dream a Little Dream '89
Prayer of the Rollerboys '91
Anything for Love '93
Blown Away '93
Just One of the Girls '93
Dream a Little Dream 2 '94
National Lampoon's Last Resort '94
Demolition High '95
Snowboard Academy '96
Crank: High Voltage '09
Decisions '10

Patricia Haines (1932-77)
Night Caller from Outer Space '66
The Virgin Witch '70

William Haines (1900-73)
Souls for Sale '23
Tell It to the Marines '26
Spring Fever '27
West Point '27
Show People '28
The Smart Set '28
Navy Blues '29
Speedway '29
Free and Easy '30 (C)
The Girl Said No '30
Are You Listening? '32
Fast Life '32
Way Out West '37

Jester Hairston (1901-2000)
The Alamo '60
I'm Gonna Git You Sucka '88

Alison Haislip (1981-)
The Indian '07
Into the Arms of Strangers '07
The Donner Party '09

Khrystyne Haje (1968-)
Scanners: The Showdown '94
Cyborg 3: The Recycler '95

Haji (1946-2013)
Faster, Pussycat! Kill! Kill! '65
Motor Psycho '65
Beyond the Valley of the Dolls '70
Supervixens '75
Ilsa, Harem Keeper of the Oil Sheiks '76

Alan Hale (1892-1950)
The Four Horsemen of the Apocalypse '21
Robin Hood '22
The Trap '22
The Sea Ghost '31
The Sin of Madelon Claudet '31

Susan Lenox: Her Fall and Rise '31
Union Depot '32
Great Expectations '34
Imitation of Life '34
It Happened One Night '34
Little Minister '34
The Lost Patrol '34
Of Human Bondage '34
The Scarlet Letter '34
The Crusades '35
The Good Fairy '35
Last Days of Pompeii '35
A Message to Garcia '36
Our Relations '36
High, Wide and Handsome '37
The Prince and the Pauper '37
Stella Dallas '37
Thin Ice '37
The Adventures of Marco Polo '38
The Adventures of Robin Hood '38
Algiers '38
Listen, Darling '38
Dodge City '39
Dust Be My Destiny '39
The Man in the Iron Mask '39
The Private Lives of Elizabeth & Essex '39
The Fighting 69th '40
Santa Fe Trail '40
The Sea Hawk '40
They Drive by Night '40
Virginia City '40
Footsteps in the Dark '41
Manpower '41
The Smiling Ghost '41
Strawberry Blonde '41
Captains of the Clouds '42
Desperate Journey '42
Gentleman Jim '42
Juke Girl '42
Action in the North Atlantic '43
Destination Tokyo '43
Thank Your Lucky Stars '43
This Is the Army '43
The Adventures of Mark Twain '44
God is My Co-Pilot '45
Roughly Speaking '45
The Man I Love '46
Night and Day '46
My Wild Irish Rose '47
Pursued '47
South of St. Louis '48
Whiplash '48
Adventures of Don Juan '49
The Inspector General '49
Rogues of Sherwood Forest '50
Stars in My Crown '50
Many Rivers to Cross '55
Thunder in Carolina '60

Alan Hale, Jr. (1918-90)
Wild Boys of the Road '33
Four Men and a Prayer '38
To the Shores of Tripoli '42
Wake Island '42
Watch on the Rhine '43
Cheyenne '47
It Happened on 5th Avenue '47
One Sunday Afternoon '48
Short Grass '50
The Underworld Story '50
The West Point Story '50
At Sword's Point '51
Big Trees '52
Captain Kidd and the Slave Girl '54
Young at Heart '54
The Indian Fighter '55
All Mine to Give '56
Canyon River '56
The Killer Is Loose '56
Battle Hymn '57
The True Story of Jesse James '57
Up Periscope '59
Hard Drivin' '60
The Crawling Hand '63
Advance to the Rear '64

There Was a Crooked Man '70
The Giant Spider Invasion '75
Rescue from Gilligan's Island '78
The Fifth Musketeer '79
The North Avenue Irregulars '79
Johnny Dangerously '84
Back to the Beach '87

Amanda Hale (1980-)
Murderland '09
The Crimson Petal and the White '12
The Invisible Woman '13

Barbara Hale (1922-)
Heavenly Days '44
West of the Pecos '45
The Boy with the Green Hair '48
Jolson Sings Again '49
The Window '49
The Jackpot '50
The First Time '52
A Lion Is in the Streets '53
Seminole '53
The Far Horizons '55
The Oklahoman '56
Seventh Cavalry '56
Buckskin '68
Airport '70
The Giant Spider Invasion '75
Flight of the Grey Wolf '76
Perry Mason Returns '85

Binnie Hale (1899-1984)
The Phantom Light '35
Love from a Stranger '37

Creighton Hale (1882-1965)
The Idol Dancer '20
Way Down East '20
Broken Hearts of Broadway '23
The Marriage Circle '24
The Cat and the Canary '27
The Great Divide '29
Sergeant York '41
Action in the North Atlantic '43
Watch on the Rhine '43

Elvi Hale (1931-)
Six Wives of Henry VIII '71
Dangerous Corner '83

Georgina Hale (1943-)
The Boy Friend '71
The Devils '71
Mahler '74
Castaway '87
Preaching to the Perverted '97

Jean Hale (1938-)
Psychomania '63
In Like Flint '67
The St. Valentine's Day Massacre '67

Jennifer Hale
The Powerpuff Girls Movie '02 (V)
Cinderella III: A Twist in Time '07 (V)
Fight to the Finish '16

Jonathan Hale (1891-1966)
The Devil Is a Sissy '36
Exiled to Shanghai '37
Saratoga '37
You Only Live Once '37
Blondie '38
Bringing Up Baby '38
Blondie Brings Up Baby '39
Blondie Meets the Boss '39
The Saint Strikes Back '39
The Story of Alexander Graham Bell '39
Blondie Has Trouble '40
Blondie Plays Cupid '40
Johnny Apollo '40
The Saint Takes Over '40
The Saint's Double Trouble '40
Blondie in Society '41
The Saint in Palm Springs '41
Blondie Goes Latin '42

Blondie Goes to College '42
Hangmen Also Die '42
Hollywood Canteen '44
Easy to Wed '46
Call Northside 777 '48
The Judge '49
Scandal Sheet '52
The Steel Trap '52
Shadow Puppets '07

Louise Closser Hale (1872-1933)
Big Boy '30
Platinum Blonde '31
The Man Who Played God '32
Movie Crazy '32
No More Orchids '32
Shanghai Express '32
The Barbarian '33
Today We Live '33
The White Sister '33

Lucy Kate Hale (1989-)
Sorority Wars '09
A Cinderella Story: Once Upon a Song '11
Truth or Dare '18
Fantasy Island '20

Sonnie Hale (1902-59)
Friday the Thirteenth '33
First a Girl '35
It's Love Again '36
London Town '46

Tony Hale (1970-)
Fortunes '05
Larry the Cable Guy: Health Inspector '06
RV '06
Stranger Than Fiction '06
Because I Said So '07
The Tale of Despereaux '08 (V)
The Year of Getting to Know Us '08
The Answer Man '09
The Goods: Live Hard, Sell Hard '09
Happythankyoumoreplease '10
Alvin and the Chipmunks: Road Chip '15
Night Owls '15
Yoga Hosers '16
Toy Story 4 '19

Brian Haley (1963-)
Baby's Day Out '94
Little Giants '94
That Darn Cat '96
McHale's Navy '97
Gran Torino '08

Jack Haley (1899-1979)
Mister Cinderella '36
Pigskin Parade '36
Danger: Love at Work '37
Pick a Star '37
Wake Up and Live '37
Alexander's Ragtime Band '38
Rebecca of Sunnybrook Farm '38
The Wizard of Oz '39
Moon over Miami '41
Beyond the Blue Horizon '42
Higher and Higher '44
One Body Too Many '44
George White's Scandals '45
Treasure of Fear '45
People Are Funny '46

Jackie Earle Haley (1961-)
The Bad News Bears '76
The Bad News Bears in Breaking Training '77
Damnation Alley '77
The Bad News Bears Go to Japan '78
Breaking Away '79
Losin' It '82
Dollman '90
Maniac Cop 3: Badge of Silence '93
All the King's Men '06
Little Children '06
Fragments '08
Semi-Pro '08
Shutter Island '09

Watchmen '09
A Nightmare on Elm Street '10
Dark Shadows '12
Lincoln '12
RoboCop '14
The Birth of a Nation '16
London Has Fallen '16

H.B. Halicki (1941-89)
Gone in 60 Seconds '74
The Junkman '82

Albert Hall (1937-)
Apocalypse Now '79
The Long, Hot Summer '86
Betrayed '88
Hearts of Darkness: A Filmmaker's Apocalypse '91
Separate but Equal '91
Malcolm X '92
Devil in a Blue Dress '95
Major Payne '95
Get On the Bus '96
Beloved '98
Swing Vote '99
Ali '01
Not Easily Broken '09

Anthony Michael Hall (1968-)
Six Pack '82
National Lampoon's Vacation '83
Sixteen Candles '84
The Breakfast Club '85
Weird Science '85
Johnny Be Good '88
Edward Scissorhands '90
Into the Sun '92
Six Degrees of Separation '93
Hail Caesar '94
Me and the Mob '94
Texas '94
Bomb Squad '97
The Killing Grounds '97
Trojan War '97
Fallen Angel '99
The Pirates of Silicon Valley '99
Happy Accidents '00 (C)
The Caveman's Valentine '01
Freddy Got Fingered '01
Hitched '01
61* '01
All About the Benjamins '02
The Dead Zone '02
Funny Valentine '05
The Dark Knight '08
Final Approach '08
Last Man Standing '11
Sexy Evil Genius '13
War Machine '17

Arch Hall, Jr. (1943-)
The Choppers '61
Eegah! '62
Wild Guitar '62
The Sadist '63
Nasty Rabbit '64
Deadwood '65

Arch (Archie) Hall, Sr. (1908-78)
Wild Guitar '62
The Thrill Killers '65

Arsenio Hall (1956-)
Amazon Women on the Moon '87
Coming to America '88
Harlem Nights '89
The Proud Family Movie '05 (V)
Igor '08 (V)
Black Dynamite '09

Brad Hall (1958-)
Troll '86
Limit Up '89
Worth Winning '89
The Guardian '90
Bye Bye, Love '94
Must Love Dogs '05

Bradley Hall
Spider '02
Far from the Madding Crowd '15

Bug Hall (1985-)
The Little Rascals '94
The Big Green '95
The Stupids '95
Honey, We Shrunk Ourselves '97
Skipped Parts '00
Get a Clue '02
Arizona Summer '03
Footsteps '03
Mortuary '05
The Day the Earth Stopped '08
American Pie Presents: Book of Love '09

Craig Hall (1974-)
The Vector File '03
Ike: Countdown to D-Day '04
Eagle *vs.* Shark '07

Delores Hall
Leap of Faith '92
Lethal Weapon 3 '92

Diane Hall (1946-)
See Diane Keaton

Evelyn Hall
Hell's Angels '30
Lovers Courageous '32

Gabriella Hall (1966-)
Sexual Roulette '96
Lolida 2000 '97
The Portrait '99
The Seductress '00

Grayson Hall (1922-85)
Satan in High Heels '61
The Night of the Iguana '64
Adam at 6 a.m. '70
House of Dark Shadows '70
Night of Dark Shadows '71

Hanna Hall (1984-)
Forrest Gump '94
Homecoming '96
The Virgin Suicides '99
Halloween '07
American Cowslip '09
Happiness Runs '10

Henry Hall (1876-1954)
Pilot X '37
Command Decision '48

Huntz Hall (1920-99)
Dead End '37
Angels with Dirty Faces '38
Crime School '38
Dead End Kids: Little Tough Guy '38
Little Tough Guy '38
Angels Wash Their Faces '39
Hell's Kitchen '39
They Made Me a Criminal '39
Junior G-Men '40
Junior G-Men of the Air '42
Mr. Wise Guy '42
Smart Alecks '42
Clancy Street Boys '43
Kid Dynamite '43
A Walk in the Sun '46
Gentle Giant '67
Valentino '77
Gas Pump Girls '79
The Escape Artist '82
Ratings Game '84
Cyclone '87

Irma P. Hall (1935-)
A Family Thing '96
Nothing to Lose '96
Buddy '97
Midnight in the Garden of Good and Evil '97
Soul Food '97
Steel '97
Beloved '98
The Love Letter '98
Patch Adams '98
A Lesson Before Dying '99
A Slipping Down Life '99
Our America '02
An Unexpected Love '03
Collateral '04
The Ladykillers '04
Tyler Perry's Meet the Browns '08

Bad Lieutenant: Port of Call New Orleans '09
Hurricane Season '09
My Son, My Son, What Have Ye Done '09

James Hall (1900-40)
Hotel Imperial '27
Four Sons '28
Eleven Men and a Girl '30
Hell's Angels '30
Millie '31

Jerry Hall (1956-)
Batman '89
R.P.M. '97
Merci Docteur Rey '04

Jon Hall (1913-79)
Charlie Chan in Shanghai '35
The Hurricane '37
Kit Carson '40
Arabian Nights '42
Invisible Agent '42
Ali Baba and the Forty Thieves '43
Cobra Woman '44
The Invisible Man's Revenge '44
The Prince of Thieves '48
Deputy Marshal '50
Hell Ship Mutiny '57
The Beach Girls and the Monster '65

Juanita Hall (1901-68)
Paradise in Harlem '40
South Pacific '58
Flower Drum Song '61

Kevin Peter Hall (1955-91)
Harry and the Hendersons '87
Predator '87
Predator 2 '90

Landon Hall
Over the Wire '95
Stolen Hearts '95
Witchcraft 9: Bitter Flesh '96

Lois Hall (1926-2006)
Dead Again '91
Kalifornia '93

Michael C. Hall (1971-)
Paycheck '03
Gamer '09
Peep World '10
The Trouble With Bliss '11
Kill Your Darlings '13
Cold in July '14
Christine '16

Natalie Hall
Love's Christmas Journey '11
The Seven Year Hitch '12

Philip Baker Hall (1931-)
The Bastard '78
Terror Out of the Sky '78
The Last Reunion '80
The Night the Bridge Fell Down '83
Secret Honor '85
The Spirit '87
Three O'Clock High '87
Blue Desert '91
Kiss of Death '94
Hard Eight '96
Hit Me '96
The Rock '96
Air Force One '97
Boogie Nights '97
Enemy of the State '98
Psycho '98
Rush Hour '98
Sour Grapes '98
The Truman Show '98
Witness to the Mob '98
The Cradle Will Rock '99
The Insider '99
Let the Devil Wear Black '99
Magnolia '99
The Talented Mr. Ripley '99
The Contender '00
Jackie Bouvier Kennedy Onassis '00
Lost Souls '00
Rules of Engagement '00
A Gentleman's Game '01

Path to War '02
The Sum of All Fears '02
Bruce Almighty '03
Die Mommie Die! '03
Dogville '03
In Good Company '04
The Amityville Horror '05
Duck '05
The Zodiac '05
Islander '06
The Matador '06
The Shaggy Dog '06
You Kill Me '07
Zodiac '07
Fired Up! '09
The Lodger '09
Wonderful World '09
All Good Things '10
People Like Us '12
Bad Words '13
The Last Word '17

Pooch Hall (1977-)
Blue Hill Avenue '01
Christmas at Water's Edge '04
Stomp the Yard 2: Homecoming '10
Jumping the Broom '11
Carter High '15

Porter Hall (1888-1953)
The Thin Man '34
The Case of the Lucky Legs '35
The General Died at Dawn '36
Petrified Forest '36
The Princess Comes Across '36
Satan Met a Lady '36
Bulldog Drummond Escapes '37
Make Way for Tomorrow '37
The Plainsman '37
Souls at Sea '37
True Confession '37
Bulldog Drummond's Peril '38
Mr. Smith Goes to Washington '39
They Shall Have Music '39
Arizona '40
His Girl Friday '40
Sullivan's Travels '41
The Desperadoes '43
Double Indemnity '44
Going My Way '44
The Great Moment '44
Miracle of Morgan's Creek '44
The Woman of the Town '44
Murder, He Says '45
Weekend at the Waldorf '45
Miracle on 34th Street '47
Unconquered '47
The Beautiful Blonde from Bashful Bend '49
Intruder in the Dust '49
Ace in the Hole '51
The Half-Breed '51
Vice Squad '53
Return to Treasure Island '54

Rebecca Hall (1982-)
The Camomile Lawn '92
The Prestige '06
Starter for 10 '06
Wide Sargasso Sea '06
Frost/Nixon '08
Vicky Cristina Barcelona '08
Dorian Gray '09
Red Riding, Part 1: 1974 '09
Everything Must Go '10
Please Give '10
The Town '10
The Awakening '11
A Bag of Hammers '11
Lay the Favorite '12
Closed Circuit '13
Iron Man 3 '13
A Promise '13
Transcendence '14
The Gift '15
The BFG '16
Christine '16
Tumbledown '16
Professor Marston and the Wonder Women '17

Holmes & Watson '18
Mirai '18
Permission '18

Regina Hall (1970-)
Disappearing Acts '00
Scary Movie '00
Scary Movie 2 '01
The Other Brother '02
Paid in Full '02
Malibu's Most Wanted '03
Scary Movie 3 '03
The Honeymooners '05
King's Ransom '05
The Elder Son '06
Scary Movie 4 '06
First Sunday '08
Law Abiding Citizen '09
Death at a Funeral '10
Mardi Gras: Spring Break '11
Think Like a Man '12
The Best Man Holiday '13
About Last Night '14
Think Like a Man Too '14
People Places Things '15
Barbershop: The Next Cut '16
When the Bough Breaks '16
Girls Trip '17
The Hate U Give '18
Support the Girls '18
Little '19
Shaft '19

Ron Hall
Raw Target '95
Vampire Assassin '05

Ruth Hall (1910-2003)
Monkey Business '31
Kid from Spain '32
Miss Pinkerton '32
The Three Musketeers '33

Scott H. Hall
Blood Feast '63
Color Me Blood Red '64

Shannah Hall
Boogey Man 2 '83
The Princess & the Call Girl '84

Shashawnee Hall (1961-)
Undercover Bridesmaid '12
Amnesiac '15

Thurston Hall (1883-1958)
The Black Room '35
Hooray for Love '35
Theodora Goes Wild '36
Amazing Dr. Clitterhouse '38
Hard to Get '38
Dancing Co-Ed '39
Each Dawn I Die '39
You Can't Cheat an Honest Man '39
The Invisible Woman '40
The Lone Wolf Meets a Lady '40
Call of the Canyon '42
Counter-Espionage '42
Crash Dive '43
I Dood It '43
The Youngest Profession '43
In Society '44
Something for the Boys '44
Colonel Effingham's Raid '45
West of the Pecos '45
Two Sisters From Boston '46
The Unfinished Dance '47
Miraculous Journey '48
Up in Central Park '48
Chain Gang '50
The WAC From Walla Walla '52

Lillian Hall-Davis (1896-1933)
The Last of the Mohicans '20
The Ring '27
The Farmer's Wife '28

Charles Hallahan (1943-97)
Nightwing '79
The Thing '82
Pale Rider '85
Vision Quest '85
True Believer '89
Body of Evidence '92

Warlock: The Armageddon '93
Wild Palms '93
The Fan '96
The Pest '96
The Rich Man's Wife '96
Dante's Peak '97

John Hallam (1941-2006)
The Offence '73
Dragonslayer '81
Lifeforce '85

Jane Hallaren (1935-)
Body Heat '81
Lianna '83
A Night in the Life of Jimmy Reardon '88

May Hallatt (1876-1969)
Black Narcissus '47
Separate Tables '58

Rod Hallett
The Shadow Within '07
The Hitman's Bodyguard '17

Tom Hallick (1941-)
The Amazing Captain Nemo '78
Hangar 18 '80

John Halliday (1880-1947)
Millie '31
Finishing School '33
The House on 56th Street '33
Perfect Understanding '33
Happiness Ahead '34
Housewife '34
Peter Ibbetson '35
Arsene Lupin Returns '38
That Certain Age '38
The Philadelphia Story '40

Lori Hallier (1959-)
My Bloody Valentine '81
The Gunfighters '87
Night of the Twisters '95
Recipe for Revenge '98
Running Wild '99
Ghost Cat '03

William (Bill) Halligan (1883-1957)
Blonde Comet '41
Robot Pilot '41

Annika Hallin (1968-)
The Girl Who Kicked the Hornet's Nest '10
The Girl Who Played With Fire '10

Brian Hallisay (1978-)
Bottoms Up '06
Hostel: Part 3 '11

Johnny Hallyday (1943-)
Detective '85
The Man on the Train '02
Crime Spree '03
Crimson Rivers 2: Angels of the Apocalypse '05
The Pink Panther 2 '09

Billy Halop (1920-76)
Dead End '37
Angels with Dirty Faces '38
Crime School '38
Dead End Kids: Little Tough Guy '38
Little Tough Guy '38
Angels Wash Their Faces '39
Dust Be My Destiny '39
Hell's Kitchen '39
They Made Me a Criminal '39
You Can't Get Away With Murder '39
Junior G-Men '40
Blues in the Night '41
Junior G-Men of the Air '42
Gas House Kids '46
Too Late for Tears '49

Luke Halpin (1947-)
Peter Pan '60
Flipper '63
Flipper's New Adventure '64
Island of the Lost '68
If It's Tuesday, This Must Be Belgium '69
Shock Waves '77

Matinee '92
Flipper '96

Brett Halsey (1933-)
Ma and Pa Kettle at Home '54
To Hell and Back '55
Atomic Submarine '59
Four Fast Guns '59
Return of the Fly '59
The Girl in Lover's Lane '60
Return to Peyton Place '61
Twice-Told Tales '63
Four Times That Night '69
Roy Colt and Winchester Jack '70
Demonia '90
Beyond Justice '92
First Degree '95

Michael Halsey
Treasure Island '89
Dollman '90
Mean Guns '97
Postmortem '98

Rosalind Halstead (1984-)
Wuthering Heights '09
The Burnt Orange Heresy '20

Julie Halston (1954-)
David Searching '97
Joe Gould's Secret '00
A Very Serious Person '06

Rodger Halston
Alien Terminator '95
Carnosaur 3: Primal Species '96

Charles Halton (1876-1959)
Come and Get It '36
Dodsworth '36
Dead End '37
Pick a Star '37
Prisoner of Zenda '37
Mad Miss Manton '38
Room Service '38
The Young in Heart '38
Dodge City '39
Golden Boy '39
Jesse James '39
Juarez '39
Nancy Drew, Reporter '39
Young Mr. Lincoln '39
Dr. Cyclops '40
Doctor Takes a Wife '40
Foreign Correspondent '40
The Shop Around the Corner '40
They Drive by Night '40
Virginia City '40
The Westerner '40
Dance Hall '41
Look Who's Laughing '41
Mr. & Mrs. Smith '41
The Smiling Ghost '41
Across the Pacific '42
Captains of the Clouds '42
In Old California '42
Saboteur '42
The Spoilers '42
To Be or Not to Be '42
Heaven Can Wait '43
Enemy of Women '44
The Thin Man Goes Home '44
Wilson '44
Rhapsody in Blue '45
A Tree Grows in Brooklyn '45
The Best Years of Our Lives '46
It's a Wonderful Life '46
If You Knew Susie '48
My Dear Secretary '49
Here Comes the Groom '51
Carrie '52
A Star Is Born '54
Friendly Persuasion '56

Courtney Halverson (1989-)
Freaky Faron '06
Love Finds a Home '09
The Hammer '10
Red Clover '12
Unfriended '15

Mie Hama (1943-)
King Kong *vs.* Godzilla '63
What's Up, Tiger Lily? '66
King Kong Escapes '67
You Only Live Twice '67

Akira Hamada
Kill! '68
Lady Snowblood: Love Song of Vengeance '74

Yuko Hamada
Gamera *vs.* Guiron '69
Shogun Assassin 2: Lightning Swords of Death '73

Jun Hamamura (1906-95)
100 Monsters '68
Shogun Assassin 2: Lightning Swords of Death '73
The Makioka Sisters '83

Veronica Hamel (1943-)
Cannonball '76
The Gathering '77
Snowblind '78
The Gathering: Part 2 '79
Taking Care of Business '90
High Stakes '93
Bone Eater '07

Alexandre Hamidi
Code Unknown '00
The Nest '02

Jayne Hamil
Vice Academy '88
Vice Academy 2 '90

Mark Hamill (1952-)
Star Wars '77
Corvette Summer '78
The Big Red One '80
The Empire Strikes Back '80
The Night the Lights Went Out in Georgia '81
Britannia Hospital '82
Return of the Jedi '83
Slipstream '89
The Guyver '91
Sleepwalkers '92
Time Runner '92
Batman: Mask of the Phantasm '93 *(V)*
Body Bags '93
Phantom 2040 Movie: The Ghost Who Walks '95 *(V)*
Village of the Damned '95
When Time Expires '97
Watchers Reborn '98
Laserhawk '99
Jay and Silent Bob Strike Back '01
Comic Book: The Movie '04
Sushi Girl '12
Kingsman: The Secret Service '15
Star Wars: The Force Awakens '15
Brigsby Bear '17
Star Wars: The Last Jedi '17
Child's Play '19
Star Wars: The Rise of Skywalker '19

Pete Hamill (1935-)
One Fine Day '96
The Insider '99

Antony (Tony) Hamilton (1952-95)
Samson and Delilah '84
Howling 4: The Original Nightmare '88
Fatal Instinct '92

Bernie Hamilton (1929-2008)
Jungle Man-Eaters '54
The Young One '61
Captain Sinbad '63
The Losers '70
Scream Blacula Scream '73
Bucktown '75

Carrie Hamilton (1963-2002)
Shag: The Movie '89
Cool World '92

Derek Hamilton
Extremedays '01
Out Cold '01
Ripper: Letter from Hell '01
Nightstalker '02
Taboo '02
To Have and to Hold '06
Angels Fall '07

Emily Hamilton (1974-)
He Died With a Falafel in His Hand '01
Perfect Victims '08

George Hamilton (1939-)
Crime and Punishment, USA '59
Home from the Hill '60
Where the Boys Are '60
Angel Baby '61
By Love Possessed '61
Light in the Piazza '61
A Thunder of Drums '61
Two Weeks in Another Town '62
Your Cheatin' Heart '64
Viva Maria! '65
The Power '68
Evel Knievel '72
Medusa '74
Once Is Not Enough '75
The Happy Hooker Goes to Washington '77
Sextette '78
From Hell to Victory '79
Love at First Bite '79
Zorro, the Gay Blade '81
Two Fathers' Justice '85
Monte Carlo '86
Poker Alice '87
The Godfather, Part 3 '90
Doc Hollywood '91
Once Upon a Crime '92
Two Fathers: Justice for the Innocent '94
Vanished '95
8 Heads in a Duffel Bag '96
Rough Riders '97
P.T. Barnum '99
Hollywood Ending '02
Too Cool for Christmas '04
The Congressman '16

Hale Hamilton (1883-1942)
Paid '30
Murder at Midnight '31
Susan Lenox: Her Fall and Rise '31
The Champ '32
Love Affair '32
Those We Love '32
One Man's Journey '33
Reform Girl '33
City Park '34
The Quitter '34
After Office Hours '35
The Nitwits '35

Jane Hamilton (1956-)
Deranged '87
Slammer Girls '87
Bloodsucking Pharoahs of Pittsburgh '90

John Hamilton (1887-1958)
The Fatal Hour '40
Flash Gordon Conquers the Universe '40
Gold Rush Maisie '40
The Saint's Double Trouble '40
I Killed That Man '42
Davy Crockett, Indian Scout '50
On the Waterfront '54

Josh Hamilton (1969-)
Sitting Bull '54
O Pioneers! '91
Alive '93
With Honors '94
Kicking and Screaming '95
Don't Look Back '96
The House of Yes '97
Blowin' Smoke '99
The '60s '99
Urbania '00
On_Line '01
The Bourne Identity '02
West of Here '02
Four and a Half Women '05
Diggers '06
Outsourced '06
Broken English '07
The Last New Yorker '07
Alexander the Last '09
Away We Go '09
J. Edgar '11
The Letter '12
Bottled Up '13
Dark Skies '13
Blaze '18
Eighth Grade '18

Judd Hamilton
Star Crash '78
Fanatic '82

Kipp Hamilton (1935-81)
Good Morning, Miss Dove '55
War of the Gargantuas '70

Linda Hamilton (1956-)
Children of the Corn '84
The Stone Boy '84
The Terminator '84
Secret Weapons '85
Black Moon Rising '86
Club Med '86
King Kong Lives '86
Mr. Destiny '90
Terminator 2: Judgment Day '91
Separate Lives '94
Silent Fall '94
The Shadow Conspiracy '96
Dante's Peak '97
The Secret Life of Girls '99
Sex & Mrs. X '00
Skeletons in the Closet '00
A Girl Thing '01
Silent Night '02
The Kid and I '05
Smile '05
Home By Christmas '06
In Your Dreams '07
Hard Times '09
Bermuda Tentacles '14
Terminator: Dark Fate '19

Lisa Gay Hamilton (1964-)
Krush Groove '85
Reversal of Fortune '90
Palookaville '95
Drunks '96
Last Breath '96
Jackie Brown '97
Beloved '98
Swing Vote '99
True Crime '99
Hamlet '01
The Sum of All Fears '02
The Truth About Charlie '02
Nine Lives '05
Honeydripper '07
Deception '08
Mother and Child '09
The Soloist '09
Take Shelter '11
Go for Sisters '13
Life of a King '13
Redemption Trail '13

Mahlon Hamilton (1880-1960)
Daddy Long Legs '19
Little Old New York '23

Margaret Hamilton (1902-85)
Broadway Bill '34
The Moon's Our Home '36
Nothing Sacred '37
You Only Live Once '37
The Adventures of Tom Sawyer '38
Four's a Crowd '38
A Slight Case of Murder '38
Angels Wash Their Faces '39
The Wizard of Oz '39
The Invisible Woman '40
My Little Chickadee '40
Play Girl '41
Meet the Stewarts '42
City Without Men '43
Guest in the House '44
George White's Scandals '45
The Sin of Harold Diddlebock '47
The Red Pony '49
Riding High '50
Wabash Avenue '50
Comin' Round the Mountain '51
People Will Talk '51
13 Ghosts '60
Brewster McCloud '70
The Anderson Tapes '71
Journey Back to Oz '71 *(V)*
The Night Strangler '72

Melinda Page Hamilton (1974-)
Sleeping Dogs Lie '06
Corporate Affairs '07
God Bless America '11

Murray Hamilton (1923-86)
The Girl He Left Behind '56
Toward the Unknown '56
Jeanne Eagels '57
Spirit of St. Louis '57
Darby's Rangers '58
Houseboat '58
No Time for Sergeants '58
Too Much, Too Soon '58
Anatomy of a Murder '59
The FBI Story '59
The Hustler '61
Papa's Delicate Condition '63
13 Frightened Girls '63
An American Dream '66
Seconds '66
The Graduate '67
The Boston Strangler '68
The Brotherhood '68
No Way to Treat a Lady '68
If It's Tuesday, This Must Be Belgium '69
The Tattered Web '71
The Way We Were '73
The Drowning Pool '75
Jaws '75
Casey's Shadow '78
Jaws 2 '78
The Amityville Horror '79
1941 '79
Brubaker '80
Mazes and Monsters '82
The Last Days of Patton '86

Neil Hamilton (1899-1984)
America '24
The Love Trap '29
Why Be Good? '29
The Dawn Patrol '30
Laughing Sinners '31
The Sin of Madelon Claudet '31
Strangers May Kiss '31
This Modern Age '31
The Animal Kingdom '32
Are You Listening? '32
Tarzan, the Ape Man '32
The Wet Parade '32
What Price Hollywood? '32
One Sunday Afternoon '33
The World Gone Mad '33
Tarzan and His Mate '34
The Daring Young Man '35
The Keeper of the Bees '35
Mutiny Ahead '35
The Saint Strikes Back '39
Betrayed '44
The Devil's Hand '61
Good Neighbor Sam '64
The Patsy '64
Batman '66

Nicholas Hamilton
Strangerland '15
Danger Close '19

Patricia Hamilton (1938-)
A House Without a Christmas Tree '72 *(V)*
Anne of Green Gables '85
Anne of Avonlea '87
The Christmas Wife '88
Anne of Green Gables: The Continuing Story '99

Richard Hamilton (1920-2004)
Greetings '68
In Country '89
Sommersby '93
Message in a Bottle '98

Suzanna Hamilton (1960-)
Brimstone & Treacle '82
1984 '84
Out of Africa '85
Wetherby '85
Duel of Hearts '92
Tale of a Vampire '92

Suzette Hamilton
Scream Bloody Murder '72
Amputee with an Axe '73

Victoria Hamilton (1971-)
Persuasion '95
King Lear '98
Mansfield Park '99
Victoria & Albert '01
Goodbye, Mr. Chips '02
Scoop '06
The Shell Seekers '06
Wide Sargasso Sea '06
French Film '08
Toast '10

Wendy Hamilton (1967-)
The Scars of Dracula '70
The Dallas Connection '94
Ski School 2 '94

Harry Hamlin (1951-)
Movie, Movie '78
Clash of the Titans '81
Making Love '82
Maxie '85
Dinner at Eight '89
Take Down '92
Allie & Me '97
Frogs for Snakes '98
Silent Predators '99
Road to Riches '01
Disappearance '02
Shoot or Be Shot '02
Strange Wilderness '08
You Lucky Dog '10
Shadow of Fear '12
Bleeding Heart '15

Jon Hamm (1971-)
We Were Soldiers '02
The Day the Earth Stood Still '08
A Single Man '09 *(V)*
Stolen '09
The A-Team '10
Howl '10
Shrek Forever After '10 *(V)*
The Town '10
Bridesmaids '11
Sucker Punch '11
Friends with Kids '12
The Congress '13 *(V)*
Million Dollar Arm '14
Minions '15 *(V)*
Keeping Up with the Joneses '16
Baby Driver '17
Marjorie Prime '17
Aardvark '18
Bad Times at the El Royale '18
Beirut '18
Nostalgia '18
Lucy in the Sky '19
The Report '19

Warren Hammack (1934-)
The Eye Creatures '65
Mars Needs Women '66
Zontar, the Thing from Venus '66

Hammer (1962-)
Last Action Hero '93 *(C)*
One Man's Justice '95

Alvin Hammer (1915-93)
A Walk in the Sun '46
Command Decision '48

Armie Hammer (1986-)
Blackout '07
The Social Network '10
J. Edgar '11
Mirror Mirror '12
The Lone Ranger '13
The Man from U.N.C.L.E. '15
The Birth of a Nation '16
Call Me by Your Name '17
Cars 3 '17 *(V)*
Final Portrait '17
Free Fire '17
Hotel Mumbai '18
On the Basis of Sex '18
Sorry to Bother You '18

Ben Hammer (1924-)
Johnny Got His Gun '71
Invasion of the Bee Girls '73

Beastmaster '82
Survival Quest '89
Crazy People '90
Subterfuge '98
The Last New Yorker '07
(Untitled) '09

John Hammil (1948-)
Crossover Dreams '85
Young Guns 2 '90
Phantoms '97

Brandon Hammond (1984-)
Tales from the Hood '95
The Fan '96
Soul Food '97
Our America '02

Darrell Hammond (1955-)
Celtic Pride '96
Blues Brothers 2000 '98
The King and I '99 (V)
Agent Cody Banks '03
New York Minute '04
Ira & Abby '06
Epic Movie '07
Netherbeast Incorporated '07
Wieners '08

Kay Hammond (1909-80)
Abraham Lincoln '30
Blithe Spirit '45
The Girl in the Red Velvet Swing '55

Nicholas Hammond (1950-)
The Sound of Music '65
Skyjacked '72
The Martian Chronicles: Part 1 '79
The Martian Chronicles: Part 3 '79
Trouble in Paradise '88
Black Cobra 2 '89
Salem's Lot '04
Stealth '05

Roger Hammond (1936-2012)
A Dangerous Man: Lawrence after Arabia '91
Lady Chatterley '92
Around the World in 80 Days '04
A Good Woman '04

Gabriella Hamori (1978-)
I Love Budapest '01
Ruben Brandt, Collector '18

Walter Hampden (1879-1955)
The Hunchback of Notre Dame '39
They Died with Their Boots On '41
Reap the Wild Wind '42
The Adventures of Mark Twain '44
Five Fingers '52
Sabrina '54
The Prodigal '55

Emily Hampshire (1981-)
Eye '96
Love Letters '99
Posers '02
The Cradle '06
It's a Boy Girl Thing '06
Snow Cake '06
The Trotsky '09
Good Neighbors '10
Hitched for the Holidays '12
The Returned '14
The Death and Life of John F. Donovan '19

Susan Hampshire (1937-)
The Three Lives of Thomasina '63
Night Must Fall '64
The Fighting Prince of Donegal '66
Those Daring Young Men in Their Jaunty Jalopies '69
David Copperfield '70
Baffled '72
Living Free '72
Neither the Sea Nor the Sand '73
The Story of David '76
Coming Home '98

Danielle Hampton (1978-)
Ginger Snaps '01
Detention '03

James Hampton (1936-)
The Longest Yard '74
W.W. and the Dixie Dancekings '75
Hawmps! '76
The Amazing Howard Hughes '77
The China Syndrome '79
Hangar 18 '80
Condorman '81
Teen Wolf '85
World War III '86
Sling Blade '96

Lionel Hampton (1908-2002)
The Benny Goodman Story '55
Force of Impulse '60

Paul Hampton (1937-)
More Dead Than Alive '68
Private Duty Nurses '71
Lady Sings the Blues '72
Hit! '73
They Came from Within '75

Maggie Han (1959-)
The Last Emperor '87
Open Season '95

Thierry Hancisse (1962-)
Gabrielle '05
The Lady in the Car with Glasses and a Gun '16

Herbie Hancock (1940-)
Round Midnight '86
Indecent Proposal '93

John Hancock (1941-92)
The Black Marble '79
In the Custody of Strangers '82
Sundown: The Vampire in Retreat '08

Lou Hancock
Evil Dead 2: Dead by Dawn '87
Miracle Mile '89

Sheila Hancock (1933-)
The Moon-Spinners '64
Night Must Fall '64
The Anniversary '68
Take a Girl Like You '70
Buster '88
Hawks '89
Three Men and a Little Lady '90
A Business Affair '93
The Buccaneers '95
Love and Death on Long Island '97
Love or Money '01
Bait '02
Yes '04
The Boy in the Striped Pajamas '08
Just Henry '11
Edie '19

Irene Handl (1901-87)
Night Train to Munich '40
The Girl in the News '41
Brief Encounter '46
The Belles of St. Trinian's '53
A Kid for Two Farthings '55
Doctor in Love '60
No Kidding '60
School for Scoundrels '60
Morgan: A Suitable Case for Treatment '66
Smashing Time '67
Wonderwall: The Movie '69
The Private Life of Sherlock Holmes '70
Confessions of a Driving Instructor '76

Chelsea Handler (1975-)
National Lampoon Presents Cattle Call '06
Hop '11
Fun Size '12
This Means War '12

Evan Handler (1961-)
Taps '81
Ruby's Dream '82
Sweet Lorraine '87
Ransom '96
Cash Crop '98
Sex and the City: The Movie '08
Sex and the City 2 '10

Taylor Handley (1984-)
The Texas Chainsaw Massacre: The Beginning '06
September Dawn '07
Skateland '10

Marina Hands (1975-)
The Barbarian Invasions '03
Tell No One '06
Change of Plans '09
Lady Chatterley '10

James Handy
The Verdict '82
Burglar '87
Bird '88
K-9 '89
Arachnophobia '90
The Rocketeer '91
False Arrest '92
Gang Related '96
K-911 '99
Unbreakable '00
15 Minutes '01
Ash Wednesday '02
Lifted '10

Scott Handy (1968-)
The Gospel of John '03
The Haunted Airman '06

Anne Haney (1934-2001)
The Bad Seed '85
The American President '95
Changing Habits '96
Liar Liar '97
Midnight in the Garden of Good and Evil '97
Psycho '98

Perla Haney-Jardine (1997-)
Dark Water '02
Kill Bill Vol. 2 '04
Spider-Man 3 '07
A Summer in Genoa '08
Untraceable '08

Helen Hanft (1934-2013)
Stardust Memories '80
Used People '92

Larry Hankin (1940-)
Escape from Alcatraz '79
Armed and Dangerous '86
Billy Madison '94
Money Talks '97
The Independent '00
Hard Ground '03

Colin Hanks (1977-)
That Thing You Do! '96
Whatever It Takes '00
Band of Brothers '01
Get Over It! '01
Orange County '02
11:14 '03
King Kong '05
Standing Still '05
Rx '06
Tenacious D in the Pick of Destiny '06
Alone With Her '07
Careless '07
The House Bunny '08
My Mom's New Boyfriend '08
Untraceable '08
The Great Buck Howard '09
Barry Munday '10
High School '10
Lucky '11
The Guilt Trip '12
Parkland '13
Super Buddies '13 (V)
Elvis & Nixon '16

Jim Hanks (1961-)
Xtro 3: Watch the Skies '95
Purgatory House '04
Black Ops '07

Steve Hanks
Hold Your Breath '12
12/12/12 '12
Echoes '15

Tom Hanks (1956-)
He Knows You're Alone '80
Mazes and Monsters '82
Bachelor Party '84
Splash '84
The Man with One Red Shoe '85
Volunteers '85
Every Time We Say Goodbye '86
The Money Pit '86
Nothing in Common '86
Dragnet '87
Big '88
Punchline '88
The 'Burbs '89
Turner and Hooch '89
The Bonfire of the Vanities '90
Joe Versus the Volcano '90
A League of Their Own '92
Radio Flyer '92 (N)
Philadelphia '93
Sleepless in Seattle '93
Forrest Gump '94
Apollo 13 '95
Toy Story '95 (V)
That Thing You Do! '96
Saving Private Ryan '98
You've Got Mail '98
The Green Mile '99
Toy Story 2 '99 (V)
Cast Away '00
Catch Me If You Can '02
Road to Perdition '02
Elvis Has Left the Building '04
The Ladykillers '04
The Polar Express '04
The Terminal '04
The Da Vinci Code '06
Charlie Wilson's War '07
The Simpsons Movie '07 (V)
Angels & Demons '09
The Great Buck Howard '09
Toy Story 3 '10 (V)
Extremely Loud and Incredibly Close '11
Larry Crowne '11
Cloud Atlas '12
Captain Phillips '13
Killing Lincoln '13 (N)
Saving Mr. Banks '13
Bridge of Spies '15
A Hologram for the King '16
Inferno '16
Ithaca '16
Sully '16
The Circle '17
The Post '17
A Beautiful Day in the Neighborhood '19
Toy Story 4 '19

Jenny Hanley (1947-)
On Her Majesty's Secret Service '69
The Scars of Dracula '70
Flesh and Blood Show '73

Jimmy Hanley (1918-70)
Boys Will Be Boys '35
Gaslight '40
Immortal Battalion '44
The Way Ahead '44
Captive Heart '47
It Always Rains on Sunday '47
The Blue Lamp '49
Boys in Brown '49
Radio Cab Murder '54
Satellite in the Sky '56

Bert Hanlon (1890-1972)
Too Busy to Work '32
Wings in the Dark '35
A Slight Case of Murder '38

Adam Hann-Byrd (1982-)
Little Man Tate '91
Jumanji '95
Diabolique '96
The Ice Storm '97
Halloween: H20 '98

Daryl Hannah (1960-)
The Fury '78
Hard Country '81
Blade Runner '82
Summer Lovers '82
The Final Terror '83
The Pope of Greenwich Village '84
Reckless '84
Splash '84
The Clan of the Cave Bear '86
Legal Eagles '86
Roxanne '87
Wall Street '87
High Spirits '88
Crimes & Misdemeanors '89
Steel Magnolias '89
Crazy People '90
Memoirs of an Invisible Man '92
Attack of the 50 Ft. Woman '93
Grumpy Old Men '93
The Little Rascals '94
Grumpier Old Men '95
The Tie That Binds '95
The Last Days of Frankie the Fly '96
Two Much '96
The Gingerbread Man '97
The Last Don '97
The Real Blonde '97
Hi-Life '98
My Favorite Martian '98
Diplomatic Siege '99
Speedway Junky '99
Wildflowers '99
Cowboy Up '00
Dancing at the Blue Iguana '00
Hide and Seek '00
Hard Cash '01
Jack and the Beanstalk: The Real Story '01
Jackpot '01
A Walk to Remember '02
Casa de los Babys '03
The Job '03
Kill Bill Vol. 1 '03
Northfork '03
The Big Empty '04
Kill Bill Vol. 2 '04
Silver City '04
Addicted to Her Love '06
Final Days of Planet Earth '06
Keeping Up with the Steins '06
All the Good Ones Are Married '07
Hearts of War '07
Dark Honeymoon '08
Kung Fu Killer '08
Shark Swarm '08
Storm Seekers '08
Vice '08
Blind Revenge '10
The Hot Flashes '13
Mother '13
Death Squad '14
Awaken '15
I Am Michael '17

John Hannah (1962-)
Faith '94
Four Weddings and a Funeral '94
The Innocent Sleep '95
Madagascar Skin '95
Romance and Rejection '96
Sliding Doors '97
The Hurricane '99
The Mummy '99
Circus '00
Pandaemonium '00
The Mummy Returns '01
I'm with Lucy '02
Ghost Son '06
The Last Legion '07
The Mummy: Tomb of the Dragon Emperor '08
Appointment With Death '10
Ping Pong Summer '14
Overboard '18

Page Hannah (1964-)
Racing with the Moon '84
Creepshow 2 '87
Shag: The Movie '89

G. Hannelius (1998-)
Spooky Buddies '11 (V)
Treasure Buddies '12 (V)

Genevieve Hannelius (1998-)
See G. Hannelius

Alyson Hannigan (1974-)
My Stepmother Is an Alien '88
Dead Man on Campus '97
American Pie '99
Boys and Girls '00
American Pie 2 '01
Rip It Off '02
American Wedding '03
Date Movie '06
American Reunion '12

Donna Hanover (1950-)
The People *vs.* Larry Flynt '96
Just the Ticket '98
Series 7: The Contenders '01

Sammi Hanratty (1995-)
American Girl: Chrissa Stands Strong '09
The Greening of Whitney Brown '11
The Lost Medallion: The Adventures of Billy Stone '13

Lawrence Hanray (1874-1947)
The Private Life of Henry VIII '33
On Approval '44

Glen Hansard
The Commitments '91
Once '06

Gale Hansen (1960-)
Dead Poets Society '89
The Finest Hour '91
Shaking the Tree '92

Gunnar Hansen (1947-)
The Texas Chainsaw Massacre '74
The Demon Lover '77
Hollywood Chainsaw Hookers '88
Freakshow '95
Mosquito '95
Hellblock 13 '97
Brutal Massacre: A Comedy '07

Holger Juul Hansen (1924-)
The Kingdom '95
The Kingdom 2 '97

Joachim Hansen (1930-2007)
Secret of the Black Trunk '62
Frozen Alive '64
Underground '70
Anne of Green Gables '85

Patti Hansen (1956-)
They All Laughed '81
Hard to Hold '84

Paul Hansen
Count Yorga, Vampire '70
The Return of Count Yorga '71

Peter Hansen (1921-)
Cavalry Charge '51
When Worlds Collide '51

Ryan Hansen (1981-)
Superhero Movie '08
Housebroken '09
Bad Actress '11
Veronica Mars '14
CHIPS '17

Valda Hansen (1932-93)
Night of the Ghouls '59
Cain's Cutthroats '71
Wham-Bam, Thank You Spaceman '75

Kit Harington (1986-)
Silent Hill: Revelation 3D '12
Pompeii '14
MI-5 '15
Seventh Son '15
Testament of Youth '15
Brimstone '17
The Death and Life of John F. Donovan '19

Tsui Hark (1951-)
Mad Mission 3 '84 (C)
Twin Dragons '92

Gordon Harker (1885-1967)
The Ring '27
Champagne '28
The Farmer's Wife '28
Rome Express '32
Boys Will Be Boys '35
The Phantom Light '35
Inspector Hornleigh '39
Things Happen at Night '48

Susannah Harker (1965-)
The Lady's Not for Burning '87
Troubles '88
A Dry White Season '89
House of Cards '90
The Crucifer of Blood '91
Faith '94
Pride and Prejudice '95
Ultraviolet '98
Heat of the Sun '99
Intimacy '00
Perfect Parents '06

John Harkins (1932-99)
Acapulco Gold '78
Absence of Malice '81
Amityville 3: The Demon '83
Birdy '84
Rampage '87
Slaves of New York '89
This Gun for Hire '90

Kenneth Harlan (1895-1967)
The Hoodlum '19
The Penalty '20
The Primitive Lover '22
Little Church Around the Corner '23
Twinkletoes '26
Paradise Island '30
San Francisco '36

Otis Harlan (1865-1940)
Loose Ankles '30
Snow White and the Seven Dwarfs '37 (V)

Jean Harlow (1911-37)
Hell's Angels '30
City Lights '31
Platinum Blonde '31
Public Enemy '31
The Secret Six '31
The Beast of the City '32
Red Dust '32
Red Headed Woman '32
Three Wise Girls '32
Bombshell '33
Dinner at Eight '33
Hold Your Man '33
The Girl from Missouri '34
China Seas '35
Reckless '35
Riff Raff '35
Libeled Lady '36
Suzy '36
Wife Versus Secretary '36
Personal Property '37
Saratoga '37
The Love Goddesses '65

Shalom Harlow (1973-)
In and Out '97
Head Over Heels '01
The Salton Sea '02
How to Lose a Guy in 10 Days '03
I Love Your Work '03
Game 6 '05

Angie Harmon (1972-)
Good Advice '01
Video Voyeur: The Susan Wilson Story '02
Agent Cody Banks '03
The Deal '05
Fun With Dick and Jane '05
End Game '06
Glass House: The Good Mother '06
Living Proof '08

Brooke Harmon (1985-)
Till Human Voices Wake Us '02
Crush '09

Deborah Harmon (1951-)
Used Cars '80
Bachelor Party '84
Prince of Bel Air '87

Jessica Harmon (1985-)
Black Christmas '06
Uncaged Heart '07
The Capture of the Green River Killer '08
Dead Rising: End Game '16

John Harmon (1905-85)
A Slight Case of Murder '38
Homicide '49

Mark Harmon (1951-)
Centennial '78
Comes a Horseman '78
Beyond the Poseidon Adventure '79
The Deliberate Stranger '86
Let's Get Harry '87
Prince of Bel Air '87
Summer School '87
The Presidio '88
Stealing Home '88
Sweet Bird of Youth '89
Worth Winning '89
Cold Heaven '92
Wyatt Earp '94
Acts of Contrition '95
Magic in the Water '95
The Last Supper '96
Casualties '97
The First to Go '97
Fear and Loathing in Las Vegas '98
From the Earth to the Moon '98
I'll Remember April '99
And Never Let Her Go '01
Crossfire Trail '01
Local Boys '02
Freaky Friday '03
Chasing Liberty '04
Weather Girl '09
Certain Prey '11

Renee Harmon (1922-2006)
The Executioner, Part 2: Frozen Scream '84
Lady Street Fighter '86
Night of Terror '87

Richard Harmon (1991-)
Judas Kiss '11
Grave Encounters 2 '12
Darkness Falls '20

Jess Harnell (1963-)
Pom Poko '94 (V)
Clifford's Really Big Movie '04 (V)

Jason Butler Harner (1970-)
Next '07
Changeling '08
The Green '11
Non-Stop '14

Ricci Harnett (1973-)
The Object of Beauty '91
A Certain Justice '99
Rise of the Footsoldier '07
Psychosis '10

Elisabeth Harnois (1979-)
One Magic Christmas '85
Where Are the Children? '85
Pretty Persuasion '05
Strangers with Candy '06
Ten Inch Hero '07
Chaos Theory '08
Keith '08
Bad Meat '11
Mars Needs Moms '11 (V)
Riddle '13

Christina Harnos (1968-)
The Rescue '88
Cold Dog Soup '89
Cool and the Crazy '94
Hellraiser 4: Bloodline '95
Hollywood Confidential '97

Gale Harold (1969-)
Falling for Grace '06
Passenger Side '09
Fertile Ground '10
Andron: The Black Labyrinth '16

Ralf Harolde (1899-1974)
Framed '30
Hook, Line and Sinker '30
Night Nurse '31
Safe in Hell '31
Smart Money '31
I'm No Angel '33
Picture Snatcher '33
Gang Busters '42
I Killed That Man '42

Frank Harper (1962-)
In the Name of the Father '93
Lock, Stock and 2 Smoking Barrels '98
Shiner '00
Lucky Break '01
Bend It Like Beckham '02
Octane '07
Berlin Job '12

Hill Harper (1966-)
Get On the Bus '96
Hav Plenty '97
The Nephew '97
Steel '97
He Got Game '98
Mama Flora's Family '98
In Too Deep '99
Loving Jezebel '99
Slaves of Hollywood '99
The Skulls '00
The Visit '00
The Badge '02
The Breed '06
Stonehenge Apocalypse '10
The Boy Next Door '15
1982 '16
All Eyez on Me '17

Jessica Harper (1949-)
Phantom of the Paradise '74
Inserts '76
Suspiria '77
Stardust Memories '80
Pennies from Heaven '81
Shock Treatment '81
My Favorite Year '82
Imagemaker '86
Blue Iguana '88
Eat a Bowl of Tea '89
Mr. Wonderful '93
Safe '95
Minority Report '02
Suspiria '18

Robert Harper (1951-2020)
Once Upon a Time in America '84
Held Hostage '91
Final Analysis '92
Running Mates '92
Molly '99

Samantha Harper
Oh! Calcutta! '72
Lookin' to Get Out '82

Shane Harper
God's Not Dead '14
God's Not Dead: A Light in Darkness '18

Tess Harper (1950-)
Amityville 3: The Demon '83
Tender Mercies '83
Flashpoint '84
A Summer to Remember '84
Promises to Keep '85
Crimes of the Heart '86
Ishtar '87
Far North '88
Her Alibi '88
Criminal Law '89
Daddy's Dyin'. . . Who's Got the Will? '90
The Man in the Moon '91
My New Gun '92
The Turning '92
Christy '94
The Jackal '97
The In Crowd '00
The Rising Place '02
Loggerheads '05
Broken Bridges '06
Jam '06
Karla '06
Kiss the Bride '07
No Country for Old Men '07
Saving Sarah Cain '07
Fatal Secrets '09
A Christmas Wish '11
Sunlight Jr. '13

Valerie Harper (1939-2019)
Freebie & the Bean '74
Chapter Two '79
The Last Married Couple in America '80
Blame It on Rio '84
The Execution '85
My Future Boyfriend '11

William Jackson Harper (1980-)
Paterson '16
Midsommar '19

Jim Harrell (1918-2000)
Don't Open the Door! '74
A Family Thing '96

Rebecca Harrell (1980-)
Prancer '89
Suspended Animation '02

Brett Harrelson (1963-)
The People vs. Larry Flynt '96
Dee Snider's Strangeland '98
From Dusk Till Dawn 2: Texas Blood Money '98

Woody Harrelson (1962-)
Wildcats '86
Eye of the Demon '87
Cool Blue '88
Doc Hollywood '91
White Men Can't Jump '92
Indecent Proposal '93
Ted & Venus '93 (C)
The Cowboy Way '94
Natural Born Killers '94
Money Train '95
Kingpin '96
The People vs. Larry Flynt '96
Sunchaser '96
Wag the Dog '97
Welcome to Sarajevo '97
The Hi-Lo Country '98
Palmetto '98
The Thin Red Line '98
Austin Powers 2: The Spy Who Shagged Me '99 (C)
EDtv '99
Play It to the Bone '99
Scorched '02
Anger Management '03
Go Further '03
After the Sunset '04
She Hate Me '04
The Big White '05
North Country '05
The Prize Winner of Defiance, Ohio '05
A Prairie Home Companion '06
A Scanner Darkly '06
Battle in Seattle '07
No Country for Old Men '07
The Walker '07
Semi-Pro '08
Seven Pounds '08
Sleepwalking '08
Surfer, Dude '08
Transsiberian '08
Defendor '09
Management '09
The Messenger '09
2012 '09
Zombieland '09
Bunraku '10
Friends With Benefits '11
Rampart '11
Game Change '12
The Hunger Games '12
Seven Psychopaths '12
Free Birds '13 (V)
The Hunger Games: Catching Fire '13
Now You See Me '13
Out of the Furnace '13
The Hunger Games: Mockingjay--Part 1 '14
The Hunger Games: Mockingjay-Part 2 '15
Triple 9 '15
The Duel '16
The Edge of Seventeen '16
Now You See Me 2 '16
The Glass Castle '17
LBJ '17
Three Billboards Outside Ebbing, Missouri '17
War for the Planet of the Apes '17
Wilson '17
Shock and Awe '18
Solo: A Star Wars Story '18
The Highwaymen '19
Midway '19
Zombieland: Double Tap '19

William Harrigan (1894-1966)
The Invisible Man '33
'G' Men '35
Whipsaw '35
Exiled to Shanghai '37
Flying Leathernecks '51

Laura Elena Harring (1964-)
The Alamo: Thirteen Days to Glory '87
Silent Night, Deadly Night 3: Better Watch Out! '89
Dead Women in Lingerie '90
The Forbidden Dance '90
Rio Diablo '93
Exit to Eden '94
Black Scorpion 2: Ground Zero '96
Mulholland Drive '01
Derailed '02
John Q '02
Loco Love '03
Willard '03
The Punisher '04
All Souls Day '05
The King '05
Ghost Son '06
Inland Empire '06
My Neighbor's Keeper '07
Nancy Drew '07
The Caller '08
Sex Ed '14

Adam Harrington (1972-)
Deep Evil '04
Too Cool for Christmas '04
Cries in the Dark '06
The Secret of Hidden Lake '06
Passchendaele '10

Desmond Harrington (1976-)
The Messenger: The Story of Joan of Arc '99
The Hole '01
My First Mister '01
Riding in Cars with Boys '01
Ghost Ship '02
We Were Soldiers '02
Wrong Turn '03
3-Way '04
Exit Speed '08
Life is Hot in Cracktown '08
Not Since You '09
Timer '09

Jay Harrington (1971-)
Octopus '00
A Little Inside '01
Why I Wore Lipstick to My Mastectomy '06

Kevin Harrington
The Dish '00
Red Hill '10

Laura Harrington (1958-)
Maximum Overdrive '86
Perfect Witness '89
The Secret '93
What's Eating Gilbert Grape '93
The Devil's Advocate '97
Paulie '98

Pat Harrington, Jr. (1929-2016)
Move Over, Darling '63
Easy Come, Easy Go '67
The President's Analyst '67
The Affair '73
Ablaze '00
These Old Broads '01

Peter Harrington
Time Chasers '95
Diamond Run '96

Richard Harrington
The Proposition '96
Cravings '06
Gwen '19

Aaron Harris
The Glory Boys '84
Returned '15

Barbara Harris (1935-)
A Thousand Clowns '65
Plaza Suite '71
Nashville '75
Family Plot '76
Freaky Friday '76
Movie, Movie '78
The North Avenue Irregulars '79
The Seduction of Joe Tynan '79
Second-Hand Hearts '81
Peggy Sue Got Married '86
Dirty Rotten Scoundrels '88
Grosse Pointe Blank '97
The Midnight Meat Train '08

Baxter Harris (1940-)
Stephen King's The Langoliers '95
Home Alone 3 '97
Species 2 '98

Brad Harris (1933-)
The Fury of Hercules '61
Samson '61
The Old Testament '62
Goliath Against the Giants '63
Kiss Kiss Kill Kill '66
Death is Nimble, Death is Quick '67
The Mad Butcher '72
The Freakmaker '73
King of Kong Island '78
Hercules '83

Cynthia Harris (1934-)
Edward and Mrs. Simpson '80
Izzy & Moe '85
Three Men and a Baby '87
I Do & I Don't '07

Danielle Harris (1977-)
Halloween 4: The Return of Michael Myers '88
Halloween 5: The Revenge of Michael Myers '89
The Killing Mind '90
Marked for Death '90
The Last Boy Scout '91
Nightmare '91
The Woman Who Loved Elvis '93
Back to Back '96
Daylight '96
Wish upon a Star '96
Urban Legend '98
Killer Bud '00
The Wild Thornberrys Movie '02 (V)
Rugrats Go Wild! '03 (V)
Halloween '07
Blood Night: The Legend of Mary Hatchet '09
Halloween II '09
Super Capers '09
The Black Waters of Echo's Pond '10
Hatchet 2 '10
Stake Land '10
ChromeSkull: Laid to Rest 2 '11
The Trouble with the Truth '11
Fatal Call '12
Camp Dread '14

Black Moon *'75*
Blue Fire Lady *'78*
The Dresser *'83*
A Handful of Dust *'88*
Clarissa *'91*
Heat of the Sun *'99*

Emily Harrison (1977-)
Curse of the Puppet Master: The Human Experiment *'98*
Valley of the Heart's Delight *'07*

George Harrison (1943-2001)
A Hard Day's Night *'64*
Help! *'65*
Yellow Submarine *'68 (V)*
Let It Be *'70*
All You Need Is Cash *'78*
Monty Python's Life of Brian *'79*
Water *'85 (C)*
Shanghai Surprise *'86 (C)*

Gregory Harrison (1950-)
Trilogy of Terror *'75*
The Gathering *'77*
Centennial *'78*
Razorback *'84*
Seduced *'85*
Oceans of Fire *'86*
North Shore *'87*
Dangerous Pursuit *'89*
Body Chemistry 2: Voice of a Stranger *'91*
It's My Party *'95*
Air Bud 2: Golden Receiver *'98*
Au Pair *'99*
Running Wild *'99*
Au Pair 2: The Fairy Tale Continues *'01*
Au Pair 3: Adventure in Paradise *'09*
Give 'Em Hell Malone *'09*
Maneater *'09*
Undercover Bridesmaid *'12*
The M Word *'14*

Jenilee Harrison (1959-)
Tank *'83*
Prime Target *'91*

Jenna Harrison
Telling Lies *'06*
Against the Dark *'08*
Chimera Strain *'19*

Kathleen Harrison (1892-1995)
The Ghoul *'34*
Night Must Fall *'37*
Bank Holiday *'38*
The Ghost Train *'41*
The Winslow Boy *'48*
A Christmas Carol *'51*
The Pickwick Papers *'54*
Cast a Dark Shadow *'55*
Let's Make Up *'55*
Where There's a Will *'55*
The Beasts of Marseilles *'57*
A Cry from the Streets *'57*

Kelvin Harrison, Jr. (1994-)
It Comes at Night *'17*
Jinn *'18*
Monsters and Men *'18*
Luce *'19*
Waves *'19*

Linda Harrison (1945-)
Planet of the Apes *'68*
Beneath the Planet of the Apes *'70*
Cocoon *'85*

Matthew Harrison (1968-)
The House Next Door *'01*
The Last Trimester *'06*
Seventeen and Missing *'06*
Judicial Indiscretion *'07*
Ace of Hearts *'08*

Michelle Harrison (1975-)
Pressure *'02*
Come as You Are *'05*
The Invisible *'07*
Luna: Spirit of the Whale *'07*
Seattle Superstorm *'12*
Stagecoach: The Texas Jack Story *'16*

Mya Harrison (1979-)
See Mya

Noel Harrison (1934-2013)
Where the Spies Are *'65*
Take a Girl Like You *'70*
Deja Vu *'98*

Rex Harrison (1908-90)
Storm in a Teacup *'37*
The Citadel *'38*
Sidewalks of London *'38*
Night Train to Munich *'40*
Major Barbara *'41*
Blithe Spirit *'45*
Anna and the King of Siam *'46*
I Live in Grosvenor Square *'46*
The Foxes of Harrow *'47*
The Ghost and Mrs. Muir *'47*
Unfaithfully Yours *'48*
The Long Dark Hall *'51*
King Richard and the Crusaders *'54*
The Reluctant Debutante *'58*
The Happy Thieves *'61*
Cleopatra *'63*
My Fair Lady *'64*
The Yellow Rolls Royce *'64*
The Agony and the Ecstasy *'65*
Doctor Dolittle *'67*
The Honey Pot *'67*
Deadly Thief *'78*
The Prince and the Pauper *'78*
Ashanti, Land of No Mercy *'79*
The Fifth Musketeer *'79*
Time to Die *'83*
Anastasia: The Mystery of Anna *'86*

Richard Harrison (1936-)
Gladiators 7 *'62*
The Invincible Gladiator *'62*
Medusa Against the Son of Hercules *'62*
Giants of Rome *'63*
Gunfight at Red Sands *'63*
Two Gladiators *'64*
Sandok *'65*
One After Another *'68*
His Name Was King *'71*
Between God, the Devil & a Winchester *'72*
Mad Dog Killer *'77*
Fireback *'78*
Terminal Force *'88*

David Harrod
The Tuskegee Airmen *'95*
The Thin Red Line *'98*

Jamie Harrold
Family Pictures *'93*
I Shot Andy Warhol *'96*
I Think I Do *'97*
Henry Hill *'00*
101 Ways (The Things a Girl Will Do to Keep Her Volvo) *'00*
Swimming *'00*
A Glimpse of Hell *'01*
The Score *'01*
The Sum of All Fears *'02*
Corn *'04*
Flannel Pajamas *'06*
The Last Winter *'06*

Kathryn Harrold (1950-)
Nightwing *'79*
The Hunter *'80*
Modern Romance *'81*
The Sender *'82*
Yes, Giorgio *'82*
Into the Night *'85*
Raw Deal *'86*
Someone to Love *'87*
Outrage *'98*
The '70s *'00*
A Woman's a Helluva Thing *'01*

John Harron (1903-39)
West-Bound Limited *'23*
The White Zombie *'32*

Robert 'Bobbie' Harron (1893-1920)
Judith of Bethulia *'14*
The Birth of a Nation *'15*
The Greatest Question *'19*
True Heart Susie *'19*

Lisa Harrow (1943-)
All Creatures Great and Small *'74*
The Final Conflict *'81*
From a Far Country: Pope John Paul II *'81*
Shaker Run *'85*
Sunday *'96*

Deborah Harry (1945-)
The Foreigner *'78*
Mr. Mike's Mondo Video *'79*
Union City *'81*
Videodrome *'83*
Forever, Lulu *'87*
Hairspray *'88*
Satisfaction *'88*
New York Stories *'89*
Tales from the Darkside: The Movie *'90*
Body Bags *'93*
Dead Beat *'94*
Heavy *'94*
Cop Land *'97*
Six Ways to Sunday *'99*
The Fluffer *'01*
All I Want *'02*
Deuces Wild *'02*
My Life Without Me *'03*
Elegy *'08*

Jackee Harry (1956-)
See Jackee

Ray Harryhausen (1920-2013)
Spies Like Us *'85*
Mighty Joe Young *'98*
Comic Book: The Movie *'04 (C)*

Margo Harshman (1986-)
Recipe for Disaster *'03*
College Road Trip *'08*
Legacy *'08*
Sorority Row *'09*

Christina Hart (1949-)
Games Girls Play *'75*
Johnny Firecloud *'75*
Helter Skelter *'76*

Christopher Hart (1961-)
The Addams Family *'91*
Addams Family Values *'93*
Idle Hands *'99*

Dianne Lee Hart
The Giant Spider Invasion *'75*
Pom Pom Girls *'76*

Dolores Hart (1938-)
Loving You *'57*
Wild Is the Wind *'57*
King Creole *'58*
The Plunderers *'60*
Where the Boys Are *'60*
Sail a Crooked Ship *'61*
Lisa *'62*

Dorothy Hart (1923-2004)
Gunfighters *'47*
The Naked City *'48*
Undertow *'49*
I Was a Communist for the FBI *'51*
Raton Pass *'51*
Loan Shark *'52*
Tarzan's Savage Fury *'52*

Hannah Hart
Dirty 30 *'16*
Electra Woman & Dyna Girl *'16*

Ian Hart (1964-)
Backbeat *'94*
The Englishman Who Went up a Hill But Came down a Mountain *'95*
Michael Collins *'96*
Robinson Crusoe *'96*
B. Monkey *'97*
The Butcher Boy *'97*
Frogs for Snakes *'98*
Monument Ave. *'98*
The End of the Affair *'99*
Spring Forward *'99*
Wonderland *'99*
Aberdeen *'00*
American Women *'00*
Born Romantic *'00*
Liam *'00*
Longitude *'00*
Harry Potter and the Sorcerer's Stone *'01*
Killing Me Softly *'01*
Strictly Sinatra *'01*
The Hound of the Baskervilles *'02*
Finding Neverland *'04*
Breakfast on Pluto *'05*
Tristram Shandy: A Cock and Bull Story *'05*
God's Own Country *'17*
Escape from Pretoria *'20*

Kevin Hart (1979-)
Paper Soldiers *'02*
Scary Movie 3 *'03*
Along Came Polly *'04*
Soul Plane *'04*
In the Mix *'05*
Scary Movie 4 *'06*
Fool's Gold *'08*
Meet Dave *'08*
Not Easily Broken *'09*
Death at a Funeral *'10*
35 and Ticking *'10*
Let Go *'11*
Think Like a Man *'12*
Grudge Match *'13*
About Last Night *'14*
Ride Along *'14*
Think Like a Man Too *'14*
Top Five *'14*
Get Hard *'15*
The Wedding Ringer *'15*
Central Intelligence *'16*
Kevin Hart: What Now? *'16*
Ride Along 2 *'16*
The Secret Life of Pets *'16*
Captain Underpants: The First Epic Movie *'17 (V)*
Jumanji: Welcome to the Jungle *'17*
The Upside *'17*
Jumanji: The Next Level *'19*
The Secret Life of Pets 2 *'19*

Linda Hart (1950-)
Gypsy *'93*
A Perfect World *'93*
Tin Cup *'96*
Crazy in Alabama *'99*
The First $20 Million is Always the Hardest *'02*

Melissa Joan Hart (1976-)
Sabrina the Teenage Witch *'96*
Two Came Back *'97*
Drive Me Crazy *'99*
Backflash *'01*
Holiday in Handcuffs *'07*
Whispers and Lies *'08*
My Fake Fiance *'09*
Nine Dead *'10*
Satin *'10*
God's Not Dead 2 *'16*

Pamela Hart
The Young Girls of Rochefort *'68*
The Proposition *'97*
Next Stop, Wonderland *'98*
Pi *'98*
Changing Lanes *'02*

Richard Hart
B.F.'s Daughter *'48*
Reign of Terror *'49*

Roxanne Hart (1952-)
The Verdict *'82*
Special Bulletin *'83*
Oh, God! You Devil *'84*
Old Enough *'84*
Highlander *'86*
Samaritan: The Mitch Snyder Story *'86*
Pulse *'88*
Once Around *'91*
Horton Foote's Alone *'97*
The Runaway *'00*
Follow the Stars Home *'01*
The Good Girl *'02*
Home Room *'02*
Moonlight Mile *'02*
The President's Man 2: A Line in the Sand *'02*

Shad Hart
Big Brother Trouble *'00*
The Reagans *'04*

Susan Hart (1941-)
The Slime People *'63*
Pajama Party *'64*
Ride the Wild Surf *'64*
Dr. Goldfoot and the Bikini Machine *'66*
Ghost in the Invisible Bikini *'66*

Teddy Hart (1897-1971)
Ma and Pa Kettle at Waikiki *'55*
Mickey One *'65*

William S. Hart (1864-1946)
Hell's Hinges *'16*
Blue Blazes Rawden *'18*
The Cradle of Courage *'20*
The Toll Gate *'20*
Three Word Brand *'21*
Tumbleweeds *'25*
Show People *'28*

Pat Hartigan (1881-1951)
Where the North Begins *'23*
Ranson's Folly *'26*

Clabe Hartley
Trancers 4: Jack of Swords *'93*
Trancers 5: Sudden Deth *'94*

Jo Hartley
This Is England *'06*
Eddie the Eagle *'16*

Justin Hartley (1977-)
Megafault *'09*
Little *'19*

Mariette Hartley (1940-)
Ride the High Country *'62*
Drums of Africa *'63*
Marnie *'64*
The Return of Count Yorga *'71*
Skyjacked *'72*
Genesis II *'73*
Nightmare at 43 Hillcrest *'74*
O'Hara's Wife *'82*
Silence of the Heart *'84*
1969 *'89*
Murder C.O.D. *'90*
Encino Man *'92*
Novel Romance *'06*

Pat Hartley
Rainbow Bridge *'71*
Edie in Ciao! Manhattan *'72*

Steven Hartley (1960-)
A Dog of Flanders *'99*
The Walker *'07*

David Hartman (1935-)
The Ballad of Josie *'67*
The Island at the Top of the World *'74*

Elizabeth Hartman (1941-87)
A Patch of Blue *'65*
The Group *'66*
You're a Big Boy Now *'66*
The Beguiled *'70*
Walking Tall *'73*
The Secret of NIMH *'82 (V)*

Margot Hartman (1933-2020)
Curse of the Living Corpse *'64*
Voyage to the Planet of Prehistoric Women *'68*

Phil Hartman (1948-98)
Cheech and Chong's Next Movie *'80*
Weekend Pass *'84*
Pee-wee's Big Adventure *'85*
Jumpin' Jack Flash *'86 (C)*
Last Resort *'86*
Three Amigos *'86*
Amazon Women on the Moon *'87*
Blind Date *'87*
Fletch Lives *'89*
How I Got into College *'89*
Quick Change *'90*
CB4: The Movie *'93*
Coneheads *'93*
Daybreak *'93 (C)*
National Lampoon's Loaded Weapon 1 *'93*
So I Married an Axe Murderer *'93 (C)*
The Crazysitter *'94*
Greedy *'94*
Houseguest *'94*
Sgt. Bilko *'95*
Jingle All the Way *'96*
The Second Civil War *'97*
Kiki's Delivery Service *'98 (V)*
Small Soldiers *'98*

Lisa Hartman Black (1956-)
Deadly Blessing *'81*
The Seventeenth Bride *'84*
Where the Boys Are '84 *'84*
Roses Are for the Rich *'87*
Full Exposure: The Sex Tape Scandals *'89*
The Return of Eliot Ness *'91*
Back to You and Me *'05*
Flicka: Country Pride *'12*

William Hartnell (1908-75)
Immortal Battalion *'44*
The Way Ahead *'44*
Appointment with Crime *'45*
Brighton Rock *'47*
Footsteps in the Fog *'55*
Carry On Sergeant *'58*
The Mouse That Roared *'59*
This Sporting Life *'63*

Rona Hartner (1973-)
The Crazy Stranger *'98*
Dad On the Run *'00*
Le Divorce *'03*
Time of the Wolf *'03*

Josh Hartnett (1978-)
The Faculty *'98*
Halloween: H20 *'98*
The Virgin Suicides *'99*
Blow Dry *'00*
Here on Earth *'00*
Black Hawk Down *'01*
O *'01*
Pearl Harbor *'01*
Town and Country *'01*
40 Days and 40 Nights *'02*
Hollywood Homicide *'03*
Wicker Park *'04*
Mozart and the Whale *'05*
Sin City *'05*
The Black Dahlia *'06*
Lucky Number Slevin *'06*
Resurrecting the Champ *'07*
30 Days of Night *'07*
August *'08*
Bunraku *'10*
Stuck Between Stations *'11*
Parts Per Billion *'14*
Wild Horses *'15*
Oh Lucy! *'17*
6 Below: Miracle on the Mountain *'17*

Joshua Harto (1979-)
The Dark Knight *'08*
Iron Man *'08*

Ryan Hartwig
The Aggression Scale *'12*
The Thompsons *'12*

Russell Harvard
There Will Be Blood *'07*
The Hammer *'11*

Rainbow Harvest (1967-)
Old Enough *'84*
Mirror, Mirror *'90*
Fever *'91*

Alex Harvey
The Long Summer of George Adams *'82*
The Parent Trap II *'86*
Gettysburg *'93*
Fire Down Below *'97*

Don Harvey (1960-)
For You I Die *'47*
The Beast *'88*
Eight Men Out *'88*
Casualties of War *'89*

Die Hard 2: Die Harder '90
Mission of the Shark '91
Prey of the Chameleon '91
American Heart '92
Men of War '94
Tank Girl '94
Last Dance '96
The Thin Red Line '98
Sparkler '99
Corn '04
Back to You and Me '05

Forrester Harvey (1890-1945)
Kongo '32
The Eagle and the Hawk '33
Thoroughbreds Don't Cry '37
The Witness Vanishes '39
The Wolf Man '41
Mrs. Miniver '42

Harry Harvey (1901-85)
The Reckless Way '36
The Spider Returns '41
I'm from Arkansas '44
Tea for Two '50
Ace in the Hole '51
The Narrow Margin '52

John Harvey (1911-82)
Four Jills in a Jeep '44
X The Unknown '56
The Stranglers of Bombay '60

Laurence Harvey (1928-73)
House of Darkness '48
Twilight Women '52
King Richard and the Crusaders '54
Romeo and Juliet '54
Storm Over the Nile '55
Three Men in a Boat '56
The Silent Enemy '58
Expresso Bongo '59
Room at the Top '59
The Alamo '60
Butterfield 8 '60
Summer and Smoke '61
The Manchurian Candidate '62
Walk on the Wild Side '62
The Ceremony '63
Of Human Bondage '64
The Outrage '64
Darling '65
Dandy in Aspic '68
The Magic Christian '69
WUSA '70
Night Watch '72

Lew Harvey
Lady of the Night '25
Big Boy '30

Paul Harvey (1882-1955)
Alibi Ike '35
The Whole Town's Talking '35
Private Number '36
Big City '37
High Flyers '37
23 1/2 Hours Leave '37
A Slight Case of Murder '38
Meet Dr. Christian '39
Arizona '40
High School '40
High Sierra '41
Out of the Fog '41
You Can't Escape Forever '42
The Bamboo Blonde '46
Easy to Wed '46
A Night in Casablanca '46
Up Goes Maisie '46
Call Northside 777 '48
John Loves Mary '48
A Southern Yankee '48
Family Honeymoon '49
Side Street '50
Excuse My Dust '51
April in Paris '52
Three for the Show '55

Rodney Harvey (1967-98)
Initiation '87
Five Corners '88
Salsa '88
My Own Private Idaho '91
Guncrazy '92

Steve Harvey (1957-)
The Fighting Temptations '03
Love Don't Cost a Thing '03
Johnson Family Vacation '04
You Got Served '04
Racing Stripes '05 (V)
Think Like a Man '12

Terence Harvey
The Phantom of the Opera '89
From Hell '01

Verna Harvey (1952-)
The Nightcomers '72
That'll Be the Day '73

Ellie Harvie (1965-)
The Mermaid Chair '06
Not My Life '06
Love Notes '07
My Baby Is Missing '07

Kazuo Hasegawa (1908-84)
Gate of Hell '54
An Actor's Revenge '63

David Haskell (1948-2000)
Godspell '73
Body Double '84

Peter Haskell (1934-2010)
The Ballad of Andy Crocker '69
The Eyes of Charles Sand '74
The Phantom of Hollywood '74
Child's Play 3 '91
Robot Wars '93

Susan Haskell (1968-)
Mrs. Winterbourne '96
Smart House '00
Black Point '01
No Turning Back '01

Iva Hasperger (1977-)
Vlad '03
Dinoshark '10

Tamer Hassan (1968-)
The Business '05
Layer Cake '05
Bonded by Blood '09
Dead Man Running '09
Wrong Turn 3: Left for Dead '09
Blood Out '10
Freerunner '10
The Double '11

O.E. Hasse (1903-78)
The Big Lift '50
Decision Before Dawn '51
I Confess '53
Betrayed '54
Above Us the Waves '55
The Elusive Corporal '62

Danny Hassel (1967-)
A Nightmare on Elm Street 4: Dream Master '88
A Nightmare on Elm Street 5: Dream Child '89

David Hasselhoff (1952-)
Revenge of the Cheerleaders '76
Star Crash '78
Cartier Affair '84
Witchery '88
Bail Out '90
Ring of the Musketeers '93
The Big Tease '99
Shaka Zulu: The Last Great Warrior '01
A Dirty Shame '04 (C)
Dodgeball: A True Underdog Story '04
The SpongeBob SquarePants Movie '04 (C)
Click '06
Kickin' It Old Skool '07 (C)
Anaconda 3: The Offspring '08
Hop '11
Piranha 3DD '11 (C)
The Christmas Consultant '12
Sharknado 3: Oh Hell No! '15
Sharknado: The 4th Awakens '16

Eddie Hassell (1990-)
The Kids Are All Right '10
Family Weekend '13

Jenny Hasselqvist (1894-1978)
One Arabian Night '20
The Atonement of Gosta Berling '24

Marilyn Hassett (1947-)
The Other Side of the Mountain '75
Shadow of the Hawk '76
Two Minute Warning '76
The Other Side of the Mountain, Part 2 '78
The Bell Jar '79
Body Count '87
Messenger of Death '88

Signe Hasso (1910-2002)
Journey for Margaret '42
Heaven Can Wait '43
House on 92nd Street '45
A Scandal in Paris '46
A Double Life '47
Where There's Life '47
Crisis '50
A Reflection of Fear '73

Bob Hastings (1925-2014)
McHale's Navy '64
Harper Valley P.T.A. '78
The Munsters' Revenge '81
Snowballing '85
Shadow Force '92

Leila Hatami (1970-)
Leila '97
Low Heights '02
Shirin '09
A Separation '11

Richard Hatch (1945-2017)
Best Friends '75
Battlestar Galactica '78
Charlie Chan and the Curse of the Dragon Queen '81
Prisoners of the Lost Universe '84
Party Line '88
Unseen Evil '99
InAlienable '08

Riley Hatch (1862-1925)
Little Old New York '23
America '24

Teri Hatcher (1964-)
The Big Picture '89
Tango and Cash '89
Dead in the Water '91
Soapdish '91
All Tied Up '92
The Cool Surface '92
Straight Talk '92
Heaven's Prisoners '95
Two Days in the Valley '96
Since You've Been Gone '97
Tomorrow Never Dies '97
Fever '99
Running Mates '00
Spy Kids '01
Momentum '03
Resurrecting the Champ '07
Coraline '09 (V)
Planes '13 (V)
Planes: Fire & Rescue '14 (V)
Sundown '16

Hurd Hatfield (1918-98)
Dragon Seed '44
Picture of Dorian Gray '45
Diary of a Chambermaid '46
The Unsuspected '47
Destination Murder '50
Tarzan and the Slave Girl '50
El Cid '61
The King of Kings '61
Mickey One '65
The Boston Strangler '68
King David '85
Crimes of the Heart '86
Her Alibi '88

Mert Hatfield
The Ballad of the Sad Cafe '91
The Last Brickmaker in America '01

Amy Hathaway
Joyride '97
Smiling Fish & Goat on Fire '99

Anne Hathaway (1982-)
The Princess Diaries '01
Nicholas Nickleby '02
The Other Side of Heaven '02
Ella Enchanted '04
The Princess Diaries 2: Royal Engagement '04
Brokeback Mountain '05
Havoc '05
Hoodwinked '05 (V)
The Devil Wears Prada '06
Becoming Jane '07
Get Smart '08
Passengers '08
Rachel Getting Married '08
Bride Wars '09
Alice in Wonderland '10
Love and Other Drugs '10
Valentine's Day '10
One Day '11
Rio '11 (V)
The Dark Knight Rises '12
Les Miserables '12
Girl Rising '13 (N)
Interstellar '14
Rio 2 '14 (V)
The Intern '15
Alice Through the Looking Glass '16
Colossal '17
Ocean's 8 '18
Dark Waters '19
The Hustle '19
Serenity '19

Noah Hathaway (1971-)
The NeverEnding Story '84
Troll '86
Sushi Girl '12

Shawn Hatosy (1975-)
In and Out '97
The Postman '97
The Faculty '98
The Thin Red Line '98
Anywhere But Here '99
Outside Providence '99
Simpatico '99
Witness Protection '99
Borstal Boy '00
Down to You '00
Tangled '01
John Q '02
The Cooler '03
Dallas 362 '03
11:14 '03
A Guy Thing '03
Soldier's Girl '03
Alpha Dog '06
Factory Girl '06
Familiar Strangers '08
The Lazarus Project '08
Nobel Son '08
Bad Lieutenant: Port of Call New Orleans '09
Public Enemies '09
Street Kings 2: Motor City '11

Eriko Hatsune (1982-)
Uzumaki '00
Apartment 1303 '07
Emperor '12

Raymond Hatton (1887-1971)
The Little American '17
Male and Female '19
The Ace of Hearts '21
Hell's Heroes '30
Road to Paradise '30
The Silver Horde '30
The Crooked Circle '32
Malay Nights '32
Polly of the Circus '32
Uptown New York '32
Day of Reckoning '33
Lady Killer '33
The Three Musketeers '33
The Daring Young Man '35
Rustlers of Red Dog '35
Steamboat Round the Bend '35
The Vigilantes Are Coming '36
The Texans '38
Kit Carson '40
Reap the Wild Wind '42
Flame of the West '45
Northwest Trail '46
Rolling Home '48
Operation Haylift '50
Kentucky Jubilee '51
The Golden Hawk '52
Day the World Ended '55
Flesh and the Spur '57
Shake, Rattle and Rock '57

Rondo Hatton (1894-1946)
The Pearl of Death '44
House of Horrors '46

Sabine Haudepin (1955-)
The Last Metro '80
Hotel America '81

Rutger Hauer (1944-2019)
Turkish Delight '73
Cold Blood '75
Katie Tippel '75
The Wilby Conspiracy '75
Soldier of Orange '78
Spetters '80
Eureka! '81
Nighthawks '81
Blade Runner '82
Fatal Error '83
The Osterman Weekend '83
Mysteries '84
Flesh and Blood '85
Ladyhawke '85
The Hitcher '86
Wanted Dead or Alive '86
Escape from Sobibor '87
The Blood of Heroes '89
Bloodhounds of Broadway '89
Blind Fury '90
Deadlock '91
Beyond Justice '92
Buffy the Vampire Slayer '92
Past Midnight '92
Split Second '92
Arctic Blue '93
Blind Side '93
Amelia Earhart: The Final Flight '94
Surviving the Game '94
Crossworlds '96
Omega Doom '96
Bleeders '97
Bone Daddy '97
Hostile Waters '97
Jack London's The Call of the Wild '97
Redline '97
Merlin '98
New World Disorder '99
Partners in Crime '99
Tactical Assault '99
The 10th Kingdom '00
Turbulence 3: Heavy Metal '00
Wilder '00
Confessions of a Dangerous Mind '02
Scorcher '02
Dracula 2: Ascension '03
Salem's Lot '04
Batman Begins '05
Dracula 3: Legacy '05
Mirror Wars: Reflection One '05
The Poseidon Adventure '05
Sin City '05
The Hunt for Eagle One: Crash Point '06
Dead Tone '07
Goal 2: Living the Dream '07
Moving McAllister '07
Bride Flight '08
Sword of War '09
Happiness Runs '10
The Heineken Kidnapping '11
Hobo With a Shotgun '11
The Mill and the Cross '11
The Rite '11
Argento's Dracula 3D '13
Il Futuro '13
Death Squad '14
The Letters '15
The Scorpion King 4: Quest for Power '15
Beyond Valkyrie: Dawn of the Fourth Reich '16
24 Hours to Live '17
Samson '18

Jonah Hauer-King
A Dog's Way Home '19
The Song of Names '19

Vicky Haughton
Her Majesty '01
Whale Rider '02
Kawa '11

Darla Haun (1964-)
Red Snow '91
Married People, Single Sex '93
Dracula: Dead and Loving It '95

Lindsey Haun (1984-)
Brave New Girl '04
Broken Bridges '06
Shrooms '07

Ullrich Haupt (1887-1931)
Tempest '28
The Iron Mask '29
Morocco '30

Cole Hauser (1975-)
School Ties '92
Dazed and Confused '93
Higher Learning '94
All Over Me '96
Gang Boys '97
Good Will Hunting '97
The Hi-Lo Country '98
Pitch Black '00
A Shot at Glory '00
Tigerland '00
Hart's War '02
White Oleander '02
Tears of the Sun '03
2 Fast 2 Furious '03
Paparazzi '04
The Cave '05
Dirty '05
The Break-Up '06
The Stone Angel '07
The Family That Preys '08
Tortured '08
Like Dandelion Dust '09
The Hit List '11
Dead Drop '13
A Good Day to Die Hard '13
Olympus Has Fallen '13
Jarhead 2: Field of Fire '14
Transcendence '14
Acts of Violence '18
Running with the Devil '19

Fay Hauser (1948-)
Jo Jo Dancer, Your Life Is Calling '86
Candyman 2: Farewell to the Flesh '94
The Hot Chick '02

Wings Hauser (1947-)
Homework '82
Vice Squad '82
Mutant '83
Code of Honor '84
A Soldier's Story '84
Jo Jo Dancer, Your Life Is Calling '86
The Long, Hot Summer '86
Nightmare at Noon '87
No Safe Haven '87
Tough Guys Don't Dance '87
The Wind '87
The Carpenter '89
The Siege of Firebase Gloria '89
The Art of Dying '90
Coldfire '90
The Killer's Edge '90
Living to Die '91
Mind, Body & Soul '92
Watchers 3 '94
Tales from the Hood '95
Gang Boys '97
The Insider '99
Avenging Angel '07
The Stone Angel '07
Rubber '10

June Haver (1926-2005)
Irish Eyes Are Smiling '44
The Dolly Sisters '46
Three Little Girls In Blue '46
Wake Up and Dream '46
Look for the Silver Lining '49
The Daughter of Rosie O'Grady '50
Love Nest '51
The Girl Next Door '53

Phyllis Haver (1899-1960)
Chicago '27
The Fighting Eagle '27
Battle of the Sexes '28

Nigel Havers (1951-)
Who Is Killing the Great Chefs of Europe? '78
Chariots of Fire '81
A Passage to India '84
Hold the Dream '86
The Charmer '87
The Death of the Heart '87
Empire of the Sun '87
The Little Princess '87
The Whistle Blower '87
Farewell to the King '89
Quiet Days in Clichy '90
Catherine Cookson's The Glass Virgin '95
Element of Doubt '96
Penelope '06

Alex Havier (1911-45)
Bataan '43
They Were Expendable '45

June Havoc (1912-2010)
My Sister Eileen '42
Hello, Frisco, Hello '43
No Time For Love '43
Home In Indiana '44
Brewster's Millions '45
Gentleman's Agreement '47
Mother Didn't Tell Me '50
Return to Salem's Lot '87

Allan Hawco (1977-)
Above and Beyond '06
Hyena Road '16

Robin Hawdon (1939-)
Bedazzled '68
Zeta One '69

Keeley Hawes (1976-)
The Moonstone '97
The Avengers '98
Our Mutual Friend '98
Retribution '98
The Last September '99
Othello '01
Wives and Daughters '01
Me & Mrs. Jones '02
Tipping the Velvet '02
Chaos & Cadavers '03
Tristram Shandy: A Cock and Bull Story '05
Under the Greenwood Tree '05
Death at a Funeral '07
Flashbacks of a Fool '08
Upstairs Downstairs '11
The Adventurer: The Curse of the Midas Box '13
The Lady Vanishes '13

Jeremy Hawk (1918-2002)
Race for Life '55
Who Done It? '56
Lucky Jim '58

Kali Hawk
Couples Retreat '09
Answers to Nothing '11
Fifty Shades of Black '16

Ethan Hawke (1971-)
Explorers '85
Dad '89
Dead Poets Society '89
Mystery Date '91
White Fang '91
A Midnight Clear '92
Waterland '92
Alive '93
Rich in Love '93
Before Sunrise '94
Floundering '94
Reality Bites '94
Search and Destroy '94
White Fang 2: The Myth of the White Wolf '94 (C)
Gattaca '97
Great Expectations '97
The Newton Boys '97
Joe the King '99
Snow Falling on Cedars '99
Hamlet '00
The Jimmy Show '01
Tape '01
Training Day '01
Waking Life '01
Before Sunset '04
Taking Lives '04
Assault on Precinct 13 '05
Lord of War '05
Fast Food Nation '06
The Hottest State '06
Before the Devil Knows You're Dead '07
What Doesn't Kill You '08
Brooklyn's Finest '09
Daybreakers '09
New York, I Love You '09
Staten Island '09
Moby Dick '11
The Woman in the Fifth '11
Sinister '12
Before Midnight '13
Getaway '13
The Purge '13
Boyhood '14
Born to Be Blue '15
Cymbeline '15
Good Kill '15
Predestination '15
Seymour: An Introduction '15
Ten Thousand Saints '15
In a Valley of Violence '16
Maggie's Plan '16
The Magnificent Seven '16
The Phenom '16
Regression '16
First Reformed '17
Maudie '17
24 Hours to Live '17
Valerian and the City of a Thousand Planets '17
Blaze '18
Juliet, Naked '18
Adopt a Highway '19
The Kid '19

John Hawkes (1959-)
Murder Rap '87
Roadracers '94
Night of the Scarecrow '95
Playing God '96
I Still Know What You Did Last Summer '98
A Slipping Down Life '99
The Perfect Storm '00
Sand '00
Hardball '01
Identity '03
Me and You and Everyone We Know '05
Miami Vice '06
Wristcutters: A Love Story '06
Zombie Strippers '08
S. Darko: A Donnie Darko Tale '09
Small Town Saturday Night '10
Winter's Bone '10
Contagion '11
Higher Ground '11
Martha Marcy May Marlene '11
Lincoln '12
The Sessions '12
Life of Crime '13
The Driftless Area '16
The Peanut Butter Falcon '19

Sydney Hawkes (1885-1965)
See Syd Chaplin

Sydney Hawkes (1926-2009)
See Syd Chaplin

Jack Hawkins (1910-73)
Phantom Fiend '35
The Fallen Idol '49
The Small Back Room '49
The Black Rose '50
No Highway in the Sky '51
The Cruel Sea '53
Malta Story '53
Angels One Five '54
Land of Fury '55
Land of the Pharaohs '55
The Prisoner '55
The Bridge on the River Kwai '57
She Played With Fire '57
Gideon's Day '58
Ben-Hur '59
The League of Gentlemen '60
Five Finger Exercise '62
Lawrence of Arabia '62
Rampage '63
Guns at Batasi '64
Zulu '64
Lord Jim '65
Lola '69
Those Daring Young Men in Their Jaunty Jalopies '69
Nicholas and Alexandra '71
When Eight Bells Toll '71
Young Winston '72
Tales That Witness Madness '73
Theatre of Blood '73

Jimmy Hawkins (1941-)
Private Hell 36 '54
Zotz! '62

Sally Hawkins (1976-)
All or Nothing '02
Tipping the Velvet '02
Byron '03
Vera Drake '04
Layer Cake '05
Persuasion '07
Happy-Go-Lucky '08
An Education '09
Happy Ever Afters '09
Made in Dagenham '10
Never Let Me Go '10
Submarine '10
Jane Eyre '11
Great Expectations '12
Blue Jasmine '13
A Brilliant Young Mind '14
Godzilla '14
Paddington '14
Maudie '17
Paddington 2 '17
The Shape of Water '17

Screamin' Jay Hawkins (1929-2000)
Two Moon Junction '88
Mystery Train '89
A Rage in Harlem '91
Dance with the Devil '97

Monte Hawley (1901-50)
The Duke Is Tops '38
Miracle in Harlem '48

Richard Hawley
Captives '94
Jane Eyre '97

Wanda (Petit) Hawley (1895-1963)
Affairs of Anatol '21
American Pluck '25
Smouldering Fires '25

Goldie Hawn (1945-)
The One and Only, Genuine, Original Family Band '68
Cactus Flower '69
There's a Girl in My Soup '70
Dollars '71
Butterflies Are Free '72
The Girl from Petrovka '74
The Sugarland Express '74
Shampoo '75
The Duchess and the Dirtwater Fox '76
Foul Play '78
Private Benjamin '80
Seems Like Old Times '80
Lovers and Liars '81
Best Friends '82
Protocol '84
Swing Shift '84
Wildcats '86
Overboard '87
Bird on a Wire '90
Deceived '91
Crisscross '92
Death Becomes Her '92
Housesitter '92
Everyone Says I Love You '96
The First Wives Club '96
The Out-of-Towners '99
Town and Country '01
The Banger Sisters '02
Snatched '17

Jill Haworth (1945-2011)
Exodus '60
In Harm's Way '65
The Ballad of Andy Crocker '69
Tower of Evil '72
The Freakmaker '73

Vinton (Hayworth) Haworth (1906-70)
Junior G-Men of the Air '42
The Pride of the Yankees '42
Spartacus '60

Elizabeth Hawthorne
The Chronicles of Narnia: The Lion, the Witch and the Wardrobe '05
Underworld: Rise of the Lycans '09
Adrift '18

Nigel Hawthorne (1929-2001)
S*P*Y*S '74
Firefox '82
Gandhi '82
The Black Cauldron '85 (V)
Demolition Man '93
The Madness of King George '94
Richard III '95
Inside '96
Twelfth Night '96
Amistad '97
Madeline '98
The Object of My Affection '98
Uncorked '98
The Winslow Boy '98
The Big Brass Ring '99
Tarzan '99 (V)
Call Me Claus '01
Victoria & Albert '01

Charles Hawtrey (1914-88)
Sabotage '36
Good Morning, Boys '37
A Canterbury Tale '44
Carry On Sergeant '58
Carry On Constable '60
Carry On Regardless '61
Carry On Cabby '63
Carry On Jack '63
Carry On Spying '64
Carry On Cleo '65
Carry On Cowboy '66
Carry On Screaming '66
Don't Lose Your Head '66
Carry On Up the Khyber '68
Carry On Again Doctor '69
Zeta One '69
Carry On Loving '70
Carry On Up the Jungle '70
Carry On at Your Convenience '71
Carry On Camping '71
Carry On Henry VIII '71
Carry On Abroad '72
Carry On Matron '72

Kay Hawtrey (1926-)
Funeral Home '82
At the Midnight Hour '95
Focus '01

Alexandra Hay (1944-93)
Skidoo '68
Model Shop '69
The Love Machine '71

Christian Hay (1944-)
L'Automobile '71
Autopsy '73

Colin Hay (1953-)
Cosi '95
Heaven's Burning '97
The Wild '06 (V)

Will Hay (1888-1949)
Boys Will Be Boys '35
Windbag the Sailor '36
Good Morning, Boys '37
Ask a Policeman '38
Hey! Hey! USA! '38

Sessue Hayakawa (1889-1973)
The Wrath of the Gods '14
Tokyo Joe '49
Three Came Home '50
House of Bamboo '55
The Bridge on the River Kwai '57
The Geisha Boy '58
Green Mansions '59
Hell to Eternity '60
The Swiss Family Robinson '60

Ashley Hayden
The Mangler '94
Pride of Africa '97

Harry Hayden (1884-1955)
The Rains Came '39
Two Sisters From Boston '46
Merton of the Movies '47
Gun Crazy '49
Double Dynamite '51

James Hayden (1954-83)
Don't Go in the Woods '81
Once Upon a Time in America '84

Josh Hayden (1992-)
My Silent Partner '06
What Comes Around '06
Christmas Caper '07

Linda Hayden (1953-)
Taste the Blood of Dracula '70
Confessions of a Window Cleaner '74
Madhouse '74
Therese: The Story of Saint Therese of Lisieux '04

Russell Hayden (1912-81)
The Frontiersmen '38
Law of the Pampas '39
The Showdown '40
Gambler's Choice '44
Lost City of the Jungle '45
Seven Were Saved '47
Rolling Home '48

Sterling Hayden (1916-86)
El Paso '49
The Asphalt Jungle '50
Denver and the Rio Grande '52
Flat Top '52
The Golden Hawk '52
Hellgate '52
The Star '52
Johnny Guitar '53
Kansas Pacific '53
Crime Wave '54
Prince Valiant '54
Suddenly '54
Shotgun '55
Top Gun '55
The Killing '56
Crime of Passion '57
The Iron Sheriff '57
Valerie '57
Zero Hour! '57
Terror in a Texas Town '58
Dr. Strangelove, or: How I Learned to Stop Worrying and Love the Bomb '64
Hard Contract '69
Loving '70
The Godfather '72
The Final Programme '73
The Long Goodbye '73
1900 '76
King of the Gypsies '78
Winter Kills '79
9 to 5 '80
The Blue and the Gray '82
Venom '82

Richard Haydn (1905-85)
Charley's Aunt '41
Thunder Birds '42
No Time For Love '43
The Green Years '46
Forever Amber '47
The Foxes of Harrow '47
Emperor Waltz '48
Sitting Pretty '48
Pride of St. Louis '52
Money from Home '53
Never Let Me Go '53
Jupiter's Darling '55
The Lost World '60
Please Don't Eat the Daisies '60
Mutiny on the Bounty '62
Clarence, the Cross-eyed Lion '65
The Sound of Music '65
Young Frankenstein '74

David Haydn-Jones
Fatal Trust '06
The Secrets of the Summer House '08
Time Bomb '08
Taken From Me: The Tiffany Rubin Story '10
Dear Santa '11

Ron Haydock (1940-77)
The Thrill Killers '65
Rat Pfink a Boo-Boo '66

Julie Haydon (1910-94)
The Conquerors '32
The Age of Innocence '34
A Family Affair '37
It's Pat: The Movie '94

Helen Haye (1874-1957)
Skin Game '31
The 39 Steps '35
The Case of the Frightened Lady '39
Spy in Black '39
Man of Evil '48

Salma Hayek (1966-)
Mi Vida Loca '94
Roadracers '94
Desperado '95
Fair Game '95
Four Rooms '95 (C)
From Dusk Till Dawn '95
Midaq Alley '95
Fled '96
Breaking Up '97
Fools Rush In '97
The Hunchback '97
The Faculty '98
54 '98
The Velocity of Gary '98
Dogma '99
Wild Wild West '99
Chain of Fools '00
Time Code '00
Traffic '00
Hotel '01
In the Time of the Butterflies '01
Frida '02
Once Upon a Time in Mexico '03
Spy Kids 3-D: Game Over '03
After the Sunset '04
Ask the Dust '06
Bandidas '06
Lonely Hearts '06
Beverly Hills Chihuahua '08 (V)
Cirque du Freak: The Vampire's Assistant '09
Grown Ups '10
Americano '11
Puss in Boots '11 (V)
Here Comes the Boom '12
The Pirates! Band of Misfits '12 (V)
Savages '12
Girl Rising '13 (N)
Grown Ups 2 '13
Everly '14
Kahlil Gibran's The Prophet '15
Some Kind of Beautiful '15
Tale of Tales '15
Septembers of Shiraz '16
Beatriz at Dinner '17
How to Be a Latin Lover '17
The Hummingbird Project '18
Drunk Parents '19
Like a Boss '20

Jeff Hayenga
Prince of Pennsylvania '88
The Unborn '91

Allison Hayes (1930-77)
Francis Joins the WACs '54
The Gunslinger '56
The Undead '57
The Unearthly '57
Zombies of Moratau '57
Attack of the 50 Foot Woman '58
Counterplot '59
The Hypnotic Eye '60
The Crawling Hand '63

Anthony Hayes (1977-)
Winter a Go-Go '65
Look Both Ways '05
Newcastle '08
The Square '08
Animal Kingdom '09
Beneath Hill 60 '10
Healing '15

Bernadene Hayes (1903-87)
Girl Loves Boy '37
Don't Gamble with Strangers '46

Billie Hayes (1932-)
Li'l Abner '59
Pufnstuf '70

George 'Gabby' Hayes (1885-1969)
Cavalier of the West '31
Boiling Point '32
Beggars in Ermine '34
The Lost City '34
Hopalong Cassidy Returns '36
The Texas Rangers '36
Borderland '37
The Plainsman '37
The Frontiersmen '38
Let Freedom Ring '39
Dark Command '40
Melody Ranch '40
Wagons Westward '40
War of the Wildcats '43
Tall in the Saddle '44
Don't Fence Me In '45
Badman's Territory '46
Great Expectations '46
My Pal Trigger '46
Under Nevada Skies '46
Home in Oklahoma '47
Lights of Old Santa Fe '47
Trail Street '47
Return of the Bad Men '48
El Paso '49

Helen Hayes (1900-93)
Arrowsmith '31
The Sin of Madelon Claudet '31
A Farewell to Arms '32
Night Flight '33
The White Sister '33
Stage Door Canteen '43
My Son John '52
Anastasia '56
Third Man on the Mountain '59 (C)
Airport '70
Herbie Rides Again '74
One of Our Dinosaurs Is Missing '75
Victory at Entebbe '76
Candleshoe '78
Agatha Christie's Murder is Easy '82
Agatha Christie's A Caribbean Mystery '83
Agatha Christie's Murder with Mirrors '85

Isaac Hayes (1942-2008)
Truck Turner '74
It Seemed Like a Good Idea at the Time '75
Escape from New York '81
Jailbait: Betrayed By Innocence '86
I'm Gonna Git You Sucka '88
Prime Target '91
Guilty as Charged '92
Posse '93 (C)
Robin Hood: Men in Tights '93
It Could Happen to You '94
Oblivion '94
Backlash: Oblivion 2 '95
Flipper '96
Uncle Sam '96
Woo '97
Six Ways to Sunday '99
South Park: Bigger, Longer and Uncut '99 (V)
Reindeer Games '00
Shaft '00
Dr. Dolittle 2 '01 (V)
Anonymous Rex '04
Hustle & Flow '05
Kill Switch '08
Return to Sleepaway Camp '08
Soul Men '08

Miss Laura Hayes
Queens of Comedy '01
Beauty Shop '05

Linda Hayes (1922-95)
Danger on the Air '38
The Girl From Mexico '39
Mexican Spitfire '40
The Mexican Spitfire Out West '40
The Saint in Palm Springs '41

Margaret (Maggie) Hayes (1916-77)
Sullivan's Travels '41
Blackboard Jungle '55
Violent Saturday '55
Omar Khayyam '57
The Case Against Brooklyn '58
Fraulein '58
Good Day for a Hanging '58
House of Women '62
13 West Street '62

Patricia Hayes (1909-98)
Super Bitch '73
The Corn Is Green '79
The NeverEnding Story '84
A Fish Called Wanda '88
Willow '88

Peter Lind Hayes (1915-98)
Playmates '41
The 5000 Fingers of Dr. T '53

Sean P. Hayes (1970-)
Billy's Hollywood Screen Kiss '98
Cats & Dogs '01 (V)
Dr. Seuss' The Cat in the Hat '03 (V)
Pieces of April '03
Win a Date with Tad Hamilton! '04
The Bucket List '07
Igor '08 (V)
Soul Men '08
Cats & Dogs: The Revenge of Kitty Galore '10
The Three Stooges '12
Monsters University '13 (V)

Tony Haygarth (1945-)
Dracula '79
A Private Function '84
A Month in the Country '87
Devices and Desires '91
Royal Deceit '94
The Infiltrator '95
Swept from the Sea '97
Chicken Run '00 (V)
Fakers '04
Under the Greenwood Tree '05
Ghostboat '06

Lisa Hayland
Novel Desires '92
Fatal Passion '94

Grace Hayle (1888-1963)
The Moon's Our Home '36
The Great Dictator '40
Loving You '57

David Hayman (1950-)
Sid & Nancy '86
Hope and Glory '87
Rob Roy '95
Behind the Lines '97
The Jackal '97
My Name Is Joe '98
The Tailor of Panama '00
Vertical Limit '00
Where the Truth Lies '05
Speed Dating '07
The Boy in the Striped Pajamas '08
Queen and Country '14

Dick Haymes (1916-80)
Du Barry Was a Lady '43
Four Jills in a Jeep '44
Irish Eyes Are Smiling '44
State Fair '45
Do You Love Me? '46
Carnival in Costa Rica '47
The Shocking Miss Pilgrim '47
One Touch of Venus '48
Up in Central Park '48
St. Benny the Dip '51
All Ashore '53
Betrayal '74

Linda Haynes (1947-)
Latitude Zero '69
The Nickel Ride '74
Rolling Thunder '77

Roberta Haynes (1929-)
The Fighter '52
Return to Paradise '53
Hell Ship Mutiny '57
The Adventurers '70

Jim Haynie (1940-)
Bitter Harvest '81
Out '82
A Death in California '85
On the Edge '86
From Hollywood to Deadwood '89
I Know My First Name Is Steven '89
Men Don't Leave '89
Too Much Sun '90
Grand Tour: Disaster in Time '92
Sleepwalkers '92
Danielle Steel's Star '93
The Bridges of Madison County '95
The Peacemaker '97
United States of Leland '03
Avenging Angel '07

Robert Hays (1947-)
Initiation of Sarah '78
Airplane! '80
The Fall of the House of Usher '80
Take This Job & Shove It '81
Airplane 2: The Sequel '82
Trenchcoat '83
Cat's Eye '85
Homeward Bound: The Incredible Journey '93
Raw Justice '93
Cyber Bandits '94
No Dessert Dad, 'Til You Mow the Lawn '94
Vanished '95
The Abduction '96
Homeward Bound 2: Lost in San Francisco '96
Dr. T & the Women '00
The Santa Trap '02

Dennis Haysbert (1954-)
Major League '89
Navy SEALS '90
Love Field '91
Mr. Baseball '92
Return to Lonesome Dove '93
Suture '93
Major League 2 '94
Heat '95
Waiting to Exhale '95
Absolute Power '97
Major League 3: Back to the Minors '98
The Minus Man '99
Random Hearts '99
The Thirteenth Floor '99
Love and Basketball '00
What's Cooking? '00
Far from Heaven '02
Sinbad: Legend of the Seven Seas '03 (V)
Jarhead '05
Breach '07
The Color of Freedom '07
The Details '11
Life of a King '13
LUV '13
Dear White People '14
Sin City: A Dame to Kill For '14
Sniper: Legacy '14
Think Like a Man Too '14
Dead Rising: End Game '16
Sniper: Ghost Shooter '16
The Dark Tower '17
Breakthrough '19

David Hayter (1969-)
The Castle of Cagliostro '80 (V)
Guyver 2: Dark Hero '94

James Hayter (1907-83)
The Fallen Idol '49
Morning Departure '50
Tom Brown's School Days '51
Four Sided Triangle '53
Beau Brummell '54
The Pickwick Papers '54
Not Tonight Darling '72

Chard Hayward (1949-)
The Killing Game '87
Violent Zone '89

Kara Hayward
Moonrise Kingdom '12
Quitters '16
To the Stars '20

Louis Hayward (1909-85)
Anthony Adverse '36
The Man in the Iron Mask '39
Dance, Girl, Dance '40
The Son of Monte Cristo '40
Ladies in Retirement '41
And Then There Were None '45
The Strange Woman '46
Black Arrow '48
Ruthless '48
Walk a Crooked Mile '48
The Pirates of Capri '49
Duffy of San Quentin '54
The Search for Bridey Murphy '56
Chuka '67

Rachel Hayward
Anything for Love '93
The Fear: Halloween Night '99
Cruel and Unusual '01
Call of the Wild '04
Unthinkable '07
The Christmas Clause '08

Susan Hayward (1918-75)
Beau Geste '39
Adam Had Four Sons '41
Reap the Wild Wind '42
Star Spangled Rhythm '42
Fighting Seabees '44
The Hairy Ape '44
Jack London '44
Canyon Passage '46
Deadline at Dawn '46
The Lost Moment '47
Smash-Up: The Story of a Woman '47
They Won't Believe Me '47
House of Strangers '49
Tulsa '49
Rawhide '50
David and Bathsheba '51
I Can Get It For You Wholesale '51
I'd Climb the Highest Mountain '51
The Lusty Men '52
The Snows of Kilimanjaro '52
With a Song in My Heart '52
White Witch Doctor '53
Demetrius and the Gladiators '54
Garden of Evil '54
I'll Cry Tomorrow '55
Soldier of Fortune '55
Untamed '55
The Conqueror '56
Top Secret Affair '57
I Want to Live! '58
Woman Obsessed '59
Ada '61
Back Street '61
The Marriage-Go-Round '61
I Thank a Fool '62
Stolen Hours '63
Where Love Has Gone '64
The Honey Pot '67
Valley of the Dolls '67
The Revengers '72

Chris Haywood (1948-)
Newsfront '78
Breaker Morant '80
Attack Force Z '84
The Coca-Cola Kid '84
Man of Flowers '84
Razorback '84
Malcolm '86
The Navigator '88
Quigley Down Under '90
Sweet Talker '91
Shine '95
Blackrock '97
Innocence '00
Jindabyne '06
Beneath Hill 60 '10
Sleeping Beauty '11

Rita Hayworth (1918-87)
Charlie Chan in Egypt '35
Paddy O'Day '35
Only Angels Have Wings '39
Angels Over Broadway '40
Blondie On a Budget '40
The Lady in Question '40
Music in My Heart '40
Susan and God '40
Blood and Sand '41
Strawberry Blonde '41
You'll Never Get Rich '41
My Gal Sal '42
Tales of Manhattan '42
You Were Never Lovelier '42
Cover Girl '44
Tonight and Every Night '45
Gilda '46
Down to Earth '47
The Lady from Shanghai '48
The Loves of Carmen '48
Affair in Trinidad '52
Miss Sadie Thompson '53
Salome '53
Fire Down Below '57
Pal Joey '57
Separate Tables '58
They Came to Cordura '59
The Happy Thieves '61
Circus World '64
The Love Goddesses '65
The Money Trap '65
The Poppy Is Also a Flower '66
The Cats '68
The Wrath of God '72

Serge Hazanavicius (1963-)
I've Loved You So Long '08
OSS 117: Lost in Rio '09
Murder on the Orient Express '10

Jayne Hazard (1922-2006)
Black Market Babies '45
Strange Illusion '45

Jonathan Haze (1929-)
Monster from the Ocean Floor '54
Day the World Ended '55
Swamp Women '55
The Gunslinger '56
Carnival Rock '57
Not of This Earth '57
Teenage Caveman '58
Little Shop of Horrors '60
The Terror '63
X: The Man with X-Ray Eyes '63
Track of the Vampire '66
The St. Valentine's Day Massacre '67

Scott Haze
Child of God '14
Venom '18

Sam Hazeldine (1972-)
Persuasion '07
Dead Mine '12
The Machine '13
Mechanic: Resurrection '16

Noni Hazlehurst (1954-)
Little Fish '05
Candy '06

Anthony Head (1954-)
And Starring Pancho Villa as Himself '03
I'll Be There '03
Imagine Me & You '06
Scoop '06
Persuasion '07
Sparkle '07
Repo! The Genetic Opera '08
The Iron Lady '11
Percy Jackson: Sea of Monsters '13
A Street Cat Named Bob '16

Jae Head
Hancock '08
The Blind Side '09

Murray Head (1946-)
A Coeur Joie '67
Sunday, Bloody Sunday '71
Madame Claude '77
White Mischief '88
Beaumarchais the Scoundrel '96

Lena Headey (1973-)
Waterland '92
Rudyard Kipling's The Jungle Book '94
Face '97
Mrs. Dalloway '97
Merlin '98
Twice upon a Yesterday '98
Gossip '99
Onegin '99
Aberdeen '00
The Gathering Storm '02
Possession '02
Ripley's Game '02
The Brothers Grimm '05
The Cave '05
Imagine Me & You '06
The Contractor '07
St. Trinian's '07
300 '07
The Broken '08
The Red Baron '08
Laid to Rest '09
Dredd '12
The Adventurer: The Curse of the Midas Box '13
The Mortal Instruments: City of Bones '13
The Purge '13
300: Rise of an Empire '13
Zipper '15
Fighting with My Family '19

Shari Headley (1964-)
Coming to America '88
The Preacher's Wife '96
Johnson Family Vacation '04
Towelhead '07

Glenne Headly (1955-2017)
Doctor Detroit '83
Fandango '85
The Purple Rose of Cairo '85
Making Mr. Right '86
Seize the Day '86
Nadine '87
Dirty Rotten Scoundrels '88
Dick Tracy '90
Mortal Thoughts '91
And the Band Played On '93
Getting Even with Dad '94
Mr. Holland's Opus '95
Sgt. Bilko '95
Bastard out of Carolina '96
Two Days in the Valley '96
Babe: Pig in the City '98 (V)
Breakfast of Champions '98
My Own Country '98
Winchell '98
The X-Files '98
The Sandy Bottom Orchestra '00
Time Code '00
Bartleby '01

A Girl Thing *'01*
What's the Worst That Could Happen? *'01*
Women *vs.* Men *'02*
Around the Bend *'04*
Confessions of a Teenage Drama Queen *'04*
Eulogy *'04*
The Moguls *'05*
Raising Flagg *'06*
Kit Kittredge: An American Girl *'08*
The Joneses *'09*
Don Jon *'13*
Just Getting Started *'17*
Making Babies *'19*

Anthony Heald (1944-)
Postcards from the Edge *'90*
The Silence of the Lambs *'91*
Whispers in the Dark *'92*
The Ballad of Little Jo *'93*
The Client *'94*
Kiss of Death *'94*
Bushwhacked *'95*
A Time to Kill *'96*
Deep Rising *'98*
8mm *'98*
Proof of Life *'00*
Red Dragon *'02*
Accepted *'06*
X-Men: The Last Stand *'06*

Elizabeth Healey
Croc *'07*
The Hive *'08*

Myron Healey (1922-2005)
Down to Earth *'47*
Elephant Stampede *'51*
Gang Busters *'55*
Jungle Moon Men *'55*
Running Target *'56*
Guns Don't Argue *'57*
The Unearthly *'57*
Apache Territory *'58*
Cavalry Command *'63*
Pulse *'88*

David Healy (1932-95)
Lust for a Vampire *'71*
The Sign of Four *'83*
Supergirl *'84*

Mary Healy (1918-)
Star Dust *'40*
The 5000 Fingers of Dr. T *'53*

Pat Healy (1971-)
Rescue Dawn *'06*
Great World of Sound *'07*
The Innkeepers *'11*
Compliance *'12*
Cheap Thrills *'14*
Carnage Park *'16*

Patricia Healy
Undertow *'04*
Mr. Fix It *'06*

Ted Healy (1896-1937)
Dancing Lady *'33*
Hollywood Party *'34*
The Casino Murder Case *'35*
Mad Love *'35*
Reckless *'35*
San Francisco *'36*
Sing, Baby, Sing *'36*
Speed *'36*
Hollywood Hotel *'37*
Varsity Show *'37*

Darin Heames
The Fear *'94*
Night of the Demons 2 *'94*
Cock & Bull Story *'03*

Amber Heard (1986-)
Friday Night Lights *'04*
North Country *'05*
All the Boys Love Mandy Lane *'06*
Remember the Daze *'07*
Spin *'07*
Never Back Down *'08*
Pineapple Express *'08*
ExTerminators *'09*
The Informers *'09*
The Joneses *'09*
The Stepfather *'09*
Zombieland *'09*
And Soon the Darkness *'10*
The River Why *'10*
The Ward *'10*
Drive Angry *'11*
The Rum Diary *'11*
Machete Kills *'13*
Paranoia *'13*
Syrup *'13*
3 Days to Kill *'14*
The Danish Girl *'15*
One More Time *'15*
The Adderall Diaries *'16*
Aquaman *'18*
London Fields *'18*

Daphne Heard (1904-83)
Macbeth *'70*
Jude the Obscure *'71*

John Heard (1945-2017)
Between the Lines *'77*
On the Yard *'79*
The Scarlet Letter *'79*
Heart Beat *'80*
Cutter's Way *'81*
Cat People *'82*
C.H.U.D. *'84*
After Hours *'85*
Heaven Help Us *'85*
The Trip to Bountiful *'85*
Beaches *'88*
Betrayed *'88*
Big *'88*
The Milagro Beanfield War *'88*
Necessity *'88*
The Seventh Sign *'88*
The Package *'89*
Awakenings *'90*
The End of Innocence *'90*
Home Alone *'90*
Deceived *'91*
Rambling Rose *'91*
Gladiator *'92*
Home Alone 2: Lost in New York *'92*
Radio Flyer *'92*
Waterland *'92*
In the Line of Fire *'93*
The Pelican Brief *'93*
Before and After *'95*
My Fellow Americans *'96*
Men *'97*
187 *'97*
Desert Blue *'98*
Executive Power *'98*
Snake Eyes *'98*
The Pact *'99*
The Witness *'99*
Animal Factory *'00*
Perfect Murder, Perfect Town *'00*
Pollock *'00*
O *'01*
The Pilot's Wife *'01*
Monday Night Mayhem *'02*
Mind the Gap *'04*
White Chicks *'04*
The Chumscrubber *'05*
The Deal *'05*
Sweet Land *'05*
Tracks *'05*
Dead Lenny *'06*
Gamers *'06*
The Guardian *'06*
Steel City *'06*
Brothers Three *'07*
The Great Debaters *'07*
The Lucky Ones *'08*
Formosa Betrayed *'09*
The Truth *'10*
A Perfect Ending *'12*
Runner Runner *'13*
Sharknado *'13*
Snake & Mongoose *'13*
Boys of Abu Ghraib *'14*
Animals *'15*
Jimmy Vestvood: Amerikan Hero *'16*
So B. It *'17*

Ann Hearn (1953-)
The Accused *'88*
Mirror, Mirror *'90*
Lorenzo's Oil *'92*
A Woman of Independent Means *'94*
The War at Home *'96*

George Hearn (1934-)
Sweeney Todd: The Demon Barber of Fleet Street *'84*
See You in the Morning *'89*
Sneakers *'92*
The Vanishing *'93*
All Dogs Go to Heaven 2 *'95 (V)*
Annie: A Royal Adventure *'95*
The Devil's Own *'96*
Barney's Great Adventure *'98*

Richard Hearne (1908-79)
Miss London Ltd. *'43*
The Time of His Life *'55*

Patty (Patricia Campbell) Hearst (1954-)
Cry-Baby *'90*
Serial Mom *'94*
Pecker *'98*
Cecil B. Demented *'00*
A Dirty Shame *'04*

Rick Hearst (1965-)
Crossing the Line *'90*
Warlock 3: The End of Innocence *'98*
Carpool Guy *'05*

Darrell Heath
Don't Be a Menace to South Central While Drinking Your Juice in the Hood *'95*
Woo *'97*

Bella Heathcote (1987-)
Beneath Hill 60 *'10*
Dark Shadows *'12*
Not Fade Away *'12*
The Curse of Downers Grove *'15*
The Neon Demon *'16*
Pride and Prejudice and Zombies *'16*
Fifty Shades Darker *'17*
Professor Marston and the Wonder Women *'17*

Thomas Heathcote (1917-86)
Above Us the Waves *'55*
Village of the Damned *'60*
Demons of the Mind *'72*
Luther *'74*

Jean Heather (1921-95)
Double Indemnity *'44*
Murder, He Says *'45*

Clifford Heatherley (1888-1937)
Champagne *'28*
Bitter Sweet *'33*
The Church Mouse *'34*

Joey Heatherton (1944-)
Twilight of Honor *'63*
Where Love Has Gone *'64*
My Blood Runs Cold *'65*
The Ballad of Andy Crocker *'69*
Bluebeard *'72*
The Happy Hooker Goes to Washington *'77*
Cry-Baby *'90*

Patricia Heaton (1958-)
Beethoven *'92*
Memoirs of an Invisible Man *'92*
The New Age *'94*
Moms' Night Out *'14*

Tom Heaton
April Fool's Day *'86*
Call of the Wild *'93*
Mermaid *'00*
Killer Bees *'02*
Mail Order Bride *'08*
Christmas in Canaan *'09*

David Heavener (1958-)
Twisted Justice *'89*
Ragin' Cajun *'90*
Prime Target *'91*
Eye of the Stranger *'93*
Kill or Be Killed *'93*
The Catcher *'98*
Outlaw Prophet *'01*

Heavy D (1967-2011)
See Dwight 'Heavy D' Myers

Anne Heche (1969-)
O Pioneers! *'91*
The Adventures of Huck Finn *'93*
Against the Wall *'94*
Girls in Prison *'94*
Milk Money *'94*
A Simple Twist of Fate *'94*
Pie in the Sky *'95*
Wild Side *'95*
Donnie Brasco *'96*
If These Walls Could Talk *'96*
The Juror *'96*
Walking and Talking *'96*
I Know What You Did Last Summer *'97*
Subway Stories *'97*
Volcano *'97*
Wag the Dog *'97*
Psycho *'98*
Return to Paradise *'98*
Six Days, Seven Nights *'98*
The Third Miracle *'99*
Beyond Suspicion *'00*
Prozac Nation *'01*
John Q *'02*
Birth *'04*
Gracie's Choice *'04*
Fatal Desire *'05*
Ghost Writer *'07*
What Love Is *'07*
Toxic Skies *'08*
Spread *'09*
The Other Guys *'10*
Cedar Rapids *'11*
Girl Fight *'11*
Rampart *'11*
That's What She Said *'12*
Wild Card *'15*
Catfight *'17*
My Friend Dahmer *'17*
Opening Night *'17*

Gina Hecht (1953-)
A Stranger's Heart *'07*
The Last Word *'08*
Seven Pounds *'08*

Jessica Hecht (1965-)
Intimate Betrayal *'96*
The Forgotten *'04*
Saving Face *'04*
Sideways *'04*
Starting Out in the Evening *'07*
Jesse Stone: Thin Ice *'09*
My Soul to Take *'10*
J. Edgar *'11*
The Sitter *'11*
The English Teacher *'13*

Paul Hecht (1941-)
Family Reunion *'81*
Last Call: The Final Chapter of F. Scott Fitzgerald *'02*

Ted Hecht (1908-69)
So Proudly We Hail *'43*
Tarzan and the Huntress *'47*

Eileen Heckart (1919-2001)
The Bad Seed *'56*
Bus Stop *'56*
Somebody Up There Likes Me *'56*
Heller in Pink Tights *'60*
Up the Down Staircase *'67*
No Way to Treat a Lady *'68*
Butterflies Are Free *'72*
Zandy's Bride *'74*
The Hiding Place *'75*
Burnt Offerings *'76*
Backstairs at the White House *'79*
Heartbreak Ridge *'86*
The First Wives Club *'96*

Jamie Hector
Max Payne *'08*
Night Catches Us *'10*

Dan Hedaya (1940-)
The Prince of Central Park *'77*
Endangered Species *'82*
The Hunger *'83*
The Adventures of Buckaroo Banzai Across the Eighth Dimension *'84*
Reckless *'84*
Tightrope *'84*
Blood Simple *'85*
Commando *'85*
Courage *'86*
Running Scared *'86*
Wise Guys *'86*
The Reluctant Agent *'89*
Joe Versus the Volcano *'90*
Pacific Heights *'90*
Tune in Tomorrow *'90*
The Addams Family *'91*
Benny & Joon *'93*
Boiling Point *'93*
For Love or Money *'93*
Mr. Wonderful *'93*
Rookie of the Year *'93*
Maverick *'94 (C)*
Clueless *'95*
Freeway *'95*
To Die For *'95*
The Usual Suspects *'95*
Daylight *'96*
The First Wives Club *'96*
Marvin's Room *'96*
Ransom *'96*
Alien: Resurrection *'97*
A Life Less Ordinary *'97*
The Second Civil War *'97*
The Extreme Adventures of Super Dave *'98*
A Night at the Roxbury *'98*
Dick *'99*
The Hurricane *'99*
The Crew *'00*
Shaft *'00*
Mulholland Drive *'01*
Quicksand *'01*
The Shaft *'01*
American Cousins *'02*
Swimfan *'02*
Robots *'05 (V)*
Strangers with Candy *'06*
The Extra Man *'10*
The Big Take *'18*

Jon Heder (1977-)
Napoleon Dynamite *'04*
Just like Heaven *'05*
The Benchwarmers *'06*
Monster House *'06 (V)*
School for Scoundrels *'06*
Blades of Glory *'07*
Mama's Boy *'07*
Moving McAllister *'07*
Surf's Up *'07 (V)*
When in Rome *'09*
Woke Up Dead *'09*
Christmas Eve *'15*
Ghost Team *'16*
The Tiger Hunter *'17*

Lucas Hedges (1996-)
The Zero Theorem *'13*
Kill the Messenger *'14*
Manchester by the Sea *'16*
Three Billboards Outside Ebbing, Missouri *'17*
Ben Is Back *'18*
Boy Erased *'18*
Mid90s *'18*
Honey Boy *'19*

David Hedison (1927-)
Enemy Below *'57*
The Fly *'58*
The Lost World *'60*
Marines, Let's Go *'61*
Live and Let Die *'73*
ffolkes *'80*
Kenny Rogers as the Gambler, Part 2: The Adventure Continues *'83*
The Naked Face *'84*
A.D. *'85*
License to Kill *'89*
Undeclared War *'91*
Fugitive Mind *'99*

Jack Hedley (1930-)
The Anniversary *'68*
Goodbye, Mr. Chips *'69*
For Your Eyes Only *'81*
New York Ripper *'82*

Garrett Hedlund (1984-)
Friday Night Lights *'04*
Troy *'04*
Four Brothers *'05*
Eragon *'06*
Death Sentence *'07*
Georgia Rule *'07*
Country Strong *'10*
Tron: Legacy *'10*
On the Road *'12*
Inside Llewyn Davis *'13*
Lullaby *'14*
Unbroken *'14*
Mojave *'15*
Pan *'15*
Billy Lynn's Long Halftime Walk *'16*
Mudbound *'17*
Triple Frontier *'19*

Tippi Hedren (1930-)
The Birds *'63*
Marnie *'64*
A Countess from Hong Kong *'67*
Harrad Experiment *'73*
Foxfire Light *'82*
In the Cold of the Night *'89*
Pacific Heights *'90*
Treacherous Beauties *'94*
Citizen Ruth *'96*
The Break Up *'98*
Footsteps *'98*
Darkwolf *'03*
Raising Genius *'04*
The Last Confederate: The Story of Robert Adams *'05*
Tribute *'09*

Astrid Heeren
Castle Keep *'69*
Silent Night, Bloody Night *'73*

Meghan Heffern (1983-)
Insecticidal *'05*
American Pie Presents: Beta House *'07*
The Shrine *'10*

Kevin Heffernan (1968-)
Super Troopers *'01*
Club Dread *'04*
The Dukes of Hazzard *'05*
Sky High *'05*
Beerfest *'06*
The Lather Effect *'06*
Strange Wilderness *'08*
The Babymakers *'12*
Super Troopers 2 *'18*

Kyle T. Heffner
Flashdance *'83*
Asylum of the Damned *'03*

Van Heflin (1910-71)
A Woman Rebels *'36*
Flight from Glory *'37*
Back Door to Heaven *'39*
Santa Fe Trail *'40*
H.M. Pulham Esquire *'41*
Grand Central Murder *'42*
Johnny Eager *'42*
Seven Sweethearts *'42*
Presenting Lily Mars *'43*
The Strange Love of Martha Ivers *'46*
Till the Clouds Roll By *'46*
Green Dolphin Street *'47*
The Possessed *'47*
Act of Violence *'48*
B.F.'s Daughter *'48*
The Three Musketeers *'48*
East Side, West Side *'49*
Madame Bovary *'49*
The Prowler *'51*
Tomahawk *'51*
My Son John *'52*
Shane *'53*
Black Widow *'54*
Battle Cry *'55*
Patterns *'56*
3:10 to Yuma *'57*
They Came to Cordura *'59*
Cry of Battle *'63*
The Greatest Story Ever Told *'65*
Stagecoach *'66*
The Man Outside *'68*
The Big Bounce *'69*
Airport *'70*

Hugh Hefner (1926-)
History of the World: Part 1 *'81*

Meek's Cutoff '10
The Crimson Petal and the White '12
Everyday '12
Treasure Island '12
Filth '13
In Secret '13
Tale of Tales '15
Stan & Ollie '18

Stephen Henderson (1949-)
Tower Heist '11
Fences '16

Ty Henderson
The Competition '80
Happy Hour '87

Daniel Hendler (1976-)
The Bottom of the Sea '03
Lost Embrace '04
The Paranoids '08

Lauri Hendler
The Child Stealer '79
High School USA '84

Tony Hendra (1941-)
This Is Spinal Tap '84
Life with Mikey '93

Christina Hendricks (1975-)
Hunger Point '03
La Cucina '07
South of Pico '07
The Family Tree '10
Life As We Know It '10
Drive '11
I Don't Know How She Does It '11
Detachment '12
Struck by Lightning '12
Ginger & Rosa '13
God's Pocket '14
Dark Places '15
Lost River '15
Bad Santa 2 '16
The Neon Demon '16
Fist Fight '17
The Strangers: Prey at Night '18
American Woman '19

Eleonore Hendricks
Boulevard '15
Heaven Knows What '15

Benjamin Hendrickson (1950-2006)
Manhunter '86
Spanking the Monkey '94

Elaine Hendrix (1970-)
Last Dance '91
Romy and Michele's High School Reunion '97
The Parent Trap '98
Molly '99
Superstar '99
Wish You Were Dead '00
Inspector Gadget 2 '02
Mr. St. Nick '02
What the #$*! Do We Know? '04
Bam Bam & Celeste '05
Coffee Date '06
Dear Lemon Lima '09
Rock Slyde: Private Eye '09
Fading of the Cries '10
Spork '10
Treasure Buddies '12 (V)
Adopt a Highway '19

Rachel Hendrix
October Baby '12
Vanished-Left Behind: Next Generation '16

Wanda Hendrix (1928-81)
Ride the Pink Horse '47
Saddle Tramp '47
Welcome Stranger '47
Miss Tatlock's Millions '48
Prince of Foxes '49
The Admiral Was a Lady '50
Captain Carey, U.S.A. '50
Sierra '50
My Outlaw Brother '51
The Last Posse '53
The Black Dakotas '54

Boy Who Caught a Crook '61
Johnny Cool '63

Gloria Hendry (1949-)
Black Caesar '73
Hell Up in Harlem '73
Live and Let Die '73
Slaughter's Big Ripoff '73
Black Belt Jones '74
Savage Sisters '74
Bare Knuckles '77
Pumpkinhead 2: Blood Wings '94

Ian Hendry (1931-84)
Room at the Top '59
Children of the Damned '63
The Hill '65
Repulsion '65
Journey to the Far Side of the Sun '69
The Southern Star '69
McKenzie Break '70
Get Carter '71
Tales from the Crypt '72
Theatre of Blood '73
Captain Kronos: Vampire Hunter '74
The Passenger '75
The Bitch '78

Mark Hengst (1964-)
Death Racers '08
Sunday School Musical '08
Countdown: Jerusalem '09

Sonja Henie (1912-69)
One in a Million '36
Thin Ice '37
Happy Landing '38
My Lucky Star '38
Iceland '42
Wintertime '43
It's a Pleasure '45

Brad William Henke (1966-)
Mr. Wrong '95
The Assassination of Richard Nixon '05
Must Love Dogs '05
The Zodiac '05
Altered '06
Hollywoodland '06
Sherrybaby '06
Around June '08
Choke '08
One Way to Valhalla '09
The Space Between '10
The Trouble With Bliss '11
Fury '14

Barry (Shabaka) Henley (1954-)
Fear of a Black Hat '94
How Stella Got Her Groove Back '98
Patch Adams '98
Life '99
Ali '01
Collateral '04
The Terminal '04
Four Brothers '05
Miami Vice '06
Stolen '12
Remember Sunday '13
Paterson '16

Georgie Henley (1995-)
The Chronicles of Narnia: The Lion, the Witch and the Wardrobe '05
The Chronicles of Narnia: Prince Caspian '08
The Chronicles of Narnia: The Voyage of the Dawn Treader '10
Perfect Sisters '14

Marilu Henner (1952-)
Between the Lines '77
Bloodbrothers '78
Hammett '82
The Man Who Loved Women '83
Cannonball Run 2 '84
Johnny Dangerously '84
Perfect '85
Rustler's Rhapsody '85
L.A. Story '91
Chains of Gold '92
Grand Larceny '92

Noises Off '92
Chasers '94
Titanic '96
Man on the Moon '99
Enemies of Laughter '00
Hitched for the Holidays '12

Jill(ian) Hennessey (1968-)
I Shot Andy Warhol '96
A Smile Like Yours '96
Most Wanted '97
Row Your Boat '98
Chutney Popcorn '99
Dead Broke '99
Komodo '99
Molly '99
Autumn in New York '00
Nuremberg '00
Two Ninas '00
Exit Wounds '01
Jackie, Ethel, Joan: The Kennedy Women '01
Love in the Time of Money '02
Wild Hogs '07

Jill Hennessy (1968-)
Lymelife '08
Small Town Murder Songs '10
Roadie '11
Dawn Rider '12

Andre Hennicke (1958-)
Antibodies '05
Sophie Scholl: The Final Days '05
Youth Without Youth '07
Jerichow '15
Victoria '15
Iceman '19

Aksel Hennie (1975-)
Max Manus: Man of War '08
Headhunters '11
Pioneer '13
Hercules '14
Last Knights '15

Shelley Hennig
Ouija '14
Unfriended '15

Eva Henning (1920-)
Devil's Wanton '49
Three Strange Loves '49

Sam Hennings (1950-)
Mission Manila '87
Seedpeople '92
Drop Zone '94

Monika Henreid
Dead Ringer '64
Omega Man '71
The California Kid '74

Paul Henreid (1908-92)
Goodbye, Mr. Chips '39
Night Train to Munich '40
Casablanca '42
Joan of Paris '42
Now, Voyager '42
Between Two Worlds '44
The Conspirators '44
The Spanish Main '45
Deception '46
Devotion '46
Song of Love '47
The Scar '48
Rope of Sand '49
A Stolen Face '52
Stolen Face '52
Tall Lie '53
Deep in My Heart '54
Ten Thousand Bedrooms '57
Holiday for Lovers '59
Never So Few '59
The Four Horsemen of the Apocalypse '62
The Madwoman of Chaillot '69
Death Among Friends '75
The Exorcist 2: The Heretic '77

David Henrie (1989-)
Arizona Summer '03
The Wizards of Waverly Place: The Movie '09
The Secret World of Arrietty '10 (V)

Lance Henriksen (1940-)
Dog Day Afternoon '75
Mansion of the Doomed '76
Network '76
Damien: Omen 2 '78
The Visitor '80
Prince of the City '81
Piranha 2: The Spawning '82
Nightmares '83
The Right Stuff '83
Savage Dawn '84
The Terminator '84
The Jagged Edge '85
Aliens '86
Near Dark '87
Deadly Intent '88
Pumpkinhead '88
The Horror Show '89
Johnny Handsome '89
Survival Quest '89
The Pit & the Pendulum '91
Stone Cold '91
Alien 3 '92
Delta Heat '92
Jennifer 8 '92
Excessive Force '93
Hard Target '93
Man's Best Friend '93
Super Mario Bros. '93
Color of Night '94
Nature of the Beast '94
No Escape '94
Baja '95
Dead Man '95
Felony '95
Powder '95
The Quick and the Dead '95
Wes Craven Presents Mind Ripper '95
Gunfighter's Moon '96
The Last Assassins '96
Face the Evil '97
Tarzan '99 (V)
Scream 3 '00
Lost Voyage '01
Antibody '02
Sasquatch '02
Unspeakable '02
The Invitation '03
The Last Cowboy '03
Mimic 3: Sentinel '03
Alien *vs.* Predator '04
Madhouse '04
Paranoia 1.0 '04
Starkweather '04
Hellraiser: Hellworld '05
Tarzan 2 '05 (V)
Abominable '06
The Da Vinci Treasure '06
Pirates of Treasure Island '06
Pumpkinhead 3: Ashes to Ashes '06
When a Stranger Calls '06 (V)
Black Ops '07
Bone Dry '07
In the Spider's Web '07
Pumpkinhead 4: Blood Feud '07
Alone in the Dark 2 '08
Appaloosa '08
Ladies of the House '08
Pistol Whipped '08
Prairie Fever '08
Screamers: The Hunting '09
The Slammin' Salmon '09
The Penitent Man '10
Beautiful Wave '11
The Dog Who Saved Halloween '11
Good Day for It '11
Scream of the Banshee '11
The Witches of Oz '11
Phantom '13
My Dog the Champion '14
Road to Paloma '14
Garm Wars: The Last Druid '15
Daylight's End '16

Stig Frode Henriksen
Dead Snow '09
Dead Snow: Red *vs.* Dead '14

Anders Henrikson (1896-1965)
Intermezzo '36
A Woman's Face '38
Miss Julie '50

Krister Henriksson (1946-)
Faithless '00
Reconstruction '03

Brian Tyree Henry
Puerto Ricans in Paris '16
Hotel Artemis '18
Spider-Man: Into the Spider-Verse '18 (V)
White Boy Rick '18
Child's Play '19
Don't Let Go '19

Buck Henry (1930-2020)
The Graduate '67
Catch-22 '70
Is There Sex After Death? '71
The Day of the Dolphin '73 (V)
The Man Who Fell to Earth '76
Heaven Can Wait '78
Old Boyfriends '79
Gloria '80
Eating Raoul '82
Aria '88
Tune in Tomorrow '90
Defending Your Life '91
The Linguini Incident '92
The Player '92
Grumpy Old Men '93
Short Cuts '93
To Die For '95 (C)
Curtain Call '97
The Real Blonde '97
Breakfast of Champions '98
I'm Losing You '98
1999 '98
Town and Country '01
The Last Shot '04

Charlotte Henry (1913-80)
Alice in Wonderland '33
March of the Wooden Soldiers '34
Charlie Chan at the Opera '36
The Mandarin Mystery '37

Gloria Henry (1923-)
Johnny Allegro '49
Miss Grant Takes Richmond '49
Kill the Umpire '50

Gloria Lynne Henry
Phantasm 3: Lord of the Dead '94
The Devil's Advocate '97
Phantasm: Ravager '16

Gregg Henry (1952-)
Pearl '78
Dummy '79
Just Before Dawn '80
Scarface '83
Body Double '84
The Patriot '86
Fair Game '89
I Know My First Name Is Steven '89
Fever '91
The Positively True Adventures of the Alleged Texas Cheerleader-Murdering Mom '93
Robin Cook's Terminal '96
Payback '98
Star Trek: Insurrection '98
The Big Brass Ring '99
Sleep Easy, Hutch Rimes '00
Ballistic: Ecks *vs.* Sever '02
Femme Fatale '02
Sin '02
Silent Partner '05
The Black Dahlia '06
In the Land of Women '06
Slither '06
United 93 '06
Super '10
The Reunion '11
Any Day Now '12
Guardians of the Galaxy '14

Lizzie Borden Took an Ax '14

Hank Henry (1906-81)
Pal Joey '57
Robin and the 7 Hoods '64

Justin Henry (1971-)
Kramer *vs.* Kramer '79
Tiger Town '83
Sixteen Candles '84
Sweet Hearts Dance '88
Andersonville '95
Chasing Destiny '00
Finding Home '03
Lost '05

Lenny Henry (1958-)
Bernard and the Genie '91
Penelope '06
The Pirates! Band of Misfits '12 (V)

Linda Henry (1963-)
Beautiful Thing '95
The Business '05

Louise Henry (1911-2011)
In Old Kentucky '35
Exclusive Story '36
Charlie Chan on Broadway '37
Hit Parade of 1937 '37

Martha Henry (1938-)
Dancing in the Dark '86
Anne of Green Gables: The Continuing Story '99
The Republic of Love '03
Clean '04

Mike Henry (1936-)
Tarzan and the Valley of Gold '65
Tarzan and the Great River '67
The Green Berets '68
More Dead Than Alive '68
Tarzan and the Jungle Boy '68
Skyjacked '72
The Longest Yard '74
Adios Amigo '75
Smokey and the Bandit '77
Smokey and the Bandit 2 '80
Smokey and the Bandit, Part 3 '83

Pat Henry (1924-82)
The Detective '68
Lady in Cement '68

Robert 'Buzzy' Henry (1931-71)
The Great Mike '44
Danny Boy '46

Thomas B(rowne). Henry (1907-80)
Beginning of the End '57
Blood of Dracula '57
The Brain from Planet Arous '57
20 Million Miles to Earth '57

Victor Henry (1943-85)
The Sorcerers '67
All Neat in Black Stockings '69

William Henry (1918-82)
China Seas '35
Tarzan Escapes '36
Double or Nothing '37
Madame X '37
Four Men and a Prayer '38
A Man to Remember '38
Dance Hall '41
Klondike Fury '42
Tornado '43
Women in Bondage '43
The Adventures of Mark Twain '44
Navy Way '44
Fury of the Congo '51
Jungle Moon Men '55
Mister Roberts '55
New Orleans Uncensored '55
The Alamo '60

Elisabeth Henry-Macari
A Bread Factory, Part One '18

A Bread Factory, Part Two '18
Daniel Henshall
The Snowtown Murders '12
The Babadook '14
Douglas Henshall (1965-)
Angels and Insects '95
Kull the Conqueror '97
Orphans '97
Sharpe's Justice '97
Twice upon a Yesterday '98
Anna Karenina '00
Gentlemen's Relish '01
Lawless Heart '01
It's All About Love '03
French Film '08
Collision '09
Dorian Gray '09
The Eagle '11
South Riding '11
The Salvation '14
Georgia Henshaw
Angus, Thongs and Perfect Snogging '08
The Hatching '16
John Henshaw (1951-)
This Is Not a Love Song '02
See No Evil: The Moors Murders '06
Going Postal '10
The Keeper '18
John Hensley
Shutter '08
Hostel: Part 3 '11
Lisa Hensley
The 13th Floor '88
Brides of Christ '91
15 Amore '98
Pamela Hensley (1950-)
Doc Savage '75
Buck Rogers in the 25th Century '79
The Nude Bomb '80
Double Exposure '82
Shuler Hensley (1967-)
The Bread, My Sweet '01
Van Helsing '04
The Legend of Zorro '05
Odd Thomas '13
Darrin Dewitt Henson (1972-)
The Salon '05
April Fools '07
Life Support '07
Blood Done Sign My Name '10
The Inheritance '10
Kiss the Bride '10
Four of Hearts '13
Black Coffee '14
Silent Cry Aloud '16
Elden (Ratliff) Henson (1977-)
The Mighty Ducks '92
D3: The Mighty Ducks '96
The Mighty '98
Idle Hands '99
She's All That '99
Manic '01
O '01
Evil Alien Conquerors '02
The Battle of Shaker Heights '03
Dumb and Dumberer: When Harry Met Lloyd '03
The Butterfly Effect '04
Deja Vu '06
Marilyn Hotchkiss' Ballroom Dancing & Charm School '06
Not Since You '09
Gladys Henson (1897-1982)
The Magnet '50
Those People Next Door '52
The Leather Boys '63
James Maury Henson (1936-90)
See Jim Henson
Jim Henson (1936-90)
The Muppet Movie '79 (V)
The Dark Crystal '82 (V)
The Muppets Take Manhattan '84 (V)
Into the Night '85 (C)
Sesame Street Presents: Follow That Bird '85 (V)
John Henson (1967-)
Stag '97
Bar Hopping '00
Nicky Henson (1945-2019)
The Conqueror Worm '68
Mosquito Squadron '70
Psychomania '73
Parting Shots '98
Love or Money '01
Me Without You '01
Blitz '11
Taraji P. Henson (1970-)
Baby Boy '01
Hair Show '04
Four Brothers '05
Hustle & Flow '05
Something New '06
Smokin' Aces '07
Talk to Me '07
The Curious Case of Benjamin Button '08
The Family That Preys '08
Hurricane Season '09
I Can Do Bad All By Myself '09
Not Easily Broken '09
Date Night '10
The Karate Kid '10
Peep World '10
Taken From Me: The Tiffany Rubin Story '10
The Good Doctor '11
Larry Crowne '11
Think Like a Man '12
No Good Deed '14
Think Like a Man Too '14
Term Life '16
Hidden Figures '17
Acrimony '18
Proud Mary '18
The Best of Enemies '19
What Men Want '19
Natasha Henstridge (1974-)
Species '95
Adrenalin: Fear the Rush '96
Maximum Risk '96
Dog Park '98
Species 2 '98
A Better Way to Die '00
Bounce '00
Caracara '00
It Had to Be You '00
Jason and the Argonauts '00
Second Skin '00
The Whole Nine Yards '00
Chilly Dogs '01
John Carpenter's Ghosts of Mars '01
Power and Beauty '02
Species 3 '04
The Whole Ten Yards '04
Widow on the Hill '05
Deception '08
Would Be Kings '08
Impact '09
The Devil's Teardrop '10
You Lucky Dog '10
The Perfect Student '11
Against the Wild '14
Home Invasion '16
Audrey Hepburn (1929-93)
The Lavender Hill Mob '51 (C)
Roman Holiday '53
Sabrina '54
War and Peace '56
Funny Face '57
Love in the Afternoon '57
Green Mansions '59
The Nun's Story '59
The Unforgiven '60
Breakfast at Tiffany's '61
The Children's Hour '61
Charade '63
My Fair Lady '64
Paris When It Sizzles '64
How to Steal a Million '66
Two for the Road '67
Wait until Dark '67
Robin and Marian '76
They All Laughed '81
Love Among Thieves '86
Always '89
Katharine Hepburn (1907-2003)
Christopher Strong '33
Little Women '33
Morning Glory '33
Little Minister '34
Spitfire '34
Alice Adams '35
Break of Hearts '35
Sylvia Scarlett '35
Mary of Scotland '36
A Woman Rebels '36
Quality Street '37
Stage Door '37
Bringing Up Baby '38
Holiday '38
The Philadelphia Story '40
Keeper of the Flame '42
Woman of the Year '42
Stage Door Canteen '43
Dragon Seed '44
Without Love '45
Undercurrent '46
The Sea of Grass '47
Song of Love '47
State of the Union '48
Adam's Rib '50
The African Queen '51
Pat and Mike '52
Summertime '55
The Iron Petticoat '56
The Rainmaker '56
Desk Set '57
Suddenly, Last Summer '59
Long Day's Journey into Night '62
Guess Who's Coming to Dinner '67
The Lion in Winter '68
The Madwoman of Chaillot '69
Trojan Women '71
Rooster Cogburn '75
Olly Olly Oxen Free '78
The Corn Is Green '79
On Golden Pond '81
Love Affair '94
One Christmas '95
Jeff Hephner
Shoot First and Pray You Live '08
The 19th Wife '10
Cole Heppell
The Sandlot 3: Heading Home '07
The Final Storm '09
Bernard Hepton (1925-)
Get Carter '71
Orde Wingate '76
Tinker, Tailor, Soldier, Spy '80
Smiley's People '82
Mansfield Park '85
The Charmer '87
The Lady's Not for Burning '87
Woman in Black '89
Emma '97
Charles Herbert (1948-)
Gun Glory '57
Colossus of New York '58
The Fly '58
13 Ghosts '60
Holmes Herbert (1882-1956)
Up the Ladder '25
A Woman of the World '25
Mr. Wu '27
When a Man Loves '27
The Kiss '29
Madame X '29
Say It With Songs '29
Untamed '29
Dr. Jekyll and Mr. Hyde '32
The Invisible Man '33
Mystery of the Wax Museum '33
Dangerous Appointment '34
The House of Secrets '37
Invisible Agent '42
Sherlock Holmes and the Secret Weapon '42
Confidential Agent '45
Command Decision '48
Hugh Herbert (1887-1952)
Hook, Line and Sinker '30
Faithless '32
Bureau of Missing Persons '33
Fashions of 1934 '34
Fog Over Frisco '34
The Merry Frinks '34
Gold Diggers of 1935 '35
A Midsummer Night's Dream '35
To Beat the Band '35
Colleen '36
One Rainy Afternoon '36
Hollywood Hotel '37
Four's a Crowd '38
Gold Diggers in Paris '38
The Great Waltz '38
Eternally Yours '39
The Black Cat '41
The Villain Still Pursued Her '41
Sherlock Holmes and the Secret Weapon '42
Kismet '44
On Our Merry Way '48
A Song Is Born '48
The Beautiful Blonde from Bashful Bend '49
Percy Herbert (1920-92)
Child in the House '56
The Bridge on the River Kwai '57
Serious Charge '59
The Guns of Navarone '61
Mysterious Island '61
Mutiny on the Bounty '62
Call Me Bwana '63
Carry On Jack '63
Carry On Cowboy '66
One Million Years B.C. '66
Too Late the Hero '70
The Fiend '71
Man in the Wilderness '71
Richard Herd (1932-2020)
Terror Out of the Sky '78
V '83
The Judas Project: The Ultimate Encounter '94
Dolores Heredia (1966-)
Rudo y Cursi '09
Bless Me, Ultima '13
Wilson Jermaine Heredia (1971-)
Rent '05
iMurders '08
Eileen Herlie (1918-2008)
Hamlet '48
Angel with the Trumpet '50
David Herlihy
Intermission '03
Veronica Guerin '03
James Leo Herlihy (1927-93)
In the French Style '63
Four Friends '81
Jacques Herlin (1932-)
Torrents of Spring '90
Of Gods and Men '10
Roberto Herlitzka (1937-)
Summer Night with Greek Profile, Almond Eyes & Scent of Basil '87
The Great Beauty '13
David Herman (1967-)
Office Space '98
Dude, Where's My Car? '00
Table One '00
Idiocracy '06
The Lather Effect '06
Jimmy Herman (1940-2013)
Dances with Wolves '90
Geronimo '93
Coyote Waits '03
Paul Herman (1946-)
The Squeeze '87
The Last Temptation of Christ '88
New York Stories '89
Somebody to Love '94
Pee-wee Herman (1952-)
See Paul (Pee-wee Herman) Reubens
Woody Herman (1913-87)
Wintertime '43
Sensations of 1945 '44
New Orleans '47
Irm Hermann (1942-2020)
The Merchant of Four Seasons '71
The Bitter Tears of Petra von Kant '72
Ali: Fear Eats the Soul '74
Fear of Fear '75
Mother Kusters Goes to Heaven '76
Peter Hermann (1967-)
In the Family '11
Chinese Puzzle '13
Philomena '13
Callie Hernandez
Blair Witch '16
The Endless '17
Jay Hernandez (1978-)
crazy/beautiful '01
The Rookie '02
Friday Night Lights '04
Torque '04
Carlito's Way: Rise to Power '05
Hostel '06
World Trade Center '06
Hostel: Part 2 '07
Live! '07
American Son '08
Lakeview Terrace '08
Nothing Like the Holidays '08
Quarantine '08
Takers '10
LOL '12
Max '15
Jonathan Hernandez (1983-)
A Million to Juan '94
My Family '94
The Hammer '07
Juan Carlos Hernandez
High Crimes '02
Carlito's Way: Rise to Power '05
Juano Hernandez (1901-70)
Intruder in the Dust '49
The Breaking Point '50
Stars in My Crown '50
Trial '55
Ransom! '56
The Mark of the Hawk '57
Something of Value '57
Sergeant Rutledge '60
The Sins of Rachel Cade '61
They Call Me Mr. Tibbs! '70
Kevin Hernandez
Expecting a Miracle '09
The Sitter '11
Get the Gringo '12
Sergio Hernandez
Johnny 100 Pesos '93
Night Across the Street '12
Gloria '13
Blake Heron (1982-)
Trilogy of Terror 2 '96
Shiloh '97
Wind River '98
Cheaters '00
We Were Soldiers '02
11:14 '03
Marcel Herrand (1897-1953)
Children of Paradise '44
Fanfan la Tulipe '51
Mark Herrier (1954-)
Porky's '82
Porky's 2: The Next Day '83
Tank '83
Porky's Revenge '85
Damon Herriman (1970-)
Rodgers & Hammerstein's South Pacific '01
100 Bloody Acres '12
The Nightingale '18
Judy & Punch '20
Aggie Herring (1876-1939)
Oliver Twist '22
That Certain Thing '28
Laura (Martinez) Herring (1964-)
See Laura Elena Harring
Edward Herrmann (1943-2014)
The Day of the Dolphin '73
The Paper Chase '73
The Great Gatsby '74
The Great Waldo Pepper '75
Eleanor & Franklin '76
Love Affair: The Eleanor & Lou Gehrig Story '77
The Betsy '78
Brass Target '78
Freedom Road '79
The North Avenue Irregulars '79
Death Valley '81
Reds '81
A Little Sex '82
Harry's War '84
Mrs. Soffel '84
The Man with One Red Shoe '85
The Purple Rose of Cairo '85
The Lost Boys '87
Overboard '87
Big Business '88
Born Yesterday '93
A Foreign Field '93
My Boyfriend's Back '93
Foreign Student '94
Richie Rich '94
Nixon '95
Pandora's Clock '96
Soul of the Game '96
Critical Care '97
Atomic Train '99
Vendetta '99
The Cat's Meow '01
Double Take '01
James Dean '01
The Shaft '01
The Emperor's Club '02
Intolerable Cruelty '03
The Aviator '04
Relative Strangers '06
Wedding Daze '06
I Think I Love My Wife '07
The Skeptic '09
Bucky Larson: Born to Be a Star '11
The Christmas Pageant '11
A Christmas Wish '11
Treasure Buddies '12
Are You Here '13
The Town That Dreaded Sundown '14
Mark Herron
8 1/2 '63
Girl in Gold Boots '69
Adam Herschman
Accepted '06
Soul Men '08
Phillipe Hersent
The White Angel '55
The Old Testament '62
Barbara Hershey (1948-)
With Six You Get Eggroll '68
Heaven With a Gun '69
The Baby Maker '70
The Liberation of L.B. Jones '70
The Pursuit of Happiness '70
Boxcar Bertha '72
Diamonds '72
Choice of Weapons '76
Flood! '76
The Last Hard Men '76
The Stunt Man '80
Americana '81
Take This Job & Shove It '81
The Entity '83
The Right Stuff '83

The Natural '84
Hannah and Her Sisters '86
Hoosiers '86
Tin Men '87
Beaches '88
The Last Temptation of Christ '88
A World Apart '88
A Killing in a Small Town '90
Tune in Tomorrow '90
Defenseless '91
The Public Eye '92
Falling Down '93
Return to Lonesome Dove '93
Splitting Heirs '93
Swing Kids '93
Abraham '94
The Last of the Dogmen '95
The Pallbearer '95
Portrait of a Lady '96
Breakfast of Champions '98
Frogs for Snakes '98
A Soldier's Daughter Never Cries '98
Passion '99
Drowning on Dry Land '00
Lantana '01
Daniel Deronda '02
Ann Rule Presents: The Stranger Beside Me '03
11:14 '03
Hunger Point '03
Riding the Bullet '04
The Bird Can't Fly '07
Love Comes Lately '07
Black Swan '10
Murder on the Orient Express '10
Answers to Nothing '11
Left to Die: The Sandra and Tammi Chase Story '12
Insidious: Chapter 2 '13
The 9th Life of Louis Drax '16

Jean Hersholt (1886-1956)
Tess of the Storm Country '22
Her Night of Romance '24
Battle of the Sexes '28
Hell Harbor '30
The Phantom of Paris '31
Private Lives '31
The Sin of Madelon Claudet '31
Susan Lenox: Her Fall and Rise '31
Are You Listening? '32
The Beast of the City '32
Emma '32
Flesh '32
Grand Hotel '32
The Mask of Fu Manchu '32
New Morals for Old '32
Skyscraper Souls '32
Dinner at Eight '33
The Cat and the Fiddle '34
Men in White '34
The Painted Veil '34
Break of Hearts '35
One in a Million '36
Heidi '37
Alexander's Ragtime Band '38
Happy Landing '38
Meet Dr. Christian '39
Mr. Moto in Danger Island '39
Courageous Dr. Christian '40
Remedy for Riches '40
Melody for Three '41
Run for Cover '55

Gerard Herter (1920-2000)
Any Gun Can Play '67
Hornets' Nest '70
Adios, Sabata '71

Louis Herthum (1956-)
Mutants '08
Journey to Promethea '10
The Last Exorcism '10
Seconds Apart '11
The Last Exorcism Part II '13

Irene Hervey (1910-98)
The Count of Monte Cristo '34
Charlie Chan in Shanghai '35
Three Godfathers '36
Destry Rides Again '39
East Side of Heaven '39
The Boys From Syracuse '40
Gang Busters '42
Night Monster '42
Mickey '48
Crash Landing '58
Play Misty for Me '71

Jason Hervey (1972-)
Ratings Game '84
Back to the Future '85
Pee-wee's Big Adventure '85
Back to School '86

Hafsia Herzi
The Rabbi's Cat '11 (V)
War Story '14

Werner Herzog (1942-)
Burden of Dreams '82
Man of Flowers '84
Julien Donkey-boy '99
Encounters at the End of the World '07 (N)
Mister Lonely '07
Cave of Forgotten Dreams '11 (N)
Into the Abyss '11 (N)
Jack Reacher '12
Happy People: A Year in the Taiga '13 (N)
Into the Inferno '16

Kam Heskin (1973-)
Blackjack '97
This Girl's Life '03
Vlad '03
Dirty Love '05
The Prince & Me 2: Royal Wedding '06
The Prince & Me 3: A Royal Honeymoon '08
The Prince & Me 4: The Elephant Adventure '10

Grant Heslov (1963-)
License to Drive '88
True Lies '94
Congo '95
Black Sheep '96
Dante's Peak '97
The Scorpion King '02
Good Night, and Good Luck '05
Sleeper Cell '05

Annelise Hesme (1976-)
Alexander '04
Avenue Montaigne '06
Priceless '06

David A(lexander) Hess (1936-2011)
Last House on the Left '72
Avalanche Express '79

Liam Hess
Edges of the Lord '01
Angus, Thongs and Perfect Snogging '08

Howard Hesseman (1940-)
A Session with The Committee '68
Billy Jack '71
Steelyard Blues '73
Private Lessons '75
Shampoo '75
The Sunshine Boys '75
The Big Bus '76
Jackson County Jail '76
Tunnelvision '76
Tarantulas: The Deadly Cargo '77
More Than Friends '78
Americathon '79
Honky Tonk Freeway '81
One Shoe Makes It Murder '82
Doctor Detroit '83
Silence of the Heart '84
This Is Spinal Tap '84
Clue '85
Police Academy 2: Their First Assignment '85
Flight of the Navigator '86
My Chauffeur '86
Amazon Women on the Moon '87
Heat '87
Murder in New Hampshire: The Pamela Smart Story '91
Home for Christmas '93
Out of Sync '95
Gridlock'd '96
About Schmidt '02
Crazy for Christmas '05
Nanny Insanity '06
The Rocker '08
Halloween II '09
Salvation Boulevard '11

Charlton Heston (1924-2008)
Dark City '50
The Greatest Show on Earth '52
Ruby Gentry '52
Arrowhead '53
Bad for Each Other '53
Pony Express '53
Naked Jungle '54
The Far Horizons '55
The Ten Commandments '56
Three Violent People '57
The Big Country '58
The Buccaneer '58
Touch of Evil '58
Ben-Hur '59
The Wreck of the Mary Deare '59
El Cid '61
Diamond Head '62
55 Days at Peking '63
The Agony and the Ecstasy '65
The Greatest Story Ever Told '65
Major Dundee '65
The War Lord '65
Khartoum '66
Counterpoint '67
Will Penny '67
Planet of the Apes '68
Beneath the Planet of the Apes '70
Julius Caesar '70
Omega Man '71
Call of the Wild '72
Skyjacked '72
Antony and Cleopatra '73
Soylent Green '73
Earthquake '74
The Three Musketeers '74
Airport '75 '75
The Four Musketeers '75
The Last Hard Men '76
Midway '76
Two Minute Warning '76
Gray Lady Down '77
The Prince and the Pauper '78
The Awakening '80
The Mountain Men '80
Mother Lode '82
Proud Men '87
A Man for All Seasons '88
Treasure Island '89
Almost an Angel '90
The Little Kidnappers '90
The Crucifer of Blood '91
Solar Crisis '92
Tombstone '93
Wayne's World 2 '93
True Lies '94
The Avenging Angel '95
In the Mouth of Madness '95
Alaska '96
Hamlet '96
Hercules '97 (N)
Any Given Sunday '99
Cats & Dogs '01 (V)
Planet of the Apes '01
Town and Country '01

Dom Hetrakul (1976-)
Mysterious Island '05
Blackbeard '06
Bangkok Dangerous '08

Sam Heughan (1980-)
First Light '10
A Princess for Christmas '11
The Spy Who Dumped Me '18
Bloodshot '20

Lori Heuring (1973-)
The In Crowd '00
Seduced: Pretty When You Cry '01
True Blue '01
The Locket '02
Taboo '02
8mm 2 '05
False Prophets '06
Wicked Little Things '07
The Poker Club '08
Cross '11

Jennifer Love Hewitt (1979-)
Home for Christmas '93
Sister Act 2: Back in the Habit '93
House Arrest '96
I Know What You Did Last Summer '97
Trojan War '97
Can't Hardly Wait '98
I Still Know What You Did Last Summer '98
Telling You '98
The Suburbans '99
The Audrey Hepburn Story '00
Heartbreakers '01
The Tuxedo '02
Garfield: The Movie '04
If Only '04
The Truth About Love '04
Confessions of a Sociopathic Social Climber '05
Garfield: A Tail of Two Kitties '06
Delgo '08 (V)
Tropic Thunder '08 (C)
Cafe '10
The Client List '10
The Lost Valentine '11
Jewtopia '12

Martin Hewitt (1958-)
Endless Love '81
Yellowbeard '83
Killer Party '86
Carnal Crimes '91
Secret Games '92
Night Fire '94
Bombshell '97

Paul Hewitt
A Perfect World '93
Hijacking Hollywood '97
Tom Clancy's Netforce '98

Sean Hewitt
The Sender '82
My Own Country '98
Battlefield Earth '00

David Hewlett (1968-)
Pin. . . '88
The Penthouse '89
Where the Heart Is '90
Desire and Hell at Sunset Motel '92
The Boys of St. Vincent '93
Cube '98
The Life Before This '99
Treed Murray '01
The Triangle '01
Cypher '02
Boa vs. Python '04
Darklight '04
Ice Men '04
A Dog's Breakfast '07
Helen '09
Splice '10
Rise of the Planet of the Apes '11
The Whistleblower '11
Haunter '13

Siobhan Hewlett (1983-)
Monsieur N. '03
Irina Palm '07

Eve Hewson
This Must Be the Place '12
Papillon '17
Robin Hood '18

Virginia Hey (1952-)
The Road Warrior '82
Bullet Down Under '94

Kirby Heyborne (1977-)
Saints and Soldiers '03
Together Again for the First Time '08

Weldon Heyburn (1910-51)
Convention Girl '35
Speed '36
Criminals Within '41
The Chinese Cat '44

Louis Jean Heydt (1905-60)
Charlie Chan at Treasure Island '39
The Great McGinty '40
Dive Bomber '41
Power Dive '41
Sleepers West '41
Thirty Seconds Over Tokyo '44
Zombies on Broadway '44
Our Vines Have Tender Grapes '45
They Were Expendable '45
The Big Sleep '46
The Kid From Cleveland '49
Roadblock '51
Island in the Sky '53

Christopher Heyerdahl (1963-)
Requiem for Murder '99
The Witness '99
Varian's War '01
Blade: Trinity '04
Catwoman '04
The Twilight Saga: New Moon '09
The Calling '14
Adopt a Highway '19
Togo '19

Herbert (Hayes) Heyes (1889-1958)
Campus Rhythm '43
Bedtime for Bonzo '51
A Place in the Sun '51
Park Row '52
The Far Horizons '55

Barton Heyman (1937-96)
The Naked Flame '68
Let's Scare Jessica to Death '71
Valdez Is Coming '71
The Exorcist '73
Cruising '80
Billy Galvin '86
Static '87
Awakenings '90
Raising Cain '92
Roadside Prophets '92
Dead Man Walking '95

Anne Heywood (1932-)
Doctor at Large '57
Upstairs and Downstairs '59
Carthage in Flames '60
The Chairman '69
I Want What I Want '72

Pat Heywood (1931-)
Girly '70
10 Rillington Place '71
Wish You Were Here '87

Sung Hi Lee (1970-)
National Lampoon's Christmas Vacation 2: Cousin Eddie's Big Island Adventure '03
The Art of War 3: Retribution '08

Edward Hibbert (1955-)
The First Wives Club '96
Friends and Family '01
A Different Loyalty '04
The Lion King 1 1/2 '04 (V)

John Benjamin Hickey (1963-)
Eddie '96
Love! Valour! Compassion! '96
Finding North '97
The Ice Storm '97
The Bone Collector '99
The General's Daughter '99
The Anniversary Party '01
Hamlet '01
Life with Judy Garland-Me and My Shadows '01
Changing Lanes '02
Flags of Our Fathers '06
Infamous '06
Freedom Writers '07
The Seeker: The Dark Is Rising '07
Living Proof '08
Big Stone Gap '15

Tom Hickey (1944-)
Nuns on the Run '90
Raining Stones '93
Possession '02
Rory O'Shea Was Here '04
Alarm '08

William Hickey (1928-97)
A Hatful of Rain '59
Invitation to a Gunfighter '64
The Boston Strangler '68
Mikey & Nicky '76
Prizzi's Honor '85
Remo Williams: The Adventure Begins '85
Walls of Glass '85
The Name of the Rose '86
One Crazy Summer '86
Hobo's Christmas '87
Bright Lights, Big City '88
National Lampoon's Christmas Vacation '89
Pink Cadillac '89
Puppet Master '89
Sea of Love '89
Any Man's Death '90
My Blue Heaven '90
Tales from the Darkside: The Movie '90
The Nightmare Before Christmas '93 (V)
Forget Paris '95
The Jerky Boys '95
Major Payne '95
Love Is All There Is '96
Twisted '96
Mouse Hunt '97

Catherine Hickland (1956-)
Witchery '88
Millions '90

Darryl Hickman (1931-)
Men of Boys Town '41
Keeper of the Flame '42
Leave Her to Heaven '45
The Devil on Wheels '47
The Happy Years '50
Lightning Strikes Twice '51
Destination Gobi '53
Island in the Sky '53
Southwest Passage '54
Tea and Sympathy '56
The Iron Sheriff '57
The Tingler '59
Johnny Shiloh '63

Dwayne Hickman (1934-)
The Sun Comes Up '49
Rally 'Round the Flag, Boys! '58
Cat Ballou '65
How to Stuff a Wild Bikini '65
Ski Party '65
Dr. Goldfoot and the Bikini Machine '66
My Dog, the Thief '69
High School USA '84
A Night at the Roxbury '98

Howard Hickman (1880-1949)
Civilization '16
Jim Hanvey, Detective '37
Gone with the Wind '39
Watch on the Rhine '43

Anthony Hickox (1959-)
Lobster Man from Mars '89
Blast '04

Adam Hicks (1992-)
Down and Derby '05
How to Eat Fried Worms '06
Lemonade Mouth '11

Catherine Hicks (1951-)
Death Valley '81
Garbo Talks '84
The Razor's Edge '84
Peggy Sue Got Married '86

Around the World in 80 Days *'89*
Hands of a Murderer *'90*
A Very Brady Sequel *'96*

Harriet Hilliard (1909-94)
See Harriet Hilliard Nelson

Candace Hilligoss (1935-)
Carnival of Souls *'62*
Curse of the Living Corpse *'64*

Ali Hillis (1978-)
All the Wrong Places *'00*
Must Love Dogs *'05*
The Ultimate Gift *'07*
Who's Your Monkey *'07*
Space Buddies *'08 (V)*
The Ultimate Life *'13*

Rib Hillis (1970-)
Dinocroc Vs. Supergator *'10*
Cowboys vs Dinosaurs *'15*

Richard Hillman (1974-2009)
Men *'97*
Bring It On *'00*
Teenage Caveman *'01*

Beverly Hills (1939-)
See Beverly (Hills) Powers

Gillian Hills (1944-)
Beat Girl *'60*
Blow-Up *'66*
Demons of the Mind *'72*

Hera Hilmar (1988-)
Mortal Engines *'18*
An Ordinary Man *'18*

Daisy Hilton (1908-69)
Freaks *'32*
Chained for Life *'51*

George Hilton (1934-2019)
Any Gun Can Play *'67*
Hallelujah for Django *'67*
The Battle of El Alamein *'68*
Liberators *'69*
Bullet for Sandoval *'70*
Dead for a Dollar *'70*
Fistful of Lead *'70*
Sartana's Here. . . Trade Your Pistol for a Coffin *'70*
The Case of the Scorpion's Tail *'71*
The Scorpion's Tail *'71*
The Case of the Bloody Iris *'72*
Day of the Maniac *'77*

Jim Hilton
All Hell Broke Loose *'09*
A Cold Day in Hell *'11*

Paris Hilton (1981-)
House of Wax *'05*
Bottoms Up *'06*
The Hottie and the Nottie *'08*
Repo! The Genetic Opera *'08*
The Dog Who Saved Christmas Vacation *'10 (V)*
The Other Guys *'10*
The Bling Ring *'13 (C)*

Paul Hilton
Wuthering Heights *'12*
Lady Macbeth *'17*

Tyler Hilton (1983-)
Walk the Line *'05*
Charlie Bartlett *'07*

Violet Hilton (1908-69)
Freaks *'32*
Chained for Life *'51*

Megan Hilty (1981-)
Bitter Feast *'10*
Legends of Oz: Dorothy's Return *'14 (V)*

Nichole Hiltz (1978-)
Amazons and Gladiators *'01*
May *'02*
All Souls Day *'05*

Aaron Himelstein (1985-)
Bachelor Party Vegas *'05*
All the Boys Love Mandy Lane *'06*
The Assistants *'09*

Madeline Hinde (1949-)
The Bloodsuckers *'70*
The Fiend *'71*

Art Hindle (1948-)
Black Christmas *'75*
Invasion of the Body Snatchers *'78*
The Brood *'79*
Octagon *'80*
Desperate Lives *'82*
Porky's *'82*
The Man Who Wasn't There *'83*
Porky's 2: The Next Day *'83*
Wild Pony *'83*
The Gunfighters *'87*
Dixie Lanes *'88*
Into the Fire *'88*
Black Horizon *'01*
The Trip *'02*
Christmas in Boston *'05*
Blind Trust *'06*
A Christmas Wedding *'06*
One Way *'06*
Lies and Crimes *'07*
Certain Prey *'11*

Earl Hindman (1942-2003)
The Taking of Pelham One Two Three *'74*
Taps *'81*
Murder in Coweta County *'83*
The Ballad of the Sad Cafe *'91*

Aisha Hinds (1975-)
Assault on Precinct 13 *'05*
Mr. Brooks *'07*
Lost Dream *'09*

Ciaran Hinds (1953-)
December Bride *'91*
Catherine Cookson's The Man Who Cried *'93*
The Affair *'95*
Mary Reilly *'95*
Persuasion *'95*
Some Mother's Son *'96*
Ivanhoe *'97*
Jane Eyre *'97*
Oscar and Lucinda *'97*
The Lost Son *'98*
Jason and the Argonauts *'00*
The Weight of Water *'00*
Road to Perdition *'02*
The Sum of All Fears *'02*
Calendar Girls *'03*
Lara Croft Tomb Raider: The Cradle of Life *'03*
The Mayor of Casterbridge *'03*
The Statement *'03*
Veronica Guerin *'03*
The Phantom of the Opera *'04*
Munich *'05*
Amazing Grace *'06*
Miami Vice *'06*
The Nativity Story *'06*
The Tiger's Tale *'06*
Margot at the Wedding *'07*
Mister Foe *'07*
There Will Be Blood *'07*
Cash *'08*
Miss Pettigrew Lives for a Day *'08*
Stop-Loss *'08*
The Tale of Despereaux *'08 (V)*
The Eclipse *'09*
Life During Wartime *'09*
Race to Witch Mountain *'09*
The Debt *'10*
Harry Potter and the Deathly Hallows, Part 1 *'10*
Harry Potter and the Deathly Hallows, Part 2 *'11*
The Rite *'11*
Tinker Tailor Soldier Spy *'11*
Ghost Rider: Spirit of Vengeance *'12*
John Carter *'12*
The Woman in Black *'12*
Closed Circuit *'13*
The Disappearance of Eleanor Rigby *'14*
McCanick *'14*
Bleed for This *'16*
Last Days in the Desert *'16*
Silence *'16*

Samuel S. Hinds (1875-1948)
Gabriel Over the White House *'33*
Rendezvous *'35*
Rhythm on the Range *'36*
The Black Legion *'37*
Double or Nothing *'37*
Navy Blue and Gold *'37*
Devil's Party *'38*
Forbidden Valley *'38*
Test Pilot *'38*
You Can't Take It with You *'38*
Young Dr. Kildare *'38*
Destry Rides Again *'39*
The Secret of Dr. Kildare *'39*
Dr. Kildare Goes Home *'40*
Adventure in Washington *'41*
Back Street *'41*
Blossoms in the Dust *'41*
Grand Central Murder *'42*
Lady in a Jam *'42*
Pardon My Sarong *'42*
Ride 'Em Cowboy *'42*
The Strange Case of Dr. Rx *'42*
Son of Dracula *'43*
Cobra Woman *'44*
Scarlet Street *'45*
The Strange Affair of Uncle Harry *'45*
Weekend at the Waldorf *'45*
It's a Wonderful Life *'46*
The Bribe *'48*

Brendan P. Hines (1976-)
Ordinary Sinner *'02*
Heavy Petting *'07*

Cheryl Hines (1965-)
Cake *'05*
Herbie: Fully Loaded *'05*
Bickford Shmeckler's Cool Ideas *'06*
Keeping Up with the Steins *'06*
RV *'06*
Waitress *'07*
Bart Got a Room *'08*
Henry Poole Is Here *'08*
Space Chimps *'08 (V)*
Labor Pains *'09*
The Ugly Truth *'09*
Cold Turkey *'13*
Life After Beth *'14*
Wilson *'17*

Damon Hines
Thunder in Carolina *'60*
The Adventures of Buckaroo Banzai Across the Eighth Dimension *'84*
Ratings Game *'84*
Barfly *'87*
Lethal Weapon *'87*
Scrooged *'88*
Lethal Weapon 2 *'89*
Lethal Weapon 3 *'92*
What's Love Got to Do with It? *'93*
Once Upon a Time . . . When We Were Colored *'95*
Lethal Weapon 4 *'98*

Gregory Hines (1946-2003)
History of the World: Part 1 *'81*
Wolfen *'81*
Deal of the Century *'83*
The Cotton Club *'84*
The Muppets Take Manhattan *'84 (C)*
White Nights *'85*
Running Scared *'86*
Off Limits *'87*
Tap *'89*
Eve of Destruction *'90*
A Rage in Harlem *'91*
Bleeding Hearts *'94*
Renaissance Man *'94*
A Stranger in Town *'95*
Waiting to Exhale *'95*
The Cherokee Kid *'96*
Good Luck *'96*
The Preacher's Wife *'96*
Trigger Happy *'96*
Subway Stories *'97*
The Tic Code *'99*
Echo of Murder *'00*
Once in the Life *'00*
Things You Can Tell Just by Looking at Her *'00*
Bojangles *'01*
The Red Sneakers *'01*

Johnny Hines (1895-1970)
Conductor 1492 *'24*
The Early Bird *'25*

Robert Hines
The Insurance Man *'86*
Hellraiser *'87*
Echoes *'88*
Devices and Desires *'91*

Ronald Hines (1929-)
Elizabeth R *'72*
We'll Meet Again *'82*
Pack of Lies *'87*

Pat Hingle (1923-2009)
No Down Payment *'57*
The Strange One *'57*
The Ugly American *'63*
Invitation to a Gunfighter *'64*
Nevada Smith *'66*
Hang 'Em High *'67*
The Ballad of Andy Crocker *'69*
Bloody Mama *'70*
WUSA *'70*
The Carey Treatment *'72*
Nightmare Honeymoon *'73*
Running Wild *'73*
The Super Cops *'74*
The Gauntlet *'77*
Tarantulas: The Deadly Cargo *'77*
Elvis: The Movie *'79*
Norma Rae *'79*
Of Mice and Men *'81*
Going Berserk *'83*
Running Brave *'83*
Sudden Impact *'83*
Brewster's Millions *'85*
Broken Badge *'85*
The Falcon and the Snowman *'85*
Maximum Overdrive *'86*
Baby Boom *'87*
The Land Before Time *'88 (V)*
Batman *'89*
The Grifters *'90*
Batman Returns *'92*
Citizen Cohn *'92*
Lightning Jack *'94*
Batman Forever *'95*
One Christmas *'95*
The Quick and the Dead *'95*
Truman *'95*
Larger Than Life *'96*
Batman and Robin *'97*
Hunter's Moon *'97*
A Thousand Acres *'97*
Muppets from Space *'99*
The Runaway *'00*
Shaft *'00*
Two Tickets to Paradise *'06*
Waltzing Anna *'06*
The List *'07*

Marin Hinkle (1966-)
Winds of Terror *'01*
The Next Big Thing *'02*
Fielder's Choice *'05*
Four and a Half Women *'05*
Rails & Ties *'07*
Turn the River *'07*
The Haunting of Molly Hartley *'08*
Quarantine *'08*
Weather Girl *'09*

Brent Hinkley (1962-)
The Silence of the Lambs *'91*
Say It Isn't So *'01*

Tommy Hinkley (1960-)
Back to the Beach *'87*
The Little Vampire *'00*

Skip Hinnant (1940-)
Fritz the Cat *'72 (V)*
Nine Lives of Fritz the Cat *'74 (V)*

Ashley Hinshaw (1988-)
About Cherry *'12*
Chronicle *'12*
LOL *'12*
Talhotblond *'12*
Snake & Mongoose *'13*
Goodbye to All That *'14*
The Pyramid *'14*

Jordan Hinson (1991-)
Glass House: The Good Mother *'06*
Breaking & Exiting *'18*
Higher Power *'18*

Darby Hinton (1957-)
Hero's Island *'62*
The Treasure of Jamaica Reef *'74*
Firecracker *'81*
Malibu Express *'85*

Ed Hinton (1919-58)
Seminole Uprising *'55*
The Dalton Girls *'57*

Michael Hinz (1939-2008)
The Bridge *'59*
Touch Me Not *'74*

Bill (William Heinzman) Hinzman (1936-2012)
Night of the Living Dead *'68*
The Majorettes *'87*
Revenge of the Living Zombies *'88*

Paul Hipp (1963-)
Bad Channels *'92*
The Funeral *'96*
Midnight in the Garden of Good and Evil *'97*
Another Day in Paradise *'98*
Cleopatra's Second Husband *'00*
More Dogs Than Bones *'00*
Waking the Dead *'00*
Teenage Caveman *'01*
Two Tickets to Paradise *'06*
South of Pico *'07*
4:44 Last Day on Earth *'11*

Mikijiro Hira (1933-)
Sword of the Beast *'65*
The Mystery of Rampo *'94*
Azumi 2 *'05*
13 Assassins *'10*

Akihiko Hirata (1927-84)
Godzilla *'54*
Samurai 2: Duel at Ichijoji Temple *'55*
Godzilla, King of the Monsters *'56*
H-Man *'59*
Mothra *'62*
King Kong *vs.* Godzilla *'63*
Son of Godzilla *'66*
Godzilla *vs.* the Cosmic Monster *'74*

Thora Hird (1911-2003)
Conspirator *'49*
The Frightened Man *'52*
Simon and Laura *'55*
Further Up the Creek *'58*
The Entertainer *'60*
Term of Trial *'63*
The Nightcomers *'72*
Consuming Passions *'88*
The Wedding Gift *'93*

Ryoko Hirosue (1980-)
Wasabi *'01*
Departures *'08*

Andy Hirsch (1966-)
Fort McCoy *'11*
Liz & Dick *'12*

Daniel Hirsch
Sky High *'84*
Zero Boys *'86*

Emile Hirsch (1985-)
The Dangerous Lives of Altar Boys *'02*
The Emperor's Club *'02*
The Mudge Boy *'03*
The Girl Next Door *'04*
Imaginary Heroes *'05*
Lords of Dogtown *'05*
Alpha Dog *'06*
The Air I Breathe *'07*
Into the Wild *'07*
Milk *'08*
Speed Racer *'08*
Taking Woodstock *'09*
The Darkest Hour *'11*
Killer Joe *'11*
The Motel Life *'12*
Twice Born *'12*
Bonnie & Clyde *'13*
Lone Survivor *'13*
Prince Avalanche *'13*
The Autopsy of Jane Doe *'16*
All Nighter *'17*
Vincent N Roxxy *'17*
Never Grow Old *'19*
Once Upon A Time... In Hollywood *'19*

Judd Hirsch (1935-)
Legend of Valentino *'75*
King of the Gypsies *'78*
Sooner or Later *'78*
Marriage Is Alive and Well *'80*
Ordinary People *'80*
Without a Trace *'83*
Teachers *'84*
Brotherly Love *'85*
Running on Empty *'88*
Independence Day *'96*
Man on the Moon *'99*
Out of the Cold *'99*
Rocky Marciano *'99*
A Beautiful Mind *'01*
Tower Heist *'11*
This Must Be the Place *'12*
Altered Minds *'13*

Lou Hirsch
Honey, I Shrunk the Kids *'89 (V)*
Thunderbirds *'04*

Robert Hirsch (1925-)
Plucking the Daisy *'56*
The Hunchback of Notre Dame *'57*
Mortal Transfer *'01*

David Julian Hirsh (1973-)
Blue Hill Avenue *'01*
Coast to Coast *'04*
St. Urbain's Horseman *'07*

Hallee Hirsh (1987-)
You've Got Mail *'98*
Spring Forward *'99*
Joe Gould's Secret *'00*
My Sister's Keeper *'02*
Speak *'04*
Happy Endings *'05*
Make the Yuletide Gay *'09*

Alice Hirson (1929-)
Miss All-American Beauty *'82*
Blind Date *'87*
StarStruck *'10*

Christianne Hirt
For the Moment *'94*
Tokyo Cowboy *'94*
Firestorm *'97*
Northern Lights *'09*

Alfred Hitchcock (1899-1980)
The Lodger *'26 (C)*
Blackmail *'29*
The Lady Vanishes *'38*
Psycho *'60*
The Birds *'63*
Family Plot *'76*
78/52: Hitchcock's Shower Scene *'17*

Michael Hitchcock (1958-)
Happy, Texas *'99*
Best in Show *'00*
A Mighty Wind *'03*
Pretty Persuasion *'05*
Danny Roane: First Time Director *'06*
Operation: Endgame *'10*

Patricia Hitchcock (1928-)
Strangers on a Train *'51*
Psycho *'60*

Chuck Hittinger (1983-)
Boogeyman 3 *'08*
Stalked at 17 *'12*
Sharknado *'13*

Ben Hiura
Kill! *'68*
Goyokin *'69*

Iben Hjejle (1971-)
Mifune *'99*
High Fidelity *'00*
The Emperor's New Clothes *'01*
Flickering Lights *'01*
Cuban Blood *'03*
The Boss of It All *'06*
Defiance *'08*
Cheri *'09*
The Eclipse *'09*
Klown *'12*

Jesse Hlubik
Roman *'06*
Violent Blue *'10*

Josie Ho (1974-)
The Cave of the Silken Web *'67*
Dead or Alive: Final *'02*
So Close *'02*
Vampire Effect *'03*
Exiled *'06*
Street Fighter: The Legend of Chun-Li *'09*
The Courier *'12*

Linda Ho
Confessions of an Opium Eater *'62*
Hillbillies in a Haunted House *'67*

Judith Hoag (1968-)
Danielle Steel's Fine Things *'90*
Teenage Mutant Ninja Turtles: The Movie *'90*
A Mother's Gift *'95*
Halloweentown *'98*
Halloweentown 2: Kalabar's Revenge *'01*
Halloweentown High *'04*
Return to Halloweentown *'06*
Sexting in Suburbia *'12*

Mitzi Hoag (1932-)
Pieces of Dreams *'70*
Deadly Game *'77*
The Girl in the Empty Grave *'77*

Ferdinand Hoang
The Quiet American *'02*
Mao's Last Dancer *'09*

Florence Hoath (1984-)
FairyTale: A True Story *'97*
The Governess *'98*
Back to the Secret Garden *'01*

Rose Hobart (1906-2000)
Liliom *'30*
East of Borneo *'31*
Dr. Jekyll and Mr. Hyde *'32*
The Shadow Laughs *'33*
Convention Girl *'35*
Susan and God *'40*
No Hands on the Clock *'41*
Conflict *'45*
Claudia and David *'46*
Cass Timberlane *'47*

Halliwell Hobbes (1877-1962)
The Bachelor Father *'31*
The Lady Refuses *'31*
Dr. Jekyll and Mr. Hyde *'32*
Love Affair *'32*
Lovers Courageous *'32*
British Agent *'34*
Cardinal Richelieu *'35*
Charlie Chan in Shanghai *'35*
You Can't Take It with You *'38*
The Earl of Chicago *'40*
Journey for Margaret *'42*
Son of Fury *'42*
To Be or Not to Be *'42*
Sherlock Holmes Faces Death *'43*
Casanova Brown *'44*
Gaslight *'44*
You Gotta Stay Happy *'48*

Chelsea Hobbs (1985-)
The Snow Queen *'02*
Clawed: The Legend of Sasquatch *'05*
More Sex and the Single Mom *'05*
The Party Never Stops *'07*

Peter Hobbs (1918-2011)
Good Neighbor Sam *'64*
Next One *'84*
In the Mood *'87*

Rebecca Hobbs
The Ugly *'96*
Siam Sunset *'99*

William Hobbs (1939-)
Captain Kronos: Vampire Hunter *'74*
The Three Musketeers *'74*

Mara Hobel (1971-)
Mommie Dearest *'81*
Broadway Damage *'98*
Personal Velocity: Three Portraits *'02*

Valerie Hobson (1917-98)
The Bride of Frankenstein *'35*
The Mystery of Edwin Drood *'35*
Werewolf of London *'35*
Secret of Stamboul *'36*
Drums *'38*
Spy in Black *'39*
Contraband *'40*
Unpublished Story *'42*
The Adventures of Tartu *'43*
Great Expectations *'46*
Blanche Fury *'48*
Interrupted Journey *'49*
Kind Hearts and Coronets *'49*
The Rocking Horse Winner *'49*
The Promoter *'52*
The Voice of Merrill *'52*

Danny Hoch (1970-)
Subway Stories *'97*
White Boyz *'99*
Black Hawk Down *'01*
Washington Heights *'02*
We Own the Night *'07*
Henry's Crime *'10*
Exposed *'16*

Kristen Hocking (1966-)
See Kristen Dalton

Kane Hodder (1955-)
Friday the 13th, Part 7: The New Blood *'88*
Friday the 13th, Part 8: Jason Takes Manhattan *'89*
Jason Goes to Hell: The Final Friday *'93*
Pumpkinhead 2: Blood Wings *'94*
Wishmaster *'97*
Watchers Reborn *'98*
Jason X *'01*
Darkwolf *'03*
Hack! *'07*
Hatchet *'07*
Bundy: A Legacy of Evil *'08*
Hatchet 2 *'10*

Aldis Hodge (1986-)
Red Sands *'09*
Straight Outta Compton *'15*
Jack Reacher: Never Go Back *'16*
Brian Banks *'18*
Clemency *'19*
The Invisible Man *'20*

Douglas Hodge (1960-)
Salome's Last Dance *'88*
Behaving Badly *'89*
Dark Obsession *'90*
Anglo-Saxon Attitudes *'92*
Middlemarch *'93*
The Way We Live Now *'02*
Vanity Fair *'04*
Scenes of a Sexual Nature *'06*
Mansfield Park *'07*
The Descent 2 *'09*
Going for Gold: The '48 Games *'12*

Diana *'13*
Gemini Man *'19*
Jonathan *'19*

Edwin Hodge (1985-)
My Teacher Ate My Homework *'98*
Coastlines *'02*
Hangman's Curse *'03*
Fighting the Odds: The Marilyn Gambrell Story *'05*
All the Boys Love Mandy Lane *'06*
The Purge *'13*
As Above, So Below *'14*
The Good Neighbor *'16*
The Purge: Election Year *'16*

Kate Hodge (1966-)
Leatherface: The Texas Chainsaw Massacre 3 *'89*
Rapid Fire *'92*
The Hidden 2 *'94*
Beach Rats *'17*

Mike Hodge (1947-)
Office Killer *'97*
Fiona *'98*
Boycott *'02*

Patricia Hodge (1946-)
The Death of the Heart *'87*
Diamond's Edge *'88*
Sunset *'88*
The Shell Seekers *'89*
The Heat of the Day *'91*
The Leading Man *'96*
The Moonstone *'97*
Lies and Whispers *'98*

Eddie Hodges (1947-)
A Hole in the Head *'59*
The Adventures of Huckleberry Finn *'60*
Summer Magic *'63*
Live a Little, Love a Little *'68*

Tom (Thomas E.) Hodges (1965-)
Lucas *'86*
Since You've Been Gone *'97*

Ty Hodges (1981-)
Blues *'08*
Krews *'10*

Earle Hodgins (1893-1964)
The Cyclone Ranger *'35*
Heroes of the Alamo *'37*
The Bashful Bachelor *'42*
Colt Comrades *'43*
Hoppy Serves a Writ *'43*

Leyland Hodgson (1894-1949)
The Eagle and the Hawk *'33*
Bedlam *'45*

John Hodiak (1914-55)
Lifeboat *'44*
Maisie Goes to Reno *'44*
Sunday Dinner for a Soldier *'44*
The Harvey Girls *'46*
Somewhere in the Night *'46*
Two Smart People *'46*
The Bribe *'48*
Command Decision *'48*
Homecoming *'48*
Battleground *'49*
Malaya *'49*
Ambush *'50*
A Lady Without Passport *'50*
The Miniver Story *'50*
Across the Wide Missouri *'51*
The People Against O'Hara *'51*
The Sellout *'51*
Battle Zone *'52*
Ambush at Tomahawk Gap *'53*
Conquest of Cochise *'53*
Dragonfly Squadron *'54*
Trial *'55*

Biddy Hodson
Loaded *'94*
Hellboy *'04*

Tyler Hoechlin (1987-)
Road to Perdition *'02*
Grizzly Rage *'07*
Hall Pass *'11*

Everybody Wants Some!! *'16*
Undrafted *'16*
Can You Keep a Secret? *'19*

Sylvia Hoeks
The Best Offer *'13*
Blade Runner 2049 *'17*
Renegades *'17*
The Girl in the Spider's Web *'18*

Hannah Hoekstra
The Canal *'14*
Hemel *'14*

Vegar Hoel (1973-)
Dead Snow *'09*
Dead Snow: Red *vs.* Dead *'14*

Heinz Hoenig
Judgment in Berlin *'88*
Antibodies *'05*

Dennis Hoey (1893-1960)
Power *'34*
Sherlock Holmes and the Secret Weapon *'42*
Son of Fury *'42*
They Came to Blow Up America *'43*
The Pearl of Death *'44*
Uncertain Glory *'44*
House of Fear *'45*
Anna and the King of Siam *'46*
Tarzan and the Leopard Woman *'46*
Golden Earrings *'47*
Where There's Life *'47*
David and Bathsheba *'51*

Abbie Hoffman (1936-89)
Born on the Fourth of July *'89*
Heavy Petting *'89*

Basil Hoffman (1938-)
Love at First Bite *'79*
Ratings Game *'84*
Communion *'89*
Lambada *'89*
The Ice Runner *'93*
Rio, I Love You *'14*

Dustin Hoffman (1937-)
The Graduate *'67*
Madigan's Millions *'67*
Midnight Cowboy *'69*
Little Big Man *'70*
Alfredo, Alfredo *'72*
Straw Dogs *'72*
Papillon *'73*
Lenny *'74*
All the President's Men *'76*
Marathon Man *'76*
Straight Time *'78*
Agatha *'79*
Kramer *vs.* Kramer *'79*
Tootsie *'82*
Death of a Salesman *'86*
Ishtar *'87*
Rain Man *'88*
Common Threads: Stories from the Quilt *'89 (N)*
Family Business *'89*
Dick Tracy *'90*
Billy Bathgate *'91*
Hook *'91*
Hero *'92*
Outbreak *'94*
American Buffalo *'95*
Sleepers *'96*
Mad City *'97*
Sphere *'97*
Wag the Dog *'97*
The Messenger: The Story of Joan of Arc *'99*
Moonlight Mile *'02*
Confidence *'03*
Runaway Jury *'03*
Finding Neverland *'04*
I Heart Huckabees *'04*
Meet the Fockers *'04*
The Lost City *'05*
Racing Stripes *'05 (V)*
Perfume: The Story of a Murderer *'06*
Stranger Than Fiction *'06*
Mr. Magorium's Wonder Emporium *'07*

Kung Fu Panda *'08 (V)*
Last Chance Harvey *'08*
The Tale of Despereaux *'08 (V)*
Barney's Version *'10*
Little Fockers *'10*
Kung Fu Panda 2 *'11 (V)*
Chef *'14*
The Cobbler *'14*
Kung Fu Panda 3 *'16*
The Meyerowitz Stories (New and Selected) *'17*
Hal *'18*

Elizabeth Hoffman (1927-)
Fear No Evil *'80*
Dante's Peak *'97*

Erika Hoffman
To Play the King *'93*
The Final Cut *'95*

Gaby Hoffman (1982-)
Field of Dreams *'89*
Uncle Buck *'89*
This Is My Life *'92*
The Man Without a Face *'93*
Sleepless in Seattle *'93*
Now and Then *'95*
Everyone Says I Love You *'96*
Volcano *'97*
All I Wanna Do *'98*
200 Cigarettes *'98*
Black and White *'99*
Coming Soon *'99*
Life During Wartime *'09*
13 *'10*
Crystal Fairy & the Magical Cactus *'13*
Goodbye World *'14*
Obvious Child *'14*
Veronica Mars *'14*
Wild *'14*

Irena A. Hoffman
Metamorphosis *'07*
Transylmania *'09*

Jackie Hoffman (1960-)
Kissing Jessica Stein *'02*
A Dirty Shame *'04*
Garden State *'04*
Robots *'05 (V)*
Queer Duck: The Movie *'06 (V)*

Jake Hoffman (1981-)
Jiminy Glick in LaLa Wood *'05*
National Lampoon's Adam & Eve *'05*
Rosencrantz & Guildenstern Are Undead *'10*
Otherhood *'19*

Jane Hoffman (1911-2004)
Up the Sandbox *'72*
Sybil *'76*
Senior Trip *'81*
Static *'87*

Linda Hoffman
The Dentist *'96*
Mission of Death *'97*
The Dentist 2: Brace Yourself *'98*
Captured *'99*

Philip Seymour Hoffman (1967-2014)
Leap of Faith *'92*
Scent of a Woman *'92*
Nobody's Fool *'94*
When a Man Loves a Woman *'94*
The Yearling *'94*
Hard Eight *'96*
Twister *'96*
The Big Lebowski *'97*
Boogie Nights *'97*
Happiness *'98*
Patch Adams *'98*
Flawless *'99*
Magnolia *'99*
The Talented Mr. Ripley *'99*
Almost Famous *'00*
State and Main *'00*
Love Liza *'02*
Punch-Drunk Love *'02*
Red Dragon *'02*
25th Hour *'02*
Cold Mountain *'03*

Owning Mahowny *'03*
Along Came Polly *'04*
Capote *'05*
Empire Falls *'05*
Mission: Impossible 3 *'06*
Strangers with Candy *'06*
Before the Devil Knows You're Dead *'07*
Charlie Wilson's War *'07*
The Savages *'07*
Doubt *'08*
Synecdoche, New York *'08*
The Invention of Lying *'09*
Mary and Max *'09*
Pirate Radio *'09*
Jack Goes Boating *'10*
The Ides of March *'11*
Moneyball *'11*
A Late Quartet *'12*
The Master *'12*
The Hunger Games: Catching Fire *'13*
God's Pocket *'14*
The Hunger Games: Mockingjay--Part 1 *'14*
A Most Wanted Man *'14*

Rick Hoffman (1970-)
Blood Work *'02*
Cellular *'04*
Hostel *'06*
The Condemned *'07*

Robert Hoffman
Eyes Behind the Stars *'72*
Joe Panther *'76*
Step Up 2 the Streets *'08*

Robert Hoffman, III (1980-)
She's the Man *'06*
Aliens in the Attic *'09*

Thom Hoffman (1957-)
The 4th Man *'79*
Orlando *'92*
Soul Assassin *'01*
Dogville *'03*
Black Book *'06*

Pato Hoffmann (1956-)
Cheyenne Warrior *'94*
The Last Winter *'06*

Robert Hoffmann (1939-)
Grand Slam *'67*
Assignment K *'68*

Susanna Hoffs (1959-)
The Allnighter *'87*
Austin Powers In Goldmember *'02 (C)*

Charlie Hofheimer (1981-)
Father's Day *'96*
Music of the Heart *'99*
Black Hawk Down *'01*
The March Sisters at Christmas *'12*

Isabella Hofmann (1958-)
The Colony *'98*
Homicide: The Movie *'00*
Midnight Bayou *'09*

Marco Hofschneider (1969-)
Europa, Europa *'91*
Foreign Student *'94*
Immortal Beloved *'94*
The Island of Dr. Moreau *'96*
Urban Legends 2: Final Cut *'00*

Bosco Hogan (1949-)
Zardoz *'73*
Count Dracula *'77*
James Joyce: A Portrait of the Artist as a Young Man *'77*
In the Name of the Father *'93*

Chris Hogan
Dancing at the Blue Iguana *'00*
On Edge *'03*

Dick Hogan (1917-95)
Action in the North Atlantic *'43*
So Proudly We Hail *'43*
Shed No Tears *'48*

Gabriel Hogan (1973-)
Head in the Clouds *'04*
Show Me *'04*
Murder in the Hamptons *'05*
Widow on the Hill *'05*
St. Urbain's Horseman *'07*
Bridal Fever *'08*
The Devil's Teardrop *'10*
Ice Soldiers *'13*
I Spit on Your Grave: Vengeance Is Mine *'15*

Heather Hogan (1985-)
The Land Before Time 2: The Great Valley Adventure *'94 (V)*
The Land Before Time 3: The Time of the Great Giving *'95 (V)*
The Land Before Time 4: Journey Through the Mists *'96 (V)*

Hulk Hogan (1953-)
Rocky 3 *'82*
No Holds Barred *'89*
Gremlins 2: The New Batch *'90*
Suburban Commando *'91*
Mr. Nanny *'93*
Thunder in Paradise *'93*
Thunder in Paradise 2 *'94*
Thunder in Paradise 3 *'94*
The Secret Agent Club *'96*
Shadow Warriors 2: Hunt for the Death Merchant *'97*
Shadow Warriors *'97*
3 Ninjas: High Noon at Mega Mountain *'97*
The Ultimate Weapon *'97*
Gnomeo & Juliet *'11 (V)*

Michael Hogan (1949-)
Coffee and Cigarettes *'03*
A Simple Curve *'05*
Battlestar Galactica: The Plan *'09*
Confined *'10*
Hunt to Kill *'10*

Pat Hogan (1920-66)
Lure of the Wilderness *'52*
Davy Crockett, King of the Wild Frontier *'55*
Savage Wilderness *'55*
Seventh Cavalry *'56*
Indian Paint *'64*

Paul Hogan (1939-)
Crocodile Dundee *'86*
Crocodile Dundee 2 *'88*
Almost an Angel *'90*
Lightning Jack *'94*
Flipper *'96*
Crocodile Dundee in Los Angeles *'01*
Strange Bedfellows *'04*

Robert Hogan (1933-)
Cry Rape! *'73*
Once an Eagle *'76*
Lady in Red *'79*
Gone Are the Days *'84*
Maze *'01*

Siobhan Fallon Hogan (1961-)
Forrest Gump *'94*
Men in Black *'97*
Krippendorf's Tribe *'98*
The Negotiator *'98*
What's the Worst That Could Happen? *'01*
Dogville *'03*
Holes *'03*
Fever Pitch *'05*
Charlotte's Web *'06*
Baby Mama *'08*
New in Town *'09*
Fred: The Movie *'10*
The House That Jack Built *'18*

Stephen Hogan
Starship Troopers 3: Marauder *'08*
The Sweeter Side of Life *'13*
The Foreigner *'17*

Susan Hogan (1951-)
The Brood *'79*
Phobia *'80*
White Fang *'91*
Impolite *'92*
A Father's Choice *'00*
Take Me Home: The John Denver Story *'00*
Everything's Gone Green *'06*
Murder on Pleasant Drive *'06*
Cleaverville *'07*
It Was One of Us *'07*
Whispers and Lies *'08*
CAT. 8 *'13*
A Very Merry Mix-Up *'13*

Ed Hogg (1979-)
Brothers of the Head *'06*
Bunny and the Bull *'09*
Anonymous *'11*

Arthur Hohl (1889-1964)
Island of Lost Souls *'32*
Brief Moment *'33*
The Sign of the Cross *'33*
The Defense Rests *'34*
Jimmy the Gent *'34*
Massacre *'34*
The Whole Town's Talking *'35*
Blondie Has Trouble *'40*
Son of Fury *'42*

Solbjorg Hojfeldt (1947-)
The Kingdom *'95*
The Kingdom 2 *'97*

Fred Holbert
Scream Bloody Murder *'72*
Amputee with an Axe *'73*

Boyd Holbrook (1981-)
Higher Ground *'11*
The Reunion *'11*
Hatfields & McCoys *'12*
Very Good Girls *'13*
Little Accidents *'14*
The Skeleton Twins *'14*
Run All Night *'15*
Cardboard Boxer *'16*
Logan *'17*
The Predator *'18*
In the Shadow of the Moon *'19*

David Holbrook
Creepshow 2 *'87*
Return to Salem's Lot *'87*

Hal Holbrook (1925-)
The Group *'66*
Wild in the Streets *'68*
The Great White Hope *'70*
Goodbye, Raggedy Ann *'71*
They Only Kill Their Masters *'72*
Magnum Force *'73*
The Girl from Petrovka *'74*
All the President's Men *'76*
Midway *'76*
Julia *'77*
Our Town *'77*
The Awakening Land *'78*
Capricorn One *'78*
The Fog *'78*
Rituals *'79*
The Kidnapping of the President *'80*
Creepshow *'82*
Girls Night Out *'83*
The Star Chamber *'83*
Behind Enemy Lines *'85*
North and South Book 1 *'85*
Dress Gray *'86*
North and South Book 2 *'86*
Wall Street *'87*
The Unholy *'88*
Day One *'89*
Fletch Lives *'89*
A Killing in a Small Town *'90*
The Firm *'93*
Carried Away *'95*
Cats Don't Dance *'97 (V)*
Eye of God *'97*
Hercules *'97 (V)*
Hush *'98*
My Own Country *'98*
The Bachelor *'99*
Men of Honor *'00*
Waking the Dead *'00*
The Majestic *'01*
Purpose *'02*
Shade *'03*
Into the Wild *'07*
Killshot *'09*
That Evening Sun *'09*
Good Day for It *'11*
Water for Elephants *'11*
Lincoln *'12*
Promised Land *'12*
Planes: Fire & Rescue *'14 (V)*

Kathryn Holcomb
Our Time *'74*
Detour to Terror *'80*

Sarah Holcomb (1960-)
National Lampoon's Animal House *'78*
Caddyshack *'80*

Alexandra Holden (1977-)
In and Out *'97*
Dancer, Texas-Pop. 81 *'98*
Sugar & Spice *'01*
Uprising *'01*
American Gun *'02*
The Hot Chick *'02*
How to Deal *'03*
Window Theory *'04*
Everything You Want *'05*
A Dead Calling *'06*
Special *'06*
A Trick of the Mind *'06*
Wasted *'06*
Working Miracles *'10*
In a World... *'13*

Fay Holden (1895-1973)
Double or Nothing *'37*
You're Only Young Once *'37*
Judge Hardy's Children *'38*
Love Finds Andy Hardy *'38*
Out West With the Hardys *'38*
Andy Hardy Gets Spring Fever *'39*
The Hardys Ride High *'39*
Judge Hardy and Son *'39*
Andy Hardy Meets Debutante *'40*
Bitter Sweet *'40*
Andy Hardy's Private Secretary *'41*
Blossoms in the Dust *'41*
H.M. Pulham Esquire *'41*
I'll Wait for You *'41*
Life Begins for Andy Hardy *'41*
Ziegfeld Girl *'41*
Andy Hardy's Double Life *'42*
The Courtship of Andy Hardy *'42*
Love Laughs at Andy Hardy *'46*
Whispering Smith *'48*
Samson and Delilah *'49*
The Big Hangover *'50*
Andy Hardy Comes Home *'58*

Frankie J. Holden (1952-)
High Tide *'87*
Introducing the Dwights *'07*

Gina Holden (1975-)
The Butterfly Effect 2 *'06*
Final Destination 3 *'06*
Trophy Wife *'06*
The Christmas Cottage *'08*
Screamers: The Hunting *'09*
A Family Thanksgiving *'10*
Jules Verne's Mysterious Island *'10*
Saw 3D: The Final Chapter *'10*
Christmas Comes Home to Canaan *'11*
Dear Santa *'11*
How to Fall in Love *'12*
LA Apocalypse *'14*

Gloria Holden (1908-91)
Dracula's Daughter *'36*
Wife Versus Secretary *'36*
The Life of Emile Zola *'37*
Hawaii Calls *'38*
Miracles for Sale *'39*

Jan Holden (1931-2005)
Fire Maidens from Outer Space *'56*
The Stranglers of Bombay *'60*

Joyce Holden (1930-)
You Never Can Tell *'51*
The Werewolf *'56*

Laurie Holden (1969-)
Expect No Mercy *'95*
The Pathfinder *'96*
The Magnificent Seven *'98*
The Majestic *'01*
Bailey's Billion$ *'05*
Fantastic Four *'05*
Silent Hill *'06*
The Mist *'07*
Meet Market *'08*
Dumb and Dumber To *'14*

Marjean Holden (1964-)
Stripped to Kill 2: Live Girls *'89*
Philadelphia Experiment 2 *'93*
Mortal Kombat 2: Annihilation *'97*
Hostage *'05*

William Holden (1862-1932)
Weary River *'29*
Framed *'30*
Three Faces East *'30*

William Holden (1918-81)
Golden Boy *'39*
Invisible Stripes *'39*
Arizona *'40*
Our Town *'40*
Texas *'41*
Meet the Stewarts *'42*
Apartment for Peggy *'48*
Man from Colorado *'49*
Miss Grant Takes Richmond *'49*
Born Yesterday *'50*
Father Is a Bachelor *'50*
Sunset Boulevard *'50*
Union Station *'50*
Force of Arms *'51*
Escape from Fort Bravo *'53*
Forever Female *'53*
The Moon Is Blue *'53*
Stalag 17 *'53*
Country Girl *'54*
Executive Suite *'54*
Sabrina *'54*
The Bridges at Toko-Ri *'55*
Love Is a Many-Splendored Thing *'55*
Picnic *'55*
The Proud and Profane *'56*
Toward the Unknown *'56*
The Bridge on the River Kwai *'57*
The Key *'58*
The Horse Soldiers *'59*
The World of Suzie Wong *'60*
The Counterfeit Traitor *'62*
Paris When It Sizzles *'64*
The Seventh Dawn *'64*
Alvarez Kelly *'66*
Casino Royale *'67*
The Devil's Brigade *'68*
The Wild Bunch *'69*
Wild Rovers *'71*
The Revengers *'72*
The Towering Inferno *'74*
Network *'76*
21 Hours at Munich *'76*
Damien: Omen 2 *'78*
Fedora *'78*
Ashanti, Land of No Mercy *'79*
Escape to Athena *'79*
When Time Ran Out *'80*
S.O.B. *'81*

Kris Holden-Ried (1973-)
Young Ivanhoe *'95*
Night of the Demons 3 *'97*
Hendrix *'00*
Touch of Pink *'04*
Waking Up Wally *'05*
Niagara Motel *'06*
Autumn Hearts: A New Beginning *'07*
A Broken Life *'07*
Girl's Best Friend *'08*
Gossip *'08*
Never Forget *'08*
Sexting *'11*
Underworld: Awakening *'12*
The Returned *'14*

Geoffrey Holder (1930-2014)
Doctor Dolittle *'67*
Krakatoa East of Java *'69*
Everything You Always Wanted to Know about Sex (But Were Afraid to Ask) *'72*
Live and Let Die *'73*
The Noah *'75 (V)*
Swashbuckler *'76*
Boomerang *'92*
Charlie and the Chocolate Factory *'05 (N)*

Meagan Holder
Bring It On: Fight to the Finish *'09*
You Again *'10*

Roy Holder (1946-)
Othello *'65*
The Land That Time Forgot *'75*

Joanna Hole
I Only Want You to Love Me *'76*
Dark Corners *'06*

Ticky Holgado (1944-2004)
Delicatessen *'92*
French Twist *'95*
And Now Ladies and Gentlemen *'02*
A Very Long Engagement *'04*

Brano Holicek (1985-)
All My Loved Ones *'00*
The Red Baron *'08*

Hope Holiday (1938-)
The Apartment *'60*
The Rounders *'65*

Andre Holland (1979-)
Sugar *'09*
Black or White *'14*
Selma *'14*
High Flying Bird *'19*

Anthony Holland (1928-88)
King of the Gypsies *'78*
All That Jazz *'79*
Oh, God! Book 2 *'80*

Edna Holland (1895-1982)
The Hunted *'48*
Blood of Dracula *'57*

Eric Holland (1933-)
Gardens of Stone *'87*
Masquerade *'88*

Jennifer Holland
Zombie Strippers *'08*
American Pie Presents: Book of Love *'09*

John Holland (1908-93)
Hell Harbor *'30*
Blonde Ice *'48*
Girl in Black Stockings *'57*
They Saved Hitler's Brain *'64*

Mary Holland
Tommy *'75*
Greener Grass *'19*

Tom Holland (1943-)
Model Shop *'69*
Stephen King's The Langoliers *'95*
The Soloist *'09*
Hatchet 2 *'10*

Tom Holland (1996-)
The Impossible *'12*
How I Live Now *'13*
Locke *'13*
Edge of Winter *'16*
The Lost City of Z *'17*
Spider-Man: Homecoming *'17*
Spider-Man: Far from Home *'19*
Spies in Disguise *'19*
Onward *'20 (V)*

Willa Holland (1991-)
Chasing 3000 *'07*
Garden Party *'08*
A Summer in Genoa *'08*
Straw Dogs *'11*
Tiger Eyes *'13*

Tom Hollander (1967-)
Bedrooms and Hallways *'98*
The Very Thought of You *'98*
Maybe Baby *'99*
Enigma *'01*
Gosford Park *'01*
Lawless Heart *'01*
Wives and Daughters *'01*
Possession *'02*
Cambridge Spies *'03*
Paparazzi *'04*
The Libertine *'05*
Pride and Prejudice *'05*
The Darwin Awards *'06*
A Good Year *'06*
Land of the Blind *'06*
Pirates of the Caribbean: Dead Man's Chest *'06*
The Company *'07*
Elizabeth: The Golden Age *'07*
Pirates of the Caribbean: At World's End *'07*
Valkyrie *'08*
In the Loop *'09*
Any Human Heart *'11*
Hanna *'11*
About Time *'13*
The Invisible Woman *'13*
Tulip Fever *'17*
A Private War *'18*

Judy Holliday (1922-65)
Adam's Rib *'50*
Born Yesterday *'50*
The Marrying Kind *'52*
It Should Happen to You *'54*
Phffft! *'54*
Full of Life *'56*
Solid Gold Cadillac *'56*
Bells Are Ringing *'60*

Kene Holliday (1949-)
The Josephine Baker Story *'90*
Great World of Sound *'07*

Polly Holliday (1937-)
All the President's Men *'76*
You Can't Take It With You *'79*
Gremlins *'84*
Konrad *'85*
Moon over Parador *'88*
Mrs. Doubtfire *'93*
Mr. Wrong *'95*
The Parent Trap *'98*
Stick It *'06*

Earl Holliman (1928-)
Destination Gobi *'53*
Broken Lance *'54*
Big Combo *'55*
The Bridges at Toko-Ri *'55*
I Died a Thousand Times *'55*
The Burning Hills *'56*
Forbidden Planet *'56*
Giant *'56*
The Rainmaker *'56*
Don't Go Near the Water *'57*
Gunfight at the O.K. Corral *'57*
Trooper Hook *'57*
Last Train from Gun Hill *'59*
The Trap *'59*
Summer and Smoke *'61*
Sons of Katie Elder *'65*
A Covenant With Death *'67*
Anzio *'68*
The Power *'68*
The Desperate Mission *'69*
Cry Panic *'74*
Alexander: The Other Side of Dawn *'77*
Sharky's Machine *'81*
Gunsmoke: Return to Dodge *'87*
Perfect Tenant *'99*

Ben Hollingsworth (1984-)
The Cutting Edge 3: Chasing the Dream *'08*
Joy Ride 3: Road Kill *'14*
Lucky in Love *'14*
Vendetta *'15*

Tommy Hollis (1954-2001)
Malcolm X '92
The Piano Lesson '94
Primary Colors '98

Ellen Hollman
Road House 2: Last Call '06
Fling '08
The Scorpion King 4: Quest for Power '15

Bridget Holloman (1958-2006)
Slumber Party '57 '76
Evils of the Night '85

Laurel Holloman (1971-)
The Incredibly True Adventure of Two Girls in Love '95
Prefontaine '96
Boogie Nights '97
The First to Go '97
The Myth of Fingerprints '97
Tumbleweeds '98
Loving Jezebel '99
Lush '01
The Rising Place '02

Josh Holloway (1969-)
Whisper '07
Stay Cool '09
Five '11
Mission: Impossible-Ghost Protocol '11
Battle of the Year '13
Paranoia '13
Sabotage '14

Julian Holloway (1944-)
Carry On Henry VIII '71
Porridge '91

Stanley Holloway (1890-1982)
Immortal Battalion '44
The Way Ahead '44
The Way to the Stars '45
Brief Encounter '46
Nicholas Nickleby '46
This Happy Breed '47
Hamlet '48
Passport to Pimlico '49
The Lavender Hill Mob '51
Beggar's Opera '54
An Alligator Named Daisy '55
My Fair Lady '64
In Harm's Way '65
Mrs. Brown, You've Got a Lovely Daughter '68
The Private Life of Sherlock Holmes '70
Flight of the Doves '71

Sterling Holloway (1905-92)
Blondie Johnson '33
Elmer the Great '33
Fast Workers '33
International House '33
Wild Boys of the Road '33
The Merry Widow '34
Strictly Dynamite '34
Doubting Thomas '35
I Live My Life '35
Life Begins at Forty '35
Career Woman '36
Join the Marines '37
Varsity Show '37
Remember the Night '40
Cheers for Miss Bishop '41
Melody Master '41
Bambi '42 (V)
The Three Caballeros '45 (V)
Sioux City Sue '46
A Walk in the Sun '46
Robin Hood of Texas '47
The Beautiful Blonde from Bashful Bend '49
Midnight Episode '50
Alice in Wonderland '51 (V)
Kentucky Rifle '55
Shake, Rattle and Rock '57
The Adventures of Huckleberry Finn '60
The Jungle Book '67 (V)
Live a Little, Love a Little '68
The Aristocats '70 (V)
The Many Adventures of Winnie the Pooh '77 (V)
Thunder and Lightning '77

Ellen Holly (1931-)
Take a Giant Step '59
Cops and Robbers '73
School Daze '88
10,000 Black Men Named George '02

Lauren Holly (1963-)
Band of the Hand '86
Seven Minutes in Heaven '86
The Adventures of Ford Fairlane '90
Fugitive Among Us '92
Dragon: The Bruce Lee Story '93
Dumb & Dumber '94
Sabrina '95
Beautiful Girls '96
Down Periscope '96
A Smile Like Yours '96
Turbulence '96
Money Kings '98
No Looking Back '98
Any Given Sunday '99
What Women Want '00
Jackie, Ethel, Joan: The Kennedy Women '01
Spirited Away '01 (V)
The Final Hit '02
King of Texas '02
Caught in the Act '04
In Enemy Hands '04
The Chumscrubber '05
Down and Derby '05
The Pleasure Drivers '05
Fatwa '06
Raising Flagg '06
Chasing 3000 '07
Before You Say 'I Do' '09
The Final Storm '09
The Least Among You '09
Call Me Mrs. Miracle '10
The Perfect Age of Rock 'n' Roll '10
You're So Cupid '10
Scream of the Banshee '11
Field of Lost Shoes '14
The Blackcoat's Daughter '17

Anna Margaret Hollyman
White Reindeer '13
Sleeping with Other People '15
Don't Leave Home '18

Ryan Hollyman
Seducing Maarya '99
The Audrey Hepburn Story '00

Anders Holm
The Intern '15
Unexpected '15
How to Be Single '16

Astrid Holm (1893-1961)
The Phantom Chariot '20
The Phantom Carriage '21
Haxan: Witchcraft through the Ages '22
Master of the House '25

Celeste Holm (1919-2012)
Three Little Girls In Blue '46
Carnival in Costa Rica '47
Gentleman's Agreement '47
Chicken Every Sunday '48
Road House '48
The Snake Pit '48
Come to the Stable '49
A Letter to Three Wives '49 (V)
All About Eve '50
Champagne for Caesar '50
The Tender Trap '55
High Society '56
Bachelor Flat '62
Cinderella '64
The Delphi Bureau: The Merchant of Death Assignment '72
Tom Sawyer '73
Backstairs at the White House '79
Three Men and a Baby '87
Still Breathing '97
Alchemy '05

Ian Holm (1931-2020)
A Midsummer Night's Dream '68
Oh! What a Lovely War '69
A Severed Head '70
Mary, Queen of Scots '71
Young Winston '72
The Homecoming '73
Juggernaut '74
Robin and Marian '76
The Man in the Iron Mask '77
March or Die '77
Holocaust '78
The Lost Boys '78
The Thief of Baghdad '78
Alien '79
S.O.S. Titanic '79
Chariots of Fire '81
Time Bandits '81
Return of the Soldier '82
Greystoke: The Legend of Tarzan, Lord of the Apes '84
Singleton's Pluck '84
Brazil '85
Dance with a Stranger '85
Dreamchild '85
Wetherby '85
Another Woman '88
Henry V '89
Hamlet '90
Naked Lunch '91
The Advocate '93
The Madness of King George '94
Mary Shelley's Frankenstein '94
Big Night '95
Loch Ness '95
Night Falls on Manhattan '96
The Sweet Hereafter '96
The Fifth Element '97
A Life Less Ordinary '97
King Lear '98
Animal Farm '99 (V)
eXistenZ '99
Beautiful Joe '00
Bless the Child '00
Esther Kahn '00
Joe Gould's Secret '00
The Last of the Blonde Bombshells '00
The Miracle Maker: The Story of Jesus '00 (V)
The Emperor's New Clothes '01
From Hell '01
Lord of the Rings: The Fellowship of the Ring '01
Lord of the Rings: The Return of the King '03
The Aviator '04
The Day After Tomorrow '04
Garden State '04
Lord of War '05
Renaissance '06
Strangers with Candy '06
O Jerusalem '07
Ratatouille '07 (V)

Clare Holman (1964-)
Catherine Cookson's The Fifteen Streets '90
Let Him Have It '91
Afraid of the Dark '92
Tom & Viv '94
Dot.Kill '05

Harry Holman (1874-1947)
Fugitive Road '34
Night Alarm '34
Mexican Spitfire at Sea '42
Swing Hostess '44

Rex Holman (1928-)
The Choppers '61
Panic in Year Zero! '62

Adrian Holmes (1974-)
Cries in the Dark '06
Ice Blues: A Donald Strachey Mystery '08
Frankie and Alice '10
Hunt to Kill '10
Vendetta '15

Arielle Holmes
Heaven Knows What '15
American Honey '16

Ashton Holmes (1978-)
A History of Violence '05
Peaceful Warrior '06
Havoc 2: Normal Adolescent Behavior '07
What We Do Is Secret '07
Wind Chill '07
Smart People '08
The Pacific '10
Cold Turkey '13
Acts of Violence '18

Emily Holmes (1977-)
Nightwatching '07
Magic Beyond Words: The JK Rowling Story '11
Independence Daysaster '13
Zodiac: Signs of the Apocalypse '14

Katie Holmes (1978-)
The Ice Storm '97
Disturbing Behavior '98
Go '99
Teaching Mrs. Tingle '99
The Gift '00
Wonder Boys '00
Abandon '02
Phone Booth '02
Pieces of April '03
The Singing Detective '03
First Daughter '04
Batman Begins '05
Thank You for Smoking '06
Mad Money '08
The Extra Man '10
The Romantics '10
Don't Be Afraid of the Dark '11
Jack and Jill '11
The Kennedys '11
The Son of No One '11
Days and Nights '14
The Giver '14
Miss Meadows '14
Woman in Gold '15
All We Had '16
Touched With Fire '16
Logan Lucky '17
Dear Dictator '18
Brahms: The Boy II '19

Luree Holmes (1942-)
Pajama Party '64
How to Stuff a Wild Bikini '65

Phillips Holmes (1909-42)
An American Tragedy '31
The Criminal Code '31
Dinner at Eight '33
Penthouse '33
Great Expectations '34

Prudence Wright Holmes
Kingpin '96
In Dreams '98

Stuart Holmes (1884-1971)
The Four Horsemen of the Apocalypse '21
The Prisoner of Zenda '22
Paint and Powder '25
When a Man Loves '27
People Will Talk '51

Taylor Holmes (1872-1959)
Boomerang '47
Nightmare Alley '47
Act of Violence '48
Copper Canyon '50
Rhubarb '51
Hoodlum Empire '52
Tobor the Great '54
Sleeping Beauty '59 (V)

Tina Holmes (1973-)
Edge of Seventeen '99
Prince of Central Park '00
Taken '02
Half Nelson '06
Shelter '07

Wendell Holmes (1915-62)
Lost Boundaries '49
Good Day for a Hanging '58
Compulsion '59
Because They're Young '60
Elmer Gantry '60
The Absent-Minded Professor '61

Karen Holness
Twitches '05
Twitches Too '07

Rosie Holotik (1946-)
Don't Look in the Basement '73
Twisted Brain '74
Encounter with the Unknown '75

Charlene Holt (1928-96)
Man's Favorite Sport? '63
Red Line 7000 '65
El Dorado '67
Wonder Woman '74

Claire Holt (1988-)
Messengers 2: The Scarecrow '09
Blue Like Jazz '12
47 Meters Down '17

David Holt (1927-2003)
Last Days of Pompeii '35
The Adventures of Tom Sawyer '38

Greyston Holt (1985-)
Hannah's Law '12
The Horses of McBride '12
Lonesome Dove Church '14

Jack Holt (1888-1951)
The Little American '17
The Smart Set '28
The Defense Rests '34
Whirlpool '34
The Littlest Rebel '35
San Francisco '36
Cat People '42
Holt of the Secret Service '42
Thunder Birds '42
They Were Expendable '45
The Chase '46
Flight to Nowhere '46
My Pal Trigger '46
Renegade Girl '46
Loaded Pistols '48
Task Force '49
Trail of Robin Hood '50
Across the Wide Missouri '51

Jim Holt (1956-)
The Monkey's Mask '00
The Prince & Me 2: Royal Wedding '06

Olivia Holt
Girl *vs.* Monster '12
Same Kind of Different as Me '17

Patrick Holt (1912-93)
Unholy Four '54
Alias John Preston '56
It Takes a Thief '60
No Blade of Grass '70
Psychomania '73

Sandrine Holt (1972-)
Black Robe '91
Rapa Nui '93
Pocahontas: The Legend '95
Once a Thief '96
Gunslinger's Revenge '98
1999 '98
Loving Jezebel '99
Mission '00
Ballistic: Ecks *vs.* Sever '02
Happy Hour '03
Resident Evil: Apocalypse '04
Fire Serpent '07
The Phantom '09
Chinese Puzzle '13

Tim Holt (1918-73)
Stella Dallas '37
Gold Is Where You Find It '38
Fifth Avenue Girl '39
Stagecoach '39
Along the Rio Grande '41
Back Street '41
The Magnificent Ambersons '42
My Darling Clementine '46
Treasure of the Sierra Madre '48
His Kind of Woman '51
The Monster That Challenged the World '57
The Yesterday Machine '63
This Stuff'll Kill Ya! '71

Ula Holt
The New Adventures of Tarzan '35
Tarzan and the Green Goddess '38

Mark Holton (1958-)
Pee-wee's Big Adventure '85
The Naked Gun: From the Files of Police Squad '88
Easy Wheels '89
A League of Their Own '92
Leprechaun '93
Convicted '04

Tenen Holtz (1877-1971)
Exit Smiling '26
The Trail of '98 '28
British Agent '34

Maria Holvoe
The Last Warrior '89
Worth Winning '89

Arabella Holzbog (1966-)
Stone Cold '91
Evil Lives '92
Carnosaur 2 '94
Red Shoe Diaries: Swimming Naked '00

Robert E. Homans (1874-1947)
Young America '32
The Scarlet Clue '45

Lluis Homar (1957-)
If They Tell You I Fell '89
Celestial Clockwork '94
What It's All About '95
Bad Education '04
The Backwoods '06
Body Armour '07
Broken Embraces '09
Julia's Eyes '10

Skip Homeier (1930-)
Tomorrow the World '44
The Gunfighter '50
The Halls of Montezuma '50
Fixed Bayonets! '51
Has Anybody Seen My Gal? '52
The Last Posse '53
Black Widow '54
Ten Wanted Men '54
The Burning Hills '56
The Tall T '57
Comanche Station '60
Johnny Shiloh '63
The Ghost and Mr. Chicken '66
The Voyage of the Yes '72

Oscar Homolka (1898-1978)
Sabotage '36
Comrade X '40
The Invisible Woman '40
Seven Sinners '40
Ball of Fire '41
Rage in Heaven '41
Mission to Moscow '43
I Remember Mama '48
The White Tower '50
The House of the Arrow '53
The Seven Year Itch '55
War and Peace '56
A Farewell to Arms '57
The Key '58
Mr. Sardonicus '61
Boys' Night Out '62
The Long Ships '64
Funeral in Berlin '66
Billion Dollar Brain '67
Dr. Jekyll and Mr. Hyde '68
Strange Case of Dr. Jekyll & Mr. Hyde '68
Assignment to Kill '69
The Madwoman of Chaillot '69
The Executioner '70

James Hong (1929-)
China Gate *'57*
The Sand Pebbles *'66*
The Carey Treatment *'72*
Chinatown *'74*
The Dynamite Brothers *'74*
Missiles of October *'74*
Go Tell the Spartans *'78*
Airplane! *'80*
Blade Runner *'82*
Yes, Giorgio *'82*
Big Trouble in Little China *'86*
The Golden Child *'86*
Black Widow *'87*
Revenge of the Nerds 2: Nerds in Paradise *'87*
The Brotherhood of the Rose *'89*
Shadowzone *'89*
Tango and Cash *'89*
The Vineyard *'89*
Caged Fury *'90*
The Two Jakes *'90*
Body Trouble *'92*
Talons of the Eagle *'92*
Wayne's World 2 *'93*
Bad Company *'94*
The Shadow *'94*
Gladiator Cop: The Swordsman 2 *'95*
The Secret Agent Club *'96*
South Beach Academy *'96*
Red Corner *'97*
Breakout *'98*
Broken Vessels *'98*
Mulan *'98 (V)*
G2: Mortal Conquest *'99*
The Art of War *'00*
Epoch *'00*
Latin Dragon *'03*
American Fusion *'05*
Balls of Fury *'07*
Shanghai Kiss *'07*
The Day the Earth Stood Still *'08*
Kung Fu Panda *'08 (V)*
Kung Fu Panda 2 *'11 (V)*
The Lost Medallion: The Adventures of Billy Stone *'13*
R.I.P.D. *'13*

Kojiro Hongo (1938-2013)
Gamera vs. Barugon *'66*
Gamera vs. Gaos *'67*
Destroy All Planets *'68*
Along with Ghosts *'69*

Shiriohona Hongsopon
The Iron Ladies *'00*
The Iron Ladies 2 *'03*

Stephanie Honore (1984-)
House of Bones *'09*
Wolvesbayne *'09*
Mirrors 2 *'10*

Stephanie Honore Sanchez (1984-)
See Stephanie Honore

Darla Hood (1931-79)
Bohemian Girl *'36*
The Bat *'59*

Don Hood (1940-2003)
Absence of Malice *'81*
Marie *'85*
Dean Koontz's Mr. Murder *'98*

Morag Hood (1942-2002)
War and Peace *'73*
A Shot at Glory *'00*

Shaun Hood
Visitor Q *'01*
Blind Eye *'06*

Joel Hookey
Visitor Q *'01*
Blind Eye *'06*

Brian Hooks (1973-)
Phat Beach *'96*
Nothin' 2 Lose *'00*
Three Strikes *'00*
Soul Plane *'04*
Dead Tone *'07*
Fool's Gold *'08*
Laughing to the Bank *'13*

Jan Hooks (1957-2014)
Pee-wee's Big Adventure *'85*
Batman Returns *'92*
Coneheads *'93*
Simon Birch *'98*
Jiminy Glick in LaLa Wood *'05*

Kevin Hooks (1958-)
Sounder *'72*
Aaron Loves Angela *'75*
Backstairs at the White House *'79*
Innerspace *'87*

Robert Hooks (1937-)
Hurry Sundown *'67*
Black Brigade *'69*
The Last of the Mobile Hotshots *'69*
Trouble Man *'72*
Aaron Loves Angela *'75*
A Woman Called Moses *'78*
Backstairs at the White House *'79*
Fast Walking *'82*
Words by Heart *'84*
The Execution *'85*
Heat Wave *'90*
Passenger 57 *'92*
Posse *'93 (C)*
Free of Eden *'98*
Seventeen Again *'00*

Ewan Hooper (1935-)
Dracula Has Risen from the Grave *'68*
Kinky Boots *'06*

Tobe Hooper (1946-)
Sleepwalkers *'92*
Body Bags *'93 (C)*

Peter Hooten (1950-)
Fantasies *'73*
Slashed Dreams *'74*
Deadly Mission *'78*
The Inglorious Bastards *'78*

William Hootkins (1948-2005)
Valentino *'77*
American Gothic *'88*
Dust Devil *'93*
Death Machine *'95*
The Omega Code *'99*
The Magnificent Ambersons *'02*
Color Me Kubrick *'05*

Joseph Hoover
Hell Is for Heroes *'62*
The Astro-Zombies *'67*

Phil Hoover
Chain Gang Women *'72*
Policewomen *'73*
Black Gestapo *'75*
Acapulco Gold *'78*

Barclay Hope (1958-)
Range of Motion *'00*
Too Cool for Christmas *'04*
Best Friends *'05*
Holiday Wishes *'06*
The Stranger Game *'06*
Trophy Wife *'06*
Charlie & Me *'08*
Storm Seekers *'08*
Toxic Skies *'08*
Patricia Cornwell's At Risk *'10*
The Christmas Consultant *'12*
The Wedding Chapel *'13*

Bob Hope (1903-2003)
The Big Broadcast of 1938 *'38*
College Swing *'38*
Give Me a Sailor *'38*
Thanks for the Memory *'38*
The Cat and the Canary *'39*
Never Say Die *'39*
The Ghost Breakers *'40*
The Road to Singapore *'40*
Caught in the Draft *'41*
Louisiana Purchase *'41*
Nothing But the Truth *'41*
The Road to Zanzibar *'41*
My Favorite Blonde *'42*
The Road to Morocco *'42*
Star Spangled Rhythm *'42*
They Got Me Covered *'43*
The Princess and the Pirate *'44*
Monsieur Beaucaire *'46*
The Road to Utopia *'46*
My Favorite Brunette *'47*
The Road to Rio *'47*
Where There's Life *'47*
The Paleface *'48*
The Great Lover *'49*
Sorrowful Jones *'49*
Fancy Pants *'50*
The Lemon Drop Kid *'51*
My Favorite Spy *'51*
Son of Paleface *'52*
Here Come the Girls *'53*
Off Limits *'53*
The Road to Bali *'53*
Scared Stiff *'53 (C)*
Casanova's Big Night *'54*
The Seven Little Foys *'55*
The Iron Petticoat *'56*
Paris Holiday *'57*
Alias Jesse James *'59*
The Facts of Life *'60*
Bachelor in Paradise *'61*
The Road to Hong Kong *'62*
Call Me Bwana *'63*
Critic's Choice *'63*
I'll Take Sweden *'65*
Boy, Did I Get a Wrong Number! *'66*
Eight on the Lam *'67*
Private Navy of Sgt. O'Farrell *'68*
How to Commit Marriage *'69*
Cancel My Reservation *'72*
The Muppet Movie *'79 (C)*

Courtney Hope (1989-)
Mob Rules *'10*
Prowl *'10*

Leslie Hope (1965-)
Sword of Gideon *'86*
Kansas *'88*
Talk Radio *'88*
The Big Slice *'90*
Doppelganger: The Evil Within *'90*
Men at Work *'90*
Sweet Killing *'93*
Fun *'94*
Paris, France *'94*
First Degree *'95*
Schemes *'95*
Conspiracy of Fear *'96*
Rowing Through *'96*
Bram Stoker's Shadowbuilder *'98*
Summer of the Monkeys *'98*
This Matter of Marriage *'98*
The Life Before This *'99*
Restless Spirits *'99*
Bruiser *'00*
The Incredible Mrs. Ritchie *'03*
An Unexpected Love *'03*
American Meltdown *'04*
Don't Cry Now *'07*
Everest *'07*
Never Back Down *'08*
Formosa Betrayed *'09*
Jesse Stone: Thin Ice *'09*

Nicholas Hope (1958-)
Bad Boy Bubby *'93*
The Goddess of 1967 *'00*
The Night We Called It a Day *'03*
Inhuman Resources *'12*

Richard Hope
Singleton's Pluck *'84*
Bellman and True *'88*
Piece of Cake *'88*

Tamara Hope (1984-)
The Sandy Bottom Orchestra *'00*
The Deep End *'01*
Shattered City: The Halifax Explosion *'03*
A Different Loyalty *'04*
Prom Queen *'04*
Saint Ralph *'04*
Shall We Dance? *'04*
The Nickel Children *'05*
Lies and Crimes *'07*
September Dawn *'07*
Shoot First and Pray You Live *'08*
Sand Serpents *'09*

Vida Hope (1918-63)
They Made Me a Fugitive *'47*
Twilight Women *'52*
Angels One Five *'54*

William Hope (1955-)
Aliens *'86*
Hellbound: Hellraiser 2 *'88*
Submerged *'05*
The Detonator *'06*
Finding Rin Tin Tin *'07*
Burton and Taylor *'13*
Spiders *'13*

Alan Hopgood (1934-)
My Brilliant Career *'79*
Road Games *'81*
Hotel de Love *'96*

Anthony Hopkins (1937-)
The Lion in Winter *'68*
The Looking Glass War *'69*
When Eight Bells Toll *'71*
Young Winston *'72*
A Doll's House *'73*
War and Peace *'73*
All Creatures Great and Small *'74*
The Girl from Petrovka *'74*
Juggernaut *'74*
QB VII *'74*
The Lindbergh Kidnapping Case *'76*
Victory at Entebbe *'76*
Audrey Rose *'77*
A Bridge Too Far *'77*
International Velvet *'78*
Magic *'78*
A Change of Seasons *'80*
The Elephant Man *'80*
Peter and Paul *'81*
The Hunchback of Notre Dame *'82*
The Bounty *'84*
A Married Man *'84*
Arch of Triumph *'85*
Guilty Conscience *'85*
Mussolini & I *'85*
84 Charing Cross Road *'86*
The Good Father *'87*
The Dawning *'88*
The Tenth Man *'88*
A Chorus of Disapproval *'89*
Desperate Hours *'90*
One Man's War *'90*
The Silence of the Lambs *'91*
Bram Stoker's Dracula *'92*
Chaplin *'92*
The Efficiency Expert *'92*
Freejack *'92*
Howard's End *'92*
The Innocent *'93*
The Remains of the Day *'93*
Shadowlands *'93*
The Trial *'93*
Legends of the Fall *'94*
The Road to Wellville *'94*
August *'95*
Nixon *'95*
Surviving Picasso *'96*
Amistad *'97*
The Edge *'97*
The Mask of Zorro *'98*
Meet Joe Black *'98*
Instinct *'99*
Titus *'99*
Dr. Seuss' How the Grinch Stole Christmas *'00 (N)*
Mission: Impossible 2 *'00*
Hannibal *'01*
Hearts in Atlantis *'01*
Bad Company *'02*
Red Dragon *'02*
The Human Stain *'03*
Alexander *'04*
Proof *'05*
The World's Fastest Indian *'05*
All the King's Men *'06*
Bobby *'06*
Beowulf *'07 (V)*
Fracture *'07*
Slipstream *'07*
The City of Your Final Destination *'09*
The Wolfman *'09*
You Will Meet a Tall Dark Stranger *'10*
The Rite *'11*
Thor *'11*
Hitchcock *'12*
360 *'12*
RED 2 *'13*
Thor: The Dark World *'13*
Noah *'14*
The Dresser *'15*
Blackway *'16*
Misconduct *'16*
Solace *'16*
Collide *'17*
Transformers: The Last Knight *'17*
The Two Popes *'19*

Bo Hopkins (1942-)
1,000 Plane Raid *'69*
The Wild Bunch *'69*
Culpepper Cattle Co. *'72*
The Getaway *'72*
American Graffiti *'73*
Man Who Loved Cat Dancing *'73*
White Lightning *'73*
The Nickel Ride *'74*
The Day of the Locust *'75*
The Killer Elite *'75*
Posse *'75*
The Invasion of Johnson County *'76*
A Small Town in Texas *'76*
Tentacles *'77*
Midnight Express *'78*
More American Graffiti *'79*
Rodeo Girl *'80*
Mutant *'83*
What Comes Around *'85*
Nightmare at Noon *'87*
Trapper County War *'89*
Big Bad John *'90*
Blood Ties *'92*
Center of the Web *'92*
The Legend of Wolf Mountain *'92*
The Ballad of Little Jo *'93*
Inside Monkey Zetterland *'93*
Cheyenne Warrior *'94*
Painted Hero *'95*
Uncle Sam *'96*
U-Turn *'97*
From Dusk Till Dawn 2: Texas Blood Money *'98*
Big Brother Trouble *'00*
Cowboy Up *'00*
A Crack in the Floor *'00*
Shade *'03*

Bruce Hopkins (1955-)
Dead Evidence *'00*
Beyond Justice *'01*
You Move You Die *'07*

Harold Hopkins (1944-2011)
Gallipoli *'81*
Resistance *'92*
Joey *'98*

Jermaine 'Huggy' Hopkins (1973-)
Juice *'92*
Phat Beach *'96*
Def Jam's How to Be a Player *'97*

Josh Hopkins (1970-)
The Pirates of Silicon Valley *'99*
Love & Sex *'00*
The Perfect Storm *'00*
The Hades Factor *'06*
The Insatiable *'06*
Pretty Ugly People *'08*
12 Men of Christmas *'09*
Lebanon, PA *'10*
A Bet's a Bet *'14*

Miriam Hopkins (1902-72)
The Smiling Lieutenant *'31*
Dr. Jekyll and Mr. Hyde *'32*
Trouble in Paradise *'32*
Design for Living *'33*
Barbary Coast *'35*
Becky Sharp *'35*
The Old Maid *'39*
Virginia City *'40*
Old Acquaintance *'43*
The Heiress *'49*
Carrie *'52*
The Children's Hour *'61*
The Chase *'66*

Paul Hopkins (1968-)
Snowboard Academy *'96*
Armistead Maupin's More Tales of the City *'97*
My First Wedding *'04*
Thrill of the Kill *'06*
The Double Life of Eleanor Kendall *'08*

Rhonda Leigh Hopkins
Cover Girl Models *'75*
Summer School Teachers *'75*

Telma Hopkins (1948-)
Trancers *'84*
Vital Signs *'90*
Trancers 3: Deth Lives *'92*
The Love Guru *'08*

Lincoln Hoppe (1971-)
Benji: Off the Leash! *'04*
Believe *'07*
Saints and Soldiers: Airborne Creed *'12*

Rolf Hoppe (1930-)
Mephisto *'81*
Spring Symphony *'86*
Schtonk *'92*
Palmetto *'98*
Go for Zucker *'05*

Dennis Hopper (1936-2010)
Rebel without a Cause *'55*
Giant *'56*
Gunfight at the O.K. Corral *'57*
Story of Mankind *'57*
The Young Land *'59*
Night Tide *'61*
Sons of Katie Elder *'65*
Planet of Blood *'66*
Queen of Blood *'66*
Cool Hand Luke *'67*
The Glory Stompers *'67*
The Trip *'67*
Head *'68*
Easy Rider *'69*
True Grit *'69*
Bloodbath *'76*
Mad Dog Morgan *'76*
Tracks *'76*
The American Friend *'77*
Apocalypse Now *'79*
Out of the Blue *'80*
Reborn *'81*
The Osterman Weekend *'83*
Rumble Fish *'83*
The Inside Man *'84*
My Science Project *'85*
Blue Velvet *'86*
Hoosiers *'86*
The Texas Chainsaw Massacre 2 *'86*
Black Widow *'87*
O.C. and Stiggs *'87*
The Pick-Up Artist *'87*
River's Edge *'87*
Straight to Hell *'87*
Blood Red *'88*
Riders of the Storm *'88*
Backtrack *'89*
Chattahoochee *'89*
Flashback *'89*
Superstar: The Life and Times of Andy Warhol *'90*
Eye of the Storm *'91*
Hearts of Darkness: A Filmmaker's Apocalypse *'91*
The Indian Runner *'91*
Boiling Point *'93*
Red Rock West *'93*
Super Mario Bros. *'93*
True Romance *'93*
Chasers *'94*
Search and Destroy *'94*
Speed *'94*
Carried Away *'95*
Waterworld *'95*
Basquiat *'96*
The Last Days of Frankie the Fly *'96*
Samson and Delilah *'96*

Home By Christmas *'06*
Legacy of Fear *'06*
Proof of Lies *'06*
Boot Camp *'07*
The Invisible *'07*
The Kate Logan Affair *'10*
Hitched for the Holidays *'12*

Adrian Hough
The Fog *'05*
The Suspect *'05*
Past Tense *'06*
Northern Lights *'09*
Dawn Rider *'12*

Julianne Hough (1988-)
Burlesque *'10*
Footloose *'11*
Rock of Ages *'12*
Safe Haven *'13*
Curve *'16*
Dirty Grandpa *'16*

James Houghton (1948-)
More American Graffiti *'79*
Superstition *'82*

Katharine Houghton (1945-)
Guess Who's Coming to Dinner *'67*
Seeds of Evil *'76*
Mr. North *'88*
Billy Bathgate *'91*
Ethan Frome *'92*

Nicholas Hoult (1989-)
About a Boy *'02*
Wah-Wah *'05*
The Weather Man *'05*
A Single Man *'09*
X-Men: First Class *'11*
Jack the Giant Slayer *'13*
Warm Bodies *'13*
X-Men: Days of Future Past *'14*
Young Ones *'14*
Dark Places *'15*
Mad Max: Fury Road *'15*
Equals *'15*
Kill Your Friends *'16*
X-Men: Apocalypse *'16*
Collide *'17*
Rebel in the Rye *'17*
The Favourite *'18*
The Current War: Director's Cut *'19*
Dark Phoenix *'19*
Tolkien *'19*
The Banker *'20*

Djimon Hounsou (1964-)
Amistad *'97*
Deep Rising *'98*
Gladiator *'00*
The Four Feathers *'02*
In America *'02*
Biker Boyz *'03*
Lara Croft Tomb Raider: The Cradle of Life *'03*
Beauty Shop *'05*
Constantine *'05*
The Island *'05*
Blood Diamond *'06*
Eragon *'06*
Never Back Down *'08*
Push *'09*
The Tempest *'10*
Elephant White *'11*
Special Forces *'11*
Guardians of the Galaxy *'14*
How to Train Your Dragon 2 *'14 (V)*
Seventh Son *'15*
The Legend of Tarzan *'16*
King Arthur: Legend of the Sword *'17*
Same Kind of Different as Me *'17*
Serenity *'19*

Eyad Hourani
Omar *'13*
The Idol *'15*

Billy House (1890-1961)
Bedlam *'45*
Egg and I *'47*
Rogues of Sherwood Forest *'50*
Where Danger Lives *'50*
People Will Talk *'51*
Santa Fe *'51*

Rachel House (1971-)
Eagle *vs.* Shark *'07*
Hunt for the Wilderpeople *'16*
Moana *'16*

Serge House
Destination: Infestation *'07*
Grace *'09*

John Houseman (1902-88)
Seven Days in May *'64*
The Paper Chase *'73*
Rollerball *'75*
Three Days of the Condor *'75*
St. Ives *'76*
Our Town *'77*
Washington: Behind Closed Doors *'77*
The Cheap Detective *'78*
The Fog *'78*
Old Boyfriends *'79*
A Christmas Without Snow *'80*
Gideon's Trumpet *'80*
My Bodyguard *'80*
Wholly Moses! *'80*
Ghost Story *'81*
The Winds of War *'83*
A.D. *'85*
Another Woman *'88*
Bright Lights, Big City *'88*
Gore Vidal's Lincoln *'88*
The Naked Gun: From the Files of Police Squad *'88*
Scrooged *'88*

Jerry Houser (1952-)
Summer of '42 *'71*
Class of '44 *'73*
Slap Shot *'77*
Magic *'78*
Forbidden Love *'82*

Allan Houston (1971-)
Black and White *'99*
Laws of Attraction *'04*

Donald Houston (1923-91)
Doctor in the House *'53*
Room at the Top *'59*
The Mark *'61*
The Prince and the Pauper *'62*
Maniac *'63*
A Study in Terror *'66*
The Viking Queen *'67*
Where Eagles Dare *'68*
Tales That Witness Madness *'73*

Gary Houston
Two Fathers: Justice for the Innocent *'94*
Proof *'05*

George Houston (1898-1944)
Captain Calamity *'36*
Let's Sing Again *'36*
The Great Waltz *'38*

Marques Houston (1981-)
Bebe's Kids *'92 (V)*
Fat Albert *'04*
You Got Served *'04*
Battlefield America *'12*

Renee Houston (1902-80)
Two Thousand Women *'44*
The Belles of St. Trinian's *'53*
Track the Man Down *'55*
A Town Like Alice *'56*
Time Without Pity *'57*
The Horse's Mouth *'58*
The Flesh and the Fiends *'60*
Repulsion *'65*

Whitney Houston (1963-2012)
The Bodyguard *'92*
Waiting to Exhale *'95*
The Preacher's Wife *'96*
Cinderella *'97*
Sparkle *'12*
Whitney *'18*

Anders (Tofting) Hove (1956-)
Subspecies *'90*
Bloodstone: Subspecies 2 *'92*
Bloodlust: Subspecies 3 *'93*
Bloodstorm: Subspecies 4 *'98*
Mifune *'99*

Adrian Hoven (1922-81)
Castle of the Creeping Flesh *'68*
Mark of the Devil *'69*
Fear of Fear *'75*
Fox and His Friends *'75*

Adam Coleman Howard
Quiet Cool *'86*
Slaves of New York *'89*

Alan Howard (1937-2015)
The Heroes of Telemark *'65*
Just Another Secret *'89*
The Cook, the Thief, His Wife & Her Lover *'90*
Death Has a Bad Reputation *'90*
A Little Piece of Sunshine *'90*
The Price of the Bride *'90*
Pride and Extreme Prejudice *'90*
Strapless *'90*
The Secret Rapture *'94*
P.D. James: Death in Holy Orders *'03*

Andrew Howard (1969-)
The Cherry Orchard *'99*
Shooters *'00*
Below *'02*
The Lion in Winter *'03*
Revolver *'05*
Hellhounds *'09*
I Spit on Your Grave *'10*
Limitless *'11*
Girls Against Boys *'12*
Hatfields & McCoys *'12*

Anne Howard (1925-91)
Great Expectations *'34*
Jane Eyre *'34*
Lloyds of London *'36*
The Prince and the Pauper *'37*
All This and Heaven Too *'40*
Little Men *'40*

Anne Marie Howard (1960-)
Prince of Darkness *'87*
Blue Streak *'99*
Shopgirl *'05*
The Weather Man *'05*

Arliss Howard (1954-)
A Killer in the Family *'83*
The Lightship *'86*
Full Metal Jacket *'87*
Tequila Sunrise *'88*
I Know My First Name Is Steven *'89*
Men Don't Leave *'89*
Somebody Has to Shoot the Picture *'90*
For the Boys *'91*
Crisscross *'92*
Ruby *'92*
The Sandlot *'93 (V)*
Tales of Erotica *'93*
Wilder Napalm *'93*
Natural Born Killers *'94*
The Infiltrator *'95*
To Wong Foo, Thanks for Everything, Julie Newmar *'95*
Beyond the Call *'96*
johns *'96*
The Man Who Captured Eichmann *'96*
The Lost World: Jurassic Park 2 *'97*
A Map of the World *'99*
You Know My Name *'99*
The Song of the Lark *'01*
Big Bad Love *'02*
Birth *'04*
Awake *'07*
The Time Traveler's Wife *'09*

Arthur Howard (1910-95)
The Reckless Way *'36*
The Belles of St. Trinian's *'53*
Another Country *'84*

Barbara Howard
Lucky Stiff *'88*
Where's Marlowe? *'98*

Bryce Dallas Howard (1981-)
Book of Love *'04*
The Village *'04*
Manderlay *'05*
As You Like It *'06*
Lady in the Water *'06*
Spider-Man 3 *'07*
The Loss of a Teardrop Diamond *'08*
Terminator Salvation *'09*
Hereafter *'10*
The Twilight Saga: Eclipse *'10*
50/50 *'11*
The Help *'11*
Jurassic World *'15*
Gold *'16*
Pete's Dragon *'16*
Jurassic World: Fallen Kingdom *'18*
Rocketman *'19*

Clint Howard (1959-)
Gentle Giant *'67*
The Wild Country *'71*
The Death of Richie *'76*
Eat My Dust *'76*
Grand Theft Auto *'77*
Rock 'n' Roll High School *'79*
Evilspeak *'82*
Night Shift *'82*
Get Crazy *'83*
Cocoon *'85*
Gung Ho *'86*
The Wraith *'87*
End of the Line *'88*
Freeway *'88*
Tango and Cash *'89*
Silent Night, Deadly Night 4: Initiation *'90*
Backdraft *'91*
Far and Away *'92*
Carnosaur *'93*
Forced to Kill *'93*
Bigfoot: The Unforgettable Encounter *'94*
Cheyenne Warrior *'94*
Leprechaun 2 *'94*
Apollo 13 *'95*
Dillinger and Capone *'95*
Ice Cream Man *'95*
Barb Wire *'96*
Body Armor *'96*
Humanoids from the Deep *'96*
That Thing You Do! *'96*
Under Oath *'97*
Chow Bella *'98*
From the Earth to the Moon *'98*
The Waterboy *'98*
Arthur's Quest *'99*
Austin Powers 2: The Spy Who Shagged Me *'99*
EDtv *'99*
The Million Dollar Kid *'99*
Ping! *'99*
Dr. Seuss' How the Grinch Stole Christmas *'00*
Austin Powers In Goldmember *'02*
Blackwoods *'02*
Beethoven's 5th *'03*
Heart of America *'03*
House of the Dead *'03*
The Missing *'03*
River's End *'05*
Curious George *'06 (V)*
Foreign Exchange *'08*
Senior Skip Day *'08*
Play the Game *'09*
Speed-Dating *'10*
Bloodrayne: The Third Reich *'11*
Blubberella *'11*

Curly Howard (1903-52)
Dancing Lady *'33*
Hollywood Party *'34*

Dennis Howard
Go Tell the Spartans *'78*
Shattered Innocence *'87*

Esther Howard (1892-1965)
Klondike Annie *'36*
Murder, My Sweet *'44*
Detour *'46*

Frank Howard (1970-)
Hard Knox *'83*
That Was Then. . . This Is Now *'85*

Jeffrey Howard
Simple Men *'92*
The Wedding Banquet *'93*

Jeremy Howard (1981-)
Sydney White *'07*
A Star for Christmas *'12*
Teenage Mutant Ninja Turtles *'14*

John Howard (1913-95)
Bulldog Drummond Comes Back *'37*
Lost Horizon *'37*
Bulldog Drummond's Peril *'38*
Bulldog Drummond's Bride *'39*
What a Life *'39*
The Invisible Woman *'40*
The Philadelphia Story *'40*
The Fighting Kentuckian *'49*
The High and the Mighty *'54*
Destination Inner Space *'66*

John Howard (1952-)
The Club *'81*
Young Einstein *'89*
The Road from Coorain *'02*
Japanese Story *'03*
Jindabyne *'06*

Joyce Howard (1922-2010)
The Night Has Eyes *'42*
Appointment with Crime *'45*

Kathleen Howard (1879-1956)
It's a Gift *'34*
The Man On the Flying Trapeze *'35*
First Love *'39*
Young People *'40*
Blossoms in the Dust *'41*
Crash Dive *'43*

Ken Howard (1944-)
Such Good Friends *'71*
1776 *'72*
Second Thoughts *'83*
The Thorn Birds *'83*
Murder in New Hampshire: The Pamela Smart Story *'91*
Oscar *'91*
The Net *'95*
At First Sight *'98*
Tactical Assault *'99*
Perfect Murder, Perfect Town *'00*
Dreamer: Inspired by a True Story *'05*
In Her Shoes *'05*
Arc *'06*
Michael Clayton *'07*
Rambo *'08*
Smother *'08*
Under Still Waters *'08*
Grey Gardens *'09*
2:13 *'09*
J. Edgar *'11*
Better Living Through Chemistry *'14*
The Judge *'14*
The Wedding Ringer *'15*

Kevyn Major Howard
Sudden Impact *'83*
Full Metal Jacket *'87*
Alien Nation *'88*

Kyle Howard (1978-)
Address Unknown *'96*
House Arrest *'96*
Baby Geniuses *'98*
Orange County *'02*
Holiday in Handcuffs *'07*

Leo Howard (1997-)
Aussie and Ted's Great Adventure *'09*
Shorts: The Adventures of the Wishing Rock *'09*
Andron: The Black Labyrinth *'16*

Leslie Howard (1893-1943)
Five and Ten *'31*
A Free Soul *'31*
The Animal Kingdom *'32*
Smilin' Through *'32*
British Agent *'34*
Of Human Bondage *'34*
The Scarlet Pimpernel *'34*
Petrified Forest *'36*
Romeo and Juliet *'36*
It's Love I'm After *'37*
Stand-In *'37*
Pygmalion *'38*
Gone with the Wind *'39*
Intermezzo *'39*
The Forty-Ninth Parallel *'41*
Spitfire *'42*

Lisa Howard (1930-65)
The Man Who Cheated Himself *'50*
Sabaka *'55*

Lisa Howard (1963-)
Bounty Hunters *'96*
Bounty Hunters 2: Hardball *'97*

Mary Howard (1913-2009)
Abe Lincoln in Illinois *'40*
Billy the Kid *'41*

Moe Howard (1897-1975)
Dancing Lady *'33*
Hollywood Party *'34*
Swing Parade of 1946 *'46*
Have Rocket Will Travel *'59*
Snow White and the Three Stooges *'61*
The Three Stooges Meet Hercules *'61*
Three Stooges in Orbit *'62*
Around the World in a Daze *'63*
Four for Texas *'63*
It's a Mad, Mad, Mad, Mad World *'63*
The Outlaws Is Coming! *'65*
Dr. Death, Seeker of Souls *'73*

Rance Howard (1928-)
Cool Hand Luke *'67*
The Wild Country *'71*
Eat My Dust *'76*
Grand Theft Auto *'77*
Far and Away *'92*
Forced to Kill *'93*
Bigfoot: The Unforgettable Encounter *'94*
Ed Wood *'94*
Ghosts of Mississippi *'96*
Psycho *'98*
A Crack in the Floor *'00*
Eye See You *'01*
The Alamo *'04*
Sister Aimee: The Aimee Semple McPherson Story *'06*
Walk Hard: The Dewey Cox Story *'07*
Play the Game *'09*
The Trial *'10*

Ron Howard (1954-)
The Journey *'59*
Door to Door Maniac *'61*
The Courtship of Eddie's Father *'62*
The Music Man *'62*
Village of the Giants *'65*
The Wild Country *'71*
American Graffiti *'73*
The Spikes Gang *'74*
The First Nudie Musical *'75*
Eat My Dust *'76*
The Shootist *'76*
Grand Theft Auto *'77*
More American Graffiti *'79*
Bitter Harvest *'81*
Return to Mayberry *'85*

The Independent *'00 (C)*
Osmosis Jones *'01 (V)*

Ronald Howard (1918-96)
The Queen of Spades *'49*
Pattern for Plunder *'62*

Shawn Michael Howard (1969-)
Sunset Park *'96*
The Rats *'01*
Boycott *'02*
The Inheritance *'10*

Shemp Howard (1895-1955)
Convention Girl *'35*
The Bank Dick *'40*
The Invisible Woman *'40*
Buck Privates *'41*
Hold That Ghost *'41*
Pittsburgh *'42*
Private Buckaroo *'42*
The Strange Case of Dr. Rx *'42*
It Ain't Hay *'43*
Strange Affair *'44*
Africa Screams *'49*

Terrence Howard (1969-)
The Jacksons: An American Dream *'92*
johns *'96*
Sunset Park *'96*
Never 2 Big *'98*
Spark *'98*
The Best Man *'99*
Big Momma's House *'00*
Love Beat the Hell Outta Me *'00*
Angel Eyes *'01*
Glitter *'01*
Intimate Affairs *'01*
Boycott *'02*
Hart's War *'02*
Biker Boyz *'03*
Ray *'04*
Animal *'05*
Crash *'05*
Four Brothers *'05*
Get Rich or Die Tryin' *'05*
Hustle & Flow *'05*
The Salon *'05*
Idlewild *'06*
August Rush *'07*
Awake *'07*
The Brave One *'07*
The Hunting Party *'07*
The Perfect Holiday *'07*
Pride *'07*
Iron Man *'08*
Fighting *'09*
The Princess and the Frog *'09 (V)*
The Ledge *'11*
The Company You Keep *'12*
Red Tails *'12*
The Best Man Holiday *'13*
Dead Man Down *'13*
House of Bodies *'13*
Lee Daniels' The Butler *'13*
Movie 43 *'13*
Prisoners *'13*
Winnie Mandela *'13*
Sabotage *'14*
St. Vincent *'14*
Cardboard Boxer *'16*

Traylor Howard (1966-)
Dirty Work *'97*
Me, Myself, and Irene *'00*
Son of the Mask *'05*

Trevor Howard (1916-88)
The Way to the Stars *'45*
Brief Encounter *'46*
I See a Dark Stranger *'46*
Green for Danger *'47*
So Well Remembered *'47*
They Made Me a Fugitive *'47*
The Third Man *'49*
The Golden Salamander *'51*
Around the World in 80 Days *'56 (C)*
Run for the Sun *'56*
Pickup Alley *'57*
The Key *'58*
Sons and Lovers *'60*
Mutiny on the Bounty *'62*
Father Goose *'64*
The Liquidator *'65*
Morituri *'65*
Operation Crossbow *'65*
Von Ryan's Express *'65*
The Poppy Is Also a Flower *'66*
Triple Cross *'67*
The Charge of the Light Brigade *'68*
Battle of Britain *'69*
Lola *'69*
The Night Visitor *'70*
Ryan's Daughter *'70*
Catch Me a Spy *'71*
Mary, Queen of Scots *'71*
Ludwig *'72*
Catholics *'73*
A Doll's House *'73*
The Offence *'73*
Craze *'74*
11 Harrowhouse *'74*
Conduct Unbecoming *'75*
Hennessy *'75*
Slavers *'77*
Superman: The Movie *'78*
Hurricane *'79*
Meteor *'79*
Staying On *'80*
Sea Wolves *'81*
Windwalker *'81*
Gandhi *'82*
The Missionary *'82*
Shaka Zulu *'83*
Sword of the Valiant *'83*
Foreign Body *'86*
The Dawning *'88*
The Unholy *'88*
White Mischief *'88*

Vanessa Howard (1948-2010)
Blood Beast Terror *'67*
Girly *'70*
The Rise and Rise of Michael Rimmer *'70*
Picture of Dorian Gray *'74*

Walker Howard
Dr. Dolittle 3 *'06*
The Black Waters of Echo's Pond *'10*

Kevin Howarth
Razor Blade Smile *'98*
The Ghost of Greville Lodge *'00*
Cold and Dark *'05*

Clark Howat (1918-2009)
The Giant Claw *'57*
Billy Jack *'71*

Brian Howe (1953-)
The Lost Skeleton of Cadavra *'01*
Catch Me If You Can *'02*
Dark Heart *'06*
The Pursuit of Happyness *'06*
RV *'06*
Gran Torino *'08*

Anthony Howell (1971-)
Wives and Daughters *'01*
The Other Boleyn Girl *'03*

C. Thomas Howell (1966-)
E.T.: The Extra-Terrestrial *'82*
The Outsiders *'83*
Tank *'83*
Grandview U.S.A. *'84*
Red Dawn *'84*
Secret Admirer *'85*
The Hitcher *'86*
Soul Man *'86*
Far Out Man *'89*
Side Out *'90*
To Protect and Serve *'92*
Gettysburg *'93*
That Night *'93*
Shameless *'94*
Hourglass *'95*
The Sweeper *'95*
The Big Fall *'96*
Pure Danger *'96*
Dilemma *'97*
Dead Fire *'98*
First Degree *'98*
Last Lives *'98*
Matter of Trust *'98*
Stalker *'98*
Avalanche *'99*
The Crimson Code *'99*
Cybercity *'99*
The Million Dollar Kid *'99*
The Prince and the Surfer *'99*
Shepherd *'99*
Dead Evidence *'00*
Burning Down the House *'01*
Killer Bees *'02*
Gods and Generals *'03*
The Hitcher 2: I've Been Waiting *'03*
Net Games *'03*
The Glass Trap *'04*
Hidalgo *'04*
The Hillside Stranglings *'04*
The Lost Angel *'04*
Crimson Force *'05*
H.G. Wells' War of the Worlds *'05*
The Keeper: The Legend of Omar Khayyam *'05*
The Poseidon Adventure *'05*
The Da Vinci Treasure *'06*
The Far Side of Jericho *'06*
The Haunting of Marsten Manor *'07*
The Day the Earth Stopped *'08*
The Pledge *'08*
War of the Worlds 2: The Next Wave *'08*
The Land That Time Forgot *'09*
Camel Spiders *'11*
Cross *'11*
Storm Rider *'13*
LBJ *'17*
A Question of Faith *'17*

Dashiell Howell (1997-)
H.G. Wells' War of the Worlds *'05*
War of the Worlds 2: The Next Wave *'08*

Hoke Howell (1930-97)
Humanoids from the Deep *'80*
Alienator *'89*
Vice Girls *'96*

Jean Howell (1927-96)
The Fast and the Furious *'54*
Crime of Passion *'57*

Kathryn Howell
Necessity *'88*
The Zodiac *'05*

Kenneth Howell (1913-66)
The Eagle and the Hawk *'33*
Junior G-Men *'40*

Peter Howell
Shadowlands *'93*
Almost Strangers *'01*

Ursula Howells (1922-2005)
Track the Man Down *'55*
Girly *'70*
Jewels *'92*

Frankie Howerd (1922-92)
The Runaway Bus *'54*
Further Up the Creek *'58*
The Great St. Trinian's Train Robbery *'66*
Carry On Doctor *'68*
Carry On Up the Jungle *'70*

Glenn Howerton (1976-)
Two Weeks *'06*
The Strangers *'08*

Reed Howes (1900-64)
The Singing Fool *'28*
Queen of the Jungle *'35*
The Clutching Hand *'36*
Custer's Last Stand *'36*
Pilot X *'37*
My Dog Shep *'46*
The Sinister Urge *'60*

Sally Ann Howes (1930-)
Thursday's Child *'43*
Dead of Night *'45*
Nicholas Nickleby *'46*
Anna Karenina *'48*
The Admirable Crichton *'57*
Chitty Chitty Bang Bang *'68*

Steve Howey (1977-)
Supercross: The Movie *'05*
DOA: Dead or Alive *'06*
Still Waiting *'08*
Bride Wars *'09*
Stan Helsing *'09*
Something Borrowed *'11*
In Your Eyes *'14*
Making Babies *'19*

Peter Howitt (1957-)
The Magician *'93*
Kiss and Tell *'96*

Billy Howle (1989-)
On Chesil Beach *'17*
Outlaw King *'18*

Noel Howlett (1901-84)
Serious Charge *'59*
Victim *'61*

Olin Howlin (1886-1959)
Satan Met a Lady *'36*
Girl of the Golden West *'38*
Nancy Drew, Reporter *'39*
Apache Rose *'47*
The Wistful Widow of Wagon Gap *'47*
Storm Rider *'57*
The Blob *'58*

Leonard Earl Howze
Barbershop *'02*
Barbershop 2: Back in Business *'04*
The Ringer *'05*

Jack Hoxie (1885-1965)
Blue Blazes Rawden *'18*
The Back Trail *'24*

Whitney Hoy (1987-)
The Final *'10*
Petals on the Wind *'14*

Carolina Hoyos
Perception *'06*
Safehouse *'08*

Cristina Hoyos (1946-)
Blood Wedding *'81*
Carmen *'83*
El Amor Brujo *'86*

Rodolfo Hoyos (1916-83)
The Brave One *'56*
California *'63*

Arthur Hoyt (1874-1953)
Going Wild *'30*
American Madness *'32*
The Devil and the Deep *'32*
His Private Secretary *'33*
The Great McGinty *'40*

John Hoyt (1905-91)
Winter Meeting *'48*
Great Dan Patch *'49*
The Lady Gambles *'49*
Trapped *'49*
The Lawless *'50*
The Lost Continent *'51*
The Black Castle *'52*
Loan Shark *'52*
Julius Caesar *'53*
Sins of Jezebel *'54*
Blackboard Jungle *'55*
The Girl in the Red Velvet Swing *'55*
The Conqueror *'56*
Death of a Scoundrel *'56*
Forever Darling *'56*
Wetbacks *'56*
Attack of the Puppet People *'58*
Riot in Juvenile Prison *'59*
Merrill's Marauders *'62*
X: The Man with X-Ray Eyes *'63*
Two On a Guillotine *'65*
Flesh Gordon *'72*

Brigitte Lin Ching Hsia (1954-)
See Brigitte Lin

Ge Hu (1982-)
The Assassin's Blade *'08*
The Wild Goose Lake *'20*

Jun Hu
Infernal Affairs 2 *'03*
Red Cliff *'08*

Kelly Hu (1968-)
Friday the 13th, Part 8: Jason Takes Manhattan *'89*
The Doors *'91*
Harley Davidson and the Marlboro Man *'91*
Surf Ninjas *'93*
Strange Days *'95*
No Way Back *'96*
The Scorpion King *'02*
Cradle 2 the Grave *'03*
X2: X-Men United *'03*
The Librarian: Quest for the Spear *'04*
Underclassman *'05*
Devil's Den *'06*
Shanghai Kiss *'07*
Dim Sum Funeral *'08*
Farmhouse *'08*
Stiletto *'08*
The Tournament *'09*
Almost Perfect *'11*
White Frog *'12*
Maximum Impact *'18*

Yi Huang
The Cave of the Silken Web *'67*
Drug War *'13*

Ying Huang
Opium and Kung-Fu Master *'84*
Madame Butterfly *'95*

Patrick Huard (1969-)
The Boys *'97*
Bon Cop Bad Cop *'06*
Funkytown *'11*
Mommy *'14*

Martin Huba (1943-)
Divided We Fall *'00*
I Served the King of England *'07*

David Huband (1958-)
Dirty Pictures *'00*
Wrong Turn *'03*
Cube: Zero *'04*
Cinderella Man *'05*

Elizabeth Hubbard (1933-)
Cold River *'81*
Center Stage *'00*

Erica Hubbard (1979-)
A Cinderella Story *'04*
Black Coffee *'14*

John Hubbard (1914-88)
Maisie *'39*
Road Show *'41*
Canal Zone *'42*
The Mummy's Tomb *'42*
There's Something About a Soldier *'43*
Mexican Hayride *'48*
Gunfight at Comanche Creek *'64*

Cork Hubbert (1952-2003)
Caveman *'81*
Legend *'86*
The Ballad of the Sad Cafe *'91*

Henry Hubchen (1947-)
Jacob the Liar *'74*
Go for Zucker *'05*

Harold Huber (1904-59)
Frisco Jenny *'32*
Girl Missing *'33*
The Defense Rests *'34*
The Gay Desperado *'36*
Klondike Annie *'36*
San Francisco *'36*
Charlie Chan at Monte Carlo *'37*
Charlie Chan on Broadway *'37*
Mr. Moto's Gamble *'38*
A Slight Case of Murder *'38*
Beau Geste *'39*
Charlie Chan in City of Darkness *'39*
You Can't Get Away With Murder *'39*
Dance, Girl, Dance *'40*
Kit Carson *'40*

Amy Huberman (1979-)
Three Wise Women *'11*
The Bachelor Weekend *'13*

Season Hubley (1951-)
Lolly-Madonna XXX *'73*
Elvis: The Movie *'79*
Hardcore *'79*
Escape from New York *'81*
Vice Squad *'82*
Agatha Christie's A Caribbean Mystery *'83*
Shakedown on the Sunset Strip *'88*
Stepfather 3: Father's Day *'92*
Kiss the Sky *'98*

Whip Hubley (1958-)
Firefighter *'86*
Top Gun *'86*
Russkies *'87*
Desire and Hell at Sunset Motel *'92*
Black Scorpion 2: Ground Zero *'96*
Daddy's Girl *'96*
Executive Decision *'96*
A Very Brady Sequel *'96*
Armistead Maupin's More Tales of the City *'97*
A Cinderella Story *'04*

Paul (Christian) Hubschmid (1917-2001)
The Beast from 20,000 Fathoms *'53*
The Day the Sky Exploded *'57*
Journey to the Lost City *'58*
Funeral in Berlin *'66*
Manon *'68*

Cooper Huckabee (1951-)
Joni *'79*
Getting Wasted *'80*
The Funhouse *'81*
The Curse *'87*
Cohen and Tate *'88*
Love Field *'91*
Gettysburg *'93*
Django Unchained *'12*

Steffany Huckaby
Death Tunnel *'05*
The Pleasure Drivers *'05*

Walter Hudd (1897-1963)
Rembrandt *'36*
Elephant Boy *'37*
I Know Where I'm Going *'45*
Cast a Dark Shadow *'55*
Sink the Bismarck *'60*

David Huddleston (1930-)
Rio Lobo *'70*
Nightmare Honeymoon *'73*
On the Run *'73*
Billy Two Hats *'74*
Blazing Saddles *'74*
McQ *'74*
Crime Busters *'78*
Smokey and the Bandit 2 *'80*
Family Reunion *'81*
The Oklahoma City Dolls *'81*
Santa Claus: The Movie *'85*
When the Bough Breaks *'86*
Frantic *'88*
The Tracker *'88*
Life with Mikey *'93*
The Big Lebowski *'97*
The Producers *'05*

Michael Huddleston (1952-)
World's Greatest Lover *'77*
Four Friends *'81*
Bad Channels *'92*
Wyatt Earp *'94*

Vanessa Anne Hudgens (1988-)
Thirteen *'03*
Thunderbirds *'04*
High School Musical *'06*
High School Musical 2 *'07*
High School Musical 3: Senior Year *'08*
Bandslam *'09*
Beastly *'11*
Sucker Punch *'11*

Journey 2: The Mysterious Island '12
The Frozen Ground '13
Machete Kills '13
Spring Breakers '13
Gimme Shelter '14
Dog Days '18
Second Act '18
The Knight Before Christmas '19
Polar '19
Bad Boys for Life '20

Reginald (Reggie) Hudlin (1961-)
She's Gotta Have It '86
Posse '93
Joe's Apartment '96 (V)

Bill Hudson (1949-)
KISS Meets the Phantom of the Park '78
Hysterical '83

Ernie Hudson (1945-)
Dolemite 2: Human Tornado '76
The Jazz Singer '80
Penitentiary 2 '82
Going Berserk '83
Spacehunter: Adventures in the Forbidden Zone '83
Ghostbusters '84
The Wrong Guys '88
Ghostbusters 2 '89
Leviathan '89
Trapper County War '89
The Hand that Rocks the Cradle '92
The Crow '93
Wild Palms '93
Airheads '94
The Cowboy Way '94
In the Army Now '94
No Escape '94
Speechless '94
Sugar Hill '94
The Basketball Diaries '95
Congo '95
The Cherokee Kid '96
The Substitute '96
Tornado! '96
Levitation '97
Mr. Magoo '97
Best of the Best: Without Warning '98
Never 2 Big '98
A Stranger in the Kingdom '98
Corrupt '99
Interceptor Force '99
Paper Bullets '99
Shark Attack '99
Stealth Fighter '99
Urban Menace '99
Miss Congeniality '00
Nowhere to Land '00
Red Letters '00
The Watcher '00
Clifford's Really Big Movie '04 (V)
Fighting the Odds: The Marilyn Gambrell Story '05
Miss Congeniality 2: Armed and Fabulous '05
Marilyn Hotchkiss' Ballroom Dancing & Charm School '06
All Hat '07
Final Approach '08
Dragonball: Evolution '09
Fatal Secrets '09
Meteor '09
Beverly Hills Chihuahua 2 '10 (V)
Smokin' Aces 2: Assassins' Ball '10
Beverly Hills Chihuahua 3: Viva La Fiesta! '12 (V)

Gary Hudson (1956-)
Martial Outlaw '93
Serial Killer '95
Black Thunder '98
Bridge of Dragons '99
Eye of the Killer '99
The Stepdaughter '00
Extreme Limits '01
My Husband's Double Life '01
The Circuit 2 '02
I Downloaded a Ghost '04
She's Too Young '04
Snakeman '05
Angels Fall '07
Termination Point '07
Sea Beast '08

Jennifer Hudson (1981-)
Dreamgirls '06
Fragments '08
The Secret Life of Bees '08
Sex and the City: The Movie '08
The Three Stooges '12
Black Nativity '13
Call Me Crazy '13
The Inevitable Defeat of Mister & Pete '13
Winnie Mandela '13
Cats '19

John Hudson (1919-96)
Return to Paradise '53
Fort Yuma '55

Kate Hudson (1979-)
Desert Blue '98
Ricochet River '98
200 Cigarettes '98
Gossip '99
About Adam '00
Almost Famous '00
Dr. T & the Women '00
The Four Feathers '02
Alex & Emma '03
How to Lose a Guy in 10 Days '03
Le Divorce '03
Raising Helen '04
The Skeleton Key '05
You, Me and Dupree '06
Fool's Gold '08
My Best Friend's Girl '08
Bride Wars '09
Nine '09
The Killer Inside Me '10
A Little Bit of Heaven '11
Something Borrowed '11
Good People '14
Wish I Was Here '14
Rock the Kasbah '15
Deepwater Horizon '16
Mother's Day '16
Marshall '17

Oliver Hudson (1976-)
The Out-of-Towners '99
The Smokers '00
Going Greek '01
New Best Friend '02
Black Christmas '06
The Breed '06
Carolina Moon '07

Rochelle Hudson (1914-72)
Mr. Skitch '33
Notorious But Nice '33
Wild Boys of the Road '33
Imitation of Life '34
Curly Top '35
Les Miserables '35
Life Begins at Forty '35
Rascals '38
Rebel without a Cause '55
Strait-Jacket '64
Alien Massacre '67

Rock Hudson (1925-85)
Winchester '73 '50
Tomahawk '51
Bend of the River '52
Has Anybody Seen My Gal? '52
Horizons West '52
The Lawless Breed '52
Back to God's Country '53
Gun Fury '53
Sea Devils '53
Seminole '53
Magnificent Obsession '54
All That Heaven Allows '55
Captain Lightfoot '55
One Desire '55
Giant '56
Written on the Wind '56
Battle Hymn '57
A Farewell to Arms '57
Something of Value '57
Tarnished Angels '57
Pillow Talk '59
Come September '61
The Last Sunset '61
Lover Come Back '61
Man's Favorite Sport? '63
Send Me No Flowers '64
Strange Bedfellows '65
A Very Special Favor '65
Seconds '66
Tobruk '66
Ice Station Zebra '68
The Undefeated '69
Darling Lili '70
Hornets' Nest '70
Pretty Maids All In a Row '71
Showdown '73
Embryo '76
Avalanche '78
The Martian Chronicles: Part 1 '79
The Martian Chronicles: Part 2 '79
The Martian Chronicles: Part 3 '79
The Mirror Crack'd '80
The Ambassador '84
The Vegas Strip Wars '84
World War III '86

Toni Hudson
Just One of the Guys '85
The Uninvited '88

William (Bill) Hudson (1925-74)
Objective, Burma! '45
The Man Who Turned to Stone '57
Attack of the 50 Foot Woman '58

Rob Huebel
Strike '07
Welcome to the Jungle '13
Night Owls '15

Justin Huen
Angel of Death '09
Hood Vengeance '09

Tenoch Huerta
Stand Clear of the Closing Doors '13
Bel Canto '18
The Motive '18
Tigers Are Not Afraid '19

Jon Huertas (1976-)
The Insatiable '06
Believers '07
Generation Kill '08
The Objective '08
Stash House '12

Matthias Hues (1959-)
Black Belt '92
Talons of the Eagle '92
Digital Man '94
Lone Tiger '94
Alone in the Woods '95
Deadly Reckoning '01

Brent Huff (1961-)
The Perils of Gwendoline '84
Nine Deaths of the Ninja '85
Armed Response '86
Falling from Grace '92
Final Justice '94
The Bad Pack '98
Submerged '00
The Glass Trap '04
Sharktopus '10

Neal Huff
Love Walked In '97
Meek's Cutoff '10
Monogamy '10
Beach Rats '17

Shawn Huff
100 Mile Rule '02
Cat City '08

David Huffman (1945-85)
Testimony of Two Men '77
F.I.S.T. '78
The Winds of Kitty Hawk '78
Ice Castles '79
The Onion Field '79
Firefox '82
St. Helen's, Killer Volcano '82
Agatha Christie's Sparkling Cyanide '83

Felicity Huffman (1962-)
Reversal of Fortune '90
Quicksand: No Escape '91
Stephen King's Golden Years '91
Hackers '95
The Spanish Prisoner '97
A Slight Case of Murder '99
Snap Decision '01
Path to War '02
Out of Order '03
Christmas With the Kranks '04
Raising Helen '04
Transamerica '05
Georgia Rule '07
Phoebe in Wonderland '08
Trust Me '13
Cake '14
Rudderless '14
Big Game '15
Otherhood '19

Logan Huffman (1989-)
A Smile as Big as the Moon '12
Bad Turn Worse '14

Daniel Hugh-Kelly (1952-)
Cujo '83
Nowhere to Hide '83
The Good Son '93
Bad Company '94
The Tuskegee Airmen '95
From the Earth to the Moon '98
Star Trek: Insurrection '98
Chill Factor '99
Passing Glory '99
Jackie, Ethel, Joan: The Kennedy Women '01

Andrew Hughes (1908-85)
Terror Beneath the Sea '66
Destroy All Monsters '68

Barnard Hughes (1915-2006)
Midnight Cowboy '69
Where's Poppa? '70
Cold Turkey '71
The Hospital '71
Rage '72
Sisters '73
Oh, God! '77
First Monday in October '81
Best Friends '82
Tron '82
Agatha Christie's A Caribbean Mystery '83
The Sky's No Limit '84
The Adventures of Huckleberry Finn '85
Maxie '85
Under the Biltmore Clock '85
Where Are the Children? '85
Hobo's Christmas '87
The Lost Boys '87
Day One '89
The Incident '89
Doc Hollywood '91
Sister Act 2: Back in the Habit '93
Primal Secrets '94
The Fantasticks '95
The Odd Couple 2 '98
The Cradle Will Rock '99

Brendan Hughes
Return to Horror High '87
To Die For '89
Howling 6: The Freaks '90
Sundown: The Vampire in Retreat '08

Carol Hughes (1910-95)
The Golden Arrow '36
Love Affair '39
Flash Gordon Conquers the Universe '40
Desperate Cargo '41
Robot Pilot '41
Home in Oklahoma '47

Charles Hughes
The Frontiersmen '38
Call of the Forest '49
Outback '71

Finola Hughes (1960-)
Staying Alive '83
Soapdish '91
Aspen Extreme '93
Prison of Secrets '97
Tycus '98
Killer Hair '09
Like Crazy '11

Frank John Hughes (1967-)
Happy Hell Night '92
Angel's Dance '99
Band of Brothers '01
Deranged '01
Catch Me If You Can '02
Kings of South Beach '07
Blue Lagoon: The Awakening '12

Geraldine Hughes (1970-)
Rocky Balboa '06
Gran Torino '08
Killing Lincoln '13

Heather Hughes
Flesh Feast '69
Blood Freak '72

Helen Hughes (1918-)
Outrageous! '77
Incubus '82
Night of the Twisters '95

Jason Hughes (1971-)
Shooters '00
Killing Me Softly '01
Plain Jane '02

Kathleen Hughes (1928-)
It Came from Outer Space '53
Cult of the Cobra '55
Three Bad Sisters '56

Kay Hughes (1914-98)
The Vigilantes Are Coming '36
The Mandarin Mystery '37

Kirsten Hughes
Jane & the Lost City '87
The Kitchen Toto '87

Lane Hughes
A Horrible Way to Die '10
V/H/S '12

Lloyd Hughes (1897-1958)
Tess of the Storm Country '22
The Sea Hawk '24
The Lost World '25
Big Boy '30
Air Eagles '31
Drums of Jeopardy '31
Blake of Scotland Yard '36
A Face in the Fog '36
Night Cargo '36

Mary Beth Hughes (1919-95)
Those Glamour Girls '39
Four Sons '40
Design for Scandal '41
The Great American Broadcast '41
Sleepers West '41
Blue, White and Perfect '42
Orchestra Wives '42
The Ox-Bow Incident '43
Men On Her Mind '44
Great Flamarion '45
I Accuse My Parents '45
The Lady Confesses '45
Rimfire '49
Close to My Heart '51
Square Dance Jubilee '51
Loophole '54

Miko Hughes (1986-)
Pet Sematary '89
Jack the Bear '93
Cops and Robbersons '94
Wes Craven's New Nightmare '94
Apollo 13 '95
Zeus and Roxanne '96
Spawn '97
Mercury Rising '98

Roddy Hughes (1891-1970)
Old Mother Riley's Jungle Treasure '51
Not So Dusty '56

Sharon Hughes
Chained Heat '83
Grotesque '87

Tom Hughes (1986-)
Cemetery Junction '10
The Lady Vanishes '13
Red Joan '19

Tresa Hughes (1929-2011)
Coming Home '78
Sarah, Plain and Tall: Skylark '93

Wendy Hughes (1952-2014)
High Rolling in a Hot Corvette '77
Newsfront '78
My Brilliant Career '79
Dangerous Summer '82
Lonely Hearts '82
Careful, He Might Hear You '84
Happy New Year '87
The Heist '89
Wild Orchid 2: Two Shades of Blue '92
Princess Caraboo '94
Paradise Road '97
The Man Who Sued God '01

D.L. Hughley (1963-)
Inspector Gadget '99 (V)
The Brothers '01
Chasing Papi '03
Scary Movie 3 '03 (C)
Soul Plane '04
Spy School '08
Cat Run '11

Andy Hui
The Cave of the Silken Web '67
Six Strong Guys '04

Kara Hui (1960-)
Legendary Weapons of China '82
8 Diagram Pole Fighter '84
Journey of the Doomed '85

Michael Hui (1942-)
Chinese Box '97
Robin-B-Hood '06

Kimberley Huie
The Paradise Virus '03
Passenger Side '09

Michiel Huisman (1981-)
Margot '09
Unmade Beds '09
The Age of Adaline '15
The Invitation '16
The Guernsey Literary & Potato Peel Pie Society '18
Irreplaceable You '18

Steve Huison (1962-)
The Full Monty '96
The Navigators '01
Chaos & Cadavers '03

Tom Hulce (1953-)
September 30, 1955 '77
National Lampoon's Animal House '78
Those Lips, Those Eyes '80
Amadeus '84
Echo Park '86
Slamdance '87
Dominick & Eugene '88
Parenthood '89
Black Rainbow '91
The Inner Circle '91
Fearless '93
Mary Shelley's Frankenstein '94
The Heidi Chronicles '95
The Hunchback of Notre Dame '96 (V)
Stranger Than Fiction '06

Otto Hulett (1898-1983)
Paula '52
Four Boys and a Gun '57

Gladys Hulette (1896-1991)
Tol'able David '21
The Family Secret '24

Dianne Hull (1949-)
Girls on the Road '73
Aloha, Bobby and Rose '74
The Onion Field '79
Christmas Evil '80
Haywire '80
The New Adventures of Pippi Longstocking '88

Henry Hull (1890-1977)
Great Expectations '34
Midnight '34
Werewolf of London '35
Boys Town '38
Three Comrades '38
Jesse James '39
Judge Hardy and Son '39
Miracles for Sale '39
Nick Carter, Master Detective '39
The Return of the Cisco Kid '39
Return of Frank James '40
High Sierra '41
Lifeboat '44
The Woman of the Town '44
Objective, Burma! '45
Deep Valley '47
High Barbaree '47
Fighter Squadron '48
Portrait of Jennie '48
Colorado Territory '49
El Paso '49
The Fountainhead '49
Great Dan Patch '49
Rimfire '49
Return of Jesse James '50
Hollywood Story '51
The Last Posse '53
The Buccaneer '58
The Sheriff of Fractured Jaw '59
Master of the World '61

Josephine Hull (1884-1957)
After Tomorrow '32
Arsenic and Old Lace '44
Harvey '50

Warren Hull (1903-74)
Hawaii Calls '38
The Spider's Web '38
The Lone Wolf Meets a Lady '40
The Spider Returns '41

Sandra Hüller (1978-)
Toni Erdmann '16
In the Aisles '19

Lachy Hulme (1971-)
The Crocodile Hunter: Collision Course '02
The Matrix Revolutions '03
Macbeth '06
John Doe: Vigilante '14

Jens Hultén (1963-)
The 100-Year-Old Man Who Climbed Out the Window and Disappeared '15
Alpha '18

George Humbert (1880-1963)
The California Trail '33
Music in My Heart '40

Benita Hume (1906-67)
Clear All Wires! '33
Power '34
Private Life of Don Juan '34
The Gay Deception '35
It Happened in New Orleans '36
Suzy '36
Tarzan Escapes '36

Mark Humphrey (1960-)
Iron Eagle 2 '88
Treacherous Beauties '94
The Wives He Forgot '06
Still Small Voices '07
Little Girl Lost: The Delimar Vera Story '08
Vipers '08

Renee Humphrey (1975-)
Fun '94
The Cure '95
Devil in a Blue Dress '95
French Kiss '95
Mallrats '95
Cadillac Ranch '96
Chicks, Man '99
The Sex Monster '99
Hard Luck '01
Jay and Silent Bob Strike Back '01

Alf Humphreys (1953-)
My Bloody Valentine '81
The Stickup '01
X2: X-Men United '03
The Suspect '05

Cecil Humphreys (1883-1947)
Accused '36
The Razor's Edge '46
Desire Me '47

William Humphreys (1874-1942)
Beau Brummel '24
The Unholy Three '25

Barry Humphries (1934-)
Bedazzled '68
Barry McKenzie Holds His Own '74
The Getting of Wisdom '77
Shock Treatment '81
Selling Hitler '91
Immortal Beloved '94
The Leading Man '96
Spice World: The Movie '97
Welcome to Woop Woop '97
Nicholas Nickleby '02
Finding Nemo '03 (V)
Mary and Max '09 (N)

Fletcher Humphrys (1976-)
The Junction Boys '02
John Doe: Vigilante '14

Hui Siu Hung
Running out of Time '99
Breaking News '04

Sammo Hung (1952-)
Enter the Dragon '73
Spooky Encounters '80
The Prodigal Son '82
Project A '83
Zu: Warriors from the Magic Mountain '83
Heart of Dragon '85
The Millionaire's Express '86
Eastern Condors '87
Dragons Forever '88
The Prisoner '90
Painted Skin '93
Mr. Nice Guy '98
Zu Warriors '01
Around the World in 80 Days '04
Three Kingdoms: Resurrection of the Dragon '08
Ip Man 2 '10
14 Blades '14

Charlie Hunnam (1980-)
Abandon '02
Nicholas Nickleby '02
Cold Mountain '03
Green Street Hooligans '05
Children of Men '06
The Ledge '11
Deadfall '12
3, 2, 1...Frankie Go Boom '12
Pacific Rim '13
Crimson Peak '15
King Arthur: Legend of the Sword '17
The Lost City of Z '17
Papillon '17
Triple Frontier '19
The Gentlemen '20
True History of the Kelly Gang '20

Arthur Hunnicutt (1911-79)
Wildcat '42
Border Incident '49
Great Dan Patch '49
Broken Arrow '50
Stars in My Crown '50
Distant Drums '51
The Red Badge of Courage '51
The Lusty Men '52
The Kettles in the Ozarks '56
The Tall T '57
Born Reckless '59
El Dorado '67
Shoot Out '71
Harry and Tonto '74
The Spikes Gang '74

Gayle Hunnicutt (1943-)
The Wild Angels '66
Marlowe '69
Fragment of Fear '70
The Love Machine '71
The Golden Bowl '72
The Legend of Hell House '73
Scorpio '73
Spiral Staircase '75
Sell Out '76
The Sellout '76
The Martian Chronicles: Part 2 '79
The Martian Chronicles: Part 3 '79
Return of the Man from U.N.C.L.E. '83
A Woman of Substance '84
Dream Lover '85
Target '85
Dream West '86

Bonnie Hunt (1961-)
Rain Man '88
Beethoven '92
Beethoven's 2nd '93
Dave '93
Only You '94
Jumanji '95
Now and Then '95
Getting Away With Murder '96
Jerry Maguire '96
Subway Stories '97
A Bug's Life '98 (V)
Kissing a Fool '98
The Green Mile '99
Random Hearts '99
Return to Me '00
Monsters, Inc. '01 (V)
Stolen Summer '02
Cheaper by the Dozen '03
Cheaper by the Dozen 2 '05
Loggerheads '05
Cars '06 (V)
I Want Someone to Eat Cheese With '06
Hurricane Season '09
Toy Story 3 '10 (V)
Cars 2 '11 (V)
Zootopia '16 (V)

Brad Hunt
Dream with the Fishes '97
Fire Down Below '97
Cherish '02
Just Add Water '07

Crystal Hunt
The Derby Stallion '05
Sydney White '07

David Hunt (1954-)
Date with an Angel '87
The Dead Pool '88
Murder on the Orient Express '01

Eleanor Hunt (1910-81)
Whoopee! '30
Yellow Cargo '36
The Gold Racket '37

Gareth Hunt (1943-2007)
A Chorus of Disapproval '89
Parting Shots '98

Helen Hunt (1963-)
Pioneer Woman '73
Rollercoaster '77
The Spell '77
Angel Dusted '81
Child Bride of Short Creek '81
Desperate Lives '82
Bill: On His Own '83
Code of Honor '84
Trancers '84
Girls Just Want to Have Fun '85
Peggy Sue Got Married '86
Project X '87
Stealing Home '88
Next of Kin '89
Trancers 2: The Return of Jack Deth '90
Murder in New Hampshire: The Pamela Smart Story '91
The Waterdance '91
Bob Roberts '92
Into the Badlands '92
Mr. Saturday Night '92
Only You '92
Trancers 3: Deth Lives '92
Kiss of Death '94
Twister '96
As Good As It Gets '97
Cast Away '00
Dr. T & the Women '00
Pay It Forward '00
What Women Want '00
The Curse of the Jade Scorpion '01
A Good Woman '04
Empire Falls '05
Bobby '06
Then She Found Me '07
Every Day '10
Soul Surfer '11
The Sessions '12
Decoding Annie Parker '13
The Miracle Season '18

Jimmy Hunt (1939-)
Song of Love '47
Family Honeymoon '49
The Capture '50
Belles on Their Toes '52
Invaders from Mars '53

Linda Hunt (1945-)
Popeye '80
The Year of Living Dangerously '82
The Bostonians '84
Dune '84
Silverado '85
Waiting for the Moon '87
She-Devil '89
Kindergarten Cop '90
If Looks Could Kill '91
Rain Without Thunder '93
Twenty Bucks '93
Ready to Wear '94
Pocahontas '95 (V)
Eat Your Heart Out '96
The Relic '96
Dragonfly '02
A Lot Like Love '05
Yours, Mine & Ours '05
Stranger Than Fiction '06

Marsha Hunt (1917-)
Those Glamour Girls '39
Irene '40
Pride and Prejudice '40
Blossoms in the Dust '41
I'll Wait for You '41
Seven Sweethearts '42
Cry Havoc '43
Lost Angel '43
Pilot No. 5 '43
Bride by Mistake '44
Music For Millions '44
The Valley of Decision '45
Carnegie Hall '47
Smash-Up: The Story of a Woman '47
Raw Deal '48
Actors and Sin '52
Bombers B-52 '57
The Plunderers '60
Johnny Got His Gun '71

Marsha A. Hunt (1946-)
Dracula A.D. 1972 '72
Britannia Hospital '82
The Sender '82
Howling 2: Your Sister Is a Werewolf '85

Martita Hunt (1900-69)
First a Girl '35
Nine Days a Queen '36
Sabotage '36
Good Morning, Boys '37
The Lady From Lisbon '42
Great Expectations '46
Anna Karenina '48
The Fan '49
The Story of Robin Hood & His Merrie Men '52
Anastasia '56
Three Men in a Boat '56
The Admirable Crichton '57
The Brides of Dracula '60
Song Without End '60
The Unsinkable Molly Brown '64
Bunny Lake Is Missing '65

Bill Hunter (1940-2011)
Newsfront '78
1915 '82
Return of Captain Invincible '83
The Hit '85
Rebel '85
Rikky and Pete '88
Strictly Ballroom '92
The Adventures of Priscilla, Queen of the Desert '94
Muriel's Wedding '94
River Street '95
Race the Sun '96
Moby Dick '98
Kangaroo Jack '02
Finding Nemo '03 (V)
The Square '08

Holly Hunter (1958-)
The Burning '82
Svengali '83
Swing Shift '84
Blood Simple '85
Broadcast News '87
Raising Arizona '87
End of the Line '88
Always '89
Miss Firecracker '89
Murder on the Bayou '91
Once Around '91
Crazy in Love '92
The Firm '93
The Piano '93
The Positively True Adventures of the Alleged Texas Cheerleader-Murdering Mom '93
Copycat '95
Crash '95
Home for the Holidays '95
A Life Less Ordinary '97
Living Out Loud '98
Woman Wanted '98
Jesus' Son '99
Harlan County War '00
O Brother Where Art Thou? '00
Things You Can Tell Just by Looking at Her '00
Time Code '00
Moonlight Mile '02
Levity '03
Thirteen '03
The Incredibles '04 (V)
Little Black Book '04
The Big White '05
Nine Lives '05
Jackie '12
Won't Back Down '12
Bonnie & Clyde '13
Top of the Lake '13
Manglehorn '15
The Big Sick '17
Incredibles 2 '18 (V)

Ian Hunter (1900-75)
Easy Virtue '27
The Ring '27
The Man From Toronto '32
The Church Mouse '34
The Girl from 10th Ave. '35
A Midsummer Night's Dream '35
The Phantom Light '35
The Devil Is a Sissy '36
Another Dawn '37
Call It a Day '37
Stolen Holiday '37
That Certain Woman '37
The Adventures of Robin Hood '38
Always Goodbye '38
The Sisters '38
Broadway Serenade '39
The Little Princess '39
Maisie '39
Tarzan Finds a Son '39
The Tower of London '39
Bitter Sweet '40
Broadway Melody of 1940 '40
Come Live With Me '40
Gallant Sons '40
The Long Voyage Home '40
Strange Cargo '40
Andy Hardy's Private Secretary '41
Billy the Kid '41
Dr. Jekyll and Mr. Hyde '41
Smilin' Through '41
Ziegfeld Girl '41
A Yank at Eton '42
Edward, My Son '49
Appointment in London '53
Pursuit of the Graf Spee '57
She Played With Fire '57
Flame Over India '59
North West Frontier '59
The Secret of Monte Cristo '61
Doctor Blood's Coffin '62

Jeffrey Hunter (1925-69)
Call Me Mister '51
Belles on Their Toes '52
Lure of the Wilderness '52
Red Skies of Montana '52
Sailor of the King '53
Princess of the Nile '54
Seven Angry Men '55
Seven Cities of Gold '55
The Great Locomotive Chase '56
The Searchers '56
Gun for a Coward '57
No Down Payment '57
The True Story of Jesse James '57
In Love and War '58
The Last Hurrah '58
Hell to Eternity '60
Sergeant Rutledge '60
The King of Kings '61
Man-Trap '61
The Longest Day '62
No Man Is an Island '62
Gold for the Caesars '63
Revenge of Sartana '65
A Guide for the Married Man '67 (C)
Private Navy of Sgt. O'Farrell '68

Kaki Hunter (1955-)
Roadie '80
Whose Life Is It Anyway? '81
Porky's '82
Porky's 2: The Next Day '83
Just the Way You Are '84
Porky's Revenge '85

Kevin Hunter
One False Move '91
Songs My Brother Taught Me '15

Kim Hunter (1922-2002)
The Seventh Victim '43
Betrayed '44
Stairway to Heaven '46
A Streetcar Named Desire '51
Requiem for a Heavyweight '56
Storm Center '56
The Young Stranger '57
Lilith '64
Planet of the Apes '68
The Swimmer '68
Beneath the Planet of the Apes '70
Escape from the Planet of the Apes '71
Bad Ronald '74
Born Innocent '74
Once an Eagle '76
Backstairs at the White House '79
Two Evil Eyes '90
Midnight in the Garden of Good and Evil '97
A Price Above Rubies '97
Out of the Cold '99

Rachel Hunter (1969-)
Two Shades of Blue '98
Just a Little Harmless Sex '99
TripFall '00
MacArthur Park '01
Rock Star '01
La Cucina '07

Strike '07
Miami Magma '11

Russell Hunter (1925-2004)
Lilli Marlene '50
American Cousins '02

Tab Hunter (1931-2018)
Island of Desire '52
The Steel Lady '53
Return to Treasure Island '54
Track of the Cat '54
Battle Cry '55
Sea Chase '55
The Burning Hills '56
The Girl He Left Behind '56
Damn Yankees '58
Lafayette Escadrille '58
They Came to Cordura '59
Operation Bikini '63
Ride the Wild Surf '64
The Loved One '65
Birds Do It '66
Hostile Guns '67
The Arousers '70
The Big Push '75
Polyester '81
Grease 2 '82
Lust in the Dust '85
Grotesque '87
Out of the Dark '88
Cameron's Closet '89

Thomas Hunter (1932-)
The Hills Run Red '67
The Vampire Happening '71

Sam Huntington (1982-)
Jungle 2 Jungle '96
Detroit Rock City '99
Not Another Teen Movie '01
Freshman Orientation '04
In Enemy Hands '04
Sleepover '04
River's End '05
Superman Returns '06
Fanboys '09
Dylan Dog: Dead of Night '11
Sully '16
Seven Stages to Achieve Eternal Bliss '20

Fred Huntley (1862-1931)
Heart o' the Hills '19
Where the North Begins '23

G.P. (Tim) Huntley, Jr. (1904-71)
The Charge of the Light Brigade '36
Beau Geste '39
They Died with Their Boots On '41
Journey for Margaret '42

Noah Huntley (1974-)
The Cyberstalking '99
28 Days Later '02

Raymond Huntley (1904-90)
Night Train to Munich '40
Immortal Battalion '44
The Way Ahead '44
I See a Dark Stranger '46
I'll Never Forget You '51
The Long Dark Hall '51
Man Bait '52
The Prisoner '55
The Mummy '59
Our Man in Havana '59
Room at the Top '59
Hostile Witness '68
Hot Millions '68

Isabelle Huppert (1953-)
Going Places '74
Violette '78
The Bronte Sisters '79
Every Man for Himself '79
Loulou '80
Coup de Torchon '81
Heaven's Gate '81
Passion '82
Entre-Nous '83
La Truite '83
Cactus '86
The Bedroom Window '87
The Story of Women '88
Madame Bovary '91
Amateur '94
Love After Love '94
The Separation '94
La Ceremonie '95
The Swindle '97
La Separation '98
Comedy of Innocence '00
Les Destinees '00
Merci pour le Chocolat '00
The Piano Teacher '01
8 Women '02
La Vie Promise '02
Time of the Wolf '03
I Heart Huckabees '04
Gabrielle '05
Comedy of Power '06
Private Property '06
Home '09
Special Treatment '10
White Material '10
My Worst Nightmare '11
Amour '12
Dead Man Down '13
The Disappearance of Eleanor Rigby '14
Elle '16
Louder Than Bombs '16
Things to Come '16
Happy End '17
Greta '18
Frankie '19

Paige Hurd (1992-)
Cradle 2 the Grave '03
Beauty Shop '05

Rachel Hurd-Wood (1990-)
Peter Pan '03
An American Haunting '05
Perfume: The Story of a Murderer '06
Dorian Gray '09
For Love or Money '19

Elizabeth Hurley (1965-)
Rowing with the Wind '88
Christabel '89
Death Has a Bad Reputation '90
Kill Cruise '90
Passenger 57 '92
Nightscare '93
Shameless '94
Sharpe's Enemy '94
Dangerous Ground '96
Samson and Delilah '96
Austin Powers: International Man of Mystery '97
My Favorite Martian '98
Permanent Midnight '98
Austin Powers 2: The Spy Who Shagged Me '99
EDtv '99
Bedazzled '00
The Weight of Water '00
Double Whammy '01
Dawg '02
Serving Sara '02
Made in Romania '10

Brandon Hurst (1866-1947)
Dr. Jekyll and Mr. Hyde '20
The Hunchback of Notre Dame '23
The Thief of Baghdad '24
The Man Who Laughs '27
Murder at Midnight '31
The Midnight Lady '32
The White Zombie '32
The Lost Patrol '34

David Hurst (1926-2019)
Tony Draws a Horse '51
Kelly's Heroes '70

Michael Hurst (1957-)
Death Warmed Up '85
Hercules the Legendary Journeys, Vol. 1: And the Amazon Women '94
Hercules the Legendary Journeys, Vol. 2: The Lost Kingdom '94
Hercules the Legendary Journeys, Vol. 3: The Circle of Fire '94
Hercules the Legendary Journeys, Vol. 4: In the Underworld '94
The Tattooist '07

Paul Hurst (1888-1953)
Tide of Empire '29
Paradise Island '30
The Public Defender '31
13th Guest '32
Hold Your Man '33
Alexander's Ragtime Band '38
Prison Break '38
Gone with the Wind '39
Caught in the Draft '41
Treasure of Fear '45

Ryan Hurst (1976-)
Remember the Titans '00
Lone Star State of Mind '02
Taken '02
We Were Soldiers '02
The Ladykillers '04
Noble Things '08
Chasing the Green '09

Veronica Hurst (1931-)
Angels One Five '54
Peeping Tom '60

John Hurt (1940-2017)
A Man for All Seasons '66
Before Winter Comes '69
Sinful Davey '69
Cry of the Penguins '71
10 Rillington Place '71
Pied Piper '72
The Ghoul '75
The Naked Civil Servant '75
The Lord of the Rings '78 (V)
Midnight Express '78
Watership Down '78 (V)
Alien '79
The Elephant Man '80
Heaven's Gate '81
History of the World: Part 1 '81
Night Crossing '81
Partners '82
The Plague Dogs '82 (V)
The Osterman Weekend '83
Champions '84
1984 '84
Success Is the Best Revenge '84
The Black Cauldron '85 (V)
The Hit '85
From the Hip '86
Jake Speed '86
Spaceballs '87
Vincent: The Life and Death of Vincent van Gogh '87 (V)
Aria '88
The Bengali Night '88
White Mischief '88
Scandal '89
The Field '90
Frankenstein Unbound '90
Little Sweetheart '90
King Ralph '91
Shades of Fear '93
Even Cowgirls Get the Blues '94
Second Best '94
Thumbelina '94 (V)
Dead Man '95
Rob Roy '95
Wild Bill '95
Brute '97
The Climb '97
Contact '97
Love and Death on Long Island '97
All the Little Animals '98
New Blood '99
Lost Souls '00
Captain Corelli's Mandolin '01
Harry Potter and the Sorcerer's Stone '01
Miranda '01
Bait '02
Dogville '03 (N)
Owning Mahowny '03
Hellboy '04
Manderlay '05 (N)
The Proposition '05
Shooting Dogs '05
The Skeleton Key '05
Valiant '05 (V)
Perfume: The Story of a Murderer '06 (N)
V for Vendetta '06
Hellboy II: The Golden Army '08
Indiana Jones and the Kingdom of the Crystal Skull '08
Outlander '08
The Oxford Murders '08
Recount '08
An Englishman in New York '09
44 Inch Chest '09
The Limits of Control '09
New York, I Love You '09
Brighton Rock '10
Harry Potter and the Deathly Hallows, Part 1 '10
Ultramarines: A Warhammer 40,000 Movie '10 (V)
Harry Potter and the Deathly Hallows, Part 2 '11
Immortals '11
Melancholia '11
Tinker Tailor Soldier Spy '11
Labyrinth '12
Charlie Countryman '13 (N)
Jayne Mansfield's Car '13
Only Lovers Left Alive '13
Hercules '14
Snowpiercer '14
Jackie '16

Mary Beth Hurt (1946-)
Interiors '78
A Change of Seasons '80
The World According to Garp '82
D.A.R.Y.L. '85
Baby Girl Scott '87
Parents '89
Slaves of New York '89
Defenseless '91
Light Sleeper '92
The Age of Innocence '93
My Boyfriend's Back '93
Six Degrees of Separation '93
From the Journals of Jean Seberg '95
Affliction '97
Bringing Out the Dead '99
Family Man '00
The Exorcism of Emily Rose '05
The Dead Girl '06
Lady in the Water '06
Perception '06
The Walker '07
Untraceable '08
Lebanon, PA '10
Young Adult '11

William Hurt (1950-)
Altered States '80
Body Heat '81
Eyewitness '81
The Big Chill '83
Gorky Park '83
Kiss of the Spider Woman '85
Children of a Lesser God '86
Broadcast News '87
The Accidental Tourist '88
Alice '90
I Love You to Death '90
The Doctor '91
Until the End of the World '91
Mr. Wonderful '93
Second Best '94
Trial by Jury '94
A Couch in New York '95
Smoke '95
Jane Eyre '96
Michael '96
Dark City '97
The Proposition '97
Lost in Space '98
One True Thing '98
The Big Brass Ring '99
The 4th Floor '99
Silent Witness '99
The Simian Line '99
Sunshine '99
Contaminated Man '00
Dune '00
The Miracle Maker: The Story of Jesus '00 (V)
A. I.: Artificial Intelligence '01
Rare Birds '01
Varian's War '01
Changing Lanes '02
Master Spy: The Robert Hanssen Story '02
Tuck Everlasting '02
The Blue Butterfly '04
The Village '04
A History of Violence '05
The King '05
Syriana '05
Beautiful Ohio '06
The Good Shepherd '06
Into the Wild '07
Mr. Brooks '07
Noise '07
The Incredible Hulk '08
Vantage Point '08
The Yellow Handkerchief '08
The Countess '09
Endgame '09
The River Why '10
Robin Hood '10
Late Bloomers '11
Moby Dick '11
Too Big to Fail '11
Bonnie & Clyde '13
The Host '13
Days and Nights '14
The Disappearance of Eleanor Rigby '14
Winter's Tale '14
The Miracle Season '18
The Last Full Measure '19

Ferlin Husky (1925-2011)
Las Vegas Hillbillys '66
Hillbillies in a Haunted House '67

Toby Huss (1966-)
Beavis and Butt-Head Do America '96 (V)
Dear God '96
Dogs: The Rise and Fall of an All-Girl Bookie Joint '96
Down Periscope '96
The Country Bears '02 (V)
Human Nature '02
Rescue Dawn '06
Balls of Fury '07
World's Greatest Dad '09
Buster's Mal Heart '17
Sword of Trust '19

Olivia Hussey (1951-)
Romeo and Juliet '68
Lost Horizon '73
Ricco '74
Black Christmas '75
The Bastard '78
Death on the Nile '78
The Cat and the Canary '79
The Man with Bogart's Face '80
Escape 2000 '81
Ivanhoe '82
Virus '82
The Last Days of Pompeii '84
The Jeweller's Shop '90
Psycho 4: The Beginning '90
Stephen King's It '90
Undeclared War '91
Ice Cream Man '95
Bloody Proof '99
Headspace '02
Seven Days of Grace '06
Tortilla Heaven '07
Three Priests '08

Ruth Hussey (1911-2005)
Madame X '37
Judge Hardy's Children '38
Another Thin Man '39
Fast and Furious '39
Maisie '39
The Women '39
Flight Command '40
Northwest Passage '40
The Philadelphia Story '40
Susan and God '40
H.M. Pulham Esquire '41
The Uninvited '44
That's My Boy '51
Stars and Stripes Forever '52
The Facts of Life '60

Francis Huster (1947-)
Another Man, Another Chance '77
The Dinner Game '98

Anjelica Huston (1951-)
The Last Tycoon '76
The Postman Always Rings Twice '81
Ice Pirates '84
This Is Spinal Tap '84
Prizzi's Honor '85
The Dead '87
Gardens of Stone '87
A Handful of Dust '88
Mr. North '88
Crimes & Misdemeanors '89
Enemies, a Love Story '89
Lonesome Dove '89
The Grifters '90
The Witches '90
The Addams Family '91
The Player '92
Addams Family Values '93
And the Band Played On '93 (C)
Family Pictures '93
Manhattan Murder Mystery '93
The Crossing Guard '94
The Perez Family '94
Buffalo Girls '95
Buffalo 66 '97
Ever After: A Cinderella Story '98
Phoenix '98
Agnes Browne '99
The Golden Bowl '00
The Man from Elysian Fields '01
Mists of Avalon '01
The Royal Tenenbaums '01
Blood Work '02
Daddy Day Care '03
Kaena: The Prophecy '03 (V)
The Life Aquatic with Steve Zissou '04
Art School Confidential '06
The Hades Factor '06
Material Girls '06
Seraphim Falls '06
These Foolish Things '06
The Darjeeling Limited '07
Martian Child '07
Choke '08
The Kreutzer Sonata '08
When in Rome '09
The Big Year '11
Thirst Street '17

Danny Huston (1962-)
Anna Karenina '96
Time Code '00
21 Grams '03
The Aviator '04
Birth '04
Silver City '04
The Constant Gardener '05
The Proposition '05
Alpha Male '06
Children of Men '06
The Hades Factor '06
Marie Antoinette '06
I Really Hate My Job '07
The Number 23 '07
30 Days of Night '07
How to Lose Friends & Alienate People '08
John Adams '08
The Kreutzer Sonata '08
Boogie Woogie '09
X-Men Origins: Wolverine '09
Clash of the Titans '10
The Conspirator '10
Edge of Darkness '10
Robin Hood '10
You Don't Know Jack '10
Hitchcock '12
Stolen '12
2 Jacks '12
Wrath of the Titans '12
The Congress '13
The Liberator '13
Big Eyes '14
Wonder Woman '17
Stan & Ollie '18
Angel Has Fallen '19

IO '19
The Professor '19

Jack Huston (1982-)
Miss Austen Regrets '07
Shrooms '07
Hemingway's Garden of Eden '08
Outlander '08
Boogie Woogie '09
Shrink '09
Mr. Nice '10
Not Fade Away '12
2 Jacks '12
American Hustle '13
Kill Your Darlings '13
Night Train to Lisbon '13
The Longest Ride '15
Ben-Hur '16
Their Finest '17
The Yellow Birds '17
Earthquake Bird '19

John Huston (1906-87)
The Cardinal '63
The Bible '66 (N)
Casino Royale '67
Candy '68
Myra Breckinridge '70
Man in the Wilderness '71
Ride to Glory '71
Battle for the Planet of the Apes '73
Chinatown '74
Breakout '75
The Wind and the Lion '75
Tentacles '77
Battleforce '78
The Hobbit '78 (V)
Jaguar Lives '79
Winter Kills '79
Wise Blood '79
The Return of the King '80 (V)
The Visitor '80
Cannery Row '82 (N)
Lovesick '83
The Black Cauldron '85 (N)
The Other Side of the Wind '18

Virginia Huston (1925-81)
Nocturne '46
Out of the Past '47
Flamingo Road '49
Tarzan's Peril '51
Flight to Mars '52
Sudden Fear '52
Knock on Wood '54

Walter Huston (1884-1950)
Abraham Lincoln '30
The Criminal Code '31
The Woman From Monte Carlo '31
American Madness '32
The Beast of the City '32
Kongo '32
Rain '32
The Wet Parade '32
Gabriel Over the White House '33
The Prizefighter and the Lady '33
Transatlantic Tunnel '35
Dodsworth '36
Of Human Hearts '38
The Devil & Daniel Webster '41
The Maltese Falcon '41
In This Our Life '42
The Shanghai Gesture '42
Yankee Doodle Dandy '42
Edge of Darkness '43
Mission to Moscow '43
The North Star '43
The Outlaw '43
Dragon Seed '44
And Then There Were None '45
Dragonwyck '46
Duel in the Sun '46
Summer Holiday '48
Treasure of the Sierra Madre '48
The Great Sinner '49
The Furies '50
December 7th: The Movie '91

Jesse Hutch
Nightmare '07
Joy Ride 3: Road Kill '14

Michael Hutchence (1960-97)
Dogs in Space '87
Frankenstein Unbound '90

Josh Hutcherson (1992-)
Miracle Dogs '03
Howl's Moving Castle '04 (V)
Kicking & Screaming '05
Little Manhattan '05
Zathura '05
RV '06
Bridge to Terabithia '07
Firehouse Dog '07
Fragments '08
Journey to the Center of the Earth '08
Cirque du Freak: The Vampire's Assistant '09
The Kids Are All Right '10
Detention '11
The Hunger Games '12
Journey 2: The Mysterious Island '12
Epic '13 (V)
The Hunger Games: Catching Fire '13
The Hunger Games: Mockingjay--Part 1 '14
Escobar: Paradise Lost '15
The Hunger Games: Mockingjay-Part 2 '15
Tragedy Girls '17

David Hutcheson (1905-76)
No Highway in the Sky '51
The Abominable Dr. Phibes '71

Geoffrey Hutchings (1939-2010)
Wish You Were Here '87
It's All About Love '03

Eleanor Hutchins
Margarita Happy Hour '01
Milk and Honey '03
Dear Lemon Lima '09

Will Hutchins (1930-)
Lafayette Escadrille '58
No Time for Sergeants '58
Claudelle Inglish '61
Merrill's Marauders '62
The Shooting '66
Spinout '66
Clambake '67
Slumber Party '57 '76
Maverick '94 (C)

Fiona Hutchinson
American Gothic '88
Rage '95

Josephine Hutchinson (1904-98)
Happiness Ahead '34
Oil for the Lamps of China '35
The Right to Live '35
Son of Frankenstein '39
Somewhere in the Night '46
Cass Timberlane '47
Adventure in Baltimore '49
Love Is Better Than Ever '52
Gun for a Coward '57
North by Northwest '59
The Adventures of Huckleberry Finn '60
Rabbit, Run '70

Kelly Hutchinson
Slippery Slope '06
Don Peyote '14

Anna Hutchison (1986-)
The Cabin in the Woods '12
Wrecker '15

Doug Hutchison (1960-)
The Green Mile '99
Bait '00
I Am Sam '01
No Good Deed '02
The Salton Sea '02
Moola '07
Punisher: War Zone '08
Give 'Em Hell Malone '09

Ken Hutchison (1943-)
The Wrath of God '72
Ladyhawke '85

Candy Hutson (1980-)
The Land Before Time 2: The Great Valley Adventure '94 (V)
The Land Before Time 3: The Time of the Great Giving '95 (V)
The Land Before Time 4: Journey Through the Mists '96 (V)

William Hutt (1920-2007)
The Statement '03
The Trojan Horse '08

Betty Hutton (1921-2007)
Star Spangled Rhythm '42
Miracle of Morgan's Creek '44
Here Come the Waves '45
The Stork Club '45
The Perils of Pauline '47
Annie Get Your Gun '50
Let's Dance '50
The Greatest Show on Earth '52
Sailor Beware '52 (C)

Brian Hutton (1935-2014)
Carnival Rock '57
The Case Against Brooklyn '58
Last Train from Gun Hill '59

Jim Hutton (1933-79)
Where the Boys Are '60
Bachelor in Paradise '61
The Honeymoon Machine '61
The Horizontal Lieutenant '62
Period of Adjustment '62
Sunday in New York '63
Looking for Love '64
The Hallelujah Trail '65
Major Dundee '65
Never Too Late '65
Walk, Don't Run '66
Who's Minding the Mint? '67
The Green Berets '68
Hellfighters '68
They Call It Murder '71
Don't Be Afraid of the Dark '73
Nightmare at 43 Hillcrest '74
Psychic Killer '75

Lauren Hutton (1943-)
Paper Lion '68
Pieces of Dreams '70
The Gambler '74
Nashville '75
Gator '76
Viva Knievel '77
A Wedding '78
American Gigolo '79
Zorro, the Gay Blade '81
Lassiter '84
Once Bitten '85
Monte Carlo '86
Malone '87
Timestalkers '87
Bulldance '88
Forbidden Sun '89
Fear '90
Millions '90
Guilty as Charged '92
My Father the Hero '93
54 '98 (C)
Just a Little Harmless Sex '99
Caracara '00
The Joneses '09

Marion Hutton (1919-87)
In Society '44
Love Happy '50

Pascale Hutton (1979-)
Hollywood Wives: The New Generation '03
Ginger Snaps: Unleashed '04
A Simple Curve '05
Disaster Zone: Volcano in New York '06
Presumed Dead '06
Tornado Valley '09

Afghan Luke '11
Behemoth '11

Robert Hutton (1920-94)
Destination Tokyo '43
Hollywood Canteen '44
The Steel Helmet '51
Big Bluff '55
Colossus of New York '58
Showdown at Boot Hill '58
Invisible Invaders '59
Naked Youth '59
Cinderfella '60
The Slime People '63
They Came from Beyond Space '67
Cry of the Banshee '70

Timothy Hutton (1960-)
Zuma Beach '78
And Baby Makes Six '79
Friendly Fire '79
Ordinary People '80
Taps '81
Daniel '83
Iceman '84
The Falcon and the Snowman '85
Turk 182! '85
Made in Heaven '87
Everybody's All American '88
Q & A '90
Torrents of Spring '90
The Dark Half '91
The Temp '93
French Kiss '95
The Last Word '95
Beautiful Girls '96
City of Industry '96
Mr. & Mrs. Loving '96
Playing God '96
The Substance of Fire '96
Money Kings '98
The General's Daughter '99
Deterrence '00
The Golden Spiders: A Nero Wolfe Mystery '00
Just One Night '00
Deliberate Intent '01
The Doorbell Rang: A Nero Wolfe Mystery '01
Winds of Terror '01
Sunshine State '02
Kinsey '04
Secret Window '04
The Good Shepherd '06
Heavens Fall '06
The Kovak Box '06
Last Holiday '06
Stephanie Daley '06
The Last Mimzy '07
When a Man Falls in the Forest '07
The Alphabet Killer '08
Lymelife '08
Reflections '08
Brief Interviews With Hideous Men '09
Broken Hill '09
The Killing Room '09
The Ghost Writer '10
Multiple Sarcasms '10
Louder Than Words '14

Eugene Hutz (1972-)
Everything is Illuminated '05
Filth and Wisdom '08

Brody Hutzler (1971-)
Totally Blonde '01
Beach Kings '08

Richard Huw
The Four Minute Mile '88
Getting It Right '89
The Buccaneers '95
A Certain Justice '99

William Huw
Merlin and the War of the Dragons '08
Sherlock Holmes '10

Judy Huxtable
The Psychopath '66
Scream and Scream Again '70

Leila Hyams (1905-77)
The Idle Rich '29
Spite Marriage '29

The Big House '30
The Bishop Murder Case '30
The Girl Said No '30
The Phantom of Paris '31
Stepping Out '31
Freaks '32
Island of Lost Souls '32
Red Headed Woman '32
Ruggles of Red Gap '35

Jacquelyn Hyde (1931-92)
Take the Money and Run '69
Hanging By a Thread '79

Jonathan Hyde (1948-)
The Death of the Heart '87
Richie Rich '94
Jumanji '95
Anaconda '96
Titanic '97
Joan of Arc '99
The Mummy '99
Attila '01
The Prince and the Pauper '01
Princess of Thieves '01
The Curse of King Tut's Tomb '06
The Contract '07

Alex Hyde-White (1959-)
The First Olympics: Athens 1896 '84
Biggles '85
Indiana Jones and the Last Crusade '89
The Phantom of the Opera '89
Murder C.O.D. '90
Pretty Woman '90
Silent Victim '92
Unknown Origin '95
Mars '96
Pursuit of Happiness '01

Wilfrid Hyde-White (1903-91)
The Man Who Knew Too Much '34
The Lady From Lisbon '42
Ghosts of Berkeley Square '47
The Forbidden Street '49
The Third Man '49
Angel with the Trumpet '50
Highly Dangerous '50
Last Holiday '50
Midnight Episode '50
The Browning Version '51
The Golden Salamander '51
Betrayed '54
Quentin Durward '55
Tarzan's Hidden Jungle '55
Tarzan and the Lost Safari '57
The Lady Is a Square '58
Carry On Nurse '59
Flame Over India '59
Libel '59
North West Frontier '59
Teenage Bad Girl '59
Two-Way Stretch '60
Ada '61
On the Double '61
In Search of the Castaways '62
My Fair Lady '64
The Liquidator '65
You Must Be Joking! '65
Bang! Bang! You're Dead! '66
The Magic Christian '69
Fragment of Fear '70
Brand New Life '72
King Solomon's Treasure '76
The Cat and the Canary '79
Oh, God! Book 2 '80
Tarzan, the Ape Man '81
The Toy '82
Fanny Hill '83
Heartburn '86

Martha Hyer (1924-2014)
Geisha Girl '52
Wild Stallion '52
Abbott and Costello Go to Mars '53
Battle of Rogue River '54
Down Three Dark Streets '54

Lucky Me '54
Sabrina '54
Francis in the Navy '55
Wyoming Renegades '55
The Delicate Delinquent '56
Battle Hymn '57
My Man Godfrey '57
Paris Holiday '57
Houseboat '58
Some Came Running '58
The Best of Everything '59
Ice Palace '60
The Right Approach '61
Bikini Beach '64
The Carpetbaggers '64
First Men in the Moon '64
Sons of Katie Elder '65
The Chase '66
Night of the Grizzly '66
Picture Mommy Dead '66
The House of 1000 Dolls '67
Once You Kiss a Stranger '69
The Day of the Wolves '71

Andre Hyland
Mr. Roosevelt '17
The Death of Dick Long '19

Diana Hyland (1936-77)
One Man's Way '63
The Boy in the Plastic Bubble '76

Frances Hyland (1927-2004)
Happy Birthday to Me '81
Broken Lullaby '94

Sarah Hyland (1990-)
Joe Gould's Secret '00
Cougars, Inc. '10
Geek Charming '11
Struck by Lightning '12
Bonnie & Clyde '13
Call Me Crazy '13
Vampire Academy '14
Satanic '15
The Wedding Year '19

Scott Hylands (1943-)
Daddy's Gone A-Hunting '69
Fools '70
Earth II '71
Earthquake '74
The Boys in Company C '77
The Winds of Kitty Hawk '78
Ordeal in the Arctic '93
Titanic '96
Ignition '01
Last Chance Cafe '06
Anna's Storm '07
Cleaverville '07
Time and Again '07
Freezer Burn: The Invasion of Laxdale '08
Beyond the Black Rainbow '10
Knockout '11
The Horses of McBride '12

Jane Hylton (1927-79)
It Always Rains on Sunday '47
The Upturned Glass '47
The Manster '59
Circus of Horrors '60

Richard Hylton (1920-62)
Lost Boundaries '49
The Halls of Montezuma '50
Fixed Bayonets! '51

Warren Hymer (1906-48)
Up the River '30
One Way Passage '32
Midnight Mary '33
20,000 Years in Sing Sing '33
Rhythm on the Range '36
San Francisco '36
Join the Marines '37
Navy Blues '37
You Only Live Once '37
Joy of Living '38
You and Me '38
Mr. Moto in Danger Island '39
Birth of the Blues '41
Mr. Wise Guy '42

Joyce Hyser (1956-)
The Hollywood Knights '80
Just One of the Guys '85

Steve Hytner (1959-)
In the Line of Fire '93
The Shadow '94
The Prophecy 2: Ashtown '97
Forces of Nature '99
Love Stinks '99
The Prophecy 3: The Ascent '99
Air Rage '01
Eurotrip '04
Bachelor Party Vegas '05

Paul Iacono (1988-)
Return to Sleepaway Camp '08
Fame '09
G.B.F. '13

Stanislav Ianevski (1985-)
Harry Potter and the Goblet of Fire '05
Hostel: Part 2 '07
Harry Potter and the Deathly Hallows, Part 1 '10

Mirta Ibarra (1946-)
Strawberry and Chocolate '93
Guantanamera '95
Mararia '98

Masato Ibu (1949-)
Empire of the Sun '87
Godzilla *vs.* Megaguirus '00
Azumi '03
Sway '06

Ice Cube (1969-)
Boyz N the Hood '91
Trespass '92
Higher Learning '94
Friday '95
The Glass Shield '95
Anaconda '96
Dangerous Ground '96
I Got the Hook-Up '98
The Players Club '98
Thicker than Water '99
Three Kings '99
Next Friday '00
John Carpenter's Ghosts of Mars '01
All About the Benjamins '02
Barbershop '02
Friday After Next '02
Barbershop 2: Back in Business '04
Torque '04
Are We There Yet? '05
XXX: State of the Union '05
Are We Done Yet? '07
First Sunday '08
The Longshots '08
The Janky Promoters '09
The Lottery Ticket '10
Rampart '11
21 Jump Street '12
The Book of Life '14 (V)
Ride Along '14
22 Jump Street '14
Barbershop: The Next Cut '16
Ride Along 2 '16
Fist Fight '17

Ice-T (1958-)
New Jack City '91
Ricochet '91
Trespass '92
Who's the Man? '93
Surviving the Game '94
Tank Girl '94
Johnny Mnemonic '95
Body Count '97
The Deli '97
Mean Guns '97
Crazy Six '98
Agent of Death '99
Corrupt '99
Final Voyage '99
Jacob Two Two Meets the Hooded Fang '99
Judgment Day '99
Leprechaun 5: In the Hood '99
Sonic Impact '99
Stealth Fighter '99
Urban Menace '99
The Wrecking Crew '99
Ablaze '00
Gangland '00
Luck of the Draw '00
Air Rage '01
Black Horizon '01
The Guardian '01
Kept '01
'R Xmas '01
Rhapsody '01
3000 Miles to Graceland '01
Ticker '01 (C)
On the Edge '02
Tracks '05
Tommy and the Cool Mule '09 (V)
The Other Guys '10 (N)
Once Upon a Time in Brooklyn '13

Etsuko Ichihara (1936-)
Black Rain '88
The Eel '96

Hayato Ichihara (1987-)
Ju-On 2 '00
All About Lily Chou-Chou '01
Onmyoji 2 '03
Negative Happy Chainsaw Edge '08
Blade of the Immortal '17

Raizo Ichikawa (1931-69)
Shin Heike Monogatari '55
Shinobi no Mono '62
Shinobi no Mono 2: Vengeance '63
Shinobi No Mono 3: Resurrection '09

Utaemon Ichikawa (1904-99)
47 Ronin, Part 1 '42
47 Ronin, Part 2 '42

Lanre Idewu
Big Bag of $ '09
Irene in Time '09
The Inheritance '10

Eric Idle (1943-)
And Now for Something Completely Different '72
Monty Python and the Holy Grail '75
All You Need Is Cash '78
Monty Python's Life of Brian '79
Monty Python's The Meaning of Life '83
Yellowbeard '83
National Lampoon's European Vacation '85 (C)
Transformers: The Movie '86 (V)
The Adventures of Baron Munchausen '89
Around the World in 80 Days '89
Nuns on the Run '90
Too Much Sun '90
Mom and Dad Save the World '92
Splitting Heirs '93
Casper '95
Mr. Toad's Wild Ride '96
An Alan Smithee Film: Burn, Hollywood, Burn '97
Quest for Camelot '98 (V)
The Secret of NIMH 2 '98 (V)
Dudley Do-Right '99
South Park: Bigger, Longer and Uncut '99 (V)
102 Dalmatians '00 (V)
Hollywood Homicide '03 (C)
National Lampoon's Christmas Vacation 2: Cousin Eddie's Big Island Adventure '03
Ella Enchanted '04 (N)
Shrek the Third '07 (V)
Delgo '08 (V)
Shrek Forever After '10 (V)

Cinnamon Idles (1975-)
Kidco '83
Sixteen Candles '84

Billy Idol (1955-)
The Doors '91
Trigger Happy '96 (C)
The Wedding Singer '97 (C)
Heavy Metal 2000 '00 (V)

Rhys Ifans (1967-)
Dancing at Lughnasa '98
Heart '99
Janice Beard '99
Notting Hill '99
Kevin & Perry Go Large '00
Little Nicky '00
Love, Honour & Obey '00
Rancid Aluminium '00
The Replacements '00
Formula 51 '01
Hotel '01
The Shipping News '01
Human Nature '02
Once Upon a Time in the Midlands '02
Danny Deckchair '03
Enduring Love '04
Vanity Fair '04
Four Last Songs '06
Garfield: A Tail of Two Kitties '06 (V)
Elizabeth: The Golden Age '07
Hannibal Rising '07
The Informers '09
Pirate Radio '09
Exit Through the Gift Shop '10 (N)
Greenberg '10
Harry Potter and the Deathly Hallows, Part 1 '10
Mr. Nice '10
Nanny McPhee Returns '10
Passion Play '10
Anonymous '11
Neverland '11
The Amazing Spider-Man '12
The Five-Year Engagement '12
Mr. Nobody '13
Serena '14
Madame Bovary '15
She's Funny That Way '15
Len & Company '16
Official Secrets '19

Hisashi Igawa (1936-)
Harakiri '62
Goyokin '69
Ran '85
Akira Kurosawa's Dreams '90
Boiling Point '90
Rhapsody in August '91
Hiroshima '95

Togo Igawa (1946-)
Incognito '97
The Last Samurai '03
The Hedgehog '09
Gambit '12

James Iglehart
Beyond the Valley of the Dolls '70
Angels Hard As They Come '71
Fighting Mad '77
Death Force '78

Eugene Iglesias (1926-)
Duel at Silver Creek '52
Hiawatha '52

Gabriel 'Fluffy' Iglesias (1976-)
The Fluffy Movie: Unity Through Laughter '14
Norm of the North '16
UglyDolls '19 (V)

Tsuyoski Ihara (1963-)
Letters from Iwo Jima '06
13 Assassins '10

Steve Ihnat (1934-72)
Hour of the Gun '67
Countdown '68
Kona Coast '68
ZigZag '70

Diasuke Iijima
Merry Christmas, Mr. Lawrence '83
Flower & Snake '04

Vladimir Ilin (1947-)
Attack on Leningrad '09
Ward No. 6 '09

Peter Illing (1899-1966)
Against the Wind '48
Bhowani Junction '56
Zarak '56
The Electronic Monster '57
The Happy Thieves '61

Annie Ilonzeh (1983-)
All Eyez on Me '17
Peppermint '18

Eriko Imai (1983-)
Andromedia '00
Onmyoji '01
Onmyoji 2 '03

Iman (1955-)
The Human Factor '79
Out of Africa '85
No Way Out '87
House Party 2: The Pajama Jam '91
L.A. Story '91
Star Trek 6: The Undiscovered Country '91
The Linguini Incident '92 (C)
Exit to Eden '94
The Deli '97

Mo'Nique Imes
Irish Jam '05
Blackbird '14

Roger Imhof (1875-1958)
David Harum '34
Life Begins at Forty '35
Riff Raff '35
Steamboat Round the Bend '35
San Francisco '36
Girl Loves Boy '37

Gary Imhoff (1952-)
The Seniors '78
Thumbelina '94 (V)

James Immekus
Boxboarders! '07
The Caretaker '08

Michael Imperioli (1966-)
Goodfellas '90
Jungle Fever '91
Bad Boys '95
The Basketball Diaries '95
Postcards from America '95
Girl 6 '96
I Shot Andy Warhol '96
Last Man Standing '96
Office Killer '97
A River Made to Drown In '97
Witness to the Mob '98
Disappearing Acts '00
Hamlet '01
Love in the Time of Money '02
My Baby's Daddy '04
Shark Tale '04 (V)
For One More Day '07
The Lovely Bones '09
Stuck Between Stations '11
The Call '13
Oldboy '13
The M Word '14
The Scribbler '14
Primal '19

Celia Imrie (1952-)
Mary Shelley's Frankenstein '94
The Return of the Native '94
A Midwinter's Tale '95
The Borrowers '97
Into the Blue '97
Hilary and Jackie '98
A Christmas Carol '99
Lucky Break '01
Station Jim '01
Daniel Deronda '02
The Gathering Storm '02
Plain Jane '02
Calendar Girls '03
Doctor Zhivago '03
Wah-Wah '05
Imagine Me & You '06
Nanny McPhee '06
The Best Exotic Marigold Hotel '12
The Love Punch '13
The Second Best Exotic Marigold Hotel '15
Finding Your Feet '18

Yoshio Inaba (1921-98)
Seven Samurai '54
Harakiri '62

John Ince (1878-1947)
Alias French Gertie '30
Headin' for Trouble '31

Ralph Ince (1887-1937)
State's Attorney '31
Malay Nights '32
The Tenderfoot '32

Annabella Incontrera (1943-)
The Assassination Bureau '69
Double Face '70
Return of Sabata '71

Frieda Inescort (1901-76)
Give Me Your Heart '36
The Great O'Malley '36
If You Could Only Cook '36
Another Dawn '37
Call It a Day '37
Tarzan Finds a Son '39
The Letter '40
Pride and Prejudice '40
Sunny '41
The Courtship of Andy Hardy '42
The Amazing Mrs. Holiday '43
Return of the Vampire '43
The Judge Steps Out '49
The Underworld Story '50
A Place in the Sun '51
The She-Creature '56

Ralph Ineson
The Witch '16
The Hurricane Heist '18
Brahms: The Boy II '19

Pedro Infante
Over the Waves '49
Pepe El Toro '53

Angelo Infanti (1939-2010)
Four Dollars of Revenge '66
Le Mans '71
A Man Called Sledge '71
The Godfather '72
The Valachi Papers '72
War Goddess '74
The Squeeze '77
The Black Stallion Returns '83
The Scarlet & the Black '83
The Assisi Underground '84
La Scorta '94
The Nest '02

Marty Ingels (1936-)
The Busy Body '67
If It's Tuesday, This Must Be Belgium '69
Instant Karma '90

Mariah Inger
The Courage to Love '00
Lost Junction '03

Randi Ingerman (1967-)
Desperate Crimes '93
Screw Loose '99

Barrie Ingham (1932-2015)
The Great Mouse Detective '86 (V)
Josh Kirby. . . Time Warrior: Chapter 3, Trapped on Toyworld '95
Josh Kirby. . . Time Warrior: Chapter 4, Eggs from 70 Million B.C. '95
Josh Kirby. . . Time Warrior: Chapter 5, Journey to the Magic Cavern '96
Josh Kirby. . . Time Warrior: Chapter 6, Last Battle for the Universe '96

John Ingle (1928-2012)
The Land Before Time 2: The Great Valley Adventure '94 (V)
The Land Before Time 3: The Time of the Great Giving '95 (V)
The Land Before Time 4: Journey Through the Mists '96 (V)
The Land Before Time 5: The Mysterious Island '97 (V)

Lee Ingleby (1976-)
Borstal Boy '00
Master and Commander: The Far Side of the World '03
Place of Execution '09

Lloyd Ingraham (1885-1956)
Scaramouche '23
Montana Moon '30
Sinister Hands '32
Peck's Bad Boy '34
Captain Calamity '36
Empty Saddles '36

David W. Ingram
Sidekick '05
Time and Again '07

Jack Ingram (1902-69)
South of Panama '41
Thundering Gunslingers '44
Lost in Alaska '52

Rex Ingram (1892-1950)
The Green Pastures '36
The Adventures of Huckleberry Finn '39
The Thief of Bagdad '40
Talk of the Town '42
Cabin in the Sky '43
Sahara '43
Dark Waters '44
The Smallest Show on Earth '48
Elmer Gantry '60
Your Cheatin' Heart '64

Frankie Ingrassia
The Positively True Adventures of the Alleged Texas Cheerleader-Murdering Mom '93
Election '99

Valeri Inkizhinov (1895-1973)
Storm over Asia '28
Journey to the Lost City '58
Samson and the 7 Miracles of the World '62

George Innes (1938-)
Danger UXB '81
Ivanhoe '82
Agatha Christie's A Caribbean Mystery '83
Master and Commander: The Far Side of the World '03

Laura Innes (1957-)
Deep Impact '98
The Good Neighbor '16

Neil Innes (1944-)
Monty Python and the Holy Grail '75
Jabberwocky '77
All You Need Is Cash '78
Monty Python's Life of Brian '79
Erik the Viking '89

Harold Innocent (1933-93)
The Canterville Ghost '86
Henry V '89
Robin Hood: Prince of Thieves '91

Annie Shizuka Inoh (1969-)
Goodbye South, Goodbye '96
Flowers of Shanghai '98
8 1/2 Women '99

Antonella Interlenghi (1960-)
Gates of Hell '80
New York Ripper '82

Franco Interlenghi (1931-)
Shoeshine '47
The Vanquished '52
I Vitelloni '53

Aharon Ipale (1951-)
Invisible: The Chronicles of Benjamin Knight '93
A Kid in Aladdin's Palace '97
The Mummy '99

Michael Irby (1972-)
The Last Castle '01
Pinero '01
Flightplan '05
Law Abiding Citizen '09

Jill Ireland (1936-90)
Three Men in a Boat '56
Robbery under Arms '57
Villa Rides '68
The Family '70
Rider on the Rain '70
Cold Sweat '71
Someone Behind the Door '71
The Mechanic '72
The Valachi Papers '72
Breakout '75
Chino '75
Hard Times '75
Breakheart Pass '76
From Noon Till Three '76
Love and Bullets '79
Death Wish 2 '82
Assassination '87

John Ireland (1914-92)
It Shouldn't Happen to a Dog '46
My Darling Clementine '46
Wake Up and Dream '46
A Walk in the Sun '46
The Gangster '47
Railroaded '47
Joan of Arc '48
Open Secret '48
Raw Deal '48
Red River '48
A Southern Yankee '48
All the King's Men '49
I Shot Jesse James '49
Mr. Soft Touch '49
Return of Jesse James '50
Little Big Horn '51
Vengeance Valley '51
The Bushwackers '52
The Fast and the Furious '54
Southwest Passage '54
Queen Bee '55
The Gunslinger '56
Gunfight at the O.K. Corral '57
Party Girl '58
Spartacus '60
Wild in the Country '61
The Ceremony '63
55 Days at Peking '63
The Fall of the Roman Empire '64
Arizona Bushwackers '67
Hate for Hate '67
Diary of a Rebel '68
Gun for 100 Graves '68
Taste of Death '68
The Adventurers '70
Dead for a Dollar '70
The House of Seven Corpses '73
The Phantom of Hollywood '74
Farewell, My Lovely '75
Maniac '77
Perfect Killer '77
Satan's Cheerleaders '77
Tomorrow Never Comes '77
Crossbar '79
Kavik the Wolf Dog '80
Mission to Glory '80
Incubus '82
The Treasure of the Amazon '85
Messenger of Death '88
Waxwork 2: Lost in Time '91

John Ireland, Jr.
Wham-Bam, Thank You Spaceman '75
Sundown: The Vampire in Retreat '08

Kathy Ireland (1963-)
Alien from L.A. '87
Mr. Destiny '90
Side Out '90
Necessary Roughness '91
Mom and Dad Save the World '92
The Player '92
National Lampoon's Loaded Weapon 1 '93
Miami Hustle '95

Marin Ireland (1979-)
28 Hotel Rooms '12
Bottled Up '13
Glass Chin '14
The Family Fang '16
Piercing '18
Light from Light '19

Vincent Irizarry (1959-)
Marie '85
Firefighter '86
Heartbreak Ridge '86
Left to Die: The Sandra and Tammi Chase Story '12
Worth: The Testimony of Johnny St. James '12

Jeremy Irons (1948-)
Love for Lydia '79
Nijinsky '80
Brideshead Revisited '81
The French Lieutenant's Woman '81
Moonlighting '82
Swann in Love '84
The Wild Duck '84
The Mission '86
Dead Ringers '88
A Chorus of Disapproval '89
Reversal of Fortune '90
Damage '92
Waterland '92
The House of the Spirits '93
M. Butterfly '93
The Lion King '94 (V)
Die Hard: With a Vengeance '95
Stealing Beauty '96
Chinese Box '97
Lolita '97
The Man in the Iron Mask '98
Dungeons and Dragons '00
Longitude '00
The Fourth Angel '01
And Now Ladies and Gentlemen '02
Callas Forever '02
Last Call: The Final Chapter of F. Scott Fitzgerald '02
The Time Machine '02
Being Julia '04
The Merchant of Venice '04
Casanova '05
Elizabeth I '05
Kingdom of Heaven '05
Eragon '06
Inland Empire '06
Appaloosa '08
The Color of Magic '08
Georgia O'Keefe '09
The Pink Panther 2 '09
Margin Call '11
The Words '12
Beautiful Creatures '13
Night Train to Lisbon '13
Assassin's Creed '16
High-Rise '16
The Man Who Knew Infinity '16

Max Irons (1985-)
Red Riding Hood '11
The Host '13
The Riot Club '15
Bitter Harvest '17
The Wife '17
Terminal '18

Nicholas Irons (1970-)
Vlad '03
Drop Dead Gorgeous '10

Michael Ironside (1950-)
Scanners '81
Visiting Hours '82
Nowhere to Hide '83
Spacehunter: Adventures in the Forbidden Zone '83
V: The Final Battle '84
The Falcon and the Snowman '85
Top Gun '86
Extreme Prejudice '87
Ford: The Man & the Machine '87
Hello Mary Lou: Prom Night 2 '87
Watchers '88
Total Recall '90
Highlander 2: The Quickening '91
Victim of Beauty '91 (C)
Guncrazy '92
Killer Image '92
The Vagrant '92
Dead Man's Revenge '93
Father Hood '93
Forced to Kill '93
Mardi Gras for the Devil '93
Point of Impact '93
Sweet Killing '93
Fortunes of War '94
The Killing Man '94
Rebel Run '94
Tokyo Cowboy '94
The Glass Shield '95
One Way Out '95
Portraits of a Killer '95
Probable Cause '95
Kids of the Round Table '96
Robin Cook's Terminal '96
Bomb Squad '97
Ivory Tower '97
Starship Troopers '97
Blood Money '98
Captive '98
Chicago Cab '98
Beyond Redemption '99
Johnny 2.0 '99
The Omega Code '99
Cause of Death '00
Crime and Punishment in Suburbia '00
Heavy Metal 2000 '00 (V)
Nuremberg '00
The Perfect Storm '00
Anti-Terrorist Cell: Manhunt '01
Children of the Corn: Revelation '01
Dead Awake '01
Extreme Honor '01
Ignition '01
Mindstorm '01
The Shaft '01
The Machinist '04
Deepwater '05
Disaster Zone: Volcano in New York '06
The Veteran '06
The Butcher '07
The Alphabet Killer '08
Mutants '08
Storm Cell '08
Surveillance '08
The Terrorist Next Door '08
Hardwired '09
Terminator Salvation '09
The Bannen Way '10
Beneath the Blue '10
Lake Placid 3 '10
Ice Soldiers '13
Stay '13
A Fighting Man '14
88 '15
The Sin Seer '15
Turbo Kid '15
Synchronicity '16

Dom Irrera (1947-)
The Big Lebowski '97
Barnyard '06 (V)

Brittney Irvin (1984-)
Angels in the Infield '00
Wilderness Love '02
National Lampoon's Holiday Reunion '03
Absolute Zero '05
Hot Rod '07
Spectacular '09
Nearlyweds '13

Jeremy Irvine (1990-)
War Horse '11
Great Expectations '12
Now Is Good '12
The Railway Man '13
A Night in Old Mexico '14
Stonewall '15
The Woman in Black 2: Angel of Death '15
The World Made Straight '15
This Beautiful Fantastic '17
Fallen '17

Amy Irving (1953-)
Carrie '76
Dynasty '76
James Dean '76
Once an Eagle '76
The Fury '78
The Competition '80
Honeysuckle Rose '80
Yentl '83
The Far Pavilions '84
Micki & Maude '84
Anastasia: The Mystery of Anna '86
Rumpelstiltskin '86
Crossing Delancey '88
Who Framed Roger Rabbit '88 (V)
A Show of Force '90
An American Tail: Fievel Goes West '91 (V)
Benefit of the Doubt '93
Carried Away '95
I'm Not Rappaport '96
Deconstructing Harry '97
The Confession '98
One Tough Cop '98
Blue Ridge Fall '99
Bossa Nova '99
The Rage: Carrie 2 '99
Traffic '00
Thirteen Conversations About One Thing '01
Tuck Everlasting '02
Hide and Seek '05
Adam '09
Unsane '18

George Irving (1874-1961)
The Divorcee '30
Eleven Men and a Girl '30
Shipmates '31
Merrily We Go to Hell '32
The Oil Raider '34
Dangerous '35
Captain January '36
The Mandarin Mystery '37
Sergeant York '41

Margaret Irving (1898-1988)
Animal Crackers '30
San Francisco '36
In Society '44

Bill Irwin (1950-)
Popeye '80
Eight Men Out '88
My Blue Heaven '90
Hot Shots! '91
Scenes from a Mall '91
Silent Tongue '92 (C)
Subway Stories '97
Illuminata '98
Just the Ticket '98
William Shakespeare's A Midsummer Night's Dream '99
Dr. Seuss' How the Grinch Stole Christmas '00
Lady in the Water '06
Rachel Getting Married '08
Higher Ground '11
Interstellar '14 (V)

Bindi Irwin (1998-)
Free Willy: Escape from Pirate's Cove '10
Return to Nim's Island '13

Boyd Irwin (1880-1957)
The Three Musketeers '21
Madam Satan '30
Meet Nero Wolfe '36
Docks of New Orleans '48

Charles Irwin (1887-1969)
Bomba on Panther Island '49
Bomba, the Jungle Boy '49
Montana '50
Charge of the Lancers '54

Steve Irwin (1962-2006)
The Crocodile Hunter: Collision Course '02
Happy Feet '06 (V)

Tom Irwin (1956-)
Deceived '91
Ladykiller '92
Mr. Jones '93
The Sandy Bottom Orchestra '00
Snow White: The Fairest of Them All '02
Exposed '03
The Bling Ring '11

Oscar Isaac (1980-)
The Nativity Story '06
PU-239 '06
Body of Lies '08
Agora '09
Robin Hood '10
Drive '11
Sucker Punch '11
W.E. '11
For Greater Glory '12
Revenge for Jolly! '12
10 Years '12
Won't Back Down '12
In Secret '13
Inside Llewyn Davis '13
A Most Violent Year '14
The Two Faces of January '14
Ex Machina '15
Mojave '15
Star Wars: The Force Awakens '15
Time to Choose '16
X-Men: Apocalypse '16
The Promise '17
Annihilation '18
At Eternity's Gate '18
Life Itself '18
Operation Finale '18
The Addams Family '19
Star Wars: The Rise of Skywalker '19
Triple Frontier '19

Jason Isaacs (1963-)
Dragonheart '96
Event Horizon '97
Armageddon '98
The Last Don 2 '98
St. Ives '98
Soldier '98
The End of the Affair '99
The Patriot '00
Black Hawk Down '01
Hotel '01
The Last Minute '01
Sweet November '01
Harry Potter and the Chamber of Secrets '02
Passionada '02
The Tuxedo '02
Windtalkers '02
Peter Pan '03
The Chumscrubber '05
Harry Potter and the Goblet of Fire '05
Nine Lives '05
Friends with Money '06
The State Within '06
Harry Potter and the Order of the Phoenix '07
Good '08
Green Zone '10
Harry Potter and the Deathly Hallows, Part 1 '10
Abduction '11
Cars 2 '11 (V)
A Single Shot '13
Sweetwater '13
Field of Lost Shoes '14
Fury '14
Rosemary's Baby '14
A Cure for Wellness '17
Look Away '18
Scoob! '20

Chris Isaak (1956-)
Married to the Mob '88
The Silence of the Lambs '91
Twin Peaks: Fire Walk with Me '92
Little Buddha '93
Grace of My Heart '96
That Thing You Do! '96
From the Earth to the Moon '98
Blue Ridge Fall '99
A Dirty Shame '04
The Informers '09

Margarita Isabel
Cronos '94
Lucia, Lucia '03

Katharine Isabelle (1981-)
Bones '01
Ginger Snaps '01
Turning Paige '01
Carrie '02
Due East '02
Insomnia '02
The Secret of Zoey '02
Falling Angels '03
Freddy vs. Jason '03
Ginger Snaps Back: The Beginning '04
Ginger Snaps: Unleashed '04
Show Me '04
Eight Days to Live '06
Everything's Gone Green '06
Another Cinderella Story '08
Mail Order Bride '08
Goodnight for Justice: Queen of Hearts '13
88 '15
Countdown '16

Madison Iseman
Goosebumps 2: Haunted Halloween '18
Annabelle Comes Home '19

Yusuke Iseya (1976-)
Black House '07
Sukiyaki Western Django '08
13 Assassins '10

Renji Ishibashi (1941-)
Dead or Alive '00
The Sea is Watching '02
One Missed Call '03
Flower & Snake '04
The Great Yokai War '05
One Missed Call 2 '05
Shinobi '05
Hana: The Tale of a Reluctant Samurai '07
Outrage '10

Ryo Ishibashi (1956-)
American Yakuza '94
Blue Tiger '94
The Crossing Guard '94
Another Lonely Hitman '95
Back to Back '96
Audition '99
Suicide Club '02
Gozu '03
The Grudge '04
Masters of Horror: Dream Cruise '07
War '07

Takaaki Ishibashi (1961-)
Major League 2 '94
Major League 3: Back to the Minors '98
Sukiyaki Western Django '08

Yuma Ishigaki
Azumi '03
Azumi 2 '05

Akira Ishihama (1935-)
The Human Condition: No Greater Love '58
Harakiri '62

Yuya Ishikawa
RoboGeisha '06
The Machine Girl '07

Kenjiro Ishimaru
Ringu 2 '99
Onmyoji '01

Dale Ishimoto (1923-2004)
King Rat '65
Beach Red '67
Midway '76

Jason Issacs
Skeletons '10
Harry Potter and the Deathly Hallows, Part 2 '11

Ravil Isyanov (1962-)
Doomsdayer '00
Octopus '00

K-19: The Widowmaker *'02*
The Good German *'06*

Juzo Itami (1933-97)
Lady Snowblood: Love Song of Vengeance *'74*
The Family Game *'83*
The Makioka Sisters *'83*

Itsuji Itao
Big Man Japan *'07*
Negative Happy Chainsaw Edge *'08*

Ayumi Ito
All About Lily Chou-Chou *'01*
Tokyo! *'09*

Emi Ito (1941-2012)
Mothra *'62*
Godzilla *vs.* Mothra *'64*
Ghidrah the Three Headed Monster *'65*

Hideaki Ito (1975-)
Onmyoji *'01*
The Princess Blade *'02*
Onmyoji 2 *'03*
Sukiyaki Western Django *'08*

Hisaya Ito (1938-)
Ghidrah the Three Headed Monster *'65*
Destroy All Monsters *'68*

Robert Ito (1931-)
Midway *'76*
The Adventures of Buckaroo Banzai Across the Eighth Dimension *'84*
Pray for Death *'85*
Once a Thief *'96*
The Omega Code *'99*

Yumi Ito (1941-)
Mothra *'62*
Godzilla *vs.* Mothra *'64*
Ghidrah the Three Headed Monster *'65*

Yunosuke Ito (1919-80)
Ikiru *'52*
The Burmese Harp *'56*
Shinobi no Mono *'62*

Jose Iturbi (1895-1980)
Music For Millions *'44*
Two Girls and a Sailor *'44*
Anchors Aweigh *'45*
Holiday in Mexico *'46*
Three Daring Daughters *'48*
That Midnight Kiss *'49*

Gregory Itzin (1948-)
Evolution *'01*
Original Sin *'01*
Life or Something Like It *'02*
DC 9/11: Time of Crisis *'04*
Forfeit *'07*
I Know Who Killed Me *'07*
Float *'08*
The Job *'09*
Lincoln *'12*

Marcel Iures (1951-)
The Peacemaker *'97*
Amen *'02*
Hart's War *'02*
The Cave *'05*
Goal! The Dream Begins *'06*

Rosalind Ivan (1880-1959)
Dead Man's Eyes *'44*
The Corn Is Green *'45*
Pursuit to Algiers *'45*
Three Strangers *'46*
The Most Wonderful Time of the Year *'08*

Zeljko Ivanek (1957-)
The Sender *'82*
Mass Appeal *'84*
Our Sons *'91*
School Ties *'92*
My Brother's Keeper *'95*
Truman *'95*
Courage Under Fire *'96*
Donnie Brasco *'96*
Infinity *'96*
White Squall *'96*
Ellen Foster *'97*
Julian Po *'97*
A Civil Action *'98*
From the Earth to the Moon *'98*
The Rat Pack *'98*
Dancer in the Dark *'99*
Homicide: The Movie *'00*
Black Hawk Down *'01*
Hannibal *'01*
Unfaithful *'02*
Dogville *'03*
The Manchurian Candidate *'04*
The Reagans *'04*
Manderlay *'05*
John Adams *'08*
Seven Psychopaths *'12*

Mark Ivanir (1968-)
Schindler's List *'93*
The Cutter *'05*
The Good Shepherd *'06*
Holy Rollers *'10*
A Late Quartet *'12*

Vlad Ivanov
4 Months, 3 Weeks and 2 Days *'07*
Police, Adjective *'09*
Graduation *'17*
Sunset *'18*

Stan Ivar
Creature *'85*
High Stakes *'93*

Terri Ivens (1967-)
Trancers 4: Jack of Swords *'93*
Trancers 5: Sudden Deth *'94*

Robert Ivers (1934-2003)
The Delicate Delinquent *'56*
G.I. Blues *'60*

Burl Ives (1909-95)
So Dear to My Heart *'49*
Sierra *'50*
East of Eden *'54*
The Power and the Prize *'56*
The Big Country *'58*
Cat on a Hot Tin Roof *'58*
Desire Under the Elms *'58*
The Day of the Outlaw *'59*
Our Man in Havana *'59*
The Brass Bottle *'63*
Summer Magic *'63*
Ensign Pulver *'64*
Those Fantastic Flying Fools *'67*
The McMasters *'70*
Baker's Hawk *'76*
Roots *'77*
The Bermuda Depths *'78*
White Dog *'82*
The Ewok Adventure *'84 (N)*
Poor Little Rich Girl: The Barbara Hutton Story *'87*
Two Moon Junction *'88*

Dana Ivey (1941-)
Explorers *'85*
Dirty Rotten Scoundrels *'88*
Postcards from the Edge *'90*
The Addams Family *'91*
Home Alone 2: Lost in New York *'92*
Addams Family Values *'93*
The Adventures of Huck Finn *'93*
Guilty as Sin *'93*
Sabrina *'95*
The Scarlet Letter *'95*
The Imposters *'98*
Simon Birch *'98*
Mumford *'99*
Disney's The Kid *'00*
Orange County *'02*
Two Weeks Notice *'02*
Legally Blonde 2: Red White & Blonde *'03*
A Very Serious Person *'06*
Rush Hour 3 *'07*
Ghost Town *'08*
The Help *'11*

Judith Ivey (1951-)
Harry & Son *'84*
The Lonely Guy *'84*
The Woman in Red *'84*
Dixie: Changing Habits *'85*
Brighton Beach Memoirs *'86*
The Long, Hot Summer *'86*
Hello Again *'87*
Sister, Sister *'87*
In Country *'89*
Decoration Day *'90*
Everybody Wins *'90*
Love Hurts *'91*
There Goes the Neighborhood *'92*
The Devil's Advocate *'97*
A Life Less Ordinary *'97*
Washington Square *'97*
Without Limits *'97*
What the Deaf Man Heard *'98*
Mystery, Alaska *'99*
Stephen King's Rose Red *'02*
Flags of Our Fathers *'06*
Pictures of Hollis Woods *'07*
Big Stone Gap *'15*

Moshe Ivgi (1953-)
Cup Final *'92*
Munich *'05*

Dana Ivgy (1982-)
Disengagement *'07*
The Secrets *'07*

Tommy 'T.V.' Ivo (1936-)
The Lost Volcano *'50*
Operation Haylift *'50*
Belles on Their Toes *'52*

Bob Ivy
Phantasm 4: Oblivion *'98*
Bubba Ho-Tep *'03*

Ryo Iwamatsu
Samurai Fiction *'99*
Zebraman *'04*

Shima Iwashita (1941-)
An Autumn Afternoon *'62*
Harakiri *'62*
Sword of the Beast *'65*
Double Suicide *'69*
Red Lion *'69*

Victor Izay (1923-)
The Astro-Zombies *'67*
Billy Jack *'71*
Blood Orgy of the She-Devils *'74*
The Trial of Billy Jack *'74*

Eddie Izzard (1962-)
The Avengers *'98*
Velvet Goldmine *'98*
Mystery Men *'99*
Circus *'00*
The Criminal *'00*
Shadow of the Vampire *'00*
The Cat's Meow *'01*
All the Queen's Men *'02*
Ocean's Twelve *'04*
Romance & Cigarettes *'05*
My Super Ex-Girlfriend *'06*
The Wild *'06 (V)*
Ocean's Thirteen *'07*
The Chronicles of Narnia: Prince Caspian *'08 (V)*
Igor *'08 (V)*
Valkyrie *'08*
Every Day *'10*
Cars 2 *'11 (V)*
Treasure Island *'12*
Rock Dog *'17*
Victoria & Abdul *'17*
Abominable *'19*

Lorenza Izzo
Aftershock *'12*
The Green Inferno *'14*
Sex Ed *'14*
Knock Knock *'15*
The Stranger *'15*
Holidays *'16*

Ja Rule (1976-)
Turn It Up *'00*
The Fast and the Furious *'01*
Half Past Dead *'02*
Scary Movie 3 *'03 (C)*
The Cookout *'04*
Assault on Precinct 13 *'05*
Back in the Day *'05*
Wrong Side of Town *'10*

Tony Jaa (1976-)
Ong-Bak *'03*
Ong Bak 2 *'08*
xXx: Return of Xander Cage *'17*
Triple Threat *'19*

Jay Jablonski
Conspiracy *'08*
Everybody Wants to Be Italian *'08*

Michael Jace (1962-)
Forrest Gump *'94*
Strange Days *'95*
The Fan *'96*
The Great White Hype *'96*
Bombshell *'97*
Boogie Nights *'97*
Thick as Thieves *'99*
Planet of the Apes *'01*
Cradle 2 the Grave *'03*
Bats: Human Harvest *'07*

Jackee (1956-)
The Reluctant Agent *'89*
The Women of Brewster Place *'89*
Ladybugs *'92*
You Got Served *'04*
The Last Days of Summer *'07*
Christmas Cupid *'10*

Ian Jacklin
Kickboxer 3: The Art of War *'92*
Expert Weapon *'93*
American Streetfighter *'96*
Capital Punishment *'96*
Warrior of Justice *'96*

Hugh Jackman (1968-)
Oklahoma! *'99*
X-Men *'00*
Kate & Leopold *'01*
Someone Like You *'01*
Swordfish *'01*
X2: X-Men United *'03*
Van Helsing *'04*
Flushed Away *'06 (V)*
The Fountain *'06*
Happy Feet *'06 (V)*
The Prestige *'06*
Scoop *'06*
X-Men: The Last Stand *'06*
Australia *'08*
Deception *'08*
X-Men Origins: Wolverine *'09*
Real Steel *'11*
Butter *'12*
Les Miserables *'12*
Rise of the Guardians *'12 (V)*
Movie 43 *'13*
Prisoners *'13*
The Wolverine *'13*
X-Men: Days of Future Past *'14*
Chappie *'15*
Pan *'15*
Eddie the Eagle *'16*
The Greatest Showman *'17*
Logan *'17*
The Front Runner *'18*
Missing Link *'19*

Andrew Jackson (1962-)
Family of Cops 2: Breach of Faith *'97*
Specimen *'97*
Bram Stoker's Shadowbuilder *'98*
The Last Don 2 *'98*
Scared Silent *'02*
We'll Meet Again *'02*
Category 6: Day of Destruction *'04*
Merlin's Apprentice *'06*
Seed *'08*

Anne Jackson (1926-)
The Journey *'59*
Tall Story *'60*
The Angel Levine *'70*
Lovers and Other Strangers *'70*
ZigZag *'70*
Nasty Habits *'77*
The Bell Jar *'79*
The Shining *'80*
Leave 'Em Laughing *'81*
A Woman Called Golda *'82*
Funny About Love *'90*
Folks! *'92*
Lucky Days *'08*

Armani Jackson
Cooties *'14*
Christmas All Over Again *'16*

Blair Jackson
Varsity Blood *'14*
Tower *'16*

Bo Jackson (1962-)
The Chamber *'96*
Imagine Me & You *'06*

Brandon T. Jackson (1984-)
April Love *'57*
Tropic Thunder *'08*
The Lottery Ticket *'10*
Operation: Endgame *'10*
Big Mommas: Like Father, Like Son *'11*
Thunderstruck *'12*
Percy Jackson: Sea of Monsters *'13*
Love by the 10th Date *'17*

Cheyenne Jackson (1975-)
United 93 *'06*
The Green *'11*
Behind the Candelabra *'13*
Love Is Strange *'14*
The One I Wrote For You *'14*

Curtis Jackson (1975-)
See 50 Cent

Dan Jackson
Odongo *'56*
Mysterious Island *'61*

Freda Jackson (1909-90)
Henry V *'44*
Great Expectations *'46*
Twilight Women *'52*
Bhowani Junction *'56*
The Brides of Dracula *'60*
Die, Monster, Die! *'65*
The Valley of Gwangi *'69*

Glenda Jackson (1936-)
Women in Love *'70*
Mary, Queen of Scots *'71*
Sunday, Bloody Sunday *'71*
Elizabeth R *'72*
A Touch of Class *'73*
Romantic Englishwoman *'75*
Nasty Habits *'77*
House Calls *'78*
Lost and Found *'79*
Hopscotch *'80*
Return of the Soldier *'82*
Beyond Therapy *'86*
Salome's Last Dance *'88*
The Rainbow *'89*
A Murder of Quality *'90*
King of the Wind *'93*

Gordon Jackson (1923-90)
Against the Wind *'48*
Whiskey Galore *'48*
Yesterday's Enemy *'59*
Trouble in the Sky *'60*
The Great Escape *'63*
The Ipcress File *'65*
Those Magnificent Men in Their Flying Machines *'65*
The Fighting Prince of Donegal *'66*
The Prime of Miss Jean Brodie *'69*
The Whistle Blower *'87*
Noble House *'88*

Howard Jackson (1900-66)
Dolemite 2: Human Tornado *'76*
Full Contact *'93*
Out for Blood *'93*

Janet Jackson (1966-)
Poetic Justice *'93*
Nutty Professor 2: The Klumps *'00*
Tyler Perry's Why Did I Get Married? *'07*
For Colored Girls *'10*
Tyler Perry's Why Did I Get Married Too *'10*

Jenie Jackson (1921-76)
Ride the High Country *'62*
How Sweet It Is! *'68*

John M. Jackson (1950-)
The Hitcher *'86*
Eve of Destruction *'90*
A Family of Spies *'90*
Sudie & Simpson *'90*
Career Opportunities *'91*
Black Widow Murders: The Blanche Taylor Moore Story *'93*
Roswell: The U.F.O. Cover-Up *'94*
The Spitfire Grill *'95*
The Invasion *'07*

Jonathan Jackson (1982-)
Camp Nowhere *'94*
Double Play *'96*
The Deep End of the Ocean *'98*
On the Edge *'00*
Skeletons in the Closet *'00*
Insomnia *'02*
Tuck Everlasting *'02*
Dirty Dancing: Havana Nights *'04*
Riding the Bullet *'04*
A Little Thing Called Murder *'06*
Kalamity *'10*

Joshua Jackson (1978-)
The Mighty Ducks *'92*
Andre *'94*
Magic in the Water *'95*
Robin of Locksley *'95*
D3: The Mighty Ducks *'96*
Apt Pupil *'97*
Ronnie and Julie *'97*
Cruel Intentions *'98*
Urban Legend *'98*
Gossip *'99*
The Skulls *'00*
Ocean's Eleven *'01 (C)*
The Safety of Objects *'01*
Lone Star State of Mind *'02*
I Love Your Work *'03*
Cursed *'04*
Americano *'05*
Racing Stripes *'05 (V)*
Venom *'05*
Aurora Borealis *'06*
Bobby *'06*
Battle in Seattle *'07*
One Week *'08*
Shutter *'08*
Lay the Favorite *'12*

Kate Jackson (1948-)
Night of Dark Shadows *'71*
Satan's School for Girls *'73*
Death at Love House *'75*
Thunder and Lightning *'77*
Making Love *'82*
Loverboy *'89*
Panic in the Skies *'96*
Miracle Dogs *'03*
A Daughter's Conviction *'06*

Leonard Jackson (1928-)
Ganja and Hess *'73*
Basket Case 2 *'90*

Mark 'Jacko' Jackson
Outback *'71*
Bullet Down Under *'94*

Mary Jackson (1910-2005)
Targets *'68*
Terror at Red Wolf Inn *'72*
Skinned Alive *'89*
A Family Thing *'96*

Mel Jackson (1970-)
Soul Food *'97*
Uninvited Guest *'99*
Little Richard *'00*
Deliver Us from Eva *'03*
Motives *'03*

Michael Jackson (1958-2009)
The Wiz *'78*
Men in Black 2 *'02 (C)*
Michael Jackson's This Is It *'09*

Neil Jackson (1976-)
Alexander *'04*
The Thirst *'06*
Push *'09*
Upstairs Downstairs *'11*

O'Shea Jackson, Jr. (1991-)
Straight Outta Compton '15
Ingrid Goes West '17
Den of Thieves '18
Just Mercy '19
Long Shot '19

Peter Jackson (1961-)
Bad Taste '88
Dead Alive '93
Hot Fuzz '07

Philip Jackson (1948-)
High Hopes '88
Bad Behavior '92
Brassed Off '96
Little Voice '98
The Intended '02
A Little Trip to Heaven '05
Fanny Hill '07
I Want Candy '07
Place of Execution '09

Quinton 'Rampage' Jackson (1978-)
Confessions of a Pit Fighter '05
Bad Guys '08
The A-Team '10
Vigilante Diaries '16

Reggie Jackson (1946-)
The Naked Gun: From the Files of Police Squad '88 (C)
Richie Rich '94 (C)
BASEketball '98
The Benchwarmers '06 (C)

Richard Lee Jackson (1979-)
Double Play '96
Madison '01
Hope Ranch '02
Bring It On Again '03
Love's Long Journey '05
Avenging Angel '07

Sammy Jackson (1937-95)
None But the Brave '65
Fastest Guitar Alive '68

Samuel L. Jackson (1948-)
Ragtime '81
Coming to America '88
School Daze '88
Betsy's Wedding '90
Def by Temptation '90
Goodfellas '90
Mo' Better Blues '90
Jungle Fever '91
Johnny Suede '92
Juice '92
Jumpin' at the Boneyard '92
Patriot Games '92
White Sands '92
Amos and Andrew '93
Jurassic Park '93
Menace II Society '93
National Lampoon's Loaded Weapon 1 '93
True Romance '93
Against the Wall '94
Fresh '94
Hail Caesar '94
Kiss of Death '94
Losing Isaiah '94
The New Age '94
Pulp Fiction '94
The Search for One-Eye Jimmy '94
Die Hard: With a Vengeance '95
Fluke '95 (V)
The Great White Hype '96
Hard Eight '96
The Long Kiss Goodnight '96
A Time to Kill '96
Tree's Lounge '96
Eve's Bayou '97
Jackie Brown '97
187 '97
Sphere '97
The Negotiator '98
Out of Sight '98 (C)
The Red Violin '98
Deep Blue Sea '99
Star Wars: Episode 1-The Phantom Menace '99
Rules of Engagement '00
Shaft '00
Unbreakable '00
The Caveman's Valentine '01
Formula 51 '01
Changing Lanes '02
No Good Deed '02
Star Wars: Episode 2-Attack of the Clones '02
XXX '02
Basic '03
S.W.A.T. '03
In My Country '04
The Incredibles '04 (V)
Kill Bill Vol. 2 '04
Twisted '04
Coach Carter '05
The Man '05
Star Wars: Episode 3-Revenge of the Sith '05
XXX: State of the Union '05
Freedomland '06
Home of the Brave '06
Snakes on a Plane '06
Black Snake Moan '07
Cleaner '07
1408 '07
Resurrecting the Champ '07
Gospel Hill '08
Iron Man '08
Jumper '08
Lakeview Terrace '08
Soul Men '08
The Spirit '08
Star Wars: The Clone Wars '08 (V)
Astro Boy '09 (V)
Inglourious Basterds '09 (N)
Mother and Child '09
Iron Man 2 '10
The Other Guys '10
Unthinkable '10
Arena '11
Captain America: The First Avenger '11
The Sunset Limited '11
Adventures in Zambezia '12
The Avengers '12
Django Unchained '12
The Good Samaritan '12
Meeting Evil '12
Oldboy '13
Turbo '13 (V)
Captain America: The Winter Soldier '14
Reasonable Doubt '14
RoboCop '14
Barely Lethal '15
Big Game '15
Chi-raq '15
The Hateful Eight '15
Kingsman: The Secret Service '15
Cell '16
The Legend of Tarzan '16
Miss Peregrine's Home for Peculiar Children '16
I Am Not Your Negro '17
Kong: Skull Island '17
Captain Marvel '19
Glass '19
The Last Full Measure '19
Shaft '19
Spider-Man: Far from Home '19
The Banker '20

Sasha Jackson
Night Junkies '07
Blue Crush 2 '11
Attack of the 50 Foot Cheerleader '12

Selmer Jackson (1888-1971)
Alibi Ike '35
Gangster's Boy '38
Brigham Young: Frontiersman '40
Johnny Apollo '40
Gangs, Inc. '41
Sergeant York '41
They Died with Their Boots On '41
The Fighting Sullivans '42
Guadalcanal Diary '43
We're Not Married '52
Mark of the Gorilla '58
The Gallant Hours '60

Sherry Jackson (1942-)
Miracle of Our Lady of Fatima '52
Trouble along the Way '53
The Adventures of Huckleberry Finn '60
Wild On the Beach '65
Cotter '72
Bare Knuckles '77
Stingray '78
Daughters of the Dust '91

Stoney Jackson (1960-)
Roller Boogie '79
Streets of Fire '84
Sweet Perfection '90
Lone Tiger '94
Black Scorpion 2: Ground Zero '96
Carnival of Wolves '96
Trippin' '99

Tom Jackson (1948-)
Spirit Rider '93
Grizzly Falls '99
Skinwalkers '07

Trevor Jackson (1996-)
Let It Shine '12
Burning Sands '17
SuperFly '18

Victoria Jackson (1959-)
Baby Boom '87
The Pick-Up Artist '87
Casual Sex? '88
Dream a Little Dream '89
Family Business '89
UHF '89
I Love You to Death '90
Wedding Bell Blues '96
Shut Up and Kiss Me '05
Midnight Clear '06
Soccer Mom '08

Oliver Jackson-Cohen (1986-)
Faster '10
What's Your Number? '11
The Raven '12
The Invisible Man '20

Irene Jacob (1966-)
Au Revoir les Enfants '87
The Double Life of Veronique '91
Trois Couleurs: Rouge '94
Beyond the Clouds '95
Othello '95
Victory '95
Incognito '97
My Life So Far '98
U.S. Marshals '98
The Big Brass Ring '99
Spy Games '99
Rio Sex Comedy '10
Dying of the Light '14

Derek Jacobi (1938-)
Othello '65
The Day of the Jackal '73
The Strauss Family '73
The Odessa File '74
The Medusa Touch '78
The Human Factor '79
Enigma '82
The Hunchback of Notre Dame '82
The Secret of NIMH '82 (V)
Philby, Burgess and MacLean: Spy Scandal of the Century '84
The Secret Garden '87
The Tenth Man '88
Henry V '89
Dead Again '91
Circle of Deceit '94
Hamlet '96
Basil '98
Love Is the Devil '98
Molokai: The Story of Father Damien '99
Gladiator '00
Jason and the Argonauts '00
Up at the Villa '00
The Wyvern Mystery '00
The Body '01
The Gathering Storm '02
Two Men Went to War '02
Underworld: Evolution '05
Nanny McPhee '06
Pinochet's Last Stand '06
The Golden Compass '07
Guantanamero '07
The Old Curiosity Shop '07
The Riddle '07
Adam Resurrected '08
Endgame '09
Margot '09
Joe Maddison's War '10
The King's Speech '10
Ironclad '11
My Week With Marilyn '11
There Be Dragons '11
Cinderella '15

Ernst Jacobi (1933-)
Germany, Pale Mother '80
Hamsun '96
The White Ribbon '09 (N)

Lou Jacobi (1913-2009)
A Kid for Two Farthings '55
The Diary of Anne Frank '59
Song Without End '60
Cotton Comes to Harlem '70
Little Murders '71
Everything You Always Wanted to Know about Sex (But Were Afraid to Ask) '72
Next Stop, Greenwich Village '76
Roseland '77
Arthur '81
My Favorite Year '82
The Boss' Wife '86
Amazon Women on the Moon '87
Avalon '90
I Don't Buy Kisses Anymore '92
I.Q. '94

Barlow Jacobs
Shotgun Stories '07
Alexander the Last '09
Dead Man's Burden '12

Danny A. Jacobs (1979-)
The Cavern '05
Bachelor Party 2: The Last Temptation '08

Gillian Jacobs (1982-)
Choke '08
Gardens of the Night '08
The Box '09
Coach '10
NoNames '10
Let Go '11
Black or White '14
Life Partners '14
The Lookalike '14
Walk of Shame '14
Hot Tub Time Machine 2 '15
Don't Think Twice '16
Visions '16
Dean '17
Life of the Party '18

Jon Jacobs (1966-)
Hard Luck '01
Welcome Says the Angel '01

Lawrence-Hilton Jacobs (1953-)
Cooley High '75
For the Love of It '80
L.A. Heat '88
Angels of the City '89
Chance '89
East L.A. Warriors '89
L.A. Vice '89
Quiet Fire '91
The Jacksons: An American Dream '92
Sublime '07
Airplane vs. Volcano '14
Playin' For Love '15

Colombe Jacobsen (1979-)
D3: The Mighty Ducks '96
Men in Black 2 '02

Finley Jacobsen
Marmaduke '10
Olympus Has Fallen '13

Eric Jacobson (1970-)
The Muppets' Wizard of Oz '05 (V)
The Muppets '11 (V)
Muppets Most Wanted '14 (V)

Peter Jacobson (1965-)
It Could Happen to You '94
A Civil Action '98
The Cradle Will Rock '99
Hit and Runway '01
61* '01
Pipe Dream '02
Domino '05
Good Night, and Good Luck '05
Failure to Launch '06
The Starter Wife '07
Transformers '07
And They're Off '11
Brightest Star '14

Shane Jacobson
Newcastle '08
The Mystery of a Hansom Cab '12

Ulla Jacobsson (1929-82)
Smiles of a Summer Night '55
Love Is a Ball '63
Zulu '64
The Heroes of Telemark '65
Fox and His Friends '75

Billy Jacoby (1969-)
Bloody Birthday '80
Beastmaster '82
Cujo '83
Just One of the Guys '85
Dr. Alien '88

Bobby Jacoby (1973-)
Iron Eagle '86
Tremors '89
The Day My Parents Ran Away '93
Night of the Demons 2 '94
Fear Runs Silent '99

Dale Jacoby (1961-)
Ring of Fire '91
Ring of Fire 2: Blood and Steel '92
Guardian Angel '94

Scott Jacoby (1956-)
Rivals '72
Bad Ronald '74
The Little Girl Who Lives down the Lane '76
Return to Horror High '87
To Die For '89

Christopher Jacot (1979-)
Merlin's Apprentice '06
Boot Camp '07
7 Things to Do Before I'm 30 '08
Come Dance at My Wedding '09

Carlos Jacott (1967-)
Kicking and Screaming '95
Mr. Jealousy '98
Bats '99
Fun With Dick and Jane '05
Jiminy Glick in LaLa Wood '05

Hattie Jacques (1924-80)
A Christmas Carol '51
Carry On Sergeant '58
The Square Peg '58
Carry On Nurse '59
Carry On Constable '60
Make Mine Mink '60
Carry On Cabby '63
Carry On Again Doctor '69
Carry On Loving '70
Carry On at Your Convenience '71
Carry On Abroad '72
Carry On Matron '72

Yves Jacques (1956-)
The Barbarian Invasions '03
La Petite Lili '03
Napoleon '03

Claude Jade (1948-2006)
Stolen Kisses '68
Bed and Board '70
Love on the Run '78

Scott Jaeck (1954-)
JAG '95
Killing Mr. Griffin '97
Washington Square '97

Richard Jaeckel (1926-97)
Guadalcanal Diary '43
A Wing and a Prayer '44
Jungle Patrol '48
Battleground '49
Sands of Iwo Jima '49
Come Back, Little Sheba '52
Hoodlum Empire '52
My Son John '52
Big Leaguer '53
Attack! '56
3:10 to Yuma '57
Cowboy '58
The Gun Runners '58
The Lineup '58
When Hell Broke Loose '58
Flaming Star '60
The Gallant Hours '60
Town without Pity '61
Once Before I Die '65
The Dirty Dozen '67
The Devil's Brigade '68
The Green Slime '68
Latitude Zero '69
Chisum '70
Sometimes a Great Notion '71
Firehouse '72
Ulzana's Raid '72
The Outfit '73
Pat Garrett & Billy the Kid '73
Born Innocent '74
The Drowning Pool '75
Walking Tall: Part 2 '75
Grizzly '76
Jaws of Death '76
Day of the Animals '77
Champions: A Love Story '78
The Dark '79
Herbie Goes Bananas '80
. . .All the Marbles '81
Cold River '81
Airplane 2: The Sequel '82
Blood Song '82
Starman '84
The Dirty Dozen: The Next Mission '85
Pacific Inferno '85
Black Moon Rising '86
Delta Force 2: Operation Stranglehold '90
Martial Outlaw '93

Frederick Jaeger (1928-2004)
Nijinsky '80
The Body in the Library '84

Sam Jaeger (1977-)
The Riverman '04
Catch and Release '07
Take Me Home '11

Oscar Jaenada
The Losers '10
The Cold Light of Day '12
The Shallows '16

Hannes Jaenicke (1960-)
Catherine the Great '95
The Heist '96
Active Stealth '99
Bandits '99
Nautilus '99
Restraining Order '99
Black Horizon '01
Extreme Limits '01
Mom's Outta Sight '01
Venomous '01
Lost Treasure '03

Sam Jaffe (1891-1984)
Scarlet Empress '34
We Live Again '34
Lost Horizon '37
Gunga Din '39
13 Rue Madeleine '46
Rope of Sand '49
The Asphalt Jungle '50
The Day the Earth Stood Still '51
I Can Get It For You Wholesale '51
Barbarian and the Geisha '58
Ben-Hur '59
A Guide for the Married Man '67 (C)
Night Gallery '69

The Dunwich Horror '70
Bedknobs and Broomsticks '71
Battle Beyond the Stars '80
Gideon's Trumpet '80

Madhur Jaffrey (1933-)
Shakespeare Wallah '65
Heat and Dust '82
Vanya on 42nd Street '94
ABCD '99
Chutney Popcorn '99
Cotton Mary '99
Partition '07
Today's Special '09

Raza Jaffrey (1975-)
The Crew '08
Cliffs of Freedom '19

Saeed Jaffrey (1929-)
The Man Who Would Be King '75
The Wilby Conspiracy '75
Hullabaloo over Georgie & Bonnie's Pictures '78
Gandhi '82
The Razor's Edge '84
The Courtesans of Bombay '85
My Beautiful Laundrette '85
The Deceivers '88
Masala '91
Chicken Tikka Masala '05

Sakina Jaffrey (1962-)
Masala '91
Chutney Popcorn '99
Cotton Mary '99
Revolution #9 '01
Raising Helen '04

Dean Jagger (1903-91)
Wings in the Dark '35
Revolt of the Zombies '36
Exiled to Shanghai '37
Brigham Young: Frontiersman '40
Western Union '41
I Escaped from the Gestapo '43
The North Star '43
Betrayed '44
I Live in Grosvenor Square '46
Pursued '47
The C-Man '49
Twelve o'Clock High '49
Dark City '50
Rawhide '50
Sierra '50
Denver and the Rio Grande '52
My Son John '52
The Robe '53
Bad Day at Black Rock '54
Executive Suite '54
Private Hell 36 '54
White Christmas '54
It's a Dog's Life '55
X The Unknown '56
Forty Guns '57
Three Brave Men '57
King Creole '58
Proud Rebel '58
The Nun's Story '59
Cash McCall '60
Elmer Gantry '60
The Honeymoon Machine '61
Parrish '61
Billy Rose's Jumbo '62
First to Fight '67
Day of the Evil Gun '68
Firecreek '68
The Kremlin Letter '70
Vanishing Point '71
The Delphi Bureau: The Merchant of Death Assignment '72
The Glass House '72
The Hanged Man '74
Hootch Country Boys '75
Visions of Evil '75
End of the World '76
The Lindbergh Kidnapping Case '76
Game of Death '79
Alligator '80
Gideon's Trumpet '80

Mick Jagger (1943-)
Gimme Shelter '70
Ned Kelly '70
Performance '70
Sympathy for the Devil '70
All You Need Is Cash '78
Burden of Dreams '82
Freejack '92
Bent '97
The Man from Elysian Fields '01
The Burnt Orange Heresy '20

Henry Jaglom (1938-)
Psych-Out '68
Sitting Ducks '80
Always '85
Someone to Love '87
New Year's Day '89
Venice, Venice '92
Last Summer In the Hamptons '96

Lisa Jakub (1978-)
Rambling Rose '91
Matinee '92
Mrs. Doubtfire '93
The Story Lady '93
The Beautician and the Beast '97
The Wicked, Wicked West '97

Adam James
Lost Battalion '01
Murder on the Orient Express '01
Mother of Tears '08
Johnny English Strikes Again '18

Anthony James (1942-2020)
Columbo: Prescription Murder '67
Sam Whiskey '69
The Teacher '74
Unforgiven '92

Austin James (1980-)
Fall Down Dead '07
The Ultimate Life '13

Brenda James
Dodson's Journey '01
The Incredible Mrs. Ritchie '03
Slither '06

Brion James (1945-99)
Blue Sunshine '78
KISS Meets the Phantom of the Park '78
Southern Comfort '81
Blade Runner '82
48 Hrs. '82
Enemy Mine '85
Flesh and Blood '85
Armed and Dangerous '86
Love Among Thieves '86
Nightmare at Noon '87
Steel Dawn '87
The Horror Show '89
Mom '89
Red Scorpion '89
Tango and Cash '89
Another 48 Hrs. '90
The Player '92
Time Runner '92
Future Shock '93
Rio Diablo '93
Striking Distance '93
Cabin Boy '94
The Last Ride '94
Nature of the Beast '94
Radioland Murders '94
Savage Land '94
The Soft Kill '94
Steel Frontier '94
Virtual Assassin '95
American Strays '96
Back in Business '96
The Killing Jar '96
Bombshell '97
The Fifth Element '97
Hunter's Moon '97
Pterodactyl Woman from Beverly Hills '97
Brown's Requiem '98
In God's Hands '98
Arthur's Quest '99

The King Is Alive '00
The Operator '01

Clifton James (1921-)
The Strange One '57
Something Wild '61
David and Lisa '62
Black Like Me '64
Cool Hand Luke '67
Will Penny '67
The Iceman Cometh '73
The Last Detail '73
Live and Let Die '73
Werewolf of Washington '73
Bank Shot '74
The Man with the Golden Gun '74
Rancho Deluxe '75
Sniper '75
The Bad News Bears in Breaking Training '77
Undercover With the KKK '78
Where Are the Children? '85
Eight Men Out '88
The Bonfire of the Vanities '90
Carolina Skeletons '92
Lone Star '95
Raising Flagg '06

Colton James (1988-)
A Memory In My Heart '99
The Cell '00
The Derby Stallion '05
National Lampoon Presents: Endless Bummer '09

Dalton James (1971-)
My Father the Hero '93
The Substitute '93

Etta James (1938-2012)
Chuck Berry: Hail! Hail! Rock 'n' Roll '87
Tap '89

Gennie James (1977-)
Broadcast News '87
The Secret Garden '87

Gerald James (1917-2006)
Hope and Glory '87
Tess of the D'Urbervilles '98

Geraldine James (1950-)
Gandhi '82
I Remember Nelson '82
The Jewel in the Crown '84
Echoes '88
The Tall Guy '89
If Looks Could Kill '91
Band of Gold '95
Moll Flanders '96
The Man Who Knew Too Little '97
Rebecca '97
Lover's Prayer '99
The Luzhin Defence '00
The Hound of the Baskervilles '02
Tom & Thomas '02
Calendar Girls '03
The Fever '04
He Knew He Was Right '04
A Harlot's Progress '06
Northanger Abbey '07 (N)
The Last Enemy '08
Sherlock Holmes '09
Made in Dagenham '10
Arthur '11
The Girl With the Dragon Tattoo '11
Sherlock Holmes: A Game of Shadows '11
Diana '13
45 Years '15
Beast '17

Godfrey James (1931-)
The Land That Time Forgot '75
At the Earth's Core '76

Harry James (1916-83)
Private Buckaroo '42
Best Foot Forward '43
Two Girls and a Sailor '44
Do You Love Me? '46
If I'm Lucky '46
The Benny Goodman Story '55

Hawthorne James
The Five Heartbeats '91
Speed '94
Heaven's Prisoners '95
Campfire Tales '98

Jesse James (1989-)
The Gingerbread Man '97
Message in a Bottle '98
A Dog of Flanders '99
Hanging Up '99
Blow '01
Fear of the Dark '02
Slap Her, She's French '02
The Butterfly Effect '04
The Amityville Horror '05
The Last Ride '12

Jessica James (1929-90)
Diner '82
I, the Jury '82
Immediate Family '89

John James (1914-60)
The Devil Bat's Daughter '46
Son of Billy the Kid '49

John James (1956-)
Secret Passions '87
Lightning: Fire from the Sky '00
Peril '00

Ken James (1948-)
Switching Channels '88
Tracked '98
The Third Miracle '99
Torso '02
Verdict in Blood '02

Kevin James (1965-)
Hitch '05
Barnyard '06 (V)
Grilled '06
Monster House '06 (V)
I Now Pronounce You Chuck and Larry '07
Paul Blart: Mall Cop '09
Grown Ups '10
The Dilemma '11
Zookeeper '11
Here Comes the Boom '12
Hotel Transylvania '12 (V)
Grown Ups 2 '13
Hotel Transylvania 2 '15 (V)
Pixels '15
Hotel Transylvania 3: Summer Vacation '18 (V)

Kevin James (1972-)
Control Alt Delete '08
Paul Blart: Mall Cop 2 '15

LeBron James (1984-)
More Than a Game '08
Smallfoot '18

Lennie James (1965-)
Among Giants '98
Lost in Space '98
Snatch '00
Lucky Break '01
24 Hour Party People '01
Sahara '05
The State Within '06
Outlaw '07
The Prisoner '09
Mob Rules '10
The Next Three Days '10
Colombiana '11
Lockout '12
Get On Up '14
Swelter '14

Liam James (1996-)
Horsemen '09
Christmas Comes Home to Canaan '11
The Way Way Back '13

Lily James (1989-)
Cinderella '15
Pride and Prejudice and Zombies '16
Baby Driver '17
Darkest Hour '17
The Exception '17
Yesterday '19

Oliver James (1980-)
What a Girl Wants '03
Raise Your Voice '04

Without a Paddle: Nature's Calling '09
Roadkill '11

Paul James
The St. Francisville Experiment '00
Cry Wolf '05
The Architect '06

Pell James (1977-)
Broken Flowers '05
The King '05
Undiscovered '05
Deceit '06
Surveillance '08
Against the Current '09
Shrink '09

Raji James (1970-)
East Is East '99
Nina's Heavenly Delights '06

Sidney James (1913-76)
The Lavender Hill Mob '51
Bad Blonde '53
The Belles of St. Trinian's '53
Norman Conquest '53
Crest of the Wave '54
Quatermass 2 '57
The Smallest Show on Earth '57
The Silent Enemy '58
Idol on Parade '59
Upstairs and Downstairs '59
Carry On Constable '60
Carry On Regardless '61
Carry On Cruising '62
What a Carve-Up! '62
Carry On Cabby '63
Carry On Cleo '65
Carry On Cowboy '66
Don't Lose Your Head '66
Carry On Up the Khyber '68
Carry On Again Doctor '69
Carry On Loving '70
Carry On Up the Jungle '70
Carry On at Your Convenience '71
Carry On Camping '71
Carry On Henry VIII '71
Carry On Abroad '72
Carry On Matron '72
Carry On Behind '75
Carry On Dick '75

Sonny James (1929-)
Las Vegas Hillbillys '66
Hillbillies in a Haunted House '67

Stephan James (1993-)
Home Again '13
When the Game Stands Tall '14
Race '16
If Beale Street Could Talk '18

Steve James (1955-93)
The Land That Time Forgot '75
The Warriors '79
Exterminator '80
The Brother from Another Planet '84
American Ninja '85
Stalking Danger '86
American Ninja 2: The Confrontation '87
Hero and the Terror '88
I'm Gonna Git You Sucka '88
Johnny Be Good '88
American Ninja 3: Blood Hunt '89
The Player '92
Bloodfist 5: Human Target '93
Weekend at Bernie's 2 '93

Theo James (1984-)
Underworld: Awakening '12
Divergent '14
Insurgent '15
Allegiant '16
The Benefactor '16
Underworld: Blood Wars '16
War on Everyone '17

Backstabbing for Beginners '18
London Fields '18

Tim James
Funnyman '94
Journey to the Center of the Earth '08

Walter James (1882-1946)
The Idol Dancer '20
The Monster '25
Battling Butler '26
The Kid Brother '27

Joyce Jameson (1932-87)
Tales of Terror '62
The Balcony '63
The Comedy of Terrors '64
Good Neighbor Sam '64
Savage Run '70
Pray TV '80
Hardbodies '84

Tadeusz Janczar (1926-97)
Kanal '56
Landscape After Battle '70

Krystyna Janda (1952-)
Man of Marble '76
Man of Iron '81
Mephisto '81
The Decalogue '88

Thomas Jane (1969-)
Buffy the Vampire Slayer '92
The Crow 2: City of Angels '96
The Last Time I Committed Suicide '96
Boogie Nights '97
Hollywood Confidential '97
The Thin Red Line '98
The Velocity of Gary '98
Deep Blue Sea '99
Molly '99
Under Suspicion '00
Original Sin '01
61* '01
The Sweetest Thing '02
Dreamcatcher '03
Stander '03
The Punisher '04
The Tripper '06
The Mist '07
Mutant Chronicles '08
Dark Country '09
Give 'Em Hell Malone '09
Killshot '09
I Melt With You '11
LOL '12
Drive Hard '14
White Bird in a Blizzard '14
Before I Wake '15
Vice '15
Standoff '16
USS Indianapolis: Men of Courage '16
1922 '17
A-X-L '18

Dong-gun Jang (1972-)
The Promise '05
Typhoon '06
Dangerous Liaisons '12

Conrad Janis (1928-)
The Duchess and the Dirtwater Fox '76
The Buddy Holly Story '78
Oh, God! Book 2 '80
Brewster's Millions '85
Mr. Saturday Night '92
The Cable Guy '96

Petr Janis
The Ninth Day '04
Hostel '06

Oleg (Yankovsky) Jankowsky (1944-2009)
The Mirror '75
The Shooting Party '77
Nostalghia '83
Mute Witness '95

Allison Janney (1959-)
Big Night '95
Private Parts '96
First Do No Harm '97
The Ice Storm '97
Julian Po '97
Celebrity '98
The Imposters '98

Richie Jen
Breaking News '04
Exiled '06

George Jenesky
See Conrad Dunn

Richard Jeni (1957-2007)
The Mask '94
An Alan Smithee Film: Burn, Hollywood, Burn '97
National Lampoon's Dad's Week Off '97

Allen Jenkins (1900-74)
Blessed Event '32
I Am a Fugitive from a Chain Gang '32
Lawyer Man '32
Blondie Johnson '33
Bureau of Missing Persons '33
Employees' Entrance '33
The Mayor of Hell '33
The Mind Reader '33
The Case of the Howling Dog '34
Happiness Ahead '34
I've Got Your Number '34
Jimmy the Gent '34
The Merry Frinks '34
Whirlpool '34
The Case of the Curious Bride '35
The Case of the Lucky Legs '35
The Irish in Us '35
Cain and Mabel '36
The Singing Kid '36
Dead End '37
Marked Woman '37
Amazing Dr. Clitterhouse '38
Gold Diggers in Paris '38
Hard to Get '38
A Slight Case of Murder '38
Swing Your Lady '38
Destry Rides Again '39
Brother Orchid '40
Dive Bomber '41
Footsteps in the Dark '41
The Gay Falcon '41
Time Out for Rhythm '41
A Date With the Falcon '42
Eyes in the Night '42
The Falcon Takes Over '42
Maisie Gets Her Man '42
Lady on a Train '45
The Big Wheel '49
Chained for Life '51
Oklahoma Annie '51
The WAC From Walla Walla '52
Robin and the 7 Hoods '64

Burgess Jenkins (1973-)
Remember the Titans '00
Unshackled '00
Fall Down Dead '07
Christmas Cupid '10
Beverly Lewis' The Shunning '11
I Am Potential '15

Carter Jenkins (1991-)
The Bad News Bears '05
Keeping Up with the Steins '06
Aliens in the Attic '09

Daniel H. Jenkins (1963-)
O.C. and Stiggs '87
The Caine Mutiny Court Martial '88
The Cradle Will Rock '99
Infested: Invasion of the Killer Bugs '02

Jackie 'Butch' Jenkins (1937-2001)
The Human Comedy '43
National Velvet '44
Our Vines Have Tender Grapes '45
My Brother Talks to Horses '47
The Bride Goes Wild '48
Summer Holiday '48

Ken Jenkins (1940-)
Matewan '87
Edge of Honor '91
Crossing the Bridge '92
And the Band Played On '93 (C)
White Mile '94
Hiroshima '95
Courage Under Fire '96
Last Man Standing '96
Home Room '02
The Sum of All Fears '02
Welcome to Paradise '07

Larry 'Flash' Jenkins (1955-)
Lookin' to Get Out '82
Fletch '85
Ferris Bueller's Day Off '86
EDtv '99

Megs Jenkins (1917-98)
Trouble in Store '53
The Gay Dog '54
Tiger Bay '59
The Innocents '61
Murder Most Foul '65
Asylum '72

Noam Jenkins
Moving Target '96
The Statement '03
The House Next Door '06
The State Within '06
All Hat '07
Adoration '08

Rebecca Jenkins (1959-)
Cowboys Don't Cry '88
Bob Roberts '92
Angels in the Infield '00
Marion Bridge '02
Whole New Thing '05
Past Sins '06
Bond of Silence '10

Richard Jenkins (1947-)
The Manhattan Project '86
On Valentine's Day '86
The Witches of Eastwick '87
Stealing Home '88
Blaze '89
Sea of Love '89
Descending Angel '90
And the Band Played On '93 (C)
Getting Out '94
It Could Happen to You '94
Trapped in Paradise '94
Wolf '94
A Couch in New York '95
Flirting with Disaster '95
The Indian in the Cupboard '95
The Boys Next Door '96
Eddie '96
Eye of God '97
Into Thin Air: Death on Everest '97
The Imposters '98
There's Something about Mary '98
The Mod Squad '99
Outside Providence '99
Random Hearts '99
Snow Falling on Cedars '99
Me, Myself, and Irene '00
What Planet Are You From? '00
The Man Who Wasn't There '01
One Night at McCool's '01
Say It Isn't So '01
Sins of the Father '01
Changing Lanes '02
Stealing Harvard '02
Cheaper by the Dozen '03
The Core '03
Intolerable Cruelty '03
The Mudge Boy '03
Shall We Dance? '04
Fun With Dick and Jane '05
North Country '05
Rumor Has It. . . '05
The Visitor '07
The Broken '08
Burn After Reading '08
Step Brothers '08
The Tale of Despereaux '08 (V)
Dear John '10
Eat, Pray, Love '10
Let Me In '10
Norman '10
Friends With Benefits '11
Hall Pass '11
The Rum Diary '11
Waiting for Forever '11
The Cabin in the Woods '12
The Company You Keep '12
Darling Companion '12
Jack Reacher '12
Killing Them Softly '12
Liberal Arts '12
A.C.O.D. '13
Turbo '13 (V)
White House Down '13
God's Pocket '14
Lullaby '14
Olive Kitteridge '14
Bone Tomahawk '15
The Hollars '16
The Shape of Water '17

Sam Jenkins (1966-)
Ed and His Dead Mother '93
Twenty Bucks '93
Fortunes of War '94
Storm Rider '13

Frank Jenks (1902-62)
First Love '39
His Girl Friday '40
Back Street '41
The Flame of New Orleans '41
Corregidor '43
His Butler's Sister '44
Strange Affair '44
Zombies on Broadway '44
That Brennan Girl '46
Kilroy Was Here '47
Woman On the Run '50

Si Jenks (1876-1970)
Captain January '36
Kentucky Jubilee '51

Michael Jenn
Another Country '84
Dance with a Stranger '85
Unleashed '05

Blake Jenner (1992-)
The Edge of Seventeen '16
Everybody Wants Some!! '16
American Animals '18

Bruce Jenner (1949-)
Can't Stop the Music '80
Grambling's White Tiger '81
The Big Tease '99

Lucinda Jenney (1954-)
The Whoopee Boys '86
Rain Man '88
Thelma & Louise '91
American Heart '92
Matinee '92
Leaving Las Vegas '95
A Stranger in Town '95
Stephen King's Thinner '96
G.I. Jane '97
Desert Blue '98
Sugar Town '99
Crime and Punishment in Suburbia '00
Thirteen Days '00
crazy/beautiful '01
The Mothman Prophecies '02
S.W.A.T. '03

Alex Jennings (1957-)
A Midsummer Night's Dream '96
The Wings of the Dove '97
The Hunley '99
The Four Feathers '02
The Queen '06
The State Within '06
Cranford '08
The Disappeared '08
Return to Cranford '09
The 39 Steps '09
The Lady Vanishes '13
The Lady in the Van '15

Brent Jennings (1951-)
The Serpent and the Rainbow '87
Nervous Ticks '93
Children of the Corn 4: The Gathering '96
Soul of the Game '96
The Fixer '97
Blue Ridge Fall '99
A Lesson Before Dying '99
Life '99
Love Songs '99
Boycott '02
My Girlfriend's Back '10
Moneyball '11

Bruce Jennings
The Falls: Testament of Love '13
The Falls: Covenant of Grace '16

Byron Jennings
A Simple Twist of Fate '94
The Ice Storm '97
Hamlet '01
Lincoln '12

Claudia Jennings (1949-79)
The Love Machine '71
The Stepmother '71
Unholy Rollers '72
Truck Stop Women '74
The Great Texas Dynamite Chase '76
Sisters of Death '76
Death Sport '78
Fast Company '78

DeWitt Jennings (1879-1937)
The Little American '17
Exit Smiling '26
The Bat Whispers '30
The Big House '30
The Criminal Code '31
The Squaw Man '31
Reform Girl '33

Juanita Jennings
Spirit Lost '96
Runaway Jury '03
The Janky Promoters '09

Waylon Jennings (1937-2002)
The Oklahoma City Dolls '81
Sesame Street Presents: Follow That Bird '85
Stagecoach '86
Maverick '94 (C)
Outlaw Justice '98

Rita Jenrette (1949-)
Zombie Island Massacre '84
End of the Line '88

Salome Jens (1935-)
Angel Baby '61
Seconds '66
Savages '72
Grace Kelly '83
A Killer in the Family '83
I'm Losing You '98
Cats & Dogs '01 (V)

Ashley Jensen (1969-)
Arthur Christmas '11 (V)
Gnomeo & Juliet '11 (V)
Hysteria '11
The Escape Artist '13
Small Time '14
Lady and the Tramp '19

David Jensen (1947-98)
A Midnight Clear '92
The Underneath '95
Schizopolis '97
Warbirds '08

Erik Jensen
Borough of Kings '98
Undermind '03
The Bronx Is Burning '07
Virtuality '09

Maren Jensen (1956-)
Battlestar Galactica '78
Deadly Blessing '81

Sarah Jayne Jensen
Center Stage: Turn It Up '08
Magic Man '10

Todd Jensen
Never Say Die '94
Alien Chaser '96
Breeders '97
Operation Delta Force 5: Random Fire '00
Target of Opportunity '04
The Cutter '05
Finding Rin Tin Tin '07
The Prince & Me 3: A Royal Honeymoon '08
Train '08

Roy Jenson (1927-2007)
The Wind and the Lion '75
The Car '77

Roy Cameron Jenson (1927-2007)
Nightmare Honeymoon '73
Demonoid, Messenger of Death '81

Sasha Jenson (1964-)
Halloween 4: The Return of Michael Myers '88
Dazed and Confused '93

Julia Jentsch (1978-)
The Edukators '04
Sophie Scholl: The Final Days '05
I Served the King of England '07
Hannah Arendt '12

Do-yeon Jeon
No Blood No Tears '02
The Housemaid '10

Ken Jeong (1969-)
Young Tiger '74
Pineapple Express '08
All About Steve '09
Couples Retreat '09
The Goods: Live Hard, Sell Hard '09
The Hangover '09
How to Make Love to a Woman '09
Despicable Me '10 (V)
Furry Vengeance '10
Vampires Suck '10
Big Mommas: Like Father, Like Son '11
The Hangover, Part 2 '11
Transformers: Dark of the Moon '11
Zookeeper '11
Despicable Me 2 '13 (V)
The Hangover, Part III '13
Pain & Gain '13
Turbo '13 (V)
Penguins of Madagascar '14 (V)
The DUFF '15
Norm of the North '16
Goosebumps 2: Haunted Halloween '18
My Spy '19

Ron Jeremy (1953-)
Orgazmo '98
Boondock Saints '99
Waiting '00

Adele Jergens (1917-2002)
She Wouldn't Say Yes '45
Down to Earth '47
The Fuller Brush Man '48
The Prince of Thieves '48
Slightly French '49
Armored Car Robbery '50
Treasure of Monte Cristo '50
Abbott and Costello Meet the Invisible Man '51
The Miami Story '54
The Cobweb '55
Day the World Ended '55
Lonesome Trail '55

Diane Jergens (1935-)
Desk Set '57
High School Confidential '58
The FBI Story '59
Island of Lost Women '59

Sterling Jerins
And So It Goes '14
Dark Places '15
No Escape '15

Tim Jerome (1943-)
Billy Bathgate '91
A Price Above Rubies '97
Thirteen Days '00

Mary Jerrold (1877-1955)
The Flemish Farm '43
Immortal Battalion '44
The Queen of Spades '49
Woman Hater '49

George Jessel (1898-1981)
The I Don't Care Girl '53
The Busy Body '67
Valley of the Dolls '67

Paul Jesson (1946-)
All or Nothing '02
Coriolanus '11
Mr. Turner '14

James Jeter (1921-2007)
Cool Hand Luke '67
The Hollywood Knights '80

Michael Jeter (1952-2003)
Ragtime '81
The Money Pit '86
Dead Bang '89
Tango and Cash '89
The Fisher King '91
Armistead Maupin's Tales of the City '93
Gypsy '93
Sister Act 2: Back in the Habit '93
Drop Zone '94
Waterworld '95
The Boys Next Door '96
Mrs. Santa Claus '96
Air Bud '97
Mouse Hunt '97
Fear and Loathing in Las Vegas '98
Patch Adams '98
Zack & Reba '98
The Green Mile '99
Jakob the Liar '99
True Crime '99
The Gift '00
South of Heaven, West of Hell '00
Jurassic Park 3 '01
Welcome to Collinwood '02
Open Range '03
The Polar Express '04

Joan Jett (1958-)
Boogie Boy '98
The Sweet Life '03
National Lampoon Presents: Endless Bummer '09

Jewel (1974-)
See Jewel Kilcher

Isabel Jewell (1909-72)
Blessed Event '32
Counsellor-at-Law '33
Day of Reckoning '33
Design for Living '33
Evelyn Prentice '34
Manhattan Melodrama '34
Shadow of Doubt '35
Big Brown Eyes '36
Career Woman '36
Go West, Young Man '36
A Tale of Two Cities '36
Lost Horizon '37
Marked Woman '37
Gone with the Wind '39
The Falcon and the Co-Eds '43
The Leopard Man '43
The Seventh Victim '43
Man in the Attic '53
The Arousers '70
Edie in Ciao! Manhattan '72

Norman Jewison (1926-)
The Stupids '95 (C)
Hal '18

Wen Jiang (1963-)
The Missing Gun '02
The Lost Bladesman '16

Igor Jijikine
Indiana Jones and the Kingdom of the Crystal Skull '08
Ruslan '09

Penn Jillette (1955-)
Tough Guys Don't Dance '87
Penn and Teller Get Killed '90
Hackers '95
Fear and Loathing in Las Vegas '98
Tim's Vermeer '13

Ann Jillian (1950-)
Gypsy '62
Mr. Mom '83

Alice in Wonderland '85
Girls of the White Orchid '85
The Ann Jillian Story '88
The Disappearance of Vonnie '94

Joyce Jillson (1945-2004)
Superchick '71
Slumber Party '57 '76

Hector Jimenez (1973-)
Killer Pad '06
Nacho Libre '06
Epic Movie '07
Gentlemen Broncos '09
Sharktopus '10
Cellmates '12
Sugar Kisses '13
Compadres '16

Lucia Jimenez (1978-)
Broken Silence '01
The Kovak Box '06

Soledad Jiminez (1874-1966)
The Cyclone Ranger '35
The Real Glory '39
For Whom the Bell Tolls '43

Elaine Jin
Yi Yi '00
Lost in Beijing '07

Courtney Jines (1992-)
Gaudi Afternoon '01
Spy Kids 3-D: Game Over '03
Because of Winn-Dixie '05

Maeve Jinkings
Neighboring Sounds '12
Aquarius '16

Christo Jivkov
David's Birthday '09
Sword of War '09

Kenzaburo Jo (1929-92)
See Tomisaburo Wakayama

Ebony Jo-Ann
Fly by Night '93
The Other Brother '02
Grown Ups '10

Suzy Joachim
Mother, May I Sleep With Danger? '96
Beyond Redemption '99
White Chicks '04

Marlene Jobert (1940-)
Masculine Feminine '66
The Thief of Paris '67
Rider on the Rain '70
Catch Me a Spy '71
Ten Days Wonder '72

Maz Jobrani (1972-)
The Medicine Show '01
13 Going on 30 '04
The Interpreter '05
Jimmy Vestvood: Amerikan Hero '16

Hans Joby
Pilot X '37
Hitler: Beast of Berlin '39

Adan Jodorowsky
Santa Sangre '90
2 Days in Paris '07

Alejandro Jodorowsky (1929-)
El Topo '71
The Holy Mountain '73
Jodorowsky's Dune '13
The Dance of Reality '14

Brontis Jodorowsky (1962-)
El Topo '71
The Dance of Reality '14

Michel Joelsas
The Year My Parents Went on Vacation '07
The Second Mother '15

Joeystarr (1967-)
See Joey Starr

Zita Johann (1904-93)
Struggle '31
The Mummy '32
Tiger Shark '32

Jóhannes Haukur Jóhannesson
Reykjavik-Rotterdam '08
Alpha '18

Colby Johannson (1978-)
NYC: Tornado Terror '08
Metal Shifters '11

David Johansen (1950-)
Married to the Mob '88
Scrooged '88
Let It Ride '89
Tales from the Darkside: The Movie '90
Desire and Hell at Sunset Motel '92
Freejack '92
Mr. Nanny '93
Naked in New York '93 (V)
Car 54, Where Are You? '94
Burnzy's Last Call '95
Cats Don't Dance '97 (V)
The Tic Code '99

Paul Johansson (1964-)
Soapdish '91
Midnight Witness '93
Ed McBain's 87th Precinct: Heatwave '97
Carnival of Souls '98
Wishmaster 2: Evil Never Dies '98
Hooded Angels '00
Dark Side '02
Edge of Madness '02
John Q '02
Novel Romance '06
A Trick of the Mind '06
Atlas Shrugged: Part 1 '11
Stonados '13

Scarlett Johansson (1984-)
Manny & Lo '96
Home Alone 3 '97
The Horse Whisperer '97
An American Rhapsody '01
Ghost World '01
The Man Who Wasn't There '01
Eight Legged Freaks '02
Girl with a Pearl Earring '03
Lost in Translation '03
A Good Woman '04
In Good Company '04
A Love Song for Bobby Long '04
The Perfect Score '04
The SpongeBob SquarePants Movie '04 (V)
The Island '05
Match Point '05
The Black Dahlia '06
The Prestige '06
Scoop '06
The Nanny Diaries '07
The Other Boleyn Girl '08
The Spirit '08
Vicky Cristina Barcelona '08
He's Just Not That Into You '09
Iron Man 2 '10
We Bought a Zoo '11
The Avengers '12
Hitchcock '12
Don Jon '13
Her '13 (V)
Under the Skin '13
Captain America: The Winter Soldier '14
Lucy '14
Avengers: Age of Ultron '15
Captain America: Civil War '16
Hail, Caesar! '16
Sing '16
Ghost in the Shell '17
Rough Night '17
Avengers: Infinity War '18
Avengers: Endgame '19
Jojo Rabbit '19
Marriage Story '19

I.S. Johar (1920-)
Flame Over India '59
North West Frontier '59

Sir Elton John (1947-)
Born to Boogie '72
Tommy '75
Spice World: The Movie '97 (C)
The Road to El Dorado '00 (N)
Kingsman: The Golden Circle '17

Gottfried John (1942-2014)
Mother Kusters Goes to Heaven '76
Fedora '78
In a Year of 13 Moons '78
The Marriage of Maria Braun '79
Mata Hari '85
Death Has a Bad Reputation '90
The Mistake '91
Abraham '94
Goldeneye '95
Institue Benjamenta or This Dream People Call Human Life '95
The Ogre '96
Proof of Life '00
Piano Tuner of Earthquakes '05

Robert John
Creatures the World Forgot '70
El Topo '71

Rosamund John (1913-98)
Spitfire '42
The Way to the Stars '45
The Upturned Glass '47

Glynis Johns (1923-)
The Forty-Ninth Parallel '41
The Adventures of Tartu '43
Vacation from Marriage '45
An Ideal Husband '47
Miranda '48
Dear Mr. Prohack '49
Appointment With Venus '51
No Highway in the Sky '51
Encore '52
The Promoter '52
Rob Roy-The Highland Rogue '53
The Sword & the Rose '53
Mad About Men '54
Land of Fury '55
All Mine to Give '56
Around the World in 80 Days '56 (C)
The Court Jester '56
Another Time, Another Place '58
The Sundowners '60
The Chapman Report '62
Papa's Delicate Condition '63
Mary Poppins '64
Dear Brigitte '65
Under Milk Wood '73
Vault of Horror '73
The Ref '93
While You Were Sleeping '95
Superstar '99

Harriette Johns (1921-90)
Edward, My Son '49
Meet Mr. Callaghan '54

Mervyn Johns (1899-1992)
The Next of Kin '42
Dead of Night '45
Captain Boycott '47
Captive Heart '47
Counterblast '48
Edward, My Son '49
A Christmas Carol '51
Tony Draws a Horse '51
The Master of Ballantrae '53
Romeo and Juliet '54
1984 '56
The Counterfeit Plan '57
Once More, With Feeling '60
Day of the Triffids '63

Stratford Johns (1925-2002)
Who Done It? '56
The Fiendish Plot of Dr. Fu Manchu '80
Great Expectations '81
Dance with a Stranger '85
Car Trouble '86
The Lair of the White Worm '88
Salome's Last Dance '88
A Demon in My View '92
Splitting Heirs '93
Neil Gaiman's NeverWhere '96

Tracy C. Johns (1963-)
She's Gotta Have It '86
Mo' Better Blues '90
New Jack City '91

Aaron Johnson (1990-)
See Aaron Taylor-Johnson

Adam Johnson (1973-)
Frozen '10
Mythica 2: The Darkspore '15
Mythica: A Quest for Heroes '15
Mythica: The Necromancer '15

A.J. (Anthony) Johnson (1967-)
House Party '90
Double Trouble '91
B.A.P.'s '97
Def Jam's How to Be a Player '97
I Got the Hook-Up '98
The Players Club '98
O '01

Alexz Johnson (1986-)
Final Destination 3 '06
House of Bodies '13

Amy Jo Johnson (1970-)
Mighty Morphin Power Rangers: The Movie '95
Turbo: A Power Rangers Movie '96
Killing Mr. Griffin '97
Cold Hearts '99
Pursuit of Happiness '01
Infested: Invasion of the Killer Bugs '02
Hard Ground '03
Fatal Trust '06
Islander '06
Magma: Volcanic Disaster '06
Veritas: Prince of Truth '07
Tiger Eyes '13

Anne-Marie Johnson (1960-)
Hollywood Shuffle '87
I'm Gonna Git You Sucka '88
Robot Jox '90
Asteroid '97
Down in the Delta '98
Pursuit of Happiness '01
About Fifty '11

Arch Johnson (1922-97)
Gun Glory '57
The Explosive Generation '61
The Cheyenne Social Club '70

Ariyan Johnson
Just Another Girl on the I.R.T. '93
Bulworth '98

Arnold Johnson (1922-2000)
Putney Swope '69
My Demon Lover '87

Arte Johnson (1929-2019)
That Funny Feeling '65
The Third Day '65
The President's Analyst '67
Charge of the Model T's '76
Love at First Bite '79
Detour to Terror '80
Making of a Male Model '83
Alice in Wonderland '85
What Comes Around '85
Evil Toons '90
Evil Spirits '91
Munchie '92
Assault of the Party Nerds 2: Heavy Petting Detective '95

Ashley Johnson (1983-)
Lionheart '90
Annie: A Royal Adventure '95
Nine Months '95
Dancer, Texas-Pop. 81 '98
Anywhere But Here '99
The Growing Pains Movie '00
What Women Want '00
Rustin '01
Growing Pains: Return of the Seavers '04
Killer Diller '04
King of the Corner '04
Nearing Grace '05
Fast Food Nation '06
Columbus Day '08
Otis '08
Alleged '10
The Help '11

Bart Johnson (1970-)
High School Musical '06
Animals '08
High School Musical 3: Senior Year '08
Murder.com '08
The Cell 2 '09
The Yankles '09
A Christmas Wish '11

Ben Johnson (1928-96)
Three Godfathers '48
Mighty Joe Young '49
She Wore a Yellow Ribbon '49
Rio Grande '50
Wagon Master '50
Fort Defiance '51
Wild Stallion '52
Shane '53
Rebel in Town '56
War Drums '57
Fort Bowie '58
One-Eyed Jacks '61
Major Dundee '65
The Rare Breed '66
Will Penny '67
The Undefeated '69
The Wild Bunch '69
Chisum '70
The Last Picture Show '71
Corky '72
The Getaway '72
Junior Bonner '72
Dillinger '73
Train Robbers '73
The Sugarland Express '74
Bite the Bullet '75
Breakheart Pass '76
Grayeagle '77
The Swarm '78
The Sacketts '79
Terror Train '80
Ruckus '81
The Shadow Riders '82
Tex '82
Champions '84
Red Dawn '84
Soggy Bottom U.S.A. '84
Wild Horses '84
Dream West '86
Let's Get Harry '87
Cherry 2000 '88
The Chase '91
Radio Flyer '92
Angels in the Outfield '94
The Evening Star '96

Beverly Johnson (1952-)
Ashanti, Land of No Mercy '79
National Lampoon's Loaded Weapon 1 '93
Def Jam's How to Be a Player '97
Crossroads '02

Bill Johnson (1916-57)
It's a Pleasure '45
Keep Your Powder Dry '45
The Texas Chainsaw Massacre 2 '86

Brad Johnson (1959-)
Nam Angels '88
Always '89
Flight of the Intruder '90
Lone Justice 2 '93
Philadelphia Experiment 2 '93
Lone Justice 3: Showdown at Plum Creek '96
Rough Riders '97
Across the Line '00
Left Behind: The Movie '00
Crossfire Trail '01
Alien Siege '05
Wild Things 3: Diamonds in the Rough '05
Safe Harbour '07

Bryce Johnson (1977-)
Bring It On Again '03
Freshman Orientation '04
Harry and Max '04
Sleeping Dogs Lie '06
Private Valentine: Blonde & Dangerous '08
Trucker '08
The Blue Tooth Virgin '09
Willow Creek '13

C. David Johnson (1955-)
The Legend of Gator Face '96
Terminal Invasion '02

Candy Johnson (1944-2012)
Beach Party '63
Bikini Beach '64
Muscle Beach Party '64
Pajama Party '64

Cecile Johnson
Strange Fruit '04
Meteor Apocalypse '10

Celia Johnson (1908-82)
In Which We Serve '43
Brief Encounter '46
This Happy Breed '47
Captain's Paradise '53
A Kid for Two Farthings '55
The Prime of Miss Jean Brodie '69
Les Miserables '78
Staying On '80

Chubby Johnson (1903-74)
Rocky Mountain '50
Back to God's Country '53
Law and Order '53

Clark Johnson (1954-)
Colors '88
Blood Brothers '93
Soul Survivor '95
Rude '96
Junior's Groove '97
Disappearing Acts '00
Homicide: The Movie '00
Love Come Down '00
Deliberate Intent '01
Boycott '02
S.W.A.T. '03 (C)
Re-Generation '04
The Sentinel '06
The Trojan Horse '08
Defendor '09
Hyena Road '16

Corey Johnson (1961-)
The Mummy '99
Endgame '01
Last Run '01
Out For a Kill '03
Hellboy '04
A Sound of Thunder '05
The Bourne Ultimatum '07
The Contract '07
The Fourth Kind '09
Ex Machina '15

Dakota Johnson (1989-)
Beastly '11
Goats '12
Date and Switch '13
Need for Speed '14
A Bigger Splash '15
Black Mass '15
Chloe & Theo '15
Cymbeline '15
Fifty Shades of Grey '15
How to Be Single '16
Fifty Shades Darker '17
Bad Times at the El Royale '18
Fifty Shades Freed '18
Suspiria '18

The Peanut Butter Falcon '19

Don Johnson (1949-)
Zachariah '70
Harrad Experiment '73
A Boy and His Dog '75
Snowblind '78
Beulah Land '80
Miami Vice '84
Soggy Bottom U.S.A. '84
The Long, Hot Summer '86
Action Force: The Movie '87 (V)
Sweet Hearts Dance '88
Dead Bang '89
The Hot Spot '90
Harley Davidson and the Marlboro Man '91
Paradise '91
Tales of the Unexpected '91
Born Yesterday '93
Guilty as Sin '93
In Pursuit of Honor '95
Tin Cup '96
Goodbye, Lover '99
Moondance Alexander '07
Machete '10
Bucky Larson: Born to Be a Star '11
A Good Old Fashioned Orgy '11
Django Unchained '12
Cold in July '14
The Other Woman '14
Brawl in Cell Block 99 '17
Vault '19

Dwayne 'The Rock' Johnson (1972-)
The Mummy Returns '01
The Scorpion King '02
The Rundown '03
Walking Tall '04
Be Cool '05
Doom '05
Gridiron Gang '06
Southland Tales '06
The Game Plan '07
Reno 911! Miami '07 (C)
Get Smart '08
Planet 51 '09 (V)
Race to Witch Mountain '09
Faster '10
The Other Guys '10
Tooth Fairy '10
You Again '10
Fast Five '11
Journey 2: The Mysterious Island '12
Fast & Furious 6 '13
G.I. Joe: Retaliation '13
Pain & Gain '13
Snitch '13
Hercules '14
Furious 7 '15
San Andreas '15
Central Intelligence '16
Moana '16
Baywatch '17
The Fate of the Furious '17
Jumanji: Welcome to the Jungle '17
Rampage '18
Skyscraper '18
Fast & Furious Presents: Hobbs & Shaw '19
Fighting with My Family '19
Jumanji: The Next Level '19

Eric Johnson (1979-)
Ginger Snaps: Unleashed '04
Marker '05
Honeymoon with Mom '06
Everest '07
My Nanny's Secret '09
Call Me Mrs. Miracle '10
Meteor Storm '10
Oh Christmas Tree! '13
Fifty Shades Darker '17
Fifty Shades Freed '18

Geordie Johnson (1953-)
A Change of Place '94
Spenser: The Judas Goat '94
Dangerous Evidence: The Lori Jackson Story '99
Charms for the Easy Life '02

The Good Witch's Charm '12

Georgann Johnson (1926-)
Murphy's Romance '85
Shattered Dreams '90

Hassan Johnson
Belly '98
Gun '10
Blood Brother '18

Helen Johnson (1954-)
The Divorcee '30
Sin Takes a Holiday '30

Jack Johnson (1987-)
Lost in Space '98
Sleep Easy, Hutch Rimes '00

Jake Johnson (1978-)
Drinking Buddies '13
Let's Be Cops '14
The Pretty One '14
Jurassic World '15
The Mummy '17
Spider-Man: Into the Spider-Verse '18 (V)
Tag '18

Jake M. Johnson (1978-)
Paper Heart '09
Ceremony '10
Safety Not Guaranteed '12

Jay Kenneth Johnson
Hack! '07
Undercover Bridesmaid '12

Jesse Johnson (1982-)
Redline '07
Killing Lincoln '13

John Johnson
Alucard '08
Skeleton Key 2: 667, the Neighbor of the Beast '08

Julie Johnson
The Islander '88
Barney's Great Adventure '98 (V)

Karl Johnson (1924-93)
Plan 9 from Outer Space '56
The Unearthly '57
Night of the Ghouls '59

Karl Johnson (1948-)
Close My Eyes '91
Wittgenstein '93
Love Is the Devil '98
Pure '02
The Chatterley Affair '06
Four Last Songs '06
The Deep Blue Sea '12

Kay Johnson (1904-75)
Billy the Kid '30
Madam Satan '30
American Madness '32
The Real Glory '39
Son of Fury '42

Kelly Johnson
Goodbye Pork Pie '81
Utu '83

Kenneth Johnson (1942-)
Major League 3: Back to the Minors '98
The Veteran '06

Kenny Johnson
The Perfect Witness '07
Few Options '11

Kurt Johnson (1952-86)
Jane Austen in Manhattan '80
Sole Survivor '84

Lamar Johnson
Full Out '15
Kings '17

Lamont Johnson (1955-)
The Brothers Rico '57
The Five Heartbeats '91
Fear of a Black Hat '94
Waiting to Exhale '95

Laura Johnson (1957-)
Opening Night '77
Nick Knight '89
Fatal Instinct '92

Red Shoe Diaries 2: Double Dare '92
Cheatin' Hearts '93
Dario Argento's Trauma '93
Judge & Jury '96
Hope Ranch '02
The Long Shot '04

Lynn-Holly Johnson (1958-)
Ice Castles '79
For Your Eyes Only '81
The Watcher in the Woods '81
Where the Boys Are '84 '84
Hyper Space '89

Mel Johnson, Jr.
Total Recall '90
Hideous '97

Melodie Johnson (1943-)
The Moonshine War '70
Rabbit, Run '70

Melody Johnson (1982-)
Jailbait! '00
Jason X '01

Michael Johnson (1939-2001)
Anne of the Thousand Days '69
Lust for a Vampire '71

Michelle Johnson (1965-)
Blame It on Rio '84
A Chorus Line '85
Gung Ho '86
Beaks: The Movie '87
Waxwork '88
Blood Ties '92
Death Becomes Her '92
Far and Away '92
Till Murder Do Us Part '92
Wishful Thinking '92
Body Shot '93
The Glimmer Man '96
Moving Target '96
Specimen '97
Fallen Angel '99

Noble Johnson (1881-1978)
The Most Dangerous Game '32
The Mummy '32
King Kong '33
The Lives of a Bengal Lancer '35
The Ghost Breakers '40
She Wore a Yellow Ribbon '49

P. Lynn Johnson
Civic Duty '06
Ice Blues: A Donald Strachey Mystery '08

Penny Johnson (1961-)
What's Love Got to Do with It? '93
Fear of a Black Hat '94
Deliberate Intent '01
DC 9/11: Time of Crisis '04

Rafer Johnson (1935-)
Pirates of Tortuga '61
Tarzan and the Great River '67
Tarzan and the Jungle Boy '68
The Last Grenade '70

Rafer Lewis Johnson (1935-)
See Rafer Johnson

Rebecca Johnson
The Trip '10
The Trip to Spain '17

Reggie Johnson
Platoon '86
Seven Hours to Judgment '88

Richard Johnson (1927-2015)
Never So Few '59
The Haunting '63
The Pumpkin Eater '64
Tomb of Ligeia '64
The Amorous Adventures of Moll Flanders '65
Operation Crossbow '65

Khartoum '66
Deadlier Than the Male '67
Fifth Day of Peace '72
Beyond the Door '75
Hennessy '75
The Comeback '77
The Four Feathers '78
The Big Alligator River '79
The Big Scam '79
Screamers '80
Zombie '80
The Great Alligator '81
Lady Jane '85
A Man for All Seasons '88
Treasure Island '89
The Crucifer of Blood '91
Anglo-Saxon Attitudes '92
The Camomile Lawn '92
Duel of Hearts '92
Lara Croft: Tomb Raider '01
The Raven '07 (N)
The Boy in the Striped Pajamas '08

Rick Johnson (1961-)
Foreign Student '94
Rustin '01

Rita Johnson (1913-65)
Smashing the Rackets '38
Broadway Serenade '39
Honolulu '39
Nick Carter, Master Detective '39
Stronger Than Desire '39
Congo Maisie '40
Edison the Man '40
Here Comes Mr. Jordan '41
The Major and the Minor '42
My Friend Flicka '43
The Naughty Nineties '45
They Won't Believe Me '47
The Big Clock '48
Sleep, My Love '48
Family Honeymoon '49
All Mine to Give '56

Robin Johnson (1964-)
Times Square '80
Splitz '84

Russell Johnson (1924-2014)
Loan Shark '52
It Came from Outer Space '53
Law and Order '53
Seminole '53
Tall Lie '53
Ride Clear of Diablo '54
Ma and Pa Kettle at Waikiki '55
Many Rivers to Cross '55
This Island Earth '55
The Space Children '58
The Horror at 37,000 Feet '73
The Bastard '78
Rescue from Gilligan's Island '78

Ryan Thomas Johnson (1976-)
Carnosaur 2 '94
Criminal Ways '03

Samuel Johnson (1978-)
Strange Fits of Passion '99
After the Deluge '03
$9.99 '08 (V)

Scott Johnson
Bodies, Rest & Motion '93
Wrong Turn 4: Bloody Beginnings '11

Shane Johnson
Black Cadillac '03
The Possession of Michael King '14

Stacii Jae Johnson
Parental Guidance '98
Da Hip Hop Witch '00

Steve Johnson
Lemora, Lady Dracula '73
Angel of H.E.A.T. '82

Tor Johnson (1903-71)
Abbott and Costello in the Foreign Legion '50
Houdini '53
Bride of the Monster '55

The Black Sleep '56
Carousel '56
Plan 9 from Outer Space '56
The Unearthly '57
Night of the Ghouls '59

Van Johnson (1916-2008)
Too Many Girls '40
Dr. Gillespie's New Assistant '42
Dr. Gillespie's Criminal Case '43
The Human Comedy '43
Madame Curie '43
Pilot No. 5 '43
Thirty Seconds Over Tokyo '44
Three Men in White '44
Two Girls and a Sailor '44
The White Cliffs of Dover '44
Between Two Women '45
Thrill of a Romance '45
Weekend at the Waldorf '45
Easy to Wed '46
High Barbaree '47
The Romance of Rosy Ridge '47
The Bride Goes Wild '48
Command Decision '48
State of the Union '48
Battleground '49
In the Good Old Summertime '49
Mother Is a Freshman '49
Scene of the Crime '49
The Big Hangover '50
The Duchess of Idaho '50
Go for Broke! '51
Invitation '51
It's a Big Country '51
Three Guys Named Mike '51
Too Young to Kiss '51
Confidentially Connie '53
Easy to Love '53
Brigadoon '54
The Caine Mutiny '54
The Last Time I Saw Paris '54
Men of the Fighting Lady '54
Siege at Red River '54
End of the Affair '55
The Pied Piper of Hamelin '57
Slander '57
Divorce American Style '67
Where Angels Go, Trouble Follows '68 (C)
Yours, Mine & Ours '68
Eagles Over London '69
The Kidnapping of the President '80
Scorpion with Two Tails '82
The Purple Rose of Cairo '85

Bobby Johnston
Body Strokes '95
Sinful Intrigue '95
DC 9/11: Time of Crisis '04

Grace Johnston
God Bless the Child '88
One Good Cop '91

Jamie Johnston
The Tenth Circle '08
Love Me '12

J.J. Johnston (1933-)
Fatal Attraction '87
Things Change '88
Mad Dog and Glory '93
Stranger by Night '94
The Fixer '97
K-911 '99
Lakeboat '00

John Dennis Johnston (1950-)
KISS Meets the Phantom of the Park '78
The Beast Within '82
Streets of Fire '84
Into Thin Air '85
Pink Cadillac '89
Big Bad John '90
Fever '91
Miracle in the Wilderness '91
Wyatt Earp '94

In Pursuit of Honor '95
Firestarter 2: Rekindled '02

Katie Johnston
Timekeeper '98
Arthur's Quest '99

Kristen Johnston (1967-)
Austin Powers 2: The Spy Who Shagged Me '99
The Flintstones in Viva Rock Vegas '00
Strangers with Candy '06
Music & Lyrics '07
Finding Bliss '09
Bad Parents '12
The Wedding Year '19

Margaret Johnston (1918-2002)
A Man About the House '47
Burn, Witch, Burn! '62
The Psychopath '66

Oliver Johnston (1888-1966)
A King in New York '57
Tomb of Ligeia '64
A Countess from Hong Kong '67

Shaun Johnston
The Christmas Blessing '05
September Dawn '07

Sue Johnston (1943-)
Imagine Me & You '06
Little Dorrit '08

Tyler Johnston (1987-)
Decoys: The Second Seduction '07
Polar Storm '09
Pressed '11

Kim Johnston-Ulrich (1955-)
Blood Ties '92
Rumpelstiltskin '96

Marilyn Joi (1945-)
Black Samurai '77
Kentucky Fried Movie '77
Hospital of Terror '78

Duncan Joiner
Some Kind of Beautiful '15
The Disappointments Room '16

Angelina Jolie (1975-)
Lookin' to Get Out '82
Cyborg 2 '93
Hackers '95
Foxfire '96
Love Is All There Is '96
Mojave Moon '96
Playing God '96
Without Evidence '96
George Wallace '97
Hell's Kitchen NYC '97
True Women '97
Gia '98
Playing by Heart '98
The Bone Collector '99
Girl, Interrupted '99
Pushing Tin '99
Gone in 60 Seconds '00
Lara Croft: Tomb Raider '01
Original Sin '01
Life or Something Like It '02
Beyond Borders '03
Lara Croft Tomb Raider: The Cradle of Life '03
Alexander '04
The Fever '04
Shark Tale '04 (V)
Sky Captain and the World of Tomorrow '04
Taking Lives '04
Mr. & Mrs. Smith '05
The Good Shepherd '06
Beowulf '07 (V)
A Mighty Heart '07
Changeling '08
Kung Fu Panda '08 (V)
Wanted '08
Salt '10
The Tourist '10
Kung Fu Panda 2 '11 (V)
Maleficent '14
By the Sea '15
Kung Fu Panda 3 '16

Maleficent: Mistress of Evil '19

Alex Jolig (1963-)
Hypersonic '02
Python 2 '02

Adrien Jolivet
Apres Lui '07
In the Arms of My Enemy '07

Vince Jolivette
The Ape '05
Sal '11

I. Stanford Jolley (1900-78)
King of the Rocketmen '49
Rimfire '49
Fort Osage '51
Wagons West '52
The Iron Sheriff '57
The Rebel Set '59
Valley of the Dragons '61

Al Jolson (1886-1950)
The Jazz Singer '27
The Singing Fool '28
Say It With Songs '29
Big Boy '30
Hallelujah, I'm a Bum '33
Wonder Bar '34
Go Into Your Dance '35
The Singing Kid '36
Rose of Washington Square '39
Swanee River '39
Rhapsody in Blue '45

Jere Jon
Unseen Evil '99
Trancers 6: Life After Deth '02

Frankie Jonas (2000-)
Ponyo '08 (V)
Camp Rock 2: The Final Jam '10
Spooky Buddies '11 (V)
Reef 2: High Tide '12

Joe Jonas (1989-)
Camp Rock '08
Jonas Brothers: The 3D Concert Experience '09
Camp Rock 2: The Final Jam '10

Kevin Jonas (1987-)
Jonas Brothers: The 3D Concert Experience '09
Camp Rock 2: The Final Jam '10

Nick Jonas (1992-)
Jonas Brothers: The 3D Concert Experience '09
Camp Rock 2: The Final Jam '10
Goat '16
Jumanji: The Next Level '19
UglyDolls '19 (V)

Wesley Jonathan (1978-)
Baadasssss! '03
Roll Bounce '05
Crossover '06
Divine Intervention '07
Remember the Daze '07
Speed-Dating '10
Make Your Move '13

Kristoffer Joner (1972-)
Hidden '09
King of Devil's Island '10
The Wave '15

Allan Jones (1908-92)
A Night at the Opera '35
Rose Marie '36
Show Boat '36
A Day at the Races '37
The Firefly '37
Everybody Sing '38
The Boys From Syracuse '40
One Night in the Tropics '40

Allison Jones
Nightjohn '96
Ellen Foster '97

Andras Jones (1968-)
Sorority Babes in the Slimeball Bowl-A-Rama '87
A Nightmare on Elm Street 4: Dream Master '88
Far from Home '89
The Demolitionist '95
The Attic Expeditions '01

Andy Jones
Rare Birds '01
Behind the Wall '08

Angela Jones (1968-)
Pulp Fiction '94
Curdled '95
The Debt '98
Pariah '98

Angus T. Jones (1993-)
See Spot Run '01
The Rookie '02
Audrey's Rain '03
Bringing Down the House '03
The Christmas Blessing '05

Ashley Jones (1976-)
The Fire Next Time '93
The Devil's Prey '01
The King's Guard '01

Barry Jones (1893-1981)
Madeleine '50
Return to Paradise '53
Brigadoon '54
Demetrius and the Gladiators '54
Prince Valiant '54
The Glass Slipper '55
War and Peace '56

Ben Jones (1941-)
Deep in the Heart '83
Primary Colors '98
Joe Gould's Secret '00

Buck Jones (1891-1942)
Lazybones '25
Forbidden Trail '32
The California Trail '33
The Ivory Handled Gun '35
Empty Saddles '36
Wagons Westward '40
Riders of Death Valley '41

Caleb Landry Jones (1989-)
X-Men: First Class '11
Antiviral '12
Byzantium '12
Contraband '12
God's Pocket '14
Queen and Country '14
Heaven Knows What '15
Stonewall '15
American Made '17
Get Out '17
Age Out '19

Carolyn Jones (1929-83)
The Big Heat '53
House of Wax '53
The Road to Bali '53
The War of the Worlds '53
The Seven Year Itch '55
The Tender Trap '55
Invasion of the Body Snatchers '56
The Man Who Knew Too Much '56
King Creole '58
Marjorie Morningstar '58
Career '59
A Hole in the Head '59
Last Train from Gun Hill '59
The Man in the Net '59
Ice Palace '60
Sail a Crooked Ship '61
How the West Was Won '63
Heaven With a Gun '69
Eaten Alive '76
Little Ladies of the Night '77

Cherry Jones (1956-)
Big Town '87
The Horse Whisperer '97
Julian Po '97
The Cradle Will Rock '99
Murder in a Small Town '99
Cora Unashamed '00
Erin Brockovich '00
The Perfect Storm '00
Divine Secrets of the Ya-Ya Sisterhood '02
Signs '02
Ocean's Twelve '04
The Village '04
24: Redemption '08
Mother and Child '09
Days and Nights '14
The Party '17
Boy Erased '18

Christopher Jones (1941-2014)
Wild in the Streets '68
The Looking Glass War '69
Ryan's Daughter '70

Christopher Jones (1982-)
Chubasco '67
You Got Served '04

Claude Earl Jones
The Girl in the Empty Grave '77
Evilspeak '82
Impulse '84
Bride of Re-Animator '89
Miracle Mile '89

Clyde Jones
Crack House '89
The Siege of Firebase Gloria '89
Delta Heat '92
Love Beat the Hell Outta Me '00
Father of Lies '07

Darby Jones (1910-86)
I Walked with a Zombie '43
Zombies on Broadway '44

Davy Jones (1945-2012)
Head '68
The Brady Bunch Movie '95 (C)

Dean Jones (1931-2015)
The Great American Pastime '56
Tea and Sympathy '56
Jailhouse Rock '57
Imitation General '58
Torpedo Run '58
Under the Yum-Yum Tree '63
That Darn Cat '65
Two On a Guillotine '65
The Ugly Dachshund '65
Any Wednesday '66
Monkeys, Go Home! '66
Blackbeard's Ghost '67
The Horse in the Gray Flannel Suit '68
The Love Bug '68
Million Dollar Duck '71
Snowball Express '72
Mr. Superinvisible '73
The Shaggy D.A. '76
Herbie Goes to Monte Carlo '77
Once Upon a Brothers Grimm '77
Born Again '78
When Every Day Was the Fourth of July '78
The Long Days of Summer '80
Other People's Money '91
Beethoven '92
Clear and Present Danger '94
That Darn Cat '96

Dick(ie) Jones (1927-2014)
The Frontiersmen '38
Nancy Drew, Reporter '39
Pinocchio '40 (V)
The Vanishing Virginian '41
Rocky Mountain '50

Doug Jones (1960-)
Hocus Pocus '93
Hellboy '04
Pan's Labyrinth '06
Fantastic Four: Rise of the Silver Surfer '07
Hellboy II: The Golden Army '08
Angel of Death '09
Gainsbourg: A Heroic Life '10
John Dies at the End '12
The Bye Bye Man '17

Duane Jones (1937-88)
Night of the Living Dead '68
Ganja and Hess '73
Beat Street '84
To Die For '89

Dylan Jones
Merlin and the War of the Dragons '08
The 7 Adventures of Sinbad '10

Eddie Jones (1937-)
Q (The Winged Serpent) '82
C.H.U.D. '84
Sneakers '92
Ed McBain's 87th Precinct: Lightning '95
Dancer, Texas-Pop. 81 '98
Return to Me '00
Seabiscuit '03
The Terminal '04

Emilia Jones
What We Did on Our Holiday '15
Brimstone '17

Evan Jones (1976-)
8 Mile '02
The Last Shot '04
Mr. 3000 '04
Jarhead '05
Glory Road '06
Rescue Dawn '06
Lucky You '07
Answer This '10
The Dry Land '10
Mirrors 2 '10
Best Man Down '12
Houdini '14

Felicity Jones (1983-)
Northanger Abbey '07
The Diary of Anne Frank '08
Flashbacks of a Fool '08
Cheri '09
Cemetery Junction '10
The Tempest '10
Albatross '11
Chalet Girls '11
Hysteria '11
Like Crazy '11
Page Eight '11
Cheerful Weather for the Wedding '12
Breathe In '13
The Invisible Woman '13
The Amazing Spider-Man 2 '14
The Theory of Everything '14
True Story '15
Inferno '16
Rogue One: A Star Wars Story '16
Collide '17
A Monster Calls '17
On the Basis of Sex '18
The Aeronauts '19

Freddie Jones (1927-2019)
Accident '67
The Bliss of Mrs. Blossom '68
Otley '68
Frankenstein Must Be Destroyed '69
Sitting Target '72
Antony and Cleopatra '73
The Satanic Rites of Dracula '73
All Creatures Great and Small '74
Juggernaut '74
Zulu Dawn '79
The Elephant Man '80
Agatha Christie's Murder is Easy '82
Firefox '82
And the Ship Sails On '83
Krull '83
Dune '84
Firestarter '84
The Black Cauldron '85 (V)
Young Sherlock Holmes '85
Consuming Passions '88
Erik the Viking '89
Wild at Heart '90
The Last Butterfly '92
Cold Comfort Farm '94
The NeverEnding Story 3: Escape from Fantasia '94
Neil Gaiman's NeverWhere '96
Prince of Poisoners: The Life and Crimes of William Palmer '98
The Count of Monte Cristo '02

Gemma Jones (1942-)
The Devils '71
The Duchess of Duke Street '78
Devices and Desires '91
Feast of July '95
Sense and Sensibility '95
Wilderness '96
Jane Eyre '97
Wilde '97
Captain Jack '98
The Winslow Boy '98
Cotton Mary '99
Longitude '00
Bridget Jones's Diary '01
Harry Potter and the Chamber of Secrets '02
Shanghai Knights '03
Bridget Jones: The Edge of Reason '04
Fragile '05
Ballet Shoes '07
The Contractor '07
Good '08
Forget Me Not '10
The Secret Diaries of Miss Anne Lister '10
You Will Meet a Tall Dark Stranger '10
The Lady Vanishes '13
Bridget Jones's Baby '16
God's Own Country '17
Rocketman '19

Gene Jones
The Sacrament '13
Uncaged '16

Gordon Jones (1911-63)
Let 'Em Have It '35
Out West With the Hardys '38
The Green Hornet '39
Flying Tigers '42
My Sister Eileen '42
The Wistful Widow of Wagon Gap '47
Trail of Robin Hood '50
Trigger, Jr. '50
Corky of Gasoline Alley '51
Island in the Sky '53
The Monster That Challenged the World '57
Shoot-out at Medicine Bend '57
McLintock! '63

Grace Jones (1948-)
Gordon's War '73
Conan the Destroyer '84
A View to a Kill '85
Vamp '86
Straight to Hell '87
Boomerang '92
Cyber Bandits '94
Shaka Zulu: The Last Great Warrior '01

Griffith Jones (1909-2007)
First a Girl '35
The Mill on the Floss '39
The Secret Four '39
Henry V '44
The Wicked Lady '45
They Made Me a Fugitive '47
Miranda '48

Henry Jones (1912-99)
The Lady Says No '51
The Bad Seed '56
The Girl Can't Help It '56
The Girl He Left Behind '56
3:10 to Yuma '57
Will Success Spoil Rock Hunter? '57
Vertigo '58
Cash McCall '60
Angel Baby '61
Never Too Late '65
Project X '68
Stay Away, Joe '68
Butch Cassidy and the Sundance Kid '69
Rabbit, Run '70
Support Your Local Gunfighter '71
Napoleon and Samantha '72
Pete 'n' Tillie '72
Balboa '82
Deathtrap '82
Arachnophobia '90
The Grifters '90

Howard Jones
Eleven Men and a Girl '30
Bloom '03

Jack Jones (1938-)
The Comeback '77
Airplane 2: The Sequel '82

James Earl Jones (1931-)
Dr. Strangelove, or: How I Learned to Stop Worrying and Love the Bomb '64
End of the Road '70
The Great White Hope '70
Deadly Hero '75
Bingo Long Traveling All-Stars & Motor Kings '76
The River Niger '76
Swashbuckler '76
The Exorcist 2: The Heretic '77
The Greatest '77
The Last Remake of Beau Geste '77
Paul Robeson '77
Piece of the Action '77
Star Wars '77
Roots: The Next Generation '79
The Bushido Blade '80
The Empire Strikes Back '80 (V)
The Guyana Tragedy: The Story of Jim Jones '80
Blood Tide '82
Conan the Barbarian '82
Flight of Dragons '82 (V)
Return of the Jedi '83
The Vegas Strip Wars '84
City Limits '85
Allan Quatermain and the Lost City of Gold '86
Soul Man '86
Gardens of Stone '87
Matewan '87
Coming to America '88
Best of the Best '89
By Dawn's Early Light '89
Field of Dreams '89
Three Fugitives '89
The Ambulance '90
Heat Wave '90
The Hunt for Red October '90
Patriot Games '92
Scorchers '92
Sneakers '92
Excessive Force '93
The Meteor Man '93
The Sandlot '93
Sommersby '93
Clean Slate '94
Clear and Present Danger '94
Jefferson in Paris '94
The Lion King '94 (V)
Naked Gun 33 1/3: The Final Insult '94 (C)
Cry, the Beloved Country '95
A Family Thing '96
Gang Related '96
Good Luck '96
Looking for Richard '96
Rebound: The Legend of Earl 'The Goat' Manigault '96
Horton Foote's Alone '97
The Second Civil War '97
The Lion King: Simba's Pride '98 (V)
Merlin '98 (V)
What the Deaf Man Heard '98
Santa and Pete '99
Summer's End '99
Undercover Angel '99

Anne Rice's The Feast of All Saints *'01*
Finder's Fee *'01*
The Reading Room *'05*
The Sandlot 2 *'05*
Star Wars: Episode 3-Revenge of the Sith *'05 (V)*
The Benchwarmers *'06 (V)*
Scary Movie 4 *'06 (N)*
Earth *'07 (N)*
Welcome Home Roscoe Jenkins *'08*
Jack and the Beanstalk *'09 (V)*
The Angriest Man in Brooklyn *'14*
Gimme Shelter *'14*

Jamison Jones
He Was a Quiet Man *'07*
Born to Ride *'11*

Janet Jones (1961-)
The Flamingo Kid *'84*
A Chorus Line *'85*
American Anthem *'86*
Police Academy 5: Assignment Miami Beach *'88*
Two Tickets to Paradise *'06*

January Jones (1978-)
Bandits *'01*
Taboo *'02*
American Wedding *'03*
Anger Management *'03*
Dirty Dancing: Havana Nights *'04*
Love's Enduring Promise *'04*
The Three Burials of Melquiades Estrada *'05*
Swedish Auto *'06*
We Are Marshall *'06*
Unknown *'11*
X-Men: First Class *'11*
Seeking Justice *'12*
Sweetwater *'13*

Jason Jones
A Beginner's Guide to Endings *'10*
The Art of the Steal *'13*

Jedda Jones
Talkin' Dirty after Dark *'91*
Jeremy's Family Reunion *'04*
Kiss the Bride *'10*

Jeffrey Jones (1946-)
Amadeus *'84*
Transylvania 6-5000 *'85*
Ferris Bueller's Day Off *'86*
Howard the Duck *'86*
If Tomorrow Comes *'86*
Hanoi Hilton *'87*
Kenny Rogers as the Gambler, Part 3: The Legend Continues *'87*
Beetlejuice *'88*
Without a Clue *'88*
Valmont *'89*
Who's Harry Crumb? *'89*
The Hunt for Red October *'90*
Mom and Dad Save the World *'92*
Stay Tuned *'92*
Ed Wood *'94*
Houseguest *'94*
The Avenging Angel *'95*
The Crucible *'96*
The Pest *'96*
The Devil's Advocate *'97*
Santa Fe *'97*
Ravenous *'99*
Sleepy Hollow *'99*
Company Man *'00*
Dr. Dolittle 2 *'01*
Heartbreakers *'01*
How High *'01*
Who's Your Caddy? *'07*

Jennifer Jones (1919-2009)
Dick Tracy *'37*
The Song of Bernadette *'43*
Since You Went Away *'44*
Love Letters *'45*
Duel in the Sun *'46*
Portrait of Jennie *'48*
Madame Bovary *'49*
Carrie *'52*
Ruby Gentry *'52*
Beat the Devil *'53*
Good Morning, Miss Dove *'55*
Love Is a Many-Splendored Thing *'55*
The Man in the Gray Flannel Suit *'56*
A Farewell to Arms *'57*
Tender Is the Night *'62*
The Towering Inferno *'74*

Jerry Jones
Dolemite *'75*
Dolemite 2: Human Tornado *'76*

Jill Jones
Graffiti Bridge *'90*
The Perfect Holiday *'07*

Jill Marie Jones (1975-)
The Longshots *'08*
Meeting Spencer *'11*

Jocelyn Jones (1950-)
The Enforcer *'76*
The Great Texas Dynamite Chase *'76*
Tourist Trap *'79*

John Jones
White Men Can't Jump *'92*
The Overbrook Brothers *'09*

John Marshall Jones (1962-)
Tapeheads *'89*
Sgt. Bilko *'95*

John Simon Jones
Mission of Death *'97*
U.S. SEALs: Dead or Alive *'02*

Julia Jones (1981-)
Black Cloud *'04*
Three Priests *'08*
Jonah Hex *'10*
The Twilight Saga: Eclipse *'10*
Wind River *'17*

Justin L. Jones
Pirates of Treasure Island *'06*
Monster *'08*

Kidada Jones (1974-)
Black and White *'99*
Thicker than Water *'99*

Kimberly (Lil' Kim) Jones (1974-)
She's All That *'99*
Juwanna Mann *'02*
Gang of Roses *'03*
Nora's Hair Salon *'04*
You Got Served *'04 (C)*

Kirk 'Sticky Fingaz' Jones (1973-)
Clockers *'95*
Dead Presidents *'95*
Ride *'98*
In Too Deep *'99*
Love Goggles *'99*
Lockdown *'00*
Next Friday *'00*
Lift *'01*
MacArthur Park *'01*
Leprechaun 6: Back 2 Tha Hood *'03*
Flight of the Phoenix *'04*
House of the Dead 2: Dead Aim *'05*
The Playaz Court *'07*
Breaking Point *'09*
A Day in the Life *'09*
The Bag Man *'14*

Larry Jones
Brotherhood of Death *'76*
Alien Invasion Arizona *'07*

Leslie Jones (1967-)
Ghostbusters *'16*
Masterminds *'16*
The Angry Birds Movie 2 *'19*

L.Q. Jones (1927-)
Battle Cry *'55*
Target Zero *'55*
Between Heaven and Hell *'56*
Love Me Tender *'56*
Santiago *'56*
Men in War *'57*
Operation Mad Ball *'57*
Buchanan Rides Alone *'58*
Torpedo Run *'58*
The Young Lions *'58*
Battle of the Coral Sea *'59*
Flaming Star *'60*
Hell Is for Heroes *'62*
Ride the High Country *'62*
Apache Rifles *'64*
Iron Angel *'64*
Stay Away, Joe *'68*
The Wild Bunch *'69*
Ballad of Cable Hogue *'70*
The McMasters *'70*
The Brotherhood of Satan *'71*
The Bravos *'72*
Richard Petty Story *'72*
A Boy and His Dog *'75*
White Line Fever *'75*
Banjo Hackett *'76*
Mother, Jugs and Speed *'76*
The Beast Within *'82*
Lone Wolf McQuade *'83*
Sacred Ground *'83*
Timerider *'83*
Bulletproof *'88*
River of Death *'90*
Lightning Jack *'94*
Casino *'95*
In Cold Blood *'96*
Tornado! *'96*
The Edge *'97*
The Mask of Zorro *'98*
The Jack Bull *'99*
The Patriot *'99*
Route 666 *'01*
A Prairie Home Companion *'06*

Marcia Mae Jones (1924-2007)
The Champ *'32*
Heidi *'37*
The Adventures of Tom Sawyer *'38*
Barefoot Boy *'38*
Mad About Music *'38*
The Little Princess *'39*
Old Swimmin' Hole *'40*
Tomboy *'40*
The Daughter of Rosie O'Grady *'50*
The Way We Were *'73*

Mark Lewis Jones
Child 44 *'15*
The Good Liar *'19*

Mark Lewis Jones (1964-)
Solomon and Gaenor *'98*
Mists of Avalon *'01*
Master and Commander: The Far Side of the World *'03*
Cravings *'06*
Framed *'10*

Marsha Jones
Hi-Jacked *'50*
Chicago Calling *'52*

Matt Jones
Home *'15 (V)*
The Layover *'17*

Michelle Jones
Tropix *'02*
Stranded *'06*

Mickey Jones (1941-2019)
National Lampoon's Vacation *'83*
Forced to Kill *'93*
Drop Zone *'94*
Sling Blade *'96*
Tin Cup *'96*

Morgan Jones (1928-2012)
Untamed Women *'52*
The Giant Claw *'57*
Not of This Earth *'57*

Nasir Jones (1973-)
Belly *'98*
Ticker *'01*
Murda Muzik *'03*
Black Nativity *'13*

Nathan Jones (1967-)
Troy *'04*
A Way of Life *'04*
Jet Li's Fearless *'06*
The Condemned *'07*
Never Back Down: No Surrender *'16*

Neal Jones (1960-)
Day at the Beach *'98*
Zombie Honeymoon *'04*

Nicholas Jones (1946-)
Crucible of Horror *'69*
A Dangerous Man: Lawrence after Arabia *'91*
Black Beauty *'94*
Horatio Hornblower: The Adventure Continues *'01*

O-lan Jones (1950-)
Miracle Mile *'89*
American Virgin *'98*

Orlando Jones (1968-)
Office Space *'98*
Liberty Heights *'99*
Waterproof *'99*
Bedazzled *'00*
Chain of Fools *'00*
The Replacements *'00*
Double Take *'01*
Evolution *'01*
Say It Isn't So *'01*
Drumline *'02*
The Time Machine *'02*
Biker Boyz *'03*
House of D *'04*
Primeval *'07*
Misconceptions *'08*
Beyond a Reasonable Doubt *'09*
Cirque du Freak: The Vampire's Assistant *'09*
Seconds Apart *'11*
Enemies Closer *'14*
The Book of Love *'16*

Paul Jones (1942-)
Privilege *'67*
Demons of the Mind *'72*

Peter Jones (1920-2000)
Man of Evil *'48*
Hot Millions *'68*

Rashida Jones (1976-)
Now You Know *'02*
Little Black Book *'04*
I Love You, Man *'09*
New in Town *'09*
Monogamy *'10*
The Social Network *'10*
The Big Year *'11*
Friends With Benefits *'11*
The Muppets *'11*
Our Idiot Brother *'11*
Celeste & Jesse Forever *'12*
Decoding Annie Parker *'13*
Cuban Fury *'14*
The Grinch *'18 (V)*
Klaus *'19*
The Sound of Silence *'19*
Spies in Disguise *'19*

Rebecca Naomi Jones
Lovesick *'14*
Ratter *'16*

Richard Jones (1946-)
Another Pair of Aces: Three of a Kind *'91*
Blue Sky *'91*
Under Siege *'92*
The Good Old Boys *'95*
Lone Star *'95*
The Newton Boys *'97*
Two for Texas *'97*
Where the Heart Is *'00*

Richard T. Jones (1972-)
Renaissance Man *'94*
The Trigger Effect *'96*
Event Horizon *'97*
Hollywood Confidential *'97*
Kiss the Girls *'97*
Incognito *'99*
The Wood *'99*
Beyond Suspicion *'00*
Lockdown *'00*
G *'02*
Moonlight Mile *'02*
Phone Booth *'02*
Twisted *'04*
Tyler Perry's Why Did I Get Married? *'07*
Vantage Point *'08*
Caught in the Crossfire *'10*
Tyler Perry's Why Did I Get Married Too *'10*
Atlas Shrugged 2: The Strike *'12*
Forgiveness *'15*
A Question of Faith *'17*

Robbie Jones
Hurricane Season *'09*
Tyler Perry's Temptation: Confessions of a Marriage Counselor *'13*

Robert Earl Jones (1911-2006)
Wild River *'60*
The Sting *'73*
Cockfighter *'74*
Cold River *'81*
Sleepaway Camp *'83*
Trading Places *'83*
The Cotton Club *'84*
Witness *'85*
Maniac Cop 2 *'90*
Rain Without Thunder *'93*

Sam Jones (1954-)
Flash Gordon *'80*
My Chauffeur *'86*
Jane & the Lost City *'87*
The Spirit *'87*
WhiteForce *'88*
One Man Force *'89*
DaVinci's War *'92*
Fist of Honor *'92*
Maximum Force *'92*
Expert Weapon *'93*
Thunder in Paradise *'93*
Hard Vice *'94*
Vegas Vice *'94*
American Strays *'96*
Where Truth Lies *'96*
T.N.T. *'98*
Dead Sexy *'01*
Strange Fruit *'04*

Sam Jones, III (1983-)
Snipes *'01*
ZigZag *'02*
For One Night *'06*
Glory Road *'06*
Home of the Brave *'06*
Safe Harbor *'09*
Krews *'10*

Sarah Jones (1983-)
Still Green *'07*
Love Finds a Home *'09*
Love Takes Wing *'09*
Mr. Jones *'14*

Shirley Jones (1934-)
Oklahoma! *'55*
Carousel *'56*
April Love *'57*
Bobbikins *'59*
Elmer Gantry *'60*
Two Rode Together *'61*
The Courtship of Eddie's Father *'62*
The Music Man *'62*
Bedtime Story *'63*
The Happy Ending *'69*
The Cheyenne Social Club *'70*
Beyond the Poseidon Adventure *'79*
Tank *'83*
Ping! *'99*
Shriek If You Know What I Did Last Friday the 13th *'00*
Manna from Heaven *'02*
Raising Genius *'04*
Grandma's Boy *'06*
Hidden Places *'06*
Carnal Innocence *'11*
Family Weekend *'13*

Simon Jones (1950-)
The Hitchhiker's Guide to the Galaxy *'81*
Monty Python's The Meaning of Life *'83*
Privates on Parade *'84*
Club Paradise *'86*
Green Card *'90*
Miracle on 34th Street *'94*
The Devil's Own *'96*
Operation Delta Force 2: Mayday *'97*
The Hitchhiker's Guide to the Galaxy *'05*

Steve Jones (1955-)
The Filth and the Fury *'99*
The Big Bounce *'04*

Tamala Jones (1974-)
Booty Call *'96*
Blue Streak *'99*
The Wood *'99*
The Ladies Man *'00*
Little Richard *'00*
Next Friday *'00*
Turn It Up *'00*
The Brothers *'01*
On the Line *'01*
Two Can Play That Game *'01*
Head of State *'03*
Nora's Hair Salon *'04*
Daddy Day Camp *'07*
What Love Is *'07*
Who's Your Caddy? *'07*
The Hustle *'08*
The Janky Promoters *'09*
35 and Ticking *'10*

Terry Jones (1942-2020)
And Now for Something Completely Different *'72*
Monty Python and the Holy Grail *'75*
Jabberwocky *'77*
Monty Python's Life of Brian *'79*
The Secret Policeman's Other Ball *'82*
Monty Python's The Meaning of Life *'83*
Erik the Viking *'89*
Mr. Toad's Wild Ride *'96*

Toby Jones (1966-)
Aristocrats *'99*
In Love and War *'01*
Love or Money *'01*
Harry Potter and the Chamber of Secrets *'02 (V)*
Elizabeth I *'05*
Amazing Grace *'06*
A Harlot's Progress *'06*
Infamous *'06*
The Painted Veil *'06*
The Mist *'07*
Nightwatching *'07*
The Old Curiosity Shop *'07*
St. Trinian's *'07*
City of Ember *'08*
Frost/Nixon *'08*
W. *'08*
Creation *'09*
Murder on the Orient Express *'10*
Sex & Drugs & Rock & Roll *'10*
Virginia *'10*
The Adventures of Tintin *'11 (V)*
Captain America: The First Avenger *'11*
Christopher and His Kind *'11*
The Rite *'11*
Tinker Tailor Soldier Spy *'11*
Your Highness *'11*
Berberian Sound Studio *'12*
The Girl *'12*
The Hunger Games *'12*
Red Lights *'12*
Snow White and the Huntsman *'12*
Titanic *'12*
By the Gun *'14*
Serena *'14*
Tale of Tales *'15*
Anthropoid *'16*
Dad's Army *'16*
Morgan *'16*
Atomic Blonde *'17*
Journey's End *'18*
First Cow *'20*

Tom Jones (1940-)
The Jerky Boys *'95 (C)*
Mars Attacks! *'96 (C)*
Agnes Browne *'99*

Tommy Lee Jones (1946-)
Eliza's Horoscope *'70*
Love Story *'70*

Alice Joyce (1890-1955)
Dancing Mothers '26
The Squall '29
Song o' My Heart '30

Brenda Joyce (1917-2009)
The Rains Came '39
Whispering Ghosts '42
Dead Man's Eyes '44
The Enchanted Forest '45
Tarzan and the Amazons '45
Little Giant '46
Tarzan and the Leopard Woman '46
Tarzan and the Huntress '47
Tarzan and the Mermaids '48
Tarzan's Magic Fountain '48

Elaine Joyce (1945-)
How to Frame a Figg '71
Motel Hell '80
Trick or Treat '86

Ella Joyce (1954-)
Set It Off '96
What About Your Friends: Weekend Getaway '02
Bubba Ho-Tep '03
Who Made the Potatoe Salad? '05
A Simple Promise '07
Preacher's Kid '10
Hopelessly in June '11
Tyler Perry's Temptation: Confessions of a Marriage Counselor '13

William Joyce (1930-98)
I Eat Your Skin '64
The Young Nurses '73

Yootha Joyce (1927-80)
Die! Die! My Darling! '65
Horrors of Burke & Hare '71

Mario Joyner (1961-)
Hangin' with the Homeboys '91
Pootie Tang '01

Michelle Joyner
Traces of Red '92
Cliffhanger '93
Painted Hero '95

Kevin Jubinville (1967-)
The Courage to Love '00
Nightwaves '03
Solar Attack '06
Demons from Her Past '07
Framed for Murder '07
Twitches Too '07
For the Love of Grace '08

Ashley Judd (1968-)
Heat '95
Norma Jean and Marilyn '95
The Passion of Darkly Noon '95
Smoke '95
Normal Life '96
A Time to Kill '96
Kiss the Girls '97
The Locusts '97
Simon Birch '98
Double Jeopardy '99
Eye of the Beholder '99
Where the Heart Is '00
Someone Like You '01
Divine Secrets of the Ya-Ya Sisterhood '02
Frida '02
High Crimes '02
De-Lovely '04
Twisted '04
Bug '06
Come Early Morning '06
Crossing Over '09
Helen '09
Tooth Fairy '10
Dolphin Tale '11
Flypaper '11
Olympus Has Fallen '13
Divergent '14
Dolphin Tale 2 '14
The Identical '14
Big Stone Gap '15
Good Kids '16
A Dog's Way Home '19

Edward Judd (1932-2009)
The Day the Earth Caught Fire '61
Stolen Hours '63
First Men in the Moon '64
The Long Ships '64
Strange Bedfellows '65
The Vengeance of She '68
Flambards '78
The Kitchen Toto '87

Naomi Judd (1946-)
More American Graffiti '79
Rio Diablo '93
Iris Johansen's The Killing Game '11
Nearlyweds '13
An Evergreen Christmas '14

Robert Judd (1986-)
Fight for Your Life '77
Crossroads '86

Charles (Judel, Judells) Judels (1882-1969)
Doorway to Hell '30
Love on the Run '36
Down Argentine Way '40
Pinocchio '40 (V)

Arline Judge (1912-74)
Girl Crazy '32
George White's Scandals of 1935 '35
One in a Million '36
Pigskin Parade '36
Wildcat '42
Girls in Chains '43
The Crawling Hand '63

Christopher Judge (1964-)
Out of Line '00
Personal Effects '05
A Dog's Breakfast '07
Stargate: Continuum '08
Stargate: The Ark of Truth '08
Age of the Hobbits '12
LA Apocalypse '14

Mike Judge (1962-)
Beavis and Butt-Head Do America '96 (V)
Office Space '98
South Park: Bigger, Longer and Uncut '99 (V)
Spy Kids 2: The Island of Lost Dreams '02
Spy Kids 3-D: Game Over '03

Heather Juergensen (1970-)
Kissing Jessica Stein '02
The Hammer '07

Arno Juerging (1947-)
Andy Warhol's Dracula '74
Andy Warhol's Frankenstein '74

Gerard Jugnot (1951-)
French Fried Vacation '79
The Chorus '04
Paris 36 '08
The Sicilian Girl '09

Aurora Julia (1942-)
See Monica Randall

Raul Julia (1940-94)
The Organization '71
Panic in Needle Park '71
Gumball Rally '76
Eyes of Laura Mars '78
The Escape Artist '82
One from the Heart '82
The Tempest '82
Kiss of the Spider Woman '85
The Morning After '86
The Alamo: Thirteen Days to Glory '87
Moon over Parador '88
Onassis '88
Tequila Sunrise '88
Romero '89
Frankenstein Unbound '90
Havana '90
Presumed Innocent '90
The Rookie '90
The Addams Family '91
Addams Family Values '93
Street Fighter '94

Janet (Johnson) Julian (1959-)
Smokey Bites the Dust '81
Humongous '82
Ghostwarrior '86
King of New York '90

Jose Julian
A Better Life '11
Spare Parts '15

Max Julien (1945-)
Uptight '68
Getting Straight '70
The Mack '73
Def Jam's How to Be a Player '97

Julissa (1944-)
Dance of Death '68
The Fear Chamber '68
The Snake People '68

Miranda July (1974-)
Me and You and Everyone We Know '05
The Future '11
Madeline's Madeline '18

Gordon Jump (1932-2003)
Conquest of the Planet of the Apes '72
Making the Grade '84

Hu Jun (1968-)
East Palace, West Palace '96
Lan Yu '01

Tito Junco (1915-83)
A Woman Without Love '51
Death in the Garden '56
The Exterminating Angel '62

Doo-hong Jung
No Blood No Tears '02
The City of Violence '06

Woo-sung Jung
Musa: The Warrior '01
The Good, the Bad, the Weird '08
Reign of Assassins '10
The King '18

Eric Jungmann (1981-)
Not Another Teen Movie '01
Monster Man '03
Happy Endings '05
Killer Pad '06
Military Intelligence and You! '06

John Junkin (1930-2006)
A Hard Day's Night '64
A Handful of Dust '88

Noah Jupe
Suburbicon '17
A Quiet Place '18
Honey Boy '19

Katy Jurado (1924-2002)
Bullfighter & the Lady '50
El Bruto '52
High Noon '52
Arrowhead '53
Broken Lance '54
Trial '55
Man from Del Rio '56
Trapeze '56
The Badlanders '58
One-Eyed Jacks '61
Barabbas '62
A Covenant With Death '67
Stay Away, Joe '68
Once Upon a Scoundrel '73
Pat Garrett & Billy the Kid '73
Children of Sanchez '79
Under the Volcano '84
The Hi-Lo Country '98

Peter Jurasik (1950-)
Tron '82
Full Exposure: The Sex Tape Scandals '89
Peter Gunn '89
Problem Child '90
The Late Shift '96

Curt Jurgens (1912-82)
And God Created Woman '57
Enemy Below '57
Bitter Victory '58
The Inn of the Sixth Happiness '58
Ferry to Hong Kong '59
The Longest Day '62
The Miracle of the White Stallions '63
Psyche 59 '64
Lord Jim '65
Target for Killing '66
The Assassination Bureau '69
Battle of Britain '69
Battle of Neretva '69
The Mephisto Waltz '71
Nicholas and Alexandra '71
Vault of Horror '73
The Twist '76
The Spy Who Loved Me '77
Smiley's People '82

Deana Jurgens (1957-)
Tin Man '83
Code Name: Zebra '84

Jet Jurgensmeyer
A Belle for Christmas '14
The Little Rascals Save the Day '14
Ferdinand '17

Carla Juri
Wetlands '13
Morris from America '16

James Robertson Justice (1905-75)
Whiskey Galore '48
David and Bathsheba '51
The Lady Says No '51
The Voice of Merrill '52
Doctor in the House '53
Rob Roy-The Highland Rogue '53
The Sword & the Rose '53
Above Us the Waves '55
An Alligator Named Daisy '55
Land of the Pharaohs '55
Storm Over the Nile '55
Doctor at Sea '56
The Iron Petticoat '56
The Beasts of Marseilles '57
Campbell's Kingdom '57
Doctor at Large '57
Upstairs and Downstairs '59
The Guns of Navarone '61
Murder She Said '61
Very Important Person '61
Guns of Darkness '62
Le Repos du Guerrier '62
Doctor in Distress '63
The Face of Fu Manchu '65
A Coeur Joie '67
Mayerling '68
Spirits of the Dead '68
Zeta One '69

Katherine Justice (1942-)
Columbo: Prescription Murder '67
Five Card Stud '68
The Stepmother '71
Frasier the Sensuous Lion '73
Captain America 2: Death Too Soon '79

Victoria Justice (1993-)
Spectacular '09
The Boy Who Cried Werewolf '10
The First Time '12
Fun Size '12

John Justin (1917-2002)
The Thief of Bagdad '40
The Sound Barrier '52
King of the Khyber Rifles '53
Crest of the Wave '54
Untamed '55
Lisztomania '75

William Justine
The Bride & the Beast '58
Trauma '62

Tony Leung Ka Fai
Jackie Chan's The Myth '05
Lost in Beijing '07

Jeff Kaake (1959-)
Border Shootout '90
D.R.E.A.M. Team '99

Hollywood Wives: The New Generation '03

Nikolaj Lie Kaas (1973-)
The Idiots '99
Flickering Lights '01
The Green Butchers '03
Reconstruction '03
Brothers '04
Adam's Apples '05
PU-239 '06
Just Another Love Story '08
Men & Chicken '15

Jane Kaczmarek (1955-)
Falling in Love '84
The Heavenly Kid '85
The Right of the People '86
D.O.A. '88
Vice Versa '88
Pleasantville '98
Reviving Ophelia '10

Christopher Kadish
Acts of Worship '01
Night Watcher '08

Piotr Kadochnikev
Ivan the Terrible, Part 1 '44
Ivan the Terrible, Part 2 '46

Charlotte Kady
Revenge of the Musketeers '94
Safe Conduct '01

Hakeem Kae-Kazim (1962-)
The Front Line '06
The Librarian: Return to King Solomon's Mines '06
Attack on Darfur '09
The Fourth Kind '09

Heather Kafka (1972-)
Three Days of Rain '02
Lovers of Hate '10

Takeshi Kaga (1950-)
Death Note '06
Death Note 2: The Last Name '07
Death Note 3: L Change the World '08

Diane Kagan
Mr. & Mrs. Bridge '90
The Living Wake '07

Kyoko Kagawa (1931-)
Sansho the Bailiff '54
The Lower Depths '57
Mothra '62

Teruyuki Kagawa (1965-)
The Mystery of Rampo '94
Sway '06
Hana: The Tale of a Reluctant Samurai '07
Sukiyaki Western Django '08
John Rabe '09
Tokyo Sonata '09
Creepy '16

David Kagen (1948-)
Friday the 13th, Part 6: Jason Lives '86
Conspiracy: The Trial of the Chicago Eight '87
Body Chemistry '90

Steve Kahan (1930-)
Lethal Weapon '87
Scrooged '88
Lethal Weapon 2 '89
Predator 2 '90
Lethal Weapon 3 '92
Demolition Man '93
Warlock: The Armageddon '93
Lethal Weapon 4 '98

Ian Kahn (1972-)
Brooklyn Lobster '05
Secrets in the Walls '10

Madeline Kahn (1942-99)
What's Up, Doc? '72
The Hideaways '73
Paper Moon '73
Blazing Saddles '74
Young Frankenstein '74
High Anxiety '77
The Adventures of Sherlock Holmes' Smarter Brother '78
The Cheap Detective '78
The Muppet Movie '79 (C)
First Family '80
Simon '80
Wholly Moses! '80
History of the World: Part 1 '81
Yellowbeard '83
City Heat '84
Clue '85
An American Tail '86 (V)
Betsy's Wedding '90
For Richer, for Poorer '92
Mixed Nuts '94
Nixon '95
A Bug's Life '98 (V)
Judy Berlin '99

Kaho
Gamera the Brave '06
Our Little Sister '16

Chen Kaige (1952-)
The Emperor and the Assassin '99
Together '02

Khalil Kain (1964-)
Juice '92
Renaissance Man '94
Love Jones '96
The Tiger Woods Story '98
Passing Glory '99
Bones '01
Baadasssss! '03

Joel Kaiser (1956-)
Home for Christmas '90
Dead Certain '92

Michael G. Kaiser
The Monster of Phantom Lake '06
Destination: Outer Space '10
Attack of the Moon Zombies '11

Oldrich Kaiser (1955-)
Dark Blue World '01
I Served the King of England '07

Suki Kaiser (1967-)
Virtual Assassin '95
Ann Rule Presents: The Stranger Beside Me '03

Elizabeth Kaitan (1960-)
Silent Night, Deadly Night 2 '87
Slave Girls from Beyond Infinity '87
Aftershock '88
Assault of the Killer Bimbos '88
Friday the 13th, Part 7: The New Blood '88
Necromancer: Satan's Servant '88
Nightwish '89
Vice Academy 3 '91
Desperate Crimes '93
Petticoat Planet '96
South Beach Academy '96
Virtual Encounters '96

Meiko Kaji (1947-)
Blind Woman's Curse '70
Lady Snowblood '73
Lady Snowblood: Love Song of Vengeance '74

Bianca Kajlich (1977-)
Halloween: Resurrection '02
30 Minutes or Less '11

Tomohiro Kaku
Ju-On 2 '00
Hana & Alice '04

Toni Kalem (1956-)
Wanderers '79
Silent Rage '82
Billy Galvin '86
American Strays '96

Patricia Kalember (1957-)
Fletch Lives '89
Jacob's Ladder '90
Big Girls Don't Cry. . . They Get Even '92
A Far Off Place '93
Degree of Guilt '95
A Time for Dancing '00
Path to War '02
Signs '02

Straight from the Heart '03
Kalamity '10
Limitless '11

Jean-Pierre Kalfon (1938-)
Weekend '67
The Valley Obscured by the Clouds '70
Condorman '81
The Cry of the Owl '87
Total Western '00
Lulu '02
Heartbeat Detector '07

Mindy Kaling (1979-)
License to Wed '07
Despicable Me '10 (V)
Inside Out '15 (V)
Ocean's 8 '18
A Wrinkle in Time '18
Late Night '19

Helena Kallianiotes (1938-)
Five Easy Pieces '70
Kansas City Bomber '72
Backtrack '89

Alexander Kalugin
Merlin's Apprentice '06
Countdown '16

Daniel Kaluuya (1989-)
Chatroom '10
Johnny English Reborn '11
Get Out '17
Queen & Slim '19

Alexander Kalyagin (1942-)
An Unfinished Piece for a Player Piano '77
A Slave of Love '78

Adhir Kalyan
Fired Up! '09
High School '10

Ivan Kamaras (1972-)
The Mark '12
The Mark 2: Redemption '13
Outpost: Rise of the Spetsnaz '13
Ruben Brandt, Collector '18

Danny Kamekona (1926-96)
The Karate Kid: Part 2 '86
Robot Jox '90
Robot Wars '93

Stanley Kamel (1943-2008)
Stonebrook '98
Running Red '99
Escape under Pressure '00
Domino '05

Antoine Kamerling (1966-2010)
Suite 16 '94
Soul Assassin '01
Dominion: Prequel to the Exorcist '05

Ryunosuke Kamiki (1993-)
The Great Yokai War '05
Big Man Japan '07
Your Name '17

Dan Kamin (1947-)
Another Pair of Aces: Three of a Kind '91
America's Dream '95
The Rookie '02

Ida Kaminska (1899-1980)
The Shop on Main Street '65
The Angel Levine '70

Kris Kamm (1964-)
Shattered Innocence '87
Born to Ride '91
When the Party's Over '91
Wyatt Earp '94
Andersonville '95

Elena Kampouris (1997-)
Men, Women & Children '14
Before I Fall '17

Melina Kanakaredes (1967-)
The Long Kiss Goodnight '96
Rounders '98
15 Minutes '01
Into the Fire '05

Percy Jackson & The Olympians: The Lightning Thief '10
Snitch '13

Anna Kanakis (1962-)
Warriors of the Wasteland '83
After the Fall of New York '85

Steve Kanaly (1946-)
The Wind and the Lion '75
Midway '76
Balboa '82
Fleshburn '84
Double Trouble '91
Eye of the Eagle 3 '91
Pumpkinhead 2: Blood Wings '94
Scorpio One '97

Jun Kaname
Black House '07
Blood '09

Sean Kanan (1966-)
The Karate Kid: Part 3 '89
Chaos Factor '00
Chasing Holden '01
Carpool Guy '05
Hack! '07

Hiroshi Kanbe (1963-)
Samurai Fiction '99
The Twilight Samurai '02

Adelaide Kane
Secrets of the Mountain '10
The Purge '13
Louder Than Words '14

Big Daddy Kane (1968-)
Gunmen '93 (C)
Posse '93
Dead Heist '07

Carol Kane (1952-)
Carnal Knowledge '71
Desperate Characters '71
Wedding in White '72
The Last Detail '73
Dog Day Afternoon '75
Hester Street '75
Harry & Walter Go to New York '76
Annie Hall '77
Valentino '77
World's Greatest Lover '77
My Sister, My Love '78
The Muppet Movie '79 (C)
When a Stranger Calls '79
Burning Rage '84
Racing with the Moon '84
Transylvania 6-5000 '85
Jumpin' Jack Flash '86
Ishtar '87
The Princess Bride '87
License to Drive '88
Scrooged '88
Sticky Fingers '88
Flashback '89
Joe Versus the Volcano '90
The Lemon Sisters '90
My Blue Heaven '90
In the Soup '92 (C)
Addams Family Values '93
Ted & Venus '93
When a Stranger Calls Back '93
The Crazysitter '94
Big Bully '95
The Pallbearer '95
American Strays '96
Sunset Park '96
Tree's Lounge '96
Gone Fishin' '97
Office Killer '97
Jawbreaker '98
Noah's Ark '99
The Tic Code '99
My First Mister '01
Love in the Time of Money '02
Audrey's Rain '03
Confessions of a Teenage Drama Queen '04
The Pacifier '05
My Girlfriend's Boyfriend '10
Sleepwalk with Me '12
Thanks for Sharing '13

Christian Kane (1974-)
Crossfire Trail '01
Life or Something Like It '02
Just Married '03
Secondhand Lions '03
Taxi '04
Four Sheets to the Wind '07
Hide '08
The Donner Party '09
Not Since You '09
Good Day for It '11
Universal Squadrons '11
50 to 1 '14

Ivan Kane
Platoon '86
Gettysburg '93
Bound '96

Marjorie 'Babe' Kane (1909-92)
The Great Gabbo '29
Be Yourself '30
Sunny Skies '30

Michael Kane
Lonely Are the Brave '62
The Gunfighters '87

Shannon Kane
Brooklyn's Finest '09
Madea's Big Happy Family '11

Tom Kane (1962-)
The Powerpuff Girls Movie '02 (V)
The Wild Thornberrys Movie '02 (V)
Rugrats Go Wild! '03 (V)
Star Wars: The Clone Wars '08 (V)
The Smurfs '11 (N)

Nobuo Kaneko (1923-95)
Ikiru '52
The Human Condition: A Soldier's Prayer '61

Takeshi Kaneshiro (1973-)
Chungking Express '95
Fallen Angels '95
House of Flying Daggers '04
Perhaps Love '05
Red Cliff '08
Warlords '08

Shin-il Kang (1960-)
Public Enemy '02
Another Public Enemy '05
Black House '07

Sung Kang (1972-)
Better Luck Tomorrow '02
The Fast and the Furious: Tokyo Drift '06
War '07
Fast Five '11
Bullet to the Head '12
Fast & Furious 6 '13

Tim Kang (1973-)
Robot Stories '03
Rambo '08

John Kani (1943-)
Killing Heat '84
Sarafina! '92
The Ghost and the Darkness '96
The Bird Can't Fly '07
Endgame '09
Coriolanus '11

Miho Kanno (1977-)
Tomie '99
Dolls '02

Lyle Kanouse (1952-)
Auto Focus '02
Caught in the Crossfire '10
House of the Rising Sun '11

China Kantner (1971-)
Airheads '94
The Stoned Age '94
The Evening Star '96

Jack Kao (1958-)
Goodbye South, Goodbye '96
Flowers of Shanghai '98
Ghosted '09

John Kapelos (1956-)
The Breakfast Club '85
Nothing in Common '86
Roxanne '87
The Boost '88
Nick Knight '89
Internal Affairs '90
Man Trouble '92
The Shadow '94
The Late Shift '96
The Deep End of the Ocean '98
Cold Blooded '00
Mimic 3: Sentinel '03
Shallow Ground '04
Stick It '06
Everybody Wants to Be Italian '08
Afternoon Delight '13

Gabe Kaplan (1945-)
Fast Break '79
Nobody's Perfekt '79

Jonathan Kaplan (1947-)
Cannonball '76
Hollywood Boulevard '76

Mady Kaplan (1956-)
The Deer Hunter '78
The Falcon and the Snowman '85

Marvin Kaplan (1927-)
Adam's Rib '50
Angels in the Outfield '51
The Severed Arm '73

Anil Kapoor (1959-)
Slumdog Millionaire '08
Mission: Impossible-Ghost Protocol '11
Total Dhamaal '19

Shashi Kapoor (1938-)
The Householder '63
Shakespeare Wallah '65
Bombay Talkie '70
Siddhartha '72
Heat and Dust '82
The Deceivers '88
In Custody '94
Gulliver's Travels '95

Valerie Kaprisky (1963-)
Breathless '83
Glam '97

Ron Karabatsos (1933-2012)
Flashdance '83
29th Street '91
The Crew '00

Amara Karan
The Darjeeling Limited '07
A Fantastic Fear of Everything '14

Mirjana Karanovic (1957-)
When Father Was Away on Business '85
Underground '95
Go West '05
Grbavica: The Land of My Dreams '06

Kim Kardashian
Disaster Movie '08
Tyler Perry's Temptation: Confessions of a Marriage Counselor '13

James Karen (1923-)
Frankenstein Meets the Space Monster '65
Hercules in New York '70
All the President's Men '76
The China Syndrome '79
Poltergeist '82
Time Walker '82
The Jagged Edge '85
Latino '85
Return of the Living Dead '85
Hardbodies 2 '86
Billionaire Boys Club '87
Wall Street '87
Return of the Living Dead 2 '88
Shattered Dreams '90
Vital Signs '90
The Willies '90
The Unborn '91

Lies Before Kisses '92
Piranha '95
Up Close and Personal '96
Joyride '97
A River Made to Drown In '97
Girl '98
Thirteen Days '00
Mulholland Drive '01
The Pursuit of Happyness '06
Dark and Stormy Night '09
Sympathy for Delicious '10

Anna Karin
Body of Influence '93
The Fear '94

Rita Karin (1919-93)
Sophie's Choice '82
Enemies, a Love Story '89
He Said, She Said '91

Anna Karina (1940-2019)
Le Petit Soldat '60
A Woman Is a Woman '60
Cleo from 5 to 7 '61
My Life to Live '62
Les Carabiniers '63
Band of Outsiders '64
Alphaville '65
Pierrot le Fou '65
Before Winter Comes '69
Bread and Chocolate '73
Regina '83
Chinese Roulette '86
The Truth About Charlie '02 (C)

Athena Karkanis
Saw 4 '07
Art of War 2: The Betrayal '08
Saw 6 '09
Sacrifice '11

Richard Karlan (1919-2004)
Captain Kidd and the Slave Girl '54
Abbott and Costello Meet the Mummy '55
Star! '68
Missiles of October '74

Olga Karlatos (1947-)
Zombie '80
Purple Rain '84

John Karlen (1933-2020)
House of Dark Shadows '70
Daughters of Darkness '71
Night of Dark Shadows '71
Melvin Purvis: G-Man '74
Trilogy of Terror '75
Impulse '84
Racing with the Moon '84
Hostage Flight '85
Babycakes '89
Surf Ninjas '93

Miriam Karlin (1925-2011)
Room at the Top '59
Ladies Who Do '63
A Clockwork Orange '71
The Attic: The Hiding of Anne Frank '88

Boris Karloff (1887-1969)
The Last of the Mohicans '20
The Bells '26
Cracked Nuts '31
The Criminal Code '31
Five Star Final '31
Frankenstein '31
The Guilty Generation '31
The Public Defender '31
Scarface '31
Smart Money '31
Tonight or Never '31
The Mask of Fu Manchu '32
The Mummy '32
The Old Dark House '32
The Black Cat '34
The Ghoul '34
The Lost Patrol '34
The Black Room '35
The Bride of Frankenstein '35
Charlie Chan at the Opera '36
The Invisible Ray '36
Mr. Wong, Detective '38

The Man They Could Not Hang '39
Mr. Wong in Chinatown '39
Mystery of Mr. Wong '39
Son of Frankenstein '39
The Tower of London '39
Black Friday '40
Doomed to Die '40
The Fatal Hour '40
You'll Find Out '40
The Boogie Man Will Get You '42
The Climax '44
House of Frankenstein '44
Bedlam '45
The Body Snatcher '45
Isle of the Dead '45
Dick Tracy Meets Gruesome '47
Lured '47
The Secret Life of Walter Mitty '47
Unconquered '47
Abbott and Costello Meet the Killer, Boris Karloff '49
The Strange Door '51
Abbott and Costello Meet Dr. Jekyll and Mr. Hyde '52
The Black Castle '52
Island Monster '53
Sabaka '55
Corridors of Blood '58
Frankenstein 1970 '58
The Haunted Strangler '58
The Raven '63
The Terror '63
Bikini Beach '64
Black Sabbath '64
The Comedy of Terrors '64
Die, Monster, Die! '65
Ghost in the Invisible Bikini '66
The Sorcerers '67
The Venetian Affair '67
The Crimson Cult '68
Dance of Death '68
The Fear Chamber '68
Mad Monster Party '68 (V)
The Snake People '68
Targets '68

Oskar Karlweis (1894-1956)
Five Fingers '52
Carry On Cabby '63

Richard Karn (1956-)
Bram Stoker's The Mummy '97
MVP2: Most Vertical Primate '01
Air Bud 4: Seventh Inning Fetch '02
Snow Buddies '08

Philipp Karner (1979-)
The Battle of Shaker Heights '03
Kiss the Bride '07

Robert Karnes (1917-79)
From Here to Eternity '53
Five Guns to Tombstone '60

Roscoe Karns (1893-1970)
Wings '27
Beggars of Life '28
Laughing Sinners '31
The Crooked Circle '32
If I Had a Million '32
Night After Night '32
One Sunday Afternoon '33
Today We Live '33
It Happened One Night '34
Twentieth Century '34
Alibi Ike '35
Front Page Woman '35
Wings in the Dark '35
Cain and Mabel '36
You and Me '38
Dancing Co-Ed '39
Frolics on Ice '39
His Girl Friday '40
Saturday's Children '40
They Drive by Night '40
Footsteps in the Dark '41
Woman of the Year '42
You Can't Escape Forever '42
Old Acquaintance '43

His Butler's Sister *'44*
Navy Way *'44*
That's My Man *'47*

Todd Karns (1921-2000)
It's a Wonderful Life *'46*
It's a Small World *'50*

Erin Karpluk (1978-)
Almost Heaven *'06*
Judicial Indiscretion *'07*
Smoke Jumpers *'08*
Mrs. Miracle *'09*
Wyvern *'09*
Christmas Lodge *'11*
Reasonable Doubt *'14*

Alex Karpovsky
Beeswax *'09*
Lovers of Hate *'10*
Tiny Furniture *'10*
Supporting Characters *'13*

Sarah Rose Karr (1984-)
Beethoven *'92*
Beethoven's 2nd *'93*

Alex Karras (1935-2012)
Paper Lion *'68*
Blazing Saddles *'74*
Babe! *'75*
Hootch Country Boys *'75*
Mad Bull *'77*
Centennial *'78*
FM *'78*
Nobody's Perfekt *'79*
Porky's *'82*
Victor/Victoria *'82*
Against All Odds *'84*

Sabine Karsenti
Silent Hunter *'94*
Battlefield Earth *'00*

Buck Kartalian (1922-)
Cool Hand Luke *'67*
Please Don't Eat My Mother *'72*
Josh Kirby. . . Time Warrior: Chapter 3, Trapped on Toyworld *'95*

Vincent Kartheiser (1979-)
Alaska *'96*
All I Wanna Do *'98*
Another Day in Paradise *'98*
Bad Seed *'00*
Crime and Punishment in Suburbia *'00*
Luckytown *'00*
The Unsaid *'01*
Alpha Dog *'06*
Elektra Luxx *'10*
In Time *'11*
A Kind of Murder *'16*
My Friend Dahmer *'17*

Claudia Karvan (1972-)
High Tide *'87*
Flynn *'96*
Passion *'99*
Strange Planet *'99*
Risk *'00*
Aquamarine *'06*
Nature's Grave *'08*
$9.99 *'08 (V)*
Daybreakers *'09*
33 Postcards *'11*

Tcheky Karyo (1953-)
Full Moon in Paris *'84*
Sorceress *'88*
The Bear *'89*
La Femme Nikita *'91*
1492: Conquest of Paradise *'92*
Sketch Artist *'92*
And the Band Played On *'93 (C)*
Red Shoe Diaries 3: Another Woman's Lipstick *'93*
Bad Boys *'95*
Foreign Land *'95*
Goldeneye *'95*
Addicted to Love *'96*
Habitat *'97*
From the Earth to the Moon *'98*
My Life So Far *'98*
Like a Fish Out of Water *'99*
The Messenger: The Story of Joan of Arc *'99*
Wing Commander *'99*
Arabian Nights *'00*
The Patriot *'00*
Saving Grace *'00*
Kiss of the Dragon *'01*
The Core *'03*
The Good Thief *'03*
Taking Lives *'04*
A Very Long Engagement *'04*
The 4 Musketeers *'05*
The Gravedancers *'06*

Alex Karzis
A Man in Uniform *'93*
Detention *'03*

Max Kasch (1985-)
Holes *'03*
Waiting *'05*
Shrooms *'07*

Lawrence Kasdan (1949-)
Into the Night *'85 (C)*
As Good As It Gets *'97 (C)*
Five Came Back *'17*

Ryo Kase (1974-)
Letters from Iwo Jima *'06*
Hana: The Tale of a Reluctant Samurai *'07*
Tokyo! *'09*
Outrage *'10*
Restless *'11*
Like Someone in Love *'13*
Our Little Sister *'16*
Bel Canto *'18*

Casey Kasem (1933-2014)
Escape from Planet Earth *'67*
The Glory Stompers *'67*
Wild Wheels *'69*
The Incredible Two-Headed Transplant *'71*
Soul Hustler *'76*
The Dark *'79*
The Return of the King *'80 (V)*
James Dean: Live Fast, Die Young *'97*
Undercover Angel *'99*

Daniel Kash (1959-)
Bone Daddy *'97*
Killing Moon *'00*
Life with Judy Garland-Me and My Shadows *'01*
Under Heavy Fire *'01*
Crown Heights *'02*
The Gospel of John *'03*
Camp Rock 2: The Final Jam *'10*
Mama *'13*

Linda Kash (1961-)
Ernest Goes to Africa *'97*
Cinderella Man *'05*
Wedding Wars *'06*

Anna Kashfi (1934-)
Battle Hymn *'57*
Cowboy *'58*

Yu Kashii
Linda Linda Linda *'05*
Death Note *'06*

Harold Kasket (1926-2002)
Moulin Rouge *'52*
The Seventh Voyage of Sinbad *'58*

Gary Kasper (1958-)
Vision Quest *'85*
Josh Kirby. . . Time Warrior: Chapter 4, Eggs from 70 Million B.C. *'95*
The Hunt for Eagle One: Crash Point *'06*

Mark Kassen (1971-)
Puncture *'11*
Before We Go *'14*

John Kassir (1957-)
Tales from the Crypt Presents Demon Knight *'94 (V)*
Pocahontas *'95 (V)*

Mathieu Kassovitz (1967-)
Cafe au Lait *'94*
The Fifth Element *'97*
Jakob the Liar *'99*
Amelie *'01*
Amen *'02*
Birthday Girl *'02*
Munich *'05*
Happy End *'17*

Daphna Kastner (1961-)
Eating *'90*
Venice, Venice *'92*
Time Code *'00*

Peter Kastner (1943-2008)
You're a Big Boy Now *'66*
Frightmare *'81*

Kurt Kasznar (1913-79)
Lovely to Look At *'52*
All the Brothers Were Valiant *'53*
Give a Girl a Break *'53*
The Great Diamond Robbery *'53*
Lili *'53*
Ride, Vaquero! *'53*
Flame of the Islands *'55*
Jump Into Hell *'55*
My Sister Eileen *'55*
Anything Goes *'56*
A Farewell to Arms *'57*
Legend of the Lost *'57*
The Journey *'59*
The Ambushers *'67*
Casino Royale *'67*

Anna (Katerina) Katarina
The Blood of Heroes *'89*
Slaves of New York *'89*
Omega Doom *'96*
The Game *'97*

Kurt Katch (1896-1958)
Ali Baba and the Forty Thieves *'43*
Background to Danger *'43*
Watch on the Rhine *'43*
The Mask of Dimitrios *'44*
Abbott and Costello Meet the Mummy *'55*

Reda Kateb
A Prophet *'09*
Fishing Without Nets *'14*
Submergence *'18*

Philippe Katerine (1968-)
Gainsbourg: A Heroic Life *'10*
Crazy Horse *'12*
Let the Sunshine In *'17*

Bernard Kates (1922-2010)
The Babe *'92*
Seedpeople *'92*

Kimberley Kates (1969-)
Chained Heat 2 *'92*
First Degree *'98*
Blue Valley Songbird *'99*
Highway *'01*

Branka Katic (1970-)
The Truth About Love *'04*
The Big Picture *'10*

Stana Katic (1978-)
Shut-Eye *'03*
Pit Fighter *'05*
Feast of Love *'07*
The Librarian: Curse of the Judas Chalice *'08*
Quantum of Solace *'08*
The Spirit *'08*
Stiletto *'08*
Would Be Kings *'08*
The Double *'11*
CBGB *'13*
Superman: Unbound *'13 (V)*

Daisuke Kato (1910-75)
Rashomon *'51*
Seven Samurai *'54*
Samurai 2: Duel at Ichijoji Temple *'55*
Yojimbo *'61*

Go Kato
Sword of the Beast *'65*
Shogun Assassin 2: Lightning Swords of Death *'73*

Kazuo Kato (1928-)
Ran *'85*
Hiroshima *'95*

Masaya Kato (1963-)
Crimebroker *'93*
The Seventh Floor *'93*
Crime Broker *'94*
Drive *'96*
Nobody *'99*
Brother *'00*

Takeshi Kato (1929-)
None But the Brave *'65*
Ran *'85*

Rosanne Katon (1954-)
The Swinging Cheerleaders *'74*
Chesty Anderson USN *'76*
The Muthers *'76*
She Devils in Chains *'76*
Motel Hell *'80*
Zapped! *'82*
Bachelor Party *'84*

Shintaro Katsu (1931-97)
Zatoichi: The Life and Opinion of Masseur Ichi *'62*
Zatoichi: Master Ichi and a Chest of Gold *'64*
Zatoichi: Zatoichi's Flashing Sword *'64*
Zatoichi: The Blind Swordsman and the Chess Expert *'65*
Zatoichi: The Blind Swordsman's Vengeance *'66*
Zatoichi: The Blind Swordsman and the Fugitives *'68*
Zatoichi *vs.* Yojimbo *'70*
Ronin Gai *'90*

Andreas Katsulas (1947-2006)
Someone to Watch Over Me *'87*
Communion *'89*
Next of Kin *'89*
Blame It on the Bellboy *'92*
The Fugitive *'93*
Path to Paradise *'97*

Nicky Katt (1970-)
The Babysitter *'95*
johns *'96*
Phantoms *'97*
Delivered *'98*
One True Thing *'98*
The Limey *'99*
Boiler Room *'00*
Way of the Gun *'00*
Waking Life *'01*
Full Frontal *'02*
Insomnia *'02*
I Love Your Work *'03*
School of Rock *'03*
Secondhand Lions *'03*
Sin City *'05*
The Brave One *'07*
Death Proof *'07*
Planet Terror *'07*
Snow Angels *'07*

William Katt (1951-)
Carrie *'76*
Big Wednesday *'78*
Butch and Sundance: The Early Days *'79*
Pippin *'81*
Baby. . . Secret of the Lost Legend *'85*
Perry Mason Returns *'85*
House *'86*
Swimsuit *'89*
Last Call *'90*
The Paperboy *'94*
Stranger by Night *'94*
Piranha *'95*
Daddy's Girl *'96*
Mother Teresa: In the Name of God's Poor *'97*
Rough Riders *'97*
Deadly Game *'98*
Jawbreaker *'98*
Twin Falls Idaho *'99*
Circuit *'02*
River's End *'05*
AVH: Alien *vs.* Hunter *'07*
Bone Eater *'07*
The Man from Earth *'07*
Mirrors 2 *'10*
Pure Country 2: The Gift *'10*
Super *'10*
Paranormal Movie *'13*
Sparks *'13*

Chris Kattan (1970-)
A Night at the Roxbury *'98*
House on Haunted Hill *'99*
Corky Romano *'01*
Monkeybone *'01*
Undercover Brother *'02*
Adam & Steve *'05*
Christmas in Wonderland *'07*
Undead or Alive *'07*
Delgo *'08 (V)*
Bollywood Hero *'09*
Scout's Honor: Badge to the Bone *'09*
Tanner Hall *'09*
Guns, Girls and Gambling *'11*
A Holiday Heist *'11*

Jerry Katz
Journey to Promethea *'10*
Wrong Side of Town *'10*

Jonathan Katz (1946-)
The Independent *'00*
Daddy Day Care *'03*

Judah Katz (1960-)
Dirty Pictures *'00*
Crown Heights *'02*

Omri Katz (1976-)
Matinee *'92*
Hocus Pocus *'93*

Adam Kaufman (1974-)
Between *'05*
Altered *'06*
Loving Leah *'09*

Andy Kaufman (1949-84)
God Told Me To *'76*
Heartbeeps *'81*

Gunther Kaufman (1947-)
Whity *'70*
In a Year of 13 Moons *'78*

Lloyd Kaufman (1945-)
Waiting *'00*
Bikini Bloodbath Christmas *'09*
Nun of That *'09*

Christine Kaufmann (1945-)
The Last Days of Pompeii *'60*
A Man Named Rocca *'61*
Town without Pity *'61*
Swordsman of Siena *'62*
Taras Bulba *'62*
Murders in the Rue Morgue *'71*
Bagdad Cafe *'88*

Joseph Kaufmann (1950-)
Johnny Got His Gun *'71*
Private Duty Nurses *'71*
Heavy Traffic *'73*

Maurice Kaufmann (1928-97)
The Giant Behemoth *'59*
Die! Die! My Darling! *'65*
The Abominable Dr. Phibes *'71*
Fright *'71*

Caroline Kava
Little Nikita *'88*
Born on the Fourth of July *'89*

Christine Kavanagh (1957-)
The Blackheath Poisonings *'92*
Catherine Cookson's The Glass Virgin *'95*
In His Life: The John Lennon Story *'00*

John Kavanagh
Bellman and True *'88*
Sharpe's Sword *'94*
Widow's Peak *'94*
Benedict Arnold: A Question of Honor *'03*
Alexander *'04*
The Black Dahlia *'06*
The Invisible Woman *'13*

Ingrid Kavelaars (1971-)
White Coats *'04*
Harm's Way *'07*
Gooby *'09*

Julie Kavner (1950-)
Katherine *'75*
Bad Medicine *'85*
Hannah and Her Sisters *'86*
Radio Days *'87*
New York Stories *'89*
Alice *'90*
Awakenings *'90*
Shadows and Fog *'92*
This Is My Life *'92*
I'll Do Anything *'93*
Forget Paris *'95*
Deconstructing Harry *'97*
Dr. Dolittle *'98 (V)*
Judy Berlin *'99*
The Lion King 1 1/2 *'04 (V)*
Click *'06*
The Simpsons Movie *'07 (V)*

Sabu Kawahara (1946-)
A Scene at Sea *'92*
The Eel *'96*

Chojuro Kawarazaki (1903-81)
47 Ronin, Part 1 *'42*
47 Ronin, Part 2 *'42*

Kunitaro Kawarazaki
47 Ronin, Part 1 *'42*
47 Ronin, Part 2 *'42*

Hiroyuki Kawase (1964-)
Godzilla *vs.* the Smog Monster *'72*
Godzilla *vs.* Megalon *'76*

Yusuke Kawazu (1935-)
The Human Condition: Road to Eternity *'59*
The Human Condition: A Soldier's Prayer *'61*
Fighting Elegy *'66*

Barnaby Kay (1967-)
Oscar and Lucinda *'97*
Conspiracy *'01*

Bernard Kay (1928-2014)
Doctor Zhivago *'65*
The Conqueror Worm *'68*
Trog *'70*

Billy Kay (1984-)
L.I.E. *'01*
The Battle of Shaker Heights *'03*

Charles Kay (1930-)
Fortunes of War *'87*
Henry V *'89*
Beautiful People *'99*
The Importance of Being Earnest *'02*
Have No Fear: The Life of Pope John Paul II *'05*

Dianne Kay (1955-)
Portrait of a Showgirl *'82*
Andy and the Airwave Rangers *'89*

Dominic Scott Kay (1996-)
Loverboy *'05*
Charlotte's Web *'06 (V)*

Lesli Kay
Forbidden Games *'95*
Petticoat Planet *'96*

Mary Ellen Kay (1929-)
Government Agents *vs.* Phantom Legion *'51*
Colorado Sundown *'52*

Melody Kay
Camp Nowhere *'94*
The NeverEnding Story 3: Escape from Fantasia *'94*

Sylvia Kay
Rapture *'65*
Outback *'71*

Yuzo Kayama (1937-)
Sanjuro *'62*
Red Beard *'65*

Caren Kaye (1951-)
Kill Castro *'80*
The Mercenaries *'80*
My Tutor *'82*
Pumpkinhead 2: Blood Wings *'94*

Danny Kaye (1913-87)
Up in Arms *'44*
Wonder Man *'45*
The Kid from Brooklyn *'46*

The Secret Life of Walter Mitty '47
A Song Is Born '48
The Inspector General '49
It's a Great Feeling '49
Hans Christian Andersen '52
Knock on Wood '54
White Christmas '54
The Court Jester '56
Merry Andrew '58
The Five Pennies '59
On the Double '61
The Madwoman of Chaillot '69

David Kaye (1964-)
Mermaid '00
3000 Miles to Graceland '01
Ratchet & Clank '16

Davy Kaye (1916-98)
Carry On Cowboy '66
The Biggest Bundle of Them All '68

Lila Kaye (1929-2012)
An American Werewolf in London '81
Camille '84
The Canterville Ghost '86
Nuns on the Run '90

Norman Kaye (1927-2007)
Lonely Hearts '82
Man of Flowers '84
Where the Green Ants Dream '84
Cactus '86
Frenchman's Farm '87
Bad Boy Bubby '93
Heaven's Burning '97
Innocence '00

Paul Kaye
It's All Gone, Pete Tong '04
The Killing Gene '07

Stubby Kaye (1918-97)
Guys and Dolls '55
Li'l Abner '59
40 Pounds of Trouble '62
Cat Ballou '65
The Way West '67
The Big Push '75
Who Framed Roger Rabbit '88

Morio Kazama (1949-)
Fall Guy '82
Samurai Fiction '99

Elia Kazan (1909-2003)
City for Conquest '40
Blues in the Night '41

Lainie Kazan (1940-)
Lady in Cement '68
Romance of a Horsethief '71
Love Affair: The Eleanor & Lou Gehrig Story '77
My Favorite Year '82
One from the Heart '82
Sunset Limousine '83
The Journey of Natty Gann '85
Lust in the Dust '85
Delta Force '86
Harry and the Hendersons '87
Beaches '88
Out of the Dark '88
29th Street '91
I Don't Buy Kisses Anymore '92
The Cemetery Club '93
Love Is All There Is '96
Allie & Me '97
The Big Hit '98
The Crew '00
If You Only Knew '00
What's Cooking? '00
My Big Fat Greek Wedding '02
Gigli '03
Tempted '03
Bratz '07
You Don't Mess with the Zohan '08
Oy Vey! My Son is Gay! '09
A Very Mary Christmas '10

Zoe Kazan (1983-)
Fracture '07
Revolutionary Road '08
The Exploding Girl '09
I Hate Valentine's Day '09
It's Complicated '09
Me and Orson Welles '09
The Private Lives of Pippa Lee '09
Happythankyoumoreplease '10
Meek's Cutoff '10
Ruby Sparks '12
Some Girl(s) '13
What If '13
In Your Eyes '14
Olive Kitteridge '14
The Pretty One '14
Our Brand is Crisis '15
The Monster '16
My Blind Brother '16
The Big Sick '17
The Ballad of Buster Scruggs '18

Robert Kazinsky
Hot Pursuit '15
For Love or Money '19

Tim Kazurinsky (1950-)
My Bodyguard '80
Somewhere in Time '80
Continental Divide '81
Police Academy 3: Back in Training '86
Police Academy 4: Citizens on Patrol '87
Hot to Trot! '88
Dinner at Eight '89
A Billion for Boris '90
Shakes the Clown '92
Poor White Trash '00
The Return of Joe Rich '11

James Keach (1947-)
Till Death Do Us Part '72
Slashed Dreams '74
Hurricane '79
The Long Riders '80
Love Letters '83
National Lampoon's Vacation '83
The Razor's Edge '84
Moving Violations '85
Wildcats '86

Stacy Keach (1941-)
The Heart Is a Lonely Hunter '68
Brewster McCloud '70
End of the Road '70
The Traveling Executioner '70
Fat City '72
Life & Times of Judge Roy Bean '72
The New Centurions '72
All the Kind Strangers '74
Luther '74
Conduct Unbecoming '75
Dynasty '76
The Killer Inside Me '76
Street People '76
Gray Lady Down '77
The Squeeze '77
Battleforce '78
Cheech and Chong's Up in Smoke '79
Mountain of the Cannibal God '79
The Ninth Configuration '79
The Long Riders '80
Cheech and Chong's Nice Dreams '81
Road Games '81
Saturday the 14th '81
The Blue and the Gray '82
Butterfly '82
That Championship Season '82
Princess Daisy '83
Mistral's Daughter '84
Class of 1999 '90
Mission of the Shark '91
Sunset Grill '92
Batman: Mask of the Phantasm '93 (V)
Body Bags '93
Raw Justice '93
Rio Diablo '93
New Crime City: Los Angeles 2020 '94
Texas '94
Young Ivanhoe '95
Escape from L.A. '96
The Pathfinder '96
Prey of the Jaguar '96
Future Fear '97
Legend of the Lost Tomb '97
American History X '98
Children of the Corn 666: Isaac's Return '99
Fear Runs Silent '99
Militia '99
The Courage to Love '00
Lightning: Fire from the Sky '00
Mercy Streets '00
Unshackled '00
Sunstorm '01
The Santa Trap '02
Miracle Dogs '03
El Padrino '04
The Hollow '04
Blackbeard '06
Come Early Morning '06
Fatal Contact: Bird Flu in America '06
Honeydripper '07
Lone Rider '08
The Nanny Express '08
Ring of Death '08
The Assistants '09
Chicago Overcoat '09
Meteor '09
Weather Wars '11
Cellmates '12
Nebraska '13
Planes '13 (V)
If I Stay '14
Planes: Fire & Rescue '14 (V)
Cell '16
Gotti '18

Stacy Keach, Sr. (1914-2003)
Missiles of October '74
Ants '77
Mission of the Shark '91

Marie Kean (1922-94)
Girl with Green Eyes '64
The Dead '87
The Lonely Passion of Judith Hearne '87

Staci Keanan (1975-)
Downhill Willie '96
You Again '10

Edward (Ed Kean, Keene) Keane (1884-1959)
The Cheat '31
A Night at the Opera '35
The Drag-Net '36
I Escaped from the Gestapo '43
A Fig Leaf for Eve '44

James Keane (1952-)
Apocalypse Now '79
Cannery Row '82
Assassination Tango '03
Annie's Point '05
Crazy Heart '09

Kerrie Keane
Incubus '82
Hot Pursuit '84
A Death in California '85
Kung Fu: The Movie '86
Distant Thunder '88
Malarek '89
Alien Nation: Millennium '96
Alien Nation: The Enemy Within '96
Steel '97

Robert Emmett Keane (1883-1981)
Born to Be Wild '38
Treasure of Fear '45
Fear in the Night '47
Susanna Pass '49

Gillian Kearney (1972-)
Catherine Cookson's The Tide of Life '96
In His Life: The John Lennon Story '00
The Other Half '06

Stephen Kearney
Rikky and Pete '88
The Nutt House '95

Billy Kearns (1923-92)
Purple Noon '60
Bed and Board '70

Gerard Kearns
Looking for Eric '09
Wasteland '13

Charles Keating (1941-2014)
Brideshead Revisited '81
The Bodyguard '92
The Thomas Crown Affair '99
Deuce Bigalow: European Gigolo '05

Dominic Keating (1962-)
Hollywood Kills '06
Species 4: The Awakening '07
Sherlock Holmes '10

Fred Keating (1897-1961)
The Captain Hates the Sea '34
I Live My Life '35
The Nitwits '35
To Beat the Band '35
The Devil on Horseback '36
Prison Train '38

Larry Keating (1896-1963)
Francis Goes to the Races '51
Too Young to Kiss '51
When Worlds Collide '51
Carson City '52
Monkey Business '52
Something for the Birds '52
Above and Beyond '53
Give a Girl a Break '53
A Lion Is in the Streets '53
She's Back on Broadway '53
Daddy Long Legs '55
Stopover Tokyo '57
The Wayward Bus '57
The Incredible Mr. Limpet '64

Buster Keaton (1895-1966)
The Saphead '21
Our Hospitality '23
Go West '25
Battling Butler '26
The General '26
The Cameraman '28
Steamboat Bill, Jr. '28
Spite Marriage '29
Doughboys '30
Free and Easy '30
Parlor, Bedroom and Bath '31
Sidewalks of New York '31
The Passionate Plumber '32
Speak Easily '32
Li'l Abner '40
New Moon '40
The Villain Still Pursued Her '41
Forever and a Day '43
Two Girls and a Sailor '44 (C)
In the Good Old Summertime '49
Sunset Boulevard '50
Limelight '52
Around the World in 80 Days '56 (C)
The Adventures of Huckleberry Finn '60
It's a Mad, Mad, Mad, Mad World '63
Pajama Party '64 (C)
Beach Blanket Bingo '65
How to Stuff a Wild Bikini '65
Sergeant Deadhead '65
A Funny Thing Happened on the Way to the Forum '66

Diane Keaton (1946-)
Lovers and Other Strangers '70
The Godfather '72
Play It Again, Sam '72
Sleeper '73
The Godfather, Part 2 '74
Love and Death '75
Harry & Walter Go to New York '76
I Will, I Will...for Now '76
Annie Hall '77
Interiors '78
Manhattan '79
Reds '81
Shoot the Moon '82
The Little Drummer Girl '84
Mrs. Soffel '84
Crimes of the Heart '86
Baby Boom '87
Radio Days '87
The Good Mother '88
The Godfather, Part 3 '90
The Lemon Sisters '90
Father of the Bride '91
Running Mates '92
Look Who's Talking Now '93 (V)
Manhattan Murder Mystery '93
Amelia Earhart: The Final Flight '94
Father of the Bride Part 2 '95
The First Wives Club '96
Marvin's Room '96
The Only Thrill '97
The Other Sister '98
Hanging Up '99
Town and Country '01
On Thin Ice '03
Something's Gotta Give '03
The Family Stone '05
Because I Said So '07
Mama's Boy '07
Mad Money '08
Smother '08
Morning Glory '10
Darling Companion '12
The Big Wedding '13
And So It Goes '14
5 Flights Up '15
Book Club '18
Hampstead '19
Poms '19

Joe Keaton (1867-1946)
Our Hospitality '23
The General '26

Michael Keaton (1951-)
Night Shift '82
Mr. Mom '83
Johnny Dangerously '84
Gung Ho '86
Touch and Go '86
The Squeeze '87
Beetlejuice '88
Clean and Sober '88
Batman '89
The Dream Team '89
Pacific Heights '90
One Good Cop '91
Batman Returns '92
Much Ado about Nothing '93
My Life '93
The Paper '94
Speechless '94
Multiplicity '96
Jackie Brown '97
Desperate Measures '98
Jack Frost '98
Out of Sight '98 (C)
A Shot at Glory '00
Quicksand '01
Live from Baghdad '03
First Daughter '04
Game 6 '05
Herbie: Fully Loaded '05
White Noise '05
Cars '06 (V)
The Last Time '06
The Company '07
The Merry Gentleman '08
Post Grad '09
The Other Guys '10
Toy Story 3 '10 (V)
Cars 2 '11 (V)
Birdman, or (The Unexpected Virtue of Ignorance) '14
Need for Speed '14
RoboCop '14
Spotlight '15
American Assassin '17
The Founder '17
Spider-Man: Homecoming '17
Dumbo '19

Caitlin Keats (1972-)
Kill Bill Vol. 2 '04
The Lather Effect '06
Women in Trouble '09
Close Range '15

Ele Keats (1973-)
Lipstick Camera '93
Mother '94
White Wolves 2: Legend of the Wild '94
Eros '04

Steven Keats (1946-94)
Hester Street '75
Black Sunday '77
The Last Dinosaur '77
The Awakening Land '78
Zuma Beach '78
Mysterious Island of Beautiful Women '79
The Executioner's Song '82
Silent Rage '82

Brian L. Keaulana (1961-)
In God's Hands '98
Riding Giants '04

Hugh Keays-Byrne (1947-)
Mad Max '80
Resistance '92
Moby Dick '98
Journey to the Center of the Earth '99
Sleeping Beauty '11
Mad Max: Fury Road '15

Arielle Kebbel (1985-)
Soul Plane '04
American Pie Presents Band Camp '05
The Kid and I '05
Aquamarine '06
The Grudge 2 '06
John Tucker Must Die '06
Forever Strong '08
The Uninvited '09
Answer This '10
Vampires Suck '10
I Melt With You '11
Mardi Gras: Spring Break '11
Think Like a Man '12
NYC Underground '13
Supporting Characters '13

Toby Kebbell (1982-)
Dead Man's Shoes '04
Control '07
RocknRolla '08
The Conspirator '10
The Sorcerer's Apprentice '10
War Horse '11
Wrath of the Titans '12
The East '13
The Escape Artist '13
Dawn of the Planet of the Apes '14
Fantastic Four '15
Ben-Hur '16
Warcraft '16
A Monster Calls '17
Destroyer '18
The Female Brain '18
The Hurricane Heist '18
Bloodshot '20

Salim Kechiouche (1979-)
Criminal Lovers '99
The String '09

Lila Kedrova (1918-2000)
Zorba the Greek '64
Torn Curtain '66
The Kremlin Letter '70
Primal Impulse '74
The Tenant '76
Tell Me a Riddle '80
Sword of the Valiant '83
Some Girls '88

James Kee
Teenage Space Vampires '99
Coast to Coast '04

Cornelius Keefe (1900-72)
The Adorable Cheat '28
Death from a Distance '36

Don Keefer (1916-2014)
Incident in an Alley '62
Sleeper '73
The Young Nurses '73
Candy Stripe Nurses '74

Andrew Keegan (1979-)
Camp Nowhere '94
Ten Things I Hate about You '99
The Broken Hearts Club '00
O '01
Teenage Caveman '01
Extreme Dating '04
Cruel World '05
A New Wave '07
Waiting for Dublin '07
Doughboys '08
The Penitent Man '10

Rose Keegan (1971-)
In a Day '06
Hope Gap '20

Howard Keel (1917-2004)
Annie Get Your Gun '50
Pagan Love Song '50
Across the Wide Missouri '51 (N)
Show Boat '51
Texas Carnival '51
Three Guys Named Mike '51
Desperate Search '52
Lovely to Look At '52
Calamity Jane '53
I Love Melvin '53
Kiss Me Kate '53
Ride, Vaquero! '53
Deep in My Heart '54
Rose Marie '54
Seven Brides for Seven Brothers '54
Jupiter's Darling '55
Kismet '55
Day of the Triffids '63
Man from Button Willow '65 (V)
Arizona Bushwackers '67
The War Wagon '67

Claire Keelan
The Trip '10
The Trip to Spain '17

Ruby Keeler (1909-93)
Footlight Parade '33
42nd Street '33
Gold Diggers of 1933 '33
Dames '34
Flirtation Walk '34
Go Into Your Dance '35
Shipmates Forever '35
Colleen '36
That's Dancing! '85

Sam Keeley
Monsters: Dark Continent '15
The Cured '18

Diane Keen (1946-)
Silver Dream Racer '83
Agatha Christie's Thirteen at Dinner '85
Jekyll and Hyde '90

Geoffrey Keen (1916-2005)
The Fallen Idol '49
The Third Man '49
Hunted '52
Scotland Yard Inspector '52
Doctor in the House '53
Genevieve '53
The Long Memory '53
Angels One Five '54
Black Glove '54
The Man Who Never Was '55
Postmark for Danger '56
Horrors of the Black Museum '59
The Scapegoat '59
Sink the Bismarck '60
A Matter of WHO '62
The Mind Benders '63
Dr. Syn, Alias the Scarecrow '64
Doctor Zhivago '65
Taste the Blood of Dracula '70
Sacco & Vanzetti '71
The Spy Who Loved Me '77
Moonraker '79
For Your Eyes Only '81
The Living Daylights '87

Malcolm Keen (1887-1970)
The Lodger '26
The Manxman '29

Monica Keena (1979-)
While You Were Sleeping '95
Ripe '97
Snow White: A Tale of Terror '97
All I Wanna Do '98
The Simian Line '99
Crime and Punishment in Suburbia '00
Freddy vs. Jason '03
Man of the House '05
The Lather Effect '06
Left in Darkness '06
Brooklyn Rules '07
Corporate Affairs '07
Loaded '08
The Narrows '08
Night of the Demons '09
Aftermath '12
40 Days and Nights '12

Caroline Keenan (1970-)
Vice Girls '96
Killer Bud '00

Will Keenan (1974-)
Tromeo & Juliet '95
Waiting '00
Margarita Happy Hour '01
Wicked Lake '08
The Ghastly Love of Johnny X '12

Tom Keene (1896-1963)
Tide of Empire '29
Our Daily Bread '34
Navy Way '44
Lights of Old Santa Fe '47
Trail of Robin Hood '50
Plan 9 from Outer Space '56

Catherine Keener (1959-)
Survival Quest '89
Johnny Suede '92
Living in Oblivion '94
Box of Moonlight '96
If These Walls Could Talk '96
Walking and Talking '96
The Real Blonde '97
8mm '98
Out of Sight '98
Your Friends & Neighbors '98
Being John Malkovich '99
Simpatico '99
Death to Smoochy '02
Full Frontal '02
Lovely & Amazing '02
Simone '02
The Ballad of Jack and Rose '05
Capote '05
The 40 Year Old Virgin '05
The Interpreter '05
Friends with Money '06
An American Crime '07
Into the Wild '07
Hamlet 2 '08
A Summer in Genoa '08
Synecdoche, New York '08
What Just Happened '08
The Soloist '09
Where the Wild Things Are '09
Cyrus '10
Percy Jackson & The Olympians: The Lightning Thief '10
Please Give '10
Trust '10
Peace, Love & Misunderstanding '11
A Late Quartet '12
The Oranges '12
Begin Again '13
Captain Phillips '13
The Croods '13 (V)
Enough Said '13
Maladies '13
War Story '14
Get Out '17
November Criminals '17
We Don't Belong Here '17
Incredibles 2 '18 (V)
Nostalgia '18
Sicario: Day of the Soldado '18

Eliott Keener (1949-99)
Angel Heart '87
Hard Target '93

Hazel Keener (1904-79)
The Freshman '25
Murder by Invitation '41

Eric Keenleyside (1957-)
The Interpreter '05
Murder on Pleasant Drive '06
Blue Smoke '07
Tell Me No Lies '07
Every Second Counts '08
November Christmas '10
Goodnight for Justice: The Measure of a Man '12
The Package '12

Matt Keeslar (1972-)
Safe Passage '94
The Run of the Country '95
The Stupids '95
Waiting for Guffman '96
The Deli '97
Mr. Magoo '97
The Last Days of Disco '98
Sour Grapes '98
Splendor '99
Dune '00
Psycho Beach Party '00
Scream 3 '00
Urbania '00
Texas Rangers '01
Stephen King's Rose Red '02
Live from Baghdad '03
Art School Confidential '06
Open Window '06
The Thirst '06
Snowglobe '07

Jared Keeso
The Party Never Stops '07
The Marine 3: Homefront '11

Jack Kehler (1946-)
Strange Invaders '83
Year of the Dragon '85
Bloodstone '88
I Love You to Death '90
Grand Canyon '91
The Last Boy Scout '91
Point Break '91
White Sands '92
The Positively True Adventures of the Alleged Texas Cheerleader-Murdering Mom '93
Across the Moon '94
Cops and Robbersons '94
Love Is a Gun '94
Wyatt Earp '94
Desert Winds '95
Waterworld '95
American Strays '96
Lost Highway '96
My Fellow Americans '96
The Big Lebowski '97
187 '97
Lethal Weapon 4 '98
Sour Grapes '98
Austin Powers 2: The Spy Who Shagged Me '99
Dudley Do-Right '99
Forces of Nature '99
The Mating Habits of the Earthbound Human '99
True Crime '99
Beyond Suspicion '00
Big Trouble '02
Love Liza '02
Men in Black 2 '02
Fever Pitch '05
Grilled '06
Invincible '06
Pineapple Express '08

Jack Kehoe (1934-2020)
Serpico '73
The Sting '73
Law and Disorder '74
The Fish that Saved Pittsburgh '79
The Pope of Greenwich Village '84
The Untouchables '87
Young Guns 2 '90
Servants of Twilight '91
Falling Down '93
Special '06

Betty Lou Keim (1938-2010)
Teenage Rebel '56
These Wilder Years '56

Claire Keim (1975-)
The Girl '01
Ripper: Letter from Hell '01
Caravaggio '07

Andrew Keir (1926-97)
Pirates of Blood River '62
Cleopatra '63
The Devil-Ship Pirates '64
Lord Jim '65
Daleks-Invasion Earth 2150 A.D. '66
Dracula, Prince of Darkness '66
The Fighting Prince of Donegal '66
The Viking Queen '67
Adam's Woman '70
The Last Grenade '70
The Night Visitor '70
Blood from the Mummy's Tomb '71
Zeppelin '71
The Thirty-Nine Steps '79
Absolution '81
Rob Roy '95

Harvey Keitel (1939-)
Who's That Knocking at My Door? '68
Mean Streets '73
Alice Doesn't Live Here Anymore '74
Shining Star '75
Buffalo Bill & the Indians '76
Mother, Jugs and Speed '76
Taxi Driver '76
The Virginia Hill Story '76
The Duellists '77
Blue Collar '78
Fingers '78
Eagle's Wing '79
Bad Timing: A Sensual Obsession '80
Death Watch '80
Saturn 3 '80
The Border '82
Corrupt '84
Falling in Love '84
Star Knight '85
The Men's Club '86
The Pick-Up Artist '87
The Last Temptation of Christ '88
The January Man '89
Two Evil Eyes '90
The Two Jakes '90
Bugsy '91
Mortal Thoughts '91
Thelma & Louise '91
Bad Lieutenant '92
Reservoir Dogs '92
Sister Act '92
Dangerous Game '93
The Piano '93
Point of No Return '93
Rising Sun '93
The Young Americans '93
Imaginary Crimes '94
Monkey Trouble '94
Pulp Fiction '94
Somebody to Love '94
Blue in the Face '95
Clockers '95
From Dusk Till Dawn '95
Get Shorty '95 (C)
Smoke '95
Ulysses' Gaze '95
City of Industry '96
Head Above Water '96
Cop Land '97
FairyTale: A True Story '97
Finding Graceland '98
Gunslinger's Revenge '98
Lulu on the Bridge '98
Shadrach '98
Holy Smoke '99
Fail Safe '00
Little Nicky '00
Prince of Central Park '00
U-571 '00
The Grey Zone '01
Taking Sides '01
Ginostra '02
Red Dragon '02
Crime Spree '03
Cuban Blood '03
National Treasure '04
Puerto Vallarta Squeeze '04
Be Cool '05
The Bridge of San Luis Rey '05
Arthur and the Invisibles '06 (V)
A Crime '06
The Stone Merchant '06
National Treasure: Book of Secrets '07
The Ministers '09
Wrong Turn at Tahoe '09
A Beginner's Guide to Endings '10
The Last Godfather '10
Fatal Honeymoon '12
The Congress '13
By the Gun '14
The Grand Budapest Hotel '14
Rio, I Love You '14
Youth '15
Chosen '16
The Comedian '16
The Last Man '19

Stella Keitel
Bad Lieutenant '92
The Life of Lucky Cucumber '08

Alexander Keith
The Capitol Conspiracy '99
Counter Measures '99

Brian Keith (1921-97)
Arrowhead '53
5 Against the House '55
The Violent Men '55
Nightfall '56
Storm Center '56
Chicago Confidential '57
Dino '57
Fort Dobbs '58
Violent Road '58
The Young Philadelphians '59
Ten Who Dared '60
Deadly Companions '61
The Parent Trap '61
Moon Pilot '62
Johnny Shiloh '63
Savage Sam '63
A Tiger Walks '64
The Hallelujah Trail '65
Those Calloways '65
Nevada Smith '66
The Rare Breed '66
The Russians Are Coming, the Russians Are Coming '66
Reflections in a Golden Eye '67
With Six You Get Eggroll '68
Krakatoa East of Java '69
McKenzie Break '70
Suppose They Gave a War and Nobody Came? '70
Scandalous John '71
The Wind and the Lion '75
The Yakuza '75
Joe Panther '76
The Longest Drive '76
Nickelodeon '76
Centennial '78
Hooper '78
Meteor '79
The Mountain Men '80
Charlie Chan and the Curse of the Dragon Queen '81
Sharky's Machine '81
World War III '86
The Alamo: Thirteen Days to Glory '87
Death Before Dishonor '87
Young Guns '88
Welcome Home '89
Escape '90
The Gambler Returns: The Luck of the Draw '93
Walking Thunder '94 (N)
Picture Windows '95
Entertaining Angels: The Dorothy Day Story '96
Rough Riders '97

David Keith (1954-)
The Rose '79
Brubaker '80
The Great Santini '80
Back Roads '81
Take This Job & Shove It '81
An Officer and a Gentleman '82
The Lords of Discipline '83
Firestarter '84
If Tomorrow Comes '86
The Whoopee Boys '86
The Curse '87
The Further Adventures of Tennessee Buck '88
Heartbreak Hotel '88
The Two Jakes '90
Raw Justice '93
Major League 2 '94
Texas '94
Gold Diggers: The Secret of Bear Mountain '95
The Indian in the Cupboard '95
Judge & Jury '96
Hot Blooded '98
Poodle Springs '98
Secre of the Andes '98
A Memory In My Heart '99
Epoch '00
Men of Honor '00
U-571 '00
Behind Enemy Lines '01
Burning Down the House '01
Sabretooth '01
The Stickup '01
World Traveler '01
Carrie '02
Daredevil '03
Deep Shock '03
Epoch: Evolution '03
Hangman's Curse '03
Raise Your Voice '04
All Souls Day '05
Locusts: The 8th Plague '05
Bottoms Up '06
In Her Line of Fire '06
Miracle Dogs Too '06
Beneath the Blue '10
Awaken '15
21 Bridges '19

Donald Keith (1903-69)
The Plastic Age '25
Dancing Mothers '26

Ian Keith (1899-1960)
The Divine Lady '29
The Great Divide '29
Abraham Lincoln '30
The Phantom of Paris '31
Queen Christina '33
The Sign of the Cross '33
The Crusades '35
Mary of Scotland '36
The White Legion '36
Corregidor '43
Five Graves to Cairo '43
The Payoff '43
The Chinese Cat '44
Nightmare Alley '47
The Black Shield of Falworth '54
It Came from Beneath the Sea '55

Penelope Keith (1940-)
The Norman Conquests, Part 1: Table Manners '78
The Norman Conquests, Part 2: Living Together '78
The Norman Conquests, Part 3: Round and Round the Garden '78
Coming Home '98

Robert Keith (1890-1966)
Boomerang '47
Woman On the Run '50
Here Comes the Groom '51
Battle Circus '53
Small Town Girl '53
Drum Beat '54
The Wild One '54
Young at Heart '54

Love Me or Leave Me '55
Between Heaven and Hell '56
Ransom! '56
Written on the Wind '56
Men in War '57
My Man Godfrey '57
The Lineup '58
Cimarron '60

Robert Keith (1921-97)
The Shadow Laughs '33
The Reformer and the Redhead '50
Rites of Passage '99

Sheila Keith (1920-2004)
Frightmare '74
The Confessional '75
The Comeback '77

Toby Keith
Broken Bridges '06
Beer for My Horses '08

Peter Keleghan (1959-)
Screwballs '83
Escape from Wildcat Canyon '99
Angels in the Infield '00
Ginger Snaps '01
Jericho Mansions '03
Niagara Motel '06

Joseph Kell (1960-)
Bone Daddy '97
White Lies '98
If I Were You '12

Robert Kellard (1915-81)
Drums of Fu Manchu '40
The Millerson Case '47

Cecil Kellaway (1893-1973)
Gunga Din '39
Wuthering Heights '39
Brother Orchid '40
The House of the Seven Gables '40
The Letter '40
Mexican Spitfire '40
The Mexican Spitfire Out West '40
The Mummy's Hand '40
Birth of the Blues '41
It Ain't Hay '43
Frenchman's Creek '44
Love Letters '45
Easy to Wed '46
Monsieur Beaucaire '46
The Postman Always Rings Twice '46
Unconquered '47
The Luck of the Irish '48
Portrait of Jennie '48
Harvey '50
Kim '50
The Reformer and the Redhead '50
Francis Goes to the Races '51
My Wife's Best Friend '52
The Beast from 20,000 Fathoms '53
Young Bess '53
Female On the Beach '55
Interrupted Melody '55
The Prodigal '55
Tammy Tell Me True '61
Zotz! '62
The Cardinal '63
Hush, Hush, Sweet Charlotte '65
Spinout '66
Fitzwilly '67
Guess Who's Coming to Dinner '67
Getting Straight '70
Quick, Let's Get Married '71

Tina Kellegher (1967-)
The Snapper '93
Scarlett '94
Happy Ever Afters '09

Tim Kelleher
Thirteen Days '00
Flash of Genius '08
Seven Pounds '08

Hiram Keller (1944-97)
Fellini Satyricon '69
Lifespan '75
A Real Young Girl '75
Countryman '83

Joel S. Keller
The Hanging Garden '97
Brotherhood of Murder '99
The Life Before This '99

Marthe Keller (1945-)
And Now My Love '74
Marathon Man '76
Black Sunday '77
Bobby Deerfield '77
Fedora '78
The Formula '80
The Amateur '82
Young Catherine '91
Women '97
Chrysalis '07
Gigantic '08
Hereafter '10
The Escape '18

Mary Page Keller (1961-)
The Colony '95
Venomous '01
Timecop 2: The Berlin Decision '03
Beginners '10

Melissa Keller (1978-)
Drop Dead Sexy '05
Impact Point '08

Barbara Kellerman (1949-)
Quatermass Conclusion '79
Sea Wolves '81
My Brother Jonathan '85
The Chronicles of Narnia '89

Sally Kellerman (1937-)
Hands of a Stranger '62
The Third Day '65
The Boston Strangler '68
April Fools '69
Brewster McCloud '70
M*A*S*H '70
Last of the Red Hot Lovers '72
Lost Horizon '73
A Reflection of Fear '73
Slither '73
The Big Bus '76
Centennial '78
A Little Romance '79
Foxes '80
Loving Couples '80
Serial '80
Dempsey '83
Moving Violations '85
Secret Weapons '85
Back to School '86
That's Life! '86
Someone to Love '87
You Can't Hurry Love '88
Limit Up '89 (C)
Doppelganger: The Evil Within '90
Victim of Beauty '91
The Player '92
Happily Ever After '93 (V)
Mirror, Mirror 2: Raven Dance '94
Ready to Wear '94
American Virgin '98
Bar Hopping '00
Verdict in Blood '02
The Boynton Beach Club '05
I Could Never Be Your Woman '06
The Prince and the Pauper '07
Delgo '08 (N)

Susan Kellerman (1944-)
Oh, Heavenly Dog! '80
Where the Buffalo Roam '80
Elvira, Mistress of the Dark '88
Last Holiday '06
In the Family '11

Barry Kelley (1908-91)
The Killer That Stalked New York '47
Ma and Pa Kettle '49
Too Late for Tears '49
The Undercover Man '49
The Asphalt Jungle '50
Right Cross '50
711 Ocean Drive '50
Southside 1-1000 '50
Francis Goes to the Races '51
The Well '51
Carrie '52
Law and Order '53
South Sea Woman '53
Buchanan Rides Alone '58
Jack the Giant Killer '62
The Manchurian Candidate '62

DeForest Kelley (1920-99)
Fear in the Night '47
House of Bamboo '55
Illegal '55
The Man in the Gray Flannel Suit '56
Gunfight at the O.K. Corral '57
The Law and Jake Wade '58
Warlock '59
Gunfight at Comanche Creek '64
Night of the Lepus '72
Star Trek: The Motion Picture '79
Star Trek 2: The Wrath of Khan '82
Star Trek 3: The Search for Spock '84
Star Trek 4: The Voyage Home '86
Star Trek 5: The Final Frontier '89
Star Trek 6: The Undiscovered Country '91

Elijah Kelley (1986-)
Hairspray '07
Strange Magic '15 (V)

Kimberly Kelley
Hard Bounty '94
Midnight Tease 2 '95

Nathalie Kelley (1985-)
The Fast and the Furious: Tokyo Drift '06
Loaded '08

Ryan Kelley (1986-)
Mean Creek '04
Still Green '07
Prayers for Bobby '09
Sexting in Suburbia '12

Sheila Kelley (1961-)
Some Girls '88
Breaking In '89
Where the Heart Is '90
The Chase '91
Pure Luck '91
Soapdish '91
Passion Fish '92
Singles '92
One Fine Day '96
Santa Fe '97
Dancing at the Blue Iguana '00
Nurse Betty '00
Matchstick Men '03
Mozart and the Whale '05
Bloodworth '10
The Guest '14

Walter Kelley (1922-)
Come Back, Little Sheba '52
Marty '55
Men in War '57

Mike Kellin (1922-83)
At War with the Army '50
Wackiest Ship in the Army '61
Hell Is for Heroes '62
Invitation to a Gunfighter '64
The Boston Strangler '68
Riot '69
The Phynx '70
Freebie & the Bean '74
The Last Porno Flick '74
God Told Me To '76
Next Stop, Greenwich Village '76
Girlfriends '78
On the Yard '79
Sleepaway Camp '83

Catherine Kellner (1970-)
Six Degrees of Separation '93
No Way Home '96
Rosewood '96
Highball '97
Day at the Beach '98
Restaurant '98
200 Cigarettes '98
Spring Forward '99
Shaft '00
Tully '00
Pearl Harbor '01
Colewell '19

Bruce Kellogg (1910-67)
They Were Expendable '45
The Golden Eye '48
Unknown World '51

John Kellogg (1916-2000)
To Be or Not to Be '42
Bad Men of Tombstone '49
Twelve o'Clock High '49
Elephant Stampede '51
The Enforcer '51
Tomorrow Is Another Day '51
The Fighting Lawman '53
The Silver Whip '53
Violets Are Blue '86

Alan Rowe Kelly (1959-)
I'll Bury You Tomorrow '02
Skinned Alive '08

Brendan Kelly (1964-)
Angels Hard As They Come '71
The Rock '96
The Lizzie McGuire Movie '03
Cellular '04

Brett Kelly (1993-)
Bad Santa '03
The Sandlot 2 '05
Unaccompanied Minors '06
Bad Santa 2 '16

Brian Kelly (1931-2005)
Flipper's New Adventure '64
Around the World Under the Sea '65

Claire Kelly (1934-98)
The Badlanders '58
Party Girl '58
Georgy Girl '66
A Guide for the Married Man '67
And Soon the Darkness '70
Dressed for Death '74

Craig Kelly (1970-)
Nightscare '93
The Young Americans '93
Collision '09

Craig G. Kelly (1907-91)
Zombies of the Stratosphere '52
Dirty Harry '71
Silence '73
Dirty Mary Crazy Larry '74

Daniel Hugh Kelly (1952-)
The Guardian '01
Mischief Night '13

Darragh Kelly
Nora '00
48 Angels '06

David Kelly (1929-2012)
Into the West '92
The Run of the Country '95
Waking Ned Devine '98
Greenfingers '00
Mean Machine '01
Agent Cody Banks 2: Destination London '04
Charlie and the Chocolate Factory '05
The Kovak Box '06
Stardust '07

David Patrick Kelly (1951-)
The Warriors '79
48 Hrs. '82
Dreamscape '84
Commando '85
The Adventures of Ford Fairlane '90
Penn and Teller Get Killed '90
Malcolm X '92
The Crow '93
Crooklyn '94
Flirting with Disaster '95
Last Man Standing '96
Cafe Society '97
Trojan War '97
In Too Deep '99
Songcatcher '99
K-PAX '01
Personal Velocity: Three Portraits '02
The Longest Yard '05
Jonah Hex '10

Frank Kelly (1938-2016)
Cowboys & Angels '04
Waiting for Dublin '07

Gene Kelly (1912-96)
For Me and My Gal '42
The Cross of Lorraine '43
Du Barry Was a Lady '43
Pilot No. 5 '43
Thousands Cheer '43
Cover Girl '44
Anchors Aweigh '45
Ziegfeld Follies '46
Living In a Big Way '47
The Pirate '48
The Three Musketeers '48
Words and Music '48
On the Town '49
Take Me Out to the Ball Game '49
Summer Stock '50
An American in Paris '51
It's a Big Country '51
The Devil Makes Three '52
Love Is Better Than Ever '52 (C)
Singin' in the Rain '52
Brigadoon '54
Crest of the Wave '54
Deep in My Heart '54
It's Always Fair Weather '55
Invitation to the Dance '56
The Happy Road '57
Les Girls '57
Marjorie Morningstar '58
Inherit the Wind '60
Let's Make Love '60
The Young Girls of Rochefort '68
Forty Carats '73
That's Entertainment '74
That's Entertainment, Part 2 '76 (N)
Viva Knievel '77
Xanadu '80
North and South Book 1 '85
Sins '85
That's Dancing! '85

Grace Kelly (1928-82)
High Noon '52
Mogambo '53
Country Girl '54
Dial 'M' for Murder '54
Rear Window '54
The Bridges at Toko-Ri '55
Green Fire '55
To Catch a Thief '55
High Society '56
The Swan '56
The Children of Theatre Street '77 (N)

Jack Kelly (1927-92)
No Room for the Groom '52
The Redhead from Wyoming '52
Drive a Crooked Road '54
Cult of the Cobra '55
The Night Holds Terror '55
To Hell and Back '55
Forbidden Planet '56
Julie '56
She Devil '57
A Fever In the Blood '61
FBI Code 98 '63
Commandos '73
The Gambler Returns: The Luck of the Draw '93

Jean Louisa Kelly (1972-)
Uncle Buck '89
The Fantasticks '95
Harvest of Fire '95
Mr. Holland's Opus '95
Stolen Women, Captured Hearts '97
A Stranger in the Kingdom '98
The Cyberstalking '99

Jim Kelly (1946-2013)
Enter the Dragon '73
Black Belt Jones '74
Golden Needles '74
Three the Hard Way '74
Take a Hard Ride '75
Hot Potato '76
Black Samurai '77
Black Eliminator '78
Kill Factor '78
One Down, Two to Go! '82

Joanne Kelly (1978-)
Playing House '06
Solar Attack '06
Closet Monster '16

Judy Kelly (1913-91)
The Private Life of Henry VIII '33
Dead of Night '45

Kitty Kelly (1902-68)
Girl Crazy '32
So Proudly We Hail '43

Dean Lennox Kelly (1975-)
Deathwatch '02
Collision '09

Lew Kelly (1879-1944)
Death from a Distance '36
Mistaken Identity '36

Lisa Robin Kelly (1970-)
Amityville Dollhouse '96
Late Last Night '99

Machine Gun Kelly
The Land '16
Viral '16

Malcolm David Kelly (1992-)
Antwone Fisher '02
You Got Served '04
Knights of the South Bronx '05

Mark Kelly (1973-)
Answers to Nothing '11
The Do-Deca-Pentathlon '12

Michael Kelly (1968-)
River Red '98
Dawn of the Dead '04
Carlito's Way: Rise to Power '05
Loggerheads '05
Invincible '06
Tooth and Nail '07
Changeling '08
Defendor '09
Did You Hear About the Morgans? '09
The Adjustment Bureau '11
Chronicle '12

Minka Kelly (1980-)
The Roommate '11
Lee Daniels' The Butler '13
The World Made Straight '15
Papa: Hemingway in Cuba '16

Moira Kelly (1968-)
Billy Bathgate '91
Chaplin '92
The Cutting Edge '92
Twin Peaks: Fire Walk with Me '92
Daybreak '93
The Lion King '94 (V)
Little Odessa '94
With Honors '94
The Tie That Binds '95
Changing Habits '96
Entertaining Angels: The Dorothy Day Story '96
Unhook the Stars '96
Love Walked In '97
Dangerous Beauty '98
Hi-Life '98
Henry Hill '00
The Safety of Objects '01
The Lion King 1 1/2 '04 (V)
Two Tickets to Paradise '06
Remember the Daze '07
A Smile as Big as the Moon '12

Morgan Kelly (1976-)
Banshee '06
Between Truth and Lies '06

The Watch *'08*
Ice Castles *'10*

Nancy Kelly (1921-95)
Frontier Marshal *'39*
Tail Spin *'39*
One Night in the Tropics *'40*
To the Shores of Tripoli *'42*
Tarzan's Desert Mystery *'43*
Tornado *'43*
Women in Bondage *'43*
Gambler's Choice *'44*
The Woman Who Came Back *'45*
The Bad Seed *'56*

Patrick Kelly (1967-)
White Coats *'04*
Twitches *'05*
Twitches Too *'07*

Patsy Kelly (1910-81)
Going Hollywood *'33*
The Girl from Missouri *'34*
Go Into Your Dance *'35*
Thanks a Million *'35*
Pigskin Parade *'36*
Private Number *'36*
Sing, Baby, Sing *'36*
Nobody's Baby *'37*
Pick a Star *'37*
Wake Up and Live *'37*
The Cowboy and the Lady *'38*
Merrily We Live *'38*
Swiss Miss *'38*
The Gorilla *'39*
Broadway Limited *'41*
Playmates *'41*
Road Show *'41*
In Old California *'42*
The Crowded Sky *'60*
Please Don't Eat the Daisies *'60*
Naked Kiss *'64*
Ghost in the Invisible Bikini *'66*
Rosemary's Baby *'68*
Freaky Friday *'76*
The North Avenue Irregulars *'79*

Paul Kelly (1899-1956)
Girl from Calgary *'32*
Star of Midnight *'35*
Murder With Pictures *'36*
Fit for a King *'37*
Join the Marines *'37*
Navy Blue and Gold *'37*
Devil's Party *'38*
Invisible Stripes *'39*
The Roaring Twenties *'39*
Flight Command *'40*
The Howards of Virginia *'40*
I'll Wait for You *'41*
Ziegfeld Girl *'41*
Flying Tigers *'42*
Tarzan's New York Adventure *'42*
Texas Legionnaires *'43*
Dead Man's Eyes *'44*
San Antonio *'45*
Crossfire *'47*
Fear in the Night *'47*
Spoilers of the North *'47*
The File on Thelma Jordon *'50*
Guilty of Treason *'50*
Side Street *'50*
The Painted Hills *'51*
Springfield Rifle *'52*
Split Second *'53*
Duffy of San Quentin *'54*
The High and the Mighty *'54*
Storm Center *'56*
The Curfew Breakers *'57*

Paula Kelly (1942-2020)
Sweet Charity *'69*
The Andromeda Strain *'71*
Trouble Man *'72*
Soylent Green *'73*
The Spook Who Sat by the Door *'73*
Jo Jo Dancer, Your Life Is Calling *'86*
The Women of Brewster Place *'89*
Once Upon a Time . . . When We Were Colored *'95*

Rae'ven (Alyia Larrymore) Kelly (1985-)
What's Love Got to Do with It? *'93*
America's Dream *'95*
A Time to Kill *'96*
Milo *'98*
Freedom Song *'00*
Preacher's Kid *'10*

Ross Kelly
Pretty Dead Things *'06*
Army of the Dead *'08*

Sam Kelly
Grown Ups *'80*
Nanny McPhee Returns *'10*

Sharon Kelly (1949-)
Dirty Mind of Young Sally *'72*
Supervixens *'75*
Ilsa, Harem Keeper of the Oil Sheiks *'76*

Tommy Kelly (1925-)
The Adventures of Tom Sawyer *'38*
Peck's Bad Boy with the Circus *'38*
Gallant Sons *'40*

Rick Kelman
Critic's Choice *'63*
The First Time *'69*

Fred Kelsey (1884-1961)
Paths to Paradise *'25*
The Red-Haired Alibi *'32*
Counter-Espionage *'42*

Linda Kelsey (1946-)
Picture of Dorian Gray *'74*
Eleanor & Franklin *'76*
Baby Girl Scott *'87*
Nutcracker: Money, Madness & Murder *'87*

Kate Kelton (1978-)
Harold and Kumar Go to White Castle *'04*
Cake *'05*

Pert Kelton (1907-68)
Sally *'29*
Annie Oakley *'35*
Hooray for Love *'35*
Cain and Mabel *'36*
Sitting On the Moon *'36*
Hit Parade of 1937 *'37*
The Music Man *'62*
The Comic *'69*

Richard Kelton (1943-78)
Silence *'73*
The Ultimate Warrior *'75*

Jonathan Keltz (1988-)
Acceptance *'09*
Playback *'12*
21 & Over *'13*

Violet Kemble-Cooper (1886-1961)
Cardinal Richelieu *'35*
Gone with the Wind *'39*

Edward Kemmer (1921-2004)
Earth *vs.* the Spider *'58*
Giant from the Unknown *'58*

Warren Kemmerling (1924-2005)
Trauma *'62*
The Cheyenne Social Club *'70*
Hit! *'73*
Eat My Dust *'76*
Family Plot *'76*
The Dark *'79*

Elizabeth Kemp (1958-)
He Knows You're Alone *'80*
Killing Hour *'84*
Eating *'90*

Gary Kemp (1960-)
The Bodyguard *'92*
Killing Zoe *'94*

Jeremy Kemp (1935-2019)
Operation Crossbow *'65*
The Blue Max *'66*
Assignment K *'68*
Darling Lili *'70*
Blockhouse *'73*
The Seven-Per-Cent Solution *'76*
Prisoner of Zenda *'79*
The Winds of War *'83*
Top Secret! *'84*
War & Remembrance *'88*
War & Remembrance: The Final Chapter *'89*
Prisoner of Honor *'91*
Duel of Hearts *'92*
The Magician *'93*
Four Weddings and a Funeral *'94*
Angels and Insects *'95*

Lindsay Kemp (1938-)
Savage Messiah *'72*
The Wicker Man *'75*
Sebastiane *'79*

Martin Kemp (1961-)
Waxwork 2: Lost in Time *'91*
Aspen Extreme *'93*
Cyber Bandits *'94*
Embrace of the Vampire *'95*
Sugar Town *'99*
Back in Business *'06*

Matty Kemp (1907-99)
Air Eagles *'31*
City Park *'34*

Tom Kemp
Crooked Arrows *'12*
Sexting in Suburbia *'12*

Will(iam) Kemp (1977-)
Van Helsing *'04*
Mindhunters *'05*
Step Up 2 the Streets *'08*
Petals on the Wind *'14*
The Scorpion King 4: Quest for Power *'15*

Will Kempe (1963-)
Metropolitan *'90*
Hit the Dutchman *'92*

Charles Kemper (1900-50)
That Hagen Girl *'47*
The Nevadan *'50*
Stars in My Crown *'50*
Where Danger Lives *'50*
On Dangerous Ground *'51*

Ellie Kemper (1980-)
Bridesmaids *'11*
Laggies *'13*
Sex Tape *'14*
They Came Together *'14*
The Secret Life of Pets *'16*

Rachel Kempson (1910-2003)
Captive Heart *'47*
Georgy Girl *'66*
The Charge of the Light Brigade *'68*
The Virgin Soldiers *'69*
Love for Lydia *'79*
Camille *'84*
Out of Africa *'85*
Deja Vu *'98*

Felicity Kendal (1946-)
Shakespeare Wallah *'65*
Valentino *'77*
The Camomile Lawn *'92*
We're Back! A Dinosaur's Story *'93 (V)*
Parting Shots *'98*

Jennifer Kendal (1934-84)
Bombay Talkie *'70*
Heat and Dust *'82*

Cy Kendall (1898-1953)
The Green Hornet *'39*
The Saint Takes Over *'40*
Billy the Kid *'41*
Johnny Eager *'42*
Tarzan's New York Adventure *'42*
Blonde for a Day *'46*

Henry Kendall (1897-1962)
Rich and Strange *'32*
Death on the Set *'35*
The Voice of Merrill *'52*

Katherine Kendall (1969-)
Swingers *'96*
Eye of the Storm *'98*
Devil in the Flesh 2 *'00*
Belladonna *'08*

Kay Kendall (1926-59)
London Town *'46*
Wings of Danger *'52*
Doctor in the House *'53*
Genevieve *'53*
The Shadow Man *'53*
Quentin Durward *'55*
Simon and Laura *'55*
Abdulla the Great *'56*
Les Girls *'57*
The Reluctant Debutante *'58*
Once More, With Feeling *'60*

Suzy Kendall (1944-)
Circus of Fear *'67*
To Sir, with Love *'67*
Up the Junction *'68*
The Bird with the Crystal Plumage *'70*
Tales That Witness Madness *'73*
Torso *'73*
Craze *'74*

Tony Kendall (1936-2009)
Hyena of London *'62*
The Whip and the Body *'63*
Kiss Kiss Kill Kill *'66*
Death is Nimble, Death is Quick *'67*
Machine Gun McCain *'69*
When the Screaming Stops *'73*
Return of the Evil Dead *'75*
Oil *'78*

William Kendall (1903-84)
Idol on Parade *'59*
Raven's Ridge *'97*

Alex Kendrick
Courageous *'11*
Overcomer *'19*

Anna Kendrick (1985-)
Camp *'03*
Rocket Science *'07*
Twilight *'08*
Elsewhere *'09*
The Marc Pease Experience *'09*
The Twilight Saga: New Moon *'09*
Up in the Air *'09*
Scott Pilgrim *vs.* the World *'10*
The Twilight Saga: Eclipse *'10*
50/50 *'11*
The Twilight Saga: Breaking Dawn, Part 1 *'11*
End of Watch *'12*
ParaNorman *'12 (V)*
Pitch Perfect *'12*
What to Expect When You're Expecting *'12*
Drinking Buddies *'13*
Cake *'14*
Happy Christmas *'14*
Into the Woods *'14*
The Last Five Years *'14*
Life After Beth *'14*
Digging for Fire *'15*
Pitch Perfect 2 *'15*
The Voices *'15*
The Accountant *'16*
Get a Job *'16*
The Hollars *'16*
Mike and Dave Need Wedding Dates *'16*
Mr. Right *'16*
Trolls *'16*
Pitch Perfect 3 *'17*
Table 19 *'17*
A Simple Favor *'18*
The Day Shall Come *'19*
Noelle *'19*
Trolls World Tour *'20*

Ellie Kendrick (1990-)
The Diary of Anne Frank *'08*
Upstairs Downstairs *'11*
Cheerful Weather for the Wedding *'12*

Alexa Kenin (1962-85)
A House Without a Christmas Tree *'72*
Honkytonk Man *'82*
Pretty in Pink *'86*

Arthur Kennedy (1914-90)
City for Conquest *'40*
High Sierra *'41*
They Died with Their Boots On *'41*
Desperate Journey *'42*
Air Force *'43*
Devotion *'46*
Boomerang *'47*
Cheyenne *'47*
Champion *'49*
Too Late for Tears *'49*
The Window *'49*
Bend of the River *'52*
The Girl in White *'52*
The Lusty Men *'52*
Rancho Notorious *'52*
Desperate Hours *'55*
The Man from Laramie *'55*
Trial *'55*
Peyton Place *'57*
Some Came Running *'58*
A Summer Place *'59*
Elmer Gantry *'60*
Claudelle Inglish *'61*
Murder She Said *'61*
Barabbas *'62*
Lawrence of Arabia *'62*
Cheyenne Autumn *'64*
Revenge of Sartana *'65*
Fantastic Voyage *'66*
Nevada Smith *'66*
A Minute to Pray, a Second to Die *'67*
Anzio *'68*
Day of the Evil Gun *'68*
Shark! *'68*
Mean Machine *'73*
Let Sleeping Corpses Lie *'74*
Emmanuelle on Taboo Island *'76*
The Sentinel *'76*
Signs of Life *'89*

Beth Kennedy
Jerome *'98*
The Tomorrow Man *'01*

David Kennedy (1964-)
Shiner *'00*
Reign of Fire *'02*
Attack Force *'06*

Deborah Kennedy
The Sum of Us *'94*
Idiot Box *'97*
The Wedding Party *'97*
Swimming Upstream *'03*

Douglas Kennedy (1915-73)
South of St. Louis *'48*
Whiplash *'48*
Chain Gang *'50*
Montana *'50*
Fort Osage *'51*
I Was an American Spy *'51*
The Lion Hunters *'51*
Safari Drums *'53*
War Paint *'53*
Sitting Bull *'54*
Wiretapper *'55*
Wyoming Renegades *'55*
Chicago Confidential *'57*
The Land Unknown *'57*

Edgar Kennedy (1890-1948)
The Better 'Ole *'26*
Hold 'Em Jail *'32*
Penguin Pool Murder *'32*
Duck Soup *'33*
Murder On the Blackboard *'34*
The Silver Streak *'34*
Twentieth Century *'34*
Cowboy Millionaire *'35*
Flirting With Danger *'35*
San Francisco *'36*
Double Wedding *'37*
True Confession *'37*
When's Your Birthday? *'37*
The Black Doll *'38*
Hey! Hey! USA! *'38*
Peck's Bad Boy with the Circus *'38*
Frolics on Ice *'39*
It's a Wonderful World *'39*
Remedy for Riches *'40*
Blondie in Society *'41*
Snuffy Smith, Yard Bird *'42*
Air Raid Wardens *'43*
The Falcon Strikes Back *'43*
It Happened Tomorrow *'44*
The Sin of Harold Diddlebock *'47*
Unfaithfully Yours *'48*
My Dream Is Yours *'49*

George Kennedy (1925-2016)
Lonely Are the Brave *'62*
Charade *'63*
McHale's Navy *'64*
Strait-Jacket *'64*
The Flight of the Phoenix *'65*
In Harm's Way *'65*
Shenandoah *'65*
Sons of Katie Elder *'65*
Mirage *'66*
The Ballad of Josie *'67*
Cool Hand Luke *'67*
The Dirty Dozen *'67*
Hurry Sundown *'67*
Bandolero! *'68*
The Boston Strangler *'68*
The Good Guys and the Bad Guys *'69*
Guns of the Magnificent Seven *'69*
Airport *'70*
Tick... Tick... Tick *'70*
ZigZag *'70*
Cahill: United States Marshal *'73*
Deliver Us From Evil *'73*
Lost Horizon *'73*
Earthquake *'74*
Thunderbolt & Lightfoot *'74*
Airport '75 *'75*
The Eiger Sanction *'75*
The Human Factor *'75*
Airport '77 *'77*
Brass Target *'78*
Death on the Nile *'78*
Backstairs at the White House *'79*
The Concorde: Airport '79 *'79*
The Double McGuffin *'79*
Just Before Dawn *'80*
Modern Romance *'81*
Search and Destroy *'81*
Virus *'82*
Bolero *'84*
The Jesse Owens Story *'84*
Savage Dawn *'84*
Delta Force *'86*
Creepshow 2 *'87*
The Gunfighters *'87*
Kenny Rogers as the Gambler, Part 3: The Legend Continues *'87*
Nightmare at Noon *'87*
The Naked Gun: From the Files of Police Squad *'88*
The Terror Within *'88*
The Uninvited *'88*
Brain Dead *'89*
Ministry of Vengeance *'89*
Hangfire *'91*
Hired to Kill *'91*
Naked Gun 2 1/2: The Smell of Fear *'91*
Final Shot: The Hank Gathers Story *'92*
Naked Gun 33 1/3: The Final Insult *'94*
Cats Don't Dance *'97 (V)*
Dennis the Menace Strikes Again *'98*
Small Soldiers *'98 (V)*
Don't Come Knocking *'05*
Three Bad Men *'05*
The Man Who Came Back *'08*
Another Happy Day *'11*

Gerard Kennedy (1932-)
Newsfront *'78*
Body Melt *'93*

Graham Kennedy (1934-2005)
Don's Party *'76*
The Odd Angry Shot *'79*
The Club *'81*
Return of Captain Invincible *'83*

Jamie Kennedy (1970-)
Scream '96
Clockwatchers '97
Scream 2 '97
Bongwater '98
Enemy of the State '98
Highway Hitcher '98
Stricken '98
Bowfinger '99
Sparkler '99
Three Kings '99
Bait '00
Boiler Room '00
Scream 3 '00
The Specials '00
Max Keeble's Big Move '01
Seduced: Pretty When You Cry '01
Sol Goode '01
Malibu's Most Wanted '03
Son of the Mask '05
Kickin' It Old Skool '07
Extreme Movie '08
Heckler '08
Finding Bliss '09
Cafe '10
Bending the Rules '12
Cupid '12
Reef 2: High Tide '12
Tyler Perry's Good Deeds '12
Bermuda Tentacles '14
The Hungover Games '14
Tremors 5: Bloodlines '15

Jayne Kennedy (1951-)
The Muthers '76
Fighting Mad '77
Death Force '78
Mysterious Island of Beautiful Women '79
Body & Soul '81

Jessica Parker Kennedy (1984-)
Another Cinderella Story '08
Bad Meat '11
Behemoth '11
Collision Earth '11
Nearlyweds '13
Deep Murder '19

Jonelle Kennedy
How U Like Me Now? '92
Fertile Ground '10

Julia Kennedy
Gossip '08
Grown Up Movie Star '10

Leon Isaac Kennedy (1949-)
Fighting Mad '77
Death Force '78
Penitentiary '79
Body & Soul '81
Penitentiary 2 '82
Lone Wolf McQuade '83
Hollywood Vice Sqaud '86
Skeleton Coast '89

Madge Kennedy (1891-1987)
The Marrying Kind '52
Three Bad Sisters '56

Merle Kennedy (1967-)
Nemesis '93
Night of the Demons 2 '94
Switchback '97
May '02
Three Days of Rain '02

Merna Kennedy (1908-44)
The Circus '28
Stepping Out '31
The Gay Buckaroo '32
The Red-Haired Alibi '32

Mimi Kennedy (1948-)
Immediate Family '89
Pump Up the Volume '90
Death Becomes Her '92
In the Loop '09
Life of Lemon '11
Midnight in Paris '11
The Five-Year Engagement '12

Patricia Kennedy (1917-2012)
The Getting of Wisdom '77
My Brilliant Career '79
Country Life '95

Patrick Kennedy (1977-)
Cambridge Spies '03
Bleak House '05
Atonement '07
The Last Station '09
Me and Orson Welles '09
The 39 Steps '09
Murder On the Home Front '13
Mr. Holmes '15

Rigg Kennedy (1942-)
R.P.M.* (*Revolutions Per Minute) '70
Girls on the Road '73
Slumber Party Massacre '82
Maid to Order '87
Dangerous Relations '93

Ryan Kennedy (1982-)
The Invisible '07
Poison Ivy 4: The Secret Society '08
Storm Cell '08
Ice Twisters '09
Super Hybrid '10
Hannah's Law '12
Nearlyweds '13
Lucky in Love '14

Sarah Kennedy
The Telephone Book '71
Working Girls '75

Sheila Kennedy
First Turn On '83
Ellie '84

Tom Kennedy (1885-1965)
Big News '29
Monkey Business '31
Hollywood Party '34
Smart Blonde '37
The Pretender '47
Invasion U.S.A. '52

Kari Kennell (1964-)
See Kari Whitman

Doug Kenney
National Lampoon's Animal House '78
Heavy Metal '81 (V)

James Kenney (1930-82)
Tough Guy '53
Above Us the Waves '55

June Kenney (1933-)
Teenage Doll '57
The Viking Women and the Sea Serpent '57
Attack of the Puppet People '58
Earth *vs.* the Spider '58
Bloodlust '59

Kerri Kenney
Waiting '00
The Comebacks '07

Sean Kenney (1942-)
The Corpse Grinders '71
Savage Abduction '73

Tom Kenny (1962-)
Shakes the Clown '92
The Powerpuff Girls Movie '02 (NV)
Comic Book: The Movie '04
The SpongeBob SquarePants Movie '04 (V)
World's Greatest Dad '09
Winnie the Pooh '11 (V)
Delhi Safari '12 (V)
Call Me Lucky '15
The SpongeBob Movie: Sponge Out of Water '15 (V)

Patsy Kensit (1968-)
The Great Gatsby '74
Monty Python and the Holy Grail '75
Silas Marner '85
Absolute Beginners '86
A Chorus of Disapproval '89
Lethal Weapon 2 '89
Bullseye! '90
Chicago Joe & the Showgirl '90
Kill Cruise '90
Timebomb '91
Blame It on the Bellboy '92
The Turn of the Screw '92
Full Eclipse '93
Dream Man '94
Angels and Insects '95
At the Midnight Hour '95
Tunnel Vision '95
Grace of My Heart '96
The Last Don 2 '98
Janice Beard '99
Speedway Junky '99
Hell's Gate '01
Strange Frequency 2 '01
Things Behind the Sun '01
Dark Side '02
Shelter Island '03
Played '06

Anne Kent
Widow's Peak '94
Catherine Cookson's The Gambling Man '98

Barbara Kent (1907-2011)
The Flesh and the Devil '27
No Man's Law '27
Feet First '30
Indiscreet '31
Pride of the Legion '32
Vanity Fair '32
Her Forgotten Past '33
Oliver Twist '33
Old Man Rhythm '35

Crauford Kent (1881-1953)
Seven Keys to Baldpate '29
Three Faces East '30
Sinister Hands '32
Tea for Two '50

Dorothea Kent (1916-90)
More Than A Secretary '36
It Happened on 5th Avenue '47

Gary Kent (1933-)
The Thrill Killers '65
Satan's Sadists '69

Jean Kent (1921-2013)
Bees in Paradise '44
Two Thousand Women '44
Caravan '46
The Magic Bow '47
Man of Evil '48
The Browning Version '51
Bonjour Tristesse '57
The Haunted Strangler '58

Julie Kent
Dancers '87
Center Stage '00

Larry Kent (1900-67)
Hangman's House '28
Seas Beneath '31
Viva Las Vegas '63

Robert Kent (1908-55)
Dimples '36
Charlie Chan at Monte Carlo '37
East Side of Heaven '39
The Phantom Creeps '39
Blonde Comet '41

Doris Kenyon (1897-1979)
Monsieur Beaucaire '24
Burning Daylight '28
Young America '32
Counsellor-at-Law '33

Gwen Kenyon (1916-99)
Tornado '43
The Great Mike '44

Marwan Kenzari (1983-)
Collide '17
Aladdin '19

Leila Kenzle (1960-)
Enemies of Laughter '00
Identity '03

Jimmy Keogh (?-2003)
The Matchmaker '97
Bloom '03

Barry Keoghan
Stay '13
The Killing of a Sacred Deer '17
American Animals '18

Riley Keough (1989-)
The Good Doctor '11
Jack and Diane '12
Kiss of the Damned '12
American Honey '16
It Comes at Night '17
Logan Lucky '17
Lovesong '17
We Don't Belong Here '17
Hold the Dark '18
Under the Silver Lake '18
Earthquake Bird '19
The Lodge '19

Ken Kercheval (1935-)
Pretty Poison '68
Rabbit, Run '70
Devil Dog: The Hound of Hell '78
Too Far to Go '79
Corporate Affairs '90
Bad Ass '09

Max Kerlow
Frida '84
Nora's Will '09

Robert Kerman
Cannibal Holocaust '80
Emerald Jungle '80

Joey Kern (1976-)
Cabin Fever '03
Grind '03
Pizza '05
The Sasquatch Gang '06
Rosencrantz & Guildenstern Are Undead '10
Beneath '13
Bloodsucking Bastards '15

Joanna Kerns (1953-)
A*P*E* '76
The Million Dollar Rip-Off '76
Broken Badge '85
Cross My Heart '88
An American Summer '90
The Great Los Angeles Earthquake '91
The Nightman '93
No Dessert Dad, 'Til You Mow the Lawn '94
Emma's Wish '98
The Growing Pains Movie '00
All Over the Guy '01
Growing Pains: Return of the Seavers '04

Bill Kerr (1922-2014)
Appointment in London '53
You Know What Sailors Are '59
Gallipoli '81
1915 '82
Pirate Movie '82
The Year of Living Dangerously '82
The Coca-Cola Kid '84
Razorback '84
Sweet Talker '91

Deborah Kerr (1921-2007)
If Winter Comes '41
Love on the Dole '41
Major Barbara '41
The Life and Death of Colonel Blimp '43
Vacation from Marriage '45
I See a Dark Stranger '46
Black Narcissus '47
The Hucksters '47
Edward, My Son '49
King Solomon's Mines '50
Quo Vadis '51
Prisoner of Zenda '52
Dream Wife '53
From Here to Eternity '53
Julius Caesar '53
Young Bess '53
End of the Affair '55
The King and I '56
The Proud and Profane '56
Tea and Sympathy '56
An Affair to Remember '57
Bonjour Tristesse '57
Heaven Knows, Mr. Allison '57
Separate Tables '58
Beloved Infidel '59
The Journey '59
The Sundowners '60
The Grass Is Greener '61
The Innocents '61
The Chalk Garden '64
The Night of the Iguana '64
Marriage on the Rocks '65
Casino Royale '67
Eye of the Devil '67
The Arrangement '69
The Gypsy Moths '69
A Woman of Substance '84
Reunion at Fairborough '85
Hold the Dream '86

E. Katherine Kerr (1937-)
Children of a Lesser God '86
Power '86
Suspect '87
The Buccaneers '95
The Siege '98
Songcatcher '99

Edward Kerr (1966-)
Above Suspicion '95
Legalese '98
Cat City '08

Frederick Kerr (1858-1933)
Frankenstein '31
Lovers Courageous '32
The Man From Toronto '32
Beauty and the Boss '33

John Kerr (1931-2013)
The Cobweb '55
Tea and Sympathy '56
South Pacific '58
The Crowded Sky '60
Girl of the Night '60
The Pit and the Pendulum '61

Kristen Kerr
Flight of the Living Dead: Outbreak on a Plane '07
Strictly Sexual '08

Linda Kerridge (1954-)
Fade to Black '80
Mixed Blood '84
Alien from L.A. '87

J.M. Kerrigan (1884-1964)
Little Old New York '23
Song o' My Heart '30
The Black Camel '31
The Lost Patrol '34
The Informer '35
Congo Maisie '40
Action in the North Atlantic '43
Fighting Seabees '44
My Cousin Rachel '52
Park Row '52
The Wild North '52
Fastest Gun Alive '56

Norman Kerry (1889-1956)
Amarilly of Clothesline Alley '18
The Hunchback of Notre Dame '23
Merry-Go-Round '23
The Phantom of the Opera '25
Air Eagles '31
The Phantom of Santa Fe '36

Brian Kerwin (1949-)
A Real American Hero '78
Hometown U.S.A. '79
Getting Wasted '80
Miss All-American Beauty '82
Wet Gold '84
Murphy's Romance '85
King Kong Lives '86
Torch Song Trilogy '88
Love Field '91
Hard Promises '92
Abandoned and Deceived '95
Gold Diggers: The Secret of Bear Mountain '95
Getting Away With Murder '96
Jack '96
The Myth of Fingerprints '97
Unlikely Angel '97
Flash '98
Mr. Jealousy '98
27 Dresses '08
The Help '11

Lance Kerwin (1960-)
Salem's Lot '79
A Killer in the Family '83
Enemy Mine '85
Fourth Wise Man '85
Final Verdict '91

William Kerwin (1927-89)
Blood Feast '63
2000 Maniacs '64
Playgirl Killer '66
A Taste of Blood '67

Ian Reed Kesler (1977-)
Poster Boy '04
Finish Line '08
Dark House '09

Jillian Kesner (1950-2007)
Firecracker '81
Beverly Hills Vamp '88

Sara Kestelman (1944-)
Zardoz '73
Lisztomania '75
Lady Jane '85

Boyd Kestner (1964-)
Lethal Lolita-Amy Fisher: My Story '92
Entertaining Angels: The Dorothy Day Story '96
The Art of Murder '99
The General's Daughter '99
Cleopatra's Second Husband '00
Hell Swarm '00
Black Hawk Down '01
The Insatiable '06

Bryan Kestner (1964-)
Fire Birds '90
In Dark Places '97

Jack Kesy
Morgan '12
Intruders '16
Blood Brother '18

Janet Key (1945-92)
Dracula A.D. 1972 '72
And Now the Screaming Starts '73

Keegan Michael Key (1971-)
Afternoon Delight '13
Let's Be Cops '14
Don't Think Twice '16
Keanu '16
Why Him? '16
The Star '17
The Predator '18
Dolemite Is My Name '19
Playing with Fire '19
Toy Story 4 '19

Christian Keyes
Black Coffee '14
The Man in 3B '16

Evelyn Keyes (1919-2008)
Gone with the Wind '39
Union Pacific '39
The Lady in Question '40
Slightly Honorable '40
Here Comes Mr. Jordan '41
Ladies in Retirement '41
The Desperadoes '43
There's Something About a Soldier '43
Strange Affair '44
The Jolson Story '46
Johnny O'Clock '47
The Killer That Stalked New York '47
Enchantment '48
Mr. Soft Touch '49
The Prowler '51
99 River Street '53
Hell's Half Acre '54
The Seven Year Itch '55
Around the World in 80 Days '56 (C)
Return to Salem's Lot '87
Wicked Stepmother '89

Irwin Keyes (1952-2015)
The Flintstones *'94*
Backlash: Oblivion 2 *'95*
Intolerable Cruelty *'03*

Skander Keynes (1991-)
The Chronicles of Narnia: The Lion, the Witch and the Wardrobe *'05*
The Chronicles of Narnia: Prince Caspian *'08*
The Chronicles of Narnia: The Voyage of the Dawn Treader *'10*

Alicia Keys (1981-)
The Nanny Diaries *'07*
Smokin' Aces *'07*
Girl Rising *'13 (N)*

Tony Kgoroge
The Bird Can't Fly *'07*
Mandela: Long Walk to Freedom *'13*

Konstantin Khabensky (1972-)
Night Watch *'04*
Day Watch *'06*
Wanted *'08*

Malika Khadijah
Sky High *'05*
ATL *'06*

Simbi Khali (1971-)
A Thin Line Between Love and Hate *'96*
We Were Soldiers *'02*

Chulpan Khamatova (1975-)
Good Bye, Lenin! *'03*
Midsummer Madness *'07*
The White Crow *'18*

Persis Khambatta (1950-98)
Conduct Unbecoming *'75*
The Wilby Conspiracy *'75*
Star Trek: The Motion Picture *'79*
Nighthawks *'81*
Warrior of the Lost World *'84*
First Strike *'85*
Deadly Intent *'88*
Phoenix the Warrior *'88*

Aamir Khan (1965-)
Earth *'98*
Lagaan: Once upon a Time in India *'01*
St. Trinian's *'07*

Irfan Khan (1967-)
The Warrior *'01*
The Namesake *'06*
A Mighty Heart *'07*
Partition *'07*
Slumdog Millionaire *'08*
Puzzle *'18*

Irrfan Khan (1967-2020)
The Amazing Spider-Man *'12*
Life of Pi *'12*
The Lunchbox *'13*
Inferno *'16*

Salman Khan (1965-)
Marigold *'07*
Zero *'18*

Julie Khaner (1957-)
Choices of the Heart: The Margaret Sanger Story *'95*
Leap! *'16*

Arsinee Khanjian (1958-)
Family Viewing *'87*
Speaking Parts *'89*
The Adjuster *'91*
Calendar *'93*
Exotica *'94*
Irma Vep *'96*
The Sweet Hereafter *'96*
Late August, Early September *'98*
Felicia's Journey *'99*
Ararat *'02*
The Lark Farm *'07*
Adoration *'08*

Rahul Khanna (1972-)
Earth *'98*
The Emperor's Club *'02*

Kulbashan Kharbanda (1944-)
Fire *'96*
Lagaan: Once upon a Time in India *'01*
Water *'05*

Sachin Khedekar
Singham *'11*
Photograph *'19*

Anupam Kher (1955-)
Bend It Like Beckham *'02*
Bride & Prejudice *'04*
The Mistress of Spices *'05*
The Other End of the Line *'08*
Silver Linings Playbook *'12*
The Big Sick *'17*
Hotel Mumbai *'18*

Kiron Kher (1955-)
Devdas *'02*
Silent Waters *'03*

Nozha Khouadra
Bye-Bye *'96*
The New Eve *'98*

Daphne Khoury
The Deadbeat Club *'04*
Fright Flick *'10*

Makram Khoury (1945-)
The Body *'01*
Free Zone *'05*
Munich *'05*
House of Saddam *'08*

Leleti Khumalo (1970-)
Sarafina! *'92*
Cry, the Beloved Country *'95*

Guy Kibbee (1882-1956)
Flying High *'31*
Laughing Sinners *'31*
Man of the World *'31*
The Conquerors *'32*
The Crowd Roars *'32*
Rain *'32*
The Strange Love of Molly Louvain *'32*
Taxi! *'32*
Two Seconds *'32*
Union Depot *'32*
Winner Take All *'32*
Footlight Parade *'33*
42nd Street *'33*
Girl Missing *'33*
Gold Diggers of 1933 *'33*
Lady for a Day *'33*
Dames *'34*
The Merry Frinks *'34*
Wonder Bar *'34*
Captain Blood *'35*
Captain January *'36*
Little Lord Fauntleroy *'36*
Jim Hanvey, Detective *'37*
The Bad Man of Brimstone *'38*
Joy of Living *'38*
Of Human Hearts *'38*
Three Comrades *'38*
Three Loves Has Nancy *'38*
Babes in Arms *'39*
It's a Wonderful World *'39*
Let Freedom Ring *'39*
Mr. Smith Goes to Washington *'39*
Chad Hanna *'40*
Our Town *'40*
Design for Scandal *'41*
It Started with Eve *'41*
Tish *'42*
Whistling in Dixie *'42*
Dixie Jamboree *'44*
The Horn Blows at Midnight *'45*
The Romance of Rosy Ridge *'47*
Fort Apache *'48*
Three Godfathers *'48*

Sandrine Kiberlain (1968-)
Beaumarchais the Scoundrel *'96*
For Sale *'98*
Seventh Heaven *'98*
Alias Betty *'01*
Apres-Vous *'03*
Mademoiselle Chambon *'09*
The Women on the Sixth Floor *'10*

Kid Cudi (1984-)
See Scott Mescudi

Kid Rock (1971-)
Joe Dirt *'01*
Biker Boyz *'03*
Larry the Cable Guy: Health Inspector *'06 (C)*

Jonathan Kidd
Seven Thieves *'60*
The 7th Commandment *'61*

Michael Kidd (1915-2007)
It's Always Fair Weather *'55*
Smile *'75*

Janet Kidder (1972-)
Dead Awake *'01*
Dark Side *'02*
Ginger Snaps: Unleashed *'04*
Knockout *'11*
Magic Beyond Words: The JK Rowling Story *'11*

Margot Kidder (1948-2018)
Quackser Fortune Has a Cousin in the Bronx *'70*
Sisters *'73*
Black Christmas *'75*
The Great Waldo Pepper *'75*
92 in the Shade *'76*
Superman: The Movie *'78*
The Amityville Horror *'79*
Mr. Mike's Mondo Video *'79*
Superman 2 *'80*
Miss Right *'81*
Some Kind of Hero *'82*
Superman 3 *'83*
Trenchcoat *'83*
Keeping Track *'86*
Superman 4: The Quest for Peace *'87*
Mob Story *'90*
To Catch a Killer *'92*
Henry & Verlin *'94*
Windrunner *'94*
Phantom 2040 Movie: The Ghost Who Walks *'95 (V)*
Young Ivanhoe *'95*
Never Met Picasso *'96*
Junior's Groove *'97*
My Teacher Ate My Homework *'98*
Tribulation *'00*
Love at First Kill *'08*
On the Other Hand, Death *'08*
Halloween II *'09*

Nicole Kidman (1967-)
BMX Bandits *'83*
Archer's Adventure *'85*
Night Master *'87*
Dead Calm *'89*
Flirting *'89*
Days of Thunder *'90*
Billy Bathgate *'91*
Far and Away *'92*
Malice *'93*
My Life *'93*
Batman Forever *'95*
To Die For *'95*
The Leading Man *'96*
Portrait of a Lady *'96*
The Peacemaker *'97*
Practical Magic *'98*
Eyes Wide Shut *'99*
Moulin Rouge *'01*
The Others *'01*
Birthday Girl *'02*
The Hours *'02*
Cold Mountain *'03*
Dogville *'03*
The Human Stain *'03*
Birth *'04*
The Stepford Wives *'04*
Bewitched *'05*
The Interpreter *'05*
Fur: An Imaginary Portrait of Diane Arbus *'06*
Happy Feet *'06 (V)*
The Golden Compass *'07*
The Invasion *'07*
Margot at the Wedding *'07*
Australia *'08*
Nine *'09*
Rabbit Hole *'10*
Just Go With It *'11*
Trespass *'11*

Hemingway & Gelhorn *'12*
The Paperboy *'12*
The Railway Man *'13*
Stoker *'13*
Before I Go to Sleep *'14*
Grace of Monaco *'14*
Paddington *'14*
Secret in Their Eyes *'15*
Strangerland *'15*
The Family Fang *'16*
Genius *'16*
Lion *'16*
The Beguiled *'17*
How To Talk To Girls At Parties *'17*
The Killing of a Sacred Deer *'17*
The Upside *'17*
Aquaman *'18*
Boy Erased *'18*
Destroyer *'18*
Bombshell *'19*
The Goldfinch *'19*

James Kidnie
Body Parts *'91*
Gate 2 *'92*
Hostile Intent *'97*
Resurrection *'99*
Swamp Devil *'08*

Richard Kiel (1939-2014)
The Phantom Planet *'61*
Eegah! *'62*
The Human Duplicators *'64*
Roustabout *'64*
The Longest Yard *'74*
Silver Streak *'76*
The Spy Who Loved Me *'77*
Force 10 from Navarone *'78*
They Went That-a-Way & That-a-Way *'78*
Moonraker *'79*
So Fine *'81*
Hysterical *'83*
Mad Mission 3 *'84*
Pale Rider *'85*
Happy Gilmore *'96*

Udo Kier (1944-)
Mark of the Devil *'69*
Andy Warhol's Dracula *'74*
Andy Warhol's Frankenstein *'74*
The Story of O *'75*
The Stationmaster's Wife *'77*
Suspiria *'77*
Medea *'88*
Seduction: The Cruel Woman *'89*
My Own Private Idaho *'91*
Zentropa *'92*
Ace Ventura: Pet Detective *'93*
For Love or Money *'93*
Breaking the Waves *'95*
Johnny Mnemonic *'95*
The Kingdom *'95*
The Adventures of Pinocchio *'96*
Barb Wire *'96*
Red Shoe Diaries 7: Burning Up *'96*
Betty *'97*
The End of Violence *'97*
The Kingdom 2 *'97*
Blade *'98*
Modern Vampires *'98*
Dancer in the Dark *'99*
End of Days *'99*
Killer Deal *'99*
Spy Games *'99*
Critical Mass *'00*
Doomsdayer *'00*
Just One Night *'00*
Life in the Fast Lane *'00*
Red Letters *'00*
Shadow of the Vampire *'00*
Invincible *'01*
The Last Minute *'01*
All the Queen's Men *'02*
Feardotcom *'02*
He Sees You When You're Sleeping *'02*
Headspace *'02*
Dogville *'03*
Evil Eyes *'04*
Modigliani *'04*
Paranoia 1.0 *'04*
Manderlay *'05*

BloodRayne *'06*
Fall Down Dead *'07*
Holly *'07*
Far Cry *'08*
Mother of Tears *'08*
My Son, My Son, What Have Ye Done *'09*
Keyhole *'11*
Melancholia *'11*
Brawl in Cell Block 99 *'17*
Puppet Master: The Littlest Reich *'18*
The Mountain *'19*

Robbie Kiger (1973-)
Table for Five *'83*
Children of the Corn *'84*
Welcome Home, Roxy Carmichael *'90*

Laura Kightlinger (1969-)
Down With Love *'03*
Anchorman: The Legend of Ron Burgundy *'04*
Kicking & Screaming *'05*
Must Love Dogs *'05*
The Shaggy Dog *'06*
Mama's Boy *'07*

Rya Kihlstedt (1970-)
The Buccaneers *'95*
Jaded *'96*
Home Alone 3 *'97*
Brave New World *'98*
Deep Impact *'98*
She Creature *'01*
Women in Trouble *'09*

Kirin Kiki
I Wish *'11*
After the Storm *'17*

Rinko Kikuchi (1981-)
Babel *'06*
The Sky Crawlers *'08*
The Brothers Bloom *'09*
Pacific Rim *'13*
Kumiko the Treasure Hunter *'14*

Rei Kikukawa (1978-)
Godzilla: Final Wars *'04*
Genghis Khan: To the Ends of the Earth and Sea *'07*

Craig Kilborn (1962-)
Old School *'03*
The Benchwarmers *'06*
The Shaggy Dog *'06*
Full of It *'07*

Percy Kilbride (1888-1964)
White Woman *'33*
George Washington Slept Here *'42*
Keeper of the Flame *'42*
The Adventures of Mark Twain *'44*
Guest in the House *'44*
The Woman of the Town *'44*
Fallen Angel *'45*
She Wouldn't Say Yes *'45*
The Southerner *'45*
State Fair *'45*
Egg and I *'47*
Welcome Stranger *'47*
Feudin', Fussin', and A-Fightin' *'48*
You Gotta Stay Happy *'48*
Ma and Pa Kettle *'49*
Mr. Soft Touch *'49*
Ma and Pa Kettle Go to Town *'50*
Riding High *'50*
Ma and Pa Kettle Back On the Farm *'51*
Ma and Pa Kettle at the Fair *'52*
Ma and Pa Kettle on Vacation *'53*
Ma and Pa Kettle at Home *'54*
Ma and Pa Kettle at Waikiki *'55*

Terence (Terry) Kilburn (1926-)
A Christmas Carol *'38*
Goodbye, Mr. Chips *'39*
They Shall Have Music *'39*
National Velvet *'44*
Fiend without a Face *'58*
Lolita *'62*

Jewel Kilcher (1974-)
Ride with the Devil *'99*
Ring of Fire *'13*

Q'orianka Kilcher (1990-)
The New World *'05*
Princess Kaiulani *'09*
Neverland *'11*
Firelight *'12*
The Power of Few *'13*

Richard Kiley (1922-99)
The Mob *'51*
Eight Iron Men *'52*
The Sniper *'52*
Pickup on South Street *'53*
Blackboard Jungle *'55*
The Phenix City Story *'55*
Night Gallery *'69*
Murder Once Removed *'71*
The Little Prince *'74*
Endless Love *'81*
The Thorn Birds *'83*
A.D. *'85*
The Adventures of Huckleberry Finn *'85*
The Bad Seed *'85*
Howard the Duck *'86 (V)*
If Tomorrow Comes *'86*
Separate but Equal *'91*
Jurassic Park *'93 (V)*
Phenomenon *'96*
Patch Adams *'98*

Victor Kilian (1891-1979)
Public Menace *'35*
Riff Raff *'35*
Adventure in Manhattan *'36*
The Road to Glory *'36*
It Happened in Hollywood *'37*
The Adventures of Tom Sawyer *'38*
Prison Break *'38*
Dr. Cyclops *'40*
Young Tom Edison *'40*
A Date With the Falcon *'42*
Rimfire *'49*
One Too Many *'51*
Unknown World *'51*

Taram Killam (1982-)
Just Married *'03*
My Best Friend's Girl *'08*

Taran Killam
Casual Encounters *'16*
Killing Gunther *'17*

Jack Kilmer
Palo Alto *'14*
Len & Company *'16*
Woodshock *'17*
Summer '03 *'18*
Hala *'19*

Val Kilmer (1959-)
Top Secret! *'84*
Real Genius *'85*
The Murders in the Rue Morgue *'86*
Top Gun *'86*
Willow *'88*
Kill Me Again *'89*
The Doors *'91*
Thunderheart *'92*
The Real McCoy *'93*
Tombstone *'93*
True Romance *'93*
Batman Forever *'95*
Heat *'95*
The Ghost and the Darkness *'96*
The Island of Dr. Moreau *'96*
The Saint *'97*
At First Sight *'98*
Prince of Egypt *'98 (V)*
Joe the King *'99*
Pollock *'00*
Red Planet *'00*
Hard Cash *'01*
The Salton Sea *'02*
The Missing *'03*
Wonderland *'03*
Alexander *'04*
Spartan *'04*
Stateside *'04*
Kiss Kiss Bang Bang *'05*
Mindhunters *'05*
Dead Man's Bounty *'06*
Deja Vu *'06*
Moscow Zero *'06*

Played '06
10th & Wolf '06
Columbus Day '08
Comanche Moon '08
Conspiracy '08
Delgo '08 (V)
Felon '08
XIII '08
2:22 '08
American Cowslip '09
Bad Lieutenant: Port of Call New Orleans '09
The Chaos Experiment '09
Hardwired '09
Streets of Blood '09
The Thaw '09
Blood Out '10
Bloodworth '10
Double Identity '10
Gun '10
MacGruber '10
The Traveler '10
5 Days of War '11
Kill the Irishman '11
7 Below '11
Breathless '12
Twixt '12
Wyatt Earp's Revenge '12
Riddle '13
Standing Up '13
Palo Alto '14
The Snowman '17
Jay and Silent Bob Reboot '19

Kevin Kilner (1958-)
Danielle Steel's Heartbeat '93
Home Alone 3 '97
Music from Another Room '97
Smart House '00
A Cinderella Story '04
Raising Helen '04
Inside '06
A Stranger's Heart '07
Julia '08
Miles from Nowhere '09
The Craigslist Killer '11

Lincoln Kilpatrick (1932-2004)
Omega Man '71
Cool Breeze '72
Fortress '93
Piranha '95

Patrick Kilpatrick (1949-)
Remo Williams: The Adventure Begins '85
Class of 1999 '90
Death Warrant '90
Scanners: The Showdown '94
3 Ninjas Knuckle Up '95
Last Stand at Saber River '96
Riot '96
Free Willy 3: The Rescue '97
The Substitute 4: Failure is Not an Option '00
Minority Report '02
Gamebox 1.0 '04
Already Dead '07
Parasomnia '08
Never Surrender '09
Assassin X '16
Black Water '18

Daniel Dae Kim (1968-)
Momentum '03
Spider-Man 2 '04
The Cave '05
The Andromeda Strain '08
Arena '11
Linsanity '13

Evan C. Kim
Go Tell the Spartans '78
The Dead Pool '88

Jacqueline Kim (1965-)
Volcano '97
Brokedown Palace '99
The Hollywood Sign '01
The Operator '01
Charlotte Sometimes '02
Red Doors '05

Joy Kim
The High and the Mighty '54
Blood Alley '55

Randall Duk Kim (1943-)
The Matrix Reloaded '03
Memoirs of a Geisha '05
Kung Fu Panda '08 (V)
Dragonball: Evolution '09
The Last Airbender '10

Bruce (Kemp) Kimball
Rebel Vixens '69
Cain's Cutthroats '71

Charles Kimbrough (1936-)
Sunday in the Park with George '86
The Good Mother '88
Switching Channels '88
The Hunchback of Notre Dame '96 (V)
The Wedding Planner '01

Clinton Kimbrough (1933-96)
Bloody Mama '70
Night Call Nurses '72

Bruce Kimmel (1947-)
The First Nudie Musical '75
Spaceship '81

Jimmy Kimmel (1967-)
Garfield: The Movie '04 (V)
The Boss Baby '17

Kenneth Kimmins (1941-)
Eleanor: First Lady of the World '82
My Best Friend Is a Vampire '88

Isao (Ko) Kimura
Seven Samurai '54
Bushido: The Cruel Code of the Samurai '63

Takuya Kimura
2046 '04
Blade of the Immortal '17

Yoshino Kimura
Masters of Horror: Dream Cruise '07
Sukiyaki Western Django '08

Aron Kincaid (1943-2011)
Ski Party '65
Ghost in the Invisible Bikini '66
Creature of Destruction '67
The Proud and the Damned '72

Danielle Kind
Posers '02
Christie's Revenge '07

Richard Kind (1956-)
All-American Murder '91
Tom and Jerry: The Movie '93 (V)
Sink or Swim '97
A Bug's Life '98 (V)
Quicksand '01
Confessions of a Dangerous Mind '02
Dog Gone Love '03
Elvis Has Left the Building '04
Bewitched '05
Raising Flagg '06
The Wild '06 (V)
Big Stan '07
The Neighbor '07
A Serious Man '09
Hereafter '10
The Search for Santa Paws '10 (V)
Toy Story 3 '10 (V)
Argo '12
Santa Paws 2: The Santa Pups '12 (V)
Obvious Child '14
All We Had '16

Kevin Kindlin
The Majorettes '87
Revenge of the Living Zombies '88
Heartstopper '92

Adrienne King (1960-)
Friday the 13th '80
Friday the 13th, Part 2 '81
Psychic Experiment '10

Aja Naomi King
Four '12
The Upside '17

Alan King (1927-2004)
The Girl He Left Behind '56
The Helen Morgan Story '57
The Anderson Tapes '71
Just Tell Me What You Want '80
Author! Author! '82
I, the Jury '82
Cat's Eye '85
Memories of Me '88
Enemies, a Love Story '89
The Bonfire of the Vanities '90
Night and the City '92
Casino '95
The Infiltrator '95
Rush Hour 2 '01
Sunshine State '02
Mind the Gap '04

Andrea King (1919-2003)
God is My Co-Pilot '45
The Beast with Five Fingers '46
The Man I Love '46
My Wild Irish Rose '47
Buccaneer's Girl '50
Dial 1119 '50
Southside 1-1000 '50
The Lemon Drop Kid '51
Red Planet Mars '52
The World in His Arms '52
Band of Angels '57
House of the Black Death '65
Blackenstein '73
The Linguini Incident '92

Atlas King
Incredibly Strange Creatures Who Stopped Living and Became Mixed-Up Zombies '63
The Thrill Killers '65

B.B. King (1925-2015)
Amazon Women on the Moon '87
Blues Brothers 2000 '98
Soul Power '08

Benjamin King (1969-)
A Little Inside '01
Spider's Web '01
A Short History of Decay '13

Brent King
A Little Thing Called Murder '06
A Warm Wind '11

Brett King (1920-99)
Battleground '49
Flying Leathernecks '51

Cammie King (1934-)
Gone with the Wind '39
Bambi '42 (V)

Charles King (1889-1944)
Behind That Curtain '29
Broadway Melody '29
Chasing Rainbows '30
The Gay Buckaroo '32

Charles 'Blackie' King (1895-1957)
Thundering Gunslingers '44
Colorado Serenade '46
Ghost of Hidden Valley '46

Charmion King (1925-2007)
Anne of Green Gables '85
Broken Lullaby '94
Jackie, Ethel, Joan: The Kennedy Women '01

Chris Thomas King (1962-)
O Brother Where Art Thou? '00
Ray '04
Kill Switch '08

Dave King (1929-2002)
The Long Good Friday '80
Revolution '85

Emmett King (1865-1953)
Barbara Frietchie '24
Pampered Youth '25

Erik King (1969-)
Casualties of War '89
Atomic Train '99
True Crime '99

Georgia King (1986-)
The Duchess '08
Little Dorrit '08
Wild Child '08
Tanner Hall '09
Tormented '09
Austenland '13
Kill Your Friends '16

Jaime King (1979-)
Blow '01
Happy Campers '01
Pearl Harbor '01
Lone Star State of Mind '02
Slackers '02
Bulletproof Monk '03
White Chicks '04
Cheaper by the Dozen 2 '05
Pretty Persuasion '05
The River King '05
Sin City '05
Two for the Money '05
Lies & Alibis '06
The Tripper '06
The Spirit '08
My Bloody Valentine 3D '09
Mother's Day '10
Waiting for Forever '11
Silent Night '12
Barely Lethal '15
Escape Plan 2: Hades '18

Jamie Thomas King (1981-)
Lost City Raiders '08
Grimm's Snow White '12

Joe King (1883-1951)
Woman in the Shadows '34
San Quentin '37
Alexander's Ragtime Band '38
Dark Town '04

Joey King (1999-)
Dr. Seuss' Horton Hears a Who! '08 (V)
Ramona and Beezus '10
Crazy, Stupid, Love. '11
The Conjuring '13
Family Weekend '13
Oz the Great and Powerful '13 (V)
White House Down '13
Outlaw Prophet: Warren Jeffs '14
Stonewall '15
Going in Style '17
Wish Upon '17
Slender Man '18
Summer '03 '18
Zeroville '19

John 'Dusty' King (1909-87)
Ace Drummond '36
Charlie Chan in Honolulu '38
The Gentleman from Arizona '39
The Hardys Ride High '39
Renegade Girl '46

Kenneth King
Polyester '81
Jade '95

Larry King (1933-)
Eddie and the Cruisers 2: Eddie Lives! '89 (C)
Dave '93 (C)
An Alan Smithee Film: Burn, Hollywood, Burn '97 (C)
America's Sweethearts '01 (C)
Shrek 2 '04 (V)
Bee Movie '07 (V)
Shrek the Third '07 (V)
Shrek Forever After '10 (V)

Mabel King (1932-99)
Ganja and Hess '73
The Wiz '78
The Jerk '79
Scrooged '88
Dead Men Don't Die '91

Matt King
Bronson '09
Malice in Wonderland '09

Morgana King (1930-)
The Godfather '72
The Godfather, Part 2 '74
A Brooklyn State of Mind '97

Perry King (1948-)
The Possession of Joel Delaney '72
Slaughterhouse Five '72
The Lords of Flatbush '74
Wild Party '74
Mandingo '75
Lipstick '76
Andy Warhol's Bad '77
The Choirboys '77
Different Story '78
Search and Destroy '81
Class of 1984 '82
Killing Hour '84
Shakedown on the Sunset Strip '88
The Prize Pulitzer '89
Danielle Steel's Kaleidoscope '90
The Man Who Lived at the Ritz '91
Switch '91
The Perfect Wife '00
The Day After Tomorrow '04
Framed for Murder '07

Regina King (1971-)
Poetic Justice '93
Higher Learning '94
Friday '95
Jerry Maguire '96
A Thin Line Between Love and Hate '96
Enemy of the State '98
How Stella Got Her Groove Back '98
Mighty Joe Young '98
Love and Action in Chicago '99
Where the Truth Lies '99
If These Walls Could Talk 2 '00
Down to Earth '01
Daddy Day Care '03
Legally Blonde 2: Red White & Blonde '03
A Cinderella Story '04
Ray '04
Miss Congeniality 2: Armed and Fabulous '05
The Ant Bully '06 (V)
Grindin' '07
Year of the Dog '07
Living Proof '08
Our Family Wedding '10
The Gabby Douglas Story '14
If Beale Street Could Talk '18

Rowena King (1970-)
Wide Sargasso Sea '92
Framed '93
To Play the King '93
Romance and Rejection '96
A Perfect Day '06
The Bucket List '07

Stephen King (1947-)
Creepshow '82
Maximum Overdrive '86
Creepshow 2 '87
Pet Sematary '89
Stephen King's Golden Years '91
Sleepwalkers '92
Stephen King's The Stand '94
Stephen King's The Langoliers '95
Stephen King's Thinner '96 (C)

Tony King (1947-)
Gordon's War '73
Hell Up in Harlem '73

Report to the Commissioner '75
Sparkle '76
Cannibal Apocalypse '80
The Last Hunter '80

Walter Woolf King (1899-1984)
Golden Dawn '30
A Night at the Opera '35
Call It a Day '37
Swiss Miss '38
Go West '40
Smart Alecks '42
Yank in Libya '42
The Helen Morgan Story '57

Wright King (1923-)
Dangerous Charter '62
King Rat '65
Invasion of the Bee Girls '73
Missiles of October '74

Yolanda King (1955-2007)
America's Dream '95
Ghosts of Mississippi '96
Selma, Lord, Selma '99

Zalman King (1942-2012)
Deadly Fieldtrip '74
Smile Jenny, You're Dead '74
Blue Sunshine '78
Galaxy of Terror '81

Walter Kingsford (1881-1958)
The White Cockatoo '35
The Invisible Ray '36
Juarez '39
The Man in the Iron Mask '39
Miracles for Sale '39
The Witness Vanishes '39
My Favorite Blonde '42

Ben Kingsley (1943-)
Hard Labour '73
Gandhi '82
Camille '84
Harem '85
Silas Marner '85
Maurice '87
Without a Clue '88
Slipstream '89
Bugsy '91
Sneakers '92
Dave '93
Schindler's List '93
Searching for Bobby Fischer '93
Death and the Maiden '94
Joseph '95
Species '95
Moses '96
Twelfth Night '96
The Assignment '97
Photographing Fairies '97
Weapons of Mass Distraction '97
The Confession '98
Parting Shots '98
Alice in Wonderland '99
Rules of Engagement '00
Sexy Beast '00
What Planet Are You From? '00
A. I.: Artificial Intelligence '01 (N)
Anne Frank: The Whole Story '01
The Triumph of Love '01
Tuck Everlasting '02
House of Sand and Fog '03
Suspect Zero '04
Thunderbirds '04
Mrs. Harris '05
Oliver Twist '05
A Sound of Thunder '05
BloodRayne '06
Lucky Number Slevin '06
The Last Legion '07
You Kill Me '07
Elegy '08
Fifty Dead Men Walking '08
The Love Guru '08
Transsiberian '08
The Wackness '08
War, Inc. '08
Shutter Island '09
Prince of Persia: The Sands of Time '10

Hugo '11
A Common Man '12
The Dictator '12
Ender's Game '13
Iron Man 3 '13
Stonehearst Asylum '13
Walking with the Enemy '13
A Birder's Guide to Everything '14
The Boxtrolls '14 (V)
Exodus: Gods and Kings '14
Night at the Museum: Secret of the Tomb '14
War Story '14
Dragonheart 3: The Sorcerer's Curse '15 (V)
Learning to Drive '15
Self/Less '15
The Walk '15
The Jungle Book '16
Collide '17
Operation Finale '18
An Ordinary Man '18
Night Hunter '19

Alex Kingston (1963-)
Carrington '95
The Infiltrator '95
Moll Flanders '96
Croupier '97
Essex Boys '99
Warrior Queen '03
Sweet Land '05
Alpha Dog '06
Crashing '07
Lost in Austen '08
Ben Hur '10
Like Crazy '11

Mark Kingston (1934-2011)
Hitler: The Last Ten Days '73
My Brother Jonathan '85

Natalie Kingston (1905-91)
Tarzan the Tiger '29
His Private Secretary '33

Amelia Kinkade (1963-)
Night of the Demons 2 '94
Night of the Demons 3 '97

Laurence Kinlan (1983-)
An Everlasting Piece '00
Ned Kelly '03
Breakfast on Pluto '05

Kathleen Kinmont (1965-)
Hardbodies '84
Fraternity Vacation '85
Halloween 4: The Return of Michael Myers '88
Phoenix the Warrior '88
Rush Week '88
Bride of Re-Animator '89
The Art of Dying '90
Final Impact '91
Night of the Warrior '91
C.I.A.: Code Name Alexa '92
Sweet Justice '92
C.I.A. 2: Target Alexa '94
Stormswept '95
That Thing You Do! '96
Gangland '00

Joel Kinnaman (1979-)
Easy Money '10
The Darkest Hour '11
The Girl With the Dragon Tattoo '11
Easy Money: Hard to Kill '12
Lola Versus '12
RoboCop '14
Child 44 '15
Run All Night '15
Edge of Winter '16
Suicide Squad '16

Greg Kinnear (1963-)
Sabrina '95
Dear God '96
A Smile Like Yours '96
As Good As It Gets '97
You've Got Mail '98
Mystery Men '99
The Gift '00
Loser '00
Nurse Betty '00
What Planet Are You From? '00
Dinner with Friends '01
Someone Like You '01
Auto Focus '02
We Were Soldiers '02
Stuck On You '03
Godsend '04
The Bad News Bears '05
Robots '05 (V)
Fast Food Nation '06
Invincible '06
Little Miss Sunshine '06
The Matador '06
Feast of Love '07
Baby Mama '08
Flash of Genius '08
Ghost Town '08
Green Zone '10
The Last Song '10
I Don't Know How She Does It '11
The Kennedys '11
Salvation Boulevard '11
Stuck in Love '12
Thin Ice '12
The English Teacher '13
Movie 43 '13
Heaven Is for Real '14
Murder of a Cat '14
Little Men '16
Brigsby Bear '17
Same Kind of Different as Me '17
Brian Banks '18
Strange But True '19

Rory Kinnear (1978-)
Secret Smile '05
Five Days '07
Mansfield Park '07
Lennon Naked '10
Women in Love '11
The Mystery of Edwin Drood '12
Broken '13
Cuban Fury '14
The Imitation Game '14
Trespass Against Us '16
Peterloo '18

Roy Kinnear (1934-88)
Help! '65
The Hill '65
How I Won the War '67
Taste the Blood of Dracula '70
Melody '71
Willy Wonka & the Chocolate Factory '71
Pied Piper '72
Juggernaut '74
The Four Musketeers '75
Herbie Goes to Monte Carlo '77
The Hound of the Baskervilles '77
The Adventures of Sherlock Holmes' Smarter Brother '78
Hawk the Slayer '81
A Man for All Seasons '88

Murray Kinnell
Old English '30
Think Fast, Mr. Moto '37

Kathy Kinney (1954-)
Parting Glances '86
Three Fugitives '89
This Boy's Life '93

Taylor Kinney (1981-)
Five '11
The Other Woman '14
The Forest '16

Terry Kinney (1954-)
Talent for the Game '91
The Last of the Mohicans '92
Body Snatchers '93
The Firm '93
JFK: Reckless Youth '93
Devil in a Blue Dress '95
The Good Old Boys '95
Fly Away Home '96
Sleepers '96
George Wallace '97
Don't Look Down '98
Oxygen '99
That Championship Season '99
The Young Girl and the Monsoon '99
House of Mirth '00
Luminous Motion '00
Save the Last Dance '01
The Laramie Project '02
The Game of Their Lives '05
Runaway '05
Turn the River '07
Promised Land '12
November Criminals '17
Mile 22 '18

Houka Kinoshita (1964-)
Ichi the Killer '01
Onmyoji '01
Shinobi '05

Leonid Kinskey (1903-98)
Duck Soup '33
Les Miserables '35
The Great Waltz '38
Outside of Paradise '38
Day-Time Wife '39
Down Argentine Way '40
Broadway Limited '41
That Night in Rio '41
Casablanca '42
I Married an Angel '42
Lady for a Night '42
Somewhere I'll Find You '42
Fighting Seabees '44
That's My Baby! '44
Can't Help Singing '45

Klaus Kinski (1926-91)
The Avenger '60
Dead Eyes of London '61
Door with the Seven Locks '62
Inn on the River '62
The Indian Scarf '63
Doctor Zhivago '65
Fighting Fists of Shanghai Joe '65
For a Few Dollars More '65
The Squeaker '65
Bang! Bang! You're Dead! '66
Target for Killing '66
Circus of Fear '67
Five for Hell '67
Five Golden Dragons '67
Grand Slam '67
Man, Pride and Vengeance '67
A Bullet for the General '68
The Cats '68
Deadly Sanctuary '68
And God Said to Cain '69
Liberators '69
Twice a Judas '69
Creature with the Blue Hand '70
Double Face '70
Night of the Assassin '70
Shoot the Living, Pray for the Dead '70
Venus in Furs '70
Web of the Spider '70
Count Dracula '71
His Name Was King '71
Slaughter Hotel '71
Aguirre, the Wrath of God '72
Primal Impulse '74
Lifespan '75
Jack the Ripper '76
Madame Claude '77
Operation Thunderbolt '77
Woyzeck '78
The French Woman '79
Nosferatu the Vampyre '79
Love and Money '80
Android '82
Burden of Dreams '82
Fitzcarraldo '82
Venom '82
Code Name: Wild Geese '84
Codename: Wildgeese '84
The Little Drummer Girl '84
Creature '85
Star Knight '85
Crawlspace '86
Timestalkers '87
Cobra Verde '88

Nastassja Kinski (1961-)
To the Devil, a Daughter '76
The Wrong Move '78
Tess '79
Cat People '82
One from the Heart '82
Boarding School '83
Moon in the Gutter '83
Paris, Texas '83
The Hotel New Hampshire '84
Maria's Lovers '84
Unfaithfully Yours '84
Harem '85
Revolution '85
Spring Symphony '86
Torrents of Spring '90
The Blonde '92
Faraway, So Close! '93
Terminal Velocity '94
Father's Day '96
Little Boy Blue '97
One Night Stand '97
Dying to Get Rich '98
The Lost Son '98
Playing by Heart '98
Savior '98
Your Friends & Neighbors '98
The Claim '00
Red Letters '00
An American Rhapsody '01
The Day the World Ended '01
Say Nothing '01
Town and Country '01
Rip It Off '02
Dangerous Liaisons '03
La Femme Musketeer '03

Nikolai Kinski (1976-)
Tortilla Soup '01
Aeon Flux '05
Klimt '06

Bruce Kirby (1928-)
Catch-22 '70
The Young Graduates '71
Armed and Dangerous '86
Throw Momma from the Train '87
Mr. Wonderful '93
Interlocked '98
Blood Money '99
2:22 '08

Bruno Kirby (1949-2006)
Cinderella Liberty '73
Harrad Experiment '73
The Godfather, Part 2 '74
Between the Lines '77
Borderline '80
Where the Buffalo Roam '80
Modern Romance '81
Birdy '84
This Is Spinal Tap '84
Flesh and Blood '85
Good Morning, Vietnam '87
Tin Men '87
Nitti: The Enforcer '88
Bert Rigby, You're a Fool '89
We're No Angels '89
When Harry Met Sally. . . '89
The Freshman '90
City Slickers '91
Golden Gate '93
The Basketball Diaries '95
Donnie Brasco '96
Sleepers '96
A Slipping Down Life '99
Spy Games '99
Stuart Little '99 (V)
American Tragedy '00
Played '06

Jay Kirby (1920-64)
Colt Comrades '43
Hoppy Serves a Writ '43
Leather Burners '43

Luke Kirby (1978-)
Lost and Delirious '01
Halloween: Resurrection '02
Mambo Italiano '03
Shattered Glass '03
Window Theory '04
All Hat '07
The Stone Angel '07
Labor Pains '09
Take This Waltz '11
The Good Samaritan '12
Touched With Fire '16

Michael Kirby (1925-97)
Keep Your Powder Dry '45
The Girl in Blue '74
Another Woman '88
Swoon '91
Shadows and Fog '92

Vanessa Kirby (1989-)
Great Expectations '11
Labyrinth '12
Wasteland '13
Queen and Country '14
The Dresser '15
Me Before You '16
Fast & Furious Presents: Hobbs & Shaw '19

Jerome Kircher
A Very Long Engagement '04
Rio Sex Comedy '10

James Kirk (1986-)
National Lampoon's Golf Punks '99
Mindstorm '01
Due East '02
A Season on the Brink '02
Talking to Heaven '02
Final Destination 2 '03
X2: X-Men United '03
Category 7: The End of the World '05
Confessions of a Sociopathic Social Climber '05
Two for the Money '05
Dr. Dolittle 3 '06
She's the Man '06
The Party Never Stops '07
Frankie and Alice '10
Behemoth '11

Joe (Joseph) Kirk (1903-75)
Smart Alecks '42
The Naughty Nineties '45
The Noose Hangs High '48
Impact '49
Abbott and Costello Go to Mars '53

Justin Kirk (1969-)
Love! Valour! Compassion! '96
Angels in America '03
Ask the Dust '06
Flannel Pajamas '06
Puccini for Beginners '06
Against the Current '09
Four Boxes '09
Elektra Luxx '10
Life Happens '11
Goats '12
Nobody Walks '12
Vamps '12
Last Love '13

Pamela Kirk (1941-)
See Pam(ela) Austin

Phyllis Kirk (1926-2006)
A Life of Her Own '50
Two Weeks with Love '50
Three Guys Named Mike '51
The Iron Mistress '52
House of Wax '53
Crime Wave '54
The Sad Sack '57

Tommy Kirk (1941-)
Old Yeller '57
The Shaggy Dog '59
The Swiss Family Robinson '60
The Absent-Minded Professor '61
Babes in Toyland '61
Bon Voyage! '62
Moon Pilot '62
The Misadventures of Merlin Jones '63
Savage Sam '63
Son of Flubber '63
Pajama Party '64
Monkey's Uncle '65
Village of the Giants '65
Ghost in the Invisible Bikini '66
Mars Needs Women '66
The Unkissed Bride '66
It's Alive! '68
Blood of Ghastly Horror '72
Attack of the 60-Foot Centerfold '95

Jemima Kirke (1985-)
Tiny Furniture '10
Untogether '19

Lola Kirke
Mistress America '15
Fallen '17
Gemini '17
Untogether '19

Sally Kirkland (1941-)
Blue '68
Coming Apart '69
Going Home '71
Cinderella Liberty '73
The Sting '73
The Way We Were '73
The Young Nurses '73
Big Bad Mama '74
Candy Stripe Nurses '74
Bite the Bullet '75
Crazy Mama '75
The Noah '75 (V)
Breakheart Pass '76
A Star Is Born '76
Hometown U.S.A. '79
Private Benjamin '80
Love Letters '83
Anna '87
Best of the Best '89
Cold Feet '89
Bullseye! '90
Heat Wave '90
Revenge '90
Superstar: The Life and Times of Andy Warhol '90
Two Evil Eyes '90
JFK '91
Hit the Dutchman '92
The Player '92
Prime Time Murder '92
Cheatin' Hearts '93
Eye of the Stranger '93
Gunmen '93
The Woman Who Loved Elvis '93
Amnesia '96
Excess Baggage '96
Brave New World '98
Dead Silence '98
Get a Clue! '98
Paranoia '98
EDtv '99
Starry Night '99
Another Woman's Husband '00
Wish You Were Dead '00
Out of the Black '01
Adam & Steve '05
Neo Ned '05
What's Up, Scarlet? '05
Coffee Date '06
Big Stan '07
Flexing with Monty '10
Cuck '19

Bryan Kirkwood (1975-)
The Devil's Prey '01
Hellbent '04
The Absent '11

Denny Kirkwood (1975-)
Groove '00
The Absent '11

Gene Kirkwood (1945-)
Hot Rods to Hell '67
Riot on Sunset Strip '67
Night and the City '92
The Crossing Guard '94

Langley Kirkwood (1973-)
In My Country '04
Invictus '09
Dredd '12

Stan Kirsch (1968-2020)
Highlander: The Gathering '92
Shallow Ground '04

Mia Kirshner (1975-)
Love and Human Remains '93
Exotica '94
The Grass Harp '95
Murder in the First '95
Anna Karenina '96
The Crow 2: City of Angels '96
Mad City '97
Out of the Cold '99

Speed of Life *'99*
Cowboys and Angels *'00*
Innocents *'00*
Not Another Teen Movie *'01*
New Best Friend *'02*
Now & Forever *'02*
The Iris Effect *'04*
The Black Dahlia *'06*
They Come Back *'07*
Miss Conception *'08*
30 Days of Night: Dark Days *'10*
The Barrens *'12*

Ken Kirzinger (1959-)
Freddy *vs.* Jason *'03*
Joy Ride 3: Road Kill *'14*
The Assignment *'17*

Terry Kiser (1939-)
Making Love *'82*
The Offspring *'87*
Friday the 13th, Part 7: The New Blood *'88*
Weekend at Bernie's *'89*
Mannequin 2: On the Move *'91*
Into the Sun *'92*
Weekend at Bernie's 2 *'93*
Forest Warrior *'95*
Mask Maker *'10*
Alien Storm *'12*
A Christmas Tree Miracle *'13*

Keiko Kishi (1932-)
Kwaidan *'64*
The Makioka Sisters *'83*

Ittoku Kishibe (1947-)
The Makioka Sisters *'83*
Onmyoji *'01*
Zatoichi *'03*
Hula Girls *'06*

Kyoko Kishida (1930-2006)
The Human Condition: A Soldier's Prayer *'61*
Shinobi no Mono *'62*
Bushido: The Cruel Code of the Samurai *'63*
Woman in the Dunes *'64*
Face of Another *'66*

Shin Kishida (1939-82)
Lady Snowblood: Love Song of Vengeance *'74*
Shogun Assassin *'80*

Goro Kishitani (1964-)
Graveyard of Honor *'02*
One Missed Call *'03*
Crows Zero *'07*

Charles Kissinger (1925-91)
Asylum of Satan *'72*
Three on a Meathook *'72*
Sheba, Baby *'75*
Grizzly *'76*

Jeremy James Kissner (1985-)
A Dog of Flanders *'99*
Brotherhood of Blood *'08*

Tawny Kitaen (1961-)
Bachelor Party *'84*
The Perils of Gwendoline *'84*
Crystal Heart *'87*
Glory Years *'87*
Happy Hour *'87*
Witchboard *'87*
Hercules the Legendary Journeys, Vol. 3: The Circle of Fire *'94*
Hercules the Legendary Journeys, Vol. 4: In the Underworld *'94*

Tsutomu Kitagawa
Godzilla *vs.* Megaguirus *'00*
Godzilla Against Mechagodzilla *'02*

Kazuki Kitamura (1969-)
The Way To Fight *'96*
Azumi *'03*
Blood and Bones *'04*
Azumi 2 *'05*
Killers *'14*

Kazuo Kitamura (1927-2007)
Tora! Tora! Tora! *'70*
Black Rain *'88*
Shinobi *'05*

Takeshi 'Beat' Kitano (1947-)
Merry Christmas, Mr. Lawrence *'83*
Violent Cop *'89*
Boiling Point *'90*
Johnny Mnemonic *'95*
Sonatine *'96*
Fireworks *'97*
Kikujiro *'99*
Taboo *'99*
Battle Royale *'00*
Brother *'00*
Zatoichi *'03*
Blood and Bones *'04*
Outrage *'10*
Ghost in the Shell *'17*

Michael Kitchen (1948-)
The Brontes of Haworth *'73*
Out of Africa *'85*
The Russia House *'90*
Enchanted April *'92*
The Guilty *'92*
To Play the King *'93*
Doomsday Gun *'94*
The Buccaneers *'95*
Goldeneye *'95*
Kidnapped *'95*
Wilderness *'96*
Mrs. Dalloway *'97*
Reckless *'97*
Reckless: The Sequel *'98*
The World Is Not Enough *'99*
Oliver Twist *'00*
Proof of Life *'00*
The Railway Children *'00*
Lorna Doone *'01*

Taylor Kitsch (1981-)
The Covenant *'06*
Snakes on a Plane *'06*
Gospel Hill *'08*
X-Men Origins: Wolverine *'09*
The Bang Bang Club *'10*
Battleship *'12*
John Carter *'12*
Savages *'12*
The Grand Seduction *'13*
Lone Survivor *'13*
The Normal Heart *'14*
American Assassin *'17*
21 Bridges *'19*

Eartha Kitt (1928-2008)
New Faces of 1952 *'54*
The Mark of the Hawk *'57*
Synanon *'65*
The Pink Chiquitas *'86*
Dragonard *'88*
Erik the Viking *'89*
Master of Dragonard Hill *'89*
Living Doll *'90*
Ernest Scared Stupid *'91*
Boomerang *'92*
Harriet the Spy *'96*
The Emperor's New Groove *'00 (V)*
Anne Rice's The Feast of All Saints *'01*
Anything But Love *'02*
Holes *'03*
Preaching to the Choir *'05*
And Then Came Love *'07*

Agnes Kittelsen (1980-)
Max Manus: Man of War *'08*
Happy, Happy *'10*
Kon-Tiki *'12*

Tory Kittles (1975-)
Big Shot: Confessions of a Campus Bookie *'02*
Frankenfish *'04*
Get Rich or Die Tryin' *'05*
Next *'07*
The Kill Hole *'12*
Steel Magnolias *'12*
American Heist *'15*
Man Down *'16*
Dragged Across Concrete *'18*

Barry Kivel
Bound *'96*
One Fine Day *'96*

Hayley Kiyoko
Lemonade Mouth *'11*
Jem and the Holograms *'15*

Alf Kjellin (1920-88)
Torment *'44*
Summer Interlude *'50*
The Iron Mistress *'52*
The Juggler *'53*

Bjorn Kjellman (1963-)
The Best Intentions *'92*
All Things Fair *'95*
Four More Years *'10*

Diego Klatenhoff
Lost Behind Bars *'06*
The Dry Land *'10*

Charles Klausmeyer
The Unnamable *'88*
The Unnamable 2: The Statement of Randolph Carter *'92*

Burghart Klaussner (1949-)
The Edukators *'04*
The White Ribbon *'09*
The Silence *'10*
13 Minutes *'17*

Uri Klauzner
Kadosh *'99*
Kippur *'00*
Free Zone *'05*

Martin Klebba (1969-)
El Matador *'03*
Pirates of the Caribbean: Dead Man's Chest *'06*
Pirates of the Caribbean: At World's End *'07*
Feast 2: Sloppy Seconds *'08*
Project X *'11*

Kristina Klebe
Proxy *'13*
Don't Kill It *'17*

Chris Klein (1979-)
American Pie *'99*
Election *'99*
Here on Earth *'00*
American Pie 2 *'01*
Say It Isn't So *'01*
Rollerball *'02*
We Were Soldiers *'02*
United States of Leland *'03*
Just Friends *'05*
The Long Weekend *'05*
American Dreamz *'06*
Full Count *'06*
Day Zero *'07*
The Good Life *'07*
Hank and Mike *'08*
Play Dead *'09*
The Six Wives of Henry Lefay *'09*
Street Fighter: The Legend of Chun-Li *'09*
Caught in the Crossfire *'10*
American Reunion *'12*
Authors Anonymous *'14*

Jonathan Klein
Green Plaid Shirt *'96*
Road Hard *'15*

Kacey Mottet Klein (1998-)
Home *'09*
Gainsbourg: A Heroic Life *'10*
Sister *'12*

Robert Klein (1942-)
The Landlord *'70*
The Owl and the Pussycat *'70*
The Pursuit of Happiness *'70*
Rivals *'72*
Hooper *'78*
The Bell Jar *'79*
Nobody's Perfekt *'79*
The Last Unicorn *'82 (V)*
Dangerous Curves *'88*
Tales from the Darkside: The Movie *'90*
Mixed Nuts *'94*
Radioland Murders *'94 (C)*
One Fine Day *'96*
Next Stop, Wonderland *'98*
Primary Colors *'98*
The Safety of Objects *'01*
People I Know *'02*
Two Weeks Notice *'02*
How to Lose a Guy in 10 Days *'03*
Ira & Abby *'06*
Reign Over Me *'07*
Demoted *'11*
National Lampoon's Dirty Movie *'11*

Silke Klein (1974-)
Tierra *'95*
Felicidades *'00*

Rudolf Klein-Rogge (1888-1955)
The Cabinet of Dr. Caligari *'19*
Destiny *'21*
Dr. Mabuse, The Gambler *'22*
Warning Shadows *'23*
Kriemhilde's Revenge *'24*
Metropolis *'26*
Spies *'28*
Crimes of Dr. Mabuse *'32*

Dennis Kleinsmith
The Cutter *'05*
Cthulhu *'08*

Luke Kleintank
Dark House *'14*
Max *'15*

Werner Klemperer (1920-2000)
Death of a Scoundrel *'56*
Kiss Them for Me *'57*
The Goddess *'58*
Judgment at Nuremberg *'61*
Operation Eichmann *'61*

Kevin Kline (1947-)
Sophie's Choice *'82*
The Big Chill *'83*
The Pirates of Penzance *'83*
Silverado *'85*
Violets Are Blue *'86*
Cry Freedom *'87*
A Fish Called Wanda *'88*
The January Man *'89*
I Love You to Death *'90*
Grand Canyon *'91*
Soapdish *'91*
Chaplin *'92*
Consenting Adults *'92*
Dave *'93*
George Balanchine's The Nutcracker *'93 (N)*
Princess Caraboo *'94*
French Kiss *'95*
Fierce Creatures *'96*
The Hunchback of Notre Dame *'96 (V)*
Looking for Richard *'96*
The Ice Storm *'97*
In and Out *'97*
Wild Wild West *'99*
William Shakespeare's A Midsummer Night's Dream *'99*
The Road to El Dorado *'00 (V)*
The Anniversary Party *'01*
Life as a House *'01*
The Emperor's Club *'02*
Orange County *'02*
De-Lovely *'04*
Jiminy Glick in LaLa Wood *'05 (C)*
As You Like It *'06*
The Pink Panther *'06*
A Prairie Home Companion *'06*
Trade *'07*
Definitely, Maybe *'08*
The Tale of Despereaux *'08 (V)*
Queen to Play *'09*
The Conspirator *'10*
The Extra Man *'10*
No Strings Attached *'11*
Darling Companion *'12*
The Last of Robin Hood *'13*
Last Vegas *'13*
My Old Lady *'14*
Ricki and the Flash *'15*
Beauty and the Beast *'17*
Dean *'17*

Richard Kline (1944-)
Liberty Heights *'99*
Treehouse Hostage *'99*
I Now Pronounce You Chuck and Larry *'07*

Heidi Kling (1962-)
The Mighty Ducks *'92*
D3: The Mighty Ducks *'96*

Brian Klugman (1975-)
Dreamland *'06*
Vacancy 2: The First Cut *'08*

Jack Klugman (1922-2012)
Twelve Angry Men *'57*
Cry Terror! *'58*
Days of Wine and Roses *'62*
I Could Go on Singing *'63*
Hail Mafia *'65*
The Detective *'68*
The Split *'68*
Goodbye, Columbus *'69*
One of My Wives Is Missing *'76*
Two Minute Warning *'76*
Around the World in 80 Days *'89*
Dear God *'96*
The Twilight of the Golds *'97*
When Do We Eat? *'05*

Heidi Klum (1973-)
Blow Dry *'00*
Ella Enchanted *'04*
Hoodwinked Too! Hood *vs.* Evil *'11 (V)*
Arctic Dogs *'19 (V)*

Vincent Klyn (1960-)
Cyborg *'89*
Dollman *'90*
Point Break *'91*
Nemesis *'93*
Urban Menace *'99*
Gangland *'00*
Mexican Blow *'02*

Skelton Knaggs (1911-55)
Bedlam *'45*
Isle of the Dead *'45*
Dick Tracy Meets Gruesome *'47*

Alexis Knapp (1989-)
Project X *'11*
Pitch Perfect *'12*
So Undercover *'13*
The Anomaly *'15*

Beau Knapp
The Signal *'14*
What Lola Wants *'15*
Dirty Lies *'16*
Crypto *'19*
Semper Fi *'19*

Evalyn Knapp (1908-81)
Mothers Cry *'30*
Smart Money *'31*
The Strange Love of Molly Louvain *'32*
A Successful Calamity *'32*
Corruption *'33*
His Private Secretary *'33*
The Perils of Pauline *'34*
Ladies Crave Excitement *'35*
Mistaken Identity *'36*

Robert Knapp (1924-2001)
Mesa of Lost Women *'52*
Outlaw's Son *'57*

Sebastian Knapp
High Plains Invaders *'09*
Sand Serpents *'09*
Son of God *'14*

Herbert Knaup (1956-)
Run Lola Run *'98*
Nuremberg *'00*
Anatomy 2 *'03*
In Darkness *'11*

Hildegarde Knef (1925-2002)
The Murderers Are Among Us *'46*
Decision Before Dawn *'51*
Diplomatic Courier *'52*
The Snows of Kilimanjaro *'52*
Unnatural *'52*
Svengali *'55*
Fedora *'78*
The Future of Emily *'85*
Witchery *'88*

David Knell (1961-)
Bitter Harvest *'81*
Spring Break *'83*
Chopper Chicks in Zombietown *'91*

Robert Knepper (1959-)
That's Life! *'86*
Renegades *'89*
Young Guns 2 *'90*
Gas Food Lodging *'92*
Where the Day Takes You *'92*
Getting Out *'94*
Absence of the Good *'99*
Love & Sex *'00*
Jackie, Ethel, Joan: The Kennedy Women *'01*
Species 3 *'04*
Good Night, and Good Luck *'05*
Hostage *'05*
Hitman *'07*
The Day the Earth Stood Still *'08*
Transporter 3 *'08*
Prison Break: The Final Break *'09*
Burning Daylight *'10*
Earth's Final Hours *'12*
R.I.P.D. *'13*
Hard Target 2 *'16*

Bobby Knight (1940-)
Blue Chips *'94 (C)*
Anger Management *'03 (C)*

Christopher Knight
Studs Lonigan *'60*
If a Man Answers *'62*

Christopher Knight (1957-)
Cotter *'72*
The Brady Bunch Movie *'95 (C)*
The Doom Generation *'95*
Madagascar: Escape 2 Africa *'08 (V)*
Letting Go *'12*

David Knight (1928-)
Across the Bridge *'57*
Missiles from Hell *'58*
Nightmare *'63*

David Edwin Knight (1972-)
Demons 2 *'87*
Who Shot Pat? *'92*

Esmond Knight (1906-87)
The Arsenal Stadium Mystery *'39*
Contraband *'40*
The Silver Fleet *'43*
A Canterbury Tale *'44*
Henry V *'44*
Black Narcissus *'47*
Hamlet *'48*
The Red Shoes *'48*
The River *'51*
Missiles from Hell *'58*
Peeping Tom *'60*
Sink the Bismarck *'60*
The Element of Crime *'84*

Fuzzy Knight (1901-76)
To the Last Man *'33*
The Old Homestead *'35*
The Trail of the Lonesome Pine *'36*
The Gold Racket *'37*
The Cowboy and the Lady *'38*
Spawn of the North *'38*
My Little Chickadee *'40*
The Shepherd of the Hills *'41*
The Adventures of Gallant Bess *'48*
Rimfire *'49*
Oklahoma Annie *'51*
Naked Hills *'56*
Hostile Guns *'67 (C)*

Gladys Knight (1944-)
Twenty Bucks *'93*
Hollywood Homicide *'03*

Unbeatable Harold '06
I Can Do Bad All By Myself '09

Jack Knight
Class of 1999 2: The Substitute '93
A Lobster Tale '06

Lily Knight (1956-)
Static '87
An Unremarkable Life '89
The Assassination of Richard Nixon '05

Matthew Knight (1994-)
The Greatest Game Ever Played '05
Intimate Stranger '06
All the Good Ones Are Married '07
Christmas in Wonderland '07
Skinwalkers '07
Finn on the Fly '09
Gooby '09
The Good Witch's Garden '09
The Grudge 3 '09
The Good Witch's Gift '10
The Good Witch's Family '11
The Good Witch's Charm '12

Michael E. Knight (1959-)
Date with an Angel '87
Hexed '93

Sandra Knight (1940-)
Frankenstein's Daughter '58
Thunder Road '58
Tower of London '62
The Terror '63
Track of the Vampire '66

Shirley Knight (1936-2020)
Ice Palace '60
The Couch '62
House of Women '62
Sweet Bird of Youth '62
Flight From Ashiya '64
The Group '66
Petulia '68
The Rain People '69
Secrets '71
Juggernaut '74
21 Hours at Munich '76
Champions: A Love Story '78
Beyond the Poseidon Adventure '79
Endless Love '81
The Sender '82
Color of Night '94
Stuart Saves His Family '94
A Good Day to Die '95
Indictment: The McMartin Trial '95
Diabolique '96
If These Walls Could Talk '96
As Good As It Gets '97
Little Boy Blue '97
75 Degrees '00
Angel Eyes '01
Divine Secrets of the Ya-Ya Sisterhood '02
My Louisiana Sky '02
P.S. Your Cat is Dead! '02
Ghost Cat '03
Grandma's Boy '06
Love and Debate '06
Open Window '06
Paul Blart: Mall Cop '09
The Private Lives of Pippa Lee '09
Listen to Your Heart '10
Our Idiot Brother '11

Sterling Knight (1989-)
17 Again '09
StarStruck '10
Transit '12

Ted (Edward) Knight (1923-86)
Psycho '60
Countdown '68
Caddyshack '80

T.R. Knight (1973-)
The Last Request '06
42 '13

Trenton Knight (1982-)
Charlie's Ghost: The Secret of Coronado '94
The Skateboard Kid 2 '94
Invisible Mom '96

Tuesday Knight (1969-)
A Nightmare on Elm Street 4: Dream Master '88
Cool and the Crazy '94
The Theory of the Leisure Class '01

Wayne Knight (1955-)
Dead Again '91
JFK '91
Basic Instinct '92
Jurassic Park '93
To Die For '95
Space Jam '96
For Richer or Poorer '97
Tarzan '99 (V)
Toy Story 2 '99 (V)
Rat Race '01
Master Spy: The Robert Hanssen Story '02
Black Cloud '04
Forfeit '07
Who's Your Monkey '07
Punisher: War Zone '08
Woke Up Dead '09

Wyatt Knight (1955-2011)
Porky's '82
Porky's 2: The Next Day '83
Porky's Revenge '85

Keira Knightley (1985-)
Oliver Twist '00
The Hole '01
Princess of Thieves '01
Bend It Like Beckham '02
Pure '02
Doctor Zhivago '03
Love Actually '03
Pirates of the Caribbean: The Curse of the Black Pearl '03
King Arthur '04
Domino '05
The Jacket '05
Pride and Prejudice '05
Pirates of the Caribbean: Dead Man's Chest '06
Atonement '07
Pirates of the Caribbean: At World's End '07
Silk '07
The Duchess '08
The Edge of Love '08
Last Night '10
London Boulevard '10
Never Let Me Go '10
A Dangerous Method '11
Neverland '11 (V)
Anna Karenina '12
Seeking a Friend for the End of the World '12
Begin Again '13
Laggies '13
The Imitation Game '14
Jack Ryan: Shadow Recruit '14
Everest '15
Collateral Beauty '16
The Nutcracker and the Four Realms '18
The Aftermath '19
Official Secrets '19

Zachery Knighton (1978-)
The Mudge Boy '03
The Hitcher '07

Ohad Knoller (1976-)
Under the Domim Tree '95
Yossi & Jagger '02
The Bubble '06
Beaufort '07
Yossi '12
A Tale of Love and Darkness '16

Sascha Knopf (1971-)
Blackmale '99
What's the Worst That Could Happen? '01
The Trade '03
He Was a Quiet Man '07

Andrew Knott (1979-)
The Secret Garden '93
Black Beauty '94
The History Boys '06

Don Knotts (1924-2006)
No Time for Sergeants '58
Wake Me When It's Over '60
It's a Mad, Mad, Mad, Mad World '63
Move Over, Darling '63
The Incredible Mr. Limpet '64
The Ghost and Mr. Chicken '66
The Reluctant Astronaut '67
The Shakiest Gun in the West '68
The Love God? '70
How to Frame a Figg '71
The Apple Dumpling Gang '75
No Deposit, No Return '76
Herbie Goes to Monte Carlo '77
Hot Lead & Cold Feet '78
The Apple Dumpling Gang Rides Again '79
Prize Fighter '79
The Private Eyes '80
Cannonball Run 2 '84
Return to Mayberry '85
Big Bully '95
Cats Don't Dance '97 (V)
Pleasantville '98
Chicken Little '05 (V)
Air Bud 6: Air Buddies '06 (V)

Marilyn Knowlden (1927-)
It Happened in New Orleans '36
Barefoot Boy '38

Beyonce Knowles (1981-)
Carmen: A Hip Hopera '01
Austin Powers In Goldmember '02
The Fighting Temptations '03
Dreamgirls '06
The Pink Panther '06
Cadillac Records '08
Obsessed '09
Epic '13 (V)

Elizabeth Knowles
Lady Godiva Rides '68
Wild Riders '71

Patric Knowles (1911-95)
The Charge of the Light Brigade '36
Give Me Your Heart '36
It's Love I'm After '37
The Adventures of Robin Hood '38
Four's a Crowd '38
The Sisters '38
How Green Was My Valley '41
The Wolf Man '41
Frankenstein Meets the Wolfman '42
Lady in a Jam '42
The Mystery of Marie Roget '42
The Strange Case of Dr. Rx '42
Who Done It? '42
Hit the Ice '43
The Bride Wore Boots '46
Monsieur Beaucaire '46
Big Steal '49
Three Came Home '50
Mutiny '52
Tarzan's Savage Fury '52
World for Ransom '54
Band of Angels '57
Auntie Mame '58
The Devil's Brigade '68
Chisum '70

Alexander Knox (1907-95)
The Four Feathers '39
Commandos Strike at Dawn '43
Wilson '44
Over 21 '45
The Judge Steps Out '49
Tokyo Joe '49
I'd Climb the Highest Mountain '51
Man in the Saddle '51
Two of a Kind '51
Paula '52
The Sleeping Tiger '54
Alias John Preston '56
Reach for the Sky '56
Chase a Crooked Shadow '58
The Vikings '58
The Wreck of the Mary Deare '59
Operation Amsterdam '60
The Longest Day '62
In the Cool of the Day '63
These Are the Damned '63
Crack in the World '65
Khartoum '66
Modesty Blaise '66
The Psychopath '66
Accident '67
Shalako '68
Villa Rides '68
Nicholas and Alexandra '71
Puppet on a Chain '72
The Chosen '77
Cry of the Innocent '80

Elyse Knox (1917-2012)
The Mummy's Tomb '42
Don Winslow of the Coast Guard '43
Hit the Ice '43
I Wouldn't Be in Your Shoes '48

Mickey Knox (1921-2013)
Killer McCoy '47
Frankenstein Unbound '90
Cemetery Man '95

Robert Knox
Scream Bloody Murder '72
Amputee with an Axe '73

Terence Knox (1946-)
Tour of Duty '87
Lucky Day '91
Children of the Corn 2: The Final Sacrifice '92
The Spy Within '94

Johnny Knoxville (1971-)
Life Without Dick '01
Big Trouble '02
Deuces Wild '02
Jackass: The Movie '02
Men in Black 2 '02
Grand Theft Parsons '03
A Dirty Shame '04
Walking Tall '04
Daltry Calhoun '05
The Dukes of Hazzard '05
Lords of Dogtown '05
The Ringer '05
Jackass Number Two '06
Jackass 3D '10
Father of Invention '11
Fun Size '12
Nature Calls '12
Small Apartments '12
Jackass Presents: Bad Grandpa '13
The Last Stand '13
Movie 43 '13
Elvis & Nixon '16
Action Point '18

Erik Knudsen (1988-)
Saw 2 '05
Youth in Revolt '10
The Barrens '12

Peggy Knudsen (1923-80)
The Big Sleep '46
Humoresque '46
Never Say Goodbye '46
A Stolen Life '46
Stallion Road '47
Copper Canyon '50
Good Morning, Miss Dove '55

Sidse Babett Knudsen
After the Wedding '06
The Duke of Burgundy '14
A Hologram for the King '16
Inferno '16
In Fabric '18

Ah-sung Ko
The Host '06
Snowpiercer '14

Philip Ko
Opium and Kung-Fu Master '84
Seeding of a Ghost '86

Mpho Koaho
Down in the Delta '98
Snipes '01
Crown Heights '02
Detention '03
Get Rich or Die Tryin' '05
It's a Boy Girl Thing '06
Saw 3 '06

Hirohoshi Kobayashi
Ichi the Killer '01
Death Note 3: L Change the World '08

Megumi Kobayashi (1977-)
Rebirth of Mothra '96
Rebirth of Mothra 2 '97

Nenji Kobayashi (1943-)
The Twilight Samurai '02
The Hidden Blade '04

Satomi Kobayashi
Godzilla vs. Mothra '92
After the Storm '17

Shigeo Kobayashi
Flower & Snake '04
The Flowers of War '11

Yukiko Kobayashi (1946-)
Destroy All Monsters '68
Yog, Monster from Space '71

Jeff Kober (1953-)
Alien Nation '88
Lucky Stiff '88
The First Power '89
Tank Girl '94
Demolition High '95
One Man's Justice '95
The Big Fall '96
Elmore Leonard's Gold Coast '97
The Colony '98
Logan's War: Bound by Honor '98
The Maker '98
Militia '99
American Tragedy '00
Lost Voyage '01
A Man Apart '03
Aces 'n Eights '08
Leave No Trace '18

Marta Kober
Friday the 13th, Part 2 '81
Children of the Night '85

Alexander Koch
Always Shine '16
Maya Dardel '17

Edward I. Koch (1924-)
New York Stories '89
Somewhere in the City '97 (C)

Marianne Koch (1931-)
Coast of Skeletons '63
A Fistful of Dollars '64
Frozen Alive '64
A Place Called Glory '66

Sebastian Koch (1962-)
The Tunnel '01
Gloomy Sunday '02
Napoleon '03
Operation Valkyrie '04
Black Book '06
The Shell Seekers '06
Albatross '11
A Good Day to Die Hard '13
Billionaire Ransom '16
Bel Canto '18
Never Look Away '18

Rebekah Kochan (1984-)
Eating Out 2: Sloppy Seconds '06
Pirates of Treasure Island '06
Freakshow '07
Eating Out 3: All You Can Eat '09
Finding Mr. Wright '11

Momoko Kochi (1932-98)
Godzilla '54
Godzilla, King of the Monsters '56

Oja Kodar (1941-)
Someone to Love '87
The Other Side of the Wind '18

Barbara Kodetova (1970-)
Dune '00
Children of Dune '03

Boris Kodjoe (1973-)
Brown Sugar '02
The Gospel '05
Madea's Family Reunion '06
Starship Troopers 3: Marauder '08
Surrogates '09
The Confidant '10
Resident Evil: Afterlife '10
Resident Evil: Retribution '12
Baggage Claim '13
Nurse 3D '13
Addicted '14

David Koechner (1962-)
A Guy Thing '03
My Boss's Daughter '03
Anchorman: The Legend of Ron Burgundy '04
Daltry Calhoun '05
The Dukes of Hazzard '05
The 40 Year Old Virgin '05
Waiting '05
Yours, Mine & Ours '05
Barnyard '06 (V)
Larry the Cable Guy: Health Inspector '06
Let's Go to Prison '06
Snakes on a Plane '06
Thank You for Smoking '06
Unaccompanied Minors '06
Balls of Fury '07
The Brothers Solomon '07
The Comebacks '07
Get Smart '08
Semi-Pro '08
Extract '09
The Goods: Live Hard, Sell Hard '09
My One and Only '09
The Perfect Game '09
Tenure '09
Brother's Justice '11
Final Destination 5 '11
Paul '11
Piranha 3DD '11
Hotel Transylvania '12 (V)
Anchorman 2: The Legend Continues '13
A Haunted House '13
Cheap Thrills '14
Krampus '15
Scout's Guide to the Zombie Apocalypse '15
Priceless '16

Frederick Koehler (1975-)
Divine Secrets of the Ya-Ya Sisterhood '02
Touched '05
Little Chenier: A Cajun Story '06
Death Race '08
Death Race 2 '10
Death Race 3: Inferno '12

Walter Koenig (1936-)
Goodbye, Raggedy Ann '71
Star Trek: The Motion Picture '79
Star Trek 2: The Wrath of Khan '82
Star Trek 3: The Search for Spock '84
Star Trek 4: The Voyage Home '86
Star Trek 5: The Final Frontier '89
Star Trek 6: The Undiscovered Country '91
Star Trek: Generations '94
Mad Cowgirl '06
Bone Eater '07
InAlienable '08

Mitsuki Koga
Godzilla-Tokyo S.O.S. '03
Shinobi '05

Michiyo Kogure (1918-90)
Shin Heike Monogatari '55
Street of Shame '56

Fumiyo Kohinata (1954-)
Ringu 2 '99
Dark Water '02
Ashura '05
Black House '07

Fred Kohler, Jr. (1912-93)
The Iron Horse '24
The Rider of Death Valley '32
Pigskin Parade '36
The Prisoner of Shark Island '36
Feudin', Fussin', and A-Fightin' '48
Daniel Boone: Trail Blazer '56

Fred Kohler, Sr. (1889-1938)
Anna Christie '23
Tide of Empire '29
Hell's Heroes '30
Fighting Caravans '31
Other Men's Women '31
The Right of Way '31
Frisco Kid '35
Mississippi '35
The Texas Rangers '36
Forbidden Valley '38

Juliane Kohler (1965-)
Aimee & Jaguar '98
Nowhere in Africa '02

Lee Kohlmar (1873-1946)
Love in Bloom '35
Death from a Distance '36

Susan Kohner (1936-)
To Hell and Back '55
Dino '57
The Gene Krupa Story '59
Imitation of Life '59

Hiroshi Koizumi (1926-2015)
Mothra '62
Matango '63
Godzilla vs. Mothra '64
Dagora, the Space Monster '65
Ghidrah the Three Headed Monster '65
Godzilla-Tokyo S.O.S. '03

Clarence (C. William) Kolb (1874-1964)
Give Me a Sailor '38
Merrily We Live '38
Honolulu '39
His Girl Friday '40
Michael Shayne: Private Detective '40
Caught in the Draft '41
Something for the Boys '44
Impact '49

Warren Kole (1977-)
Cougar Club '07
Mother's Day '10

Roman Kolinka (1986-)
Eden '14
Things to Come '16

Henry Kolker (1870-1947)
The Devil and the Deep '32
Jewel Robbery '32
Baby Face '33
The Power and the Glory '33
Rasputin and the Empress '33
The Ghost Walks '34
Charlie Chan in Paris '35
Mad Love '35
Sitting On the Moon '36
The Cowboy and the Lady '38
The Real Glory '39
Union Pacific '39

Tetsu Komai (1894-1970)
The Princess Comes Across '36
The Real Glory '39

Jacek Koman
Romulus, My Father '07
Son of a Gun '14
Judy & Punch '20

Rich Komenich
Henry: Portrait of a Serial Killer 2: Mask of Sanity '96
The Amityville Horror '05

Liliana Komorowska (1956-)
Martial Outlaw '93
The Assignment '97
The Art of War '00
Extreme Ops '02

Maja Komorowska (1937-)
Maids of Wilko '79
Year of the Quiet Sun '84
The Decalogue '88

Karin Konoval (1961-)
We'll Meet Again '02
Alone in the Dark '05
The Tooth Fairy '06
War for the Planet of the Apes '17

Phyllis Konstam (1907-76)
Murder '30
Skin Game '31

Louis Koo (1970-)
Zu Warriors '01
Robin-B-Hood '06
Flash Point '07
Drug War '13
Out of the Inferno '13
The White Storm '13
Call of Heroes '16

Guich Koock (1944-)
American Ninja '85
Square Dance '87
Picasso Trigger '89

Kool Moe Dee (1962-)
Storm Trooper '98
Crossroads '02

Thomas Kopache (1945-)
Stigmata '99
Ten 'Til Noon '06
A Stranger's Heart '07
Love Finds a Home '09

Bernie Kopell (1933-)
Good Neighbor Sam '64
The Loved One '65
Get Smart, Again! '89
Bug Buster '99
The Cutter '05
Get Smart '08

Karen Kopins (1961-)
Creator '85
Once Bitten '85
Jake Speed '86

Michael Kopsa (1956-)
Past Sins '06
Ba'al: The Storm God '08
Impact '09
Stonehenge Apocalypse '10

Aya Koren (1979-)
Yossi & Jagger '02
Bonjour Monsieur Shlomi '03

Tinsel Korey
Hybrid '07
Black Box '12

Harmony Korine (1974-)
Last Days '05
Manglehorn '15

Jon Korkes (1965-)
Catch-22 '70
Little Murders '71
The Day of the Dolphin '73
Jaws of Satan '81
Syngenor '90

Baltasar Kormakur (1966-)
Devil's Island '96
101 Reykjavik '00
No Such Thing '01
Reykjavik-Rotterdam '08

Harvey Korman (1927-2008)
Lord Love a Duck '66
April Fools '69
Blazing Saddles '74
Huckleberry Finn '74
High Anxiety '77
Americathon '79
Herbie Goes Bananas '80
History of the World: Part 1 '81
Curse of the Pink Panther '83
Gone Are the Days '84
Alice in Wonderland '85
The Longshot '86
Munchies '87
The Flintstones '94 (V)
Radioland Murders '94 (C)
Dracula: Dead and Loving It '95
Jingle All the Way '96
The Secret of NIMH 2 '98 (V)
The Flintstones in Viva Rock Vegas '00

Mary Kornman (1915-73)
College Humor '33
The Quitter '34
Queen of the Jungle '35

Alix Koromzay (1969-)
Nightwatch '96
Children of the Corn 666: Isaac's Return '99
The Haunting '99
Mimic 2 '01
Blood Work '02
Tre '06

Charlie Korsmo (1978-)
Men Don't Leave '89
Dick Tracy '90
Heat Wave '90
The Doctor '91
Hook '91
What about Bob? '91
Can't Hardly Wait '98

Robert F. (Bob) Kortman (1887-1967)
The Devil Horse '26
Island of Lost Souls '32
The Lone Defender '32
Robinson Crusoe of Clipper Island '36

Fritz Kortner (1892-1970)
Warning Shadows '23
The Hands of Orlac '25
Pandora's Box '28
Somewhere in the Night '46
Woman in Brown '48

Charles Korvin (1907-98)
The Killer That Stalked New York '47
Berlin Express '48
Tarzan's Savage Fury '52
Ship of Fools '65

Dina Korzun (1971-)
Forty Shades of Blue '05
Cold Souls '09
Farewell '09

Graham Kosakoski (1982-)
Best Friends '05
Grizzly Rage '07
Unthinkable '07

Sylva Koscina (1933-94)
Hercules '58
Hercules Unchained '59
Uncle Was a Vampire '59
Swordsman of Siena '62
Hot Enough for June '64
Juliet of the Spirits '65
Deadlier Than the Male '67
Deadly Sanctuary '68
A Lovely Way to Die '68
The Secret War of Harry Frigg '68
Hornets' Nest '70
The Italian Connection '73
Lisa and the Devil '75

Martin Kosleck (1907-94)
Foreign Correspondent '40
Underground '41
All Through the Night '42
Berlin Correspondent '42
Pursuit to Algiers '45
House of Horrors '46
Something Wild '61
Hitler '62
The Flesh Eaters '64
36 Hours '64

Paul Koslo (1944-)
The Losers '70
Omega Man '71
Vanishing Point '71
Joe Kidd '72
Welcome Home, Soldier Boys '72
Rooster Cogburn '75
Maniac '77
Roots: The Next Generation '79
A Night in the Life of Jimmy Reardon '88
Robot Jox '90
Xtro 2: The Second Encounter '91
Chained Heat 2 '92
Judge & Jury '96

David Kossoff (1919-2005)
A Kid for Two Farthings '55
Svengali '55
1984 '56
Who Done It? '56
The House of the Seven Hawks '59
The Mouse That Roared '59
The Two Faces of Dr. Jekyll '60
The Mouse on the Moon '62

Mitchell Kosterman (1958-)
Cruel and Unusual '01
Safe Harbor '06

Maria Kosti (1951-)
Exorcism '74
Night of the Death Cult '75

Goran Kostic
In the Land of Blood and Honey '11
The Last Days on Mars '13

Kane (Takeshi) Kosugi (1974-)
Revenge of the Ninja '83
Nine Deaths of the Ninja '85
Pray for Death '85
DOA: Dead or Alive '06

Sho Kosugi (1948-)
Enter the Ninja '81
Revenge of the Ninja '83
Nine Deaths of the Ninja '85
Pray for Death '85
Rage of Honor '87
Black Eagle '88
Blind Fury '90
Ninja Assassin '09

Yoshio Kosugi (1903-68)
Seven Samurai '54
The Human Condition: No Greater Love '58

Elias Koteas (1961-)
Gardens of Stone '87
Some Kind of Wonderful '87
Blood Red '88
Full Moon in Blue Water '88
Tucker: The Man and His Dream '88
Malarek '89
Almost an Angel '90
Desperate Hours '90
Look Who's Talking, Too '90
Teenage Mutant Ninja Turtles: The Movie '90
The Adjuster '91
Cyborg 2 '93
Teenage Mutant Ninja Turtles 3 '93
Camilla '94
Exotica '94
Power of Attorney '94
Crash '95
The Prophecy '95
Sugartime '95
Hit Me '96
Apt Pupil '97
Fallen '97
Gattaca '97
Living Out Loud '98
The Thin Red Line '98
Dancing at the Blue Iguana '00
Lost Souls '00
Novocaine '01
Shot in the Heart '01
Ararat '02
Collateral Damage '02
Harrison's Flowers '02
Simone '02
The Greatest Game Ever Played '05
Prisoner '07
Shooter '07
Skinwalkers '07
Zodiac '07
The Curious Case of Benjamin Button '08
Dark Streets '08
Defendor '09
The Fourth Kind '09
The Haunting in Connecticut '09
Shutter Island '09
Two Lovers '09
The Killer Inside Me '10
Let Me In '10
My Own Love Song '10
3 Backyards '10
Dream House '11
A Very Harold & Kumar Christmas '11
The Last Days on Mars '13
Winnie Mandela '13
Devil's Knot '14

Yaphet Kotto (1939-)
Nothing but a Man '64
Five Card Stud '68
The Thomas Crown Affair '68
Man & Boy '71
Across 110th Street '72
Housewife '72
Live and Let Die '73
Truck Turner '74
Friday Foster '75
Report to the Commissioner '75
Drum '76
Monkey Hustle '77
Raid on Entebbe '77
Blue Collar '78
Alien '79
Brubaker '80
Fighting Back '82
The Star Chamber '83
The Park Is Mine '85
Warning Sign '85
Eye of the Tiger '86
The Running Man '87
Midnight Run '88
Ministry of Vengeance '89
Freddy's Dead: The Final Nightmare '91
Hangfire '91
Almost Blue '93
Extreme Justice '93
The Puppet Masters '94
Out of Sync '95
Two If by Sea '95
Homicide: The Movie '00
Stiletto Dance '01
Witless Protection '08

Adam Kotz (1962-)
Touching Evil '97
Shot Through the Heart '98
All the King's Men '99
Suspicion '03
Nightwatching '07

Hubert Kounde (1970-)
Cafe au Lait '94
Hate '95
How I Killed My Father '03
The Constant Gardener '05

Nancy Kovack (1935-)
Diary of a Madman '63
Jason and the Argonauts '63
Frankie and Johnny '65
The Outlaws Is Coming! '65
Tarzan and the Valley of Gold '65
The Silencers '66

Ernie Kovacs (1919-62)
Operation Mad Ball '57
Bell, Book and Candle '58
It Happened to Jane '59
Our Man in Havana '59
North to Alaska '60
Strangers When We Meet '60
Wake Me When It's Over '60
Sail a Crooked Ship '61

Lajos Kovacs (1944-)
Woyzeck '94
Kontroll '03

Martin Kove (1946-)
Last House on the Left '72
Death Race 2000 '75
The Karate Kid '84
Rambo: First Blood, Part 2 '85
The Karate Kid: Part 2 '86
Steele Justice '87
Higher Ground '88
The Karate Kid: Part 3 '89
Future Shock '93
To Be the Best '93
Wyatt Earp '94
Judge & Jury '96
Mercenary '96
Grizzly Mountain '97
Shadow Warriors 2: Hunt for the Death Merchant '97
Shadow Warriors '97
Top of the World '97
Nowhere Land '98
Final Payback '99
Timelock '99
Crocodile 2: Death Swamp '01
Extreme Honor '01
Under Heavy Fire '01
Con Games '02
Devil's Knight '03
Hard Ground '03
Alien Lockdown '04
Crooked '05
7 Mummies '06
Ballistica '10
Bare Knuckles '10
Our Wild Hearts '13
Assassin X '16
Traded '16

Shigeru Koyama (1929-)
Kill! '68
Black Rain '89
Red Shadow '01
Azumi 2 '05

Koyuki (1976-)
Pulse '01
Alive '02
The Last Samurai '03

Harley Jane Kozak (1957-)
Parenthood '89
When Harry Met Sally. . . '89
Arachnophobia '90
Side Out '90
All I Want for Christmas '91
Necessary Roughness '91
The Favor '92
The Amy Fisher Story '93
The Android Affair '95
Magic in the Water '95
Titanic '96
Dark Planet '97
The Lovemaster '97
Emma's Wish '98
I Spit on Your Grave: Vengeance Is Mine '15

Danila Kozlovsky (1985-)
Vampire Academy '14
Hardcore Henry '15

Linda Kozlowski (1958-)
Crocodile Dundee '86
Crocodile Dundee 2 '88
Almost an Angel '90
The Neighbor '93
Village of the Damned '95
Crocodile Dundee in Los Angeles '01

Jeroen Krabbe (1944-)
Soldier of Orange '78
The 4th Man '79
Jumpin' Jack Flash '86 (C)
No Mercy '86
Code Name: Dancer '87
The Living Daylights '87
Crossing Delancey '88
A World Apart '88
Scandal '89
A Family of Spies '90
The Punisher '90
The Prince of Tides '91
Robin Hood '91
For a Lost Soldier '93
The Fugitive '93
Farinelli '94

Immortal Beloved '94
The Disappearance of Garcia Lorca '96
The Odyssey '97
Dangerous Beauty '98
Ever After: A Cinderella Story '98
Left Luggage '98
Only Love '98
An Ideal Husband '99
Jesus '00
The Sky Is Falling '00
Ocean's Twelve '04
Deuce Bigalow: European Gigolo '05
Transporter 3 '08

Jane Krakowski (1966-)
National Lampoon's Vacation '83
No Big Deal '83
Dance with Me '98
Go '99
The Flintstones in Viva Rock Vegas '00
Ice Age '02 (V)
Marci X '03
Alfie '04
Mom at Sixteen '05
Pretty Persuasion '05
Open Season '06 (V)
Surf's Up '07 (V)
Kit Kittredge: An American Girl '08
Open Season 2 '08 (V)
The Rocker '08
Cirque du Freak: The Vampire's Assistant '09

Chris Kramer (1975-)
Stranger in My Bed '05
Circle of Friends '06
Her Fatal Flaw '06
Afghan Knights '07

Clare Kramer (1974-)
Bring It On '00
The Gravedancers '06
The Thirst '06
Endure '10

Eric Allen Kramer (1962-)
Robin Hood: Men in Tights '93
The Colony '98
American Wedding '03
Grilled '06
LA Apocalypse '14

Grant Kramer (1961-)
See Grant Cramer

Jeffrey Kramer (1945-)
Hollywood Boulevard '76
Jaws 2 '78
Halloween 2: The Nightmare Isn't Over! '81

Stephanie Kramer (1956-)
The Man with Two Brains '83
Twin Sisters '91
The Cutting Edge: Going for the Gold '05

Fran Kranz (1981-)
The Village '04
Whirlygirl '04
The Night of the White Pants '06
The TV Set '06
Careless '07
Wieners '08
The Cabin in the Woods '12
Much Ado About Nothing '13
Last Weekend '14
Murder of a Cat '14
Bloodsucking Bastards '15
Mojave '15

John Krasinski (1979-)
Kinsey '04
Duane Hopwood '05
Jarhead '05
The Holiday '06
License to Wed '07
A New Wave '07
Shrek the Third '07 (V)
Smiley Face '07
Leatherheads '08
Away We Go '09
Brief Interviews With Hideous Men '09
It's Complicated '09
Monsters *vs.* Aliens '09 (V)
Something Borrowed '11
Big Miracle '12
Nobody Walks '12
Promised Land '12
Aloha '15
Kahlil Gibran's The Prophet '15
The Hollars '16
13 Hours: The Secret Soldiers of Benghazi '16
Animal Crackers '17
Born in China '17
Detroit '17
A Quiet Place '18

Brian Krause (1969-)
An American Summer '90
December '91
Return to the Blue Lagoon '91
Sleepwalkers '92
Naked Souls '95
Within the Rock '96
Return to Cabin by the Lake '01
Ties That Bind '06
Loch Ness Terror '07
Protecting the King '07
Supernova '09
Growth '10
You're So Cupid '10
Camel Spiders '11
Stalked at 17 '12
Red Sky '14

Louisa Krause (1986-)
The Babysitters '07
Toe to Toe '09
Bluebird '13
Dog Eat Dog '16
Donald Cried '16
Skin '18

Peter Krause (1965-)
Lovelife '97
We Don't Live Here Anymore '04
Civic Duty '06
Beastly '11
Night Owls '15

Werner Krauss (1884-1959)
The Cabinet of Dr. Caligari '19
Othello '22
Joyless Street '25
Secrets of a Soul '25
Tartuffe '25
Variety '25
Jud Suess '40

Lenny Kravitz (1964-)
The Brave One '07
Precious: Based on the Novel 'Push' by Sapphire '09
The Hunger Games '12
The Hunger Games: Catching Fire '13
Lee Daniels' The Butler '13

Zoë Kravitz (1988-)
Birds of America '08
The Greatest '09
It's Kind of a Funny Story '10
X-Men: First Class '11
Yelling to the Sky '11
After Earth '13
Divergent '14
Dope '15
Gemini '17
Rough Night '17
Vincent N Roxxy '17
Fantastic Beasts: The Crimes of Grindelwald '18
Kin '18

Nicolette Krebitz (1972-)
Bandits '99
The Tunnel '01
All the Queen's Men '02

Nathan Kress (1992-)
Babe: Pig in the City '98 (V)
Gym Teacher: The Movie '08
Game of Your Life '11

Thomas Kretschmann (1962-)
Stalingrad '94
The Stendahl Syndrome '95
Total Reality '97
Esther '98
Green Sails '00
U-571 '00
Blade 2 '02
The Pianist '02
Downfall '04
Head in the Clouds '04
In Enemy Hands '04
Karate Dog '04
Resident Evil: Apocalypse '04
Have No Fear: The Life of Pope John Paul II '05
King Kong '05
The Celestine Prophecy '06
Grimm Love '06
Eichmann '07
In Tranzit '07
Next '07
Hellboy II: The Golden Army '08 (V)
Transsiberian '08
Valkyrie '08
Wanted '08
The Young Victoria '09
The Sinking of the Laconia '10
The Big Bang '11
Cars 2 '11 (V)
Hostel: Part 3 '11
Argento's Dracula 3D '13
Hitman: Agent 47 '15
Jungle '17
A Taxi Driver '17
Dragged Across Concrete '18

Kurt Kreuger (1916-2006)
Sahara '43
Dark Corner '46
Unfaithfully Yours '48

Kristin Kreuk (1982-)
Snow White: The Fairest of Them All '02
Eurotrip '04
Partition '07
Street Fighter: The Legend of Chun-Li '09
Ben Hur '10

David Kriegel
Alive '93
Speed '94

Vicky Krieps
Hanna '11
Phantom Thread '17

Alice Krige (1954-)
A Tale of Two Cities '80
Chariots of Fire '81
Ghost Story '81
King David '85
Wallenberg: A Hero's Story '85
Dream West '86
Barfly '87
Haunted Summer '88
See You in the Morning '89
Ladykiller '92
Sleepwalkers '92
Sharpe's Honour '94
Institue Benjamenta or This Dream People Call Human Life '95
Joseph '95
Hidden in America '96
Star Trek: First Contact '96
Habitat '97
The Twilight of the Ice Nymphs '97
Molokai: The Story of Father Damien '99
The Little Vampire '00
Attila '01
Dinotopia '02
Reign of Fire '02
Children of Dune '03
The Line of Beauty '06
Lonely Hearts '06
Silent Hill '06
The Contract '07
Persuasion '07
Ten Inch Hero '07
Page Eight '11

Johannes Krisch
360 '12
In the Fade '17

Sylvia Kristel (1952-2012)
Emmanuelle '74
Private Lessons '75
Emmanuelle, the Joys of a Woman '76
Game of Seduction '76
Good-bye, Emmanuelle '77
The Concorde: Airport '79 '79
The Fifth Musketeer '79
The Nude Bomb '80
Lady Chatterley's Lover '81
Private School '83
Emmanuelle 4 '84
Mysteries '84
The Big Bet '85
Mata Hari '85
Red Heat '85
Dracula's Widow '88

Marta Kristen (1945-)
Savage Sam '63
Beach Blanket Bingo '65
Terminal Island '73
Battle Beyond the Stars '80
Body Count '97
Lost in Space '98 (C)

Kris Kristofferson (1936-)
Blume in Love '73
Pat Garrett & Billy the Kid '73
Alice Doesn't Live Here Anymore '74
Bring Me the Head of Alfredo Garcia '74
The Sailor Who Fell from Grace with the Sea '76
A Star Is Born '76
Vigilante Force '76
Semi-Tough '77
Convoy '78
Freedom Road '79
Heaven's Gate '81
Rollover '81
Flashpoint '84
Songwriter '84
Blood and Orchids '86
Last Days of Frank & Jesse James '86
Stagecoach '86
Trouble in Mind '86
Big Top Pee-wee '88
The Tracker '88
Millennium '89
Welcome Home '89
Another Pair of Aces: Three of a Kind '91
Miracle in the Wilderness '91
Original Intent '91
Christmas in Connecticut '92
Cheatin' Hearts '93
Lone Star '95
Pharoah's Army '95
Fire Down Below '97
Two for Texas '97
Blade '98
Dance with Me '98
The Land Before Time 6: The Secret of Saurus Rock '98 (V)
Outlaw Justice '98
Payback '98
A Soldier's Daughter Never Cries '98
Tom Clancy's Netforce '98
Limbo '99
Molokai: The Story of Father Damien '99
Perfect Murder, Perfect Town '00
Chelsea Walls '01
Eye See You '01
Planet of the Apes '01
Blade 2 '02
Blade: Trinity '04
Silver City '04
Dreamer: Inspired by a True Story '05
The Jacket '05
The Wendell Baker Story '05
Disappearances '06
Fast Food Nation '06
Lords of the Street '08
Snow Buddies '08 (V)
For Sale by Owner '09
He's Just Not That Into You '09
The Last Rites of Ransom Pride '09
Powder Blue '09
Bloodworth '10
Dolphin Tale '11
The Greening of Whitney Brown '11
Deadfall '12
Joyful Noise '12
The Motel Life '12
Angels Sing '13
Dolphin Tale 2 '14
Traded '16

Berry Kroeger (1912-91)
Act of Violence '48
Gun Crazy '49
Guilty of Treason '50
Battles of Chief Pontiac '52
Blood Alley '55
Yellowneck '55
Man in the Vault '56
Seven Thieves '60
The Incredible Two-Headed Transplant '71
Demon Seed '77

Joachim Krol (1957-)
Run Lola Run '98
The Princess and the Warrior '00
Anne Frank: The Whole Story '01
Gloomy Sunday '02

Nick Kroll (1978-)
A Good Old Fashioned Orgy '11
Joshy '16
Loving '16
My Blind Brother '16
Captain Underpants: The First Epic Movie '17 (V)
The House '17
Operation Finale '18
The Addams Family '19

Josef Kroner (1924-98)
The Shop on Main Street '65
Another Way '82

Margareta Krook (1925-2001)
Persona '66
Gossip '00

Michael Kropsa (1956-)
Takedown '10
Earth's Final Hours '12

David Kross (1990-)
The Reader '08
Into the White '12
The Keeper '18

Chad Krowchuk (1982-)
Heck's Way Home '95
Poltergeist: The Legacy '96
Collision Earth '11

Frank Krueger
The Pink Conspiracy '07
Break '09

Alma Kruger (1871-1960)
100 Men and a Girl '37
The Great Waltz '38
The Toy Wife '38
Calling Dr. Gillespie '42
Dr. Gillespie's New Assistant '42
Dr. Gillespie's Criminal Case '43
Three Men in White '44
Between Two Women '45
A Scandal in Paris '46
Dark Delusion '47
Forever Amber '47

Christiane Kruger (1945-)
Double Face '70
Little Mother '71
Le Dernier Combat '84
Anne of Green Gables '85

Diane Kruger (1976-)
The Target '02
Whatever You Say '02
National Treasure '04
Troy '04
Wicker Park '04
Joyeux Noel '05
The Color of Freedom '07
The Hunting Party '07
National Treasure: Book of Secrets '07
Inglourious Basterds '09
Inhale '10
Special Forces '11
Unknown '11
Farewell, My Queen '12
The Host '13
Mr. Nobody '13
The Better Angels '14
Disorder '16
Fathers and Daughters '16
The Infiltrator '16
In the Fade '17
Welcome to Marwen '18
The Operative '19

Hardy Kruger (1928-)
Liane, Jungle Goddess '56
One That Got Away '57
Taxi for Tobruk '60
Hatari! '62
The Flight of the Phoenix '65
The Defector '66
Battle of Neretva '69
Red Tent '69
The Secret of Santa Vittoria '69
What the Peeper Saw '72
Death Merchants '73
Barry Lyndon '75
A Bridge Too Far '77
Blue Fin '78
Wild Geese '78
Wrong Is Right '82
The Inside Man '84
Operation Valkyrie '04

Otto Kruger (1885-1974)
Gallant Lady '33
The Prizefighter and the Lady '33
Turn Back the Clock '33
Chained '34
Men in White '34
Treasure Island '34
Dracula's Daughter '36
They Won't Forget '37
Thanks for the Memory '38
Another Thin Man '39
Dr. Ehrlich's Magic Bullet '40
The Man I Married '40
The Big Boss '41
Saboteur '42
Corregidor '43
Tarzan's Desert Mystery '43
Cover Girl '44
Murder, My Sweet '44
The Woman Who Came Back '45
Wonder Man '45
Lulu Belle '48
Smart Woman '48
711 Ocean Drive '50
Payment on Demand '51
High Noon '52
Black Widow '54
Colossus of New York '58
The Young Philadelphians '59
Cash McCall '60

David Krumholtz (1978-)
Addams Family Values '93
Life with Mikey '93
The Santa Clause '94
The Ice Storm '97
Slums of Beverly Hills '98
Liberty Heights '99
Ten Things I Hate about You '99
The Mexican '01
Sidewalks of New York '01
Big Shot: Confessions of a Campus Bookie '02
The Santa Clause 2 '02
Scorched '02
You Stupid Man '02
Kill the Poor '03
Harold and Kumar Go to White Castle '04
Looking for Kitty '04
Ray '04
Guess Who '05
Bobby '06

Tenacious D in the Pick of Destiny '06
Live! '07
Walk Hard: The Dewey Cox Story '07
Harold & Kumar Escape from Guantanamo Bay '08
A Very Harold & Kumar Christmas '11
Casual Encounters '16
Ghost Team '16

Gene Krupa (1909-73)
Ball of Fire '41
The Glenn Miller Story '54
The Benny Goodman Story '55

Olek Krupa (1955-)
Mac '93
Home Alone 3 '97
Kicked in the Head '97
Blue Streak '99
No Vacancy '99
Thirteen Days '00
Behind Enemy Lines '01
The Italian Job '03
Burn After Reading '08

Jack Kruschen (1922-2002)
Abbott and Costello Go to Mars '53
A Blueprint for Murder '53
Money from Home '53
The War of the Worlds '53
The Night Holds Terror '55
Soldier of Fortune '55
Julie '56
Cry Terror! '58
The Decks Ran Red '58
The Angry Red Planet '59
The Apartment '60
The Last Voyage '60
Where the Boys Are '60
Cape Fear '61
Follow That Dream '61
The Ladies' Man '61
Lover Come Back '61
McLintock! '63
Dear Brigitte '65
Caprice '67
Freebie & the Bean '74
Satan's Cheerleaders '77
Cheaters '84

Michelle Krusiec (1974-)
Nixon '95
Final Encounter '00
Sweet Home Alabama '02
Daddy Day Care '03
Dumb and Dumberer: When Harry Met Lloyd '03
Duplex '03
Cursed '04
Saving Face '04
Far North '07
What Happens in Vegas '08
Four of Hearts '13
The Invitation '16

Nikolai Kryuchkov (1911-94)
The Patriots '33
Ballad of a Soldier '60

Feng Ku (1930-)
Have Sword, Will Travel '69
The Heroic Ones '70
Sword Masters: Brothers Five '70
Sword Masters: Web of Death '76
The Brave Archer '77
Five Deadly Venoms '78
Bat Without Wings '80
Black Magic '06
The Magic Blade '08

Wen Chung Ku (1909-81)
Intimate Confessions of a Chinese Courtesan '72
King Boxer '72
Black Magic '06

Akira Kubo (1936-)
Throne of Blood '57
Matango '63
Son of Godzilla '66
Destroy All Monsters '68
Godzilla *vs.* Monster Zero '68
Kill! '68

Yog, Monster from Space '71

Naoko Kubo
Zatoichi: Zatoichi's Flashing Sword '64
Kill! '68

Marc Kudisch (1966-)
Bye Bye Birdie '95
Break-In '06
Unsane '18

Youki Kudoh (1971-)
Mystery Train '89
Picture Bride '94
Heaven's Burning '97
Snow Falling on Cedars '99
Memoirs of a Geisha '05
Rush Hour 3 '07

Lisa Kudrow (1963-)
Mother '96
Clockwatchers '97
Romy and Michele's High School Reunion '97
Analyze This '98
The Opposite of Sex '98
Hanging Up '99
Lucky Numbers '00
All Over the Guy '01
Dr. Dolittle 2 '01 (V)
Analyze That '02
Bark! '02
Marci X '03
Wonderland '03
Happy Endings '05
P.S. I Love You '07
Bandslam '09
Hotel for Dogs '09
Paper Man '09
Powder Blue '09
Easy A '10
Neighbors '14
The Boss Baby '17
Table 19 '17
Booksmart '19

Yoshiko Kuga (1931-)
The Idiot '51
Shin Heike Monogatari '55

Nikolina Kujaca
Dust '01
The Great Water '04

Nutsa Kukhianidze (1983-)
The Good Thief '03
Bad City '06

Agata Kulesza (1971-)
Ida '13
Dark Crimes '16
The Innocents '16
Cold War '18

Vladimir Kulich (1956-)
Firestorm '97
The 13th Warrior '99
Smokin' Aces '07
The Equalizer '14

Joanna Kulig (1982-)
Elles '11
The Woman in the Fifth '11
The Innocents '16
Cold War '18

Jarl Kulle (1927-97)
Secrets of Women '52
Smiles of a Summer Night '55
Fanny and Alexander '83
Babette's Feast '87

Nancy Kulp (1921-91)
Forever Darling '56
The Three Faces of Eve '57
Two Little Bears '61
Who's Minding the Store? '63
The Patsy '64
Strange Bedfellows '65
The Aristocats '70 (V)
The Return of the Beverly Hillbillies '81

Will Kuluva (1917-90)
Abandoned '47
Crime in the Streets '56
Odds Against Tomorrow '59
Missiles of October '74

William J. Kulzer
Shadows Run Black '84
Lust for Freedom '87

Mitchell Kummen
Lucky Christmas '11
Interrogation '16

Magda Kun (1912-45)
Old Mother Riley in Paris '38
Dead of Night '45

Vusi Kunene (1956-)
Cry, the Beloved Country '95
The King Is Alive '00
Queen's Messenger II '01

Jun Kunimura (1955-)
Audition '99
Ichi the Killer '01
Kill Bill Vol. 1 '03
Hana: The Tale of a Reluctant Samurai '07
Outrage '10
The Wailing '16

Mila Kunis (1983-)
Get Over It! '01
American Psycho 2: All American Girl '02
Boot Camp '07
Moving McAllister '07
Tony n' Tina's Wedding '07
Forgetting Sarah Marshall '08
Max Payne '08
Extract '09
Black Swan '10
The Book of Eli '10
Date Night '10
Friends With Benefits '11
Ted '12
Blood Ties '13
Oz the Great and Powerful '13
Third Person '13
The Angriest Man in Brooklyn '14
Jupiter Ascending '15
Bad Moms '16
A Bad Moms Christmas '17
The Spy Who Dumped Me '18
Wonder Park '19

William Kunstler (1919-95)
The Doors '91
Malcolm X '92 (C)

Doris Kunstmann (1944-)
Hitler: The Last Ten Days '73
Inside Out '75

Simon Kunz
The Parent Trap '98
The Affair of the Necklace '01

Nina Kunzendorf (1971-)
Rosenstrasse '03
Operation Valkyrie '04
Phoenix '14

Sakari Kuosmanen (1956-)
Night on Earth '91
The Man Without a Past '02
The Other Side of Hope '17

Chiaki Kuriyama (1984-)
Battle Royale '00
Kill Bill Vol. 1 '03
Kill Bill Vol. 2 '04
Azumi 2 '05
The Great Yokai War '05
The Sky Crawlers '08

Susumu Kurobe (1939-)
Destroy All Monsters '68
Goyokin '69
Latitude Zero '69

Meisa Kuroki
One Missed Call 3: Final '06
Crows Zero '07

Akbar Kurtha
My Son the Fanatic '97
Syriana '05

Alwyn Kurts (1915-2000)
Tim '79
The Efficiency Expert '92

Mehmet Kurtulus (1972-)
The Tunnel '01
Head On '04

Marcia Jean Kurtz
Once Upon a Time in America '84
Find Me Guilty '06
Inside Man '06
Big Fan '09

Swoosie Kurtz (1944-)
Slap Shot '77
Marriage Is Alive and Well '80
The World According to Garp '82
Agatha Christie's A Caribbean Mystery '83
Against All Odds '84
Guilty Conscience '85
True Stories '86
Wildcats '86
Bright Lights, Big City '88
Dangerous Liaisons '88
Vice Versa '88
The Image '89
A Shock to the System '90
Stanley and Iris '90
And the Band Played On '93 (C)
The Positively True Adventures of the Alleged Texas Cheerleader-Murdering Mom '93
Reality Bites '94
Betrayed: A Story of Three Women '95
One Christmas '95
Storybook '95
Citizen Ruth '96
Armistead Maupin's More Tales of the City '97
Liar Liar '97
Cruel Intentions '98
My Own Country '98
White River '99
Sleep Easy, Hutch Rimes '00
Bubble Boy '01
Get Over It! '01
The Rules of Attraction '02
Duplex '03
Category 7: The End of the World '05
Living Proof '08
An Englishman in New York '09

Katy Kurtzman (1965-)
Child of Glass '78
When Every Day Was the Fourth of July '78

Kurupt (1972-)
Half Past Dead '02
Dark Blue '03
Hollywood Homicide '03
I Accidentally Domed Your Son '04
Johnson Family Vacation '04 (C)
Cut Off '06
Vice '08

Olga Kurylenko (1979-)
Paris, je t'aime '06
Hitman '07
Max Payne '08
Quantum of Solace '08
Centurion '10
There Be Dragons '11
Erased '12
To the Wonder '12
Oblivion '13
The November Man '14
Vampire Academy '14
Momentum '15
The Water Diviner '15
A Perfect Day '16
Gun Shy '17
The Courier '19
15 Minutes of War '19

Clyde Kusatsu (1948-)
Midway '76
Black Sunday '77
The Choirboys '77
Go Tell the Spartans '78
Lookin' to Get Out '82
Bird on a Wire '90

Dream Lover '93
In the Line of Fire '93
Made in America '93
Top Dog '95
Paradise Road '97
American Pie '99
American Tragedy '00
Hollywood Homicide '03
United States of Leland '03
The Interpreter '05
Shopgirl '05
Pandemic '07
Harold & Kumar Escape from Guantanamo Bay '08

Richard Kuss (1927-99)
The Deer Hunter '78
Warlock '91

Dylan Kussman (1971-)
Dead Poets Society '89
Wild Hearts Can't Be Broken '91
Way of the Gun '00
Wild Things 2 '04
Ten 'Til Noon '06

Emir Kusturica (1954-)
Underground '95 (C)
The Widow of Saint-Pierre '00
The Good Thief '03
Farewell '09

Ashton Kutcher (1978-)
Down to You '00
Dude, Where's My Car? '00
Texas Rangers '01
Cheaper by the Dozen '03
Just Married '03
My Boss's Daughter '03
The Butterfly Effect '04
A Lot Like Love '05
Guess Who '05
Bobby '06
The Guardian '06
Open Season '06 (V)
What Happens in Vegas '08
Personal Effects '09
Spread '09
Killers '10
Valentine's Day '10
New Year's Eve '11
No Strings Attached '11
Jobs '13

Alexander Kuznitsov (1959-)
The Ice Runner '93
Agent Red '00

Mimi Kuzyk (1952-)
Miles to Go '86
The Kiss '88
Dead Silence '96
Family of Cops 2: Breach of Faith '97
Thrill Seekers '99
The Golden Spiders: A Nero Wolfe Mystery '00
Lost and Delirious '01
The Human Stain '03
A Different Loyalty '04
The Final Cut '04
I Do (But I Don't) '04
A Christmas Wedding '06

Hoi-Shan Kwan (1925-2006)
Shaolin & Wu Tang '81
Hard-Boiled '92

Nancy Kwan (1939-)
The World of Suzie Wong '60
Flower Drum Song '61
A Wild Affair '63
Fate Is the Hunter '64
Lt. Robin Crusoe, U.S.N. '66
The Wrecking Crew '68
The Girl Who Knew Too Much '69
The McMasters '70
Project: Kill! '77
Night Creature '79
Walking the Edge '83
Cold Dog Soup '89
Dragon: The Bruce Lee Story '93

Rosamund Kwan (1962-)
Operation Condor 2: The Armour of the Gods '86

Shanghai Express '86
Once Upon a Time in China '91
Once Upon a Time in China II '92
Once Upon a Time in China III '93
Big Shot's Funeral '01

Ryan Kwanten (1976-)
The Junction Boys '02
Flicka '06
Dead Silence '07
Griff the Invisible '10
Legend of the Guardians: The Owls of Ga'Hoole '10 (V)
Red Hill '10
Not Suitable for Children '12
7500 '12
Knights of Badassdom '13
The Right Kind Of Wrong '13
Northman: A Viking Saga '15
Flight 7500 '16
The Hurricane Heist '18

Aaron Kwok (1965-)
Legend of the Liquid Sword '93
Wind and Cloud: The Storm Riders '04

Philip Kwok (1951-)
The Brave Archer '77
Five Deadly Venoms '78
Heaven & Hell '78
House of Traps '81
The Brave Archer and His Mate '82
Hard-Boiled '92
The Phantom Lover '95

Burt Kwouk (1930-2016)
The Terror of the Tongs '61
Casino Royale '67
The Chairman '69
The Pink Panther Strikes Again '76
Revenge of the Pink Panther '78
Trail of the Pink Panther '82
Plenty '85
Empire of the Sun '87
Son of the Pink Panther '93
Kiss of the Dragon '01
Beyond Borders '03

Gerald Kyd (1973-)
The Defender '04
Legacy '10

Sam Kydd (1915-82)
Radio Cab Murder '54
Too Late the Hero '70
Eye of the Needle '81

Machiko Kyo (1924-2019)
Rashomon '51
Ugetsu '53
Gate of Hell '54
Street of Shame '56
The Teahouse of the August Moon '56
Drifting Weeds '59
Face of Another '66

Kay Kyser (1905-95)
You'll Find Out '40
Playmates '41
Stage Door Canteen '43
Swing Fever '43
Thousands Cheer '43
Carolina Blues '44

Jake La Botz
Rambo '08
Close Range '15

David La Haye (1966-)
The Courage to Love '00
Ginger Snaps Back: The Beginning '04

Barbara La Marr
The Prisoner of Zenda '22
Souls for Sale '23

Jake La Motta (1921-)
See Jake LaMotta

Alison La Placa (1959-)
Fletch '85
Voyage of the Rock Aliens '87

Laura La Plante (1904-96)
Smouldering Fires *'25*
Skinner's Dress Suit *'26*
The Cat and the Canary *'27*
The Love Trap *'29*
Arizona *'31*
God's Gift to Women *'31*
Lonely Wives *'31*
The Sea Ghost *'31*
Hold Your Man *'33*
The Church Mouse *'34*

Rod La Rocque (1898-1969)
The Ten Commandments *'23*
The Fighting Eagle *'27*
Show People *'28*
Our Modern Maidens *'29*
Let Us Be Gay *'30*
One Romantic Night *'30*
S.O.S. Iceberg *'33*
The Drag-Net *'36*
The Hunchback of Notre Dame *'39*
Beyond Tomorrow *'40*
Meet John Doe *'41*

Rita La Roy (1907-93)
The Love Trap *'29*
Sin Takes a Holiday *'30*
The Mandarin Mystery *'37*

Jack La Rue (1902-84)
A Farewell to Arms *'32*
Lawyer Man *'32*
The Kennel Murder Case *'33*
To the Last Man *'33*
Headline Woman *'35*
Dancing Pirate *'36*
Yellow Cargo *'36*
Captains Courageous *'37*
Footsteps in the Dark *'41*
Paper Bullets *'41*
The Payoff *'43*
The Road to Utopia *'46*
Robin and the 7 Hoods *'64*
The Young Nurses *'73*

Eriq La Salle (1962-)
Cut and Run *'85*
Coming to America *'88*
Jacob's Ladder *'90*
Color of Night *'94*
DROP Squad *'94*
Rebound: The Legend of Earl 'The Goat' Manigault *'96*
Crazy as Hell *'02*
One Hour Photo *'02*
Biker Boyz *'03*
Inside Out *'05*
Johnny Was *'05*
Megafault *'09*
Relative Stranger *'09*

Lucille La Verne (1872-1945)
See Lucille LaVerne

John La Zar (1946-)
See John Lazar

Barbara Laage (1920-88)
The Happy Road *'57*
Therese & Isabelle *'67*
Bed and Board *'70*

Nadine Labaki
Caramel *'07*
Rio, I Love You *'14*
The Idol *'15*

Samuel Labarthe (1952-)
Le Divorce *'03*
Strayed *'03*

Patrick Labbe (1970-)
The Boys *'97*
The High Cost of Living *'10*

Ariane Labed
Fidelio: Alice's Odyssey *'14*
Mary Magdalene *'19*

Patti LaBelle (1944-)
A Soldier's Story *'84*
Unnatural Causes *'86*
Preaching to the Choir *'05*
Why I Wore Lipstick to My Mastectomy *'06*
Cover *'08*

Rob LaBelle
RV *'06*
Ice Quake *'10*

Shia LaBeouf (1986-)
The Battle of Shaker Heights *'03*
Charlie's Angels: Full Throttle *'03*
Dumb and Dumberer: When Harry Met Lloyd *'03*
Holes *'03*
I, Robot *'04*
Constantine *'05*
The Greatest Game Ever Played *'05*
Bobby *'06*
A Guide to Recognizing Your Saints *'06*
Disturbia *'07*
Surf's Up *'07 (V)*
Transformers *'07*
Eagle Eye *'08*
Indiana Jones and the Kingdom of the Crystal Skull *'08*
New York, I Love You *'09*
Transformers: Revenge of the Fallen *'09*
Wall Street 2: Money Never Sleeps *'10*
Transformers: Dark of the Moon *'11*
The Company You Keep *'12*
Lawless *'12*
Charlie Countryman *'13*
Nymphomaniac, Volume 1 *'13*
Fury *'14*
American Honey *'16*
Man Down *'16*
Borg *vs.* McEnroe *'17*
Honey Boy *'19*
The Peanut Butter Falcon *'19*

Tyler Labine (1978-)
Flyboys *'06*
Control Alt Delete *'08*
Tucker & Dale *vs.* Evil *'10*
A Good Old Fashioned Orgy *'11*
Rise of the Planet of the Apes *'11*
Best Man Down *'12*
Someone Marry Barry *'12*
Cottage Country *'13*
The Boss *'16*
Escape Room *'19*

Matthew Laborteaux (1966-)
A Woman under the Influence *'74*
Tarantulas: The Deadly Cargo *'77*
King of the Gypsies *'78*
Deadly Friend *'86*
Shattered Spirits *'86*

Patrick Laborteaux (1965-)
Prince of Bel Air *'87*
Heathers *'89*
3 Ninjas *'92*
JAG *'95*

Elina Labourdette (1919-)
The Ladies of the Bois de Bologne *'44*
Lola *'61*

Catherine Lacey (1904-79)
The Lady Vanishes *'38*
Cottage to Let *'41*
The Servant *'63*
The Sorcerers *'67*
The Private Life of Sherlock Holmes *'70*

Ingrid Lacey (1958-)
A Woman's Guide to Adultery *'93*
Funnyman *'94*
In Love and War *'96*

Margaret Lacey (1910-88)
Seance on a Wet Afternoon *'64*
Diamonds Are Forever *'71*
Our Town *'03*

Ronald Lacey (1935-91)
The Fearless Vampire Killers *'67*
Take a Girl Like You *'70*
Crucible of Terror *'72*
Disciple of Death *'72*
Nijinsky *'80*
Raiders of the Lost Ark *'81*
Firefox *'82*
The Hound of the Baskervilles *'83*
The Adventures of Buckaroo Banzai Across the Eighth Dimension *'84*
Making the Grade *'84*
Flesh and Blood *'85*
The Lone Runner *'88*

Stephen Lack (1946-)
Scanners *'81*
Perfect Strangers *'84*
Dead Ringers *'88*
All the Vermeers in New York *'91*

Elizabeth Lackey (1971-)
Blood Crime *'02*
Boa *'02*

Peter Lacroix
The Silencer *'99*
Anna's Storm *'07*

Jake Lacy
Obvious Child *'14*
Carol *'15*
Diane *'18*
Rampage *'18*
Ode to Joy *'19*
Otherhood *'19*

Preston Lacy (1969-)
Jackass Number Two *'06*
The Life of Lucky Cucumber *'08*
Jackass 3D *'10*
A Holiday Heist *'11*

Alan Ladd (1913-64)
Island of Lost Souls *'32 (C)*
Hitler: Beast of Berlin *'39*
The Howards of Virginia *'40*
The Black Cat *'41*
Citizen Kane *'41*
Gangs, Inc. *'41*
Paper Bullets *'41*
They Met in Bombay *'41*
The Glass Key *'42*
Joan of Paris *'42*
Star Spangled Rhythm *'42*
This Gun for Hire *'42*
China *'43*
Salty O'Rourke *'45*
The Blue Dahlia *'46*
Calcutta *'47*
My Favorite Brunette *'47*
Saigon *'47*
Whispering Smith *'48*
Branded *'50*
Captain Carey, U.S.A. *'50*
Appointment With Danger *'51*
The Iron Mistress *'52*
Shane *'53*
Drum Beat *'54*
Saskatchewan *'54*
The McConnell Story *'55*
Santiago *'56*
The Badlanders *'58*
Deep Six *'58*
Proud Rebel *'58*
The Man in the Net *'59*
One Foot in Hell *'60*
Duel of Champions *'61*
13 West Street *'62*
The Carpetbaggers *'64*

Cheryl Ladd (1951-)
Satan's School for Girls *'73*
The Treasure of Jamaica Reef *'74*
Now and Forever *'82*
Grace Kelly *'83*
Purple Hearts *'84*
A Death in California *'85*
Millennium *'89*
Jekyll and Hyde *'90*
Danielle Steel's Changes *'91*
Poison Ivy *'92*
The Haunting of Lisa *'96*
Permanent Midnight *'98*
A Dog of Flanders *'99*
Though None Go With Me *'06*
Holiday Baggage *'08*
Love's Everlasting Courage *'11*
Santa Paws 2: The Santa Pups *'12*
Unforgettable *'17*

David Ladd (1947-)
A Dog of Flanders *'59*
Misty *'61*
Catlow *'71*
Raw Meat *'72*
Jonathan Livingston Seagull *'73 (V)*
The Treasure of Jamaica Reef *'74*

Diane Ladd (1935-)
The Wild Angels *'66*
Rebel Rousers *'69*
Alice Doesn't Live Here Anymore *'74*
Chinatown *'74*
Embryo *'76*
All Night Long *'81*
Desperate Lives *'82*
Grace Kelly *'83*
Something Wicked This Way Comes *'83*
I Married a Centerfold *'84*
Black Widow *'87*
National Lampoon's Christmas Vacation *'89*
Wild at Heart *'90*
A Kiss Before Dying *'91*
Rambling Rose *'91*
Carnosaur *'93*
The Cemetery Club *'93*
Father Hood *'93*
Hush Little Baby *'93*
Mother *'94*
Citizen Ruth *'96*
Ghosts of Mississippi *'96*
Family of Cops 2: Breach of Faith *'97*
James Dean: Live Fast, Die Young *'97*
Get a Clue! *'98*
Primary Colors *'98*
Daddy & Them *'99*
Forever Together *'00*
28 Days *'00*
A Long Way Home *'01*
Talking to Heaven *'02*
Gracie's Choice *'04*
The World's Fastest Indian *'05*
Come Early Morning *'06*
Inland Empire *'06*
When I Find the Ocean *'06*
Montana Sky *'07*
Jake's Corner *'08*
American Cowslip *'09*

Jordan Ladd (1975-)
Embrace of the Vampire *'95*
Stand-Ins *'97*
Never Been Kissed *'99*
The Specials *'00*
Cabin Fever *'03*
Dog Gone Love *'03*
Club Dread *'04*
Madhouse *'04*
Waiting *'05*
Death Proof *'07*
Hostel: Part 2 *'07*
It Was One of Us *'07*
Grace *'09*

Walter Ladengast (1899-1980)
Every Man for Himself & God Against All *'75*
Nosferatu the Vampyre *'79*

John Lafayette
White Sands *'92*
Loverboy *'05*

Pat Laffan
The Snapper *'93*
American Women *'00*
How Harry Became a Tree *'01*
Intermission *'03*

Patricia Laffan (1919-)
Quo Vadis *'51*
Devil Girl from Mars *'54*

James Lafferty (1985-)
A Season on the Brink *'02*
S. Darko: A Donnie Darko Tale *'09*
Oculus *'14*

Laurent Lafitte (1973-)
Little White Lies *'10*
Birdsong *'12*
The Love Punch *'13*
Bright Days Ahead *'14*
Elle *'16*

Art LaFleur (1943-)
The Hollywood Knights *'80*
Jekyll & Hyde. . . Together Again *'82*
Trancers *'84*
Zone Troopers *'84*
Rampage *'87*
Oscar *'91*
Forever Young *'92*
Jack the Bear *'93*
The Sandlot *'93*
Man of the House *'95*
First Kid *'96*
Hijacking Hollywood *'97*
Lewis and Clark and George *'97*
The Replacements *'00*
Beethoven's 4th *'01*
The Santa Clause 2 *'02*
Ace Ventura Jr.: Pet Detective *'08*
Bad Guys *'08*
The Rig *'10*
A Snow Globe Christmas *'13*

Sarah Lafleur
Terminal Invasion *'02*
Lake Placid 2 *'07*

Bernadette LaFont (1938-2013)
Le Beau Serge *'58*
Les Bonnes Femmes *'60*
The Thief of Paris *'67*
Catch Me a Spy *'71*
Violette *'78*
The Perils of Gwendoline *'84*
Waiting for the Moon *'87*
Dingo *'90*
Son of Gascogne *'95*
Genealogies of a Crime *'97*
I Do *'06*
A Cat in Paris *'11 (V)*

Roc Lafortune (1956-)
The Boys *'97*
The Minion *'98*
The List *'99*

Matt Lagan
Princess of Mars *'09*
Airline Disaster *'10*
2010: Moby Dick *'10*

Alicia Lagano (1979-)
The Truth About Jane *'00*
Believe in Me *'06*

Marika Lagercrantz (1954-)
All Things Fair *'95*
Gossip *'00*
The Girl With the Dragon Tattoo *'09*

Caroline Lagerfelt (1947-)
Iron Eagle *'86*
Glam *'97*
August *'08*
Altered Minds *'13*

Valerie Lagrange (1942-)
A Man and a Woman *'66*
Weekend *'67*
Queen to Play *'09*

Ernesto Laguardia (1959-)
Like A Bride *'94*
Esmeralda Comes by Night *'98*

Brigitte Lahaie (1955-)
The Grapes of Death *'78*
Night of the Hunted *'80*
Faceless *'88*

Emma Lahana (1984-)
Alien Agent *'07*
Seven Deadly Sins *'10*
Debbie Macomber's Trading Christmas *'11*

Bert Lahr (1895-1967)
Flying High *'31*
Josette *'38*
Just Around the Corner *'38*
The Wizard of Oz *'39*
Ship Ahoy *'42*
Meet the People *'44*
Rose Marie *'54*
The Night They Raided Minsky's *'69*

Christine Lahti (1950-)
And Justice for All *'79*
The Henderson Monster *'80*
Whose Life Is It Anyway? *'81*
The Executioner's Song *'82*
Swing Shift *'84*
Just Between Friends *'86*
Housekeeping *'87*
Running on Empty *'88*
Gross Anatomy *'89*
Miss Firecracker *'89*
Funny About Love *'90*
Crazy from the Heart *'91*
The Doctor *'91*
The Good Fight *'92*
Leaving Normal *'92*
Hideaway *'94*
Pie in the Sky *'95*
Subway Stories *'97*
Trial by Media *'00*
The Pilot's Wife *'01*
Women *vs.* Men *'02*
Out of the Ashes *'03*
Yonkers Joe *'08*
Obsessed *'09*
Touchback *'11*
Hateship Loveship *'13*
Petunia *'13*
Safelight *'15*
Touched With Fire *'16*

Leon Lai (1966-)
Wicked City *'92*
Fallen Angels *'95*
Infernal Affairs 3 *'03*
Seven Swords *'07*
An Empress and the Warriors *'08*

Me Me Lai (1952-)
Au Pair Girls *'72*
Crucible of Terror *'72*
Emerald Jungle *'80*
The Element of Crime *'84*

Leah Lail (1966-)
Something About Sex *'98*
Late Last Night *'99*

Robin Laing (1976-)
Relative Strangers *'99*
Borstal Boy *'00*
Dr. Bell and Mr. Doyle: The Dark Beginnings of Sherlock Holmes *'00*
Joyeux Noel *'05*

Stuart Laing (1969-)
Lawless Heart *'01*
Cambridge Spies *'03*

Jenny Laird (1917-2001)
Black Narcissus *'47*
Village of the Damned *'60*

Arthur Lake (1905-87)
Skinner's Dress Suit *'26*
On with the Show *'29*
The Silver Streak *'34*
Exiled to Shanghai *'37*
23 1/2 Hours Leave *'37*
Blondie *'38*
Blondie Brings Up Baby *'39*
Blondie Meets the Boss *'39*
Blondie Takes a Vacation *'39*
Blondie Has Trouble *'40*
Blondie On a Budget *'40*
Blondie Plays Cupid *'40*
Blondie in Society *'41*
Blondie Goes Latin *'42*
Blondie Goes to College *'42*

Don Lake (1956-)
Big Town *'87*
Best in Show *'00*

Florence Lake (1904-80)
Romance *'30*
Quality Street *'37*
Next Time I Marry *'38*
Crash Dive *'43*

Ricki Lake (1968-)
Hairspray *'88*
Working Girl *'88*
Babycakes *'89*
Cookie *'89*
Cry-Baby *'90*
Last Exit to Brooklyn *'90*
The Chase *'91*
Buffy the Vampire Slayer *'92*
Where the Day Takes You *'92*
Inside Monkey Zetterland *'93*
Skinner *'93*
Cabin Boy *'94*
Serial Mom *'94*
Mrs. Winterbourne *'96*
Cecil B. Demented *'00*
A Dirty Shame *'04 (C)*
Loving Leah *'09*
Gemini *'17*

Sanoe Lake (1979-)
Blue Crush *'02*
Cruel World *'05*
Creature of Darkness *'09*

Veronica Lake (1919-73)
Sullivan's Travels *'41*
The Glass Key *'42*
Star Spangled Rhythm *'42*
This Gun for Hire *'42*
So Proudly We Hail *'43*
The Blue Dahlia *'46*
Ramrod *'47*
Saigon *'47*
Slattery's Hurricane *'49*
Flesh Feast *'69*

Martijn Lakemeier
Winter in Wartime *'10*
It's All So Quiet *'13*

Christine Lakin (1979-)
Boltneck *'98*
Mystery Kids *'99*
Dark Mirror *'07*
The Hottie and the Nottie *'08*
Super Capers *'09*
Caught in the Crossfire *'10*
You Again *'10*
Small Town Santa *'14*

Padma Lakshmi (1970-)
Glitter *'01*
The Mistress of Spices *'05*
Sharpe's Challenge *'06*

Lalaine
Her Best Move *'07*
Ninja's Creed *'09*

Nicole LaLiberte
Kaboom *'11*
Girls Against Boys *'12*

James Lally (1956-)
Working Girl *'88*
Critical Care *'97*

Michael David Lally (1942-)
The Nesting *'80*
Cool World *'92*

Mick (Michael) Lally (1945-2010)
Circle of Friends *'94*
The Secret of Roan Inish *'94*
The Secret of Kells *'09 (V)*

Ben Lam
So Close *'02*
Flash Point *'07*

Ching-Ying Lam (1952-97)
The Prodigal Son *'82*
Heroes Shed No Tears *'86*
Mr. Vampire *'86*

Ka-tung Lam (1967-)
Infernal Affairs 3 *'03*
Exiled *'06*
Drug War *'13*

Suet Lam (1964-)
Full Time Killer *'01*
Dog Bite Dog *'06*
Exiled *'06*
Running Out of Time 2 *'06*
Croczilla *'12*
Drug War *'13*

Maurice LaMarche (1958-)
Pom Poko *'94 (V)*
Hey Arnold! The Movie *'02 (V)*
Team America: World Police *'04 (V)*
Inspector Gadget's Biggest Caper Ever *'05 (V)*
Barnyard *'06 (V)*
Queer Duck: The Movie *'06 (V)*
Zootopia *'16 (V)*

Hedy Lamarr (1913-2000)
Ecstasy *'33*
Algiers *'38*
Boom Town *'40*
Come Live With Me *'40*
Comrade X *'40*
I Take This Woman *'40*
H.M. Pulham Esquire *'41*
Ziegfeld Girl *'41*
Crossroads *'42*
Tortilla Flat *'42*
The Conspirators *'44*
The Heavenly Body *'44*
Experiment Perilous *'45*
Her Highness and the Bellboy *'45*
The Strange Woman *'46*
Dishonored Lady *'47*
Samson and Delilah *'49*
Copper Canyon *'50*
A Lady Without Passport *'50*
My Favorite Spy *'51*
Loves of Three Queens *'54*
Story of Mankind *'57*

Phil LaMarr (1967-)
Bio-Dome *'96*
Free Enterprise *'98*
Shark Tale *'04 (V)*

Jean LaMarre
Malcolm X *'92*
Fresh *'94*
Deadly Voyage *'96*

Fernando Lamas (1915-82)
The Law and the Lady *'51*
Rich, Young and Pretty *'51*
Dangerous When Wet *'53*
The Girl Who Had Everything *'53*
Rose Marie *'54*
The Lost World *'60*
Revenge of the Musketeers *'63*
Kill a Dragon *'67*
Violent Ones *'68*
100 Rifles *'69*
Murder on Flight 502 *'75*
The Cheap Detective *'78*

Lorenzo Lamas (1958-)
Grease *'78*
Detour to Terror *'80*
Body Rock *'84*
Final Impact *'91*
Night of the Warrior *'91*
C.I.A.: Code Name Alexa *'92*
The Swordsman *'92*
C.I.A. 2: Target Alexa *'94*
Gladiator Cop: The Swordsman 2 *'95*
Terminal Justice: Cybertech P.D. *'95*
The Rage *'96*
Mask of Death *'97*
The Debt *'98*
The Muse *'99 (C)*
Undercurrent *'99*
The Circuit 2 *'02*
Hope Ranch *'02*
Dark Waters *'03*
Latin Dragon *'03*
The Paradise Virus *'03*
Alien 3000 *'04*
Deep Evil *'04*
Lethal *'04*
Raptor Island *'04*
Sci-Fighter *'04*
Blood Angels *'05*
18 Fingers of Death *'05*
30,000 Leagues Under the Sea *'07*
Mega Shark Vs. Giant Octopus *'09*

Debra Lamb (1963-)
Beverly Hills Vamp *'88*
Stripped to Kill 2: Live Girls *'89*
Evil Spirits *'91*
The G-String Horror *'12*

Larry Lamb (1947-)
Buster *'88*
A Little Piece of Sunshine *'90*
Fool's Gold: The Story of the Brink's-Mat Robbery *'92*
Essex Boys *'99*

Adam Lamberg (1984-)
The Lizzie McGuire Movie *'03*
When Do We Eat? *'05*

Anne Louise Lambert (1955-)
Picnic at Hanging Rock *'75*
The Draughtsman's Contract *'82*
Lilian's Story *'95*
Napoleon *'96 (V)*

Christopher Lambert (1957-)
Greystoke: The Legend of Tarzan, Lord of the Apes *'84*
Love Songs *'84*
Subway *'85*
Highlander *'86*
The Sicilian *'87*
To Kill a Priest *'89*
Highlander 2: The Quickening *'91*
Highlander: The Gathering *'92*
Fortress *'93*
Gunmen *'93*
Knight Moves *'93*
Highlander: The Final Dimension *'94*
The Hunted *'94*
Mortal Kombat 1: The Movie *'95*
The Road Killers *'95*
Adrenalin: Fear the Rush *'96*
North Star *'96*
Mean Guns *'97*
Nirvana *'97*
Beowulf *'98*
Fortress 2: Re-Entry *'99*
Resurrection *'99*
Highlander: Endgame *'00*
Druids *'01*
The Target *'02*
Day of Wrath *'06*
Metamorphosis *'07*
White Material *'10*

Jack Lambert (1899-1976)
The Ghost Goes West *'36*
Hue and Cry *'47*

Jack Lambert (1920-2002)
The Unsuspected *'47*
Stars in My Crown *'50*
99 River Street *'53*
Kiss Me Deadly *'55*
Run for Cover *'55*
The Day of the Outlaw *'59*
Neither the Sea Nor the Sand *'73*

Paul Lambert (1922-97)
The Windsplitter *'71*
Missiles of October *'74*
Soldier's Revenge *'84*

Ellie Lambetti (1926-83)
Girl in Black *'56*
A Matter of Dignity *'57*

Lloyd Lamble (1914-2008)
The Belles of St. Trinian's *'53*
Sea Wife *'57*

Vassili Lambrinos (1926-)
Island of Love *'63*
That Man Bolt *'73*
Last Rites *'88*

Anne Lambton (1954-)
American History X *'98*
Love Is the Devil *'98*
A Different Loyalty *'04*

Duncan Lamont (1918-78)
The Golden Coach *'52*
Quentin Durward *'55*
Murder at the Gallop *'63*
The Devil-Ship Pirates *'64*
The Evil of Frankenstein *'64*
Frankenstein Created Woman *'66*
The Creeping Flesh *'72*

Maurice Lamont
Zero Tolerance *'93*
Crooked *'05*

Molly Lamont (1910-2000)
The Third Clue *'34*
The Awful Truth *'37*
Somewhere I'll Find You *'42*
The Devil Bat's Daughter *'46*
So Goes My Love *'46*

Jake LaMotta (1921-)
The Hustler *'61*
Hangmen *'87*
Mob War *'88*

John Lamotta
Revenge of the Ninja *'83*
Showdown *'94*

Dorothy Lamour (1914-96)
Dixiana *'30*
High, Wide and Handsome *'37*
The Hurricane *'37*
Swing High, Swing Low *'37*
The Big Broadcast of 1938 *'38*
Her Jungle Love *'38*
Spawn of the North *'38*
Chad Hanna *'40*
Johnny Apollo *'40*
The Road to Singapore *'40*
Caught in the Draft *'41*
The Road to Zanzibar *'41*
Beyond the Blue Horizon *'42*
The Road to Morocco *'42*
Star Spangled Rhythm *'42*
They Got Me Covered *'43*
The Road to Utopia *'46*
My Favorite Brunette *'47*
The Road to Rio *'47*
Lulu Belle *'48*
On Our Merry Way *'48*
Slightly French *'49*
Here Comes the Groom *'51 (C)*
The Greatest Show on Earth *'52*
The Road to Bali *'53*
The Road to Hong Kong *'62*
Donovan's Reef *'63*
Pajama Party *'64*
The Love Goddesses *'65*
Creepshow 2 *'87*

Lisa Lampanelli (1961-)
Larry the Cable Guy: Health Inspector *'06*
Delta Farce *'07*

Jutta Lampe (1937-)
Sisters, Or the Balance of Happiness *'79*
Rosenstrasse *'03*

Zohra Lampert (1937-)
Splendor in the Grass *'61*
A Fine Madness *'66*
Bye Bye Braverman *'67*
Let's Scare Jessica to Death *'71*
Opening Night *'77*
Alphabet City *'84*
Teachers *'84*
Izzy & Moe *'85*
Stanley and Iris *'90*

Charles Lampkin (1913-89)
Five *'51*
Rider on a Dead Horse *'62*

Chus (Maria Jesus) Lampreave (1930-)
What Have I Done to Deserve This? *'85*
Matador *'86*
The Flower of My Secret *'95*
Volver *'06*
Chef's Special *'08*

Alexandra Lamy (1971-)
Ricky *'09*
Cinderella *'12 (V)*
Retour Chez Ma Mere *'16*

Katherine LaNasa (1966-)
The Campaign *'12*
The Frozen Ground *'13*
Jayne Mansfield's Car *'13*
The Squeeze *'15*

Sarah Lancashire (1964-)
Gentlemen's Relish *'01*
Oliver Twist *'07*
When Did You Last See Your Father? *'07*
Wuthering Heights *'09*
The Dresser *'15*

Ann Lancaster (1920-70)
Hot Millions *'68*
The Railway Children *'70*

Burt Lancaster (1913-94)
The Killers *'46*
Brute Force *'47*
Criss Cross *'48*
I Walk Alone *'48*
Sorry, Wrong Number *'48*
Rope of Sand *'49*
The Flame & the Arrow *'50*
Mister 880 *'50*
Jim Thorpe: All American *'51*
Vengeance Valley *'51*
Come Back, Little Sheba *'52*
Crimson Pirate *'52*
From Here to Eternity *'53*
His Majesty O'Keefe *'53*
South Sea Woman *'53*
Three Sailors and a Girl *'53*
Vera Cruz *'53*
Apache *'54*
The Kentuckian *'55*
The Rose Tattoo *'55*
The Rainmaker *'56*
Trapeze *'56*
Gunfight at the O.K. Corral *'57*
Sweet Smell of Success *'57*
Run Silent, Run Deep *'58*
Separate Tables *'58*
Elmer Gantry *'60*
The Unforgiven *'60*
Judgment at Nuremberg *'61*
The Young Savages *'61*
Birdman of Alcatraz *'62*
The Leopard *'63*
The List of Adrian Messenger *'63*
Seven Days in May *'64*
The Hallelujah Trail *'65*
The Train *'65*
The Professionals *'66*
The Scalphunters *'68*
The Swimmer *'68*
Castle Keep *'69*
The Gypsy Moths *'69*
Airport *'70*
Lawman *'71*
Valdez Is Coming *'71*
Ulzana's Raid *'72*
Executive Action *'73*
Scorpio *'73*
Conversation Piece *'75*
Buffalo Bill & the Indians *'76*
The Cassandra Crossing *'76*
Moses *'76*
1900 *'76*
Victory at Entebbe *'76*
The Island of Dr. Moreau *'77*
Go Tell the Spartans *'78*
Zulu Dawn *'79*
Atlantic City *'81*
The Skin *'81*
Local Hero *'83*
The Osterman Weekend *'83*
Barnum *'86*
Tough Guys *'86*
Rocket Gibraltar *'88*
Field of Dreams *'89*
The Jeweller's Shop *'90*
The Phantom of the Opera *'90*
Separate but Equal *'91*

James Lancaster
Gettysburg *'93*
Leprechaun 2 *'94*

Sarah Lancaster (1980-)
Smother *'08*
Oh Christmas Tree! *'13*
The Stray *'17*

Stuart Lancaster (1920-2000)
Faster, Pussycat! Kill! Kill! *'65*
Born Losers *'67*
Mantis in Lace *'68*
Beneath the Valley of the Ultra-Vixens *'79*

James Lance (1975-)
The Search for John Gissing *'01*
Mr. Right *'06*
Bronson *'09*
The Look of Love *'13*

Elsa Lanchester (1902-86)
The Private Life of Henry VIII *'33*
The Bride of Frankenstein *'35*
David Copperfield *'35*
Naughty Marietta *'35*
The Ghost Goes West *'36*
Rembrandt *'36*
Beachcomber *'38*
Ladies in Retirement *'41*
Son of Fury *'42*
Tales of Manhattan *'42*
Forever and a Day *'43*
Lassie, Come Home *'43*
The Razor's Edge *'46*
The Spiral Staircase *'46*
The Bishop's Wife *'47*
The Big Clock *'48*
Come to the Stable *'49*
The Inspector General *'49*
The Secret Garden *'49*
Buccaneer's Girl *'50*
Mystery Street *'50*
Androcles and the Lion *'52*
Hell's Half Acre *'54*
The Glass Slipper *'55*
Witness for the Prosecution *'57*
Bell, Book and Candle *'58*
Pajama Party *'64*
That Darn Cat *'65*
Blackbeard's Ghost *'67*
Easy Come, Easy Go *'67*
My Dog, the Thief *'69*
Murder by Death *'76*
Die Laughing *'80*

Micheline Lanctot (1947-)
The Apprenticeship of Duddy Kravitz *'74*
Good Neighbors *'10*

Addie Land (1988-)
Evergreen *'04*
The Sasquatch Gang *'06*

Geoffrey Land
Against a Crooked Sky *'75*
Black Heat *'76*
Hospital of Terror *'78*

Paul Land (1956-)
Idolmaker *'80*
Spring Break *'83*

David Landau (1878-1935)
Street Scene *'31*
False Faces *'32*
Horse Feathers *'32*
Lawyer Man *'32*
Polly of the Circus *'32*
The Purchase Price *'32*
Taxi! *'32*
Union Depot *'32*
Gabriel Over the White House *'33*
One Man's Journey *'33*
The Man with Two Faces *'34*

Juliet Landau (1965-)
Direct Hit *'93*
Ed Wood *'94*
Theodore Rex *'95*
Going Shopping *'05*
Hack! *'07*
Haunted Echoes *'08*
InSight *'11*
Dark Hearts *'12*

Martin Landau (1928-2017)
The Gazebo *'59*
North by Northwest *'59*
Pork Chop Hill *'59*
Cleopatra *'63*
The Hallelujah Trail *'65*
They Call Me Mr. Tibbs! *'70*
Black Gunn *'72*
A Town Called Hell *'72*
Destination Moonbase Alpha *'75*
Meteor *'79*
The Fall of the House of Usher *'80*
Without Warning *'80*
Alone in the Dark *'82*
The Being *'83*
Kung Fu: The Movie *'86*
Cyclone *'87*
Death Blow *'87*
Lethal Victims *'87*
Run If You Can *'87*
Sweet Revenge *'87*
Tucker: The Man and His Dream *'88*
By Dawn's Early Light *'89*
Crimes & Misdemeanors *'89*
Firehead *'90*
Mistress *'91*
Eye of the Stranger *'93*
Intersection *'93*
Sliver *'93*
12:01 *'93*
Ed Wood *'94*
City Hall *'95*
Joseph *'95*
The Adventures of Pinocchio *'96*
B.A.P.'s *'97*
Rounders *'98*
The X-Files *'98*
Bonanno: A Godfather's Story *'99*
EDtv *'99*
Sleepy Hollow *'99 (C)*
Ready to Rumble *'00*
Shiner *'00*
The Majestic *'01*
Hollywood Homicide *'03*
City of Ember *'08*
Lovely, Still *'08*
9 *'09 (V)*
Mitch Albom's Have a Little Faith *'11*
Mysteria *'11*
Frankenweenie *'12 (V)*
Anna Nicole *'13*
Outlaw Prophet: Warren Jeffs *'14*
Remember *'15*

Amy Landecker (1969-)
Project Almanac *'15*
Beatriz at Dinner *'17*
A Kid Like Jake *'18*

Dinsdale Landen (1932-2003)
Mosquito Squadron *'70*
Morons from Outer Space *'85*
Catherine Cookson's The Wingless Bird *'97*

David Lander (1947-)
The Tell-Tale Heart *'60*
Used Cars *'80*
The Man with One Red Shoe *'85*
Funland *'89*
A League of Their Own *'92*
Tom and Jerry: The Movie *'93 (V)*
Ava's Magical Adventure *'94*
The Modern Adventures of Tom Sawyer *'99*
Scary Movie *'00*

Audrey Landers (1959-)
A Chorus Line *'85*
Bachelor Party 2: The Last Temptation *'08*

Harry Landers (1921-)
The C-Man *'49*
Phantom from Space *'53*
Drive a Crooked Road *'54*
The Indian Fighter *'55*
The Gallant Hours *'60*

Judy Landers (1958-)
The Yum-Yum Girls *'78*
The Black Marble *'79*
Doin' Time *'85*
Armed and Dangerous *'86*
Dr. Alien *'88*
Club Fed *'90*
Expert Weapon *'93*

Michael Landes (1972-)
An American Summer *'90*
Dream for an Insomniac *'96*
Final Destination 2 *'03*
Last Chance Harvey *'08*
Possession *'08*
Homecoming *'09*
Just Wright *'10*
My Girlfriend's Boyfriend *'10*
11-11-11 *'11*

Steve Landesberg (1936-2010)
Mission of the Shark *'91*
Home for Christmas *'93*
The Crazysitter *'94*
The Souler Opposite *'97*
Forgetting Sarah Marshall *'08*

Janet Landgard
The Swimmer *'68*
Land Raiders *'69*

Sonny Landham (1941-)
Southern Comfort *'81*
48 Hrs. *'82*
Fleshburn *'84*
The Dirty Dozen: The Next Mission *'85*
Predator *'87*
Lock Up *'89*
Best of the Best 2 *'93*

Elissa Landi (1904-48)
The Sign of the Cross *'33*
The Count of Monte Cristo *'34*
After the Thin Man *'36*
Corregidor *'43*

Marla Landi (1933-)
Across the Bridge *'57*
First Man into Space *'59*
Pirates of Blood River *'62*

Sal Landi (1951-)
Savage Streets *'83*
Xtro 3: Watch the Skies *'95*
The Indian *'07*

D.W. Landingham
Omega Cop *'90*
Karate Cop *'91*

Carole Landis (1919-48)
One Million B.C. *'40*
Dance Hall *'41*
I Wake Up Screaming *'41*
Moon over Miami *'41*
Road Show *'41*
Topper Returns *'41*
My Gal Sal *'42*
Orchestra Wives *'42*
Wintertime *'43*
Four Jills in a Jeep *'44*
It Shouldn't Happen to a Dog *'46*
A Scandal in Paris *'46*
Out of the Blue *'47*

Cullen Landis (1895-1975)
Soul of the Beast *'23*
Pampered Youth *'25*

Forrest Landis (1994-)
Cheaper by the Dozen *'03*
Benji: Off the Leash! *'04*
Cheaper by the Dozen 2 *'05*
Spy School *'08*

Jessie Royce Landis (1904-72)
Mother Didn't Tell Me *'50*
To Catch a Thief *'55*
The Girl He Left Behind *'56*
The Swan *'56*
My Man Godfrey *'57*
North by Northwest *'59*
Bon Voyage! *'62*
Boys' Night Out *'62*
Critic's Choice *'63*
Gidget Goes to Rome *'63*
Airport *'70*

John Landis (1950-)
Battle for the Planet of the Apes *'73*
Schlock *'73*
Death Race 2000 *'75*
The Blues Brothers *'80 (C)*
The Muppets Take Manhattan *'84 (C)*
Spontaneous Combustion *'89*
Darkman *'90*
Body Chemistry 2: Voice of a Stranger *'91*
Sleepwalkers *'92*
Venice, Venice *'92*
Diamonds *'99*
Freeway 2: Confessions of a Trickbaby *'99*
The Scenesters *'09*

Margaret Landis (1891-1981)
Amarilly of Clothesline Alley *'18*
The Confession *'20*

Monte Landis (1933-)
The Mouse That Roared *'59*
Targets *'68*
Candy Stripe Nurses *'74*
Young Frankenstein *'74*
Yellowbeard *'83*

Nina Landis
Rikky and Pete *'88*
Komodo *'99*

Joe Lando (1961-)
Alien Nation: The Enemy Within *'96*
No Code of Conduct *'98*
Counterstrike *'03*
Shockwave *'06*
Meteor Apocalypse *'10*

Hal Landon, Jr. (1941-)
Eraserhead *'78*
Bill & Ted's Bogus Journey *'91*

Laurene Landon (1957-)
I, the Jury *'82*
It's Alive 3: Island of the Alive *'87*
Maniac Cop *'88*
Wicked Stepmother *'89*
The Ambulance *'90*
Maniac Cop 2 *'90*

Michael Landon (1936-91)
God's Little Acre *'58*
High School Confidential *'58*
The Errand Boy *'61*
Little House on the Prairie *'74*

Avice Landone (1910-76)
An Alligator Named Daisy *'55*
Carve Her Name with Pride *'58*

Ali Landry (1973-)
Outta Time *'01*
Repli-Kate *'01*
Bella *'06*

Karen Landry
The Personals *'83*
Heartbreak Hotel *'88*
Roadracers *'94*

Margaret Landry (1922-2005)
Gildersleeve on Broadway *'43*
The Leopard Man *'43*

Mike Landry
The Last International Playboy *'08*
Rosencrantz & Guildenstern Are Undead *'10*

Tamara Landry (1962-)
Bikini House Calls *'96*
Bikini Med School *'98*

Valerie Landsburg (1958-)
Thank God It's Friday *'78*
The Triangle Factory Fire Scandal *'79*

Abbe Lane (1932-)
Ride Clear of Diablo *'54*
Americano *'55*
Twilight Zone: The Movie *'83*

Allan 'Rocky' Lane (1904-73)
Night Nurse *'31*
Charlie Chan at the Olympics *'37*
Trail of Robin Hood *'50*

Charles Lane (1869-1945)
Dr. Jekyll and Mr. Hyde *'20*
The White Sister *'23*
Romola *'25*
The Winning of Barbara Worth *'26*
Sadie Thompson *'28*

Charles Lane (1905-2007)
Twentieth Century *'34*
Mr. Smith Goes to Washington *'39*
The Invisible Woman *'40*
Rhythm on the River *'40*
I Wake Up Screaming *'41*
Call Northside 777 *'48*
Borderline *'50*
The Affairs of Dobie Gillis *'53*
The Juggler *'53*
Teacher's Pet *'58*
The Mating Game *'59*
Papa's Delicate Condition *'63*
Good Neighbor Sam *'64*
Billie *'65*
Little Dragons *'80*
Strange Behavior *'81*
Strange Invaders *'83*
Sunset Limousine *'83*
The Winds of War *'83*
Murphy's Romance *'85*
Date with an Angel *'87*
War & Remembrance *'88*

Colin Lane
Broken Harvest *'94*
The Blood Oranges *'97*

Diane Lane (1965-)
A Little Romance *'79*
Child Bride of Short Creek *'81*
National Lampoon Goes to the Movies *'81*
Ladies and Gentlemen, the Fabulous Stains *'82*
Miss All-American Beauty *'82*
Six Pack *'82*
The Outsiders *'83*
Rumble Fish *'83*
The Cotton Club *'84*
Streets of Fire *'84*
Big Town *'87*
Lonesome Dove *'89*
Descending Angel *'90*
Vital Signs *'90*
Chaplin *'92*
My New Gun *'92*
Indian Summer *'93*
Knight Moves *'93*
Judge Dredd *'95*
Oldest Confederate Widow Tells All *'95*
A Streetcar Named Desire *'95*
Wild Bill *'95*
Jack *'96*
Trigger Happy *'96*
Murder at 1600 *'97*
The Only Thrill *'97*
Gunshy *'98*
My Dog Skip *'99*
The Virginian *'99*
A Walk on the Moon *'99*
The Perfect Storm *'00*
The Glass House *'01*
Hardball *'01*
Unfaithful *'02*
Under the Tuscan Sun *'03*
Fierce People *'05*
Must Love Dogs *'05*
Hollywoodland *'06*
Jumper *'08*
Nights in Rodanthe *'08*
Untraceable *'08*
Killshot *'09*
Secretariat *'10*

Cinema Verite *'11*
Man of Steel *'13*
Every Secret Thing *'15*
Trumbo *'15*
Batman v Superman: Dawn of Justice *'16*
Mark Felt: The Man Who Brought Down the White House *'17*
Paris Can Wait *'17*
Serenity *'19*

Frederic Lane (1959-)
See Frederic Lehne

Lenita Lane (1901-95)
The Mad Magician *'54*
The Bat *'59*

Lola Lane (1909-81)
Murder On a Honeymoon *'35*
Death from a Distance *'36*
Hollywood Hotel *'37*
Marked Woman *'37*
Four Daughters *'38*
Daughters Courageous *'39*
Four Wives *'39*
Four Mothers *'41*
Buckskin Frontier *'43*
Deadline at Dawn *'46*

Lupino Lane (1892-1959)
The Love Parade *'29*
Golden Dawn *'30*

Mike Lane (1933-)
The Harder They Fall *'56*
Ulysses Against the Son of Hercules *'61*
A Name for Evil *'70*
Zebra Force *'76*
Code Name: Zebra *'84*
Cold War Killers *'86*

Nathan Lane (1956-)
Ironweed *'87*
Joe Versus the Volcano *'90*
Frankie and Johnny *'91*
He Said, She Said *'91*
Life with Mikey *'93*
The Lion King *'94 (V)*
The Birdcage *'95*
Jeffrey *'95*
The Boys Next Door *'96*
Mouse Hunt *'97*
At First Sight *'98*
The Lion King: Simba's Pride *'98 (V)*
Stuart Little *'99 (V)*
Isn't She Great *'00*
Love's Labour's Lost *'00*
Titan A.E. *'00 (V)*
Trixie *'00*
Austin Powers In Goldmember *'02*
Nicholas Nickleby *'02*
Stuart Little 2 *'02 (V)*
Disney's Teacher's Pet *'04 (V)*
The Lion King 1 1/2 *'04 (V)*
Win a Date with Tad Hamilton! *'04*
The Producers *'05*
Swing Vote *'08*
Astro Boy *'09 (V)*
Mirror Mirror *'12*
The English Teacher *'13*
Carrie Pilby *'17*
The Vanishing of Sidney Hall *'17*

Nora Lane (1905-48)
Sally *'29*
Borderland *'37*
The Gentleman from Arizona *'39*

Priscilla Lane (1917-95)
Varsity Show *'37*
Brother Rat *'38*
Cowboy from Brooklyn *'38*
Four Daughters *'38*
Daughters Courageous *'39*
Dust Be My Destiny *'39*
Four Wives *'39*
The Roaring Twenties *'39*
Brother Rat and a Baby *'40*
Blues in the Night *'41*
Four Mothers *'41*
Saboteur *'42*

Silver Queen *'42*
Arsenic and Old Lace *'44*

Richard Lane (1899-1982)
Mr. Moto in Danger Island *'39*
Stronger Than Desire *'39*
Two Girls on Broadway *'40*
Sunny *'41*
Time Out for Rhythm *'41*
Arabian Nights *'42*
Junior G-Men of the Air *'42*
Ride 'Em Cowboy *'42*
Air Force *'43*
Mr. Winkle Goes to War *'44*
Sioux City Sue *'46*
Take Me Out to the Ball Game *'49*
The Jackie Robinson Story *'50*

Rosemary Lane (1914-74)
Hollywood Hotel *'37*
Varsity Show *'37*
Four Daughters *'38*
Gold Diggers in Paris *'38*
Blackwell's Island *'39*
Daughters Courageous *'39*
Four Wives *'39*
Oklahoma Kid *'39*
The Boys From Syracuse *'40*
Four Mothers *'41*
Time Out for Rhythm *'41*

Sara Malakul Lane (1982-)
Belly of the Beast *'03*
Sharktopus *'10*
12/12/12 *'12*
Cowboys vs Dinosaurs *'15*
Scout's Guide to the Zombie Apocalypse *'15*
Sun Choke *'16*

Sasha Lane (1995-)
American Honey *'16*
Hearts Beat Loud *'18*

Sirpa Lane (1952-99)
The Beast *'75*
The Beast in Space *'80*

Eric Laneuville (1952-)
Omega Man *'71*
Love at First Bite *'79*
Fear of a Black Hat *'94*

Doreen Lang (1918-99)
Missiles of October *'74*
Almost an Angel *'90*

Harold Lang (1923-70)
Cloudburst *'51*
Blackout *'54*

Judith Lang
The Trip *'67*
Count Yorga, Vampire *'70*

June Lang (1917-2005)
Bonnie Scotland *'35*
Captain January *'36*
The Road to Glory *'36*
Nancy Steele Is Missing *'37*
Wee Willie Winkie *'37*
International Settlement *'38*

k.d. lang (1961-)
Salmonberries *'91*
The Last Don *'97*
Eye of the Beholder *'99*

Matthew Lang
The Rules of Attraction *'02*
We Were Soldiers *'02*

Perry Lang (1959-)
Zuma Beach *'78*
Alligator *'80*
The Big Red One *'80*
Body & Soul *'81*
O'Hara's Wife *'82*
Spring Break *'83*
Jocks *'87*
Eight Men Out *'88*
Mortuary Academy *'91*
Sunshine State *'02*

Robert Lang (1934-2004)
Cider with Rosie *'99*
Mrs. Palfrey at the Claremont *'05*

Stephen Lang (1952-)
Band of the Hand *'86*
Death of a Salesman *'86*

Manhunter '86
Project X '87
Last Exit to Brooklyn '90
Another You '91
The Hard Way '91
Gettysburg '93
Guilty as Sin '93
Tombstone '93
The Amazing Panda Adventure '95
Tall Tale: The Unbelievable Adventures of Pecos Bill '95
Gang in Blue '96
An Occasional Hell '96
The Shadow Conspiracy '96
Fire Down Below '97
Niagara, Niagara '97
Escape: Human Cargo '98
A Town Has Turned to Dust '98
The Proposal '00
Trixie '00
After the Storm '01
Eye See You '01
Gods and Generals '03
The I Inside '04
The Treatment '06
Save Me '07
Avatar '09
From Mexico With Love '09
The Men Who Stare at Goats '09
Christina '10
White Irish Drinkers '10
Conan the Barbarian '11
The Girl On the Train '13
In the Blood '13
Officer Down '13
Pawn '13
Pioneer '13
A Good Marriage '14
Gutshot Straight '14
Jarhead 2: Field of Fire '14
The Nut Job '14 (V)
Beyond Valkyrie: Dawn of the Fourth Reich '16
Don't Breathe '16

Glenn Langan (1917-91)
Something for the Boys '44
Hangover Square '45
Dragonwyck '46
The Snake Pit '48
Treasure of Monte Cristo '50
Hangman's Knot '52
One Girl's Confession '53

Harry Langdon (1884-1944)
Strong Man '26
Tramp, Tramp, Tramp '26
Mad About Money '37

Libby Langdon (1954-)
Federal Hill '94
A Shot at Glory '00
Corn '04

Lillian Langdon (1884-1944)
Daddy Long Legs '19
His Majesty, the American '19

Sue Ane Langdon (1936-)
Roustabout '64
Frankie and Johnny '65
The Rounders '65
When the Boys Meet the Girls '65
A Fine Madness '66
Hold On! '66
A Guide for the Married Man '67
The Cheyenne Social Club '70
Without Warning '80
Zapped! '82

Allison Lange (1978-)
Christina's House '99
Out of the Black '01
The Hillside Stranglings '04
Single White Female 2: The Psycho '05
Alone in the Dark 2 '08

Artie Lange (1967-)
Dirty Work '97
The Bachelor '99
The 4th Floor '99
Lost and Found '99
Boat Trip '03
Old School '03
Beer League '06
Waltzing Anna '06

Carl Lange (1909-99)
Again, the Ringer '64
The Torture Chamber of Dr. Sadism '69
Creature with the Blue Hand '70

Hope Lange (1931-2003)
Bus Stop '56
Peyton Place '57
The True Story of Jesse James '57
In Love and War '58
The Young Lions '58
The Best of Everything '59
Pocketful of Miracles '61
Wild in the Country '61
Love Is a Ball '63
The Love Bug '68
Death Wish '74
Fer-De-Lance '74
Beulah Land '80
I Am the Cheese '83
A Nightmare on Elm Street 2: Freddy's Revenge '85
Blue Velvet '86
Ford: The Man & the Machine '87
Tune in Tomorrow '90

Jessica Lange (1949-)
King Kong '76
All That Jazz '79
How to Beat the High Cost of Living '80
The Postman Always Rings Twice '81
Frances '82
Tootsie '82
Cat on a Hot Tin Roof '84
Country '84
Sweet Dreams '85
Crimes of the Heart '86
Everybody's All American '88
Far North '88
Men Don't Leave '89
Music Box '89
Blue Sky '91
Cape Fear '91
O Pioneers! '91
Night and the City '92
Losing Isaiah '94
Rob Roy '95
A Streetcar Named Desire '95
Cousin Bette '97
A Thousand Acres '97
Hush '98
Titus '99
Prozac Nation '01
Big Fish '03
Masked and Anonymous '03
Normal '03
Broken Flowers '05
Don't Come Knocking '05
Bonneville '06
Grey Gardens '09
The Vow '12
In Secret '13
The Gambler '14
Wild Oats '16

Jack Langedijk (1956-)
Evil Judgment '85
Blind Fear '89
Dead End '98
The Pact '99
Left Behind: The Movie '00
One Way Out '02

Frank Langella (1938-)
The Twelve Chairs '70
The Wrath of God '72
The Seagull '75
Dracula '79
Those Lips, Those Eyes '80
Sphinx '81
The Men's Club '86
Masters of the Universe '87
And God Created Woman '88
Body of Evidence '92
1492: Conquest of Paradise '92
Dave '93
Bad Company '94
Brainscan '94
Doomsday Gun '94
Junior '94
Cutthroat Island '95
Eddie '96
Moses '96
Lolita '97
I'm Losing You '98
Small Soldiers '98 (V)
The Ninth Gate '99
Innocents '00 (C)
Jason and the Argonauts '00
Stardom '00
Sweet November '01
House of D '04
Back in the Day '05
Good Night, and Good Luck '05
How You Look to Me '05
Superman Returns '06
Starting Out in the Evening '07
The Caller '08
Frost/Nixon '08
The Tale of Despereaux '08 (V)
The Box '09
All Good Things '10
Wall Street 2: Money Never Sleeps '10
Unknown '11
Robot & Frank '12
The Time Being '12
Muhammad Ali's Greatest Fight '13
Draft Day '14
Grace of Monaco '14
Parts Per Billion '14
Captain Fantastic '16
The Driftless Area '16

Heather Langenkamp (1964-)
A Nightmare on Elm Street '84
A Nightmare on Elm Street 3: Dream Warriors '87
Shocker '89
Wes Craven's New Nightmare '94
The Demolitionist '95
Fugitive Mind '99

A.J. (Allison Joy) Langer (1974-)
The People under the Stairs '91
The Ghost Brigade '93
Escape from L.A. '96
Meet the Deedles '98
On Edge '03

Frances Langford (1913-2005)
Born to Dance '36
Hit Parade of 1937 '37
Dreaming Out Loud '40
Too Many Girls '40
Yankee Doodle Dandy '42
Career Girl '44
Dixie Jamboree '44
Radio Stars on Parade '45
The Bamboo Blonde '46
Melody Time '48 (V)
Deputy Marshal '50

Chris Langham (1949-)
The Big Tease '99
Black Pond '11

Wallace (Wally) Langham (1965-)
Children of the Night '85
The Chocolate War '88
God's Lonely Man '96
On Edge '03
I Want Someone to Eat Cheese With '06
Little Miss Sunshine '06
The Great Buck Howard '09
The Social Network '10
Somewhere Slow '14

Amanda Langlet (1967-)
Pauline at the Beach '83
A Summer's Tale '96
Triple Agent '04

Lisa Langlois (1959-)
Class of 1984 '82
The Man Who Wasn't There '83
Truth or Die '86
The Nest '88

Margaret Langrick (1971-)
My American Cousin '85
Harry and the Hendersons '87

Caroline Langrishe (1958-)
Eagle's Wing '79
Sharpe's Regiment '96
Sharpe's Justice '97
Parting Shots '98
Rogue Trader '98
Cleopatra '99

Murray Langston
Night Patrol '85
Wishful Thinking '92

Brooke Langton (1970-)
Swingers '96
Playing Mona Lisa '00
The Replacements '00
The Benchwarmers '06
Primeval '07

David Langton (1912-94)
Quintet '79
The Whistle Blower '87

Jeff Langton
Final Impact '91
Maximum Force '92

Paul Langton (1913-80)
Thirty Seconds Over Tokyo '44
They Were Expendable '45
For You I Die '47
The Snow Creature '54
The Big Knife '55
Murder Is My Beat '55
To Hell and Back '55
Chicago Confidential '57
The Incredible Shrinking Man '57
It! The Terror from Beyond Space '58
The Cosmic Man '59

Nicholas Lanier (1974-)
Witchouse 2: Blood Coven '00
Hit Parade '10

Guy Lankester
Tower of the Firstborn '98
Pandaemonium '00

Kim Lankford (1955-)
Malibu Beach '78
Octagon '80
Terror Among Us '81
Cameron's Closet '89
Street Corner Justice '96

Bouli Lanners (1965-)
Special Treatment '10
Rust and Bone '12

George Lannes (1895-1983)
Moulin Rouge '52
Operation Abduction '58

Les Lannom (1946-)
Centennial '78
Stingray '78
Southern Comfort '81

Jenya Lano
Deathlands: Homeward Bound '03
Stealing Candy '04
Ten 'Til Noon '06

Victor Lanoux (1936-)
Cousin, Cousine '76
Dog Day '83
National Lampoon's European Vacation '85
Scene of the Crime '87

Angela Lansbury (1925-)
If Winter Comes '41
Gaslight '44
National Velvet '44
Picture of Dorian Gray '45
The Harvey Girls '46
The Private Affairs of Bel Ami '47
Tenth Avenue Angel '47
State of the Union '48
The Three Musketeers '48
Samson and Delilah '49
The Red Danube '50
Mutiny '52
A Lawless Street '55
The Court Jester '56
The Long, Hot Summer '58
The Reluctant Debutante '58
Breath of Scandal '60
All Fall Down '62
Blue Hawaii '62
The Manchurian Candidate '62
In the Cool of the Day '63
Dear Heart '64
The World of Henry Orient '64
The Amorous Adventures of Moll Flanders '65
The Greatest Story Ever Told '65
Harlow '65
Mister Buddwing '66
Bedknobs and Broomsticks '71
Death on the Nile '78
The Lady Vanishes '79
The Mirror Crack'd '80
The Last Unicorn '82 (V)
The Pirates of Penzance '83
The First Olympics: Athens 1896 '84
Lace '84
Sweeney Todd: The Demon Barber of Fleet Street '84
The Company of Wolves '85
The Shell Seekers '89
Beauty and the Beast '91 (V)
Mrs. Santa Claus '96
Anastasia '97 (V)
Nanny McPhee '06
Mr. Popper's Penguins '11
The Grinch '18 (V)

David Lansbury (1961-)
Gas Food Lodging '92
Truman '95
A Stranger in the Kingdom '98
Cupid & Cate '00
From Other Worlds '04
Valley Inn '14

Joi Lansing (1928-72)
Easter Parade '48
Julia Misbehaves '48
Neptune's Daughter '49
Two Tickets to Broadway '51
Singin' in the Rain '52
The Brave One '56
Hot Cars '56
Touch of Evil '58 (C)
Atomic Submarine '59
A Hole in the Head '59
Hillbillies in a Haunted House '67
Bigfoot '70

Robert Lansing (1929-94)
The 4D Man '59
Under the Yum-Yum Tree '63
Namu, the Killer Whale '66
The Grissom Gang '71
Killer by Night '72
Empire of the Ants '77
Acapulco Gold '78
The Nest '88

Matt Lanter (1983-)
The Cutting Edge 3: Chasing the Dream '08
Disaster Movie '08
Star Wars: The Clone Wars '08 (V)
WarGames: The Dead Code '08
Vampires Suck '10
The Roommate '11
USS Indianapolis: Men of Courage '16

Virginia Lantry
Ain't No Way Back '89
No Way Back '90

Gerard Lanvin (1950-)
The Taste of Others '00
Mesrine: Part 2-Public Enemy Number 1 '08
Point Blank '10

Mario Lanza (1921-59)
That Midnight Kiss '49
The Toast of New Orleans '50
The Great Caruso '51
Because You're Mine '52
Serenade '56
The Seven Hills of Rome '58

Fabio Lanzoni (1961-)
See Fabio

Anthony LaPaglia (1959-)
Nitti: The Enforcer '88
Slaves of New York '89
Betsy's Wedding '90
He Said, She Said '91
One Good Cop '91
29th Street '91
Innocent Blood '92
Whispers in the Dark '92
So I Married an Axe Murderer '93
The Client '94
Mixed Nuts '94
Bulletproof Heart '95
Empire Records '95
Commandments '96
Paperback Romance '96
Tree's Lounge '96
Phoenix '98
Lansky '99
Summer of Sam '99
Sweet and Lowdown '99
Autumn in New York '00
Company Man '00
House of Mirth '00
The Bank '01
Dead Heat '01
Lantana '01
The Guys '02
I'm with Lucy '02
The Salton Sea '02
Happy Hour '03
Winter Solstice '04
The Architect '06
Happy Feet '06 (V)
Played '06
$9.99 '08 (V)
Legend of the Guardians: The Owls of Ga'Hoole '10 (V)
Crazy Kind of Love '12
Underground: The Julian Assange Story '12
A Good Marriage '14
Annabelle: Creation '17
The Assignment '17

Jonathan LaPaglia (1969-)
Under Hellgate Bridge '99
Plain Truth '04
Attack of the Gryphon '07
A Beautiful Life '08
The Hit List '11
Pioneer '13
The Reckoning '14

Daniel Lapaine (1971-)
Muriel's Wedding '94
Polish Wedding '97
Dangerous Beauty '98
1999 '98
Brokedown Palace '99
The 10th Kingdom '00
Tales from the Crypt Presents Ritual '02
Shanghai '09

Andrzej Lapicki (1924-)
Everything for Sale '68
The Deluge '73

Peter Lapis
Death Blow '87
Undeclared War '91

Jane Lapotaire (1944-)
Crescendo '69
The Asphyx '72
Eureka! '81
Surviving Picasso '96
Shooting Fish '98

Alexandra Maria Lara (1978-)
The Tunnel *'01*
Doctor Zhivago *'03*
The Company *'07*
Control *'07*
I Really Hate My Job *'07*
Youth Without Youth *'07*
The Reader *'08*
The City of Your Final Destination *'09*
Farewell *'09*
Rush *'13*
Geostorm *'17*

Joe Lara (1962-)
American Cyborg: Steel Warrior *'94*
Steel Frontier *'94*
Hologram Man *'95*
Live Wire: Human Timebomb *'95*
Warhead *'96*
Doomsdayer *'00*

Farid Larbi
Of Gods and Men *'10*
Free Men *'12*

John Larch (1914-2005)
The Phenix City Story *'55*
The Killer Is Loose *'56*
Man from Del Rio *'56*
7 Men From Now *'56*
The Careless Years *'57*
Man in the Shadow *'57*
Quantez *'57*
The Wrecking Crew *'68*
Cannon for Cordoba *'70*
Dirty Harry *'71*
Play Misty for Me *'71*
Santee *'73*
Bad Ronald *'74*
Winter Kill *'74*
The Amityville Horror *'79*

Vincent Laresca (1974-)
Juice *'92*
Money Train *'95*
Music from Another Room *'97*
Ripe *'97*
Forever Mine *'99*
Just One Time *'00*
Hard Cash *'01*
Empire *'02*
The Aviator *'04*
El Cantante *'06*
The Fast and the Furious: Tokyo Drift *'06*
.45 *'06*
Unthinkable *'10*

Corey Large (1975-)
Window Theory *'04*
Chasing Ghosts *'05*
Toxic *'07*
Loaded *'08*
The Penthouse *'10*

Jordana Largy
Takedown *'10*
Rememory *'17*

Sheila Larken (1944-)
Cave-In! *'79*
Behind the Mask *'99*

Bryan Larkin (1973-)
Born on the Fourth of July *'89*
She-Devil *'89*
Outpost: Rise of the Spetsnaz *'13*

Chris Larkin (1967-)
Angels and Insects *'95*
Shackleton *'02*
Hitler: The Rise of Evil *'03*
Master and Commander: The Far Side of the World *'03*
Friends & Crocodiles *'05*
Mysterious Island *'05*

Linda Larkin (1970-)
Aladdin *'92 (V)*
The Return of Jafar *'94 (V)*
Aladdin and the King of Thieves *'96 (V)*

Ben Larned (1994-)
Tattoo, a Love Story *'02*
The Five *'10*

Mary Laroche (1920-99)
The Lineup *'58*
Run Silent, Run Deep *'58*
Gidget *'59*
Psychomania *'73*

Michele Laroque (1960-)
Nelly et Monsieur Arnaud *'95*
Ma Vie en Rose *'97*
The Closet *'00*
The Neighbor *'07*

Scott LaRose
Booty Call *'96*
Comic Book: The Movie *'04*

Pierre Larquey (1884-1962)
The Murderer Lives at Number 21 *'42*
Le Corbeau *'43*

Tito Larriva (1953-)
True Stories *'86*
Just a Little Harmless Sex *'99*
Machete *'10*

John Larroquette (1947-)
The Texas Chainsaw Massacre *'74 (N)*
Altered States *'80*
Heart Beat *'80*
Green Ice *'81*
Stripes *'81*
Cat People *'82*
Twilight Zone: The Movie *'83*
Choose Me *'84*
Meatballs 2 *'84*
Star Trek 3: The Search for Spock *'84*
Summer Rental *'85*
Blind Date *'87*
Second Sight *'89*
Tune in Tomorrow *'90*
Richie Rich *'94*
Isn't She Great *'00*
The 10th Kingdom *'00*
Walter and Henry *'01*
Beethoven's 5th *'03*
Recipe for Disaster *'03*
The Texas Chainsaw Massacre *'03 (N)*
Kill Your Darlings *'06*
Southland Tales *'06*
The Storm *'09*

Larry the Cable Guy (1963-)
Cars *'06*
Larry the Cable Guy: Health Inspector *'06*
Delta Farce *'07*
Witless Protection *'08*
Cars 2 *'11 (V)*
Tooth Fairy 2 *'12*
Tyler Perry's A Madea Christmas *'13*
Jingle All the Way 2 *'14*
Cars 3 *'17 (V)*

Ham Larsen
Further Adventures of the Wilderness Family, Part 2 *'77*
Mountain Family Robinson *'79*

Keith Larsen (1924-2006)
Flat Top *'52*
Hiawatha *'52*
Fort Vengeance *'53*
War Paint *'53*

Thomas Bo Larsen (1963-)
The Celebration *'98*
The Hunt *'13*

Bobby Larson (1930-2002)
Leather Burners *'43*
The Underdog *'43*

Brie Larson (1989-)
Sleepover *'04*
Hoot *'06*
Housebroken *'09*
Just Peck *'09*
Tanner Hall *'09*
Greenberg *'10*
Scott Pilgrim *vs.* the World *'10*
Rampart *'11*
The Trouble With Bliss *'11*
21 Jump Street *'12*
Short Term 12 *'13*
The Spectacular Now *'13*
The Gambler *'14*
Room *'15*
Trainwreck *'15*
Free Fire *'17*
The Glass Castle *'17*
Kong: Skull Island *'17*
Captain Marvel *'19*
Just Mercy *'19*

Darrell Larson (1950-)
The Student Nurses *'70*
Mike's Murder *'84*
City Limits *'85*
Hero *'92*
Stuart Saves His Family *'94*
Shadrach *'98*
Stepmom *'98*

Jack Larson
Battle Zone *'52*
Superman Returns *'06*

Wolf Larson (1959-)
Expect No Mercy *'95*
The Heist *'96*
Storm Chasers: Revenge of the Twister *'98*
Crash & Byrnes *'99*
Shakedown *'02*

Ali Larter (1976-)
Varsity Blues *'98*
Drive Me Crazy *'99*
Giving It Up *'99*
House on Haunted Hill *'99*
Final Destination *'00*
American Outlaws *'01*
Jay and Silent Bob Strike Back *'01*
Legally Blonde *'01*
Final Destination 2 *'03*
3-Way *'04*
A Lot Like Love *'05*
Confess *'05*
Marigold *'07*
National Lampoon's The Stoned Aged *'07*
Resident Evil: Extinction *'07*
Crazy *'08*
Obsessed *'09*
Resident Evil: Afterlife *'10*
Lovesick *'14*
Resident Evil: The Final Chapter *'16*

Eva LaRue (1966-)
Crash and Burn *'90*
Cries in the Dark *'06*
Lakeview Terrace *'08*

Frank LaRue (1878-1960)
Sidewalks of New York *'31*
Forbidden Trail *'32*

Jack LaRue (1902-84)
Virtue *'32*
Charlie Chan in Panama *'40*
Gangs, Inc. *'41*
Ringside Maisie *'41*
No Orchids for Miss Blandish *'48*

Lash LaRue (1917-96)
Master Key *'44*
Son of Billy the Kid *'49*
Alien Outlaw *'85*
The Dark Power *'85*

Robert LaSardo (1963-)
Waterworld *'95*
Gang Related *'96*
Tiger Heart *'96*
Under Oath *'97*
Running Woman *'98*
Mercy Streets *'00*
Latin Dragon *'03*
Dirty *'05*
Never Down *'06*
Autopsy *'08*
Death Race *'08*
Caged Animal *'10*
Tomorrow You're Gone *'12*
The Human Centipede 3: The Final Sequence *'15*

Dieter Laser (1942-2020)
The Lost Honor of Katharina Blum *'75*
The Human Centipede: First Sequence *'10*

Nick Lashaway
Humble Pie *'07*
My Soul to Take *'10*

Harris Laskawy
Necessity *'88*
Murder C.O.D. *'90*

Michael Laskin (1951-)
The Personals *'83*
Eight Men Out *'88*
Passion Fish *'92*
Limbo *'99*
Bounce *'00*

Kathleen Lasky
Lethal Lolita-Amy Fisher: My Story *'92*
Getting Gotti *'94*

Tommy Lasorda (1927-)
Americathon *'79 (C)*
Ladybugs *'92*
Homeward Bound 2: Lost in San Francisco *'96 (V)*

Dagmar Lassander (1943-)
Hatchet for the Honeymoon *'70*
The Frightened Woman *'71*
The Black Cat *'81*

Louise Lasser (1939-)
Take the Money and Run *'69*
Bananas *'71*
Such Good Friends *'71*
Everything You Always Wanted to Know about Sex (But Were Afraid to Ask) *'72*
Slither *'73*
Blood Rage *'87*
Frankenhooker *'90*
Modern Love *'90*
Sudden Manhattan *'96*
Happiness *'98*
Mystery Men *'99*
Requiem for a Dream *'00*
National Lampoon's Gold Diggers *'04*

Sarah Lassez
Roosters *'95*
The Blackout *'97*
In Pursuit *'00*
Mad Cowgirl *'06*

Rolf Lassgard (1955-)
The White Lioness *'96*
Under the Sun *'98*
Gossip *'00*
After the Wedding *'06*
A Man Called Ove *'15*
Downsizing *'17*

Sydney Lassick (1922-2003)
Carrie *'76*
The Billion Dollar Hobo *'78*
Alligator *'80*
Night Patrol *'85*
Curse 2: The Bite *'88*
Tale of Two Sisters *'89*
The Art of Dying *'90*
Committed *'91*
Cool As Ice *'91*
Deep Cover *'92*
Shakes the Clown *'92*
Freeway *'95*
American Vampire *'97*

Hana Laszlo (1953-)
Free Zone *'05*
Adam Resurrected *'08*

Lyle Latell (1904-67)
Men On Her Mind *'44*
Dick Tracy Meets Gruesome *'47*

Dick Latessa (1929-)
Izzy & Moe *'85*
Stigmata *'99*
The Event *'03*
Alfie *'04*
The Great New Wonderful *'06*
The Last New Yorker *'07*

Anne Latham
Mind Warp *'72*
Thieves Like Us *'74*

Louise Latham (1922-)
Marnie *'64*
Adam at 6 a.m. *'70*
Dying Room Only *'73*
White Lightning *'73*
The Awakening Land *'78*
Backstairs at the White House *'79*
Lois Gibbs and the Love Canal *'82*
Mass Appeal *'84*
Crazy from the Heart *'91*
Love Field *'91*
Paradise *'91*
In Cold Blood *'96*

Philip Latham (1929-)
The Devil-Ship Pirates *'64*
Dracula, Prince of Darkness *'66*

Sanaa Lathan (1971-)
Blade *'98*
The Best Man *'99*
The Wood *'99*
Catfish in Black Bean Sauce *'00*
Disappearing Acts *'00*
Love and Basketball *'00*
Brown Sugar *'02*
Out of Time *'03*
Alien *vs.* Predator *'04*
Something New *'06*
The Family That Preys *'08*
A Raisin in the Sun *'08*
Powder Blue *'09*
Wonderful World *'09*
Contagion *'11*
The Best Man Holiday *'13*
Repentance *'14*
The Perfect Guy *'15*
Approaching the Unknown *'16*
American Assassin *'17*

Louise Latimer (1913-73)
Murder On a Bridle Path *'36*
The Plot Thickens *'36*

Frank Latimore (1925-98)
In the Meantime, Darling *'44*
The Dolly Sisters *'46*
The Razor's Edge *'46*
Shock! *'46*
13 Rue Madeleine *'46*
Three Little Girls In Blue *'46*
The Sergeant *'68*
Patton *'70*

Jacob Latimore (1996-)
Vanishing on 7th Street *'10*
Black Nativity *'13*
Sleight *'17*
Like a Boss *'20*

Matt Lattanzi (1959-)
Rich and Famous *'81*
My Tutor *'82*
Roxanne *'87*

Andy Lau (1961-)
As Tears Go By *'88*
Days of Being Wild *'91*
The Legend of Drunken Master *'94*
Running out of Time *'99*
Full Time Killer *'01*
Infernal Affairs *'02*
Infernal Affairs 3 *'03*
Running on Karma *'03*
House of Flying Daggers *'04*
Battle of the Warriors *'06*
Three Kingdoms: Resurrection of the Dragon *'08*
Warlords *'08*
What Women Want *'10*
A Simple Life *'11*
The Great Wall *'17*

Carina Lau (1965-)
Project A: Part 2 *'87*
Days of Being Wild *'91*
Ashes of Time *'94*
Infernal Affairs 2 *'03*
Infernal Affairs 3 *'03*
2046 *'04*
Ashes of Time Redux *'08*

Ching-Wan Lau (1964-)
Running Out of Time 2 *'06*
The Great Magician *'11*
The White Storm *'13*
Call of Heroes *'16*

Damian Lau (1949-)
Last Hurrah for Chivalry *'78*
Duel to the Death *'82*
The Heroic Trio *'93*
Jet Li's The Enforcer *'95*
Three Kingdoms: Resurrection of the Dragon *'08*

Frederick Lau
The Wave *'08*
Victoria *'15*

Tak-Wah Lau (1961-)
See Andy Lau

Chantal Lauby
Mr. Average *'06*
You and Me *'06*

Chester Lauck (1902-80)
Dreaming Out Loud *'40*
The Bashful Bachelor *'42*
So This Is Washington *'43*

Philippe Laudenbach (1936-)
Confidentially Yours *'83*
Of Gods and Men *'10*

Andrew Lauer (1965-)
Never on Tuesday *'88*
Screamers *'96*
I'll Be Home for Christmas *'98*
Gun Shy *'00*
H.G. Wells' War of the Worlds *'05*
King of the Lost World *'06*
Badge of Faith *'15*

Jack Laufer (1954-)
And the Band Played On *'93 (C)*
Lost in Yonkers *'93*
The Man Who Captured Eichmann *'96*
The Learning Curve *'01*

John Laughlin (1953-)
Crimes of Passion *'84*
Footloose *'84*
The Hills Have Eyes, Part 2 *'84*
Agatha Christie's Murder with Mirrors *'85*
Midnight Crossing *'87*
Motorama *'91*
The Lawnmower Man *'92*
Sexual Malice *'93*
Night Fire *'94*
Back to Back *'96*
Storm Trooper *'98*
Love's Abiding Joy *'06*

Tom Laughlin (1931-2013)
South Pacific *'58*
Tall Story *'60*
Born Losers *'67*
Billy Jack *'71*
The Trial of Billy Jack *'74*
Billy Jack Goes to Washington *'77*

Charles Laughton (1899-1962)
Piccadilly *'29*
The Devil and the Deep *'32*
If I Had a Million *'32*
Island of Lost Souls *'32*
The Old Dark House *'32*
The Private Life of Henry VIII *'33*
The Sign of the Cross *'33*
White Woman *'33*
The Barretts of Wimpole Street *'34*
Les Miserables *'35*
Mutiny on the Bounty *'35*
Ruggles of Red Gap *'35*
Rembrandt *'36*
Beachcomber *'38*
Sidewalks of London *'38*
The Hunchback of Notre Dame *'39*
Jamaica Inn *'39*
It Started with Eve *'41*
Stand by for Action *'42*
Tales of Manhattan *'42*
Forever and a Day *'43*
This Land Is Mine *'43*
The Canterville Ghost *'44*
Because of Him *'45*
Captain Kidd *'45*

The Paradine Case *'47*
Arch of Triumph *'48*
The Big Clock *'48*
The Bribe *'48*
Man on the Eiffel Tower *'48*
The Strange Door *'51*
Abbott and Costello Meet Captain Kidd *'52*
Hobson's Choice *'53*
Salome *'53*
Young Bess *'53*
Witness for the Prosecution *'57*
Spartacus *'60*
Advise and Consent *'62*

S. John Launer (1919-2006)
The Werewolf *'56*
Crime of Passion *'57*

Cyndi Lauper (1953-)
Vibes *'88*
Life with Mikey *'93*

Matthew Laurance (1950-)
Eddie and the Cruisers *'83*
Eddie and the Cruisers 2: Eddie Lives! *'89*

Mitchell Laurance (1950-)
Stepfather 2: Make Room for Daddy *'89*
Syngenor *'90*
The Hand that Rocks the Cradle *'92*

Carole Laure (1948-)
The Apprentice *'71*
Sweet Movie *'75*
Born for Hell *'76*
Get Out Your Handkerchiefs *'78*
Victory *'81*

Stan Laurel (1890-1965)
Pardon Us *'31*
Pack Up Your Troubles *'32*
The Devil's Brother *'33*
Sons of the Desert *'33*
Hollywood Party *'34*
March of the Wooden Soldiers *'34*
Bonnie Scotland *'35*
Bohemian Girl *'36*
Our Relations *'36*
Pick a Star *'37*
Way Out West *'37*
Block-heads *'38*
Swiss Miss *'38*
The Flying Deuces *'39*
Great Guns *'41*
Air Raid Wardens *'43*
Nothing But Trouble *'44*
Utopia *'51*

Ashley Lauren (1966-)
See Ashley Laurence

Greg Lauren (1970-)
Boys Life *'94*
The Prophet's Game *'99*
Friends and Family *'01*

Rod Lauren (1940-2007)
Black Zoo *'63*
The Crawling Hand *'63*
The Gun Hawk *'63*
Once Before I Die *'65*

Tammy Lauren (1969-)
The Last Flight of Noah's Ark *'80*
Wishmaster *'97*

Val Lauren
Landspeed *'01*
Sal *'11*

Veronica Lauren (1980-)
Homeward Bound: The Incredible Journey *'93*
Homeward Bound 2: Lost in San Francisco *'96*

Ashley Laurence (1966-)
Hellraiser *'87*
Hellbound: Hellraiser 2 *'88*
Hellraiser 3: Hell on Earth *'92*
Mikey *'92*
Lurking Fear *'94*
Untamed Love *'94*
Felony *'95*
Outside the Law *'95*
Triplecross *'95*
Warlock 3: The End of Innocence *'98*
Cypress Edge *'99*
Hellraiser: Hellseeker *'02*
Lightning Bug *'04*
Chill *'06*

Michael Laurence
The Operator *'01*
Room 314 *'07*

Oona Laurence (2002-)
Lamb *'16*
Pete's Dragon *'16*
The Beguiled *'17*

James Laurenson (1940-)
Pink Floyd: The Wall *'82*
Sharpe's Mission *'96*
Sharpe's Regiment *'96*
Sharpe's Siege *'96*
The Cat's Meow *'01*
Three Blind Mice *'02*
Ghostboat *'06*

Phil Laurenson (1946-2009)
The Wizard of Gore *'70*
The Gore-Gore Girls *'72*

Agnes Laurent (1936-2010)
Girl in His Pocket *'57*
The Nude Set *'57*
The Twilight Girls *'57*

Jacqueline Laurent
Judge Hardy's Children *'38*
Le Jour Se Leve *'39*

Melanie Laurent (1983-)
The Beat My Heart Skipped *'05*
Paris *'08*
The Concert *'09*
Inglourious Basterds *'09*
Beginners *'10*
Enemy *'13*
Night Train to Lisbon *'13*
Now You See Me *'13*
By the Sea *'15*
Operation Finale *'18*
6 Underground *'19*

Joan Laurer (1969-2016)
Frank McKlusky, C.I. *'02*
Cougar Club *'07*

Joanie Marie Laurer (1969-2016)
See Joan Laurer

Dan Lauria (1947-)
Stakeout *'87*
In the Line of Duty: Ambush in Waco *'93*
Independence Day *'96*
Dogwatch *'97*
Prison of Secrets *'97*
Wide Awake *'97*
Dean Koontz's Mr. Murder *'98*
From the Earth to the Moon *'98*
Ricochet River *'98*
True Friends *'98*
Fear Runs Silent *'99*
Full Disclosure *'00*
Hangman *'00*
Big Momma's House 2 *'06*
The Bronx Is Burning *'07*
Dead Air *'08*
Dear Me: A Blogger's Tale *'08*
Finish Line *'08*
The Spirit *'08*
Alien Trespass *'09*
Donna on Demand *'09*
Life of Lemon *'11*

Hugh Laurie (1959-)
Strapless *'90*
Peter's Friends *'92*
All or Nothing at All *'93*
Sense and Sensibility *'95*
101 Dalmatians *'96*
The Borrowers *'97*
Cousin Bette *'97*
Spice World: The Movie *'97*
The Man in the Iron Mask *'98*
Maybe Baby *'99*
Stuart Little *'99*
Life with Judy Garland-Me and My Shadows *'01*
Stuart Little 2 *'02*
Flight of the Phoenix *'04*
Valiant *'05 (V)*
Stuart Little 3: Call of the Wild *'06 (V)*
Street Kings *'08*
Monsters *vs.* Aliens *'09 (V)*
Arthur Christmas *'11 (V)*
Hop *'11 (V)*
The Oranges *'12*
Tomorrowland *'15*

John Laurie (1897-1980)
Juno and the Paycock *'30*
The 39 Steps *'35*
Nine Days a Queen *'36*
Edge of the World *'37*
The Four Feathers *'39*
Henry V *'44*
Immortal Battalion *'44*
Mine Own Executioner *'47*
Hamlet *'48*
Man of Evil *'48*
Madeleine *'50*
No Trace *'50*
Encore *'52*
Love in Pawn *'53*
Devil Girl from Mars *'54*
Campbell's Kingdom *'57*
The Reptile *'66*

Piper Laurie (1932-)
Francis Goes to the Races *'51*
Has Anybody Seen My Gal? *'52*
No Room for the Groom *'52*
Son of Ali Baba *'52*
The Mississippi Gambler *'53*
Dawn at Socorro *'54*
Until They Sail *'57*
Days of Wine and Roses *'58*
The Hustler *'61*
Carrie *'76*
Ruby *'77*
Tim *'79*
The Thorn Birds *'83*
Return to Oz *'85*
Children of a Lesser God *'86*
Promise *'86*
Tiger Warsaw *'87*
Dream a Little Dream *'89*
Other People's Money *'91*
Storyville *'92*
Dario Argento's Trauma *'93*
Rich in Love *'93*
Wrestling Ernest Hemingway *'93*
The Crossing Guard *'94*
The Grass Harp *'95*
Dean Koontz's Intensity *'97*
Horton Foote's Alone *'97*
The Faculty *'98*
Inherit the Wind *'99*
St. Patrick's Day *'99*
Possessed *'00*
The Last Brickmaker in America *'01*
Eulogy *'04*
The Dead Girl *'06*
Hounddog *'08*
Saving Grace B. Jones *'09*
Hesher *'10*

Lucie Laurier (1975-)
Strip Search *'97*
Stiletto Dance *'01*
Seducing Doctor Lewis *'03*
Bon Cop Bad Cop *'06*

Ed Lauter (1940-2013)
The Last American Hero *'73*
Lolly-Madonna XXX *'73*
The Longest Yard *'74*
Breakheart Pass *'76*
Family Plot *'76*
King Kong *'76*
Magic *'78*
Undercover With the KKK *'78*
Death Hunt *'81*
Eureka! *'81*
The Amateur *'82*
In the Custody of Strangers *'82*
Big Score *'83*
Cujo *'83*
Timerider *'83*
Cartier Affair *'84*
Lassiter *'84*
Death Wish 3 *'85*
Girls Just Want to Have Fun *'85*
Real Genius *'85*
The Last Days of Patton *'86*
Youngblood *'86*
Yuri Nosenko, KGB *'86*
Revenge of the Nerds 2: Nerds in Paradise *'87*
The Rocketeer *'91*
Stephen King's Golden Years *'91*
School Ties *'92*
Extreme Justice *'93*
True Romance *'93*
Digital Man *'94*
Trial by Jury *'94*
Leaving Las Vegas *'95*
Mulholland Falls *'95*
The Sweeper *'95*
Mercenary *'96*
Allie & Me *'97*
A Bright Shining Lie *'98*
Dollar for the Dead *'98*
Malicious Intent *'99*
Thirteen Days *'00*
Seabiscuit *'03*
Starship Troopers 2: Hero of the Federation *'04*
Art Heist *'05*
Into the Fire *'05*
The Longest Yard *'05*
Venice Underground *'05*
Seraphim Falls *'06*
Camille *'07*
The Number 23 *'07*
The Prince and the Pauper *'07*
Expecting a Miracle *'09*
The Frankenstein Syndrome *'10*
The Artist *'11*
Carnal Innocence *'11*
The Fitzgerald Family Christmas *'12*
Trouble with the Curve *'12*
The Town That Dreaded Sundown *'14*

Harry Lauter (1914-90)
The Fighting Lawman *'53*
The Crooked Web *'55*
The Werewolf *'56*
Tarzan's Fight for Life *'58*
Escape from the Planet of the Apes *'71*

Kathrin Lautner (1959-)
The Last Riders *'90*
Night of the Wilding *'90*
Final Impact *'91*
Two Bits & Pepper *'95*

Taylor Lautner (1992-)
The Adventures of Sharkboy and Lavagirl in 3-D *'05*
Cheaper by the Dozen 2 *'05*
Twilight *'08*
The Twilight Saga: New Moon *'09*
The Twilight Saga: Eclipse *'10*
Valentine's Day *'10*
Abduction *'11*
The Twilight Saga: Breaking Dawn, Part 1 *'11*
The Twilight Saga: Breaking Dawn, Part 2 *'12*
Grown Ups 2 *'13*
Tracers *'15*

Rene Lavan (1968-)
Bitter Sugar *'96*
Christmas With the Kranks *'04*
Dirty Dancing: Havana Nights *'04*

Dominque Lavanant (1944-)
French Fried Vacation *'79*
Hotel America *'81*
Three Men and a Cradle *'85*
The Monster *'96*

Denis Lavant (1961-)
Boy Meets Girl *'84*
Mauvais Sang *'86*
The Lovers on the Bridge *'91*
Beau Travail *'98*
A Very Long Engagement *'04*
Mister Lonely *'07*
Holy Motors *'12*
The Mountain *'19*

Lucille LaVerne (1872-1945)
An American Tragedy *'31*
Alias the Doctor *'32*
Pilgrimage *'33*
Kentucky Kernels *'34*
Snow White and the Seven Dwarfs *'37 (V)*

Daliah Lavi (1942-)
The Return of Dr. Mabuse *'61*
Two Weeks in Another Town *'62*
The Whip and the Body *'63*
Apache's Last Battle *'64*
Lord Jim *'65*
The Silencers *'66*
Those Fantastic Flying Fools *'67*

Gabriele Lavia (1942-)
Deep Red: Hatchet Murders *'75*
Zeder *'83*
Revenge of the Dead *'84*

Avril Lavigne (1984-)
Fast Food Nation *'06*
The Flock *'07*

Linda Lavin (1937-)
The Muppets Take Manhattan *'84 (C)*
I Want to Go Home *'89*
See You in the Morning *'89*
A Short History of Decay *'13*

Marc Lavoine (1962-)
L'Enfer *'93*
The Good Thief *'03*

Adam LaVorgna (1981-)
I'll Be Home for Christmas *'98*
Outside Providence *'99*

John Phillip Law (1937-2008)
The Russians Are Coming, the Russians Are Coming *'66*
Hurry Sundown *'67*
Barbarella *'68*
Danger: Diabolik *'68*
The Sergeant *'68*
Skidoo *'68*
Death Rides a Horse *'69*
The Love Machine *'71*
Golden Voyage of Sinbad *'73*
Spiral Staircase *'75*
The Cassandra Crossing *'76*
African Rage *'78*
Tarzan, the Ape Man *'81*
American Commandos *'84*
Attack Force Z *'84*
Night Train to Terror *'84*
Space Mutiny *'88*
Alienator *'89*
My Magic Dog *'97*
CQ *'01*

Jude Law (1972-)
Shopping *'93*
Bent *'97 (C)*
Gattaca *'97*
I Love You, I Love You Not *'97*
Midnight in the Garden of Good and Evil *'97*
Music from Another Room *'97*
Wilde *'97*
Final Cut *'98*
Immortality *'98*
eXistenZ *'99*
The Talented Mr. Ripley *'99*
Enemy at the Gates *'00*
Love, Honour & Obey *'00*
A. I.: Artificial Intelligence *'01*
Road to Perdition *'02*
Cold Mountain *'03*
Alfie *'04*
The Aviator *'04*
Closer *'04*
I Heart Huckabees *'04*
Lemony Snicket's A Series of Unfortunate Events *'04*
Sky Captain and the World of Tomorrow *'04*
All the King's Men *'06*
Breaking and Entering *'06*
The Holiday *'06*
My Blueberry Nights *'07*
Sleuth *'07*
The Imaginarium of Doctor Parnassus *'09*
Sherlock Holmes *'09*
Repo Men *'10*
Contagion *'11*
Hugo *'11*
Sherlock Holmes: A Game of Shadows *'11*
Anna Karenina *'12*
Rise of the Guardians *'12 (V)*
360 *'12*
Dom Hemingway *'13*
Side Effects *'13*
Black Sea *'14*
The Grand Budapest Hotel *'14*
Spy *'15*
Genius *'16*
King Arthur: Legend of the Sword *'17*
Fantastic Beasts: The Crimes of Grindelwald *'18*
Vox Lux *'18*
Captain Marvel *'19*
The Rhythm Section *'19*

Phyllida Law (1932-)
Hitler: The Last Ten Days *'73*
Peter's Friends *'92*
All or Nothing at All *'93*
Much Ado about Nothing *'93*
Before the Rain *'94*
Anna Karenina *'96*
Emma *'96*
The Winter Guest *'97*
The Magical Legend of the Leprechauns *'99*
The Time Machine *'02*
Two Men Went to War *'02*
Brush with Fate *'03*
A Little Trip to Heaven *'05*
Day of Wrath *'06*
Miss Potter *'06*
Pinochet's Last Stand *'06*
Miss Austen Regrets *'07*
The Waiting Room *'07*

Betty Lawford (1912-60)
Old English *'30*
Gallant Lady *'33*
Love Before Breakfast *'36*

Christopher Lawford (1955-)
Mr. North *'88*
The Russia House *'90*
The Abduction *'96*
Kiss Me, Guido *'97*
The Confession *'98*
Mary, Mother of Jesus *'99*
The 6th Day *'00*
Thirteen Days *'00*
Counterstrike *'03*
The World's Fastest Indian *'05*

Ningali Lawford (1967-2019)
Rabbit-Proof Fence *'02*
Last Cab to Darwin *'16*

Peter Lawford (1923-84)
Mrs. Miniver *'42*
Thunder Birds *'42*
A Yank at Eton *'42*
Immortal Sergeant *'43*
Sahara *'43*
The Canterville Ghost *'44*
The White Cliffs of Dover *'44*
Picture of Dorian Gray *'45*
Son of Lassie *'45*
Two Sisters From Boston *'46*
Good News *'47*
It Happened in Brooklyn *'47*
My Brother Talks to Horses *'47*

Easter Parade '48
Julia Misbehaves '48
On an Island with You '48
Little Women '49
The Red Danube '50
Royal Wedding '51
The Australian Story '52
The Hour of 13 '52
It Should Happen to You '54
Never So Few '59
Exodus '60
Ocean's 11 '60
Advise and Consent '62
The Longest Day '62
Sergeants 3 '62
Dead Ringer '64
Harlow '65
A Man Called Adam '66
Salt & Pepper '68
Skidoo '68
April Fools '69
One More Time '70
A Step Out of Line '71
They Only Kill Their Masters '72
The Phantom of Hollywood '74
Fantasy Island '76
Mysterious Island of Beautiful Women '79
Body & Soul '81

Lucy Lawless (1968-)
Hercules the Legendary Journeys, Vol. 1: And the Amazon Women '94
Spider-Man '02 (C)
Eurotrip '04
Boogeyman '05
Vampire Bats '05
Bedtime Stories '08
Angel of Death '09

Kian Lawley (1995-)
Before I Fall '17
Monster Party '18

Sean Lawlor (1954-2008)
Red Roses and Petrol '03
30,000 Leagues Under the Sea '07
Mega Shark Vs. Giant Octopus '09
The Black Waters of Echo's Pond '10

Jody Lawrance (1930-86)
The Family Secret '51
All Ashore '53
The Purple Gang '59

Andrew (Andy) Lawrence (1988-)
Jack Frost '98
The Least of These '08
Miles from Nowhere '09

Barbara Lawrence (1930-30)
The Street with No Name '48
A Letter to Three Wives '49
The Star '52
Oklahoma! '55
Kronos '57
Man in the Shadow '57

Bruno Lawrence (1941-95)
Smash Palace '82
Treasure of the Yankee Zephyr '83
Utu '83
Heart of the Stag '84
The Quiet Earth '85
Initiation '87
Rikky and Pete '88
The Efficiency Expert '92
Jack Be Nimble '94

Carol Lawrence (1932-)
New Faces of 1952 '54
Summer of Fear '78
Shattered Image '93

Carolyn Lawrence (1964-)
Jimmy Neutron: Boy Genius '01 (V)
The SpongeBob SquarePants Movie '04 (V)

Colin Lawrence
To Have and to Hold '06
Eve of Destruction '13

Delphi Lawrence (1926-2002)
Murder on Approval '56
The Man Who Could Cheat Death '59
Frozen Alive '64

Elizabeth Lawrence (1922-2000)
Sleeping with the Enemy '91
The Crucible '96
Unbreakable '00

Gertrude Lawrence (1898-1952)
Rembrandt '36
Stage Door Canteen '43

Hanna Mangan Lawrence
Acolytes '08
The Reckoning '14

Jennifer Lawrence (1990-)
The Devil You Know '05
The Burning Plain '08
The Poker House '09
Winter's Bone '10
The Beaver '11
Like Crazy '11
X-Men: First Class '11
House at the End of the Street '12
The Hunger Games '12
Silver Linings Playbook '12
American Hustle '13
The Hunger Games: Catching Fire '13
The Hunger Games: Mockingjay--Part 1 '14
Serena '14
X-Men: Days of Future Past '14
The Hunger Games: Mockingjay-Part 2 '15
Passengers '16
X-Men: Apocalypse '16
mother! '17
Red Sparrow '18
Dark Phoenix '19

Joey Lawrence (1976-)
See Joseph Lawrence

John Lawrence (1931-92)
The Asphyx '72
They Live '88

Joseph Lawrence (1976-)
Summer Rental '85
Oliver & Company '88 (V)
Pulse '88
Chains of Gold '92
Radioland Murders '94 (C)
Tequila Body Shots '99
Urban Legends 2: Final Cut '00
Confessions of a Sociopathic Social Climber '05
Killer Pad '06
Rest Stop '06
Together Again for the First Time '08
My Fake Fiance '09
The Dog Who Saved Halloween '11 (V)
The Dog Who Saved the Holidays '12 (V)
Hitched for the Holidays '12
Arlo the Burping Pig '16
Emma's Chance '16
Christmas All Over Again '16

Marc Lawrence (1910-2005)
San Quentin '37
The Spider's Web '38
Invisible Stripes '39
Brigham Young: Frontiersman '40
Johnny Apollo '40
This Gun for Hire '42
Tampico '44
Cloak and Dagger '46
Key Largo '48
Jigsaw '49
Abbott and Costello in the Foreign Legion '50
The Asphalt Jungle '50
Johnny Cool '63
Krakatoa East of Java '69
Dream No Evil '70
Frasier the Sensuous Lion '73
Pigs '73
The Man with the Golden Gun '74
Marathon Man '76
Foul Play '78
Goin' Coconuts '78
King of Kong Island '78
Cataclysm '81
Night Train to Terror '84
The Big Easy '87
Ruby '92
Gotti '96
The Shipping News '01

Mark Christopher Lawrence (1964-)
Fear of a Black Hat '94
That Darn Cat '96
Lost Treasure '03

Martin Lawrence (1965-)
House Party '90
House Party 2: The Pajama Jam '91
Talkin' Dirty after Dark '91
Boomerang '92
You So Crazy '94
Bad Boys '95
Nothing to Lose '96
A Thin Line Between Love and Hate '96
Blue Streak '99
Life '99
Big Momma's House '00
Black Knight '01
What's the Worst That Could Happen? '01
Bad Boys 2 '03
National Security '03
Rebound '05
Big Momma's House 2 '06
Open Season '06 (V)
Wild Hogs '07
College Road Trip '08
Welcome Home Roscoe Jenkins '08
Death at a Funeral '10
Big Mommas: Like Father, Like Son '11
Bad Boys for Life '20

Matthew Lawrence (1980-)
Tales from the Darkside: The Movie '90
Mrs. Doubtfire '93
All I Wanna Do '98
Angels in the Endzone '98
Boltneck '98
Kiki's Delivery Service '98 (V)
The Hot Chick '02
The Comebacks '07
Creature of Darkness '09

Michael Lawrence
Othello '52
The Price of Milk '00

Peter Lee Lawrence (1943-73)
Gun for 100 Graves '68
Special Forces '68

Rosina Lawrence (1913-97)
Charlie Chan's Secret '35
Mister Cinderella '36
Nobody's Baby '37
Pick a Star '37
Way Out West '37

Scott Lawrence
Timecop '94
Equals '16

Sharon Lawrence (1961-)
Degree of Guilt '95
The Heidi Chronicles '95
The Only Thrill '97
Aftershock: Earthquake in New York '99
Gossip '99
Lies & Alibis '06
The Capture of the Green River Killer '08
The Perfect Family '11
Middle of Nowhere '12
Born to Race: Fast Track '14

Stephanie Lawrence
Buster '88
The Phantom of the Opera '89

Steve Lawrence (1935-)
The Blues Brothers '80 (C)
The Lonely Guy '84
Alice in Wonderland '85
Blues Brothers 2000 '98
The Yards '00
Ocean's Eleven '01 (C)

Steven Anthony Lawrence (1990-)
Cheaper by the Dozen '03
Kicking & Screaming '05
Rebound '05

Vicki Lawrence (1949-)
Hannah Montana: The Movie '09
Annie Claus is Coming to Town '11

Bianca Lawson (1979-)
Boltneck '98
Anne Rice's The Feast of All Saints '01
Bones '01
Save the Last Dance '01
Breakin' All The Rules '04

Denis Lawson (1947-)
Local Hero '83
Return of the Jedi '83
Horatio Hornblower '99
Bleak House '05
Jekyll '07
Perfect Sense '11
The Machine '13

Greg Lawson (1957-)
Hollywood Wives: The New Generation '03
I Dream of Murder '06
Carolina Moon '07
Northern Lights '09
Merry In-Laws '12

Leigh Lawson (1945-)
Brother Sun, Sister Moon '73
Disraeli '79
Tess '79
Agatha Christie's Murder is Easy '82
Sword of the Valiant '83
Lace '84
Madame Sousatzka '88
Tears in the Rain '88
O Pioneers! '91
Battling for Baby '92
Back to the Secret Garden '01
Being Julia '04
Casanova '05

Linda Lawson
Night Tide '61
Apache Rifles '64

Maggie Lawson (1980-)
Heart of a Stranger '02
Winter Break '02
Cleaner '07
Hostile Makeover '09
Killer Hair '09

Priscilla Lawson (1914-58)
Girl of the Golden West '38
Flash Gordon: Rocketship '40

Richard Lawson (1947-)
Scream Blacula Scream '73
Sugar Hill '74
Homeboy '75
Fist '76
Coming Home '78
Poltergeist '82
Streets of Fire '84
Johnnie Gibson F.B.I. '87
The Reluctant Agent '89
Pandora's Clock '96
How Stella Got Her Groove Back '98
Blue Hill Avenue '01
Black Listed '03
Christmas at Water's Edge '04

Sarah Lawson (1928-)
You Know What Sailors Are '59
Island of the Burning Doomed '67
The Devil Rides Out '68

Shannon Lawson
Heck's Way Home '95
Anne of Green Gables: The Continuing Story '99
Possessed '00
Last Call: The Final Chapter of F. Scott Fitzgerald '02
Scared Silent '02

Wilfred Lawson (1900-66)
Pygmalion '38
The Night Has Eyes '42
Thursday's Child '43
Man of Evil '48
The Prisoner '55
War and Peace '56
Room at the Top '59

Marlene Lawston (1998-)
Flightplan '05
Dan in Real Life '07

Alex Lawther
Goodbye Christopher Robin '17
Freak Show '18

Chas Lawther
Love Letters '99
Urban Legends 2: Final Cut '00

Frank Lawton (1904-69)
Skin Game '31
Cavalcade '33
David Copperfield '35
Devil Doll '36
The Invisible Ray '36
The Mill on the Floss '39
The Secret Four '39
The Winslow Boy '48
A Night to Remember '58

Evelyn Laye (1900-96)
Theatre of Death '67
Say Hello to Yesterday '71

KiKi Layne
If Beale Street Could Talk '18
Native Son '19

John Lazar (1946-)
Beyond the Valley of the Dolls '70
Every Girl Should Have One '78
Deathstalker 2: Duel of the Titans '87
Eddie Presley '92
Attack of the 60-Foot Centerfold '95
Night of the Scarecrow '95
Over the Wire '95

Justin Lazard (1966-)
The Big Fall '96
Species 2 '98
The Brutal Truth '99
Universal Soldier: The Return '99

Eugene (Yevgeny) Lazarev (1937-)
The Ice Runner '93
The Saint '97
The Sum of All Fears '02
Pearl Diver '04
Lord of War '05

George Lazenby (1939-)
On Her Majesty's Secret Service '69
Who Saw Her Die? '72
Kentucky Fried Movie '77
Black Eliminator '78
Kill Factor '78
Saint Jack '79
Gettysburg '93
Twinsitters '95
Four Dogs Playing Poker '00
Spider's Web '01
Winter Break '02

Bruce Le
Bruce Lee Fights Back from the Grave '76
Infra-Man '76

Cung Le (1972-)
Pandorum '09
Dragon Eyes '12
The Man with the Iron Fists '12
The Grandmaster '13

Hiep Thi Le (1970-)
Heaven and Earth '93
Green Dragon '01

Becky Le Beau (1962-)
See Becky LeBeau

Islid Le Besco (1982-)
Girls Can't Swim '99
Sade '00
A Song of Innocence '05
The Good Heart '09

Maiwenn Le Besco (1976-)
The Fifth Element '97
High Tension '03

Samuel Le Bihan (1965-)
Trois Couleurs: Rouge '94
Capitaine Conan '96
For Sale '98
Venus Beauty Institute '98
Total Western '00
Brotherhood of the Wolf '01
He Loves Me . . . He Loves Me Not '02
Mesrine: Part 2-Public Enemy Number 1 '08

Charlotte Le Bon (1986-)
The Hundred-Foot Journey '14
The Walk '15
Anthropoid '16
The Take '16
The Promise '17

Gene Le Brock (1961-)
Fortress of Amerikka '89
Metamorphosis '90

Kelly Le Brock (1960-)
The Woman in Red '84
Weird Science '85
Hard to Kill '89
Hard Bounty '94
Wrongfully Accused '98

Bernard Le Coq (1950-)
Van Gogh '92
Capitaine Conan '96
The Bridesmaid '04
Hidden '05
Joyeux Noel '05
Times Have Been Better '06

Jake Le Doux (1985-)
See Jake LeDoux

Steve Le Marquand (1967-)
Vertical Limit '00
Rodgers & Hammerstein's South Pacific '01

John Le Mesurier (1912-83)
Jack the Ripper '60
Invasion Quartet '61
Very Important Person '61
Hot Enough for June '64
Where the Spies Are '65
Bang! Bang! You're Dead! '66
Eye of the Devil '67
Salt & Pepper '68
Confessions of a Window Cleaner '74
Jabberwocky '77
The Adventures of Sherlock Holmes' Smarter Brother '78
The Fiendish Plot of Dr. Fu Manchu '80
Brideshead Revisited '81
A Married Man '84

Paul Le Person (1931-2005)
The Thief of Paris '67
Phantom of Liberty '74

Nicholas Le Prevost (1947-)
The Girl in a Swing '89
The Camomile Lawn '92
P.D. James: The Murder Room '04
Half Broken Things '07

Miss Conception '08
Return to Cranford '09
Made in Romania '10

Sylvestria Le Touzel (1958-)
Mansfield Park '85
Catherine Cookson's The Gambling Man '98
Amazing Grace '06
Northanger Abbey '07
Happy-Go-Lucky '08
Appropriate Adult '11
Secret State '12

Nicholas Lea (1962-)
Xtro 2: The Second Encounter '91
Once a Thief '96
Kiss Tomorrow Goodbye '00
Vertical Limit '00
Ignition '01
The Impossible Elephant '02
Moving Malcolm '03
Threshold '03
Category 7: The End of the World '05
Deadly Isolation '05
American Venus '07
Shattered '07
Vice '08

Ron Lea
The Neighbor '93
A Map of the World '99
Sea People '00
A Different Loyalty '04
The Phantom '09
The Stranger '10
Goodnight for Justice '11

Britt Leach
The California Kid '74
Baby Boom '87

Rosemary Leach (1935-)
That'll Be the Day '73
Disraeli '79
The Seventeenth Bride '84
A Room with a View '86
The Charmer '87
The Hawk '93
The Buccaneers '95
Berkeley Square '98
Catherine Cookson's Tilly Trotter '99

Cloris Leachman (1926-)
Kiss Me Deadly '55
The Rack '56
Butch Cassidy and the Sundance Kid '69
Lovers and Other Strangers '70
WUSA '70
The Last Picture Show '71
Brand New Life '72
Charley and the Angel '73
Dillinger '73
Dying Room Only '73
Daisy Miller '74
Death Sentence '74
Young Frankenstein '74
Crazy Mama '75
Someone I Touched '75
High Anxiety '77
Backstairs at the White House '79
The Muppet Movie '79 (C)
The North Avenue Irregulars '79
S.O.S. Titanic '79
Herbie Goes Bananas '80
History of the World: Part 1 '81
The Victory '81
Miss All-American Beauty '82
Dixie: Changing Habits '85
Walk Like a Man '87
Prancer '89
Danielle Steel's Fine Things '90
Texasville '90
The Beverly Hillbillies '93
My Boyfriend's Back '93
Double Double Toil and Trouble '94
A Troll in Central Park '94 (V)
Now and Then '95
Beavis and Butt-Head Do America '96 (V)
Hanging Up '99
The Iron Giant '99 (V)
Music of the Heart '99
Manna from Heaven '02
Alex & Emma '03
Bad Santa '03
Spanglish '04
The Longest Yard '05
Mrs. Harris '05
Sky High '05
Beerfest '06
Scary Movie 4 '06
Lake Placid 2 '07
Ponyo '08 (V)
The Women '08
American Cowslip '09
Inglourious Basterds '09
Love Takes Wing '09
New York, I Love You '09
A Very Mary Christmas '10
You Again '10
The Fields '11
Gambit '12
The Oogieloves in the Big Balloon Adventure '12
Adult World '13
The Croods '13 (V)
The Wedding Ringer '15
I Can Only Imagine '18

Richard Leacock
The Note '07
That Russell Girl '08

Viv Leacock (1974-)
I Spy '02
White Coats '04
The Stranger '10

Sharon Leal (1972-)
Face the Music '00
Dreamgirls '06
This Christmas '07
Tyler Perry's Why Did I Get Married? '07
Linewatch '08
Soul Men '08
Tyler Perry's Why Did I Get Married Too '10
The Last Letter '13
Addicted '14
Freedom '14
1982 '16

Michael Learned (1939-)
A Christmas Without Snow '80
Nurse '80
Power '86
Roots: The Gift '88
Murder in New Hampshire: The Pamela Smart Story '91
Dragon: The Bruce Lee Story '93
Loggerheads '05
American Girl: Chrissa Stands Strong '09

Denis Leary (1957-)
Demolition Man '93
Gunmen '93
Judgment Night '93
National Lampoon's Loaded Weapon 1 '93
The Ref '93
The Sandlot '93
Who's the Man? '93
Natural Born Killers '94
The Neon Bible '95
Operation Dumbo Drop '95
Two If by Sea '95
Underworld '96
Love Walked In '97
The Matchmaker '97
The Real Blonde '97
The Second Civil War '97
Subway Stories '97
Suicide Kings '97
Wag the Dog '97
Wide Awake '97
A Bug's Life '98 (V)
Monument Ave. '98
Small Soldiers '98
Jesus' Son '99
Silent Witness '99
The Thomas Crown Affair '99
True Crime '99
Company Man '00
Lakeboat '00
Sand '00
Double Whammy '01
Final '01
Dawg '02
Ice Age '02 (V)
The Secret Lives of Dentists '02
Ice Age: The Meltdown '06 (V)
Recount '08
Ice Age: Dawn of the Dinosaurs '09 (V)
The Amazing Spider-Man '12
Ice Age: Continental Drift '12 (V)
Draft Day '14
Freaks of Nature '15
Ice Age: Collision Course '16

Timothy Leary (1920-96)
Cheech and Chong's Nice Dreams '81 (C)
Shocker '89
Roadside Prophets '92
Ted & Venus '93 (C)
Conceiving Ada '97

Rex Lease (1901-66)
Sunny Skies '30
Cavalcade of the West '36
The Clutching Hand '36
Custer's Last Stand '36
Lightnin' Bill Carson '36
Ten Laps to Go '36
Heroes of the Alamo '37
Lost in Alaska '52

Jean-Pierre Leaud (1944-)
The 400 Blows '59
The Testament of Orpheus '59
Alphaville '65
The Joy of Knowledge '65
Pierrot le Fou '65
Masculine Feminine '66
La Chinoise '67
Weekend '67
Stolen Kisses '68
Porcile '69
Bed and Board '70
Two English Girls '72
Day for Night '73
Last Tango in Paris '73
Love on the Run '78
Detective '85
36 Fillete '88
Irma Vep '96
What Time Is It There? '01 (C)

Becky LeBeau (1962-)
Not of This Earth '88
The Malibu Beach Vampires '91

Madeleine LeBeau (1923-2016)
Casablanca '42
Paris After Dark '43
8 1/2 '63

Pierre Lebeau (1954-)
The Boys '97
Bon Cop Bad Cop '06

Ivan Lebedeff (1894-1953)
They Had to See Paris '29
The Lady Refuses '31
Made On Broadway '33
The Merry Frinks '34
Goin' to Town '35
Sweepstake Annie '35
The Golden Arrow '36
Love on the Run '36

Karen LeBlanc
Crazy for Christmas '05
Mobile Homes '19

Matt LeBlanc (1967-)
The Ghost Brigade '93
Red Shoe Diaries 3: Another Woman's Lipstick '93
Showdown '94
Ed '96
Lost in Space '98
Charlie's Angels '00
All the Queen's Men '02
Charlie's Angels: Full Throttle '03
Lovesick '14

Sadie LeBlanc (1977-)
The Secrets of the Summer House '08
Hostile Makeover '09
Killer Hair '09

Brian Leckner (1967-)
Sgt. Bilko '95
Joy Ride '01

Michael LeClair
Anatomy of a Seduction '79
Leave 'Em Laughing '81

Ginette LeClerc (1912-92)
Le Corbeau '43
Le Plaisir '52

Jean LeClerc (1948-)
Whispers '89
Blown Away '93

Katie Leclerc (1986-)
Beverly Lewis' The Confession '13
Holiday Breakup '16

Vincent Leclerc
Affinity '08
The Fall of the American Empire '19

Cyril Lecomte
The Girl '01
Chrysalis '07

Sofia Ledarp (1974-)
The Girl Who Kicked the Hornet's Nest '10
The Girl Who Played With Fire '10

Friedrich Ledebur (1900-86)
Moby Dick '56
The 27th Day '57

Erwin Leder (1951-)
Das Boot '81
Underworld '03

Francis Lederer (1899-2000)
Pandora's Box '28
Romance in Manhattan '34
The Gay Deception '35
One Rainy Afternoon '36
Confessions of a Nazi Spy '39
Midnight '39
The Man I Married '40
The Bridge of San Luis Rey '44
Diary of a Chambermaid '46
Captain Carey, U.S.A. '50
The Ambassador's Daughter '56
Return of Dracula '58
Terror Is a Man '59

Brandy Ledford (1969-)
Zebra Lounge '01
We'll Meet Again '02
Ice Men '04

Heath Ledger (1979-2008)
Two Hands '98
Ten Things I Hate about You '99
The Patriot '00
A Knight's Tale '01
Monster's Ball '01
The Four Feathers '02
Ned Kelly '03
The Order '03
Brokeback Mountain '05
The Brothers Grimm '05
Casanova '05
Lords of Dogtown '05
Candy '06
I'm Not There '07
The Dark Knight '08
The Imaginarium of Doctor Parnassus '09

Jake LeDoux (1985-)
Summer's End '99
Love Come Down '00

Virginie Ledoyen (1976-)
La Ceremonie '95
A Single Girl '96
Jeanne and the Perfect Guy '98
Late August, Early September '98
A Soldier's Daughter Never Cries '98
The Beach '00
8 Women '02
Bon Voyage '03
The Backwoods '06
The Valet '06
Holly '07
Shall We Kiss? '07
The Army of Crime '10
Farewell, My Queen '12

Angelica Lee
Re-Cycle '06
Out of the Inferno '13

Anna Lee (1913-2004)
First a Girl '35
The Passing of the Third Floor Back '35
King Solomon's Mines '37
Non-Stop New York '37
The Secret Four '39
How Green Was My Valley '41
Flying Tigers '42
Hangmen Also Die '42
Commandos Strike at Dawn '43
Summer Storm '44
Bedlam '45
The Ghost and Mrs. Muir '47
Fort Apache '48
Gideon's Day '58
The Crimson Kimono '59
The Horse Soldiers '59
Jack the Giant Killer '62
What Ever Happened to Baby Jane? '62
The Sound of Music '65
In Like Flint '67
Eleanor & Franklin '76

Belinda Lee (1935-61)
The Belles of St. Trinian's '53
Blackout '54
The Runaway Bus '54
Footsteps in the Fog '55
No Smoking '55
Who Done It? '56

Bernard Lee (1908-81)
The Blue Lamp '49
The Fallen Idol '49
The Third Man '49
Last Holiday '50
Morning Departure '50
Appointment With Venus '51
Beat the Devil '53
Sailor of the King '53
Crest of the Wave '54
The Purple Plain '54
Across the Bridge '57
The Spanish Gardener '57
Trouble in the Sky '60
Dr. No '62
From Russia with Love '63
Goldfinger '64
Thunderball '65
You Only Live Twice '67
On Her Majesty's Secret Service '69
Diamonds Are Forever '71
10 Rillington Place '71
Live and Let Die '73
Frankenstein and the Monster from Hell '74
The Man with the Golden Gun '74
The Spy Who Loved Me '77
Moonraker '79

Bobby Lee (1972-)
Kickin' It Old Skool '07
Pineapple Express '08

Brandon Lee (1965-93)
Kung Fu: The Movie '86
Legacy of Rage '86
Laser Mission '90
Showdown in Little Tokyo '91
Rapid Fire '92
The Crow '93

Bruce Lee (1940-73)
Marlowe '69
Chinese Connection '73
Enter the Dragon '73
Fists of Fury '73
Return of the Dragon '73
Chinese Connection 2 '77
Game of Death '79

Byung-hun Lee (1970-)
JSA: Joint Security Area '00
The Good, the Bad, the Weird '08
G.I. Joe: The Rise of Cobra '09
I Saw the Devil '10
RED 2 '13
The Age of Shadows '16
The Magnificent Seven '16

Canada Lee (1907-52)
Lifeboat '44
Body and Soul '47
Lost Boundaries '49

Carl Lee (1926-86)
The Connection '61
Superfly '72
Gordon's War '73

Casey Lee
Parental Guidance '98
White Chicks '04

China Lee (1942-)
What's Up, Tiger Lily? '66
Good Times '67

Christian Lee
Invasion Earth: The Aliens Are Here! '87
Kung Fu Killer '08

Christopher Lee (1922-2015)
Hamlet '48
Scott of the Antarctic '48
Captain Horatio Hornblower '51
Crimson Pirate '52
Moulin Rouge '52
Storm Over the Nile '55
Alias John Preston '56
The Accursed '57
The Curse of Frankenstein '57
Night Ambush '57
She Played With Fire '57
Bitter Victory '58
Corridors of Blood '58
The Horror of Dracula '58
Missiles from Hell '58
A Tale of Two Cities '58
The Hound of the Baskervilles '59
The Man Who Could Cheat Death '59
The Mummy '59
Uncle Was a Vampire '59
Beat Girl '60
The Hands of Orlac '60
Horror Hotel '60
The Two Faces of Dr. Jekyll '60
Scream of Fear '61
The Terror of the Tongs '61
The Longest Day '62
Pirates of Blood River '62
Sherlock Holmes and the Deadly Necklace '62
The Whip and the Body '63
Castle of the Living Dead '64
The Devil-Ship Pirates '64
The Gorgon '64
Hercules in the Haunted World '64
The Face of Fu Manchu '65
She '65
The Skull '65
The Virgin of Nuremberg '65
Brides of Fu Manchu '66
Dracula, Prince of Darkness '66
Rasputin the Mad Monk '66
Circus of Fear '67
Five Golden Dragons '67
Island of the Burning Doomed '67
Theatre of Death '67
The Vengeance of Fu Manchu '67

The Castle of Fu Manchu '68
The Crimson Cult '68
The Devil Rides Out '68
Dracula Has Risen from the Grave '68
Kiss and Kill '68
The Magic Christian '69
The Oblong Box '69
The Torture Chamber of Dr. Sadism '69
One More Time '70 (C)
The Private Life of Sherlock Holmes '70
The Scars of Dracula '70
Scream and Scream Again '70
Taste the Blood of Dracula '70
Count Dracula '71
The House that Dripped Blood '71
I, Monster '71
The Creeping Flesh '72
Dracula A.D. 1972 '72
Hannie Caulder '72
Horror Express '72
Nothing But the Night '72
Raw Meat '72
The Satanic Rites of Dracula '73
The Man with the Golden Gun '74
The Three Musketeers '74
The Four Musketeers '75
The Wicker Man '75
End of the World '76
Keeper '76
To the Devil, a Daughter '76
Airport '77 '77
Circle of Iron '78
Return from Witch Mountain '78
Captain America 2: Death Too Soon '79
Jaguar Lives '79
1941 '79
The Passage '79
Once Upon a Spy '80
Serial '80
An Eye for an Eye '81
The Last Unicorn '82 (V)
The Salamander '82
Return of Captain Invincible '83
Shaka Zulu '83
The Far Pavilions '84
Howling 2: Your Sister Is a Werewolf '85
Rosebud Beach Hotel '85
Jocks '87
The Land of Faraway '87
Around the World in 80 Days '89
Murder Story '89
Treasure Island '89
Gremlins 2: The New Batch '90
Sherlock Holmes and the Incident at Victoria Falls '91
Detonator '93
Funnyman '94 (C)
Police Academy 7: Mission to Moscow '94
The Stupids '95
Moses '96
Ivanhoe '97
The Odyssey '97
Russell Mulcahy's Tale of the Mummy '99
Sleepy Hollow '99
Lord of the Rings: The Fellowship of the Ring '01
Lord of the Rings: The Two Towers '02
Star Wars: Episode 2-Attack of the Clones '02
Charlie and the Chocolate Factory '05
Crimson Rivers 2: Angels of the Apocalypse '05
Star Wars: Episode 3-Revenge of the Sith '05
Tim Burton's Corpse Bride '05 (V)
The Golden Compass '07
The Color of Magic '08 (V)
Star Wars: The Clone Wars '08 (V)
Boogie Woogie '09
Glorious 39 '09
The Heavy '09
Triage '09
Alice in Wonderland '10
The Resident '10
Hugo '11
Frankenweenie '12 (V)
The Hobbit: An Unexpected Journey '12
Night Train to Lisbon '13
The Hobbit: The Battle of the Five Armies '14

Cinque Lee (1966-)
Mystery Train '89
Coffee and Cigarettes '03
Rapturious '07

Cosette Lee (1910-76)
Deranged '74
The Fly '86

Danny Lee (1952-)
Infra-Man '76
The Mighty Peking Man '77
Sword Masters: The Battle Wizard '77
City on Fire '87
The Killer '90
Organized Crime & Triad Bureau '93

Davey Lee
The Singing Fool '28
Say It With Songs '29

David Lee
Operation Delta Force 5: Random Fire '00
Steamboy '05 (V)

Dixie Lee (1911-52)
Manhattan Love Song '34
Love in Bloom '35

Dorothy Lee (1911-99)
Rio Rita '29
Half-Shot at Sunrise '30
Hook, Line and Sinker '30
Caught Plastered '31
Cracked Nuts '31
Girl Crazy '32
The Old Homestead '35
The Rainmakers '35

Elizabeth Lee
Something Weird '68
Organized Crime & Triad Bureau '93

Eric Lee (1948-)
Ring of Fire '91
Out for Blood '93

Gwen Lee (1904-61)
A Lady of Chance '28
Laugh, Clown, Laugh '28
Untamed '29
Chasing Rainbows '30
Lord Byron of Broadway '30

Gypsy Rose Lee (1914-70)
You Can't Have Everything '37
My Lucky Star '38
Sally, Irene and Mary '38
Screaming Mimi '58
The Trouble with Angels '66
The Over-the-Hill Gang '69

Hacken Lee
The Cave of the Silken Web '67
Six Strong Guys '04

James Kyson Lee
Asian Stories '06
Shutter '08

Jason Lee (1970-)
Mallrats '95
Chasing Amy '97
Weapons of Mass Distraction '97
Enemy of the State '98
Kissing a Fool '98
Dogma '99
Mumford '99
Almost Famous '00
Heartbreakers '01
Jay and Silent Bob Strike Back '01
Vanilla Sky '01
Big Trouble '02
Stealing Harvard '02
Dreamcatcher '03
A Guy Thing '03
I Love Your Work '03
The Incredibles '04 (V)
Jersey Girl '04
The Ballad of Jack and Rose '05
Drop Dead Sexy '05
Clerks 2 '06
Monster House '06 (V)
Alvin and the Chipmunks '07
Underdog '07 (V)
Alvin and the Chipmunks: The Squeakuel '09
Columbus Circle '10
Cop Out '10
Alvin and the Chipmunks: Chipwrecked '11
Alvin and the Chipmunks: Road Chip '15
Growing Up Smith '17

Jason Scott Lee (1966-)
Back to the Future, Part 2 '89
Dragon: The Bruce Lee Story '93
Map of the Human Heart '93
Rapa Nui '93
Rudyard Kipling's The Jungle Book '94
Soldier '98
Russell Mulcahy's Tale of the Mummy '99
Arabian Nights '00
Lilo & Stitch '02 (V)
Dracula 2: Ascension '03
Timecop 2: The Berlin Decision '03
Dracula 3: Legacy '05
Lilo & Stitch 2: Stitch Has a Glitch '05 (V)
Only the Brave '06
Balls of Fury '07
Seventh Son '15
Crouching Tiger, Hidden Dragon: Sword of Destiny '16

Jeong-jin Lee
Seoul Raiders '05
Pieta '13

Jesse Lee (1984-)
Matinee '92
The Brady Bunch Movie '95
From the Mixed-Up Files of Mrs. Basil E. Frankweiler '95
A Very Brady Sequel '96

Joanna Lee (1931-2003)
Plan 9 from Outer Space '56
Making the Grade '84

John Edward Lee (1981-)
Flesh Wounds '10
Asian Connection '16

Joie Lee (1962-)
She's Gotta Have It '86
School Daze '88
Mo' Better Blues '90
Crooklyn '94
Coffee and Cigarettes '03

Jon Kit Lee (1967-)
The Corruptor '99
Romeo Must Die '00

Julia Lee
Asylum of the Damned '03
The Hillside Stranglings '04

Kaiulani Lee (1950-)
Cujo '83
Before and After '95
Hush '98

Kang-sheng Lee (1968-)
The Hole '98
What Time Is It There? '01
Goodbye, Dragon Inn '03
Stray Dogs '13

Ki Hong Lee
Maze Runner: The Scorch Trials '15
Wish Upon '17
Maze Runner: The Death Cure '18

Laura Lee (1910-)
Eleven Men and a Girl '30
Going Wild '30

Lila Lee (1901-73)
Male and Female '19
Blood and Sand '22
Midnight Girl '25
The Adorable Cheat '28
The Unholy Three '30
False Faces '32
Stand Up and Cheer '34
Whirlpool '34

Margaret Lee (1943-)
Fire Monsters Against the Son of Hercules '62
Casanova '70 '65
Secret Agent Super Dragon '66
Action Man '67
Circus of Fear '67
Five for Hell '67
Five Golden Dragons '67
The Cats '68
Dorian Gray '70
Venus in Furs '70
Slaughter Hotel '71

Mark Lee (1958-)
Gallipoli '81
The Everlasting Secret Family '88
Sahara '95
Nowhere to Land '00
The Junction Boys '02

Mary Lee (1925-96)
Nancy Drew, Reporter '39
South of the Border '39
Ridin' on a Rainbow '41

Michele Lee (1942-)
How to Succeed in Business without Really Trying '67
The Love Bug '68
The Comic '69
Only with Married Men '74
The Fatal Image '90
Along Came Polly '04

Moon Lee (1965-)
Zu: Warriors from the Magic Mountain '83
Mr. Vampire '86

Nelson Lee (1975-)
Virtuality '09
All Saints '17

Peggy Lee (1920-2002)
Stage Door Canteen '43
The Jazz Singer '52
Lady and the Tramp '55 (V)
Pete Kelly's Blues '55

Reggie Lee
Frankenfish '04
Drag Me to Hell '09

Robine Lee (1974-)
Hav Plenty '97
Deliver Us from Eva '03
National Security '03
13 Going on 30 '04
Seven Pounds '08
Hotel for Dogs '09

RonReaco Lee (1977-)
Glory '89
The Return of the Swamp Thing '89
How I Spent My Summer Vacation '97
Jacked Up '01
Killer Diller '04
Guess Who '05
Madea Goes to Jail '09

Ruta Lee (1935-)
Witness for the Prosecution '57
Operation Eichmann '61
Sergeants 3 '62
The Gun Hawk '63
Escape from Planet Earth '67
Sweet Bird of Youth '89
Funny Bones '94
Christmas Do-Over '06

Sam Lee (1975-)
Biozombie '98
Gen-X Cops '99
Ping Pong '02
Dog Bite Dog '06

Serena Lee
Our America '02
Crimes of Fashion '04

Shannon Lee (1969-)
High Voltage '98
Epoch '00
The Gay Bed and Breakfast of Terror '07

Sheryl Lee (1967-)
Wild at Heart '90
Jersey Girl '92
Twin Peaks: Fire Walk with Me '92
Red Shoe Diaries 4: Auto Erotica '93
Backbeat '94
Don't Do It '94
Fall Time '94
Guinevere '94
Follow the River '95
Homage '95
Notes from Underground '95
Bliss '96
Mother Night '96
The Blood Oranges '97
David '97
John Carpenter's Vampires '97
Kiss the Sky '98
Angel's Dance '99
Hitched '01
Children On Their Birthdays '02
Paradise, Texas '05
The Secrets of Comfort House '06
Winter's Bone '10
Texas Killing Fields '11

Sophie Lee (1968-)
Muriel's Wedding '94
The Castle '97
Holy Smoke '99
Bootmen '00
He Died With a Falafel in His Hand '01

Spike Lee (1957-)
She's Gotta Have It '86
School Daze '88
Do the Right Thing '89
Mo' Better Blues '90
Jungle Fever '91
Malcolm X '92
Crooklyn '94
DROP Squad '94
Girl 6 '96
Summer of Sam '99
Lisa Picard Is Famous '01 (C)
Red Hook Summer '12
Pavarotti '19

Stan Lee (1922-)
The Ambulance '90
Mallrats '95 (C)
Daredevil '03 (C)
Hulk '03 (C)
Comic Book: The Movie '04 (C)
Fantastic Four '05
Big Hero 6 '14 (V)

Stephen Lee (1955-2014)
Purple Hearts '84
Dolls '87
The Pit & the Pendulum '91
Me and the Mob '94

Sung-jae Lee (1970-)
Attack the Gas Station '99
Barking Dogs Never Bite '00
Public Enemy '02

Tommy Lee (1901-76)
The Sand Pebbles '66
Rooster Cogburn '75

Tommy Lee (1962-)
The New Guy '02 (C)
10th & Wolf '06

Waise Lee (1959-)
A Better Tomorrow, Part 1 '86
A Bullet in the Head '90
Wing Chun '94
Running out of Time '99
Infernal Affairs 3 '03

Will Yun Lee (1971-)
What's Cooking? '00
Die Another Day '02
Torque '04
Elektra '05
5 Star Day '10
Setup '11
Where the Road Meets the Sun '11
Total Recall '12
Make Your Move '13
The Wolverine '13

William Gregory Lee (1972-)
In Enemy Hands '04
Domain '18

Yu-won Lee
Attack the Gas Station '99
Take Care of My Cat '01

Caroline Lee-Johnson
A Woman's Guide to Adultery '93
The Defender '04

Allen Leech (1981-)
Cowboys & Angels '04
Grand Piano '13
In Fear '13
The Imitation Game '14

Andrea Leeds (1914-74)
Come and Get It '36
Stage Door '37
The Goldwyn Follies '38
Letter of Introduction '38
The Real Glory '39
Swanee River '39
They Shall Have Music '39

Phil Leeds (1916-98)
Saturday the 14th Strikes Back '88
Enemies, a Love Story '89
Ghost '90
Frankie and Johnny '91
He Said, She Said '91
Lost and Found '99

Erica Leerhsen (1976-)
Book of Shadows: Blair Witch 2 '00
Anything Else '03
The Texas Chainsaw Massacre '03
Little Athens '05
Wrong Turn 2: Dead End '07
Organizm '08
Magic in the Moonlight '14

Lindsay Leese
Comfort and Joy '03
Coast to Coast '04

Scott Leet (1962-)
Out in Fifty '99
The Frankenstein Syndrome '10

Jane Leeves (1961-)
Mr. Write '92
Miracle on 34th Street '94
James and the Giant Peach '96 (V)
Pandora's Clock '96
The Event '03
Garfield: A Tail of Two Kitties '06 (V)
National Lampoon Presents: Endless Bummer '09

Philippe Lefebvre
Whatever You Say '02
OSS 117: Cairo, Nest of Spies '06
Retour Chez Ma Mere '16

Adam LeFevre (1950-)
Return of the Secaucus 7 '80
Hearts in Atlantis '01
L.I.E. '01
Tadpole '02
Arthur and the Invisibles '06
I Do & I Don't '07
The Lifeguard '13
Gold '16

Rachelle Lefevre (1979-)
Dead Awake '01
The Legend of Butch & Sundance '04
The River King '05

Prom Wars *'08*
The Summit *'08*
Twilight *'08*
The Twilight Saga: New Moon *'09*
Barney's Version *'10*
The Pool Boys *'10*
The Caller *'11*
Reclaim *'14*
Edge of Winter *'16*

Rene Lefevre (1898-1991)
Le Million *'31*
The Crime of Monsieur Lange *'36*

Christian Leffler
A Girl, 3 Guys and a Gun *'01*
Madhouse *'04*

Dave Legano
Bonded by Blood *'09*
Command Performance *'09*

Lance LeGault (1935-2012)
French Quarter *'78*
Kenny Rogers as the Gambler *'80*
Stripes *'81*
Welcome to Spring Break *'88*
Shadow Force *'92*
Roadracers *'94*
Home on the Range *'04 (V)*

Sheila LeGay (1911-2003)
See Sheila Mannors

Phoebe Legere
The Toxic Avenger, Part 2 *'89*
The Toxic Avenger, Part 3: The Last Temptation of Toxie *'89*

Alison Leggatt (1904-90)
Waterloo Road *'45*
This Happy Breed *'47*
Never Take Candy From a Stranger *'60*
Day of the Triffids *'63*

Michael Legge (1978-)
Angela's Ashes *'99*
Cowboys & Angels *'04*
The Bachelor Weekend *'13*

Annie Legras (1947-)
See Anny (Annie Legras) Duperey

James LeGros (1962-)
Ratings Game *'84*
*batteries not included *'87*
Phantasm 2 *'88*
Drugstore Cowboy *'89*
Leather Jackets *'90*
Blood & Concrete: A Love Story *'91*
Point Break *'91*
Guncrazy *'92*
My New Gun *'92*
Singles *'92*
Where the Day Takes You *'92*
Nervous Ticks *'93*
Bad Girls *'94*
Don't Do It *'94*
Floundering *'94*
Living in Oblivion *'94*
The Low Life *'95*
Safe *'95*
Infinity *'96*
Serial Bomber *'96*
Wishful Thinking *'96*
The Myth of Fingerprints *'97*
Enemy of the State *'98*
Highway Hitcher *'98*
Psycho *'98*
If You Only Knew *'00*
World Traveler *'01*
Big Shot: Confessions of a Campus Bookie *'02*
Lovely & Amazing *'02*
Scotland, PA *'02*
Catch That Kid *'04*
Straight into Darkness *'04*
November *'05*
Sleeper Cell *'05*
The Last Winter *'06*
Trust the Man *'06*
Sherman's Way *'08*
Vantage Point *'08*
Bitter Feast *'10*
Skateland *'10*
Mildred Pierce *'11*
Big Miracle *'12*
A Birder's Guide to Everything *'14*
The Young Kieslowski *'15*
Certain Women *'16*
Wildling *'18*

John Leguizamo (1964-)
Casualties of War *'89*
Die Hard 2: Die Harder *'90*
Hangin' with the Homeboys *'91*
Out for Justice *'91*
Regarding Henry *'91*
Whispers in the Dark *'92*
Carlito's Way *'93*
Super Mario Bros. *'93*
A Pyromaniac's Love Story *'95*
To Wong Foo, Thanks for Everything, Julie Newmar *'95*
Executive Decision *'96*
The Fan *'96*
The Pest *'96*
William Shakespeare's Romeo and Juliet *'96*
Body Count *'97*
A Brother's Kiss *'97*
Spawn *'97*
Dr. Dolittle *'98 (V)*
Frogs for Snakes *'98*
Joe the King *'99*
Summer of Sam *'99*
Arabian Nights *'00*
Titan A.E. *'00 (V)*
King of the Jungle *'01*
Moulin Rouge *'01*
What's the Worst That Could Happen? *'01*
Collateral Damage *'02*
Empire *'02*
Ice Age *'02 (V)*
Point of Origin *'02*
Spun *'02*
ZigZag *'02*
Undefeated *'03*
Cronicas *'04*
Assault on Precinct 13 *'05*
George A. Romero's Land of the Dead *'05*
The Honeymooners *'05*
Sueno *'05*
The Groomsmen *'06*
Ice Age: The Meltdown *'06 (V)*
Lies & Alibis *'06*
The Babysitters *'07*
Where God Left His Shoes *'07*
The Happening *'08*
Miracle at St. Anna *'08*
Nothing Like the Holidays *'08*
Righteous Kill *'08*
Gamer *'09*
Ice Age: Dawn of the Dinosaurs *'09*
The Ministers *'09*
Vanishing on 7th Street *'10*
The Lincoln Lawyer *'11*
Ice Age: Continental Drift *'12 (V)*
One for the Money *'12*
Kick-Ass 2 *'13*
Walking with Dinosaurs 3D *'13 (V)*
Chef *'14*
Fugly! *'14*
John Wick *'14*
Ride Along *'14*
Cymbeline *'15*
Experimenter *'15*
Meadowland *'15*
Sisters *'15*
The Hollow Point *'16*
Ice Age: Collision Course *'16*
The Infiltrator *'16*
Stealing Cars *'16*
Nancy *'18*
Playing with Fire *'19*
The Sun Is Also a Star *'19*

Kristen Lehman (1972-)
Bleeders *'97*
Dog Park *'98*
Way of the Gun *'00*
Verdict in Blood *'02*
The Sentinel *'06*

Kristin Lehman (1972-)
Playing House *'06*
The Loft *'14*

Beatrix Lehmann (1903-79)
Psyche 59 *'64*
The Cat and the Canary *'79*
Love for Lydia *'79*

Carla Lehmann (1917-90)
Cottage to Let *'41*
Candlelight in Algeria *'44*

Frederic Lehne (1959-)
Ordinary People *'80*
The Children Nobody Wanted *'81*
Coward of the County *'81*
Billionaire Boys Club *'87*
Amityville 4: The Evil Escapes *'89*
This Gun for Hire *'90*
Dream Lover *'93*
Man's Best Friend *'93*
Balloon Farm *'97*
Terror Tract *'00*
Octopus 2: River of Fear *'02*

John Lehne
Griffin and Phoenix: A Love Story *'76*
Ladies and Gentlemen, the Fabulous Stains *'82*

Meme Lei (1952-)
See Me Me Lai

Ron Leibman (1937-2019)
The Hot Rock *'70*
Where's Poppa? *'70*
Slaughterhouse Five *'72*
The Super Cops *'74*
Norma Rae *'79*
Up the Academy *'80*
Zorro, the Gay Blade *'81*
Romantic Comedy *'83*
Rhinestone *'84*
Seven Hours to Judgment *'88*
Night Falls on Manhattan *'96*
Don King: Only in America *'97*
Just the Ticket *'98*
Auto Focus *'02*
Dummy *'02*
Personal Velocity: Three Portraits *'02*
Garden State *'04*
A Little Help *'11*

Hudson (Heidi) Leick (1969-)
Dangerous Cargo *'96*
Something About Sex *'98*
Chill Factor *'99*
Shockwave *'06*

Don Leifert (1951-2010)
The Alien Factor *'78*
Fiend *'83*
Galaxy Invader *'85*
Deadly Neighbor *'91*

Barbara Leigh (1946-)
The Student Nurses *'70*
Pretty Maids All In a Row *'71*
Junior Bonner *'72*
Boss *'74*

Cassandra Leigh (1964-)
Midnight Tease *'94*
Alien Terminator *'95*

Chyler Leigh (1982-)
Not Another Teen Movie *'01*
The 19th Wife *'10*
Brake *'12*

Janet Leigh (1926-2004)
If Winter Comes *'41*
The Romance of Rosy Ridge *'47*
Act of Violence *'48*
The Hills of Home *'48*
Words and Music *'48*
The Doctor and the Girl *'49*
Holiday Affair *'49*
Little Women *'49*
The Red Danube *'50*
That Forsyte Woman *'50*
Angels in the Outfield *'51*
It's a Big Country *'51*
Two Tickets to Broadway *'51*
Fearless Fagan *'52*
Scaramouche *'52*
Confidentially Connie *'53*
Houdini *'53*
The Naked Spur *'53*
The Black Shield of Falworth *'54*
Living It Up *'54*
Prince Valiant *'54*
My Sister Eileen *'55*
Pete Kelly's Blues *'55*
Jet Pilot *'57*
Touch of Evil *'58*
The Vikings *'58*
The Perfect Furlough *'59*
Psycho *'60*
Who Was That Lady? *'60*
The Manchurian Candidate *'62*
Bye, Bye, Birdie *'63*
An American Dream *'66*
Harper *'66*
Grand Slam *'67*
Hello Down There *'69*
Night of the Lepus *'72*
The Fog *'78*
Boardwalk *'79*
Halloween: H20 *'98*

Jennifer Jason Leigh (1962-)
Eyes of a Stranger *'81*
Fast Times at Ridgemont High *'82*
Wrong Is Right *'82*
Easy Money *'83*
Grandview U.S.A. *'84*
Flesh and Blood *'85*
Girls of the White Orchid *'85*
The Hitcher *'86*
The Men's Club *'86*
Sister, Sister *'87*
The Big Picture *'89*
Buried Alive *'90*
Last Exit to Brooklyn *'90*
Miami Blues *'90*
Backdraft *'91*
Crooked Hearts *'91*
Rush *'91*
Single White Female *'92*
The Hudsucker Proxy *'93*
Short Cuts *'93*
Dolores Claiborne *'94*
Mrs. Parker and the Vicious Circle *'94*
Georgia *'95*
Kansas City *'95*
Bastard out of Carolina *'96*
A Thousand Acres *'97*
Washington Square *'97*
The Love Letter *'98*
eXistenZ *'99*
The King Is Alive *'00*
Skipped Parts *'00*
The Anniversary Party *'01*
The Quickie *'01*
Hey Arnold! The Movie *'02 (V)*
Road to Perdition *'02*
In the Cut *'03*
The Machinist *'04*
Palindromes *'04*
The Jacket *'05*
Margot at the Wedding *'07*
Synecdoche, New York *'08*
Greenberg *'10*
Hateship Loveship *'13*
Kill Your Darlings *'13*
The Moment *'13*
The Spectacular Now *'13*
The Hateful Eight *'15*
Anomalisa *'16*
Amityville: The Awakening *'17*
Good Time *'17*
LBJ *'17*
Annihilation *'18*
White Boy Rick *'18*

John Leigh (1965-)
Stickmen *'01*
Kidnapped *'05*

Nelson Leigh (1905-85)
World Without End *'56*
Bombers B-52 *'57*
The Gallant Hours *'60*
Ma Barker's Killer Brood *'60*

Spencer Leigh (1963-)
Caravaggio *'86*
The Last of England *'87*
Smart Money *'88*

Steven Leigh (1964-)
Deadly Bet *'91*
To Be the Best *'93*
Sword of Honor *'94*

Suzanna Leigh (1945-)
Boeing Boeing *'65*
Paradise, Hawaiian Style *'66*
Deadlier Than the Male *'67*
The Fiend *'71*
Lust for a Vampire *'71*

Vivien Leigh (1913-67)
Dark Journey *'37*
Fire Over England *'37*
Storm in a Teacup *'37*
Sidewalks of London *'38*
Gone with the Wind *'39*
21 Days *'40*
Waterloo Bridge *'40*
That Hamilton Woman *'41*
Caesar and Cleopatra *'46*
Anna Karenina *'48*
A Streetcar Named Desire *'51*
Roman Spring of Mrs. Stone *'61*
Ship of Fools *'65*

Barbara Leigh-Hunt (1935-)
Frenzy *'72*
The Plague Dogs *'82 (V)*
Paper Mask *'91*
Pride and Prejudice *'95*
A Merry War *'97*
Longitude *'00*
Wives and Daughters *'01*

Laura Leighton (1968-)
Seven Girlfriends *'00*
We'll Meet Again *'02*
A Deadly Encounter *'04*
Love Notes *'07*
Daniel's Daughter *'08*

Margaret Leighton (1922-76)
The Winslow Boy *'48*
Under Capricorn *'49*
Waltz of the Toreadors *'62*
The Best Man *'64*
The Loved One *'65*
The Madwoman of Chaillot *'69*
The Go-Between *'71*
X, Y & Zee *'72*
From Beyond the Grave *'73*
Choice of Weapons *'76*

Harald Leipnitz (1926-2000)
River of Evil *'64*
Thunder at the Border *'66*

Frederick Leister (1885-1970)
Spellbound *'41*
Green Grow the Rushes *'51*
The Time of His Life *'55*

David Leisure (1950-)
You Can't Hurry Love *'88*
Hollywood Safari *'96*
Gangster World *'98*
Ten Things I Hate about You *'99*
Three Strikes *'00*
Elvis Has Left the Building *'04*

Donovan Leitch (1967-)
And God Created Woman *'88*
The Blob *'88*
The In Crowd *'88*
Cutting Class *'89*
Glory *'89*
Dark Horse *'92*
Gas Food Lodging *'92*
I Shot Andy Warhol *'96*
One Night Stand *'97*
Love Kills *'98*
Big City Blues *'99*
The '60s *'99*

Matthew Leitch (1975-)
AKA *'02*
The Detonator *'06*

Virginia Leith (1925-2019)
Black Widow *'54*
Violent Saturday *'55*
Toward the Unknown *'56*
The Brain that Wouldn't Die *'63*

Tyron Leitso (1976-)
Dinotopia *'02*
Snow White: The Fairest of Them All *'02*
House of the Dead *'03*
Seed *'08*

Jeremy Lelliott (1982-)
Disappearance *'02*
Lady Jayne Killer *'03*

Gilles Lellouche (1972-)
Tell No One *'06*
Mesrine: Part 1-Killer Instinct *'08*
Paris *'08*
Little White Lies *'10*
Point Blank *'10*
My Piece of the Pie *'11*
Therese *'12*
The Clearstream Affair *'15*
The Connection *'15*

Philippe Lemaire (1927-2004)
Cartouche *'62*
Death is Nimble, Death is Quick *'67*

Braeden Lemasters (1996-)
Love's Unending Legacy *'07*
The Stepfather *'09*
A Christmas Story 2 *'12*

Paul LeMat (1945-)
Firehouse *'72*
American Graffiti *'73*
Aloha, Bobby and Rose *'74*
Citizens Band *'77*
More American Graffiti *'79*
Melvin and Howard *'80*
Death Valley *'81*
Rock & Rule *'83 (V)*
Strange Invaders *'83*
The Burning Bed *'85*
Hanoi Hilton *'87*
Secret Witness *'88*
Blind Witness *'89*
Easy Wheels *'89*
Puppet Master *'89*
Sensation *'94*
American History X *'98*
Big Bad Love *'02*
The Long Shot *'04*

Harvey Lembeck (1923-82)
Stalag 17 *'53*
The Command *'54*
Between Heaven and Hell *'56*
Sail a Crooked Ship *'61*
Beach Party *'63*
Bikini Beach *'64*
Pajama Party *'64*
Beach Blanket Bingo *'65*
How to Stuff a Wild Bikini *'65*
Sergeant Deadhead *'65*
Fireball 500 *'66*
Ghost in the Invisible Bikini *'66*

Michael Lembeck (1948-)
The Boys in Company C *'77*
The In-Laws *'79*
Conspiracy: The Trial of the Chicago Eight *'87*
Danielle Steel's Heartbeat *'93*

Kris Lemche (1978-)
Ginger Snaps *'01*
A Simple Curve *'05*
Final Destination 3 *'06*
Rosencrantz & Guildenstern Are Undead *'10*
The Frankenstein Theory *'13*
They're Watching *'16*

Stephanie Lemelin (1979-)
Anonymous Rex '04
Raising Flagg '06

Valerie Lemercier (1964-)
The Visitors '95
Friday Night '02
Avenue Montaigne '06

Rachel Lemieux
Mommy '95
Mommy 2: Mommy's Day '96

Anthony Lemke
Ricky Nelson: Original Teen Idol '99
Do or Die '03
A Deadly Encounter '04
False Pretenses '04
Legacy of Fear '06
Proof of Lies '06
A Life Interrupted '07
Wide Awake '07
The Phantom '09
You Lucky Dog '10
Who Is Simon Miller? '11
Exploding Sun '13

Tutte Lemkow (1924-91)
Moulin Rouge '52
The Siege of Sidney Street '60
The Guns of Navarone '61
Inspector Clouseau '68

Steve Lemme (1968-)
Super Troopers '01
Club Dread '04
The Dukes of Hazzard '05
Beerfest '06
The Slammin' Salmon '09
Super Troopers 2 '18

Julia Lemmertz (1963-)
The 3 Marias '03
From Beginning to End '09

Chris Lemmon (1954-)
The Happy Hooker Goes Hollywood '80
Just Before Dawn '80
Swing Shift '84
That's Life! '86
Going Undercover '88
Dad '89
Corporate Affairs '90
Firehead '90
Lena's Holiday '90
Thunder in Paradise '93
Thunder in Paradise 2 '94
Thunder in Paradise 3 '94
Wishmaster '97
Best of the Best: Without Warning '98
Just the Ticket '98
Land of the Free '98

Jack Lemmon (1925-2001)
It Should Happen to You '54
Phffft! '54
Mister Roberts '55
My Sister Eileen '55
Three for the Show '55
Fire Down Below '57
Operation Mad Ball '57
Bell, Book and Candle '58
Cowboy '58
It Happened to Jane '59
Some Like It Hot '59
The Apartment '60
Wackiest Ship in the Army '61
Days of Wine and Roses '62
The Notorious Landlady '62
Irma La Douce '63
Under the Yum-Yum Tree '63
Good Neighbor Sam '64
How to Murder Your Wife '64
The Great Race '65
The Fortune Cookie '66
Luv '67
The Odd Couple '68
April Fools '69
The Out-of-Towners '70
Avanti! '72
Save the Tiger '73
The Front Page '74
Prisoner of Second Avenue '74
Airport '77 '77
The China Syndrome '79
Missing '82
Mass Appeal '84
Macaroni '85
That's Life! '86
The Murder of Mary Phagan '87
Long Day's Journey into Night '88
Dad '89
JFK '91
For Richer, for Poorer '92
Glengarry Glen Ross '92
The Player '92
Grumpy Old Men '93
A Life in the Theater '93
Short Cuts '93
The Grass Harp '95
Grumpier Old Men '95
Getting Away With Murder '96
Hamlet '96
My Fellow Americans '96
Out to Sea '97
The Long Way Home '98
The Odd Couple 2 '98
Inherit the Wind '99
Tuesdays with Morrie '99
The Legend of Bagger Vance '00

Kasi Lemmons (1961-)
School Daze '88
Vampire's Kiss '88
The Silence of the Lambs '91
Candyman '92
Hard Target '93
DROP Squad '94
Fear of a Black Hat '94
Til There Was You '96

Genevieve Lemon
Sweetie '89
The Piano '93
Billy's Holiday '95

Ute Lemper (1963-)
Bogus '96
A River Made to Drown In '97
Appetite '98

Mark Lenard (1928-96)
Noon Sunday '75
Star Trek: The Motion Picture '79
Star Trek 3: The Search for Spock '84
Star Trek 4: The Voyage Home '86
Star Trek 6: The Undiscovered Country '91

Jorge Lendeborg, Jr.
The Land '16
Bumblebee '18

Vanessa Lengies (1985-)
Ratz '99
The Perfect Man '05
Waiting '05
Stick It '06
Foreign Exchange '08
Still Waiting '08

Tom Lenk (1976-)
Window Theory '04
My Girlfriend's Boyfriend '10

Nels Lennarson (1972-)
Best Friends '05
Lesser Evil '06
The Obsession '06
Good People, Bad Things '08
The Traveler '10

Bárbara Lennie (1984-)
Magical Girl '14
Everybody Knows '18

Harry J. Lennix (1964-)
The Five Heartbeats '91
Bob Roberts '92
Mo' Money '92
Get On the Bus '96
Titus '99
Love and Basketball '00
Collateral Damage '02
Keep the Faith, Baby '02
Pumpkin '02
Black Listed '03
The Human Stain '03
The Matrix Reloaded '03
The Matrix Revolutions '03
Barbershop 2: Back in Business '04
Ray '04
Suspect Zero '04
Resurrecting the Champ '07
Stomp the Yard '07
Man of Steel '13

Jarrett Lennon (1982-)
Servants of Twilight '91
Short Cuts '93
Amityville Dollhouse '96

John Lennon (1940-80)
A Hard Day's Night '64
Help! '65
How I Won the War '67
Yellow Submarine '68 *(V)*
The Magic Christian '69
Let It Be '70
Chuck Berry: Hail! Hail! Rock 'n' Roll '87

Julian Lennon (1963-)
Chuck Berry: Hail! Hail! Rock 'n' Roll '87
The Linguini Incident '92 *(C)*
Leaving Las Vegas '95

Maria Lennon
Oktober '98
Bloom '03

Thomas Lennon (1970-)
A Guy Thing '03
How to Lose a Guy in 10 Days '03
Le Divorce '03
Heights '04
Conversations with Other Women '05
Herbie: Fully Loaded '05
The Hitchhiker's Guide to the Galaxy '05 *(V)*
Balls of Fury '07
Reno 911! Miami '07
Hancock '08
17 Again '09
Bad Teacher '11
Cedar Rapids '11
A Very Harold & Kumar Christmas '11
What's Your Number? '11
The Dark Knight Rises '12
What to Expect When You're Expecting '12
Monster Trucks '16
Dog Days '18
Puppet Master: The Littlest Reich '18

Annie Lennox (1954-)
Revolution '85
Edward II '92

Jay Leno (1950-)
Americathon '79
What's Up, Hideous Sun Demon? '83
Collision Course '89
Dave '93 *(C)*
We're Back! A Dinosaur's Story '93 *(V)*
The Flintstones '94 *(C)*
Calendar Girls '03 *(C)*
Stuck On You '03 *(C)*
Ice Age: The Meltdown '06 *(V)*
Igor '08 *(V)*

Rosetta LeNoire (1911-2002)
Fritz the Cat '72 *(V)*
The Father Clements Story '87

Anne LeNy
La Petite Lili '03
The Intouchables '12

Lotte Lenya (1899-1981)
The Threepenny Opera '31
Roman Spring of Mrs. Stone '61
From Russia with Love '63
Semi-Tough '77

Kay Lenz (1953-)
Lisa, Bright and Dark '73
White Line Fever '75
Great Scout & Cathouse Thursday '76
Moving Violation '76
Rich Man, Poor Man '76
Initiation of Sarah '78
The Passage '79
Fast Walking '82
Prisoners of the Lost Universe '84
House '86
Death Wish 4: The Crackdown '87
Stripped to Kill '87
Fear '88
Physical Evidence '89
Falling from Grace '92
Gunfighter's Moon '96
A Gun, a Car, a Blonde '97

Rick Lenz (1939-)
Cactus Flower '69
Scandalous John '71
Little Dragons '80

Melissa Leo (1960-)
Always '85
Silent Witness '85
Streetwalkin' '85
Deadtime Stories '86
Carolina Skeletons '92
Venice, Venice '92
Scarlett '94
Last Summer In the Hamptons '96
The 24 Hour Woman '99
Homicide: The Movie '00
21 Grams '03
From Other Worlds '04
American Gun '05
Confess '05
Hide and Seek '05
Runaway '05
The Three Burials of Melquiades Estrada '05
Stephanie Daley '06
Black Irish '07
The Cake Eaters '07
Mr. Woodcock '07
Racing Daylight '07
According to Greta '08
The Alphabet Killer '08
Frozen River '08
Lullaby '08
Righteous Kill '08
Dear Lemon Lima '09
Don McKay '09
Conviction '10
The Fighter '10
The Space Between '10
Welcome to the Rileys '10
Mildred Pierce '11
Red State '11
Seven Days in Utopia '11
Why Stop Now '12
Bottled Up '13
Charlie Countryman '13
Oblivion '13
Olympus Has Fallen '13
Prisoners '13
The Angriest Man in Brooklyn '14
The Equalizer '14
Veronika Decides to Die '15
London Has Fallen '16
Snowden '16
Novitiate '17
The Equalizer 2 '18
Furlough '18

Leon (1962-)
Colors '88
The Five Heartbeats '91
Bad Attitude '93
Cliffhanger '93
Cool Runnings '93
Above the Rim '94
Once Upon a Time . . . When We Were Colored '95
Waiting to Exhale '95
Pure Danger '96
Spirit Lost '96
The Temptations '98
Bats '99
Friends & Lovers '99
Mr. Rock 'n' Roll: The Alan Freed Story '99
Little Richard '00
The Brooklyn Heist '08
Cover '08

Carlos Leon (1966-)
The Woodsman '04
The Cry: La Llorona '07
The Echo '08
Tricks of a Woman '08
Immigration Tango '11

Loles Leon (1950-)
Tie Me Up! Tie Me Down! '90
The Girl of Your Dreams '99

Valerie Leon (1943-)
Zeta One '69
Blood from the Mummy's Tomb '71
The Spy Who Loved Me '77
Never Say Never Again '83

Jack E. Leonard (1911-73)
Three Sailors and a Girl '53
The Fat Spy '66

Joshua Leonard (1975-)
The Blair Witch Project '99
In the Weeds '00
Men of Honor '00
Mission '00
Sacrifice '00
Scorched '02
Live from Baghdad '03
Two Days '03
Madhouse '04
Shooting Livien '05
The Shaggy Dog '06
20 Years After '08
Humpday '09
Bitter Feast '10
Higher Ground '11
Shark Night 3D '11
If I Stay '14
The Town That Dreaded Sundown '14
Unsane '18

Lu Leonard (1927-2004)
Shadowzone '89
Circuitry Man '90

Robert Sean Leonard (1969-)
The Manhattan Project '86
My Best Friend Is a Vampire '88
Dead Poets Society '89
Mr. & Mrs. Bridge '90
The Age of Innocence '93
Married to It '93
Much Ado about Nothing '93
Swing Kids '93
Safe Passage '94
Killer: A Journal of Murder '95
The Boys Next Door '96
I Love You, I Love You Not '97
Ground Control '98
The Last Days of Disco '98
Chelsea Walls '01
Driven '01
A Glimpse of Hell '01
Tape '01
A Painted House '03
The I Inside '04

Sheldon Leonard (1907-97)
Tall, Dark and Handsome '41
Week-End in Havana '41
Tortilla Flat '42
City Without Men '43
Passport to Suez '43
Gambler's Choice '44
To Have & Have Not '44
Uncertain Glory '44
Zombies on Broadway '44
Captain Kidd '45
Radio Stars on Parade '45
Decoy '46
It's a Wonderful Life '46
Somewhere in the Night '46
Sinbad, the Sailor '47
Violence '47
Open Secret '48
Force of Evil '49
Abbott and Costello Meet the Invisible Man '51
Chained for Life '51
Young Man With Ideas '52
Breakdown '53
Money from Home '53
Guys and Dolls '55
Brink's Job '78

Marco Leonardi (1971-)
Cinema Paradiso '88
Like Water for Chocolate '93
Manhattan Merenque! '95
The Stendahl Syndrome '95
David '97
The Five Senses '99
From Dusk Till Dawn 3: The Hangman's Daughter '99
Texas Rangers '01
Once Upon a Time in Mexico '03
The Last Man '19

Al Leong (1952-)
Lethal Weapon '87
Die Hard '88
Bill & Ted's Excellent Adventure '89
Hard Hunted '92
The Shadow '94

Isabella Leong (1978-)
The Eye 3 '05
The Mummy: Tomb of the Dragon Emperor '08

Tea Leoni (1966-)
A League of Their Own '92
Wyatt Earp '94
Bad Boys '95
Flirting with Disaster '95
Deep Impact '98
Family Man '00
Life in the Fast Lane '00
Jurassic Park 3 '01
Hollywood Ending '02
People I Know '02
House of D '04
Spanglish '04
Fun With Dick and Jane '05
You Kill Me '07
Ghost Town '08
The Smell of Success '09
Tower Heist '11

Demitri Leonidas
Tormented '09
Centurion '10

Stephanie Leonidas (1984-)
Yes '04
MirrorMask '05
Crusade: A March through Time '06
Dracula '06

Chauncey Leopardi (1981-)
Huck and the King of Hearts '93
The Sandlot '93
Houseguest '94
The Big Green '95
ShadowZone: The Undead Express '96
The Sandlot 3: Heading Home '07

Philippe Leotard (1940-2001)
Two English Girls '72
La Balance '82
Le Choc '82

Robert Lepage (1957-)
Jesus of Montreal '89
Stardom '00
Far Side of the Moon '03

Sarah Le Picard
The Hedgehog '09
Things to Come '16

Gerald Lepkowski
American Cousins '02
Sisters of War '10

Gregoire Leprince-Ringuet (1987-)
Strayed '03
In the Arms of My Enemy '07
Love Songs '07
The Beautiful Person '08
The Army of Crime '10
Black Heaven '10
The Princess of Montpensier '10

Logan Lerman (1992-)
The Patriot '00
What Women Want '00
Riding in Cars with Boys '01
A Painted House '03
The Butterfly Effect '04
Hoot '06
Meet Bill '07
The Number 23 '07
3:10 to Yuma '07
Gamer '09
My One and Only '09
Percy Jackson & The Olympians: The Lightning Thief '10
The Three Musketeers '11
The Perks of Being a Wallflower '12
Stuck in Love '12
Percy Jackson: Sea of Monsters '13
Fury '14
Noah '14
Indignation '16
The Vanishing of Sidney Hall '17
Sgt. Stubby: An American Hero '18

Ken Lerner (1948-)
Relentless '89
Unlawful Entry '92
Mother's Boys '94
Relentless 4 '94
Senseless '98

Michael Lerner (1941-)
The Candidate '72
Firehouse '72
Busting '74
Missiles of October '74
Outlaw Blues '77
The Postman Always Rings Twice '81
National Lampoon's Class Reunion '82
Strange Invaders '83
The Execution '85
Anguish '88
Eight Men Out '88
Harlem Nights '89
Any Man's Death '90
Maniac Cop 2 '90
Barton Fink '91
Omen 4: The Awakening '91
Newsies '92
Amos and Andrew '93
Blank Check '93
No Escape '94
Radioland Murders '94
The Road to Wellville '94
A Pyromaniac's Love Story '95
No Way Back '96
The Beautician and the Beast '97
For Richer or Poorer '97
Celebrity '98
Godzilla '98
My Favorite Martian '98
Safe Men '98
Attention Shoppers '99
The Mod Squad '99
Russell Mulcahy's Tale of the Mummy '99
Mockingbird Don't Sing '01
Elf '03
29 Palms '03
Poster Boy '04
When Do We Eat? '05
The Last Time '06
Love and Other Disasters '06
Yonkers Joe '08
Life During Wartime '09
The Bannen Way '10
Pete Smalls Is Dead '10
Atlas Shrugged: Part 1 '11

Sam Lerner (1992-)
Envy '04
Monster House '06 (V)
Project Almanac '15

Adelaide Leroux (1982-)
Flanders '06
Seraphine '08
Home '09

Baby LeRoy
It's a Gift '34
The Old-Fashioned Way '34

Phillippe LeRoy (1930-)
Le Trou '59
Castle of the Living Dead '64
Une Femme Mariee '64
A Married Woman '65
The Frightened Woman '71
Caliber 9 '72
The Night Porter '74
Three Men and a Cradle '85
Vatel '00
Mother of Tears '08

Bethel Leslie (1929-99)
A Rage to Live '65
Ironweed '87
Long Day's Journey into Night '88
In Cold Blood '96
Message in a Bottle '98

Ewen Leslie (1980-)
Sleeping Beauty '11
The Daughter '15
The Nightingale '18

Joan Leslie (1925-)
Love Affair '39
High Sierra '41
Sergeant York '41
The Wagons Roll at Night '41
The Male Animal '42
Yankee Doodle Dandy '42
The Hard Way '43
The Sky's the Limit '43
Thank Your Lucky Stars '43
This Is the Army '43
Hollywood Canteen '44
Rhapsody in Blue '45
Man in the Saddle '51
Hellgate '52
Woman They Almost Lynched '53

Nan Leslie (1926-2000)
Desperate '47
The Woman on the Beach '47
The Bamboo Saucer '68

Rose Leslie (1987-)
Honeymoon '14
The Last Witch Hunter '15
Morgan '16

William Leslie (1925-2005)
The Lineup '58
The Couch '62

Jalil Lespert (1976-)
Sade '00
Le Petit Lieutenant '05
The Escape '18

Mimi Lesseos (1964-)
Final Impact '91
Pushed to the Limit '92
Beyond Fear '93
Personal Vendetta '96

Anton Lesser (1952-)
Moses '96
Vanity Fair '99
Almost Strangers '01
Charlotte Gray '01
Lorna Doone '01
River Queen '05
Miss Potter '06
The Escape Artist '13
Disobedience '17

Len Lesser (1922-2011)
Shack Out on 101 '55
How to Stuff a Wild Bikini '65
Kelly's Heroes '70
Grandma's House '88
Ain't No Way Back '89
Baadasssss! '03

Ben Lessy (1902-92)
The Jackie Robinson Story '50
Pajama Party '64
That Funny Feeling '65

Adrian Lester (1968-)
Primary Colors '98
Maybe Baby '99
Born Romantic '00
Jason and the Argonauts '00
Love's Labour's Lost '00
Dust '01
The Day After Tomorrow '04
As You Like It '06
Scenes of a Sexual Nature '06
Starting Out in the Evening '07
Doomsday '08
Case 39 '10
Euphoria '19

Bruce Lester (1912-2008)
Boy Meets Girl '38
The Witness Vanishes '39
The Letter '40
Golden Earrings '47
Charade '53

Buddy Lester (1917-2002)
Ocean's 11 '60
Sergeants 3 '62
The Nutty Professor '63
The Patsy '64
Cracking Up '83

Jack Lester
Crackerjack '38
Deadwood '65

Mark Lester (1958-)
Fahrenheit 451 '66
Our Mother's House '67
Oliver! '68
Eye Witness '70
Black Beauty '71
Melody '71
Who Slew Auntie Roo? '71
What the Peeper Saw '72
The Prince and the Pauper '78

Ron Lester (1970-2016)
Good Burger '97
Varsity Blues '98
Not Another Teen Movie '01

James Lesure (1970-)
The Ring 2 '05
Loveless in Los Angeles '07

Lori Lethin (1955-)
Bloody Birthday '80
Brotherly Love '85
Return to Horror High '87

Jared Leto (1971-)
Cool and the Crazy '94
How to Make an American Quilt '95
The Last of the High Kings '96
Prefontaine '96
Switchback '97
Basil '98
The Thin Red Line '98
Urban Legend '98
American Psycho '99
Black and White '99
Fight Club '99
Girl, Interrupted '99
Sunset Strip '99
Requiem for a Dream '00
Highway '01
Panic Room '02
Alexander '04
Lord of War '05
Lonely Hearts '06
Chapter 27 '07
Dallas Buyers Club '13
Mr. Nobody '13
Suicide Squad '16

Matt Letscher (1970-)
Lovelife '97
The Mask of Zorro '98
John John in the Sky '00
Jackie, Ethel, Joan: The Kennedy Women '01
Madison '01
King of Texas '02
Gods and Generals '03
Identity '03
Super Sucker '03
Towelhead '07
Amish Grace '10

Dan Lett
Paris, France '94
Under the Piano '95
Blind Faith '98
The Life Before This '99
Get a Clue '02

David Letterman (1947-)
Cabin Boy '94 (C)
Beavis and Butt-Head Do America '96 (V)
I'm Still Here '10

Al Lettieri (1928-75)
The Getaway '72
The Godfather '72
Pulp '72
The Deadly Trackers '73
The Don Is Dead '73
McQ '74
Mr. Majestyk '74

Tracy Letts (1965-)
Christine '16
Imperium '16
Indignation '16
Wiener-Dog '16
The Lovers '17
The Post '17

Katie Leung (1987-)
Harry Potter and the Goblet of Fire '05
Harry Potter and the Order of the Phoenix '07

Ken Leung (1970-)
Red Dragon '02
Saw '04
Sucker Free City '05
Falling for Grace '06
X-Men: The Last Stand '06
Shanghai Kiss '07

Tony Leung Chiu-Wai (1962-)
A Bullet in the Head '90
Hard-Boiled '92
Ashes of Time '94
Chungking Express '95
Cyclo '95
Happy Together '96
Flowers of Shanghai '98
Gorgeous '99
In the Mood for Love '00
Tokyo Raiders '00
Hero '02
Infernal Affairs 3 '03
2046 '04
Lust, Caution '07
Ashes of Time Redux '08
Red Cliff '08
The Great Magician '11
The Grandmaster '13

Tony Leung Ka-Fai (1958-)
Journey of the Doomed '85
Prison on Fire '87
A Better Tomorrow, Part 3 '89
The Prisoner '90
The Lover '92
Ashes of Time '94
Double Vision '02
Three . . . Extremes '04
Ashes of Time Redux '08
Iron Road '08

Oscar Levant (1906-72)
Rhythm on the River '40
Humoresque '46
Romance on the High Seas '48
The Barkleys of Broadway '49
An American in Paris '51
The Band Wagon '53
The I Don't Care Girl '53
The Cobweb '55

Francois Levantal (1960-)
Hate '95
Murderous Maids '00
A Very Long Engagement '04
Dante 01 '08
Prey '10

Calvin Levels (1954-)
A Christmas Without Snow '80
Adventures in Babysitting '87
Johnny Suede '92
Point of No Return '93
Hellbound '94
Within the Rock '96
Black Listed '03

Sam Levene (1905-80)
Mad Miss Manton '38
Shopworn Angel '38
Golden Boy '39
Shadow of the Thin Man '41
Action in the North Atlantic '43
I Dood It '43
Whistling in Brooklyn '43
The Purple Heart '44
The Killers '46
Boomerang '47
Killer McCoy '47
Babe Ruth Story '48
Dial 1119 '50
Three Sailors and a Girl '53
Designing Woman '57
Sweet Smell of Success '57
A Dream of Kings '69
Such Good Friends '71
God Told Me To '76

Elyse Levesque (1985-)
Family in Hiding '06
How I Married My High School Crush '07
Unthinkable '07
Storm Cell '08

Joanna 'JoJo' Levesque (1990-)
Aquamarine '06
RV '06
True Confessions of a Hollywood Starlet '08

Marcel Levesque (1877-1962)
Les Vampires '15
Judex '16
The Fantastic Night '42

Mariette Levesque
Snowballin' '71
Tanya's Island '81

Paul Levesque (1969-)
The Chaperone '11
Inside Out '11

Elliot Levey
Filth and Wisdom '08
MI-5 '15

Zachary Levi (1980-)
Big Momma's House 2 '06
Spiral '07
Wieners '08
Alvin and the Chipmunks: The Squeakuel '09
Stuntmen '09
Tangled '10 (V)
Remember Sunday '13
The Star '17
Shazam! '19

Margarita Levieva (1980-)
The Invisible '07
Noise '07
Spread '09
Knights of Badassdom '13
Future World '18

John Levin
Zoltan. . . Hound of Dracula '78
Bounce '00

Zoe Levin
Beneath the Harvest Sky '14
Palo Alto '14

Adam Levine
Begin Again '13
The Clapper '18

Floyd Levine
Ice '93
Watchers Reborn '98

Ilana Levine (1963-)
Just Looking '99
Anything But Love '02
Tanner on Tanner '04

Jerry Levine (1957-)
Iron Eagle '86
Casual Sex? '88
Born on the Fourth of July '89
Ghosts of Mississippi '96

Lawrence Michael Levine
V/H/S/2 '13
Always Shine '16

Samm Levine (1982-)
Not Another Teen Movie '01
Club Dread '04
Home on the Range '04 (V)
Pulse '06
Inglourious Basterds '09

Ted Levine (1957-)
Ironweed '87
Love at Large '89
The Silence of the Lambs '91
Detonator '93
The Last Outlaw '93
Nowhere to Run '93
Bullet '94
The Mangler '94
Georgia '95
Heat '95
Ellen Foster '97
Flubber '97
Mad City '97
Switchback '97
From the Earth to the Moon '98
Moby Dick '98
Wild Wild West '99
Harlan County War '00
Ali '01
Evolution '01
The Fast and the Furious '01
Joy Ride '01 (V)
The Truth About Charlie '02
Wonderland '03
Birth '04
The Manchurian Candidate '04
The Hills Have Eyes '06
American Gangster '07
The Assassination of Jesse James by the Coward Robert Ford '07
Deep Dark Canyon '12
A Single Shot '13
Gutshot Straight '14
Bleed for This '16

Connor Christopher Levins (1999-)
Eight Below '06
The Betrayed '08
The Most Wonderful Time of the Year '08

Barry Levinson (1942-)
History of the World: Part 1 '81
Jimmy Hollywood '94 (C)
Quiz Show '94
Bee Movie '07 (V)
Muhammad Ali's Greatest Fight '13

Steve Levitt (1960-)
Last Resort '86
Hunk '87
The Incredible Hulk Returns '88

Uta Levka (1942-)
Carmen, Baby '66
Scream and Scream Again '70

Liron Levo (1972-)
Kippur '00
Disengagement '07
This Must Be the Place '12

Ariel Levy (1984-)
Aftershock '12
The Green Inferno '14
The Stranger '15

Eugene Levy (1946-)
Heavy Metal '81 (V)
Going Berserk '83
National Lampoon's Vacation '83
Splash '84
Armed and Dangerous '86
Club Paradise '86
Father of the Bride '91
Stay Tuned '92
I Love Trouble '94
Father of the Bride Part 2 '95
Multiplicity '96
Waiting for Guffman '96
Almost Heroes '97
American Pie '99
The Secret Life of Girls '99

Best in Show '00
The Ladies Man '00
American Pie 2 '01
Down to Earth '01
Repli-Kate '01
Serendipity '01
Like Mike '02
American Wedding '03
Bringing Down the House '03
Dumb and Dumberer: When Harry Met Lloyd '03
A Mighty Wind '03
New York Minute '04
American Pie Presents Band Camp '05
Cheaper by the Dozen 2 '05
The Man '05
American Pie Presents: The Naked Mile '06
Curious George '06 (V)
For Your Consideration '06
Over the Hedge '06 (V)
American Pie Presents: Beta House '07
American Pie Presents: Book of Love '09
Astro Boy '09 (V)
Gooby '09
Night at the Museum: Battle of the Smithsonian '09
Taking Woodstock '09
American Reunion '12
Goon '12
Madea's Witness Protection '12

Jane Levy (1989-)
Fun Size '12
Evil Dead '13
About Alex '14
Don't Breathe '16
Monster Trucks '16
I Don't Feel at Home in This World Anymore '17
Pretenders '19

Ori Levy
Before Winter Comes '69
The Chairman '69
Moon Zero Two '70
The Sellout '76
Operation Thunderbolt '77

William Levy
Addicted '14
Tyler Perry's The Single Moms' Club '14
Resident Evil: The Final Chapter '16

James Lew (1952-)
Private Wars '93
Boogie Boy '98
High Voltage '98
Deep Core '00
18 Fingers of Death '05

Jose Lewgoy (1920-2003)
Fitzcarraldo '82
Kiss of the Spider Woman '85
Cobra Verde '88

Al Lewis (1923-2006)
Munster, Go Home! '66
They Shoot Horses, Don't They? '69
The Night Strangler '72
Used Cars '80
The Munsters' Revenge '81
Married to the Mob '88
Car 54, Where Are You? '94
South Beach Academy '96

Ben Lewis (1894-1970)
Stir of Echoes 2: The Homecoming '07
That Russell Girl '08
Scott Pilgrim vs. the World '10
The Shrine '10

Bubba Lewis (1989-)
Miracle Run '04
To Save a Life '10

Charlotte Lewis (1967-)
The Golden Child '86
Sketch Artist '92
Storyville '92
Excessive Force '93
Men of War '94
Embrace of the Vampire '95
Red Shoe Diaries 6: How I Met My Husband '95
Navajo Blues '97

Clea Lewis (1965-)
The Rich Man's Wife '96
Ice Age: The Meltdown '06 (V)
Confessions of a Shopaholic '09

Damian Lewis (1971-)
Robinson Crusoe '96
Band of Brothers '01
Dreamcatcher '03
Keane '04
Friends & Crocodiles '05
Much Ado About Nothing '05
An Unfinished Life '05
Alex Rider: Operation Stormbreaker '06
The Situation '06
Assassin in Love '07
The Escapist '08
Your Highness '11
The Sweeney '12
Romeo & Juliet '13
Our Kind of Traitor '16
Run This Town '20

David Lewis (1916-2000)
The Apartment '60
Lake Placid '99
Personal Effects '09
Polar Storm '09

David Lewis (1976-)
How It All Went Down '03
Christmas Caper '07
Making Mr. Right '08
The Killing Machine '09
No Men Beyond This Point '15

Dawnn Lewis (1961-)
I'm Gonna Git You Sucka '88
Race to Freedom: The Story of the Underground Railroad '94
The 10th Kingdom '00
Let It Shine '12

Diana Lewis (1919-97)
Andy Hardy Meets Debutante '40
Go West '40
Somewhere I'll Find You '42
Whistling in Dixie '42
Cry Havoc '43

Fiona Lewis (1946-)
The Fearless Vampire Killers '67
Doctor Phibes Rises Again '72
Dracula '73
Lisztomania '75
Drum '76
Stunts '77
Wanda Nevada '79
Strange Behavior '81
Strange Invaders '83
Innerspace '87

Gary Lewis (1958-)
Carla's Song '97
Orphans '97
My Name Is Joe '98
Postmortem '98
Billy Elliot '00
Gangs of New York '02
Pure '02
Warrior Queen '03
Yes '04
Joyeux Noel '05
Eragon '06
Goal! The Dream Begins '06
Valhalla Rising '09
Not Another Happy Ending '13

Geoffrey Lewis (1935-2015)
Culpepper Cattle Co. '72
Moon of the Wolf '72
Welcome Home, Soldier Boys '72
Macon County Line '74
Thunderbolt & Lightfoot '74
The Great Waldo Pepper '75
Smile '75
The Wind and the Lion '75
The Return of a Man Called Horse '76
Every Which Way But Loose '78
When Every Day Was the Fourth of July '78
Any Which Way You Can '80
Bronco Billy '80
Heaven's Gate '81
I, the Jury '82
Return of the Man from U.N.C.L.E. '83
Night of the Comet '84
Lust in the Dust '85
Maximum Security '87
Out of the Dark '88
Fletch Lives '89
Pink Cadillac '89
Tango and Cash '89
Double Impact '91
The Lawnmower Man '92
The Man Without a Face '93
Only the Strong '93
Point of No Return '93
Army of One '94
Maverick '94
National Lampoon's Last Resort '94
White Fang 2: The Myth of the White Wolf '94
An Occasional Hell '96
Trilogy of Terror 2 '96
Midnight in the Garden of Good and Evil '97
Rough Riders '97
The Prophet's Game '99
Way of the Gun '00
Sunstorm '01
A Light in the Darkness '02
A Painted House '03
The Devil's Rejects '05
Down in the Valley '05
The Fallen Ones '05
The Butcher '07
Wicked Little Things '07
Miss Nobody '10

George Lewis (1903-95)
Captain Calamity '36
Zorro's Black Whip '44
Border River '47
The Big Sombrero '49
The Sign of Zorro '60
Indian Paint '64

Gus Lewis (1993-)
Asylum '05
Batman Begins '05

Harry Lewis (1920-)
Bomba on Panther Island '49
Gun Crazy '49

Huey Lewis (1950-)
Back to the Future '85 (C)
Short Cuts '93
Shadow of Doubt '98
Duets '00

Jason Lewis (1971-)
The Attic '06
For One Night '06
My Faraway Bride '06
Bobby Z '07
Mr. Brooks '07
Sex and the City: The Movie '08
Tribute '09
Sex and the City 2 '10
Sexting '11

Jazsmin Lewis (1976-)
Barbershop '02
Barbershop 2: Back in Business '04
Divine Intervention '07
Three Can Play That Game '07
The Perfect Man '11
She's Not Our Sister '11

Jean Ann Lewis (1930-2011)
See Eve Brent

Jenifer Lewis (1957-)
What's Love Got to Do with It? '93
Corrina, Corrina '94
Renaissance Man '94
Girl 6 '96
The Preacher's Wife '96
The Mighty '98
Jackie's Back '99
Partners '99
Cast Away '00
Dancing in September '00
Little Richard '00
The Brothers '01
Juwanna Mann '02
The Cookout '04
Nora's Hair Salon '04
Shark Tale '04 (V)
Cars '06 (V)
Madea's Family Reunion '06
Dirty Laundry '07
Who's Your Caddy? '07
Tyler Perry's Meet the Browns '08
Not Easily Broken '09
The Princess and the Frog '09 (V)
Hereafter '10
Think Like a Man Too '14
Playin' For Love '15

Jenny Lewis (1976-)
Troop Beverly Hills '89
The Wizard '89
Runaway Father '91
Runaway Daughters '94
Foxfire '96
Little Boy Blue '97

Jerry Lewis (1926-2017)
My Friend Irma '49
At War with the Army '50
My Friend Irma Goes West '50
The Stooge '51
That's My Boy '51
Jumping Jacks '52
Sailor Beware '52
The Caddy '53
Money from Home '53
The Road to Bali '53
Scared Stiff '53
Living It Up '54
Artists and Models '55
You're Never Too Young '55
The Delicate Delinquent '56
Hollywood or Bust '56
Pardners '56
Rock-A-Bye Baby '57
The Sad Sack '57
The Geisha Boy '58
The Bellboy '60
Cinderfella '60
The Errand Boy '61
The Ladies' Man '61
It's Only Money '62
It's a Mad, Mad, Mad, Mad World '63
The Nutty Professor '63
Who's Minding the Store? '63
Disorderly Orderly '64
The Patsy '64
Boeing Boeing '65
The Family Jewels '65
Don't Raise the Bridge, Lower the River '68
Which Way to the Front? '70
King of Comedy '82
Cracking Up '83
Cookie '89
Mr. Saturday Night '92
Arizona Dream '94
Funny Bones '94

Jerry Lee Lewis (1935-)
High School Confidential '58
Chuck Berry: Hail! Hail! Rock 'n' Roll '87

Joe Lewis (1943-)
Jaguar Lives '79
Force: Five '81

Joe E. Lewis (1902-71)
Private Buckaroo '42
Lady in Cement '68

Johnny Lewis (1983-2012)
Raise Your Voice '04
Aliens vs. Predator: Requiem '07
Palo Alto '07
Felon '08

Judah Lewis
Demolition '15
The Babysitter '17
Summer of 84 '18

Juliette Lewis (1973-)
My Stepmother Is an Alien '88
Meet the Hollowheads '89
National Lampoon's Christmas Vacation '89
Too Young to Die '90
Cape Fear '91
Crooked Hearts '91
Husbands and Wives '92
Kalifornia '93
Romeo Is Bleeding '93
That Night '93
What's Eating Gilbert Grape '93
Mixed Nuts '94
Natural Born Killers '94
The Basketball Diaries '95
From Dusk Till Dawn '95
Strange Days '95
The Evening Star '96
The Other Sister '98
The 4th Floor '99
Way of the Gun '00
Gaudi Afternoon '01
Picture Claire '01
Enough '02
Hysterical Blindness '02
My Louisiana Sky '02
Cold Creek Manor '03
Old School '03
Chasing Freedom '04
Starsky & Hutch '04
Daltry Calhoun '05
Aurora Borealis '06
Grilled '06
Catch and Release '07
Whip It '09
Conviction '10
Due Date '10
The Switch '10
Sympathy for Delicious '10
The Hangover, Part 2 '11
Hick '11
August: Osage County '13
Hellion '13
Open Road '13
Nerve '16
Ma '19

Leigh Lewis
Revelation '00
Tribulation '00

Matthew Lewis (1989-)
The Legend of Wolf Mountain '92
Harry Potter and the Sorcerer's Stone '01
Harry Potter and the Goblet of Fire '05
Harry Potter and the Deathly Hallows, Part 1 '10
Wasteland '13

Michael Lewis (1939-)
Gruesome Twosome '67
Signs of Life '89

Mitchell Lewis (1880-1956)
The Red Lily '24
Kongo '32
The Wizard of Oz '39
Billy the Kid '41
Cairo '42

Monica Lewis (1922-2015)
Excuse My Dust '51
Everything I Have is Yours '52
The Concorde: Airport '79 '79

Phill Lewis (1968-)
Brother Future '91
City Slickers '91
Once Upon a Time . . . When We Were Colored '95 (N)
Spent '00
I Spy '02
Elvis Has Left the Building '04
Pretty Ugly People '08

Ralph Lewis (1872-1937)
The Birth of a Nation '15
The Hoodlum '19
When the Clouds Roll By '19
Outside the Law '21

Richard Lewis (1947-)
The Wrong Guys '88
Once Upon a Crime '92
The Return of Spinal Tap '92 (C)
Robin Hood: Men in Tights '93
Wagons East '94
Leaving Las Vegas '95
Drunks '96
Hugo Pool '97
Vamps '12
She's Funny That Way '15

Robert Lewis (1909-97)
Son of Lassie '45
Monsieur Verdoux '47
Hello Again '87
Misbegotten '98

Robert Q. Lewis (1921-91)
An Affair to Remember '57
Good Neighbor Sam '64
Ski Party '65

Ronald Lewis (1928-82)
Storm Over the Nile '55
Helen of Troy '56
Robbery under Arms '57
The Wind Cannot Read '58
Conspiracy of Hearts '60
Stop Me Before I Kill! '60
Mr. Sardonicus '61
Scream of Fear '61
Billy Budd '62
Friends '71

Russell Scott Lewis
Boys Life '94
Green Plaid Shirt '96

Tommy (Tom E.) Lewis (1958-)
The Chant of Jimmie Blacksmith '78
The Proposition '05
Red Hill '10

Vera Lewis (1873-1956)
The Man On the Flying Trapeze '35
Paddy O'Day '35
Missing Girls '36

Vicki Lewis (1960-)
Mouse Hunt '97
Breakfast of Champions '98
Godzilla '98
Pushing Tin '99
Finding Nemo '03 (V)
California Dreaming '07
Alpha and Omega '10 (V)

Johan Leysen (1950-)
Hail Mary '85
The Music Teacher '88
The Gambler '97
Brotherhood of the Wolf '01
The American '10
Young & Beautiful '13

Drue Leyton
Charlie Chan in London '34
Charlie Chan at the Circus '36

John Leyton (1939-)
The Great Escape '63
Guns at Batasi '64
Seaside Swingers '65
Von Ryan's Express '65
Krakatoa East of Java '69
Schizo '77

Sara Lezana
Gunfight at Red Sands '63
Revenge of Sartana '65

Thierry Lhermitte (1952-)
French Fried Vacation '79
Until September '84
Grosse Fatigue '94 (C)
An American Werewolf in Paris '97
The Dinner Game '98
The Closet '00
And Now Ladies and Gentlemen '02
Le Divorce '03
Mr. Average '06
The French Minister '13

Baotian Li (1946-)
Ju Dou '90
Shanghai Triad '95

Bin Li (1982-)
Beijing Bicycle '01
The Road Home '01
Li Bingbing (1973-)
Seventeen Years '99
Silver Hawk '04
The Forbidden Kingdom '08
1911 '11
Resident Evil: Retribution '12
Transformers: Age of Extinction '14
The Meg '18
Bruce Li (1950-)
Chinese Connection 2 '77
Counter Attack '84
Gong Li (1965-)
Ju Dou '90
Raise the Red Lantern '91
The Story of Qiu Ju '91
Farewell My Concubine '93
To Live '94
Shanghai Triad '95
Temptress Moon '96
Chinese Box '97
The Emperor and the Assassin '99
Zhou Yu's Train '02
Eros '04
2046 '04
Memoirs of a Geisha '05
Curse of the Golden Flower '06
Miami Vice '06
Hannibal Rising '07
Shanghai '09
What Women Want '10
Coming Home '14
Jet Li (1963-)
Once Upon a Time in China '91
Once Upon a Time in China II '92
Once Upon a Time in China III '93
Twin Warriors '93
The Bodyguard from Beijing '94
Fist of Legend '94
Jet Li's The Enforcer '95
Meltdown '95
Black Mask '96
Contract Killer '98
Lethal Weapon 4 '98
Romeo Must Die '00
Kiss of the Dragon '01
The One '01
Hero '02
Cradle 2 the Grave '03
Unleashed '05
Jet Li's Fearless '06
War '07
The Forbidden Kingdom '08
The Mummy: Tomb of the Dragon Emperor '08
Warlords '08
The Expendables '10
The Expendables 2 '12
The Sorcerer and the White Snake '13
The Expendables 3 '14
Lily Li (1950-)
8 Diagram Pole Fighter '84
Black Magic '06
The Magic Blade '08
Xuejian Li (1954-)
Shanghai Triad '95
The Emperor and the Assassin '99
Happy Times '00
Yi-min Li
Heaven & Hell '78
7 Grand Masters '04
Yuan Li
What Women Want '10
Empire of Assassins '11
Fan Liao
The Final Master '15
Ash Is Purest White '18
The Wild Goose Lake '20
Peter Paul Liapis
Lethal Victims '87
Ghoulies 4 '93

Liberace (1919-87)
Sincerely Yours '55
The Loved One '65
Liana Liberato (1995-)
Safe Harbour '07
Trust '10
Trespass '11
Erased '12
Stuck in Love '12
Free Ride '13
The Best of Me '14
Dear Eleanor '16
Novitiate '17
Johan Libereau (1984-)
Cold Showers '05
The Witnesses '07
Cosmos '16
Anne Libert (1946-)
Virgin among the Living Dead '71
Rites of Frankenstein '72
Richard Libertini (1933-)
Catch-22 '70
I Wonder Who's Killing Her Now? '76
The In-Laws '79
Popeye '80
Sharky's Machine '81
Deal of the Century '83
Going Berserk '83
All of Me '84
Unfaithfully Yours '84
Fletch '85
Fourth Wise Man '85
Big Trouble '86
Fletch Lives '89
Awakenings '90
The Bonfire of the Vanities '90
DuckTales the Movie: Treasure of the Lost Lamp '90 (V)
And You Thought Your Parents Were Weird! '91 (V)
Nell '94
Lethal Weapon 4 '98
Telling You '98
The 4th Tenor '02
Grilled '06
A Grandpa for Christmas '07
Everybody Wants to Be Italian '08
Richard Liberty (1932-)
The Crazies '73
Day of the Dead '85
Landon Liboiron (1992-)
Don't Cry Now '07
Altitude '10
Daydream Nation '10
Girl in Progress '12
Alain Libolt (1943-)
Army of Shadows '69
The Lady and the Duke '01
Domain '09
Jeremy Licht (1971-)
Lois Gibbs and the Love Canal '82
Twilight Zone: The Movie '83
Next One '84
Mitchell Lichtenstein (1956-)
Streamers '83
The Wedding Banquet '93
Jeff(rey) Licon (1985-)
Mysterious Skin '04
Alien Raiders '08
Chuck Liddell
Bobby Z '07
Riot '15
G. Gordon Liddy (1930-)
When Nature Calls '85
Camp Cucamonga: How I Spent My Summer Vacation '90
Anders Danielsen Lie (1979-)
Reprise '06
Oslo, August 31st '11
Fidelio: Alice's Odyssey '14
Approaching the Unknown '16

Personal Shopper '17
22 July '18
Mimi Lieber (1956-)
Last Resort '86
Wilder Napalm '93
The Thing About My Folks '05
Jaeden Lieberher (2003-)
St. Vincent '14
The Confirmation '16
The Book of Henry '17
It '17
Michael Liebman
The Painted Lady '97
2 by 4 '98
Harry Liedtke (1882-1945)
Passion '19
One Arabian Night '20
The Finances of the Grand Duke '24
Jan Josef Liefers
The Baader Meinhof Complex '08
Simon and the Oaks '12
Jennifer Lien (1974-)
American History X '98
SLC Punk! '99
Albert Lieven (1906-71)
Night Train to Munich '40
The Life and Death of Colonel Blimp '43
Sarah Lieving
King of the Lost World '06
666: The Child '06
The Apocalypse '07
Invasion of the Pod People '07
Mega Shark *vs.* Crocosaurus '10
500 MPH Storm '13
Tina Lifford
Colors '88
Grand Canyon '91
America's Dream '95
Mandela and de Klerk '97
Letters from a Killer '98
The Temptations '98
The '70s '00
Amy's O '02
Blood Work '02
Hostage '05
Urban Legends: Bloody Mary '05
John Light (1972-)
Intimate Affairs '01
Purpose '02
Benedict Arnold: A Question of Honor '03
Cambridge Spies '03
The Lion in Winter '03
Heights '04
Dresden '06
Partition '07
Judith Light (1949-)
Ira & Abby '06
Save Me '07
Last Weekend '14
Cody Lightning (1986-)
Smoke Signals '98
Manic '01
Four Sheets to the Wind '07
Crystle Lightning (1981-)
3 Ninjas Knuckle Up '95
American Pie Presents Band Camp '05
Marilyn Lightstone (1940-)
Wild Pony '83
Anne of Green Gables '85
Abraxas: Guardian of the Universe '90
Grand Tour: Disaster in Time '92
Lil Duval
More Money More Family '15
Meet the Blacks '16
Lil' Kim (1974-)
See Kimberly (Lil' Kim) Jones

Lil' Romeo (1989-)
Honey '03
Internet Dating '08
Dennis (Denis) Lill (1942-)
Lillie '79
Bad Blood '81
Element of Doubt '96
Matthew Lillard (1970-)
Serial Mom '94
Animal Room '95
Hackers '95
Tarantella '95
Scream '96
The Curve '97
Without Limits '97
Dish Dogs '98
Senseless '98
Telling You '98
She's All That '99
SLC Punk! '99
Spanish Judges '99
Wing Commander '99
Love's Labour's Lost '00
Finder's Fee '01
Summer Catch '01
13 Ghosts '01
Scooby-Doo '02
The Perfect Score '04
Scooby-Doo 2: Monsters Unleashed '04
Wicker Park '04
Without a Paddle '04
Bickford Shmeckler's Cool Ideas '06
The Groomsmen '06
What Love Is '07
Spooner '08
All's Faire in Love '09
National Lampoon Presents: Endless Bummer '09
Home Run Showdown '10
The Pool Boys '10
The Descendants '11
Trouble with the Curve '12
Return to Nim's Island '13
Beatrice Lillie (1898-1989)
Exit Smiling '26
On Approval '44
Around the World in 80 Days '56 (C)
Thoroughly Modern Millie '67
Rachael Lillis (1969-)
Pokemon: The First Movie '99 (V)
Pokemon 3: The Movie '01 (V)
Sophia Lillis (2002-)
It '17
Nancy Drew and the Hidden Staircase '19
Evangeline Lilly (1979-)
Afterwards '08
The Hurt Locker '08
Real Steel '11
The Hobbit: The Desolation of Smaug '13
The Hobbit: The Battle of the Five Armies '14
Ant-Man '15
Ant-Man and the Wasp '18
Morgan Lily (2000-)
Henry Poole Is Here '08
Love's Everlasting Courage '11
Jennifer Lim
Hostel '06
When Evil Calls '06
Kay Tong Lim
Dragon: The Bruce Lee Story '93
Kung Fu Killer '08
Brigitte Lin (1954-)
Zu: Warriors from the Magic Mountain '83
Fantasy Mission Force '84
Police Story '85
Dream Lovers '86
The Bride with White Hair '93
The Bride with White Hair 2 '93
Ashes of Time '94

Chungking Express '95
Ashes of Time Redux '08
Chen Chi Lin (1955-)
Sword Masters: The Battle Wizard '77
Heaven & Hell '78
Ching-hsai Lin (1954-)
See Brigitte Lin
Kelly Lin (1975-)
Full Time Killer '01
Zu Warriors '01
Running Out of Time 2 '06
Boarding Gate '07
Kay Linaker (1914-2008)
Charlie Chan at Monte Carlo '37
Charlie Chan's Murder Cruise '40
Men On Her Mind '44
Aida Linares
Clueless '95
U-Turn '97
Abbey Lincoln (1930-2010)
The Girl Can't Help It '56
Nothing but a Man '64
For Love of Ivy '68
Mo' Better Blues '90
Andrew Lincoln (1973-)
Boston Kickout '95
The Woman in White '97
Gangster No. 1 '00
Love Actually '03
Enduring Love '04
Scenes of a Sexual Nature '06
These Foolish Things '06
Wuthering Heights '09
Heartbreaker '10
Elmo Lincoln (1889-1952)
The Adventures of Tarzan '21
Tarzan's New York Adventure '42 (C)
Pamela Lincoln (1937-2019)
The Tingler '59
Anatomy of a Psycho '61
Alyvia Alyn Lind
Blended '14
Dolly Parton's Coat of Many Colors '15
Emily Alyn Lind (2002-)
Enter the Void '09
November Christmas '10
Sundays at Tiffany's '10
Who Is Clark Rockefeller? '10
Dear Dumb Diary '13
The Haunting in Connecticut 2: Ghosts of Georgia '13
Gillian Lind (1904-83)
Dynasty of Fear '72
And Now the Screaming Starts '73
Heather Lind
Mistress America '15
Stealing Cars '16
Traci Lind (1968-)
Club Med '86
Fright Night 2 '88
Survival Quest '89
Class of 1999 '90
The Handmaid's Tale '90
My Boyfriend's Back '93
The Road to Wellville '94
Wolverine '96
The End of Violence '97
No Strings Attached '98
Red Meat '98
Boguslaw Linda (1952-)
Danton '82
The Decalogue '88
Dead Man's Bounty '06
Chad Lindberg (1976-)
Black Circle Boys '97
October Sky '99
The Fast and the Furious '01
The Rookie '02

National Lampoon's Adam & Eve '05
Punk Love '06
Push '06
Crimes of the Past '09
I Spit on Your Grave '10
Gunnel Lindblom (1931-)
The Seventh Seal '56
The Virgin Spring '59
Hunger '66
Eric Linden (1909-94)
The Crowd Roars '32
Sweepings '33
Ah, Wilderness! '35
Ladies Crave Excitement '35
Let 'Em Have It '35
Career Woman '36
A Family Affair '37
Girl Loves Boy '37
Romance of the Limberlost '38
Frolics on Ice '39
Gone with the Wind '39
Criminals Within '41
Hal Linden (1931-)
The Colony '95
Out to Sea '97
Jennie Linden (1939-)
Nightmare '63
A Severed Head '70
Women in Love '70
Marta Linden (1903-90)
Stand by for Action '42
A Yank at Eton '42
The Youngest Profession '43
Maisie Goes to Reno '44
See Here, Private Hargrove '44
Cec Linder (1921-92)
Lolita '62
Goldfinger '64
A Touch of Class '73
Vengeance Is Mine '74
Christa Linder
Kiss Kiss Kill Kill '66
Night of a Thousand Cats '72
Viveca Lindfors (1920-95)
Adventures of Don Juan '49
Night Unto Night '49
Backfire '50
Dark City '50
No Sad Songs For Me '50
This Side of the Law '50
Four in a Jeep '51
Moonfleet '55
Run for Cover '55
The Halliday Brand '57
The Story of Ruth '60
The King of Kings '61
These Are the Damned '63
Coming Apart '69
The Way We Were '73
Bell from Hell '74
Girlfriends '78
A Wedding '78
The Hand '81
Creepshow '82
Divorce Wars: A Love Story '82
Secret Weapons '85
The Sure Thing '85
The Ann Jillian Story '88
Exorcist 3: Legion '90
Zandalee '91
The Linguini Incident '92
Stargate '94
Last Summer In the Hamptons '96
Peter Lindgren (1915-81)
I Am Curious (Yellow) '67
The New Land '72
Thure Lindhardt (1974-)
Eddie the Sleepwalking Cannibal '12
Keep the Lights On '12
Riki Lindhome (1979-)
Million Dollar Baby '04
My Best Friend's Girl '08
The Last House on the Left '09

Natacha Lindinger (1970-)
Double Team '97
Coco Chanel & Igor Stravinsky '09

Audra Lindley (1918-97)
The Heartbreak Kid '72
Best Friends '82
Cannery Row '82
Desert Hearts '86
Spellbinder '88
Troop Beverly Hills '89
The New Age '94
Sudden Death '95

Carl Michael Lindner (1988-)
Slappy and the Stinkers '97
The Extreme Adventures of Super Dave '98
Krippendorf's Tribe '98

Delroy Lindo (1952-)
More American Graffiti '79
Mountains of the Moon '90
Bright Angel '91
Malcolm X '92
Blood In . . . Blood Out: Bound by Honor '93
Mr. Jones '93
Crooklyn '94
Broken Arrow '95
Clockers '95
Get Shorty '95
Feeling Minnesota '96
Ransom '96
Soul of the Game '96
The Winner '96
The Devil's Advocate '97
First Time Felon '97
A Life Less Ordinary '97
The Book of Stars '99
The Cider House Rules '99
Pros & Cons '99
Gone in 60 Seconds '00
Romeo Must Die '00
Heist '01
The Last Castle '01
The One '01
The Core '03
Domino '05
Sahara '05
Wondrous Oblivion '06
This Christmas '07
Up '09 (V)
The Big Bang '11
Do You Believe? '15
Point Break '15
Da 5 Bloods '20

Olga Lindo (1899-1968)
Things Happen at Night '48
The Hidden Room '49
The Twenty Questions Murder Mystery '50

Vincent Lindon (1959-)
Betty Blue '86
A Man in Love '87
Seventh Heaven '98
Chaos '01
Friday Night '02
La Moustache '05
Mademoiselle Chambon '09
Augustine '12
Diary of a Chambermaid '16

Margaret Lindsay (1910-81)
Baby Face '33
Cavalcade '33
The House on 56th Street '33
Lady Killer '33
Fog Over Frisco '34
Bordertown '35
The Case of the Curious Bride '35
Dangerous '35
Frisco Kid '35
'G' Men '35
The Green Light '37
Slim '37
Garden of the Moon '38
Gold Is Where You Find It '38
Jezebel '38
Hell's Kitchen '39
The House of the Seven Gables '40
The Spoilers '42
Her Sister's Secret '46
Cass Timberlane '47
B.F.'s Daughter '48
The Restless Years '58
Please Don't Eat the Daisies '60

Nigel Lindsay
Four Lions '10
Alan Partridge '13

Robert Lindsay (1949-)
That'll Be the Day '73
Bert Rigby, You're a Fool '89
Strike It Rich '90
G.B.H. '91
Fierce Creatures '96
Horatio Hornblower '99
Oliver Twist '00
Horatio Hornblower: The Adventure Continues '01
Wimbledon '04
Friends & Crocodiles '05
Gideon's Daughter '05

George Lindsey (1933-)
Robin Hood '73 (V)
Return to Mayberry '85

Joseph Lindsey
Amongst Friends '93
Caught Up '98

Blake Lindsley (1973-)
Swingers '96
Starship Troopers '97
Trial by Media '00
Coastlines '02
Plain Dirty '04

Angela Lindvall (1979-)
CQ '01
Kiss Kiss Bang Bang '05
Life Blood '09

Helga Line (1932-)
The Blancheville Monster '63
Hercules and the Tyrants of Babylon '64
Nightmare Castle '65
Horror Express '72
Horror Rises from the Tomb '72
When the Screaming Stops '73
Death Will Have Your Eyes '74
Black Venus '83

Richard Lineback (1952-)
Beyond the Next Mountain '87
Natural Born Killers '94
Speed '94
Tin Cup '96
Twister '96
The Jackal '97
The Baby Dance '98
Meet the Deedles '98
Varsity Blues '98
Dangerous Evidence: The Lori Jackson Story '99
Ready to Rumble '00

Stephi Lineburg (1982-)
Richie Rich '94
Zoe '01

Rosaleen Linehan (1937-)
Sharpe's Gold '94
The Matchmaker '97
The Hi-Lo Country '98
About Adam '00

Bai Ling (1966-)
The Crow '93
Red Corner '97
Somewhere in the City '97
Row Your Boat '98
Anna and the King '99
Wild Wild West '99
The Breed '01
The Lost Empire '01
Code Hunter '02
Point of Origin '02
The Beautiful Country '04
My Baby's Daddy '04
She Hate Me '04
Three . . . Extremes '04
Edmond '05
The Gene Generation '07
Living & Dying '07
Toxic '07
A Beautiful Life '08
Dim Sum Funeral '08
The Hustle '08
Crank: High Voltage '09
Chain Letter '10
The Confidant '10
Love Ranch '10
Magic Man '10
Knockdown '11
Age of the Hobbits '12

Paul (Link) Linke (1948-)
Motel Hell '80
Parenthood '89

Hamish Linklater (1976-)
Groove '00
The Future '11
Lola Versus '12
42 '13
Redemption Trail '13
The Angriest Man in Brooklyn '14
Magic in the Moonlight '14
The Big Short '15
One More Time '15

Richard Linklater (1960-)
Slacker '91
The Underneath '95
Beavis and Butt-Head Do America '96 (V)
Waking Life '01
Side by Side '12

Art Linkletter (1912-2010)
People Are Funny '46
Champagne for Caesar '50

Cody Linley (1989-)
My Dog Skip '99
Hoot '06
R.L. Stine's The Haunting Hour: Don't Even Think About It '07
Forget Me Not '09
My Dog the Champion '14

Rex Linn (1956-)
Cliffhanger '93
Drop Zone '94
Wyatt Earp '94
Breakdown '96
Ghosts of Mississippi '96
Tin Cup '96
The Postman '97
The Odd Couple 2 '98
Rush Hour '98
Crossfire Trail '01
Cheaper by the Dozen '03
The Hunted '03
After the Sunset '04
The Zodiac '05
Appaloosa '08

Mark Linn-Baker (1954-)
Manhattan '79
My Favorite Year '82
Noises Off '92
Adam '09
How Do You Know '10

Laura Linney (1964-)
Armistead Maupin's Tales of the City '93
Dave '93
A Simple Twist of Fate '94
Congo '95
Primal Fear '96
Absolute Power '97
Armistead Maupin's More Tales of the City '97
The Truman Show '98
Love Letters '99
You Can Count On Me '99
House of Mirth '00
Running Mates '00
Lush '01
Maze '01
The Laramie Project '02
The Mothman Prophecies '02
The Life of David Gale '03
Love Actually '03
Mystic River '03
Kinsey '04
P.S. '04
The Exorcism of Emily Rose '05
The Squid and the Whale '05
Driving Lessons '06
The Hottest State '06
Jindabyne '06
Man of the Year '06
Breach '07
The Nanny Diaries '07
The Savages '07
John Adams '08
The Other Man '08
The City of Your Final Destination '09
Morning '10
Sympathy for Delicious '10
The Details '11
Hyde Park on Hudson '12
Mr. Holmes '15
Genius '16
Sully '16
Teenage Mutant Ninja Turtles: Out of the Shadows '16

Richard Lintern
Lost Souls '98
Clapham Junction '07
The Bank Job '08
Unmade Beds '09

Louise Linton
The Echo '08
Intruder '16

Joanne Linville (1928-)
Scorpio '73
From the Dead of Night '89
James Dean '01

Larry Linville (1939-2000)
The Night Stalker '71
The Stepmother '71
School Spirit '85
Earth Girls Are Easy '89
Rock 'n' Roll High School Forever '91
No Dessert Dad, 'Til You Mow the Lawn '94

Alex D. Linz (1989-)
Vanished '95
The Cable Guy '96
One Fine Day '96
Home Alone 3 '97
The Dress Code '99
Tarzan '99 (V)
Bounce '00
Titan A.E. '00 (V)
Max Keeble's Big Move '01
Race to Space '01
Choose Connor '07

Lio (1962-)
Love After Love '94
Carnage '02

Therese Liotard (1949-)
The Disenchanted '90
My Father's Glory '91
My Mother's Castle '91

Ray Liotta (1955-)
Something Wild '86
Dominick & Eugene '88
Field of Dreams '89
Goodfellas '90
Women & Men: In Love There Are No Rules '91
Article 99 '92
Unlawful Entry '92
Corrina, Corrina '94
No Escape '94
Operation Dumbo Drop '95
Turbulence '96
Unforgettable '96
Cop Land '97
Phoenix '98
The Rat Pack '98
Forever Mine '99
Inferno '99
Muppets from Space '99
A Rumor of Angels '00
Blow '01
Hannibal '01
Heartbreakers '01
John Q '02
Narc '02
Point of Origin '02
Identity '03
The Last Shot '04
Revolver '05
Slow Burn '05
Even Money '06
Local Color '06
Battle in Seattle '07
Bee Movie '07 (V)
Chasing 3000 '07
Smokin' Aces '07
Wild Hogs '07
Hero Wanted '08
In the Name of the King: A Dungeon Siege Tale '08
The Line '08
Crossing Over '09
Observe and Report '09
Powder Blue '09
Charlie St. Cloud '10
Crazy on the Outside '10
Date Night '10
Snowmen '10
Youth in Revolt '10
The Details '11
The Entitled '11
The River Murders '11
The Son of No One '11
Street Kings 2: Motor City '11
Breathless '12
The Iceman '12
Killing Them Softly '12
The Devil's in the Details '13
Pawn '13
The Place Beyond the Pines '13
Better Living Through Chemistry '14
The Identical '14
Kill the Messenger '14
Revenge of the Green Dragons '14
Blackway '16
Marriage Story '19

Daniele Liotti (1971-)
Mad Love '01
Doctor Zhivago '03

Tommy Lioutas (1983-)
How I Married My High School Crush '07
A Life Interrupted '07
The Circuit '08
Will You Merry Me? '08

Eugene Lipinski (1956-)
Moonlighting '82
Riders of the Storm '88
Restless Spirits '99
Bless the Child '00
The Recruit '03
The Lost Angel '04
Alice '09

Maureen Lipman (1946-)
Up the Junction '68
Educating Rita '83
The Little Princess '87
Carry On Columbus '92
Captain Jack '98
Solomon and Gaenor '98
Oklahoma! '99
The Pianist '02
Lighthouse Hill '04

Jonathan Lipnicki (1990-)
Jerry Maguire '96
Stuart Little '99
The Little Vampire '00
Like Mike '02
Stuart Little 2 '02
Arlo the Burping Pig '16
Altitude '17

David Lipper
Bug Buster '99
Last Run '01
Federal Protection '02
Threshold '03
I Do (But I Don't) '04

Sarah K. Lippmann
Addicted to Murder 2: Tainted Blood '97
Addicted to Murder 3: Bloodlust '99

Dennis Lipscomb (1942-2014)
Union City '81
Sister, Sister '87
Retribution '88

James Lipton
Bolt '08
Igor '08 (V)

Peggy Lipton (1946-2019)
I'm Gonna Git You Sucka '88
Kinjite: Forbidden Subjects '89
Fatal Charm '92
Twin Peaks: Fire Walk with Me '92
The Postman '97
Intern '00
The '70s '00
Skipped Parts '00
Jackpot '01
When in Rome '09
A Dog's Purpose '17

LisaRaye (1967-)
The Players Club '98
The Wood '99
All About You '01
Civil Brand '02
Gang of Roses '03
Beauty Shop '05

Joe Lisi (1950-)
Come See the Paradise '90
Traces of Red '92
Kiss of Death '94

Virna Lisi (1936-2014)
Eva '62
The Black Tulip '64
How to Murder Your Wife '64
Bambole '65
Casanova '70 '65
Assault on a Queen '66
The 25th Hour '67
Carbon Copy '69
The Secret of Santa Vittoria '69
Bluebeard '72
Night Flight from Moscow '73
Miss Right '81
La Cicada '83
I Love N.Y. '87
Queen Margot '94
Balzac: A Life of Passion '99

Natalie Lisinska
My Neighbor's Secret '09
Fairfield Road '10

Pavel Liska (1972-)
Up and Down '04
Something Like Happiness '05
The Country Teacher '08

Leon Lissek (1927-)
Blockhouse '73
The Unbearable Lightness of Being '88
Bloodmoon '90

Peyton List (1998-)
The Greatest Game Ever Played '05
Deep Winter '08
Shuttle '09
Bereavement '10
Secrets in the Walls '10
Diary of a Wimpy Kid 2: Rodrick Rules '11
Diary of a Wimpy Kid: Dog Days '12
The Dog Who Saved the Holidays '12 (V)
Meeting Evil '12

Spencer List (1998-)
Bereavement '10
Bringing Up Bobby '11
Night Has Settled '14

Francis Lister (1899-1951)
Cardinal Richelieu '35
Clive of India '35
The Return of the Scarlet Pimpernel '37

Moira Lister (1923-2007)
Love Story '44
Grand National Night '53
The Limping Man '53
Trouble in Store '53
The Yellow Rolls Royce '64
The Double Man '67
Not Now Darling '73
The 10th Kingdom '00

Tommy (Tiny) Lister (1958-)
Beverly Hills Cop 2 '87
Extreme Prejudice '87
No Holds Barred '89
9 1/2 Ninjas '90
Posse '93
Immortal Combat '94
Men of War '94
Friday '95
Hologram Man '95
Things to Do in Denver When You're Dead '95
Phat Beach '96
Body Count '97
The Fifth Element '97
Jackie Brown '97
I Got the Hook-Up '98
Never 2 Big '98
The Players Club '98
Wishmaster 2: Evil Never Dies '98
Judgment Day '99
Supreme Sanction '99
Circus '00
Little Nicky '00
Next Friday '00
Keepin' It Real '01
The Wash '01
Austin Powers In Goldmember '02
Asylum of the Damned '03
Confidence '03
Blast '04
El Padrino '04
My Baby's Daddy '04
Never Die Alone '04
Who Made the Potatoe Salad? '05
Bone Dry '07
The Dark Knight '08
Hard Times '09
First Dog '10
Hopelessly in June '11
The Human Centipede 3: The Final Sequence '15

Zoe Lister-Jones (1982-)
The Wedding Bros. '08
Breaking Upwards '09
Shadows and Lies '10
Stuck Between Stations '11
Band Aid '17

Litefoot (1969-)
The Indian in the Cupboard '95
Kull the Conqueror '97
Mortal Kombat 2: Annihilation '97
The Song of Hiawatha '97
Adaptation '02

John Litel (1892-1972)
The Black Legion '37
Amazing Dr. Clitterhouse '38
Gold Is Where You Find It '38
Nancy Drew-Detective '38
A Slight Case of Murder '38
Nancy Drew, Reporter '39
Nancy Drew-Trouble Shooter '39
Wings of the Navy '39
You Can't Get Away With Murder '39
Castle on the Hudson '40
The Fighting 69th '40
Flight Angels '40
It All Came True '40
The Big Boss '41
They Died with Their Boots On '41
Invisible Agent '42
The Mystery of Marie Roget '42
Boss of Big Town '43
So Proudly We Hail '43
Submarine Base '43
Where Are Your Children? '44
San Antonio '45
Northwest Trail '46
Cass Timberlane '47
Outpost in Morocco '49
Woman in Hiding '49
The Fuller Brush Girl '50
The Groom Wore Spurs '51
Sitting Bull '54

John Lithgow (1945-)
Dealing: Or the Berkeley-to-Boston Forty-Brick Lost-Bag Blues '72
Obsession '76
All That Jazz '79
Blow Out '81
I'm Dancing as Fast as I Can '82
The World According to Garp '82
The Day After '83
Terms of Endearment '83
Twilight Zone: The Movie '83
The Adventures of Buckaroo Banzai Across the Eighth Dimension '84
Footloose '84
Mesmerized '84
2010: The Year We Make Contact '84
Santa Claus: The Movie '85
The Manhattan Project '86
Resting Place '86
Baby Girl Scott '87
Harry and the Hendersons '87
Distant Thunder '88
Out Cold '89
Traveling Man '89
Memphis Belle '90
Ricochet '91
Raising Cain '92
Cliffhanger '93
Love, Cheat & Steal '93
The Pelican Brief '93
A Good Man in Africa '94
Princess Caraboo '94
Silent Fall '94
World War II: When Lions Roared '94
Hollow Point '95
My Brother's Keeper '95
The Tuskegee Airmen '95
Homegrown '97
Johnny Skidmarks '97
A Civil Action '98
Rugrats in Paris: The Movie '00 *(V)*
Shrek '01 *(V)*
Orange County '02
Kinsey '04
Confessions of a Shopaholic '09
Leap Year '10
Rise of the Planet of the Apes '11
The Campaign '12
This Is 40 '12
The Homesman '14
Interstellar '14
Love Is Strange '14
Miss Sloane '16
Beatriz at Dinner '17
Daddy's Home 2 '17
Bombshell '19
Late Night '19
Pet Sematary '19
The Tomorrow Man '19

Paulie (Litowsky) Litt (1995-)
Eternal Sunshine of the Spotless Mind '04
Jersey Girl '04
Speed Racer '08

Cleavon Little (1939-92)
Cotton Comes to Harlem '70
Homecoming: A Christmas Story '71
Vanishing Point '71
Blazing Saddles '74
Greased Lightning '77
Once Upon a Brothers Grimm '77
FM '78
High Risk '81
Double Exposure '82
The Salamander '82
Toy Soldiers '84
Once Bitten '85
Gore Vidal's Lincoln '88
Fletch Lives '89
Perfect Harmony '91
Separate but Equal '91

Kim Little
Social Intercourse '01
H.G. Wells' War of the Worlds '05
666: The Child '06
The Apocalypse '07
30,000 Leagues Under the Sea '07
War of the Worlds 2: The Next Wave '08
Countdown: Jerusalem '09

Michelle Little
My Demon Lover '87
Apollo 13 '95

Natasha Little (1969-)
Vanity Fair '99
The Criminal '00
Greenfingers '00
Another Life '01
Byron '03
Vanity Fair '04
A Congregation of Ghosts '09
Mr. Nobody '13

Rich Little (1938-)
Happy Hour '87
The Late Shift '96

Sacheen Little Feather (1947-)
The Trial of Billy Jack '74
Johnny Firecloud '75

Little JJ (1990-)
Beauty Shop '05
Yours, Mine & Ours '05
The Janky Promoters '09

Little Nell (1953-)
See Nell Campbell

Little Richard (1935-)
The Girl Can't Help It '56
Down and Out in Beverly Hills '86
Last Action Hero '93 *(C)*
The Pickle '93 *(C)*
Why Do Fools Fall in Love? '98
Mystery, Alaska '99 *(C)*

Lucien Littlefield (1895-1960)
The Sheik '21
Tumbleweeds '25
Torrent '26
Twinkletoes '26
The Cat and the Canary '27
My Best Girl '27
The Great Divide '29
Seven Keys to Baldpate '29
Clancy in Wall Street '30
Reducing '31
Pride of the Legion '32
Shopworn '32
Strangers of the Evening '32
The Bitter Tea of General Yen '33
Chance at Heaven '33
Skyway '33
Kiss and Make Up '34
The Man On the Flying Trapeze '35
Sweepstake Annie '35
Let's Sing Again '36
The Moon's Our Home '36
Wide Open Faces '38
One Body Too Many '44
Zorro's Black Whip '44
Treasure of Fear '45
Lights of Old Santa Fe '47
Susanna Pass '49

Gary Littlejohn
Angels Hard As They Come '71
Bury Me an Angel '71
Badlands '74

Chia Hui Liu (1955-)
The 36th Chamber of Shaolin '78
Shaolin & Wu Tang '81
8 Diagram Pole Fighter '84
Heroes of the East '08
Kill 'Em All '12

Chia-Liang Liu
Legendary Weapons of China '82
Seven Swords '07

Chia Yung Liu
Master of the Flying Guillotine '75
The 36th Chamber of Shaolin '78
Legendary Weapons of China '82

Emily Liu
All About You '01
The Trouble with Romance '09

Ernest Liu
From Dusk Till Dawn '95
Get a Clue! '98

Gordon (Chia Hui) Liu (1955-)
Legendary Weapons of China '82
Kill Bill Vol. 1 '03
Kill Bill Vol. 2 '04

Jim Liu
The Farewell '19
Ip Man 4: The Finale '19

Lucy Liu (1968-)
City of Industry '96
Flypaper '97
Payback '98
The Mating Habits of the Earthbound Human '99
Molly '99
Play It to the Bone '99
Charlie's Angels '00
Shanghai Noon '00
Hotel '01
Ballistic: Ecks *vs.* Sever '02
Chicago '02
Cypher '02
Charlie's Angels: Full Throttle '03
Kill Bill Vol. 1 '03
Kill Bill Vol. 2 '04
Mulan 2 '04 *(V)*
Domino '05
Lucky Number Slevin '06
Code Name: The Cleaner '07
Rise: Blood Hunter '07
Watching the Detectives '07
Kung Fu Panda '08 *(V)*
The Year of Getting to Know Us '08
Marry Me '10
Kung Fu Panda 2 '11 *(V)*
Someday This Pain Will Be Useful to You '11
The Trouble With Bliss '11
Detachment '12
The Man with the Iron Fists '12
The Tale of the Princess Kaguya '13 *(V)*

Matty Liu
In God's Hands '98
Off the Lip '04

Peiqi Liu
Shadow Magic '00
Together '02

Rene Liu (1970-)
The Personals '98
Double Vision '02

Tony Liu (1952-)
Enter the Dragon '73
The Duel of the Century '81

Ye Liu (1978-)
Purple Butterfly '03
Blood Brothers '07
Dark Matter '07
City of Life and Death '09

Yifei Liu
The Assassins '12
The Four '12

Boris Livanov
Ten Days That Shook the World '27
Baltic Deputy '37

Blake Lively (1987-)
The Sisterhood of the Traveling Pants '05
Accepted '06
Elvis and Annabelle '07
Simon Says '07
The Sisterhood of the Traveling Pants 2 '08
New York, I Love You '09
The Private Lives of Pippa Lee '09
The Town '10
Green Lantern '11
Hick '11
Savages '12
The Age of Adaline '15
Café Society '16
The Shallows '16
All I See Is You '17
A Simple Favor '18
The Rhythm Section '19

Eric Lively (1981-)
American Pie '99
Crash Course '00
Uprising '01
Speak '04
The Breed '06
The Butterfly Effect 2 '06
Live! '07
Sex and Breakfast '07
Deep Winter '08
24: Redemption '08
Tyler Perry's A Madea Christmas '13

Ernie Lively (1947-)
The Legend of Cryin' Ryan '98
Senseless '98
The Sisterhood of the Traveling Pants 2 '08

Jason Lively (1968-)
National Lampoon's European Vacation '85
Night of the Creeps '86
Ghost Chase '88
Rock 'n' Roll High School Forever '91
Maximum Force '92

Robin (Robyn) Lively (1972-)
The Karate Kid: Part 3 '89
Teen Witch '89
Crazy from the Heart '91
Strike '07
Murder.com '08
Who Is Simon Miller? '11

Roger Livesey (1906-76)
Lorna Doone '34
Men of the Sea '35
Drums '38
The Girl in the News '41
The Life and Death of Colonel Blimp '43
I Know Where I'm Going '45
Stairway to Heaven '46
Green Grow the Rushes '51
The Master of Ballantrae '53
The Entertainer '60
The League of Gentlemen '60
Of Human Bondage '64

Barry Livingston (1953-)
Easy Wheels '89
Invisible Mom '96
Steel Sharks '97
Invisible Mom 2 '99
Final Approach '08
You Don't Mess with the Zohan '08
Expecting a Miracle '09

John Livingston (1970-)
Betrayed: A Story of Three Women '95
Mr. Wrong '95
Dogtown '97
Where's Marlowe? '98
The Stickup '01
Dopamine '03
The Hungover Games '14

Margaret Livingston (1900-84)
Up the Ladder '25
Sunrise '27
Seven Keys to Baldpate '29
The Lady Refuses '31

Robert 'Bob' Livingston (1904-88)
The Bold Caballero '36
Three Godfathers '36
The Vigilantes Are Coming '36
Don't Fence Me In '45
Grand Canyon Trail '48
I Spit on Your Corpse '74
Blazing Stewardesses '75

Ron Livingston (1967-)
Swingers '96
Campfire Tales '98
Office Space '98
The Big Brass Ring '99
Body Shots '99
Beat '00
A Rumor of Angels '00
Two Ninas '00
Band of Brothers '01
Adaptation '02
Buying the Cow '02
The Cooler '03
44 Minutes: The North Hollywood Shootout '03
King of the Ants '03
Little Black Book '04
Winter Solstice '04
Pretty Persuasion '05
Relative Strangers '06
American Crude '07
Holly '07
Music Within '07
The Time Traveler's Wife '09
Dinner for Schmucks '10
Going the Distance '10
Game Change '12
The Odd Life of Timothy Green '12
The Conjuring '13
Drinking Buddies '13
Parkland '13
The Pretty One '14
James White '15
The 5th Wave '16
Lucky '17
Tully '18
The Man Who Killed Hitler and Then the Bigfoot '19

Shelby Livingston
Nude on the Moon '61
2000 Maniacs '64

Stanley Livingston (1950-)
Private Parts '72
Attack of the 60-Foot Centerfold '95

Kari Lizer (1961-)
Smokey Bites the Dust '81
Private School '83

LL Cool J (1968-)
Krush Groove '85
The Hard Way '91
Toys '92
Out of Sync '95
Woo '97
Caught Up '98
Halloween: H20 '98
Any Given Sunday '99
Deep Blue Sea '99
In Too Deep '99
Charlie's Angels '00
Kingdom Come '01
Rollerball '02
Deliver Us from Eva '03
Rugrats Go Wild! '03 *(V)*
S.W.A.T. '03
Edison Force '05
Mindhunters '05
Slow Burn '05
Last Holiday '06
The Deal '08

Desmond Llewelyn (1914-99)
From Russia with Love '63
Goldfinger '64
Thunderball '65
You Only Live Twice '67
On Her Majesty's Secret Service '69
Diamonds Are Forever '71
The Man with the Golden Gun '74
The Spy Who Loved Me '77
Moonraker '79
For Your Eyes Only '81
A View to a Kill '85
The Living Daylights '87
License to Kill '89
Goldeneye '95

Tomorrow Never Dies '97
The World Is Not Enough '99

Christopher Lloyd (1938-)
One Flew Over the Cuckoo's Nest '75
Three Warriors '77
Goin' South '78
The Black Marble '79
Lady in Red '79
The Onion Field '79
Legend of the Lone Ranger '81
National Lampoon Goes to the Movies '81
The Postman Always Rings Twice '81
Mr. Mom '83
To Be or Not to Be '83
The Adventures of Buckaroo Banzai Across the Eighth Dimension '84
Star Trek 3: The Search for Spock '84
Back to the Future '85
Clue '85
Walk Like a Man '87
Eight Men Out '88
Track 29 '88
Who Framed Roger Rabbit '88
Back to the Future, Part 2 '89
The Dream Team '89
Back to the Future, Part 3 '90
DuckTales the Movie: Treasure of the Lost Lamp '90 (V)
The Addams Family '91
Suburban Commando '91
Addams Family Values '93
Dennis the Menace '93
Twenty Bucks '93
Angels in the Outfield '94
Camp Nowhere '94
The Pagemaster '94 (V)
Radioland Murders '94
Things to Do in Denver When You're Dead '95
Cadillac Ranch '96
Changing Habits '96
Anastasia '97 (V)
The Real Blonde '97
Angels in the Endzone '98
Baby Geniuses '98
It Came from the Sky '98
My Favorite Martian '98
Premonition '98
Quicksilver Highway '98
Alice in Wonderland '99
Chasing Destiny '00
Wish You Were Dead '00
When Good Ghouls Go Bad '01
Wit '01
Hey Arnold! The Movie '02 (V)
Interstate 60 '02
A Perfect Day '06
Flakes '07
Fly Me to the Moon '08
The Tale of Despereaux '08 (V)
Call of the Wild 3D '09
Jack and the Beanstalk '09
Meteor '09
Santa Buddies '09
Piranha 3D '10
Snowmen '10
The Chateau Meroux '11
InSight '11
Piranha 3DD '11
The Witches of Oz '11
Excuse Me for Living '12
The Oogieloves in the Big Balloon Adventure '12
Blood Lake '14
The One I Wrote For You '14
Zodiac: Signs of the Apocalypse '14
88 '15
Boundaries '18

Doris Lloyd (1896-1968)
The Black Bird '26
Exit Smiling '26
Old English '30
The Bachelor Father '31
A Shot in the Dark '35
The Black Doll '38
Vigil in the Night '40
Journey for Margaret '42
The Constant Nymph '43
The Invisible Man's Revenge '44
The Time Machine '60

Emily Lloyd (1970-)
Wish You Were Here '87
Cookie '89
In Country '89
Chicago Joe & the Showgirl '90
A River Runs Through It '92
Scorchers '92
Welcome to Sarajevo '97
Boogie Boy '98

Emily Ann Lloyd (1984-)
Annie: A Royal Adventure '95
Apollo 13 '95

Eric Lloyd (1986-)
The Santa Clause '94
Abandoned and Deceived '95
Dunston Checks In '95
Deconstructing Harry '97
Luminous Motion '00
The Santa Clause 2 '02
The Santa Clause 3: The Escape Clause '06

George Lloyd (1897-1967)
San Quentin '37
I Accuse My Parents '45
White Pongo '45

Harold Lloyd (1893-1971)
Safety Last '23
Girl Shy '24
The Freshman '25
The Kid Brother '27
Speedy '28
Feet First '30
Movie Crazy '32
Milky Way '36
The Sin of Harold Diddlebock '47

Harry Lloyd (1983-)
Great Expectations '11
The Iron Lady '11
The Riot Club '15

Hugh Lloyd (1923-2008)
August '95
Cider with Rosie '99

Jake Lloyd (1989-)
Jingle All the Way '96
Unhook the Stars '96
Virtual Obsession '98
Star Wars: Episode 1-The Phantom Menace '99
Madison '01
Race to Space '01

Jeremy Lloyd (1930-2014)
Just for Fun '63
Doctor in Clover '66
Murder on the Orient Express '74

Jimmy Lloyd (1918-88)
The Story of G.I. Joe '45
The Jolson Story '46
Key Witness '47
Miss Grant Takes Richmond '49

John Bedford Lloyd (1956-)
Sweet Lorraine '87
Tough Guys Don't Dance '87
Crossing Delancey '88
The Abyss '89
Waiting for the Light '90
Philadelphia '93
Fair Game '95
Killer: A Journal of Murder '95
Super Troopers '01
The Bourne Supremacy '04
The Killing Floor '06
Muhammad Ali's Greatest Fight '13

Kathleen Lloyd (1948-)
Missouri Breaks '76
The Car '77
Skateboard '77
It's Alive 2: It Lives Again '78
The Jayne Mansfield Story '80

Norman Lloyd (1914-)
Saboteur '42
The Southerner '45
The Green Years '46
A Walk in the Sun '46
Buccaneer's Girl '50
Audrey Rose '77
The Nude Bomb '80
Jaws of Satan '81
Amityville 4: The Evil Escapes '89
The Adventures of Rocky & Bullwinkle '00
Fail Safe '00
The Song of the Lark '01
In Her Shoes '05

Sabrina Lloyd (1970-)
Father Hood '93
Dopamine '03
On Edge '03
The Breakup Artist '04
The Last Request '06
Racing Daylight '07

Sue Lloyd (1939-2011)
Hysteria '64
The Ipcress File '65
Ned Kelly '70
Innocent Bystanders '72
The Bitch '78

Ben Lloyd-Hughes
Great Expectations '12
Divergent '14

Max Lloyd-Jones
The Sandlot 2 '05
Flicka: Country Pride '12

Charles Lloyd-Pack (1905-83)
The Horror of Dracula '58
The Terror of the Tongs '61
Victim '61
The Reptile '66
Bedazzled '68
If. . . '69

Roger Lloyd-Pack (1944-2014)
Fright '71
The Young Poisoner's Handbook '94
Harry Potter and the Goblet of Fire '05
The History of Mr. Polly '07

Carmen (Lee) Llywelyn (1973-)
Chasing Amy '97
The Mod Squad '99
Never Been Kissed '99
Cowboys and Angels '00

Candy Lo (1974-)
The Cave of the Silken Web '67
Time and Tide '00
The Eye '02

Chi Muoi Lo
The Relic '96
Catfish in Black Bean Sauce '00

Lieh Lo (1939-2002)
The Magnificent Trio '66
Sword Masters: Brothers Five '70
King Boxer '72
Sword Masters: Web of Death '76
Chinese Connection 2 '77
The 36th Chamber of Shaolin '78
Black Magic '06
The Magic Blade '08

Meng Lo (1952-)
Five Deadly Venoms '78
Heaven & Hell '78
Five Element Ninjas '82

Monica Lo
Belly of the Beast '03
Legacy '08

Selina Lo
The Prince & Me 4: The Elephant Adventure '10
The Scorpion King 3: Battle for Redemption '11

Tony Lo Bianco (1936-)
Champions: A Love Story '78
Death Has a Bad Reputation '90
The Last Request '06
Kill the Irishman '11

Luigi Lo Cascio (1967-)
Light of My Eyes '01
Best of Youth '03
Don't Tell '05

Enrico Lo Verso (1964-)
The Stolen Children '92
Farinelli '94
La Scorta '94
Lamerica '95
Moses '96
Hannibal '01
Baaria '09

Tony LoBianco (1936-)
Honeymoon Killers '70
The French Connection '71
Escape from Death Row '73
The Seven-Ups '73
The Story of Jacob & Joseph '74
Mean Frank and Crazy Tony '75
God Told Me To '76
Bloodbrothers '78
F.I.S.T. '78
Separate Ways '82
City Heat '84
The Ann Jillian Story '88
City of Hope '91
Teamster Boss: The Jackie Presser Story '92
Boiling Point '93
Nixon '95
The Juror '96
Bomb Squad '97
Sworn to Justice '97
Mafia! '98
Rocky Marciano '99
Friends and Family '01
Endangered Species '02
Mary Higgins Clark: Lucky Day '02

Stephen Lobo (1973-)
The Wedding Date '05
Afghan Luke '11

Amy Locane (1971-)
Lost Angels '89
Cry-Baby '90
Blue Sky '91
School Ties '92
Airheads '94
Carried Away '95
Prefontaine '96
Bram Stoker's The Mummy '97
Going All the Way '97
Love to Kill '97
Bongwater '98
Implicated '98
Route 9 '98
Hell's Gate '01
Secretary '02

Carol Locatell
Convict Women '74
Thunder County '74

David Lochary (1944-77)
Pink Flamingos '72
Female Trouble '74

Felix Locher (1882-1969)
Curse of the Faceless Man '58
Frankenstein's Daughter '58

Hannah Lochner (1993-)
Encrypt '03
The Devil's Mercy '07
Harm's Way '07
In God's Country '07
Jack and Jill vs. the World '08

Bruce Locke
RoboCop 3 '91
Lone Tiger '94

Philip Locke (1928-2004)
And the Ship Sails On '83
Tom & Viv '94
Othello '95

Ryan Locke (1975-)
Supercross: The Movie '05
The New Twenty '08

Sondra Locke (1944-)
The Heart Is a Lonely Hunter '68
A Reflection of Fear '73
The Outlaw Josey Wales '76
Death Game '77
The Gauntlet '77
Seducers '77
Shadow of Chikara '77
Every Which Way But Loose '78
Friendship, Secrets and Lies '79
Any Which Way You Can '80
Bronco Billy '80
Second Coming of Suzanne '80
Sudden Impact '83
Ratboy '86
Tales of the Unexpected '91
The Prophet's Game '99

Spencer Locke (1991-)
Monster House '06 (V)
Resident Evil: Extinction '07
Detention '11

Anne Lockhart (1953-)
Lisa, Bright and Dark '73
Slashed Dreams '74
Joyride '77
Troll '86
Big Bad John '90
Bug Buster '99

Calvin Lockhart (1934-2007)
Dark of the Sun '68
Cotton Comes to Harlem '70
Halls of Anger '70
Honeybaby '74
Uptown Saturday Night '74
The Beast Must Die '75
Let's Do It Again '75
The Baron '88
Coming to America '88
Predator 2 '90

Emma Lockhart (1994-)
Looking for Comedy in the Muslim World '06
Ace Ventura Jr.: Pet Detective '08

Gene Lockhart (1891-1957)
The Devil Is a Sissy '36
The Gorgeous Hussy '36
Something to Sing About '36
Wedding Present '36
Algiers '38
Blondie '38
A Christmas Carol '38
Of Human Hearts '38
The Story of Alexander Graham Bell '39
Abe Lincoln in Illinois '40
Dr. Kildare Goes Home '40
Edison the Man '40
His Girl Friday '40
Billy the Kid '41
The Devil & Daniel Webster '41
Meet John Doe '41
One Foot in Heaven '41
They Died with Their Boots On '41
Hangmen Also Die '42
Juke Girl '42
You Can't Escape Forever '42
The Desert Song '43
Mission to Moscow '43
Northern Pursuit '43
Action in Arabia '44
Going My Way '44
House on 92nd Street '45
Leave Her to Heaven '45
A Scandal in Paris '46
The Strange Woman '46
Cynthia '47
The Foxes of Harrow '47
Her Husband's Affairs '47
Honeymoon '47
Miracle on 34th Street '47
The Shocking Miss Pilgrim '47
Apartment for Peggy '48
That Wonderful Urge '48
The Inspector General '49
Madame Bovary '49
Red Light '49
The Big Hangover '50
I'd Climb the Highest Mountain '51
Rhubarb '51
Hoodlum Empire '52
Confidentially Connie '53
Francis Covers the Big Town '53
World for Ransom '54
Carousel '56
The Man in the Gray Flannel Suit '56

June Lockhart (1925-)
All This and Heaven Too '40
Adam Had Four Sons '41
Sergeant York '41
Meet Me in St. Louis '44
The White Cliffs of Dover '44
Keep Your Powder Dry '45
Son of Lassie '45
Easy to Wed '46
The Yearling '46
T-Men '47
Time Limit '57
Lassie's Great Adventure '62
Butterfly '82
Strange Invaders '83
Troll '86
The Big Picture '89
Dead Women in Lingerie '90
The Gift of Love '90
Sleep with Me '94
The Colony '95
Lost in Space '98 (C)
Au Pair 2: The Fairy Tale Continues '01
Holiday in Handcuffs '07

Heather Locklear (1961-)
Firestarter '84
The Return of Swamp Thing '89
The Return of the Swamp Thing '89
The Big Slice '90
The Great American Sex Scandal '94
The First Wives Club '96
Money Talks '97
Looney Tunes: Back in Action '03
Uptown Girls '03
The Perfect Man '05
Angels Fall '07
Flirting with Forty '09
Flying By '09
Hannah Montana: The Movie '09
He Loves Me '11
Scary Movie 5 '13

Loryn Locklin
Taking Care of Business '90
Fortress '93

Gary Lockwood (1937-)
Tall Story '60
Wild in the Country '61
The Magic Sword '62
It Happened at the World's Fair '63
Firecreek '68
They Came to Rob Las Vegas '68
2001: A Space Odyssey '68
Model Shop '69
R.P.M.* (*Revolutions Per Minute) '70
Earth II '71
Project: Kill! '77
The Incredible Journey of Dr. Meg Laurel '79
Night of the Scarecrow '95

Julia Lockwood
Teenage Bad Girl '59
No Kidding '60

Margaret Lockwood (1911-90)
Lorna Doone '34
Men of the Sea '35

Dr. Syn '37
Bank Holiday '38
The Lady Vanishes '38
The Stars Look Down '39
Susannah of the Mounties '39
Night Train to Munich '40
The Girl in the News '41
The Man in Grey '43
Give Us the Moon '44
Love Story '44
The Wicked Lady '45
Highly Dangerous '50
Trouble in the Glen '54
Cast a Dark Shadow '55
The Slipper and the Rose '76

Thomas Lockyer
Teenagers from Outer Space '59
Incognito '97
The Scarlet Tunic '97
Ultraviolet '98
Jesus '00
Dog Soldiers '01
The Defender '04

Barbara Loden (1932-80)
Wild River '60
Splendor in the Grass '61
Iron Cowboy '68
Wanda '70

John Loder (1898-1988)
The Private Life of Henry VIII '33
Lorna Doone '34
The Silent Passenger '35
Sabotage '36
Dr. Syn '37
King Solomon's Mines '37
Non-Stop New York '37
Confirm or Deny '41
How Green Was My Valley '41
Old Acquaintance '43
The Hairy Ape '44
Passage to Marseilles '44
The Woman Who Came Back '45
Dishonored Lady '47

Kathryn Loder (1940-78)
The Big Doll House '71
Foxy Brown '74

Kesun Loder (1993-)
Fielder's Choice '05
A Smile as Big as the Moon '12

David Lodge (1921-2003)
Two-Way Stretch '60
Trial & Error '62
Oh! What a Lovely War '69
What's Good for the Goose '69
The Railway Children '70
Edge of Sanity '89

John Lodge (1903-85)
Seas Beneath '31
Scarlet Empress '34
The Little Colonel '35
Bank Holiday '38
The Witchmaker '69

Bret Loehr (1993-)
Identity '03
Veritas: Prince of Truth '07

Jocelyne Loewen
Chaos Theory '08
Making Mr. Right '08

Fiona Loewi (1975-)
Love and Death on Long Island '97
Blackheart '98
Invasion! '99
Killer Bees '02

Jeanette Loff (1906-42)
My Friend from India '27
Party Girl '30
St. Louis Woman '34

Jacob Lofland
Mud '12
Little Accidents '14

Spencer Lofranco
At Middleton '13
Jamesy Boy '14
Gotti '18

Arthur Loft (1897-1947)
Blue, White and Perfect '42
Woman in the Window '44
It's a Pleasure '45
Lights of Old Santa Fe '47

Cecilia Loftus (1876-1943)
Lucky Partners '40
The Black Cat '41

Janice Logan (1915-65)
What a Life '39
Dr. Cyclops '40

Paul Logan (1973-)
Bram Stoker's Way of the Vampire '05
Megafault '09
The Terminators '09
Ballistica '10
Mega Piranha '10
200 MPH '11

Phyllis Logan (1956-)
The Doctor and the Devils '85
The Kitchen Toto '87
Secrets and Lies '95
Invasion: Earth '98
All the King's Men '99

Ricky Dean Logan (1967-)
Back to the Future, Part 2 '89
Back to the Future, Part 3 '90
Freddy's Dead: The Final Nightmare '91

Robert F. Logan (1941-)
Across the Great Divide '76
The Adventures of the Wilderness Family '76
Further Adventures of the Wilderness Family, Part 2 '77
Snowbeast '77
Sea Gypsies '78
Mountain Family Robinson '79
Death Ray 2000 '81
Man Outside '88

Stanley Logan (1885-1953)
That Forsyte Woman '50
Double Crossbones '51

Robert Loggia (1930-2015)
Somebody Up There Likes Me '56
The Garment Jungle '57
Cop Hater '58
The Lost Missile '58
Cattle King '63
The Greatest Story Ever Told '65
Arthur Hailey's The Moneychangers '76
Revenge of the Pink Panther '78
The Ninth Configuration '79
S.O.B. '81
An Officer and a Gentleman '82
Trail of the Pink Panther '82
A Woman Called Golda '82
Curse of the Pink Panther '83
Psycho 2 '83
Scarface '83
The Jagged Edge '85
Prizzi's Honor '85
Armed and Dangerous '86
Over the Top '86
That's Life! '86
The Believers '87
Conspiracy: The Trial of the Chicago Eight '87
Hot Pursuit '87
Big '88
Oliver & Company '88 (V)
Relentless '89
Triumph of the Spirit '89
Opportunity Knocks '90
The Marrying Man '91
Necessary Roughness '91
Afterburn '92
Gladiator '92
Innocent Blood '92
Lifepod '93
Mercy Mission '93
Wild Palms '93
Bad Girls '94
Coldblooded '94
I Love Trouble '94
White Mile '94
Man with a Gun '95
Picture Windows '95
Independence Day '96
Lost Highway '96
Mistrial '96
Pandora's Clock '96
Smilla's Sense of Snow '96
Flypaper '97
National Lampoon's The Don's Analyst '97
The Proposition '97
Wide Awake '97
American Virgin '98
Holy Man '98
Bonanno: A Godfather's Story '99
Joan of Arc '99
The Suburbans '99
Return to Me '00
The Deal '05
Forget About It '06
Rain '06
The Least of These '08
Shrink '09
Fake '10
Harvest '10
Tim and Eric's Billion Dollar Movie '12
An Evergreen Christmas '14

Donal Logue (1966-)
Sneakers '92
And the Band Played On '93 (C)
Gettysburg '93
Baja '95
The Crew '95
Dear God '96
Metro '96
Glam '97
Blade '98
A Bright Shining Lie '98
The Thin Red Line '98
The Big Tease '99
The Million Dollar Hotel '99
Runaway Bride '99
The Patriot '00
Reindeer Games '00
Steal This Movie! '00
The Tao of Steve '00
The Chateau '01
Comic Book Villains '02
American Splendor '03
Confidence '03
Two Days '03
Just like Heaven '05
Almost Heaven '06
Citizen Duane '06
The Groomsmen '06
The Ex '07
Ghost Rider '07
The Good Life '07
Purple Violets '07
Zodiac '07
Max Payne '08
The Lodger '09
Charlie St. Cloud '10
Kill for Me '12
Reef 2: High Tide '12
Silent Night '12
CBGB '13

Lindsay Lohan (1986-)
The Parent Trap '98
Life-Size '00
Get a Clue '02
Freaky Friday '03
Confessions of a Teenage Drama Queen '04
Mean Girls '04
Herbie: Fully Loaded '05
Bobby '06
Just My Luck '06
A Prairie Home Companion '06
Chapter 27 '07
Georgia Rule '07
I Know Who Killed Me '07
Labor Pains '09
Machete '10
Liz & Dick '12
The Canyons '13
Scary Movie 5 '13

Svea Lohde (1992-)
Rosenstrasse '03
Summer of '04 '06

Alison Lohman (1979-)
The Thirteenth Floor '99
White Oleander '02
Big Fish '03
Matchstick Men '03
The Big White '05
Where the Truth Lies '05
Flicka '06
Beowulf '07 (V)
Things We Lost in the Fire '07
Drag Me to Hell '09
Gamer '09

Marie Lohr (1890-1975)
Pygmalion '38
The Magic Bow '47
Counterblast '48
A Town Like Alice '56

Florence Loiret-Caille (1975-)
Time of the Wolf '03
The Intruder '04
Let It Rain '08

Kristanna Loken (1979-)
Gangland '00 (C)
Terminator 3: Rise of the Machines '03
Dark Kingdom: The Dragon King '04
BloodRayne '06
Lime Salted Love '06
In the Name of the King: A Dungeon Siege Tale '08
Attack on Darfur '09
National Lampoon's The Legend of Awesomest Maximus '11
S.W.A.T.: Firefight '11
Bounty Killer '13

Gina Lollobrigida (1927-)
Fanfan la Tulipe '51
Young Caruso '51
Beauties of the Night '52
Beat the Devil '53
Bread, Love and Dreams '53
Trapeze '56
The Hunchback of Notre Dame '57
Never So Few '59
Solomon and Sheba '59
Where the Hot Wind Blows '59
Come September '61
Imperial Venus '63
Bambole '65
Strange Bedfellows '65
Private Navy of Sgt. O'Farrell '68
Bad Man's River '72

Guido Lollobrigida (1929-)
Man, Pride and Vengeance '67
A Long Ride From Hell '68
Crime Boss '72

Herbert Lom (1917-2012)
Appointment with Crime '45
The Black Rose '50
Night and the City '50
The Golden Salamander '51
Hell Is Sold Out '51
The Ladykillers '55
War and Peace '56
Fire Down Below '57
Chase a Crooked Shadow '58
Flame Over India '59
North West Frontier '59
Third Man on the Mountain '59
Spartacus '60
The Frightened City '61
Mysterious Island '61
The Phantom of the Opera '62
Tiara Tahiti '62
The Horse Without a Head '63
A Shot in the Dark '64
Bang! Bang! You're Dead! '66
Gambit '66
Villa Rides '68
Assignment to Kill '69
Journey to the Far Side of the Sun '69
Mark of the Devil '69
99 Women '69
Dorian Gray '70
Count Dracula '71
Murders in the Rue Morgue '71
Asylum '72
And Now the Screaming Starts '73
Return of the Pink Panther '74
Ten Little Indians '75
The Pink Panther Strikes Again '76
Revenge of the Pink Panther '78
The Lady Vanishes '79
Hopscotch '80
The Man with Bogart's Face '80
Peter and Paul '81
Trail of the Pink Panther '82
Curse of the Pink Panther '83
Dead Zone '83
Lace '84
King Solomon's Mines '85
Skeleton Coast '89
River of Death '90
The Devil's Daughter '91
Son of the Pink Panther '93

Herbert Lomas (1887-1961)
The Ghost Goes West '36
The Ghost Train '41
Intent to Kill '58

Noah Lomax
Playing for Keeps '12
99 Homes '14

Carole Lombard (1908-42)
Big News '29
The Racketeer '29
Man of the World '31
No Man of Her Own '32
No More Orchids '32
Virtue '32
Brief Moment '33
The Eagle and the Hawk '33
Supernatural '33
White Woman '33
Lady by Choice '34
Now and Forever '34
Twentieth Century '34
We're Not Dressing '34
Hands Across the Table '35
Love Before Breakfast '36
My Man Godfrey '36
The Princess Comes Across '36
Nothing Sacred '37
Swing High, Swing Low '37
True Confession '37
In Name Only '39
Made for Each Other '39
Vigil in the Night '40
Mr. & Mrs. Smith '41
To Be or Not to Be '42

Karina Lombard (1969-)
Wide Sargasso Sea '92
The Firm '93
Legends of the Fall '94
Last Man Standing '96
Kull the Conqueror '97
Footsteps '98

Louise Lombard (1970-)
Esther '98
After the Rain '99
Russell Mulcahy's Tale of the Mummy '99
Hidalgo '04

Louis Lombardi (1968-)
Amongst Friends '93
Beverly Hills Cop 3 '94
The Immortals '95
The Usual Suspects '95
Father's Day '96
Suicide Kings '97
The Crew '00
The Animal '01
3000 Miles to Graceland '01
Deuces Wild '02
Confidence '03
Doughboys '08

Roberto Lombardi
Abduction '07
Dead Collections '12

Michelle Lombardo
All In '06
Calvin Marshall '09

Domenick Lombardozzi (1976-)
The Young Girl and the Monsoon '99
Just One Time '00
Love in the Time of Money '02
S.W.A.T. '03
Carlito's Way: Rise to Power '05
Find Me Guilty '06
How Do You Know '10
God's Pocket '14
Bridge of Spies '15

Ulli Lommel (1944-)
Love Is Colder Than Death '69
The American Soldier '70
Beware of a Holy Whore '70
Whity '70
World on a Wire '73
Effi Briest '74
Boogey Man 2 '83
Chinese Roulette '86

Tadeusz Lomnicki (1927-92)
A Generation '54
Innocent Sorcerers '60
Man of Marble '76

Banlop Lomnoi
Tropical Malady '04
Cemetery of Splendor '15

Beba Loncar (1943-)
The Long Ships '64
Pussycat, Pussycat, I Love You '70
Don't Look in the Attic '81

Alexandra London
Van Gogh '92
Les Destinees '00

Daniel London (1970-)
Patch Adams '98
Four Dogs Playing Poker '00
Minority Report '02
Old Joy '06
The Bridge to Nowhere '09

Jason London (1972-)
December '91
The Man in the Moon '91
Blood Ties '92
Dazed and Confused '93
Fall Time '94
Safe Passage '94
My Teacher's Wife '95
To Wong Foo, Thanks for Everything, Julie Newmar '95
If These Walls Could Talk '96
Serial Bomber '96
Broken Vessels '98
The Rage: Carrie 2 '99
The Hound of the Baskervilles '00
Jason and the Argonauts '00
Poor White Trash '00
Spent '00
Out Cold '01
Dracula 2: Ascension '03
Grind '03
Identity Theft: The Michelle Brown Story '04
Dracula 3: Legacy '05
Out of the Woods '05
Axe '06
Glass House: The Good Mother '06
Showdown at Area 51 '07
Who's Your Monkey '07
All Roads Lead Home '08
Killer Movie '08
The Devil's Tomb '09
Monsterwolf '10
Area 51 '11
Weather Wars '11

Black Box *'12*
Fatal Call *'12*
Awaken *'15*
Urban Country *'18*

Jeremy London (1972-)
White Wolves 2: Legend of the Wild *'94*
The Babysitter *'95*
Mallrats *'95*
A Mother's Gift *'95*
Levitation *'97*
Journey to the Center of the Earth *'99*
Gods and Generals *'03*
Kiss Me Again *'06*
Ba'al: The Storm God *'08*
Chasing the Green *'09*
Lost Dream *'09*
The Terminators *'09*
Wolvesbayne *'09*
Drop Dead Gorgeous *'10*
The Dinner Party *'20*

Julie London (1926-2000)
Nabonga *'44*
The Red House *'47*
Task Force *'49*
The Girl Can't Help It *'56*
Man of the West *'58*
Saddle the Wind *'58*
The Wonderful Country *'59*
The George Raft Story *'61*

Lauren London (1984-)
ATL *'06*
This Christmas *'07*
I Love You, Beth Cooper *'09*

Lisa London (1957-)
H.O.T.S. *'79*
Lethal Victims *'87*
Savage Beach *'89*

Tom London (1889-1963)
Westward Bound *'30*
Call of the Wilderness *'32*
The Miracle Rider *'35*
Fighting Seabees *'44*
Zorro's Black Whip *'44*
Tribute to a Bad Man *'56*

Tony London (1961-)
Sid & Nancy *'86*
24 Hours in London *'00*

John Lone (1952-)
Americathon *'79*
Iceman *'84*
Year of the Dragon *'85*
The Last Emperor *'87*
The Moderns *'88*
M. Butterfly *'93*
The Hunted *'94*
The Shadow *'94*
Rush Hour 2 *'01*
War *'07*

Keith Loneker (1971-)
Out of Sight *'98*
Lakeview Terrace *'08*
Leatherheads *'08*

Audrey Long (1922-2014)
Desperate *'47*
The Adventures of Gallant Bess *'48*
Miraculous Journey *'48*
Stage Struck *'48*
David Harding, Counterspy *'50*
Cavalry Scout *'51*

Derek Long
The Gay Bed and Breakfast of Terror *'07*
Bio-dead *'09*
Make the Yuletide Gay *'09*

Howie Long (1960-)
Broken Arrow *'95*
Firestorm *'97*
Dollar for the Dead *'98*
3000 Miles to Graceland *'01*

Jackie Long (1981-)
ATL *'06*
The Comebacks *'07*
A Cross to Bear *'12*
Bodied *'17*

Jodi Long (1954-)
Patty Hearst *'88*
Amos and Andrew *'93*

Justin Long (1978-)
Happy Campers *'01*
Jeepers Creepers *'01*
Crossroads *'02*
Dodgeball: A True Underdog Story *'04*
Raising Genius *'04*
Herbie: Fully Loaded *'05*
Waiting *'05*
Accepted *'06*
The Break-Up *'06*
Dreamland *'06*
Idiocracy *'06*
The Sasquatch Gang *'06*
Alvin and the Chipmunks *'07 (V)*
Just Add Water *'07*
Live Free or Die Hard *'07*
Walk Hard: The Dewey Cox Story *'07*
Still Waiting *'08*
Strange Wilderness *'08*
Zack and Miri Make a Porno *'08*
Alvin and the Chipmunks: The Squeakuel *'09 (V)*
Drag Me to Hell *'09*
He's Just Not That Into You *'09*
Planet 51 *'09 (V)*
Taking Chances *'09*
After.life *'10*
Alpha and Omega *'10 (V)*
The Conspirator *'10*
Going the Distance *'10*
Youth in Revolt *'10*
Alvin and the Chipmunks: Chipwrecked *'11 (V)*
Best Man Down *'12*
For a Good Time, Call... *'12*
10 Years *'12*
A Case of You *'13*
Movie 43 *'13*
Walking with Dinosaurs 3D *'13 (V)*
Comet *'14*
The Lookalike *'14*
Tusk *'14*
Alvin and the Chipmunks: Road Chip *'15*
Frank & Lola *'16*
Ghost Team *'16*

Lisa Long
Mysterious Skin *'04*
Back to You and Me *'05*

Lotus Long (1909-90)
Mr. Wong in Chinatown *'39*
Mystery of Mr. Wong *'39*

Mark Long
Stormy Monday *'88*
7 Grand Masters *'04*

Matt Long (1980-)
Deceit *'06*
Ghost Rider *'07*
Sydney White *'07*
Homecoming *'09*

Nia Long (1970-)
Boyz N the Hood *'91*
Made in America *'93*
Friday *'95*
Love Jones *'96*
Soul Food *'97*
Never 2 Big *'98*
The Best Man *'99*
In Too Deep *'99*
Stigmata *'99*
Big Momma's House *'00*
Boiler Room *'00*
The Broken Hearts Club *'00*
Held Up *'00*
If These Walls Could Talk 2 *'00*
Baadasssss! *'03*
Alfie *'04*
Are We There Yet? *'05*
Big Momma's House 2 *'06*
Are We Done Yet? *'07*
Premonition *'07*
Mooz-Lum *'10*
The Best Man Holiday *'13*
Tyler Perry's The Single Moms' Club *'14*
The Banker *'20*

Richard Long (1927-74)
The Stranger *'46*
Tomorrow Is Forever *'46*
Egg and I *'47*
Criss Cross *'48*
Ma and Pa Kettle *'49*
Kansas Raiders *'50*
Ma and Pa Kettle Go to Town *'50*
Ma and Pa Kettle Back On the Farm *'51*
Cult of the Cobra *'55*
House on Haunted Hill *'58*
Follow the Boys *'63*

Shelley Long (1949-)
A Small Circle of Friends *'80*
Caveman *'81*
Losin' It *'82*
Night Shift *'82*
Irreconcilable Differences *'84*
The Money Pit *'86*
Hello Again *'87*
Outrageous Fortune *'87*
Troop Beverly Hills *'89*
Don't Tell Her It's Me *'90*
The Brady Bunch Movie *'95*
A Very Brady Sequel *'96*
Dr. T & the Women *'00*
The Santa Trap *'02*
Honeymoon with Mom *'06*
Holiday Engagement *'11*
Best Man Down *'12*
The Dog Who Saved the Holidays *'12*
Merry In-Laws *'12*
Strawberry Summer *'12*
The Wedding Chapel *'13*

Tom Long (1968-2020)
Two Hands *'98*
Strange Planet *'99*
The Dish *'00*
Risk *'00*
Do or Die *'01*

Walter Long (1879-1952)
The Birth of a Nation *'15*
The Little American *'17*
The Sheik *'21*
Blood and Sand *'22*
Moran of the Lady Letty *'22*
Little Church Around the Corner *'23*
Yankee Clipper *'27*

John Longden (1900-71)
Blackmail *'29*
Juno and the Paycock *'30*
Young and Innocent *'37*
Alias John Preston *'56*
Quatermass 2 *'57*

Terence Longdon (1922-2011)
Another Time, Another Place *'58*
Carry On Sergeant *'58*

Jane Longenecker
The Coroner *'98*
Dinocroc *'04*

Cody Longo (1988-)
Bring It On: Fight to the Finish *'09*
Piranha 3D *'10*

Tony Longo (1961-2015)
Fletch *'85*
Bloodhounds of Broadway *'89*
Worth Winning *'89*
The Last Boy Scout *'91*
Suburban Commando *'91*
Rapid Fire *'92*
Houseguest *'94*
Hard Luck *'01*
The Cooler *'03*
Jake's Corner *'08*

Eva Longoria (1975-)
Senorita Justice *'03*
Harsh Times *'05*
The Sentinel *'06*
Lower Learning *'08*
Over Her Dead Body *'08*
Without Men *'11*
The Baytown Outlaws *'12*
A Dark Truth *'12*
For Greater Glory *'12*
Any Day *'15*
Visions *'16*

Dog Days *'18*
Overboard *'18*
Dora and the Lost City of Gold *'19*

Robert Longstreet
Great World of Sound *'07*
5 Time Champion *'11*
Take Shelter *'11*
This is Martin Bonner *'13*

Emily Longstreth (1967-)
Private Resort *'84*
The Big Picture *'89*
Too Young to Die *'90*

Michael (Michel) Lonsdale (1931-)
Is Paris Burning? *'66*
The Bride Wore Black *'68*
Stolen Kisses *'68*
Murmur of the Heart *'71*
The Day of the Jackal *'73*
Phantom of Liberty *'74*
Mr. Klein *'76*
Moonraker *'79*
The Passage *'79*
Enigma *'82*
The Holcroft Covenant *'85*
The Name of the Rose *'86*
Souvenir *'88*
The Remains of the Day *'93*
Nelly et Monsieur Arnaud *'95*
Ronin *'98*
5x2 *'04*
Munich *'05*
Goya's Ghosts *'06*
Heartbeat Detector *'07*
Agora *'09*
Of Gods and Men *'10*
Free Men *'12*

Leon Lontoc (1908-74)
The Hunters *'58*
The Gallant Hours *'60*

Richard Loo (1903-83)
The Bitter Tea of General Yen *'33*
Mr. Wong in Chinatown *'39*
Across the Pacific *'42*
China *'43*
The Purple Heart *'44*
Back to Bataan *'45*
God is My Co-Pilot *'45*
Seven Were Saved *'47*
Malaya *'49*
I Was an American Spy *'51*
The Steel Helmet *'51*
Five Fingers *'52*
Love Is a Many-Splendored Thing *'55*
Battle Hymn *'57*
Confessions of an Opium Eater *'62*
The Sand Pebbles *'66*
Chandler *'71*
The Man with the Golden Gun *'74*

Michael (Mike) Lookinland (1960-)
Stephen King's The Stand *'94*
The Brady Bunch Movie *'95 (C)*

Nancy Loomis (1949-)
Assault on Precinct 13 *'76*
Halloween *'78*

Theodore Loos (1883-1954)
Kriemhilde's Revenge *'24*
Metropolis *'26*
M *'31*

Tanya Lopert (1942-)
Navajo Joe *'67*
Tales of Ordinary Madness *'83*
Changing Times *'04*

Carmen Lopez
Curdled *'95*
Our Song *'01*

George Lopez (1961-)
Bread and Roses *'00*
Real Women Have Curves *'02*
The Adventures of Sharkboy and Lavagirl in 3-D *'05*

Balls of Fury *'07*
Tortilla Heaven *'07*
Beverly Hills Chihuahua *'08 (V)*
Henry Poole Is Here *'08*
Swing Vote *'08*
Mr. Troop Mom *'09*
Beverly Hills Chihuahua 2 *'10 (V)*
Marmaduke *'10 (V)*
The Spy Next Door *'10*
Valentine's Day *'10*
Rio *'11 (V)*
The Smurfs *'11 (V)*
Beverly Hills Chihuahua 3: Viva La Fiesta! *'12 (V)*
Rio 2 *'14 (V)*
Spare Parts *'15*
El Chicano *'19*

Jennifer Lopez (1970-)
My Family *'94*
Money Train *'95*
Anaconda *'96*
Blood & Wine *'96*
Jack *'96*
Selena *'96*
U-Turn *'97*
Antz *'98 (V)*
Out of Sight *'98*
The Cell *'00*
Angel Eyes *'01*
The Wedding Planner *'01*
Enough *'02*
Maid in Manhattan *'02*
Gigli *'03*
Jersey Girl *'04*
Shall We Dance? *'04*
Monster-in-Law *'05*
An Unfinished Life *'05*
Bordertown *'06*
El Cantante *'06*
The Back-Up Plan *'10*
Ice Age: Continental Drift *'12 (V)*
What to Expect When You're Expecting *'12*
Parker *'13*
The Boy Next Door *'15*
Home *'15 (V)*
Lila & Eve *'15*
Ice Age: Collision Course *'16*
Second Act *'18*
Hustlers *'19*

Kamala Lopez (1964-)
Born in East L.A. *'87*
Dollman *'90*
Crazy from the Heart *'91*
Erotique *'94*

Mario Lopez (1973-)
Breaking the Surface: The Greg Louganis Story *'96*
Absolution *'97*
Killing Mr. Griffin *'97*
Depraved *'98*
Eastside *'99*
Big Brother Trouble *'00*
A Crack in the Floor *'00*
Outta Time *'01*
The Street King *'02*
Holiday in Handcuffs *'07*
The Dog Who Saved Christmas *'09 (V)*
The Dog Who Saved Christmas Vacation *'10 (V)*
The Dog Who Saved Easter *'15 (V)*
The Dog Who Saved Summer *'15*

Perry Lopez (1929-2008)
Battle Cry *'55*
Mister Roberts *'55*
Violent Road *'58*
Taras Bulba *'62*
McLintock! *'63*
Kelly's Heroes *'70*
Chinatown *'74*
The Two Jakes *'90*

Priscilla Lopez (1948-)
Chutney Popcorn *'99*
Center Stage *'00*
Maid in Manhattan *'02*
Tony n' Tina's Wedding *'07*
Humor Me *'17*

Sal Lopez (1954-)
Full Metal Jacket *'87*
American Me *'92*
The Fire Next Time *'93*
Selena *'96*
Luminarias *'99*
Price of Glory *'00*
El Padrino *'04*
Silver City *'04*
ESL: English as a Second Language *'05*
Comanche Moon *'08*

Seidy Lopez
Mi Vida Loca *'94*
Solo *'96*
Depraved *'98*
The Stray *'00*
Gabriela *'01*

Sergi Lopez (1965-)
Western *'96*
Caresses *'97*
The New Eve *'98*
An Affair of Love *'99*
Between Your Legs *'99*
Lisboa *'99*
With a Friend Like Harry *'00*
Jet Lag *'02*
Dirty Pretty Things *'03*
Pan's Labyrinth *'06*
Ricky *'09*
The Prey *'11*
A Perfect Day *'16*

Trini Lopez (1937-)
The Poppy Is Also a Flower *'66*
The Dirty Dozen *'67*
Antonio *'73*

Pilar Lopez de Ayala (1978-)
Mad Love *'01*
The Bridge of San Luis Rey *'05*
In the City of Sylvia *'07*
The Strange Case of Angelica *'10*
Intruders *'11*
Night Has Settled *'14*

Sophie Lorain (1957-)
Home Team *'98*
The Sign of Four *'01*
Mambo Italiano *'03*

Isabel Lorca
Lightning: The White Stallion *'86*
She's Having a Baby *'88*

Theodore Lorch (1880-1947)
The Last of the Mohicans *'20*
The Better 'Ole *'26*

Jack Lord (1920-98)
The Court Martial of Billy Mitchell *'55*
Tip On a Dead Jockey *'57*
God's Little Acre *'58*
Man of the West *'58*
The Hangman *'59*
Dr. No *'62*

Marjorie Lord (1918-)
Forty Naughty Girls *'37*
High Flyers *'37*
On Again-Off Again *'37*
Johnny Come Lately *'43*
Sherlock Holmes in Washington *'43*
Chain Gang *'50*
The Lost Volcano *'50*
Boy, Did I Get a Wrong Number! *'66*

Quinn Lord (1999-)
Trick 'r Treat *'08*
Call Me Mrs. Miracle *'10*
Daydream Nation *'10*
In Their Skin *'12*

Stephen Lord (1972-)
Lethal Dose *'03*
Pulse *'03*
The Shepherd: Border Patrol *'08*
Mrs. Lowry & Son *'19*

Traci Lords (1968-)
Not of This Earth '88
Fast Food '89
Cry-Baby '90
Shock 'Em Dead '90
Raw Nerve '91
A Time to Die '91
Laser Moon '92
Desperate Crimes '93
Ice '93
Skinner '93
Stephen King's The Tommyknockers '93
Dragstrip Girl '94
Plughead Rewired: Circuitry Man 2 '94
Serial Mom '94
The Nutt House '95
Blade '98
Boogie Boy '98
Extramarital '98
D.R.E.A.M. Team '99
Me & Will '99
The Killing Club '01
Black Mask 2: City of Masks '02
Deathlands: Homeward Bound '03
Crazy Eights '06
Novel Romance '06
Zack and Miri Make a Porno '08
Princess of Mars '09
Excision '12

Donna Loren (1947-)
Bikini Beach '64
Muscle Beach Party '64
Pajama Party '64

Sophia Loren (1934-)
Quo Vadis '51
Attila '54
The Gold of Naples '54
Neapolitan Carousel '54
Too Bad She's Bad '54
Two Nights with Cleopatra '54
Legend of the Lost '57
The Pride and the Passion '57
Desire Under the Elms '58
Houseboat '58
The Key '58
Black Orchid '59
Breath of Scandal '60
Heller in Pink Tights '60
It Started in Naples '60
The Millionairess '60
El Cid '61
Two Women '61
Boccaccio '70 '62
Madame Sans-Gene '62
The Fall of the Roman Empire '64
Marriage Italian Style '64
Yesterday, Today and Tomorrow '64
Lady L '65
The Love Goddesses '65
Operation Crossbow '65
Arabesque '66
A Countess from Hong Kong '67
More Than a Miracle '67
The Priest's Wife '71
Man of La Mancha '72
Get Rita '75
Lady of the Evening '75
The Cassandra Crossing '76
A Special Day '77
Brass Target '78
Blood Feud '79
Firepower '79
Courage '86
Ready to Wear '94
Grumpier Old Men '95
Between Strangers '02
Nine '09

Livio Lorenzon (1923-71)
Pirates of the Coast '61
Gladiators 7 '62
The Invincible Gladiator '62
Hercules and the Tyrants of Babylon '64
Last Gun '64
Challenge of the Gladiator '65
Go With God Gringo '66
Cjamango '67
The Good, the Bad and the Ugly '67

Susanne Loret
Uncle Was a Vampire '59
Atom Age Vampire '61

Louise Lorimer (1898-1995)
Gangster's Boy '38
Japanese War Bride '52
30 '59

Teala Loring (1922-2007)
Delinquent Daughters '44
Black Market Babies '45
Gas House Kids '46
Wife Wanted '46

James Lorinz (1964-)
Street Trash '87
Frankenhooker '90
Last Exit to Brooklyn '90
Me and the Mob '94
The Jerky Boys '95
The Sweet Life '03

Jean-Pierre Lorit (1960-)
Jeanne la Pucelle '94
Trois Couleurs: Rouge '94
The White Countess '05
Outside the Law '10

Marion Lorne (1883-1968)
Strangers on a Train '51
The Graduate '67

Louise Lorraine (1901-81)
The Adventures of Tarzan '21
Exit Smiling '26

Suzi Lorraine
Dead Collections '12
Solid State '12

Peter Lorre (1904-64)
M '31
F.P. 1 Doesn't Answer '33
The Man Who Knew Too Much '34
Mad Love '35
The Secret Agent '36
Nancy Steele Is Missing '37
Thank you, Mr. Moto '37
Think Fast, Mr. Moto '37
Mr. Moto's Gamble '38
Mr. Moto in Danger Island '39
Mr. Moto's Last Warning '39
Strange Cargo '40
You'll Find Out '40
The Maltese Falcon '41
Mr. District Attorney '41
They Met in Bombay '41
All Through the Night '42
The Boogie Man Will Get You '42
Casablanca '42
Invisible Agent '42
Background to Danger '43
The Constant Nymph '43
The Cross of Lorraine '43
Arsenic and Old Lace '44
The Conspirators '44
Hollywood Canteen '44
The Mask of Dimitrios '44
Passage to Marseilles '44
Confidential Agent '45
The Beast with Five Fingers '46
Black Angel '46
The Chase '46
Three Strangers '46
The Verdict '46
My Favorite Brunette '47
Rope of Sand '49
Quicksand '50
Beat the Devil '53
20,000 Leagues under the Sea '54
Around the World in 80 Days '56 (C)
Hell Ship Mutiny '57
The Sad Sack '57
Silk Stockings '57
Story of Mankind '57
The Big Circus '59
Voyage to the Bottom of the Sea '61
Five Weeks in a Balloon '62
Tales of Terror '62
The Raven '63
The Comedy of Terrors '64
Muscle Beach Party '64
The Patsy '64

Joan Lorring (1926-2014)
The Corn Is Green '45
Three Strangers '46
The Verdict '46
The Gangster '47
The Other Love '47
Good Sam '48
The Big Night '51
Stranger on the Prowl '52

Diana Lorys (1940-)
The Awful Dr. Orlof '62
Revenge of Sartana '65
The Texican '66
Lightning Bolt '67
Fangs of the Living Dead '68
Villa Rides '68

Donald Losby
Critic's Choice '63
Your Cheatin' Heart '64

Susanne Lothar (1960-2012)
Funny Games '97
The Piano Teacher '01
The Reader '08
Murder on the Orient Express '10

Eb Lottimer (1951-)
Stripped to Kill 2: Live Girls '89
Streets '90
The Finest Hour '91
Futurekick '91
Beyond the Call of Duty '92
Bloodfist 7: Manhunt '95
Termination Man '97
Diamondbacks '99

Caity Lotz (1986-)
The Pact '12
Battle of the Year '13
The Machine '13

Alexander Lou
Ninja in the U.S.A. '88
Ninja the Battalion '90

Louanne (1970-)
The Long Days of Summer '80
Oh, God! Book 2 '80
A Night in the Life of Jimmy Reardon '88

Lance Loud (1950-2001)
Armistead Maupin's Tales of the City '93
Inside Monkey Zetterland '93

Dorothy Loudon (1933-2003)
Garbo Talks '84
Midnight in the Garden of Good and Evil '97

Jackie Loughery (1930-)
Abbott and Costello Go to Mars '53
Pardners '56
D.I. '57

Lori Loughlin (1964-)
Amityville 3: The Demon '83
The New Kids '85
Secret Admirer '85
Back to the Beach '87
The Night Before '88
Doing Time on Maple Drive '92
To Grandmother's House We Go '94 (C)
Abandoned and Deceived '95
Critical Mass '00
Moondance Alexander '07
Old Dogs '09
Soldier Love Story '10
Garage Sale Mystery '13
When Calls the Heart '13

Jonathan Loughran (1966-)
Anger Management '03
Grandma's Boy '06
Death Proof '07
I Now Pronounce You Chuck and Larry '07
The House Bunny '08

Bill Louie
The Bodyguard '76
Fist of Fear, Touch of Death '80

Joe Louis (1914-81)
The Spirit of Youth '37
This Is the Army '43

Justin Louis (1967-)
Hello Mary Lou: Prom Night 2 '87
The Big Slice '90
Blood & Donuts '95
National Lampoon's Dad's Week Off '97
Everything Put Together '00
Stiletto Dance '01
Dawn of the Dead '04
Shooter '07
The Andromeda Strain '08
True Confessions of a Hollywood Starlet '08
Grey Gardens '09

Patrick Louis
Lansdown '01
Cinderella Man '05

Willard Louis (1882-1926)
Robin Hood '22
Beau Brummel '24
Don Juan '26

Louis C.K. (1967-)
Welcome Home Roscoe Jenkins '08
The Secret Life of Pets '16

Julia Louis-Dreyfus (1961-)
Troll '86
National Lampoon's Christmas Vacation '89
Jack the Bear '93
Father's Day '96
Deconstructing Harry '97
A Bug's Life '98 (V)
Animal Farm '99 (V)
Gepetto '00
Enough Said '13
Planes '13 (V)
Downhill '20
Onward '20 (V)

Anita Louise (1915-70)
Millie '31
The Woman Between '31
The Phantom of Crestwood '32
Judge Priest '34
Anthony Adverse '36
Call It a Day '37
The Green Light '37
That Certain Woman '37
Marie Antoinette '38
The Sisters '38
The Gorilla '39
The Little Princess '39
Reno '39
Those Glamour Girls '39
Wagons Westward '40
The Villain Still Pursued Her '41
Casanova Brown '44
Love Letters '45
The Bandit of Sherwood Forest '46

Tina Louise (1934-)
God's Little Acre '58
The Day of the Outlaw '59
The Hangman '59
The Trap '59
The Wrecking Crew '68
The Good Guys and the Bad Guys '69
The Happy Ending '69
How to Commit Marriage '69
The Stepford Wives '75
Friendship, Secrets and Lies '79
Evils of the Night '85
O.C. and Stiggs '87
Dixie Lanes '88
Johnny Suede '92

Todd Louiso (1970-)
Apollo 13 '95
8 Heads in a Duffel Bag '96
Jerry Maguire '96
The Rock '96
High Fidelity '00
School for Scoundrels '06
Snakes on a Plane '06
Thank You for Smoking '06
A Bag of Hammers '11

Tim Lounibos
Erotique '94
Steel Sharks '97
Life Tastes Good '99

Sam Louwyck
Bullhead '11
The Wonders '15

Demi Lovato (1992-)
Camp Rock '08
Princess Protection Program '09
Camp Rock 2: The Final Jam '10
Smurfs: The Lost Village '17 (V)

Alan Love
That Sinking Feeling '79
The Apple '80

Bessie Love (1898-1986)
Intolerance '16
The Lost World '25
Dress Parade '27
Broadway Melody '29
The Idle Rich '29
Chasing Rainbows '30
Roman Spring of Mrs. Stone '61
A Wild Affair '63
The Poppy Is Also a Flower '66
Catlow '71
Sunday, Bloody Sunday '71
Vampyres '74

Courtney Love (1964-)
Sid & Nancy '86
Straight to Hell '87
Tapeheads '89
Basquiat '96
Feeling Minnesota '96
The People vs. Larry Flynt '96
200 Cigarettes '98
Man on the Moon '99
Beat '00
Trapped '02

Darlene Love (1938-)
Lethal Weapon '87
Lethal Weapon 2 '89
Lethal Weapon 3 '92
Lethal Weapon 4 '98
Holiday Rush '19

Darris Love (1980-)
Sucker Free City '05
The Janky Promoters '09

Faizon Love (1968-)
Bebe's Kids '92 (V)
Fear of a Black Hat '94
The Players Club '98
Inhumanity '00
The Replacements '00
Three Strikes '00
Made '01
Blue Crush '02
Elf '03
Wonderland '03
Torque '04
Animal '05
Idlewild '06
Just My Luck '06
The Perfect Holiday '07
Who's Your Caddy? '07
Couples Retreat '09
A Day in the Life '09
Big Mommas: Like Father, Like Son '11
Zookeeper '11 (V)

Lucretia Love
The She-Beast '65
Go With God Gringo '66
The Arena '73

Montagu Love (1877-1943)
Don Juan '26
King of Kings '27
The Divine Lady '29
Inside the Lines '30
The Midnight Lady '32
Vanity Fair '32
His Double Life '33
Clive of India '35
The Crusades '35
Lloyds of London '36
One in a Million '36
Sing, Baby, Sing '36
A Damsel in Distress '37
The Prince and the Pauper '37
Prisoner of Zenda '37
The Adventures of Robin Hood '38
Gunga Din '39
Juarez '39
All This and Heaven Too '40
Dr. Ehrlich's Magic Bullet '40
The Mark of Zorro '40
The Son of Monte Cristo '40
Lady for a Night '42
Sherlock Holmes and the Voice of Terror '42
The Constant Nymph '43
Devotion '46

Mother Love (1953-)
Armistead Maupin's Tales of the City '93
Mr. Nanny '93
The Surgeon '94
Twinsitters '95

Suzanna Love
Cocaine Cowboys '79
The Boogey Man '80
Brainwaves '82
Boogey Man 2 '83
Devonsville Terror '83
Olivia '83

Victor Love (1957-)
Heaven Is a Playground '91
Final Shot: The Hank Gathers Story '92
Gang Related '96
A Gun, a Car, a Blonde '97

Frank Lovejoy (1914-62)
Breakthrough '50
In a Lonely Place '50
Three Secrets '50
Force of Arms '51
Goodbye My Fancy '51
I Was a Communist for the FBI '51
I'll See You in My Dreams '51
The Winning Team '52
The Hitch-Hiker '53
House of Wax '53
She's Back on Broadway '53
The System '53
Men of the Fighting Lady '54
Americano '55
The Crooked Web '55
Shack Out on 101 '55
Strategic Air Command '55
Julie '56
Three Brave Men '57
Cole Younger, Gunfighter '58

Aiden Lovekamp
Paranormal Activity 4 '12
The Invitation '16

Jacqueline Lovell (1974-)
Femalien '96
Head of the Family '96
Exotic House of Wax '97
Hideous '97
Lolida 2000 '97

Pedro Lovell (1945-)
Rocky '76
Rocky Balboa '06

Raymond Lovell (1900-53)
Contraband '40
Candlelight in Algeria '44
Immortal Battalion '44
Appointment with Crime '45

Ray Lovelock (1950-)
Fiddler on the Roof '71
Let Sleeping Corpses Lie '74
Autopsy '75
Live Like a Cop, Die Like a Man '76
Meet Him and Die '76
From Hell to Victory '79

Patrice Lovely
Tyler Perry's Hell Hath No Fury Like a Woman Scorned: The Play *'14*
Boo! A Madea Halloween *'16*
Boo 2! A Madea Halloween *'17*
A Madea Family Funeral *'19*

Ed Lover (1963-)
Gunmen *'93 (C)*
Who's the Man? *'93*

Dorothy Lovett (1915-98)
Courageous Dr. Christian *'40*
Remedy for Riches *'40*

Lyle Lovett (1957-)
The Player *'92*
Short Cuts *'93*
Ready to Wear *'94*
Bastard out of Carolina *'96*
Fear and Loathing in Las Vegas *'98*
The Opposite of Sex *'98*
Cookie's Fortune *'99*
The New Guy *'02*
The Open Road *'09 (C)*
Angels Sing *'13*

Ophelia Lovibond (1986-)
Nowhere Boy *'09*
4.3.2.1 *'10*
The Autopsy of Jane Doe *'16*
Tommy's Honour *'17*
Timmy Failure: Mistakes Were Made *'20*

Jon Lovitz (1957-)
Jumpin' Jack Flash *'86*
Last Resort *'86*
Three Amigos *'86*
Big *'88*
My Stepmother Is an Alien *'88*
Mr. Destiny *'90*
An American Tail: Fievel Goes West *'91 (V)*
A League of Their Own *'92*
Mom and Dad Save the World *'92*
National Lampoon's Loaded Weapon 1 *'93*
City Slickers 2: The Legend of Curly's Gold *'94*
Trapped in Paradise *'94*
The Great White Hype *'96*
High School High *'96*
The Wedding Singer *'97*
Happiness *'98*
Lost and Found *'99*
Little Nicky *'00*
Sand *'00*
Small Time Crooks *'00*
Cats & Dogs *'01 (V)*
Good Advice *'01*
Rat Race *'01*
3000 Miles to Graceland *'01*
Adam Sandler's 8 Crazy Nights *'02 (V)*
Dickie Roberts: Former Child Star *'03*
The Stepford Wives *'04*
Bailey's Billion$ *'05 (V)*
The Producers *'05*
The Benchwarmers *'06*
I Could Never Be Your Woman *'06*
Casino Jack *'10*
Jewtopia *'12*

Celia Lovsky (1897-1979)
Captain Carey, U.S.A. *'50*
Rhapsody *'54*
Rumble on the Docks *'56*
I, Mobster *'58*
36 Hours *'64*

Victor Low (1962-)
Character *'97*
Everybody's Famous! *'00*
Love at First Kill *'08*

Jack Lowden (1990-)
Denial *'16*
Dunkirk *'17*
Tommy's Honour *'17*
Mary Queen of Scots *'18*
Fighting with My Family *'19*

Alex Lowe (1968-)
Peter's Friends *'92*
Haunted *'95*

Alice Lowe
Sightseers *'12*
Sometimes Always Never *'19*

Arthur Lowe (1915-82)
Kind Hearts and Coronets *'49*
This Sporting Life *'63*
If. . . *'69*
Fragment of Fear *'70*
The Rise and Rise of Michael Rimmer *'70*
The Ruling Class *'72*
No Sex Please-We're British *'73*
O Lucky Man! *'73*
Theatre of Blood *'73*
Adolf Hitler: My Part in His Downfall *'74*
Sweet William *'79*

Barry Lowe
Cash on Demand *'61*
Sands of the Kalahari *'65*

Chad Lowe (1968-)
Silence of the Heart *'84*
April Morning *'88*
True Blood *'89*
Nobody's Perfect *'90*
Floating *'97*
In the Presence of Mine Enemies *'97*
Quiet Days in Hollywood *'97*
Take Me Home: The John Denver Story *'00*
Acceptable Risk *'01*
Unfaithful *'02*
Fielder's Choice *'05*

Crystal Lowe (1981-)
Children of the Corn: Revelation *'01*
Insomnia *'02*
Blood Angels *'05*
Black Christmas *'06*
Final Destination 3 *'06*
Wrong Turn 2: Dead End *'07*
Yeti *'08*
Signed, Sealed, Delivered for Christmas *'14*
Rampage: President Down *'16*

Edmund Lowe (1890-1971)
The Eyes of Youth *'19*
Barbara Frietchie *'24*
Chandu the Magician *'32*
Dinner at Eight *'33*
Bombay Mail *'34*
Every Day's a Holiday *'38*
The Witness Vanishes *'39*
I Love You Again *'40*
Men Against the Sky *'40*
Klondike Fury *'42*
Dillinger *'45*
The Enchanted Forest *'45*
Good Sam *'48*
Wings of Eagles *'57*
Heller in Pink Tights *'60*

Harrison Lowe
Geronimo *'93*
Buffalo Soldiers *'97*

Rob Lowe (1964-)
Class *'83*
The Outsiders *'83*
The Hotel New Hampshire *'84*
Oxford Blues *'84*
St. Elmo's Fire *'85*
About Last Night. . . *'86*
Youngblood *'86*
Illegally Yours *'87*
Square Dance *'87*
Masquerade *'88*
Bad Influence *'90*
The Dark Backward *'91*
The Finest Hour *'91*
Wayne's World *'92*
Frank and Jesse *'94*
Stephen King's The Stand *'94*
First Degree *'95*
Mulholland Falls *'95 (C)*
Tommy Boy *'95*
Contact *'97*
Hostile Intent *'97*
Living in Peril *'97*
Crazy Six *'98*
For Hire *'98*
Outrage *'98*
Atomic Train *'99*
Austin Powers 2: The Spy Who Shagged Me *'99*
Dead Silent *'99*
Escape under Pressure *'00*
Proximity *'00*
The Specials *'00*
The Christmas Shoes *'02*
View from the Top *'03*
Salem's Lot *'04*
The Christmas Blessing *'05*
Jiminy Glick in LaLa Wood *'05 (C)*
Secret Smile *'05*
A Perfect Day *'06*
Thank You for Smoking *'06*
Stir of Echoes 2: The Homecoming *'07*
The Invention of Lying *'09*
I Melt With You *'11*
Drew Peterson: Untouchable *'12*
Behind the Candelabra *'13*
Killing Kennedy *'13*
Knife Fight *'13*
Prosecuting Casey Anthony *'13*
Sex Tape *'14*
Monster Trucks *'16*
How to Be a Latin Lover *'17*
Holiday in the Wild *'19*

Robert Hepler Lowe (1964-)
See Rob Lowe

Sophie Lowe (1990-)
Beautiful Kate *'09*
Adore *'13*
Autumn Blood *'14*
What Lola Wants *'15*
Blow The Man Down *'19*

Susan Lowe (1948-)
Female Trouble *'74*
Desperate Living *'77*
Polyester *'81*
Hairspray *'88*
Serial Mom *'94*

Bob Lowell
An American Romance *'44*
Mom & Dad *'47*

Carey Lowell (1961-)
Club Paradise *'86*
License to Kill *'89*
The Guardian *'90*
Sleepless in Seattle *'93*
Leaving Las Vegas *'95*
Fierce Creatures *'96*

Chris Lowell (1984-)
Graduation *'07*
Spin *'07*
Up in the Air *'09*
The Help *'11*
Brightest Star *'14*
Veronica Mars *'14*
Complete Unknown *'16*

Helen Lowell (1866-1937)
The Goose and the Gander *'35*
Living on Velvet *'35*

Curt Lowens (1925-2017)
A Midnight Clear *'92*
Invisible: The Chronicles of Benjamin Knight *'93*
Mandroid *'93*
The Cutter *'05*

Elina Lowensohn (1966-)
Simple Men *'92*
Amateur *'94*
Nadja *'95*
Basquiat *'96*
I'm Not Rappaport *'96*
Jane Doe *'96*
In the Presence of Mine Enemies *'97*
Immortality *'98*
Six Ways to Sunday *'99*
Get Well Soon *'01*
Quicksand *'01*
Dark Water *'02*
Fay Grim *'06*
Declaration of War *'11*

Yuri Lowenthal
The Pirates Who Don't Do Anything: A VeggieTales Movie *'08 (V)*
The Wild Life *'16*

Britt Lower
Mr. Roosevelt *'17*
Domain *'18*

Andrew Lowery (1970-)
A Family of Spies *'90*
School Ties *'92*
JFK: Reckless Youth *'93*
My Boyfriend's Back *'93*
Color of Night *'94*
Conspiracy of Fear *'96*

Robert Lowery (1914-71)
Drums Along the Mohawk *'39*
Charlie Chan's Murder Cruise *'40*
Four Sons *'40*
Murder over New York *'40*
Campus Rhythm *'43*
Rhythm Parade *'43*
Tarzan's Desert Mystery *'43*
Navy Way *'44*
Gas House Kids *'46*
House of Horrors *'46*
Call of the Forest *'49*
The Rise and Fall of Legs Diamond *'60*
Young Guns of Texas *'62*
Johnny Reno *'66*
The Undertaker and His Pals *'67*

Klaus Lowitsch (1936-2002)
World on a Wire *'73*
The Odessa File *'74*
Cross of Iron *'76*
Despair *'78*
The Marriage of Maria Braun *'79*
Gotcha! *'85*
Extreme Ops *'02*

Siegfried Lowitz (1915-99)
The Invisible Dr. Mabuse *'62*
Again, the Ringer *'64*

Allen Lowman
Bonnie and Clyde *vs.* Dracula *'08*
The Invoking 2 *'15*

Jessica Lowndes (1988-)
To Have and to Hold *'06*
Autopsy *'08*
The Haunting of Molly Hartley *'08*
Altitude *'10*
The Prince *'14*
Abattoir *'17*

Lynn Lowry (1947-)
Score *'72*
The Crazies *'73*
They Came from Within *'75*
Fighting Mad *'76*
Sugar Cookies *'77*
Beyond the Dunwich Horror *'08*
Basement Jack *'09*

Morton Lowry (1914-87)
Dawn Patrol *'38*
Hudson's Bay *'40*
Counter-Espionage *'42*
Immortal Sergeant *'43*
The Most Wonderful Time of the Year *'08*

Sam Lowry (1963-)
See Steven Soderbergh

T.J. Lowther (1986-)
A Perfect World *'93*
Mad Love *'95*
One Christmas *'95*

Myrna Loy (1905-93)
Don Juan *'26*
The Jazz Singer *'27*
The Great Divide *'29*
The Squall *'29*
The Truth About Youth *'30*
Arrowsmith *'31*
The Animal Kingdom *'32*
Emma *'32*
Love Me Tonight *'32*
The Mask of Fu Manchu *'32*
New Morals for Old *'32*
Vanity Fair *'32*
The Wet Parade *'32*
The Barbarian *'33*
Night Flight *'33*
Penthouse *'33*
The Prizefighter and the Lady *'33*
Broadway Bill *'34*
Evelyn Prentice *'34*
Manhattan Melodrama *'34*
Men in White *'34*
The Thin Man *'34*
Whipsaw *'35*
Wings in the Dark *'35*
After the Thin Man *'36*
The Great Ziegfeld *'36*
Libeled Lady *'36*
Wife Versus Secretary *'36*
Double Wedding *'37*
Parnell *'37*
Test Pilot *'38*
Too Hot to Handle *'38*
Another Thin Man *'39*
The Rains Came *'39*
I Love You Again *'40*
Third Finger, Left Hand *'40*
Love Crazy *'41*
Shadow of the Thin Man *'41*
The Thin Man Goes Home *'44*
The Best Years of Our Lives *'46*
So Goes My Love *'46*
The Bachelor and the Bobby-Soxer *'47*
Song of the Thin Man *'47*
Mr. Blandings Builds His Dream House *'48*
The Red Pony *'49*
Cheaper by the Dozen *'50*
Belles on Their Toes *'52*
The Ambassador's Daughter *'56*
From the Terrace *'60*
Airport '75 *'75*
Ants *'77*
The End *'78*
Just Tell Me What You Want *'80*
Summer Solstice *'81*

Florencia Lozano (1969-)
Perfect Stranger *'07*
The Ministers *'09*

Margarita Lozano (1931-)
Viridiana *'61*
The Night of the Shooting Stars *'82*
Kaos *'85*
Jean de Florette *'87*
Manon of the Spring *'87*
Night Sun *'90*

Feng Lu (1953-)
Five Deadly Venoms *'78*
House of Traps *'81*

Liping Lu (1961-)
The Blue Kite *'93*
Shadow Magic *'00*

Lisa Lu (1927-)
Rider on a Dead Horse *'62*
Demon Seed *'77*
The Joy Luck Club *'93*
I Love Trouble *'94*
Dim Sum Funeral *'08*

Leem Lubany
Omar *'13*
Saint Judy *'19*

Lou Lubin (1895-1973)
Betrayed *'44*
The Clown *'53*

Arthur Lucan (1887-1954)
Old Mother Riley in Paris *'38*
Old Mother Riley, MP *'39*
Old Mother Riley's Ghosts *'41*
Old Mother Riley's New Venture *'49*
Old Mother Riley, Headmistress *'50*
Old Mother Riley's Jungle Treasure *'51*
My Son, the Vampire *'52*

George Lucas (1944-)
Hearts of Darkness: A Filmmaker's Apocalypse *'91*
Hugh Hefner: Playboy, Activist and Rebel *'09*

Isabel Lucas (1985-)
Daybreakers *'09*
The Waiting City *'09*
Immortals *'11*

Ivan Lucas
Ernest in the Army *'97*
Mama Africa *'02*

Jessica Lucas (1985-)
The Covenant *'06*
Amusement *'08*
Cloverfield *'08*
Big Mommas: Like Father, Like Son *'11*
Evil Dead *'13*
Pompeii *'14*
That Awkward Moment *'14*

Josh(ua) Lucas (1971-)
No Money Down *'97*
Cash Crop *'98*
American Psycho *'99*
The Weight of Water *'00*
A Beautiful Mind *'01*
The Deep End *'01*
Session 9 *'01*
Coastlines *'02*
Sweet Home Alabama *'02*
Hulk *'03*
Secondhand Lions *'03*
Wonderland *'03*
Around the Bend *'04*
Undertow *'04*
Empire Falls *'05*
Stealth *'05*
An Unfinished Life *'05*
Glory Road *'06*
Poseidon *'06*
Death in Love *'08*
Peacock *'09*
Stolen *'09*
Daydream Nation *'10*
Life As We Know It *'10*
Shadows and Lies *'10*
Hide Away *'11*
J. Edgar *'11*
The Lincoln Lawyer *'11*
Red Dog *'11*
Stolen *'12*
Big Sur *'13*
Space Warriors *'13*
Little Accidents *'14*
The Mend *'15*
Breakthrough *'19*
Ford v Ferrari *'19*

Laurent Lucas (1965-)
Pola X *'99*
With a Friend Like Harry *'00*
Who Killed Bambi? *'03*
Lemming *'05*
The Kate Logan Affair *'10*
Raw *'17*
The Demons *'19*

Lisa Lucas (1961-)
A House Without a Christmas Tree *'72*
Forbidden Love *'82*

Matt Lucas (1974-)
Cold and Dark *'05*
Astro Boy *'09 (V)*
Alice in Wonderland *'10*
Gnomeo & Juliet *'11 (V)*
Small Apartments *'12*
In Secret *'13*
Missing Link *'19*

Peter J. Lucas (1962-)
Dangerous Cargo *'96*
Heart of Stone *'01*
Inland Empire *'06*
The Perfect Sleep *'08*
Life *'15*

Wilfred Lucas (1871-1940)
Through the Back Door *'21*
Dishonored *'31*
Mile a Minute Love *'37*

William Lucas (1925-)
X The Unknown '56
The Marked One '63
Susan Lucci (1946-)
Invitation to Hell '84
Anastasia: The Mystery of Anna '86
Secret Passions '87
French Silk '94
Angela Luce (1938-)
The Decameron '70
'Tis a Pity She's a Whore '73
Enrique Lucero (1920-89)
Tarzan and the Valley of Gold '65
The Woman Hunter '72
The Evil That Men Do '84
Fabrice Luchini (1951-)
Perceval '78
Full Moon in Paris '84
Beaumarchais the Scoundrel '96
On Guard! '03
Intimate Strangers '04
Moliere '07
The Girl From Monaco '08
Paris '08
The Women on the Sixth Floor '10
Bicycling With Moliere '13
Gemma Bovery '15
Shannon Lucio (1980-)
Starkweather '04
Graduation '07
Fireflies in the Garden '08
Shadow on the Mesa '13
The Perfect Guy '15
Laurence Luckinbill (1934-)
The Boys in the Band '70
Such Good Friends '71
The Delphi Bureau: The Merchant of Death Assignment '72
Death Sentence '74
The Money '75
The Lindbergh Kidnapping Case '76
The Promise '79
Not for Publication '84
Cocktail '88
Messenger of Death '88
Star Trek 5: The Final Frontier '89
William Lucking (1941-)
Hell's Belles '69
Doc Savage '75
Kung Fu: The Movie '86
Naked Lie '89
The Trigger Effect '96
The Last Best Sunday '98
K-PAX '01
The Rundown '03
Contraband '12
Ludacris (1977-)
See Chris Bridges
Barbara Luddy (1908-79)
Lady and the Tramp '55 (V)
Sleeping Beauty '59 (V)
Patrick Ludlow (1903-96)
Gangway '37
Old Mother Riley, MP '39
Alexander Ludwig (1992-)
The Seeker: The Dark Is Rising '07
Race to Witch Mountain '09
The Hunger Games '12
When the Game Stands Tall '14
The Final Girls '15
Blackway '16
Bad Boys for Life '20
Pamela Ludwig
Over the Edge '79
Rush Week '88
Salem Ludwig (1915-2007)
I Love You, Alice B. Toklas! '68
Family Business '89
Laurette Luez (1928-99)
D.O.A. '49
Prehistoric Women '50
African Treasure '52
Lorna Luft (1952-)
Grease 2 '82
Where the Boys Are '84 '84
Life with Judy Garland-Me and My Shadows '01 (C)
Bela Lugosi (1882-1956)
Midnight Girl '25
The Black Camel '31
Dracula '31
Chandu the Magician '32
Island of Lost Souls '32
The White Zombie '32
The Death Kiss '33
International House '33
Whispering Shadow '33
The Black Cat '34
Chandu on the Magic Island '34
Return of Chandu '34
The Invisible Ray '36
Shadow of Chinatown '36
S.O.S. Coast Guard '37
The Gorilla '39
The Human Monster '39
Ninotchka '39
The Phantom Creeps '39
Son of Frankenstein '39
Black Friday '40
The Saint's Double Trouble '40
You'll Find Out '40
The Black Cat '41
The Devil Bat '41
The Invisible Ghost '41
The Wolf Man '41
Frankenstein Meets the Wolfman '42
The Ghost of Frankenstein '42
Night Monster '42
Return of the Vampire '43
One Body Too Many '44
Zombies on Broadway '44
The Body Snatcher '45
Abbott and Costello Meet Frankenstein '48
Bela Lugosi Meets a Brooklyn Gorilla '52
My Son, the Vampire '52
Glen or Glenda? '53
Bride of the Monster '55
The Black Sleep '56
Plan 9 from Outer Space '56
James Luisi (1928-2002)
Cry Rape! '73
The Take '74
Contract on Cherry Street '77
Stunts '77
The Dark Ride '78
Fade to Black '80
Murphy's Law '86
Feds '88
Florian Lukas (1973-)
Good Bye, Lenin! '03
North Face '08
Into the White '12
Paul Lukas (1887-1971)
Downstairs '32
Little Women '33
The Casino Murder Case '35
Dodsworth '36
Dinner at the Ritz '37
The Lady Vanishes '38
Confessions of a Nazi Spy '39
The Mutiny of the Elsinore '39
The Ghost Breakers '40
Strange Cargo '40
Watch on the Rhine '43
Address Unknown '44
Uncertain Glory '44
Experiment Perilous '45
Deadline at Dawn '46
Whispering City '47
Berlin Express '48
Kim '50
20,000 Leagues under the Sea '54
The Four Horsemen of the Apocalypse '62
Tender Is the Night '62
55 Days at Peking '63
Fun in Acapulco '63
Lord Jim '65
Paul Lukather (1926-)
Dinosaurus! '60
Hands of a Stranger '62
Benny Luke (1939-2013)
La Cage aux Folles '78
La Cage aux Folles 2 '81
La Cage aux Folles 3: The Wedding '86
Derek Luke (1974-)
Antwone Fisher '02
Biker Boyz '03
Pieces of April '03
Friday Night Lights '04
Spartan '04
Catch a Fire '06
Glory Road '06
Lions for Lambs '07
Definitely, Maybe '08
Miracle at St. Anna '08
Madea Goes to Jail '09
Notorious '09
Sparkle '12
Baggage Claim '13
Self/Less '15
Jorge Luke (1942-2012)
The Revengers '72
Ulzana's Raid '72
Shark Hunter '79
The Evil That Men Do '84
The Treasure of the Amazon '85
Salvador '86
Keye Luke (1904-91)
Charlie Chan in Paris '35
Charlie Chan in Shanghai '35
Mad Love '35
Charlie Chan at the Circus '36
Charlie Chan at the Opera '36
Charlie Chan at the Race Track '36
Charlie Chan at Monte Carlo '37
Charlie Chan at the Olympics '37
Charlie Chan on Broadway '37
The Good Earth '37
International Settlement '38
Mr. Moto's Gamble '38
The Green Hornet '39
No, No Nanette '40
Across the Pacific '42
Dr. Gillespie's New Assistant '42
Dr. Gillespie's Criminal Case '43
Salute to the Marines '43
Three Men in White '44
Between Two Women '45
Dark Delusion '47
Sleep, My Love '48
Hell's Half Acre '54
The Chairman '69
Kung Fu '72
Noon Sunday '75
Cocaine and Blue Eyes '83
Gremlins '84
Kung Fu: The Movie '86
Dead Heat '88
The Mighty Quinn '89
Alice '90
Gremlins 2: The New Batch '90
Adrian Lukis (1958-)
Pride and Prejudice '95
Nightwatching '07
Wolfgang Lukschy (1905-83)
Dead Eyes of London '61
Frozen Alive '64
24 Hours to Kill '65
Folco Lulli (1912-70)
Variety Lights '51
Nobody's Children '52
Submarine Attack '54
Wages of Fear '55
The Mercenaries '62
Revenge of the Musketeers '63
The Organizer '64
Lightning Bolt '67
Pierro Lulli (1923-91)
Hercules and the Black Pirate '60
Fury of Achilles '62
The Beast of Babylon Against the Son of Hercules '63
Two Gladiators '64
Challenge of the Gladiator '65
The Triumph of Hercules '66
Cjamango '67
Fistful of Lead '70
Nora Lum (1989-)
Crazy Rich Asians '18
Ocean's 8 '18
The Farewell '19
Lum & Abner (1902-80)
See Chester Lauck
Lum & Abner (1906-78)
See Norris Goff
Carl Lumbly (1951-)
Escape from Alcatraz '79
The Adventures of Buckaroo Banzai Across the Eighth Dimension '84
The Bedroom Window '87
Everybody's All American '88
Judgment in Berlin '88
Pacific Heights '90
To Sleep with Anger '90
Brother Future '91
South Central '92
America's Dream '95
Nightjohn '96
Buffalo Soldiers '97
Little Richard '00
Men of Honor '00
The Alphabet Killer '08
Sidney Lumet (1924-2011)
One Third of a Nation '39
Running on Empty '88
Joanna Lumley (1946-)
On Her Majesty's Secret Service '69
The Satanic Rites of Dracula '73
Curse of the Pink Panther '83
Weather in the Streets '84
Shirley Valentine '89
Cold Comfort Farm '94
Innocent Lies '95
James and the Giant Peach '96 (V)
Coming Home '98
Parting Shots '98
A Rather English Marriage '98
Maybe Baby '99
Whispers: An Elephant's Tale '00 (V)
The Cat's Meow '01
Ella Enchanted '04
Eurotrip '04
Doogal '05 (V)
Tim Burton's Corpse Bride '05 (V)
Boogie Woogie '09
The Making of a Lady '12
The Wolf of Wall Street '13
Absolutely Fabulous: The Movie '16
Finding Your Feet '18
Dayton Lummis (1903-88)
Loophole '54
The First Texan '56
Barbara Luna (1939-)
Mail Order Bride '63
Synanon '65
Firecreek '68
The Gatling Gun '72
The Hanged Man '74
Diego Luna (1979-)
Y Tu Mama Tambien '01
Frida '02
John Carpenter Presents Vampires: Los Muertos '02
Nicotina '03
Open Range '03
Criminal '04
Dirty Dancing: Havana Nights '04
The Terminal '04
Mister Lonely '07
Milk '08
Rudo y Cursi '09
Casa de mi Padre '12
Contraband '12
Elysium '13
The Book of Life '14 (V)
Blood Father '16
Rogue One: A Star Wars Story '16
Flatliners '17
Gabriel Luna (1982-)
Transpecos '16
Hala '19
Terminator: Dark Fate '19
Art Lund (1915-90)
Black Caesar '73
The Last American Hero '73
Bucktown '75
Jana Lund (1933-91)
Loving You '57
Frankenstein 1970 '58
John Lund (1913-92)
The Perils of Pauline '47
Miss Tatlock's Millions '48
My Friend Irma '49
The Duchess of Idaho '50
My Friend Irma Goes West '50
Woman They Almost Lynched '53
Dakota Incident '56
Wackiest Ship in the Army '61
If a Man Answers '62
Lucille Lund (1913-2002)
The Black Cat '34
Prison Shadows '36
Nicole Lund
The Legend of Wolf Mountain '92
Grizzly Mountain '97
Richard Lund
Treasure of Arne '19
Dragonquest '09
Zoe Lund (1962-99)
See Zoe Tamerlis
Dolph Lundgren (1957-)
Rocky 4 '85
A View to a Kill '85
Masters of the Universe '87
Red Scorpion '89
I Come in Peace '90
The Punisher '90
Cover-Up '91
Showdown in Little Tokyo '91
Universal Soldier '92
Army of One '94
Hidden Assassin '94
Men of War '94
Pentathlon '94
Johnny Mnemonic '95
Blackjack '97
Silent Trigger '97
The Minion '98
The Peacekeeper '98
Bridge of Dragons '99
The Last Warrior '99
Storm Catcher '99
Sweepers '99
Agent Red '00
Jill the Ripper '00
Hidden Agenda '01
Detention '03
Retrograde '03
The Defender '04
The Russian Specialist '05
Diamond Dogs '07
Missionary Man '07
Command Performance '09
Direct Contact '09
The Killing Machine '09
Universal Soldier: Regeneration '09
The Expendables '10
In the Name of the King 2: Two Worlds '11
The Expendables 2 '12
One In the Chamber '12
The Package '12
Stash House '12
Universal Soldier: Day of Reckoning '12
Ambushed '13
Battle of the Damned '14
The Expendables 3 '14
Riot '15
Kindergarten Cop 2 '16
Altitude '17
Don't Kill It '17
Black Water '18
Creed II '18
William Lundigan (1914-75)
Danger on the Air '38
Wives under Suspicion '38
Three Smart Girls Grow Up '39
East of the River '40
The Fighting 69th '40
Andy Hardy's Double Life '42
The Courtship of Andy Hardy '42
Dr. Gillespie's Criminal Case '43
Salute to the Marines '43
Dishonored Lady '47
Pinky '49
State Department File 649 '49
Mother Didn't Tell Me '50
Elopement '51
I'd Climb the Highest Mountain '51
Love Nest '51
Terror Ship '54
The White Orchid '54
Vic Lundin (1930-2013)
Ma Barker's Killer Brood '60
Two for the Seesaw '62
Promises! Promises! '63
Robinson Crusoe on Mars '64
Steve Lundquist (1961-)
Return of the Killer Tomatoes! '88
Killer Tomatoes Strike Back '90
Killer Tomatoes Eat France '91
Gary Lundy
Senior Skip Day '08
National Lampoon's The Legend of Awesomest Maximus '11
Jessica Lundy (1966-)
Bright Lights, Big City '88
Caddyshack 2 '88
Vampire's Kiss '88
Single White Female '92
I Love Trouble '94
The Stupids '95
RocketMan '97
Something About Sex '98
Just a Little Harmless Sex '99
Kenneth Lundy (1922-53)
Junior G-Men '40
Sioux City Sue '46
Jamie Luner (1971-)
Confessions of Sorority Girls '94
The St. Tammany Miracle '94
Sacrifice '00
Threshold '03
Stranger in My Bed '05
The Suspect '05
Nuclear Hurricane '07
Stalked at 17 '12
Walking the Halls '12
Emma Lung (1982-)
The Boys Are Back '09
Crush '09
Triangle '09

Fei Lung
Master of the Flying Guillotine '75
7 Grand Masters '04

Sihung Lung (1930-2002)
Pushing Hands '92
The Wedding Banquet '93
Eat Drink Man Woman '94
Crouching Tiger, Hidden Dragon '00

Ti Lung (1946-)
Duel of Fists '71
A Better Tomorrow, Part 1 '86
The Legend of Drunken Master '94

Tien Hsiang Lung
House of Traps '81
Five Element Ninjas '82

Cherie Lunghi (1952-)
Excalibur '81
Oliver Twist '82
The Sign of Four '83
King David '85
The Mission '86
The Lady's Not for Burning '87
To Kill a Priest '89
The Man Who Lived at the Ritz '91
Mary Shelley's Frankenstein '94
The Buccaneers '95
Jack and Sarah '95
The Canterville Ghost '96
An Alan Smithee Film: Burn, Hollywood, Burn '97
Horatio Hornblower '99
Back to the Secret Garden '01
Love's Kitchen '11

Stephen Lunsford
Bratz '07
Beneath the Darkness '12

Kathleen Luong (1976-)
Two Days in the Valley '96
Missing Brendan '03

Roldano Lupi (1909-89)
The Mongols '60
The Giant of Metropolis '61

Ida Lupino (1914-95)
Search for Beauty '34
Peter Ibbetson '35
The Gay Desperado '36
One Rainy Afternoon '36
Artists and Models '37
The Adventures of Sherlock Holmes '39
They Drive by Night '40
High Sierra '41
Ladies in Retirement '41
Out of the Fog '41
Life Begins at Eight-Thirty '42
Moontide '42
Forever and a Day '43
The Hard Way '43
Thank Your Lucky Stars '43
Hollywood Canteen '44
Devotion '46
The Man I Love '46
Deep Valley '47
Escape Me Never '47
Road House '48
Lust for Gold '49
Woman in Hiding '49
On Dangerous Ground '51
The Bigamist '53
Private Hell 36 '54
The Big Knife '55
Women's Prison '55
While the City Sleeps '56
Junior Bonner '72
Devil's Rain '75
Food of the Gods '76
My Boys Are Good Boys '78

Alberto Lupo (1924-84)
The Giant of Marathon '60
Herod the Great '60
Atom Age Vampire '61
The Lion of Thebes '64
The Agony and the Ecstasy '65
Django Shoots First '74

Patti LuPone (1949-)
King of the Gypsies '78
Fighting Back '82
Witness '85
Wise Guys '86
Driving Miss Daisy '89
Bonanno: A Godfather's Story '99
Just Looking '99
Summer of Sam '99
The 24 Hour Woman '99
Cold Blooded '00
State and Main '00
Heist '01
City by the Sea '02
Monday Night Mayhem '02
Cliffs of Freedom '19

Robert LuPone (1946-)
Palookaville '95
American Tragedy '00

Federico Luppi (1936-)
Funny, Dirty Little War '83
A Place in the World '92
Cronos '94
Extasis '96
Hombres Armados '97
Martin (Hache) '97
Autumn Sun '98
Lisboa '99
The Devil's Backbone '01
Swindled '04

John Lupton (1926-93)
All the Brothers Were Valiant '53
Escape from Fort Bravo '53
Battle Cry '55
Diane '55
The Man in the Net '59
The Rebel Set '59
Three Came to Kill '61
Jesse James Meets Frankenstein's Daughter '65
Private Parts '72

Peter Lupus (1932-)
Hercules and the Tyrants of Babylon '64
Muscle Beach Party '64
Challenge of the Gladiator '65

Luis Luque (1956-)
What Your Eyes Don't See '99
Manhunt '01

Evan Lurie (1954-)
Ring of Fire 2: Blood and Steel '92
American Kickboxer 2: To the Death '93
T-Force '94
Hologram Man '95
Shadow Warriors '95
Mortal Challenge '97

John Lurie (1952-)
Stranger than Paradise '84
Down by Law '86
The Last Temptation of Christ '88
Blue in the Face '95
New Rose Hotel '98

Billy Lush (1981-)
Generation Kill '08
Norman '10
Straw Dogs '11

Aaron Lustig (1956-)
Bad Channels '92
The Shadow '94
Stuart Saves His Family '94
Pinocchio's Revenge '96
Tuesdays with Morrie '99

William Lustig (1955-)
Maniac '80
Darkman '90
Army of Darkness '92

Eric Lutes (1962-)
Bram Stoker's The Mummy '97
The Twelve Dogs of Christmas '05
Adventures of a Teenage Dragonslayer '10

Bobbi Sue (Bobby Sue) Luther (1978-)
Laid to Rest '09
Night of the Demons '09
Made in Romania '10

Alfred Lutter (1962-)
The Bad News Bears '76
The Bad News Bears in Breaking Training '77

Alex Lutz
OSS 117: Lost in Rio '09
Meet the Guilbys '15

Kellan Lutz (1985-)
Stick It '06
Ghosts of Goldfield '07
Deep Winter '08
Twilight '08
The Twilight Saga: New Moon '09
Meskada '10
A Nightmare on Elm Street '10
The Twilight Saga: Eclipse '10
Arena '11
Immortals '11
Love, Wedding, Marriage '11
The Twilight Saga: Breaking Dawn, Part 1 '11
A Warrior's Heart '11
Java Heat '13
Syrup '13
The Expendables 3 '14
The Legend of Hercules '14
Experimenter '15
Extraction '15
What Men Want '19

Matilda Anna Ingrid Lutz
Revenge '17
Rings '17

Noemie Lvovsky (1964-)
My Wife is an Actress '01
Farewell, My Queen '12
Summertime '16

Elena Lyadova
Elena '11
Leviathan '14

Troels Lyby (1966-)
The Idiots '99
What We Become '16

Pasha D. Lychnikoff
Rage '14
Siberia '18

Brent Lydic
Flu Birds '08
Hansel & Gretel '13

Desi Lydic
Out at the Wedding '07
Stan Helsing '09

Gary Lydon (1954-)
The Last September '99
Calvary '14

James Lydon (1923-)
Cynthia '47
When Willie Comes Marching Home '50
Corky of Gasoline Alley '51
Gasoline Alley '51

Jimmy Lydon (1923-)
Back Door to Heaven '39
Little Men '40
Tom Brown's School Days '40
Strange Illusion '45
Life with Father '47
The Magnificent Yankee '50
Island in the Sky '53

John (Johnny Rotten) Lydon (1956-)
Corrupt '84
The Filth and the Fury '99
The Independent '00

Emma Rayne Lyle
Why Stop Now '12
Hamlet & Hutch '14

Leslie Lyles
My Teacher's Wife '95
Coming Soon '99
Slippery Slope '06

Dorothy Lyman (1947-)
Camp Cucamonga: How I Spent My Summer Vacation '90
I Love Trouble '94

Kaiwi Lyman
Robinson Crusoe: The Great Blitzkrieg '08
The Outsider '19

Will Lyman (1948-)
Floating '97
The Siege '98
American Meltdown '04
Little Children '06 (N)
What Doesn't Kill You '08

Alfred Lynch (1931-2003)
The Password Is Courage '62
The Hill '65
The Sea Gull '68
Blockhouse '73

David Lynch (1946-)
Twin Peaks: Fire Walk with Me '92
Nadja '95 (C)
Side by Side '12
Lucky '17

Evanna Lynch (1991-)
Harry Potter and the Order of the Phoenix '07
Harry Potter and the Deathly Hallows, Part 1 '10

Finbar Lynch (1959-)
King Lear '98
To Kill a King '03

Jane Lynch (1960-)
Exposed '03
A Mighty Wind '03
Sleepover '04
Bam Bam & Celeste '05
The 40 Year Old Virgin '05
Eye of the Dolphin '06
For Your Consideration '06
Talladega Nights: The Ballad of Ricky Bobby '06
Alvin and the Chipmunks '07
Ghost Writer '07
I Do & I Don't '07
Walk Hard: The Dewey Cox Story '07
Another Cinderella Story '08
The Rocker '08
Role Models '08
Space Chimps '08 (V)
Spring Breakdown '08
Julie & Julia '09
Mr. Troop Mom '09
Post Grad '09
Weather Girl '09
Shrek Forever After '10 (V)
Paul '11
The Three Stooges '12
Wreck-It Ralph '12 (V)
Afternoon Delight '13
Escape From Planet Earth '13 (V)
Mascots '16
Ralph Breaks the Internet '18 (V)

Jimmy Lynch
Avenging Disco Godfather '76
Dolemite 2: Human Tornado '76

John Lynch (1961-)
Hardware '90
Edward II '92
In the Name of the Father '93
The Secret Garden '93
Princess Caraboo '94
The Secret of Roan Inish '94
Moll Flanders '96
Some Mother's Son '96
Sliding Doors '97
The Quarry '98
The Seventh Stream '01
Evelyn '02
Alien Hunter '03
Conspiracy of Silence '03
The Bridge of San Luis Rey '05
Lassie '05
Hard Times '09

Black Death '10
Paul '11
Labyrinth '12
Private Peaceful '12
Mobius '13
Paul, Apostle of Christ '18

John Carroll Lynch (1963-)
Fargo '96
Face/Off '97
A Thousand Acres '97
Volcano '97
From the Earth to the Moon '98
Restaurant '98
Tuesdays with Morrie '99
Bubble Boy '01
The Good Girl '02
Confidence '03
Gothika '03
Live from Baghdad '03
Catch That Kid '04
Mozart and the Whale '05
Looking for Comedy in the Muslim World '06
Full of It '07
Things We Lost in the Fire '07
Zodiac '07
Gran Torino '08
Love Happens '09
Hesher '10
Highland Park '13
Camp X-Ray '14
The Pretty One '14
The Founder '17

Kate Lynch (1959-)
Meatballs '79
Def-Con 4 '85
Lethal Lolita-Amy Fisher: My Story '92
Coast to Coast '04

Kelly Lynch (1959-)
Bright Lights, Big City '88
Cocktail '88
Drugstore Cowboy '89
Road House '89
Warm Summer Rain '89
Desperate Hours '90
Curly Sue '91
Three of Hearts '93
Imaginary Crimes '94
Heaven's Prisoners '95
Virtuosity '95
White Man's Burden '95
Persons Unknown '96
Cold Around the Heart '97
Homegrown '97
Mr. Magoo '97
Brotherhood of Murder '99
Charlie's Angels '00
Joe Somebody '01
The Slaughter Rule '01
Dallas 362 '03
Homeless to Harvard: The Liz Murray Story '03
Cyber Seduction: His Secret Life '05
The Jacket '05
Havoc 2: Normal Adolescent Behavior '07
Passion Play '10
Kaboom '11
Glass Chin '14
The Frontier '16

Ken Lynch (1910-90)
I Married a Monster from Outer Space '58
Run Silent, Run Deep '58
Pork Chop Hill '59

Mark Lynch
The Other Half '06
Dance of the Dead '08

Pauline Lynch
Trainspotting '95
Attila '01

Richard Lynch (1940-2012)
Scarecrow '73
The Premonition '75
God Told Me To '76
Death Sport '78
The Formula '80
Sword & the Sorcerer '82
Savage Dawn '84
Cut and Run '85
Invasion U.S.A. '85

Aftershock '88
Bad Dreams '88
The Baron '88
Little Nikita '88
One Man Force '89
Alligator 2: The Mutation '90
The Forbidden Dance '90
Lockdown '90
Puppet Master 3: Toulon's Revenge '90
Trancers 2: The Return of Jack Deth '90
Maximum Force '92
Lone Tiger '94
Terrified '94
Cyborg 3: The Recycler '95
Destination Vegas '95
Midnight Confessions '95
Werewolf '95
Diamond Run '96
Warrior of Justice '96
Under Oath '97
Eastside '99
Dark Fields '09
Laid to Rest '09

Ross Lynch
Teen Beach Movie '13
My Friend Dahmer '17

Susan Lynch (1971-)
The Secret of Roan Inish '94
Ivanhoe '97
Kings in Grass Castles '97
Amongst Women '98
Waking Ned Devine '98
Beautiful Creatures '00
Nora '00
From Hell '01
The Mapmaker '01
Casa de los Babys '03
Red Roses and Petrol '03
16 Years of Alcohol '03
Enduring Love '04
Duane Hopwood '05
Hard Times '09
The Race '09
The Unloved '09
The Secret Diaries of Miss Anne Lister '10
Great Expectations '11
Bad Day for the Cut '17

Helen Lynd (1902-92)
Hats Off '37
So Proudly We Hail '43

Paul Lynde (1926-82)
New Faces of 1952 '54
Bye, Bye, Birdie '63
Son of Flubber '63
Under the Yum-Yum Tree '63
Send Me No Flowers '64
Beach Blanket Bingo '65
The Glass Bottom Boat '66
How Sweet It Is! '68
Journey Back to Oz '71 (V)
Gidget Gets Married '72
Charlotte's Web '73 (V)
The Villain '79

Nicholas Lyndhurst (1961-)
Stalag Luft '93
Gulliver's Travels '95
David Copperfield '99

Amy Lyndon
Big City Blues '99
Slaves of Hollywood '99

Simon Lyndon (1971-)
Blackrock '97
Chopper '00

Carol Lynley (1942-2019)
Holiday for Lovers '59
The Last Sunset '61
Return to Peyton Place '61
The Cardinal '63
Under the Yum-Yum Tree '63
Bunny Lake Is Missing '65
Blood Island '68
Once You Kiss a Stranger '69
The Night Stalker '71
Beware! The Blob '72
Cotter '72
The Poseidon Adventure '72
Four Deuces '75
Fantasy Island '76

Flood! '76
The Beasts Are On the Streets '78
The Cat and the Canary '79
Balboa '82
Vigilante '83
Howling 6: The Freaks '90
Neon Signs '96
Drowning on Dry Land '00
Ann Lynn (1933-)
Flame in the Streets '61
Black Torment '64
Estate of Insanity '64
A Shot in the Dark '64
Four in the Morning '65
Betty Lynn (1926-)
Mother Is a Freshman '49
Cheaper by the Dozen '50
Payment on Demand '51
Return to Mayberry '85
Diana Lynn (1924-71)
The Major and the Minor '42
Miracle of Morgan's Creek '44
The Bride Wore Boots '46
Every Girl Should Be Married '48
Ruthless '48
My Friend Irma '49
My Friend Irma Goes West '50
Rogues of Sherwood Forest '50
Bedtime for Bonzo '51
The People Against O'Hara '51
Track of the Cat '54
The Kentuckian '55
You're Never Too Young '55
Emmett Lynn (1897-1958)
Along the Rio Grande '41
Tomorrow We Live '42
Swing Hostess '44
George Lynn (1906-64)
To Be or Not to Be '42
The Werewolf '56
The Man Who Turned to Stone '57
Jeffrey Lynn (1909-95)
Four Daughters '38
Daughters Courageous '39
Four Wives '39
The Roaring Twenties '39
All This and Heaven Too '40
The Fighting 69th '40
It All Came True '40
My Love Came Back '40
Four Mothers '41
Underground '41
For the Love of Mary '48
Whiplash '48
A Letter to Three Wives '49
Lost Lagoon '58
Tony Rome '67
Jenny Lynn
Ticket of Leave Man '37
The Greed of William Hart '48
Jonathan Lynn (1943-)
Three Men and a Little Lady '90
Greedy '94
Meredith Scott Lynn (1970-)
I Love You, Don't Touch Me! '97
Billy's Hollywood Screen Kiss '98
Forces of Nature '99
Standing on Fishes '99
Hollywood Homicide '03
When Do We Eat? '05
How to Go Out on a Date in Queens '06
Sheri Lynn
Bikini Bloodbath '06
Bikini Bloodbath Carwash '08
Bikini Bloodbath Christmas '09
Theresa Lynn (1964-)
Vampire Vixens from Venus '94
Psycho Sisters '98
Melanie Lynskey (1977-)
Heavenly Creatures '94
Ever After: A Cinderella Story '98
The Cherry Orchard '99
Coyote Ugly '00
Shooters '00
Abandon '02
Stephen King's Rose Red '02
Sweet Home Alabama '02
Serial Slayer '03
Shattered Glass '03
Say Uncle '05
Flags of Our Fathers '06
Comanche Moon '08
Away We Go '09
The Informant! '09
Leaves of Grass '09
Up in the Air '09
Touchback '11
Win Win '11
Hello I Must Be Going '12
The Perks of Being a Wallflower '12
Seeking a Friend for the End of the World '12
Goodbye to All That '14
Happy Christmas '14
They Came Together '14
The Intervention '16
I Don't Feel at Home in This World Anymore '17
XX '17
Ben Lyon (1901-79)
Alias French Gertie '30
Hell's Angels '30
Indiscreet '31
Night Nurse '31
The Crooked Circle '32
Girl Missing '33
I Cover the Waterfront '33
Crimson Romance '34
Mad About Money '37
Earle Lyon (1926-)
Lonesome Trail '55
Silver Star '55
Sue Lyon (1946-2019)
Lolita '62
The Night of the Iguana '64
Flim-Flam Man '67
Tony Rome '67
Four Rode Out '69
Evel Knievel '72
Autopsy '73
End of the World '76
The Invisible Strangler '76
Alligator '80
Wendy Lyon
Anne of Green Gables '85
Hello Mary Lou: Prom Night 2 '87
Natasha Lyonne (1979-)
Everyone Says I Love You '96
Krippendorf's Tribe '98
Modern Vampires '98
Slums of Beverly Hills '98
American Pie '99
But I'm a Cheerleader '99
Detroit Rock City '99
Freeway 2: Confessions of a Trickbaby '99
If These Walls Could Talk 2 '00
American Pie 2 '01
Fast Sofa '01
The Grey Zone '01
Kate & Leopold '01
Scary Movie 2 '01
Comic Book Villains '02
Night at the Golden Eagle '02
ZigZag '02
Die Mommie Die! '03
Party Monster '03
Blade: Trinity '04
Madhouse '04
Robots '05 (V)
Tricks of a Woman '08
Loving Leah '09
Outrage Born in Terror '09
4:44 Last Day on Earth '11
American Reunion '12
Girl Most Likely '12
The Rambler '13
Addicted to Fresno '15
The Intervention '16
Jack Goes Home '16
Show Dogs '18
Cliff Lyons (1901-74)
She Wore a Yellow Ribbon '49
The Horse Soldiers '59
Elena Lyons (1973-)
Face the Music '00
Club Dread '04
James Lyons (1960-2007)
Poison '91
Frisk '95
Postcards from America '95
I Shot Andy Warhol '96
Jennifer Lyons (1977-)
Tiger Heart '96
Tequila Body Shots '99
Killer Pad '06
Transylmania '09
Robert F. Lyons (1939-)
Getting Straight '70
Shoot Out '71
The Todd Killings '71
Murphy's Law '86
American Eagle '90
Counter Measures '99
The Omega Code '99
Annie's Point '05
Tom Lyons
Burn! '70
Factotum '06
Stefan Lysenko
The Stray '00
Dark Waters '03
Monika M.
Nekromantik '87
Nekromantik 2 '91
Tzi Ma (1962-)
Rapid Fire '92
Golden Gate '93
Chain Reaction '96
Dante's Peak '97
Red Corner '97
Rush Hour '98
Catfish in Black Bean Sauce '00
The Quiet American '02
The Ladykillers '04
Red Doors '05
Akeelah and the Bee '06
Rush Hour 3 '07
Formosa Betrayed '09
A Good Man '14
The Farewell '19
Moussa Maaskri
Two Brothers '04
Collision '13
Theo Maassen
Miss Minoes '01
Nothing to Lose '08
Byron Mabe (1932-2001)
The Defilers '65
The Doberman Gang '72
Ricky Mabe (1983-)
Little Men '98
Believe '99
Zack and Miri Make a Porno '08
Hoax for the Holidays '10
Kate Maberly (1982-)
The Secret Garden '93
Gulliver's Travels '95
Stephen King's The Langoliers '95
Murderous Intent '06
Boogeyman 3 '08
Rites of Passage '12
Standing Up '13
Eric Mabius (1971-)
Welcome to the Dollhouse '95
I Shot Andy Warhol '96
Lawn Dogs '96
Black Circle Boys '97
Around the Fire '98
Cruel Intentions '98
The Minus Man '99
Splendor '99
Wirey Spindell '99
The Crow: Salvation '00
On the Borderline '01
Tempted '01
Resident Evil '02
The Job '03
Venice Underground '05
Voodoo Moon '05
A Christmas Wedding '06
Nature of the Beast '07
Where the Road Meets the Sun '11
How to Fall in Love '12
Signed, Sealed, Delivered for Christmas '14
Moms (Jackie) Mabley (1894-1975)
Boardinghouse Blues '48
Killer Diller '48
Amazing Grace '74
Luke Mably (1976-)
The Prince & Me '04
Color Me Kubrick '05
Deceit '06
The Prince & Me 2: Royal Wedding '06
Exam '09
Chosen '16
Sunny Mabrey (1975-)
The New Guy '02
Species 3 '04
One Last Thing '05
XXX: State of the Union '05
Snakes on a Plane '06
Final Approach '08
San Saba '08
Not Since You '09
Bernie Mac (1958-2008)
Above the Rim '94
House Party 3 '94
Friday '95
Booty Call '96
Get On the Bus '96
Def Jam's How to Be a Player '97
Don King: Only in America '97
The Players Club '98
Life '99
Ocean's Eleven '01
What's the Worst That Could Happen? '01
Bad Santa '03
Charlie's Angels: Full Throttle '03
Head of State '03
Mr. 3000 '04
Ocean's Twelve '04
Guess Who '05
Inspector Gadget's Biggest Caper Ever '05 (V)
Ocean's Thirteen '07
Pride '07
Transformers '07
Madagascar: Escape 2 Africa '08 (V)
Soul Men '08
Old Dogs '09
Anne MacAdams (1925-2003)
Common Law Wife '63
Don't Look in the Basement '73
Vincent Macaigne
Eden '14
The Innocents '16
Non-Fiction '18
Cal Macaninch (1969-)
A Mind to Murder '96
Dear Frankie '04
Hayes Macarthur (1977-)
The Game Plan '07
National Lampoon's The Stoned Aged '07
Life As We Know It '10
The Babymakers '12
Bachelorette '12
Someone Marry Barry '12
James MacArthur (1937-2010)
The Young Stranger '57
Third Man on the Mountain '59
Kidnapped '60
The Swiss Family Robinson '60
The Interns '62
Cry of Battle '63
Spencer's Mountain '63
Battle of the Bulge '65
Bedford Incident '65
Hang 'Em High '67
The Love-Ins '67
The Night the Bridge Fell Down '83
Storm Chasers: Revenge of the Twister '98
Charles Macaulay (1927-99)
Blacula '72
The Big Red One '80
Marc Macaulay (1957-)
Cop and a Half '93
Holy Man '98
Wild Things '98
Cleaner '07
Monsterwolf '10
Nine Dead '10
Donald MacBride (1889-1957)
Room Service '38
Blondie Takes a Vacation '39
Charlie Chan at Treasure Island '39
The Girl From Mexico '39
The Invisible Woman '40
Michael Shayne: Private Detective '40
Murder over New York '40
The Saint's Double Trouble '40
High Sierra '41
The Mexican Spitfire Sees a Ghost '42
A Night to Remember '42
Buck Privates Come Home '47
Egg and I '47
Catriona MacCall (1954-)
See Katherine (Katriona) MacColl
Ralph Macchio (1961-)
Up the Academy '80
The Outsiders '83
The Karate Kid '84
Teachers '84
Crossroads '86
The Karate Kid: Part 2 '86
Distant Thunder '88
The Karate Kid: Part 3 '89
Too Much Sun '90
My Cousin Vinny '92
Naked in New York '93
The Secret of NIMH 2 '98 (V)
Forever Together '00
Beer League '06
Rosencrantz & Guildenstern Are Undead '10
Holiday Spin '12
Aldo Maccione (1935-)
Lady of the Evening '75
Loves & Times of Scaramouche '76
The Chambermaid on the Titanic '97
Katherine (Katriona) MacColl (1954-)
Gates of Hell '80
The Beyond '82
The House by the Cemetery '83
Simon MacCorkindale (1952-2010)
Death on the Nile '78
Quatermass Conclusion '79
The Riddle of the Sands '79
Cabo Blanco '81
The Manions of America '81
Sword & the Sorcerer '82
Jaws 3 '83
At the Midnight Hour '95
Family of Cops '95
The Girl Next Door '98
Blind Revenge '10
Allie MacDonald (1988-)
Jodi Picoult's Salem Falls '11
The Barrens '12
And Now a Word From Our Sponsor '13
Stage Fright '14
Ann-Marie MacDonald (1958-)
I've Heard the Mermaids Singing '87
Better Than Chocolate '99
Bill MacDonald
The Corruptor '99
Mercy '00
Defending Our Kids: The Julie Posey Story '03
Christopher Macdonald
The Dukes of Hazzard: The Beginning '06
The Collection '12
Danielle MacDonald
Every Secret Thing '15
Patti Cake$ '17
Skin '18
Edmund MacDonald (1908-51)
Prison Break '38
The Strange Case of Dr. Rx '42
The Lady Confesses '45
Detour '46
Ian MacDonald (1914-78)
Montana '50
This Woman Is Dangerous '52
Taza, Son of Cochise '54
J. Farrell MacDonald (1875-1952)
Sunrise '27
Song o' My Heart '30
The Truth About Youth '30
The Easiest Way '31
Other Men's Women '31
Sporting Blood '31
The Squaw Man '31
No Man of Her Own '32
Pride of the Legion '32
13th Guest '32
Under Eighteen '32
The Working Man '33
Romance in Manhattan '34
The Irish in Us '35
Riff Raff '35
Exclusive Story '36
Slim '37
The Gentleman from Arizona '39
Susannah of the Mounties '39
Snuffy Smith, Yard Bird '42
Panhandle '48
Whispering Smith '48
James MacDonald
Cinderella '50 (V)
Sour Grapes '98
Phone Booth '02
Hollywood Homicide '03
Jeanette MacDonald (1901-65)
The Love Parade '29
Lottery Bride '30
Monte Carlo '30
Love Me Tonight '32
One Hour with You '32
The Cat and the Fiddle '34
The Merry Widow '34
Naughty Marietta '35
Rose Marie '36
San Francisco '36
The Firefly '37
Maytime '37
Girl of the Golden West '38
Sweethearts '38
Broadway Serenade '39
Bitter Sweet '40
New Moon '40
Smilin' Through '41
Cairo '42
I Married an Angel '42

Three Daring Daughters *'48*
The Sun Comes Up *'49*

Jennifer MacDonald
Clean, Shaven *'93*
Alien Chaser *'96*
Headless Body in Topless Bar *'96*
Campfire Tales *'98*

Kelly Macdonald (1976-)
Trainspotting *'95*
Stella Does Tricks *'96*
Cousin Bette *'97*
The Loss of Sexual Innocence *'98*
My Life So Far *'98*
Splendor *'99*
Two Family House *'99*
Gosford Park *'01*
Strictly Sinatra *'01*
Brush with Fate *'03*
Intermission *'03*
State of Play *'03*
Finding Neverland *'04*
The Girl in the Cafe *'05*
Lassie *'05*
Tristram Shandy: A Cock and Bull Story *'05*
Nanny McPhee *'06*
No Country for Old Men *'07*
Choke *'08*
In the Electric Mist *'08*
The Merry Gentleman *'08*
Skellig: The Owl Man *'09*
The Decoy Bride *'11*
Anna Karenina *'12*
Brave *'12 (V)*
T2 Trainspotting *'17*
Holmes & Watson *'18*
Puzzle *'18*

Norm MacDonald (1963-)
Billy Madison *'94*
The People *vs.* Larry Flynt *'96*
Dirty Work *'97*
Dr. Dolittle *'98 (V)*
Screwed *'00*
Dr. Dolittle 2 *'01 (V)*
Deuce Bigalow: European Gigolo *'05*
Senior Skip Day *'08*
Grown Ups *'10*

Ray Macdonald
Babes on Broadway *'41*
The Eye 3 *'05*

Scott MacDonald
Straight into Darkness *'04*
Jarhead *'05*

Shauna Macdonald (1981-)
Shattered City: The Halifax Explosion *'03*
Saint Ralph *'04*
The Descent *'05*
The Descent 2 *'09*
Harriet the Spy: Blog Wars *'10*
Filth *'13*

Wallace MacDonald (1891-1978)
The Sea Hawk *'24*
Pampered Youth *'25*

William Macdonald
Personal Effects *'05*
Hollow Man 2 *'06*
To Have and to Hold *'06*
White Noise 2: The Light *'07*
Mail Order Bride *'08*

Lewis MacDougall (2002-)
A Monster Calls *'17*
Boundaries *'18*

Andie MacDowell (1958-)
Greystoke: The Legend of Tarzan, Lord of the Apes *'84*
St. Elmo's Fire *'85*
sex, lies and videotape *'89*
Green Card *'90*
Hudson Hawk *'91*
The Object of Beauty *'91*
Women & Men: In Love There Are No Rules *'91*
Deception *'92*
The Player *'92*
Groundhog Day *'93*
Short Cuts *'93*
Bad Girls *'94*
Four Weddings and a Funeral *'94*
Unstrung Heroes *'95*
Michael *'96*
Multiplicity *'96*
The End of Violence *'97*
Just the Ticket *'98*
Shadrach *'98*
Muppets from Space *'99*
The Muse *'99*
Dinner with Friends *'01*
Town and Country *'01*
Crush *'02*
Ginostra *'02*
Harrison's Flowers *'02*
Beauty Shop *'05*
Tara Road *'05*
Barnyard *'06 (V)*
The Six Wives of Henry Lefay *'09*
As Good As Dead *'10*
Daydream Nation *'10*
The 5th Quarter *'10*
Happiness Runs *'10*
Patricia Cornwell's At Risk *'10*
Patricia Cornwell's The Front *'10*
Footloose *'11*
Monte Carlo *'11*
Mighty Fine *'12*
Ready or Not *'19 (C)*

Sterling Macer (1963-)
Dragon: The Bruce Lee Story *'93*
The Beast *'96*
Double Take *'01*

Angus MacFadyen (1963-)
The Lost Language of Cranes *'92*
Braveheart *'95*
The Brylcreem Boys *'96*
Still Breathing *'97*
Warriors of Virtue *'97*
The Rat Pack *'98*
The Cradle Will Rock *'99*
Titus *'99*
Jason and the Argonauts *'00*
Second Skin *'00*
Styx *'00*
A Woman's a Helluva Thing *'01*
Divine Secrets of the Ya-Ya Sisterhood *'02*
Equilibrium *'02*
The Pleasure Drivers *'05*
Blackbeard *'06*
Fatwa *'06*
.45 *'06*
Saw 3 *'06*
Killer Wave *'07*
Redline *'07*
Impulse *'08*
San Saba *'08*
Shadowheart *'09*
Pound of Flesh *'10*
We Bought a Zoo *'11*
Copperhead *'13*

Matthew Macfadyen (1974-)
Almost Strangers *'01*
Enigma *'01*
The Way We Live Now *'02*
Pride and Prejudice *'05*
Middletown *'06*
Death at a Funeral *'07*
Frost/Nixon *'08*
Incendiary *'08*
Little Dorrit *'08*
Pillars of the Earth *'10*
Robin Hood *'10*
Any Human Heart *'11*
The Three Musketeers *'11*
Anna Karenina *'12*
The Nutcracker and the Four Realms *'18*

Seth MacFarlane (1973-)
Hellboy II: The Golden Army *'08 (V)*
Tooth Fairy *'10*
Movie 43 *'13*
A Million Ways to Die In the West *'14*
Ted 2 *'15 (V)*
Sing *'16*

Moyna MacGill (1895-1975)
Gaslight *'40*
Frenchman's Creek *'44*
The Strange Affair of Uncle Harry *'45*
Three Daring Daughters *'48*

Niall MacGinnis (1913-78)
Edge of the World *'37*
Henry V *'44*
Captain Boycott *'47*
Anna Karenina *'48*
No Highway in the Sky *'51*
Martin Luther *'53*
Betrayed *'54*
Helen of Troy *'56*
Lust for Life *'56*
Curse of the Demon *'57*
Tarzan's Greatest Adventure *'59*
Never Take Candy From a Stranger *'60*
Sword of Sherwood Forest *'60*
Jason and the Argonauts *'63*
The War Lord *'65*
The Viking Queen *'67*
Krakatoa East of Java *'69*

Jack MacGowran (1918-73)
The Quiet Man *'52*
The Giant Behemoth *'59*
Doctor Zhivago *'65*
Lord Jim *'65*
Cul de Sac *'66*
The Fearless Vampire Killers *'67*
Age of Consent *'69*
Wonderwall: The Movie *'69*
Start the Revolution without Me *'70*
The Exorcist *'73*

Tara MacGowran (1964-)
Las Vegas Serial Killer *'86*
The Dawning *'88*

Ali MacGraw (1939-)
Goodbye, Columbus *'69*
Love Story *'70*
The Getaway *'72*
Convoy *'78*
Just Tell Me What You Want *'80*
The Winds of War *'83*
Glam *'97 (C)*

Justina Machado (1972-)
Sticks *'98*
Final Destination 2 *'03*
Torque *'04*
Fatal Contact: Bird Flu in America *'06*
Little Fugitive *'06*
The Accidental Husband *'08*
In the Electric Mist *'08*
The Call *'13*

Gabriel Macht (1972-)
The Audrey Hepburn Story *'00*
101 Ways (The Things a Girl Will Do to Keep Her Volvo) *'00*
American Outlaws *'01*
Behind Enemy Lines *'01*
Bad Company *'02*
Grand Theft Parsons *'03*
The Recruit *'03*
A Love Song for Bobby Long *'04*
Archangel *'05*
The Good Shepherd *'06*
Because I Said So *'07*
The Spirit *'08*
One Way to Valhalla *'09*
Whiteout *'09*
Middle Men *'10*
A Bag of Hammers *'11*
S.W.A.T.: Firefight *'11*

Stephen Macht (1942-)
The Choirboys *'77*
Nightwing *'79*
Galaxina *'80*
Killjoy *'81*
Agatha Christie's A Caribbean Mystery *'83*
The Monster Squad *'87*
Blind Witness *'89*
Graveyard Shift *'90*
Amityville 1992: It's About Time *'92*
Trancers 3: Deth Lives *'92*
Trancers 4: Jack of Swords *'93*
Trancers 5: Sudden Deth *'94*
Watchers Reborn *'98*
DC 9/11: Time of Crisis *'04*

Angus MacInnes (1947-)
Outland *'81*
The Sender *'82*
Strange Brew *'83*
High Plains Invaders *'09*

Jacqueline MacInnes-Wood
Nightmare at the End of the Hall *'08*
Final Destination 5 *'11*

Keegan Macintosh (1984-)
Henry & Verlin *'94*
At the Midnight Hour *'95*

Martha MacIsaac (1984-)
In God's Country *'07*
Superbad *'07*
The Last House on the Left *'09*
The Thaw *'09*
Hoax for the Holidays *'10*

Daniel MacIvor (1962-)
Beefcake *'99*
The Five Senses *'99*
Whole New Thing *'05*

Charles Emmet Mack (1900-27)
Dream Street *'21*
America *'24*
A Woman of the World *'25*
The First Auto *'27*
Old San Francisco *'27*

Helen Mack (1913-86)
Struggle *'31*
The California Trail *'33*
Son of Kong *'33*
Kiss and Make Up *'34*
She *'35*
Milky Way *'36*
Fit for a King *'37*
King of the Newsboys *'38*
His Girl Friday *'40*
Power Dive *'41*

Wayne Mack (1924-93)
Crypt of Dark Secrets *'76*
Mardi Gras Massacre *'78*

Dorothy Mackaill (1903-90)
Shore Leave *'25*
Ranson's Folly *'26*
The Great Divide *'29*
Bright Lights *'30*
Kept Husbands *'31*
Party Husband *'31*
The Reckless Hour *'31*
Safe in Hell *'31*
Love Affair *'32*
No Man of Her Own *'32*
Curtain at Eight *'33*

Barry Mackay (1906-85)
Gangway *'37*
Sailing Along *'38*

Fulton Mackay (1922-87)
Nothing But the Night *'72*
Local Hero *'83*
Defense of the Realm *'85*
Porridge *'91*

George MacKay (1992-)
The Old Curiosity Shop *'07*
The Boys Are Back *'09*
The Best of Men *'12*
Private Peaceful *'12*
How I Live Now *'13*
Pride *'14*
1917 *'19*
Ophelia *'19*
True History of the Kelly Gang *'20*

John MacKay
Rocket Attack U.S.A. *'58*
Assault of the Rebel Girls *'59*
Krush Groove *'85*
I Was a Teenage TV Terrorist *'87*
Alligator Eyes *'90*
Trust *'90*
Simple Men *'92*
Niagara, Niagara *'97*
The Rook *'99*

Kenneth MacKenna (1899-1962)
Sin Takes a Holiday *'30*
Those We Love *'32*
Judgment at Nuremberg *'61*
13 West Street *'62*

Alastair Mackenzie (1970-)
The Shell Seekers *'06*
Tonight You're Mine *'11*
The Sweeter Side of Life *'13*

Evan Mackenzie
Ghoulies 3: Ghoulies Go to College *'91*
Children of the Night *'92*

Georgia Mackenzie (1973-)
Possession *'02*
The Kovak Box *'06*

J.C. MacKenzie (1970-)
Final *'01*
The Aviator *'04*
The Return *'06*

Joyce MacKenzie (1929-)
Destination Murder *'50*
Mother Didn't Tell Me *'50*
Tarzan and the She-Devil *'53*

Mary MacKenzie (1922-66)
Stolen Face *'52*
The Master Plan *'55*

Patch MacKenzie (1942-)
Goodbye, Norma Jean *'75*
Black Eliminator *'78*
Graduation Day *'81*

David Mackey
Tooth Fairy 2 *'12*
Kate Plays Christine *'16*

Doon Mackichan (1962-)
The Borrowers *'97*
Breaking the Bank *'14*
Draw on Sweet Night *'15*

Allison Mackie (1960-)
Lurking Fear *'94*
Schemes *'95*
Steve Martini's Undue Influence *'96*
The Souler Opposite *'97*
Original Sin *'01*
The Gymnast *'06*

Anthony Mackie (1978-)
8 Mile *'02*
Brother to Brother *'04*
Haven *'04*
Million Dollar Baby *'04*
She Hate Me *'04*
The Man *'05*
Sucker Free City *'05*
Crossover *'06*
Freedomland *'06*
Half Nelson *'06*
Heavens Fall *'06*
We Are Marshall *'06*
Eagle Eye *'08*
The Hurt Locker *'08*
Notorious *'09*
Night Catches Us *'10*
The Adjustment Bureau *'11*
Real Steel *'11*
Abraham Lincoln: Vampire Hunter *'12*
Man on a Ledge *'12*
Gangster Squad *'13*
The Inevitable Defeat of Mister & Pete *'13*
Pain & Gain *'13*
Runner Runner *'13*
Black or White *'14*
Captain America: The Winter Soldier *'14*
Playing It Cool *'14*
Repentance *'14*
Love the Coopers *'15*
The Night Before *'15*
Our Brand is Crisis *'15*
Shelter *'15*
Triple 9 *'15*
Captain America: Civil War *'16*
The Hate U Give *'18*
IO *'19*
Miss Bala *'19*
The Banker *'20*

Simmone MacKinnon (1973-)
Attila *'01*
Python 2 *'02*
Dark Waters *'03*
Deep Shock *'03*

Steven Mackintosh (1967-)
The Buddha of Suburbia *'92*
The Return of the Native *'94*
Blue Juice *'95*
Different for Girls *'96*
Twelfth Night *'96*
The Ebb-Tide *'97*
Lock, Stock and 2 Smoking Barrels *'98*
Our Mutual Friend *'98*
The Criminal *'00*
Lady Audley's Secret *'00*
The Mother *'03*
The Other Boleyn Girl *'03*
Underworld: Evolution *'05*
Sugarhouse *'07*
The Escapist *'08*
Good *'08*
Underworld: Rise of the Lycans *'09*
Inside Men *'12*
The Sweeney *'12*

Jim MacKrell (1937-)
Just Between Friends *'86*
Cannibal Women in the Avocado Jungle of Death *'89*

Andrew MacLachlan
Monty Python's Life of Brian *'79*
Monty Python's The Meaning of Life *'83*
A Fish Called Wanda *'88*
The Adventures of Baron Munchausen *'89*
Erik the Viking *'89*

Janet MacLachlan (1933-2010)
Halls of Anger *'70*
Tick... Tick... Tick *'70*
Sounder *'72*
Murphy's Law *'86*

Kyle MacLachlan (1959-)
Dune *'84*
Blue Velvet *'86*
The Hidden *'87*
Don't Tell Her It's Me *'90*
The Doors *'91*
Twin Peaks: Fire Walk with Me *'92*
Where the Day Takes You *'92*
Rich in Love *'93*
The Trial *'93*
Against the Wall *'94*
The Flintstones *'94*
Roswell: The U.F.O. Cover-Up *'94*
Showgirls *'95*
The Trigger Effect *'96*
Trigger Happy *'96*
One Night Stand *'97*
Route 9 *'98*
Hamlet *'00*
The Spring *'00*
Time Code *'00*
Xchange *'00*
Me Without You *'01*
Miranda *'01*
Northfork *'03*
The Librarian: Quest for the Spear *'04*
Touch of Pink *'04*
Mysterious Island *'05*
The Sisterhood of the Traveling Pants 2 *'08*
Mao's Last Dancer *'09*
The Smell of Success *'09*
Peace, Love & Misunderstanding *'11*
Breathe In *'13*
The House with a Clock in Its Walls *'18*
Giant Little Ones *'19*

Shirley MacLaine (1934-)
Artists and Models *'55*
The Trouble with Harry *'55*

Around the World in 80 Days *'56*
The Matchmaker *'58*
The Sheepman *'58*
Some Came Running *'58*
Career *'59*
The Apartment *'60*
Can-Can *'60*
Ocean's 11 *'60*
All in a Night's Work *'61*
The Children's Hour *'61*
My Geisha *'62*
Two for the Seesaw *'62*
Irma La Douce *'63*
The Yellow Rolls Royce *'64*
Gambit *'66*
Woman Times Seven *'67*
The Bliss of Mrs. Blossom *'68*
Sweet Charity *'69*
Two Mules for Sister Sara *'70*
Desperate Characters *'71*
The Possession of Joel Delaney *'72*
The Turning Point *'77*
Being There *'79*
A Change of Seasons *'80*
Loving Couples *'80*
Terms of Endearment *'83*
Cannonball Run 2 *'84*
That's Dancing! *'85*
Madame Sousatzka *'88*
Steel Magnolias *'89*
Postcards from the Edge *'90*
Waiting for the Light *'90*
Used People *'92*
Wrestling Ernest Hemingway *'93*
Guarding Tess *'94*
The Evening Star *'96*
Mrs. Winterbourne *'96*
A Smile Like Yours *'96 (C)*
The Dress Code *'99*
Joan of Arc *'99*
These Old Broads *'01*
Carolina *'03*
Bewitched *'05*
In Her Shoes *'05*
Rumor Has It. . . *'05*
Closing the Ring *'07*
Coco Chanel *'08*
Valentine's Day *'10*
Bernie *'12*
The Secret Life of Walter Mitty *'13*
Elsa & Fred *'14*
Wild Oats *'16*
The Last Word *'17*
The Little Mermaid *'18*
Noelle *'19*

Barton MacLane (1902-69)
To the Last Man *'33*
Black Fury *'35*
The Case of the Lucky Legs *'35*
Frisco Kid *'35*
'G' Men *'35*
Go Into Your Dance *'35*
Stranded *'35*
The Prince and the Pauper *'37*
San Quentin *'37*
Smart Blonde *'37*
You Only Live Once *'37*
Bullets or Ballots *'38*
Gold Is Where You Find It *'38*
Prison Break *'38*
You and Me *'38*
Mutiny in the Big House *'39*
Stand Up and Fight *'39*
Come Live With Me *'40*
Melody Ranch *'40*
Dr. Jekyll and Mr. Hyde *'41*
High Sierra *'41*
The Maltese Falcon *'41*
Manpower *'41*
Western Union *'41*
All Through the Night *'42*
Big Street *'42*
Bombardier *'43*
The Underdog *'43*
Nabonga *'44*
The Spanish Main *'45*
Tarzan and the Amazons *'45*
Treasure of Fear *'45*
Cheyenne *'47*
Tarzan and the Huntress *'47*
The Dude Goes West *'48*
Treasure of the Sierra Madre *'48*
Unknown Island *'48*
Let's Dance *'50*
Drums in the Deep South *'51*
The Half-Breed *'51*
Kansas Pacific *'53*
Silver Star *'55*
Backlash *'56*
Wetbacks *'56*
Three Violent People *'57*
The Geisha Boy *'58*
Noose for a Gunman *'60*
Arizona Bushwackers *'67*
Buckskin *'68*

John Maclaren (1951-)
Ties That Bind *'06*
Metal Tornado *'11*

Gavin MacLeod (1931-)
Compulsion *'59*
Pork Chop Hill *'59*
High Time *'60*
Twelve Hours to Kill *'60*
War Hunt *'62*
McHale's Navy *'64*
The Sand Pebbles *'66*
The Party *'68*
1,000 Plane Raid *'69*
Kelly's Heroes *'70*
Only with Married Men *'74*
Scruples *'80*

Micheal MacLiammoir (1899-1978)
Othello *'52*
The Kremlin Letter *'70*
What's the Matter with Helen? *'71*

Aline MacMahon (1899-1991)
Five Star Final *'31*
One Way Passage *'32*
Gold Diggers of 1933 *'33*
Heroes for Sale *'33*
The Merry Frinks *'34*
Ah, Wilderness! *'35*
I Live My Life *'35*
Back Door to Heaven *'39*
Out of the Fog *'41*
Tish *'42*
Dragon Seed *'44*
Guest in the House *'44*
The Search *'48*
The Flame & the Arrow *'50*
The Eddie Cantor Story *'53*
The Man from Laramie *'55*
I Could Go on Singing *'63*

Will MacMillan (1944-)
The Crazies *'73*
The Sister-in-Law *'74*
The Enforcer *'76*
Tin Man *'83*
Salvador *'86*
Aspen Extreme *'93*
Bad Girls *'94*
Monarch of the Moon *'05*

Fred MacMurray (1908-91)
Alice Adams *'35*
The Bride Comes Home *'35*
The Gilded Lily *'35*
Hands Across the Table *'35*
The Princess Comes Across *'36*
The Texas Rangers *'36*
The Trail of the Lonesome Pine *'36*
Maid of Salem *'37*
Swing High, Swing Low *'37*
True Confession *'37*
Men with Wings *'38*
Sing You Sinners *'38*
My Love For Yours *'39*
Remember the Night *'40*
Too Many Husbands *'40*
Dive Bomber *'41*
Above Suspicion *'43*
No Time For Love *'43*
Double Indemnity *'44*
Murder, He Says *'45*
Egg and I *'47*
The Miracle of the Bells *'48*
On Our Merry Way *'48*
Family Honeymoon *'49*
Borderline *'50*
The Moonlighter *'53*
The Caine Mutiny *'54*
Pushover *'54*
The Far Horizons *'55*
The Rains of Ranchipur *'55*
There's Always Tomorrow *'56*
Gun for a Coward *'57*
Quantez *'57*
Good Day for a Hanging *'58*
The Shaggy Dog *'59*
The Apartment *'60*
The Absent-Minded Professor *'61*
Bon Voyage! *'62*
Son of Flubber *'63*
Kisses for My President *'64*
Follow Me, Boys! *'66*
The Happiest Millionaire *'67*
Charley and the Angel *'73*
Beyond the Bermuda Triangle *'75*
The Swarm *'78*

Alan MacNaughton (1920-2002)
Bond of Fear *'56*
Victim *'61*
Frankenstein Created Woman *'66*
How Many Miles to Babylon? *'82*
The Insurance Man *'86*
A Very British Coup *'88*

Robert MacNaughton (1966-)
E.T.: The Extra-Terrestrial *'82*
I Am the Cheese *'83*

Patrick Macnee (1922-2015)
A Christmas Carol *'51*
Les Girls *'57*
The Bloodsuckers *'70*
King Solomon's Treasure *'76*
Dead of Night *'77*
Battlestar Galactica *'78*
The Howling *'81*
Sea Wolves *'81*
Spaceship *'81*
Rehearsal for Murder *'82*
Young Doctors in Love *'82*
Return of the Man from U.N.C.L.E. *'83*
This Is Spinal Tap *'84*
A View to a Kill *'85*
Club Med *'86*
Down Under *'86 (N)*
Waxwork *'88*
Around the World in 80 Days *'89*
Lobster Man from Mars *'89*
Chill Factor *'90*
Sherlock Holmes and the Incident at Victoria Falls *'91*
Waxwork 2: Lost in Time *'91*
The Gambler Returns: The Luck of the Draw *'93*
Thunder in Paradise *'93*
Thunder in Paradise 2 *'94*
The Avengers *'98 (C)*

Laine MacNeil
Diary of a Wimpy Kid 2: Rodrick Rules *'11*
Diary of a Wimpy Kid: Dog Days *'12*

Meredith MacNeill (1975-)
The Queen's Sister *'05*
Confetti *'06*

Peter MacNeill
Crash *'95*
Closer and Closer *'96*
The Hanging Garden *'97*
Dangerous Evidence: The Lori Jackson Story *'99*
Killer Deal *'99*
Sex & Mrs. X *'00*
Angel Eyes *'01*
Steve Martini's The Judge *'01*
Who is Cletis Tout? *'02*
Killer Instinct: From the Files of Agent Candice DeLong *'03*
A History of Violence *'05*
Above and Beyond *'06*
Something Beneath *'07*
Celine *'08*
The Good Witch *'08*
The Good Witch's Garden *'09*
The Good Witch's Gift *'10*
The Journey Home *'14*

Tress MacNeille (1951-)
Pom Poko *'94 (V)*
Kiki's Delivery Service *'98 (V)*
The Rugrats Movie *'98 (V)*
Hey Arnold! The Movie *'02 (V)*
Rugrats Go Wild! *'03 (V)*
Cinderella III: A Twist in Time *'07 (V)*

Peter MacNichol (1954-)
Dragonslayer *'81*
Sophie's Choice *'82*
Heat *'87*
Ghostbusters 2 *'89*
Hard Promises *'92*
Housesitter *'92*
Addams Family Values *'93*
Radioland Murders *'94 (C)*
Roswell: The U.F.O. Cover-Up *'94*
Dracula: Dead and Loving It *'95*
Bean *'97*
Baby Geniuses *'98*
The Secret of NIMH 2 *'98 (V)*
Breakin' All The Rules *'04*
Stuart Little 3: Call of the Wild *'06*
24: Redemption *'08*
Battleship *'12*
Game Change *'12*

Alex MacNicoll
My All American *'15*
Last Rampage *'17*

Elle Macpherson (1964-)
Alice *'90*
Sirens *'94*
If Lucy Fell *'95*
Jane Eyre *'96*
The Mirror Has Two Faces *'96*
Batman and Robin *'97*
The Edge *'97*
A Girl Thing *'01*

George MacQuarrie
The Idol Dancer *'20*
The Love Flower *'20*

Alex MacQueen
The Hide *'08*
In the Loop *'09*
Youth *'15*

Duncan MacRae (1905-67)
Our Man in Havana *'59*
Casino Royale *'67*

Gordon MacRae (1921-86)
Look for the Silver Lining *'49*
Backfire *'50*
The Daughter of Rosie O'Grady *'50*
Tea for Two *'50*
The West Point Story *'50*
On Moonlight Bay *'51*
Starlift *'51*
By the Light of the Silvery Moon *'53*
The Desert Song *'53*
Three Sailors and a Girl *'53*
Oklahoma! *'55*
Carousel *'56*

Carol MacReady
Agatha Christie's Murder is Easy *'82*
102 Dalmatians *'00*
Wondrous Oblivion *'06*

George Macready (1999-73)
Counter-Attack *'45*
The Bandit of Sherwood Forest *'46*
Gilda *'46*
Down to Earth *'47*
The Swordsman *'47*
The Big Clock *'48*
Black Arrow *'48*
Johnny Allegro *'49*
Knock on Any Door *'49*
A Lady Without Passport *'50*
The Nevadan *'50*
Rogues of Sherwood Forest *'50*
Detective Story *'51*
Tarzan's Peril *'51*
The Green Glove *'52*
Julius Caesar *'53*
The Stranger Wore a Gun *'53*
Vera Cruz *'53*
Duffy of San Quentin *'54*
Paths of Glory *'57*
Taras Bulba *'62*
Two Weeks in Another Town *'62*
Dead Ringer *'64*
The Human Duplicators *'64*
Seven Days in May *'64*
Where Love Has Gone *'64*
The Great Race *'65*
Night Gallery *'69*
Tora! Tora! Tora! *'70*
The Return of Count Yorga *'71*

Bruce MacVittie (1956-)
Stonewall *'95*
Hi-Life *'98*
Where the Money Is *'00*
2B Perfectly Honest *'04*
Just Like the Son *'06*

Bill Macy (1922-2019)
Oh! Calcutta! *'72*
The Late Show *'77*
The Jerk *'79*
Serial *'80*
My Favorite Year *'82*
Bad Medicine *'85*
Movers and Shakers *'85*
Sibling Rivalry *'90*
The Doctor *'91*
Analyze This *'98*
Surviving Christmas *'04*
The Holiday *'06*
Mr. Woodcock *'07*

William H. Macy (1950-)
The Awakening Land *'78*
Somewhere in Time *'80*
Things Change *'88*
Homicide *'91*
A Private Matter *'92*
Benny & Joon *'93*
Searching for Bobby Fischer *'93*
Twenty Bucks *'93*
Being Human *'94*
The Client *'94*
Evolver *'94 (V)*
Oleanna *'94*
Andersonville *'95*
Mr. Holland's Opus *'95*
Murder in the First *'95*
Down Periscope *'96*
Fargo *'96*
Ghosts of Mississippi *'96*
Hit Me *'96*
Air Force One *'97*
Boogie Nights *'97*
Wag the Dog *'97*
A Civil Action *'98*
Jerry and Tom *'98*
Pleasantville *'98*
Psycho *'98*
The Secret of NIMH 2 *'98 (V)*
Happy, Texas *'99*
Magnolia *'99*
Mystery Men *'99*
A Slight Case of Murder *'99*
Panic *'00*
State and Main *'00*
Focus *'01*
Jurassic Park 3 *'01*
Welcome to Collinwood *'02*
The Cooler *'03*
Out of Order *'03*
Seabiscuit *'03*
Cellular *'04*
In Enemy Hands *'04*
Spartan *'04*
Stealing Sinatra *'04*
Edmond *'05*
Sahara *'05*
Bobby *'06*
Everyone's Hero *'06 (V)*
Thank You for Smoking *'06*
He Was a Quiet Man *'07*
Wild Hogs *'07*
Bart Got a Room *'08*
The Deal *'08*
The Maiden Heist *'08*
The Tale of Despereaux *'08 (V)*
Shorts: The Adventures of the Wishing Rock *'09*
Dirty Girl *'10*
Marmaduke *'10*
The Lincoln Lawyer *'11*
The Sessions *'12*
Ernest & Celestine *'13 (V)*
A Single Shot *'13*
Cake *'14*
Rudderless *'14*
Room *'15*
Blood Father *'16*
Stealing Cars *'16*

Ciaran Madden (1947-)
The Beast Must Die *'75*
A Married Man *'84*
Fortunes of War *'87*
Ivanhoe *'97*

Peter Madden (1904-76)
Missiles from Hell *'58*
Kiss of the Vampire *'62*
The Loneliness of the Long Distance Runner *'62*
Doctor Zhivago *'65*
Frankenstein Created Woman *'66*

Richard Madden (1986-)
Chatroom *'10*
Birdsong *'12*
A Promise *'13*
Cinderella *'15*
The Take *'16*
Rocketman *'19*

Victor Maddern (1926-93)
Sailor of the King *'53*
The Shadow Man *'53*
Terror on a Train *'53*
Child in the House *'56*
All at Sea *'57*
Blood of the Vampire *'58*
I'm All Right Jack *'59*
Carry On Spying *'64*

Anna Madeley (1977-)
The Secret Life of Mrs. Beeton *'06*
The Old Curiosity Shop *'07*
Affinity *'08*
The Secret Diaries of Miss Anne Lister *'10*

Rebecca Mader (1977-)
Mimic 3: Sentinel *'03*
The Devil Wears Prada *'06*
Great World of Sound *'07*
The Men Who Stare at Goats *'09*
Ceremony *'10*
Cougars, Inc. *'10*
The Rainbow Tribe *'11*

Amy Madigan (1950-)
The Ambush Murders *'82*
Love Child *'82*
Love Letters *'83*
Nowhere to Hide *'83*
Places in the Heart *'84*
Streets of Fire *'84*
Alamo Bay *'85*
Twice in a Lifetime *'85*
Prince of Pennsylvania *'88*
Field of Dreams *'89*
Uncle Buck *'89*
The Dark Half *'91*
Lucky Day *'91*
Female Perversions *'96*
Riders of the Purple Sage *'96*
A Bright Shining Lie *'98*
Pollock *'00*
A Time for Dancing *'00*
Shot in the Heart *'01*
The Sleepy Time Gal *'01*
The Laramie Project *'02*
Winter Passing *'05*
Murder on Pleasant Drive *'06*
Gone Baby Gone *'07*
Living Proof *'08*
Virginia *'10*
That's What I Am *'11*

The Lifeguard '13
American Woman '19

James Madio (1975-)
Hero '92
The Basketball Diaries '95
Band of Brothers '01
Searching for Bobby D '05
The Box '07
Doughboys '08
No God, No Master '12

Bailee Madison (1999-)
Bridge to Terabithia '07
Conviction '10
Don't Be Afraid of the Dark '11
An Invisible Sign '11
Just Go With It '11
Cowgirls 'n Angels '12
Parental Guidance '12
A Taste of Romance '12
Smart Cookies '13
Northpole '14
The Strangers: Prey at Night '18

Elina Madison (1976-)
LIP Service '99
Creepshow III '06
Death Racers '08

Guy Madison (1922-96)
Since You Went Away '44
Till the End of Time '46
Honeymoon '47
Massacre River '49
Drums in the Deep South '51
The Command '54
5 Against the House '55
Savage Wilderness '55
Executioner of Venice '63
Apache's Last Battle '64
Bang Bang Kid '67
Superargo '67
Special Forces '68
Hell Commandos '69
Computer Wizard '77
Where's Willie? '77

Noel Madison (1897-1975)
Doorway to Hell '30
Me and My Gal '32
Symphony of Six Million '32
Cocaine Fiends '36
Missing Girls '36
Gangway '37
The House of Secrets '37
Climbing High '38
Crackerjack '38
Sailing Along '38
Charlie Chan in City of Darkness '39
Footsteps in the Dark '41
Secret Agent of Japan '42

Ruth Madoc (1943-)
Agatha Christie's The Pale Horse '96
Very Annie Mary '00

Madonna (1959-)
Desperately Seeking Susan '85
Shanghai Surprise '86
Who's That Girl? '87
Bloodhounds of Broadway '89
Dick Tracy '90
Truth or Dare '91
Body of Evidence '92
A League of Their Own '92
Shadows and Fog '92
Dangerous Game '93
Blue in the Face '95
Four Rooms '95
Evita '96
Girl 6 '96
The Next Best Thing '00
Die Another Day '02
Swept Away '02
Arthur and the Invisibles '06 (V)

Rob Madrid
Black Thunder '98
Moscow Heat '04

Al Madrigal
Lies and Illusions '09
The Way Back '20

Michael Madsen (1958-)
One for the Road '82
The Natural '84
Racing with the Moon '84
Iguana '89
Kill Me Again '89
The End of Innocence '90
The Doors '91
Thelma & Louise '91
Beyond the Law '92
Fatal Instinct '92
Reservoir Dogs '92
Straight Talk '92
Trouble Bound '92
Almost Blue '93
Final Combination '93
Free Willy '93
The Getaway '93
Money for Nothing '93
Season of Change '94
Wyatt Earp '94
Free Willy 2: The Adventure Home '95
Man with a Gun '95
Mulholland Falls '95
Species '95
Donnie Brasco '96
The Last Days of Frankie the Fly '96
Red Line '96
The Winner '96
Diary of a Serial Killer '97
Executive Target '97
Love to Kill '97
The Florentine '98
The Maker '98
The Sender '98
Species 2 '98
Trail of a Serial Killer '98
Agent of Death '99
Supreme Sanction '99
Voodoo Dawn '99
Choke '00
High Noon '00
The Inspectors 2: A Shred of Evidence '00
Luck of the Draw '00
Sacrifice '00
The Stray '00
Extreme Honor '01
L.A.P.D.: To Protect and Serve '01
Die Another Day '02
44 Minutes: The North Hollywood Shootout '03
Kill Bill Vol. 1 '03
My Boss's Daughter '03
Kill Bill Vol. 2 '04
Chasing Ghosts '05
L.A. Dicks '05
The Last Drop '05
Sin City '05
All In '06
BloodRayne '06
Scary Movie 4 '06
UKM: The Ultimate Killing Machine '06
Afghan Knights '07
Boarding Gate '07
Crash and Burn '07
Croc '07
Living & Dying '07
Tooth and Nail '07
Deep Winter '08
Hell Ride '08
Last Hour '08
Lost Treasure of the Maya '08
Vice '08
The Bleeding '09
Break '09
Outrage Born in Terror '09
Road of No Return '09
Shannon's Rainbow '09
The Tomb '09
The Big I Am '10
The Killing Jar '10
Terror Trap '10
A Cold Day in Hell '11
Loosies '11
Beyond the Trophy '12
A Sierra Nevada Gunfight '13
Death Squad '14
Vigilante Diaries '16
Trading Paint '19
Welcome to Acapulco '19

Virginia Madsen (1961-)
Dune '84
Creator '85
Fire with Fire '86
Modern Girls '86
Slamdance '87
Zombie High '87
Gotham '88
Hot to Trot! '88
Mr. North '88
The Heart of Dixie '89
The Hot Spot '90
Highlander 2: The Quickening '91
Victim of Love '91
Candyman '92
Blue Tiger '94
The Prophecy '95
Ghosts of Mississippi '96
The Apocalypse Watch '97
John Grisham's The Rainmaker '97
The Florentine '98
The Haunting '99
Full Disclosure '00
Crossfire Trail '01
Just Ask My Children '01
American Gun '02
Tempted '03
Brave New Girl '04
Sideways '04
Firewall '06
A Prairie Home Companion '06
Stuart Little 3: Call of the Wild '06 (V)
The Astronaut Farmer '07
The Number 23 '07
Ripple Effect '07
Diminished Capacity '08
The Haunting in Connecticut '09
Father of Invention '11
Red Riding Hood '11
Crazy Kind of Love '12
The Magic of Belle Isle '12
Anna Nicole '13
The Hot Flashes '13

Aki Maeda (1985-)
Battle Royale '00
Azumi 2 '05
Linda Linda Linda '05

Beverly (Bibari) Maeda (1948-)
Face of Another '66
Son of Godzilla '66

Christian Maelen
I Think I Do '97
Wisegirls '02
This Thing of Ours '03
Remedy '05

Mia Maestro (1978-)
Tango '98
For Love or Country: The Arturo Sandoval Story '00
Time Code '00
In the Time of the Butterflies '01
Frida '02
The Motorcycle Diaries '04
Deepwater '05
Poseidon '06
The Box '07
The Summit '08
The Music Never Stopped '11
The Speed of Thought '11
Some Girl(s) '13

Stella Maeve (1989-)
Harold '08
Accused at 17 '09
The Runaways '10

Roma Maffia (1958-)
Disclosure '94
The Heidi Chronicles '95
Nick of Time '95
Mistrial '96
Kiss the Girls '97
Route 9 '98
Double Jeopardy '99
Things You Can Tell Just by Looking at Her '00
Holes '03
Ghost Image '07
Yonkers Joe '08

The Blue Tooth Virgin '09
The Call '13

Dominic Mafham (1968-)
Our Mutual Friend '98
Shooting Fish '98
The Scarlet Pimpernel '99

Pancho Magalona (1926-98)
Merrill's Marauders '62
The Hook '63

John Magaro (1983-)
My Soul to Take '10
Down the Shore '11
Liberal Arts '12
Not Fade Away '12
War Machine '17
Overlord '18
First Cow '20

Robbie Magasiva
Stickmen '01
The Tattooist '07

Cass Magda
Hawk's Vengeance '96
Blade Boxer '97

Daniel Magder (1991-)
A Deadly Encounter '04
Sticks and Stones '08
Knockout '11

Patrick Magee (1922-82)
Dementia 13 '63
Seance on a Wet Afternoon '64
Zulu '64
Die, Monster, Die! '65
Masque of the Red Death '65
The Skull '65
Portrait in Terror '66
Anzio '68
Hard Contract '69
Cromwell '70
A Clockwork Orange '71
The Fiend '71
Trojan Women '71
Asylum '72
Demons of the Mind '72
Young Winston '72
And Now the Screaming Starts '73
The Final Programme '73
Luther '74
Barry Lyndon '75
Telefon '77
The Bronte Sisters '79
The Black Cat '81
Chariots of Fire '81
The Monster Club '85

Jad Mager (1969-)
Blue Flame '93
Big City Blues '99

Brandon Maggart (1933-)
Christmas Evil '80
Dressed to Kill '80
The World According to Garp '82
Running Mates '92

Pupella Maggio (1910-99)
The Valachi Papers '72
Amarcord '74

Santiago Magill (1977-)
City of M '01
I Love You Baby '01

Benoît Magimel (1974-)
Les Voleurs '96
A Single Girl '96
Children of the Century '99
The Piano Teacher '01
The Nest '02
The Bridesmaid '04
Crimson Rivers 2: Angels of the Apocalypse '05
A Girl Cut in Two '07
Little White Lies '10
Special Forces '11
The Connection '15

Philippe Magnan (1948-)
The Widow of Saint-Pierre '00
Farewell '09

Anna Magnani (1907-73)
Open City '45
Bellissima '51
The Golden Coach '52
The Rose Tattoo '55
Wild Is the Wind '57
And the Wild, Wild Women '59
The Fugitive Kind '60
Mamma Roma '62
The Secret of Santa Vittoria '69
L'Automobile '71
Fellini's Roma '72 (C)

Donna Magnani
29th Street '91
Epoch '00

Pierre Magnier (1869-1959)
La Roue '23
Cyrano de Bergerac '25

Ann Magnuson (1956-)
The Hunger '83
Perfect Strangers '84
Desperately Seeking Susan '85
Making Mr. Right '86
A Night in the Life of Jimmy Reardon '88
Tequila Sunrise '88
Checking Out '89
Heavy Petting '89
Love at Large '89
Cabin Boy '94
Tank Girl '94
Before and After '95
Levitation '97
Still Breathing '97
From the Earth to the Moon '98
Small Soldiers '98
Kitchen Privileges '00
Love & Sex '00
The Caveman's Valentine '01
Glitter '01
Night at the Golden Eagle '02
Panic Room '02
United States of Leland '03
One More Time '15

Billy Magnussen (1985-)
Blood Night: The Legend of Mary Hatchet '09
Happy Tears '09
Twelve '10
Damsels in Distress '11
The Lost Valentine '11
Into the Woods '14
Ingrid Goes West '17
Game Night '18
The Oath '18

Kate Magowan (1975-)
It's All Gone, Pete Tong '04
Stardust '07
A Lonely Place to Die '11

Pierre Maguelon (1933-2010)
Bed and Board '70
Cyrano de Bergerac '90

Kathleen Maguire
Edge of the City '57
Flipper '63

Tobey Maguire (1975-)
Revenge of the Red Baron '93
Deconstructing Harry '97
The Ice Storm '97
Joyride '97
Fear and Loathing in Las Vegas '98
Pleasantville '98
The Cider House Rules '99
Ride with the Devil '99
Wonder Boys '00
Cats & Dogs '01 (V)
Spider-Man '02
Seabiscuit '03
Spider-Man 2 '04
The Good German '06
Spider-Man 3 '07
Tropic Thunder '08 (C)
Brothers '09
The Details '11
The Great Gatsby '13

Labor Day '13
Pawn Sacrifice '15
The Boss Baby '17

Derek Magyar
Boy Culture '06
Train '08

Valerie Mahaffey (1953-)
Women of Valor '86
Code Name: Dancer '87
National Lampoon's Senior Trip '95
Jungle 2 Jungle '96
Seabiscuit '03
My First Wedding '04
Summer Eleven '10
Crazy Eyes '12
If I Were You '12
Sully '16

George Maharis (1928-)
The Mugger '58
Exodus '60
The Satan Bug '65
A Covenant With Death '67
Land Raiders '69
Come Die With Me '75
Murder on Flight 502 '75
Return to Fantasy Island '77
Sword & the Sorcerer '82

Annet Mahendru
Escape From Tomorrow '13
Penguins of Madagascar '14 (V)

Bill Maher (1956-)
Club Med '86
House 2: The Second Story '87
Cannibal Women in the Avocado Jungle of Death '89
Pizza Man '91
Religulous '08
Hugh Hefner: Playboy, Activist and Rebel '09

Joseph Maher (1934-98)
Under the Rainbow '81
The Evil That Men Do '84
Funny Farm '88
My Stepmother Is an Alien '88
Sister Act '92
I.Q. '94
The Shadow '94
Bulletproof Heart '95
Surviving Picasso '96

Sean Maher (1975-)
Brian's Song '01
The Dive from Clausen's Pier '05
Serenity '05
Wedding Wars '06
Much Ado About Nothing '13

Grace Mahlaba
Bopha! '93
Being Human '94

Bruce Mahler (1950-)
Funland '89
Police Academy 6: City under Siege '89

Shiek Mahmud-Bey
Joe's Apartment '96
Night Falls on Manhattan '96
Path to Paradise '97
Mercy Streets '00
Buffalo Soldiers '01
Leprechaun 6: Back 2 Tha Hood '03

Michael Mahonen (1964-)
By Way of the Stars '92
Captured '99

Brian Mahoney
Red Snow '91
Boondock Saints '99

Jock Mahoney (1919-89)
Cow Town '50
The Nevadan '50
Battle Hymn '57
The Land Unknown '57
Tarzan the Magnificent '60
Three Blondes in His Life '61
Tarzan Goes to India '62
California '63

Tarzan's Three Challenges '63
The Walls of Hell '64
The Glory Stompers '67
Bad Bunch '76

John Mahoney (1940-2018)
The Manhattan Project '86
Trapped in Silence '86
Moonstruck '87
Suspect '87
Tin Men '87
Betrayed '88
Eight Men Out '88
Frantic '88
Dinner at Eight '89
The Image '89
Say Anything '89
The Russia House '90
Barton Fink '91
Love Hurts '91
Article 99 '92
The Hudsucker Proxy '93
In the Line of Fire '93
Striking Distance '93
Reality Bites '94
The American President '95
Primal Fear '96
She's the One '96
Antz '98 (V)
The Iron Giant '99 (V)
The Broken Hearts Club '00
Atlantis: The Lost Empire '01 (V)
Dan in Real Life '07
Flipped '10

Simona Maicanescu
Dante 01 '08
Splice '10

Aïssa Maïga (1975-)
Russian Dolls '05
Paris, je t'aime '06
Mood Indigo '13
The Boy Who Harnessed the Wind '19

Steven Mailer (1966-)
Reversal of Fortune '90
Quiet Days in Hollywood '97
Red Meat '98
24 Nights '99

Robert Mailhouse (1962-)
Just a Little Harmless Sex '99
A Secret Affair '99
All I Want for Christmas '07
The Christmas Pageant '11

Caludette Maille
Like Water for Chocolate '93
Like A Bride '94

Robert Maillet
The Big Bang '11
Septic Man '14

Laurie Main (1929-2012)
Private Parts '72
Tarzan, the Ape Man '81

Marjorie Main (1890-1975)
Dead End '37
Stella Dallas '37
Dead End Kids: Little Tough Guy '38
Little Tough Guy '38
Romance of the Limberlost '38
Angels Wash Their Faces '39
They Shall Have Music '39
The Women '39
Dark Command '40
I Take This Woman '40
Susan and God '40
Honky Tonk '41
The Shepherd of the Hills '41
A Woman's Face '41
Tish '42
We Were Dancing '42
Heaven Can Wait '43
Johnny Come Lately '43
Murder, He Says '45
The Harvey Girls '46
Undercurrent '46
Egg and I '47
The Wistful Widow of Wagon Gap '47
Feudin', Fussin', and A-Fightin' '48
Ma and Pa Kettle '49
Ma and Pa Kettle Go to Town '50
Summer Stock '50
It's a Big Country '51
The Law and the Lady '51
Ma and Pa Kettle Back On the Farm '51
Mr. Imperium '51
The Belle of New York '52
Ma and Pa Kettle at the Fair '52
Ma and Pa Kettle on Vacation '53
The Long, Long Trailer '54
Ma and Pa Kettle at Home '54
Rose Marie '54
Ma and Pa Kettle at Waikiki '55
Friendly Persuasion '56
The Kettles in the Ozarks '56
The Kettles on Old MacDonald's Farm '57

Giorgio Maiocchi
The Iron Ladies '00
The Iron Ladies 2 '03

Guy Mairesse (1924-)
The Diabolical Dr. Z '65
A Reason to Live, a Reason to Die '73

Valerie Mairesse (1955-)
The Sacrifice '86
One to Another '06

Marne Maitland (1920-45)
Bhowani Junction '56
The Stranglers of Bombay '60
The Terror of the Tongs '61
The Reptile '66
Fellini's Roma '72

Tina Majorino (1985-)
Andre '94
Corrina, Corrina '94
When a Man Loves a Woman '94
Waterworld '95
Santa Fe '97
True Women '97
Alice in Wonderland '99
Napoleon Dynamite '04
Think Tank '06
What We Do Is Secret '07
Veronica Mars '14

Austin Majors (1995-)
Treasure Planet '02 (V)
The Ant Bully '06 (V)

Jonathan Majors
Captive State '19
The Last Black Man in San Francisco '19
Da 5 Bloods '20

Lee Majors (1939-)
Strait-Jacket '64
Will Penny '67
The Ballad of Andy Crocker '69
The Bionic Woman '75
The Agency '81
Last Chase '81
Scrooged '88
Keaton's Cop '90
Trojan War '97
Out Cold '01
Big Fat Liar '02
Arizona Summer '03
The Trail to Hope Rose '04
When I Find the Ocean '06
The Brothers Solomon '07

Heike Makatsch (1971-)
Obsession '97
Aimee & Jaguar '98
Love Actually '03

Miriam Makeba
Sarafina! '92
Soul Power '08

Chris Makepeace (1964-)
My Bodyguard '80
Last Chase '81
Mazes and Monsters '82
Vamp '86
Captive Hearts '87
Synapse '95

Kuroudo Maki
A Scene at Sea '92
Brother '00

Yoko Maki (1962-)
The Princess Blade '02
The Grudge '04
Sway '06
Like Father, Like Son '13
After the Storm '17

Wendy Makkena (1958-)
Eight Men Out '88
Sister Act '92
Sister Act 2: Back in the Habit '93
Camp Nowhere '94
Serving in Silence: The Margarethe Cammermeyer Story '95
Air Bud '97
Finding North '97
The Bling Ring '11

Mako (1933-2006)
The Ugly Dachshund '65
The Sand Pebbles '66
Private Navy of Sgt. O'Farrell '68
The Streets of San Francisco '72
The Island at the Top of the World '74
The Killer Elite '75
Battle Creek Brawl '80
The Big Brawl '80
An Eye for an Eye '81
Under the Rainbow '81
Conan the Barbarian '82
Testament '83
Conan the Destroyer '84
Girls of the White Orchid '85
Armed Response '86
Kung Fu: The Movie '86
Tucker: The Man and His Dream '88
Fatal Mission '89
An Unremarkable Life '89
Pacific Heights '90
Taking Care of Business '90
Rising Sun '93
A Dangerous Place '94
Highlander: The Final Dimension '94
Riot in the Streets '96
Seven Years in Tibet '97
Sworn to Justice '97
Rugrats in Paris: The Movie '00 (V)
Pearl Harbor '01
Bulletproof Monk '03
Memoirs of a Geisha '05
Rise: Blood Hunter '07
TMNT: Teenage Mutant Ninja Turtles '07 (V)

Lawrence Makoare (1968-)
Die Another Day '02
Lord of the Rings: The Return of the King '03

Khoury J. Makram (1945-)
See Makram Khoury

Mala (1906-52)
Robinson Crusoe of Clipper Island '36
Call of the Yukon '38

Patrick Malahide (1945-)
The Singing Detective '86
A Month in the Country '87
December Bride '91
Middlemarch '93
Two Deaths '94
Cutthroat Island '95
Kidnapped '95
The Long Kiss Goodnight '96
Til There Was You '96
The Beautician and the Beast '97
Deacon Brodie '98
Miracle at Midnight '98
All the King's Men '99
Fortress 2: Re-Entry '99
Heaven '99
Ordinary Decent Criminal '99
Captain Corelli's Mandolin '01
Victoria & Albert '01
Goodbye, Mr. Chips '02
Eurotrip '04
Elizabeth I '05
Friends & Crocodiles '05
Sahara '05
Murderous Intent '06
Five Days '07
Brideshead Revisited '08
Into the Storm '09
A Short Stay in Switzerland '09
The 39 Steps '09

Rick Malambri (1982-)
Universal Soldiers '07
Step Up 3D '10
A Holiday Heist '11

Christophe MaLavoy (1952-)
The Cry of the Owl '87
Madame Bovary '91

Paolo Malco (1947-)
New York Ripper '82
Scorpion with Two Tails '82
The House by the Cemetery '83

Romany Malco (1968-)
Urban Menace '99
The Chateau '01
The Tuxedo '02
The 40 Year Old Virgin '05
The Ex '07
Baby Mama '08
The Love Guru '08
Saint John of Las Vegas '09
A Little Bit of Heaven '11
Think Like a Man Too '14
Almost Christmas '16
When the Bough Breaks '16
Holiday Rush '19

Christopher Malcolm (1946-2014)
We'll Meet Again '82
Daphne '07

Graeme Malcolm
In the Blood '06
Rosencrantz & Guildenstern Are Undead '10

Robyn Malcolm (1965-)
Perfect Strangers '03
Boogeyman '05

Paula Malcomson (1970-)
Hamlet '00
Caprica '09
The Hunger Games '12

Karl Malden (1912-2009)
13 Rue Madeleine '46
Boomerang '47
Kiss of Death '47
The Gunfighter '50
The Halls of Montezuma '50
Where the Sidewalk Ends '50
The Sellout '51
A Streetcar Named Desire '51
Diplomatic Courier '52
Operation Secret '52
Ruby Gentry '52
I Confess '53
On the Waterfront '54
Baby Doll '56
Bombers B-52 '57
Fear Strikes Out '57
The Hanging Tree '59
Pollyanna '60
One-Eyed Jacks '61
Parrish '61
All Fall Down '62
Birdman of Alcatraz '62
Gypsy '62
How the West Was Won '63
Cheyenne Autumn '64
Dead Ringer '64
The Cincinnati Kid '65
The Adventures of Bullwhip Griffin '66
Murderers' Row '66
Nevada Smith '66
Billion Dollar Brain '67
Hotel '67
Blue '68
Hot Millions '68
Patton '70
The Cat o' Nine Tails '71
Wild Rovers '71
The Streets of San Francisco '72
Ricco '74
Beyond the Poseidon Adventure '79
Meteor '79
Miracle on Ice '81
The Sting 2 '83
Alice in Wonderland '85
Billy Galvin '86
Nuts '87

Ruth Maleczech (1939-2013)
Anna '87
In the Soup '92
The Ballad of Little Jo '93

Irina Maleeva
Kidnap Syndicate '76
Union City '81

Rami Malek (1981-)
Night at the Museum '06
The Pacific '10
Short Term 12 '13
Da Sweet Blood of Jesus '14
Need for Speed '14
Buster's Mal Heart '17
Papillon '17
Bohemian Rhapsody '18

Jonathan Malen (1987-)
Possessed '00
Charlie Bartlett '07

Arthur Malet (1927-2013)
King Rat '65
Munster, Go Home! '66
Halloween '78
The Black Cauldron '85 (V)
Hook '91
A Little Princess '95

Laurent Malet (1955-)
Querelle '83
Sword of Gideon '86

Ryan Malgarini (1992-)
Freaky Friday '03
United States of Leland '03
The Young Kieslowski '15

Wendie Malick (1950-)
Scrooged '88
The American President '95
Trojan War '97
Jerome '98
Take My Advice: The Ann & Abby Story '99
The Emperor's New Groove '00 (V)
Strange Frequency 2 '01
Manna from Heaven '02
On Edge '03
Raising Genius '04
Racing Stripes '05
Waiting '05
Will You Merry Me? '08
Alvin and the Chipmunks: The Squeakuel '09
Confessions of a Shopaholic '09
Adventures of a Teenage Dragonslayer '10
Knucklehead '10
About Fifty '11
What Happens Next '11

Keram Malicki-Sanchez (1974-)
Cherry Falls '00
Happy Campers '01

Art Malik (1952-)
The Jewel in the Crown '84
The Living Daylights '87
City of Joy '92
Year of the Comet '92
True Lies '94
Uncovered '94
A Kid in King Arthur's Court '95
Booty Call '96
Path to Paradise '97
Catherine Cookson's Colour Blind '98
Cleopatra '99
Tempo '03
Fakers '04
Nina's Heavenly Delights '06
Franklyn '08
The Wolfman '09
Upstairs Downstairs '11

Kevork Malikyan (1942-)
Belly of the Beast '03
Flight of the Phoenix '04

Joshua Malina (1966-)
In the Line of Fire '93
The American President '95
Bulworth '98
From the Earth to the Moon '98
View from the Top '03
The First Time '12
The Young Kieslowski '15

Judith Malina (1926-2015)
Enemies, a Love Story '89
Awakenings '90
The Addams Family '91
The Deli '97
Music from Another Room '97
Let It Snow '99

Ross Malinger (1984-)
Eve of Destruction '90
Late for Dinner '91
Sleepless in Seattle '93
Bye Bye, Love '94
Sudden Death '95
Little Bigfoot '96
Toothless '97
Club Vampire '98

Cylia Malki (1976-)
Daughter of Keltoum '01
La Moustache '05

Sam Malkin
Blood Relations '87
Caribe '87

John Malkovich (1953-)
The Killing Fields '84
Places in the Heart '84
Death of a Salesman '86
Making Mr. Right '86
Empire of the Sun '87
The Glass Menagerie '87
Dangerous Liaisons '88
The Sheltering Sky '90
The Object of Beauty '91
Queens Logic '91
Jennifer 8 '92
Of Mice and Men '92
Shadows and Fog '92
Alive '93 (N)
In the Line of Fire '93
Beyond the Clouds '95
The Convent '95
Mary Reilly '95
Mulholland Falls '95
The Ogre '96
Portrait of a Lady '96
Con Air '97
The Man in the Iron Mask '98
Rounders '98
Being John Malkovich '99
The Messenger: The Story of Joan of Arc '99
RKO 281 '99
Time Regained '99
I'm Going Home '00
Shadow of the Vampire '00
Hotel '01
Knockaround Guys '01
Ripley's Game '02
Johnny English '03
Napoleon '03
Color Me Kubrick '05
The Hitchhiker's Guide to the Galaxy '05
The Libertine '05
Art School Confidential '06
Eragon '06
Klimt '06
Beowulf '07 (V)
In Tranzit '07
Afterwards '08
Burn After Reading '08
Changeling '08
Disgrace '08

Gardens of the Night *'08*
Mutant Chronicles *'08*
The Great Buck Howard *'09*
Jonah Hex *'10*
RED *'10*
Secretariat *'10*
Transformers: Dark of the Moon *'11*
RED 2 *'13*
Warm Bodies *'13*
Cesar Chavez *'14*
Penguins of Madagascar *'14 (V)*
Cut Bank *'15*
Deepwater Horizon *'16*
Bullet Head *'17*
Unlocked *'17*
The Wilde Wedding *'17*
Extremely Wicked, Shockingly Evil and Vile *'19*
Velvet Buzzsaw *'19*

Miles Malleson (1888-1969)
Nine Days a Queen *'36*
The Thief of Bagdad *'40*
Unpublished Story *'42*
Dead of Night *'45*
Kind Hearts and Coronets *'49*
A Christmas Carol *'51*
The Golden Salamander *'51*
Captain's Paradise *'53*
The Horror of Dracula *'58*
The Brides of Dracula *'60*
Peeping Tom *'60*

Perry Mallette
Going Back *'83*
Thou Shalt Not Kill. . .Except *'87*

Soren Malling
A Hijacking *'13*
Men & Chicken *'15*
A War *'15*
Domino *'19*
The Vanishing *'19*

Rory Mallinson (1903-76)
For You I Die *'47*
Seminole Uprising *'55*

Brian Mallon
Gettysburg *'93*
Gods and Generals *'03*

Matt Malloy (1963-)
Surviving Desire *'91*
In the Company of Men *'96*
Cookie's Fortune *'99*
Drop Dead Gorgeous *'99*
Election *'99*
Dr. T & the Women *'00*
Everything Put Together *'00*
Running Mates *'00*
The Great Gatsby *'01*
Changing Lanes *'02*
Elephant *'03*
United States of Leland *'03*
Spartan *'04*
Tanner on Tanner *'04*
Wedding Daze *'06*
Morning Glory *'10*

Tom Malloy (1974-)
Gravesend *'97*
The Attic *'06*
The Alphabet Killer *'08*
Love N' Dancing *'09*

Jan Malmsjo (1932-)
Scenes from a Marriage *'73*
Fanny and Alexander *'83*

Birger Malmsten (1920-91)
Night Is My Future *'47*
Three Strange Loves *'49*
Summer Interlude *'50*
To Joy *'50*
The Silence *'63*

Bonz Malone
Slam *'98*
White Boyz *'99*
Bomb the System *'05*

Dorothy Malone (1925-2018)
The Big Sleep *'46*
Night and Day *'46*
The Killer That Stalked New York *'47*
One Sunday Afternoon *'48*
South of St. Louis *'48*
Colorado Territory *'49*
Convicted *'50*
The Nevadan *'50*
The Bushwackers *'52*
Law and Order *'53*
Scared Stiff *'53*
The Fast and the Furious *'54*
Loophole *'54*
Private Hell 36 *'54*
Pushover *'54*
Young at Heart *'54*
Artists and Models *'55*
Battle Cry *'55*
Sincerely Yours *'55*
Pillars of the Sky *'56*
Written on the Wind *'56*
Man of a Thousand Faces *'57*
Quantez *'57*
Tarnished Angels *'57*
Tip On a Dead Jockey *'57*
Too Much, Too Soon *'58*
Warlock *'59*
The Last Voyage *'60*
The Last Sunset *'61*
Beach Party *'63*
Winter Kills *'79*
Day Time Ended *'80*
Basic Instinct *'92*

Jena Malone (1984-)
Bastard out of Carolina *'96*
Hidden in America *'96*
Contact *'97*
Ellen Foster *'97*
Stepmom *'98*
The Book of Stars *'99*
For Love of the Game *'99*
Cheaters *'00*
Donnie Darko *'01*
Life as a House *'01*
The Badge *'02*
The Dangerous Lives of Altar Boys *'02*
Cold Mountain *'03*
Hitler: The Rise of Evil *'03*
United States of Leland *'03*
Corn *'04*
Howl's Moving Castle *'04 (V)*
Saved! *'04*
The Ballad of Jack and Rose *'05*
Pride and Prejudice *'05*
Four Last Songs *'06*
The Go-Getter *'07*
Into the Wild *'07*
The Ruins *'08*
The Messenger *'09*
5 Star Day *'10*
Sucker Punch *'11*
Hatfields & McCoys *'12*
The Hunger Games: Catching Fire *'13*
The Wait *'13*
Inherent Vice *'14*
Time Out of Mind *'14*
The Neon Demon *'16*
Nocturnal Animals *'16*
Lovesong *'17*
The Public *'18*

Nancy Malone (1935-)
Fright *'56*
Man Who Loved Cat Dancing *'73*

Patrick Malone (1969-)
Grand Canyon *'91*
Rock 'n' Roll High School Forever *'91*
Hostage High *'97*
Face the Music *'00*

Michael Maloney (1957-)
Henry V *'89*
Truly, Madly, Deeply *'91*
A Midwinter's Tale *'95*
Othello *'95*
Hamlet *'96*
The Painted Lady *'97*
Me & Mrs. Jones *'02*
P.D. James: The Murder Room *'04*
Pinochet's Last Stand *'06*
The Young Victoria *'09*

Nadine Malouf
May in Summer *'13*
May in the Summer *'13*

Natassia Malthe (1974-)
Call Me: The Rise and Fall of Heidi Fleiss *'04*
Bound by Lies *'05*
Confessions of a Sociopathic Social Climber *'05*
DOA: Dead or Alive *'06*
BloodRayne 2: Deliverance *'07*
Alone in the Dark 2 *'08*
Slave *'09*
Bloodrayne: The Third Reich *'11*
In the Name of the King 2: Two Worlds *'11*
Vikingdom *'13*
Alpha *'18*

Leonard Maltin (1950-)
Gremlins 2: The New Batch *'90*
Forgotten Silver *'96*

Barbara Mamabolo (1986-)
Dangerous Evidence: The Lori Jackson Story *'99*
Brave New Girl *'04*

Peter Mamakos (1918-2008)
My Gun Is Quick *'57*
Fort Bowie *'58*

Tony Mamet
Lakeboat *'00*
Spartan *'04*

Zosia Mamet (1988-)
The Kids Are All Right *'10*
Bleeding Heart *'15*

Robert Mammone
Heaven's Burning *'97*
Salem's Lot *'04*
The Great Raid *'05*
The Condemned *'07*

Alex Man (1957-)
Hong Kong 1941 *'84*
Journey of the Doomed *'85*

Ross Manarchy
Dark Waters *'03*
Darklight *'04*

Biff Manard (1939-)
Zone Troopers *'84*
Trancers 2: The Return of Jack Deth *'90*

Michael Manasseri (1974-)
License to Drive *'88*
Sunstorm *'01*

Melissa Manchester (1951-)
The Great Mouse Detective *'86 (V)*
For the Boys *'91*

Al Mancini (1932-2007)
The Dirty Dozen *'67*
Mission Manila *'87*
My Summer Story *'94*

Ray 'Boom Boom' Mancini (1961-)
Oceans of Fire *'86*
The Dirty Dozen: The Fatal Mission *'88*
Backstreet Dreams *'90*
Timebomb *'91*
Wishful Thinking *'92*
The Search for One-Eye Jimmy *'94*
Body and Soul *'98*
Redbelt *'08*

Nick Mancuso (1948-)
The House on Garibaldi Street *'79*
Nightwing *'79*
Ticket to Heaven *'81*
Mother Lode *'82*
Blame It on the Night *'84*
Love Songs *'84*
Lena's Holiday *'90*
Lies Before Kisses *'92*
Rapid Fire *'92*
Wild Palms *'93*
Under Siege 2: Dark Territory *'95*
Young Ivanhoe *'95*
The Invader *'96*
Marquis de Sade *'96*
Provocateur *'96*
Against the Law *'98*
Loving Evangeline *'98*
Matter of Trust *'98*
Misbegotten *'98*
Captured *'99*
The Pact *'99*
Total Recall 2070: Machine Dreams *'99*
Revelation *'00*
Tribulation *'00*
Firefight *'03*
Call of the Wild *'04*
Today You Die *'05*
Blind Eye *'06*
What Comes Around *'06*
Vanessa *'07*
Contract Killers *'08*
Rise of the Gargoyles *'09*
Violent Blue *'10*

Robert Mandan (1932-2018)
You Can't Take It With You *'79*
Return of the Rebels *'81*
Zapped! *'82*
National Lampoon's Last Resort *'94*
The Nutt House *'95 (C)*

Howie Mandel (1955-)
Gremlins *'84 (V)*
A Fine Mess *'86*
Walk Like a Man *'87*
Little Monsters *'89*
Gremlins 2: The New Batch *'90 (V)*
Shake, Rattle & Rock! *'94*
Tribulation *'00*

Miles Mander (1888-1946)
The Pleasure Garden *'25*
Murder *'30*
Matinee Idol *'33*
The Private Life of Henry VIII *'33*
Don Quixote *'35*
Slave Ship *'37*
Kidnapped *'38*
Mad Miss Manton *'38*
Suez *'38*
The Little Princess *'39*
The Three Musketeers *'39*
The Tower of London *'39*
Wuthering Heights *'39*
Primrose Path *'40*
To Be or Not to Be *'42*
Five Graves to Cairo *'43*
Guadalcanal Diary *'43*
Return of the Vampire *'43*
Murder, My Sweet *'44*
The Pearl of Death *'44*
Scarlet Claw *'44*
The White Cliffs of Dover *'44*
Picture of Dorian Gray *'45*

Michael Mando
The Pregnancy Project *'12*
The Hummingbird Project *'18*

Barbara Mandrell (1948-)
Concrete Cowboys *'79*
Burning Rage *'84*

Neil Mandt (1969-)
Hijacking Hollywood *'97*
Arthur's Quest *'99*
Last Stop for Paul *'08*

Aasif Mandvi (1966-)
ABCD *'99*
American Chai *'01*
The Mystic Masseur *'01*
Spider-Man 2 *'04*
Sorry, Haters *'05*
The War Within *'05*
Music & Lyrics *'07*
The Proposal *'09*
Today's Special *'09*
It's Kind of a Funny Story *'10*
The Last Airbender *'10*
Dark Horse *'11*
Margin Call *'11*
Premium Rush *'12*
Ruby Sparks *'12*
The Internship *'13*
Million Dollar Arm *'14*

Costas Mandylor (1965-)
Triumph of the Spirit *'89*
The Doors *'91*
Mobsters *'91*
Soapdish *'91*
Almost Dead *'94*
Delta of Venus *'95*
Fist of the North Star *'95*
Portraits of a Killer *'95*
Venus Rising *'95*
Virtuosity *'95*
Just Write *'97*
Stand-Ins *'97*
Shelter *'98*
Bonanno: A Godfather's Story *'99*
Stealth Fighter *'99*
Gangland *'00*
Dinocroc *'04*
The Game of Their Lives *'05*
Disaster Zone: Volcano in New York *'06*
Saw 3 *'06*
Nobody *'07*
Saw 4 *'07*
Saw 5 *'08*
In the Eyes of a Killer *'09*
Saw 6 *'09*
Hyenas *'10*
Saw 3D: The Final Chapter *'10*
Sinners and Saints *'10*

Louis Mandylor (1966-)
The Quest *'96*
Mafia! *'98*
Rogue Force *'99*
Price of Glory *'00*
My Big Fat Greek Wedding *'02*
Gang of Roses *'03*
Lady Jayne Killer *'03*
The Game of Their Lives *'05*
Redline *'07*
Silent Venom *'08*
In the Eyes of a Killer *'09*
Wrong Turn at Tahoe *'09*
Bare Knuckles *'10*
The Frankenstein Syndrome *'10*
One In the Chamber *'12*
Code of Honor *'16 (C)*
Daylight's End *'16*
My Big Fat Greek Wedding 2 *'16*

Tyler Mane (1966-)
X-Men *'00*
How to Make a Monster *'01*
Black Mask 2: City of Masks *'02*
Troy *'04*
The Devil's Rejects *'05*
Halloween *'07*
Halloween II *'09*

Marshall Manesh (1950-)
Kazaam *'96*
Car Babes *'06*
Pirates of the Caribbean: At World's End *'07*
A Girl Walks Home Alone at Night *'14*
Jimmy Vestvood: Amerikan Hero *'16*

Jeanne Manet
Slightly French *'49*
Operation Mad Ball *'57*

Larry Manetti (1943-)
Magnum P.I.: Don't Eat the Snow in Hawaii *'80*
C.I.A. 2: Target Alexa *'94*
Body Chemistry 4: Full Exposure *'95*
Back to You and Me *'05*

Nino Manfredi (1921-2004)
Bambole *'65*
Bread and Chocolate *'73*
We All Loved Each Other So Much *'77*
Cafe Express *'83*

Stephen Mangan (1972-)
Confetti *'06*
Postman Pat: The Movie *'14 (V)*

Joe Manganiello (1976-)
Spider-Man *'02*
Spider-Man 3 *'07*
Behind Enemy Lines 3: Colombia *'08*
Impact Point *'08*
Magic Mike *'12*
What to Expect When You're Expecting *'12*
Sabotage *'14*
Magic Mike XXL *'15*
Tumbledown *'16*
Smurfs: The Lost Village *'17 (V)*
Drunk Parents *'19*

Anthony Mangano
Point Break *'91*
8 Heads in a Duffel Bag *'96*
All Saint's Day *'98*

Silvana Mangano (1930-89)
Bitter Rice *'49*
The Gold of Naples *'54*
Mambo *'55*
Ulysses *'55*
Barabbas *'62*
Oedipus Rex *'67*
Teorema *'68*
The Decameron *'70*
Death in Venice *'71*
Ludwig *'72*
Conversation Piece *'75*
Dune *'84*

Alec Mango (1911-89)
Race for Life *'55*
The Seventh Voyage of Sinbad *'58*

Camryn Manheim (1961-)
Sudden Impact *'83*
David Searching *'97*
Romy and Michele's High School Reunion *'97*
Wide Awake *'97*
Happiness *'98*
The Tic Code *'99*
The 10th Kingdom *'00*
What Planet Are You From? *'00*
A Girl Thing *'01*
Dark Water *'02*
Scary Movie 3 *'03*
Twisted *'04*
An Unfinished Life *'05*
Marilyn Hotchkiss' Ballroom Dancing & Charm School *'06*
Slipstream *'07*
Jesse Stone: Thin Ice *'09*
Just Peck *'09*
Love Hurts *'09*
The Pregnancy Pact *'10*
Fort McCoy *'11*
The Hot Flashes *'13*
The Makeover *'13*
Cop Car *'15*
Return to Sender *'15*
All About Nina *'18*

Karin Mani
Alley Cat *'84*
Avenging Angel *'85*

Sunita Mani
Madeline's Madeline *'18*
Can You Keep a Secret? *'19*

Jim Maniaci
Timebomb *'91*
The Rock *'96*

Cindy Manion
Preppies *'82*
The Toxic Avenger *'86*

Sebastian Maniscalco (1973-)
Cruise *'18*
Green Book *'18*

Blu Mankuma (1948-)
Watchers *'88*
Bliss *'96*
Dead Silence *'96*
Dean Koontz's Intensity *'97*
Premonition *'98*
Atomic Train *'99*
Mermaid *'00*
Halloweentown 2: Kalabar's Revenge *'01*
Johnson County War *'02*

Jasper, Texas '03
Fierce People '05
Connor's War '06
Presumed Dead '06
Tin Man '07
The Final Storm '09
Smoke Screen '10

Alakina Mann (1990-)
The Others '01
Girl with a Pearl Earring '03

Byron Mann (1967-)
Street Fighter '94
Red Corner '97
The Corruptor '99
Belly of the Beast '03
Catwoman '04
Sniper 3 '04
Blonde and Blonder '07
Mercenary: Absolution '15
Skyscraper '18

Danny Mann (1951-)
Babe '95 (V)
Balto '95 (V)
Pocahontas '95 (V)
Babe: Pig in the City '98 (V)
Open Season 2 '08 (V)
Open Season 3 '10 (V)

David Mann
Tyler Perry's Meet the Browns '08
Madea Goes to Jail '09

Gabriel Mann (1972-)
American Virgin '98
High Art '98
Kiss of Fire '98
No Vacancy '99
Outside Providence '99
Cherry Falls '00
Sleep Easy, Hutch Rimes '00
Buffalo Soldiers '01
Josie and the Pussycats '01
Things Behind the Sun '01
Abandon '02
The Bourne Identity '02
The Life of David Gale '03
The Bourne Supremacy '04
A Lot Like Love '05
Born Killers '05
Dominion: Prequel to the Exorcist '05
Don't Come Knocking '05
Love and Mary '07
Valley of the Heart's Delight '07
Dark Streets '08
Fake '10
Psych: 9 '10
The Rainbow Tribe '11

Hank Mann (1887-1971)
Spite Marriage '29
City Lights '31

John Mann (1962-)
Turbulence 3: Heavy Metal '00
Underworld: Evolution '05
Personal Effects '09

Leonard Mann (1947-)
Night School '81
Corrupt '84
Cut and Run '85

Leslie Mann (1972-)
The Cable Guy '96
Last Man Standing '96
She's the One '96
Things I Never Told You '96
George of the Jungle '97
Big Daddy '99
Time Code '00
Perfume '01
Orange County '02
Stealing Harvard '02
The 40 Year Old Virgin '05
Knocked Up '07
Drillbit Taylor '08
Funny People '09
17 Again '09
Shorts: The Adventures of the Wishing Rock '09
I Love You Phillip Morris '10
The Change-Up '11
Rio '11 (V)
ParaNorman '12 (V)
This Is 40 '12
The Bling Ring '13
Mr. Peabody & Sherman '14 (V)
The Other Woman '14
Rio 2 '14 (V)
The Comedian '16
How to Be Single '16
Blockers '18
Welcome to Marwen '18

Peter Mann
Frankenstein Conquers the World '64
The Lively Set '64

Robert Mann
Assault of the Party Nerds '89
Black Christmas '06

Tamela Mann (1966-)
Tyler Perry's Meet the Browns '08
Madea Goes to Jail '09
Madea's Big Happy Family '11

Terrence Mann (1951-)
A Chorus Line '85
Critters '86
Critters 2: The Main Course '88
Critters 4 '91
Mrs. Santa Claus '96
True Women '97

Thomas Mann (1991-)
Project X '11
Fun Size '12
As Cool As I Am '13
Beautiful Creatures '13
Me and Earl and the Dying Girl '15
Amityville: The Awakening '17
The Land of Steady Habits '18
The Highwaymen '19
Them That Follow '19

Yanka (Doris Keating) Mann
Pagan Island '60
Flesh Feast '69

Guido Mannari
Driver's Seat '73
Cop in Blue Jeans '78

David Manners (1901-98)
Mothers Cry '30
The Truth About Youth '30
Dracula '31
The Last Flight '31
The Miracle Woman '31
The Mummy '32
They Call It Sin '32
Three Broadway Girls '32
Beauty and the Boss '33
The Death Kiss '33
Torch Singer '33
The Black Cat '34
The Mystery of Edwin Drood '35

Sheila Manners (1911-2003)
See Sheila Mannors

Lucie Mannheim (1899-1976)
The 39 Steps '35
East Meets West '36
High Command '37
Bunny Lake Is Missing '65

Ettore Manni (1927-79)
Attila '54
Two Nights with Cleopatra '54
Giants of Rome '63
Gold for the Caesars '63
Hercules and the Captive Women '63
Mademoiselle '66
Untamable Angelique '67
Angelique and the Sultan '68
The Battle of El Alamein '68
Meet Him and Die '76
Street People '76
City of Women '81

Vic Manni
29th Street '91
Trapped in Paradise '94

Sarah Manninen (1977-)
Eternal '04
Touch the Top of the World '06
Never Forget '08

Irene Manning (1912-2004)
The Big Shot '42
Yankee Doodle Dandy '42
The Desert Song '43

Marilyn Manning
Eegah! '62
The Sadist '63

Taryn Manning (1978-)
crazy/beautiful '01
Crossroads '02
8 Mile '02
Cold Mountain '03
A Lot Like Love '05
Hustle & Flow '05
Banshee '06
The Breed '06
Unbeatable Harold '06
Cult '07
Weirdsville '07
Jack and Jill vs. the World '08
The Devil's Tomb '09
The Job '09
Last Resort '09
Love Ranch '10
The Perfect Age of Rock 'n' Roll '10
Redemption Road '10
Waking Madison '10
The Speed of Thought '11
Experimenter '15

Sheila Mannors (1911-2003)
Cocaine Fiends '36
King of the Newsboys '38
Nancy Drew, Reporter '39

Dinah Manoff (1958-)
The Possessed '77
Grease '78
Ordinary People '80
Backfire '88
Child's Play '88
Bloodhounds of Broadway '89
Welcome Home, Roxy Carmichael '90
The Lost Child '00

Miki (Predrag) Manojlovic (1950-)
When Father Was Away on Business '85
Tito and Me '92
Underground '95
Portraits Chinois '96
Artemisia '97
Cabaret Balkan '98
Criminal Lovers '99
Mortal Transfer '01
Irina Palm '07

Grigori Manoukov
Triple Agent '04
Coco Chanel & Igor Stravinsky '09

J.P. Manoux (1969-)
Eurotrip '04
Knocked Up '07
Minutemen '08
Secrets of Eden '12

Jayne Mansfield (1932-67)
Illegal '55
Pete Kelly's Blues '55
The Girl Can't Help It '56
The Burglar '57
Kiss Them for Me '57
The Wayward Bus '57
Will Success Spoil Rock Hunter? '57
The Sheriff of Fractured Jaw '59
It Takes a Thief '60
The Loves of Hercules '60
The George Raft Story '61
Panic Button '62
Promises! Promises! '63
Dog Eat Dog '64
The Fat Spy '66
Las Vegas Hillbillys '66
A Guide for the Married Man '67 (C)
Single Room Furnished '68

Alan Manson (1920-2002)
The Rain People '69
Let's Scare Jessica to Death '71
Whiffs '75

Amy Manson
Blood Monkey '07
Pumpkinhead 4: Blood Feud '07
Edie '19

Ted Manson (1926-2008)
Gordy '95
Crystal River '08

Paul Mantee (1931-2013)
Robinson Crusoe on Mars '64
The Manitou '78
Lurking Fear '94

Gina Mantegna (1990-)
Uncle Nino '03
In the Land of Women '06
Unaccompanied Minors '06
The Neighbor '07

Joe Mantegna (1947-)
Elvis: The Movie '79
Second Thoughts '83
Critical Condition '86
The Money Pit '86
Three Amigos '86
House of Games '87
Suspect '87
Things Change '88
Alice '90
The Godfather, Part 3 '90
Bugsy '91
Homicide '91
Queens Logic '91
Body of Evidence '92
Searching for Bobby Fischer '93
Airheads '94
Baby's Day Out '94
State of Emergency '94
Above Suspicion '95
An Eye for an Eye '95
For Better or Worse '95
Forget Paris '95
Albino Alligator '96
Persons Unknown '96
Stephen King's Thinner '96
Underworld '96
Up Close and Personal '96
The Last Don '97
Body and Soul '98
Celebrity '98
For Hire '98
Hoods '98
Jerry and Tom '98
The Last Don 2 '98
The Rat Pack '98
The Wonderful Ice Cream Suit '98
Liberty Heights '99
My Little Assassin '99
The Runner '99
Lakeboat '00 (C)
More Dogs Than Bones '00
Thin Air '00
Turbulence 3: Heavy Metal '00
The Trumpet of the Swan '01 (V)
Women vs. Men '02
Uncle Nino '03
Stateside '04
Edmond '05
The Kid and I '05
Nine Lives '05
Cougar Club '07
Elvis and Annabelle '07
The Simpsons Movie '07 (V)
Hank and Mike '08
The Last Hit Man '08
Redbelt '08
Witless Protection '08
The Assistants '09
Cars 2 '11 (V)
Compulsion '13

Bronwen Mantel
Pin. . . '88
Gothika '03

Henriette Mantel (1958-)
The Brady Bunch Movie '95
A Very Brady Sequel '96

Joe Mantell (1915-2010)
Marty '55
Storm Center '56
The Birds '63
Chinatown '74
The Two Jakes '90

Michael Mantell
Eight Men Out '88
City of Hope '91
The Night We Never Met '93
Chain of Command '00
Gun Shy '00
Secretary '02
Ocean's Thirteen '07

Doreen Mantle (1930-)
The Duchess of Duke Street '78
Late Bloomers '11

Randolph Mantooth (1945-)
Agent Red '00
Fire Serpent '07

Jason Mantzoukas (1972-)
Sleeping with Other People '15
Dirty Grandpa '16
The House '17
The Long Dumb Road '19

Robert Manuel
Rififi '54
Life Is a Bed of Roses '83

Lesley Manville (1956-)
Grown Ups '80
Dance with a Stranger '85
High Hopes '88
High Season '88
Secrets and Lies '95
The Painted Lady '97
Topsy Turvy '99
All or Nothing '02
Plain Jane '02
Perfect Parents '06
Sparkle '07
A Christmas Carol '09 (V)
Another Year '10
Womb '10
An Adventure in Space and Time '13
Romeo & Juliet '13
Maleficent '14
Phantom Thread '17
Hampstead '19
Ordinary Love '20

Linda Manz (1961-)
Days of Heaven '78
Wanderers '79
Out of the Blue '80
Gummo '97

Ralph Manza (1921-2000)
The Hunters '58
Too Soon to Love '60

Dagmar Manzel (1958-)
Coming Out '89
The Mistake '91
John Rabe '09

Alec Mapa (1965-)
Connie and Carla '04
Sharpay's Fabulous Adventure '11

Marla Maples (1963-)
Happiness '98
Black and White '99
Loving Annabelle '06

William Mapother (1965-)
In the Bedroom '01
The Grudge '04
Suspect Zero '04
The Zodiac '05
The Lather Effect '06
Moola '07
Hurt '09
Another Earth '11
Citizen Gangster '11
A Warrior's Heart '11
Drew Peterson: Untouchable '12

Adele Mara (1923-2010)
Robin Hood of Texas '47
Sands of Iwo Jima '49
Curse of the Faceless Man '58

Kate Mara (1983-)
Random Hearts '99
Brokeback Mountain '05
Urban Legends: Bloody Mary '05
We Are Marshall '06
Zoom '06
Full of It '07
Shooter '07
Transsiberian '08
The Open Road '09
Happythankyoumoreplease '10
Iron Man 2 '10
127 Hours '10
Peep World '10
Ironclad '11
10 Years '12
Transcendence '14
Captive '15
Fantastic Four '15
The Martian '15
Man Down '16
Morgan '16
Chappaquiddick '17
The Heyday of the Insensitive Bastards '17
Megan Leavey '17

Mary Mara (1960-)
Love Potion #9 '92
Mr. Saturday Night '92
Bound '96
Lloyd '00
K-PAX '01
Swedish Auto '06

Rooney Mara (1985-)
Dare '09
Tanner Hall '09
The Winning Season '09
A Nightmare on Elm Street '10
The Social Network '10
The Girl With the Dragon Tattoo '11
Ain't Them Bodies Saints '13
Her '13
Side Effects '13
Trash '14
Carol '15
Pan '15
Kubo and the Two Strings '16
Lion '16
The Discovery '17
A Ghost Story '17
Song to Song '17
Una '17
Don't Worry, He Won't Get Far on Foot '18
Mary Magdalene '19

Jean Marais (1913-98)
Beauty and the Beast '46
Orpheus '49
Elena and Her Men '56
Girl in His Pocket '57
White Nights '57
The Testament of Orpheus '59
The Rape of the Sabines '61
Donkey Skin '70
Peau D'Ane '71
Stealing Beauty '96

Josie Maran (1978-)
The Aviator '04
Little Black Book '04
Van Helsing '04
The Gravedancers '06

Arash Marandi
A Girl Walks Home Alone at Night '14
Under the Shadow '16

Laura Marano (1995-)
The Perfect Date '19
Saving Zoe '19

Marcel Marceau (1923-2007)
Barbarella '68
Shanks '74
Silent Movie '76

Sophie Marceau (1966-)
La Boum '81
Fort Saganne '84
Police '85
Revenge of the Musketeers '94
Beyond the Clouds '95
Braveheart '95
Anna Karenina '96
Firelight '97
Lost and Found '99
William Shakespeare's A Midsummer Night's Dream '99
The World Is Not Enough '99
Belphegor: Phantom of the Louvre '01
Alex & Emma '03

Elspeth March (1911-99)
Quo Vadis '51
Roman Spring of Mrs. Stone '61
The Three Lives of Thomasina '63 (V)
Psyche 59 '64
Woman Times Seven '67
Goodbye, Mr. Chips '69

Fredric March (1897-1975)
Dr. Jekyll and Mr. Hyde '32
Merrily We Go to Hell '32
Smilin' Through '32
Design for Living '33
The Eagle and the Hawk '33
The Sign of the Cross '33
The Barretts of Wimpole Street '34
Death Takes a Holiday '34
We Live Again '34
Anna Karenina '35
Les Miserables '35
Anthony Adverse '36
Mary of Scotland '36
The Road to Glory '36
Nothing Sacred '37
A Star Is Born '37
Susan and God '40
One Foot in Heaven '41
So Ends Our Night '41
The Adventures of Mark Twain '44
Tomorrow the World '44
The Best Years of Our Lives '46
Christopher Columbus '49
Death of a Salesman '51
It's a Big Country '51
Man on a Tightrope '53
Executive Suite '54
Alexander the Great '55
The Bridges at Toko-Ri '55
Desperate Hours '55
The Man in the Gray Flannel Suit '56
Middle of the Night '59
Inherit the Wind '60
Seven Days in May '64
Hombre '67
Tick... Tick... Tick '70
The Iceman Cometh '73

Jane March (1973-)
The Lover '92
Color of Night '94
Provocateur '96
Circle of Passion '97
Tarzan and the Lost City '98
Dracula: The Dark Prince '01
The Stone Merchant '06
Grimm's Snow White '12
Jack the Giant Killer '13
The Sweeter Side of Life '13

Stephanie March (1974-)
Head of State '03
Mr. & Mrs. Smith '05
Falling for Grace '06
Flannel Pajamas '06
Jesse Stone: Night Passage '06
The Treatment '06
The Invention of Lying '09

Georges Marchal (1920-97)
Death in the Garden '56
The Colossus of Rhodes '61
Ulysses Against the Son of Hercules '61
Belle de Jour '67

Corinne Marchand (1937-)
Cleo from 5 to 7 '61
Borsalino '70

Guy Marchand (1937-)
Cousin, Cousine '76
Loulou '80
Coup de Torchon '81
Entre-Nous '83
New World '95
Inside Paris '06
Paid '06
Apres Lui '07

Nancy Marchand (1928-2000)
The Hospital '71
Killjoy '81
Agatha Christie's Sparkling Cyanide '83
The Bostonians '84
North and South Book 2 '86
The Naked Gun: From the Files of Police Squad '88
Regarding Henry '91
Brain Donors '92
Sabrina '95
Dear God '96

Josh Marchette (1973-)
Floating '97
Tequila Body Shots '99

Ron Marchini (1945-)
Death Machines '76
Omega Cop '90
Karate Cop '91

David Marciano (1960-)
Harlem Nights '89
Kiss Shot '89
The Last Don '97
The Last Don 2 '98
Few Options '11

Vanessa Marcil (1968-)
The Rock '96
Nice Guys Sleep Alone '99
Code Hunter '02
The Nanny Express '08
The Bannen Way '10

Joseph Marco
Gladiators 7 '62
The Invincible Gladiator '62

Paul Marco (1927-2006)
Bride of the Monster '55
Plan 9 from Outer Space '56
Night of the Ghouls '59

Andre Marcon (1948-)
Jeanne la Pucelle '94
Les Destinees '00
La Vie Promise '02
Around a Small Mountain '09
Rapt '09
Marguerite '16
Things to Come '16

Saverio Marconi
Padre Padrone '77
Contraband '80

Lisa Marcos (1982-)
Diary of a Mad Black Woman '05
King's Ransom '05

Ted Marcoux (1962-)
Ghost in the Machine '93
The Nightman '93
Andersonville '95

Andrea Marcovicci (1948-)
Cry Rape! '73
Smile Jenny, You're Dead '74
The Front '76
The Concorde: Airport '79 '79
The Hand '81
Spacehunter: Adventures in the Forbidden Zone '83
The Stuff '85
The Canterville Ghost '86
Someone to Love '87

Jack the Bear '93
Irene in Time '09

James A. Marcus (1867-1937)
Oliver Twist '22
The Eagle '25
The Texas Streak '26
Sadie Thompson '28
Billy the Kid '30

Jeff Marcus (1960-)
Alien Nation: Dark Horizon '94
Alien Nation: Millennium '96

Rachel Marcus
Booky's Crush '09
The Devil's Teardrop '10
The Dogfather '10

Richard Marcus (1945-)
Enemy Mine '85
Deadly Friend '86
Cannibal Campout '88

Stephen Marcus (1962-)
Lock, Stock and 2 Smoking Barrels '98
Sorted '04
The Greatest Game Ever Played '05
Interview With a Hitman '12

Jordan Marder (1973-)
Lord of Illusions '95
American History X '98

Tom Mardirosian (1947-)
Presumed Innocent '90
The Dark Half '91

Ivano Marescotti (1946-)
The Monster '96
King Arthur '04
The Moon & the Stars '07

Bam Margera (1979-)
Jackass: The Movie '02
Jackass Number Two '06
Jackass 3D '10

Margo (1917-85)
Winterset '36
Lost Horizon '37
The Leopard Man '43
Viva Zapata! '52
I'll Cry Tomorrow '55
Who's Got the Action? '63

Janet Margolin (1943-93)
David and Lisa '62
Morituri '65
Nevada Smith '66
Take the Money and Run '69
Planet Earth '74
Annie Hall '77
Last Embrace '79
The Triangle Factory Fire Scandal '79
Distant Thunder '88
Ghostbusters 2 '89
Murder C.O.D. '90

Stuart Margolin (1940-)
Kelly's Heroes '70
Death Wish '74
The Big Bus '76
Futureworld '76
Days of Heaven '78
S.O.B. '81
Class '83
A Killer in the Family '83
Running Hot '83
A Fine Mess '86
Iron Eagle 2 '88
Guilty by Suspicion '91
Impolite '92
To Grandmother's House We Go '94

Mark Margolis (1939-)
Scarface '83
Descending Angel '90
Where the Rivers Flow North '94
Pi '98
Jakob the Liar '99
The Thomas Crown Affair '99
Dinner Rush '00
The Tailor of Panama '00
Hardball '01
Headspace '02

Infested: Invasion of the Killer Bugs '02
2B Perfectly Honest '04
Stay '05
The Fountain '06
The Courier '12
Stand Up Guys '12
Noah '14
Nasty Baby '15
My Big Fat Greek Wedding 2 '16

Miriam Margolyes (1941-)
I Love You to Death '90
The Butcher's Wife '91
The Age of Innocence '93
Ed and His Dead Mother '93
Cold Comfort Farm '94
Immortal Beloved '94
Babe '95 (V)
Balto '95 (V)
Different for Girls '96
James and the Giant Peach '96 (V)
William Shakespeare's Romeo and Juliet '96
Mulan '98 (V)
Dreaming of Joseph Lees '99
End of Days '99
Sunshine '99
Vanity Fair '99
Cats & Dogs '01
Harry Potter and the Chamber of Secrets '02
Being Julia '04
Chasing Liberty '04
Ladies in Lavender '04
Modigliani '04
Flushed Away '06 (V)
Happy Feet '06 (V)
The Dukes '07
How to Lose Friends & Alienate People '08
Blind Revenge '10
Legend of the Guardians: The Owls of Ga'Hoole '10 (V)
The Man Who Invented Christmas '17

David Margulies (1937-)
All That Jazz '79
Dressed to Kill '80
Ghostbusters '84
9 1/2 Weeks '86
Running on Empty '88
Ghostbusters 2 '89
Funny About Love '90
Last Breath '96
Looking for an Echo '99
Bought and Sold '03
Roadie '11
The Girl On the Train '13

Julianna Margulies (1966-)
Out for Justice '91
Traveller '96
The Newton Boys '97
Paradise Road '97
A Price Above Rubies '97
The Big Day '99
Dinosaur '00 (V)
What's Cooking? '00
The Man from Elysian Fields '01
Mists of Avalon '01
Evelyn '02
Ghost Ship '02
Hitler: The Rise of Evil '03
Beautiful Ohio '06
The Darwin Awards '06
Snakes on a Plane '06
City Island '09
Stand Up Guys '12

Ali Marhyar
Black Heaven '10
Elles '11
As Above, So Below '14

A. L. Mariaux (1930-2013)
See Jess (Jesus) Franco

Constance Marie (1965-)
My Family '94
Selena '96
The Last Marshal '99
Tortilla Soup '01
Puss in Boots '11 (V)

Lisa Marie (1968-)
Dead and Buried '81
Ed Wood '94
Mars Attacks! '96
Breast Men '97
Frogs for Snakes '98
Sleepy Hollow '99
Tail Lights Fade '99
The Beatnicks '00
Silent Night '12
We are Still Here '15

Jean-Pierre Marielle (1932-)
The Women '68
Four Flies on Grey Velvet '72
Coup de Torchon '81
Menage '86
Tous les Matins du Monde '92
La Petite Lili '03
The Da Vinci Code '06
Micmacs '09
Phantom Boy '16

Eli Marienthal (1986-)
Jack Frost '98
Slums of Beverly Hills '98
American Pie '99
The Iron Giant '99 (V)
American Pie 2 '01
Jay and Silent Bob Strike Back '01
The Country Bears '02
Confessions of a Teenage Drama Queen '04

Cheech Marin (1946-)
Expecting a Miracle '09
The Perfect Game '09
Pure Country 2: The Gift '10
Cars 2 '11 (V)
Hoodwinked Too! Hood *vs.* Evil '11 (V)
Cheech & Chong's Animated Movie! '13 (V)

Jacques Marin (1919-2001)
Forbidden Games '52
Duke of the Derby '62
The Train '65
How to Steal a Million '66
The Night of the Following Day '69
Darling Lili '70
Shaft in Africa '73
The Island at the Top of the World '74

Richard 'Cheech' Marin (1946-)
Cheech and Chong's Up in Smoke '79
Cheech and Chong's Next Movie '80
Cheech and Chong's Nice Dreams '81
Cheech and Chong: Things Are Tough All Over '82
Cheech and Chong: Still Smokin' '83
Yellowbeard '83
Cheech and Chong's The Corsican Brothers '84
After Hours '85 (C)
Echo Park '86
Born in East L.A. '87
Fatal Beauty '87
Oliver & Company '88 (V)
Far Out Man '89
Ghostbusters 2 '89
The Shrimp on the Barbie '90
Ferngully: The Last Rain Forest '92 (V)
Ring of the Musketeers '93
Charlie's Ghost: The Secret of Coronado '94
The Cisco Kid '94
The Lion King '94 (V)
A Million to Juan '94 (C)
Desperado '95
From Dusk Till Dawn '95
The Great White Hype '96
Tin Cup '96
Paulie '98
Luminarias '99
Picking Up the Pieces '99
Spy Kids '01

Spy Kids 2: The Island of Lost Dreams '02
Good Boy! '03 (V)
Once Upon a Time in Mexico '03
Spy Kids 3-D: Game Over '03
Christmas With the Kranks '04
The Lion King 1 1/2 '04 (V)
Underclassman '05
Cars '06 (V)
Beverly Hills Chihuahua '08 (V)
Race to Witch Mountain '09
Machete '10
Toy Story 3 '10 (V)

Rikki Marin
Cheech and Chong: Things Are Tough All Over '82
Cheech and Chong's The Corsican Brothers '84

Ed Marinaro (1950-)
Queens Logic '91
Lethal Lolita-Amy Fisher: My Story '92
Panic in the Skies '96
Deadly Game '98
Urban Legends: Bloody Mary '05
Yeti '08
An L.A. Minute '18

Anamaria Marinca (1978-)
4 Months, 3 Weeks and 2 Days '07
The Last Enemy '08
The Countess '09
Five Minutes of Heaven '09
Europa Report '13
The Girl with All the Gifts '17

Sonny Marinelli (1967-)
Boss of Bosses '99
Dot.Kill '05

Ethier Crispin Marini (1893-1953)
See Chris-Pin (Ethier Crispin Martini) Martin

Ken Marino (1968-)
Prince of the City '81
Alphabet City '84
Joe Somebody '01
Love for Rent '05
Diggers '06
The Ten '07
Role Models '08
Wanderlust '12
In a World... '13
Veronica Mars '14
Goosebumps '15

George F. Marion, Sr. (1860-1945)
Anna Christie '23
Evangeline '29
Anna Christie '30
The Big House '30
Hook, Line and Sinker '30
Death from a Distance '36

Paul Marion (1915-2011)
So Dark the Night '46
Fury of the Congo '51
Harem Girl '52
Fort Vengeance '53

Howard Marion-Crawford (1914-69)
The Singing Princess '49
Paid to Kill '54
The Face of Fu Manchu '65
The Castle of Fu Manchu '68
The Charge of the Light Brigade '68
Kiss and Kill '68

Mona Maris (1903-91)
Seas Beneath '31
The Passionate Plumber '32
Kiss and Make Up '34
Love on the Run '36
Underground '41
Berlin Correspondent '42
A Date With the Falcon '42
I Married an Angel '42
The Falcon in Mexico '44
Heartbeat '46

The Smiling Ghost '41
Captains of the Clouds '42
You Can't Escape Forever '42
Background to Danger '43
The Constant Nymph '43
Paris After Dark '43
Strange Impersonation '46
Whispering Smith '48

Bryan Marshall (1938-2019)
Mosquito Squadron '70
The Long Good Friday '80
Return to Snowy River '88

Connie Marshall (1933-2001)
Sunday Dinner for a Soldier '44
Wake Up and Dream '46
Daisy Kenyon '47
Mother Wore Tights '47
The Green Promise '49
Kill the Umpire '50

David Anthony Marshall
Another 48 Hrs. '90
The Demolitionist '95

Dodie Marshall
Spinout '66
Easy Come, Easy Go '67

Don Marshall (1936-)
The Thing with Two Heads '72
Terminal Island '73

E.G. Marshall (1910-98)
13 Rue Madeleine '46
Call Northside 777 '48
Broken Lance '54
The Caine Mutiny '54
Pushover '54
The Silver Chalice '54
The Left Hand of God '55
The Mountain '56
Twelve Angry Men '57
The Buccaneer '58
Compulsion '59
The Journey '59
Cash McCall '60
Town without Pity '61
The Chase '66
Is Paris Burning? '66
The Poppy Is Also a Flower '66
The Bridge at Remagen '69
The Littlest Angel '69
The Pursuit of Happiness '70
Tora! Tora! Tora! '70
Pursuit '72
Interiors '78
The Lazarus Syndrome '79
Superman 2 '80
Creepshow '82
Eleanor: First Lady of the World '82
Kennedy '83
My Chauffeur '86
Power '86
Saigon: Year of the Cat '87
National Lampoon's Christmas Vacation '89
Two Evil Eyes '90
Consenting Adults '92
Russian Roulette '93
Stephen King's The Tommyknockers '93
Nixon '95
Oldest Confederate Widow Tells All '95
Absolute Power '97
Miss Evers' Boys '97

Garry Marshall (1934-2016)
Lost in America '85
Jumpin' Jack Flash '86 (C)
Soapdish '91
A League of Their Own '92
Hocus Pocus '93 (C)
Dear God '96 (C)
The Twilight of the Golds '97
Never Been Kissed '99
Forever Together '00
The Hollywood Sign '01 (C)
Orange County '02
Devil's Knight '03
Chicken Little '05 (V)
Keeping Up with the Steins '06
Finding Bliss '09
Race to Witch Mountain '09

Herbert Marshall (1890-1966)
The Letter '29
Murder '30
Blonde Venus '32
Trouble in Paradise '32
Four Frightened People '34
The Painted Veil '34
Riptide '34
The Good Fairy '35
Girl's Dormitory '36
If You Could Only Cook '36
A Woman Rebels '36
Angel '37
Breakfast for Two '37
Always Goodbye '38
Mad About Music '38
Foreign Correspondent '40
The Letter '40
Adventure in Washington '41
Kathleen '41
The Little Foxes '41
When Ladies Meet '41
Forever and a Day '43
The Moon and Sixpence '43
Young Ideas '43
Andy Hardy's Blonde Trouble '44
The Enchanted Cottage '45
Crack-Up '46
Duel in the Sun '46
The Razor's Edge '46
High Wall '47
The Secret Garden '49
The Underworld Story '50
Angel Face '52
The Black Shield of Falworth '54
GOG '54
The Virgin Queen '55
The Weapon '56
The Fly '58
A Fever In the Blood '61
The Caretakers '63
The Third Day '65

James Marshall (1967-)
A Few Good Men '92
Gladiator '92
Twin Peaks: Fire Walk with Me '92
Don't Do It '94
Vibrations '94
Soccer Dog: The Movie '98
Luck of the Draw '00
The Shaft '01
Alien Lockdown '04
Come as You Are '05

Ken Marshall (1950-)
The Skin '81
Krull '83
Feds '88

Kris Marshall (1973-)
Deathwatch '02
The Four Feathers '02
Doctor Zhivago '03
Love Actually '03
The Merchant of Venice '04
Death at a Funeral '07
Easy Virtue '08
A Few Best Men '11

Marion Marshall (1929-)
I Was a Male War Bride '49
The Stooge '51
Sailor Beware '52

Paula Marshall (1964-)
Hellraiser 3: Hell on Earth '92
Warlock: The Armageddon '93
The New Age '94
A Family Thing '96
That Old Feeling '96
A Gun, a Car, a Blonde '97
Cheaper by the Dozen '03
I Know Who Killed Me '07

Penny Marshall (1943-)
Evil Roy Slade '71
More Than Friends '78
Movers and Shakers '85
The Hard Way '91
Hocus Pocus '93 (C)
Get Shorty '95 (C)
Stateside '04
Looking for Comedy in the Muslim World '06
Alice Upside Down '07
Everybody Wants to Be Italian '08

Peter Marshall (1926-)
Return of Jesse James '50
The Rookie '59
A Guide for the Married Woman '78
Americathon '79 (C)

Sarah Marshall (1933-2014)
Lord Love a Duck '66
The People vs. Jean Harris '81
French Silk '94

Trudy Marshall (1920-2004)
The Fighting Sullivans '42
Crash Dive '43
Key Witness '47
Mark of the Gorilla '58

Tully Marshall (1864-1943)
Broken Hearts of Broadway '23
He Who Gets Slapped '24
The Merry Widow '25
Smouldering Fires '25
Torrent '26
Twinkletoes '26
The Cat and the Canary '27
The Trail of '98 '28
Queen Kelly '29
The Big Trail '30
One Night at Susie's '30
Fighting Caravans '31
The Beast of the City '32
Red Dust '32
Strangers of the Evening '32
Corruption '33
This Gun for Hire '42

William Marshall (1917-94)
Tomorrow We Live '42
State Fair '45
That Brennan Girl '46

William Marshall (1924-2003)
Demetrius and the Gladiators '54
The Boston Strangler '68
ZigZag '70
Blacula '72
Scream Blacula Scream '73

Logan Marshall-Green (1976-)
Devil '10
Prometheus '12
Cold Comes the Night '14
Madame Bovary '15
The Invitation '16
Upgrade '18

Christina Marsillach (1963-)
Every Time We Say Goodbye '86
Opera '88

James Marsters (1962-)
Strange Frequency 2 '01
P.S. I Love You '07
Shadow Puppets '07
The Capture of the Green River Killer '08
Dragonball: Evolution '09
High Plains Invaders '09
A Bread Factory, Part One '18
A Bread Factory, Part Two '18

Nathaniel Marston (1975-)
Love Is All There Is '96
Ordinary Sinner '02

Lynn(e) Marta (1946-)
Joe Kidd '72
Richard Petty Story '72
Genesis II '73

Judy Marte (1983-)
Raising Victor Vargas '03
On the Outs '05

Henri Marteau (1933-2005)
La Femme Infidele '69
Indochine '92

K.C. Martel (1967-)
The Amityville Horror '79
The Munsters' Revenge '81
E.T.: The Extra-Terrestrial '82
White Water Summer '87

Chris Martell
Gruesome Twosome '67
Flesh Feast '69
Scream, Baby, Scream '69

Donna Martell (1927-)
Abbott and Costello Meet the Killer, Boris Karloff '49
Elephant Stampede '51
Give a Girl a Break '53
Ten Wanted Men '54

Gillian Martell
Oliver Twist '85
Cause Celebre '87

Jaeden Martell
The Lodge '19
Low Tide '19

Pietro Martellanza
Lola Colt '67
Ringo, the Lone Rider '68

Cynthia Martells
A Modern Affair '94
Broken Trust '95
The Wood '99
Paid in Full '02

Barbara Marten
The Debt '03
Florence Nightingale '08

Mona Martenson
The Atonement of Gosta Berling '24
Laila '29

Francois Marthouret (1943-)
Sitcom '97
The Lady and the Duke '01
La Petite Jerusalem '05

Andrea Martin (1947-)
Black Christmas '75
Club Paradise '86
Worth Winning '89
Too Much Sun '90
All I Want for Christmas '91
Gypsy '93
Ted & Venus '93 (C)
Bogus '96
Wag the Dog '97
The Secret of NIMH 2 '98 (V)
Believe '99
Hedwig and the Angry Inch '00
Loser '00
All Over the Guy '01
Jimmy Neutron: Boy Genius '01 (V)
My Big Fat Greek Wedding '02
New York Minute '04
The Producers '05
Black Christmas '06
Brother Bear 2 '06 (V)
St. Urbain's Horseman '07
Breaking Upwards '09
Diane '18

Andrew Martin
Hallowed '05
Medium Raw: Night of the Wolf '10

Anna Maxwell Martin (1977-)
Bleak House '05
Becoming Jane '07
South Riding '11
The Bletchley Circle '13
Death Comes to Pemberley '13

Barney Martin (1923-2005)
Arthur '81
Arthur 2: On the Rocks '88

Chris-Pin (Ethier Crispin Martini) Martin (1893-1953)
The California Trail '33
The Texans '38
The Cisco Kid and the Lady '39
Stagecoach '39
Charlie Chan in Panama '40
Down Argentine Way '40
Rimfire '49

Chris William Martin (1975-)
Emile '03
The Terrorist Next Door '08
The Unquiet '08

Christopher Martin (1962-)
House Party '90
Class Act '91
House Party 2: The Pajama Jam '91
House Party 3 '94

Damon Martin
Ghoulies 2 '87
Amityville 1992: It's About Time '92

Dan Martin (1951-)
Sleepwalkers '92
Groom Lake '02

Dean Martin (1917-95)
My Friend Irma '49
At War with the Army '50
My Friend Irma Goes West '50
The Stooge '51
That's My Boy '51
Jumping Jacks '52
Sailor Beware '52
The Caddy '53
Money from Home '53
The Road to Bali '53
Scared Stiff '53
Living It Up '54
Artists and Models '55
You're Never Too Young '55
Hollywood or Bust '56
Pardners '56
Ten Thousand Bedrooms '57
Some Came Running '58
The Young Lions '58
Career '59
Rio Bravo '59
Bells Are Ringing '60
Ocean's 11 '60
Who Was That Lady? '60
Ada '61
All in a Night's Work '61
Sergeants 3 '62
Four for Texas '63
Toys in the Attic '63
Who's Got the Action? '63
Kiss Me, Stupid! '64
Robin and the 7 Hoods '64
Marriage on the Rocks '65
Sons of Katie Elder '65
Murderers' Row '66
The Silencers '66
Texas Across the River '66
The Ambushers '67
Rough Night in Jericho '67
Bandolero! '68
Five Card Stud '68
The Wrecking Crew '68
Airport '70
Showdown '73
Mr. Ricco '75
Cannonball Run '81
Cannonball Run 2 '84
That's Dancing! '85

Demetri Martin (1973-)
Taking Woodstock '09
Contagion '11
Take Me Home Tonight '11
In a World... '13
Dean '17

Dewey Martin (1923-)
Kansas Raiders '50
The Thing '51
Men of the Fighting Lady '54
Desperate Hours '55
Land of the Pharaohs '55
The Proud and Profane '56
Ten Thousand Bedrooms '57
Savage Sam '63
Seven Alone '75

Dick Martin (1922-2008)
The Glass Bottom Boat '66
Carbon Copy '81
Air Bud 2: Golden Receiver '98
The Trial of Old Drum '00
Bartleby '01

Duane Martin (1965-)
Above the Rim '94
Down Periscope '96
Scream 2 '97
Woo '97
Deliver Us from Eva '03

Duke Martin
Across to Singapore '28
The Lost Zeppelin '29

D'Urville Martin (1938-84)
Watermelon Man '70
Final Comedown '72
Hell Up in Harlem '73
Boss '74
Dolemite '75
Sheba, Baby '75
Death Journey '76
Big Score '83

Edie Martin (1880-1964)
Genevieve '53
The Ladykillers '55

George Martin (1929-2010)
Falling in Love '84
Crossing Delancey '88
Drunks '96
One Fine Day '96

Gilbert Martin
Rob Roy '95
Beautiful People '99

Gregory Mars Martin (1971-)
See Mars Callahan

Helen Martin (1909-2000)
A Hero Ain't Nothin' but a Sandwich '78
Dummy '79
Hollywood Shuffle '87
Doc Hollywood '91
House Party 2: The Pajama Jam '91
Don't Be a Menace to South Central While Drinking Your Juice in the Hood '95
I Got the Hook-Up '98

Ivan Martin
Prey for Rock and Roll '03
Funny Valentine '05
Monogamy '10

Jared Martin (1941-2017)
Second Coming of Suzanne '80
The New Gladiators '83
Quiet Cool '86
Twinsitters '95

Jesse L. Martin (1969-)
Rent '05
The Cake Eaters '07
Peter and Vandy '09
Puncture '11
Joyful Noise '12

John Martin (1951-)
Black Roses '88
The Underneath '95

Jose Martin
Four Dollars of Revenge '66
The Castle of Fu Manchu '68

Justin Martin
Bloody Murder '99
A Raisin in the Sun '08

Kellie Martin (1975-)
Secret Witness '88
Troop Beverly Hills '89
Matinee '92
Christy '94
A Goofy Movie '94 (V)
Hidden in Silence '96
Mystery Woman: Mystery Weekend '05
No Brother of Mine '07
The Jensen Project '10
Smooch '11
The Christmas Ornament '13
Dear Viola '14

Kiel Martin (1944-90)
Panic in Needle Park '71
Trick Baby '72
Child Bride of Short Creek '81

Lewis Martin (1894-1969)
Ace in the Hole '51
No Escape '53
The War of the Worlds '53
Men of the Fighting Lady '54

Lock Martin (1916-59)
The Day the Earth Stood Still '51
Invaders from Mars '53

Marion Martin (1918-85)
The Man in the Iron Mask '39
Big Store '41
The Mexican Spitfire's Baby '41
Mexican Spitfire at Sea '42
The Great Mike '44

Mary Martin (1913-90)
Rhythm on the River '40
Birth of the Blues '41
Star Spangled Rhythm '42
Night and Day '46
Peter Pan '60

Meaghan Jette Martin
Camp Rock '08
Dear Lemon Lima '09
Camp Rock 2: The Final Jam '10

Mel Martin (1947-)
Love for Lydia '79
White Hunter, Black Heart '90
Poldark '96

Millicent Martin (1934-)
Libel '59
Invasion Quartet '61
Those Magnificent Men in Their Flying Machines '65
Alfie '66
Mrs. Palfrey at the Claremont '05
Return to Halloweentown '06

Nan Martin (1927-2010)
The Mugger '58
Toys in the Attic '63
For Love of Ivy '68
Goodbye, Columbus '69
The Young Nurses '73
A Nightmare on Elm Street 3: Dream Warriors '87
Proud Men '87
Big Eden '00
Cast Away '00
Shallow Hal '01
The Song of the Lark '01

Pamela Sue Martin (1953-)
Our Time '74
Lady in Red '79
Torchlight '85
Eye of the Demon '87
A Cry in the Wild '90

Pepper Martin (1936-)
Angels from Hell '68
The Longest Yard '74
Scream '83

Richard Martin (1917-94)
West of the Pecos '45
The Bamboo Blonde '46
Four Fast Guns '59

Ross Martin (1920-81)
Conquest of Space '55
Colossus of New York '58
Experiment in Terror '62
The Ceremony '63
Dying Room Only '73
Wild, Wild West Revisited '79
More Wild, Wild West '80

Rudolf Martin (1967-)
Fall '97
Bedazzled '00
Dracula: The Dark Prince '01
Swordfish '01
The Home Front '02
River's End '05
Hyenas '10

Sandy Martin (1950-)
Vendetta '85
Barfly '87
Sparkler '99

Skip Martin (1928-84)
Masque of the Red Death '65
Horror Hospital '73

Sonequa Martin
Toe to Toe '09
Yelling to the Sky '11

Stacy Martin (1991-)
Nymphomaniac, Volume 1 '13
The Childhood of a Leader '16
The Lady in the Car with Glasses and a Gun '16
Vox Lux '18

Steve Martin (1945-)
Sgt. Pepper's Lonely Hearts Club Band '78
The Jerk '79
The Kids Are Alright '79
The Muppet Movie '79 (C)
Pennies from Heaven '81
Dead Men Don't Wear Plaid '82
The Man with Two Brains '83
All of Me '84
The Lonely Guy '84
Movers and Shakers '85
Little Shop of Horrors '86
Three Amigos '86
Planes, Trains & Automobiles '87
Roxanne '87
Dirty Rotten Scoundrels '88
Parenthood '89
My Blue Heaven '90
Father of the Bride '91
Grand Canyon '91
L.A. Story '91
Housesitter '92
Leap of Faith '92
And the Band Played On '93 (C)
Mixed Nuts '94
A Simple Twist of Fate '94
Father of the Bride Part 2 '95
Sgt. Bilko '95
The Spanish Prisoner '97
Prince of Egypt '98 (V)
Bowfinger '99
The Out-of-Towners '99
Joe Gould's Secret '00
Novocaine '01
Bringing Down the House '03
Cheaper by the Dozen '03
Looney Tunes: Back in Action '03
Cheaper by the Dozen 2 '05
Jiminy Glick in LaLa Wood '05 (C)
Shopgirl '05
The Pink Panther '06
Baby Mama '08
It's Complicated '09
The Pink Panther 2 '09
The Big Year '11
Home '15 (V)
Love the Coopers '15 (V)

Strother Martin (1919-80)
The Asphalt Jungle '50
Rhubarb '51
Kiss Me Deadly '55
Attack! '56
Black Patch '57
The Horse Soldiers '59
The Man Who Shot Liberty Valance '62
McLintock! '63
Invitation to a Gunfighter '64
Shenandoah '65
Cool Hand Luke '67
Butch Cassidy and the Sundance Kid '69
True Grit '69
The Wild Bunch '69
Ballad of Cable Hogue '70
The Brotherhood of Satan '71
Hannie Caulder '72
Pocket Money '72
Sssssss '73
Hard Times '75
Rooster Cogburn '75
Slap Shot '77
The Champ '79
Cheech and Chong's Up in Smoke '79
Love and Bullets '79
Nightwing '79
The Villain '79

Tony Martin (1912-2012)
Pigskin Parade '36
You Can't Have Everything '37
Kentucky Moonshine '38
Sally, Irene and Mary '38
Music in My Heart '40
Big Store '41
Ziegfeld Girl '41
Till the Clouds Roll By '46
Two Tickets to Broadway '51
Easy to Love '53
Here Come the Girls '53
Hit the Deck '55
Quincannon, Frontier Scout '56

Tony (Anthony) Martin (1953-)
A Cry in the Dark '88
The Interview '98
Inspector Gadget 2 '02
The Incredible Journey of Mary Bryant '05
Candy '06

Margo Martindale (1951-)
Lorenzo's Oil '92
Nobody's Fool '94
Dead Man Walking '95
Ghosts of Mississippi '96
Marvin's Room '96
Critical Care '97
Eye of God '97
In Dreams '98
Twilight '98
Earthly Possessions '99
Ride with the Devil '99
Proof of Life '00
28 Days '00
The Hours '02
The Human Stain '03
It's All About Love '03
An Unexpected Love '03
Million Dollar Baby '04
Paris, je t'aime '06
Wedding Daze '06
Rails & Ties '07
Rocket Science '07
Superheroes '07
Walk Hard: The Dewey Cox Story '07
Management '09
Orphan '09
The Winning Season '09
Main Street '10
Secretariat '10
Win Win '11
August: Osage County '13
Beautiful Creatures '13
Bluebird '13
Heaven Is for Real '14
The Hollars '16
Blow The Man Down '19

Edward Martindel (1876-1955)
The Duchess of Buffalo '26
The Singing Fool '28
Why Be Good? '29
Golden Dawn '30

Daniel Martine
Cause of Death '90
Time Barbarians '90

Elsa Martinelli (1935-)
The Indian Fighter '55
Blood and Roses '61
Hatari! '62
Rampage '63
The Trial '63
The V.I.P.'s '63
Hail Mafia '65
10th Victim '65
Madigan's Millions '67
Maroc 7 '67
Woman Times Seven '67
Candy '68
Manon '68

Belle Starr '79
Once Upon a Crime '92

Alessandra Martines (1963-)
And Now Ladies and Gentlemen '02
Towards Zero '07

A. Martinez (1948-)
The Cowboys '72
Once Upon a Scoundrel '73
The Take '74
Joe Panther '76
Centennial '78
Born in East L.A. '87
Powwow Highway '89
She-Devil '89
One Night Stand '95
The Cherokee Kid '96
Wind River '98
A Memory In My Heart '99
What's Cooking? '00
Ordinary Sinner '02
Killer Instinct: From the Files of Agent Candice DeLong '03
Once Upon a Wedding '05
Little Girl Lost: The Delimar Vera Story '08
The Terminators '09
Mega Python Vs. Gatoroid '11

Adrian Martinez
Corn '04
Mail Order Wife '04
Just Like the Son '06
Casa de mi Padre '12
Focus '15
White Girl '16

Benito Martinez (1971-)
Kill Your Darlings '06
Not Forgotten '09
The Dry Land '10
Mandrake '10
Bless Me, Ultima '13

Fele Martinez (1975-)
Open Your Eyes '97
Lovers of the Arctic Circle '98
Darkness '02
Bad Education '04

Joaquin Martinez (1932-2012)
Jeremiah Johnson '72
The Cowboy Way '94

Nacho Martinez (1952-96)
Law of Desire '86
Matador '86

Nathalia Martinez
Terranova '91
Death Race '08

Olivier Martinez (1966-)
The Horseman on the Roof '95
The Chambermaid on the Titanic '97
Before Night Falls '00
Angel of Death '02
Unfaithful '02
The Roman Spring of Mrs. Stone '03
S.W.A.T. '03
Taking Lives '04
Blood & Chocolate '07
Cybergeddon '12
Dark Tide '12
Paul, Apostle of Christ '18

Petra Martinez (1940-)
Bad Education '04
Sleep Tight '11

Raul Martinez
The Damned '06
Illegal Business '06

Vanessa Martinez (1979-)
Limbo '99
Casa de los Babys '03

Vincent Martinez
Confusion of Genders '00
Twisted Souls '05

Maximillian Martini (1969-)
Saving Private Ryan '98
Caught in the Act '04

The Great Raid '05
Redbelt '08
Mandrake '10
Colombiana '11
He Loves Me '11
Sabotage '14
Eli '19

Steven Martini (1978-)
Major Payne '95
Smiling Fish & Goat on Fire '99

Susanna Martinkova (1946-)
Diary of a Rebel '68
Ring of Death '69

Al Martino (1927-2009)
The Godfather '72
The Godfather, Part 3 '90

Orlando Martins (1899-1985)
Simba '55
Call Me Bwana '63

Christian Martyn (2000-)
Home Alone: The Holiday Heist '12
Be My Valentine '13

Peter Martyn (1925-55)
Mad About Men '54
No Smoking '55

Elizabeth Marvel (1969-)
Burn After Reading '08
Pretty Bird '08
A Dog Year '09
Holy Rollers '10
True Grit '10
The Congressman '16
The Phenom '16
The Meyerowitz Stories (New and Selected) '17
Swallow '20

Lee Marvin (1924-87)
Union Station '50
Duel at Silver Creek '52
Eight Iron Men '52
Hangman's Knot '52
We're Not Married '52
The Big Heat '53
The Glory Brigade '53
Gun Fury '53
Seminole '53
The Stranger Wore a Gun '53
Bad Day at Black Rock '54
The Caine Mutiny '54
The Wild One '54
I Died a Thousand Times '55
Pete Kelly's Blues '55
Shack Out on 101 '55
Violent Saturday '55
Attack! '56
Pillars of the Sky '56
The Rack '56
7 Men From Now '56
Raintree County '57
Missouri Traveler '58
The Comancheros '61
The Man Who Shot Liberty Valance '62
Donovan's Reef '63
The Killers '64
Cat Ballou '65
Ship of Fools '65
The Professionals '66
The Dirty Dozen '67
The Meanest Men in the West '67
Point Blank '67
Hell in the Pacific '69
Paint Your Wagon '69
Monte Walsh '70
Pocket Money '72
Prime Cut '72
Emperor of the North Pole '73
The Iceman Cometh '73
The Klansman '74
The Spikes Gang '74
Great Scout & Cathouse Thursday '76
Avalanche Express '79
The Big Red One '80
Death Hunt '81
Dog Day '83
Gorky Park '83

The Dirty Dozen: The Next Mission '85
Delta Force '86

Brett Marx (1964-)
The Bad News Bears '76
The Bad News Bears in Breaking Training '77
The Bad News Bears Go to Japan '78

Chico Marx (1886-1961)
The Cocoanuts '29
Animal Crackers '30
Monkey Business '31
Horse Feathers '32
Duck Soup '33
A Night at the Opera '35
A Day at the Races '37
Room Service '38
At the Circus '39
Go West '40
Big Store '41
A Night in Casablanca '46
Love Happy '50

Groucho Marx (1890-1977)
The Cocoanuts '29
Animal Crackers '30
Monkey Business '31
Horse Feathers '32
Duck Soup '33
A Night at the Opera '35
A Day at the Races '37
Room Service '38
At the Circus '39
Go West '40
Big Store '41
A Night in Casablanca '46
Copacabana '47
Love Happy '50
Double Dynamite '51
Story of Mankind '57
Will Success Spoil Rock Hunter? '57 (C)
Skidoo '68

Harpo Marx (1888-1964)
The Cocoanuts '29
Animal Crackers '30
Monkey Business '31
Horse Feathers '32
Duck Soup '33
A Night at the Opera '35
A Day at the Races '37
Room Service '38
At the Circus '39
Go West '40
Big Store '41
Stage Door Canteen '43
A Night in Casablanca '46
Love Happy '50
Story of Mankind '57

Zeppo Marx (1901-79)
The Cocoanuts '29
Animal Crackers '30
Monkey Business '31
Horse Feathers '32
Duck Soup '33

Franca Marzi (1926-89)
Island Monster '53
Nights of Cabiria '57

Ron Masak (1936-)
Tora! Tora! Tora! '70
Harper Valley P.T.A. '78

Masako (1964-2015)
Ringu '98
Ringu 2 '99
Ringu 0 '01

Tohoru Masamune
Warbirds '08
Teenage Mutant Ninja Turtles '14

Masasa
Kingdom Come '01
Team America: World Police '04 (V)

Pierrino Mascarino
Summer Rental '85
Timekeeper '98
Uncle Nino '03

Marino (Martin) Mase (1939-)
Les Carabiniers '63
The Boss '73
Zorro '74

Kidnap Syndicate *'76*
Live Like a Cop, Die Like a Man *'76*
The Belly of an Architect *'91*

Vladimir Mashkov (1963-)
The Thief *'97*
Dancing at the Blue Iguana *'00*
Behind Enemy Lines *'01*
The Quickie *'01*
The Edge *'10*
Mission: Impossible-Ghost Protocol *'11*
The Duelist *'16*

Corinne Masiero
Rust and Bone *'12*
Queens of the Ring *'13*

Giulietta Masina (1921-94)
Variety Lights *'51*
The White Sheik *'52*
La Strada *'54*
Il Bidone *'55*
Nights of Cabiria *'57*
And the Wild, Wild Women *'59*
Juliet of the Spirits *'65*
The Madwoman of Chaillot *'69*
Ginger & Fred *'86*

Ace Mask (1948-)
Not of This Earth *'88*
The Return of the Swamp Thing *'89*
Transylvania Twist *'89*

Neil Maskell (1976-)
Bonded by Blood *'09*
Kill List *'12*
Wasteland *'13*
Open Windows *'14 (V)*
Hyena *'15*

Virginia Maskell
Doctor in Love *'60*
Interlude *'68*

Tatiana Maslany (1985-)
Ginger Snaps: Unleashed *'04*
Trapped *'06*
An Old-Fashioned Thanksgiving *'08*
Hardwired *'09*
Grown Up Movie Star *'10*
Certain Prey *'11*
The Entitled *'11*
Violet & Daisy *'11*
Picture Day *'13*
Cas & Dylan *'15*
Woman in Gold *'15*
The Other Half *'17*
Stronger *'17*
Destroyer *'18*

Connie Mason (1937-)
Blood Feast *'63*
2000 Maniacs *'64*

Elliot Mason (1888-1949)
The Ghost Goes West *'36*
On Approval *'44*

Hilary Mason (1917-2006)
Macbeth *'70*
Don't Look Now *'73*
Dolls *'87*
Robot Jox *'90*

Jackie Mason (1931-)
The Jerk *'79*
History of the World: Part 1 *'81*
Caddyshack 2 *'88*

James Mason (1890-1954)
The Plainsman *'37*
The Upturned Glass *'47*
The Passage *'79*

James Mason (1909-84)
Secret of Stamboul *'36*
Fire Over England *'37*
High Command *'37*
The Return of the Scarlet Pimpernel *'37*
The Mill on the Floss *'39*
The Night Has Eyes *'42*
The Man in Grey *'43*
Candlelight in Algeria *'44*
The Wicked Lady *'45*
Odd Man Out *'47*
Man of Evil *'48*
Caught *'49*
East Side, West Side *'49*
Madame Bovary *'49*
Reckless Moment *'49*
The Desert Fox *'51*
Pandora and the Flying Dutchman *'51*
Five Fingers *'52*
Prisoner of Zenda *'52*
Charade *'53*
The Desert Rats *'53*
Julius Caesar *'53*
The Story of Three Loves *'53*
Prince Valiant *'54*
A Star Is Born *'54*
20,000 Leagues under the Sea *'54*
Forever Darling *'56*
Island in the Sun *'57*
Cry Terror! *'58*
The Decks Ran Red *'58*
Journey to the Center of the Earth *'59*
North by Northwest *'59*
The Trials of Oscar Wilde *'60*
The Marriage-Go-Round *'61*
Escape From Zahrain *'62*
Hero's Island *'62*
Lolita *'62*
Tiara Tahiti *'62*
The Fall of the Roman Empire *'64*
The Pumpkin Eater *'64*
Genghis Khan *'65*
Lord Jim *'65*
The Blue Max *'66*
Georgy Girl *'66*
Duffy *'68*
Mayerling *'68*
The Sea Gull *'68*
Age of Consent *'69*
Cold Sweat *'71*
Bad Man's River *'72*
Child's Play *'72*
The Last of Sheila *'73*
Mackintosh Man *'73*
The Destructors *'74*
11 Harrowhouse *'74*
Inside Out *'75*
Mandingo *'75*
Cross of Iron *'76*
Kidnap Syndicate *'76*
Street War *'76*
Voyage of the Damned *'76*
Jesus of Nazareth *'77*
The Boys from Brazil *'78*
Heaven Can Wait *'78*
Murder by Decree *'79*
Salem's Lot *'79*
Water Babies *'79*
ffolkes *'80*
Dangerous Summer *'82*
Evil under the Sun *'82*
Ivanhoe *'82*
The Verdict *'82*
Yellowbeard *'83*
The Assisi Underground *'84*
A.D. *'85*
The Shooting Party *'85*

Laurence Mason
The Crow *'93*
Hackers *'95*
Parallel Sons *'95*
Ali *'01*

Leroy Mason (1903-47)
Lightning Hutch *'26*
The Viking *'28*
Children of the Wild *'37*

Madison Mason
Thirteen Days *'00*
Amish Grace *'10*

Marsha Mason (1942-)
Blume in Love *'73*
Cinderella Liberty *'73*
Audrey Rose *'77*
The Goodbye Girl *'77*
The Cheap Detective *'78*
Chapter Two *'79*
Promises in the Dark *'79*
Only When I Laugh *'81*
Lois Gibbs and the Love Canal *'82*
Max Dugan Returns *'83*
Heartbreak Ridge *'86*
Trapped in Silence *'86*
Dinner at Eight *'89*
The Image *'89*
Stella *'89*
Drop Dead Fred *'91*
I Love Trouble *'94*
Broken Trust *'95*
Nick of Time *'95*
Two Days in the Valley *'96*
Restless Spirits *'99*
Life with Judy Garland-Me and My Shadows *'01*
Bride & Prejudice *'04*
The Long Shot *'04*

Mike Mason
The Monster of Phantom Lake *'06*
It Came From Another World *'07*

Pamela Mason (1922-96)
Charade *'53*
Sex Kittens Go to College *'60*
Door to Door Maniac *'61*
Navy *vs.* the Night Monsters *'66*

Tom Mason (1949-)
Apocalypse Now *'79*
Mississippi Burning *'88*
Men Don't Leave *'89*
The Amy Fisher Story *'93*
Looking for an Echo *'99*
Runaway Bride *'99*
Brooklyn Lobster *'05*

Varvara O. Massalitinova
Alexander Nevsky *'38*
My Childhood *'38*

Lea Massari (1933-)
L'Avventura *'60*
The Colossus of Rhodes *'61*
Murmur of the Heart *'71*
Les Rendez-vous D'Anna *'78*
Christ Stopped at Eboli *'79*

Michael Massee (1955-)
The Crow *'93*
Sahara *'95*
Tales from the Hood *'95*
Lost Highway *'96*
One Fine Day *'96*
Playing God *'96*
The Last Don *'97*
The Theory of the Leisure Class *'01*
Momentum *'03*
Catwoman *'04*

Osa Massen (1914-2006)
A Woman's Face *'41*
Iceland *'42*
Background to Danger *'43*
The Master Race *'44*
Night Unto Night *'49*
Rocketship X-M *'50*

Anna Massey (1937-2011)
Gideon's Day *'58*
Peeping Tom *'60*
Bunny Lake Is Missing *'65*
Frenzy *'72*
A Doll's House *'73*
Vault of Horror *'73*
The Corn Is Green *'79*
Sweet William *'79*
I Remember Nelson *'82*
Another Country *'84*
The Little Drummer Girl *'84*
Mansfield Park *'85*
Foreign Body *'86*
A Tale of Two Cities *'89*
The Tall Guy *'89*
Impromptu *'90*
Mountains of the Moon *'90*
Angels and Insects *'95*
Haunted *'95*
Driftwood *'97*
Captain Jack *'98*
Deja Vu *'98*
A Respectable Trade *'98*
Dark Blue World *'01*
The Importance of Being Earnest *'02*
Possession *'02*
Agatha Christie: A Life in Pictures *'04*
The Machinist *'04*
Mrs. Palfrey at the Claremont *'05*
Pinochet's Last Stand *'06*
Oliver Twist *'07*
Affinity *'08*
The Oxford Murders *'08*
Tess of the D'Urbervilles *'08*

Athena Massey (1967-)
Undercover *'94*
Virtual Combat *'95*
Red Shoe Diaries: Strip Poker *'96*
Termination Man *'97*
Harold Robbins' Body Parts *'99*

Daniel Massey (1933-98)
Upstairs and Downstairs *'59*
The Entertainer *'60*
Star! *'68*
Fragment of Fear *'70*
Mary, Queen of Scots *'71*
The Golden Bowl *'72*
Vault of Horror *'73*
The Cat and the Canary *'79*
Victory *'81*
Dance with a Stranger *'85*
Scandal *'89*
G.B.H. *'91*
Catherine Cookson's The Man Who Cried *'93*
In the Name of the Father *'93*
Samson and Delilah *'96*
The Miracle Maker: The Story of Jesus *'00 (V)*

Edith Massey (1918-84)
Pink Flamingos *'72*
Female Trouble *'74*
Desperate Living *'77*
Polyester *'81*

Ilona Massey (1910-74)
Rosalie *'38*
Balalaika *'39*
Melody Master *'41*
Frankenstein Meets the Wolfman *'42*
Invisible Agent *'42*
Holiday in Mexico *'46*
Love Happy *'50*

Kyle Massey
Beethoven's Christmas Adventure *'11*
Contest *'13*

Raymond Massey (1896-1983)
The Speckled Band *'31*
The Old Dark House *'32*
The Scarlet Pimpernel *'34*
Things to Come *'36*
Under the Red Robe *'36*
Fire Over England *'37*
The Hurricane *'37*
Prisoner of Zenda *'37*
Drums *'38*
Abe Lincoln in Illinois *'40*
Santa Fe Trail *'40*
Dangerously We Live *'41*
The Forty-Ninth Parallel *'41*
Desperate Journey *'42*
Reap the Wild Wind *'42*
Action in the North Atlantic *'43*
Arsenic and Old Lace *'44*
Woman in the Window *'44*
God is My Co-Pilot *'45*
Stairway to Heaven *'46*
The Possessed *'47*
Barricade *'49*
The Fountainhead *'49*
Chain Lightning *'50*
David and Bathsheba *'51*
Carson City *'52*
The Desert Song *'53*
East of Eden *'54*
Battle Cry *'55*
Seven Angry Men *'55*
Omar Khayyam *'57*
How the West Was Won *'63*
MacKenna's Gold *'69*

Paul Massie (1932-2011)
Libel *'59*
Sapphire *'59*
The Two Faces of Dr. Jekyll *'60*

Leonide Massine
The Red Shoes *'48*
Neapolitan Carousel *'54*

Chris Massoglia (1992-)
A Plumm Summer *'08*
Cirque du Freak: The Vampire's Assistant *'09*

Mena Massoud (1991-)
Aladdin *'19*
Run This Town *'20*

Valerio Mastandrea
The Nest *'02*
Giulia Doesn't Date at Night *'09*
The Face of an Angel *'14*

Master P (1967-)
Foolish *'99*
No Tomorrow *'99*
Gone in 60 Seconds *'00*
Lockdown *'00*
Dark Blue *'03*
Hollywood Homicide *'03*
Scary Movie 3 *'03 (C)*
Toxic *'07*
Internet Dating *'08*
Soccer Mom *'08*

Ben Masters (1947-)
Mandingo *'75*
Dream Lover *'85*
The Deliberate Stranger *'86*
Kate's Secret *'86*
Making Mr. Right *'86*
Noble House *'88*
Running Mates *'92*

Chase Masterson (1963-)
Married People, Single Sex *'93*
Sometimes They Come Back. . . For More *'99*
Terminal Invasion *'02*
Comic Book: The Movie *'04 (C)*
Manticore *'05*

Christopher K. Masterson (1980-)
Campfire Tales *'98*
Girl *'98*
Dragonheart: A New Beginning *'00*
Scary Movie 2 *'01*
MTV's Wuthering Heights *'03*
The Art of Travel *'08*

Danny Masterson (1976-)
Bye Bye, Love *'94*
Star Kid *'97*
The Faculty *'98*
Dracula 2000 *'00*
Comic Book Villains *'02*
Puff, Puff, Pass *'06*
Smiley Face *'07*
The Brooklyn Heist *'08*
Yes Man *'08*
The Bridge to Nowhere *'09*
Wake *'09*
California Solo *'12*
Urge *'16*

Fay Masterson (1974-)
The Power of One *'92*
The Man Without a Face *'93*
Cops and Robbersons *'94*
Eyes Wide Shut *'99*
The Lost Skeleton of Cadavra *'01*
Johnson County War *'02*
Rancid *'04*
Sorted *'04*
Amish Grace *'10*

Mary Stuart Masterson (1966-)
The Stepford Wives *'75*
Heaven Help Us *'85*
At Close Range *'86*
Gardens of Stone *'87*
Some Kind of Wonderful *'87*
Mr. North *'88*
Chances Are *'89*
Immediate Family *'89*
Funny About Love *'90*
Fried Green Tomatoes *'91*
Benny & Joon *'93*
Married to It *'93*
Bad Girls *'94*
Radioland Murders *'94*
Bed of Roses *'95*
Heaven's Prisoners *'95*
Lily Dale *'96*
Dogtown *'97*
Digging to China *'98*
The Florentine *'98*
The Book of Stars *'99*
Leo *'02*
West of Here *'02*
Something the Lord Made *'04*
The Sisters *'05*
The Insurgents *'06*

Peter Masterson (1934-)
The Exorcist *'73*
Man on a Swing *'74*
The Stepford Wives *'75*
Gardens of Stone *'87*

Mary Elizabeth Mastrantonio (1958-)
Scarface *'83*
The Color of Money *'86*
Slamdance *'87*
The Abyss *'89*
The January Man *'89*
Class Action *'91*
Robin Hood: Prince of Thieves *'91*
Consenting Adults *'92*
White Sands *'92*
Three Wishes *'95*
Two Bits *'96*
My Life So Far *'98*
Limbo *'99*
Witness Protection *'99*
The Perfect Storm *'00*
That Russell Girl *'08*

Chiara Mastroianni (1972-)
Ma Saison Preferee *'93*
For Sale *'98*
Time Regained *'99*
Carnage *'02*
Love Songs *'07*
Persepolis *'07 (V)*
Towards Zero *'07*
A Christmas Tale *'08*
Making Plans for Lena *'09*
Americano *'11*
Beloved *'11*
Chicken With Plums *'11*
Augustine *'12*

Marcello Mastroianni (1923-96)
Too Bad She's Bad *'54*
White Nights *'57*
Big Deal on Madonna Street *'58*
Where the Hot Wind Blows *'59*
Adua and Her Friends *'60*
La Dolce Vita *'60*
La Notte *'60*
Divorce-Italian Style *'62*
8 1/2 *'63*
Marriage Italian Style *'64*
The Organizer *'64*
Yesterday, Today and Tomorrow *'64*
Casanova '70 *'65*
10th Victim *'65*
The Poppy Is Also a Flower *'66*
Shoot Loud, Louder, I Don't Understand! *'66*
The Priest's Wife *'71*
Fellini's Roma *'72 (C)*
La Grande Bouffe *'73*
Massacre in Rome *'73*
Get Rita *'75*
Lady of the Evening *'75*
A Special Day *'77*
We All Loved Each Other So Much *'77*
Blood Feud *'79*
A Slightly Pregnant Man *'79*
City of Women *'81*
The Skin *'81*
Beyond Obsession *'82*
Gabriela *'84*
Henry IV *'85*
Macaroni *'85*
Ginger & Fred *'86*
Intervista *'87*
A Fine Romance *'92*
Used People *'92*

I Don't Want to Talk About It '94
Ready to Wear '94
Beyond the Clouds '95
One Hundred and One Nights '95
Voyage to the Beginning of the World '96

Alessandra Mastronardi
To Rome with Love '12
Life '15

Shoichiro Masumoto
Azumi '03
Azumi 2 '05

Richard Masur (1948-)
Semi-Tough '77
Betrayal '78
Who'll Stop the Rain? '78
East of Eden '80
Heaven's Gate '81
The Thing '82
Adam '83
Nightmares '83
Risky Business '83
Timerider '83
Under Fire '83
Wild Horses '84
The Burning Bed '85
Mean Season '85
My Science Project '85
Hard Lessons '86
Heartburn '86
When the Bough Breaks '86
The Believers '87
Roses Are for the Rich '87
Walker '87
Higher Ground '88
License to Drive '88
Rent-A-Cop '88
Shoot to Kill '88
Far from Home '89
Flashback '89
Stephen King's It '90
My Girl '91
Encino Man '92
And the Band Played On '93
The Man Without a Face '93
Six Degrees of Separation '93
My Girl 2 '94
Forget Paris '95
Hiroshima '95
My Brother's Keeper '95
Multiplicity '96
Steve Martini's Undue Influence '96
Fire Down Below '97
Play It to the Bone '99
61* '01
Palindromes '04
Lovely by Surprise '07
Tumbledown '16

Orestes Matacena
The Mask '94
Last Stand '00

Clelia Matania (1918-81)
Neapolitan Carousel '54
The Seven Hills of Rome '58
Don't Look Now '73

Heather Matarazzo (1982-)
Welcome to the Dollhouse '95
Hurricane Streets '96
The Deli '97
The Devil's Advocate '97
All I Wanna Do '98
54 '98
Blue Moon '00
Company Man '00
Scream 3 '00
The Princess Diaries '01
Sorority Boys '02
Freshman Orientation '04
The Princess Diaries 2: Royal Engagement '04
Saved! '04
Believe in Me '06
Hostel: Part 2 '07
Sisters '15

Kari Matchett (1970-)
Cube 2: Hypercube '02
Cypher '02
Men with Brooms '02
Civic Duty '06
Intimate Stranger '06
The National Tree '09
Meteor Storm '10
The Horses of McBride '12
Maudie '17

Julian Mateos (1938-96)
Return of the Magnificent Seven '66
Hellbenders '67
Four Rode Out '69

Edouard Mathe (1886-1934)
Les Vampires '15
Judex '16

Aubrey Mather (1885-1958)
The Silent Passenger '35
Sabotage '36
Mrs. Miniver '42
Hello, Frisco, Hello '43
Jane Eyre '44
House of Fear '45
Adventures of Don Juan '49
That Forsyte Woman '50

George Mather (1920-97)
Hell Bound '57
Ring of Terror '62

Marie Matheron (1959-)
Western '96
Come Undone '00
Inspector Bellamy '09

Jerry Mathers (1948-)
The Trouble with Harry '55
Shadow on the Window '57
Back to the Beach '87
Down the Drain '89
Larry the Cable Guy: Health Inspector '06 (C)

Marshall Mathers, III (1972-)
See Eminem

Hans Matheson (1975-)
Poldark '96
Stella Does Tricks '96
Les Miserables '97
Still Crazy '98
Bodywork '99
Mists of Avalon '01
Deathwatch '02
Doctor Zhivago '03
Tess of the D'Urbervilles '08
Sherlock Holmes '09
300: Rise of an Empire '13

Judy Matheson (1945-)
Twins of Evil '71
Crucible of Terror '72
Flesh and Blood Show '73

Michelle Matheson (1971-)
Howling 6: The Freaks '90
Test Tube Teens from the Year 2000 '93
Threesome '94

Tim Matheson (1947-)
Yours, Mine & Ours '68
How to Commit Marriage '69
Magnum Force '73
The Longest Drive '76
Mary White '77
National Lampoon's Animal House '78
The Apple Dumpling Gang Rides Again '79
1941 '79
A Little Sex '82
To Be or Not to Be '83
Impulse '84
Up the Creek '84
Fletch '85
Eye of the Demon '87
Buried Alive '90
Drop Dead Fred '91
Quicksand: No Escape '91
Sometimes They Come Back '91
Solar Crisis '92
Midnight Heat '95
Black Sheep '96
A Very Brady Sequel '96
Deadly Game '98
Forever Love '98
She's All That '99
The Story of Us '99
Jackie Bouvier Kennedy Onassis '00
National Lampoon's Van Wilder '02
Don't Come Knocking '05
Redline '07
Behind Enemy Lines 3: Colombia '08
Child's Play '19

Suleka Mathew
Touch of Pink '04
Final Days of Planet Earth '06

Carmen Mathews (1911-95)
A Rage to Live '65
Sounder '72

Carole Mathews (1920-2014)
Massacre River '49
Swamp Women '55
Showdown at Boot Hill '58
Strange Awakening '58

George Mathews (1911-84)
Yankee Buccaneer '52
The Great Diamond Robbery '53
The Man with the Golden Arm '55

Hrothgar Mathews (1964-)
A Decent Proposal '06
Family in Hiding '06
Second Sight '07

Kerwin Mathews (1926-2007)
5 Against the House '55
The Garment Jungle '57
The Seventh Voyage of Sinbad '58
Tarawa Beachhead '58
The Three Worlds of Gulliver '59
Man On a String '60
The 3 Worlds of Gulliver '60
The Devil at 4 O'Clock '61
Jack the Giant Killer '62
Pirates of Blood River '62
Maniac '63
Waltz King '63
Battle Beneath the Earth '68
Octaman '71
Nightmare in Blood '75
Killer Likes Candy '78

Thom Mathews (1958-)
Friday the 13th, Part 6: Jason Lives '86
Alien from L.A. '87
Return of the Living Dead 2 '88
Heatseeker '95

Marion Mathie (1925-2012)
Lolita '62
Dracula Has Risen from the Grave '68

Samantha Mathis (1970-)
Pump Up the Volume '90
Ferngully: The Last Rain Forest '92 (V)
This Is My Life '92
The Music of Chance '93
Super Mario Bros. '93
The Thing Called Love '93
Little Women '94
The American President '95
Broken Arrow '95
How to Make an American Quilt '95
Jack and Sarah '95
Sweet Jane '98
American Psycho '99
The Simian Line '99
Mermaid '00
Mists of Avalon '01
The Punisher '04
Salem's Lot '04
Absolution '05
Kids in America '05
Touched '05
Believe in Me '06
Local Color '06
For One More Day '07
A Stranger's Heart '07
Buried '10
Lebanon, PA '10
The New Daughter '10
Order of Chaos '10
Unanswered Prayers '10
Atlas Shrugged 2: The Strike '12
Boarding School '18

Cameron Mathison (1969-)
The Christmas Ornament '13
The Surrogate '13
My Gal Sunday '14

Jacques Mathou
Betty Blue '86
The Hairdresser's Husband '92
Year of the Comet '92
Ridicule '96

Marie Matiko (1971-)
The Art of War '00
Counterstrike '03
Gang of Roses '03
Date Movie '06

Elisa Matilla
Why Do They Call It Love When They Mean Sex? '92
Km. 0 '00

Marlee Matlin (1965-)
Children of a Lesser God '86
Walker '87
Bridge to Silence '89
The Linguini Incident '92
The Player '92
Hear No Evil '93
It's My Party '95
Dead Silence '96
Two Shades of Blue '98
When Justice Fails '98
Where the Truth Lies '99
What the #$*! Do We Know? '04
Sweet Nothing in My Ear '08
Excision '12

Norman Matlock
Sweet Revenge '76
Wilma '77
Crooklyn '94

John Matshikiza (1954-2008)
Mandela '87
Dust Devil '93
Yankee Zulu '95

Chieko Matsubara (1945-)
Black Tight Killers '66
Dolls '02

Eiko Matsuda (1947-)
In the Realm of the Senses '76
Sweet Evil '95

Ryuhei Matsuda (1983-)
Taboo '99
Blue Spring '01
9 Souls '03
Nightmare Detective '06

Yusaku Matsuda (1950-89)
The Family Game '83
Black Rain '89

Kayo Matsuo (1943-)
Gate of Flesh '64
Shogun Assassin '80

Suzuki Matsuo
Ichi the Killer '01
RoboGeisha '06

Yutaka Matsushige (1963-)
Rasen '98
Ringu '98
The Princess Blade '02
One Missed Call '03
Blood and Bones '04
Shinobi '05
Miss Hokusai '16

Nanako Matsushima (1973-)
Rasen '98
Ringu '98
Ringu 2 '99

Ken'ichi Matsuyama (1985-)
Death Note '06
Death Note 2: The Last Name '07
Genghis Khan: To the Ends of the Earth and Sea '07
Death Note 3: L Change the World '08

Takashi Matsuyama
Stray Dog '91
Ju-On 2 '00

Keiko Matsuzaka (1952-)
Fall Guy '82
Dr. Akagi '98
The Happiness of the Katakuris '01

Niall Matter (1980-)
Loch Ness Terror '07
Dr. Dolittle 4: Tail to the Chief '08
The Secrets of the Summer House '08

Eva Mattes (1954-)
The Bitter Tears of Petra von Kant '72
Stroszek '77
In a Year of 13 Moons '78
Woyzeck '78
Germany, Pale Mother '80
Enemy at the Gates '00

Walter Matthau (1920-2000)
The Indian Fighter '55
The Kentuckian '55
A Face in the Crowd '57
King Creole '58
Onionhead '58
Ride a Crooked Trail '58
Strangers When We Meet '60
Lonely Are the Brave '62
Charade '63
Island of Love '63
Who's Got the Action? '63
Ensign Pulver '64
Fail-Safe '64
The Fortune Cookie '66
Mirage '66
A Guide for the Married Man '67
Candy '68
The Odd Couple '68
Cactus Flower '69
Hello, Dolly! '69
Kotch '71
A New Leaf '71
Plaza Suite '71
Pete 'n' Tillie '72
Charley Varrick '73
Earthquake '74
The Front Page '74
The Laughing Policeman '74
The Taking of Pelham One Two Three '74
The Sunshine Boys '75
The Bad News Bears '76
California Suite '78
Casey's Shadow '78
House Calls '78
Hopscotch '80
Little Miss Marker '80
First Monday in October '81
Survivors '83
Movers and Shakers '85
The Couch Trip '87
The Incident '89
JFK '91
Dennis the Menace '93
Grumpy Old Men '93
I.Q. '94
The Grass Harp '95
Grumpier Old Men '95
I'm Not Rappaport '96
Out to Sea '97
The Odd Couple 2 '98
Hanging Up '99

Ulrich Matthes (1959-)
Winter Sleepers '97
Downfall '04
The Ninth Day '04

A.E. Matthews (1869-1960)
Immortal Battalion '44
The Forbidden Street '49
Made in Heaven '52
Penny Princess '52
Carry On Admiral '57

Al Matthews (1942-)
The Sender '82
Aliens '86

Dakin Matthews (1940-)
Nuts '87
My Brother's Wife '89
Naked Lie '89
Child's Play 3 '91
In a Stranger's Hand '92
And the Band Played On '93 (C)
The Temp '93
The Swan Princess '94 (V)
White Mile '94
Bean '97
Rough Riders '97
From the Earth to the Moon '98
The Siege '98
The Muse '99
Thirteen Days '00
True Grit '10
Lincoln '12

Dave Matthews (1967-)
Because of Winn-Dixie '05
Lake City '08
You Don't Mess with the Zohan '08
Just Go With It '11

DeLane Matthews (1961-)
From the Earth to the Moon '98
Running Red '99

Denise Katrina Matthews (1959-2016)
See Vanity

Francis Matthews (1927-2014)
Bhowani Junction '56
Corridors of Blood '58
The Revenge of Frankenstein '58
Murder Ahoy '64
Dracula, Prince of Darkness '66
Rasputin the Mad Monk '66

Jessie Matthews (1907-81)
The Man From Toronto '32
There Goes the Bride '32
Friday the Thirteenth '33
The Good Companions '33
First a Girl '35
It's Love Again '36
Gangway '37
Head Over Heels '37
Climbing High '38
Sailing Along '38
Forever and a Day '43
Candles at Nine '44
The Hound of the Baskervilles '77

Junius Matthews
The Sword in the Stone '63 (V)
The Many Adventures of Winnie the Pooh '77 (V)

Layton Matthews
Alien 51 '04
Necromentia '09

Lester Matthews (1900-75)
Werewolf of London '35
Across the Pacific '42
The Invisible Man's Revenge '44
Objective, Burma! '45
Dark Delusion '47
Rogues of Sherwood Forest '50
Operation Secret '52
Man in the Attic '53
Charge of the Lancers '54
Jungle Man-Eaters '54
King Richard and the Crusaders '54
The Far Horizons '55

Liesl Matthews (1984-)
A Little Princess '95
Air Force One '97

Melina Matthews
Panzer '13
The Returned '14

Sinead Matthews (1980-)
Half Broken Things '07
Happy-Go-Lucky '08
Nanny McPhee Returns '10

Terumi Matthews (1965-)
The Sticky Fingers of Time '97
The Waiting Game '99
Michael Matthias
The Bleeding '09
Caught in the Crossfire '10
Martha Mattox
The Family Secret '24
Torrent '26
Robin Mattson (1956-)
Namu, the Killer Whale '66
Island of the Lost '68
Bonnie's Kids '73
Candy Stripe Nurses '74
Captain America '79
Helena Mattsson (1984-)
Species 4: The Awakening '07
Surrogates '09
Iron Man 2 '10
Guns, Girls and Gambling '11
Code of Honor '16
Victor Mature (1915-99)
No, No Nanette '40
One Million B.C. '40
I Wake Up Screaming '41
My Gal Sal '42
Seven Days' Leave '42
The Shanghai Gesture '42
My Darling Clementine '46
Kiss of Death '47
Cry of the City '48
Easy Living '49
Samson and Delilah '49
Wabash Avenue '50
Androcles and the Lion '52
Million Dollar Mermaid '52
Something for the Birds '52
The Glory Brigade '53
The Robe '53
Betrayed '54
Demetrius and the Gladiators '54
The Egyptian '54
Savage Wilderness '55
Violent Saturday '55
Zarak '56
The Long Haul '57
Pickup Alley '57
The Big Circus '59
Timbuktu '59
The Tartars '61
After the Fox '66
Head '68
Samson and Delilah '84
John Matuszak (1950-89)
Semi-Tough '77
North Dallas Forty '79
Caveman '81
Ice Pirates '84
The Goonies '85
Down the Drain '89
One Man Force '89
Amy Matysio
Stranded '13
Wolfcop '15
Johanna (Hannerl) Matz (1932-)
Party Girls for Sale '54
They Were So Young '55
The Life and Loves of Mozart '59
Tony Maudsley (1968-)
The Intended '02
Strange Relations '02
Vanity Fair '04
Place of Execution '09
Wayne Maunder (1935-)
Porky's '82
Crazy Horse and Custer: 'The Untold Story' '90
Sarah Maur-Thorp
Edge of Sanity '89
River of Death '90
Carmen Maura (1945-)
Dark Habits '84
What Have I Done to Deserve This? '85
Law of Desire '86
Matador '86
Women on the Verge of a Nervous Breakdown '88
How to Be a Woman and Not Die in the Attempt '91
Women '97
Lisboa '99
800 Bullets '02
Valentin '02
Free Zone '05
Volver '06
Hemingway's Garden of Eden '08
Tetro '09
The Women on the Sixth Floor '10
Let My People Go! '11
Nicole Maurey (1925-)
Diary of a Country Priest '50
The Weapon '56
The House of the Seven Hawks '59
The Jayhawkers '59
The Scapegoat '59
High Time '60
Day of the Triffids '63
Claire Maurier (1929-)
The 400 Blows '59
Sweet Ecstasy '62
Angelique: The Road to Versailles '65
La Cage aux Folles '78
Un Air de Famille '96
Amelie '01
My Afternoons with Marguerite '10
Eve Mauro (1986-)
Wicked Lake '08
The Chaos Experiment '09
The Kane Files '10
Osombie '12
The Surrogate '13
Mythica: The Iron Crown '16
Gerda Maurus (1903-68)
Spies '28
Woman in the Moon '29
Gary Mavers (1964-)
Body & Soul '93
The Unknown Soldier '98
Abigail Mavity (1993-)
Coastlines '02
Love Begins '11
The Ultimate Life '13
Freya Mavor
The Lady in the Car with Glasses and a Gun '16
The Keeper '18
Joseph Mawle (1974-)
The Secret Life of Mrs. Beeton '06
Clapham Junction '07
Red Riding, Part 2: 1980 '09
Heartless '10
Murder on the Orient Express '10
The Awakening '11
Women in Love '11
Birdsong '12
Dawn Maxey (1966-)
Normal Life '96
That Thing You Do! '96
Ringmaster '98
The Killing Club '01
Raising Flagg '06
Chenoa Maxwell (1969-)
Hav Plenty '97
G '02
Edwin Maxwell (1886-1948)
The Taming of the Shrew '29
Waterfront '44
Swamp Fire '46
Woman in Brown '48
Frank Maxwell (1916-2004)
Ada '61
Shame '61
The Haunted Palace '63
Jack Maxwell
Irene in Time '09
Born to Ride '11
John Maxwell (1918-82)
Honky Tonk '41
Boss of Big Town '43
The Payoff '43
The Prowler '51
Cage of Evil '60
Julia Maxwell
Don't Cry Now '07
Lost Holiday: The Jim & Suzanne Shemwell Story '07
Earth's Final Hours '12
Larry Maxwell (1953-96)
Poison '91
Public Access '93
Lois Maxwell (1927-2007)
That Hagen Girl '47
Scotland Yard Inspector '52
Twilight Women '52
Submarine Attack '54
Satellite in the Sky '56
Kill Me Tomorrow '57
Time Without Pity '57
Face of Fire '59
Dr. No '62
Lolita '62
From Russia with Love '63
The Haunting '63
Goldfinger '64
Thunderball '65
You Only Live Twice '67
On Her Majesty's Secret Service '69
Diamonds Are Forever '71
Live and Let Die '73
The Man with the Golden Gun '74
The Spy Who Loved Me '77
Moonraker '79
For Your Eyes Only '81
A View to a Kill '85
Eternal Evil '87
Hard to Forget '98
The Fourth Angel '01
Marilyn Maxwell (1922-72)
Stand by for Action '42
Salute to the Marines '43
Swing Fever '43
Lost in a Harem '44
Three Men in White '44
Between Two Women '45
High Barbaree '47
Race Street '48
Summer Holiday '48
Champion '49
Key to the City '50
The Lemon Drop Kid '51
Off Limits '53
Rock-A-Bye Baby '57
Critic's Choice '63
The Lively Set '64
Arizona Bushwackers '67
Michael Maxwell (1962-)
Offensive Behaviour '04
Slave '09
Roberta Maxwell (1942-)
The Changeling '80
Lois Gibbs and the Love Canal '82
Psycho 3 '86
Philadelphia '93
Dead Man Walking '95
Mistrial '96
The Postman '97
Last Night '98
Full Disclosure '00
Gracie's Choice '04
Brokeback Mountain '05
The Mermaid Chair '06
Hungry Hearts '15
Elaine May (1932-)
Luv '67
A New Leaf '71
California Suite '78
Small Time Crooks '00
Jodhi May (1975-)
A World Apart '88
The Last of the Mohicans '92
Sister My Sister '94
The Gambler '97
Aristocrats '99
The Aristocrats '99
The Turn of the Screw '99
House of Mirth '00
Daniel Deronda '02
Tipping the Velvet '02
The Mayor of Casterbridge '03
The Other Boleyn Girl '03
Friends & Crocodiles '05
On a Clear Day '05
Land of the Blind '06
Nightwatching '07
Defiance '08
Flashbacks of a Fool '08
Emma '09
The Scapegoat '12
Ginger & Rosa '13
Mathilda May (1965-)
Lifeforce '85
The Cry of the Owl '87
Grosse Fatigue '94 (C)
Prince Brat and the Whipping Boy '95
The Jackal '97
Only Love '98
A Girl Cut in Two '07
Rik Mayall (1958-2014)
An American Werewolf in London '81
Eye of the Needle '81
Shock Treatment '81
Drop Dead Fred '91
Carry On Columbus '92
Jesus Christ Superstar '00
Chilly Dogs '01
Valiant '05 (V)
Melusine Mayance
Ricky '09
Sarah's Key '10
Anthony (Jose, J. Antonio, J.A.) Mayans (1939-)
Sex Is Crazy '79
Zombie Lake '80
Revenge in the House of Usher '82
Eddie Mayehoff (1909-92)
The Stooge '51
That's My Boy '51
Artists and Models '55
How to Murder Your Wife '64
Jose Mayens (1939-)
See Anthony (Jose, J. Antonio, J.A.) Mayans
Chip (Christopher) Mayer (1954-2011)
Liar Liar '97
Fugitive Champion '99
Rob Mayes (1985-)
The American Mall '08
Acceptance '09
Ice Castles '10
John Dies at the End '12
Meddling Mom '13
NYC Underground '13
Burning Blue '14
Lauren C. Mayhew (1985-)
Raise Your Voice '04
Frat Party '09
Peter Mayhew (1944-)
Star Wars '77
The Empire Strikes Back '80
Return of the Jedi '83
Comic Book: The Movie '04 (C)
Star Wars: Episode 3-Revenge of the Sith '05
Bill Maynard (1928-)
Adolf Hitler: My Part in His Downfall '74
Confessions of a Window Cleaner '74
Confessions of a Driving Instructor '76
John Maynard (1959-)
Dark Universe '93
Biohazard: The Alien Force '95
Ken Maynard (1895-1973)
False Faces '32
Mystery Mountain '34
Kermit Maynard (1897-1971)
The Showdown '40
Billy the Kid '41
Thundering Gunslingers '44
Trail of Robin Hood '50
Terence Maynard (1969-)
Terror in the Mall '98
Reign of Fire '02
Revolver '05
All Things to All Men '13
Belinda Mayne (1954-)
Alien 2 on Earth '80
Don't Open Till Christmas '84
White Fire '84
Ferdinand 'Ferdy' Mayne (1916-98)
Echo Murders '45
Made in Heaven '52
Captain's Paradise '53
White Fire '53
Our Man in Havana '59
The Fearless Vampire Killers '67
Where Eagles Dare '68
The Magic Christian '69
The Adventurers '70
The Vampire Lovers '70
The Walking Stick '70
The Vampire Happening '71
When Eight Bells Toll '71
Au Pair Girls '72
Frightmare '81
Hawk the Slayer '81
Yellowbeard '83
Night Train to Terror '84
Howling 2: Your Sister Is a Werewolf '85
Benefit of the Doubt '93
Juliette Mayniel (1936-)
The Cousins '59
The Horror Chamber of Dr. Faustus '59
Les Cousins '59
The Trojan Horse '62
Assassination in Rome '65
The Bloodstained Shadow '78
Alfredo Mayo (1911-85)
The Hunt '65
Bell from Hell '74
Frank Mayo (1886-1963)
Souls for Sale '23
Wild Oranges '24
Doughboys '30
The Phantom of Santa Fe '36
Tim Tyler's Luck '37
Across the Pacific '42
Virginia Mayo (1920-2005)
Jack London '44
The Princess and the Pirate '44
Wonder Man '45
The Best Years of Our Lives '46
The Kid from Brooklyn '46
Out of the Blue '47
The Secret Life of Walter Mitty '47
A Song Is Born '48
Colorado Territory '49
The Girl from Jones Beach '49
Red Light '49
White Heat '49
Backfire '50
The Flame & the Arrow '50
The West Point Story '50
Along the Great Divide '51
Captain Horatio Hornblower '51
Painting the Clouds With Sunshine '51
The Iron Mistress '52
She's Working Her Way Through College '52
She's Back on Broadway '53
South Sea Woman '53
King Richard and the Crusaders '54
The Silver Chalice '54
Pearl of the South Pacific '55
Story of Mankind '57
Fort Dobbs '58
Westbound '58
Runaways '75
French Quarter '78
Evil Spirits '91
Midnight Witness '93
Whitman Mayo (1930-2001)
Of Mice and Men '81
Boyz N the Hood '91
Waterproof '99
Boycott '02
Karen Mayo-Chandler (1958-2006)
Death Feud '89
Stripped to Kill 2: Live Girls '89
Melanie Mayron (1952-)
Harry and Tonto '74
Car Wash '76
Great Smokey Roadblock '76
You Light Up My Life '77
Girlfriends '78
Playing for Time '80
Heartbeeps '81
Missing '82
Wallenberg: A Hero's Story '85
The Boss' Wife '86
Sticky Fingers '88
Checking Out '89
My Blue Heaven '90
Ordeal in the Arctic '93
Toothless '97
Range of Motion '00
Daniel Mays (1978-)
All or Nothing '02
Vera Drake '04
Middletown '06
Half Broken Things '07
The Bank Job '08
Shifty '08
Red Riding, Part 3: 1983 '09
Made in Dagenham '10
Nanny McPhee Returns '10
Treasure Island '12
Mr. Nobody '13
The Limehouse Golem '17
Fisherman's Friends '19
1917 '19
The Rhythm Section '19
Jayma Mays (1979-)
Epic Movie '07
Paul Blart: Mall Cop '09
The Smurfs '11
The Smurfs 2 '13
Last Weekend '14
Jefferson Mays (1965-)
The Big Brass Ring '99
Alfie '04
The Notorious Bettie Page '06
Joshua Gibran Mayweather (1981-)
Camp Nowhere '94
Candyman 2: Farewell to the Flesh '94
Bob Maza (1939-2000)
Reckless Kelly '93
Back of Beyond '95
Jason Maza (1987-)
Fish Tank '09
Outside Bet '12
Debi Mazar (1964-)
Goodfellas '90
Jungle Fever '91
Little Man Tate '91
In the Soup '92
Beethoven's 2nd '93
Inside Monkey Zetterland '93
Money for Nothing '93
Bad Love '95
Batman Forever '95
Empire Records '95
Girl 6 '96
Things I Never Told You '96
Tree's Lounge '96
Meet Wally Sparks '97
She's So Lovely '97
Space Truckers '97
Frogs for Snakes '98
Hush '98
Witness to the Mob '98
The Insider '99
Life in the Fast Lane '00

More Dogs Than Bones *'00*
The Tuxedo *'02*
Collateral *'04*
Be Cool *'05*
Edmond *'05*
Lies & Alibis *'06*
A Beautiful Life *'08*
The Women *'08*
Home Alone: The Holiday Heist *'12*
Entourage *'15*

Monet Mazur (1976-)
Angel Eyes *'01*
The Learning Curve *'01*
Comic Book Villains *'02*
40 Days and 40 Nights *'02*
Stark Raving Mad *'02*
Just Married *'03*
Torque *'04*
Whirlygirl *'04*
Monster-in-Law *'05*
Stoned *'05*
Live! *'07*
The House Bunny *'08*
The Last International Playboy *'08*
Dead Man Running *'09*

Mike Mazurki (1907-90)
The Shanghai Gesture *'42*
The Canterville Ghost *'44*
Murder, My Sweet *'44*
Abbott and Costello in Hollywood *'45*
Killer Dill *'47*
Nightmare Alley *'47*
Sinbad, the Sailor *'47*
Unconquered *'47*
I Walk Alone *'48*
The Noose Hangs High *'48*
Come to the Stable *'49*
Neptune's Daughter *'49*
Rope of Sand *'49*
Dark City *'50*
Night and the City *'50*
Criminal Lawyer *'51*
Blood Alley *'55*
New Orleans Uncensored *'55*
Man in the Vault *'56*
Hell Ship Mutiny *'57*
Some Like It Hot *'59*
The Errand Boy *'61*
Donovan's Reef *'63*
Cheyenne Autumn *'64*
The McCullochs *'75*
Challenge To Be Free *'76*
Doin' Time *'85*

Paul Mazursky (1930-2014)
Blackboard Jungle *'55*
Alex in Wonderland *'70*
Harry and Tonto *'74 (C)*
A Star Is Born *'76*
A Man, a Woman, and a Bank *'79*
History of the World: Part 1 *'81*
Into the Night *'85*
Moon over Parador *'88*
Punchline *'88*
Enemies, a Love Story *'89*
Man Trouble *'92*
Love Affair *'94*
Faithful *'95 (C)*
Miami Rhapsody *'95*
Touch *'96*
Two Days in the Valley *'96*
Weapons of Mass Distraction *'97*
Antz *'98 (V)*
Why Do Fools Fall in Love? *'98*
Crazy in Alabama *'99*
A Slight Case of Murder *'99*
Big Shot's Funeral *'01*
Coast to Coast *'04*
National Lampoon Presents Cattle Call *'06*

Marcello Mazzarello (1965-)
Time Regained *'99*
Felicidades *'00*
The Sicilian Girl *'09*

Joseph Mazzello (1983-)
Presumed Innocent *'90*
Jersey Girl *'92*
Radio Flyer *'92*
Jurassic Park *'93*
Shadowlands *'93*
The River Wild *'94*
The Cure *'95*
Three Wishes *'95*
The Lost World: Jurassic Park 2 *'97*
Star Kid *'97*
Simon Birch *'98*
The Sensation of Sight *'06*
The Pacific *'10*
The Social Network *'10*
G.I. Joe: Retaliation *'13*
Undrafted *'16*
Bohemian Rhapsody *'18*

Gugu Mbatha-Raw (1983-)
Larry Crowne *'11*
Belle *'13*
Odd Thomas *'13*
Beyond the Lights *'14*
Concussion *'15*
Free State of Jones *'16*
Miss Sloane *'16*
The Whole Truth *'16*
Fast Color *'18*
Irreplaceable You *'18*
Farming *'19*
Motherless Brooklyn *'19*

M.C. Lyte (1970-)
Fly by Night *'93*
An Alan Smithee Film: Burn, Hollywood, Burn *'97*
Civil Brand *'02*

Rachel McAdams (1978-)
The Hot Chick *'02*
Mean Girls *'04*
The Notebook *'04*
The Family Stone *'05*
Red Eye *'05*
Wedding Crashers *'05*
Married Life *'07*
The Lucky Ones *'08*
Sherlock Holmes *'09*
State of Play *'09*
The Time Traveler's Wife *'09*
Morning Glory *'10*
Midnight in Paris *'11*
Sherlock Holmes: A Game of Shadows *'11*
To the Wonder *'12*
The Vow *'12*
About Time *'13*
Passion *'13*
A Most Wanted Man *'14*
Aloha *'15*
Every Thing Will Be Fine *'15*
Southpaw *'15*
Spotlight *'15*
Doctor Strange *'16*
The Little Prince *'16*
Disobedience *'17*
Game Night *'18*

Andni McAfee (1979-)
Conagher *'91*
The Land Before Time 5: The Mysterious Island *'97 (V)*
The Land Before Time 6: The Secret of Saurus Rock *'98 (V)*
Land Before Time 7: The Stone of Cold Fire *'00 (V)*

Scott McAfee (1981-)
The Land Before Time 2: The Great Valley Adventure *'94 (V)*
The Land Before Time 3: The Time of the Great Giving *'95 (V)*
The Land Before Time 4: Journey Through the Mists *'96 (V)*

Des McAleer (1952-)
Four Days in July *'85*
Hidden Agenda *'90*
Butterfly Kiss *'94*
Kings in Grass Castles *'97*
When the Sky Falls *'99*

Lisa McAllister
Pumpkinhead 3: Ashes to Ashes *'06*
Dead Cert *'10*

Ray McAnally (1926-89)
Sea of Sand *'58*
Danny Boy *'82*
The Mission *'86*
No Surrender *'86*
The Fourth Protocol *'87*
A Perfect Spy *'88*
Taffin *'88*
A Very British Coup *'88*
My Left Foot *'89*
We're No Angels *'89*

Kelly McAndrew
Superheroes *'07*
In the Family *'11*

Marianne McAndrew (1942-)
Hello, Dolly! *'69*
The Bat People *'74*

Aidan McArdle
The Duchess *'08*
Late Bloomers *'11*

Alex McArthur (1957-)
Silent Witness *'85*
Rampage *'87*
Ed McBain's 87th Precinct: Lightning *'95*
Kiss the Girls *'97*
Lady Killer *'97*
Devil in the Flesh *'98*
Route 666 *'01*
Suspended Animation *'02*
Stealing Candy *'04*
Lost Colony: The Legend of Roanoke *'07*
Hydra *'09*

Alphonso McAuley (1984-)
Fat Albert *'04*
Glory Road *'06*
Pride *'07*
Cat Run *'11*

Callan McAuliffe
Flipped *'10*
Beneath the Harvest Sky *'14*

James McAvoy (1979-)
Bright Young Things *'03*
Children of Dune *'03*
State of Play *'03*
Rory O'Shea Was Here *'04*
Wimbledon *'04*
The Chronicles of Narnia: The Lion, the Witch and the Wardrobe *'05*
The Last King of Scotland *'06*
Penelope *'06*
Starter for 10 *'06*
Atonement *'07*
Becoming Jane *'07*
Wanted *'08*
The Last Station *'09*
The Conspirator *'10*
Arthur Christmas *'11 (V)*
Gnomeo & Juliet *'11 (V)*
X-Men: First Class *'11*
Filth *'13*
Trance *'13*
Welcome to the Punch *'13*
The Disappearance of Eleanor Rigby *'14*
X-Men: Days of Future Past *'14*
Victor Frankenstein *'15*
Split *'16*
X-Men: Apocalypse *'16*
Atomic Blonde *'17*
Sherlock Gnomes *'18*
Submergence *'18*
Dark Phoenix *'19*
Glass *'19*
It Chapter Two *'19*

May McAvoy (1899-1984)
Lady Windermere's Fan *'25*
Ben-Hur *'26*
The Jazz Singer *'27*
Gun Glory *'57*

Diane McBain (1941-)
Claudelle Inglish *'61*
Parrish *'61*
Black Gold *'62*
The Caretakers *'63*
Mary, Mary *'63*
A Distant Trumpet *'64*
Spinout *'66*
Thunder Alley *'67*
The Sidehackers *'69*
Wicked, Wicked *'73*
Monster *'78*
Puppet Master 5: The Final Chapter *'94*

Tom McBeath (1958-)
Firestorm *'97*
Off Season *'01*
The Bad Son *'07*
Lost in the Dark *'07*

Daron McBee (1961-)
The Killing Zone *'90*
T-Force *'94*
Mortal Kombat 2: Annihilation *'97*
The Base 2: Guilty as Charged *'00*
The Cutter *'05*

Jack McBrayer (1973-)
Walk Hard: The Dewey Cox Story *'07*
Forgetting Sarah Marshall *'08*
Cats & Dogs: The Revenge of Kitty Galore *'10*
Despicable Me *'10 (V)*
Wreck-It Ralph *'12 (V)*
Movie 43 *'13*
Cooties *'14*
Smurfs: The Lost Village *'17 (V)*
Ralph Breaks the Internet *'18 (V)*

Chi McBride (1961-)
What's Love Got to Do with It? *'93*
The Frighteners *'96*
Hoodlum *'96*
Mercury Rising *'98*
Dancing in September *'00*
Disney's The Kid *'00*
Gone in 60 Seconds *'00*
Narc *'02*
Paid in Full *'02*
Undercover Brother *'02*
Cradle 2 the Grave *'03*
I, Robot *'04*
The Terminal *'04*
Roll Bounce *'05*
Waiting *'05*
Annapolis *'06*
Let's Go to Prison *'06*
The Brothers Solomon *'07*
American Son *'08*
First Sunday *'08*
Who Do You Love *'08*
The Family Tree *'10*

Danny McBride (1976-)
All the Real Girls *'03*
The Heartbreak Kid *'07*
Hot Rod *'07*
The Foot Fist Way *'08*
Pineapple Express *'08*
Tropic Thunder *'08*
Land of the Lost *'09*
Up in the Air *'09*
Despicable Me *'10 (V)*
Due Date *'10*
30 Minutes or Less *'11*
Your Highness *'11*
This Is the End *'13*
Don Verdean *'15*
The Angry Birds Movie *'16*
Alien: Covenant *'17*
Arizona *'18*
Zeroville *'19*

Jon McBride (1960-)
Cannibal Campout *'88*
Blades *'89*
Woodchipper Massacre *'89*
Feeders *'96*
Terror House *'97*

Simon McBurney (1957-)
Mesmer *'94*
The Manchurian Candidate *'04*
Friends with Money *'06*
The Last King of Scotland *'06*
Body of Lies *'08*
The Duchess *'08*
Boogie Woogie *'09*
Jane Eyre *'11*
Tinker Tailor Soldier Spy *'11*
Magic in the Moonlight *'14*
The Theory of Everything *'14*

Debra McCabe
Saw 3 *'06*
Sticks and Stones *'08*

Richard McCabe (1960-)
Heat of the Sun *'99*
Notting Hill *'99*
Master and Commander: The Far Side of the World *'03*
The Constant Gardener *'05*
The Best of Men *'12*

Ruth McCabe
My Left Foot *'89*
The Snapper *'93*
Talk of Angels *'96*
American Women *'00*
An Everlasting Piece *'00*
Rory O'Shea Was Here *'04*
Breakfast on Pluto *'05*
Wake Wood *'10*
Philomena *'13*

Tony McCabe (?-1968)
Suburban Roulette *'67*
Something Weird *'68*

James McCaffrey (1959-)
Burnzy's Last Call *'95*
Schemes *'95*
The Tic Code *'99*
American Splendor *'03*
Fresh Cut Grass *'04*
Feel the Noise *'07*
Camp Hell *'10*
Meskada *'10*
The Pregnancy Pact *'10*
Compliance *'12*
The Suspect *'14*
The Big Take *'18*

Frances Lee McCain (1944-)
Real Life *'79*
Tex *'82*
Gremlins *'84*
Broken Badge *'85*
Patch Adams *'98*

Catriona McCall (1954-)
See Katherine (Katriona) MacColl

Mitzi McCall (1932-)
You're Never Too Young *'55*
The Opposite Sex and How to Live With Them *'93*
World's Greatest Dad *'09*

Ross McCall (1976-)
Lethal Dose *'03*
Green Street Hooligans *'05*
Green Street Hooligans 2 *'09*

Irish McCalla (1929-2002)
She Demons *'58*
Hands of a Stranger *'62*

Holt McCallany (1964-)
Creepshow 2 *'87*
Alien 3 *'92*
The Search for One-Eye Jimmy *'94*
The Peacemaker *'97*
Rough Riders *'97*
Three Kings *'99*
Kiss Tomorrow Goodbye *'00*
Men of Honor *'00*
Out of Line *'00*
Below *'02*
The Upside of Anger *'05*
Vantage Point *'08*
Bound by a Secret *'09*
The Losers *'10*
Bullet to the Head *'12*
Hijacked *'12*
Crush *'13*
Gangster Squad *'13*
Blackhat *'15*

Lon (Bud) McCallister (1923-2005)
Stage Door Canteen *'43*
Home In Indiana *'44*
The Red House *'47*
Thunder In the Valley *'47*
The Big Cat *'49*
The Story of Seabiscuit *'49*

David McCallum (1933-)
Robbery under Arms *'57*
A Night to Remember *'58*
Billy Budd *'62*
The Great Escape *'63*
Around the World Under the Sea *'65*
Mosquito Squadron *'70*
King Solomon's Treasure *'76*
The Watcher in the Woods *'81*
Return of the Man from U.N.C.L.E. *'83*
Behind Enemy Lines *'85*
The Wind *'87*
The Haunting of Morella *'91*
The Man Who Lived at the Ritz *'91*
Shattered Image *'93*
Mortal Challenge *'97*
Coming Home *'98*

Joanna McCallum
Testament of Youth *'79*
Tom & Viv *'94*

John McCallum (1918-2010)
It Always Rains on Sunday *'47*
Miranda *'48*
Derby Day *'52*
The Long Memory *'53*

Macon McCalman (1932-2005)
Fleshburn *'84*
Doc Hollywood *'91*

Mercedes McCambridge (1918-2004)
All the King's Men *'49*
Lightning Strikes Twice *'51*
Johnny Guitar *'53*
Giant *'56*
A Farewell to Arms *'57*
Touch of Evil *'58 (C)*
Suddenly, Last Summer *'59*
Cimarron *'60*
Angel Baby *'61*
Deadly Sanctuary *'68*
99 Women *'69*
Killer by Night *'72*
Sixteen *'72*
The Exorcist *'73 (V)*
The Concorde: Airport '79 *'79*
The Sacketts *'79*
Echoes *'83*

Tom McCamus (1955-)
A Man in Uniform *'93*
Choices of the Heart: The Margaret Sanger Story *'95*
First Degree *'95*
The Sweet Hereafter *'96*
The Passion of Ayn Rand *'99*
Torso *'02*
Confessions of a Teenage Drama Queen *'04*
Ginger Snaps Back: The Beginning *'04*
Siblings *'04*
Waking Up Wally *'05*
Shake Hands With the Devil *'07*
Cairo Time *'09*
The Good Samaritan *'12*

Chuck McCann (1934-2018)
The Heart Is a Lonely Hunter *'68*
Jennifer On My Mind *'71*
The Projectionist *'71*
The Girl Most Likely to. . . *'73*
Foul Play *'78*
They Went That-a-Way & That-a-Way *'78*
C.H.O.M.P.S. *'79*
Rosebud Beach Hotel *'85*
Thrashin' *'86*
Cameron's Closet *'89*
DuckTales the Movie: Treasure of the Lost Lamp *'90 (V)*
Storyville *'92*
Citizen Jane *'09*

Donal McCann (1943-99)
Sinful Davey '69
Out of Africa '85
The Dead '87
Rawhead Rex '87
December Bride '91
Stealing Beauty '96
The Nephew '97
The Serpent's Kiss '97
Illuminata '98

Martin McCann (1983-)
Closing the Ring '07
My Boy Jack '07
The Pacific '10
Killing Bono '11
Stand Off '11
A Brilliant Young Mind '14

Rory McCann (1969-)
Alexander '04
Beowulf & Grendel '06
The Crew '08

Sean McCann (1935-2019)
Unnatural Causes '86
Guilty as Sin '93
The Air Up There '94
Trapped in Paradise '94
Iron Eagle 4 '95
Gang in Blue '96
Affliction '97
Tracked '98
Miracle '04
The Reagans '04
A Separate Peace '04
The River King '05
A Dad for Christmas '06
Wedding Wars '06

Brian McCardie (1965-)
Kidnapped '95
Rob Roy '95
The Ghost and the Darkness '96
Speed 2: Cruise Control '97
200 Cigarettes '98
Rip It Off '02
The Damned United '09
Titanic '12

Andrew McCarthy (1962-)
The Beniker Gang '83
Class '83
Heaven Help Us '85
St. Elmo's Fire '85
Pretty in Pink '86
Less Than Zero '87
Mannequin '87
Waiting for the Moon '87
Fresh Horses '88
Kansas '88
Weekend at Bernie's '89
Quiet Days in Clichy '90
Year of the Gun '91
Only You '92
The Joy Luck Club '93
Weekend at Bernie's 2 '93
Dream Man '94
Mrs. Parker and the Vicious Circle '94
Night of the Running Man '94
Mulholland Falls '95
Escape Clause '96
The Heist '96
Things I Never Told You '96
Stag '97
I'm Losing You '98
Beyond Redemption '99
New Waterford Girl '99
New World Disorder '99
Jackie Bouvier Kennedy Onassis '00
Nowhere in Sight '01
Anything But Love '02
The Secret of Zoey '02
Straight from the Heart '03
2B Perfectly Honest '04
The Spiderwick Chronicles '08
The National Tree '09
Camp Hell '10
The Good Guy '10
Main Street '10
Come Dance With Me '12

Francis X. (Frank) McCarthy (1942-)
Dead Men Don't Wear Plaid '82
The Man with Two Brains '83
Nightwaves '03

James McCarthy
Oktober '98
To End All Wars '01

Jenny McCarthy (1972-)
Things to Do in Denver When You're Dead '95
BASEketball '98
Diamonds '99
Python '00
Scream 3 '00
Crazy Little Thing '02
Scary Movie 3 '03 (C)
Dirty Love '05
John Tucker Must Die '06
Santa Baby '06
Wieners '08
Witless Protection '08
Hugh Hefner: Playboy, Activist and Rebel '09
Santa Baby 2: Santa Maybe '09

Kevin McCarthy (1914-2010)
Death of a Salesman '51
Drive a Crooked Road '54
The Gambler from Natchez '54
Stranger on Horseback '55
Invasion of the Body Snatchers '56
40 Pounds of Trouble '62
The Best Man '64
A Big Hand for the Little Lady '66
Mirage '66
Hotel '67
Ace High '68
Operation Heartbeat '69
Kansas City Bomber '72
Dan Candy's Law '73
Order to Kill '73
The Seagull '75
Buffalo Bill & the Indians '76
Invasion of the Body Snatchers '78
Piranha '78
Hero at Large '80
Portrait of an Escort '80
Those Lips, Those Eyes '80
The Howling '81
My Tutor '82
Making of a Male Model '83
Twilight Zone: The Movie '83
Invitation to Hell '84
Ratings Game '84
The Midnight Hour '86
Innerspace '87
Poor Little Rich Girl: The Barbara Hutton Story '87
Fast Food '89
UHF '89
The Rose and the Jackal '90
Texas Guns '90
Ghoulies 3: Ghoulies Go to College '91
The Distinguished Gentleman '92
Matinee '92
Just Cause '94
Loving Annabelle '06

Lin McCarthy (1918-2002)
Yellowneck '55
D.I. '57

Melissa McCarthy (1970-)
The Nines '07
Pretty Ugly People '08
The Back-Up Plan '10
Life As We Know It '10
Bridesmaids '11
The Hangover, Part III '13
The Heat '13
Identity Thief '13
St. Vincent '14
Tammy '14
Spy '15
The Boss '16
Ghostbusters '16
Can You Ever Forgive Me? '18
The Happytime Murders '18
Life of the Party '18
The Kitchen '19

Molly McCarthy
The Great St. Louis Bank Robbery '59
Blast of Silence '61
The Flamingo Kid '84

Neil McCarthy (1932-85)
Zulu '64
The Hill '65
Where Eagles Dare '68

Nobu McCarthy (1934-2002)
The Geisha Boy '58
Wake Me When It's Over '60
The Karate Kid: Part 2 '86
Pacific Heights '90

Sheila McCarthy (1956-)
I've Heard the Mermaids Singing '87
Die Hard 2: Die Harder '90
Bright Angel '91
Paradise '91
Beautiful Dreamers '92
A Private Matter '92
A Woman of Independent Means '94
The Awakening '95
House Arrest '96
Armistead Maupin's More Tales of the City '97 (C)
My Teacher Ate My Homework '98
You Know My Name '99
Rare Birds '01
The Rats '01
The Lathe of Heaven '02
Being Julia '04
Confessions of a Teenage Drama Queen '04
The Day After Tomorrow '04
Bailey's Billion$ '05
Cow Belles '06
The Stone Angel '07
Antiviral '12
A Fighting Man '14
Isabelle '19

Steven McCarthy
The Crossing '00
Picture Day '13

Thomas (Tom) McCarthy (1966-)
Meet the Parents '00
Good Night, and Good Luck '05
Beautiful Ohio '06
Flags of Our Fathers '06
The Great New Wonderful '06
Year of the Dog '07
Duplicity '09
Mammoth '09
2012 '09
Jack Goes Boating '10
Mayor Cupcake '11

Paul McCarthy-Boyington
Altered '06
The Human Race '14
Kill or Be Killed '15

Jesse McCartney (1987-)
The Biggest Fan '02
Alvin and the Chipmunks '07 (V)
Dr. Seuss' Horton Hears a Who! '08 (V)
Keith '08
Alvin and the Chipmunks: The Squeakquel '09 (V)
Alvin and the Chipmunks: Chipwrecked '11 (V)
Chernobyl Diaries '12
Alvin and the Chipmunks: Road Chip '15
88 '15

Linda McCartney (1941-98)
Give My Regards to Broad Street '84
Eat the Rich '87

Paul McCartney (1942-)
A Hard Day's Night '64
Help! '65
Yellow Submarine '68 (V)
Let It Be '70
Give My Regards to Broad Street '84
Eat the Rich '87
George Harrison: Living in the Material World '11

Rod McCary (1941-)
The Christine Jorgensen Story '70
Night of the Demons 2 '94

Constance McCashin (1947-)
The Two Worlds of Jenny Logan '79
Nightmare at Bittercreek '91

Charles McCaughan
Heat and Dust '82
Slaves of New York '89
Impulse '90

Nikki McCauley
American Warships '01
American Warship '12

Peggy McCay (1930-)
The Case Against Brooklyn '58
FBI Code 98 '63

China McClain (1998-)
Daddy's Little Girls '07
Blood Brother '18

Lauryn McClain (1997-)
Daddy's Little Girls '07
Haunt '19

Saundra McClain
Mr. & Mrs. Bridge '90
The Sixth Man '97

Rue McClanahan (1934-2010)
Five Minutes to Love '63
Hollywood after Dark '65
Modern Love '90
Baby of the Bride '91
Dear God '96
Out to Sea '97
Starship Troopers '97
A Saintly Switch '99
Miracle Dogs '03
Back to You and Me '05

Brandon Jay McClaren
Yeti '08
Tucker & Dale vs. Evil '10

Michael (Mick) McCleery (1959-)
Harry and Tonto '74
Addicted to Murder '95
Addicted to Murder 2: Tainted Blood '97
If I Die Before I Wake '98
Addicted to Murder 3: Bloodlust '99

Catherine McClements (1965-)
Better Than Sex '00
After the Deluge '03

Reiley McClendon
Accused at 17 '09
Safe Harbor '09
Time Trap '17

Belinda McClory (1968-)
The Matrix '99
Acolytes '08

Sean McClory (1924-2003)
The Daughter of Rosie O'Grady '50
The Quiet Man '52
Charade '53
Island in the Sky '53
Man in the Attic '53
Them! '54
Diane '55
The King's Thief '55
Valley of the Dragons '61
Roller Boogie '79
My Chauffeur '86

Leigh McCloskey (1955-)
Alexander: The Other Side of Dawn '77
The Bermuda Depths '78
Inferno '80
Fraternity Vacation '85
Just One of the Guys '85
Cameron's Closet '89

Doug McClure (1934-95)
Enemy Below '57
Because They're Young '60
The Unforgiven '60
The Lively Set '64
Shenandoah '65
Colditz: Escape of the Birdmen '71
The Land That Time Forgot '75
At the Earth's Core '76
The People That Time Forgot '77
Humanoids from the Deep '80
House Where Evil Dwells '82
52 Pick-Up '86
Prime Suspect '88
Tapeheads '89
Battling for Baby '92
The Gambler Returns: The Luck of the Draw '93
Maverick '94 (C)

Kandyse McClure (1980-)
Carrie '02
Hollywood Wives: The New Generation '03
Children of the Corn '09

Marc McClure (1957-)
I Wanna Hold Your Hand '78
Superman: The Movie '78
Superman 2 '80
Strange Behavior '81
Superman 3 '83
Supergirl '84
Back to the Future '85
Superman 4: The Quest for Peace '87
After Midnight '89
Back to the Future, Part 3 '90
Apollo 13 '95
That Thing You Do! '96
Landspeed '01

Molly McClure (1919-2008)
Daddy's Dyin'. . . Who's Got the Will? '90
Pure Country '92
Finding North '97

Tane McClure (1958-)
Caged Hearts '95
Lap Dancing '95
Midnight Tease 2 '95
Stripshow '95
Scorned 2 '96
Sexual Roulette '96
Death and Desire '97

Vicky McClure
This Is England '06
Redemption '13

Edie McClurg (1951-)
Carrie '76
Cheech and Chong's Next Movie '80
Eating Raoul '82
The Secret of NIMH '82 (V)
Mr. Mom '83
Cheech and Chong's The Corsican Brothers '84
Back to School '86
Ferris Bueller's Day Off '86
Planes, Trains & Automobiles '87
Elvira, Mistress of the Dark '88
She's Having a Baby '88
The Little Mermaid '89 (V)
A River Runs Through It '92
Airborne '93
Flubber '97
A Bug's Life '98 (V)
Master of Disguise '02
Air Bud 5: Buddy Spikes Back '03
Dickie Roberts: Former Child Star '03
Home on the Range '04 (V)
Everything You Want '05

Stephen McCole
Orphans '97
The Acid House '98
Postmortem '98
Rushmore '98
A Lonely Place to Die '11

Warren McCollum (1918-87)
Reefer Madness '38
The Great Commandment '41

Matt McColm (1965-)
Body Armor '96
Subterfuge '98
The Matrix Reloaded '03
Cellular '04

Lorissa McComas (1970-2009)
Lap Dancing '95
Stormswept '95
Hard As Nails '01

Heather McComb (1977-)
New York Stories '89
Stay Tuned '92
God's Lonely Man '96
Apt Pupil '97
Blowin' Smoke '99
If These Walls Could Talk 2 '00
Steel City '06
Shark Swarm '08
Chasing the Green '09
Supernova '09

Matthew McConaughey (1969-)
Dazed and Confused '93
Boys on the Side '94
Lone Star '95
The Texas Chainsaw Massacre 4: The Next Generation '95
Glory Daze '96 (C)
Larger Than Life '96
Scorpion Spring '96
A Time to Kill '96
Amistad '97
Contact '97
The Newton Boys '97
EDtv '99
U-571 '00
Thirteen Conversations About One Thing '01
The Wedding Planner '01
Frailty '02
Reign of Fire '02
How to Lose a Guy in 10 Days '03
Tiptoes '03
Paparazzi '04 (C)
Sahara '05
Two for the Money '05
Failure to Launch '06
We Are Marshall '06
Fool's Gold '08
Surfer, Dude '08
Tropic Thunder '08
Ghosts of Girlfriends Past '09
Killer Joe '11
The Lincoln Lawyer '11
Bernie '12
Magic Mike '12
Mud '12
The Paperboy '12
Dallas Buyers Club '13
The Wolf of Wall Street '13
Interstellar '14
Free State of Jones '16
Gold '16
Kubo and the Two Strings '16
The Sea of Trees '16
Sing '16
The Dark Tower '17
White Boy Rick '18
The Beach Bum '19
Between Two Ferns '19
Serenity '19
The Gentlemen '20

Elias McConnell
Elephant '03
Paris, je t'aime '06

John McConnell (1958-)
Delta Heat '92
The Ladykillers '04

Judith McConnell (1944-)
The Thirsty Dead '74
The Weather Man '05

John McCook (1944-)
Scorned 2 '96
The Invincible Iron Man '07 (V)

AnnaLynne McCord (1987-)
The Haunting of Molly Hartley '08
Fired Up! '09
Blood Out '10
Gun '10
Excision '12
Officer Down '13
Gutshot Straight '14

Kent McCord (1942-)
Airplane 2: The Sequel '82
Predator 2 '90
Return of the Living Dead 3 '93

Catherine McCormack (1972-)
Loaded '94
Braveheart '95
North Star '96
Dancing at Lughnasa '98
Dangerous Beauty '98
Deacon Brodie '98
Born Romantic '00
A Rumor of Angels '00
Shadow of the Vampire '00
The Tailor of Panama '00
The Weight of Water '00
Spy Game '01
A Sound of Thunder '05
Renaissance '06 (V)
The Moon & the Stars '07
28 Weeks Later '07
The Song of Names '19

Eric McCormack (1963-)
Call of the Wild '93
Free Enterprise '98
Holy Man '98
The Audrey Hepburn Story '00
The Sisters '05
The Andromeda Strain '08
Alien Trespass '09
My One and Only '09
Who Is Clark Rockefeller? '10
Sexting '11
Barricade '12
Knife Fight '13

Gary McCormack
The Acid House '98
Sweet Sixteen '02
Valhalla Rising '09

Mary McCormack (1969-)
Private Parts '96
The Alarmist '98
Cash Crop '98
Deep Impact '98
The Big Tease '99
Mystery, Alaska '99
True Crime '99
The Broken Hearts Club '00
Gun Shy '00
High Heels and Low Lifes '01
K-PAX '01
Madison '01
World Traveler '01
Full Frontal '02
Dickie Roberts: Former Child Star '03
Right at Your Door '06
1408 '07
Drone '17

Patty McCormack (1945-)
All Mine to Give '56
The Bad Seed '56
The Adventures of Huckleberry Finn '60
The Explosive Generation '61
Bug '75
Invitation to Hell '84
Saturday the 14th Strikes Back '88
Mommy '95
Mommy 2: Mommy's Day '96
Silent Predators '99
Acceptable Risk '01
Shallow Ground '04

A Christmas Proposal '08
Soda Springs '11

Will McCormack (1974-)
American Outlaws '01
Abandon '02
Celeste & Jesse Forever '12

Carolyn McCormick (1959-)
Enemy Mine '85
Rain Without Thunder '93
You Know My Name '99

Gilmer McCormick (1947-)
Godspell '73
Silent Night, Deadly Night '84

Maureen McCormick (1956-)
Pony Express Rider '76
Idolmaker '80
Texas Lightning '81
Return to Horror High '87
Panic in the Skies '96
Dogtown '97
The Million Dollar Kid '99
Snow White: A Deadly Summer '12

Merrill McCormick (1892-1953)
Robin Hood '22
Call of the Coyote '34

Myron McCormick (1908-62)
One Third of a Nation '39
Jigsaw '49
Not as a Stranger '55
Three for the Show '55
No Time for Sergeants '58
The Iceman Cometh '60
The Hustler '61

Pat McCormick (1927-2005)
If You Don't Stop It. . . You'll Go Blind '77
Smokey and the Bandit '77
A Wedding '78
Smokey and the Bandit 2 '80
Under the Rainbow '81
Smokey and the Bandit, Part 3 '83
Doin' Time '85
Frost/Nixon '08

Sierra McCormick (1997-)
The Dog Who Saved Christmas '09
A Nanny for Christmas '10
Ramona and Beezus '10
Some Kind of Hate '15
The Vast of Night '20

Grayson McCouch (1968-)
Armageddon '98
Momentum '03

Emer McCourt
Riff Raff '92
Boston Kickout '95

Malachy McCourt (1931-)
Q (The Winged Serpent) '82
JFK: Reckless Youth '93
Ash Wednesday '02
The Guru '02

Alec McCowen (1925-)
One That Got Away '57
Time Without Pity '57
A Night to Remember '58
The Silent Enemy '58
The Witches '66
Frenzy '72
Travels with My Aunt '72
Hanover Street '79
Forever Young '85
Cry Freedom '87
Personal Services '87
Henry V '89
The Age of Innocence '93
Longitude '00
Gangs of New York '02

Larry McCoy
Bulletproof '96
The Players Club '98

Lisa Ray McCoy (1967-)
See LisaRaye

Matt McCoy (1958-)
Fraternity Vacation '85
Police Academy 5: Assignment Miami Beach '88
Deepstar Six '89
Police Academy 6: City under Siege '89
The Cool Surface '92
The Hand that Rocks the Cradle '92
Bigfoot: The Unforgettable Encounter '94
Hard Bounty '94
Hard Drive '94
The Soft Kill '94
Synapse '95
The Apocalypse '96
Little Bigfoot '96
L.A. Confidential '97
Monsoon '97
Tales of the Kama Sutra 2: Monsoon '98
Forever Together '00
Rangers '00
Beethoven's 4th '01
National Security '03
Abominable '06
The Town That Banned Christmas '06

Sandra McCoy (1979-)
Cry Wolf '05
Wild Things 3: Diamonds in the Rough '05

Sylvester McCoy (1943-)
Doctor Who '96
The Hobbit: An Unexpected Journey '12

Mark McCracken (1960-)
Matinee '92
Pumpkinhead 2: Blood Wings '94
We Were Soldiers '02

Paul McCrane (1961-)
Fame '80
Purple Hearts '84
RoboCop '87
From the Earth to the Moon '98

Darius McCrary (1976-)
Big Shots '87
Don King: Only in America '97
15 Minutes '01
Kingdom Come '01
John Carpenter Presents Vampires: Los Muertos '02
Transformers '07 (V)
Next Day Air '09

Jody McCrea (1934-2009)
Force of Impulse '60
Young Guns of Texas '62
Beach Party '63
Operation Bikini '63
Bikini Beach '64
Muscle Beach Party '64
Pajama Party '64
Beach Blanket Bingo '65
How to Stuff a Wild Bikini '65
The Glory Stompers '67
Cry Blood, Apache '70

Joel McCrea (1905-90)
The Silver Horde '30
Kept Husbands '31
Bird of Paradise '32
The Most Dangerous Game '32
Chance at Heaven '33
One Man's Journey '33
Barbary Coast '35
Adventure in Manhattan '36
Come and Get It '36
Dead End '37
Internes Can't Take Money '37
Three Blind Mice '38
They Shall Have Music '39
Union Pacific '39
Foreign Correspondent '40
Primrose Path '40
Sullivan's Travels '41
The Great Man's Lady '42
The Palm Beach Story '42
The More the Merrier '43
Buffalo Bill '44

The Great Moment '44
The Virginian '46
Border River '47
Ramrod '47
Saddle Tramp '47
Four Faces West '48
South of St. Louis '48
Colorado Territory '49
The Outriders '50
Stars in My Crown '50
The San Francisco Story '52
Stranger on Horseback '55
The First Texan '56
The Oklahoman '56
Trooper Hook '57
Fort Massacre '58
Lafayette Escadrille '58
The Gunfight at Dodge City '59
Ride the High Country '62
Cry Blood, Apache '70

Helen McCrory (1968-)
Uncovered '94
Dad Savage '97
Split Second '99
Anna Karenina '00
Charlotte Gray '01
Dead Gorgeous '02
Enduring Love '04
Casanova '05
The Queen '06
Becoming Jane '07
Flashbacks of a Fool '08
Fantastic Mr. Fox '09 (V)
Harry Potter and the Half-Blood Prince '09
The Special Relationship '10
Harry Potter and the Deathly Hallows, Part 2 '11
Hugo '11
Skyfall '12
A Little Chaos '14
The Woman in Black 2: Angel of Death '15

Bruce McCulloch (1961-)
Kids in the Hall: Brain Candy '96
Dog Park '98
Dick '99

Ian McCulloch (1939-)
Doctor Butcher M.D. '80
Zombie '80
Alien Contamination '81

Kyle McCulloch
Tales from the Gimli Hospital '88
Careful '92

Julie McCullough (1965-)
Big Bad Mama 2 '87
The St. Tammany Miracle '94

Mathew McCurley (1982-)
Little Giants '94
The Secret Agent Club '96

John McCurry (1928-89)
The Last Mile '59
Fritz the Cat '72 (V)

Bill McCutcheon (1924-2002)
Santa Claus Conquers the Martians '64
Family Business '89
Steel Magnolias '89
Mr. Destiny '90
Tune in Tomorrow '90

Etta McDaniel
Mile a Minute Love '37
Mokey '42

Hattie McDaniel (1895-1952)
Blonde Venus '32
I'm No Angel '33
Alice Adams '35
China Seas '35
Harmony Lane '35
The Little Colonel '35
The Bride Walks Out '36
Libeled Lady '36
Show Boat '36
Saratoga '37
True Confession '37
Carefree '38
Mad Miss Manton '38

Shopworn Angel '38
Gone with the Wind '39
The Great Lie '41
They Died with Their Boots On '41
George Washington Slept Here '42
In This Our Life '42
The Male Animal '42
Johnny Come Lately '43
Since You Went Away '44
Never Say Goodbye '46
Mickey '48
Family Honeymoon '49

James McDaniel (1958-)
Malcolm X '92
Out of Time '00
Deliberate Intent '01
Sunshine State '02
Taken '02
Steel City '06
War Eagle, Arkansas '07
Organizm '08
Hostile Makeover '09
Killer Hair '09

Charlie McDermott (1990-)
Disappearances '06
Frozen River '08
Safe Harbor '09
Bond of Silence '10
Hot Tub Time Machine '10
Morning '10

Dean McDermott (1966-)
The Wall '99
Brian's Song '01
Open Range '03
Saving God '08
Santa Baby 2: Santa Maybe '09

Dylan McDermott (1961-)
Hamburger Hill '87
Blue Iguana '88
Steel Magnolias '89
Twister '89
Hardware '90
Where Sleeping Dogs Lie '91
Into the Badlands '92
Jersey Girl '92
In the Line of Fire '93
The Cowboy Way '94
Miracle on 34th Street '94
Home for the Holidays '95
Til There Was You '96
Three to Tango '99
Texas Rangers '01
Party Monster '03
Wonderland '03
Edison Force '05
The Mistress of Spices '05
The Tenants '06
Unbeatable Harold '06
The Messengers '07
Mercy '09
The Campaign '12
Nobody Walks '12
The Perks of Being a Wallflower '12
Olympus Has Fallen '13
Freezer '14

Hugh McDermott (1906-72)
No Orchids for Miss Blandish '48
Lilli Marlene '50
Devil Girl from Mars '54

Marc McDermott (1881-1929)
He Who Gets Slapped '24
Kiki '26
The Temptress '26

Ruth McDevitt (1895-1976)
The Parent Trap '61
The Birds '63
Love Is a Ball '63
The Shakiest Gun in the West '68
Change of Habit '69

Ian McDiarmid (1944-)
The Awakening '80
Annie: A Royal Adventure '95
Touching Evil '97
All the King's Men '99
Sleepy Hollow '99

Star Wars: Episode 1-The Phantom Menace '99
Star Wars: Episode 2-Attack of the Clones '02
Elizabeth I '05
Star Wars: Episode 3-Revenge of the Sith '05

Amber McDonald
You Tell Me '06
Without a Paddle: Nature's Calling '09

Audra McDonald (1970-)
Annie '99
Having Our Say: The Delany Sisters' First 100 Years '99
The Last Debate '00
Wit '01
It Runs in the Family '03
A Raisin in the Sun '08

Bruce McDonald (1959-)
Roadkill '89
Hard Core Logo 2 '10

Christopher McDonald (1955-)
Grease 2 '82
Breakin' '84
Where the Boys Are '84 '84
The Boys Next Door '85
Chances Are '89
Thelma & Louise '91
Conflict of Interest '92
Wild Orchid 2: Two Shades of Blue '92
Benefit of the Doubt '93
Fatal Instinct '93
Grumpy Old Men '93
Monkey Trouble '94
Quiz Show '94
Terminal Velocity '94
Best of the Best 3: No Turning Back '95
Fair Game '95
My Teacher's Wife '95
The Tuskegee Airmen '95
Celtic Pride '96
Happy Gilmore '96
House Arrest '96
Jaded '96
Lawn Dogs '96
The Rich Man's Wife '96
A Smile Like Yours '96
Unforgettable '96
Dirty Work '97
The Eighteenth Angel '97
Flubber '97
Into Thin Air: Death on Everest '97
Leave It to Beaver '97
The Faculty '98
The Iron Giant '99 (V)
SLC Punk! '99
The Perfect Storm '00
Requiem for a Dream '00
The Skulls '00
61* '01
The Theory of the Leisure Class '01
Children On Their Birthdays '02
Grind '03
Broken Flowers '05
Rumor Has It. . . '05
American Pie Presents: The Naked Mile '06
American Pie Presents: Beta House '07
Awake '07
Kickin' It Old Skool '07
The House Bunny '08
Mad Money '08
Player 5150 '08
Spooner '08
Superhero Movie '08
Splinterheads '09
Barry Munday '10
Cat Run '11
Lemonade Mouth '11
Not Fade Away '12
About Last Night '14
The Squeeze '15
Exposed '16
Deep Murder '19

Country Joe McDonald (1942-)
Zachariah '70
Armistead Maupin's Tales of the City '93
Deanne McDonald
The Monster of Phantom Lake '06
It Came From Another World '07
Francis McDonald (1891-1968)
The Confession '20
Battling Butler '26
The Notorious Lady '27
Morocco '30
Call of the Wilderness '32
The Prisoner of Shark Island '36
The Kansan '43
Zorro's Black Whip '44
Spoilers of the North '47
Fort Massacre '58
Garry McDonald (1948-)
Pirate Movie '82
Moulin Rouge '01
Rabbit-Proof Fence '02
The Rage In Placid Lake '03
The Shepherd: Border Patrol '08
Grace McDonald (1918-99)
Gung Ho! '43
It Ain't Hay '43
Jeff (Jeffrey) McDonald (1963-)
Spirit of '76 '91
Sugar Town '99
Kevin McDonald (1961-)
National Lampoon's Senior Trip '95
Kids in the Hall: Brain Candy '96
The Godson '98
Lilo & Stitch '02 (V)
Lilo & Stitch 2: Stitch Has a Glitch '05 (V)
Sky High '05
Leroy and Stitch '06 (V)
Marie McDonald (1923-65)
Tornado '43
Guest in the House '44
Getting Gertie's Garter '45
It's a Pleasure '45
Living In a Big Way '47
Tell It to the Judge '49
The Geisha Boy '58
Promises! Promises! '63
Michael McDonald
The Nutcracker Prince '91 (V)
Outing Riley '04
Miriam McDonald (1987-)
She's Too Young '04
Poison Ivy 4: The Secret Society '08
Sea Beast '08
Peter McDonald (1972-)
Captain Jack '98
Felicia's Journey '99
Blow Dry '00
Nora '00
When Brendan Met Trudy '00
The Bachelor Weekend '13
Ryan McDonald (1984-)
The Ballad of Jack and Rose '05
Resurrecting the Champ '07
Art of War 2: The Betrayal '08
The Private Lives of Pippa Lee '09
William McDonald
Don't Look Down '98
Subhuman '04
Ryan McDonell (1983-)
Snakehead Terror '04
Eight Days to Live '06
Meltdown '06
Destination: Infestation '07
Rampage: President Down '16

Mary McDonnell (1952-)
Matewan '87
Tiger Warsaw '87
Dances with Wolves '90
Grand Canyon '91
Passion Fish '92
Sneakers '92
Blue Chips '94
Independence Day '96
Evidence of Blood '97
Behind the Mask '99
Mumford '99
A Father's Choice '00
Donnie Darko '01
Crazy Like a Fox '04
Margin Call '11
Scream 4 '11
Mary (Elizabeth) McDonough (1961-)
A Day for Thanks on Walton's Mountain '82
Snowballing '85
Mom '89
The Locket '02
Neal McDonough (1966-)
Blue River '95
Star Trek: First Contact '96
Balloon Farm '97
Robin Cook's Invasion '97
Ravenous '99
Band of Brothers '01
The Killing Club '01
Minority Report '02
Timeline '03
Walking Tall '04
Flags of Our Fathers '06
The Guardian '06
The Last Time '06
Brothers Three '07
The Hitcher '07
I Know Who Killed Me '07
Tin Man '07
88 Minutes '08
Forever Strong '08
Traitor '08
Street Fighter: The Legend of Chun-Li '09
Ticking Clock '10
Captain America: The First Avenger '11
The Marine 3: Homefront '11
The Philly Kid '12
Company of Heroes '13
RED 2 '13
Bad Country '14
Paul Blart: Mall Cop 2 '15
1922 '17
Proud Mary '18
Shannon McDonough
It Came From Another World '07
Attack of the Moon Zombies '11
Jake McDorman (1986-)
Aquamarine '06
Bring It On: All or Nothing '06
The Craigslist Killer '11
American Sniper '14
Frances McDormand (1957-)
Blood Simple '85
Raising Arizona '87
Mississippi Burning '88
Chattahoochee '89
Darkman '90
Hidden Agenda '90
The Butcher's Wife '91
Crazy in Love '92
Passed Away '92
Short Cuts '93
Beyond Rangoon '95
The Good Old Boys '95
Lone Star '95
Palookaville '95
Fargo '96
Hidden in America '96
Primal Fear '96
Talk of Angels '96
Johnny Skidmarks '97
Paradise Road '97
Madeline '98
Almost Famous '00
Wonder Boys '00
The Man Who Wasn't There '01

City by the Sea '02
Laurel Canyon '02
Something's Gotta Give '03
Aeon Flux '05
North Country '05
Friends with Money '06
Burn After Reading '08
Miss Pettigrew Lives for a Day '08
Transformers: Dark of the Moon '11
Madagascar 3: Europe's Most Wanted '12 (V)
Moonrise Kingdom '12
Promised Land '12
This Must Be the Place '12
Olive Kitteridge '14
The Good Dinosaur '15
Three Billboards Outside Ebbing, Missouri '17
Betty McDowall (1933-93)
Time Lock '57
Jack the Ripper '60
Ballad in Blue '66
Roddy McDowall (1928-98)
Confirm or Deny '41
How Green Was My Valley '41
Man Hunt '41
Son of Fury '42
Lassie, Come Home '43
My Friend Flicka '43
The Keys of the Kingdom '44
The White Cliffs of Dover '44
Holiday in Mexico '46
Kidnapped '48
Macbeth '48
Everybody's Dancin' '50
The Longest Day '62
Cleopatra '63
The Greatest Story Ever Told '65
Inside Daisy Clover '65
The Loved One '65
That Darn Cat '65
The Third Day '65
The Adventures of Bullwhip Griffin '66
The Defector '66
Lord Love a Duck '66
The Cool Ones '67
Five Card Stud '68
Planet of the Apes '68
Night Gallery '69
Bedknobs and Broomsticks '71
Escape from the Planet of the Apes '71
Pretty Maids All In a Row '71
Conquest of the Planet of the Apes '72
Life & Times of Judge Roy Bean '72
The Poseidon Adventure '72
Battle for the Planet of the Apes '73
The Legend of Hell House '73
Dirty Mary Crazy Larry '74
Funny Lady '75
Mean Johnny Barrows '75
Embryo '76
Flood! '76
Sixth and Main '77
The Cat from Outer Space '78
Circle of Iron '78
Laserblast '78
The Thief of Baghdad '78
The Martian Chronicles: Part 2 '79
The Martian Chronicles: Part 3 '79
The Return of the King '80 (V)
Charlie Chan and the Curse of the Dragon Queen '81
Class of 1984 '82
Evil under the Sun '82
Alice in Wonderland '85
Fright Night '85
Dead of Winter '87
Overboard '87
Fright Night 2 '88

Around the World in 80 Days '89
The Big Picture '89
Cutting Class '89
Shakma '89
Double Trouble '91
Mirror, Mirror 2: Raven Dance '94
The Grass Harp '95
It's My Party '95
Star Hunter '95
Unknown Origin '95
Last Summer In the Hamptons '96
Rudyard Kipling's the Second Jungle Book: Mowgli and Baloo '97
Unlikely Angel '97
A Bug's Life '98 (V)
Claire McDowell (1877-1966)
Heart o' the Hills '19
West-Bound Limited '23
The Big Parade '25
Ben-Hur '26
The Show Off '26
Central Airport '33
Wild Boys of the Road '33
Malcolm McDowell (1943-)
If. . . '69
A Clockwork Orange '71
O Lucky Man! '73
Royal Flash '75
Voyage of the Damned '76
She Fell Among Thieves '78
The Passage '79
Time After Time '79
Caligula '80
Britannia Hospital '82
Cat People '82
Blue Thunder '83
Cross Creek '83
Get Crazy '83
Monte Carlo '86
The Caller '87
Sunset '88
Class of 1999 '90
Jezebel's Kiss '90
Moon 44 '90
The Player '92
Bopha! '93
Night Train to Venice '93
Milk Money '94
Star Trek: Generations '94
The Surgeon '94
Tank Girl '94
Cyborg 3: The Recycler '95
Fist of the North Star '95
Kids of the Round Table '96
Where Truth Lies '96
Hugo Pool '97
Mr. Magoo '97
2103: Deadly Wake '97
The First 9 1/2 Weeks '98
My Life So Far '98
Gangster No. 1 '00
Island of the Dead '00
St. Patrick: The Irish Legend '00
Just Visiting '01
Princess of Thieves '01
The Void '01
Between Strangers '02
Firestarter 2: Rekindled '02
I Spy '02
The Company '03
I'll Sleep When I'm Dead '03
Red Roses and Petrol '03
Tempo '03
Bobby Jones: Stroke of Genius '04
Hidalgo '04
Mirror Wars: Reflection One '05
The Curse of King Tut's Tomb '06
Cut Off '06
Halloween '07
The List '07
Bolt '08
Coco Chanel '08
Delgo '08 (V)
Doomsday '08
Halloween II '09
Suck '09
Barry Munday '10
The Book of Eli '10
Easy A '10

Golf in the Kingdom '10
Pound of Flesh '10
The Artist '11
Antiviral '12
Excision '12
Home Alone: The Holiday Heist '12
Silent Hill: Revelation 3D '12
Silent Night '12
Vamps '12
Sanitarium '13
Free Fall '14
Some Kind of Beautiful '15
Roger Corman's Death Race 2050 '17
Nelson McDowell (1870-1947)
The Last of the Mohicans '20
Oliver Twist '22
Randy McDowell
Dance of the Dead '08
Paranormal Activity '09
Trevyn McDowell (1967-)
Middlemarch '93
Mary Shelley's Frankenstein '94
Michael McElhatton (1963-)
Blow Dry '00
Intermission '03
Perrier's Bounty '09
Parked '10
The Autopsy of Jane Doe '16
The Zookeeper's Wife '17
Rob McElhenney (1977-)
Latter Days '04
The Tollbooth '04
Ian McElhinney (1948-)
The Playboys '92
A Woman's Guide to Adultery '93
Hamlet '96
The Mapmaker '01
The Front Line '06
Jack McElhone (1994-)
Young Adam '03
Dear Frankie '04
Natascha (Natasha) McElhone (1971-)
The Devil's Own '96
Surviving Picasso '96
Mrs. Dalloway '97
Ronin '98
The Truman Show '98
Contaminated Man '00
Love's Labour's Lost '00
Killing Me Softly '01
Feardotcom '02
Laurel Canyon '02
Solaris '02
City of Ghosts '03
The Other Boleyn Girl '03
Big Nothing '06
The Company '07
The Secret of Moonacre '08
Romeo & Juliet '13
Mr. Church '16
Dominique McElligott (1986-)
Moon '09
Blackthorn '11
John McEnery (1943-)
Bartleby '70
The Land That Time Forgot '75
Schizo '77
A.D. '85
The Buddha of Suburbia '92
Black Beauty '94
Merlin '98
Tess of the D'Urbervilles '98
Peter McEnery (1940-)
Victim '61
The Moon-Spinners '64
The Fighting Prince of Donegal '66
The Game Is Over '66
Tales That Witness Madness '73
Primal Impulse '74
The Cat and the Canary '79
Florence Nightingale '85

Annie McEnroe (1955-)
The Hand '81
Warlords of the 21st Century '82
Purple Hearts '84
Howling 2: Your Sister Is a Werewolf '85
True Stories '86
Cop '88
John McEnroe (1959-)
Mr. Deeds '02 (C)
Anger Management '03 (C)
Reba McEntire (1955-)
Tremors '89
The Gambler Returns: The Luck of the Draw '93
The Man from Left Field '93
Is There Life Out There? '94
Buffalo Girls '95
Forever Love '98
One Night at McCool's '01
Charlotte's Web '06 (V)
The Fox and the Hound 2 '06 (V)
Spies in Disguise '19
Barry McEvoy
Gloria '98
An Everlasting Piece '00
Geraldine McEwan (1932-2015)
No Kidding '60
The Prime of Miss Jean Brodie '78
Foreign Body '86
Henry V '89
Oranges Are Not the Only Fruit '89
Robin Hood: Prince of Thieves '91
Moses '96
The Love Letter '99
Titus '99
Contaminated Man '00
Love's Labour's Lost '00
Food of Love '02
The Magdalene Sisters '02
Pure '02
Carrie's War '04
Vanity Fair '04
Davenia McFadden (1961-)
Double Jeopardy '99
Smokin' Aces '07
Gates (Cheryl) McFadden (1949-)
Taking Care of Business '90
Star Trek: Generations '94
Star Trek: First Contact '96
Star Trek: Insurrection '98
Star Trek: Nemesis '02
Make the Yuletide Gay '09
Joseph McFadden (1975-)
The Crow Road '96
Dad Savage '97
Cranford '08
George 'Spanky' McFarland (1928-93)
Day of Reckoning '33
Kentucky Kernels '34
The Trail of the Lonesome Pine '36
Peck's Bad Boy with the Circus '38
The Aurora Encounter '85
Hayley McFarland
An American Crime '07
Fragments '08
Colin McFarlane (1961-)
Fragile '05
The Dark Knight '08
Douglas McFerran
Sliding Doors '97
Antitrust '00
Johnny English '03
Mark McGann (1961-)
Let Him Have It '91
Catherine the Great '95
Samson and Delilah '96
Endgame '01
Shackleton '02
Paul McGann (1959-)
Withnail and I '87
Dealers '89

The Rainbow '89
Paper Mask '91
Afraid of the Dark '92
Alien 3 '92
Catherine the Great '95
Doctor Who '96
The One That Got Away '96
FairyTale: A True Story '97
Our Mutual Friend '98
Horatio Hornblower: The Adventure Continues '01
Queen of the Damned '02
Kidnapped '05
Vampire Killers '09

Darren McGavin (1922-2006)
Queen for a Day '51
The Court Martial of Billy Mitchell '55
The Man with the Golden Arm '55
Summertime '55
The Delicate Delinquent '56
The Case Against Brooklyn '58
The Night Stalker '71
The Night Strangler '72
Richard Petty Story '72
No Deposit, No Return '76
Airport '77 '77
The Martian Chronicles: Part 1 '79
The Martian Chronicles: Part 2 '79
The Martian Chronicles: Part 3 '79
Hangar 18 '80
A Christmas Story '83
Power, Passion & Murder '83
The Baron and the Kid '84
The Natural '84
Turk 182! '85
Raw Deal '86
Dead Heat '88
Sunset '88
Around the World in 80 Days '89
By Dawn's Early Light '89
Captain America '89
Blood & Concrete: A Love Story '91
Perfect Harmony '91
Happy Hell Night '92
Billy Madison '94
Smalltime '96

Patrick McGaw (1967-)
Amongst Friends '93
The Basketball Diaries '95
Scorpion Spring '96
Dream with the Fishes '97

Jack McGee (1949-)
Crash and Burn '90
The Last Days of Frankie the Fly '96
The Quest '96
Chairman of the Board '97
Treehouse Hostage '99
Bread and Roses '00
21 '08
The International '09
The Fighter '10

Vic McGee
Horrors of the Red Planet '64
Alien Massacre '67
Gallery of Horrors '67

Vonetta McGee (1945-2010)
Blacula '72
The Norliss Tapes '73
Shaft in Africa '73
The Eiger Sanction '75
Repo Man '83
To Sleep with Anger '90
Brother Future '91
You Must Remember This '92
Johnny B. '00

Johnny Rae McGhee
Project X '87
Love Field '91

William (Bill) McGhee (1930-2007)
Don't Look in the Basement '73
1918 '85

Bruce McGill (1950-)
Citizens Band '77
National Lampoon's Animal House '78
The Hand '81
Silkwood '83
Tough Enough '83
Into the Night '85
No Mercy '86
Wildcats '86
Waiting for the Moon '87
End of the Line '88
Out Cold '89
Three Fugitives '89
The Last Boy Scout '91
My Cousin Vinny '92
Play Nice '92
Black Widow Murders: The Blanche Taylor Moore Story '93
Timecop '94
The Good Old Boys '95
Black Sheep '96
Lawn Dogs '96
Rosewood '96
Ground Control '98
Letters from a Killer '98
A Dog of Flanders '99
The Insider '99
Deep Core '00
The Legend of Bagger Vance '00
Running Mates '00
Ali '01
Exit Wounds '01
Shallow Hal '01
61* '01
Path to War '02
The Sum of All Fears '02
Legally Blonde 2: Red White & Blonde '03
Live from Baghdad '03
Matchstick Men '03
Runaway Jury '03
Collateral '04
Cinderella Man '05
Elizabethtown '05
Slow Burn '05
Behind Enemy Lines 2: Axis of Evil '06
The Good Life '07
Humble Pie '07
The Lookout '07
Valley of the Heart's Delight '07
Kings of the Evening '08
Recount '08
Vantage Point '08
From Mexico With Love '09
Held Hostage '09
Law Abiding Citizen '09
Obsessed '09
The Perfect Game '09
Fair Game '10
For Greater Glory '12
Lincoln '12
Unconditional '12
Ride Along '14
Run All Night '15

Everett McGill (1945-)
Brubaker '80
Union City '81
Quest for Fire '82
Dune '84
Silver Bullet '85
Heartbreak Ridge '86
Iguana '89
License to Kill '89
Drug Wars: The Camarena Story '90
Jezebel's Kiss '90
The People under the Stairs '91
Under Siege 2: Dark Territory '95
My Fellow Americans '96

Paul McGillion (1969-)
A Dog's Breakfast '07
Loch Ness Terror '07
Mom, Dad and Her '08
Confined '10
Finding a Family '10
The Traveler '10
Christmas Magic '11
Magic Beyond Words: The JK Rowling Story '11
Metal Shifters '11
Witchslayer Gretl '12

Kelly McGillis (1957-)
Code of Honor '84
Witness '85
Top Gun '86
Made in Heaven '87
The Accused '88
The House on Carroll Street '88
Winter People '89
Cat Chaser '90
The Babe '92
The Wicked, Wicked West '97
At First Sight '98
Ground Control '98
Storm Chasers: Revenge of the Twister '98
Morgan's Ferry '99
The Settlement '99
The Monkey's Mask '00
Stake Land '10
The Innkeepers '11
We Are What We Are '13

John C. McGinley (1959-)
Platoon '86
Wall Street '87
Talk Radio '88
Fat Man and Little Boy '89
Lost Angels '89
Highlander 2: The Quickening '91
Point Break '91
Article 99 '92
A Midnight Clear '92
Hear No Evil '93
The Last Outlaw '93
Car 54, Where Are You? '94
Mother's Boys '94
On Deadly Ground '94
Surviving the Game '94
Wagons East '94
Born to Be Wild '95
Seven '95
Mother '96
Nothing to Lose '96
The Rock '96
Set It Off '96
Dean Koontz's Intensity '97
Flypaper '97
Truth or Consequences, N.M. '97
Office Space '98
The Pentagon Wars '98
Any Given Sunday '99
The Jack Bull '99
Three to Tango '99
Get Carter '00
The Animal '01
Highway '01
Crazy as Hell '02
Stealing Harvard '02
Identity '03
Two Tickets to Paradise '06
Are We Done Yet? '07
Wild Hogs '07
42 '13
Kid Cannabis '14
The Belko Experiment '17
The Good Catholic '17
Benched '18

Sean McGinley (1956-)
The Field '90
Braveheart '95
Michael Collins '96
Trojan Eddie '96
The Butcher Boy '97
The General '98
American Women '00
The Claim '00
Dr. Bell and Mr. Doyle: The Dark Beginnings of Sherlock Holmes '00
Conspiracy of Silence '03
Dead Bodies '03
Freeze Frame '04
On a Clear Day '05
The Tiger's Tale '06

Ted McGinley (1958-)
Making of a Male Model '83
Revenge of the Nerds '84
Physical Evidence '89
Revenge of the Nerds 3: The Next Generation '92
Covert Assassin '94
Revenge of the Nerds 4: Nerds in Love '94
Major League 3: Back to the Minors '98
Dick '99
Face the Music '00
Daybreak '01
The Note '07
The Note 2: Taking a Chance on Love '09
The Note 3: Notes from the Heart Healer '12
Do You Believe? '15
A-X-L '18
God's Not Dead: A Light in Darkness '18

Scott McGinnis (1958-)
Joy Sticks '83
Making the Grade '84
Odd Jobs '85
You Can't Hurry Love '88

Boris McGiver (1962-)
Little Odessa '94
Connie and Carla '04

John McGiver (1912-75)
Love in the Afternoon '57
The Gazebo '59
Bachelor in Paradise '61
Breakfast at Tiffany's '61
The Manchurian Candidate '62
Mr. Hobbs Takes a Vacation '62
Period of Adjustment '62
Johnny Cool '63
Man's Favorite Sport? '63
Take Her, She's Mine '63
Who's Got the Action? '63
Who's Minding the Store? '63
Made in Paris '65
Marriage on the Rocks '65
The Glass Bottom Boat '66
Fitzwilly '67
Midnight Cowboy '69
Lawman '71
Mame '74

Mike McGlone (1972-)
The Brothers McMullen '94
Ed '96
She's the One '96
Subway Stories '97
One Tough Cop '98
The Bone Collector '99
Dinner Rush '00
Hardball '01
Fortunes '05
The War Within '05
Bad City '06
The Fitzgerald Family Christmas '12

Frank McGlynn (1866-1951)
America '24
Custer's Last Stand '36
The Prisoner of Shark Island '36

Patrick McGoohan (1928-2009)
Zarak '56
All Night Long '62
The Quare Fellow '62
The Three Lives of Thomasina '63
Dr. Syn, Alias the Scarecrow '64
Ice Station Zebra '68
The Moonshine War '70
Mary, Queen of Scots '71
Silver Streak '76
The Man in the Iron Mask '77
Brass Target '78
Escape from Alcatraz '79
Scanners '81
Jamaica Inn '82
Baby. . . Secret of the Lost Legend '85
Three Sovereigns for Sarah '85
Braveheart '95
The Phantom '96
A Time to Kill '96
Treasure Planet '02 (V)

Barry McGovern (1948-)
Joe Versus the Volcano '90
Braveheart '95
Driftwood '97
Miracle at Midnight '98

Elizabeth McGovern (1961-)
Ordinary People '80
Ragtime '81
Lovesick '83
Once Upon a Time in America '84
Racing with the Moon '84
The Bedroom Window '87
She's Having a Baby '88
Johnny Handsome '89
The Handmaid's Tale '90
A Shock to the System '90
Tune in Tomorrow '90
Women & Men: Stories of Seduction '90
The Favor '92
Broken Trust '95
The Wings of the Dove '97
Twice upon a Yesterday '98
The Scarlet Pimpernel '99
The Scarlet Pimpernel 2: Mademoiselle Guillotine '99
The Scarlet Pimpernel 3: The Kidnapped King '99
House of Mirth '00
Buffalo Soldiers '01
Daphne '07
A Room With a View '08
Appointment With Death '10
Kick-Ass '10
Angels Crest '11
Cheerful Weather for the Wedding '12
Unexpected '15
The Wife '17

Michael McGovern
Mosquito Squadron '70
Dirty Games '89

Terence McGovern (1942-)
Americathon '79
DuckTales the Movie: Treasure of the Lost Lamp '90 (V)

Daniel McGowan
In His Life: The John Lennon Story '00
If a Tree Falls: A Story of the Earth Liberation Front '11

James McGowan (1960-)
All the Good Ones Are Married '07
Christie's Revenge '07
Lies and Crimes '07
The Good Witch's Gift '10

Rose McGowan (1973-)
Encino Man '92
The Doom Generation '95
Bio-Dome '96
Scream '96
Going All the Way '97
Lewis and Clark and George '97
Phantoms '97
Devil in the Flesh '98
Jawbreaker '98
Southie '98
The Last Stop '99
Ready to Rumble '00
Monkeybone '01
Road to Riches '01
The Black Dahlia '06
Death Proof '07
Planet Terror '07
Fifty Dead Men Walking '08
Machete '10
Conan the Barbarian '11
The Pastor's Wife '11

Tom McGowan (1959-)
Mrs. Parker and the Vicious Circle '94
The Birdcage '95
As Good As It Gets '97 (C)
Bean '97
Dog Gone Love '03
Just Peck '09

Zach McGowan
The Hunt for Eagle One: Crash Point '06
Seal Team '08

Michael McGrady (1960-)
The Babe '92
Operation Delta Force 2: Mayday '97
The Deep End of the Ocean '98
The Perfect Family '11
Rage '14

Walter McGrail (1888-1970)
Where the North Begins '23
Night Nurse '31
The Green Hornet '39

Brian McGrath
Falling for a Dancer '98
A Love Divided '01

Derek McGrath (1951-)
She's Out of Control '89
Freaked '93
Stuart Bliss '98
Full of It '07
Wide Awake '07
Daniel's Daughter '08
Fairfield Road '10
Christmas Magic '11

Douglas McGrath (1958-)
Porky's '82
Pale Rider '85
Company Man '00

Gulliver McGrath
Dark Shadows '12
Lincoln '12

Katie McGrath (1983-)
A Princess for Christmas '11
W.E. '11
Labyrinth '12

Matt McGrath (1969-)
Desperate Hours '90
Bob Roberts '92
Last Breath '96
The Imposters '98
1999 '98
Boys Don't Cry '99
The Broken Hearts Club '00
The Notorious Bettie Page '06

Charles McGraw (1914-80)
The Killers '46
T-Men '47
Border Incident '49
Armored Car Robbery '50
Ma and Pa Kettle Go to Town '50
Side Street '50
His Kind of Woman '51
Roadblock '51
The Narrow Margin '52
One Minute to Zero '52
War Paint '53
Loophole '54
The Bridges at Toko-Ri '55
Toward the Unknown '56
The Defiant Ones '58
Saddle the Wind '58
The Man in the Net '59
The Wonderful Country '59
Cimarron '60
Spartacus '60
The Horizontal Lieutenant '62
The Birds '63
The Busy Body '67
In Cold Blood '67
Tell Them Willie Boy Is Here '69
Chandler '71
Johnny Got His Gun '71
A Boy and His Dog '75
The Killer Inside Me '76

Melinda McGraw (1963-)
Wrongfully Accused '98
Nutty Professor 2: The Klumps '00
The Dark Knight '08
Meeting Spencer '11
Mitch Albom's Have a Little Faith '11

Tim McGraw (1967-)
Black Cloud '04
Friday Night Lights '04

Flicka '06
Four Christmases '08
The Blind Side '09
Country Strong '10
Dirty Girl '10
Tomorrowland '15
The Shack '17

Michael McGreevey (1948-)
Death of a Gunfighter '69
The Strongest Man in the World '75

Angela Punch McGregor (1953-)
The Chant of Jimmie Blacksmith '78
Newsfront '78
The Island '80
Survivor '80
We of the Never Never '82
The Efficiency Expert '92

Charles McGregor (1922-96)
Superfly '72
The Baron '88

Ewan McGregor (1971-)
Being Human '94
Shallow Grave '94
Blue Juice '95
The Pillow Book '95
Trainspotting '95
Brassed Off '96
Emma '96
Nightwatch '96
A Life Less Ordinary '97
The Serpent's Kiss '97
Little Voice '98
Rogue Trader '98
Velvet Goldmine '98
Eye of the Beholder '99
Star Wars: Episode 1-The Phantom Menace '99
Nora '00
Black Hawk Down '01
Moulin Rouge '01
Star Wars: Episode 2-Attack of the Clones '02
Big Fish '03
Down With Love '03
Young Adam '03
The Island '05
Robots '05 (V)
Star Wars: Episode 3-Revenge of the Sith '05
Stay '05
Valiant '05 (V)
Alex Rider: Operation Stormbreaker '06
Miss Potter '06
Scenes of a Sexual Nature '06
Deception '08
Incendiary '08
Amelia '09
Angels & Demons '09
The Men Who Stare at Goats '09
Beginners '10
The Ghost Writer '10
I Love You Phillip Morris '10
Nanny McPhee Returns '10
Perfect Sense '11
Salmon Fishing in the Yemen '11
Haywire '12
The Impossible '12
August: Osage County '13
Jack the Giant Slayer '13
Son of a Gun '14
Mortdecai '15
American Pastoral '16
Jane Got a Gun '16
Last Days in the Desert '16
Miles Ahead '16
Our Kind of Traitor '16
Beauty and the Beast '17
T2 Trainspotting '17
Christopher Robin '18
Doctor Sleep '19
Birds of Prey: And the Fantabulous Emancipation of One Harley Quinn '20

Jane McGregor (1983-)
Slap Her, She's French '02
Citizen Duane '06
That Beautiful Somewhere '06
American Venus '07

Malcolm McGregor (1892-1945)
Lady of the Night '25
Smouldering Fires '25
The Reckless Way '36

Kate McGregor-Stewart (1944-)
A Midsummer Night's Sex Comedy '82
Critical Condition '86
Scrooged '88
Father of the Bride '91
The Shadow '94
Father of the Bride Part 2 '95
Safe '95
In and Out '97
The Maker '98
Pavilion of Women '01
The Sleepy Time Gal '01
School of Rock '03
Failure to Launch '06

Matthew McGrory (1973-2005)
Big Fish '03
The Devil's Rejects '05

Aislin McGuckin (1974-)
Trojan Eddie '96
The Nephew '97
The Unknown Soldier '98

Barry McGuire (1930-)
The President's Analyst '67
Werewolves on Wheels '71

Biff McGuire (1926-)
The Phenix City Story '55
Werewolf of Washington '73
Midway '76
Child of Glass '78

Don McGuire (1919-99)
The Man I Love '46
The Fuller Brush Man '48
Armored Car Robbery '50
Double Dynamite '51

Dorothy McGuire (1916-2001)
Claudia '43
The Enchanted Cottage '45
A Tree Grows in Brooklyn '45
Claudia and David '46
The Spiral Staircase '46
Till the End of Time '46
Gentleman's Agreement '47
Mister 880 '50
Mother Didn't Tell Me '50
Invitation '51
Three Coins in the Fountain '54
Trial '55
Friendly Persuasion '56
Old Yeller '57
The Remarkable Mr. Pennypacker '59
A Summer Place '59
The Swiss Family Robinson '60
Susan Slade '61
Summer Magic '63
The Greatest Story Ever Told '65
Flight of the Doves '71
Jonathan Livingston Seagull '73 (V)
Rich Man, Poor Man '76
Little Women '78
The Incredible Journey of Dr. Meg Laurel '79
Between the Darkness and the Dawn '85
The Last Best Year '90

Harp McGuire (1921-66)
Cage of Evil '60
Incident in an Alley '62

John McGuire (1910-80)
Steamboat Round the Bend '35
Charlie Chan at the Circus '36
The Invisible Ghost '41
Sands of Iwo Jima '49

Kathryn McGuire (1903-78)
Midnight Faces '26
The Lost Zeppelin '29

Mary McGuire
Seven Days' Leave '42
Higher and Higher '44

Michael McGuire (1934-)
Report to the Commissioner '75
The Long Days of Summer '80
The Ordeal of Dr. Mudd '80
Jekyll & Hyde. . . Together Again '82
Bird '88

Victor McGuire (1964-)
The Phantom of the Opera '04
Midsummer Madness '07

Joel McHale (1971-)
Open Season 2 '08 (V)
The Informant! '09
The Big Year '11
Spy Kids 4: All the Time in the World '11
What's Your Number? '11
Ted '12
Deliver Us From Evil '14
The Happytime Murders '18

Stephen McHattie (1947-)
Search for the Gods '75
James Dean '76
Moving Violation '76
Tomorrow Never Comes '77
Centennial '78
Death Valley '81
Belizaire the Cajun '86
Caribe '87
Sticky Fingers '88
Bloodhounds of Broadway '89
Geronimo: An American Legend '93
Beverly Hills Cop 3 '94
Convict Cowboy '95
The Climb '97
The Highway Man '99
Secretary '02
Twist '03
Absolution '05
A History of Violence '05
Jesse Stone: Stone Cold '05
The Rocket '05
Jesse Stone: Death in Paradise '06
Jesse Stone: Night Passage '06
Poor Man's Game '06
All Hat '07
Killer Wave '07
300 '07
The Summit '08
XIII '08
The Trojan Horse '08
Would Be Kings '08
Jesse Stone: Thin Ice '09
Pontypool '09
Summer's Moon '09
Watchmen '09
Jesse Stone: No Remorse '10
Red: Werewolf Hunter '10
Who Is Clark Rockefeller? '10
The Entitled '11
Immortals '11
Jesse Stone: Innocents Lost '11
Eddie the Sleepwalking Cannibal '12
Jesse Stone: Benefit of the Doubt '12
The Tall Man '12
Haunter '13
Lizzie Borden Took an Ax '14
Born to Be Blue '15
Awakening the Zodiac '17
Come to Daddy '20

Frank McHugh (1898-1981)
The Dawn Patrol '30
Going Wild '30
Corsair '31
Millie '31
The Crowd Roars '32
One Way Passage '32
Parachute Jumper '32
The Strange Love of Molly Louvain '32
Elmer the Great '33
The House on 56th Street '33
Mystery of the Wax Museum '33
Fashions of 1934 '34
Happiness Ahead '34
Here Comes the Navy '34
Gold Diggers of 1935 '35
The Irish in Us '35
Boy Meets Girl '38
Bullets or Ballots '38
Four Daughters '38
Swing Your Lady '38
Daughters Courageous '39
Dodge City '39
Dust Be My Destiny '39
Four Wives '39
The Roaring Twenties '39
Wings of the Navy '39
City for Conquest '40
The Fighting 69th '40
I Love You Again '40
Virginia City '40
Back Street '41
Four Mothers '41
Manpower '41
All Through the Night '42
Her Cardboard Lover '42
Going My Way '44
State Fair '45
Carnegie Hall '47
Mighty Joe Young '49
Miss Grant Takes Richmond '49
My Son John '52
A Lion Is in the Streets '53
There's No Business Like Show Business '54
The Last Hurrah '58
A Tiger Walks '64
Easy Come, Easy Go '67

David McIlwraith
Outrageous! '77
Millennium '89
Gunfighter's Moon '96
Cruel Intentions 2 '99
Caracara '00
DC 9/11: Time of Crisis '04
Hollow Man 2 '06

Tim (McInnerny) McInnery (1956-)
Wetherby '85
A Very British Coup '88
FairyTale: A True Story '97
Rogue Trader '98
Notting Hill '99
Longitude '00
102 Dalmatians '00
The Emperor's New Clothes '01
Casanova '05
The Line of Beauty '06
Severance '06
Black Death '10

William McInnes (1963-)
Do or Die '01
Look Both Ways '05
Irresistible '06

John McIntire (1907-91)
Saddle Tramp '47
Call Northside 777 '48
Francis the Talking Mule '49
Scene of the Crime '49
Ambush '50
The Asphalt Jungle '50
No Sad Songs For Me '50
Winchester '73 '50
The Tanks Are Coming '51
Westward the Women '51
You're In the Navy Now '51
Horizons West '52
The Lawless Breed '52
The World in His Arms '52
A Lion Is in the Streets '53
The Mississippi Gambler '53
War Arrow '53
Apache '54
Far Country '55
The Kentuckian '55
The Phenix City Story '55
The Phenix City Story '55
The Scarlet Coat '55
Stranger on Horseback '55
Backlash '56
The Mark of the Hawk '57
The Tin Star '57
The Gunfight at Dodge City '59
Elmer Gantry '60
Flaming Star '60
Psycho '60
Who Was That Lady? '60
Summer and Smoke '61
Two Rode Together '61
Rough Night in Jericho '67
Herbie Rides Again '74
Rooster Cogburn '75
The Fox and the Hound '81 (V)
Honkytonk Man '82
Cloak & Dagger '84
Heroes of the Heart '94

Tim McIntire (1943-86)
Shenandoah '65
1,000 Plane Raid '69
The Sterile Cuckoo '69
Aloha, Bobby and Rose '74
Smile Jenny, You're Dead '74
A Boy and His Dog '75 (V)
Gumball Rally '76
The Choirboys '77
Fast Walking '82
Sacred Ground '83

Burr McIntosh (1862-1942)
Way Down East '20
The Adorable Cheat '28
That Certain Thing '28

Neve McIntosh (1972-)
Lady Audley's Secret '00
The Hound of the Baskervilles '02
Spring 1941 '08

Pollyanna McIntosh (1979-)
Exam '09
The Woman '11

Marvin J. McIntyre
Fandango '85
Wilder Napalm '93
Born to Be Wild '95

Stephen McIntyre
Fear X '03
High Life '09
Small Town Murder Songs '10

Rose McIver (1988-)
The Lovely Bones '09
Brightest Star '14
Petals on the Wind '14

Susan McIver (1951-)
I Spit on Your Corpse '74
Smokey and the Bandit '77

Christian McKay (1973-)
Me and Orson Welles '09
Appointment With Death '10
Mr. Nice '10
The Road to Coronation Street '10
I Melt With You '11
Draw on Sweet Night '15
Chicklit '16
The Leisure Seeker '17

Scott McKay (1915-87)
Guest in the House '44
Thirty Seconds Over Tokyo '44
Creature of Destruction '67
Christmas Evil '80

Wanda McKay (1916-96)
Corregidor '43
The Monster Maker '44
Raiders of Ghost City '44
Kilroy Was Here '47
The Golden Eye '48

Michael McKean (1947-)
More Than Friends '78
Used Cars '80
Young Doctors in Love '82
This Is Spinal Tap '84
Clue '85
D.A.R.Y.L. '85
Jumpin' Jack Flash '86 (C)
Planes, Trains & Automobiles '87
Short Circuit 2 '88
The Big Picture '89
Earth Girls Are Easy '89
Flashback '89
Book of Love '91
Man Trouble '92
Memoirs of an Invisible Man '92
The Return of Spinal Tap '92
Coneheads '93
Across the Moon '94
Airheads '94
Radioland Murders '94
The Brady Bunch Movie '95
Edie & Pen '95 (C)
The Sunshine Boys '95
Jack '96
Nothing to Lose '96
That Darn Cat '96
Final Justice '98
Highway Hitcher '98
No Strings Attached '98
Small Soldiers '98 (V)
Teaching Mrs. Tingle '99
True Crime '99
Beautiful '00
Best in Show '00
Little Nicky '00
My First Mister '01
Never Again '01
Auto Focus '02
The Guru '02
100 Mile Rule '02
Slap Her, She's French '02
And Starring Pancho Villa as Himself '03
A Mighty Wind '03
The Producers '05
For Your Consideration '06
Joshua '07
Surf's Up '07 (V)
Whatever Works '09
Pure Country 2: The Gift '10
10 Rules for Sleeping Around '13

Donna McKechnie (1940-)
The Little Prince '74
Every Little Step '08

Gina McKee (1964-)
Naked '93
Element of Doubt '96
Croupier '97
Notting Hill '99
Wonderland '99
Divine Secrets of the Ya-Ya Sisterhood '02
The Reckoning '03
MirrorMask '05
Scenes of a Sexual Nature '06
Atonement '07
The Old Curiosity Shop '07
When Did You Last See Your Father? '07
In the Loop '09
Secret State '12
Jimmy P. '13

John McKee (1916-2013)
Above and Beyond '53
Big Leaguer '53
Strategic Air Command '55
The Gallant Hours '60
Cape Fear '61
The Hallelujah Trail '65
Monte Walsh '70
MacArthur '77

Lafe (Lafayette) McKee (1872-1959)
Boiling Point '32
The Gay Buckaroo '32
The Dude Bandit '33
City Park '34
Law of the Wild '34
The Quitter '34
The Keeper of the Bees '35
The Miracle Rider '35
Rustlers of Red Dog '35
Lightnin' Bill Carson '36

Lonette McKee (1954-)
Detroit 9000 '73
Sparkle '76
Which Way Is Up? '77
Cuba '79
The Cotton Club '84

Pauline McLynn (1962-)
Angela's Ashes '99
An Everlasting Piece '00
When Brendan Met Trudy '00

Ed McMahon (1923-2009)
Slaughter's Big Ripoff '73
Fun with Dick and Jane '77
Butterfly '82
Just Write '97 (C)

Horace McMahon (1906-71)
Navy Blues '37
King of the Newsboys '38
Melody Ranch '40
Birth of the Blues '41
Detective Story '51
Abbott and Costello Go to Mars '53
My Sister Eileen '55
The Delicate Delinquent '56
The Detective '68

Julian McMahon (1968-)
Chasing Sleep '00
Fantastic Four '05
Fantastic Four: Rise of the Silver Surfer '07
Premonition '07
Prisoner '07
Meet Market '08
RED '10
Faces in the Crowd '11
Fire With Fire '12
Paranoia '13

Cody McMains (1985-)
Bring It On '00
Madison '01
Not Another Teen Movie '01

Don McManus (1959-)
True Colors '91
The 6th Day '00
Frenemy '09
Just Peck '09
For a Good Time, Call... '12
Grand Piano '13

James McManus
The Big Empty '98
La Cucaracha '99
Black Dynamite '09

Michael McManus (1962-)
Captain America '79
Poltergeist '82
Funland '89
Speaking Parts '89
Hard to Forget '98

John McMartin (1929-)
Sweet Charity '69
Dream Lover '85
Legal Eagles '86
Gore Vidal's Lincoln '88
Roots: The Gift '88
Day One '89
Little Sweetheart '90
A Shock to the System '90
Separate but Equal '91
The Dish '00
Kinsey '04
No Reservations '07

Niles McMaster
Bloodsucking Freaks '75
Alice Sweet Alice '76

Ciaran McMenamin (1975-)
David Copperfield '99
The Trench '99
The Last Minute '01
To End All Wars '01

Kenneth McMillan (1932-89)
The Taking of Pelham One Two Three '74
Bloodbrothers '78
Girlfriends '78
Salem's Lot '79
Borderline '80
Carny '80
Hide in Plain Sight '80
Eyewitness '81
Heartbeeps '81
Ragtime '81
True Confessions '81
Whose Life Is It Anyway? '81
In the Custody of Strangers '82
Partners '82
Dune '84
Killing Hour '84
The Pope of Greenwich Village '84
Protocol '84
Reckless '84
Cat's Eye '85
Dixie: Changing Habits '85
Runaway Train '85
Armed and Dangerous '86
Malone '87
Three Fugitives '89

Richard McMillan
M. Butterfly '93
Ordeal in the Arctic '93
Bram Stoker's Shadowbuilder '98
The Sandy Bottom Orchestra '00
Cube: Zero '04
A Different Loyalty '04

Ross McMillan
The Twilight of the Ice Nymphs '97
The Saddest Music in the World '03

W.G. McMillan (1944-)
See Will MacMillan

James McMullan (1929-)
Shenandoah '65
Sex Through a Window '72

Sam McMurray (1952-)
Union City '81
C.H.U.D. '84
Raising Arizona '87
L.A. Story '91
Stone Cold '91
Getting Even with Dad '94
Slappy and the Stinkers '97
Drop Dead Gorgeous '99
The Mod Squad '99
Lucky Numbers '00
Lone Star State of Mind '02
Stealing Sinatra '04
Lake Placid 2 '07
Holiday Engagement '11

Mercedes McNab (1980-)
Addams Family Values '93
Savage Land '94
White Wolves 3: Cry of the White Wolf '98
Hatchet '07
The Pink Conspiracy '07
Medium Raw: Night of the Wolf '10

Barbara McNair (1934-2007)
Change of Habit '69
They Call Me Mr. Tibbs! '70
Venus in Furs '70
The Organization '71
Neon Signs '96

Scoot McNairy (1977-)
Monsters '10
Killing Them Softly '12
12 Years a Slave '13
Black Sea '14
Frank '14
Non-Stop '14
The Rover '14
Our Brand is Crisis '15
Lamb '16
Aftermath '17
Destroyer '18
The Parts You Lose '19

Kevin McNally (1956-)
Poldark 2 '75
Cry Freedom '87
Jekyll and Hyde '90
Abraham '94
When the Sky Falls '99
Conspiracy '01
High Heels and Low Lifes '01
Shackleton '02
Johnny English '03
Pirates of the Caribbean: The Curse of the Black Pearl '03
De-Lovely '04
The Phantom of the Opera '04
Bloodlines '05
Irish Jam '05
Pirates of the Caribbean: Dead Man's Chest '06
Pirates of the Caribbean: At World's End '07
Valkyrie '08
Pirates of the Caribbean: On Stranger Tides '11

Stephen McNally (1913-94)
Dr. Gillespie's New Assistant '42
For Me and My Gal '42
Keeper of the Flame '42
Air Raid Wardens '43
An American Romance '44
Thirty Seconds Over Tokyo '44
Magnificent Doll '46
Up Goes Maisie '46
Criss Cross '48
The Lady Gambles '49
Woman in Hiding '49
No Way Out '50
Winchester '73 '50
Battle Zone '52
The Black Castle '52
Diplomatic Courier '52
Duel at Silver Creek '52
Split Second '53
A Bullet Is Waiting '54
Violent Saturday '55
Tribute to a Bad Man '56
The Fiend Who Walked the West '58
Panic in the City '68
Once You Kiss a Stranger '69
Black Gunn '72
Hi-Riders '77

Terrance McNally (1939-)
Earth Girls Are Easy '89
Tap '89

Brian McNamara (1960-)
Detective Sadie & Son '84
Short Circuit '86
The Betty Ford Story '87
Billionaire Boys Club '87
Arachnophobia '90
Mystery Date '91
When the Party's Over '91
Where the Truth Lies '99
The Ghost of Spoon River '00
The Gunman '03
Caught in the Act '04
Secret Lives of Second Wives '08

Katherine McNamara
Jr. Detective Agency '09
Girl vs. Monster '12
Contest '13

Maggie McNamara (1929-78)
The Moon Is Blue '53
Three Coins in the Fountain '54
The Cardinal '63

Pat McNamara (1933-)
Commandments '96
The Daytrippers '96
Ash Wednesday '02

William McNamara (1965-)
Opera '88
Stealing Home '88
Dream a Little Dream '89
Texasville '90
Wildflower '91
Doing Time on Maple Drive '92
Chasers '94
Radio Inside '94
Surviving the Game '94
Copycat '95
Storybook '95
The Brylcreem Boys '96
Natural Enemy '96
Glam '97
Stag '97
Implicated '98
Ringmaster '98
Sweet Jane '98
Paper Bullets '99
Time Lapse '01
The Bleeding '09
Day of the Mummy '14

Penny McNamee
Salem's Lot '04
See No Evil '06

Howard McNear (1905-69)
Escape from Fort Bravo '53
The Errand Boy '61
Follow That Dream '61
Fun in Acapulco '63
Kiss Me, Stupid! '64

Ian McNeice (1950-)
The Lonely Passion of Judith Hearne '87
Valmont '89
The Russia House '90
The Blackheath Poisonings '92
Year of the Comet '92
Funny Bones '94
No Escape '94
Ace Ventura: When Nature Calls '95
The Englishman Who Went up a Hill But Came down a Mountain '95
The Beautician and the Beast '97
A Life Less Ordinary '97
A Certain Justice '99
The Cherry Orchard '99
David Copperfield '99
Dune '00
The Body '01
Conspiracy '01
The Fourth Angel '01
Chaos & Cadavers '03
Children of Dune '03
I'll Be There '03
Around the World in 80 Days '04
Freeze Frame '04
The Hitchhiker's Guide to the Galaxy '05 (V)
Oliver Twist '05
White Noise '05
The Black Dahlia '06
The Mystery of Edwin Drood '12

Claudia McNeil (1916-93)
A Raisin in the Sun '61
Cry Panic '74

Kate McNeil (1959-)
The House on Sorority Row '83
Monkey Shines '88
Sudden Death '95
Escape Clause '96

Jimmy (James Vincent) McNichol (1961-)
Champions: A Love Story '78
Smokey Bites the Dust '81

Kristy McNichol (1962-)
The End '78
My Old Man '79
The Night the Lights Went Out in Georgia '81
Only When I Laugh '81
Pirate Movie '82
White Dog '82
Just the Way You Are '84
Dream Lover '85
Women of Valor '86
Two Moon Junction '88
You Can't Hurry Love '88
Baby of the Bride '91

Kevin McNulty (1955-)
Impolite '92
Anything for Love '93
The NeverEnding Story 3: Escape from Fantasia '94
Timecop '94
Titanic '96
A Date With Darkness '03
Past Sins '06
Meteor Storm '10

Matthew McNulty (1982-)
See No Evil: The Moors Murders '06
Little Ashes '09
Messengers 2: The Scarecrow '09
Return to Cranford '09
Toast '10

Ryan McPartlin (1975-)
Super Capers '09
Game Time: Tackling the Past '11
Holly's Holiday '12
The Right Kind Of Wrong '13

Sandy McPeak (1935-97)
Ode to Billy Joe '76
Tarantulas: The Deadly Cargo '77

Marnie McPhail (1966-)
RFK '02
Scared Silent '02
The Greatest Game Ever Played '05
Stir of Echoes 2: The Homecoming '07

Katharine McPhee (1984-)
The House Bunny '08
Shark Night 3D '11
You May Not Kiss the Bride '12
In My Dreams '14

Kris McQuade (1952-)
The Coca-Cola Kid '84
Two Friends '86
Resistance '92
Strictly Ballroom '92
Billy's Holiday '95
Better Than Sex '00
Ned Kelly '03
December Boys '07

Butterfly McQueen (1911-95)
Gone with the Wind '39
I Dood It '43
Duel in the Sun '46
Killer Diller '48
Amazing Grace '74
The Adventures of Huckleberry Finn '85
The Mosquito Coast '86

Chad McQueen (1960-)
Skateboard '77
The Karate Kid '84
Where the Red Fern Grows: Part 2 '92
Death Ring '93
Firepower '93
Sexual Malice '93
Indecent Behavior 2 '94
New York Cop '94
Number One Fan '94
Red Line '96
Trail of a Serial Killer '98

Evert McQueen
Malibu Shark Attack '09
Absolute Deception '13

Justus E. McQueen (1927-)
See L.Q. Jones

Steve McQueen (1930-80)
Somebody Up There Likes Me '56
The Blob '58
Never Love a Stranger '58
The Great St. Louis Bank Robbery '59
Never So Few '59
The Magnificent Seven '60
The Honeymoon Machine '61
Hell Is for Heroes '62
War Lover '62
The Great Escape '63
Soldier in the Rain '63
Baby, the Rain Must Fall '64
The Cincinnati Kid '65
Nevada Smith '66
The Sand Pebbles '66
Bullitt '68
The Thomas Crown Affair '68
The Reivers '69
Le Mans '71
The Getaway '72
Junior Bonner '72
Papillon '73
The Towering Inferno '74
An Enemy of the People '77
The Hunter '80
Tom Horn '80
Minutemen '08

Alan McRae
The Slayer '82
3 Ninjas '92
3 Ninjas: High Noon at Mega Mountain '97

Elizabeth McRae
The Incredible Mr. Limpet '64
The Conversation '74

Frank McRae (1944-)
Cannery Row '82
National Lampoon's Vacation '83
Hostage Flight '85
*batteries not included '87
Farewell to the King '89
License to Kill '89
Lock Up '89
Sketch Artist '92
Last Action Hero '93
National Lampoon's Loaded Weapon 1 '93
Lightning Jack '94
Asteroid '97

Hilton McRae (1949-)
The Secret Rapture '94
Bobby Jones: Stroke of Genius '04

Leslie McRae
Girl in Gold Boots '69
Blood Orgy of the She-Devils '74

Gerald McRaney (1947-)
Night of Bloody Horror '69
Mind Warp '72
The Haunting Passion '83
The NeverEnding Story '84
American Justice '86
Hobo's Christmas '87
A Nightmare Come True '97
Take Me Home: The John Denver Story '00
Danger Beneath the Sea '02
Ike: Countdown to D-Day '04
Saving Shiloh '06
Get Low '09
The A-Team '10
The Best of Me '14
Dolly Parton's Coat of Many Colors '15
Focus '15
The Disappointments Room '16

Peter McRobbie (1943-)
Johnny Suede '92
And the Band Played On '93 (C)
The Neon Bible '95
Kill by Inches '99
Corn '04
Brokeback Mountain '05
The Notorious Bettie Page '06
Lincoln '12
The Visit '15

Ian McShane (1942-)
Battle of Britain '69
If It's Tuesday, This Must Be Belgium '69
Pussycat, Pussycat, I Love You '70
Villain '71
Sitting Target '72
The Last of Sheila '73
The Terrorists '74
Disraeli '79
The Fifth Musketeer '79
High Tide '80
Grace Kelly '83
A.D. '85
Torchlight '85
The Murders in the Rue Morgue '86
War & Remembrance '88
War & Remembrance: The Final Chapter '89
Grand Larceny '92
D.R.E.A.M. Team '99
Sexy Beast '00
Agent Cody Banks '03
Nemesis Game '03

Nine Lives *'05*
Scoop *'06*
We Are Marshall *'06*
The Golden Compass *'07 (V)*
Hot Rod *'07*
The Seeker: The Dark Is Rising *'07*
Shrek the Third *'07 (V)*
Death Race *'08*
Kung Fu Panda *'08 (V)*
Coraline *'09 (V)*
44 Inch Chest *'09*
Case 39 *'10*
Pillars of the Earth *'10*
Pirates of the Caribbean: On Stranger Tides *'11*
Snow White and the Huntsman *'12*
Jack the Giant Slayer *'13*
Cuban Fury *'14*
Hercules *'14*
John Wick *'14*
The Hollow Point *'16*
John Wick: Chapter 3-Parabellum *'19*

Jamie McShane
Landspeed *'01*
In My Pocket *'11*
The Meanest Man in Texas *'19*

Jenny (Jennifer) McShane (1974-)
Hit the Dutchman *'92*
Never Say Die *'94*
Terminal Impact *'95*
The Rage *'96*
Monsoon *'97*
Stag *'97*
Tales of the Kama Sutra 2: Monsoon *'98*
Shark Attack *'99*
The Watcher *'00*
Shark Attack 3: Megalodon *'02*

Kitty McShane (1898-1964)
Old Mother Riley in Paris *'38*
Old Mother Riley, MP *'39*
Old Mother Riley's Ghosts *'41*
Old Mother Riley's New Venture *'49*
Old Mother Riley, Headmistress *'50*
Old Mother Riley's Jungle Treasure *'51*

Michael McShane (1955-)
Robin Hood: Prince of Thieves *'91*
Richie Rich *'94*
Tom and Huck *'95*
A Bug's Life *'98 (V)*
Office Space *'98*
Drop Dead Gorgeous *'99*
Treasure Planet *'02 (V)*
Kaena: The Prophecy *'03 (V)*
Memron *'04*
Happily N'Ever After *'07 (V)*

Gerard McSorley (1950-)
In the Name of the Father *'93*
An Awfully Big Adventure *'94*
Widow's Peak *'94*
Moondance *'95*
Michael Collins *'96*
Some Mother's Son *'96*
The Boxer *'97*
Felicia's Journey *'99*
Ordinary Decent Criminal *'99*
Bloody Sunday *'01*
Dead Bodies *'03*
Veronica Guerin *'03*
Rory O'Shea Was Here *'04*
The Constant Gardener *'05*
The Front Line *'06*
Middletown *'06*

Virginia McSweeney (1898-1968)
See Virginia Valli

Graham McTavish (1961-)
Rambo *'08*
Green Street Hooligans 2 *'09*
Pandemic *'09*
The Wicker Tree *'10*
Colombiana *'11*
Creed *'15*

Janet McTeer (1961-)
Hawks *'89*
Catherine Cookson's The Black Velvet Gown *'92*
Emily Bronte's Wuthering Heights *'92*
Carrington *'95*
Tumbleweeds *'98*
Songcatcher *'99*
The King Is Alive *'00*
Waking the Dead *'00*
The Intended *'02*
Tideland *'05*
As You Like It *'06*
Daphne *'07*
Five Days *'07*
Sense & Sensibility *'07*
Into the Storm *'09*
Albert Nobbs *'11*
Cat Run *'11*
Hannah Arendt *'12*
The Woman in Black *'12*
The Exception *'17*

Patrick McVey (1910-73)
The Detective *'68*
Desperate Characters *'71*

Tyler McVey (1912-2003)
From Here to Eternity *'53*
The Gallant Hours *'60*

Daniel McVicar (1958-)
Guardian Angel *'94*
Alone in the Woods *'95*

Margaret McWade (1872-1956)
The Confession *'20*
Mr. Deeds Goes to Town *'36*
Theodora Goes Wild *'36*

Robert McWade (1872-1938)
Feet First *'30*
Kept Husbands *'31*
Movie Crazy *'32*
The Phantom of Crestwood *'32*
Hard to Handle *'33*
Healer *'36*
Next Time We Love *'36*

Jillian McWhirter
After Midnight *'89*
Beyond the Call of Duty *'92*
Stranglehold *'94*
Bloodfist 7: Manhunt *'95*
Last Man Standing *'95*
Rage *'95*
The Dentist 2: Brace Yourself *'98*
Progeny *'98*

Caroline McWilliams (1945-2010)
Into Thin Air *'85*
Mermaids *'90*

Anne Meacham (1925-2006)
Lilith *'64*
Seizure *'74*

Courtland Mead (1987-)
The Little Rascals *'94*
Tom and Huck *'95*
Emma's Wish *'98*

Taylor Mead (1924-2013)
Superstar: The Life and Times of Andy Warhol *'90*
Frogs for Snakes *'98*
Coffee and Cigarettes *'03*

Emily Meade (1989-)
My Soul to Take *'10*
Twelve *'10*
Trespass *'11*
Bluebird *'13*
Nerve *'16*
Trial by Fire *'18*

Julia Meade
Tammy Tell Me True *'61*
Zotz! *'62*

Audrey Meadows (1922-96)
That Touch of Mink *'62*
Take Her, She's Mine *'63*

Jayne Meadows (1920-2015)
Lady in the Lake *'46*
Song of the Thin Man *'47*
Enchantment *'48*
The Luck of the Irish *'48*
David and Bathsheba *'51*
James Dean *'76*
Norman, Is That You? *'76*
Miss All-American Beauty *'82*
Ratings Game *'84*
City Slickers *'91*
The Player *'92*
Casino *'95*
The Story of Us *'99*

Joyce Meadows (1933-)
The Brain from Planet Arous *'57*
Flesh and the Spur *'57*
The Girl in Lover's Lane *'60*
Zebra in the Kitchen *'65*

Stephen Meadows
A Cry in the Wild *'90*
The End of Innocence *'90*

Tim Meadows (1961-)
It's Pat: The Movie *'94*
The Ladies Man *'00*
The Cookout *'04*
Mean Girls *'04*
The Benchwarmers *'06*
Shredderman Rules *'07*
Walk Hard: The Dewey Cox Story *'07*
Aliens in the Attic *'09*
Grown Ups *'10*
Jack and Jill *'11*
Mean Girls 2 *'11*
Grown Ups 2 *'13*
Chasing Ghosts *'14*
Popstar: Never Stop Never Stopping *'16*

Ray Meagher (1944-)
The Chant of Jimmie Blacksmith *'78*
The Odd Angry Shot *'79*
Breaker Morant *'80*
Nowhere to Hide *'83*

Colm Meaney (1953-)
Die Hard 2: Die Harder *'90*
The Commitments *'91*
Far and Away *'92*
Into the West *'92*
The Last of the Mohicans *'92*
The Snapper *'93*
The Road to Wellville *'94*
Scarlett *'94*
The Englishman Who Went up a Hill But Came down a Mountain *'95*
The Van *'95*
War of the Buttons *'95*
The Last of the High Kings *'96*
Claire Dolan *'97*
Con Air *'97*
Owd Bob *'97*
Monument Ave. *'98*
The Magical Legend of the Leprechauns *'99*
Mystery, Alaska *'99*
This Is My Father *'99*
How Harry Became a Tree *'01*
King of Texas *'02*
The Boys and Girl From County Clare *'03*
Intermission *'03*
Layer Cake *'05*
Five Fingers *'06*
The Hades Factor *'06*
A Lobster Tale *'06*
Kings *'07*
Three and Out *'08*
Alice *'09*
The Damned United *'09*
Law Abiding Citizen *'09*
The Race *'09*
Alleged *'10*
The Conspirator *'10*
Parked *'10*
Stand Off *'11*
Bel Ami *'12*
Alan Partridge *'13*
Free Birds *'13 (V)*

One Chance *'13*
Norm of the North *'16*
Tolkien *'19*

Kevin Meaney (1957-)
Plump Fiction *'97*
Shut Up and Kiss Me *'05*

Russell Means (1939-2012)
The Last of the Mohicans *'92*
Natural Born Killers *'94*
Wagons East *'94*
Windrunner *'94*
Buffalo Girls *'95*
The Pathfinder *'96*
The Song of Hiawatha *'97*
Black Cat Run *'98*
Wind River *'98*
Cowboy Up *'00*
29 Palms *'03*
Black Cloud *'04*
Pathfinder *'07*
Unearthed *'07*
Tiger Eyes *'13*

Anne Meara (1929-2015)
Lovers and Other Strangers *'70*
The Out-of-Towners *'70*
Nasty Habits *'77*
Fame *'80*
The Longshot *'86*
Awakenings *'90*
Heavyweights *'94*
Kiss of Death *'94*
Reality Bites *'94 (C)*
The Search for One-Eye Jimmy *'94*
The Daytrippers *'96*
Southie *'98*
A Fish in the Bathtub *'99*
Judy Berlin *'99*
The Independent *'00*
Get Well Soon *'01*
Like Mike *'02*
Night at the Museum *'06*

Derek Mears (1972-)
Friday the 13th *'09*
The Aggression Scale *'12*
Hansel & Gretel: Witch Hunters *'12*

Michael Mears (1957-)
Sharpe's Rifles *'93*
The Old Curiosity Shop *'94*
Sharpe's Legend *'97*
Sylvia *'03*

Scott Mechlowicz (1981-)
Eurotrip *'04*
Mean Creek *'04*
Peaceful Warrior *'06*
Cat Run *'11*
Waiting for Forever *'11*

Julio Oscar Mechoso (1955-)
Bad Boys *'95*
White Squall *'96*
Switchback *'97*
Krippendorf's Tribe *'98*
Virus *'98*
All the Pretty Horses *'00*
Heartbreakers *'01*
Jurassic Park 3 *'01*
Pumpkin *'02*
Assassination Tango *'03*
The Legend of Zorro *'05*
The Lost City *'05*
The Go-Getter *'07*
Planet Terror *'07*
The Janky Promoters *'09*
Beyond the Blackboard *'11*
Justice for Natalee *'11*

Elli Medeiros
Lulu *'02*
Lion's Den *'08*

Kay Medford (1920-80)
Swing Shift Maisie *'43*
Butterfield 8 *'60*
Girl of the Night *'60*
The Rat Race *'60*
A Fine Madness *'66*
The Busy Body *'67*
Funny Girl *'68*
Lola *'69*
More Than Friends *'78*
Windows *'80*

Harriet Medin (1914-2005)
The Horrible Dr. Hichcock *'62*
The Ghost *'63*
The Whip and the Body *'63*
Blood and Black Lace *'64*

Ofelia Medina (1950-)
Frida *'84*
Innocent Voices *'04*

Patricia Medina (1920-2012)
Dinner at the Ritz *'37*
Spitfire *'42*
The Secret Heart *'46*
The Foxes of Harrow *'47*
The Three Musketeers *'48*
Francis the Talking Mule *'49*
Abbott and Costello in the Foreign Legion *'50*
The Jackpot *'50*
The Magic Carpet *'51*
Desperate Search *'52*
Mr. Arkadin *'55*
Missiles from Hell *'58*
Snow White and the Three Stooges *'61*
The Killing of Sister George *'69*
Latitude Zero *'69*
The Big Push *'75*

Frank Medrano (1954-)
The Fan *'96*
Sleepers *'96*
Suicide Kings *'97*
The Apostate *'98*
Kissing a Fool *'98*
The Replacement Killers *'98*
Telling You *'98*
Winchell *'98*
Shade *'03*

Michael Medwin (1923-2020)
Four in a Jeep *'51*
Genevieve *'53*
Above Us the Waves *'55*
24 Hours to Kill *'65*
A Countess from Hong Kong *'67*

Geoff Meed (1965-)
100 Million BC *'08*
Miss March *'09*
Airline Disaster *'10*
6 Guns *'10*

Donald Meek (1878-1946)
The Merry Widow *'34*
Mrs. Wiggs of the Cabbage Patch *'34*
Murder at the Vanities *'34*
Barbary Coast *'35*
The Gilded Lily *'35*
The Informer *'35*
Peter Ibbetson *'35*
The Whole Town's Talking *'35*
And So They Were Married *'36*
One Rainy Afternoon *'36*
Pennies from Heaven *'36*
Breakfast for Two *'37*
Maid of Salem *'37*
Toast of New York *'37*
The Adventures of Tom Sawyer *'38*
Having a Wonderful Time *'38*
Little Miss Broadway *'38*
You Can't Take It with You *'38*
Blondie Takes a Vacation *'39*
Hollywood Cavalcade *'39*
Jesse James *'39*
Nick Carter, Master Detective *'39*
Stagecoach *'39*
Young Mr. Lincoln *'39*
Come Live With Me *'40*
Dr. Ehrlich's Magic Bullet *'40*
Hullabaloo *'40*
My Little Chickadee *'40*
Phantom Raiders *'40*
Return of Frank James *'40*
Sky Murder *'40*
Star Dust *'40*
Design for Scandal *'41*
A Woman's Face *'41*
Keeper of the Flame *'42*
Maisie Gets Her Man *'42*
Tortilla Flat *'42*
Air Raid Wardens *'43*
Du Barry Was a Lady *'43*
Lost Angel *'43*
They Got Me Covered *'43*
Bathing Beauty *'44*
Maisie Goes to Reno *'44*
The Thin Man Goes Home *'44*
Two Girls and a Sailor *'44*
Because of Him *'45*
Colonel Effingham's Raid *'45*
State Fair *'45*
Magic Town *'47*

Jeffrey Meek (1959-)
Winter People *'89*
Heart Condition *'90*
The St. Tammany Miracle *'94*
Breaking the Surface: The Greg Louganis Story *'96*
Timelock *'99*

George Meeker (1904-84)
Four Sons *'28*
Emma *'32*
Chance at Heaven *'33*
Double Harness *'33*
Dark Hazard *'34*
Murder On a Honeymoon *'35*
The Rainmakers *'35*
Danger on the Air *'38*
Frolics on Ice *'39*
Michael Shayne: Private Detective *'40*
High Sierra *'41*
Dead Man's Eyes *'44*
Seven Doors to Death *'44*
Black Market Babies *'45*
I Accuse My Parents *'45*
Apache Rose *'47*
The Invisible Monster *'50*

Ralph Meeker (1920-88)
Four in a Jeep *'51*
Code Two *'53*
Jeopardy *'53*
The Naked Spur *'53*
Big House, U.S.A. *'55*
Kiss Me Deadly *'55*
Paths of Glory *'57*
Ada *'61*
Something Wild *'61*
Wall of Noise *'63*
The Dirty Dozen *'67*
Gentle Giant *'67*
The St. Valentine's Day Massacre *'67*
The Detective *'68*
I Walk the Line *'70*
The Anderson Tapes *'71*
The Night Stalker *'71*
Birds of Prey *'72*
Mind Snatchers *'72*
Cry Panic *'74*
Brannigan *'75*
Johnny Firecloud *'75*
The Alpha Incident *'76*
Food of the Gods *'76*
Hi-Riders *'77*
My Boys Are Good Boys *'78*
Winter Kills *'79*
Without Warning *'80*

Justin Meeks
The Wild Man of the Navidad *'08*
Kill or Be Killed *'15*

Leighton Meester (1986-)
Hangman's Curse *'03*
Flourish *'06*
Inside *'06*
Remember the Daze *'07*
Killer Movie *'08*
Country Strong *'10*
Date Night *'10*
Going the Distance *'10*
Monte Carlo *'11*
The Roommate *'11*
The Oranges *'12*
That's My Boy *'12*
By the Gun *'14*
The Judge *'14*
Life Partners *'14*
Semper Fi *'19*

Armand Meffre (1929-2009)
Here Comes Santa Claus '84
Jean de Florette '87
Manon of the Spring '87

John Megna (1953-95)
To Kill a Mockingbird '62
Go Tell the Spartans '78

Don Megowan (1922-81)
A Lawless Street '55
The Creature Walks among Us '56
Gun the Man Down '56
The Werewolf '56
The Jayhawkers '59
Creation of the Humanoids '62
Tarzan and the Valley of Gold '65
The Devil's Brigade '68

Blanche Mehaffey (1907-68)
A Woman of the World '25
The Texas Streak '26
Devil Monster '46

Tobias Mehler (1976-)
Sabrina the Teenage Witch '96
Wishmaster 3: Beyond the Gates of Hell '01
Carrie '02

Yan-Fang Mei (1963-2003)
See Anita (Yim-Fong) Mui

Armin Meier (1943-78)
Fear of Fear '75
Mother Kusters Goes to Heaven '76

Shane Meier (1977-)
Andre '94
Outrage '98
Silver Wolf '98
Call of the Wild '04

Thomas Meighan (1879-1936)
The Forbidden City '18
Male and Female '19
Why Change Your Wife? '20
The Canadian '26
Peck's Bad Boy '34

John Meillon (1934-89)
Billy Budd '62
Outback '71
Walkabout '71
The Cars That Ate Paris '74
Inn of the Damned '74
Ride a Wild Pony '75
Crocodile Dundee '86
Frenchman's Farm '87
Crocodile Dundee 2 '88

Kurt Meisel (1912-94)
Wozzeck '47
Party Girls for Sale '54
The Odessa File '74

Kathryn Meisle (1960-)
Basket Case 2 '90
Rosewood '96
Bereavement '10

Gunter Meisner (1926-94)
Willy Wonka & the Chocolate Factory '71
In a Glass Cage '86

Bent Mejding (1937-)
Reptilicus '62
Just Another Love Story '08

Gerardo Mejia (1965-)
Can't Buy Me Love '87
Winners Take All '87
Colors '88
A Million to Juan '94
Somebody to Love '94
Loco Love '03
Sundown: The Vampire in Retreat '08

Fred Melamed (1956-)
A Serious Man '09
In a World... '13
Lemon '17

Mariangela Melato (1941-2013)
Seduction of Mimi '72
Love and Anarchy '73
Swept Away. . . '75
So Fine '81
Dancers '87
Summer Night with Greek Profile, Almond Eyes & Scent of Basil '87

Lauritz Melchior (1890-1973)
Thrill of a Romance '45
Two Sisters From Boston '46
This Time for Keeps '47
Luxury Liner '48

Wendel Meldrum (1959-)
Beautiful Dreamers '92
City Boy '93
Hush Little Baby '93
National Lampoon's Dad's Week Off '97

Nicholas Mele
Capone '89
A Nightmare on Elm Street 5: Dream Child '89
Impulse '90

Ron Melendez (1974-)
Children of the Corn 3: Urban Harvest '95
Wild Things 3: Diamonds in the Rough '05

Jill Melford (1934-)
Blackout '54
Edge of Sanity '89

Joe Melia (1935-2012)
Four in the Morning '65
Privates on Parade '84

Claude Melki (1939-94)
Six in Paris '68
A Slightly Pregnant Man '79

Gilbert Melki (1958-)
Monsieur Ibrahim '03
Changing Times '04
Intimate Strangers '04
Angel-A '05
Cote d'Azur '05
Mr. Average '06

Joseph Mell (1915-77)
36 Hours '64
Lord Love a Duck '66

Marisa Mell (1939-92)
Secret Agent Super Dragon '66
Danger: Diabolik '68
Death Will Have Your Eyes '74
Mad Dog Killer '77
Mad Dog '84

Randle Mell (1951-)
Grand Canyon '91
Wyatt Earp '94
Cookie's Fortune '99

John Cougar Mellencamp (1951-)
Falling from Grace '92
Lone Star State of Mind '02

Harry Melling (1989-)
Harry Potter and the Sorcerer's Stone '01
The Keeper '18

Tamara Mello (1976-)
She's All That '99
Tortilla Soup '01

Andree Melly (1932-2020)
The Belles of St. Trinian's '53
The Brides of Dracula '60

Christopher Meloni (1961-)
Bound '96
The Souler Opposite '97
Runaway Bride '99
Wet Hot American Summer '01
Murder in Greenwich '02
Harold and Kumar Go to White Castle '04
Gym Teacher: The Movie '08
Harold & Kumar Escape from Guantanamo Bay '08
Nights in Rodanthe '08
Carriers '09
National Lampoon's Dirty Movie '11
42 '13
Man of Steel '13
Awful Nice '14
Sin City: A Dame to Kill For '14
Small Time '14
They Came Together '14
White Bird in a Blizzard '14
The Diary of a Teenage Girl '15
I Am Wrath '16
Marauders '16
Almost Friends '17

Charles Melton
The Sun Is Also a Star '19
Bad Boys for Life '20

Frank Melton (1907-51)
David Harum '34
Stand Up and Cheer '34
365 Nights in Hollywood '34

Sid Melton (1917-2011)
Girls in Chains '43
Hi-Jacked '50
The Lost Continent '51
Savage Drums '51
The Steel Helmet '51
Lady Sings the Blues '72
Hit! '73

Murray Melvin (1932-)
Alfie '66
Kaleidoscope '66
Start the Revolution without Me '70
The Devils '71
Lisztomania '75
Let Him Have It '91
The Emperor's New Clothes '01
The Phantom of the Opera '04

Rachel Melvin
Seven Deadly Sins '10
Dumb and Dumber To '14

Nasser Memarzia
Millions '05
The Situation '06

George Memmoli (1938-85)
Mean Streets '73
Phantom of the Paradise '74
Hot Potato '76

Carlos Mencia (1967-)
29 Palms '03
The Heartbreak Kid '07
Our Family Wedding '10

Stephen Mendel
Scanners: The Showdown '94
Midnight Heat '95
The Terminal '04

Ben Mendelsohn (1969-)
The Year My Voice Broke '87
Quigley Down Under '90
The Efficiency Expert '92
Metal Skin '94
Sirens '94
Cosi '95
Idiot Box '97
Vertical Limit '00
The New World '05
Australia '08
$9.99 '08 (V)
Animal Kingdom '09
Beautiful Kate '09
Knowing '09
Needle '10
Trespass '11
The Dark Knight Rises '12
Killing Them Softly '12
Adore '13
The Place Beyond the Pines '13
Starred Up '13
Black Sea '14
Exodus: Gods and Kings '14
Guns for Hire '15
Lost River '15
Mississippi Grind '15
Slow West '15
Rogue One: A Star Wars Story '16
Darkest Hour '17
Una '17
The Land of Steady Habits '18
Ready Player One '18
Robin Hood '18
Captain Marvel '19
The King '19
Untogether '19

David Mendenhall (1971-)
Over the Top '86
Streets '90

Eva Mendes (1974-)
Children of the Corn 5: Fields of Terror '98
Urban Legends 2: Final Cut '00
Exit Wounds '01
Training Day '01
All About the Benjamins '02
Once Upon a Time in Mexico '03
Out of Time '03
Stuck On You '03
2 Fast 2 Furious '03
Hitch '05
The Wendell Baker Story '05
Trust the Man '06
Cleaner '07
Ghost Rider '07
Live! '07
We Own the Night '07
The Spirit '08
The Women '08
Bad Lieutenant: Port of Call New Orleans '09
Last Night '10
The Other Guys '10
Girl in Progress '12
Holy Motors '12
The Place Beyond the Pines '13

Gerry Mendicino (1950-)
DC 9/11: Time of Crisis '04
The Dogfather '10

Joey Mendicino
Rest Stop '06
Rest Stop: Don't Look Back '08

Stephen Mendillo (1942-)
Slap Shot '77
King of the Gypsies '78
Ethan Frome '92
The First Wives Club '96
The Invincible Iron Man '07 (V)

Bridgit Mendler (1992-)
The Clique '08
Alvin and the Chipmunks: The Squeakuel '09
Labor Pains '09
Beverly Hills Chihuahua 2 '10 (V)
The Secret World of Arrietty '10 (V)
Lemonade Mouth '11

Maria Luisa Mendonca (1970-)
Carandiru '03
The 3 Marias '03

Natalie Mendoza (1978-)
Moulin Rouge '01
Rodgers & Hammerstein's South Pacific '01
The Descent '05
The Great Raid '05

Victor Manuel Mendoza (1913-95)
Susana '51
Garden of Evil '54
Cowboy '58
The Wonderful Country '59

Gonzalo Menendez (1971-)
The Lost City '05
Fantastic Four: Rise of the Silver Surfer '07
Act of Valor '12

Alex Meneses (1965-)
Living in Peril '97
The Flintstones in Viva Rock Vegas '00
44 Minutes: The North Hollywood Shootout '03
Fire From Below '09
Wrong Turn at Tahoe '09

Alex Menglet (1956-)
Zone 39 '96
He Died With a Falafel in His Hand '01

Adolphe Menjou (1890-1963)
The Sheik '21
Through the Back Door '21
The Marriage Circle '24
Morocco '30
The Easiest Way '31
The Front Page '31
A Farewell to Arms '32
Forbidden '32
Morning Glory '33
Little Miss Marker '34
Gold Diggers of 1935 '35
Milky Way '36
One in a Million '36
Sing, Baby, Sing '36
Cafe Metropole '37
100 Men and a Girl '37
Stage Door '37
A Star Is Born '37
The Goldwyn Follies '38
Letter of Introduction '38
Golden Boy '39
Road Show '41
Roxie Hart '42
Syncopation '42
You Were Never Lovelier '42
Hi Diddle Diddle '43
Step Lively '44
Heartbeat '46
The Hucksters '47
State of the Union '48
My Dream Is Yours '49
To Please a Lady '50
Across the Wide Missouri '51
The Tall Target '51
The Sniper '52
Man on a Tightrope '53
The Ambassador's Daughter '56
Bundle of Joy '56
Paths of Glory '57
Pollyanna '60

Shepard Menken (1921-99)
The Red Menace '49
The Great Caruso '51

Laura Mennell (1980-)
Personal Effects '05
Montana Sky '07
The Christmas Clause '08
Ruslan '09

Denis Menochet (1976-)
Inglourious Basterds '09
Murder on the Orient Express '10
Special Forces '11

Peter Mensah (1959-)
Jason X '01
Tears of the Sun '03
Hidalgo '04
The Incredible Hulk '08

Oleg Menshikov (1960-)
Burnt by the Sun '94
Prisoner of the Mountains '96
East-West '99

Vladimir Menshov
Night Watch '04
Day Watch '06

Idina Menzel (1971-)
The Tollbooth '04
Rent '05
Ask the Dust '06
Enchanted '07
Frozen '13 (V)
Frozen II '19

Heather Menzies (1949-)
The Sound of Music '65
Ssssssss '73
Piranha '78
Captain America '79

Robert Menzies (1955-)
Cactus '86
Innocence '00

Tobias Menzies (1974-)
Casino Royale '06
Anton Chekhov's The Duel '09
Forget Me Not '10
Any Human Heart '11
Black Sea '14
Underworld: Blood Wars '16

Christian Meoli (1972-)
Alive '93
The Low Life '95
The Song of the Lark '01

Julino Mer
Under the Domim Tree '95
The Last Warrior '99

Kad Merad (1964-)
The Chorus '04
Paris 36 '08
22 Bullets '10
The Well-Digger's Daughter '11

Doro Merande (1898-1975)
Mr. Belvedere Rings the Bell '51
The Man with the Golden Arm '55
The Seven Year Itch '55
The Gazebo '59
Kiss Me, Stupid! '64
The Russians Are Coming, the Russians Are Coming '66

Alex Meraz (1985-)
The Twilight Saga: Eclipse '10
Never Back Down 2: The Beatdown '11

Hector Mercado (1949-)
Nomads '86
Leather Jacket Love Story '98

Beryl Mercer (1862-1939)
All Quiet on the Western Front '30
The Matrimonial Bed '30
The Man in Possession '31
The Miracle Woman '31
Public Enemy '31
Lovers Courageous '32
Smilin' Through '32
Young America '32
Cavalcade '33
Supernatural '33
Jane Eyre '34

Frances Mercer (1915-2000)
Smashing the Rackets '38
Society Lawyer '39

Mae Mercer (1932-2008)
Dirty Harry '71
Frogs '72
The Swinging Cheerleaders '74
Pretty Baby '78

Matt Mercer (1982-)
Among Brothers '05
Contracted '13
Airplane *vs.* Volcano '14
Beyond the Gates '16

Matthew Mercer
Mythica 2: The Darkspore '15
Mythica: The Necroromancer '15
Resident Evil: Vendetta '17

Stephen Merchant (1974-)
Tooth Fairy '10
Gnomeo & Juliet '11 (V)
I Give It a Year '13
Movie 43 '13
Logan '17
Table 19 '17
The Girl in the Spider's Web '18

Tamzin Merchant (1987-)
Pride and Prejudice *'05*
Princess Kaiulani *'09*
Jane Eyre *'11*
Red Faction: Origins *'11*
The Mystery of Edwin Drood *'12*
Murder On the Home Front *'13*
Dragonheart 3: The Sorcerer's Curse *'15*

Vivien Merchant (1929-82)
Alfie *'66*
Accident *'67*
Frenzy *'72*
The Homecoming *'73*
The Offence *'73*
Under Milk Wood *'73*

Michele Mercier (1939-)
Shoot the Piano Player *'62*
Angelique *'64*
Black Sabbath *'64*
Angelique: The Road to Versailles *'65*
Casanova '70 *'65*
Angelique and the King *'66*
Untamable Angelique *'67*
Angelique and the Sultan *'68*
Web of the Spider *'70*
Call of the Wild *'72*

Melina Mercouri (1925-94)
Stella *'55*
Where the Hot Wind Blows *'59*
Never on Sunday *'60*
Phaedra *'61*
Topkapi *'64*
Once Is Not Enough *'75*
Nasty Habits *'77*

Monique Mercure (1930-2020)
The Odyssey of the Pacific *'82*
Naked Lunch *'91*
The Red Violin *'98*
When Justice Fails *'98*

Micole Mercurio (1938-)
Colors *'88*
While You Were Sleeping *'95*
Bandits *'01*

Paul Mercurio (1963-)
Strictly Ballroom *'92*
Exit to Eden *'94*
Back of Beyond *'95*
Cosi *'95 (C)*
Joseph *'95*
Dark Planet *'97*
The First 9 1/2 Weeks *'98*

Burgess Meredith (1908-97)
Winterset *'36*
Idiot's Delight *'39*
Of Mice and Men *'39*
Castle on the Hudson *'40*
Second Chorus *'40*
That Uncertain Feeling *'41*
Tom, Dick, and Harry *'41*
The Story of G.I. Joe *'45*
Diary of a Chambermaid *'46*
Magnificent Doll *'46*
Mine Own Executioner *'47*
Man on the Eiffel Tower *'48*
On Our Merry Way *'48*
Jigsaw *'49 (C)*
Advise and Consent *'62*
The Cardinal *'63*
In Harm's Way *'65*
Batman *'66*
A Big Hand for the Little Lady *'66*
Madame X *'66*
Hurry Sundown *'67*
Torture Garden *'67*
Skidoo *'68*
Stay Away, Joe *'68*
Hard Contract *'69*
MacKenna's Gold *'69*
There Was a Crooked Man *'70*
Such Good Friends *'71*
Beware! The Blob *'72*
Probe *'72*
Golden Needles *'74*
The Day of the Locust *'75*
The Hindenburg *'75*
Burnt Offerings *'76*
92 in the Shade *'76*
Rocky *'76*
The Sentinel *'76*
The Amazing Captain Nemo *'78*
Foul Play *'78*
Great Bank Hoax *'78*
Magic *'78*
The Manitou *'78*
Rocky 2 *'79*
Final Assignment *'80*
When Time Ran Out *'80*
Clash of the Titans *'81*
Last Chase *'81*
True Confessions *'81*
Rocky 3 *'82*
Twilight Zone: The Movie *'83*
Wet Gold *'84*
Santa Claus: The Movie *'85*
Action Force: The Movie *'87 (V)*
Full Moon in Blue Water *'88*
Rocky 5 *'90*
State of Grace *'90*
Grumpy Old Men *'93*
Across the Moon *'94*
Camp Nowhere *'94*
Grumpier Old Men *'95*

Don Meredith (1938-2010)
Terror on the 40th Floor *'74*
Banjo Hackett *'76*
Mayday at 40,000 Feet *'76*
Undercover With the KKK *'78*
Terror Among Us *'81*
Three Days of Rain *'02*

Ifan Meredith
Metroland *'97*
The Mill on the Floss *'97*

Iris Meredith (1915-80)
The Spider's Web *'38*
Green Archer *'40*

Judi Meredith (1936-2014)
Jack the Giant Killer *'62*
Planet of Blood *'66*
Queen of Blood *'66*

Lee Meredith (1947-)
The Producers *'68*
The Sunshine Boys *'75*

Luc Merenda (1943-)
Le Mans *'71*
Shoot First, Die Later *'74*
The Cheaters *'76*
Kidnap Syndicate *'76*

Stanislas Merhar (1971-)
Dry Cleaning *'97*
The Count of Monte Cristo *'99*
Almost Peaceful *'02*
Merci Docteur Rey *'04*
Almayer's Folly *'12*

Jalal Merhi (1967-)
Tiger Claws *'91*
Talons of the Eagle *'92*
Fearless Tiger *'94*
Expect No Mercy *'95*
The Circuit 2 *'02*

Macha Meril (1940-)
Une Femme Mariee *'64*
A Married Woman *'65*
The Defector *'66*
Deep Red: Hatchet Murders *'75*
Night Train Murders *'75*
Beau Pere *'81*
Vagabond *'85*
Chinese Roulette *'86*
Meeting Venus *'91*

Eda Reiss Merin (1913-98)
The Reluctant Agent *'89*
Don't Tell Mom the Babysitter's Dead *'91*
For Better or Worse *'95*

Aitor Merino (1972-)
If They Tell You I Fell *'89*
Deserter *'02*

Michele Meritz
Le Beau Serge *'58*
Classe Tous Risque *'60*

Philip Merivale (1886-1946)
Rage in Heaven *'41*
Lady for a Night *'42*
This Above All *'42*
Lost Angel *'43*
Nothing But Trouble *'44*

Lee Meriwether (1935-)
The 4D Man *'59*
Batman *'66*
Namu, the Killer Whale *'66*
The Undefeated *'69*
Brothers O'Toole *'73*
The Ultimate Gift *'07*
Touching Home *'08*
The Ultimate Life *'13*

Una Merkel (1903-86)
Abraham Lincoln *'30*
The Bat Whispers *'30*
The Maltese Falcon *'31*
Private Lives *'31*
Huddle *'32*
Red Headed Woman *'32*
They Call It Sin *'32*
Bombshell *'33*
Clear All Wires! *'33*
Day of Reckoning *'33*
42nd Street *'33*
Midnight Mary *'33*
Evelyn Prentice *'34*
The Merry Widow *'34*
Broadway Melody of 1936 *'35*
Riff Raff *'35*
Born to Dance *'36*
Speed *'36*
Saratoga *'37*
True Confession *'37*
Destry Rides Again *'39*
On Borrowed Time *'39*
The Bank Dick *'40*
The Road to Zanzibar *'41*
The Bride Goes Wild *'48*
Kill the Umpire *'50*
My Blue Heaven *'50*
Golden Girl *'51*
Rich, Young and Pretty *'51*
With a Song in My Heart *'52*
I Love Melvin *'53*
The Kentuckian *'55*
The Kettles in the Ozarks *'56*
The Mating Game *'59*
The Parent Trap *'61*
Summer and Smoke *'61*
Summer Magic *'63*
A Tiger Walks *'64*
Spinout *'66*

S. Epatha Merkerson (1952-)
She's Gotta Have It *'86*
Radio *'03*
Jersey Girl *'04*
Black Snake Moan *'07*
Girl, Positive *'07*
Slipstream *'07*
Mother and Child *'09*
The Six Wives of Henry Lefay *'09*
Lincoln *'12*
Peeples *'13*
The Gabby Douglas Story *'14*

Maurizio Merli (1940-89)
Street War *'76*
Fearless *'77*
Mannaja: A Man Called Blade *'77*

Jan Merlin (1925-2019)
Screaming Eagles *'56*
Cole Younger, Gunfighter *'58*
Gunfight at Comanche Creek *'64*
Take the Money and Run *'69*
Twilight People *'72*

Joanna Merlin (1931-)
Fame *'80*
Baby It's You *'82*
Mystic Pizza *'88*
Class Action *'91*
Two Bits *'96*
City of Angels *'98*

Maria Luisa Merlo
The Mighty Ursus *'61*
Ursus in the Valley of the Lions *'62*

Ethel Merman (1909-84)
Kid Millions *'34*
We're Not Dressing *'34*
Alexander's Ragtime Band *'38*
Happy Landing *'38*
Stage Door Canteen *'43*
There's No Business Like Show Business *'54*
It's a Mad, Mad, Mad, Mad World *'63*
Journey Back to Oz *'71 (V)*
Airplane! *'80*

Mary Merrall (1890-1973)
Dead of Night *'45*
Nicholas Nickleby *'46*
They Made Me a Fugitive *'47*
The Belles of St. Trinian's *'53*

Charlotte Merriam (1906-72)
Pampered Youth *'25*
Night Nurse *'31*
Alimony Madness *'33*

Dina Merrill (1923-2017)
Desk Set *'57*
Operation Petticoat *'59*
Butterfield 8 *'60*
The Sundowners *'60*
Twenty Plus Two *'61*
The Young Savages *'61*
The Courtship of Eddie's Father *'62*
I'll Take Sweden *'65*
Running Wild *'73*
The Greatest *'77*
A Wedding *'78*
Anna to the Infinite Power *'84*
Hot Pursuit *'84*
Caddyshack 2 *'88*
Fear *'90*
True Colors *'91*
The Player *'92*
Suture *'93*
Open Season *'95*
The Other Sister *'98*
Shade *'03*

Frank Merrill (1893-1966)
The Adventures of Tarzan *'21*
Tarzan the Tiger *'29*

Gary Merrill (1915-90)
Slattery's Hurricane *'49*
Twelve o'Clock High *'49*
All About Eve *'50*
Mother Didn't Tell Me *'50*
Where the Sidewalk Ends *'50*
Decision Before Dawn *'51*
Another Man's Poison *'52*
The Girl in White *'52*
Phone Call from a Stranger *'52*
A Blueprint for Murder *'53*
The Black Dakotas *'54*
Witness to Murder *'54*
Crash Landing *'58*
Missouri Traveler *'58*
The Wonderful Country *'59*
Mysterious Island *'61*
Catacombs *'64*
Around the World Under the Sea *'65*
Destination Inner Space *'66*
Clambake *'67*
The Last Challenge *'67*
The Power *'68*
Then Came Bronson *'68*
Huckleberry Finn *'74*

Ryan Merriman (1983-)
The Deep End of the Ocean *'98*
Just Looking *'99*
Lansky *'99*
Smart House *'00*
Dangerous Child *'01*
Halloween: Resurrection *'02*
Spin *'04*
The Ring 2 *'05*
Final Destination 3 *'06*
Home of the Giants *'07*
Backwoods *'08*
Comanche Moon *'08*
Wild Cherry *'09*
The 5th Quarter *'10*
Dose of Reality *'12*
42 *'13*
Independence Daysaster *'13*
The Congressman *'16*
Domain *'18*

Clive Merrison (1945-)
An Awfully Big Adventure *'94*
Heavenly Creatures *'94*
The English Patient *'96*
Photographing Fairies *'97*
The History Boys *'06*

George Merritt (1890-1977)
Young and Innocent *'37*
The Secret Four *'39*
I, Monster *'71*

Theresa Merritt (1922-98)
The Serpent and the Rainbow *'87*
Voodoo Dawn *'89*
Billy Madison *'94*

Jane Merrow (1941-)
Catacombs *'64*
The System *'64*
The Girl Getters *'66*
Island of the Burning Doomed *'67*
The Lion in Winter *'68*
Adam's Woman *'70*
Hands of the Ripper *'71*
The Horror at 37,000 Feet *'73*

Susan Merson
Lost in Yonkers *'93*
American Meltdown *'04*

John Merton (1901-59)
Lightnin' Bill Carson *'36*
Zorro's Fighting Legion *'39*

William Mervyn (1912-76)
Murder Ahoy *'64*
The Railway Children *'70*
The Ruling Class *'72*

Scott Mescudi (1984-)
Need for Speed *'14*
James White *'15*
Vincent N Roxxy *'17*

John Mese (1963-)
Excessive Force 2: Force on Force *'95*
Night of the Scarecrow *'95*
Red Dirt *'99*

Daniel Mesguich (1952-)
The Musketeer *'01*
Le Divorce *'03*

Roxane Mesquida (1981-)
Sheitan *'06*
Rubber *'10*
Kaboom *'11*
Kiss of the Damned *'12*

Hannes Messemer (1924-91)
The Great Escape *'63*
The Defector *'66*
The Odessa File *'74*

Donald E. Messick (1926-97)
The Hobbit *'78 (V)*
Flight of Dragons *'82 (V)*
Jetsons: The Movie *'90 (V)*

Marc Messier (1947-)
A Wind from Wyoming *'94*
The Boys *'97*

Chris Messina (1974-)
Ira & Abby *'06*
Towelhead *'07*
Humboldt County *'08*
Made of Honor *'08*
Vicky Cristina Barcelona *'08*
Away We Go *'09*
Brief Interviews With Hideous Men *'09*
Julie & Julia *'09*
Devil *'10*
Greenberg *'10*
Monogamy *'10*
An Invisible Sign *'11*
Like Crazy *'11*
The Trouble With Bliss *'11*
Celeste & Jesse Forever *'12*
The Giant Mechanical Man *'12*
Ruby Sparks *'12*
28 Hotel Rooms *'12*
Cake *'14*
Manglehorn *'15*
Live by Night *'16*
Blame *'17*

Francesco Messina
In the Soup *'92*
13 Moons *'02*

Debra Messing (1968-)
A Walk in the Clouds *'95*
McHale's Navy *'97*
Jesus *'00*
Hollywood Ending *'02*
The Mothman Prophecies *'02*
Along Came Polly *'04*
Garfield: The Movie *'04 (V)*
The Wedding Date *'05*
Open Season *'06 (V)*
Lucky You *'07*
Purple Violets *'07*
The Starter Wife *'07*
Nothing Like the Holidays *'08*
The Women *'08*
Searching *'18*

Buddy Messinger
The Hoodlum *'19*
A Lady of Chance *'28*

Johnny Messner (1970-)
Finding Home *'03*
Tears of the Sun *'03*
Anacondas: The Hunt for the Blood Orchid *'04*
Spartan *'04*
The Whole Ten Yards *'04*
Hostage *'05*
Running Scared *'06*
Believers *'07*
The Art of Travel *'08*
Loaded *'08*
The Poker Club *'08*
Remarkable Power *'08*
Ring of Death *'08*
Bad Ass *'09*
Wrong Turn at Tahoe *'09*
Soldier Love Story *'10*
Arena *'11*
Kill 'Em All *'12*
The Outsider *'14*
Condemned *'15*
Decommissioned *'16*
Weaponized *'16*
American Violence *'17*

George Metaxa (1899-1950)
Doctor Takes a Wife *'40*
Submarine Base *'43*
The Mask of Dimitrios *'44*

Laurie Metcalf (1955-)
Desperately Seeking Susan *'85*
Execution of Raymond Graham *'85*
Making Mr. Right *'86*
Uncle Buck *'89*
Internal Affairs *'90*
Pacific Heights *'90*
JFK *'91*
Mistress *'91*
Blink *'93*
Leaving Las Vegas *'95*
Toy Story *'95 (V)*
Dear God *'96*
Balloon Farm *'97*
Scream 2 *'97*
U-Turn *'97*
Always Outnumbered Always Outgunned *'98*
Bulworth *'98*
Chicago Cab *'98*
Runaway Bride *'99*
Toy Story 2 *'99 (V)*
Treasure Planet *'02 (V)*
Beer League *'06*
Steel City *'06*
Georgia Rule *'07*
Meet the Robinsons *'07 (V)*

Toy Story 3 *'10 (V)*
Lady Bird *'17*

Mark Metcalf (1946-)
Julia *'77*
National Lampoon's Animal House *'78*
The Final Terror *'83*
One Crazy Summer *'86*
Mr. North *'88*
Rage *'95*
The Stupids *'95*
Hijacking Hollywood *'97*
Drive Me Crazy *'99*

Jesse Metcalfe (1978-)
John Tucker Must Die *'06*
Insanitarium *'08*
Loaded *'08*
The Other End of the Line *'08*
Beyond a Reasonable Doubt *'09*
Fairfield Road *'10*
Dead Rising: End Game *'16*
Escape Plan 2: Hades *'18*

Ken Metcalfe
TNT Jackson *'75*
Nam Angels *'88*
Savage Justice *'88*

Aaron Michael Metchik (1980-)
Trading Mom *'94*
The Baby-Sitters' Club *'95*

Asher Metchik (1986-)
Trading Mom *'94*
Milo *'98*

Saul Meth
Deadly Weapons *'70*
Double Agent 73 *'80*

Method Man (1971-)
Belly *'98*
How High *'01*
Garden State *'04*
My Baby's Daddy *'04*
Soul Plane *'04*
Venom *'05*
Meet the Spartans *'08*
The Wackness *'08*
Sinners and Saints *'10*
The Mortician *'11*
The Sitter *'11*
Keanu *'16*
Paterson *'16*

Mayo Methot (1904-51)
Corsair *'31*
Virtue *'32*
Counsellor-at-Law *'33*
The Mind Reader *'33*
Goodbye Love *'34*
Jimmy the Gent *'34*
Marked Woman *'37*

Svetlana Metkina (1974-)
The Second Front *'05*
Bobby *'06*

Art Metrano (1936-)
Rocket Attack U.S.A. *'58*
The Heartbreak Kid *'72*
They Only Kill Their Masters *'72*
Slaughter's Big Ripoff *'73*
Prisoner in the Middle *'74*
How to Beat the High Cost of Living *'80*
Breathless *'83*
Malibu Express *'85*
Police Academy 2: Their First Assignment *'85*
Police Academy 3: Back in Training *'86*

Nancy Mette
Matewan *'87*
Meet the Hollowheads *'89*

Omar Metwally (1974-)
Munich *'05*
Rendition *'07*
The City of Your Final Destination *'09*
Virtuality *'09*
Miral *'10*
Non-Stop *'14*

Belinda Metz (1960-)
The Suspect *'05*
Eight Below *'06*

Jim Metzler (1951-)
Squeeze Play *'79*
Four Friends *'81*
Tex *'82*
River's Edge *'87*
Hot to Trot! *'88*
976-EVIL *'88*
Old Gringo *'89*
Circuitry Man *'90*
One False Move *'91*
French Silk *'94*
Plughead Rewired: Circuitry Man 2 *'94*
Children of the Corn 3: Urban Harvest *'95*
Cadillac Ranch *'96*
A Gun, a Car, a Blonde *'97*
St. Patrick's Day *'99*
The Doe Boy *'01*
Sundown: The Vampire in Retreat *'08*

Paul Meurisse (1912-79)
Diabolique *'55*
The Monocle *'64*
Le Deuxieme Souffle *'66*
Army of Shadows *'69*
Gypsy *'75*
Le Gitan *'75*

Anne-Laure Meury
The Aviator's Wife *'80*
Boyfriends & Girlfriends *'88*

Jason Mewes (1974-)
Clerks *'94*
Mallrats *'95*
Chasing Amy *'97*
Dogma *'99*
Scream 3 *'00*
Jay and Silent Bob Strike Back *'01*
R.S.V.P. *'02*
The Pleasure Drivers *'05*
Bottoms Up *'06*
Clerks 2 *'06*
The Tripper *'06*
Netherbeast Incorporated *'07*
Zack and Miri Make a Porno *'08*
The Last Godfather *'10*
Vigilante Diaries *'16*
Jay and Silent Bob Reboot *'19*
Madness in the Method *'19*

Bess Meyer
The Inner Circle *'91*
All I Want for Christmas *'07*

Breckin Meyer (1974-)
Betrayed: A Story of Three Women *'95*
Clueless *'95*
Prefontaine *'96*
Touch *'96*
Dancer, Texas-Pop. 81 *'98*
54 *'98*
Go *'99*
Tail Lights Fade *'99*
Road Trip *'00*
Josie and the Pussycats *'01 (C)*
Kate & Leopold *'01*
Rat Race *'01*
Blast *'04*
Garfield: The Movie *'04*
Herbie: Fully Loaded *'05*
Rebound *'05*
Caffeine *'06*
Garfield: A Tail of Two Kitties *'06*
Blue State *'07*
Corporate Affairs *'07*
Stag Night *'08*
Ghosts of Girlfriends Past *'09*

Brendan Meyer
Girl *vs.* Monster *'12*
The Guest *'14*

Dina Meyer (1968-)
Johnny Mnemonic *'95*
Dragonheart *'96*
Starship Troopers *'97*
Nowhere Land *'98*
Poodle Springs *'98*
Bats *'99*
Stranger than Fiction *'99*
Eye See You *'01*

Time Lapse *'01*
Federal Protection *'02*
Star Trek: Nemesis *'02*
Unspeakable *'02*
Saw *'04*
His and Her Christmas *'05*
Saw 2 *'05*
Wild Things 3: Diamonds in the Rough *'05*
Crazy Eights *'06*
Imaginary Playmate *'06*
Saw 3 *'06*
Decoys: The Second Seduction *'07*
Fatal Secrets *'09*
Piranha 3D *'10*
Golden Shoes *'15*

Emile Meyer (1910-87)
Shane *'53*
Drums Across the River *'54*
Riot in Cell Block 11 *'54*
Blackboard Jungle *'55*
The Girl in the Red Velvet Swing *'55*
Stranger on Horseback *'55*
Gun the Man Down *'56*
The Case Against Brooklyn *'58*
The Fiend Who Walked the West *'58*
Good Day for a Hanging *'58*
The Lineup *'58*
King of the Wild Stallions *'59*

Hans Meyer (1925-2020)
Le Magnifique *'76*
Mauvais Sang *'86*
Brotherhood of the Wolf *'01*

Michael Meyer (1957-)
Virtual Desire *'95*
The Biggest Fan *'02*

Russ Meyer (1922-2004)
Motor Psycho *'65*
Amazon Women on the Moon *'87*

Torben Meyer (1884-1975)
Thin Ice *'37*
Sullivan's Travels *'41*
The Matchmaker *'58*
Judgment at Nuremberg *'61*

Ari Meyers (1969-)
License to Kill *'84*
Shakma *'89*
Dark Horse *'92*

Harry Meyers (1886-1938)
See Harry C. (Henry) Myers

Josh Meyers
How to Make Love to a Woman *'09*
Going to America *'15*

Seth Meyers (1973-)
American Dreamz *'06*
Perception *'06*
Spring Breakdown *'08*
I Don't Know How She Does It *'11*
New Year's Eve *'11*

Gerard Meylan (1952-)
Nenette and Boni *'96*
Marius and Jeannette *'97*
The Town Is Quiet *'00*
Lulu *'02*
Rapt *'09*

Michelle Meyrink (1962-)
Valley Girl *'83*
Revenge of the Nerds *'84*
One Magic Christmas *'85*
Real Genius *'85*
Permanent Record *'88*

Giovanna Mezzogiorno (1974-)
The Last Kiss *'01*
Facing Windows *'03*
Don't Tell *'05*
Vincere *'09*

Vittorio Mezzogiorno (1942-94)
Three Brothers *'80*
Cafe Express *'83*
L'Homme Blesse *'83*
Moon in the Gutter *'83*

Robert Miano (1942-)
Chained Heat *'83*
Donnie Brasco *'96*
Matter of Trust *'98*
Smoke Signals *'98*
Thick as Thieves *'99*
Dungeons and Dragons *'00*
Loser *'00*
Luckytown *'00*
The Stickup *'01*
Today You Die *'05*
The Indian *'07*
The Still Life *'07*
Safehouse *'08*
2:22 *'08*
Giallo *'09*
Mysteria *'11*
Beyond the Trophy *'12*

Cora Miao (1958-)
Dim Sum: A Little Bit of Heart *'85*
Eat a Bowl of Tea *'89*

Tien Miao (1925-2005)
The Hole *'98*
What Time Is It There? *'01*
Goodbye, Dragon Inn *'03*

Gertrude Michael (1911-64)
I'm No Angel *'33*
Cleopatra *'34*
Murder at the Vanities *'34*
Murder On the Blackboard *'34*
Search for Beauty *'34*
The Last Outpost *'35*
Where Are Your Children? *'44*
Flamingo Road *'49*
Caged *'50*

Ralph Michael (1907-94)
Dead of Night *'45*
A Night to Remember *'58*
Children of the Damned *'63*
The Heroes of Telemark *'65*
Murder Most Foul *'65*

Sean Michael (1988-)
See Sean Michael Afable

Sean Cameron Michael (1969-)
Allan Quartermain and the Temple of Skulls *'08*
The Natalee Holloway Story *'09*

Dario Michaelis (1927-)
I, Vampiri *'56*
The Day the Sky Exploded *'57*

Al Michaels (1944-)
Homeward Bound 2: Lost in San Francisco *'96 (V)*
BASEketball *'98*

Bret Michaels (1963-)
In God's Hands *'98*
No Code of Conduct *'98*

Dolores Michaels (1933-2001)
April Love *'57*
Time Limit *'57*
The Wayward Bus *'57*
The Fiend Who Walked the West *'58*
One Foot in Hell *'60*
Battle at Bloody Beach *'61*

Julie Michaels
Road House *'89*
Jason Goes to Hell: The Final Friday *'93*

Mimi Michaels (1983-)
Sister Aimee: The Aimee Semple McPherson Story *'06*
Boogeyman 3 *'08*
Meteor *'09*
ChromeSkull: Laid to Rest 2 *'11*

Nicola Michaels (1934-)
See Niki Dantine

Joel Michaely
Cruel World *'05*
Cult *'07*

AJ Michalka
Angels in Stardust *'14*
Weepah Way for Now *'15*

Alyson Michalka (1989-)
Cow Belles *'06*
Bandslam *'09*
Easy A *'10*
The Roommate *'11*
Weepah Way for Now *'15*

Amanda (A.J.) Michalka (1991-)
Cow Belles *'06*
Secretariat *'10*
Jodi Picoult's Salem Falls *'11*
Super 8 *'11*
Grace Unplugged *'13*

Jeff Michalski
Star Maps *'97*
The Laundromat *'19*

Nicki Micheaux
Ringmaster *'98*
Lowlife *'18*

Dominique Michel (1932-)
The Decline of the American Empire *'86*
The Barbarian Invasions *'03*

Marc Michel (1932-)
Le Trou *'59*
Lola *'61*
Umbrellas of Cherbourg *'64*

Marcella Michelangeli
And God Said to Cain *'69*
Padre Padrone *'77*

Lea Michele (1986-)
Glee: The 3D Concert Movie *'11*
New Year's Eve *'11*
Legends of Oz: Dorothy's Return *'14 (V)*

Michael Michele (1966-)
New Jack City *'91*
The Sixth Man *'97*
The Substitute 2: School's Out *'97*
Homicide: The Movie *'00*
Ali *'01*
Dark Blue *'03*
How to Lose a Guy in 10 Days *'03*
Relative Stranger *'09*

Helena Michell (1963-)
Piece of Cake *'88*
Devices and Desires *'91*

Keith Michell (1928-)
All Night Long *'62*
Seven Seas to Calais *'62*
The Executioner *'70*
Six Wives of Henry VIII *'71*
The Story of Jacob & Joseph *'74*
The Story of David *'76*
Ruddigore *'82*
The Deceivers *'88*

Anne Michelle (1952-)
The Virgin Witch *'70*
House of Whipcord *'75*
French Quarter *'78*

Janee Michelle
Scream Blacula Scream *'73*
The House on Skull Mountain *'74*

Shelley Michelle (1962-)
Bikini Summer *'91*
Sunset Strip *'91*
Married People, Single Sex *'93*

Maria Michi (1921-80)
Open City *'45*
Paisan *'46*
Last Tango in Paris *'73*

Kate Micucci (1980-)
When in Rome *'09*
Don't Think Twice *'16*
The Little Hours *'17*
Seven Stages to Achieve Eternal Bliss *'20*

Tracy Middendorf (1970-)
Wes Craven's New Nightmare *'94*

Ed McBain's 87th Precinct: Lightning *'95*
The Assassination of Richard Nixon *'05*
Just Add Water *'07*
Boy Wonder *'10*
Reaching for the Moon *'13*

Thomas Middleditch (1982-)
Splinterheads *'09*
Fun Size *'12*
The Bronze *'15*
Joshy *'16*
Captain Underpants: The First Epic Movie *'17 (V)*
Replicas *'18*

Frank Middlemass (1919-2006)
The Island *'80*
Oliver Twist *'85*
The Bretts *'88*

Charles Middleton (1879-1949)
An American Tragedy *'31*
The Miracle Woman *'31*
The Strange Love of Molly Louvain *'32*
Too Busy to Work *'32*
Duck Soup *'33*
David Harum *'34*
Mrs. Wiggs of the Cabbage Patch *'34*
Murder at the Vanities *'34*
The Miracle Rider *'35*
Empty Saddles *'36*
Rocketship *'36*
Dick Tracy Returns *'38*
Flash Gordon: Mars Attacks the World *'39*
Oklahoma Kid *'39*
Flash Gordon Conquers the Universe *'40*
Flash Gordon: Rocketship *'40*
Western Union *'41*
Northwest Trail *'46*

Guy Middleton (1906-73)
A Man About the House *'47*
The Belles of St. Trinian's *'53*
Oh! What a Lovely War *'69*

Ray Middleton (1908-84)
Lady for a Night *'42*
Lady from Louisiana *'42*
I Dream of Jeannie *'52*

Robert Middleton (1911-77)
Desperate Hours *'55*
The Court Jester *'56*
Love Me Tender *'56*
Tarnished Angels *'57*
The Law and Jake Wade *'58*
Career *'59*
Gold of the Seven Saints *'61*
Cattle King *'63*
Harrad Experiment *'73*

Tuppence Middleton (1987-)
Tormented *'09*
Skeletons *'10*
Cleanskin *'12*
The Lady Vanishes *'13*
Trap for Cinderella *'13*
Jupiter Ascending *'15*
MI-5 *'15*
The Current War: Director's Cut *'19*
Downton Abbey *'19*
Fisherman's Friends *'19*

Dale Midkiff (1959-)
Streetwalkin' *'85*
Nightmare Weekend *'86*
Pet Sematary *'89*
Love Potion #9 *'92*
Ed McBain's 87th Precinct: Heatwave *'97*
Toothless *'97*
The Magnificent Seven *'98*
Air Bud 3: World Pup *'00*
Another Woman's Husband *'00*
The Crow: Salvation *'00*
Route 666 *'01*
Video Voyeur: The Susan Wilson Story *'02*
Love Comes Softly *'03*

Love's Enduring Promise *'04*
Torn Apart *'04*
Back to You and Me *'05*
Love's Abiding Joy *'06*
Boxboarders! *'07*
Flight of the Living Dead: Outbreak on a Plane *'07*
Love's Unending Legacy *'07*
Love's Unfolding Dream *'07*
2012: Doomsday *'08*

Bette Midler (1945-)
Hawaii *'66*
The Rose *'79*
Jinxed *'82*
Down and Out in Beverly Hills *'86*
Ruthless People *'86*
Outrageous Fortune *'87*
Beaches *'88*
Big Business *'88*
Oliver & Company *'88 (V)*
Stella *'89*
For the Boys *'91*
Scenes from a Mall *'91*
Gypsy *'93*
Hocus Pocus *'93*
Get Shorty *'95 (C)*
The First Wives Club *'96*
That Old Feeling *'96*
Drowning Mona *'00*
Isn't She Great *'00*
What Women Want *'00*
The Stepford Wives *'04*
Then She Found Me *'07*
The Women *'08*
Cats & Dogs: The Revenge of Kitty Galore *'10 (V)*
Parental Guidance *'12*
Freak Show *'18*

Danny Midwinter
Blackbeard *'06*
Anacondas: Trail of Blood *'09*
Interview With a Hitman *'12*
The Rise of the Krays *'16*

Toshiro Mifune (1920-97)
Drunken Angel *'48*
A Quiet Duel *'49*
Stray Dog *'49*
Scandal *'50*
The Idiot *'51*
Rashomon *'51*
Seven Samurai *'54*
I Live in Fear *'55*
Samurai 1: Musashi Miyamoto *'55*
Samurai 2: Duel at Ichijoji Temple *'55*
Samurai 3: Duel at Ganryu Island *'56*
The Lower Depths *'57*
Throne of Blood *'57*
The Hidden Fortress *'58*
Rikisha-Man *'58*
The Bad Sleep Well *'60*
Yojimbo *'61*
High & Low *'62*
Sanjuro *'62*
Red Beard *'65*
Grand Prix *'66*
Samurai Rebellion *'67*
Sword of Doom *'67*
Hell in the Pacific *'69*
Red Lion *'69*
Samurai Banners *'69*
Zatoichi *vs.* Yojimbo *'70*
Red Sun *'71*
Midway *'76*
1941 *'79*
Winter Kills *'79*
Shogun *'80*
Picture Bride *'94 (C)*

R.A. Mihailoff
Leatherface: The Texas Chainsaw Massacre 3 *'89*
Pumpkinhead 2: Blood Wings *'94*
Hatchet 2 *'10*

Tatsuya Mihashi (1923-2004)
The Burmese Harp *'56*
High & Low *'62*
None But the Brave *'65*
What's Up, Tiger Lily? *'66*
Tora! Tora! Tora! *'70*

Dolls *'02*
Black House *'07*

Dash Mihok (1974-)
Telling You *'98*
The Thin Red Line *'98*
White Boyz *'99*
The Perfect Storm *'00*
Finder's Fee *'01*
The Guru *'02*
Basic *'03*
Dark Blue *'03*
Connie and Carla *'04*
The Day After Tomorrow *'04*
Death Valley *'04*
Hustle *'04*
Kiss Kiss Bang Bang *'05*
Hollywoodland *'06*
10th & Wolf *'06*
Firehouse Dog *'07*
I Am Legend *'07*
Loveless in Los Angeles *'07*
Superheroes *'07*
The Longshots *'08*
Punisher: War Zone *'08*
Lifted *'10*
The Mortician *'11*
On the Inside *'11*
Trespass *'11*
Silver Linings Playbook *'12*
Before I Wake *'15*

Joshua Mikel
Extraction *'15*
Intruders *'16*
Only *'20*

Ted V. Mikels (1929-)
Addicted to Murder 2: Tainted Blood *'97 (C)*
Mark of the Astro-Zombies *'02*
Astro-Zombies M4: Invaders from Cyberspace *'12*

Nikita Mikhalkov (1945-)
An Unfinished Piece for a Player Piano *'77*
Siberiade *'79*
Burnt by the Sun *'94*
12 *'07*

Mads Mikkelsen (1965-)
Pusher *'96*
Flickering Lights *'01*
Wilbur Wants to Kill Himself *'02*
The Green Butchers *'03*
King Arthur *'04*
Adam's Apples *'05*
After the Wedding *'06*
Casino Royale *'06*
Coco Chanel & Igor Stravinsky *'09*
Valhalla Rising *'09*
Clash of the Titans *'10*
The Three Musketeers *'11*
A Royal Affair *'12*
Charlie Countryman *'13*
The Hunt *'13*
The Salvation *'14*
Men & Chicken *'15*
Doctor Strange *'16*
Arctic *'18*
At Eternity's Gate *'18*
Polar *'19*

Izabella Miko (1981-)
Coyote Ugly *'00*
The Forsaken *'01*
The House of Usher *'06*
Save the Last Dance 2 *'06*
Crashing *'07*
Dark Streets *'08*
Clash of the Titans *'10*
Double Identity *'10*
The Frontier *'16*

Rentaro Mikuni (1923-2013)
Samurai 1: Musashi Miyamoto *'55*
The Burmese Harp *'56*
Harakiri *'62*
Kwaidan *'64*
Vengeance Is Mine *'79*
Rikyu *'90*

Frank Milan
The Gold Racket *'37*
Joy of Living *'38*

Lita Milan (1933-)
The Ride Back *'57*
I, Mobster *'58*
The Left-Handed Gun *'58*
Never Love a Stranger *'58*

Alyssa Milano (1972-)
Old Enough *'84*
Commando *'85*
The Canterville Ghost *'86*
Conflict of Interest *'92*
Where the Day Takes You *'92*
Confessions of Sorority Girls *'94*
Double Dragon *'94*
Embrace of the Vampire *'95*
Poison Ivy 2: Lily *'95*
Fear *'96*
Glory Daze *'96*
Body Count *'97*
Hugo Pool *'97*
Goldrush: A Real Life Alaskan Adventure *'98*
Dickie Roberts: Former Child Star *'03*
Pathology *'08*
Wisegal *'08*
My Girlfriend's Boyfriend *'10*
Sundays at Tiffany's *'10*
Alvin and the Chipmunks: Chipwrecked *'11*
Hall Pass *'11*

Axel Milberg (1956-)
Operation Valkyrie *'04*
Hannah Arendt *'12*
Wetlands *'13*

David Milbern (1967-)
See David Millbern

Oliver Milburn (1973-)
Loaded *'94*
Tess of the D'Urbervilles *'98*
Me Without You *'01*
The Descent *'05*

David Milchard (1974-)
A Valentine Carol *'07*
Finn on the Fly *'09*

Ben Miles (1967-)
Three Blind Mice *'02*
Under the Greenwood Tree *'05*
V for Vendetta *'06*
Ninja Assassin *'09*
Red Joan *'19*

Bernard Miles (1907-91)
In Which We Serve *'43*
Great Expectations *'46*
Nicholas Nickleby *'46*
Never Let Me Go *'53*
The Man Who Knew Too Much *'56*
She Played With Fire *'57*
The Smallest Show on Earth *'57*
Sapphire *'59*

Elaine Miles (1960-)
Smoke Signals *'98*
The Business of Fancydancing *'02*
Wyvern *'09*

Joanna Miles (1940-)
Born Innocent *'74*
Bug *'75*
The Ultimate Warrior *'75*
The Orphan *'79*
Rosencrantz & Guildenstern Are Dead *'90*
The Avenging Angel *'95*
Horton Foote's Alone *'97*
Crossfire Trail *'01*
Monte Walsh *'03*
Sex and Breakfast *'07*
Jesse Stone: Thin Ice *'09*

Kate Miles
The Truth About Love *'04*
Longford *'06*

Kevin Miles
The Cars That Ate Paris *'74*
The Chant of Jimmie Blacksmith *'78*

Lillian Miles (1907-72)
The Old Homestead *'35*
Reefer Madness *'38*

Maria Miles
Catherine Cookson's The Cinder Path *'94*
Cold Comfort Farm *'94*

Peter Miles (1938-2002)
Family Honeymoon *'49*
The Red Pony *'49*
Trigger, Jr. *'50*

Rosalind Miles
Shaft's Big Score *'72*
The Black Six *'74*
I Spit on Your Corpse *'74*

Sarah Miles (1941-)
The Ceremony *'63*
The Servant *'63*
Term of Trial *'63*
Those Magnificent Men in Their Flying Machines *'65*
Blow-Up *'66*
I Was Happy Here *'66*
Ryan's Daughter *'70*
The Hireling *'73*
Man Who Loved Cat Dancing *'73*
Dynasty *'76*
The Sailor Who Fell from Grace with the Sea *'76*
The Big Sleep *'78*
Venom *'82*
Hope and Glory *'87*
Queenie *'87*
White Mischief *'88*

Sherry Miles (1952-)
The Todd Killings *'71*
The Velvet Vampire *'71*
Jailbreakin' *'72*

Sylvia Miles (1924-2019)
Parrish *'61*
Psychomania *'63*
Midnight Cowboy *'69*
Heat *'72*
Farewell, My Lovely *'75*
The Sentinel *'76*
Deadly Thief *'78*
The Funhouse *'81*
Evil under the Sun *'82*
No Big Deal *'83*
Crossing Delancey *'88*
She-Devil *'89*
Sleeping Beauty *'89*
Superstar: The Life and Times of Andy Warhol *'90*

Vera Miles (1929-)
Tall Lie *'53*
The Searchers *'56*
The Wrong Man *'56*
The FBI Story *'59*
Psycho *'60*
Back Street *'61*
The Man Who Shot Liberty Valance *'62*
A Tiger Walks *'64*
Those Calloways *'65*
Follow Me, Boys! *'66*
Gentle Giant *'67*
Hellfighters *'68*
Kona Coast *'68*
Baffled *'72*
Molly & Lawless John *'72*
One Little Indian *'73*
The Castaway Cowboy *'74*
Fire *'77*
Brainwaves *'82*
Mazes and Monsters *'82*
Psycho 2 *'83*
The Initiation *'84*
Into the Night *'85*
Separate Lives *'94*

Kim Milford (1950-88)
Corvette Summer *'78*
Laserblast *'78*

Penelope Milford (1948-)
Coming Home *'78*
Take This Job & Shove It *'81*
The Golden Seal *'83*
The Burning Bed *'85*
Heathers *'89*
Henry: Portrait of a Serial Killer 2: Mask of Sanity *'96*
Normal Life *'96*

Christina Milian (1981-)
American Pie *'99*
Love Don't Cost a Thing *'03*

Be Cool *'05*
Man of the House *'05*
Pulse *'06*
Snowglobe *'07*
Bring It On: Fight to the Finish *'09*
Christmas Cupid *'10*
A Snow Globe Christmas *'13*

Tomas Milian (1933-)
Boccaccio '70 *'62*
The Big Gundown *'66*
Beatrice Cenci *'69*
Companeros *'70*
Counter Punch *'71*
Don't Torture a Duckling *'72*
Sonny and Jed *'73*
Cop in Blue Jeans *'78*
Identification of a Woman *'82*
Cat Chaser *'90*
Drug Wars: The Camarena Story *'90*
Havana *'90*
Revenge *'90*
JFK *'91*
The Cowboy Way *'94*
Amistad *'97*
Fools Rush In *'97*
For Love or Country: The Arturo Sandoval Story *'00*
Traffic *'00*
The Yards *'00*
Washington Heights *'02*
The Lost City *'05*

Ivana Milicevic (1974-)
Head Over Heels *'01*
Just like Heaven *'05*
Casino Royale *'06*
Running Scared *'06*
Witless Protection *'08*
Beneath the Blue *'10*

Cristin Milioti
Sleepwalk with Me *'12*
The Wolf of Wall Street *'13*

Frank Military
Nutcracker: Money, Madness & Murder *'87*
Dead Bang *'89*
Everybody Wins *'90*
The Last Castle *'01*

John Miljan (1892-1960)
Yankee Clipper *'27*
Speedway *'29*
Untamed *'29*
The Voice of the City *'29*
Our Blushing Brides *'30*
Paid *'30*
Show Girl in Hollywood *'30*
The Unholy Three *'30*
The Woman Racket *'30*
Politics *'31*
Possessed *'31*
The Secret Six *'31*
Susan Lenox: Her Fall and Rise *'31*
Are You Listening? *'32*
Emma *'32*
Flesh *'32*
Kid from Spain *'32*
The Rich Are Always With Us *'32*
The Nuisance *'33*
Belle of the Nineties *'34*
The Ghost Walks *'34*
Whirlpool *'34*
Charlie Chan in Paris *'35*
Mississippi *'35*
Fast and Furious *'39*
Boss of Big Town *'43*
The Fallen Sparrow *'43*
I Accuse My Parents *'45*
Run for Cover *'55*

Hugh Millais (1929-2009)
McCabe & Mrs. Miller *'71*
Images *'72*
The Dogs of War *'81*

Robyn Millan
The Witchmaker *'69*
Murph the Surf *'75*

Victor Millan (1920-2009)
Terror in a Texas Town *'58*
Touch of Evil *'58*
The FBI Story *'59*
Boulevard Nights *'79*

Gloria Milland (1940-)
Fury of Achilles *'62*
Goliath Against the Giants *'63*
Revenge of the Musketeers *'63*
Hate for Hate *'67*

Ray Milland (1905-86)
Ambassador Bill *'31*
The Bachelor Father *'31*
Blonde Crazy *'31*
Charlie Chan in London *'34*
We're Not Dressing *'34*
The Gilded Lily *'35*
Next Time We Love *'36*
Three Smart Girls *'36*
Bulldog Drummond Escapes *'37*
Easy Living *'37*
Her Jungle Love *'38*
Men with Wings *'38*
Beau Geste *'39*
Doctor Takes a Wife *'40*
Irene *'40*
The Major and the Minor *'42*
Reap the Wild Wind *'42*
Star Spangled Rhythm *'42*
Forever and a Day *'43*
Ministry of Fear *'44*
The Uninvited *'44*
The Lost Weekend *'45*
Golden Earrings *'47*
The Big Clock *'48*
Copper Canyon *'50*
A Life of Her Own *'50*
Close to My Heart *'51*
Rhubarb *'51*
Something to Live For *'52*
The Thief *'52*
Let's Do It Again *'53*
Dial 'M' for Murder *'54*
The Girl in the Red Velvet Swing *'55*
Three Brave Men *'57*
Panic in Year Zero! *'62*
Premature Burial *'62*
X: The Man with X-Ray Eyes *'63*
Hostile Witness *'68*
Love Story *'70*
Quick, Let's Get Married *'71*
The Big Game *'72*
Embassy *'72*
Frogs *'72*
The Thing with Two Heads *'72*
Escape to Witch Mountain *'75*
The Last Tycoon *'76*
Mayday at 40,000 Feet *'76*
Rich Man, Poor Man *'76*
Slavers *'77*
Swiss Conspiracy *'77*
Blackout *'78*
Oil *'78*
Oliver's Story *'78*
Cave-In! *'79*
Spree *'79*
The Attic *'80*

Harry Millard (1928-69)
The Last Mile *'59*
Thunder in Dixie *'65*

David Millbern (1967-)
Bikini Summer *'91*
Gods and Monsters *'98*
The Paradise Virus *'03*
Chupacabra Terror *'05*
Christmas Do-Over *'06*
In Her Line of Fire *'06*
Ice Spiders *'07*
Nuclear Hurricane *'07*

David Millburn (1967-)
See David Millbern

Allan Miller (1929-)
Pearl *'78*
Murder C.O.D. *'90*
Warlock *'91*

Allison Miller (1985-)
Devil's Due *'14*
Always Woodstock *'15*

Andrew Miller
The Last of the Dogmen *'95*
Cube *'98*

Ann Miller (1919-2004)
Room Service *'38*
You Can't Take It with You *'38*
Melody Ranch *'40*
Too Many Girls *'40*
Time Out for Rhythm *'41*
Carolina Blues *'44*
Easter Parade *'48*
On the Town *'49*
Watch the Birdie *'50*
Texas Carnival *'51*
Lovely to Look At *'52*
Kiss Me Kate *'53*
Small Town Girl *'53*
Deep in My Heart *'54*
Hit the Deck *'55*
The Great American Pastime *'56*
The Opposite Sex *'56*
Mulholland Drive *'01*

Annette Miller
The Imported Bridegroom *'89*
Lift *'01*

Aubree Miller (1979-)
The Ewok Adventure *'84*
The Ewoks: Battle for Endor *'85*

Barry Miller (1958-)
Saturday Night Fever *'77*
Fame *'80*
The Chosen *'81*
Roommate *'84*
Peggy Sue Got Married *'86*
The Last Temptation of Christ *'88*
Love at Large *'89*
The Pickle *'93*
Love Affair *'94*
Flawless *'99*

Ben Miller (1966-)
Johnny English *'03*
The Prince & Me *'04*

Blaise Miller
The Scenesters *'09*
It's a Disaster *'12*

Bodil Miller (1928-)
Ma and Pa Kettle on Vacation *'53*
Reptilicus *'62*

Brendan Miller (1985-)
The Last Days of Summer *'07*
Red Sands *'09*
Project X *'11*

Charles F. Miller (1891-1955)
The Spider Returns *'41*
Call Northside 777 *'48*

Cheryl Miller (1943-)
Clarence, the Cross-eyed Lion *'65*
Dr. Death, Seeker of Souls *'73*

Chris Miller
Madagascar: Escape 2 Africa *'08 (V)*
Penguins of Madagascar *'14 (V)*

Christa Miller (1964-)
Smiling Fish & Goat on Fire *'99*
The Operator *'01*
The Andromeda Strain *'08*

Colleen Miller (1932-)
Man in the Shadow *'57*
Gunfight at Comanche Creek *'64*

C.T. Miller (1951-)
Friend of the Family *'95*
Lap Dancing *'95*

Dax Miller
Blood Surf *'00*
The Convent *'00*

Dean Miller (1924-2004)
Because You're Mine *'52*
Everything I Have is Yours *'52*

Dennis Miller (1953-)
The Everlasting Secret Family *'88*
Disclosure *'94*
The Net *'95*
Never Talk to Strangers *'95*
Tales from the Crypt Presents Bordello of Blood *'96*
Murder at 1600 *'97*
Joe Dirt *'01*
What Happens in Vegas *'08*

Denny Miller (1934-)
The Party *'68*
Buck and the Preacher *'72*

Dick Miller (1928-)
The Gunslinger *'56*
Carnival Rock *'57*
Not of This Earth *'57*
The Undead *'57*
War of the Satellites *'58*
A Bucket of Blood *'59*
Atlas *'60*
Little Shop of Horrors *'60*
Premature Burial *'62*
The Terror *'63*
X: The Man with X-Ray Eyes *'63*
The Wild Angels *'66*
The St. Valentine's Day Massacre *'67*
The Trip *'67*
Night Call Nurses *'72*
The Young Nurses *'73*
Big Bad Mama *'74*
Candy Stripe Nurses *'74*
Truck Turner *'74*
Crazy Mama *'75*
Cannonball *'76*
Hollywood Boulevard *'76*
New York, New York *'77*
Piranha *'78*
Lady in Red *'79*
Rock 'n' Roll High School *'79*
Used Cars *'80*
Heartbeeps *'81*
The Howling *'81*
All the Right Moves *'83*
Get Crazy *'83*
Heart Like a Wheel *'83*
Twilight Zone: The Movie *'83*
Gremlins *'84*
The Terminator *'84*
After Hours *'85*
Explorers *'85*
Chopping Mall *'86*
Night of the Creeps *'86*
Amazon Women on the Moon *'87*
Innerspace *'87*
Project X *'87*
Far from Home *'89*
Under the Boardwalk *'89*
Evil Toons *'90*
Gremlins 2: The New Batch *'90*
Motorama *'91*
Amityville 1992: It's About Time *'92*
Matinee *'92*
Unlawful Entry *'92*
Batman: Mask of the Phantasm *'93 (V)*
Runaway Daughters *'94*
Shake, Rattle & Rock! *'94*
Tales from the Crypt Presents Demon Knight *'94*
Small Soldiers *'98*

Eve Miller (1933-77)
April in Paris *'52*
Big Trees *'52*
The Winning Team *'52*
Kansas Pacific *'53*

Ezra Miller (1992-)
Afterschool *'08*
City Island *'09*
Every Day *'10*
Another Happy Day *'11*
We Need to Talk About Kevin *'11*
The Perks of Being a Wallflower *'12*
Madame Bovary *'15*
The Stanford Prison Experiment *'15*
Justice League *'17*
Fantastic Beasts: The Crimes of Grindelwald *'18*

Gabrielle Miller (1973-)
The Silencer *'99*
Debbie Macomber's Trading Christmas *'11*

Geri Miller
Flesh *'68*
Trash *'70*

J. Matthew Miller
Open Cam *'05*
2 Minutes Later *'07*

Jason Miller (1939-2001)
The Exorcist *'73*
The Nickel Ride *'74*
A Home of Our Own *'75*
The Dain Curse *'78*
The Ninth Configuration *'79*
The Henderson Monster *'80*
Monsignor *'82*
That Championship Season *'82*
Toy Soldiers *'84*
Exorcist 3: Legion *'90*
Rudy *'93*
Mommy *'95*
Finding Home *'03*

Jeremy Miller (1976-)
The Willies *'90*
The Growing Pains Movie *'00*
Growing Pains: Return of the Seavers *'04*

Joel McKinnon Miller
The Swan Princess *'94 (V)*
Friday After Next *'02*

John Miller
Undefeatable *'94*
Ratcatcher *'99*

Johnny Miller
Byron *'03*
The Flying Scotsman *'06*

Jonny Lee Miller (1972-)
Hackers *'95*
Trainspotting *'95*
Larry McMurtry's Dead Man's Walk *'96*
Afterglow *'97*
Behind the Lines *'97*
Plunkett & Macleane *'98*
Retribution *'98*
Mansfield Park *'99*
Dracula 2000 *'00*
Love, Honour & Obey *'00*
Aeon Flux *'05*
Melinda and Melinda *'05*
Mindhunters *'05*
Emma *'09*
Endgame *'09*
Byzantium *'12*
Dark Shadows *'12*
T2 Trainspotting *'17*

Joshua John Miller (1974-)
Near Dark *'87*
River's Edge *'87*
Teen Witch *'89*
Class of 1999 *'90*
And You Thought Your Parents Were Weird! *'91*
The Wizard of Gore *'07*

Kathleen Miller (1945-)
Strange New World *'75*
Fighting Mad *'76*
Coming Home *'78*

Kelly Miller
George of the Jungle *'97*
Newsbreak *'00*

Kristen Miller (1976-)
Team America: World Police *'04 (V)*
The Fallen Ones *'05*
Single White Female 2: The Psycho *'05*
All In *'06*

Kristine Miller (1925-)
Jungle Patrol *'48*
Too Late for Tears *'49*
High Lonesome *'50*

Larry Miller (1953-)
Three Fugitives *'89*
Almost an Angel *'90*
Pretty Woman *'90*
Suburban Commando *'91*
Carry On Columbus *'92*
The Favor *'92*
Dream Lover *'93*
Undercover Blues *'93*
Corrina, Corrina *'94*
Radioland Murders *'94*
Dear God *'96*
Waiting for Guffman *'96*
Chairman of the Board *'97*
For Richer or Poorer *'97*
Carnival of Souls *'98*
The Big Tease *'99*
The Minus Man *'99*
Pros & Cons *'99*
Ten Things I Hate about You *'99*
Best in Show *'00*
Nutty Professor 2: The Klumps *'00*
Max Keeble's Big Move *'01*
The Princess Diaries *'01*
What's the Worst That Could Happen? *'01*
A Mighty Wind *'03*
Final Approach *'04*
The Princess Diaries 2: Royal Engagement *'04*
Kiss Kiss Bang Bang *'05*
Life of the Party *'05*
The Ant Bully *'06 (V)*
Keeping Up with the Steins *'06*
Bee Movie *'07 (V)*
Blonde Ambition *'07*
The Final Season *'07*
The Other End of the Line *'08*
Senior Skip Day *'08*
Alpha and Omega *'10 (V)*
Valentine's Day *'10*

Levi Miller (2002-)
Pan *'15*
Better Watch Out *'17*
A Wrinkle in Time *'18*

Linda Miller (1942-)
King Kong Escapes *'67*
Alice Sweet Alice *'76*

Logan Miller (1992-)
Scout's Guide to the Zombie Apocalypse *'15*
The Good Neighbor *'16*
Before I Fall *'17*
Being Frank *'19*
Escape Room *'19*
Prey *'19*

Mandy Miller
Child in the House *'56*
The Snorkel *'58*

Marci Miller
American Fable *'17*
Roger Corman's Death Race 2050 *'17*

Marilyn Miller (1898-1936)
Sally *'29*
Sunny *'30*

Mark Miller (1925-)
Ginger in the Morning *'73*
Savannah Smiles *'82*
Love Field *'91*

Martin Miller (1899-1969)
Frenzy *'46*
Libel *'59*
Peeping Tom *'60*
The Phantom of the Opera *'62*
Children of the Damned *'63*

Marvin Miller (1913-85)
Dead Reckoning *'47*
Red Planet Mars *'52*
Off Limits *'53*
Forbidden Planet *'56 (V)*
The Day the Earth Froze *'59 (N)*
Sleeping Beauty *'59 (V)*
Kiss Daddy Goodbye *'81*

McKaley Miller
Where Hope Grows *'15*
Ma *'19*

Mindi Miller (1950-)
Hell Up in Harlem *'73*
Hercules *'83*
Sacred Ground *'83*
Body Double *'84*
Amazons *'86*
The Big Turnaround *'88*
Caged Fury *'90*

Mirta Miller (1948-)
Dr. Jekyll and the Wolfman *'71*
Dracula's Great Love *'72*
Cria Cuervos *'76*

Omar Benson Miller (1978-)
8 Mile *'02*
Undefeated *'03*
Shall We Dance? *'04*
Get Rich or Die Tryin' *'05*
Gordon Glass *'07*
Grindin' *'07*
Things We Lost in the Fire *'07*
The Express *'08*
Miracle at St. Anna *'08*
Blood Done Sign My Name *'10*
1982 *'16*

Patsy Ruth Miller (1905-95)
The Sheik *'21*
The Hunchback of Notre Dame *'23*
The First Auto *'27*
Lonely Wives *'31*

Penelope Ann Miller (1964-)
Adventures in Babysitting *'87*
Big Top Pee-wee *'88*
Biloxi Blues *'88*
Dead Bang *'89*
Downtown *'89*
Our Town *'89*
Awakenings *'90*
The Freshman *'90*
Kindergarten Cop *'90*
Other People's Money *'91*
Chaplin *'92*
The Gun in Betty Lou's Handbag *'92*
Year of the Comet *'92*
Carlito's Way *'93*
The Shadow *'94*
The Relic *'96*
The Last Don *'97*
Little City *'97*
The Break Up *'98*
Ruby Bridges *'98*
Rocky Marciano *'99*
Along for the Ride *'00*
Full Disclosure *'00*
Killing Moon *'00*
Along Came a Spider *'01*
A Woman's a Helluva Thing *'01*
Dead in a Heartbeat *'02*
Scared Silent *'02*
National Lampoon's Holiday Reunion *'03*
Rudy: The Rudy Giulani Story *'03*
Carry Me Home *'04*
Personal Effects *'05*
Blonde Ambition *'07*
The Messengers *'07*
Free Style *'09*
Saving Grace B. Jones *'09*
Flipped *'10*
The Artist *'11*
Think of Me *'11*
About Sunny *'12*
The Birth of a Nation *'16*

Percy Miller (1967-)
See Master P

Rebecca Miller (1962-)
The Murder of Mary Phagan *'87*
Consenting Adults *'92*
Wind *'92*
The Pickle *'93*
Mrs. Parker and the Vicious Circle *'94*

Roger Miller (1936-92)
Robin Hood *'73 (V)*
Lucky Luke *'94 (V)*

Sarah Jane Miller
Mommy *'95*
Mommy 2: Mommy's Day *'96*

Sherry Miller (1955-)
Sabrina the Teenage Witch *'96*
This Matter of Marriage *'98*
Tribulation *'00*
A Killing Spring *'02*
Too Young to Be a Dad *'02*
It's a Boy Girl Thing *'06*
Ice Blues: A Donald Strachey Mystery *'08*

Sidney Miller (1916-2004)
Rafter Romance *'33*
Boys Town *'38*
Men of Boys Town *'41*

Sienna Miller (1981-)
Alfie *'04*
Casanova *'05*
Layer Cake *'05*
Factory Girl *'06*
Camille *'07*
Interview *'07*
Stardust *'07*
The Edge of Love *'08*
The Mysteries of Pittsburgh *'08*
G.I. Joe: The Rise of Cobra *'09*
The September Issue *'09*
The Girl *'12*
2 Jacks *'12*
A Case of You *'13*
Just Like a Woman *'13*
American Sniper *'14*
Foxcatcher *'14*
Burnt *'15*
Mississippi Grind *'15*
Unfinished Business *'15*
High-Rise *'16*
Live by Night *'16*
The Lost City of Z *'17*
The Catcher Was a Spy *'18*
American Woman *'19*
21 Bridges *'19*

Stacey Miller
The Ape *'05*
The Broken Tower *'11*
Sal *'11*

Stephen E. Miller (1947-)
Jane Doe *'83*
The Stepfather *'87*
Air Bud *'97*
The Bouquet *'13*

Tangi Miller (1970-)
The Other Brother *'02*
Leprechaun 6: Back 2 Tha Hood *'03*
Love and Other Four Letter Words *'07*
My Girlfriend's Back *'10*

T.J. Miller (1981-)
Cloverfield *'08*
Gulliver's Travels *'10*
She's Out of My League *'10*
Yogi Bear *'10*
Our Idiot Brother *'11*
Big Hero 6 *'14 (V)*
How to Train Your Dragon 2 *'14 (V)*
Transformers: Age of Extinction *'14*
Office Christmas Party *'16*
The Emoji Movie *'17 (V)*
Ready Player One *'18*
Underwater *'20*

Ty Miller (1964-)
Trancers 4: Jack of Swords *'93*
Trancers 5: Sudden Deth *'94*

Walter Miller (1892-1940)
The Galloping Ghost *'31*
Blessed Event *'32*
The Lone Defender *'32*
Shadow of the Eagle *'32*
Tailspin Tommy *'34*
The Ivory Handled Gun *'35*
Rustlers of Red Dog *'35*
Night Cargo *'36*

Wentworth Miller (1972-)
Dinotopia '02
The Human Stain '03
Underworld '03
Stealth '05 (V)
Prison Break: The Final Break '09
Resident Evil: Afterlife '10
The Loft '14

Andra Millian
Stacy's Knights '83
Nightfall '88

James Millican (1910-55)
Spoilers of the North '47
The Adventures of Gallant Bess '48
Man from Colorado '49
Rimfire '49
Cavalry Scout '51
I Was a Communist for the FBI '51
Carson City '52
Scandal Sheet '52
The Winning Team '52
A Lion Is in the Streets '53
Top Gun '55

Deanna Milligan (1972-)
Suspicious River '00
Whispers and Lies '08

Dustin Milligan (1985-)
The Butterfly Effect 2 '06
Eight Days to Live '06
In the Land of Women '06
The Messengers '07
Eva '09
Extract '09
The Entitled '11
Shark Night 3D '11
Love at the Christmas Table '12

Spike Milligan (1918-2002)
Down Among the Z Men '52
Goon Movie '52
Invasion Quartet '61
Postman's Knock '62
The Bed Sitting Room '69
The Magic Christian '69
Rentadick '72
Adolf Hitler: My Part in His Downfall '74
The Hound of the Baskervilles '77
Monty Python's Life of Brian '79

Angie Milliken (1964-)
Dead Heart '96
Solo '06
The Condemned '07

Ben Milliken
Beautiful Wave '11
Blue Crush 2 '11

Alley Mills (1951-)
Going Berserk '83
A Golden Christmas '09
Satin '10
A Golden Christmas 2: The Second Tail '11

Barbara Mills
Chain Gang Women '72
Sweet Georgia '72

Brooke Mills (1949-)
Dream No Evil '70
The Big Doll House '71
The Student Teachers '73

Donna Mills (1940-)
Play Misty for Me '71
Beyond the Bermuda Triangle '75
Murph the Surf '75
Fire '77
Hanging By a Thread '79
Alice in Wonderland '85
Runaway Father '91
False Arrest '92
Too Cool for Christmas '04
Ladies of the House '08

Eddie Mills (1972-)
Dancer, Texas-Pop. 81 '98
Heartwood '98
Winter Break '02
The Trade '03

Hayley Mills (1946-)
Tiger Bay '59
Pollyanna '60
The Parent Trap '61
In Search of the Castaways '62
Summer Magic '63
The Chalk Garden '64
The Moon-Spinners '64
That Darn Cat '65
The Trouble with Angels '66
Africa Texas Style '67 (C)
Take a Girl Like You '70
Cry of the Penguins '71
Endless Night '71
The Flame Trees of Thika '81
The Parent Trap II '86
Back Home '90
A Troll in Central Park '94 (V)
2B Perfectly Honest '04
Angel in the House '11

John Mills (1908-2005)
Nine Days a Queen '36
The Green Cockatoo '37
Goodbye, Mr. Chips '39
Cottage to Let '41
In Which We Serve '43
We Dive at Dawn '43
Waterloo Road '45
The Way to the Stars '45
Great Expectations '46
So Well Remembered '47
This Happy Breed '47
Scott of the Antarctic '48
Morning Departure '50
Hobson's Choice '53
The Long Memory '53
Above Us the Waves '55
The Colditz Story '55
End of the Affair '55
Around the World in 80 Days '56 (C)
War and Peace '56
Tiger Bay '59
The Swiss Family Robinson '60
Tunes of Glory '60
Flame in the Streets '61
Tiara Tahiti '62
The Chalk Garden '64
King Rat '65
Operation Crossbow '65
The Wrong Box '66
Africa Texas Style '67
Chuka '67
Oh! What a Lovely War '69
Adam's Woman '70
Ryan's Daughter '70
Young Winston '72
Oklahoma Crude '73
The Human Factor '75
Choice of Weapons '76
The Big Sleep '78
Quatermass Conclusion '79
The Thirty-Nine Steps '79
Zulu Dawn '79
Gandhi '82
A Woman of Substance '84
Agatha Christie's Murder with Mirrors '85
Hold the Dream '86
When the Wind Blows '86 (V)
Who's That Girl? '87
Around the World in 80 Days '89
The Lady and the Highwayman '89
A Tale of Two Cities '89
Frankenstein '93
Martin Chuzzlewit '94
Hamlet '96

Judson Mills (1969-)
Joyride '97
Major League 3: Back to the Minors '98
Chill Factor '99
The President's Man 2: A Line in the Sand '02

Juliet Mills (1941-)
Carry On Jack '63
The Rare Breed '66
Oh! What a Lovely War '69
Avanti! '72

Jonathan Livingston Seagull '73 (V)
QB VII '74
Beyond the Door '75
Once an Eagle '76
Alexander: The Other Side of Dawn '77
Waxwork 2: Lost in Time '91
The Other Sister '98
Running for Grace '18

Mort Mills (1920-93)
Ride a Crooked Trail '58
Touch of Evil '58
Return of the Gunfighter '67

Stephanie Mills (1979-)
Hunger Point '03
Come Dance With Me '12

Zach Mills
Mr. Magorium's Wonder Emporium '07
Kit Kittredge: An American Girl '08

Bill Milner (1995-)
Son of Rambow '07
Is Anybody There? '08
Skellig: The Owl Man '09
Sex & Drugs & Rock & Roll '10
The Lodgers '17
Apostle '18

Martin Milner (1931-2015)
Life with Father '47
The Halls of Montezuma '50
Battle Zone '52
Belles on Their Toes '52
The Captive City '52
My Wife's Best Friend '52
Destination Gobi '53
Francis in the Navy '55
Mister Roberts '55
Pete Kelly's Blues '55
Screaming Eagles '56
Gunfight at the O.K. Corral '57
Sweet Smell of Success '57
Too Much, Too Soon '58
Compulsion '59
Sex Kittens Go to College '60
13 Ghosts '60
Zebra in the Kitchen '65
Valley of the Dolls '67
Columbo: Murder by the Book '71
Hurricane '74
Flood! '76

Aaron Milo
Eating Out 4: Drama Camp '11
Eating Out: The Open Weekend '11

Sandra Milo (1933-)
Adua and Her Friends '60
Classe Tous Risque '60
Herod the Great '60
Vanina Vanini '61
8 1/2 '63
Juliet of the Spirits '65
Bang Bang Kid '67
Dead for a Dollar '70
Incantato '03
Generale Della Rovere '09

Andy Milonakis (1976-)
Waiting '05
Killer Pad '06
Who's Your Caddy? '07
Still Waiting '08
Wieners '08

Sofia Milos (1965-)
Double Bang '01
Passionada '02

Ernest Milton (1890-1974)
The Scarlet Pimpernel '34
It's Love Again '36
Alice in Wonderland '50

Gerald Milton (1923-2005)
China Gate '57
Counterplot '59
Underworld U.S.A. '61

Mantoyo Mimasu
47 Ronin, Part 1 '42
47 Ronin, Part 2 '42

Yvette Mimieux (1942-)
The Time Machine '60
Where the Boys Are '60
Light in the Piazza '61
Diamond Head '62
The Four Horsemen of the Apocalypse '62
Toys in the Attic '63
Monkeys, Go Home! '66
Dark of the Sun '68
The Picasso Summer '69
Skyjacked '72
Neptune Factor '73
Hit Lady '74
Legend of Valentino '75
Jackson County Jail '76
Snowbeast '77
Devil Dog: The Hound of Hell '78
The Black Hole '79
Forbidden Love '82

Nico Minardos (1930-2011)
Holiday for Lovers '59
Twelve Hours to Kill '60

Leo Minaya (1984-)
Manito '03
How the Garcia Girls Spent Their Summer '05
Morgan '12

Christiane Minazzoli (1931-)
The Story of O '75
Betty '92

Esther Minciotti (1883-1962)
Marty '55
Full of Life '56

Sal Mineo (1939-76)
Rebel without a Cause '55
Crime in the Streets '56
Giant '56
Rock, Pretty Baby '56
Somebody Up There Likes Me '56
Dino '57
Tonka '58
The Gene Krupa Story '59
Exodus '60
Escape From Zahrain '62
The Longest Day '62
Cheyenne Autumn '64
Krakatoa East of Java '69
Escape from the Planet of the Apes '71

Jan Miner (1917-2004)
Lenny '74
Mermaids '90

Rachel Miner (1980-)
Bully '01
Circadian Rhythm '05
Little Athens '05
The Black Dahlia '06
Fatwa '06
Love and Debate '06
Cult '07
The Still Life '07
Tooth and Nail '07
Hide '08
The Butterfly Effect 3: Revelation '09
Area 51 '11
Life of Lemon '11
In Their Skin '12

Ming Na (1963-)
The Joy Luck Club '93
Star Quest '94
Street Fighter '94
One Night Stand '97
Mulan '98 (V)
Final Fantasy: The Spirits Within '01 (V)
Mulan 2 '04 (V)
Push '09
The Darkness '16

Max Minghella (1985-)
Bee Season '05
Syriana '05
Art School Confidential '06
Elvis and Annabelle '07
How to Lose Friends & Alienate People '08
Agora '09
Brief Interviews With Hideous Men '09

The Social Network '10
The Darkest Hour '11
The Ides of March '11
10 Years '12
Horns '13
The Internship '13
About Alex '14
Into the Forest '16

Elvira Minguez (1965-)
The Dancer Upstairs '02
The Reckoning '03
Che '08

Birgit Minichmayr (1977-)
Taking Sides '01
The Crown Prince '06
Falling '06
Midsummer Madness '07
Cherry Blossoms '08
Everyone Else '09

Claudette Mink (1971-)
Killer Deal '99
Children of the Corn: Revelation '01
Best Friends '05
Tamara '05
Shattered '07

Liza Minnelli (1946-)
In the Good Old Summertime '49
The Sterile Cuckoo '69
Journey Back to Oz '71 (V)
Cabaret '72
A Matter of Time '76
Silent Movie '76
New York, New York '77
Arthur '81
King of Comedy '82
The Muppets Take Manhattan '84 (C)
That's Dancing! '85
Arthur 2: On the Rocks '88
Rent-A-Cop '88
Jackie's Back '99
The Oh in Ohio '06
Sex and the City 2 '10 (C)

Dylan Minnette
Alexander and the Terrible, Horrible, No Good, Very Bad Day '14
Goosebumps '15
Don't Breathe '16

Byron Keith Minns
South Central '92
Black Dynamite '09

Kylie Minogue (1968-)
Street Fighter '94
Bio-Dome '96
Cut '00 (C)
Moulin Rouge '01
Doogal '05 (V)
Holy Motors '12
Jack and Diane '12
Swinging Safari '19

Bob Minor (1942-)
The Swinging Cheerleaders '74
Black Eliminator '78

Kelly Jo Minter (1966-)
Summer School '87
Miracle Mile '89
A Nightmare on Elm Street 5: Dream Child '89
Popcorn '89
The People under the Stairs '91
Tapped Out '03

Kristin Minter (1965-)
Cool As Ice '91
There Goes My Baby '92
Flashfire '94
The Apostate '98
Tick Tock '00
The Bread, My Sweet '01

Christopher Mintz-Plasse (1989-)
Superbad '07
Role Models '08
Year One '09
How to Train Your Dragon '10 (V)
Kick-Ass '10
Marmaduke '10 (V)
Fright Night '11

Pitch Perfect '12
Kick-Ass 2 '13
The To Do List '13
How to Train Your Dragon 2 '14 (V)
Neighbors '14
Trolls '16

Frank Minucci (1943-)
A Brother's Kiss '97
Tar '97
Friends and Family '01

Juan Minujin (1975-)
Zama '17
The Two Popes '19

Fabrizio Mioni (1930-)
Hercules '58
Get Yourself a College Girl '64

Miou-Miou (1950-)
The Mad Adventures of Rabbi Jacob '73
Going Places '74
Dog Day '83
Entre-Nous '83
Menage '86
Dry Cleaning '97
Women '97
The Science of Sleep '06
The Concert '09

Brigitte Mira (1910-2005)
Tenderness of the Wolves '73
Ali: Fear Eats the Soul '74
Every Man for Himself & God Against All '75
Fear of Fear '75
Mother Kusters Goes to Heaven '76
Chinese Roulette '86

Irene Miracle (1954-)
Night Train Murders '75
Inferno '80
Puppet Master '89

Evan Mirand
Brotherhood of Justice '86
My Best Friend Is a Vampire '88
Megalodon '03

Aurora Miranda (1915-2005)
Phantom Lady '44
The Three Caballeros '45 (V)

Carmen Miranda (1909-55)
Down Argentine Way '40
That Night in Rio '41
Week-End in Havana '41
Springtime in the Rockies '42
The Gang's All Here '43
Greenwich Village '44
Something for the Boys '44
Doll Face '46
If I'm Lucky '46
Copacabana '47
A Date with Judy '48
Nancy Goes to Rio '50
Scared Stiff '53

Isa Miranda (1909-82)
La Ronde '51
Summertime '55
Dog Eat Dog '64
Dorian Gray '70
Roy Colt and Winchester Jack '70
Twitch of the Death Nerve '71
The Night Porter '74

Pia Miranda (1973-)
Garage Days '03
The Boxer and the Bombshell '08

Robert Miranda
Sister Act '92
Lost in Yonkers '93
What's Love Got to Do with It? '93
Gotti '96
Steel Sharks '97
Black Thunder '98
The Rat Pack '98
Blue Streak '99

Soledad Miranda (1943-72)
Sound of Horror *'64*
Count Dracula *'71*

Ilyena Vasilievna Mironov (1945-)
See Dame Helen Mirren

Dame Helen Mirren (1945-)
A Midsummer Night's Dream *'68*
Age of Consent *'69*
Savage Messiah *'72*
O Lucky Man! *'73*
S.O.S. Titanic *'79*
Caligula *'80*
The Fiendish Plot of Dr. Fu Manchu *'80*
Hussy *'80*
The Long Good Friday *'80*
Excalibur *'81*
Priest of Love *'81*
2010: The Year We Make Contact *'84*
Coming Through *'85*
White Nights *'85*
The Mosquito Coast *'86*
Cause Celebre *'87*
The Cook, the Thief, His Wife & Her Lover *'90*
The Comfort of Strangers *'91*
Where Angels Fear to Tread *'91*
Prime Suspect *'92*
The Hawk *'93*
The Madness of King George *'94*
Royal Deceit *'94*
Losing Chase *'96*
Some Mother's Son *'96*
Critical Care *'97*
The Painted Lady *'97*
Prince of Egypt *'98 (V)*
The Passion of Ayn Rand *'99*
Teaching Mrs. Tingle *'99*
Greenfingers *'00*
The Pledge *'00*
Gosford Park *'01*
Last Orders *'01*
No Such Thing *'01*
Calendar Girls *'03*
The Roman Spring of Mrs. Stone *'03*
The Clearing *'04*
Raising Helen *'04*
Elizabeth I *'05*
The Hitchhiker's Guide to the Galaxy *'05 (V)*
The Queen *'06*
Shadowboxer *'06*
National Treasure: Book of Secrets *'07*
Inkheart *'09*
The Last Station *'09*
State of Play *'09*
Brighton Rock *'10*
The Debt *'10*
Legend of the Guardians: The Owls of Ga'Hoole *'10 (V)*
Love Ranch *'10*
RED *'10*
The Tempest *'10*
Arthur *'11*
Hitchcock *'12*
Monsters University *'13 (V)*
Phil Spector *'13*
RED 2 *'13*
The Hundred-Foot Journey *'14*
Eye in the Sky *'15*
Trumbo *'15*
Woman in Gold *'15*
Collateral Beauty *'16*
The Leisure Seeker *'17*
The Nutcracker and the Four Realms *'18*
Winchester *'18*
Anna *'19*
Fast & Furious Presents: Hobbs & Shaw *'19*
The Good Liar *'19*

Masao Mishima (1906-73)
The Human Condition: No Greater Love *'58*
Harakiri *'62*

Tom Mison
Mysterious Island *'05*
One Day *'11*

Dorian Missick (1976-)
Two Weeks Notice *'02*
Lucky Number Slevin *'06*
Mama's Boy *'07*
Mooz-Lum *'10*
Deliver Us From Evil *'14*
Jinn *'18*

Ralph Misske (1959-)
Head On *'04*
The Red Baron *'08*

Karen Mistal
Return of the Killer Tomatoes! *'88*
Cannibal Women in the Avocado Jungle of Death *'89*

Mr. T (1952-)
Penitentiary 2 *'82*
Rocky 3 *'82*
D.C. Cab *'84*
Freaked *'93*
Cloudy with a Chance of Meatballs *'09 (V)*

Mr. Wiggles (1977-)
See Chris Bridges

Jimi Mistry (1973-)
East Is East *'99*
Born Romantic *'00*
The Mystic Masseur *'01*
The Guru *'02*
Dead Fish *'04*
Ella Enchanted *'04*
Touch of Pink *'04*
The Truth About Love *'04*
Blood Diamond *'06*
Partition *'07*
RocknRolla *'08*
Exam *'09*

Yoshiko Mita
Bushido: The Cruel Code of the Samurai *'63*
Revenge *'64*

Ann Mitchell
A Matador's Mistress *'08*
The Deep Blue Sea *'12*

Beverley Mitchell (1981-)
Saw 2 *'05*
The Dog Who Saved Easter *'15*

Brian Stokes Mitchell (1957-)
Double Platinum *'99*
Call Me Claus *'01*
Ruby's Bucket of Blood *'01*
One Last Thing *'05*

Cameron Mitchell (1918-94)
They Were Expendable *'45*
High Barbaree *'47*
The Adventures of Gallant Bess *'48*
Homecoming *'48*
Death of a Salesman *'51*
The Sellout *'51*
Flight to Mars *'52*
Japanese War Bride *'52*
How to Marry a Millionaire *'53*
Man on a Tightrope *'53*
Powder River *'53*
Desiree *'54*
Garden of Evil *'54*
House of Bamboo *'55*
Love Me or Leave Me *'55*
Strange Lady in Town *'55*
The Tall Men *'55*
All Mine to Give *'56*
Carousel *'56*
No Down Payment *'57*
Face of Fire *'59*
Three Came to Kill *'61*
Conquest of the Normans *'62*
Caesar the Conqueror *'63*
The Invaders *'63*
Blood and Black Lace *'64*
Dog Eat Dog *'64*
Last Gun *'64*
Knives of the Avenger *'65*
Minnesota Clay *'65*
Ride in the Whirlwind *'66*
Hombre *'67*
Nightmare in Wax *'69*
Rebel Rousers *'69*
The Andersonville Trial *'70*
The Big Game *'72*
Buck and the Preacher *'72*
The Delphi Bureau: The Merchant of Death Assignment *'72*
Slaughter *'72*
The Hanged Man *'74*
The Klansman *'74*
Medusa *'74*
Flood! *'76*
The Longest Drive *'76*
Haunts *'77*
Return to Fantasy Island *'77*
Slavers *'77*
Viva Knievel *'77*
The Bastard *'78*
Supersonic Man *'78*
The Swarm *'78*
The Toolbox Murders *'78*
Hanging By a Thread *'79*
The Last Reunion *'80*
Silent Scream *'80*
Without Warning *'80*
Cataclysm *'81*
The Demon *'81*
Frankenstein Island *'81*
Raw Force *'81*
Texas Lightning *'81*
Code of Honor *'82*
My Favorite Year *'82*
Killpoint *'84*
Night Train to Terror *'84*
Mission. . . Kill *'85*
Hollywood Cop *'87*
The Offspring *'87*
Killers *'88*
Memorial Valley Massacre *'88*
Space Mutiny *'88*
Easy Kill *'89*
Crossing the Line *'90*
Jack-O *'95*

Charlotte Mitchell (1926-2012)
Village of the Damned *'60*
Persuasion *'71*

Chuck 'Porky' Mitchell (1928-92)
Penitentiary *'79*
Porky's *'82*
Porky's Revenge *'85*
Ghost Chase *'88*

Daryl (Chill) Mitchell (1965-)
Fly by Night *'93*
Sgt. Bilko *'95*
A Thin Line Between Love and Hate *'96*
Quiet Days in Hollywood *'97*
Toothless *'97*
Home Fries *'98*
Galaxy Quest *'99*
Ten Things I Hate about You *'99*
Lucky Numbers *'00*
Black Knight *'01*
The Country Bears *'02*
13 Moons *'02*
Inside Man *'06*

Donna Mitchell
Psycho 4: The Beginning *'90*
Two Bits *'96*
Mona Lisa Smile *'03*
Bomb the System *'05*
St. Vincent *'14*

E. Roger Mitchell (1971-)
How I Spent My Summer Vacation *'97*
Boycott *'02*
A Smile as Big as the Moon *'12*

Elizabeth Mitchell (1970-)
Gia *'98*
Molly *'99*
Frequency *'00*
Double Bang *'01*
The Santa Clause 2 *'02*
Running Scared *'06*
The Santa Clause 3: The Escape Clause *'06*
Answers to Nothing *'11*
Prosecuting Casey Anthony *'13*
The Purge: Election Year *'16*

Ewing Mitchell (1910-88)
Cavalry Charge *'51*
Above and Beyond *'53*

Gordon Mitchell (1923-2003)
The Giant of Metropolis *'61*
Fury of Achilles *'62*
Ali Baba and the Seven Saracens *'64*
Erik, the Viking *'65*
Fighting Fists of Shanghai Joe *'65*
Beyond the Law *'68*
Django and Sartana; It's the End *'70*
Frankenstein '80 *'79*

Grant Mitchell (1874-1957)
No Man of Her Own *'32*
A Successful Calamity *'32*
Central Airport *'33*
Heroes for Sale *'33*
20,000 Years in Sing Sing *'33*
Wild Boys of the Road *'33*
The Case of the Howling Dog *'34*
365 Nights in Hollywood *'34*
Gold Diggers of 1935 *'35*
The Secret Bride *'35*
Seven Keys to Baldpate *'35*
Next Time We Love *'36*
The Last Gangster *'37*
Hell's Kitchen *'39*
The Grapes of Wrath *'40*
It All Came True *'40*
My Love Came Back *'40*
Footsteps in the Dark *'41*
The Great Lie *'41*
The Man Who Came to Dinner *'41*
One Foot in Heaven *'41*
Cairo *'42*
Meet the Stewarts *'42*
My Sister Eileen *'42*
The Amazing Mrs. Holiday *'43*
Laura *'44*
See Here, Private Hargrove *'44*
Conflict *'45*
Easy to Wed *'46*
It Happened on 5th Avenue *'47*

Heather Mitchell (1958-)
The Everlasting Secret Family *'88*
Proof *'91*
A Little Bit of Soul *'97*
Rogue *'07*

James Mitchell (1920-2010)
Border Incident *'49*
Colorado Territory *'49*
The Devil's Doorway *'50*

Jason Mitchell
Straight Outta Compton *'15*
Detroit *'17*
SuperFly *'18*
The Mustang *'19*

John Cameron Mitchell (1963-)
Book of Love *'91*
David Searching *'97*
Hedwig and the Angry Inch *'00*

Julien Mitchell (1888-1954)
Vigil in the Night *'40*
Echo Murders *'45*

Kel Mitchell (1978-)
Good Burger *'97*
Mystery Men *'99*
The Adventures of Rocky & Bullwinkle *'00*
Clifford's Really Big Movie *'04 (V)*
Ganked *'05*

Kenneth Mitchell (1974-)
Charms for the Easy Life *'02*
Miracle *'04*
Home of the Giants *'07*

Kirsty Mitchell (1974-)
A Shot at Glory *'00*
Lighthouse Hill *'04*
Almost Heaven *'06*
Lake Placid 3 *'10*
Mercenaries *'11*
The Leisure Seeker *'17*

Laurie Mitchell (1922-)
Queen of Outer Space *'58*
Missile to the Moon *'59*

Leigh Mitchell
Scream Bloody Murder *'72*
Amputee with an Axe *'73*

Maia Mitchell
Teen Beach Movie *'13*
Never Goin' Back *'18*

Mary Mitchell (1940-)
Panic in Year Zero! *'62*
Dementia 13 *'63*
Spider Baby *'64*

Millard Mitchell (1900-53)
A Double Life *'47*
Twelve o'Clock High *'49*
Convicted *'50*
The Gunfighter *'50*
Mister 880 *'50*
Winchester '73 *'50*
Singin' in the Rain *'52*
Here Come the Girls *'53*
The Naked Spur *'53*

Penelope Mitchell
6 Plots *'12*
The Curse of Downers Grove *'15*
Curve *'16*
Look Away *'18*
Hellboy *'19*

Radha Mitchell (1973-)
High Art *'98*
Cleopatra's Second Husband *'00*
Cowboys and Angels *'00*
Everything Put Together *'00*
Pitch Black *'00*
Dead Heat *'01*
Nobody's Baby *'01*
Uprising *'01*
Phone Booth *'02*
Visitors *'03*
Finding Neverland *'04*
Man on Fire *'04*
Melinda and Melinda *'05*
Mozart and the Whale *'05*
PU-239 *'06*
Silent Hill *'06*
Feast of Love *'07*
Rogue *'07*
The Children of Huang Shi *'08*
Henry Poole Is Here *'08*
The Code *'09*
The Crazies *'09*
Surrogates *'09*
The Waiting City *'09*
Silent Hill: Revelation 3D *'12*
Big Sur *'13*
The Frozen Ground *'13*
Olympus Has Fallen *'13*
Standing Up *'13*
Bird People *'14*
Fugly! *'14*
The Darkness *'16*
The Shack *'17*

Red Mitchell (1964-94)
Forever Evil *'87*
8 Seconds *'94*

Sasha Mitchell (1967-)
Kickboxer 2: The Road Back *'90*
Kickboxer 3: The Art of War *'92*
Class of 1999 2: The Substitute *'93*
Kickboxer 4: The Aggressor *'94*
Gangland *'00*
Luck of the Draw *'00*

Scoey Mitchell (1930-)
The Voyage of the Yes *'72*
Jo Jo Dancer, Your Life Is Calling *'86*

Silas Weir Mitchell (1969-)
Johnson County War *'02*
The Whole Ten Yards *'04*
Prairie Fever *'08*
Circle *'10*

Thomas Mitchell (1892-1962)
Adventure in Manhattan *'36*
Theodora Goes Wild *'36*
The Hurricane *'37*
Lost Horizon *'37*
Make Way for Tomorrow *'37*
Gone with the Wind *'39*
The Hunchback of Notre Dame *'39*
Mr. Smith Goes to Washington *'39*
Only Angels Have Wings *'39*
Stagecoach *'39*
Angels Over Broadway *'40*
The Long Voyage Home *'40*
Our Town *'40*
Out of the Fog *'41*
The Black Swan *'42*
The Fighting Sullivans *'42*
Joan of Paris *'42*
Moontide *'42*
Tales of Manhattan *'42*
This Above All *'42*
Bataan *'43*
Immortal Sergeant *'43*
The Outlaw *'43*
Buffalo Bill *'44*
Dark Waters *'44*
The Keys of the Kingdom *'44*
Wilson *'44*
Dark Mirror *'46*
It's a Wonderful Life *'46*
High Barbaree *'47*
The Romance of Rosy Ridge *'47*
The Big Wheel *'49*
High Noon *'52*
While the City Sleeps *'56*
By Love Possessed *'61*
Pocketful of Miracles *'61*

Warren Mitchell (1926-)
The Crawling Eye *'58*
Postman's Knock *'62*
Help! *'65*
The Assassination Bureau *'69*
Moon Zero Two *'70*
Jabberwocky *'77*
Foreign Body *'86*

Yvonne Mitchell (1925-79)
The Queen of Spades *'49*
Sapphire *'59*
Tiger Bay *'59*
Conspiracy of Hearts *'60*
The Trials of Oscar Wilde *'60*
Crucible of Horror *'69*
Demons of the Mind *'72*

Ilan Mitchell-Smith (1969-)
Weird Science *'85*
The Chocolate War *'88*
Journey to the Center of the Earth *'88*
Identity Crisis *'90*

Bentley Mitchum (1967-)
Promises to Keep *'85*
Demonic Toys *'90*
Chained Heat 3: Hell Mountain *'98*
On the Border *'98*
Delta Force One-The Lost Patrol *'99*
Shark Attack *'99*
Conviction *'02*
U.S. SEALs: Dead or Alive *'02*
Walking Tall: The Payback *'07*

Chris Mitchum (1943-)
Rio Lobo *'70*
Big Jake *'71*
Mean Machine *'73*
Ricco *'74*
The Last Hard Men *'76*
Stingray *'78*
Day Time Ended *'80*
American Commandos *'84*

The Executioner, Part 2: Frozen Scream *'84*
Promises to Keep *'85*
Angel of Death *'86*
Aftershock *'88*
Faceless *'88*
Death Feud *'89*
Tombstone *'93*
Biohazard: The Alien Force *'95*
Lethal Seduction *'97*
Diamondbacks *'99*

James Mitchum (1941-)
Young Guns of Texas *'62*
The Money Trap *'65*

Jim Mitchum (1941-)
Thunder Road *'58*
Ride the Wild Surf *'64*
In Harm's Way *'65*
Maniac *'77*
Blackout *'78*
Monster *'78*
Code Name: Zebra *'84*
Hollywood Cop *'87*
Fatal Mission *'89*

John Mitchum (1919-2001)
The Devil's Sleep *'51*
Bigfoot *'70*
Dirty Harry *'71*
The Hanged Man *'74*
The Enforcer *'76*
The Outlaw Josey Wales *'76*

Julie Mitchum (1914-2003)
The High and the Mighty *'54*
House on Haunted Hill *'58*

Robert Mitchum (1917-97)
Colt Comrades *'43*
Gung Ho! *'43*
Hopalong Cassidy: Riders of the Deadline *'43*
Hoppy Serves a Writ *'43*
The Human Comedy *'43*
Leather Burners *'43*
Betrayed *'44*
Johnny Doesn't Live Here Any More *'44*
Thirty Seconds Over Tokyo *'44*
The Story of G.I. Joe *'45*
West of the Pecos *'45*
The Locket *'46*
Till the End of Time *'46*
Undercurrent *'46*
Crossfire *'47*
Desire Me *'47*
Out of the Past *'47*
Pursued *'47*
Big Steal *'49*
Holiday Affair *'49*
The Red Pony *'49*
Where Danger Lives *'50*
His Kind of Woman *'51*
My Forbidden Past *'51*
The Racket *'51*
Angel Face *'52*
The Lusty Men *'52*
Macao *'52*
One Minute to Zero *'52*
White Witch Doctor *'53*
River of No Return *'54*
Track of the Cat *'54*
The Night of the Hunter *'55*
Not as a Stranger *'55*
Enemy Below *'57*
Fire Down Below *'57*
Heaven Knows, Mr. Allison *'57*
The Hunters *'58*
Thunder Road *'58*
The Wonderful Country *'59*
Home from the Hill *'60*
The Sundowners *'60*
Cape Fear *'61*
The Grass Is Greener *'61*
The Longest Day *'62*
Two for the Seesaw *'62*
The List of Adrian Messenger *'63*
Rampage *'63*
El Dorado *'67*
The Way West *'67*
Anzio *'68*
Five Card Stud *'68*
Villa Rides *'68*
The Good Guys and the Bad Guys *'69*
Ryan's Daughter *'70*
Going Home *'71*
The Wrath of God *'72*
Farewell, My Lovely *'75*
The Yakuza *'75*
The Last Tycoon *'76*
Midway *'76*
The Big Sleep *'78*
The Agency *'81*
One Shoe Makes It Murder *'82*
That Championship Season *'82*
A Killer in the Family *'83*
The Winds of War *'83*
The Ambassador *'84*
Maria's Lovers *'84*
North and South Book 1 *'85*
Promises to Keep *'85*
Reunion at Fairborough *'85*
Mr. North *'88*
Scrooged *'88*
War & Remembrance *'88*
The Brotherhood of the Rose *'89*
War & Remembrance: The Final Chapter *'89*
Thompson's Last Run *'90*
Cape Fear *'91*
Tombstone *'93 (N)*
Woman of Desire *'93*
Dead Man *'95*
James Dean: Live Fast, Die Young *'97*

Rhona Mitra (1976-)
A Kid in Aladdin's Palace *'97*
Beowulf *'98*
Get Carter *'00*
Sweet Home Alabama *'02*
Highwaymen *'03*
The Life of David Gale *'03*
The Number 23 *'07*
Shooter *'07*
Skinwalkers *'07*
Doomsday *'08*
Stolen *'09*
Underworld: Rise of the Lycans *'09*
Hard Target 2 *'16*

Koji Mitsui (1910-79)
The Hidden Fortress *'58*
Woman in the Dunes *'64*

Madhur Mittal
Slumdog Millionaire *'08*
Million Dollar Arm *'14*

Asumi Miwa (1982-)
Uzumaki *'00*
The Great Yokai War *'05*

Tom Mix (1880-1940)
In the Days of the Thundering Herd & the Law & the Outlaw *'14*
The Rider of Death Valley *'32*
The Miracle Rider *'35*

Katy Mixon (1981-)
The Quiet *'05*
Four Christmases *'08*
All About Steve *'09*
State of Play *'09*
Drive Angry *'11*
Take Shelter *'11*
Minions *'15 (V)*

Seiji Miyaguchi (1913-85)
Early Summer *'51*
Seven Samurai *'54*
The Human Condition: No Greater Love *'58*
Pale Flower *'64*

Kuniko Miyake (1916-92)
Early Summer *'51*
Good Morning *'59*

Nobuko Miyamoto (1945-)
The Funeral *'84*
Tampopo *'86*
A Taxing Woman *'87*

Hiroyuki Miyasako
The Great Yokai War *'05*
Black House *'07*

Rie Miyazawa (1973-)
The Twilight Samurai *'02*
Ashura *'05*
Hana: The Tale of a Reluctant Samurai *'07*

Junko Miyazono (1943-)
Legends of the Poisonous Seductress 1: Female Demon Ohyaku *'68*
Legends of the Poisonous Seductress 2: Quick Draw Okatsu *'69*
Legends of the Poisonous Seductress 3: Okatsu the Fugitive *'69*

Eric Miyeni
Cry, the Beloved Country *'95*
Dangerous Ground *'96*

Kim Miyori (1951-)
When the Bough Breaks *'86*
The Big Picture *'89*
The Punisher *'90*
Body Shot *'93*
Journey to the Center of the Earth *'93*
Metro *'96*
The Grudge 2 *'06*

Eiko Miyoshi (1894-1963)
No Regrets for Our Youth *'46*
I Live in Fear *'55*
Samurai 1: Musashi Miyamoto *'55*
The Hidden Fortress *'58*

Isaac Mizrahi (1961-)
For Love or Money *'93*
Celebrity *'98 (C)*
Hollywood Ending *'02*

Kenji Mizuhashi (1975-)
Moonlight Whispers *'99*
Pulse *'01*

Kumi Mizuno (1937-)
Matango *'63*
Frankenstein Conquers the World *'64*
Godzilla *vs.* the Sea Monster *'66*
What's Up, Tiger Lily? *'66*
Godzilla *vs.* Monster Zero *'68*
War of the Gargantuas *'70*

Genevieve Mnich (1942-)
Beau Pere *'81*
Seraphine *'08*

Payman Moaadi
A Separation *'11*
Camp X-Ray *'14*

Mary Ann Mobley (1939-2014)
Get Yourself a College Girl *'64*
Girl Happy *'65*
Harum Scarum *'65*
My Dog, the Thief *'69*
Crazy Horse and Custer: 'The Untold Story' *'90*

Roger Mobley (1949-)
Boy Who Caught a Crook *'61*
Jack the Giant Killer *'62*
Emil and the Detectives *'64*

Moby (1965-)
Pittsburgh *'06*
Suck *'09*

Colin Mochrie
Kit Kittredge: An American Girl *'08*
Oh Christmas Tree! *'13*

Laurie Mock
Hot Rods to Hell *'67*
Riot on Sunset Strip *'67*

Tony Mockus, Sr.
Backdraft *'91*
Charming Billy *'98*

Matthew Modine (1959-)
Baby It's You *'82*
Private School *'83*
Streamers *'83*
Birdy *'84*
The Hotel New Hampshire *'84*
Mrs. Soffel *'84*
Vision Quest *'85*
Full Metal Jacket *'87*
Orphans *'87*
The Gamble *'88*
Married to the Mob *'88*
Gross Anatomy *'89*
Memphis Belle *'90*
Pacific Heights *'90*
Wind *'92*
And the Band Played On *'93*
Short Cuts *'93*
The Browning Version *'94*
Bye Bye, Love *'94*
Jacob *'94*
Cutthroat Island *'95*
Fluke *'95*
The Blackout *'97*
The Real Blonde *'97*
The Maker *'98*
What the Deaf Man Heard *'98*
Any Given Sunday *'99*
Flowers for Algernon *'00*
The American *'01*
In the Shadows *'01*
Jack and the Beanstalk: The Real Story *'01*
Nobody's Baby *'01*
Redeemer *'02*
Hitler: The Rise of Evil *'03*
Hollywood North *'03*
Le Divorce *'03*
Opa! *'05*
Transporter 2 *'05*
Kettle of Fish *'06*
The Neighbor *'07*
Hemingway's Garden of Eden *'08*
Sex & Lies in Sin City: The Ted Binion Scandal *'08*
Frenemy *'09*
The Trial *'10*
Too Big to Fail *'11*
The Dark Knight Rises *'12*
Girl in Progress *'12*
CAT. 8 *'13*
Family Weekend *'13*
Jobs *'13*
The Confirmation *'16*
47 Meters Down *'17*
The Heyday of the Insensitive Bastards *'17*

Ruby Modine (1990-)
Happy Death Day *'17*
Satanic Panic *'19*

Gaston Modot (1887-1970)
Under the Roofs of Paris *'29*
Grand Illusion *'37*
The Rules of the Game *'39*
Children of Paradise *'44*
Casque d'Or *'52*

Ralph (Ralf) Moeller (1959-)
Best of the Best 2 *'93*
The Viking Sagas *'95*
The Bad Pack *'98*
Gladiator *'00*
The Scorpion King *'02*
The Paradise Virus *'03*
Dark Kingdom: The Dragon King *'04*
El Padrino *'04*
Beerfest *'06*
Pathfinder *'07*
Alone in the Dark 2 *'08*
Far Cry *'08*
Seed *'08*

Katherine Moenning (1977-)
Everybody's Fine *'09*
The Lincoln Lawyer *'11*

Donald Moffat (1930-)
Rachel, Rachel *'68*
The Great Northfield Minnesota Raid *'72*
Showdown *'73*
Mary White *'77*
Promises in the Dark *'79*
Winter Kills *'79*
The Long Days of Summer *'80*
The Thing *'82*
The Right Stuff *'83*
License to Kill *'84*
Alamo Bay *'85*
The Best of Times *'86*
The Bourne Identity *'88*
Far North *'88*
Necessary Parties *'88*
The Unbearable Lightness of Being *'88*
Music Box *'89*
The Bonfire of the Vanities *'90*
Danielle Steel's Kaleidoscope *'90*
Class Action *'91*
Regarding Henry *'91*
Housesitter *'92*
Teamster Boss: The Jackie Presser Story *'92*
Armistead Maupin's Tales of the City *'93*
Love, Cheat & Steal *'93*
Clear and Present Danger *'94*
Is There Life Out There? *'94*
Trapped in Paradise *'94*
The Evening Star *'96*
A Smile Like Yours *'96*
Cookie's Fortune *'99*
61* *'01*

Jane Moffat
Come Dance With Me *'12*
Mama *'13*

Graham Moffatt (1919-65)
Windbag the Sailor *'36*
Good Morning, Boys *'37*
Ask a Policeman *'38*

D.W. Moffett (1954-)
An Early Frost *'85*
Black Widow *'87*
Danielle Steel's Fine Things *'90*
In the Deep Woods *'91*
Falling Down *'93*
Rough Magic *'95*
Stealing Beauty *'96*
Molly *'99*
A Song From the Heart *'99*
Traffic *'00*
Kill Me Later *'01*
Thirteen *'03*
An Unexpected Love *'03*
Twisted *'04*
Skateland *'10*

Gregory Moffett
Let's Dance *'50*
Robot Monster *'53*

Michelle Moffett
Hired to Kill *'91*
Deathstalker 4: Match of Titans *'92*

Sharyn Moffett (1936-)
The Body Snatcher *'45*
The Judge Steps Out *'49*

Jerry Mofokeng
Mandela and de Klerk *'97*
Tsotsi *'05*

Carl Mohner (1916-2005)
Rififi *'54*
It Takes a Thief *'60*
Sink the Bismarck *'60*
Last Gun *'64*
Wanted: Babysitter *'75*

Gerald Mohr (1914-68)
Charlie Chan at Treasure Island *'39*
Love Affair *'39*
Hunt the Man Down *'50*
Detective Story *'51*
Sirocco *'51*
Duel at Silver Creek *'52*
Invasion U.S.A. *'52*
The Ring *'52*
The Sniper *'52*
Son of Ali Baba *'52*
The Eddie Cantor Story *'53*
Money from Home *'53*
Raiders of the Seven Seas *'53*
Dragonfly Squadron *'54*
Terror in the Haunted House *'58*
The Angry Red Planet *'59*

Jay Mohr (1970-)
For Better or Worse *'95*
Jerry Maguire *'96*
Picture Perfect *'96*
Suicide Kings *'97*
From the Earth to the Moon *'98*
Mafia! *'98*
Paulie *'98 (V)*
Playing by Heart *'98*
Small Soldiers *'98*
200 Cigarettes *'98*
Go *'99*
Cherry Falls *'00*
Pay It Forward *'00*
Dean Koontz's Black River *'01*
The Adventures of Pluto Nash *'02*
Simone *'02*
Seeing Other People *'04*
Are We There Yet? *'05*
King's Ransom *'05*
Christmas Do-Over *'06*
Even Money *'06*
The Groomsmen *'06*
Street Kings *'08*
Hereafter *'10*
A Christmas Wedding Tail *'11 (V)*
The Incredible Burt Wonderstone *'13*
Road Hard *'15*
All About Nina *'18*

Wotan Wilke Mohring (1967-)
The Experiment *'01*
Antibodies *'05*
The Silence *'10*

Richard Moir (1950-)
The Odd Angry Shot *'79*
Wrangler *'88*
Welcome to Woop Woop *'97*

Marisa Moitzi (1939-92)
See Marisa Mell

Jose Mojica Marins (1929-)
At Midnight, I'll Take Your Soul *'63*
Awakenings of the Beast *'68*

Karen Mok (1970-)
Fallen Angels *'95*
Black Mask *'96*
So Close *'02*
Vampire Effect *'03*
Man of Tai Chi *'13*

Zakes Mokae (1934-2009)
The Comedians *'67*
Agatha Christie's A Caribbean Mystery *'83*
Cry Freedom *'87*
The Serpent and the Rainbow *'87*
Dad *'89*
A Dry White Season *'89*
Gross Anatomy *'89*
Body Parts *'91*
A Rage in Harlem *'91*
Dust Devil *'93*
Vampire in Brooklyn *'95*
Waterworld *'95*
Krippendorf's Tribe *'98*

Gretchen Mol (1972-)
The Funeral *'96*
The Last Time I Committed Suicide *'96*
Music from Another Room *'97*
Celebrity *'98*
Finding Graceland *'98*
New Rose Hotel *'98*
Rounders *'98*
The Cradle Will Rock *'99*
Forever Mine *'99*
Just Looking *'99*
Sweet and Lowdown *'99*
The Thirteenth Floor *'99*
Get Carter *'00*
The Magnificent Ambersons *'02*
The Shape of Things *'03*
The Notorious Bettie Page *'06*
Puccini for Beginners *'06*
American Loser *'07*
The Ten *'07*
3:10 to Yuma *'07*
The Memory Keeper's Daughter *'08*
An American Affair *'09*
Tenure *'09*

Laggies '13
Manchester by the Sea '16

Alfred Molina (1953-)
The Big Scam '79
Meantime '81
Raiders of the Lost Ark '81
Ladyhawke '85
Prick Up Your Ears '87
Not Without My Daughter '90
American Friends '91
Enchanted April '92
The Trial '93
Maverick '94
The Perez Family '94
White Fang 2: The Myth of the White Wolf '94
Before and After '95
Dead Man '95
Species '95
Anna Karenina '96
Mojave Moon '96
Scorpion Spring '96
Boogie Nights '97
The Man Who Knew Too Little '97
The Imposters '98
The Impostors '98
Pete's Meteor '98
The Treat '98
Dudley Do-Right '99
Chocolat '00
The Miracle Maker: The Story of Jesus '00 (V)
Murder on the Orient Express '01
Texas Rangers '01
Frida '02
Undertaking Betty '02
Coffee and Cigarettes '03
Identity '03
Luther '03
My Life Without Me '03
Cronicas '04
Spider-Man 2 '04
Steamboy '05 (V)
As You Like It '06
The Da Vinci Code '06
The Hoax '06
The Company '07
The Moon & the Stars '07
Silk '07
Nothing Like the Holidays '08
An Education '09
The Lodger '09
The Pink Panther 2 '09
Prince of Persia: The Sands of Time '10
The Sorcerer's Apprentice '10
The Tempest '10
Abduction '11
Rango '11 (V)
Monsters University '13 (V)
The Truth About Emanuel '13
Love Is Strange '14
The Normal Heart '14
Return to Zero '14
Swelter '14
Kahlil Gibran's The Prophet '15
Secret in Their Eyes '15
Little Men '16
Whiskey Tango Foxtrot '16
Don't Let Go '19
Saint Judy '19

Angela Molina (1955-)
That Obscure Object of Desire '77
1492: Conquest of Paradise '92
Live Flesh '97
Carnage '02
The Lark Farm '07
Baaria '09

Jacinto (Jack) Molina (1934-2009)
See Paul Naschy

Mariano Vidal Molina (1925-96)
White Comanche '68
Curse of the Devil '73

Rolando Molina (1971-)
Next Friday '00
crazy/beautiful '01

Charles Moll (1943-)
Cataclysm '81
Night Train to Terror '84

Georgia Moll (1938-)
Island of Love '63
Contempt '64

Richard Moll (1943-)
Hard Country '81
Sword & the Sorcerer '82
Dungeonmaster '83
Metalstorm: The Destruction of Jared Syn '83
Savage Journey '83
House '86
Wicked Stepmother '89
Highlander: The Gathering '92
National Lampoon's Loaded Weapon 1 '93
The Flintstones '94
No Dessert Dad, 'Til You Mow the Lawn '94
Storybook '95
The Secret Agent Club '96
Living in Peril '97
Boltneck '98
Dish Dogs '98
Evolution '01
Scary Movie 2 '01
Spiders 2: Breeding Ground '01
The Biggest Fan '02
Headless Horseman '07
The Christmas Cottage '08

Jordi Molla (1968-)
Second Skin '99
Blow '01
Bad Boys 2 '03
The Alamo '04
The Stone Merchant '06
Caravaggio '07
Elizabeth: The Golden Age '07
Che '08
Bunraku '10
Inhale '10
Knight and Day '10
Colombiana '11
There Be Dragons '11
Riddick '13
Criminal '16
Speed Kills '18

Jenny Mollen (1979-)
Return of the Living Dead: Rave to the Grave '05
National Lampoon Presents Cattle Call '06
My Best Friend's Girl '08
Amateur Night '16

Roland Moller
Land of Mine '15
Papillon '17

Clothilde Mollet
Amelie '01
The Page Turner '06

Dearbhla Molloy (1946-)
G.B.H. '91
Bloom '03

Janel Moloney (1969-)
The Souler Opposite '97
The Leisure Seeker '17

Robert Moloney
Hollywood Wives: The New Generation '03
Touch the Top of the World '06
Secrets of an Undercover Wife '07
Storm Cell '08
Ice Twisters '09
Rags '12

Jason Momoa (1979-)
Tempted '03
Conan the Barbarian '11
Bullet to the Head '12
Road to Paloma '14
The Bad Batch '17
Aquaman '18

Kaori Momoi (1952-)
Memoirs of a Geisha '05
The Sun '05
Sukiyaki Western Django '08
Emperor '12

Sloane Momsen (1996-)
Dr. Seuss' How the Grinch Stole Christmas '00
We Were Soldiers '02
Daddy Day Care '03

Taylor Momsen (1993-)
Dr. Seuss' How the Grinch Stole Christmas '00
We Were Soldiers '02
Paranoid Park '07
Underdog '07

Janelle Monáe (1985-)
Hidden Figures '17
Welcome to Marwen '18
Harriet '19
Lady and the Tramp '19
UglyDolls '19 (V)

Cameron Monaghan (1993-)
Jamie Marks is Dead '13
Vampire Academy '14
Amityville: The Awakening '17

Dominic Monaghan (1976-)
Lord of the Rings: The Fellowship of the Ring '01
Lord of the Rings: The Two Towers '02
Lord of the Rings: The Return of the King '03
The Purifiers '04
Shooting Livien '05
I Sell the Dead '09
X-Men Origins: Wolverine '09
Molly Moon and The Incredible Book of Hypnotism '15

Michelle Monaghan (1976-)
It Runs in the Family '03
The Bourne Supremacy '04
Winter Solstice '04
Kiss Kiss Bang Bang '05
Mr. & Mrs. Smith '05
North Country '05
Mission: Impossible 3 '06
Gone Baby Gone '07
The Heartbreak Kid '07
Eagle Eye '08
Made of Honor '08
Trucker '08
Due Date '10
Somewhere '10
Machine Gun Preacher '11
Source Code '11
Tomorrow You're Gone '12
The Best of Me '14
Better Living Through Chemistry '14
Playing It Cool '14
Pixels '15
Patriots Day '17
Sleepless '17
The Vanishing of Sidney Hall '17
Saint Judy '19

Dan Monahan (1955-)
Porky's '82
Porky's 2: The Next Day '83
Porky's Revenge '85
Stephen King's The Night Flier '96

Jeff Monahan
One Way Out '95
Bruiser '00

Richard Monahan (1924-93)
Fixed Bayonets! '51
The Steel Helmet '51
Untamed Women '52

Karen Moncrieff (1963-)
Midnight Witness '93
Xtro 3: Watch the Skies '95

Julie Mond
Exit Speed '08
Rest Stop: Don't Look Back '08
Love Begins '11

Love's Everlasting Courage '11
Strawberry Summer '12

Merwin Mondesir (1976-)
Bones '01
Godsend '04

Isabela Moner (2001-)
Instant Family '18
Sicario: Day of the Soldado '18
Dora and the Lost City of Gold '19

Richard Monette (1944-2008)
Dancing in the Dark '86
Hello Mary Lou: Prom Night 2 '87

William V. Mong
The Girl Said No '30
Her Forgotten Past '33

Corbett Monica (1930-98)
The Grasshopper '69
The Passing of Evil '70

Andrea Monier
Are You Scared 2 '09
The Black Water Vampire '13
Day of the Mummy '14
All Hallow's Eve 2 '15

Mo'Nique (1967-)
Three Strikes '00
Queens of Comedy '01
Two Can Play That Game '01
Half Past Dead '02
Good Fences '03
Hair Show '04
Soul Plane '04
Domino '05
Beerfest '06
Phat Girlz '06
Shadowboxer '06
Welcome Home Roscoe Jenkins '08
Precious: Based on the Novel 'Push' by Sapphire '09

Wendy Moniz (1969-)
Tuesdays with Morrie '99
Wheelman '17

Debra Monk (1949-)
Bed of Roses '95
Extreme Measures '96
The First Wives Club '96
The Devil's Advocate '97
Ellen Foster '97
Center Stage '00
The Doorbell Rang: A Nero Wolfe Mystery '01
Dark Water '02
Eloise at the Plaza '03
Milwaukee, Minnesota '03
Palindromes '04
Plain Dirty '04
The Producers '05

Sophie Monk (1979-)
Date Movie '06
Spring Breakdown '08
Life Blood '09
National Lampoon's The Legend of Awesomest Maximus '11

Bob Monkhouse (1928-2003)
Carry On Sergeant '58
Dentist In the Chair '60
All or Nothing at All '93

Kathy Monks
Invasion for Flesh and Blood '94
Flesh Eaters from Outer Space '05

Yvonne Monlaur (1939-)
The Brides of Dracula '60
Circus of Horrors '60
The Terror of the Tongs '61
Ladies' Man '62
License to Kill '64

Alex Monner
[REC] 3: Genesis '12
Summer Camp '16

Carlo Monni (1943-)
Berlinguer I Love You '77
The Tesseract '03

Lawrence Monoson (1964-)
Last American Virgin '82
Mask '85
And the Band Played On '93 (C)

Maika Monroe
The Guest '14
It Follows '15
Independence Day: Resurgence '16
The Scent of Rain & Lightening '17
Greta '18
I'm Not Here '19
Villains '19

Marilyn Monroe (1926-62)
All About Eve '50
The Asphalt Jungle '50
The Fireball '50
Love Happy '50
As Young As You Feel '51
Let's Make It Legal '51
Love Nest '51
Clash by Night '52
Don't Bother to Knock '52
Monkey Business '52
Niagara '52
We're Not Married '52
Gentlemen Prefer Blondes '53
How to Marry a Millionaire '53
River of No Return '54
There's No Business Like Show Business '54
The Seven Year Itch '55
Bus Stop '56
The Prince and the Showgirl '57
Some Like It Hot '59
Let's Make Love '60
The Misfits '61
The Love Goddesses '65

Meredith Monroe (1969-)
Full Ride '02
New Best Friend '02
Not My Life '06
Tornado Valley '09
Born Bad '11

Mircea Monroe (1982-)
All Souls Day '05
Fast Girl '07
One Long Night '07
Finding Bliss '09
Into the Blue 2: The Reef '09
The Black Waters of Echo's Pond '10
Growth '10

Steve Monroe (1972-)
Can't Hardly Wait '98
Inherit the Wind '99
Cast Away '00
Miss Congeniality '00
Going Greek '01
The Santa Trap '02
House of the Dead 2: Dead Aim '05
School for Scoundrels '06

Renzo Montagnani (1930-77)
The Libertine '69
The Mad Adventures of Rabbi Jacob '73

Felicity Montagu
I Want Candy '07
Alan Partridge '13

Lee Montague (1927-)
Moulin Rouge '52
You Must Be Joking! '65
Brother Sun, Sister Moon '73
Mahler '74
Madame Sousatzka '88
Jekyll and Hyde '90

Monte Montague (1891-1959)
Radio Patrol '37
Along the Rio Grande '41

Carlos Montalban
Beyond All Limits '59
Bananas '71

Paolo Montalban (1973-)
Cinderella '97
American Adobo '02
The Great Raid '05

Ricardo Montalban (1920-2009)
On an Island with You '48
Battleground '49
Border Incident '49
Neptune's Daughter '49
Mystery Street '50
Right Cross '50
Two Weeks with Love '50
Across the Wide Missouri '51
My Man and I '52
Sayonara '57
Love Is a Ball '63
Cheyenne Autumn '64
The Money Trap '65
Alice Through the Looking Glass '66
Madame X '66
The Singing Nun '66
Blue '68
Iron Cowboy '68
Black Water Gold '69
The Desperate Mission '69
Sweet Charity '69
Escape from the Planet of the Apes '71
Ride to Glory '71
Conquest of the Planet of the Apes '72
Train Robbers '73
Wonder Woman '74
Fantasy Island '76
Joe Panther '76
Return to Fantasy Island '77
Mission to Glory '80
Star Trek 2: The Wrath of Khan '82
Cannonball Run 2 '84
The Naked Gun: From the Files of Police Squad '88
Spy Kids 2: The Island of Lost Dreams '02
Spy Kids 3-D: Game Over '03
The Ant Bully '06 (V)

Lenny Montana (1926-92)
The Godfather '72
Fingers '78
They Went That-a-Way & That-a-Way '78
Defiance '79
The Jerk '79
Battle Creek Brawl '80
Below the Belt '80
The Big Brawl '80
. . .All the Marbles '81
Blood Song '82
Evilspeak '82

Yves Montand (1921-91)
Napoleon '55
Wages of Fear '55
The Wide Blue Road '57
Where the Hot Wind Blows '59
Let's Make Love '60
My Geisha '62
Grand Prix '66
Is Paris Burning? '66
La Guerre Est Finie '66
Z '69
Le Cercle Rouge '70
On a Clear Day You Can See Forever '70
Cesar & Rosalie '72
Lovers Like Us '75
The Savage '75
Delusions of Grandeur '76
Jean de Florette '87
Manon of the Spring '87

Ted Monte
Attack of the 60-Foot Centerfold '95
Turbulent Skies '10

Cory Monteith (1982-2013)
Kraken: Tentacles of the Deep '06
Hybrid '07

Hannibal '01
The Shipping News '01
World Traveler '01
Far from Heaven '02
The Hours '02
The Forgotten '04
Laws of Attraction '04
Marie and Bruce '04
The Prize Winner of Defiance, Ohio '05
Children of Men '06
Freedomland '06
Trust the Man '06
I'm Not There '07
Next '07
Savage Grace '07
Blindness '08
Chloe '09
The Private Lives of Pippa Lee '09
A Single Man '09
Elektra Luxx '10 (C)
The Kids Are All Right '10
Crazy, Stupid, Love. '11
Being Flynn '12
Game Change '12
What Maisie Knew '12
Carrie '13
Don Jon '13
The English Teacher '13
6 Souls '13
The Hunger Games: Mockingjay--Part 1 '14
Maps to the Stars '14
Non-Stop '14
Still Alice '14
Freeheld '15
Seventh Son '15
Maggie's Plan '16
Kingsman: The Golden Circle '17
Suburbicon '17
Wonderstruck '17
Bel Canto '18
Gloria Bell '18
After the Wedding '19

Kaycee Moore
Killer of Sheep '77
Daughters of the Dust '91

Kenya Moore (1971-)
Senseless '98
No Turning Back '01
I Know Who Killed Me '07
The Confidant '10

Kieron Moore (1924-2007)
A Man About the House '47
Mine Own Executioner '47
Anna Karenina '48
David and Bathsheba '51
Recoil '53
Satellite in the Sky '56
The Key '58
Darby O'Gill & the Little People '59
The Day They Robbed the Bank of England '60
The Siege of Sidney Street '60
Doctor Blood's Coffin '62
I Thank a Fool '62
The 300 Spartans '62
Day of the Triffids '63
The Thin Red Line '64
Crack in the World '65
Son of a Gunfighter '65
Arabesque '66

Lisa Bronwyn Moore (1940-)
Bleeders '97
The Education of Little Tree '97
A Walk on the Moon '99
The Courage to Love '00
Isn't She Great '00
The Sum of All Fears '02
Mambo Italiano '03
The Aviator '04
The Reagans '04
I'm Not There '07

Mandy Moore (1984-)
The Princess Diaries '01
All I Want '02
A Walk to Remember '02
How to Deal '03
Chasing Liberty '04
Saved! '04
Racing Stripes '05 (V)
Romance & Cigarettes '05
American Dreamz '06
Brother Bear 2 '06 (V)
Southland Tales '06
Because I Said So '07
Dedication '07
License to Wed '07
Tangled '10 (V)
Love, Wedding, Marriage '11
Swinging With the Finkels '11
Christmas In Conway '13
47 Meters Down '17
The Darkest Minds '18
I'm Not Here '19
Midway '19

Margo Moore (1931-2000)
Wake Me When It's Over '60
The George Raft Story '61

Mary Tyler Moore (1936-2017)
Thoroughly Modern Millie '67
Change of Habit '69
Ordinary People '80
Six Weeks '82
Just Between Friends '86
Gore Vidal's Lincoln '88
The Last Best Year '90
Flirting with Disaster '95
Keys to Tulsa '96
Against the Current '09

Matt Moore (1888-1960)
Traffic in Souls '13
20,000 Leagues under the Sea '16
Pride of the Clan '18
White Tiger '23
The Unholy Three '25
Penrod and Sam '31
That Forsyte Woman '50
An Affair to Remember '57
I Bury the Living '58
Devon's Ghost: Legend of the Bloody Boy '05

Melba Moore (1945-)
All Dogs Go to Heaven '89 (V)
The Fighting Temptations '03

Melissa Moore (1963-)
The Killing Zone '90
Evil Lives '92
Sorority House Massacre 2: Nighty Nightmare '92
Stormswept '95

Michael Moore (1954-)
Roger & Me '89
Canadian Bacon '94 (C)
The Big One '98 (N)
The Insider '99
Lucky Numbers '00
The Fever '04
Capitalism: A Love Story '09
Where to Invade Next '15
Fahrenheit 11/9 '18

Norma Moore (1935-)
Fear Strikes Out '57
Unwed Mother '58

Owen Moore (1886-1939)
The Black Bird '26
The Red Mill '27
She Done Him Wrong '33

Pauline Moore (1914-2001)
Charlie Chan at the Olympics '37
Love Is News '37
Three Blind Mice '38
Charlie Chan at Treasure Island '39
The Three Musketeers '39

R.J. (Geoffrey) Moore (1966-)
Hard Hunted '92
Fit to Kill '93

Roger Moore (1927-2017)
Mutiny Ahead '35
The Last Time I Saw Paris '54
Diane '55
Interrupted Melody '55
The King's Thief '55
Gold of the Seven Saints '61
The Rape of the Sabines '61
The Sins of Rachel Cade '61
The Man Who Haunted Himself '70
Live and Let Die '73
The Man with the Golden Gun '74
Street People '76
The Spy Who Loved Me '77
Wild Geese '78
Escape to Athena '79
Moonraker '79
ffolkes '80
Cannonball Run '81
For Your Eyes Only '81
Sea Wolves '81
Octopussy '83
The Naked Face '84
A View to a Kill '85
Bullseye! '90
The Quest '96
Spice World: The Movie '97
D.R.E.A.M. Team '99
The Enemy '01
Boat Trip '03
Cats & Dogs: The Revenge of Kitty Galore '10
A Princess for Christmas '11

Rudy Ray Moore (1937-2008)
Dolemite '75
Avenging Disco Godfather '76
Dolemite 2: Human Tornado '76
Devil's Son-in-Law '77
Monkey Hustle '77
Vampire Assassin '05

Sam Moore (1935-)
Tapeheads '89
Night at the Golden Eagle '02

Shameik Moore
Dope '15
Spider-Man: Into the Spider-Verse '18 (V)
Let It Snow '19

Shemar Moore (1970-)
Mama Flora's Family '98
Never 2 Big '98
The Brothers '01
Motives '03
Diary of a Mad Black Woman '05
The Bounce Back '16

Stephan Campbell Moore (1977-)
Bright Young Things '03
A Good Woman '04
Amazing Grace '06
The History Boys '06
Season of the Witch '10

Stephen Moore (1937-2019)
Clockwise '86
Under Suspicion '92
Prince of Poisoners: The Life and Crimes of William Palmer '98
A Short Stay in Switzerland '09

Stephen Campbell Moore (1977-)
He Knew He Was Right '04
Ben Hur '10
Just Henry '11
Moonwalkers '16
The Ones Below '16
Red Joan '19

Tedde Moore
A Christmas Story '83
Mistletoe Over Manhattan '11

Terry Moore (1929-)
Gaslight '44
Since You Went Away '44
Mighty Joe Young '49
The Great Rupert '50
Two of a Kind '51
Come Back, Little Sheba '52
Beneath the 12-Mile Reef '53
King of the Khyber Rifles '53
Man on a Tightrope '53
Daddy Long Legs '55
Shack Out on 101 '55
Between Heaven and Hell '56
Postmark for Danger '56
Peyton Place '57
Cast a Long Shadow '59
Why Must I Die? '60
Kill Factor '78
Death Blow '87
Lethal Victims '87
Beverly Hills Brats '89
Second Chances '98
Kill Your Darlings '06
The Still Life '07

Toby Moore (1977-)
Murder in Greenwich '02
A Separate Peace '04

Tom Moore (1883-1955)
The Woman Racket '30
Ten Laps to Go '36

Victor Moore (1876-1962)
Gold Diggers of 1937 '36
Swing Time '36
Make Way for Tomorrow '37
She's Got Everything '37
Louisiana Purchase '41
Star Spangled Rhythm '42
Carolina Blues '44
Ziegfeld Follies '46
It Happened on 5th Avenue '47
On Our Merry Way '48
A Kiss in the Dark '49
We're Not Married '52
The Seven Year Itch '55

Vivienne Moore
Emma '72
Miss Conception '08

Agnes Moorehead (1906-74)
Citizen Kane '41
Big Street '42
The Magnificent Ambersons '42
Government Girl '43
The Youngest Profession '43
Dragon Seed '44
Jane Eyre '44
Mrs. Parkington '44
Since You Went Away '44
Tomorrow the World '44
Her Highness and the Bellboy '45
Keep Your Powder Dry '45
Our Vines Have Tender Grapes '45
Dark Passage '47
The Lost Moment '47
Johnny Belinda '48
Summer Holiday '48
The Great Sinner '49
The Stratton Story '49
Caged '50
Show Boat '51
Scandal at Scourie '53
The Story of Three Loves '53
Magnificent Obsession '54
All That Heaven Allows '55
The Left Hand of God '55
Untamed '55
The Conqueror '56
The Opposite Sex '56
Pardners '56
Jeanne Eagels '57
Raintree County '57
Story of Mankind '57
The True Story of Jesse James '57
The Bat '59
Pollyanna '60
Bachelor in Paradise '61
Twenty Plus Two '61
How the West Was Won '63
Who's Minding the Store? '63
Hush, Hush, Sweet Charlotte '65
Alice Through the Looking Glass '66
The Singing Nun '66
The Ballad of Andy Crocker '69
What's the Matter with Helen? '71
Dear Dead Delilah '72
Charlotte's Web '73 (V)

Natalie Moorhead (1901-92)
Hook, Line and Sinker '30
Illicit '31
Three Wise Girls '32
Corruption '33
The Mind Reader '33
The Thin Man '34

Danny Mora
The Eye '08
We Have Your Husband '11

Tiriel Mora (1958-)
The Castle '97
Garage Days '03

Hattie Morahan
Sense & Sensibility '07
Mr. Holmes '15

Esai Morales (1962-)
Bad Boys '83
La Bamba '87
The Principal '87
Bloodhounds of Broadway '89
Freejack '92
Rapa Nui '93
Don't Do It '94
In the Army Now '94
My Family '94
The Disappearance of Garcia Lorca '96
Scorpion Spring '96
Dogwatch '97
The Wonderful Ice Cream Suit '98
Atomic Train '99
Paid in Full '02
American Fusion '05
Once Upon a Wedding '05
Fast Food Nation '06
How to Go Out on a Date in Queens '06
The Line '08
Caprica '09
Gun Hill Road '11
We Have Your Husband '11
Atlas Shrugged 2: The Strike '12
Seattle Superstorm '12
Jarhead 2: Field of Fire '14
Playin' For Love '15
Spare Parts '15
Never Back Down: No Surrender '16

Natalie Morales
Going the Distance '10
Battle of the Sexes '17

Natalie Leticia Morales (1972-)
See Natalie Morales

Santos Morales
The Boys in Company C '77
Hot to Trot! '88

Dan Moran
Rick '03
Winter of Frozen Dreams '08

Dolores Moran (1924-82)
Old Acquaintance '43
To Have & Have Not '44
The Horn Blows at Midnight '45
The Man I Love '46

Dylan Moran (1971-)
Shaun of the Dead '04
Tristram Shandy: A Cock and Bull Story '05
Run, Fatboy, Run '07
The Decoy Bride '11
Calvary '14

Erin Moran (1960-2017)
How Sweet It Is! '68
Watermelon Man '70
Lisa, Bright and Dark '73
Galaxy of Terror '81
Not Another B Movie '10

Jackie Moran (1923-90)
And So They Were Married '36
The Adventures of Tom Sawyer '38
Barefoot Boy '38
Mad About Music '38
Buck Rogers Conquers the Universe '39
Old Swimmin' Hole '40
Tomboy '40
Since You Went Away '44

Lois Moran (1909-90)
Feu Mathias Pascal '26
Behind That Curtain '29
West of Broadway '31

Mercedes Morán (1955-)
Holy Girl '04
Neruda '16

Nick Moran (1969-)
Lock, Stock and 2 Smoking Barrels '98
Miss Monday '98
New Blood '99
The Proposal '00
Rancid Aluminium '00
Another Life '01
The Musketeer '01
Chaos & Cadavers '03
Silent Partner '05
Don't Knock Twice '17
Avengement '19

Pat Moran
Pink Flamingos '72
Female Trouble '74
Desperate Living '77

Patrick Moran (1960-)
Dark Universe '93
Biohazard: The Alien Force '95

Peggy Moran (1918-2002)
The Mummy's Hand '40
One Night in the Tropics '40
Spring Parade '40
Seven Sweethearts '42

Polly Moran (1883-1952)
So This Is College '29
Chasing Rainbows '30
The Girl Said No '30
Paid '30
Politics '31
Reducing '31
The Passionate Plumber '32
Hollywood Party '34
Adam's Rib '50

Rob Moran (1963-)
Dumb & Dumber '94
Kingpin '96
There's Something about Mary '98
Me, Myself, and Irene '00
Shallow Hal '01
You're Next '13

Rick Moranis (1953-)
Strange Brew '83
Ghostbusters '84
Hockey Night '84
Streets of Fire '84
Brewster's Millions '85
Club Paradise '86
Head Office '86
Little Shop of Horrors '86
Spaceballs '87
Ghostbusters 2 '89
Honey, I Shrunk the Kids '89
Parenthood '89
My Blue Heaven '90
Honey, I Blew Up the Kid '92
Splitting Heirs '93
The Flintstones '94
Little Giants '94
Big Bully '95
Honey, We Shrunk Ourselves '97
Brother Bear '03 (V)
Brother Bear 2 '06 (V)

Richard Morant (1945-2011)
Mahler '74
Poldark '75
Scandal '89

Laura Morante (1956-)
The Son's Room '00
The Dancer Upstairs '02
Empire of the Wolves '05
Avenue Montaigne '06

Private Fears in Public Places '06
Moliere '07
Romeo & Juliet '13

Kestie Morassi (1978-)
Dirty Deeds '02
Strange Bedfellows '04
Wolf Creek '05

Kenneth More (1914-82)
Scott of the Antarctic '48
Morning Departure '50
Appointment With Venus '51
No Highway in the Sky '51
Doctor in the House '53
Genevieve '53
Never Let Me Go '53
The Adventures of Sadie '55
Reach for the Sky '56
The Admirable Crichton '57
A Night to Remember '58
Flame Over India '59
North West Frontier '59
The Sheriff of Fractured Jaw '59
Sink the Bismarck '60
The Longest Day '62
Dark of the Sun '68
Battle of Britain '69
Scrooge '70
The Slipper and the Rose '76
Where Time Began '77
Leopard in the Snow '78
Unidentified Flying Oddball '79
A Tale of Two Cities '80

Jeanne Moreau (1928-)
Grisbi '53
Hijack Highway '55
Frantic '58
The 400 Blows '59
The Lovers '59
Dangerous Liaisons '60
La Notte '60
Eva '62
Jules and Jim '62
The Trial '63
Diary of a Chambermaid '64
The Fire Within '64
The Yellow Rolls Royce '64
The Train '65
Viva Maria! '65
Mademoiselle '66
Chimes at Midnight '67
The Bride Wore Black '68
Alex in Wonderland '70 (C)
Monte Walsh '70
Nathalie Granger '72
Going Places '74
The Last Tycoon '76
Mr. Klein '76
La Truite '83
Querelle '83
La Femme Nikita '91
Until the End of the World '91
The Lover '92 (N)
A Foreign Field '93
Map of the Human Heart '93
Beyond the Clouds '95
Catherine the Great '95
I Love You, I Love You Not '97
Ever After: A Cinderella Story '98 (C)
Balzac: A Life of Passion '99
Go West '05 (C)
Time to Leave '05
Disengagement '07
One Day You'll Understand '08

Marguerite Moreau (1977-)
Wet Hot American Summer '01
Firestarter 2: Rekindled '02
The Locket '02
Queen of the Damned '02
Runaway Jury '03
Two Days '03
Off the Lip '04
Beverly Hills Chihuahua '08 (V)
Wake '09
Douchebag '10
Easier With Practice '10

Sylvie Moreau (1964-)
The Widow of Saint-Pierre '00
Familia '05

Yolande Moreau (1953-)
Vagabond '85
Amelie '01
Paris, je t'aime '06
Seraphine '08
Micmacs '09
Mammuth '10
Cinderella '12 (V)
The Brand New Testament '15

Francois Morel (1959-)
A Model Employee '02
Towards Zero '07
The Rabbi's Cat '11 (V)

Mantan Moreland (1902-73)
The Spirit of Youth '37
Next Time I Marry '38
King of the Zombies '41
The Mexican Spitfire Sees a Ghost '42
The Strange Case of Dr. Rx '42
The Chinese Cat '44
Meeting at Midnight '44
Pin-Up Girl '44
The Jade Mask '45
The Scarlet Clue '45
Shadows Over Chinatown '46
The Trap '46
The Chinese Ring '47
Docks of New Orleans '48
The Golden Eye '48
Shanghai Chest '48
Spider Baby '64
The Young Nurses '73

Andre Morell (1909-78)
Madeleine '50
A Stolen Face '52
Stolen Face '52
The Man Who Never Was '55
The Bridge on the River Kwai '57
The Giant Behemoth '59
The Hound of the Baskervilles '59
Cash on Demand '61
Plague of the Zombies '66
Dark of the Sun '68
10 Rillington Place '71

Rina Morelli (1908-76)
The Inveterate Bachelor '58
The Leopard '63
The Innocent '76

Sean Morelli (1970-)
Mark of the Astro-Zombies '02
Astro-Zombies M3: Cloned '10
Astro-Zombies M4: Invaders from Cyberspace '12

Antonio Moreno (1887-1967)
The Temptress '26
It '27
Captain from Castile '47
Creature from the Black Lagoon '54
Saskatchewan '54
The Searchers '56

Catalina Sandino Moreno (1981-)
Maria Full of Grace '04
Fast Food Nation '06
The Hottest State '06
Journey to the End of the Night '06
Paris, je t'aime '06
Che '08
The Twilight Saga: Eclipse '10
Magic Magic '13
Swelter '14

Rene L. Moreno (1969-)
Tequila Body Shots '99
Band of Brothers '01

Rita Moreno (1931-)
Pagan Love Song '50
The Toast of New Orleans '50
Cattle Town '52
The Ring '52
Singin' in the Rain '52
Fort Vengeance '53
Garden of Evil '54
Seven Cities of Gold '55
Untamed '55
The King and I '56
Summer and Smoke '61
West Side Story '61
Cry of Battle '63
Marlowe '69
The Night of the Following Day '69
Popi '69
Carnal Knowledge '71
The Ritz '76
Anatomy of a Seduction '79
The Four Seasons '81
Portrait of a Showgirl '82
Italian Movie '93
I Like It Like That '94
Angus '95
Slums of Beverly Hills '98
Blue Moon '00
Pinero '01
Casa de los Babys '03
King of the Corner '04

David Moretti
Murder.com '08
Finding Mr. Wright '11

Michele Moretti (1977-)
Wild Reeds '94
Apres-Vous '03
The Names of Love '10
Declaration of War '11

Nanni Moretti (1953-)
Caro Diario '93
The Son's Room '00
Quiet Chaos '08
Mia Madre '16

Chloë Grace Moretz (1997-)
The Amityville Horror '05
Big Momma's House 2 '06
Wicked Little Things '07
The Eye '08
(500) Days of Summer '09
Jack and the Beanstalk '09
Not Forgotten '09
Diary of a Wimpy Kid '10
Kick-Ass '10
Let Me In '10
Hick '11
Hugo '11
Texas Killing Fields '11
Dark Shadows '12
Carrie '13
Girl Rising '13 (N)
Kick-Ass 2 '13
Laggies '13
The Tale of the Princess Kaguya '13 (V)
The Equalizer '14
If I Stay '14
Clouds of Sils Maria '15
The 5th Wave '16
Neighbors 2: Sorority Rising '16
November Criminals '17
Greta '18
The Miseducation of Cameron Post '18
Suspiria '18
The Addams Family '19

George Morfogen (1933-)
Yuri Nosenko, KGB '86
Twenty Bucks '93

Diogo Morgado
Born to Race: Fast Track '14
Son of God '14

Boyd 'Red' Morgan (1915-88)
Gun Duel In Durango '57
The Adventures of Buckaroo Banzai Across the Eighth Dimension '84

Brit Morgan (1987-)
The Frozen '12
Friend Request '16

Chesty Morgan (1928-)
Deadly Weapons '70
Double Agent 73 '80

Cindy Morgan (1954-)
Caddyshack '80
Tron '82

Colin Morgan (1986-)
Parked '10
Legend '15

Debbi (Deborah) Morgan (1956-)
Mandingo '75
Monkey Hustle '77
The Jesse Owens Story '84
Eve's Bayou '97
Asunder '99
The Hurricane '99
She's All That '99
Love and Basketball '00
The Runaway '00
Woman, Thou Art Loosed '04
Back in the Day '05
Coach Carter '05

Dennis Morgan (1910-94)
The Great Ziegfeld '36
The Fighting 69th '40
Flight Angels '40
Kitty Foyle '40
Captains of the Clouds '42
In This Our Life '42
The Desert Song '43
The Hard Way '43
Thank Your Lucky Stars '43
Christmas in Connecticut '45
God is My Co-Pilot '45
Cheyenne '47
My Wild Irish Rose '47
One Sunday Afternoon '48
It's a Great Feeling '49
Perfect Strangers '50
Pretty Baby '50
Painting the Clouds With Sunshine '51
Raton Pass '51
Cattle Town '52
This Woman Is Dangerous '52
The Gun That Won the West '55
Pearl of the South Pacific '55

Frank Morgan (1890-1949)
Hallelujah, I'm a Bum '33
The Nuisance '33
The Cat and the Fiddle '34
The Good Fairy '35
I Live My Life '35
Naughty Marietta '35
Dancing Pirate '36
Dimples '36
The Great Ziegfeld '36
The Emperor's Candlesticks '37
The Last of Mrs. Cheyney '37
Saratoga '37
The Crowd Roars '38
Paradise for Three '38
Rosalie '38
Sweethearts '38
Balalaika '39
Broadway Serenade '39
The Wizard of Oz '39
Boom Town '40
Broadway Melody of 1940 '40
Hullabaloo '40
The Mortal Storm '40
The Shop Around the Corner '40
Honky Tonk '41
The Vanishing Virginian '41
Tortilla Flat '42
The Human Comedy '43
Thousands Cheer '43
Casanova Brown '44
The White Cliffs of Dover '44
Courage of Lassie '46
Summer Holiday '48
The Three Musketeers '48
Any Number Can Play '49
The Great Sinner '49
The Stratton Story '49
Key to the City '50

Gary Morgan (1950-)
The California Kid '74
The Power Within '95
Storybook '95

Harry (Henry) Morgan (1915-2011)
Orchestra Wives '42
To the Shores of Tripoli '42
Crash Dive '43
The Ox-Bow Incident '43
A Wing and a Prayer '44
State Fair '45
Dragonwyck '46
It Shouldn't Happen to a Dog '46
The Gangster '47
The Big Clock '48
Race Street '48
The Smallest Show on Earth '48
Holiday Affair '49
Red Light '49
Dark City '50
Appointment With Danger '51
The Well '51
Bend of the River '52
High Noon '52
Scandal Sheet '52
Torch Song '53
The Glenn Miller Story '54
Far Country '55
The Teahouse of the August Moon '56
It Started with a Kiss '59
Inherit the Wind '60
Murder, Inc. '60
How the West Was Won '63
Frankie and Johnny '65
What Did You Do in the War, Daddy? '66
Flim-Flam Man '67
Support Your Local Sheriff '69
The Barefoot Executive '71
Scandalous John '71
Support Your Local Gunfighter '71
Snowball Express '72
Charley and the Angel '73
Sidekicks '74
The Apple Dumpling Gang '75
The Shootist '76
The Bastard '78
The Cat from Outer Space '78
The Apple Dumpling Gang Rides Again '79
Backstairs at the White House '79
Roots: The Next Generation '79
Wild, Wild West Revisited '79
Agatha Christie's Sparkling Cyanide '83
M*A*S*H: Goodbye, Farewell & Amen '83
Dragnet '87
The Incident '89

Helen Morgan (1900-41)
Applause '29
Marie Galante '34
Go Into Your Dance '35
Show Boat '36

Jaye P. Morgan (1931-)
Night Patrol '85
Confessions of a Dangerous Mind '02 (C)

Jeffrey Dean Morgan (1966-)
Undercover '94
Six: The Mark Unleashed '04
Jam '06
Live! '07
P.S. I Love You '07
The Accidental Husband '08
Shanghai '09
Taking Woodstock '09
Watchmen '09
The Losers '10
The Resident '10
Peace, Love & Misunderstanding '11

Texas Killing Fields '11
The Courier '12
The Possession '12
The Salvation '14
Guns for Hire '15
Desierto '16
Solace '16
Rampage '18

Joseph Morgan (1981-)
Alexander '04
Ben Hur '10
Angels Crest '11
Immortals '11

Melissa Morgan (1926-2007)
See Liz Renay

Michael Morgan
The Gun That Won the West '55
Homework '82

Michele Morgan (1920-)
Joan of Paris '42
Heart of a Nation '43
Higher and Higher '44
Passage to Marseilles '44
The Chase '46
Fabiola '48
The Fallen Idol '49
The Lost Command '66
Bulworth '98
The Other Brother '02

Nancy Morgan (1949-)
Grand Theft Auto '77
Americathon '79
Backstairs at the White House '79
Pray TV '80
The Nest '88
Danielle Steel's Heartbeat '93
Lucky Luke '94

Ralph Morgan (1882-1956)
Strange Interlude '32
The Kennel Murder Case '33
The Power and the Glory '33
Rasputin and the Empress '33
Little Men '34
Condemned to Live '35
Magnificent Obsession '35
Little Miss Nobody '36
Speed '36
Mannequin '37
Out West With the Hardys '38
Fast and Loose '39
Adventure in Washington '41
Dick Tracy *vs.* Crime Inc. '41
Gang Busters '42
Klondike Fury '42
Night Monster '42
Enemy of Women '44
The Monster Maker '44
Black Market Babies '45
Song of the Thin Man '47

Rob Morgan
Mudbound '17
Monsters and Men '18
The Last Black Man in San Francisco '19

Shelley Taylor Morgan
My Tutor '82
Malibu Express '85

Stafford Morgan
The Alpha Incident '76
The Capture of Bigfoot '79

Terence Morgan (1921-2005)
Svengali '55
The Scamp '57
Tread Softly Stranger '58

Tracy Morgan (1968-)
A Thin Line Between Love and Hate '96
Half-Baked '97
30 Years to Life '01
Frank McKlusky, C.I. '02
Head of State '03
Are We There Yet? '05
The Longest Yard '05
Little Man '06

First Sunday '08
G-Force '09 (V)
Cop Out '10
Death at a Funeral '10
The Son of No One '11
Why Stop Now '12
Top Five '14
Fist Fight '17
The Clapper '18
What Men Want '19

Trevor Morgan (1986-)
Barney's Great Adventure '98
I'll Remember April '99
The Sixth Sense '99
A Rumor of Angels '00
The Glass House '01
Jurassic Park 3 '01
The Rookie '02
Uncle Nino '03
Mean Creek '04
The Prize Winner of Defiance, Ohio '05
Local Color '06
Chasing 3000 '07
Beneath the Dark '10
Brotherhood '10

Vanessa Morgan (1992-)
Frankie and Alice '10
Harriet the Spy: Blog Wars '10
Geek Charming '11
Pimp '18

Wendy Morgan
High Tide '80
The Mirror Crack'd '80
Edie '19

Maia Morgenstern (1962-)
Ulysses' Gaze '95
The Passion of the Christ '04

Stephanie Morgenstern (1965-)
The Sweet Hereafter '96
P.T. Barnum '99
Maelstrom '00

Masayuki Mori (1911-73)
The Idiot '51
Rashomon '51
Ugetsu '53
The Bad Sleep Well '60
When a Woman Ascends the Stairs '60
Bushido: The Cruel Code of the Samurai '63

Naoko Mori (1971-)
Spice World: The Movie '97
Lennon Naked '10

Cathy Moriarty (1960-)
Raging Bull '80
Neighbors '81
Kindergarten Cop '90
Soapdish '91
The Gun in Betty Lou's Handbag '92
The Mambo Kings '92
Matinee '92
Another Stakeout '93
Me and the Kid '93
Pontiac Moon '94
Runaway Daughters '94 (C)
Casper '95
Forget Paris '95
Foxfire '96
A Brother's Kiss '97
Cop Land '97
Dream with the Fishes '97
Hugo Pool '97
Digging to China '98
Gloria '98
P.U.N.K.S. '98
But I'm a Cheerleader '99
Crazy in Alabama '99
The Crimson Code '99
New Waterford Girl '99
Prince of Central Park '00
Analyze That '02
The Bounty Hunter '10
Once Upon a Time in Brooklyn '13
Patti Cake$ '17

Erin Moriarty
The Kings of Summer '13
Blood Father '16

The Miracle Season '18
Monster Party '18

James Moriarty
Someone to Watch Over Me '87
Ten Benny '98

Michael Moriarty (1941-)
Hickey & Boggs '72
Bang the Drum Slowly '73
The Last Detail '73
Report to the Commissioner '75
Holocaust '78
Who'll Stop the Rain? '78
The Winds of Kitty Hawk '78
Too Far to Go '79
Reborn '81
Q (The Winged Serpent) '82
Odd Birds '85
Pale Rider '85
The Stuff '85
Troll '86
Hanoi Hilton '87
It's Alive 3: Island of the Alive '87
Return to Salem's Lot '87
Nitti: The Enforcer '88
A Good Day to Die '95
Courage Under Fire '96
Shiloh '97
Woman Wanted '98
The Art of Murder '99
Shiloh 2: Shiloh Season '99
Cold Blooded '00
Out of Line '00
Along Came a Spider '01
James Dean '01
Mindstorm '01
Taken '02
Talking to Heaven '02
12 Hours to Live '06

P. H. Moriarty (1939-)
The Long Good Friday '80
Lock, Stock and 2 Smoking Barrels '98
Dune '00
Children of Dune '03
The Riddle '07

Tara Morice (1964-)
Strictly Ballroom '92
Metal Skin '94
Salem's Lot '04
Oranges and Sunshine '10

Philippe Morier-Genoud (1944-)
Confidentially Yours '83
Au Revoir les Enfants '87
Cyrano de Bergerac '90
Trois Couleurs: Blanc '94
Time Regained '99
Safe Conduct '01

Johnny Morina (1981-)
The Boys of St. Vincent '93
The Other Side of the Law '95
Kids of the Round Table '96
Home Team '98
Nico the Unicorn '98

Yoshiyuki Morishita
Wild Zero '00
The Happiness of the Katakuris '01

Patricia Morison (1915-)
Beyond the Blue Horizon '42
The Fallen Sparrow '43
Silver Skates '43
Where Are Your Children? '44
Without Love '45
Dressed to Kill '46
Song of the Thin Man '47
Tarzan and the Huntress '47
The Prince of Thieves '48
Song Without End '60

Alanis Morissette (1974-)
Dogma '99
Jay and Silent Bob Strike Back '01 (C)

Noriyuki 'Pat' Morita (1932-2005)
Thoroughly Modern Millie '67

The Shakiest Gun in the West '68
Evil Roy Slade '71
Cancel My Reservation '72
I Wonder Who's Killing Her Now? '76
Midway '76
For the Love of It '80
When Time Ran Out '80
The Karate Kid '84
The Vegas Strip Wars '84
Alice in Wonderland '85
Night Patrol '85
The Karate Kid: Part 2 '86
Captive Hearts '87
Collision Course '89
The Karate Kid: Part 3 '89
Lena's Holiday '90
Do or Die '91
Honeymoon in Vegas '92
Miracle Beach '92
Even Cowgirls Get the Blues '94
The Next Karate Kid '94
Timemaster '95
King Cobra '98
Mulan '98 (V)
Desert Heat '99
I'll Remember April '99
The Biggest Fan '02
Elvis Has Left the Building '04
Karate Dog '04
American Fusion '05
Down and Derby '05
18 Fingers of Death '05

Pat Morita
Mulan 2 '04 (V)
Ninja's Creed '09

Louisa Moritz (1946-)
Death Race 2000 '75
One Flew Over the Cuckoo's Nest '75
Six-Pack Annie '75
True Confessions '81
Last American Virgin '82
Chained Heat '83

Henning Moritzen (1928-2012)
Cries and Whispers '72
Sofie '92
The Celebration '98

Yuko Moriyama (1968-)
Zeram '91
Zeram 2 '94

Karen Morley (1909-2003)
Politics '31
Scarface '31
The Sin of Madelon Claudet '31
Are You Listening? '32
Flesh '32
The Mask of Fu Manchu '32
Mata Hari '32
The Phantom of Crestwood '32
Dinner at Eight '33
Gabriel Over the White House '33
Our Daily Bread '34
The Littlest Rebel '35
Healer '36
Framed '47

Robert Morley (1908-92)
Marie Antoinette '38
Major Barbara '41
I Live in Grosvenor Square '46
Ghosts of Berkeley Square '47
The Small Back Room '49
The African Queen '51
Beat the Devil '53
Beau Brummell '54
Quentin Durward '55
Around the World in 80 Days '56 (C)
The Doctor's Dilemma '58
The Journey '59
Libel '59
Ladies Who Do '63
Murder at the Gallop '63
Take Her, She's Mine '63
Hot Enough for June '64
Of Human Bondage '64
Topkapi '64

The Alphabet Murders '65
Genghis Khan '65
The Loved One '65
Those Magnificent Men in Their Flying Machines '65
A Study in Terror '66
Woman Times Seven '67
Hot Millions '68
Lola '69
Sinful Davey '69
Cromwell '70
When Eight Bells Toll '71
Theatre of Blood '73
Who Is Killing the Great Chefs of Europe? '78
The Human Factor '79
Oh, Heavenly Dog! '80
The Great Muppet Caper '81
High Road to China '83
Loophole '83
Second Time Lucky '84
Alice in Wonderland '85
The Wind '87
War & Remembrance '88
Around the World in 80 Days '89
The Lady and the Highwayman '89
War & Remembrance: The Final Chapter '89
A Troll in Central Park '94 (V)

Stanley Morner (1910-94)
See Dennis Morgan

Mike Moroff (1961-)
Angel Town '89
The Cage '89
The Wonderful Ice Cream Suit '98
My Little Assassin '99
The Crew '00
Three Bad Men '05

Michael Morra (1948-2001)
See Rockets Redglare

Geoff Morrell (1958-)
Marking Time '03
Rogue '07
Cloudstreet '11

Adrian Morris (1903-41)
Radio Patrol '37
Angels with Dirty Faces '38

Anita Morris (1944-94)
The Hotel New Hampshire '84
Maria's Lovers '84
Absolute Beginners '86
Blue City '86
Ruthless People '86
Aria '88
18 Again! '88
Bloodhounds of Broadway '89
A Sinful Life '89
Home for Christmas '93
Me and the Kid '93
Radioland Murders '94

Aubrey Morris (1930-2015)
Night Caller from Outer Space '66
A Clockwork Orange '71
Lisztomania '75
Lifeforce '85
She Creature '01

Barboura Morris (1932-75)
Teenage Doll '57
A Bucket of Blood '59
The Wasp Woman '59
Atlas '60
The Haunted Palace '63
X: The Man with X-Ray Eyes '63
The St. Valentine's Day Massacre '67
The Trip '67
The Dunwich Horror '70

Beth Morris (1949-)
Crucible of Terror '72
That'll Be the Day '73

Chester Morris (1901-70)
Alibi '29
The Bat Whispers '30
The Big House '30
The Divorcee '30

Corsair '31
Red Headed Woman '32
Blondie Johnson '33
Three Godfathers '36
Flight from Glory '37
Smashing the Rackets '38
Wagons Westward '40
No Hands on the Clock '41
Canal Zone '42
Wrecking Crew '42
Tornado '43
Gambler's Choice '44
The She-Creature '56
The Great White Hope '70

David Morris (1924-)
Charlie and the Chocolate Factory '05
Mr. Right '06

Dorothy Morris (1922-2011)
Seven Sweethearts '42
Bataan '43
Thirty Seconds Over Tokyo '44
Macabre '58

Garrett Morris (1937-)
Where's Poppa? '70
The Anderson Tapes '71
Cooley High '75
The Stuff '85
Motorama '91
Children of the Night '92
Almost Blue '93
Black Scorpion '95
Black Scorpion 2: Ground Zero '96
Twin Falls Idaho '99
Little Richard '00
Jackpot '01
The Salon '05
Dog Gone '08
Valley of the Sun '11

Greg Morris (1934-96)
Killer by Night '72
Vegas '78

Haviland (Haylie) Morris (1959-)
Sixteen Candles '84
Who's That Girl? '87
Gremlins 2: The New Batch '90
Larry McMurtry's Dead Man's Walk '96
Home Alone 3 '97
Rick '03
Cherry Crush '07

Howard Morris (1919-2005)
40 Pounds of Trouble '62
The Nutty Professor '63
High Anxiety '77
The Many Adventures of Winnie the Pooh '77 (V)
History of the World: Part 1 '81
The Munsters' Revenge '81
Portrait of a Showgirl '82
Splash '84
End of the Line '88
Life Stinks '91
Tom and Jerry: The Movie '93 (V)
The Wonderful Ice Cream Suit '98

Iona Morris (1957-)
Rain Without Thunder '93
Next Time '99

Jane Morris
Nothing in Common '86
Pretty Woman '90
Frankie and Johnny '91

Jeff Morris (1934-2004)
Kelly's Heroes '70
Payday '73
The Crossing Guard '94

John Morris (1984-)
Toy Story '95 (V)
Toy Story 2 '99 (V)
Toy Story 3 '10 (V)

Jonathan Morris (1960-)
The Fantasticks '95
Vampire Journals '96
Bloodstorm: Subspecies 4 '98

Judy Morris (1947-)
Plumber '79
Razorback '84

Julian Morris (1983-)
Whirlygirl '04
Cry Wolf '05
Donkey Punch '08
Sorority Row '09
Beyond '11
Dragonheart 3: The Sorcerer's Curse '15

Kathryn Morris (1969-)
Sleepstalker: The Sandman's Last Rites '94
Inherit the Wind '99
Hell Swarm '00
And Never Let Her Go '01
Minority Report '02
Mindhunters '05
Resurrecting the Champ '07
Assassination of a High School President '08
Cougars, Inc. '10
Moneyball '11
The Sweeter Side of Life '13
Bone Tomahawk '15
The Perfect Guy '15

Kirk Morris (1942-)
Maciste in Hell '60
Devil of the Desert Against the Son of Hercules '62
Hercules, Samson and Ulysses '64

Mary Morris (1915-88)
Victoria the Great '37
The Thief of Bagdad '40

Phil Morris (1959-)
Clay Pigeons '98
Devil in the Flesh '98
Incognito '99
Atlantis: The Lost Empire '01 (V)
Comic Book: The Movie '04 (C)
Bottoms Up '06
Meet the Spartans '08

Wayne Morris (1914-59)
Kid Galahad '37
Brother Rat '38
Brother Rat and a Baby '40
Flight Angels '40
The Smiling Ghost '41
Deep Valley '47
The Voice of the Turtle '47
John Loves Mary '48
A Kiss in the Dark '49
Task Force '49
The Bushwackers '52
The Fighting Lawman '53
Lonesome Trail '55
Lord of the Jungle '55
The Master Plan '55
Paths of Glory '57
Plunder Road '57

Ann Morrison
Close to My Heart '51
Battle Circus '53

James Morrison
The One '01
Seeds of Destruction '11

Jennifer (Jenny) Morrison (1979-)
Intersection '93
Stir of Echoes '99
Urban Legends 2: Final Cut '00
Big Shot: Confessions of a Campus Bookie '02
Grind '03
Surviving Christmas '04
Mr. & Mrs. Smith '05
Flourish '06
Big Stan '07
Star Trek '09
Table for Three '09
Bringing Ashley Home '11
Warrior '11
Alpha Alert '13
Some Girl(s) '13
The Darkness '16
SuperFly '18

William R. Moses (1959-)
Alien from L.A. '87
Mystic Pizza '88
Almost Dead '94
Fun '94
The Cold Equations '96
The Fiance '96
The Nurse '97
Emma's Wish '98
Wicked '98
Alone with a Stranger '99
Chain of Command '00
The Perfect Wife '00
75 Degrees '00
Christmas Child '03
Hangman's Curse '03
The Derby Stallion '05
The Sitter '07
Accused at 17 '09
We Have Your Husband '11

Nthati Moshesh (1969-)
Pride of Africa '97
Cape of Good Hope '04

Moni Moshonov (1951-)
Late Marriage '01
We Own the Night '07
Two Lovers '09
A Tale of Love and Darkness '16

Michael Mosley (1978-)
The Big Bad Swim '06
The Insurgents '06
Goodbye Baby '07
Room 314 '07
Hot Pursuit '15
A Crooked Somebody '18

Roger E. Mosley (1938-)
The Mack '73
The River Niger '76
The Greatest '77
Magnum P.I.: Don't Eat the Snow in Hawaii '80
Pray TV '80
Heart Condition '90
Zora Is My Name! '90
Unlawful Entry '92
Pentathlon '94
A Thin Line Between Love and Hate '96
Letters from a Killer '98

Arnold Moss (1910-89)
The Loves of Carmen '48
Border Incident '49
Reign of Terror '49
My Favorite Spy '51
Viva Zapata! '52
Jump Into Hell '55
The 27th Day '57

Carrie-Anne Moss (1967-)
The Soft Kill '94
Sabotage '96
The Matrix '99
New Blood '99
Chocolat '00
The Crew '00
Memento '00
Red Planet '00
The Matrix Reloaded '03
The Matrix Revolutions '03
Suspect Zero '04
The Chumscrubber '05
Fido '06
Snow Cake '06
Disturbia '07
Normal '07
Fireflies in the Garden '08
Love Hurts '09
Unthinkable '10
Silent Hill: Revelation 3D '12
Compulsion '13
Knife Fight '13
Pompeii '14
The Bye Bye Man '17

Colin Moss
The World Unseen '07
Holiday in the Wild '19

Cullen Moss (1981-)
Ball of Wax '03
Blood Done Sign My Name '10
Dear John '10
99 Homes '14

Elisabeth Moss (1982-)
Midnight's Child '93
Imaginary Crimes '94
Separate Lives '94
A Thousand Acres '97
Earthly Possessions '99
Girl, Interrupted '99
Mumford '99
Heart of America '03
The Missing '03
Virgin '03
The Attic '06
Day Zero '07
El Camino '08
Did You Hear About the Morgans? '09
Get Him to the Greek '10
Darling Companion '12
On the Road '12
Top of the Lake '13
Listen Up Philip '14
The One I Love '14
Meadowland '15
Queen of Earth '15
Truth '15
High-Rise '16
Chuck '17
The Square '17
The Seagull '18
Her Smell '19
The Kitchen '19
Us '19
The Invisible Man '20

Jesse Moss (1983-)
Ginger Snaps '01
Final Destination 3 '06
Partition '07
Mom, Dad and Her '08
Free Style '09
Merlin and the Book of Beasts '09
The Uninvited '09
Wild Cherry '09
Tucker & Dale *vs.* Evil '10
Seeds of Destruction '11
Extraterrestrial '14
Wolfcop '15

Stewart Moss (1937-)
In Harm's Way '65
Dr. Death, Seeker of Souls '73
The Bat People '74
Missiles of October '74

Tegan Moss (1985-)
Sea People '00
Video Voyeur: The Susan Wilson Story '02
Inspector Gadget's Biggest Caper Ever '05 (V)
Eight Days to Live '06
Seventeen and Missing '06
The Bad Son '07
Scar '07
NYC: Tornado Terror '08
7 Things to Do Before I'm 30 '08
The Unquiet '08
Dr. Dolittle: Million Dollar Mutts '09
Free Style '09
November Christmas '10

Ebon Moss-Bachrach (1978-)
Winter Solstice '04
The Lake House '06
Evening '07
American Virgin '09
Breaking Upwards '09
The Marc Pease Experience '09
Higher Ground '11
The Big Take '18

Ido Mosseri
You Don't Mess with the Zohan '08
Bucky Larson: Born to Be a Star '11

Donny Most (1953-)
Crazy Mama '75
EDtv '99
The Great Buck Howard '09
The Yankles '09

Josh Mostel (1946-)
The King of Marvin Gardens '72
Jesus Christ, Superstar '73
Harry and Tonto '74
Deadly Hero '75
Sophie's Choice '82
Star 80 '83
Almost You '85
The Money Pit '86
Matewan '87
Radio Days '87
Wall Street '87
Heavy Petting '89
City of Hope '91
City Slickers '91
Little Man Tate '91
The Chase '93
Billy Madison '94
City Slickers 2: The Legend of Curly's Gold '94
The Basketball Diaries '95
Great Expectations '97
Rounders '98
Big Daddy '99

Zero Mostel (1915-77)
Du Barry Was a Lady '43
Panic in the Streets '50
The Enforcer '51
Mr. Belvedere Rings the Bell '51
The Model and the Marriage Broker '51
Sirocco '51
A Funny Thing Happened on the Way to the Forum '66
The Producers '68
The Angel Levine '70
The Hot Rock '70
Marco '73
Once Upon a Scoundrel '73
Foreplay '75
The Front '76
Watership Down '78 (V)

Masahiro Motoki (1965-)
The Mystery of Rampo '94
Departures '08

Zeze Motta (1944-)
Quilombo '84
Tieta of Agreste '96
Orfeu '99

Greg Mottola (1964-)
Celebrity '98 (C)
Hollywood Ending '02

Anna Mouglalis (1978-)
Merci pour le Chocolat '00
Coco Chanel & Igor Stravinsky '09
Gainsbourg: A Heroic Life '10
Kiss of the Damned '12
Jealousy '13

John Moulder-Brown (1953-)
First Love '70
Vampire Circus '71
Killing Heat '84
Rumpelstiltskin '86

Anson Mount (1973-)
Tully '00
Urban Legends 2: Final Cut '00
City by the Sea '02
Crossroads '02
Poolhall Junkies '02
The Battle of Shaker Heights '03
In Her Shoes '05
All the Boys Love Mandy Lane '06
The Two Mr. Kissels '08
Last Night '10
Hick '11
Straw Dogs '11
Seal Team Six: The Raid on Osama Bin Laden '12
Non-Stop '14
The Forger '15
Mr. Right '16
Visions '16

Wagner Moura (1976-)
Carandiru '03
Elysium '13
Trash '14

Benjamin Mouton (1965-)
The Whole Wide World '96
All the Real Girls '03

Movita (1915-2015)
Mutiny on the Bounty '35
Captain Calamity '36
Panic in Echo Park '77

Alan Mowbray (1896-1969)
God's Gift to Women '31
The Man in Possession '31
Jewel Robbery '32
The Man From Yesterday '32
Her Secret '33
A Study in Scarlet '33
Charlie Chan in London '34
The Girl from Missouri '34
The Gay Deception '35
It Happened in New Orleans '36
Mary of Scotland '36
My Man Godfrey '36
Hollywood Hotel '37
On the Avenue '37
Stand-In '37
Merrily We Live '38
Never Say Die '39
Music in My Heart '40
I Wake Up Screaming '41
That Hamilton Woman '41
That Uncertain Feeling '41
The Villain Still Pursued Her '41
Panama Hattie '42
We Were Dancing '42
A Yank at Eton '42
Holy Matrimony '43
So This Is Washington '43
His Butler's Sister '44
My Darling Clementine '46
Captain from Castile '47
Lured '47
Merton of the Movies '47
The Prince of Thieves '48
Abbott and Costello Meet the Killer, Boris Karloff '49
My Dear Secretary '49
Ma and Pa Kettle at Home '54
The King's Thief '55
The King and I '56
A Majority of One '56
The Man Who Knew Too Much '56

Jack Mower (1890-1965)
Mystery Squadron '33
The Phantom of Santa Fe '36

Patrick Mower (1938-)
The Devil Rides Out '68
The Bloodsuckers '70
Cry of the Banshee '70
Catch Me a Spy '71
Carry On England '76

Tamera Mowry (1978-)
Seventeen Again '00
The Hot Chick '02
Twitches '05
Twitches Too '07
Double Wedding '10

Tia Mowry (1978-)
Seventeen Again '00
The Hot Chick '02
Twitches '05
Twitches Too '07
Double Wedding '10

Andrew Moxham (1976-)
Water's Edge '03
Black Mountain Side '16

Stephen Moyer (1969-)
Comic Act '98
Ultraviolet '98
Catherine Cookson's The Secret '00
Princess of Thieves '01
Uprising '01
Undiscovered '05
The Starter Wife '07
88 Minutes '08
Restraint '08
Open House '10
The Caller '11
The Double '11
Priest '11
The Barrens '12
Devil's Knot '14
Detour '17 (C)

Bridget Moynahan (1971-)
Coyote Ugly '00
In the Weeds '00
Serendipity '01
The Sum of All Fears '02
The Recruit '03
I, Robot '04
Lord of War '05
Gray Matters '06
Noise '07
Ramona and Beezus '10
Battle: Los Angeles '11
John Wick '14
The Journey Home '14
Small Time '14

Bobby Moynihan
When in Rome '09
Delivery Man '13

Dragomir Mrsic
Easy Money '10
Easy Money: Hard to Kill '12

David Mucci
Prom Night '80
Unforgiven '92

Leonard Mudie (1883-1965)
The Mummy '32
Charlie Chan's Murder Cruise '40
Elephant Stampede '51
African Treasure '52
Bomba and the Jungle Girl '52
Safari Drums '53
The Golden Idol '54
Killer Leopard '54
Lord of the Jungle '55
Timbuktu '59

Cookie Mueller (1949-89)
Pink Flamingos '72
Female Trouble '74
Desperate Living '77
Polyester '81

Maureen Mueller
The New Age '94
Oldest Confederate Widow Tells All '95
Larger Than Life '96

Armin Mueller-Stahl (1930-)
Jacob the Liar '74
Lola '81
Colonel Redl '84
Angry Harvest '85
Lethal Obsession '87
Midnight Cop '88
Music Box '89
Avalon '90
Night on Earth '91
The Power of One '92
The House of the Spirits '93
Holy Matrimony '94
A Pyromaniac's Love Story '95
Shine '95
Theodore Rex '95
The Ogre '96
The Game '97
In the Presence of Mine Enemies '97
The Peacemaker '97
The X-Files '98
Inferno '99
Jakob the Liar '99
The Third Miracle '99
The Thirteenth Floor '99
Jesus '00
The Story of an African Farm '04
Local Color '06
Eastern Promises '07
Angels & Demons '09
Attack on Leningrad '09
The International '09

Marianne Muellerleile (1948-)
Curse 2: The Bite '88
A Smile Like Yours '96
Return to Me '00

Ulrich Muhe (1953-2007)
Benny's Video '92
Funny Games '97
Straight Shooter '99
Amen '02

Anita (Yim-Fong) Mui (1963-2003)
A Better Tomorrow, Part 3 '89
Miracles '89
The Executioners '93
The Heroic Trio '93
The Legend of Drunken Master '94
Jet Li's The Enforcer '95
Rumble in the Bronx '96

Esther Muir (1903-95)
A Day at the Races '37
On Again-Off Again '37

Gavin Muir (1900-72)
Charlie Chan at the Race Track '36
Mary of Scotland '36
Passport to Suez '43
Sherlock Holmes Faces Death '43
House of Fear '45
Abbott and Costello Meet the Invisible Man '51
Thunder on the Hill '51
Island of Lost Women '59
Night Tide '61

Jean Muir (1911-96)
Oil for the Lamps of China '35
Orchids to You '35
The White Cockatoo '35
White Fang '36
The Lone Wolf Meets a Lady '40
The Constant Nymph '43

Oliver Muirhead (1947-)
The Duke '99
MVP: Most Valuable Primate '00
Like Crazy '11

Diana Muldaur (1938-)
The Other '72
McQ '74
Planet Earth '74

Patrick Muldoon (1968-)
Rage and Honor 2: Hostile Takeover '93
Starship Troopers '97
The Arrival 2 '98
Black Cat Run '98
Wicked '98
The Crimson Code '99
Stigmata '99
Chain of Command '00
Hell's Gate '01
Blackwoods '02
Project Viper '02
Whacked! '02
Heart of America '03
A Boyfriend for Christmas '04
Military Intelligence and You! '06
Miracle Dogs Too '06
Ice Spiders '07
Christmas Town '08
The Chaos Experiment '09
The 7 Adventures of Sinbad '10
Turbulent Skies '10
Born to Ride '11
Spiders '13
The Dog Who Saved Easter '15
The Dog Who Saved Summer '15
A Horse Tale '15
Robo-Dog '15

Rhys Muldoon (1965-)
Danny Deckchair '03
33 Postcards '11

Kate Mulgrew (1955-)
Lovespell '79
A Time for Miracles '80
The Manions of America '81
A Stranger Is Watching '82
Remo Williams: The Adventure Begins '85
Throw Momma from the Train '87
Roots: The Gift '88
Danielle Steel's Daddy '91
Camp Nowhere '94

Fuyuki Murakami (1911-2007)
Godzilla *'54*
Godzilla, King of the Monsters *'56*
Godzilla *vs.* Monster Zero *'68*

Katsumi Muramatsu
Ringu *'98*
Ringu 2 *'99*

Takehiro Murata (1960-)
Godzilla *vs.* Mothra *'92*
Okoge *'93*
Godzilla 2000 *'99*
When the Last Sword is Drawn *'02*

George Murcell (1925-98)
Year of the Gun *'91*
Cutthroat Island *'95*

Enrique Murciano (1973-)
Speed 2: Cruise Control *'97*
Traffic *'00*
Black Hawk Down *'01*
The Lost City *'05*
Miss Congeniality 2: Armed and Fabulous *'05*
How to Go Out on a Date in Queens *'06*
Marry Me *'10*
Dawn of the Planet of the Apes *'14*

Vince Murdocco (1966-)
Flesh Gordon 2: Flesh Gordon Meets the Cosmic Cheerleaders *'90*
Ring of Fire *'91*
Ring of Fire 2: Blood and Steel *'92*

George Murdock (1930-2012)
The Bravos *'72*
Breaker! Breaker! *'77*
Grand Tour: Disaster in Time *'92*
Firepower *'93*
Scorpio One *'97*
Spider's Web *'01*
Orange County *'02*
Serial Killing 101 *'04*

Jack Murdock (1922-2001)
Altered States *'80*
Rain Man *'88*

Tim Murdock
Thirty Seconds Over Tokyo *'44*
They Were Expendable *'45*

Caterina Murino (1977-)
Casino Royale *'06*
Hemingway's Garden of Eden *'08*
XIII *'08*
The Prey *'11*
Voice from the Stone *'17*

Christopher Murney (1943-)
The Last Dragon *'85*
Maximum Overdrive *'86*
Barton Fink *'91*

Peter Murnik (1965-)
Body Parts *'91*
Golden Gate *'93*
Andersonville *'95*
Rowing Through *'96*
Hard Rain *'97*

Aaron Murphy (1992-)
Rain *'01*
Boogeyman *'05*
The World's Fastest Indian *'05*

Annette Murphy (1967-)
Star Maps *'97*
Race *'99*

Audie Murphy (1924-71)
Kansas Raiders *'50*
Sierra *'50*
The Red Badge of Courage *'51*
Duel at Silver Creek *'52*
Drums Across the River *'54*
Ride Clear of Diablo *'54*
To Hell and Back *'55*
Night Passage *'57*
The Gun Runners *'58*
Ride a Crooked Trail *'58*
Cast a Long Shadow *'59*
No Name on the Bullet *'59*
The Unforgiven *'60*
Battle at Bloody Beach *'61*
Apache Rifles *'64*
Gunfight at Comanche Creek *'64*
The Quick Gun *'64*
Arizona Raiders *'65*
The Texican *'66*
40 Guns to Apache Pass *'67*

Ben Murphy (1942-)
1,000 Plane Raid *'69*
Time Walker *'82*
The Winds of War *'83*

Brittany Murphy (1977-2009)
Clueless *'95*
Freeway *'95*
Drive *'96*
The Prophecy 2: Ashtown *'97*
Bongwater *'98*
Phoenix *'98*
Zack & Reba *'98*
The Devil's Arithmetic *'99*
Drop Dead Gorgeous *'99*
Girl, Interrupted *'99*
Cherry Falls *'00*
Trixie *'00*
Don't Say a Word *'01*
Riding in Cars with Boys *'01*
Sidewalks of New York *'01*
Summer Catch *'01*
8 Mile *'02*
Spun *'02*
Good Boy! *'03 (V)*
Just Married *'03*
Uptown Girls *'03*
Little Black Book *'04*
Sin City *'05*
The Dead Girl *'06*
The Groomsmen *'06*
Happy Feet *'06 (V)*
Love and Other Disasters *'06*
The Ramen Girl *'08*
Across the Hall *'09*
Deadline *'09*
Megafault *'09*
Tribute *'09*
Abandoned *'10*

Charlie (Charles Q.) Murphy (1959-2017)
Harlem Nights *'89*
CB4: The Movie *'93*
King's Ransom *'05*
Roll Bounce *'05*
The Perfect Holiday *'07*
Unearthed *'07*
The Hustle *'08*
The Lottery Ticket *'10*

Cillian Murphy (1976-)
On the Edge *'00*
Disco Pigs *'01*
How Harry Became a Tree *'01*
28 Days Later *'02*
The Way We Live Now *'02*
Girl with a Pearl Earring *'03*
Intermission *'03*
Batman Begins *'05*
Breakfast on Pluto *'05*
Red Eye *'05*
The Wind That Shakes the Barley *'06*
Sunshine *'07*
Watching the Detectives *'07*
The Dark Knight *'08*
The Edge of Love *'08*
Peacock *'09*
Perrier's Bounty *'09*
Inception *'10*
In Time *'11*
Retreat *'11*
The Dark Knight Rises *'12*
Red Lights *'12*
Broken *'13*
Transcendence *'14*
In the Heart of the Sea *'15*
Anthropoid *'16*
Free Fire *'17*
The Party *'17*
Anna *'19*

Donald Murphy (1910-95)
Shack Out on 101 *'55*
Frankenstein's Daughter *'58*
Lord Love a Duck *'66*

Donna Murphy (1959-)
Star Trek: Insurrection *'98*
The Astronaut's Wife *'99*
Center Stage *'00*
The Last Debate *'00*
Spider-Man 2 *'04*
The Nanny Diaries *'07*
Sherman's Way *'08*
Tangled *'10 (V)*
Dark Horse *'11*
Higher Ground *'11*
House of Versace *'13*

Dwain Murphy
How She Move *'08*
Saving God *'08*

Eddie Murphy (1961-)
48 Hrs. *'82*
Trading Places *'83*
Best Defense *'84*
Beverly Hills Cop *'84*
The Golden Child *'86*
Beverly Hills Cop 2 *'87*
Coming to America *'88*
Harlem Nights *'89*
Another 48 Hrs. *'90*
Boomerang *'92*
The Distinguished Gentleman *'92*
Beverly Hills Cop 3 *'94*
Vampire in Brooklyn *'95*
Metro *'96*
The Nutty Professor *'96*
Dr. Dolittle *'98*
Holy Man *'98*
Mulan *'98 (V)*
Bowfinger *'99*
Life *'99*
Nutty Professor 2: The Klumps *'00*
Dr. Dolittle 2 *'01*
Shrek *'01 (V)*
The Adventures of Pluto Nash *'02*
I Spy *'02*
Showtime *'02*
Daddy Day Care *'03*
The Haunted Mansion *'03*
Shrek 2 *'04 (V)*
Dreamgirls *'06*
Norbit *'07*
Shrek the Third *'07 (V)*
Meet Dave *'08*
Imagine That *'09*
Shrek Forever After *'10 (V)*
Tower Heist *'11*
A Thousand Words *'12*
Mr. Church *'16*
Dolemite Is My Name *'19*

George Murphy (1902-92)
Kid Millions *'34*
Public Menace *'35*
Broadway Melody of 1938 *'37*
Letter of Introduction *'38*
Little Miss Broadway *'38*
Broadway Melody of 1940 *'40*
Little Nellie Kelly *'40*
Two Girls on Broadway *'40*
Ringside Maisie *'41*
Tom, Dick, and Harry *'41*
For Me and My Gal *'42*
The Mayor of 44th Street *'42*
Bataan *'43*
This Is the Army *'43*
Broadway Rhythm *'44*
Show Business *'44*
Step Lively *'44*
Up Goes Maisie *'46*
Cynthia *'47*
Tenth Avenue Angel *'47*
Battleground *'49*
Border Incident *'49*
It's a Big Country *'51*
Walk East on Beacon *'52*

Jack Murphy
Peter Pan *'24*
The Texas Streak *'26*

Johnny Murphy
The Commitments *'91*
War of the Buttons *'95*

Kim Murphy (1974-)
Houseguest *'94*
Campfire Tales *'98*
The In Crowd *'00*

Mary Murphy (1931-2011)
Carrie *'52*
Houdini *'53*
The Mad Magician *'54*
Sitting Bull *'54*
The Wild One *'54*
Desperate Hours *'55*
The Electronic Monster *'57*
Crime and Punishment, USA *'59*
40 Pounds of Trouble *'62*

Maurice Murphy (1913-78)
Faithless *'32*
Pilgrimage *'33*
Tailspin Tommy *'34*
Abe Lincoln in Illinois *'40*

Michael Murphy (1938-)
Double Trouble *'67*
Countdown *'68*
That Cold Day in the Park *'69*
Brewster McCloud *'70*
Count Yorga, Vampire *'70*
M*A*S*H *'70*
McCabe & Mrs. Miller *'71*
The Autobiography of Miss Jane Pittman *'74*
Phase 4 *'74*
Nashville *'75*
The Front *'76*
Great Bank Hoax *'78*
An Unmarried Woman *'78*
Manhattan *'79*
Strange Behavior *'81*
The Year of Living Dangerously *'82*
Cloak & Dagger *'84*
Mesmerized *'84*
Salvador *'86*
The Caine Mutiny Court Martial *'88*
Tanner '88 *'88*
Shocker *'89*
Batman Returns *'92*
Folks! *'92*
Clean Slate *'94*
Kansas City *'95*
Breaking the Surface: The Greg Louganis Story *'96*
The Day Reagan Was Shot *'01*
Footsteps *'03*
Live from Baghdad *'03*
Heights *'04*
Silver City *'04*
Tanner on Tanner *'04*
Away From Her *'06*
Playing House *'06*
X-Men: The Last Stand *'06*
According to Greta *'08*
The Trotsky *'09*
White House Down *'13*

Rosemary Murphy (1925-2014)
To Kill a Mockingbird *'62*
Any Wednesday *'66*
Walking Tall *'73*
Eleanor & Franklin *'76*
Julia *'77*
The Attic *'80*
For the Boys *'91*
The Tuskegee Airmen *'95*
Message in a Bottle *'98*
Dust *'01*

Timothy Murphy
Shallow Ground *'04*
National Treasure: Book of Secrets *'07*

Timothy V. Murphy
The Frankenstein Theory *'13*
Road to Paloma *'14*
Cuck *'19*

William Murphy
The Story of G.I. Joe *'45*
Sands of Iwo Jima *'49*

Barbara Murray (1929-2014)
Boys in Brown *'49*
Tony Draws a Horse *'51*
Another Man's Poison *'52*
The Frightened Man *'52*
Campbell's Kingdom *'57*
A Cry from the Streets *'57*
The Bretts *'88*

Beverly Murray
Cathy's Curse *'77*
The Carpenter *'89*

Bill Murray (1950-)
All You Need Is Cash *'78*
Meatballs *'79*
Mr. Mike's Mondo Video *'79*
Caddyshack *'80*
Where the Buffalo Roam *'80*
Stripes *'81*
Tootsie *'82*
Ghostbusters *'84*
The Razor's Edge *'84*
Little Shop of Horrors *'86*
Scrooged *'88*
Ghostbusters 2 *'89*
Quick Change *'90*
What about Bob? *'91*
Groundhog Day *'93*
Mad Dog and Glory *'93*
Ed Wood *'94*
Kingpin *'96*
Larger Than Life *'96*
Space Jam *'96*
The Man Who Knew Too Little *'97*
Rushmore *'98*
Wild Things *'98*
The Cradle Will Rock *'99*
Charlie's Angels *'00*
Hamlet *'00*
Osmosis Jones *'01*
The Royal Tenenbaums *'01*
Coffee and Cigarettes *'03 (C)*
Lost in Translation *'03*
Garfield: The Movie *'04 (V)*
The Life Aquatic with Steve Zissou *'04*
Broken Flowers *'05*
The Lost City *'05*
Garfield: A Tail of Two Kitties *'06 (V)*
City of Ember *'08*
Get Smart *'08*
Fantastic Mr. Fox *'09 (V)*
Get Low *'09*
The Limits of Control *'09*
Zombieland *'09*
Passion Play *'10*
A Glimpse Inside the Mind of Charles Swan III *'12*
Hyde Park on Hudson *'12*
Moonrise Kingdom *'12*
The Monuments Men *'13*
The Grand Budapest Hotel *'14 (C)*
Olive Kitteridge *'14*
St. Vincent *'14*
Aloha *'15*
Rock the Kasbah *'15*
The Jungle Book *'16*
Isle of Dogs *'18 (V)*
The Dead Don't Die *'19*

Billy Murray
Essex Boys *'99*
Dead Cert *'10*

Brian Murray (1937-)
Bob Roberts *'92*
Treasure Planet *'02 (V)*
Nearing Grace *'05*
My Dog Tulip *'09 (V)*
In the Family *'11*

Chad Michael Murray (1981-)
A Long Way Home *'01*
Freaky Friday *'03*
A Cinderella Story *'04*
House of Wax *'05*
Home of the Brave *'06*
Christmas Cupid *'10*
Fruitvale Station *'13*
The Haunting in Connecticut 2: Ghosts of Georgia *'13*
Tyler Perry's A Madea Christmas *'13*
Left Behind *'14*
To Write Love On Her Arms *'14*
Outlaws and Angels *'16*

Charles Murray (1872-1941)
The Wizard of Oz *'25*
Clancy in Wall Street *'30*

David Murray (1970-)
Veronica Guerin *'03*
Cowboys & Angels *'04*

Don Murray (1929-)
Bus Stop *'56*
A Hatful of Rain *'59*
One Foot in Hell *'60*
The Hoodlum Priest *'61*
Advise and Consent *'62*
One Man's Way *'63*
Baby, the Rain Must Fall *'64*
The Viking Queen *'67*
Conquest of the Planet of the Apes *'72*
Cotter *'72*
Deadly Hero *'75*
Endless Love *'81*
Justin Morgan Had a Horse *'81*
Return of the Rebels *'81*
I Am the Cheese *'83*
License to Kill *'84*
Peggy Sue Got Married *'86*
Scorpion *'86*
Made in Heaven *'87*

Doug Murray
Harriet the Spy: Blog Wars *'10*
Home Alone: The Holiday Heist *'12*

Duane Murray
Bugs *'03*
The Journey Home *'14*

Forbes Murray (1844-1982)
The Spider's Web *'38*
Leather Burners *'43*

Hannah Murray (1989-)
Chatroom *'10*
Womb *'10*
The Numbers Station *'13*
God Help the Girl *'14*
Lily & Kat *'15*

Jaime Murray (1977-)
Botched *'07*
The Deaths of Ian Stone *'07*
Fright Night 2: New Blood *'13*

James Murray (1901-36)
Frisco Jenny *'32*
Baby Face *'33*
Central Airport *'33*

James Murray (1975-)
All the King's Men *'99*
Under the Greenwood Tree *'05*

Jan Murray (1916-2006)
The Busy Body *'67*
Tarzan and the Great River *'67*
Thunder Alley *'67*
Which Way to the Front? *'70*
The Day of the Wolves *'71*
Banjo Hackett *'76*

Jillian Murray (1984-)
Forget Me Not *'09*
The Graves *'10*
Wild Things: Foursome *'10*
Cougar Hunting *'11*
The Squeeze *'15*

Joel Murray (1963-)
One Crazy Summer *'86*
Scrooged *'88*
The Cable Guy *'96*
Hatchet *'07*
God Bless America *'11*
Bloodsucking Bastards *'15*

John Murray
True Confession *'37*
Moving Violations *'85*

Ken Murray (1903-88)
The Marshal's Daughter *'53*
The Man Who Shot Liberty Valance *'62*
Follow Me, Boys! *'66*

Mae Murray (1889-1965)
A Mormon Maid *'17*
The Merry Widow *'25*

Rodion Nakhapetov
A Slave of Love *'78*
Border Blues *'03*

Laith Nakli (1969-)
Amira & Sam *'15*
The Wall *'17*

Reggie Nalder (1911-91)
Mark of the Devil *'69*
The Bird with the Crystal Plumage *'70*
Mark of the Devil 2 *'72*
Zoltan. . . Hound of Dracula *'78*
Salem's Lot *'79*

Nita Naldi (1897-1961)
Dr. Jekyll and Mr. Hyde *'20*
Blood and Sand *'22*
The Ten Commandments *'23*
Cobra *'25*
The Pleasure Garden *'25*

James Nam
The Heroic Ones *'70*
King Boxer *'72*

Leonardo Nam (1979-)
The Perfect Score *'04*
The Fast and the Furious: Tokyo Drift *'06*
Vantage Point *'08*
He's Just Not That Into You *'09*

Joe Namath (1943-)
C.C. & Company *'70*
Avalanche Express *'79*
Marriage Is Alive and Well *'80*

Yu Nan
Diamond Dogs *'07*
The Expendables 2 *'12*

Jack Nance (1943-96)
Breaker! Breaker! *'77*
Eraserhead *'78*
Dune *'84*
Ghoulies *'84*
Blue Velvet *'86*
Barfly *'87*
Colors *'88*
The Hot Spot *'90*
Wild at Heart *'90*
Motorama *'91*
Meatballs 4 *'92*
Across the Moon *'94*
The Demolitionist *'95*
Voodoo *'95*
Little Witches *'96*
Lost Highway *'96*
The Secret Agent Club *'96*

Kumail Nanjiani (1978-)
The Late Bloomer *'16*
The Big Sick *'17*
Fist Fight *'17*
Men in Black: International *'19*
Stuber *'19*
The Lovebirds *'20*

Isabelle Nanty (1962-)
Amelie *'01*
Cinderella *'12 (V)*

Sennia Nanua
The Girl with All the Gifts *'17*
Frankie *'19*

Igal Naor
Munich *'05*
Rendition *'07*
House of Saddam *'08*
300: Rise of an Empire *'13*
The Women's Balcony *'16*

Yigal Naor
Bonjour Monsieur Shlomi *'03*
The Infidel *'10*

Neriah Napaul (1972-)
The Bikini Car Wash Company *'90*
The Bikini Car Wash Company 2 *'92*

Alan Napier (1903-88)
The Secret Four *'39*
The House of the Seven Gables *'40*
Cat People *'42*
Action in Arabia *'44*
The Hairy Ape *'44*
Ministry of Fear *'44*
Thirty Seconds Over Tokyo *'44*
The Uninvited *'44*
Hangover Square *'45*
Isle of the Dead *'45*
House of Horrors *'46*
A Scandal in Paris *'46*
Three Strangers *'46*
Forever Amber *'47*
Lured *'47*
Criss Cross *'48*
Tarzan's Magic Fountain *'48*
Across the Wide Missouri *'51*
The Great Caruso *'51*
The Strange Door *'51*
Tarzan's Peril *'51*
The Mole People *'56*
Until They Sail *'57*
Island of Lost Women *'59*
Journey to the Center of the Earth *'59*
Wild in the Country *'61*
Premature Burial *'62*
The Sword in the Stone *'63 (V)*
Marnie *'64*
36 Hours *'64*
The Loved One *'65*
Batman *'66*
Come Die With Me *'75*
The Bastard *'78*

Charles Napier (1936-2011)
Beyond the Valley of the Dolls *'70*
Supervixens *'75*
Citizens Band *'77*
Last Embrace *'79*
The Blues Brothers *'80*
In Search of a Golden Sky *'84*
Rambo: First Blood, Part 2 *'85*
Something Wild *'86*
Night Stalker *'87*
The Incredible Hulk Returns *'88*
Married to the Mob *'88*
One Man Force *'89*
Ernest Goes to Jail *'90*
Future Zone *'90*
The Grifters *'90*
Miami Blues *'90*
The Silence of the Lambs *'91*
Center of the Web *'92*
Return to Frogtown *'92*
Body Shot *'93*
Raw Justice *'93*
Skeeter *'93*
Felony *'95*
Hard Justice *'95*
Jury Duty *'95*
3 Ninjas Knuckle Up *'95*
The Cable Guy *'96*
Riot *'96*
Austin Powers: International Man of Mystery *'97*
Hunter's Moon *'97*
Steel *'97*
Austin Powers 2: The Spy Who Shagged Me *'99*
The Big Tease *'99*
Cypress Edge *'99*
Nutty Professor 2: The Klumps *'00*
Extreme Honor *'01*
Dinocroc *'04*
Annapolis *'06*
The Goods: Live Hard, Sell Hard *'09*
Life Blood *'09*

Jessica Napier (1979-)
Love Serenade *'96*
Cut *'00*
The Alice *'04*

Marshall Napier
The Navigator *'88*
Strange Planet *'99*
Griff the Invisible *'10*

Russell Napier (1910-75)
Unholy Four *'54*
The Mark *'61*

Tony Nappo
Better Than Chocolate *'99*
Hank and Mike *'08*
The Dogfather *'10*

Tony Nardi (1958-)
Speaking Parts *'89*
Bonanno: A Godfather's Story *'99*

Daniela Nardini (1968-)
Reckless *'97*
Sirens *'02*

Tom Nardini (1945-)
Winter a Go-Go *'65*
Africa Texas Style *'67*

Kathrine Narducci (1965-)
A Bronx Tale *'93*
Two Family House *'99*
Cruise *'18*
Capone *'20*

Darling Narita
Bang *'95*
Pups *'99*

Mikio Narita
Zatoichi: The Blind Swordsman and the Chess Expert *'65*
Cops *vs.* Thugs *'75*

Nas (1973-)
See Nasir Jones

Nas (1973-)
See Nasir Jones

Arthur J. Nascarella (1944-)
Cop Land *'97*
Bringing Out the Dead *'99*
Wisegirls *'02*
The Cooler *'03*
Remedy *'05*
The Groomsmen *'06*
Running Scared *'06*

Paul Naschy (1934-2009)
Dracula *vs.* Frankenstein *'69*
The Fury of the Wolfman *'70*
The Werewolf *vs.* the Vampire Woman *'70*
Dr. Jekyll and the Wolfman *'71*
Dracula's Great Love *'72*
The Hanging Woman *'72*
Horror Rises from the Tomb *'72*
Vengeance of the Zombies *'72*
Curse of the Devil *'73*
The Rue Morgue Massacres *'73*
The Devil's Possessed *'74*
Exorcism *'74*
Inquisition *'76*
The Craving *'80*
Human Beasts *'80*

Chris Nash
Mischief *'85*
Silent Witness *'85*

Kevin Nash
DOA: Dead or Alive *'06*
Almighty Thor *'11*
Magic Mike XXL *'15*

Marilyn Nash (1926-2011)
The Rains Came *'39*
Monsieur Verdoux *'47*
Unknown World *'51*

Mary Nash (1885-1976)
Easy Living *'37*
Heidi *'37*
Charlie Chan in Panama *'40*
Gold Rush Maisie *'40*
The Philadelphia Story *'40*
Calling Dr. Gillespie *'42*
Cobra Woman *'44*
In the Meantime, Darling *'44*

Niecy Nash (1970-)
Cookie's Fortune *'99*
Guess Who *'05*
Code Name: The Cleaner *'07*
Reno 911! Miami *'07*
Not Easily Broken *'09*

Noreen Nash (1924-)
The Devil on Wheels *'47*
Phantom from Space *'53*

Kais Nashef
Paradise Now *'05*
American East *'07*

Danae Nason
Invasion of the Pod People *'07*
2012: Doomsday *'08*

Frank Nasso (1984-)
Prince of Central Park *'00*
Dot.Kill *'05*

Marie-Jose Nat (1940-2019)
Love and the Frenchwoman *'60*
Embassy *'72*

Adam Nathan
Parting Glances *'86*
I Was a Teenage TV Terrorist *'87*

Stephen Nathan (1948-)
1776 *'72*
The First Nudie Musical *'75*
You Light Up My Life *'77*

Louis Natheaux (1984-42)
Dress Parade *'27*
Weary River *'29*
Sinister Hands *'32*
Captain Calamity *'36*

Zoe Nathenson (1969-)
Those Glory, Glory Days *'83*
Mona Lisa *'86*
The Raggedy Rawney *'90*

Jonathan Nation
Death Racers *'08*
War of the Worlds 2: The Next Wave *'08*
Mega Shark Vs. Giant Octopus *'09*
6 Guns *'10*
All Hallow's Eve 2 *'15*

Francesca 'Kitten' Natividad (1948-)
Beneath the Valley of the Ultra-Vixens *'79*
My Tutor *'82*
Doin' Time *'85*
Eddie Presley *'92*
Night at the Golden Eagle *'02*

Yui Natsukawa (1968-)
Gonin 2 *'96*
When the Last Sword is Drawn *'02*
Hana: The Tale of a Reluctant Samurai *'07*

Mari Natsuki (1952-)
The Hunted *'94*
Samurai Fiction *'99*
Ping Pong *'02*

Yosuke Natsuki (1936-)
Dagora, the Space Monster *'65*
Ghidrah the Three Headed Monster *'65*

Isao Natsuyagi (1940-)
Goyokin *'69*
The Wolves *'82*

Mildred Natwick (1905-94)
The Long Voyage Home *'40*
The Enchanted Cottage *'45*
Yolanda and the Thief *'45*
The Kissing Bandit *'48*
Three Godfathers *'48*
She Wore a Yellow Ribbon *'49*
Cheaper by the Dozen *'50*
Against All Flags *'52*
The Quiet Man *'52*
The Trouble with Harry *'55*
The Court Jester *'56*
Teenage Rebel *'56*
Tammy and the Bachelor *'57*
Barefoot in the Park *'67*
If It's Tuesday, This Must Be Belgium *'69*
A House Without a Christmas Tree *'72*
Daisy Miller *'74*
You Can't Take It With You *'79*
Kiss Me Goodbye *'82*
Dangerous Liaisons *'88*

Myron Natwick
Project Vampire *'93*
DC 9/11: Time of Crisis *'04*
Shallow Ground *'04*
Ice Blues: A Donald Strachey Mystery *'08*

David Naughton (1951-)
Midnight Madness *'80*
An American Werewolf in London *'81*
Separate Ways *'82*
Hot Dog. . . The Movie! *'83*
Not for Publication *'84*
Boy in Blue *'86*
Amityville: A New Generation *'93*
Body Bags *'93*
Ice Cream Man *'95*
Mirror, Mirror 3: The Voyeur *'96*
A Crack in the Floor *'00*
Big Bad Wolf *'06*
Brutal Massacre: A Comedy *'07*
A Thousand Cuts *'12*

James Naughton (1945-)
The Paper Chase *'73*
A Stranger Is Watching *'82*
Between the Darkness and the Dawn *'85*
Cat's Eye *'85*
The Glass Menagerie *'87*
The Good Mother *'88*
Necessity *'88*
First Kid *'96*
The First Wives Club *'96*
Oxygen *'99*
The Truth About Jane *'00*
Fascination *'04*
The Devil Wears Prada *'06*
Factory Girl *'06*
Suburban Girl *'07*

Naturi Naughton (1984-)
Fame *'09*
Notorious *'09*
The Lottery Ticket *'10*

Demetrius Navarro
187 *'97*
The Wash *'01*
Purple Heart *'05*

John P. Navin, Jr. (1968-)
Taps *'81*
Losin' It *'82*

Borivoj Navratil (1933-)
The Girl of Your Dreams *'99*
Last Stand *'00*

Lola Naymark (1987-)
Monsieur Ibrahim *'03*
The Army of Crime *'10*

Alla Nazimova (1879-1945)
Escape *'40*
Blood and Sand *'41*
The Bridge of San Luis Rey *'44*
Since You Went Away *'44*

Amedeo Nazzari (1907-79)
Chains *'49*
Nobody's Children *'52*
The White Angel *'55*
Nights of Cabiria *'57*
Journey Beneath the Desert *'61*
Nefertiti, Queen of the Nile *'64*
The Valachi Papers *'72*

Ne-Yo (1979-)
Stomp the Yard *'07*
Battle: Los Angeles *'11*
Red Tails *'12*

Anna Neagle (1904-86)
Bitter Sweet *'33*
Victoria the Great *'37*
Sixty Glorious Years *'38*
Nurse Edith Cavell *'39*
Irene *'40*
No, No Nanette *'40*
Sunny *'41*
Forever and a Day *'43*
I Live in Grosvenor Square *'46*
Spring in Park Lane *'48*
The Lady With the Lamp *'51*
Derby Day *'52*
Let's Make Up *'55*
The Lady Is a Square *'58*
Teenage Bad Girl *'59*

Billie Neal (1955-99)
Down by Law *'86*
Mortal Thoughts *'91*
Consenting Adults *'92*

Diane Neal (1976-)
Dracula 2: Ascension *'03*
Dracula 3: Legacy *'05*
My Fake Fiance *'09*

Dylan Neal (1969-)
Prom Night 3: The Last Kiss *'89*
The President's Man *'00*
Landspeed *'01*
40 Days and 40 Nights *'02*
Chupacabra Terror *'05*
Vampire Bats *'05*
Cradle of Lies *'06*
No Brother of Mine *'07*
Storm Seekers *'08*
The Traveler *'10*
He Loves Me *'11*
Fifty Shades of Grey *'15*

Edwin Neal (1945-)
The Texas Chainsaw Massacre *'74*
Future Kill *'85*

Elise Neal (1966-)
Rosewood *'96*
Def Jam's How to Be a Player *'97*
Money Talks *'97*
Scream 2 *'97*
Restaurant *'98*
Mission to Mars *'00*
Brian's Song *'01*
Paid in Full *'02*
The Rising Place *'02*
Hustle & Flow *'05*
The Perfect Man *'11*
Aaliyah: The Princess of R&B *'14*

Patricia Neal (1926-2010)
John Loves Mary *'48*
The Fountainhead *'49*
The Breaking Point *'50*
Bright Leaf *'50*
Three Secrets *'50*
The Day the Earth Stood Still *'51*
Raton Pass *'51*
Diplomatic Courier *'52*
Something for the Birds *'52*
Stranger from Venus *'54*
A Face in the Crowd *'57*
Breakfast at Tiffany's *'61*
Hud *'63*
Psyche 59 *'64*
In Harm's Way *'65*
The Subject Was Roses *'68*
Homecoming: A Christmas Story *'71*
The Night Digger *'71*
Love Affair: The Eleanor & Lou Gehrig Story *'77*
The Bastard *'78*
All Quiet on the Western Front *'79*
The Passage *'79*
Ghost Story *'81*
An Unremarkable Life *'89*
Heidi *'93*
Cookie's Fortune *'99*
Flying By *'09*

Rome Neal
Hamlet *'00*
Pinero *'01*

Tom Neal (1914-72)
Andy Hardy Meets Debutante *'40*
Courageous Dr. Christian *'40*
There's Something About a Soldier *'43*
Detour *'46*
My Dog Shep *'46*
Great Jesse James Raid *'49*

Mohawk '56
Pardners '56
Outlaw's Son '57
The Pied Piper of Hamelin '57
Untamed Youth '57

Novella Nelson (1939-)
Manny & Lo '96
Mercy '96
A Perfect Murder '98
Antwone Fisher '02
Dear Wendy '05
Preaching to the Choir '05
The Inheritance '10

Ozzie Nelson (1906-75)
Big Street '42
People Are Funny '46
The Impossible Years '68

Peter Gill Nelson
V '83
Eye of the Eagle 3 '91

Portia Nelson (1921-2001)
The Sound of Music '65
The Other '72

Ricky Nelson (1940-85)
The Story of Three Loves '53
Rio Bravo '59
Wackiest Ship in the Army '61
The Over-the-Hill Gang '69

Ruth Nelson (1905-92)
Wilson '44
Humoresque '46
The Sea of Grass '47
3 Women '77
A Christmas Without Snow '80
The Haunting Passion '83

Sandra Nelson (1962-)
Life as a House '01
De-Lovely '04

Sean Nelson (1980-)
Fresh '94
American Buffalo '95
A Stranger in the Kingdom '98
The Wood '99
The Corner '00
My Effortless Brilliance '08
The Freebie '10
Stake Land '10

Tim Blake Nelson (1964-)
The Thin Red Line '98
O Brother Where Art Thou? '00
Cherish '02
The Good Girl '02
Minority Report '02
Holes '03
2 Brothers & a Bride '03
Wonderland '03
The Last Shot '04
Meet the Fockers '04
Scooby-Doo 2: Monsters Unleashed '04
The Big White '05
The Moguls '05
Syriana '05
Come Early Morning '06
The Darwin Awards '06
Fido '06
Hoot '06
The Astronaut Farmer '07
The Incredible Hulk '08
American Violet '09
Leaves of Grass '09
Saint John of Las Vegas '09
Flypaper '11
Yelling to the Sky '11
Big Miracle '12
Detachment '12
Lincoln '12
Snake & Mongoose '13
Child of God '14
Kill the Messenger '14
The Ballad of Buster Scruggs '18
Just Mercy '19

Tommy Nelson
And Then Came Love '07
Meek's Cutoff '10

Tracy Nelson (1963-)
Yours, Mine & Ours '68
Maria's Lovers '84
Down and Out in Beverly Hills '86
Kate's Secret '86
The Night Caller '97
Perfect Tenant '99
Perfect Game '00
The Perfect Nanny '00
Killer Bees '02
A Grandpa for Christmas '07
Deadly Shift '08

Willie Nelson (1933-)
The Electric Horseman '79
Honeysuckle Rose '80
Thief '81
Barbarosa '82
Songwriter '84
Amazons '86
Last Days of Frank & Jesse James '86
Stagecoach '86
Texas Guns '90
Another Pair of Aces: Three of a Kind '91
Gone Fishin' '97
Half-Baked '97
Wag the Dog '97
Outlaw Justice '98
Austin Powers 2: The Spy Who Shagged Me '99 (C)
The Big Bounce '04
The Dukes of Hazzard '05
The Dukes of Hazzard: The Beginning '06
Blonde Ambition '07
Fighting with Anger '07
Beer for My Horses '08
Surfer, Dude '08
Angels Sing '13

Corin 'Corky' Nemec (1971-)
Tucker: The Man and His Dream '88
I Know My First Name Is Steven '89
Solar Crisis '92
Drop Zone '94
Stephen King's The Stand '94
White Wolves 2: Legend of the Wild '94
Operation Dumbo Drop '95
The War at Home '96
The First to Go '97
Killer Bud '00
Brother's Keeper '02
Mosquito Man '05
The Boston Strangler: The Untold Story '08
Bundy: A Legacy of Evil '08
Cop Dog '08
National Lampoon Presents RoboDoc '08
Sea Beast '08
House of Bones '09
Dragon Wasps '12
Rise of the Dinosaurs '13

Neil Nephew (1939-78)
Mad Dog Coll '61
The Young Savages '61
Panic in Year Zero! '62

Francesca Neri (1964-)
Flight of the Innocent '93
Outrage '93
Live Flesh '97
Hannibal '01
Collateral Damage '02

Rosalba Neri (1939-)
Hercules and the Black Pirate '60
Conquest of Mycene '63
The Lion of Thebes '64
Three Avengers '64
Johnny Yuma '66
The Castle of Fu Manchu '68
Amuck! '71
Slaughter Hotel '71
Lady Frankenstein '72
The Arena '73
Devil's Wedding Night '73

David Nerman
The Scorpio Factor '90
Witchboard 3: The Possession '95
The Minion '98
The Witness Files '00
Nightwaves '03

Franco Nero (1941-)
The War of the Planets '65
Wild, Wild Planet '65
The Bible '66
Texas, Adios '66
Camelot '67
Man, Pride and Vengeance '67
Django '68
Battle of Neretva '69
A Quiet Place in the Country '69
Ring of Death '69
Companeros '70
The Virgin and the Gypsy '70
Confessions of a Police Captain '72
Fifth Day of Peace '72
Street Law '74
How to Kill a Judge '75
Legend of Valentino '75
21 Hours at Munich '76
Last Four Days '77
Force 10 from Navarone '78
Shark Hunter '79
The Man with Bogart's Face '80
Enter the Ninja '81
The Salamander '82
Querelle '83
Day of the Cobra '84
The Last Days of Pompeii '84
Wagner: The Complete Epic '85
Challenge to White Fang '86
Django Strikes Again '87
Die Hard 2: Die Harder '90
Young Catherine '91
The Innocent Sleep '95
Talk of Angels '96
David '97
The Painted Lady '97
Letters to Juliet '10
Django Unchained '12

Toni Nero
Silent Night, Deadly Night '84
No Dead Heroes '87

Caroline Neron (1973-)
Strip Search '97
Eternal '04
Rise of the Gargoyles '09

Cathleen Nesbitt (1888-1982)
The Passing of the Third Floor Back '35
Nicholas Nickleby '46
Man of Evil '48
Black Widow '54
Desiree '54
An Affair to Remember '57
Separate Tables '58
The Parent Trap '61
Villain '71
Family Plot '76

Derren Nesbitt (1935-)
Victim '61
Kill or Cure '62
The Blue Max '66
Where Eagles Dare '68
Horrors of Burke & Hare '71
Innocent Bystanders '72
Not Now Darling '73

James Nesbitt (1965-)
Welcome to Sarajevo '97
Waking Ned Devine '98
Bloody Sunday '01
Lucky Break '01
Match Point '05
Millions '05
Jekyll '07
Five Minutes of Heaven '09
The Way '10
Coriolanus '11

Alex Nesic (1976-)
Sleeper Cell '05
From Mexico With Love '09

Michael Nesmith (1942-)
Head '68
Tapeheads '89

Ottola Nesmith (1889-1972)
Return of the Vampire '43
Witness for the Prosecution '57

Loni Nest (1915-2008)
The Golem '20
Joyless Street '25

Lois Nettleton (1927-2008)
Period of Adjustment '62
Mail Order Bride '63
The Bamboo Saucer '68
The Good Guys and the Bad Guys '69
The Man in the Glass Booth '75
Washington: Behind Closed Doors '77
Centennial '78
Deadly Blessing '81
The Best Little Whorehouse in Texas '82
Butterfly '82
Soggy Bottom U.S.A. '84
Brass '85
Mirror, Mirror 2: Raven Dance '94
The Christmas Card '06

Alex Neuberger (1992-)
Running Scared '06
Underdog '07

Martin Neufeld
Relative Fear '95
Silent Night '02

Dorothy Neumann (1912-94)
The Undead '57
The Ghost of Dragstrip Hollow '59
The Terror '63
Get Yourself a College Girl '64
Private Parts '72

Jenny Neumann
Hell Night '81
Delos Adventure '86

Alex Neustaedter
Ithaca '16
Walking Out '17
A-X-L '18
Low Tide '19

Thierry Neuvic (1970-)
Code Unknown '00
Hereafter '10

Bebe Neuwirth (1958-)
Say Anything '89
Green Card '90
Bugsy '91
Malice '93
Wild Palms '93
All Dogs Go to Heaven 2 '95 (V)
Jumanji '95
The Adventures of Pinocchio '96
The Associate '96
Celebrity '98
The Faculty '98
Liberty Heights '99
Summer of Sam '99
Cupid & Cate '00
Tadpole '02
How to Lose a Guy in 10 Days '03
Le Divorce '03
The Big Bounce '04
Game 6 '05
Adopt a Sailor '08
Fame '09

Chantal Neuwirth
A Very Long Engagement '04
Gabrielle '05

Suzanne Neve (1939-)
Naked Evil '66
Portrait of a Lady '67
Mosquito Squadron '70

Aaron Neville (1941-)
Zandalee '91
Posse '93 (C)
The Last Ride '94

John Neville (1925-2011)
Billy Budd '62
A Study in Terror '66
The Adventures of Baron Munchausen '89
Journey to the Center of the Earth '93
Baby's Day Out '94
Little Women '94
The Road to Wellville '94
Dangerous Minds '95
Sabotage '96
Behind the Lines '97
The Fifth Element '97
My Teacher Ate My Homework '98
Urban Legend '98
The X-Files '98
The Duke '99
Goodbye, Lover '99
Sunshine '99
Spider '02
Hollywood North '03
Moving Malcolm '03
The Statement '03
Separate Lies '05

Brooke Nevin (1982-)
Running Wild '99
Too Cool for Christmas '04
A Daughter's Conviction '06
The Comebacks '07
Sherman's Way '08
Come Dance at My Wedding '09
Infestation '09

Robyn Nevin (1942-)
The Chant of Jimmie Blacksmith '78
The Irishman '78
Careful, He Might Hear You '84
Resistance '92
The Matrix Revolutions '03
Top of the Lake '13

Claudette Nevins (1937-)
The Mask '61
The Possessed '77
More Than Friends '78
. . .All the Marbles '81
Tuff Turf '85
Sleeping with the Enemy '91
Sweet Evil '95
Star Trek: Insurrection '98

Alexander Nevsky (1971-)
Red Serpent '02
Moscow Heat '04
Treasure Raiders '07
Magic Man '10
Maximum Impact '18

Derek Newark (1933-98)
The Blue Max '66
The Offence '73
Bellman and True '88

George Newbern (1964-)
Adventures in Babysitting '87
Switching Channels '88
Doppelganger: The Evil Within '90
Father of the Bride '91
Father of the Bride Part 2 '95
The Evening Star '96
Friends & Lovers '99
The Simple Life of Noah Dearborn '99
If These Walls Could Talk 2 '00
Crazy Eights '06
What Comes Around '06
A Dennis the Menace Christmas '07
Fireflies in the Garden '08
Saw 6 '09
Santa Paws 2: The Santa Pups '12

William 'Billy' Newell (1894-1967)
Sitting On the Moon '36
The Mandarin Mystery '37
Escape from Fort Bravo '53

Bob Newhart (1929-)
Hell Is for Heroes '62
Hot Millions '68
Catch-22 '70
On a Clear Day You Can See Forever '70
Cold Turkey '71
The Rescuers '77 (V)
First Family '80
Little Miss Marker '80
Marathon '80
The Rescuers Down Under '90 (V)
In and Out '97
Elf '03
Legally Blonde 2: Red White & Blonde '03
The Librarian: Quest for the Spear '04
The Librarian: Return to King Solomon's Mines '06
The Librarian: Curse of the Judas Chalice '08
Five '11

Jamison Newlander (1970-)
The Lost Boys '87
Lost Boys: The Thirst '10

Anthony Newlands (1926-95)
Circus of Fear '67
Scream and Scream Again '70

Anthony Newley (1931-99)
Oliver Twist '48
Those People Next Door '52
Above Us the Waves '55
X The Unknown '56
Fire Down Below '57
The Lady Is a Square '58
Idol on Parade '59
Doctor Dolittle '67
Sweet November '68
It Seemed Like a Good Idea at the Time '75
Alice in Wonderland '85
Stagecoach '86
The Garbage Pail Kids Movie '87

Alec Newman (1974-)
Catherine Cookson's The Rag Nymph '96
Dr. Bell and Mr. Doyle: The Dark Beginnings of Sherlock Holmes '00
Dune '00
Children of Dune '03
Four Corners of Suburbia '05
The Gene Generation '07
Moonlight Serenade '09
A Lonely Place to Die '11

Barry Newman (1938-)
Vanishing Point '71
Amy '81
Daylight '96
Brown's Requiem '98
Bowfinger '99
Goodbye, Lover '99
The Limey '99
Good Advice '01
True Blue '01
40 Days and 40 Nights '02
What the #$*! Do We Know? '04
Grilled '06

Daniel Newman (1981-)
Shopping '93
Riddler's Moon '98
Endgame '01
Children of the Corn '09
Road Trip: Beer Pong '09

Jaime Ray Newman (1978-)
Under the Mistletoe '06
Sex and Breakfast '07
Altered Minds '13

Laraine Newman (1952-)
Tunnelvision '76
Mr. Mike's Mondo Video '79
Wholly Moses! '80
Perfect '85
Invaders from Mars '86
Problem Child 2 '91

Denise Nickerson (1957-2019)
Willy Wonka & the Chocolate Factory *'71*
Smile *'75*

Michael A. (M.A.) Nickles (1968-)
Hamburger Hill *'87*
Wayne's World 2 *'93*
Baja *'95*
Desert Winds *'95*

Sarah Nicklin
Beyond the Dunwich Horror *'08*
Nun of That *'09*

Julia Nickson-Soul (1958-)
Rambo: First Blood, Part 2 *'85*
Glitch! *'88*
Noble House *'88*
Around the World in 80 Days *'89*
The Chinatown Murders: Man against the Mob *'89*
China Cry *'91*
K2: The Ultimate High *'92*
Amityville: A New Generation *'93*
Double Dragon *'94*
White Tiger *'95*
Life Tastes Good *'99*
Dim Sum Funeral *'08*

Alex Nicol (1919-2001)
Tomahawk *'51*
Law and Order *'53*
The Redhead from Wyoming *'53*
Black Glove *'54*
Dawn at Socorro *'54*
The Man from Laramie *'55*
Sincerely Yours *'55*
Look in Any Window *'61*
A Matter of WHO *'62*
A*P*E* *'76*

Danielle Nicolet
Ticking Clock *'10*
Red Faction: Origins *'11*
Believe *'16*
Central Intelligence *'16*

Jackson Nicoll (2003-)
The Fighter *'10*
Fun Size *'12*
Jackass Presents: Bad Grandpa *'13*

Daria Nicolodi (1950-)
Deep Red: Hatchet Murders *'75*
Shock *'79*
Unsane *'82*
Creepers *'85*
Macaroni *'85*
Opera *'88*
Scarlet Diva *'00*
Mother of Tears *'08*

Michael Nicolosi
Dream a Little Dream 2 *'94*
Things to Do in Denver When You're Dead *'95*
Persons Unknown *'96*
Hell's Kitchen NYC *'97*

Niko Nicotera
Blackbeard *'06*
The Curse of King Tut's Tomb *'06*

Lachlan Nieboer (1981-)
Into the White *'12*
Identicals *'16*

Brigitte Nielsen (1963-)
Red Sonja *'85*
Rocky 4 *'85*
Cobra *'86*
Beverly Hills Cop 2 *'87*
Bye Bye Baby *'88*
Chained Heat 2 *'92*
Body Count *'95*
Snowboard Academy *'96*
Doomsdayer *'00*

Connie Nielsen (1965-)
The Devil's Advocate *'97*
Rushmore *'98*
Soldier *'98*
Gladiator *'00*
Innocents *'00*
Mission to Mars *'00*
Demonlover *'02*
One Hour Photo *'02*
Basic *'03*
The Hunted *'03*
Brothers *'04*
Convicted *'04*
The Great Raid *'05*
The Ice Harvest *'05*
Battle in Seattle *'07*
A Shine of Rainbows *'09*
Perfect Sense *'11*
Return to Zero *'14*
3 Days to Kill *'14*
The Runner *'15*
Wonder Woman *'17*

Hans Nielsen (1911-65)
Sherlock Holmes and the Deadly Necklace *'62*
Strangler of Blackmoor Castle *'63*

Leslie Nielsen (1926-2010)
Forbidden Planet *'56*
The Opposite Sex *'56*
Ransom! *'56*
Tammy and the Bachelor *'57*
The Sheepman *'58*
Harlow *'65*
Counterpoint *'67*
Gunfight in Abilene *'67*
The Reluctant Astronaut *'67*
Four Rode Out *'69*
How to Commit Marriage *'69*
Resurrection of Zachary Wheeler *'71*
They Call It Murder *'71*
Day of the Animals *'77*
Project: Kill! *'77*
Sixth and Main *'77*
Viva Knievel *'77*
Backstairs at the White House *'79*
Cave-In! *'79*
Airplane! *'80*
Prom Night *'80*
Spaceship *'81*
Creepshow *'82*
Foxfire Light *'82*
Wrong Is Right *'82*
The Night the Bridge Fell Down *'83*
The Patriot *'86*
Soul Man *'86*
Nuts *'87*
Dangerous Curves *'88*
The Naked Gun: From the Files of Police Squad *'88*
Repossessed *'90*
All I Want for Christmas *'91*
Naked Gun 2 1/2: The Smell of Fear *'91*
Surf Ninjas *'93*
Naked Gun 33 1/3: The Final Insult *'94*
Dracula: Dead and Loving It *'95*
Spy Hard *'96*
Mr. Magoo *'97*
Wrongfully Accused *'98*
Camouflage *'00*
2001: A Space Travesty *'00*
Chilly Dogs *'01*
Men with Brooms *'02*
Scary Movie 3 *'03*
Scary Movie 4 *'06*
An American Carol *'08*
Superhero Movie *'08*
Stan Helsing *'09*

Benny Nieves
Double Take *'01*
Lost Treasure *'03*

Joe Nieves
Gamers *'06*
Sun Choke *'16*

Anjul Nigam (1965-)
The First $20 Million is Always the Hardest *'02*
Bad Words *'13*
Growing Up Smith *'17*

Jane Nigh (1925-93)
Operation Haylift *'50*
Fort Osage *'51*

Rebecca Night
Fanny Hill *'07*
Wuthering Heights *'09*

Bill Nighy (1949-)
Agatha Christie's Thirteen at Dinner *'85*
The Phantom of the Opera *'89*
Being Human *'94*
Alive and Kicking *'96*
FairyTale: A True Story *'97*
Still Crazy *'98*
Blow Dry *'00*
Longitude *'00*
Lawless Heart *'01*
Lucky Break *'01*
AKA *'02*
I Capture the Castle *'02*
Love Actually *'03*
State of Play *'03*
Underworld *'03*
He Knew He Was Right *'04*
Shaun of the Dead *'04*
The Constant Gardener *'05*
Doogal *'05 (V)*
Gideon's Daughter *'05*
The Girl in the Cafe *'05*
The Hitchhiker's Guide to the Galaxy *'05*
Underworld: Evolution *'05*
Alex Rider: Operation Stormbreaker *'06*
Flushed Away *'06 (V)*
Notes on a Scandal *'06*
Pirates of the Caribbean: Dead Man's Chest *'06*
Hot Fuzz *'07*
Pirates of the Caribbean: At World's End *'07*
Valkyrie *'08*
Astro Boy *'09 (V)*
G-Force *'09*
Glorious 39 *'09*
Pirate Radio *'09*
Underworld: Rise of the Lycans *'09*
Harry Potter and the Deathly Hallows, Part 1 *'10*
Wild Target *'10*
Arthur Christmas *'11 (V)*
Chalet Girls *'11*
Harry Potter and the Deathly Hallows, Part 2 *'11*
Page Eight *'11*
Rango *'11 (V)*
The Best Exotic Marigold Hotel *'12*
Total Recall *'12*
Wrath of the Titans *'12*
About Time *'13*
I, Frankenstein *'13*
Jack the Giant Slayer *'13*
Pride *'14*
The Second Best Exotic Marigold Hotel *'15*
Dad's Army *'16*
Norm of the North *'16*
Their Finest *'17*
The Bookshop *'18*
Pokémon Detective Pikachu *'19*
Sometimes Always Never *'19*
Emma *'20*
Hope Gap *'20*

Mary Nighy (1984-)
Marie Antoinette *'06*
Tormented *'09*

Esko Nikkari (1938-2006)
The Winter War *'89*
The Match Factory Girl *'90*

Jan Niklas (1947-)
Colonel Redl *'84*
Anastasia: The Mystery of Anna *'86*
The Rose Garden *'89*
The House of the Spirits *'93*
Plain Truth *'04*

Valery (Valeri Nikolayev) Nikolaev (1965-)
Aberration *'97*
The Saint *'97*
U-Turn *'97*
The Terminal *'04*

Tony Nikolakopoulos
Head On *'98*
Criminal Ways *'03*

Anna Q. Nilsson (1888-1974)
Regeneration *'15*
The Toll Gate *'20*

Inger Nilsson (1959-)
Pippi Goes on Board *'69*
Pippi Longstocking *'69*
Pippi in the South Seas *'70*
Pippi on the Run *'70*

Maj-Britt Nilsson (1924-2006)
Summer Interlude *'50*
To Joy *'50*
Secrets of Women *'52*

Derek Nimmo (1930-99)
Coast of Skeletons *'63*
One of Our Dinosaurs Is Missing *'75*

Leonard Nimoy (1931-2015)
Rhubarb *'51*
Kid Monk Baroni *'52*
Zombies of the Stratosphere *'52*
Them! *'54*
The Balcony *'63*
Catlow *'71*
Baffled *'72*
Invasion of the Body Snatchers *'78*
Star Trek: The Motion Picture *'79*
Star Trek 2: The Wrath of Khan *'82*
A Woman Called Golda *'82*
Star Trek 3: The Search for Spock *'84*
Star Trek 4: The Voyage Home *'86*
Transformers: The Movie *'86 (V)*
Star Trek 5: The Final Frontier *'89*
Never Forget *'91*
Star Trek 6: The Undiscovered Country *'91*
The Pagemaster *'94 (V)*
David *'97*
Brave New World *'98*
Atlantis: The Lost Empire *'01 (V)*
Star Trek *'09*
Transformers: Dark of the Moon *'11 (V)*
Adventures in Zambezia *'12*

Chaicham Nimpulsawasdi
The Iron Ladies *'00*
The Iron Ladies 2 *'03*

Najwa Nimri (1972-)
Open Your Eyes *'97*
Lovers of the Arctic Circle *'98*
Before Night Falls *'00*
Sex and Lucia *'01*
The Method *'05*

Pierre Niney (1989-)
Black Heaven *'10*
Romantics Anonymous *'10*
Frantz *'17*

Yvette Nipar (1964-)
Run If You Can *'87*
Ski Patrol *'89*
Doctor Mordrid: Master of the Unknown *'90*
Submerged *'00*
Black Horizon *'01*
Kept *'01*

Joe Nipote
Casper *'95 (V)*
Soul's Midnight *'06*

Naomi Nishida (1972-)
Godzilla 2000 *'99*
The Happiness of the Katakuris *'01*

Toshiyuki Nishida (1947-)
The Ramen Girl *'08*
A Letter to Momo *'11 (V)*
Emperor *'12*

Hidetoshi Nishijima (1971-)
Dolls *'02*
Black House *'07*
The Wind Rises *'13 (V)*
Creepy *'16*

Ko Nishimura
Yojimbo *'61*
Legends of the Poisonous Seductress 2: Quick Draw Okatsu *'69*
Lady Snowblood *'73*

Ronald Nitschke (1950-)
The Innocent *'93*
Sons of Trinity *'95*

Barbara Niven (1953-)
Hired to Kill *'91*
Lone Tiger *'94*
Psycho Cop 2 *'94*
Depraved *'98*
Alone with a Stranger *'99*
Serial Killing 101 *'04*
Back to You and Me *'05*
Stranger in My Bed *'05*
Double Cross *'06*
Redline *'07*
A Valentine Carol *'07*
Moonlight & Mistletoe *'08*
Accused at 17 *'09*
Summer's Moon *'09*
A Perfect Ending *'12*

David Niven (1909-83)
Barbary Coast *'35*
The Charge of the Light Brigade *'36*
Dodsworth *'36*
Rose Marie *'36*
Dinner at the Ritz *'37*
Prisoner of Zenda *'37*
Bluebeard's Eighth Wife *'38*
Dawn Patrol *'38*
Four Men and a Prayer *'38*
Three Blind Mice *'38*
Bachelor Mother *'39*
Eternally Yours *'39*
Raffles *'39*
The Real Glory *'39*
Wuthering Heights *'39*
Spitfire *'42*
Immortal Battalion *'44*
The Way Ahead *'44*
Magnificent Doll *'46*
Stairway to Heaven *'46*
The Bishop's Wife *'47*
The Other Love *'47*
Enchantment *'48*
A Kiss in the Dark *'49*
The Toast of New Orleans *'50*
Appointment With Venus *'51*
Happy Go Lovely *'51*
The Lady Says No *'51*
The Moon Is Blue *'53*
The King's Thief *'55*
Around the World in 80 Days *'56*
Birds & the Bees *'56*
Bonjour Tristesse *'57*
My Man Godfrey *'57*
Oh, Men! Oh, Women! *'57*
Separate Tables *'58*
Please Don't Eat the Daisies *'60*
The Guns of Navarone *'61*
Guns of Darkness *'62*
Bedtime Story *'63*
55 Days at Peking *'63*
The Pink Panther *'64*
Lady L *'65*
Where the Spies Are *'65*
Casino Royale *'67*
Eye of the Devil *'67*
The Impossible Years *'68*
Before Winter Comes *'69*
The Brain *'69*
Murder by Death *'76*
No Deposit, No Return *'76*
Candleshoe *'78*
Death on the Nile *'78*
The Big Scam *'79*
Escape to Athena *'79*
Sea Wolves *'81*
Trail of the Pink Panther *'82*
Curse of the Pink Panther *'83*

Kip Niven (1945-)
Magnum Force *'73*
Midway *'76*

Alessandro Nivola (1972-)
Face/Off *'97*
Best Laid Plans *'99*
Mansfield Park *'99*
Love's Labour's Lost *'00*
Time Code *'00*
Jurassic Park 3 *'01*
Laurel Canyon *'02*
Carolina *'03*
The Clearing *'04*
Junebug *'05*
The Sisters *'05*
The Darwin Awards *'06*
Goal! The Dream Begins *'06*
The Company *'07*
Goal 2: Living the Dream *'07*
Grace Is Gone *'07*
The Eye *'08*
$5 a Day *'08*
Who Do You Love *'08*
Coco Before Chanel *'09*
Howl *'10*
Janie Jones *'10*
American Hustle *'13*
Ginger & Rosa *'13*
Devil's Knot *'14*
A Most Violent Year *'14*
Disobedience *'17*
The Art of Self-Defense *'19*

Tommy Nix
Roadracers *'94*
Sin City *'05*

Allan Nixon (1920-95)
Prehistoric Women *'50*
Mesa of Lost Women *'52*

Cynthia Nixon (1966-)
I Am the Cheese *'83*
Amadeus *'84*
The Manhattan Project *'86*
Tanner '88 *'88*
Let It Ride *'89*
Marvin's Room *'96*
Igby Goes Down *'02*
Tanner on Tanner *'04*
Little Manhattan *'05*
One Last Thing *'05*
The Babysitters *'07*
Lymelife *'08*
Sex and the City: The Movie *'08*
An Englishman in New York *'09*
Sex and the City 2 *'10*
Rampart *'11*
5 Flights Up *'15*
James White *'15*
The Only Living Boy in New York *'17*
A Quiet Passion *'17*

Derek Lee Nixon
Outrage Born in Terror *'09*
The Jerk Theory *'11*

DeVaughn Nixon
The Bodyguard *'92*
Prom *'11*

Kimberly Nixon (1985-)
Angus, Thongs and Perfect Snogging *'08*
Cranford *'08*
Easy Virtue *'08*
Wild Child *'08*
Black Death *'10*

Marion (Marian) Nixon (1904-83)
Say It With Songs *'29*
After Tomorrow *'32*
Too Busy to Work *'32*
Winner Take All *'32*
Chance at Heaven *'33*
Doctor Bull *'33*
Pilgrimage *'33*
Strictly Dynamite *'34*
Sweepstake Annie *'35*
Captain Calamity *'36*
The Drag-Net *'36'*
The Reckless Way *'36*

Marni Nixon (1930-)
The Sound of Music *'65*
I Think I Do *'97*
Mulan *'98 (V)*

Mojo Nixon (1956-)
Rock 'n' Roll High School Forever '91
Super Mario Bros. '93
Stephanie Niznik (1967-2019)
Epoch '00
Spiders 2: Breeding Ground '01
Kenneth Nkosi
Tsotsi '05
White Wedding '10
Keith Nobbs (1979-)
Phone Booth '02
The Pacific '10
Weakness '10
Chelsea Noble (1964-)
Instant Karma '90
The Growing Pains Movie '00
Left Behind: The Movie '00
Growing Pains: Return of the Seavers '04
Christian Noble (1961-)
Illegal Affairs '96
Human Desires '97
James Noble (1922-)
Dempsey '83
When the Bough Breaks '86
Chances Are '89
John Noble (1948-)
The Monkey's Mask '00
Lord of the Rings: The Return of the King '03
One Night with the King '06
Running Scared '06
Superman: Unbound '13 (V)
Nancy Lee Noble
Just for the Hell of It '68
She-Devils on Wheels '68
Ray Noble (1907-78)
A Damsel in Distress '37
Here We Go Again! '42
Bernard Noel (1926-70)
The Fire Within '64
Une Femme Mariee '64
A Married Woman '65
Chris Noel (1941-)
Get Yourself a College Girl '64
The Glory Stompers '67
The Tormentors '71
Magali Noel (1932-2015)
Elena and Her Men '56
La Dolce Vita '60
Amarcord '74
Les Rendez-vous D'Anna '78
Ulrich Noethen (1959-)
The Harmonists '99
Downfall '04
Yumiko Nogawa (1944-)
Gate of Flesh '64
Zatoichi: The Blind Swordsman and the Fugitives '68
The Sea is Watching '02
Natalija Nogulich (1950-)
Sister, Sister '87
The Guardian '90
Homicide '91
Hoffa '92
Confessions of Sorority Girls '94
Jean Pierre Noher (1956-)
Valentin '02
From Beginning to End '09
Philippe Noiret (1930-2006)
Zazie dans le Metro '61
Lady L '65
Night of the Generals '67
Woman Times Seven '67
The Assassination Bureau '69
Justine '69
Topaz '69
Murphy's War '71
The Holes '72
The Clockmaker '73
La Grande Bouffe '73
Night Flight from Moscow '73
The Desert of the Tartars '76
Who Is Killing the Great Chefs of Europe? '78
Three Brothers '80
Coup de Torchon '81
Fort Saganne '84
Cinema Paradiso '88
Life and Nothing But '89
I Don't Kiss '91
Grosse Fatigue '94
The Postman '94
Revenge of the Musketeers '94
On Guard! '03
Bob Nolan (1908-80)
Lights of Old Santa Fe '47
Melody Time '48 (V)
Doris Nolan (1916-98)
Holiday '38
Follies Girl '43
Jeannette Nolan (1911-98)
Abandoned '47
Saddle Tramp '47
Macbeth '48
No Sad Songs For Me '50
Hangman's Knot '52
A Lawless Street '55
Seventh Cavalry '56
Tribute to a Bad Man '56
April Love '57
The Halliday Brand '57
Psycho '60 (V)
The Man Who Shot Liberty Valance '62
My Blood Runs Cold '65
The Reluctant Astronaut '67
Babe! '75
The Rescuers '77 (V)
The Awakening Land '78
The Manitou '78
The Fox and the Hound '81 (V)
Cloak & Dagger '84
The Horse Whisperer '97
John Nolan (1933-2000)
The Terror '79
Following '99
Kathleen Nolan (1933-)
The Iron Sheriff '57
No Time to Be Young '57
Amy '81
Lloyd Nolan (1902-85)
'G' Men '35
Big Brown Eyes '36
The Texas Rangers '36
Internes Can't Take Money '37
Every Day's a Holiday '38
House Across the Bay '40
Johnny Apollo '40
The Man I Married '40
Michael Shayne: Private Detective '40
Blues in the Night '41
Sleepers West '41
Blue, White and Perfect '42
Just Off Broadway '42
Bataan '43
Guadalcanal Diary '43
House on 92nd Street '45
A Tree Grows in Brooklyn '45
Lady in the Lake '46
Somewhere in the Night '46
Two Smart People '46
The Street with No Name '48
Easy Living '49
The Sun Comes Up '49
The Lemon Drop Kid '51
Island in the Sky '53
The Last Hunt '56
Santiago '56
Toward the Unknown '56
Peyton Place '57
A Hatful of Rain '59
Girl of the Night '60
Portrait in Black '60
Susan Slade '61
The Girl Hunters '63
Circus World '64
Never Too Late '65
An American Dream '66
The Double Man '67
Ice Station Zebra '68
Airport '70
Earthquake '74
My Boys Are Good Boys '78
It Came Upon a Midnight Clear '84
Hannah and Her Sisters '86
Tom Nolan (1948-)
School Spirit '85
Voyage of the Rock Aliens '87
Amaury Nolasco (1970-)
Mr. 3000 '04
The Benchwarmers '06
Transformers '07
Max Payne '08
Street Kings '08
Armored '09
Prison Break: The Final Break '09
The Rum Diary '11
A Good Day to Die Hard '13
In the Blood '13
Small Time '14
Michelle Nolden
Cybermutt '02
Men with Brooms '02
Rudy: The Rudy Giulani Story '03
Show Me '04
All Hat '07
Would Be Kings '08
The Time Traveler's Wife '09
Come Dance With Me '12
Haunter '13
Jacques Nolot (1943-)
I Don't Kiss '91
Nenette and Boni '96
Artemisia '97
Under the Sand '00
Before I Forget '07
Nick Nolte (1941-)
The California Kid '74
Death Sentence '74
Winter Kill '74
Rich Man, Poor Man '76
The Deep '77
Who'll Stop the Rain? '78
North Dallas Forty '79
Heart Beat '80
Cannery Row '82
48 Hrs. '82
Under Fire '83
Teachers '84
Down and Out in Beverly Hills '86
Extreme Prejudice '87
Farewell to the King '89
New York Stories '89
Three Fugitives '89
Another 48 Hrs. '90
Everybody Wins '90
Q & A '90
Cape Fear '91
The Prince of Tides '91
Lorenzo's Oil '92
The Player '92
I'll Do Anything '93
Blue Chips '94
I Love Trouble '94
Jefferson in Paris '94
Mulholland Falls '95
Mother Night '96
Nightwatch '96
Affliction '97
Afterglow '97
U-Turn '97
Breakfast of Champions '98
The Thin Red Line '98
Simpatico '99
The Golden Bowl '00
Trixie '00
Intimate Affairs '01
The Good Thief '03
Hulk '03
Northfork '03
The Beautiful Country '04
Clean '04
Hotel Rwanda '04
A Few Days in September '06
Over the Hedge '06 (V)
Paris, je t'aime '06
Peaceful Warrior '06
Chicago 10 '07 (V)
The Mysteries of Pittsburgh '08
The Spiderwick Chronicles '08 (V)
Tropic Thunder '08
Cats & Dogs: The Revenge of Kitty Galore '10
My Own Love Song '10
Arthur '11
Warrior '11
Zookeeper '11 (V)
Gangster Squad '13
Hateship Loveship '13
Parker '13
The Trials of Cate McCall '13
Noah '14
Return to Sender '15
A Walk in the Woods '15
The Padre '18
Eugene Nomura
Azumi 2 '05
Genghis Khan: To the Ends of the Earth and Sea '07
Hironobu Nomura (1965-)
Flower & Snake '04
Executive Koala '06
Mansai Nomura (1966-)
Onmyoji '01
Onmyoji 2 '03
The Wind Rises '13 (V)
Takashi Nomura
Ran '85
Suicide Club '02
John Ford Noonan (1943-)
Adventures in Babysitting '87
Flirting with Disaster '96
Kelly Noonan
Border Lost '08
iCrime '11
Beneath '13
Road to Paloma '14
Tom Noonan (1951-)
Wolfen '81
The Man with One Red Shoe '85
Manhunter '86
The Monster Squad '87
Mystery Train '89
RoboCop 2 '90
Last Action Hero '93
What Happened Was. . . '94
Heat '95
The Wife '95
Phoenix '98
The Astronaut's Wife '99
The Pledge '00
Knockaround Guys '01
Eight Legged Freaks '02
Seraphim Falls '06
Snow Angels '07
The Alphabet Killer '08
Synecdoche, New York '08
The House of the Devil '09
Anomalisa '16
Wonderstruck '17
Tommy Noonan (1921-68)
Jungle Patrol '48
Adam's Rib '50
Return of Jesse James '50
Gentlemen Prefer Blondes '53
A Star Is Born '54
Violent Saturday '55
The Ambassador's Daughter '56
The Rookie '59
Promises! Promises! '63
Three Nuts in Search of a Bolt '64
Nora-Jane Noone (1984-)
The Magdalene Sisters '02
The Descent '05
Legend of the Bog '08
Identicals '16
Peter Noone
Hold On! '66
Mrs. Brown, You've Got a Lovely Daughter '68
Ghita Norby (1935-)
The Inheritance '76
Babette's Feast '87 (N)
The Best Intentions '92
Sofie '92
The Kingdom '95
Like It Never Was Before '95
Hamsun '96
The Kingdom 2 '97
Everlasting Moments '08
O'Horten '09
Jauja '14
Jeffrey Nordling (1962-)
And the Band Played On '93 (C)
Journey to the Center of the Earth '93
Holy Matrimony '94
A Stranger in Town '95
D3: The Mighty Ducks '96
True Women '97
Turbulence 2: Fear of Flying '99
Just Ask My Children '01
Wilderness Love '02
Flicka '06
Surfer, Dude '08
Love Hurts '09
Mrs. Washington Goes to Smith '09
Carsten Norgaard (1963-)
Red Shoe Diaries 6: How I Met My Husband '95
Alien vs. Predator '04
Eduardo Noriega (1916-2007)
Seven Cities of Gold '55
Tarzan and the Valley of Gold '65
The In-Laws '79
Zorro, the Gay Blade '81
Eduardo Noriega (1973-)
Open Your Eyes '97
Burnt Money '00
The Devil's Backbone '01
The Method '05
Transsiberian '08
Vantage Point '08
The Last Stand '13
Sweetwater '13
Beauty and the Beast '14
Felix Noriego (1930-)
Battle Cry '55
To Hell and Back '55
Lucille Norman (1921-98)
Painting the Clouds With Sunshine '51
Carson City '52
Maidie Norman (1913-98)
Bright Road '53
What Ever Happened to Baby Jane? '62
Sixteen '72
Susan Norman
Poison '91
Safe '95
Zack Norman
Tracks '76
Sitting Ducks '80
Romancing the Stone '84
Cadillac Man '90
Venice, Venice '92
Babyfever '94
Festival at Cannes '02
Mabel Normand (1894-1930)
Tillie's Punctured Romance '14
Mickey '17
Extra Girl '23
David Norona (1972-)
Mrs. Santa Claus '96
Twisted '96
Though None Go With Me '06
Aaron Norris (1951-)
Overkill '96
The Cutter '05
Bruce Norris (1960-)
A Civil Action '98
The Sixth Sense '99
Chuck Norris (1940-)
Return of the Dragon '73
The Student Teachers '73
Breaker! Breaker! '77
Good Guys Wear Black '78
Force of One '79
Game of Death '79
Octagon '80
An Eye for an Eye '81
Forced Vengeance '82
Silent Rage '82
Lone Wolf McQuade '83
Missing in Action '84
Code of Silence '85
Invasion U.S.A. '85
Missing in Action 2: The Beginning '85
Delta Force '86
Firewalker '86
Braddock: Missing in Action 3 '88
Hero and the Terror '88
Delta Force 2: Operation Stranglehold '90
The Hitman '91
Walker: Texas Ranger: One Riot, One Ranger '93
Hellbound '94
Forest Warrior '95
Top Dog '95
Logan's War: Bound by Honor '98
The President's Man '00
The President's Man 2: A Line in the Sand '02
Dodgeball: A True Underdog Story '04 (C)
The Cutter '05
The Expendables 2 '12
Dean Norris (1963-)
Hard to Kill '89
Lethal Weapon 2 '89
The Lawnmower Man '92
Starship Troopers '97
Without Limits '97
My Little Assassin '99
The Cell '00
Three Strikes '00
Linewatch '08
How Do You Know '10
The Frozen Ground '13
Men, Women & Children '14
Small Time '14
Remember '15
Secret in Their Eyes '15
The Book of Henry '17
Beirut '18
Death Wish '18
Scary Stories to Tell in the Dark '19
Edward Norris (1911-2002)
They Won't Forget '37
The Lady in Question '40
Road Show '41
The Man with Two Lives '42
Career Girl '44
Men On Her Mind '44
Decoy '46
Inside the Walls of Folsom Prison '51
Hermione Norris (1968-)
Born Romantic '00
Separate Lies '05
Mike Norris (1962-)
Born American '86
Delta Force 3: The Killing Game '91
Death Ring '93
Carnival of Wolves '96
Delta Force One-The Lost Patrol '99
Marilyn Norry
The Bad Son '07
Beyond the Black Rainbow '10
Alan North (1920-2000)
Billy Galvin '86
Highlander '86
Glory '89
Lean on Me '89
Crazy People '90
The Jerky Boys '95
I'll Take You There '99
Jay North (1952-)
Zebra in the Kitchen '65
The Teacher '74

J.J. North (1964-)
Vampire Vixens from Venus *'94*
Attack of the 60-Foot Centerfold *'95*
Hellblock 13 *'97*
Psycho Sisters *'98*

Robert North
The Green Years *'46*
Blades *'89*

Sheree North (1933-2005)
No Down Payment *'57*
In Love and War *'58*
Destination Inner Space *'66*
Then Came Bronson *'68*
The Gypsy Moths *'69*
The Trouble with Girls (and How to Get into It) *'69*
Lawman *'71*
The Organization *'71*
Charley Varrick *'73*
Winter Kill *'74*
Breakout *'75*
The Shootist *'76*
Telefon *'77*
Maniac Cop *'88*
Cold Dog Soup *'89*
Defenseless *'91*
Dying to Get Rich *'98*

Ted North (1916-75)
Chad Hanna *'40*
Thunder Birds *'42*
Men On Her Mind *'44*
The Unsuspected *'47*

Jeremy Northam (1961-)
Emily Bronte's Wuthering Heights *'92*
Carrington *'95*
The Net *'95*
A Village Affair *'95*
Emma *'96*
Mimic *'97*
Gloria *'98*
The Winslow Boy *'98*
Happy, Texas *'99*
An Ideal Husband *'99*
The Golden Bowl *'00*
Enigma *'01*
Gosford Park *'01*
Cypher *'02*
Possession *'02*
The Singing Detective *'03*
The Statement *'03*
Bobby Jones: Stroke of Genius *'04*
Tristram Shandy: A Cock and Bull Story *'05*
The Invasion *'07*
Dean Spanley *'08*
Creation *'09*
Glorious 39 *'09*
Eye in the Sky *'15*
Our Kind of Traitor *'16*

Ryan Northcott (1980-)
Mystery, Alaska *'99*
Ripper: Letter from Hell *'01*

Michael P. Northey
Return to Cabin by the Lake *'01*
Killer Bees *'02*

Alex Norton (1950-)
Gregory's Girl *'80*
Hidden City *'87*
Squanto: A Warrior's Tale *'94*
Orphans *'97*
Beautiful Creatures *'00*
The Count of Monte Cristo *'02*
Pirates of the Caribbean: Dead Man's Chest *'06*

Barry Norton (1909-56)
Dishonored *'31*
Dracula Spanish Version *'31*
Captain Calamity *'36*
Devil Monster *'46*

Edgar Norton (1868-1953)
The Love Parade *'29*
The Lady Refuses *'31*
Dr. Jekyll and Mr. Hyde *'32*
Thirty Day Princess *'34*
Son of Frankenstein *'39*

Edward Norton (1969-)
Everyone Says I Love You *'96*
The People *vs.* Larry Flynt *'96*
Primal Fear *'96*
American History X *'98*
Rounders *'98*
Fight Club *'99*
Keeping the Faith *'00*
The Score *'01*
Death to Smoochy *'02*
Frida *'02*
Red Dragon *'02*
25th Hour *'02*
The Italian Job *'03*
Down in the Valley *'05*
Kingdom of Heaven *'05*
The Illusionist *'06*
The Painted Veil *'06*
The Incredible Hulk *'08*
Pride and Glory *'08*
The Invention of Lying *'09*
Leaves of Grass *'09*
Stone *'10*
The Bourne Legacy *'12*
Moonrise Kingdom *'12*
Birdman, or (The Unexpected Virtue of Ignorance) *'14*
The Grand Budapest Hotel *'14*
Collateral Beauty *'16*
Isle of Dogs *'18 (V)*
Motherless Brooklyn *'19*

Jack Norton (1889-1958)
Finishing School *'33*
The Bank Dick *'40*

James Norton
Cheerful Weather for the Wedding *'12*
Belle *'13*

James Norton (1985-)
Death Comes to Pemberley *'13*
Northman: A Viking Saga *'15*
Flatliners *'17*
Hampstead *'19*

Jim Norton (1938-)
Hidden Agenda *'90*
Memoirs of an Invisible Man *'92*
Midnight's Child *'93*
Conspiracy of Silence *'03*
Driving Lessons *'06*
The Boy in the Striped Pajamas *'08*
The Eclipse *'09*
The Boy *'16*

Ken Norton (1943-2013)
Mandingo *'75*
Drum *'76*
Oceans of Fire *'86*
Dirty Work *'97*
The Man Who Came Back *'08*

Richard Norton (1950-)
Gymkata *'85*
The Millionaire's Express *'86*
China O'Brien *'88*
Hyper Space *'89*
Lady Dragon *'92*
Rage and Honor *'92*
Raiders of the Sun *'92*
Cyber-Tracker *'93*
Direct Hit *'93*
Rage and Honor 2: Hostile Takeover *'93*
Under the Gun *'95*
Black Thunder *'98*
Mr. Nice Guy *'98*
Nautilus *'99*
Amazons and Gladiators *'01*

Brandy Norwood (1979-)
Cinderella *'97*
I Still Know What You Did Last Summer *'98*
Double Platinum *'99*
Osmosis Jones *'01 (V)*
Tyler Perry's Temptation: Confessions of a Marriage Counselor *'13*

Desiree Nosbuch
Killer Deal *'99*
Contaminated Man *'00*

Jack Noseworthy (1969-)
Encino Man *'92*
Alive *'93*
S.F.W. *'94*
The Brady Bunch Movie *'95*
Barb Wire *'96*
Breakdown *'96*
Event Horizon *'97*
Idle Hands *'99*
Murder at Devil's Glen *'99*
Cecil B. Demented *'00*
U-571 *'00*
Undercover Brother *'02*
Unconditional Love *'03*
Poster Boy *'04*
Phat Girlz *'06*
A Dennis the Menace Christmas *'07*
Aces 'n Eights *'08*
Pretty Ugly People *'08*
Surrogates *'09*
Killing Kennedy *'13*

Ralph Nossek (1923-2011)
Chicago Joe & the Showgirl *'90*
Citizen X *'95*
My Life in Ruins *'09*

Chris Noth (1954-)
Smithereens *'82*
Baby Boom *'87*
Where Are My Children? *'94*
Burnzy's Last Call *'95*
Cold Around the Heart *'97*
Rough Riders *'97*
The Confession *'98*
A Texas Funeral *'99*
Cast Away *'00*
Double Whammy *'01*
The Glass House *'01*
Steve Martini's The Judge *'01*
Searching for Paradise *'02*
Mr. 3000 *'04*
The Perfect Man *'05*
Sex and the City: The Movie *'08*
My One and Only *'09*
Sex and the City 2 *'10*
3, 2, 1...Frankie Go Boom *'12*
Lovelace *'13*
Elsa & Fred *'14*
White Girl *'16*

Michael Nouri (1945-)
Contract on Cherry Street *'77*
Flashdance *'83*
Imagemaker *'86*
The Hidden *'87*
Thieves of Fortune *'89*
Shattered Dreams *'90*
Danielle Steel's Changes *'91*
Psychic *'91*
DaVinci's War *'92*
No Escape, No Return *'93*
American Yakuza *'94*
Fortunes of War *'94*
The Hidden 2 *'94*
Hologram Man *'95*
To the Limit *'95*
Overkill *'96*
This Matter of Marriage *'98*
Finding Forrester *'00*
61* *'01*
Lovely & Amazing *'02*
Terminal Error *'02*
Klepto *'03*
The Terminal *'04*
The Boynton Beach Club *'05*
Invincible *'06*
Last Holiday *'06*
The Proposal *'09*

Allen Nourse
Pushover *'54*
Cell 2455, Death Row *'55*

Benjamin Joseph Manaly Novak (1979-)
See B.J. Novak

B.J. Novak (1979-)
Knocked Up *'07*
Inglourious Basterds *'09*
Saving Mr. Banks *'13*
The Founder *'17*

John Novak (1955-)
Wishmaster 3: Beyond the Gates of Hell *'01*
Wishmaster 4: The Prophecy Fulfilled *'02*
Last Chance Cafe *'06*
The Secrets of Comfort House *'06*

Kayvan Novak
Four Lions *'10*
Cuban Fury *'14*

Kim Novak (1933-)
Phffft! *'54*
Pushover *'54*
5 Against the House *'55*
The Man with the Golden Arm *'55*
Picnic *'55*
The Eddy Duchin Story *'56*
Jeanne Eagels *'57*
Pal Joey *'57*
Bell, Book and Candle *'58*
Vertigo *'58*
Middle of the Night *'59*
Strangers When We Meet *'60*
Boys' Night Out *'62*
The Notorious Landlady *'62*
Kiss Me, Stupid! *'64*
Of Human Bondage *'64*
The Amorous Adventures of Moll Flanders *'65*
The Legend of Lylah Clare *'68*
Tales That Witness Madness *'73*
The Third Girl from the Left *'73*
The White Buffalo *'77*
The Mirror Crack'd *'80*
Liebestraum *'91*

Mel Novak (1942-)
Cat in the Cage *'68*
Family Reunion *'79*
Expert Weapon *'93*
Capital Punishment *'96*
Vampire Assassin *'05*

Bojana Novakovic (1981-)
Marking Time *'03*
Solo *'06*
Devil *'10*
Edge of Darkness *'10*
Burning Man *'11*
Not Suitable for Children *'12*
Generation Um... *'13*

Ramon Novarro (1899-1968)
The Prisoner of Zenda *'22*
Scaramouche *'23*
The Red Lily *'24*
Ben-Hur *'26*
Across to Singapore *'28*
The Flying Fleet *'29*
The Pagan *'29*
Huddle *'32*
Mata Hari *'32*
The Barbarian *'33*
The Cat and the Fiddle *'34*
Big Steal *'49*
Crisis *'50*
The Outriders *'50*
Heller in Pink Tights *'60*

Tamar Novas (1986-)
The Sea Inside *'04*
Broken Embraces *'09*

Don Novello (1943-)
Tucker: The Man and His Dream *'88*
New York Stories *'89*
The Godfather, Part 3 *'90*
Spirit of '76 *'91*
Armistead Maupin's Tales of the City *'93*
Casper *'95 (C)*
One Night Stand *'95*
Jack *'96*
Just the Ticket *'98*
The Adventures of Rocky & Bullwinkle *'00*
Just One Night *'00*
Atlantis: The Lost Empire *'01 (V)*

Ivor Novello (1893-1951)
The Lodger *'26*
Phantom Fiend *'35*

Jay Novello (1904-82)
Cattle Town *'52*
Miracle of Our Lady of Fatima *'52*
Operation Secret *'52*
Ma and Pa Kettle on Vacation *'53*
Crime Wave *'54*
The Mad Magician *'54*
The Prodigal *'55*
Sabaka *'55*
The Pride and the Passion *'57*
Escape From Zahrain *'62*
Harum Scarum *'65*
What Did You Do in the War, Daddy? *'66*

Tom Novembre (1959-)
An American Werewolf in Paris *'97*
The Ice Rink *'99*

Nancho Novo (1958-)
Tierra *'95*
Lovers of the Arctic Circle *'98*

Jarmila Novotna (1908-94)
The Search *'48*
The Great Caruso *'51*

Tuva Novotny (1979-)
Stoned *'05*
Eat, Pray, Love *'10*
A War *'15*
Borg *vs.* McEnroe *'17*
Exit Plan *'20*

Jerzy Nowak (1923-)
Trois Couleurs: Blanc *'94*
The Healer *'02*

Tom Nowicki
Nightjohn *'96*
Flash *'98*
Kiss of Fire *'98*
Conjurer *'08*
Game of Your Life *'11*

Joanna Noyes
Bleeders *'97*
The Reaper *'97*
Nightwaves *'03*

Bruce Nozick
Hit the Dutchman *'92*
Tuesdays with Morrie *'99*
Gale Force *'01*

Winston Ntshona (1941-)
A Dry White Season *'89*
Tarzan and the Lost City *'98*

Danny Nucci (1968-)
The Children of Times Square *'86*
Book of Love *'91*
Crimson Tide *'95*
Homage *'95*
Roosters *'95*
The Big Squeeze *'96*
Eraser *'96*
The Rock *'96*
That Old Feeling *'96*
Love Walked In *'97*
Titanic *'97*
Codename: Jaguar *'98*
Friends & Lovers *'99*
American Cousins *'02*
Firestarter 2: Rekindled *'02*
Break a Leg *'03*
The Sandlot 3: Heading Home *'07*
Backwoods *'08*

Carole Nugent
Belles on Their Toes *'52*
Lost, Lonely, and Vicious *'59*

Eddie Nugent (1904-95)
The Flying Fleet *'29*
Vagabond Lover *'29*
Night Nurse *'31*
Prison Shadows *'36*

Edward J. Nugent (1904-95)
Clancy in Wall Street *'30*
This Day and Age *'33*
Just My Luck *'35*
The Old Homestead *'35*
Two Minutes to Play *'37*

Elliott Nugent (1900-80)
So This Is College *'29*
Romance *'30*
The Unholy Three *'30*
The Last Flight *'31*
Welcome Stranger *'47 (C)*

J.C. Nugent
Navy Blues *'29*
Love in the Rough *'30*

Judy Nugent
There's Always Tomorrow *'56*
High School Caesar *'60*

Ted Nugent
Tapeheads *'89*
Beer for My Horses *'08*

Yoichi Numata (1924-2006)
Ringu *'98*
Ringu 2 *'99*
The Princess Blade *'02*

Miguel A. Nunez, Jr. (1964-)
Return of the Living Dead *'85*
Harlem Nights *'89*
Lethal Weapon 3 *'92*
For Richer or Poorer *'97*
Life *'99*
If You Only Knew *'00*
MacArthur Park *'01*
The Adventures of Pluto Nash *'02*
Juwanna Mann *'02*
Scooby-Doo *'02*
Kickin' It Old Skool *'07*
Christmas in Compton *'12*

Oscar Nunez (1958-)
Without Men *'11*
Prosecuting Casey Anthony *'13*
Miss Stevens *'16*

Osmar Nunez
Beethoven's Big Break *'08*
The Proposal *'09*

Bill Nunn (1953-)
School Daze *'88*
Do the Right Thing *'89*
Def by Temptation *'90*
Mo' Better Blues *'90*
New Jack City *'91*
Regarding Henry *'91*
Sister Act *'92*
Blood Brothers *'93*
National Lampoon's Loaded Weapon 1 *'93*
Canadian Bacon *'94*
Candyman 2: Farewell to the Flesh *'94*
The Last Seduction *'94*
The Affair *'95*
Money Train *'95*
Things to Do in Denver When You're Dead *'95*
True Crime *'95*
Bulletproof *'96*
Extreme Measures *'96*
Mr. & Mrs. Loving *'96*
Ellen Foster *'97*
Kiss the Girls *'97*
Mad City *'97*
Always Outnumbered Always Outgunned *'98*
He Got Game *'98*
The Legend of 1900 *'98*
Quicksilver Highway *'98*
Foolish *'99*
Passing Glory *'99*
The Tic Code *'99*
Lockdown *'00*
The Substitute 4: Failure is Not an Option *'00*
People I Know *'02*
Spider-Man *'02*
Runaway Jury *'03*
Spider-Man 2 *'04*
Firehouse Dog *'07*
Spider-Man 3 *'07*
A Raisin in the Sun *'08*
Won't Back Down *'12*

Teri Nunn (1961-)
Thank God It's Friday *'78*
Follow That Car *'80*

Maila Nurmi (1921-2008)
See Vampira

Loredana Nusciak (1942-)
Gladiators 7 *'62*
Django *'68*

Mike Nussbaum (1923-)
House of Games *'87*
Things Change *'88*
Osso Bucco *'08*

Jeff Nuttal (1933-2004)
Robin Hood *'91*
Captives *'94*
Beaumarchais the Scoundrel *'96*

Tarah Nutter
Without Warning *'80*
Bitter Harvest *'81*

France Nuyen (1939-)
In Love and War *'58*
South Pacific *'58*
Diamond Head *'62*
Black Water Gold *'69*
The Big Game *'72*
The Horror at 37,000 Feet *'73*
Return to Fantasy Island *'77*
China Cry *'91*
The Joy Luck Club *'93*
A Smile Like Yours *'96*

N!xau (1944-2003)
The Gods Must Be Crazy *'84*
The Gods Must Be Crazy 2 *'89*

Carrie Nye (1937-2006)
The Group *'66*
Creepshow *'82*
Hello Again *'87*

Carroll Nye (1901-74)
The Flying Fleet *'29*
The Squall *'29*
Lottery Bride *'30*
Gone with the Wind *'39*

Louis Nye (1933-2005)
The Facts of Life *'60*
Sex Kittens Go to College *'60*
The Wheeler Dealers *'63*
Good Neighbor Sam *'64*
A Guide for the Married Man *'67 (C)*
Charge of the Model T's *'76*
Harper Valley P.T.A. *'78*
Alice in Wonderland *'85*
O.C. and Stiggs *'87*

Andy Nyman (1966-)
Severance *'06*
Death at a Funeral *'07*
Black Death *'10*
A Shaun the Sheep Movie: Farmageddon *'19*

Lena Nyman (1944-2011)
I Am Curious (Yellow) *'67*
Autumn Sonata *'78*

Lupita Nyong'o (1983-)
12 Years a Slave *'13*
Non-Stop *'14*
The Jungle Book *'16*
Queen of Katwe *'16*
Black Panther *'18*
Little Monsters *'19*
Us *'19*

Michael Nyqvist (1960-)
As It Is In Heaven *'04*
London Voodoo *'04*
Mother of Mine *'05*
Arn: The Knight Templar *'07*
Downloading Nancy *'08*
The Girl With the Dragon Tattoo *'09*
The Girl Who Kicked the Hornet's Nest *'10*
The Girl Who Played With Fire *'10*
Abduction *'11*
Mission: Impossible-Ghost Protocol *'11*
Europa Report *'13*

Days and Nights *'14*
John Wick *'14*
The Girl in the Book *'15*
Frank & Lola *'16*
I.T. *'16*
Hunter Killer *'18*

Sophie Nyweide
Mammoth *'09*
An Invisible Sign *'11*

Pascal Nzonzi
Night on Earth *'91*
Lumumba *'01*

Henry O (1927-)
Dragonheart: A New Beginning *'00*
Romeo Must Die *'00*
Shanghai Noon *'00*
The Lost Empire *'01*
A Thousand Years of Good Prayers *'07*

Jack Oakie (1903-78)
If I Had a Million *'32*
Uptown New York *'32*
College Humor *'33*
The Eagle and the Hawk *'33*
Murder at the Vanities *'34*
The Call of the Wild *'35*
Colleen *'36*
The Texas Rangers *'36*
Toast of New York *'37*
The Great Dictator *'40*
Little Men *'40*
Young People *'40*
The Great American Broadcast *'41*
Iceland *'42*
Hello, Frisco, Hello *'43*
Wintertime *'43*
It Happened Tomorrow *'44*
Sweet and Low-Down *'44*
Tomahawk *'51*
Around the World in 80 Days *'56 (C)*
The Wonderful Country *'59*
The Rat Race *'60*
Lover Come Back *'61*

Simon Oakland (1922-83)
I Want to Live! *'58*
Murder, Inc. *'60*
Psycho *'60*
The Rise and Fall of Legs Diamond *'60*
Who Was That Lady? *'60*
Follow That Dream *'61*
West Side Story *'61*
Wall of Noise *'63*
The Satan Bug *'65*
The Sand Pebbles *'66*
Chubasco *'67*
Tony Rome *'67*
Bullitt *'68*
On a Clear Day You Can See Forever *'70*
Chato's Land *'71*
The Night Stalker *'71*
The Night Strangler *'72*
Emperor of the North Pole *'73*

Vivien Oakland (1895-1958)
The Matrimonial Bed *'30*
The Tenderfoot *'32*
Mile a Minute Love *'37*

Wheeler Oakman (1890-1949)
Outside the Law *'21*
On with the Show *'29*
Boiling Point *'32*
The Lost Jungle *'34*
Death from a Distance *'36*
Pilot X *'37*

Simon Oates (1932-2009)
Doomwatch *'72*
Jewels *'92*

Warren Oates (1928-82)
The Rise and Fall of Legs Diamond *'60*
Hero's Island *'62*
Ride the High Country *'62*
Mail Order Bride *'63*
Shenandoah *'65*
Return of the Magnificent Seven *'66*
The Shooting *'66*
In the Heat of the Night *'67*

Welcome to Hard Times *'67*
The Split *'68*
The Wild Bunch *'69*
There Was a Crooked Man *'70*
Chandler *'71*
Hired Hand *'71*
Two Lane Blacktop *'71*
Dillinger *'73*
Tom Sawyer *'73*
Badlands *'74*
Bring Me the Head of Alfredo Garcia *'74*
Cockfighter *'74*
Race with the Devil *'75*
The White Dawn *'75*
Dixie Dynamite *'76*
Drum *'76*
92 in the Shade *'76*
Prime Time *'77*
Sleeping Dogs *'77*
Brink's Job *'78*
Gunfire *'78*
And Baby Makes Six *'79*
My Old Man *'79*
1941 *'79*
East of Eden *'80*
Stripes *'81*
The Blue and the Gray *'82*
The Border *'82*
Blue Thunder *'83*
Tough Enough *'83*

Barack Obama (1961-)
2016: Obama's America *'12*
Fahrenheit 11/9 *'18*

Barack H. Obama (1961-)
See Barack Obama

Barack Hussein Obama (1961-)
See Barack Obama

Barry Obama (1961-)
See Barack Obama

Philip Ober (1902-82)
The Magnificent Yankee *'50*
Come Back, Little Sheba *'52*
The Clown *'53*
From Here to Eternity *'53*
Scandal at Scourie *'53*
Beloved Infidel *'59*
The Mating Game *'59*
North by Northwest *'59*
The Facts of Life *'60*
The Ghost and Mr. Chicken *'66*

Robert Ober (1881-1950)
The Big Parade *'25*
The Idle Rich *'29*

Merle Oberon (1911-79)
The Private Life of Henry VIII *'33*
Private Life of Don Juan *'34*
The Scarlet Pimpernel *'34*
Folies Bergere de Paris *'35*
The Cowboy and the Lady *'38*
The Divorce of Lady X *'38*
Wuthering Heights *'39*
That Uncertain Feeling *'41*
Forever and a Day *'43*
Stage Door Canteen *'43*
Dark Waters *'44*
A Song to Remember *'45*
Night Song *'47*
Berlin Express *'48*
Deep in My Heart *'54*
Desiree *'54*
The Price of Fear *'56*
Hotel *'67*

Bill Oberst, Jr. (1965-)
Beverly Lewis' The Shunning *'11*
Born Bad *'11*
Abraham Lincoln *vs.* Zombies *'12*
The Black Water Vampire *'13*
Zombieworld *'15*

Jacqueline Obradors (1966-)
Six Days, Seven Nights *'98*
Deuce Bigalow: Male Gigolo *'99*
Atlantis: The Lost Empire *'01 (V)*

Tortilla Soup *'01*
A Man Apart *'03*

Claudio Obregon (1935-2010)
Midaq Alley *'95*
Esmeralda Comes by Night *'98*

Rodrigo Obregon
Django Strikes Again *'87*
Hard Ticket to Hawaii *'87*
Picasso Trigger *'89*
Savage Beach *'89*
Hard Hunted *'92*
Enemy Gold *'93*
Fit to Kill *'93*

Hugh O'Brian (1925-)
Return of Jesse James *'50*
Rocketship X-M *'50*
Little Big Horn *'51*
Vengeance Valley *'51*
The Lawless Breed *'52*
Son of Ali Baba *'52*
Man from the Alamo *'53*
Broken Lance *'54*
Drums Across the River *'54*
Saskatchewan *'54*
There's No Business Like Show Business *'54*
The Brass Legend *'56*
The Fiend Who Walked the West *'58*
Alias Jesse James *'59 (C)*
Assassination in Rome *'65*
In Harm's Way *'65*
Love Has Many Faces *'65*
Africa Texas Style *'67*
Probe *'72*
Murder on Flight 502 *'75*
Fantasy Island *'76*
The Shootist *'76*
Twins *'88*
The Gambler Returns: The Luck of the Draw *'93*

Austin O'Brien (1981-)
Last Action Hero *'93*
My Girl 2 *'94*
The Baby-Sitters' Club *'95*
Lawnmower Man 2: Beyond Cyberspace *'95*
Bounty *'09*

Chris O'Brien
Private Hell 36 *'54*
The Gun That Won the West *'55*

Clay O'Brien (1961-)
The Cowboys *'72*
Cahill: United States Marshal *'73*
One Little Indian *'73*

Conan O'Brien (1963-)
Queer Duck: The Movie *'06 (V)*
The Great Buck Howard *'09 (C)*
Conan O'Brien Can't Stop *'11*

Dave O'Brien (1912-69)
Reefer Madness *'38*
The Devil Bat *'41*
The Spider Returns *'41*

Donald O'Brien (1930-2003)
The Train *'65*
Mannaja: A Man Called Blade *'77*
Doctor Butcher M.D. *'80*

Dylan O'Brien (1991-)
The First Time *'12*
The Internship *'13*
The Maze Runner *'14*
Maze Runner: The Scorch Trials *'15*
Deepwater Horizon *'16*
American Assassin *'17*
Bumblebee *'18 (V)*
Maze Runner: The Death Cure *'18*

Edmond O'Brien (1915-85)
The Hunchback of Notre Dame *'39*
The Amazing Mrs. Holiday *'43*
The Killers *'46*

A Double Life *'47*
Fighter Squadron *'48*
For the Love of Mary *'48*
D.O.A. *'49*
White Heat *'49*
The Admiral Was a Lady *'50*
Backfire *'50*
Between Midnight and Dawn *'50*
711 Ocean Drive *'50*
Two of a Kind *'51*
Denver and the Rio Grande *'52*
The Bigamist *'53*
The Hitch-Hiker *'53*
Julius Caesar *'53*
The Barefoot Contessa *'54*
Pete Kelly's Blues *'55*
D-Day, the Sixth of June *'56*
The Girl Can't Help It *'56*
1984 *'56*
The Rack *'56*
Stopover Tokyo *'57*
The World Was His Jury *'58*
Up Periscope *'59*
The Last Voyage *'60*
Birdman of Alcatraz *'62*
The Longest Day *'62*
The Man Who Shot Liberty Valance *'62*
Moon Pilot *'62*
Rio Conchos *'64*
Seven Days in May *'64*
Synanon *'65*
Fantastic Voyage *'66*
To Commit a Murder *'67*
The Wild Bunch *'69*
Dream No Evil *'70*
The Love God? *'70*
They Only Kill Their Masters *'72*
Lucky Luciano *'74*
99 & 44/100 Dead *'74*

Eugene O'Brien (1880-1966)
Rebecca of Sunnybrook Farm *'17*
Fine Manners *'26*

George O'Brien (1900-85)
The Iron Horse *'24*
Sunrise *'27*
Noah's Ark *'28*
The Painted Desert *'31*
Seas Beneath *'31*
Daniel Boone *'34*
Cowboy Millionaire *'35*
Windjammer *'37*
My Wild Irish Rose *'47*
She Wore a Yellow Ribbon *'49*
Cheyenne Autumn *'64*

Gerry O'Brien
Veronica Guerin *'03*
Speed Dating *'07*

Hugh O'Brien (1925-)
Back to God's Country *'53*
Seminole *'53*

Joan O'Brien (1936-)
Operation Petticoat *'59*
The Alamo *'60*
It's Only Money *'62*
Samar *'62*
It Happened at the World's Fair *'63*
Get Yourself a College Girl *'64*

Kieran O'Brien (1973-)
Bellman and True *'88*
Cracker: Brotherly Love *'95*
Virtual Sexuality *'99*
Jason and the Argonauts *'00*
Bloodlines *'05*
Tristram Shandy: A Cock and Bull Story *'05*
Goal! The Dream Begins *'06*

Margaret O'Brien (1937-)
Journey for Margaret *'42*
Dr. Gillespie's Criminal Case *'43*
Lost Angel *'43*
Thousands Cheer *'43*
The Canterville Ghost *'44*
Jane Eyre *'44*
Meet Me in St. Louis *'44*
Music For Millions *'44*

Our Vines Have Tender Grapes *'45*
Tenth Avenue Angel *'47*
Little Women *'49*
The Secret Garden *'49*
Heller in Pink Tights *'60*
Amy *'81*

Mark O'Brien (1984-)
Grown Up Movie Star *'10*
Arrival *'16*
The Front Runner *'18*
Ready or Not *'19*

Maureen O'Brien (1943-)
The Lost Boys *'78*
Falling for a Dancer *'98*
American Women *'00*

Myles O'Brien
Scorned 2 *'96*
Sexual Roulette *'96*

Niall O'Brien (1946-2009)
Lovespell *'79*
Excalibur *'81*
Rawhead Rex *'87*
Broken Harvest *'94*
Secret of the Cave *'06*

Pat O'Brien (1899-1983)
Flying High *'31*
The Front Page *'31*
American Madness *'32*
Hell's House *'32*
Virtue *'32*
Bombshell *'33*
Bureau of Missing Persons *'33*
The World Gone Mad *'33*
Flirtation Walk *'34*
Here Comes the Navy *'34*
I've Got Your Number *'34*
In Caliente *'35*
The Irish in Us *'35*
Oil for the Lamps of China *'35*
China Clipper *'36*
The Great O'Malley *'36*
San Quentin *'37*
Slim *'37*
Angels with Dirty Faces *'38*
Boy Meets Girl *'38*
Cowboy from Brooklyn *'38*
Garden of the Moon *'38*
Castle on the Hudson *'40*
The Fighting 69th *'40*
Flowing Gold *'40*
Knute Rockne: All American *'40*
Slightly Honorable *'40*
Torrid Zone *'40*
Broadway *'42*
Bombardier *'43*
His Butler's Sister *'44*
Crack-Up *'46*
The Boy with the Green Hair *'48*
A Dangerous Profession *'49*
The Fireball *'50*
Criminal Lawyer *'51*
Kill Me Tomorrow *'57*
The Last Hurrah *'58*
Some Like It Hot *'59*
The Over-the-Hill Gang *'69*
The End *'78*
Ragtime *'81*

Peter O'Brien (1960-)
The Grand Duel *'73*
Hotel de Love *'96*
The Return *'06*

Richard O'Brien (1942-)
Pieces of Dreams *'70*
The Rocky Horror Picture Show *'75*
Shock Treatment *'81*
Dark City *'97*
Spice World: The Movie *'97*
Dungeons and Dragons *'00*
Elvira's Haunted Hills *'02*
Night Train *'09*

Shauna O'Brien (1970-)
Friend of the Family *'95*
Over the Wire *'95*
Body Armor *'96*
Friend of the Family 2 *'96*
Fugitive Rage *'96*
The Seductress *'00*
Baberellas *'03*

Tom O'Brien (1965-)
The Big Easy '87
The Accused '88

Virginia O'Brien (1921-2001)
Big Store '41
Lady Be Good '41
Panama Hattie '42
Ship Ahoy '42
Du Barry Was a Lady '43
Thousands Cheer '43
Meet the People '44
Two Girls and a Sailor '44
The Harvey Girls '46
Till the Clouds Roll By '46
Merton of the Movies '47

Erin O'Brien-Moore (1902-79)
His Greatest Gamble '34
Little Men '34
Seven Keys to Baldpate '35
The Black Legion '37
The Green Light '37
Destination Moon '50
The Family Secret '51

Pat O'Bryan
976-EVIL '88
Relentless '89
976-EVIL 2: The Astral Factor '91

Sean O'Bryan (1963-)
The Twilight of the Golds '97
I'll Be Home for Christmas '98
Nice Guys Sleep Alone '99
The Princess Diaries '01
Big Fat Liar '02
A Place Called Home '04
The Princess Diaries 2: Royal Engagement '04
Raising Helen '04

Brian F. O'Byrne (1967-)
Amongst Women '98
An Everlasting Piece '00
Bandits '01
Disco Pigs '01
The Mapmaker '01
Intermission '03
Million Dollar Baby '04
The New World '05
Bug '06
Before the Devil Knows You're Dead '07
No Reservations '07
Brooklyn's Finest '09
The International '09
Mildred Pierce '11

Ric Ocasek (1949-)
Made in Heaven '87 (C)
Hairspray '88

Ilaria Occhini (1934-2019)
Damon and Pythias '62
Loose Cannons '10

Andrea Occhipinti (1957-)
New York Ripper '82
A Blade in the Dark '83
Conquest '83
Bolero '84

P.J. Ochlan
Little Man Tate '91
Quigley '03

Jesus Ochoa (1959-)
Nicotina '03
Innocent Voices '04
Man on Fire '04

Uwe Ochsenknecht (1956-)
Das Boot '81
Schtonk '92
Kaspar Hauser '93
Luther '03

Arthur O'Connell (1908-81)
Citizen Kane '41
Open Secret '48
Picnic '55
Bus Stop '56
The Man in the Gray Flannel Suit '56
Solid Gold Cadillac '56
April Love '57
Operation Mad Ball '57
Man of the West '58
Anatomy of a Murder '59
Gidget '59
Operation Petticoat '59
Cimarron '60
Follow That Dream '61
Misty '61
Pocketful of Miracles '61
A Thunder of Drums '61
7 Faces of Dr. Lao '63
Kissin' Cousins '64
Your Cheatin' Heart '64
Monkey's Uncle '65
The Third Day '65
Birds Do It '66
Fantastic Voyage '66
The Silencers '66
The Reluctant Astronaut '67
The Power '68
There Was a Crooked Man '70
The Last Valley '71
They Only Kill Their Masters '72
Huckleberry Finn '74
The Hiding Place '75

Charlie O'Connell (1975-)
Derby '71
Dude, Where's My Car? '00
The Devil's Prey '01
Kraken: Tentacles of the Deep '06
2-Headed Shark Attack '12
Mischief Night '13

Deirdre O'Connell
Pastime '91
Cool World '92
Falling from Grace '92
Straight Talk '92
Fearless '93
Murder in a Small Town '99
Hearts in Atlantis '01
Imaginary Heroes '05
Winter Passing '05
Stephanie Daley '06
American Loser '07
What Happens in Vegas '08
Diane '18

Jack O'Connell (1990-)
Harry Brown '09
United '11
The Liability '12
Private Peaceful '12
Starred Up '13
300: Rise of an Empire '13
'71 '14
Unbroken '14
Money Monster '16
Tulip Fever '17
Trial by Fire '18
Seberg '19

Jerry O'Connell (1974-)
Stand by Me '86
Blue River '95
Hole in the Sky '95
Jerry Maguire '96
Joe's Apartment '96
Scream 2 '97
Can't Hardly Wait '98
What the Deaf Man Heard '98
Body Shots '99
The '60s '99
Mission to Mars '00
Tomcats '01
Buying the Cow '02
Kangaroo Jack '02
Yours, Mine & Ours '05
Baby on Board '08
Midnight Bayou '09
Obsessed '09
Piranha 3D '10
The Lookalike '14
Space Station 76 '14
Veronica Mars '14
Deep Murder '19

Patrick O'Connell (1934-)
McKenzie Break '70
We'll Meet Again '82

Raoul O'Connell
Boys Life '94
Frisk '95

Taaffe O'Connell
Caged Fury '80
Galaxy of Terror '81

Carroll O'Connor (1924-2001)
A Fever In the Blood '61
Parrish '61
Lonely Are the Brave '62
Cleopatra '63
In Harm's Way '65
Hawaii '66
What Did You Do in the War, Daddy? '66
Point Blank '67
Waterhole Number 3 '67
The Devil's Brigade '68
For Love of Ivy '68
Death of a Gunfighter '69
Marlowe '69
Doctors' Wives '70
Kelly's Heroes '70
Law and Disorder '74
Brass '85
The Father Clements Story '87
Return to Me '00

Derrick O'Connor (1941-2018)
Hope and Glory '87
Dealers '89
Lethal Weapon 2 '89
How to Make an American Quilt '95
Deep Rising '98
End of Days '99
Daredevil '03

Donald O'Connor (1925-2003)
Sing You Sinners '38
Beau Geste '39
Private Buckaroo '42
Something in the Wind '47
Feudin', Fussin', and A-Fightin' '48
Francis the Talking Mule '49
Double Crossbones '51
Francis Goes to the Races '51
Francis Goes to West Point '52
Singin' in the Rain '52
Francis Covers the Big Town '53
I Love Melvin '53
Francis Joins the WACs '54
There's No Business Like Show Business '54
Francis in the Navy '55
Anything Goes '56
That Funny Feeling '65
Ragtime '81
Alice in Wonderland '85
Toys '92
Out to Sea '97

Frances O'Connor (1967-)
A Little Bit of Soul '97
The Wedding Party '97
Mansfield Park '99
About Adam '00
Bedazzled '00
A. I.: Artificial Intelligence '01
The Importance of Being Earnest '02
Windtalkers '02
Timeline '03
Book of Love '04
Darwin's Darkest Hour '09
Best Man Down '12
The Hunter '12
Jayne Mansfield's Car '13
The Truth About Emanuel '13
The Conjuring 2 '16

Glynnis O'Connor (1956-)
Kid Vengeance '75
Someone I Touched '75
The Boy in the Plastic Bubble '76
Ode to Billy Joe '76
Our Town '77
California Dreaming '79
Those Lips, Those Eyes '80
Night Crossing '81
Johnny Dangerously '84
The Deliberate Stranger '86
Ellen Foster '97
New Best Friend '02
Graduation '07

Hazel O'Connor (1955-)
Breaking Glass '80
Car Trouble '86

John Carroll O'Connor (1924-2001)
See Carroll O'Connor

Josh O'Connor
God's Own Country '17
Hope Gap '20

Kevin J. O'Connor (1963-)
Let's Scare Jessica to Death '71
Special Effects '85
Peggy Sue Got Married '86
The Caine Mutiny Court Martial '88
The Moderns '88
Love at Large '89
Signs of Life '89
Steel Magnolias '89
Hero '92
Canadian Bacon '94
Color of Night '94
No Escape '94
Lord of Illusions '95
Virtuosity '95
Hit Me '96
Black Cat Run '98
Deep Rising '98
Gods and Monsters '98
Chill Factor '99
The Mummy '99
Van Helsing '04
Kettle of Fish '06
Seraphim Falls '06
Flight of the Living Dead: Outbreak on a Plane '07
There Will Be Blood '07

Renee O'Connor (1971-)
Darkman 2: The Return of Durant '94
Hercules the Legendary Journeys, Vol. 2: The Lost Kingdom '94
Follow the River '95
Alien Apocalypse '05
Boogeyman 2 '07
2010: Moby Dick '10
A Question of Faith '17

Robert Emmett O'Connor (1885-1962)
Alias French Gertie '30
Up the River '30
Kid from Spain '32
Picture Snatcher '33
A Night at the Opera '35

Simon O'Connor
Heavenly Creatures '94
You Wont Miss Me '09

Sinead O'Connor (1966-)
Emily Bronte's Wuthering Heights '92
The Butcher Boy '97

Tim O'Connor (1927-)
Across 110th Street '72
The Groundstar Conspiracy '72
Sssssss '73
Winter Kill '74
Naked Gun 2 1/2: The Smell of Fear '91

Una O'Connor (1880-1959)
Cavalcade '33
The Invisible Man '33
The Barretts of Wimpole Street '34
Chained '34
Stingaree '34
The Bride of Frankenstein '35
David Copperfield '35
The Informer '35
Lloyds of London '36
Personal Property '37
The Adventures of Robin Hood '38
It All Came True '40
The Sea Hawk '40
Strawberry Blonde '41
Holy Matrimony '43
This Land Is Mine '43
The Canterville Ghost '44
Christmas in Connecticut '45
Witness for the Prosecution '57

Hugh O'Conor (1975-)
Lamb '85
My Left Foot '89
The Young Poisoner's Handbook '94
Chocolat '00
Deathwatch '02
Bloom '03
Flick '07
Speed Dating '07
Waiting for Dublin '07
Three Wise Women '11
The Bachelor Weekend '13

Erika Oda (1979-)
After Life '98
Alive '02

Joe Odagiri (1976-)
Azumi '03
Bright Future '03
Blood and Bones '04
Princess Raccoon '05
Shinobi '05
Sway '06
I Wish '11

Megumi Odaka (1972-)
Godzilla *vs.* SpaceGodzilla '94
Godzilla *vs.* Destroyah '95

Denis O'Dea (1905-78)
The Fallen Idol '49
Under Capricorn '49
Treasure Island '50
Captain Horatio Hornblower '51
The Long Dark Hall '51
Niagara '52
Mogambo '53
Captain Lightfoot '55
Esther and the King '60

Jimmy O'Dea (1899-1965)
The Rising of the Moon '57
Darby O'Gill & the Little People '59

Judith O'Dea (1945-)
Night of the Living Dead '68
Serial Slayer '03

Deborah Odell
Protection '01
Godsend '04
She's Too Young '04
All the Good Ones Are Married '07
Time Bomb '08

Jennifer O'Dell (1974-)
Window Theory '04
Slayer '06
Nevermore '07

Tony O'Dell
The Karate Kid '84
Chopping Mall '86

Bob Odenkirk (1962-)
Wayne's World 2 '93
Clean Slate '94
The Cable Guy '96
The Truth about Cats and Dogs '96
Waiting for Guffman '96
Sink or Swim '97
Danny Roane: First Time Director '06
Operation: Endgame '10
The Giant Mechanical Man '12
Nebraska '13
The Spectacular Now '13
The Post '17

Christophe Odent
First Name: Carmen '83
Safe Conduct '01

Devon Odessa (1974-)
The Omega Code '99
Mad Cowgirl '06

Odetta (1930-2008)
The Autobiography of Miss Jane Pittman '74
The Fire Next Time '93 (C)

Leslie Odom, Jr. (1981-)
Murder on the Orient Express '17
Harriet '19
Only '20

Anthony O'Donnell (1948-)
Nuts in May '76
Agatha Christie: A Life in Pictures '04
Assassin in Love '07

Cathy O'Donnell (1925-70)
The Best Years of Our Lives '46
The Amazing Mr. X '48
They Live by Night '49
The Miniver Story '50
Side Street '50
Detective Story '51
The Man from Laramie '55
Terror in the Haunted House '58
Ben-Hur '59

Chris O'Donnell (1970-)
Men Don't Leave '89
Blue Sky '91
Fried Green Tomatoes '91
Scent of a Woman '92
School Ties '92
The Three Musketeers '93
Circle of Friends '94
Batman Forever '95
Mad Love '95
The Chamber '96
In Love and War '96
Batman and Robin '97
The Bachelor '99
Cookie's Fortune '99
Vertical Limit '00
29 Palms '03
Kinsey '04
The Sisters '05
The Company '07
Kit Kittredge: An American Girl '08
Max Payne '08
Cats & Dogs: The Revenge of Kitty Galore '10
A Little Help '11

David O'Donnell (1974-)
Lime Salted Love '06
Magma: Volcanic Disaster '06
A Christmas Proposal '08
Dear Me: A Blogger's Tale '08
12 Christmas Wishes For My Dog '11

Erin O'Donnell (1971-)
Incident in an Alley '62
Saintly Sinners '62
Hell's Bloody Devils '70

Keir O'Donnell (1978-)
Wedding Crashers '05
Flakes '07
Pathology '08
Paul Blart: Mall Cop '09
Taking Chances '09
When in Rome '09
A Case of You '13

Rosie O'Donnell (1962-)
A League of Their Own '92
Another Stakeout '93
Sleepless in Seattle '93
Car 54, Where Are You? '94
Exit to Eden '94
The Flintstones '94
Now and Then '95
Beautiful Girls '96
Harriet the Spy '96
A Very Brady Sequel '96 (C)
The Twilight of the Golds '97
Wide Awake '97
Tarzan '99 (V)
America '09

Colin O'Donoghue (1981-)
The Rite '11
Storage 24 '12
Carrie Pilby '17

Chris O'Dowd (1979-)
Pirate Radio '09
Bridesmaids '11
The Crimson Petal and the White '12
Friends with Kids '12
3, 2, 1...Frankie Go Boom '12
Epic '13 (V)

Calvary *'14*
Cuban Fury *'14*
St. Vincent *'14*
The Program *'15*
Mascots *'16*
Miss Peregrine's Home for Peculiar Children *'16*
Loving Vincent *'17*
Juliet, Naked *'18*

Martha O'Driscoll (1922-98)
Judge Hardy and Son *'39*
Reap the Wild Wind *'42*
The Fallen Sparrow *'43*
Here Come the Co-Eds *'45*
House of Dracula *'45*
Carnegie Hall *'47*

Adepero Oduye
Pariah *'11*
Steel Magnolias *'12*

Steve Oedekerk (1961-)
Kung Pow! Enter the Fist *'02*
Barnyard *'06 (V)*

Gregoire Oestermann
Look at Me *'04*
I Do *'06*
The Intouchables *'12*

Conor O'Farrell (1956-)
Baby of the Bride *'91*
From the Earth to the Moon *'98*
Stir of Echoes *'99*

George Offerman, Jr. (1917-63)
Calling Dr. Kildare *'39*
The Fighting Sullivans *'42*
A Walk in the Sun *'46*

Nick Offerman (1970-)
Treasure Island *'99*
Groove *'00*
Miss Congeniality 2: Armed and Fabulous *'05*
November *'05*
Sin City *'05*
Wristcutters: A Love Story *'06*
The Go-Getter *'07*
Taking Chances *'09*
All Good Things *'10*
Casa de mi Padre *'12*
Smashed *'12*
Somebody Up There Likes Me *'12*
Date and Switch *'13*
Ernest & Celestine *'13 (V)*
In a World... *'13*
The Kings of Summer *'13*
We're the Millers *'13*
The Lego Movie *'14 (V)*
22 Jump Street *'14*
Danny Collins *'15*
Me and Earl and the Dying Girl *'15*
A Walk in the Woods *'15*
My Life as a Zucchini *'16 (V)*
The Founder *'17*
The Hero *'17*
Hearts Beat Loud *'18*
The House of Tomorrow *'18*
Nostalgia *'18*

Deborah Offner (1951-)
Streetwalkin' *'85*
Unlawful Entry *'92*

Damian O'Flynn (1907-82)
Wake Island *'42*
Crack-Up *'46*
The Devil on Wheels *'47*
Daniel Boone: Trail Blazer *'56*

Jakob Oftebro
Kon-Tiki *'12*
In Order of Disappearance *'14*

Issey Ogata (1952-)
Yi Yi *'00*
The Sun *'05*

Ken Ogata (1937-2008)
Vengeance Is Mine *'79*
Samurai Reincarnation *'81*
Virus *'82*
The Ballad of Narayama *'83*
Mishima: A Life in Four Chapters *'85*
The Pillow Book *'95*
Gonin 2 *'96*
The Hidden Blade *'04*

Mayumi Ogawa (1939-)
Zatoichi: The Blind Swordsman's Vengeance *'66*
Vengeance Is Mine *'79*

Bulle Ogier (1939-)
The Valley Obscured by the Clouds *'70*
The Discreet Charm of the Bourgeoisie *'72*
Maitresse *'76*
Tricheurs *'84*
Son of Gascogne *'95*
Irma Vep *'96*
Somewhere in the City *'97*
Shattered Image *'98*
Venus Beauty Institute *'98*
Merci Docteur Rey *'04*
Belle Toujours *'06*
The Duchess of Langeais *'07*

Ian Ogilvy (1943-)
The She-Beast *'65*
The Sorcerers *'67*
The Conqueror Worm *'68*
Wuthering Heights *'70*
And Now the Screaming Starts *'73*
From Beyond the Grave *'73*
No Sex Please-We're British *'73*
Death Becomes Her *'92*
Eddie Presley *'92*
Puppet Master 5: The Final Chapter *'94*
Fugitive Mind *'99*

Jorgo Ognenovski
Warrior of Justice *'96*
Stalked *'99*

Dean O'Gorman (1976-)
Young Hercules *'97*
When Love Comes *'98*
Beyond Justice *'01*
The Legend of Bloody Mary *'08*
Kawa *'11*

Gail O'Grady (1963-)
Nobody's Perfect *'90*
Celtic Pride *'96*
That Old Feeling *'96*
Deuce Bigalow: Male Gigolo *'99*
Another Woman's Husband *'00*
Lip Service *'00*
Sleep Easy, Hutch Rimes *'00*
Hope Ranch *'02*
Lucky Seven *'03*
Sex and the Single Mom *'03*
More Sex and the Single Mom *'05*
All I Want for Christmas *'07*
The Sitter *'07*
An American Carol *'08*
Circle *'10*
ChromeSkull: Laid to Rest 2 *'11*
Shadow on the Mesa *'13*

Nivek Ogre
Repo! The Genetic Opera *'08*
2001 Maniacs: Field of Screams *'10*

Shun Oguri (1982-)
Azumi *'03*
Azumi 2 *'05*
Crows Zero *'07*

Sandra Oh (1971-)
Double Happiness *'94*
Bean *'97*
Last Night *'98*
Guinevere *'99*
Dancing at the Blue Iguana *'00*
Waking the Dead *'00*
The Princess Diaries *'01*
Big Fat Liar *'02*
Long Life, Happiness and Prosperity *'02*
Break a Leg *'03*
Rick *'03*
Under the Tuscan Sun *'03*
Mulan 2 *'04 (V)*
Sideways *'04*
Cake *'05*
Sorry, Haters *'05*
Hard Candy *'06*
The Night Listener *'06*
Defendor *'09*
Rabbit Hole *'10*
Ramona and Beezus *'10*
Tammy *'14*
Catfight *'17*

Soon-Teck Oh (1943-)
The Man with the Golden Gun *'74*
East of Eden *'80*
Missing in Action 2: The Beginning *'85*
A Home of Our Own *'93*
Beverly Hills Ninja *'96*
Mulan *'98 (V)*
Yellow *'98*
True Blue *'01*

Michael O'Hagan (1941-)
For Love or Country: The Arturo Sandoval Story *'00*
Quicksand *'01*

Brian O'Halloran (1969-)
Clerks *'94*
Mallrats *'95*
Chasing Amy *'97*
Jay and Silent Bob Strike Back *'01*
Clerks 2 *'06*
Brutal Massacre: A Comedy *'07*
How Do You Know *'10*

Jack O'Halloran (1943-)
Farewell, My Lovely *'75*
King Kong *'76*
Superman: The Movie *'78*
Superman 2 *'80*
Dragnet *'87*
Hero and the Terror *'88*

George O'Hanlon (1917-89)
The Joe McDoakes Collection *'42*
Heading for Heaven *'47*
The Tanks Are Coming *'51*
Cattle Town *'52*
Jetsons: The Movie *'90 (V)*

George O'Hanlon, Jr. (1953-)
Our Time *'74*
Where Have All the People Gone? *'74*
The Evil *'78*

Catherine O'Hara (1954-)
Rock & Rule *'83 (V)*
After Hours *'85*
Heartburn *'86*
Beetlejuice *'88*
Betsy's Wedding *'90*
Dick Tracy *'90*
Home Alone *'90*
Home Alone 2: Lost in New York *'92*
There Goes the Neighborhood *'92*
The Nightmare Before Christmas *'93 (V)*
The Paper *'94*
A Simple Twist of Fate *'94*
Wyatt Earp *'94*
Tall Tale: The Unbelievable Adventures of Pecos Bill *'95*
The Last of the High Kings *'96*
Waiting for Guffman *'96*
Home Fries *'98*
Late Last Night *'99*
The Life Before This *'99*
Best in Show *'00*
Orange County *'02*
A Mighty Wind *'03*
Lemony Snicket's A Series of Unfortunate Events *'04*
Surviving Christmas *'04*
Chicken Little *'05 (V)*
Game 6 *'05*
Brother Bear 2 *'06 (V)*
For Your Consideration *'06*
Monster House *'06 (V)*
Over the Hedge *'06 (V)*
Penelope *'06*
Away We Go *'09*
Where the Wild Things Are *'09 (V)*
Killers *'10*
Temple Grandin *'10*
Frankenweenie *'12 (V)*
A.C.O.D. *'13*
The Right Kind Of Wrong *'13*

David O'Hara (1965-)
Braveheart *'95*
Some Mother's Son *'96*
The Matchmaker *'97*
Oliver Twist *'97*
Fever *'99*
Janice Beard *'99*
Jesus *'00*
Crossfire Trail *'01*
Made *'01*
Stander *'03*
Hotel Rwanda *'04*
Tristan & Isolde *'06*
Doomsday *'08*
Wanted *'08*
Attack on Darfur *'09*
Golf in the Kingdom *'10*
Stand Off *'11*

Jenny O'Hara (1942-)
Last Song *'80*
Career Opportunities *'91*
Angie *'94*
Robin Cook's Terminal *'96*
Wishmaster *'97*
The Truth About Jane *'00*
Mystic River *'03*
Forty Shades of Blue *'05*
Devil *'10*

Maureen O'Hara (1920-2015)
The Hunchback of Notre Dame *'39*
Jamaica Inn *'39*
Dance, Girl, Dance *'40*
How Green Was My Valley *'41*
The Black Swan *'42*
To the Shores of Tripoli *'42*
The Fallen Sparrow *'43*
Immortal Sergeant *'43*
This Land Is Mine *'43*
Buffalo Bill *'44*
The Spanish Main *'45*
Do You Love Me? *'46*
The Foxes of Harrow *'47*
Miracle on 34th Street *'47*
Sinbad, the Sailor *'47*
Sitting Pretty *'48*
The Forbidden Street *'49*
Rio Grande *'50*
At Sword's Point *'51*
Against All Flags *'52*
The Australian Story *'52*
The Quiet Man *'52*
The Redhead from Wyoming *'53*
War Arrow *'53*
Lady Godiva *'55*
The Long Gray Line *'55*
Wings of Eagles *'57*
Our Man in Havana *'59*
Deadly Companions *'61*
The Parent Trap *'61*
Mr. Hobbs Takes a Vacation *'62*
McLintock! *'63*
Spencer's Mountain *'63*
The Rare Breed *'66*
Big Jake *'71*
Only the Lonely *'91*
The Christmas Box *'95*

Denis O'Hare (1962-)
River Red *'98*
The Anniversary Party *'01*
Garden State *'04*
Angel Rodriguez *'05*
Derailed *'05*
Stephanie Daley *'06*
American Loser *'07*
The Babysitters *'07*
Charlie Wilson's War *'07*
A Mighty Heart *'07*
Changeling *'08*
Milk *'08*
Pretty Bird *'08*
Quarantine *'08*
Duplicity *'09*
An Englishman in New York *'09*
The Proposal *'09*
Edge of Darkness *'10*
The Eagle *'11*
C.O.G. *'13*
Dallas Buyers Club *'13*
The Normal Heart *'14*
The Pyramid *'14*
The Town That Dreaded Sundown *'14*
Lizzie *'18*
The Day Shall Come *'19*
Swallow *'20*

Michael O'Hare (1952-2012)
The Promise *'79*
C.H.U.D. *'84*

Caitlin (Kathleen Heaney) O'Heaney (1953-)
He Knows You're Alone *'80*
Savage Weekend *'80*

Jim O'Heir
Road Hard *'15*
Logan Lucky *'17*

Cornelia Hayes O'Herlihy
The Old Curiosity Shop *'94*
Mother Teresa: In the Name of God's Poor *'97*
Rudyard Kipling's the Second Jungle Book: Mowgli and Baloo *'97*

Dan O'Herlihy (1919-2005)
Odd Man Out *'47*
Kidnapped *'48*
Macbeth *'48*
At Sword's Point *'51*
Actors and Sin *'52*
Invasion U.S.A. *'52*
Operation Secret *'52*
Sword of Venus *'53*
The Black Shield of Falworth *'54*
Robinson Crusoe *'54*
The Virgin Queen *'55*
Home Before Dark *'58*
The Young Land *'59*
One Foot in Hell *'60*
The King of the Roaring '20s: The Story of Arnold Rothstein *'61*
Fail-Safe *'64*
100 Rifles *'69*
The People *'71*
The Carey Treatment *'72*
The Tamarind Seed *'74*
Banjo Hackett *'76*
Deadly Game *'77*
MacArthur *'77*
Death Ray 2000 *'81*
Halloween 3: Season of the Witch *'82*
The Last Starfighter *'84*
The Whoopee Boys *'86*
The Dead *'87*
RoboCop *'87*
A Waltz Through the Hills *'88*
RoboCop 2 *'90*
Love, Cheat & Steal *'93*
The Rat Pack *'98*

Gavan O'Herlihy (1954-)
The California Kid *'74*
A Wedding *'78*
Willow *'88*
Hidden Assassin *'94*
Seven Days of Grace *'06*
The Descent 2 *'09*

Nils Ohlund
Come Undone *'00*
You'll Get Over It *'02*

Carol Ohmart (1927-)
House on Haunted Hill *'58*
Born Reckless *'59*
Naked Youth *'59*
One Man's Way *'63*
Spider Baby *'64*

John O'Hurley (1954-)
Mirror Images *'91*
The Power Within *'95*
Firetrap *'01*
Race to Space *'01*
Knuckle Sandwich *'04*
Beethoven's Christmas Adventure *'11*

Tony Oller
Field of Vision *'11*
Beneath the Darkness *'12*

Berta Ojea
The Devil's Backbone *'01*
The Women on the Sixth Floor *'10*

Masi Oka (1974-)
Balls of Fury *'07*
Get Smart *'08*
Spies in Disguise *'19*

Eiji Okada (1920-95)
Hiroshima, Mon Amour *'59*
The Ugly American *'63*
Woman in the Dunes *'64*
Face of Another *'66*
Lady Snowblood *'73*

Mariko Okada (1933-)
Samurai 2: Duel at Ichijoji Temple *'55*
Samurai 3: Duel at Ganryu Island *'56*
An Autumn Afternoon *'62*

Henry Okawa (1905-71)
The Bridge on the River Kwai *'57*
The Wind Cannot Read *'58*

Dennis O'Keefe (1908-68)
Cimarron *'31*
Libeled Lady *'36*
The Bad Man of Brimstone *'38*
You'll Find Out *'40*
Broadway Limited *'41*
Mr. District Attorney *'41*
Topper Returns *'41*
Hangmen Also Die *'42*
Hi Diddle Diddle *'43*
The Leopard Man *'43*
Fighting Seabees *'44*
Sensations of 1945 *'44*
Brewster's Millions *'45*
Getting Gertie's Garter *'45*
Doll Face *'46*
Abandoned *'47*
Dishonored Lady *'47*
T-Men *'47*
Raw Deal *'48*
Walk a Crooked Mile *'48*
Cover Up *'49*
Great Dan Patch *'49*
Woman On the Run *'50*
Everything I Have is Yours *'52*
All Hands on Deck *'61*
The Naked Flame *'68*

Doug O'Keefe (1966-)
Specimen *'97*
The Invitation *'03*

Jodi Lyn O'Keefe (1978-)
Halloween: H20 *'98*
She's All That *'99*
The Crow: Salvation *'00*
Devil in the Flesh 2 *'00*
Whatever It Takes *'00*
Prison Break: The Final Break *'09*

Michael O'Keefe (1955-)
Gray Lady Down *'77*
Caddyshack *'80*
The Great Santini *'80*
Nate and Hayes *'83*
The Slugger's Wife *'85*
The Whoopee Boys *'86*
Ironweed *'87*
Bridge to Silence *'89*
Fear *'90*
Too Young to Die *'90*
Nina Takes a Lover *'94*
Edie & Pen *'95 (C)*
Three Wishes *'95*
Ghosts of Mississippi *'96*
Just One Night *'00*
The Glass House *'01*
Prancer Returns *'01*
The Hot Chick *'02*
Defending Our Kids: The Julie Posey Story *'03*
An American Crime *'07*
Cherry Crush *'07*

Michael Clayton '07
Frozen River '08
American Violet '09
A Thousand Cuts '12
The Wait '13

Miles O'Keeffe (1954-)
Tarzan, the Ape Man '81
Ator the Fighting Eagle '83
Sword of the Valiant '83
Campus Man '87
The Drifter '88
The Lone Runner '88
Waxwork '88
Cartel '90
Relentless 2: Dead On '91
Zero Tolerance '93
Silent Hunter '94
Pocahontas: The Legend '95
Diamondbacks '99
Out of the Black '01
Clawed: The Legend of Sasquatch '05

Don O'Kelly (1924-66)
Frontier Uprising '61
The Hostage '67

Donal O'Kelly (1958-)
The Van '95
Bloom '03
Kings '07

Tim O'Kelly
Targets '68
The Passing of Evil '70

Megumi Okina (1979-)
Red Shadow '01
Ju-On: The Grudge '03
Shutter '08

Denjiro Okochi (1898-1962)
Sanshiro Sugata '43
No Regrets for Our Youth '46

Sophie Okonedo (1968-)
Ace Ventura: When Nature Calls '95
Dirty Pretty Things '03
Hotel Rwanda '04
Aeon Flux '05
Alex Rider: Operation Stormbreaker '06
Scenes of a Sexual Nature '06
Martian Child '07
Oliver Twist '07
The Secret Life of Bees '08
After Earth '13
The Escape Artist '13
Wild Rose '18

Eiji Okuda (1950-)
The Pianist '91
The Sea is Watching '02

Enuka Okuma (1976-)
House of the Dead '03
What Color Is Love? '08

Yuji Okumoto (1959-)
The Karate Kid: Part 2 '86
True Believer '89
Bloodfist 5: Human Target '93
Nemesis '93
Robot Wars '93
Hard Justice '95
Mean Guns '97
I'll Remember April '99
Partners '99
The Base 2: Guilty as Charged '00
The Crow: Wicked Prayer '05
Only the Brave '06

Olafur Darri Olafsson (1973-)
101 Reykjavik '00
Beowulf & Grendel '06
The Last Witch Hunter '15
The Vanishing '19

Warner Oland (1880-1938)
Don Juan '26
Tell It to the Marines '26
Twinkletoes '26
The Jazz Singer '27
Old San Francisco '27
When a Man Loves '27
The Black Camel '31
Dishonored '31
Drums of Jeopardy '31
Shanghai Express '32
Charlie Chan in London '34
The Painted Veil '34
Charlie Chan in Egypt '35
Charlie Chan in Paris '35
Charlie Chan in Shanghai '35
Charlie Chan's Secret '35
Werewolf of London '35
Charlie Chan at the Circus '36
Charlie Chan at the Opera '36
Charlie Chan at the Race Track '36
Charlie Chan at Monte Carlo '37
Charlie Chan at the Olympics '37
Charlie Chan on Broadway '37

Ken Olandt
April Fool's Day '86
Summer School '87
Leprechaun '93
Digital Man '94
Darkdrive '98
Interceptor Force '99
Velocity Trap '99

Daniel Olbrychski (1945-)
Everything for Sale '68
Landscape After Battle '70
The Deluge '73
Land of Promise '74
Maids of Wilko '79
The Tin Drum '79
La Truite '83
The Decalogue '88
The Unbearable Lightness of Being '88
Salt '10

William Oldham (1970-)
Matewan '87
Old Joy '06
Wendy and Lucy '08

Gary Oldman (1958-)
Meantime '81
Sid & Nancy '86
Prick Up Your Ears '87
Track 29 '88
Chattahoochee '89
Criminal Law '89
Rosencrantz & Guildenstern Are Dead '90
State of Grace '90
JFK '91
Bram Stoker's Dracula '92
Romeo Is Bleeding '93
True Romance '93
Immortal Beloved '94
The Professional '94
Murder in the First '95
The Scarlet Letter '95
Basquiat '96
Air Force One '97
The Fifth Element '97
Lost in Space '98
Quest for Camelot '98 (V)
The Contender '00
Jesus '00
Hannibal '01
Nobody's Baby '01
Interstate 60 '02
Sin '02
Tiptoes '03
Dead Fish '04
Harry Potter and the Prisoner of Azkaban '04
Batman Begins '05
Harry Potter and the Goblet of Fire '05
The Backwoods '06
Harry Potter and the Order of the Phoenix '07
The Dark Knight '08
A Christmas Carol '09 (V)
Planet 51 '09 (V)
Rain Fall '09
The Unborn '09
The Book of Eli '10
Countdown to Zero '10 (N)
Guns, Girls and Gambling '11
Harry Potter and the Deathly Hallows, Part 2 '11
Kung Fu Panda 2 '11 (V)
Red Riding Hood '11
Tinker Tailor Soldier Spy '11
The Dark Knight Rises '12
Lawless '12
Paranoia '13
Dawn of the Planet of the Apes '14
RoboCop '14
Child 44 '15
Criminal '16
Man Down '16
Darkest Hour '17
The Hitman's Bodyguard '17
The Space Between Us '17
Hunter Killer '18
The Courier '19
Killers Anonymous '19
The Laundromat '19
Mary '19

Brandon Olds
The Sandlot 3: Heading Home '07
To Be Fat Like Me '07

Gabriel Olds (1974-)
Andersonville '95
Animal Room '95
Without Limits '97
A Town Has Turned to Dust '98
Urbania '00
Now & Forever '02
Life of the Party '05
Open House '10

Matt O'Leary (1987-)
Domestic Disturbance '01
Frailty '02
Spy Kids 2: The Island of Lost Dreams '02
Spy Kids 3-D: Game Over '03
Havoc '05
Brick '06
Death Sentence '07
American Son '08
Mother's Day '10
Natural Selection '11
Fat Kid Rules the World '12
Natural Selection '12

William O'Leary (1957-)
Flight of Black Angel '91
Hot Shots! '91
In the Line of Duty: Ambush in Waco '93
Candyman 2: Farewell to the Flesh '94

Craig Olejnik (1979-)
Margaret's Museum '95
Obituary '06

Larisa Oleynik (1981-)
The Baby-Sitters' Club '95
Ten Things I Hate about You '99
100 Girls '00
A Time for Dancing '00
Pope Dreams '06
Together Again for the First Time '08

Ken Olin (1954-)
Queens Logic '91
Dead by Sunset '95
Til There Was You '96

Lena Olin (1955-)
The Unbearable Lightness of Being '88
Enemies, a Love Story '89
Havana '90
Mr. Jones '93
Romeo Is Bleeding '93
The Night and the Moment '94
Night Falls on Manhattan '96
Polish Wedding '97
Mystery Men '99
The Ninth Gate '99
Chocolat '00
Ignition '01
Darkness '02
Queen of the Damned '02
Hollywood Homicide '03
United States of Leland '03
Casanova '05
The Devil You Know '05
Awake '07
The Reader '08
Remember Me '10
Night Train to Lisbon '13
Maya Dardel '17

Ingrid Oliu
Stand and Deliver '88
Real Women Have Curves '02

Luis Oliva
The Christmas Choir '08
The Cutting Edge 3: Chasing the Dream '08

Barret Oliver (1973-)
Invitation to Hell '84
The NeverEnding Story '84
Cocoon '85
D.A.R.Y.L. '85
The Secret Garden '87
Cocoon: The Return '88

Charles Oliver (1907-83)
The Green Cockatoo '37
Ask a Policeman '38
The Hooded Terror '38

Christian Oliver (1972-)
Eat Your Heart Out '96
Kept '01
The Good German '06
Subject Two '06
Speed Racer '08
Tribute '09

David Oliver (1962-92)
Night of the Creeps '86
The Horror Show '89
Miracle in the Wilderness '91

Edna May Oliver (1883-1942)
Half-Shot at Sunrise '30
Cimarron '31
Cracked Nuts '31
The Conquerors '32
Hold 'Em Jail '32
Penguin Pool Murder '32
Little Women '33
Murder On the Blackboard '34
David Copperfield '35
Murder On a Honeymoon '35
No More Ladies '35
Romeo and Juliet '36
A Tale of Two Cities '36
Parnell '37
Little Miss Broadway '38
Paradise for Three '38
Rosalie '38
Drums Along the Mohawk '39
Nurse Edith Cavell '39
The Story of Vernon and Irene Castle '39
Pride and Prejudice '40

Gordon Oliver (1911-95)
The Case of the Stuttering Bishop '37
San Quentin '37
Blondie '38
Follies Girl '43
Heavenly Days '44
The Spiral Staircase '46

John Oliver
The Love Guru '08
The Lion King '19

Michael Oliver (1981-)
Problem Child '90
Problem Child 2 '91

Rochelle Oliver
1918 '85
On Valentine's Day '86
Courtship '87
An Unremarkable Life '89
Scent of a Woman '92

Stephen Oliver
Motor Psycho '65
Angels from Hell '68
Werewolves on Wheels '71
Cycle Psycho '72
Savage Abduction '73

Susan Oliver (1937-90)
The Gene Krupa Story '59
Butterfield 8 '60
The Caretakers '63
Disorderly Orderly '64
Guns of Diablo '64
Looking for Love '64
Your Cheatin' Heart '64
The Love-Ins '67
Black Brigade '69
Ginger in the Morning '73

Vic Oliver
He Found a Star '41
Give Us the Moon '44

Robert Oliveri (1978-)
Honey, I Shrunk the Kids '89
Edward Scissorhands '90
Honey, I Blew Up the Kid '92

Laurence Olivier (1907-89)
Perfect Understanding '33
As You Like It '36
I Stand Condemned '36
Fire Over England '37
The Divorce of Lady X '38
Wuthering Heights '39
Pride and Prejudice '40
Rebecca '40
21 Days '40
The Forty-Ninth Parallel '41
That Hamilton Woman '41
Henry V '44
This Happy Breed '47 (N)
Hamlet '48
Carrie '52
Beggar's Opera '54
Richard III '55
The Prince and the Showgirl '57
The Entertainer '60
Spartacus '60
Term of Trial '63
Bunny Lake Is Missing '65
Othello '65
Khartoum '66
Romeo and Juliet '68 (N)
The Shoes of the Fisherman '68
Battle of Britain '69
Oh! What a Lovely War '69
David Copperfield '70
Nicholas and Alexandra '71
Sleuth '72
The Merchant of Venice '73
Marathon Man '76
The Seven-Per-Cent Solution '76
A Bridge Too Far '77
Jesus of Nazareth '77
The Betsy '78
The Boys from Brazil '78
Dracula '79
A Little Romance '79
The Jazz Singer '80
Brideshead Revisited '81
Clash of the Titans '81
The Bounty '84
The Last Days of Pompeii '84
Wagner: The Complete Epic '85
Ebony Tower '86
A Voyage 'Round My Father '89
Sky Captain and the World of Tomorrow '04

Paul Olivier (1876-1948)
A Nous la Liberte '31
Le Million '31

Dawn Olivieri
Devil's Den '06
Hydra '09
Traffik '18

Silvio Oliviero
Graveyard Shift '87
Gotti '96

America Olivo
Circle '10
Maniac '12

Walter Olkewicz (1948-)
Can I Do It. . . Till I Need Glasses? '77
1941 '79
The Client '94
The Good Old Boys '95
Meeting Daddy '98
Milo '98

Edward James Olmos (1947-)
Wolfen '81
Zoot Suit '81
Blade Runner '82
Virus '82
Stand and Deliver '88
Triumph of the Spirit '89
Talent for the Game '91
American Me '92
A Million to Juan '94
My Family '94 (N)
Roosters '95
Caught '96
The Disappearance of Garcia Lorca '96
Larry McMurtry's Dead Man's Walk '96
Selena '96
Hollywood Confidential '97
The Wonderful Ice Cream Suit '98
Bonanno: A Godfather's Story '99
Gossip '99
The Wall '99
The Road to El Dorado '00 (V)
In the Time of the Butterflies '01
Steve Martini's The Judge '01
Splinter '06
Beverly Hills Chihuahua '08 (V)
Battlestar Galactica: The Plan '09
I'm Still Here '10
The Green Hornet '11
Filly Brown '12
Go for Sisters '13
2 Guns '13
Coco '17
A Dog's Way Home '19

Gertrude (Olmstead) Olmsted (1904-75)
California Straight Ahead '25
Cobra '25
The Monster '25
Torrent '26
Mr. Wu '27

Alex O'Loughlin (1976-)
Feed '05
The Incredible Journey of Mary Bryant '05
The Invisible '07
Whiteout '09
The Back-Up Plan '10

Gerald S. O'Loughlin (1921-2015)
Cop Hater '58
A Hatful of Rain '59
Ensign Pulver '64
A Fine Madness '66
In Cold Blood '67
Desperate Characters '71
The Valachi Papers '72
Detour to Terror '80
Frances '82
Crimes of Passion '84
Quicksilver '86
Three Strikes '00

Ashley (Fuller) Olsen (1986-)
Double Double Toil and Trouble '94
To Grandmother's House We Go '94
How the West Was Fun '95
It Takes Two '95
Billboard Dad '98
Charlie's Angels: Full Throttle '03 (C)
New York Minute '04

Elizabeth Olsen (1989-)
Martha Marcy May Marlene '11
Peace, Love & Misunderstanding '11
Liberal Arts '12
Red Lights '12
Silent House '12
In Secret '13
Kill Your Darlings '13

Oldboy '13
Very Good Girls '13
Godzilla '14
Ingrid Goes West '17
Wind River '17

Eric Christian Olsen (1977-)
Not Another Teen Movie '01
The Hot Chick '02
Local Boys '02
Dumb and Dumberer: When Harry Met Lloyd '03
Cellular '04
Death Valley '04
Beerfest '06
The Comebacks '07
License to Wed '07
Fired Up! '09
The Six Wives of Henry Lefay '09
Sunshine Cleaning '09
The Back-Up Plan '10
The Thing '11

Mary-Kate Olsen (1986-)
Double Double Toil and Trouble '94
To Grandmother's House We Go '94
How the West Was Fun '95
It Takes Two '95
Billboard Dad '98
Charlie's Angels: Full Throttle '03 (C)
New York Minute '04
The Wackness '08
Beastly '11

Merlin Olsen (1940-2010)
The Undefeated '69
Mitchell '75

Moroni Olsen (1899-1954)
Annie Oakley '35
Seven Keys to Baldpate '35
Mary of Scotland '36
Mummy's Boys '36
Snow White and the Seven Dwarfs '37 (V)
Kentucky '38
Allegheny Uprising '39
Rose of Washington Square '39
Susannah of the Mounties '39
Brigham Young: Frontiersman '40
East of the River '40
Dangerously We Live '41
The Glass Key '42
Reunion in France '42
Air Force '43
Ali Baba and the Forty Thieves '43
Buffalo Bill '44
Cobra Woman '44
Notorious '46
High Wall '47
The Long Night '47
The Possessed '47
Call Northside 777 '48
The Fountainhead '49
Task Force '49
Father of the Bride '50
Father's Little Dividend '51
The Long, Long Trailer '54

Richard Olsen
Wildflower '91
Stephen King's The Night Flier '96

James Olson (1930-)
The Strange One '57
Rachel, Rachel '68
Crescendo '69
Moon Zero Two '70
The Andromeda Strain '71
Paper Man '71
The Groundstar Conspiracy '72
Missiles of October '74
Someone I Touched '75
Strange New World '75
The Spell '77
My Sister, My Love '78
Cave-In! '79
Ragtime '81
Amityville 2: The Possession '82
Commando '85

Jeff Olson
Benji: Off the Leash! '04
Believe '07

Kaitlin Olson (1975-)
Weather Girl '09
Leap Year '10
Finding Dory '16

Nancy Olson (1928-)
Sunset Boulevard '50
Union Station '50
Force of Arms '51
Big Jim McLain '52
The Boy From Oklahoma '54
Battle Cry '55
Pollyanna '60
The Absent-Minded Professor '61
Son of Flubber '63
Snowball Express '72
Airport '75 '75
Making Love '82

Ty Olsson (1974-)
Her Sister's Keeper '06
Christmas Caper '07
Second Sight '07
High Noon '09
Behemoth '11
Iris Johansen's The Killing Game '11
Smart Cookies '13
12 Rounds 3: Lockdown '15

Timothy Olyphant (1968-)
The First Wives Club '96
Ellen Foster '97
Scream 2 '97
When Trumpets Fade '98
Go '99
No Vacancy '99
Beyond Suspicion '00
The Broken Hearts Club '00
Gone in 60 Seconds '00
Rock Star '01
The Safety of Objects '01
Coastlines '02
Dreamcatcher '03
A Man Apart '03
The Girl Next Door '04
Catch and Release '07
Hitman '07
Live Free or Die Hard '07
Meet Bill '07
Stop-Loss '08
The Crazies '09
High Life '09
A Perfect Getaway '09
Elektra Luxx '10
I Am Number Four '11
Rango '11 (V)
This Is Where I Leave You '14
Mother's Day '16

Bingo O'Malley
Two Evil Eyes '90
Bob Roberts '92

Daragh O'Malley
Sharpe's Eagle '93
Sharpe's Rifles '93
Sharpe's Battle '94
Sharpe's Company '94
Sharpe's Enemy '94
Sharpe's Gold '94
Sharpe's Honour '94
Sharpe's Sword '94
Sharpe's Mission '96
Sharpe's Regiment '96
Sharpe's Siege '96
Sharpe's Justice '97
Sharpe's Revenge '97
Sharpe's Waterloo '97
The Magnificent Seven '98
Cleopatra '99
Longitude '00
Sharpe's Challenge '06
Sharpe's Peril '08

J. Pat O'Malley (1901-85)
Lassie, Come Home '43
Witness for the Prosecution '57
101 Dalmatians '61 (V)
Hey There, It's Yogi Bear '64 (V)
The Jungle Book '67 (V)
Star! '68

Michael O'Malley (1966-)
28 Days '00
The Perfect Man '05
Meet Dave '08
Eat, Pray, Love '10
Cedar Rapids '11

Mike O'Malley (1966-)
Behind the Candelabra '13
R.I.P.D. '13
So Undercover '13

Pat O'Malley (1891-1966)
Mothers Cry '30
Evelyn Prentice '34
The Perils of Pauline '34
The Miracle Rider '35
Fighting Marines '36
The Adventures of Ichabod and Mr. Toad '49 (V)
Invasion of the Body Snatchers '56

Rex O'Malley (1901-76)
Camille '36
Midnight '39

Jason O'Mara (1972-)
Resident Evil: Extinction '07
One for the Money '12
Wakefield '17

Kate O'Mara (1939-2014)
The Horror of Frankenstein '70
The Vampire Lovers '70

Omarion (1984-)
See Omari (Omarion) Grandberry

Judd Omen (1940-)
Howling 2: Your Sister Is a Werewolf '85
Pee-wee's Big Adventure '85
Dollman '90

Afemo Omilami (1950-)
DROP Squad '94
Bringing Out the Dead '99
Drumline '02
Hounddog '08
Beneath the Dark '10
Blood Done Sign My Name '10

Pat O'Moore (1909-83)
Sahara '43
The Two Mrs. Carrolls '47

Andy On (1976-)
Black Mask 2: City of Masks '02
The Kumite '03
Three Kingdoms: Resurrection of the Dragon '08
The Lost Bladesman '16

Ryan O'Nan
The Dry Land '10
Joint Body '11
Altered Minds '13

Anny Ondra (1903-87)
Blackmail '29
The Manxman '29

Anne O'Neal (1893-1971)
Open Secret '48
Gun Crazy '49

Frederick O'Neal (1905-92)
Tarzan's Peril '51
Take a Giant Step '59
The Sins of Rachel Cade '61
Free, White, and 21 '62

Griffin O'Neal (1964-)
The Escape Artist '82
April Fool's Day '86
The Children of Times Square '86
The Wraith '87
Assault of the Killer Bimbos '88
Ghoulies 3: Ghoulies Go to College '91
Evil Lives '92

Patrice O'Neal (1969-2011)
Scary Movie 4 '06
Nature Calls '12

Patrick O'Neal (1927-94)
The Black Shield of Falworth '54
The Mad Magician '54
From the Terrace '60
In Harm's Way '65
King Rat '65
Alvarez Kelly '66
A Fine Madness '66
Assignment to Kill '69
Castle Keep '69
El Condor '70
The Kremlin Letter '70
Corky '72
Silent Night, Bloody Night '73
The Way We Were '73
The Stepford Wives '75
Perry Mason Returns '85
The Stuff '85
New York Stories '89
Alice '90
Q & A '90
For the Boys '91
Under Siege '92

Ron O'Neal (1937-2004)
Superfly '72
Freedom Road '79
When a Stranger Calls '79
St. Helen's, Killer Volcano '82
Red Dawn '84
Hero and the Terror '88
Hyper Space '89
Original Gangstas '96
On the Edge '02

Ryan O'Neal (1941-)
The Big Bounce '69
Love Story '70
Wild Rovers '71
What's Up, Doc? '72
Paper Moon '73
Barry Lyndon '75
Nickelodeon '76
A Bridge Too Far '77
The Driver '78
Oliver's Story '78
The Main Event '79
Green Ice '81
So Fine '81
Partners '82
Irreconcilable Differences '84
Tough Guys Don't Dance '87
Chances Are '89
Faithful '95
An Alan Smithee Film: Burn, Hollywood, Burn '97
Sink or Swim '97
Zero Effect '97
Coming Soon '99
The List '99
Epoch '00
People I Know '02
Malibu's Most Wanted '03
Freelancers '12

Shaquille O'Neal (1972-)
Blue Chips '94
Kazaam '96
Good Burger '97 (C)
Steel '97
Scary Movie 4 '06
Grown Ups 2 '13
Blended '14
Uncle Drew '18

Tatum O'Neal (1963-)
Paper Moon '73
The Bad News Bears '76
Nickelodeon '76
International Velvet '78
Circle of Two '80
Basquiat '96
The Home Front '02
My Brother '06
Saving Grace B. Jones '09
The Runaways '10

Ty O'Neal (1978-)
D2: The Mighty Ducks '94
Bug Buster '99
American Outlaws '01

Barbara O'Neil (1910-80)
Stella Dallas '37
The Toy Wife '38
Gone with the Wind '39
The Tower of London '39
All This and Heaven Too '40
I Remember Mama '48
Secret Beyond the Door '48
Whirlpool '49
Angel Face '52
Flame of the Islands '55

Nance O'Neil (1875-1965)
Ladies of Leisure '30
Cimarron '31
The Royal Bed '31

Sally O'Neil (1908-68)
Battling Butler '26
Battle of the Sexes '28
On with the Show '29
Convention Girl '35

Chris O'Neill (1945-97)
Backbeat '94
2 by 4 '98

Con O'Neill (1966-)
The Last Seduction 2 '98
Telstar: The Joe Meek Story '08
Margot '09

Dick O'Neill (1928-98)
Gamera, the Invincible '66
Pretty Poison '68
The Taking of Pelham One Two Three '74
Prime Time '77
The Jerk '79
Wolfen '81
The Mosquito Coast '86
She's Out of Control '89
Dark Justice '91
My Summer Story '94

Ed O'Neill (1946-)
Deliverance '72
Cruising '80
Disorganized Crime '89
K-9 '89
The Adventures of Ford Fairlane '90
Sibling Rivalry '90
Dutch '91
Wayne's World '92
Wayne's World 2 '93
Blue Chips '94
Little Giants '94
Prefontaine '96
The Spanish Prisoner '97
The Bone Collector '99
Lucky Numbers '00
The 10th Kingdom '00
Nobody's Baby '01
Spartan '04
Finding Dory '16

Henry O'Neill (1891-1961)
America '24
Lady Killer '33
I've Got Your Number '34
Massacre '34
Black Fury '35
Living on Velvet '35
The Secret Bride '35
It Happened in New Orleans '36
The Green Light '37
Amazing Dr. Clitterhouse '38
Confessions of a Nazi Spy '39
Four Wives '39
Juarez '39
Castle on the Hudson '40
Billy the Kid '41
Honky Tonk '41
Men of Boys Town '41
Shadow of the Thin Man '41
Johnny Eager '42
Stand by for Action '42
Air Raid Wardens '43
Lost Angel '43
Whistling in Brooklyn '43
The Heavenly Body '44
Nothing But Trouble '44
The Virginian '46
Holiday Affair '49
Scandal Sheet '52

Jennifer O'Neill (1948-)
Rio Lobo '70
Such Good Friends '71
Summer of '42 '71
The Carey Treatment '72
Lady Ice '73
Whiffs '75
The Innocent '76
Force of One '79
Scanners '81
A.D. '85
I Love N.Y. '87
Full Exposure: The Sex Tape Scandals '89
Committed '91
Discretion Assured '93
Bad Love '95
Last Ounce of Courage '12

Kel O'Neill
XX/XY '02
Domino '05
Stephanie Daley '06
Redacted '07

Maggie O'Neill (1962-)
Under Suspicion '92
Invasion: Earth '98
Little Devil '07
Mansfield Park '07

Maire O'Neill (1887-1952)
Juno and the Paycock '30
Sidewalks of London '38

Michael O'Neill (1947-)
The Gun in Betty Lou's Handbag '92
Sunchaser '96
Dancer, Texas-Pop. 81 '98
Dreamcatcher '03
Seabiscuit '03
Transformers '07

Terry O'Neill (1948-)
Dragonheart '96
Kull the Conqueror '97

Alannah Ong
Double Happiness '94
New York Minute '04

Onimaru
Blue Spring '01
9 Souls '03

Yoko Ono (1933-)
The Magic Christian '69
Let It Be '70

Peter Onorati
Fire Birds '90
Goodfellas '90
Camp Nowhere '94
RocketMan '97
Shelter '98
True Friends '98
Tycus '98
The Art of Murder '99
Just Looking '99
Dancing in September '00
Ordinary Sinner '02
Circle '10

Lupe Ontiveros (1942-2012)
El Norte '83
My Family '94
Selena '96
As Good As It Gets '97
Candyman 3: Day of the Dead '98
Picking Up the Pieces '99
Chuck & Buck '00
Gabriela '01
Storytelling '01
Mr. St. Nick '02
Passionada '02
Real Women Have Curves '02
A Girl Like Me: The Gwen Araujo Story '06
Dark Mirror '07
Tortilla Heaven '07
Beverly Hills Chihuahua 2 '10
Our Family Wedding '10

Michael Ontkean (1946-)
Peacekillers '71
The Witching '72
Girls on the Road '73
Slap Shot '77
Making Love '82
Just the Way You Are '84
The Right of the People '86
The Allnighter '87
Maid to Order '87
Clara's Heart '88

Postcards from the Edge *'90*
Nico the Unicorn *'98*
Summer of the Monkeys *'98*
Just a Little Harmless Sex *'99*
Green Sails *'00*
A Killing Spring *'02*
Ghost Cat *'03*

Amanda Ooms (1964-)
Wilderness *'96*
Everlasting Moments *'08*

Dhobi Oparei
Thunderbirds *'04*
Seven Seconds *'05*

David Opatoshu (1918-96)
The Light Ahead *'39*
Exodus *'60*
Guns of Darkness *'62*
Tarzan and the Valley of Gold *'65*
The Defector *'66*
Torn Curtain *'66*
Death of a Gunfighter *'69*
Romance of a Horsethief *'71*
Who'll Stop the Rain? *'78*
Americathon *'79*

Anne Openshaw
Ricky Nelson: Original Teen Idol *'99*
Narc *'02*
We'll Meet Again *'02*

Alan Oppenheimer (1930-)
Star! *'68*
The Groundstar Conspiracy *'72*
The Bionic Woman *'75*
Helter Skelter *'76*
Invisible: The Chronicles of Benjamin Knight *'93*
Trancers 4: Jack of Swords *'93*
Trancers 5: Sudden Deth *'94*

Don Opper (1949-)
Android *'82*
Critters *'86*
Critters 2: The Main Course *'88*
Critters 3 *'91*
Critters 4 *'91*

Terry O'Quinn (1952-)
Mahler *'74*
Heaven's Gate *'81*
Mrs. Soffel *'84*
Places in the Heart *'84*
Mischief *'85*
Silver Bullet *'85*
SpaceCamp *'86*
Women of Valor *'86*
Black Widow *'87*
The Stepfather *'87*
Pin. . . *'88*
Young Guns *'88*
Stepfather 2: Make Room for Daddy *'89*
Blind Fury *'90*
Company Business *'91*
Prisoners of the Sun *'91*
The Rocketeer *'91*
The Cutting Edge *'92*
The Good Fight *'92*
Take Down *'92*
Amityville: A New Generation *'93*
Lipstick Camera *'93*
Tombstone *'93*
Visions of Murder *'93*
JAG *'95*
Shadow Warriors *'95*
Ghosts of Mississippi *'96*
Primal Fear *'96*
The Shadow Conspiracy *'96*
Breast Men *'97*
The X-Files *'98*
Murder in a Small Town *'99*
Rated X *'00*
American Outlaws *'01*
Winds of Terror *'01*
Hometown Legend *'02*
The Locket *'02*
Old School *'03*
Taken From Me: The Tiffany Rubin Story *'10*

Rita Ora (1990-)
Fifty Shades of Grey *'15*
Fifty Shades Freed *'18*

Steve Oram
The Canal *'14*
In Fabric *'18*

Marek Oravec (1983-)
Get Lucky *'13*
The Guernsey Literary & Potato Peel Pie Society *'18*

Geraldine O'Rawe (1969-)
Circle of Friends *'94*
Some Mother's Son *'96*
Amongst Women *'98*
Disco Pigs *'01*

Jerry Orbach (1935-2004)
Cop Hater *'58*
Mad Dog Coll *'61*
Foreplay *'75*
Prince of the City *'81*
Brewster's Millions *'85*
Dream West *'86*
F/X *'86*
Imagemaker *'86*
Love Among Thieves *'86*
Dirty Dancing *'87*
I Love N.Y. *'87*
Someone to Watch Over Me *'87*
Crimes & Misdemeanors *'89*
Dead Women in Lingerie *'90*
Last Exit to Brooklyn *'90*
Beauty and the Beast *'91 (V)*
Delirious *'91*
Out for Justice *'91*
Toy Soldiers *'91 (C)*
Mr. Saturday Night *'92*
Straight Talk *'92*
Universal Soldier *'92*
Aladdin and the King of Thieves *'96 (V)*
Prince of Central Park *'00*

Roy Orbison (1936-88)
Fastest Guitar Alive *'68*
Roadie *'80*
Chuck Berry: Hail! Hail! Rock 'n' Roll *'87*

Melissa Ordway (1983-)
Miami Magma *'11*
Tales of an Ancient Empire *'11*
The Outsider *'14*

Ahna O'Reilly (1985-)
The Help *'11*
The Time Being *'12*
Lucky Them *'13*
All I See Is You *'17*

Cyril O'Reilly (1958-)
Porky's *'82*
Porky's 2: The Next Day *'83*
Purple Hearts *'84*
Navy SEALS *'90*
The Cool Surface *'92*
Philadelphia Experiment 2 *'93*
Bloodfist 7: Manhunt *'95*
Air Rage *'01*

Genevieve O'Reilly
The State Within *'06*
Forget Me Not *'10*

Fereshteh Sadr Orfani
The White Balloon *'95*
The Circle *'00*

Liana Orfei (1937-)
Mill of the Stone Women *'60*
The Giant of Metropolis *'61*
Pirates of the Coast *'61*
The Tartars *'61*
The Avenger *'62*
Damon and Pythias *'62*
Hercules, Samson and Ulysses *'64*
Nefertiti, Queen of the Nile *'64*
Casanova '70 *'65*

Moira Orfei (1931-)
The Mighty Ursus *'61*
Mole Men Against the Son of Hercules *'61*
Ursus in the Valley of the Lions *'62*
The Beast of Babylon Against the Son of Hercules *'63*
Two Gladiators *'64*
The Triumph of Hercules *'66*
The Scent of a Woman *'75*

Silvio Orlando (1957-)
Children of Hannibal *'98*
Not of This World *'99*
The Son's Room *'00*
Light of My Eyes *'01*

Julia Ormond (1965-)
Traffik *'90*
Young Catherine *'91*
Captives *'94*
Legends of the Fall *'94*
First Knight *'95*
Sabrina *'95*
Smilla's Sense of Snow *'96*
Animal Farm *'99 (V)*
The Prime Gig *'00*
Varian's War *'01*
Resistance *'03*
Inland Empire *'06*
I Know Who Killed Me *'07*
Che *'08*
The Curious Case of Benjamin Button *'08*
Kit Kittredge: An American Girl *'08*
Surveillance *'08*
Temple Grandin *'10*
The Wronged Man *'10*
Albatross *'11*
The Green *'11*
The Music Never Stopped *'11*
My Week With Marilyn *'11*
The East *'13*
Rememory *'17*

Alan Ormsby (1944-)
Children Shouldn't Play with Dead Things *'72*
Deathdream *'72*

Anya Ormsby
Children Shouldn't Play with Dead Things *'72*
Thunder County *'74*

Ed O'Ross (1946-)
Ruby's Dream *'82*
Full Metal Jacket *'87*
The Hidden *'87*
Lethal Weapon *'87*
Red Heat *'88*
Another 48 Hrs. *'90*
Play Nice *'92*
Universal Soldier *'92*
Hoodlum *'96*
Dark Planet *'97*
Navajo Blues *'97*
Mindstorm *'01*
Curious George *'06 (V)*
Delta Farce *'07*
Nobody *'07*

Heather O'Rourke (1975-88)
Poltergeist *'82*
Poltergeist 2: The Other Side *'86*
Poltergeist 3 *'88*

Ashley Rose Orr (1990-)
Child Star: The Shirley Temple Story *'01*
Carry Me Home *'04*

Christopher Orr
D3: The Mighty Ducks *'96*
Robin Cook's Invasion *'97*

Leland Orser (1960-)
Excess Baggage *'96*
Independence Day *'96*
Alien: Resurrection *'97*
Saving Private Ryan *'98*
Very Bad Things *'98*
The Bone Collector *'99*
Resurrection *'99*
Brother's Keeper *'02*
Confidence *'03*
Daredevil *'03*
Runaway Jury *'03*
Twisted *'04*
The Good German *'06*
Taken *'08*
Give 'Em Hell Malone *'09*
Morning *'10*
Taken 2 *'12*
The Guest *'14*
Faults *'15*
Taken 3 *'15*

Marina Orsini (1967-)
Battle of the Worlds *'61*
Eddie and the Cruisers 2: Eddie Lives! *'89*
Steel Toes *'06*

Umberto Orsini (1934-)
Mademoiselle *'66*
The Family *'70*
Cesar & Rosalie *'72*
Emmanuelle, the Joys of a Woman *'76*
Good-bye, Emmanuelle *'77*

Dyana Ortelli
Alienator *'89*
Luminarias *'99*

David Orth
In Her Mother's Footsteps *'06*
The Stranger Game *'06*

Frank Orth (1880-1962)
Nancy Drew-Detective *'38*
I Wake Up Screaming *'41*
The Great Rupert *'50*

Zak Orth (1970-)
My Teacher's Wife *'95*
In and Out *'97*
Rose Hill *'97*
When Trumpets Fade *'98*
Down to You *'00*
Loser *'00*
Wet Hot American Summer *'01*
Kill the Poor *'03*
The Baxter *'05*
Prime *'05*
Peter and Vandy *'09*
(Untitled) *'09*
Monogamy *'10*

Ana Ortiz (1971-)
Mr. St. Nick *'02*
Tortilla Heaven *'07*
Little Girl Lost: The Delimar Vera Story *'08*

Antonio Ortiz (1999-)
Knights of the South Bronx *'05*
Just Like the Son *'06*
Illegal Tender *'07*

Humberto Ortiz (1979-)
Dollman *'90*
Arcade *'93*

John Ortiz (1968-)
Riot in the Streets *'96*
The Last Marshal *'99*
Narc *'02*
El Cantante *'06*
Miami Vice *'06*
Take the Lead *'06*
Aliens *vs.* Predator: Requiem *'07*
American Gangster *'07*
Pride and Glory *'08*
Jack Goes Boating *'10*
Silver Linings Playbook *'12*
A Woman, A Part *'17*
Bumblebee *'18*
Peppermint *'18*
Replicas *'18*
Horse Girl *'20*

Shalim Ortiz (1979-)
The Art of Travel *'08*
Expecting a Miracle *'09*

Meaghan Ory (1982-)
Decoys *'04*
Her Sister's Keeper *'06*
Merlin's Apprentice *'06*
Blonde and Blonder *'07*
Nightmare *'07*
Dark House *'09*

Romano Orzari (1964-)
Wilder *'00*
Stiletto Dance *'01*
Silent Night *'02*
Wolves in the Snow *'02*
Bugs *'03*
The Last Hit Man *'08*

Takao Osawa
All About Lily Chou-Chou *'01*
Ichi *'08*

Andrew Osborn (1912-85)
Spaceways *'53*
Angels One Five *'54*
Blackout *'54*

Bud Osborne (1884-1964)
Battling with Buffalo Bill *'31*
Rustlers of Red Dog *'35*
Bride of the Monster *'55*
Tribute to a Bad Man *'56*
Gun Glory *'57*
Night of the Ghouls *'59*

Holmes Osborne (1947-)
That Thing You Do! *'96*
Affliction *'97*
From the Earth to the Moon *'98*
Crazy in Alabama *'99*
Election *'99*
The Mod Squad *'99*
Donnie Darko *'01*
The Quiet American *'02*
Waking Up in Reno *'02*
Cheaper by the Dozen *'03*
Identity *'03*
A Lot Like Love *'05*
Dreamer: Inspired by a True Story *'05*
Southland Tales *'06*
Meet Bill *'07*
The Box *'09*

John Osborne (1929-94)
Get Carter *'71*
The Power of One *'92*

Kent Osborne
Hannah Takes the Stairs *'07*
All the Light in the Sky *'13*

Vivienne Osborne (1896-1961)
Two Seconds *'32*
Supernatural *'33*
No More Ladies *'35*
Follow Your Heart *'36*
Let's Sing Again *'36*
Primrose Path *'40*

Ozzy Osbourne (1948-)
Trick or Treat *'86*
The Jerky Boys *'95*
Austin Powers In Goldmember *'02 (C)*
Gnomeo & Juliet *'11 (V)*

Sharon Osbourne (1952-)
Garfield: A Tail of Two Kitties *'06 (V)*
It's a Boy Girl Thing *'06*

Henry Oscar (1891-1969)
The Man Who Knew Too Much *'34*
The Return of the Scarlet Pimpernel *'37*
The Four Feathers *'39*
The Greed of William Hart *'48*
Postmark for Danger *'56*
The Spaniard's Curse *'58*
The Brides of Dracula *'60*

Per Oscarsson (1927-2010)
Hunger *'66*
Dandy in Aspic *'68*
The Night Visitor *'70*
Endless Night *'71*
The Last Valley *'71*
Secrets *'71*
The New Land *'72*
Blockhouse *'73*
The Girl Who Kicked the Hornet's Nest *'10*
The Girl Who Played With Fire *'10*

Kevin O'Shea (1915-)
The Purple Heart *'44*
A Wing and a Prayer *'44*

Michael O'Shea (1906-73)
Lady of Burlesque *'43*
Jack London *'44*
Something for the Boys *'44*
It's a Pleasure *'45*
Violence *'47*
Smart Woman *'48*
The Big Wheel *'49*
Parole, Inc. *'49*
The Underworld Story *'50*
Fixed Bayonets! *'51*
The Model and the Marriage Broker *'51*
Bloodhounds of Broadway *'52*

Milo O'Shea (1926-2013)
Carry On Cabby *'63*
Ulysses *'67*
Barbarella *'68*
Romeo and Juliet *'68*
The Angel Levine *'70*
Sacco & Vanzetti *'71*
Theatre of Blood *'73*
Peter Lundy and the Medicine Hat Stallion *'77*
Arabian Adventure *'79*
A Time for Miracles *'80*
The Verdict *'82*
The Purple Rose of Cairo *'85*
Broken Vows *'87*
The Dream Team *'89*
Opportunity Knocks *'90*
Only the Lonely *'91*
The Playboys *'92*
The Butcher Boy *'97*
The Matchmaker *'97*
Swing Vote *'99*

Tessie O'Shea (1913-95)
Immortal Battalion *'44*
London Town *'46*
The Russians Are Coming, the Russians Are Coming *'66*
Dr. Jekyll and Mr. Hyde *'68*

Karen Oshima
One Missed Call *'03*
One Missed Call 2 *'05*

Yukari Oshima (1963-)
The Millionaire's Express *'86*
Supercop 2 *'93*

Shugo Oshinari
All About Lily Chou-Chou *'01*
Blue Spring *'01*

Emily Osment (1992-)
Sarah, Plain and Tall: Winter's End *'99*
Spy Kids 2: The Island of Lost Dreams *'02*
Spy Kids 3-D: Game Over *'03*
R.L. Stine's The Haunting Hour: Don't Even Think About It *'07*
Soccer Mom *'08*
Hannah Montana: The Movie *'09*
Beverly Hills Chihuahua 2 *'10 (V)*
Cyberbully *'11*

Haley Joel Osment (1988-)
Forrest Gump *'94*
Bogus *'96*
Last Stand at Saber River *'96*
I'll Remember April *'99*
The Sixth Sense *'99*
Pay It Forward *'00*
A. I.: Artificial Intelligence *'01*
Edges of the Lord *'01*
The Country Bears *'02 (V)*
The Jungle Book 2 *'03 (V)*
Secondhand Lions *'03*
Home of the Giants *'07*
I'll Follow You Down *'13*
Sex Ed *'14*
Tusk *'14*
The World Made Straight *'15*
Almost Friends *'17*

Cliff Osmond (1937-2012)
Kiss Me, Stupid! *'64*
The Fortune Cookie *'66*
Sweet Sugar *'72*
Invasion of the Bee Girls *'73*
Joe Panther *'76*
Hangar 18 *'80*
In Search of a Golden Sky *'84*

Donny Osmond (1957-)
Goin' Coconuts *'78*
Mulan *'98 (V)*

Rena Owen
Once Were Warriors '94
When Love Comes '98
Soul Assassin '01
Nemesis Game '03
Players '03
A Beautiful Life '08
The Last Witch Hunter '15

Seena Owen (1894-1966)
Intolerance '16
Queen Kelly '29

Stefania LaVie Owen
All We Had '16
The Beach Bum '19

Tudor Owen (1898-1979)
My Cousin Rachel '52
Most Dangerous Man Alive '61

Ciaran Owens (1985-)
Agnes Browne '99
Angela's Ashes '99

Dana Elaine Owens (1970-)
See Queen Latifah

Eamon Owens (1983-)
The Butcher Boy '97
The General '98
St. Patrick: The Irish Legend '00
The Boys and Girl From County Clare '03

Patricia Owens (1925-2000)
No Down Payment '57
Sayonara '57
The Fly '58
The Gun Runners '58
The Law and Jake Wade '58
Hell to Eternity '60

Monroe Owsley (1900-37)
Ten Cents a Dance '31
This Modern Age '31
Call Her Savage '32
Brief Moment '33
Goin' to Town '35
Mister Cinderella '36
Hit Parade of 1937 '37

Catherine Oxenberg (1961-)
The Lair of the White Worm '88
K-9000 '89
Swimsuit '89
Charles & Diana: A Palace Divided '93
Treacherous Beauties '94
Heaven Before I Die '96
Boys Will Be Boys '97
Deadly Game '98
The Collectors '99
The Omega Code '99
Frozen in Fear '00
Road Rage '01
Sanctimony '01
The Vector File '03
The Dog Who Saved Christmas Vacation '10

Ed Oxenbould
Alexander and the Terrible, Horrible, No Good, Very Bad Day '14
The Visit '15
Better Watch Out '17
Wildlife '18

David Oxley (1920-85)
Ill Met By Moonlight '57
Night Ambush '57
House of the Living Dead '73

David Oyelowo (1976-)
A Sound of Thunder '05
As You Like It '06
Five Days '07
A Raisin in the Sun '08
Sweet Nothing in My Ear '08
Who Do You Love '08
Small Island '09
96 Minutes '11
Jack Reacher '12
Lincoln '12
Middle of Nowhere '12
The Paperboy '12
Red Tails '12
Lee Daniels' The Butler '13
A Most Violent Year '14
Selma '14
Captive '15
Five Nights in Maine '16
Nina '16
Queen of Katwe '16
A United Kingdom '17
Gringo '18
Don't Let Go '19

Frank Oz (1944-)
The Muppet Movie '79 (V)
The Blues Brothers '80 (C)
The Empire Strikes Back '80
An American Werewolf in London '81
The Great Muppet Caper '81 (V)
The Dark Crystal '82 (V)
Return of the Jedi '83 (V)
The Muppets Take Manhattan '84 (V)
Sesame Street Presents: Follow That Bird '85 (V)
Spies Like Us '85
Innocent Blood '92
The Muppet Christmas Carol '92 (V)
Muppet Treasure Island '96 (V)
Blues Brothers 2000 '98
Muppets from Space '99 (V)
Star Wars: Episode 1-The Phantom Menace '99 (V)
Monsters, Inc. '01 (V)
Star Wars: Episode 2-Attack of the Clones '02 (V)
Star Wars: Episode 3-Revenge of the Sith '05 (V)
Zathura '05 (V)

Frank Richard Oz (1944-)
See Frank Oz

Eitaro (Sakae, Saka Ozawa) Ozawa (1909-88)
Ugetsu '53
The Human Condition: No Greater Love '58

Sakae (Saka) Ozawa (1909-88)
See Eitaro (Sakae, Saka Ozawa) Ozawa

Shoichi Ozawa
The Pornographers '66
The Ballad of Narayama '83
Black Rain '88

Yuya Ozeki (1996-)
Ju-On: The Grudge '03
The Grudge '04

Jack Paar (1918-2004)
Easy Living '49
Love Nest '51

Johnny Pacar (1981-)
Purgatory House '04
Love Hurts '09
Playback '12

Jackson Pace
Queen Sized '08
A Walk in My Shoes '10

Judy Pace (1942-)
Cotton Comes to Harlem '70
Brian's Song '71
Cool Breeze '72
Frogs '72
The Slams '73

Lee Pace (1979-)
Soldier's Girl '03
The White Countess '05
The Fall '06
The Good Shepherd '06
Infamous '06
Miss Pettigrew Lives for a Day '08
Possession '08
A Single Man '09
Ceremony '10
Marmaduke '10
The Resident '10
Lincoln '12
Guardians of the Galaxy '14
The Hobbit: The Battle of the Five Armies '14
The Program '15
Revolt '17

Tom Pace
The Astro-Zombies '67
Girl in Gold Boots '69
Blood Orgy of the She-Devils '74

Frederico Pacifici (1955-)
Flight of the Innocent '93
Fluke '95

Al Pacino (1940-)
Panic in Needle Park '71
The Godfather '72
Scarecrow '73
Serpico '73
The Godfather, Part 2 '74
Dog Day Afternoon '75
Bobby Deerfield '77
And Justice for All '79
Cruising '80
Author! Author! '82
Scarface '83
Revolution '85
Sea of Love '89
Dick Tracy '90
The Godfather, Part 3 '90
Frankie and Johnny '91
Glengarry Glen Ross '92
Scent of a Woman '92
Carlito's Way '93
City Hall '95
Heat '95
Donnie Brasco '96
Looking for Richard '96
Two Bits '96
The Devil's Advocate '97
Any Given Sunday '99
The Insider '99
Insomnia '02
People I Know '02
Simone '02
Gigli '03
The Recruit '03
The Merchant of Venice '04
Two for the Money '05
Ocean's Thirteen '07
88 Minutes '08
Righteous Kill '08
You Don't Know Jack '10
Jack and Jill '11
The Son of No One '11
Stand Up Guys '12
Phil Spector '13
Danny Collins '15
Manglehorn '15
Misconduct '16
Hangman '17
The Pirates of Somalia '17
The Irishman '19

Kinsey Packard
Infestation '09
Circle '10

David Packer (1962-)
You Can't Hurry Love '88
No Strings Attached '98
The Killing Club '01

Joanna Pacula (1957-)
Gorky Park '83
Not Quite Paradise '86
Death Before Dishonor '87
Escape from Sobibor '87
The Kiss '88
Sweet Lies '88
Marked for Death '90
Tombstone '93
Warlock: The Armageddon '93
Deep Red '94
Timemaster '95
Heaven Before I Die '96 (C)
The Haunted Sea '97
My Giant '98
Virus '98
The White Raven '98
The Art of Murder '99
Crash & Byrnes '99
The Hit '01
El Padrino '04
Moscow Heat '04
The Cutter '05
Forget About It '06

Jared Padalecki (1982-)
A Little Inside '01
New York Minute '04
Cry Wolf '05
House of Wax '05
The Christmas Cottage '08
Friday the 13th '09

Sarah Padden (1881-1967)
The Midnight Lady '32
The Power and the Glory '33
Exiled to Shanghai '37
Three Comrades '38
Murder by Invitation '41
The Mad Monster '42
Snuffy Smith, Yard Bird '42
My Dog Shep '46

Manuel Padilla, Jr. (1955-2008)
Tarzan and the Valley of Gold '65
Tarzan and the Great River '67

Pilar Padilla
Bread and Roses '00
In the Time of the Butterflies '01

Lea Padovani (1920-91)
Three Steps North '51
Barrier of the Law '54

Deepika Padukone
xXx: Return of Xander Cage '17
Padmaavat '18

Dira Paes (1969-)
The Emerald Forest '85
Chronically Unfeasible '00
Mango Yellow '02

David Paetkau (1978-)
Final Destination 2 '03
National Lampoon's Holiday Reunion '03

Michael J. Pagan (1985-)
How Stella Got Her Groove Back '98
The Gospel '05
See No Evil '06

Anita Page (1910-2008)
Our Dancing Daughters '28
Broadway Melody '29
The Flying Fleet '29
Navy Blues '29
Our Modern Maidens '29
Speedway '29
Free and Easy '30
Our Blushing Brides '30
The Easiest Way '31
Reducing '31
Sidewalks of New York '31
Are You Listening? '32
Skyscraper Souls '32
Under Eighteen '32

Dallas Page (1956-)
Ready to Rumble '00
The Devil's Rejects '05
Splinter '06

Ellen Page (1987-)
Ghost Cat '03
I Downloaded a Ghost '04
Hard Candy '06
X-Men: The Last Stand '06
An American Crime '07
Juno '07
The Stone Angel '07
The Tracey Fragments '07
Smart People '08
Peacock '09
Whip It '09
Inception '10
Super '10
To Rome with Love '12
The East '13
Freeheld '15
Into the Forest '16
My Life as a Zucchini '16 (V)
Flatliners '17
The Cured '18

Gale Page (1911-83)
Amazing Dr. Clitterhouse '38
Crime School '38
Four Daughters '38
Daughters Courageous '39
Four Wives '39
You Can't Get Away With Murder '39
Knute Rockne: All American '40
They Drive by Night '40
Four Mothers '41

Genevieve Page (1927-)
Fanfan la Tulipe '51
Girl in His Pocket '57
Song Without End '60
El Cid '61
Youngblood Hawke '64
Belle de Jour '67
Decline and Fall...of a Birdwatcher '68
Mayerling '68
The Private Life of Sherlock Holmes '70
Buffet Froid '79

Geraldine Page (1924-87)
Hondo '53
Summer and Smoke '61
Sweet Bird of Youth '62
Toys in the Attic '63
Dear Heart '64
You're a Big Boy Now '66
The Happiest Millionaire '67
Whatever Happened to Aunt Alice? '69
The Beguiled '70
Pete 'n' Tillie '72
The Day of the Locust '75
Nasty Habits '77
The Rescuers '77 (V)
Interiors '78
Honky Tonk Freeway '81
I'm Dancing as Fast as I Can '82
Harry's War '84
The Pope of Greenwich Village '84
The Adventures of Huckleberry Finn '85
The Bride '85
The Trip to Bountiful '85
Walls of Glass '85
White Nights '85

Harrison Page (1941-)
Beyond the Valley of the Dolls '70
Backstairs at the White House '79
Lionheart '90
Carnosaur '93

Joanna Page (1978-)
David Copperfield '99
Very Annie Mary '00
Love Actually '03

Joy Page (1924-2008)
Casablanca '42
Kismet '44
Conquest of Cochise '53

Ken Page (1954-)
The Nightmare Before Christmas '93 (V)
The Alamo '04

LaWanda Page (1920-2002)
Zapped! '82
Mausoleum '83
Shakes the Clown '92
The Meteor Man '93
Friday '95

Michelle Page (1987-)
I Know Who Killed Me '07
Together Again for the First Time '08

Patti Page (1927-2013)
Elmer Gantry '60
Dondi '61
Boys' Night Out '62

Sam Page (1976-)
Falling Up '08
Finish Line '08
Slave '09
Annie Claus is Coming to Town '11

Justin Pagel
Street Gun '96
Thugs '96

Debra Paget (1933-)
Cry of the City '48
House of Strangers '49
Broken Arrow '50
Bird of Paradise '51
Belles on Their Toes '52
Stars and Stripes Forever '52
Demetrius and the Gladiators '54
The Gambler from Natchez '54
Prince Valiant '54
Princess of the Nile '54
Seven Angry Men '55
The Last Hunt '56
Love Me Tender '56
The Ten Commandments '56
Omar Khayyam '57
Journey to the Lost City '58
Why Must I Die? '60
Most Dangerous Man Alive '61
The Mercenaries '62
Tales of Terror '62
The Haunted Palace '63

Nicola Pagett (1945-)
The Viking Queen '67
Operation Daybreak '75
Oliver's Story '78
Privates on Parade '84
A Woman of Substance '84
An Awfully Big Adventure '94

Liana Pai
The Siege '98
Happy Accidents '00

Allison Paige
The Dog Lover '16
Bennett's War '19

Janis Paige (1922-)
Hollywood Canteen '44
Cheyenne '47
One Sunday Afternoon '48
Romance on the High Seas '48
Winter Meeting '48
This Side of the Law '50
Silk Stockings '57
Please Don't Eat the Daisies '60
Bachelor in Paradise '61
The Caretakers '63
Follow the Boys '63

Mabel Paige (1880-1954)
Murder, He Says '45
Nocturne '46
The Scar '48

Peter Paige (1969-)
Our America '02
Say Uncle '05

Robert Paige (1910-87)
Cain and Mabel '36
Smart Blonde '37
Golden Gloves '40
Pardon My Sarong '42
Son of Dracula '43
Can't Help Singing '45
Blonde Ice '48
The Green Promise '49
Abbott and Costello Go to Mars '53
The Marriage-Go-Round '61

Yasmin Paige
Wondrous Oblivion '06
Ballet Shoes '07
Submarine '10

Geraldine Pailhas (1971-)
Don Juan DeMarco '94
Suite 16 '94
5x2 '04
They Came Back '04
Young & Beautiful '13

Didier Pain (1947-)
My Father's Glory '91
My Mother's Castle '91
On Guard! '03

Heidi Paine
Alien Seed '89
Wizards of the Demon Sword '94

Josh Pais (1964-)
Music of the Heart '99
Swimming '00
Phone Booth '02
Scotland, PA '02
Year of the Dog '07

Assassination of a High School President *'08*
Gentlemen Broncos *'09*
Leaves of Grass *'09*
Syrup *'13*
That Awkward Moment *'14*

Nestor Paiva (1905-66)
Prison Train *'38*
Beau Geste *'39*
Hold That Ghost *'41*
The Falcon in Mexico *'44*
The Purple Heart *'44*
The Road to Utopia *'46*
Double Dynamite *'51*
The Great Caruso *'51*
Five Fingers *'52*
Creature from the Black Lagoon *'54*
Revenge of the Creature *'55*
Tarantula *'55*
The Mole People *'56*
The Case Against Brooklyn *'58*
Frontier Uprising *'61*
The Four Horsemen of the Apocalypse *'62*
Girls! Girls! Girls! *'62*
California *'63*
They Saved Hitler's Brain *'64*
Jesse James Meets Frankenstein's Daughter *'65*

Ivica Pajer
David and Goliath *'61*
Caesar the Conqueror *'63*

Maria Pakulnis (1956-)
No End *'84*
The Decalogue *'88*

Holly Palance (1950-)
The Omen *'76*
The Best of Times *'86*

Jack Palance (1919-2006)
The Halls of Montezuma *'50*
Panic in the Streets *'50*
Sudden Fear *'52*
Arrowhead *'53*
Man in the Attic *'53*
Shane *'53*
The Silver Chalice *'54*
The Big Knife *'55*
I Died a Thousand Times *'55*
Attack! *'56*
Requiem for a Heavyweight *'56*
The Lonely Man *'57*
Beyond All Limits *'59*
The Mongols *'60*
Revak the Rebel *'60*
Barabbas *'62*
Contempt *'64*
Alice Through the Looking Glass *'66*
The Professionals *'66*
Kill a Dragon *'67*
Torture Garden *'67*
Deadly Sanctuary *'68*
Dr. Jekyll and Mr. Hyde *'68*
Strange Case of Dr. Jekyll & Mr. Hyde *'68*
They Came to Rob Las Vegas *'68*
Companeros *'70*
The Horsemen *'70*
The McMasters *'70*
Monte Walsh *'70*
Chato's Land *'71*
Dracula *'73*
Oklahoma Crude *'73*
Craze *'74*
Four Deuces *'75*
God's Gun *'75*
Great Adventure *'75*
Rulers of the City *'76*
The Sensuous Nurse *'76*
Portrait of a Hitman *'77*
Rulers of the City *'77*
Cop in Blue Jeans *'78*
Cocaine Cowboys *'79*
The Last Ride of the Dalton Gang *'79*
Unknown Powers *'80*
Without Warning *'80*
Hawk the Slayer *'81*
Alone in the Dark *'82*
Black Cobra *'83*
Bagdad Cafe *'88*
Gor *'88*
Young Guns *'88*
Batman *'89*
Tango and Cash *'89*
City Slickers *'91*
Solar Crisis *'92*
Cyborg 2 *'93*
City Slickers 2: The Legend of Curly's Gold *'94*
Cops and Robbersons *'94*
The Swan Princess *'94 (V)*
Buffalo Girls *'95*
Sarah, Plain and Tall: Winter's End *'99*
Treasure Island *'99*
Prancer Returns *'01*
Talking to Heaven *'02*

Joe Palese
Sinners *'89*
The Box *'03*

David Palffy (1969-)
He Sees You When You're Sleeping *'02*
House of the Dead *'03*
Criminal Intent *'05*
Beyond Sherwood Forest *'09*

Adrianne Palicki (1983-)
7 Mummies *'06*
Women in Trouble *'09*
Elektra Luxx *'10*
Legion *'10*
G.I. Joe: Retaliation *'13*
John Wick *'14*

Ron Palillo (1949-2012)
Doin' Time *'85*
Hellgate *'89*
Committed *'91*

Michael Palin (1943-)
John Cleese on How to Irritate People *'68*
And Now for Something Completely Different *'72*
Monty Python and the Holy Grail *'75*
Jabberwocky *'77*
All You Need Is Cash *'78*
Monty Python's Life of Brian *'79*
Time Bandits *'81*
The Missionary *'82*
The Secret Policeman's Other Ball *'82*
Monty Python's The Meaning of Life *'83*
A Private Function *'84*
Brazil *'85*
A Fish Called Wanda *'88*
American Friends *'91*
G.B.H. *'91*
Fierce Creatures *'96*
Mr. Toad's Wild Ride *'96*

Anna Palk (1943-90)
Fahrenheit 451 *'66*
The Frozen Dead *'66*
The Nightcomers *'72*

Aleksa Palladino (1980-)
Manny & Lo *'96*
Wrestling with Alligators *'98*
The Adventures of Sebastian Cole *'99*
Red Dirt *'99*
Storytelling *'01*
Before the Devil Knows You're Dead *'07*
Wrong Turn 2: Dead End *'07*

Erik Palladino (1968-)
Can't Hardly Wait *'98*
U-571 *'00*
Finder's Fee *'01*
Life Without Dick *'01*
Latter Days *'04*
Alchemy *'05*
L.A. Dicks *'05*
The Thirst *'06*
Crash and Burn *'07*
Return to House on Haunted Hill *'07*
Buried *'10*
Deadly Honeymoon *'10*
The New Daughter *'10*
Answers to Nothing *'11*
The Speed of Thought *'11*

Kumar Pallana (1918-2013)
The Royal Tenenbaums *'01*
The Terminal *'04*
Bomb the System *'05*
Another Earth *'11*

Jana Pallaske (1979-)
Extreme Ops *'02*
Phantom Pain *'09*

Anita Pallenberg (1944-)
Barbarella *'68*
Candy *'68*
Dillinger Is Dead *'69*
Performance *'70*
Mister Lonely *'07*
Cheri *'09*
4:44 Last Day on Earth *'11*

Eugene Pallette (1889-1954)
The Birth of a Nation *'15*
Intolerance *'16*
The Three Musketeers *'21*
Chicago *'27*
The Love Parade *'29*
Shanghai Express *'32*
Strangers of the Evening *'32*
The Kennel Murder Case *'33*
Made On Broadway *'33*
Strictly Dynamite *'34*
Bordertown *'35*
Steamboat Round the Bend *'35*
The Ghost Goes West *'36*
The Golden Arrow *'36*
My Man Godfrey *'36*
Stowaway *'36*
100 Men and a Girl *'37*
Topper *'37*
The Adventures of Robin Hood *'38*
First Love *'39*
Mr. Smith Goes to Washington *'39*
Wife, Husband and Friend *'39*
The Mark of Zorro *'40*
Young Tom Edison *'40*
The Bride Came C.O.D. *'41*
The Lady Eve *'41*
Big Street *'42*
Lady in a Jam *'42*
The Male Animal *'42*
Silver Queen *'42*
The Gang's All Here *'43*
Heaven Can Wait *'43*
It Ain't Hay *'43*
The Kansan *'43*
Slightly Dangerous *'43*
Heavenly Days *'44*
In the Meantime, Darling *'44*
Pin-Up Girl *'44*
Sensations of 1945 *'44*
Step Lively *'44*
Suspense *'46*

Joseph Pallister
Bikini Bistro *'94*
Broadcast Bombshells *'95*

Gabriella Pallotta (1938-)
Il Grido *'57*
The Mongols *'60*
Hero of Rome *'63*

Adam Pally (1982-)
Night Owls *'15*
Joshy *'16*
Band Aid *'17*

Andrea Palma
Tarzan and the Mermaids *'48*
The Criminal Life of Archibaldo de la Cruz *'55*

Mimmo Palmara (1928-81)
The Last Days of Pompeii *'60*
The Trojan Horse *'62*
Three Avengers *'64*
Two Gladiators *'64*
A Long Ride From Hell *'68*

Betsy Palmer (1929-2015)
The Long Gray Line *'55*
Mister Roberts *'55*
Queen Bee *'55*
The Tin Star *'57*
Friday the 13th *'80*
Friday the 13th, Part 2 *'81*
The Fear: Halloween Night *'99*
Waltzing Anna *'06*

Byron Palmer (1920-2009)
Man in the Attic *'53*
Ma and Pa Kettle at Waikiki *'55*

Geoffrey Palmer (1927-)
A Fish Called Wanda *'88*
Christabel *'89*
A Question of Attribution *'91*
Stalag Luft *'93*
Mrs. Brown *'97*
Tomorrow Never Dies *'97*
Peter Pan *'03*
He Knew He Was Right *'04*
The Pink Panther 2 *'09*
W.E. *'11*
Going for Gold: The '48 Games *'12*

Gregg (Hunter) Palmer (1927-)
Francis Goes to West Point *'52*
Taza, Son of Cochise *'54*
To Hell and Back *'55*
The Creature Walks among Us *'56*
From Hell It Came *'57*
Zombies of Moratau *'57*
The Rebel Set *'59*
Most Dangerous Man Alive *'61*

Gretchen Palmer (1961-)
Chopper Chicks in Zombietown *'91*
I Got the Hook-Up *'98*

Hubbel Palmer (1977-)
The Sasquatch Gang *'06*
Humble Pie *'07*
Cafe *'10*

Keke Palmer (1993-)
Knights of the South Bronx *'05*
Akeelah and the Bee *'06*
Madea's Family Reunion *'06*
Cleaner *'07*
Jump In! *'07*
The Longshots *'08*
Shrink *'09*
Abducted: The Carlina White Story *'12*
Ice Age: Continental Drift *'12 (V)*
Joyful Noise *'12*
Rags *'12*
The Trip to Bountiful *'14*
Pimp *'18*

Lewis Lemperuer Palmer
Don't Tell *'05*
The Disappeared *'08*

Lilli Palmer (1914-86)
The Secret Agent *'36*
Good Morning, Boys *'37*
Crackerjack *'38*
Chamber of Horrors *'40*
Cloak and Dagger *'46*
Body and Soul *'47*
The Long Dark Hall *'51*
Conspiracy of Hearts *'60*
The Counterfeit Traitor *'62*
The Miracle of the White Stallions *'63*
The Amorous Adventures of Moll Flanders *'65*
Hard Contract *'69*
Murders in the Rue Morgue *'71*
What the Peeper Saw *'72*
The Boys from Brazil *'78*
The Holcroft Covenant *'85*

Maria Palmer (1924-81)
Days of Glory *'43*
By the Light of the Silvery Moon *'53*

Rebecca Palmer
Intimacy *'00*
Blood Trails *'06*

Renzo Palmer (1929-88)
Eagles Over London *'69*
Street Law *'74*
How to Kill a Judge *'75*

Teresa Palmer (1986-)
The Grudge 2 *'06*
December Boys *'07*
Bedtime Stories *'08*
Restraint *'08*
I Am Number Four *'11*
Take Me Home Tonight *'11*
Wish You Were Here *'12*
Warm Bodies *'13*
Parts Per Billion *'14*
Cut Bank *'15*
Point Break *'15*
Triple 9 *'15*
The Choice *'16*
Lights Out *'16*
Berlin Syndrome *'17*

Zoie Palmer (1977-)
Godsend *'04*
The Reagans *'04*
Gospel of Deceit *'06*

Chazz Palminteri (1952-)
Oscar *'91*
Innocent Blood *'92*
There Goes the Neighborhood *'92*
A Bronx Tale *'93*
Bullets over Broadway *'94*
The Perez Family *'94*
Faithful *'95*
Jade *'95*
The Last Word *'95*
Mulholland Falls *'95*
The Usual Suspects *'95*
Diabolique *'96*
Analyze This *'98*
Hurlyburly *'98*
Scarred City *'98*
Boss of Bosses *'99*
Excellent Cadavers *'99*
Stuart Little *'99 (V)*
Down to Earth *'01*
Poolhall Junkies *'02*
One Last Ride *'03*
Noel *'04*
Animal *'05*
Hoodwinked *'05 (V)*
In the Mix *'05*
Arthur and the Invisibles *'06 (V)*
A Guide to Recognizing Your Saints *'06*
Little Man *'06*
Push *'06*
Running Scared *'06*
Body Armour *'07*
The Dukes *'07*
Jolene *'08*
Once More With Feeling *'08*
Yonkers Joe *'08*
Mighty Fine *'12*
The Oogieloves in the Big Balloon Adventure *'12*
Taken for Ransom *'13*
Vault *'19*

Carlos Palomino (1949-)
Die Watching *'93*
Geronimo: An American Legend *'93*

Brooke Palsson
Breakaway *'02*
Keyhole *'11*

Gwyneth Paltrow (1973-)
Hook *'91*
Deadly Relations *'93*
Flesh and Bone *'93*
Malice *'93*
Jefferson in Paris *'94*
Mrs. Parker and the Vicious Circle *'94*
Moonlight and Valentino *'95*
The Pallbearer *'95*
Seven *'95*
Emma *'96*
Hard Eight *'96*
Great Expectations *'97*
Sliding Doors *'97*
Hush *'98*
A Perfect Murder *'98*
Shakespeare in Love *'98*
The Talented Mr. Ripley *'99*
Bounce *'00*
Duets *'00*
The Anniversary Party *'01*
The Royal Tenenbaums *'01*
Shallow Hal *'01*
Austin Powers In Goldmember *'02 (C)*
Possession *'02*
Sylvia *'03*
View from the Top *'03*
Sky Captain and the World of Tomorrow *'04*
Proof *'05*
Infamous *'06*
Running with Scissors *'06*
The Good Night *'07*
Iron Man *'08*
Two Lovers *'09*
Country Strong *'10*
Iron Man 2 *'10*
Contagion *'11*
Glee: The 3D Concert Movie *'11*
The Avengers *'12*
Iron Man 3 *'13*
Thanks for Sharing *'13*
Mortdecai *'15*
Spider-Man: Homecoming *'17*

Luciana Paluzzi (1937-)
Journey to the Lost City *'58*
Carlton Browne of the F.O. *'59*
Return to Peyton Place *'61*
Muscle Beach Party *'64*
Thunderball *'65*
Chuka *'67*
One-Eyed Soldiers *'67*
The Venetian Affair *'67*
The Green Slime *'68*
Captain Nemo and the Underwater City *'69*
99 Women *'69*
Black Gunn *'72*
The Italian Connection *'73*
Manhunt *'73*
The Klansman *'74*
Medusa *'74*
War Goddess *'74*

Rebecca Pan
Days of Being Wild *'91*
In the Mood for Love *'00*
Chinese Odyssey 2002 *'02*

Danielle Panabaker (1987-)
Sex and the Single Mom *'03*
Empire Falls *'05*
Mom at Sixteen *'05*
Sky High *'05*
Yours, Mine & Ours *'05*
Home of the Giants *'07*
Mr. Brooks *'07*
The Crazies *'09*
Friday the 13th *'09*
The Ward *'10*
Weakness *'10*
Beverly Lewis' The Shunning *'11*
Piranha 3DD *'11*
Girls Against Boys *'12*
Nearlyweds *'13*

Kay Panabaker (1990-)
Moondance Alexander *'07*
Nancy Drew *'07*
The Prince and the Pauper *'07*
Fame *'09*
Secrets in the Walls *'10*
Cyberbully *'11*
Beverly Hills Chihuahua 3: Viva La Fiesta! *'12 (V)*

Sylvia Panacione
8213: Gacy House *'10*
Kill Katie Malone *'10*

Jafar Panahi (1960-)
This is Not a Film *'10*
Closed Curtain *'13*
Jafar Panahi's Taxi *'15*

Alessandra Panaro (1939-2019)
Rocco and His Brothers *'60*
Ulysses Against the Son of Hercules *'61*
Conquest of Mycene *'63*
Executioner of Venice *'63*

Michael Panes (1963-)
The Anniversary Party *'01*
Fabled *'02*
Broken English *'07*

Watching the Detectives '07
(Untitled) '09

Hayden Panettiere (1989-)
A Bug's Life '98 (V)
Dinosaur '00 (V)
Remember the Titans '00
The Affair of the Necklace '01
Joe Somebody '01
Normal '03
Raising Helen '04
Ice Princess '05
Lies My Mother Told Me '05
Racing Stripes '05
The Architect '06
Bring It On: All or Nothing '06
Shanghai Kiss '07
Fireflies in the Garden '08
The Good Student '08
The Cove '09
I Love You, Beth Cooper '09
Alpha and Omega '10 (V)
Amanda Knox: Murder on Trail in Italy '11
Hoodwinked Too! Hood vs. Evil '11 (V)
Scream 4 '11

Jansen Panettiere (1994-)
The Last Days of Summer '07
The Perfect Game '09
The Lost Medallion: The Adventures of Billy Stone '13

Andrew Pang
The Corruptor '99
Petty Crimes '02

Franklin Pangborn (1889-1958)
Exit Smiling '26
Getting Gertie's Garter '27
My Friend from India '27
Design for Living '33
Flying Down to Rio '33
Manhattan Love Song '34
Strictly Dynamite '34
My Man Godfrey '36
Easy Living '37
Hats Off '37
It Happened in Hollywood '37
The Mandarin Mystery '37
A Star Is Born '37
Bluebeard's Eighth Wife '38
Carefree '38
Four's a Crowd '38
Just Around the Corner '38
Vivacious Lady '38
Fifth Avenue Girl '39
The Bank Dick '40
Christmas in July '40
Spring Parade '40
The Flame of New Orleans '41
Never Give a Sucker an Even Break '41
Sullivan's Travels '41
The Palm Beach Story '42
Holy Matrimony '43
The Great Moment '44
Hail the Conquering Hero '44
His Butler's Sister '44
The Sin of Harold Diddlebock '47
Romance on the High Seas '48

Ty Panitz (1999-)
Yours, Mine & Ours '05
Because I Said So '07
Santa Buddies '09 (V)
Spooky Buddies '11 (V)
Treasure Buddies '12 (V)
Super Buddies '13 (V)

Archie Panjabi (1972-)
East Is East '99
Bend It Like Beckham '02
The Constant Gardener '05
A Good Year '06
A Mighty Heart '07
Traitor '08
The Infidel '10

Stuart Pankin (1946-)
The Hollywood Knights '80
Dirt Bike Kid '86
Fatal Attraction '87
Love at Stake '87
Second Sight '89
Arachnophobia '90
Life Stinks '91
Mannequin 2: On the Move '91
The Vagrant '92
Father and Scout '94
I Love Trouble '94
Squanto: A Warrior's Tale '94
Honey, We Shrunk Ourselves '97
Chasing Destiny '00
Miss Cast Away '04
Hopelessly in June '11

John Pankow (1954-)
To Live & Die in L.A. '85
Johnny Be Good '88
Monkey Shines '88
Talk Radio '88
Mortal Thoughts '91
Year of the Gun '91
A Stranger Among Us '92
The Object of My Affection '98
Bride Wars '09
The Extra Man '10
Morning Glory '10

Taapsee Pannu
Badla '19
Mission Mangal '19

Vithaya Pansringarm
The Prince & Me 4: The Elephant Adventure '10
Only God Forgives '13
A Prayer Before Dawn '18

Joe Pantoliano (1951-)
More Than Friends '78
Idolmaker '80
Eddie and the Cruisers '83
The Final Terror '83
Risky Business '83
The Goonies '85
Mean Season '85
Running Scared '86
Empire of the Sun '87
La Bamba '87
Scenes from the Goldmine '87
The Squeeze '87
The In Crowd '88
Midnight Run '88
Downtown '89
El Diablo '90
The Last of the Finest '90
Zandalee '91
Used People '92
The Fugitive '93
Me and the Kid '93
Three of Hearts '93
Baby's Day Out '94
The Spy Within '94
Bad Boys '95
The Immortals '95
The Last Word '95
Steal Big, Steal Little '95
Bound '96
Natural Enemy '96
Top of the World '97
Hoods '98
The Taxman '98
U.S. Marshals '98
Black and White '99
The Life Before This '99
The Matrix '99
New Blood '99
A Better Way to Die '00
Memento '00
Ready to Rumble '00
Cats & Dogs '01 (V)
The Adventures of Pluto Nash '02
Bad Boys 2 '03
Daredevil '03
The Moguls '05
Racing Stripes '05 (V)
Second Best '05
Canvas '06
Deceit '06
Larry the Cable Guy: Health Inspector '06
Wedding Daze '06
Falling Up '08
Deadly Impact '09
The Job '09
Cats & Dogs: The Revenge of Kitty Galore '10 (V)
Loosies '11
The Identical '14

Cecile Paoli (1961-)
Riders '88
Sharpe's Revenge '97
Sharpe's Waterloo '97

Connor Paolo (1990-)
Alexander '04
Snow Angels '07
Camp Hell '10
Stake Land '10
Friend Request '16

Tom Papa
The Haunted World of El Superbeasto '09 (V)
The Informant! '09

Michael (Mike) Papajohn (1964-)
Predator 2 '90
The Last Boy Scout '91
The Babe '92
The Indian in the Cupboard '95
Naked Souls '95
Eraser '96
Spawn '97
My Giant '98
For Love of the Game '99
Charlie's Angels '00
The Animal '01
Rustin '01
Spider-Man '02
Whacked! '02
The Last Shot '04
I Know Who Killed Me '07
Spider-Man 3 '07
The Hit List '11

Melanie Papalia (1984-)
Confined '10
Super Hybrid '10
Smiley '12
Extraterrestrial '14

Irene Papas (1926-)
Attila '54
Tribute to a Bad Man '56
The Guns of Navarone '61
The Moon-Spinners '64
Zorba the Greek '64
The Brotherhood '68
Anne of the Thousand Days '69
A Dream of Kings '69
Z '69
Trojan Women '71
Don't Torture a Duckling '72
1931: Once Upon a Time in New York '72
Moses '76
Iphigenia '77
The Message '77
Christ Stopped at Eboli '79
Lion of the Desert '81
The Assisi Underground '84
Into the Night '85
High Season '88
Jacob '94
Party '96
The Odyssey '97
Yerma '99
Captain Corelli's Mandolin '01

Lionel Pape (1877-1944)
Outside of Paradise '38
Raffles '39

Ike Pappas (1933-)
Moon over Parador '88
The Package '89

Anna Paquin (1982-)
The Piano '93
Fly Away Home '96
Jane Eyre '96
Amistad '97
Hurlyburly '98
It's the Rage '99
She's All That '99
A Walk on the Moon '99
Almost Famous '00
Finding Forrester '00
X-Men '00
Buffalo Soldiers '01
Darkness '02
25th Hour '02
X2: X-Men United '03
The Squid and the Whale '05
Steamboy '05 (V)
X-Men: The Last Stand '06
Blue State '07
Bury My Heart at Wounded Knee '07
Trick 'r Treat '08
Open House '10
The Romantics '10
Scream 4 '11
Free Ride '13
Straight A's '13
Tell It to the Bees '19

Vanessa Paradis (1972-)
The Girl on the Bridge '98
Heartbreaker '10
A Monster in Paris '11
Fading Gigolo '13

John Paragon (1954-)
Eating Raoul '82
Pee-wee's Big Adventure '85
Elvira, Mistress of the Dark '88
UHF '89

Kiri Paramore
Flirting '89
Doing Time for Patsy Cline '97
Ned Kelly '03

Rawiri Paratene
Whale Rider '02
The Legend of Johnny Lingo '03

J.D. Pardo (1980-)
Hope Ranch '02
A Cinderella Story '04
Supercross: The Movie '05
A Girl Like Me: The Gwen Araujo Story '06
The Burning Plain '08

Michael Parducci
Gravesend '97
Hit and Runway '01

Kip Pardue (1975-)
Remember the Titans '00
Driven '01
Road to Riches '01
The Rules of Attraction '02
Devil's Pond '03
Thirteen '03
This Girl's Life '03
American Crime '04
The Heart Is Deceitful Above All Things '04
The Iris Effect '04
Imaginary Heroes '05
Loggerheads '05
Undiscovered '05
Wasted '06
Ripple Effect '07
South of Pico '07
The Wizard of Gore '07
Princess: A Modern Fairytale '08
Remarkable Power '08
Stag Night '08
Bitter/Sweet '09
The Trouble with Romance '09
Answer This '10
Hostel: Part 3 '11
Beyond Valkyrie: Dawn of the Fourth Reich '16
American Fable '17

Jessica Pare (1980-)
Stardom '00
Lost and Delirious '01
Posers '02
Wicker Park '04
Suck '09
The Way of the West '11

Michael Paré (1958-)
Eddie and the Cruisers '83
The Philadelphia Experiment '84
Streets of Fire '84
Eddie and the Cruisers 2: Eddie Lives! '89
Moon 44 '90
Into the Sun '92
Point of Impact '93
Solar Force '94
Triplecross '95
Village of the Damned '95
Bad Moon '96
Carver's Gate '96
Sworn Enemies '96
Falling Fire '97
Mission of Death '97
Strip Search '97
2103: Deadly Wake '97
The Debt '98
Hope Floats '98
In the Dead of Space '99
Peril '00
Sanctimony '01
Blackwoods '02
Red Serpent '02
Heart of America '03
Komodo vs. Cobra '05
BloodRayne '06
BloodRayne 2: Deliverance '07
Alone in the Dark 2 '08
Dark World '08
Far Cry '08
100 Feet '08
The Perfect Sleep '08
Seed '08
Tunnel Rats '08
Direct Contact '09
Rampage '09
Bloodrayne: The Third Reich '11
Blubberella '11
The Lincoln Lawyer '11
Tales of an Ancient Empire '11
Gone '12
Maximum Conviction '12
SWAT: Unit 887 '15
Decommissioned '16
Traded '16
Puppet Master: The Littlest Reich '18

Marisa Paredes (1946-)
Dark Habits '84
In a Glass Cage '86
High Heels '91
The Flower of My Secret '95
Deep Crimson '96
Talk of Angels '96
Doctor Chance '97
Life Is Beautiful '98
All About My Mother '99
The Devil's Backbone '01
Four Last Songs '06
The Skin I Live In '11

Mila Parely (1917-2012)
The Rules of the Game '39
Beauty and the Beast '46
Le Plaisir '52

Monique Parent (1965-)
Play Time '94
Dark Secrets '95
Masseuse '95
Midnight Confessions '95
Stripshow '95
Illegal Affairs '96
Mirror, Mirror 3: The Voyeur '96
James Dean: Live Fast, Die Young '97
Tender Flesh '97
The Catcher '98
The Pornographer '00
Cuck '19

Flavio Parenti
I Am Love '09
To Rome with Love '12

Judy Parfitt (1935-)
The Mind of Mr. Soames '70
The Jewel in the Crown '84
The Charmer '87
Maurice '87
Getting It Right '89
Dark Obsession '90
The Blackheath Poisonings '92
Midnight's Child '93
Dolores Claiborne '94
Element of Doubt '96
September '96
Wilde '97
Berkeley Square '98
Ever After: A Cinderella Story '98
Girl with a Pearl Earring '03
Asylum '05
Little Dorrit '08
Dean Spanley '08
The Moth Diaries '11
W.E. '11

Woodrow Parfrey (1922-84)
Sam Whiskey '69
Dirty Harry '71
Oklahoma Crude '73
The Outlaw Josey Wales '76
Backstairs at the White House '79

Anne Parillaud (1960-)
La Femme Nikita '91
Innocent Blood '92
Map of the Human Heart '93
Six Days, Six Nights '94
The Man in the Iron Mask '98
Shattered Image '98
Sex is Comedy '02

Jerry Paris (1925-86)
The Glass Wall '53
The Caine Mutiny '54
Drive a Crooked Road '54
The Wild One '54
Good Morning, Miss Dove '55
Marty '55
D-Day, the Sixth of June '56
Zero Hour! '57
Evil Roy Slade '71 (C)

Billy Parish
Talisman '98
Phobic '02

Sarah Parish (1968-)
Sirens '02
Much Ado About Nothing '05
The Wedding Date '05
Hatfields & McCoys '12

Annie Parisse (1975-)
How to Lose a Guy in 10 Days '03
Monster-in-Law '05
Prime '05
Definitely, Maybe '08
My Own Love Song '10
The Pacific '10
And So It Goes '14

Andrea Parisy
Greed In the Sun '64
Slogan '69

Ji-yeon Park
Memento Mori '00
Time '06
The Housemaid '10

Kris Park
I Love You, I Love You Not '97
Drive Me Crazy '99
Ordinary Sinner '02

Megan Park (1986-)
She's Too Young '04
Charlie Bartlett '07
The Perfect Teacher '10
A Cinderella Story: Once Upon a Song '11
What If '13

Randall Park
American Fusion '05
The People I've Slept With '09
Amigo Undead '15
Always Be My Maybe '19

Ray Park (1974-)
Star Wars: Episode 1-The Phantom Menace '99
X-Men '00
Ballistic: Ecks vs. Sever '02
Slayer '06
What We Do Is Secret '07
G.I. Joe: The Rise of Cobra '09
G.I. Joe: Retaliation '13
Jinn '14

Reg Park (1928-2007)
Hercules and the Captive Women '63
Hercules in the Haunted World '64

Hercules, Prisoner of Evil '64

Sydney Park (1997-)
Spork '10
Wish Upon '17

Lar Park-Lincoln (1961-)
Children of the Night '85
House 2: The Second Story '87
Friday the 13th, Part 7: The New Blood '88

Evan Dexter Parke (1968-)
The Cider House Rules '99
Planet of the Apes '01
Brother's Keeper '02
Nightstalker '02
King Kong '05
All Roads Lead Home '08

MacDonald Parke (1891-1960)
No Orchids for Miss Blandish '48
Summertime '55
The Mouse That Roared '59
Never Take Candy From a Stranger '60

Anthony Ray Parker (1958-)
The Matrix '99
The Marine '06
TKO '06
Fast Lane '08

Cecil Parker (1897-1971)
Storm in a Teacup '37
The Lady Vanishes '38
The Stars Look Down '39
Caesar and Cleopatra '46
Captain Boycott '47
The Magic Bow '47
Dear Mr. Prohack '49
Under Capricorn '49
Tony Draws a Horse '51
The Ladykillers '55
The Court Jester '56
The Admirable Crichton '57
A Tale of Two Cities '58
The Wreck of the Mary Deare '59
The Pure Hell of St. Trinian's '61
Carry On Jack '63
Heavens Above '63
Lady L '65
A Study in Terror '66

Cecilia Parker (1914-93)
The Lost Jungle '34
Ah, Wilderness! '35
Naughty Marietta '35
A Family Affair '37
Girl Loves Boy '37
You're Only Young Once '37
Judge Hardy's Children '38
Love Finds Andy Hardy '38
Out West With the Hardys '38
Andy Hardy Gets Spring Fever '39
The Hardys Ride High '39
Judge Hardy and Son '39
Andy Hardy Meets Debutante '40
Gambling Daughters '41
Andy Hardy's Double Life '42
The Courtship of Andy Hardy '42
Grand Central Murder '42
Seven Sweethearts '42
Andy Hardy Comes Home '58

Corey Parker (1965-)
Biloxi Blues '88
How I Got into College '89
White Palace '90
The Lost Language of Cranes '92
Mr. & Mrs. Loving '96

Eleanor Parker (1922-2013)
Mission to Moscow '43
Between Two Worlds '44
Hollywood Canteen '44
Pride of the Marines '45
Never Say Goodbye '46
Escape Me Never '47
The Voice of the Turtle '47
It's a Great Feeling '49
Caged '50
Chain Lightning '50
Three Secrets '50
Detective Story '51
Scaramouche '52
Above and Beyond '53
Escape from Fort Bravo '53
Naked Jungle '54
Interrupted Melody '55
The Man with the Golden Arm '55
Many Rivers to Cross '55
The King and Four Queens '56
A Hole in the Head '59
Home from the Hill '60
Return to Peyton Place '61
Panic Button '62
The Sound of Music '65
An American Dream '66
Tiger and the Pussycat '67
Warning Shot '67
Hans Brinker '69
Maybe I'll Come Home in the Spring '71
Fantasy Island '76
The Bastard '78
She's Dressed to Kill '79
Once Upon a Spy '80

Ellen Parker
Cop Hater '58
The Lost Missile '58

Erica Parker (1978-)
See Erica Durance

F. William Parker (1941-)
Hard Eight '96
Jack Frost '97
Warm Blooded Killers '01

Fess Parker (1924-2010)
Island in the Sky '53
Them! '54
Battle Cry '55
Davy Crockett, King of the Wild Frontier '55
Davy Crockett and the River Pirates '56
The Great Locomotive Chase '56
Westward Ho, the Wagons! '56
Old Yeller '57
Alias Jesse James '59 (C)
The Hangman '59
The Jayhawkers '59
Hell Is for Heroes '62

Jameson Parker (1947-)
Anatomy of a Seduction '79
The Gathering: Part 2 '79
A Small Circle of Friends '80
Callie and Son '81
White Dog '82
Agatha Christie's A Caribbean Mystery '83
American Justice '86
Who Is Julia? '86
Prince of Darkness '87

Jean Parker (1915-2005)
Gabriel Over the White House '33
Lady for a Day '33
Little Women '33
Made On Broadway '33
Rasputin and the Empress '33
Operator 13 '34
The Ghost Goes West '36
The Texas Rangers '36
Romance of the Limberlost '38
The Flying Deuces '39
Beyond Tomorrow '40
Flying Blind '41
No Hands on the Clock '41
Power Dive '41
Tomorrow We Live '42
Wrecking Crew '42
Bluebeard '44
Dead Man's Eyes '44
Navy Way '44
One Body Too Many '44
Rolling Home '48
The Gunfighter '50
A Lawless Street '55

Kim Parker
Fire Maidens from Outer Space '56
Fiend without a Face '58

Lara Parker (1937-)
Hi, Mom! '70
Night of Dark Shadows '71
Race with the Devil '75
The Lazarus Syndrome '79
Foxfire Light '82

Mary-Louise Parker (1964-)
Signs of Life '89
Longtime Companion '90
Fried Green Tomatoes '91
Grand Canyon '91
Mr. Wonderful '93
Naked in New York '93
Boys on the Side '94
Bullets over Broadway '94
The Client '94
Sugartime '95
Portrait of a Lady '96
Legalese '98
The Maker '98
The Five Senses '99
Goodbye, Lover '99
Let the Devil Wear Black '99
The Simple Life of Noah Dearborn '99
Cupid & Cate '00
Master Spy: The Robert Hanssen Story '02
Pipe Dream '02
Red Dragon '02
Angels in America '03
Miracle Run '04
Saved! '04
Romance & Cigarettes '05
The Assassination of Jesse James by the Coward Robert Ford '07
The Spiderwick Chronicles '08
Howl '10
RED '10
Solitary Man '10
Christmas In Conway '13
RED 2 '13
R.I.P.D. '13
Jamesy Boy '14
Golden Exits '17
Red Sparrow '18

Michael Parker (1969-)
Kill Line '91
My Own Private Idaho '91

Molly Parker (1972-)
Anything for Love '93
Hole in the Sky '95
Kissed '96
Dean Koontz's Intensity '97
In the Shadows '98
The Five Senses '99
Sunshine '99
Wonderland '99
Suspicious River '00
Waking the Dead '00
The Center of the World '01
Last Wedding '01
Rare Birds '01
The War Bride '01
Marion Bridge '02
Max '02
Men with Brooms '02
Pure '02
Break a Leg '03
The Confessor '04
Nine Lives '05
Hollywoodland '06
Who Loves the Sun '06
The Wicker Man '06
Trigger '10
That's What I Am '11
Hemingway & Gelhorn '12
Outlaw Prophet: Warren Jeffs '14
The 9th Life of Louis Drax '16
1922 '17
Madeline's Madeline '18

Nate Parker (1979-)
Blood Done Sign My Name '10
Arbitrage '12
Red Hook Summer '12
Red Tails '12
Ain't Them Bodies Saints '13
About Alex '14
Beyond the Lights '14
Non-Stop '14
Every Secret Thing '15
The Birth of a Nation '16

Nathaniel Parker (1962-)
Piece of Cake '88
Hamlet '90
Catherine Cookson's The Black Candle '92
Wide Sargasso Sea '92
Squanto: A Warrior's Tale '94
Othello '95
A Village Affair '95
Beverly Hills Ninja '96
David '97
Far from the Madding Crowd '97
Into Thin Air: Death on Everest '97
Lover's Prayer '99
Vanity Fair '99
The Haunted Mansion '03
Bleak House '05
The Great Debaters '07
Pride '07
Stardust '07
The Secret Life of Bees '08
Land Girls '09
Malice in Wonderland '09
The Perfect Host '10

Nicole Parker
Harlem Aria '99
Disaster Movie '08

Nicole Ari Parker
The Incredibly True Adventure of Two Girls in Love '95
Boogie Nights '97
The End of Violence '97
Spark '98
200 Cigarettes '98
Blue Streak '99
Loving Jezebel '99
Dancing in September '00
Remember the Titans '00
Brown Sugar '02
King's Ransom '05
Welcome Home Roscoe Jenkins '08
Imagine That '09
35 and Ticking '10
Repentance '14

Noelle Parker (1971-)
The Whoopee Boys '86
Ernest Saves Christmas '88
Lethal Lolita-Amy Fisher: My Story '92
Newsbreak '00

Paula Jai Parker (1969-)
Tales from the Hood '95
Sprung '96
Woo '97
The Breaks '99
30 Years to Life '01
Phone Booth '02
My Baby's Daddy '04
She Hate Me '04
Animal '05
Hustle & Flow '05
The Proud Family Movie '05 (V)
Cover '08

Sachi (MacLaine) Parker (1956-)
Peggy Sue Got Married '86
Welcome Home, Roxy Carmichael '90

Sarah Jessica Parker (1965-)
Footloose '84
Girls Just Want to Have Fun '85
Somewhere Tomorrow '85
Flight of the Navigator '86
L.A. Story '91
Honeymoon in Vegas '92
Hocus Pocus '93
Striking Distance '93
Ed Wood '94
If Lucy Fell '95
Miami Rhapsody '95
The Sunshine Boys '95
Extreme Measures '96
The First Wives Club '96
Mars Attacks! '96
The Substance of Fire '96
Til There Was You '96
Dudley Do-Right '99
State and Main '00
Life Without Dick '01
The Family Stone '05
Failure to Launch '06
Strangers with Candy '06
Sex and the City: The Movie '08
Smart People '08
Did You Hear About the Morgans? '09
Sex and the City 2 '10
I Don't Know How She Does It '11
New Year's Eve '11
Escape From Planet Earth '13 (V)
All Roads Lead to Rome '15

Suzy Parker (1932-2003)
Funny Face '57
Kiss Them for Me '57
The Best of Everything '59
The Interns '62
Flight From Ashiya '64

Trey Parker (1969-)
Cannibal! The Musical '96
BASEketball '98
Orgazmo '98
South Park: Bigger, Longer and Uncut '99 (V)
Team America: World Police '04 (V)
Despicable Me 3 '17 (V)

Ursula Parker
Lightning Bolt '67
The Son of No One '11

Willard Parker (1912-96)
A Slight Case of Murder '38
You Gotta Stay Happy '48
Great Jesse James Raid '49
Slightly French '49
David Harding, Counterspy '50

Gerard Parkes (1924-2014)
The Apprentice '71
Speaking Parts '89
It Takes Two '95

Shaun Parkes
Human Traffic '99
The Mummy Returns '01
Small Island '09

Barbara Parkins (1942-)
Valley of the Dolls '67
The Kremlin Letter '70
The Mephisto Waltz '71
Asylum '72
Puppet on a Chain '72
Testimony of Two Men '77
Calendar Girl Murders '84
To Catch a King '84

Art Parkinson (2001-)
Dracula Untold '14
Kubo and the Two Strings '16

Craig Parkinson
Control '07
The Unloved '09
Wild Rose '18

Katherine Parkinson
Easy Virtue '08
Pirate Radio '09
The Guernsey Literary & Potato Peel Pie Society '18

Bert Parks (1914-92)
Shining Star '75
The Freshman '90

Catherine Parks (1956-)
Friday the 13th, Part 3 '82
Body of Influence '93

James Parks (1968-)
You Know My Name '99
Spent '00
The Listening '06
Death Proof '07
Noble Things '08

Larry Parks (1914-75)
Blondie Goes to College '42
The Boogie Man Will Get You '42
Canal Zone '42
You Were Never Lovelier '42
Destroyer '43
Counter-Attack '45
The Jolson Story '46
Down to Earth '47
Her Husband's Affairs '47
The Swordsman '47
Jolson Sings Again '49
Love Is Better Than Ever '52

Michael Parks (1940-2017)
The Bible '66
Then Came Bronson '68
The Last Hard Men '76
The Private Files of J. Edgar Hoover '77
Sidewinder One '77
ffolkes '80
Hard Country '81
Savannah Smiles '82
Welcome to Spring Break '88
The Hitman '91
Storyville '92
Death Wish 5: The Face of Death '94
Stranger by Night '94
From Dusk Till Dawn '95
Julian Po '97
Niagara, Niagara '97
Wicked '98
From Dusk Till Dawn 3: The Hangman's Daughter '99
Big Bad Love '02
Kill Bill Vol. 1 '03
Kill Bill Vol. 2 '04
The Listening '06
The Assassination of Jesse James by the Coward Robert Ford '07
The Dead One '07
Death Proof '07
Planet Terror '07
Noble Things '08
Three Priests '08
Machete '10
Smokin' Aces 2: Assassins' Ball '10
Red State '11
Django Unchained '12
We Are What We Are '13
Tusk '14
Blood Father '16

Tammy Parks (1965-)
Play Time '94
Attack of the 60-Foot Centerfold '95

Trina Parks
Diamonds Are Forever '71
The Muthers '76

Van Dyke Parks (1943-)
The Two Jakes '90
Broken Trail '06

Parkyakarkus (Harry Einstein) (1904-58)
New Faces of 1937 '37
Yank in Libya '42

Steve Parlavecchio (1970-)
Amongst Friends '93
Bandwagon '95
The First to Go '97

Dita Parlo (1906-71)
Hungarian Rhapsody '28
L'Atalante '34
Grand Illusion '37

Julie-Marie Parmentier (1981-)
Murderous Maids '00
The Town Is Quiet '00
Around a Small Mountain '09
Evolution '16

Charles Parnell
Mind the Gap '04
Pariah '11

Chris Parnell (1967-)
Evil Alien Conquerors '02
Anchorman: The Legend of Ron Burgundy '04

I'm Reed Fish '06
Ira & Abby '06
Hot Rod '07
Walk Hard: The Dewey Cox Story '07
Harold '08
Labor Pains '09
Paper Man '09
Answer This '10
The Dogfather '10

Emory Parnell (1892-1979)
Casanova Brown '44
Miracle of Morgan's Creek '44
Colonel Effingham's Raid '45
Blonde Ice '48
Chain Gang '50
Trail of Robin Hood '50
Ma and Pa Kettle Back On the Farm '51
Lost in Alaska '52
Ma and Pa Kettle at the Fair '52
Safari Drums '53
Battle of Rogue River '54
Ma and Pa Kettle at Home '54
The Rocket Man '54
Pardners '56
Man of the West '58

Mark Parra
The Unnamable '88
Crooked '05

Jim Parrack (1981-)
Sal '11
Child of God '14
Fury '14
Priceless '16

Marriam Parris
Club Vampire '98
Maryam '00

Teyonah Parris
Dear White People '14
Chi-raq '15
Where Children Play '15
Five Nights in Maine '16
If Beale Street Could Talk '18
The Photograph '20

Helen Parrish (1924-59)
The Big Trail '30
Dead End Kids: Little Tough Guy '38
Little Tough Guy '38
Mad About Music '38
First Love '39
Three Smart Girls Grow Up '39
You'll Find Out '40
Overland Mail '42

Hunter Parrish (1987-)
Down in the Valley '05
RV '06
It's Complicated '09
Paper Man '09
The Space Between '10
Still Alice '14

Janel Parrish (1988-)
Bratz '07
Triple Dog '09
To All the Boys I've Loved Before '18
To All the Boys: P.S. I Still Love You '20

Julie Parrish (1940-2003)
Fireball 500 '66
Paradise, Hawaiian Style '66
The Doberman Gang '72

Leslie Parrish (1935-)
Li'l Abner '59
The Manchurian Candidate '62
For Love or Money '63
Sex and the Single Girl '64
The Giant Spider Invasion '75
The Invisible Strangler '76

Frederick Parslow
The Last Wave '77
Wrangler '88

Estelle Parsons (1927-)
Bonnie & Clyde '67
Rachel, Rachel '68
Don't Drink the Water '69
I Never Sang for My Father '70
I Walk the Line '70
Watermelon Man '70
For Pete's Sake '74
Foreplay '75
Backstairs at the White House '79
Dick Tracy '90
A Private Matter '92
Looking for Richard '96
That Darn Cat '96
The Love Letter '98
Empire Falls '05
Diane '18

Jim Parsons (1973-)
Garden State '04
The Great New Wonderful '06
The Big Year '11
The Normal Heart '14
Wish I Was Here '14
Home '15 (V)
Hidden Figures '17
A Kid Like Jake '18

Karyn Parsons (1966-)
Class Act '91
Gulliver's Travels '95
Major Payne '95
Mixing Nia '98
The Ladies Man '00
13 Moons '02

Michael Parsons
Raiders of Leyte Gulf '63
Beach Red '67

Mike Parsons
The Walls of Hell '64
The Ravagers '65

Nancy Parsons (1942-2001)
Motel Hell '80
Porky's '82
Porky's 2: The Next Day '83
Sudden Impact '83
Porky's Revenge '85
Ladybugs '92

Percy Parsons (1878-1944)
Blackmail '29
The Good Companions '33
Power '34

Dolly Parton (1946-)
9 to 5 '80
The Best Little Whorehouse in Texas '82
Rhinestone '84
Steel Magnolias '89
Straight Talk '92
The Beverly Hillbillies '93 (C)
Unlikely Angel '97
Blue Valley Songbird '99
Jackie's Back '99
Frank McKlusky, C.I. '02
Hannah Montana: The Movie '09
Gnomeo & Juliet '11 (V)
Joyful Noise '12

Ross Partridge (1968-)
Amityville: A New Generation '93
Baghead '08
Feed the Fish '09
Lamb '16
Stray '19

Adam Pascal (1970-)
SLC Punk! '99
School of Rock '03
Rent '05

Christine Pascal (1953-96)
The Clockmaker '73
The Best Way '76
Maids of Wilko '79

Pedro Pascal (1975-)
Bloodsucking Bastards '15
The Great Wall '17
The Equalizer 2 '18
Triple Frontier '19

Isabelle Pasco (1966-)
Prospero's Books '91
Invisible Circus '00

Richard Pasco (1926-2014)
Room at the Top '59
Sword of Sherwood Forest '60
The Gorgon '64
Rasputin the Mad Monk '66
The Watcher in the Woods '81
Mrs. Brown '97

Adrian Pasdar (1965-)
Top Gun '86
Near Dark '87
Cookie '89
Torn Apart '89
The Lost Capone '90
Vital Signs '90
Carlito's Way '93
The Ghost Brigade '93
A Mother's Gift '95
The Pompatus of Love '95
A Brother's Kiss '97
The Big Day '99
Secondhand Lions '03
Home Movie '08
Seeds of Destruction '11

Ralitsa Paskaleva
In the Name of the King 3: The Last Mission '14
Jarhead 2: Field of Fire '14

Pier Paolo Pasolini (1922-75)
Oedipus Rex '67
The Decameron '70
The Canterbury Tales '71

Steven Pasquale (1976-)
Aliens *vs.* Predator: Requiem '07
Marry Me '10
Coma '12
American Son '19

David Pasquesi
I Want Someone to Eat Cheese With '06
Strangers with Candy '06

Cyndi Pass
Deadbolt '92
Serial Killer '95
The Night Caller '97

Mary Kay Pass
Kansas City Bomber '72
Hospital of Terror '78

George Pastell (1923-76)
The Gambler & the Lady '52
The Mummy '59
The Stranglers of Bombay '60
The High Bright Sun '65

Reagan Pasternak (1977-)
Jailbait! '00
Verdict in Blood '02
Cake '05
A Christmas Wedding '06
Just Buried '07

Earl Pastko (1965-)
Highway 61 '91
The Sweet Hereafter '96
Subhuman '04
Just Business '08
The Way of the West '11

Vincent Pastore (1946-)
True Love '89
Awakenings '90
Goodfellas '90
Carlito's Way '93
It Could Happen to You '94
The Jerky Boys '95
Money Train '95
Gotti '96
Walking and Talking '96
West New York '96
Mafia! '98
Witness to the Mob '98
Hitman's Journal '99
The Hurricane '99
A Slight Case of Murder '99
Under Hellgate Bridge '99
Blue Moon '00
Made '01
American Cousins '02
Deuces Wild '02
Serving Sara '02
A Tale of Two Pizzas '03
This Thing of Ours '03
Shark Tale '04 (V)
Bachelor Party Vegas '05
Remedy '05
Revolver '05
The Last Request '06
The Devil's Dominoes '07
College Road Trip '08
Doughboys '08
Looking for Palladin '08
Return to Sleepaway Camp '08
Tricks of a Woman '08
Oy Vey! My Son is Gay! '09
Street Boss '09
Once Upon a Time in Brooklyn '13

Robert Pastorelli (1954-2004)
Beverly Hills Cop 2 '87
Dances with Wolves '90
Folks! '92
Sister Act 2: Back in the Habit '93
Striking Distance '93
The Yarn Princess '94
Eraser '96
Michael '96
A Simple Wish '97
Modern Vampires '98
Bait '00
Rodgers & Hammerstein's South Pacific '01
Women *vs.* Men '02
Be Cool '05

Willie Pastrano (1935-97)
Wild Rebels '71
Alligator Alley '72

Patachou (1918-)
French Can-Can '55
Belphegor: Phantom of the Louvre '01

Michael Pataki (1938-2010)
The Sidehackers '69
The Baby '72
Grave of the Vampire '72
The Bat People '74
The Last Porno Flick '74
When Every Day Was the Fourth of July '78
Zoltan. . . Hound of Dracula '78
Love at First Bite '79
The Onion Field '79
Dead and Buried '81
Delinquent School Girls '84
Remo Williams: The Adventure Begins '85
Rocky 4 '85
American Anthem '86
Death House '88
Halloween 4: The Return of Michael Myers '88

Elsa Pataky (1976-)
Beyond Re-Animator '03
Snakes on a Plane '06
Giallo '09
Give 'Em Hell Malone '09
Mr. Nice '10
Where the Road Meets the Sun '11
Fast & Furious 6 '13

Wally Patch (1888-1970)
The Private Life of Henry VIII '33
Don Quixote '35
Bank Holiday '38
Inspector Hornleigh '39
Night Train to Munich '40
Cottage to Let '41

Michael Pate (1920-2008)
The Strange Door '51
Thunder on the Hill '51
Five Fingers '52
Hondo '53
Houdini '53
Julius Caesar '53
King Richard and the Crusaders '54
A Lawless Street '55
The Killer Is Loose '56
The Oklahoman '56
Seventh Cavalry '56
Westbound '58
Green Mansions '59
Tower of London '62
California '63
McLintock! '63
The Singing Nun '66
Return of Captain Invincible '83
Howling 3: The Marsupials '87

Dev Patel (1990-)
Slumdog Millionaire '08
The Last Airbender '10
About Cherry '12
The Best Exotic Marigold Hotel '12
Chappie '15
The Second Best Exotic Marigold Hotel '15
Lion '16
The Man Who Knew Infinity '16
Only Yesterday '16
Hotel Mumbai '18
The Wedding Guest '18

Harish Patel
Run, Fatboy, Run '07
Today's Special '09

Himesh Patel
The Aeronauts '19
Yesterday '19

Bill Paterson (1945-)
The Ploughman's Lunch '83
The Killing Fields '84
A Private Function '84
Defense of the Realm '85
Dutch Girls '87
Hidden City '87
The Adventures of Baron Munchausen '89
The Rachel Papers '89
Traffik '90
The Witches '90
The Object of Beauty '91
Truly, Madly, Deeply '91
Chaplin '92
The Crow Road '96
Spice World: The Movie '97
Hilary and Jackie '98
Retribution '98
Heart '99
Wives and Daughters '01
Crush '02
Doctor Zhivago '03
Miss Potter '06
Little Dorrit '08
Into the Storm '09

Vinay Pathak
Water '05
Luka Chuppi '19

Mandy Patinkin (1952-)
French Postcards '79
Last Embrace '79
Ragtime '81
Daniel '83
Yentl '83
Maxie '85
Sunday in the Park with George '86
The Princess Bride '87
Alien Nation '88
The House on Carroll Street '88
Dick Tracy '90
Impromptu '90
The Doctor '91
True Colors '91
The Music of Chance '93
Squanto: A Warrior's Tale '94
Hombres Armados '97
The Hunchback '97
Lulu on the Bridge '98
Pinero '01
Wish I Was Here '14
Wonder '17
Life Itself '18

Tatjana Patitz (1966-)
Rising Sun '93
Restraining Order '99

Angela Paton (1930-)
Dirty Harry '71
Groundhog Day '93
Trapped in Paradise '94
American Wedding '03
United States of Leland '03
The Final Season '07

Jason Patric (1966-)
Solarbabies '86
The Lost Boys '87
The Beast '88
After Dark, My Sweet '90
Frankenstein Unbound '90
Rush '91
Geronimo: An American Legend '93
The Journey of August King '95
Sleepers '96
Incognito '97
Speed 2: Cruise Control '97
Your Friends & Neighbors '98
Narc '02
The Alamo '04
Walker Payne '06
Expired '07
Downloading Nancy '08
My Sister's Keeper '09
The Losers '10
Keyhole '11
The Outsider '14
The Prince '14
Home Invasion '16
The Yellow Birds '17

Butch Patrick (1953-)
Two Little Bears '61
Munster, Go Home! '66

Dennis Patrick (1918-2002)
Joe '70
Dear Dead Delilah '72
Missiles of October '74
Choices '81
The Air Up There '94

Dorothy Patrick (1922-87)
High Wall '47
New Orleans '47
711 Ocean Drive '50
Torch Song '53
Violent Saturday '55

Gail Patrick (1911-80)
To the Last Man '33
Death Takes a Holiday '34
Murder at the Vanities '34
Mississippi '35
No More Ladies '35
Murder With Pictures '36
My Man Godfrey '36
Artists and Models '37
Stage Door '37
Mad About Music '38
Wives under Suspicion '38
Reno '39
Doctor Takes a Wife '40
Gallant Sons '40
My Favorite Wife '40
Kathleen '41
Love Crazy '41
We Were Dancing '42
Women in Bondage '43
Brewster's Millions '45
Claudia and David '46

Lee Patrick (1911-82)
Fisherman's Wharf '39
Invisible Stripes '39
Saturday's Children '40
Dangerously We Live '41
Footsteps in the Dark '41
The Maltese Falcon '41
The Smiling Ghost '41
In This Our Life '42
Somewhere I'll Find You '42
Gambler's Choice '44
Mrs. Parkington '44
Keep Your Powder Dry '45
Caged '50
The Fuller Brush Girl '50
The Lawless '50
Vertigo '58
Pillow Talk '59
Summer and Smoke '61
7 Faces of Dr. Lao '63

Marcus Patrick (1974-)
Descent '07
Love and Other Four Letter Words '07
Violent Tendencies '10

Nigel Patrick (1913-81)
The Jack of Diamonds *'49*
Morning Departure *'50*
The Browning Version *'51*
Pandora and the Flying Dutchman *'51*
Encore *'52*
The Sound Barrier *'52*
Grand National Night *'53*
The Pickwick Papers *'54*
Raintree County *'57*
Sapphire *'59*
The League of Gentlemen *'60*
The Trials of Oscar Wilde *'60*
Battle of Britain *'69*
The Virgin Soldiers *'69*
The Executioner *'70*
Mackintosh Man *'73*

Robert Patrick (1958-)
Behind Enemy Lines *'85*
Eye of the Eagle *'87*
Die Hard 2: Die Harder *'90*
Terminator 2: Judgment Day *'91*
The Cool Surface *'92*
Body Shot *'93*
Fire in the Sky *'93*
Last Action Hero *'93 (C)*
Zero Tolerance *'93*
Double Dragon *'94*
Striptease *'96*
Cop Land *'97*
The Only Thrill *'97*
The Faculty *'98*
Forgotten City *'98*
From Dusk Till Dawn 2: Texas Blood Money *'98*
Rogue Force *'99*
Tactical Assault *'99*
A Texas Funeral *'99*
All the Pretty Horses *'00*
Angels Don't Sleep Here *'00*
Mexico City *'00*
Backflash *'01*
Eye See You *'01*
Spy Kids *'01*
Texas Rangers *'01*
Charlie's Angels: Full Throttle *'03*
Ladder 49 *'04*
Walk the Line *'05*
Firewall *'06*
Flags of Our Fathers *'06*
The Marine *'06*
Balls of Fury *'07*
Bridge to Terabithia *'07*
Autopsy *'08*
Strange Wilderness *'08*
Alien Trespass *'09*
The Men Who Stare at Goats *'09*
The Black Waters of Echo's Pond *'10*
Caged Animal *'10*
Good Day for It *'11*
Mafia *'11*
Red Faction: Origins *'11*
S.W.A.T.: Firefight *'11*
Safe House *'12*
Trouble with the Curve *'12*
Gangster Squad *'13*
Identity Thief *'13*
Jayne Mansfield's Car *'13*
Lovelace *'13*
Endless Love *'14*
Hellions *'15*
Last Rampage *'17*
Tone-Deaf *'19*

Brendan Patricks
The Curse of King Tut's Tomb *'06*
Three Wise Women *'11*

Luana Patten (1938-96)
So Dear to My Heart *'49*
Rock, Pretty Baby *'56*
Johnny Tremain & the Sons of Liberty *'58*
A Thunder of Drums *'61*
Follow Me, Boys! *'66*

Elizabeth Patterson (1875-1966)
Miss Pinkerton *'32*
No Man of Her Own *'32*
Hold Your Man *'33*
Go West, Young Man *'36*
Bluebeard's Eighth Wife *'38*
Sing You Sinners *'38*
Bulldog Drummond's Bride *'39*
The Cat and the Canary *'39*
Michael Shayne: Private Detective *'40*
Remember the Night *'40*
Tobacco Road *'41*
The Vanishing Virginian *'41*
Her Cardboard Lover *'42*
My Sister Eileen *'42*
The Sky's the Limit *'43*
Colonel Effingham's Raid *'45*
Lady on a Train *'45*
Welcome Stranger *'47*
Intruder in the Dust *'49*
Pal Joey *'57*
Tall Story *'60*

James Patterson (1932-72)
Lilith *'64*
Castle Keep *'69*

Jay Patterson (1954-)
Heaven Help Us *'85*
Nadine *'87*
Street Smart *'87*
D.O.A. *'88*
Nobody's Fool *'94*
Excessive Force 2: Force on Force *'95*

Kenneth Patterson (1911-90)
Hard, Fast and Beautiful *'51*
Private Hell 36 *'54*

Lee Patterson (1929-2007)
Above Us the Waves *'55*
Spin a Dark Web *'56*
The Counterfeit Plan *'57*
Time Lock *'57*
The Spaniard's Curse *'58*
Jack the Ripper *'60*
The 3 Worlds of Gulliver *'60*
The Ceremony *'63*
Chato's Land *'71*
Bullseye! *'90*

Marne(tte) Patterson (1980-)
Camp Nowhere *'94*
Pope Dreams *'06*
Ghosts of Goldfield *'07*
Remember the Daze *'07*
Wild Things: Foursome *'10*

Merritt Patterson (1990-)
Radio Rebel *'12*
Unbroken: Path to Redemption *'18*

Neva Patterson (1920-2010)
Solid Gold Cadillac *'56*
An Affair to Remember *'57*
Desk Set *'57*
Too Much, Too Soon *'58*
David and Lisa *'62*
V *'83*
Women of Valor *'86*

Pat Patterson
Moonshine Mountain *'64*
Gas-s-s-s! *'70*
The Body Shop *'72*

Ross Patterson (1977-)
Strike *'07*
Garden Party *'08*
Stuntmen *'09*

Sarah Patterson (1972-)
The Company of Wolves *'85*
Snow White *'89*
Do I Love You? *'02*
Tick Tock Lullaby *'07*

Scott Patterson (1958-)
Alien Nation: Dark Horizon *'94*
Little Big League *'94*
Her Best Move *'07*
Saw 4 *'07*
Saw 5 *'08*
Boys of Abu Ghraib *'14*

Robert Pattinson (1986-)
Dark Kingdom: The Dragon King *'04*
Harry Potter and the Goblet of Fire *'05*
The Haunted Airman *'06*
The Bad Mother's Handbook *'07*
How to Be *'08*
Twilight *'08*
Little Ashes *'09*
The Twilight Saga: New Moon *'09*
Remember Me *'10*
The Twilight Saga: Eclipse *'10*
The Twilight Saga: Breaking Dawn, Part 1 *'11*
Water for Elephants *'11*
Bel Ami *'12*
Cosmopolis *'12*
The Twilight Saga: Breaking Dawn, Part 2 *'12*
Maps to the Stars *'14*
The Rover *'14*
Life *'15*
The Childhood of a Leader *'16*
Good Time *'17*
The Lost City of Z *'17*
Damsel *'18*
High Life *'18*
The Lighthouse *'19*

Antwan Andre Patton (1975-)
ATL *'06*
Idlewild *'06*
Who's Your Caddy? *'07*

Mark Patton (1964-)
Anna to the Infinite Power *'84*
A Nightmare on Elm Street 2: Freddy's Revenge *'85*

Paula Patton (1975-)
Deja Vu *'06*
Idlewild *'06*
Mirrors *'08*
Swing Vote *'08*
Precious: Based on the Novel 'Push' by Sapphire *'09*
Just Wright *'10*
Jumping the Broom *'11*
Mission: Impossible-Ghost Protocol *'11*
Baggage Claim *'13*
2 Guns *'13*
About Last Night *'14*
Warcraft *'16*
Traffik *'18*

Stephanie Patton (1993-)
Mortuary *'05*
Nanny Insanity *'06*

Will Patton (1954-)
Variety *'83*
After Hours *'85*
Desperately Seeking Susan *'85*
Belizaire the Cajun *'86*
No Way Out *'87*
Wildfire *'88*
Signs of Life *'89*
Everybody Wins *'90*
A Shock to the System *'90*
In the Deep Woods *'91*
Murder on the Bayou *'91*
The Rapture *'91*
Cold Heaven *'92*
In the Soup *'92*
Romeo Is Bleeding *'93*
The Client *'94*
The Puppet Masters *'94*
Copycat *'95*
The Spitfire Grill *'95*
Fled *'96*
Inventing the Abbotts *'97*
The Postman *'97*
Armageddon *'98*
Breakfast of Champions *'98*
Entrapment *'99*
Jesus' Son *'99*
Gone in 60 Seconds *'00*
Remember the Titans *'00*
Trixie *'00*
The Mothman Prophecies *'02*
The Last Ride *'04*
The Punisher *'04*
Road House 2: Last Call *'06*
Code Name: The Cleaner *'07*
The List *'07*
A Mighty Heart *'07*
The Loss of a Teardrop Diamond *'08*
Lucky Days *'08*
Wendy and Lucy *'08*
American Violet *'09*
Brooklyn's Finest *'09*
The Canyon *'09*
The Fourth Kind *'09*
Princess Kaiulani *'09*
Meek's Cutoff *'10*
Waking Madison *'10*
The November Man *'14*
The Scent of Rain & Lightening *'17*

Tina Ona Paukstelis (1970-)
The Unearthing *'93*
Aswang *'03*

Aaron Paul (1979-)
Whatever It Takes *'00*
K-PAX *'01*
The Last House on the Left *'09*
Smashed *'12*
Decoding Annie Parker *'13*
Hellion *'13*
Exodus: Gods and Kings *'14*
A Long Way Down *'14*
Need for Speed *'14*
Eye in the Sky *'15*
Triple 9 *'15*
Come and Find Me *'16*
Fathers and Daughters *'16*
The 9th Life of Louis Drax *'16*
Welcome Home *'18*
American Woman *'19*
The Parts You Lose *'19*

Adrian Paul (1959-)
Highlander: The Gathering *'92*
Dead Men Can't Dance *'97*
Dying to Get Rich *'98*
Premonition *'98*
Highlander: Endgame *'00*
The Breed *'01*
The Void *'01*
Code Hunter *'02*
Nemesis Game *'03*
Moscow Heat *'04*
Seance *'06*
Highlander: The Source *'07*
Lost Colony: The Legend of Roanoke *'07*
Eyeborgs *'09*
The Heavy *'09*
AE: Apocalypse Earth *'13*
Beverly Lewis' The Confession *'13*
Apocalypse Pompeii *'14*

Alexandra Paul (1963-)
Christine *'84*
Just the Way You Are *'84*
American Flyers *'85*
Dragnet *'87*
Millions *'90*
Prey of the Chameleon *'91*
Sunset Grill *'92*
Detonator *'93*
Cyber Bandits *'94*
The Paperboy *'94*
Detonator 2: Night Watch *'95*
Piranha *'95*
Spectre *'96*
Fallen Angel *'99*
Facing the Enemy *'00*
Green Sails *'00*
A Woman Hunted *'03*
Disaster Zone: Volcano in New York *'06*
Gospel of Deceit *'06*
Trapped *'06*
Demons from Her Past *'07*
Murder.com *'08*
Betrayed at 17 *'11*
Love at the Christmas Table *'12*

David Paul (1957-2020)
Double Trouble *'91*
Twinsitters *'95*

Don Michael Paul
Lovelines *'84*
Brotherhood of Justice *'86*
Alien from L.A. *'87*
Winners Take All *'87*
The Heart of Dixie *'89*
Robot Wars *'93*
Half Past Dead *'02*

Peter Paul
Double Trouble *'91*
Twinsitters *'95*

Richard Paul (1940-98)
Eating Raoul *'82*
Not for Publication *'84*
Bloodfist 3: Forced to Fight *'92*
The People *vs.* Larry Flynt *'96*

Richard Joseph Paul (1962-)
Under the Boardwalk *'89*
Oblivion *'94*
Vampirella *'96*

Scott Paulin (1950-)
Forbidden World *'82*
The Right Stuff *'83*
A Soldier's Story *'84*
Teen Wolf *'85*
Tricks of the Trade *'88*
Capone *'89*
Captain America *'89*
From Hollywood to Deadwood *'89*
Turner and Hooch *'89*
Pump Up the Volume *'90*
My Little Assassin *'99*
Just Ask My Children *'01*
The Heart Specialist *'06*
Invasion *'07*
Final Approach *'08*

Marcus T. Paulk (1986-)
Another Cinderella Story *'08*
The Rig *'10*

Morgan Paull (1944-2012)
Patton *'70*
The Last Hard Men *'76*
Fade to Black *'80*

Gaston Pauls (1972-)
What Your Eyes Don't See *'99*
Felicidades *'00*
Nine Queens *'00*

Albert Paulsen (1929-2004)
The Manchurian Candidate *'62*
Missiles of October *'74*
The Arab Conspiracy *'76*

Pat Paulsen (1927-97)
Foreplay *'75*
Harper Valley P.T.A. *'78*
Ellie *'84*
Night Patrol *'85*

Rob Paulsen (1956-)
A Goofy Movie *'94 (V)*
The Land Before Time 2: The Great Valley Adventure *'94 (V)*
The Land Before Time 3: The Time of the Great Giving *'95 (V)*
The Land Before Time 4: Journey Through the Mists *'96 (V)*
The Land Before Time 5: The Mysterious Island *'97 (V)*
Land Before Time 7: The Stone of Cold Fire *'00 (V)*
Jimmy Neutron: Boy Genius *'01 (V)*
Disney's Teacher's Pet *'04 (V)*
The Ant Bully *'06 (V)*
Barnyard *'06 (V)*
The Fox and the Hound 2 *'06 (V)*
Leroy and Stitch *'06 (V)*

Jay Paulson (1978-)
Go *'99*
Imaginary Heroes *'05*
The Marc Pease Experience *'09*
Black Rock *'12*

Sarah Paulson (1974-)
Levitation *'97*
The Long Way Home *'98*
The Other Sister *'98*
Held Up *'00*
What Women Want *'00*
Down With Love *'03*
A Christmas Wedding *'06*
Diggers *'06*
Griffin & Phoenix *'06*
The Notorious Bettie Page *'06*
The Spirit *'08*
November Christmas *'10*
Martha Marcy May Marlene *'11*
Game Change *'12*
Mud *'12*
The Time Being *'12*
12 Years a Slave *'13*
Carol *'15*
The Runner *'15*
Blue Jay *'16*
The Post *'17*
Rebel in the Rye *'17*
Ocean's 8 *'18*
Glass *'19*

Rodolphe Pauly (1983-)
Merci pour le Chocolat *'00*
Close to Leo *'02*
Before Sunset *'04*
A Very Long Engagement *'04*
The Romance of Astrea and Celadon *'07*

Aleks Paunovic (1969-)
Fireball *'09*
In the Name of the King 2: Two Worlds *'11*
Chupacabra *vs.* the Alamo *'13*
Eve of Destruction *'13*
Kindergarten Cop 2 *'16*
Siberia *'18*

Marisa Pavan (1932-)
What Price Glory? *'52*
Down Three Dark Streets *'54*
Drum Beat *'54*
Diane *'55*
The Rose Tattoo *'55*
The Man in the Gray Flannel Suit *'56*
Solomon and Sheba *'59*
A Slightly Pregnant Man *'79*

Muriel Pavlow (1921-)
Doctor in the House *'53*
Malta Story *'53*
Simon and Laura *'55*
Eyewitness *'56*
Doctor at Large *'57*
Murder She Said *'61*

Lennox Pawle (1872-1936)
David Copperfield *'35*
Sylvia Scarlett *'35*

Edward Pawley (1901-88)
Dead End Kids: Little Tough Guy *'38*
Romance of the Limberlost *'38*

William Pawley
Bad Girl *'31*
After Tomorrow *'32*

Adam Pawlikowski (1925-76)
Ashes and Diamonds *'58*
Lotna *'64*

James Pax
The Chinatown Murders: Man against the Mob *'89*
In Love and War *'91*

Katina Paxinou (1900-73)
For Whom the Bell Tolls *'43*
Confidential Agent *'45*
Inheritance *'47*
Prince of Foxes *'49*
Rocco and His Brothers *'60*
Zita *'68*

Bill Paxton (1955-2017)
Crazy Mama *'75*
The Lords of Discipline *'83*
Impulse *'84*
Streets of Fire *'84*
The Terminator *'84*
Commando *'85*
Weird Science *'85*

Aliens '86
Near Dark '87
Brain Dead '89
Next of Kin '89
Slipstream '89
The Last of the Finest '90
Navy SEALS '90
Predator 2 '90
The Dark Backward '91
One False Move '91
Trespass '92
The Vagrant '92
Boxing Helena '93
Future Shock '93
Indian Summer '93
Tombstone '93
Frank and Jesse '94
True Lies '94
Apollo 13 '95
The Evening Star '96
The Last Supper '96
Traveller '96
Twister '96
Titanic '97
A Bright Shining Lie '98
Mighty Joe Young '98
A Simple Plan '98
U-571 '00
Vertical Limit '00
Frailty '02
Resistance '03
Spy Kids 3-D: Game Over '03
Club Dread '04
Haven '04
Thunderbirds '04
The Good Life '07
Hatfields & McCoys '12
Haywire '12
2 Guns '13
Edge of Tomorrow '14
Million Dollar Arm '14
Nightcrawler '14
Term Life '16
Mean Dreams '17

Sara Paxton (1988-)
Sleepover '04
Aquamarine '06
Return to Halloweentown '06
The Party Never Stops '07
Sydney White '07
Superhero Movie '08
The Last House on the Left '09
The Innkeepers '11
Shark Night 3D '11
Blue-Eyed Butcher '12
Boys of Abu Ghraib '14
Cheap Thrills '14
Love & Air Sex '14

Johnny Paycheck (1938-2003)
Take This Job & Shove It '81 (C)
Sweet Country Road '83
Heroes of the Heart '94

David Paymer (1954-)
Howard the Duck '86
No Way Out '87
Crazy People '90
City Slickers '91
Mr. Saturday Night '92
Heart and Souls '93
Searching for Bobby Fischer '93
City Slickers 2: The Legend of Curly's Gold '94
Quiz Show '94
The American President '95
City Hall '95
Get Shorty '95
Nixon '95
Carpool '96
Gang Related '96
Unforgettable '96
Amistad '97
The Sixth Man '97
Mighty Joe Young '98
Payback '98
Chill Factor '99
The Hurricane '99
Mumford '99
Partners '99
Bait '00
Bounce '00
Enemies of Laughter '00
For Love or Country: The Arturo Sandoval Story '00
State and Main '00
Bartleby '01
Focus '01
Joe and Max '02
RFK '02
Alex & Emma '03
In Good Company '04
Spartan '04
Marilyn Hotchkiss' Ballroom Dancing & Charm School '06
School of Life '06
Ocean's Thirteen '07
Resurrecting the Champ '07
Redbelt '08
Drag Me to Hell '09
The Five-Year Engagement '12
Twixt '12

Allen Payne (1968-)
New Jack City '91
CB4: The Movie '93
Jason's Lyric '94
The Tuskegee Airmen '95
Vampire in Brooklyn '95
A Price Above Rubies '97
The Perfect Storm '00
Blue Hill Avenue '01
30 Years to Life '01

Bruce Payne (1958-)
Howling 6: The Freaks '90
Switch '91
Passenger 57 '92
Full Eclipse '93
The Cisco Kid '94
One Man's Justice '95
Kounterfeit '96
Face the Evil '97
Warlock 3: The End of Innocence '98
Cleopatra '99
Sweepers '99
Britannic '00
Dungeons and Dragons '00
Highlander: Endgame '00
Ripper: Letter from Hell '01
Asylum of the Damned '03
Paranoia 1.0 '04
Prowl '10
Getaway '13

Carl Anthony Payne, II (1969-)
Ed '96
The Breaks '99
Feast 2: Sloppy Seconds '08

Dan Payne (1972-)
Mulligans '08
Secret Lives of Second Wives '08
Ruslan '09
A Family Thanksgiving '10
The Hunters '13

Eric Payne
She's Gotta Have It '86
Gridlock'd '96

John Payne (1912-89)
Dodsworth '36
Hats Off '37
College Swing '38
Garden of the Moon '38
Wings of the Navy '39
Star Dust '40
The Great American Broadcast '41
Remember the Day '41
Week-End in Havana '41
Iceland '42
Springtime in the Rockies '42
To the Shores of Tripoli '42
Hello, Frisco, Hello '43
The Dolly Sisters '46
The Razor's Edge '46
Wake Up and Dream '46
Miracle on 34th Street '47
El Paso '49
Kansas City Confidential '52
99 River Street '53
Raiders of the Seven Seas '53
Silver Lode '54
Tennessee's Partner '55
The Boss '56
Rebel in Town '56
Slightly Scarlet '56

Laurence Payne (1919-2009)
Ill Met By Moonlight '57
The Crawling Eye '58
The Tell-Tale Heart '60
Vampire Circus '71

Tom Payne
Miss Pettigrew Lives for a Day '08
Wuthering Heights '09
IO '19

Waylon Malloy Payne (1972-)
Walk the Line '05
Ghost Image '07
Crazy '08

Amanda Pays (1959-)
Cold Room '84
Oxford Blues '84
A.D. '85
Agatha Christie's Thirteen at Dinner '85
Off Limits '87
Leviathan '89
The Flash '90
Hollywood Confidential '97
Spacejacked '98
Subterfuge '98
Ablaze '00
The Santa Trap '02

Barbara Payton (1927-67)
Great Jesse James Raid '49
Trapped '49
Kiss Tomorrow Goodbye '50
Only the Valiant '50
Bride of the Gorilla '51
Drums in the Deep South '51
Bad Blonde '53
Four Sided Triangle '53
Murder Is My Beat '55

Christian Payton (1965-)
To Sir, With Love 2 '96
The Temptations '98

Khary Payton (1972-)
Latter Days '04
National Lampoon's The Legend of Awesomest Maximus '11
Teen Titans Go! To the Movies '18 (V)

Pamela Payton-Wright (1941-2019)
Resurrection '80
In Dreams '98

Adriana Paz
Rudo y Cursi '09
The Motive '18

Nello Pazzafini
Fort Yuma Gold '66
A Long Ride From Hell '68

Rock Peace (1953-)
Attack of the Killer Tomatoes '77
Return of the Killer Tomatoes! '88
Killer Tomatoes Strike Back '90

Mary Peach (1934-)
Room at the Top '59
Ballad in Blue '66
Disraeli '79

Trevor Peacock (1931-)
The Insurance Man '86
For Roseanna '96
Neil Gaiman's NeverWhere '96
A Christmas Carol '99
Fred Claus '07
Quartet '12

Maxine Peake (1974-)
See No Evil: The Moors Murders '06
Red Riding, Part 2: 1980 '09
The Secret Diaries of Miss Anne Lister '10
Private Peaceful '12
Run & Jump '13
The Theory of Everything '14
Peterloo '18
Gwen '19

Adele Pearce (1915-2009)
See Pamela Blake

Alice Pearce (1913-66)
The Belle of New York '52
Dear Brigitte '65
The Glass Bottom Boat '66

Guy Pearce (1967-)
The Adventures of Priscilla, Queen of the Desert '94
Flynn '96
L.A. Confidential '97
Ravenous '99
A Slipping Down Life '99
Memento '00
Rules of Engagement '00
The Count of Monte Cristo '02
The Hard Word '02
Till Human Voices Wake Us '02
The Time Machine '02
Two Brothers '04
The Proposition '05
Factory Girl '06
Death Defying Acts '07
First Snow '07
Bedtime Stories '08
Fragments '08
The Hurt Locker '08
Traitor '08
Animal Kingdom '09
In Her Skin '09
The Road '09
The King's Speech '10
Don't Be Afraid of the Dark '11
Mildred Pierce '11
33 Postcards '11
Lawless '12
Lockout '12
Prometheus '12
Seeking Justice '12
Breathe In '13
Hateship Loveship '13
Iron Man 3 '13
The Rover '14
Results '15
Equals '16
Genius '16
Brimstone '17
The Catcher Was a Spy '18
Spinning Man '18
Domino '19
Swinging Safari '19

Jacqueline Pearce (1943-)
Plague of the Zombies '66
The Reptile '66
Don't Raise the Bridge, Lower the River '68
White Mischief '88
Princess Caraboo '94

Mary Vivian Pearce (1947-)
Pink Flamingos '72
Female Trouble '74
Desperate Living '77
Polyester '81
Hairspray '88
Cry-Baby '90
Serial Mom '94

Slade Pearce (1995-)
Yours, Mine & Ours '05
Air Bud 6: Air Buddies '06

Aaron Pearl (1972-)
The Spring '00
All I Want '02
Anna's Storm '07
Lost Holiday: The Jim & Suzanne Shemwell Story '07
Love Notes '07
Montana Sky '07
Growing the Big One '09
Takedown '10

Barry Pearl (1950-)
Grease '78
Avenging Angel '85

Corey Pearson (1974-)
Going Greek '01
Jiminy Glick in LaLa Wood '05

James Anthony Pearson
Kidnapped '05
Control '07

Neil Pearson (1959-)
The Secret Rapture '94
Fever Pitch '96
Bridget Jones: The Edge of Reason '04
The State Within '06

Virginia Pearson (1886-1958)
The Phantom of the Opera '25
The Wizard of Oz '25
Lightning Hutch '26

Harold (Hal) Peary (1908-85)
Look Who's Laughing '41
Here We Go Again! '42
Seven Days' Leave '42
Gildersleeve on Broadway '43
Wetbacks '56
Clambake '67

Sierra Pecheur
3 Women '77
Bronco Billy '80
Kalifornia '93

Bob Peck (1945-99)
Edge of Darkness '86
The Kitchen Toto '87
Slipstream '89
Catherine Cookson's The Black Velvet Gown '92
Jurassic Park '93
Smilla's Sense of Snow '96
Surviving Picasso '96
FairyTale: A True Story '97
The Miracle Maker: The Story of Jesus '00 (V)

Cecilia Peck (1958-)
Wall Street '87
My Best Friend Is a Vampire '88
Torn Apart '89
Blue Flame '93

Ethan Peck
Adopt a Sailor '08
Tennessee '08

George Peck
Dawn of the Mummy '82
Curse of the Puppet Master: The Human Experiment '98

Gregory Peck (1916-2003)
Days of Glory '43
The Keys of the Kingdom '44
Spellbound '45
The Valley of Decision '45
Duel in the Sun '46
The Yearling '46
Gentleman's Agreement '47
The Paradine Case '47
Yellow Sky '48
The Great Sinner '49
Twelve o'Clock High '49
The Gunfighter '50
Only the Valiant '50
Captain Horatio Hornblower '51
David and Bathsheba '51
The Snows of Kilimanjaro '52
The World in His Arms '52
Roman Holiday '53
Night People '54
The Purple Plain '54
The Man in the Gray Flannel Suit '56
Moby Dick '56
Designing Woman '57
The Big Country '58
The Bravados '58
Beloved Infidel '59
On the Beach '59
Pork Chop Hill '59
Cape Fear '61
The Guns of Navarone '61
To Kill a Mockingbird '62
Captain Newman, M.D. '63
How the West Was Won '63
Behold a Pale Horse '64
Arabesque '66
Mirage '66
The Chairman '69
MacKenna's Gold '69
Marooned '69
The Stalking Moon '69
I Walk the Line '70
Shoot Out '71
Billy Two Hats '74
The Omen '76
MacArthur '77
The Boys from Brazil '78
Sea Wolves '81
The Blue and the Gray '82
The Scarlet & the Black '83
Amazing Grace & Chuck '87
Old Gringo '89
Cape Fear '91
Other People's Money '91
Moby Dick '98

J. Eddie Peck
Curse 2: The Bite '88
Lambada '89
To Grandmother's House We Go '94
Blind Heat '00

Josh Peck (1986-)
Max Keeble's Big Move '01
Mean Creek '04
Ice Age: The Meltdown '06 (V)
Special '06
Drillbit Taylor '08
The Wackness '08
Aliens in the Attic '09 (V)
Ice Age: Dawn of the Dinosaurs '09 (V)
What Goes Up '09
ATM '12
Ice Age: Continental Drift '12 (V)
Battle of the Year '13

Tony Peck (1956-)
Brenda Starr '86
Poor Little Rich Girl: The Barbara Hutton Story '87
Hard Hunted '92
Fit to Kill '93
The Magic Bubble '93
Die Hard: With a Vengeance '95
Carnosaur 3: Primal Species '96

Sam Peckinpah (1925-84)
Invasion of the Body Snatchers '56
Gunfire '78
The Visitor '80

Chris Pederson (1963-)
Suburbia '83
Platoon '86
Point Break '91

Tom Pedi (1913-96)
The Iceman Cometh '60
The Iceman Cometh '73

Luciana Pedraza
Assassination Tango '03
Wild Horses '15

David Peel (1920-82)
The Brides of Dracula '60
The Hands of Orlac '60

Jordan Peele (1979-)
Keanu '16
Captain Underpants: The First Epic Movie '17 (V)

Aubrey Peeples
Rage '14
Jem and the Holograms '15

Nia Peeples (1961-)
North Shore '87
Deepstar Six '89
Swimsuit '89
I Don't Buy Kisses Anymore '92
Return to Lonesome Dove '93
Robin Cook's Terminal '96
Tower of Terror '97
Blues Brothers 2000 '98
Poodle Springs '98
Alone with a Stranger '99
Half Past Dead '02
Inside Out '05
Connor's War '06

Citizen Jane '09
Werewolf: The Beast Among Us '12

Joan Peers (1911-75)
Applause '29
Rain or Shine '30

Amanda Peet (1972-)
Grind '96
One Fine Day '96
She's the One '96
Ellen Foster '97
1999 '98
Southie '98
Body Shots '99
Isn't She Great '00
Two Ninas '00
Whipped '00
The Whole Nine Yards '00
Saving Silverman '01
Changing Lanes '02
High Crimes '02
Igby Goes Down '02
Identity '03
Something's Gotta Give '03
The Whole Ten Yards '04
A Lot Like Love '05
Melinda and Melinda '05
Syriana '05
Griffin & Phoenix '06
The Ex '07
Martian Child '07
$5 a Day '08
What Doesn't Kill You '08
The X Files: I Want to Believe '08
Battle for Terra '09 (V)
2012 '09
Gulliver's Travels '10
Please Give '10
Identity Thief '13
Trust Me '13
The Way Way Back '13

Simon Pegg (1970-)
Shaun of the Dead '04
George A. Romero's Land of the Dead '05
Big Nothing '06
Mission: Impossible 3 '06
The Good Night '07
Hot Fuzz '07
Run, Fatboy, Run '07
How to Lose Friends & Alienate People '08
Ice Age: Dawn of the Dinosaurs '09 (V)
Star Trek '09
Burke & Hare '10
The Chronicles of Narnia: The Voyage of the Dawn Treader '10 (V)
The Adventures of Tintin '11 (V)
Mission: Impossible-Ghost Protocol '11
Paul '11
Star Trek: Into Darkness '13
The World's End '13
The Boxtrolls '14 (V)
A Fantastic Fear of Everything '14
Hector and the Search for Happiness '14
Mission: Impossible Rogue Nation '15
Star Trek: Beyond '16
Absolutely Anything '17
Mission: Impossible-Fallout '18
Terminal '18

Luke Pegler
See No Evil '06
The Condemned '07

Mary Beth Peil (1940-)
The Odd Couple 2 '98
The Reagans '04
The List '07
Mirrors '08
Contest '13
The Song of Sway Lake '18

Ashley Peldon
Deceived '91
Cats Don't Dance '97 (V)
Get a Clue! '98
Night Skies '07
Float '08
Aliens in the Attic '09 (V)

Courtney Peldon (1981-)
Wild Grizzly '99
Mortuary '05
National Lampoon's Adam & Eve '05
InAlienable '08

Pele (1940-)
Victory '81
Hot Shot '86

Lisa Pelikan (1954-)
Julia '77
Ghoulies '84
Swing Shift '84
Lionheart '90
Return to the Blue Lagoon '91
Into the Badlands '92

Valentine Pelka (1957-)
Hold the Dream '86
Rowing with the Wind '88
First Knight '95
Ivanhoe '97
The Last of the Blonde Bombshells '00
Under the Tuscan Sun '03
8mm 2 '05
Double Identity '10

Oana Pellea (1962-)
High Tension '03
I Really Hate My Job '07
Fire & Ice: The Dragon Chronicles '08

Raymond Pellegrin (1925-2007)
Napoleon '55
Bitter Victory '58
Imperial Venus '63
Le Deuxieme Souffle '66
Taste of Death '68
Beatrice Cenci '69
Shoot First, Die Later '74
Street War '76

Frank Pellegrino (1957-)
Tarantella '95
Friends and Family '01

Mark Pellegrino (1965-)
Blood & Concrete: A Love Story '91
Prayer of the Rollerboys '91
Midnight Witness '93
Drowning Mona '00
Mulholland Drive '01
Say It Isn't So '01
The Hunted '03
Twisted '04
Capote '05
Caffeine '06
The Number 23 '07
An American Affair '09
2:13 '09
Bad Meat '11
Joint Body '11
Bad Turn Worse '14
Beirut '18

Clara Peller (1903-87)
Moving Violations '85
The Stuff '85

Michelle-Barbara Pelletier
P.T. Barnum '99
Twist '03

Mark Pellington (1962-)
Jerry Maguire '96
Almost Famous '00

Matti Pellonpaa (1951-95)
Ariel '89
Night on Earth '91

Markku Peltola (1956-2007)
The Man Without a Past '02
Jade Warrior '06

Nicola Peltz
The Last Airbender '10
Transformers: Age of Extinction '14

Meeno Peluce (1970-)
The Amityville Horror '79
Nightstalker '81

Ron Pember (1934-)
The Land That Time Forgot '75
Bullshot '83

Johnny Pemberton
Action Point '18
Tone-Deaf '19

Steve Pemberton (1967-)
Lassie '05
Under the Greenwood Tree '05
The Bad Mother's Handbook '07
Mr. Bean's Holiday '07
Going Postal '10

George Pembroke (1900-72)
Buried Alive '39
Gangs, Inc. '41
Paper Bullets '41
I Killed That Man '42

Candela Pena (1973-)
Running Out of Time '94
All About My Mother '99
Take My Eyes '03
Torremolinos 73 '03

Elizabeth Pena (1959-2014)
Times Square '80
They All Laughed '81
Thief '81
Crossover Dreams '85
Down and Out in Beverly Hills '86
*batteries not included '87
La Bamba '87
Vibes '88
Blue Steel '90
Drug Wars: The Camarena Story '90
Jacob's Ladder '90
The Waterdance '91
Fugitive Among Us '92
Across the Moon '94
Free Willy 2: The Adventure Home '95
Lone Star '95
The Second Civil War '97
Dee Snider's Strangeland '98
Highway Hitcher '98
Rush Hour '98
Seven Girlfriends '00
On the Borderline '01
Things Behind the Sun '01
Tortilla Soup '01
Impostor '02
ZigZag '02
The Incredibles '04 (V)
How the Garcia Girls Spent Their Summer '05
The Lost City '05
Sueno '05
Transamerica '05
Adrift in Manhattan '07
Dragon Wars '07
Goal 2: Living the Dream '07
Love Comes Lately '07
Nothing Like the Holidays '08
Racing for Time '08
The Perfect Family '11
The Song of Sway Lake '18

Julio Pena (1912-72)
The Werewolf vs. the Vampire Woman '70
Horror Express '72

Michael Peña (1976-)
Running Free '94
Bellyfruit '99
Buffalo Soldiers '01
United States of Leland '03
Crash '05
Little Athens '05
World Trade Center '06
Lions for Lambs '07
Shooter '07
The Lucky Ones '08
My Son, My Son, What Have Ye Done '09
Observe and Report '09
Everything Must Go '10
Battle: Los Angeles '11
The Good Doctor '11
The Lincoln Lawyer '11
30 Minutes or Less '11
Tower Heist '11
End of Watch '12
American Hustle '13
Gangster Squad '13
Turbo '13 (V)
Cesar Chavez '14
Fury '14
Collateral Beauty '16
CHIPS '17
War on Everyone '17
Ant-Man and the Wasp '18
The Mule '18
12 Strong '18
Dora and the Lost City of Gold '19
Fantasy Island '20

Alexa PenaVega (1988-)
See Alexa Vega

Oaklee Pendergast
The Impossible '12
The Woman in Black 2: Angel of Death '15

Austin Pendleton (1940-)
Petulia '68
Skidoo '68
Catch-22 '70
What's Up, Doc? '72
The Front Page '74
Great Smokey Roadblock '76
Starting Over '79
Simon '80
Short Circuit '86
Hello Again '87
Mr. & Mrs. Bridge '90
The Ballad of the Sad Cafe '91
My Cousin Vinny '92
Mr. Nanny '93
My Boyfriend's Back '93
Rain Without Thunder '93
Guarding Tess '94
Home for the Holidays '95
The Mirror Has Two Faces '96
Trial and Error '96
Two Days in the Valley '96
Amistad '97
A River Made to Drown In '97
The 4th Floor '99
Joe the King '99
A Beautiful Mind '01
Finding Nemo '03 (V)
Uptown Girls '03
Christmas With the Kranks '04
Bad City '06
The Notorious Bettie Page '06
Raising Flagg '06
Lovely by Surprise '07
Wall Street 2: Money Never Sleeps '10
The Sound of Silence '19

Nat Pendleton (1895-1967)
Blonde Crazy '31
Horse Feathers '32
Penthouse '33
The Sign of the Cross '33
The Defense Rests '34
Manhattan Melodrama '34
The Thin Man '34
Reckless '35
The Great Ziegfeld '36
Gangway '37
Arsene Lupin Returns '38
Shopworn Angel '38
Swing Your Lady '38
Young Dr. Kildare '38
At the Circus '39
Calling Dr. Kildare '39
It's a Wonderful World '39
The Secret of Dr. Kildare '39
Dr. Kildare's Crisis '40
Dr. Kildare's Strange Case '40
Flight Command '40
Northwest Passage '40
Phantom Raiders '40
Calling Dr. Gillespie '42
Dr. Gillespie's New Assistant '42
Dr. Gillespie's Criminal Case '43
Swing Fever '43

Buck Privates Come Home '47

Susan Penhaligon (1949-)
No Sex Please-We're British '73
The Confessional '75
The Land That Time Forgot '75
Count Dracula '77
Nasty Habits '77
Leopard in the Snow '78
Patrick '78
Soldier of Orange '78

Bruce Penhall (1957-)
Picasso Trigger '89
Savage Beach '89
Do or Die '91
Hard Hunted '92
Enemy Gold '93
Fit to Kill '93

Tahmoh Penikett (1975-)
Wildfire 7: The Inferno '02
Lesser Evil '06
Trick 'r Treat '08
Riverworld '10
Painkillers '15

Lea Penman (1895-1962)
Fancy Pants '50
We're No Angels '55

Christopher Penn (1965-2006)
All the Right Moves '83
Rumble Fish '83
Footloose '84
Pale Rider '85
At Close Range '86
Best of the Best '89
Leather Jackets '90
Futurekick '91
Mobsters '91
Reservoir Dogs '92
Beethoven's 2nd '93
Best of the Best 2 '93
Josh and S.A.M. '93
The Music of Chance '93
The Pickle '93
Short Cuts '93
True Romance '93
Imaginary Crimes '94
Fist of the North Star '95
Mulholland Falls '95
To Wong Foo, Thanks for Everything, Julie Newmar '95
The Boys Club '96
The Funeral '96
Deceiver '97
The Florentine '98
One Tough Cop '98
Trail of a Serial Killer '98
Cement '99
American Pie 2 '01
Corky Romano '01
Murder by Numbers '02
Stealing Harvard '02
Shelter Island '03
After the Sunset '04
Starsky & Hutch '04
The Darwin Awards '06
Holly '07

Kal Penn (1977-)
National Lampoon's Van Wilder '02
Love Don't Cost a Thing '03
Malibu's Most Wanted '03
Ball & Chain '04
Harold and Kumar Go to White Castle '04
A Lot Like Love '05
Bachelor Party Vegas '05
Dancing in Twilight '05
Son of the Mask '05
The Namesake '06
National Lampoon's Van Wilder 2: The Rise of Taj '06
Superman Returns '06
Epic Movie '07
Harold & Kumar Escape from Guantanamo Bay '08
A Very Harold & Kumar Christmas '11
Better Off Single '16
The Layover '17

Leonard Penn (1907-75)
Girl of the Golden West '38
Judge Hardy's Children '38
Streets of Sin '49

Matthew Penn
Playing for Keeps '86
Delta Force 3: The Killing Game '91

Sean Penn (1960-)
Taps '81
Fast Times at Ridgemont High '82
Bad Boys '83
Crackers '84
Racing with the Moon '84
The Falcon and the Snowman '85
At Close Range '86
Shanghai Surprise '86
Colors '88
Cool Blue '88 (C)
Judgment in Berlin '88
Casualties of War '89
We're No Angels '89
State of Grace '90
Carlito's Way '93
Dead Man Walking '95
The Game '97
Hugo Pool '97
She's So Lovely '97
U-Turn '97
Hurlyburly '98
The Thin Red Line '98
Sweet and Lowdown '99
Before Night Falls '00
Up at the Villa '00
The Weight of Water '00
I Am Sam '01
It's All About Love '03
Mystic River '03
21 Grams '03
The Assassination of Richard Nixon '05
The Interpreter '05
All the King's Men '06
Milk '08
What Just Happened '08
Crossing Over '09
Fair Game '10
The Tree of Life '11
This Must Be the Place '12
Gangster Squad '13
The Secret Life of Walter Mitty '13
The Gunman '15
The Professor and the Madman '19

Larry Pennell (1928-2013)
The Far Horizons '55
Seven Angry Men '55
The FBI Story '59
The Fear: Halloween Night '99
Bubba Ho-Tep '03

Nicholas Pennell (1939-95)
Rasputin the Mad Monk '66
Cry of the Penguins '71

Joe Penner (1904-41)
New Faces of 1937 '37
The Boys From Syracuse '40

Jonathan Penner (1962-)
A Fool and His Money '88
Bloodfist 7: Manhunt '95
Down Periscope '96
The Last Supper '96
Wedding Bell Blues '96
Let the Devil Wear Black '99
Cleopatra's Second Husband '00

Jack Pennick (1895-1964)
Stagecoach '39
Sergeant York '41
Lady from Louisiana '42
They Were Expendable '45
She Wore a Yellow Ribbon '49
The Beast from 20,000 Fathoms '53
Mister Roberts '55
The Horse Soldiers '59
The Alamo '60

Collins Pennie
Fame '09
Stomp the Yard 2: Homecoming '10

Chris Pennock (1944-)
The Great Texas Dynamite Chase '76
Frances '82
Running Woman '98

Joe Penny (1956-)
Bloody Birthday '80
Blood Vows: The Story of a Mafia Wife '87
Roses Are for the Rich '87
The Disappearance of Vonnie '94
Family of Cops 2: Breach of Faith '97
Family of Cops 3 '98
The Prophet's Game '99
Anti-Terrorist Cell: Manhunt '01
Betrayed at 17 '11

Sydney Penny (1971-)
Pale Rider '85
News at Eleven '86
Bernadette '90
Hidden Places '06

John Penrose (1914-83)
Kind Hearts and Coronets '49
The Shadow Man '53

Rupert Penry-Jones (1970-)
Hilary and Jackie '98
Virtual Sexuality '99
Charlotte Gray '01
The Four Feathers '02
Cambridge Spies '03
Casanova '05
Match Point '05
Persuasion '07
The 39 Steps '09
Treasure Island '12
Vita & Virginia '19

Del Pentacost (1963-)
Coyote Ugly '00
O Brother Where Art Thou? '00

George Peppard (1928-94)
The Strange One '57
Pork Chop Hill '59
Home from the Hill '60
Breakfast at Tiffany's '61
How the West Was Won '63
The Carpetbaggers '64
Operation Crossbow '65
The Third Day '65
The Blue Max '66
Tobruk '66
Rough Night in Jericho '67
Cannon for Cordoba '70
The Executioner '70
The Bravos '72
The Groundstar Conspiracy '72
Damnation Alley '77
From Hell to Victory '79
Torn Between Two Lovers '79
Battle Beyond the Stars '80
Treasure of the Yankee Zephyr '83
The Chinatown Murders: Man against the Mob '89
Night of the Fox '90
The Tigress '93

Barbara Pepper (1915-69)
Our Daily Bread '34
Last Outlaw '36
Mummy's Boys '36
Rogue's Tavern '36
Wide Open Faces '38
Girls in Chains '43
Murder, He Says '45
Kiss Me, Stupid! '64

Barry Pepper (1970-)
Dead Silence '96
Firestorm '97
Enemy of the State '98
Saving Private Ryan '98
The Green Mile '99
Battlefield Earth '00
We All Fall Down '00
Knockaround Guys '01
61* '01
25th Hour '02
We Were Soldiers '02
The Snow Walker '03
The Three Burials of Melquiades Estrada '05
Flags of Our Fathers '06
Seven Pounds '08
Like Dandelion Dust '09
Princess Kaiulani '09
Casino Jack '10
True Grit '10
When Love Is Not Enough: The Lois Wilson Story '10
The Kennedys '11
Broken City '13
The Lone Ranger '13
Snitch '13
Kill the Messenger '14
Monster Trucks '16
Crawl '19

Marilia Pera (1943-)
Pixote '81
Mixed Blood '84
Tieta of Agreste '96
Central Station '98

Piper Perabo (1976-)
White Boyz '99
The Adventures of Rocky & Bullwinkle '00
Coyote Ugly '00
Lost and Delirious '01
Slap Her, She's French '02
Cheaper by the Dozen '03
George and the Dragon '04
The I Inside '04
The Cave '05
Cheaper by the Dozen 2 '05
Edison Force '05
Imagine Me & You '06
Perception '06
The Prestige '06
10th & Wolf '06
Because I Said So '07
First Snow '07
Beverly Hills Chihuahua '08
The Lazarus Project '08
Carriers '09
Looper '12
Black Butterfly '17
Angel Has Fallen '19

Ed Peranio
Female Trouble '74
Desperate Living '77

Jeroen Perceval
Bullhead '11
Borgman '13
The Ardennes '17

Daniel Percival (1980-)
National Lampoon's Van Wilder 2: The Rise of Taj '06
Lost in Austen '08

Lance Percival (1933-)
Postman's Knock '62
Yellow Submarine '68 (V)

Eileen Percy (1901-73)
Within the Law '23
Spring Fever '27

Esme Percy (1887-1957)
Bitter Sweet '33
Accused '36
21 Days '40
Dead of Night '45

Wayne Pere
An American Summer '90
Soundman '99
Mandrake '10
Mirrors 2 '10

Missy Peregrym (1982-)
Call Me: The Rise and Fall of Heidi Fleiss '04
Stick It '06
Wide Awake '07
Cybergeddon '12

Tony Perenski (1959-)
The Texas Chainsaw Massacre 4: The Next Generation '95
The Underneath '95
Varsity Blues '98

Jose Perez (1940-)
Short Eyes '79
One Shoe Makes It Murder '82
Courage '86
Miami Blues '90

Manny Perez (1969-)
Washington Heights '02
Bella '06
El Cantante '06
Yellow '06
Illegal Tender '07
The Ministers '09
Love Is Strange '14

Marco Perez
Amores Perros '00
Trade '07
Desierto '16

Rosie Perez (1964-)
Do the Right Thing '89
Night on Earth '91
White Men Can't Jump '92
Fearless '93
Untamed Heart '93
It Could Happen to You '94
Somebody to Love '94
A Brother's Kiss '97
Dance with the Devil '97
Subway Stories '97
The 24 Hour Woman '99
The Road to El Dorado '00 (V)
King of the Jungle '01
Human Nature '02
Widows '02
Just Like the Son '06
Pineapple Express '08
Pete Smalls Is Dead '10
Won't Back Down '12
Fugly! '14
Five Nights in Maine '16

Timothy Paul Perez
Relax. . . It's Just Sex! '98
The Street King '02

Tony Perez
Right at Your Door '06
Close Range '15

Vincent Perez (1964-)
Cyrano de Bergerac '90
Indochine '92
Queen Margot '94
Beyond the Clouds '95
The Crow 2: City of Angels '96
Talk of Angels '96
Swept from the Sea '97
Shot Through the Heart '98
Those Who Love Me Can Take the Train '98
The Treat '98
Time Regained '99
I Dreamed of Africa '00
Bride of the Wind '01
Queen of the Damned '02
On Guard! '03
Arn: The Knight Templar '07
Inhale '10
The Aeronauts '19

Walter Perez (1982-)
Fame '09
The Pregnancy Project '12
Sanitarium '13
Bodied '17

Francois Perier (1919-2002)
Orpheus '49
Gervaise '56
Nights of Cabiria '57
The Testament of Orpheus '59
The Organizer '64
Le Samourai '67
Z '69
Le Cercle Rouge '70
Just Before Nightfall '71
Stavisky '74

Sergio Peris-Mencheta
You and Me '06
Love Ranch '10
Rambo: Last Blood '19

Anthony Perkins (1932-92)
The Actress '53
Friendly Persuasion '56
Fear Strikes Out '57
The Lonely Man '57
The Tin Star '57
Desire Under the Elms '58
The Matchmaker '58
Green Mansions '59
On the Beach '59
Psycho '60
Tall Story '60
Phaedra '61
The Trial '63
Ravishing Idiot '64
Is Paris Burning? '66
Pretty Poison '68
Catch-22 '70
WUSA '70
Someone Behind the Door '71
Life & Times of Judge Roy Bean '72
Ten Days Wonder '72
Murder on the Orient Express '74
Mahogany '75
Les Miserables '78
The Black Hole '79
Winter Kills '79
ffolkes '80
Psycho 2 '83
Crimes of Passion '84
The Glory Boys '84
Psycho 3 '86
Napoleon and Josephine: A Love Story '87
Edge of Sanity '89
Psycho 4: The Beginning '90
In the Deep Woods '91
A Demon in My View '92

Elizabeth Perkins (1960-)
About Last Night. . . '86
From the Hip '86
Big '88
Sweet Hearts Dance '88
Love at Large '89
Avalon '90
Enid Is Sleeping '90
The Doctor '91
He Said, She Said '91
Indian Summer '93
The Flintstones '94
Miracle on 34th Street '94
Moonlight and Valentino '95
From the Earth to the Moon '98
I'm Losing You '98
Crazy in Alabama '99
If These Walls Could Talk 2 '00
28 Days '00
Cats & Dogs '01
All I Want '02
My Sister's Keeper '02
Finding Nemo '03 (V)
Speak '04
Fierce People '05
Jiminy Glick in LaLa Wood '05
Kids in America '05
Must Love Dogs '05
The Ring 2 '05
The Thing About My Folks '05
Hop '11

Emily Perkins (1977-)
Ginger Snaps '01
Prozac Nation '01
Ginger Snaps Back: The Beginning '04
Ginger Snaps: Unleashed '04
She's the Man '06
Another Cinderella Story '08

Kathleen Rose Perkins
The Pact '12
A Short History of Decay '13

Millie Perkins (1938-)
The Diary of Anne Frank '59
Wild in the Country '61
Ensign Pulver '64
Ride in the Whirlwind '66
The Shooting '66
Wild in the Streets '68
Cockfighter '74
Witch Who Came from the Sea '76
The Haunting Passion '83
Table for Five '83
License to Kill '84
A.D. '85
At Close Range '86
Wall Street '87
Two Moon Junction '88
Pistol: The Birth of a Legend '90
The Chamber '96
The Lost City '05

Osgood Perkins (1892-1937)
Scarface '31
Gold Diggers of 1937 '36

Oz (Osgood) Perkins, II (1974-)
Psycho 2 '83
Six Degrees of Separation '93
Wolf '94
Legally Blonde '01
Secretary '02
Quigley '03
La Cucina '07

Ron Perkins
Ed McBain's 87th Precinct: Lightning '95
Spider-Man '02

Max Perlich (1968-)
Ferris Bueller's Day Off '86
Can't Buy Me Love '87
Drugstore Cowboy '89
The Butcher's Wife '91
Rush '91
Born Yesterday '93
Cliffhanger '93
Dead Beat '94
Maverick '94
Shake, Rattle & Rock! '94
Terrified '94
Georgia '95
Beautiful Girls '96
Homeward Bound 2: Lost in San Francisco '96
Gummo '97
Truth or Consequences, N.M. '97
Freeway 2: Confessions of a Trickbaby '99
Goodbye, Lover '99
House on Haunted Hill '99
Sometimes They Come Back. . . For More '99
Homicide: The Movie '00
The Independent '00
Blow '01
Sol Goode '01
Deuces Wild '02
The Missing '03
Punk Love '06
7 Mummies '06
Protecting the King '07
InSight '11

Rhea Perlman (1948-)
Ratings Game '84
Enid Is Sleeping '90
Class Act '91
There Goes the Neighborhood '92
Ted & Venus '93
We're Back! A Dinosaur's Story '93 (V)
Canadian Bacon '94
To Grandmother's House We Go '94
Carpool '96
Matilda '96
Sunset Park '96
Houdini '98
10 Items or Less '06
Love Comes Lately '07
Beethoven's Big Break '08
The Christmas Choir '08
I'll See You in My Dreams '15

Ron Perlman (1950-)
Quest for Fire '82
Ice Pirates '84
The Name of the Rose '86
Sleepwalkers '92
The Adventures of Huck Finn '93
Romeo Is Bleeding '93
When the Bough Breaks '93
Cronos '94
Police Academy 7: Mission to Moscow '94
Sensation '94
Acts of Contrition '95
The City of Lost Children '95
Fluke '95
Phantom 2040 Movie: The Ghost Who Walks '95 (V)
Body Armor '96
The Island of Dr. Moreau '96
The Last Supper '96
Alien: Resurrection '97
Betty '97
The Second Civil War '97
Frogs for Snakes '98
Houdini '98
The Magnificent Seven '98
A Town Has Turned to Dust '98
Happy, Texas '99
Supreme Sanction '99
Enemy at the Gates '00
Price of Glory '00
Titan A.E. '00 (V)
The Trial of Old Drum '00
The King's Guard '01
The Shaft '01
Blade 2 '02
Shakedown '02
Star Trek: Nemesis '02
Hoodlum & Son '03
Comic Book: The Movie '04 (C)
Hellboy '04
The Second Front '05
Tarzan 2 '05 (V)
How to Go Out on a Date in Queens '06
The Last Winter '06
Local Color '06
Hellboy II: The Golden Army '08
In the Name of the King: A Dungeon Siege Tale '08
Mutant Chronicles '08
Outlander '08
Dark Country '09
The Devil's Tomb '09
I Sell the Dead '09
The Job '09
Bunraku '10
Killer by Nature '10
Marmaduke '10 (V)
Season of the Witch '10
Tangled '10
Conan the Barbarian '11
Drive '11
The Scorpion King 3: Battle for Redemption '11
3, 2, 1...Frankie Go Boom '12
Pacific Rim '13
13 Sins '13
The Book of Life '14 (V)
Kid Cannabis '14
Stonewall '15
Moonwalkers '16
Chuck '17

Florence Pernel (1966-)
Trois Couleurs: Bleu '93
Trois Couleurs: Blanc '94 (C)

J.W. Perra
Head of the Family '96
Goobers! '97

Gigi Perreau (1941-)
Song of Love '47
Family Honeymoon '49
For Heaven's Sake '50
Has Anybody Seen My Gal? '52
Dance with Me, Henry '56
The Man in the Gray Flannel Suit '56
There's Always Tomorrow '56
Look in Any Window '61
Hell on Wheels '67
Journey to the Center of Time '67

Paul Perri (1953-)
Delta Force 2: Operation Stranglehold '90
Hellraiser 4: Bloodline '95
Without Evidence '96

Mireille Perrier (1959-)
Boy Meets Girl '84
Mauvais Sang '86
Chocolat '88
Toto le Heros '91
The Ice Rink '99
Point Blank '10
Olivier Perrier (1940-)
Les Destinees '00
Read My Lips '01
Blame It on Fidel '06
Of Gods and Men '10
Pierre Perrier (1984-)
Cold Showers '05
One to Another '06
Jack Perrin (1896-1967)
Midnight Faces '26
The Story of Vernon and Irene Castle '39
New Moon '40
The North Star '43
Ten Wanted Men '54
Them! '54
The Court Martial of Billy Mitchell '55
Sunrise at Campobello '60
Jacques Perrin (1941-)
The Girl with a Suitcase '60
The Young Girls of Rochefort '68
Z '69
Donkey Skin '70
Peau D'Ane '71
Black and White in Color '76
The Desert of the Tartars '76
Love Songs '84
Cinema Paradiso '88
Flight of the Innocent '93
Brotherhood of the Wolf '01
Winged Migration '01 (N)
The Chorus '04
Le Petit Lieutenant '05
Oceans '09 (N)
Maxence Perrin (1996-)
The Chorus '04
Paris 36 '08
Valerie Perrine (1943-)
Slaughterhouse Five '72
The Last American Hero '73
Lenny '74
Mr. Billion '77
Superman: The Movie '78
The Electric Horseman '79
Can't Stop the Music '80
Superman 2 '80
The Agency '81
The Border '82
Water '85
Maid to Order '87
Sweet Bird of Youth '89
Bright Angel '91
Boiling Point '93
The Break '95
Curtain Call '97
Brown's Requiem '98
What Women Want '00
The Moguls '05
Harold Perrineau, Jr. (1963-)
Smoke '95
Blood & Wine '96
William Shakespeare's Romeo and Juliet '96
The Edge '97
The Best Man '99
Woman on Top '00
On_Line '01
The Matrix Reloaded '03
The Matrix Revolutions '03
28 Weeks Later '07
Felon '08
Gardens of the Night '08
The Killing Jar '10
30 Days of Night: Dark Days '10
Seeking Justice '12
Transit '12
The Best Man Holiday '13
Go for Sisters '13
Sexy Evil Genius '13
Snitch '13
Cold Brook '18
Joe Perrino (1982-)
Sleepers '96
The Bumblebee Flies Anyway '98
The Mighty '98
Leslie Perrins (1902-62)
The Living Dead '33
The Silent Passenger '35
Nine Days a Queen '36
Michel Perron
Battlefield Earth '00
The Sign of Four '01
Lost Junction '03
Francois Perrot (1924-)
Le Choc '82
Life and Nothing But '89
Alex Ross Perry
The Color Wheel '11
Joshy '16
Felton Perry (1945-)
Night Call Nurses '72
Magnum Force '73
Walking Tall '73
Sudden Death '77
RoboCop '87
Checking Out '89
RoboCop 2 '90
RoboCop 3 '91
Dumb & Dumber '94
Jane Perry
In the Spider's Web '07
Greta '18
Jeff(rey) Perry (1955-)
Wild Things '98
Diminished Capacity '08
Lizzie '18
Trial by Fire '18
Jeffrey S. (Jeff) Perry
Oxford Blues '84
The Chronicles of Narnia '89
Joan Perry (1911-96)
Meet Nero Wolfe '36
Maisie Was a Lady '41
John Bennett Perry
Only When I Laugh '81
Fools Rush In '97
George of the Jungle '97
Protecting the King '07
Loaded '08
Katy Perry (1984-)
The Smurfs '11 (V)
Katy Perry: Part of Me '12
The Smurfs 2 '13 (V)
Luke Perry (1966-)
Buffy the Vampire Slayer '92
8 Seconds '94
American Strays '96
Last Breath '96
Normal Life '96
Riot in the Streets '96
The Fifth Element '97
Robin Cook's Invasion '97
The Florentine '98
Attention Shoppers '99
Storm Tracker '99
The Enemy '01
The Triangle '01
Johnson County War '02
Descent '05
Dishdogz '05
Supernova '05
Alice Upside Down '07
The Sandlot 3: Heading Home '07
The Pledge '08
Silent Venom '08
A Very Merry Daughter of the Bride '08
Angel and the Badman '09
The Final Storm '09
Jr. Detective Agency '09
The Storm '09
Good Intentions '10
Redemption Road '10
Goodnight for Justice '11
Goodnight for Justice: The Measure of a Man '12
Goodnight for Justice: Queen of Hearts '13
Matthew Perry (1969-)
A Night in the Life of Jimmy Reardon '88
She's Out of Control '89
Deadly Relations '93
Almost Heroes '97
Fools Rush In '97
Three to Tango '99
The Whole Nine Yards '00
Serving Sara '02
The Whole Ten Yards '04
Numb '07
Birds of America '08
17 Again '09
Megahn Perry (1977-)
The Convent '00
The Perfect Host '10
Rod Perry (1941-)
Black Godfather '74
Black Gestapo '75
Roger Perry (1933-2018)
Follow the Boys '63
Count Yorga, Vampire '70
The Return of Count Yorga '71
The Thing with Two Heads '72
Roller Boogie '79
Tyler Perry (1969-)
Diary of a Mad Black Woman '05
Madea's Family Reunion '06
Tyler Perry's Why Did I Get Married? '07
The Family That Preys '08
Tyler Perry's Meet the Browns '08
I Can Do Bad All By Myself '09
Madea Goes to Jail '09
Star Trek '09
Tyler Perry's Why Did I Get Married Too '10
Madea's Big Happy Family '11
Alex Cross '12
Madea's Witness Protection '12
Tyler Perry's Good Deeds '12
Tyler Perry's A Madea Christmas '13
Gone Girl '14
Tyler Perry's The Single Moms' Club '14
Boo! A Madea Halloween '16
Boo 2! A Madea Halloween '17
A Madea Family Funeral '19
Mikael Persbrandt (1963-)
Gossip '00
Everlasting Moments '08
In a Better World '10
The Salvation '14
Maria Perschy (1938-2004)
The Password Is Courage '62
Man's Favorite Sport? '63
633 Squadron '64
The Mad Executioners '65
Kiss Kiss Kill Kill '66
The Castle of Fu Manchu '68
The Rue Morgue Massacres '73
Exorcism '74
Betty Joan Perske (1924-2014)
See Lauren Bacall
Lisa Jane Persky (1955-)
KISS Meets the Phantom of the Park '78
The Great Santini '80
American Pop '81 (V)
Breathless '83
The Cotton Club '84
The Sure Thing '85
Peggy Sue Got Married '86
The Big Easy '87
Great Balls of Fire '89
When Harry Met Sally. . . '89
The Last of the Finest '90
Vital Signs '90
Coneheads '93
Pontiac Moon '94
Female Perversions '96
An American Rhapsody '01
My First Mister '01
Grilled '06
Nehemiah Persoff (1919-)
On the Waterfront '54
The Wrong Man '56
Men in War '57
The Badlanders '58
Al Capone '59
The Day of the Outlaw '59
Green Mansions '59
Some Like It Hot '59
The Comancheros '61
The Hook '63
Fate Is the Hunter '64
Panic in the City '68
The Power '68
The Girl Who Knew Too Much '69
Deadly Harvest '72
Missiles of October '74
The Stranger Within '74
Voyage of the Damned '76
The Henderson Monster '80
Yentl '83
An American Tail '86 (V)
The Last Temptation of Christ '88
Twins '88
An American Tail: Fievel Goes West '91 (V)
Raphael Personnaz (1981-)
The Princess of Montpensier '10
Special Forces '11
The French Minister '13
The New Girlfriend '14
Essy Persson (1941-)
I, a Woman '66
Therese & Isabelle '67
Mission Stardust '68
Cry of the Banshee '70
Maria Persson (1959-)
Pippi Goes on Board '69
Pippi Longstocking '69
Pippi in the South Seas '70
Pippi on the Run '70
Jon Pertwee (1919-96)
Ladies Who Do '63
Carry On Screaming '66
The House that Dripped Blood '71
Sean Pertwee (1964-)
Clarissa '91
Shopping '93
Blue Juice '95
Deadly Voyage '96
Stiff Upper Lips '96
Event Horizon '97
Soldier '98
Cleopatra '99
Russell Mulcahy's Tale of the Mummy '99
Love, Honour & Obey '00
7 Days to Live '00
Dog Soldiers '01
Formula 51 '01
The Last Drop '05
Goal! The Dream Begins '06
When Evil Calls '06
Botched '07
Goal 2: Living the Dream '07
Mutant Chronicles '08
Ultramarines: A Warhammer 40,000 Movie '10 (V)
Alien Uprising '12
Berlin Job '12
Jorge Perugorria (1965-)
Strawberry and Chocolate '93
Guantanamera '95
Things I Left in Havana '97
Che '08
Frank Pesce
Vigilante '83
29th Street '91
Trapped in Paradise '94
Night Vision '97
Joe Pesci (1943-)
Family Enforcer '76
Raging Bull '80
Eureka! '81
I'm Dancing as Fast as I Can '82
Ruby's Dream '82
Easy Money '83
Once Upon a Time in America '84
Backtrack '89 (C)
Lethal Weapon 2 '89
Betsy's Wedding '90
Goodfellas '90
Home Alone '90
JFK '91
The Super '91
Home Alone 2: Lost in New York '92
Lethal Weapon 3 '92
My Cousin Vinny '92
The Public Eye '92
A Bronx Tale '93 (C)
Jimmy Hollywood '94
With Honors '94
Casino '95
8 Heads in a Duffel Bag '96
Gone Fishin' '97
Lethal Weapon 4 '98
The Good Shepherd '06
Love Ranch '10
The Irishman '19
Lisa Pescia
Body Chemistry '90
Body Chemistry 2: Voice of a Stranger '91
Donna Pescow (1954-)
Saturday Night Fever '77
Glory Years '87
Ivory Tower '97
Partners '99
Eric Peter-Kaiser (1981-)
Miracle '04
Basement Jack '09
Melissa Peterman (1971-)
Recipe for Disaster '03
Here Comes the Boom '12
Bernadette Peters (1948-)
The Longest Yard '74
Silent Movie '76
Vigilante Force '76
The Jerk '79
The Martian Chronicles: Part 2 '79
The Martian Chronicles: Part 3 '79
Heartbeeps '81
Pennies from Heaven '81
Annie '82
Sunday in the Park with George '86
Pink Cadillac '89
Slaves of New York '89
Alice '90
Impromptu '90
The Last Best Year '90
Anastasia '97 (V)
Cinderella '97
The Odyssey '97
What the Deaf Man Heard '98
Let It Snow '99
Bobbie's Girl '02
It Runs in the Family '03
Living Proof '08
Legends of Oz: Dorothy's Return '14 (V)
Brock Peters (1927-2005)
Carmen Jones '54
To Kill a Mockingbird '62
The Pawnbroker '65
Ace High '68
The McMasters '70
Slaughter's Big Ripoff '73
Soylent Green '73
Framed '75
Agatha Christie's A Caribbean Mystery '83
Star Trek 4: The Voyage Home '86
Alligator 2: The Mutation '90
Star Trek 6: The Undiscovered Country '91
The Secret '93
The Locket '02
10,000 Black Men Named George '02
The Wild Thornberrys Movie '02 (V)
Clarke Peters (1952-)
Outland '81
Mona Lisa '86
The Corner '00
Freedomland '06
Endgame '09
Legacy '10
Red Hook Summer '12
The Best of Me '14
The Benefactor '16
Division 19 '19
Harriet '19
Da 5 Bloods '20
Evan Peters (1987-)
Never Back Down '08
Remarkable Power '08
Kick-Ass '10
Never Back Down 2: The Beatdown '11
Adult World '13
X-Men: Days of Future Past '14
The Lazarus Effect '15
Safelight '15
The Pirates of Somalia '17
American Animals '18
House Peters, Jr. (1916-2008)
Red Planet Mars '52
Black Patch '57
Man From God's Country '58
Jean Peters (1926-2000)
Captain from Castile '47
Deep Waters '48
Love That Brute '50
As Young As You Feel '51
Lure of the Wilderness '52
Niagara '52
Viva Zapata! '52
A Blueprint for Murder '53
Pickup on South Street '53
Apache '54
Broken Lance '54
Three Coins in the Fountain '54
A Man Called Peter '55
Arthur Hailey's The Moneychangers '76
Peter and Paul '81
Luan Peters (1946-)
Twins of Evil '71
Not Tonight Darling '72
Flesh and Blood Show '73
Land of the Minotaur '77
Mattie Peters
Within Our Gates '20
Barbara Frietchie '24
Molly Peters (1942-)
Thunderball '65
Target for Killing '66
Rick Peters (1967-)
Night of the Demons 2 '94
American Virgin '98
This Matter of Marriage '98
Robert Peters (1961-)
Baadasssss! '03
From Other Worlds '04
Unbeatable Harold '06
Russell Peters (1970-)
The Con Artist '10
The Clapper '18
Scott Peters (1930-94)
The Girl Hunters '63
They Saved Hitler's Brain '64
Susan Peters (1921-52)
Andy Hardy's Double Life '42
The Big Shot '42
Dr. Gillespie's New Assistant '42
Random Harvest '42
Tish '42
Young Ideas '43
Keep Your Powder Dry '45
Werner Peters (1918-71)
The Counterfeit Traitor '62
The Phantom of Soho '64
36 Hours '64
A Fine Madness '66

The Bird with the Crystal Plumage '70
Chris Petersen
When Every Day Was the Fourth of July '78
Little Dragons '80
Colin Petersen
A Cry from the Streets '57
The Scamp '57
Ellen Dorrit Petersen
Blind '14
Thelma '17
Oscar Petersen
The Quarry '98
Mama Africa '02
Pat Petersen (1966-)
Little Dragons '80
Cold River '81
Stewart Petersen (1960-)
Where the Red Fern Grows '74
Against a Crooked Sky '75
Seven Alone '75
Pony Express Rider '76
William L. Petersen (1953-)
To Live & Die in L.A. '85
Manhunter '86
Amazing Grace & Chuck '87
Cousins '89
Young Guns 2 '90
Hard Promises '92
Passed Away '92
Return to Lonesome Dove '93
Mulholland Falls '95 (C)
The Beast '96
Fear '96
Gunshy '98
Kiss the Sky '98
The Rat Pack '98
The Contender '00
The Skulls '00
Alan C. Peterson
Deathlands: Homeward Bound '03
Obituary '06
Dress to Kill '07
Second Sight '07
The Other Woman '08
Carny '09
The Case for Christmas '11
Amanda Peterson (1971-2015)
Explorers '85
Can't Buy Me Love '87
Fatal Charm '92
Windrunner '94
Annika Peterson
Frederick Forsyth's Icon '05
The Man from Earth '07
Bob Peterson (1961-)
Monsters, Inc. '01 (V)
Finding Nemo '03 (V)
Up '09 (V)
Cassandra Peterson (1951-)
Working Girls '75
Balboa '82
Jekyll & Hyde. . . Together Again '82
Pee-wee's Big Adventure '85
Echo Park '86
Elvira, Mistress of the Dark '88
Ted & Venus '93 (C)
Elvira's Haunted Hills '02
Dorothy Peterson (1900-79)
Mothers Cry '30
Party Husband '31
Penrod and Sam '31
The Beast of the City '32
Forbidden '32
I'm No Angel '33
Reform Girl '33
Peck's Bad Boy '34
Girl Loves Boy '37
Too Many Husbands '40
Air Force '43
Woman in the Window '44
That Hagen Girl '47

Gil Peterson (1936-)
The Cool Ones '67
Mind Warp '72
Kimberlee Peterson (1980-)
Homecoming '96
Legend of the Lost Tomb '97
Seth Peterson (1970-)
Hard Ground '03
Hate Crime '05
Edward Petherbridge (1936-)
An Awfully Big Adventure '94
Gulliver's Travels '95
Isabelle Petit-Jacques
The Girl on the Bridge '98
The Man on the Train '02
Martin Petitguyot
Don't Let Me Die on a Sunday '98
Nocturama '17
Hortense Petra
Hold On! '66
Riot on Sunset Strip '67
Ian Petrella (1974-)
A Christmas Story '83
Crimes of Passion '84
Alexei Petrenko (1938-)
Rasputin '85
12 '07
Into the Storm '09
Mario Petri (1922-85)
Fury of Achilles '62
The Beast of Babylon Against the Son of Hercules '63
Hercules and the Tyrants of Babylon '64
Hay Petrie (1895-1948)
The Private Life of Henry VIII '33
The Ghost Goes West '36
Crimes at the Dark House '39
The Four Feathers '39
Spy in Black '39
Contraband '40
21 Days '40
Spellbound '41
A Canterbury Tale '44
On Approval '44
Great Expectations '46
Howard Petrie (1906-68)
Border River '47
Rocky Mountain '50
Susan Petrie
Vengeance Is Mine '74
They Came from Within '75
Snapshot '77
Dan Petronijevic (1981-)
Absolution '05
Cottage Country '13
Marisa Petroro (1972-)
No Witness '04
Everybody Wants to Be Italian '08
Joanna Pettet (1942-)
The Group '66
Casino Royale '67
Night of the Generals '67
Blue '68
The Best House in London '69
Pioneer Woman '73
The Evil '78
Cry of the Innocent '80
Double Exposure '82
Christopher Pettiet (1976-2000)
Point Break '91
Carried Away '95
Brian Pettifer (1953-)
If. . . '69
Conspiracy '01
Valarie Pettiford (1960-)
Glitter '01
Stomp the Yard '07
Why Am I Doing This? '09

Frank Pettingell (1891-1966)
Sailing Along '38
Gaslight '40
Value for Money '55
Trial & Error '62
Madison Pettis (1998-)
The Game Plan '07
Free Style '09
The Search for Santa Paws '10
Lori Petty (1963-)
Cadillac Man '90
Point Break '91
A League of Their Own '92
Free Willy '93
In the Army Now '94
Tank Girl '94
The Glass Shield '95
Serial Bomber '96
Blood Money '98
Relax. . . It's Just Sex! '98
Firetrap '01
MacArthur Park '01
Route 666 '01
Prey for Rock and Roll '03
Karate Dog '04 (V)
Chasing 3000 '07
Richard Petty (1937-)
Speedway '68 (C)
Richard Petty Story '72
Cars '06 (V)
Tom Petty (1950-)
Made in Heaven '87 (C)
The Postman '97
George Harrison: Living in the Material World '11
Alex Pettyfer (1990-)
Alex Rider: Operation Stormbreaker '06
Wild Child '08
Tormented '09
Beastly '11
I Am Number Four '11
In Time '11
Magic Mike '12
Lee Daniels' The Butler '13
Endless Love '14
Elvis & Nixon '16
Angelique Pettyjohn (1943-92)
Clambake '67
Mad Doctor of Blood Island '68
Hell's Belles '69
G.I. Executioner '71
Repo Man '83
Bio Hazard '85
Katija Pevec (1988-)
Air Bud 5: Buddy Spikes Back '03
Yours, Mine & Ours '05
Joseph Pevney (1911-2008)
Nocturne '46
Body and Soul '47
The Street with No Name '48
The Plunderers '60
Penny Peyser (1951-)
The Frisco Kid '79
The In-Laws '79
Messenger of Death '88
Dedee Pfeiffer (1964-)
The Midnight Hour '86
Vamp '86
The Horror Show '89
Red Surf '90
Falling Down '93
Up Close and Personal '96
Seventeen and Missing '06
AVH: Alien *vs.* Hunter '07
The Prince and the Pauper '07
Fix '08
Michelle Pfeiffer (1958-)
Falling in Love Again '80
The Hollywood Knights '80
Callie and Son '81
Charlie Chan and the Curse of the Dragon Queen '81
The Children Nobody Wanted '81

Grease 2 '82
Power, Passion & Murder '83
Scarface '83
Into the Night '85
Ladyhawke '85
Sweet Liberty '86
Amazon Women on the Moon '87
The Witches of Eastwick '87
Dangerous Liaisons '88
Married to the Mob '88
Tequila Sunrise '88
The Fabulous Baker Boys '89
The Russia House '90
Frankie and Johnny '91
Love Field '91
Batman Returns '92
The Age of Innocence '93
Wolf '94
Dangerous Minds '95
One Fine Day '96
To Gillian on Her 37th Birthday '96
Up Close and Personal '96
A Thousand Acres '97
The Deep End of the Ocean '98
Prince of Egypt '98 (V)
The Story of Us '99
William Shakespeare's A Midsummer Night's Dream '99
What Lies Beneath '00
I Am Sam '01
White Oleander '02
Sinbad: Legend of the Seven Seas '03 (V)
I Could Never Be Your Woman '06
Hairspray '07
Stardust '07
Cheri '09
Personal Effects '09
New Year's Eve '11
Dark Shadows '12
People Like Us '12
The Family '13
mother! '17
Where Is Kyra? '17
Maleficent: Mistress of Evil '19
JoAnn Pflug (1940-)
M*A*S*H '70
Catlow '71
A Step Out of Line '71
They Call It Murder '71
Scream of the Wolf '74
Liz Phair (1967-)
Cherish '02
Seeing Other People '04
Linh Dan Pham (1974-)
Indochine '92
The Beat My Heart Skipped '05
Dante 01 '08
Mr. Nobody '13
Joe Phelan (1946-)
See Joe Estevez
Peter Phelps (1960-)
Zone 39 '96
Lantana '01
Ned Kelly '03
The Square '08
Terry Pheto
Tsotsi '05
Mandela: Long Walk to Freedom '13
Mekhi Phifer (1974-)
Clockers '95
High School High '96
Hell's Kitchen NYC '97
Soul Food '97
I Still Know What You Did Last Summer '98
A Lesson Before Dying '99
Uninvited Guest '99
Shaft '00
Brian's Song '01
Carmen: A Hip Hopera '01
O '01
8 Mile '02
Impostor '02
The Other Brother '02

Paid in Full '02
Honey '03
Dawn of the Dead '04
Slow Burn '05
Puff, Puff, Pass '06
This Christmas '07
Nora's Hair Salon 2: A Cut Above '08
A Day in the Life '09
Flypaper '11
Last Man Standing '11
A Day Late and a Dollar Short '14
Divergent '14
The Suspect '14
Insurgent '15
John Philbin (1960-)
North Shore '87
The Four Minute Mile '88
Point Break '91
The Crew '95
Mary Philbin (1903-93)
Merry-Go-Round '23
The Phantom of the Opera '25
The Man Who Laughs '27
Regis Philbin (1931-)
The Bad News Bears Go to Japan '78
Sextette '78
Night and the City '92 (C)
Dudley Do-Right '99
Cheaper by the Dozen '03 (C)
The Breakup Artist '04 (C)
Shrek the Third '07 (V)
Shrek Forever After '10 (V)
James Philbrook (1924-82)
Sound of Horror '64
The Thin Red Line '64
Son of a Gunfighter '65
Dominic Philie
The Boys '97
For Hire '98
Gerard Philipe (1922-59)
Devil in the Flesh '46
La Chartreuse de Parme '48
Fanfan la Tulipe '51
La Ronde '51
Beauties of the Night '52
Fever Mounts at El Pao '59
Dangerous Liaisons '60
Busy Philipps (1979-)
The Smokers '00
Home Room '02
White Chicks '04
Made of Honor '08
Reef 2: High Tide '12
A Case of You '13
The Gift '15
Gina Philips (1970-)
Jeepers Creepers '01
Chronicle of the Raven '04
Love and Debate '06
Jeepers Creepers 3 '17
Lee Philips (1927-99)
Peyton Place '57
The Hunters '58
Psychomania '63
Mary (Phillips) Philips (1900-75)
A Farewell to Arms '32
Leave Her to Heaven '45
Prince Valiant '54
Ryan Phillipe (1974-)
The I Inside '04
Reclaim '14
Ryan Phillippe (1974-)
White Squall '96
Homegrown '97
I Know What You Did Last Summer '97
Little Boy Blue '97
Cruel Intentions '98
54 '98
Playing by Heart '98
Antitrust '00
Company Man '00
Way of the Gun '00
Gosford Park '01
Igby Goes Down '02
Crash '05

Five Fingers '06
Flags of Our Fathers '06
Breach '07
Franklyn '08
Stop-Loss '08
The Bang Bang Club '10
MacGruber '10
The Lincoln Lawyer '11
Setup '11
Revenge for Jolly! '12
Straight A's '13
Wish Upon '17
Angie Phillips
Manny & Lo '96
Duets '00
Anne Lise Phillips
Walking on Water '02
Animal Kingdom '09
Barney (Bernard) Phillips (1913-82)
A Blueprint for Murder '53
The Sand Pebbles '66
Savage Run '70
Bijou Phillips (1980-)
Black and White '99
Almost Famous '00
Bully '01
Fast Sofa '01
Tart '01
Pulse '03
Havoc '05
Venom '05
Hostel: Part 2 '07
Spin '07
What We Do Is Secret '07
The Wizard of Gore '07
Choke '08
Dark Streets '08
The Bridge to Nowhere '09
Wake '09
Black Limousine '10
Bill (William) Phillips (1908-57)
Thirty Seconds Over Tokyo '44
Chain Gang '50
The Last Hunt '56
Bobbie Phillips (1972-)
Back in Action '94
Hail Caesar '94
Ring of Fire 3: Lion Strike '94
American Virgin '98
Carnival of Souls '98
Red Shoe Diaries: Luscious Lola '00
Chynna Phillips (1968-)
Caddyshack 2 '88
The Prize Pulitzer '89
Say Anything '89
Bye Bye Birdie '95
Conrad Phillips (1925-)
Sons and Lovers '60
Murder She Said '61
Eddie (Edward) Phillips (1899-1965)
The Love Light '21
Lightning Hutch '26
Big Boy '30
Her Forgotten Past '33
Ethan Phillips (1955-)
Bloodhounds of Broadway '89
Glory '89
Lean on Me '89
Green Card '90
The Shadow '94
From the Earth to the Moon '98
The Island '05
The Babysitters '07
California Dreaming '07
Gina Phillips
My Baby Is Missing '07
Hijacked '12
Grace Phillips
All the Vermeers in New York '91
Truth or Consequences, N.M. '97
The New Yorker '98

Graham Phillips
Evan Almighty '07
Goats '12

Jeffrey Daniel Phillips
The Lords of Salem '13
31 '16
3 from Hell '19

John Phillips (1915-95)
Black Angel '46
Village of the Damned '60
The Mummy's Shroud '67

Jonathan Phillips (1962-)
Clarissa '91
Dead Gorgeous '02
Bronson '09

Julianne Phillips (1960-)
Seven Hours to Judgment '88
Sweet Lies '88
Fletch Lives '89
Skin Deep '89
Acts of Contrition '95
Big Bully '95
Allie & Me '97

Kate Phillips (1914-2008)
See Kay Linaker

Kevin Phillips (1981-)
Rock the Paint '05
Pride '07
Sinners and Saints '10

Leslie Phillips (1924-)
The Limping Man '53
The Smallest Show on Earth '57
Carry On Constable '60
Doctor in Love '60
No Kidding '60
Very Important Person '61
Doctor in Clover '66
Maroc 7 '67
Not Now Darling '73
Empire of the Sun '87
Scandal '89
Mountains of the Moon '90
Carry On Columbus '92
August '95
Agatha Christie's The Pale Horse '96
The Canterville Ghost '96
Lara Croft: Tomb Raider '01
Color Me Kubrick '05
Millions '05 (C)
Venus '06

Lou Diamond Phillips (1962-)
La Bamba '87
Dakota '88
Stand and Deliver '88
Young Guns '88
Disorganized Crime '89
The First Power '89
Renegades '89
A Show of Force '90
Young Guns 2 '90
The Dark Wind '91
Extreme Justice '93
Dangerous Touch '94
Sioux City '94
Courage Under Fire '96
Another Day in Paradise '98
The Big Hit '98
Bats '99
Brokedown Palace '99
In a Class of His Own '99
Picking Up the Pieces '99
Supernova '99
A Better Way to Die '00
Hangman '00
Red Water '01
Route 666 '01
Lone Hero '02
Stark Raving Mad '02
Hollywood Homicide '03
The Trail to Hope Rose '04
The Triangle '05
Death Toll '07
Termination Point '07
Che '08
Lone Rider '08
Never Forget '08
Angel and the Badman '09
Carny '09
Love Takes Wing '09
Takedown '10
Metal Tornado '11
Filly Brown '12
Sanitarium '13
The 33 '15
Urban Country '18

MacKenzie Phillips (1959-)
American Graffiti '73
Eleanor & Franklin '76
More American Graffiti '79
Love Child '82
Kate's Secret '86
True Friends '98
The Jacket '05

Margaret 'Peg' Phillips (1918-2002)
Dogfight '91
How the West Was Fun '95

Michelle Phillips (1944-)
Dillinger '73
The California Kid '74
Valentino '77
The French Atlantic Affair '79
Secrets of a Married Man '84
American Anthem '86
Let It Ride '89
Scissors '91
Army of One '94
Harry and Max '04
Kids in America '05
Unbeatable Harold '06

Nathan Phillips (1980-)
One Perfect Day '04
Wolf Creek '05
Snakes on a Plane '06
Redline '07
Chernobyl Diaries '12

Robert Phillips (1925-)
The Killers '64
Cat Ballou '65
The Dirty Dozen '67
Hour of the Gun '67
MacKenna's Gold '69
Slaughter '72
Detroit 9000 '73
Adios Amigo '75
Mitchell '75
The Killing of a Chinese Bookie '76
The Car '77

Robin Phillips (1942-)
Decline and Fall...of a Birdwatcher '68
David Copperfield '70

Sally Phillips (1970-)
Bridget Jones's Diary '01
Bridget Jones: The Edge of Reason '04

Samantha (Sam) Phillips (1966-)
Phantasm 2 '88
Sexual Malice '93
The Dallas Connection '94

Sian Phillips (1933-)
Young Cassidy '65
Goodbye, Mr. Chips '69
Murphy's War '71
Nijinsky '80
Tinker, Tailor, Soldier, Spy '80
Clash of the Titans '81
How Many Miles to Babylon? '82
Smiley's People '82
Dune '84
The Doctor and the Devils '85
The Ewoks: Battle for Endor '85
Valmont '89
Heidi '93
Ivanhoe '97
Aristocrats '99 (N)
The Aristocrats '99
Attila '01
P.D. James: The Murder Room '04

Wendy Phillips (1953-)
Midnight Run '88
Bugsy '91

Grace Phipps (1992-)
Teen Beach Movie '13
Some Kind of Hate '15
Tales of Halloween '15

Max Phipps (1939-2000)
The Road Warrior '82
Nate and Hayes '83
Return of Captain Invincible '83

Nicholas Phipps (1913-80)
Spring in Park Lane '48
Captain's Paradise '53
Doctor in Love '60

William Phipps (1922-)
Cinderella '50 (V)
Five '51
Flat Top '52
Loan Shark '52
The War of the Worlds '53
Lord of the Jungle '55
Cavalry Command '63

Joaquin Rafael (Leaf) Phoenix (1974-)
SpaceCamp '86
Russkies '87
Secret Witness '88
Parenthood '89
To Die For '95
Inventing the Abbotts '97
U-Turn '97
Clay Pigeons '98
8mm '98
Return to Paradise '98
Gladiator '00
Quills '00
The Yards '00
Buffalo Soldiers '01
Signs '02
Brother Bear '03 (V)
It's All About Love '03
Hotel Rwanda '04
Ladder 49 '04
The Village '04
Walk the Line '05
Reservation Road '07
We Own the Night '07
Two Lovers '09
I'm Still Here '10
The Master '12
Her '13
The Immigrant '13
Inherent Vice '14
You Were Never Really Here '17
Don't Worry, He Won't Get Far on Foot '18
The Sisters Brothers '18
Joker '19
Mary Magdalene '19

Rain Phoenix (1972-)
Even Cowgirls Get the Blues '94
Spent '00
O '01
Harry and Max '04
Kids in America '05

River Phoenix (1970-93)
Explorers '85
The Mosquito Coast '86
Stand by Me '86
Little Nikita '88
A Night in the Life of Jimmy Reardon '88
Running on Empty '88
Indiana Jones and the Last Crusade '89
I Love You to Death '90
Dogfight '91
My Own Private Idaho '91
Silent Tongue '92
Sneakers '92
The Thing Called Love '93

Summer Phoenix (1978-)
Kate's Secret '86
Girl '98
SLC Punk! '99
Dinner Rush '00
Esther Kahn '00
The Believer '01

Tanit Phoenix (1984-)
Death Race 2 '10
Lost Boys: The Thirst '10
Death Race 3: Inferno '12

Jesdaporn Pholdee (1977-)
The Iron Ladies '00
The Iron Ladies 2 '03
The Eye 2 '04

Maurice Pialat (1925-2003)
This Man Must Die '70
A Nos Amours '84

Jason Pai Piao
The Duel of the Century '81
Holy Flame of the Martial World '83

Ben Piazza (1934-91)
A Dangerous Age '57
The Hanging Tree '59
Nightwing '79
Scene of the Crime '85
Clean and Sober '88
Guilty by Suspicion '91

Vincent Piazza (1976-)
Goodbye Baby '07
Rocket Science '07
Jersey Boys '14
The Intervention '16

Robert Picardo (1953-)
The Howling '81
Explorers '85
Back to School '86
Legend '86
Innerspace '87
Munchies '87
976-EVIL '88
Gremlins 2: The New Batch '90
Motorama '91
Matinee '92
Fatal Deception: Mrs. Lee Harvey Oswald '93
Revenge of the Nerds 4: Nerds in Love '94
Runaway Daughters '94
Wagons East '94
White Mile '94
Menno's Mind '96
Star Trek: First Contact '96
Small Soldiers '98
Chasing the Green '09
Mega Shark *vs.* Crocosaurus '10
Monsterwolf '10
Beethoven's Christmas Adventure '11
Atlas Shrugged 2: The Strike '12

Michel Piccoli (1925-2020)
Death in the Garden '56
Le Doulos '61
Contempt '64
Diary of a Chambermaid '64
Lady L '65
The Game Is Over '66
La Guerre Est Finie '66
Belle de Jour '67
Danger: Diabolik '68
The Milky Way '68
The Young Girls of Rochefort '68
Dillinger Is Dead '69
Topaz '69
The Discreet Charm of the Bourgeoisie '72
Ten Days Wonder '72
La Grande Bouffe '73
Phantom of Liberty '74
Wedding in Blood '74
Mado '76
Atlantic City '81
Beyond Obsession '82
Passion '82
Dangerous Moves '84
Mauvais Sang '86
La Belle Noiseuse '90
One Hundred and One Nights '95
Beaumarchais the Scoundrel '96
Party '96
Traveling Companion '96
Genealogies of a Crime '97
Passion in the Desert '97
I'm Going Home '00
Belle Toujours '06
The Duchess of Langeais '07
You Ain't Seen Nothin' Yet '12

Paul Picerni (1922-2011)
Breakthrough '50
Force of Arms '51
I Was a Communist for the FBI '51
Inside the Walls of Folsom Prison '51
The Tanks Are Coming '51
Cattle Town '52
Mara Maru '52
Operation Secret '52
House of Wax '53
She's Back on Broadway '53
The System '53
Drive a Crooked Road '54
Lord of the Jungle '55
To Hell and Back '55
Wiretapper '55
The Big Caper '57
The Brothers Rico '57
The Scalphunters '68

Irving Pichel (1891-1954)
An American Tragedy '31
The Cheat '31
Oliver Twist '33
British Agent '34
Fog Over Frisco '34
Dracula's Daughter '36
Dick Tracy '37
Join the Marines '37
How Green Was My Valley '41 (N)

Joe Pichler (1987-)
Varsity Blues '98
Shiloh 2: Shiloh Season '99
Beethoven's 3rd '00
Beethoven's 4th '01
When Good Ghouls Go Bad '01
Children On Their Birthdays '02

John Pickard (1913-93)
Government Agents *vs.* Phantom Legion '51
Hellgate '52
Above and Beyond '53
The Fighting Lawman '53
Seminole Uprising '55
War Drums '57

Raymond Pickard (1982-)
The Canterville Ghost '96
The Borrowers '97

Sorrels Pickard (1940-2003)
Running Hot '83
Hardbodies '84

James Pickens, Jr. (1954-)
Ghosts of Mississippi '96
Gridlock'd '96
RocketMan '97
Liberty Heights '99
A Slight Case of Murder '99
Home Room '02
Venom '05
Just Wright '10

Slim Pickens (1919-83)
Rocky Mountain '50
Colorado Sundown '52
The Story of Will Rogers '52
Gun Brothers '56
The Sheepman '58
One-Eyed Jacks '61
A Thunder of Drums '61
Dr. Strangelove, or: How I Learned to Stop Worrying and Love the Bomb '64
In Harm's Way '65
Major Dundee '65
Stagecoach '66
Flim-Flam Man '67
Rough Night in Jericho '67
Never a Dull Moment '68
The Desperate Mission '69
Ballad of Cable Hogue '70
Ride to Glory '71
The Cowboys '72
The Getaway '72
Ginger in the Morning '73
Pat Garrett & Billy the Kid '73
Poor Pretty Eddie '73
Blazing Saddles '74
The Apple Dumpling Gang '75
Babe! '75
Rancho Deluxe '75
White Line Fever '75
Banjo Hackett '76
Hawmps! '76
Pony Express Rider '76
Mr. Billion '77
Shadow of Chikara '77
The White Buffalo '77
The Swarm '78
Undercover With the KKK '78
Beyond the Poseidon Adventure '79
1941 '79
Honeysuckle Rose '80
Tom Horn '80
The Howling '81
Crazy Horse and Custer: 'The Untold Story' '90

Marc Pickering (1985-)
Sleepy Hollow '99
Cashback '06

Cindy Pickett (1947-)
Cocaine and Blue Eyes '83
Hysterical '83
Ferris Bueller's Day Off '86
The Men's Club '86
Hot to Trot! '88
Deepstar Six '89
I Know My First Name Is Steven '89
Crooked Hearts '91
Original Intent '91
Sleepwalkers '92
Son-in-Law '93
Evolver '94
Painted Hero '95
The Stepdaughter '00
Hate Crime '05
The Village Barbershop '08

Jay Pickett (1961-)
Abandoned '10
The Perfect Student '11
Soda Springs '11

Jack Pickford (1896-1933)
The Man Who Had Everything '20
The Bat '26
Exit Smiling '26

Mary Pickford (1893-1979)
The Little American '17
Rebecca of Sunnybrook Farm '17
Amarilly of Clothesline Alley '18
Pride of the Clan '18
Stella Maris '18
Daddy Long Legs '19
Heart o' the Hills '19
The Hoodlum '19
Suds '20
The Love Light '21
Through the Back Door '21
Tess of the Storm Country '22
Sparrows '26
My Best Girl '27
The Taming of the Shrew '29

Christina Pickles (1935-)
Seizure '74
Revenge of the Nerds 4: Nerds in Love '94
William Shakespeare's Romeo and Juliet '96
Weapons of Mass Distraction '97
The Wedding Singer '97
Angels Don't Sleep Here '00
Sol Goode '01
The Family Holiday '07

Vivian Pickles (1933-)
Harold and Maude '71
Sunday, Bloody Sunday '71
Elizabeth R '72
Candleshoe '78

Ronald Pickup (1940-)
Nijinsky '80
Ivanhoe '82
Camille '84
The Mission '86
Fortunes of War '87
The Attic: The Hiding of Anne Frank '88
Behaving Badly '89

Jekyll and Hyde *'90*
A Murder of Quality *'90*
The Rector's Wife *'94*
Scarlett *'94*
Ivanhoe *'97*
Horatio Hornblower *'99*
The Christmas Miracle of Jonathan Toomey *'07*
The Best Exotic Marigold Hotel *'12*
The Second Best Exotic Marigold Hotel *'15*

Molly Picon (1898-1992)
Come Blow Your Horn *'63*
Fiddler on the Roof *'71*
For Pete's Sake *'74*
Murder on Flight 502 *'75*
Cannonball Run *'81*
Cannonball Run 2 *'84*

Jim Piddock (1956-)
Traces of Red *'92*
She Creature *'01*
A Different Loyalty *'04*
Love for Rent *'05*
For Your Consideration *'06*
The Seeker: The Dark Is Rising *'07*
Falling Up *'08*
The Cold Light of Day *'12*
The Five-Year Engagement *'12*
Kill Your Friends *'16*

Rebecca Pidgeon (1965-)
The Dawning *'88*
Homicide *'91*
The Spanish Prisoner *'97*
The Winslow Boy *'98*
State and Main *'00*
Heist *'01*
Edmond *'05*
Shopgirl *'05*
Jesse Stone: Sea Change *'07*
Cat City *'08*
How to Be *'08*
Redbelt *'08*
RED *'10*
Phil Spector *'13*

Walter Pidgeon (1897-1984)
Going Wild *'30*
Big Brown Eyes *'36*
Saratoga *'37*
Girl of the Golden West *'38*
Listen, Darling *'38*
Shopworn Angel *'38*
Too Hot to Handle *'38*
Nick Carter, Master Detective *'39*
Society Lawyer *'39*
Stronger Than Desire *'39*
Dark Command *'40*
Flight Command *'40*
House Across the Bay *'40*
Phantom Raiders *'40*
Sky Murder *'40*
Blossoms in the Dust *'41*
Design for Scandal *'41*
How Green Was My Valley *'41*
If Winter Comes *'41*
Man Hunt *'41*
Mrs. Miniver *'42*
Madame Curie *'43*
Mrs. Parkington *'44*
Weekend at the Waldorf *'45*
Holiday in Mexico *'46*
The Secret Heart *'46*
Cass Timberlane *'47 (C)*
Command Decision *'48*
Julia Misbehaves *'48*
The Miniver Story *'50*
The Red Danube *'50*
That Forsyte Woman *'50*
Quo Vadis *'51 (N)*
The Sellout *'51*
The Bad and the Beautiful *'52*
Million Dollar Mermaid *'52*
Dream Wife *'53*
Scandal at Scourie *'53*
Deep in My Heart *'54*
Executive Suite *'54*
The Last Time I Saw Paris *'54*
Men of the Fighting Lady *'54*
The Glass Slipper *'55 (N)*
Hit the Deck *'55*
Forbidden Planet *'56*
The Rack *'56*
These Wilder Years *'56*
Voyage to the Bottom of the Sea *'61*
Advise and Consent *'62*
Big Red *'62*
Cinderella *'64*
Funny Girl *'68*
Skyjacked *'72*
Harry in Your Pocket *'73*
Neptune Factor *'73*
Murder on Flight 502 *'75*
The Lindbergh Kidnapping Case *'76*
Two Minute Warning *'76*
Sextette *'78*

Jacques Pieller
Time Regained *'99*
The Town Is Quiet *'00*

Claude Pieplu (1923-2006)
Phantom of Liberty *'74*
Wedding in Blood *'74*
The Best Way *'76*

Bradley Michael Pierce (1982-)
Beauty and the Beast *'91 (V)*
Jumanji *'95*
The Borrowers *'97*

Brock Pierce (1938-)
First Kid *'96*
Legend of the Lost Tomb *'97*

Charles B. Pierce (1938-)
Grayeagle *'77*
Boggy Creek II *'83*

Chonda Pierce
12 Christmas Wishes For My Dog *'11*
All Saints *'17*

David Hyde Pierce (1959-)
Bright Lights, Big City *'88*
Crossing Delancey *'88*
Vampire's Kiss *'88*
The Fisher King *'91*
Little Man Tate *'91*
Wolf *'94*
Nixon *'95*
A Bug's Life *'98 (V)*
Jackie's Back *'99*
The Mating Habits of the Earthbound Human *'99 (N)*
Chain of Fools *'00*
Isn't She Great *'00*
Osmosis Jones *'01 (V)*
Wet Hot American Summer *'01*
Full Frontal *'02*
Treasure Planet *'02 (V)*
Down With Love *'03*
Hellboy *'04 (V)*
The Perfect Host *'10*

Jill Pierce
Darkroom *'90*
Cyborg Soldier *'94*
Omega Doom *'96*

Justin Pierce (1975-2000)
Kids *'95*
A Brother's Kiss *'97*
Blackmale *'99*
Next Friday *'00*

Norman Pierce (1900-)
Ticket of Leave Man *'37*
The Four Feathers *'39*

Stack Pierce
Night Call Nurses *'72*
A Rage in Harlem *'91*

Tony Pierce
Trancers 3: Deth Lives *'92*
Big Bully *'95*

Wendell Pierce (1966-)
The Money Pit *'86*
Family Business *'89*
Bye Bye, Love *'94*
It Could Happen to You *'94*
Hackers *'95*
Waiting to Exhale *'95*
Get On the Bus *'96*
Bulworth *'98*
The 24 Hour Woman *'99*
Brown Sugar *'02*
A Hole in One *'04*
Land of Plenty *'04*
Ray *'04*
Stay Alive *'06*
I Think I Love My Wife *'07*
Life Support *'07*
Night Catches Us *'10*
The Mortician *'11*
Four *'12*
Parker *'13*
Elsa & Fred *'14*
The Runner *'15*
Piercing *'18*
Burning Cane *'19*
Clemency *'19*

Eric Pierpoint (1950-)
Alien Nation: Dark Horizon *'94*
Alien Nation: Body and Soul *'95*
Alien Nation: Millennium *'96*
Alien Nation: The Enemy Within *'96*
Little Witches *'96*
Where Truth Lies *'96*
Liar Liar *'97*

Frederic Pierrot (1960-)
For Ever Mozart *'96*
Artemisia *'97*
The Girl from Paris *'02*
Monsieur N. *'03*
They Came Back *'04*
A Song of Innocence *'05*
I've Loved You So Long *'08*
Let It Rain *'08*
Sarah's Key *'10*

Sarah Pierse
The Navigator *'88*
Heavenly Creatures *'94*

Emma Pierson (1981-)
Bloodlines *'05*
Little Dorrit *'08*

Geoffrey Pierson (1949-)
Necessary Parties *'88*
Venomous *'01*
Spartan *'04*
Sleeping Dogs Lie *'06*
J. Edgar *'11*

Sasha Pieterse (1996-)
The Adventures of Sharkboy and Lavagirl in 3-D *'05*
Geek Charming *'11*
G.B.F. *'13*
Inherent Vice *'14*

Angela Pietropinto
Goodfellas *'90*
Honeymoon in Vegas *'92*
It Could Happen to You *'94*
Welcome to the Dollhouse *'95*
Finding North *'97*
Shaft *'00*
A Tale of Two Pizzas *'03*

Amy Pietz (1969-)
Adventures of a Teenage Dragonslayer *'10*
Stalked at 17 *'12*

Cara Pifko (1976-)
I Me Wed *'07*
For the Love of Grace *'08*

Roger Pigaut (1919-89)
Untamable Angelique *'67*
Angelique and the Sultan *'68*

Alexandra Pigg (1962-)
Smart Money *'88*
Bullseye! *'90*
Chicago Joe & the Showgirl *'90*
Strapless *'90*

Tim Pigott-Smith (1946-)
The Lost Boys *'78*
The Hunchback of Notre Dame *'82*
I Remember Nelson *'82*
The Jewel in the Crown *'84*
The Remains of the Day *'93*
Bloody Sunday *'01*
The Four Feathers *'02*
Johnny English *'03*
Alexander *'04*
V for Vendetta *'06*
RED 2 *'13*
Houdini *'14*
Victoria & Abdul *'17*

Luciano Pigozzi (1927-)
See Alan Collins

Rosamund Pike (1979-)
Die Another Day *'02*
The Devil You Know *'05*
Doom *'05*
The Libertine *'05*
Pride and Prejudice *'05*
Fracture *'07*
An Education *'09*
Surrogates *'09*
Barney's Version *'10*
Made in Dagenham *'10*
The Big Year *'11*
Women in Love *'11*
Jack Reacher *'12*
Wrath of the Titans *'12*
The World's End *'13*
Gone Girl *'14*
Hector and the Search for Happiness *'14*
A Long Way Down *'14*
Return to Sender *'15*
What We Did on Our Holiday *'15*
Hostiles *'17*
A United Kingdom *'17*
Beirut *'18*
A Private War *'18*
7 Days in Entebbe *'18*

Joe Pilato (1949-)
Day of the Dead *'85*
Married People, Single Sex *'93*
Fatal Passion *'94*

Nova Pilbeam (1919-2015)
The Man Who Knew Too Much *'34*
Nine Days a Queen *'36*
Young and Innocent *'37*
The Next of Kin *'42*
Counterblast *'48*

Mitch Pileggi (1952-)
On the Line *'84*
Shocker *'89*
The X-Files *'98*
Gun Shy *'00*
Recount *'08*
The X Files: I Want to Believe *'08*
Super Storm *'12*

Lorraine Pilkington (1974-)
The Last of the High Kings *'96*
The Nephew *'97*
Human Traffic *'99*
In a Day *'06*

Alison Pill (1985-)
What Katy Did *'99*
Baby *'00*
Skipped Parts *'00*
The Pilot's Wife *'01*
Pieces of April *'03*
An Unexpected Love *'03*
Confessions of a Teenage Drama Queen *'04*
Plain Truth *'04*
A Separate Peace *'04*
Dear Wendy *'05*
Dan in Real Life *'07*
Milk *'08*
One Way to Valhalla *'09*
Pillars of the Earth *'10*
Scott Pilgrim vs. the World *'10*
Midnight in Paris *'11*
Goon *'12*
To Rome with Love *'12*
Cooties *'14*
Goon: Last of the Enforcers *'17*

Drew Pillsbury
Jerome *'98*
About Fifty *'11*

Soren Pilmark (1955-)
The Kingdom *'95*
The Kingdom 2 *'97*
Flickering Lights *'01*

Daniel Pilon (1940-)
Snowballin' *'71*
Brannigan *'75*
Poltergeist: The Legacy *'96*
Suspicious Minds *'96*
The Ultimate Weapon *'97*
The Collectors *'99*
Left Behind: The Movie *'00*
Sex & Mrs. X *'00*
Shoot 'Em Up *'07*

Donald Pilon (1941-)
The Pyx *'73*
Keeping Track *'86*
A Wind from Wyoming *'94*

Silvia Pinal (1931-)
Viridiana *'61*
The Exterminating Angel *'62*
Vintage Model *'92*

Jimmy Pinchak
All I Want for Christmas *'07*
Let Me In *'10*

Bronson Pinchot (1959-)
Risky Business *'83*
Beverly Hills Cop *'84*
The Flamingo Kid *'84*
After Hours *'85*
Second Sight *'89*
Blame It on the Bellboy *'92*
True Romance *'93*
Beverly Hills Cop 3 *'94*
The Great American Sex Scandal *'94*
It's My Party *'95*
Stephen King's The Langoliers *'95*
Courage Under Fire *'96*
The First Wives Club *'96*
Slappy and the Stinkers *'97*
All New Adventures of Laurel and Hardy: For Love or Mummy *'98*
Quest for Camelot *'98 (V)*
Out of the Cold *'99*
Second Best *'05*
Pure Country 2: The Gift *'10*
You and I *'11*
The Strike *'16*

Chris Pine (1980-)
The Princess Diaries 2: Royal Engagement *'04*
Blind Dating *'06*
Just My Luck *'06*
Smokin' Aces *'07*
Carriers *'09*
Star Trek *'09*
Small Town Saturday Night *'10*
Unstoppable *'10*
People Like Us *'12*
Rise of the Guardians *'12 (V)*
This Means War *'12*
Star Trek: Into Darkness *'13*
Horrible Bosses 2 *'14*
Into the Woods *'14*
Jack Ryan: Shadow Recruit *'14*
Z for Zachariah *'15*
The Finest Hours *'16*
Hell or High Water *'16*
Star Trek: Beyond *'16*
Wonder Woman *'17*
Outlaw King *'18*

Larry Pine (1945-)
Hullabaloo over Georgie & Bonnie's Pictures *'78*
Anna *'87*
Vanya on 42nd Street *'94*
Dead Man Walking *'95*
Sunday *'96*
A Stranger in the Kingdom *'98*
Let It Snow *'99*
The Shipping News *'01*
2 Brothers & a Bride *'03*
The Clearing *'04*
Islander *'06*
Outsourced *'06*
Chasing the Green *'09*
Jimmy P. *'13*

Phillip Pine (1920-2006)
The Phantom from 10,000 Leagues *'56*
Men in War *'57*
The Lost Missile *'58*
Murder by Contract *'58*

Robert Pine (1941-)
Munster, Go Home! *'66*
Empire of the Ants *'77*
Mysterious Two *'82*
Independence Day *'96*
Body Count *'97*
Lost Voyage *'01*
The Long Shot *'04*
All I Want for Christmas *'07*
Love's Unfolding Dream *'07*

Daniella Pineda (1981-)
Mr. Roosevelt *'17*
Jurassic World: Fallen Kingdom *'18*
Mercy Black *'19*

Miguel Pinero (1946-88)
Short Eyes *'79*
Alphabet City *'84*
Almost You *'85*

John Pinette (1962-)
Simon Sez *'99*
My 5 Wives *'00*

Joe Pingue
Obituary *'06*
Antiviral *'12*

Pink (1979-)
See Alecia Moore

Jada Pinkett Smith (1971-)
Menace II Society *'93*
The Inkwell *'94*
Jason's Lyric *'94*
A Low Down Dirty Shame *'94*
Tales from the Crypt Presents Demon Knight *'94*
If These Walls Could Talk *'96*
The Nutty Professor *'96*
Set It Off *'96*
Scream 2 *'97*
Woo *'97*
Princess Mononoke *'98 (V)*
Return to Paradise *'98*
Bamboozled *'00*
Ali *'01*
Kingdom Come *'01*
The Matrix Reloaded *'03*
The Matrix Revolutions *'03*
Collateral *'04*
Madagascar *'05 (V)*
Reign Over Me *'07*
The Human Contract *'08*
Madagascar: Escape 2 Africa *'08 (V)*
The Women *'08*
Madagascar 3: Europe's Most Wanted *'12 (V)*
Bad Moms *'16*
Girls Trip *'17*

Tonya Pinkins (1962-)
Above the Rim *'94*
Fading Gigolo *'13*
Aardvark *'18*

Rob Pinkston (1988-)
The Derby Stallion *'05*
The Sasquatch Gang *'06*
Extreme Movie *'08*

Ryan Pinkston (1988-)
Full of It *'07*
College *'08*
Extreme Movie *'08*
Foreign Exchange *'08*
Cougars, Inc. *'10*

Arnold Pinnock (1967-)
Twitches *'05*
Twitches Too *'07*
A Day Late and a Dollar Short *'14*
Dear Viola *'14*

Nicholas Pinnock
Monsters: Dark Continent *'15*
The Last Tree *'19*

Danny Pino (1974-)
Between *'05*
Flicka *'06*
Rx *'06*
The Burning Plain *'08*
Across the Hall *'09*

Liberty Stands Still *'02*
ZigZag *'02*
Pieces of April *'03*
Kinsey *'04*
Casanova *'05*
The Ice Harvest *'05*
Loverboy *'05*
The Bronx Is Burning *'07*
Martian Child *'07*
The Ten *'07*
Frost/Nixon *'08*
2012 *'09*
Year One *'09*
Love and Other Drugs *'10*
Please Give *'10*
X-Men: First Class *'11*
The Oranges *'12*
Ginger & Rosa *'13*
Lucky Them *'13*
Chef *'14*
Kill the Messenger *'14*
Legends of Oz: Dorothy's Return *'14 (V)*
Cut Bank *'15*
The 9th Life of Louis Drax *'16*
Shut In *'16*
The Ticket *'17*

Victoria Platt (1972-)
Winchell *'98*
My Girlfriend's Back *'10*

Dylan Playfair
Grave Encounters 2 *'12*
Mr. Hockey: The Gordie Howe Story *'13*

Alice Playten (1947-2011)
Legend *'86*
Doug's 1st Movie *'99 (V)*

Aubrey Plaza (1984-)
Funny People *'09*
Scott Pilgrim *vs.* the World *'10*
A Glimpse Inside the Mind of Charles Swan III *'12*
Safety Not Guaranteed *'12*
10 Years *'12*
Monsters University *'13 (V)*
The To Do List *'13*
About Alex *'14*
Life After Beth *'14*
Playing It Cool *'14*
Addicted to Fresno *'15*
Dirty Grandpa *'16*
Mike and Dave Need Wedding Dates *'16*
Ingrid Goes West *'17*
The Little Hours *'17*
Child's Play *'19*

Angela Pleasence (1941-)
Six Wives of Henry VIII *'71*
A Christmas Carol *'84*
The Favor, the Watch, & the Very Big Fish *'92*
September *'96*
Appointment With Death *'10*

Donald Pleasence (1919-95)
Value for Money *'55*
1984 *'56*
Look Back in Anger *'58*
A Tale of Two Cities *'58*
Circus of Horrors *'60*
The Flesh and the Fiends *'60*
The Hands of Orlac *'60*
Lisa *'62*
What a Carve-Up! *'62*
The Great Escape *'63*
The Greatest Story Ever Told *'65*
The Hallelujah Trail *'65*
Cul de Sac *'66*
Fantastic Voyage *'66*
Eye of the Devil *'67*
Night of the Generals *'67*
Will Penny *'67*
You Only Live Twice *'67*
The Madwoman of Chaillot *'69*
Soldier Blue *'70*
Outback *'71*
THX 1138 *'71*
Innocent Bystanders *'72*
Pied Piper *'72*
Raw Meat *'72*
Wedding in White *'72*
Dr. Jekyll and Mr. Hyde *'73*
The Freakmaker *'73*
From Beyond the Grave *'73*
Tales That Witness Madness *'73*
Barry McKenzie Holds His Own *'74*
Escape to Witch Mountain *'75*
Hearts of the West *'75*
I Don't Want to Be Born *'75*
Choice of Weapons *'76*
The Last Tycoon *'76*
The Eagle Has Landed *'77*
Land of the Minotaur *'77*
Oh, God! *'77*
Telefon *'77*
Tomorrow Never Comes *'77*
The Bastard *'78*
Halloween *'78*
Power Play *'78*
Sgt. Pepper's Lonely Hearts Club Band *'78*
All Quiet on the Western Front *'79*
Dracula *'79*
Gold of the Amazon Women *'79*
Jaguar Lives *'79*
Night Creature *'79*
Escape from New York *'81*
Halloween 2: The Nightmare Isn't Over! *'81*
Alone in the Dark *'82*
Devonsville Terror *'83*
Frankenstein's Great Aunt Tillie *'83*
Treasure of the Yankee Zephyr *'83*
The Ambassador *'84*
To Kill a Stranger *'84*
Warrior of the Lost World *'84*
Arch of Triumph *'85*
Creepers *'85*
Mansfield Park *'85*
The Monster Club *'85*
The Treasure of the Amazon *'85*
Django Strikes Again *'87*
Prince of Darkness *'87*
Deep Cover *'88*
Halloween 4: The Return of Michael Myers *'88*
Buried Alive *'89*
Casablanca Express *'89*
Halloween 5: The Revenge of Michael Myers *'89*
Millions *'90*
River of Death *'90*
Shadows and Fog *'92*
The Advocate *'93*
Guinevere *'94*
Halloween 6: The Curse of Michael Myers *'95*

Andrew Pleavin (1968-)
Attack of the Gryphon *'07*
Witchville *'10*

Jesse Plemons (1988-)
Children On Their Birthdays *'02*
Like Mike *'02*
Observe and Report *'09*
Happiness Runs *'10*
Meeting Spencer *'11*
Paul *'11*
The Master *'12*
The Program *'15*
Other People *'16*
American Made *'17*
The Discovery *'17*
The Irishman *'19*

John Pleshette (1942-)
The Trial of Lee Harvey Oswald *'77*
Burning Rage *'84*
Shattered Innocence *'87*
Eye of the Stranger *'93*
James Dean *'01*

Suzanne Pleshette (1937-2008)
The Geisha Boy *'58*
40 Pounds of Trouble *'62*
Rome Adventure *'62*
The Birds *'63*
Wall of Noise *'63*
A Distant Trumpet *'64*
Fate Is the Hunter *'64*
Youngblood Hawke *'64*
A Rage to Live *'65*
The Ugly Dachshund *'65*
The Adventures of Bullwhip Griffin *'66*
Mister Buddwing *'66*
Nevada Smith *'66*
Blackbeard's Ghost *'67*
The Power *'68*
If It's Tuesday, This Must Be Belgium *'69*
Suppose They Gave a War and Nobody Came? *'70*
Support Your Local Gunfighter *'71*
Legend of Valentino *'75*
The Shaggy D.A. *'76*
Hot Stuff *'80*
Oh, God! Book 2 *'80*
Dixie: Changing Habits *'85*
Alone in the Neon Jungle *'87*
The Queen of Mean *'90*
Battling for Baby *'92*
The Lion King: Simba's Pride *'98 (V)*
Spirited Away *'01 (V)*

George Plimpton (1927-2003)
The Detective *'68*
Rio Lobo *'70*
Reds *'81*
Volunteers *'85*
A Fool and His Money *'88*
Easy Wheels *'89*
Little Man Tate *'91*
Just Cause *'94*
Good Will Hunting *'97*
Just Visiting *'01*
Soul Power *'08*

Martha Plimpton (1970-)
Rollover *'81*
The Goonies *'85*
The Mosquito Coast *'86*
Another Woman *'88*
Running on Empty *'88*
Parenthood *'89*
Stanley and Iris *'90*
Samantha *'92*
Daybreak *'93*
Inside Monkey Zetterland *'93*
Josh and S.A.M. *'93*
Mrs. Parker and the Vicious Circle *'94*
My Life's in Turnaround *'94 (C)*
Beautiful Girls *'96*
I Shot Andy Warhol *'96*
I'm Not Rappaport *'96*
Last Summer In the Hamptons *'96*
Eye of God *'97*
Music from Another Room *'97*
Pecker *'98*
200 Cigarettes *'98*
The Sleepy Time Gal *'01*
Remember Me *'10*
Small Town Murder Songs *'10*

Pete Ploszek
Teenage Mutant Ninja Turtles *'14*
Teenage Mutant Ninja Turtles: Out of the Shadows *'16*

Jack Plotnick (1968-)
Chairman of the Board *'97*
Gods and Monsters *'98*
Say It Isn't So *'01*
Down With Love *'03*
Sleeping Dogs Lie *'06*
Remarkable Power *'08*
Rubber *'10*
Sharpay's Fabulous Adventure *'11*

Anna-Louise Plowman (1972-)
Cambridge Spies *'03*
The Foreigner *'03*
6 Bullets *'12*

Melinda Plowman
Chicago Calling *'52*
Billy the Kid Versus Dracula *'66*

Hilda Plowright (1890-1973)
Separate Tables *'58*
36 Hours *'64*

Joan Plowright (1929-)
Time Without Pity *'57*
The Entertainer *'60*
The Merchant of Venice *'73*
Equus *'77*
Brimstone & Treacle *'82*
Britannia Hospital *'82*
Revolution *'85*
Drowning by Numbers *'87*
Avalon *'90*
I Love You to Death *'90*
Enchanted April *'92*
Dennis the Menace *'93*
Last Action Hero *'93 (C)*
The Return of the Native *'94*
Widow's Peak *'94*
Mr. Wrong *'95*
A Pyromaniac's Love Story *'95*
The Scarlet Letter *'95*
Jane Eyre *'96*
101 Dalmatians *'96*
Surviving Picasso *'96*
Dance with Me *'98*
Tea with Mussolini *'99*
Dinosaur *'00 (V)*
Back to the Secret Garden *'01*
Callas Forever *'02*
Rock My World *'02*
Bringing Down the House *'03*
I Am David *'04*
Mrs. Palfrey at the Claremont *'05*
Curious George *'06 (V)*
The Spiderwick Chronicles *'08*
Tea with the Dames *'18*

Eve Plumb (1958-)
Alexander: The Other Side of Dawn *'77*
Little Women *'78*
The Night the Bridge Fell Down *'83*
I'm Gonna Git You Sucka *'88*
. . .And God Spoke *'94*
Blue Ruin *'13*

Amanda Plummer (1957-)
The World According to Garp *'82*
Daniel *'83*
The Hotel New Hampshire *'84*
Courtship *'87*
Made in Heaven *'87*
Static *'87*
Joe Versus the Volcano *'90*
The Fisher King *'91*
Freejack *'92*
Last Light *'93*
Needful Things *'93*
So I Married an Axe Murderer *'93*
Butterfly Kiss *'94*
Pulp Fiction *'94*
Freeway *'95*
The Prophecy *'95*
Under the Piano *'95*
Don't Look Back *'96*
Drunks *'96*
Hercules *'97 (V)*
A Simple Wish *'97*
8 1/2 Women *'99*
The Million Dollar Hotel *'99*
7 Days to Live *'00*
Get a Clue *'02*
Triggermen *'02*
Mimic 3: Sentinel *'03*
My Life Without Me *'03*
Satan's Little Helper *'04*
Affinity *'08*
Red *'08*
The Hunger Games: Catching Fire *'13*

Arthur Christopher Orme Plummer (1929-)
See Christopher Plummer

Charlie Plummer
King Jack *'16*
All the Money in the World *'17*
The Dinner *'17*
Lean on Pete *'17*

Christopher Plummer (1929-)
The Fall of the Roman Empire *'64*
Inside Daisy Clover *'65*
The Sound of Music *'65*
Night of the Generals *'67*
Triple Cross *'67*
Battle of Britain *'69*
The Pyx *'73*
Return of the Pink Panther *'74*
Conduct Unbecoming *'75*
The Man Who Would Be King *'75*
Spiral Staircase *'75*
Arthur Hailey's The Moneychangers *'76*
International Velvet *'78*
The Silent Partner *'78*
Star Crash *'78*
Hanover Street *'79*
Murder by Decree *'79*
Somewhere in Time *'80*
Eyewitness *'81*
The Amateur *'82*
Prototype *'83*
The Scarlet & the Black *'83*
The Thorn Birds *'83*
Dreamscape *'84*
Lily in Love *'85*
An American Tail *'86 (V)*
The Boss' Wife *'86*
Boy in Blue *'86*
Dragnet *'87*
I Love N.Y. *'87*
Souvenir *'88*
Firehead *'90*
Red Blooded American Girl *'90*
Where the Heart Is *'90*
Star Trek 6: The Undiscovered Country *'91*
Young Catherine *'91*
Impolite *'92*
Malcolm X *'92 (C)*
Rock-a-Doodle *'92 (V)*
Dolores Claiborne *'94*
Wolf *'94*
12 Monkeys *'95*
Conspiracy of Fear *'96*
Blackheart *'98*
Winchell *'98*
Hidden Agenda *'99*
The Insider *'99*
American Tragedy *'00*
Dracula 2000 *'00*
Full Disclosure *'00*
Nuremberg *'00*
Possessed *'00*
A Beautiful Mind *'01*
Lucky Break *'01*
Ararat *'02*
Nicholas Nickleby *'02*
Cold Creek Manor *'03*
The Gospel of John *'03 (N)*
Alexander *'04*
National Treasure *'04*
Must Love Dogs *'05*
The New World *'05*
Syriana *'05*
Inside Man *'06*
The Lake House *'06*
Already Dead *'07*
Autumn Hearts: A New Beginning *'07*
Closing the Ring *'07*
The Summit *'08*
The Imaginarium of Doctor Parnassus *'09*
The Last Station *'09*
My Dog Tulip *'09 (V)*
9 *'09 (V)*
Up *'09 (V)*
Beginners *'10*
Barrymore *'11*
The Girl With the Dragon Tattoo *'11*
Priest *'11*
Muhammad Ali's Greatest Fight *'13*
Elsa & Fred *'14*
Hector and the Search for Happiness *'14*
Danny Collins *'15*
The Forger *'15*
Remember *'15*
All the Money in the World *'17*
The Exception *'17*
The Man Who Invented Christmas *'17*
Boundaries *'18*
Cliffs of Freedom *'19*

Glenn Plummer (1961-)
Colors *'88*
Pastime *'91*
South Central *'92*
Menace II Society *'93*
Speed *'94*
Convict Cowboy *'95*
Showgirls *'95*
Strange Days *'95*
Things to Do in Denver When You're Dead *'95*
Smalltime *'96*
The Substitute *'96*
Up Close and Personal *'96*
One Night Stand *'97*
Speed 2: Cruise Control *'97*
Interceptor Force *'99*
Spy Games *'99*
The Corner *'00*
Love Beat the Hell Outta Me *'00*
Rangers *'00*
MacArthur Park *'01*
Rhapsody *'01*
Ruby's Bucket of Blood *'01*
Poolhall Junkies *'02*
The Salton Sea *'02*
Baadasssss! *'03*
Shade *'03*
The Day After Tomorrow *'04*
Saw 2 *'05*
The Longshots *'08*
The Janky Promoters *'09*
Teeth and Blood *'15*

Gerard Plunkett
Two for the Money *'05*
Eight Below *'06*

Maryann Plunkett
Peter and Vandy *'09*
Blue Valentine *'10*
The Family Fang *'16*
A Beautiful Day in the Neighborhood *'19*

Werner Pochath (1939-93)
Shark Hunter *'79*
Laser Mission *'90*
Devil Hunter *'08*

Denis Podalydes (1963-)
Children of the Century *'99*
Comedy of Innocence *'00*
Mortal Transfer *'01*
Safe Conduct *'01*
Almost Peaceful *'02*
You Ain't Seen Nothin' Yet *'12*

Rossana Podesta (1934-2013)
Ulysses *'55*
Helen of Troy *'56*
Santiago *'56*
Sodom and Gomorrah *'62*
The Virgin of Nuremberg *'65*

Fernando Poe, Jr. (1939-2004)
The Walls of Hell *'64*
The Ravagers *'65*

Amy Poehler (1971-)
Wet Hot American Summer *'01*
Envy *'04*
Mean Girls *'04*
Tenacious D in the Pick of Destiny *'06*
Blades of Glory *'07*
The Ex *'07*
Mr. Woodcock *'07*
Shrek the Third *'07 (V)*
Baby Mama *'08*

Dr. Seuss' Horton Hears a Who! '08 (V)
Hamlet 2 '08
Spring Breakdown '08
Alvin and the Chipmunks: The Squeakuel '09 (V)
Monsters vs. Aliens '09 (V)
The Secret World of Arrietty '10 (V)
Alvin and the Chipmunks: Chipwrecked '11 (V)
Hoodwinked Too! Hood vs. Evil '11 (V)
Are You Here '13
Free Birds '13 (V)
They Came Together '14
Inside Out '15 (V)
Sisters '15
The House '17

Benoit Poelvoorde (1964-)
Man Bites Dog '91
Coco Before Chanel '09
Romantics Anonymous '10
My Worst Nightmare '11
The Brand New Testament '15

Clarence Poesy (1982-)
Harry Potter and the Goblet of Fire '05
In Bruges '08

Clemence Poesy (1982-)
127 Hours '10
Birdsong '12
Last Love '13
The Ones Below '16
Final Portrait '17
Resistance '20

Massimo Poggio (1970-)
Facing Windows '03
David's Birthday '09

Kathryn Pogson
The Company of Wolves '85
Millions '05

Ken Pogue (1934-)
Keeping Track '86
Dead of Winter '87
Where the Heart Is '90
The Hitman '91
The Amy Fisher Story '93
Bad Moon '96
In the Lake of the Woods '96
National Lampoon's Dad's Week Off '97
The Jack Bull '99
Out of Time '00
The 6th Day '00
Crossfire Trail '01
Johnson County War '02
The Mermaid Chair '06
A Dog Named Christmas '09

Eric Pohlmann (1913-79)
Blackout '50
The Gambler & the Lady '52
Moulin Rouge '52
The Belles of St. Trinian's '53
Mogambo '53
Terror Street '54
The House of the Seven Hawks '59
Carry On Spying '64
Where the Spies Are '65

Clementine Poidatz (1981-)
Frontier of Dawn '08
Shut In '16

Larry Poindexter (1959-)
American Ninja 2: The Confrontation '87
Sorceress '94
Body Chemistry 4: Full Exposure '95
Steel Sharks '97
Black Horizon '01
Poison '01
S.W.A.T. '03

Priscilla Pointer (1924-)
The Onion Field '79
The Competition '80
Honeysuckle Rose '80
Mysterious Two '82
The Falcon and the Snowman '85
Blue Velvet '86
Rumpelstiltskin '86
A Nightmare on Elm Street 3: Dream Warriors '87
The Magic Bubble '93
Carried Away '95

Jean Poiret (1926-92)
The Last Metro '80
Cop Au Vin '85

Kim Poirier (1980-)
Dawn of the Dead '04
Decoys '04
Decoys: The Second Seduction '07
How I Married My High School Crush '07

Earl C. Poitier (1974-)
Remember the Titans '00
Drumline '02

Sidney Poitier
No Way Out '50
Blackboard Jungle '55
Goodbye, My Lady '56
Band of Angels '57
Edge of the City '57
The Mark of the Hawk '57
Something of Value '57
The Defiant Ones '58
Paris Blues '61
A Raisin in the Sun '61
Pressure Point '62
Lilies of the Field '63
The Long Ships '64
Bedford Incident '65
The Greatest Story Ever Told '65
A Patch of Blue '65
The Slender Thread '65
Duel at Diablo '66
Guess Who's Coming to Dinner '67
In the Heat of the Night '67
To Sir, with Love '67
For Love of Ivy '68
Brother John '70
They Call Me Mr. Tibbs! '70
The Organization '71
Buck and the Preacher '72
Uptown Saturday Night '74
Let's Do It Again '75
The Wilby Conspiracy '75
Piece of the Action '77
Little Nikita '88
Shoot to Kill '88
Separate but Equal '91
Sneakers '92
A Good Day to Die '95
To Sir, With Love 2 '96
The Jackal '97
Mandela and de Klerk '97
Free of Eden '98
The Simple Life of Noah Dearborn '99
The Last Brickmaker in America '01

Sydney Tamiia Poitier (1973-)
Free of Eden '98
Noah's Ark '99
True Crime '99
MacArthur Park '01
Nine Lives '05
Death Proof '07
Blues '08

Kristoffer Polaha (1977-)
Atlas Shrugged 3: Who Is John Galt? '14
Where Hope Grows '15
Run the Race '19

Dascha Polanco
The Cobbler '14
Joy '15

Simon Poland
Alien from L.A. '87
Nemesis 4: Cry of Angels '97

Anna Maria Polani
Hercules against the Moon Men '64
Hercules and the Tyrants of Babylon '64

Roman Polanski (1933-)
A Generation '54
Innocent Sorcerers '60
The Fearless Vampire Killers '67
The Magic Christian '69
Andy Warhol's Dracula '74 (C)
Chinatown '74
The Tenant '76
Grosse Fatigue '94 (C)
A Pure Formality '94
Zemsta '02
Rush Hour 3 '07

Victor Poletti
And the Ship Sails On '83
Meeting Venus '91

Maurice Poli (1933-)
Sandokan the Great '63
Five Dolls for an August Moon '70
Kidnapped '74

Mark Polish (1970-)
Twin Falls Idaho '99
The Good Thief '03
Northfork '03
The Bridge of San Luis Rey '05
The Astronaut Farmer '07
The Smell of Success '09
Stay Cool '09

Michael Polish (1970-)
Twin Falls Idaho '99
The Good Thief '03
The Bridge of San Luis Rey '05

Jon Polito (1950-2016)
Fire with Fire '86
Highlander '86
The Freshman '90
Leather Jackets '90
Miller's Crossing '90
Barton Fink '91
The Crow '93
Blankman '94
Girls in Prison '94
Bushwhacked '95
Fluke '95
Homeward Bound 2: Lost in San Francisco '96 (V)
The Big Lebowski '97
Music from Another Room '97
Robin Cook's Invasion '97
Nowhere Land '98
Angel's Dance '99
Russell Mulcahy's Tale of the Mummy '99
The Adventures of Rocky & Bullwinkle '00
Homicide: The Movie '00
The Man Who Wasn't There '01
Mimic 2 '01
Women vs. Men '02
The Box '03
The Singing Detective '03
29 Palms '03
The Last Shot '04
The Family Plan '05
The Honeymooners '05
Big Nothing '06
Grilled '06
Stiffs '06
American Gangster '07
Cougar Club '07
The Wedding Bros. '08
Citizen Jane '09
The Last Godfather '10
Venus and Vegas '10
Atlas Shrugged: Part 1 '11
Son of Morning '11
Big Eyes '14

Haydee Politoff (1946-)
La Collectionneuse '67
Dracula's Great Love '72

Vic Polizos (1947-)
C.H.U.D. '84
Harlem Nights '89
Winchell '98
Light It Up '99

Oscar Polk (1899-1949)
The Green Pastures '36
Gone with the Wind '39

Stephen Polk (1960-)
Destination Vegas '95
Drowning on Dry Land '00
Cherish '02
Holiday Baggage '08

Ben Pollack (1903-71)
The Glenn Miller Story '54
The Benny Goodman Story '55

Kevin Pollack (1957-)
Otis '08
2:13 '09
Columbus Circle '10

Sydney Pollack (1934-2008)
War Hunt '62
Tootsie '82
Death Becomes Her '92
Husbands and Wives '92
The Player '92
A Civil Action '98
Eyes Wide Shut '99
Random Hearts '99
Changing Lanes '02
The Interpreter '05
Avenue Montaigne '06
Michael Clayton '07
Made of Honor '08

Cheryl Pollak (1967-)
The Dark Side of the Sun '88
My Best Friend Is a Vampire '88
Swimsuit '89
Pump Up the Volume '90
Crossing the Bridge '92
Betty '97
Art House '98
No Strings Attached '98

Kevin Pollak (1957-)
Willow '88
Avalon '90
Another You '91
L.A. Story '91
Ricochet '91
A Few Good Men '92
Grumpy Old Men '93
Indian Summer '93
The Opposite Sex and How to Live With Them '93
Wayne's World 2 '93
Canadian Bacon '94
Clean Slate '94
Casino '95
Grumpier Old Men '95
Miami Rhapsody '95
The Usual Suspects '95
House Arrest '96
That Thing You Do! '96
National Lampoon's The Don's Analyst '97
Truth or Consequences, N.M. '97
From the Earth to the Moon '98
Hoods '98
Ruby Bridges '98
Deal of a Lifetime '99
End of Days '99
She's All That '99
Deterrence '00
Steal This Movie! '00
The Whole Nine Yards '00
Dr. Dolittle 2 '01
3000 Miles to Graceland '01
The Wedding Planner '01
Frank McKlusky, C.I. '02
Juwanna Mann '02
The Santa Clause 2 '02
Stolen Summer '02
The Whole Ten Yards '04
Hostage '05
Niagara Motel '06
The Santa Clause 3: The Escape Clause '06 (C)
Numb '07
Picture This! '08
Cop Out '10
Middle Men '10
The Big Year '11
The Magic of Belle Isle '12
Grace Unplugged '13
The One I Wrote For You '14
War Dogs '16
The Tiger Hunter '17

Tracy Pollan (1960-)
Baby It's You '82
Bright Lights, Big City '88
Promised Land '88
Danielle Steel's Fine Things '90
A Stranger Among Us '92
The Natalee Holloway Story '09
Justice for Natalee '11

Daphne Pollard (1890-1978)
The Lady Refuses '31
Bonnie Scotland '35
Our Relations '36

Michael J. Pollard (1939-2019)
The Wild Angels '66
Bonnie & Clyde '67
Caprice '67
Hannibal Brooks '69
Dirty Little Billy '72
Vengeance Is Mine '74
Between the Lines '77
Melvin and Howard '80
The Patriot '86
Roxanne '87
American Gothic '88
Riders of the Storm '88
Scrooged '88
Fast Food '89
Next of Kin '89
Night Visitor '89
Sleepaway Camp 3: Teenage Wasteland '89
Tango and Cash '89
The Art of Dying '90
Dick Tracy '90
I Come in Peace '90
Motorama '91
Split Second '92
Skeeter '93
Trigger Happy '96 (C)
The Odyssey '97
Tumbleweeds '98
Along for the Ride '00
Out of the Black '01
House of 1000 Corpses '03

Snub Pollard (1886-1962)
Just My Luck '35
The White Legion '36
The Errand Boy '61

Sarah Polley (1979-)
Big Town '87
Babar: The Movie '88 (V)
The Adventures of Baron Munchausen '89
Exotica '94
The Sweet Hereafter '96
The Hanging Garden '97
Junior's Groove '97
Last Night '98
White Lies '98
eXistenZ '99
Go '99
Guinevere '99
The Life Before This '99
The Claim '00
Love Come Down '00
The Weight of Water '00
No Such Thing '01
The Event '03
My Life Without Me '03
Dawn of the Dead '04
The I Inside '04
Siblings '04
Don't Come Knocking '05
Beowulf & Grendel '06
John Adams '08
Splice '10
Trigger '10
Mr. Nobody '13

David Pollock (1961-)
The Bad News Bears '76
The Bad News Bears in Breaking Training '77
The Bad News Bears Go to Japan '78

Eileen Pollock (1947-)
Four Days in July '85
Far and Away '92

Ellen Pollock (1903-97)
Non-Stop New York '37
The Time of His Life '55
Not So Dusty '56
Horror Hospital '73

Teri Polo (1969-)
The Phantom of the Opera '90
Born to Ride '91
Mystery Date '91
Passed Away '92
Aspen Extreme '93
Golden Gate '93
The House of the Spirits '93
Quick '93
The Arrival '96
Meet the Parents '00
Domestic Disturbance '01
The Unsaid '01
Beyond Borders '03
Straight from the Heart '03
Meet the Fockers '04
Legacy of Fear '06
Full of It '07
Expecting a Miracle '09
The Storm '09
2:13 '09
Little Fockers '10
Beyond '11
We Have Your Husband '11
A Taste of Romance '12
Taken for Ransom '13
Authors Anonymous '14
Outlaws and Angels '16

John Polson (1965-)
Dangerous Game '90
Sirens '94
The Sum of Us '94
Back of Beyond '95
Idiot Box '97
Mission: Impossible 2 '00

Max Pomeranc (1984-)
Searching for Bobby Fischer '93
Fluke '95

Ellen Pompeo (1969-)
In the Weeds '00
Moonlight Mile '02
Old School '03
Undermind '03
Eternal Sunshine of the Spotless Mind '04
Art Heist '05
Life of the Party '05

Carlos Ponce (1972-)
Deuce Bigalow: European Gigolo '05
Break-In '06
Just My Luck '06
Stranded '06
Vanished '06
Couples Retreat '09

Eusebio Poncela (1947-)
Cannibal Man '71
Law of Desire '86
Matador '86
A Shadow You Soon Will Be '94
Martin (Hache) '97
Intacto '01
800 Bullets '02

Jenjira Pongpas
Uncle Boonmee Who Can Recall His Past Lives '10
Cemetery of Splendor '15

Merce Pons (1966-)
Caresses '97
Km. 0 '00

Vimala Pons
Around a Small Mountain '09
40 Love '15

Chris Pontius (1974-)
Jackass: The Movie '02
Jackass Number Two '06
Jackass 3D '10
Somewhere '10

Aaron Poole
Small Town Murder Songs '10
The Last Will and Testament of Rosalind Leigh '12
Cas & Dylan '15
Foresaken '16

The Scent of Rain & Lightening '17
The Void '17

Olaf Pooley (1916-)
Naked Evil '66
Crucible of Horror '69

Bray Poor
Anima '98
Two Ninas '00

Imogen Poots (1989-)
Miss Austen Regrets '07
Cracks '09
Centurion '10
Chatroom '10
Waking Madison '10
Christopher and His Kind '11
Fright Night '11
Jane Eyre '11
Greetings from Tim Buckley '12
A Late Quartet '12
Filth '13
The Look of Love '13
Jimi: All Is by My Side '14
A Long Way Down '14
Need for Speed '14
That Awkward Moment '14
She's Funny That Way '15
Frank & Lola '16
Sweet Virginia '17
Age Out '19
The Art of Self-Defense '19
Black Christmas '19
Mobile Homes '19

Iggy Pop (1947-)
Sid & Nancy '86
Cry-Baby '90
Hardware '90
Tank Girl '94
Dead Man '95
The Crow 2: City of Angels '96
Snow Day '00
Coffee and Cigarettes '03
Suck '09

Carly Pope (1980-)
Finder's Fee '01
Nemesis Game '03
Eighteen '04
White Coats '04
Window Theory '04
Recipe for a Perfect Christmas '05
Two for the Money '05
Beneath '07
Itty Bitty Titty Committee '07
Yeti '08
Stuntmen '09
Sexting '11
S.W.A.T.: Firefight '11
Ambushed '13

Valentin Popescu (1955-)
Ryna '05
Aurora '10

Paul Popowich (1973-)
Vlad '03
Fatal Trust '06
I Me Wed '07

Marc Poppel
Damned River '89
Separate Lives '94

Anna Popplewell (1988-)
Dirty Tricks '00
The Little Vampire '00
The Chronicles of Narnia: The Lion, the Witch and the Wardrobe '05
The Chronicles of Narnia: Prince Caspian '08
The Chronicles of Narnia: The Voyage of the Dawn Treader '10

Paul Popplewell (1977-)
24 Hour Party People '01
Tyrannosaur '11

Albert 'Poppy' Popwell (1926-99)
The Joe Louis Story '53
The Harder They Fall '56
Coogan's Bluff '68
Dirty Harry '71
Fuzz '72
Charley Varrick '73
Cleopatra Jones '73
Cleopatra Jones & the Casino of Gold '75
The Enforcer '76
The Buddy Holly Story '78
Sudden Impact '83
Who's That Girl? '87
The Siege of Firebase Gloria '89
Wild at Heart '90
Scissors '91

Paul Porcasi
Morocco '30
The Devil and the Deep '32

Colleen Porch
Bending All the Rules '02
Starship Troopers 2: Hero of the Federation '04
All In '06
S.I.S. '08

Marc Porel (1949-83)
Don't Torture a Duckling '72
The Innocent '76
Live Like a Cop, Die Like a Man '76

Paulina Porizkova (1965-)
Anna '87
Her Alibi '88
Arizona Dream '94
Female Perversions '96
Wedding Bell Blues '96
Long Time Since '97
Partners in Crime '99
Intern '00
Dark Asylum '01
Second Best '05

Maria Poroshina (1973-)
Night Watch '04
Day Watch '06

Louise Portal (1950-)
The Klutz '73
The Decline of the American Empire '86
The Barbarian Invasions '03
Heading South '05

Robert Portal (1967-)
Stiff Upper Lips '96
Mrs. Dalloway '97
In Your Dreams '07
Welcome to the Punch '13

Adina Porter
The Fluffer '01
Think of Me '11

Billy Porter (1969-)
Twisted '96
The Broken Hearts Club '00
Intern '00
Like a Boss '20

Brett Porter (1956-)
Firehead '90
Stiletto Dance '01

Don Porter (1912-96)
Night Monster '42
Who Done It? '42
Buck Privates Come Home '47
711 Ocean Drive '50
The Racket '51
Our Miss Brooks '56
Bachelor in Paradise '61
Live a Little, Love a Little '68
The Candidate '72
The Norliss Tapes '73
Mame '74
The Legend of Lizzie Borden '75

Eric Porter (1928-95)
The Fall of the Roman Empire '64
The Pumpkin Eater '64
The Heroes of Telemark '65
Kaleidoscope '66
Macbeth '70
Hands of the Ripper '71
Antony and Cleopatra '73
Hitler: The Last Ten Days '73
Hennessy '75
The Thirty-Nine Steps '79
Oliver Twist '85

Ian Porter
The Defender '04
Gulliver's Travels '10

Jean Porter (1922-)
The Youngest Profession '43
Bathing Beauty '44
Abbott and Costello in Hollywood '45
Kentucky Jubilee '51

Mackenzie Porter (1990-)
The Other Woman '08
The Horses of McBride '12
Seattle Superstorm '12

Robert Porter
The Jesus Trip '71
Deadly Fieldtrip '74

Scott Porter (1979-)
Speed Racer '08
Bandslam '09
The Good Guy '10
The To Do List '13

Susie Porter (1971-)
Idiot Box '97
Welcome to Woop Woop '97
Two Hands '98
Better Than Sex '00
Bootmen '00
The Monkey's Mask '00
Sisters of War '10

Blanca Portillo (1963-)
Goya's Ghosts '06
Volver '06
Broken Embraces '09

Eric Portman (1903-69)
The Crimes of Stephen Hawke '36
Murder in the Old Red Barn '36
Moonlight Sonata '38
The Forty-Ninth Parallel '41
One of Our Aircraft Is Missing '41
We Dive at Dawn '43
A Canterbury Tale '44
The Colditz Story '55
Child in the House '56
Bedford Incident '65
The Whisperers '66
Assignment to Kill '69

Natalie Portman (1981-)
The Professional '94
Heat '95
Beautiful Girls '96
Everyone Says I Love You '96
Mars Attacks! '96
Anywhere But Here '99
Star Wars: Episode 1-The Phantom Menace '99
Where the Heart Is '00
Star Wars: Episode 2-Attack of the Clones '02
Cold Mountain '03
Closer '04
Garden State '04
Free Zone '05
Star Wars: Episode 3-Revenge of the Sith '05
Goya's Ghosts '06
Paris, je t'aime '06
V for Vendetta '06
Mr. Magorium's Wonder Emporium '07
My Blueberry Nights '07
The Other Boleyn Girl '08
Brothers '09
New York, I Love You '09
Black Swan '10
Hesher '10
No Strings Attached '11
Thor '11
Your Highness '11
Thor: The Dark World '13
Knight of Cups '15
Jackie '16
Jane Got a Gun '16
A Tale of Love and Darkness '16
Song to Song '17
Annihilation '18
Vox Lux '18
The Death and Life of John F. Donovan '19
Lucy in the Sky '19

Richard Portnow (1947-)
Good Morning, Vietnam '87
Meet the Hollowheads '89
Say Anything '89
Kindergarten Cop '90
Barton Fink '91
Sister Act '92
S.F.W. '94
Trial by Jury '94
Man of the House '95
Going Postal '98
Desert Thunder '99
Ghost Dog: The Way of the Samurai '99
The Substitute 3: Winner Takes All '99
Witness Protection '99
The Ghost of Spoon River '00
Happy Accidents '00
Double Bang '01
Double Down '01
Find Me Guilty '06
The Indian '07
Perfect Stranger '07
Tony n' Tina's Wedding '07

Elika Portnoy
Tricks of a Woman '08
Immigration Tango '11
Assassin's Bullet '12

Brian Posehn (1966-)
Pom Poko '94 (V)
The Devil's Rejects '05
The Haunted World of El Superbeasto '09 (V)
Uncle Nick '15

Nicola Posener
Mythica 2: The Darkspore '15
Mythica: A Quest for Heroes '15
Mythica: The Necromancer '15

Parker Posey (1968-)
Armistead Maupin's Tales of the City '93
Dazed and Confused '93
Party Girl '94
Sleep with Me '94
The Doom Generation '95
Frisk '95
Kicking and Screaming '95
Basquiat '96
The Daytrippers '96
Drunks '96
Waiting for Guffman '96
Armistead Maupin's More Tales of the City '97 (C)
Clockwatchers '97
The House of Yes '97
Henry Fool '98
You've Got Mail '98
Best in Show '00
Scream 3 '00
The Anniversary Party '01
Josie and the Pussycats '01
Personal Velocity: Three Portraits '02
The Sweetest Thing '02
The Event '03
A Mighty Wind '03
Blade: Trinity '04
Laws of Attraction '04
Adam & Steve '05
Fay Grim '06
For Your Consideration '06
The Oh in Ohio '06
Superman Returns '06
Broken English '07
The Eye '08
Spring Breakdown '08
Happy Tears '09
Inside Out '11
Hemingway & Gelhorn '12
And Now a Word From Our Sponsor '13
Highland Park '13
Grace of Monaco '14
Mascots '16
Columbus '17

Tyler Posey (1991-)
Inside Out '05
Veritas: Prince of Truth '07
Legendary '10
White Frog '12
Truth or Dare '18

Markie Post (1950-)
Scene of the Crime '85
Tricks of the Trade '88
I've Been Waiting for You '98
There's Something about Mary '98
Holiday in Handcuffs '07

Mikey Post
Rest Stop '06
Rest Stop: Don't Look Back '08

William Post, Jr. (1901-89)
Sherlock Holmes and the Secret Weapon '42
Ship Ahoy '42
House on 92nd Street '45
Call Northside 777 '48

Pete Postlethwaite (1946-2011)
A Private Function '84
Distant Voices, Still Lives '88
To Kill a Priest '89
Hamlet '90
The Last of the Mohicans '92
Split Second '92
Waterland '92
In the Name of the Father '93
Martin Chuzzlewit '94
Sharpe's Company '94
Sharpe's Enemy '94
Suite 16 '94
The Usual Suspects '95
Brassed Off '96
Crimetime '96
Dragonheart '96
James and the Giant Peach '96 (V)
William Shakespeare's Romeo and Juliet '96
Amistad '97
Brute '97
The Lost World: Jurassic Park 2 '97
The Serpent's Kiss '97
Among Giants '98
Alice in Wonderland '99
Animal Farm '99
Butterfly Collectors '99
When the Sky Falls '99
Cowboy Up '00
The Shipping News '01
Between Strangers '02
Dark Water '02
Triggermen '02
Gone Dark '03
Shattered City: The Halifax Explosion '03
Strange Bedfellows '04
Aeon Flux '05
The Constant Gardener '05
Red Mercury '05
Ghost Son '06
The Omen '06
Closing the Ring '07
Valley of the Heart's Delight '07
The Town '10
Killing Bono '11

Tom Poston (1921-2007)
Zotz! '62
Soldier in the Rain '63
Cold Turkey '71
Up the Academy '80
Carbon Copy '81
Krippendorf's Tribe '98
The Story of Us '99
Beethoven's 5th '03
The Princess Diaries 2: Royal Engagement '04

Victor Potel (1889-1947)
Anna Christie '23
Doughboys '30
Paradise Island '30
Miracle of Morgan's Creek '44

Franka Potente (1974-)
Run Lola Run '98
Anatomy '00
The Princess and the Warrior '00
Blow '01
Storytelling '01
All I Want '02
The Bourne Identity '02
I Love Your Work '03
The Bourne Supremacy '04
Eichmann '07
Romulus, My Father '07
Che '08
Shanghai '09
The Sinking of the Laconia '10

Christian Potenza (1972-)
Hendrix '00
Reel Love '11

Brian Poth (1975-)
Venomous '01
Dog Gone Love '03
Angel of Death '09

Alex Potocean
4 Months, 3 Weeks and 2 Days '07
The Way Back '10

Chris Potter (1960-)
The Waiting Game '98
Arachnid '01
The Pacifier '05
Thrill of the Kill '06
She Drives Me Crazy '07
The Good Witch '08
The Good Witch's Garden '09
The Good Witch's Gift '10
The Good Witch's Family '11
The Good Witch's Charm '12

Madeleine Potter (1958-)
The Bostonians '84
Hello Again '87
Bloodhounds of Broadway '89
Slaves of New York '89
Two Evil Eyes '90
The Golden Bowl '00
Caught in the Act '04
The White Countess '05

Martin Potter (1944-)
Fellini Satyricon '69
The Only Way '70

Monica Potter (1971-)
Con Air '97
Without Limits '97
A Cool, Dry Place '98
Patch Adams '98
The Very Thought of You '98
Along Came a Spider '01
Head Over Heels '01
I'm with Lucy '02
Saw '04
Lower Learning '08
The Last House on the Left '09

Ryan Potter (1995-)
Big Hero 6 '14 (V)
Underdog Kids '15
Running for Grace '18

Andrew Lee Potts (1979-)
Dead Fish '04
Return to House on Haunted Hill '07
Alice '09
The Hatching '16

Annie Potts (1952-)
Corvette Summer '78
King of the Gypsies '78
Crimes of Passion '84
Ghostbusters '84
It Came Upon a Midnight Clear '84
Jumpin' Jack Flash '86
Pretty in Pink '86
Ghostbusters 2 '89
Who's Harry Crumb? '89
Texasville '90
Toy Story '95 (V)
Toy Story 2 '99 (V)
Defending Our Kids: The Julie Posey Story '03
Elvis Has Left the Building '04
Queen Sized '08
Marry Me '10
Toy Story 4 '19

Her Fatal Flaw '06
Kraken: Tentacles of the Deep '06
Hush Little Baby '07
What Love Is '07
Brotherhood of Blood '08
Journey to the Center of the Earth '08
Mongolian Death Worm '10
Soda Springs '11
F6 Twister '12
June '15
The Last Heist '16

George Pravda (1918-85)
Frankenstein Must Be Destroyed '69
The Duchess of Duke Street '78

Joana Preiss
Inside Paris '06
Boarding Gate '07
Raw '17

Wolfgang Preiss (1910-2002)
Mill of the Stone Women '60
The Thousand Eyes of Dr. Mabuse '60
The Return of Dr. Mabuse '61
The Invisible Dr. Mabuse '62
Testament of Dr. Mabuse '62
The Mad Executioners '65
The Train '65
Von Ryan's Express '65
Hannibal Brooks '69
Raid on Rommel '71
A Bridge Too Far '77

June Preisser (1920-84)
Babes in Arms '39
Judge Hardy and Son '39
Gallant Sons '40
Strike Up the Band '40

Albert Prejean (1893-1979)
Italian Straw Hat '27
Under the Roofs of Paris '29
Princess Tam Tam '35

Otto Preminger (1906-86)
Margin for Error '43
They Got Me Covered '43
Stalag 17 '53
The Hobbit '78 (V)

Luis Prendes (1913-98)
The Mighty Ursus '61
Ursus in the Valley of the Lions '62
White Comanche '68

Jordan Prentice (1973-)
Weirdsville '07
In Bruges '08
The Night Before the Night Before Christmas '10
The 11th Hour '14

Paula Prentiss
Where the Boys Are '60
Bachelor in Paradise '61
The Honeymoon Machine '61
The Horizontal Lieutenant '62
Follow the Boys '63
Man's Favorite Sport? '63
The World of Henry Orient '64
In Harm's Way '65
What's New Pussycat? '65
Catch-22 '70
Born to Win '71
Last of the Red Hot Lovers '72
The Parallax View '74
The Stepford Wives '75
The Black Marble '79
Friendship, Secrets and Lies '79
Saturday the 14th '81
Mrs. Winterbourne '96
Hard Four '07

Laura Prepon (1980-)
Slackers '02
Lightning Bug '04
Come Early Morning '06
Karla '06
Iris Johansen's The Killing Game '11
The Kitchen '12
Lay the Favorite '12
The Hero '17

Guy Prescott (1914-98)
The Pharaoh's Curse '57
The Hypnotic Eye '60

Judy Prescott
Hit and Runway '01
Islander '06

Robert Prescott
Bachelor Party '84
Real Genius '85
Michael Clayton '07

Micheline Presle (1922-)
The Fantastic Night '42
Devil in the Flesh '46
American Guerrilla in the Philippines '50
If a Man Answers '62
The Prize '63
Hail Mafia '65
The King of Hearts '66
A Slightly Pregnant Man '79
I Want to Go Home '89
A Chef in Love '96
Bad Company '99
Transfixed '01

Brian Presley (1977-)
Guarding Eddy '04
Home of the Brave '06
Borderland '07
Touchback '11

Elvis Presley (1935-77)
Love Me Tender '56
Jailhouse Rock '57
Loving You '57
King Creole '58
Flaming Star '60
G.I. Blues '60
Follow That Dream '61
Wild in the Country '61
Blue Hawaii '62
Girls! Girls! Girls! '62
Kid Galahad '62
Fun in Acapulco '63
It Happened at the World's Fair '63
Viva Las Vegas '63
Kissin' Cousins '64
Roustabout '64
Frankie and Johnny '65
Girl Happy '65
Harum Scarum '65
Tickle Me '65
Paradise, Hawaiian Style '66
Spinout '66
Clambake '67
Double Trouble '67
Easy Come, Easy Go '67
Live a Little, Love a Little '68
Speedway '68
Stay Away, Joe '68
Change of Habit '69
Charro! '69
The Trouble with Girls (and How to Get into It) '69
This Is Elvis '81

Priscilla Presley (1945-)
The Naked Gun: From the Files of Police Squad '88
The Adventures of Ford Fairlane '90
Naked Gun 2 1/2: The Smell of Fear '91
Naked Gun 33 1/3: The Final Insult '94

Harve Presnell (1933-2009)
The Unsinkable Molly Brown '64
When the Boys Meet the Girls '65
Paint Your Wagon '69
Fargo '96
Larger Than Life '96
The Whole Wide World '96
Face/Off '97
Julian Po '97
A Bright Shining Lie '98
Patch Adams '98
Saving Private Ryan '98
Family Man '00
The Legend of Bagger Vance '00
Escanaba in da Moonlight '01
Jackie, Ethel, Joan: The Kennedy Women '01
Mr. Deeds '02
Old School '03
Super Sucker '03
Flags of Our Fathers '06
Bait Shop '08

Nathalie Press (1980-)
My Summer of Love '05
Red Road '06
In Tranzit '07
Nightwatching '07
Fifty Dead Men Walking '08

Jaime Pressly (1977-)
Absolution '97
Poison Ivy 3: The New Seduction '97
Ringmaster '98
100 Girls '00
Poor White Trash '00
Joe Dirt '01
Not Another Teen Movie '01
Ticker '01
Tomcats '01
Survival Island '02
Karate Dog '04
Torque '04
Bachelor Party Vegas '05
Cruel World '05
DOA: Dead or Alive '06
Dr. Seuss' Horton Hears a Who! '08 (V)
I Love You, Man '09
Beauty & the Briefcase '10
Smoke Screen '10
Venus and Vegas '10
The Oogieloves in the Big Balloon Adventure '12
A Haunted House 2 '14
Making the Rules '14

Lawrence Pressman (1939-)
The Hellstrom Chronicle '71
Shaft '71
Winter Kill '74
The Man in the Glass Booth '75
Rich Man, Poor Man '76
The Gathering '77
The Trial of Lee Harvey Oswald '77
The Gathering: Part 2 '79
Rehearsal for Murder '82
The Winds of War '83
The Deliberate Stranger '86
Hanoi Hilton '87
White Hot: The Mysterious Murder of Thelma Todd '91
Angus '95
The Late Shift '96
Sunchaser '96
Trial and Error '96
The Maker '98
Mighty Joe Young '98
American Pie '99
American Wedding '03
DC 9/11: Time of Crisis '04
American Dreamz '06
The Far Side of Jericho '06

Jason Presson (1971-)
The Stone Boy '84
Explorers '85
The Lady in White '88
Saturday the 14th Strikes Back '88

Jude Gerard Prest
Airline Disaster '10
Mega Piranha '10

Jo Prestia (1960-)
The Dreamlife of Angels '98
Irreversible '02

Billy Preston (1946-2006)
Let It Be '70
Blame It on the Night '84

Carrie Preston (1967-)
Transamerica '05
Lovely by Surprise '07
Towelhead '07
Doubt '08
Ready? OK! '08
Duplicity '09
That Evening Sun '09
A Bag of Hammers '11
5 Flights Up '15

Cynthia (Cyndy, Cindy) Preston (1968-)
The Darkside '87
Pin. . . '88
Prom Night 3: The Last Kiss '89
Black Fox: The Price of Peace '94
The Ultimate Weapon '97
Premonition '98
Total Recall 2070: Machine Dreams '99
Facing the Enemy '00
The Thin Blue Lie '00
The Event '03
Nanny Insanity '06
Lone Rider '08

J.A. Preston (1957-)
The Spook Who Sat by the Door '73
Body Heat '81
Remo Williams: The Adventure Begins '85
Fire Birds '90
A Few Good Men '92
Harvest of Fire '95

Kelly Preston (1962-2020)
Metalstorm: The Destruction of Jared Syn '83
Christine '84
Mischief '85
Secret Admirer '85
52 Pick-Up '86
SpaceCamp '86
Amazon Women on the Moon '87
Love at Stake '87
Spellbinder '88
Twins '88
Only You '92
Cheyenne Warrior '94
Love Is a Gun '94
From Dusk Till Dawn '95
Addicted to Love '96
Citizen Ruth '96
Jerry Maguire '96
Nothing to Lose '96
Holy Man '98
Jack Frost '98
Daddy & Them '99
For Love of the Game '99
Bar Hopping '00
Battlefield Earth '00
Dr. Seuss' The Cat in the Hat '03
View from the Top '03
What a Girl Wants '03
Convicted '04
Eulogy '04
Sky High '05
Broken Bridges '06
Death Sentence '07
The Tenth Circle '08
Old Dogs '09
Casino Jack '10
The Last Song '10
Gotti '18

Mike (Michael) Preston (1938-)
The Road Warrior '82
Metalstorm: The Destruction of Jared Syn '83
Hot Pursuit '84

Robert Preston (1918-87)
Beau Geste '39
Union Pacific '39
Reap the Wild Wind '42
This Gun for Hire '42
Wake Island '42
Whispering Smith '48
The Lady Gambles '49
Tulsa '49
Best of the Badmen '50
Cloudburst '51
My Outlaw Brother '51
Savage Wilderness '55
The Music Man '62
How the West Was Won '63
Island of Love '63
Child's Play '72
Junior Bonner '72
Mame '74
Semi-Tough '77
S.O.B. '81
Rehearsal for Murder '82
Victor/Victoria '82
The Last Starfighter '84

Wayde Preston (1929-92)
A Long Ride From Hell '68
Today We Kill, Tomorrow We Die '71
Smokey & the Judge '80

Giancarlo Prete (1942-2001)
Street Law '74
Warriors of the Wasteland '83

Daniel Prevost (1939-)
The Dinner Game '98
Whatever You Say '02

Marie Prevost (1898-1937)
The Marriage Circle '24
Getting Gertie's Garter '27
The Flying Fool '29
Ladies of Leisure '30
Paid '30
Party Girl '30
Hell Divers '31
The Sin of Madelon Claudet '31
Sporting Blood '31
Three Wise Girls '32
Hands Across the Table '35
Ten Laps to Go '36

Augustus Prew (1987-)
The Secret of Moonacre '08
Charlie St. Cloud '10
Copperhead '13

Alessandro Preziosi (1973-)
The Lark Farm '07
Loose Cannons '10

Alan Price (1941-)
Don't Look Back '67
O Lucky Man! '73
Oh, Alfie '75

Connor Price (1994-)
Cinderella Man '05
Booky's Crush '09
Cancel Christmas '11

Dennis Price (1915-73)
A Canterbury Tale '44
Echo Murders '45
Caravan '46
The Magic Bow '47
Kind Hearts and Coronets '49
I'll Never Forget You '51
Eight Witnesses '54
She Played With Fire '57
The Naked Truth '58
The Millionairess '60
School for Scoundrels '60
Tunes of Glory '60
Victim '61
Kill or Cure '62
What a Carve-Up! '62
The V.I.P.'s '63
The Wrong Arm of the Law '63
Murder Most Foul '65
The Horror of Frankenstein '70
Venus in Furs '70
Twins of Evil '71
Pulp '72
Rites of Frankenstein '72
The Screaming Dead '72
Horror Hospital '73
Theatre of Blood '73

Felicity Price
Wish You Were Here '12
The Duel '16

Lindsay Price (1976-)
No Turning Back '01
Club Dread '04
The Secrets of the Summer House '08

Marc Price (1968-)
Trick or Treat '86
The Rescue '88
Killer Tomatoes Eat France '91

Molly Price (1966-)
Jersey Girl '92
Kiss Me, Guido '97
Chasing Sleep '00
The Devil You Know '05
What Goes Up '09
How Do You Know '10

Nancy Price (1880-1970)
The Speckled Band '31
Madonna of the Seven Moons '45
The Three Weird Sisters '48

Oliver Price
Parasite '03
Dark Corners '06

Richard Price (1949-)
Wanderers '79
Shocker '89
Night and the City '92 (C)
Ransom '96 (C)

Stanley Price (1892-1955)
Rimfire '49
The Invisible Monster '50

Vincent Price (1911-93)
The Private Lives of Elizabeth & Essex '39
The Tower of London '39
Brigham Young: Frontiersman '40
The House of the Seven Gables '40
Hudson's Bay '40
The Invisible Man Returns '40
The Song of Bernadette '43
The Keys of the Kingdom '44
Laura '44
Wilson '44
Leave Her to Heaven '45
A Royal Scandal '45
Dragonwyck '46
Shock! '46
The Long Night '47
Abbott and Costello Meet Frankenstein '48 (V)
The Bribe '48
The Three Musketeers '48
Up in Central Park '48
Champagne for Caesar '50
Baron of Arizona '51
His Kind of Woman '51
House of Wax '53
Casanova's Big Night '54
The Mad Magician '54
Serenade '56
The Ten Commandments '56
While the City Sleeps '56
Story of Mankind '57
The Fly '58
House on Haunted Hill '58
The Bat '59
The Big Circus '59
Return of the Fly '59
The Tingler '59
The Fall of the House of Usher '60
Master of the World '61
The Pit and the Pendulum '61
Confessions of an Opium Eater '62
Tales of Terror '62
Tower of London '62
Beach Party '63
Diary of a Madman '63
The Haunted Palace '63
The Raven '63
Twice-Told Tales '63
The Comedy of Terrors '64
The Last Man on Earth '64
Nefertiti, Queen of the Nile '64
Tomb of Ligeia '64
Masque of the Red Death '65
Dr. Goldfoot and the Bikini Machine '66
The House of 1000 Dolls '67
The Jackals '67
The Conqueror Worm '68
More Dead Than Alive '68
Spirits of the Dead '68 (N)
The Oblong Box '69
The Trouble with Girls (and How to Get into It) '69

Ainslie Pryor (1921-58)
The Girl in the Red Velvet Swing *'55*
The Last Hunt *'56*
Ransom! *'56*

Nicholas Pryor (1935-)
The Happy Hooker *'75*
Smile *'75*
Gumball Rally *'76*
Damien: Omen 2 *'78*
The Fish that Saved Pittsburgh *'79*
East of Eden *'80*
Last Song *'80*
Risky Business *'83*
The Falcon and the Snowman *'85*
Into Thin Air *'85*
Morgan Stewart's Coming Home *'87*
Brain Dead *'89*
Hoffa *'92*
Hail Caesar *'94*
American Tragedy *'00*

Richard Pryor (1940-2005)
The Busy Body *'67*
Wild in the Streets *'68*
Black Brigade *'69*
Dynamite Chicken *'70*
Lady Sings the Blues *'72*
Hit! *'73*
The Mack *'73*
Uptown Saturday Night *'74*
Adios Amigo *'75*
Bingo Long Traveling All-Stars & Motor Kings *'76*
Car Wash *'76*
Silver Streak *'76*
Greased Lightning *'77*
Which Way Is Up? *'77*
Blue Collar *'78*
California Suite *'78*
The Wiz *'78*
Stir Crazy *'80*
Wholly Moses! *'80*
Bustin' Loose *'81*
Some Kind of Hero *'82*
The Toy *'82*
Superman 3 *'83*
Brewster's Millions *'85*
Critical Condition *'86*
Jo Jo Dancer, Your Life Is Calling *'86*
Moving *'88*
Harlem Nights *'89*
See No Evil, Hear No Evil *'89*
Another You *'91*
Lost Highway *'96*
Trigger Happy *'96 (C)*

Roger Pryor (1901-74)
Belle of the Nineties *'34*
Lady by Choice *'34*
Headline Woman *'35*
To Beat the Band *'35*
Missing Girls *'36*
Sitting On the Moon *'36*
The Man They Could Not Hang *'39*
The Lone Wolf Meets a Lady *'40*
Flying Blind *'41*
Gambling Daughters *'41*
Power Dive *'41*
South of Panama *'41*
Identity Unknown *'45*

Wojtek Psoniak (1942-)
See Wojciech Pszoniak

Wojciech Pszoniak (1942-)
Land of Promise *'74*
Danton *'82*
Angry Harvest *'85*
Chaos *'01*

Wojtek Pszoniak (1942-)
See Wojciech Pszoniak

Lou Taylor Pucci (1985-)
Personal Velocity: Three Portraits *'02*
The Chumscrubber *'05*
Empire Falls *'05*
Thumbsucker *'05*
The Go-Getter *'07*
Explicit Ills *'08*
The Answer Man *'09*
Brief Interviews With Hideous Men *'09*
Carriers *'09*
Horsemen *'09*
The Informers *'09*
Brotherhood *'10*
The Music Never Stopped *'11*
Evil Dead *'13*
Spring *'15*

Vladimir Pucholt (1942-)
Black Peter *'63*
Loves of a Blonde *'65*

Danny Pudi
Road Trip: Beer Pong *'09*
Smurfs: The Lost Village *'17 (V)*
The Tiger Hunter *'17*

Tito Puente (1925-2000)
Radio Days *'87*
The Mambo Kings *'92*

Florence Pugh (1996-)
Lady Macbeth *'17*
Outlaw King *'18*
Fighting with My Family *'19*
Little Women *'19*
Midsommar *'19*

Robert Pugh (1950-)
Danger UXB *'81*
Nighthawks *'81*
Thicker Than Water *'93*
Priest *'94*
A Mind to Murder *'96*
Enigma *'01*
Sword of Honour *'01*
The Intended *'02*
Undertaking Betty *'02*
Master and Commander: The Far Side of the World *'03*
Bloodlines *'05*
Kinky Boots *'06*
Longford *'06*
Framed *'10*

Willard Pugh (1959-)
The Color Purple *'85*
A Rage in Harlem *'91*
Eddie Presley *'92*
CB4: The Movie *'93*
Puppet Master 5: The Final Chapter *'94*
Alien Storm *'12*

Frank Puglia (1892-1975)
Romola *'25*
Charlie Chan in Panama *'40*
The Fatal Hour *'40*
Billy the Kid *'41*
Casablanca *'42*
Ali Baba and the Forty Thieves *'43*
For Whom the Bell Tolls *'43*
Without Reservations *'46*
Captain Carey, U.S.A. *'50*
The Bandits of Corsica *'53*
The Steel Lady *'53*
The Burning Hills *'56*
Serenade *'56*
20 Million Miles to Earth *'57*
Girls! Girls! Girls! *'62*

Aldo Puglisi (1935-)
Marriage Italian Style *'64*
Seduced and Abandoned *'64*

Ian Puleston-Davies (1958-)
Strange Relations *'02*
Ghostboat *'06*
Tess of the D'Urbervilles *'08*

Benjamin Pullen (1972-)
An Ideal Husband *'99*
Intern *'00*

Keisha Knight Pulliam (1979-)
What About Your Friends: Weekend Getaway *'02*
Motives *'03*
Christmas at Water's Edge *'04*
Beauty Shop *'05*
The Gospel *'05*
Death Toll *'07*
Madea Goes to Jail *'09*

Bill Pullman (1953-)
Ruthless People *'86*
The Serpent and the Rainbow *'87*
Spaceballs *'87*
The Accidental Tourist *'88*
Rocket Gibraltar *'88*
Brain Dead *'89*
Cold Feet *'89*
Sibling Rivalry *'90*
Bright Angel *'91*
Going Under *'91*
Liebestraum *'91*
Crazy in Love *'92*
The Favor *'92*
A League of Their Own *'92*
Newsies *'92*
Singles *'92*
Malice *'93*
Nervous Ticks *'93*
Sleepless in Seattle *'93*
Sommersby *'93*
The Last Seduction *'94*
Wyatt Earp *'94*
Casper *'95*
Mr. Wrong *'95*
While You Were Sleeping *'95*
Independence Day *'96*
Lost Highway *'96*
Mistrial *'96*
The End of Violence *'97*
Zero Effect *'97*
Brokedown Palace *'99*
The Guilty *'99*
Lake Placid *'99*
Spy Games *'99*
The Virginian *'99*
Lucky Numbers *'00*
Titan A.E. *'00 (V)*
Ignition *'01*
Igby Goes Down *'02*
Rick *'03*
29 Palms *'03*
The Grudge *'04*
Dear Wendy *'05*
Scary Movie 4 *'06*
You Kill Me *'07*
Nobel Son *'08*
Phoebe in Wonderland *'08*
Surveillance *'08*
Peacock *'09*
The Killer Inside Me *'10*
Rio Sex Comedy *'10*
Bringing Up Bobby *'11*
Too Big to Fail *'11*
Lola Versus *'12*
May in Summer *'13*
May in the Summer *'13*
The Equalizer *'14*
Independence Day: Resurgence *'16*
The Ballad of Lefty Brown *'17*
LBJ *'17*
Walking Out *'17*
The Equalizer 2 *'18*
Dark Waters *'19*

Lewis Pullman (1993-)
The Strangers: Prey at Night *'18*
Them That Follow *'19*

Lindsay Pulsipher
Hatfields & McCoys *'12*
The Rambler *'13*
God Bless the Broken Road *'18*

Lara Pulver (1980-)
Legacy *'10*
Underworld: Blood Wars *'16*

Lucy Punch (1977-)
Being Julia *'04*
St. Trinian's *'07*
(Untitled) *'09*
Dinner for Schmucks *'10*
You Will Meet a Tall Dark Stranger *'10*
Bad Teacher *'11*
A Good Old Fashioned Orgy *'11*
A Little Bit of Heaven *'11*
Take Me Home Tonight *'11*
The Giant Mechanical Man *'12*
Someone Marry Barry *'12*
Stand Up Guys *'12*
Cottage Country *'13*

Bernard Punsley (1923-2004)
Dead End *'37*
Angels with Dirty Faces *'38*
Crime School *'38*
Dead End Kids: Little Tough Guy *'38*
Angels Wash Their Faces *'39*
Hell's Kitchen *'39*
Junior G-Men *'40*
Junior G-Men of the Air *'42*

Bruno Punzalan
Mad Doctor of Blood Island *'68*
Beast of Blood *'71*

Mario Pupella
Angela *'02*
The Sicilian Girl *'09*

Romano Puppo (?-1994)
The Big Alligator River *'79*
The Great Alligator *'81*

Dick Purcell (1908-44)
Navy Blues *'37*
Slim *'37*
Blackwell's Island *'39*
Flying Blind *'41*
King of the Zombies *'41*
No Hands on the Clock *'41*
Captain America *'44*

Dominic Purcell (1970-)
Scenes of the Crime *'01*
Blade: Trinity *'04*
3-Way *'04*
The Gravedancers *'06*
Primeval *'07*
Blood Creek *'09*
Prison Break: The Final Break *'09*
House of the Rising Sun *'11*
Killer Elite *'11*
Straw Dogs *'11*
Hijacked *'12*
Ice Soldiers *'13*
Officer Down *'13*
Vikingdom *'13*
The Bag Man *'14*
A Fighting Man *'14*
In the Name of the King 3: The Last Mission *'14*

Dylan Purcell (1983-)
Clawed: The Legend of Sasquatch *'05*
Parasomnia *'08*

Irene Purcell (1896-1972)
The Man in Possession *'31*
The Passionate Plumber *'32*

James Purcell
Another Woman *'94*
Sabotage *'96*

Leah Purcell (1970-)
Lantana *'01*
Somersault *'04*
The Proposition *'05*
Jindabyne *'06*

Lee Purcell (1957-)
Adam at 6 a.m. *'70*
Dirty Little Billy *'72*
The Witching *'72*
Mr. Majestyk *'74*
The Amazing Howard Hughes *'77*
Big Wednesday *'78*
Summer of Fear *'78*
Kenny Rogers as the Gambler *'80*
Stir Crazy *'80*
Homework *'82*
Eddie Macon's Run *'83*
Valley Girl *'83*
Jailbait: Betrayed By Innocence *'86*
The Incredible Hulk Returns *'88*

Noel Purcell (1900-85)
Captain Boycott *'47*
Appointment With Venus *'51*
Encore *'52*
Grand National Night *'53*
Land of Fury *'55*
Lust for Life *'56*
The Rising of the Moon *'57*
Merry Andrew *'58*
No Kidding *'60*
Mutiny on the Bounty *'62*

Reginald Purdell (1896-1953)
Candles at Nine *'44*
Love Story *'44*
Two Thousand Women *'44*
Brighton Rock *'47*

Edmund Purdom (1924-2009)
Athena *'54*
The Egyptian *'54*
The Student Prince *'54*
The King's Thief *'55*
The Prodigal *'55*
Herod the Great *'60*
Nefertiti, Queen of the Nile *'64*
The Yellow Rolls Royce *'64*
Dr. Frankenstein's Castle of Freaks *'74*
Rulers of the City *'76*
Rulers of the City *'77*
Ator the Fighting Eagle *'83*
Don't Open Till Christmas *'84*
After the Fall of New York *'85*

Carolyn Purdy-Gordon (1947-)
Re-Animator *'84*
From Beyond *'86*
Dolls *'87*

James Purefoy
Feast of July *'95*
Catherine Cookson's The Tide of Life *'96*
The Tenant of Wildfell Hall *'96*
A Dance to the Music of Time *'97*
Bedrooms and Hallways *'98*
Dead of Night *'99*
Mansfield Park *'99*
Maybe Baby *'99*
A Knight's Tale *'01*
Resident Evil *'02*
The Mayor of Casterbridge *'03*
George and the Dragon *'04*
Vanity Fair *'04*
Beau Brummell: This Charming Man *'06*
The Summit *'08*
Ironclad *'11*
John Carter *'12*
Wicked Blood *'13*
Momentum *'15*
Equity *'16*
Fisherman's Friends *'19*

Om Puri (1950-2017)
Gandhi *'82*
City of Joy *'92*
In Custody *'94*
Wolf *'94*
The Ghost and the Darkness *'96*
My Son the Fanatic *'97*
Such a Long Journey *'98*
East Is East *'99*
The Mystic Masseur *'01*
Code 46 *'03*
Charlie Wilson's War *'07*
The Hundred-Foot Journey *'14*

Linda Purl
Crazy Mama *'75*
Eleanor & Franklin *'76*
Little Ladies of the Night *'77*
Testimony of Two Men *'77*
The Manions of America *'81*
Visiting Hours *'82*
The Last Days of Pompeii *'84*
Viper *'88*
Spies, Lies and Naked Thighs *'91*
Mighty Joe Young *'98*
Perfect Tenant *'99*
Fear of the Dark *'02*
Criminal Intent *'05*
Stalked at 17 *'12*

Ella Purnell
Never Let Me Go *'10*
Intruders *'11*

Alycia Purrott (1983-)
Jailbait! *'00*
The Cutting Edge 3: Chasing the Dream *'08*

Alexandra Purvis (1988-)
Poltergeist: The Legacy *'96*
Ronnie and Julie *'97*
A Song From the Heart *'99*
Now & Forever *'02*

Keely Purvis (1992-)
X2: X-Men United *'03*
Girl Fight *'11*

Roberto Purvis (1971-)
Red Riding Hood *'03*
The Moon & the Stars *'07*

Jeff Pustil
The Killing Man *'94*
Real Time *'08*

John Putch (1961-)
Angel Dusted *'81*
Jaws 3 *'83*
Curfew *'88*
Camp Nowhere *'94*
Same River Twice *'97*
The Souler Opposite *'97*

Hanna Putnam
Nightmare Man *'06*
Feast 2: Sloppy Seconds *'08*

Bruno Putzulu (1967-)
L'Appat *'94*
In Praise of Love *'01*
Lulu *'02*
Monsieur N. *'03*

Denver Pyle (1920-97)
Too Late for Tears *'49*
Oklahoma Annie *'51*
Johnny Guitar *'53*
Ride Clear of Diablo *'54*
To Hell and Back *'55*
Top Gun *'55*
Naked Hills *'56*
Seventh Cavalry *'56*
Fort Massacre *'58*
Cast a Long Shadow *'59*
The Horse Soldiers *'59*
King of the Wild Stallions *'59*
The Alamo *'60*
The Man Who Shot Liberty Valance *'62*
Mail Order Bride *'63*
The Rounders *'65*
Shenandoah *'65*
Bonnie & Clyde *'67*
Bandolero! *'68*
Escape to Witch Mountain *'75*
Hawmps! *'76*
Legend of the Northwest *'78*
Maverick *'94 (C)*

Missi Pyle (1972-)
As Good As It Gets *'97*
Galaxy Quest *'99*
Trick *'99*
Josie and the Pussycats *'01*
BachelorMan *'03*
Big Fish *'03*
Bringing Down the House *'03*
Exposed *'03*
Along Came Polly *'04*
Anchorman: The Legend of Ron Burgundy *'04*
Dodgeball: A True Underdog Story *'04*
50 First Dates *'04*
Soul Plane *'04*
Charlie and the Chocolate Factory *'05*
Alex Rider: Operation Stormbreaker *'06*
Just My Luck *'06*
American Crude *'07*
Entry Level *'07*
Live! *'07*
Harold & Kumar Escape from Guantanamo Bay *'08*
Meet Market *'08*
Pretty Ugly People *'08*
Soccer Mom *'08*
Spring Breakdown *'08*

Taking Chances *'09*
Barry Munday *'10*
Miss Nobody *'10*
The Artist *'11*
A Cinderella Story: Once Upon a Song *'11*
Gone Girl *'14*
A Haunted House 2 *'14*
Uncle Nick *'15*
Captain Fantastic *'16*
Emma's Chance *'16*
Miles *'17*
Traffik *'18*

Natasha Pyne
The Devil-Ship Pirates *'64*
Madhouse *'74*

John Pyper-Ferguson (1964-)
Bird on a Wire *'90*
Showdown at Williams Creek *'91*
Killer Image *'92*
Drive *'96*
Hard Core Logo *'96*
For Richer or Poorer *'97*
The Waiting Game *'98*
I'll Take You There *'99*
Black Dawn *'05*
Everest *'07*
Conviction *'10*
A Night for Dying Tigers *'10*
Born 2 Race *'11*
Hannah's Law *'12*

Maggie Q (1979-)
Naked Weapon *'03*
Mission: Impossible 3 *'06*
Balls of Fury *'07*
Live Free or Die Hard *'07*
Deception *'08*
Three Kingdoms: Resurrection of the Dragon *'08*
New York, I Love You *'09*
Operation: Endgame *'10*
Priest *'11*
Divergent *'14*
Fantasy Island *'20*

Q-Tip (1970-)
Love Goggles *'99*
She Hate Me *'04*
Beats, Rhymes and Life: The Travels of a Tribe Called Quest *'11*

Gregory (GQ) Qaiyum (1976-)
See GQ

Shaobo Qin (1982-)
Ocean's Eleven *'01*
Ocean's Twelve *'04*
Ocean's Thirteen *'07*

Xu Qing (1969-)
Life on a String *'90*
The Emperor's Shadow *'96*

Yun Qu
Jet Li's Fearless *'06*
Stomp the Yard *'07*

John Quade (1938-2009)
The Last Hard Men *'76*
The Outlaw Josey Wales *'76*
Peter Lundy and the Medicine Hat Stallion *'77*
Fury to Freedom: The Life Story of Raul Ries *'85*
The Tracker *'88*
And You Thought Your Parents Were Weird! *'91*

Stephen Quadros
Shock 'Em Dead *'90*
C.I.A.: Code Name Alexa *'92*

Dennis Quaid (1954-)
I Never Promised You a Rose Garden *'77*
September 30, 1955 *'77*
The Seniors *'78*
Breaking Away *'79*
The Long Riders *'80*
All Night Long *'81*
Bill *'81*
Caveman *'81*
The Night the Lights Went Out in Georgia *'81*
Bill: On His Own *'83*
Jaws 3 *'83*
The Right Stuff *'83*
Tough Enough *'83*
Dreamscape *'84*
Enemy Mine *'85*
The Big Easy *'87*
Innerspace *'87*
Suspect *'87*
D.O.A. *'88*
Everybody's All American *'88*
Great Balls of Fire *'89*
Come See the Paradise *'90*
Postcards from the Edge *'90*
Flesh and Bone *'93*
Undercover Blues *'93*
Wilder Napalm *'93*
Wyatt Earp *'94*
Something to Talk About *'95*
Dragonheart *'96*
Gang Related *'96*
Switchback *'97*
The Parent Trap *'98*
Playing by Heart *'98*
Savior *'98*
Any Given Sunday *'99*
Frequency *'00*
Traffic *'00*
Dinner with Friends *'01*
Far from Heaven *'02*
The Rookie *'02*
Cold Creek Manor *'03*
The Alamo *'04*
The Day After Tomorrow *'04*
Flight of the Phoenix *'04*
In Good Company *'04*
Yours, Mine & Ours *'05*
American Dreamz *'06*
The Express *'08*
Smart People *'08*
Vantage Point *'08*
Battle for Terra *'09 (V)*
G.I. Joe: The Rise of Cobra *'09*
Horsemen *'09*
Pandorum *'09*
Legion *'10*
The Special Relationship *'10*
Footloose *'11*
Soul Surfer *'11*
Beneath the Darkness *'12*
Playing for Keeps *'12*
What to Expect When You're Expecting *'12*
The Words *'12*
Movie 43 *'13*
Truth *'15*
A Dog's Purpose *'17*
I Can Only Imagine *'18*
Kin *'18*
A Dog's Journey *'19*
The Intruder *'19*
Pretenders *'19*

Jack Quaid (1992-)
The Hunger Games *'12*
Ithaca *'16*
Plus One *'19*

Randy Quaid (1950-)
The Last Picture Show *'71*
What's Up, Doc? *'72*
The Last Detail *'73*
Lolly-Madonna XXX *'73*
Paper Moon *'73*
The Apprenticeship of Duddy Kravitz *'74*
Breakout *'75*
Bound for Glory *'76*
Missouri Breaks *'76*
The Choirboys *'77*
Three Warriors *'77*
Midnight Express *'78*
The Last Ride of the Dalton Gang *'79*
Foxes *'80*
The Guyana Tragedy: The Story of Jim Jones *'80*
The Long Riders *'80*
Heartbeeps *'81*
Of Mice and Men *'81*
National Lampoon's Vacation *'83*
The Slugger's Wife *'85*
Fool for Love *'86*
No Man's Land *'87*
The Wraith *'87*
Caddyshack 2 *'88*
Moving *'88*
Bloodhounds of Broadway *'89*
Cold Dog Soup *'89*
National Lampoon's Christmas Vacation *'89*
Out Cold *'89*
Parents *'89*
Days of Thunder *'90*
Quick Change *'90*
Texasville *'90*
Frankenstein *'93*
Freaked *'93*
Bye Bye, Love *'94*
Curse of the Starving Class *'94*
Major League 2 *'94*
The Paper *'94*
Larry McMurtry's Streets of Laredo *'95*
Get On the Bus *'96*
Independence Day *'96*
Kingpin *'96*
Last Dance *'96*
Vegas Vacation *'96*
Hard Rain *'97*
Protector *'97*
P.U.N.K.S. *'98*
Bug Buster *'99*
The Magical Legend of the Leprechauns *'99*
Purgatory *'99*
The Adventures of Rocky & Bullwinkle *'00*
Mail to the Chief *'00*
Sand *'00*
The Thin Blue Lie *'00*
The Day the World Ended *'01*
The Adventures of Pluto Nash *'02*
Frank McKlusky, C.I. *'02*
Black Cadillac *'03*
Carolina *'03*
Grind *'03*
Milwaukee, Minnesota *'03*
National Lampoon's Christmas Vacation 2: Cousin Eddie's Big Island Adventure *'03*
Category 6: Day of Destruction *'04*
Home on the Range *'04 (V)*
Brokeback Mountain *'05*
Category 7: The End of the World *'05*
The Ice Harvest *'05*
Goya's Ghosts *'06*
Real Time *'08*
Balls Out: Gary the Tennis Coach *'09*

John Qualen (1899-1987)
Our Daily Bread *'34*
365 Nights in Hollywood *'34*
Black Fury *'35*
Charlie Chan in Paris *'35*
Angels Over Broadway *'40*
Blondie On a Budget *'40*
The Grapes of Wrath *'40*
His Girl Friday *'40*
Knute Rockne: All American *'40*
The Long Voyage Home *'40*
The Devil & Daniel Webster *'41*
Out of the Fog *'41*
Casablanca *'42*
The Jungle Book *'42*
Larceny, Inc. *'42*
Tortilla Flat *'42*
Swing Shift Maisie *'43*
An American Romance *'44*
Dark Waters *'44*
Captain Kidd *'45*
The Fugitive *'48*
The Scar *'48*
Big Steal *'49*
Woman On the Run *'50*
The High and the Mighty *'54*
Passion *'54*
Sea Chase *'55*
The Searchers *'56*
Revolt in the Big House *'58*
Terror in the Haunted House *'58*
The Man Who Shot Liberty Valance *'62*
7 Faces of Dr. Lao *'63*
Cheyenne Autumn *'64*
I'll Take Sweden *'65*
A Patch of Blue *'65*
Those Calloways *'65*

Margaret Qualley
The Nice Guys *'16*
Novitiate *'17*
Donnybrook *'18*
IO *'19*
Native Son *'19*
Once Upon A Time... In Hollywood *'19*
Seberg *'19*
Strange But True *'19*

DJ Qualls
Road Trip *'00*
Chasing Holden *'01*
Comic Book Villains *'02*
Lone Star State of Mind *'02*
The New Guy *'02*
The Core *'03*
Hustle & Flow *'05*
Little Athens *'05*
I'm Reed Fish *'06*
Delta Farce *'07*
Familiar Strangers *'08*
All About Steve *'09*
Road Trip: Beer Pong *'09*
Last Day of Summer *'10*
Buster's Mal Heart *'17*

Jonathan Ke Quan (1971-)
The Goonies *'85*
Breathing Fire *'91*

Robert Quarry (1925-2009)
Soldier of Fortune *'55*
Crime of Passion *'57*
Count Yorga, Vampire *'70*
WUSA *'70*
The Return of Count Yorga *'71*
Doctor Phibes Rises Again *'72*
Madhouse *'74*
Sugar Hill *'74*
Cyclone *'87*
Phantom Empire *'87*
Warlords *'88*
Alienator *'89*
Evil Spirits *'91*
Teenage Exorcist *'93*

Hugh Quarshie (1954-)
Melissa *'97*
The Church *'98*
Star Wars: Episode 1-The Phantom Menace *'99*
To Walk with Lions *'99*
Conspiracy of Silence *'03*
Small Island *'09 (N)*

Nina Quartero (1908-85)
The Bachelor Father *'31*
The Cyclone Ranger *'35*
The Phantom of Santa Fe *'36*

Philip Quast (1957-)
Napoleon *'96 (V)*
Ultraviolet *'98*
Me & Mrs. Jones *'02*
Introducing the Dwights *'07*
The Devil's Double *'11*

Simon Quaterman
The Scorpion King 2: Rise of a Warrior *'08*
The Devil Inside *'12*

James Quattrochi (1961-)
True Friends *'98*
Wanted *'98*

Anna Quayle (1932-2019)
A Hard Day's Night *'64*
Casino Royale *'67*
Smashing Time *'67*
Chitty Chitty Bang Bang *'68*

Anthony Quayle (1913-89)
Hamlet *'48*
The Wrong Man *'56*
Pursuit of the Graf Spee *'57*
Serious Charge *'59*
Tarzan's Greatest Adventure *'59*
It Takes a Thief *'60*
The Guns of Navarone *'61*
Damn the Defiant *'62*
Lawrence of Arabia *'62*
East of Sudan *'64*
The Fall of the Roman Empire *'64*
Operation Crossbow *'65*
A Study in Terror *'66*
Anne of the Thousand Days *'69*
Before Winter Comes *'69*
MacKenna's Gold *'69*
Everything You Always Wanted to Know about Sex (But Were Afraid to Ask) *'72*
QB VII *'74*
The Tamarind Seed *'74*
Moses *'76*
The Story of David *'76*
21 Hours at Munich *'76*
The Chosen *'77*
The Eagle Has Landed *'77*
Murder by Decree *'79*
Masada *'81*
Lace *'84*
The Last Days of Pompeii *'84*
The Bourne Identity *'88*
Buster *'88*

Queen Kong (1951-)
See Deanna (Dee) Booher

Queen Latifah (1970-)
House Party 2: The Pajama Jam *'91*
Jungle Fever *'91*
My Life *'93*
Hoodlum *'96*
Set It Off *'96*
Sphere *'97*
Living Out Loud *'98*
Mama Flora's Family *'98*
The Bone Collector *'99*
Brown Sugar *'02*
Chicago *'02*
The Country Bears *'02*
Talking to Heaven *'02*
Bringing Down the House *'03*
Scary Movie 3 *'03*
Barbershop 2: Back in Business *'04*
The Cookout *'04*
Taxi *'04*
Beauty Shop *'05*
The Muppets' Wizard of Oz *'05*
Ice Age: The Meltdown *'06 (V)*
Last Holiday *'06*
Stranger Than Fiction *'06*
Arctic Tale *'07 (N)*
Hairspray *'07*
Life Support *'07*
The Perfect Holiday *'07*
Mad Money *'08*
The Secret Life of Bees *'08*
What Happens in Vegas *'08*
Ice Age: Dawn of the Dinosaurs *'09 (V)*
Just Wright *'10*
Valentine's Day *'10*
The Dilemma *'11*
Ice Age: Continental Drift *'12 (V)*
Joyful Noise *'12*
Steel Magnolias *'12*
House of Bodies *'13*
Ice Age: Collision Course *'16*
Girls Trip *'17*

Valerie Quennessen (1957-89)
French Postcards *'79*
Conan the Barbarian *'82*
Summer Lovers *'82*

John Quentin
The Terrorists *'74*
Blue *'93 (N)*
Wittgenstein *'93*
The Stendahl Syndrome *'95*

Rosette Quere (1959-)
See Rosette

Mae Questel (1908-98)
A Majority of One *'56*
It's Only Money *'62*
Who Framed Roger Rabbit *'88 (V)*
National Lampoon's Christmas Vacation *'89*
New York Stories *'89*

Hugues Quester (1948-)
A Tale of Springtime *'89*
Trois Couleurs: Bleu *'93*

Diana Quick (1946-)
The Duellists *'77*
Brideshead Revisited *'81*
The Price of the Bride *'90*
The Leading Man *'96*
Heat of the Sun *'99*
AKA *'02*

Charles Quigley (1906-64)
Charlie Chan's Secret *'35*
A Woman's Face *'41*

Juanita Quigley (1931-)
The Vanishing Virginian *'41*
A Yank at Eton *'42*

Linnea Quigley (1958-)
Cheech and Chong's Nice Dreams *'81*
Nightstalker *'81*
The Black Room *'82*
Savage Streets *'83*
Return of the Living Dead *'85*
Creepozoids *'87*
Nightmare Sisters *'87*
Sorority Babes in the Slimeball Bowl-A-Rama *'87*
Hollywood Chainsaw Hookers *'88*
Night of the Demons *'88*
Vice Academy *'88*
Assault of the Party Nerds *'89*
Vice Academy 2 *'90*
Virgin High *'90*
Innocent Blood *'92*
Pumpkinhead 2: Blood Wings *'94*
Assault of the Party Nerds 2: Heavy Petting Detective *'95*
Jack-O *'95*
Boogie Boy *'98*
Death Mask *'98*
Kolobos *'99*

Pearce Quigley
Millions *'05*
Peterloo *'18*

Rita Quigley (1923-2008)
Susan and God *'40*
The Trap *'46*

Tim Quill
Hamburger Hill *'87*
Hiding Out *'87*
Thou Shalt Not Kill. . .Except *'87*
Staying Together *'89*
Army of Darkness *'92*
A Plumm Summer *'08*

Eddie Quillan (1907-90)
Girl Crazy *'32*
Mutiny on the Bounty *'35*
Big City *'37*
The Mandarin Mystery *'37*
Young Mr. Lincoln *'39*
The Grapes of Wrath *'40*
Flying Blind *'41*
It Ain't Hay *'43*
Move Over, Darling *'63*

Denis Quilley (1927-2003)
Murder on the Orient Express *'74*
In This House of Brede *'75*
Privates on Parade *'84*
A.D. *'85*
Foreign Body *'86*
The Shell Seekers *'89*
A Dangerous Man: Lawrence after Arabia *'91*
Mister Johnson *'91*

Veronica Quilligan (1956-)
Lisztomania *'75*
Danny Boy *'82*
Halfmoon *'95*

Richard Quine (1920-89)
Babes on Broadway *'41*
Dr. Gillespie's New Assistant *'42*
For Me and My Gal *'42*
My Sister Eileen *'42*
Tish *'42*

Kathleen Quinlan
American Graffiti '73
Where Have All the People Gone? '74
Lifeguard '76
Airport '77 '77
I Never Promised You a Rose Garden '77
The Promise '79
Hanky Panky '82
Twilight Zone: The Movie '83
The Last Winter '84
Children of the Night '85
Warning Sign '85
Dreams Lost, Dreams Found '87
Clara's Heart '88
Man Outside '88
Sunset '88
The Doors '91
Last Light '93
Trial by Jury '94
Apollo 13 '95
Breakdown '96
In the Lake of the Woods '96
Lawn Dogs '96
Zeus and Roxanne '96
Event Horizon '97
A Civil Action '98
My Giant '98
The Battle of Shaker Heights '03
El Padrino '04
The Riverman '04
The Hills Have Eyes '06
Breach '07
Harm's Way '07
Humble Pie '07
Made of Honor '08
Elektra Luxx '10
The River Why '10
Horns '13
Chimera Strain '19

Maeve Quinlan (1964-)
Totally Blonde '01
Heart of America '03
Net Games '03
A Boyfriend for Christmas '04
The Drone Virus '04
The Nickel Children '05
Not Easily Broken '09

Abby Quinn
Landline '17
After the Wedding '19

Aidan Quinn (1959-)
Reckless '84
Desperately Seeking Susan '85
An Early Frost '85
The Mission '86
Stakeout '87
Crusoe '89
Perfect Witness '89
Avalon '90
The Handmaid's Tale '90
The Lemon Sisters '90
The Playboys '92
A Private Matter '92
Benny & Joon '93
Blink '93
Legends of the Fall '94
Mary Shelley's Frankenstein '94
The Stars Fell on Henrietta '94
Haunted '95
Commandments '96
Looking for Richard '96
Michael Collins '96
The Assignment '97
In Dreams '98
Practical Magic '98
Music of the Heart '99
Songcatcher '99
This Is My Father '99
Two of Us '00
The Prince and the Pauper '01
Evelyn '02
Stolen Summer '02
Benedict Arnold: A Question of Honor '03
Bobby Jones: Stroke of Genius '04
Convicted '04
Miracle Run '04
Empire Falls '05
Nine Lives '05
Bury My Heart at Wounded Knee '07
Dark Matter '07
Wild Child '08
The Eclipse '09
Handsome Harry '09
A Shine of Rainbows '09
Across the Line: The Exodus of Charlie Wright '10
The 5th Quarter '10
Flipped '10
Jonah Hex '10
Sarah's Key '10
The Greening of Whitney Brown '11
Unknown '11
Allegiance '12
The Horses of McBride '12
If I Were You '12
Rushlights '13
Stay '13

Anthony Quinn (1915-2001)
The Plainsman '37
Waikiki Wedding '37
Union Pacific '39
City for Conquest '40
The Ghost Breakers '40
The Road to Singapore '40
Blood and Sand '41
They Died with Their Boots On '41
The Black Swan '42
Larceny, Inc. '42
The Road to Morocco '42
Guadalcanal Diary '43
The Ox-Bow Incident '43
Buffalo Bill '44
Irish Eyes Are Smiling '44
Back to Bataan '45
Sinbad, the Sailor '47
Tycoon '47
Against All Flags '52
Viva Zapata! '52
The World in His Arms '52
Ride, Vaquero! '53
Seminole '53
Attila '54
La Strada '54
Seven Cities of Gold '55
Ulysses '55
Lust for Life '56
Man from Del Rio '56
The Hunchback of Notre Dame '57
The Ride Back '57
Wild Is the Wind '57
Black Orchid '59
Last Train from Gun Hill '59
Warlock '59
Heller in Pink Tights '60
Portrait in Black '60
The Guns of Navarone '61
Barabbas '62
Lawrence of Arabia '62
Requiem for a Heavyweight '62
Behold a Pale Horse '64
The Visit '64
Zorba the Greek '64
The Lost Command '66
The 25th Hour '67
The Shoes of the Fisherman '68
A Dream of Kings '69
The Secret of Santa Vittoria '69
Flap '70
R.P.M.* (*Revolutions Per Minute) '70
Walk in the Spring Rain '70
Across 110th Street '72
The Don Is Dead '73
The Destructors '74
The Inheritance '76
The Switch '76
Jesus of Nazareth '77
The Message '77
African Rage '78
The Greek Tycoon '78
Children of Sanchez '79
The Passage '79
The Con Artists '80
High Risk '81
Lion of the Desert '81
The Salamander '82
Regina '83
A Man of Passion '88
Onassis '88
The Old Man and the Sea '90
Revenge '90
Jungle Fever '91
Mobsters '91
Only the Lonely '91
Last Action Hero '93
Hercules the Legendary Journeys, Vol. 1: And the Amazon Women '94
Hercules the Legendary Journeys, Vol. 2: The Lost Kingdom '94
Hercules the Legendary Journeys, Vol. 3: The Circle of Fire '94
Hercules the Legendary Journeys, Vol. 4: In the Underworld '94
Somebody to Love '94
A Walk in the Clouds '95
Gotti '96
Avenging Angelo '02

Anthony Tyler Quinn (1962-)
Abandoned and Deceived '95
Silent Venom '08
American Bandits: Frank and Jesse James '10

Bill Quinn (1912-94)
Backstairs at the White House '79
Bustin' Loose '81
Dead and Buried '81
Twilight Zone: The Movie '83

Colin Quinn (1959-)
Crocodile Dundee 2 '88
Who's the Man? '93
Harold '08
Grown Ups '10
Trainwreck '15

Daniel Quinn (1956-2015)
Conagher '91
Scanners: The Showdown '94
A Reason to Believe '95
Wolverine '96
Spiders 2: Breeding Ground '01
Miracle at Sage Creek '05
Raising Flagg '06

Ed Quinn (1968-)
Blood Out '10
Behemoth '11
The Caller '11
The Rainbow Tribe '11
12 Disasters '12
Werewolf: The Beast Among Us '12
Navy Seals *vs.* Zombies '15

Edward Quinn (1968-)
Starship Troopers 2: Hero of the Federation '04
House of the Dead 2: Dead Aim '05
The Neighbor '07

Francesco Quinn (1963-2011)
Platoon '86
The Old Man and the Sea '90
Dead Certain '92
Red Shoe Diaries 5: Weekend Pass '95
Top Dog '95
Cannes Man '96
Rough Riders '97
Nowhere Land '98
Vlad '03
Afghan Knights '07
The Pledge '08
4 Single Fathers '09
Justice for Natalee '11
Transformers: Dark of the Moon '11 *(V)*

Glenn Quinn (1970-2002)
Dr. Giggles '92
Live Nude Girls '95
Campfire Tales '98
R.S.V.P. '02

James W. Quinn
Witchboard '87
Endangered Species '02

J.C. Quinn (1940-2004)
Heartbreak Ridge '86
Barfly '87
The Abyss '89
Turner and Hooch '89
All-American Murder '91
Prayer of the Rollerboys '91
The Babe '92
Crisscross '92
Hit Me '96
Primary Colors '98

Kevin Quinn
GhostWatcher '02
Wild Country '05

Louis Quinn (1915-88)
High School Big Shot '59
Superchick '71
Unholy Rollers '72

Martha Quinn (1959-)
Eddie and the Cruisers 2: Eddie Lives! '89 *(C)*
Tapeheads '89
Chopper Chicks in Zombietown '91
Motorama '91
Bad Channels '92
The Return of Spinal Tap '92 *(C)*

Molly C. Quinn (1993-)
My One and Only '09
Hansel & Gretel Get Baked '13
Superman: Unbound '13 *(V)*
We're the Millers '13
Last Rampage '17

Pat Quinn (1937-)
Alice's Restaurant '69
Zachariah '70
Clean and Sober '88

Patricia Quinn (1944-)
The Rocky Horror Picture Show '75
Shock Treatment '81
Monty Python's The Meaning of Life '83
The Lords of Salem '13

Terry Quinn
The Two Faces of Dr. Jekyll '60
The Witching '72

Adolfo 'Shabba Doo' Quinones (1955-)
Breakin' 2: Electric Boogaloo '84
Breakin' '84
Lambada '89

Jonathan Quint
Floating '97
Silicon Towers '99

Zachary Quinto (1977-)
Star Trek '09
Margin Call '11
What's Your Number? '11
Star Trek: Into Darkness '13
Hitman: Agent 47 '15
Snowden '16
Star Trek: Beyond '16
I Am Michael '17
Aardvark '18
High Flying Bird '19

Sophie Quinton (1976-)
Who Killed Bambi? '03
Nobody Else But You '11

Kristen Quintrall
The Apocalypse '07
Universal Soldiers '07

Pauline Quirke (1959-)
The Sculptress '97
David Copperfield '99
Carrie's War '04

Jocelyn Quivrin (1979-2009)
Empire of the Wolves '05
The Romance of Astrea and Celadon '07
Cash '08

Beulah Quo (1923-2002)
Girls! Girls! Girls! '62
The Seventh Dawn '64

Nguyen Nhu Quynh
Cyclo '95
The Vertical Ray of the Sun '00

Ellie Raab (1977-)
The Fabulous Baker Boys '89
Eyes of an Angel '91

Kurt Raab (1946-88)
Why Does Herr R. Run Amok? '69
The American Soldier '70
Beware of a Holy Whore '70
Tenderness of the Wolves '73
Fox and His Friends '75
Satan's Brew '76
The Stationmaster's Wife '77
Tricheurs '84
Angry Harvest '85
Mussolini & I '85

Birgitte Raaberg (1954-)
The Kingdom '95
The Kingdom 2 '97

Francisco Rabal (1926-2001)
The Wide Blue Road '57
Viridiana '61
The Eclipse '62
Belle de Jour '67
Long Days of Revenge '67
Diary of a Rebel '68
Eagles Over London '69
Sorcerer '77
City of the Walking Dead '80
Reborn '81
Tie Me Up! Tie Me Down! '90
Talk of Angels '96
Goya in Bordeaux '99

Lily Rabe (1982-)
A Crime '06
No Reservations '07
The Toe Tactic '08
What Just Happened '08
All Good Things '10
Weakness '10
Redemption Trail '13
Pawn Sacrifice '15
Miss Stevens '16
Golden Exits '17
Vice '18
Finding Steve McQueen '19
Fractured '19

Pamela Rabe (1959-)
Sirens '94
Cosi '95
Paradise Road '97
The Well '97

Olivier Rabourdin (1959-)
Kings and Queen '04
Taken '08
Of Gods and Men '10
Nobody Else But You '11
Augustine '12

Francine Racette (1947-)
Four Flies on Grey Velvet '72
Mr. Klein '76
Au Revoir les Enfants '87

Alan Rachins (1942-)
Always '85
Heart Condition '90
Star Quest '94
Showgirls '95
Leave It to Beaver '97
Meet Wally Sparks '97
Any Day Now '12

Victoria Racimo (1950-)
G.I. Executioner '71
Search for the Gods '75
Prophecy '79
Ernest Goes to Camp '87
White Fang 2: The Myth of the White Wolf '94

Kurt Rackelmann (1910-73)
First Spaceship on Venus '60
Carbide and Sorrel '63

Damaine Radcliff
Glory Road '06
Step Up '06

Daniel Radcliffe (1989-)
David Copperfield '99
The Tailor of Panama '00
Harry Potter and the Sorcerer's Stone '01
Harry Potter and the Chamber of Secrets '02
Harry Potter and the Prisoner of Azkaban '04
Harry Potter and the Goblet of Fire '05
December Boys '07
Harry Potter and the Order of the Phoenix '07
My Boy Jack '07
Harry Potter and the Half-Blood Prince '09
Harry Potter and the Deathly Hallows, Part 1 '10
Harry Potter and the Deathly Hallows, Part 2 '11
The Woman in Black '12
Horns '13
Kill Your Darlings '13
What If '13
Victor Frankenstein '15
Imperium '16
Now You See Me 2 '16
Swiss Army Man '16
Jungle '17
Playmobil: The Movie '19
Escape from Pretoria '20

Rosemary Radcliffe
Anne of Green Gables '85
Anne of Green Gables: The Continuing Story '99

Ronald Radd
The Iceman Cometh '60
The Kremlin Letter '70

Basil Radford (1897-1952)
There Goes the Bride '32
Young and Innocent '37
The Lady Vanishes '38
Night Train to Munich '40
The Girl in the News '41
Unpublished Story '42
Dead of Night '45
The Way to the Stars '45
Captive Heart '47
Whiskey Galore '48
The Winslow Boy '48
Passport to Pimlico '49

Natalie Radford (1966-)
JFK: Reckless Youth '93
Spenser: The Judas Goat '94
The Android Affair '95
P.T. Barnum '99
Agent Red '00
Killing Moon '00
Last Call: The Final Chapter of F. Scott Fitzgerald '02

Giovanni Lambardo Radice (1954-)
Cannibal Apocalypse '80
Deadly Impact '84

Gilda Radner (1946-89)
The Last Detail '73
All You Need Is Cash '78
Mr. Mike's Mondo Video '79
First Family '80
Hanky Panky '82
The Woman in Red '84
Movers and Shakers '85
Haunted Honeymoon '86

Josh Radnor (1974-)
Happythankyoumoreplease '10
Liberal Arts '12
Afternoon Delight '13

Jerzy Radziwilowicz (1950-)
Man of Marble '76
Man of Iron '81
Passion '82
No End '84
The Story of Marie and Julien '03

Joy '15
Point Break '15
Gold '16
Hands of Stone '16
Bright '17
Furlough '18

Efren Ramirez (1973-)
Napoleon Dynamite '04
Crank '06
Employee of the Month '06
Moola '07
Crank: High Voltage '09
National Lampoon's Ratko: The Dictator's Son '09
Casa de mi Padre '12

Frank Ramirez
Smith! '69
Code of Honor '82

Marisa Ramirez (1977-)
All Souls Day '05
Prosecuting Casey Anthony '13

Harold Ramis (1944-2014)
Heavy Metal '81 (V)
Stripes '81
Ghostbusters '84
Baby Boom '87
Stealing Home '88
Ghostbusters 2 '89
Airheads '94
Love Affair '94
As Good As It Gets '97
I'm with Lucy '02
Orange County '02
The Last Kiss '06
Knocked Up '07
Walk Hard: The Dewey Cox Story '07
Year One '09

Haley Ramm (1992-)
Flightplan '05
Yours, Mine & Ours '05
X-Men: The Last Stand '06
Walking Tall: Lone Justice '07
Bond of Silence '10
Skateland '10

Eulalia Ramon (1959-)
Outrage '93
Goya in Bordeaux '99

Rudy Ramos (1950-)
Open House '86
Quicksilver '86
Colors '88
The Spy Within '94

Charlotte Rampling (1946-)
Georgy Girl '66
The Damned '69
Asylum '72
Corky '72
'Tis a Pity She's a Whore '73
Zardoz '73
The Night Porter '74
Farewell, My Lovely '75
Orca '77
Stardust Memories '80
The Verdict '82
Max, Mon Amour '86
Angel Heart '87
D.O.A. '88
Hammers over the Anvil '91
The Wings of the Dove '97
The Cherry Orchard '99
Great Expectations '99
Aberdeen '00
Signs & Wonders '00
Under the Sand '00
The Fourth Angel '01
My Uncle Silas '01
Spy Game '01
I'll Sleep When I'm Dead '03
The Statement '03
Swimming Pool '03
Heading South '05
Lemming '05
Basic Instinct 2 '06
Angel '07
Babylon A.D. '08
Deception '08
The Duchess '08
Life During Wartime '09
Never Let Me Go '10
Rio Sex Comedy '10
Charlotte Rampling: The Look '11
Melancholia '11
The Mill and the Cross '11
Cleanskin '12
Night Train to Lisbon '13
45 Years '15
Assassin's Creed '16
The Sense of an Ending '17
The Little Stranger '18
Red Sparrow '18
Euphoria '19

Anne Ramsay
Honky Tonk Freeway '81
The Town That Banned Christmas '06

Bruce Ramsay (1966-)
Alive '93
Dead Beat '94
Killing Zoe '94
The New Age '94
Curdled '95
Hellraiser 4: Bloodline '95
Hit Me '96
Bonanno: A Godfather's Story '99
Island of the Dead '00
Jericho Mansions '03
What Comes Around '06
Nightmare '07
Riverworld '10
Doomsday Prophecy '11

Remak Ramsay (1937-)
Mr. & Mrs. Bridge '90
Addicted to Love '96

Bobby Ramsen
Hell Up in Harlem '73
It's Alive 2: It Lives Again '78

Anne Ramsey (1929-88)
The Boy in the Plastic Bubble '76
Goin' South '78
The Black Marble '79
The Goonies '85
Deadly Friend '86
Throw Momma from the Train '87
Dr. Hackenstein '88
Meet the Hollowheads '89

David Ramsey
Pay It Forward '00
Hair Show '04
Fatal Contact: Bird Flu in America '06
Mother and Child '09

Laura Ramsey (1982-)
Cruel World '05
Venom '05
The Covenant '06
She's the Man '06
The Ruins '08
Shrink '09
Middle Men '10
Kill the Irishman '11
Are You Here '13
Pulling Strings '13

Logan Ramsey (1921-2000)
The Hoodlum Priest '61
Head '68
The Beast Within '82
Dr. Hackenstein '88

Marion Ramsey (1947-)
Police Academy 3: Back in Training '86
Police Academy 5: Assignment Miami Beach '88
Police Academy 6: City under Siege '89

Natalie Ramsey (1975-)
Children of the Corn 666: Isaac's Return '99
Cruel Intentions 3 '04

Wes Ramsey (1977-)
Latter Days '04
Slippery Slope '06
Brotherhood of Blood '08
Dark Honeymoon '08

Stacey Linn Ramsower
Tank Girl '94
The Baby-Sitters' Club '95
The Quick and the Dead '95

Nick Ramus (1952-2007)
Geronimo '93
3 Ninjas Knuckle Up '95

Frederica Ranchi (1939-)
The Wide Blue Road '57
Son of Samson '62

Sally Rand
The Fighting Eagle '27
Getting Gertie's Garter '27

Monica Randal (1942-)
See Monica Randall

Addison Randall (1949-)
Chance '89
Deadly Breed '89

Frankie Randall
Wild On the Beach '65
The Day of the Wolves '71

Josh Randall
Wild Things: Foursome '10
Knockdown '11
2: Voodoo Academy '12

Lexi (Faith) Randall (1980-)
Sarah, Plain and Tall '91
Heidi '93
Sarah, Plain and Tall: Skylark '93
The Stars Fell on Henrietta '94
The War '94
Sarah, Plain and Tall: Winter's End '99

Meg Randall (1926-)
Abandoned '47
Ma and Pa Kettle '49
Ma and Pa Kettle Go to Town '50
Ma and Pa Kettle Back On the Farm '51

Monica Randall (1942-)
Commando Attack '67
Cria Cuervos '76
Inquisition '76

Stacie Randall
Eddie Presley '92
Trancers 4: Jack of Swords '93
Dream a Little Dream 2 '94
Trancers 5: Sudden Deth '94
Excessive Force 2: Force on Force '95

Tony Randall (1920-2004)
No Down Payment '57
Oh, Men! Oh, Women! '57
Will Success Spoil Rock Hunter? '57
The Mating Game '59
Pillow Talk '59
The Adventures of Huckleberry Finn '60
Let's Make Love '60
Lover Come Back '61
Boys' Night Out '62
The Brass Bottle '63
Island of Love '63
7 Faces of Dr. Lao '63
Robin and the 7 Hoods '64
Send Me No Flowers '64
The Alphabet Murders '65
Bang! Bang! You're Dead! '66
Hello Down There '69
The Littlest Angel '69
Everything You Always Wanted to Know about Sex (But Were Afraid to Ask) '72
King of Comedy '82
Gremlins 2: The New Batch '90 (V)
Fatal Instinct '93
Down With Love '03

Steven Randazzo
Jungle Fever '91
In the Soup '92
Mac '93
The Wedding Bros. '08

Monica Randel (1942-)
See Monica Randall

Ron Randell (1918-2005)
The Loves of Carmen '48
Counterspy Meets Scotland Yard '50
1,000 Years From Now '52
The Mississippi Gambler '53
Quincannon, Frontier Scout '56
The She-Creature '56
Girl in Black Stockings '57
Most Dangerous Man Alive '61
Follow the Boys '63
Gold for the Caesars '63

Theresa Randle (1967-)
Jungle Fever '91
Malcolm X '92
CB4: The Movie '93
Beverly Hills Cop 3 '94
Sugar Hill '94
Bad Boys '95
Girl 6 '96
Space Jam '96
Spawn '97
Bad Boys 2 '03
The Hunt for Eagle One: Crash Point '06

Anders Randolf (1870-1930)
See Anders Randolph

Anders Randolph (1870-1930)
The Idol Dancer '20
The Love Flower '20
Ranson's Folly '26
Old San Francisco '27
The Viking '28
The Kiss '29
Son of the Gods '30

Donald Randolph (1906-93)
Harem Girl '52
The Mad Magician '54
Over-Exposed '56
The Deadly Mantis '57
My Gun Is Quick '57

Jane Randolph (1915-2009)
Cat People '42
The Falcon Strikes Back '43
Curse of the Cat People '44
Railroaded '47
Abbott and Costello Meet Frankenstein '48
Open Secret '48

John Randolph (1915-2004)
Seconds '66
Pretty Poison '68
There Was a Crooked Man '70
Escape from the Planet of the Apes '71
A Step Out of Line '71
Conquest of the Planet of the Apes '72
Serpico '73
Missiles of October '74
King Kong '76
The Winds of Kitty Hawk '78
Backstairs at the White House '79
Frances '82
Prizzi's Honor '85
The Right of the People '86
National Lampoon's Christmas Vacation '89
Iron Maze '91
A Foreign Field '93
A Price Above Rubies '97
You've Got Mail '98
Sunset Strip '99

Katherine Randolph (1983-)
Girl Play '04
Black Ops '07

Lillian Randolph (1898-1980)
The Mexican Spitfire Sees a Ghost '42
Magic '78

Ty Randolph (1950-)
See Mindi Miller

Windsor Taylor Randolph (1950-)
See Mindi Miller

Salvo Randone (1906-91)
The Mercenaries '62
10th Victim '65
Spirits of the Dead '68
Fellini Satyricon '69

Joe Ranft (1960-2005)
A Bug's Life '98 (V)
Toy Story 2 '99 (V)
Finding Nemo '03 (V)
Cars '06 (V)

Liam Ranger
The Final Cut '04
Best Friends '05
The Stranger Game '06

Kevin Rankin (1976-)
The Chaperone '11
Congratulations '13
Dallas Buyers Club '13
Skyscraper '18

Kenny Ransom
There Goes My Baby '92
The Crocodile Hunter: Collision Course '02

Tim Ransom (1963-)
Vital Signs '90
Courage Under Fire '96

Prunella Ransome (1943-)
Far from the Madding Crowd '67
Man in the Wilderness '71

James Ransone (1979-)
The Good Humor Man '05
Generation Kill '08
The Son of No One '11
Starlet '12
Oldboy '13
Sinister 2 '15
Tangerine '15
In a Valley of Violence '16
Mr. Right '16

Noomi Rapace (1979-)
The Girl With the Dragon Tattoo '09
The Girl Who Kicked the Hornet's Nest '10
The Girl Who Played With Fire '10
Sherlock Holmes: A Game of Shadows '11
Prometheus '12
Dead Man Down '13
Passion '13
The Drop '14
Child 44 '15
Bright '17
Unlocked '17
Close '19

Michael Rapaport (1970-)
Zebrahead '92
Hand Gun '93
Money for Nothing '93
True Romance '93
Higher Learning '94
Kiss of Death '94
The Scout '94
The Basketball Diaries '95
Mighty Aphrodite '95
The Pallbearer '95
Beautiful Girls '96
Metro '96
A Brother's Kiss '97
Cop Land '97
Kicked in the Head '97
Subway Stories '97
Palmetto '98
Deep Blue Sea '99
Bamboozled '00
Chain of Fools '00
Kiss Toledo Goodbye '00
Lucky Numbers '00
Men of Honor '00
The 6th Day '00
Small Time Crooks '00
Dr. Dolittle 2 '01 (V)
King of the Jungle '01
Comic Book Villains '02
Triggermen '02
This Girl's Life '03
29 Palms '03
Hitch '05
Grilled '06
Special '06
Assassination of a High School President '08
Big Fan '09
A Day in the Life '09
Inside Out '11
Kiss of the Damned '12
My Man Is a Loser '14

June Raphael (1980-)
Year One '09
The Dry Land '10
Going the Distance '10

June Diane Raphael (1980-)
Weakness '10
Ass Backwards '13
Unfinished Business '15
Long Shot '19

Anthony Rapp (1971-)
Adventures in Babysitting '87
Far from Home '89
School Ties '92
Dazed and Confused '93
Six Degrees of Separation '93
David Searching '97
Man of the Century '99
Road Trip '00
A Beautiful Mind '01
Rent '05
Danny Roane: First Time Director '06

David Rappaport (1952-90)
Mysteries '84
The Bride '85
Peter Gunn '89

Michael Rappaport (1970-)
Push '06
The Heat '13

Sheeri Rappaport (1977-)
Little Witches '96
Serial Slayer '03
United States of Leland '03
Seeing Other People '04

Kseniya Rappoport (1974-)
The Unknown Woman '06
The Double Hour '09

Eva Ras (1941-)
Man Is Not a Bird '65
The Love Affair, or The Case of the Missing Switchboard Operator '67
It Rains In My Village '68

Renato Rascel (1912-91)
The Seven Hills of Rome '58
Uncle Was a Vampire '59
The Secret of Santa Vittoria '69

David Rasche (1944-)
Manhattan '79
Honky Tonk Freeway '81
Made in Heaven '87 (C)
Secret Witness '88
An Innocent Man '89
Wicked Stepmother '89
Bingo '91
Delirious '91
Twenty Bucks '93
Bigfoot: The Unforgettable Encounter '94
A Million to Juan '94 (C)
That Old Feeling '96
The Big Tease '99
Friends & Lovers '99
The Settlement '99
Hostage Hotel '00
Divine Secrets of the Ya-Ya Sisterhood '02
Exposed '03
Just Married '03
Final Approach '04
Off the Lip '04
Perception '06
The Sentinel '06
Burn After Reading '08
Blue Eyes '09
Crimes of the Past '09
In the Loop '09
Men in Black 3 '12
Petunia '13

Amira & Sam '15
Swallow '20
Jim Rash
Sky High '05
The Way Way Back '13
Phylicia Rashad (1948-)
Once Upon a Time . . . When We Were Colored '95
Free of Eden '98
Loving Jezebel '99
The Visit '00
The Old Settler '01
A Raisin in the Sun '08
For Colored Girls '10
Frankie and Alice '10
Just Wright '10
Steel Magnolias '12
Tyler Perry's Good Deeds '12
Creed '15
Creed II '18
Sharif Rashed
Crooklyn '94
Blue in the Face '95
Hell's Kitchen NYC '97
Alexia Rasmussen
Listen to Your Heart '10
California Solo '12
Kilimanjaro '13
Proxy '13
Last Weekend '14
Rie Rasmussen (1976-)
Femme Fatale '02
Angel-A '05
Fritz Rasp (1891-1976)
Metropolis '26
The Love of Jeanne Ney '27
Spies '28
Diary of a Lost Girl '29
The Threepenny Opera '31
Ivan Rassimov (1938-2003)
Planet of the Vampires '65
Cjamango '67
Your Vice is a Closed Room and Only I Have the Key '72
Shock '79
Emerald Jungle '80
Rada Rassimov (1938-)
The Good, the Bad and the Ugly '67
Torture Chamber of Baron Blood '72
Silvestre Rasuk (1987-)
Raising Victor Vargas '03
Toe to Toe '09
Victor Rasuk (1984-)
Raising Victor Vargas '03
Haven '04
Lords of Dogtown '05
Bonneville '06
I'm Reed Fish '06
Adrift in Manhattan '07
Feel the Noise '07
Che '08
Stop-Loss '08
Being Flynn '12
Fifty Shades of Grey '15
Thalmus Rasulala (1939-91)
Blacula '72
Cool Breeze '72
Adios Amigo '75
Bucktown '75
Friday Foster '75
Mr. Ricco '75
The Last Hard Men '76
Born American '86
Above the Law '88
Bulletproof '88
The Package '89
New Jack City '91
Mom and Dad Save the World '92
Mikhail Rasumny (1890-1956)
Wake Island '42
For Whom the Bell Tolls '43
Anna and the King of Siam '46
The Kissing Bandit '48
The Pirates of Capri '49
Hot Blood '56
Emily Ratajkowski
We Are Your Friends '15
Cruise '18
I Feel Pretty '18
Welcome Home '18
Jeremy Ratchford (1965-)
Prom Night 3: The Last Kiss '89
Fly Away Home '96
The Crew '00
Angel Eyes '01
One Angry Juror '10
Basil Rathbone (1892-1967)
The Last of Mrs. Cheyney '29
The Bishop Murder Case '30
Sin Takes a Holiday '30
Anna Karenina '35
Captain Blood '35
David Copperfield '35
Last Days of Pompeii '35
The Garden of Allah '36
Private Number '36
Romeo and Juliet '36
A Tale of Two Cities '36
Love from a Stranger '37
Make a Wish '37
The Adventures of Marco Polo '38
The Adventures of Robin Hood '38
Dawn Patrol '38
The Adventures of Sherlock Holmes '39
The Hound of the Baskervilles '39
Son of Frankenstein '39
The Tower of London '39
The Mark of Zorro '40
Rhythm on the River '40
The Black Cat '41
Crossroads '42
Sherlock Holmes and the Secret Weapon '42
Sherlock Holmes and the Voice of Terror '42
Above Suspicion '43
Sherlock Holmes Faces Death '43
Sherlock Holmes in Washington '43
Bathing Beauty '44
Frenchman's Creek '44
The Pearl of Death '44
Scarlet Claw '44
House of Fear '45
Pursuit to Algiers '45
Dressed to Kill '46
Heartbeat '46
The Adventures of Ichabod and Mr. Toad '49 (N)
The Woman in Green '49
Casanova's Big Night '54
We're No Angels '55
The Black Sleep '56
The Court Jester '56
The Last Hurrah '58
The Magic Sword '62
Tales of Terror '62
The Comedy of Terrors '64
Voyage to the Prehistoric Planet '65
Ghost in the Invisible Bikini '66
Planet of Blood '66
Queen of Blood '66
Hillbillies in a Haunted House '67
Jackson Rathbone (1984-)
Twilight '08
Dread '09
Hurt '09
S. Darko: A Donnie Darko Tale '09
The Twilight Saga: New Moon '09
The Last Airbender '10
The Twilight Saga: Eclipse '10
The Twilight Saga: Breaking Dawn, Part 1 '11
Cowgirls 'n Angels '12
Samson '18
Benjamin Ratner
Bounty Hunters '96
Firestorm '97
Ignition '01
Last Wedding '01
Ann Rule Presents: The Stranger Beside Me '03
Moving Malcolm '03
Gregory Ratoff (1897-1960)
Skyscraper Souls '32
Symphony of Six Million '32
I'm No Angel '33
Sweepings '33
The Road to Glory '36
Sing, Baby, Sing '36
Cafe Metropole '37
Gateway '38
Sally, Irene and Mary '38
All About Eve '50
Abdulla the Great '56
The Sun Also Rises '57
Exodus '60
Once More, With Feeling '60
Devin Ratray (1977-)
Home Alone '90
Home Alone 2: Lost in New York '92
Surrogates '09
Heather Rattray (1965-)
Across the Great Divide '76
Further Adventures of the Wilderness Family, Part 2 '77
Sea Gypsies '78
Mountain Family Robinson '79
Basket Case 2 '90
John Ratzenberger (1947-)
A Bridge Too Far '77
The Bitch '78
The Empire Strikes Back '80
Motel Hell '80
Outland '81
Ragtime '81
Gandhi '82
House 2: The Second Story '87
Timestalkers '87
Camp Cucamonga: How I Spent My Summer Vacation '90
Toy Story '95 (V)
That Darn Cat '96
One Night Stand '97
A Bug's Life '98 (V)
Under Pressure '98
Toy Story 2 '99 (V)
Tick Tock '00
Monsters, Inc. '01 (V)
Spirited Away '01 (V)
Finding Nemo '03 (V)
Cars '06 (V)
Ratatouille '07 (V)
The Village Barbershop '08
WALL-E '08 (V)
Up '09 (V)
Toy Story 3 '10 (V)
Cars 2 '11 (V)
Super Buddies '13
Coco '17
Andrea Rau (1949-)
Daughters of Darkness '71
Beyond Erotica '74
Melissa Rauch
The Bronze '15
Ode to Joy '19
Siegfried Rauch (1932-)
Death is Nimble, Death is Quick '67
Patton '70
The Uranium Conspiracy '78
The Big Red One '80
Alien Contamination '81
Sons of Trinity '95
Drew Rausch
Bigfoot: The Lost Coast Tapes '12
Curve '16
Rick Ravanello (1967-)
Out of Line '00
The Cave '05
Imaginary Playmate '06
The Christmas Clause '08
Smoke Jumpers '08
Garage Sale Mystery '13
Gina Ravarra (1966-)
See Gina Ravera
Raven (1985-)
Queen '93
Dr. Dolittle '98
Dr. Dolittle 2 '01
The Cheetah Girls '03
The Princess Diaries 2: Royal Engagement '04
The Cheetah Girls 2 '06
Everyone's Hero '06 (V)
For One Night '06
College Road Trip '08
Revenge of the Bridesmaids '10
Mike Raven (1924-97)
I, Monster '71
Lust for a Vampire '71
Crucible of Terror '72
Disciple of Death '72
Raven-Symone (1985-)
See Raven
Christopher Ravenscroft (1946-)
Henry V '89
A Mind to Murder '96
Kim Raver (1969-)
Mind the Gap '04
Haunting Sarah '05
Night at the Museum '06
Bond of Silence '10
Lorna Raver
Drag Me to Hell '09
The Caller '11 (V)
Gina Ravera (1966-)
Showgirls '95
Soul of the Game '96
Kiss the Girls '97
Soul Food '97
The Temptations '98
The Great Debaters '07
Dax Ravina
Weirdsville '07
The Dogfather '10
Paresh Rawal (1950-)
American Chai '01
Uri: The Surgical Strike '19
Navi Rawat (1977-)
House of Sand and Fog '03
Feast '06
Loveless in Los Angeles '07
Undead or Alive '07
The Collection '12
Adrian Rawlins (1958-)
Woman in Black '89
Breaking the Waves '95
Wilbur Wants to Kill Himself '02
The Old Curiosity Shop '07
The Woman in Black 2: Angel of Death '15
Herbert Rawlinson (1885-1953)
Convention Girl '35
Blake of Scotland Yard '36
Robinson Crusoe of Clipper Island '36
Flash Gordon Conquers the Universe '40
I Killed That Man '42
The Panther's Claw '42
Smart Alecks '42
Colt Comrades '43
Nabonga '44
Jail Bait '54
Lou Rawls (1933-2006)
Showdown '94
Don King: Only in America '97
Still Breathing '97
Motel Blue '98
Watchers Reborn '98
Aldo Ray (1926-91)
The Marrying Kind '52
Pat and Mike '52
Let's Do It Again '53
Miss Sadie Thompson '53
Battle Cry '55
Three Stripes in the Sun '55
We're No Angels '55
Nightfall '56
Men in War '57
God's Little Acre '58
The Day They Robbed the Bank of England '60
Dead Heat on a Merry-Go-Round '66
What Did You Do in the War, Daddy? '66
Kill a Dragon '67
Riot on Sunset Strip '67
Welcome to Hard Times '67
The Green Berets '68
The Power '68
Angel Unchained '70
Gone with the West '72
The Centerfold Girls '74
The Dynamite Brothers '74
Inside Out '75
Psychic Killer '75
Seven Alone '75
Bad Bunch '76
Haunts '77
Black Eliminator '78
The Glove '78
Kill Factor '78
Little Moon & Jud McGraw '78
The Lucifer Complex '78
Mission to Glory '80
Nightstalker '81
The Secret of NIMH '82 (V)
Frankenstein's Great Aunt Tillie '83
Bog '84
The Executioner, Part 2: Frozen Scream '84
To Kill a Stranger '84
Bio Hazard '85
Evils of the Night '85
Hollywood Cop '87
Star Slammer '87
Blood Red '88
Shock 'Em Dead '90
Andrew Ray (1939-2003)
The Mudlark '50
Gideon's Day '58
Serious Charge '59
Anthony Ray
Men in War '57
Shadows '60
Charles Ray (1891-1943)
Getting Gertie's Garter '27
The Garden of Eden '28
Just My Luck '35
Connie Ray (1956-)
Idle Hands '99
How to Deal '03
Bobby Jones: Stroke of Genius '04
Ice Princess '05
Flourish '06
Thank You for Smoking '06
Frankie Ray
Carnival Rock '57
Invasion of the Star Creatures '63
James Ray (1932-88)
Mass Appeal '84
She's Having a Baby '88
Joey Ray
Blonde Comet '41
The Old Man and the Sea '58
Lisa Ray (1972-)
Ball & Chain '04
Water '05
All Hat '07
The World Unseen '07
Defendor '09
Michel Ray (1944-)
The Brave One '56
The Tin Star '57
The Space Children '58
Lawrence of Arabia '62
Nicholas Ray (1911-79)
The American Friend '77
Hair '79
Rene Ray (1911-93)
Tiger Bay '33
The Passing of the Third Floor Back '35
The Green Cockatoo '37
Bank Holiday '38
They Made Me a Fugitive '47
Twilight Women '52
Conner Rayburn (1999-)
The Invention of Lying '09
Old Dogs '09
Martha Raye (1916-94)
Rhythm on the Range '36
Double or Nothing '37
Waikiki Wedding '37
The Big Broadcast of 1938 '38
College Swing '38
Give Me a Sailor '38
Never Say Die '39
The Boys From Syracuse '40
Keep 'Em Flying '41
Four Jills in a Jeep '44
Pin-Up Girl '44
Monsieur Verdoux '47
Billy Rose's Jumbo '62
Pufnstuf '70
The Concorde: Airport '79 '79
Pippin '81
Alice in Wonderland '85
Bill Raymond
Sudden Death '77
City of Hope '91
My New Gun '92
The Crow '93
Where the Rivers Flow North '94
A Stranger in the Kingdom '98
Spring Forward '99
A Death in the Family '02
Dogville '03
A Hole in One '04
Cyril Raymond (1897-1973)
Spy in Black '39
Brief Encounter '46
The Jack of Diamonds '49
Angels One Five '54
Gary Raymond (1935-)
Look Back in Anger '58
Jason and the Argonauts '63
Scarlett '94
Gene Raymond (1908-98)
Red Dust '32
Brief Moment '33
Flying Down to Rio '33
The House on 56th Street '33
Sadie McKee '34
Hooray for Love '35
Seven Keys to Baldpate '35
The Woman in Red '35
The Bride Walks Out '36
Love on a Bet '36
She's Got Everything '37
Mr. & Mrs. Smith '41
Smilin' Through '41
The Locket '46
Hit the Deck '55
Plunder Road '57
The Best Man '64
Paula Raymond (1924-2003)
Adam's Rib '50
Crisis '50
The Devil's Doorway '50
The Duchess of Idaho '50
The Sellout '51
The Tall Target '51
Texas Carnival '51
The Bandits of Corsica '53
The Beast from 20,000 Fathoms '53
King Richard and the Crusaders '54
The Gun That Won the West '55
Blood of Dracula's Castle '69
Robin Raymond (1916-94)
Girls in Chains '43
The Glass Wall '53
High School Confidential '58

Usher Raymond (1978-)
The Faculty *'98*
Light It Up *'99*
She's All That *'99*
Gepetto *'00*
Texas Rangers *'01*
In the Mix *'05*
Justin Bieber: Never Say Never *'11*
Hands of Stone *'16*

Tania Raymonde (1988-)
Children On Their Birthdays *'02*
Chasing 3000 *'07*
Foreign Exchange *'08*
Still Waiting *'08*
Elsewhere *'09*
Wild Cherry *'09*
Blue Like Jazz *'12*
Crazy Eyes *'12*
Texas Chainsaw 3D *'13*
Dirty Lies *'16*
Cliffs of Freedom *'19*

Adam Rayner
The Whale *'13*
Tracers *'15*

Michael Raynor
Federal Hill *'94*
A Brother's Kiss *'97*
The Waiting Game *'99*

Peggy Rea (1921-2011)
In Country *'89*
Love Field *'91*
Made in America *'93*

Stephen Rea (1946-)
Danny Boy *'82*
The Company of Wolves *'85*
The Doctor and the Devils *'85*
Four Days in July *'85*
Life Is Sweet *'90*
Bad Behavior *'92*
The Crying Game *'92*
Angie *'94*
Interview with the Vampire *'94*
Princess Caraboo *'94*
Ready to Wear *'94*
Citizen X *'95*
Fever Pitch *'96*
The Last of the High Kings *'96*
Michael Collins *'96*
Trojan Eddie *'96*
The Butcher Boy *'97*
Sink or Swim *'97*
In Dreams *'98*
Still Crazy *'98*
The End of the Affair *'99*
Guinevere *'99*
The Life Before This *'99*
This Is My Father *'99*
On the Edge *'00*
The Musketeer *'01*
Snow in August *'01*
Evelyn *'02*
Feardotcom *'02*
Bloom *'03*
The Confessor *'04*
The I Inside *'04*
Breakfast on Pluto *'05*
River Queen *'05*
Tara Road *'05*
V for Vendetta *'06*
The Devil's Mercy *'07*
The Reaping *'07*
Stuck *'07*
The Heavy *'09*
Nothing Personal *'09*
Ondine *'09*
Blackthorn *'11*
Roadkill *'11*
Stella Days *'12*
Underworld: Awakening *'12*
Werewolf: The Beast Among Us *'12*
Black '47 *'18*

Barbara Read (1917-63)
Three Smart Girls *'36*
Make Way for Tomorrow *'37*
Key Witness *'47*

James Read (1953-)
The Initiation *'84*
Lace 2 *'85*
North and South Book 1 *'85*
North and South Book 2 *'86*
Poor Little Rich Girl: The Barbara Hutton Story *'87*
Beaches *'88*
Eight Men Out *'88*
Walking Thunder *'94*
Harvest of Fire *'95*
A Lot Like Love *'05*

Rufus Read
Happiness *'98*
Double Parked *'00*

Jonathan Readwin
Dread *'09*
Stoner Express *'16*

Nancy Reagan (1921-2016)
See Nancy Davis

Ronald Reagan (1911-2004)
Boy Meets Girl *'38*
Brother Rat *'38*
Cowboy from Brooklyn *'38*
Angels Wash Their Faces *'39*
Dark Victory *'39*
Hell's Kitchen *'39*
Brother Rat and a Baby *'40*
Knute Rockne: All American *'40*
Santa Fe Trail *'40*
The Bad Man *'41*
Kings Row *'41*
Desperate Journey *'42*
Juke Girl *'42*
This Is the Army *'43*
Stallion Road *'47*
That Hagen Girl *'47*
The Voice of the Turtle *'47*
John Loves Mary *'48*
The Girl from Jones Beach *'49*
It's a Great Feeling *'49*
Night Unto Night *'49*
Bedtime for Bonzo *'51*
Cavalry Charge *'51*
Storm Warning *'51*
She's Working Her Way Through College *'52*
The Winning Team *'52*
Law and Order *'53*
Cattle Queen of Montana *'54*
Tennessee's Partner *'55*
Hellcats of the Navy *'57*
The Killers *'64*

Portia Realer
Keepin' It Real *'01*
Makin' Baby *'02*

John Reardon (1975-)
Merlin's Apprentice *'06*
Blue Smoke *'07*
A Valentine Carol *'07*
Make It Happen *'08*
7 Things to Do Before I'm 30 *'08*
Bringing Ashley Home *'11*

John Henry Reardon (1975-)
See John Reardon

Marjorie Reardon (1921-84)
See Marjorie (Reardon) Riordan

Elizabeth Reaser (1975-)
Mind the Gap *'04*
The Family Stone *'05*
Stay *'05*
Sweet Land *'05*
Puccini for Beginners *'06*
Purple Violets *'07*
Twilight *'08*
Against the Current *'09*
The Twilight Saga: New Moon *'09*
The Twilight Saga: Eclipse *'10*
The Art of Getting By *'11*
The Twilight Saga: Breaking Dawn, Part 1 *'11*
Young Adult *'11*
Liberal Arts *'12*
The Twilight Saga: Breaking Dawn, Part 2 *'12*
Bonnie & Clyde *'13*
Ouija: Origin of Evil *'16*

Rex Reason (1928-)
Taza, Son of Cochise *'54*
Lady Godiva *'55*
This Island Earth *'55*
The Creature Walks among Us *'56*
Band of Angels *'57*

Sady Rebbot (1935-94)
My Life to Live *'62*
Friends *'71*

James Rebhorn (1948-2014)
He Knows You're Alone *'80*
Lorenzo's Oil *'92*
Scent of a Woman *'92*
White Sands *'92*
Carlito's Way *'93*
JFK: Reckless Youth *'93*
Sarah, Plain and Tall: Skylark *'93*
8 Seconds *'94*
I Love Trouble *'94*
The Buccaneers *'95*
If Lucy Fell *'95*
Independence Day *'96*
Mistrial *'96*
My Fellow Americans *'96*
Up Close and Personal *'96*
The Game *'97*
A Bright Shining Lie *'98*
From the Earth to the Moon *'98*
Snow Falling on Cedars *'99*
The Talented Mr. Ripley *'99*
The Adventures of Rocky & Bullwinkle *'00*
Meet the Parents *'00*
The Adventures of Pluto Nash *'02*
Far from Heaven *'02*
Scotland, PA *'02*
Cold Mountain *'03*
Head of State *'03*
The Trade *'03*
The Last Shot *'04*
How to Eat Fried Worms *'06*
Anamorph *'07*
Bernard and Doris *'08*
Comanche Moon *'08*
An American Affair *'09*
The Box *'09*
Don McKay *'09*
The International *'09*
Real Steel *'11*
Coma *'12*
The Perfect Wedding *'12*
Sleepwalk with Me *'12*

Donnamarie Recco
Analyze This *'98*
Analyze That *'02*

Winston Reckert (1949-2012)
See Winston Rekert

Paco Reconti
Men Men Men *'95*
I Am David *'04*

Max Records
Where the Wild Things Are *'09*
The Sitter *'11*

Jeff Rector (1958-)
The Black Gate *'95*
Dinosaur Valley Girls *'96*
Friend of the Family 2 *'96*
Rapid Assault *'99*

Lois Red Elk
Three Warriors *'77*
Skins *'02*

Lance Reddick (1962-)
The Siege *'98*
I Dreamed of Africa *'00*
Don't Say a Word *'01*
Bad City *'06*
Tennessee *'08*
The Way of War *'08*
Won't Back Down *'12*
White House Down *'13*
The Guest *'14*
Faults *'15*

Keith Reddin (1956-)
Lolita *'97*
Eye of the Storm *'98*

Brian Reddy
Dante's Peak *'97*
Lost Souls *'00*
O Brother Where Art Thou? *'00*

Helen Reddy (1941-)
Airport '75 *'75*
Pete's Dragon *'77*
The Perfect Host *'10*

Quinn (K.) Redeker (1936-)
The Three Stooges Meet Hercules *'61*
Spider Baby *'64*
The Christine Jorgensen Story *'70*
The Slams *'73*

Dennis Redfield (1943-)
Private Duty Nurses *'71*
The McCullochs *'75*
Pulse *'88*

Mark Redfield
Despiser *'03*
Come Hell or High Water *'08*

William Redfield (1927-76)
Conquest of Space *'55*
The Proud and Profane *'56*
The Connection *'61*
Morituri *'65*
Fantastic Voyage *'66*
The Hot Rock *'70*
A New Leaf *'71*
Death Wish *'74*
For Pete's Sake *'74*
One Flew Over the Cuckoo's Nest *'75*

Amy Redford (1970-)
Giving It Up *'99*
The Last Confederate: The Story of Robert Adams *'05*
This Revolution *'05*
When I Find the Ocean *'06*

Robert Redford (1936-)
The Iceman Cometh *'60*
War Hunt *'62*
Inside Daisy Clover *'65*
The Chase *'66*
This Property Is Condemned *'66*
Barefoot in the Park *'67*
Butch Cassidy and the Sundance Kid *'69*
Downhill Racer *'69*
Tell Them Willie Boy Is Here *'69*
The Hot Rock *'70*
The Candidate *'72*
Jeremiah Johnson *'72*
The Sting *'73*
The Way We Were *'73*
The Great Gatsby *'74*
The Great Waldo Pepper *'75*
Three Days of the Condor *'75*
All the President's Men *'76*
A Bridge Too Far *'77*
The Electric Horseman *'79*
Brubaker *'80*
The Natural *'84*
Out of Africa *'85*
Legal Eagles *'86*
Havana *'90*
Incident at Oglala: The Leonard Peltier Story *'92* *(N)*
Sneakers *'92*
Indecent Proposal *'93*
Up Close and Personal *'96*
The Horse Whisperer *'97*
The Last Castle *'01*
Spy Game *'01*
The Clearing *'04*
An Unfinished Life *'05*
Charlotte's Web *'06 (V)*
Lions for Lambs *'07*
Buck *'11*
The Company You Keep *'12*
All is Lost *'13*
Captain America: The Winter Soldier *'14*
Truth *'15*
A Walk in the Woods *'15*
Pete's Dragon *'16*
The Discovery *'17*
Earth: One Amazing Day *'17*
The Old Man & the Gun *'18*

Rockets Redglare (1948-2001)
After Hours *'85*
Down by Law *'86*
Shakedown *'88*
Cookie *'89*
Mystery Train *'89*
In the Soup *'92*

Corin Redgrave (1939-2010)
The Charge of the Light Brigade *'68*
Oh! What a Lovely War *'69*
When Eight Bells Toll *'71*
Excalibur *'81*
In the Name of the Father *'93*
Four Weddings and a Funeral *'94*
Persuasion *'95*
The Ice House *'97*
The Woman in White *'97*
Ultraviolet *'98*
Enigma *'01*
Close Your Eyes *'02*
Plain Jane *'02*
To Kill a King *'03*
Enduring Love *'04*

Jemma Redgrave (1965-)
The Buddha of Suburbia *'92*
Howard's End *'92*
Diana: Her True Story *'93*
The Acid House *'98*
I'll Be There *'03*
Lassie *'05*
Like Father Like Son *'05*
Mansfield Park *'07*

Lynn Redgrave (1943-2010)
Tom Jones *'63*
Girl with Green Eyes *'64*
Georgy Girl *'66*
Smashing Time *'67*
The Last of the Mobile Hotshots *'69*
The Virgin Soldiers *'69*
Everything You Always Wanted to Know about Sex (But Were Afraid to Ask) *'72*
The National Health *'73*
The Turn of the Screw *'74*
The Happy Hooker *'75*
The Big Bus *'76*
Centennial *'78*
Sooner or Later *'78*
Rehearsal for Murder *'82*
The Bad Seed *'85*
Morgan Stewart's Coming Home *'87*
Getting It Right *'89*
What Ever Happened To. . . *'93*
The Great American Sex Scandal *'94*
Shine *'95*
Toothless *'97*
All I Wanna Do *'98*
Gods and Monsters *'98*
White Lies *'98*
Deeply *'99*
A Season for Miracles *'99*
The Simian Line *'99*
The Next Best Thing *'00*
How to Kill Your Neighbor's Dog *'01*
Varian's War *'01*
My Sister's Keeper *'02*
Spider *'02*
The Wild Thornberrys Movie *'02 (V)*
Peter Pan *'03*
Unconditional Love *'03*
Kinsey *'04*
The White Countess *'05*
The Jane Austen Book Club *'07*
Confessions of a Shopaholic *'09*
My Dog Tulip *'09 (V)*

Michael Redgrave (1908-85)
Climbing High *'38*
The Lady Vanishes *'38*
The Stars Look Down *'39*
Dead of Night *'45*
The Way to the Stars *'45*
Captive Heart *'47*
Secret Beyond the Door *'48*
The Browning Version *'51*
The Importance of Being Earnest *'52*
Dam Busters *'55*
Mr. Arkadin *'55*
1984 *'56*
The Happy Road *'57*
Time Without Pity *'57*
The Wreck of the Mary Deare *'59*
The Innocents *'61*
The Loneliness of the Long Distance Runner *'62*
The Heroes of Telemark *'65*
The Hill *'65*
Young Cassidy *'65*
Alice in Wonderland *'66*
Heidi *'67*
The 25th Hour *'67*
Assignment K *'68*
Battle of Britain *'69*
Goodbye, Mr. Chips *'69*
Oh! What a Lovely War *'69*
The Go-Between *'71*
Nicholas and Alexandra *'71*
Dr. Jekyll and Mr. Hyde *'73*

Vanessa Redgrave (1937-)
Blow-Up *'66*
A Man for All Seasons *'66*
Morgan: A Suitable Case for Treatment *'66*
Camelot *'67*
The Charge of the Light Brigade *'68*
The Sea Gull *'68*
Oh! What a Lovely War *'69*
A Quiet Place in the Country *'69*
The Devils *'71*
Mary, Queen of Scots *'71*
Trojan Women *'71*
Murder on the Orient Express *'74*
Out of Season *'75*
The Seven-Per-Cent Solution *'76*
Julia *'77*
Agatha *'79*
Yanks *'79*
Playing for Time *'80*
The Bostonians *'84*
Three Sovereigns for Sarah *'85*
Wagner: The Complete Epic *'85*
Wetherby *'85*
Prick Up Your Ears *'87*
Consuming Passions *'88*
A Man for All Seasons *'88*
The Ballad of the Sad Cafe *'91*
Young Catherine *'91*
Howard's End *'92*
The House of the Spirits *'93*
Shades of Fear *'93*
What Ever Happened To. . . *'93*
Little Odessa *'94*
Mother's Boys *'94*
A Month by the Lake *'95*
Looking for Richard *'96*
Mission: Impossible *'96*
Smilla's Sense of Snow *'96*
Mrs. Dalloway *'97*
Wilde *'97*
Deep Impact *'98*
Deja Vu *'98*
Lulu on the Bridge *'98*
The Cradle Will Rock *'99*
Girl, Interrupted *'99*
If These Walls Could Talk 2 *'00*
The Pledge *'00*
A Rumor of Angels *'00*
Jack and the Beanstalk: The Real Story *'01*
The Gathering Storm *'02*
The Locket *'02*
Byron *'03*
Good Boy! *'03 (V)*
The Fever *'04*
Merci Docteur Rey *'04 (C)*
The Keeper: The Legend of Omar Khayyam *'05*
The White Countess *'05*

Point Break '91
Bram Stoker's Dracula '92
Freaked '93 (C)
Little Buddha '93
Much Ado about Nothing '93
Even Cowgirls Get the Blues '94
Speed '94
Johnny Mnemonic '95
A Walk in the Clouds '95
Chain Reaction '96
Feeling Minnesota '96
The Last Time I Committed Suicide '96
The Devil's Advocate '97
The Matrix '99
The Gift '00
The Replacements '00
The Watcher '00
Hardball '01
Sweet November '01
The Matrix Reloaded '03
The Matrix Revolutions '03
Something's Gotta Give '03
Constantine '05
Ellie Parker '05 (C)
Thumbsucker '05
The Lake House '06
A Scanner Darkly '06
The Day the Earth Stood Still '08
Street Kings '08
Bollywood Hero '09 (C)
The Private Lives of Pippa Lee '09
Henry's Crime '10
Side by Side '12 (N)
47 Ronin '13
Generation Um... '13
Man of Tai Chi '13
John Wick '14
Knock Knock '15
Exposed '16
The Neon Demon '16
The Whole Truth '16
The Bad Batch '17
John Wick: Chapter 2 '17
Destination Wedding '18
Replicas '18
Siberia '18
Always Be My Maybe '19
John Wick: Chapter 3-Parabellum '19

Kynaston Reeves (1893-1971)
Phantom Fiend '35
Penny Princess '52
Fiend without a Face '58
Hot Millions '68

Lisa Reeves
Pom Pom Girls '76
Snowblind '78

Perrey Reeves (1970-)
Child's Play 3 '91
Red Shoe Diaries: Luscious Lola '00
Old School '03
An American Affair '09

Phil Reeves (1946-)
Election '99
13 Going on 30 '04
Taking Chances '09

Richard Reeves (1912-67)
Loophole '54
Running Target '56
Collision '09

Saskia Reeves
A Woman of Substance '84
Close My Eyes '91
December Bride '91
Butterfly Kiss '94
Different for Girls '96
A Christmas Carol '99
Heart '99
Dune '00
Suspicion '03
The Tesseract '03
Page Eight '11

Scott Reeves (1966-)
Friday the 13th, Part 8: Jason Takes Manhattan '89
Edge of Honor '91
Pride '07

Steve Reeves (1926-2000)
Athena '54
Jail Bait '54
Hercules '58
Hercules Unchained '59
The Giant of Marathon '60
Goliath and the Barbarians '60
The Last Days of Pompeii '60
The Avenger '62
Pirates of the Seven Seas '62
The Slave '62
The Trojan Horse '62
Sandokan the Great '63
A Long Ride From Hell '68

Steve Reevis (1962-)
The Last of the Dogmen '95
Fargo '96
Wild Grizzly '99
The Missing '03
Monsterwolf '10

Joe Regalbuto (1949-)
Divorce Wars: A Love Story '82
Missing '82
Invitation to Hell '84
Lassiter '84
The Queen of Mean '90
Mockingbird Don't Sing '01

Jayne Regan (1909-2000)
Thank you, Mr. Moto '37
Mr. Moto's Gamble '38

Laura Regan
Someone Like You '01
Wes Craven Presents: They '02
Hollow Man 2 '06
Dead Silence '07
How to be a Serial Killer '08
Atlas Shrugged 3: Who Is John Galt? '14

Phil Regan (1906-96)
In Caliente '35
Hit Parade of 1937 '37
Manhattan Merry-Go-Round '37
Outside of Paradise '38
Las Vegas Nights '41
Swing Parade of 1946 '46

Vincent Regan (1965-)
Invasion: Earth '98
Black Knight '01
Troy '04
300 '07
Bonded by Blood '09
Eva '09
The Big I Am '10
Berlin Job '12
Lockout '12

George Regas (1890-1940)
The Love Light '21
The Lives of a Bengal Lancer '35
The Charge of the Light Brigade '36
Beau Geste '39
Gunga Din '39
The Rains Came '39

Duncan Regehr (1952-)
The Last Days of Pompeii '84
The Monster Squad '87
Timemaster '95
The Haunting of Lisa '96
Air Bud 3: World Pup '00
Blood Surf '00
Presumed Dead '06
Nightmare at the End of the Hall '08

Benoit Regent (1953-94)
Trois Couleurs: Bleu '93
Trois Couleurs: Rouge '94 (C)

Serge Reggiani (1922-2004)
La Ronde '51
Casque d'Or '52
Les Miserables '57
Le Doulos '61
Mauvais Sang '86

Nadja Regin (1921-93)
From Russia with Love '63
Goldfinger '64

Paul Regina (1956-2006)
Adam '83
It's My Party '95
Prey of the Jaguar '96

Patrick Regis
Blackbeard '06
Anaconda 3: The Offspring '08

Meg Register
Demonia '90
Boxing Helena '93

Carola Regnier (1946-)
Seduction: The Cruel Woman '89
Rosenstrasse '03

Charles Regnier (1914-2001)
Angelique '64
Angelique: The Road to Versailles '65

Natacha Regnier (1974-)
The Dreamlife of Angels '98
Criminal Lovers '99
How I Killed My Father '03
The Prey '11
Capital '12

Rehan
The Living Corpse '03
Hell's Ground '08

Frank Reicher (1875-1965)
King Kong '33
South of the Border '39
Dr. Cyclops '40
To Be or Not to Be '42
Watch on the Rhine '43

Wolfgang Reichmann (1932-91)
Signs of Life '68
Woyzeck '78

Alex Reid (1975-)
Arachnid '01
The Honeymooners '03
The Descent '05

Anne Reid (1935-)
Catherine Cookson's The Wingless Bird '97
Liam '00
The Mother '03
A Little Trip to Heaven '05
The Bad Mother's Handbook '07
Affinity '08
Angel in the House '11
Upstairs Downstairs '11
Unfinished Song '12

Audrey Reid
Dancehall Queen '97
Third World Cop '99

Beryl Reid (1920-96)
The Belles of St. Trinian's '53
Trial & Error '62
Inspector Clouseau '68
Star! '68
The Assassination Bureau '69
The Killing of Sister George '69
Beast in the Cellar '70
Doctor Phibes Rises Again '72
No Sex Please-We're British '73
Psychomania '73
Joseph Andrews '77
Carry On Emmanuelle '78
Tinker, Tailor, Soldier, Spy '80
Smiley's People '82
Yellowbeard '83
The Doctor and the Devils '85
Duel of Hearts '92

Carl Benton Reid (1893-1973)
The Little Foxes '41
The Killer That Stalked New York '47
The Fuller Brush Girl '50
In a Lonely Place '50
Criminal Lawyer '51
The Great Caruso '51
Carbine Williams '52
The Story of Will Rogers '52
Escape from Fort Bravo '53
The Command '54
The Egyptian '54
One Desire '55
The First Texan '56
Battle Hymn '57
Time Limit '57
Tarzan's Fight for Life '58
The Trap '59
The Gallant Hours '60
Pressure Point '62

Christopher Reid (1964-)
House Party '90
Class Act '91
House Party 2: The Pajama Jam '91
House Party 3 '94
War of the Worlds 2: The Next Wave '08

Elliott Reid (1920-2013)
Young Ideas '43
Gentlemen Prefer Blondes '53
Inherit the Wind '60
Move Over, Darling '63
The Thrill of It All! '63
Follow Me, Boys! '66
Blackbeard's Ghost '67

Fiona Reid (1951-)
Blood & Donuts '95
Bogus '96
My Big Fat Greek Wedding '02
Prom Queen '04
Breakfast With Scot '07
One Week '08

Frances Reid (1914-2010)
Seconds '66
The Affair '73

Kate Reid (1930-93)
One Plus One '61
This Property Is Condemned '66
The Andromeda Strain '71
Death Among Friends '75
Crossbar '79
Circle of Two '80
Atlantic City '81
Execution of Raymond Graham '85
Heaven Help Us '85
Death of a Salesman '86
Fire with Fire '86
Signs of Life '89
The Last Best Year '90
Deceived '91
Teamster Boss: The Jackie Presser Story '92

Michael Earl Reid
Army of Darkness '92
Asylum of the Damned '03

R.D. Reid
Dirty Pictures '00
Dawn of the Dead '04
The Night Before the Night Before Christmas '10

Sam Reid (1987-)
Anonymous '11
Inhuman Resources '12
Belle '13
The Railway Man '13
'71 '14
The Limehouse Golem '17

Sheila Reid (1937-)
Othello '65
Zero Population Growth '72
The Winter Guest '97

Storm Reid (2003-)
Sleight '17
A Wrinkle in Time '18
Don't Let Go '19
The Invisible Man '20

Tara Reid (1975-)
The Big Lebowski '97
Around the Fire '98
Girl '98
Urban Legend '98
American Pie '99
Body Shots '99
Murder at Devil's Glen '99
Dr. T & the Women '00
American Pie 2 '01
Josie and the Pussycats '01
Just Visiting '01
National Lampoon's Van Wilder '02
Devil's Pond '03
My Boss's Daughter '03
Alone in the Dark '05
The Crow: Wicked Prayer '05
Incubus '05
Knots '05
Silent Partner '05
Strike '07
Senior Skip Day '08
Vipers '08
The Fields '11
American Reunion '12
Sharknado '13
The Hungover Games '14
Sharknado 2: The Second One '14
Sharknado 3: Oh Hell No! '15
Sharknado: The 4th Awakens '16

Taylor Anne Reid (1990-)
The 6th Day '00
FBI: Negotiator '05
The Suspect '05

Tim Reid (1944-)
Dead Bang '89
The Fourth War '90
Stephen King's It '90
You Must Remember This '92
Race to Freedom: The Story of the Underground Railroad '94
For Real '02
The Reading Room '05

Wallace Reid (1891-1923)
The Birth of a Nation '15
Affairs of Anatol '21

Timothy Reifsnyder (1986-)
Wide Awake '97
Hearts in Atlantis '01

Halina Reijn (1975-)
Zus & Zo '01
Black Book '06

Charles Nelson Reilly (1931-2007)
Cannonball Run 2 '84
Body Slam '87
All Dogs Go to Heaven '89 (V)
Rock-a-Doodle '92 (V)
A Troll in Central Park '94 (V)
Boys Will Be Boys '97

Georgina Reilly (1986-)
Pontypool '09
Eddie the Sleepwalking Cannibal '12

Hugh Reilly (1916-98)
Lassie's Great Adventure '62
Chuka '67

John C. Reilly (1965-)
Touch and Go '86
Casualties of War '89
We're No Angels '89
Days of Thunder '90
State of Grace '90
Hoffa '92
What's Eating Gilbert Grape '93
Dolores Claiborne '94
The River Wild '94
Boys '95
Georgia '95
Hard Eight '96
Nightwatch '96
Boogie Nights '97
Chicago Cab '98
The Thin Red Line '98
For Love of the Game '99
Magnolia '99
Never Been Kissed '99
The Settlement '99
The Perfect Storm '00
The Anniversary Party '01
Chicago '02
Dark Water '02
Gangs of New York '02
The Good Girl '02
The Hours '02
Anger Management '03
The Aviator '04
Criminal '04
A Prairie Home Companion '06
Talladega Nights: The Ballad of Ricky Bobby '06
Tenacious D in the Pick of Destiny '06
Walk Hard: The Dewey Cox Story '07
Year of the Dog '07
The Promotion '08
Step Brothers '08
Cirque du Freak: The Vampire's Assistant '09
9 '09 (V)
Cyrus '10
The Extra Man '10
Carnage '11
Cedar Rapids '11
Terri '11
We Need to Talk About Kevin '11
Wreck-It Ralph '12 (V)
Bears '14 (N)
Guardians of the Galaxy '14
Life After Beth '14
Entertainment '15
Tale of Tales '15
The Lobster '16
Sing '16
Kong: Skull Island '17
The Little Hours '17
Holmes & Watson '18
Ralph Breaks the Internet '18 (V)
The Sisters Brothers '18
Stan & Ollie '18

Kelly Reilly (1977-)
Poldark '96
Last Orders '01
L'Auberge Espagnole '02
Dead Bodies '03
The Libertine '05
Mrs. Henderson Presents '05
Pride and Prejudice '05
Russian Dolls '05
Me and Orson Welles '09
Sherlock Holmes '09
Triage '09
Citizen Gangster '11
Sherlock Holmes: A Game of Shadows '11
Flight '12
Chinese Puzzle '13
A Single Shot '13
Calvary '14
Heaven Is for Real '14
The Take '16
Eli '19

Robert Reilly
Lilith '64
Frankenstein Meets the Space Monster '65

Gary Reineke (1926-)
The Golden Spiders: A Nero Wolfe Mystery '00
Spider '02

Carl Reiner (1922-2020)
The Gazebo '59
Gidget Goes Hawaiian '61
It's a Mad, Mad, Mad, Mad World '63
The Thrill of It All! '63
The Russians Are Coming, the Russians Are Coming '66
A Guide for the Married Man '67 (C)
The End '78
The Jerk '79 (C)
Dead Men Don't Wear Plaid '82
Summer School '87 (C)
Spirit of '76 '91
Slums of Beverly Hills '98
The Adventures of Rocky & Bullwinkle '00

Ocean's Eleven '01
Good Boy! '03 (V)
Ocean's Twelve '04
Ocean's Thirteen '07

Rob Reiner (1947-)
Halls of Anger '70
Where's Poppa? '70
More Than Friends '78
The Jerk '79 (C)
This Is Spinal Tap '84
Throw Momma from the Train '87
Postcards from the Edge '90
Spirit of '76 '91
The Return of Spinal Tap '92 (C)
Sleepless in Seattle '93
Bullets over Broadway '94
Bye Bye, Love '94
Mixed Nuts '94
For Better or Worse '95 (C)
The First Wives Club '96
Trigger Happy '96 (C)
Primary Colors '98
EDtv '99
The Muse '99 (C)
The Story of Us '99
Alex & Emma '03
Dickie Roberts: Former Child Star '03 (C)
Everyone's Hero '06 (V)
The Wolf of Wall Street '13
Shock and Awe '18

Robert Reiner (1947-)
See Rob Reiner

Tracy Reiner (1964-)
Jumpin' Jack Flash '86 (C)
Nothing in Common '86
New Year's Day '89
When Harry Met Sally. . . '89
Frankie and Johnny '91
A League of Their Own '92
Apollo 13 '95

Judge Reinhold (1957-)
Stripes '81
Fast Times at Ridgemont High '82
The Lords of Discipline '83
Beverly Hills Cop '84
Gremlins '84
Roadhouse 66 '84
Head Office '86
Ruthless People '86
Beverly Hills Cop 2 '87
Vice Versa '88
Rosalie Goes Shopping '89
Daddy's Dyin'. . . Who's Got the Will? '90
Enid Is Sleeping '90
A Soldier's Tale '91
Zandalee '91
Beverly Hills Cop 3 '94
The Santa Clause '94
Homegrown '97 (C)
Boltneck '98
Last Lives '98
Tom Clancy's Netforce '98
Ping! '99
Beethoven's 3rd '00
Enemies of Laughter '00
Newsbreak '00
Beethoven's 4th '01
Dead in a Heartbeat '02
The Santa Clause 2 '02
Whacked! '02
National Lampoon's Holiday Reunion '03
Clifford's Really Big Movie '04 (V)
The Hollow '04
Sheeba '05
The Santa Clause 3: The Escape Clause '06
Swing Vote '08
I Am Potential '15

Ann Reinking (1949-)
All That Jazz '79
Annie '82
Micki & Maude '84

Diana Reis
The Dive from Clausen's Pier '05
Maneater '07
What If God Were the Sun? '07
Taken in Broad Daylight '09

Michelle Reis (1970-)
Fallen Angels '95
Flowers of Shanghai '98

Geri Reischl (1959-)
The Brotherhood of Satan '71
I Dismember Mama '74

Hans Reiser (1919-92)
Secret of the Black Trunk '62
The Great Escape '63

Paul Reiser (1957-)
Diner '82
Sunset Limousine '83
Beverly Hills Cop '84
Odd Jobs '85
Aliens '86
Beverly Hills Cop 2 '87
Cross My Heart '88
Crazy People '90
The Marrying Man '91
Mr. Write '92
Bye Bye, Love '94
The Story of Us '99
One Night at McCool's '01
Purpose '02
Strange Relations '02
Women vs. Men '02
The Thing About My Folks '05
Life After Beth '14
Whiplash '14
Miles '17
War on Everyone '17

Robbie Reist (1964-)
See Robbie (Reist) Rist

David Reivers
Jump In! '07
Free Style '09

Winston Rekert (1949-2012)
Agnes of God '85
Eternal Evil '87
Toby McTeague '87
Loving Evangeline '98
The Last Stop '99
A Date With Darkness '03
Savage Island '03
The Secret of Hidden Lake '06
Art of War 2: The Betrayal '08
NYC: Tornado Terror '08
Smoke Jumpers '08
Phantom Racer '09
Goodnight for Justice '11

James Remar (1953-)
The Warriors '79
Cruising '80
Windwalker '81
48 Hrs. '82
The Cotton Club '84
The Clan of the Cave Bear '86
Quiet Cool '86
Rent-A-Cop '88
The Dream Team '89
Drugstore Cowboy '89
Tales from the Darkside: The Movie '90
Deadlock '91
White Fang '91
Fatal Charm '92
Blink '93
Fatal Instinct '93
The Tigress '93
Across the Moon '94
Boys on the Side '94
Miracle on 34th Street '94
Renaissance Man '94
The Surgeon '94
One Good Turn '95
The Phantom '96
The Quest '96
Born Bad '97
Mortal Kombat 2: Annihilation '97
Psycho '98
Blowback '99
D.R.E.A.M. Team '99
Rites of Passage '99
The Base 2: Guilty as Charged '00
Hellraiser 5: Inferno '00
What Lies Beneath '00
The Guardian '01
Duplex '03
Fear X '03
Lady Jayne Killer '03
2 Fast 2 Furious '03
American Meltdown '04
Blade: Trinity '04
The Girl Next Door '04
Ike: Countdown to D-Day '04
Ratatouille '07 (V)
Sharpshooter '07
Pineapple Express '08
The Christmas Hope '09
The Unborn '09
Gun '10
RED '10
All Superheroes Must Die '11
Arena '11
Setup '11
Transformers: Dark of the Moon '11 (V)
Django Unchained '12
Horns '13
Decommissioned '16
The Dog Lover '16
USS Indianapolis: Men of Courage '16
The Blackcoat's Daughter '17

Erika Remberg (1932-)
Circus of Horrors '60
The Lickerish Quartet '70

George Remes
Police, Adjective '09
Born to Raise Hell '10

Lee Remick (1935-91)
A Face in the Crowd '57
The Long, Hot Summer '58
Anatomy of a Murder '59
Wild River '60
Days of Wine and Roses '62
Experiment in Terror '62
The Wheeler Dealers '63
Baby, the Rain Must Fall '64
The Hallelujah Trail '65
The Detective '68
No Way to Treat a Lady '68
Hard Contract '69
A Severed Head '70
Sometimes a Great Notion '71
QB VII '74
Touch Me Not '74
Hennessy '75
Hustling '75
The Omen '76
Telefon '77
The Medusa Touch '78
The Europeans '79
Torn Between Two Lovers '79
The Competition '80
Haywire '80
Mistral's Daughter '84
Nutcracker: Money, Madness & Murder '87
Around the World in 80 Days '89
Bridge to Silence '89

Leah Remini (1970-)
Old School '03
Second Act '18

Bert Remsen (1925-99)
Pork Chop Hill '59
Dead Ringer '64
McCabe & Mrs. Miller '71
Thieves Like Us '74
Nashville '75
Sweet Hostage '75
Tarantulas: The Deadly Cargo '77
Uncle Joe Shannon '78
A Wedding '78
Joni '79
Carny '80
Second-Hand Hearts '81
Lookin' to Get Out '82
Burning Rage '84
I Married a Centerfold '84
Code of Silence '85
Eye of the Tiger '86
Tai-Pan '86
Terrorvision '86
Who Is Julia? '86
Curfew '88
Miss Firecracker '89
Daddy's Dyin'. . . Who's Got the Will? '90
Peacemaker '90
Evil Spirits '91
Only the Lonely '91
Maverick '94 (C)
Humanoids from the Deep '96
Sundown: The Vampire in Retreat '08

Kerry Remsen
Ghoulies 2 '87
Pumpkinhead '88

Albert Remy (1912-67)
Children of Paradise '44
The 400 Blows '59
Shoot the Piano Player '62
The Train '65

Ronald Remy
No Man Is an Island '62
Mad Doctor of Blood Island '68

Richie Ren (1966-)
Silver Hawk '04
Seoul Raiders '05

Duncan Renaldo (1904-80)
Ten Laps to Go '36
Mile a Minute Love '37
Two Minutes to Play '37
Zorro Rides Again '37
Spawn of the North '38
South of the Border '39
Down Mexico Way '41
South of Panama '41
For Whom the Bell Tolls '43
Fighting Seabees '44
The Capture '50

Tito Renaldo
For Whom the Bell Tolls '43
The Story of G.I. Joe '45

Simone Renant (1911-2004)
Jenny Lamour '47
Bedevilled '55
Dangerous Liaisons '60

Mercedes Renard
Break-In '06
Meddling Mom '13

Francis Renaud (1967-)
Pigalle '95
Perfect Love '96
The 36th Precinct '04
Chrysalis '07

Isabelle Renauld (1966-)
Perfect Love '96
Eternity and a Day '97
Murderous Maids '00
Monsieur Ibrahim '03
Prey '10

Georges Renavent (1894-1969)
Rio Rita '29
East of Borneo '31
Mara Maru '52

Liz Renay (1926-2007)
Nasty Rabbit '64
Deadwood '65
The Thrill Killers '65
Lady Godiva Rides '68
Blackenstein '73
Desperate Living '77
Mark of the Astro-Zombies '02

Mark Rendall (1988-)
The Impossible Elephant '02
The Interrogation of Michael Crowe '02
A Different Loyalty '04
Spirit Bear: The Simon Jackson Story '05
Charlie Bartlett '07
30 Days of Night '07
The Exploding Girl '09
My One and Only '09
The Bird Men '13

Robert Rendel (1885-1944)
Her Night of Romance '24
The Four Feathers '39

Victor Rendina (1916-85)
The Godfather '72
The Man Who Wasn't There '83
Racing with the Moon '84

Salvatore Rendino
Miami Beach Cops '93
Devoured '14

Chelsea Rendon
No Turning Back '01
The Infiltrators '20

Liz Rene (1926-2007)
See Liz Renay

Lyne Renee (1979-)
Love at First Kill '08
The Hessen Conspiracy '09
An L.A. Minute '18

Zoe Renee
Jinn '18
Nancy Drew and the Hidden Staircase '19

Brad Renfro (1982-2008)
The Client '94
The Cure '95
Tom and Huck '95
Sleepers '96
Telling Lies in America '96
Apt Pupil '97
Skipped Parts '00
Bully '01
Ghost World '01
Happy Campers '01
Tart '01
The Theory of the Leisure Class '01
Deuces Wild '02
The Job '03
The Jacket '05
10th & Wolf '06

Jeremie Renier (1981-)
La Promesse '96
Criminal Lovers '99
Brotherhood of the Wolf '01
The Child '05
Private Property '06
In Bruges '08
Lorna's Silence '08
Summer Hours '08
A Heavenly Vintage '09
Potiche '10
The Kid with a Bike '11
Neither Heaven Nor Earth '16
The Unknown Girl '17
Frankie '19

Yannick Renier (1975-)
Private Property '06
Love Songs '07
Born in 68 '08

Yves Renier (1942-)
The Other Side of the Law '95
Mortal Transfer '01

Serge Renko
Triple Agent '04
The Romance of Astrea and Celadon '07

Patrick Renna (1979-)
The Sandlot '93
Son-in-Law '93
The Big Green '95
Blue River '95
Address Unknown '96
P.U.N.K.S. '98
Life Blood '09

Deborah Rennard (1959-)
Land of Doom '84
Lionheart '90

Jeremy Renner (1971-)
A Nightmare Come True '97
Fish in a Barrel '01
Dahmer '02
S.W.A.T. '03
A Little Trip to Heaven '05
Neo Ned '05
North Country '05
12 and Holding '05
The Assassination of Jesse James by the Coward Robert Ford '07
28 Weeks Later '07
The Hurt Locker '08
The Town '10
Mission: Impossible-Ghost Protocol '11
The Avengers '12
The Bourne Legacy '12
Hansel & Gretel: Witch Hunters '12
American Hustle '13
The Immigrant '13
Kill the Messenger '14
Mission: Impossible Rogue Nation '15
Arrival '16
Wind River '17
Tag '18
Arctic Dogs '19 (V)

Callum Keith Rennie (1960-)
Double Happiness '94
Hard Core Logo '96
Last Night '98
eXistenZ '99
The Highway Man '99
The Last Stop '99
The Life Before This '99
Memento '00
Suspicious River '00
Picture Claire '01
Now & Forever '02
Slap Shot 2: Breaking the Ice '02
Torso '02
Falling Angels '03
Blade: Trinity '04
Whole New Thing '05
Code Name: The Cleaner '07
The Invisible '07
Normal '07
Shattered '07
Tin Man '07
The X Files: I Want to Believe '08
Battlestar Galactica: The Plan '09
Case 39 '10
Hoax for the Holidays '10
Trigger '10
Born to Be Blue '15
The Young and Prodigious T.S. Spivet '15
Into the Forest '16
Jigsaw '17
Mobile Homes '19

Michael Rennie (1909-71)
The Wicked Lady '45
The Black Rose '50
The Day the Earth Stood Still '51
I'll Never Forget You '51
Five Fingers '52
Phone Call from a Stranger '52
Dangerous Crossing '53
King of the Khyber Rifles '53
The Robe '53
Sailor of the King '53
Demetrius and the Gladiators '54
Desiree '54
Princess of the Nile '54
Mambo '55
The Rains of Ranchipur '55
Seven Cities of Gold '55
Soldier of Fortune '55
Teenage Rebel '56
Omar Khayyam '57
Missiles from Hell '58
Third Man on the Mountain '59
The Lost World '60
Mary, Mary '63
Commando Attack '67
Hotel '67
The Battle of El Alamein '68
The Devil's Brigade '68
The Power '68
Dracula vs. Frankenstein '69
Die Screaming, Marianne '73

Ginette Reno (1946-)
Leolo '92
Mambo Italiano '03

Jean Reno (1948-)
Le Dernier Combat '84
Subway '85
The Big Blue '88

La Femme Nikita '91
The Professional '94
Beyond the Clouds '95
French Kiss '95
The Visitors '95
For Roseanna '96
Mission: Impossible '96
Godzilla '98
Ronin '98
The Crimson Rivers '01
Just Visiting '01
Wasabi '01
Jet Lag '02
Rollerball '02
Hotel Rwanda '04
Crimson Rivers 2: Angels of the Apocalypse '05
Empire of the Wolves '05
The Tiger and the Snow '05
The Da Vinci Code '06
Flushed Away '06 (V)
Flyboys '06
The Pink Panther '06
Cash '08
Armored '09
Couples Retreat '09
The Pink Panther 2 '09
Ultimate Heist '09
22 Bullets '10
Margaret '11
Alex Cross '12
Days and Nights '14
Hector and the Search for Happiness '14
The Last Face '17

John Reno
Bloodspell '87
Mirror of Death '87

Kelly Reno (1966-)
The Black Stallion '79
The Black Stallion Returns '83

Pierre Renoir (1885-1952)
La Marseillaise '37
Children of Paradise '44

Sophie Renoir
Le Beau Mariage '82
Boyfriends & Girlfriends '88

Robin Renucci (1956-)
Children of the Century '99
Taking Sides '01
The Dreamers '03
Comedy of Power '06

Andrea Renzi (1963-)
His Secret Life '01
The Spectator '04

Eva Renzi (1944-2005)
Funeral in Berlin '66
The Bird with the Crystal Plumage '70
Night of the Assassin '70

Maggie Renzi (1951-)
Return of the Secaucus 7 '80
The Brother from Another Planet '84
Matewan '87
Eight Men Out '88
City of Hope '91
Passion Fish '92

Lisa Repo Martell (1971-)
Scared Silent '02
Touch of Pink '04

Stafford Repp (1918-74)
Plunder Road '57
Batman '66

Antonio Resines (1954-)
How to Be a Woman and Not Die in the Attempt '91
The Girl of Your Dreams '99
Two Tough Guys '03
Cell 211 '09

Frank Ressel (1925-85)
Blood and Black Lace '64
Sabata '69

Dale Resteghini (1968-)
Colorz of Rage '97
Da Hip Hop Witch '00

Tommy Rettig (1941-96)
For Heaven's Sake '50
Elopement '51
Paula '52
The 5000 Fingers of Dr. T '53
The Egyptian '54
River of No Return '54
The Cobweb '55

Raoul Retzer (1919-74)
The Vampire Happening '71
2069: A Sex Odyssey '78

Gloria Reuben (1964-)
Timecop '94
Nick of Time '95
Inferno '99
Cold Blooded '00
Shaft '00
Anne Rice's The Feast of All Saints '01
Little John '02
Life Support '07
Jesse Stone: Innocents Lost '11
Jesse Stone: Benefit of the Doubt '12
Lincoln '12
Admission '13
Reasonable Doubt '14

Paul (Pee-wee Herman) Reubens (1952-)
The Blues Brothers '80 (C)
Cheech and Chong's Next Movie '80
Cheech and Chong's Nice Dreams '81
Meatballs 2 '84
Pee-wee's Big Adventure '85
Flight of the Navigator '86 (V)
Back to the Beach '87
Big Top Pee-wee '88
Batman Returns '92
Buffy the Vampire Slayer '92
The Nightmare Before Christmas '93 (V)
Dunston Checks In '95
Matilda '96
Buddy '97
Dr. Dolittle '98 (V)
Mystery Men '99
South of Heaven, West of Hell '00
Blow '01
Disney's Teacher's Pet '04 (V)
The Tripper '06
Life During Wartime '09
The Smurfs '11 (V)

Thekla Reuten (1975-)
Everybody's Famous! '00
Rosenstrasse '03
Highlander: The Source '07
In Bruges '08
The American '10
Hidden '11

Amber Rose Revah
From Paris With Love '10
The Mystery of Edwin Drood '12

Anne Revere (1903-90)
The Howards of Virginia '40
Remember the Day '41
The Falcon Takes Over '42
Meet the Stewarts '42
Old Acquaintance '43
The Song of Bernadette '43
The Keys of the Kingdom '44
National Velvet '44
Sunday Dinner for a Soldier '44
The Thin Man Goes Home '44
Don Juan Quilligan '45
Fallen Angel '45
Dragonwyck '46
Body and Soul '47
Forever Amber '47
Gentleman's Agreement '47
The Shocking Miss Pilgrim '47
Deep Waters '48
Secret Beyond the Door '48
A Place in the Sun '51

Dorothy Revier (1904-93)
The Black Camel '31
Green Eyes '34
Circumstantial Evidence '35

Clive Revill (1930-)
Bunny Lake Is Missing '65
A Fine Madness '66
Kaleidoscope '66
Modesty Blaise '66
The Double Man '67
Fathom '67
The Assassination Bureau '69
The Buttercup Chain '70
The Private Life of Sherlock Holmes '70
A Severed Head '70
Avanti! '72
The Legend of Hell House '73
The Little Prince '74
One of Our Dinosaurs Is Missing '75
The Empire Strikes Back '80
Zorro, the Gay Blade '81
Rumpelstiltskin '86
Let Him Have It '91
Dracula: Dead and Loving It '95
The Thief and the Cobbler '96 (V)
Possums '99
Deadly Shift '08

Tony Revolori (1996-)
The Grand Budapest Hotel '14
Dope '15
Lowriders '17
Table 19 '17
The Long Dumb Road '19
The Sound of Silence '19

Simon Rex (1974-)
Shriek If You Know What I Did Last Friday the 13th '00
The Forsaken '01
Going Greek '01
Scary Movie 3 '03
Karate Dog '04
Scary Movie 4 '06
Scary Movie 5 '13

Alejandro Rey (1930-87)
Solomon and Sheba '59
Battle at Bloody Beach '61
Fun in Acapulco '63
Synanon '65
The Stepmother '71
The Ninth Configuration '79
Grace Kelly '83
Moscow on the Hudson '84
Terrorvision '86

Antonia Rey (1927-)
King of the Gypsies '78
Tarantella '95

Fernando Rey (1917-94)
The Miracle of Marcelino '55
Viridiana '61
The Castilian '63
The Ceremony '63
Goliath Against the Giants '63
Son of a Gunfighter '65
Attack of the Robots '66
Chimes at Midnight '67
Navajo Joe '67
Villa Rides '68
Guns of the Magnificent Seven '69
The Adventurers '70
Cold Eyes of Fear '70
Companeros '70
The French Connection '71
The Discreet Charm of the Bourgeoisie '72
A Town Called Hell '72
Antony and Cleopatra '73
Autopsy '73
French Connection 2 '75
The Desert of the Tartars '76
Insanity '76
Seven Beauties '76
That Obscure Object of Desire '77
Quintet '79
Cabo Blanco '81
Monsignor '82
A.D. '85
The Hit '85
Star Knight '85
Angel of Death '86
Moon over Parador '88
1492: Conquest of Paradise '92

Mony Rey
Mademoiselle '66
Not Without My Daughter '90

Cisco Reyes
Next Day Air '09
Decisions '10

Ernie Reyes, Jr. (1972-)
Teenage Mutant Ninja Turtles 2: The Secret of the Ooze '91
Surf Ninjas '93
White Wolves 2: Legend of the Wild '94
Rush Hour 2 '01
Poolhall Junkies '02
The Rundown '03
Indiana Jones and the Kingdom of the Crystal Skull '08

Judy Reyes (1967-)
Washington Heights '02
Little Girl Lost: The Delimar Vera Story '08
The Poker Club '08
Gun Hill Road '11
Without Men '11
The Pregnancy Project '12

Julian Reyes (1961-)
Point Break '91
Mi Vida Loca '94

Kamar Reyes (1967-)
See Kamar De Los Reyes

Natalia Reyes (1987-)
Birds of Passage '18
Terminator: Dark Fate '19

Patricia Reyes Spindola (1953-)
Frida '02
Between '05

Dominique Reymond (1957-)
Come Undone '00
Les Destinees '00
Demonlover '02
Summer Hours '08

Janine Reynaud (1930-)
Castle of the Creeping Flesh '68
The Case of the Scorpion's Tail '71
The Scorpion's Tail '71

Amanda Reyne
Landspeed '01
Hypersonic '02

Burt Reynolds (1936-2018)
Angel Baby '61
Operation C.I.A. '65
Navajo Joe '67
Iron Cowboy '68
Shark! '68
Impasse '69
100 Rifles '69
Sam Whiskey '69
Savage Run '70
Deliverance '72
Everything You Always Wanted to Know about Sex (But Were Afraid to Ask) '72
Fuzz '72
Man Who Loved Cat Dancing '73
Shamus '73
White Lightning '73
The Longest Yard '74
The Hustle '75
W.W. and the Dixie Dancekings '75
Gator '76
Nickelodeon '76
Silent Movie '76
Semi-Tough '77
Smokey and the Bandit '77
The End '78
Hooper '78
Starting Over '79
Smokey and the Bandit 2 '80
Cannonball Run '81
Sharky's Machine '81
Best Friends '82
The Best Little Whorehouse in Texas '82
The Man Who Loved Women '83
Smokey and the Bandit, Part 3 '83 (C)
Stroker Ace '83
Cannonball Run 2 '84
City Heat '84
Stick '85
Sherman's March '86 (C)
Heat '87
Malone '87
Rent-A-Cop '88
Switching Channels '88
All Dogs Go to Heaven '89 (V)
Breaking In '89
Physical Evidence '89
Modern Love '90
The Player '92 (C)
Cop and a Half '93
The Man from Left Field '93
The Cherokee Kid '96
Citizen Ruth '96
Striptease '96
Trigger Happy '96
Bean '97
Boogie Nights '97
Hunter's Moon '97
Meet Wally Sparks '97
Raven '97
Crazy Six '98
Big City Blues '99
Mystery, Alaska '99
Pups '99
Waterproof '99
The Crew '00
Hostage Hotel '00
Driven '01
The Hollywood Sign '01
Tempted '01
The Final Hit '02
Johnson County War '02
Snapshots '02
Hard Ground '03
Without a Paddle '04
The Dukes of Hazzard '05
The Longest Yard '05
Broken Bridges '06
End Game '06
Forget About It '06
Grilled '06
Deal '08
Delgo '08 (V)
In the Name of the King: A Dungeon Siege Tale '08
Reel Love '11
Hamlet & Hutch '14
The Last Movie Star '17

Craig Reynolds (1907-49)
Smart Blonde '37
The Gentleman from Arizona '39

Debbie Reynolds (1932-2016)
The Daughter of Rosie O'Grady '50
Three Little Words '50
Two Weeks with Love '50
Mr. Imperium '51
Singin' in the Rain '52
Skirts Ahoy! '52
The Affairs of Dobie Gillis '53
Give a Girl a Break '53
I Love Melvin '53
Athena '54
Susan Slept Here '54
Hit the Deck '55
The Tender Trap '55
Bundle of Joy '56
The Catered Affair '56
Tammy and the Bachelor '57
The Gazebo '59
It Started with a Kiss '59
The Mating Game '59
Say One for Me '59
The Rat Race '60
The Second Time Around '61
How the West Was Won '63
Mary, Mary '63
The Unsinkable Molly Brown '64
The Singing Nun '66
Divorce American Style '67
How Sweet It Is! '68
What's the Matter with Helen? '71
Charlotte's Web '73 (V)
Detective Sadie & Son '84
Battling for Baby '92
The Bodyguard '92 (C)
Heaven and Earth '93
Mother '96
Wedding Bell Blues '96 (C)
In and Out '97
Halloweentown '98
Kiki's Delivery Service '98 (V)
Zack & Reba '98
Rugrats in Paris: The Movie '00 (V)
Halloweentown 2: Kalabar's Revenge '01
These Old Broads '01
Connie and Carla '04 (C)
Halloweentown High '04
Return to Halloweentown '06
One for the Money '12
Behind the Candelabra '13

Gene Reynolds (1923-2020)
In Old Chicago '37
Boys Town '38
Love Finds Andy Hardy '38
They Shall Have Music '39
Gallant Sons '40
Adventure in Washington '41
Andy Hardy's Private Secretary '41
Life Begins for Andy Hardy '41
Junior G-Men of the Air '42
Jungle Patrol '48
Country Girl '54
Down Three Dark Streets '54

Jacob Reynolds (1983-)
Gummo '97
The Aggression Scale '12

Jordan Reynolds (1994-)
Tommy and the Cool Mule '09
Adventures of a Teenage Dragonslayer '10

Marjorie Reynolds (1916-97)
Gone with the Wind '39
Mr. Wong in Chinatown '39
Doomed to Die '40
The Fatal Hour '40
Holiday Inn '42
Ministry of Fear '44
Monsieur Beaucaire '46
The Time of Their Lives '46
Bad Men of Tombstone '49
His Kind of Woman '51

Michael J. Reynolds (1939-)
The Big Turnaround '88
Wicked City '89 (V)
A Secret Affair '99
Out For a Kill '03

Nicola Reynolds (1974-)
Human Traffic '99
Framed '10

Peter Reynolds (1925-75)
The Vanquished '52
Devil Girl from Mars '54
The Hands of Orlac '60
It Takes a Thief '60

Robert Reynolds
Tunnel Vision '95
Element of Doubt '96
The Watch '08

Russell Reynolds
Countdown: Jerusalem '09
Dragonquest '09

Ryan Reynolds (1976-)
Sabrina the Teenage Witch '96

The Alarmist *'98*
Boltneck *'98*
Coming Soon *'99*
Dick *'99*
We All Fall Down *'00*
Finder's Fee *'01*
Buying the Cow *'02*
National Lampoon's Van Wilder *'02*
The In-Laws *'03*
Blade: Trinity *'04*
Harold and Kumar Go to White Castle *'04*
The Amityville Horror *'05*
Just Friends *'05*
Waiting *'05*
School of Life *'06*
The Nines *'07*
Smokin' Aces *'07*
Chaos Theory *'08*
Definitely, Maybe *'08*
Fireflies in the Garden *'08*
Adventureland *'09*
Paper Man *'09*
The Proposal *'09*
X-Men Origins: Wolverine *'09*
Buried *'10*
The Change-Up *'11*
Green Lantern *'11*
Safe House *'12*
The Croods *'13 (V)*
R.I.P.D. *'13*
Turbo *'13 (V)*
The Captive *'14*
Mississippi Grind *'15*
Self/Less *'15*
The Voices *'15*
Woman in Gold *'15*
Criminal *'16*
Deadpool *'16*
The Hitman's Bodyguard *'17*
Life *'17*
Deadpool 2 *'18*
Pokémon Detective Pikachu *'19 (V)*
6 Underground *'19*

Simon Reynolds (1969-)
Gate 2 *'92*
The Prize Winner of Defiance, Ohio *'05*
The Two Mr. Kissels *'08*

William Reynolds (1931-)
Carrie *'52*
Francis Goes to West Point *'52*
Has Anybody Seen My Gal? *'52*
Son of Ali Baba *'52*
All That Heaven Allows *'55*
Cult of the Cobra *'55*
There's Always Tomorrow *'56*
The Land Unknown *'57*
FBI Code 98 *'63*
A Distant Trumpet *'64*

Jack Reynor
Transformers: Age of Extinction *'14*
Sing Street *'16*
Kin *'18*
Midsommar *'19*

Ving Rhames (1959-)
Patty Hearst *'88*
The Long Walk Home *'89*
Flight of the Intruder *'90*
Jacob's Ladder *'90*
Homicide *'91*
The People under the Stairs *'91*
Dave *'93*
The Saint of Fort Washington *'93*
DROP Squad *'94*
Kiss of Death *'94*
Pulp Fiction *'94*
Ed McBain's 87th Precinct: Lightning *'95*
Dangerous Ground *'96*
Mission: Impossible *'96*
Rosewood *'96*
Striptease *'96*
Body Count *'97*
Con Air *'97*
Don King: Only in America *'97*
Out of Sight *'98*
Bringing Out the Dead *'99*
Entrapment *'99*
American Tragedy *'00*
Holiday Heart *'00*
Mission: Impossible 2 *'00*
Baby Boy *'01*
Final Fantasy: The Spirits Within *'01 (V)*
Sins of the Father *'01*
Lilo & Stitch *'02 (V)*
Little John *'02*
RFK *'02*
Sin *'02*
Undisputed *'02*
Dark Blue *'03*
Dawn of the Dead *'04*
Animal *'05*
Back in the Day *'05*
Idlewild *'06*
Mission: Impossible 3 *'06*
Animal 2 *'07*
A Broken Life *'07*
I Now Pronounce You Chuck and Larry *'07*
Saving God *'08*
The Bridge to Nowhere *'09*
Echelon Conspiracy *'09*
Give 'Em Hell Malone *'09*
The Goods: Live Hard, Sell Hard *'09*
Phantom Punch *'09*
Surrogates *'09*
The Tournament *'09*
Caged Animal *'10*
Death Race 2 *'10*
Operation: Endgame *'10*
Piranha 3D *'10 (C)*
Mafia *'11*
Mission: Impossible-Ghost Protocol *'11*
Piranha 3DD *'11*
The River Murders *'11*
7 Below *'11*
Death Race 3: Inferno *'12*
Won't Back Down *'12*
Armed Response *'13*
Force of Execution *'13*
Percentage *'13*
A Day Late and a Dollar Short *'14*
Jamesy Boy *'14*
Mission: Impossible Rogue Nation *'15*
Mission: Impossible-Fallout *'18*

Caroline Rhea (1964-)
Christmas With the Kranks *'04*
The Perfect Man *'05*
Fast Girl *'07*
To Be Fat Like Me *'07*
Love N' Dancing *'09*
The Christmas Consultant *'12*

Phillip Rhee (1960-)
Best of the Best *'89*
Best of the Best 2 *'93*
Best of the Best 3: No Turning Back *'95*
Best of the Best: Without Warning *'98*
Underdog Kids *'15*

Simon Rhee (1957-)
Best of the Best *'89*
Best of the Best 2 *'93*
The Substitute 4: Failure is Not an Option *'00*
Landspeed *'01*
Kung Pow! Enter the Fist *'02*

Iwan Rheon
Wasteland *'13*
Mission of Honor *'19*

Ashlie Rhey (1961-)
Bikini Drive-In *'94*
Midnight Tease *'94*
Play Time *'94*

Rhianna (1988-)
Battleship *'12*
Home *'15 (V)*

Julian Rhind-Tutt (1968-)
The Madness of King George *'94*
Reckless *'97*
Heat of the Sun *'99*
The Trench *'99*
Lara Croft: Tomb Raider *'01*
Miranda *'01*
To Kill a King *'03*
The River King *'05*
Oliver Twist *'07*
The Shadow in the North *'07*
Gambit *'12*
The Lady Vanishes *'13*

Barbara Rhoades (1946-)
The Shakiest Gun in the West *'68*
Up the Sandbox *'72*
Scream Blacula Scream *'73*
The Choirboys *'77*
The Goodbye Girl *'77*
Serial *'80*

Bobby Rhodes (1947-)
The Last Hunter *'80*
Demons 2 *'87*

Brian Rhodes (1947-)
Nemesis Game *'03*
DC 9/11: Time of Crisis *'04*

Christopher Rhodes
The Lady Is a Square *'58*
Gorgo *'61*

Cynthia Rhodes (1956-)
Flashdance *'83*
Staying Alive *'83*
Runaway *'84*
Dirty Dancing *'87*

Dane Rhodes
A Love Song for Bobby Long *'04*
Ticking Clock *'10*

Donnelly Rhodes (1937-2018)
Gunfight in Abilene *'67*
The Penthouse *'89*
Showdown at Williams Creek *'91*
Big and Hairy *'98*
Pressure *'02*
Wilderness Love *'02*
Past Tense *'06*
Loch Ness Terror *'07*
Goblin *'10*
Hunt to Kill *'10*
Marley & Me: The Puppy Years *'11*
Metal Shifters *'11*
Barricade *'12*
12 Disasters *'12*

Erik Rhodes (1906-90)
The Gay Divorcee *'34*
Charlie Chan in Paris *'35*
Old Man Rhythm *'35*
Top Hat *'35*

Grandon Rhodes (1904-87)
Magnificent Doll *'46*
Revenge of the Creature *'55*

Hari Rhodes (1932-92)
The Nun and the Sergeant *'62*
Drums of Africa *'63*
Shock Corridor *'63*
Earth II *'71*
Conquest of the Planet of the Apes *'72*
Detroit 9000 *'73*
Mayday at 40,000 Feet *'76*
Coma *'78*
A Woman Called Moses *'78*
Backstairs at the White House *'79*

Kim Rhodes
Beethoven's Christmas Adventure *'11*
Atlas Shrugged 2: The Strike *'12*

Marjorie Rhodes (1903-79)
Those People Next Door *'52*
Decameron Nights *'53*
Hands of the Ripper *'71*

Trevante Rhodes (1990-)
Moonlight *'16*
Burning Sands *'17*
The Predator *'18*
12 Strong *'18*

Madlyn Rhue (1935-2003)
A Majority of One *'56*
Escape From Zahrain *'62*
Kenner *'73*

Busta Rhymes (1972-)
The Rugrats Movie *'98 (V)*
Finding Forrester *'00*
Shaft *'00*
Halloween: Resurrection *'02*
Narc *'02*
Full Clip *'06*

Matthew Rhys (1974-)
Heart *'99*
Titus *'99*
Shooters *'00*
Very Annie Mary *'00*
Deathwatch *'02*
The Lost World *'02*
Fakers *'04*
Sorted *'04*
Beau Brummell: This Charming Man *'06*
Love and Other Disasters *'06*
Virgin Territory *'07*
The Edge of Love *'08*
The Mystery of Edwin Drood *'12*
The Scapegoat *'12*
Death Comes to Pemberley *'13*
A Beautiful Day in the Neighborhood *'19*

Paul Rhys (1963-)
Vincent & Theo *'90*
Chaplin *'92*
Nina Takes a Lover *'94*
A Dance to the Music of Time *'97*
King Lear *'98*
Food of Love *'02*
Hellraiser: Deader *'05*
Great Expectations *'11*

Phillip Rhys (1974-)
The Fear: Halloween Night *'99*
Flatland *'02*
The Space Between *'10*

John Rhys-Davies (1944-)
Shogun *'80*
Raiders of the Lost Ark *'81*
Sphinx *'81*
Ivanhoe *'82*
Victor/Victoria *'82*
Sword of the Valiant *'83*
Kim *'84*
King Solomon's Mines *'85*
The Living Daylights *'87*
Higher Ground *'88*
Noble House *'88*
War & Remembrance *'88*
Waxwork *'88*
Indiana Jones and the Last Crusade *'89*
The Trial of the Incredible Hulk *'89*
Tusks *'89*
War & Remembrance: The Final Chapter *'89*
The High Crusade *'92*
The Lost World *'92*
The Seventh Coin *'92*
Sunset Grill *'92*
The Unnamable 2: The Statement of Randolph Carter *'92*
Return to the Lost World *'93*
Ring of the Musketeers *'93*
Catherine the Great *'95*
Aladdin and the King of Thieves *'96 (V)*
Glory Daze *'96*
The Great White Hype *'96*
Marquis de Sade *'96*
Cats Don't Dance *'97 (V)*
Secre of the Andes *'98*
Au Pair *'99*
Delta Force One-The Lost Patrol *'99*
Britannic *'00*
Lord of the Rings: The Fellowship of the Ring *'01*
Sabretooth *'01*
Endangered Species *'02*
Lord of the Rings: The Two Towers *'02 (V)*
Scorcher *'02*
Coronado *'03*
Helen of Troy *'03*
The Jungle Book 2 *'03 (V)*
La Femme Musketeer *'03*
Lord of the Rings: The Return of the King *'03*
The Medallion *'03*
Vlad *'03*
Dragon Storm *'04*
The Lost Angel *'04*
The Princess Diaries 2: Royal Engagement *'04*
Chupacabra Terror *'05*
The Game of Their Lives *'05*
One Night with the King *'06*
Anaconda 3: The Offspring *'08*
Fire & Ice: The Dragon Chronicles *'08*
In the Name of the King: A Dungeon Siege Tale *'08*
Kiss Me Deadly *'08*
Anacondas: Trail of Blood *'09*
31 North 62 East *'09*
Medium Raw: Night of the Wolf *'10*
Ferocious Planet *'11*
Three Wise Women *'11*
Apocalypse Pompeii *'14*
Golden Shoes *'15*

Jonathan Rhys Meyers (1977-)
Killer Tongue *'96*
Michael Collins *'96*
Samson and Delilah *'96*
Telling Lies in America *'96*
B. Monkey *'97*
The Governess *'98*
The Loss of Sexual Innocence *'98*
The Maker *'98*
Velvet Goldmine *'98*
Ride with the Devil *'99*
Titus *'99*
Prozac Nation *'01*
Tangled *'01*
Bend It Like Beckham *'02*
The Magnificent Ambersons *'02*
The Lion in Winter *'03*
Pulse *'03*
The Tesseract *'03*
Alexander *'04*
Vanity Fair *'04*
Match Point *'05*
Mission: Impossible 3 *'06*
August Rush *'07*
The Children of Huang Shi *'08*
From Paris With Love *'10*
Albert Nobbs *'11*
The Mortal Instruments: City of Bones *'13*
6 Souls *'13*
Stonewall *'15*
Black Butterfly *'17*

Serge Riaboukine
Angel-A *'05*
Sleepless Night *'11*

Candice Rialson (1951-2006)
Candy Stripe Nurses *'74*
Summer School Teachers *'75*
Chatterbox *'76*
Hollywood Boulevard *'76*

Renie Riano (1899-1971)
Nancy Drew-Detective *'38*
Nancy Drew-Trouble Shooter *'39*

Jacques Riberolles (1929-82)
Please Not Now! *'61*
The Young Girls of Rochefort *'68*

Giovanni Ribisi (1974-)
That Thing You Do! *'96*
The Postman *'97*
The Other Sister *'98*
Saving Private Ryan *'98*
It's the Rage *'99*
The Mod Squad *'99*
The Virgin Suicides *'99 (N)*
Boiler Room *'00*
The Gift *'00*
Gone in 60 Seconds *'00*
Heaven *'01*
Shot in the Heart *'01*
Basic *'03*
Cold Mountain *'03*
I Love Your Work *'03*
Lost in Translation *'03*
Flight of the Phoenix *'04*
Sky Captain and the World of Tomorrow *'04*
The Big White *'05*
The Dead Girl *'06*
The Dog Problem *'06*
10th & Wolf *'06*
Perfect Stranger *'07*
Avatar *'09*
Public Enemies *'09*
Columbus Circle *'10*
Middle Men *'10*
The Rum Diary *'11*
Contraband *'12*
Ted *'12*
Gangster Squad *'13*
A Million Ways to Die In the West *'14*
Meadowland *'15*
Results *'15*
Papa: Hemingway in Cuba *'16*
The Bad Batch *'17*

Marissa Ribisi (1974-)
Armistead Maupin's Tales of the City *'93*
Dazed and Confused *'93*
Changing Habits *'96*
True Crime *'99*

Christina Ricci (1980-)
Mermaids *'90*
The Addams Family *'91*
The Hard Way *'91*
Addams Family Values *'93*
The Cemetery Club *'93*
Casper *'95*
Gold Diggers: The Secret of Bear Mountain *'95*
Now and Then *'95*
Bastard out of Carolina *'96*
The Last of the High Kings *'96*
That Darn Cat *'96*
Buffalo 66 *'97*
The Ice Storm *'97*
Desert Blue *'98*
Fear and Loathing in Las Vegas *'98*
The Opposite of Sex *'98*
Pecker *'98*
Small Soldiers *'98 (V)*
200 Cigarettes *'98*
No Vacancy *'99*
Sleepy Hollow *'99*
Bless the Child *'00*
The Man Who Cried *'00*
All Over the Guy *'01*
Miranda *'01*
Prozac Nation *'01*
The Gathering *'02*
The Laramie Project *'02*
Pumpkin *'02*
Anything Else *'03*
I Love Your Work *'03*
Monster *'03*
Cursed *'04*
Home of the Brave *'06*
Penelope *'06*
Black Snake Moan *'07*
Speed Racer *'08*
All's Faire in Love *'09*
New York, I Love You *'09*
After.life *'10*
Alpha and Omega *'10 (V)*
Bucky Larson: Born to Be a Star *'11*
Bel Ami *'12*
War Flowers *'12*
Around the Block *'13*
The Smurfs 2 *'13 (V)*
Lizzie Borden Took an Ax *'14*
Distorted *'18*

Alex Rice (1972-)
Skinwalker *'02*
Coyote Waits *'03*
The New World *'05*

Angourie Rice
The Nice Guys '16
Every Day '18

Brett Rice (1954-)
Final Cut '88
Bobby Jones: Stroke of Genius '04
Conjurer '08
Endure '10
Prime of Your Life '10
Hope Springs '12
Norman Rockwell's Shuffleton's Barbershop '13

Florence Rice (1911-74)
Double Wedding '37
Navy Blue and Gold '37
Fast Company '38
Paradise for Three '38
Sweethearts '38
At the Circus '39
Miracles for Sale '39
Stand Up and Fight '39
Phantom Raiders '40
Mr. District Attorney '41
Boss of Big Town '43

Frank Rice (1892-1936)
Forbidden Trail '32
The Ivory Handled Gun '35
The Gore-Gore Girls '72

Joan Rice (1930-97)
The Story of Robin Hood & His Merrie Men '52
His Majesty O'Keefe '53
The Horror of Frankenstein '70

Mandy Rice-Davies (1944-)
Black Venus '83
Absolute Beginners '86

Claude Rich (1929-)
Murder By Two '60
The Burning Court '62
The Elusive Corporal '62
Monsieur Gangster '63
Is Paris Burning? '66
The Bride Wore Black '68
Revenge of the Musketeers '94
Capitaine Conan '96
Balzac: A Life of Passion '99
La Buche '00

Delphine Rich
Bad Company '99
Mr. Average '06

Irene Rich (1891-1988)
The Trap '22
Beau Brummel '24
They Had to See Paris '29
Beau Ideal '31
Five and Ten '31
The Champ '32
Held for Murder '32
That Certain Age '38
The Lady in Question '40
The Mortal Storm '40
Angel and the Badman '47

Cliff Richard (1940-)
Expresso Bongo '59
Serious Charge '59

Emily Richard (1948-)
The Life and Adventures of Nicholas Nickleby '81
Empire of the Sun '87

Jean-Louis Richard (1927-2012)
The Last Metro '80
Le Professionnel '81
Le Choc '82
La Sentinelle '92
Jeanne la Pucelle '94
After Sex '97

Nathalie Richard (1963-)
Irma Vep '96
Confusion of Genders '00
Le Divorce '03

Pierre Richard (1934-)
The Daydreamer '70
The Tall Blond Man with One Black Shoe '72
La Chevre '81
Les Comperes '83
A Chef in Love '96
Lost in Paris '17

Robert Ri'chard (1983-)
In His Father's Shoes '97
Light It Up '99
Anne Rice's The Feast of All Saints '01
Coach Carter '05
House of Wax '05
The Comebacks '07
The Man in 3B '16

Addison Richards (1887-1964)
Our Daily Bread '34
The Black Legion '37
Smart Blonde '37
The Fighting Sullivans '42
The Man with Two Lives '42
Air Force '43
Fighting Seabees '44
Since You Went Away '44
Black Market Babies '45
The Millerson Case '47
Call Northside 777 '48
A Southern Yankee '48
Davy Crockett, Indian Scout '50
Fort Yuma '55
The Broken Star '56
Saintly Sinners '62

Ann Richards (1917-2006)
An American Romance '44
Love Letters '45
Badman's Territory '46
Lost Honeymoon '47
Sorry, Wrong Number '48
Breakdown '53

Ariana Richards (1979-)
Prancer '89
Tremors '89
Spaced Invaders '90
Grand Tour: Disaster in Time '92
Jurassic Park '93
Angus '95
The Lost World: Jurassic Park 2 '97
Tremors 3: Back to Perfection '01

Beah Richards (1926-2000)
Take a Giant Step '59
The Miracle Worker '62
Gone Are the Days '63
Purlie Victorious '63
Guess Who's Coming to Dinner '67
Hurry Sundown '67
Roots: The Next Generation '79
A Christmas Without Snow '80
Drugstore Cowboy '89
Beloved '98

Dakota Blue Richards
The Golden Compass '07
The Secret of Moonacre '08
Chicklit '16

Denise Richards (1971-)
National Lampoon's Loaded Weapon 1 '93
Starship Troopers '97
Wild Things '98
Drop Dead Gorgeous '99
Tail Lights Fade '99
The World Is Not Enough '99
Good Advice '01
Valentine '01
Empire '02
The Third Wheel '02
Undercover Brother '02
You Stupid Man '02
Love Actually '03
Scary Movie 3 '03
Elvis Has Left the Building '04
I Do (But I Don't) '04
Edmond '05
Blonde and Blonder '07
Jolene '08
Finding Bliss '09
Cougars, Inc. '10
Blue Lagoon: The Awakening '12
Madea's Witness Protection '12
Altitude '17
American Violence '17
The ToyBox '18

Evan Richards (1970-)
Down and Out in Beverly Hills '86
Rock 'n' Roll High School Forever '91
Society '92
Mute Witness '95

Grant Richards (1911-63)
Four Skulls of Jonathan Drake '59
Twelve Hours to Kill '60

Jeff Richards (1922-89)
Kill the Umpire '50
Angels in the Outfield '51
Above and Beyond '53
Battle Circus '53
Big Leaguer '53
Code Two '53
Crest of the Wave '54
Seven Brides for Seven Brothers '54
It's a Dog's Life '55
Born Reckless '59
Island of Lost Women '59
The Secret of the Purple Reef '60

Keith Richards (1915-87)
Gimme Shelter '70
The Kids Are Alright '79
Chuck Berry: Hail! Hail! Rock 'n' Roll '87

Kim Richards (1964-)
Escape to Witch Mountain '75
Assault on Precinct 13 '76
Devil Dog: The Hound of Hell '78
Return from Witch Mountain '78
Meatballs 2 '84
Tuff Turf '85
Black Snake Moan '07

Kyle Richards (1969-)
Eaten Alive '76
Halloween '78
The Watcher in the Woods '81
Curfew '88

Lisa Richards
The Prince of Central Park '77
Eating '90

Michael Richards (1949-)
Ratings Game '84
Transylvania 6-5000 '85
UHF '89
Problem Child '90
Coneheads '93
So I Married an Axe Murderer '93 (C)
Airheads '94
Unstrung Heroes '95
Trial and Error '96
Bee Movie '07 (V)

Michele Lamar Richards (1954-)
The Bodyguard '92
Top Dog '95

Paul Richards (1934-)
Pushover '54
Four Fast Guns '59
Beach Girls '82
Kiss Daddy Goodnight '87

Cameron Richardson (1979-)
The Good Humor Man '05
Supercross: The Movie '05
Alvin and the Chipmunks '07
Familiar Strangers '08
Women in Trouble '09

Derek Richardson (1976-)
Dumb and Dumberer: When Harry Met Lloyd '03
Hostel '06

Haley Lu Richardson (1995-)
F6 Twister '12
The Bronze '15
The Young Kieslowski '15
The Edge of Seventeen '16
Split '16
Columbus '17
Support the Girls '18
Five Feet Apart '19

Ian Richardson (1934-2007)
A Midsummer Night's Dream '68
Tinker, Tailor, Soldier, Spy '80
The Hound of the Baskervilles '83
The Sign of Four '83
Brazil '85
Mountbatten: The Last Viceroy '86
Cry Freedom '87
The Fourth Protocol '87
Troubles '88
House of Cards '90
The Phantom of the Opera '90
The Plot to Kill Hitler '90
Rosencrantz & Guildenstern Are Dead '90
Year of the Comet '92
M. Butterfly '93
To Play the King '93
A Change of Place '94
Catherine the Great '95
The Final Cut '95
B.A.P.'s '97
Dark City '97
Incognito '97
The Woman in White '97
A Knight in Camelot '98
The King and I '99 (V)
Dr. Bell and Mr. Doyle: The Dark Beginnings of Sherlock Holmes '00
102 Dalmatians '00
From Hell '01
Joyeux Noel '05
Hogfather '06 (V)
Becoming Jane '07

Jackie Richardson
Another Woman '94
Under the Piano '95

Jay Richardson
Gator King '70
The Newlydeads '87
Hollywood Chainsaw Hookers '88
Alienator '89
Slashdance '89
Bad Girls from Mars '90
Vice Academy 2 '90
Original Intent '91
Vice Academy 3 '91
Mind, Body & Soul '92
Teenage Exorcist '93
Wizards of the Demon Sword '94
Attack of the 60-Foot Centerfold '95
Fugitive Rage '96
Illegal Affairs '96

Joely Richardson (1965-)
The Charge of the Light Brigade '68
Wetherby '85
Drowning by Numbers '87
Behaving Badly '89
King Ralph '91
Lady Chatterley '92
Shining Through '92
I'll Do Anything '93
Sister My Sister '94
Loch Ness '95
101 Dalmatians '96
Event Horizon '97
In the Shadows '98
Wrestling with Alligators '98
Maybe Baby '99
The Patriot '00
Return to Me '00
The Affair of the Necklace '01
Fallen Angel '03
The Fever '04
Lies My Mother Told Me '05
Fatal Contact: Bird Flu in America '06
The Christmas Miracle of Jonathan Toomey '07
The Last Mimzy '07
Anonymous '11
The Girl With the Dragon Tattoo '11
Red Lights '12
Thanks for Sharing '13
Endless Love '14
Vampire Academy '14
Maggie '15
Papa: Hemingway in Cuba '16
Fallen '17
Color Out of Space '19

John Richardson (1934-)
Black Sunday '60
Pirates of Tortuga '61
She '65
One Million Years B.C. '66
Execution '68
The Vengeance of She '68
Torso '73
War in Space '77
Frankenstein '80 '79
Cosmos: War of the Planets '80

Kevin M. Richardson (1964-)
Pom Poko '94 (V)
Bound '96
Whispers: An Elephant's Tale '00 (V)
The Country Bears '02 (V)
Lilo & Stitch '02 (V)
The Wild Thornberrys Movie '02 (V)
The Matrix Revolutions '03
Leroy and Stitch '06 (V)
Queer Duck: The Movie '06 (V)
The Wild '06 (V)
Star Wars: The Clone Wars '08 (V)
La Mission '09

Lee Richardson (1926-99)
Prizzi's Honor '85
The Believers '87
Sweet Lorraine '87
Tiger Warsaw '87
The Fly 2 '89
Q & A '90
A Stranger Among Us '92
Sarah, Plain and Tall: Skylark '93

Marie Richardson (1959-)
Eyes Wide Shut '99
Faithless '00
Gossip '00
Evil '03

Miranda Richardson (1958-)
A Woman of Substance '84
Dance with a Stranger '85
The Death of the Heart '87
Eat the Rich '87
Empire of the Sun '87
Twisted Obsession '90
The Crying Game '92
Damage '92
Enchanted April '92
The Night and the Moment '94
Tom & Viv '94
Kansas City '95
The Evening Star '96
The Apostle '97
A Dance to the Music of Time '97
The Designated Mourner '97
Merlin '98
St. Ives '98
Alice in Wonderland '99
The Big Brass Ring '99
Jacob Two Two Meets the Hooded Fang '99
The King and I '99 (V)
Sleepy Hollow '99
Chicken Run '00 (V)
Get Carter '00
The Miracle Maker: The Story of Jesus '00 (V)
The Hours '02
Snow White: The Fairest of Them All '02
Spider '02
Falling Angels '03
The Rage In Placid Lake '03
The Phantom of the Opera '04
The Prince & Me '04
Gideon's Daughter '05
Harry Potter and the Goblet of Fire '05
Wah-Wah '05
Merlin's Apprentice '06
Paris, je t'aime '06
Southland Tales '06
Fred Claus '07
The Young Victoria '09
Harry Potter and the Deathly Hallows, Part 1 '10
Made in Dagenham '10
Belle '13
Churchill '17
Stronger '17

Natasha Richardson (1963-2009)
Gothic '87
A Month in the Country '87
Patty Hearst '88
Fat Man and Little Boy '89
The Handmaid's Tale '90
The Comfort of Strangers '91
The Favor, the Watch, & the Very Big Fish '92
Past Midnight '92
Nell '94
Widow's Peak '94
The Parent Trap '98
Blow Dry '00
Chelsea Walls '01
Maid in Manhattan '02
Waking Up in Reno '02
Asylum '05
The White Countess '05
Evening '07
Wild Child '08
The Wildest Dream: The Conquest of Everest '10 (V)

Patricia Richardson (1951-)
Christmas Evil '80
In Country '89
Steve Martini's Undue Influence '96
Ulee's Gold '97
Blonde '01
Dead Simple '01
California Dreaming '07
Lost Dream '09
The Jensen Project '10
Beautiful Wave '11
Bringing Ashley Home '11
Black Box '12
Smart Cookies '13

Ralph Richardson (1902-83)
The Ghoul '34
Things to Come '36
The Man Who Could Work Miracles '37
Thunder in the City '37
The Citadel '38
The Divorce of Lady X '38
The Four Feathers '39
The Silver Fleet '43
Anna Karenina '48
The Fallen Idol '49
The Heiress '49
The Sound Barrier '52
Richard III '55
Our Man in Havana '59
Exodus '60
Long Day's Journey into Night '62
The 300 Spartans '62
Doctor Zhivago '65
Khartoum '66
The Wrong Box '66
Chimes at Midnight '67 (N)
Battle of Britain '69
The Bed Sitting Room '69
The Looking Glass War '69
Oh! What a Lovely War '69
Who Slew Auntie Roo? '71
Tales from the Crypt '72
A Doll's House '73
O Lucky Man! '73
The Man in the Iron Mask '77
Watership Down '78 (V)
Dragonslayer '81
Time Bandits '81

Give My Regards to Broad Street '84
Greystoke: The Legend of Tarzan, Lord of the Apes '84
Wagner: The Complete Epic '85

Regina Richardson
Tightrope '84
Nine Deaths of the Ninja '85

Russell Richardson
Ancient Evil: Scream of the Mummy '00
Tigerland '00
The Rookie '02

Sy Richardson (1941-)
Fairy Tales '76
Repo Man '83
Straight to Hell '87
Bad Dreams '88
Colors '88
They Live '88
Backtrack '89
Tapeheads '89
Three Fugitives '89
Ring of Fire 2: Blood and Steel '92
Floundering '94

LaTanya Richardson Jackson (1949-)
Losing Isaiah '94
When a Man Loves a Woman '94
Julian Po '97
U.S. Marshals '98
Introducing Dorothy Dandridge '99
The Fighting Temptations '03
Kill Bill Vol. 2 '04
Freedomland '06
The Watsons Go to Birmingham '13

Salli Richardson-Whitfield (1967-)
How U Like Me Now? '92
Posse '93
Gargoyles, The Movie: The Heroes Awaken '94 (V)
A Low Down Dirty Shame '94
Sioux City '94
The Great White Hype '96
Soul of the Game '96
True Women '97
Never 2 Big '98
Antwone Fisher '02
Biker Boyz '03
Anacondas: The Hunt for the Blood Orchid '04
I Am Legend '07
Black Dynamite '09
Playin' For Love '15
The Sin Seer '15

Carole Richert
Tous les Matins du Monde '92
The Night and the Moment '94

William Richert (1942-)
My Own Private Idaho '91
The Man in the Iron Mask '97
Manic '01

Julian Richings (1956-)
Cube '98
The Claim '00
My Life Without Me '03
Wrong Turn '03
Shoot 'Em Up '07
The Tracey Fragments '07
Hard Core Logo 2 '10
Septic Man '14

Charles Richman (1865-1940)
Struggle '31
In Old Kentucky '35

Peter Mark Richman (1927-)
The Strange One '57
Black Orchid '59
Dempsey '83
Friday the 13th, Part 8: Jason Takes Manhattan '89
Naked Gun 2 1/2: The Smell of Fear '91
Poolhall Junkies '02
Mysteria '11

B.L. Richmond (1955-)
See Branscombe Richmond

Branscombe Richmond (1955-)
DaVinci's War '92
Vegas Vice '94
To the Limit '95
The Scorpion King '02
Black Cloud '04
Born to Ride '11

Deon Richmond (1978-)
Trippin' '99
Scream 3 '00
Not Another Teen Movie '01
National Lampoon's Van Wilder '02
Hatchet '07

Kane Richmond (1906-73)
Cavalier of the West '31
Politics '31
Stepping Out '31
Huddle '32
The Lost City '34
The Reckless Way '36
The Return of the Cisco Kid '39
Tail Spin '39
Charlie Chan in Panama '40
Play Girl '41
Action in the North Atlantic '43
Black Market Babies '45
Don't Gamble with Strangers '46
Stage Struck '48

Warner Richmond (1886-1948)
Chicago '27
Big News '29
Corruption '33
The Lost Jungle '34
The Gold Racket '37
Colorado Serenade '46

Andy Richter (1966-)
The Positively True Adventures of the Alleged Texas Cheerleader-Murdering Mom '93
Cabin Boy '94
Dr. T & the Women '00
Dr. Dolittle 2 '01
Pootie Tang '01
Scary Movie 2 '01
Big Trouble '02
Frank McKlusky, C.I. '02
Elf '03
My Boss's Daughter '03
New York Minute '04
Seeing Other People '04
Madagascar '05 (V)
Talladega Nights: The Ballad of Ricky Bobby '06
Madagascar: Escape 2 Africa '08 (V)
Semi-Pro '08
Aliens in the Attic '09
Conan O'Brien Can't Stop '11
Madagascar 3: Europe's Most Wanted '12 (V)

Deborah Richter (1961-)
Hot Moves '84
Square Dance '87
Promised Land '88
Cyborg '89

Jason James Richter (1980-)
Free Willy '93
Cops and Robbersons '94
The NeverEnding Story 3: Escape from Fantasia '94
Free Willy 2: The Adventure Home '95
Free Willy 3: The Rescue '97
Ricochet River '98
Laserhawk '99

Paul Richter (1896-1961)
The Indian Tomb '21
Dr. Mabuse, The Gambler '22
Kriemhilde's Revenge '24
Siegfried '24

Chelsea Ricketts
Crooked Arrows '12
From Above '13

Don Rickles (1926-2017)
Run Silent, Run Deep '58
The Rat Race '60
X: The Man with X-Ray Eyes '63
Bikini Beach '64
Muscle Beach Party '64
Pajama Party '64
Beach Blanket Bingo '65
Where It's At '69
Kelly's Heroes '70
For the Love of It '80
Keaton's Cop '90
Innocent Blood '92
Casino '95
Toy Story '95 (V)
Dirty Work '97
Dennis the Menace Strikes Again '98
Quest for Camelot '98 (V)
Toy Story 2 '99 (V)
Toy Story 3 '10 (V)

Alan Rickman (1946-2016)
Therese Raquin '80
Die Hard '88
The January Man '89
Quigley Down Under '90
Close My Eyes '91
Robin Hood: Prince of Thieves '91
Truly, Madly, Deeply '91
Bob Roberts '92
An Awfully Big Adventure '94
Mesmer '94
Sense and Sensibility '95
Michael Collins '96
Dark Harbor '98
Dogma '99
Galaxy Quest '99
Blow Dry '00
Harry Potter and the Sorcerer's Stone '01
The Search for John Gissing '01
Harry Potter and the Chamber of Secrets '02
Love Actually '03
Harry Potter and the Prisoner of Azkaban '04
Something the Lord Made '04
Harry Potter and the Goblet of Fire '05
The Hitchhiker's Guide to the Galaxy '05 (V)
Perfume: The Story of a Murderer '06
Snow Cake '06
Harry Potter and the Order of the Phoenix '07
Sweeney Todd: The Demon Barber of Fleet Street '07
Nobel Son '08
Harry Potter and the Half-Blood Prince '09
Alice in Wonderland '10
Harry Potter and the Deathly Hallows, Part 1 '10
The Wildest Dream: The Conquest of Everest '10 (V)
Harry Potter and the Deathly Hallows, Part 2 '11
Gambit '12
CBGB '13
Lee Daniels' The Butler '13
A Promise '13
A Little Chaos '14
Eye in the Sky '15

Maria Ricossa
Bojangles '01
The In-Laws '03
Sex and the Single Mom '03
Absolution '05
The Note '07
The Note 2: Taking a Chance on Love '09

Stephane Rideau (1976-)
Wild Reeds '94
Full Speed '96
Sitcom '97
Come Undone '00
Our Paradise '11

John Ridgely (1909-68)
Air Force '43
Destination Tokyo '43
Arsenic and Old Lace '44
God is My Co-Pilot '45
Pride of the Marines '45
The Big Sleep '46
The Man I Love '46
My Reputation '46
Cry Wolf '47
Nora Prentiss '47
The Possessed '47
That's My Man '47
Border Incident '49
Task Force '49
The Lost Volcano '50
Cavalry Charge '51
Fort Osage '51
Room for One More '51

Robert Ridgely (1931-96)
Prime Time '77
Beverly Hills Cop 2 '87
Philadelphia '93
Robin Hood: Men in Tights '93
Hard Eight '96
Boogie Nights '97

Stanley Ridges (1891-1951)
Internes Can't Take Money '37
Dust Be My Destiny '39
Each Dawn I Die '39
Let Us Live '39
Nick Carter, Master Detective '39
Union Pacific '39
Black Friday '40
Mr. District Attorney '41
Sergeant York '41
They Died with Their Boots On '41
The Big Shot '42
To Be or Not to Be '42
Air Force '43
Tarzan Triumphs '43
The Master Race '44
Wilson '44
Because of Him '45
God is My Co-Pilot '45
Mr. Ace '46
The Possessed '47
Task Force '49
No Way Out '50
The Groom Wore Spurs '51

Freddy Ridgeway
A Blueprint for Murder '53
Fangs of the Wild '54

Fritzi Ridgeway
Getting Gertie's Garter '27
Hell's Heroes '30

Daisy Ridley (1992-)
Star Wars: The Force Awakens '15
The Eagle Huntress '16
Only Yesterday '16
Murder on the Orient Express '17
Star Wars: The Last Jedi '17
Peter Rabbit '18 (V)
Ophelia '19
Star Wars: The Rise of Skywalker '19

Harry Riebauer (1921-99)
The Great Escape '63
Strangler of Blackmoor Castle '63

Leni Riefenstahl (1902-2003)
The Blue Light '32
S.O.S. Iceberg '33
Tiefland '44

Eden Riegel (1981-)
Prince of Egypt '98 (V)
Henry Hill '00

Peter Riegert (1947-)
National Lampoon's Animal House '78
Americathon '79
National Lampoon Goes to the Movies '81
Local Hero '83
News at Eleven '86
A Man in Love '87
The Stranger '87
Crossing Delancey '88
A Shock to the System '90
The Object of Beauty '91
Oscar '91
Passed Away '92
Barbarians at the Gate '93
Gypsy '93
Bleeding Hearts '94
Coldblooded '94
The Mask '94
The Infiltrator '95
Pie in the Sky '95
Infinity '96
The Baby Dance '98
Hi-Life '98
Jerry and Tom '98
In the Weeds '00
Passion of Mind '00
Traffic '00
Bojangles '01
How to Kill Your Neighbor's Dog '01
King of the Corner '04
White Irish Drinkers '10
We Bought a Zoo '11
At Middleton '13
American Pastoral '16

Richard Riehle (1948-)
Glory '89
Body of Evidence '92
Hero '92
Of Mice and Men '92
The Public Eye '92
Lone Justice 2 '93
Holy Matrimony '94
Lightning Jack '94
A Stranger in Town '95
Ghosts of Mississippi '96
Soul of the Game '96
Desperate Measures '98
Lethal Weapon 4 '98
Office Space '98
Au Pair '99
Deuce Bigalow: Male Gigolo '99
Bandits '01
The Fluffer '01
Say It Isn't So '01
Home on the Range '04 (V)
Mysterious Skin '04
Palindromes '04
The Twelve Dogs of Christmas '05
Midnight Clear '06
Hatchet '07
The Man from Earth '07
Red '08
Messengers 2: The Scarecrow '09
Growth '10
Killer by Nature '10
The Search for Santa Paws '10
Dead Man's Burden '12
Treasure Buddies '12
Girl Meets Boy '13
Texas Chainsaw 3D '13
Amnesiac '15

Katja Riemann (1963-)
Balzac: A Life of Passion '99
Bandits '99
The Harmonists '99
Rosenstrasse '03
Blood & Chocolate '07

Max Riemelt (1984-)
Before the Fall '04
The Wave '08
Free Fall '13
Berlin Syndrome '17

Beth Riesgraf (1978-)
Intruders '16
In Search of Fellini '17

Adam Rifkin (1966-)
The Dark Backward '91
Something About Sex '98 (C)
Welcome to Hollywood '00
National Lampoon's The Stoned Aged '07

Richard Rifkin
Assault of the Party Nerds '89
Eragon '06

Ron Rifkin (1939-)
Silent Running '71
The Chosen '81
Ratings Game '84
Courage '86
Manhattan Murder Mystery '93
Wolf '94
Norma Jean and Marilyn '95
I'm Not Rappaport '96
Last Summer In the Hamptons '96
The Substance of Fire '96
L.A. Confidential '97
The Negotiator '98
Boiler Room '00
Flowers for Algernon '00
Keeping the Faith '00
Deliberate Intent '01
The Majestic '01
Dragonfly '02
The Sum of All Fears '02
Pulse '06
Peep World '10

Jorge (George) Rigaud (1905-84)
The Castilian '63
Grand Slam '67
The Case of the Bloody Iris '72
Horror Express '72

Edward Rigby (1879-1951)
Lorna Doone '34
Young and Innocent '37
Convoy '40

Terence Rigby (1937-2008)
Get Carter '71
The Homecoming '73
High Tide '80
Tinker, Tailor, Soldier, Spy '80
The Young Americans '93
Plunkett & Macleane '98
Essex Boys '99
Mona Lisa Smile '03
Color Me Kubrick '05
Flick '07

Diana Rigg (1938-)
A Midsummer Night's Dream '68
The Assassination Bureau '69
On Her Majesty's Secret Service '69
Julius Caesar '70
The Hospital '71
Theatre of Blood '73
In This House of Brede '75
A Little Night Music '77
The Great Muppet Caper '81
Evil under the Sun '82
Bleak House '85
The Worst Witch '86
Snow White '89
Unexplained Laughter '89
A Good Man in Africa '94
Moll Flanders '96
Samson and Delilah '96
Rebecca '97
Parting Shots '98
Speedy Death '99
The American '01
Victoria & Albert '01
The Painted Veil '06
Breathe '17

Rebecca Rigg (1967-)
Fortress '85
The Efficiency Expert '92
Tunnel Vision '95
Ellie Parker '05

Chris Riggi (1985-)
Vampires Suck '10
Lily & Kat '15

Rob Riggle (1970-)
The Goods: Live Hard, Sell Hard '09
Furry Vengeance '10
Going the Distance '10
Killers '10
The Other Guys '10

Big Miracle '12
Dr. Seuss' The Lorax '12 (V)
Nature Calls '12
21 Jump Street '12
Dumb and Dumber To '14
Let's Be Cops '14
Absolutely Anything '17
Midnight Sun '18

Mitchell Riggs
Spin the Bottle '97
Kaaterskill Falls '01

Amanda Righetti (1983-)
Return to House on Haunted Hill '07
Friday the 13th '09
The Chateau Meroux '11
Shadow of Fear '12

Massimo Righi
Black Sabbath '64
Blood and Black Lace '64

Alex(andre) Rignault (1901-85)
The Horror Chamber of Dr. Faustus '59
Numero Deux '75

Rihanna (1988-)
Valerian and the City of a Thousand Planets '17
Ocean's 8 '18

Lucia Rijker (1967-)
The Dreamers '03
Million Dollar Baby '04

Brad Rijn
Smithereens '82
Perfect Strangers '84
Special Effects '85

Robin Riker (1952-)
Alligator '80
Body Chemistry 2: Voice of a Stranger '91
Stepmonster '92
Holly's Holiday '12

Amber Riley (1986-)
Nobody's Fool '18
Infamous '20

Charlotte Riley (1981-)
Easy Virtue '08
The Take '09
Wuthering Heights '09
London Has Fallen '16

Cheryl 'Pepsii' Riley
Colorz of Rage '97
Tyler Perry's Hell Hath No Fury Like a Woman Scorned: The Play '14

Jack Riley (1935-)
McCabe & Mrs. Miller '71
Attack of the Killer Tomatoes '77
Night Patrol '85
The Rugrats Movie '98 (V)
Rugrats in Paris: The Movie '00 (V)
Rugrats Go Wild! '03 (V)

Jeannine Riley (1940-)
The Comic '69
Electra Glide in Blue '73
Wackiest Wagon Train in the West '77

Larry Riley (1953-92)
Crackers '84
A Soldier's Story '84

Madison Riley
Without a Paddle: Nature's Calling '09
The Prankster '10

Michael Riley (1962-)
To Catch a Killer '92
Because Why? '93
. . .And God Spoke '94
Race to Freedom: The Story of the Underground Railroad '94
French Kiss '95
Heck's Way Home '95
Pale Saints '97
The Interrogation of Michael Crowe '02
The Way We Live Now '02
Homeless to Harvard: The Liz Murray Story '03
Cube: Zero '04
St. Urbain's Horseman '07
The Tenth Circle '08

Sam Riley (1980-)
Control '07
Franklyn '08
Brighton Rock '10
13 '10
Byzantium '12
On the Road '12
Maleficent '14
Pride and Prejudice and Zombies '16
Free Fire '17
Maleficent: Mistress of Evil '19
Sometimes Always Never '19

Talulah Riley (1985-)
Pride and Prejudice '05
St. Trinian's '07
The Legend of Fritton's Gold '09
Bloodshot '20

Tom Riley (1981-)
A Few Days in September '06
I Want Candy '07
Return to House on Haunted Hill '07
Happy Ever Afters '09
Appointment With Death '10

Walter Rilla (1894-1980)
The Finances of the Grand Duke '24
The Scarlet Pimpernel '34
Victoria the Great '37
Sixty Glorious Years '38
Candlelight in Algeria '44
The Golden Salamander '51
Frozen Alive '64

LeAnn Rimes (1982-)
Northern Lights '09
Good Intentions '10
Reel Love '11

Shane Rimmer (1929-)
Dr. Strangelove, or: How I Learned to Stop Worrying and Love the Bomb '64
S*P*Y*S '74
The People That Time Forgot '77
Dreamchild '85
Out of Africa '85
Reunion at Fairborough '85
Crusoe '89
Space Truckers '97

Cyril Ring (1892-1967)
The Cocoanuts '29
I Wake Up Screaming '41

Molly Ringwald (1968-)
The Tempest '82
Spacehunter: Adventures in the Forbidden Zone '83
Sixteen Candles '84
The Breakfast Club '85
Pretty in Pink '86
The Pick-Up Artist '87
For Keeps '88
Fresh Horses '88
Betsy's Wedding '90
Strike It Rich '90
Women & Men: Stories of Seduction '90
Stephen King's The Stand '94
Baja '95
Office Killer '97
Since You've Been Gone '97 (C)
The Brutal Truth '99
Requiem for Murder '99
Teaching Mrs. Tingle '99
Cowboy Up '00
Cut '00
In the Weeds '00
The Wives He Forgot '06
Jem and the Holograms '15
King Cobra '16
Siberia '18

Scott Rinker (1971-)
Shoot or Be Shot '02
Gamers '06

Lisa Rinna (1963-)
Robot Wars '93
Vanished '95
Another Woman's Husband '00

David Rintoul (1948-)
Pride and Prejudice '85
Horatio Hornblower: The Adventure Continues '01

Nicole Rio
Sorority House Massacre '86
Zero Boys '86

Marjorie (Reardon) Riordan (1921-84)
Stage Door Canteen '43
Pursuit to Algiers '45
Three Strangers '46

Emily Rios (1989-)
Quinceanera '06
The Winning Season '09
Big Mommas: Like Father, Like Son '11

Lalo Rios (1927-73)
The Lawless '50
The Ring '52
Big Leaguer '53

Vincent Riotta (1959-)
Car Trouble '86
Belly of the Beast '03
Under the Tuscan Sun '03
Amanda Knox: Murder on Trail in Italy '11
Black Butterfly '17

Marc Rioufol
Before I Forget '07
The Special Relationship '10

Kelly Ripa (1970-)
Cheaper by the Dozen '03 (C)
Delgo '08 (V)
Fly Me to the Moon '08 (V)

Maurice Ripke (1966-)
Killing Down '06
Living & Dying '07
Mad Bad '07

Fay Ripley (1966-)
Mute Witness '95
For Roseanna '96
Dead Gorgeous '02

Michael Ripper (1913-2000)
Eye Witness '49
Quatermass 2 '57
The Mummy '59
The Brides of Dracula '60
The Curse of the Werewolf '61
Pirates of Blood River '62
The Devil-Ship Pirates '64
Plague of the Zombies '66
The Reptile '66
Dracula Has Risen from the Grave '68
Girly '70
The Scars of Dracula '70
Taste the Blood of Dracula '70
The Creeping Flesh '72
No Surrender '86

Leon Rippy (1949-)
Track 29 '88
The Hot Spot '90
Moon 44 '90
Young Guns 2 '90
Eye of the Storm '91
Beyond the Law '92
Kuffs '92
Stargate '94
Eight Legged Freaks '02
The Life of David Gale '03
The Alamo '04
Gridiron Gang '06

Maurice Risch (1943-)
The Last Metro '80
Beau Pere '81

Elisabeth Risdon (1887-1958)
Theodora Goes Wild '36
Make Way for Tomorrow '37
Mannequin '37
The Girl From Mexico '39
Mexican Spitfire '40
The Mexican Spitfire Out West '40
High Sierra '41
The Mexican Spitfire's Baby '41
Mexican Spitfire at Sea '42
The Mexican Spitfire Sees a Ghost '42
Reap the Wild Wind '42
The Amazing Mrs. Holiday '43
The Romance of Rosy Ridge '47
Bunco Squad '50
Guilty of Treason '50
Scaramouche '52

Andrea Riseborough (1981-)
The Secret Life of Mrs. Beeton '06
Brighton Rock '10
W.E. '11
Shadow Dancer '12
Oblivion '13
Welcome to the Punch '13
Birdman, or (The Unexpected Virtue of Ignorance) '14
Battle of the Sexes '17
Mandy '18
Nancy '18

Michael Risley (1969-)
Revolution #9 '01
The Poker Club '08

Michael Rispoli (1960-)
Night and the City '92
While You Were Sleeping '95
Homeward Bound 2: Lost in San Francisco '96
Volcano '97
Rounders '98
Scarred City '98
Snake Eyes '98
Summer of Sam '99
The Third Miracle '99
Two Family House '99
Death to Smoochy '02
Mr. 3000 '04
One Last Thing '05
The Weather Man '05
Invincible '06
Black Irish '07
The Bronx Is Burning '07
Yonkers Joe '08
The Taking of Pelham 123 '09
Kick-Ass '10
The Last Godfather '10
The Reunion '11
The Rum Diary '11
Rob the Mob '14

Roberto Risso (1925-2010)
Bread, Love and Dreams '53
Fury of Achilles '62
Gladiator of Rome '63
Revenge of the Musketeers '63

Robbie (Reist) Rist (1964-)
He Is My Brother '75
Iron Eagle '86
She's Out of Control '89
Teenage Mutant Ninja Turtles: The Movie '90 (V)
Unseen Evil '99

Lazar Ristovski (1952-)
Tito and Me '92
Underground '95
King of Thieves '04
The November Man '14

Steven Ritch (1921-95)
Seminole Uprising '55
The Werewolf '56
Plunder Road '57
City of Fear '59

Cyril Ritchard (1897-1977)
Blackmail '29
Piccadilly '29
Peter Pan '60
Half a Sixpence '67
Hans Brinker '69
The Hobbit '78 (V)

Bob Ritchie (1971-)
See Kid Rock

Clint Ritchie (1938-2009)
The St. Valentine's Day Massacre '67
Peacekillers '71

Jill Ritchie (1974-)
Face the Music '00
Breakin' All The Rules '04
D.E.B.S. '04
Seeing Other People '04
Herbie: Fully Loaded '05
Little Athens '05

Alan Ritchson
Teenage Mutant Ninja Turtles '14
The Wedding Ringer '15
Teenage Mutant Ninja Turtles: Out of the Shadows '16

Blake Ritson (1978-)
AKA '02
Mansfield Park '07
God on Trial '08
Dead Man Running '09
Emma '09
Upstairs Downstairs '11

Huntley Ritter
Dark Heart '06
September Dawn '07

Jason Ritter (1980-)
Mumford '99
Swimfan '02
Freddy vs. Jason '03
Raise Your Voice '04
Happy Endings '05
Full Count '06
The Wicker Man '06
The Deal '08
Good Dick '08
W. '08
Peter and Vandy '09
The Dry Land '10
Morning '10
The Perfect Age of Rock 'n' Roll '10
A Bag of Hammers '11
The Perfect Family '11
Free Samples '12
About Alex '14
Always Woodstock '15
7 Minutes '15
The Intervention '16
The Tale '18

John Ritter (1948-2003)
The Barefoot Executive '71
Evil Roy Slade '71
Scandalous John '71
The Other '72
The Stone Killer '73
Nickelodeon '76
Americathon '79
Hero at Large '80
Wholly Moses! '80
They All Laughed '81
Flight of Dragons '82 (V)
Sunset Limousine '83
Letting Go '85
Unnatural Causes '86
Real Men '87
Tricks of the Trade '88
My Brother's Wife '89
Skin Deep '89
Problem Child '90
Stephen King's It '90
Problem Child 2 '91
Noises Off '92
Stay Tuned '92
Danielle Steel's Heartbeat '93
The Colony '95
Mercenary '96
Sling Blade '96
A Gun, a Car, a Blonde '97
Sink or Swim '97
Bride of Chucky '98
It Came from the Sky '98
Shadow of Doubt '98
The Million Dollar Kid '99
Panic '00
Terror Tract '00
TripFall '00
Tadpole '02
Bad Santa '03
Clifford's Really Big Movie '04 (V)

Krysten Ritter (1981-)
The Last International Playboy '08
What Happens in Vegas '08
Confessions of a Shopaholic '09
How to Make Love to a Woman '09
Woke Up Dead '09
She's Out of My League '10
Killing Bono '11
Life Happens '11
Vamps '12
Big Eyes '14
Listen Up Philip '14
Veronica Mars '14
The Hero '17

Paul Ritter
On a Clear Day '05
Their Finest '17

Thelma Ritter (1905-69)
Miracle on 34th Street '47
A Letter to Three Wives '49
All About Eve '50
Perfect Strangers '50
As Young As You Feel '51
The Model and the Marriage Broker '51
With a Song in My Heart '52
Pickup on South Street '53
Titanic '53
Rear Window '54
Daddy Long Legs '55
The Proud and Profane '56
A Hole in the Head '59
Pillow Talk '59
The Misfits '61
The Second Time Around '61
Birdman of Alcatraz '62
For Love or Money '63
How the West Was Won '63
Move Over, Darling '63
A New Kind of Love '63
Boeing Boeing '65

Tyson Ritter (1984-)
The House Bunny '08
Miss You Already '15

Al Ritz (1901-65)
One in a Million '36
On the Avenue '37
The Goldwyn Follies '38
Kentucky Moonshine '38
The Gorilla '39
The Three Musketeers '39

Harry Ritz (1906-86)
One in a Million '36
On the Avenue '37
The Goldwyn Follies '38
Kentucky Moonshine '38
The Gorilla '39
The Three Musketeers '39
Blazing Stewardesses '75 (C)
Silent Movie '76

Jimmy Ritz (1903-85)
One in a Million '36
On the Avenue '37
The Goldwyn Follies '38
Kentucky Moonshine '38
The Gorilla '39
The Three Musketeers '39
Blazing Stewardesses '75 (C)

Emmanuelle Riva (1927-)
Hiroshima, Mon Amour '59
Kapo '59
Adua and Her Friends '60
Leon Morin, Priest '61
Trois Couleurs: Bleu '93 (C)
Amour '12
Lost in Paris '17

Carlos Rivas (1928-2003)
The King and I '56
The Black Scorpion '57

They Saved Hitler's Brain *'64*
True Grit *'69*

Geoffrey Rivas
Luminarias *'99*
Running Red *'99*

Naike Rivelli (1974-)
The Count of Monte Cristo *'99*
Ancient Relic *'02*

Chita Rivera (1933-)
Sweet Charity *'69*
Once Upon a Brothers Grimm *'77*
Pippin *'81*
Mayflower Madam *'87*

Emilio Rivera (1961-)
The Base 2: Guilty as Charged *'00*
El Matador *'03*
El Padrino *'04*
Next Day Air *'09*
Act of Valor *'12*
The Devil's in the Details *'13*
Hitman: Agent 47 *'15*

Mabel Rivera (1952-)
The Sea Inside *'04*
The Orphanage *'07*

Rene Rivera
Rangers *'00*
Break a Leg *'03*
Lost Treasure *'03*

George Rivero (1938-)
See Jorge (George) Rivero

Jorge (George) Rivero (1938-)
Rio Lobo *'70*
Soldier Blue *'70*
The Last Hard Men *'76*
Priest of Love *'81*
Conquest *'83*
Ice *'93*
Werewolf *'95*
Warrior of Justice *'96*

Joan Rivers (1933-2014)
The Muppets Take Manhattan *'84 (C)*
Spaceballs *'87*
Serial Mom *'94*
Napoleon *'96 (V)*
Intern *'00*
Whispers: An Elephant's Tale *'00 (V)*
Joan Rivers: A Piece of Work *'10*

Victor Rivers (1955-)
Blood In . . . Blood Out: Bound by Honor *'93*
A Million to Juan *'94*
Two for Texas *'97*
What's Cooking? *'00*

Mia Riverton (1978-)
Alien 51 *'04*
Red Doors *'05*

Jorge Rivier (1938-)
See Jorge (George) Rivero

George Riviere (1924-)
Journey Beneath the Desert *'61*
Castle of Blood *'64*
The Virgin of Nuremberg *'65*

George(s) Riviere (1938-)
See Jorge (George) Rivero

Julien Riviere
Les Voleurs *'96*
Ma Vie en Rose *'97*

Marie Riviere (1956-)
The Aviator's Wife *'80*
Summer *'86*
Girls Can't Swim *'99*
The Lady and the Duke *'01*
Time to Leave *'05*

George Riviya (1938-)
See Jorge (George) Rivero

Gianni Rizzo (1925-92)
Three Avengers *'64*
Desert Commandos *'67*
Mission Stardust *'68*
Sabata *'69*

Alexandra Roach (1987-)
The Iron Lady *'11*
Private Peaceful *'12*
One Chance *'13*
Trap for Cinderella *'13*

Bert Roach (1891-1971)
Smouldering Fires *'25*
San Francisco *'36*
The Great Waltz *'38*

Brian Roach
Eye of the Beast *'07*
Taken in Broad Daylight *'09*

Daryl Roach
Watchers 3 *'94*
Gang Boys *'97*

Martin Roach (1962-)
The Wall *'99*
Blue Hill Avenue *'01*
Cube: Zero *'04*
Cradle of Lies *'06*

Linus Roache (1964-)
Priest *'94*
The Wings of the Dove *'97*
Shot Through the Heart *'98*
Siam Sunset *'99*
Pandaemonium *'00*
The Gathering Storm *'02*
Hart's War *'02*
RFK *'02*
Beyond Borders *'03*
The Chronicles of Riddick *'04*
The Forgotten *'04*
Batman Begins *'05*
12 and Holding *'05*
Find Me Guilty *'06*
Before the Rains *'07*
Yonkers Joe *'08*
The Making of a Lady *'12*
Titanic *'12*
Non-Stop *'14*
Mandy *'18*
Division 19 *'19*

Adam Roarke (1938-96)
Hell's Angels on Wheels *'67*
Hell's Belles *'69*
The Losers *'70*
Frogs *'72*
Dirty Mary Crazy Larry *'74*
Four Deuces *'75*
The Stunt Man *'80*
Beach Girls *'82*
Sioux City *'94*

Jason Robards, Jr. (1922-2000)
The Journey *'59*
The Iceman Cometh *'60*
By Love Possessed *'61*
Long Day's Journey into Night *'62*
Tender Is the Night *'62*
A Thousand Clowns *'65*
Any Wednesday *'66*
A Big Hand for the Little Lady *'66*
Divorce American Style *'67*
Hour of the Gun *'67*
The St. Valentine's Day Massacre *'67*
Once Upon a Time in the West *'68*
The Night They Raided Minsky's *'69*
Ballad of Cable Hogue *'70*
Fools *'70*
Julius Caesar *'70*
Tora! Tora! Tora! *'70*
Johnny Got His Gun *'71*
Murders in the Rue Morgue *'71*
A House Without a Christmas Tree *'72*
A Boy and His Dog *'75*
All the President's Men *'76*
Julia *'77*
Washington: Behind Closed Doors *'77*
Comes a Horseman *'78*
Hurricane *'79*
Haywire *'80*
Melvin and Howard *'80*
Raise the Titanic *'80*
Cabo Blanco *'81*
Legend of the Lone Ranger *'81*
Burden of Dreams *'82*
The Day After *'83*
Max Dugan Returns *'83*
Something Wicked This Way Comes *'83*
The Long, Hot Summer *'86*
Square Dance *'87*
Bright Lights, Big City *'88*
The Christmas Wife *'88*
The Good Mother *'88*
Dream a Little Dream *'89*
Parenthood *'89*
Quick Change *'90*
Black Rainbow *'91*
Storyville *'92*
The Adventures of Huck Finn *'93*
Heidi *'93*
Philadelphia *'93*
The Trial *'93*
The Enemy Within *'94*
Little Big League *'94*
The Paper *'94*
Crimson Tide *'95 (C)*
A Thousand Acres *'97*
Beloved *'98*
Enemy of the State *'98*
Heartwood *'98*
Magnolia *'99*

Jason Robards, Sr. (1892-1963)
Caught Plastered *'31*
Crimson Romance *'34*
The Miracle Rider *'35*
Fighting Marines *'36*
The Fatal Hour *'40*
Bedlam *'45*
Isle of the Dead *'45*
Desperate *'47*
Trail Street *'47*
Mr. Blandings Builds His Dream House *'48*
Return of the Bad Men *'48*
Rimfire *'49*
Death Merchants *'73*

Sam Robards (1961-)
The Tempest *'82*
Fandango *'85*
Into Thin Air *'85*
Not Quite Paradise *'86*
Bright Lights, Big City *'88*
Casualties of War *'89*
The Ballad of Little Jo *'93*
Mrs. Parker and the Vicious Circle *'94*
Ready to Wear *'94*
Beautiful Girls *'96*
The Man Who Captured Eichmann *'96*
Dinner and Driving *'97*
American Beauty *'99*
Bounce *'00*
A. I.: Artificial Intelligence *'01*
Hamlet *'01*
Life as a House *'01*
Obsessed *'02*
Catch That Kid *'04*
Awake *'07*
Perestroika *'09*
The Rebound *'09*
The Art of Getting By *'11*
Where Is Kyra? *'17*

Andrew Robb
Dreamcatcher *'03*
School of Life *'06*

AnnaSophia Robb (1993-)
Because of Winn-Dixie *'05*
Charlie and the Chocolate Factory *'05*
Bridge to Terabithia *'07*
The Reaping *'07*
Jumper *'08*
Sleepwalking *'08*
Spy School *'08*
Race to Witch Mountain *'09*
The Space Between *'10*
Soul Surfer *'11*
The Way Way Back *'13*
Jack of the Red Hearts *'15*
Down a Dark Hall *'18*
Freak Show *'18*

Daniel Robb (1929-)
See Christopher Plummer

David Robb (1947-)
The Flame Trees of Thika *'81*
Dangerous Corner *'83*
Wallenberg: A Hero's Story *'85*
The Man Who Lived at the Ritz *'91*
The Crow Road *'96*
Behind the Lines *'97*

R.D. Robb (1972-)
A Christmas Story *'83*
Eight Days a Week *'97*

Margot Robbie (1990-)
About Time *'13*
The Wolf of Wall Street *'13*
Focus *'15*
Z for Zachariah *'15*
The Legend of Tarzan *'16*
Suicide Squad *'16*
Whiskey Tango Foxtrot *'16*
Goodbye Christopher Robin *'17*
I, Tonya *'17*
Mary Queen of Scots *'18*
Terminal *'18*
Bombshell *'19*
Once Upon A Time... In Hollywood *'19*
Birds of Prey: And the Fantabulous Emancipation of One Harley Quinn *'20*

Amy Robbins (1971-)
Rudyard Kipling's the Second Jungle Book: Mowgli and Baloo *'97*
All the Little Animals *'98*
Strange Relations *'02*

Gale Robbins (1921-80)
In the Meantime, Darling *'44*
Race Street *'48*
The Barkleys of Broadway *'49*
Between Midnight and Dawn *'50*
The Fuller Brush Girl *'50*
Three Little Words *'50*
The Belle of New York *'52*
The Girl in the Red Velvet Swing *'55*
Parasite *'82*

Marty Robbins (1925-82)
Hell on Wheels *'67*
Road to Nashville *'67*

Ryan Robbins (1972-)
Horsey *'99*
Passengers *'08*
Wrecked *'10*
Apollo 18 *'11*
Kill for Me *'12*
Goodnight for Justice: Queen of Hearts *'13*
Reasonable Doubt *'14*

Skeeter Bill Robbins (1887-1933)
Boiling Point *'32*
The Dude Bandit *'33*

Tim Robbins (1958-)
No Small Affair *'84*
Toy Soldiers *'84*
Fraternity Vacation *'85*
The Sure Thing *'85*
Howard the Duck *'86*
Top Gun *'86*
Bull Durham *'88*
Five Corners *'88*
Erik the Viking *'89*
Miss Firecracker *'89*
Tapeheads *'89*
Twister *'89*
Cadillac Man *'90*
Jacob's Ladder *'90*
Jungle Fever *'91*
Bob Roberts *'92*
The Player *'92*
The Hudsucker Proxy *'93*
Short Cuts *'93*
I.Q. *'94*
Ready to Wear *'94*
The Shawshank Redemption *'94*
Nothing to Lose *'96*
Arlington Road *'99*
Austin Powers 2: The Spy Who Shagged Me *'99*
Antitrust *'00*
High Fidelity *'00*
Mission to Mars *'00*
Human Nature *'02*
The Truth About Charlie *'02*
Code 46 *'03*
Mystic River *'03*
Anchorman: The Legend of Ron Burgundy *'04*
War of the Worlds *'05*
Zathura *'05*
Catch a Fire *'06*
Tenacious D in the Pick of Destiny *'06*
Noise *'07*
City of Ember *'08*
The Lucky Ones *'08*
Cinema Verite *'11*
Green Lantern *'11*
Back to 1942 *'12*
Life of Crime *'13*
Thanks for Sharing *'13*
A Perfect Day *'16*
Marjorie Prime *'17*
Dark Waters *'19*

Richard Rober (1910-52)
Call Northside 777 *'48*
Task Force *'49*
Backfire *'50*
Dial 1119 *'50*
The File on Thelma Jordon *'50*
Sierra *'50*
The Woman on Pier 13 *'50*
Man in the Saddle *'51*
The Well *'51*
The Devil Makes Three *'52*
Kid Monk Baroni *'52*
Outlaw Women *'52*
Jet Pilot *'57*

Lyda Roberti (1906-38)
Kid from Spain *'32*
Three-Cornered Moon *'33*
Torch Singer *'33*
George White's Scandals of 1935 *'35*
Nobody's Baby *'37*

Allene Roberts (1928-2019)
The Red House *'47*
Bomba on Panther Island *'49*
Union Station *'50*

Arthur Roberts (1938-)
Revenge of the Ninja *'83*
Not of This Earth *'88*
The Capitol Conspiracy *'99*
Behind Your Eyes *'11*

Bart Roberts (1928-)
See Rex Reason

Beverly Roberts (1914-2009)
China Clipper *'36*
The Singing Kid *'36*
Call of the Yukon *'38*
Buried Alive *'39*

Bret Roberts
Nightstalker *'02*
Cock & Bull Story *'03*
Rampage: The Hillside Strangler Murders *'04*
Crooked *'05*
Beach Kings *'08*
S. Darko: A Donnie Darko Tale *'09*
The Off Hours *'11*
Appetites *'15*

Christian Roberts (1944-)
To Sir, with Love *'67*
The Anniversary *'68*
The Adventurers *'70*
The Mind of Mr. Soames *'70*

Clete Roberts (1912-84)
The Story of G.I. Joe *'45*
Man On a String *'60 (N)*

Conrad Roberts
The Mosquito Coast *'86*
The Serpent and the Rainbow *'87*
The Million Dollar Hotel *'99*
The Scorpion King *'02*

Craig Roberts
Submarine *'10*
Kill Your Friends *'16*

Dallas Roberts (1970-)
A Home at the End of the World *'04*
Walk the Line *'05*
Winter Passing *'05*
Flicka *'06*
The Notorious Bettie Page *'06*
Joshua *'07*
Lovely by Surprise *'07*
3:10 to Yuma *'07*
Shrink *'09*
The Factory *'10*
The River Why *'10*
The Grey *'12*
Dallas Buyers Club *'13*
Shadow People *'13*
My Friend Dahmer *'17*

Daniel Roberts
Walking on Water *'02*
Valiant *'05 (V)*

David Roberts
Me Myself I *'99*
Fool's Gold *'08*
The Square *'08*

Doris Roberts (1925-2016)
Honeymoon Killers *'70*
The Taking of Pelham One Two Three *'74*
Hester Street *'75*
Number One with a Bullet *'87*
National Lampoon's Christmas Vacation *'89*
Simple Justice *'89*
Used People *'92*
The Night We Never Met *'93*
My Giant *'98*
A Fish in the Bathtub *'99*
All Over the Guy *'01*
Dickie Roberts: Former Child Star *'03*
A Time to Remember *'03*
Grandma's Boy *'06*
I-See-You.Com *'06*
Keeping Up with the Steins *'06*
Aliens in the Attic *'09*
Mrs. Miracle *'09*
Play the Game *'09*
Call Me Mrs. Miracle *'10*
Madea's Witness Protection *'12*
The Little Rascals Save the Day *'14*

Douglas Roberts
Pumpkinhead 3: Ashes to Ashes *'06*
Attack of the Gryphon *'07*

Eliza Roberts
Dead End *'98*
First Dog *'10*
The M Word *'14*

Emma Roberts (1991-)
Blow *'01*
Aquamarine *'06*
Nancy Drew *'07*
Lymelife *'08*
Wild Child *'08*
Hotel for Dogs *'09*
The Winning Season *'09*
4.3.2.1 *'10*
It's Kind of a Funny Story *'10*
Twelve *'10*
Valentine's Day *'10*
Virginia *'10*
The Art of Getting By *'11*
Scream 4 *'11*
Adult World *'13*
We're the Millers *'13*
Palo Alto *'14*
Nerve *'16*
The Blackcoat's Daughter *'17*
I Am Michael *'17*
Billionaire Boys Club *'18*
UglyDolls *'19 (V)*

Eric Roberts (1956-)
King of the Gypsies *'78*
Raggedy Man *'81*

Star 80 '83
The Coca-Cola Kid '84
The Pope of Greenwich Village '84
Runaway Train '85
Nobody's Fool '86
Blood Red '88
Best of the Best '89
The Ambulance '90
Descending Angel '90
The Lost Capone '90
Lonely Hearts '91
Final Analysis '92
Fugitive Among Us '92
Best of the Best 2 '93
Love, Cheat & Steal '93
Babyfever '94
Firefall '94
Love Is a Gun '94
Nature of the Beast '94
Sensation '94
The Specialist '94
Heaven's Prisoners '95
The Immortals '95
It's My Party '95
American Strays '96
Doctor Who '96
In Cold Blood '96
Most Wanted '97
The Odyssey '97
The Prophecy 2: Ashtown '97
Bitter Sweet '98
Dead End '98
T.N.T. '98
Two Shades of Blue '98
Agent of Death '99
Heaven's Fire '99
Hitman's Run '99
La Cucaracha '99
Lansky '99
Purgatory '99
Restraining Order '99
Wildflowers '99
The Beatnicks '00
Cecil B. Demented '00
Frozen in Fear '00
Luck of the Draw '00
Mercy Streets '00
No Alibi '00
Race Against Time '00
TripFall '00
Fast Sofa '01
The King's Guard '01
The Long Ride Home '01
Mindstorm '01
Sanctimony '01
Stiletto Dance '01
Breakaway '02
Con Games '02
Endangered Species '02
Spun '02
Border Blues '03
Break a Leg '03
National Security '03
Final Approach '04
Miss Cast Away '04
Six: The Mark Unleashed '04
Fatal Desire '05
DOA: Dead or Alive '06
A Guide to Recognizing Your Saints '06
One Way '06
Phat Girlz '06
The Butcher '07
Pandemic '07
Sister's Keeper '07
Cyclops '08
Dark Honeymoon '08
The Dark Knight '08
Depth Charge '08
Witless Protection '08
The Chaos Experiment '09
Crimes of the Past '09
Ninja's Creed '09
Project Solitude: Buried Alive '09
Rock Slyde: Private Eye '09
The Tomb '09
Bed & Breakfast '10
Enemies Among Us '10
The Expendables '10
First Dog '10
Hunt to Kill '10
Sharktopus '10
Jesse '11
Silver Case '11
Christmas in Compton '12
Deadline '12
The Mark '12
Snow White: A Deadly Summer '12
Stealing Las Vegas '12
Worth: The Testimony of Johnny St. James '12
The Hot Flashes '13
Lovelace '13
The Mark 2: Redemption '13
Paranormal Movie '13
Revelation Road: The Beginning of the End '13
A Bet's a Bet '14
Camp Dread '14
Inherent Vice '14
Cowboys vs Dinosaurs '15
The Human Centipede 3: The Final Sequence '15
The Condemned 2 '16

Ewan Roberts (1914-83)
Curse of the Demon '57
Day of the Triffids '63

Florence Roberts (1860-1940)
Kept Husbands '31
Make Me a Star '32
Torch Singer '33
Harmony Lane '35

Ian Roberts (1952-)
The Power of One '92
Terminal Impact '95
Mandela and de Klerk '97
Tarzan and the Lost City '98
Wah-Wah '05

Jeremy Roberts (1954-)
Jungle Boy '96
The Thirteenth Floor '99
Herbie: Fully Loaded '05

J.H. Roberts (1884-1961)
Nine Days a Queen '36
Young and Innocent '37
Spitfire '42

Joe Roberts
Shakespeare in Love '98
Cider with Rosie '99

Joe Roberts (1871-1923)
The Primitive Lover '22
Our Hospitality '23

Judith Roberts
Dead Silence '07
You Were Never Really Here '17

Judith Anna Roberts
Eraserhead '78
The Nanny Diaries '07

Julia Roberts (1967-)
Firehouse '87
Blood Red '88
Mystic Pizza '88
Satisfaction '88
Steel Magnolias '89
Flatliners '90
Pretty Woman '90
Dying Young '91
Hook '91
Sleeping with the Enemy '91
The Player '92
The Pelican Brief '93
I Love Trouble '94
Ready to Wear '94
Mary Reilly '95
Something to Talk About '95
Everyone Says I Love You '96
Michael Collins '96
Conspiracy Theory '97
My Best Friend's Wedding '97
Stepmom '98
Notting Hill '99
Runaway Bride '99
Erin Brockovich '00
America's Sweethearts '01
The Mexican '01
Ocean's Eleven '01
Confessions of a Dangerous Mind '02
Full Frontal '02
Mona Lisa Smile '03
Closer '04
Ocean's Twelve '04
The Ant Bully '06 (V)
Charlotte's Web '06 (V)
Charlie Wilson's War '07
Fireflies in the Garden '08
Duplicity '09
Eat, Pray, Love '10
Valentine's Day '10
Larry Crowne '11
Mirror Mirror '12
August: Osage County '13
The Normal Heart '14
Secret in Their Eyes '15
Money Monster '16
Mother's Day '16
Wonder '17
Ben Is Back '18

Kimberly Roberts
Vice Girls '96
Range of Motion '00
Get a Clue '02

Leonard Roberts (1972-)
Love Jones '96
The '60s '99
Drumline '02
Joe and Max '02
Red Sands '09

Lynne Roberts (1922-78)
Frolics on Ice '39
High School '40
Sioux City Sue '46
Robin Hood of Texas '47
Hunt the Man Down '50

Mark Roberts (1921-2006)
Shed No Tears '48
Posse '75
Bulletproof '96

Michael D. Roberts (1947-)
Heartbreaker '83
Ice Pirates '84
Rain Man '88

Pascale Roberts (1930-2019)
The Peking Blond '68
Friends '71
Marius and Jeannette '97
The Town Is Quiet '00

Pernell Roberts (1928-2010)
The Sheepman '58
Ride Lonesome '59
The Errand Boy '61
Four Rode Out '69
The Bravos '72
Paco '75
Sniper '75
Around the World in 80 Days '89

Rachel Roberts (1927-80)
Our Man in Havana '59
Saturday Night and Sunday Morning '60
This Sporting Life '63
The Reckoning '69
Doctors' Wives '70
Wild Rovers '71
Baffled '72
O Lucky Man! '73
Murder on the Orient Express '74
Picnic at Hanging Rock '75
Foul Play '78
When a Stranger Calls '79
Yanks '79
Charlie Chan and the Curse of the Dragon Queen '81

Rick Roberts (1965-)
Love and Human Remains '93
And Never Let Her Go '01
Student Seduction '03
Descent '05
Haunting Sarah '05
More Sex and the Single Mom '05
Man of the Year '06
The Note '07
Phantom Punch '09
Pontypool '09
The Night Before the Night Before Christmas '10

Roy Roberts (1900-75)
The Fighting Sullivans '42
Guadalcanal Diary '43
Colonel Effingham's Raid '45
He Walked by Night '48
Force of Evil '49
Borderline '50
The Enforcer '51
Santa Fe '51
Battles of Chief Pontiac '52
Wyoming Renegades '55
The Boss '56
The King and Four Queens '56
I'll Take Sweden '65
The Strongest Man in the World '75

Sebastien Roberts (1972-)
One Way '06
Black Swarm '07
Ice Blues: A Donald Strachey Mystery '08

Shawn Roberts (1984-)
Ghost Cat '03
Diary of the Dead '07
I Love You, Beth Cooper '09
Edge of Darkness '10
Resident Evil: Afterlife '10
Reel Love '11
Resident Evil: Retribution '12
Wyatt Earp's Revenge '12
Resident Evil: The Final Chapter '16

Stephen Roberts (1917-99)
GOG '54
Diary of a Madman '63

Tanya Roberts (1955-)
Fingers '78
The Yum-Yum Girls '78
Zuma Beach '78
California Dreaming '79
Tourist Trap '79
Beastmaster '82
Sheena '84
A View to a Kill '85
Body Slam '87
Inner Sanctum '91

Ted Jan Roberts (1979-)
Magic Kid '92
A Dangerous Place '94
Magic Kid 2 '94
The Power Within '95
Hollywood Safari '96
Tiger Heart '96

Thayer Roberts
The Chinese Ring '47
This Is Not a Test '62

Theodore Roberts (1861-1928)
Suds '20
Affairs of Anatol '21
The Ten Commandments '23

Tony Roberts (1939-)
Million Dollar Duck '71
Star Spangled Girl '71
Play It Again, Sam '72
Serpico '73
The Taking of Pelham One Two Three '74
Lovers Like Us '75
The Savage '75
The Lindbergh Kidnapping Case '76
Annie Hall '77
Just Tell Me What You Want '80
Stardust Memories '80
A Midsummer Night's Sex Comedy '82
Amityville 3: The Demon '83
Hannah and Her Sisters '86
Seize the Day '86
Radio Days '87
18 Again! '88
Popcorn '89
Our Sons '91
Switch '91
Dead Broke '99

Tracey Roberts (1914-2002)
Fort Defiance '51
Queen for a Day '51
Actors and Sin '52
Murder Is My Beat '55
The Prodigal '55
The Naked Flame '68

Wink Roberts (1955-)
The First Time '69
The Day It Came to Earth '77

Alex Robertson
Wide Sargasso Sea '06
Fanny Hill '07
First Light '10

Britt Robertson (1990-)
The Family Tree '10
The First Time '12
The Longest Ride '15
Tomorrowland '15
Jack Goes Home '16
Mr. Church '16
A Dog's Purpose '17
The Space Between Us '17

Brittany Robertson (1990-)
Dan in Real Life '07
Frank '07
The Tenth Circle '08
Triple Dog '09

Cliff Robertson (1925-2011)
Picnic '55
Days of Wine and Roses '58
Battle of the Coral Sea '59
Gidget '59
All in a Night's Work '61
Underworld U.S.A. '61
The Interns '62
PT 109 '63
Sunday in New York '63
The Best Man '64
633 Squadron '64
Love Has Many Faces '65
The Honey Pot '67
Charly '68
The Devil's Brigade '68
Too Late the Hero '70
The Great Northfield Minnesota Raid '72
Man on a Swing '74
Out of Season '75
Three Days of the Condor '75
Midway '76
Obsession '76
Washington: Behind Closed Doors '77
Dominique '79
Brainstorm '83
Class '83
Star 80 '83
Shaker Run '85
Ford: The Man & the Machine '87
Malone '87
Wild Hearts Can't Be Broken '91
Wind '92
Renaissance Man '94 (C)
Escape from L.A. '96
Race '99
Mach 2 '00
Spider-Man '02
13th Child: Legend of the Jersey Devil '02
Riding the Bullet '04
Spider-Man 2 '04
Spider-Man 3 '07

Dale Robertson (1923-2013)
Call Me Mister '51
Golden Girl '51
City of Bad Men '53
The Silver Whip '53
The Gambler from Natchez '54
Sitting Bull '54
Dakota Incident '56
Coast of Skeletons '63
Man from Button Willow '65 (V)
One-Eyed Soldiers '67
Melvin Purvis: G-Man '74
The Last Ride of the Dalton Gang '79

Finlay Robertson
In a Day '06
The Disappeared '08

Francoise Robertson
Armistead Maupin's More Tales of the City '97
The Minion '98
We All Fall Down '00
Ties That Bind '06

Iain Robertson (1981-)
Plunkett & Macleane '98
Basic Instinct 2 '06

Jenny Robertson (1963-)
Bull Durham '88
The Nightman '93
The Boys Next Door '96
Twitches '05
Balls of Fury '07

Kathleen Robertson (1973-)
Blown Away '93
Dog Park '98
Splendor '99
Beautiful '00
Psycho Beach Party '00
Scary Movie 2 '01
Torso '02
XX/XY '02
Hollywoodland '06
Tin Man '07
The Terrorist Next Door '08
Not Since You '09
A Night for Dying Tigers '10
Seal Team Six: The Raid on Osama Bin Laden '12
Mr. Hockey: The Gordie Howe Story '13

Kimmy Robertson (1954-)
Beauty and the Beast '91 (V)
Leprechaun 2 '94
Speed 2: Cruise Control '97

Luke Robertson
Levity '03
A Stand Up Guy '16

Robbie Robertson (1943-)
Carny '80
The Crossing Guard '94

Steven Robertson (1980-)
Rory O'Shea Was Here '04
Joyeux Noel '05
Murderland '09
The Bletchley Circle '13

Willard Robertson (1886-1948)
The Rider of Death Valley '32
Virtue '32
Supernatural '33
Tugboat Annie '33
Whirlpool '34
Dante's Inferno '35
The Old Homestead '35
Brigham Young: Frontiersman '40
Remember the Night '40
Air Force '43

William Robertson
Operator 13 '34
Deep Valley '47

James Robertson-Justice
Doctor in Love '60
Doctor in Clover '66

Paul Robeson (1898-1976)
Body and Soul '24
Emperor Jones '33
Sanders of the River '35
Show Boat '36
Song of Freedom '36
Big Fella '37
King Solomon's Mines '37
Jericho '38
Tales of Manhattan '42

George Robey (1869-1954)
Don Quixote '35
Henry V '44

Wendy Robie (1953-)
The People under the Stairs '91
The Attic Expeditions '01
Were the World Mine '08

Kim Robillard (1955-)
Rain Man '88
Breakdown '96
The Fan '96
Home Fries '98
Ali '01

Dany Robin (1927-95)
Waltz of the Toreadors '62
Follow the Boys '63
Don't Lose Your Head '66
The Best House in London '69

Michel Robin (1930-)
La Chevre '81
Merci pour le Chocolat '00
Farewell, My Queen '12

Herb Robins
The Thrill Killers '65
The Worm Eaters '77

Laila Robins (1959-)
Planes, Trains & Automobiles '87
An Innocent Man '89
Welcome Home, Roxy Carmichael '90
Live Nude Girls '95
Female Perversions '96
The Blood Oranges '97
Oxygen '99
True Crime '99
Searching for Paradise '02
Slippery Slope '06
Multiple Sarcasms '10

Mikul Robins
Witchcraft 9: Bitter Flesh '96
Witchcraft 11: Sisters in Blood '00
The Bagman '02

Oliver Robins (1971-)
Poltergeist '82
Poltergeist 2: The Other Side '86

Andrew (Andy) Robinson (1942-)
Dirty Harry '71
Charley Varrick '73
Someone I Touched '75
Mask '85
Cobra '86
Hellraiser '87
Shoot to Kill '88
Child's Play 3 '91
Prime Target '91
Fatal Charm '92
Into the Badlands '92
There Goes My Baby '92
Trancers 3: Deth Lives '92
Pumpkinhead 2: Blood Wings '94
Running Woman '98

Ann (Robin) Robinson
The Glass Wall '53
The War of the Worlds '53
Dragnet '54
Gun Brothers '56
Gun Duel In Durango '57
Attack from Mars '88
War of the Worlds '05

Bill Robinson (1878-1949)
Dixiana '30
The Little Colonel '35
The Littlest Rebel '35
Just Around the Corner '38
Rebecca of Sunnybrook Farm '38
Stormy Weather '43

Bruce Robinson (1946-)
The Story of Adele H. '75
Still Crazy '98

Bumper Robinson (1974-)
The Spirit '87
The Old Settler '01
Flatland '02
Death Valley '04

Charles Robinson (1945-)
Shenandoah '65
The Brotherhood of Satan '71
Daring Dobermans '73
Sugar Hill '74
Black Gestapo '75
Murder C.O.D. '90
Set It Off '96
Land of the Free '98
The Playaz Court '07
The House Bunny '08

Chris Robinson (1938-)
Because They're Young '60
13 West Street '62
Revenge Is My Destiny '71
Stanley '72
Thunder County '74
Women's Prison Escape '74
Amy '81
Savannah Smiles '82
Viper '88

Craig Robinson (1971-)
Daddy's Little Girls '07
Dragon Wars '07
Knocked Up '07
Walk Hard: The Dewey Cox Story '07
Pineapple Express '08
Zack and Miri Make a Porno '08
Fanboys '09
Miss March '09
Post Grad '09
Hot Tub Time Machine '10
Shrek Forever After '10 (V)
Peeples '13
This Is the End '13
Hot Tub Time Machine 2 '15
Morris from America '16
Table 19 '17
Tragedy Girls '17
Timmy Failure: Mistakes Were Made '20

Craig Phillip Robinson (1971-)
See Craig Robinson

Dar Robinson (1947-86)
Stick '85
Cyclone '87

Dewey Robinson (1898-1950)
Her Forgotten Past '33
Missing Girls '36
The Lady Confesses '45

Eartha D. Robinson (1960-)
Daughters of the Dust '91
The Old Settler '01

Edward G. Robinson (1893-1973)
Little Caesar '30
Five Star Final '31
Smart Money '31
The Hatchet Man '32
Tiger Shark '32
Two Seconds '32
The Little Giant '33
Dark Hazard '34
The Man with Two Faces '34
Barbary Coast '35
The Whole Town's Talking '35
Kid Galahad '37
The Last Gangster '37
Thunder in the City '37
Amazing Dr. Clitterhouse '38
Bullets or Ballots '38
A Slight Case of Murder '38
Confessions of a Nazi Spy '39
Brother Orchid '40
Dr. Ehrlich's Magic Bullet '40
Manpower '41
Larceny, Inc. '42
Tales of Manhattan '42
Destroyer '43
Double Indemnity '44
Mr. Winkle Goes to War '44
Tampico '44
Woman in the Window '44
Our Vines Have Tender Grapes '45
Scarlet Street '45
The Stranger '46
The Red House '47
Key Largo '48
House of Strangers '49
It's a Great Feeling '49
Actors and Sin '52
Big Leaguer '53
Vice Squad '53
A Bullet for Joey '55
Illegal '55
The Violent Men '55
A Hole in the Head '59
Seven Thieves '60
My Geisha '62
Two Weeks in Another Town '62
The Prize '63
Cheyenne Autumn '64
Good Neighbor Sam '64
The Outrage '64
Robin and the 7 Hoods '64
The Cincinnati Kid '65
Grand Slam '67
The Biggest Bundle of Them All '68
Never a Dull Moment '68
The Peking Blond '68
MacKenna's Gold '69
Operation Heartbeat '69
Soylent Green '73

Frances Robinson (1916-71)
Tim Tyler's Luck '37
Forbidden Valley '38
Smilin' Through '41

Jay Robinson (1930-)
The Robe '53
Demetrius and the Gladiators '54
The Virgin Queen '55
My Man Godfrey '57
Everything You Always Wanted to Know about Sex (But Were Afraid to Ask) '72
Three the Hard Way '74
Partners '82
Transylvania Twist '89
Sinatra '92

Joe Robinson (1927-)
A Kid for Two Farthings '55
Thor and the Amazon Women '60
The Invaders '63
Diamonds Are Forever '71

John Robinson
Zero Patience '94
Cyber Seduction: His Secret Life '05
Killer Wave '07
Just Business '08
Sticks and Stones '08

John Robinson (1908-79)
Ghost Ship '53
The Doctor's Dilemma '58
The Longest Day '62
Nothing But the Night '72

John Robinson (1985-)
Elephant '03
Lords of Dogtown '05
Seraphim Falls '06
Remember the Daze '07
Transformers '07
Wendy and Lucy '08
Intruder '16

Karen Robinson
My Teacher Ate My Homework '98
My Louisiana Sky '02
Jasper, Texas '03
Student Seduction '03
Lars and the Real Girl '07

Keith D. Robinson (1976-)
Fat Albert '04
Dreamgirls '06
This Christmas '07
Dear John '10
35 and Ticking '10

Leon Robinson (1962-)
Sole Survivor '84
Streetwalkin' '85
Band of the Hand '86
The Father Clements Story '87
Buffalo Soldiers '01
And Then There Was You '13

Leonard Robinson
The Bronx Is Burning '07
Speed-Dating '10

Linette Robinson
The Wall '99
Blue Hill Avenue '01

Madeleine Robinson (1916-2008)
Duke of the Derby '62
Mission to Venice '63
Camille Claudel '89

Nick Robinson
Goodnight, Mr. Tom '99
The Kings of Summer '13
Being Charlie '16
The 5th Wave '16

Nick Robinson (1995-)
Everything, Everything '17
Love, Simon '18
Native Son '19
Strange But True '19

Paul Michael Robinson (1963-)
Friend of the Family 2 '96
The Capitol Conspiracy '99
Kept '01

Roger Robinson (1940-)
Burnzy's Last Call '95
Brother to Brother '04
H. '15

Sherry Robinson
Gruesome Twosome '67
Hot Summer in Barefoot County '74

'Sugar Ray' Robinson (1921-89)
Candy '68
The Detective '68
Paper Lion '68

Wendy Raquel Robinson (1967-)
Ringmaster '98
Miss Congeniality '00
Two Can Play That Game '01
Rebound '05
Something New '06
35 and Ticking '10
Mysterious Ways '15

Zuleikha Robinson (1977-)
Hidalgo '04
The Merchant of Venice '04
The Namesake '06

Holly Robinson Peete (1964-)
Howard the Duck '86
The Jacksons: An American Dream '92
Speed-Dating '10
21 Jump Street '12

Rudy Robles (1910-70)
The Real Glory '39
Across the Pacific '42

Flora Robson (1902-84)
Catherine the Great '34
Fire Over England '37
Invisible Stripes '39
Wuthering Heights '39
The Sea Hawk '40
Two Thousand Women '44
Saratoga Trunk '45
Caesar and Cleopatra '46
Black Narcissus '47
Malta Story '53
Romeo and Juliet '54
55 Days at Peking '63
Murder at the Gallop '63
Guns at Batasi '64
Those Magnificent Men in Their Flying Machines '65
Young Cassidy '65
Eye of the Devil '67
Blood Island '68
Beast in the Cellar '70
Fragment of Fear '70
Les Miserables '78
A Tale of Two Cities '80

May Robson (1858-1942)
Chicago '27
Red Headed Woman '32
Strange Interlude '32
Dancing Lady '33
Dinner at Eight '33
Lady for a Day '33
One Man's Journey '33
Lady by Choice '34
Anna Karenina '35
Reckless '35
It Happened in New Orleans '36
Wife Versus Secretary '36
A Star Is Born '37
The Adventures of Tom Sawyer '38
Bringing Up Baby '38
Four Daughters '38
The Texans '38
Daughters Courageous '39
Four Wives '39
Nurse Edith Cavell '39
Irene '40
Four Mothers '41
Playmates '41
Joan of Paris '42

Wayne Robson (1946-2011)
Two If by Sea '95
Affliction '97
Cube '98
Harlan County War '00
Wrong Turn '03
Welcome to Mooseport '04

Erica Roby
The Apocalypse '07
Invasion of the Pod People '07

Patricia Roc (1915-2003)
Love Story '44
Two Thousand Women '44
Madonna of the Seven Moons '45
The Wicked Lady '45
Canyon Passage '46
So Well Remembered '47
Man on the Eiffel Tower '48

Daniela Rocca (1938-95)
Colossus and the Amazon Queen '60
The Giant of Marathon '60
Revenge of the Barbarians '60
Divorce-Italian Style '62
The Mercenaries '62

Stefania Rocca (1971-)
Solomon '98
The Talented Mr. Ripley '99
Jesus '00
Love's Labour's Lost '00
Heaven '01
Operation Valkyrie '04
Don't Tell '05
The 4 Musketeers '05

Alex Rocco (1936-2015)
Motor Psycho '65
The St. Valentine's Day Massacre '67
Blood Mania '70
Wild Riders '71
The Godfather '72
Stanley '72
Bonnie's Kids '73
Detroit 9000 '73
Slither '73
Three the Hard Way '74
Hustling '75
Herbie Goes Bananas '80
The Stunt Man '80
The Entity '83
Gotcha! '85
Return to Horror High '87
Scenes from the Goldmine '87
The Lady in White '88
Dream a Little Dream '89
The Spy Within '94
That Thing You Do! '96
Just Write '97
A Bug's Life '98 (V)
Dudley Do-Right '99
Goodbye, Lover '99
The Wedding Planner '01
Big Shot: Confessions of a Campus Bookie '02
The Country Bears '02
The Job '03
Find Me Guilty '06
Jam '06
Smokin' Aces '07

Mario Roccuzzo
Earth vs. the Spider '01
One Last Ride '03

Kali Rocha (1971-)
Meet the Parents '00
Gods and Generals '03
Meet the Fockers '04
The Family Plan '05
29th & Gay '05
Ripple Effect '07
Ready? OK! '08
Timer '09
Space Station 76 '14

Eugene Roche (1928-2004)
Cotton Comes to Harlem '70
They Might Be Giants '71
Slaughterhouse Five '72
W '74
Winter Kill '74
Mr. Ricco '75
The Late Show '77
The Possessed '77
Corvette Summer '78
Foul Play '78
The Winds of Kitty Hawk '78
The Child Stealer '79
You Can't Take It With You '79
Cocaine and Blue Eyes '83
Oh, God! You Devil '84
When a Man Loves a Woman '94

Sebastien Roche (1964-)
Merlin '98
The Hunley '99
The Crossing '00
What We Do Is Secret '07
24: Redemption '08
Happy Tears '09
The Adventures of Tintin '11 (V)
Beverly Hills Chihuahua 3: Viva La Fiesta! '12

Suzzy Roche
Almost You '85
Crossing Delancey '88

Jean Rochefort (1930-)
Angelique '64
Angelique: The Road to Versailles '65
Angelique and the King '66
A Coeur Joie '67
The Tall Blond Man with One Black Shoe '72
The Clockmaker '73
Escape from Death Row '73
Mean Frank and Crazy Tony '75
Innocents with Dirty Hands '76
Who Is Killing the Great Chefs of Europe? '78
The Hairdresser's Husband '92
Ready to Wear '94
Ridicule '96
The Count of Monte Cristo '99
The Closet '00
The Man on the Train '02
Tell No One '06
Mr. Bean's Holiday '07

Spencer Rochfort (1966-)
Motel Blue '98
A Decent Proposal '06

Debbie Rochon (1968-)
Vampire's Kiss '88
Broadcast Bombshells '95
Tromeo & Juliet '95
Hellblock 13 '97
American Nightmare '00
Witchouse 3: Demon Fire '01
Blood Relic '05
Bikini Bloodbath '06
Rapturious '07
Bikini Bloodbath Carwash '08
Bikini Bloodbath Christmas '09
Nun of That '09
Psychic Experiment '10
Solid State '12
Phobia '13
Varsity Blood '14

Lela Rochon (1964-)
Harlem Nights '89
Waiting to Exhale '95

The Chamber '96
Gang Related '96
Mr. & Mrs. Loving '96
The Big Hit '98
Knock Off '98
Ruby Bridges '98
Why Do Fools Fall in Love? '98
Any Given Sunday '99
Fatal Secrets '09
Blood Done Sign My Name '10

Chris Rock (1966-)
Beverly Hills Cop 2 '87
I'm Gonna Git You Sucka '88
New Jack City '91
Boomerang '92
CB4: The Movie '93
Coneheads '93
The Immortals '95
Beverly Hills Ninja '96
Dr. Dolittle '98 (V)
Lethal Weapon 4 '98
Dogma '99
Nurse Betty '00
A. I.: Artificial Intelligence '01 (V)
Down to Earth '01
Jay and Silent Bob Strike Back '01
Osmosis Jones '01 (V)
Pootie Tang '01
Bad Company '02
Head of State '03
Paparazzi '04 (C)
The Longest Yard '05
Madagascar '05 (V)
Bee Movie '07 (V)
I Think I Love My Wife '07
Madagascar: Escape 2 Africa '08 (V)
Good Hair '09
Death at a Funeral '10
Grown Ups '10
Madagascar 3: Europe's Most Wanted '12 (V)
What to Expect When You're Expecting '12
Grown Ups 2 '13
Top Five '14

Crissy Rock (1958-)
Ladybird, Ladybird '93
Butterfly Collectors '99

Tony Rock
Life Support '07
Three Can Play That Game '07

Rock, The (1972-)
See Dwayne 'The Rock' Johnson

Charles Rocket (1949-2005)
Fraternity Vacation '85
Earth Girls Are Easy '89
How I Got into College '89
Dances with Wolves '90
Delirious '91
Hocus Pocus '93
Wild Palms '93
Dumb & Dumber '94
It's Pat: The Movie '94
Steal Big, Steal Little '95
Tom and Huck '95
Father's Day '96
The Killing Grounds '97
Shade '03

Rick Rockwell (1956-)
Killer Tomatoes Strike Back '90
Killer Tomatoes Eat France '91

Sam Rockwell (1968-)
Clownhouse '88
Last Exit to Brooklyn '90
Happy Hell Night '92
The Search for One-Eye Jimmy '94
Box of Moonlight '96
Glory Daze '96
Lawn Dogs '96
Mercy '96
Jerry and Tom '98
Safe Men '98
Galaxy Quest '99
The Green Mile '99
William Shakespeare's A Midsummer Night's Dream '99
Charlie's Angels '00
Heist '01
Confessions of a Dangerous Mind '02
Welcome to Collinwood '02
Matchstick Men '03
The Hitchhiker's Guide to the Galaxy '05
The Assassination of Jesse James by the Coward Robert Ford '07
Joshua '07
Snow Angels '07
Choke '08
Frost/Nixon '08
Everybody's Fine '09
G-Force '09 (V)
Gentlemen Broncos '09
Moon '09
The Winning Season '09
Conviction '10
Iron Man 2 '10
Cowboys & Aliens '11
The Sitter '11
Seven Psychopaths '12
A Case of You '13
Laggies '13
A Single Shot '13
Trust Me '13
The Way Way Back '13
Better Living Through Chemistry '14
Don Verdean '15
Poltergeist '15
Mr. Right '16
Three Billboards Outside Ebbing, Missouri '17
Woman Walks Ahead '17
Blue Iguana '18
Vice '18
The Best of Enemies '19
Jojo Rabbit '19
Richard Jewell '19

Jay Rodan (1974-)
The Caveman's Valentine '01
Lost Battalion '01
The Triumph of Love '01
Callas Forever '02
Monsieur N. '03
The Game of Their Lives '05

Ziva Rodann (1935-)
The Pharaoh's Curse '57
Teenage Doll '57
Last Train from Gun Hill '59
The Giants of Thessaly '60
Samar '62

James Roday (1976-)
Coming Soon '99
Repli-Kate '01
Don't Come Knocking '05
The Dukes of Hazzard '05
Christmas Eve '15

Marcia Rodd (1940-)
Little Murders '71
Citizens Band '77

Ebbe Rode (1910-98)
Gertrud '64
Babette's Feast '87

Karel Roden (1962-)
15 Minutes '01
Blade 2 '02
Bulletproof Monk '03
The Bourne Supremacy '04
Dead Fish '04
Hellboy '04
The Last Drop '05
Dead Man's Bounty '06
Running Scared '06
Mr. Bean's Holiday '07
RocknRolla '08
Orphan '09
Cat Run '11
A Lonely Place to Die '11

Shmuel Rodensku (1904-89)
The Odessa File '74
The Sellout '76

Kate Rodger
Chained Heat 3: Hell Mountain '98
Last Stand '00

Struan Rodger (1956-)
The Waiting Time '99
Sherlock: Case of Evil '02

Anton Rodgers (1933-2007)
Disraeli '79
Lillie '79
Agatha Christie's Murder with Mirrors '85
Dirty Rotten Scoundrels '88
Impromptu '90
The Merchant of Venice '04
Longford '06

Michael E. Rodgers (1969-)
Uncorked '98
Last Stand '00
Auto Focus '02
The Triangle '05
Sinner '07

Dennis Rodman (1961-)
Double Team '97
Simon Sez '99
Cutaway '00
The Comebacks '07

John Rodney
Pursued '47
Fighter Squadron '48

Michael Rodrick (1970-)
Desolation Angels '95
Under Hellgate Bridge '99
Revolution #9 '01

Adam Rodriguez (1975-)
Love and Debate '06
I Can Do Bad All By Myself '09
Caught in the Crossfire '10
About Last Night '14
Lovesick '14
Magic Mike XXL '15

Elizabeth Rodriguez
Miami Vice '06
Pound of Flesh '10

Estelita Rodriguez (1928-66)
The Golden Stallion '49
Susanna Pass '49

Freddy Rodriguez (1975-)
Dead Presidents '95
A Walk in the Clouds '95
The Pest '96
For Love or Country: The Arturo Sandoval Story '00
Rip It Off '02
Chasing Papi '03
Dallas 362 '03
Players '03
Dreamer: Inspired by a True Story '05
Harsh Times '05
Havoc '05
Bobby '06
Lady in the Water '06
Poseidon '06
Planet Terror '07
Nothing Like the Holidays '08
Seal Team Six: The Raid on Osama Bin Laden '12

Genesis Rodriguez (1987-)
Casa de mi Padre '12
Man on a Ledge '12
Hours '13
Identity Thief '13
The Last Stand '13
Big Hero 6 '14 (V)
Tusk '14

Gina Rodriguez
Filly Brown '12
Deepwater Horizon '16
The Star '17
Annihilation '18

Gina Rodriguez
Miss Bala '19
Someone Great '19
Scoob! '20

Marco Rodriguez (1953-)
Internal Affairs '90
The Rookie '90
The Crow '93
. . .And the Earth Did Not Swallow Him '94
Serial Killer '95
Angel Blue '97
Two for Texas '97
Unspeakable '02
Hamlet 2 '08

Mel Rodriguez (1973-)
The Three Burials of Melquiades Estrada '05
Lakeview Terrace '08
Overboard '18
Onward '20 (V)

Michelle Rodriguez (1978-)
Girlfight '99
The Fast and the Furious '01
3 A.M. '01
Blue Crush '02
Resident Evil '02
S.W.A.T. '03
BloodRayne '06
The Breed '06
Battle in Seattle '07
Avatar '09
Fast & Furious '09
Machete '10
Battle: Los Angeles '11
Fast & Furious 6 '13
Machete Kills '13
Turbo '13 (V)
Furious 7 '15
The Assignment '17
The Fate of the Furious '17
Widows '18

Paul Rodriguez (1955-)
Quicksilver '86
The Whoopee Boys '86
Born in East L.A. '87
Made in America '93
A Million to Juan '94
Rough Magic '95
Race '99
Mambo Cafe '00
Price of Glory '00
Ali '01
Crocodile Dundee in Los Angeles '01
Rat Race '01
Tortilla Soup '01
Blood Work '02
Baadasssss! '03
A Cinderella Story '04
The World's Fastest Indian '05
One Long Night '07
Beverly Hills Chihuahua '08 (V)
Cats & Dogs: The Revenge of Kitty Galore '10
Without Men '11

Raini Rodriguez
Paul Blart: Mall Cop '09
Paul Blart: Mall Cop 2 '15

Ramon Rodriguez (1979-)
Bella '06
Surfer, Dude '08
Battle: Los Angeles '11
Need for Speed '14
Megan Leavey '17

Rebel Rodriguez (1999-)
Planet Terror '07
Shorts: The Adventures of the Wishing Rock '09

Rico Rodriguez (1998-)
Babysitters Beware '08
The Heyday of the Insensitive Bastards '17

Valente Rodriguez (1961-)
The Big Squeeze '96
Ed '96

Norman Rodway (1929-2001)
Four in the Morning '65
Chimes at Midnight '67
Coming Through '85
The Bretts '88
The Empty Mirror '99

Alex Roe (1990-)
Rings '17
Forever My Girl '18

Channon Roe (1969-)
Persons Unknown '96
Girl '98
Rampage: The Hillside Strangler Murders '04
Behind Enemy Lines 3: Colombia '08

Matt Roe (1952-2003)
Puppet Master '89
Last Call '90

Owen Roe
Intermission '03
Alarm '08

Daniel Roebuck (1963-)
Cave Girl '85
River's Edge '87
Disorganized Crime '89
The Killing Mind '90
Eddie Presley '92
The Fugitive '93
The Cold Equations '96
The Late Shift '96
Money Talks '97
U.S. Marshals '98
Final Destination '00
Double Take '01
A Glimpse of Hell '01
We Were Soldiers '02
Agent Cody Banks '03
Agent Cody Banks 2: Destination London '04
Straight into Darkness '04
Confessions of a Sociopathic Social Climber '05
The Devil's Rejects '05
Flourish '06
Shredderman Rules '07
Flash of Genius '08
Dark and Stormy Night '09
Woke Up Dead '09
That's What I Am '11
Let There Be Light '17

Sarah Roemer (1984-)
Wristcutters: A Love Story '06
Disturbia '07
Falling Up '08
Fired Up! '09
The Con Artist '10
Waking Madison '10

William Roerick (1912-95)
Not of This Earth '57
The Wasp Woman '59
The Love Machine '71

Emily Roeske
Halloweentown '98
Halloweentown 2: Kalabar's Revenge '01

Maurice Roeves (1937-2020)
Ulysses '67
Oh! What a Lovely War '69
When Eight Bells Toll '71
Danger UXB '81
Hidden Agenda '90
The Big Man: Crossing the Line '91
The Last of the Mohicans '92
Moses '96
David '97
The Acid House '98
Forgive and Forget '99
Beautiful Creatures '00
Mister Foe '07
The Damned United '09

Seth Rogen (1982-)
The 40 Year Old Virgin '05
You, Me and Dupree '06
Knocked Up '07
Shrek the Third '07 (V)
Superbad '07
Dr. Seuss' Horton Hears a Who! '08 (V)
Kung Fu Panda '08 (V)
Pineapple Express '08
The Spiderwick Chronicles '08 (V)
Zack and Miri Make a Porno '08
Funny People '09
Monsters vs. Aliens '09 (V)
Observe and Report '09
50/50 '11
The Green Hornet '11
Kung Fu Panda 2 '11 (V)
Paul '11 (V)
Take This Waltz '11
The Guilt Trip '12
This Is the End '13
The Interview '14
Neighbors '14
The Night Before '15
Steve Jobs '15
Neighbors 2: Sorority Rising '16
Sausage Party '16
The Disaster Artist '17
Long Shot '19
Zeroville '19

Austin Rogers (1994-)
How to Eat Fried Worms '06
Ace Ventura Jr.: Pet Detective '08

Bill Rogers (1930-2004)
Shanty Tramp '67
A Taste of Blood '67

Charles 'Buddy' Rogers (1904-99)
My Best Girl '27
Wings '27
Old Man Rhythm '35
The Mexican Spitfire's Baby '41
Mexican Spitfire at Sea '42
The Mexican Spitfire Sees a Ghost '42

Clyde Rogers (1929-2005)
See Rik van Nutter

David Clayton Rogers (1977-)
The Legend of Butch & Sundance '04
The Pregnancy Pact '10
Revenge of the Bridesmaids '10
Uncanny '15

Ginger Rogers (1911-95)
Suicide Fleet '31
The Tenderfoot '32
13th Guest '32
You Said a Mouthful '32
Chance at Heaven '33
Finishing School '33
Flying Down to Rio '33
42nd Street '33
Gold Diggers of 1933 '33
Rafter Romance '33
The Gay Divorcee '34
Romance in Manhattan '34
Upperworld '34
Roberta '35
Star of Midnight '35
Top Hat '35
Follow the Fleet '36
Swing Time '36
Shall We Dance '37
Stage Door '37
Carefree '38
Having a Wonderful Time '38
Vivacious Lady '38
Bachelor Mother '39
Fifth Avenue Girl '39
The Story of Vernon and Irene Castle '39
Kitty Foyle '40
Lucky Partners '40
Primrose Path '40
Tom, Dick, and Harry '41
The Major and the Minor '42
Once Upon a Honeymoon '42
Roxie Hart '42
Tales of Manhattan '42
I'll Be Seeing You '44
Weekend at the Waldorf '45
Heartbeat '46
Magnificent Doll '46
The Barkleys of Broadway '49
Perfect Strangers '50
The Groom Wore Spurs '51
Storm Warning '51
Monkey Business '52
We're Not Married '52
Forever Female '53

Black Widow '54
Teenage Rebel '56
Oh, Men! Oh, Women! '57
Cinderella '64
Quick, Let's Get Married '71
That's Dancing! '85

Graham Rogers
Crazy Kind of Love '12
Love & Mercy '15

Helen Rogers
24 Exposures '13
Body '15

Ingrid Rogers (1968-)
Carlito's Way '93
The Capture of the Green River Killer '08
On Strike for Christmas '10

Jean Rogers (1916-91)
Ace Drummond '36
Rocketship '36
Flash Gordon: Mars Attacks the World '39
Brigham Young: Frontiersman '40
Charlie Chan in Panama '40
Flash Gordon: Rocketship '40
Design for Scandal '41
Dr. Kildare's Victory '42
Swing Shift Maisie '43
Whistling in Brooklyn '43

Kasey Rogers
Denver and the Rio Grande '52
The Naked Flame '68

Kenny Rogers (1938-)
Kenny Rogers as the Gambler '80
Coward of the County '81
Six Pack '82
Kenny Rogers as the Gambler, Part 2: The Adventure Continues '83
Wild Horses '84
Kenny Rogers as the Gambler, Part 3: The Legend Continues '87
The Return of Spinal Tap '92 (C)
The Gambler Returns: The Luck of the Draw '93
Rio Diablo '93

Kylie Rogers
Space Station 76 '14
Miracles From Heaven '16

Michael Rogers (1964-)
Children of the Corn: Revelation '01
Past Tense '06
In the Spider's Web '07

Mimi Rogers (1956-)
Divorce Wars: A Love Story '82
Gung Ho '86
Someone to Watch Over Me '87
Street Smart '87
The Mighty Quinn '89
Desperate Hours '90
The Rousters '90
Deadlock '91
The Doors '91
The Rapture '91
Dark Horse '92
Ladykiller '92
The Player '92
Shooting Elizabeth '92
White Sands '92
Far from Home: The Adventures of Yellow Dog '94
Monkey Trouble '94
Bulletproof Heart '95
The Mirror Has Two Faces '96
Tree's Lounge '96
Austin Powers: International Man of Mystery '97
Weapons of Mass Distraction '97
Lost in Space '98
Virtual Obsession '98
Cruel Intentions 2 '99
The Devil's Arithmetic '99
Seven Girlfriends '00
Ginger Snaps '01
Charms for the Easy Life '02
Dumb and Dumberer: When Harry Met Lloyd '03
The Gunman '03
The Door in the Floor '04
Seeing Other People '04
Dancing in Twilight '05
Jesse Stone: Stone Cold '05
Big Nothing '06
The Stranger Game '06
Falling Up '08
Storm Cell '08
Abandoned '10
Order of Chaos '10
Lucky '11
For a Good Time, Call... '12
Hope Springs '12
Captive '15
The Wedding Ringer '15
Weepah Way for Now '15

Paul Rogers (1917-2013)
Beau Brummell '54
Svengali '55
Our Man in Havana '59
The Trials of Oscar Wilde '60
The Mark '61
Billy Budd '62
Stolen Hours '63
A Midsummer Night's Dream '68
The Looking Glass War '69
The Reckoning '69
The Homecoming '73
Edwin '84
The Tenth Man '88
The Return of the Native '94

Reg Rogers (1964-)
I'll Take You There '99
Runaway Bride '99
Attila '01
Analyze That '02
Lovely by Surprise '07

Roy Rogers (1912-98)
Under Western Stars '38
Dark Command '40
Hands Across the Border '43
Idaho '43
Texas Legionnaires '43
Don't Fence Me In '45
My Pal Trigger '46
Under Nevada Skies '46
Apache Rose '47
Home in Oklahoma '47
Lights of Old Santa Fe '47
Grand Canyon Trail '48
Melody Time '48
Under California Stars '48
The Golden Stallion '49
Susanna Pass '49
Bells of Coronado '50
Trail of Robin Hood '50
Trigger, Jr. '50
Son of Paleface '52
Alias Jesse James '59 (C)

Tristan Rogers (1946-)
Flesh and Blood Show '73
The Rescuers Down Under '90 (V)
Evil Lives '92

Wayne Rogers (1933-2015)
Cool Hand Luke '67
WUSA '70
Pocket Money '72
The Killing Time '87
Ghosts of Mississippi '96
Miracle Dogs '03

Will Rogers (1879-1935)
They Had to See Paris '29
Ambassador Bill '31
Too Busy to Work '32
Doctor Bull '33
Mr. Skitch '33
David Harum '34
Judge Priest '34
Doubting Thomas '35
In Old Kentucky '35
Life Begins at Forty '35
Steamboat Round the Bend '35

Will Rogers, Jr. (1911-93)
The Story of Will Rogers '52
The Eddie Cantor Story '53
The Boy From Oklahoma '54

Ron Rogge (1968-)
Valley of the Heart's Delight '07
Animals '08
Christmas Mail '10

Franz Rogowski
Victoria '15
Happy End '17
Transit '18
In the Aisles '19

Elisabeth Rohm (1973-)
FBI: Negotiator '05
Miss Congeniality 2: Armed and Fabulous '05
Ghost Image '07
The Kreutzer Sonata '08
San Saba '08
Crimes of the Past '09
Lake Placid: The Final Chapter '12
Transit '12
American Hustle '13
Chlorine '13
Hidden Away '13
Joy '15

Maria Rohm (1945-)
The House of 1000 Dolls '67
Kiss and Kill '68
Dorian Gray '70
Venus in Furs '70
Count Dracula '71

Clayton Rohner
Just One of the Guys '85
April Fool's Day '86
Bat 21 '88
I, Madman '89
Nightwish '89
Naked Souls '95
The Relic '96
Where's Marlowe? '98
The Big Day '99
Sometimes They Come Back. . . For More '99
Coronado '03

Geza Rohrig
Son of Saul '15
To Dust '19

Alba Rohrwacher (1979-)
Days and Clouds '07
My Brother Is an Only Child '07
I Am Love '09
Hungry Hearts '15
The Wonders '15
Happy as Lazzaro '18

Sophie Rois (1961-)
The Inheritors '98
3 '10

Gustavo Rojo (1923-)
Tarzan and the Mermaids '48
It Started with a Kiss '59
Apache's Last Battle '64
The Valley of Gwangi '69

Helena Rojo (1944-)
Aguirre, the Wrath of God '72
Mary, Mary, Bloody Mary '76

Maria Rojo (1943-)
Candy Stripe Nurses '74
Break of Dawn '88
Homework '90
Midaq Alley '95
Esmeralda Comes by Night '98

Roxie Roker (1929-95)
Making of a Male Model '83
Amazon Women on the Moon '87

Will Rokos
Monster's Ball '01
Evil Remains '04

Gilbert Roland (1905-94)
The Plastic Age '25
Call Her Savage '32
A Parisian Romance '32
The Passionate Plumber '32
She Done Him Wrong '33
Gateway '38
Juarez '39
The Sea Hawk '40
Captain Kidd '45
The Dude Goes West '48
Malaya '49
Bullfighter & the Lady '50
Crisis '50
The Furies '50
The Torch '50
The Bad and the Beautiful '52
Miracle of Our Lady of Fatima '52
Beneath the 12-Mile Reef '53
Thunder Bay '53
Around the World in 80 Days '56 (C)
Three Violent People '57
The Big Circus '59
Samar '62
Cheyenne Autumn '64
The Poppy Is Also a Flower '66
Any Gun Can Play '67
Go Kill and Come Back '68
Between God, the Devil & a Winchester '72
Running Wild '73
Islands in the Stream '77
The Sacketts '79
Cabo Blanco '81
Barbarosa '82

Erik Rolf
Counter-Attack '45
Davy Crockett, Indian Scout '50

Guy Rolfe (1911-2003)
King of the Khyber Rifles '53
Young Bess '53
Yesterday's Enemy '59
The Stranglers of Bombay '60
Mr. Sardonicus '61
The Alphabet Murders '65
And Now the Screaming Starts '73
Dolls '87
Puppet Master 3: Toulon's Revenge '90
Puppet Master 4 '93
Puppet Master 5: The Final Chapter '94
Retro Puppet Master '99

Kirsten Rolffes (1928-2000)
Sofie '92
The Kingdom '95
The Kingdom 2 '97

Esther Rolle (1920-98)
Age Old Friends '89
Driving Miss Daisy '89
The Mighty Quinn '89
A Raisin in the Sun '89
House of Cards '92
To Dance with the White Dog '93
Scarlett '94
How to Make an American Quilt '95
My Fellow Americans '96
Rosewood '96
Down in the Delta '98

Henry Rollins (1961-)
The Chase '93
Heat '95
Johnny Mnemonic '95
Lost Highway '96
Jack Frost '98
Morgan's Ferry '99
Scenes of the Crime '01
Time Lapse '01
The New Guy '02 (C)
Bad Boys 2 '03
Feast '06
Lies & Alibis '06
Wrong Turn 2: Dead End '07
The Devil's Tomb '09
Suck '09
He Never Died '15
The Last Heist '16

Howard E. Rollins, Jr. (1950-96)
King '78
Ragtime '81
A Soldier's Story '84
The Children of Times Square '86
Johnnie Gibson F.B.I. '87
The House of Dies Drear '88
Drunks '96

Rose Rollins (1978-)
13 Moons '02
Undisputed '02

Mark Rolston (1956-)
Aliens '86
Lethal Weapon 2 '89
Prancer '89
A Sinful Life '89
Survival Quest '89
Body of Evidence '92
Black Widow Murders: The Blanche Taylor Moore Story '93
The Shawshank Redemption '94
Best of the Best 3: No Turning Back '95
Daylight '96
Eraser '96
Humanoids from the Deep '96
George Wallace '97
Hard Rain '97
From the Earth to the Moon '98
Letters from a Killer '98
Rush Hour '98
Wicked Ways '99
Scorcher '02
The Departed '06
Protecting the King '07
You've Got a Friend '07
Backwoods '08
Not Forgotten '09
Saw 6 '09
Whitney '15

Yvonne Romain (1938-)
The Curse of the Werewolf '61
The Frightened City '61
Devil Doll '64
Double Trouble '67
The Last of Sheila '73

Candice Roman
The Big Bird Cage '72
Unholy Rollers '72

Freddie Roman (1937-)
Sweet Lorraine '87
Finding North '97

Leticia Roman (1941-)
G.I. Blues '60
Gold of the Seven Saints '61
Pirates of Tortuga '61
The Girl Who Knew Too Much '63

Ruth Roman (1924-99)
Since You Went Away '44
Good Sam '48
Barricade '49
Champion '49
The Window '49
Three Secrets '50
Invitation '51
Lightning Strikes Twice '51
Strangers on a Train '51
Tomorrow Is Another Day '51
Mara Maru '52
Young Man With Ideas '52
Down Three Dark Streets '54
Far Country '55
Rebel in Town '56
Bitter Victory '58
Look in Any Window '61
Love Has Many Faces '65
The Baby '72
The Killing Kind '73
Impulse '74
Day of the Animals '77
The Sacketts '79
Echoes '83

Susan (Suzan) Roman (1957-)
Weekend with the Babysitter '70
Rabid '77
Rock & Rule '83 (V)

Viviane Romance (1909-91)
Princess Tam Tam '35
Any Number Can Win '63

Beatrice Romand (1952-)
Claire's Knee '71
Le Beau Mariage '82
Summer '86

Carla Romanelli
Fighting Fists of Shanghai Joe '65
Steppenwolf '74

Andy Romano (1941-)
Get Christie Love! '74
Over the Edge '79
Pump Up the Volume '90
Afterburn '92
Unlawful Entry '92
Drop Zone '94
Under Siege 2: Dark Territory '95
Eraser '96
Ghosts of Mississippi '96
Two Bits '96

Christy Carlson Romano (1984-)
Looking for an Echo '99
The Cutting Edge: Going for the Gold '05
The Cutting Edge 3: Chasing the Dream '08
Wolvesbayne '09
Mirrors 2 '10
Christmas All Over Again '16

Lou Romano (1972-)
Ratatouille '07 (V)
Toy Story 3 '10 (V)

Ray Romano (1957-)
Ice Age '02 (V)
Eulogy '04
Welcome to Mooseport '04
Grilled '06
Ice Age: The Meltdown '06 (V)
The Last Word '08
Ice Age: Dawn of the Dinosaurs '09 (V)
Ice Age: Continental Drift '12 (V)
Rob the Mob '14
Ice Age: Collision Course '16
The Big Sick '17
Paddleton '19

Renato Romano (1940-)
The Bird with the Crystal Plumage '70
Dorian Gray '70
Frankenstein '80 '79

Stephanie Romanov (1969-)
Sunset Strip '99
Thirteen Days '00
Last Night '10

Richard Romanus (1943-)
Mean Streets '73
Wizards '77 (V)
Sitting Ducks '80
Heavy Metal '81 (V)
Protocol '84
Murphy's Law '86
The Couch Trip '87
Oscar '91
To Protect and Serve '92
Point of No Return '93
Cops and Robbersons '94

Robert Romanus (1956-)
Fast Times at Ridgemont High '82
Bad Medicine '85
Pulse '88
The Resurrected '91
Route 30 '08

Lina Romay (1919-2010)
Love Laughs at Andy Hardy '46
Honeymoon '47

Lina Romay (1954-2012)
Rites of Frankenstein '72
Female Vampire '73
The Perverse Countess '73
Jack the Ripper '76
Ilsa, the Wicked Warden '78
Sex Is Crazy '79

Revenge in the House of Usher '82
Tender Flesh '97

Sydne Rome (1951-)
Sundance and the Kid '69
Order to Kill '73
Wanted: Babysitter '75
The Twist '76

Cesar Romero (1907-94)
The Shadow Laughs '33
The Thin Man '34
Cardinal Richelieu '35
Clive of India '35
The Devil Is a Woman '35
The Good Fairy '35
Rendezvous '35
Love Before Breakfast '36
Wee Willie Winkie '37
Always Goodbye '38
Happy Landing '38
My Lucky Star '38
Charlie Chan at Treasure Island '39
The Cisco Kid and the Lady '39
Frontier Marshal '39
The Little Princess '39
The Return of the Cisco Kid '39
Wife, Husband and Friend '39
Dance Hall '41
The Great American Broadcast '41
Tall, Dark and Handsome '41
Week-End in Havana '41
Orchestra Wives '42
Springtime in the Rockies '42
Tales of Manhattan '42
Coney Island '43
Wintertime '43
Captain from Castile '47
Carnival in Costa Rica '47
Deep Waters '48
Julia Misbehaves '48
The Beautiful Blonde from Bashful Bend '49
Love That Brute '50
Happy Go Lovely '51
The Lost Continent '51
FBI Girl '52
Jungle '52
Scotland Yard Inspector '52
The Shadow Man '53
Vera Cruz '53
Americano '55
Around the World in 80 Days '56 (C)
Ocean's 11 '60
If a Man Answers '62
The Castilian '63
Donovan's Reef '63
Marriage on the Rocks '65
Sergeant Deadhead '65
Two On a Guillotine '65
Batman '66
Madigan's Millions '67
Hot Millions '68
Skidoo '68
The Computer Wore Tennis Shoes '69
Latitude Zero '69
Now You See Him, Now You Don't '72
The Proud and the Damned '72
The Big Push '75
The Strongest Man in the World '75
Mission to Glory '80
Lust in the Dust '85
Simple Justice '89
Mortuary Academy '91

Fernanda Romero
The Eye '08
Creature of Darkness '09

George A. Romero (1940-2017)
Night of the Living Dead '68
Martin '77
Dawn of the Dead '78

Joanelle Romero
Powwow Highway '89
Miracle in the Wilderness '91

Ned Romero (1926-)
I Will Fight No More Forever '75
Children of the Corn 2: The Final Sacrifice '92
The Magnificent Seven '98
The Lost Child '00

Rebecca Romijn (1972-)
Austin Powers 2: The Spy Who Shagged Me '99 (C)
X-Men '00
Femme Fatale '02
Rollerball '02
Simone '02
X2: X-Men United '03
Godsend '04
The Punisher '04
Lies & Alibis '06
X-Men: The Last Stand '06
Lake City '08
The Con Artist '10
Possessing Piper Rose '11
Tyler Perry's Good Deeds '12
Satanic Panic '19

Tiny Ron (1947-)
The Rocketeer '91
Alien Nation: Body and Soul '95
Alien Nation: The Enemy Within '96

Paul Ronan (1965-)
The Devil's Own '96
Bloom '03
Speed Dating '07

Saoirse Ronan (1994-)
I Could Never Be Your Woman '06
Atonement '07
The Christmas Miracle of Jonathan Toomey '07
Death Defying Acts '07
City of Ember '08
The Lovely Bones '09
The Way Back '10
Hanna '11
Violet & Daisy '11
Byzantium '12
The Host '13
How I Live Now '13
The Grand Budapest Hotel '14
Brooklyn '15
Lost River '15
Weepah Way for Now '15 (V)
Lady Bird '17
On Chesil Beach '17
Mary Queen of Scots '18
The Seagull '18
Little Women '19

Maurice Ronet (1927-83)
Carve Her Name with Pride '58
Frantic '58
Purple Noon '60
The Fire Within '64
The Lost Command '66
Who's Got the Black Box? '67
How Sweet It Is! '68
The Women '68
La Femme Infidele '69
La Piscine '69
Swimming Pool '70
Don Juan (Or If Don Juan Were a Woman) '73
Beau Pere '81
Sphinx '81

Fabrizio Rongione (1973-)
Rosetta '99
The Child '05
Lorna's Silence '08
Two Days, One Night '14

Linda Ronstadt (1946-)
FM '78
The Pirates of Penzance '83
Chuck Berry: Hail! Hail! Rock 'n' Roll '87

Linda Maria Ronstadt (1946-)
See Linda Ronstadt

Michael Roof (1976-2009)
Black Hawk Down '01
XXX '02
The Dukes of Hazzard '05
XXX: State of the Union '05

Michael Rooker (1955-)
Above the Law '88
Eight Men Out '88
Mississippi Burning '88
Music Box '89
Sea of Love '89
Days of Thunder '90
Henry: Portrait of a Serial Killer '90
The Dark Half '91
JFK '91
Afterburn '92
Cliffhanger '93
Tombstone '93
Mallrats '95
Back to Back '96
Bastard out of Carolina '96
Keys to Tulsa '96
Rosewood '96
The Trigger Effect '96
Deceiver '97
The Song of Hiawatha '97
Bram Stoker's Shadowbuilder '98
Brown's Requiem '98
The Replacement Killers '98
The Bone Collector '99
Rogue Force '99
Wicked Ways '99
Here on Earth '00
Newsbreak '00
The 6th Day '00
Table One '00
Replicant '01
Undisputed '02
The Box '03
On Thin Ice '03
Chasing Ghosts '05
Full Count '06
Slither '06
Whisper '07
Jumper '08
The Lena Baker Story '08
The Marine 2 '09
Meteor '09
Super Capers '09
Super '10
Cell 213 '11
Mysteria '11
Guardians of the Galaxy '14

Mickey Rooney (1920-2014)
Manhattan Melodrama '34
Ah, Wilderness! '35
A Midsummer Night's Dream '35
Riff Raff '35
The Devil Is a Sissy '36
Healer '36
Little Lord Fauntleroy '36
Captains Courageous '37
A Family Affair '37
Live, Love and Learn '37
Slave Ship '37
Thoroughbreds Don't Cry '37
You're Only Young Once '37
Boys Town '38
Judge Hardy's Children '38
Love Finds Andy Hardy '38
Out West With the Hardys '38
The Adventures of Huckleberry Finn '39
Andy Hardy Gets Spring Fever '39
Babes in Arms '39
The Hardys Ride High '39
Judge Hardy and Son '39
Mickey the Great '39
Andy Hardy Meets Debutante '40
Strike Up the Band '40
Young Tom Edison '40
Andy Hardy's Private Secretary '41
Babes on Broadway '41
Life Begins for Andy Hardy '41
Men of Boys Town '41
Andy Hardy's Double Life '42
The Courtship of Andy Hardy '42
A Yank at Eton '42
Girl Crazy '43
The Human Comedy '43
Thousands Cheer '43
Andy Hardy's Blonde Trouble '44
National Velvet '44
Love Laughs at Andy Hardy '46
Killer McCoy '47
Summer Holiday '48
Words and Music '48
The Big Wheel '49
The Fireball '50
Quicksand '50
My Outlaw Brother '51
All Ashore '53
Off Limits '53
A Slight Case of Larceny '53
The Atomic Kid '54
Drive a Crooked Road '54
The Bridges at Toko-Ri '55
Francis in the Haunted House '56
Operation Mad Ball '57
Andy Hardy Comes Home '58
The Last Mile '59
Breakfast at Tiffany's '61
Everything's Ducky '61
The King of the Roaring '20s: The Story of Arnold Rothstein '61
Requiem for a Heavyweight '62
It's a Mad, Mad, Mad, Mad World '63
The Secret Invasion '64
How to Stuff a Wild Bikini '65
24 Hours to Kill '65
Skidoo '68
The Comic '69
Evil Roy Slade '71
Journey Back to Oz '71 (V)
Manipulator '71
Pulp '72
Convict Women '74
Thunder County '74
Women's Prison Escape '74
Rachel's Man '75
The Domino Principle '77
Pete's Dragon '77
The Black Stallion '79
Bill '81
The Fox and the Hound '81 (V)
Leave 'Em Laughing '81
Senior Trip '81
The Odyssey of the Pacific '82
Bill: On His Own '83
It Came Upon a Midnight Clear '84
Lightning: The White Stallion '86
Erik the Viking '89
Home for Christmas '90
Silent Night, Deadly Night 5: The Toymaker '91
The Legend of Wolf Mountain '92
Little Nemo: Adventures in Slumberland '92 (V)
Maximum Force '92
Sweet Justice '92
The Gambler Returns: The Luck of the Draw '93
The Magic Voyage '93 (V)
Revenge of the Red Baron '93
Boys Will Be Boys '97
Babe: Pig in the City '98
The Last Confederate: The Story of Robert Adams '05
Night at the Museum '06
Lost Stallions: The Journey Home '08
Night at the Museum: Secret of the Tomb '14

Ted Rooney
It Happened to Jane '59
Celtic Pride '96
The Kill Hole '12

Tim Rooney (1947-2006)
Village of the Giants '65
Riot on Sunset Strip '67

Jeff Roop (1973-)
Widow on the Hill '05
Final Draft '07
Before You Say 'I Do' '09
Reel Love '11

Fay Roope (1893-1961)
The System '53
Ma and Pa Kettle at Waikiki '55

Jemima Rooper (1981-)
Owd Bob '97
The Railway Children '00
Snapshots '02
A Sound of Thunder '05
The Black Dahlia '06
Kinky Boots '06
Lost in Austen '08
One Chance '13

Camilla Overbye Roos (1969-)
On the Border '98
The Guilty '99

Buddy Roosevelt (1898-1973)
Westward Bound '30
Tribute to a Bad Man '56

Amanda Root (1963-)
Catherine Cookson's The Man Who Cried '93
Persuasion '95
Jane Eyre '96
Deep in the Heart (of Texas) '98
Anna Karenina '00
Daniel Deronda '02

Bonnie Root (1975-)
Coming Soon '99
In the Weeds '00
Don't Tell '05
Rails & Ties '07

Stephen (Steve) Root (1951-)
Crocodile Dundee 2 '88
Monkey Shines '88
Black Rain '89
Ghost '90
Guilty by Suspicion '91
RoboCop 3 '91
Stephen King's Golden Years '91
V.I. Warshawski '91
Buffy the Vampire Slayer '92
Till Murder Do Us Part '92
Dave '93
Extreme Justice '93
Bye Bye, Love '94
Night of the Scarecrow '95
Pandora's Clock '96
From the Earth to the Moon '98
Krippendorf's Tribe '98
Office Space '98
Bicentennial Man '99
O Brother Where Art Thou? '00
The Country Bears '02 (V)
Ice Age '02 (V)
Finding Nemo '03 (V)
Anchorman: The Legend of Ron Burgundy '04
Dodgeball: A True Underdog Story '04
Jersey Girl '04
The Ladykillers '04
Raising Genius '04
Surviving Christmas '04
Just Friends '05
Ice Age: The Meltdown '06 (V)
Idiocracy '06
Leatherheads '08
Mad Money '08
Over Her Dead Body '08
Bob Funk '09
The Men Who Stare at Goats '09
The Soloist '09
Everything Must Go '10
Unthinkable '10
Cedar Rapids '11
Rango '11 (V)
Red State '11
Son of Morning '11
Big Miracle '12
Sweetwater '13
Mike and Dave Need Wedding Dates '16
Miles '17

Noel Roquevert (1892-1973)
The Murderer Lives at Number 21 '42
Le Corbeau '43
Fanfan la Tulipe '51
Nana '55

Hayden Rorke (1910-87)
Double Crossbones '51
Francis Goes to the Races '51
The Law and the Lady '51
Wild Stallion '52
Above and Beyond '53
South Sea Woman '53
Spencer's Mountain '63

Rosanna Rory (1927-)
The Big Boodle '57
Big Deal on Madonna Street '58

Tom Rosales (1948-)
Detour to Terror '80
Bail Out '90
John Carpenter's Vampires '97

Tony Rosato (1954-)
Switching Channels '88
The Good Fight '92

Francoise Rosay (1891-1974)
Bizarre Bizarre '39
September Affair '50
The Red Inn '51
Nobody's Children '52

Alan Roscoe (1886-1933)
The Texas Streak '26
Rain or Shine '30

Anika Noni Rose (1972-)
From Justin to Kelly '03
Dreamgirls '06
Just Add Water '07
The Starter Wife '07
The Princess and the Frog '09 (V)
For Colored Girls '10
Bag of Bones '11
Mitch Albom's Have a Little Faith '11
As Cool As I Am '13
The Watsons Go to Birmingham '13
A Day Late and a Dollar Short '14
Everything, Everything '17

Felissa Rose
Sleepaway Camp '83
Return to Sleepaway Camp '08
Camp Dread '14

Gabrielle Rose (1954-)
Family Viewing '87
Speaking Parts '89
The Adjuster '91
Timecop '94
The Sweet Hereafter '96
The Five Senses '99
Beneath '07
Cleaverville '07
Lost Boys: The Tribe '08
On the Other Hand, Death '08
Courage '09
Grace '09
He Loves Me '11
If I Stay '14
Maudie '17

George Rose (1920-88)
Track the Man Down '55
All at Sea '57
A Night to Remember '58
The Flesh and the Fiends '60

Jack the Ripper '60
A New Leaf '71
The Hideaways '73
The Pirates of Penzance '83

Jamie Rose (1960-)
Tightrope '84
Chopper Chicks in Zombietown '91

Laurie Rose (1948-)
The Abductors '72
Hot Box '72
Working Girls '75

Nectar Rose (1974-)
The Hazing '04
Roman '06

Roger Rose
Ski Patrol '89
Comic Book: The Movie '04

Sherrie Rose (1966-)
Maximum Force '92
New Crime City: Los Angeles 2020 '94
Black Scorpion 2: Ground Zero '96
The Nurse '97
Devil in the Flesh '98
Me & Will '99

Rose Marie (1923-)
Top Banana '54
Dead Heat on a Merry-Go-Round '66
Don't Worry, We'll Think of a Title '66
Witchboard '87
Shriek If You Know What I Did Last Friday the 13th '00

Roseanne (1952-)
She-Devil '89
Look Who's Talking, Too '90 (V)
Backfield in Motion '91
Freddy's Dead: The Final Nightmare '91
The Woman Who Loved Elvis '93
Even Cowgirls Get the Blues '94 (C)
Blue in the Face '95
Home on the Range '04 (V)

John Roselius
Devil in a Blue Dress '95
JAG '95
Con Air '97

Romy Rosemont
John John in the Sky '00
Shopgirl '05
An American Crime '07
A Taste of Romance '12

Beatrice Rosen
Sharpe's Peril '08
The Big I Am '10

Sam Rosen
Four Boxes '09
Stuck Between Stations '11

Michael Rosenbaum (1972-)
Urban Legend '98
Sweet November '01
Poolhall Junkies '02
Sorority Boys '02
Bringing Down the House '03
Racing Stripes '05 (V)
Kickin' It Old Skool '07
Catch.44 '11
Father of Invention '11
Hit and Run '12
Back in the Day '14

Alan Rosenberg (1950-)
Wanderers '79
Promise '86
After Midnight '89
Capone '89
Miracle Mile '89
Impulse '90
In a Stranger's Hand '92
Steve Martini's Undue Influence '96
The Temptations '98
Crash Course '00
Righteous Kill '08

Maxie 'Slapsie' Rosenbloom (1903-76)
Amazing Dr. Clitterhouse '38
Mr. Moto's Gamble '38
Each Dawn I Die '39
Louisiana Purchase '41
Ringside Maisie '41
The Boogie Man Will Get You '42
To the Shores of Tripoli '42
Swing Fever '43
Irish Eyes Are Smiling '44
Abbott and Costello Meet the Keystone Kops '54
Hollywood or Bust '56
I Married a Monster from Outer Space '58
The Bellboy '60

Saskia Rosendahl
Lore '13
Never Look Away '18

George Rosener (1879-1945)
Alias the Doctor '32
Union Depot '32

Ben Rosenfield
Greetings from Tim Buckley '12
Jamesy Boy '14

Grant Rosenmeyer (1991-)
The Royal Tenenbaums '01
Come As You Are '20

Rick Rosenthal (1949-)
Distant Thunder '88
Halloween: Resurrection '02 (C)

Jose Roseto
The Damned '06
Illegal Business '06

Rosette (1959-)
Pauline at the Beach '83
Summer '86

Jose Rosette (1975-)
I Got Five on It '05
Machined '06
San Franpsycho '06

Stelvio Rosi (1938-)
Hell Commandos '69
The Hanging Woman '72

Bodil Rosing (1877-1941)
Sunrise '27
Why Be Good? '29
Downstairs '32

Justin Rosniak
Sweet Talker '91
Animal Kingdom '09

Annie Ross (1930-)
Dressed for Death '74
Yanks '79
Superman 3 '83
Basket Case 2 '90
Pump Up the Volume '90
Basket Case 3: The Progeny '92
Short Cuts '93

Anthony Ross (1909-55)
Between Midnight and Dawn '50
Perfect Strangers '50
Country Girl '54

Betsy King Ross (1921-89)
Fighting with Kit Carson '33
The Phantom Empire '35

Charlotte Ross (1968-)
Foreign Student '94
Love and a .45 '94
Savage Land '94
Christmas in Paradise '07
Live! '07
Montana Sky '07
Moola '07
Ring of Death '08

Chelcie Ross (1942-)
Keep My Grave Open '80
Above the Law '88
Major League '89
Bill & Ted's Bogus Journey '91
The Last Boy Scout '91
Basic Instinct '92
Amos and Andrew '93
Rudy '93
Chain Reaction '96
Charming Billy '98
A Simple Plan '98
The Gift '00
Madison '01
The Majestic '01
Snap Decision '01
Waking Up in Reno '02
A Little Thing Called Murder '06
Drag Me to Hell '09
Formosa Betrayed '09
Fertile Ground '10
The Dilemma '11
The Last Rites of Joe May '11

David Ross (1945-)
Splitting Heirs '93
Mary Reilly '95
Six Ways to Sunday '99
Vanity Fair '99
Oliver Twist '00
Station Jim '01

David W. Ross
Love the Hard Way '01
Quinceanera '06
I Do '13

Diana Ross (1944-)
Lady Sings the Blues '72
Mahogany '75
The Wiz '78
Double Platinum '99

Evan Ross (1988-)
ATL '06
Life Support '07
Pride '07
According to Greta '08
Gardens of the Night '08
Life is Hot in Cracktown '08
Linewatch '08
The Family Tree '10
Mooz-Lum '10
96 Minutes '11
Jeff, Who Lives at Home '12
NYC Underground '13

Gene Ross (1930-)
Don't Look in the Basement '73
Don't Open the Door! '74
Encounter with the Unknown '75
Keep My Grave Open '80
Halloween 4: The Return of Michael Myers '88
Lost Highway '96

Govind Raja Ross
Flame Over India '59
North West Frontier '59

Herbert Ross (1927-2001)
Goodbye, Mr. Chips '69
Play It Again, Sam '72

Howard Ross (1941-)
Hercules Against the Mongols '63
Diary of a Rebel '68
Five Dolls for an August Moon '70
Sergeant Klems '71
The Legend of the Wolf Woman '77
New York Ripper '82
The New Gladiators '83

Howard (Red) Ross (1941-)
See Howard Ross

Hugh Ross (1945-)
For Love of the Game '99
The Assassination of Jesse James by the Coward Robert Ford '07 (N)
Bronson '09

Joe E. Ross
Revenge Is My Destiny '71
Slumber Party '57 '76

Katharine Ross (1940-)
Shenandoah '65
Mister Buddwing '66
The Singing Nun '66
Games '67
The Graduate '67
Hellfighters '68
Butch Cassidy and the Sundance Kid '69
Tell Them Willie Boy Is Here '69
Fools '70
Get to Know Your Rabbit '72
They Only Kill Their Masters '72
Pigs '73
The Stepford Wives '75
Voyage of the Damned '76
The Betsy '78
The Swarm '78
The Legacy '79
The Final Countdown '80
Rodeo Girl '80
The Shadow Riders '82
Wrong Is Right '82
Conagher '91
Donnie Darko '01
Eye of the Dolphin '06
The Hero '17

Kimberly Ross (1959-2006)
The Last Starfighter '84
Nightmare at Noon '87
Pumpkinhead '88

Lee Ross (1971-)
The Guilty '92
Secrets and Lies '95
Metroland '97
Dreaming of Joseph Lees '99
Secret Society '00
Goal! The Dream Begins '06
Centurion '10

Lonny Ross
Good Luck Chuck '07
The Rocker '08

Marion Ross (1928-)
Forever Female '53
The Proud and Profane '56
Teacher's Pet '58
Grand Theft Auto '77
Pearl '78
The Evening Star '96
Hidden in Silence '96
The Last Best Sunday '98
Superhero Movie '08

Matt Ross (1970-)
Face/Off '97
American Psycho '99
Pushing Tin '99
Just Visiting '01
Stephen King's Rose Red '02
The Aviator '04
Good Night, and Good Luck '05
Last Holiday '06
Turn the River '07
Ring of Fire '13

Merrie Lynn Ross
The Lucifer Complex '78
Class of 1984 '82

Michael Ross (1911-93)
D.O.A. '49
Captain Kidd and the Slave Girl '54
Attack of the 50 Foot Woman '58

Ricco Ross (1960-)
The Dirty Dozen: The Next Mission '85
Aliens '86

Shavar Ross (1971-)
Friday the 13th, Part 5: A New Beginning '85
The House of Dies Drear '88

Shirley Ross (1913-75)
San Francisco '36
Waikiki Wedding '37
The Big Broadcast of 1938 '38
Thanks for the Memory '38

Stanley Ralph Ross (1936-2000)
Candy Stripe Nurses '74
Babe: Pig in the City '98 (V)

Ted Ross (1934-2002)
The Wiz '78
Arthur '81
Arthur 2: On the Rocks '88
Stealing Home '88

Tracee Ellis Ross (1972-)
I-See-You.Com '06
Daddy's Little Girls '07
Life Support '07
Labor Pains '09
Little '19

Yolonda Ross
Antwone Fisher '02
United States of Leland '03
Go for Sisters '13
Whitney '15
The Bad Batch '17

Gavin Rossdale (1965-)
Constantine '05
The Game of Their Lives '05
How to Rob a Bank '07
The Bling Ring '13

Isabella Rossellini (1952-)
A Matter of Time '76
White Nights '85
Blue Velvet '86
Tough Guys Don't Dance '87
Red Riding Hood '88
Cousins '89
Wild at Heart '90
Death Becomes Her '92
Fearless '93
The Innocent '93
The Pickle '93 (C)
Immortal Beloved '94
Wyatt Earp '94
Big Night '95
The Funeral '96
The Odyssey '97
The Imposters '98
Left Luggage '98
Merlin '98
The Sky Is Falling '00
Empire '02
Roger Dodger '02
Monte Walsh '03
Napoleon '03
The Saddest Music in the World '03
Heights '04
King of the Corner '04
The Architect '06
Brand Upon the Brain! '06 (N)
Infamous '06
Infected '08
My Dog Tulip '09 (V)
The Phantom '09
Two Lovers '09
Keyhole '11
Late Bloomers '11
Enemy '13
Joy '15
Vita & Virginia '19

Carol Rossen (1937-)
The Stepford Wives '75
The Fury '78

Leo Rossi (1946-)
Heart Like a Wheel '83
River's Edge '87
The Accused '88
Relentless '89
Maniac Cop 2 '90
Relentless 2: Dead On '91
Where the Day Takes You '92
Raw Justice '93
Relentless 3 '93
Beyond Desire '94
Relentless 4 '94
Felony '95
In Cold Blood '96
Wedding Bell Blues '96
Analyze This '98
Sticks '98
True Friends '98
Crackerjack 3 '00
One Night at McCool's '01
The Business of Fancydancing '02
The Last Letter '04

Mick Rossi
Played '06
2:22 '08

Theo Rossi
Last Resort '09
Red Sands '09

When the Bough Breaks '16
Lowriders '17
Rattlesnake '19
Vault '19

Eleanora Rossi-Drago (1925-2007)
David and Goliath '61
Camille 2000 '69
Dorian Gray '70

Giacomo 'Jack' Rossi-Stuart (1925-94)
The Avenger '62
Gunfight at Red Sands '63
The Last Man on Earth '64
Knives of the Avenger '65
Planet on the Prowl '65
Kill, Baby, Kill '66
The Snow Devils '67
Diary of a Rebel '68
Hornets' Nest '70
Kill Django '71
The Night Evelyn Came Out of the Grave '71
Zorro '74
Reactor '78

Norman Rossington (1928-99)
Carry On Sergeant '58
Saturday Night and Sunday Morning '60
Lawrence of Arabia '62
A Hard Day's Night '64
The Charge of the Light Brigade '68
Man in the Wilderness '71
Raw Meat '72
Let Him Have It '91

Ronato Rossini (1941-)
See Howard Ross

Leonard Rossiter (1926-84)
King Rat '65
Otley '68
2001: A Space Odyssey '68
Luther '74
The Pink Panther Strikes Again '76
Britannia Hospital '82
Water '85

Angelo Rossitto (1908-91)
Mesa of Lost Women '52
Brain of Blood '71
Dracula vs. Frankenstein '71
Mad Max: Beyond Thunderdome '85
The Offspring '87

Rick Rossovich (1957-)
Losin' It '82
The Lords of Discipline '83
Streets of Fire '84
The Terminator '84
Warning Sign '85
The Morning After '86
Top Gun '86
Let's Get Harry '87
Roxanne '87
Spellbinder '88
Navy SEALS '90
The Gambler Returns: The Luck of the Draw '93
Tropical Heat '93
New Crime City: Los Angeles 2020 '94
Black Scorpion '95
Legend of the Lost Tomb '97
Truth or Consequences, N.M. '97
Telling You '98
Killer Deal '99
Miracle in Lane Two '00

Emmy Rossum (1986-)
Songcatcher '99
An American Rhapsody '01
Passionada '02
Mystic River '03
The Day After Tomorrow '04
The Phantom of the Opera '04
Poseidon '06
Dare '09
Dragonball: Evolution '09
Beautiful Creatures '13
Comet '14

Carlo Rota (1961-)
32 Short Films about Glenn Gould '93
Boondock Saints '99
Saw 5 '08
Brick Mansions '14

Andrea Roth (1967-)
The Good Fight '92
Seedpeople '92
A Change of Place '94
Crossworlds '96
Executive Power '98
Hidden Agenda '99
The Stepdaughter '00
Sasquatch '02
Wilderness Love '02
Chasing Christmas '05
Crazy for Christmas '05
Bridal Fever '08
Secret Lives of Second Wives '08
The Collector '09
Courage '09
A Golden Christmas '09
The Skeptic '09

Cecilia (Celia) Roth (1956-)
The Stranger '87
A Place in the World '92
Martin (Hache) '97
All About My Mother '99
Second Skin '99
Lucia, Lucia '03
I'm So Excited '13

Cooper Roth
Super Buddies '13 *(V)*
Cooties '14

Eli Roth (1972-)
Cabin Fever '03
2001 Maniacs '05
Death Proof '07
Don't Look Up '08
Inglourious Basterds '09
Aftershock '12

Gene Roth (1903-76)
Earth *vs.* the Spider '58
She Demons '58

Joanna Roth (1965-)
Rosencrantz & Guildenstern Are Dead '90
The Real Charlotte '91

Lillian Roth (1910-80)
The Love Parade '29
Animal Crackers '30
Madam Satan '30
Alice Sweet Alice '76

Martha Roth
Massacre '56
The Man and the Monster '65

Nick Roth (1985-)
Brave New Girl '04
Berkeley '05

Tim Roth (1961-)
Meantime '81
Agatha Christie's Murder with Mirrors '85
The Hit '85
Return to Waterloo '85
A World Apart '88
To Kill a Priest '89
The Cook, the Thief, His Wife & Her Lover '90
Rosencrantz & Guildenstern Are Dead '90
Vincent & Theo '90
Jumpin' at the Boneyard '92
The Perfect Husband '92
Reservoir Dogs '92
Bodies, Rest & Motion '93
Captives '94
Little Odessa '94
Pulp Fiction '94
Four Rooms '95
Rob Roy '95
Everyone Says I Love You '96
Gridlock'd '96
Hoodlum '96
No Way Home '96
Deceiver '97
The Legend of 1900 '98
The Million Dollar Hotel '99
Lucky Numbers '00
Vatel '00
Invincible '01
The Musketeer '01
Planet of the Apes '01
Dark Water '02
Killing Emmett Young '02
To Kill a King '03
The Beautiful Country '04
Silver City '04
Don't Come Knocking '05
Even Money '06
Funny Games '07
Virgin Territory '07
Youth Without Youth '07
The Incredible Hulk '08
Skellig: The Owl Man '09
Pete Smalls Is Dead '10
Arbitrage '12
The Liability '12
Broken '13
Mobius '13
Grace of Monaco '14
Selma '14
Hardcore Henry '15
Chronic '16
Mr. Right '16
600 Miles '16
The Padre '18
Luce '19
The Song of Names '19

Jessica Rothe (1987-)
Lily & Kat '15
Happy Death Day '17
Forever My Girl '18
Happy Death Day 2U '19
Valley Girl '20

Adam Rothenberg
Mad Money '08
Tennessee '08

Jessica A. Rothenberg (1987-)
See Jessica Rothe

Teryl Rothery (1962-)
Mr. Rice's Secret '00
Video Voyeur: The Susan Wilson Story '02
Threshold '03
The Twelve Days of Christmas Eve '04
The Sandlot 2 '05
Whisper '07
White Noise 2: The Light '07
Battle of the Bulbs '10
Iris Johansen's The Killing Game '11
Flicka: Country Pride '12

Will Rothhaar (1987-)
Hearts in Atlantis '01
Killing Kennedy '13

John Rothman (1949-)
The Boost '88
Gettysburg '93
Copycat '95
Hostile Waters '97
The Siege '98
Say It Isn't So '01
Welcome to Mooseport '04
Brooklyn Lobster '05

Cynthia Rothrock (1957-)
The Millionaire's Express '86
China O'Brien '88
Tiger Claws '91
Lady Dragon '92
Rage and Honor '92
Rage and Honor 2: Hostile Takeover '93
Guardian Angel '94
Undefeatable '94
Night Vision '97
Sworn to Justice '97
Sci-Fighter '04

Paolo Rotondo
The Ugly '96
Stickmen '01

Vincent Rottiers (1986-)
I'm Glad My Mother Is Alive '09
Renoir '12
Dheepan '16
Nocturama '17

Brigitte Rouan (1946-)
After Sex '97
Time of the Wolf '03
Love Songs '07

Alida Rouffe (1874-1949)
Fanny '32
Cesar '36

Richard Roundtree (1942-)
Shaft '71
Diamonds '72
Embassy '72
Firehouse '72
Shaft's Big Score '72
Shaft in Africa '73
Earthquake '74
Man Friday '75
Portrait of a Hitman '77
Escape to Athena '79
An Eye for an Eye '81
One Down, Two to Go! '82
Q (The Winged Serpent) '82
Big Score '83
The Baron and the Kid '84
City Heat '84
Killpoint '84
A.D. '85
Jocks '87
Opposing Force '87
Angel 3: The Final Chapter '88
Maniac Cop '88
Party Line '88
Bad Jim '89
Crack House '89
Night Visitor '89
A Time to Die '91
Bloodfist 3: Forced to Fight '92
Christmas in Connecticut '92
Amityville: A New Generation '93
Body of Influence '93
Once Upon a Time . . . When We Were Colored '95
Seven '95
Theodore Rex '95
Original Gangstas '96
George of the Jungle '97
Steel '97
Having Our Say: The Delany Sisters' First 100 Years '99
Antitrust '00
Shaft '00
Corky Romano '01
Joe and Max '02
Boat Trip '03
Brick '06
Final Approach '08
Ladies of the House '08
Speed Racer '08
The Confidant '10
Shaft '19

Robert Rounseville (1914-74)
The Tales of Hoffmann '51
Carousel '56

Mickey Rourke (1955-)
1941 '79
Fade to Black '80
Body Heat '81
Eureka! '81
Heaven's Gate '81
Diner '82
Rumble Fish '83
The Pope of Greenwich Village '84
Year of the Dragon '85
9 1/2 Weeks '86
Angel Heart '87
Barfly '87
Prayer for the Dying '87
Homeboy '88
Johnny Handsome '89
Desperate Hours '90
Wild Orchid '90
Harley Davidson and the Marlboro Man '91
White Sands '92
Francesco '93
The Last Outlaw '93
Bullet '94
Fall Time '94
The Last Ride '94
Another 9 1/2 Weeks '96
Buffalo 66 '97
Double Team '97
John Grisham's The Rainmaker '97
Point Blank '98
Out in Fifty '99
Animal Factory '00
Get Carter '00
The Pledge '00
Picture Claire '01
They Crawl '01
Spun '02
Once Upon a Time in Mexico '03
Man on Fire '04
Domino '05
Sin City '05
Alex Rider: Operation Stormbreaker '06
The Wrestler '08
The Informers '09
Killshot '09
The Expendables '10
Iron Man 2 '10
Passion Play '10
13 '10
Immortals '11
The Courier '12
Generation Iron '13
Java Heat '13
Sin City: A Dame to Kill For '14
Weaponized '16
Nightmare Cinema '19

Eddie Rouse
Pandorum '09
Being Flynn '12

Graham Rouse (1934-)
Ride a Wild Pony '75
The Odd Angry Shot '79

Mitch Rouse
Sweethearts '97
Call Me Crazy '13

Anne Roussel (1960-)
The Music Teacher '88
Wolves in the Snow '02

Myriem Roussel (1962-)
First Name: Carmen '83
Hail Mary '85

Nathalie Roussel
My Father's Glory '91
My Mother's Castle '91

Jean-Paul Roussillon (1931-)
Baxter '89
The Girl from Paris '02
A Christmas Tale '08

Brandon Routh (1979-)
Superman Returns '06
Fling '08
Life is Hot in Cracktown '08
Zack and Miri Make a Porno '08
Stuntmen '09
Table for Three '09
Miss Nobody '10
Scott Pilgrim *vs.* the World '10
Unthinkable '10
Dylan Dog: Dead of Night '11
Crooked Arrows '12

Jordan Routledge
East Is East '99
Gabriel & Me '01

Jean-Paul Rouve (1967-)
A Very Long Engagement '04
La Vie en Rose '07
Nobody Else But You '11

Catherine Rouvel (1939-)
Borsalino '70
La Rupture '70
Black and White in Color '76
Va Savoir '01

Jean-Louis Roux (1923-)
The Third Miracle '99
The Courage to Love '00

Jack Rovello (1994-)
The Hours '02
Lonesome Jim '06

Dominic Rowan (1971-)
David '97
Emma '97

Kelly Rowan (1965-)
The Gate '87
Black Fox: Good Men and Bad '94
Candyman 2: Farewell to the Flesh '94
187 '97
Loving Evangeline '98
Three to Tango '99
Proximity '00
The Truth About Jane '00
Greenmail '01
Eight Days to Live '06
In God's Country '07
Jack and Jill *vs.* the World '08
Cyberbully '11

Brad Rowe (1970-)
Billy's Hollywood Screen Kiss '98
Stonebrook '98
Body Shots '99
Christina's House '99
The '70s '00
Fish Without a Bicycle '03
Lucky Seven '03
Four Corners of Suburbia '05
Love for Rent '05
Shut Up and Kiss Me '05
The Insatiable '06
Though None Go With Me '06
Vanished '06
Shelter '07
Carnal Innocence '11
A Christmas Wedding Tail '11
Your Love Never Fails '11

Charlie Rowe
Never Let Me Go '10
Neverland '11

Leanne Rowe (1982-)
Warrior Queen '03
Oliver Twist '05

Misty Rowe (1950-)
Goodbye, Norma Jean '75
The Man with Bogart's Face '80
Double Exposure '82
Meatballs 2 '84

Nicholas (Nick) Rowe (1966-)
Young Sherlock Holmes '85
Sharpe's Enemy '94
Longitude '00
The Infinite Worlds of H.G. Wells '01
Shackleton '02
A Waste of Shame '05
Beau Brummell: This Charming Man '06
A Harlot's Progress '06
Anton Chekhov's The Duel '09
Shanghai '09

Rosie Rowell (1965-)
Kiss and Tell '96
Gabriel & Me '01

Victoria Rowell (1959-)
The Distinguished Gentleman '92
Dumb & Dumber '94
Barb Wire '96
Anne Rice's The Feast of All Saints '01
Black Listed '03
Motives '03
Home of the Brave '06
Of Boys and Men '08

Henry Rowland (1914-84)
36 Hours '64
Supervixens '75
Beneath the Valley of the Ultra-Vixens '79

Kelly Rowland
Freddy *vs.* Jason '03
Love by the 10th Date '17

Oscar Rowland
Promised Land '88
Bats '99

Paige Rowland (1967-)
Riot '96
Doomsdayer '00

Rodney Rowland (1964-)
Dancing at the Blue Iguana '00
The 6th Day '00
I Know Who Killed Me '07

Steve Rowland (1932-)
Gun Glory '57
Naked Youth '59

David Rowlands
Husbands '70
Minnie and Moskowitz '71

Gena Rowlands (1930-)
Lonely Are the Brave '62
Tony Rome '67
Faces '68
Machine Gun McCain '69
Minnie and Moskowitz '71
A Woman under the Influence '74
Two Minute Warning '76
Opening Night '77
Brink's Job '78
Gloria '80
The Tempest '82
An Early Frost '85
The Betty Ford Story '87
Another Woman '88
Night on Earth '91
Once Around '91
Crazy in Love '92
Ted & Venus '93 *(C)*
The Neon Bible '95
Something to Talk About '95
Unhook the Stars '96
She's So Lovely '97
Hope Floats '98
The Mighty '98
Paulie '98
Playing by Heart '98
The Weekend '00
Charms for the Easy Life '02
Hysterical Blindness '02
The Incredible Mrs. Ritchie '03
The Notebook '04
Taking Lives '04
The Skeleton Key '05
Paris, je t'aime '06
Broken English '07
What If God Were the Sun? '07
Parts Per Billion '14 *(C)*

Richard Roxburgh (1962-)
Billy's Holiday '95
Children of the Revolution '95
Doing Time for Patsy Cline '97
Oscar and Lucinda '97
The Wedding Party '97
In the Winter Dark '98
The Last September '99
Passion '99
Mission: Impossible 2 '00
Blonde '01
Moulin Rouge '01
The Hound of the Baskervilles '02
The Road from Coorain '02
The League of Extraordinary Gentlemen '03
Van Helsing '04
Fragile '05
Stealth '05
Murderous Intent '06
The Silence '06
The Diplomat '08
Legend of the Guardians: The Owls of Ga'Hoole '10 *(V)*
Sanctum '11
Danger Close '19

Deep Roy
Alien from L.A. '87
Charlie and the Chocolate Factory '05
Tim Burton's Corpse Bride '05 *(V)*
Star Trek '09

Transformers: Revenge of the Fallen '09

Lise Roy (1924-)
The Boys of St. Vincent '93
The Courage to Love '00

Maxim Roy (1972-)
Stalker '98
Cause of Death '00
Dead Awake '01
Hidden Agenda '01
Federal Protection '02
Rudy: The Rudy Giulani Story '03
A Woman Hunted '03
Murder in the Hamptons '05
The Wives He Forgot '06
Infected '08
Picture This! '08
WarGames: The Dead Code '08
Would Be Kings '08
CAT. 8 '13
The Fall of the American Empire '19

Allan Royal (1944-)
The Pirates of Silicon Valley '99
DC 9/11: Time of Crisis '04
The Good Witch '08

Lionel Royce (1886-1946)
Charlie Chan in Panama '40
The Road to Zanzibar '41
South of Panama '41
My Favorite Blonde '42
White Pongo '45

Roselyn Royce
Sizzle Beach U.S.A. '74
Retrievers '82

Selena Royle (1904-83)
The Fighting Sullivans '42
Mrs. Parkington '44
Thirty Seconds Over Tokyo '44
Courage of Lassie '46
The Green Years '46
The Harvey Girls '46
Cass Timberlane '47
The Romance of Rosy Ridge '47
A Date with Judy '48
The Smallest Show on Earth '48
Summer Holiday '48
The Heiress '49
My Dream Is Yours '49
The Big Hangover '50
The Damned Don't Cry '50
Robot Monster '53

William Royle (1887-1940)
Mr. Wong in Chinatown '39
Mutiny in the Big House '39
The Rains Came '39

Andre Royo (1968-)
G '02
August '08
Super '10
Aftermath '12
The Spectacular Now '13
Lila & Eve '15

Spela Rozin (1945-)
Son of Hercules in the Land of Darkness '63
The Secret Invasion '64

Christian Rub (1887-1956)
100 Men and a Girl '37
Pinocchio '40 (V)

Jan Rubes (1920-2009)
Blood Relations '87
Dead of Winter '87
The Kiss '88
Blind Fear '89
Courage Mountain '89
Descending Angel '90
Class Action '91
Deceived '91
By Way of the Stars '92
D2: The Mighty Ducks '94
Mesmer '94
Serving in Silence: The Margarethe Cammermeyer Story '95
Flood: A River's Rampage '97

Music from Another Room '97
The White Raven '98
Believe '99
The Republic of Love '03

Benny Rubin (1899-1986)
It's a Great Life '29
Lord Byron of Broadway '30
Love in the Rough '30
Sunny Skies '30
Sunny '41
The Bashful Bachelor '42
Mr. Wise Guy '42
The Noose Hangs High '48
Torch Song '53
The Tender Trap '55

Jennifer Rubin (1962-)
A Nightmare on Elm Street 3: Dream Warriors '87
Bad Dreams '88
Blueberry Hill '88
Permanent Record '88
Victim of Beauty '91
A Woman, Her Men and Her Futon '92
The Crush '93
Stranger by Night '94
Saints and Sinners '95
Little Witches '96
Screamers '96
The Wasp Woman '96
Kisses in the Dark '97
Plump Fiction '97
Last Lives '98
Deal of a Lifetime '99
Amazons and Gladiators '01
Beyond Justice '01
Sanctimony '01
Transmorphers: Fall of Man '09

Daphne Rubin-Vega (1969-)
Wild Things '98
Flawless '99
Virgin '03
Jack Goes Boating '10

Saul Rubinek (1948-)
The Agency '81
Ticket to Heaven '81
Young Doctors in Love '82
Against All Odds '84
Wall Street '87
The Bonfire of the Vanities '90
Man Trouble '92
Unforgiven '92
And the Band Played On '93
The Quarrel '93
True Romance '93
Undercover Blues '93
Getting Even with Dad '94
I Love Trouble '94
The Android Affair '95
Hiroshima '95
Nixon '95
Open Season '95
Synapse '95
Blackjack '97
Pale Saints '97
Bad Manners '98
Dick '99
The Contender '00
Family Man '00
The Golden Spiders: A Nero Wolfe Mystery '00
Lakeboat '00
The Doorbell Rang: A Nero Wolfe Mystery '01
Rush Hour 2 '01
Triggermen '02
And Starring Pancho Villa as Himself '03
Baadasssss! '03
Hollywood North '03
The Singing Detective '03
Call Me: The Rise and Fall of Heidi Fleiss '04
Coast to Coast '04
White Coats '04
Jesse Stone: Night Passage '06
A Broken Life '07
Jesse Stone: Sea Change '07
War '07
Julia '08
The Trojan Horse '08

Oy Vey! My Son is Gay! '09
The Trotsky '09
Barney's Version '10
Jesse Stone: No Remorse '10
Jesse Stone: Innocents Lost '11
Jesse Stone: Benefit of the Doubt '12
The Song of Names '19

Giulia Rubini (1935-)
David and Goliath '61
Journey Beneath the Desert '61

Sergio Rubini (1959-)
Intervista '87
The Blonde '92
A Pure Formality '94
Nirvana '97
The Count of Monte Cristo '99
The Talented Mr. Ripley '99
The Passion of the Christ '04

John Rubinstein (1946-)
The Trouble with Girls (and How to Get into It) '69
Getting Straight '70
Zachariah '70
The Car '77
The French Atlantic Affair '79
She's Dressed to Kill '79
Killjoy '81
Someone to Watch Over Me '87
Another Stakeout '93
Norma Jean and Marilyn '95
Mercy '96
Perfect Murder, Perfect Town '00
Choose Connor '07
Atlas Shrugged 2: The Strike '12
Hello I Must Be Going '12

Ronen Rubinstein
It Felt Like Love '14
Condemned '15
Some Kind of Hate '15

Zelda Rubinstein (1936-2010)
Under the Rainbow '81
Poltergeist '82
Sixteen Candles '84
Poltergeist 2: The Other Side '86
Anguish '88
Poltergeist 3 '88
Teen Witch '89
Little Witches '96
The Wild Card '03

Richard Ruccolo (1972-)
Luck of the Draw '00
All Over the Guy '01
Deranged '01
A Nanny for Christmas '10

Alan Ruck
Hard Knox '83
Ferris Bueller's Day Off '86
Three Fugitives '89
Young Guns 2 '90
Speed '94
Star Trek: Generations '94
Twister '96
From the Earth to the Moon '98
Everything Put Together '00
Cheaper by the Dozen '03
Goodbye Baby '07
Kickin' It Old Skool '07
Ghost Town '08
InAlienable '08
I Love You, Beth Cooper '09
Extraordinary Measures '10
Carnage Park '16

Lamman Rucker
Tyler Perry's Why Did I Get Married? '07
Tyler Perry's Meet the Browns '08
Black Coffee '14
The Man in 3B '16

Paul Rudd (1969-)
Beulah Land '80
Last Song '80

Family Reunion '81
Runaway Daughters '94
Clueless '95
Halloween 6: The Curse of Michael Myers '95
Overnight Delivery '96
William Shakespeare's Romeo and Juliet '96
The Locusts '97
The Object of My Affection '98
200 Cigarettes '98
The Cider House Rules '99
The Chateau '01
The Great Gatsby '01
Wet Hot American Summer '01
The Shape of Things '03
Two Days '03
Anchorman: The Legend of Ron Burgundy '04
P.S. '04
The Baxter '05
The 40 Year Old Virgin '05
Diggers '06
I Could Never Be Your Woman '06
Night at the Museum '06
The Oh in Ohio '06
The Ex '07
Knocked Up '07
Reno 911! Miami '07
The Ten '07
Walk Hard: The Dewey Cox Story '07
Forgetting Sarah Marshall '08
Over Her Dead Body '08
Role Models '08
I Love You, Man '09
Monsters vs. Aliens '09 (V)
Year One '09
Dinner for Schmucks '10
How Do You Know '10
Our Idiot Brother '11
This Is 40 '12
Wanderlust '12
Admission '13
Anchorman 2: The Legend Continues '13
Prince Avalanche '13
They Came Together '14
Ant-Man '15
The Fundamentals of Caring '16
The Little Prince '16
Ant-Man and the Wasp '18
The Catcher Was a Spy '18

John Ruddock (1897-1981)
The Fallen Idol '49
Martin Luther '53
Lawrence of Arabia '62

Herbert Rudley (1911-2006)
Abe Lincoln in Illinois '40
Rhapsody in Blue '45
Decoy '46
A Walk in the Sun '46
The Scar '48
Artists and Models '55
The Black Sleep '56
The Young Lions '58
Beloved Infidel '59
The Jayhawkers '59

Lars Rudolph (1966-)
The Inheritors '98
The Princess and the Warrior '00

Maya Rudolph (1972-)
Chuck & Buck '00
Duplex '03
50 First Dates '04
Idiocracy '06
A Prairie Home Companion '06
Shrek the Third '07 (V)
Away We Go '09
Bollywood Hero '09 (C)
Grown Ups '10
Shrek Forever After '10 (V)
Bridesmaids '11
Zookeeper '11 (V)
Friends with Kids '12
Grown Ups 2 '13
Turbo '13 (V)
The Way Way Back '13
Big Hero 6 '14 (V)

Inherent Vice '14
The Nut Job '14 (V)
Sisters '15
Strange Magic '15 (V)
The Angry Birds Movie '16
Maggie's Plan '16
The Emoji Movie '17 (V)
My Entire High School Sinking Into the Sea '17
The Nut Job 2: Nutty by Nature '17
The Happytime Murders '18
Life of the Party '18
The Willoughbys '20

Joshua Rudoy (1975-)
Harry and the Hendersons '87
Flatliners '90

Sara Rue (1979-)
A Slipping Down Life '99
Gypsy 83 '01
The Ring '02
Danny Roane: First Time Director '06
Nightmare at the End of the Hall '08
Not Since You '09
Dorfman in Love '11
My Future Boyfriend '11

Belen Rueda (1965-)
The Sea Inside '04
The Orphanage '07

Mercedes Ruehl (1948-)
The Warriors '79
84 Charing Cross Road '86
Heartburn '86
Radio Days '87
Big '88
Married to the Mob '88
Slaves of New York '89
Crazy People '90
Another You '91
The Fisher King '91
Last Action Hero '93
Lost in Yonkers '93
Indictment: The McMartin Trial '95
For Roseanna '96
Subway Stories '97
Gia '98
The Minus Man '99
Out of the Cold '99
The Lost Child '00
More Dogs Than Bones '00
What's Cooking? '00
Widows '02
Mom at Sixteen '05
A Girl Like Me: The Gwen Araujo Story '06
Loving Leah '09
Banner 4th of July '13

Mark Ruffalo (1967-)
Mirror, Mirror 3: The Voyeur '96
Houdini '98
Safe Men '98
Committed '99
A Fish in the Bathtub '99
Ride with the Devil '99
You Can Count On Me '99
The Last Castle '01
Windtalkers '02
XX/XY '02
In the Cut '03
My Life Without Me '03
View from the Top '03
Collateral '04
Eternal Sunshine of the Spotless Mind '04
13 Going on 30 '04
We Don't Live Here Anymore '04
Just like Heaven '05
Rumor Has It. . . '05
All the King's Men '06
Apartment 12 '06
Chicago 10 '07 (V)
Reservation Road '07
Zodiac '07
Blindness '08
What Doesn't Kill You '08
The Brothers Bloom '09
Shutter Island '09
Where the Wild Things Are '09
Date Night '10

The Kids Are All Right '10
Sympathy for Delicious '10
Margaret '11
The Avengers '12
Begin Again '13
Now You See Me '13
Thanks for Sharing '13
Foxcatcher '14
Infinitely Polar Bear '14
The Normal Heart '14
Avengers: Age of Ultron '15
Spotlight '15
Now You See Me 2 '16
Avengers: Infinity War '18
Avengers: Endgame '19
Dark Waters '19

Leonora Ruffo (1935-2007)
Goliath and the Dragon '61
Hercules in the Haunted World '64

Rufus (1942-)
Metroland '97
Amelie '01

Adamo Ruggiero (1986-)
Make the Yuletide Gay '09
Dear Viola '14

Charlie Ruggles (1886-1970)
The Smiling Lieutenant '31
If I Had a Million '32
Love Me Tonight '32
One Hour with You '32
This Is the Night '32
Trouble in Paradise '32
Goodbye Love '34
No More Ladies '35
Ruggles of Red Gap '35
Bringing Up Baby '38
Balalaika '39
The Invisible Woman '40
No Time For Comedy '40
A Stolen Life '46
It Happened on 5th Avenue '47
My Brother Talks to Horses '47
Ramrod '47
Look for the Silver Lining '49
All in a Night's Work '61
The Parent Trap '61
Papa's Delicate Condition '63
Son of Flubber '63
The Ugly Dachshund '65
Follow Me, Boys! '66

Vyto Ruginis (1956-)
Descending Angel '90
Clean Slate '94
The Devil's Advocate '97
A Thousand Acres '97
The Fast and the Furious '01
The Glass House '01

Yayan Ruhian
The Raid: Redemption '11
Yakuza Apocalypse '15

Heinz Ruhmann (1902-94)
Ship of Fools '65
Faraway, So Close! '93

Barbara Ruick (1932-74)
Above and Beyond '53
The Affairs of Dobie Gillis '53
Carousel '56

Anthony Michael Ruivivar (1970-)
White Fang 2: The Myth of the White Wolf '94
Race the Sun '96
Starship Troopers '97
Speed of Life '99
Swimming '00
The Adjustment Bureau '11

Janice Rule (1931-2003)
Goodbye My Fancy '51
Starlift '51
Gun for a Coward '57
Bell, Book and Candle '58
Invitation to a Gunfighter '64
Alvarez Kelly '66
The Chase '66
The Ambushers '67
Welcome to Hard Times '67

The Swimmer '68
Doctors' Wives '70
Gumshoe '72
3 Women '77
Missing '82
American Flyers '85

Olesya Rulin (1986-)
Halloweentown High '04
Urban Legends: Bloody Mary '05
High School Musical 3: Senior Year '08
Flying By '09
A Very Mary Christmas '10
A Thousand Cuts '12
Family Weekend '13

Sig Rumann (1884-1967)
Marie Galante '34
The World Moves On '34
A Night at the Opera '35
The Wedding Night '35
The Bold Caballero '36
The Princess Comes Across '36
A Day at the Races '37
Nothing Sacred '37
On the Avenue '37
Thank you, Mr. Moto '37
Thin Ice '37
Think Fast, Mr. Moto '37
The Great Waltz '38
Paradise for Three '38
Never Say Die '39
Ninotchka '39
Only Angels Have Wings '39
Bitter Sweet '40
Comrade X '40
Dr. Ehrlich's Magic Bullet '40
Love Crazy '41
That Uncertain Feeling '41
The Wagons Roll at Night '41
Berlin Correspondent '42
China Girl '42
To Be or Not to Be '42
Tarzan Triumphs '43
They Came to Blow Up America '43
House of Frankenstein '44
It Happened Tomorrow '44
Summer Storm '44
The Dolly Sisters '46
A Night in Casablanca '46
Emperor Waltz '48
Border Incident '49
Father Is a Bachelor '50
The World in His Arms '52
Houdini '53
Ma and Pa Kettle on Vacation '53
Stalag 17 '53
Living It Up '54
Wings of Eagles '57
The Errand Boy '61
36 Hours '64

Bob Rumnock
Deranged '01
Conspiracy '08

Jenny Runacre (1946-)
Husbands '70
The Canterbury Tales '71
The Creeping Flesh '72
The Final Programme '73
The Passenger '75
Hussy '80

Damon Runyan
On the Other Hand, Death '08
Whispers and Lies '08

Tygh Runyan (1976-)
Antitrust '00
Cruel and Unusual '01
Emile '03
Twist '03
Holiday Wishes '06
Normal '07
A Night for Dying Tigers '10
The Hunt for the I-5 Killer '11
Treasure Buddies '12
When Calls the Heart '13
Making the Rules '14

Jennifer Runyon (1960-)
Up the Creek '84
The Falcon and the Snowman '85
18 Again! '88
The In Crowd '88
A Man Called Sarge '90
Carnosaur '93

Ying Ruocheng (1929-2003)
The Last Emperor '87
Little Buddha '93

RuPaul (1960-)
See RuPaul Charles

Debra Jo Rupp (1951-)
Disney's Teacher's Pet '04 (V)
Kickin' It Old Skool '07
Spooky Buddies '11 (V)
Congratulations '13

Troy Ruptash
Leaving Metropolis '02
A Marine Story '10

Al Ruscio (1924-2013)
Al Capone '59
The Naked Flame '68
The Cage '89
Romero '89
Boss of Bosses '99

Elizabeth Ruscio (1955-)
The Positively True Adventures of the Alleged Texas Cheerleader-Murdering Mom '93
Glory Daze '96
Letters from a Killer '98
The Clearing '04

Barbara Rush (1927-)
When Worlds Collide '51
It Came from Outer Space '53
The Black Shield of Falworth '54
Magnificent Obsession '54
Taza, Son of Cochise '54
Captain Lightfoot '55
No Down Payment '57
Oh, Men! Oh, Women! '57
The Young Lions '58
The Young Philadelphians '59
Strangers When We Meet '60
Come Blow Your Horn '63
Robin and the 7 Hoods '64
Hombre '67
Moon of the Wolf '72
Superdad '73
The Eyes of Charles Sand '74
The Night the Bridge Fell Down '83

Deborah Rush (1954-)
Honky Tonk Freeway '81
The Purple Rose of Cairo '85
Family Business '89
Parents '89
In and Out '97
Three to Tango '99
The Good Girl '02
American Wedding '03
Half Nelson '06
Strangers with Candy '06
Women Who Kill '17

Geoffrey Rush (1951-)
Storm Boy
Children of the Revolution '95
Shine '95
Twisted '96
Les Miserables '97
A Little Bit of Soul '97
Oscar and Lucinda '97 (N)
Elizabeth '98
Shakespeare in Love '98
House on Haunted Hill '99
Mystery Men '99
Quills '00
The Tailor of Panama '00
Lantana '01
The Banger Sisters '02
Frida '02
Finding Nemo '03 (V)
Intolerable Cruelty '03
Ned Kelly '03
Pirates of the Caribbean: The Curse of the Black Pearl '03
Swimming Upstream '03
Munich '05
Candy '06
Elizabeth: The Golden Age '07
Pirates of the Caribbean: At World's End '07
$9.99 '08 (V)
Brand New Day '10
The King's Speech '10
Legend of the Guardians: The Owls of Ga'Hoole '10 (V)
Green Lantern '11 (V)
Pirates of the Caribbean: On Stranger Tides '11
The Best Offer '13
The Book Thief '13
The Daughter '15
Minions '15 (V)
Final Portrait '17
Pirates of the Caribbean: Dead Men Tell No Tales '17

Odeya Rush
The Giver '14
Goosebumps '15
Almost Friends '17
Lady Bird '17
Dear Dictator '18
Spinning Man '18
Let It Snow '19

Claire Rushbrook (1970-)
Secrets and Lies '95
Spice World: The Movie '97
Plunkett & Macleane '98
Shiner '00
Close Your Eyes '02
Collision '09
Great Expectations '11

Jared Rushton (1974-)
Big '88
The Lady in White '88
Honey, I Shrunk the Kids '89
A Cry in the Wild '90
Pet Sematary 2 '92

William Rushton (1937-96)
Flight of the Doves '71
Consuming Passions '88

Joseph Ruskin (1924-2013)
The Gypsy Warriors '78
Captain America '79
Prizzi's Honor '85
Saturday the 14th Strikes Back '88
Cyber-Tracker '93
Firepower '93
King Cobra '98
Smokin' Aces '07

Morgan Rusler
The Tomorrow Man '01
Solaris '02
Trapped: Buried Alive '02

Robert Rusler (1965-)
A Nightmare on Elm Street 2: Freddy's Revenge '85
Thrashin' '86
Vamp '86
Shag: The Movie '89
Sometimes They Come Back '91

Tim Russ (1956-)
Final Combination '93
Journey to the Center of the Earth '93
The Oh in Ohio '06
Unbeatable Harold '06
Live Free or Die Hard '07
Mother '13
Asteroid vs. Earth '14

William Russ (1950-)
Cruising '80
The Right Stuff '83
Beer '85
Blood and Orchids '86
The Long, Hot Summer '86
Wanted Dead or Alive '86
Dead of Winter '87
The Unholy '88
Disorganized Crime '89
Crazy from the Heart '91
Pastime '91
Traces of Red '92
Aspen Extreme '93
American History X '98
California Solo '12

Alex Russell (1987-)
Wasted on the Young '10
Chronicle '12
Carrie '13
Jungle '17
Goldstone '18

Andy Russell (1919-92)
The Stork Club '45
Copacabana '47

Betsy Russell (1963-)
Private School '83
Avenging Angel '85
Tomboy '85
Cheerleader Camp '88
The Prize Pulitzer '89
Trapper County War '89
Delta Heat '92
The Break '95
Saw 3 '06
Saw 4 '07
Saw 5 '08
Saw 6 '09
Chain Letter '10
Mandrake '10
Saw 3D: The Final Chapter '10

Bing (Neil) Russell (1926-2003)
Good Day for a Hanging '58
The Horse Soldiers '59
Stakeout '62
Billy the Kid Versus Dracula '66
Satan's School for Girls '73
Elvis: The Movie '79

Bryan Russell (1952-)
Emil and the Detectives '64
The Adventures of Bullwhip Griffin '66

Clive Russell (1945-)
Cracker: Brotherly Love '95
Margaret's Museum '95
Neil Gaiman's NeverWhere '96
Oscar and Lucinda '97
Bodywork '99
Great Expectations '99
The 13th Warrior '99
The Railway Children '00
The Emperor's New Clothes '01
Mists of Avalon '01
The Mayor of Casterbridge '03
The Wicker Tree '10
Outpost: Black Sun '12

Elizabeth Russell (1916-2002)
Cat People '42
Curse of the Cat People '44
Bedlam '45

Gail Russell (1925-61)
The Uninvited '44
Salty O'Rourke '45
Angel and the Badman '47
Calcutta '47
The Smallest Show on Earth '48
El Paso '49
Great Dan Patch '49
Wake of the Red Witch '49
The Lawless '50
7 Men From Now '56

Grayson Russell (1998-)
Talladega Nights: The Ballad of Ricky Bobby '06
Diary of a Wimpy Kid 2: Rodrick Rules '11
Marley & Me: The Puppy Years '11 (V)
The Rainbow Tribe '11
Space Warriors '13

Harold Russell (1914-2002)
The Best Years of Our Lives '46
Dogtown '97

Jane Russell (1921-2011)
The Outlaw '43
The Paleface '48
Double Dynamite '51
His Kind of Woman '51
Macao '52
Son of Paleface '52
Gentlemen Prefer Blondes '53
The Road to Bali '53
The Tall Men '55
Hot Blood '56
Fate Is the Hunter '64 (C)
Johnny Reno '66
Born Losers '67

John Russell (1921-91)
The Blue Bird '40
Don Juan Quilligan '45
Forever Amber '47
Saddle Tramp '47
Yellow Sky '48
Slattery's Hurricane '49
Undertow '49
Man in the Saddle '51
Oklahoma Annie '51
Hoodlum Empire '52
The Sun Shines Bright '53
The Dalton Girls '57
Hell Bound '57
Untamed Youth '57
Fort Massacre '58
Rio Bravo '59
Hostile Guns '67
Buckskin '68
Cannon for Cordoba '70
Blood Legacy '73
Noon Sunday '75
Runaways '75
The Outlaw Josey Wales '76
The Changeling '80
Pale Rider '85

Karen Russell
Vice Academy '88
Easy Wheels '89
Shock 'Em Dead '90
Dead Certain '92

Ken Russell (1927-2011)
The Russia House '90
Tales of Erotica '93
Brothers of the Head '06 (C)
Mr. Nice '10

Keri Russell (1976-)
Honey, I Blew Up the Kid '92
The Curve '97
Eight Days a Week '97
We Were Soldiers '02
The Upside of Anger '05
Grimm Love '06
Mission: Impossible 3 '06
August Rush '07
Waitress '07
Bedtime Stories '08
Leaves of Grass '09
Extraordinary Measures '10
Goats '12
Austenland '13
Dark Skies '13
Dawn of the Planet of the Apes '14
Free State of Jones '16

Kimberly Russell (1964-)
Hangin' with the Homeboys '91
Sugar Hill '94
Prison of Secrets '97

Kirsten Russell
Virgil Bliss '01
Milk and Honey '03

Kurt Russell (1951-)
It Happened at the World's Fair '63
Guns of Diablo '64
Follow Me, Boys! '66
The Horse in the Gray Flannel Suit '68
The One and Only, Genuine, Original Family Band '68
The Computer Wore Tennis Shoes '69
The Barefoot Executive '71
Now You See Him, Now You Don't '72
Charley and the Angel '73
Superdad '73
Search for the Gods '75
Sniper '75
The Strongest Man in the World '75
The Longest Drive '76
Elvis: The Movie '79
Used Cars '80
Escape from New York '81
The Fox and the Hound '81 (V)
The Thing '82
Silkwood '83
Swing Shift '84
Mean Season '85
The Best of Times '86
Big Trouble in Little China '86
Overboard '87
Tequila Sunrise '88
Tango and Cash '89
Winter People '89
Backdraft '91
Captain Ron '92
Unlawful Entry '92
Tombstone '93
Stargate '94
Breakdown '96
Escape from L.A. '96
Executive Decision '96
Soldier '98
3000 Miles to Graceland '01
Vanilla Sky '01
Interstate 60 '02 (C)
Dark Blue '03
Miracle '04
Dreamer: Inspired by a True Story '05
Jiminy Glick in LaLa Wood '05 (C)
Sky High '05
Poseidon '06
Death Proof '07
Touchback '11
The Art of the Steal '13
Bone Tomahawk '15
The Hateful Eight '15
Deepwater Horizon '16
Guardians of the Galaxy Vol. 2 '17
Crypto '19

Lucy Russell (1972-)
Following '99
The Lady and the Duke '01
Tristan & Isolde '06
Angel '07

Nipsey Russell (1918-2005)
The Wiz '78
Posse '93 (C)
Car 54, Where Are You? '94

Robert Russell (?-2008)
Bedazzled '68
The Conqueror Worm '68
Dune '00

Rosalind Russell (1908-76)
Evelyn Prentice '34
The Casino Murder Case '35
China Seas '35
Forsaking All Others '35
Reckless '35
Rendezvous '35
Live, Love and Learn '37
Night Must Fall '37
The Citadel '38
Four's a Crowd '38
Fast and Loose '39
The Women '39
His Girl Friday '40
No Time For Comedy '40
Design for Scandal '41
They Met in Bombay '41
My Sister Eileen '42
Roughly Speaking '45
She Wouldn't Say Yes '45
The Guilt of Janet Ames '47
Tell It to the Judge '49
Never Wave at a WAC '52
Picnic '55
A Majority of One '56
Auntie Mame '58
Five Finger Exercise '62
Gypsy '62
The Trouble with Angels '66
Where Angels Go, Trouble Follows '68

Bad Day at Black Rock '54
Escape to Burma '55
House of Bamboo '55
The Tall Men '55
Men in War '57
God's Little Acre '58
The Day of the Outlaw '59
Odds Against Tomorrow '59
Ice Palace '60
The King of Kings '61
Billy Budd '62
The Longest Day '62
Battle of the Bulge '65
The Crooked Road '65
The Professionals '66
The Busy Body '67
The Dirty Dozen '67
Hour of the Gun '67
A Minute to Pray, a Second to Die '67
Anzio '68
Captain Nemo and the Underwater City '69
The Wild Bunch '69
Lawman '71
The Love Machine '71
Executive Action '73
The Iceman Cometh '73
Lolly-Madonna XXX '73
The Outfit '73

Sheila Ryan (1921-75)
Great Guns '41
Something for the Boys '44
Getting Gertie's Garter '45
Railroaded '47
Jungle Manhunt '51

Thomas Ryan
Body Count '87
The Relic '96

Thomas Jay Ryan (1962-)
Henry Fool '98
The Legend of Bagger Vance '00
Eternal Sunshine of the Spotless Mind '04
Fay Grim '06
Dream Boy '08

Tim Ryan (1899-1956)
Detour '46
Shanghai Chest '48
From Here to Eternity '53

Will Ryan (1939-)
An American Tail '86 (V)
The Land Before Time '88 (V)
Thumbelina '94 (V)

Derek Rydall (1968-)
Night Visitor '89
Phantom of the Mall: Eric's Revenge '89
Popcorn '89

Georg Rydeberg (1907-83)
A Woman's Face '38
Hour of the Wolf '68

Bobby Rydell (1942-)
Bye, Bye, Birdie '63
Marco Polo, Jr. '72 (V)
Mr. Rock 'n' Roll: The Alan Freed Story '99 (C)

Christopher Rydell (1963-)
Gotcha! '85
Blood and Sand '89
How I Got into College '89
Side Out '90
For the Boys '91
In the Deep Woods '91
Dario Argento's Trauma '93
Flesh and Bone '93

Mark Rydell (1929-)
Crime in the Streets '56
The Long Goodbye '73
Punchline '88
Havana '90
James Dean '01
Hollywood Ending '02

Alfred Ryder (1919-95)
T-Men '47
True Grit '69
Probe '72

Winona Ryder (1971-)
Lucas '86
Square Dance '87
Beetlejuice '88
Great Balls of Fire '89
Heathers '89
1969 '89
Edward Scissorhands '90
Mermaids '90
Welcome Home, Roxy Carmichael '90
Night on Earth '91
Bram Stoker's Dracula '92
The Age of Innocence '93
The House of the Spirits '93
Little Women '94
Reality Bites '94
Boys '95
How to Make an American Quilt '95
The Crucible '96
Looking for Richard '96
Alien: Resurrection '97
Celebrity '98
Girl, Interrupted '99
Autumn in New York '00
Lost Souls '00
Mr. Deeds '02
Simone '02 (C)
The Darwin Awards '06
A Scanner Darkly '06
Sex and Death 101 '07
The Ten '07
The Last Word '08
The Informers '09
The Private Lives of Pippa Lee '09
Star Trek '09
Stay Cool '09
Black Swan '10
When Love Is Not Enough: The Lois Wilson Story '10
The Dilemma '11
Frankenweenie '12 (V)
The Iceman '12
The Letter '12
Homefront '13
Experimenter '15
Author: The JT LeRoy Story '16
Destination Wedding '18

Joseph Rye
Born to Lose '99
Alien vs. Predator '04

Patrick Ryecart (1952-)
Camille '84
Lace 2 '85
Silas Marner '85
The Bretts '88
Coming Home '98
Parting Shots '98

Georgina Rylance (1979-)
Hellraiser: Deader '05
Seven Seconds '05
Pulse 2: Afterlife '08

Juliet Rylance (1979-)
Sinister '12
Days and Nights '14

Mark Rylance (1960-)
Wallenberg: A Hero's Story '85
Prospero's Books '91
Angels and Insects '95
Institue Benjamenta or This Dream People Call Human Life '95
Intimacy '00
The Other Boleyn Girl '08
Blitz '11
Days and Nights '14
Bridge of Spies '15
The Gunman '15
The BFG '16

Ryo (1973-)
Alive '02
Azumi '03
Black House '07

Chishu Ryu (1904-93)
Late Spring '49
Early Summer '51
Tokyo Story '53
Twenty-Four Eyes '54
Equinox Flower '58
Good Morning '59
The Human Condition: A Soldier's Prayer '61
An Autumn Afternoon '62
Akira Kurosawa's Dreams '90

Daisuke Ryu (1957-)
Ran '85
Nezulla the Rat Monster '02

RZA (1966-)
Coffee and Cigarettes '03
Scary Movie 3 '03 (C)
Derailed '05
American Gangster '07
Life is Hot in Cracktown '08
Funny People '09
Due Date '10
The Next Three Days '10
The Man with the Iron Fists '12
Brick Mansions '14

Bruno S (1932-2010)
Every Man for Himself & God Against All '75
Stroszek '77

Daryl Sabara (1992-)
Spy Kids '01
Spy Kids 2: The Island of Lost Dreams '02
Spy Kids 3-D: Game Over '03
The Polar Express '04 (V)
Keeping Up with the Steins '06
Havoc 2: Normal Adolescent Behavior '07
Her Best Move '07
A Christmas Carol '09 (V)
World's Greatest Dad '09
Machete '10
Spy Kids 4: All the Time in the World '11
The Green Inferno '14

Joe Sabatino
Asylum of the Damned '03
Going to America '15

Antonio Sabato, Jr. (1972-)
Jailbreakers '94
Wolverine '96
The Big Hit '98
High Voltage '98
Fatal Error '99
The Base 2: Guilty as Charged '00
Chaos Factor '00
Mindstorm '01
Hypersonic '02
Bugs '03
Testosterone '03
Destination: Infestation '07
Drifter '09
Princess of Mars '09

Antonio (Tony) Sabato (1943-)
Hate for Hate '67
Beyond the Law '68
Twice a Judas '69
Black Lemons '70
Crime Boss '72
New Mafia Boss '72
Seven Blood-Stained Orchids '72
Reactor '78
Crimebusters '79
High Voltage '98

Ernie Sabella (1949-)
The Lion King '94 (V)
The Lion King: Simba's Pride '98 (V)
The Lion King 1 1/2 '04 (V)
Listen to Your Heart '10

Kyle Sabihy (1983-)
Analyze This '98
Analyze That '02

Patrick Sabongui (1975-)
High Noon '09
Merlin and the Book of Beasts '09
Drone '17

Marcel Sabourin (1935-)
The Hitman '91
Lilies '96

Sabu (1924-63)
Elephant Boy '37
Drums '38
The Thief of Bagdad '40
Arabian Nights '42
The Jungle Book '42
Cobra Woman '44
Black Narcissus '47
Savage Drums '51
Jungle Hell '55
Rampage '63
A Tiger Walks '64

Robin Sachs (1951-2013)
Cold War Killers '86
Deadly Recruits '86
Galaxy Quest '99
Megalodon '03
Northfork '03

Salli Sachse (1943-)
Devil's Angels '67
The Trip '67

Katee Sackhoff (1980-)
Halloween: Resurrection '02
How I Married My High School Crush '07
The Last Sentinel '07
White Noise 2: The Light '07
The Haunting in Connecticut 2: Ghosts of Georgia '13
Riddick '13
Sexy Evil Genius '13
Oculus '14
Don't Knock Twice '17

Michael Sacks (1948-)
Slaughterhouse Five '72
The Sugarland Express '74

Gordon Sackville (1872-1926)
Slow as Lightning '23
Lightning Hutch '26

Jose Sacristan (1937-)
A Place in the World '92
Magical Girl '14

Keiji Sada (1926-64)
The Human Condition: No Greater Love '58
The Human Condition: Road to Eternity '59
An Autumn Afternoon '62

Benjamin Sadler (1971-)
Dresden '06
Caravaggio '07
Impact '09

Nicholas Sadler
Idle Hands '99
True Grit '10

William Sadler (1950-)
Project X '87
Hard to Kill '89
Die Hard 2: Die Harder '90
The Hot Spot '90
Bill & Ted's Bogus Journey '91
Rush '91
Trespass '92
Freaked '93
Roadracers '94
The Shawshank Redemption '94
Tales from the Crypt Presents Demon Knight '94
Poltergeist: The Legacy '96
Solo '96
RocketMan '97
Disturbing Behavior '98
The Green Mile '99
The Battle of Shaker Heights '03
Kinsey '04
Confess '05
Devour '05
Purple Heart '05
Jimmy & Judy '06
August Rush '07
The Mist '07
A New Wave '07
The Good Student '08
Jesse Stone: Thin Ice '09
Shadowheart '09
Jesse Stone: No Remorse '10
Last Day of Summer '10
The Pacific '10
Jesse Stone: Innocents Lost '11
Greetings from Tim Buckley '12
Jesse Stone: Benefit of the Doubt '12
Iron Man 3 '13
Machete Kills '13
Riddle '13
Freedom '14
The Suspect '14

Thomas Sadoski (1976-)
Wild '14
I Smile Back '15
The Last Word '17

Tom Sadoski (1976-)
Loser '00
Happy Hour '03
The New Twenty '08

Jonathan Sadowski (1979-)
She's the Man '06
Spring Breakdown '08
Chernobyl Diaries '12

Isabelle Sadoyan (1928-)
Trois Couleurs: Bleu '93
Summer Hours '08

Chris Sadrinna (1975-)
Garage Days '03
Bad Bush '09

Marianne Saegebrecht (1945-)
Bagdad Cafe '88
Moon over Parador '88
Rosalie Goes Shopping '89
The War of the Roses '89
Dust Devil '93
Left Luggage '98

Hinako Saeki
Rasen '98
Uzumaki '00

Libuse Safrankova (1953-)
Kolya '96
All My Loved Ones '00

Elizabeth Sagal (1961-)
Flashdance '83
Howard the Duck '86

Joe Sagal (1957-)
The Return of the Swamp Thing '89
Lost Treasure '03
Retrograde '03

Katey Sagal (1954-)
The Good Mother '88
Smart House '00 (V)
I'm Reed Fish '06
Housebroken '09
Jack and the Beanstalk '09
Always Woodstock '15
Bleed for This '16

Bill Sage (1962-)
The Maldonado Miracle '03
Heavens Fall '06
Blue Blood '07
The New Twenty '08
Tennessee '08
Handsome Harry '09
Boy Wonder '10
The Green '11
Bad Parents '12
We Are What We Are '13
Born to Race: Fast Track '14
Fender Bender '16
The Dinner Party '20

Halston Sage (1993-)
Paper Towns '15
Scout's Guide to the Zombie Apocalypse '15
Before I Fall '17

Willard Sage (1922-74)
The Tender Trap '55
The Brass Legend '56
Dirty Little Billy '72

William Sage (1962-)
Simple Men '92
Boys '95
High Art '98
American Psycho '99
Double Parked '00
Urbania '00
Desert Saints '01
Sin '02
Mysterious Skin '04

Melissa Sagemiller (1974-)
Get Over It! '01
Soul Survivors '01
Sorority Boys '02
The Clearing '04
Sleeper Cell '05
Standing Still '05
The Guardian '06
Mr. Woodcock '07

Ray Sager
Blast-Off Girls '67
Gruesome Twosome '67
Just for the Hell of It '68
The Wizard of Gore '70
This Stuff'll Kill Ya! '71
The Gore-Gore Girls '72

Bob Saget (1956-)
Father and Scout '94
To Grandmother's House We Go '94 (C)
New York Minute '04 (C)

Tami Sagher
Don't Think Twice '16
Women Who Kill '17

Ludivine Sagnier (1979-)
Water Drops on Burning Rocks '99
My Wife is an Actress '01
8 Women '02
La Petite Lili '03
Peter Pan '03
Swimming Pool '03
Paris, je t'aime '06
A Girl Cut in Two '07
Love Songs '07
Moliere '07
A Secret '07
Mesrine: Part 2-Public Enemy Number 1 '08
Love Crime '10
Beloved '11
The Devil's Double '11
A Monster in Paris '11
Love is in the Air '13

Ken Sagoes (1967-)
Death by Dialogue '88
A Nightmare on Elm Street 4: Dream Master '88

Luis Saguar (1956-2009)
Against the Wall '04
Silver City '04
Everything Strange and New '09

Elena Sahagun
Teenage Exorcist '93
Firetrap '01

Kenji Sahara (1932-)
Rodan '56
The Mysterians '58
H-Man '59
Mothra '62
King Kong vs. Godzilla '63
Matango '63
Godzilla vs. Mothra '64
Ghidrah the Three Headed Monster '65
Son of Godzilla '66
Destroy All Monsters '68
Godzilla's Revenge '69
War of the Gargantuas '70
Yog, Monster from Space '71

Fridtjov Saheim
Cold Prey II '08
The Wave '15

Mort Sahl (1927-)
In Love and War '58
Johnny Cool '63
Don't Make Waves '67

Morton Lyon Sahl (1927-)
See Mort Sahl

Amir Ali Said (1996-)
Game 6 '05
Inside Man '06

Eva Marie Saint (1924-)
On the Waterfront '54
Raintree County '57
A Hatful of Rain '59
North by Northwest '59
Exodus '60
All Fall Down '62
36 Hours '64
The Sandpiper '65
Grand Prix '66
The Russians Are Coming, the Russians Are Coming '66

The Stalking Moon '69
Loving '70
Cancel My Reservation '72
Jane Doe '83
The Last Days of Patton '86
Nothing in Common '86
Danielle Steel's Palomino '91
Titanic '96
I Dreamed of Africa '00
Because of Winn-Dixie '05
Don't Come Knocking '05
Superman Returns '06
Winter's Tale '14

Michael St. Clair (1921-2001)
Von Ryan's Express '65
Our Man Flint '66

Julie St. Claire (1970-)
Extreme Limits '01
Stealing Candy '04
Dark World '08

Patrick St. Esprit
Lost Treasure '03
Blue Lagoon: The Awakening '12

Michael St. Gerard (1961-)
Hairspray '88
Great Balls of Fire '89
Replikator: Cloned to Kill '94

Soledad St. Hilaire (1950-)
crazy/beautiful '01
Real Women Have Curves '02
The Maldonado Miracle '03

Raymond St. Jacques (1930-90)
Mister Buddwing '66
The Comedians '67
The Green Berets '68
Uptight '68
Cotton Comes to Harlem '70
Cool Breeze '72
Final Comedown '72
Search for the Gods '75
The Private Files of J. Edgar Hoover '77
Kill Castro '80
The Mercenaries '80
The Evil That Men Do '84
They Live '88
Glory '89
Voodoo Dawn '89
Timebomb '91

Susan St. James (1946-)
Where Angels Go, Trouble Follows '68
Outlaw Blues '77
Love at First Bite '79
S.O.S. Titanic '79
How to Beat the High Cost of Living '80
Carbon Copy '81

Al 'Fuzzy' St. John (1892-1963)
His Private Secretary '33
A Face in the Fog '36
Call of the Yukon '38
Dead Men Walk '43
Thundering Gunslingers '44
Ghost of Hidden Valley '46
My Dog Shep '46
Son of Billy the Kid '49

Betta St. John (1929-)
All the Brothers Were Valiant '53
Dream Wife '53
The Student Prince '54
Tarzan's Hidden Jungle '55
Alias John Preston '56
Tarzan and the Lost Safari '57
Corridors of Blood '58
The Snorkel '58
Horror Hotel '60
Tarzan the Magnificent '60

Howard St. John (1905-74)
Shockproof '49
Born Yesterday '50
Counterspy Meets Scotland Yard '50
David Harding, Counterspy '50
711 Ocean Drive '50
The Sun Sets at Dawn '50
The Big Night '51
Close to My Heart '51
Goodbye My Fancy '51
I Died a Thousand Times '55
Illegal '55
The Tender Trap '55
Li'l Abner '59
Lover Come Back '61
Strait-Jacket '64
Strange Bedfellows '65

Jill St. John (1940-)
Holiday for Lovers '59
The Remarkable Mr. Pennypacker '59
The Lost World '60
Roman Spring of Mrs. Stone '61
Tender Is the Night '62
Come Blow Your Horn '63
Who's Minding the Store? '63
The Liquidator '65
Eight on the Lam '67
Tony Rome '67
Diamonds Are Forever '71
Sitting Target '72
Around the World in 80 Days '89
The Player '92
The Trip '02
Northpole '14

Julia St. John
G.B.H. '91
The Blackheath Poisonings '92

Michelle St. John
Geronimo '93
Spirit Rider '93
Pocahontas '95 (V)
Smoke Signals '98
The Business of Fancydancing '02

Trevor St. John (1971-)
Dogtown '97
The King's Guard '01
In the Family '11
Finding Normal '13

Michael St. Michaels (1944-)
The Video Dead '87
The Greasy Strangler '16

Guylaine St. Onge
Mary Higgins Clark: Lucky Day '02
Do or Die '03

Matthew St. Patrick (1968-)
Steel Sharks '97
War '07
Alien Raiders '08

Irma St. Paule (1927-2007)
Fever '99
Where the Money Is '00

John St. Polis (1873-1946)
The Four Horsemen of the Apocalypse '21
Paint and Powder '25
The Phantom of the Opera '25
Why Be Good? '29
Party Girl '30
Alias the Doctor '32
Symphony of Six Million '32
Notorious But Nice '33
Death from a Distance '36

Lucile Saint-Simon (1937-)
The Hands of Orlac '60
Les Bonnes Femmes '60

James Saito (1955-)
The Adventures of Buckaroo Banzai Across the Eighth Dimension '84
Blood and Orchids '86
Henry Fool '98
Robot Stories '03
The Sea of Trees '16
Always Be My Maybe '19

Tatsuo Saito (1902-68)
I Was Born But. . . '32
Three Stripes in the Sun '55
My Geisha '62

Tak Sakaguchi (1975-)
Versus '00
Azumi '03
Azumi 2 '05
Death Trance '05
Shinobi '05

Sachio Sakai (1925-98)
Samurai 2: Duel at Ichijoji Temple '55
Godzilla, King of the Monsters '56
Godzilla's Revenge '69

Hideo Sakaki
Versus '00
Alive '02
Azumi '03

S.Z. Sakall (1884-1955)
My Love Came Back '40
Spring Parade '40
Ball of Fire '41
The Devil & Miss Jones '41
That Night in Rio '41
Casablanca '42
Seven Sweethearts '42
Yankee Doodle Dandy '42
Wintertime '43
Hollywood Canteen '44
Christmas in Connecticut '45
San Antonio '45
Wonder Man '45
The Dolly Sisters '46
Never Say Goodbye '46
Cynthia '47
Romance on the High Seas '48
Whiplash '48
In the Good Old Summertime '49
Look for the Silver Lining '49
My Dream Is Yours '49
The Daughter of Rosie O'Grady '50
Montana '50
Tea for Two '50
It's a Big Country '51
Lullaby of Broadway '51
Painting the Clouds With Sunshine '51
Small Town Girl '53
The Student Prince '54

Ryuichi Sakamoto (1952-)
Merry Christmas, Mr. Lawrence '83
The Last Emperor '87
New Rose Hotel '98

Sumiko Sakamoto (1936-)
The Pornographers '66
The Ballad of Narayama '83

Amy Sakasitz (1985-)
Dennis the Menace '93
A Home of Our Own '93
Mad Love '95
House Arrest '96

Harold Sakata (1920-82)
Goldfinger '64
The Wrestler '73
Impulse '74
Jaws of Death '76
Black Eliminator '78
Goin' Coconuts '78
Kill Factor '78

Nancy Sakovich (1961-)
The Jesse Ventura Story '99
Category 6: Day of Destruction '04
Coast to Coast '04

Gene Saks (1921-2015)
A Thousand Clowns '65
Prisoner of Second Avenue '74
The One and Only '78
A Fine Romance '92
I.Q. '94
Nobody's Fool '94
Deconstructing Harry '97

Yoshiko Sakuma (1939-)
Samurai Banners '69
The Makioka Sisters '83

Rosa Salazar
Night Owls '15
Alita: Battle Angel '19

Theresa Saldana (1954-2016)
I Wanna Hold Your Hand '78
Defiance '79
Raging Bull '80
The Evil That Men Do '84
The Night Before '88
Angel Town '89
Thrill Seekers '99

Zoe Saldana (1978-)
Center Stage '00
Get Over It! '01
Snipes '01
Crossroads '02
Drumline '02
Pirates of the Caribbean: The Curse of the Black Pearl '03
Haven '04
The Terminal '04
Guess Who '05
The Heart Specialist '06
Vantage Point '08
Avatar '09
The Skeptic '09
Star Trek '09
Death at a Funeral '10
The Losers '10
Takers '10
Colombiana '11
The Words '12
Blood Ties '13
Out of the Furnace '13
Star Trek: Into Darkness '13
The Book of Life '14 (V)
Guardians of the Galaxy '14
Infinitely Polar Bear '14
Rosemary's Baby '14
Live by Night '16
Nina '16
Star Trek: Beyond '16
Guardians of the Galaxy Vol. 2 '17

Charles 'Chic' Sale (1885-1936)
Treasure Island '34
You Only Live Once '37

Dahlia Salem (1971-)
Return to Cabin by the Lake '01
Her Sister's Keeper '06
Love Finds a Home '09

Kario Salem (1955-)
Centennial '78
Triumph of the Spirit '89
1492: Conquest of Paradise '92
Killing Zoe '94

Pamela Salem (1950-)
Never Say Never Again '83
Quicksand '01

Meredith Salenger (1970-)
The Journey of Natty Gann '85
April Morning '88
The Kiss '88
A Night in the Life of Jimmy Reardon '88
Dream a Little Dream '89
Edge of Honor '91
Dead Beat '94
Village of the Damned '95
Glory Daze '96 (C)
No Code of Conduct '98
Bug Buster '99
Lake Placid '99
The Third Wheel '02
Out of the Woods '05

Enrico Maria Salerno (1926-94)
The Queens '66
The Bird with the Crystal Plumage '70
Night Train Murders '75
The Cheaters '76

Soupy Sales (1926-2009)
Two Little Bears '61
Critic's Choice '63
Birds Do It '66
. . .And God Spoke '94

John Salew (1897-1961)
Kind Hearts and Coronets '49
Black Glove '54

Diane Salinger (1951-)
Creature '85
Pee-wee's Big Adventure '85
The Morning After '86
The Butcher's Wife '91
Venice, Venice '92
The Magic Bubble '93
One Night Stand '95
The Scarlet Letter '95
Last Summer In the Hamptons '96
The Kid with the X-Ray Eyes '99
Rest Stop '06
20 Years After '08
Dark House '09
Freedom '14

Emmanuel Salinger (1964-)
La Sentinelle '92
One Hundred and One Nights '95
My Sex Life. . . Or How I Got into an Argument '96
Kill by Inches '99
Triple Agent '04

Justin Salinger
Rise of the Gargoyles '09
Ray & Liz '19

Matt Salinger (1960-)
Blood and Orchids '86
Power '86
Captain America '89
Babyfever '94
Fortunes of War '94
Bigger Than the Sky '05
Black Dawn '05

Jason Salkey (1962-)
Sharpe's Rifles '93
The Turn of the Screw '99

Celine Sallette (1980-)
A Burning Hot Summer '11
Capital '12
Rust and Bone '12
The Connection '15

John Salley (1964-)
Bad Boys '95
Eddie '96
Coast to Coast '04
Mr. 3000 '04 (C)
The Comebacks '07 (C)

Peter Sallis (1921-2017)
The Curse of the Werewolf '61
Taste the Blood of Dracula '70
Wallace & Gromit in The Curse of the Were-Rabbit '05 (V)

Tomi Salmela (1957-)
The Winter War '89
Night on Earth '91

Gustavo Salmeron (1970-)
Twice upon a Yesterday '98
Body Armour '07

Albert Salmi (1928-90)
The Bravados '58
The Unforgiven '60
Wild River '60
The Outrage '64
The Ambushers '67
Hour of the Gun '67
The Meanest Men in the West '67
Menace on the Mountain '70
Lawman '71
The Take '74
Empire of the Ants '77
Viva Knievel '77
Undercover With the KKK '78
Kill Castro '80
The Mercenaries '80
Dragonslayer '81
Love Child '82
St. Helen's, Killer Volcano '82
Superstition '82
Hard to Hold '84
Born American '86
Breaking In '89

Colin Salmon (1962-)
Captives '94
Tomorrow Never Dies '97
Immortality '98
The World Is Not Enough '99
Anti-Terrorist Cell: Manhunt '01
Die Another Day '02
Dinotopia '02
Resident Evil '02
The Statement '03
Alien *vs.* Predator '04
Freeze Frame '04
Punisher: War Zone '08
Exam '09
Resident Evil: Retribution '12

Sonya Salomaa (1974-)
Firefight '03
House of the Dead '03
Blood Angels '05
The Stranger Game '06
Ties That Bind '06
Christmas Caper '07
Malibu Shark Attack '09
Secrets of Eden '12

Lea Salonga (1971-)
My Neighbor Totoro '88 (V)
Aladdin '92 (V)
Mulan '98 (V)

Frank S. Salsedo
Creepshow 2 '87
Magic in the Water '95

Jennifer Salt (1944-)
Hi, Mom! '70
Play It Again, Sam '72
Sisters '73
Terror Among Us '81

Gino Saltamerenda
The Bicycle Thief '48
Young Caruso '51

Montserrat Salvador
If They Tell You I Fell '89
Caresses '97

Chris Salvatore (1985-)
Eating Out 3: All You Can Eat '09
Eating Out 4: Drama Camp '11

Renato Salvatori (1933-88)
Big Deal on Madonna Street '58
And the Wild, Wild Women '59
Era Notte a Roma '60
Rocco and His Brothers '60
The Organizer '64
Burn! '70
La Cicada '83

Andy Samberg (1978-)
Hot Rod '07
Space Chimps '08 (V)
Cloudy with a Chance of Meatballs '09 (V)
Friends With Benefits '11
What's Your Number? '11
Celeste & Jesse Forever '12
Hotel Transylvania '12 (V)
That's My Boy '12
Cloudy with a Chance of Meatballs 2 '13 (V)
Hotel Transylvania 2 '15 (V)
Popstar: Never Stop Never Stopping '16
Storks '16
Hotel Transylvania 3: Summer Vacation '18 (V)

Aldo Sambrell (1931-2010)
Son of a Gunfighter '65
The Texican '66
Navajo Joe '67
Kill Django '71
The Last Run '71
Emmanuelle in the Country '78

Udo Samel (1953-)
Kaspar Hauser '93
The Piano Teacher '01
Go for Zucker '05

Madeleine Sami
Perfect Strangers '03
Come to Daddy '20

Richard Sammel (1960-)
The Nest '02
Sniper Reloaded '11
3 Days to Kill '14

Emma Samms (1960-)
Arabian Adventure '79
The Lady and the Highwayman '89
The Shrimp on the Barbie '90
Delirious '91
Star Quest '94
Treacherous Beauties '94
Humanoids from the Deep '96
Supernova '05

Mercedes Sampietro (1947-)
Second Skin '99
Broken Silence '01

Candy Samples (1940-)
Flesh Gordon '72 (C)
Beneath the Valley of the Ultra-Vixens '79

Angus Sampson (1979-)
Insidious '10
100 Bloody Acres '12
Insidious: Chapter 3 '15
Insidious: The Last Key '18

Cindy Sampson (1978-)
Mama Africa '02
Proof of Lies '06
The Christmas Choir '08
Swamp Devil '08
High Plains Invaders '09
The Shrine '10

Paul Sampson
If You Only Knew '00
Deuces Wild '02
Whacked! '02

Robert Sampson (1933-)
Gates of Hell '80
Re-Animator '84
Netherworld '90
Robot Jox '90

Will Sampson (1935-87)
One Flew Over the Cuckoo's Nest '75
Buffalo Bill & the Indians '76
The Outlaw Josey Wales '76
Orca '77
The White Buffalo '77
Vegas '78
Fish Hawk '79
Insignificance '85
Poltergeist 2: The Other Side '86

Jeffrey D. Sams (1966-)
Fly by Night '93
Waiting to Exhale '95
Just Write '97
Rose Hill '97
Soul Food '97

Russell Sams (1977-)
The Rules of Attraction '02
The Flock '07

Ekaterina Samsonov
The Ticket '17
You Were Never Really Here '17

Xavier Samuel (1983-)
Newcastle '08
Anonymous '11
A Few Best Men '11
Adore '13
Plush '13
Healing '15
Mr. Church '16

Laura San Giacomo (1962-)
sex, lies and videotape '89
Pretty Woman '90
Quigley Down Under '90
Vital Signs '90
Once Around '91
Under Suspicion '92
Where the Day Takes You '92 (V)
Nina Takes a Lover '94
Stephen King's The Stand '94
Stuart Saves His Family '94
The Apocalypse '96
Eat Your Heart Out '96
Suicide Kings '97
Havoc '05
Talhotblond '12
Honey Boy '19

Alberto San Juan
Km. 0 '00
Sleep Tight '11

Olga San Juan (1927-2009)
Blue Skies '46
One Touch of Venus '48
The Beautiful Blonde from Bashful Bend '49

Conrado San Martin (1921-)
The Colossus of Rhodes '61
The Awful Dr. Orloff '62
Long Days of Revenge '67

Hiroyuki (Henry) Sanada (1960-)
Samurai Reincarnation '81
Royal Warriors '86
Rasen '98
Ringu '98
Ringu 2 '99
Onmyoji '01
The Twilight Samurai '02
The Last Samurai '03
The Promise '05
The White Countess '05
Rush Hour 3 '07
Sunshine '07
Speed Racer '08
The City of Your Final Destination '09
47 Ronin '13
The Railway Man '13
The Wolverine '13
Mr. Holmes '15
Life '17

Jaime Sanchez (1938-)
The Pawnbroker '65
Beach Red '67
The Wild Bunch '69
Pinero '01

Kiele Sanchez (1977-)
Migrating Forms '00
Insanitarium '08
A Perfect Getaway '09
Redemption Road '10
30 Days of Night: Dark Days '10
The Purge: Anarchy '14

Lucia Sanchez (1969-)
Sitcom '97
Carnage '02

Marisol Padilla Sanchez (1973-)
Dementia '98
Fever '99
Traffic '00

Otto Sanchez
Bad Boys 2 '03
Kill the Poor '03
Push '06

Paul Sanchez
Platoon '86
Navy SEALS '90

Pedro Sanchez (1924-95)
Go With God Gringo '66
Any Gun Can Play '67
Cjamango '67
Beatrice Cenci '69
Sabata '69
Adios, Sabata '71
Return of Sabata '71
White Fang and the Hunter '85
Night and the City '92

Roberto Sanchez
Mating Dance '08
Beneath Us '20

Roselyn Sanchez (1973-)
Rush Hour 2 '01
Nightstalker '02
Basic '03
Boat Trip '03
Chasing Papi '03
Edison Force '05
Underclassman '05
Yellow '06
The Game Plan '07
Rush Hour 3 '07
The Perfect Sleep '08
Venus and Vegas '10
Act of Valor '12
Traffik '18

Susi Sanchez
A Love to Keep '07
The Milk of Sorrow '09

Victoria Sanchez (1976-)
Codename: Jaguar '98
P.T. Barnum '99
Eternal '04
The Watch '08

Aitana Sanchez-Gijon (1968-)
Rowing with the Wind '88
The Perfect Husband '92
Mouth to Mouth '95
A Walk in the Clouds '95
The Chambermaid on the Titanic '97
Love Walked In '97
Jealousy '99
Yerma '99
I'm Not Scared '03
The Machinist '04
The Backwoods '06

Fernando (Fernand) Sancho (1916-90)
Hate for Hate '67
Orloff and the Invisible Man '70
Dr. Orloff and the Invisible Man '72
Return of the Evil Dead '75

Jose Sancho (1944-)
Live Flesh '97
Arachnid '01

Paul Sand (1935-)
Once Upon a Brothers Grimm '77
Great Bank Hoax '78
You Can't Take It With You '79
Can't Stop the Music '80
Second Coming of Suzanne '80
Wholly Moses! '80
Teen Wolf Too '87
Chuck & Buck '00
Sweet Land '05

Dominique Sanda (1951-)
First Love '70
The Conformist '71
The Garden of the Finzi-Continis '71
Mackintosh Man '73
Steppenwolf '74
The Inheritance '76
1900 '76
Damnation Alley '77
Cabo Blanco '81
I, the Worst of All '90
Joseph '95
The Crimson Rivers '01

Walter Sande (1906-71)
Don Winslow of the Navy '43
Nocturne '46
The Red House '47
The Woman on the Beach '47
Blonde Ice '48
Bomba and the Jungle Girl '52
Canyon River '56
Gun Brothers '56
The Gallant Hours '60
Noose for a Gunman '60
The Quick Gun '64
I'll Take Sweden '65

Casey Sander (1956-)
Mystery Woman: Mystery Weekend '05
16 Blocks '06

Eivind Sander
Hidden '09
Headhunters '11

Otto Sander (1941-2013)
The Marquise of O '76
Wings of Desire '88
Faraway, So Close! '93

John Sanderford
The Alchemist '81
Leprechaun '93

Ashton Sanders
Moonlight '16
The Equalizer 2 '18
Captive State '19
Native Son '19

Cedric Sanders
The Least Among You '09
Domain '18

Chris (Christopher) Sanders (1962-)
Lilo & Stitch '02 (V)
Lilo & Stitch 2: Stitch Has a Glitch '05 (V)
Leroy and Stitch '06 (V)
The Croods '13 (V)

Dirk Sanders (1934-2002)
Black Tights '60
Pierrot le Fou '65

George Sanders (1906-72)
Lloyds of London '36
Love Is News '37
Slave Ship '37
Four Men and a Prayer '38
International Settlement '38
Allegheny Uprising '39
Confessions of a Nazi Spy '39
Mr. Moto's Last Warning '39
Nurse Edith Cavell '39
The Saint in London '39
The Saint Strikes Back '39
Bitter Sweet '40
Foreign Correspondent '40
The House of the Seven Gables '40
Rebecca '40
The Saint Takes Over '40
The Saint's Double Trouble '40
The Son of Monte Cristo '40
The Gay Falcon '41
Man Hunt '41
Rage in Heaven '41
The Saint in Palm Springs '41
Sundown '41
The Black Swan '42
A Date With the Falcon '42
The Falcon Takes Over '42
Her Cardboard Lover '42
Son of Fury '42
Tales of Manhattan '42
The Moon and Sixpence '43
Paris After Dark '43
They Came to Blow Up America '43
This Land Is Mine '43
Action in Arabia '44
Summer Storm '44
Hangover Square '45
Picture of Dorian Gray '45
The Strange Affair of Uncle Harry '45
A Scandal in Paris '46
The Strange Woman '46
Forever Amber '47
The Ghost and Mrs. Muir '47
Lured '47
The Private Affairs of Bel Ami '47
The Fan '49
Samson and Delilah '49
All About Eve '50
I Can Get It For You Wholesale '51
Assignment: Paris '52
Ivanhoe '52
Voyage in Italy '53
King Richard and the Crusaders '54
Witness to Murder '54
Jupiter's Darling '55
The King's Thief '55
Moonfleet '55
The Scarlet Coat '55
Death of a Scoundrel '56
While the City Sleeps '56
Rock-A-Bye Baby '57
Solomon and Sheba '59
The Last Voyage '60
Trouble in the Sky '60
Village of the Damned '60
In Search of the Castaways '62
A Shot in the Dark '64
The Amorous Adventures of Moll Flanders '65
The Quiller Memorandum '66
Good Times '67
The Jungle Book '67 (V)
Warning Shot '67
The Best House in London '69
The Kremlin Letter '70
Night of the Assassin '70
Endless Night '71
Doomwatch '72
Psychomania '73

Henry Sanders (1942-)
Killer of Sheep '77
Rocky Balboa '06
Blues '08

Hugh Sanders (1911-66)
The Damned Don't Cry '50
The Magnificent Yankee '50
Storm Warning '51
That's My Boy '51
Tomorrow Is Another Day '51
The Fighter '52
Pride of St. Louis '52
City of Bad Men '53

Jay O. Sanders (1953-)
Assault of the Killer Bimbos '88
Glory '89
Mr. Destiny '90
JFK '91
Meeting Venus '91
V.I. Warshawski '91
My Boyfriend's Back '93
Angels in the Outfield '94
Kiss of Death '94
The Big Green '95
Three Wishes '95
Daylight '96
For Richer or Poorer '97
Kiss the Girls '97
The Matchmaker '97
The Confession '98
The Odd Couple 2 '98
Tumbleweeds '98
Wrestling with Alligators '98
Boss of Bosses '99
Earthly Possessions '99
The Jack Bull '99
Music of the Heart '99
Dead Dog '00
Along Came a Spider '01
The Last Brickmaker in America '01
My Husband's Double Life '01
The Salem Witch Trials '02
Widows '02
The Day After Tomorrow '04
Shooting Livien '05
Half Nelson '06
Wedding Daze '06
Revolutionary Road '08
I Hate Valentine's Day '09
The Undying '09
Green Lantern '11
A Novel Romance '11

Will Sanderson (1980-)
Blackwoods '02
Heart of America '03
House of the Dead '03
Deep Evil '04
Alone in the Dark '05
BloodRayne '06
In the Name of the King: A Dungeon Siege Tale '08
Seed '08

William Sanderson (1948-)
Fight for Your Life '77
The Onion Field '79
Savage Weekend '80
Raggedy Man '81
Blade Runner '82
City Heat '84
Fletch '85
Mirror, Mirror '90
Sometimes They Come Back '91
Return to Lonesome Dove '93
Mirror, Mirror 2: Raven Dance '94
Wagons East '94
Andersonville '95
Forest Warrior '95
Hologram Man '95
Phoenix '95
Last Man Standing '96
Lone Justice 3: Showdown at Plum Creek '96
George Wallace '97
Nice Guys Sleep Alone '99
Crossfire Trail '01
Gods and Generals '03
Monte Walsh '03
Beyond the Wall of Sleep '06
Disappearances '06
Pretty Ugly People '08

Elizabeth Sandifer (1962-)
Animal Instincts 2 '94
Indecent Behavior 2 '94

Adam Sandler (1966-)
Going Overboard '89
Shakes the Clown '92
Coneheads '93
Airheads '94
Billy Madison '94
Mixed Nuts '94
Bulletproof '96
Happy Gilmore '96
Dirty Work '97
The Wedding Singer '97
The Waterboy '98
Big Daddy '99
Little Nicky '00
Adam Sandler's 8 Crazy Nights '02 (V)
The Hot Chick '02 (C)
Mr. Deeds '02
Punch-Drunk Love '02
Anger Management '03
50 First Dates '04
Spanglish '04
Deuce Bigalow: European Gigolo '05
The Longest Yard '05
Click '06
I Now Pronounce You Chuck and Larry '07
Reign Over Me '07
Bedtime Stories '08
You Don't Mess with the Zohan '08
Funny People '09
Grown Ups '10
Jack and Jill '11
Just Go With It '11
Zookeeper '11 (V)
Hotel Transylvania '12 (V)
That's My Boy '12
Grown Ups 2 '13
Blended '14
The Cobbler '14
Men, Women & Children '14
Hotel Transylvania 2 '15 (V)
Pixels '15
The Meyerowitz Stories (New and Selected) '17
Hotel Transylvania 3: Summer Vacation '18 (V)
Uncut Gems '19

Miguel (Michael) Sandoval (1951-)
Howard the Duck '86
Walker '87
El Diablo '90
Jungle Fever '91
White Sands '92
Clear and Present Danger '94
Girls in Prison '94
Fair Game '95
Mrs. Winterbourne '96
Scorpion Spring '96
Up Close and Personal '96
The Fixer '97
Route 9 '98
The Crew '00
Thin Air '00
Things You Can Tell Just by Looking at Her '00
Blow '01
Ballistic: Ecks vs. Sever '02
Collateral Damage '02
Human Nature '02
Nine Lives '05

Michael Sarne (1940-)
Seaside Swingers '65
A Coeur Joie '67
Head Over Heels '67

Michael Sarrazin (1940-2011)
Flim-Flam Man '67
The Sweet Ride '68
They Shoot Horses, Don't They? '69
The Pursuit of Happiness '70
Sometimes a Great Notion '71
The Groundstar Conspiracy '72
Harry in Your Pocket '73
For Pete's Sake '74
Gumball Rally '76
Loves & Times of Scaramouche '76
Beulah Land '80
Fighting Back '82
The Seduction '82
The Train Killer '83
Keeping Track '86
Captive Hearts '87
Malarek '89
Lena's Holiday '90
The Arrival 2 '98
The Peacekeeper '98
Feardotcom '02
The Christmas Choir '08

Peter Sarsgaard (1971-)
The Man in the Iron Mask '98
Boys Don't Cry '99
Kitchen Privileges '00
The Center of the World '01
Empire '02
K-19: The Widowmaker '02
The Salton Sea '02
Shattered Glass '03
Unconditional Love '03
Garden State '04
Kinsey '04
The Dying Gaul '05
Flightplan '05
Jarhead '05
The Skeleton Key '05
Rendition '07
Year of the Dog '07
Elegy '08
In the Electric Mist '08
The Mysteries of Pittsburgh '08
An Education '09
Orphan '09
Knight and Day '10
Green Lantern '11
Robot & Frank '12 (V)
Blue Jasmine '13
Lovelace '13
Night Moves '13
Very Good Girls '13
Experimenter '15
Pawn Sacrifice '15
Jackie '16
The Sound of Silence '19

Gailard Sartain (1946-)
The Hollywood Knights '80
Roadie '80
Hard Country '81
Trouble in Mind '86
Ernest Goes to Camp '87
Mississippi Burning '88
Blaze '89
Ernest Goes to Jail '90
The Grifters '90
The Chase '91
Fried Green Tomatoes '91
Guilty by Suspicion '91
Stop! or My Mom Will Shoot '92
The Real McCoy '93
Walker: Texas Ranger: One Riot, One Ranger '93
Getting Even with Dad '94
Speechless '94
Wagons East '94
Open Season '95
The Spitfire Grill '95
All New Adventures of Laurel and Hardy: For Love or Mummy '98
The Patriot '99
The Pirates of Silicon Valley '99
The Replacements '00
Ali '01
Elizabethtown '05

Fabio Sartor (1954-)
The Luzhin Defence '00
The Fallen '05

Katsuhiko Sasakai (1944-)
Godzilla vs. Megalon '76
Terror of Mechagodzilla '78

Katrin Sass (1956-)
Good Bye, Lenin! '03
The Silence '10

Jacqueline Sassard (1940-)
Pirates of the Seven Seas '62
Accident '67
Les Biches '68

Will Sasso (1975-)
Brown's Requiem '98
Drop Dead Gorgeous '99
College Road Trip '08
Lower Learning '08
Life As We Know It '10
National Lampoon's The Legend of Awesomest Maximus '11
The Three Stooges '12
The Right Kind Of Wrong '13
Hit By Lightning '14
Klaus '19
Irresistible '20

Catya (Cat) Sassoon (1968-2002)
Tuff Turf '85
Dance with Death '91
Bloodfist 4: Die Trying '92

Ines Sastre (1973-)
Beyond the Clouds '95
The Best Man '97
The Count of Monte Cristo '99
Druids '01
The Lost City '05

Tura Satana (1938-2011)
Faster, Pussycat! Kill! Kill! '65
The Astro-Zombies '67
The Doll Squad '73
Mark of the Astro-Zombies '02

Hitomi Sato (1979-)
Rasen '98
Ringu '98
Ringu 2 '99

Kei Sato (1928-2010)
Harakiri '62
Onibaba '64
Zatoichi: The Blind Swordsman's Vengeance '66
Kuroneko '68

Koichi Sato (1960-)
Goyokin '69
Rasen '98
Inugami '01
When the Last Sword is Drawn '02
Sukiyaki Western Django '08

Kenpachiro Satsuma (1947-)
Godzilla vs. Mothra '92
Godzilla vs. SpaceGodzilla '94
Godzilla vs. Destroyah '95

Paul Satterfield (1960-)
Creepshow 2 '87
Mystery Woman: Mystery Weekend '05

Daniel Serafini Sauli
Brooklyn Lobster '05
You Belong to Me '07

Cliff Saunders
Deathlands: Homeward Bound '03
Outlander '08

Jennifer Saunders (1958-)
A Midwinter's Tale '95
Muppet Treasure Island '96
Spice World: The Movie '97
Shrek 2 '04 (V)
Coraline '09 (V)
Minions '15 (V)
Absolutely Fabulous: The Movie '16

Lori Saunders (1941-)
Track of the Vampire '66
Wackiest Wagon Train in the West '77

Mary Jane Saunders (1943-)
Sorrowful Jones '49
Father Is a Bachelor '50

Russel Savadier
Alien from L.A. '87
Lullaby '08

Andrea Savage
Step Brothers '08
Summer '03 '18

Ann Savage (1921-2008)
The More the Merrier '43
Passport to Suez '43
Treasure of Fear '45
Detour '46
Renegade Girl '46
Pygmy Island '50

Ben Savage (1980-)
Little Monsters '89
Big Girls Don't Cry. . . They Get Even '92
Wild Palms '93
Car Babes '06
Palo Alto '07
Lake Effects '12
Girl Meets Boy '13

Fred Savage (1976-)
The Boy Who Could Fly '86
The Princess Bride '87
Vice Versa '88
Little Monsters '89
The Wizard '89
Austin Powers In Goldmember '02
The Rules of Attraction '02
Welcome to Mooseport '04

John Savage (1949-)
Bad Company '72
The Killing Kind '73
Steelyard Blues '73
All the Kind Strangers '74
The Sister-in-Law '74
The Deer Hunter '78
Hair '79
The Onion Field '79
Inside Moves '80
The Amateur '82
Maria's Lovers '84
Soldier's Revenge '84
Silent Witness '85
Salvador '86
Caribe '87
Do the Right Thing '89
Any Man's Death '90
The Godfather, Part 3 '90
Daybreak '93
Shattered Image '93
Carnosaur 2 '94
C.I.A. 2: Target Alexa '94
The Crossing Guard '94
Killing Obsession '94
One Good Turn '95
American Strays '96
Amnesia '96
Hollywood Safari '96
Where Truth Lies '96
White Squall '96
Hostile Intent '97
Little Boy Blue '97
Club Vampire '98
Lost Souls '98
Message in a Bottle '98
The Thin Red Line '98
Christina's House '99
The Jack Bull '99
Summer of Sam '99
The Virginian '99
Burning Down the House '01
Alien Lockdown '04
Confessions of a Pit Fighter '05
Iowa '05
The New World '05
The Attic '06
The Drop '06
Kill Your Darlings '06
The Golden Boys '08
Handsome Harry '09
Bed & Breakfast '10
Bereavement '10
Open Road '13
A Sierra Nevada Gunfight '13
Bermuda Tentacles '14
The Lookalike '14

Martin Savage
Topsy Turvy '99
Another Year '10

Dany Saval (1940-)
Moon Pilot '62
Boeing Boeing '65

George Savalas (1926-85)
The Family '70
Kelly's Heroes '70
Alice in Wonderland '85

Telly Savalas (1924-94)
Cape Fear '61
Mad Dog Coll '61
The Young Savages '61
Birdman of Alcatraz '62
The Interns '62
Johnny Cool '63
Love Is a Ball '63
Battle of the Bulge '65
Genghis Khan '65
The Greatest Story Ever Told '65
The Slender Thread '65
The Dirty Dozen '67
The Scalphunters '68
The Assassination Bureau '69
Land Raiders '69
MacKenna's Gold '69
On Her Majesty's Secret Service '69
The Family '70
Kelly's Heroes '70
Mongo's Back In Town '71
Pretty Maids All In a Row '71
Crime Boss '72
Horror Express '72
New Mafia Boss '72
Pancho Villa '72
A Town Called Hell '72
A Reason to Live, a Reason to Die '73
Sonny and Jed '73
Inside Out '75
Lisa and the Devil '75
Capricorn One '78
Beyond the Poseidon Adventure '79
Escape to Athena '79
The French Atlantic Affair '79
The Muppet Movie '79 (C)
Fake Out '82
Cannonball Run 2 '84
Cartier Affair '84
Alice in Wonderland '85
The Dirty Dozen: The Deadly Mission '87
The Dirty Dozen: The Fatal Mission '88
Faceless '88

Souleymane Sy Savane
Behind the Wall '08
Goodbye Solo '08
Machine Gun Preacher '11

Doug Savant (1964-)
Trick or Treat '86
Masquerade '88
Red Surf '90
Shaking the Tree '92
Maniac Cop 3: Badge of Silence '93
Robin Cook's Terminal '96
Godzilla '98
What Color Is Love? '08

John Savident
Impromptu '90
Mountains of the Moon '90
Brain Donors '92
Middlemarch '93
Othello '95

Tom Savini (1946-)
Martin '77
Dawn of the Dead '78
Maniac '80
Knightriders '81
Creepshow '82
Creepshow 2 '87
Heartstopper '92
Innocent Blood '92
The Demolitionist '95
From Dusk Till Dawn '95
Children of the Living Dead '00
Demon Lust '01
Dawn of the Dead '04
The Absence of Light '06
Beyond the Wall of Sleep '06
Planet Terror '07
Machete '10

Lunetta Savino
Saturn in Opposition '07
Loose Cannons '10

Camille Saviola (1950-)
Stuart Saves His Family '94
Sunset Park '96

Devon Sawa (1978-)
Little Giants '94
Night of the Twisters '95
Robin of Locksley '95
The Boys Club '96
Wild America '97
Around the Fire '98
A Cool, Dry Place '98
The Guilty '99
Idle Hands '99
SLC Punk! '99
Final Destination '00
Extreme Ops '02
Slackers '02
Extreme Dating '04
Devil's Den '06
Creature of Darkness '09
Endure '10
The Philly Kid '12
Life on the Line '16
The Fanatic '19

Kenji Sawada (1948-)
Samurai Reincarnation '81
Mishima: A Life in Four Chapters '85
The Happiness of the Katakuris '01
Sabu '04

Keiko Sawai (1945-)
Frankenstein Conquers the World '64
Godzilla vs. Monster Zero '68

Julia Sawalha (1968-)
Martin Chuzzlewit '94
A Midwinter's Tale '95
Pride and Prejudice '95
Mr. Toad's Wild Ride '96
Chicken Run '00 (V)
Cranford '08
Absolutely Fabulous: The Movie '16

Nadim Sawalha (1935-)
The Wind and the Lion '75
The Awakening '80
Cleopatra '99
The Nativity Story '06
Incendies '10

Ikio Sawamura (1905-75)
Yojimbo '61
Godzilla's Revenge '69
War of the Gargantuas '70

Cassandra Sawtell
Imaginary Playmate '06
Nightmare '07

Joe Sawyer (1906-82)
Frisco Kid '35
Navy Blues '37
Frontier Marshal '39
You Can't Get Away With Murder '39
Tarzan's Desert Mystery '43

Joseph (Joe) Sawyer (1906-82)
College Humor '33
The Informer '35
Murder With Pictures '36
Petrified Forest '36
The Black Legion '37
San Quentin '37
Confessions of a Nazi Spy '39
The Roaring Twenties '39
Melody Ranch '40
They Died with Their Boots On '41
Wrecking Crew '42
The Outlaw '43
Tornado '43
Raiders of Ghost City '44
The Naughty Nineties '45
Operation Haylift '50
Comin' Round the Mountain '51
The Kettles in the Ozarks '56
The Killing '56

John Saxon (1935-)
Rock, Pretty Baby '56
The Unguarded Moment '56
The Reluctant Debutante '58
The Restless Years '58
The Plunderers '60
Portrait in Black '60
The Unforgiven '60
Mr. Hobbs Takes a Vacation '62
War Hunt '62
The Cardinal '63
The Girl Who Knew Too Much '63
The Ravagers '65
The Appaloosa '66
Night Caller from Outer Space '66
Planet of Blood '66
Queen of Blood '66
Death of a Gunfighter '69
Joe Kidd '72
Enter the Dragon '73
Planet Earth '74
Black Christmas '75
Mitchell '75
Strange New World '75
Once an Eagle '76
Raid on Entebbe '77
Swiss Conspiracy '77
Deadly Thief '78
Fast Company '78
The Glove '78
The Electric Horseman '79
Battle Beyond the Stars '80
Beyond Evil '80
Cannibal Apocalypse '80
Scorpion with Two Tails '82
Unsane '82
Wrong Is Right '82
Big Score '83
A Nightmare on Elm Street '84
Prisoners of the Lost Universe '84
Half Slave, Half Free '85
Hands of Steel '86
A Nightmare on Elm Street 3: Dream Warriors '87
Aftershock '88
Criminal Act '88
Death House '88
Welcome to Spring Break '88
My Mom's a Werewolf '89
Crossing the Line '90
Animal Instincts '92
Hellmaster '92
Maximum Force '92
No Escape, No Return '93
Beverly Hills Cop 3 '94
Killing Obsession '94
Wes Craven's New Nightmare '94
From Dusk Till Dawn '95
Final Payback '99
Outta Time '01

Vin Saxon (1940-77)
See Ron Haydock

Charlie Saxton
Bandslam '09
Twelve '10

Diane Sayer (1938-2001)
Kitten with a Whip '64
The Strangler '64

Philip Sayer (1947-89)
Xtro '83
Slayground '84
A.D. '85

Alexei Sayle (1952-)
Selling Hitler '91
Carry On Columbus '92
Reckless Kelly '93
Tipping the Velvet '02
The Thief Lord '06

John Sayles (1950-)
Piranha '78
Return of the Secaucus 7 '80
The Howling '81 (C)
Lianna '83 (C)
The Brother from Another Planet '84 (C)
Hard Choices '84
Something Wild '86
Unnatural Causes '86
Matewan '87
Eight Men Out '88
City of Hope '91
Matinee '92
Straight Talk '92
My Life's in Turnaround '94 (C)
Gridlock'd '96
Girlfight '99

Morgan Saylor (1994-)
Jamie Marks is Dead '13
Being Charlie '16
White Girl '16
Blow The Man Down '19

Syd Saylor (1895-1962)
The Light of Western Stars '30
The Lost Jungle '34
Prison Shadows '36
Abbott and Costello Meet the Invisible Man '51

Kyu Sazanka (1914-71)
Fires on the Plain '59
Yojimbo '61

Leonardo Sbaraglia (1970-)
Burnt Money '00
Intacto '01
Carmen '03
Wild Tales '14
Pain and Glory '19

Raphael Sbarge (1964-)
Risky Business '83
My Science Project '85
Vision Quest '85
Billionaire Boys Club '87
Back to Hannibal: The Return of Tom Sawyer and Huckleberry Finn '90
Final Verdict '91
Murder 101 '91
Carnosaur '93
The Hidden 2 '94
Independence Day '96
Message in a Bottle '98
Quicksilver Highway '98
Home Room '02

Mattia Sbragia (1952-)
Year of the Gun '91
Heaven '01
The Passion of the Christ '04

Greta Scacchi (1960-)
Heat and Dust '82
Camille '84
The Coca-Cola Kid '84
Defense of the Realm '85
Ebony Tower '86
A Man in Love '87
White Mischief '88
Presumed Innocent '90
Fires Within '91
Shattered '91
The Player '92
Desire '93
The Browning Version '94
Jefferson in Paris '94
Cosi '95 (C)
Country Life '95
Emma '96
The Odyssey '97
The Serpent's Kiss '97
The Red Violin '98
Cotton Mary '99
Love and Rage '99
Daniel Deronda '02
Festival at Cannes '02
Beyond the Sea '04
Flightplan '05
Broken Trail '06
Miss Austen Regrets '07
Brideshead Revisited '08
The Trojan Horse '08

Gia Scala (1934-72)
The Price of Fear '56
The Big Boodle '57
Don't Go Near the Water '57
The Garment Jungle '57
Tip On a Dead Jockey '57
Ride a Crooked Trail '58
The Tunnel of Love '58
Battle of the Coral Sea '59
The Guns of Navarone '61

Prunella Scales (1932-)
Room at the Top '59
The Lonely Passion of Judith Hearne '87
Consuming Passions '88
A Chorus of Disapproval '89
A Question of Attribution '91
Howard's End '92
An Awfully Big Adventure '94
The Rector's Wife '94
Second Best '94
Wolf '94
Stiff Upper Lips '96
Emma '97
The Ghost of Greville Lodge '00
Station Jim '01
The Shell Seekers '06

Jack Scalia (1950-)
Fear City '85
Club Med '86
Runaway Father '91
Shattered Image '93
T-Force '94
Storybook '95
Act of War '96
Dark Breed '96
The Silencers '96
Under Oath '97
Chained Heat 3: Hell Mountain '98
First Degree '98
Silent Predators '99
Hollywood Wives: The New Generation '03
Red Eye '05
End Game '06
Honeymoon with Mom '06
Kraken: Tentacles of the Deep '06
Nuclear Hurricane '07
The Dog Who Saved the Holidays '12
Jersey Shore Shark Attack '12

Riccardo Scamarcio (1979-)
Loose Cannons '10
John Wick: Chapter 2 '17
Welcome Home '18
Loro '19

Tiare Scanda (1974-)
I Love You Baby '01
Tod@s Caen '19

Carlo Scandiuzzi
Red Snow '91
Killing Zoe '94
Darkdrive '98

Joanna Scanlan
Girl with a Pearl Earring '03
The Invisible Woman '13

Eliza Scanlen
Little Women '19
Babyteeth '20

Kevin Scannell
Shoot to Kill '88
Don't Tell Her It's Me '90
Backfield in Motion '91

Michelle Scarabelli (1955-)
Age Old Friends '89
Deadbolt '92
Alien Nation: Dark Horizon '94
Alien Nation: Body and Soul '95
The Colony '95
Alien Nation: Millennium '96
Alien Nation: The Enemy Within '96

Tecla Scarano
Marriage Italian Style '64
Yesterday, Today and Tomorrow '64

Sam Scarber (1949-)
Shocker '89
Dark Heart '06

Adrian Scarborough (1968-)
Vera Drake '04
The History Boys '06
Upstairs Downstairs '11

Margaret Scarborough
Sunstorm '01
Loco Love '03

Don Scardino (1948-)
Squirm '76
Cruising '80
He Knows You're Alone '80

Hal Scardino (1984-)
Searching for Bobby Fischer '93
The Indian in the Cupboard '95
Marvin's Room '96

Alan Scarfe (1946-)
Cathy's Curse '77
The Deserters '83
Keeping Track '86
Iron Eagle 2 '88
Back in Business '96
Once a Thief '96
The Wrong Guy '96
Sanctuary '98

Jonathan Scarfe (1975-)
Eye '96
The Morrison Murders '96
White Lies '98
Blood Money '99
Liberty Stands Still '02
Above and Beyond '06
Proof of Lies '06
Carolina Moon '07
Hearts of War '07
Vipers '08
One Angry Juror '10

Renato Scarpa (1939-)
St. Michael Had a Rooster '72
The Postman '94
For Roseanna '96

Diana Scarwid (1955-)
The Possessed '77
Pretty Baby '78
Inside Moves '80
Mommie Dearest '81
Desperate Lives '82
Rumble Fish '83
Silkwood '83
Strange Invaders '83
Brenda Starr '86
Extremities '86
Psycho 3 '86
JFK: Reckless Youth '93
The Cure '95
Gold Diggers: The Secret of Bear Mountain '95
The Neon Bible '95
Truman '95
Bastard out of Carolina '96
If These Walls Could Talk '96
From the Earth to the Moon '98
Ruby Bridges '98
Dirty Pictures '00
What Lies Beneath '00
Path to War '02
A Guy Thing '03
Party Monster '03
The Clearing '04
Local Color '06
Valley of the Heart's Delight '07
Dream Boy '08
Tribute '09

Cassie Scerbo (1990-)
Bring It On: In It to Win It '07
Soccer Mom '08
Teen Spirit '11
Sharknado '13

David Schaal
Down Terrace '10
Mrs. Lowry & Son '19

Kirsten Schaal (1978-)
Going the Distance '10
Shrek Forever After '10 (V)
Toy Story 3 '10 (V)
Valentine's Day '10

Kristen Schaal (1978-)
Welcome to the Jungle '13
A Walk in the Woods '15
Boundaries '18
My Spy '19

Wendy Schaal (1954-)
Where the Boys Are '84 '84
Creature '85
Innerspace '87
Munchies '87
Going Under '91
Small Soldiers '98
Loving Annabelle '06

Johnathon Schaech (1969-)
The Doom Generation '95
How to Make an American Quilt '95
Poison Ivy 2: Lily '95
That Thing You Do! '96
Welcome to Woop Woop '97
Finding Graceland '98
Houdini '98
Hush '98
The Brutal Truth '99
Splendor '99
Caracara '00
If You Only Knew '00
The Forsaken '01
How to Kill Your Neighbor's Dog '01
Sol Goode '01
Blood Crime '02
8mm 2 '05
Little Chenier: A Cajun Story '06
Road House 2: Last Call '06
Angels Fall '07
Organizm '08
The Poker Club '08
Prom Night '08
Quarantine '08
Sex & Lies in Sin City: The Ted Binion Scandal '08
Laid to Rest '09
Takers '10
ChromeSkull: Laid to Rest 2 '11
7500 '12
Phantom '13
The Legend of Hercules '14
Vice '15
Marauders '16
Arsenal '17
Reprisal '18

Joshua Schaefer
No Dessert Dad, 'Til You Mow the Lawn '94
johns '96
Eight Days a Week '97

Eric Schaeffer (1962-)
My Life's in Turnaround '94
If Lucy Fell '95
Fall '97
Gunshy '98
Wirey Spindell '99
One Night at McCool's '01
Mind the Gap '04
After Fall, Winter '11

Natalie Schafer (1900-91)
Keep Your Powder Dry '45
Wonder Man '45
The Other Love '47
The Time of Your Life '48
Caught '49
The Girl Next Door '53
Female On the Beach '55
Forever Darling '56
Oh, Men! Oh, Women! '57
Susan Slade '61
Rescue from Gilligan's Island '78

William Schallert (1922-)
The Man from Planet X '51
Flat Top '52
Invasion U.S.A. '52
1,000 Years From Now '52
Sword of Venus '53
The High and the Mighty '54
Them! '54
The Gunslinger '56
The Incredible Shrinking Man '57
Man in the Shadow '57
Tarnished Angels '57
The Gallant Hours '60
Lonely Are the Brave '62
Speedway '68
The Computer Wore Tennis Shoes '69
Sam Whiskey '69
Colossus: The Forbin Project '70
Death Sentence '74
The Strongest Man in the World '75
Grace Kelly '83
Twilight Zone: The Movie '83
Innerspace '87
War & Remembrance '88
The Incident '89
War & Remembrance: The Final Chapter '89
Held Hostage '91
House Party 2: The Pajama Jam '91
Matinee '92
Shake, Rattle & Rock! '94
Bag of Bones '11

Mike Schank
American Movie '99
Storytelling '01

Tom Schanley (1961-)
Footsteps '98
Lone Rider '08
A Better Life '11

Heidi Schanz (1973-)
Body Language '95
Mixing Nia '98
Universal Soldier: The Return '99

Sabrina Scharf
Hell's Angels on Wheels '67
Easy Rider '69

Alexander Scheer (1976-)
Eight Miles High '07
Carlos '10

Paul Scheer
Army of One '16
Opening Night '17
Summer '03 '18

Roy Scheider (1932-2008)
Curse of the Living Corpse '64
Paper Lion '68
Loving '70
The French Connection '71
Klute '71
The Seven-Ups '73
Jaws '75
Marathon Man '76
Sorcerer '77
Jaws 2 '78
All That Jazz '79
Last Embrace '79
Still of the Night '82
Blue Thunder '83
Tiger Town '83
2010: The Year We Make Contact '84
Mishima: A Life in Four Chapters '85 (N)
52 Pick-Up '86
The Men's Club '86
Cohen and Tate '88
The Fourth War '90
The Russia House '90
Somebody Has to Shoot the Picture '90
Naked Lunch '91
Romeo Is Bleeding '93
Covert Assassin '94
Plato's Run '96
The Rage '96
Executive Target '97
John Grisham's The Rainmaker '97
The Myth of Fingerprints '97
The Peacekeeper '98
Silver Wolf '98
The White Raven '98
RKO 281 '99
Angels Don't Sleep Here '00
Chain of Command '00
The Doorway '00
Daybreak '01
Time Lapse '01
King of Texas '02
Love Thy Neighbor '02
Red Serpent '02
Dracula 2: Ascension '03
The Punisher '04
Dracula 3: Legacy '05
Blue Blood '07
Chicago 10 '07 (V)
Hearts of War '07
Dark Honeymoon '08

Raynor Scheine (1942-)
The War '94
The Rookie '02
The Sentinel '06
A Stranger's Heart '07
Lincoln '12

Clemens Scheitz
Heart of Glass '74
Stroszek '77

Catherine Schell (1944-)
On Her Majesty's Secret Service '69
Moon Zero Two '70
Return of the Pink Panther '74
Gulliver's Travels '77

Maria Schell (1926-2005)
Angel with the Trumpet '50
Napoleon '55
Gervaise '56
White Nights '57
The Brothers Karamazov '58
The Hanging Tree '59
Cimarron '60
The Mark '61
99 Women '69
The Odessa File '74
The Twist '76
Voyage of the Damned '76
Samson and Delilah '84

Maximilian Schell (1930-2014)
The Young Lions '58
Judgment at Nuremberg '61
Five Finger Exercise '62
Topkapi '64
Counterpoint '67
Heidi '67
Krakatoa East of Java '69
First Love '70
The Odessa File '74
The Man in the Glass Booth '75
Cross of Iron '76
St. Ives '76
A Bridge Too Far '77
Julia '77
Avalanche Express '79
The Black Hole '79
The Chosen '81
The Assisi Underground '84
The Rose Garden '89
The Freshman '90
Young Catherine '91
A Far Off Place '93
Abraham '94
Little Odessa '94
Telling Lies in America '96
The Thorn Birds: The Missing Years '96
The Eighteenth Angel '97
John Carpenter's Vampires '97
Deep Impact '98
Left Luggage '98
Joan of Arc '99
The Song of the Lark '01
Festival at Cannes '02
Coast to Coast '04
The Shell Seekers '06
The Brothers Bloom '09

Ronnie Schell (1931-)
Gus '76
Jetsons: The Movie '90 (V)
August Schellenberg (1936-2013)
Black Robe '91
Free Willy '93
Geronimo '93
Iron Will '93
Getting Gotti '94
Free Willy 2: The Adventure Home '95
Free Willy 3: The Rescue '97
True Heart '97
High Noon '00
Out of Time '00
The Unsaid '01
Tremors 4: The Legend Begins '04
The New World '05
Eight Below '06
Bury My Heart at Wounded Knee '07
Missionary Man '07
David Scheller (1972-)
Extreme Ops '02
Eight Miles High '07
The Lost Samaritan '08
Mary Kate Schellhardt (1978-)
What's Eating Gilbert Grape '93
Apollo 13 '95
Wolfgang Schenck (1934-)
Tenderness of the Wolves '73
World on a Wire '73
Effi Briest '74
Jean Schertler
Pecker '98
Runaway Bride '99
Rosanna Schiaffino (1939-2009)
Two Weeks in Another Town '62
The Long Ships '64
Vincent Schiavelli (1948-2005)
One Flew Over the Cuckoo's Nest '75
Fast Times at Ridgemont High '82
Night Shift '82 (V)
The Adventures of Buckaroo Banzai Across the Eighth Dimension '84
Amadeus '84
Ratings Game '84
Better Off Dead '85
Cold Feet '89
Valmont '89
Ghost '90
Waiting for the Light '90
Batman Returns '92
Miracle Beach '92
Lurking Fear '94
Lord of Illusions '95
Prince Brat and the Whipping Boy '95
3 Ninjas Knuckle Up '95
Back to Back '96
The People *vs.* Larry Flynt '96
Two Much '96
Tomorrow Never Dies '97
Milo '98
Desert Heat '99
Man on the Moon '99
The Prince and the Surfer '99
Treehouse Hostage '99
Three Strikes '00
Death to Smoochy '02
The 4th Tenor '02
Hey Arnold! The Movie '02 (V)
Snow White: The Fairest of Them All '02
Baadasssss! '03
Richard Schiff (1955-)
Hoffa '92
City Hall '95
The Trigger Effect '96
The Lost World: Jurassic Park 2 '97
Deep Impact '98
Dr. Dolittle '98
Living Out Loud '98
The Pentagon Wars '98
Crazy in Alabama '99
Forces of Nature '99
Heaven '99
Along for the Ride '00
Gun Shy '00
Lucky Numbers '00
Whatever It Takes '00
I Am Sam '01
What's the Worst That Could Happen? '01
People I Know '02
Ray '04
Civic Duty '06
Last Chance Harvey '08
The Infidel '10
Made in Dagenham '10
Solitary Man '10
Johnny English Reborn '11
Knife Fight '13
Man of Steel '13
Clemency '19
Claudia Schiffer (1970-)
Richie Rich '94 (C)
The Blackout '97
Black and White '99
Friends & Lovers '99
In Pursuit '00
Life Without Dick '01
Love Actually '03
Joseph Schildkraut (1895-1964)
Wandering Jew '20
Orphans of the Storm '21
The Road to Yesterday '25
King of Kings '27
Cleopatra '34
The Crusades '35
The Garden of Allah '36
The Life of Emile Zola '37
Slave Ship '37
Souls at Sea '37
The Baroness and the Butler '38
Marie Antoinette '38
Suez '38
Idiot's Delight '39
The Man in the Iron Mask '39
The Rains Came '39
The Three Musketeers '39
Phantom Raiders '40
The Shop Around the Corner '40
Flame of the Barbary Coast '45
Monsieur Beaucaire '46
The Diary of Anne Frank '59
Adrian Schiller
Son of God '14
A Cure for Wellness '17
Gus Schilling (1908-57)
Citizen Kane '41
It's a Pleasure '45
The Lady from Shanghai '48
Gasoline Alley '51
Taylor Schilling (1984-)
Atlas Shrugged: Part 1 '11
Argo '12
The Lucky One '12
Stay '13
The Overnight '15
The Public '18
The Prodigy '19
Tom Schilling (1982-)
Before the Fall '04
Generation War '13
Vivian Schilling (1968-)
Soultaker '90
Project: Eliminator '91
The Legend of Wolf Mountain '92
Future Shock '93
Savage Land '94
Sebastian Schipper
3 '10
The 11th Hour '14
Steve Schirripa (1957-)
Something About Sex '98
Must Love Dogs '05
Open Season 2 '08 (V)
The Hungry Ghosts '09
My Fake Fiance '09
Open Season 3 '10 (V)
Kill the Irishman '11
Charlie Schlatter (1966-)
Bright Lights, Big City '88
18 Again! '88
Heartbreak Hotel '88
All-American Murder '91
Police Academy 7: Mission to Moscow '94
Ed '96
Miss Cast Away '04
Out at the Wedding '07
Kyle Schmid (1984-)
The Cheetah Girls '03
Sex and the Single Mom '03
Cyber Seduction: His Secret Life '05
The Sisterhood of the Traveling Pants '05
Joy Ride 2: Dead Ahead '08
The Thaw '09
Dark Hearts '12
88 '15
10 Minutes Gone '19
Kevin G. Schmidt (1988-)
The Butterfly Effect '04
Catch That Kid '04
Cheaper by the Dozen 2 '05
Wolfgang Schmidt (1938-2009)
See Ray Dennis Steckler
Wrenn Schmidt
Preservation '14
The Good Catholic '17
Christiane Schmidtmer (1940-2003)
Boeing Boeing '65
The Big Doll House '71
The Giant Spider Invasion '75
Sybille Schmitz (1909-55)
Diary of a Lost Girl '29
Vampyr '31
F.P. 1 Doesn't Answer '33
Stefan Schnabel (1912-99)
Houdini '53
The 27th Day '57
The Mugger '58
Two Weeks in Another Town '62
Anna '87
Stella Schnabel
You Wont Miss Me '09
Miral '10
Noah Schnapp
The Peanuts Movie '15
Abe '20
Monica Schnarre (1971-)
The Death Merchant '91
Waxwork 2: Lost in Time '91
Fearless Tiger '94
Bulletproof Heart '95
Dead Fire '98
The Peacekeeper '98
Turbulence 3: Heavy Metal '00
Love on the Side '04
Ashley Schneider
Autopsy '08
American Virgin '09
Dan Schneider (1966-)
Better Off Dead '85
The Big Picture '89
Happy Together '89
Good Burger '97
Helmuth Schneider (1920-72)
Captain Sinbad '63
Angelique and the Sultan '68
Fifth Day of Peace '72
John Schneider (1960-)
Smokey and the Bandit '77
Eddie Macon's Run '83
Stagecoach '86
Christmas Comes to Willow Creek '87
The Curse '87
Ministry of Vengeance '89
Texas '94
Night of the Twisters '95
True Women '97
Lightning: Fire from the Sky '00
Snow Day '00
Collier & Co.: Hot Pursuit '06
Lake Placid 2 '07
Sydney White '07
You've Got a Friend '07
Conjurer '08
Shark Swarm '08
Come Dance at My Wedding '09
Wild Things: Foursome '10
WWJD: What Would Jesus Do? '10
Your Love Never Fails '11
October Baby '12
Lauren Schneider
Among Brothers '05
Creature '11
Maria Schneider (1952-2011)
Last Tango in Paris '73
The Passenger '75
Wanted: Babysitter '75
Mama Dracula '80
Jane Eyre '96
Michael Schneider (1939-)
The Last Winter '84
Schindler's List '93
Niels Schneider
I Killed My Mother '09
Heartbeats '11
Gemma Bovery '15
Dark Diamond '16
Paul Schneider (1976-)
All the Real Girls '03
How to Lose Your Lover '04
Elizabethtown '05
The Family Stone '05
The Assassination of Jesse James by the Coward Robert Ford '07
Lars and the Real Girl '07
Away We Go '09
Bright Star '09
Beloved '11
Water for Elephants '11
The Babymakers '12
Goodbye to All That '14
The Daughter '15
Rob Schneider (1963-)
Home Alone 2: Lost in New York '92
The Beverly Hillbillies '93
Demolition Man '93
Surf Ninjas '93
Judge Dredd '95
The Adventures of Pinocchio '96
Down Periscope '96
Dying to Get Rich '98
Knock Off '98
The Waterboy '98
Big Daddy '99
Deuce Bigalow: Male Gigolo '99
Muppets from Space '99
Little Nicky '00
The Animal '01
Adam Sandler's 8 Crazy Nights '02 (V)
The Hot Chick '02
Mr. Deeds '02
Around the World in 80 Days '04
50 First Dates '04
Deuce Bigalow: European Gigolo '05
The Longest Yard '05
The Benchwarmers '06
Click '06
Grandma's Boy '06
American Crude '07
Big Stan '07
I Now Pronounce You Chuck and Larry '07
You Don't Mess with the Zohan '08
American Virgin '09
Wild Cherry '09
Grown Ups '10
You May Not Kiss the Bride '12
Norm of the North '16
Romy Schneider (1938-82)
Boccaccio '70 '62
The Trial '63
Good Neighbor Sam '64
What's New Pussycat? '65
Triple Cross '67
Otley '68
La Piscine '69
Swimming Pool '70
Assassination of Trotsky '72
Cesar & Rosalie '72
Ludwig '72
The Last Train '74
Innocents with Dirty Hands '76
Mado '76
Death Watch '80
Ben Schnetzer
Pride '14
Goat '16
Warcraft '16
7 Days in Entebbe '18
Andrea Schober (1964-)
The Merchant of Four Seasons '71
Chinese Roulette '86
Michael Schoeffling (1960-)
Racing with the Moon '84
Sixteen Candles '84
Sylvester '85
Vision Quest '85
Belizaire the Cajun '86
Let's Get Harry '87
Slaves of New York '89
Longtime Companion '90
Mermaids '90
Wild Hearts Can't Be Broken '91
Jill Schoelen (1963-)
D.C. Cab '84
Hot Moves '84
That Was Then. . . This Is Now '85
Billionaire Boys Club '87
The Stepfather '87
Curse 2: The Bite '88
Cutting Class '89
The Phantom of the Opera '89
Popcorn '89
There Goes My Baby '92
When a Stranger Calls Back '93
Margareta Schoen (1895-1985)
Kriemhilde's Revenge '24
Siegfried '24
Matthias Schoenaerts (1977-)
Left Bank '08
Bullhead '11
Rust and Bone '12
Blood Ties '13
The Drop '14
A Little Chaos '14
The Loft '14
A Bigger Splash '15
The Danish Girl '15
Far from the Madding Crowd '15
Disorder '16
Red Sparrow '18
A Hidden Life '19
The Mustang '19
Ingeborg (Inge) Schoener (1935-)
Mark of the Devil '69
Mr. Superinvisible '73
Andrew Schofield (1958-)
Sid & Nancy '86
G.B.H. '91
Liam '00
Annabel Schofield (1963-)
Dragonard '88
Solar Crisis '92
Body Armor '96
David Schofield (1951-)
An American Werewolf in London '81
Jekyll and Hyde '90
Band of Gold '95
Anna Karenina '96
Gladiator '00
The Musketeer '01
Pirates of the Caribbean: Dead Man's Chest '06
Tom Scholte
Goldrush: A Real Life Alaskan Adventure '98
Last Wedding '01
Jason Schombing (1963-)
3 Ninjas Kick Back '94
Timecop '94
Robin Cook's Invasion '97
K-9 3: P.I. '01
A Job to Kill For '06
Held Hostage '09
The Stranger '10
The Eleventh Victim '12
Reiner Schone (1942-)
Return of Sabata '71
The Gunfighters '87
Crash Dive '96
Mortal Kombat 2: Annihilation '97
My Little Assassin '99
Frank Schorpion
Dead End '98
Random Encounter '98
Escape from Wildcat Canyon '99
No Alibi '00
Dead Awake '01
A Deadly Encounter '04
Too Young to Marry '07
The Secrets of the Summer House '08
Fugitive at 17 '12
Bob Schott (1949-)
In the Line of Fire '93
Out for Blood '93
Head of the Family '96
Maria Schrader (1965-)
Burning Life '94
Aimee & Jaguar '98
Rosenstrasse '03
In Darkness '11
Lisa Schrage
Hello Mary Lou: Prom Night 2 '87
Food of the Gods: Part 2 '88
Bitty Schram (1968-)
A League of Their Own '92
Caught '96
One Fine Day '96
Kissing a Fool '98
Cleopatra's Second Husband '00
You've Got a Friend '07
John Schrapnel
G.B.H. '91
Sparkle '07
Avery Schreiber (1935-2002)
Galaxina '80
Silent Scream '80
Caveman '81
Hunk '87
Saturday the 14th Strikes Back '88
Robin Hood: Men in Tights '93
Liev Schreiber (1967-)
Mixed Nuts '94
Party Girl '94
Buffalo Girls '95
The Sunshine Boys '95
The Daytrippers '96
Ransom '96
Scream '96
Walking and Talking '96
Phantoms '97
Scream 2 '97
Since You've Been Gone '97 (C)
Sphere '97
Twilight '98
The Hurricane '99
Jakob the Liar '99

RKO 281 *'99*
Spring Forward *'99*
A Walk on the Moon *'99*
Hamlet *'00*
Scream 3 *'00*
Kate & Leopold *'01*
The Sum of All Fears *'02*
Hitler: The Rise of Evil *'03*
The Manchurian Candidate *'04*
The Omen *'06*
The Painted Veil *'06*
Chicago 10 *'07 (V)*
Defiance *'08*
Taking Woodstock *'09*
X-Men Origins: Wolverine *'09*
Every Day *'10*
Repo Men *'10*
Salt *'10*
Goon *'12*
Fading Gigolo *'13*
The Last Days on Mars *'13*
Lee Daniels' The Butler *'13*
Money for Nothing: Inside the Federal Reserve *'13 (N)*
A Perfect Man *'13*
Pawn Sacrifice *'15*
Spotlight *'15*
Chuck *'17*
Goon: Last of the Enforcers *'17*

Pablo Schreiber (1978-)
The Mudge Boy *'03*
A Painted House *'03*
The Manchurian Candidate *'04*
Into the Fire *'05*
Nights in Rodanthe *'08*
Breaking Upwards *'09*
Happythankyoumoreplease *'10*
Allegiance *'12*
Preservation *'14*
13 Hours: The Secret Soldiers of Benghazi *'16*
Den of Thieves *'18*

Rick Schroder (1970-)
The Champ *'79*
The Last Flight of Noah's Ark *'80*
Across the Tracks *'89*
Lonesome Dove *'89*
There Goes My Baby *'92*
Call of the Wild *'93*
Return to Lonesome Dove *'93*
Texas *'94*
Crimson Tide *'95*
Hostage High *'97*
Murder at Devil's Glen *'99*
Lost Battalion *'01*
Poolhall Junkies *'02*
Black Cloud *'04*
Face of Terror *'04*
The Andromeda Strain *'08*
Journey to the Center of the Earth *'08*
Blood Done Sign My Name *'10*
Goodnight for Justice: Queen of Hearts *'13*
Our Wild Hearts *'13*
Dolly Parton's Coat of Many Colors *'15*

Barbet Schroeder (1941-)
Six in Paris *'68*
Paris, je t'aime *'06*
The Duchess of Langeais *'07*

Carly Schroeder (1990-)
The Lizzie McGuire Movie *'03*
Mean Creek *'04*
Eye of the Dolphin *'06*
Firewall *'06*
Gracie *'07*
Forget Me Not *'09*
Prayers for Bobby *'09*

Steven Schub (1967-)
Caught *'96*
Footsteps *'98*
No Vacancy *'99*
The Thirteenth Floor *'99*
Devil's Den *'06*

Karin Schubert (1944-)
Cold Eyes of Fear *'70*
Delusions of Grandeur *'76*

John Schuck (1940-)
Brewster McCloud *'70*
M*A*S*H *'70*
McCabe & Mrs. Miller *'71*
Thieves Like Us *'74*
Butch and Sundance: The Early Days *'79*
Star Trek 4: The Voyage Home *'86*
The New Adventures of Pippi Longstocking *'88*
My Mom's a Werewolf *'89*
Second Sight *'89*
Star Trek 6: The Undiscovered Country *'91*
Holy Matrimony *'94*
Tales from the Crypt Presents Demon Knight *'94*
The Trial of Old Drum *'00*
The Curse of the Jade Scorpion *'01*

Rudolf Schuendler (1906-88)
The American Friend *'77*
Suspiria *'77*

Erik Markus Schuetz
Mercury Man *'06*
The Sanctuary *'09*

Amanda Schull (1978-)
Center Stage *'00*
Mao's Last Dancer *'09*
Sorority Wars *'09*
I Am Wrath *'16*

Rebecca Schull (1929-)
My Life *'93*
That Darn Cat *'96*
Analyze This *'98*
The Odd Couple 2 *'98*
Flannel Pajamas *'06*

Dwight Schultz (1947-)
Alone in the Dark *'82*
Fat Man and Little Boy *'89*
The Long Walk Home *'89*
The Temp *'93*
Star Trek: First Contact *'96*
The A-Team *'10 (C)*

Sarah Ann Schultz
Lies and Illusions *'09*
Tales of an Ancient Empire *'11*

Matt Schulze (1972-)
Dementia *'98*
The Fast and the Furious *'01*
Blade 2 *'02*
The Transporter *'02*
Out of Reach *'04*
Torque *'04*
Final Move *'06*
7 Mummies *'06*
The Flock *'07*
Mr. Brooks *'07*
Fast Five *'11*

Paul Schulze (1962-)
Laws of Gravity *'92*
Hand Gun *'93*
Grind *'96*
Drowning Mona *'00*
Don't Say a Word *'01*
Panic Room *'02*
Rambo *'08*

Wendy Schumacher (1971-)
Animal Instincts 3: The Seductress *'95*
Star Hunter *'95*
Fugitive Rage *'96*
Scorned 2 *'96*

Amy Schumer (1981-)
Trainwreck *'15*
Snatched *'17*
Thank You for Your Service *'17*
I Feel Pretty *'18*

Reinhold Schunzel (1886-1954)
The Threepenny Opera *'31*
Notorious *'46*
Golden Earrings *'47*
Woman in Brown *'48*

Katharina Schuttler
Free Fall *'13*
13 Minutes *'17*

Maurice Schutz (1866-1955)
Passion of Joan of Arc *'28*
Vampyr *'31*

Lonnie Schuyler
Cybernator *'91*
Beneath the Mississippi *'08*

Ben Schwartz (1981-)
Peep World *'10*
The Walk *'15*
The Intervention *'16*
Outside In *'17*
Blue Iguana *'18*
Sonic the Hedgehog *'20 (V)*

Maurice Schwartz (1891-1960)
Bird of Paradise *'51*
Salome *'53*

Scott Schwartz (1968-)
The Toy *'82*
A Christmas Story *'83*
Kidco *'83*
Bridge of Dragons *'99*
Lost Treasure *'03*
Alien 3000 *'04*

Jason Schwartzman (1980-)
Rushmore *'98*
CQ *'01*
Simone *'02*
Slackers *'02*
Spun *'02*
I Heart Huckabees *'04*
Bewitched *'05*
The Hitchhiker's Guide to the Galaxy *'05*
Shopgirl *'05*
Marie Antoinette *'06*
The Darjeeling Limited *'07*
Walk Hard: The Dewey Cox Story *'07*
Fantastic Mr. Fox *'09 (V)*
Funny People *'09*
The Marc Pease Experience *'09*
Scott Pilgrim *vs.* the World *'10*
A Glimpse Inside the Mind of Charles Swan III *'12*
Moonrise Kingdom *'12*
Saving Mr. Banks *'13*
Big Eyes *'14*
The Grand Budapest Hotel *'14 (C)*
Listen Up Philip *'14*
The Overnight *'15*
Golden Exits *'17*
My Entire High School Sinking Into the Sea *'17*
The Polka King *'18*
Klaus *'19*

Simon Schwarz (1971-)
The Inheritors *'98*
North Face *'08*

Arnold Schwarzenegger (1947-)
Hercules in New York *'70*
The Long Goodbye *'73 (C)*
Stay Hungry *'76*
The Villain *'79*
The Jayne Mansfield Story *'80*
Conan the Barbarian *'82*
Conan the Destroyer *'84*
The Terminator *'84*
Commando *'85*
Red Sonja *'85*
Raw Deal *'86*
Predator *'87*
The Running Man *'87*
Red Heat *'88*
Twins *'88*
Kindergarten Cop *'90*
Total Recall *'90*
Terminator 2: Judgment Day *'91*
Dave *'93 (C)*
Last Action Hero *'93*
Junior *'94*
True Lies *'94*
Eraser *'96*
Jingle All the Way *'96*
Batman and Robin *'97*
End of Days *'99*
The 6th Day *'00*
Collateral Damage *'02*
The Rundown *'03 (C)*
Terminator 3: Rise of the Machines *'03*
Around the World in 80 Days *'04*
The Expendables *'10*
The Expendables 2 *'12*
Escape Plan *'13*
The Last Stand *'13*
The Expendables 3 *'14*
Sabotage *'14*
Maggie *'15*
Terminator Genisys *'15*
Aftermath *'17*
Killing Gunther *'17*
Terminator: Dark Fate *'19*

Patrick Schwarzenegger
Scout's Guide to the Zombie Apocalypse *'15*
Midnight Sun *'18*

Eric Schweig (1967-)
The Last of the Mohicans *'92*
Pontiac Moon *'94*
Squanto: A Warrior's Tale *'94*
Follow the River *'95*
Tom and Huck *'95*
Larry McMurtry's Dead Man's Walk *'96*
Big Eden *'00*
Skins *'02*
The Missing *'03*
Mr. Barrington *'03*
It Waits *'05*
Not Like Everyone Else *'06*
Bury My Heart at Wounded Knee *'07*
Casino Jack *'10*

Til Schweiger (1963-)
Brute *'97*
The Replacement Killers *'98*
SLC Punk! *'99*
Driven *'01*
Intimate Affairs *'01*
Joe and Max *'02*
What to Do in Case of Fire *'02*
Lara Croft Tomb Raider: The Cradle of Life *'03*
In Enemy Hands *'04*
King Arthur *'04*
Deuce Bigalow: European Gigolo *'05*
One Way *'06*
Already Dead *'07*
Body Armour *'07*
Far Cry *'08*
The Red Baron *'08*
Inglourious Basterds *'09*
Phantom Pain *'09*
New Year's Eve *'11*
The Three Musketeers *'11*
The Courier *'12*
This Means War *'12*
Charlie Countryman *'13*

Matthias Schweighofer
The Red Baron *'08*
Resistance *'20*

Jan Schweiterman (1972-)
Good Burger *'97*
Warlock 3: The End of Innocence *'98*

Benji Schwimmer
Leading Ladies *'10*
Holiday Spin *'12*

David Schwimmer (1966-)
Flight of the Intruder *'90*
Crossing the Bridge *'92*
The Pallbearer *'95*
Apt Pupil *'97*
Breast Men *'97*
Since You've Been Gone *'97*
Kissing a Fool *'98*
Six Days, Seven Nights *'98*
It's the Rage *'99*
Picking Up the Pieces *'99*
Band of Brothers *'01*
Hotel *'01*
Uprising *'01*
Duane Hopwood *'05*
Madagascar *'05 (V)*
Big Nothing *'06*
Madagascar: Escape 2 Africa *'08 (V)*
Nothing But the Truth *'08*
The Iceman *'12*
Madagascar 3: Europe's Most Wanted *'12 (V)*

Rusty Schwimmer (1962-)
Jason Goes to Hell: The Final Friday *'93*
Lone Justice 2 *'93*
A Little Princess *'95*
Lone Justice 3: Showdown at Plum Creek *'96*
Twister *'96*
Prison of Secrets *'97*
John John in the Sky *'00*
The Perfect Storm *'00*
Runaway Jury *'03*
Mozart and the Whale *'05*
North Country *'05*
Broken Trail *'06*
The Hawk Is Dying *'06*
American Fable *'17*

Hanna Schygulla (1943-)
Gods of the Plague *'69*
Love Is Colder Than Death *'69*
Why Does Herr R. Run Amok? *'69*
Beware of a Holy Whore *'70*
Whity *'70*
The Merchant of Four Seasons *'71*
The Bitter Tears of Petra von Kant *'72*
Effi Briest *'74*
The Wrong Move *'78*
The Marriage of Maria Braun *'79*
Passion *'82*
Sheer Madness *'84*
Barnum *'86*
Delta Force *'86*
Forever, Lulu *'87*
Dead Again *'91*
Golem: The Petrified Garden *'93*
Lea *'96*
The Girl of Your Dreams *'99*
The Edge of Heaven *'07*

Fausto Maria Sciarappa
The Girl by the Lake *'07*
Me, Myself and Her *'16*

Yvonne Scio (1969-)
Redline *'97*
Sorority Boys *'02*

Steve Scionti
Mom's Outta Sight *'01*
Megalodon *'03*

Annabella Sciorra (1960-)
True Love *'89*
Cadillac Man *'90*
Internal Affairs *'90*
Reversal of Fortune *'90*
The Hard Way *'91*
Jungle Fever *'91*
The Hand that Rocks the Cradle *'92*
Whispers in the Dark *'92*
Mr. Wonderful *'93*
The Night We Never Met *'93*
Romeo Is Bleeding *'93*
The Cure *'95*
The Innocent Sleep *'95*
The Funeral *'96*
Underworld *'96*
Asteroid *'97*
Cop Land *'97*
Highball *'97*
Little City *'97*
Mr. Jealousy *'98*
New Rose Hotel *'98*
What Dreams May Come *'98*
Above Suspicion *'00*
Once in the Life *'00*
King of the Jungle *'01*
American Crime *'04*
Chasing Liberty *'04*
Identity Theft: The Michelle Brown Story *'04*
12 and Holding *'05*
Find Me Guilty *'06*

Edith Scob (1937-)
The Horror Chamber of Dr. Faustus *'59*
The Burning Court *'62*
The Milky Way *'68*
Time Regained *'99*
Comedy of Innocence *'00*
Brotherhood of the Wolf *'01*
The Man on the Train *'02*
Bon Voyage *'03*
Heartbeat Detector *'07*
Summer Hours *'08*
Holy Motors *'12*
Things to Come *'16*

Brittany Scobie
Something Beneath *'07*
High Life *'09*

Kaya Scodelario (1992-)
Moon *'09*
Now Is Good *'12*
Twenty8k *'12*
Wuthering Heights *'12*
The Truth About Emanuel *'13*
The Maze Runner *'14*
Maze Runner: The Scorch Trials *'15*
Pirates of the Caribbean: Dead Men Tell No Tales *'17*
Maze Runner: The Death Cure *'18*
Crawl *'19*
Extremely Wicked, Shockingly Evil and Vile *'19*

Paul Scofield (1922-2008)
Carve Her Name with Pride *'58*
The Train *'65*
A Man for All Seasons *'66*
Bartleby *'70*
Scorpio *'73*
The Attic: The Hiding of Anne Frank *'88*
Henry V *'89*
Hamlet *'90*
Martin Chuzzlewit *'94*
Quiz Show *'94*
The Crucible *'96*
Animal Farm *'99 (V)*

Tracy Scoggins (1953-)
Toy Soldiers *'84*
Demonic Toys *'90*
Watchers 2 *'90*
Timebomb *'91*
Alien Intruder *'93*
Dollman vs Demonic Toys *'93*
The Great American Sex Scandal *'94*
A Crack in the Floor *'00*
Asylum of the Damned *'03*
The Cutter *'05*
The Strange Case of Dr. Jekyll and Mr. Hyde *'06*

Peter Scolari (1954-)
Rosebud Beach Hotel *'85*
Corporate Affairs *'90*
Perfect Harmony *'91*
Ticks *'93*
Camp Nowhere *'94*
That Thing You Do! *'96*
From the Earth to the Moon *'98*
The Polar Express *'04*
A Plumm Summer *'08*
Larry Crowne *'11*

Martin Scorsese (1942-)
Boxcar Bertha *'72*
Cannonball *'76*
Taxi Driver *'76*
After Hours *'85 (C)*
Round Midnight *'86*
Akira Kurosawa's Dreams *'90*
Guilty by Suspicion *'91*
The Age of Innocence *'93*
Quiz Show *'94*
Search and Destroy *'94 (C)*
The Muse *'99 (C)*
Gangs of New York *'02 (C)*

Shark Tale '04 (V)
Side by Side '12

Nicolette Scorsese (1954-)
Aspen Extreme '93
Boxing Helena '93

Izabela Scorupco (1970-)
Goldeneye '95
Vertical Limit '00
Reign of Fire '02
Exorcist: The Beginning '04
Cougar Club '07

Adam Scott (1973-)
High Crimes '02
Two Days '03
The Aviator '04
Off the Lip '04
Torque '04
Monster-in-Law '05
The Matador '06
The Return '06
Who Loves the Sun '06
Corporate Affairs '07
August '08
Lovely, Still '08
Step Brothers '08
Passenger Side '09
The Vicious Kind '09
Leap Year '10
Operation: Endgame '10
Piranha 3D '10
Our Idiot Brother '11
Bachelorette '12
Friends with Kids '12
The Guilt Trip '12
A.C.O.D. '13
The Secret Life of Walter Mitty '13
Hot Tub Time Machine 2 '15
Krampus '15
The Overnight '15
Sleeping with Other People '15
My Blind Brother '16
Flower '18

Alan Randolph Scott
Murder By Two '60
Night on Earth '91

Alex Scott (1929-2015)
Fahrenheit 451 '66
The Abominable Dr. Phibes '71
The Asphyx '72
Romper Stomper '92

Andrew Scott (1976-)
Nora '00
The American '01
Dead Bodies '03
Anton Chekhov's The Duel '09
Lennon Naked '10
The Scapegoat '12
The Bachelor Weekend '13
Locke '13
Pride '14
Victor Frankenstein '15
Denial '16
This Beautiful Fantastic '17

April Scott (1979-)
The Dukes of Hazzard: The Beginning '06
Living Will '10
The Penthouse '10

Ashley Scott (1977-)
Evil Remains '04
Walking Tall '04
Into the Blue '05
Lost '05
Strange Wilderness '08
12 Rounds '09
Christmas Mail '10

Audrey P. Scott (2002-)
Think of Me '11
About Sunny '12
Goodbye to All That '14

Campbell Scott (1961-)
Ain't No Way Back '89
Longtime Companion '90
No Way Back '90
The Sheltering Sky '90
Dead Again '91
Dying Young '91
Singles '92
The Innocent '93
Mrs. Parker and the Vicious Circle '94
Big Night '95
The Daytrippers '96
The Spanish Prisoner '97
Hi-Life '98
The Imposters '98
The Love Letter '98
Invasion! '99
Spring Forward '99
Follow the Stars Home '01
Hamlet '01
Lush '01
The Pilot's Wife '01
Roger Dodger '02
The Secret Lives of Dentists '02
Saint Ralph '04
Duma '05
The Dying Gaul '05
The Exorcism of Emily Rose '05
Loverboy '05
Final Days of Planet Earth '06
Crashing '07
Music & Lyrics '07
One Week '08 (N)
Phoebe in Wonderland '08
Handsome Harry '09
The Amazing Spider-Man '12
Still Mine '13

Debralee Scott (1953-2005)
Dirty Harry '71
Lisa, Bright and Dark '73
Our Time '74
Police Academy '84

Donovan Scott (1946-)
Zorro, the Gay Blade '81
Savannah Smiles '82
Sheena '84
Blast from the Past '98
I Know Who Killed Me '07

Dougray Scott (1965-)
Another 9 1/2 Weeks '96
The Crow Road '96
Behind the Lines '97
Deep Impact '98
Ever After: A Cinderella Story '98
Arabian Nights '00
Mission: Impossible 2 '00
Enigma '01
Dark Water '02
Ripley's Game '02
To Kill a King '03
The Truth About Love '04
Hitman '07
The Diplomat '08
Dr. Jekyll and Mr. Hyde '08
Love's Kitchen '11
My Week With Marilyn '11
There Be Dragons '11
A Thousand Kisses Deep '11
United '11
Death Race 3: Inferno '12
Last Passenger '14
Taken 3 '15

Fred Scott (1902-91)
Rodeo Rhythm '42
The Black Six '74

George C. Scott (1927-99)
Anatomy of a Murder '59
The Hanging Tree '59
The Hustler '61
The List of Adrian Messenger '63
Dr. Strangelove, or: How I Learned to Stop Worrying and Love the Bomb '64
The Yellow Rolls Royce '64
The Bible '66
Flim-Flam Man '67
Petulia '68
Patton '70
The Hospital '71
The Last Run '71
They Might Be Giants '71
The New Centurions '72
Rage '72
The Day of the Dolphin '73
Oklahoma Crude '73
Bank Shot '74
Savage Is Loose '74
The Hindenburg '75
Islands in the Stream '77
Movie, Movie '78
The Prince and the Pauper '78
Hardcore '79
The Changeling '80
The Formula '80
Taps '81
Oliver Twist '82
A Christmas Carol '84
Firestarter '84
Choices '86
The Last Days of Patton '86
The Murders in the Rue Morgue '86
Pals '87
Descending Angel '90
Exorcist 3: Legion '90
The Rescuers Down Under '90 (V)
Malice '93
Angus '95
Prince Brat and the Whipping Boy '95
Titanic '96
Gloria '98
Inherit the Wind '99
Rocky Marciano '99

Gordon Scott (1926-2007)
Tarzan's Hidden Jungle '55
Tarzan and the Lost Safari '57
Tarzan and the Trappers '58
Tarzan's Fight for Life '58
Tarzan's Greatest Adventure '59
Tarzan the Magnificent '60
Samson and the 7 Miracles of the World '62
The Beast of Babylon Against the Son of Hercules '63
Conquest of Mycene '63
Gladiator of Rome '63
Hero of Rome '63

Jacqueline Scott (1932-)
Macabre '58
Death of a Gunfighter '69
Duel '71
Charley Varrick '73
Empire of the Ants '77

Janette Scott (1938-)
Helen of Troy '56
The Lady Is a Square '58
School for Scoundrels '60
Paranoiac '62
Day of the Triffids '63

Jason-Shane Scott (1976-)
The Pit and the Pendulum '09
Sniper: Special Ops '16

Jill Scott (1972-)
Tyler Perry's Why Did I Get Married? '07
Hounddog '08
Tyler Perry's Why Did I Get Married Too '10
Steel Magnolias '12
Baggage Claim '13
Get On Up '14

John Scott (1930-)
The Tell-Tale Heart '60
Horror of Party Beach '64

Judith Scott (1958-)
Burn, Witch, Burn! '62
Soul Survivor '95
A Nightmare Come True '97
Flightplan '05
Guess Who '05

Kathryn Leigh Scott (1943-)
House of Dark Shadows '70
Come Die With Me '75
The Last Days of Patton '86
Parasomnia '08

Keith Scott (1954-)
George of the Jungle '97 (N)
The Adventures of Rocky & Bullwinkle '00 (V)

Ken Scott (1928-86)
Stopover Tokyo '57
The Fiend Who Walked the West '58
Woman Obsessed '59
Pirates of Tortuga '61
Raiders from Beneath the Sea '64
Fantastic Voyage '66

Kente Scott (1977-)
They Call Me Sirr '00
Antwone Fisher '02

Kimberly Scott (1961-)
The Abyss '89
Flatliners '90
Batman Forever '95
Toothless '97
Bellyfruit '99
K-PAX '01
United States of Leland '03
Guess Who '05

Larry B. Scott (1961-)
Wilma '77
A Hero Ain't Nothin' but a Sandwich '78
The Karate Kid '84
Revenge of the Nerds '84
That Was Then. . . This Is Now '85
The Children of Times Square '86
Iron Eagle '86
SpaceCamp '86
Extreme Prejudice '87
Revenge of the Nerds 2: Nerds in Paradise '87
Fear of a Black Hat '94
Revenge of the Nerds 4: Nerds in Love '94
The Bad Pack '98

Lizabeth Scott (1922-2015)
The Strange Love of Martha Ivers '46
Dead Reckoning '47
I Walk Alone '48
Easy Living '49
Too Late for Tears '49
Dark City '50
The Racket '51
Two of a Kind '51
A Stolen Face '52
Stolen Face '52
Bad for Each Other '53
Scared Stiff '53
Silver Lode '54
The Weapon '56
Loving You '57
Pulp '72

Margaretta Scott (1912-2005)
Things to Come '36
The Return of the Scarlet Pimpernel '37
The Girl in the News '41
Counterblast '48
Man of Evil '48
Crescendo '69

Martha Scott (1914-2003)
The Howards of Virginia '40
Our Town '40
Cheers for Miss Bishop '41
One Foot in Heaven '41
Hi Diddle Diddle '43
War of the Wildcats '43
So Well Remembered '47
Desperate Hours '55
The Ten Commandments '56
Sayonara '57
Ben-Hur '59
The Turning Point '77
Adam '83

Naomi Scott (1993-)
Lemonade Mouth '11
Power Rangers '17
Aladdin '19
Charlie's Angels '19

Pippa Scott (1935-)
Petulia '68
Cold Turkey '71
Bad Ronald '74

Randolph Scott (1898-1987)
Hot Saturday '32
Island of Lost Souls '32 (C)
A Successful Calamity '32
Supernatural '33
To the Last Man '33
Roberta '35
She '35
Follow the Fleet '36
Go West, Young Man '36
The Last of the Mohicans '36
High, Wide and Handsome '37
Rebecca of Sunnybrook Farm '38
The Texans '38
Frontier Marshal '39
Jesse James '39
Susannah of the Mounties '39
My Favorite Wife '40
Virginia City '40
Western Union '41
Pittsburgh '42
The Spoilers '42
To the Shores of Tripoli '42
Bombardier '43
The Desperadoes '43
Gung Ho! '43
Captain Kidd '45
Abilene Town '46
Badman's Territory '46
Gunfighters '47
Trail Street '47
Return of the Bad Men '48
The Nevadan '50
Man in the Saddle '51
Santa Fe '51
Carson City '52
Hangman's Knot '52
The Stranger Wore a Gun '53
Ten Wanted Men '54
A Lawless Street '55
Rage at Dawn '55
7 Men From Now '56
Seventh Cavalry '56
Decision at Sundown '57
Shoot-out at Medicine Bend '57
The Tall T '57
Buchanan Rides Alone '58
Westbound '58
Ride Lonesome '59
Comanche Station '60
Ride the High Country '62

Reid Scott (1977-)
Amusement '08
Under the Eiffel Tower '18
Venom '18
Black and Blue '19
Late Night '19

Seann William Scott (1976-)
American Pie '99
Dude, Where's My Car? '00
Final Destination '00
Road Trip '00
American Pie 2 '01
Evolution '01
Jay and Silent Bob Strike Back '01
Stark Raving Mad '02
American Wedding '03
Bulletproof Monk '03
Old School '03
The Rundown '03
The Dukes of Hazzard '05
Ice Age: The Meltdown '06 (V)
Southland Tales '06
American Loser '07
Mr. Woodcock '07
The Promotion '08
Role Models '08
Balls Out: Gary the Tennis Coach '09
Ice Age: Dawn of the Dinosaurs '09 (V)
Planet 51 '09 (V)
Cop Out '10
American Reunion '12
Goon '12
Ice Age: Continental Drift '12 (V)
Just Before I Go '15
Goon: Last of the Enforcers '17
Bloodline '19

Shaley Scott
The Apocalypse '07
Invasion of the Pod People '07
Transmorphers '07

Stefanie Scott
Insidious: Chapter 3 '15
Jem and the Holograms '15
I.T. '16
At First Light '18
Mary '19

Terry Scott (1927-94)
Carry On Sergeant '58
Carry On Up the Khyber '68
Carry On Loving '70
Carry On Up the Jungle '70
Carry On Matron '72

Timothy Scott (1938-95)
Love Me Deadly '73
Fried Green Tomatoes '91
Return to Lonesome Dove '93

Tom Everett Scott (1970-)
That Thing You Do! '96
An American Werewolf in Paris '97
Dead Man on Campus '97
One True Thing '98
River Red '98
Inherit the Wind '99
Invasion! '99
The Love Letter '99
Boiler Room '00
National Lampoon's Van Wilder '02
Because I Said So '07
Race to Witch Mountain '09
Tanner Hall '09
The Devil's Teardrop '10
Mars Needs Moms '11 (V)
Parental Guidance '12
Santa Paws 2: The Santa Pups '12 (V)
Independence Daysaster '13
Enemies Closer '14
Diary of a Wimpy Kid: The Long Haul '17

William Lee Scott (1973-)
The Opposite of Sex '98
Black and White '99
October Sky '99
Gone in 60 Seconds '00
Pearl Harbor '01
Dumb and Dumberer: When Harry Met Lloyd '03
Identity '03
The Butterfly Effect '04
Killer Diller '04
The Go-Getter '07
Farmhouse '08
Nine Dead '10
Burning Blue '14

Zachary Scott (1914-65)
The Mask of Dimitrios '44
Mildred Pierce '45
The Southerner '45
Cass Timberlane '47
Stallion Road '47
Ruthless '48
South of St. Louis '48
Whiplash '48
Flamingo Road '49
Pretty Baby '50
Let's Make It Legal '51
Lightning Strikes Twice '51
Wings of Danger '52
Appointment in Honduras '53
Flame of the Islands '55
Shotgun '55
The Counterfeit Plan '57
The Young One '61
It's Only Money '62

Kristin Scott Thomas (1960-)
Under the Cherry Moon '86
A Handful of Dust '88
The Tenth Man '88
Framed '90
Bitter Moon '92
Body & Soul '93
Four Weddings and a Funeral '94
Angels and Insects '95
Gulliver's Travels '95
The Pompatus of Love '95
Richard III '95
The English Patient '96
The Horse Whisperer '97
Sweet Revenge '98

Random Hearts '99
Up at the Villa '00
Gosford Park '01
Life as a House '01
Keeping Mum '05
Tell No One '06
The Valet '06
The Golden Compass '07 (V)
The Walker '07
Easy Virtue '08
I've Loved You So Long '08
The Other Boleyn Girl '08
Confessions of a Shopaholic '09
Nowhere Boy '09
Love Crime '10
Sarah's Key '10
Salmon Fishing in the Yemen '11
The Woman in the Fifth '11
Bel Ami '12
The Invisible Woman '13
Only God Forgives '13
My Old Lady '14
Darkest Hour '17
The Party '17
Tomb Raider '18

Serena Scott Thomas (1961-)
Diana: Her True Story '93
Relax. . . It's Just Sex! '98
The World Is Not Enough '99
Hostage '05
The Thirst '06
William & Kate '11

Andrea Scotti (1931-)
Atom Age Vampire '61
The Beast of Babylon Against the Son of Hercules '63
Hercules vs. the Sons of the Sun '64
The Legend of the Wolf Woman '77

Nick Scotti (1966-)
Kiss Me, Guido '97
The Last Request '06
Perception '06

Vito Scotti (1918-96)
Two Weeks in Another Town '62
Von Ryan's Express '65
What Did You Do in the War, Daddy? '66
The McCullochs '75
I Wonder Who's Killing Her Now? '76

Alexander Scourby (1913-85)
Affair in Trinidad '52
The Big Heat '53
The Glory Brigade '53
The Redhead from Wyoming '53
Man On a String '60
Seven Thieves '60
The Stuff '85

Rory Scovel
Dean '17
I Feel Pretty '18

Don Scribner
Slave Girls from Beyond Infinity '87
Rapid Assault '99

Angus Scrimm (1926-2016)
Amputee with an Axe '73
Phantasm '79
Phantasm 2 '88
Transylvania Twist '89
Subspecies '90
Mindwarp '91
Phantasm 3: Lord of the Dead '94
Vampirella '96
Phantasm 4: Oblivion '98
Automatons '06
I Sell the Dead '09
Phantasm: Ravager '16

Linda Scruggs
Las Vegas Lady '76
The Million Dollar Rip-Off '76

Matthew Scurfield (1948-)
A Murder of Quality '90
Bait '02
A Different Loyalty '04

Sandra Seacat (1936-)
Promised Land '88
The New Age '94
Crazy in Alabama '99

Susan Seaforth Hayes (1943-)
California '63
Billie '65

Steven Seagal (1952-)
Above the Law '88
Hard to Kill '89
Marked for Death '90
Out for Justice '91
Under Siege '92
On Deadly Ground '94
Under Siege 2: Dark Territory '95
Executive Decision '96
The Glimmer Man '96
Fire Down Below '97
My Giant '98 (C)
The Patriot '99
Exit Wounds '01
Ticker '01
Half Past Dead '02
Belly of the Beast '03
The Foreigner '03
Out For a Kill '03
Out of Reach '04
Black Dawn '05
Submerged '05
Today You Die '05
Attack Force '06
Shadow Man '06
Urban Justice '07
Against the Dark '08
Kill Switch '08
Pistol Whipped '08
The Keeper '09
Ruslan '09
Born to Raise Hell '10
Machete '10
Maximum Conviction '12
Force of Execution '13
A Good Man '14
Gutshot Straight '14
Mercenary: Absolution '15
Asian Connection '16
Code of Honor '16
Contract to Kill '16
End of a Gun '16
Sniper: Special Ops '16

Jenny Seagrove (1957-)
Local Hero '83
Nate and Hayes '83
A Woman of Substance '84
Hold the Dream '86
A Chorus of Disapproval '89
Bullseye! '90
The Guardian '90
Sherlock Holmes and the Incident at Victoria Falls '91
Zoe '01

Elizabeth Seal (1933-)
Radio Cab Murder '54
Trouble in the Sky '60
Vampire Circus '71

Douglas Seale (1913-99)
Ernest Saves Christmas '88
Almost an Angel '90
Mr. Destiny '90
Aladdin '92 (V)

Orlando Seale (1973-)
Everything You Want '05
Caffeine '06
Miss Conception '08

Franklyn Seales (1952-90)
The Onion Field '79
Southern Comfort '81

Alison Sealy-Smith
Haunting Sarah '05
You Kill Me '07

Nick Searcy (1959-)
The War '94
From the Earth to the Moon '98
Cast Away '00
Head of State '03

Runaway Jury '03
The Assassination of Richard Nixon '05
The Dead Girl '06
Flicka '06
An American Crime '07
The Comebacks '07
Welcome to Paradise '07
Eagle Eye '08
The Ugly Truth '09
Blood Done Sign My Name '10
The Expendables '10
The Last Song '10
The Best of Enemies '19

Jackie Searl (1921-91)
No Greater Glory '34
Peck's Bad Boy '34
Dead End Kids: Little Tough Guy '38
That Certain Age '38

Fred F. Sears (1913-57)
Down to Earth '47
Counterspy Meets Scotland Yard '50

Heather Sears (1935-94)
Room at the Top '59
Sons and Lovers '60
The Phantom of the Opera '62
Black Torment '64
Estate of Insanity '64

Teddy Sears (1977-)
The Client List '10
Drew Peterson: Untouchable '12
Curve '16

Michael Seater
On Thin Ice '03
She Drives Me Crazy '07

James Seay (1914-92)
Close to My Heart '51
Phantom from Space '53
Captain Kidd and the Slave Girl '54
Return to Treasure Island '54
Man in the Vault '56
Beginning of the End '57

Heidi Lenhart Seban (1973-)
Au Pair '99
Au Pair 2: The Fairy Tale Continues '01
Au Pair 3: Adventure in Paradise '09

Dorothy Sebastian (1906-57)
Our Dancing Daughters '28
The Single Standard '29
Spite Marriage '29
Montana Moon '30
Our Blushing Brides '30

Lobo Sebastian
187 '97
Next Friday '00
Dirty '05
The Longest Yard '05
Crash and Burn '07
Columbus Day '08

Jean Seberg (1938-79)
Bonjour Tristesse '57
Saint Joan '57
Breathless '59
The Mouse That Roared '59
In the French Style '63
Lilith '64
A Fine Madness '66
Who's Got the Black Box? '67
Paint Your Wagon '69
Airport '70

Douta Seck
Xala '75
Sugar Cane Alley '83

Harry Secombe (1921-2001)
Down Among the Z Men '52
Goon Movie '52

Kyle Secor (1957-)
The Heart of Dixie '89
City Slickers '91

Sleeping with the Enemy '91
Silent Victim '92
Untamed Heart '93
Drop Zone '94
Beat '00
Homicide: The Movie '00

Jon Seda (1970-)
Gladiator '92
Carlito's Way '93
I Like It Like That '94
12 Monkeys '95
Dear God '96
Mistrial '96
Primal Fear '96
Selena '96
Sunchaser '96
Homicide: The Movie '00
Price of Glory '00
Thin Air '00
Double Bang '01
Love the Hard Way '01
The Street King '02
Undisputed '02
Bad Boys 2 '03
One Long Night '07
The Pacific '10
Bullet to the Head '12

Amy Sedaris (1961-)
Maid in Manhattan '02
Elf '03
My Baby's Daddy '04
Bewitched '05
Chicken Little '05 (V)
Stay '05
I Want Someone to Eat Cheese With '06
Strangers with Candy '06
Shrek the Third '07 (V)
Snow Angels '07
Gym Teacher: The Movie '08
Dance Flick '09
Jennifer's Body '09
Old Dogs '09
Tanner Hall '09
Shrek Forever After '10 (V)
Puss in Boots '11 (V)
Goodbye to All That '14
Ghost Team '16
My Life as a Zucchini '16 (V)

Margaret Seddon (1872-1968)
Little Church Around the Corner '23
Smilin' Through '32
Mr. Deeds Goes to Town '36

Kyra Sedgwick (1965-)
Tai-Pan '86
Kansas '88
Born on the Fourth of July '89
Mr. & Mrs. Bridge '90
Women & Men: In Love There Are No Rules '91
Singles '92
Family Pictures '93
Heart and Souls '93
The Low Life '95
Murder in the First '95
Something to Talk About '95
Losing Chase '96
Phenomenon '96
Critical Care '97
What's Cooking? '00
Behind the Red Door '02
Just a Kiss '02
Personal Velocity: Three Portraits '02
Secondhand Lions '03
Something the Lord Made '04
The Woodsman '04
Loverboy '05
The Game Plan '07
Gamer '09
Man on a Ledge '12
The Possession '12
Chlorine '13
Reach Me '14
Time Out of Mind '14
The Edge of Seventeen '16
Villains '19

Robert Sedgwick
Morgan Stewart's Coming Home '87
Tune in Tomorrow '90

Kailin See
Lies My Mother Told Me '05
Decoys: The Second Seduction '07

Miriam Seegar (1907-2011)
Seven Keys to Baldpate '29
Clancy in Wall Street '30
The Woman Between '31
Strangers of the Evening '32

Pete Seeger
Alice's Restaurant '69
Hugh Hefner: Playboy, Activist and Rebel '09

Andrew Seeley
Another Cinderella Story '08
The Shortcut '09

George Segal (1934-)
Invitation to a Gunfighter '64
King Rat '65
Ship of Fools '65
The Lost Command '66
The Quiller Memorandum '66
Who's Afraid of Virginia Woolf? '66
Bye Bye Braverman '67
The St. Valentine's Day Massacre '67
No Way to Treat a Lady '68
The Bridge at Remagen '69
The Southern Star '69
The Hot Rock '70
Loving '70
The Owl and the Pussycat '70
Where's Poppa? '70
Born to Win '71
Blume in Love '73
A Touch of Class '73
The Terminal Man '74
Russian Roulette '75
The Duchess and the Dirtwater Fox '76
Fun with Dick and Jane '77
Rollercoaster '77
Who Is Killing the Great Chefs of Europe? '78
Lost and Found '79
The Last Married Couple in America '80
Carbon Copy '81
Cold Room '84
Stick '85
Look Who's Talking '89
For the Boys '91
Direct Hit '93
Look Who's Talking Now '93
Army of One '94
Following Her Heart '94
The Babysitter '95
Flirting with Disaster '95
It's My Party '95
To Die For '95 (C)
The Cable Guy '96
The Mirror Has Two Faces '96
Houdini '98
Heights '04
Fielder's Choice '05
Three Days to Vegas '07
Love and Other Drugs '10
Elsa & Fred '14

Zohra Segal (1912-2014)
See Zohra Sehgal

Pamela Segall (1966-)
After Midnight '89
Say Anything '89
Gate 2 '92
Bed of Roses '95
Sgt. Bilko '95
Eat Your Heart Out '96
Plump Fiction '97
Kiki's Delivery Service '98 (V)
Disney's Teacher's Pet '04 (V)

Noah Segan (1983-)
Adam & Steve '05
Brick '06
Still Green '07
What We Do Is Secret '07
Cabin Fever 2: Spring Fever '08
Deadgirl '08
Love at First Kill '08

Chain Letter '10
The Frozen '12
The Mind's Eye '16

Paolo Seganti (1965-)
L.A. Confidential '97
Still Breathing '97
Tea with Mussolini '99
Sex & Mrs. X '00
Cradle 2 the Grave '03
Carnera: The Walking Mountain '08

Jason Segel (1980-)
Dead Man on Campus '97
SLC Punk! '99
Slackers '02
11:14 '03
The Good Humor Man '05
Forgetting Sarah Marshall '08
I Love You, Man '09
Despicable Me '10 (V)
Gulliver's Travels '10
Bad Teacher '11
The Muppets '11
The Five-Year Engagement '12
Jeff, Who Lives at Home '12
This Is 40 '12
Sex Tape '14
The End of the Tour '15
The Discovery '17

Santiago Segura (1965-)
Dance with the Devil '97
The Girl of Your Dreams '99
Blade 2 '02
Agent Cody Banks 2: Destination London '04
A Matador's Mistress '08
The Last Circus '10

Zohra Sehgal (1912-2014)
The Courtesans of Bombay '85
Masala '91
The Mystic Masseur '01
Chicken Tikka Masala '05

Emmanuelle Seigner (1966-)
Frantic '88
Bitter Moon '92
Nirvana '97
R.P.M. '97
Place Vendome '98
Buddy Boy '99
The Ninth Gate '99
Happily Ever After '04
Four Last Songs '06
The Diving Bell and the Butterfly '07
La Vie en Rose '07
Change of Plans '09
Giallo '09
Venus in Fur '13

Louis Seigner (1903-95)
The Eclipse '62
Mr. Klein '76

Mathilde Seigner (1968-)
Dry Cleaning '97
The Man I Love '97
Venus Beauty Institute '98
Time Regained '99
With a Friend Like Harry '00
Alias Betty '01
The Girl from Paris '02
Retour Chez Ma Mere '16

Koudous Seihon
Mediterranea '15
A Ciambra '17

Amy Seimetz (1987-)
Alexander the Last '09
Bitter Feast '10
A Horrible Way to Die '10
Tiny Furniture '10
The Off Hours '11
The Sacrament '13
Upstream Color '13
You're Next '13
Lean on Pete '17
Pet Sematary '19

Jerry Seinfeld (1954-)
Ratings Game '84
Bee Movie '07 (V)

Rapulana Seiphemo (1967-)
Tarzan and the Lost City *'98*
Tsotsi *'05*
White Wedding *'10*

John Seitz (1892-1979)
The Prowler *'81*
Hard Choices *'84*
Five Corners *'88*
The Bread, My Sweet *'01*

Owen Sejake
In My Country *'04*
Shake Hands With the Devil *'07*

Johnny Sekka (1934-2006)
Flame in the Streets *'61*
East of Sudan *'64*
Khartoum *'66*
The Southern Star *'69*
The Bloodsuckers *'70*
The Message *'77*

David Selby (1941-)
Night of Dark Shadows *'71*
Up the Sandbox *'72*
The Girl in Blue *'74*
The Super Cops *'74*
Washington: Behind Closed Doors *'77*
Rich and Famous *'81*
Dying Young *'91*
Grave Secrets: The Legacy of Hilltop Drive *'92*
Intersection *'93*
D3: The Mighty Ducks *'96*
Headless Body in Topless Bar *'96*
White Squall *'96*
Horton Foote's Alone *'97*
End Game *'06*
Inhale *'10*
The Social Network *'10*

Nicholas Selby (1925-2011)
A Midsummer Night's Dream *'68*
Macbeth *'71*
House of Cards *'90*

Sarah Selby (1905-80)
Battle Circus *'53*
Battle Cry *'55*
An Affair to Remember *'57*
No Time to Be Young *'57*
Stopover Tokyo *'57*

Tony Selby (1938-)
The Conqueror Worm *'68*
Adolf Hitler: My Part in His Downfall *'74*

Marian Seldes (1928-2014)
Crime and Punishment, USA *'59*
Fingers *'78*
Tom and Huck *'95*
Truman *'95*
Affliction *'97*
Home Alone 3 *'97*
Digging to China *'98*
The Haunting *'99*
Duets *'00*
If These Walls Could Talk 2 *'00*
Town and Country *'01*
Hollywood Ending *'02*
Mona Lisa Smile *'03*
Ballets Russes *'05*
Home *'08*
The Extra Man *'10*

William (Bill) Self (1921-2010)
The Story of G.I. Joe *'45*
The Thing *'51*

Edgar Selge (1948-)
The Experiment *'01*
The Debt *'07*

Elizabeth Sellars (1921-2019)
Madeleine *'50*
Cloudburst *'51*
Hunted *'52*
The Long Memory *'53*
Recoil *'53*
Desiree *'54*
The Day They Robbed the Bank of England *'60*
Never Let Go *'60*
The Chalk Garden *'64*
The Mummy's Shroud *'67*
A Voyage 'Round My Father *'89*

Connie Sellecca (1955-)
The Bermuda Depths *'78*
Captain America 2: Death Too Soon *'79*
She's Dressed to Kill *'79*
The Brotherhood of the Rose *'89*
The Wild Stallion *'09*

Tom Selleck (1945-)
Myra Breckinridge *'70*
Daughters of Satan *'72*
Terminal Island *'73*
Midway *'76*
Coma *'78*
The Gypsy Warriors *'78*
Concrete Cowboys *'79*
The Sacketts *'79*
Magnum P.I.: Don't Eat the Snow in Hawaii *'80*
Divorce Wars: A Love Story *'82*
The Shadow Riders *'82*
High Road to China *'83*
Lassiter *'84*
Runaway *'84*
Three Men and a Baby *'87*
Her Alibi *'88*
An Innocent Man *'89*
Quigley Down Under *'90*
Three Men and a Little Lady *'90*
Folks! *'92*
Mr. Baseball *'92*
Broken Trust *'95*
Open Season *'95*
Last Stand at Saber River *'96*
In and Out *'97*
The Love Letter *'99*
Running Mates *'00*
Crossfire Trail *'01*
Monte Walsh *'03*
Ike: Countdown to D-Day *'04*
Jesse Stone: Stone Cold *'05*
Jesse Stone: Death in Paradise *'06*
Jesse Stone: Night Passage *'06*
Jesse Stone: Sea Change *'07*
Meet the Robinsons *'07 (V)*
Jesse Stone: Thin Ice *'09*
Jesse Stone: No Remorse *'10*
Killers *'10*
Jesse Stone: Innocents Lost *'11*
Jesse Stone: Benefit of the Doubt *'12*

Peter Sellers (1925-80)
Down Among the Z Men *'52*
Goon Movie *'52*
The Ladykillers *'55*
The Smallest Show on Earth *'57*
The Naked Truth *'58*
Tom Thumb *'58*
Carlton Browne of the F.O. *'59*
I'm All Right Jack *'59*
The Mouse That Roared *'59*
The Millionairess *'60*
Never Let Go *'60*
Two-Way Stretch *'60*
Lolita *'62*
The Road to Hong Kong *'62*
Trial & Error *'62*
Waltz of the Toreadors *'62*
Heavens Above *'63*
The Wrong Arm of the Law *'63*
Dr. Strangelove, or: How I Learned to Stop Worrying and Love the Bomb *'64*
The Pink Panther *'64*
A Shot in the Dark *'64*
The World of Henry Orient *'64*
What's New Pussycat? *'65*
After the Fox *'66*
Alice in Wonderland *'66*
The Wrong Box *'66*
The Bobo *'67*
Casino Royale *'67*
Woman Times Seven *'67*
I Love You, Alice B. Toklas! *'68*
The Party *'68*
The Magic Christian *'69*
Hoffman *'70*
There's a Girl in My Soup *'70*
Blockhouse *'73*
The Optimists *'73*
Return of the Pink Panther *'74*
Murder by Death *'76*
The Pink Panther Strikes Again *'76*
Revenge of the Pink Panther *'78*
Being There *'79*
Prisoner of Zenda *'79*
The Fiendish Plot of Dr. Fu Manchu *'80*
Trail of the Pink Panther *'82*

Sabrina Sellers (1963-)
See Sabrina Siani

Charles Sellon (1870-1937)
The Monster *'25*
Vagabond Lover *'29*
Behind Office Doors *'31*
Make Me a Star *'32*
Bright Eyes *'34*
In Old Kentucky *'35*
Life Begins at Forty *'35*

Morton Selten (1860-1939)
The Ghost Goes West *'36*
The Thief of Bagdad *'40*

David Selvas (1971-)
Caresses *'97*
Beloved/Friend *'99*

Katy Selverstone (1918-2006)
Seven Girlfriends *'00*
Divine Secrets of the Ya-Ya Sisterhood *'02*

Clarissa Selwynne (1886-1948)
The Love Trap *'29*
Jane Eyre *'34*

Milton Selzer (1918-2006)
The Legend of Lylah Clare *'68*
The Evil *'78*
The Triangle Factory Fire Scandal *'79*
Tapeheads *'89*

Aparna Sen (1945-)
Bombay Talkie *'70*
Hullabaloo over Georgie & Bonnie's Pictures *'78*

Nandana Sen (1967-)
Seducing Maarya *'99*
The War Within *'05*
Marigold *'07*

Paola Senatore (1949-)
Mean Machine *'73*
Emerald Jungle *'80*

Koreya Senda (1904-94)
Gate of Hell *'54*
H-Man *'59*
Face of Another *'66*
Tora! Tora! Tora! *'70*

Joe Seneca (1914-96)
Wilma *'77*
The Verdict *'82*
Half Slave, Half Free *'85*
Crossroads *'86*
Samaritan: The Mitch Snyder Story *'86*
The Blob *'88*
School Daze *'88*
Mo' Better Blues *'90*
Murder on the Bayou *'91*
Mississippi Masala *'92*
The Saint of Fort Washington *'93*

Noriko Sengoku (1922-)
Godzilla *vs.* Monster Zero *'68*
Okoge *'93*

Andrew Sensenig
The Last Exorcism Part II *'13*
Upstream Color *'13*
We are Still Here *'15*

Martin Sensmeier
The Magnificent Seven *'16*
Wind River *'17*

Marc Senter
Cabin Fever 2: Spring Fever *'08*
Wicked Lake *'08*
Red White & Blue *'10*

Heyon-a Seong (1975-)
Cello *'05*
Time *'06*

Peter Serafinowicz (1972-)
Shaun of the Dead *'04*
Couples Retreat *'09*
An Ordinary Man *'18*

Carmen Serano
Urban Justice *'07*
Deadly Impact *'09*

Greg Serano (1972-)
Absolution *'97*
Beer for My Horses *'08*
Conspiracy *'08*

Massimo Serato (1916-89)
The Pirates of Capri *'49*
Loves of Three Queens *'54*
David and Goliath *'61*
Hero of Rome *'63*
The Lion of Thebes *'64*
Challenge of the Gladiator *'65*
10th Victim *'65*
Wild, Wild Planet *'65*
Camille 2000 *'69*
Sergeant Klems *'71*
Don't Look Now *'73*
The Bloodstained Shadow *'78*

Rade Serbedzija (1946-)
Before the Rain *'94*
The Truce *'96*
Polish Wedding *'97*
The Saint *'97*
Lies and Whispers *'98*
Mighty Joe Young *'98*
Eyes Wide Shut *'99*
Stigmata *'99*
Mission: Impossible 2 *'00*
Snatch *'00*
Space Cowboys *'00*
Quicksand *'01*
Rodgers & Hammerstein's South Pacific *'01*
The Quiet American *'02*
Eurotrip *'04*
The Fever *'04*
The Fog *'05*
Go West *'05*
The Keeper: The Legend of Omar Khayyam *'05*
The Elder Son *'06*
Moscow Zero *'06*
Battle in Seattle *'07*
Shooter *'07*
The Eye *'08*
Quarantine *'08*
The Code *'09*
Middle Men *'10*
In the Land of Blood and Honey *'11*
Taken 2 *'12*
The Legend of Hercules *'14*

Ivan Sergei (1971-)
Gunfighter's Moon *'96*
Mother, May I Sleep With Danger? *'96*
Once a Thief *'96*
The Opposite of Sex *'98*
The Big Day *'99*
Playing Mona Lisa *'00*
The Break-Up *'06*
Santa Baby *'06*
High Noon *'09*
Sundays at Tiffany's *'10*
Jewtopia *'12*
Hidden Away *'13*

Brian Sergent (1959-)
Meet the Feebles *'89 (V)*
Eagle *vs.* Shark *'07*
Slow West *'15*

Yahoo Serious (1953-)
Young Einstein *'89*
Reckless Kelly *'93*
Mr. Accident *'99*

Andy Serkis (1964-)
Stella Does Tricks *'96*
Career Girls *'97*
Among Giants *'98*
The Jolly Boys' Last Stand *'00*
Oliver Twist *'00*
Pandaemonium *'00*
Shiner *'00*
Lord of the Rings: The Fellowship of the Ring *'01*
24 Hour Party People *'01*
Deathwatch *'02*
Lord of the Rings: The Two Towers *'02 (V)*
Lord of the Rings: The Return of the King *'03*
13 Going on 30 *'04*
King Kong *'05*
Alex Rider: Operation Stormbreaker *'06*
Flushed Away *'06 (V)*
Longford *'06*
The Prestige *'06*
Extraordinary Rendition *'07*
Sugarhouse *'07*
Little Dorrit *'08*
Inkheart *'09*
Brighton Rock *'10*
Burke & Hare *'10*
Sex & Drugs & Rock & Roll *'10*
The Adventures of Tintin *'11 (V)*
Rise of the Planet of the Apes *'11*
The Hobbit: An Unexpected Journey *'12 (V)*
Dawn of the Planet of the Apes *'14*
War for the Planet of the Apes *'17*
Mowgli: Legend of the Jungle *'18*
Long Shot *'19*

Assumpta Serna (1957-)
Matador *'86*
I, the Worst of All *'90*
Wild Orchid *'90*
Sharpe's Eagle *'93*
Sharpe's Rifles *'93*
Hidden Assassin *'94*
Sharpe's Company *'94*
Sharpe's Enemy *'94*
The Craft *'96*
Piano Tuner of Earthquakes *'05*
Uncertainty *'08*

Pepe Serna (1944-)
The Student Nurses *'70*
Shoot Out *'71*
Sniper *'75*
Tarantulas: The Deadly Cargo *'77*
The Jerk *'79*
Scarface *'83*
The Adventures of Buckaroo Banzai Across the Eighth Dimension *'84*
Fandango *'85*
Break of Dawn *'88*
Bad Jim *'89*
The Rookie *'90*
American Me *'92*
A Million to Juan *'94*
Devil's Knight *'03*
Latin Dragon *'03*
The Black Dahlia *'06*

Jacques Sernas (1925-2015)
The Golden Salamander *'51*
Barrier of the Law *'54*
Jump Into Hell *'55*
Helen of Troy *'56*
La Dolce Vita *'60*
The Slave *'62*
55 Days at Peking *'63*
Fort Yuma Gold *'66*
Hornets' Nest *'70*

Raymond Serra (1931-2003)
Alphabet City *'84*
Splitz *'84*
Sugar Hill *'94*
Gotti *'96*
Wannabes *'01*

Diego Serrano (1973-)
Mixing Nia *'98*
The 24 Hour Woman *'99*

Julieta Serrano (1933-)
Dark Habits *'84*
Matador *'86*
Women on the Verge of a Nervous Breakdown *'88*
Tie Me Up! Tie Me Down! *'90*
Caresses *'97*
A Love to Keep *'07*
Pain and Glory *'19*

Nestor Serrano
Brenda Starr *'86*
The Money Pit *'86*
Lethal Weapon 2 *'89*
Hangin' with the Homeboys *'91*
I Love Trouble *'94*
Bad Boys *'95*
City Hall *'95*
The Negotiator *'98*
Bringing Out the Dead *'99*
The Insider *'99*
Bait *'00*
City by the Sea *'02*
Empire *'02*
Showtime *'02*
Runaway Jury *'03*
Undefeated *'03*
The Day After Tomorrow *'04*
Sueno *'05*
Definitely, Maybe *'08*
Secretariat *'10*
Act of Valor *'12*

Rosa Maria Serrano (1964-)
See Rosie Perez

Christian Serratos (1990-)
Twilight *'08*
The Twilight Saga: New Moon *'09*
The Twilight Saga: Eclipse *'10*
96 Minutes *'11*

Michel Serrault (1928-2007)
Diabolique *'55*
Love on a Pillow *'62*
The King of Hearts *'66*
The Holes *'72*
La Cage aux Folles *'78*
The Associate *'79*
Buffet Froid *'79*
La Cage aux Folles 2 *'81*
La Cage aux Folles 3: The Wedding *'86*
Nelly et Monsieur Arnaud *'95*
Beaumarchais the Scoundrel *'96*
Artemisia *'97*
The Swindle *'97*
Belphegor: Phantom of the Louvre *'01*
The Girl from Paris *'02*
Joyeux Noel *'05*

Henri Serre (1931-)
Jules and Jim *'62*
The Fire Within *'64*

Ignacio Serricchio
Keith *'08*
The Wedding Ringer *'15*

Jean Servais (1910-76)
Le Plaisir *'52 (N)*
Rififi *'54*
Fever Mounts at El Pao *'59*
Murder at 45 R.P.M. *'65*
Black Jesus *'68*
They Came to Rob Las Vegas *'68*
The Devil's Nightmare *'71*

What Planet Are You From? '00
Town and Country '01
Over the Hedge '06 (V)
Trust the Man '06
Iron Man 2 '10

Sara Shane (1928-)
The King and Four Queens '56
Three Bad Sisters '56
Tarzan's Greatest Adventure '59

Michael Shaner
Bloodfist '89
Traveller '96

Amelia Shankley (1972-)
Dreamchild '85
The Little Princess '87

Don Shanks (1950-)
Halloween 5: The Revenge of Michael Myers '89
Spirit of the Eagle '90
The Legend of Wolf Mountain '92
3 Ninjas Knuckle Up '95

Michael Shanks (1970-)
Terror Train '80
Suspicious River '00
Under the Mistletoe '06
Judicial Indiscretion '07
Megasnake '07
The Lost Treasure of the Grand Canyon '08
Stargate: Continuum '08
Stargate: The Ark of Truth '08
Christmas Lodge '11
Faces in the Crowd '11
The Pastor's Wife '11
Red Riding Hood '11
Tactical Force '11
The Bouquet '13
Mr. Hockey: The Gordie Howe Story '13

Fay Shannon (1918-)
See Fay McKenzie

Frank Shannon (1874-1959)
Flash Gordon Conquers the Universe '40
Flash Gordon: Rocketship '40

Harry Shannon (1890-1964)
Citizen Kane '41
The Saint in Palm Springs '41
Idaho '43
The Red House '47
Feudin', Fussin', and A-Fightin' '48
Cow Town '50
The Jackie Robinson Story '50
The Underworld Story '50
Witness to Murder '54
Written on the Wind '56
Man or Gun '58
Summer and Smoke '61

Martin Shannon
Back Against the Wall '00
Chicago Overcoat '09

Michael Shannon (1974-)
Chicago Cab '98
Pearl Harbor '01
Vanilla Sky '01
8 Mile '02
High Crimes '02
Kangaroo Jack '02
Bad Boys 2 '03
Grand Theft Parsons '03
Dead Birds '04
The Woodsman '04
Bug '06
Let's Go to Prison '06
World Trade Center '06
Before the Devil Knows You're Dead '07
Lucky You '07
Shotgun Stories '07
Revolutionary Road '08
Bad Lieutenant: Port of Call New Orleans '09
The Greatest '09
The Missing Person '09
My Son, My Son, What Have Ye Done '09
Jonah Hex '10
The Runaways '10
13 '10
The Broken Tower '11
Machine Gun Preacher '11
Return '11
Take Shelter '11
The Iceman '12
Mud '12
Premium Rush '12
Man of Steel '13
99 Homes '14
Young Ones '14
Freeheld '15
Complete Unknown '16
Elvis & Nixon '16
Frank & Lola '16
Loving '16
Midnight Special '16
Nocturnal Animals '16
The Shape of Water '17
12 Strong '18
What They Had '18
The Current War: Director's Cut '19
Knives Out '19

Michael J. Shannon (1943-)
We'll Meet Again '82
Pride and Extreme Prejudice '90
Detonator 2: Night Watch '95

Molly Shannon (1964-)
The Phantom of the Opera '89
Dinner and Driving '97
Analyze This '98
A Night at the Roxbury '98
Never Been Kissed '99
Superstar '99
Dr. Seuss' How the Grinch Stole Christmas '00
My 5 Wives '00
Osmosis Jones '01
Serendipity '01
Wet Hot American Summer '01
American Splendor '03
Good Boy! '03
My Boss's Daughter '03
The Twelve Days of Christmas Eve '04
Gray Matters '06
Little Man '06
Marie Antoinette '06
Scary Movie 4 '06
Talladega Nights: The Ballad of Ricky Bobby '06
Evan Almighty '07
More of Me '07
Year of the Dog '07
Igor '08 (V)
Snow Buddies '08
What Goes Up '09
Hotel Transylvania '12 (V)
Scary Movie 5 '13
Life After Beth '14
Addicted to Fresno '15
Other People '16
Miles '17
Horse Girl '20

Peggy Shannon (1907-41)
False Faces '32
Girl Missing '33
Turn Back the Clock '33
The Case of the Lucky Legs '35

Polly Shannon (1973-)
The Girl Next Door '98
Hard to Forget '98
The Triangle '01
Men with Brooms '02
Do or Die '03
Jesse Stone: Stone Cold '05
Jesse Stone: Night Passage '06
Hide '08
Hydra '09

Richard Shannon (1920-89)
The Bridges at Toko-Ri '55
The Space Children '58

Vicellous Shannon (1971-)
The Hurricane '99
Dancing in September '00
Freedom Song '00
Hart's War '02
Annapolis '06
Animal 2 '07
Distorted '18

Bing Shao
Rhapsody of Spring '98
The Lost Bladesman '16

Brighton Sharbino
Miracles From Heaven '16
Growing Up Smith '17
Urban Country '18

Saxon Sharbino
Trust Me '13
Poltergeist '15

Omar Sharif (1932-2015)
Lawrence of Arabia '62
Behold a Pale Horse '64
The Fall of the Roman Empire '64
The Yellow Rolls Royce '64
Doctor Zhivago '65
Genghis Khan '65
More Than a Miracle '67
Night of the Generals '67
Funny Girl '68
Mayerling '68
MacKenna's Gold '69
The Horsemen '70
The Last Valley '71
Juggernaut '74
The Tamarind Seed '74
Crime & Passion '75
Funny Lady '75
Ashanti, Land of No Mercy '79
Oh, Heavenly Dog! '80
Green Ice '81
The Far Pavilions '84
Top Secret! '84
Anastasia: The Mystery of Anna '86
Beyond Justice '92
Grand Larceny '92
Catherine the Great '95
Gulliver's Travels '95
Heaven Before I Die '96 (C)
The 13th Warrior '99
Shaka Zulu: The Last Great Warrior '01
Monsieur Ibrahim '03
Hidalgo '04
The Crown Prince '06
One Night with the King '06
10,000 B.C. '08 (N)
The Last Templar '09

David Shark (1962-)
See David 'Shark' Fralick

Ray Sharkey (1953-93)
Who'll Stop the Rain? '78
Heart Beat '80
Idolmaker '80
Love and Money '80
Some Kind of Hero '82
Regina '83
Body Rock '84
Behind Enemy Lines '85
No Mercy '86
Wise Guys '86
Capone '89
Relentless 2: Dead On '91
Zebrahead '92
Cop and a Half '93
Urban Crossfire '94

Kunal Sharma (1987-)
The Cheetah Girls: One World '08
The Kids Are All Right '10
Red Line '13

Suraj Sharma
Life of Pi '12
Million Dollar Arm '14
Happy Death Day 2U '19
Killerman '19

Alex Sharp
How To Talk To Girls At Parties '17
The Hustle '19

Lesley Sharp (1960-)
Rita, Sue & Bob Too '87
The Rachel Papers '89
Close My Eyes '91
Naked '93
Priest '94
The Full Monty '96
Great Expectations '99
From Hell '01
Carrie's War '04
The Diary of Anne Frank '08
Return to Cranford '09

Timm Sharp (1978-)
Stark Raving Mad '02
King of the Ants '03
Americano '05
The New Romantic '18

Albert Sharpe (1885-1970)
Up in Central Park '48
Adventure in Baltimore '49
Brigadoon '54
Darby O'Gill & the Little People '59
The Day They Robbed the Bank of England '60

Cornelia Sharpe (1943-)
Serpico '73
Busting '74
The Arab Conspiracy '76
Venom '82

Karen Sharpe (1934-)
Bomba and the Jungle Girl '52
Man in the Vault '56
Tarawa Beachhead '58

Isaac Sharry (1968-)
Dad On the Run '00
Ultimate Heist '09

Melanie Shatner (1964-)
Star Trek 5: The Final Frontier '89
Syngenor '90
Unknown Origin '95

William Shatner (1931-)
The Brothers Karamazov '58
The Explosive Generation '61
Judgment at Nuremberg '61
Shame '61
The Outrage '64
Incubus '65
White Comanche '68
The Andersonville Trial '70
The People '71
The Horror at 37,000 Feet '73
Pioneer Woman '73
Big Bad Mama '74
Impulse '74
Devil's Rain '75
Kingdom of the Spiders '77
Testimony of Two Men '77
The Bastard '78
Little Women '78
Star Trek: The Motion Picture '79
The Kidnapping of the President '80
Airplane 2: The Sequel '82
Star Trek 2: The Wrath of Khan '82
Visiting Hours '82
Secrets of a Married Man '84
Star Trek 3: The Search for Spock '84
Star Trek 4: The Voyage Home '86
Broken Angel '88
Star Trek 5: The Final Frontier '89
Bill & Ted's Bogus Journey '91
Star Trek 6: The Undiscovered Country '91
Family of Strangers '93
National Lampoon's Loaded Weapon 1 '93
Star Trek: Generations '94
TekWar '94
Double Play '96
Free Enterprise '98
Land of the Free '98
Miss Congeniality '00
Osmosis Jones '01 (V)
American Psycho 2: All American Girl '02
Groom Lake '02
Shoot or Be Shot '02
Showtime '02
Dodgeball: A True Underdog Story '04
Miss Congeniality 2: Armed and Fabulous '05
Over the Hedge '06 (V)
The Wild '06 (V)
Everest '07
Escape From Planet Earth '13 (V)
A Christmas Horror Story '15

Shari Shattuck (1960-)
Number One with a Bullet '87
Tainted '88
The Uninvited '88
Body Chemistry 3: Point of Seduction '93
Out for Blood '93

Grant Shaud (1961-)
Wall Street '87
The Distinguished Gentleman '92
From the Earth to the Moon '98
The Crow: Salvation '00
Waltzing Anna '06

Charles Shaughnessy (1955-)
Something About Sex '98
Get a Clue '02
Kids in America '05
Soldiers of Change '06
Deadly Shift '08
The Tale of Despereaux '08 (V)
Love's Christmas Journey '11
Mardi Gras: Spring Break '11
Liz & Dick '12

Mickey Shaughnessy (1920-85)
From Here to Eternity '53
Conquest of Space '55
The Burglar '57
Designing Woman '57
Jailhouse Rock '57
The Sheepman '58
Edge of Eternity '59
The Hangman '59
The Adventures of Huckleberry Finn '60
Sex Kittens Go to College '60
Dondi '61
The King of the Roaring '20s: The Story of Arnold Rothstein '61
Pocketful of Miracles '61
My Dog, the Thief '69
Primal Scream '87

Billy Joe Shaver (1939-)
The Apostle '97
Bait Shop '08

Helen Shaver (1951-)
Outrageous! '77
In Praise of Older Women '78
The Amityville Horror '79
Harry Tracy '83
The Osterman Weekend '83
Best Defense '84
The Park Is Mine '85
The Color of Money '86
Desert Hearts '86
The Believers '87
The Land Before Time '88 (V)
Zebrahead '92
Morning Glory '93
That Night '93
Born to Be Wild '95
Open Season '95
The Craft '96
Poltergeist: The Legacy '96
Rowing Through '96
Tremors 2: Aftershocks '96
We All Fall Down '00
Tremors 3: Back to Perfection '01
Numb '07
A Very Merry Daughter of the Bride '08

Anabel Shaw (1921-2010)
Shock! '46
Gun Crazy '49
To Hell and Back '55

Artie Shaw
Dancing Co-Ed '39
Second Chorus '40

Bobbi Shaw (1943-)
Pajama Party '64
Beach Blanket Bingo '65
How to Stuff a Wild Bikini '65
Ski Party '65
Ghost in the Invisible Bikini '66

C. Montague Shaw (1884-1968)
The Rains Came '39
Zorro's Fighting Legion '39
Holt of the Secret Service '42
Thunder Birds '42

Crystal Shaw
Hardbodies '84
Laser Moon '92

Fiona Shaw (1958-)
My Left Foot '89
Mountains of the Moon '90
Three Men and a Little Lady '90
Super Mario Bros. '93
Undercover Blues '93
Persuasion '95
Anna Karenina '96
Jane Eyre '96
The Butcher Boy '97
The Avengers '98
The Last September '99
RKO 281 '99
Harry Potter and the Sorcerer's Stone '01
The Seventh Stream '01
The Triumph of Love '01
Close Your Eyes '02
Harry Potter and the Chamber of Secrets '02
The Black Dahlia '06
Catch and Release '07
Fracture '07
Harry Potter and the Order of the Phoenix '07
Dorian Gray '09
Harry Potter and the Half-Blood Prince '09
The Tree of Life '11
The English Teacher '13 (N)

Frances Shaw
Someone Marry Barry '12
The Pretty One '14

Frankie Shaw
Explicit Ills '08
Falling Up '08
Stronger '17

Joe Norman Shaw (1957-)
Lies My Mother Told Me '05
Lost Holiday: The Jim & Suzanne Shemwell Story '07
Moondance Alexander '07
Made in Romania '10

John Shaw
The Foursome '06
Wyvern '09

Lindsey Shaw (1989-)
Teen Spirit '11
Love Me '12

Martin Shaw (1945-)
Macbeth '71
Golden Voyage of Sinbad '73
Operation Daybreak '75
The Hound of the Baskervilles '83
The Last Place on Earth '85
The Scarlet Pimpernel '99

The War at Home '96
Hostile Waters '97
Spawn '97
Truth or Consequences, N.M. '97
Gunfighter '98
Monument Ave. '98
No Code of Conduct '98
A Stranger in the Kingdom '98
D.R.E.A.M. Team '99
Lost and Found '99
Storm Tracker '99
A Texas Funeral '99
Thrill Seekers '99
O '01
Catch Me If You Can '02
Bobby '06
Bordertown '06
The Departed '06
Talk to Me '07
Echelon Conspiracy '09
Imagine That '09
Love Happens '09
The Way '10
The Double '11
The Amazing Spider-Man '12
Stella Days '12
The Whale '13
Selma '14
Trash '14
The Vessel '16

Michael Sheen (1969-)
Mary Reilly '95
Othello '95
Wilde '97
The Four Feathers '02
Bright Young Things '03
Timeline '03
Underworld '03
Laws of Attraction '04
Kingdom of Heaven '05
Underworld: Evolution '05
Blood Diamond '06
The Queen '06
Music Within '07
Frost/Nixon '08
The Damned United '09
The Twilight Saga: New Moon '09
Underworld: Rise of the Lycans '09
Alice in Wonderland '10
Beautiful Boy '10
The Special Relationship '10
Tron: Legacy '10
Unthinkable '10
Few Options '11
Midnight in Paris '11
The Twilight Saga: Breaking Dawn, Part 1 '11
Jesus Henry Christ '12
The Twilight Saga: Breaking Dawn, Part 2 '12
Admission '13
The Adventurer: The Curse of the Midas Box '13
Kill the Messenger '14
Passengers '16
Brad's Status '17
Home Again '17
Norman '17
Dolittle '20
How to Build a Girl '20

Ruth Sheen (1952-)
High Hopes '88
The Young Poisoner's Handbook '94
All or Nothing '02
Vera Drake '04
Another Year '10
Heartless '10
Mr. Turner '14

Craig Sheffer (1960-)
That Was Then. . . This Is Now '85
Fire with Fire '86
Some Kind of Wonderful '87
Voyage of the Rock Aliens '87
Split Decisions '88
Babycakes '89
Instant Karma '90
Nightbreed '90
Blue Desert '91
Eye of the Storm '91
A River Runs Through It '92
Fire in the Sky '93
Fire on the Amazon '93
The Program '93
The Desperate Trail '94
Sleep with Me '94
In Pursuit of Honor '95
The Road Killers '95
Bliss '96
Head Above Water '96
Flypaper '97
Miss Evers' Boys '97
Executive Power '98
The Fall '98
Shadow of Doubt '98
Turbulence 2: Fear of Flying '99
Deep Core '00
Hellraiser 5: Inferno '00
Turbulence 3: Heavy Metal '00
Maze '01
Tales from the Crypt Presents Ritual '02
Dracula 2: Ascension '03
The Second Front '05
Long Lost Son '06
Love Lies Bleeding '07
While She Was Out '08
The Mark '12
The Mark 2: Redemption '13
Code of Honor '16

Jeremy Sheffield (1966-)
Merlin '98
The Wedding Date '05
The Children '08

John(ny) Sheffield (1931-2010)
Tarzan Finds a Son '39
Tarzan's Secret Treasure '41
Tarzan's New York Adventure '42
Tarzan Triumphs '43
Tarzan's Desert Mystery '43
Tarzan and the Amazons '45
Tarzan and the Leopard Woman '46
Tarzan and the Huntress '47
Bomba on Panther Island '49
Bomba, the Jungle Boy '49
Bomba and the Hidden City '50
The Lost Volcano '50
Elephant Stampede '51
The Lion Hunters '51
African Treasure '52
Bomba and the Jungle Girl '52
Safari Drums '53
The Golden Idol '54
Killer Leopard '54
Lord of the Jungle '55

Reginald (Reggie, Reggy) Sheffield (1901-57)
Old English '30
Gunga Din '39

Kate Lyn Sheil
Sun Don't Shine '12
The Sacrament '13
Kate Plays Christine '16
Buster's Mal Heart '17

David S. Sheiner
Battle Creek Brawl '80
News at Eleven '86

Gene Sheldon (1908-82)
The Dolly Sisters '46
Toby Tyler '59
The Sign of Zorro '60

Irit Sheleg
Fill the Void '12
The Wedding Plan '17

Tom Shell
Surf Nazis Must Die '87
Beverly Hills Vamp '88
Teenage Exorcist '93

Stephen Shellen (1957-)
The Stepfather '87
Casual Sex? '88
Murder One '88
Damned River '89
Victim of Beauty '91
A River Runs Through It '92
Dr. Jekyll and Ms. Hyde '95
Rude '96
Luscious '97

Barbara Shelley (1932-)
Blood of the Vampire '58
Bobbikins '59
Village of the Damned '60
Postman's Knock '62
Blind Corner '63
The Gorgon '64
Dracula, Prince of Darkness '66
Rasputin the Mad Monk '66

Carol(e) Shelley (1939-)
The Odd Couple '68
The Aristocats '70 (V)
Robin Hood '73 (V)
The Whoopee Boys '86
Hercules '97 (V)
Bewitched '05

Rachel Shelley (1969-)
Photographing Fairies '97
B.U.S.T.E.D. '99
Dead of Night '99
Lagaan: Once upon a Time in India '01
Gray Matters '06
The Children '08

Adrienne Shelly (1966-2006)
Trust '90
The Unbelievable Truth '90
Big Girls Don't Cry. . . They Get Even '92
Hexed '93
Sleep with Me '94
The Road Killers '95
Grind '96
Sudden Manhattan '96
Wrestling with Alligators '98
I'll Take You There '99
Dead Dog '00
Revolution #9 '01
Factotum '06
Waitress '07

Anne Shelton
Miss London Ltd. '43
Bees in Paradise '44

Deborah Shelton (1948-)
Mysterious Island of Beautiful Women '79
Body Double '84
Hunk '87
Plughead Rewired: Circuitry Man 2 '94
Surprise, Surprise '09

John Shelton (1917-72)
Ghost City '32
Whispering Ghosts '42
The Time of Their Lives '46
Sins of Jezebel '54

Joy Shelton (1922-2000)
Bees in Paradise '44
Waterloo Road '45
Norman Conquest '53

Lynn Shelton (1946-2020)
Humpday '09
The Off Hours '11

Marley Shelton (1974-)
Grand Canyon '91
The Sandlot '93
Lured Innocence '97
Trojan War '97
Warriors of Virtue '97
Pleasantville '98
Too Smooth '98
The Bachelor '99
Never Been Kissed '99
Bubble Boy '01
On the Borderline '01
Sugar & Spice '01
Valentine '01
Just a Kiss '02
Dallas 362 '03
Grand Theft Parsons '03
Uptown Girls '03
Don't Come Knocking '05
Sin City '05
American Dreamz '06
The Last Kiss '06
Death Proof '07
Planet Terror '07
The Mighty Macs '09
A Perfect Getaway '09
(Untitled) '09
Women in Trouble '09
Elektra Luxx '10
Scream 4 '11

Uriah Shelton
The Nanny Express '08
Lifted '10
Enter the Warriors Gate '17

Parry Shen (1973-)
Shrieker '97
Better Luck Tomorrow '02
The New Guy '02
The Hazing '04
The Gene Generation '07
Hatchet '07
Hatchet 2 '10

Paul Shenar (1936-89)
Scarface '83
Brass '85
Dream Lover '85
Raw Deal '86
The Bedroom Window '87
Best Seller '87
The Big Blue '88

Alexander Fu Sheng
The Chinatown Kid '78
The Brave Archer and His Mate '82

Ben Shenkman (1968-)
Pi '98
Chasing Sleep '00
Table One '00
Roger Dodger '02
Angels in America '03
Just like Heaven '05
Must Love Dogs '05
Breakfast With Scot '07
Then She Found Me '07
Brief Interviews With Hideous Men '09
Blue Valentine '10
Breathe In '13
Concussion '13

Dax Shepard (1975-)
Without a Paddle '04
Zathura '05
Employee of the Month '06
Idiocracy '06
Let's Go to Prison '06
The Comebacks '07
Baby Mama '08
Smother '08
When in Rome '09
The Freebie '10
Brother's Justice '11
Hit and Run '12
The Judge '14
This Is Where I Leave You '14
CHIPS '17

Hilary Shepard (1961-)
Peacemaker '90
Avalanche '99

Jewel Shepard (1958-)
My Tutor '82
Return of the Living Dead '85
Scenes from the Goldmine '87
Scanners: The Showdown '94

Patty (Patti) Shepard (1945-2013)
Dracula *vs.* Frankenstein '69
The Werewolf *vs.* the Vampire Woman '70
Crypt of the Living Dead '73
Curse of the Devil '73

Sam Shepard (1943-2017)
Days of Heaven '78
Resurrection '80
Raggedy Man '81
Frances '82
The Right Stuff '83
Country '84
Crimes of the Heart '86
Fool for Love '86
Baby Boom '87
Steel Magnolias '89
Bright Angel '91
Defenseless '91
Thunderheart '92
The Pelican Brief '93
Safe Passage '94
The Good Old Boys '95
Larry McMurtry's Streets of Laredo '95
Lily Dale '96
Curtain Call '97
The Only Thrill '97
Purgatory '99
Snow Falling on Cedars '99
All the Pretty Horses '00
Hamlet '00
The Pledge '00
Black Hawk Down '01
Shot in the Heart '01
Swordfish '01
Leo '02
The Notebook '04
Don't Come Knocking '05
Stealth '05
Bandidas '06
Charlotte's Web '06 (V)
The Return '06
Walker Payne '06
The Assassination of Jesse James by the Coward Robert Ford '07
The Accidental Husband '08
Felon '08
Brothers '09
Fair Game '10
Inhale '10
Blackthorn '11
Darling Companion '12
Killing Them Softly '12
Mud '12
Safe House '12
August: Osage County '13
Cold in July '14
Savannah '14
Ithaca '16
Midnight Special '16
In Dubious Battle '17

Quinn Shephard (1995-)
Unaccompanied Minors '06
Blame '17
Midnight Sun '18
The Miseducation of Cameron Post '18

Chaz Lamar Shepherd (1977-)
Set It Off '96
The Temptations '98

Cybill Shepherd (1950-)
The Last Picture Show '71
The Heartbreak Kid '72
Daisy Miller '74
Taxi Driver '76
A Guide for the Married Woman '78
Americathon '79
The Lady Vanishes '79
Secrets of a Married Man '84
Moonlighting '85
Seduced '85
The Long, Hot Summer '86
Chances Are '89
Alice '90
Texasville '90
Once Upon a Crime '92
Married to It '93
The Last Word '95
Due East '02
Open Window '06
High Noon '09
Mrs. Washington Goes to Smith '09
Barry Munday '10
The Client List '10
Listen to Your Heart '10
Do You Believe? '15

Elizabeth Shepherd (1936-)
Blind Corner '63
Tomb of Ligeia '64
Hell Boats '70
Verdict in Blood '02

Jack Shepherd (1940-)
All Neat in Black Stockings '69
The Virgin Soldiers '69
Count Dracula '77
Escape from Sobibor '87
No Escape '94
The Scarlet Tunic '97
Wonderland '99
Charlotte Gray '01
Lorna Doone '01
The Other Boleyn Girl '03
God on Trial '08

Jean Shepherd (1921-99)
A Christmas Story '83 (CN)
My Summer Story '94 (N)

John Shepherd
Friday the 13th, Part 5: A New Beginning '85
Banzai Runner '86

Scott Shepherd
And So It Goes '14
Bridge of Spies '15
Hostiles '17

Sherri Shepherd (1967-)
Beauty Shop '05
Guess Who '05
Who's Your Caddy? '07
Madagascar: Escape 2 Africa '08 (V)
Precious: Based on the Novel 'Push' by Sapphire '09
Abducted: The Carlina White Story '12
One for the Money '12
Brian Banks '18

Simon Shepherd (1956-)
Henry V '89
Emily Brontë's Wuthering Heights '92
Tales of Erotica '93
Catherine Cookson's Tilly Trotter '99

Steve John Shepherd (1973-)
Forgive and Forget '99
Virtual Sexuality '99
Me Without You '01
The Bad Mother's Handbook '07

Suzanne Shepherd
The Jerky Boys '95
Palookaville '95
Lolita '97
A Dirty Shame '04
Harold '08
Where Is Kyra? '17

W. Morgan Shepherd (1932-)
See William Morgan Sheppard

Tiffany Shepis (1979-)
The Hazing '04
Abominable '06
Nightmare Man '06
Bonnie and Clyde *vs.* Dracula '08
Home Sick '08
The Frankenstein Syndrome '10

Michael Shepley (1907-61)
Henry V '44
Mine Own Executioner '47

Delia Sheppard (1961-)
Witchcraft 2: The Temptress '90
Mirror Images '91
Animal Instincts '92
Secret Games '92
Dinocroc Vs. Supergator '10

Mark Sheppard (1964-)
In the Name of the Father '93
Out of the Cold '99
Lost Voyage '01
Deep Shock '03
Megalodon '03
Evil Eyes '04

Paula Sheppard (1957-)
Alice Sweet Alice '76
Liquid Sky '83

William Morgan Sheppard (1932-)
The Duellists '77
Shogun '80
Hawk the Slayer '81
Sea Wolves '81
Lassiter '84
Elvira, Mistress of the Dark '88
Wild at Heart '90

Pizza '05
The Cake Eaters '07
5 Flights Up '15
Puerto Ricans in Paris '16

Dinah Shore (1917-94)
Thank Your Lucky Stars '43
Up in Arms '44
Till the Clouds Roll By '46
Fun & Fancy Free '47 *(N)*
Oh, God! '77

Pauly Shore (1968-)
18 Again! '88
Phantom of the Mall: Eric's Revenge '89
Encino Man '92
Son-in-Law '93
In the Army Now '94
Jury Duty '95
Bio-Dome '96
The Bogus Witch Project '00
The Wash '01
Adopted '09
Opposite Day '09

Columbus Short (1982-)
Accepted '06
Save the Last Dance 2 '06
Stomp the Yard '07
This Christmas '07
Cadillac Records '08
Quarantine '08
Armored '09
Whiteout '09
Death at a Funeral '10
The Losers '10
Stomp the Yard 2: Homecoming '10
American Violence '17

Dorothy Short (1915-63)
Assassin of Youth '35
Savage Fury '35
Reefer Madness '38

Florence Short (1889-1946)
The Love Flower '20
Way Down East '20

Martin Short (1950-)
Lost and Found '79
Sunset Limousine '83
Three Amigos '86
Innerspace '87
Cross My Heart '88
The Big Picture '89
Three Fugitives '89
Father of the Bride '91
Pure Luck '91
Captain Ron '92
Clifford '92
The Return of Spinal Tap '92 *(C)*
We're Back! A Dinosaur's Story '93 *(V)*
The Pebble and the Penguin '94 *(V)*
Father of the Bride Part 2 '95
Jungle 2 Jungle '96
Mars Attacks! '96
A Simple Wish '97
Merlin '98
Prince of Egypt '98 *(V)*
Alice in Wonderland '99
Mumford '99
Get Over It! '01
Jimmy Neutron: Boy Genius '01 *(V)*
Treasure Planet '02 *(V)*
Jiminy Glick in LaLa Wood '05
The Santa Clause 3: The Escape Clause '06
The Spiderwick Chronicles '08 *(V)*
Hoodwinked Too! Hood *vs.* Evil '11 *(V)*
Frankenweenie '12 *(V)*
Inherent Vice '14
Legends of Oz: Dorothy's Return '14 *(V)*
The Willoughbys '20

Richard Short
Delirious '06
Cafe '10

Ken Shorter (1945-)
Ned Kelly '70
Dragonheart: A New Beginning '00

Pat Shortt (1966-)
American Women '00
Life's a Breeze '14

Robin Shou (1960-)
Beverly Hills Ninja '96
Mortal Kombat 2: Annihilation '97
18 Fingers of Death '05
DOA: Dead or Alive '06
Street Fighter: The Legend of Chun-Li '09

Frida Show (1979-)
Lost Colony: The Legend of Roanoke '07
Contract Killers '08
Cyclops '08

Grant Show (1962-)
A Woman, Her Men and Her Futon '92
Texas '94
The Alchemists '99
Encrypt '03
Sex and the Single Mom '03
More Sex and the Single Mom '05
The Natalee Holloway Story '09
Born 2 Race '11
Justice for Natalee '11
The Possession '12

Max (Casey Adams) Showalter (1917-2000)
My Wife's Best Friend '52
Niagara '52
What Price Glory? '52
Dangerous Crossing '53
Destination Gobi '53
Down Three Dark Streets '54
Night People '54
Bus Stop '56
The Indestructible Man '56
The Monster That Challenged the World '57
Summer and Smoke '61
Move Over, Darling '63
Fate Is the Hunter '64
Lord Love a Duck '66
Racing with the Moon '84
Sixteen Candles '84

Michael Showalter (1970-)
Wet Hot American Summer '01
The Baxter '05
Four and a Half Women '05

Kathy Shower (1953-)
The Further Adventures of Tennessee Buck '88
American Kickboxer 2: To the Death '93
Sexual Malice '93
To the Limit '95

John Shrapnel (1942-2020)
How to Get Ahead in Advertising '89
Two Deaths '94
Gladiator '00
The Body '01
K-19: The Widowmaker '02
Troy '04
Elizabeth: The Golden Age '07
Mirrors '08

Lex Shrapnel (1979-)
Thunderbirds '04
Seal Team 8: Behind Enemy Lines '14

Kin Shriner (1953-)
Vendetta '85
Angel 3: The Final Chapter '88
Hoot '06

Sonny Shroyer (1935-)
Payday '73
The Longest Yard '74
Gator '76
Smokey and the Bandit '77
They Went That-a-Way & That-a-Way '78

The Devil & Max Devlin '81
Forrest Gump '94
Bastard out of Carolina '96
The Gingerbread Man '97
John Grisham's The Rainmaker '97
Wild America '97
The Runaway '00
The Rosa Parks Story '02
A Love Song for Bobby Long '04

Qi Shu (1976-)
Gorgeous '99
So Close '02
The Eye 2 '04
Seoul Raiders '05
Blood Brothers '07
Journey to the West '14
The Assassin '15

Karin Shubert (1944-)
See Karin Schubert

Andrew Shue (1967-)
The Karate Kid '84
John Grisham's The Rainmaker '97
Gracie '07

Elisabeth Shue (1963-)
The Karate Kid '84
Link '86
Adventures in Babysitting '87
Cocktail '88
Back to the Future, Part 2 '89
Back to the Future, Part 3 '90
The Marrying Man '91
Soapdish '91
Heart and Souls '93
Twenty Bucks '93
Blind Justice '94
Radio Inside '94
Leaving Las Vegas '95
The Underneath '95
The Trigger Effect '96
Cousin Bette '97
Deconstructing Harry '97
The Saint '97
Palmetto '98
Molly '99
Hollow Man '00
Leo '02
Tuck Everlasting '02 *(N)*
Mysterious Skin '04
Dreamer: Inspired by a True Story '05
Hide and Seek '05
Gracie '07
Hamlet 2 '08
Don McKay '09
Janie Jones '10
Piranha 3D '10
Waking Madison '10
Chasing Mavericks '12
Hope Springs '12
House at the End of the Street '12
Death Wish '18

Richard B. Shull (1929-99)
The Anderson Tapes '71
Slither '73
Sssssss '73
Cockfighter '74
The Big Bus '76
The Pack '77
Heartbeeps '81
Splash '84
Unfaithfully Yours '84
Housesitter '92
Trapped in Paradise '94

Constance Shulman (1958-)
Doug's 1st Movie '99 *(V)*
Sweet and Lowdown '99

Harry Shum, Jr. (1982-)
Step Up 3D '10
White Frog '12
Revenge of the Green Dragons '14
Crouching Tiger, Hidden Dragon: Sword of Destiny '16

Iris Shunn (1915-80)
See Iris Meredith

Antonina Shuranova (1936-)
War and Peace '68
An Unfinished Piece for a Player Piano '77

Daryl Shuttleworth (1960-)
In Her Mother's Footsteps '06
Safe Harbor '06
Shock to the System '06
Secrets of an Undercover Wife '07
Ice Blues: A Donald Strachey Mystery '08
On the Other Hand, Death '08
Goodnight for Justice '11

M. Night Shyamalan (1970-)
Signs '02
Lady in the Water '06

Christopher Shyer
K-9 3: P.I. '01
The Invitation '03
Category 6: Day of Destruction '04
Fierce People '05
Big Bad Wolf '06

Sabrina Siani (1963-)
Ator the Fighting Eagle '83
Conquest '83

Jane Sibbett (1962-)
The Resurrected '91
It Takes Two '95
The Arrival 2 '98
Au Pair '99
The Town That Banned Christmas '06

Clement Sibony (1976-)
Dad On the Run '00
He Loves Me . . . He Loves Me Not '02
Finding Altamira '16

Joseph R. Sicari
Night School '81
Stiffs '06

Barbara Sicuranza
Margarita Happy Hour '01
The Sweet Life '03

Alexander Siddig (1965-)
A Dangerous Man: Lawrence after Arabia '91
Vertical Limit '00
Reign of Fire '02
Kingdom of Heaven '05
Syriana '05
The Nativity Story '06
The Last Legion '07
Doomsday '08
Cairo Time '09
Miral '10
May in Summer '13
May in the Summer '13
Submergence '18

Nawazuddin Siddiqui
The Lunchbox '13
Photograph '19

Gabourey Sidibe
Yelling to the Sky '11
White Bird in a Blizzard '14

Gabourney 'Gabby' Sidibe (1983-)
Precious: Based on the Novel 'Push' by Sapphire '09
Tower Heist '11
Life Partners '14

George Sidney (1916-2002)
Rafter Romance '33
Manhattan Melodrama '34

Sylvia Sidney (1910-99)
An American Tragedy '31
Street Scene '31
Merrily We Go to Hell '32
Thirty Day Princess '34
Fury '36
Sabotage '36
The Trail of the Lonesome Pine '36
Dead End '37
You Only Live Once '37

You and Me '38
One Third of a Nation '39
The Wagons Roll at Night '41
Blood on the Sun '45
Mr. Ace '46
Summer Wishes, Winter Dreams '73
Death at Love House '75
God Told Me To '76
I Never Promised You a Rose Garden '77
Raid on Entebbe '77
Snowbeast '77
Damien: Omen 2 '78
Hammett '82
Corrupt '84
An Early Frost '85
Pals '87
Beetlejuice '88
Used People '92
Mars Attacks! '96

Drew Sidora (1985-)
Never Die Alone '04
White Chicks '04
She's Not Our Sister '11

James Sie (1962-)
Strawberry Fields '97
The Invincible Iron Man '07 *(V)*

Jennifer Siebel (Newsom) (1974-)
April Fool's Day '08
The Trouble with Romance '09
Tales of an Ancient Empire '11

Charles Siebert (1938-)
Tarantulas: The Deadly Cargo '77
Blue Sunshine '78

Jim Siedow (1920-2003)
The Texas Chainsaw Massacre '74
The Texas Chainsaw Massacre 2 '86

Bernard Siegel (1868-1940)
Laugh, Clown, Laugh '28
Beau Ideal '31

Donald Siegel (1912-91)
Invasion of the Body Snatchers '56
Play Misty for Me '71 *(C)*
Invasion of the Body Snatchers '78
Into the Night '85 *(C)*

Jake Siegel
American Pie Presents: The Naked Mile '06
American Pie Presents: Beta House '07

George Siegmann (1882-1928)
The Birth of a Nation '15
The Three Musketeers '21
Oliver Twist '22
Anna Christie '23
Scaramouche '23
Hotel Imperial '27
The Man Who Laughs '27
The Red Mill '27
Uncle Tom's Cabin '27

Casey Siemaszko (1961-)
Class '83
Silence of the Heart '84
Back to the Future '85
Secret Admirer '85
Miracle of the Heart: A Boys Town Story '86
Stand by Me '86
Gardens of Stone '87
Three O'Clock High '87
Biloxi Blues '88
Young Guns '88
Back to the Future, Part 2 '89
Breaking In '89
The Big Slice '90
The Chase '91
Of Mice and Men '92
Milk Money '94
My Life's in Turnaround '94 *(C)*

Black Scorpion '95
Bliss '96
Mistrial '96
Rose Hill '97
Limbo '99
Stephen King's The Storm of the Century '99
The Crew '00
Waltzing Anna '06
Killing Kennedy '13

Nina Siemaszko (1970-)
License to Drive '88
Tucker: The Man and His Dream '88
Sinatra '92
Wild Orchid 2: Two Shades of Blue '92
Red Shoe Diaries 3: Another Woman's Lipstick '93
The Saint of Fort Washington '93
Twenty Bucks '93
Airheads '94
Power of Attorney '94
The American President '95
Armistead Maupin's More Tales of the City '97
Suicide Kings '97
Goodbye, Lover '99
Jakob the Liar '99
Sleep Easy, Hutch Rimes '00
Mystery Woman: Mystery Weekend '05
The Haunting of Molly Hartley '08

Gregory Sierra (1941-)
Pocket Money '72
The Wrath of God '72
The Night the Bridge Fell Down '83
Miami Vice '84
Code Name: Dancer '87
Let's Get Harry '87
Deep Cover '92
Honey, I Blew Up the Kid '92
Hot Shots! Part Deux '93
Mafia! '98
The Wonderful Ice Cream Suit '98
Blood Money '99

Maggie Siff (1974-)
Push '09
Concussion '13
The 5th Wave '16
A Woman, A Part '17

Rocco Siffredi (1964-)
Romance '99
Anatomy of Hell '04

Beanie Sigel (1974-)
Paper Soldiers '02
State Property 2 '05

Jamie-Lynn Sigler (1981-)
Call Me: The Rise and Fall of Heidi Fleiss '04
Extreme Dating '04
Beneath the Dark '10
Son of Morning '11
Jewtopia '12
I Do '13

Tom Signorelli (1939-2010)
The St. Valentine's Day Massacre '67
The Trip '67
Kelly's Heroes '70
Big Bad Mama '74
The Last Porno Flick '74
Alice Sweet Alice '76
One Down, Two to Go! '82
Crossover Dreams '85

Simone Signoret (1921-85)
Against the Wind '48
La Ronde '51
Casque d'Or '52
Diabolique '55
Death in the Garden '56
Room at the Top '59
Adua and Her Friends '60
Term of Trial '63
Ship of Fools '65
Is Paris Burning? '66
Games '67
The Sea Gull '68

Army of Shadows '69
Widow Couderc '74

Ingvar Sigurdsson (1963-)
Beowulf & Grendel '06
Reykjavik-Rotterdam '08

Caroline Sihol (1949-)
Confidentially Yours '83
Tous les Matins du Monde '92
A Girl Cut in Two '07

Cynthia Sikes (1954-)
Ladies and Gentlemen, the Fabulous Stains '82
The Man Who Loved Women '83
Oceans of Fire '86
Love Hurts '91
Possums '99
Going Shopping '05

James B. Sikking (1934-)
The Strangler '64
Von Ryan's Express '65
Point Blank '67
Charro! '69
Daddy's Gone A-Hunting '69
The New Centurions '72
Scorpio '73
The Terminal Man '74
The Electric Horseman '79
The Competition '80
Ordinary People '80
Outland '81
The Star Chamber '83
Star Trek 3: The Search for Spock '84
Up the Creek '84
Morons from Outer Space '85
Dress Gray '86
Around the World in 80 Days '89
The Brotherhood of the Rose '89
Narrow Margin '90
Doing Time on Maple Drive '92
The Pelican Brief '93
In Pursuit of Honor '95
Nowhere to Land '00
Fever Pitch '05
Made of Honor '08

Joe Sikora (1976-)
The Watcher '00
Normal '03
Night Skies '07

Vic Silayan
Project: Kill! '77
The Last Reunion '80

Tusse Silberg
The Company of Wolves '85
Hidden City '87
Citizen X '95

Jerome Silberman (1933-2016)
See Gene Wilder

Johannes Silberschneider (1958-)
The Girl of Your Dreams '99
Bride of the Wind '01

Vira (Vera) Silenti (1931-)
Maciste in Hell '60
Son of Samson '62

Caroline Silhol (1949-)
See Caroline Sihol

silkk the Shocker
Corrupt '99
More Money More Family '15

Felix Silla
Don't Be Afraid of the Dark '73
Little Cigars '73

Karen Sillas (1963-)
Simple Men '92
What Happened Was. . . '94
The Beast '96
Female Perversions '96
Sour Grapes '98
75 Degrees '00

Douglas Sills (1960-)
The Swan Princess 2: Escape from Castle Mountain '97 (V)
Deuce Bigalow: European Gigolo '05

Milton Sills (1882-1930)
The Sea Hawk '24
Burning Daylight '28

Darien Sills-Evans (1974-)
Preaching to the Choir '05
The Reception '05

Augustin Silva
Crystal Fairy & the Magical Cactus '13
Magic Magic '13

David Silva (1917-76)
The First Texan '56
El Topo '71

Geno Silva (1948-)
Geronimo '93
A Man Apart '03

Henry Silva (1928-)
The Tall T '57
The Bravados '58
The Law and Jake Wade '58
Ride a Crooked Trail '58
Green Mansions '59
A Hatful of Rain '59
The Jayhawkers '59
Cinderfella '60
Ocean's 11 '60
The Manchurian Candidate '62
Sergeants 3 '62
Johnny Cool '63
The Secret Invasion '64
Hail Mafia '65
The Hills Run Red '67
Never a Dull Moment '68
The Desperados '70
Man & Boy '71
Cry of a Prostitute: Love Kills '72
The Boss '73
Hired to Kill '73
The Italian Connection '73
Manhunt '73
Contract on Cherry Street '77
Buck Rogers in the 25th Century '79
Crimebusters '79
Love and Bullets '79
Thirst '79
Alligator '80
Sharky's Machine '81
Wrong Is Right '82
Chained Heat '83
Cannonball Run 2 '84
Code of Silence '85
Lust in the Dust '85
Above the Law '88
Bulletproof '88
The Harvest '92
Trigger Happy '96
The End of Violence '97
Backlash '99
Ghost Dog: The Way of the Samurai '99
Ocean's Eleven '01 (C)

Maria Silva (1941-)
The Awful Dr. Orloff '62
Curse of the Devil '73

Sebastian Silva (1979-)
Crystal Fairy & the Magical Cactus '13
Nasty Baby '15

Trinidad Silva (1950-88)
Alambrista! '77
The Jerk '79
Crackers '84
Colors '88
The Night Before '88
UHF '89

Aldo Silvani (1891-1964)
Chains '49
La Strada '54
Nights of Cabiria '57

Leonor Silveira (1970-)
Abraham's Valley '93
The Convent '95
Party '96

Voyage to the Beginning of the World '96
I'm Going Home '00
Eccentricities of a Blonde-Haired Girl '10
The Strange Case of Angelica '10

Fawn Silver
Orgy of the Dead '65
Terror in the Jungle '68

Joe Silver (1922-89)
The Apprenticeship of Duddy Kravitz '74
They Came from Within '75
Rabid '77
You Light Up My Life '77
Boardwalk '79
Almost You '85
Switching Channels '88

Noah Silver (1994-)
Jamie Marks is Dead '13
Down a Dark Hall '18

Ron Silver (1946-2009)
Tunnelvision '76
Semi-Tough '77
Betrayal '78
Best Friends '82
Silent Rage '82
The Entity '83
Lovesick '83
Silkwood '83
Garbo Talks '84
Oh, God! You Devil '84
Romancing the Stone '84
Trapped in Silence '86 (C)
Billionaire Boys Club '87
A Father's Revenge '88
Enemies, a Love Story '89
Blue Steel '90
Reversal of Fortune '90
Live Wire '92
Mr. Saturday Night '92
Blind Side '93
Lifepod '93
Married to It '93
Timecop '94
A Woman of Independent Means '94
Danger Zone '95
The Arrival '96
Girl 6 '96
ShadowZone: The Undead Express '96
The White Raven '98
Black & White '99
Ratz '99
American Tragedy '00
Cutaway '00
Ali '01
Festival at Cannes '02
Master Spy: The Robert Hanssen Story '02
Spliced '03
Red Mercury '05
Find Me Guilty '06
The Ten '07

Veronique Silver (1931-)
The Woman Next Door '81
Life Is a Bed of Roses '83

Frank Silvera (1914-70)
The Fighter '52
Miracle of Our Lady of Fatima '52
Killer's Kiss '55
Crime and Punishment, USA '59
Toys in the Attic '63
The St. Valentine's Day Massacre '67
Valdez Is Coming '71

Jay Silverheels (1912-80)
Lust for Gold '49
Broken Arrow '50
The Story of Will Rogers '52
War Arrow '53
The Black Dakotas '54
Drums Across the River '54
Saskatchewan '54
Lone Ranger '56
Alias Jesse James '59 (C)
Indian Paint '64
True Grit '69
Man Who Loved Cat Dancing '73
Santee '73

Daniela Silverio
Identification of a Woman '82
Oriana '85

David Michael Silverman (1966-)
Copycat '95
Metro '96

Jonathan Silverman (1966-)
Brighton Beach Memoirs '86
Caddyshack 2 '88
Stealing Home '88
Traveling Man '89
Weekend at Bernie's '89
Class Action '91
Death Becomes Her '92
For Richer, for Poorer '92
12:01 '93
Weekend at Bernie's 2 '93
Little Big League '94
The Inspectors '98
The Odd Couple 2 '98
Something About Sex '98
Just a Little Harmless Sex '99
The Inspectors 2: A Shred of Evidence '00
Lip Service '00
The Medicine Show '01
These Old Broads '01
Bobbie's Girl '02
The Cookout '04
Coffee Date '06
Jam '06
Beethoven's Big Break '08
Swinging With the Finkels '11
A Bet's a Bet '14

Robert A. Silverman
The Brood '79
Scanners '81
Naked Lunch '91

Sarah Silverman (1970-)
What Planet Are You From? '00
School of Rock '03
I Want Someone to Eat Cheese With '06
School for Scoundrels '06
Saint John of Las Vegas '09
Peep World '10
Take This Waltz '11
Wreck-It Ralph '12 (V)
A Million Ways to Die In the West '14
I Smile Back '15
Popstar: Never Stop Never Stopping '16
Battle of the Sexes '17
The Book of Henry '17
Ralph Breaks the Internet '18 (V)

Mary Silvers (1941-)
See Maria Silva

Phil Silvers (1912-85)
Lady Be Good '41
Tom, Dick, and Harry '41
All Through the Night '42
Just Off Broadway '42
My Gal Sal '42
Roxie Hart '42
Coney Island '43
Lady Takes a Chance '43
Cover Girl '44
Four Jills in a Jeep '44
Something for the Boys '44
Don Juan Quilligan '45
If I'm Lucky '46
Summer Stock '50
Lucky Me '54
Top Banana '54
40 Pounds of Trouble '62
It's a Mad, Mad, Mad, Mad World '63
A Funny Thing Happened on the Way to the Forum '66
Follow That Camel '67
A Guide for the Married Man '67 (C)
The Boatniks '70
The Strongest Man in the World '75
The Cheap Detective '78

The Happy Hooker Goes Hollywood '80

Sid Silvers (1904-76)
Broadway Melody of 1936 '35
Born to Dance '36

Andrew Silverstein (1957-)
Making the Grade '84
Private Resort '84
Night Patrol '85
Pretty in Pink '86
Amazon Women on the Moon '87
Casual Sex? '88
The Adventures of Ford Fairlane '90
No Contest '94
Jury Duty '95 (C)
Foolish '99
My 5 Wives '00
One Night at McCool's '01
Blue Jasmine '13

Alicia Silverstone (1976-)
The Crush '93
Cool and the Crazy '94
Hideaway '94
The Babysitter '95
Clueless '95
New World '95
True Crime '95
Excess Baggage '96
Batman and Robin '97
Blast from the Past '98
Love's Labour's Lost '00
Rock My World '02
Scorched '02
Scooby-Doo 2: Monsters Unleashed '04
Beauty Shop '05
Alex Rider: Operation Stormbreaker '06
The Art of Getting By '11
Butter '12
Vamps '12
Ass Backwards '13
Angels in Stardust '14
Catfight '17
Diary of a Wimpy Kid: The Long Haul '17
The Killing of a Sacred Deer '17
The Lodge '19

Ben Silverstone (1979-)
The Browning Version '94
Lolita '97
Get Real '99

Armando Silvestre
Hiawatha '52
The White Orchid '54
Night of the Bloody Apes '68
The Killing Zone '90
The Last Riders '90

Victoria Silvstedt (1974-)
Out Cold '01
Boat Trip '03

Alastair Sim (1900-76)
Gangway '37
Climbing High '38
Sailing Along '38
Inspector Hornleigh '39
Cottage to Let '41
Waterloo Road '45
Captain Boycott '47
Green for Danger '47
Hue and Cry '47
Stage Fright '50
A Christmas Carol '51
The Belles of St. Trinian's '53
Geordie '55
Blue Murder at St. Trinian's '56
The Doctor's Dilemma '58
The Millionairess '60
School for Scoundrels '60
The Ruling Class '72
Royal Flash '75
The Littlest Horse Thieves '76
Rogue Male '76

Gerald Sim (1925-2014)
King Rat '65
The Whisperers '66

Dr. Jekyll and Sister Hyde '71
No Sex Please-We're British '73

Sheila Sim (1922-)
A Canterbury Tale '44
Dear Mr. Prohack '49
Pandora and the Flying Dutchman '51

Silvio Simac (1973-)
Black Mask 2: City of Masks '02
DOA: Dead or Alive '06

Jon Simanton
Turbo: A Power Rangers Movie '96
The Creeps '97

John Simm (1970-)
Boston Kickout '95
Forgive and Forget '99
Human Traffic '99
Wonderland '99
Miranda '01
24 Hour Party People '01
State of Play '03
Brothers of the Head '06
Skellig: The Owl Man '09
Everyday '12

Millicent Simmonds
Wonderstruck '17
A Quiet Place '18

Chelan Simmons (1982-)
Snakehead Terror '04
Chupacabra Terror '05
Final Destination 3 '06
Good Luck Chuck '07
Ice Twisters '09
Malibu Shark Attack '09
Tucker & Dale *vs.* Evil '10

Dick Simmons (1913-2003)
Pilot No. 5 '43
Undercover Maisie '47
Above and Beyond '53
Battle Circus '53
Men of the Fighting Lady '54

Gene Simmons (1949-)
KISS Meets the Phantom of the Park '78
Runaway '84
Trick or Treat '86
Wanted Dead or Alive '86
Red Surf '90
Detroit Rock City '99
Wish You Were Dead '00
The New Guy '02 (C)
Extract '09
Hugh Hefner: Playboy, Activist and Rebel '09

Henry Simmons (1970-)
Let It Snow '99
A Gentleman's Game '01
Taxi '04
The Insurgents '06
Madea's Family Reunion '06
South of Pico '07
Georgia O'Keefe '09
World's Greatest Dad '09
No Good Deed '14

Jaason Simmons (1970-)
Frankenstein Reborn '98
Highway Hitcher '98
Sharknado '13

Jean Simmons (1929-2010)
Give Us the Moon '44
Great Expectations '46
Black Narcissus '47
Inheritance '47
Hamlet '48
Androcles and the Lion '52
Angel Face '52
The Actress '53
The Robe '53
Young Bess '53
A Bullet Is Waiting '54
Desiree '54
The Egyptian '54
Footsteps in the Fog '55
Guys and Dolls '55
Until They Sail '57
The Big Country '58
Home Before Dark '58
Elmer Gantry '60
Spartacus '60

The Grass Is Greener '61
Mister Buddwing '66
Divorce American Style '67
Heidi '67
Rough Night in Jericho '67
The Happy Ending '69
Say Hello to Yesterday '71
The Dain Curse '78
Dominique '79
The Thorn Birds '83
North and South Book 1 '85
North and South Book 2 '86
The Dawning '88
Going Undercover '88
How to Make an American Quilt '95
Final Fantasy: The Spirits Within '01 (V)
Howl's Moving Castle '04 (V)

J.K. Simmons (1955-)
The Ref '93
Pom Poko '94 (V)
Extreme Measures '96
The First Wives Club '96
The Jackal '97
Love Walked In '97
Celebrity '98
The Cider House Rules '99
For Love of the Game '99
The Gift '00
Hit and Runway '01
The Mexican '01
Spider-Man '02
Off the Map '03
Hidalgo '04
The Ladykillers '04
Spider-Man 2 '04
Harsh Times '05
Thank You for Smoking '06
The Astronaut Farmer '07
Bury My Heart at Wounded Knee '07
First Snow '07
Juno '07
Postal '07
Spider-Man 3 '07
Burn After Reading '08
The Way of War '08
Aliens in the Attic '09 (V)
Extract '09
I Love You, Man '09
Jennifer's Body '09
New in Town '09
Up in the Air '09
The Vicious Kind '09
A Beginner's Guide to Endings '10
Crazy on the Outside '10
The Good Doctor '11
An Invisible Sign '11
The Music Never Stopped '11
Young Adult '11
Contraband '12
The Words '12
Dark Skies '13
Jobs '13
Ava & Lala '14
Barefoot '14
Murder of a Cat '14
Whiplash '14
The Meddler '15
The Rewrite '15
Terminator Genisys '15
The Accountant '16
Kung Fu Panda 3 '16
La La Land '16
Zootopia '16 (V)
All Nighter '17
Patriots Day '17
Renegades '17
Rock Dog '17
The Snowman '17
Worlds Apart '17
The Front Runner '18
I'm Not Here '19
Klaus '19
21 Bridges '19

Johnny Simmons (1986-)
The Greatest '09
Hotel for Dogs '09
Jennifer's Body '09
The Conspirator '10
The Perks of Being a Wallflower '12
The To Do List '13

The Stanford Prison Experiment '15
The Late Bloomer '16
The Phenom '16
Transpecos '16

Kimora Lee Simmons (1975-)
Beauty Shop '05
Waist Deep '06

Lili Simmons
Fat Kid Rules the World '12
Bone Tomahawk '15
Dirty Lies '16

Pat Simmons
The Giant Gila Monster '59
My Science Project '85

Peter Simmons
Renaissance Man '94
Best of the Best 3: No Turning Back '95
Sand '00

Joey Simmrin (1981-)
Little Giants '94
Nine Months '95
Star Kid '97

Ginny Simms (1913-94)
Playmates '41
Hit the Ice '43
Broadway Rhythm '44
Night and Day '46

Heather Alicia Simms (1970-)
Broken Flowers '05
You Belong to Me '07
Red Hook Summer '12

Larry Simms (1934-2009)
Blondie '38
Blondie Brings Up Baby '39
Blondie Meets the Boss '39
Blondie Takes a Vacation '39
Blondie Has Trouble '40
Blondie On a Budget '40
Blondie Plays Cupid '40
Blondie in Society '41
Blondie Goes Latin '42
Blondie Goes to College '42

Adam Simon (1962-)
Bob Roberts '92
The Haunting in Connecticut '09

Cliff Simon
Operation Delta Force 5: Random Fire '00
Stargate: Continuum '08

Michel Simon (1895-1975)
Feu Mathias Pascal '26
Passion of Joan of Arc '28
Boudu Saved from Drowning '32
L'Atalante '34
Bizarre Bizarre '39
Fabiola '48
Saadia '53
The Head '59
The Train '65
The Two of Us '68

Paul Simon (1941-)
Annie Hall '77
All You Need Is Cash '78
One Trick Pony '80

Robert F. Simon (1908-92)
Where the Sidewalk Ends '50
The Black Dakotas '54
The Court Martial of Billy Mitchell '55
The Catered Affair '56
Edge of the City '57
Compulsion '59

Simone Simon (1911-2005)
Girl's Dormitory '36
Josette '38
La Bete Humaine '38
The Devil & Daniel Webster '41
Cat People '42
Curse of the Cat People '44
Johnny Doesn't Live Here Any More '44
La Ronde '51
Le Plaisir '52

Hannah Simone (1980-)
Band Aid '17
Killing Gunther '17

Mathieu Simonet (1975-)
Merci pour le Chocolat '00
Days of Glory '06

Timothy Simons
Irreplaceable You '18
The Hustle '19

Ryan Simpkins (1998-)
Sherrybaby '06
Gardens of the Night '08
Surveillance '08
A Single Man '09
Space Warriors '13
The House '17

Ty Simpkins (2001-)
Insidious '10
The Next Three Days '10
Insidious: Chapter 2 '13
Meadowland '15

Ivan Simpson (1875-1951)
Inside the Lines '30
Safe in Hell '31
The Man Who Played God '32
Her Secret '33
British Agent '34

Jessica Simpson (1980-)
The Dukes of Hazzard '05
Employee of the Month '06
Blonde Ambition '07
Private Valentine: Blonde & Dangerous '08

Jimmi Simpson (1975-)
Loser '00
Stephen King's Rose Red '02
D.E.B.S. '04
Herbie: Fully Loaded '05
Stay Alive '06
Good Intentions '10
The Big Bang '11
The Truth About Emanuel '13
Under the Silver Lake '18

O.J. Simpson (1947-)
The Klansman '74
The Towering Inferno '74
The Cassandra Crossing '76
Roots '77
Capricorn One '78
Firepower '79
Detour to Terror '80
Cocaine and Blue Eyes '83
The Naked Gun: From the Files of Police Squad '88
Naked Gun 2 1/2: The Smell of Fear '91
C.I.A.: Code Name Alexa '92
Naked Gun 33 1/3: The Final Insult '94

Russell Simpson (1880-1959)
The First Auto '27
Abraham Lincoln '30
San Francisco '36
The Grapes of Wrath '40
Three Faces West '40
They Were Expendable '45
My Dog Shep '46
Saddle Tramp '47
Ma and Pa Kettle at the Fair '52
The Sun Shines Bright '53
The Horse Soldiers '59

Jeremy Sims
Idiot Box '97
Last Cab to Darwin '16 (V)

Joan Sims (1930-2001)
The Belles of St. Trinian's '53
Carry On Admiral '57
Upstairs and Downstairs '59
Carry On Constable '60
Carry On Regardless '61
Carry On Cleo '65
Carry On Cowboy '66
Carry On Screaming '66
Doctor in Clover '66
Don't Lose Your Head '66
Carry On Up the Khyber '68
Carry On Again Doctor '69
Carry On Loving '70
Carry On Up the Jungle '70
Carry On at Your Convenience '71
Carry On Camping '71
Carry On Henry VIII '71
Carry On Abroad '72
Carry On Matron '72
Carry On Behind '75
Carry On Dick '75
One of Our Dinosaurs Is Missing '75
The Canterville Ghost '96
The Last of the Blonde Bombshells '00

Molly Sims (1973-)
Starsky & Hutch '04
The Benchwarmers '06
Yes Man '08
Fired Up! '09
Venus and Vegas '10

Sylvia Sims
Hostile Witness '68
The Queen '06

Frank Sinatra (1915-98)
Higher and Higher '44
Step Lively '44
Anchors Aweigh '45
Till the Clouds Roll By '46
It Happened in Brooklyn '47
The Kissing Bandit '48
The Miracle of the Bells '48
On the Town '49
Take Me Out to the Ball Game '49
Double Dynamite '51
From Here to Eternity '53
Suddenly '54
Young at Heart '54
Guys and Dolls '55
The Man with the Golden Arm '55
Not as a Stranger '55
The Tender Trap '55
Around the World in 80 Days '56 (C)
High Society '56
Pal Joey '57
The Pride and the Passion '57
Kings Go Forth '58
Some Came Running '58
A Hole in the Head '59
Never So Few '59
Can-Can '60
Ocean's 11 '60
The Devil at 4 O'Clock '61
The Manchurian Candidate '62
Sergeants 3 '62
Come Blow Your Horn '63
Four for Texas '63
The List of Adrian Messenger '63
Paris When It Sizzles '64
Robin and the 7 Hoods '64
Marriage on the Rocks '65
None But the Brave '65
Von Ryan's Express '65
Assault on a Queen '66
Cast a Giant Shadow '66
Tony Rome '67
The Detective '68
Lady in Cement '68
That's Entertainment '74
Contract on Cherry Street '77
The First Deadly Sin '80
Cannonball Run 2 '84
Who Framed Roger Rabbit '88 (V)

Frank Sinatra, Jr. (1944-2016)
A Man Called Adam '66
Pepper and His Wacky Taxi '72
Code Name: Zebra '84
Cool World '92
Hollywood Homicide '03

Nancy Sinatra (1940-)
Get Yourself a College Girl '64
Marriage on the Rocks '65
Ghost in the Invisible Bikini '66

The Wild Angels '66
Speedway '68

Sinbad
Necessary Roughness '91
Coneheads '93
The Meteor Man '93
Houseguest '94
The Cherokee Kid '96
First Kid '96
Homeward Bound 2: Lost in San Francisco '96 (V)
Jingle All the Way '96
Good Burger '97
Crazy as Hell '02

Gordon John Sinclair (1962-)
Gregory's Girl '80
Erik the Viking '89
The Brylcreem Boys '96

Hugh Sinclair (1903-62)
The Secret Four '39
The Saint Meets the Tiger '43
The Rocking Horse Winner '49
No Trace '50

Jaz Sinclair
When the Bough Breaks '16
Slender Man '18

Madge Sinclair (1938-95)
Cornbread, Earl & Me '75
Convoy '78
Uncle Joe Shannon '78
Coming to America '88
The End of Innocence '90
Queen '93
The Lion King '94 (V)

Donald Sinden (1923-2014)
Doctor in the House '53
Mogambo '53
Mad About Men '54
Above Us the Waves '55
An Alligator Named Daisy '55
Simba '55
Eyewitness '56
Doctor at Large '57
You Know What Sailors Are '59
The Captain's Table '60
The Siege of Sidney Street '60
Villain '71
Rentadick '72
The National Health '73
The Island at the Top of the World '74
The Canterville Ghost '96

Jeremy Sinden (1950-96)
Danger UXB '81
Fortunes of War '87
The Innocent '93

Ngai Sing (1967-)
See Collin Chou

Campbell Singer (1909-76)
Scotland Yard Inspector '52
The Square Peg '58
The Hands of Orlac '60

Lori Singer (1957-)
Footloose '84
The Falcon and the Snowman '85
The Man with One Red Shoe '85
Trouble in Mind '86
Summer Heat '87
Storm and Sorrow '90
Warlock '91
Sunset Grill '92
Short Cuts '93
The Last Ride '94

Marc Singer (1948-)
Go Tell the Spartans '78
Roots: The Next Generation '79
The Two Worlds of Jenny Logan '79
Beastmaster '82
V '83
V: The Final Battle '84
In the Cold of the Night '89
Body Chemistry '90
Dead Space '90

A Man Called Sarge '90
Watchers 2 '90
Sweet Justice '92
Street Corner Justice '96
L.A.P.D.: To Protect and Serve '01
Lesser Evil '06
Eagle Eye '08
Dragonquest '09

Steve Singer
Ms. 45 '81
Hit and Runway '01
Palindromes '04

Penny Singleton (1908-2003)
Love in the Rough '30
Blondie '38
Boy Meets Girl '38
Garden of the Moon '38
Hard to Get '38
Outside of Paradise '38
Swing Your Lady '38
Blondie Brings Up Baby '39
Blondie Meets the Boss '39
Blondie Takes a Vacation '39
Blondie Has Trouble '40
Blondie On a Budget '40
Blondie Plays Cupid '40
Blondie in Society '41
Blondie Goes Latin '42
Blondie Goes to College '42
Jetsons: The Movie '90 (V)

Linda Sini (1926-)
The War of the Planets '65
Sartana's Here. . . Trade Your Pistol for a Coffin '70

Gary Sinise (1955-)
My Name Is Bill W. '89
A Midnight Clear '92
Of Mice and Men '92
Jack the Bear '93
Forrest Gump '94
Stephen King's The Stand '94
Apollo 13 '95
The Quick and the Dead '95
Truman '95
Albino Alligator '96
Ransom '96
George Wallace '97
Snake Eyes '98
The Dress Code '99
The Green Mile '99
It's the Rage '99
That Championship Season '99
Mission to Mars '00
Reindeer Games '00
A Gentleman's Game '01
Impostor '02
Path to War '02
Fallen Angel '03
The Human Stain '03
The Big Bounce '04
The Forgotten '04
Open Season '06 (V)

Karolin Siol (1949-)
See Caroline Sihol

Jennifer Sipes
Walking Tall: Lone Justice '07
Brotherhood '10

Shaun Sipos (1981-)
Lost Dream '09
Rampage '09

Sir Lancelot (1903-2001)
I Walked with a Zombie '43
Zombies on Broadway '44

Joseph Siravo (1957-)
Carlito's Way '93
Walking and Talking '96
Wisegirls '02

Nirut Sirichanya
Ong Bak 2 '08
The Hangover, Part 2 '11

G. Anthony 'Tony' Sirico (1942-)
The Pick-Up Artist '87
Backtrack '89
Cookie '89
Goodfellas '90
Gotti '96
It Had to Be You '00

Joseph Sirola (1929-)
Cry Rape! '73
Seizure '74
The Super Cops '74

Michael Sirow
Burning Blue '14
Infamous '20

Marina Sirtis (1955-)
Blind Date '84
Death Wish 3 '85
Waxwork 2: Lost in Time '91
Gargoyles, The Movie: The Heroes Awaken '94 (V)
Star Trek: Generations '94
Star Trek: First Contact '96
Star Trek: Insurrection '98
Star Trek: Nemesis '02
Terminal Error '02
Net Games '03
InAlienable '08
Green Street Hooligans 2 '09
The Grudge 3 '09
31 North 62 East '09

Tomer Sisley
You and Me '06
Sleepless Night '11

Sisqo (1978-)
Get Over It! '01
Snow Dogs '02
Pieces of April '03

Jeremy Sisto (1974-)
Grand Canyon '91
Hideaway '94
Clueless '95
The Crew '95
Moonlight and Valentino '95
White Squall '96
Suicide Kings '97
Without Limits '97
Bongwater '98
Playing by Heart '98
The '60s '99
Dead Dog '00
Jesus '00
Angel Eyes '01
May '02
Now You Know '02
Thirteen '03
Wrong Turn '03
In Enemy Hands '04
Paranoia 1.0 '04
A Lot Like Love '05
The Nickel Children '05
Population 436 '06
The Thirst '06
Waitress '07
Gardens of the Night '08
Into Temptation '09
Rosencrantz & Guildenstern Are Undead '10
Robot & Frank '12
As Cool As I Am '13
The Other Side of the Door '16

Rocco Sisto (1953-)
After Hours '85
Truth or Die '86
Red Riding Hood '88
Innocent Blood '92

Tim Sitarz
Outta Time '01
Axe '06

Emil Sitka (1915-98)
Three Stooges in Orbit '62
The Outlaws Is Coming! '65

Jules Sitruk
Son of Rambow '07
The Other Son '12

Olivier Sitruk
L'Appat '94
Coco Chanel '08

Phomsit Sitthijamroenkhun
The Iron Ladies '00
The Iron Ladies 2 '03

Sutthipong Sitthijamroenkhun
The Iron Ladies '00
The Iron Ladies 2 '03

Nancy Sivak
Last Wedding '01
Imaginary Playmate '06

Frank Sivero (1952-)
The Godfather, Part 2 '74
Ratings Game '84
Goodfellas '90
Fist of Honor '92
Cop and a Half '93
Foolish '99

Jamie Sives (1973-)
Wilbur Wants to Kill Himself '02
On a Clear Day '05
Love and Other Disasters '06
Mister Foe '07
Triage '09
Wild Rose '18

Eva Six
Beach Party '63
Operation Bikini '63

Sean Six
Alien Nation: Dark Horizon '94
Alien Nation: Body and Soul '95
Alien Nation: Millennium '96
Alien Nation: The Enemy Within '96

Veronica Sixtos
The Prankster '10
Hostile Border '16

Kevin Sizemore (1972-)
A Christmas Tree Miracle '13
Believe '16

Tom Sizemore
Born on the Fourth of July '89
Blue Steel '90
Flight of the Intruder '90
Guilty by Suspicion '91
Harley Davidson and the Marlboro Man '91
Point Break '91
Where Sleeping Dogs Lie '91
Passenger 57 '92
Heart and Souls '93
Striking Distance '93
True Romance '93
Natural Born Killers '94
Wyatt Earp '94
Bad Love '95
Devil in a Blue Dress '95
Heat '95
Strange Days '95
The Relic '96
Enemy of the State '98
The Florentine '98
Saving Private Ryan '98
Witness to the Mob '98
Bringing Out the Dead '99
Play It to the Bone '99
Witness Protection '99
Red Planet '00
Black Hawk Down '01
Pearl Harbor '01
Sins of the Father '01
Ticker '01
Big Trouble '02
Swindle '02
Dreamcatcher '03
Hustle '04
Paparazzi '04
Born Killers '05
The Nickel Children '05
Splinter '06
A Broken Life '07
Protecting the King '07
Toxic '07
American Son '08
The Last Lullaby '08
Red '08
Stiletto '08
Bad Ass '09
Cross '11
Cellmates '12
Chlorine '13
Company of Heroes '13
Seal Team 8: Behind Enemy Lines '14
SWAT: Unit 887 '15
Beyond Valkyrie: Dawn of the Fourth Reich '16
Traded '16
USS Indianapolis: Men of Courage '16
Weaponized '16

Gunnar Sjoberg (1909-71)
June Night '40
Brink of Life '57

Helen Sjoholm (1970-)
As It Is In Heaven '04
Simon and the Oaks '12

Victor Sjostrom (1879-1960)
The Outlaw and His Wife '17
The Phantom Carriage '21
To Joy '50
Wild Strawberries '57

George Skaff (1930-95)
The Incredible Petrified World '58
Frogs '72

Jimmie F. Skaggs (1944-2004)
Puppet Master '89
The Lost Capone '90
Backlash: Oblivion 2 '95

Lilia Skala (1900-94)
Lilies of the Field '63
Caprice '67
Charly '68
Probe '72
Deadly Hero '75
Heartland '81
Flashdance '83
Testament '83
House of Games '87

Alexander Skarsgård (1976-)
The Last Drop '05
Kill Your Darlings '06
Generation Kill '08
13 '10
Melancholia '11
Straw Dogs '11
Battleship '12
What Maisie Knew '12
The East '13
The Giver '14
The Diary of a Teenage Girl '15
The Legend of Tarzan '16
War on Everyone '17
Hold the Dark '18
The Hummingbird Project '18
The Aftermath '19

Bill Skarsgård (1990-)
Simon and the Oaks '12
It '17
Villains '19

Gustaf Skarsgard (1980-)
Evil '03
The Way Back '10
Kon-Tiki '12

Stellan Skarsgard (1951-)
The Unbearable Lightness of Being '88
The Ox '91
Wind '92
Good Evening, Mr. Wallenberg '93
The Slingshot '93
Breaking the Waves '95
Zero Degrees Kelvin '95
Amistad '97
Good Will Hunting '97
Insomnia '97
My Son the Fanatic '97
Ronin '98
Savior '98
Deep Blue Sea '99
Aberdeen '00
Harlan County War '00
Passion of Mind '00
Signs & Wonders '00
Time Code '00
The Glass House '01
Taking Sides '01
No Good Deed '02
City of Ghosts '03
Dogville '03
Helen of Troy '03
Exorcist: The Beginning '04
King Arthur '04
Dominion: Prequel to the Exorcist '05
Beowulf & Grendel '06
Goya's Ghosts '06
Kill Your Darlings '06
Pirates of the Caribbean: Dead Man's Chest '06
Arn: The Knight Templar '07
The Killing Gene '07
Pirates of the Caribbean: At World's End '07
God on Trial '08
Mamma Mia! '08
Angels & Demons '09
Boogie Woogie '09
Frankie and Alice '10
King of Devil's Island '10
A Somewhat Gentle Man '10
The Girl With the Dragon Tattoo '11
Melancholia '11
Thor '11
The Avengers '12
Nymphomaniac, Volume 1 '13
The Railway Man '13
Romeo & Juliet '13
Thor: The Dark World '13
Hector and the Search for Happiness '14
In Order of Disappearance '14
Nymphomaniac: Volume II '14
Our Kind of Traitor '16
Borg vs. McEnroe '17
Mamma Mia! Here We Go Again '18

Rachel (Racheal) Skarsten (1985-)
Fear of the Dark '02
In My Dreams '14

Brigitte Skay
Four Times That Night '69
Zeta One '69

Hal Skelly (1891-1934)
Struggle '31
The Shadow Laughs '33

Daniel Skelton
Eating Out 3: All You Can Eat '09
Eating Out 4: Drama Camp '11
Eating Out: The Open Weekend '11

Red Skelton (1913-97)
Having a Wonderful Time '38
Flight Command '40
Dr. Kildare's Wedding Day '41
Lady Be Good '41
The People vs. Dr. Kildare '41
Whistling in the Dark '41
Maisie Gets Her Man '42
Panama Hattie '42
Ship Ahoy '42
Whistling in Dixie '42
Du Barry Was a Lady '43
I Dood It '43
Thousands Cheer '43
Whistling in Brooklyn '43
Bathing Beauty '44
Ziegfeld Follies '46
Merton of the Movies '47
The Fuller Brush Man '48
A Southern Yankee '48
Neptune's Daughter '49
The Fuller Brush Girl '50 (C)
Three Little Words '50
Watch the Birdie '50
Excuse My Dust '51
Texas Carnival '51
Lovely to Look At '52
The Clown '53
The Great Diamond Robbery '53
Half a Hero '53
Around the World in 80 Days '56 (C)
Ocean's 11 '60
Those Magnificent Men in Their Flying Machines '65

Tom Skerritt (1933-)
War Hunt '62
M*A*S*H '70
Colditz: Escape of the Birdmen '71
Wild Rovers '71
Fuzz '72
Big Bad Mama '74
Thieves Like Us '74
Devil's Rain '75
The Turning Point '77
Alien '79
Cheech and Chong's Up in Smoke '79
Ice Castles '79
Dangerous Summer '82
Fighting Back '82
Dead Zone '83
Calendar Girl Murders '84
Miles to Go '86
The Parent Trap II '86
SpaceCamp '86
Top Gun '86
Big Town '87
Maid to Order '87
Opposing Force '87
Poker Alice '87
Wisdom '87
Poltergeist 3 '88
The Heist '89
Steel Magnolias '89
The Rookie '90
Nightmare at Bittercreek '91
Poison Ivy '92
A River Runs Through It '92
Singles '92 (C)
Wild Orchid 2: Two Shades of Blue '92
Knight Moves '93
Contact '97
Two for Texas '97
The Other Sister '98
Smoke Signals '98
What the Deaf Man Heard '98
Aftershock: Earthquake in New York '99
High Noon '00
Jackie Bouvier Kennedy Onassis '00
Trial by Media '00
Greenmail '01
Texas Rangers '01
Path to War '02
Tears of the Sun '03
Category 7: The End of the World '05
Bonneville '06
Mammoth '06
Killer Wave '07
Beer for My Horses '08
Dr. Jekyll and Mr. Hyde '08
The Trojan Horse '08
For Sale by Owner '09
Whiteout '09
Redemption Road '10
Soda Springs '11
Your Love Never Fails '11
At Middleton '13
Lucky '17

Anita Skinner
Girlfriends '78
Sole Survivor '84

Claire Skinner (1965-)
Life Is Sweet '90
Naked '93
The Return of the Native '94
Catherine Cookson's The Wingless Bird '97
A Dance to the Music of Time '97
Second Sight '99
Sleepy Hollow '99
Almost Strangers '01
Sense & Sensibility '07
When Did You Last See Your Father? '07

Cornelia Otis Skinner (1899-1979)
The Uninvited '44
The Girl in the Red Velvet Swing '55

Keith Skinner (1949-)
Mademoiselle '66
The Slipper and the Rose '76

Graham Skipper
Beyond the Gates '16
The Mind's Eye '16

Pat Skipper
Chain of Command '00
Ed Gein '01

Alison Skipworth (1863-1952)
Raffles '30
Tonight or Never '31
If I Had a Million '32
Night After Night '32
The Song of Songs '33
The Captain Hates the Sea '34
Here is My Heart '34
The Casino Murder Case '35
Dangerous '35
The Devil Is a Woman '35
Doubting Thomas '35
The Girl from 10th Ave. '35
The Gorgeous Hussy '36
The Princess Comes Across '36
Satan Met a Lady '36
Stolen Holiday '37
King of the Newsboys '38
Wide Open Faces '38

Espen Skjonberg (1924-)
The Last Lieutenant '94
O'Horten '09

Jerzy Skolimowski (1938-)
Innocent Sorcerers '60
White Nights '85
Big Shots '87
Eastern Promises '07

Tiera Skovbye
The Miracle Season '18
Summer of 84 '18

Ed Skrein
Northman: A Viking Saga '15
The Transporter Refueled '15
Deadpool '16
Alita: Battle Angel '19
Midway '19

Jennifer Sky (1977-)
Never Die Alone '04
Meet Market '08

Azura Skye (1981-)
Dementia '98
28 Days '00
Bandits '01
Carolina '03
The Wendell Baker Story '05
Heavens Fall '06
Love and Debate '06
Wristcutters: A Love Story '06
What We Do Is Secret '07
One Missed Call '08
20 Years After '08

Ione Skye (1970-)
Napoleon and Josephine: A Love Story '87
River's Edge '87
A Night in the Life of Jimmy Reardon '88
The Rachel Papers '89
Say Anything '89
Gas Food Lodging '92
Guncrazy '92
Samantha '92
Girls in Prison '94
Four Rooms '95
Dream for an Insomniac '96
Tower of the Firstborn '98
Went to Coney Island on a Mission from God. . . Be Back by Five '98
Fever Pitch '05
The Lather Effect '06
12 Hours to Live '06
The Santa Incident '10
Dear Eleanor '16

Tristen Skylar (1971-)
Kidco '83
Cadillac Man '90
Book of Shadows: Blair Witch 2 '00

Demian Slade (1972-)
Better Off Dead '85
Back to the Beach '87

Max Elliott Slade (1980-)
3 Ninjas '92
3 Ninjas Kick Back '94
Apollo 13 '95
3 Ninjas Knuckle Up '95

Jenny Slate (1982-)
The Longest Week '14
Obvious Child '14
Joshy '16
My Blind Brother '16
The Secret Life of Pets '16
Zootopia '16 (V)
Gifted '17
Landline '17
Aardvark '18
The Polka King '18
The Secret Life of Pets 2 '19

Jeremy Slate (1926-2006)
G.I. Blues '60
Girls! Girls! Girls! '62
I'll Take Sweden '65
Born Losers '67
The Devil's Brigade '68
Hell's Angels '69 '69
Hell's Belles '69
The Hooked Generation '69
True Grit '69
Alligator Alley '72
The Centerfold Girls '74
Summer of Fear '78
Dead Pit '89
The Lawnmower Man '92

Christian Slater (1969-)
Legend of Billie Jean '85
The Name of the Rose '86
Tucker: The Man and His Dream '88
Beyond the Stars '89
Gleaming the Cube '89
Heathers '89
The Wizard '89
Pump Up the Volume '90
Tales from the Darkside: The Movie '90
Young Guns 2 '90
Mobsters '91
Robin Hood: Prince of Thieves '91
Star Trek 6: The Undiscovered Country '91
Ferngully: The Last Rain Forest '92 (V)
Kuffs '92
Where the Day Takes You '92
True Romance '93
Untamed Heart '93
Interview with the Vampire '94
Jimmy Hollywood '94
Bed of Roses '95
Broken Arrow '95
Murder in the First '95
Hard Rain '97
Julian Po '97
Basil '98
Very Bad Things '98
The Contender '00
Hard Cash '01
3000 Miles to Graceland '01
Who is Cletis Tout? '02
Windtalkers '02
The Confessor '04
Alone in the Dark '05
The Deal '05
Mindhunters '05
Bobby '06
Hollow Man 2 '06
He Was a Quiet Man '07
Love Lies Bleeding '07
Slipstream '07
Igor '08 (V)
Dolan's Cadillac '09
Lies and Illusions '09
Guns, Girls and Gambling '11
The River Murders '11
Sacrifice '11
Without Men '11
Assassin's Bullet '12
Bullet to the Head '12
Dawn Rider '12
El Gringo '12
Freaky Deaky '12
Playback '12
Rites of Passage '12
Nymphomaniac, Volume 1 '13
The Power of Few '13
Stranded '13
Way of the Wicked '14
The Adderall Diaries '16
King Cobra '16
The Wife '17
The Public '18

Helen Slater (1963-)
Supergirl '84
Legend of Billie Jean '85
Ruthless People '86
The Secret of My Success '87
Sticky Fingers '88
Happy Together '89
City Slickers '91
12:01 '93
Lassie '94
No Way Back '96
Toothless '97
Nowhere in Sight '01
Seeing Other People '04
Beautiful Wave '11
The Curse of Downers Grove '15

John Slater (1916-75)
It Always Rains on Sunday '47
Bad Blonde '53
The Long Memory '53

Ryan Slater (1983-)
The Amazing Panda Adventure '95
Hell's Kitchen NYC '97
Home Team '98

John Slattery (1962-)
Lily Dale '96
Cash Crop '98
From the Earth to the Moon '98
Red Meat '98
Where's Marlowe? '98
Bad Company '02
A Death in the Family '02
Mona Lisa Smile '03
Dirty Dancing: Havana Nights '04
Flags of Our Fathers '06
The Situation '06
Charlie Wilson's War '07
Reservation Road '07
Underdog '07
Iron Man 2 '10
The Adjustment Bureau '11
Return '11
Bluebird '13
Ant-Man '15
Spotlight '15
Churchill '17

Richard X. Slattery (1925-97)
Black Eye '74
Trained to Kill, U.S.A. '75
Zebra Force '76

Tony Slattery (1959-)
Peter's Friends '92
Heaven's a Drag '94

Tod Slaughter (1885-1956)
The Crimes of Stephen Hawke '36
Demon Barber of Fleet Street '36
Murder in the Old Red Barn '36
Ticket of Leave Man '37
The Hooded Terror '38
Sexton Blake and the Hooded Terror '38
Crimes at the Dark House '39
The Face at the Window '39
The Greed of William Hart '48

Darla Slavens (1964-)
See Darla Haun

Jonathan Slavin
Free Enterprise '98
Hard Pill '05

Millie Slavin
The People *vs.* Jean Harris '81
One Night Stand '95

Bobby Slayton (1955-)
Get Shorty '95
The Rat Pack '98
Bandits '01
The Third Wheel '02

Martha Sleeper
Huddle '32
Spitfire '34

Haaz Sleiman
The Visitor '07
Dorfman in Love '11
3022 '19

Victor Slezak (1957-)
Beyond Rangoon '95
The Bridges of Madison County '95
One Tough Cop '98
The Siege '98
Lost Souls '00
The Cat's Meow '01
The Notorious Bettie Page '06
Happy Tears '09

Walter Slezak (1902-83)
Once Upon a Honeymoon '42
The Fallen Sparrow '43
This Land Is Mine '43
Lifeboat '44
The Princess and the Pirate '44
Step Lively '44
Cornered '45
The Spanish Main '45
Born to Kill '47
Sinbad, the Sailor '47
The Pirate '48
The Inspector General '49
Abbott and Costello in the Foreign Legion '50
Bedtime for Bonzo '51
People Will Talk '51
Confidentially Connie '53
White Witch Doctor '53
Ten Thousand Bedrooms '57
Come September '61
Emil and the Detectives '64
24 Hours to Kill '65
A Very Special Favor '65
Black Beauty '71
Treasure Island '72

Grace Slick (1939-)
Gimme Shelter '70
Jackie's Back '99

Jonathan Slinger
The Last September '99
A Thousand Kisses Deep '11

Amy Sloan (1978-)
The Aviator '04
Pterodactyl '05

Paul Sloan
Stiletto '08
Vigilante Diaries '16

Everett Sloane (1909-65)
Citizen Kane '41
The Lady from Shanghai '48
Prince of Foxes '49
The Men '50
Bird of Paradise '51
The Enforcer '51
The Sellout '51
Sirocco '51
Way of a Gaucho '52
The Big Knife '55
Lust for Life '56
Patterns '56
Somebody Up There Likes Me '56
The Gun Runners '58
Marjorie Morningstar '58
Home from the Hill '60
Disorderly Orderly '64
The Patsy '64

Lindsay Sloane (1977-)
Bring It On '00
Dog Gone Love '03
The In-Laws '03
The TV Set '06
The Accidental Husband '08
Over Her Dead Body '08
The Six Wives of Henry Lefay '09
The Other Guys '10
She's Out of My League '10
A Good Old Fashioned Orgy '11
Endings, Beginnings '20

Micah Sloat
Paranormal Activity '09
Paranormal Activity 2 '10

Ptolemy Slocum
(Untitled) '09
Wild Oats '16

Joey Slotnick (1968-)
A League of Their Own '92
Twister '96
Dinner and Driving '97
Since You've Been Gone '97
Blast from the Past '98
The Pirates of Silicon Valley '99
Hollow Man '00
I Want Someone to Eat Cheese With '06
Made in Romania '10

James Sloyan (1940-)
The Million Dollar Rip-Off '76
Callie and Son '81
Prime Suspect '82
Billionaire Boys Club '87
Code Name: Dancer '87
Danielle Steel's Changes '91

Marya Small
American Pop '81 (V)
Zapped! '82

Sharon Small (1967-)
Dear Frankie '04
Murderland '09

Jimmy Smallhorne
2 by 4 '98
When the Sky Falls '99

Amy Smart (1976-)
Starship Troopers '97
Campfire Tales '98
Dee Snider's Strangeland '98
High Voltage '98
Varsity Blues '98
Outside Providence '99
Road Trip '00
The '70s '00
Rat Race '01
Interstate 60 '02
Scotland, PA '02
The Battle of Shaker Heights '03
Blind Horizon '04
The Butterfly Effect '04
Starsky & Hutch '04
Win a Date with Tad Hamilton! '04
Bigger Than the Sky '05
Just Friends '05
Crank '06
Peaceful Warrior '06
Mirrors '08
Seventh Moon '08
Crank: High Voltage '09
Love N' Dancing '09
Columbus Circle '10
House of the Rising Sun '11
The Reunion '11
7500 '12
Bad Country '14
Tyler Perry's The Single Moms' Club '14
Flight 7500 '16

Dee Smart
Back of Beyond '95
Welcome to Woop Woop '97

Jean Smart (1951-)
Fire with Fire '86
Maximum Security '87
Project X '87
Mistress '91
Homeward Bound: The Incredible Journey '93
Scarlett '94
The Yarn Princess '94
The Yearling '94
The Brady Bunch Movie '95
Edie & Pen '95 (C)
A Stranger in Town '95
Steve Martini's Undue Influence '96
A Change of Heart '98
The Odd Couple 2 '98
Guinevere '99
Disney's The Kid '00
Snow Day '00
Sweet Home Alabama '02
Audrey's Rain '03
Bringing Down the House '03
Killer Instinct: From the Files of Agent Candice DeLong '03
Garden State '04
Lucky You '07
Hero Wanted '08
Barry Munday '10
Youth in Revolt '10
William & Catherine: A Royal Romance '11
Hope Springs '12
When Calls the Heart '13
Miss Meadows '14
Life Itself '18

Richard Smedley
Brain of Blood '71
The Abductors '72

Hana Smekalova (1919-78)
See Florence Marly

Ron Smerczak (1949-2019)
Jackie Chan's Who Am I '98
Operation Delta Force 5: Random Fire '00
Queen's Messenger II '01

Laura Smet (1983-)
The Bridesmaid '04
Gilles' Wife '04
Towards Zero '07
Frontier of Dawn '08

Robert Smigel (1960-)
Happy Gilmore '96
Little Nicky '00 (V)

Michael Smiley (1963-)
In the Spider's Web '07
Outpost '07
Down Terrace '10
Kill List '12
A Field in England '14
Free Fire '17

Tava Smiley (1971-)
A Girl, 3 Guys and a Gun '01
Outta Time '01
Timecop 2: The Berlin Decision '03

Yakov Smirnoff (1951-)
The Adventures of Buckaroo Banzai Across the Eighth Dimension '84
Brewster's Millions '85
Heartburn '86
The Money Pit '86

Kodi Smit-McPhee (1996-)
Romulus, My Father '07
The Road '09
Let Me In '10
ParaNorman '12 (V)
The Congress '13
Romeo & Juliet '13
A Birder's Guide to Everything '14
Dawn of the Planet of the Apes '14
Young Ones '14
Slow West '15
Alpha '18

Alexis Smith (1921-93)
Dive Bomber '41
The Smiling Ghost '41
Gentleman Jim '42
The Constant Nymph '43
The Adventures of Mark Twain '44
Hollywood Canteen '44
Conflict '45
The Horn Blows at Midnight '45
Rhapsody in Blue '45
San Antonio '45
Night and Day '46
Stallion Road '47
The Two Mrs. Carrolls '47
South of St. Louis '48
Whiplash '48
Any Number Can Play '49
Montana '50
Here Comes the Groom '51
Split Second '53
The Sleeping Tiger '54
The Young Philadelphians '59
Once Is Not Enough '75
The Little Girl Who Lives down the Lane '76
Casey's Shadow '78
La Truite '83
A Death in California '85
Dress Gray '86
Tough Guys '86
The Age of Innocence '93

Allison Smith (1969-)
Wildflower '91
Jason Goes to Hell: The Final Friday '93
A Reason to Believe '95
Terror Tract '00

Amber Smith (1971-)
Mars '96
Red Shoe Diaries 7: Burning Up '96
Def Jam's How to Be a Player '97
L.A. Confidential '97

Andrew Smith
Quicksilver '86
Blackbeard '06

Anna Deavere Smith (1950-)
Dave '93
The American President '95
The Human Stain '03
Cry Wolf '05
Life Support '07
Rachel Getting Married '08

Anna Nicole Smith (1967-2007)
Naked Gun 33 1/3: The Final Insult '94
Skyscraper '95
To the Limit '95

Arjay Smith (1983-)
The Day After Tomorrow '04
Be Kind Rewind '08
Vacancy 2: The First Cut '08

Art Smith (1899-1973)
Ride the Pink Horse '47
Letter from an Unknown Woman '48
Caught '49
In a Lonely Place '50
The Next Voice You Hear '50
The Painted Hills '51

Benjamin Smith (1995-)
Second Sight '99
Bob the Butler '05

Brandon Smith (1952-)
Powder '95
Jeepers Creepers '01
Slap Her, She's French '02
The Alamo '04
Paradise, Texas '05
Bernie '12

Brian J. Smith
Hate Crime '05
Murder on the Orient Express '10
Red Faction: Origins '11

Britta Smith
In the Name of the Father '93
Moll Flanders '96
A Certain Justice '99
American Women '00
The Magdalene Sisters '02
Bloom '03

Brooke Smith (1967-)
The Silence of the Lambs '91
Vanya on 42nd Street '94
Kansas City '95
Last Summer In the Hamptons '96

Series 7: The Contenders '01
Bad Company '02
In Her Shoes '05
Fair Game '10

Bubba Smith (1945-2011)
Stroker Ace '83
Police Academy '84
Police Academy 2: Their First Assignment '85
Police Academy 3: Back in Training '86
Police Academy 4: Citizens on Patrol '87
Police Academy 5: Assignment Miami Beach '88
Police Academy 6: City under Siege '89
Fist of Honor '92
Full Clip '06

Sir C. Aubrey Smith (1863-1948)
The Bachelor Father '31
The Man in Possession '31
The Phantom of Paris '31
But the Flesh Is Weak '32
Love Me Tonight '32
No More Orchids '32
Polly of the Circus '32
Trouble in Paradise '32
The Barbarian '33
Bombshell '33
Curtain at Eight '33
Queen Christina '33
Cleopatra '34
Scarlet Empress '34
We Live Again '34
China Seas '35
Clive of India '35
The Crusades '35
The Gilded Lily '35
The Lives of a Bengal Lancer '35
The Right to Live '35
Transatlantic Tunnel '35
The Garden of Allah '36
Little Lord Fauntleroy '36
Lloyds of London '36
The Hurricane '37
Prisoner of Zenda '37
Thoroughbreds Don't Cry '37
Wee Willie Winkie '37
Four Men and a Prayer '38
Kidnapped '38
Sixty Glorious Years '38
Another Thin Man '39
Balalaika '39
East Side of Heaven '39
Eternally Yours '39
The Four Feathers '39
Beyond Tomorrow '40
Rebecca '40
Waterloo Bridge '40
Maisie Was a Lady '41
Forever and a Day '43
Madame Curie '43
The Adventures of Mark Twain '44
Sensations of 1945 '44
The White Cliffs of Dover '44
And Then There Were None '45
An Ideal Husband '47
Unconquered '47

Cedric Smith (1943-)
Anne of Green Gables '85
The Penthouse '89
JFK: Reckless Youth '93
Witchboard 3: The Possession '95
Sea People '00
The Gospel of John '03

Chad Smith
Tears of the Sun '03
Hostage '05

Charles Martin Smith (1953-)
Culpepper Cattle Co. '72
Fuzz '72
American Graffiti '73
Pat Garrett & Billy the Kid '73
The Spikes Gang '74
No Deposit, No Return '76
The Campus Corpse '77
The Buddy Holly Story '78
More American Graffiti '79
Herbie Goes Bananas '80
Never Cry Wolf '83
Starman '84
The Untouchables '87
The Hot Spot '90
Deep Cover '92
And the Band Played On '93
I Love Trouble '94
Roswell: The U.F.O. Cover-Up '94
Speechless '94
Larry McMurtry's Streets of Laredo '95
The Beast '96
Dead Silence '96
Wedding Bell Blues '96
Deep Impact '98
P.T. Barnum '99
Lucky You '07
Still Small Voices '07
Jack and Jill *vs.* the World '08

Cheryl 'Rainbeaux' Smith (1955-2002)
Lemora, Lady Dracula '73
Caged Heat '74
The Swinging Cheerleaders '74
Farewell, My Lovely '75
Drum '76
Massacre at Central High '76
Pom Pom Girls '76
Revenge of the Cheerleaders '76
Slumber Party '57 '76
Incredible Melting Man '77
Laserblast '78
Cheech and Chong's Up in Smoke '79
Melvin and Howard '80
Parasite '82
Vice Squad '82

Connie Smith (1941-)
Hell on Wheels '67
Road to Nashville '67

Constance Smith (1928-2003)
Lure of the Wilderness '52
Red Skies of Montana '52
Man in the Attic '53

Cotter Smith (1949-)
Broken Badge '85
Cameron's Closet '89
K-9 '89
Midnight's Child '93
Ride the Wild Fields '00
X2: X-Men United '03
Burning Blue '14

Cynthia Smith
Benji '74
For the Love of Benji '77

Cyril Smith (1892-1963)
Friday the Thirteenth '33
Appointment with Crime '45
Old Mother Riley, Headmistress '50
A Stolen Face '52

Daniel E. Smith
Heimat 2 '92
John Q '02

David Lee Smith
Divine Secrets of the Ya-Ya Sisterhood '02
The Man from Earth '07

Douglas Smith (1985-)
Hangman's Curse '03
Rock the Paint '05
Citizen Duane '06
Remember the Daze '07
Percy Jackson: Sea of Monsters '13
Ouija '14
Stage Fright '14

Dylan Smith
Murder on the Orient Express '01
One Hour Photo '02
Eddie the Sleepwalking Cannibal '12

Ebbe Roe Smith
Big Bad Mama 2 '87
The Big Easy '87
Tapeheads '89

Eddie Bo Smith, Jr.
Stir of Echoes '99
The Courage to Love '00

Ella Smith (1983-)
The Voices '15
Ray & Liz '19

Ethel Smith (1910-96)
Bathing Beauty '44
Melody Time '48 (V)

Geraldine Smith (1949-)
Flesh '68
Mixed Blood '84

Gregory Edward Smith (1983-)
Harriet the Spy '96
The Climb '97
Krippendorf's Tribe '98
My Teacher Ate My Homework '98
Small Soldiers '98
The Patriot '00
American Outlaws '01
Just Ask My Children '01
Book of Love '04
Kids in America '05
Nearing Grace '05
Boot Camp '07
Closing the Ring '07
The Seeker: The Dark Is Rising '07
Guns '08
Hobo With a Shotgun '11
In My Pocket '11

Harley Quinn Smith (1999-)
Holidays '16
Yoga Hosers '16
Jay and Silent Bob Reboot '19

Hillary Bailey Smith (1957-)
Love Potion #9 '92
Last Breath '96

Howard Smith (1893-1968)
Call Northside 777 '48
State of the Union '48
I Bury the Living '58
No Time for Sergeants '58
The Brass Bottle '63

Izaak Smith
Aaliyah: The Princess of R&B '14
A Fighting Man '14

Jaclyn Smith (1945-)
Goodbye, Columbus '69
The Adventurers '70
Probe '72
Deja Vu '84
Florence Nightingale '85
The Bourne Identity '88
Danielle Steel's Kaleidoscope '90
Lies Before Kisses '92
Charlie's Angels: Full Throttle '03

Jacob Smith (1990-)
Dragonfly '02
Cheaper by the Dozen '03
Cheaper by the Dozen 2 '05

Jaden Smith (1998-)
The Pursuit of Happyness '06
The Day the Earth Stood Still '08
The Karate Kid '10
Justin Bieber: Never Say Never '11
After Earth '13

James Todd Smith (1968-)
See LL Cool J

Jamie Renee Smith (1987-)
Children of the Corn 4: The Gathering '96
Dante's Peak '97
MVP: Most Valuable Primate '00

Jason Alan Smith (1976-)
Crazy '08
The Lightkeepers '09

Jennifer Schwalbach Smith (1971-)
Jay and Silent Bob Strike Back '01
Jersey Girl '04
Clerks 2 '06

John Smith (1931-95)
We're No Angels '55
Ghost Town '56
Hot Rod Girl '56
Quincannon, Frontier Scout '56
Rebel in Town '56
The Kettles on Old MacDonald's Farm '57
Island of Lost Women '59

Julie K. Smith (1967-)
The Dallas Connection '94
Return to Savage Beach '97
Baberellas '03

Justice Smith (1995-)
Paper Towns '15
Every Day '18
Jurassic World: Fallen Kingdom '18
Pokémon Detective Pikachu '19

Kavan Smith (1970-)
Mission to Mars '00
Stark Raving Mad '02
Talking to Heaven '02
Nightmare at the End of the Hall '08
Growing the Big One '09
Red: Werewolf Hunter '10
Iris Johansen's The Killing Game '11
Metal Shifters '11

Kellita Smith (1969-)
Hair Show '04
King's Ransom '05
Roll Bounce '05
Feel the Noise '07
Three Can Play That Game '07
She's Not Our Sister '11

Ken Smith
Nora Prentiss '47
Paula '52

Kent Smith (1907-85)
Back Door to Heaven '39
Cat People '42
This Land Is Mine '43
Curse of the Cat People '44
The Spiral Staircase '46
Magic Town '47
The Voice of the Turtle '47
The Fountainhead '49
The Damned Don't Cry '50
This Side of the Law '50
Sayonara '57
The Badlanders '58
Imitation General '58
The Mugger '58
Party Girl '58
Strangers When We Meet '60
The Balcony '63
Games '67
Kona Coast '68
Assignment to Kill '69
Death of a Gunfighter '69
The Night Stalker '71
Pete 'n' Tillie '72
Probe '72
The Affair '73
Die Sister, Die! '74

Kerr Smith (1972-)
Final Destination '00
The Forsaken '01
Hit and Runway '01
Pressure '02
Cruel Intentions 3 '04
My Bloody Valentine 3D '09

Kevin Smith (1963-2002)
Young Hercules '97
Dead Evidence '00
Beyond Justice '01

Kevin Smith (1970-)
Clerks '94 (C)
Mallrats '95
Chasing Amy '97
Dogma '99
Scream 3 '00
Jay and Silent Bob Strike Back '01
Daredevil '03
Comic Book: The Movie '04 (C)
Clerks 2 '06
Catch and Release '07
Live Free or Die Hard '07
Jay and Silent Bob Reboot '19
Madness in the Method '19

Kim Smith (1983-)
Oh! What a Lovely War '69
National Lampoon's Van Wilder '02
Catwoman '04

Kurtwood Smith (1943-)
RoboCop '87
Rambo 3 '88
Dead Poets Society '89
The Heart of Dixie '89
True Believer '89
Quick Change '90
Company Business '91
Star Trek 6: The Undiscovered Country '91
Shadows and Fog '92
Boxing Helena '93
The Crush '93
Fortress '93
The Last of the Dogmen '95
To Die For '95
Citizen Ruth '96
Prefontaine '96
A Time to Kill '96
A Bright Shining Lie '98
The Magnificent Seven '98
Shelter '98
Entry Level '07
Cedar Rapids '11

Lane Smith (1936-2005)
The Last American Hero '73
Network '76
Blue Collar '78
Frances '82
Prime Suspect '82
Dress Gray '86
If Tomorrow Comes '86
Air America '90
The Distinguished Gentleman '92
False Arrest '92
The Mighty Ducks '92
My Cousin Vinny '92
Son-in-Law '93
The Scout '94
The Spy Within '94
From the Earth to the Moon '98
The Hi-Lo Country '98
Why Do Fools Fall in Love? '98
Inherit the Wind '99
The Legend of Bagger Vance '00
Winds of Terror '01

Lauren Lee Smith (1980-)
The Last Kiss '06
One Way '06
Normal '07
Pathology '08
Trick 'r Treat '08
Helen '09
A Night for Dying Tigers '10

Lewis Smith (1956-)
Southern Comfort '81
The Final Terror '83
The Adventures of Buckaroo Banzai Across the Eighth Dimension '84
The Heavenly Kid '85
North and South Book 2 '86
Diary of a Hitman '91
Wyatt Earp '94

Lionel Mark Smith (1946-2008)
Galaxina '80
King of the Ants '03
Spartan '04
Edmond '05

Liz Smith (1921-)
A Private Function '84
Apartment Zero '88
A Merry War '97
Sweet Revenge '98
A Christmas Carol '99
Dead Cool '04
Charlie and the Chocolate Factory '05
Keeping Mum '05
Oliver Twist '05
Wallace & Gromit in The Curse of the Were-Rabbit '05 (V)
Flick '07

Lois Smith (1930-)
Strange Lady in Town '55
Five Easy Pieces '70
Reckless '84
Black Widow '87
Green Card '90
Fried Green Tomatoes '91
Hard Promises '92
Falling Down '93
Sarah, Plain and Tall: Skylark '93
Holy Matrimony '94
Dead Man Walking '95
How to Make an American Quilt '95
Truman '95
Larger Than Life '96
Twister '96
Tumbleweeds '98
The Eternal '99
The Pledge '00
Minority Report '02
2 Brothers & a Bride '03
P.S. '04
Sweet Land '05
Griffin & Phoenix '06
Hollywoodland '06
Little Fugitive '06
Turn the River '07
Diminished Capacity '08
A Dog Year '09
Please Give '10
Roadie '11
The Odd Life of Timothy Green '12
Marjorie Prime '17

Loring Smith (1895-1981)
Shadow of the Thin Man '41
Close-Up '48
The Clown '53
Ma and Pa Kettle at Waikiki '55
Hurry Sundown '67

Madeleine Smith (1949-)
The Vampire Lovers '70
Live and Let Die '73
Frankenstein and the Monster from Hell '74

Madolyn Smith (1957-)
Urban Cowboy '80
Rehearsal for Murder '82
All of Me '84
2010: The Year We Make Contact '84
If Tomorrow Comes '86
The Caller '87
Funny Farm '88
The Plot to Kill Hitler '90
The Rose and the Jackal '90
The Super '91

Maggie Smith (1934-)
The V.I.P.'s '63
The Pumpkin Eater '64
Othello '65
Young Cassidy '65
The Honey Pot '67
Hot Millions '68
Oh! What a Lovely War '69
The Prime of Miss Jean Brodie '69
Travels with My Aunt '72
Love and Pain and the Whole Damn Thing '73
Murder by Death '76
California Suite '78
Death on the Nile '78
Clash of the Titans '81
Quartet '81
Evil under the Sun '82
The Missionary '82
A Private Function '84

Lily in Love *'85*
A Room with a View *'86*
The Lonely Passion of Judith Hearne *'87*
Hook *'91*
Sister Act *'92*
The Secret Garden *'93*
Sister Act 2: Back in the Habit *'93*
Richard III *'95*
The First Wives Club *'96*
Curtain Call *'97*
Washington Square *'97*
All the King's Men *'99*
David Copperfield *'99*
The Last September *'99*
Tea with Mussolini *'99*
Gosford Park *'01*
Harry Potter and the Sorcerer's Stone *'01*
Divine Secrets of the Ya-Ya Sisterhood *'02*
Harry Potter and the Chamber of Secrets *'02*
My House in Umbria *'03*
Harry Potter and the Prisoner of Azkaban *'04*
Ladies in Lavender *'04*
Harry Potter and the Goblet of Fire *'05*
Keeping Mum *'05*
Becoming Jane *'07*
Harry Potter and the Order of the Phoenix *'07*
Harry Potter and the Half-Blood Prince *'09*
Harry Potter and the Deathly Hallows, Part 1 *'10*
Nanny McPhee Returns *'10*
Gnomeo & Juliet *'11 (V)*
Harry Potter and the Deathly Hallows, Part 2 *'11*
The Best Exotic Marigold Hotel *'12*
Quartet *'12*
My Old Lady *'14*
The Lady in the Van *'15*
The Second Best Exotic Marigold Hotel *'15*
Tea with the Dames *'18*
Downton Abbey *'19*

Mark Coles Smith
Around the Block *'13*
Last Cab to Darwin *'16*

Matt Smith (1982-)
Outsourced *'06*
Ruby in the Smoke *'06*
The Shadow in the North *'07*
Womb *'10*
Christopher and His Kind *'11*
Going for Gold: The '48 Games *'12*
Lost River *'15*
Patient Zero *'18*
Official Secrets *'19*

Maurice Smith (1961-)
Miami Connection *'87*
Bloodfist 2 *'90*
Double Whammy *'01*

Mel Smith (1952-2013)
Slayground *'84*
Morons from Outer Space *'85*
National Lampoon's European Vacation *'85*
The Princess Bride *'87*
Brain Donors *'92*
Twelfth Night *'96*
The Riddle *'07*

Melanie Smith (1962-)
Trancers 3: Deth Lives *'92*
Night Hunter *'95*

Michael Bailey Smith (1957-)
Ice *'93*
Black Mask 2: City of Masks *'02*
In Hell *'03*
Monster Man *'03*
The Hills Have Eyes *'06*
The Hills Have Eyes 2 *'07*
Bus Driver *'16*

Oliver Smith
Hellraiser *'87*
Hellbound: Hellraiser 2 *'88*

Patricia Smith (1930-2011)
Spirit of St. Louis *'57*
Save the Tiger *'73*

Paul Smith (1936-2012)
Loving You *'57*
Madron *'70*
Midnight Express *'78*
Popeye *'80*
Mortuary *'81*
The Salamander *'82*
Pieces *'83*
Dune *'84*
Jungle Warriors *'84*
Red Sonja *'85*
Haunted Honeymoon *'86*
Gor *'88*
Caged Fury *'90*
Crossing the Line *'90*
Maverick *'94*

Queenie Smith
Mississippi *'35*
The Great Rupert *'50*

Quinn Smith
The Bad News Bears *'76*
The Bad News Bears in Breaking Training *'77*

Rachele Brooke Smith
Center Stage: Turn It Up *'08*
Bring It On: Fight to the Finish *'09*
Centerstage: On Pointe *'16*

Rebekah Louise Smith
The Watcher *'00*
No Sleep 'Til Madison *'02*

Rex Smith (1955-)
Sooner or Later *'78*
The Pirates of Penzance *'83*
The Trial of the Incredible Hulk *'89*
Collier & Co.: Hot Pursuit *'06*
Pope Dreams *'06*

Riley Smith (1978-)
Wild Grizzly *'99*
Voodoo Academy *'00*
Eight Legged Freaks *'02*
Full Ride *'02*
Radio *'03*
New York Minute *'04*
Graduation *'07*
Make It Happen *'08*
Universal Squadrons *'11*
Christmas In Conway *'13*

Robin Smith
Bopha! *'93*
Never Say Die *'94*

Roger Smith (1932-)
Man of a Thousand Faces *'57*
No Time to Be Young *'57*
Operation Mad Ball *'57*
Auntie Mame *'58*
Crash Landing *'58*

Roger Guenveur Smith (1955-)
Deep Cover *'92*
Tales from the Hood *'95*
Get On the Bus *'96*
Summer of Sam *'99*
Final Destination *'00*
Hamlet *'01*
All About the Benjamins *'02*
Shade *'03*
Cover *'08*
Fighting *'09*

Russell Smith
Bloom *'03*
Botched *'07*

Sam Smith
Oliver Twist *'00*
Wondrous Oblivion *'06*
Jirga *'19*

Samantha Smith (1969-)
Love's Unending Legacy *'07*
Love's Unfolding Dream *'07*
Transformers *'07*

Savannah Smith (1943-)
The Long Riders *'80*
The Oklahoma City Dolls *'81*
Code of Honor *'84*

Everybody's All American *'88*

Sean Smith (1987-)
Atomic Train *'99*
The King and I *'99 (V)*
Children of the Corn: Revelation *'01*

Seth Smith (1982-)
The Climb *'97*
Home Alone 3 *'97*

Shawn Smith (1922-95)
The Land Unknown *'57*
It! The Terror from Beyond Space *'58*

Shawnee Smith (1969-)
Summer School *'87*
The Blob *'88*
Who's Harry Crumb? *'89*
Desperate Hours *'90*
Stephen King's The Stand *'94*
The Low Life *'95*
Bombshell *'97*
Dogtown *'97*
Breakfast of Champions *'98*
Carnival of Souls *'98*
A Slipping Down Life *'99*
Saw *'04*
The Island *'05*
Saw 2 *'05*
Saw 3 *'06*
Secrets of an Undercover Wife *'07*
Saw 5 *'08*
The Grudge 3 *'09*
Saw 6 *'09*
Grace Unplugged *'13*
Believe *'16*

Sheridan Smith (1981-)
Quartet *'12*
The Scapegoat *'12*

Stacy Smith
Heart of a Stranger *'02*
Marion Bridge *'02*

Sydney Smith (1909-78)
Valerie *'57*
No Time for Sergeants *'58*
The Gallant Hours *'60*

Tasha Smith (1971-)
The Corner *'00*
The Whole Ten Yards *'04*
Daddy's Little Girls *'07*
Love and Other Four Letter Words *'07*
Tyler Perry's Why Did I Get Married? *'07*
The Longshots *'08*
Couples Retreat *'09*
Tyler Perry's Why Did I Get Married Too *'10*
Addicted *'14*

Will Smith (1968-)
Where the Day Takes You *'92*
Made in America *'93*
Six Degrees of Separation *'93*
Bad Boys *'95*
Independence Day *'96*
Men in Black *'97*
Enemy of the State *'98*
Wild Wild West *'99*
The Legend of Bagger Vance *'00*
Ali *'01*
Men in Black 2 *'02*
Bad Boys 2 *'03*
I, Robot *'04*
Jersey Girl *'04 (C)*
Shark Tale *'04 (V)*
Hitch *'05*
The Pursuit of Happyness *'06*
I Am Legend *'07*
Hancock *'08*
Seven Pounds *'08*
Men in Black 3 *'12*
After Earth *'13*
Winter's Tale *'14*
Concussion *'15*
Focus *'15*
Collateral Beauty *'16*
Suicide Squad *'16*
Aladdin *'19*

Gemini Man *'19*
Bad Boys for Life *'20*

Willard Smith (1968-)
See Will Smith

William (Bill) Smith (1933-)
Atlantis, the Lost Continent *'61*
Mail Order Bride *'63*
Run, Angel, Run! *'69*
Angels Die Hard *'70*
C.C. & Company *'70*
The Losers *'70*
Chrome and Hot Leather *'71*
Grave of the Vampire *'72*
The Deadly Trackers *'73*
Invasion of the Bee Girls *'73*
Black Samson *'74*
Boss *'74*
Death Among Friends *'75*
The Ultimate Warrior *'75*
Hollywood Man *'76*
Fast Company *'78*
The Frisco Kid *'79*
Any Which Way You Can *'80*
Conan the Barbarian *'82*
Red Dawn *'84*
Mean Season *'85*
Eye of the Tiger *'86*
Maniac Cop *'88*
Memorial Valley Massacre *'88*
Deadly Breed *'89*
East L.A. Warriors *'89*
Emperor of the Bronx *'89*
L.A. Vice *'89*
Cartel *'90*
The Last Riders *'90*
Spirit of the Eagle *'90*
Neon Signs *'96*
The Shooter *'97*
Broken Vessels *'98*

Willow Smith (2000-)
I Am Legend *'07*
Kit Kittredge: An American Girl *'08*
Dr. Seuss' The Lorax *'12 (V)*

Yeardley Smith (1964-)
Heaven Help Us *'85*
Legend of Billie Jean *'85*
Maximum Overdrive *'86*
City Slickers *'91*
We're Back! A Dinosaur's Story *'93 (V)*
As Good As It Gets *'97*
Just Write *'97*
The Simpsons Movie *'07 (V)*
High School *'10*

J. Smith-Cameron (1957-)
Harriet the Spy *'96*
In and Out *'97*
The Rage: Carrie 2 *'99*
Margaret *'11*
Christine *'16*
Nancy *'18*

Jamie Smith-Jackson (1948-)
Lisa, Bright and Dark *'73*
Satan's School for Girls *'73*
Bug *'75*

William (Bill) Smithers (1927-)
Attack! *'56*
Trouble Man *'72*
Scorpio *'73*
Death Sport *'78*

Bill Smitrovich (1947-)
A Killing Affair *'85*
Silver Bullet *'85*
Renegades *'89*
Crazy People *'90*
Nick of Time *'95*
Ghosts of Mississippi *'96*
Independence Day *'96*
The Trigger Effect *'96*
Air Force One *'97*
Around the Fire *'98*
Dean Koontz's Mr. Murder *'98*
Futuresport *'98*
The '60s *'99*
The Golden Spiders: A Nero Wolfe Mystery *'00*
Kiss Toledo Goodbye *'00*
Thirteen Days *'00*
The Reagans *'04*

The Game of Their Lives *'05*
Mrs. Harris *'05*
Heavens Fall *'06*
The Contract *'07*
Eagle Eye *'08*
Flash of Genius *'08*
Iron Man *'08*
The Last Lullaby *'08*
Seven Pounds *'08*
The November Man *'14*

Jimmy Smits (1955-)
Running Scared *'86*
The Believers *'87*
Old Gringo *'89*
Vital Signs *'90*
Fires Within *'91*
Switch *'91*
Stephen King's The Tommyknockers *'93*
The Cisco Kid *'94*
My Family *'94*
The Last Word *'95*
The Million Dollar Hotel *'99*
Bless the Child *'00*
Price of Glory *'00*
Star Wars: Episode 2-Attack of the Clones *'02*
Star Wars: Episode 3-Revenge of the Sith *'05*
The Jane Austen Book Club *'07*
Mother and Child *'09*

Sonja Smits (1958-)
The Pit *'81*
Videodrome *'83*
Life with Judy Garland-Me and My Shadows *'01*
How to Deal *'03*
Owning Mahowny *'03*
A Different Loyalty *'04*
Siblings *'04*
One Way *'06*

Jurnee Smollett (1986-)
Eve's Bayou *'97*
Selma, Lord, Selma *'99*
Ruby's Bucket of Blood *'01*
Roll Bounce *'05*
The Great Debaters *'07*
Tyler Perry's Temptation: Confessions of a Marriage Counselor *'13*
Birds of Prey: And the Fantabulous Emancipation of One Harley Quinn *'20*

J.B. Smoove (1965-)
Pootie Tang *'01*
Mr. Deeds *'02*
The Sitter *'11*
We Bought a Zoo *'11*
The Smurfs 2 *'13 (V)*
Top Five *'14*
The Polka King *'18*

Dick Smothers (1939-)
Tales of the Unexpected *'91*
Casino *'95*
The Informant! *'09 (C)*

Tom Smothers (1937-)
Alice Through the Looking Glass *'66*
Get to Know Your Rabbit *'72*
The Kids Are Alright *'79*
Serial *'80*
The Informant! *'09 (C)*

Cobie Smulders (1982-)
The Long Weekend *'05*
The Slammin' Salmon *'09*
The Avengers *'12*
Delivery Man *'13*
Safe Haven *'13*
Captain America: The Winter Soldier *'14*
They Came Together *'14*
Results *'15*
Unexpected *'15*
The Intervention *'16*
Jack Reacher: Never Go Back *'16*
Killing Gunther *'17*

Victoria Smurfit (1974-)
The Run of the Country *'95*
Romance and Rejection *'96*
Ivanhoe *'97*
Berkeley Square *'98*
About a Boy *'02*

Bulletproof Monk *'03*
The Shell Seekers *'06*

Kasia Smutniak (1979-)
Carnera: The Walking Mountain *'08*
Quiet Chaos *'08*
Sword of War *'09*
From Paris With Love *'10*
Loro *'19*

Ann Smyrner (1934-)
Reptilicus *'62*
Death is Nimble, Death is Quick *'67*
The House of 1000 Dolls *'67*
Beyond the Law *'68*

Sarah Smyth (1982-)
Student Seduction *'03*
Alien Trespass *'09*
Duke *'12*

Yuliya Snigir (1983-)
A Good Day to Die Hard *'13*
Freezer *'14*

Wesley Snipes (1962-)
Wildcats *'86*
Major League *'89*
King of New York *'90*
Mo' Better Blues *'90*
Jungle Fever *'91*
New Jack City *'91*
The Waterdance *'91*
Passenger 57 *'92*
White Men Can't Jump *'92*
Boiling Point *'93*
Demolition Man *'93*
Rising Sun *'93*
Drop Zone *'94*
Sugar Hill *'94*
America's Dream *'95*
Money Train *'95*
To Wong Foo, Thanks for Everything, Julie Newmar *'95*
Waiting to Exhale *'95 (C)*
The Fan *'96*
Murder at 1600 *'97*
One Night Stand *'97*
Blade *'98*
Down in the Delta *'98*
Futuresport *'98*
U.S. Marshals *'98*
The Art of War *'00*
Disappearing Acts *'00*
Blade 2 *'02*
Liberty Stands Still *'02*
Undisputed *'02*
ZigZag *'02*
Blade: Trinity *'04*
Seven Seconds *'05*
The Detonator *'06*
The Contractor *'07*
Art of War 2: The Betrayal *'08*
Brooklyn's Finest *'09*
Game of Death *'10*
The Expendables 3 *'14*
Chi-raq *'15*
The Recall *'17*

Carrie Snodgress (1946-2004)
Rabbit, Run *'70*
The Fury *'78*
The Attic *'80*
A Night in Heaven *'83*
Nadia *'84*
Pale Rider *'85*
Murphy's Law *'86*
Blueberry Hill *'88*
Across the Tracks *'89*
Chill Factor *'90*
The Rose and the Jackal *'90*
Blue Sky *'91*
Mission of the Shark *'91*
The Ballad of Little Jo *'93*
8 Seconds *'94*
Phantom 2040 Movie: The Ghost Who Walks *'95 (V)*
White Man's Burden *'95*
A Stranger in the Kingdom *'98*
Wild Things *'98*
Bartleby *'01*
Ed Gein *'01*
The Forsaken *'01*

Sarah Snook (1987-)
Not Suitable for Children '12
Predestination '15
Steve Jobs '15
The Dressmaker '16
Winchester '18

Snoop Dogg (1971-)
Half-Baked '97
Caught Up '98
Ride '98 (C)
Urban Menace '99
The Wrecking Crew '99
Baby Boy '01
Bones '01
Training Day '01
The Wash '01
Malibu's Most Wanted '03 (V)
Old School '03 (C)
Soul Plane '04
Starsky & Hutch '04
Racing Stripes '05 (V)
Arthur and the Invisibles '06 (V)
The Tenants '06
Falling Up '08
The Big Bang '11
Turbo '13 (V)
Future World '18
The Beach Bum '19

Brittany Snow (1986-)
The Pacifier '05
John Tucker Must Die '06
All the Good Ones Are Married '07
Hairspray '07
On the Doll '07
Finding Amanda '08
Prom Night '08
The Vicious Kind '09
Janie Jones '10
96 Minutes '11
Pitch Perfect '12
Call Me Crazy '13
Petunia '13
Syrup '13
Always Woodstock '15
Pitch Perfect 2 '15
Bushwick '17
Hangman '17
Pitch Perfect 3 '17
Someone Great '19

Raven Snow
Delta of Venus '95
Red Shoe Diaries 6: How I Met My Husband '95

Victoria Snow
Buffalo Jump '90
My Husband's Double Life '01
Waking Up Wally '05

Arlen Dean Snyder
Yanks '79
Heartbreak Ridge '86
Internal Affairs '90
Marked for Death '90
Mommy 2: Mommy's Day '96
Cora Unashamed '00

Dana Snyder
Aqua Teen Hunger Force Colon Movie Film for Theaters '07 (V)
Open Season 3 '10 (V)

Drew Snyder (1946-)
Night School '81
Firestarter '84
Izzy & Moe '85
Dance with Death '91
Project: Eliminator '91
Separate Lives '94

Suzanne Snyder (1962-)
Killer Klowns from Outer Space '88
The Night Before '88
Retribution '88
Return of the Living Dead 2 '88

Michele (Michael) Soavi (1957-)
Alien 2 on Earth '80
Gates of Hell '80
A Blade in the Dark '83
Creepers '85
Demons '86

Barry Sobel
Punchline '88
Doc Hollywood '91
I Love Trouble '94
That Thing You Do! '96

Leelee Sobieski (1983-)
A Horse for Danny '95
Jungle 2 Jungle '96
Deep Impact '98
A Soldier's Daughter Never Cries '98
Eyes Wide Shut '99
Joan of Arc '99
Never Been Kissed '99
Here on Earth '00
The Glass House '01
Joy Ride '01
My First Mister '01
Uprising '01
Max '02
Dangerous Liaisons '03
The Elder Son '06
Heavens Fall '06
The Wicker Man '06
88 Minutes '08
In the Name of the King: A Dungeon Siege Tale '08
Finding Bliss '09
Night Train '09
Public Enemies '09
Branded '12

Ron Soble (1932-2002)
True Grit '69
The Beast Within '82

Maria Socas (1959-)
Soldier's Revenge '84
The Warrior & the Sorceress '84
Deathstalker 2: Duel of the Titans '87

Michael Socha (1987-)
Twenty8k '12
The Keeper '18
Killers Anonymous '19

Kristina Soderbaum (1912-2001)
Jud Suess '40
Kolberg '45
Night Train to Venice '93

Steven Soderbergh (1963-)
Schizopolis '97
Waking Life '01
Side by Side '12

Camilla Soeberg (1966-)
Twist & Shout '84
Erotique '94
Mouse Hunt '97
The Empty Mirror '99

Barry Soetoro (1961-)
See Barack Obama

Abraham Sofaer (1896-1988)
Quo Vadis '51
Elephant Walk '54
Naked Jungle '54
Bhowani Junction '56
Captain Sinbad '63

Rena Sofer (1968-)
Twinsitters '95
Keeping the Faith '00
Traffic '00
Carrie '02
The Secret of Hidden Lake '06
Rock Slyde: Private Eye '09
The Devil's Teardrop '10

Andre Sogliuzzo
The Polar Express '04
Open Season 3 '10 (V)

Peter Sohn
Ratatouille '07 (V)
Monsters University '13 (V)

Sonja Sohn
Slam '98
Step Up 2 the Streets '08
Domain '18

Hans Sohnker (1903-81)
Sherlock Holmes and the Deadly Necklace '62
The Phantom of Soho '64

Sojin (1884-1954)
The Thief of Baghdad '24
Seven Samurai '54

Marilyn Sokol (1937-)
The Goodbye Girl '77
Foul Play '78
Something Short of Paradise '79
Lucky Days '08

Marla Sokoloff (1980-)
Dude, Where's My Car? '00
Whatever It Takes '00
Sugar & Spice '01
A Date With Darkness '03
Freshman Orientation '04
Love on the Side '04
The Tollbooth '04
Christmas in Boston '05
Crazylove '05
Maneater '09
Meteor '09
Play the Game '09
Gift of the Magi '10
The Chateau Meroux '11

Vladimir Sokoloff (1889-1962)
The Lower Depths '36
Conquest '37
The Real Glory '39
Comrade X '40
Crossroads '42
The Road to Morocco '42
For Whom the Bell Tolls '43
Cloak and Dagger '46
A Scandal in Paris '46
Two Smart People '46
Baron of Arizona '51
Beyond the Time Barrier '60
Mr. Sardonicus '61
Taras Bulba '62

Kyung-gu Sol
Public Enemy '02
Another Public Enemy '05

Miguel Angel Sola (1950-)
Funny, Dirty Little War '83
A Shadow You Soon Will Be '94
Tango '98

Simonetta Solder
Mother of Tears '08
One Kiss '16

Andres Soler
Over the Waves '49
El Bruto '52

Paul Soles (1930-)
Ticket to Heaven '81
The Score '01

P.J. Soles (1950-)
The Boy in the Plastic Bubble '76
Carrie '76
The Possessed '77
Halloween '78
Zuma Beach '78
Rock 'n' Roll High School '79
Stripes '81
Sweet Dreams '85
Alienator '89
Little Bigfoot '96
Jawbreaker '98
The Devil's Rejects '05
The Tooth Fairy '06
Alone in the Dark 2 '08

Magaly Solier (1986-)
The Milk of Sorrow '09
Blackthorn '11

Cristian Solimeno (1975-)
Highlander: The Source '07
Mother of Tears '08
Perfect Hideout '08

Yulia Solntseva (1901-89)
Aelita: Queen of Mars '24
The Cigarette Girl of Mosselprom '24
Earth '30

Ksenia Solo
Defending Our Kids: The Julie Posey Story '03
In Search of Fellini '17

Bruce Solomon (1944-)
Children Shouldn't Play with Dead Things '72
Foul Play '78
Night of the Creeps '86
Auto Focus '02

Charles Solomon, Jr.
1918 '85
Witchcraft 2: The Temptress '90
Witchcraft 4: Virgin Heart '92
Cadillac Ranch '96
The Strangers '98
Poor White Trash '00
Missionary Man '07

Anatoli (Otto) Solonitzin (1934-82)
Andrei Rublev '66
Solaris '72
Stalker '79

Elena Solovei (1947-)
An Unfinished Piece for a Player Piano '77
A Slave of Love '78
Oblomov '81

Laura Soltis (1961-)
Double Cross '06
Home By Christmas '06
Secret Lives of Second Wives '08

Yanti Somer
Reactor '78
Cosmos: War of the Planets '80

Ian Somerhalder (1978-)
Life as a House '01
The Rules of Attraction '02
In Enemy Hands '04
Pulse '06
The Sensation of Sight '06
Marco Polo '07
Lost City Raiders '08
The Lost Samaritan '08
Fireball '09
How to Make Love to a Woman '09
The Tournament '09
Wake '09
The Anomaly '15

Kristi Somers (1962-)
Hardbodies '84
Tomboy '85

Suzanne Somers (1946-)
American Graffiti '73
Ants '77
Zuma Beach '78
Serial Mom '94
Say It Isn't So '01

Bonnie Somerville (1974-)
Sleep Easy, Hutch Rimes '00
Without a Paddle '04
Wedding Wars '06
The Search for Santa Paws '10
Holiday Engagement '11
7 Below '11
Treasure Buddies '12 (V)

Geraldine Somerville (1967-)
Catherine Cookson's The Black Velvet Gown '92
Cracker: Men Should Weep '94
Cracker: To Be a Somebody '94
Cracker: Brotherly Love '95
Haunted '95
Aristocrats '99
The Aristocrats '99
Gosford Park '01
Daphne '07
Titanic '12

Phyllis Somerville (1943-)
Swimfan '02
Little Children '06
The Brooklyn Heist '08
The Curious Case of Benjamin Button '08
The Mighty Macs '09
Weakness '10
The Double '13

Julie Sommars (1941-)
Herbie Goes to Monte Carlo '77
Cave-In! '79

Elke Sommer (1940-)
Daniella by Night '61
Sweet Ecstasy '62
The Prize '63
A Shot in the Dark '64
Bambole '65
The Money Trap '65
Boy, Did I Get a Wrong Number! '66
Deadlier Than the Male '67
The Venetian Affair '67
They Came to Rob Las Vegas '68
The Wrecking Crew '68
Zeppelin '71
Probe '72
Torture Chamber of Baron Blood '72
Carry On Behind '75
Lisa and the Devil '75
Ten Little Indians '75
The Invisible Strangler '76
Meet Him and Die '76
Swiss Conspiracy '77
The Big Scam '79
The Double McGuffin '79
Prisoner of Zenda '79
Lily in Love '85
No One Cries Forever '85
Anastasia: The Mystery of Anna '86

Josef Sommer (1934-)
Dirty Harry '71
The Scarlet Letter '79
Hide in Plain Sight '80
Absence of Malice '81
Reds '81
Rollover '81
Still of the Night '82
Agatha Christie's Sparkling Cyanide '83
Silkwood '83
Iceman '84
Execution of Raymond Graham '85
Target '85
Witness '85
Yuri Nosenko, KGB '86
The Betty Ford Story '87
Dracula's Widow '88
Bloodhounds of Broadway '89
Bridge to Silence '89
Chances Are '89
The Mighty Ducks '92
Shadows and Fog '92
Malice '93
The Enemy Within '94
Nobody's Fool '94
Moonlight and Valentino '95
Strange Days '95
Hidden in America '96
Mistrial '96
The Proposition '97
Patch Adams '98
Family Man '00
The Next Best Thing '00
Shaft '00
Searching for Paradise '02
The Sum of All Fears '02
The Elephant King '06
X-Men: The Last Stand '06
The Invasion '07
Stop-Loss '08

Kostas Sommer
The Boston Strangler: The Untold Story '08
Drifter '09

Rich Sommer (1978-)
The Devil Wears Prada '06
The Giant Mechanical Man '12

Helga Sommerfeld (1941-91)
The Phantom of Soho '64
24 Hours to Kill '65

Jennifer Sommerfield
Destination Vegas '95
Megalodon '03

Joanie Sommers
Everything's Ducky '61
The Lively Set '64

Sommore (1966-)
Queens of Comedy '01
Friday After Next '02

Gale Sondergaard (1899-1985)
Anthony Adverse '36
The Life of Emile Zola '37
Maid of Salem '37
The Cat and the Canary '39
Juarez '39
Never Say Die '39
The Blue Bird '40
The Letter '40
The Mark of Zorro '40
The Black Cat '41
My Favorite Blonde '42
A Night to Remember '42
Isle of Forgotten Sins '43
The Climax '44
The Invisible Man's Revenge '44
Anna and the King of Siam '46
The Time of Their Lives '46
The Road to Rio '47
East Side, West Side '49
The Return of a Man Called Horse '76
Echoes '83

Brenda Song (1988-)
Get a Clue '02
Like Mike '02
College Road Trip '08
Special Delivery '08
The Social Network '10

Kang-ho Song (1967-)
No. 3 '97
The Quiet Family '98
The Foul King '00
JSA: Joint Security Area '00
Sympathy for Mr. Vengeance '02
The Host '06
The Good, the Bad, the Weird '08
Thirst '09
Snowpiercer '14
The Age of Shadows '16
A Taxi Driver '17
Parasite '19

Steph Song (1984-)
Everything's Gone Green '06
Dim Sum Funeral '08
The Thaw '09
Maximum Conviction '12

Trey Songz (1984-)
Texas Chainsaw 3D '13
Blood Brother '18

Karan Soni
Safety Not Guaranteed '12
Deadpool '16
Corporate Animals '19

Paul Sonkkila
The Interview '98
The Hard Word '02

Michael Sonye
Sorority Babes in the Slimeball Bowl-A-Rama '87 (V)
Surf Nazis Must Die '87

Jack Soo (1916-79)
Flower Drum Song '61
The Green Berets '68
Return from Witch Mountain '78

Brandon Soo Hoo (1995-)
Tropic Thunder '08
G.I. Joe: The Rise of Cobra '09

Veena Sood
Touch of Pink '04
Nina's Heavenly Delights '06
Compulsion '08
Possession '08

Nikki SooHoo (1988-)
Stick It *'06*
Bring It On: Fight to the Finish *'09*
Bahar Soomekh (1975-)
Saw 3 *'06*
Just Like a Woman *'13*
Lucille Soong (1938-)
Nora's Hair Salon 2: A Cut Above *'08*
Nine Dead *'10*
Michael Sopkiw (1954-)
After the Fall of New York *'85*
Massacre in Dinosaur Valley *'85*
Agnes Soral (1960-)
Blitz *'85*
Window to Paris *'95*
Kevin Sorbo (1958-)
Hercules the Legendary Journeys, Vol. 1: And the Amazon Women *'94*
Hercules the Legendary Journeys, Vol. 2: The Lost Kingdom *'94*
Hercules the Legendary Journeys, Vol. 3: The Circle of Fire *'94*
Hercules the Legendary Journeys, Vol. 4: In the Underworld *'94*
Kull the Conqueror *'97*
Last Chance Cafe *'06*
Avenging Angel *'07*
Something Beneath *'07*
Walking Tall: Lone Justice *'07*
Walking Tall: The Payback *'07*
Meet the Spartans *'08*
Never Cry Werewolf *'08*
Prairie Fever *'08*
Fire From Below *'09*
Tommy and the Cool Mule *'09*
Flesh Wounds *'10*
The Santa Suit *'10*
Coffin *'11*
Soul Surfer *'11*
Tales of an Ancient Empire *'11*
Abel's Field *'12*
Black Box *'12*
Fatal Call *'12*
Shadow on the Mesa *'13*
Storm Rider *'13*
God's Not Dead *'14*
Mythica: A Quest for Heroes *'15*
Mythica: The Iron Crown *'16*
Let There Be Light *'17*
Alberto Sordi (1920-2003)
The White Sheik *'52*
I Vitelloni *'53*
Two Nights with Cleopatra *'54*
A Farewell to Arms *'57*
And the Wild, Wild Women *'59*
Mafioso *'62*
Those Magnificent Men in Their Flying Machines *'65*
The Queens *'66*
Jean Sorel (1934-)
Bambole *'65*
The Queens *'66*
Belle de Jour *'67*
Kill Me Quick, I'm Cold *'67*
A Lizard in a Woman's Skin *'71*
Short Night of Glass Dolls *'71*
Louise Sorel (1940-)
Plaza Suite *'71*
Get Christie Love! *'74*
When Every Day Was the Fourth of July *'78*
Mazes and Monsters *'82*
Nancy Sorel (1964-)
In the Lake of the Woods *'96*
I Love You, Don't Touch Me! *'97*

Ted (Theodore) Sorel (1936-2010)
Network *'76*
From Beyond *'86*
Basket Case 2 *'90*
Me and the Mob *'94*
Linda Sorensen (1942-)
Kavik the Wolf Dog *'80*
Relative Fear *'95*
The Mountain Between Us *'17*
Ricky Sorenson (1946-94)
Tarzan and the Trappers *'58*
Tarzan's Fight for Life *'58*
The Sword in the Stone *'63 (V)*
Joseph Julian Soria
Hamlet 2 *'08*
The Purge: Election Year *'16*
Charo Soriano (1928-)
Dracula's Great Love *'72*
Orgy of the Vampires *'73*
Takashi Sorimachi
Full Time Killer *'01*
Genghis Khan: To the Ends of the Earth and Sea *'07*
Arleen (Arlene) Sorkin (1956-)
I Don't Buy Kisses Anymore *'92*
It's Pat: The Movie *'94*
Comic Book: The Movie *'04*
Lodovico Sorret (1951-)
See Tom Noonan
Mira Sorvino (1967-)
Amongst Friends *'93*
Tales of Erotica *'93*
Barcelona *'94*
New York Cop *'94*
Quiz Show *'94*
Blue in the Face *'95*
The Buccaneers *'95*
Mighty Aphrodite *'95*
Norma Jean and Marilyn *'95*
Tarantella *'95*
Beautiful Girls *'96*
Mimic *'97*
Romy and Michele's High School Reunion *'97*
At First Sight *'98*
Lulu on the Bridge *'98*
The Replacement Killers *'98*
Free Money *'99*
Summer of Sam *'99*
The Great Gatsby *'01*
The Grey Zone *'01*
The Triumph of Love *'01*
Angel of Death *'02*
Between Strangers *'02*
Wisegirls *'02*
Gods and Generals *'03*
The Final Cut *'04*
Human Trafficking *'05*
The Hades Factor *'06*
Attack on Leningrad *'09*
The Last Templar *'09*
Like Dandelion Dust *'09*
Multiple Sarcasms *'10*
Angels Crest *'11*
Trade of Innocents *'12*
Space Warriors *'13*
Ava & Lala *'14*
Perfect Sisters *'14*
Chloe & Theo *'15*
Do You Believe? *'15*
Exposed *'16*
Quitters *'16*
6 Below: Miracle on the Mountain *'17*
Look Away *'18*
Stuber *'19*
Paul Sorvino (1939-)
Where's Poppa? *'70*
Cry Uncle *'71*
Panic in Needle Park *'71*
The Day of the Dolphin *'73*
A Touch of Class *'73*
The Gambler *'74*
I Will, I Will...for Now *'76*
Oh, God! *'77*
Bloodbrothers *'78*
Brink's Job *'78*
Dummy *'79*
Lost and Found *'79*

Cruising *'80*
Reds *'81*
I, the Jury *'82*
That Championship Season *'82*
The Stuff *'85*
Turk 182! *'85*
A Fine Mess *'86*
Jailbait: Betrayed By Innocence *'86*
Dick Tracy *'90*
Goodfellas *'90*
Nightmare *'91*
The Rocketeer *'91*
The Firm *'93*
Nixon *'95*
Escape Clause *'96*
Love Is All There Is *'96*
William Shakespeare's Romeo and Juliet *'96*
Dogwatch *'97*
Money Talks *'97*
Most Wanted *'97*
Bulworth *'98*
Houdini *'98*
Knock Off *'98*
Dead Broke *'99*
Harlem Aria *'99*
That Championship Season *'99*
Cheaters *'00*
The Thin Blue Lie *'00*
Perfume *'01*
See Spot Run *'01*
Hey Arnold! The Movie *'02 (V)*
The Cooler *'03*
Mambo Italiano *'03*
Mr. 3000 *'04*
Mr. Fix It *'06*
Last Hour *'08*
Repo! The Genetic Opera *'08*
Doc West *'09*
Santa Baby 2: Santa Maybe *'09*
Triggerman *'09*
The Wild Stallion *'09*
Kill the Irishman *'11*
Jersey Shore Shark Attack *'12*
The Hybrids Family *'16*
Roberto Sosa (1970-)
Cabeza de Vaca *'90*
Highway Patrolman *'91*
Lolo *'92*
Hombres Armados *'97*
Pulling Strings *'13*
Nina Sosanya
Casanova *'05*
Wide Sargasso Sea *'06*
Shannyn Sossamon (1978-)
A Knight's Tale *'01*
40 Days and 40 Nights *'02*
The Rules of Attraction *'02*
The Order *'03*
Chasing Ghosts *'05*
Devour *'05*
Kiss Kiss Bang Bang *'05*
Undiscovered *'05*
The Holiday *'06*
Wristcutters: A Love Story *'06*
Catacombs *'07*
Life is Hot in Cracktown *'08*
One Missed Call *'08*
The Heavy *'09*
Sinister 2 *'15*
Paul Soter (1969-)
Super Troopers *'01*
Club Dread *'04*
Beerfest *'06*
The Slammin' Salmon *'09*
Super Troopers 2 *'18*
Ann Sothern (1909-2001)
Kid Millions *'34*
Folies Bergere de Paris *'35*
Hooray for Love *'35*
Danger: Love at Work *'37*
She's Got Everything *'37*
Fast and Furious *'39*
Maisie *'39*
Brother Orchid *'40*
Congo Maisie *'40*
Gold Rush Maisie *'40*

Lady Be Good *'41*
Maisie Was a Lady *'41*
Ringside Maisie *'41*
Maisie Gets Her Man *'42*
Panama Hattie *'42*
Cry Havoc *'43*
Swing Shift Maisie *'43*
Maisie Goes to Reno *'44*
Up Goes Maisie *'46*
Undercover Maisie *'47*
Words and Music *'48*
The Judge Steps Out *'49*
A Letter to Three Wives *'49*
Nancy Goes to Rio *'50*
The Blue Gardenia *'53*
The Best Man *'64*
Lady in a Cage *'64*
Chubasco *'67*
The Killing Kind *'73*
Golden Needles *'74*
Crazy Mama *'75*
The Manitou *'78*
Little Dragons *'80*
The Whales of August *'87*
Talisa Soto (1967-)
License to Kill *'89*
The Mambo Kings *'92*
Don Juan DeMarco *'94*
Mortal Kombat 1: The Movie *'95*
Sunchaser *'96*
Vampirella *'96*
Flypaper *'97*
Mortal Kombat 2: Annihilation *'97*
Island of the Dead *'00*
Pinero *'01*
Ballistic: Ecks *vs.* Sever *'02*
La Mission *'09*
Zinedine Soualem
Roman de Gare *'07*
The Names of Love *'10*
Kath Soucie (1967-)
The Rugrats Movie *'98 (V)*
Rugrats in Paris: The Movie *'00 (V)*
Return to Never Land *'02 (V)*
Piglet's Big Movie *'03 (V)*
Rugrats Go Wild! *'03 (V)*
Clifford's Really Big Movie *'04 (V)*
Happily N'Ever After *'07 (V)*
Space Chimps *'08 (V)*
Masami Souda
Rica *'72*
Rica 3: Juvenile's Lullaby *'73*
David Soul (1943-)
Johnny Got His Gun *'71*
Magnum Force *'73*
Dog Pound Shuffle *'75*
Little Ladies of the Night *'77*
Salem's Lot *'79*
The Manions of America *'81*
World War III *'86*
Hanoi Hilton *'87*
Through Naked Eyes *'87*
In the Line of Duty: The FBI Murders *'88*
In the Cold of the Night *'89*
Grave Secrets: The Legacy of Hilltop Drive *'92*
Pentathlon *'94*
Terror in the Mall *'98*
Starsky & Hutch *'04 (C)*
Farewell *'09*
Nicholas Soussanin
The Last Command *'28*
A Parisian Romance *'32*
Renee Soutendijk (1957-)
The 4th Man *'79*
Spetters *'80*
Cold Room *'84*
Eve of Destruction *'90*
A Perfect Man *'13*
J.D. Souther
To Cross the Rubicon *'91*
Deadline *'12*
Charles Southwood (1937-)
Fistful of Lead *'70*
Roy Colt and Winchester Jack *'70*

Sartana's Here. . . Trade Your Pistol for a Coffin *'70*
Ben Soutten
The Crimes of Stephen Hawke *'36*
The Mutiny of the Elsinore *'39*
Jane Sowerby
How It All Went Down *'03*
Secrets of an Undercover Wife *'07*
Ania Sowinski
Extraordinary Rendition *'07*
Draw on Sweet Night *'15*
Catherine Spaak (1945-)
Le Trou *'59*
Il Sorpasso *'63*
Circle of Love *'64*
Hotel *'67*
The Libertine *'69*
The Cat o' Nine Tails *'71*
Counter Punch *'71*
Arthur Space (1908-83)
Magnificent Doll *'46*
The Red House *'47*
A Southern Yankee *'48*
Miss Grant Takes Richmond *'49*
African Treasure *'52*
Terror at Red Wolf Inn *'72*
Sissy Spacek (1949-)
Prime Cut *'72*
Ginger in the Morning *'73*
Badlands *'74*
Katherine *'75*
Carrie *'76*
3 Women *'77*
Coal Miner's Daughter *'80*
Heart Beat *'80*
Raggedy Man *'81*
Missing *'82*
The Man with Two Brains *'83 (V)*
The River *'84*
Marie *'85*
Crimes of the Heart *'86*
'night, Mother *'86*
Violets Are Blue *'86*
The Long Walk Home *'89*
JFK *'91*
Hard Promises *'92*
A Private Matter *'92*
Trading Mom *'94*
The Good Old Boys *'95*
The Grass Harp *'95*
Larry McMurtry's Streets of Laredo *'95*
Beyond the Call *'96*
If These Walls Could Talk *'96*
Affliction *'97*
Blast from the Past *'98*
The Straight Story *'99*
In the Bedroom *'01*
Last Call: The Final Chapter of F. Scott Fitzgerald *'02*
Tuck Everlasting *'02*
A Home at the End of the World *'04*
An American Haunting *'05*
Nine Lives *'05*
North Country *'05*
The Ring 2 *'05*
Gray Matters *'06*
Hot Rod *'07*
Pictures of Hollis Woods *'07*
Four Christmases *'08*
Lake City *'08*
Get Low *'09*
The Help *'11*
Deadfall *'12*
The Old Man & the Gun *'18*
Kevin Spacey (1959-)
Heartburn *'86*
The Murder of Mary Phagan *'87*
Long Day's Journey into Night *'88*
Rocket Gibraltar *'88*
Working Girl *'88*
Dad *'89*
See No Evil, Hear No Evil *'89*
Henry & June *'90*
Consenting Adults *'92*

Glengarry Glen Ross *'92*
Iron Will *'93*
The Ref *'93*
Doomsday Gun *'94*
Outbreak *'94*
Swimming with Sharks *'94*
Seven *'95*
The Usual Suspects *'95*
Looking for Richard *'96*
A Time to Kill *'96*
L.A. Confidential *'97*
Midnight in the Garden of Good and Evil *'97*
A Bug's Life *'98 (V)*
Hurlyburly *'98*
The Negotiator *'98*
American Beauty *'99*
Ordinary Decent Criminal *'99*
The Big Kahuna *'00*
Pay It Forward *'00*
K-PAX *'01*
The Shipping News *'01*
Austin Powers In Goldmember *'02 (C)*
The Life of David Gale *'03*
United States of Leland *'03*
Beyond the Sea *'04*
Edison Force *'05*
Superman Returns *'06*
Fred Claus *'07*
Recount *'08*
Telstar: The Joe Meek Story *'08*
21 *'08*
The Men Who Stare at Goats *'09*
Moon *'09 (V)*
Shrink *'09*
Casino Jack *'10*
Father of Invention *'11*
Horrible Bosses *'11*
Margin Call *'11*
Horrible Bosses 2 *'14*
NOW: In the Wings on a World Stage *'14*
Elvis & Nixon *'16*
Nine Lives *'16*
Baby Driver *'17*
Rebel in the Rye *'17*
Billionaire Boys Club *'18*
David Spade (1964-)
Coneheads *'93*
P.C.U. *'94*
Tommy Boy *'95*
Beavis and Butt-Head Do America *'96 (V)*
Black Sheep *'96*
8 Heads in a Duffel Bag *'96*
A Very Brady Sequel *'96*
The Rugrats Movie *'98 (V)*
Senseless *'98*
Lost and Found *'99*
The Emperor's New Groove *'00 (V)*
Loser *'00*
Joe Dirt *'01*
Dickie Roberts: Former Child Star *'03*
Racing Stripes *'05 (V)*
The Benchwarmers *'06*
Grandma's Boy *'06*
Grown Ups *'10*
Jack and Jill *'11*
Hotel Transylvania *'12 (V)*
Grown Ups 2 *'13*
Hotel Transylvania 3: Summer Vacation *'18 (V)*
James Spader (1960-)
Endless Love *'81*
A Killer in the Family *'83*
The New Kids *'85*
Tuff Turf *'85*
Pretty in Pink *'86*
Baby Boom *'87*
Less Than Zero *'87*
Mannequin *'87*
Wall Street *'87*
The Rachel Papers *'89*
sex, lies and videotape *'89*
Bad Influence *'90*
White Palace *'90*
True Colors *'91*
Bob Roberts *'92*
Storyville *'92*
Dream Lover *'93*
The Music of Chance *'93*

Stargate *'94*
Wolf *'94*
Crash *'95*
Keys to Tulsa *'96*
Two Days in the Valley *'96*
Critical Care *'97*
Curtain Call *'97*
Driftwood *'97*
Supernova *'99*
Slow Burn *'00*
The Watcher *'00*
The Stickup *'01*
Secretary *'02*
Alien Hunter *'03*
I Witness *'03*
Shorts: The Adventures of the Wishing Rock *'09*
The Homesman *'14*

Joshua Spafford (1972-)
XX/XY *'02*
Robot Stories *'03*

Douglas Spain (1974-)
Riot in the Streets *'96*
Star Maps *'97*
The Last Best Sunday *'98*
Ricochet River *'98*
What's Cooking? *'00*
Nightstalker *'02*
44 Minutes: The North Hollywood Shootout *'03*
The Reading Room *'05*
Still Green *'07*
Fix *'08*

Fay Spain (1932-83)
Dragstrip Girl *'57*
Teenage Doll *'57*
God's Little Acre *'58*
Al Capone *'59*
Black Gold *'62*
Hercules and the Captive Women *'63*
Welcome to Hard Times *'67*
The Godfather, Part 2 *'74*

Rafe Spall (1983-)
Green Street Hooligans *'05*
The Chatterley Affair *'06*
Dracula *'06*
Wide Sargasso Sea *'06*
Hot Fuzz *'07*
A Room With a View *'08*
Anonymous *'11*
One Day *'11*
Life of Pi *'12*
Prometheus *'12*
I Give It a Year *'13*
What If *'13*
A Brilliant Young Mind *'14*
Jurassic World: Fallen Kingdom *'18*
Men in Black: International *'19*

Timothy Spall (1957-)
Home Sweet Home *'82*
Dutch Girls *'87*
Gothic *'87*
Crusoe *'89*
Life Is Sweet *'90*
The Sheltering Sky *'90*
White Hunter, Black Heart *'90*
Secrets and Lies *'95*
Hamlet *'96*
Immortality *'98*
Our Mutual Friend *'98*
Still Crazy *'98*
Shooting the Past *'99*
Topsy Turvy *'99*
Chicken Run *'00 (V)*
Intimacy *'00*
Love's Labour's Lost *'00*
Vatel *'00*
Lucky Break *'01*
Rock Star *'01*
Vacuuming Completely Nude in Paradise *'01*
Vanilla Sky *'01*
All or Nothing *'02*
Nicholas Nickleby *'02*
The Last Samurai *'03*
My House in Umbria *'03*
Harry Potter and the Prisoner of Azkaban *'04*
Lemony Snicket's A Series of Unfortunate Events *'04*
Harry Potter and the Goblet of Fire *'05*
Death Defying Acts *'07*
Enchanted *'07*
Oliver Twist *'07*
Sweeney Todd: The Demon Barber of Fleet Street *'07*
Appaloosa *'08*
A Room With a View *'08*
The Damned United *'09*
Harry Potter and the Half-Blood Prince *'09*
Heartless *'10*
The King's Speech *'10*
Wake Wood *'10*
Christmas Angel *'11*
Assassin's Bullet *'12*
Ginger & Rosa *'13*
The Love Punch *'13*
Upside Down *'13*
Wasteland *'13*
Mr. Turner *'14*
Denial *'16*
The Party *'17*
Early Man *'18*
Finding Your Feet *'18*
Mrs. Lowry & Son *'19*

Ignazio Spalla (1924-95)
See Pedro Sanchez

Joe Spano (1946-)
American Graffiti *'73*
Warlock Moon *'73*
The Enforcer *'76*
Brotherhood of Justice *'86*
Fever *'91*
Apollo 13 *'95*
Primal Fear *'96*
From the Earth to the Moon *'98*
Logan's War: Bound by Honor *'98*
Texas Rangers *'01*
Hart's War *'02*
Hollywoodland *'06*

Vincent Spano (1962-)
The Double McGuffin *'79*
Over the Edge *'79*
Senior Trip *'81*
Baby It's You *'82*
The Black Stallion Returns *'83*
Rumble Fish *'83*
Alphabet City *'84*
Maria's Lovers *'84*
Creator *'85*
And God Created Woman *'88*
City of Hope *'91*
Oscar *'91*
Afterburn *'92*
Alive *'93*
Indian Summer *'93*
The Tie That Binds *'95*
A Brooklyn State of Mind *'97*
No Strings Attached *'98*
The Prophecy 3: The Ascent *'99*
The Rats *'01*
Texas Rangers *'01*
Deathlands: Homeward Bound *'03*
Her Fatal Flaw *'06*
Nevermore *'07*
Pandemic *'07*
The Prince and the Pauper *'07*
Lone Rider *'08*
Fatal Secrets *'09*

Adrian Sparks
My Stepmother Is an Alien *'88*
Papa: Hemingway in Cuba *'16*

Jordin Sparks (1989-)
Sparkle *'12*
The Inevitable Defeat of Mister & Pete *'13*
Left Behind *'14*
God Bless the Broken Road *'18*

Ned Sparks (1883-1957)
Corsair *'31*
Kept Husbands *'31*
The Crusader *'32*
42nd Street *'33*
Going Hollywood *'33*
Gold Diggers of 1933 *'33*
Lady for a Day *'33*
Hi, Nellie! *'34*
Imitation of Life *'34*
Marie Galante *'34*
George White's Scandals of 1935 *'35*
The Bride Walks Out *'36*
One in a Million *'36*
Wake Up and Live *'37*
Hawaii Calls *'38*

Paul Sparks (1971-)
Return *'11*
Trust Me *'13*
Stealing Cars *'16*
Thoroughbreds *'17*
The Lovebirds *'20*

Camilla Sparv (1943-)
Dead Heat on a Merry-Go-Round *'66*
Murderers' Row *'66*
Assignment K *'68*
Downhill Racer *'69*

Dan Speaker
Glitch! *'88*
Wizards of the Demon Sword *'94*

Jeff Speakman (1958-)
The Perfect Weapon *'91*
Plato's Run *'96*
Scorpio One *'97*
Land of the Free *'98*
Running Red *'99*
Timelock *'99*
The Gunman *'03*

Bernard Spear (1919-2003)
Bedazzled *'68*
Yentl *'83*

Hannah Spearritt (1981-)
Agent Cody Banks 2: Destination London *'04*
Seed of Chucky *'04*

Aaron Spears
Blue Hill Avenue *'01*
Makin' Baby *'02*

Aries Spears (1975-)
The Pest *'96*
Jiminy Glick in LaLa Wood *'05*

Britney Spears (1981-)
Austin Powers In Goldmember *'02 (C)*
Crossroads *'02*
Fahrenheit 9/11 *'04*

Eddie Spears (1982-)
The Slaughter Rule *'01*
Black Cloud *'04*

Michael Spears
Shadowheart *'09*
The Ballad of Lefty Brown *'17*

David Speck
Other Voices, Other Rooms *'95*
Crazy in Alabama *'99*

Morgan Spector
Burning Blue *'14*
A Vigilante *'19*

Carol Speed (1945-)
The Big Bird Cage *'72*
Bummer *'73*
The Mack *'73*
Black Samson *'74*
Avenging Disco Godfather *'76*

Scott Speedman (1975-)
Dead Silence *'96*
Duets *'00*
Dark Blue *'03*
My Life Without Me *'03*
Underworld *'03*
The 24th Day *'04*
Underworld: Evolution *'05*
XXX: State of the Union *'05*
Anamorph *'07*
Weirdsville *'07*
Adoration *'08*
The Strangers *'08*
The Last Rites of Ransom Pride *'09*
Barney's Version *'10*
Good Neighbors *'10*
Citizen Gangster *'11*
The Moth Diaries *'11*
Underworld: Awakening *'12*
The Vow *'12*
Barefoot *'14*
The Captive *'14*
The Monster *'16*
Run This Town *'20*

Hermann Speelmanns (1904-60)
F.P. 1 Doesn't Answer *'33*
Baron Munchausen *'43*

Hugo Speer (1969-)
The Full Monty *'96*
Mainline Run *'98*
Do or Die *'01*
Deathwatch *'02*
The Debt *'03*
Warrior Queen *'03*
The Interpreter *'05*
Fanny Hill *'07*

Martin Speer
The Hills Have Eyes *'77*
The Dark Ride *'78*

Lester 'Rasta' Speight
Norbit *'07*
Faster *'10*

Richard Speight, Jr. (1970-)
Ernest Goes to Camp *'87*
Demonic Toys *'90*
Independence Day *'96*
Menno's Mind *'96*
Speed 2: Cruise Control *'97*
Band of Brothers *'01*
Love for Rent *'05*

Dona Speir (1964-)
Hard Ticket to Hawaii *'87*
Picasso Trigger *'89*
Savage Beach *'89*
Guns *'90*
Do or Die *'91*
Hard Hunted *'92*
Fit to Kill *'93*

Steve Speirs (1965-)
Eragon *'06*
Assassin in Love *'07*
Sharpe's Peril *'08*

Ed Speleers (1988-)
Eragon *'06*
Witchville *'10*
A Lonely Place to Die *'11*
Plastic *'14*
For Love or Money *'19*

Tori Spelling (1973-)
Last Action Hero *'93 (C)*
Mother, May I Sleep With Danger? *'96*
The House of Yes *'97*
Scream 2 *'97 (C)*
Perpetrators of the Crime *'98*
Trick *'99*
Scary Movie 2 *'01*
Sol Goode *'01*
Evil Alien Conquerors *'02*
How to Lose Your Lover *'04*
The Family Plan *'05*
Kiss the Bride *'07*
Cthulhu *'08*

Peter Spellos
Bound *'96*
Men in Black 2 *'02*

Sharon Spelman
Deadly Game *'77*
Terror Among Us *'81*

Georgina Spelvin (1936-)
I Spit on Your Corpse *'74*
Police Academy *'84*
Next Year in Jerusalem *'98*

Bruce Spence (1945-)
The Road Warrior *'82*
Where the Green Ants Dream *'84*
Mad Max: Beyond Thunderdome *'85*
The Year My Voice Broke *'87*
Rikky and Pete *'88*
. . .Almost *'90*
The Shrimp on the Barbie *'90*
Sweet Talker *'91*
Dark City *'97*
Moby Dick *'98*
Inspector Gadget 2 *'02*
Queen of the Damned *'02*
Finding Nemo *'03 (V)*
The Matrix Revolutions *'03*
Star Wars: Episode 3-Revenge of the Sith *'05*
Aquamarine *'06*
Solo *'06*
Australia *'08*
The Chronicles of Narnia: The Voyage of the Dawn Treader *'10*
Backtrack *'16*

Paul J. Spence
It's All Gone, Pete Tong *'04*
Freezer Burn: The Invasion of Laxdale *'08*

Sebastian Spence (1969-)
The Boys of St. Vincent *'93*
Family of Cops *'95*
Family of Cops 2: Breach of Faith *'97*
Firestorm *'97*
Family of Cops 3 *'98*
Category 7: The End of the World *'05*
Criminal Intent *'05*
Third Man Out: A Donald Strachey Mystery *'05*
The Obsession *'06*
Shock to the System *'06*
To Have and to Hold *'06*
Dress to Kill *'07*
Uncaged Heart *'07*
Daniel's Daughter *'08*
Ice Blues: A Donald Strachey Mystery *'08*
NYC: Tornado Terror *'08*
On the Other Hand, Death *'08*
Stonados *'13*

Abigail Spencer (1981-)
Cowboys & Aliens *'11*
Chasing Mavericks *'12*
This Means War *'12*
The Haunting in Connecticut 2: Ghosts of Georgia *'13*
Kilimanjaro *'13*
This Is Where I Leave You *'14*
The Forger *'15*
The Heyday of the Insensitive Bastards *'17*

Bud Spencer (1929-)
Ace High *'68*
Beyond the Law *'68*
Boot Hill *'69*
The Five Man Army *'69*
Today We Kill, Tomorrow We Die *'71*
Four Flies on Grey Velvet *'72*
They Call Me Trinity *'72*
All the Way, Boys *'73*
A Reason to Live, a Reason to Die *'73*
Trinity Is Still My Name *'75*
Crime Busters *'78*
I'm for the Hippopotamus *'79*
Troublemakers *'94*

Chaske Spencer (1975-)
Skins *'02*
The Twilight Saga: New Moon *'09*
The Twilight Saga: Eclipse *'10*
Woman Walks Ahead *'17*

Chris Spencer (1968-)
Don't Be a Menace to South Central While Drinking Your Juice in the Hood *'95*
The Sixth Man *'97*
All About You *'01*
Sin *'02*

Douglas Spencer (1910-60)
The Thing *'51*
The Glass Wall *'53*
Trouble along the Way *'53*
River of No Return *'54*
Cole Younger, Gunfighter *'58*
Saddle the Wind *'58*

George Spencer
Massage Parlor Murders *'73*
If You Don't Stop It. . . You'll Go Blind *'77*

Jesse Spencer (1979-)
P.D. James: Death in Holy Orders *'03*
Swimming Upstream *'03*
Uptown Girls *'03*
Flourish *'06*

John Spencer (1946-2005)
Echoes *'83*
Black Rain *'89*
Simple Justice *'89*
Presumed Innocent *'90*
Forget Paris *'95*
Albino Alligator *'96*
The Rock *'96*
Cafe Society *'97*
Cold Around the Heart *'97*
Cop Land *'97*
The Negotiator *'98*
Twilight *'98*
Ravenous *'99*

Octavia Spencer (1970-)
Pretty Ugly People *'08*
The Help *'11*
Smashed *'12*
Fruitvale Station *'13*
Black or White *'14*
Get On Up *'14*
Snowpiercer *'14*
Allegiant *'16*
The Great Gilly Hopkins *'16*
Zootopia *'16 (V)*
Gifted *'17*
Hidden Figures *'17*
The Shack *'17*
The Shape of Water *'17*
A Kid Like Jake *'18*
Luce *'19*
Ma *'19*
Onward *'20 (V)*

Tara Spencer-Nairn (1978-)
Don't Look Down *'98*
New Waterford Girl *'99*
Wishmaster 4: The Prophecy Fulfilled *'02*
Waking Up Wally *'05*
Final Draft *'07*

Stephen Spender
Legacy of Fear *'06*
Tell Me No Lies *'07*

Volker Spengler (1939-2020)
Satan's Brew *'76*
The Stationmaster's Wife *'77*
Despair *'78*
In a Year of 13 Moons *'78*
Veronika Voss *'82*
Chinese Roulette *'86*
The Ogre *'96*

Jeremy Spenser (1937-)
Kind Hearts and Coronets *'49*
Summertime *'55*
The Prince and the Showgirl *'57*

Wendie Jo Sperber (1958-2005)
I Wanna Hold Your Hand *'78*
1941 *'79*
Used Cars *'80*
Bachelor Party *'84*
Back to the Future *'85*
Moving Violations *'85*
Back to the Future, Part 3 *'90*
Mr. Write *'92*

Alessandro Sperduti
Heaven *'01*
I Am David *'04*

John Speredakos (1962-)
Wendigo *'01*
I Sell the Dead *'09*
Bitter Feast *'10*
The Mind's Eye *'16*

Jason Spevack (1997-)
Crazy for Christmas *'05*
Sunshine Cleaning *'09*
Ramona and Beezus *'10*
Jesus Henry Christ *'12*

Jane Spidell
Men with Brooms *'02*
Gospel of Deceit *'06*

Scott Spiegel (1957-)
Evil Dead *'83*
Evil Dead 2: Dead by Dawn *'87*
Thou Shalt Not Kill. . .Except *'87*
The Dead Next Door *'89*
Skinned Alive *'89*
Darkman *'90*

David Spielberg (1939-)
Prime Time *'77*
The Henderson Monster *'80*
Christine *'84*
The Stranger *'87*
Alice *'90*
Silent Predators *'99*

Steven Spielberg (1947-)
The Blues Brothers *'80 (C)*
Austin Powers In Goldmember *'02 (C)*
Five Came Back *'17*

Laurent Spielvogel (1955-)
French Kiss *'95*
The Monster *'96*

Jacques Spiesser (1947-)
Black and White in Color *'76*
La Truite *'83*
Baxter *'89*
Priceless *'06*

Mickey Spillane (1918-2006)
The Girl Hunters *'63*
Mommy *'95*
Mommy 2: Mommy's Day *'96*

Petra Spindler
Lethal Target *'99*
Last Stand *'00*

Joe Spinell (1938-89)
The Godfather *'72*
Cops and Robbers *'73*
The Godfather, Part 2 *'74*
Rocky *'76*
Taxi Driver *'76*
Star Crash *'78*
Winter Kills *'79*
Cruising *'80*
Forbidden Zone *'80*
Little Dragons *'80*
Maniac *'80*
Nighthawks *'81*
Fanatic *'82*
Night Shift *'82*
One Down, Two to Go! *'82*
Big Score *'83*
Vigilante *'83*
Walking the Edge *'83*
The Children of Times Square *'86*
The Whoopee Boys *'86*
The Pick-Up Artist *'87*
Rapid Fire *'89*

Stephen Spinella (1956-)
And the Band Played On *'93 (C)*
Tarantella *'95*
Virtuosity *'95*
Love! Valour! Compassion! *'96*
David Searching *'97*
Great Expectations *'97*
The Jackal *'97*
What the Deaf Man Heard *'98*
Ravenous *'99*
Bubble Boy *'01*
Our Town *'03*
Connie and Carla *'04*
And Then Came Love *'07*
Milk *'08*
Rubber *'10*
Lincoln *'12*
Can You Ever Forgive Me? *'18*

Brent Spiner (1949-)
Crazy from the Heart *'91*
Star Trek: Generations *'94*
Independence Day *'96*
Phenomenon *'96*
Star Trek: First Contact *'96*
Out to Sea *'97*
Star Trek: Insurrection *'98*
Introducing Dorothy Dandridge *'99*
South Park: Bigger, Longer and Uncut *'99 (V)*
Gepetto *'00*
A Girl Thing *'01*
Master of Disguise *'02*
Star Trek: Nemesis *'02*
An Unexpected Love *'03*
The Aviator *'04*
Material Girls *'06*

Victor Spinetti (1932-2012)
A Wild Affair *'63*
A Hard Day's Night *'64*
Help! *'65*
Start the Revolution without Me *'70*
The Little Prince *'74*
Return of the Pink Panther *'74*
Voyage of the Damned *'76*

Tracy Spiridakos (1988-)
Secret Lives of Second Wives *'08*
Goblin *'10*
Kill for Me *'12*

Jordana Spiro (1977-)
Must Love Dogs *'05*
Alone With Her *'07*
Living & Dying *'07*
The Goods: Live Hard, Sell Hard *'09*
Trespass *'11*
To the Stars *'20*

Kevin Blair Spirtas (1963-)
The Hills Have Eyes, Part 2 *'84*
Friday the 13th, Part 7: The New Blood *'88*
Bloodstone: Subspecies 2 *'92*
Bloodlust: Subspecies 3 *'93*
Green Plaid Shirt *'96*
Albino Farm *'09*

Angelo Spizzirri (1974-2007)
The Rookie *'02*
The Pleasure Drivers *'05*
Underclassman *'05*

Gregory Sporleder (1964-)
A League of Their Own *'92*
True Romance *'93*
The Rock *'96*
Twister *'96*
Clay Pigeons *'98*
Uncorked *'98*
Black Hawk Down *'01*

Greg Spottiswood (1964-)
JFK: Reckless Youth *'93*
The Snow Walker *'03*
DC 9/11: Time of Crisis *'04*
Ice Men *'04*

G.D. Spradlin (1920-2011)
Hell's Angels '69 *'69*
Zabriskie Point *'70*
The Godfather, Part 2 *'74*
One on One *'77*
Apocalypse Now *'79*
North Dallas Forty *'79*
The Formula *'80*
The Jayne Mansfield Story *'80*
Wrong Is Right *'82*
The Lords of Discipline *'83*
Tank *'83*
Dream West *'86*
Resting Place *'86*
Nutcracker: Money, Madness & Murder *'87*
The War of the Roses *'89*
Carolina Skeletons *'92*
Canadian Bacon *'94*
Ed Wood *'94*
Nick of Time *'95*
The Long Kiss Goodnight *'96*
Riders of the Purple Sage *'96*
Dick *'99*

Charlie Spradling (1968-)
Mirror, Mirror *'90*
Puppet Master 2 *'90*
Wild at Heart *'90*
Bad Channels *'92*
To Sleep with a Vampire *'92*
Angel of Destruction *'94*
Johnny Skidmarks *'97*
Spent *'00*

Elizabeth Spriggs (1929-2008)
Oranges Are Not the Only Fruit *'89*
Impromptu *'90*
Anglo-Saxon Attitudes *'92*
Sense and Sensibility *'95*
The Secret Agent *'96*
Paradise Road *'97*
A Christmas Carol *'99*
Is Anybody There? *'08*

Ashley Springer
Dare *'09*
Chloe & Theo *'15*

Jerry Springer (1944-)
Ringmaster *'98*
Austin Powers 2: The Spy Who Shagged Me *'99 (C)*
The Defender *'04*

Rick Springfield (1949-)
Hard to Hold *'84*
Nick Knight *'89*
A Change of Place *'94*
Legion *'98*
Ricki and the Flash *'15*

Bruce Springsteen (1949-)
Chuck Berry: Hail! Hail! Rock 'n' Roll *'87*
High Fidelity *'00*
Springsteen & I *'13*
Western Stars *'19*

Pamela Springsteen (1962-)
Fast Times at Ridgemont High *'82*
Reckless *'84*
My Science Project *'85*
Dixie Lanes *'88*
Sleepaway Camp 2: Unhappy Campers *'88*
Sleepaway Camp 3: Teenage Wasteland *'89*

Cole Sprouse (1992-)
Big Daddy *'99*
The Heart Is Deceitful Above All Things *'04*
The Prince and the Pauper *'07*
Five Feet Apart *'19*

Dylan Sprouse (1992-)
Big Daddy *'99*
The Heart Is Deceitful Above All Things *'04*
The Prince and the Pauper *'07*
Snow Buddies *'08 (V)*

Sam Spruell (1977-)
Snow White and the Huntsman *'12*
Starred Up *'13*
Good People *'14*
Taken 3 *'15*
Outlaw King *'18*

Morgan Spurlock (1970-)
Where in the World Is Osama Bin Laden? *'06*
POM Wonderful Presents: The Greatest Movie Ever Sold *'11*
Super Size Me 2: Holy Chicken! *'19*

Dina Spybey (1965-)
Big Night *'95*
The First Wives Club *'96*
Striptease *'96*
An Alan Smithee Film: Burn, Hollywood, Burn *'97*
Julian Po *'97*
Isn't She Great *'00*
Full Frontal *'02*
Freaky Friday *'03*
The Haunted Mansion *'03*
Just like Heaven *'05*

June Squibb (1929-)
About Schmidt *'02*
Welcome to Mooseport *'04*
A Stranger's Heart *'07*
Nebraska *'13*
I'll See You in My Dreams *'15*
Love the Coopers *'15*
Table 19 *'17*
Blow The Man Down *'19*

Katherine Squire (1903-95)
Studs Lonigan *'60*
Ride in the Whirlwind *'66*

Ronald Squire (1886-1958)
Woman Hater *'49*
No Highway in the Sky *'51*
Encore *'52*
My Cousin Rachel *'52*
Footsteps in the Fog *'55*
Sea Wife *'57*

Rebecca Staab (1961-)
Love Potion #9 *'92*
T.N.T. *'98*
The Substitute 3: Winner Takes All *'99*
Safe Harbour *'07*
A Perfect Ending *'12*

Kelly Stables (1978-)
The Ring 2 *'05*
Telling Lies *'06*
Together Again for the First Time *'08*
Santa Baby 2: Santa Maybe *'09*
A Golden Christmas 2: The Second Tail *'11*

Chris Stack
Roger Dodger *'02*
School of Rock *'03*

Robert Stack (1919-2003)
First Love *'39*
The Mortal Storm *'40*
To Be or Not to Be *'42*
A Date with Judy *'48*
Fighter Squadron *'48*
Miss Tatlock's Millions *'48*
Bullfighter & the Lady *'50*
My Outlaw Brother *'51*
Conquest of Cochise *'53*
War Paint *'53*
The High and the Mighty *'54*
Good Morning, Miss Dove *'55*
House of Bamboo *'55*
Written on the Wind *'56*
Tarnished Angels *'57*
The Last Voyage *'60*
The Caretakers *'63*
Is Paris Burning? *'66*
Action Man *'67*
Murder on Flight 502 *'75*
1941 *'79*
Airplane! *'80*
Uncommon Valor *'83*
Big Trouble *'86*
Transformers: The Movie *'86 (V)*
Caddyshack 2 *'88*
Dangerous Curves *'88*
Joe Versus the Volcano *'90*
The Return of Eliot Ness *'91*
Beavis and Butt-Head Do America *'96 (V)*
BASEketball *'98*
Mumford *'99*
Killer Bud *'00*

William Stack (1882-1949)
Mary of Scotland *'36*
Pennies from Heaven *'36*

James Stacy (1936-)
Winter a Go-Go *'65*
Paper Man *'71*
Posse *'75*
Double Exposure *'82*
Something Wicked This Way Comes *'83*

John Stacy
Too Bad She's Bad *'54*
The Big Game *'72*

Lewis J. Stadlen (1947-)
Savages *'72*
Between the Lines *'77*
In and Out *'97*
The Imposters *'98*

Michael Stadvec
The Dentist *'96*
The Chosen One: Legend of the Raven *'98*

Frederick Stafford (1928-79)
The Battle of El Alamein *'68*
Eagles Over London *'69*
Topaz *'69*
The Legend of the Wolf Woman *'77*

Jon Stafford
Full Metal Jacket *'87*
Munchies *'87*
Crossing the Line *'90*

Michelle Stafford
Lethal Force *'00*
3 Days Gone *'08*

Sandra Staggs
Getting It *'06*
Area 51 *'15*

Nick Stahl (1979-)
The Man Without a Face *'93*
Safe Passage *'94*
Blue River *'95*
Tall Tale: The Unbelievable Adventures of Pecos Bill *'95*
Eye of God *'97*
Disturbing Behavior *'98*
The Thin Red Line *'98*
Lover's Prayer *'99*
Soundman *'99*
Sunset Strip *'99*
Bully *'01*
In the Bedroom *'01*
The Sleepy Time Gal *'01*
Taboo *'02*
Bookies *'03*
Terminator 3: Rise of the Machines *'03*
Twist *'03*
Sin City *'05*
The Night of the White Pants *'06*
How to Rob a Bank *'07*
Quid Pro Quo *'08*
Sleepwalking *'08*
My One and Only *'09*
Kalamity *'10*
Meskada *'10*
Mirrors 2 *'10*
Afghan Luke *'11*
On the Inside *'11*
The Speed of Thought *'11*

Richard Stahl (1932-2006)
Five Easy Pieces *'70*
The Student Nurses *'70*
Beware! The Blob *'72*
Private School *'83*

Michael Stahl-David (1982-)
Cloverfield *'08*
Girls Against Boys *'12*
In Your Eyes *'14*
Love & Air Sex *'14*
The Light of the Moon *'17*

Philip Stainton (1908-61)
Mogambo *'53*
Who Done It? *'56*

Brent Stait (1959-)
Call of the Wild *'93*
Sea Beast *'08*
Stonehenge Apocalypse *'10*

Jewel Staite (1982-)
Serenity *'05*
Widow on the Hill *'05*
Call Me Mrs. Miracle *'10*
Mothman *'10*
Doomsday Prophecy *'11*
The Christmas Ornament *'13*

Marion Stalens
The Lovers on the Bridge *'91*
Trois Couleurs: Rouge *'94*

James Staley (1948-)
American Dreamer *'84*
Protocol *'84*
Sweet Dreams *'85*
Robot Wars *'93*

Joan Staley (1940-2019)
Valley of the Dragons *'61*
Roustabout *'64*
The Ghost and Mr. Chicken *'66*

Mia Stallard (1996-)
Inhale *'10*
Paul *'11*

Jerry Stallion
See Jerome Eden

Frank Stallone (1950-)
The Pink Chiquitas *'86*
Barfly *'87*
Death Blow *'87*
Lethal Victims *'87*
Fear *'88*
Midnight Cop *'88*
Prime Suspect *'88*
Death Feud *'89*
Easy Kill *'89*
Hudson Hawk *'91*

Sage Stallone (1976-2012)
Rocky 5 *'90*
Daylight *'96*
Chaos *'05*
Moscow Zero *'06*

Sylvester Stallone (1946-)
Bananas *'71*
The Italian Stallion *'73*
The Lords of Flatbush *'74*
Prisoner of Second Avenue *'74*
Death Race 2000 *'75*
Farewell, My Lovely *'75*
Cannonball *'76*
Rocky *'76*
F.I.S.T. *'78*
Paradise Alley *'78*
Rocky 2 *'79*
Nighthawks *'81*
Victory *'81*
First Blood *'82*
Rocky 3 *'82*
Rhinestone *'84*
Rambo: First Blood, Part 2 *'85*
Rocky 4 *'85*
Cobra *'86*
Over the Top *'86*
Rambo 3 *'88*
Lock Up *'89*
Tango and Cash *'89*
Rocky 5 *'90*
Oscar *'91*
Stop! or My Mom Will Shoot *'92*
Cliffhanger *'93*
Demolition Man *'93*
The Specialist *'94*
Assassins *'95*
Judge Dredd *'95*
Daylight *'96*
An Alan Smithee Film: Burn, Hollywood, Burn *'97 (C)*
Cop Land *'97*
Antz *'98 (V)*
Get Carter *'00*
Driven *'01*
Eye See You *'01*
Avenging Angelo *'02*
Shade *'03*
Spy Kids 3-D: Game Over *'03*
Rocky Balboa *'06*
Rambo *'08*
The Expendables *'10*
Zookeeper *'11 (V)*
Bullet to the Head *'12*
The Expendables 2 *'12*
Escape Plan *'13*
Grudge Match *'13*
The Expendables 3 *'14*
Reach Me *'14*
Creed *'15*
Creed II *'18*
Escape Plan 2: Hades *'18*
Rambo: Last Blood *'19*

Anne Stallybrass (1938-)
Six Wives of Henry VIII *'71*
The Strauss Family *'73*
Diana: Her True Story *'93*

Lynn Stalmaster
Flying Leathernecks *'51*
The Steel Helmet *'51*
Hal *'18*

David Stambaugh (1961-)
The Bad News Bears *'76*
The Bad News Bears in Breaking Training *'77*
The Bad News Bears Go to Japan *'78*

Josh Stamberg (1970-)
Fracture *'07*
Afternoon Delight *'13*

Lauren Stamile (1976-)
The Blue Tooth Virgin *'09*
Midnight Bayou *'09*

John Stamos (1963-)
Alice in Wonderland *'85*
Born to Ride *'91*
The Reagans *'04*
Knots *'05*
Wedding Wars *'06*
A Raisin in the Sun *'08*
The Two Mr. Kissels *'08*
Father of Invention *'11*
Secrets of Eden *'12*
My Man Is a Loser *'14*

Terence Stamp (1938-)
Billy Budd *'62*
Term of Trial *'63*
The Collector *'65*
Modesty Blaise *'66*
Far from the Madding Crowd *'67*
Blue *'68*
Iron Cowboy *'68*
Spirits of the Dead *'68*
Teorema *'68*
The Mind of Mr. Soames *'70*
Insanity *'76*
Superman: The Movie *'78*
The Thief of Baghdad *'78*
Superman 2 *'80*
The Hit *'85*
Alamut Ambush *'86*
Cold War Killers *'86*
Deadly Recruits *'86*
Legal Eagles *'86*
Link *'86*
The Sicilian *'87*
Wall Street *'87*
Alien Nation *'88*
Young Guns *'88*
The Real McCoy *'93*
The Adventures of Priscilla, Queen of the Desert *'94*
Bliss *'96*
Love Walked In *'97*
Kiss the Sky *'98*
Bowfinger *'99*
The Limey *'99*
Star Wars: Episode 1-The Phantom Menace *'99*
Red Planet *'00*
My Wife is an Actress *'01*
Fellini: I'm a Born Liar *'03*
The Haunted Mansion *'03*
My Boss's Daughter *'03*
Dead Fish *'04*
Elektra *'05*
These Foolish Things *'06*
September Dawn *'07*
Get Smart *'08*
Valkyrie *'08*
Wanted *'08*
Yes Man *'08*
Ultramarines: A Warhammer 40,000 Movie *'10 (V)*
The Adjustment Bureau *'11*
Unfinished Song *'12*
The Art of the Steal *'13*
Big Eyes *'14*
Bitter Harvest *'17*

Enid Stamp-Taylor
Candlelight in Algeria *'44*
The Wicked Lady *'45*

Sebastian Stan (1982-)
Red Doors *'05*
The Architect *'06*
The Covenant *'06*
Spread *'09*
Hot Tub Time Machine *'10*
Captain America: The First Avenger *'11*
The Apparition *'12*
Gone *'12*
Labyrinth *'12*
Captain America: The Winter Soldier *'14*
The Bronze *'15*
The Martian *'15*
Captain America: Civil War *'16*
I, Tonya *'17*
Destroyer *'18*
I'm Not Here *'19*
The Last Full Measure *'19*
Endings, Beginnings *'20*

George Stanchev
Shark Attack 3: Megalodon *'02*
U.S. SEALs: Dead or Alive *'02*

Wadeck Stanczak (1961-)
Rendez-vous *'85*
Scene of the Crime *'87*

Clive Standen
Everest *'15*
Patient Zero *'18*
Vault *'19*

Lionel Stander (1908-94)
Hooray for Love *'35*
I Live My Life *'35*
If You Could Only Cook *'36*
Meet Nero Wolfe *'36*
Mr. Deeds Goes to Town *'36*
More Than A Secretary *'36*
The Last Gangster *'37*
A Star Is Born *'37*
The Crowd Roars *'38*
Ice Follies of 1939 *'39*
Guadalcanal Diary *'43*
The Sin of Harold Diddlebock *'47*
Call Northside 777 *'48*
Unfaithfully Yours *'48*
St. Benny the Dip *'51*
Blast of Silence *'61 (N)*
The Loved One *'65*
Cul de Sac *'66*
Beyond the Law *'68*
Dandy in Aspic *'68*
Once Upon a Time in the West *'68*
Boot Hill *'69*
Caliber 9 *'72*
1931: Once Upon a Time in New York *'72*
Pulp *'72*
Treasure Island *'72*
The Cassandra Crossing *'76*
New York, New York *'77*
The Squeeze *'80*
Cookie *'89*
Wicked Stepmother *'89*

Guy Standing (1873-1937)
The Eagle and the Hawk *'33*
Death Takes a Holiday *'34*
Now and Forever *'34*
The Lives of a Bengal Lancer *'35*
I'd Give My Life *'36*
Lloyds of London *'36*
Bulldog Drummond Comes Back *'37*
Bulldog Drummond Escapes *'37*

John Standing (1934-)
King Rat *'65*
The Psychopath *'66*
Walk, Don't Run *'66*
Rogue Male *'76*
The Legacy *'79*
To Catch a King *'84*
Riders *'88*
Chaplin *'92*
Gulliver's Travels *'95*
The Man Who Knew Too Little *'97*
Mrs. Dalloway *'97*
The Woman in White *'97*
Rogue Trader *'98*
8 1/2 Women *'99*
Longitude *'00*
A Good Woman *'04*
Lassie *'05*
Before the Rains *'07*
I Want Candy *'07*
The Shadow in the North *'07*
Queen and Country *'14*

Wyndham Standing (1880-1963)
The Early Bird *'25*
The Canadian *'26*
Billy the Kid *'30*

Lakeith Stanfield (1991-)
Short Term 12 *'13*
Miles Ahead *'16*
Crown Heights *'17*
The Girl in the Spider's Web *'18*
Sorry to Bother You *'18*
Someone Great *'19*
Uncut Gems *'19*
The Photograph *'20*

Lakeith Lee Stanfield (1991-)
See Lakeith Stanfield

Aaron Stanford (1976-)
Tadpole *'02*
Rick *'03*
X2: X-Men United *'03*
Spartan *'04*
Winter Solstice *'04*
Runaway *'05*
Standing Still *'05*
The Hills Have Eyes *'06*
X-Men: The Last Stand *'06*
The Cake Eaters *'07*
Flakes *'07*
How I Got Lost *'09*

Arnold Stang (1918-2009)
Seven Days' Leave *'42*
The Man with the Golden Arm *'55*
Dondi *'61*
Hercules in New York *'70*
Marco Polo, Jr. *'72 (V)*
Ghost Dad *'90*
Dennis the Menace *'93*

Maya Stange
XX/XY *'02*
Garage Days *'03*

Florence Stanley (1924-2003)
Trouble Bound *'92*
A Goofy Movie *'94 (V)*
Trapped in Paradise *'94*
The Odd Couple 2 *'98*
Atlantis: The Lost Empire *'01 (V)*
Down With Love *'03*

Forrest Stanley (1889-1969)
Up the Ladder *'25*
Arizona *'31*
The Rider of Death Valley *'32*

Jack Stanley (1991-)
Carrie's War *'04*
The Hitchhiker's Guide to the Galaxy *'05*

Kim Stanley (1925-2001)
The Goddess *'58*
To Kill a Mockingbird *'62 (N)*
Seance on a Wet Afternoon *'64*
Operation Heartbeat *'69*
Frances *'82*
The Right Stuff *'83*
Cat on a Hot Tin Roof *'84*

Mark Stanley
Dark River *'18*
Hellboy *'19*

Paul Stanley (1952-)
KISS Meets the Phantom of the Park *'78*
Detroit Rock City *'99*

Claire Stansfield (1964-)
The Swordsman *'92*
Best of the Best 2 *'93*
Drop Zone *'94*
Sensation *'94*
Red Shoe Diaries 5: Weekend Pass *'95*
Wes Craven Presents Mind Ripper *'95*
Darkdrive *'98*
Sweepers *'99*

Andrew Stanton (1965-)
Toy Story 2 *'99 (V)*
Finding Nemo *'03 (V)*

Harry Dean Stanton (1926-2017)
Proud Rebel *'58*
The Adventures of Huckleberry Finn *'60*
Hero's Island *'62*
Ride in the Whirlwind *'66*
Cool Hand Luke *'67*
The Hostage *'67*
Day of the Evil Gun *'68*
Rebel Rousers *'69*
Kelly's Heroes *'70*
Two Lane Blacktop *'71*
Dillinger *'73*
Pat Garrett & Billy the Kid *'73*
Cockfighter *'74*
The Godfather, Part 2 *'74*
Zandy's Bride *'74*
Farewell, My Lovely *'75*
Rancho Deluxe *'75*
Missouri Breaks *'76*
92 in the Shade *'76*
Straight Time *'78*
Alien *'79*
The Black Marble *'79*
The Rose *'79*
Wise Blood *'79*
Death Watch *'80*
Private Benjamin *'80*
Escape from New York *'81*
One from the Heart *'82*
Young Doctors in Love *'82*
Paris, Texas *'83*
Repo Man *'83*
Christine *'84*
Red Dawn *'84*
One Magic Christmas *'85*
Fool for Love *'86*
Pretty in Pink *'86*
Slamdance *'87*
The Last Temptation of Christ *'88*
Mr. North *'88*
Dream a Little Dream *'89*
Twister *'89*
The Fourth War *'90*
Wild at Heart *'90*
Man Trouble *'92*
Twin Peaks: Fire Walk with Me *'92*
Against the Wall *'94*
Blue Tiger *'94*
Never Talk to Strangers *'95*
Down Periscope *'96*
Larry McMurtry's Dead Man's Walk *'96*
Fire Down Below *'97*
She's So Lovely *'97*
Fear and Loathing in Las Vegas *'98*
The Mighty *'98*
The Green Mile *'99*
The Straight Story *'99*
The Man Who Cried *'00*
The Pledge *'00*
Sand *'00*
Ginostra *'02*
Sonny *'02*
Anger Management *'03*
The Big Bounce *'04*
The Wendell Baker Story *'05*
Alpha Dog *'06*
Inland Empire *'06*
You, Me and Dupree *'06*
The Good Life *'07*
Alice *'09*
The Open Road *'09*
Rango *'11 (V)*
The Avengers *'12*
This Must Be the Place *'12*
Lucky *'17*

Helene Stanton (1925-)
Jungle Moon Men *'55*
New Orleans Uncensored *'55*
The Phantom from 10,000 Leagues *'56*

John Stanton (1944-)
Tai-Pan *'86*
Day of the Panther *'88*
Rent-A-Cop *'88*

Paul Stanton (1884-1955)
The People *vs.* Dr. Kildare *'41*
Whistling in the Dark *'41*
Across the Pacific *'42*

Robert Stanton (1963-)
Abbott and Costello in Hollywood *'45*
I Eat Your Skin *'64*
Bob Roberts *'92*
Dennis the Menace *'93*
Red Corner *'97*
Washington Square *'97*
Mercury Rising *'98*
Next Stop, Wonderland *'98*
The Quiet American *'02*
Head of State *'03*
Find Me Guilty *'06*
Confessions of a Shopaholic *'09*

Barbara Stanwyck (1907-90)
Ladies of Leisure *'30*
Illicit *'31*
The Miracle Woman *'31*
Night Nurse *'31*
Ten Cents a Dance *'31*
Forbidden *'32*
The Purchase Price *'32*
Shopworn *'32*
Baby Face *'33*
The Bitter Tea of General Yen *'33*
Annie Oakley *'35*
The Secret Bride *'35*
The Woman in Red *'35*
The Bride Walks Out *'36*
A Message to Garcia *'36*
Breakfast for Two *'37*
Internes Can't Take Money *'37*
Stella Dallas *'37*
Always Goodbye *'38*
Mad Miss Manton *'38*
Golden Boy *'39*
Union Pacific *'39*
Remember the Night *'40*
Ball of Fire *'41*
The Lady Eve *'41*
Meet John Doe *'41*
The Great Man's Lady *'42*
Lady of Burlesque *'43*
Double Indemnity *'44*
Hollywood Canteen *'44*
Christmas in Connecticut *'45*
The Bride Wore Boots *'46*
My Reputation *'46*
The Strange Love of Martha Ivers *'46*
Cry Wolf *'47*
The Other Love *'47*
The Two Mrs. Carrolls *'47*
B.F.'s Daughter *'48*
Sorry, Wrong Number *'48*
East Side, West Side *'49*
The Lady Gambles *'49*
The File on Thelma Jordon *'50*
The Furies *'50*
To Please a Lady *'50*
The Man With a Cloak *'51*
Clash by Night *'52*
All I Desire *'53*
Jeopardy *'53*
The Moonlighter *'53*
Titanic *'53*
Cattle Queen of Montana *'54*
Executive Suite *'54*
Witness to Murder *'54*
Escape to Burma *'55*
The Violent Men *'55*
There's Always Tomorrow *'56*
These Wilder Years *'56*
Crime of Passion *'57*
Forty Guns *'57*
Trooper Hook *'57*
Walk on the Wild Side *'62*
Roustabout *'64*
The Thorn Birds *'83*

Jean Stapleton (1923-2013)
Damn Yankees *'58*
Bells Are Ringing *'60*
Something Wild *'61*
Up the Down Staircase *'67*
Cold Turkey *'71*
Klute *'71*
You Can't Take It With You *'79*
Eleanor: First Lady of the World *'82*
Lily Dale *'96*
Michael *'96*
You've Got Mail *'98*
Baby *'00*
Pursuit of Happiness *'01*

Kevin Stapleton
Carver's Gate *'96*
Cyclops *'08*

Maureen Stapleton (1925-2006)
The Fugitive Kind *'60*
Bye, Bye, Birdie *'63*
Airport *'70*
The Cosmic Eye *'71 (V)*
Plaza Suite *'71*
Queen of the Stardust Ballroom *'75*
The Gathering *'77*
Interiors *'78*
The Gathering: Part 2 *'79*
Lost and Found *'79*
Angel Dusted *'81*
The Fan *'81*
Reds *'81*
Johnny Dangerously *'84*
Cocoon *'85*
Heartburn *'86*
The Money Pit *'86*
Made in Heaven *'87*
Nuts *'87*
Sweet Lorraine *'87*
Cocoon: The Return *'88*
Passed Away *'92*
Trading Mom *'94*
Addicted to Love *'96*
Dead Silence *'98 (C)*

Nicola Stapleton (1974-)
Courage Mountain *'89*
Urban Ghost Story *'98*

Sullivan Stapleton (1977-)
River Street *'95*
Darkness Falls *'03*
December Boys *'07*
Animal Kingdom *'09*
300: Rise of an Empire *'13*
Renegades *'17*

Richard Stapley (1923-2010)
The Strange Door *'51*
Target Zero *'55*
D-Day, the Sixth of June *'56*

Don Stark (1954-)
Evilspeak *'82*
Bloodfist 5: Human Target *'93*

Graham Stark (1922-2013)
Alfie *'66*
Salt & Pepper *'68*
Blind Date *'87*

Jonathan Stark (1952-)
Fright Night *'85*
House 2: The Second Story *'87*
Project X *'87*

Koo Stark (1956-)
The Rocky Horror Picture Show *'75*
Eat the Rich *'87*

Anthony Starke (1963-)
18 Again! *'88*
Return of the Killer Tomatoes! *'88*
Repossessed *'90*
The Magnificent Seven *'98*
Baby on Board *'08*

Pauline Starke (1901-77)
Little Church Around the Corner *'23*
Captain Salvation *'27*
The Viking *'28*

Beau Starr (1944-)
Fletch *'85*
Summer School *'87*
Halloween 4: The Return of Michael Myers *'88*
Halloween 5: The Revenge of Michael Myers *'89*
Goodfellas *'90*
Trial by Jury *'94*
Devil in a Blue Dress *'95*
Never Talk to Strangers *'95*
Hoodlum *'96*

Prisoner of Love '99
The Golden Spiders: A Nero Wolfe Mystery '00
Mercy '00
The Thin Blue Lie '00
Where the Truth Lies '05
Time and Again '07

Fredro Starr (1971-)
Sunset Park '96
Ride '98
Light It Up '99
Save the Last Dance '01
Torque '04
My Brother '06
The Next Hit '08
A Day in the Life '09

Joey Starr (1967-)
Polisse '11
Sleepless Night '11

Martin Starr (1979-)
Knocked Up '07
Walk Hard: The Dewey Cox Story '07
Adventureland '09
Deep Dark Canyon '12
Save the Date '12
The Lifeguard '13
Dead Snow: Red vs. Dead '14
Amira & Sam '15
I'll See You in My Dreams '15

Mike Starr (1950-)
Cruising '80
The Money Pit '86
Goodfellas '90
Last Exit to Brooklyn '90
Billy Bathgate '91
The Bodyguard '92
Mad Dog and Glory '93
Mardi Gras for the Devil '93
Dumb & Dumber '94
Ed Wood '94
Trial by Jury '94
Two If by Sea '95
Hoodlum '96
The Deli '97
Path to Paradise '97
A River Made to Drown In '97
Frogs for Snakes '98
Gloria '98
Murder in a Small Town '99
Tempted '01
3 A.M. '01
The Next Big Thing '02
Elvis Has Left the Building '04
Jersey Girl '04
The Black Dahlia '06
Hot Tamale '06
Jesse Stone: Night Passage '06
Doughboys '08
Lone Rider '08
Osso Bucco '08
Chicago Overcoat '09
I Hate Valentine's Day '09
Wrong Turn at Tahoe '09
Kill the Irishman '11

Ringo Starr (1940-)
A Hard Day's Night '64
Help! '65
Candy '68
Yellow Submarine '68 (V)
The Magic Christian '69
Let It Be '70
The Point '71 (N)
200 Motels '71
Born to Boogie '72
That'll Be the Day '73
Lisztomania '75
Sextette '78
The Kids Are Alright '79
Caveman '81
Princess Daisy '83
Give My Regards to Broad Street '84
Alice in Wonderland '85
Water '85 (C)
George Harrison: Living in the Material World '11

Charles Starrett (1903-86)
The Mask of Fu Manchu '32
Mr. Skitch '33
Dangerous Appointment '34
Green Eyes '34
The Silver Streak '34
Make a Million '35
A Shot in the Dark '35

Jack Starrett (1936-89)
Angels from Hell '68
Hell's Bloody Devils '70
The Losers '70
First Blood '82
Nightwish '89

David Starzyk (1961-)
A Boyfriend for Christmas '04
Haunted Echoes '08
Bring It On: Fight to the Finish '09

Todd Stashwick
You, Me and Dupree '06
Kim Possible '19

Jason Statham (1967-)
Lock, Stock and 2 Smoking Barrels '98
Snatch '00
Turn It Up '00
John Carpenter's Ghosts of Mars '01
Mean Machine '01
The One '01
The Transporter '02
The Italian Job '03
Cellular '04
London '05
Revolver '05
Transporter 2 '05
Crank '06
War '07
The Bank Job '08
Death Race '08
In the Name of the King: A Dungeon Siege Tale '08
Transporter 3 '08
Crank: High Voltage '09
The Expendables '10
13 '10
Blitz '11
Gnomeo & Juliet '11 (V)
Killer Elite '11
The Mechanic '11
The Expendables 2 '12
Homefront '13
Parker '13
Redemption '13
The Expendables 3 '14
Furious 7 '15
Spy '15
Wild Card '15
Mechanic: Resurrection '16
The Fate of the Furious '17
The Meg '18
Fast & Furious Presents: Hobbs & Shaw '19

Chelsea Staub (1988-)
Bratz '07
Minutemen '08

Liz Stauber (1979-)
Teaching Mrs. Tingle '99
Three Kings '99
Almost Famous '00
Kitchen Privileges '00
The Tollbooth '04
The Village '04

Imelda Staunton (1956-)
Peter's Friends '92
Deadly Advice '93
Much Ado about Nothing '93
Citizen X '95
Sense and Sensibility '95
Twelfth Night '96
Shakespeare in Love '98
David Copperfield '99
Chicken Run '00 (V)
Another Life '01
Crush '02
Cambridge Spies '03
I'll Be There '03
Vera Drake '04
Nanny McPhee '06
Shadow Man '06
Freedom Writers '07
Harry Potter and the Order of the Phoenix '07
How About You '07
Cranford '08
Three and Out '08
Return to Cranford '09
Taking Woodstock '09
Another Year '10
Harry Potter and the Deathly Hallows, Part 1 '10
Arthur Christmas '11 (V)
The Awakening '11
The Girl '12
The Pirates! Band of Misfits '12 (V)
Maleficent '14
Pride '14
Finding Your Feet '18
Downton Abbey '19

Mary Stavin (1957-)
House '86
Open House '86
The Opponent '89

Alison Steadman (1946-)
Hard Labour '73
Nuts in May '76
Abigail's Party '77
Champions '84
A Private Function '84
Coming Through '85
Clockwise '86
The Adventures of Baron Munchausen '89
Shirley Valentine '89
Life Is Sweet '90
Blame It on the Bellboy '92
Pride and Prejudice '95
Secrets and Lies '95 (C)
Fanny Hill '07

Catherine Steadman
Mansfield Park '07
Outpost: Black Sun '12

John Steadman (1909-93)
The Hills Have Eyes '77
Fade to Black '80

Red Steagall (1937-)
Benji the Hunted '87
Big Bad John '90

Rick Stear (1972-)
Went to Coney Island on a Mission from God. . . Be Back by Five '98
Astoria '00

Michael Stearns (1940-)
Chrome and Hot Leather '71
Chain Gang Women '72
Battle for the Planet of the Apes '73

Peter Stebbings (1971-)
No Alibi '00
Re-Generation '04
Jack and Jill vs. the World '08
Never Cry Werewolf '08
S.I.S. '08

Ray Dennis Steckler (1938-2009)
Eegah! '62
Wild Guitar '62
Wild Ones on Wheels '62
Incredibly Strange Creatures Who Stopped Living and Became Mixed-Up Zombies '63
The Thrill Killers '65

Myrtle Stedman (1885-1938)
In the Days of the Thundering Herd & the Law & the Outlaw '14
Sex '20
Beau Ideal '31

Alan Steel (1935-2015)
The Fury of Hercules '61
Samson '61
Hercules against the Moon Men '64
Samson and His Mighty Challenge '64

Amy Steel (1960-)
Friday the 13th, Part 2 '81
April Fool's Day '86
Walk Like a Man '87
What Ever Happened To. . . '93

Anthony Steel (1920-2001)
The Mudlark '50
Another Man's Poison '52
Malta Story '53
The Master of Ballantrae '53
Storm Over the Nile '55
Valerie '57
Revenge of the Barbarians '60
Tiger of the Seven Seas '62
Massacre in Rome '73
The Story of O '75

Barbara Steele (1937-)
Black Sunday '60
La Dolce Vita '60
The Pit and the Pendulum '61
The Horrible Dr. Hichcock '62
8 1/2 '63
The Ghost '63
Castle of Blood '64
The Monocle '64
Nightmare Castle '65
The She-Beast '65
An Angel for Satan '66
Terror Creatures from the Grave '66
The Crimson Cult '68
Caged Heat '74
They Came from Within '75
Piranha '78
Pretty Baby '78
Silent Scream '80
The Winds of War '83
The Capitol Conspiracy '99

Bob Steele (1907-88)
Mystery Squadron '33
Of Mice and Men '39
City for Conquest '40
The Big Sleep '46
Northwest Trail '46
The Enforcer '51
Pardners '56
Giant from the Unknown '58
Atomic Submarine '59
Pork Chop Hill '59
Rio Bravo '59

Brian Steele (1956-)
Doom '05
Underworld: Evolution '05
Hellboy II: The Golden Army '08

Don Steele (1936-97)
Death Race 2000 '75
Rock 'n' Roll High School '79
Eating Raoul '82

Freddie (Fred) Steele (1912-84)
Hail the Conquering Hero '44
The Story of G.I. Joe '45
Black Angel '46
Call Northside 777 '48

Jadrien Steele (1974-)
The Mosquito Coast '86
The Secret Garden '87

Karen Steele (1931-88)
Marty '55
Decision at Sundown '57
Westbound '58
Ride Lonesome '59
The Rise and Fall of Legs Diamond '60

Pippa Steele (1948-92)
The Vampire Lovers '70
Lust for a Vampire '71

Sarah Steele (1988-)
Spanglish '04
The Good Student '08
Please Give '10
The To Do List '13

Tommy Steele (1936-)
Half a Sixpence '67
The Happiest Millionaire '67
Finian's Rainbow '68

Vernon Steele
The Witness Vanishes '39
They Were Expendable '45

Jessica Steen (1965-)
Dream to Believe '85
Trial and Error '96
Dogwatch '97
Armageddon '98
Smart House '00
Slap Shot 2: Breaking the Ice '02
The Paradise Virus '03
Vipers '08

Paprika Steen (1964-)
The Celebration '98
Mifune '99
Adam's Apples '05
Forty Shades of Blue '05
Skeletons '10
Keep the Lights On '12

Mary Steenburgen (1953-)
Goin' South '78
Time After Time '79
Melvin and Howard '80
Ragtime '81
A Midsummer Night's Sex Comedy '82
Cross Creek '83
Romantic Comedy '83
One Magic Christmas '85
Dead of Winter '87
The Whales of August '87
The Attic: The Hiding of Anne Frank '88
End of the Line '88
The Long Walk Home '89 (N)
Miss Firecracker '89
Parenthood '89
Back to the Future, Part 3 '90
The Butcher's Wife '91
Clifford '92
Philadelphia '93
What's Eating Gilbert Grape '93
My Family '94
My Summer Story '94
Pontiac Moon '94
The Grass Harp '95
Gulliver's Travels '95
Nixon '95
Powder '95
Noah's Ark '99
Wish You Were Dead '00
I Am Sam '01
Life as a House '01
Nobody's Baby '01
The Trumpet of the Swan '01 (V)
Sunshine State '02
Talking to Heaven '02
Casa de los Babys '03
Elf '03
The Dead Girl '06
Marilyn Hotchkiss' Ballroom Dancing & Charm School '06
The Brave One '07
Elvis and Anabelle '07
Numb '07
Four Christmases '08
In the Electric Mist '08
Nobel Son '08
Step Brothers '08
Did You Hear About the Morgans? '09
The Open Road '09
The Proposal '09
Dirty Girl '10
Last Vegas '13
The Tale of the Princess Kaguya '13 (V)
The One I Love '14
A Walk in the Woods '15
The Book of Love '16
The Discovery '17
Book Club '18

Eddie Steeples (1973-)
Wristcutters: A Love Story '06
I Know Who Killed Me '07
Home Alone: The Holiday Heist '12

Simonetta Stefanelli (1954-)
The Godfather '72
Three Brothers '80

Leslie Stefanson (1971-)
An Alan Smithee Film: Burn, Hollywood, Burn '97
Delivered '98
The General's Daughter '99
Beautiful '00
Unbreakable '00
Desert Saints '01
Jackie, Ethel, Joan: The Kennedy Women '01
The Stickup '01
Alien Hunter '03
The Hunted '03

Anthony Steffen (1929-2006)
An Angel for Satan '66
Ringo's Mark of Vengeance '67
The Gentleman Killer '69
The Night Evelyn Came Out of the Grave '71
Escape from Hell '79
Savage Island '85

Katie Stegeman
Contracted '13
Roadside '15

Mark Steger
The Pact '12
Mr. Jones '14

Bernice Stegers
Macabre '80
City of Women '81
Xtro '83
To Play the King '93
Little Lord Fauntleroy '95
My Life in Ruins '09

Edgar Stehli (1884-1973)
No Name on the Bullet '59
Loving '70

Rod Steiger (1925-2002)
On the Waterfront '54
The Big Knife '55
The Court Martial of Billy Mitchell '55
Oklahoma! '55
The Harder They Fall '56
Jubal '56
Across the Bridge '57
Cry Terror! '58
Al Capone '59
Seven Thieves '60
The Mark '61
The Longest Day '62
13 West Street '62
Doctor Zhivago '65
The Loved One '65
The Pawnbroker '65
In the Heat of the Night '67
No Way to Treat a Lady '68
The Sergeant '68
The Illustrated Man '69
A Fistful of Dynamite '72
Lolly-Madonna XXX '73
Lucky Luciano '74
Hennessy '75
Innocents with Dirty Hands '76
Last Four Days '77
Portrait of a Hitman '77
F.I.S.T. '78
The Amityville Horror '79
Klondike Fever '79
Love and Bullets '79
The Chosen '81
Lion of the Desert '81
The Glory Boys '84
The Naked Face '84
Sword of Gideon '86
Catch the Heat '87
American Gothic '88
The January Man '89
The Ballad of the Sad Cafe '91
Guilty as Charged '92
The Player '92
Sinatra '92
Armistead Maupin's Tales of the City '93
The Neighbor '93
The Specialist '94
Choices of the Heart: The Margaret Sanger Story '95
Dalva '95
In Pursuit of Honor '95
Carpool '96

Mars Attacks! '96
Incognito '97
The Kid '97
Shiloh '97
Truth or Consequences, N.M. '97
Body and Soul '98
Modern Vampires '98
Crazy in Alabama '99
Cypress Edge '99
End of Days '99
The Hurricane '99
Shiloh 2: Shiloh Season '99
Frozen in Fear '00
The Hollywood Sign '01
Poolhall Junkies '02

Ben Stein (1944-)
Ferris Bueller's Day Off '86
Planes, Trains & Automobiles '87
Ghostbusters 2 '89
Honeymoon in Vegas '92
Mr. Write '92
Dave '93
The Mask '94
My Girl 2 '94
Casper '95
Miami Rhapsody '95

Margaret Sophie Stein (1956-)
Enemies, a Love Story '89
Sarah, Plain and Tall '91
Sarah, Plain and Tall: Skylark '93

Miriam Stein
Young Goethe in Love '11
Generation War '13

Saul Stein
New Jersey Drive '95
Grind '96
Open Water '03

David Steinberg (1942-)
The End '78
Something Short of Paradise '79
Hugh Hefner: Playboy, Activist and Rebel '09
Transylmania '09

John Steiner (1941-)
Massacre in Rome '73
Mannaja: A Man Called Blade '77
Shock '79
Caligula '80
The Last Hunter '80
Ark of the Sun God '82
Unsane '82
Yor, the Hunter from the Future '83
The Lone Runner '88
Sinbad of the Seven Seas '89

Sherry Steiner (1948-)
Asylum of Satan '72
Three on a Meathook '72
Heaven Help Us '85

Hailee Steinfeld (1996-)
True Grit '10
Begin Again '13
Ender's Game '13
Hateship Loveship '13
Romeo & Juliet '13
3 Days to Kill '14
Barely Lethal '15
The Keeping Room '15
Pitch Perfect 2 '15
The Edge of Seventeen '16
Term Life '16
Pitch Perfect 3 '17
Bumblebee '18
Spider-Man: Into the Spider-Verse '18 (V)

Jake Steinfeld (1958-)
Home Sweet Home '80
Tough Guys '86

Richard Steinmetz (1959-)
Liquid Dreams '92
Skyscraper '95
The One '01

Robert J. Steinmiller, Jr. (1978-)
Bingo '91
Jack the Bear '93
The Ref '93
Rudy '93

William (Bill) Steis (1945-95)
Demon of Paradise '87
Eye of the Eagle '87
Raiders of the Sun '92

Anna Sten (1908-93)
We Live Again '34
The Wedding Night '35
Exile Express '39
The Man I Married '40
So Ends Our Night '41
They Came to Blow Up America '43
Soldier of Fortune '55
The Nun and the Sergeant '62

Amandla Stenberg (1998-)
Colombiana '11
The Hunger Games '12
Everything, Everything '17
The Darkest Minds '18
The Hate U Give '18

Leni Stengel (1901-82)
Beau Ideal '31
Cracked Nuts '31

Yutte Stensgaard (1946-)
Zeta One '69
Scream and Scream Again '70
Lust for a Vampire '71

Karel Stepanek (1899-1981)
Counterblast '48
The Fallen Idol '49
Walk East on Beacon '52
Never Let Me Go '53
The Accursed '57
Sink the Bismarck '60
Devil Doll '64
The Frozen Dead '66

Nicole Stephane (1923-2007)
Les Enfants Terrible '50
Carve Her Name with Pride '58

Susan Stephen (1931-2000)
A Stolen Face '52
Value for Money '55
White Huntress '57

Darryl Stephens
Boy Culture '06
Noah's Arc: Jumping the Broom '08

Harvey Stephens (1901-86)
The Cheat '31
Evelyn Prentice '34
After Office Hours '35
Let 'Em Have It '35
The Murder Man '35
Orchids to You '35
Whipsaw '35
Maid of Salem '37
The Texans '38
Beau Geste '39
Oklahoma Kid '39
You Can't Get Away With Murder '39
Abe Lincoln in Illinois '40
Sergeant York '41
The Courtship of Andy Hardy '42
Cell 2455, Death Row '55
The Girl in the Red Velvet Swing '55

Heather Stephens (1971-)
Forever Love '98
Blue Ridge Fall '99
Tomcats '01
Messengers 2: The Scarecrow '09

James Stephens (1951-)
First Monday in October '81
Mysterious Two '82

Martin Stephens (1949-)
Village of the Damned '60
The Innocents '61

Nancy Stephens (1945-)
Halloween '78
Halloween: H20 '98

Perry Stephens (1958-2005)
Norma Jean and Marilyn '95
Two Bits & Pepper '95
Grizzly Mountain '97

Robert Stephens (1931-95)
Pirates of Tortuga '61
Lisa '62
Morgan: A Suitable Case for Treatment '66
The Prime of Miss Jean Brodie '69
The Private Life of Sherlock Holmes '70
The Asphyx '72
Travels with My Aunt '72
Luther '74
Empire of the Sun '87
Fortunes of War '87
High Season '88
Henry V '89
The Bonfire of the Vanities '90
Afraid of the Dark '92
Chaplin '92
Searching for Bobby Fischer '93
The Secret Rapture '94

Toby Stephens (1969-)
The Camomile Lawn '92
The Tenant of Wildfell Hall '96
Twelfth Night '96
Cousin Bette '97
Photographing Fairies '97
Onegin '99
Almost Strangers '01
The Great Gatsby '01
Die Another Day '02
Possession '02
Cambridge Spies '03
Napoleon '03
The Queen's Sister '05
Dark Corners '06
Jane Eyre '06
Severance '06
Sharpe's Challenge '06
Wired '08
All Things to All Men '13
The Machine '13

Bob Stephenson
Friends with Money '06
The Ex '07
Making Babies '19

Henry Stephenson (1871-1956)
The Animal Kingdom '32
Red Headed Woman '32
Double Harness '33
If I Were Free '33
Stingaree '34
Thirty Day Princess '34
Mutiny on the Bounty '35
Rendezvous '35
The Charge of the Light Brigade '36
Give Me Your Heart '36
Conquest '37
The Emperor's Candlesticks '37
The Prince and the Pauper '37
The Baroness and the Butler '38
Marie Antoinette '38
Suez '38
The Old Maid '39
Tarzan Finds a Son '39
Down Argentine Way '40
Spring Parade '40
Lady from Louisiana '42
Rings on Her Fingers '42
This Above All '42
Mr. Lucky '43
Tarzan and the Amazons '45
Heartbeat '46
Her Sister's Secret '46
Song of Love '47
Oliver Twist '48

James Stephenson (1889-1941)
Boy Meets Girl '38
Nancy Drew-Detective '38
Beau Geste '39
King of the Underworld '39
The Letter '40
The Sea Hawk '40

John Stephenson (1923-)
Teenage Rebel '56
The Careless Years '57

Mark Kinsey Stephenson
The Unnamable '88
The Unnamable 2: The Statement of Randolph Carter '92

Pamela Stephenson (1949-)
The Comeback '77
History of the World: Part 1 '81
Superman 3 '83

Craig Stepp
Indecent Behavior 2 '94
Play Time '94

Ford Sterling (1883-1939)
He Who Gets Slapped '24
Wild Oranges '24
The Show Off '26
Sally '29
Show Girl in Hollywood '30
Headline Woman '35

Jan Sterling (1923-2004)
Tycoon '47
Johnny Belinda '48
Caged '50
Mystery Street '50
Union Station '50
Ace in the Hole '51
Appointment With Danger '51
Rhubarb '51
Sky Full of Moon '52
Pony Express '53
Split Second '53
The High and the Mighty '54
Female On the Beach '55
Women's Prison '55
The Harder They Fall '56
1984 '56
High School Confidential '58
Backstairs at the White House '79
First Monday in October '81

Maury Sterling (1971-)
Come as You Are '05
Smokin' Aces '07
The A-Team '10
Coherence '13

Mindy Sterling (1953-)
Austin Powers: International Man of Mystery '97
Austin Powers 2: The Spy Who Shagged Me '99
Drop Dead Gorgeous '99
Totally Blonde '01
Austin Powers In Goldmember '02
The Twelve Dogs of Christmas '05
Ice Age: The Meltdown '06 (V)
Nanny Insanity '06
The Dog Who Saved Christmas '09
The Dog Who Saved Christmas Vacation '10
The Dog Who Saved Halloween '11
Mars Needs Moms '11 (V)

Philip Sterling (1922-98)
Come Die With Me '75
Baby Broker '81
Death of the Incredible Hulk '90
My Giant '98

Robert Sterling (1917-2006)
I'll Wait for You '41
Ringside Maisie '41
Dr. Kildare's Victory '42
Johnny Eager '42
Somewhere I'll Find You '42
The Secret Heart '46
Bunco Squad '50
Return to Peyton Place '61
Voyage to the Bottom of the Sea '61

Tisha Sterling (1944-)
Village of the Giants '65
Coogan's Bluff '68
Betrayal '74
The Killer Inside Me '76
Kiss Me...Kill Me '76
The Whales of August '87

Daniel Stern (1957-)
Breaking Away '79
Starting Over '79
It's My Turn '80
One Trick Pony '80
Stardust Memories '80
Honky Tonk Freeway '81
Diner '82
I'm Dancing as Fast as I Can '82
Blue Thunder '83
Get Crazy '83
C.H.U.D. '84
Ratings Game '84
The Boss' Wife '86
Hannah and Her Sisters '86
Born in East L.A. '87
D.O.A. '88
The Milagro Beanfield War '88
Leviathan '89
Little Monsters '89
Coupe de Ville '90
Home Alone '90
My Blue Heaven '90
City Slickers '91
Home Alone 2: Lost in New York '92
Rookie of the Year '93
City Slickers 2: The Legend of Curly's Gold '94
Bushwhacked '95
Celtic Pride '96
Very Bad Things '98
Dead Simple '01
Bachelor Party Vegas '05
The Last Time '06
Otis '08
Whip It '09
Battle of the Bulbs '10
The Next Three Days '10
A Christmas Story 2 '12

Howard Stern (1954-)
Ryder P.I. '86
Private Parts '96

Miroslava Stern
The Criminal Life of Archibaldo de la Cruz '55
Stranger on Horseback '55

Selma Stern
Made of Honor '08
Smother '08

Tom Stern (1940-)
Angels from Hell '68
The Devil's Brigade '68
Hell's Angels '69 '69
Freaked '93 (C)

Frances Sternhagen (1930-)
Fedora '78
Starting Over '79
Outland '81
Prototype '83
Romantic Comedy '83
Resting Place '86
Bright Lights, Big City '88
Communion '89
See You in the Morning '89
Misery '90
Sibling Rivalry '90
Doc Hollywood '91
Stephen King's Golden Years '91
Raising Cain '92
Curtain Call '97
Julie & Julia '09
And So It Goes '14

Florian Stetter
Sophie Scholl: The Final Days '05
Beloved Sisters '14

Steve-O
Jackass Number Two '06
Jackass 3D '10

Jean-Francois Stevenin (1944-)
Small Change '76
For Sale '98
Total Western '00
Brotherhood of the Wolf '01
The Man on the Train '02
On Guard! '03
The Limits of Control '09
My Afternoons with Marguerite '10
Let My People Go! '11
Bright Days Ahead '14
The Last Diamond '14

Robinson Stevenin (1981-)
Bad Company '99
Transfixed '01
La Petite Lili '03
The Army of Crime '10

Sagamore Stevenin
Romance '99
Coco Chanel '08

Amber Stevens
Tyler Perry's Why Did I Get Married Too '10
22 Jump Street '14

Andrew Stevens (1955-)
Las Vegas Lady '76
Massacre at Central High '76
Vigilante Force '76
The Boys in Company C '77
Day of the Animals '77
The Bastard '78
The Fury '78
Death Hunt '81
Miracle on Ice '81
Forbidden Love '82
The Seduction '82
Ten to Midnight '83
The Terror Within '88
Down the Drain '89
Tusks '89
Red Blooded American Girl '90
Munchie '92
Body Chemistry 3: Point of Seduction '93
The Skateboard Kid 2 '94
Body Chemistry 4: Full Exposure '95
Scorned 2 '96
The Shooter '97
Black Horizon '01

Brinke Stevens (1954-)
Slumber Party Massacre '82
Sole Survivor '84
Nightmare Sisters '87
Slave Girls from Beyond Infinity '87
Sorority Babes in the Slimeball Bowl-A-Rama '87
Grandma's House '88
Warlords '88
Phantom of the Mall: Eric's Revenge '89
Transylvania Twist '89
Bad Girls from Mars '90
Haunting Fear '91
Teenage Exorcist '93
Jack-O '95
Masseuse '95
Mommy '95
Mommy 2: Mommy's Day '96
Hybrid '97
The Kid with the X-Ray Eyes '99
American Nightmare '00
Demon Lust '01
Mom's Outta Sight '01
Witchouse 3: Demon Fire '01
Mark of the Astro-Zombies '02

Charles Stevens (1893-1964)
Mark of Zorro '20
The Three Musketeers '21
The California Trail '33
Call of the Coyote '34
Frontier Marshal '39
Overland Mail '42
Buffalo Bill Rides Again '47
Ambush '50

Connie Stevens (1938-)
Rock-A-Bye Baby *'57*
Parrish *'61*
Susan Slade *'61*
Palm Springs Weekend *'63*
Never Too Late *'65*
Two On a Guillotine *'65*
The Littlest Angel *'69*
The Grissom Gang *'71*
Scruples *'80*
Back to the Beach *'87*
Tapeheads *'89*
Love Is All There Is *'96*
James Dean: Live Fast, Die Young *'97*

Craig Stevens (1918-2000)
Dive Bomber *'41*
The Hidden Hand *'42*
Since You Went Away *'44*
God is My Co-Pilot *'45*
Humoresque *'46*
The Man I Love *'46*
Night Unto Night *'49*
Where the Sidewalk Ends *'50*
Drums in the Deep South *'51*
Abbott and Costello Meet Dr. Jekyll and Mr. Hyde *'52*
Phone Call from a Stranger *'52*
The Deadly Mantis *'57*
Buchanan Rides Alone *'58*
S.O.B. *'81*
La Truite *'83*

Dan Stevens (1982-)
Dracula *'06*
The Line of Beauty *'06*
Sense & Sensibility *'07*
Vamps *'12*
Summer in February *'13*
The Guest *'14*
Night at the Museum: Secret of the Tomb *'14*
A Walk Among the Tombstones *'14*
Criminal Activities *'15*
Beauty and the Beast *'17*
Colossal *'17*
The Man Who Invented Christmas *'17*
Marshall *'17*
The Ticket *'17*
Apostle *'18*
Permission *'18*
Her Smell *'19*
Lucy in the Sky *'19*
The Call of the Wild *'20*

Fisher Stevens (1963-)
The Burning *'82*
The Flamingo Kid *'84*
My Science Project *'85*
Short Circuit *'86*
Short Circuit 2 *'88*
Reversal of Fortune *'90*
The Marrying Man *'91*
Mystery Date *'91*
When the Party's Over *'91*
Bob Roberts *'92*
Super Mario Bros. *'93*
Nina Takes a Lover *'94*
Only You *'94*
Hackers *'95*
The Tic Code *'99*
Undisputed *'02*
Undiscovered *'05*
Factotum *'06*
Kettle of Fish *'06*
Awake *'07*
The Experiment *'10*
Fake *'10*
Henry's Crime *'10*
Rio Sex Comedy *'10*
The Grand Budapest Hotel *'14 (C)*

G.W. Stevens
Landspeed *'01*
Parasite *'03*

Inger Stevens (1934-70)
The Buccaneer *'58*
Cry Terror! *'58*
A Guide for the Married Man *'67*
Hang 'Em High *'67*
Firecreek *'68*
Five Card Stud *'68*
Madigan *'68*
A Dream of Kings *'69*
Savage Run *'70*

Joe Stevens
American Outlaws *'01*
The Alamo *'04*

K.T. Stevens (1919-94)
Address Unknown *'44*
Port of New York *'49*
Vice Squad *'53*
Jungle Hell *'55*
Missile to the Moon *'59*
They're Playing with Fire *'84*

Mark Stevens (1915-94)
Objective, Burma! *'45*
Dark Corner *'46*
The Snake Pit *'48*
The Street with No Name *'48*
Between Midnight and Dawn *'50*
Mutiny *'52*
Fate Is the Hunter *'64*
Frozen Alive *'64*
The Fury of the Wolfman *'70*

Onslow Stevens (1902-77)
Counsellor-at-Law *'33*
Bombay Mail *'34*
Murder With Pictures *'36*
Flight from Glory *'37*
Hands Across the Border *'43*
House of Dracula *'45*
Angel on My Shoulder *'46*
Walk a Crooked Mile *'48*
Bomba, the Jungle Boy *'49*
One Too Many *'51*
The San Francisco Story *'52*
A Lion Is in the Streets *'53*
Fangs of the Wild *'54*
Them! *'54*
Tribute to a Bad Man *'56*
Mark of the Gorilla *'58*
Tarawa Beachhead *'58*
The Couch *'62*

Paul Stevens (1921-86)
Exodus *'60*
The Mask *'61*
Rage *'72*
Get Christie Love! *'74*

Rise Stevens (1913-2013)
The Chocolate Soldier *'41*
Going My Way *'44*

Ronnie Stevens (1925-2002)
Dentist In the Chair *'60*
The Parent Trap *'98*

Ruthelma Stevens (1903-84)
Scarlet Empress *'34*
Orchids to You *'35*

Stella Stevens (1938-)
Li'l Abner *'59*
Man-Trap *'61*
Too Late Blues *'61*
The Courtship of Eddie's Father *'62*
Girls! Girls! Girls! *'62*
The Nutty Professor *'63*
Advance to the Rear *'64*
Synanon *'65*
The Silencers *'66*
Where Angels Go, Trouble Follows *'68*
The Mad Room *'69*
Ballad of Cable Hogue *'70*
Slaughter *'72*
A Town Called Hell *'72*
Cleopatra Jones & the Casino of Gold *'75*
Kiss Me...Kill Me *'76*
Las Vegas Lady *'76*
Nickelodeon *'76*
The Manitou *'78*
Friendship, Secrets and Lies *'79*
Chained Heat *'83*
Power, Passion & Murder *'83*
The Longshot *'86*
Monster in the Closet *'86*
Down the Drain *'89*
Mom *'89*
Last Call *'90*
Eye of the Stranger *'93*
Hard Drive *'94*
Body Chemistry 4: Full Exposure *'95*
The Nutt House *'95 (C)*
Star Hunter *'95*
Virtual Combat *'95*
In Cold Blood *'96*
Invisible Mom *'96*
By Dawn's Early Light *'00*
The Long Ride Home *'01*
The Glass Trap *'04*

Warren Stevens (1919-2012)
Red Skies of Montana *'52*
The I Don't Care Girl *'53*
The Barefoot Contessa *'54*
Women's Prison *'55*
Forbidden Planet *'56*
The Price of Fear *'56*
The Case Against Brooklyn *'58*
Intent to Kill *'58*
Man or Gun *'58*
No Name on the Bullet *'59*
The Sweet Ride *'68*
The Trail to Hope Rose *'04*

Cynthia Stevenson (1962-)
The Reluctant Agent *'89*
The Player *'92*
Forget Paris *'95*
Home for the Holidays *'95*
Live Nude Girls *'95*
Air Bud 2: Golden Receiver *'98*
From the Earth to the Moon *'98*
Happiness *'98*
Air Bud 4: Seventh Inning Fetch *'02*
Agent Cody Banks *'03*
Air Bud 5: Buddy Spikes Back *'03*
Agent Cody Banks 2: Destination London *'04*
A Little Thing Called Murder *'06*
Full of It *'07*
Snow Buddies *'08*
Will You Merry Me? *'08*
I Love You, Beth Cooper *'09*
Case 39 *'10*
Tiger Eyes *'13*

Houseley Stevenson (1879-1953)
Somewhere in the Night *'46*
Kidnapped *'48*
Sierra *'50*
The Sun Sets at Dawn *'50*

Jessica Stevenson (1972-)
Bridget Jones: The Edge of Reason *'04*
Shaun of the Dead *'04*
Confetti *'06*
Four Last Songs *'06*
Pinochet's Last Stand *'06*
Son of Rambow *'07*

Juliet Stevenson (1956-)
Drowning by Numbers *'87*
Truly, Madly, Deeply *'91*
The Trial *'93*
The Secret Rapture *'94*
Emma *'96*
Cider with Rosie *'99*
The Search for John Gissing *'01*
Bend It Like Beckham *'02*
Food of Love *'02*
Nicholas Nickleby *'02*
The Road from Coorain *'02*
Mona Lisa Smile *'03*
Being Julia *'04*
Red Mercury *'05*
Breaking and Entering *'06*
Infamous *'06*
When Did You Last See Your Father? *'07*
The Secret of Moonacre *'08*
Place of Execution *'09*
Triage *'09*
Diana *'13*
The Letters *'15*

McLean Stevenson (1929-96)
The Cat from Outer Space *'78*
Armistead Maupin's Tales of the City *'93*

Parker Stevenson (1952-)
Our Time *'74*
Lifeguard *'76*
Stroker Ace *'83*
North and South Book 2 *'86*
Not of This Earth *'96*
Legion *'98*
Terror Peak *'03*

Ray Stevenson (1964-)
The Return of the Native *'94*
Catherine Cookson's The Tide of Life *'96*
King Arthur *'04*
Outpost *'07*
Punisher: War Zone *'08*
Cirque du Freak: The Vampire's Assistant *'09*
The Book of Eli *'10*
Kill the Irishman *'11*
Thor *'11*
The Three Musketeers *'11*
G.I. Joe: Retaliation *'13*
Jayne Mansfield's Car *'13*
Divergent *'14*
Big Game *'15*
The Transporter Refueled *'15*
Cold Skin *'18*
Final Score *'18*

Robert Stevenson (1905-86)
Fangs of the Wild *'54*
Zero Hour! *'57*

Tom Stevenson (1910-2004)
Across the Pacific *'42*
The Hidden Hand *'42*
Gaslight *'44*

Venetia Stevenson (1938-)
Darby's Rangers *'58*
The Day of the Outlaw *'59*
Island of Lost Women *'59*
Horror Hotel *'60*

Alexandra Stewart (1938-)
Exodus *'60*
Tarzan the Magnificent *'60*
The Fire Within *'64*
Mickey One *'65*
Zeppelin *'71*
Day for Night *'73*
The Destructors *'74*
Black Moon *'75*
In Praise of Older Women *'78*
The Agency *'81*
Last Chase *'81*
Sans Soleil *'82 (N)*
Son of Gascogne *'95*
Under the Sand *'00*

Amy Stewart
Another Woman *'94*
Trucks *'97*

Athole Stewart (1879-1940)
The Speckled Band *'31*
Accused *'36*

Booboo Stewart (1994-)
The Conrad Boys *'06*
666: The Child *'06*
White Frog *'12*
Space Warriors *'13*
An Evergreen Christmas *'14*
He Never Died *'15*
Tales of Halloween *'15*

Byron Stewart (1956-)
Grambling's White Tiger *'81*
How U Like Me Now? *'92*

Cameron Deane Stewart
A Walk in My Shoes *'10*
Beverly Lewis' The Confession *'13*

Catherine Mary Stewart (1959-)
The Apple *'80*
Nighthawks *'81*
The Last Starfighter *'84*
Night of the Comet *'84*
Mischief *'85*
Sins *'85*
Scenes from the Goldmine *'87*
Weekend at Bernie's *'89*
Perfect Harmony *'91*
Psychic *'91*
Ordeal in the Arctic *'93*
Number One Fan *'94*
The Reaper *'97*
Dead Silent *'99*
The Attic *'06*
Sharpshooter *'07*

Charlotte Stewart (1941-)
Eraserhead *'78*
Tremors *'89*
Dark Angel: The Ascent *'94*
Tremors 3: Back to Perfection *'01*

David J. Stewart
Carnival Rock *'57*
Murder, Inc. *'60*

Elaine Stewart (1930-2011)
The Bad and the Beautiful *'52*
Code Two *'53*
A Slight Case of Larceny *'53*
Young Bess *'53*
Brigadoon *'54*
Night Passage *'57*
The Rise and Fall of Legs Diamond *'60*
Most Dangerous Man Alive *'61*

Evelyn Stewart (1942-)
Murder Mansion *'70*
The Scorpion's Tail *'71*
Django Shoots First *'74*

Ewan Stewart (1957-)
Rob Roy *'95*
Stella Does Tricks *'96*
The Big Brass Ring *'99*
American Women *'00*
Conspiracy *'01*

Frank Stewart
Galactic Gigolo *'87*
Psychos in Love *'87*
Cemetery High *'89*

French Stewart (1964-)
Glory Daze *'96*
McHale's Navy *'97*
Love Stinks *'99*
Clockstoppers *'02*
Inspector Gadget 2 *'02*
Duck *'05*
The Flock *'07*
Grindin' *'07*
Pandemic *'07*
Dog Gone *'08*
Surveillance *'08*
Give 'Em Hell Malone *'09*
Opposite Day *'09*
30 Nights of Paranormal Activity with the Devil Inside the Girl with the Dragon Tattoo *'12*

James Stewart (1908-97)
The Murder Man *'35*
After the Thin Man *'36*
Born to Dance *'36*
The Gorgeous Hussy *'36*
Next Time We Love *'36*
Rose Marie *'36*
Speed *'36*
Wife Versus Secretary *'36*
The Last Gangster *'37*
Navy Blue and Gold *'37*
Of Human Hearts *'38*
Shopworn Angel *'38*
Vivacious Lady *'38*
You Can't Take It with You *'38*
Destry Rides Again *'39*
Ice Follies of 1939 *'39*
It's a Wonderful World *'39*
Made for Each Other *'39*
Mr. Smith Goes to Washington *'39*
Come Live With Me *'40*
The Mortal Storm *'40*
No Time For Comedy *'40*
The Philadelphia Story *'40*
The Shop Around the Corner *'40*
Pot o' Gold *'41*
Ziegfeld Girl *'41*
It's a Wonderful Life *'46*
Magic Town *'47*
Call Northside 777 *'48*
On Our Merry Way *'48*
Rope *'48*
You Gotta Stay Happy *'48*
Malaya *'49*
The Stratton Story *'49*
Broken Arrow *'50*
Harvey *'50*
The Jackpot *'50*
Winchester '73 *'50*
No Highway in the Sky *'51*
Bend of the River *'52*
Carbine Williams *'52*
The Greatest Show on Earth *'52*
The Naked Spur *'53*
Thunder Bay *'53*
The Glenn Miller Story *'54*
Rear Window *'54*
Far Country *'55*
The Man from Laramie *'55*
Strategic Air Command *'55*
The Man Who Knew Too Much *'56*
Night Passage *'57*
Spirit of St. Louis *'57*
Bell, Book and Candle *'58*
Vertigo *'58*
Anatomy of a Murder *'59*
The FBI Story *'59*
Two Rode Together *'61*
The Man Who Shot Liberty Valance *'62*
Mr. Hobbs Takes a Vacation *'62*
How the West Was Won *'63*
Take Her, She's Mine *'63*
Cheyenne Autumn *'64 (C)*
Dear Brigitte *'65*
The Flight of the Phoenix *'65*
Shenandoah *'65*
The Rare Breed *'66*
Bandolero! *'68*
Firecreek *'68*
The Cheyenne Social Club *'70*
The Shootist *'76*
Airport '77 *'77*
The Big Sleep *'78*
North and South Book 2 *'86*
An American Tail: Fievel Goes West *'91 (V)*

Johna Stewart (1979-)
Address Unknown *'96*
Young Hercules *'97*

Jon Stewart (1962-)
Wishful Thinking *'96*
Half-Baked *'97*
Since You've Been Gone *'97 (C)*
The Faculty *'98*
Playing by Heart *'98*
Big Daddy *'99*
Jay and Silent Bob Strike Back *'01*
Death to Smoochy *'02*

Josh Stewart (1977-)
Full Count *'06*
The Collector *'09*
Law Abiding Citizen *'09*
Beneath the Dark *'10*
The Collection *'12*
Alpha Alert *'13*

Kate McGregor Stewart (1944-)
See Kate McGregor-Stewart

Kellee Stewart
Guess Who *'05*
Love by the 10th Date *'17*

Kristen Stewart (1990-)
The Safety of Objects *'01*
Panic Room *'02*
Cold Creek Manor *'03*
Catch That Kid *'04*
Speak *'04*
Fierce People *'05*
Zathura *'05*
In the Land of Women *'06*
The Cake Eaters *'07*
Into the Wild *'07*
The Messengers *'07*
Twilight *'08*
What Just Happened *'08*
The Yellow Handkerchief *'08*
Adventureland *'09*

Billionaire Boys Club '87
Born to Ride '91
Breast Men '97
The Nurse '97
Stag '97

Malcolm Stoddard (1948-)
Luther '74
Catherine Cookson's The Girl '96
Coming Home '98

Austin Stoker (1934-)
Battle for the Planet of the Apes '73
Twisted Brain '74
Sheba, Baby '75
Assault on Precinct 13 '76
Time Walker '82
The Uninvited '88

Barry Stokes
Alien Prey '78
Spaced Out '80

Christian Stokes
Lake Dead '07
Few Options '11

Matthew Stokoe
Hollow '11
Devil's Pass '13

Oliver Stokowski (1962-)
Regular Guys '96
The Experiment '01

Mink Stole (1947-)
Pink Flamingos '72
Female Trouble '74
Desperate Living '77
Polyester '81
Hairspray '88
Cry-Baby '90
Liquid Dreams '92
Serial Mom '94
Leather Jacket Love Story '98 (C)
Pecker '98
But I'm a Cheerleader '99
Cecil B. Demented '00
Shriek If You Know What I Did Last Friday the 13th '00
A Dirty Shame '04
Girl Play '04
Ring of Darkness '04
Eating Out 2: Sloppy Seconds '06
Out at the Wedding '07
Eating Out 3: All You Can Eat '09
Eating Out 4: Drama Camp '11

Shirley Stoler (1929-99)
Honeymoon Killers '70
A Real Young Girl '75
Seven Beauties '76
The Deer Hunter '78
Splitz '84
Shakedown '88
Sticky Fingers '88
Frankenhooker '90
Miami Blues '90
Malcolm X '92

Erik Stolhanske (1968-)
Super Troopers '01
Club Dread '04
Beerfest '06
The Slammin' Salmon '09
Super Troopers 2 '18

Corey Stoll (1976-)
A Girl Like Me: The Gwen Araujo Story '06
Midnight in Paris '11
The Time Being '12
C.O.G. '13
Decoding Annie Parker '13
Glass Chin '14
The Good Lie '14
Non-Stop '14
This Is Where I Leave You '14
Ant-Man '15
Dark Places '15
First Man '18
The Seagull '18
The Report '19

Gunther Stoll (1924-77)
The Castle of Fu Manchu '68
Double Face '70
Cold Blood '75

Fred Stoller (1958-)
Dumb & Dumber '94
Downhill Willie '96
Chairman of the Board '97
Rebound '05

Eric Stoltz (1961-)
Fast Times at Ridgemont High '82
A Killer in the Family '83
Running Hot '83
Code Name: Emerald '85
Mask '85
The New Kids '85
Lionheart '87
Sister, Sister '87
Some Kind of Wonderful '87
Haunted Summer '88
The Fly 2 '89
Our Town '89
Say Anything '89
Memphis Belle '90
The Waterdance '91
Singles '92 (C)
Bodies, Rest & Motion '93
Naked in New York '93
Killing Zoe '94
Little Women '94
Pulp Fiction '94
Sleep with Me '94
Fluke '95
Kicking and Screaming '95
The Prophecy '95
Rob Roy '95
Anaconda '96
Don't Look Back '96
Grace of My Heart '96
Inside '96
Jerry Maguire '96 (C)
Keys to Tulsa '96
Two Days in the Valley '96
Highball '97
Hi-Life '98
Mr. Jealousy '98
A Murder of Crows '99
The Passion of Ayn Rand '99
The Simian Line '99
House of Mirth '00
Harvard Man '01
Things Behind the Sun '01
The Rules of Attraction '02
Happy Hour '03
Out of Order '03
The Butterfly Effect '04
The Honeymooners '05
The Triangle '05
The Lather Effect '06
Caprica '09
Fort McCoy '11
5 to 7 '15

Lena Stolze (1956-)
The Nasty Girl '90
Relative Strangers '99
Rosenstrasse '03
Vision '09

Peter Stomare
Boot Camp '07
Insanitarium '08

Christopher Stone (1940-95)
The Grasshopper '69
The Passing of Evil '70
Love Me Deadly '73
Prisoner in the Middle '74
The Howling '81
The Junkman '82
Cujo '83

Danton Stone
Crazy People '90
He Said, She Said '91
Once Around '91
McHale's Navy '97
Series 7: The Contenders '01

Emma Stone (1988-)
Superbad '07
The House Bunny '08
The Rocker '08
Ghosts of Girlfriends Past '09
Paper Man '09
Zombieland '09
Easy A '10
Marmaduke '10 (V)
Crazy, Stupid, Love. '11
The Help '11
The Amazing Spider-Man '12
The Croods '13 (V)
Gangster Squad '13
Movie 43 '13
The Amazing Spider-Man 2 '14
Birdman, or (The Unexpected Virtue of Ignorance) '14
Magic in the Moonlight '14
Aloha '15
La La Land '16
Battle of the Sexes '17
The Favourite '18
Zombieland: Double Tap '19

Fred Stone (1873-1959)
Alice Adams '35
The Trail of the Lonesome Pine '36
The Westerner '40

George E. Stone (1903-67)
Weary River '29
Cimarron '31
Five Star Final '31
The Woman From Monte Carlo '31
The Last Mile '32
Taxi! '32
The Vampire Bat '32
42nd Street '33
Frisco Kid '35
Make a Million '35
A Slight Case of Murder '38
You and Me '38
Broadway Limited '41
Road Show '41
Treasure of Fear '45
Jungle Hell '55

Harold J. Stone (1911-2005)
X: The Man with X-Ray Eyes '63
Girl Happy '65
The St. Valentine's Day Massacre '67
Legend of Valentino '75
The McCullochs '75
Mitchell '75

Jennifer Stone (1933-)
The Wizards of Waverly Place: The Movie '09
Harriet the Spy: Blog Wars '10
Mean Girls 2 '11

Julia Stone
Sirens '94
The Year Dolly Parton Was My Mom '11

Julian Stone (1962-)
National Lampoon's Christmas Vacation 2: Cousin Eddie's Big Island Adventure '03
Black Dawn '05
Bed & Breakfast '10

Leonard Stone (1923-2011)
Willy Wonka & the Chocolate Factory '71
Once Upon a Spy '80
Blood Money '99

Lewis Stone (1879-1953)
Nomads of the North '20
The Prisoner of Zenda '22
Scaramouche '23
The Lost World '25
The Notorious Lady '27
Wild Orchids '28
Madame X '29
Their Own Desire '29
The Big House '30
Romance '30
The Phantom of Paris '31
The Secret Six '31
The Sin of Madelon Claudet '31
Grand Hotel '32
The Mask of Fu Manchu '32
Mata Hari '32
New Morals for Old '32
Red Headed Woman '32
The Wet Parade '32
Bureau of Missing Persons '33
Queen Christina '33
The White Sister '33
The Girl from Missouri '34
Treasure Island '34
China Seas '35
David Copperfield '35
Shipmates Forever '35
Suzy '36
Three Godfathers '36
You're Only Young Once '37
The Bad Man of Brimstone '38
Judge Hardy's Children '38
Love Finds Andy Hardy '38
Out West With the Hardys '38
Andy Hardy Gets Spring Fever '39
The Hardys Ride High '39
Ice Follies of 1939 '39
Judge Hardy and Son '39
Andy Hardy Meets Debutante '40
Andy Hardy's Private Secretary '41
Life Begins for Andy Hardy '41
Andy Hardy's Double Life '42
The Courtship of Andy Hardy '42
Andy Hardy's Blonde Trouble '44
Love Laughs at Andy Hardy '46
State of the Union '48
Any Number Can Play '49
The Sun Comes Up '49
Key to the City '50
Stars in My Crown '50
Angels in the Outfield '51
Prisoner of Zenda '52
Scaramouche '52
All the Brothers Were Valiant '53

Marianne Stone (1922-2009)
Terror Street '54
Lolita '62

Matt Stone (1971-)
Cannibal! The Musical '96
BASEketball '98
Orgazmo '98
South Park: Bigger, Longer and Uncut '99 (V)
Team America: World Police '04 (V)

Melanie Stone
Mythica 2: The Darkspore '15
Mythica: A Quest for Heroes '15
Mythica: The Necromancer '15
Mythica: The Iron Crown '16
Little Women '18

Michael Stone
The Quick and the Dead '95
Bloody Murder '99

Milburn Stone (1904-80)
Sherlock Holmes Faces Death '43
Master Key '44
Phantom Lady '44
Heading for Heaven '47
Killer Dill '47
The Green Promise '49
The Judge '49
Branded '50
The Fireball '50
Roadblock '51
The Atomic City '52
Arrowhead '53
Pickup on South Street '53
The Sun Shines Bright '53
Siege at Red River '54

Natalie Stone
30,000 Leagues Under the Sea '07
Allan Quartermain and the Temple of Skulls '08

Oliver Stone (1946-)
Midnight Express '78
The Hand '81 (C)
Scarface '83
Platoon '86
Wall Street '87
Born on the Fourth of July '89 (C)
Dave '93 (C)
Wild Palms '93 (C)
South of the Border '09 (N)

Philip Stone (1924-2003)
Hitler: The Last Ten Days '73
The Shining '80
A Certain Justice '99

Sam Oz Stone
Rock the Paint '05
The Box '09

Sharon Stone (1958-)
Deadly Blessing '81
Calendar Girl Murders '84
Irreconcilable Differences '84
The Vegas Strip Wars '84
King Solomon's Mines '85
Allan Quatermain and the Lost City of Gold '86
Cold Steel '87
Police Academy 4: Citizens on Patrol '87
Above the Law '88
Action Jackson '88
Tears in the Rain '88
War & Remembrance '88
Beyond the Stars '89
Blood and Sand '89
War & Remembrance: The Final Chapter '89
Total Recall '90
Diary of a Hitman '91
He Said, She Said '91
Scissors '91
Where Sleeping Dogs Lie '91
Year of the Gun '91
Basic Instinct '92
Intersection '93
Last Action Hero '93 (C)
Sliver '93
The Specialist '94
Casino '95
The Quick and the Dead '95
Diabolique '96
Last Dance '96
Sphere '97
Antz '98 (V)
Gloria '98
The Mighty '98
The Muse '99
Picking Up the Pieces '99
Simpatico '99
Beautiful Joe '00
If These Walls Could Talk 2 '00
Cold Creek Manor '03
Catwoman '04
A Different Loyalty '04
Broken Flowers '05
Jiminy Glick in LaLa Wood '05 (C)
Alpha Dog '06
Basic Instinct 2 '06
Bobby '06
When a Man Falls in the Forest '07
$5 a Day '08
The Year of Getting to Know Us '08
Streets of Blood '09
Border Run '12
Fading Gigolo '13
Lovelace '13

Skyler Stone
Housebroken '09
Hostel: Part 3 '11

Stuart Stone (1977-)
The Boys Club '96
Donnie Darko '01
Joy Ride '01
Endure '10

Terry Stone
Rise of the Footsoldier '07
Bonded by Blood '09

Jo Stone-Fewings
All the King's Men '99
Wondrous Oblivion '06

Alyson Stoner (1993-)
Cheaper by the Dozen '03
Cheaper by the Dozen 2 '05
Alice Upside Down '07
Camp Rock '08
Camp Rock 2: The Final Jam '10
Step Up 3D '10
Step Up: All In '14

Sherri Stoner (1965-)
Impulse '84
Lovelines '84
Reform School Girls '86

Eric Stonestreet (1971-)
Identity Thief '13
The Loft '14
The Secret Life of Pets '16
The Secret Life of Pets 2 '19

Paolo Stoppa (1906-88)
Miracle in Milan '51
Beauties of the Night '52
The Gold of Naples '54
Neapolitan Carousel '54
Where the Hot Wind Blows '59
The Leopard '63

Ed Stoppard (1974-)
The Little Vampire '00
The Pianist '02
Any Human Heart '11
Upstairs Downstairs '11
Branded '12

Arthur Storch
The Strange One '57
Girl of the Night '60

Larry Storch (1923-)
Who Was That Lady? '60
40 Pounds of Trouble '62
Captain Newman, M.D. '63
Sex and the Single Girl '64
That Funny Feeling '65
A Very Special Favor '65
The Woman Hunter '72
Airport '75 '75
Without Warning '80
S.O.B. '81
Flight of Dragons '82 (V)
I Don't Buy Kisses Anymore '92
Funny Valentine '05

June Storey (1918-91)
First Love '39
South of the Border '39
Dance Hall '41
The Strange Woman '46

Adam Storke (1962-)
Mystic Pizza '88
The Phantom of the Opera '90
Death Becomes Her '92
Lifepod '93
Stephen King's The Stand '94
A Mother's Gift '95
Rough Riders '97
Johnson County War '02

Dirk Storm (1953-)
See Kevin Nealon

Gale Storm (1922-2009)
Gambling Daughters '41
Smart Alecks '42
Campus Rhythm '43
Rhythm Parade '43
Where Are Your Children? '44
Swing Parade of 1946 '46
Abandoned '47
It Happened on 5th Avenue '47
The Dude Goes West '48
Stampede '49
Between Midnight and Dawn '50
The Underworld Story '50

James Storm (1943-)
Night of Dark Shadows '71
Scream of the Wolf '74
Trilogy of Terror '75
Ants '77

KaDee Strickland (1975-)
Anything Else '03
Something's Gotta Give '03
Anacondas: The Hunt for the Blood Orchid '04
The Grudge '04
Fever Pitch '05
Knots '05
Walker Payne '06
American Gangster '07
The Flock '07
The Family That Preys '08

Ray Stricklyn (1928-2002)
Return of Dracula '58
The Remarkable Mr. Pennypacker '59
The Plunderers '60

David Striesow (1973-)
The Counterfeiters '07
Yella '07
Vision '09
3 '10

Reshad Strik
Don't Look Up '08
Newcastle '08

Anita Strindberg (1944-)
The Case of the Scorpion's Tail '71
A Lizard in a Woman's Skin '71
The Scorpion's Tail '71
Who Saw Her Die? '72
Your Vice is a Closed Room and Only I Have the Key '72

Sherry Stringfield (1967-)
Burnzy's Last Call '95
54 '98
Autumn in New York '00
Dead Simple '01
Forfeit '07
The Stepfather '09
Who Is Clark Rockefeller? '10
Beverly Lewis' The Shunning '11
Born 2 Race '11
Beverly Lewis' The Confession '13
The Dog Lover '16

Elaine Stritch (1925-2014)
A Farewell to Arms '57
Three Violent People '57
The Perfect Furlough '59
September '88
Out to Sea '97
Krippendorf's Tribe '98
Autumn in New York '00
Screwed '00
Small Time Crooks '00
Monster-in-Law '05
Romance & Cigarettes '05
ParaNorman '12 (V)
Elaine Stritch: Shoot Me '14

Woody Strode (1914-94)
The Lion Hunters '51
Tarzan's Fight for Life '58
Pork Chop Hill '59
The Last Voyage '60
Sergeant Rutledge '60
Spartacus '60
The Sins of Rachel Cade '61
The Man Who Shot Liberty Valance '62
Tarzan's Three Challenges '63
Genghis Khan '65
The Professionals '66
Black Jesus '68
Once Upon a Time in the West '68
Shalako '68
Boot Hill '69
Ride to Glory '71
The Gatling Gun '72
The Revengers '72
Hired to Kill '73
The Italian Connection '73
Manhunt '73
Loaded Guns '75
Kingdom of the Spiders '77
Oil '78
Jaguar Lives '79
Kill Castro '80
The Mercenaries '80
Scream '83
Vigilante '83
Jungle Warriors '84
Lust in the Dust '85
Murder on the Bayou '91
Storyville '92
Posse '93 (C)

Phoebe Strole
Hamlet 2 '08
Sorority Wars '09

Edson Stroll (1930-2011)
Snow White and the Three Stooges '61
Three Stooges in Orbit '62

Freddie Stroma
A Cinderella Story: Once Upon a Song '11
Pitch Perfect '12
Extraterrestrial '14

Brenda Strong (1960-)
Black Dog '98
The Deep End of the Ocean '98
Undercurrent '99
Terror Tract '00
Exposed '03
Missing Brendan '03
Starship Troopers 2: Hero of the Federation '04
The Kid and I '05
Family in Hiding '06
A Plumm Summer '08

Danny Strong (1974-)
Perpetrators of the Crime '98
Shriek If You Know What I Did Last Friday the 13th '00
Veritas: Prince of Truth '07
Bad Guys '08

Jeremy Strong (1978-)
Humboldt County '08
The Romantics '10
Lincoln '12
Robot & Frank '12
Parkland '13
The Judge '14
Molly's Game '17
The Gentlemen '20

Johnny Strong (1974-)
The Glimmer Man '96
Get Carter '00
Black Hawk Down '01
The Fast and the Furious '01
Sinners and Saints '10
Daylight's End '16

Mark Strong (1963-)
Fever Pitch '96
Sharpe's Mission '96
Emma '97
Twice upon a Yesterday '98
Sunshine '99
Anna Karenina '00
To End All Wars '01
It's All About Love '03
Oliver Twist '05
Revolver '05
Syriana '05
Scenes of a Sexual Nature '06
Tristan & Isolde '06
Stardust '07
Sunshine '07
Babylon A.D. '08
Body of Lies '08
Flashbacks of a Fool '08
Good '08
Miss Pettigrew Lives for a Day '08
RocknRolla '08
Endgame '09
Sherlock Holmes '09
The Young Victoria '09
Kick-Ass '10
Robin Hood '10
The Way Back '10
Day of the Falcon '11
The Eagle '11
Green Lantern '11
The Guard '11
Tinker Tailor Soldier Spy '11
John Carter '12
Zero Dark Thirty '12
Welcome to the Punch '13
Before I Go to Sleep '14
The Imitation Game '14
Kingsman: The Secret Service '15
Approaching the Unknown '16
The Brothers Grimsby '16
Miss Sloane '16
Kingsman: The Golden Circle '17
The Catcher Was a Spy '18
Shazam! '19

Michael Strong (1924-80)
The Iceman Cometh '60
Point Blank '67
Patton '70
Queen of the Stardust Ballroom '75

Natalie Strong
Bob Roberts '92
The Player '92
Short Cuts '93
Mrs. Parker and the Vicious Circle '94

Rider Strong (1979-)
Benefit of the Doubt '93
My Giant '98
The Pact '99
Cabin Fever '03
Death Valley '04
Paradise, Texas '05
Borderland '07
Tooth and Nail '07
Cabin Fever 2: Spring Fever '08
Spy School '08
The Penthouse '10

Tara Strong (1973-)
Family Pictures '93
The Rugrats Movie '98 (V)
Rugrats in Paris: The Movie '00 (V)
Spirited Away '01 (V)
Ice Age '02 (V)
The Powerpuff Girls Movie '02 (V)
Rugrats Go Wild! '03 (V)
Delhi Safari '12 (V)
Animal Crackers '17
Teen Titans Go! To the Movies '18 (V)

Don Stroud (1943-)
Games '67
Coogan's Bluff '68
Madigan '68
Angel Unchained '70
Bloody Mama '70
Tick... Tick... Tick '70
Joe Kidd '72
Slaughter's Big Ripoff '73
Murph the Surf '75
Hollywood Man '76
The Killer Inside Me '76
The Choirboys '77
Sudden Death '77
The Buddy Holly Story '78
The Amityville Horror '79
The Night the Lights Went Out in Georgia '81
Search and Destroy '81
Armed and Dangerous '86
Down the Drain '89
Hyper Space '89
Twisted Justice '89
Cartel '90
Prime Target '91
Return to Frogtown '92
Dillinger and Capone '95
Unknown Origin '95
Little Bigfoot '96
Dance with the Devil '97
The Haunted Sea '97
Wild America '97
Django Unchained '12

Duke Stroud
Children of the Corn 3: Urban Harvest '95
Human Desires '97

Jessica Stroup (1986-)
The Hills Have Eyes 2 '07
Prom Night '08
Homecoming '09

Henry Strozier
The Curve '97
Thirteen Days '00

Shepperd Strudwick (1907-83)
Fast Company '38
Congo Maisie '40
Dr. Kildare's Strange Case '40
Flight Command '40
Remember the Day '41
Rings on Her Fingers '42
Enchantment '48
Fighter Squadron '48
All the King's Men '49
The Red Pony '49
Let's Dance '50
Three Husbands '50
A Place in the Sun '51
Beyond a Reasonable Doubt '56
Psychomania '63
Cops and Robbers '73

Joe Strummer (1952-2002)
Straight to Hell '87
Mystery Train '89
Doctor Chance '97

Lusia Strus
50 First Dates '04
Restless '11

Sally Struthers (1947-)
Five Easy Pieces '70
The Getaway '72
A Gun in the House '81
Alice in Wonderland '85
Out of the Black '01
Baadasssss! '03

Carel Struycken (1948-)
The Ewoks: Battle for Endor '85
The Witches of Eastwick '87
The Addams Family '91
Servants of Twilight '91
Addams Family Values '93
Oblivion '94
Backlash: Oblivion 2 '95
Men in Black '97

Barbara Stuart (1930-2011)
Marines, Let's Go '61
A Family Affair '01

Cassie Stuart
Dolls '87
Hidden City '87

Eric Stuart (1967-)
Pokemon: The First Movie '99 (V)
Pokemon 3: The Movie '01 (V)
Yu-Gi-Oh! The Movie: Pyramid of Light '04 (V)

Gloria Stuart (1910-2010)
The Old Dark House '32
Street of Women '32
The Invisible Man '33
Sweepings '33
Here Comes the Navy '34
Gold Diggers of 1935 '35
Professional Soldier '35
The Prisoner of Shark Island '36
Rebecca of Sunnybrook Farm '38
The Three Musketeers '39
Enemy of Women '44
The Two Worlds of Jenny Logan '79
My Favorite Year '82
Titanic '97
The Love Letter '99
The Million Dollar Hotel '99
Land of Plenty '04

James Patrick Stuart (1968-)
Gettysburg '93
The Man Who Came Back '08
A Taste of Romance '12

James R. Stuart (1925-94)
See Giacomo 'Jack' Rossi-Stuart

Jason Stuart
Coffee Date '06
Finding Mr. Wright '11

John Stuart (1898-1979)
The Pleasure Garden '25
Hindle Wakes '27
The Mistress of Atlantis '32
Old Mother Riley's Ghosts '41
Candles at Nine '44
Madonna of the Seven Moons '45
House of Darkness '48
Alias John Preston '56
The Mummy '59
Sink the Bismarck '60
Village of the Damned '60
Lone Tiger '94

Katie Stuart (1985-)
Summer of the Monkeys '98
Too Young to Be a Dad '02
X2: X-Men United '03
Wild Things 2 '04
Spirit Bear: The Simon Jackson Story '05
Tamara '05
Blackout '07
Lost Dream '09

Randy Stuart (1924-96)
Sitting Pretty '48
I Was a Male War Bride '49
I Can Get It For You Wholesale '51
Room for One More '51
The Incredible Shrinking Man '57
Man From God's Country '58

Harry Stubbs (1874-1950)
Alibi '29
Stepping Out '31

Imogen Stubbs (1961-)
A Summer Story '88
Erik the Viking '89
True Colors '91
Jack and Sarah '95
Sense and Sensibility '95
Twelfth Night '96
Dead Cool '04

Stephen Stucker (1947-86)
Airplane! '80
Airplane 2: The Sequel '82
Trading Places '83
Delinquent School Girls '84

Sophie Stuckey
Close Your Eyes '02
The Woman in Black '12

Wes Studi (1947-)
Dances with Wolves '90
The Doors '91
The Last of the Mohicans '92
Geronimo: An American Legend '93
Lone Justice 2 '93
Street Fighter '94
Heat '95
Larry McMurtry's Streets of Laredo '95
The Killing Jar '96
Lone Justice 3: Showdown at Plum Creek '96
Deep Rising '98
Wind River '98
Mystery Men '99
Soundman '99
Skinwalker '02
SuperFire '02
Undisputed '02
Coyote Waits '03
A Thief of Time '04
Animal '05
Miracle at Sage Creek '05
The New World '05
Bury My Heart at Wounded Knee '07
Comanche Moon '08
El Camino '08
Older Than America '08
Three Priests '08
Avatar '09
Call of the Wild 3D '09
The Undying '09
A Million Ways to Die In the West '14
Planes: Fire & Rescue '14 (V)
The Condemned 2 '16

Michael Stuhlbarg (1968-)
The Hunley '99
Afterschool '08
A Serious Man '09
Hugo '11
Hitchcock '12
Lincoln '12
Men in Black 3 '12
Pawn Sacrifice '15
Arrival '16
Miss Sloane '16
Call Me by Your Name '17
The Shape of Water '17

Jerzy Stuhr (1947-)
Camera Buff '79
The Decalogue '88
Trois Couleurs: Blanc '94

Neil Stuke (1967-)
Twice upon a Yesterday '98
Robert Louis Stevenson's The Game of Death '99
Circus '00

Geoff Stults (1977-)
D.E.B.S. '04
Confessions of an American Bride '05
In the Mix '05
Wedding Crashers '05
The Express '08
I Hope They Serve Beer in Hell '09
She's Out of My League '10
Life Happens '11
A Bet's a Bet '14
Unforgettable '17

George Stults (1975-)
Night Skies '07
Hydra '09
American Bandits: Frank and Jesse James '10

Malcolm Stumpf
The Next Best Thing '00
Wild Tigers I Have Known '06

Wolfgang Stumpf (1909-83)
The Bridge '59
Signs of Life '68

Preston Sturges (1898-1959)
Star Spangled Rhythm '42
Paris Holiday '57

Shannon Sturges (1968-)
Tornado! '96
Convict 762 '98
Terror in the Mall '98
Silent Predators '99
The Perfect Wife '00
Cradle of Lies '06
The Wives He Forgot '06
A Christmas Proposal '08

Jim Sturgess (1978-)
Across the Universe '07
Fifty Dead Men Walking '08
The Other Boleyn Girl '08
21 '08
Crossing Over '09
Heartless '10
Legend of the Guardians: The Owls of Ga'Hoole '10 (V)
The Way Back '10
One Day '11
Cloud Atlas '12
The Best Offer '13
Stonehearst Asylum '13
Upside Down '13
Geostorm '17
London Fields '18

Gary Sturgis (1966-)
Daddy's Little Girls '07
Pride '07

Thomas Sturridge (1985-)
Gulliver's Travels '95
Being Julia '04
A Waste of Shame '05
Brothers of the Head '06
Murderous Intent '06

Pirate Radio '09
Waiting for Forever '11

Tom Sturridge (1985-)
On the Road '12
Effie Gray '15
Far from the Madding Crowd '15

Joris Stuyck (1952-)
We'll Meet Again '82
Sinatra '92

Trudie Styler (1954-)
Poldark 2 '75
Fair Game '89
Me Without You '01
Alpha Male '06
Living Proof '08

Harry Styles
One Direction: This Is Us '13
Dunkirk '17

Emma Suarez (1964-)
Against the Wind '90
Vacas '91
Tierra '95
Julieta '16

Jeremy Suarez (1990-)
Brother Bear '03 (V)
The Ladykillers '04
Brother Bear 2 '06 (V)
Adventures in Zambezia '12

Jose Suarez (1919-81)
Carthage in Flames '60
Texas, Adios '66

Tara Subkoff (1972-)
Freeway '95
All Over Me '96
As Good As It Gets '97
Black Circle Boys '97
The Last Days of Disco '98
American Pie '99
The Cell '00
Teenage Caveman '01
Undermind '03
Anchorman: The Legend of Ron Burgundy '04
The Notorious Bettie Page '06

Michel Subor (1935-)
Le Petit Soldat '60
Please Not Now! '61
Beau Travail '98
The Intruder '04
White Material '10

David Suchet (1946-)
Agatha Christie's Thirteen at Dinner '85
The Falcon and the Snowman '85
Iron Eagle '86
Cause Celebre '87
Harry and the Hendersons '87
A World Apart '88
To Kill a Priest '89
Deadly Voyage '96
Executive Decision '96
Moses '96
Sunday '96
A Perfect Murder '98
Solomon '98
RKO 281 '99
Wing Commander '99
Victoria & Albert '01
The Way We Live Now '02
The In-Laws '03
Live from Baghdad '03
Dracula '06
Flushed Away '06 (V)
Flood '07
The Bank Job '08
Appointment With Death '10
Going Postal '10
Murder on the Orient Express '10
Great Expectations '11
Hidden '11

Brooklyn Sudano (1981-)
Rain '06
5 Star Day '10

Kohl Sudduth (1974-)
Cora Unashamed '00
Jesse Stone: Stone Cold '05
Jesse Stone: Death in Paradise '06
Jesse Stone: Night Passage '06
Jesse Stone: Sea Change '07
Jesse Stone: Thin Ice '09
Jesse Stone: No Remorse '10
Jesse Stone: Innocents Lost '11
Jesse Stone: Benefit of the Doubt '12

Skipp (Robert L.) Sudduth (1956-)
Money Train '95
George Wallace '97
54 '98
Ronin '98
Flawless '99

Jason Sudeikis (1975-)
Meet Bill '07
Watching the Detectives '07
The Rocker '08
What Happens in Vegas '08
The Bounty Hunter '10
Going the Distance '10
A Good Old Fashioned Orgy '11
Hall Pass '11
Horrible Bosses '11
The Campaign '12
Epic '13 (V)
Movie 43 '13
We're the Millers '13
Horrible Bosses 2 '14
Sleeping with Other People '15
The Angry Birds Movie '16
The Book of Love '16
Masterminds '16
Race '16
Tumbledown '16
Colossal '17
Permission '18
The Angry Birds Movie 2 '19
Booksmart '19

Lam Suet (1954-)
The Mission '99
Breaking News '04
Kung Fu Hustle '04

Ichiro Sugai (1907-73)
Early Summer '51
Sansho the Bailiff '54

Shun Sugata (1955-)
Organ '96
Ichi the Killer '01
Pulse '01
Alive '02
The Last Samurai '03

Bunta Sugawara
Cops vs. Thugs '75
The Great Yokai War '05

Aya Sugimoto (1968-)
Flower & Snake '04
Flower & Snake 2 '05
Blood '09

Haruko Sugimura (1905-97)
No Regrets for Our Youth '46
Late Spring '49
Early Summer '51
Tokyo Story '53
Drifting Weeds '59

Barbara Sukowa (1950-)
Lola '81
The Sicilian '87
Zentropa '92
M. Butterfly '93
Johnny Mnemonic '95
Office Killer '97
Lost Souls '98
The Cradle Will Rock '99
The Third Miracle '99
Urbania '00
Thirteen Conversations About One Thing '01
Vision '09
Hannah Arendt '12

Jessica Sula (1994-)
Split '16
The Lovers '17

Ania Suli
Fun '94
Stuart Bliss '98

Ali Suliman (1977-)
Paradise Now '05
The Kingdom '07
Lemon Tree '08
The Attack '13

Gregg Sulkin
White Frog '12
Don't Hang Up '17

Margaret Sullavan (1911-60)
The Good Fairy '35
The Moon's Our Home '36
Next Time We Love '36
The Shining Hour '38
Shopworn Angel '38
Three Comrades '38
The Mortal Storm '40
The Shop Around the Corner '40
Back Street '41
So Ends Our Night '41
Cry Havoc '43
No Sad Songs For Me '50

Barry Sullivan (1912-94)
The Woman of the Town '44
Getting Gertie's Garter '45
Suspense '46
Framed '47
The Gangster '47
Smart Woman '48
Any Number Can Play '49
Bad Men of Tombstone '49
A Life of Her Own '50
Nancy Goes to Rio '50
The Outriders '50
Tension '50
Cause for Alarm '51
Mr. Imperium '51
Payment on Demand '51
Three Guys Named Mike '51
The Bad and the Beautiful '52
Skirts Ahoy! '52
Jeopardy '53
Loophole '54
The Miami Story '54
Queen Bee '55
Strategic Air Command '55
Julie '56
Texas Lady '56
Forty Guns '57
Another Time, Another Place '58
The Purple Gang '59
Light in the Piazza '61
My Blood Runs Cold '65
Planet of the Vampires '65
An American Dream '66
Buckskin '68
Shark! '68
Night Gallery '69
Tell Them Willie Boy Is Here '69
Yuma '70
Kung Fu '72
Earthquake '74
Hurricane '74
The Human Factor '75
Take a Hard Ride '75
Oh, God! '77
The Bastard '78

Billy L. Sullivan (1980-)
Little Big League '94
The Big Green '95

Brad Sullivan (1931-2008)
Slap Shot '77
Cold River '81
Funny Farm '88
Guilty by Suspicion '91
The Prince of Tides '91
True Colors '91
Sister Act 2: Back in the Habit '93
Bushwhacked '95
The Jerky Boys '95

Camille Sullivan (1975-)
Cries in the Dark '06
Normal '07
Sea Beast '08
Ice Twisters '09
Goblin '10
The Traveler '10
The Marine 3: Homefront '11
Ice Soldiers '13

Charlotte Sullivan (1983-)
The House Next Door '06
Population 436 '06
Defendor '09
Citizen Gangster '11
The Kennedys '11

David Sullivan
Primer '04
Karma Police '08

Don Sullivan (1938-)
Teenage Zombies '58
The Giant Gila Monster '59
The Rebel Set '59

Elliott Sullivan (1907-74)
Action in the North Atlantic '43
Vampyres '74

Erik Per Sullivan (1991-)
Armageddon '98
The Cider House Rules '99
Joe Dirt '01
Wendigo '01
Unfaithful '02
Finding Nemo '03 (V)
Christmas With the Kranks '04

Francis L. Sullivan (1903-56)
Great Expectations '34
Power '34
The Mystery of Edwin Drood '35
Non-Stop New York '37
The Secret Four '39
21 Days '40
The Lady From Lisbon '42
Caesar and Cleopatra '46
Great Expectations '46
Oliver Twist '48
Christopher Columbus '49
Night and the City '50
My Favorite Spy '51
Behave Yourself! '52
The Prodigal '55

Jean Sullivan (1923-2003)
Uncertain Glory '44
Squirm '76

Jenny Sullivan (1947-)
The Other '72
Katherine '75

Larry Sullivan (1970-)
The Trip '02
Pretty Ugly People '08
Aftermath '17

Nicole Sullivan (1970-)
Bar Hopping '00
The Third Wheel '02
Guess Who '05
The Ant Bully '06 (V)
Meet the Robinsons '07 (V)
Black Dynamite '09
Let It Shine '12

Paul Sullivan
Shoot the Living, Pray for the Dead '70
I'll Believe You '07

Ruth Sullivan
Beyond the Dunwich Horror '08
Nun of That '09

Sean Gregory Sullivan
Howling 6: The Freaks '90
RFK '02

Susan Sullivan (1942-)
Midway '76
The Incredible Hulk '77
The Dark Ride '78
Cave-In! '79
Marriage Is Alive and Well '80
The Ordeal of Dr. Mudd '80
My Best Friend's Wedding '97
Two Came Back '97

Tim Sullivan
2001 Maniacs '05
2001 Maniacs: Field of Screams '10

Tomas D. Sullivan
Cocaine Cowboys '79
Intermission '03

Cree Summer (1969-)
The Rugrats Movie '98 (V)
Atlantis: The Lost Empire '01 (V)
Rugrats Go Wild! '03 (V)
Clifford's Really Big Movie '04 (V)

Eleanor Summerfield (1921-2001)
Black Glove '54
Blackout '54

Slim Summerville (1892-1946)
The Texas Streak '26
The Beloved Rogue '27
All Quiet on the Western Front '30
The Farmer Takes a Wife '35
Life Begins at Forty '35
Captain January '36
White Fang '36
Love Is News '37
Kentucky Moonshine '38
Rebecca of Sunnybrook Farm '38
Jesse James '39
Gold Rush Maisie '40
Tobacco Road '41
Western Union '41
I'm from Arkansas '44

Ashleigh Sumner
And Then Came Lola '09
I Want to Get Married '11

Bart Sumner (1964-)
Video Violence '87
Video Violence Part 2. . . The Exploitation! '87

Mickey Sumner (1984-)
Girl Most Likely '12
CBGB '13
Frances Ha '13
The Mend '15

Peter Sumner (1942-)
Ned Kelly '70
The Chant of Jimmie Blacksmith '78

Donald (Don) Sumpter (1943-)
Rosencrantz & Guildenstern Are Dead '90
The Blackheath Poisonings '92
The Buddha of Suburbia '92
Enigma '01
K-19: The Widowmaker '02
The Constant Gardener '05
Eastern Promises '07
Into the Storm '09
The Girl With the Dragon Tattoo '11

Jeremy Sumpter (1989-)
Frailty '02
Local Boys '02
Peter Pan '03
Cyber Seduction: His Secret Life '05
The Sasquatch Gang '06
Calvin Marshall '09
Death and Cremation '10
You're So Cupid '10
Excision '12
Into the Storm '14
The Squeeze '15
Billionaire Ransom '16

Tika Sumpter (1980-)
Stomp the Yard 2: Homecoming '10
Sparkle '12
Tyler Perry's A Madea Christmas '13
My Man Is a Loser '14
Ride Along '14
Ride Along 2 '16
Southside with You '16
Nobody's Fool '18
Sonic the Hedgehog '20

Betty Sun (1982-)
Jet Li's Fearless '06
Iron Road '08

Chien Sun (1955-)
Five Deadly Venoms '78
Heaven & Hell '78
Sword Masters: Two Champions of Shaolin '80
House of Traps '81

Honglei Sun (1970-)
The Road Home '01
Zhou Yu's Train '02
Blood Brothers '07
Mongol '07
Seven Swords '07
A Woman, a Gun and a Noodle Shop '10
Drug War '13

Li Sun
The Lost Bladesman '16
Shadow '18

Hideo Sunazuka
Godzilla vs. the Sea Monster '66
Blind Woman's Curse '70

Clinton Sundberg (1906-87)
Undercurrent '46
Undercover Maisie '47
In the Good Old Summertime '49
Annie Get Your Gun '50
Father Is a Bachelor '50
Two Weeks with Love '50
As Young As You Feel '51
The Belle of New York '52
The Thief and the Cobbler '96 (V)

Par Sundberg (1957-)
Pippi Goes on Board '69
Pippi Longstocking '69
Pippi in the South Seas '70
Pippi on the Run '70

Bjorn Sundquist (1948-)
Shipwrecked '90
The Last Lieutenant '94
Zero Degrees Kelvin '95
The Other Side of Sunday '96
Dead Snow '09

Gerry Sundquist (1955-93)
Alexandria. . . Why? '78
Great Expectations '81
Don't Open Till Christmas '84

Daniel Sunjata (1971-)
Anne Rice's The Feast of All Saints '01
Brother to Brother '04
The Devil Wears Prada '06
The Bronx Is Burning '07
Ghosts of Girlfriends Past '09
Patricia Cornwell's At Risk '10
Patricia Cornwell's The Front '10
Weakness '10
The Dark Knight Rises '12
Gone '12
One for the Money '12
Generation Um... '13

Ethan Suplee (1976-)
Mallrats '95
Chasing Amy '97
American History X '98
Desert Blue '98
Remember the Titans '00
Road Trip '00
Blow '01
Evolution '01
The First $20 Million is Always the Hardest '02
John Q '02
Cold Mountain '03
The Butterfly Effect '04
Without a Paddle '04
Art School Confidential '06
Clerks 2 '06
Unstoppable '10
Rise of the Zombies '12
The Wolf of Wall Street '13
Walk of Shame '14
True Story '15
The Trust '16
The Hunt '20

Helene Surgere (1928-)
My Life on Ice *'02*
Intimate Strangers *'04*

Nicolas Surovy (1944-)
Anastasia: The Mystery of Anna *'86*
Forever Young *'92*
12:01 *'93*
The Man Who Captured Eichmann *'96*
All Over the Guy *'01*

Tammin Sursok (1983-)
Aquamarine *'06*
Albino Farm *'09*
Spectacular *'09*
10 Rules for Sleeping Around *'13*

Todd Susman (1947-)
Star Spangled Girl *'71*
Portrait of an Escort *'80*
Beverly Hills Cop 2 *'87*
Only the Strong *'93*

Kevin Sussman (1970-)
Wet Hot American Summer *'01*
Little Black Book *'04*
Heavy Petting *'07*
Insanitarium *'08*
Made of Honor *'08*
Killers *'10*

Matthew Sussman
Illuminata *'98*
13 Moons *'02*

David Sutcliffe (1969-)
Testosterone *'03*
Under the Tuscan Sun *'03*
Cake *'05*
Happy Endings *'05*
His and Her Christmas *'05*
Murder in the Hamptons *'05*
Towards Darkness *'07*
Misconceptions *'08*
Sticks and Stones *'08*
Before You Say 'I Do' *'09*
On Strike for Christmas *'10*
Super Storm *'12*

Paul Sutera (1979-)
Problem Child 2 *'91*
The Brady Bunch Movie *'95*
A Very Brady Sequel *'96*

Catherine Sutherland (1974-)
Turbo: A Power Rangers Movie *'96*
The Cell *'00*

Donald Sutherland (1935-)
Castle of the Living Dead *'64*
Bedford Incident *'65*
Die! Die! My Darling! *'65*
The Dirty Dozen *'67*
Interlude *'68*
The Split *'68*
Alex in Wonderland *'70*
Kelly's Heroes *'70*
M*A*S*H *'70*
Start the Revolution without Me *'70*
Johnny Got His Gun *'71*
Klute *'71*
Little Murders *'71*
Dan Candy's Law *'73*
Don't Look Now *'73*
Lady Ice *'73*
Steelyard Blues *'73*
S*P*Y*S *'74*
The Day of the Locust *'75*
1900 *'76*
The Eagle Has Landed *'77*
Kentucky Fried Movie *'77*
Invasion of the Body Snatchers *'78*
National Lampoon's Animal House *'78*
The Great Train Robbery *'79*
A Man, a Woman, and a Bank *'79*
Murder by Decree *'79*
Ordinary People *'80*
Eye of the Needle *'81*
Max Dugan Returns *'83*
Crackers *'84*
Heaven Help Us *'85*
Revolution *'85*
A Dry White Season *'89*
Lock Up *'89*
Lost Angels *'89*
Backdraft *'91*
JFK *'91*
Quicksand: No Escape *'91*
Buffy the Vampire Slayer *'92*
Benefit of the Doubt *'93*
Six Degrees of Separation *'93*
Disclosure *'94*
Outbreak *'94*
The Puppet Masters *'94*
Citizen X *'95*
Hollow Point *'95*
Oldest Confederate Widow Tells All *'95*
Natural Enemy *'96*
The Shadow Conspiracy *'96*
A Time to Kill *'96*
The Assignment *'97*
Fallen *'97*
Without Limits *'97*
Virus *'98*
Behind the Mask *'99*
Free Money *'99*
The Hunley *'99*
Instinct *'99*
The Art of War *'00*
Panic *'00*
Space Cowboys *'00*
Big Shot's Funeral *'01*
Final Fantasy: The Spirits Within *'01 (V)*
Uprising *'01*
Path to War *'02*
Cold Mountain *'03*
Fellini: I'm a Born Liar *'03*
The Italian Job *'03*
Salem's Lot *'04*
American Gun *'05*
An American Haunting *'05*
Fierce People *'05*
Human Trafficking *'05*
Pride and Prejudice *'05*
Ask the Dust *'06*
Aurora Borealis *'06*
Beerfest *'06*
Land of the Blind *'06*
Reign Over Me *'07*
Fool's Gold *'08*
Astro Boy *'09 (V)*
The Con Artist *'10*
Pillars of the Earth *'10*
The Eagle *'11*
Horrible Bosses *'11*
The Man on the Train *'11*
The Mechanic *'11*
Assassin's Bullet *'12*
Dawn Rider *'12*
The Hunger Games *'12*
Treasure Island *'12*
The Best Offer *'13*
The Hunger Games: Catching Fire *'13*
The Calling *'14*
The Hunger Games: Mockingjay--Part 1 *'14*
Forsaken *'15*
The Hunger Games: Mockingjay-Part 2 *'15*
Foresaken *'16*
Milton's Secret *'16*
The Leisure Seeker *'17*
Ad Astra *'19*
The Burnt Orange Heresy *'20*

Kiefer Sutherland (1966-)
Max Dugan Returns *'83*
At Close Range *'86*
Brotherhood of Justice *'86*
Stand by Me *'86*
Trapped in Silence *'86*
The Killing Time *'87*
The Lost Boys *'87*
Bright Lights, Big City *'88*
Promised Land *'88*
Young Guns *'88*
Flashback *'89*
1969 *'89*
Renegades *'89*
Chicago Joe & the Showgirl *'90*
Flatliners *'90*
Young Guns 2 *'90*
The Nutcracker Prince *'91 (V)*
Article 99 *'92*
A Few Good Men *'92*
Twin Peaks: Fire Walk with Me *'92*
Last Light *'93*
The Three Musketeers *'93*
The Vanishing *'93*
The Cowboy Way *'94*
An Eye for an Eye *'95*
Freeway *'95*
The Last Days of Frankie the Fly *'96*
A Time to Kill *'96*
Dark City *'97*
Truth or Consequences, N.M. *'97*
The Break Up *'98*
Ground Control *'98*
Woman Wanted *'98*
Eye of the Killer *'99*
Picking Up the Pieces *'99*
Beat *'00*
Cowboy Up *'00*
The Right Temptation *'00*
Dead Heat *'01*
Desert Saints *'01*
To End All Wars *'01*
Behind the Red Door *'02*
Phone Booth *'02*
Taking Lives *'04*
Jiminy Glick in LaLa Wood *'05 (C)*
River Queen *'05*
The Sentinel *'06*
The Wild *'06 (V)*
Mirrors *'08*
24: Redemption *'08*
Monsters *vs.* Aliens *'09 (V)*
Twelve *'10 (N)*
Melancholia *'11*
Pompeii *'14*
Forsaken *'15*
Foresaken *'16*
Where Is Kyra? *'17*

Kristine Sutherland
Honey, I Shrunk the Kids *'89*
The Perfect Wedding *'12*

Rossif Sutherland (1978-)
Red Doors *'05*
Poor Man's Game *'06*
High Life *'09*
The Con Artist *'10*
Hellions *'15*
Hyena Road *'16*
Backstabbing for Beginners *'18*

Sarah Sutherland (1988-)
Beneath the Harvest Sky *'14*
Chronic *'16*

Dolores Sutton (1927-2009)
The Mugger *'58*
Where Angels Go, Trouble Follows *'68*

Dudley Sutton (1933-)
The Leather Boys *'63*
Cry of the Penguins *'71*
The Devils *'71*
Edward II *'92*
Orlando *'92*

Frank Sutton (1923-74)
Marty *'55*
Four Boys and a Gun *'57*
Town without Pity *'61*
Hurricane *'74*

Grady Sutton (1908-95)
Alice Adams *'35*
The Man On the Flying Trapeze *'35*
Two Minutes to Play *'37*
Waikiki Wedding *'37*
Three Loves Has Nancy *'38*
The Bank Dick *'40*
Flying Blind *'41*
The Bashful Bachelor *'42*
The More the Merrier *'43*
My Dog Shep *'46*
Paradise, Hawaiian Style *'66*

John Sutton (1908-63)
Bulldog Drummond's Bride *'39*
The Tower of London *'39*
Hudson's Bay *'40*
The Invisible Man Returns *'40*
A Yank in the R.A.F. *'41*
My Gal Sal *'42*
Thunder Birds *'42*
Tonight We Raid Calais *'43*
Jane Eyre *'44*
Claudia and David *'46*
Captain from Castile *'47*
Mickey *'48*
David and Bathsheba *'51*
Payment on Demand *'51*
The Second Woman *'51*
Five Fingers *'52 (N)*
The Golden Hawk *'52*
My Cousin Rachel *'52*
The Bat *'59*
Beloved Infidel *'59*
Return of the Fly *'59*

Michael Sutton (1971-)
Wanted *'98*
Dracula: The Dark Prince *'01*
Hypersonic *'02*

Mena Suvari (1979-)
American Virgin *'98*
American Beauty *'99*
American Pie *'99*
Atomic Train *'99*
The Rage: Carrie 2 *'99*
Loser *'00*
American Pie 2 *'01*
The Musketeer *'01*
Sugar & Spice *'01*
Sonny *'02*
Spun *'02*
Trauma *'04*
Beauty Shop *'05*
Domino *'05*
Edmond *'05*
Rumor Has It. . . *'05*
Standing Still *'05*
Caffeine *'06*
The Dog Problem *'06*
Factory Girl *'06*
Brooklyn Rules *'07*
Stuck *'07*
Hemingway's Garden of Eden *'08*
The Mysteries of Pittsburgh *'08*
Sex & Lies in Sin City: The Ted Binion Scandal *'08*
American Reunion *'12*
You May Not Kiss the Bride *'12*
A Bet's a Bet *'14*

Taro Suwa (1954-)
Ju-On 2 *'00*
Uzumaki *'00*
The Machine Girl *'07*

Janet Suzman (1939-)
Macbeth *'70*
A Day in the Death of Joe Egg *'71*
Nicholas and Alexandra *'71*
Voyage of the Damned *'76*
The House on Garibaldi Street *'79*
Nijinsky *'80*
Priest of Love *'81*
The Draughtsman's Contract *'82*
And the Ship Sails On *'83*
Mountbatten: The Last Viceroy *'86*
The Singing Detective *'86*
A Dry White Season *'89*
Nuns on the Run *'90*
Leon the Pig Farmer *'93*
Max *'02*
The Color of Magic *'08*

Anne Suzuki (1987-)
Hana & Alice *'04*
Steamboy *'05 (V)*

Kyoka Suzuki
Blood and Bones *'04*
Zebraman *'04*

Semyon Svashenko (1904-69)
Zvenigora *'28*
Arsenal *'29*
Earth *'30*

Tore Svennberg (1858-1941)
The Phantom Chariot *'20*
The Phantom Carriage *'21*
A Woman's Face *'38*

Bo Svenson (1941-)
The Bravos *'72*
Frankenstein *'73*
The Great Waldo Pepper *'75*
Walking Tall: Part 2 *'75*
Portrait of a Hitman *'77*
Snowbeast *'77*
Walking Tall: The Final Chapter *'77*
Deadly Mission *'78*
The Inglorious Bastards *'78*
Gold of the Amazon Women *'79*
North Dallas Forty *'79*
Virus *'82*
Deadly Impact *'84*
Delta Force *'86*
Heartbreak Ridge *'86*
The Manhunt *'86*
Delta Force Commando *'87*
The Dirty Dozen: The Deadly Mission *'87*
Curse 2: The Bite *'88*
Andy and the Airwave Rangers *'89*
Beyond the Door 3 *'91*
Steele's Law *'91*
Private Obsession *'94*
Savage Land *'94*
Steel Frontier *'94*
Speed 2: Cruise Control *'97*
Crackerjack 3 *'00*
Kill Bill Vol. 2 *'04*
Inglourious Basterds *'09*
The Killing Machine *'09*
The 7 Adventures of Sinbad *'10*

Bob Swaim (1943-)
La Balance *'82*
Spies Like Us *'85*

Dominique Swain (1980-)
Face/Off *'97*
Lolita *'97*
Girl *'98*
Intern *'00*
The Smokers *'00*
Dead in the Water *'01*
Happy Campers *'01*
Tart *'01*
New Best Friend *'02*
Pumpkin *'02*
The Job *'03*
Plain Dirty *'04*
Devour *'05*
All In *'06*
Alpha Dog *'06*
Fall Down Dead *'07*
The Pacific and Eddy *'07*
The Brooklyn Heist *'08*
Noble Things *'08*
Prairie Fever *'08*
Stiletto *'08*
Stuntmen *'09*
A Horse Tale *'15*

Mack Swain (1876-1935)
Tillie's Punctured Romance *'14*
The Gold Rush *'25*
Torrent *'26*
The Beloved Rogue *'27*
The Chaplin Revue *'58*

Tim Swain
Between Something & Nothing *'08*
The Boy With the Sun in His Eyes *'09*

Serinda Swan (1984-)
Hostile Makeover *'09*
Creature *'11*
Recoil *'11*
Jinn *'14*

Joe Swanberg (1981-)
Nights and Weekends *'08*
A Horrible Way to Die *'10*
V/H/S *'12*
Proxy *'13*
The Sacrament *'13*
White Reindeer *'13*
You're Next *'13*
Happy Christmas *'14*

Hilary Swank (1974-)
Buffy the Vampire Slayer *'92*
The Next Karate Kid *'94*
Kounterfeit *'96*
Sometimes They Come Back. . . Again *'96*
Quiet Days in Hollywood *'97*
Heartwood *'98*
Boys Don't Cry *'99*
The Gift *'00*
The Affair of the Necklace *'01*
Insomnia *'02*
The Core *'03*
11:14 *'03*
Million Dollar Baby *'04*
The Black Dahlia *'06*
Freedom Writers *'07*
P.S. I Love You *'07*
The Reaping *'07*
Birds of America *'08*
Amelia *'09*
Conviction *'10*
The Resident *'10*
New Year's Eve *'11*
Mary and Martha *'13*
The Homesman *'14*
Spark: A Space Tail *'17 (V)*
What They Had *'18*
The Hunt *'20*

Brenda Swanson
Scanners: The Showdown *'94*
Secret Games 3 *'94*

Gary Swanson (1946-)
Vice Squad *'82*
Coldfire *'90*
The Guardian *'90*

Gloria Swanson (1897-1983)
Male and Female *'19*
Why Change Your Wife? *'20*
Affairs of Anatol *'21*
Beyond the Rocks *'22*
Fine Manners *'26*
Sadie Thompson *'28*
Queen Kelly *'29*
Indiscreet *'31*
Tonight or Never *'31*
Perfect Understanding *'33*
Sunset Boulevard *'50*
The Love Goddesses *'65*
Airport '75 *'75*

Jackie Swanson (1963-)
Lethal Weapon *'87*
Oblivion *'94*

Kristy Swanson (1969-)
Deadly Friend *'86*
Ferris Bueller's Day Off *'86*
Pretty in Pink *'86*
Flowers in the Attic *'87*
Hot Shots! *'91*
Mannequin 2: On the Move *'91*
Buffy the Vampire Slayer *'92*
The Chase *'93*
The Program *'93*
Higher Learning *'94*
8 Heads in a Duffel Bag *'96*
The Phantom *'96*
Ground Control *'98*
Meeting Daddy *'98*
Big Daddy *'99*
Supreme Sanction *'99*
Dude, Where's My Car? *'00*
Red Water *'01*
Soul Assassin *'01*
Zebra Lounge *'01*
Bound by Lies *'05*
A Christmas Wish *'11*
Swamp Shark *'11*
The Bouquet *'13*
Storm Rider *'13*
A Belle for Christmas *'14*

Maureen Swanson (1932-2011)
Moulin Rouge *'52*
A Town Like Alice *'56*
Robbery under Arms *'57*
The Spanish Gardener *'57*

Rochelle Swanson (1963-)
Hard Bounty *'94*
Indecent Behavior 2 *'94*
Night Fire *'94*

Secret Games 3 *'94*
On the Border *'98*

Nick Swardson (1976-)
Art School Confidential *'06*
The Benchwarmers *'06*
Click *'06*
Grandma's Boy *'06*
Blades of Glory *'07*
I Now Pronounce You Chuck and Larry *'07*
Reno 911! Miami *'07*
You Don't Mess with the Zohan *'08*
Bucky Larson: Born to Be a Star *'11*
Jack and Jill *'11*
Just Go With It *'11*
30 Minutes or Less *'11*
Grown Ups 2 *'13*
A Haunted House *'13*
Back in the Day *'14*

Don Swayze (1958-)
Death Blow *'87*
Lethal Victims *'87*
The Tracker *'88*
Trapper County War *'89*
Edge of Honor *'91*
Body of Influence *'93*
Death Ring *'93*
Eye of the Stranger *'93*
Forced to Kill *'93*
Sexual Malice *'93*
The Prophet's Game *'99*
Lady Jayne Killer *'03*
Prairie Fever *'08*

Patrick Swayze (1952-2009)
Return of the Rebels *'81*
The Outsiders *'83*
Uncommon Valor *'83*
Grandview U.S.A. *'84*
Red Dawn *'84*
North and South Book 1 *'85*
North and South Book 2 *'86*
Youngblood *'86*
Dirty Dancing *'87*
Steel Dawn *'87*
Tiger Warsaw *'87*
Next of Kin *'89*
Road House *'89*
Ghost *'90*
Point Break *'91*
City of Joy *'92*
Father Hood *'93*
Tall Tale: The Unbelievable Adventures of Pecos Bill *'95*
Three Wishes *'95*
To Wong Foo, Thanks for Everything, Julie Newmar *'95*
Black Dog *'98*
Letters from a Killer *'98*
Along for the Ride *'00*
Donnie Darko *'01*
Green Dragon *'01*
Waking Up in Reno *'02*
11:14 *'03*
Dirty Dancing: Havana Nights *'04*
George and the Dragon *'04*
Frederick Forsyth's Icon *'05*
Keeping Mum *'05*
The Fox and the Hound 2 *'06 (V)*
Christmas in Wonderland *'07*
Powder Blue *'09*

Heidi Swedberg (1966-)
Hot Shots! *'91*
Father and Scout *'94*
75 Degrees *'00*

Bob Sweeney (1918-92)
South Sea Woman *'53*
Toby Tyler *'59*

Conor Sweeney
Manborg *'11*
Father's Day *'12*

D.B. Sweeney (1961-)
Fire with Fire *'86*
Gardens of Stone *'87*
No Man's Land *'87*
Eight Men Out *'88*
Lonesome Dove *'89*
Leather Jackets *'90*
Memphis Belle *'90*
Blue Desert *'91*
Heaven Is a Playground *'91*
The Cutting Edge *'92*
A Day in October *'92*
Fire in the Sky *'93*
Hear No Evil *'93*
Roommates *'95*
Spawn *'97*
The Book of Stars *'99*
Introducing Dorothy Dandridge *'99*
Dinosaur *'00 (V)*
The Weekend *'00*
Greenmail *'01*
Hardball *'01*
SuperFire *'02*
Brother Bear *'03 (V)*
Speak *'04*
Two Tickets to Paradise *'06*
Yellow *'06*
Entry Level *'07*
Miracle at St. Anna *'08*
Stiletto *'08*
K-11 *'11*
Swamp Shark *'11*
Atlas Shrugged 2: The Strike *'12*
Taken 2 *'12*
12 Dogs of Christmas: Great Puppy Rescue *'12*
Free Fall *'14*
Extraction *'15*
The Resurrection of Gavin Stone *'17*

Garry Sweeney
The Acid House *'98*
A Lonely Place to Die *'11*

Joseph Sweeney (1884-1963)
The Man in the Gray Flannel Suit *'56*
Twelve Angry Men *'57*

Julia Sweeney (1959-)
Honey, I Blew Up the Kid *'92*
Coneheads *'93*
It's Pat: The Movie *'94*
Pulp Fiction *'94*
Stuart Saves His Family *'94*
Vegas Vacation *'96 (C)*
God Said 'Ha!' *'99*
Stuart Little *'99*
Thick as Thieves *'99*
Beethoven's 3rd *'00*
Whatever It Takes *'00*
Beethoven's 4th *'01*
Clockstoppers *'02*
Don't Come Knocking *'05*

Steve Sweeney (1949-)
Nil by Mouth *'96*
Lock, Stock and 2 Smoking Barrels *'98*
Beautiful People *'99*

Sydney Sweeney (1997-)
Spiders *'13*
Angels in Stardust *'14*
Along Came the Devil *'18*
Under the Silver Lake *'18*

Blanche Sweet (1895-1986)
Avenging Conscience *'14*
Judith of Bethulia *'14*
Anna Christie *'23*
Show Girl in Hollywood *'30*
The Silver Horde *'30*
The Woman Racket *'30*

Dolph Sweet (1920-85)
Finian's Rainbow *'68*
Cops and Robbers *'73*
Sisters *'73*
Amazing Grace *'74*
The Bad News Bears in Breaking Training *'77*
Go Tell the Spartans *'78*
Wanderers *'79*
Reds *'81*

Gary Sweet (1957-)
The Dreaming *'88*
Macbeth *'06*
The Chronicles of Narnia: The Voyage of the Dawn Treader *'10*
Fatal Honeymoon *'12*
Adore *'13*

Vonte Sweet (1971-)
Menace II Society *'93*
American Strays *'96*
Restaurant *'98*

Yousef (Joe) Sweid
The Bubble *'06*
Inch'Allah *'12*

Eliza Swenson (1982-)
King of the Lost World *'06*
Transmorphers *'07*
The Witches of Oz *'11*

Inga Swenson (1932-)
The Miracle Worker *'62*
Earth II *'71*
North and South Book 1 *'85*
Nutcracker: Money, Madness & Murder *'87*

Jeep Swenson (1957-97)
Bulletproof *'96*
Batman and Robin *'97*

Karl Swenson (1908-78)
The Hanging Tree *'59*
No Name on the Bullet *'59*
Flaming Star *'60*
The Gallant Hours *'60*
Judgment at Nuremberg *'61*
Lonely Are the Brave *'62*
The Sword in the Stone *'63 (V)*
Seconds *'66*
Brighty of the Grand Canyon *'67*

Tommy Swerdlow (1962-)
Real Genius *'85*
Howard the Duck *'86*
Hamburger Hill *'87*
Child's Play *'88*

Josef Swickard (1866-1940)
The Four Horsemen of the Apocalypse *'21*
The Wizard of Oz *'25*
Old San Francisco *'27*
The Lone Defender *'32*
Caryl of the Mountains *'36*
Custer's Last Stand *'36*

Clive Swift (1936-)
Frenzy *'72*
Raw Meat *'72*
Pack of Lies *'87*
The Aristocrats *'99*

David Swift (1919-2001)
Good Neighbor Sam *'64*
No Sex Please-We're British *'73*

Francie Swift (1969-)
Last Breath *'96*
Fall *'97*
The Great Gatsby *'01*

Jeremy Swift (1960-)
Vanity Fair *'99*
Gosford Park *'01*
Oliver Twist *'05*
Fred Claus *'07*
Anton Chekhov's The Duel *'09*

Paul Swift (1934-94)
Pink Flamingos *'72*
Female Trouble *'74*

Taylor Swift (1989-)
Valentine's Day *'10*
Dr. Seuss' The Lorax *'12 (V)*
The Giver *'14*
Cats *'19*

Nora Swinburne (1902-2000)
Perfect Understanding *'33*
Man of Evil *'48*
Quo Vadis *'51*
The River *'51*
Betrayed *'54*
Helen of Troy *'56*
Strange Awakening *'58*

Tilda Swinton (1960-)
Caravaggio *'86*
The Last of England *'87*
Edward II *'92*
Orlando *'92*
Blue *'93 (N)*
Wittgenstein *'93*
Female Perversions *'96*
Conceiving Ada *'97*
Love Is the Devil *'98*
The War Zone *'98*
The Beach *'00*
The Deep End *'01*
Vanilla Sky *'01*
Adaptation *'02*
The Statement *'03*
Young Adam *'03*
Broken Flowers *'05*
The Chronicles of Narnia: The Lion, the Witch and the Wardrobe *'05*
Constantine *'05*
Thumbsucker *'05*
Deep Water *'06 (V)*
Stephanie Daley *'06*
Michael Clayton *'07*
Burn After Reading *'08*
The Chronicles of Narnia: Prince Caspian *'08*
The Curious Case of Benjamin Button *'08*
Julia *'08*
I Am Love *'09*
The Limits of Control *'09*
We Need to Talk About Kevin *'11*
Moonrise Kingdom *'12*
Only Lovers Left Alive *'13*
The Grand Budapest Hotel *'14*
Snowpiercer *'14*
A Bigger Splash *'15*
Doctor Strange *'16*
Okja *'17*
Suspiria *'18*
The Souvenir *'19*

Amanda Swisten (1978-)
American Wedding *'03*
The Girl Next Door *'04*

Loretta Swit (1937-)
Freebie & the Bean *'74*
Race with the Devil *'75*
Friendship, Secrets and Lies *'79*
S.O.B. *'81*
M*A*S*H: Goodbye, Farewell & Amen *'83*
Beer *'85*
The Execution *'85*
A Killer Among Friends *'92*

Bill Switzer
Mail to the Chief *'00*
Mr. Rice's Secret *'00*

Carl 'Alfalfa' Switzer (1926-59)
The Great Mike *'44*
Gas House Kids *'46*
It's a Wonderful Life *'46*
Cause for Alarm *'51*
Pat and Mike *'52*
Island in the Sky *'53*
The High and the Mighty *'54*
Track of the Cat *'54*
Between Heaven and Hell *'56*

Ken Swofford (1933-)
Bless the Beasts and Children *'71*
Skyjacked *'72*
Black Roses *'88*
Disney's Teacher's Pet *'04 (V)*

Tracy Brooks Swope (1953-)
The Big Picture *'89*
The Power of One *'92*
White Wolves 3: Cry of the White Wolf *'98*
Counter Measures *'99*

Omar Sy (1978-)
The Intouchables *'12*
Mood Indigo *'13*
Good People *'14*
Samba *'14*
Inferno *'16*
Arctic Dogs *'19 (V)*
The Call of the Wild *'20*

Meera Syal (1961-)
Forgive and Forget *'99*
Jekyll *'07*
Yesterday *'19*

Sabrina Syan (1963-)
See Sabrina Siani

Basil Sydney (1894-1968)
The Third Clue *'34*
Accused *'36*
Hamlet *'48*
Angel with the Trumpet *'50*
Treasure Island *'50*
Salome *'53*
Dam Busters *'55*
Sea Wife *'57*
The Three Worlds of Gulliver *'59*
The Hands of Orlac *'60*

Brenda Sykes (1949-)
Black Gunn *'72*
Cleopatra Jones *'73*
Mandingo *'75*

Eric Sykes (1923-2012)
Very Important Person *'61*
Kill or Cure *'62*
Heavens Above *'63*
The Liquidator *'65*
Those Daring Young Men in Their Jaunty Jalopies *'69*
The Others *'01*

Wanda Sykes (1964-)
Pootie Tang *'01*
Monster-in-Law *'05*
Barnyard *'06 (V)*
Brother Bear 2 *'06 (V)*
Clerks 2 *'06*
My Super Ex-Girlfriend *'06*
Over the Hedge *'06 (V)*
Evan Almighty *'07*
Ice Age: Continental Drift *'12 (V)*
The Hot Flashes *'13*
Snatched *'17*

Harold Sylvester (1949-)
Fast Break *'79*
Uncommon Valor *'83*
Vision Quest *'85*
Innerspace *'87*
The Reluctant Agent *'89*
In the Deep Woods *'91*
The Sixth Man *'97*
Trippin' *'99*
Missing Brendan *'03*
For One Night *'06*

William Sylvester (1923-95)
Appointment in London *'53*
Unholy Four *'54*
Postmark for Danger *'56*
Gorgo *'61*
Blind Corner *'63*
Devil Doll *'64*
Beast of Morocco *'66*
2001: A Space Odyssey *'68*

Kari Sylway (1940-)
Cries and Whispers *'72*
Face to Face *'76*

Peter Symonds
Lawless Heart *'01*
Sharpe's Challenge *'06*

Robert Symonds (1926-2007)
Ice Pirates *'84*
Rumpelstiltskin *'86*
Mandroid *'93*

Sylvia Syms (1934-)
Expresso Bongo *'59*
Ferry to Hong Kong *'59*
Teenage Bad Girl *'59*
Conspiracy of Hearts *'60*
The World of Suzie Wong *'60*
Flame in the Streets *'61*
Victim *'61*
The Quare Fellow *'62*
East of Sudan *'64*
Asylum *'72*
The Tamarind Seed *'74*
A Chorus of Disapproval *'89*
Shirley Valentine *'89*
Shining Through *'92*
Catherine Cookson's The Glass Virgin *'95*
I'll Sleep When I'm Dead *'03*
What a Girl Wants *'03*
Collision *'09*

Del Synnott
Othello *'01*
Princess of Thieves *'01*

Laszlo Szabo (1936-)
Le Petit Soldat *'60*
Alphaville *'65*
Adoption *'75*
The Last Metro *'80*
Passion *'82*
The Unbearable Lightness of Being *'88*
Esther Kahn *'00*

Pawel Szajda (1982-)
Under the Tuscan Sun *'03*
Venom *'05*
Generation Kill *'08*
The Haunting of Sharon Tate *'19*

Grazyna Szapolowska (1953-)
Another Way *'82*
No End *'84*

Keith Szarabajka (1952-)
Protocol *'84*
Marie *'85*
Billy Galvin *'86*
Stephen King's Golden Years *'91*
A Perfect World *'93*
Andre *'94*
We Were Soldiers *'02*

Eric Szmanda
Little Athens *'05*
Shadow of Fear *'12*

Jessica Szohr (1985-)
Piranha 3D *'10*
I Don't Know How She Does It *'11*
Love, Wedding, Marriage *'11*
Art Machine *'12*
The Internship *'13*
Pawn *'13*
Brightest Star *'14*
Lucky in Love *'14*
Two Night Stand *'14*

Stephanie Szostak (1975-)
Motherhood *'09*
Dinner for Schmucks *'10*
We Bought a Zoo *'11*
R.I.P.D. *'13*
Gimme Shelter *'14*
Hit By Lightning *'14*

Magda Szubanski (1961-)
Babe *'95*
Babe: Pig in the City *'98*
The Crocodile Hunter: Collision Course *'02*
Happy Feet *'06 (V)*
Brand New Day *'10*

Oleg Tabakov (1935-)
An Unfinished Piece for a Player Piano *'77*
Oblomov *'81*
Taking Sides *'01*

Tomoko Tabata (1980-)
Blood and Bones *'04*
Sabu *'04*
Hana: The Tale of a Reluctant Samurai *'07*

Kristopher Tabori (1952-)
The Glass House *'72*
Girlfriends *'78*
Last Summer In the Hamptons *'96*

Tabu (1970-)
The Namesake *'06*
Life of Pi *'12*

Jorma Taccone (1977-)
Hot Rod *'07*
Land of the Lost *'09*
Popstar: Never Stop Never Stopping *'16*

Hiroshi Tachikawa
Yojimbo *'61*
Matango *'63*

Sydney Tafler (1916-79)
It Always Rains on Sunday *'47*
Fire Maidens from Outer Space *'56*
The Way Out *'56*

The Counterfeit Plan *'57*
Carve Her Name with Pride *'58*
Sink the Bismarck *'60*
Alfie *'66*
The Adventurers *'70*

Cary-Hiroyuki Tagawa (1950-)
The Last Warrior *'89*
Showdown in Little Tokyo *'91*
American Me *'92*
Nemesis *'93*
Rising Sun *'93*
Picture Bride *'94*
Danger Zone *'95*
Mortal Kombat 1: The Movie *'95*
White Tiger *'95*
The Phantom *'96*
Provocateur *'96*
John Carpenter's Vampires *'97*
Top of the World *'97*
Tom Clancy's Netforce *'98*
Bridge of Dragons *'99*
The Art of War *'00*
Planet of the Apes *'01*
Elektra *'05*
Memoirs of a Geisha *'05*
Hachiko: A Dog's Tale *'09*
The Tomb *'09*

Aron Tager
Protection *'01*
Homeless to Harvard: The Liz Murray Story *'03*

Rita Taggart (1949-)
Coming Home *'78*
Used Cars *'80*
Torchlight *'85*
The Horror Show *'89*
Coupe de Ville *'90*
Crossing the Bridge *'92*
Limbo *'99*

Sharon Taggart (1947-)
The Last Picture Show *'71*
Harrad Experiment *'73*

Said Taghmaoui (1973-)
Hate *'95*
Hideous Kinky *'99*
Three Kings *'99*
Crime Spree *'03*
The Good Thief *'03*
Hidalgo *'04*
Spartan *'04*
Five Fingers *'06*
O Jerusalem *'07*
House of Saddam *'08*
Traitor *'08*
Vantage Point *'08*
G.I. Joe: The Rise of Cobra *'09*
My Brother the Devil *'12*
At First Light *'18*

Alice Taglioni (1976-)
The Valet *'06*
Cash *'08*
The Prey *'11*

Sharmila Tagore (1946-)
The World of Apu *'59*
Devi *'60*
Mississippi Masala *'92*

Tomorowo Taguchi (1957-)
Tetsuo: The Iron Man *'92*
The Eel *'96*
Tetsuo 2: Body Hammer *'97*
Tomie *'99*
Andromedia *'00*

Charlie Tahan (1996-)
I Am Legend *'07*
Nights in Rodanthe *'08*
Charlie St. Cloud *'10*
Frankenweenie *'12 (V)*
Life of Crime *'13*
Love Is Strange *'14*
Super Dark Times *'17*
Poms *'19*

Faran Tahir (1964-)
ABCD *'99*
Manticore *'05*
Iron Man *'08*
Star Trek *'09*
Jinn *'14*
Mr. Jones *'14*

Marissa Tait (1979-)
Witchouse *'99*
The Biggest Fan *'02*

Tristan Tait (1971-)
Larry McMurtry's Streets of Laredo *'95*
Rose Hill *'97*

Taj Mahal (1942-)
Sounder *'72*
Bill & Ted's Bogus Journey *'91*
Songcatcher *'99*
Killer Diller *'04*

Yoshifumi Tajima (1918-2009)
Godzilla *vs.* Mothra *'64*
Destroy All Monsters *'68*
Godzilla's Revenge *'69*
War of the Gargantuas *'70*

Miiko Taka (1932-)
Sayonara *'57*
Walk, Don't Run *'66*

Hitoshi Takagi
Lady Snowblood *'73*
Rica 2: Lonely Wanderer *'73*

Ken Takakura (1931-2014)
Too Late the Hero *'70*
The Yakuza *'75*
Black Rain *'89*
Mr. Baseball *'92*
Riding Alone for Thousands of Miles *'05*

Sophia Takal
V/H/S *'12*
All the Light in the Sky *'13*
24 Exposures *'13*

Hideko Takamine (1924-)
Twenty-Four Eyes *'54*
When a Woman Ascends the Stairs *'60*

Micko Takamine (1918-90)
47 Ronin, Part 1 *'42*
Phoenix *'78*

Rin Takanashi
Like Someone in Love *'13*
Killers *'14*

Hassei Takano
Uzumaki *'00*
Masked Rider-The First *'05*

Akira Takarada (1934-)
Godzilla *'54*
Godzilla, King of the Monsters *'56*
Godzilla *vs.* Mothra *'64*
King Kong Escapes *'67*
Godzilla *vs.* Monster Zero *'68*
Latitude Zero *'69*
Godzilla: Final Wars *'04*

Reiko Takashima
The Hidden Blade *'04*
Azumi 2 *'05*

Tadao Takashima (1930-2019)
Atragon *'63*
King Kong *vs.* Godzilla *'63*
Frankenstein Conquers the World *'64*
Son of Godzilla *'66*

Shinji Takeda (1972-)
Taboo *'99*
The Happiness of the Katakuris *'01*
Pulse *'01*

George Takei (1940-)
Ice Palace *'60*
Red Line 7000 *'65*
An American Dream *'66*
The Green Berets *'68*
Star Trek: The Motion Picture *'79*
Star Trek 2: The Wrath of Khan *'82*
Star Trek 3: The Search for Spock *'84*
Star Trek 4: The Voyage Home *'86*
Star Trek 5: The Final Frontier *'89*
Prisoners of the Sun *'91*
Star Trek 6: The Undiscovered Country *'91*
Oblivion *'94*
Backlash: Oblivion 2 *'95*
Mulan *'98 (V)*
Bug Buster *'99*
DC 9/11: Time of Crisis *'04*
Mulan 2 *'04 (V)*
The Great Buck Howard *'09 (C)*
Larry Crowne *'11*
Free Birds *'13 (V)*
Ava & Lala *'14*
Kubo and the Two Strings *'16*

Naoto Takenaka (1956-)
The Mystery of Rampo *'94*
Shall We Dance? *'96*
The Happiness of the Katakuris *'01*
Red Shadow *'01*
Ping Pong *'02*
Azumi *'03*
The Great Yokai War *'05*
RoboGeisha *'06*
Hara-Kiri: Death of a Samurai *'11*

Beat Takeshi (1947-)
See Takeshi 'Beat' Kitano

Riki Takeuchi (1964-)
Fudoh: The New Generation *'96*
Nobody *'99*
Dead or Alive 2 *'00*
Dead or Alive *'00*
Dead or Alive: Final *'02*
Big Man Japan *'07*
Tokyo Tribe *'15*

Yuko Takeuchi
Ringu *'98*
Death Trance *'05*
Creepy *'16*

Osamu Takizawa (1906-2000)
Fires on the Plain *'59*
Zatoichi *vs.* Yojimbo *'70*

Oleg Taktarov (1967-)
15 Minutes *'01*
Red Serpent *'02*
Rollerball *'02*
44 Minutes: The North Hollywood Shootout *'03*
Righteous Kill *'08*

Alona Tal
College *'08*
Kalamity *'10*
Opening Night *'17*

Ana Claudia Talancon (1980-)
The Crime of Father Amaro *'02*
Sueno *'05*
Alone With Her *'07*
One Missed Call *'08*

Odette Talazac
The Rules of the Game *'39*
The Murderer Lives at Number 21 *'42*

Charlie Talbert (1978-)
Angus *'95*
Bachelor Party Vegas *'05*
20 Years After *'08*

Lyle Talbot (1902-96)
No More Orchids *'32*
The Purchase Price *'32*
13th Guest *'32*
Girl Missing *'33*
20,000 Years in Sing Sing *'33*
Fog Over Frisco *'34*
The Case of the Lucky Legs *'35*
Oil for the Lamps of China *'35*
Go West, Young Man *'36*
The Singing Kid *'36*
Second Honeymoon *'37*
Call of the Yukon *'38*
Gateway *'38*
Gambler's Choice *'44*
One Body Too Many *'44*
Sensations of 1945 *'44*
Up in Arms *'44*
Strange Impersonation *'46*
Parole, Inc. *'49*
She Shoulda Said No *'49*
Atom Man *vs.* Superman *'50*
Fury of the Congo *'51*
Jungle Manhunt *'51*
One Too Many *'51*
African Treasure *'52*
Mesa of Lost Women *'52*
Untamed Women *'52*
Glen or Glenda? *'53*
Captain Kidd and the Slave Girl *'54*
Jail Bait *'54*
Plan 9 from Outer Space *'56*
Guns Don't Argue *'57*
High School Confidential *'58*
City of Fear *'59*
Sunrise at Campobello *'60*

Nita Talbot (1930-)
Who's Got the Action? *'63*
Girl Happy *'65*
That Funny Feeling *'65*
A Very Special Favor *'65*
The Cool Ones *'67*
They Call It Murder *'71*
Frightmare *'81*
Night Shift *'82*
Chained Heat *'83*
Fraternity Vacation *'85*
Puppet Master 2 *'90*
Amityville 1992: It's About Time *'92*

Gloria Talbott (1931-2000)
All That Heaven Allows *'55*
We're No Angels *'55*
Cyclops *'56*
The Oklahoman *'56*
The Daughter of Dr. Jekyll *'57*
The Kettles on Old MacDonald's Farm *'57*
I Married a Monster from Outer Space *'58*
Alias Jesse James *'59*
The Leech Woman *'59*
Arizona Raiders *'65*

Michael Talbott (1955-)
Miami Vice *'84*
Racing with the Moon *'84*

Hal Taliaferro (1895-1980)
Along the Rio Grande *'41*
Hoppy Serves a Writ *'43*
Leather Burners *'43*

Michael 'Bear' Taliferro (1961-2006)
Life *'99*
Blue Hill Avenue *'01*
Half Past Dead *'02*
Rude Boy: The Jamaican Don *'03*
You Got Served *'04*

Steve Talley (1981-)
Beyond the Blackboard *'11*
Deadline *'12*

Steven Talley (1981-)
American Pie Presents: The Naked Mile *'06*
American Pie Presents: Beta House *'07*
Van Wilder: Freshman Year *'08*

Patricia Tallman (1957-)
Night of the Living Dead *'90*
Army of Darkness *'92*
Dead Air *'08*

Constance Talmadge (1900-73)
Intolerance *'16*
The Primitive Lover *'22*
Her Night of Romance *'24*
Her Sister from Paris *'25*
The Duchess of Buffalo *'26*

Norma Talmadge (1895-1957)
The Forbidden City *'18*
Within the Law *'23*
Kiki *'26*

William Talman (1915-68)
Armored Car Robbery *'50*
The Woman on Pier 13 *'50*
One Minute to Zero *'52*
The Hitch-Hiker *'53*
Big House, U.S.A. *'55*
The Ballad of Josie *'67*

Alix Talton
The Deadly Mantis *'57*
Carnival of Crime *'62*

Patrick Tam (1968-)
Zu Warriors *'01*
Ip Man 3 *'16*

Shawn Tam
The Cave of the Silken Web *'67*
The Kumite *'03*

Tetsuro Tamba (1922-2006)
Harakiri *'62*
The Seventh Dawn *'64*
You Only Live Twice *'67*
Goyokin *'69*
Under the Flag of the Rising Sun *'72*
Hunter in the Dark *'80*
The Happiness of the Katakuris *'01*

Carlo Tamberlani (1899-1980)
The Fury of Hercules *'61*
The Old Testament *'62*
The Trojan Horse *'62*
Caesar the Conqueror *'63*
Three Avengers *'64*

Nando Tamberlani (1896-1967)
Fury of Achilles *'62*
The Trojan Horse *'62*
Hercules against the Moon Men *'64*

Amber Tamblyn (1983-)
The Ring *'02*
The Sisterhood of the Traveling Pants *'05*
The Grudge 2 *'06*
Stephanie Daley *'06*
Blackout *'07*
Havoc 2: Normal Adolescent Behavior *'07*
Spiral *'07*
The Sisterhood of the Traveling Pants 2 *'08*
Spring Breakdown *'08*
That Russell Girl *'08*
Beyond a Reasonable Doubt *'09*
Main Street *'10*
127 Hours *'10*
Django Unchained *'12*

Russ Tamblyn (1934-)
Gun Crazy *'49*
The Kid From Cleveland *'49*
Samson and Delilah *'49*
Father of the Bride *'50*
Father's Little Dividend *'51*
The Winning Team *'52*
Seven Brides for Seven Brothers *'54*
Hit the Deck *'55*
Many Rivers to Cross *'55*
Fastest Gun Alive *'56*
The Last Hunt *'56*
Don't Go Near the Water *'57*
Peyton Place *'57*
High School Confidential *'58*
Tom Thumb *'58*
Cimarron *'60*
West Side Story *'61*
Follow the Boys *'63*
The Haunting *'63*
How the West Was Won *'63*
The Long Ships *'64*
Son of a Gunfighter *'65*
Satan's Sadists *'69*
War of the Gargantuas *'70*
Dracula *vs.* Frankenstein *'71*
Black Heat *'76*
Cyclone *'87*
Phantom Empire *'87*
Aftershock *'88*
Necromancer: Satan's Servant *'88*
Running Mates *'92*
Cabin Boy *'94*
Wizards of the Demon Sword *'94*
Attack of the 60-Foot Centerfold *'95*
Invisible Mom *'96*
My Magic Dog *'97*
Inherit the Wind *'99*
Django Unchained *'12*

Jeffrey Tambor (1944-)
And Justice for All *'79*
A Gun in the House *'81*
Saturday the 14th *'81*
The Man Who Wasn't There *'83*
Mr. Mom *'83*
Brenda Starr *'86*
Desert Hearts *'86*
Three O'Clock High *'87*
City Slickers *'91*
Life Stinks *'91*
Pastime *'91*
Article 99 *'92*
Crossing the Bridge *'92*
Heavyweights *'94*
Radioland Murders *'94*
Big Bully *'95*
My Teacher's Wife *'95*
The Man Who Captured Eichmann *'96*
Weapons of Mass Distraction *'97*
Dr. Dolittle *'98*
Meet Joe Black *'98*
There's Something about Mary *'98*
Girl, Interrupted *'99*
Muppets from Space *'99*
Teaching Mrs. Tingle *'99*
Dr. Seuss' How the Grinch Stole Christmas *'00*
Pollock *'00*
Get Well Soon *'01*
Never Again *'01*
Eloise at the Plaza *'03*
Malibu's Most Wanted *'03*
My Boss's Daughter *'03*
Eurotrip *'04*
Hellboy *'04*
The SpongeBob SquarePants Movie *'04 (V)*
The Muppets' Wizard of Oz *'05*
Slipstream *'07*
Hellboy II: The Golden Army *'08*
The Hangover *'09*
The Invention of Lying *'09*
Monsters *vs.* Aliens *'09 (V)*
Operation: Endgame *'10*
Tangled *'10 (V)*
Flypaper *'11*
Lucky *'11*
Meeting Spencer *'11*
Paul *'11*
Win Win *'11*
Branded *'12*
The Hangover, Part III *'13*
Phil Spector *'13*
Apartment Troubles *'15*
The D Train *'15*
The Accountant *'16*
The Death of Stalin *'17*

Zoe Tamerlis (1962-99)
Ms. 45 *'81*
Special Effects *'85*
Bad Lieutenant *'92*

Akim Tamiroff (1899-1972)
The Merry Widow *'34*
China Seas *'35*
The Gay Deception *'35*
The Last Outpost *'35*
The Lives of a Bengal Lancer *'35*
The General Died at Dawn *'36*
High, Wide and Handsome *'37*
Spawn of the North *'38*
Union Pacific *'39*
The Great McGinty *'40*
The Corsican Brothers *'42*
Tortilla Flat *'42*
Five Graves to Cairo *'43*
For Whom the Bell Tolls *'43*
The Bridge of San Luis Rey *'44*

The Favor '92
Cop and a Half '93
Steal Big, Steal Little '95
To Die For '95
Last Summer In the Hamptons '96
One Fine Day '96
Betty '97
George of the Jungle '97
Just Write '97
Next Stop, Wonderland '98
The Truman Show '98
Happy Accidents '00
Keeping the Faith '00
Mail to the Chief '00
The Day Reagan Was Shot '01
Legally Blonde '01
Home Room '02
Spy Kids 2: The Island of Lost Dreams '02
Spy Kids 3-D: Game Over '03
D.E.B.S. '04
The Wedding Date '05
Baby Mama '08

Jack Taylor (1936-)
Night of the Sorcerers '70
Dr. Jekyll and the Wolfman '71
Female Vampire '73
Orgy of the Vampires '73
Where Time Began '77
The Ninth Gate '99

James Taylor (1948-)
Two Lane Blacktop '71
TMNT: Teenage Mutant Ninja Turtles '07 *(V)*

James Arnold Taylor (1969-)
Star Wars: The Clone Wars '08 *(V)*
Robo-Dog '15
Ratchet & Clank '16
Animal Crackers '17

Jana Taylor
Hell's Angels on Wheels '67
Dreamscape '84

Jayceon Taylor (1979-)
See The Game

Jennifer Taylor
Arlo the Burping Pig '16
Emma's Chance '16
God's Not Dead: A Light in Darkness '18

Jeremy Ray Taylor
It '17
Goosebumps 2: Haunted Halloween '18

Joan Taylor (1929-2012)
War Paint '53
Rose Marie '54
Fort Yuma '55
Earth *vs.* the Flying Saucers '56
Omar Khayyam '57
20 Million Miles to Earth '57
War Drums '57

Joanna Taylor
Post Impact '04
Back in Business '06

John Taylor (1960-)
The Seventh Sign '88
Sugar Town '99
Four Dogs Playing Poker '00
The Ringer '05

Joseph Lyle Taylor (1964-)
Borough of Kings '98
The Breakup Artist '04
Dead Man's Burden '12

Joyce Taylor (1932-)
The FBI Story '59
Atlantis, the Lost Continent '61
The Windsplitter '71

Kent Taylor (1906-87)
I'm No Angel '33
White Woman '33
David Harum '34
Death Takes a Holiday '34
Mrs. Wiggs of the Cabbage Patch '34
Ramona '36
The Gracie Allen Murder Case '39
I Take This Woman '40
Men Against the Sky '40
Two Girls on Broadway '40
Gang Busters '42
Payment on Demand '51
Track the Man Down '55
Ghost Town '56
The Phantom from 10,000 Leagues '56
Slightly Scarlet '56
The Iron Sheriff '57
Fort Bowie '58
The Crawling Hand '63
Brides of the Beast '68
Satan's Sadists '69
Hell's Bloody Devils '70
Brain of Blood '71
Angels' Wild Women '72
Blood of Ghastly Horror '72
I Spit on Your Corpse '74

Kirk Taylor
Streetwalkin' '85
Full Metal Jacket '87

Lawrence Taylor (1959-)
Mercy Streets '00
In Hell '03
The Comebacks '07 *(C)*

Lili Taylor (1967-)
Mystic Pizza '88
Say Anything '89
A Family of Spies '90
Bright Angel '91
Dogfight '91
Rudy '93
Short Cuts '93
Arizona Dream '94
Mrs. Parker and the Vicious Circle '94
Ready to Wear '94
Four Rooms '95
Girls Town '95
I Shot Andy Warhol '96
Ransom '96
Things I Never Told You '96
Kicked in the Head '97
Subway Stories '97
The Imposters '98
Pecker '98
The Haunting '99
A Slipping Down Life '99
High Fidelity '00
Anne Frank: The Whole Story '01
Gaudi Afternoon '01
Casa de los Babys '03
Live from Baghdad '03
Factotum '06
The Notorious Bettie Page '06
The Secret '07
Starting Out in the Evening '07
The Promotion '08
Brooklyn's Finest '09
About Cherry '12
Being Flynn '12
The Courier '12
Blood Ties '13
The Cold Lands '13
The Conjuring '13
Eli '19

Lindsay Taylor (1989-)
Hellraiser 5: Inferno '00
Accused at 17 '09
Walking the Halls '12

Marjorie Taylor (1912-74)
The Crimes of Stephen Hawke '36
Ticket of Leave Man '37
The Face at the Window '39

Mark L. Taylor (1954-)
Arachnophobia '90
Eight Days a Week '97

Meshach Taylor (1947-2014)
Damien: Omen 2 '78
The Howling '81
The Beast Within '82
Explorers '85
House of Games '87
Mannequin '87
Class Act '91
Mannequin 2: On the Move '91
Double Double Toil and Trouble '94
The Secret of NIMH 2 '98 *(V)*
Friends and Family '01
Hyenas '10

Mirelly Taylor
Kiss Me Again '06
Underdog Kids '15

Natascha Taylor (1971-)
See Natascha (Natasha) McElhone

Noah Taylor (1969-)
The Year My Voice Broke '87
Flirting '89
The Nostradamus Kid '92
Shine '95
Almost Famous '00
Life in the Fast Lane '00
He Died With a Falafel in His Hand '01
Lara Croft: Tomb Raider '01
Vanilla Sky '01
Max '02
The Sleeping Dictionary '02
Lara Croft Tomb Raider: The Cradle of Life '03
Charlie and the Chocolate Factory '05
The New World '05
The Proposition '05
The New Daughter '10
Red White & Blue '10
Submarine '10
Lawless '12
Edge of Tomorrow '14
Predestination '15

Rachael Taylor (1984-)
See No Evil '06
Transformers '07
Deception '08
The Legend of Bloody Mary '08
Shutter '08
Ghost Machine '09
Splinterheads '09
The Darkest Hour '11
Red Dog '11
The Loft '14
Finding Steve McQueen '19

Regina Taylor (1960-)
Lean on Me '89
A Good Day to Die '95
Courage Under Fire '96
A Family Thing '96
The Keeper '96
Spirit Lost '96
Hostile Waters '97
The Negotiator '98
Cora Unashamed '00
Who Is Clark Rockefeller? '10

Renee Taylor (1933-)
The Errand Boy '61
The Detective '68
Jennifer On My Mind '71
Last of the Red Hot Lovers '72
The End of Innocence '90
White Palace '90
Delirious '91
Love Is All There Is '96
61* '01
Alfie '04
National Lampoon's Gold Diggers '04
The Boynton Beach Club '05
Ice Age: The Meltdown '06 *(V)*
Pandemic '07
Life During Wartime '09
Opposite Day '09
The Rainbow Tribe '11

Rip Taylor (1931-2019)
Cheech and Chong: Things Are Tough All Over '82
DuckTales the Movie: Treasure of the Lost Lamp '90 *(V)*
Indecent Proposal '93
Tom and Jerry: The Movie '93 *(V)*
Wayne's World 2 '93
Private Obsession '94
Alex & Emma '03

Robert Taylor (1911-69)
Broadway Melody of 1936 '35
Magnificent Obsession '35
Camille '36
The Gorgeous Hussy '36
Private Number '36
Broadway Melody of 1938 '37
Personal Property '37
The Crowd Roars '38
Three Comrades '38
Stand Up and Fight '39
Flight Command '40
Waterloo Bridge '40
Billy the Kid '41
When Ladies Meet '41
Her Cardboard Lover '42
Johnny Eager '42
Stand by for Action '42
Bataan '43
Undercurrent '46
High Wall '47
The Bribe '48
Conspirator '49
Ambush '50
The Devil's Doorway '50
Quo Vadis '51
Westward the Women '51
Ivanhoe '52
Above and Beyond '53
All the Brothers Were Valiant '53
I Love Melvin '53
Knights of the Round Table '53
Ride, Vaquero! '53
Many Rivers to Cross '55
Quentin Durward '55
D-Day, the Sixth of June '56
The Last Hunt '56
The Power and the Prize '56
Tip On a Dead Jockey '57
The Law and Jake Wade '58
Party Girl '58
Saddle the Wind '58
The Hangman '59
The House of the Seven Hawks '59
Cattle King '63
The Miracle of the White Stallions '63
Return of the Gunfighter '67
Where Angels Go, Trouble Follows '68 *(C)*

Robert Taylor (1963-)
The Matrix '99
Vertical Limit '00
The Hard Word '02
Focus '15
What Lola Wants '15

Rod Taylor (1929-2015)
Long John Silver '54
Top Gun '55
The Catered Affair '56
Giant '56
World Without End '56
Raintree County '57
Separate Tables '58
Colossus and the Amazon Queen '60
The Time Machine '60
101 Dalmatians '61 *(V)*
Seven Seas to Calais '62
The Birds '63
Sunday in New York '63
The V.I.P.'s '63
Fate Is the Hunter '64
36 Hours '64
Do Not Disturb '65
The Liquidator '65
Young Cassidy '65
The Glass Bottom Boat '66
Chuka '67
Hotel '67
Dark of the Sun '68
Zabriskie Point '70
The Deadly Trackers '73
Train Robbers '73
Cry of the Innocent '80
Time to Die '83
Danielle Steel's Palomino '91
Open Season '95
Welcome to Woop Woop '97
Inglourious Basterds '09

Russi Taylor (1944-)
DuckTales the Movie: Treasure of the Lost Lamp '90 *(V)*
Jetsons: The Movie '90 *(V)*
Babe: Pig in the City '98 *(V)*
Cinderella III: A Twist in Time '07 *(V)*

Tamara Taylor (1970-)
Nightstalker '81
Senseless '98
Introducing Dorothy Dandridge '99
Diary of a Mad Black Woman '05
Gordon Glass '07

Tammy Taylor
Lovelines '84
Meatballs 2 '84

Tom Taylor (2001-)
The Dark Tower '17
The Kid Who Would Be King '19

Vanessa Taylor
Femalien '96
Femalien 2 '98

Vaughn Taylor (1910-83)
Francis Goes to the Races '51
Jailhouse Rock '57
Andy Hardy Comes Home '58
The Lineup '58
The Gallant Hours '60

Veronica Taylor
Pokemon: The First Movie '99 *(V)*
Pokemon 3: The Movie '01 *(V)*

Wally Taylor (1931-2012)
Cool Breeze '72
Shaft's Big Score '72
Night of the Creeps '86

Zara Taylor
Past Tense '06
No Brother of Mine '07

Scout Taylor-Compton (1989-)
Sleepover '04
Halloween '07
Love's Unfolding Dream '07
Wicked Little Things '07
April Fool's Day '08
Halloween II '09
Life Blood '09
Obsessed '09
Triple Dog '09
Love Ranch '10
The Runaways '10
Dirty Lies '16
Flight 7500 '16

Aaron Taylor-Johnson (1990-)
Tom & Thomas '02
Shanghai Knights '03
Dead Cool '04
The Illusionist '06
The Thief Lord '06
Angus, Thongs and Perfect Snogging '08
The Greatest '09
Nowhere Boy '09
Chatroom '10
Kick-Ass '10
Albert Nobbs '11
Anna Karenina '12
Savages '12
Kick-Ass 2 '13
Godzilla '14
Nocturnal Animals '16
The Wall '17
Outlaw King '18

Anya Taylor-Joy
Morgan '16
Split '16
The Witch '16
Thoroughbreds '17
Glass '19
Playmobil: The Movie '19
Emma '20

Leigh Taylor-Young (1945-)
I Love You, Alice B. Toklas! '68
The Big Bounce '69
The Adventurers '70
The Buttercup Chain '70
The Horsemen '70
Soylent Green '73
Can't Stop the Music '80
Marathon '80
Looker '81
The Jagged Edge '85
Secret Admirer '85
Napoleon and Josephine: A Love Story '87
Accidents '89
Bliss '96
Slackers '02
Klepto '03
Coffee Date '06

Jun Tazaki (1910-85)
Seven Samurai '54
Atragon '63
King Kong *vs.* Godzilla '63
Destroy All Monsters '68
Godzilla *vs.* Monster Zero '68
War of the Gargantuas '70
Ran '85

Ludmilla Tcherina (1924-2004)
The Red Shoes '48
Sins of Rome '54

Kiri Te Kanawa (1944-)
Don Giovanni '79
Meeting Venus '91 *(V)*

Phil Tead (1893-1974)
Music in My Heart '40
Fangs of the Wild '54

Anthony Teague (1940-89)
How to Succeed in Business without Really Trying '67
The Trouble with Girls (and How to Get into It) '69

Marshall Teague (1953-)
The Shadow Riders '82
Road House '89
Guardian Angel '94
The Colony '95
The Bad Pack '98
Across the Line '00
Crime and Punishment in Suburbia '00
U.S. Seals 2 '01
What Matters Most '01
Special Forces '03
The Cutter '05
Universal Squadrons '11
Last Ounce of Courage '12

Ray Teal (1902-76)
Hollywood Canteen '44
The Bandit of Sherwood Forest '46
The Best Years of Our Lives '46
Ace in the Hole '51
Distant Drums '51
Tomorrow Is Another Day '51
The Captive City '52
Carrie '52
Cattle Town '52
Jumping Jacks '52
Ambush at Tomahawk Gap '53
The Command '54
The Burning Hills '56
Band of Angels '57
Saddle the Wind '58
Judgment at Nuremberg '61

Owen Teale (1961-)
Catherine Cookson's The Fifteen Streets '90
Robin Hood '91
The Hawk '93
Wilderness '96
The Cherry Orchard '99
Cleopatra '99
Conspiracy '01
The Last Legion '07

Conway Tearle (1878-1938)
Stella Maris '18
Dancing Mothers '26
The Lost Zeppelin '29

The Truth About Youth '30
Held for Murder '32
Hurricane Express '32
Vanity Fair '32
Day of Reckoning '33
Stingaree '34
Headline Woman '35
Desert Guns '36
Klondike Annie '36

Godfrey Tearle (1884-1953)
The 39 Steps '35
East Meets West '36
One of Our Aircraft Is Missing '41

Verree Teasdale (1904-87)
Skyscraper Souls '32
Goodbye Love '34
Milky Way '36
Come Live With Me '40
I Take This Woman '40

Sandor Tecsy (1946-)
Angel Blue '97
Fever '99

Paola Tedesco
Crime Boss '72
New Mafia Boss '72

Travis Tedford (1988-)
The Little Rascals '94
Slappy and the Stinkers '97
The Final '10

Brian Tee (1977-)
The Fast and the Furious: Tokyo Drift '06
The Wolverine '13
The Gabby Douglas Story '14

Jill Teed
Impolite '92
Mission to Mars '00
X2: X-Men United '03
He Loves Me '11

Maureen Teefy (1954-)
Fame '80
Supergirl '84

Aimee Teegarden (1989-)
Call of the Wild 3D '09
Beautiful Wave '11
Prom '11
Beneath the Darkness '12
Rings '17

Blair Tefkin (1959-)
A Sinful Life '89
Dream Lover '93

Aaron Teich (1961-)
Bloodspell '87
Darkroom '90

Virgilio Teixeira (1917-2010)
The Happy Thieves '61
Saul and David '64
The Magnificent Two '67
Tricheurs '84

Fernando Tejero
Torremolinos 73 '03
Chef's Special '08

April Telek (1975-)
Man in the Mirror: The Michael Jackson Story '04
His and Her Christmas '05
Love at the Thanksgiving Day Parade '12

Zoe Telford (1973-)
Beau Brummell: This Charming Man '06
The Waiting Room '07
Place of Execution '09

Olive Tell
The Right of Way '31
Scarlet Empress '34

Miles Teller (1987-)
Rabbit Hole '10
Footloose '11
Project X '11
The Spectacular Now '13
21 & Over '13
Divergent '14
That Awkward Moment '14
Two Night Stand '14
Whiplash '14
Fantastic Four '15
Insurgent '15
Allegiant '16
Bleed for This '16
Get a Job '16
War Dogs '16
Only the Brave '17
Thank You for Your Service '17

Muzaffer Tema
12 to the Moon '60
The Deathless Devil '05

Sybil Temchen (1979-)
Floating '97
Restaurant '98
Ten Benny '98
Body Shots '99
Nice Guys Sleep Alone '99
The Passion of Ayn Rand '99
Lip Service '00

Juno Temple (1989-)
Notes on a Scandal '06
Atonement '07
St. Trinian's '07
The Other Boleyn Girl '08
Wild Child '08
Cracks '09
Glorious 39 '09
The Legend of Fritton's Gold '09
Dirty Girl '10
Greenberg '10
Kaboom '11
Killer Joe '11
The Three Musketeers '11
The Dark Knight Rises '12
Jack and Diane '12
Small Apartments '12
Afternoon Delight '13
Horns '13
Lovelace '13
Magic Magic '13
Mr. Nobody '13
Maleficent '14
Black Mass '15
Far from the Madding Crowd '15
Safelight '15
Len & Company '16
Wonder Wheel '17
Pretenders '19

Lew Temple (1967-)
The Devil's Rejects '05
Domino '05
The Texas Chainsaw Massacre: The Beginning '06
Waitress '07
The Killing Jar '10
Wicked Blood '13
The Endless '17
Kidnap '17

Shirley Temple (1928-2014)
The Red-Haired Alibi '32
To the Last Man '33
Baby, Take a Bow '34
Bright Eyes '34
Little Miss Marker '34
Now and Forever '34
Stand Up and Cheer '34
Curly Top '35
The Little Colonel '35
The Littlest Rebel '35
Captain January '36
Dimples '36
Stowaway '36
Heidi '37
Wee Willie Winkie '37
Just Around the Corner '38
Little Miss Broadway '38
Rebecca of Sunnybrook Farm '38
The Little Princess '39
Susannah of the Mounties '39
The Blue Bird '40
Young People '40
Kathleen '41
I'll Be Seeing You '44
Since You Went Away '44
The Bachelor and the Bobby-Soxer '47
Honeymoon '47
That Hagen Girl '47
Fort Apache '48
Adventure in Baltimore '49
The Story of Seabiscuit '49

Sybil Temtchine (1970-)
The Cavern '05
The Undying '09

Natalia Tena (1984-)
Harry Potter and the Deathly Hallows, Part 1 '10
Tonight You're Mine '11
10,000 Km '14

Harry Tenbrook (1887-1960)
A Slight Case of Murder '38
They Were Expendable '45

John Tench
The Suspect '05
The Secrets of Comfort House '06
The Killing Machine '09

David Tennant (1971-)
The Last September '99
Bright Young Things '03
He Knew He Was Right '04
Casanova '05
Harry Potter and the Goblet of Fire '05
Secret Smile '05
Glorious 39 '09
The Legend of Fritton's Gold '09
The Decoy Bride '11
Fright Night '11
United '11
The Pirates! Band of Misfits '12 (V)
The Escape Artist '13
Spies of Warsaw '13
Postman Pat: The Movie '14 (V)
What We Did on Our Holiday '15
Bad Samaritan '18
Mary Queen of Scots '18

Emily Tennant (1990-)
Killer Bees '02
Wilderness Love '02
Destination: Infestation '07
Triple Dog '09
Battle of the Bulbs '10
Frankie and Alice '10
Christmas Comes Home to Canaan '11
Way of the Wicked '14

Victoria Tennant (1950-)
Inseminoid '80
The Dogs of War '81
Dempsey '83
The Winds of War '83
All of Me '84
The Holcroft Covenant '85
Best Seller '87
Flowers in the Attic '87
War & Remembrance '88
War & Remembrance: The Final Chapter '89
Whispers '89
The Handmaid's Tale '90
L.A. Story '91
Edie & Pen '95 (C)
Bram Stoker's The Mummy '97
Irene in Time '09

Anne Tenney
Dead Heart '96
The Castle '97

Jon Tenney (1961-)
Guilty by Suspicion '91
Tombstone '93
Lassie '94
Free Willy 2: The Adventure Home '95
The Phantom '96
Fools Rush In '97
Homegrown '97
Lovelife '97
Music from Another Room '97
The Twilight of the Golds '97
You Can Count On Me '99
Looking for Comedy in the Muslim World '06
The Stepfather '09
Rabbit Hole '10
Green Lantern '11
Hide Away '11
As Cool As I Am '13
The Best of Me '14
Love the Coopers '15

William Tepper (1948-)
Miss Right '81
Bachelor Party '84

Johanna Ter Steege (1961-)
The Vanishing '88
Vincent & Theo '90
Meeting Venus '91
Immortal Beloved '94
Paradise Road '97

Shinobu Terajima
Riding Alone for Thousands of Miles '05
Oh Lucy! '17

Susumu Terajima (1963-)
Fireworks '97
After Life '98
Brother '00
Ichi the Killer '01
Blood and Bones '04
Flower & Snake '04
Steamboy '05 (V)
Gamera the Brave '06
Black House '07
Hana: The Tale of a Reluctant Samurai '07

Akira Terao (1947-)
Ran '85
Akira Kurosawa's Dreams '90
Casshern '04
Black House '07

Lee Tergesen (1965-)
The Killing Mind '90
Point Break '91
Shaft '00
Shot in the Heart '01
Bark! '02
Monster '03
Extreme Dating '04
A Thief of Time '04
The Texas Chainsaw Massacre: The Beginning '06
Generation Kill '08

Studs Terkel (1912-2008)
Long Shadows '86
Eight Men Out '88

John Terlesky (1961-)
Chopping Mall '86
The Allnighter '87
Deathstalker 2: Duel of the Titans '87
Damned River '89
When He's Not a Stranger '89
Battling for Baby '92

Scott Terra (1987-)
Shadrach '98
Eight Legged Freaks '02
Daredevil '03

John Canada Terrell
She's Gotta Have It '86
Def by Temptation '90
The Five Heartbeats '91

Ken Terrell (1907-66)
The Indestructible Man '56
The Brain from Planet Arous '57
Attack of the 50 Foot Woman '58

Alice Terry (1899-1987)
The Four Horsemen of the Apocalypse '21
The Prisoner of Zenda '22
Scaramouche '23
The Magician '26

Don Terry (1902-88)
Overland Mail '42
Don Winslow of the Coast Guard '43
Don Winslow of the Navy '43

John Terry (1950-)
Hawk the Slayer '81
Full Metal Jacket '87
In Country '89
A Killing in a Small Town '90
The Resurrected '91
Of Mice and Men '92
Iron Will '93
Betrayed: A Story of Three Women '95
The Big Green '95
Dead by Sunset '95
A Change of Heart '98
Blue Valley Songbird '99
Steve Martini's The Judge '01
Zodiac '07
The Way of War '08
Nine Dead '10

Kim Terry
Slugs '87
Rushmore '98

Nigel Terry (1945-2015)
The Lion in Winter '68
Excalibur '81
Deja Vu '84
Caravaggio '86
Edward II '92
Blue '93 (N)
The Ebb-Tide '97
Far from the Madding Crowd '97
The Emperor's New Clothes '01
Feardotcom '02
Red Mercury '05
Blackbeard '06

Phillip Terry (1909-93)
Wake Island '42
Bataan '43
George White's Scandals '45
The Lost Weekend '45
The Leech Woman '59
The Explosive Generation '61

Ruth Terry (1920-)
Alexander's Ragtime Band '38
Blondie Goes Latin '42
Call of the Canyon '42
Hands Across the Border '43
Texas Legionnaires '43

William Terry
Stage Door Canteen '43
Johnny Doesn't Live Here Any More '44

Terry-Thomas (1911-89)
Blue Murder at St. Trinian's '56
Lucky Jim '58
The Naked Truth '58
Tom Thumb '58
Carlton Browne of the F.O. '59
I'm All Right Jack '59
Too Many Crooks '59
Make Mine Mink '60
School for Scoundrels '60
Bachelor Flat '62
Kill or Cure '62
A Matter of WHO '62
The Mouse on the Moon '62
It's a Mad, Mad, Mad, Mad World '63
A Wild Affair '63
How to Murder Your Wife '64
Strange Bedfellows '65
Those Magnificent Men in Their Flying Machines '65
You Must Be Joking! '65
Bang! Bang! You're Dead! '66
La Grande Vadrouille '66
Munster, Go Home! '66
A Guide for the Married Man '67 (C)
Those Fantastic Flying Fools '67
Danger: Diabolik '68
Don't Raise the Bridge, Lower the River '68
How Sweet It Is! '68
Those Daring Young Men in Their Jaunty Jalopies '69
The Abominable Dr. Phibes '71
Doctor Phibes Rises Again '72
Robin Hood '73 (V)
Vault of Horror '73

Laurent Terzieff (1935-2010)
Araya '59 (N)
Kapo '59
Vanina Vanini '61
A Coeur Joie '67
Head Over Heels '67
The Milky Way '68
Medea '70
Detective '85

Venus Terzo
Circle of Friends '06
Meltdown '06

Robert Tessier (1934-2000)
Born Losers '67
The Glory Stompers '67
Cry Blood, Apache '70
The Velvet Vampire '71
The Longest Yard '74
Star Crash '78
The Villain '79
Sword & the Sorcerer '82
Avenging Angel '85
No Safe Haven '87
Future Force '89
Nightwish '89

Desmond Tester (1919-2002)
Nine Days a Queen '36
Sabotage '36
Non-Stop New York '37

Fabio Testi (1941-)
One Fine Day, When Django Met Sartana '70
The Garden of the Finzi-Continis '71
'Tis a Pity She's a Whore '73
Revolver '75
Stateline Motel '75
The Inheritance '76
Gunfire '78
The Uranium Conspiracy '78
Contraband '80
The Ambassador '84
Mussolini & I '85
Iguana '89

Sylvie Testud (1971-)
Beyond Silence '96
Murderous Maids '00
The Chateau '01
A Loving Father '02
La France '07
La Vie en Rose '07
The Scapegoat '12
24 Days '14
Final Portrait '17
Suspiria '18

Lauren Tewes (1953-)
Eyes of a Stranger '81
Camp Cucamonga: How I Spent My Summer Vacation '90
Magic Kid '92
The Doom Generation '95

Tia Texada (1971-)
From Dusk Till Dawn '95
Paulie '98
The Thirteenth Floor '99
Bait '00
Nurse Betty '00
Glitter '01
Thirteen Conversations About One Thing '01
Crazy as Hell '02
Phone Booth '02
Spartan '04

Gilda Texter (1946-)
Angels Hard As They Come '71
Vanishing Point '71

Maurice Teynac (1915-92)
Bedevilled '55
In the French Style '63
Ash Wednesday '73

Elizabeth Thai (1979-)
Saved! '04
Mr. Troop Mom '09

Eric Thal (1965-)
The Gun in Betty Lou's Handbag '92
A Stranger Among Us '92

Six Degrees of Separation '93
The Puppet Masters '94
Samson and Delilah '96
Wishful Thinking '96
Mixing Nia '98
Prisoner of Love '99
Snow Falling on Cedars '99
The Shaft '01

Katharina Thalbach (1954-)
The Second Awakening of Christa Klages '78
The Tin Drum '79
Good Evening, Mr. Wallenberg '93
Kaspar Hauser '93
King of Thieves '04

Byron Thames (1969-)
Blame It on the Night '84
Seven Minutes in Heaven '86
Not Another B Movie '10

Heather Thatcher (1896-1987)
But the Flesh Is Weak '32
Beau Geste '39
Son of Fury '42
The Moon and Sixpence '43

Torin Thatcher (1905-81)
Sabotage '36
Young and Innocent '37
Old Mother Riley, MP '39
Great Expectations '46
Affair in Trinidad '52
Crimson Pirate '52
The Snows of Kilimanjaro '52
The Desert Rats '53
Houdini '53
The Robe '53
The Black Shield of Falworth '54
Knock on Wood '54
Diane '55
Lady Godiva '55
Love Is a Many-Splendored Thing '55
Helen of Troy '56
Band of Angels '57
Witness for the Prosecution '57
Darby's Rangers '58
The Seventh Voyage of Sinbad '58
Jack the Giant Killer '62
Drums of Africa '63
Dr. Jekyll and Mr. Hyde '68

Hilmar Thate (1931-)
The Gleiwitz Case '61
Divided Heaven '64
Veronika Voss '82
The Ninth Day '04

John Thaw (1942-2002)
The Last Grenade '70
Macbeth '70
Killing Heat '84
Cry Freedom '87
A Year in Provence '89
Chaplin '92
Into the Blue '97
Goodnight, Mr. Tom '99
The Waiting Time '99

Phyllis Thaxter (1919-2012)
Thirty Seconds Over Tokyo '44
Weekend at the Waldorf '45
Living In a Big Way '47
The Sea of Grass '47
Tenth Avenue Angel '47
Act of Violence '48
The Breaking Point '50
Jim Thorpe: All American '51
Operation Secret '52
She's Working Her Way Through College '52
Springfield Rifle '52
Women's Prison '55
The World of Henry Orient '64
Superman: The Movie '78
Three Sovereigns for Sarah '85

Brynn Thayer (1949-)
Hero and the Terror '88
The Tracker '88
The Bannen Way '10

Lorna Thayer
The Beast With a Million Eyes '56
Five Easy Pieces '70

Maria Thayer (1975-)
Accepted '06
Strangers with Candy '06
Forgetting Sarah Marshall '08
Annie Claus is Coming to Town '11
Night of the Living Deb '14

Max (Michael) Thayer (1946-)
Ilsa, Harem Keeper of the Oil Sheiks '76
Planet of the Dinosaurs '80
Retrievers '82
No Dead Heroes '87

Marcello Thedford
An Alan Smithee Film: Burn, Hollywood, Burn '97
Freedom Song '00

Darryl Theirse (1967-2009)
I Love You, Don't Touch Me! '97
Crocodile 2: Death Swamp '01

Brooke Theiss (1969-)
A Nightmare on Elm Street 4: Dream Master '88
Quicksand '01

Brother Theodore (1906-2001)
Massage Parlor Murders '73
The Hobbit '78 (V)
The 'Burbs '89

Fabianne Therese
The Aggression Scale '12
Southbound '16

Christa Theret (1991-)
Renoir '12
Marguerite '16
Non-Fiction '18

Charlize Theron (1975-)
That Thing You Do! '96
Trial and Error '96
Two Days in the Valley '96
The Devil's Advocate '97
Hollywood Confidential '97
Celebrity '98
Mighty Joe Young '98
The Astronaut's Wife '99
The Cider House Rules '99
The Legend of Bagger Vance '00
Men of Honor '00
Reindeer Games '00
The Yards '00
The Curse of the Jade Scorpion '01
15 Minutes '01
Sweet November '01
Trapped '02
Waking Up in Reno '02
The Italian Job '03
Monster '03
Head in the Clouds '04
Aeon Flux '05
North Country '05
Battle in Seattle '07
In the Valley of Elah '07
The Burning Plain '08
Hancock '08
Sleepwalking '08
Astro Boy '09 (N)
The Road '09
Young Adult '11
Prometheus '12
Snow White and the Huntsman '12
A Million Ways to Die In the West '14
Dark Places '15
Mad Max: Fury Road '15
The Huntsman: Winter's War '16
Kubo and the Two Strings '16

Atomic Blonde '17
The Last Face '17
Gringo '18
Tully '18
The Addams Family '19
Bombshell '19
Long Shot '19

Justin Theroux (1971-)
Body Count '97
Frogs for Snakes '98
American Psycho '99
Dead Broke '99
The Broken Hearts Club '00
Mulholland Drive '01
Charlie's Angels: Full Throttle '03
Duplex '03
The Baxter '05
Inland Empire '06
The Legend of Lucy Keyes '06
Miami Vice '06
Strangers with Candy '06
Broken English '07
The Ten '07
John Adams '08
Tropic Thunder '08
Megamind '10 (V)
Your Highness '11
Wanderlust '12
The Girl on the Train '16
The LEGO Ninjago Movie '17 (V)
On the Basis of Sex '18
The Spy Who Dumped Me '18
Lady and the Tramp '19

Ernest Thesiger (1879-1961)
The Old Dark House '32
The Ghoul '34
The Bride of Frankenstein '35
Henry V '44
A Christmas Carol '51
The Robe '53
Quentin Durward '55
Value for Money '55
Who Done It? '56

Londale Theus
Supernova '09
Dreams and Shadows '10

David Thewlis (1963-)
The Life and Adventures of Nicholas Nickleby '81
Life Is Sweet '90
Naked '93
Black Beauty '94
Restoration '94
Total Eclipse '95
Dragonheart '96
The Island of Dr. Moreau '96
James and the Giant Peach '96 (V)
The Big Lebowski '97
Seven Years in Tibet '97
Besieged '98
Gangster No. 1 '00
The Miracle Maker: The Story of Jesus '00 (V)
Dinotopia '02
Timeline '03
Harry Potter and the Prisoner of Azkaban '04
Kingdom of Heaven '05
The New World '05
Basic Instinct 2 '06
The Omen '06
Harry Potter and the Order of the Phoenix '07
The Boy in the Striped Pajamas '08
Harry Potter and the Half-Blood Prince '09
Harry Potter and the Deathly Hallows, Part 1 '10
London Boulevard '10
Mr. Nice '10
Anonymous '11
Harry Potter and the Deathly Hallows, Part 2 '11
The Lady '11
War Horse '11
The Fifth Estate '13
RED 2 '13
Stonehearst Asylum '13
The Zero Theorem '13

Queen and Country '14
The Theory of Everything '14
Veronika Decides to Die '15
Anomalisa '16
Regression '16
The Mercy '19

Jack Thibeau (1946-)
Apocalypse Now '79
Escape from Alcatraz '79
Ms. 45 '81
Sudden Impact '83
Lethal Weapon '87

Debi Thibeault
Galactic Gigolo '87
Psychos in Love '87
Cemetery High '89

Alan Thicke (1947-2016)
Scene of the Crime '85
And You Thought Your Parents Were Weird! '91 (V)
Stepmonster '92
The Great American Sex Scandal '94
Demolition High '95
Open Season '95
The Growing Pains Movie '00
Carolina '03
Hollywood North '03
Growing Pains: Return of the Seavers '04
National Lampoon Presents RoboDoc '08
The Goods: Live Hard, Sell Hard '09

Max Thieriot (1988-)
Catch That Kid '04
The Pacifier '05
The Astronaut Farmer '07
Nancy Drew '07
Jumper '08
Kit Kittredge: An American Girl '08
Chloe '09
The Family Tree '10
My Soul to Take '10
House at the End of the Street '12

Mélanie Thierry (1981-)
The Legend of 1900 '98
Twisted Souls '05
Chrysalis '07
Babylon A.D. '08
The Princess of Montpensier '10
Unforgivable '11
The Zero Theorem '13
A Perfect Day '16

Tiffani(-Amber) Thiessen (1974-)
A Killer Among Friends '92
Son-in-Law '93
From Dusk Till Dawn 2: Texas Blood Money '98
Love Stinks '99
Speedway Junky '99
The Ladies Man '00
Shriek If You Know What I Did Last Friday the 13th '00
Hollywood Ending '02
Pandemic '07
Cyborg Soldier '08
Northpole '14

Kevin Thigpen
Just Another Girl on the I.R.T. '93
Tar '97

Lynne Thigpen (1948-2003)
Godspell '73
The Warriors '79
Streets of Fire '84
Lean on Me '89
Impulse '90
Separate but Equal '91
Article 99 '92
Bob Roberts '92
Naked in New York '93
Just Cause '94
The Paper '94
The Boys Next Door '96
Bicentennial Man '99
The Insider '99

Random Hearts '99
Shaft '00
Trial by Media '00
Novocaine '01
Anger Management '03

Chief Ted Thin Elk (1919-97)
Thunderheart '92
Walking Thunder '94

Roy Thinnes (1938-)
Journey to the Far Side of the Sun '69
The Horror at 37,000 Feet '73
The Norliss Tapes '73
Satan's School for Girls '73
Airport '75 '75
The Hindenburg '75
Rush Week '88
Robin Cook's Terminal '96
Bar Hopping '00

Olivia Thirlby (1986-)
Juno '07
The Secret '07
Snow Angels '07
Uncertainty '08
The Wackness '08
The Answer Man '09
Breaking Upwards '09
New York, I Love You '09
What Goes Up '09
The Darkest Hour '11
No Strings Attached '11
Being Flynn '12
Dredd '12
Nobody Walks '12
5 to 7 '15
Just Before I Go '15
The Wedding Ringer '15

Victorie Thivisol (1991-)
Ponette '95
Chocolat '00

Alex Thomas
The Players Club '98
The Wash '01

Betty Thomas (1948-)
Jackson County Jail '76
Homework '82
Troop Beverly Hills '89

B.J. Thomas
Jory '72
Jake's Corner '08

Damien Thomas (1942-)
Twins of Evil '71
The Message '77
Shogun '80

Danny Thomas (1914-91)
The Unfinished Dance '47
Call Me Mister '51
I'll See You in My Dreams '51
The Jazz Singer '52
Journey Back to Oz '71 (V)

Dave Thomas (1949-)
Stripes '81
Strange Brew '83
Sesame Street Presents: Follow That Bird '85
Love at Stake '87
Moving '88
Cold Sweat '93
Coneheads '93
Beethoven's 5th '03
Brother Bear '03 (V)
Love on the Side '04
White Coats '04
Brother Bear 2 '06 (V)

David Jean Thomas
The Drone Virus '04
Sister's Keeper '07

Eddie Kaye Thomas (1980-)
American Pie '99
Black and White '99
The Rage: Carrie 2 '99
More Dogs Than Bones '00
American Pie 2 '01
Freddy Got Fingered '01
Stolen Summer '02
Taboo '02
Winter Break '02
American Wedding '03

Harold and Kumar Go to White Castle '04
Dirty Love '05
Blind Dating '06
Wasted '06
Nature of the Beast '07
Harold & Kumar Escape from Guantanamo Bay '08
Venus and Vegas '10
American Reunion '12
Petunia '13

Frank M. Thomas, Sr. (1889-1989)
Charlie Chan in Egypt '35
Mummy's Boys '36
Breakfast for Two '37
A Man to Remember '38

Frankie Thomas, Jr. (1921-2006)
Tim Tyler's Luck '37
Boys Town '38
Nancy Drew-Detective '38
Angels Wash Their Faces '39
Nancy Drew, Reporter '39
Nancy Drew-Trouble Shooter '39
The Major and the Minor '42

Gareth Thomas
Super Bitch '73
Made in Romania '10

Heather Thomas (1957-)
Zapped! '82
Cyclone '87
Ford: The Man & the Machine '87
The Dirty Dozen: The Fatal Mission '88
Red Blooded American Girl '90
My Giant '98

Henry Thomas (1971-)
Raggedy Man '81
E.T.: The Extra-Terrestrial '82
Cloak & Dagger '84
Murder One '88
Valmont '89
Psycho 4: The Beginning '90
A Taste for Killing '92
Fire in the Sky '93
Curse of the Starving Class '94
Legends of the Fall '94
Indictment: The McMartin Trial '95
Riders of the Purple Sage '96
Bombshell '97
Hijacking Hollywood '97
Niagara, Niagara '97
Suicide Kings '97
Moby Dick '98
Fever '99
A Good Baby '99
All the Pretty Horses '00
Dead in the Water '01
The Quickie '01
Gangs of New York '02
I Capture the Castle '02
I'm with Lucy '02
11:14 '03
Dead Birds '04
Plain Dirty '04
Ghost Writer '07
Don't Look Up '08
Dear John '10
The Last Ride '12
Big Sur '13
Ouija: Origin of Evil '16

Jake Thomas (1990-)
A. I.: Artificial Intelligence '01
The Lizzie McGuire Movie '03
National Lampoon's Christmas Vacation 2: Cousin Eddie's Big Island Adventure '03
Aces 'n Eights '08
Betrayed at 17 '11

James Thomas (1948-)
Charlie Chan in Egypt '35
Ice Men '04
Behind the Wall '08

The Double Life of Eleanor Kendall '08
National Lampoon Presents: Endless Bummer '09
Be My Valentine '13

Jameson Thomas (1888-1939)
The Farmer's Wife '28
Piccadilly '29
Night Birds '31
No More Orchids '32
Three Wise Girls '32
Brief Moment '33
Beggars in Ermine '34
Jane Eyre '34

Jay Thomas (1948-)
C.H.U.D. '84
Straight Talk '92
Mr. Holland's Opus '95
A Smile Like Yours '96
Killing Mr. Griffin '97
Trial by Media '00
Dragonfly '02
The Santa Clause 2 '02
Disney's Teacher's Pet '04 (V)
The Santa Clause 3: The Escape Clause '06 (C)
The Pool Boys '10

Jeffrey Thomas
Forgotten Silver '96 (N)
Adrift '18

Jonathan Taylor Thomas (1981-)
The Lion King '94 (V)
Pom Poko '94 (V)
Man of the House '95
Tom and Huck '95
The Adventures of Pinocchio '96
Wild America '97
I'll Be Home for Christmas '98
Speedway Junky '99

Khleo Thomas (1989-)
Baadasssss! '03
Holes '03
Walking Tall '04
Dirty '05
Roll Bounce '05

Larry Thomas
Postal '07
Not Another B Movie '10

Lyn Thomas (1929-2004)
Space Master X-7 '58
Noose for a Gunman '60
Three Came to Kill '61

Marcus Thomas
Cowboy Up '00
Drowning Mona '00
Noel '04
Bigger Than the Sky '05
The Gravedancers '06
You Kill Me '07

Marlo Thomas (1937-)
Held Hostage '91
The Real Blonde '97
Playing Mona Lisa '00
Deceit '04
LOL '12

Melissa Thomas
Brides of Christ '91
Swimming Upstream '03

Michelle Rene Thomas (1970-)
Coneheads '93
Dazed and Confused '93
Major League 2 '94
The Last Word '95
The Last Don '97
The Last Don 2 '98
National Lampoon's Van Wilder '02

Patrick Thomas
Eddie Presley '92
The Witness '99

Philip Michael Thomas (1949-)
Stigma '73
Homeboy '75
Mr. Ricco '75
Streetfight '75
Fist '76
Sparkle '76
The Beasts Are On the Streets '78
Miami Vice '84

Richard Thomas (1951-)
Winning '69
Homecoming: A Christmas Story '71
The Todd Killings '71
September 30, 1955 '77
All Quiet on the Western Front '79
Roots: The Next Generation '79
Battle Beyond the Stars '80
Berlin Tunnel 21 '81
Hobson's Choice '83
Andy and the Airwave Rangers '89
Stephen King's It '90
Mission of the Shark '91
Stalking Laura '93
The Christmas Box '95
Flood: A River's Rampage '97
Big and Hairy '98
The Million Dollar Kid '99
Wonder Boys '00
Annie's Point '05
Taking Woodstock '09

Robin Thomas (1949-)
About Last Night. . . '86
Summer School '87
From the Dead of Night '89
Amityville Dollhouse '96
Star Maps '97
Halloweentown '98
Halloweentown 2: Kalabar's Revenge '01
The Banger Sisters '02
Clockstoppers '02
Missing Brendan '03

Ron Thomas
The Big Bet '85
Night Screams '87

Ross Thomas (1981-)
The Cutting Edge: Going for the Gold '05
American Pie Presents: The Naked Mile '06
Shelter '07
Soul Surfer '11

Rufus Thomas (1917-2001)
Mystery Train '89
Cookie's Fortune '99

Sarah Megan Thomas
Backwards '12
Equity '16

Sean Patrick Thomas (1970-)
Cruel Intentions '98
Dracula 2000 '00
Save the Last Dance '01
Barbershop '02
Halloween: Resurrection '02
Barbershop 2: Back in Business '04
A Raisin in the Sun '08
Barbershop: The Next Cut '16

Sian Thomas (1953-)
The Wedding Gift '93
A Mind to Murder '96
Half Broken Things '07

C.J. Thomason
Brotherhood 2: The Young Warlocks '01
Aftermath '12

Marsha Thomason (1976-)
Black Knight '01
Pure '02
The Haunted Mansion '03
My Baby's Daddy '04
The Nickel Children '05
Caffeine '06
Into the Blue 2: The Reef '09

William Thomason
Test Tube Babies '48
The Devil's Sleep '51

Florence Thomassin (1966-)
Beaumarchais the Scoundrel '96
Cold Showers '05
Mesrine: Part 1-Killer Instinct '08

Tim Thomerson (1946-)
A Wedding '78
Carny '80
Fade to Black '80
Jekyll & Hyde. . . Together Again '82
Some Kind of Hero '82
Metalstorm: The Destruction of Jared Syn '83
Uncommon Valor '83
Rhinestone '84
Trancers '84
Zone Troopers '84
Volunteers '85
Iron Eagle '86
Glory Years '87
Near Dark '87
Cherry 2000 '88
The Wrong Guys '88
Who's Harry Crumb? '89
Air America '90
Dollman '90
Trancers 2: The Return of Jack Deth '90
Vietnam, Texas '90
Bad Channels '92
Eddie Presley '92
The Harvest '92
Prime Time Murder '92
Trancers 3: Deth Lives '92
Die Watching '93
Dollman vs Demonic Toys '93
Nemesis '93
Trancers 4: Jack of Swords '93
The Cisco Kid '94
Trancers 5: Sudden Deth '94
When Time Expires '97
Fear and Loathing in Las Vegas '98
The Crimson Code '99
Unseen Evil '99
Gangland '00
Submerged '00
The Devil's Prey '01
Gale Force '01
They Crawl '01
Shoot or Be Shot '02
Final Approach '04
Bottoms Up '06
Christmas Do-Over '06
Forget About It '06
Left in Darkness '06
The Strange Case of Dr. Jekyll and Mr. Hyde '06
Wicked Lake '08
Abandoned '10

Al Thompson
A Season on the Brink '02
Love Don't Cost a Thing '03

Anna Thompson (1953-)
See Anna Thomson

Bill Thompson (1913-71)
Peter Pan '53 (V)
Lady and the Tramp '55 (V)
The Aristocats '70 (V)

Bobb'e J. Thompson (1996-)
Snow '04
Columbus Day '08
Of Boys and Men '08
Role Models '08
Cloudy with a Chance of Meatballs '09 (V)
Snowmen '10

Brian Thompson (1959-)
Fright Night 2 '88
Nightwish '89
Doctor Mordrid: Master of the Unknown '90
Lionheart '90
Moon 44 '90
Hired to Kill '91
Rage and Honor '92
Dragonheart '96
Mortal Kombat 2: Annihilation '97
Perfect Target '98
Epoch '00
Jason and the Argonauts '00
Epoch: Evolution '03
Dragonquest '09

Charles P. Thompson
Teenage Caveman '58
Hot Rods to Hell '67

Christopher Thompson (1966-)
The Count of Monte Cristo '99
La Buche '00
The Luzhin Defence '00
Change of Plans '09

Elizabeth Thompson
The Car '77
Metropolitan '90

Emma Thompson (1959-)
Fortunes of War '87
Henry V '89
Look Back in Anger '89
The Tall Guy '89
Impromptu '90
Dead Again '91
Howard's End '92
Peter's Friends '92
In the Name of the Father '93
Much Ado about Nothing '93
My Father the Hero '93 (C)
The Remains of the Day '93
Junior '94
Carrington '95
Sense and Sensibility '95
The Winter Guest '97
Primary Colors '98
Maybe Baby '99
Wit '01
Treasure Planet '02 (V)
Angels in America '03
Love Actually '03
Harry Potter and the Prisoner of Azkaban '04
Imagining Argentina '04
Nanny McPhee '06
Stranger Than Fiction '06
Harry Potter and the Order of the Phoenix '07
Brideshead Revisited '08
Last Chance Harvey '08
An Education '09
Pirate Radio '09
Nanny McPhee Returns '10
Harry Potter and the Deathly Hallows, Part 2 '11
Brave '12 (V)
Men in Black 3 '12
Beautiful Creatures '13
The Love Punch '13
Saving Mr. Banks '13
Burnt '15
Effie Gray '15
A Walk in the Woods '15
Bridget Jones's Baby '16
The Meyerowitz Stories (New and Selected) '17
The Children Act '18
Johnny English Strikes Again '18
Last Christmas '19
Late Night '19

Fred Dalton Thompson (1942-)
Marie '85
No Way Out '87
Feds '88
Days of Thunder '90
Die Hard 2: Die Harder '90
The Hunt for Red October '90
Cape Fear '91
Class Action '91
Curly Sue '91
Aces: Iron Eagle 3 '92
Thunderheart '92
White Sands '92 (C)
Barbarians at the Gate '93
Born Yesterday '93
In the Line of Fire '93
Baby's Day Out '94
Racing Stripes '05 (V)
Looking for Comedy in the Muslim World '06
Bury My Heart at Wounded Knee '07
Alleged '10
Secretariat '10
The Last Ride '12

Greg Thompson
Ghost of the Needle '03
Dark Remains '05

Hugh Thompson
Recipe for Revenge '98
The Christmas Shoes '02
The Christmas Blessing '05
The Memory Keeper's Daughter '08

Jack Thompson (1940-)
Outback '71
The Chant of Jimmie Blacksmith '78
Breaker Morant '80
Bad Blood '81
The Club '81
The Man from Snowy River '82
Merry Christmas, Mr. Lawrence '83
Flesh and Blood '85
Trouble in Paradise '88
Deception '92
Resistance '92
Wind '92
A Far Off Place '93
The Sum of Us '94
Excess Baggage '96
Last Dance '96
The Thorn Birds: The Missing Years '96
Midnight in the Garden of Good and Evil '97
Under the Lighthouse Dancing '97
Original Sin '01
Rodgers & Hammerstein's South Pacific '01
Star Wars: Episode 2-Attack of the Clones '02
The Assassination of Richard Nixon '05
Feed '05
The Good German '06
December Boys '07
Australia '08
Leatherheads '08
Mao's Last Dancer '09
Don't Be Afraid of the Dark '11
Around the Block '13
The Light Between Oceans '16

Jody Thompson (1976-)
In Her Mother's Footsteps '06
The Secrets of Comfort House '06
Alien Trespass '09
Barricade '12

Kay Thompson (1903-98)
Manhattan Merry-Go-Round '37
Funny Face '57

Kenan Thompson (1978-)
D2: The Mighty Ducks '94
Heavyweights '94
Good Burger '97
The Adventures of Rocky & Bullwinkle '00
Love Don't Cost a Thing '03
My Boss's Daughter '03
Barbershop 2: Back in Business '04
Fat Albert '04
Snakes on a Plane '06
Space Chimps '08 (V)
Stan Helsing '09
The Smurfs '11 (V)
The Magic of Belle Isle '12
Rock Dog '17
Wonder Park '19

Kevin Thompson
Spaced Invaders '90
Battle Planet '08

Lea Thompson (1961-)
All the Right Moves '83
Jaws 3 '83
Red Dawn '84
Back to the Future '85
Howard the Duck '86
SpaceCamp '86
Some Kind of Wonderful '87
Casual Sex? '88
Going Undercover '88
Back to the Future, Part 2 '89
Back to the Future, Part 3 '90
Article 99 '92
The Beverly Hillbillies '93
Dennis the Menace '93
The Substitute Wife '94
California Dreaming '07
A Life Interrupted '07
The Christmas Clause '08
Exit Speed '08
Final Approach '08
Senior Skip Day '08
Spy School '08
Fatal Secrets '09
Splinterheads '09
Adventures of a Teenage Dragonslayer '10
Game of Your Life '11
J. Edgar '11
Mayor Cupcake '11
The Trouble with the Truth '11
Love at the Christmas Table '12
Thin Ice '12
Left Behind '14
Ping Pong Summer '14
The Dog Lover '16
Little Women '18

Marshall Thompson (1925-92)
The Purple Heart '44
The Clock '45
They Were Expendable '45
The Secret Heart '46
The Romance of Rosy Ridge '47
Words and Music '48
Battleground '49
The Devil's Doorway '50
Dial 1119 '50
Mystery Street '50
Stars in My Crown '50 (N)
The Tall Target '51
The Caddy '53
Cult of the Cobra '55
Good Morning, Miss Dove '55
To Hell and Back '55
East of Kilimanjaro '57
Fiend without a Face '58
It! The Terror from Beyond Space '58
First Man into Space '59
No Man Is an Island '62
Clarence, the Cross-eyed Lion '65
George! '70
The Turning Point '77
Bog '84

Miles Thompson
Me and You and Everyone We Know '05
Foreign Exchange '08

Natalie Thompson (1921-2000)
Ringside Maisie '41
The Vanishing Virginian '41

Peter Thompson (1920-2001)
The Wistful Widow of Wagon Gap '47
The Happy Years '50
Santa Fe '51

Reece Thompson (1988-)
Talking to Heaven '02
Dreamcatcher '03
National Lampoon's Holiday Reunion '03
The Sandlot 2 '05
Rocket Science '07
Afterwards '08
Assassination of a High School President '08
Bloodworth '10
Ceremony '10
Daydream Nation '10

Rex Thompson (1942-)
Young Bess '53
All Mine to Give '56

The Eddy Duchin Story *'56*
The King and I *'56*

Sada Thompson (1929-2011)
Desperate Characters *'71*
Our Town *'77*
The Adventures of Huckleberry Finn *'85*
Queen *'93*
Indictment: The McMartin Trial *'95*

Sarah Thompson (1979-)
Cruel Intentions 2 *'99*
The Pink Conspiracy *'07*
Babysitter Wanted *'08*
A Christmas Proposal *'08*
Dear Me: A Blogger's Tale *'08*
Break *'09*
A Nanny for Christmas *'10*
12 Christmas Wishes For My Dog *'11*

Scott Thompson (1959-)
Kids in the Hall: Brain Candy *'96*
Armistead Maupin's More Tales of the City *'97 (C)*
Hijacking Hollywood *'97*
Loser *'00*
Tart *'01*
My Baby's Daddy *'04*
Prom Queen *'04*
The Pacifier *'05*

Scottie Thompson (1981-)
Skyline *'10*
Lake Effects *'12*
The Lookalike *'14*
Before I Wake *'15*

Shawn Thompson
Hairspray *'88*
Future Fear *'97*
Bram Stoker's Shadowbuilder *'98*

Sophie Thompson
Four Weddings and a Funeral *'94*
Persuasion *'95*
Emma *'96*
Dancing at Lughnasa *'98*
Relative Values *'99*
Gosford Park *'01*
A Harlot's Progress *'06*
A Room With a View *'08*
Eat, Pray, Love *'10*

Susanna Thompson (1958-)
Little Giants *'94*
America's Dream *'95*
Ghosts of Mississippi *'96*
Random Hearts *'99*
High Noon *'00*
Dragonfly *'02*
The Ballad of Jack and Rose *'05*

Tessa Thompson (1983-)
Cracker: Brotherly Love *'95*
The Initiation of Sarah *'06*
When a Stranger Calls *'06*
Make It Happen *'08*
Everyday Black Man *'10*
For Colored Girls *'10*
Dear White People *'14*
Selma *'14*
Creed *'15*
War on Everyone *'17*
Creed II *'18*
Furlough *'18*
Sorry to Bother You *'18*
Lady and the Tramp *'19*
Men in Black: International *'19*

Victoria Thompson (1946-)
Harrad Experiment *'73*
Harrad Summer *'74*

Wesley Thompson
Smiling Fish & Goat on Fire *'99*
Infestation *'09*

Tracie Thoms (1975-)
Rent *'05*
The Devil Wears Prada *'06*
Death Proof *'07*
Sex and Breakfast *'07*
Looper *'12*
Meeting Evil *'12*

Ulrich Thomsen (1963-)
The Inheritance *'76*
Angel of the Night *'98*
The Celebration *'98*
The World Is Not Enough *'99*
The Weight of Water *'00*
Flickering Lights *'01*
Killing Me Softly *'01*
Mostly Martha *'01*
Max *'02*
Brothers *'04*
Adam's Apples *'05*
Kingdom of Heaven *'05*
The Company *'07*
Hitman *'07*
Opium: Diary of a Madwoman *'07*
The Broken *'08*
The International *'09*
Centurion *'10*
In a Better World *'10*
Season of the Witch *'10*
The Silence *'10*
The Thing *'11*
The Notebook *'13*
Mortdecai *'15*

Sally Thomsett (1950-)
The Railway Children *'70*
Straw Dogs *'72*

Anna Thomson (1953-)
Unforgiven *'92*
The Crow *'93*
Angela *'94*
Angus *'95*
Other Voices, Other Rooms *'95*
Outside the Law *'95*
Drunks *'96*
I Shot Andy Warhol *'96*
Jaded *'96*
Cafe Society *'97*
Fiona *'98*
Six Ways to Sunday *'99*
Water Drops on Burning Rocks *'99*
Intern *'00*

Cassi Thomson
Cop Dog *'08*
Left Behind *'14*

Erik Thomson (1967-)
The Alice *'04*
Somersault *'04*
The Black Balloon *'09*
The Boys Are Back *'09*

Gordon Thomson (1945-)
The Fiance *'96*
Ladies of the House *'08*

Helen Thomson
Bloodmoon *'90*
Nowhere to Land *'00*

Kenneth Thomson (1899-1967)
White Gold *'28*
Broadway Melody *'29*
Say It With Songs *'29*
Fast Life *'32*
Held for Murder *'32*
Movie Crazy *'32*
The Little Giant *'33*

Kim Thomson (1960-)
The Tall Guy *'89*
Hands of a Murderer *'90*
Jekyll and Hyde *'90*
Murder 101 *'91*
The Princess Diaries 2: Royal Engagement *'04*

R.H. Thomson (1947-)
Ticket to Heaven *'81*
Ford: The Man & the Machine *'87*
The Quarrel *'93*
Bone Daddy *'97*
The Twilight of the Ice Nymphs *'97*
P.T. Barnum *'99*
Bugs *'03*
Population 436 *'06*
Who Loves the Sun *'06*
Chloe *'09*
Clara *'19*

Scott Thomson (1957-)
Fast Times at Ridgemont High *'82*
Ghoulies *'84*
Blast from the Past *'98*

Jon Mikl Thor
Rock 'n' Roll Nightmare *'85*
Zombie Nightmare *'86*

Jim Thorburn
Deep Evil *'04*
The Deal *'05*
The Last Trimester *'06*
Merlin and the Book of Beasts *'09*

Kelly Thordsen (1917-78)
The Fearmakers *'58*
Sweet Bird of Youth *'62*
The Misadventures of Merlin Jones *'63*
Shenandoah *'65*
The Ugly Dachshund *'65*
Boy, Did I Get a Wrong Number! *'66*
Texas Across the River *'66*
Blackbeard's Ghost *'67*
Good Times *'67*
The Boatniks *'70*
Now You See Him, Now You Don't *'72*
Charley and the Angel *'73*
The Parallax View *'74*

Frankie Thorn (1964-)
Bad Lieutenant *'92*
Liquid Dreams *'92*

Bill Thornbury (1952-)
Phantasm *'79*
Phantasm 3: Lord of the Dead *'94*
Phantasm 4: Oblivion *'98*

Sybil Thorndike (1882-1976)
Nine Days a Queen *'36*
Major Barbara *'41*
Nicholas Nickleby *'46*
The Forbidden Street *'49*
Stage Fright *'50*
The Lady With the Lamp *'51*
The Prince and the Showgirl *'57*

Angela Thorne (1939-)
Oh! What a Lovely War *'69*
The Lady's Not for Burning *'87*

Bella Thorne (1997-)
Blended *'14*
Alvin and the Chipmunks: Road Chip *'15*
The DUFF *'15*
Boo! A Madea Halloween *'16*
Amityville: The Awakening *'17*
The Babysitter *'17*
Midnight Sun *'18*
Infamous *'20*

Callie (Calliope) Thorne (1969-)
Giving It Up *'99*
Wirey Spindell *'99*
Double Parked *'00*
Homicide: The Movie *'00*
Whipped *'00*
Revolution #9 *'01*
Sidewalks of New York *'01*
Analyze That *'02*
Washington Heights *'02*
Four and a Half Women *'05*
Delirious *'06*
David & Layla *'07*
Watching the Detectives *'07*
Nice Guy Johnny *'10*

Dyanne Thorne (1936-2020)
Point of Terror *'71*
Wham-Bam, Thank You Spaceman *'75*
Ilsa, Harem Keeper of the Oil Sheiks *'76*
Ilsa, the Wicked Warden *'78*

William Thorne
The Gold Racket *'37*
Silent Night, Deadly Night 5: The Toymaker *'91*

Courtney Thorne-Smith (1967-)
Lucas *'86*
Revenge of the Nerds 2: Nerds in Paradise *'87*
Summer School *'87*
Side Out *'90*
Chairman of the Board *'97*
The Lovemaster *'97*
Sorority Wars *'09*

Billy Bob Thornton (1955-)
Chopper Chicks in Zombietown *'91*
One False Move *'91*
The Ghost Brigade *'93*
Indecent Proposal *'93*
Tombstone *'93*
Floundering *'94*
On Deadly Ground *'94*
Dead Man *'95*
Sling Blade *'96*
The Winner *'96*
An Alan Smithee Film: Burn, Hollywood, Burn *'97 (C)*
The Apostle *'97*
A Gun, a Car, a Blonde *'97*
Homegrown *'97*
U-Turn *'97*
Armageddon *'98*
Primary Colors *'98*
Princess Mononoke *'98 (V)*
A Simple Plan *'98*
Daddy & Them *'99*
Pushing Tin *'99*
South of Heaven, West of Hell *'00*
Bandits *'01*
The Man Who Wasn't There *'01*
Monster's Ball *'01*
The Badge *'02*
Waking Up in Reno *'02*
Bad Santa *'03*
Intolerable Cruelty *'03*
Levity *'03*
Love Actually *'03*
The Alamo *'04*
Friday Night Lights *'04*
The Bad News Bears *'05*
The Ice Harvest *'05*
School for Scoundrels *'06*
The Astronaut Farmer *'07*
Mr. Woodcock *'07*
Eagle Eye *'08*
The Informers *'09*
The Smell of Success *'09*
Faster *'10*
Puss in Boots *'11 (V)*
The Baytown Outlaws *'12*
Jayne Mansfield's Car *'13*
Parkland *'13*
The Judge *'14*
Cut Bank *'15*
Our Brand is Crisis *'15*
Bad Santa 2 *'16*
Whiskey Tango Foxtrot *'16*
London Fields *'18*

David Thornton (1953-)
Diamond Run *'90*
Unhook the Stars *'96*
Home Alone 3 *'97*
Office Killer *'97*
She's So Lovely *'97*
High Art *'98*
Hush *'98*
The Last Days of Disco *'98*
Dead Dog *'00*
John Q *'02*
100 Mile Rule *'02*
Swept Away *'02*
XX/XY *'02*
Alpha Dog *'06*
My Sister's Keeper *'09*

Noley Thornton (1983-)
Danielle Steel's Fine Things *'90*
Heidi *'93*

Sigrid Thornton (1959-)
The Night After Halloween *'79*
The Man from Snowy River *'82*
1915 *'82*
Nevil Shute's The Far Country *'85*
Return to Snowy River *'88*
Over the Hill *'93*
Inspector Gadget 2 *'02*

Sven-Ole Thorsen (1944-)
Abraxas: Guardian of the Universe *'90*
Dragon: The Bruce Lee Story *'93*
Mallrats *'95*
The Viking Sagas *'95*
Kull the Conqueror *'97*
Foolish *'99*
Gladiator *'00*
The Sum of All Fears *'02*
In Enemy Hands *'04*

Linda Thorson (1947-)
Curtains *'83*
Walls of Glass *'85*
The Other Sister *'98*
Half Past Dead *'02*
Straight into Darkness *'04*
The Wives He Forgot *'06*

Russ Thorson (1906-82)
Tarawa Beachhead *'58*
36 Hours *'64*
My Blood Runs Cold *'65*

Cyrille Thouvenin (1976-)
Confusion of Genders *'00*
Dangerous Liaisons *'03*

David Threlfall (1953-)
Kiss of Death *'77*
A Murder of Quality *'90*
The Russia House *'90*
Diana: Her True Story *'93*
Mary, Mother of Jesus *'99*
Conspiracy *'01*
Master and Commander: The Far Side of the World *'03*
The Queen's Sister *'05*
Elizabeth: The Golden Age *'07*
Nowhere Boy *'09*

Frank Thring, Jr. (1926-94)
Mad Max: Beyond Thunderdome *'85*
Howling 3: The Marsupials *'87*

Michelle Thrush
Skins *'02*
Jimmy P. *'13*

Ingrid Thulin (1926-2003)
Brink of Life *'57*
Wild Strawberries *'57*
The Magician *'58*
The Four Horsemen of the Apocalypse *'62*
The Winter Light *'62*
The Silence *'63*
La Guerre Est Finie *'66*
Hour of the Wolf *'68*
The Damned *'69*
The Rite *'69*
Short Night of Glass Dolls *'71*
Cries and Whispers *'72*
The Cassandra Crossing *'76*
Moses *'76*

Chief Thundercloud (1899-1955)
Annie Oakley *'35*
Rustlers of Red Dog *'35*
Renegade Girl *'46*
Call of the Forest *'49*
Ambush *'50*

Nick Thune
Urge *'16*
Mr. Roosevelt *'17*

Bill (Billy) Thurman (1920-95)
Curse of the Swamp Creature *'66*
Night Fright *'67*
It's Alive! *'68*
The Last Picture Show *'71*
Creature from Black Lake *'76*
Slumber Party *'57 '76*
Mountaintop Motel Massacre *'86*

Dechen Thurman (1973-)
I Think I Do *'97*
Hamlet *'00*

Uma Thurman (1970-)
Kiss Daddy Goodnight *'87*
Dangerous Liaisons *'88*
Johnny Be Good *'88*
The Adventures of Baron Munchausen *'89*
Henry & June *'90*
Where the Heart Is *'90*
Robin Hood *'91*
Final Analysis *'92*
Jennifer 8 *'92*
Mad Dog and Glory *'93*
Even Cowgirls Get the Blues *'94*
Pulp Fiction *'94*
A Month by the Lake *'95*
Beautiful Girls *'96*
The Truth about Cats and Dogs *'96*
Batman and Robin *'97*
Gattaca *'97*
Les Miserables *'97*
The Avengers *'98*
Sweet and Lowdown *'99*
The Golden Bowl *'00*
Vatel *'00*
Chelsea Walls *'01*
Tape *'01*
Hysterical Blindness *'02*
Kill Bill Vol. 1 *'03*
Paycheck *'03*
Kill Bill Vol. 2 *'04*
Be Cool *'05*
Prime *'05*
The Producers *'05*
My Super Ex-Girlfriend *'06*
The Life Before Her Eyes *'07*
The Accidental Husband *'08*
My Zinc Bed *'08*
Motherhood *'09*
Ceremony *'10*
Percy Jackson & The Olympians: The Lightning Thief *'10*
Bel Ami *'12*
Playing for Keeps *'12*
Movie 43 *'13*
Nymphomaniac, Volume 1 *'13*
Burnt *'15*
Down a Dark Hall *'18*
The House That Jack Built *'18*

Sophie Thursfield
Oranges Are Not the Only Fruit *'89*
Sister My Sister *'94*

Nick Thurston
Reviving Ophelia *'10*
White Irish Drinkers *'10*

Brenton Thwaites (1989-)
Blue Lagoon: The Awakening *'12*
The Giver *'14*
Maleficent *'14*
Oculus *'14*
The Signal *'14*
Son of a Gun *'14*
Gods of Egypt *'16*

Greta Thyssen (1933-)
Terror Is a Man *'59*
Three Blondes in His Life *'61*
Journey to the Seventh Planet *'62*

Lung Ti (1946-)
Have Sword, Will Travel *'69*
The Heroic Ones *'70*
The Delightful Forest *'72*
Black Magic *'06*
The Magic Blade *'08*

Ben Tibber (1990-)
A Christmas Carol *'99*
I Am David *'04*

Gerard Tichy (1920-92)
Gladiators 7 *'62*
The Blancheville Monster *'63*
Doctor Zhivago *'65*
Four Dollars of Revenge *'66*
Hatchet for the Honeymoon *'70*
The Hanging Woman *'72*
Ricco *'74*

Nancy Ticotin
Ransom '96
The Tavern '00

Rachel Ticotin (1958-)
King of the Gypsies '78
Fort Apache, the Bronx '81
Critical Condition '86
When the Bough Breaks '86
Total Recall '90
F/X 2: The Deadly Art of Illusion '91
One Good Cop '91
Spies, Lies and Naked Thighs '91
Where the Day Takes You '92
Falling Down '93
Don Juan DeMarco '94
Natural Born Killers '94
Steal Big, Steal Little '95
Turbulence '96
Con Air '97
First Time Felon '97
Aftershock: Earthquake in New York '99
Malicious Intent '99
Forever Together '00
Full Disclosure '00
Desert Saints '01
Something's Gotta Give '03
Man on Fire '04
The Sisterhood of the Traveling Pants '05
The Burning Plain '08
The Eye '08

Max Tidof
Burning Life '94
The Harmonists '99

Andrea Tidona
Best of Youth '03
The Listening '06

Dov Tiefenbach (1981-)
Jason X '01
Detention '03

Fernando Tielve
The Devil's Backbone '01
Unmade Beds '09

Feng Tien
Sword Masters: Brothers Five '70
King Boxer '72

James Tien
Chinese Connection '73
Half a Loaf of Kung Fu '78

Ni Tien (1948-)
Sword Masters: The Battle Wizard '77
Corpse Mania '81
Black Magic '06
The Magic Blade '08

Andrew Tiernan (1965-)
Edward II '92
The Guilty '92
Playing God '96
Face '97
The Scarlet Tunic '97
Horatio Hornblower '99
The Criminal '00
Red Siren '02
A Waste of Shame '05
300 '07
Murderland '09
Dead Cert '10
Mr. Nice '10
300: Rise of an Empire '13

Patricia Tiernan
Battle Circus '53
Zero Hour! '57

Brigid Tierney
The Paperboy '94
Affliction '97
Twist '03

Gene Tierney (1920-91)
Hudson's Bay '40
Return of Frank James '40
Sundown '41
Tobacco Road '41
China Girl '42
Rings on Her Fingers '42
The Shanghai Gesture '42
Son of Fury '42
Thunder Birds '42
Heaven Can Wait '43
Laura '44
Leave Her to Heaven '45
Dragonwyck '46
The Razor's Edge '46
The Ghost and Mrs. Muir '47
That Wonderful Urge '48
Whirlpool '49
Night and the City '50
Where the Sidewalk Ends '50
Close to My Heart '51
Way of a Gaucho '52
Never Let Me Go '53
Black Widow '54
The Egyptian '54
The Left Hand of God '55
Advise and Consent '62
Toys in the Attic '63
Scruples '80

Jacob Tierney (1979-)
Pin. . . '88
Josh and S.A.M. '93
The Neon Bible '95
Dead End '98
The Life Before This '99
This Is My Father '99
Poor White Trash '00
St. Urbain's Horseman '07

Lawrence Tierney (1919-2002)
The Ghost Ship '43
Back to Bataan '45
Dillinger '45
Born to Kill '47
Best of the Badmen '50
The Bushwackers '52
The Greatest Show on Earth '52
Andy Warhol's Bad '77
Midnight '81
The Prowler '81
Prizzi's Honor '85
Silver Bullet '85
Murphy's Law '86
The Offspring '87
Tough Guys Don't Dance '87
City of Hope '91
The Death Merchant '91
Eddie Presley '92
Reservoir Dogs '92
Wizards of the Demon Sword '94
Southie '98

Malcolm Tierney (1938-2014)
House of Cards '90
The Apocalypse Watch '97

Maura Tierney (1965-)
Dead Women in Lingerie '90
White Sands '92
Fly by Night '93
The Temp '93
Primal Fear '96
Liar Liar '97
Primary Colors '98
Forces of Nature '99
Instinct '99
Oxygen '99
Insomnia '02
Scotland, PA '02
Melvin Goes to Dinner '03
Welcome to Mooseport '04
Danny Roane: First Time Director '06
Diggers '06
All the Good Ones Are Married '07
Baby Mama '08
Finding Amanda '08
Semi-Pro '08
Nature Calls '12
Beautiful Boy '18

Jonathan Tiersten
Sleepaway Camp '83
Return to Sleepaway Camp '08

Tiffany (1971-)
Jetsons: The Movie '90 (V)
Mega Piranha '10
Mega Python Vs. Gatoroid '11

Angelo Tiffe
Sword of Honor '94
3 Ninjas Kick Back '94

Pamela Tiffin (1942-)
One, Two, Three '61
Summer and Smoke '61
State Fair '62
The Lively Set '64
The Hallelujah Trail '65
Harper '66
Viva Max '69

Ken Tigar (1942-)
The Betty Ford Story '87
Phantasm 2 '88
Rage '95
Hollywood Safari '96
Little Bigfoot '96
The Underground '97

Kevin Tighe (1944-)
Matewan '87
Eight Men Out '88
K-9 '89
Lost Angels '89
Road House '89
Another 48 Hrs. '90
Bright Angel '91
City of Hope '91
Newsies '92
School Ties '92
Geronimo: An American Legend '93
A Man in Uniform '93
What's Eating Gilbert Grape '93
Men of War '94
The Avenging Angel '95
In Cold Blood '96
Race the Sun '96
Winchell '98
The Big Day '99
Mumford '99
Stephen King's Rose Red '02
The Deal '05
Today You Die '05
My Bloody Valentine 3D '09

Ramon Tikaram (1967-)
Kama Sutra: A Tale of Love '96
Ruby in the Smoke '06
Wired '08

Zeffie Tilbury (1863-1950)
The Single Standard '29
Werewolf of London '35
Give Me Your Heart '36
The Grapes of Wrath '40
Tobacco Road '41

Lucas Till (1990-)
Not Like Everyone Else '06
Dance of the Dead '08
Hannah Montana: The Movie '09
The Lost & Found Family '09
All Superheroes Must Die '11
Battle: Los Angeles '11
X-Men: First Class '11
Dark Hearts '12
Crush '13
Paranoia '13
Stoker '13
The Curse of Downers Grove '15
The Disappointments Room '16
Monster Trucks '16
Sins of Our Youth '16

Nadja Tiller (1929-)
The Rough and the Smooth '59
The Burning Court '62
Tonio Kroger '65
Dead Are Alive '72
Wanted: Babysitter '75

Mel Tillis (1932-)
The Villain '79
Smokey and the Bandit 2 '80

Jennifer Tilly (1958-)
No Small Affair '84
Moving Violations '85
He's My Girl '87
High Spirits '88
The Fabulous Baker Boys '89
Far from Home '89
Let It Ride '89
Scorchers '92
The Getaway '93
Made in America '93
Bullets over Broadway '94
Bird of Prey '95
Edie & Pen '95
Embrace of the Vampire '95
Man with a Gun '95
The Pompatus of Love '95
American Strays '96
Bound '96
House Arrest '96
The Wrong Guy '96
Liar Liar '97
Music from Another Room '97
Bride of Chucky '98
Hoods '98
Relax. . . It's Just Sex! '98
The Dress Code '99
The Muse '99 (C)
Silent Witness '99
Stuart Little '99 (V)
The Crew '00
Dancing at the Blue Iguana '00
Hide and Seek '00
The Cat's Meow '01
Fast Sofa '01
Monsters, Inc. '01 (V)
The Magnificent Ambersons '02
The Haunted Mansion '03
Hollywood North '03
Jericho Mansions '03
El Padrino '04
Home on the Range '04 (V)
Love on the Side '04
Saint Ralph '04
Seed of Chucky '04 (V)
Bailey's Billion$ '05
Second Best '05
Tideland '05
The Initiation of Sarah '06
Bart Got a Room '08
The Caretaker '08
Deal '08
American Girl: Chrissa Stands Strong '09
Made in Romania '10

Meg Tilly (1960-)
One Dark Night '82
Tex '82
The Big Chill '83
Psycho 2 '83
Impulse '84
Agnes of God '85
Masquerade '88
The Girl in a Swing '89
Valmont '89
The Two Jakes '90
Leaving Normal '92
Body Snatchers '93
Primal Secrets '94
Sleep with Me '94

Charlene Tilton (1958-)
Freaky Friday '76
The Fall of the House of Usher '80
Border Shootout '90
Ragin' Cajun '90
Deadly Bet '91
Problem Child 2 '91
Center of the Web '92
Totally Blonde '01
#1 Cheerleader Camp '10

Martha Tilton (1915-2006)
Sunny '41
Swing Hostess '44
The Benny Goodman Story '55
Bereavement '10

Justin Timberlake (1981-)
Edison Force '05
Alpha Dog '06
Southland Tales '06
Black Snake Moan '07
Shrek the Third '07 (V)
The Love Guru '08
The Open Road '09
Shrek Forever After '10 (V)
The Social Network '10
Yogi Bear '10 (V)
Bad Teacher '11
Friends With Benefits '11
In Time '11
Trouble with the Curve '12
Inside Llewyn Davis '13
Runner Runner '13
Trolls '16
Wonder Wheel '17
Trolls World Tour '20

Corbin Timbrook
Forbidden Sins '99
Alien 3000 '04

Filippo Timi
Saturn in Opposition '07
The Double Hour '09
Vincere '09

Patharawarin Timkul
Bangkok Dangerous '00
The Sanctuary '09

Addison Timlin (1991-)
Derailed '05
Afterschool '08
Best Man Down '12
Odd Thomas '13
Love & Air Sex '14
That Awkward Moment '14
The Town That Dreaded Sundown '14
Little Sister '16
Fallen '17

Cali Timmins (1963-)
The Heist '96
Heaven's Fire '99

Patti Tindall
Machined '06
The Frankenstein Syndrome '10
The Graves '10

Charles 'Bud' Tingwell (1923-2009)
The Desert Rats '53
Murder She Said '61
Murder at the Gallop '63
Murder Ahoy '64
Murder Most Foul '65
Dracula, Prince of Darkness '66
Breaker Morant '80
Malcolm '86
A Cry in the Dark '88
The Castle '97
Innocence '00
Ned Kelly '03
Irresistible '06

Tinkerbell
Time of Favor '00
Eyes Wide Open '09

Gabriele Tinti (1932-91)
Journey Beneath the Desert '61
Ulysses Against the Son of Hercules '61
Cannon for Cordoba '70
Lisa and the Devil '75
Delusions of Grandeur '76
Emmanuelle in the Country '78
Emmanuelle, the Queen '79
Emmanuelle's Daughter '79
Love Camp '81
Caged Women '84

Analeigh Tipton (1988-)
Crazy, Stupid, Love. '11
Damsels in Distress '11
Warm Bodies '13
Two Night Stand '14
Mississippi Grind '15
Viral '16
All Nighter '17

Itay Tiran
The Debt '07
Lebanon '09
Demon '16

Jamie Tirelli (1945-)
Lotto Land '95
Girlfight '99
Bella '06
The Groomsmen '06
Yellow '06
Sugar '09

Ashley Tisdale (1985-)
High School Musical 2 '07
High School Musical 3: Senior Year '08
Picture This! '08
Aliens in the Attic '09
Sharpay's Fabulous Adventure '11
Scary Movie 5 '13
Amateur Night '16

Adair Tishler
Ten Inch Hero '07
American Girl: Chrissa Stands Strong '09

Jean Tissier (1896-1973)
The Murderer Lives at Number 21 '42
The Hunchback of Notre Dame '57
Please Not Now! '61

Christopher Titus (1964-)
Scar '07
Remarkable Power '08
Bad Parents '12

Chapman To (1972-)
The Cave of the Silken Web '67
Infernal Affairs 2 '03
Infernal Affairs 3 '03
The Beautiful Country '04
Six Strong Guys '04

James Toback (1944-)
Fingers '78
Black and White '99
Giving It Up '99
When Will I Be Loved '04
Never Down '06 (C)

Joel Tobeck (1971-)
Perfect Strangers '03
Little Fish '05
Eagle vs. Shark '07
Accidents Happen '09

Kenneth Tobey (1919-2002)
I Was a Male War Bride '49
The Thing '51
Angel Face '52
The Beast from 20,000 Fathoms '53
The Bigamist '53
Down Three Dark Streets '54
Davy Crockett, King of the Wild Frontier '55
It Came from Beneath the Sea '55
The Great Locomotive Chase '56
The Man in the Gray Flannel Suit '56
The Search for Bridey Murphy '56
Gunfight at the O.K. Corral '57
Wings of Eagles '57
Cry Terror! '58
40 Guns to Apache Pass '67
Missiles of October '74
The Howling '81
Strange Invaders '83
Night of the Creeps '86
Innerspace '87
Freeway '88
Gremlins 2: The New Batch '90
Desire and Hell at Sunset Motel '92
Honey, I Blew Up the Kid '92
Single White Female '92
Body Shot '93

George Tobias (1901-80)
The Hunchback of Notre Dame '39
City for Conquest '40
East of the River '40
Music in My Heart '40
Saturday's Children '40
Torrid Zone '40
The Bride Came C.O.D. '41
Out of the Fog '41
Sergeant York '41
Strawberry Blonde '41
Captains of the Clouds '42
Juke Girl '42
My Sister Eileen '42
Yankee Doodle Dandy '42
Air Force '43
Mission to Moscow '43
This Is the Army '43

Between Two Worlds '44
The Mask of Dimitrios '44
Passage to Marseilles '44
Objective, Burma! '45
Nobody Lives Forever '46
My Wild Irish Rose '47
Sinbad, the Sailor '47
The Judge Steps Out '49
The Set-Up '49
Rawhide '50
Southside 1-1000 '50
The Magic Carpet '51
The Seven Little Foys '55
Silk Stockings '57
A New Kind of Love '63

Heather Tobias (1953-)
High Hopes '88
Beautiful People '99

Oliver Tobias (1947-)
Romance of a Horsethief '71
'Tis a Pity She's a Whore '73
King Arthur, the Young Warlord '75
Young Warlord '75
The Stud '78
Arabian Adventure '79
The Big Scam '79
Mata Hari '85
Broken Lullaby '94
The Brylcreem Boys '96
Breeders '97
Darkness Falls '98
Grizzly Falls '99

Dan Tobin (1910-82)
Woman of the Year '42
Undercurrent '46
The Big Clock '48

Genevieve Tobin (1901-95)
One Hour with You '32
Perfect Understanding '33
Dark Hazard '34
Kiss and Make Up '34
The Case of the Lucky Legs '35
The Goose and the Gander '35
The Woman in Red '35
Petrified Forest '36
No Time For Comedy '40

Jason J. Tobin
Yellow '98
Better Luck Tomorrow '02
The Fast and the Furious: Tokyo Drift '06

Lawrence Tobin
Shanty Tramp '67
A Taste of Blood '67

Stephen Tobolowsky (1951-)
Keep My Grave Open '80
Nobody's Fool '86
Spaceballs '87
Mississippi Burning '88
Breaking In '89
Great Balls of Fire '89
Bird on a Wire '90
Funny About Love '90
Mirror, Mirror '90
Deadlock '91
Thelma & Louise '91
Basic Instinct '92
Hero '92
Memoirs of an Invisible Man '92
Single White Female '92
Sneakers '92
Where the Day Takes You '92
Groundhog Day '93
Josh and S.A.M. '93
Radioland Murders '94
Dr. Jekyll and Ms. Hyde '95
Murder in the First '95
The Glimmer Man '96
An Alan Smithee Film: Burn, Hollywood, Burn '97
Mr. Magoo '97
Black Dog '98
One Man's Hero '98
Bossa Nova '99
The Insider '99
Memento '00
The Prime Gig '00
Sleep Easy, Hutch Rimes '00
The Day the World Ended '01
Dean Koontz's Black River '01
The Operator '01
Adaptation '02
The Country Bears '02
Love Liza '02
Freaky Friday '03
National Security '03
Garfield: The Movie '04
Little Black Book '04
Win a Date with Tad Hamilton! '04
Failure to Launch '06
Pope Dreams '06
The Sasquatch Gang '06
Boxboarders! '07
Loveless in Los Angeles '07
Wild Hogs '07
Beethoven's Big Break '08
The Time Traveler's Wife '09
Buried '10
The Last Ride '12
Fractured '19

Brian Tochi (1963-)
Revenge of the Nerds '84
Teenage Mutant Ninja Turtles: The Movie '90 (V)
The Player '92

Erika Toda (1988-)
Death Note '06
Death Note 2: The Last Name '07
Death Note 3: L Change the World '08
Blade of the Immortal '17

Ann Todd (1909-93)
Stronger Than Desire '39
Remember the Day '41
Vacation from Marriage '45
The Paradine Case '47
Madeleine '50
The Sound Barrier '52
Time Without Pity '57
Scream of Fear '61
The Fiend '71
The Human Factor '79

Ann E. Todd (1931-2020)
Intermezzo '39
How Green Was My Valley '41
Pride of the Marines '45
Three Daring Daughters '48
Cover Up '49
The Lion Hunters '51

Beverly Todd (1946-)
Brother John '70
Clara's Heart '88
Lean on Me '89
Animal '05
Crash '05
The Bucket List '07
The Lena Baker Story '08
Taken From Me: The Tiffany Rubin Story '10

Hallie Todd (1962-)
The Lizzie McGuire Movie '03
National Lampoon's Holiday Reunion '03

James Todd (1908-68)
The Luck of the Irish '48
Trapped '49
High School Confidential '58

Kate Todd
Grizzly Rage '07
Saving God '08

Lisa Todd (1954-)
The Doll Squad '73
Blood Hook '86

Mabel Todd (1907-77)
Hollywood Hotel '37
Varsity Show '37
The Cowboy and the Lady '38
Garden of the Moon '38
Gold Diggers in Paris '38

Richard Todd (1919-2009)
Interrupted Journey '49
Lightning Strikes Twice '51
The Story of Robin Hood & His Merrie Men '52
Rob Roy-The Highland Rogue '53
The Sword & the Rose '53
Dam Busters '55
A Man Called Peter '55
The Virgin Queen '55
D-Day, the Sixth of June '56
Saint Joan '57
Chase a Crooked Shadow '58
Intent to Kill '58
Never Let Go '60
The Longest Day '62
Coast of Skeletons '63
The Love-Ins '67
Dorian Gray '70
Asylum '72
Bloodbath '76
The Big Sleep '78

Russell Todd (1958-)
Chopping Mall '86
Border Shootout '90

Thelma Todd (1905-35)
Corsair '31
The Maltese Falcon '31
Monkey Business '31
Call Her Savage '32
Horse Feathers '32
Speak Easily '32
This Is the Night '32
Counsellor-at-Law '33
The Devil's Brother '33
Palooka '34
Bohemian Girl '36

Tony Todd (1954-)
Platoon '86
Colors '88
Voodoo Dawn '89
Night of the Living Dead '90
Candyman '92
The Crow '93
Excessive Force '93
Black Fox: Good Men and Bad '94
Black Fox: The Price of Peace '94
Candyman 2: Farewell to the Flesh '94
Burnzy's Last Call '95
The Rock '96
Sabotage '96
True Women '97
Wishmaster '97
Bram Stoker's Shadowbuilder '98
Candyman 3: Day of the Dead '98
Caught Up '98
Never 2 Big '98
Final Destination '00
Final Destination 2 '03
Heart of the Beholder '05
The Eden Formula '06
Final Destination 3 '06 (V)
The Strange Case of Dr. Jekyll and Mr. Hyde '06
Hatchet '07
The Man from Earth '07
Shadow Puppets '07
iMurders '08
24: Redemption '08
Are You Scared 2 '09
Transformers: Revenge of the Fallen '09 (V)
The Graves '10
Hatchet 2 '10
Final Destination 5 '11
Sushi Girl '12

Bruno Todeschini (1962-)
La Sentinelle '92
Those Who Love Me Can Take the Train '98
Va Savoir '01
A Model Employee '02
La Petite Jerusalem '05
Delicacy '12

Bora Todorovic (1930-)
Time of the Gypsies '90
Underground '95

Chotaro Togin
Godzilla vs. the Sea Monster '66
Godzilla's Revenge '69

Ugo Tognazzi (1922-90)
Barbarella '68
Porcile '69
La Grande Bouffe '73
La Cage aux Folles '78
La Cage aux Folles 2 '81
La Cage aux Folles 3: The Wedding '86

Niall Toibin (1929-2019)
Lovespell '79
Rawhead Rex '87

Hannah Tointon (1987-)
The Children '08
Walking with the Enemy '13

Jacques Toja (1929-96)
Angelique '64
Angelique: The Road to Versailles '65
Angelique and the King '66

Marilyn Tokuda
My Tutor '82
The Cage '89
Farewell to the King '89
Strawberry Fields '97

Yu Tokui
Shall We Dance? '96
Dark Water '02

Michael (Lawrence) Tolan (1924-2011)
The Enforcer '51
Inside the Walls of Folsom Prison '51
All That Jazz '79
Half Slave, Half Free '85
Presumed Innocent '90

Berlinda Tolbert
Harlem Nights '89
Strange Fruit '04

Fabiola Toledo
A Blade in the Dark '83
Demons '86

Goya Toledo (1969-)
Mararia '98
Amores Perros '00

Sidney Toler (1874-1947)
Madame X '29
Blonde Venus '32
Speak Easily '32
Massacre '34
Operator 13 '34
Spitfire '34
Upperworld '34
The Call of the Wild '35
The Daring Young Man '35
Orchids to You '35
The Gorgeous Hussy '36
Our Relations '36
Three Godfathers '36
Double Wedding '37
Charlie Chan in Honolulu '38
Wide Open Faces '38
Charlie Chan at Treasure Island '39
Charlie Chan in City of Darkness '39
Law of the Pampas '39
Charlie Chan in Panama '40
Charlie Chan's Murder Cruise '40
Murder over New York '40
A Night to Remember '42
Adventures of Smilin' Jack '43
Isle of Forgotten Sins '43
The Chinese Cat '44
Meeting at Midnight '44
The Jade Mask '45
The Scarlet Clue '45
Dangerous Money '46
Shadows Over Chinatown '46
The Trap '46

John Toles-Bey
A Rage in Harlem '91
Leap of Faith '92
Waterworld '95
Extreme Measures '96
K-PAX '01
Joe and Max '02

James Tolkan (1931-)
Back to the Future '85
Split Decisions '88
Viper '88
Back to the Future, Part 2 '89
Family Business '89
Ministry of Vengeance '89
Second Sight '89
Back to the Future, Part 3 '90
Dick Tracy '90
Opportunity Knocks '90
Hangfire '91
Problem Child 2 '91
Bloodfist 4: Die Trying '92
Sketch Artist '92
Boiling Point '93
Beyond Betrayal '94
Underworld '96
Heavens Fall '06

Allison Tolman
Krampus '15
Barracuda '17
Killing Gunther '17

Marilu Tolo (1944-)
Marriage Italian Style '64
The Triumph of Hercules '66
Roy Colt and Winchester Jack '70
Confessions of a Police Captain '72
Commandos '73
Killer Likes Candy '78
Scorpion with Two Tails '82

David Tom (1978-)
Stay Tuned '92
Swing Kids '93
Walking Thunder '94
The Hazing '04
Love Begins '11

Lauren Tom (1961-)
The Joy Luck Club '93
Mr. Jones '93
When a Man Loves a Woman '94
Catfish in Black Bean Sauce '00
Bad Santa '03
Disney's Teacher's Pet '04 (V)
Mulan 2 '04 (V)

Layne Tom, Jr.
Charlie Chan at the Olympics '37
Charlie Chan in Honolulu '38

Nicholle Tom (1978-)
Beethoven '92
Beethoven's 2nd '93
Season of Change '94

Dara Tomanovich
Amnesia '96
Back in Business '96
Bio-Dome '96
Perfect Target '98

Jeana Tomasina (1955-)
Beach Girls '82
Up the Creek '84

Concetta Tomei (1945-)
The Betty Ford Story '87
Don't Tell Mom the Babysitter's Dead '91
In Love and War '91
Twenty Bucks '93
The Muse '99

Marisa Tomei (1964-)
Oscar '91
Zandalee '91
Chaplin '92
My Cousin Vinny '92
Untamed Heart '93
Only You '94
The Paper '94
The Perez Family '94
Four Rooms '95
Unhook the Stars '96
A Brother's Kiss '97
Since You've Been Gone '97 (C)
Welcome to Sarajevo '97
My Own Country '98
Only Love '98
Slums of Beverly Hills '98
Happy Accidents '00
The Watcher '00
What Women Want '00
In the Bedroom '01
King of the Jungle '01
Someone Like You '01
The Guru '02
Just a Kiss '02
The Wild Thornberrys Movie '02 (V)
Anger Management '03
Alfie '04
Loverboy '05
Factotum '06
Marilyn Hotchkiss' Ballroom Dancing & Charm School '06
Before the Devil Knows You're Dead '07
Wild Hogs '07
War, Inc. '08
The Wrestler '08
Cyrus '10
Crazy, Stupid, Love. '11
The Ides of March '11
The Lincoln Lawyer '11
Salvation Boulevard '11
Parental Guidance '12
Love Is Strange '14
The Big Short '15
Love the Coopers '15
The Rewrite '15
Spare Parts '15
Spider-Man: Homecoming '17
The First Purge '18
Spider-Man: Far from Home '19

Frances Tomelty (1948-)
Bullshot '83
Lamb '85
Bellman and True '88
A Perfect Spy '88
The Field '90
Cheri '09

Joseph Tomelty (1911-95)
The Sound Barrier '52
Devil Girl from Mars '54
Bedevilled '55
The Atomic Man '56
A Night to Remember '58

Akihiro Tomikawa (1968-)
Lone Wolf and Cub 4 '72
Lone Wolf and Cub '72
Lone Wolf and Cub: Baby Cart at the River Styx '72
Lone Wolf and Cub: Baby Cart to Hades '72
Shogun Assassin 2: Lightning Swords of Death '73

Tamlyn Tomita (1966-)
The Karate Kid: Part 2 '86
Come See the Paradise '90
Vietnam, Texas '90
The Joy Luck Club '93
Picture Bride '94
Four Rooms '95
The Killing Jar '96
Life Tastes Good '99
Soundman '99
Robot Stories '03
The Day After Tomorrow '04
Only the Brave '06
Pandemic '07
Why Am I Doing This? '09

Sara Tomko
2012: Doomsday '08
The Terminators '09

Lily Tomlin (1939-)
Nashville '75
The Late Show '77
9 to 5 '80
The Incredible Shrinking Woman '81
All of Me '84
Big Business '88
Search for Signs of Intelligent Life in the Universe '91
The Player '92
Shadows and Fog '92
And the Band Played On '93
The Beverly Hillbillies '93
Short Cuts '93
Blue in the Face '95
The Celluloid Closet '95 (N)
Flirting with Disaster '95

Getting Away With Murder '96
Krippendorf's Tribe '98
Tea with Mussolini '99
Disney's The Kid '00
Orange County '02
I Heart Huckabees '04
The Ant Bully '06 (V)
A Prairie Home Companion '06
The Walker '07
Ponyo '08 (V)
The Pink Panther 2 '09
Admission '13
Grandma '15

David Tomlinson (1917-2000)
Miranda '48
Made in Heaven '52
Three Men in a Boat '56
Carry On Admiral '57
Further Up the Creek '58
Tom Jones '63
Mary Poppins '64
The Liquidator '65
Bedknobs and Broomsticks '71
Water Babies '79
The Fiendish Plot of Dr. Fu Manchu '80

Eleanor Tomlinson (1992-)
Angus, Thongs and Perfect Snogging '08
The Lost Future '10
Death Comes to Pemberley '13
Jack the Giant Slayer '13

Ricky Tomlinson (1939-)
Riff Raff '92
Raining Stones '93
Butterfly Kiss '94
Cracker: Brotherly Love '95
Preaching to the Perverted '97
Formula 51 '01
Once Upon a Time in the Midlands '02

Jorma Tommila
Rare Exports: A Christmas Tale '10
Big Game '15

Onni Tommila
Rare Exports: A Christmas Tale '10
Big Game '15

Angel Tompkins (1942-)
Prime Cut '72
Probe '72
The Don Is Dead '73
Little Cigars '73
The Teacher '74
Walking Tall: Part 2 '75
Alligator '80
Murphy's Law '86
Crack House '89
Relentless '89

Matthew Tompkins
Killing Down '06
Missionary Man '07

Stephen Tompkinson (1965-)
Brassed Off '96
Oktober '98

Franchot Tone (1905-68)
Bombshell '33
Dancing Lady '33
Gabriel Over the White House '33
Midnight Mary '33
Today We Live '33
The Girl from Missouri '34
Sadie McKee '34
The World Moves On '34
Dangerous '35
The Lives of a Bengal Lancer '35
Mutiny on the Bounty '35
No More Ladies '35
Reckless '35
Exclusive Story '36
The Gorgeous Hussy '36
Love on the Run '36
Suzy '36
The Unguarded Hour '36
The Bride Wore Red '37
Quality Street '37
They Gave Him a Gun '37
Three Comrades '38
Three Loves Has Nancy '38
Fast and Furious '39
Five Graves to Cairo '43
Pilot No. 5 '43
Dark Waters '44
His Butler's Sister '44
Phantom Lady '44
Because of Him '45
Her Husband's Affairs '47
Honeymoon '47
Lost Honeymoon '47
Every Girl Should Be Married '48
Man on the Eiffel Tower '48
Jigsaw '49
Here Comes the Groom '51
Advise and Consent '62
In Harm's Way '65
Mickey One '65

Tone Loc (1966-)
The Adventures of Ford Fairlane '90
Bebe's Kids '92 (V)
Ferngully: The Last Rain Forest '92 (V)
Ace Ventura: Pet Detective '93
Blank Check '93
Posse '93
Surf Ninjas '93
Heat '95
Freedom Strike '98
Titan A.E. '00 (V)
Rhapsody '01
They Crawl '01
Code Hunter '02

Jacqueline Tong
How to Get Ahead in Advertising '89
Angel '07

Philip Tonge (1897-1959)
Track of the Cat '54
Witness for the Prosecution '57
Macabre '58
Invisible Invaders '59

Eijiro Tono (1907-94)
The Human Condition: No Greater Love '58
Yojimbo '61
Bushido: The Cruel Code of the Samurai '63
Pale Flower '64
Kill! '68
Tora! Tora! Tora! '70

Taiji Tonoyama (1915-89)
Rica 2: Lonely Wanderer '73
Rica 3: Juvenile's Lullaby '73

Regis Toomey (1902-91)
Alibi '29
Framed '30
The Light of Western Stars '30
Other Men's Women '31
Shopworn '32
Under Eighteen '32
Laughing at Life '33
Murder On the Blackboard '34
'G' Men '35
Shadow of Doubt '35
The Phantom Creeps '39
Union Pacific '39
Arizona '40
Dive Bomber '41
Meet John Doe '41
They Died with Their Boots On '41
Destroyer '43
Phantom Lady '44
Raiders of Ghost City '44
Spellbound '45
Strange Illusion '45
The Big Sleep '46
Her Sister's Secret '46
The Bishop's Wife '47
Magic Town '47
I Wouldn't Be in Your Shoes '48
Come to the Stable '49
Cry Danger '51
Never Wave at a WAC '52
Island in the Sky '53
Drums Across the River '54
The High and the Mighty '54
Guys and Dolls '55
Top Gun '55
The Curfew Breakers '57
Warlock '59
The Last Sunset '61
Change of Habit '69

Geoffrey Toone (1910-2005)
Zero Hour! '57
Once More, With Feeling '60
The Terror of the Tongs '61

Gordon Tootoosis (1941-2011)
Dan Candy's Law '73
Call of the Wild '93
Spirit Rider '93
Legends of the Fall '94
Pocahontas '95 (V)
Pocahontas: The Legend '95
The Song of Hiawatha '97
Big Bear '98
Black Point '01
The Doe Boy '01
Nobody's Baby '01
Zoe '01
Now & Forever '02
Open Season '06 (V)
That Beautiful Somewhere '06
Bury My Heart at Wounded Knee '07
Hybrid '07
Doomsday Prophecy '11
Guns, Girls and Gambling '11

Shawn Toovey (1983-)
The Fire Next Time '93
Flash '98

Jean Topart (1922-2012)
The Testament of Dr. Cordelier '59
Action Man '67
Cop Au Vin '85

Travis Tope
Little Accidents '14
Men, Women & Children '14
The Town That Dreaded Sundown '14
Viral '16

Velibor Topic (1970-)
Second in Command '05
Sharpe's Peril '08
Outpost: Rise of the Spetsnaz '13

Topol (1935-)
Sallah '63
Cast a Giant Shadow '66
Before Winter Comes '69
Fiddler on the Roof '71
The House on Garibaldi Street '79
Flash Gordon '80
For Your Eyes Only '81
The Winds of War '83
Queenie '87
War & Remembrance '88
War & Remembrance: The Final Chapter '89
Left Luggage '98

Chaim Topol (1935-)
See Topol

Amanda Topping
Stargate: Continuum '08
Stargate: The Ark of Truth '08

Sahaphap Tor
The Iron Ladies '00
The Iron Ladies 2 '03

Juan Torena (1898-1983)
Captain Calamity '36
American Guerrilla in the Philippines '50

Hal Torey (1915-89)
Earth vs. the Spider '58
Invisible Invaders '59

Peter Tork (1942-)
Head '68
The Brady Bunch Movie '95 (C)

Mel Torme (1925-99)
Good News '47
Words and Music '48
The Fearmakers '58
A Man Called Adam '66
Naked Gun 2 1/2: The Smell of Fear '91 (C)
The Return of Spinal Tap '92 (C)

John Tormey (1937-)
Ghost Dog: The Way of the Samurai '99
Joe Gould's Secret '00

Angelica Torn (1964-)
Wrestling with Alligators '98
Domestic Disturbance '01
Ruby's Bucket of Blood '01
The Golden Boys '08
Lucky Days '08
The Hungry Ghosts '09

Rip Torn (1931-2019)
Baby Doll '56
Time Limit '57
Pork Chop Hill '59
The King of Kings '61
Hero's Island '62
Sweet Bird of Youth '62
Critic's Choice '63
The Cincinnati Kid '65
You're a Big Boy Now '66
Beach Red '67
Coming Apart '69
Tropic of Cancer '70
Cotter '72
Slaughter '72
Payday '73
The Man Who Fell to Earth '76
Nasty Habits '77
The Private Files of J. Edgar Hoover '77
Betrayal '78
Coma '78
The Seduction of Joe Tynan '79
One Trick Pony '80
Heartland '81
Airplane 2: The Sequel '82
Beastmaster '82
Jinxed '82
A Stranger Is Watching '82
Cross Creek '83
Cat on a Hot Tin Roof '84
City Heat '84
Flashpoint '84
Songwriter '84
Beer '85
The Execution '85
Summer Rental '85
Dream West '86
Extreme Prejudice '87
Nadine '87
April Morning '88
By Dawn's Early Light '89
Cold Feet '89
Sweet Bird of Youth '89
Another Pair of Aces: Three of a Kind '91
Defending Your Life '91
RoboCop 3 '91
Beautiful Dreamers '92
Beyond the Law '92
Dolly Dearest '92
Hard Promises '92
Canadian Bacon '94
Where the Rivers Flow North '94
For Better or Worse '95 (C)
How to Make an American Quilt '95
Down Periscope '96
Trial and Error '96
Balloon Farm '97
Hercules '97 (V)
Men in Black '97
Senseless '98
The Insider '99
Passing Glory '99
Wonder Boys '00
Freddy Got Fingered '01
Men in Black 2 '02
Dodgeball: A True Underdog Story '04
Eulogy '04
Welcome to Mooseport '04
Forty Shades of Blue '05
The Sisters '05
Yours, Mine & Ours '05
Marie Antoinette '06
Zoom '06
Bee Movie '07 (V)
Three Days to Vegas '07
Turn the River '07
August '08
The Golden Boys '08
Lucky Days '08
American Cowslip '09
Happy Tears '09
National Lampoon's The Legend of Awesomest Maximus '11
3 Weeks to Daytona '11

Mari Torocsik (1935-)
Love '71
Electra, My Love '74
Forbidden Relations '83

Ane Dahl Torp (1975-)
Dead Snow '09
The Wave '15

Ingrid Torrance (1969-)
Act of War '96
Criminal Intent '05
Under the Mistletoe '06
Impulse '08

Kirk Torrance
Stickmen '01
The Dark Horse '14

David Torrence (1864-1951)
Tess of the Storm Country '22
Raffles '30
The Bachelor Father '31
The Mask of Fu Manchu '32
A Successful Calamity '32
Jane Eyre '34

Ernest Torrence (1878-1933)
Tol'able David '21
The Hunchback of Notre Dame '23
Peter Pan '24
Captain Salvation '27
King of Kings '27
Across to Singapore '28
Steamboat Bill, Jr. '28
Speedway '29
Untamed '29
Fighting Caravans '31
Shipmates '31
Sporting Blood '31
I Cover the Waterfront '33

Nate Torrence (1977-)
Get Smart '08
My Best Friend's Girl '08
She's Out of My League '10
Zootopia '16 (V)

Pip Torrens (1960-)
A Handful of Dust '88
Incognito '97
To End All Wars '01
Shackleton '02
Valiant '05 (V)
Pinochet's Last Stand '06
Miss Austen Regrets '07
Easy Virtue '08

Ana Torrent (1966-)
Spirit of the Beehive '73
Cria Cuervos '76
Blood and Sand '89
Vacas '91
The Other Boleyn Girl '08
There Be Dragons '11

Diego Torres
A Shadow You Soon Will Be '94
The Caretaker '08

Fernanda Torres (1965-)
One Man's War '90
Foreign Land '95
Four Days in September '97
House of Sand '05

Gina Torres
The Matrix Reloaded '03
The Matrix Revolutions '03
Hair Show '04
Serenity '05
Five Fingers '06
Jam '06
I Think I Love My Wife '07
South of Pico '07

Jose Torres
Diary of a Rebel '68
Death Rides a Horse '69

Liz Torres (1947-)
Lena's Holiday '90
Bloodfist 4: Die Trying '92
A Million to Juan '94 (C)
Storm Chasers: Revenge of the Twister '98
The Wonderful Ice Cream Suit '98

Raquel Torres (1908-87)
White Shadows in the South Seas '29
Duck Soup '33

Philippe Torreton (1965-)
Capitaine Conan '96
It All Starts Today '99
Monsieur N. '03
District 13: Ultimatum '09
Mood Indigo '13

Guy Torry (1969-)
American History X '98
Ride '98
Life '99
Trippin' '99
The '70s '00
The Animal '01
Don't Say a Word '01
Runaway Jury '03

Joe Torry (1965-)
Poetic Justice '93
Tales from the Hood '95
Back in Business '96
Sprung '96
Lockdown '00
Motives '03
Hair Show '04
Getting Played '05
The Boston Strangler: The Untold Story '08
The Dog Who Saved Christmas '09
Why Am I Doing This? '09

Nico Tortorella
Scream 4 '11
Trespass '11

Silvia Tortosa (1947-)
Horror Express '72
When the Screaming Stops '73

Jose Torvay (1910-73)
Border Incident '49
Borderline '50
My Outlaw Brother '51
The Hitch-Hiker '53
Green Fire '55

Luis Tosar (1971-)
Jealousy '99
Angel of Death '02
Mondays in the Sun '02
Take My Eyes '03
Miami Vice '06
Cell 211 '09
The Limits of Control '09
Even the Rain '10
Mr. Nice '10
Sleep Tight '11
A Night in Old Mexico '14

Luigi Tosi
The Black Devils of Kali '55
David and Goliath '61

Toto (1898-1967)
Big Deal on Madonna Street '58
The Hawks & the Sparrows '67

Merle Tottenham (1901-59)
Cavalcade '33
Night Must Fall '37
Bank Holiday '38
This Happy Breed '47

Audrey Totter (1918-2013)
Lady in the Lake '46
The Postman Always Rings Twice '46
High Wall '47
Any Number Can Play '49
The Set-Up '49
Tension '50
The Sellout '51
Assignment: Paris '52
FBI Girl '52
Woman They Almost Lynched '53
Women's Prison '55
Man or Gun '58
The Carpetbaggers '64
Chubasco '67

Shaun Toub (1963-)
Maryam '00
Land of Plenty '04
Crash '05
The Nativity Story '06
The Kite Runner '07
Iron Man '08
The Last Airbender '10
Setup '11
Papa: Hemingway in Cuba '16
War Dogs '16

Elias Toufexis
Decoys '04
Sand Serpents '09

Tamara Toumanova (1919-96)
Days of Glory '43
Invitation to the Dance '56
The Private Life of Sherlock Holmes '70

Sheila Tousey (1960-)
Silent Tongue '92
Thunderheart '92
Slaughter of the Innocents '93
The Song of Hiawatha '97
Christmas in the Clouds '01
Skinwalker '02
Coyote Waits '03

Lorraine Toussaint
Breaking In '89
Point of No Return '93
Bleeding Hearts '94
Mother's Boys '94
America's Dream '95
Dangerous Minds '95
If These Walls Could Talk '96
Jaded '96
Nightjohn '96
The Soloist '09
Middle of Nowhere '12
Selma '14
Fast Color '18

Roland Toutain (1905-77)
Liliom '35
The Rules of the Game '39

Lupita Tovar (1910-)
Dracula Spanish Version '31
South of the Border '39
The Westerner '40

Russell Tovey (1981-)
The History Boys '06
Little Dorrit '08
The Good Liar '19

Harry Towb (1925-2009)
The Blue Max '66
All Neat in Black Stockings '69

Michael Tower
The Apocalypse '07
Invasion of the Pod People '07

Constance Towers (1933-)
The Horse Soldiers '59
Sergeant Rutledge '60
Shock Corridor '63
Naked Kiss '64
Sylvester '85
A Perfect Murder '98

Tom Towler
Henry: Portrait of a Serial Killer '90
Night of the Living Dead '90
The Pit & the Pendulum '91
Blood In . . . Blood Out: Bound by Honor '93
Mad Dog and Glory '93
Girls in Prison '94
Gridlock'd '96
Normal Life '96
Groom Lake '02
House of 1000 Corpses '03
The Devil's Rejects '05
Home Sick '08

Aline Towne (1929-96)
Highway 301 '50
The Invisible Monster '50
Radar Men from the Moon '52
The Steel Trap '52
Zombies of the Stratosphere '52

Katharine Towne (1978-)
She's All That '99
What Lies Beneath '00
Evolution '01
Mulholland Drive '01
Sol Goode '01
Town and Country '01
Lethal Dose '03
Something New '06

Robert Towne (1936-)
Villa Rides '68
The Pick-Up Artist '87

Harry Townes (1914-2001)
Screaming Mimi '58
The Warrior & the Sorceress '84

Colleen Townsend
Chicken Every Sunday '48
When Willie Comes Marching Home '50

Jill Townsend (1945-)
The Golden Bowl '72
Sitting Target '72
Oh, Alfie '75
Poldark 2 '75
Poldark '75
The Awakening '80

Najarra Townsend (1989-)
Me and You and Everyone We Know '05
Dawning '09
Supernova '09
Contracted '13
Going to America '15

Patrice Townsend
Sitting Ducks '80
Always '85

Robert Townsend (1957-)
The Warriors '79
A Soldier's Story '84
Streets of Fire '84
American Flyers '85
Odd Jobs '85
Ratboy '86
Hollywood Shuffle '87
I'm Gonna Git You Sucka '88
The Mighty Quinn '89
The Five Heartbeats '91
The Meteor Man '93
The Taxman '98
Love Songs '99
Black Listed '03
Of Boys and Men '08
Playin' For Love '15

Stanley Townsend
The Nativity Story '06
Wondrous Oblivion '06
Hard Times '09
Killing Bono '11
Burton and Taylor '13
Florence Foster Jenkins '16
The Current War: Director's Cut '19

Stuart Townsend (1972-)
Trojan Eddie '96
Shooting Fish '98
Wonderland '99
About Adam '00
Queen of the Damned '02
Trapped '02
The League of Extraordinary Gentlemen '03
Shade '03
Head in the Clouds '04
Chaos Theory '08

Tammy Townsend
The Pest '96
Preacher's Kid '10

Pete Townshend (1945-)
Tommy '75
The Kids Are Alright '79
The Secret Policeman's Other Ball '82

Etsushi Toyokawa (1962-)
No Way Back '96
The Great Yokai War '05
Hula Girls '06

Fausto Tozzi (1921-78)
East of Kilimanjaro '57
The Return of Dr. Mabuse '61
Swordsman of Siena '62
Knives of the Avenger '65
The Valachi Papers '72
Escape from Death Row '73
Street War '76

Giorgio Tozzi (1923-)
South Pacific '58 (V)
Torn Between Two Lovers '79

Ian Tracey (1964-)
Timecop '94
Man with a Gun '95
Liberty Stands Still '02
Emile '03
Owning Mahowny '03
Call Me: The Rise and Fall of Heidi Fleiss '04
Ice Men '04
Civic Duty '06
Iron Road '08
Donovan's Echo '11

Keenan Tracey
The Hunters '13
Independence Daysaster '13

Jeff Trachta (1960-)
Interlocked '98
Poison '01

Michelle Trachtenberg (1985-)
Harriet the Spy '96
Inspector Gadget '99
A Father's Choice '00
Forever Together '00
Eurotrip '04
Mysterious Skin '04
The Dive from Clausen's Pier '05
Ice Princess '05
Beautiful Ohio '06
Black Christmas '06
Kickin' It Old Skool '07
The Circuit '08
Against the Current '09
17 Again '09
Cop Out '10
Take Me Home Tonight '11
Killing Kennedy '13
Sexy Evil Genius '13
The Scribbler '14

Keegan Connor Tracy (1971-)
Out of Line '00
Blackwoods '02
Final Destination 2 '03
Her Fatal Flaw '06
The Net 2.0 '06
Dead Rising: End Game '16

Lee Tracy (1898-1968)
Liliom '30
Blessed Event '32
Doctor X '32
The Strange Love of Molly Louvain '32
Bombshell '33
Clear All Wires! '33
Dinner at Eight '33
The Nuisance '33
Turn Back the Clock '33
The Payoff '43
The Best Man '64

Spencer Tracy (1900-67)
Up the River '30
Me and My Gal '32
Young America '32
The Power and the Glory '33
20,000 Years in Sing Sing '33
Marie Galante '34
Dante's Inferno '35
The Murder Man '35
Riff Raff '35
Whipsaw '35
Fury '36
Libeled Lady '36
San Francisco '36
Big City '37
Captains Courageous '37
Mannequin '37
They Gave Him a Gun '37
Boys Town '38
Test Pilot '38
Boom Town '40
Edison the Man '40
I Take This Woman '40
Northwest Passage '40
Dr. Jekyll and Mr. Hyde '41
Men of Boys Town '41
Keeper of the Flame '42
Tortilla Flat '42
Woman of the Year '42
Thirty Seconds Over Tokyo '44
Without Love '45
Cass Timberlane '47
The Sea of Grass '47
State of the Union '48
Edward, My Son '49
Malaya '49
Adam's Rib '50
Father of the Bride '50
Father's Little Dividend '51
The People Against O'Hara '51
Pat and Mike '52
The Actress '53
Bad Day at Black Rock '54
Broken Lance '54
The Mountain '56
Desk Set '57
The Last Hurrah '58
The Old Man and the Sea '58
Inherit the Wind '60
The Devil at 4 O'Clock '61
Judgment at Nuremberg '61
How the West Was Won '63
It's a Mad, Mad, Mad, Mad World '63
Guess Who's Coming to Dinner '67

William Tracy (1917-67)
Gallant Sons '40
Strike Up the Band '40
Tobacco Road '41
George Washington Slept Here '42
To the Shores of Tripoli '42

Mary Ellen Trainor (1952-2015)
Romancing the Stone '84
The Stone Boy '84
The Goonies '85
Lethal Weapon '87
The Monster Squad '87
Action Jackson '88
Die Hard '88
Scrooged '88
Ghostbusters 2 '89
Lethal Weapon 2 '89
Fire Birds '90
Grand Canyon '91
Ricochet '91
Death Becomes Her '92
Kuffs '92
Lethal Weapon 3 '92
Forrest Gump '94
Greedy '94
Little Giants '94
Congo '95
Executive Decision '96
Lethal Weapon 4 '98
Anywhere But Here '99
Amy's O '02
Cake: A Wedding Story '07

Sam Trammell (1969-)
Wrestling with Alligators '98
Beat '00
Undermind '03
Anonymous Rex '04
Aliens vs. Predator: Requiem '07
What If God Were the Sun? '07
Guns, Girls and Gambling '11
Crazy Kind of Love '12
The Fault In Our Stars '14
I Am Wrath '16
Imperium '16

Billinger C. Tran
Green Dragon '01
We Were Soldiers '02

Silvano Tranquilli (1925-97)
The Horrible Dr. Hichcock '62
Castle of Blood '64

Cordula Trantow (1942-)
The Bridge '59
Hitler '62

Sophie Traub
Daltry Calhoun '05
Tenderness '08

Helen Traubel (1899-1972)
Deep in My Heart '54
The Ladies' Man '61

Daniel J. Travanti (1940-)
St. Ives '76
Adam '83
Midnight Crossing '87
Millennium '89
Just Cause '94
To Sir, With Love 2 '96
The Wasp Woman '96

Bill Travers (1922-94)
The Browning Version '51
Romeo and Juliet '54
Footsteps in the Fog '55
Geordie '55
Bhowani Junction '56
The Smallest Show on Earth '57
Gorgo '61
Invasion Quartet '61
Born Free '66
Duel at Diablo '66
A Midsummer Night's Dream '68
An Elephant Called Slowly '69
Ring of Bright Water '69
Christian the Lion '76
The First Olympics: Athens 1896 '84

Henry Travers (1874-1965)
The Invisible Man '33
The Sisters '38
Dark Victory '39
Dodge City '39
On Borrowed Time '39
The Rains Came '39
You Can't Get Away With Murder '39
Edison the Man '40
Primrose Path '40
The Bad Man '41
Ball of Fire '41
High Sierra '41
I'll Wait for You '41
Mrs. Miniver '42
Random Harvest '42
Madame Curie '43
The Moon is Down '43
Shadow of a Doubt '43
Dragon Seed '44
The Bells of St. Mary's '45
The Naughty Nineties '45
Thrill of a Romance '45
It's a Wonderful Life '46
The Yearling '46
The Girl from Jones Beach '49

Linden Travers (1913-2001)
The Lady Vanishes '38
No Orchids for Miss Blandish '48

Susan Travers (1939-)
Peeping Tom '60
The Snake Woman '61
The Abominable Dr. Phibes '71

Greg Travis
Paradise '91
Landspeed '01

June Travis (1914-2008)
The Case of the Black Cat '36
Exiled to Shanghai '37
Join the Marines '37
The Star '52
Monster a Go-Go! '65

Kylie Travis (1966-)
Retroactive '97
Gia '98
Sanctuary '98

Nancy Travis (1961-)
Three Men and a Baby '87
Eight Men Out '88
Married to the Mob '88
Air America '90
Internal Affairs '90
Loose Cannons '90
Three Men and a Little Lady '90
Chaplin '92
Passed Away '92
So I Married an Axe Murderer '93
The Vanishing '93
Greedy '94
Body Language '95
Fluke '95
Bogus '96
Beyond Suspicion '00
Running Mates '00
Stephen King's Rose Red '02
The Sisterhood of the Traveling Pants '05
The Jane Austen Book Club '07
The Party Never Stops '07
Safe Harbor '09
The Pregnancy Pact '10
A Walk in My Shoes '10

Randy Travis (1959-)
Dead Man's Revenge '93
Frank and Jesse '94
Texas '94
Edie & Pen '95 (C)
Boys Will Be Boys '97
Fire Down Below '97
John Grisham's The Rainmaker '97
The Shooter '97
Black Dog '98
T.N.T. '98
The Million Dollar Kid '99
White River '99
John John in the Sky '00
The Trial of Old Drum '00
The Long Ride Home '01
Texas Rangers '01

Richard Travis (1913-89)
The Man Who Came to Dinner '41
The Big Shot '42
Operation Haylift '50
One Too Many '51
Mesa of Lost Women '52
The Girl in the Red Velvet Swing '55
Missile to the Moon '59

Stacey Travis (1966-)
Dr. Hackenstein '88
Earth Girls Are Easy '89
Hardware '90
The Super '91
Dracula Rising '93
Only the Strong '93
Playing God '96
The Only Thrill '97
The Muse '99
Sleep Easy, Hutch Rimes '00
Submerged '00
Traffic '00
What Planet Are You From? '00
Bandits '01
Ghost World '01
Heartbreakers '01
Intolerable Cruelty '03
Two Days '03
Soul Plane '04
Venom '05

The Great Buck Howard '09
Easy A '10
A Christmas Story 2 '12

Tony Travis
The Beatniks '60
Flesh Gordon 2: Flesh Gordon Meets the Cosmic Cheerleaders '90

Ella Bleu Travolta (2000-)
Old Dogs '09
The Poison Rose '19

Joey Travolta (1950-)
Amazon Women on the Moon '87
American Born '89
Sinners '89
DaVinci's War '92
To the Limit '95
Dangerous Cargo '96

John Travolta (1954-)
Devil's Rain '75
The Boy in the Plastic Bubble '76
Carrie '76
Saturday Night Fever '77
Grease '78
Urban Cowboy '80
Blow Out '81
Staying Alive '83
Two of a Kind '83
Perfect '85
Look Who's Talking '89
Look Who's Talking, Too '90
Eyes of an Angel '91
Shout '91
Chains of Gold '92
Look Who's Talking Now '93
Pulp Fiction '94
Broken Arrow '95
Get Shorty '95
White Man's Burden '95
Michael '96
Phenomenon '96
Face/Off '97
Mad City '97
She's So Lovely '97
A Civil Action '98
Primary Colors '98
The Thin Red Line '98
The General's Daughter '99
Battlefield Earth '00
Lucky Numbers '00
Domestic Disturbance '01
Swordfish '01
Austin Powers In Goldmember '02 (C)
Basic '03
Ladder 49 '04
A Love Song for Bobby Long '04
The Punisher '04
Be Cool '05
Lonely Hearts '06
Hairspray '07
Wild Hogs '07
Bolt '08 (V)
Old Dogs '09
The Taking of Pelham 123 '09
From Paris With Love '10
Savages '12
Killing Season '13
The Forger '15
I Am Wrath '16
In a Valley of Violence '16
Life on the Line '16
Gotti '18
Speed Kills '18
The Fanatic '19
The Poison Rose '19
Trading Paint '19

Susan Traylor
The New Age '94
Sleep with Me '94
To Die For '95
Bastard out of Carolina '96
She's So Lovely '97
Broken Vessels '98
Greenberg '10

Joel Thomas Traywick
Nightjohn '96
Sub Down '97

Treach (1970-)
Jason's Lyric '94
Conviction '02

Empire '02
Today You Die '05
Connor's War '06
The Art of War 3: Retribution '08

Arthur Treacher (1894-1975)
Hollywood Party '34
Curly Top '35
The Daring Young Man '35
David Copperfield '35
I Live My Life '35
Magnificent Obsession '35
A Midsummer Night's Dream '35
No More Ladies '35
The Woman in Red '35
Mister Cinderella '36
Satan Met a Lady '36
Stowaway '36
Heidi '37
Thin Ice '37
Mad About Music '38
My Lucky Star '38
The Little Princess '39
Irene '40
Star Spangled Rhythm '42
The Amazing Mrs. Holiday '43
In Society '44
National Velvet '44
Delightfully Dangerous '45
Love That Brute '50

Emerson Treacy (1900-67)
Give Me a Sailor '38
The Prowler '51
A Star Is Born '54

Harry Treadaway (1984-)
Brothers of the Head '06
Control '07
City of Ember '08
The Disappeared '08
Fish Tank '09
Albatross '11
Honeymoon '14

Luke Treadaway (1984-)
Heartless '10
Tonight You're Mine '11
Berlin Job '12
Cheerful Weather for the Wedding '12
Get Lucky '13
Wasteland '13
A Street Cat Named Bob '16

Luke Treadway
Brothers of the Head '06
Attack the Block '11

Michael Treanor (1979-)
3 Ninjas '92
3 Ninjas Knuckle Up '95

Terri Treas (1957-)
The Nest '88
The Terror Within '88
Frankenstein Unbound '90 (V)
Rage and Honor '92
Home for Christmas '93
Alien Nation: Dark Horizon '94
Alien Nation: Body and Soul '95
Yankee Zulu '95
Alien Nation: Millennium '96
Alien Nation: The Enemy Within '96
Lady Killer '97

Robert Trebor (1953-)
52 Pick-Up '86
Hercules the Legendary Journeys, Vol. 2: The Lost Kingdom '94
Raise Your Voice '04
Jiminy Glick in LaLa Wood '05

David Tree (1915-2009)
Drums '38
Pygmalion '38

Dorothy Tree (1906-92)
East of Fifth Avenue '33
The Woman in Red '35
Three Godfathers '36
Charlie Chan in City of Darkness '39

Confessions of a Nazi Spy '39
Mystery of Mr. Wong '39
Abe Lincoln in Illinois '40
The Asphalt Jungle '50

Mary Treen (1907-89)
They Gave Him a Gun '37
First Love '39
Hands Across the Border '43
So Proudly We Hail '43
Casanova Brown '44
Don Juan Quilligan '45
It's a Wonderful Life '46
Strange Impersonation '46
The Sad Sack '57
I Married a Monster from Outer Space '58
Paradise, Hawaiian Style '66

Yann Tregouet (1975-)
Trois Couleurs: Bleu '93
Artemisia '97
Born in 68 '08
The Army of Crime '10

Danny Trejo (1944-)
From Dusk Till Dawn '95
Anaconda '96
Con Air '97
Dilemma '97
From Dusk Till Dawn 2: Texas Blood Money '98
Point Blank '98
The Replacement Killers '98
Six Days, Seven Nights '98
Desert Heat '99
From Dusk Till Dawn 3: The Hangman's Daughter '99
Soundman '99
Animal Factory '00
Reindeer Games '00
Bubble Boy '01
Spy Kids '01
Nightstalker '02
Spy Kids 2: The Island of Lost Dreams '02
13 Moons '02
XXX '02
Once Upon a Time in Mexico '03
Spy Kids 3-D: Game Over '03
Anchorman: The Legend of Ron Burgundy '04
The Big Empty '04
All Souls Day '05
Chasing Ghosts '05
The Crow: Wicked Prayer '05
The Devil's Rejects '05
Lost '05
Danny Roane: First Time Director '06
7 Mummies '06
Sherrybaby '06
Slayer '06
Delta Farce '07
Halloween '07
Urban Justice '07
Alone in the Dark 2 '08
Babysitters Beware '08
Jake's Corner '08
The Line '08
Eyeborgs '09
Death Race 2 '10
The Killing Jar '10
Machete '10
Predators '10
House of the Rising Sun '11
Recoil '11
Spy Kids 4: All the Time in the World '11
A Very Harold & Kumar Christmas '11
Violet & Daisy '11
Death Race 3: Inferno '12
Rise of the Zombies '12
Force of Execution '13
In the Blood '13
Machete Kills '13
The Book of Life '14 (V)
Voodoo Possession '14
Reaper '15
Maximum Impact '18
The Outsider '19

Christine Tremarco (1977-)
Priest '94
Five Days '07

Les Tremayne (1913-2003)
Francis Goes to West Point '52
Dream Wife '53
I Love Melvin '53
The War of the Worlds '53
A Man Called Peter '55
Forbidden Planet '56 (N)
The Unguarded Moment '56
The Monolith Monsters '57
The Angry Red Planet '59
Say One for Me '59
The Gallant Hours '60
King Kong vs. Godzilla '63 (N)
The Slime People '63
Creature of Destruction '67

Jacob Tremblay (2006-)
Room '15
Shut In '16
The Book of Henry '17
Wonder '17
The Predator '18
The Death and Life of John F. Donovan '19
Good Boys '19

Johanne-Marie Tremblay (1950-)
Jesus of Montreal '89
The Barbarian Invasions '03

Ken Tremblett (1965-)
The Guilty '99
My Neighbor's Keeper '07
The Betrayed '08
Midnight Sun '18

Jonathan Trent (1984-)
Addicted to Her Love '06
Alone With Her '07

Philip Trent
The Power and the Glory '33
Paper Bullets '41

Ricardo Trepa
Belle Toujours '06
Eccentricities of a Blonde-Haired Girl '10
The Strange Case of Angelica '10

Adam Trese (1969-)
The Good Fight '92
Laws of Gravity '92
Palookaville '95
The Underneath '95
Polish Wedding '97
Cowboys and Angels '00
40 Days and 40 Nights '02
2B Perfectly Honest '04
Silent House '12

Frederick Treves (1925-2012)
Paper Mask '91
Shameless '94
A Certain Justice '99

Leonardo Treviglio
Sebastiane '79
Stealing Beauty '96

Austin Trevor (1897-1978)
The Silent Passenger '35
Sabotage '36
Night Train to Munich '40

Claire Trevor (1909-2000)
Baby, Take a Bow '34
Dante's Inferno '35
Career Woman '36
Dead End '37
Second Honeymoon '37
Amazing Dr. Clitterhouse '38
Allegheny Uprising '39
Stagecoach '39
Dark Command '40
Honky Tonk '41
Texas '41
Crossroads '42
The Desperadoes '43
Murder, My Sweet '44
The Woman of the Town '44
Crack-Up '46
Born to Kill '47
Babe Ruth Story '48
Key Largo '48
Raw Deal '48
Best of the Badmen '50
Borderline '50

Hard, Fast and Beautiful '51
Hoodlum Empire '52
My Man and I '52
The Stranger Wore a Gun '53
The High and the Mighty '54
Man Without a Star '55
The Mountain '56
Marjorie Morningstar '58
Two Weeks in Another Town '62
How to Murder Your Wife '64
Kiss Me Goodbye '82

Jack Trevor (1890-1976)
Secrets of a Soul '25
Champagne '28

Paula Trickey (1966-)
Carnal Crimes '91
The Base '99
Past Tense '06

Ivan Triesault (1898-1980)
Border River '47
Golden Earrings '47
Johnny Allegro '49
Five Fingers '52
Jet Pilot '57
Von Ryan's Express '65

Leopoldo Trieste (1917-2003)
The White Sheik '52
I Vitelloni '53
Divorce-Italian Style '62
Seduced and Abandoned '64
Don't Look Now '73
Henry IV '85
Cinema Paradiso '88

Sergej Trifunovic (1972-)
Savior '98
3 A.M. '01
Love '05

Sarah Trigger (1968-)
El Diablo '90
Bill & Ted's Bogus Journey '91
Grand Canyon '91
Paradise '91
Pet Sematary 2 '92
Deadfall '93
Sleepless in Seattle '93
Don't Do It '94
P.C.U. '94
Acts of Contrition '95
Things to Do in Denver When You're Dead '95
Good Luck '96

Jerry Trimble (1961-)
Breathing Fire '91
Full Contact '93
One Man Army '93
Stranglehold '94

Jasmine Trinca (1981-)
The Son's Room '00
Best of Youth '03
The Gunman '15

Jean-Louis Trintignant (1930-)
And God Created Woman '57
Dangerous Liaisons '60
Journey Beneath the Desert '61
Il Sorpasso '63
Angelique: The Road to Versailles '65
Is Paris Burning? '66
A Man and a Woman '66
Les Biches '68
The Man Who Lies '68
The Libertine '69
My Night at Maud's '69
Z '69
The Conformist '71
The Last Train '74
The Desert of the Tartars '76
Confidentially Yours '83
Under Fire '83
Rendez-vous '85
A Man and a Woman: 20 Years Later '86
Trois Couleurs: Rouge '94
The City of Lost Children '95 (V)

Those Who Love Me Can Take the Train '98
Amour '12
Happy End '17

Marie Trintignant (1962-2003)
The Story of Women '88
Betty '92
Ponette '95
Portraits Chinois '96
Harrison's Flowers '02

Pankaj Tripathi
Luka Chuppi '19
Extraction '20

Louis Tripp (1974-)
The Gate '87
Gate 2 '92

Jeanne Tripplehorn (1963-)
Basic Instinct '92
The Firm '93
The Night We Never Met '93
Reality Bites '94 (C)
Waterworld '95
Til There Was You '96
Office Killer '97
Sliding Doors '97
Monument Ave. '98
Very Bad Things '98
Mickey Blue Eyes '99
Relative Values '99
Steal This Movie! '00
Time Code '00
Brother's Keeper '02
Swept Away '02
The Moguls '05
Fragments '08
Grey Gardens '09
Crazy on the Outside '10
Morning '10
Five '11
A Perfect Man '13

Jan Triska (1936-)
World War II: When Lions Roared '94
Andersonville '95
The People vs. Larry Flynt '96
Apt Pupil '97
Ronin '98
The Omega Code '99
Up and Down '04

Elisabeth Trissenaar (1944-)
The Stationmaster's Wife '77
In a Year of 13 Moons '78
Angry Harvest '85

Dorothy Tristan (1942-)
End of the Road '70
Scarecrow '73
Man on a Swing '74
Griffin and Phoenix: A Love Story '76
Down and Out in Beverly Hills '86
The Looking Glass '16

Travis Tritt (1963-)
Rio Diablo '93
The Cowboy Way '94 (C)
Outlaw Justice '98
Forever My Girl '18

Margot Trooger (1923-94)
Again, the Ringer '64
Pippi Goes on Board '69
Pippi Longstocking '69

Jason Trost
All Superheroes Must Die '11
The FP '12

Audrey Trotter
The Unsuspected '47
A Bullet for Joey '55

Kate Trotter (1953-)
Beyond Borders '03
Plain Truth '04
Cheaters' Club '06

Michael Trotter
Road Trip: Beer Pong '09
Jamesy Boy '14

Tariq Trotter
Explicit Ills '08
Night Catches Us '10

David Troughton (1950-)
The Norman Conquests, Part 1: Table Manners '78
The Norman Conquests, Part 2: Living Together '78
The Norman Conquests, Part 3: Round and Round the Garden '78
Dance with a Stranger '85
Sharpe's Eagle '93
Sharpe's Rifles '93
All the King's Men '99
Cider with Rosie '99
Chicklit '16

Michael Troughton (1955-)
Testament of Youth '79
Speedy Death '99

Patrick Troughton (1920-87)
The Gorgon '64
The Viking Queen '67
The Scars of Dracula '70
Frankenstein and the Monster from Hell '74
The Omen '76

Sam Troughton (1977-)
Sylvia '03
Alien vs. Predator '04

Bobby Troup
First to Fight '67
M*A*S*H '70

Tom Troupe (1928-)
The Devil's Brigade '68
Kelly's Heroes '70
My Own Private Idaho '91

Charles Trowbridge (1882-1967)
The Gorgeous Hussy '36
Libeled Lady '36
Crime School '38
The Fatal Hour '40
Johnny Apollo '40
The Mummy's Hand '40
Sergeant York '41
Wake Island '42
Fighting Seabees '44
Colonel Effingham's Raid '45
They Were Expendable '45
Don't Gamble with Strangers '46
Key Witness '47
Tarzan and the Huntress '47
Tycoon '47

Phillip Troy (1964-)
Ice '93
To Be the Best '93

Verne Troyer (1969-2018)
Austin Powers 2: The Spy Who Shagged Me '99
Bubble Boy '01
Hard Cash '01
Austin Powers In Goldmember '02
Postal '07
College '08
The Love Guru '08
The Imaginarium of Doctor Parnassus '09
My Son, My Son, What Have Ye Done '09

Michael Trubshawe (1905-85)
The Guns of Navarone '61
Bedazzled '68

Michael Trucco (1970-)
A Girl, 3 Guys and a Gun '01
Wishmaster 4: The Prophecy Fulfilled '02
Next '07
Battlestar Galactica: The Plan '09
Meteor Storm '10

John Trudell (1946-)
Thunderheart '92
Smoke Signals '98

Rachel True (1966-)
Embrace of the Vampire '95
The Craft '96
Half-Baked '97
Groove '00
New Best Friend '02
The Perfect Holiday '07
Mother '13
Blood Lake '14

Jim True-Frost (1966-)
Singles '92
The Hudsucker Proxy '93
Normal Life '96
Affliction '97
Off the Map '03
Slippery Slope '06
Diminished Capacity '08

Ernest Truex (1890-1973)
The Adventures of Marco Polo '38
It's a Wonderful World '39
His Girl Friday '40
All Mine to Give '56

Francois Truffaut (1932-84)
The 400 Blows '59
The Wild Child '70
Day for Night '73
Small Change '76
Close Encounters of the Third Kind '77
The Green Room '78

Joe Lo Truglio (1970-)
Beer League '06
Paul '11
Wanderlust '12

Raoul Trujillo (1955-)
The Adjuster '91
Black Fox: The Price of Peace '94
Paris, France '94
Frankenfish '04
The New World '05
Apocalypto '06
Tin Man '07
Moby Dick '11
Neverland '11
Riddick '13

Ralph Truman (1900-77)
The Silent Passenger '35
The Challenge '38
Henry V '44
Treasure Island '50
The Man Who Knew Too Much '56
The Spaniard's Curse '58

Donald Trump (1946-)
Home Alone 2: Lost in New York '92
Celebrity '98 (C)

Natalie Trundy (1940-2019)
The Careless Years '57
Beneath the Planet of the Apes '70
Escape from the Planet of the Apes '71
Conquest of the Planet of the Apes '72
Battle for the Planet of the Apes '73
Huckleberry Finn '74

Tom Tryon (1926-91)
Screaming Eagles '56
Three Violent People '57
I Married a Monster from Outer Space '58
The Story of Ruth '60
Marines, Let's Go '61
The Longest Day '62
Moon Pilot '62
The Cardinal '63
In Harm's Way '65

Eric Tsang (1953-)
Supercop 2 '93
Contract Killer '98
The Accidental Spy '01
Infernal Affairs '02
Infernal Affairs 2 '03
Infernal Affairs 3 '03

Kenneth Tsang (1934-)
The Cave of the Silken Web '67
The Killer '90
Once a Thief '90
Supercop '92
The Replacement Killers '98
Rush Hour 2 '01
Die Another Day '02
Memoirs of a Geisha '05
Formosa Betrayed '09

Nicholas Tse (1980-)
Gen-X Cops '99
Time and Tide '00
New Police Story '04
The Promise '05
Dragon Tiger Gate '07

Lyudmila Tselikovskaya (1919-92)
Ivan the Terrible, Part 1 '44
Ivan the Terrible, Part 2 '46

Chang Tseng (1932-)
Dr. Jekyll & Mr. Hyde '99
Long Life, Happiness and Prosperity '02

Nikolai Tseretelli
Aelita: Queen of Mars '24
The Cigarette Girl of Mosselprom '24

Yee Jee Tso
Doctor Who '96
Antitrust '00

Irene Tsu (1910-89)
How to Stuff a Wild Bikini '65
Paradise, Hawaiian Style '66
Caprice '67
The Green Berets '68
Island of the Lost '68

Mikiko Tsubouchi (1940-)
Shinobi no Mono 2: Vengeance '63
100 Monsters '68
Gamera vs. Zigra '71

Yoshio Tsuchiya (1927-)
Seven Samurai '54
Yojimbo '61
Matango '63
Frankenstein Conquers the World '64
Red Beard '65
Destroy All Monsters '68
Godzilla vs. Monster Zero '68
Kill! '68
Yog, Monster from Space '71

Kanji Tsuda (1965-)
The Great Yokai War '05
Gamera the Brave '06
Blood '09
Tokyo Sonata '09

Elvis Tsui (1961-)
Shaolin & Wu Tang '81
Prison on Fire 2 '91
Butterfly Sword '93

Shinya Tsukamoto (1960-)
Tetsuo: The Iron Man '92
Ichi the Killer '01
Nightmare Detective '06

Yoko Tsukasa
Yojimbo '61
Goyokin '69

Masane Tsukayama (1944-)
Rica '72
Steamboy '05 (V)

Satoshi Tsumabaki
Sabu '04
Dororo '07

Satoshi Tsumabuki
The Assassin '15
The World of Kanako '15

Gotaro Tsunashima (1973-)
Japanese Story '03
The Great Raid '05

Kazue Tsunogae
Adrenaline Drive '99
Ringu 0 '01

Yuriy Tsurilo
Hard to Be a God '13
The Last Warrior '18

Shingo Tsurumi
Rasen '98
Dead or Alive '00

Barry Tubb
Mask '85
Top Gun '86
Billionaire Boys Club '87
Warm Summer Rain '89
Guilty by Suspicion '91
Return to Lonesome Dove '93

William Tubbs (1907-53)
Paisan '46
Three Steps North '51
Wages of Fear '55

Marcelo Tubert
Tremors 2: Aftershocks '96
Tortilla Heaven '07

Christine Tucci (1967-)
K-911 '99
Big Fat Liar '02
Straight from the Heart '03

Maria Tucci (1941-)
Touch and Go '86
To Die For '95
Once More With Feeling '08

Michael Tucci (1950-)
Grease '78
The Man Who Captured Eichmann '96

Nicholas Tucci (1981-2020)
You're Next '13
Most Beautiful Island '17

Stanley Tucci (1960-)
Monkey Shines '88
Slaves of New York '89
Quick Change '90
Billy Bathgate '91
Men of Respect '91
Beethoven '92
In the Soup '92
Prelude to a Kiss '92
The Public Eye '92
The Pelican Brief '93
Undercover Blues '93
It Could Happen to You '94
Kiss of Death '94
A Modern Affair '94
Somebody to Love '94
Big Night '95
Jury Duty '95
Sex and the Other Man '95
The Daytrippers '96
Deconstructing Harry '97
The Eighteenth Angel '97
A Life Less Ordinary '97
The Alarmist '98
The Imposters '98
The Impostors '98
Winchell '98
In Too Deep '99
William Shakespeare's A Midsummer Night's Dream '99
Joe Gould's Secret '00
America's Sweethearts '01
Conspiracy '01
Sidewalks of New York '01
The Whole Shebang '01
Big Trouble '02
Maid in Manhattan '02
Road to Perdition '02
The Core '03
Shall We Dance? '04
Spin '04
The Terminal '04
Robots '05 (V)
The Devil Wears Prada '06
Four Last Songs '06
The Hoax '06
Lucky Number Slevin '06
Blind Date '08
Kit Kittredge: An American Girl '08
Space Chimps '08 (V)
Swing Vote '08
The Tale of Despereaux '08 (V)
What Just Happened '08
Julie & Julia '09
The Lovely Bones '09
Burlesque '10
Easy A '10
Captain America: The First Avenger '11
Magic Trip: Ken Kesey's Search for a Kool Place '11 (N)
Margin Call '11
Gambit '12
The Hunger Games '12
The Hunger Games: Catching Fire '13
Jack the Giant Slayer '13
Percy Jackson: Sea of Monsters '13
Some Velvet Morning '13
The Hunger Games: Mockingjay--Part 1 '14
A Little Chaos '14
Mr. Peabody & Sherman '14 (V)
Transformers: Age of Extinction '14
Wild Card '15
The Children Act '18
Patient Zero '18
Show Dogs '18 (V)
Night Hunter '19

Jessica Tuck (1963-)
Mr. Write '92
Lifepod '93
Revenge of the Nerds 4: Nerds in Love '94
Batman Forever '95
Billboard Dad '98
Secretary '02
A Decent Proposal '06
The Last Days of Summer '07
Sharpay's Fabulous Adventure '11

Chris Tucker (1971-)
House Party 3 '94
Dead Presidents '95
Friday '95
The Fifth Element '97
Jackie Brown '97
Money Talks '97
Rush Hour '98
Rush Hour 2 '01
Rush Hour 3 '07
Silver Linings Playbook '12
Billy Lynn's Long Halftime Walk '16

Forrest Tucker (1919-86)
The Westerner '40
Robot Pilot '41
Canal Zone '42
Counter-Espionage '42
Keeper of the Flame '42
Never Say Goodbye '46
The Yearling '46
Gunfighters '47
The Big Cat '49
Sands of Iwo Jima '49
The Nevadan '50
Hoodlum Empire '52
Pony Express '53
Trouble in the Glen '54
Rage at Dawn '55
The Abominable Snowman '57
Three Violent People '57
Auntie Mame '58
The Crawling Eye '58
Fort Massacre '58
Counterplot '59
Chisum '70
Cancel My Reservation '72
The McCullochs '75
Once an Eagle '76
Wackiest Wagon Train in the West '77
Walking Tall: The Final Chapter '77
A Real American Hero '78
Timestalkers '87

Jonathan Tucker (1982-)
Two If by Sea '95
Sleepers '96
The Virgin Suicides '99
100 Girls '00
The Deep End '01
The Texas Chainsaw Massacre '03
Criminal '04
Stateside '04
Hostage '05
Pulse '06
Cherry Crush '07
In the Valley of Elah '07
The Ruins '08
An Englishman in New York '09
Meskada '10
The Next Three Days '10
Veronika Decides to Die '15

Larry Tucker (1933-2001)
Blast of Silence '61
Shock Corridor '63
Angels Hard As They Come '71

Michael Tucker (1945-)
Eyes of Laura Mars '78
Diner '82
The Purple Rose of Cairo '85
Radio Days '87
Tin Men '87
Checking Out '89
Day One '89
Too Young to Die '90
For Love or Money '93
D2: The Mighty Ducks '94
Til There Was You '96

Richard Tucker (1884-1942)
Wings '27
Painted Faces '29
The Squall '29
The Bat Whispers '30
The Plot Thickens '36
Two Minutes to Play '37

Sophie Tucker (1884-1966)
Broadway Melody of 1938 '37
Thoroughbreds Don't Cry '37
Sensations of 1945 '44

Tanya Tucker (1958-)
Follow That Car '80
Hard Country '81

Alan Tudyk (1971-)
Patch Adams '98
28 Days '00
Hearts in Atlantis '01
A Knight's Tale '01
Ice Age '02 (V)
Dodgeball: A True Underdog Story '04
I, Robot '04
Serenity '05
Ice Age: The Meltdown '06 (V)
Death at a Funeral '07
Knocked Up '07
3:10 to Yuma '07
Meet Market '08
Tucker & Dale vs. Evil '10
Transformers: Dark of the Moon '11
Wreck-It Ralph '12 (V)
Big Hero 6 '14 (V)
Rogue One: A Star Wars Story '16
Zootopia '16 (V)

Sonny Tufts (1911-70)
Government Girl '43
So Proudly We Hail '43
Here Come the Waves '45
The Virginian '46
Easy Living '49
Cat Women of the Moon '53
No Escape '53
The Seven Year Itch '55
Easy Come, Easy Go '67

Ulrich Tukur (1957-)
My Mother's Courage '95
Taking Sides '01
Amen '02
Solaris '02
Operation Valkyrie '04
The Lives of Others '06
North Face '08
Seraphine '08
John Rabe '09
The White Ribbon '09

Tom Tully (1908-82)
Destination Tokyo '43
Northern Pursuit '43
I'll Be Seeing You '44
Lady in the Lake '46
Till the End of Time '46
The Virginian '46
Killer McCoy '47
Where the Sidewalk Ends '50
Texas Carnival '51
Tomahawk '51
The Jazz Singer '52
Love Is Better Than Ever '52

Lure of the Wilderness '52
The Moon Is Blue '53
Trouble along the Way '53
The Caine Mutiny '54
Love Me or Leave Me '55
Soldier of Fortune '55
Coogan's Bluff '68

Frans Tumbuan
Rage and Honor 2: Hostile Takeover '93
Java Heat '13

Tommy Tune (1939-)
Hello, Dolly! '69
The Boy Friend '71

Bill Tung (1933-2006)
Police Story '85
Jackie Chan's First Strike '96
Rumble in the Bronx '96

Jennifer Tung (1973-)
The President's Man '00
Kung Pow! Enter the Fist '02
The President's Man 2: A Line in the Sand '02

Tamara Tunie (1959-)
Rebound: The Legend of Earl 'The Goat' Manigault '96
The Devil's Advocate '97
Eve's Bayou '97 (N)
Snake Eyes '98
The Caveman's Valentine '01
Flight '12

Robin Tunney (1972-)
Encino Man '92
JFK: Reckless Youth '93
Empire Records '95
The Craft '96
Riders of the Purple Sage '96
Julian Po '97
Niagara, Niagara '97
End of Days '99
Supernova '99
Vertical Limit '00
Intimate Affairs '01
Cherish '02
The Secret Lives of Dentists '02
The In-Laws '03
Paparazzi '04
Runaway '05
The Zodiac '05
Hollywoodland '06
Open Window '06
August '08
The Burning Plain '08
The Two Mr. Kissels '08
Passenger Side '09
My All American '15
Horse Girl '20

James Tupper (1965-)
Love's Long Journey '05
Invisible '06
Love's Abiding Joy '06
Pictures of Hollis Woods '07
Toxic Skies '08
The Gambler, the Girl and the Gunslinger '09
Me and Orson Welles '09
Girl Fight '11
Playing for Keeps '12
Beneath Us '20

Arlene Tur
Final Engagement '07
Eat, Pray, Love '10

Robert Turano
Federal Hill '94
One Way Out '95
Brooklyn Rules '07

Paige Turco (1965-)
Teenage Mutant Ninja Turtles 2: The Secret of the Ooze '91
Teenage Mutant Ninja Turtles 3 '93
Vibrations '94
The Pompatus of Love '95
Astoria '00
Dead Dog '00
Urbania '00
Invincible '06
Waltzing Anna '06
The Game Plan '07
The Stepfather '09
Taking Chance '09
Secrets of the Mountain '10

Paolo Turco
The Lickerish Quartet '70
Bread and Chocolate '73

Thomas Turgoose
This Is England '06
The Hatching '16
Avengement '19

Ann Turkel
Paper Lion '68
99 & 44/100 Dead '74
The Cassandra Crossing '76
Portrait of a Hitman '77
Humanoids from the Deep '80
Death Ray 2000 '81
The Fear '94

Joe Turkel (1927-)
The Killing '56
Paths of Glory '57
The Case Against Brooklyn '58
King Rat '65
Village of the Giants '65
The Sand Pebbles '66
The Desperados '70
Cycle Psycho '72
The Shining '80
Blade Runner '82

Gregg Turkington
Entertainment '15
Mister America '19

Glynn Turman (1947-)
Cooley High '75
J.D.'s Revenge '76
The River Niger '76
Centennial '78
A Hero Ain't Nothin' but a Sandwich '78
Penitentiary 2 '82
Gremlins '84
Secrets of a Married Man '84
Deep Cover '92
Race to Freedom: The Story of the Underground Railroad '94
Rebound: The Legend of Earl 'The Goat' Manigault '96
Buffalo Soldiers '97
Subterfuge '98
Light It Up '99
Freedom Song '00
Men of Honor '00
The Visit '00
Sahara '05

John Turnbull (1880-1956)
The Private Life of Henry VIII '33
The Passing of the Third Floor Back '35
The 39 Steps '35
Nine Days a Queen '36
Man of Evil '48

Aidan Turner (1983-)
Alarm '08
The Mortal Instruments: City of Bones '13
The Hobbit: The Battle of the Five Armies '14
Love Is Blind '19
The Man Who Killed Hitler and Then the Bigfoot '19

Bree Turner (1977-)
Bring It On Again '03
Just My Luck '06
Firehouse Dog '07
The Ugly Truth '09
Take Me Home '11

Callum Turner
Queen and Country '14
The Only Living Boy in New York '17
Mobile Homes '19

Glynn Turner (1947-)
Kings of the Evening '08
John Dies at the End '12

Guinevere Turner (1968-)
Go Fish '94
Chasing Amy '97
Preaching to the Perverted '97
The Watermelon Woman '97
American Psycho '99
Dogma '99
Pipe Dream '02
Itty Bitty Titty Committee '07
The Owls '09

Janine Turner (1962-)
Young Doctors in Love '82 (C)
Monkey Shines '88
Steel Magnolias '89
The Ambulance '90
Cliffhanger '93
Leave It to Beaver '97
Stolen Women, Captured Hearts '97
Fatal Error '99
A Secret Affair '99
Dr. T & the Women '00
Miracle Dogs Too '06
The Night of the White Pants '06

Jessica Turner
All or Nothing at All '93
Karma Police '08

Jim Turner (1952-)
Kid Colter '85
Joe's Apartment '96
Off the Lip '04
Bewitched '05

John Turner (1932-)
The Giant Behemoth '59
Black Torment '64
Estate of Insanity '64
Captain Nemo and the Underwater City '69
The Slipper and the Rose '76

Kathleen Turner (1954-)
Body Heat '81
The Man with Two Brains '83
Crimes of Passion '84
Romancing the Stone '84
The Jewel of the Nile '85
Prizzi's Honor '85
Peggy Sue Got Married '86
The Accidental Tourist '88
Switching Channels '88
Who Framed Roger Rabbit '88 (V)
Honey, I Shrunk the Kids '89 (V)
The War of the Roses '89
V.I. Warshawski '91
House of Cards '92
Naked in New York '93
Undercover Blues '93
Serial Mom '94
Moonlight and Valentino '95
The Real Blonde '97
A Simple Wish '97
Baby Geniuses '98
Legalese '98
Love and Action in Chicago '99
The Virgin Suicides '99
Beautiful '00
Prince of Central Park '00
Monster House '06 (V)
Marley & Me '08
The Perfect Family '11
Nurse 3D '13
Dumb and Dumber To '14

Kristopher Turner
The Brotherhood 3: The Young Demons '02
A Dad for Christmas '06
An Old-Fashioned Thanksgiving '08
Without a Paddle: Nature's Calling '09

Lana Turner (1920-95)
The Great Garrick '37
They Won't Forget '37
Love Finds Andy Hardy '38
Calling Dr. Kildare '39
Dancing Co-Ed '39
Those Glamour Girls '39
Two Girls on Broadway '40
Dr. Jekyll and Mr. Hyde '41
Honky Tonk '41
Ziegfeld Girl '41
Johnny Eager '42
Somewhere I'll Find You '42
Slightly Dangerous '43
Keep Your Powder Dry '45
Weekend at the Waldorf '45
The Postman Always Rings Twice '46
Cass Timberlane '47
Green Dolphin Street '47
Homecoming '48
The Three Musketeers '48
A Life of Her Own '50
Mr. Imperium '51
The Bad and the Beautiful '52
Betrayed '54
Diane '55
The Prodigal '55
The Rains of Ranchipur '55
Sea Chase '55
Peyton Place '57
Another Time, Another Place '58
Imitation of Life '59
Portrait in Black '60
Bachelor in Paradise '61
By Love Possessed '61
Who's Got the Action? '63
Love Has Many Faces '65
Madame X '66

Lawrence Turner
Mirrors 2 '10
Nine Dead '10

Morgan Turner (1999-)
Mildred Pierce '11
Quitters '16

Sophie Turner
Barely Lethal '15
X-Men: Apocalypse '16
Time Freak '18
Dark Phoenix '19

Ted Turner (1938-)
Gettysburg '93
Gods and Generals '03 (C)

Tina Turner (1939-)
Gimme Shelter '70
Tommy '75
Mad Max: Beyond Thunderdome '85

Travis Turner
Marley & Me: The Puppy Years '11
A Princess for Christmas '11

Tyrin Turner (1971-)
Menace II Society '93
Little Boy Blue '97
Belly '98

Zara Turner (1968-)
Sliding Doors '97
The Waiting Time '99

Maude Turner Gordon (1868-1940)
The Early Bird '25
The Last of Mrs. Cheyney '29
Sally '29

Ben Turpin (1874-1940)
Make Me a Star '32
Law of the Wild '34

Kett Turton (1982-)
Gypsy 83 '01
Falling Angels '03
Heart of America '03
Show Me '04
A Simple Curve '05
Firewall '06

Aida Turturro (1962-)
True Love '89
Jersey Girl '92
Tales of Erotica '93
Angie '94
Junior '94
Money Train '95
Sleepers '96
Celebrity '98
Illuminata '98
Bringing Out the Dead '99
Deep Blue Sea '99
Hitman's Journal '99
The 24 Hour Woman '99
24 Nights '99
Crocodile Dundee in Los Angeles '01
Sidewalks of New York '01
2B Perfectly Honest '04
Romance & Cigarettes '05
Rob the Mob '14

John Turturro (1957-)
Desperately Seeking Susan '85
To Live & Die in L.A. '85
The Color of Money '86
Gung Ho '86
Hannah and Her Sisters '86
The Sicilian '87
Five Corners '88
Backtrack '89
Do the Right Thing '89
Miller's Crossing '90
Mo' Better Blues '90
State of Grace '90
Barton Fink '91
Jungle Fever '91
Men of Respect '91
Brain Donors '92
Fearless '93
Mac '93
Being Human '94
Quiz Show '94
Search and Destroy '94
The Search for One-Eye Jimmy '94
Clockers '95
Sugartime '95
Unstrung Heroes '95
Box of Moonlight '96
Girl 6 '96
Grace of My Heart '96
The Truce '96
The Big Lebowski '97
He Got Game '98
Illuminata '98
Rounders '98
The Cradle Will Rock '99
Company Man '00
The Luzhin Defence '00
The Man Who Cried '00
O Brother Where Art Thou? '00
Monkeybone '01 (V)
Thirteen Conversations About One Thing '01
Collateral Damage '02
Mr. Deeds '02
Monday Night Mayhem '02
Anger Management '03
Fear X '03
Secret Window '04
She Hate Me '04
2B Perfectly Honest '04
A Few Days in September '06
The Good Shepherd '06
The Bronx Is Burning '07
Margot at the Wedding '07
Slipstream '07
Transformers '07
Miracle at St. Anna '08
What Just Happened '08
You Don't Mess with the Zohan '08
The Taking of Pelham 123 '09
Transformers: Revenge of the Fallen '09
Cars 2 '11 (V)
Transformers: Dark of the Moon '11
Fading Gigolo '13
Exodus: Gods and Kings '14
God's Pocket '14
Mia Madre '16
Landline '17
Gloria Bell '18

Nicholas Turturro (1962-)
Mo' Better Blues '90
Jungle Fever '91
Mac '93
Federal Hill '94
The Search for One-Eye Jimmy '94
Excess Baggage '96
The Shadow Conspiracy '96
Witness to the Mob '98
Hellraiser 5: Inferno '00
Big Shot: Confessions of a Campus Bookie '02
Monday Night Mayhem '02
The Hillside Stranglings '04
The Hollow '04
The Longest Yard '05
Trapped '06
I Now Pronounce You Chuck and Larry '07
Phantom Punch '09
Street Boss '09
Paul Blart: Mall Cop 2 '15

Rita Tushingham (1942-)
The Leather Boys '63
Girl with Green Eyes '64
Doctor Zhivago '65
The Knack '65
Smashing Time '67
The Bed Sitting Room '69
Dressed for Death '74
The Human Factor '75
Rachel's Man '75
Mysteries '84
Dream to Believe '85
An Awfully Big Adventure '94
Being Julia '04

Dorothy Tutin (1930-2001)
The Importance of Being Earnest '52
Beggar's Opera '54
A Tale of Two Cities '58
Six Wives of Henry VIII '71
Savage Messiah '72
Agatha Christie's Murder with Mirrors '85
The Shooting Party '85
Anglo-Saxon Attitudes '92
Body & Soul '93
Shades of Fear '93
Scarlett '94
Alive and Kicking '96

Tracy Tutor
Expose '97
No Vacancy '99

Lurene Tuttle (1906-86)
Homecoming '48
Goodbye My Fancy '51
Room for One More '51
Tomorrow Is Another Day '51
Don't Bother to Knock '52
Niagara '52
The Affairs of Dobie Gillis '53
The Glass Slipper '55
Sincerely Yours '55
Untamed Youth '57
Ma Barker's Killer Brood '60
The Fortune Cookie '66
The Ghost and Mr. Chicken '66
The Manitou '78

Aaron Tveit (1983-)
Howl '10
Better Off Single '16
Undrafted '16
Out of Blue '19

Shannon Tweed (1957-)
Hot Dog. . . The Movie! '83
Of Unknown Origin '83
Cannibal Women in the Avocado Jungle of Death '89
In the Cold of the Night '89
Night Visitor '89
Twisted Justice '89
Last Call '90
The Firing Line '91
Cold Sweat '93
Hard Vice '94
Indecent Behavior 2 '94
Night Fire '94
No Contest '94
Vegas Vice '94
Body Chemistry 4: Full Exposure '95
Face the Evil '97
Human Desires '97
Shadow Warriors 2: Hunt for the Death Merchant '97
Shadow Warriors '97
Dead by Dawn '98
Naked Lies '98
Forbidden Sins '99
The Rowdy Girls '00
Wish You Were Dead '00

Dead Sexy '01
Hugh Hefner: Playboy, Activist and Rebel '09

Helen Twelvetrees (1907-58)
Millie '31
The Painted Desert '31
State's Attorney '31

Twiggy (1949-)
The Boy Friend '71
W '74
Butterfly Ball '76
The Blues Brothers '80 (C)
The Doctor and the Devils '85
Club Paradise '86
Madame Sousatzka '88
Body Bags '93

Anne Twomey (1951-)
Behind Enemy Lines '85
Deadly Friend '86
Last Rites '88
The Scout '94
Picture Perfect '96
The Confession '98

Alexandra Tydings (1972-)
Red Shoe Diaries 7: Burning Up '96
Sunchaser '96

Aisha Tyler (1970-)
The Santa Clause 2 '02
Never Die Alone '04
For One Night '06
.45 '06
The Santa Clause 3: The Escape Clause '06 (C)
Balls of Fury '07
Death Sentence '07
Bedtime Stories '08
Meet Market '08
The Babymakers '12

Beverly Tyler (1927-2005)
The Green Years '46
My Brother Talks to Horses '47
The Fireball '50
Chicago Confidential '57

Harry Tyler (1888-1961)
Pennies from Heaven '36
Bedtime for Bonzo '51

Liv Tyler (1977-)
Heavy '94
Silent Fall '94
Empire Records '95
Stealing Beauty '96
That Thing You Do! '96
Inventing the Abbotts '97
U-Turn '97
Armageddon '98
Plunkett & Macleane '98
Cookie's Fortune '99
Onegin '99
Dr. T & the Women '00
Lord of the Rings: The Fellowship of the Ring '01
One Night at McCool's '01
Lord of the Rings: The Two Towers '02
Lord of the Rings: The Return of the King '03
Jersey Girl '04
Lonesome Jim '06
Reign Over Me '07
The Incredible Hulk '08
Smother '08
The Strangers '08
Super '10
The Ledge '11
Robot & Frank '12
Jamie Marks is Dead '13
Mademoiselle C '13
Space Station 76 '14
Wildling '18

Tom Tyler (1903-54)
Battling with Buffalo Bill '31
Phantom of the West '31
Last Outlaw '36
Stagecoach '39
The Mummy's Hand '40
The Westerner '40
She Wore a Yellow Ribbon '49

Hunter Tylo (1962-)
A Place Called Home '04
Down and Derby '05

Judy Tylor (1979-)
My 5 Wives '00
Freshman Orientation '04
Dead Tone '07
What Love Is '07

George Tyne (1917-2008)
Objective, Burma! '45
A Walk in the Sun '46
Call Northside 777 '48
Open Secret '48
Sands of Iwo Jima '49

Charles Tyner (1925-)
Cool Hand Luke '67
The Cheyenne Social Club '70
Harold and Maude '71
Jeremiah Johnson '72
Emperor of the North Pole '73
The Longest Yard '74
Planes, Trains & Automobiles '87
Pulse '88

Tyrese (1978-)
See Tyrese Gibson

Susan Tyrrell (1945-2012)
Shoot Out '71
Fat City '72
Zandy's Bride '74
The Killer Inside Me '76
Andy Warhol's Bad '77
Another Man, Another Chance '77
Islands in the Stream '77
September 30, 1955 '77
Forbidden Zone '80
Fast Walking '82
Liar's Moon '82
Fire and Ice '83 (V)
Tales of Ordinary Madness '83
Angel '84
Avenging Angel '85
Flesh and Blood '85
The Offspring '87
Poker Alice '87
Big Top Pee-wee '88
Far from Home '89
Tapeheads '89
Cry-Baby '90
Rockula '90
Thompson's Last Run '90
Motorama '91
The Demolitionist '95
Powder '95
Relax. . . It's Just Sex! '98
Buddy Boy '99

Barbara Tyson (1964-)
Ratz '99
Resurrection '99
Beautiful Joe '00
K-9 3: P.I. '01

Cathy Tyson (1965-)
Mona Lisa '86
The Serpent and the Rainbow '87
The Lost Language of Cranes '92
Priest '94
Band of Gold '95

Cicely Tyson (1924-)
A Man Called Adam '66
The Heart Is a Lonely Hunter '68
Sounder '72
The Autobiography of Miss Jane Pittman '74
The River Niger '76
Roots '77
Wilma '77
A Hero Ain't Nothin' but a Sandwich '78
King '78
A Woman Called Moses '78
The Concorde: Airport '79 '79
Bustin' Loose '81
Samaritan: The Mitch Snyder Story '86
The Women of Brewster Place '89
Heat Wave '90
Fried Green Tomatoes '91
Oldest Confederate Widow Tells All '95
Hoodlum '96
Riot in the Streets '96
Always Outnumbered Always Outgunned '98
Mama Flora's Family '98
Aftershock: Earthquake in New York '99
A Lesson Before Dying '99
Life '99
The Rosa Parks Story '02
Because of Winn-Dixie '05
Diary of a Mad Black Woman '05
Madea's Family Reunion '06
Relative Stranger '09
Tyler Perry's Why Did I Get Married Too '10
The Help '11
Alex Cross '12
The Haunting in Connecticut 2: Ghosts of Georgia '13
The Trip to Bountiful '14

Michael G. Tyson (1966-)
See Mike Tyson

Mike Tyson (1966-)
Black and White '99
Crocodile Dundee in Los Angeles '01 (C)
Tyson '08
The Hangover '09

Mike Tyson (1966-)
Ip Man 3 '16
A Madea Family Funeral '19

Pamela Tyson
Jungle Fever '91
What's Love Got to Do with It? '93
Last Dance '96

Richard Tyson (1961-)
Three O'Clock High '87
Two Moon Junction '88
Kindergarten Cop '90
The Babe '92
Red Shoe Diaries 3: Another Woman's Lipstick '93
Pharoah's Army '95
Kingpin '96
Monsoon '97
Tales of the Kama Sutra 2: Monsoon '98
There's Something about Mary '98
Desert Thunder '99
Liar's Poker '99
Battlefield Earth '00
Lethal Force '00
Black Hawk Down '01
Firetrap '01
Moscow Heat '04
The Trail to Hope Rose '04
Big Bad Wolf '06
When I Find the Ocean '06
Flight of the Living Dead: Outbreak on a Plane '07
Jake's Corner '08
Lost Treasure of the Maya '08
Shoot First and Pray You Live '08
3 Days Gone '08
Magic Man '10

Galina Tyunina
Night Watch '04
Day Watch '06

Margaret Tyzack (1931-2011)
2001: A Space Odyssey '68
Quatermass Conclusion '79
The King's Whore '90
Mrs. Dalloway '97
Our Mutual Friend '98
Match Point '05

Alanna Ubach (1975-)
Airborne '93
Freeway '95
johns '96
Clockwatchers '97
Blue Moon '00
Crazy Little Thing '02
Legally Blonde 2: Red White & Blonde '03
Meet the Fockers '04
Waiting '05
Still Waiting '08
Coco '17
Gloria Bell '18

Ryohei Uchida (1931-84)
The Human Condition: Road to Eternity '59
Blind Woman's Curse '70
Rica '72

Fabiana Udenio (1964-)
Hardbodies 2 '86
Summer School '87
Bride of Re-Animator '89
Austin Powers: International Man of Mystery '97
The Godson '98

Bob Uecker (1934-)
Major League '89
Major League 2 '94
Homeward Bound 2: Lost in San Francisco '96 (V)
Major League 3: Back to the Minors '98

Kichijiro Ueda (1904-72)
Rashomon '51
Seven Samurai '54
The Hidden Fortress '58
Gamera vs. Gaos '67

Ken Uehara
Mothra '62
Atragon '63

Misa(ko) Uehara (1937-)
The Hidden Fortress '58
Ju-On: The Grudge '03

Kenjiro Uemura (1914-79)
A Quiet Duel '49
The Human Condition: Road to Eternity '59

Aya Ueto
Azumi '03
Azumi 2 '05

Unax Ugalde
There Be Dragons '11
Argento's Dracula 3D '13

Leslie Uggams (1943-)
Two Weeks in Another Town '62
Skyjacked '72
Poor Pretty Eddie '73
Roots '77
Backstairs at the White House '79
Sugar Hill '94
Toe to Toe '09

Nadja Uhl (1972-)
The Legend of Rita '99
What to Do in Case of Fire '02
The Baader Meinhof Complex '08
Cherry Blossoms '08

Gisela Uhlen (1919-2007)
The Indian Scarf '63
The Marriage of Maria Braun '79
Toto le Heros '91

Ana Ularu
Anacondas: Trail of Blood '09
Werewolf: The Beast Among Us '12
Serena '14
Chosen '16
Siberia '18

Emilie Ullerup (1984-)
Witchslayer Gretl '12
Step Dogs '13
Death Do Us Part '14

Gaspard Ulliel (1984-)
Strayed '03
A Very Long Engagement '04
Paris, je t'aime '06
Hannibal Rising '07
A Heavenly Vintage '09
Ultimate Heist '09
The Princess of Montpensier '10

Raviv (Ricky) Ullman (1986-)
The Big Bad Swim '06
Havoc 2: Normal Adolescent Behavior '07
Prom Wars '08

Tracey Ullman (1959-)
Give My Regards to Broad Street '84
Plenty '85
Jumpin' Jack Flash '86 (C)
I Love You to Death '90
Happily Ever After '93 (V)
I'll Do Anything '93
Robin Hood: Men in Tights '93
Bullets over Broadway '94
Ready to Wear '94
Panic '00
Small Time Crooks '00
A Dirty Shame '04
Tim Burton's Corpse Bride '05 (V)
I Could Never Be Your Woman '06
The Tale of Despereaux '08 (V)
Into the Woods '14

Liv Ullmann (1939-)
Persona '66
Hour of the Wolf '68
The Shame '68
The Night Visitor '70
The Passion of Anna '70
Cold Sweat '71
Cries and Whispers '72
The New Land '72
Forty Carats '73
Lost Horizon '73
Scenes from a Marriage '73
Zandy's Bride '74
Face to Face '76
A Bridge Too Far '77
Autumn Sonata '78
The Serpent's Egg '78
Dangerous Moves '84
The Wild Duck '84
The Rose Garden '89
The Ox '91
Saraband '03

Tristan Ulloa (1970-)
The Nameless '99
Km. 0 '00
Sex and Lucia '01
The 4 Musketeers '05

Skeet Ulrich (1970-)
Boys '95
Albino Alligator '96
The Craft '96
Last Dance '96
Scream '96
Touch '96
As Good As It Gets '97
The Newton Boys '97
Chill Factor '99
Ride with the Devil '99
Chilly Dogs '01
Nobody's Baby '01
Soul Assassin '01
Armored '09
For Sale by Owner '09
50 to 1 '14

Fred Ulysse
Making Plans for Lena '09
Prey '10

Mark Umbers (1973-)
A Good Woman '04
Blackbeard '06
These Foolish Things '06

Miyoshi Umeki (1929-2007)
Sayonara '57
Flower Drum Song '61
The Horizontal Lieutenant '62

Edward Underdown (1908-89)
Wings of the Morning '37
Inspector Hornleigh '39
The Voice of Merrill '52
Beat the Devil '53
Recoil '53
The Shadow Man '53
Pattern for Plunder '62
Beast of Morocco '66

Blair Underwood (1964-)
Krush Groove '85
Heat Wave '90
Dangerous Relations '93
Posse '93
Just Cause '94
Mistrial '96
Set It Off '96
Soul of the Game '96
Deep Impact '98
Mama Flora's Family '98
Asunder '99
Rules of Engagement '00
Full Frontal '02
G '02
Malibu's Most Wanted '03
The Hades Factor '06
The Hit '06
Madea's Family Reunion '06
Something New '06
The Art of Getting By '11
The Trip to Bountiful '14
Juanita '19

Jay Underwood (1968-)
The Boy Who Could Fly '86
Desert Bloom '86
Promised Land '88
Uncle Buck '89
Sleepstalker: The Sandman's Last Rites '94
A Reason to Believe '95
Afterglow '97
The Nurse '97
Stalker '98
Possums '99
Dancing in September '00

Billy Unger (1995-)
Opposite Day '09
You Again '10
The Lost Medallion: The Adventures of Billy Stone '13

Deborah Kara Unger (1966-)
Prisoners of the Sun '91
Whispers in the Dark '92
Highlander: The Final Dimension '94
Crash '95
Keys to Tulsa '96
No Way Home '96
The Game '97
Payback '98
The Rat Pack '98
The Hurricane '99
Sunshine '99
Luminous Motion '00
Signs & Wonders '00
The Weekend '00
Between Strangers '02
Leo '02
The Salton Sea '02
Emile '03
Fear X '03
Hollywood North '03
Stander '03
Thirteen '03
A Love Song for Bobby Long '04
Paranoia 1.0 '04
White Noise '05
Lies & Alibis '06
Silent Hill '06
Shake Hands With the Devil '07
88 Minutes '08
Angel and the Badman '09
Takedown '10
The Way '10
A Dark Truth '12
The Good Samaritan '12
Silent Hill: Revelation 3D '12

Joe Unger
Go Tell the Spartans '78
Leatherface: The Texas Chainsaw Massacre 3 '89

Gabrielle Union (1972-)
She's All That '99
Ten Things I Hate about You '99
Bring It On '00
The Brothers '01
Two Can Play That Game '01
Abandon '02
Welcome to Collinwood '02
Bad Boys 2 '03

Cradle 2 the Grave '03
Deliver Us from Eva '03
Breakin' All The Rules '04
Something the Lord Made '04
The Honeymooners '05
Neo Ned '05
Say Uncle '05
Running with Scissors '06
The Box '07
Daddy's Little Girls '07
The Perfect Holiday '07
Cadillac Records '08
Meet Dave '08
Flight '12
Think Like a Man '12
Tyler Perry's Good Deeds '12
Think Like a Man Too '14
Top Five '14
Sleepless '17
Breaking In '18

Misty Upham (1982-2014)
Frozen River '08
August: Osage County '13

Kate Upton
The Other Woman '14
The Layover '17

Johann Urb (1977-)
All In '06
The Bank Job '07
The Hottie and the Nottie '08
Strictly Sexual '08
Dorfman in Love '11
Resident Evil: Retribution '12

Karl Urban (1972-)
The Price of Milk '00
Ghost Ship '02
Lord of the Rings: The Two Towers '02
Lord of the Rings: The Return of the King '03
The Bourne Supremacy '04
The Chronicles of Riddick '04
Doom '05
Pathfinder '07
Comanche Moon '08
Star Trek '09
And Soon the Darkness '10
RED '10
Priest '11
Dredd '12
Riddick '13
Star Trek: Into Darkness '13
Walking with Dinosaurs 3D '13 (V)
The Loft '14
Star Trek: Beyond '16
Acts of Vengeance '17
Hangman '17

James Urbaniak (1963-)
The Sticky Fingers of Time '97
Henry Fool '98
Sweet and Lowdown '99
American Splendor '03
Plain Dirty '04
Fortunes '05
Fay Grim '06
Cinema Verite '11

Roberto Urbina
Towards Darkness '07
Hostile Border '16

Mary Ure (1933-75)
Storm Over the Nile '55
Look Back in Anger '58
Sons and Lovers '60
The Mind Benders '63
Where Eagles Dare '68
A Reflection of Fear '73

Minerva Urecal (1894-1966)
Murder by Invitation '41
Niagara '52

Fabio Urena
The Bronx War '90
Return of the Living Dead 3 '93

Justin Urich (1978-)
Winter Break '02
Monster Man '03
Serial Killing 101 '04
Perfect Victims '08

Robert Urich (1946-2002)
Magnum Force '73
Vegas '78
Endangered Species '82
Ice Pirates '84
Invitation to Hell '84
Mistral's Daughter '84
Turk 182! '85
April Morning '88
Lonesome Dove '89
In a Stranger's Hand '92
Deadly Relations '93
Spenser: Ceremony '93
Spenser: A Savage Place '94
Spenser: Pale Kings & Princes '94
Spenser: The Judas Goat '94
Captains Courageous '95
A Horse for Danny '95
A Long Way Home '01
The President's Man 2: A Line in the Sand '02

Michael Urie (1980-)
Beverly Hills Chihuahua '08 (V)
The Decoy Bride '11
Petunia '13

Robert Urquhart (1922-95)
The House of the Arrow '53
The Curse of Frankenstein '57
White Huntress '57
The Kitchen Toto '87

Benny 'The Jet' Urquidez (1952-)
Down the Drain '89
Grosse Pointe Blank '97

Saro Urzi
Seduced and Abandoned '64
Who's Got the Black Box? '67

Jun Usami (1911-81)
Late Spring '49
Tora! Tora! Tora! '70

Usher (1978-)
See Usher Raymond

Guy Usher (1883-1944)
Make a Million '35
Prison Break '38

Jessie T. Usher
Independence Day: Resurgence '16
Shaft '19

Peter Ustinov (1921-2004)
One of Our Aircraft Is Missing '41
Immortal Battalion '44
Quo Vadis '51
Le Plaisir '52 (N)
Beau Brummell '54
The Egyptian '54
Lola Montes '55
We're No Angels '55
Spartacus '60
The Sundowners '60
Billy Budd '62
Topkapi '64
Lady L '65 (C)
Blackbeard's Ghost '67
The Comedians '67
Hot Millions '68
Viva Max '69
Robin Hood '73 (V)
One of Our Dinosaurs Is Missing '75
Logan's Run '76
The Treasure of Matecumbe '76
The Last Remake of Beau Geste '77
Death on the Nile '78
The Thief of Baghdad '78
Ashanti, Land of No Mercy '79
Charlie Chan and the Curse of the Dragon Queen '81
The Great Muppet Caper '81
Evil under the Sun '82
Agatha Christie's Thirteen at Dinner '85
Around the World in 80 Days '89
Lorenzo's Oil '92
The Old Curiosity Shop '94
Stiff Upper Lips '96
Alice in Wonderland '99
Animal Farm '99 (V)
The Bachelor '99
Victoria & Albert '01
Luther '03

Ken Utsui
Atomic Rulers of the World '65
Evil Brain from Outer Space '65

Iko Uwais
The Raid: Redemption '11
Headshot '17
Mile 22 '18
Stuber '19
Triple Threat '19

Kari Vaananen (1953-)
Night on Earth '91
Ambush '99

Brenda Vaccaro (1939-)
Midnight Cowboy '69
Where It's At '69
Going Home '71
Summertree '71
Honor Thy Father '73
Once Is Not Enough '75
Airport '77 '77
Capricorn One '78
The First Deadly Sin '80
The Guyana Tragedy: The Story of Jim Jones '80
Pride of Jesse Hallum '81
Zorro, the Gay Blade '81
Supergirl '84
Water '85
Cookie '89
Following Her Heart '94
Love Affair '94
The Mirror Has Two Faces '96
Sonny '02
The Boynton Beach Club '05
You Don't Know Jack '10

Annette (Stroyberg) Vadim (1936-2005)
Dangerous Liaisons '60
Blood and Roses '61

David Vadim
Little Odessa '94
Air Force One '97
Exit Wounds '01

Roger Vadim (1928-2000)
Edie in Ciao! Manhattan '72
Into the Night '85

Dan Vadis (1938-87)
Son of Hercules in the Land of Darkness '63
Fort Yuma Gold '66
The Triumph of Hercules '66
Death is Nimble, Death is Quick '67
Bronco Billy '80

Vera Vague (1905-74)
See Barbara Jo Allen

Lester Vail (1900-59)
Beau Ideal '31
Dance Fools Dance '31
The Woman Between '31

Charlotte Valandrey (1968-)
Orlando '92
My Life and Times with Antonin Artaud '93

Birgitta Valberg (1916-)
The Virgin Spring '59
The Shame '68

Serge-Henri Valcke (1946-)
The Quarry '98
No Man's Land '01
Soul Assassin '01

Wilmer Valderrama (1980-)
Party Monster '03
Clifford's Really Big Movie '04 (V)
The Darwin Awards '06
Fast Food Nation '06
Unaccompanied Minors '06
The Dead One '07
Columbus Day '08
The Dry Land '10
From Prada to Nada '11
Larry Crowne '11
The Adderall Diaries '16

Jerry Vale (1932-2014)
Goodfellas '90
Casino '95

Virginia Vale (1920-2006)
Blonde Comet '41
South of Panama '41

Carlos Valencia
In the Blood '06
Towards Darkness '07

Vladimir Valenta (1923-2001)
Closely Watched Trains '66
Vengeance Is Mine '74
The Unbearable Lightness of Being '88

Deborah Valente
The Devil's Mercy '07
Cell 213 '11

Barbara Valentin (1940-2002)
Carmen, Baby '66
World on a Wire '73

Anthony Valentine (1939-)
Dangerous Corner '83
Robin Hood. . . The Legend: Robin Hood and the Sorcerer '83
Riders '88
Body & Soul '93
Two Men Went to War '02

Gary Valentine (1961-)
The Dog Who Saved Christmas '09
The Dog Who Saved Christmas Vacation '10
The Dog Who Saved Halloween '11
The Dog Who Saved the Holidays '12
The Dog Who Saved Summer '15

Karen Valentine (1947-)
Return to Fantasy Island '77
Hot Lead & Cold Feet '78
The North Avenue Irregulars '79
Jane Doe '83
Children in the Crossfire '84
The Power Within '95

Scott Valentine (1958-)
Deadtime Stories '86
True Stories '86
My Demon Lover '87
Dangerous Pursuit '89
To Sleep with a Vampire '92
The Unborn 2 '94
Object of Obsession '95
Phantom 2040 Movie: The Ghost Who Walks '95 (V)
Carnosaur 3: Primal Species '96
Mars '96
Paranoia '98
Airline Disaster '10

Rudolph Valentino (1895-1926)
The Married Virgin '18
The Eyes of Youth '19
The Four Horsemen of the Apocalypse '21
The Sheik '21
Beyond the Rocks '22
Blood and Sand '22
Moran of the Lady Letty '22
Monsieur Beaucaire '24
Cobra '25
The Eagle '25

Lili Valenty
Wild Is the Wind '57
Girls! Girls! Girls! '62

Tasia Valenza (1968-)
Crackers '84
Rappin' '85

Daniel Valenzuela
The Road '00
La Leon '07

Laura Valenzuela
Madame Sans-Gene '62
Make Your Bets Ladies '65

Jeanne Valerie (1941-)
Dangerous Liaisons '60
Desert Commandos '67

Joan Valerie (1911-83)
Children of the Wild '37
Day-Time Wife '39
Michael Shayne: Private Detective '40

Fanny Valette
La Petite Jerusalem '05
Moliere '07

Rosa Valetti (1878-1937)
Tartuffe '25
The Blue Angel '30
M '31

Frederick Valk (1895-1956)
Night Train to Munich '40
Dead of Night '45
Frenzy '46
Bad Blonde '53
Zarak '56

Kitty Vallacher
Grave of the Vampire '72
The Legend of Frank Woods '77

Riccardo Valle
The Awful Dr. Orloff '62
Hercules *vs.* the Sons of the Sun '64

Rudy Vallee (1901-86)
Vagabond Lover '29
Glorifying the American Girl '30
International House '33
Gold Diggers in Paris '38
Time Out for Rhythm '41
The Palm Beach Story '42
People Are Funny '46
The Bachelor and the Bobby-Soxer '47
The Sin of Harold Diddlebock '47
I Remember Mama '48
So This Is New York '48
Unfaithfully Yours '48
The Beautiful Blonde from Bashful Bend '49
Mother Is a Freshman '49
My Dear Secretary '49
The Admiral Was a Lady '50
How to Succeed in Business without Really Trying '67
Live a Little, Love a Little '68
Slashed Dreams '74

Amber Valletta (1974-)
Family Man '00
What Lies Beneath '00
Max Keeble's Big Move '01
Duplex '03
Hitch '05
Transporter 2 '05
The Last Time '06
Dead Silence '07
Premonition '07
Gamer '09
The Spy Next Door '10

Mark Valley (1964-)
George Wallace '97
The Siege '98
The Next Best Thing '00
Jericho '01
Stolen '12
Gun Shy '17

Alida Valli (1921-2006)
We the Living '42
The Paradine Case '47
The Miracle of the Bells '48
The Third Man '49
Senso '54
Il Grido '57
The Night Heaven Fell '57
The Wide Blue Road '57
The Horror Chamber of Dr. Faustus '59
The Happy Thieves '61
The Castilian '63
Oedipus Rex '67
Beyond Erotica '74
Lisa and the Devil '75
The Cassandra Crossing '76
1900 '76
Berlinguer I Love You '77
Suspiria '77
Le Jupon Rouge '87
A Month by the Lake '95
Angel of Death '02

Frankie Valli (1937-)
Modern Love '90
Witness to the Mob '98

Romolo Valli (1925-80)
The Girl with a Suitcase '60
The Leopard '63
The Garden of the Finzi-Continis '71
A Fistful of Dynamite '72
Bobby Deerfield '77

Virginia Valli (1898-1968)
The Shock '23
Wild Oranges '24
The Pleasure Garden '25
Up the Ladder '25
The Lost Zeppelin '29

Rick Vallin (1919-77)
The Panther's Claw '42
Corregidor '43
Dangerous Money '46
Jungle Manhunt '51
The Magic Carpet '51
The Fighting Lawman '53

Raf Vallone (1917-2002)
Bitter Rice '49
El Cid '61
Phaedra '61
Two Women '61
The Secret Invasion '64
Harlow '65
Nevada Smith '66
The Italian Job '69
Cannon for Cordoba '70
The Kremlin Letter '70
A Gunfight '71
Honor Thy Father '73
Ricco '74
The Human Factor '75
The Girl in Room 2A '76
The Other Side of Midnight '77
The Greek Tycoon '78
An Almost Perfect Affair '79
Lion of the Desert '81
I Remember Nelson '82
The Scarlet & the Black '83
Time to Die '83
The Godfather, Part 3 '90

Lee Valmassy
All Superheroes Must Die '11
The FP '12

Maria Valverde (1987-)
Cracks '09
Exodus: Gods and Kings '14
Guernica '16
The Limehouse Golem '17

Vampira (1921-2008)
Plan 9 from Outer Space '56
Night of the Ghouls '59

Bobby Van (1930-80)
The Affairs of Dobie Gillis '53
Kiss Me Kate '53
Small Town Girl '53
Navy *vs.* the Night Monsters '66
Escape from Planet Earth '67
Lost Horizon '73

Willeke Van Ammelrooy (1944-)
Fatal Error '83
Antonia's Line '95
The Lake House '06

Joan Van Ark (1943-)
Frogs '72
The Last Dinosaur '77
Shakedown on the Sunset Strip '88
Net Games '03

Ingrid van Bergen (1931-)
The Avenger '60
The Vampire Happening '71
Lewis Van Bergen
Rage of Honor '87
Bugsy '91
False Arrest '92
Pinocchio's Revenge '96
The Relic '96
Mabel van Buren (1878-47)
The Four Horsemen of the Apocalypse '21
Beyond the Rocks '22
Emily Van Camp (1986-)
A Different Loyalty '04
The Ring 2 '05
Black Irish '07
Lee Van Cleef (1925-89)
High Noon '52
Kansas City Confidential '52
The Lawless Breed '52
The Bandits of Corsica '53
The Beast from 20,000 Fathoms '53
Vice Squad '53
Big Combo '55
The Conqueror '56
Pardners '56
Tribute to a Bad Man '56
China Gate '57
Gunfight at the O.K. Corral '57
The Tin Star '57
The Bravados '58
The Young Lions '58
Ride Lonesome '59
The Man Who Shot Liberty Valance '62
For a Few Dollars More '65
The Big Gundown '66
The Good, the Bad and the Ugly '67
Beyond the Law '68
Death Rides a Horse '69
Sabata '69
El Condor '70
Captain Apache '71
Return of Sabata '71
Bad Man's River '72
New Mafia Boss '72
Commandos '73
Escape from Death Row '73
The Grand Duel '73
God's Gun '75
Kid Vengeance '75
Mean Frank and Crazy Tony '75
Take a Hard Ride '75
Perfect Killer '77
The Rip Off '78
Octagon '80
The Squeeze '80
Escape from New York '81
Code Name: Wild Geese '84
Codename: Wildgeese '84
Armed Response '86
Thieves of Fortune '89
Rob van Dam
Black Mask 2: City of Masks '02
Wrong Side of Town '10
Sniper: Special Ops '16
Jean-Claude Van Damme (1960-)
Black Eagle '88
Bloodsport '88
Cyborg '89
Kickboxer '89
Death Warrant '90
Lionheart '90
Double Impact '91
Universal Soldier '92
Hard Target '93
Last Action Hero '93 (C)
Nowhere to Run '93
Street Fighter '94
Timecop '94
Sudden Death '95
Maximum Risk '96
The Quest '96
Double Team '97
Knock Off '98
Legionnaire '98
Desert Heat '99
Universal Soldier: The Return '99
Replicant '01
Derailed '02
In Hell '03
Second in Command '05
The Shepherd: Border Patrol '08
Universal Soldier: Regeneration '09
Kung Fu Panda 2 '11 (V)
Alien Uprising '12
Dragon Eyes '12
The Expendables 2 '12
6 Bullets '12
Universal Soldier: Day of Reckoning '12
Welcome to the Jungle '13
Enemies Closer '14
Swelter '14
Kickboxer: Vengeance '16
Black Water '18
We Die Young '19
Monique Van De Ven (1952-)
Turkish Delight '73
Katie Tippel '75
James Van Der Beek (1977-)
Angus '95
I Love You, I Love You Not '97
Cash Crop '98
Varsity Blues '98
Jay and Silent Bob Strike Back '01 (C)
Texas Rangers '01
The Rules of Attraction '02
Standing Still '05
Danny Roane: First Time Director '06
Eye of the Beast '07
Final Draft '07
Formosa Betrayed '09
Mrs. Miracle '09
Stolen '09
The Storm '09
Taken in Broad Daylight '09
The Big Bang '11
Jodi Picoult's Salem Falls '11
Backwards '12
Claire Van Der Boom (1983-)
The Square '08
Red Hill '10
Sisters of War '10
Anneliese van der Pol
Bratz '07
Vampires Suck '10
Nadine Van Der Velde (1962-)
Critters '86
Munchies '87
After Midnight '89
Diana Van Der Vlis (1935-2001)
Girl in Black Stockings '57
X: The Man with X-Ray Eyes '63
Lovespell '79
Frederique van der Wal (1967-)
Two Girls and a Guy '98
Wild Wild West '99
Trish Van Devere (1943-)
Where's Poppa? '70
The Last Run '71
The Day of the Dolphin '73
Harry in Your Pocket '73
Savage Is Loose '74
Movie, Movie '78
The Changeling '80
The Hearse '80
Hollywood Vice Sqaud '86
Messenger of Death '88
Caspar Van Dien
The Fallen Ones '05
500 MPH Storm '13
Casper Van Dien (1968-)
James Dean: Live Fast, Die Young '97
NightScreams '97
Starship Troopers '97
Modern Vampires '98
On the Border '98
Tarzan and the Lost City '98
The Collectors '99
The Omega Code '99
Partners '99
Shark Attack '99
Sleepy Hollow '99
Thrill Seekers '99
Chasing Destiny '00
Cutaway '00
Python '00
Road Rage '01
Sanctimony '01
Under Heavy Fire '01
Danger Beneath the Sea '02
The Vector File '03
Maiden Voyage: Ocean Hijack '04
Personal Effects '05
The Curse of King Tut's Tomb '06
Meltdown '06
Slayer '06
Aces 'n Eights '08
Starship Troopers 3: Marauder '08
The Dog Who Saved Christmas Vacation '10
Turbulent Skies '10
Born to Ride '11
F6 Twister '12
Fugitive at 17 '12
Lake Effects '12
June '15
Dead Water '19
Mamie Van Doren (1931-)
Francis Joins the WACs '54
Girl in Black Stockings '57
Untamed Youth '57
High School Confidential '58
Teacher's Pet '58
Born Reckless '59
Sex Kittens Go to College '60
Vice Raid '60
Three Nuts in Search of a Bolt '64
Las Vegas Hillbillys '66
Navy vs. the Night Monsters '66
Voyage to the Planet of Prehistoric Women '68
Slackers '02
John van Dreelen (1922-92)
13 Ghosts '60
Von Ryan's Express '65
Granville Van Dusen (1944-)
Dynasty '76
A Death in California '85
The Rose and the Jackal '90
Jennifer Van Dyck (1962-)
States of Control '98
Series 7: The Contenders '01
Michael Clayton '07
Barry Van Dyke (1951-)
Ants '77
Foxfire Light '82
6 Guns '10
Strawberry Summer '12
Carey Van Dyke
6 Guns '10
Mega Python Vs. Gatoroid '11
Conny Van Dyke (1945-)
Hell's Angels '69 '69
Framed '75
W.W. and the Dixie Dancekings '75
Dick Van Dyke (1925-)
Bye, Bye, Birdie '63
Mary Poppins '64
Lt. Robin Crusoe, U.S.N. '66
Divorce American Style '67
Fitzwilly '67
Chitty Chitty Bang Bang '68
Never a Dull Moment '68
The Comic '69
Cold Turkey '71
Dick Tracy '90
Curious George '06 (V)
Night at the Museum '06
Night at the Museum: Battle of the Smithsonian '09
Night at the Museum: Secret of the Tomb '14
Jerry Van Dyke (1931-2018)
The Courtship of Eddie's Father '62
McLintock! '63
Death Blow '87
Lethal Victims '87
Run If You Can '87
Phillip Van Dyke (1984-)
Halloweentown '98
The Modern Adventures of Tom Sawyer '99
Halloweentown 2: Kalabar's Revenge '01
Shane Van Dyke (1979-)
Transmorphers: Fall of Man '09
6 Guns '10
Titanic 2 '10
Peter Van Eyck (1911-69)
Five Graves to Cairo '43
Address Unknown '44
Sailor of the King '53
A Bullet for Joey '55
Jump Into Hell '55
Wages of Fear '55
Run for the Sun '56
The Snorkel '58
The Thousand Eyes of Dr. Mabuse '60
Dr. Mabuse vs. Scotland Yard '64
The Spy Who Came in from the Cold '65
Assignment to Kill '69
John Van Eyssen (1922-95)
Four Sided Triangle '53
Quatermass 2 '57
The Horror of Dracula '58
Jo Van Fleet (1919-96)
East of Eden '54
I'll Cry Tomorrow '55
The Rose Tattoo '55
The King and Four Queens '56
Gunfight at the O.K. Corral '57
Wild River '60
Cool Hand Luke '67
I Love You, Alice B. Toklas! '68
Satan's School for Girls '73
The Tenant '76
Harry Van Gorkum
Dragonheart: A New Beginning '00
Escape under Pressure '00
Face the Music '00
Avenging Angelo '02
The Foreigner '03
The Last Legion '07
Kevin Van Hentenryck (1953-)
Basket Case '82
Brain Damage '88
Basket Case 2 '90
Basket Case 3: The Progeny '92
Brian Van Holt (1969-)
Whipped '00
Black Hawk Down '01
Windtalkers '02
Basic '03
Confidence '03
S.W.A.T. '03
House of Wax '05
Man of the House '05
Patrick Van Horn (1969-)
Swingers '96
Ivory Tower '97
Free Enterprise '98
Three to Tango '99
Pursuit of Happiness '01
Carice van Houten (1976-)
Miss Minoes '01
Black Book '06
Body of Lies '08
Valkyrie '08
Black Death '10
Repo Men '10
Intruders '11
Jackie '12
Race '16
Brimstone '17
Domino '19
Fedja Van Huet (1973-)
Character '97
The Delivery '99
Rosenstrasse '03
Erland van Lidth (1953-87)
Wanderers '79
Stir Crazy '80
The Running Man '87
Rik van Nutter (1929-2005)
Assignment Outer Space '61
Thunderball '65
Nina Van Pallandt (1932-)
The Long Goodbye '73
A Wedding '78
American Gigolo '79
Quintet '79
Cutter's Way '81
Sword & the Sorcerer '82
Jungle Warriors '84
Dick Van Patten (1928-2015)
Psychomania '63
Charly '68
Zachariah '70
Beware! The Blob '72
Joe Kidd '72
Soylent Green '73
Superdad '73
Westworld '73
The Strongest Man in the World '75
Freaky Friday '76
Gus '76
High Anxiety '77
The Midnight Hour '86
Spaceballs '87
The New Adventures of Pippi Longstocking '88
Body Trouble '92
Robin Hood: Men in Tights '93
A Dangerous Place '94
Demolition High '95
Love Is All There Is '96
Big Brother Trouble '00
Groom Lake '02
The Santa Trap '02
Opposite Day '09
Grace Van Patten (1996-)
The Meyerowitz Stories (New and Selected) '17
The Wilde Wedding '17
Under the Silver Lake '18
James Van Patten (1956-)
Freaky Friday '76
Roller Boogie '79
The Dirty Dozen: The Deadly Mission '87
Hyper Space '89
Twisted Justice '89
A Thousand Cuts '12
Joyce Van Patten (1934-)
The Goddess '58
I Love You, Alice B. Toklas! '68
The Trouble with Girls (and How to Get into It) '69
Pussycat, Pussycat, I Love You '70
Housewife '72
Thumb Tripping '72
Mame '74
The Stranger Within '74
Winter Kill '74
The Bad News Bears '76
Eleanor: First Lady of the World '82
The Falcon and the Snowman '85
St. Elmo's Fire '85
Billy Galvin '86
Crawlspace '86
The Rumor Mill '86
Monkey Shines '88
Grown Ups '10
This Must Be the Place '12
Nels Van Patten (1955-)
Grotesque '87
Summer School '87
Mirror Images '91
Timothy Van Patten (1959-)
Class of 1984 '82
Zone Troopers '84
Dress Gray '86
The Wrong Guys '88
Vincent Van Patten (1957-)
The Bravos '72
Charley and the Angel '73
Chino '75
Rock 'n' Roll High School '79
Spree '79
Hell Night '81
The Victory '81
The Dirty Dozen: The Deadly Mission '87
The Break '95
Mario Van Peebles (1957-)
Sweet Sweetback's Baadasssss Song '71
Children of the Night '85
Rappin' '85
South Bronx Heroes '85
Heartbreak Ridge '86
Hot Shot '86
Last Resort '86
Jaws: The Revenge '87
Identity Crisis '90
New Jack City '91
Full Eclipse '93
Gunmen '93
Posse '93
Highlander: The Final Dimension '94
Urban Crossfire '94
Panther '95
Gang in Blue '96
Riot in the Streets '96
Solo '96
Protector '97
Stag '97
Crazy Six '98
Love Kills '98
Mama Flora's Family '98
Blowback '99
Judgment Day '99
Raw Nerve '99
Sally Hemings: An American Scandal '00
Ali '01
American Warships '01
The Guardian '01
10,000 Black Men Named George '02
Baadasssss! '03
44 Minutes: The North Hollywood Shootout '03
Carlito's Way: Rise to Power '05
Sharpshooter '07
Across the Line: The Exodus of Charlie Wright '10
Multiple Sarcasms '10
American Warship '12
Run the Race '19
Megan Van Peebles (1958-2006)
Sweet Sweetback's Baadasssss Song '71
South Bronx Heroes '85
Melvin Van Peebles (1932-)
Sweet Sweetback's Baadasssss Song '71
O.C. and Stiggs '87
Boomerang '92
Posse '93 (C)
Terminal Velocity '94
Fist of the North Star '95
Gang in Blue '96
Riot in the Streets '96
Love Kills '98
Freakonomics '10 (N)
Redemption Road '10
Peeples '13
Luis van Rooten (1906-73)
My Favorite Spy '51
Curse of the Faceless Man '58
Contagion '11

Gus Van Sant (1952-)
Jay and Silent Bob Strike Back *'01 (C)*
The Canyons *'13*

Edward Van Sloan (1881-1964)
Dracula *'31*
Frankenstein *'31*
The Mummy *'32*
The Death Kiss *'33*
Death Takes a Holiday *'34*
Manhattan Melodrama *'34*
Air Hawks *'35*
A Shot in the Dark *'35*
The Woman in Red *'35*
Dracula's Daughter *'36*
Danger on the Air *'38*
The Mask of Diijon *'46*

Alan Van Sprang (1971-)
Steal This Movie! *'00*
Narc *'02*
Do or Die *'03*
The Gospel of John *'03*
Confessions of an American Bride *'05*
Guns *'08*
Phantom Punch *'09*

Deborah Van Valkenburgh (1952-)
The Warriors *'79*
Streets of Fire *'84*
Rampage *'87*
Mean Guns *'97*
Free Enterprise *'98*
Chasing Destiny *'00*
Firestarter 2: Rekindled *'02*
The Devil's Rejects *'05*
Mystery Woman: Mystery Weekend *'05*
Backwoods *'08*

Monique Van Vooren (1927-)
Tarzan and the She-Devil *'53*
Ash Wednesday *'73*
Andy Warhol's Frankenstein *'74*
Sugar Cookies *'77*

Yorick Van Wageningen (1964-)
Deserter *'02*
Beyond Borders *'03*
The Chronicles of Riddick *'04*
The New World *'05*
The Way *'10*
Winter in Wartime *'10*
The Girl With the Dragon Tattoo *'11*
Blackhat *'15*

Travis Van Winkle (1982-)
Accepted *'06*
Transformers *'07*
Meet the Spartans *'08*
Friday the 13th *'09*
A Star for Christmas *'12*

Steve Van Wormer (1969-)
The Extreme Adventures of Super Dave *'98*
Meet the Deedles *'98*
Groove *'00*

Philip Van Zandt (1904-58)
Citizen Kane *'41*
Sherlock Holmes and the Secret Weapon *'42*
Wake Island *'42*
Tarzan Triumphs *'43*
Tarzan's Desert Mystery *'43*
Counter-Attack *'45*
Decoy *'46*
Don't Gamble with Strangers *'46*
Walk a Crooked Mile *'48*
Woman in Brown *'48*
Where Danger Lives *'50*
GOG *'54*
The Pride and the Passion *'57*

Louis Vanaria
This Thing of Ours *'03*
Searching for Bobby D *'05*
Stiffs *'06*

Emily VanCamp (1986-)
Carriers *'09*
Ben Hur *'10*
Norman *'10*
Beyond the Blackboard *'11*
The Girl in the Book *'15*

Courtney B. Vance (1960-)
Hamburger Hill *'87*
The Hunt for Red October *'90*
Beyond the Law *'92*
The Adventures of Huck Finn *'93*
Holy Matrimony *'94*
The Piano Lesson *'94*
Race to Freedom: The Story of the Underground Railroad *'94*
The Affair *'95*
Dangerous Minds *'95*
Panther *'95*
The Tuskegee Airmen *'95*
The Boys Next Door *'96*
The Last Supper *'96*
The Preacher's Wife *'96*
Blind Faith *'98*
Cookie's Fortune *'99*
Love and Action in Chicago *'99*
Space Cowboys *'00*
Eye See You *'01*
Nothing But the Truth *'08*
Hurricane Season *'09*
Extraordinary Measures *'10*
Final Destination 5 *'11*
Joyful Noise *'12*
Let It Shine *'12*
Office Christmas Party *'16*
Ben Is Back *'18*
The Photograph *'20*

Danitra Vance (1959-94)
Sticky Fingers *'88*
Limit Up *'89*
The War of the Roses *'89*
Little Man Tate *'91*
Jumpin' at the Boneyard *'92*

Sheila Vand (1985-)
A Girl Walks Home Alone at Night *'14*
Women Who Kill *'17*
Aardvark *'18*
We the Animals *'18*

Musetta Vander (1963-)
Backlash: Oblivion 2 *'95*
Project Shadowchaser 3000 *'95*
Mortal Kombat 2: Annihilation *'97*
Gunshy *'98*
Wild Wild West *'99*
O Brother Where Art Thou? *'00*
Kicking & Screaming *'05*
Mosquito Man *'05*
What's Up, Scarlet? *'05*
Breaking Point *'09*
Transylmania *'09*

Jean Vander Pyl (1919-99)
Jetsons: The Movie *'90 (V)*
The Flintstones *'94 (C)*

Alexandra Vandernoot (1965-)
Highlander: The Gathering *'92*
The Dinner Game *'98*
The Closet *'00*
The Crown Prince *'06*

Laura Vandervoort (1984-)
Into the Blue 2: The Reef *'09*
Riverworld *'10*
The Entitled *'11*
Ted *'12*

Titos Vandis (1917-2003)
Never on Sunday *'60*
Island of Love *'63*
Once Upon a Scoundrel *'73*
Black Samson *'74*
Smile *'75*
Piece of the Action *'77*

Pierre Vaneck (1931-2010)
A Man Named Rocca *'61*
Is Paris Burning? *'66*

Othello *'95*
The Science of Sleep *'06*

Charles Vanel (1892-1989)
Diabolique *'55*
To Catch a Thief *'55*
Wages of Fear *'55*
Death in the Garden *'56*
Three Brothers *'80*

Vanilla Ice (1967-)
Cool As Ice *'91*
Teenage Mutant Ninja Turtles 2: The Secret of the Ooze *'91*
That's My Boy *'12*

Vanity (1959-2016)
Terror Train *'80*
Tanya's Island *'81*
The Last Dragon *'85*
52 Pick-Up *'86*
Action Jackson *'88*
DaVinci's War *'92*
Highlander: The Gathering *'92*
South Beach *'92*

Renata Vanni (1909-2004)
Westward the Women *'51*
The Lady in White *'88*

Joanne Vannicola (1968-)
Love and Human Remains *'93*
Iron Eagle 4 *'95*

Luigi Vannucchi (1930-78)
Johnny Yuma *'66*
Red Tent *'69*
Lovers Like Us *'75*
The Savage *'75*

Shantel VanSanten (1985-)
The Final Destination *'09*
In My Pocket *'11*
You and I *'11*

Victor Varconi (1891-1976)
Chicago *'27*
King of Kings *'27*
The Divine Lady *'29*
The Black Camel *'31*
Safe in Hell *'31*
Dancing Pirate *'36*
Big City *'37*
King of the Newsboys *'38*
My Favorite Blonde *'42*
For Whom the Bell Tolls *'43*
Unconquered *'47*
The Man Who Turned to Stone *'57*

Nia Vardalos (1962-)
My Big Fat Greek Wedding *'02*
Connie and Carla *'04*
I Hate Valentine's Day *'09*
My Life in Ruins *'09*
For a Good Time, Call... *'12*
My Big Fat Greek Wedding 2 *'16*

Evelyn Varden (1895-1958)
When Willie Comes Marching Home *'50*
Elopement *'51*
Athena *'54*
The Night of the Hunter *'55*
The Bad Seed *'56*

Norma Varden (1898-1989)
Boys Will Be Boys *'35*
East Meets West *'36*
Windbag the Sailor *'36*
National Velvet *'44*
The White Cliffs of Dover *'44*
Fancy Pants *'50*
Thunder on the Hill *'51*
Jupiter's Darling *'55*
Witness for the Prosecution *'57*
13 Frightened Girls *'63*
The Sound of Music *'65*
A Very Special Favor *'65*

Leonor Varela (1972-)
Cleopatra *'99*
The Tailor of Panama *'00*
Texas Rangers *'01*
Blade 2 *'02*
Innocent Voices *'04*
Americano *'05*

The Curse of King Tut's Tomb *'06*
Goal 2: Living the Dream *'07*
Where God Left His Shoes *'07*
Hell Ride *'08*
Balls Out: Gary the Tennis Coach *'09*
Wrong Turn at Tahoe *'09*
Monsterwolf *'10*
Odd Thomas *'13*
Captive *'15*
Alpha *'18*

Matias Varela
Storm *'05*
Easy Money *'10*
Easy Money: Hard to Kill *'12*
Point Break *'15*

Daniele Vargas
Sandok *'65*
Django: Last Killer *'67*

Eli Vargas
The Last Days of Summer *'07*
Cesar Chavez *'14*

Jacob Vargas (1971-)
The Children of Times Square *'86*
The Principal *'87*
Gas Food Lodging *'92*
Airborne *'93*
Mi Vida Loca *'94*
My Family *'94*
Selena *'96*
Romy and Michele's High School Reunion *'97*
The Hi-Lo Country *'98*
Next Friday *'00*
Traffic *'00*
Dr. Dolittle 2 *'01 (V)*
RFK *'02*
Flight of the Phoenix *'04*
Jarhead *'05*
The Wendell Baker Story *'05*
Bobby *'06*
Bobby Z *'07*
The Hills Have Eyes 2 *'07*
Love Lies Bleeding *'07*
Death Race *'08*
Devil *'10*

John Vargas (1959-)
Unnatural Causes *'86*
In Dark Places *'97*
Primary Colors *'98*
The Last Cowboy *'03*

Valentina Vargas (1964-)
Dirty Games *'89*
The Tigress *'93*
Hellraiser 4: Bloodline *'95*
Faces in the Crowd *'11*
Night Across the Street *'12*

Beatrice Varley (1896-1964)
Young and Innocent *'37*
Bees in Paradise *'44*
Waterloo Road *'45*
Horrors of the Black Museum *'59*
Room at the Top *'59*

John Varley (1915-)
In Which We Serve *'43*
The Life and Death of Colonel Blimp *'43*

Indira Varma (1973-)
Kama Sutra: A Tale of Love *'96*
Bride & Prejudice *'04*
A Waste of Shame *'05*
Basic Instinct 2 *'06*

Jim Varney (1949-2000)
Dr. Otto & the Riddle of the Gloom Beam *'86*
Ernest Goes to Camp *'87*
Ernest Saves Christmas *'88*
Fast Food *'89*
Ernest Goes to Jail *'90*
The Rousters *'90*
Ernest Scared Stupid *'91*
The Beverly Hillbillies *'93*
Wilder Napalm *'93*
Slam Dunk Ernest *'95*
Toy Story *'95 (V)*
Snowboard Academy *'96*

Ernest Goes to Africa *'97*
Ernest in the Army *'97*
3 Ninjas: High Noon at Mega Mountain *'97*
Daddy & Them *'99*
Toy Story 2 *'99 (V)*
Treehouse Hostage *'99*
Atlantis: The Lost Empire *'01 (V)*

Roland Varno (1908-96)
Gunga Din *'39*
To Be or Not to Be *'42*
Return of the Vampire *'43*

Shelly Varod
Command Performance *'09*
Spiders *'13*

Diane Varsi (1937-92)
Peyton Place *'57*
Compulsion *'59*
Wild in the Streets *'68*
Bloody Mama *'70*
Johnny Got His Gun *'71*
The People *'71*
I Never Promised You a Rose Garden *'77*

Michael Vartan (1968-)
Fiorile *'93*
The Pallbearer *'95*
The Curve *'97*
The Myth of Fingerprints *'97*
Never Been Kissed *'99*
It Had to Be You *'00*
The Next Best Thing *'00*
Sand *'00*
Mists of Avalon *'01*
One Hour Photo *'02*
Monster-in-Law *'05*
Rogue *'07*
Jolene *'08*
Colombiana *'11*
Demoted *'11*

Vagelis Vartan
Emmanuelle, the Queen *'79*
Emmanuelle's Daughter *'79*

Luiz Carlos Vasconcelos (1954-)
Me You Them *'00*
Behind the Sun *'01*
Carandiru *'03*

Raicho Vasilev
Diamond Dogs *'07*
Command Performance *'09*

Nelson Vasquez
Pinero *'01*
El Cantante *'06*

Roberta Vasquez (1963-)
Easy Wheels *'89*
Picasso Trigger *'89*
The Rookie *'90*
Do or Die *'91*
Hard Hunted *'92*
Fit to Kill *'93*

Yul Vasquez
The Wedding Bros. *'08*
Salvation Boulevard *'11*

Liz Vassey (1972-)
Pursuit of Happiness *'01*
Man of the House *'05*
Sexting in Suburbia *'12*

Sofia Vassilieva (1992-)
Eloise at the Plaza *'03*
Day Zero *'07*
Hurt *'09*
My Sister's Keeper *'09*
Call Me Crazy *'13*

Frankie Vaughan (1928-99)
The Lady Is a Square *'58*
Let's Make Love *'60*
The Right Approach *'61*

Greg Vaughan (1973-)
Poison Ivy 3: The New Seduction *'97*
Children of the Corn 5: Fields of Terror *'98*
Love's Christmas Journey *'11*

Paris Vaughan (1961-)
Heat Wave *'90*
Buffy the Vampire Slayer *'92*
Les Miserables *'97*

Peter Vaughan (1923-)
Die! Die! My Darling! *'65*
Hammerhead *'68*
The Man Outside *'68*
Pied Piper *'72*
Savage Messiah *'72*
Straw Dogs *'72*
Blockhouse *'73*
Mackintosh Man *'73*
Valentino *'77*
Time Bandits *'81*
The Razor's Edge *'84*
Bleak House *'85*
Brazil *'85*
Haunted Honeymoon *'86*
Mountains of the Moon *'90*
Porridge *'91*
Prisoner of Honor *'91*
The Remains of the Day *'93*
Circle of Deceit *'94*
The Crucible *'96*
The Secret Agent *'96*
Face *'97*
Our Mutual Friend *'98*
An Ideal Husband *'99*
Longitude *'00*
Lorna Doone *'01*
The Mother *'03*
Death at a Funeral *'07*
Is Anybody There? *'08*

Ned Vaughn (1964-)
Wind *'92*
Courage Under Fire *'96*
Life *'99*

Robert Vaughn (1932-2016)
No Time to Be Young *'57*
Good Day for a Hanging *'58*
Teenage Caveman *'58*
Unwed Mother *'58*
The Young Philadelphians *'59*
The Magnificent Seven *'60*
The Caretakers *'63*
The Glass Bottom Boat *'66 (C)*
The Venetian Affair *'67*
Bullitt *'68*
The Bridge at Remagen *'69*
Julius Caesar *'70*
The Mind of Mr. Soames *'70*
The Woman Hunter *'72*
The Towering Inferno *'74*
Wanted: Babysitter *'75*
Kiss Me...Kill Me *'76*
Demon Seed *'77 (V)*
Washington: Behind Closed Doors *'77*
Brass Target *'78*
Centennial *'78*
The Lucifer Complex *'78*
Backstairs at the White House *'79*
Battle Beyond the Stars *'80*
Hangar 18 *'80*
Kill Castro *'80*
The Mercenaries *'80*
S.O.B. *'81*
Virus *'82*
Return of the Man from U.N.C.L.E. *'83*
Superman 3 *'83*
Black Moon Rising *'86*
Delta Force *'86*
Prince of Bel Air *'87*
Buried Alive *'89*
Skeleton Coast *'89*
Transylvania Twist *'89*
Nobody's Perfect *'90*
River of Death *'90*
Going Under *'91*
Joe's Apartment *'96*
Menno's Mind *'96*
BASEketball *'98*
Motel Blue *'98*
The Sender *'98*
Virtual Obsession *'98*
An American Affair *'99*
Lethal Force *'00*
Pootie Tang *'01*
Happy Hour *'03*
Hoodlum & Son *'03*
2B Perfectly Honest *'04*
Excuse Me for Living *'12*
Gold Star *'17*

Terri J. Vaughn
Dirty Laundry *'07*
Three Can Play That Game *'07*

Vince Vaughn (1970-)
Rudy *'93*
Swingers *'96*
The Locusts *'97*
The Lost World: Jurassic Park 2 *'97*
Clay Pigeons *'98*
A Cool, Dry Place *'98*
Psycho *'98*
Return to Paradise *'98*
The Cell *'00*
The Prime Gig *'00*
South of Heaven, West of Hell *'00*
Domestic Disturbance *'01*
Made *'01*
I Love Your Work *'03*
Old School *'03*
Anchorman: The Legend of Ron Burgundy *'04*
Dodgeball: A True Underdog Story *'04*
Paparazzi *'04 (C)*
Starsky & Hutch *'04*
Be Cool *'05*
Mr. & Mrs. Smith *'05*
Thumbsucker *'05*
Wedding Crashers *'05*
The Break-Up *'06*
Vince Vaughn's Wild West Comedy Show *'06 (C)*
Fred Claus *'07*
Into the Wild *'07*
Four Christmases *'08*
Couples Retreat *'09*
The Dilemma *'11*
Lay the Favorite *'12*
The Watch *'12*
A Case of You *'13*
Delivery Man *'13*
The Internship *'13*
Unfinished Business *'15*
Hacksaw Ridge *'16*
Term Life *'16*
Brawl in Cell Block 99 *'17*
Dragged Across Concrete *'18*

Emmanuelle Vaugier (1976-)
The Fear: Halloween Night *'99*
My 5 Wives *'00*
Mindstorm *'01*
Return to Cabin by the Lake *'01*
Ripper: Letter from Hell *'01*
40 Days and 40 Nights *'02*
Secondhand Lions *'03*
Water's Edge *'03*
Call Me: The Rise and Fall of Heidi Fleiss *'04*
House of the Dead 2: Dead Aim *'05*
Saw 2 *'05*
What Comes Around *'06*
Blonde and Blonder *'07*
Unearthed *'07*
Bachelor Party 2: The Last Temptation *'08*
Far Cry *'08*
Dolan's Cadillac *'09*
Mirrors 2 *'10*
A Nanny for Christmas *'10*
Where the Road Meets the Sun *'11*
Absolute Deception *'13*
Hidden Away *'13*
The Wedding Chapel *'13*

Sophie Vavasseur (1992-)
Evelyn *'02*
Resident Evil: Apocalypse *'04*
Northanger Abbey *'07*

Dana Vavrova (1967-2009)
Brother of Sleep *'95*
The Harmonists *'99*

Ron Vawter (1949-94)
Sudden Death *'77*
sex, lies and videotape *'89*
Internal Affairs *'90*
The Silence of the Lambs *'91*
Swoon *'91*
Philadelphia *'93*

Yul Vazquez
Fly by Night *'93*
Fresh *'94*
Runaway Bride *'99*
Bad Boys 2 *'03*
War of the Worlds *'05*
The Box *'07*
Music Within *'07*
The A-Team *'10*
Kill the Messenger *'14*
The Infiltrator *'16*

Alex Veadov (1962-)
Black Horizon *'01*
We Own the Night *'07*
Act of Valor *'12*

Alexa Vega (1988-)
Little Giants *'94*
Nine Months *'95*
Ghosts of Mississippi *'96*
The Glimmer Man *'96*
Twister *'96*
The Deep End of the Ocean *'98*
Tom Clancy's Netforce *'98*
Ride the Wild Fields *'00*
Follow the Stars Home *'01*
Spy Kids *'01*
Spy Kids 2: The Island of Lost Dreams *'02*
Spy Kids 3-D: Game Over *'03*
Sleepover *'04*
Remember the Daze *'07*
Repo! The Genetic Opera *'08*
Broken Hill *'09*
Cafe *'10*
From Prada to Nada *'11*
Spy Kids 4: All the Time in the World *'11*
The Pregnancy Project *'12*
The Hunters *'13*
Machete Kills *'13*
Wicked Blood *'13*
Spare Parts *'15*

Isela Vega (1939-)
The Fear Chamber *'68*
Bring Me the Head of Alfredo Garcia *'74*
Drum *'76*
Joshua *'76*
Barbarosa *'82*

Makenzie Vega (1994-)
Saw *'04*
Sin City *'05*
In the Land of Women *'06*
Just My Luck *'06*
X-Men: The Last Stand *'06*
Fender Bender *'16*

Paz Vega (1976-)
Sex and Lucia *'01*
Carmen *'03*
Spanglish *'04*
10 Items or Less *'06*
The Lark Farm *'07*
The Human Contract *'08*
The Spirit *'08*
Not Forgotten *'09*
The Six Wives of Henry Lefay *'09*
Triage *'09*
Cat Run *'11*
Grace of Monaco *'14*
Kill the Messenger *'14*
All Roads Lead to Rome *'15*
Acts of Vengeance *'17*
Rambo: Last Blood *'19*

Conrad Veidt (1893-1943)
The Cabinet of Dr. Caligari *'19*
The Indian Tomb *'21*
The Hands of Orlac *'25*
The Beloved Rogue *'27*
The Man Who Laughs *'27*
Rome Express *'32*
F.P. 1 *'33*
Power *'34*
The Passing of the Third Floor Back *'35*
Under the Red Robe *'36*
Dark Journey *'37*
Spy in Black *'39*
Contraband *'40*
Escape *'40*
The Thief of Bagdad *'40*
Whistling in the Dark *'41*
A Woman's Face *'41*
All Through the Night *'42*
Casablanca *'42*
Above Suspicion *'43*

Manuela Velasco (1975-)
[Rec] *'07*
[Rec] 2 *'09*
[REC] 4: Apocalyse *'14*

Patricia Velasquez (1971-)
Beowulf *'98*
Committed *'99*
The Mummy *'99*
No Vacancy *'99*
The Mummy Returns *'01*
Fidel *'02*
The Twelve Days of Christmas Eve *'04*
Mindhunters *'05*
Almighty Thor *'11*

Nadine Velazquez
Kings of South Beach *'07*
War *'07*
The Bounce Back *'16*

Teresa Velazquez (1942-98)
Night of a Thousand Cats *'72*
The Killer Must Kill Again *'75*

Eddie Velez (1958-)
Children of the Night *'85*
Doin' Time *'85*
Split Decisions *'88*
Romero *'89*
Rooftops *'89*
Drug Wars: The Camarena Story *'90*
Under Oath *'97*
Running Woman *'98*
A Father's Choice *'00*
The Hunted *'03*
White Chicks *'04*
Black Dawn *'05*

Lauren Velez (1964-)
I Like It Like That *'94*
I Think I Do *'97*
Prince of Central Park *'00*

Lupe Velez (1908-44)
The Gaucho *'27*
Hell Harbor *'30*
The Squaw Man *'31*
Kongo *'32*
Hollywood Party *'34*
Palooka *'34*
Strictly Dynamite *'34*
High Flyers *'37*
Mad About Money *'37*
The Girl From Mexico *'39*
Mexican Spitfire *'40*
The Mexican Spitfire Out West *'40*
The Mexican Spitfire's Baby *'41*
Playmates *'41*
Mexican Spitfire at Sea *'42*
The Mexican Spitfire Sees a Ghost *'42*

Reginald VelJohnson (1952-)
Ghostbusters *'84*
Remo Williams: The Adventure Begins *'85*
Die Hard *'88*
Die Hard 2: Die Harder *'90*
Posse *'93*
The Great American Sex Scandal *'94*

Evelyn Venable (1913-93)
David Harum *'34*
Death Takes a Holiday *'34*
Mrs. Wiggs of the Cabbage Patch *'34*
Alice Adams *'35*
Harmony Lane *'35*
The Little Colonel *'35*
Vagabond Lady *'35*
The Frontiersmen *'38*
Pinocchio *'40 (V)*

Venantino Venantini (1930-)
The Priest's Wife *'71*
Contraband *'80*
Final Justice *'84*

Veronique Vendell (1942-)
Barbarella *'68*
Cross of Iron *'76*

Amy Veness (1876-1960)
Windbag the Sailor *'36*
This Happy Breed *'47*
Man of Evil *'48*
Madeleine *'50*

Ingrid Veninger
Hush Little Baby *'93*
Re-Generation *'04*

Lenny Venito (1969-)
Money for Nothing *'93*
Just the Ticket *'98*
Rounders *'98*
Witness to the Mob *'98*
Men in Black 2 *'02*
Gigli *'03*
Shark Tale *'04 (V)*
Duane Hopwood *'05*
War of the Worlds *'05*
The Wild *'06 (V)*
The Brave One *'07*
4 Single Fathers *'09*
How Do You Know *'10*

Chick Vennera (1947-)
Thank God It's Friday *'78*
Yanks *'79*
High Risk *'81*
Last Rites *'88*
The Milagro Beanfield War *'88*
Alone in the Woods *'95*
Body Chemistry 4: Full Exposure *'95*
Tycus *'98*
Active Stealth *'99*
The Glass Trap *'04*

Diane Venora (1952-)
Wolfen *'81*
The Cotton Club *'84*
A.D. *'85*
F/X *'86*
Ironweed *'87*
Bird *'88*
Heat *'95*
Three Wishes *'95*
The Substitute *'96*
Surviving Picasso *'96*
William Shakespeare's Romeo and Juliet *'96*
The Jackal *'97*
The Insider *'99*
Looking for an Echo *'99*
The 13th Warrior *'99*
True Crime *'99*
The Young Girl and the Monsoon *'99*
Hamlet *'00*
Stateside *'04*
Touched *'05*
Stiletto *'08*
The Ministers *'09*
All Good Things *'10*

Juliana Venter
Hooded Angels *'00*
The Harvesters *'19*

Wanda Ventham (1935-)
Blood Beast Terror *'67*
Captain Kronos: Vampire Hunter *'74*
Asylum *'05*

John Ventimiglia (1963-)
Angela *'94*
Girls Town *'95*
The Funeral *'96*
Row Your Boat *'98*
Personal Velocity: Three Portraits *'02 (N)*
The War Within *'05*
The Hungry Ghosts *'09*
The Missing Person *'09*
Rosencrantz & Guildenstern Are Undead *'10*
Flypaper *'11*

Milo Ventimiglia (1977-)
She's All That *'99*
Winter Break *'02*
Cursed *'04*
Rocky Balboa *'06*
Pathology *'08*
Armored *'09*
Gamer *'09*
Order of Chaos *'10*
Kiss of the Damned *'12*
That's My Boy *'12*
Killing Season *'13*
Wild Card *'15*
Second Act *'18*
The Art of Racing in the Rain *'19*

Vincent Ventresca (1966-)
Love & Sex *'00*
The Learning Curve *'01*
Madison *'01*
Mammoth *'06*
My Neighbor's Secret *'09*
Bad Actress *'11*

Cassie Ventura
Step Up 2 the Streets *'08*
Honey 3: Dare to Dance *'16*

Jesse Ventura (1951-)
Predator *'87*
The Running Man *'87*
Abraxas: Guardian of the Universe *'90*
Repossessed *'90*
Ricochet *'91*
Demolition Man *'93*

Lino Ventura (1919-87)
Grisbi *'53*
Classe Tous Risque *'60*
Taxi for Tobruk *'60*
Monsieur Gangster *'63*
The Great Spy Chase *'64*
Greed In the Sun *'64*
Le Deuxieme Souffle *'66*
The Last Adventure *'67*
Army of Shadows *'69*
The Valachi Papers *'72*
Happy New Year *'73*
The Medusa Touch *'78*
Sword of Gideon *'86*

Richard Venture (1923-)
The Onion Field *'79*
Missing *'82*
Heartbreak Ridge *'86*
Scent of a Woman *'92*
Truman *'95*
Red Corner *'97*
Series 7: The Contenders *'01*

Silvana Venturelli
A Long Ride From Hell *'68*
Camille 2000 *'69*
The Lickerish Quartet *'70*

Billy Vera (1944-)
The Adventures of Buckaroo Banzai Across the Eighth Dimension *'84*
The Doors *'91*

Victoria Vera (1953-)
Monster Dog *'82*
A Man of Passion *'88*

Vera-Ellen (1920-81)
Wonder Man *'45*
Three Little Girls In Blue *'46*
Carnival in Costa Rica *'47*
Words and Music *'48*
On the Town *'49*
Love Happy *'50*
Three Little Words *'50*
Happy Go Lovely *'51*
The Belle of New York *'52*
Big Leaguer *'53*
White Christmas *'54*

Eduardo Verastegui
Chasing Papi *'03*
Bella *'06*
Paul Blart: Mall Cop 2 *'15*

Lotte Verbeek (1982-)
Nothing Personal *'09*
The Fault In Our Stars *'14*
Division 19 *'19*

Natalia Verbeke (1975-)
The Son of the Bride *'01*
Dot the I *'03*
The Method *'05*
Guantanamero *'07*
The Women on the Sixth Floor *'10*

Gwen Verdon (1925-2000)
Damn Yankees *'58*
The Cotton Club *'84*
Cocoon *'85*
Nadine *'87*
Cocoon: The Return *'88*
Alice *'90*
Oldest Confederate Widow Tells All *'95*
In Cold Blood *'96*
Marvin's Room *'96*
The Dress Code *'99*

Carlo Verdone (1950-)
Iris Blond *'98*
The Great Beauty *'13*

Bruno Verdoni
Suspicious River *'00*
Her Sister's Keeper *'06*

Maribel Verdu (1970-)
Belle Epoque *'92*
Goya in Bordeaux *'99*
Y Tu Mama Tambien *'01*
Jericho Mansions *'03*
Pan's Labyrinth *'06*
Tetro *'09*

Elena Verdugo (1925-)
The Moon and Sixpence *'43*
House of Frankenstein *'44*
Little Giant *'46*
The Big Sombrero *'49*
Cyrano de Bergerac *'50*
The Lost Volcano *'50*

Peter Vere-Jones
Bad Taste *'88*
Meet the Feebles *'89 (V)*

Ben Vereen (1946-)
Gas-s-s-s! *'70*
Funny Lady *'75*
Roots *'77*
All That Jazz *'79*
Pippin *'81*
The Jesse Owens Story *'84*
A.D. *'85*
Once Upon a Forest *'93 (V)*
Why Do Fools Fall in Love? *'98*
I'll Take You There *'99*
Anne Rice's The Feast of All Saints *'01*
Idlewild *'06*
And Then Came Love *'07*

Sofia Vergara (1972-)
Big Trouble *'02*
Chasing Papi *'03*
The 24th Day *'04*
Four Brothers *'05*
Grilled *'06*
Tyler Perry's Meet the Browns *'08*
Happy Feet Two *'11 (V)*
New Year's Eve *'11*
The Smurfs *'11 (V)*
The Three Stooges *'12*
Escape From Planet Earth *'13 (V)*
Fading Gigolo *'13*
Machete Kills *'13*
The Smurfs 2 *'13*
Chef *'14*
Hot Pursuit *'15*
Wild Card *'15*
The Female Brain *'18*

Julian Vergov
Antibody *'02*
Hypersonic *'02*

Tom Verica (1964-)
Die Hard 2: Die Harder *'90*
800 Leagues Down the Amazon *'93*
From the Earth to the Moon *'98*
Princess Protection Program *'09*

Dany Verissimo
District B13 *'04*
Gradiva *'06*

Bernard Verley (1939-)
The Milky Way *'68*
Chloe in the Afternoon *'72*
Phantom of Liberty *'74*
Helas pour Moi *'94*
The Color of Lies *'99*

Francoise Verley
Chloe in the Afternoon *'72*
The Monkey's Mask *'00*

Harold Vermilyea (1889-1958)
Emperor Waltz '48
Sorry, Wrong Number '48
Denise Vernac (1916-84)
The Mask of Dijon '46
Unnatural '52
Karen Verne (1918-67)
Kings Row '41
Underground '41
All Through the Night '42
Sherlock Holmes and the Secret Weapon '42
Guy Verney (1915-70)
This Happy Breed '47
Martin Luther '53
Adam Vernier (1972-)
Black Cadillac '03
Bring It On: In It to Win It '07
Pierre Vernier (1931-)
Betty '92
Under the Sand '00
Jerry Verno (1895-1975)
The 39 Steps '35
Non-Stop New York '37
Young and Innocent '37
Old Mother Riley in Paris '38
The Belles of St. Trinian's '53
Kaili Vernoff
Ratter '16
Thoroughbreds '17
Anne Vernon (1924-)
Terror on a Train '53
Umbrellas of Cherbourg '64
Therese & Isabelle '67
Conrad Vernon (1968-)
Shrek '01 (V)
Shrek 2 '04 (V)
Shrek the Third '07 (V)
Madagascar: Escape 2 Africa '08 (V)
Penguins of Madagascar '14 (V)
Glenn Vernon (1923-99)
Bedlam '45
I Bury the Living '58
Howard Vernon (1914-96)
Bob le Flambeur '55
The Awful Dr. Orloff '62
Alphaville '65
The Diabolical Dr. Z '65
The Train '65
Triple Cross '67
Castle of the Creeping Flesh '68
Orloff and the Invisible Man '70
Virgin among the Living Dead '71
Dr. Orloff and the Invisible Man '72
Rites of Frankenstein '72
The Screaming Dead '72
The Perverse Countess '73
Zombie Lake '80
Revenge in the House of Usher '82
Faceless '88
John Vernon (1932-2005)
Point Blank '67
Justine '69
Tell Them Willie Boy Is Here '69
Dirty Harry '71
Charley Varrick '73
The Questor Tapes '74
W '74
Brannigan '75
Sweet Movie '75
The Outlaw Josey Wales '76
The Virginia Hill Story '76
A Special Day '77
National Lampoon's Animal House '78
Herbie Goes Bananas '80
Chained Heat '83
Curtains '83
Savage Streets '83
Jungle Warriors '84
Doin' Time '85
Fraternity Vacation '85
Ernest Goes to Camp '87
Deadly Stranger '88
Dixie Lanes '88
I'm Gonna Git You Sucka '88
Killer Klowns from Outer Space '88
Bail Out '90
Mob Story '90
Kate Vernon (1961-)
Alphabet City '84
Roadhouse 66 '84
Mob Story '90
Malcolm X '92
Dangerous Touch '94
Probable Cause '95
Blackjack '97
Flood: A River's Rampage '97
The Secret Life of Girls '99
The Family Plan '05
Last Chance Cafe '06
School of Life '06
Battlestar Galactica: The Plan '09
Red Faction: Origins '11
Richard Vernon (1925-97)
Village of the Damned '60
Cash on Demand '61
Just for Fun '63
The Servant '63
A Hard Day's Night '64
Tomb of Ligeia '64
The Satanic Rites of Dracula '73
The Duchess of Duke Street '78
The Human Factor '79
Wally Vernon (1905-70)
Happy Landing '38
Broadway Serenade '39
Square Dance Jubilee '51
Bloodhounds of Broadway '52
Cec Verrell
Eye of the Eagle '87
Hell Comes to Frogtown '88
Three of Hearts '93
Marie Versini
Brides of Fu Manchu '66
Thunder at the Border '66
Odile Versois (1930-80)
To Paris with Love '55
Cartouche '62
Veruschka (1939-)
Blow-Up '66
The Bride '85
Arie Verveen (1976-)
Caught '96
The Thin Red Line '98
Running Free '00
Sin '02
Cabin Fever '03
Red Roses and Petrol '03
Plain Dirty '04
Sin City '05
Across the Hall '09
Fire With Fire '12
Viktor Verzhbitsky
Night Watch '04
Day Watch '06
Bruno VeSota (1922-76)
The Egyptian '54
The Wild One '54
The Gunslinger '56
Carnival Rock '57
Teenage Doll '57
The Undead '57
A Bucket of Blood '59
The Wasp Woman '59
The Choppers '61
The Haunted Palace '63
Hell's Angels on Wheels '67
Edy Vessel (1940-)
Seven Seas to Calais '62
The Trojan Horse '62
Tricia Vessey (1972-)
Bean '97
The Alarmist '98
Coming Soon '99
Ghost Dog: The Way of the Samurai '99
On the Edge '00
Town and Country '01
Karin Viard (1966-)
Delicatessen '92
The Separation '94
La Separation '98
The New Eve '98
Children of the Century '99
Time Out '01
Change of Plans '09
Potiche '10
My Piece of the Pie '11
Polisse '11
Lolo '15
Ronan Vibert (1964-)
The Buccaneers '95
The Scarlet Pimpernel '99
The Scarlet Pimpernel 2: Mademoiselle Guillotine '99
The Scarlet Pimpernel 3: The Kidnapped King '99
Shadow of the Vampire '00
The Cat's Meow '01
Tristan & Isolde '06
Hatfields & McCoys '12
Sid Vicious (1957-79)
Mr. Mike's Mondo Video '79
The Filth and the Fury '99
Nicole Vicius
Last Days '05
Itty Bitty Titty Committee '07
How I Got Lost '09
Douchebag '10
Sound of My Voice '11
Martha Vickers (1925-71)
The Falcon in Mexico '44
The Big Sleep '46
The Man I Love '46
Ruthless '48
Big Bluff '55
The Burglar '57
Four Fast Guns '59
Yvette Vickers (1936-2011)
Attack of the 50 Foot Woman '58
Beach Party '63
Evil Spirits '91
Charles Victor (1896-1965)
Contraband '40
The Lady From Lisbon '42
The Frightened Man '52
Made in Heaven '52
Those People Next Door '52
The Pit and the Pendulum '61
Henry Victor (1892-1945)
The Beloved Rogue '27
Seas Beneath '31
Freaks '32
The Mummy '32
Tiger Bay '33
King of the Zombies '41
Blue, White and Perfect '42
Sherlock Holmes and the Secret Weapon '42
To Be or Not to Be '42
Katherine Victor (1923-2004)
Mesa of Lost Women '52
Teenage Zombies '58
House of the Black Death '65
SuperGuy: Behind the Cape '02
Piero Vida
Execution '68
Dead for a Dollar '70
Christina Vidal (1981-)
Life with Mikey '93
Freaky Friday '03
See No Evil '06
Magic Man '10
Gore Vidal (1925-2012)
Fellini's Roma '72 (C)
Bob Roberts '92
With Honors '94
The Shadow Conspiracy '96
Gattaca '97
Henri Vidal (1919-59)
Fabiola '48
Attila '54
Voulez-Vous Danser avec Moi? '59
Lisa Vidal (1965-)
I Like It Like That '94
Fall '97
The Wonderful Ice Cream Suit '98
Active Stealth '99
Chasing Papi '03
Dark Mirror '07
Gala Videnovic (1969-)
Hey, Babu Riba '88
Happy Hell Night '92
Steven Vidler (1960-)
The Good Wife '86
Encounter at Raven's Gate '88
Wrangler '88
Napoleon '96 (V)
Two Hands '98
Child Star: The Shirley Temple Story '01
The Crocodile Hunter: Collision Course '02
Salem's Lot '04
See No Evil '06
Susan Vidler (1972-)
Naked '93
The Woman in White '97
Wilbur Wants to Kill Himself '02
Florence Vidor (1895-1977)
Barbara Frietchie '24
The Marriage Circle '24
King Vidor (1894-1982)
Show People '28 (C)
Love and Money '80
Asia Vieira (1982-)
The Good Mother '88
Omen 4: The Awakening '91
Vince Vieluf (1970-)
An American Werewolf in Paris '97
Clay Pigeons '98
Rat Race '01
Grind '03
Death Valley '04
Firewall '06
Vesa Vierikko (1956-)
The Winter War '89
The Match Factory Girl '90
Abe Vigoda (1921-2016)
The Godfather '72
The Godfather, Part 2 '74
The Cheap Detective '78
The Stuff '85
Look Who's Talking '89
Prancer '89
Joe Versus the Volcano '90
Keaton's Cop '90
Fist of Honor '92
Batman: Mask of the Phantasm '93 (V)
Sugar Hill '94
Jury Duty '95
Love Is All There Is '96
Underworld '96
A Brooklyn State of Mind '97
Good Burger '97
Just the Ticket '98
Witness to the Mob '98
Crime Spree '03
Herb Vigran (1910-86)
Murder by Invitation '41
Bedtime for Bonzo '51
The Star '52
Robert Viharo (1942-)
Valley of the Dolls '67
Villa Rides '68
Bare Knuckles '77
Hide in Plain Sight '80
Night Stalker '87
Romero '89
Coldfire '90
Alicia Vikander (1988-)
Anna Karenina '12
A Royal Affair '12
The Fifth Estate '13
Son of a Gun '14
The Danish Girl '15
Ex Machina '15
The Man from U.N.C.L.E. '15
Seventh Son '15
Testament of Youth '15
Jason Bourne '16
The Light Between Oceans '16
Tulip Fever '17
Submergence '18
Tomb Raider '18
Earthquake Bird '19
Euphoria '19
Jordi Vilches (1979-)
Nico and Dani '00
Two Tough Guys '03
Marthe Villalonga (1932-)
The Big Red One '80
Three Men and a Cradle '85
Ma Saison Preferee '93
Frank Villard
Operation Abduction '58
Duke of the Derby '62
Tom Villard (1954-94)
Heartbreak Ridge '86
One Crazy Summer '86
Popcorn '89
Swimsuit '89
My Girl '91
Carlos Villarias
Dracula Spanish Version '31
The California Trail '33
Daniel Villarreal (1960-)
American Me '92
Speed '94
J.R. Villarreal (1992-)
Akeelah and the Bee '06
Bobby Z '07
Herve Villechaize (1943-93)
Greaser's Palace '72
The Man with the Golden Gun '74
Seizure '74
Return to Fantasy Island '77
The One and Only '78
Forbidden Zone '80
Two Moon Junction '88
James Villemaire (1966-)
Gate 2 '92
Matinee '92
Dead Silence '96
Fernando Villena
Planet of the Vampires '65
Earthquake in Chile '74
Jacques Villeret (1951-2005)
Bolero '82
The Favor, the Watch, & the Very Big Fish '92
The Dinner Game '98
Christopher Villiers (1960-)
Top Secret! '84
First Knight '95
James Villiers (1933-98)
Eva '62
These Are the Damned '63
King and Country '64
The Nanny '65
Repulsion '65
Otley '68
Blood from the Mummy's Tomb '71
Asylum '72
The Ruling Class '72
The Scarlet Pimpernel '82
Fortunes of War '87
House of Cards '90
Mountains of the Moon '90
Let Him Have It '91
Uncovered '94
Jay Villiers (1961-)
Henry V '89
The Sculptress '97
Pruitt Taylor Vince (1960-)
Barfly '87
Mississippi Burning '88
I Know My First Name Is Steven '89
Come See the Paradise '90
Jacob's Ladder '90
City Slickers 2: The Legend of Curly's Gold '94
Heavy '94
Natural Born Killers '94
Nobody's Fool '94
Beautiful Girls '96
The End of Violence '97
The Legend of 1900 '98
Mumford '99
The Cell '00
Nurse Betty '00
Simone '02
13 Moons '02
Trapped '02
Identity '03
Monster '03
Constantine '05
Drop Dead Sexy '05
Captivity '07
When a Man Falls in the Forest '07
The Echo '08
In the Electric Mist '08
Don McKay '09
The Smell of Success '09
Jules Verne's Mysterious Island '10
Creature '11
Drive Angry '11
Flypaper '11
On the Inside '11
Brake '12 (V)
Beautiful Creatures '13
13 Sins '13
The Devil's Candy '17
Gotti '18
Alex Vincent (1982-)
Child's Play '88
Child's Play 2 '90
Allen Vincent (1903-79)
Street of Women '32
Mystery of the Wax Museum '33
A Family Affair '37
Brian Vincent (1970-)
Animal Room '95
Black Dog '98
Under Hellgate Bridge '99
Blue Moon '00
Cerina Vincent (1979-)
Cabin Fever '03
It Waits '05
7 Mummies '06
Return to House on Haunted Hill '07
Everybody Wants to Be Italian '08
Frank Vincent (1939-)
Raging Bull '80
Goodfellas '90
Last Exit to Brooklyn '90
Jungle Fever '91
Federal Hill '94
Gotti '96
Grind '96
She's the One '96
West New York '96
Cop Land '97
The Deli '97
Ten Benny '98
Tom Clancy's Netforce '98
Witness to the Mob '98
Under Hellgate Bridge '99
Undercurrent '99
The Crew '00
Gun Shy '00
If You Only Knew '00
Snipes '01
A Tale of Two Pizzas '03
This Thing of Ours '03
The Last Request '06
Chicago Overcoat '09
Helene Vincent (1943-)
I Don't Kiss '91
Trois Couleurs: Bleu '93
Ma Vie en Rose '97
The Count of Monte Cristo '99
Jan-Michael Vincent (1944-)
The Undefeated '69
Going Home '71
The Mechanic '72
Deliver Us From Evil '73

The World's Greatest Athlete *'73*
Bite the Bullet *'75*
White Line Fever *'75*
Shadow of the Hawk *'76*
Vigilante Force *'76*
Damnation Alley *'77*
Big Wednesday *'78*
Hooper *'78*
Defiance *'79*
Hard Country *'81*
The Winds of War *'83*
Born in East L.A. *'87*
Alienator *'89*
Demonstone *'89*
Dirty Games *'89*
Hangfire *'91*
Haunting Fear *'91*
Raw Nerve *'91*
Xtro 2: The Second Encounter *'91*
Animal Instincts *'92*
Beyond the Call of Duty *'92*
Midnight Witness *'93*
Body Count *'95*
Ice Cream Man *'95*
Red Line *'96*
Buffalo 66 *'97*

June Vincent (1920-2008)
The Climax *'44*
Can't Help Singing *'45*
Here Come the Co-Eds *'45*
Black Angel *'46*
Shed No Tears *'48*
Counterspy Meets Scotland Yard *'50*
Colorado Sundown *'52*
The WAC From Walla Walla *'52*

Virginia Vincent (1918-2013)
I Want to Live! *'58*
Return of Dracula *'58*
Sweet November *'68*
The Baby *'72*
The Hills Have Eyes *'77*

Lee Ving (1950-)
Flashdance *'83*
Get Crazy *'83*
Streets of Fire *'84*
Clue *'85*
Scenes from the Goldmine *'87*

Helen Vinson (1907-99)
I Am a Fugitive from a Chain Gang *'32*
Jewel Robbery *'32*
Lawyer Man *'32*
They Call It Sin *'32*
The Little Giant *'33*
The Power and the Glory *'33*
Broadway Bill *'34*
The Captain Hates the Sea *'34*
Transatlantic Tunnel *'35*
The Wedding Night *'35*
Live, Love and Learn *'37*
Torrid Zone *'40*
Nothing But the Truth *'41*
The Thin Man Goes Home *'44*

Sharni Vinson (1983-)
Step Up 3D *'10*
Blue Crush 2 *'11*
Patrick *'13*
You're Next *'13*

Alan Vint (1944-2006)
The McMasters *'70*
Panic in Needle Park *'71*
Unholy Rollers *'72*
Welcome Home, Soldier Boys *'72*
Badlands *'74*
Macon County Line *'74*
Sniper *'75*

Jesse Vint (1940-)
Pigs *'73*
Macon County Line *'74*
Bug *'75*
Bobbie Jo and the Outlaw *'76*
Death Sport *'78*
Forbidden World *'82*
Dempsey *'83*
On the Line *'84*
I Come in Peace *'90*
Merchants of War *'90*

Gustav Vintas
Lethal Weapon *'87*
Vampire at Midnight *'88*
And You Thought Your Parents Were Weird! *'91*
Zero Tolerance *'93*

Arthur Vinton (1889-1963)
Blondie Johnson *'33*
Skyway *'33*
Circumstantial Evidence *'35*

Bobby Vinton (1935-)
Big Jake *'71*
Train Robbers *'73*

Ultra Violet (1935-)
Simon, King of the Witches *'71*
Superstar: The Life and Times of Andy Warhol *'90*

Ian Virgo (1981-)
Band of Brothers *'01*
Black Hawk Down *'01*
Extreme Dating *'04*
Witchville *'10*

Denise Virieux
Northern Extremes *'93*
Diamond Girl *'98*

Sal Viscuso (1948-)
M*A*S*H *'70 (V)*
The Taking of Pelham One Two Three *'74*
Spaceballs *'87*

Nana Visitor (1957-)
The Spirit *'87*
They Are Among Us *'04*
Babysitter Wanted *'08*
Swing Vote *'08*
Friday the 13th *'09*
A Bread Factory, Part One *'18*
A Bread Factory, Part Two *'18*

Goran Visnjic (1972-)
Welcome to Sarajevo *'97*
Practical Magic *'98*
Rounders *'98*
Committed *'99*
The Deep End *'01*
Close Your Eyes *'02*
Ice Age *'02 (V)*
Elektra *'05*
Helen *'09*
Beginners *'10*
The Girl With the Dragon Tattoo *'11*
K-11 *'11*
Dark Hearts *'12*
The Journey Home *'14*

Morné Visser (1971-)
Cape of Good Hope *'04*
The Forgiven *'18*
The Harvesters *'19*

Antonella Vitale
Opera *'88*
The Church *'98*

Joseph (Joe) Vitale (1901-94)
Zombies on Broadway *'44*
The Stranger Wore a Gun *'53*
A Bullet for Joey *'55*
Alias Jesse James *'59*
Apache Rifles *'64*

Lidia Vitale
Best of Youth *'03*
Giulia Doesn't Date at Night *'09*

Milly Vitale (1932-2006)
The Juggler *'53*
The Seven Little Foys *'55*
War and Peace *'56*
Missiles from Hell *'58*
Revak the Rebel *'60*

Elisabeth Vitali
Western *'96*
Paris 36 *'08*

Keith Vitali
Revenge of the Ninja *'83*
American Kickboxer 1 *'91*

Vitamin C (1969-)
See Colleen (Ann) Fitzpatrick

Simonetta Vitelli
Django and Sartana; It's the End *'70*
Dr. Frankenstein's Castle of Freaks *'74*

Joe (Johnny) Viterelli (1941-2004)
State of Grace *'90*
Mobsters *'91*
Ruby *'92*
The Firm *'93*
Bullets over Broadway *'94*
The Crossing Guard *'94*
Heaven's Prisoners *'95*
American Strays *'96*
Eraser *'96*
Out to Sea *'97*
Analyze This *'98*
Mafia! *'98*
Mickey Blue Eyes *'99*
See Spot Run *'01*
Shallow Hal *'01*
Wannabes *'01*
Analyze That *'02*
Serving Sara *'02*

Antoine Vitez (1930-90)
My Night at Maud's *'69*
The Green Room *'78*

Monica Vitti (1931-)
La Notte *'60*
L'Avventura *'60*
The Eclipse *'62*
The Red Desert *'64*
Bambole *'65*
Modesty Blaise *'66*
The Queens *'66*
Kill Me Quick, I'm Cold *'67*
Phantom of Liberty *'74*
An Almost Perfect Affair *'79*

Kelly Vitz (1988-)
Sky High *'05*
Nancy Drew *'07*

Viva (1938-)
Edie in Ciao! Manhattan *'72*
Play It Again, Sam *'72*
Forbidden Zone *'80*
Superstar: The Life and Times of Andy Warhol *'90*

Edgar Vivar
Guardians of the Lost Code *'10 (V)*
Tod@s Caen *'19*

Floyd Vivino (1951-)
Good Morning, Vietnam *'87*
Crazy People *'90*

Marina Vlady (1938-)
Double Agents *'59*
Two or Three Things I Know about Her *'66*
Chimes at Midnight *'67*
Son of Gascogne *'95*

Sam Vlahos (1935-2011)
Powwow Highway *'89*
The Big Squeeze *'96*
Christmas in the Clouds *'01*

Clara Voda
Aurora *'10*
If I Want to Whistle, I Whistle *'10*

Sandra Voe (1936-)
Body & Soul *'93*
Breaking the Waves *'95*
The Winter Guest *'97*
Janice Beard *'99*

Emmett Vogan (1893-1969)
The Oil Raider *'34*
San Quentin *'37*
Robot Pilot *'41*
A Fig Leaf for Eve *'44*
The Lady Confesses *'45*
Dangerous Money *'46*

Jurgen Vogel
Rosenstrasse *'03*
The Wave *'08*
Iceman *'19*

Mike Vogel (1979-)
Grind *'03*
MTV's Wuthering Heights *'03*
The Texas Chainsaw Massacre *'03*
Havoc *'05*
The Sisterhood of the Traveling Pants *'05*
Supercross: The Movie *'05*
Caffeine *'06*
Poseidon *'06*
The Deaths of Ian Stone *'07*
Cloverfield *'08*
Across the Hall *'09*
Open Graves *'09*
Blue Valentine *'10*
She's Out of My League *'10*
The Help *'11*
What's Your Number? *'11*
In My Dreams *'14*
McCanick *'14*
The Case for Christ *'17*

Mitch Vogel (1956-)
Menace on the Mountain *'70*
Born Innocent *'74*

Ruediger Vogler (1942-)
The Wrong Move *'78*
Night Sun *'90*
Until the End of the World *'91*
Faraway, So Close! *'93*
Lisbon Story *'94*

Stephanie Vogt
The Forest *'16*
Sniper: Ghost Shooter *'16*

Jon Voight (1938-)
Hour of the Gun *'67*
Midnight Cowboy *'69*
Catch-22 *'70*
Deliverance *'72*
The All-American Boy *'73*
The Odessa File *'74*
Coming Home *'78*
The Champ *'79*
Lookin' to Get Out *'82*
Table for Five *'83*
Runaway Train *'85*
Desert Bloom *'86*
The Last of His Tribe *'92*
Return to Lonesome Dove *'93*
Convict Cowboy *'95*
Heat *'95*
Anaconda *'96*
Mission: Impossible *'96*
Rosewood *'96*
Boys Will Be Boys *'97*
The Fixer *'97*
John Grisham's The Rainmaker *'97*
Most Wanted *'97*
U-Turn *'97*
Enemy of the State *'98*
The General *'98*
Varsity Blues *'98*
A Dog of Flanders *'99*
Noah's Ark *'99*
Ali *'01*
Jack and the Beanstalk: The Real Story *'01*
Lara Croft: Tomb Raider *'01*
Pearl Harbor *'01*
Uprising *'01*
Zoolander *'01*
Holes *'03*
Jasper, Texas *'03*
Karate Dog *'04*
The Manchurian Candidate *'04*
National Treasure *'04*
Superbabies: Baby Geniuses 2 *'04*
Glory Road *'06*
Bratz *'07*
National Treasure: Book of Secrets *'07*
September Dawn *'07*
Transformers *'07*
An American Carol *'08*
Four Christmases *'08*
Pride and Glory *'08*
Tropic Thunder *'08 (C)*
24: Redemption *'08*
Beyond *'11*
Getaway *'13*
Same Kind of Different as Me *'17*

Vicki Volante
Blood of Dracula's Castle *'69*
Hell's Bloody Devils *'70*
Horror of the Blood Monsters *'70*
Brain of Blood *'71*
Angels' Wild Women *'72*

Ingrid Vold
Time Barbarians *'90*
To Sleep with a Vampire *'92*

Katie Volding (1989-)
Au Pair *'99*
Au Pair 2: The Fairy Tale Continues *'01*
Au Pair 3: Adventure in Paradise *'09*

Gian Marie Volonte (1933-94)
The Girl with a Suitcase *'60*
Journey Beneath the Desert *'61*
A Fistful of Dollars *'64*
For a Few Dollars More *'65*
A Bullet for the General *'68*
Le Cercle Rouge *'70*
Sacco & Vanzetti *'71*
Lucky Luciano *'74*
Christ Stopped at Eboli *'79*

Philippe Volter (1959-2005)
The Music Teacher *'88*
Cyrano de Bergerac *'90*
The Double Life of Veronique *'91*
Trois Couleurs: Bleu *'93*
The Five Senses *'99*
Resistance *'03*

Daniel von Bargen (1950-2015)
The Silence of the Lambs *'91*
Before and After *'95*
Lord of Illusions *'95*
Truman *'95*
Stephen King's Thinner *'96*
The Postman *'97*
The Faculty *'98*
The General's Daughter *'99*
Universal Soldier: The Return *'99*
Disney's The Kid *'00*
O Brother Where Art Thou? *'00*
Shaft *'00*
The Majestic *'01*
Super Troopers *'01*
Coastlines *'02*
Simone *'02*

Tomas von Bromssen (1943-)
My Life As a Dog *'85*
All Things Fair *'95*

Erik von Detten (1982-)
Top Dog *'95*
Toy Story *'95 (V)*
Leave It to Beaver *'97*
The Princess Diaries *'01*
Girl, Positive *'07*

Lenny Von Dohlen (1958-)
Tender Mercies *'83*
Under the Biltmore Clock *'85*
Billy Galvin *'86*
Dracula's Widow *'88*
Leaving Normal *'92*
Bird of Prey *'95*
One Good Turn *'95*
Entertaining Angels: The Dorothy Day Story *'96*
Home Alone 3 *'97*

Theodore von Eltz (1894-1964)
Paint and Powder *'25*
No Man's Law *'27*
Beyond Victory *'31*
The Midnight Lady *'32*
The Red-Haired Alibi *'32*
Strangers of the Evening *'32*
Behind the Green Lights *'35*
Jim Hanvey, Detective *'37*

Clement von Franckenstein
Body Parts *'94*
Command Performance *'09*

Loni von Friedl (1943-)
The Blue Max *'66*
Journey to the Far Side of the Sun *'69*

Ira von Furstenberg (1940-)
See Ira Furstenberg

Wilhelm von Homburg (1940-2004)
The Devil's Brigade *'68*
The Wrecking Crew *'68*
Stroszek *'77*
Die Hard *'88*
Ghostbusters 2 *'89*
The Package *'89*
Eye of the Storm *'91*
Night of the Warrior *'91*
Diggstown *'92*
In the Mouth of Madness *'95*

Heidi von Palleske (1960-)
Dead Ringers *'88*
Blind Fear *'89*
Falling Fire *'97*
Strip Search *'97*
2103: Deadly Wake *'97*
Cybercity *'99*
Shepherd *'99*

Stefanie von Pfetten (1973-)
Posers *'02*
A Date With Darkness *'03*
The Invitation *'03*
Decoys *'04*
The Twelve Days of Christmas Eve *'04*
Meltdown *'06*
One Way *'06*
Christmas Caper *'07*
Holiday Switch *'07*
Termination Point *'07*
The Killing Machine *'09*
Seeds of Destruction *'11*
Goodnight for Justice: The Measure of a Man *'12*

Gustav von Seyffertitz (1863-1943)
Sherlock Holmes *'22*
The Bells *'26*
Don Juan *'26*
Sparrows *'26*
The Gaucho *'27*
The Mysterious Lady *'28*
Ambassador Bill *'31*
Dishonored *'31*
Rasputin and the Empress *'33*
She *'35*

Erich von Stroheim (1885-1957)
The Birth of a Nation *'15*
Intolerance *'16*
Blind Husbands *'19*
Foolish Wives *'22*
The Great Gabbo *'29*
Three Faces East *'30*
Crimson Romance *'34*
Fugitive Road *'34*
Grand Illusion *'37*
So Ends Our Night *'41*
Five Graves to Cairo *'43*
The North Star *'43*
Great Flamarion *'45*
The Mask of Diijon *'46*
Portrait of an Assassin *'49*
Sunset Boulevard *'50*
Unnatural *'52*
Napoleon *'55*

Max von Sydow (1929-)
Miss Julie *'50*
The Seventh Seal *'56*
Brink of Life *'57*
Wild Strawberries *'57*
The Magician *'58*
The Virgin Spring *'59*
Through a Glass Darkly *'61*
The Winter Light *'62*
The Greatest Story Ever Told *'65*
Hawaii *'66*
The Quiller Memorandum *'66*

Tony Leung Chiu Wai
Butterfly Sword *'93*
Cyclo *'95*

Edward (Robert Towne) Wain (1934-)
Creature from the Haunted Sea *'60*
The Last Woman on Earth *'61*

James Wainwright (1938-99)
Joe Kidd *'72*
A Woman Called Moses *'78*
Warlords of the 21st Century *'82*
Survivors *'83*
Mission Manila *'87*

Loudon Wainwright, III (1946-)
The Slugger's Wife *'85*
Jacknife *'89*
Big Fish *'03*
Elizabethtown *'05*
The 40 Year Old Virgin *'05*

Liam Waite (1971-)
Malicious Intent *'99*
Simpatico *'99*
Second Skin *'00*
John Carpenter's Ghosts of Mars *'01*
King of Texas *'02*
Vampire Bats *'05*

Ralph Waite (1928-2014)
Cool Hand Luke *'67*
A Lovely Way to Die *'68*
Five Easy Pieces *'70*
Chato's Land *'71*
The Grissom Gang *'71*
Lawman *'71*
Trouble Man *'72*
Girls on the Road *'73*
The Stone Killer *'73*
A Day for Thanks on Walton's Mountain *'82*
Crash and Burn *'90*
The Bodyguard *'92*
Cliffhanger *'93*
Sioux City *'94*
Homeward Bound 2: Lost in San Francisco *'96 (V)*
Sunshine State *'02*
Silver City *'04*
Ace Ventura Jr.: Pet Detective *'08*

Thomas G. Waites (1955-)
And Justice for All *'79*
On the Yard *'79*
The Warriors *'79*
The Thing *'82*
The Clan of the Cave Bear *'86*

Taika Waititi (1975-)
What We Do in the Shadows *'14*
Jojo Rabbit *'19*
Seven Stages to Achieve Eternal Bliss *'20*

Tom Waits (1949-)
The Outsiders *'83*
Rumble Fish *'83*
The Cotton Club *'84*
Down by Law *'86*
Ironweed *'87*
Shakedown *'88*
Cold Feet *'89*
Mystery Train *'89 (V)*
Queens Logic *'91*
Bram Stoker's Dracula *'92*
Short Cuts *'93*
Mystery Men *'99*
Coffee and Cigarettes *'03*
Domino *'05*
The Tiger and the Snow *'05*
Wristcutters: A Love Story *'06*
The Imaginarium of Doctor Parnassus *'09*
Seven Psychopaths *'12*
Twixt *'12 (N)*
The Ballad of Buster Scruggs *'18*
The Old Man & the Gun *'18*
The Dead Don't Die *'19*

Akiko Wakabayashi (1939-)
King Kong *vs.* Godzilla *'63*
Dagora, the Space Monster *'65*
Ghidrah the Three Headed Monster *'65*
What's Up, Tiger Lily? *'66*
You Only Live Twice *'67*

Ayako Wakao (1933-)
Drifting Weeds *'59*
An Actor's Revenge *'63*
Shinobi No Mono 3: Resurrection *'09*

Tomisaburo Wakayama (1929-92)
Shinobi no Mono *'62*
Shinobi no Mono 2: Vengeance *'63*
Zatoichi: Master Ichi and a Chest of Gold *'64*
Legends of the Poisonous Seductress 1: Female Demon Ohyaku *'68*
Lone Wolf and Cub 4 *'72*
Lone Wolf and Cub *'72*
Lone Wolf and Cub: Baby Cart at the River Styx *'72*
Lone Wolf and Cub: Baby Cart to Hades *'72*
Shogun Assassin 2: Lightning Swords of Death *'73*
The Bad News Bears Go to Japan *'78*
Phoenix *'78*
Shogun Assassin *'80*

Amr Waked (1973-)
Salmon Fishing in the Yemen *'11*
Lucy *'14*

Charity Wakefield
Sense & Sensibility *'07*
Any Human Heart *'11*

Hugh Wakefield (1888-1971)
The Man Who Knew Too Much *'34*
Blithe Spirit *'45*

Rhys Wakefield (1988-)
The Black Balloon *'09*
Sanctum *'11*
Nobody Walks *'12*
The Purge *'13*
Endless Love *'14*
Cardboard Boxer *'16*

Anton Walbrook (1900-67)
Victoria the Great *'37*
Sixty Glorious Years *'38*
Gaslight *'40*
The Forty-Ninth Parallel *'41*
The Life and Death of Colonel Blimp *'43*
The Red Shoes *'48*
The Queen of Spades *'49*
La Ronde *'51*
Lola Montes *'55*
Saint Joan *'57*

Raymond Walburn (1887-1969)
The Count of Monte Cristo *'34*
The Defense Rests *'34*
Lady by Choice *'34*
Thanks a Million *'35*
Born to Dance *'36*
Mister Cinderella *'36*
Mr. Deeds Goes to Town *'36*
High, Wide and Handsome *'37*
Thin Ice *'37*
Gateway *'38*
Let Freedom Ring *'39*
Christmas in July *'40*
Flowing Gold *'40*
Third Finger, Left Hand *'40*
Confirm or Deny *'41*
Louisiana Purchase *'41*
The Desperadoes *'43*
Hail the Conquering Hero *'44*
Heavenly Days *'44*
Key to the City *'50*
Riding High *'50*
Short Grass *'50*

Hynden Walch
Sudden Manhattan *'96*
Teen Titans Go! To the Movies *'18 (V)*

Gregory Walcott (1928-2015)
Above and Beyond *'53*
Battle Cry *'55*
Plan 9 from Outer Space *'56*
Texas Lady *'56*
Joe Kidd *'72*
Prime Cut *'72*
The Last American Hero *'73*
Midway *'76*
Ed Wood *'94*

Lynette Walden
The Silencer *'92*
Almost Blue *'93*

Robert Walden (1943-)
Bloody Mama *'70*
Murderer's Keep *'70*
Everything You Always Wanted to Know about Sex (But Were Afraid to Ask) *'72*
Our Time *'74*
Blue Sunshine *'78*

Katie Walder
Safe Harbour *'07*
Shelter *'07*

Shawna Waldron (1982-)
Little Giants *'94*
The American President *'95*
A Change of Heart *'98*
A Long Way Home *'01*
Poison Ivy 4: The Secret Society *'08*

Ethel Wales (1898-1952)
My Friend from India *'27*
Loose Ankles *'30*

Wally Wales (1895-1980)
The Miracle Rider *'35*
Rustlers of Red Dog *'35*
Adventures of Red Ryder *'40*
Fighting Seabees *'44*

Sonya Walger (1974-)
All the King's Men *'99*
Heat of the Sun *'99*
Noah's Ark *'99*
The Search for John Gissing *'01*
The Librarian: Quest for the Spear *'04*
Caffeine *'06*
Sweet Nothing in My Ear *'08*
Cold Turkey *'13*

Christopher Walken (1943-)
The Anderson Tapes *'71*
Mind Snatchers *'72*
Next Stop, Greenwich Village *'76*
The Sentinel *'76*
Annie Hall *'77*
Roseland *'77*
The Deer Hunter *'78*
Last Embrace *'79*
The Dogs of War *'81*
Heaven's Gate *'81*
Pennies from Heaven *'81*
Brainstorm *'83*
Dead Zone *'83*
A View to a Kill *'85*
At Close Range *'86*
Deadline *'87*
Biloxi Blues *'88*
Homeboy *'88*
The Milagro Beanfield War *'88*
Communion *'89*
King of New York *'90*
All-American Murder *'91*
The Comfort of Strangers *'91*
Mistress *'91*
Sarah, Plain and Tall *'91*
Batman Returns *'92*
A Business Affair *'93*
Sarah, Plain and Tall: Skylark *'93*
True Romance *'93*
Wayne's World 2 *'93*
Pulp Fiction *'94*
Search and Destroy *'94*
Nick of Time *'95*
The Prophecy *'95*
Things to Do in Denver When You're Dead *'95*
Wild Side *'95*
Basquiat *'96*
Excess Baggage *'96*
The Funeral *'96*
Last Man Standing *'96*
Touch *'96*
Mouse Hunt *'97*
The Prophecy 2: Ashtown *'97*
Suicide Kings *'97*
Antz *'98 (V)*
Blast from the Past *'98*
Illuminata *'98*
New Rose Hotel *'98*
The Eternal *'99*
The External *'99*
The Prophecy 3: The Ascent *'99*
Sarah, Plain and Tall: Winter's End *'99*
Sleepy Hollow *'99*
Vendetta *'99*
Kiss Toledo Goodbye *'00*
The Affair of the Necklace *'01*
America's Sweethearts *'01*
Joe Dirt *'01*
Catch Me If You Can *'02*
The Country Bears *'02*
Kangaroo Jack *'02*
Poolhall Junkies *'02*
Scotland, PA *'02*
Undertaking Betty *'02*
Gigli *'03*
The Rundown *'03*
Around the Bend *'04*
Envy *'04*
Man on Fire *'04*
The Stepford Wives *'04*
Domino *'05*
Romance & Cigarettes *'05*
Wedding Crashers *'05*
Click *'06*
Man of the Year *'06*
Balls of Fury *'07*
Hairspray *'07*
$5 a Day *'08*
The Maiden Heist *'08*
Dark Horse *'11*
Kill the Irishman *'11*
A Late Quartet *'12*
Seven Psychopaths *'12*
Stand Up Guys *'12*
The Power of Few *'13*
Jersey Boys *'14*
Peter Pan Live! *'14*
One More Time *'15*
The Family Fang *'16*
Nine Lives *'16*

Ally Walker (1961-)
The Seventh Coin *'92*
Singles *'92*
Universal Soldier *'92*
When the Bough Breaks *'93*
Bed of Roses *'95*
While You Were Sleeping *'95*
Kazaam *'96*
Happy, Texas *'99*
Toe to Toe *'09*
Wonderful World *'09*

Amanda Walker
Heat and Dust *'82*
Charles & Diana: A Palace Divided *'93*
7 Days to Live *'00*

Andrew W. Walker (1979-)
Steel Toes *'06*
The Way of the West *'11*
God Bless the Broken Road *'18*

Benjamin Walker (1982-)
Abraham Lincoln: Vampire Hunter *'12*
Muhammad Ali's Greatest Fight *'13*
In the Heart of the Sea *'15*
The Choice *'16*
Love Is Blind *'19*

Bill (William) Walker (1896-1992)
Boy Who Caught a Crook *'61*
The Mask *'61*

Catherine Walker (1975-)
Conspiracy of Silence *'03*
Northanger Abbey *'07*
Ferocious Planet *'11*

Charlotte Walker (1876-1958)
Midnight Girl *'25*
Three Faces East *'30*

Cheryl Walker (1918-71)
Stage Door Canteen *'43*
Identity Unknown *'45*
Larceny in her Heart *'46*

Clint Walker (1927-)
Fort Dobbs *'58*
Gold of the Seven Saints *'61*
None But the Brave *'65*
Night of the Grizzly *'66*
The Dirty Dozen *'67*
More Dead Than Alive *'68*
Sam Whiskey *'69*
Yuma *'70*
Deadly Harvest *'72*
Pancho Villa *'72*
Scream of the Wolf *'74*
Baker's Hawk *'76*
Snowbeast *'77*
The White Buffalo *'77*
Mysterious Island of Beautiful Women *'79*
The Gambler Returns: The Luck of the Draw *'93*
Small Soldiers *'98 (V)*

Dreama Walker (1986-)
Gran Torino *'08*
Seven Deadly Sins *'10*
Compliance *'12*
The Kitchen *'12*

Eamonn Walker (1962-)
Once in the Life *'00*
Unbreakable *'00*
Othello *'01*
Tears of the Sun *'03*
Duma *'05*
Lord of War *'05*
Cadillac Records *'08*
Blood and Bone *'09*
The Messenger *'09*
Legacy *'10*
A Lonely Place to Die *'11*

Eric Walker (1970-)
The Ewok Adventure *'84*
The Ewoks: Battle for Endor *'85*
And You Thought Your Parents Were Weird! *'91*
Kicking & Screaming *'05*

Fiona Walker (1944-)
Jude the Obscure *'71*
The Asphyx *'72*
The Norman Conquests, Part 1: Table Manners *'78*
The Norman Conquests, Part 2: Living Together *'78*
The Norman Conquests, Part 3: Round and Round the Garden *'78*

Helen Walker (1920-68)
Brewster's Millions *'45*
Murder, He Says *'45*
People Are Funny *'46*
Nightmare Alley *'47*
Call Northside 777 *'48*
Impact *'49*
Big Combo *'55*

Jimmie Walker (1947-)
Let's Do It Again *'75*
The Concorde: Airport '79 *'79*
Airplane! *'80*
Doin' Time *'85*
Water *'85*
Invasion of the Space Preachers *'90*
Open Season *'95*

Justin Walker
Absolution *'97*
Born Bad *'97*
Boltneck *'98*

Kathryn Walker (1943-)
A House Without a Christmas Tree *'72*
Slap Shot *'77*
Girlfriends *'78*
The Winds of Kitty Hawk *'78*
Family Reunion *'81*
Neighbors *'81*
Special Bulletin *'83*
The Murder of Mary Phagan *'87*
Dangerous Game *'90*

Kerry Walker (1948-)
The Piano *'93*
Cosi *'95*
A Little Bit of Soul *'97*

Lathrop Walker
The Penitent Man *'10*
ECCO *'19*

Matthew (Matt) Walker (1942-)
Child's Play 3 *'91*
Misbegotten *'98*
Blackwoods *'02*
Dead in a Heartbeat *'02*
Ginger Snaps Back: The Beginning *'04*
The Princess Diaries 2: Royal Engagement *'04*
Alone in the Dark *'05*
FBI: Negotiator *'05*
Doomsday Prophecy *'11*

Nancy Walker (1921-92)
Best Foot Forward *'43*
Girl Crazy *'43*
Broadway Rhythm *'44*
Lucky Me *'54*
Forty Carats *'73*
Murder by Death *'76*

Nicholas Walker
Amnesia *'96*
Body Count *'97*

Nicola Walker (1970-)
Touching Evil *'97*
Shiner *'00*
Thunderbirds *'04*
Shooting Dogs *'05*
Inside Men *'12*

Paul Walker (1973-2013)
Meet the Deedles *'98*
Pleasantville *'98*
Varsity Blues *'98*
She's All That *'99*
The Skulls *'00*
The Fast and the Furious *'01*
Joy Ride *'01*
Timeline *'03*
2 Fast 2 Furious *'03*
Noel *'04*
Into the Blue *'05*
Eight Below *'06*
Flags of Our Fathers *'06*
Running Scared *'06*
Bobby Z *'07*
The Lazarus Project *'08*
Fast & Furious *'09*
Takers *'10*
Fast Five *'11*
Fast & Furious 6 *'13*
Hours *'13*
Vehicle 19 *'13*
Brick Mansions *'14*
Furious 7 *'15*

Polly Walker (1966-)
Lorna Doone *'90*
A Dangerous Man: Lawrence after Arabia *'91*
Enchanted April *'92*
Patriot Games *'92*
Sliver *'93*
The Trial *'93*
Restoration *'94*
Emma *'96*
For Roseanna *'96*
Robinson Crusoe *'96*
Talk of Angels *'96*
Brute *'97*
Curtain Call *'97*
The Gambler *'97*
Dark Harbor *'98*
8 1/2 Women *'99*
Eye of the Killer *'99*
Eye See You *'01*

Savage Messiah '02
The Mayor of Casterbridge '03
State of Play '03
Scenes of a Sexual Nature '06
Caprica '09
John Carter '12

Ray Walker (1904-80)
Skyway '33
Goodbye Love '34
The Dark Hour '36
The Blue Gardenia '53

Robert Walker (1888-1954)
Headin' for Trouble '31
The Sea of Grass '47

Robert Walker (1918-51)
Bataan '43
Madame Curie '43
See Here, Private Hargrove '44
Since You Went Away '44
Thirty Seconds Over Tokyo '44
The Clock '45
Her Highness and the Bellboy '45
Till the Clouds Roll By '46
Song of Love '47
One Touch of Venus '48
Strangers on a Train '51
Vengeance Valley '51
My Son John '52

Robert Walker, Jr. (1940-2019)
The Ceremony '63
The Hook '63
Ensign Pulver '64
The War Wagon '67
Easy Rider '69
Beware! The Blob '72
Charms '73
AngKor: Cambodia Express '81
Devonsville Terror '83
Olivia '83

Sarah Walker
Man of Flowers '84
Housekeeping '87

Tippy Walker (1947-)
The World of Henry Orient '64
Jennifer On My Mind '71
The Jesus Trip '71

Walter Walker (1901-75)
American Madness '32
No Man of Her Own '32

Zena Walker (1934-2003)
The Marked One '63
The Dresser '83

Katie Wall
Marking Time '03
Introducing the Dwights '07
My Year Without Sex '09

Max Wall (1894-1990)
Jabberwocky '77
Strike It Rich '90

Aria Wallace (1996-)
The Perfect Man '05
Christmas in Paradise '07

Basil Wallace
Marked for Death '90
Deadlock '91
Return of the Living Dead 3 '93
Caught Up '98
Joy Ride '01
Blood Diamond '06

David Wallace (1957-)
Humongous '82
Mazes and Monsters '82

Dee Wallace (1948-)
The Stepford Wives '75
The Hills Have Eyes '77
10 '79
The Howling '81
E.T.: The Extra-Terrestrial '82
Cujo '83
The Sky's No Limit '84
Hostage Flight '85
Secret Admirer '85
Critters '86
Popcorn '89
Alligator 2: The Mutation '90
Discretion Assured '93
Huck and the King of Hearts '93
Runaway Daughters '94
The Skateboard Kid 2 '94
Best of the Best 3: No Turning Back '95
The Frighteners '96
Invisible Mom '96
Black Circle Boys '97
Invisible Mom 2 '99
Killer Instinct '00
Out of the Black '01
Headspace '02
Boo! '05
Voodoo Moon '05
The Eden Formula '06
Bone Dry '07
Halloween '07
Babysitters Beware '08
Dark Fields '09
The House of the Devil '09
Extraordinary Measures '10
Pound of Flesh '10
Collision Course '12
Grand Piano '13
Hansel & Gretel '13
The Lords of Salem '13

George Wallace (1952-)
Batman Forever '95
Three Strikes '00
The Wash '01
The Ladykillers '04

George D. Wallace (1917-2005)
Border River '47
Radar Men from the Moon '52
Forbidden Planet '56
The Swinging Cheerleaders '74
Defending Your Life '91
A Rage in Harlem '91
Diggstown '92
Bicentennial Man '99
Forces of Nature '99

Jack Wallace (1933-2020)
Assignment Outer Space '61 (N)
Things Change '88
The Bear '89
The Fixer '97
Lakeboat '00
Breakaway '02
Edmond '05

Jean Wallace (1923-90)
Jigsaw '49
Big Combo '55
Sword of Lancelot '63
Beach Red '67
No Blade of Grass '70

Marcia Wallace (1942-2013)
Pray TV '80
My Mom's a Werewolf '89
Big Stan '07
The Simpsons Movie '07 (V)

Mike Wallace (1918-2012)
Hugh Hefner: Playboy, Activist and Rebel '09
Mike Wallace Is Here '19

Morgan Wallace (1881-1953)
Up the River '30
Safe in Hell '31
The House of Secrets '37
Honky Tonk '41

Myron Leon Wallace (1918-2012)
See Mike Wallace

Toby Wallace
Return to Nim's Island '13
Babyteeth '20

William Wallace (1971-)
The Vector File '03
Cake: A Wedding Story '07

Dee Wallace Stone (1948-)
See Dee Wallace

Eli Wallach (1915-2014)
Baby Doll '56
The Lineup '58
The Magnificent Seven '60
Seven Thieves '60
The Misfits '61
How the West Was Won '63
Kisses for My President '64
The Moon-Spinners '64
Genghis Khan '65
Lord Jim '65
How to Steal a Million '66
The Poppy Is Also a Flower '66
The Good, the Bad and the Ugly '67
Ace High '68
A Lovely Way to Die '68
The Brain '69
MacKenna's Gold '69
The Angel Levine '70
ZigZag '70
Romance of a Horsethief '71
Cinderella Liberty '73
Stateline Motel '75
The Sentinel '76
The Deep '77
The Domino Principle '77
Nasty Habits '77
Circle of Iron '78
Girlfriends '78
Movie, Movie '78
Winter Kills '79
The Hunter '80
Pride of Jesse Hallum '81
The Executioner's Song '82
The Salamander '82
Tough Guys '86
The Impossible Spy '87
Nuts '87
The Godfather, Part 3 '90
The Two Jakes '90
Mistress '91
Article 99 '92
Night and the City '92
Teamster Boss: The Jackie Presser Story '92
The Associate '96
Two Much '96
Keeping the Faith '00
Monday Night Mayhem '02
King of the Corner '04
The Holiday '06
Mama's Boy '07
New York, I Love You '09
The Ghost Writer '10
Wall Street 2: Money Never Sleeps '10

Deborah Walley (1943-2001)
Gidget Goes Hawaiian '61
Bon Voyage! '62
Summer Magic '63
Beach Blanket Bingo '65
Sergeant Deadhead '65
Ski Party '65
Dr. Goldfoot and the Bikini Machine '66
Ghost in the Invisible Bikini '66
Spinout '66
The Severed Arm '73
Benji '74

David Walliams
Stoned '05
Tristram Shandy: A Cock and Bull Story '05
Stardust '07

Annabelle Wallis (1984-)
The Lost Future '10
Annabelle '14
Come and Find Me '16
The Mummy '17

Quvenzhane Wallis (2003-)
Beasts of the Southern Wild '12
Annie '14
Kahlil Gibran's The Prophet '15
Fathers and Daughters '16

Shani Wallis (1941-)
Oliver! '68
The Pebble and the Penguin '94 (N)

Tom Walls (1883-1949)
Crackerjack '38
Love Story '44
Spring in Park Lane '48

Amanda Walsh (1981-)
These Girls '05
Full of It '07
WarGames: The Dead Code '08

Angela Walsh
Distant Voices, Still Lives '88
Catherine Cookson's The Man Who Cried '93

Arthur Walsh (1923-95)
They Were Expendable '45
Courage of Lassie '46
You Gotta Stay Happy '48
The Last Hurrah '58
Mystic Pizza '88

Dermot Walsh (1924-2002)
The Frightened Man '52
Ghost Ship '53
Bond of Fear '56
The Flesh and the Fiends '60
It Takes a Thief '60
The Tell-Tale Heart '60

Dylan Walsh (1963-)
Betsy's Wedding '90
Where the Heart Is '90
Arctic Blue '93
Nobody's Fool '94
Radio Inside '94
Congo '95
Changing Habits '96
Men '97
Eden '98
Final Voyage '99
Blood Work '02
Power Play '02
We Were Soldiers '02
Edmond '05
The Lake House '06
Just Add Water '07
Lost Holiday: The Jim & Suzanne Shemwell Story '07
The Stepfather '09
Secretariat '10
Authors Anonymous '14

Eileen Walsh (1977-)
Janice Beard '99
The Magdalene Sisters '02

George Walsh (1889-1981)
American Pluck '25
Me and My Gal '32

Gwynyth Walsh (1958-)
The Crush '93
2103: Deadly Wake '97
MXP: Most Xtreme Primate '03
Holiday Wishes '06
Nightmare '07
Sea Beast '08
Storm Seekers '08

J.T. Walsh (1943-98)
Hard Choices '84
Power '86
Good Morning, Vietnam '87
House of Games '87
Tin Men '87
Tequila Sunrise '88
Things Change '88
The Big Picture '89
Dad '89
Crazy People '90
The Grifters '90
Narrow Margin '90
The Russia House '90
Backdraft '91
Defenseless '91
Iron Maze '91
A Few Good Men '92
Hoffa '92
Sniper '92
Morning Glory '93
National Lampoon's Loaded Weapon 1 '93
Needful Things '93
Red Rock West '93
Blue Chips '94
The Client '94
The Last Seduction '94
Miracle on 34th Street '94
Outbreak '94
Silent Fall '94
The Babysitter '95
Black Day Blue Night '95
The Low Life '95
Nixon '95
Breakdown '96
Executive Decision '96
Gang in Blue '96
Persons Unknown '96
Sling Blade '96
The Negotiator '98
Pleasantville '98
Hidden Agenda '99

Kate Walsh (1967-)
Henry: Portrait of a Serial Killer 2: Mask of Sanity '96
Normal Life '96
Family Man '00
Under the Tuscan Sun '03
After the Sunset '04
Bewitched '05
Inside Out '05
Kicking & Screaming '05
Veritas: Prince of Truth '07
One Way to Valhalla '09
Legion '10
Angels Crest '11
The Perks of Being a Wallflower '12
Any Day '15
Just Before I Go '15
3022 '19

Kay Walsh (1914-2005)
Secret of Stamboul '36
In Which We Serve '43
This Happy Breed '47
Oliver Twist '48
Last Holiday '50
The Magnet '50
Stage Fright '50
Encore '52
Hunted '52
Young Bess '53
Cast a Dark Shadow '55
The Horse's Mouth '58
Tunes of Glory '60
Greyfriars Bobby '61
The Witches '66

M. Emmet Walsh (1935-)
Alice's Restaurant '69
The Traveling Executioner '70
Escape from the Planet of the Apes '71
They Might Be Giants '71
The Gambler '74
The Invasion of Johnson County '76
Nickelodeon '76
Slap Shot '77
Straight Time '78
The Jerk '79
Brubaker '80
East of Eden '80
Ordinary People '80
Reds '81
Blade Runner '82
Cannery Row '82
Fast Walking '82
Grandview U.S.A. '84
Missing in Action '84
The Pope of Greenwich Village '84
Blood Simple '85
Fletch '85
Back to School '86
The Best of Times '86
Critters '86
The Deliberate Stranger '86
Resting Place '86
The Right of the People '86
Wildcats '86
Broken Vows '87
Harry and the Hendersons '87
Raising Arizona '87
Clean and Sober '88
The Milagro Beanfield War '88
Sunset '88
The Brotherhood of the Rose '89
Chattahoochee '89
The Mighty Quinn '89
Red Scorpion '89
Narrow Margin '90
Killer Image '92
White Sands '92
The Music of Chance '93
Wilder Napalm '93
Camp Nowhere '94
The Glass Shield '95
Panther '95
Portraits of a Killer '95
Probable Cause '95
Relative Fear '95
Albino Alligator '96
The Killing Jar '96
A Time to Kill '96
William Shakespeare's Romeo and Juliet '96
Chairman of the Board '97
My Best Friend's Wedding '97
Retroactive '97
Twilight '98
The Iron Giant '99 (V)
Me & Will '99
Wild Wild West '99
Poor White Trash '00
Christmas in the Clouds '01
Snow Dogs '02
Christmas With the Kranks '04
Racing Stripes '05
Big Stan '07
Haunted Echoes '08
Sherman's Way '08
Sundown: The Vampire in Retreat '08
Don McKay '09
Jr. Detective Agency '09
Youth in Revolt '10
The Odd Life of Timothy Green '12
Calvary '14
The Scorpion King 4: Quest for Power '15

Maiara Walsh (1988-)
Mean Girls 2 '11
The Starving Games '13
Summer Camp '16

Mary Walsh (1952-)
New Waterford Girl '99
Mambo Italiano '03
Gossip '08
Crackie '09
The Grand Seduction '13

Matt Walsh (1964-)
Semi-Pro '08
Cyrus '10
Into the Storm '14
Brigsby Bear '17
Under the Eiffel Tower '18
The Perfect Date '19

Percy Walsh (1888-1952)
Thursday's Child '43
The Golden Salamander '51

Raoul Walsh (1887-1980)
The Birth of a Nation '15
Sadie Thompson '28

Susan Walsh (1948-2009)
Pink Flamingos '72
Female Trouble '74

Sydney Walsh (1961-)
A Nightmare on Elm Street 2: Freddy's Revenge '85
To Die For '89
Three Men and a Little Lady '90
Point Break '91
MacArthur Park '01

Vincent Walsh (1972-)
Shattered City: The Halifax Explosion '03
Bridal Fever '08
The Two Mr. Kissels '08
The Young Messiah '16

Leanna (Leeanna) Walsman (1979-)
Star Wars: Episode 2-Attack of the Clones '02
$9.99 '08 (V)

Ray Walston (1918-2001)
Kiss Them for Me '57
Damn Yankees '58
South Pacific '58
Say One for Me '59
The Apartment '60

Portrait in Black *'60*
Tall Story *'60*
Who's Minding the Store? *'63*
Kiss Me, Stupid! *'64*
Caprice *'67*
The Sting *'73*
Silver Streak *'76*
The Happy Hooker Goes to Washington *'77*
The Fall of the House of Usher *'80*
Popeye *'80*
Galaxy of Terror *'81*
Fast Times at Ridgemont High *'82*
O'Hara's Wife *'82*
Private School *'83*
Johnny Dangerously *'84*
From the Hip *'86*
Blood Relations *'87*
O.C. and Stiggs *'87*
A Man of Passion *'88*
Saturday the 14th Strikes Back *'88*
I Know My First Name Is Steven *'89*
Popcorn *'89*
Ski Patrol *'89*
Of Mice and Men *'92*
The Player *'92*
Stephen King's The Stand *'94*
House Arrest *'96*
Get a Clue! *'98*
My Favorite Martian *'98*
Swing Vote *'99*

Harriet Walter (1950-)
The Good Father *'87*
The Advocate *'93*
Sense and Sensibility *'95*
A Merry War *'97*
Bedrooms and Hallways *'98*
The Governess *'98*
Onegin *'99*
Atonement *'07*
Ballet Shoes *'07*
Cheri *'09*
The Young Victoria *'09*
The Sense of an Ending *'17*

Jessica Walter (1941-)
Lilith *'64*
The Group *'66*
Bye Bye Braverman *'67*
Play Misty for Me *'71*
They Call It Murder *'71*
Hurricane *'74*
Victory at Entebbe *'76*
She's Dressed to Kill *'79*
Miracle on Ice *'81*
The Flamingo Kid *'84*
The Execution *'85*
Tapeheads *'89*
Ghost in the Machine *'93*
P.C.U. *'94*
Slums of Beverly Hills *'98*
Dummy *'02*
I Do (But I Don't) *'04*
Unaccompanied Minors *'06*

Lisa Ann Walter (1963-)
Eddie *'96*
The Parent Trap *'98*
Bruce Almighty *'03*
Shall We Dance? *'04*
War of the Worlds *'05*
Entry Level *'07*

Tracey Walter (1947-)
Mad Bull *'77*
Raggedy Man *'81*
Repo Man *'83*
Timerider *'83*
Conan the Destroyer *'84*
At Close Range *'86*
Something Wild *'86*
Married to the Mob *'88*
Out of the Dark *'88*
Batman *'89*
Under the Boardwalk *'89*
The Two Jakes *'90*
Young Guns 2 *'90*
City Slickers *'91*
Mortuary Academy *'91*
The Silence of the Lambs *'91*
Liquid Dreams *'92*
Buffalo Girls *'95*
Drive *'96*
Larger Than Life *'96*
Matilda *'96*
Wild America *'97*
Drowning Mona *'00*
Erin Brockovich *'00*
How High *'01*
I Spit on Your Grave *'10*

Alexander Walters
Wildfire 7: The Inferno *'02*
That's What I Am *'11*

Ashley Walters (1982-)
Get Rich or Die Tryin' *'05*
House of 9 *'05*
Goal! The Dream Begins *'06*
The Killing Gene *'07*
Sugarhouse *'07*
Small Island *'09*
Inside Men *'12*

Hal Walters (1891-1941)
Sabotage *'36*
The Four Feathers *'39*

Julie Walters (1950-)
Educating Rita *'83*
She'll Be Wearing Pink Pajamas *'84*
Car Trouble *'86*
Personal Services *'87*
Prick Up Your Ears *'87*
Buster *'88*
G.B.H. *'91*
The Wedding Gift *'93*
Sister My Sister *'94*
Melissa *'97*
Lover's Prayer *'99*
Billy Elliot *'00*
Oliver Twist *'00*
Harry Potter and the Sorcerer's Stone *'01*
Harry Potter and the Chamber of Secrets *'02*
Strange Relations *'02*
Calendar Girls *'03*
Harry Potter and the Prisoner of Azkaban *'04*
Wah-Wah *'05*
Driving Lessons *'06*
Ruby in the Smoke *'06*
Becoming Jane *'07*
Harry Potter and the Order of the Phoenix *'07*
Filth *'08*
Mamma Mia! *'08*
Harry Potter and the Half-Blood Prince *'09*
A Short Stay in Switzerland *'09*
Gnomeo & Juliet *'11 (V)*
Brave *'12 (V)*
One Chance *'13*
Paddington *'14*
Brooklyn *'15*
Effie Gray *'15*
Film Stars Don't Die in Liverpool *'17*
Mary Poppins Returns *'18*
Wild Rose *'18*

Laurie Walters (1947-)
Harrad Experiment *'73*
Warlock Moon *'73*
Harrad Summer *'74*

Luana Walters (1912-63)
Assassin of Youth *'35*
Shadow of Chinatown *'36*
Blondie Plays Cupid *'40*

Lucia Walters
Double Cross *'06*
A Job to Kill For *'06*

Melora Walters (1960-)
Twenty Bucks *'93*
American Strays *'96*
Hard Eight *'96*
Boogie Nights *'97*
Magnolia *'99*
Desert Saints *'01*
Wisegirls *'02*
Cold Mountain *'03*
The Big Empty *'04*
The Butterfly Effect *'04*
Brothers Three *'07*
Hurt *'09*
The River Murders *'11*
The Young Kieslowski *'15*
The Lovers *'17*

Stephen Walters
Layer Cake *'05*
Franklyn *'08*

Susan Walters (1963-)
Russkies *'87*
Defending Your Life *'91*
Two Came Back *'97*
Where the Truth Lies *'99*
Framed for Murder *'07*

Thorley Walters (1913-91)
Blue Murder at St. Trinian's *'56*
Who Done It? *'56*
Invasion Quartet *'61*
Murder She Said *'61*
The Pure Hell of St. Trinian's *'61*
The Phantom of the Opera *'62*
Sherlock Holmes and the Deadly Necklace *'62*
Dracula, Prince of Darkness *'66*
Frankenstein Created Woman *'66*
Frankenstein Must Be Destroyed *'69*
Bartleby *'70*
Cry of the Penguins *'71*
Vampire Circus *'71*
The People That Time Forgot *'77*
The Adventures of Sherlock Holmes' Smarter Brother *'78*
The Sign of Four *'83*
The Little Drummer Girl *'84*

Henry B. Walthall (1878-1936)
Avenging Conscience *'14*
Judith of Bethulia *'14*
The Birth of a Nation *'15*
The Raven *'15*
The Confession *'20*
The Plastic Age *'25*
Wings *'27*
Abraham Lincoln *'30*
Chandu the Magician *'32*
Me and My Gal *'32*
Strange Interlude *'32*
Her Forgotten Past *'33*
Laughing at Life *'33*
Beggars in Ermine *'34*
City Park *'34*
Judge Priest *'34*
Men in White *'34*
The Scarlet Letter *'34*
Dante's Inferno *'35*
Last Outlaw *'36*
A Tale of Two Cities *'36*

David Walton
Fired Up! *'09*
The Makeover *'13*

Douglas Walton (1910-61)
Charlie Chan in London *'34*
The Lost Patrol *'34*
The Bride of Frankenstein *'35*
Mary of Scotland *'36*
Raffles *'39*
Murder, My Sweet *'44*

Mark Walton
Home on the Range *'04 (V)*
Bolt *'08 (V)*

Christoph Waltz (1956-)
Jacob *'94*
Inglourious Basterds *'09*
Carnage *'11*
The Green Hornet *'11*
The Three Musketeers *'11*
Water for Elephants *'11*
Django Unchained *'12*
Epic *'13 (V)*
The Zero Theorem *'13*
Big Eyes *'14*
Horrible Bosses 2 *'14*
The Legend of Tarzan *'16*
Downsizing *'17*
Alita: Battle Angel *'19*

Lisa Waltz (1961-)
Brighton Beach Memoirs *'86*
Pet Sematary 2 *'92*
The Odd Couple 2 *'98*
Starry Night *'99*

Patrick Waltz
The Sun Sets at Dawn *'50*
Queen of Outer Space *'58*

Chi Keung Wan
Infernal Affairs 2 *'03*
Infernal Affairs 3 *'03*

Lau Ching Wan (1964-)
Black Mask *'96*
Running out of Time *'99*

Siu-Lun Wan (1964-)
Legend of the Liquid Sword *'93*
So Close *'02*

Sam Wanamaker (1919-93)
Taras Bulba *'62*
The Spy Who Came in from the Cold *'65*
Those Magnificent Men in Their Flying Machines *'65*
Warning Shot *'67*
Spiral Staircase *'75*
Sell Out *'76*
The Sellout *'76*
Voyage of the Damned *'76*
From Hell to Victory *'79*
The Competition *'80*
Private Benjamin *'80*
Detective Sadie & Son *'84*
Irreconcilable Differences *'84*
The Aviator *'85*
Raw Deal *'86*
Baby Boom *'87*
Superman 4: The Quest for Peace *'87*
Judgment in Berlin *'88*
The Shell Seekers *'89*
Guilty by Suspicion *'91*
Pure Luck *'91*
City of Joy *'92 (C)*
Covert Assassin *'94*

Zoe Wanamaker (1949-)
Poor Little Rich Girl: The Barbara Hutton Story *'87*
The Raggedy Rawney *'90*
Tales of the Unexpected *'91*
The Blackheath Poisonings *'92*
Prime Suspect *'92*
The Widowing of Mrs. Holroyd *'95*
A Dance to the Music of Time *'97*
Swept from the Sea *'97*
Wilde *'97*
David Copperfield *'99*
The Magical Legend of the Leprechauns *'99*
Harry Potter and the Sorcerer's Stone *'01*
A Waste of Shame *'05*
The Old Curiosity Shop *'07*
My Week With Marilyn *'11*

Chung Wang
Have Sword, Will Travel *'69*
The Heroic Ones *'70*

Faye Wang (1969-)
See Faye Wong

Hongwei Wang
Balzac and the Little Chinese Seamstress *'02*
Old Stone *'16*

Hsieh Wang
Infra-Man *'76*
Sword Masters: Web of Death *'76*

Joey Wang (1967-)
Butterfly Sword *'93*
Painted Skin *'93*

Li Wang
House of Traps *'81*
The Brave Archer and His Mate *'82*

Lung-Wai Wang
Master of the Flying Guillotine *'75*
Shaolin & Wu Tang *'81*

Lung Wei Wang (1949-)
Five Deadly Venoms *'78*
The Master *'80*
8 Diagram Pole Fighter *'84*

Peter Wang
Chan Is Missing *'82*
A Great Wall *'86*

Yu Wang (1943-)
The Magnificent Trio *'66*
The One-Armed Swordsman *'67*
Golden Swallow *'68*
Master of the Flying Guillotine *'75*

Zhiwen Wang (1966-)
The Emperor and the Assassin *'99*
Together *'02*
Battle of the Warriors *'06*

Percy Waram (1881-1961)
Ministry of Fear *'44*
The Big Hangover *'50*

David Warbeck (1941-97)
Twins of Evil *'71*
The Sex Thief *'74*
The Last Hunter *'80*
The Black Cat *'81*
Ark of the Sun God *'82*
The Beyond *'82*
Razor Blade Smile *'98*

John Warburton (1887-1981)
Cavalcade *'33*
Nothing But Trouble *'44*
The White Cliffs of Dover *'44*
Confidential Agent *'45*
Saratoga Trunk *'45*
Tarzan and the Huntress *'47*
Secret File of Hollywood *'62*
King Rat *'65*

Patrick Warburton (1964-)
Dragonard *'88*
Angels in the Infield *'00*
The Dish *'00*
The Emperor's New Groove *'00 (V)*
Scream 3 *'00*
Joe Somebody *'01*
Big Trouble *'02*
Men in Black 2 *'02*
Home on the Range *'04 (V)*
Chicken Little *'05 (V)*
Hoodwinked *'05 (V)*
Rebound *'05*
Sky High *'05 (V)*
Open Season *'06 (V)*
The Wild *'06 (V)*
Bee Movie *'07 (V)*
Happily N'Ever After *'07 (V)*
I'll Believe You *'07*
Underdog *'07*
Get Smart *'08*
Space Chimps *'08 (V)*
Rock Slyde: Private Eye *'09*
Hoodwinked Too! Hood *vs.* Evil *'11 (V)*
Ted *'12*
Movie 43 *'13*
Mr. Peabody & Sherman *'14 (V)*
Playing It Cool *'14*

Amelita Ward (1923-87)
Clancy Street Boys *'43*
The Falcon and the Co-Eds *'43*
The Falcon in Danger *'43*

Brendan Ward
Taps *'81*
South Bronx Heroes *'85*

Burt Ward (1945-)
Batman *'66*
Virgin High *'90*
Assault of the Party Nerds 2: Heavy Petting Detective *'95*

David Oren Ward (1972-99)
Pariah *'98*
Witchouse *'99*

Donal Lardner Ward (1964-)
My Life's in Turnaround *'94*
The Suburbans *'99*

Fred Ward (1942-)
Escape from Alcatraz *'79*
Carny *'80*
Southern Comfort *'81*
The Right Stuff *'83*
Silkwood *'83*
Timerider *'83*
Uncommon Valor *'83*
Swing Shift *'84*
Remo Williams: The Adventure Begins *'85*
Secret Admirer *'85*
Off Limits *'87*
Big Business *'88*
Prince of Pennsylvania *'88*
Backtrack *'89*
Tremors *'89*
Henry & June *'90*
Miami Blues *'90*
Bob Roberts *'92*
The Player *'92*
Thunderheart *'92*
Short Cuts *'93*
Naked Gun 33 1/3: The Final Insult *'94*
Chain Reaction *'96*
Tremors 2: Aftershocks *'96*
First Do No Harm *'97*
Best Men *'98*
Dangerous Beauty *'98*
Forgotten City *'98*
Invasion: Earth *'98*
The Crimson Code *'99*
Chaos Factor *'00*
Circus *'00*
The Crow: Salvation *'00*
Full Disclosure *'00*
Jackie Bouvier Kennedy Onassis *'00*
Road Trip *'00*
Corky Romano *'01*
Joe Dirt *'01*
Summer Catch *'01*
Abandon *'02*
Enough *'02*
Sweet Home Alabama *'02*
Coast to Coast *'04*
The Last Ride *'04*
Feast of Love *'07*
Exit Speed *'08*
Armored *'09*
Farewell *'09*
Management *'09*
The Wild Stallion *'09*
2 Guns *'13*

Gemma Ward (1987-)
The Strangers *'08*
The Black Balloon *'09*
Pirates of the Caribbean: On Stranger Tides *'11*

John Ward (1924-95)
Robinson Crusoe of Clipper Island *'36*
Holt of the Secret Service *'42*

Jonathan Ward (1970-)
White Water Summer *'87*
Mac and Me *'88*
Ferngully: The Last Rain Forest *'92 (V)*

Kelly Ward (1956-)
Grease *'78*
The Big Red One *'80*

Lucille Ward (1907-69)
California Straight Ahead *'25*
A Woman of the World *'25*

Lyman Ward (1941-)
Great Smokey Roadblock *'76*
Creature *'85*
Ferris Bueller's Day Off *'86*
Planes, Trains & Automobiles *'87*
Mikey *'92*
Sleepwalkers *'92*
Serial Killer *'95*
Independence Day *'96*
The Secret Agent Club *'96*

Maitland Ward (1977-)
Dish Dogs *'98*
White Chicks *'04*

Mary B. Ward
Hangin' with the Homeboys *'91*
Surviving Desire *'91*

Matt Ward
Christmas in Canaan '09
Christmas Comes Home to Canaan '11

Megan Ward (1969-)
Trancers 2: The Return of Jack Deth '90
Amityville 1992: It's About Time '92
Encino Man '92
Trancers 3: Deth Lives '92
Arcade '93
Freaked '93
P.C.U. '94
Glory Daze '96
Joe's Apartment '96
Don't Look Down '98
Rated X '00
Tick Tock '00
Murder Without Conviction '04

Paddy Ward
Waking Ned Devine '98
Casanova '05

Penelope Dudley Ward (1919-82)
I Stand Condemned '36
The Citadel '38
The Case of the Frightened Lady '39

Rachel Ward (1957-)
Night School '81
Sharky's Machine '81
Dead Men Don't Wear Plaid '82
The Final Terror '83
The Thorn Birds '83
Against All Odds '84
Fortress '85
The Good Wife '86
How to Get Ahead in Advertising '89
After Dark, My Sweet '90
Wide Sargasso Sea '92
Twisted '96
On the Beach '00
And Never Let Her Go '01
Bobbie's Girl '02
Johnson County War '02
Blackbeard '06

Richard Ward (1915-79)
Across 110th Street '72
Mandingo '75
The Jerk '79

Roger Ward (1936-)
Mad Max '80
Quigley Down Under '90

Roy Ward
The Forbidden Quest '93
The Ugly '96

Sandy Ward (1926-2005)
The Velvet Vampire '71
Cujo '83
Tank '83
The Chinatown Murders: Man against the Mob '89
Blue Desert '91
Delta Force 3: The Killing Game '91

Sela Ward (1956-)
Nothing in Common '86
Hello Again '87
Steele Justice '87
The Fugitive '93
My Fellow Americans '96
54 '98
Runaway Bride '99
The Badge '02
The Day After Tomorrow '04
Dirty Dancing: Havana Nights '04
The Guardian '06
The Stepfather '09
Gone Girl '14
Independence Day: Resurgence '16

Simon Ward (1941-2012)
Frankenstein Must Be Destroyed '69
Young Winston '72
Dracula '73
Hitler: The Last Ten Days '73
All Creatures Great and Small '74
The Three Musketeers '74
The Four Musketeers '75
The Chosen '77
The Four Feathers '78
Dominique '79
Zulu Dawn '79
Supergirl '84
The Monster Club '85

Skip Ward (1932-2003)
Road Racers '59
The Mad Room '69

Sophie Ward (1964-)
Young Sherlock Holmes '85
A Summer Story '88
The Shell Seekers '89
Waxwork 2: Lost in Time '91
A Demon in My View '92
Emily Brontë's Wuthering Heights '92
A Village Affair '95
The Big Fall '96
Clive Barker's Book of Blood '08
Land Girls '09
Jane Eyre '11

Susan Ward (1976-)
The In Crowd '00
Shallow Hal '01
Wild Things 2 '04
Cruel World '05
Toxic '07
Order of Chaos '10

Tom Ward (1971-)
Moll Flanders '96
The Infinite Worlds of H.G. Wells '01
The Lost World '02
Death Comes to Pemberley '13

Wally Ward (1965-)
See Wallace (Wally) Langham

Warwick Ward (1891-1967)
Variety '25
The Informer '29

Zack (Zach) Ward (1970-)
A Christmas Story '83
Star Hunter '95
Ed '96
Brotherhood of Murder '99
Malicious Intent '99
Almost Famous '00
April's Shower '03
L.A. Twister '04
Resident Evil: Apocalypse '04
Hollywood Kills '06
BloodRayne 2: Deliverance '07
Postal '07
Transformers '07
Alone in the Dark 2 '08
Battle Planet '08
The Devil's Tomb '09
In My Pocket '11
Blood Lake '14

Jennifer Ward-Lealand
Dangerous Orphans '86
The Ugly '96

Luke Ward-Wilinson
The Christmas Miracle of Jonathan Toomey '07
Sharpe's Peril '08

Anthony Warde (1908-75)
The Spider Returns '41
I Escaped from the Gestapo '43
Where Are Your Children? '44
Stage Struck '48

Harlan Warde (1917-80)
Money Madness '47
The Man Who Cheated Himself '50
Flying Leathernecks '51
Loan Shark '52
Above and Beyond '53
Julie '56

Jack Warden (1920-2006)
From Here to Eternity '53
Edge of the City '57
Twelve Angry Men '57
Darby's Rangers '58
Run Silent, Run Deep '58
Wake Me When It's Over '60
Escape From Zahrain '62
Donovan's Reef '63
The Thin Red Line '64
Bye Bye Braverman '67
Brian's Song '71
Summertree '71
Man Who Loved Cat Dancing '73
The Apprenticeship of Duddy Kravitz '74
Billy Two Hats '74
Shampoo '75
Raid on Entebbe '77
The White Buffalo '77
Death on the Nile '78
Heaven Can Wait '78
And Justice for All '79
Being There '79
Beyond the Poseidon Adventure '79
The Champ '79
Used Cars '80
Carbon Copy '81
The Great Muppet Caper '81
So Fine '81
The Verdict '82
Hobson's Choice '83
Crackers '84
A.D. '85
Alice in Wonderland '85
The Aviator '85
The Presidio '88
September '88
Everybody Wins '90
Judgment '90
Problem Child '90
Robert Kennedy and His Times '90
Problem Child 2 '91
Night and the City '92
Passed Away '92
Guilty as Sin '93
Bullets over Broadway '94
Mighty Aphrodite '95
Things to Do in Denver When You're Dead '95
While You Were Sleeping '95
Ed '96
Chairman of the Board '97
Dirty Work '97
The Island on Bird Street '97
Bulworth '98
A Dog of Flanders '99
The Replacements '00

Geoffrey Wardwell (1900-55)
The Challenge '38
Crimes at the Dark House '39

Helen Ware (1877-1939)
One Night at Susie's '30
The Reckless Hour '31

Herta Ware (1917-2005)
Cocoon '85
Dakota '88
Crazy in Love '92
Top Dog '95
St. Patrick's Day '99

Irene Ware (1910-93)
Chandu the Magician '32
The Dark Hour '36

Linda Ware
Gangs, Inc. '41
Paper Bullets '41

Kierston Wareing (1976-)
Fish Tank '09
The Take '09
Inside Men '12
The Liability '12
Avengement '19

Chris Warfield (1927-96)
Dangerous Charter '62
Incident in an Alley '62
Diary of a Madman '63

Marsha Warfield (1954-)
D.C. Cab '84
Mask '85
The Whoopee Boys '86

Andy Warhol (1928-87)
Driver's Seat '73
Cocaine Cowboys '79

Raymond Waring (1977-)
Lucky Break '01
Yes '04

Billy Warlock (1961-)
Hot Shot '86
Swimsuit '89
Society '92
Panic in the Skies '96
Steel Sharks '97

Kimberly Warnat
Silver Wolf '98
Eight Days to Live '06
The Bad Son '07

Amelia Warner (1982-)
Lorna Doone '01
Aeon Flux '05
Stoned '05
Winter Passing '05
Alpha Male '06
The Echo '08

David Warner (1941-)
Tom Jones '63
Morgan: A Suitable Case for Treatment '66
A Midsummer Night's Dream '68
The Sea Gull '68
Ballad of Cable Hogue '70
Straw Dogs '72
A Doll's House '73
From Beyond the Grave '73
Cross of Iron '76
The Omen '76
Holocaust '78
The Concorde: Airport '79 '79
Nightwing '79
S.O.S. Titanic '79
The Thirty-Nine Steps '79
Time After Time '79
The Island '80
Masada '81
Time Bandits '81
Tron '82
The Man with Two Brains '83
A Christmas Carol '84
The Company of Wolves '85
Mr. North '88
My Best Friend Is a Vampire '88
Waxwork '88
Star Trek 5: The Final Frontier '89
Star Trek 6: The Undiscovered Country '91
Teenage Mutant Ninja Turtles 2: The Secret of the Ooze '91
The Lost World '92
The Unnamable 2: The Statement of Randolph Carter '92
Body Bags '93
Return to the Lost World '93
Wild Palms '93
Ice Cream Man '95
In the Mouth of Madness '95
Naked Souls '95
The Leading Man '96
Money Talks '97
Scream 2 '97
Titanic '97
Houdini '98
Wing Commander '99
Back to the Secret Garden '01
Horatio Hornblower: The Adventure Continues '01
Planet of the Apes '01
Ladies in Lavender '04
Straight into Darkness '04
Hogfather '06
Perfect Parents '06
Albert's Memorial '09
Black Death '10
A Thousand Kisses Deep '11

H.B. Warner (1876-1958)
King of Kings '27
The Divine Lady '29
Liliom '30
The Reckless Hour '31
The Crusader '32
The Phantom of Crestwood '32
Supernatural '33
Night Alarm '34
Mr. Deeds Goes to Town '36
A Tale of Two Cities '36
Lost Horizon '37
Victoria the Great '37
The Adventures of Marco Polo '38
The Toy Wife '38
You Can't Take It with You '38
Bulldog Drummond's Bride '39
Let Freedom Ring '39
Mr. Smith Goes to Washington '39
The Rains Came '39
The Devil & Daniel Webster '41
Topper Returns '41
The Corsican Brothers '42
Yank in Libya '42
Boss of Big Town '43
Women in Bondage '43
Action in Arabia '44
Enemy of Women '44
It's a Wonderful Life '46
Strange Impersonation '46
High Wall '47
The Judge Steps Out '49
Savage Drums '51
The Ten Commandments '56

Jack Warner (1895-1981)
Captive Heart '47
Hue and Cry '47
It Always Rains on Sunday '47
Against the Wind '48
The Blue Lamp '49
Boys in Brown '49
A Christmas Carol '51
Those People Next Door '52
The Ladykillers '55
The Quatermass Experiment '56
Carve Her Name with Pride '58

Julie Warner (1965-)
Doc Hollywood '91
Mr. Saturday Night '92
Indian Summer '93
The Puppet Masters '94
Tommy Boy '95
Wedding Bell Blues '96
Dean Koontz's Mr. Murder '98
Stick It '06
Uncaged Heart '07
Forever Strong '08

Malcolm Jamal Warner (1970-)
The Father Clements Story '87
Drop Zone '94
The Tuskegee Airmen '95
Restaurant '98
Fool's Gold '08

Barry Warren (1933-94)
Kiss of the Vampire '62
The Devil-Ship Pirates '64
Frankenstein Created Woman '66

C. Denier Warren (1889-1971)
Old Mother Riley in Paris '38
Lolita '62

E. Alyn (Fred) Warren (1874-1940)
Abraham Lincoln '30
Son of the Gods '30
Tarzan the Fearless '33

Estella Warren (1978-)
Driven '01
Planet of the Apes '01
Tangled '01
Kangaroo Jack '02
The Cooler '03
Evil Remains '04
Lies and Crimes '07
Blue Seduction '09
Beauty and the Beast: A Dark Tale '10
Takedown '10
The Stranger Within '13
Decommissioned '16

Gloria Warren (1926-)
Dangerous Money '46
Don't Gamble with Strangers '46
Bells of San Fernando '47

Jennifer Warren (1941-)
The Swap '71
Night Moves '75
Banjo Hackett '76
Another Man, Another Chance '77
Slap Shot '77
Champions: A Love Story '78
Ice Castles '79
Mutant '83

Jennifer Leigh Warren (1969-)
The Crossing Guard '94
Grace of My Heart '96
Matter of Trust '98
Sour Grapes '98

Katherine Warren (1905-65)
The Prowler '51
Battles of Chief Pontiac '52
The Caine Mutiny '54

Kenneth J. Warren (1929-73)
I, Monster '71
The Creeping Flesh '72
Demons of the Mind '72

Kiersten Warren (1965-)
Independence Day '96
Bicentennial Man '99
Liberty Heights '99
Duets '00
Circuit '02
Divine Secrets of the Ya-Ya Sisterhood '02
Black Cadillac '03
The Snow Walker '03
Hoot '06
The Christmas Cottage '08
Acceptance '09

Lesley Ann Warren (1946-)
Cinderella '64
The Happiest Millionaire '67
The One and Only, Genuine, Original Family Band '68
Legend of Valentino '75
Harry & Walter Go to New York '76
Betrayal '78
Pearl '78
Beulah Land '80
Portrait of a Showgirl '82
Victor/Victoria '82
A Night in Heaven '83
Treasure of the Yankee Zephyr '83
Choose Me '84
Songwriter '84
Clue '85
Burglar '87
Cop '88
Worth Winning '89
A Family of Spies '90
Life Stinks '91
Pure Country '92
Color of Night '94
Bird of Prey '95
Joseph '95
Natural Enemy '96
Going All the Way '97
Love Kills '98
The Limey '99
Twin Falls Idaho '99
Trixie '00
The Quickie '01
Secretary '02
Recipe for Disaster '03
Deepwater '05
When Do We Eat? '05
Miracle Dogs Too '06
Stiffs '06
10th & Wolf '06

Bound by a Secret *'09*
A Little Help *'11*

Marc Warren (1967-)
Boston Kickout *'95*
Hidden in Silence *'96*
Dad Savage *'97*
Band of Brothers *'01*
State of Play *'03*
Green Street Hooligans *'05*
Hellraiser: Deader *'05*
Dracula *'06*
Hogfather *'06*
Ballet Shoes *'07*
Wanted *'08*

Michael Warren (1946-)
Norman, Is That You? *'76*
Heaven Is a Playground *'91*
Storyville *'92*
Buffalo Soldiers *'97*
Trippin' *'99*
Species 3 *'04*

Harold Warrender (1903-53)
Contraband *'40*
Conspirator *'49*
Pandora and the Flying Dutchman *'51*

Ruth Warrick (1915-2005)
Citizen Kane *'41*
The Corsican Brothers *'42*
Guest in the House *'44*
Mr. Winkle Goes to War *'44*
Arch of Triumph *'48*
Great Dan Patch *'49*
Let's Dance *'50*
Three Husbands *'50*
One Too Many *'51*

David Warrilow (1934-95)
Bright Lights, Big City *'88*
Barton Fink *'91*

Dan Warry-Smith (1982-)
The Legend of Gator Face *'96*
My Teacher Ate My Homework *'98*

David Warshofsky (1961-)
Personal Velocity: Three Portraits *'02*
Running Scared *'06*
The Future *'11*
Captain Phillips *'13*
Wilson *'17*

John Warwick (1905-72)
Ticket of Leave Man *'37*
The Face at the Window *'39*
Horrors of the Black Museum *'59*

Richard Warwick (1945-97)
If. . . *'69*
Sebastiane *'79*

Robert Warwick (1878-1964)
The Royal Bed *'31*
The Woman From Monte Carlo *'31*
Whispering Shadow *'33*
A Shot in the Dark *'35*
Whipsaw *'35*
The Bold Caballero *'36*
The Awful Truth *'37*
Gangster's Boy *'38*
Sullivan's Travels *'41*
A Woman's Face *'41*
Tarzan and the Slave Girl *'50*
The Star *'52*
It Started with a Kiss *'59*

Mona Washbourne (1903-88)
Cast a Dark Shadow *'55*
The Brides of Dracula *'60*
My Fair Lady *'64*
Night Must Fall *'64*
The Collector *'65*
The Third Day *'65*
Mrs. Brown, You've Got a Lovely Daughter *'68*
If. . . *'69*
Fragment of Fear *'70*
Driver's Seat *'73*
O Lucky Man! *'73*
Therese Raquin *'80*
Brideshead Revisited *'81*

Beverly Washburn (1943-)
Old Yeller *'57*
Spider Baby *'64*
Pit Stop *'67*

Bryant Washburn (1889-1963)
The Wizard of Oz *'25*
Kept Husbands *'31*
Savage Fury *'35*
The Spider Returns *'41*

Carl Washington
I Got Five on It *'05*
Illegal Business *'06*

Denzel Washington (1954-)
Wilma *'77*
Carbon Copy *'81*
License to Kill *'84*
A Soldier's Story *'84*
Hard Lessons *'86*
Power *'86*
Cry Freedom *'87*
Glory *'89*
The Mighty Quinn *'89*
Heart Condition *'90*
Mo' Better Blues *'90*
Ricochet *'91*
Malcolm X *'92*
Mississippi Masala *'92*
Much Ado about Nothing *'93*
The Pelican Brief *'93*
Philadelphia *'93*
Crimson Tide *'95*
Devil in a Blue Dress *'95*
Virtuosity *'95*
Courage Under Fire *'96*
The Preacher's Wife *'96*
Fallen *'97*
He Got Game *'98*
The Siege *'98*
The Bone Collector *'99*
The Hurricane *'99*
Remember the Titans *'00*
Training Day *'01*
Antwone Fisher *'02*
John Q *'02*
Out of Time *'03*
Man on Fire *'04*
The Manchurian Candidate *'04*
Deja Vu *'06*
Inside Man *'06*
American Gangster *'07*
The Great Debaters *'07*
The Taking of Pelham 123 *'09*
The Book of Eli *'10*
Unstoppable *'10*
Flight *'12*
Safe House *'12*
2 Guns *'13*
The Equalizer *'14*
Fences *'16*
The Magnificent Seven *'16*
Roman J. Israel, Esq. *'17*
The Equalizer 2 *'18*

Fredi Washington (1903-94)
Emperor Jones *'33*
Imitation of Life *'34*

Gene Washington (1947-)
The Black Six *'74*
Lady Cocoa *'75*

Isaiah Washington, IV (1963-)
Crooklyn *'94*
Clockers *'95*
Get On the Bus *'96*
Girl 6 *'96*
Love Jones *'96*
Mr. & Mrs. Loving *'96*
Always Outnumbered Always Outgunned *'98*
Bulworth *'98*
Mixing Nia *'98*
Out of Sight *'98*
A Texas Funeral *'99*
True Crime *'99*
Dancing in September *'00*
Romeo Must Die *'00*
Exit Wounds *'01*
Ghost Ship *'02*
Welcome to Collinwood *'02*
Hollywood Homicide *'03*
This Girl's Life *'03*
Dead Birds *'04*

Wild Things 2 *'04*
The Moguls *'05*
The Least of These *'08*
Hurricane Season *'09*
The Trials of Cate McCall *'13*
Blackbird *'14*
The Sin Seer *'15*

Jascha Washington (1989-)
Big Momma's House *'00*
My Sister's Keeper *'02*
Last Holiday *'06*
The Final *'10*

John David Washington
BlacKkKlansman *'18*
Monsters and Men *'18*

Kerry Washington (1977-)
Lift *'01*
Our Song *'01*
Save the Last Dance *'01*
Bad Company *'02*
Sin *'02*
The Human Stain *'03*
United States of Leland *'03*
Against the Ropes *'04*
Ray *'04*
She Hate Me *'04*
Fantastic Four *'05*
Mr. & Mrs. Smith *'05*
The Dead Girl *'06*
The Last King of Scotland *'06*
Little Man *'06*
Fantastic Four: Rise of the Silver Surfer *'07*
I Think I Love My Wife *'07*
Lakeview Terrace *'08*
Life is Hot in Cracktown *'08*
Miracle at St. Anna *'08*
Mother and Child *'09*
For Colored Girls *'10*
Night Catches Us *'10*
The Details *'11*
Django Unchained *'12*
A Thousand Words *'12*
Girl Rising *'13 (N)*
Peeples *'13*
American Son *'19*

Mia Wasikowska (1989-)
Rogue *'07*
Defiance *'08*
Amelia *'09*
That Evening Sun *'09*
Alice in Wonderland *'10*
The Kids Are All Right *'10*
Albert Nobbs *'11*
Jane Eyre *'11*
Restless *'11*
Lawless *'12*
The Double *'13*
Only Lovers Left Alive *'13*
Stoker *'13*
Maps to the Stars *'14*
Tracks *'14*
Crimson Peak *'15*
Madame Bovary *'15*
Alice Through the Looking Glass *'16*
Damsel *'18*
Piercing *'18*
Judy & Punch *'20*

Ted Wass (1952-)
The Triangle Factory Fire Scandal *'79*
Curse of the Pink Panther *'83*
Oh, God! You Devil *'84*
Sheena *'84*
The Canterville Ghost *'86*
The Longshot *'86*
Danielle Steel's Star *'93*

Alexi Wasser
Cabin Fever 2: Spring Fever *'08*
Return to Sender *'15*

Jerry Wasserman (1945-)
FBI: Negotiator *'05*
Family in Hiding *'06*
Unthinkable *'07*
NYC: Tornado Terror *'08*

Craig Wasson (1954-)
The Boys in Company C *'77*
Rollercoaster *'77*
Go Tell the Spartans *'78*

Carny *'80*
Four Friends *'81*
Ghost Story *'81*
Second Thoughts *'83*
Body Double *'84*
The Men's Club *'86*
A Nightmare on Elm Street 3: Dream Warriors *'87*
Malcolm X *'92*
Strapped *'93*
Harvest of Fire *'95*
The Last Best Sunday *'98*
Velocity Trap *'99*
Epoch *'00*
Escape under Pressure *'00*
The Pornographer *'00*
Boa *'02*
Puerto Vallarta Squeeze *'04*

Stephen Wastell
The Eden Formula *'06*
The Strange Case of Dr. Jekyll and Mr. Hyde *'06*

Atsuro Watabe (1968-)
Inugami *'01*
Zebraman *'04*
Ashura *'05*
The Flowers of War *'11*

Gedde Watanabe (1955-)
Sixteen Candles *'84*
Volunteers *'85*
Gung Ho *'86*
Vamp *'86*
UHF *'89*
Booty Call *'96*
That Thing You Do! *'96*
Mulan *'98 (V)*
EDtv *'99*
Guinevere *'99*
Alfie *'04*
Mulan 2 *'04 (V)*
Two for the Money *'05*
Forgetting Sarah Marshall *'08*
Not Forgotten *'09*

Hiroyuki Watanabe (1955-)
Ringu *'98*
Everly *'14*

Ken(saku) Watanabe (1959-)
Tampopo *'86*
The Last Samurai *'03*
Batman Begins *'05*
Memoirs of a Geisha *'05*
Letters from Iwo Jima *'06*
Cirque du Freak: The Vampire's Assistant *'09*
Shanghai *'09*
Inception *'10*
Godzilla *'14*
Transformers: Age of Extinction *'14 (V)*
The Sea of Trees *'16*
Bel Canto *'18*
Godzilla: King of the Monsters *'19*
Pokémon Detective Pikachu *'19*

Tetsu Watanabe (1951-)
Sonatine *'96*
Fireworks *'97*

Suki Waterhouse (1992-)
The Bad Batch *'17*
Future World *'18*
Jonathan *'19*

Dennis Waterman (1948-)
Up the Junction *'68*
The Scars of Dracula *'70*
Fright *'71*
Man in the Wilderness *'71*
Circle of Deceit *'94*
Back in Business *'06*

Felicity Waterman
Lena's Holiday *'90*
Miracle Beach *'92*
Hard Bounty *'94*
Titanic *'96*
Freedom Strike *'98*

Ida Waterman (1852-1941)
Amarilly of Clothesline Alley *'18*
Stella Maris *'18*

Willard Waterman (1915-95)
Rhubarb *'51*
Half a Hero *'53*
Hollywood or Bust *'56*
Get Yourself a College Girl *'64*

Dina Waters (1965-)
See Dina Spybey

Drew Waters (1973-)
Mongolian Death Worm *'10*
The Hit List *'11*
The Ultimate Life *'13*

Ethel Waters (1896-1977)
Cairo *'42*
Tales of Manhattan *'42*
Cabin in the Sky *'43*
Stage Door Canteen *'43*
Pinky *'49*
The Member of the Wedding *'52*

Harry Waters, Jr.
Back to the Future *'85*
Back to the Future, Part 2 *'89*

John Waters (1946-)
Pink Flamingos *'72 (N)*
Something Wild *'86*
Hairspray *'88 (C)*
Serial Mom *'94 (V)*
Pecker *'98 (V)*
Sweet and Lowdown *'99*
Seed of Chucky *'04*
Excision *'12*

John Waters (1948-)
The Getting of Wisdom *'77*
Breaker Morant *'80*
Attack Force Z *'84*
The Mystery of a Hansom Cab *'12*
Return to Nim's Island *'13*

Katherine Waterston (1980-)
The Babysitters *'07*
Inherent Vice *'14*
Queen of Earth *'15*
Sleeping with Other People *'15*
Fantastic Beasts and Where to Find Them *'16*
Alien: Covenant *'17*
Fantastic Beasts: The Crimes of Grindelwald *'18*
Mid90s *'18*

Sam Waterston (1940-)
Savages *'72*
The Great Gatsby *'74*
Rancho Deluxe *'75*
Sweet Revenge *'76*
Capricorn One *'78*
Interiors *'78*
Eagle's Wing *'79*
Friendly Fire *'79*
Sweet William *'79*
Hopscotch *'80*
Heaven's Gate *'81*
Dempsey *'83*
The Killing Fields *'84*
Warning Sign *'85*
Hannah and Her Sisters *'86*
Just Between Friends *'86*
Gore Vidal's Lincoln *'88*
September *'88*
Crimes & Misdemeanors *'89*
Welcome Home *'89*
The Man in the Moon *'91*
The Enemy Within *'94*
Serial Mom *'94*
The Journey of August King *'95*
The Shadow Conspiracy *'96*
Miracle at Midnight *'98*
Le Divorce *'03*
On the Basis of Sex *'18*

Gwen Watford (1927-94)
The Fall of the House of Usher *'49*
Never Take Candy From a Stranger *'60*
Taste the Blood of Dracula *'70*
In This House of Brede *'75*
The Body in the Library *'84*

Pierre Watkin (1889-1960)
The Road to Singapore *'40*
The Great Mike *'44*
Over 21 *'45*
Little Giant *'46*
Sioux City Sue *'46*
Swamp Fire *'46*
The Hunted *'48*
Atom Man *vs.* Superman *'50*
The Stranger Wore a Gun *'53*

Gerard Watkins
Love Me if You Dare *'03*
Taken *'08*

Jason Watkins
Confetti *'06*
The Man Who Killed Don Quixote *'18*

Michaela Watkins (1971-)
The Back-Up Plan *'10*
Afternoon Delight *'13*
In a World... *'13*
Lazy Eye *'16*
Under the Eiffel Tower *'18*
Brittany Runs a Marathon *'19*
Sword of Trust *'19*
The Way Back *'20*

Royale Watkins (1969-)
Speed 2: Cruise Control *'97*
Deliver Us from Eva *'03*

Tuc Watkins (1966-)
I Think I Do *'97*
The Mummy *'99*
Miracle in Lane Two *'00*

Deborah Watling (1948-)
That'll Be the Day *'73*
Danger UXB *'81*

Jack Watling (1923-2001)
Immortal Battalion *'44*
Under Capricorn *'49*
The Admirable Crichton *'57*
A Night to Remember *'58*
Sink the Bismarck *'60*
The Nanny *'65*

Leonor Watling (1975-)
My Mother Likes Women *'02*
Talk to Her *'02*
My Life Without Me *'03*
Cronicas *'04*
Paris, je t'aime *'06*
The Oxford Murders *'08*
If I Were You *'12*

Cynthia Watros (1968-)
Mercy Streets *'00*
P.S. Your Cat is Dead! *'02*
American Crude *'07*
Avenging Angel *'07*
Frank *'07*
Calvin Marshall *'09*
A Smile as Big as the Moon *'12*

Alberta Watson (1955-2015)
Women of Valor *'86*
The Hitman *'91*
Spanking the Monkey *'94*
Hackers *'95*
Gotti *'96*
The Sweet Hereafter *'96*
The Girl Next Door *'98*
Deeply *'99*
The Life Before This *'99*
Hedwig and the Angry Inch *'00*
Tart *'01*
The Prince & Me *'04*
Away From Her *'06*
Citizen Duane *'06*
A Lobster Tale *'06*
The Lookout *'07*
Helen *'09*

Barry Watson (1974-)
Teaching Mrs. Tingle *'99*
Sorority Boys *'02*
Love on the Side *'04*
Boogeyman *'05*
The Chateau Meroux *'11*
My Future Boyfriend *'11*

Bob Watson
In Hot Pursuit *'77*
Tough Enough *'83*

Bobby Watson (1888-1965)
Captains Courageous '37
Frolics on Ice '39
The Band Wagon '53

Bobs Watson (1930-99)
Show Boat '36
In Old Chicago '37
On Borrowed Time '39
The Story of Alexander Graham Bell '39
Dreaming Out Loud '40

Debbie Watson (1949-)
Munster, Go Home! '66
The Cool Ones '67

Emily Watson (1967-)
Breaking the Waves '95
The Boxer '97
Metroland '97
The Mill on the Floss '97
Hilary and Jackie '98
Angela's Ashes '99
The Cradle Will Rock '99
The Luzhin Defence '00
Trixie '00
Gosford Park '01
Equilibrium '02
Punch-Drunk Love '02
Red Dragon '02
The Proposition '05
Separate Lies '05
Tim Burton's Corpse Bride '05 (V)
Wah-Wah '05
Crusade: A March through Time '06
Miss Potter '06
The Water Horse: Legend of the Deep '07
Fireflies in the Garden '08
The Memory Keeper's Daughter '08
Synecdoche, New York '08
Cold Souls '09
Cemetery Junction '10
Oranges and Sunshine '10
Appropriate Adult '11
War Horse '11
Anna Karenina '12
Belle '13
The Book Thief '13
Some Girl(s) '13
The Theory of Everything '14
The Dresser '15
Molly Moon and The Incredible Book of Hypnotism '15
A Royal Night Out '15
On Chesil Beach '17

Emma Watson (1990-)
Harry Potter and the Sorcerer's Stone '01
Harry Potter and the Chamber of Secrets '02
Harry Potter and the Prisoner of Azkaban '04
Harry Potter and the Goblet of Fire '05
Ballet Shoes '07
Harry Potter and the Order of the Phoenix '07
The Tale of Despereaux '08 (V)
Harry Potter and the Half-Blood Prince '09
Harry Potter and the Deathly Hallows, Part 1 '10
Harry Potter and the Deathly Hallows, Part 2 '11
My Week With Marilyn '11
The Perks of Being a Wallflower '12
The Bling Ring '13
This Is the End '13
Noah '14
Regression '16
Beauty and the Beast '17
The Circle '17
Little Women '19

Jack Watson (1915-99)
Peeping Tom '60
The Gorgon '64
The Hill '65
Night Caller from Outer Space '66
The Devil's Brigade '68
McKenzie Break '70
Tower of Evil '72
King Arthur, the Young Warlord '75
Young Warlord '75
Schizo '77

James A. Watson, Jr. (1945-)
Halls of Anger '70
Sex Through a Window '72
Backstairs at the White House '79

Lucile Watson (1879-1962)
Rhythm on the Range '36
Made for Each Other '39
The Women '39
Waterloo Bridge '40
Footsteps in the Dark '41
The Great Lie '41
Mr. & Mrs. Smith '41
Rage in Heaven '41
Watch on the Rhine '43
The Thin Man Goes Home '44
Uncertain Glory '44
My Reputation '46
Never Say Goodbye '46
The Razor's Edge '46
Tomorrow Is Forever '46
Emperor Waltz '48
Julia Misbehaves '48
That Wonderful Urge '48
Let's Dance '50
My Forbidden Past '51

Mills Watson (1940-)
Tick... Tick... Tick '70
Dirty Little Billy '72
Cujo '83

Minor Watson (1889-1965)
Charlie Chan in Paris '35
Dead End '37
Navy Blue and Gold '37
That Certain Woman '37
Abe Lincoln in Illinois '40
Gallant Sons '40
Mr. District Attorney '41
They Died with Their Boots On '41
Western Union '41
The Big Shot '42
To the Shores of Tripoli '42
Woman of the Year '42
Action in the North Atlantic '43
Crash Dive '43
Guadalcanal Diary '43
Princess O'Rourke '43
That's My Baby! '44
A Southern Yankee '48
The Jackie Robinson Story '50
Mister 880 '50
As Young As You Feel '51
My Son John '52
The Star '52
The Ambassador's Daughter '56

Muse Watson (1948-)
Something to Talk About '95
Rosewood '96
I Know What You Did Last Summer '97
From Dusk Till Dawn 2: Texas Blood Money '98
I Still Know What You Did Last Summer '98
If I Die Before I Wake '98
Austin Powers 2: The Spy Who Shagged Me '99
Morgan's Ferry '99
Songcatcher '99
The Last Cowboy '03
A Day Without a Mexican '04
Dead Birds '04
Frankenfish '04
Down in the Valley '05
Iowa '05
Small Town Saturday Night '10
Meeting Evil '12
The Last Exorcism Part II '13

Shari Watson (1971-)
Ali '01
The Wash '01

Tom Watson (1932-2001)
Lafayette Escadrille '58
Fahrenheit 451 '66
The Winter Guest '97

Woody Watson (1949-99)
All-American Murder '91
Sarah, Plain and Tall: Skylark '93
Texas '94

Wylie Watson (1889-1966)
The 39 Steps '35
The Saint Meets the Tiger '43
Brighton Rock '47
Things Happen at Night '48
The Magnet '50
The Sundowners '60

Vernee Watson-Johnson (1954-)
Trick Baby '72
The Boy in the Plastic Bubble '76
Norman, Is That You? '76
No Turning Back '01
Antwone Fisher '02
Home Room '02
The Ant Bully '06 (V)
Clemency '19

Richard Wattis (1912-75)
Made in Heaven '52
My Son, the Vampire '52
The Belles of St. Trinian's '53
Doctor in the House '53
Norman Conquest '53
The Time of His Life '55
The Abominable Snowman '57
The Prince and the Showgirl '57
Libel '59
Very Important Person '61

Jonathan Watton
Between Truth and Lies '06
They Come Back '07
Just Business '08

Charles Watts (1912-66)
Outlaw's Son '57
Something Wild '61

Johanna Watts
American Warships '01
American Warship '12

Naomi Watts (1968-)
Brides of Christ '91
Tank Girl '94
Children of the Corn 4: The Gathering '96
Persons Unknown '96
Under the Lighthouse Dancing '97
Dangerous Beauty '98
Strange Planet '99
The Wyvern Mystery '00
Mulholland Drive '01
The Shaft '01
The Outsider '02
The Ring '02
Undertaking Betty '02
Le Divorce '03
Ned Kelly '03
21 Grams '03
I Heart Huckabees '04
We Don't Live Here Anymore '04
The Assassination of Richard Nixon '05
Ellie Parker '05
King Kong '05
The Ring 2 '05
Stay '05
Inland Empire '06 (V)
The Painted Veil '06
Eastern Promises '07
Funny Games '07
The International '09
Mother and Child '09
Fair Game '10
You Will Meet a Tall Dark Stranger '10
Dream House '11
J. Edgar '11
The Impossible '12
Adore '13
Diana '13
Movie 43 '13
Sunlight Jr. '13
Birdman, or (The Unexpected Virtue of Ignorance) '14
St. Vincent '14
While We're Young '14
Demolition '15
Allegiant '16
The Sea of Trees '16
Shut In '16
The Book of Henry '17
Chuck '17
The Glass Castle '17
3 Generations '17
Luce '19
Ophelia '19
The Wolf Hour '19

Ruby Wax (1953-)
Shock Treatment '81
The Borrowers '97

Al Waxman (1935-2001)
Vengeance Is Mine '74
Wild Horse Hank '79
Atlantic City '81
Class of 1984 '82
Clown Murders '83
Switching Channels '88
Collision Course '89
Malarek '89
Millennium '89
Mob Story '90
The Hitman '91
Teamster Boss: The Jackie Presser Story '92
Iron Eagle 4 '95
Bogus '96
Gotti '96
The Assignment '97
Critical Care '97
A Saintly Switch '99
The Thin Blue Lie '00
Life with Judy Garland-Me and My Shadows '01

Eileen Way (1911-94)
Sea Wife '57
All Passion Spent '86
Queen of Hearts '89

Tony Way
Down Terrace '10
The Girl With the Dragon Tattoo '11
Identicals '16
For Love or Money '19
Ray & Liz '19

Damon Wayans (1960-)
Beverly Hills Cop '84
Hollywood Shuffle '87
Roxanne '87
Colors '88
I'm Gonna Git You Sucka '88
Punchline '88
Earth Girls Are Easy '89
Look Who's Talking, Too '90 (V)
The Last Boy Scout '91
Mo' Money '92
Last Action Hero '93 (C)
Blankman '94
Major Payne '95
Bulletproof '96
Celtic Pride '96
The Great White Hype '96
Harlem Aria '99
Bamboozled '00
Marci X '03

Damon Wayans, Jr. (1982-)
Dance Flick '09
Marmaduke '10 (V)
The Other Guys '10
Someone Marry Barry '12
Big Hero 6 '14 (V)
Let's Be Cops '14
How to Be Single '16

Keenen Ivory Wayans (1958-)
Hollywood Shuffle '87
I'm Gonna Git You Sucka '88
A Low Down Dirty Shame '94
Don't Be a Menace to South Central While Drinking Your Juice in the Hood '95 (C)
The Glimmer Man '96
Most Wanted '97
Scary Movie '00
Dance Flick '09

Kim Wayans (1961-)
I'm Gonna Git You Sucka '88
Juwanna Mann '02
Pariah '11

Marlon Wayans (1972-)
Mo' Money '92
Above the Rim '94
Don't Be a Menace to South Central While Drinking Your Juice in the Hood '95
The Sixth Man '97
Senseless '98
Dungeons and Dragons '00
Requiem for a Dream '00
Scary Movie '00
Scary Movie 2 '01
The Ladykillers '04
White Chicks '04
Little Man '06
Norbit '07
Dance Flick '09
G.I. Joe: The Rise of Cobra '09
A Haunted House '13
The Heat '13
A Haunted House 2 '14
Fifty Shades of Black '16

Shawn Wayans (1971-)
Don't Be a Menace to South Central While Drinking Your Juice in the Hood '95
New Blood '99
Scary Movie '00
Scary Movie 2 '01
White Chicks '04
Little Man '06
Dance Flick '09

Kristina Wayborn (1950-)
Octopussy '83
Hostage Flight '85
The Frankenstein Syndrome '10

David Wayne (1914-95)
Portrait of Jennie '48
Adam's Rib '50
My Blue Heaven '50
The Reformer and the Redhead '50
As Young As You Feel '51
We're Not Married '52
With a Song in My Heart '52
How to Marry a Millionaire '53
The I Don't Care Girl '53
The Tender Trap '55
Naked Hills '56
The Sad Sack '57
The Three Faces of Eve '57
The Andromeda Strain '71
Huckleberry Finn '74
The Apple Dumpling Gang '75
An American Christmas Carol '79
Poker Alice '87
The Gift of Love '90

John Wayne (1907-79)
The Big Trail '30
Arizona '31
Hurricane Express '32
Shadow of the Eagle '32
Baby Face '33
His Private Secretary '33
The Three Musketeers '33
Allegheny Uprising '39
Stagecoach '39
Dark Command '40
The Long Voyage Home '40
Seven Sinners '40
Three Faces West '40
The Shepherd of the Hills '41
Flying Tigers '42
In Old California '42
Lady for a Night '42
Lady from Louisiana '42
Pittsburgh '42
Reap the Wild Wind '42
Reunion in France '42
The Spoilers '42
Lady Takes a Chance '43
War of the Wildcats '43
Fighting Seabees '44
Tall in the Saddle '44
Back to Bataan '45
Dakota '45
Flame of the Barbary Coast '45
They Were Expendable '45
Without Reservations '46
Angel and the Badman '47
Tycoon '47
Fort Apache '48
Red River '48
Three Godfathers '48
The Fighting Kentuckian '49
Sands of Iwo Jima '49
She Wore a Yellow Ribbon '49
Wake of the Red Witch '49
Rio Grande '50
Flying Leathernecks '51
Big Jim McLain '52
The Quiet Man '52
Hondo '53
Island in the Sky '53
Trouble along the Way '53
The High and the Mighty '54
Blood Alley '55
Sea Chase '55
The Conqueror '56
The Searchers '56
Jet Pilot '57
Legend of the Lost '57
Wings of Eagles '57
Barbarian and the Geisha '58
The Horse Soldiers '59
Rio Bravo '59
The Alamo '60
North to Alaska '60
The Comancheros '61
Hatari! '62
The Longest Day '62
The Man Who Shot Liberty Valance '62
Donovan's Reef '63
How the West Was Won '63
McLintock! '63
Circus World '64
The Greatest Story Ever Told '65
In Harm's Way '65
Sons of Katie Elder '65
Cast a Giant Shadow '66
El Dorado '67
The War Wagon '67
The Green Berets '68
Hellfighters '68
True Grit '69
The Undefeated '69
Chisum '70
Rio Lobo '70
Big Jake '71
Cancel My Reservation '72 (C)
The Cowboys '72
Cahill: United States Marshal '73
Train Robbers '73
McQ '74
Brannigan '75
Rooster Cogburn '75
The Shootist '76

John Ethan Wayne (1961-)
Scream '83
The Manhunt '86

Michael Wayne (1934-2003)
Alley Cat '84
Rapid Fire '89

Naunton Wayne (1901-70)
The Lady Vanishes '38
Night Train to Munich '40
Dead of Night '45
The Hidden Room '49
Obsession '49
Passport to Pimlico '49
Highly Dangerous '50
You Know What Sailors Are '59

Nina Wayne (1943-)
Dead Heat on a Merry-Go-Round '66
The Comic '69

Patricia Wayne (1926-74)
Eye Witness '49
The Long Dark Hall '51

Patrick Wayne (1939-)
Mister Roberts '55
The Searchers '56
The Young Land '59
The Alamo '60
McLintock! '63
Shenandoah '65
The Green Berets '68
Big Jake '71
Ride to Glory '71
The Gatling Gun '72
Beyond Atlantis '73
The Bears & I '74
The People That Time Forgot '77
Sinbad and the Eye of the Tiger '77
Rustler's Rhapsody '85
Revenge '86
Her Alibi '88
Young Guns '88
Chill Factor '90

Randy Wayne (1981-)
The Dukes of Hazzard: The Beginning '06
Dream Boy '08
Foreign Exchange '08
Frat Party '09
To Save a Life '10
The Trial '10
Cougar Hunting '11
Hold Your Breath '12
Android Cop '14

Jake Weary
Altitude '10
Fred: The Movie '10
It Follows '15

Michael Weatherly (1968-)
Asteroid '97
The Colony '98
The Last Days of Disco '98
Cabin by the Lake '00
The Substitute 4: Failure is Not an Option '00
The Hitman Diaries '09

Shawn Weatherly (1960-)
Police Academy 3: Back in Training '86
Party Line '88
Shadowzone '89
Thieves of Fortune '89
Amityville 1992: It's About Time '92
Rustin '01

Carl Weathers (1948-)
Bucktown '75
Friday Foster '75
Rocky '76
Semi-Tough '77
The Bermuda Depths '78
Force 10 from Navarone '78
Rocky 2 '79
Death Hunt '81
Rocky 3 '82
Rocky 4 '85
Predator '87
Action Jackson '88
Hurricane Smith '92
Dangerous Passion '95
Happy Gilmore '96
Shadow Warriors 2: Hunt for the Death Merchant '97
Shadow Warriors '97
American Warships '01
Alien Siege '05
The Sasquatch Gang '06
The Comebacks '07
American Warship '12

Blayne Weaver (1976-)
Manic '01
Return to Never Land '02 (V)
Weather Girl '09

Dennis Weaver (1924-2006)
Horizons West '52
The Lawless Breed '52
Law and Order '53
The Redhead from Wyoming '53
War Arrow '53
Seven Angry Men '55
Touch of Evil '58
The Gallant Hours '60
Duel at Diablo '66
Gentle Giant '67
Duel '71
A Man Called Sledge '71
What's the Matter with Helen? '71
Centennial '78
Pearl '78
The Ordeal of Dr. Mudd '80
Cocaine: One Man's Seduction '83
Two Bits & Pepper '95
Stolen Women, Captured Hearts '97
Escape from Wildcat Canyon '99
The Virginian '99
High Noon '00
Submerged '00
Home on the Range '04 (V)

Doodles Weaver (1911-83)
The Errand Boy '61
The Ladies' Man '61
Road to Nashville '67
Cancel My Reservation '72 (C)
Runaways '75

Fritz Weaver (1926-)
Fail-Safe '64
Walk in the Spring Rain '70
The Day of the Dolphin '73
The Legend of Lizzie Borden '75
Marathon Man '76
Black Sunday '77
Demon Seed '77
Holocaust '78
The Martian Chronicles: Part 2 '79
The Martian Chronicles: Part 3 '79
Jaws of Satan '81
Creepshow '82
A Death in California '85
Dream West '86
Power '86
My Name Is Bill W. '89
Broken Trust '95
The Thomas Crown Affair '99
Muhammad Ali's Greatest Fight '13

Jacki Weaver (1947-)
Picnic at Hanging Rock '75
Cosi '95
Animal Kingdom '09
Silver Linings Playbook '12
Parkland '13
Stoker '13
Magic in the Moonlight '14
Reclaim '14
The Voices '15
Equals '16
Last Cab to Darwin '16
Goldstone '18
Irreplaceable You '18
The Polka King '18
Out of Blue '19
Poms '19

Jason Weaver (1979-)
The Jacksons: An American Dream '92
Freedom Song '00
Drumline '02
The Ladykillers '04
ATL '06
Jada '08

Lee Weaver (1930-)
My Brother's Wife '89
O Brother Where Art Thou? '00
The Box '03
Swedish Auto '06

Marjorie Weaver (1913-94)
Second Honeymoon '37
Kentucky Moonshine '38
Sally, Irene and Mary '38
Three Blind Mice '38
The Cisco Kid and the Lady '39
Young Mr. Lincoln '39
Charlie Chan's Murder Cruise '40
Michael Shayne: Private Detective '40
Murder over New York '40
Just Off Broadway '42

Michael Weaver (1971-)
Super Troopers '01
Club Dread '04
The Greatest Game Ever Played '05

Sigourney Weaver (1949-)
Alien '79
Madman '79
Eyewitness '81
The Year of Living Dangerously '82
Deal of the Century '83
Ghostbusters '84
Aliens '86
Half Moon Street '86
Gorillas in the Mist '88
Working Girl '88
Ghostbusters 2 '89
Alien 3 '92
1492: Conquest of Paradise '92
Dave '93
Death and the Maiden '94
Copycat '95
Jeffrey '95
Alien: Resurrection '97
The Ice Storm '97
Snow White: A Tale of Terror '97
Galaxy Quest '99
A Map of the World '99
Company Man '00
Heartbreakers '01
Big Bad Love '02 (V)
The Guys '02
Tadpole '02
Holes '03
The Village '04
Imaginary Heroes '05
Infamous '06
Snow Cake '06
The TV Set '06
Happily N'Ever After '07 (V)
Baby Mama '08
Be Kind Rewind '08
The Tale of Despereaux '08 (N)
Vantage Point '08
WALL-E '08 (V)
Avatar '09
Prayers for Bobby '09
Crazy on the Outside '10
You Again '10
Abduction '11
Cedar Rapids '11
Paul '11
Rampart '11
The Cold Light of Day '12
Red Lights '12
Vamps '12
Exodus: Gods and Kings '14
A Monster Calls '17

Hugo Weaving (1960-)
The Right Hand Man '87
Proof '91
Reckless Kelly '93
The Adventures of Priscilla, Queen of the Desert '94
Babe '95 (V)
Bedrooms and Hallways '98
The Interview '98
The Matrix '99
Strange Planet '99
Lord of the Rings: The Fellowship of the Ring '01
Lord of the Rings: The Two Towers '02
After the Deluge '03
Lord of the Rings: The Return of the King '03
The Matrix Reloaded '03
The Matrix Revolutions '03
Little Fish '05
Happy Feet '06 (V)
V for Vendetta '06
Transformers '07 (V)
The Boxer and the Bombshell '08
Last Ride '09
Transformers: Revenge of the Fallen '09 (V)
The Wolfman '09
Legend of the Guardians: The Owls of Ga'Hoole '10 (V)
Oranges and Sunshine '10
Captain America: The First Avenger '11
Happy Feet Two '11 (V)
Transformers: Dark of the Moon '11 (V)
Cloud Atlas '12
The Hobbit: An Unexpected Journey '12
The Hobbit: The Battle of the Five Armies '14
Healing '15
Strangerland '15
The Dressmaker '16
Hacksaw Ridge '16
Black '47 '18
Mortal Engines '18

Samara Weaving
The Babysitter '17
Mayhem '17
Ready or Not '19

Alan Webb (1906-82)
The Pumpkin Eater '64
King Rat '65
The Great Train Robbery '79

Chloe Webb (1956-)
Sid & Nancy '86
Twins '88
Heart Condition '90
The Belly of an Architect '91
Lucky Day '91
Queens Logic '91
Armistead Maupin's Tales of the City '93
Love Affair '94
The Newton Boys '97
She's So Lovely '97
Repo Chick '09

Clifton Webb (1889-1966)
Laura '44
Dark Corner '46
The Razor's Edge '46
Sitting Pretty '48
Cheaper by the Dozen '50
For Heaven's Sake '50
Elopement '51
Mr. Belvedere Rings the Bell '51
Stars and Stripes Forever '52
Mr. Scoutmaster '53
Titanic '53
Three Coins in the Fountain '54
The Man Who Never Was '55
Holiday for Lovers '59
The Remarkable Mr. Pennypacker '59

Danny (Daniel) Webb (1958-)
Death Wish 4: The Crackdown '87
Henry V '89
Alien 3 '92
A Woman's Guide to Adultery '93
Love and Death on Long Island '97
Frenchman's Creek '98
Terror in the Mall '98
Shiner '00
Take Me '01
The Hound of the Baskervilles '02
Attack Force '06
Land Girls '09
Never Grow Old '19

David Webb
Lethal Ninja '93
Ghost Image '07

Haley Webb (1985-)
The Final Destination '09
Rushlights '13

Jack Webb (1920-82)
He Walked by Night '48
Dark City '50
The Halls of Montezuma '50
The Men '50
Sunset Boulevard '50
Appointment With Danger '51
You're In the Navy Now '51
Dragnet '54
Pete Kelly's Blues '55
D.I. '57
30 '59

Richard Webb (1915-93)
Out of the Past '47
Sands of Iwo Jima '49
The Invisible Monster '50
Distant Drums '51
I Was a Communist for the FBI '51
Starlift '51
Carson City '52
Mara Maru '52
This Woman Is Dangerous '52
Three Hours to Kill '54
Beware! The Blob '72

Rita Webb (1904-81)
Zeta One '69
Frenzy '72

Veronica Webb (1965-)
Jungle Fever '91
In Too Deep '99

Daniel Webber (1988-)
Danger Close '19
Escape from Pretoria '20

Diane Webber (1932-2008)
The Mermaids of Tiburon '62
Sinthia: The Devil's Doll '70

Mark Webber (1980-)
Drive Me Crazy '99
White Boyz '99
Snow Day '00
Chelsea Walls '01
Storytelling '01
Hollywood Ending '02
The Laramie Project '02
People I Know '02
The Rising Place '02
Winter Solstice '04
Bomb the System '05
Broken Flowers '05
Dear Wendy '05
The Hottest State '06
Just Like the Son '06
The Good Life '07
Shrink '09
Gift of the Magi '10
For a Good Time, Call... '12
Save the Date '12
Laggies '13
13 Sins '13
Goodbye World '14
Happy Christmas '14
Green Room '15
Uncanny '15
The Scent of Rain & Lightening '17

Robert Webber (1924-89)
Highway 301 '50
Twelve Angry Men '57
The Nun and the Sergeant '62
Hysteria '64
The Sandpiper '65
The Third Day '65
Dead Heat on a Merry-Go-Round '66
The Silencers '66
The Dirty Dozen '67
Don't Make Waves '67
Manon '68
The Big Bounce '69
The Great White Hope '70
Dollars '71
Bring Me the Head of Alfredo Garcia '74
Midway '76
The Choirboys '77
Casey's Shadow '78
Revenge of the Pink Panther '78
10 '79
Private Benjamin '80
S.O.B. '81
Wrong Is Right '82
Assassin '86
Nuts '87

Timothy Webber
Terror Train '80
Toby McTeague '87
The Boys of St. Vincent '93
Cypher '02
Past Sins '06
Bringing Ashley Home '11

Amy Weber (1970-)
Forbidden Games '95
Art House '98
Kolobos '99
Crackerjack 3 '00
Transmorphers '07

Jacques Weber (1949-)
Cyrano de Bergerac '90
Beaumarchais the Scoundrel '96

Jake Weber (1964-)
Dangerous Beauty '98
Meet Joe Black '98
What the Deaf Man Heard '98
Pushing Tin '99
The Cell '00
U-571 '00
Wendigo '01
Leo '02
Love Thy Neighbor '02
100 Mile Rule '02
Dawn of the Dead '04
The Haunting of Molly Hartley '08
Redemption Trail '13
Learning to Drive '15

Stanley Weber (1986-)
Murder on the Orient Express '10
Therese '12
Not Another Happy Ending '13

Steven Weber (1961-)
Hamburger Hill '87
Single White Female '92
The Temp '93
Dracula: Dead and Loving It '95
Jeffrey '95
Leaving Las Vegas '95
At First Sight '98
The Break Up '98
Sour Grapes '98
Late Last Night '99
Love Letters '99
Sleep Easy, Hutch Rimes '00
Time Code '00
The Twelve Days of Christmas Eve '04
Inside Out '05
Choose Connor '07
More of Me '07
Farmhouse '08
My One and Only '09
A Little Bit of Heaven '11
Son of Morning '11
Duke '12
Eve of Destruction '13
The Perfection '19

Derek Webster
Josh Kirby. . .Time Warrior: Chapter 1, Planet of the Dino-Knights '95
Josh Kirby. . . Time Warrior: Chapter 3, Trapped on Toyworld '95
Josh Kirby. . . Time Warrior: Chapter 4, Eggs from 70 Million B.C. '95
Josh Kirby. . . Time Warrior: Chapter 5, Journey to the Magic Cavern '96
Josh Kirby. . . Time Warrior: Chapter 6, Last Battle for the Universe '96
Flight of the Living Dead: Outbreak on a Plane '07

Victor Webster (1973-)
Wishmaster 4: The Prophecy Fulfilled '02
Dirty Love '05
Hostile Makeover '09
Killer Hair '09
The Scorpion King 3: Battle for Redemption '11
A Good Man '14

Battle of Neretva *'69*
The Southern Star *'69*
Catch-22 *'70*
The Kremlin Letter *'70*
Start the Revolution without Me *'70*
A Safe Place *'71*
Get to Know Your Rabbit *'72*
Ten Days Wonder *'72*
Treasure Island *'72*
The Witching *'72*
Ten Little Indians *'75*
Voyage of the Damned *'76*
Battleforce *'78 (N)*
The Double McGuffin *'79 (V)*
The Muppet Movie *'79 (C)*
Shogun *'80 (N)*
History of the World: Part 1 *'81 (N)*
Butterfly *'82*
Scene of the Crime *'85 (N)*
Transformers: The Movie *'86 (V)*
Someone to Love *'87*
Don Quixote *'92*

Virginia Welles (1925-)
Dynamite *'49*
Francis in the Haunted House *'56*

Tom Welling (1977-)
Cheaper by the Dozen *'03*
Cheaper by the Dozen 2 *'05*
The Fog *'05*
Parkland *'13*

Titus Welliver (1961-)
The Lost Capone *'90*
Zero Tolerance *'93*
The Big Fall *'96*
Rough Riders *'97*
Once in the Life *'00*
Blonde *'01*
Biker Boyz *'03*
Twisted *'04*
Assault on Precinct 13 *'05*
Gone Baby Gone *'07*
The Narrows *'08*
Handsome Harry *'09*
The Town *'10*
Argo *'12*
Man on a Ledge *'12*

William Wellman, Jr. (1937-)
High School Confidential *'58*
Lafayette Escadrille *'58*
Born Losers *'67*
It's Alive *'74*
The Trial of Billy Jack *'74*
Curfew *'88*
The Prodigal Planet *'88*

William A. Wellman (1896-1975)
Wings *'27*
Winter a Go-Go *'65*

Carole Wells (1942-)
The House of Seven Corpses *'73*
Funny Lady *'75*

Dawn Wells (1938-)
Return to Boggy Creek *'77*
Rescue from Gilligan's Island *'78*
Evil Lives *'92*
Super Sucker *'03*

Dolly Wells
Dr. Bell and Mr. Doyle: The Dark Beginnings of Sherlock Holmes *'00*
45 Years *'15*

Dolores Wells (1937-)
Beach Party *'63*
Bikini Beach *'64*
Muscle Beach Party *'64*

Jacqueline Wells (1914-2001)
See Julie Bishop

John Wells (1936-98)
Rentadick *'72*
Consuming Passions *'88*
Princess Caraboo *'94*

Stuart Wells (1982-)
Billy Elliot *'00*
The Reckoning *'03*

Tico Wells
The Five Heartbeats *'91*
All About You *'01*
Sister's Keeper *'07*

Tracy Wells (1971-)
After Midnight *'89*
Mirror, Mirror 2: Raven Dance *'94*

Vernon Wells (1945-)
The Road Warrior *'82*
Commando *'85*
Innerspace *'87*
Nam Angels *'88*
Circle of Fear *'89*
American Eagle *'90*
Circuitry Man *'90*
Crossing the Line *'90*
The Shrimp on the Barbie *'90*
Undeclared War *'91*
Plughead Rewired: Circuitry Man 2 *'94*
Stranglehold *'94*
Hard Justice *'95*
Space Truckers *'97*
Beneath Loch Ness *'01*
King of the Ants *'03*
The Strange Case of Dr. Jekyll and Mr. Hyde *'06*
Rise of the Dinosaurs *'13*
Cowboys vs Dinosaurs *'15*

John Welsh (1904-85)
Lucky Jim *'58*
The Revenge of Frankenstein *'58*
The Moonstone *'72*
The Duchess of Duke Street *'78*

Kenneth Welsh (1942-)
Of Unknown Origin *'83*
Another Woman *'88*
Crocodile Dundee 2 *'88*
The Big Slice *'90*
The Last Best Year *'90*
The Good Fight *'92*
Another Woman *'94*
Death Wish 5: The Face of Death *'94*
Getting Gotti *'94*
Legends of the Fall *'94*
Timecop *'94*
Choices of the Heart: The Margaret Sanger Story *'95*
Hiroshima *'95*
Margaret's Museum *'95*
Portraits of a Killer *'95*
Dead Silence *'96*
Escape Clause *'96*
Rowing Through *'96*
The Wrong Guy *'96*
Habitat *'97*
Vendetta *'99*
The Hound of the Baskervilles *'00*
Love Come Down *'00*
The Day Reagan Was Shot *'01*
Deliberate Intent *'01*
Focus *'01*
The Sign of Four *'01*
Eloise at the Plaza *'03*
The Aviator *'04*
The Day After Tomorrow *'04*
Miracle *'04*
Bailey's Billion$ *'05*
The Exorcism of Emily Rose *'05*
The Fog *'05*
Four Brothers *'05*
Above and Beyond *'06*
The Hades Factor *'06*
Silk *'07*
Adoration *'08*
The Trojan Horse *'08*
A Very Merry Daughter of the Bride *'08*
Survival of the Dead *'09*
The Art of the Steal *'13*
Surfacing *'14*
The Void *'17*

Margaret Welsh
Smooth Talk *'85*
Mr. & Mrs. Bridge *'90*
American Heart *'92*
A Killer Among Friends *'92*

William Welsh (1870-1946)
Traffic in Souls *'13*
20,000 Leagues under the Sea *'16*

Ariadne Welter (1931-99)
The Criminal Life of Archibaldo de la Cruz *'55*
The Devil's Hand *'61*

Hsueh-erh Wen (1960-)
The Master *'80*
Sword Masters: Two Champions of Shaolin *'80*
Holy Flame of the Martial World *'83*

Jiang Wen
The Emperor's Shadow *'96*
Devils on the Doorstep *'00*

Ming-Na Wen (1963-)
See Ming Na

Lara Wendel (1965-)
Unsane *'82*
Intervista *'87*

Alan J. Wendl
Hairspray *'88*
Serial Mom *'94*

George Wendt (1948-)
My Bodyguard *'80*
Somewhere in Time *'80*
Jekyll & Hyde. . . Together Again *'82*
Dreamscape *'84*
No Small Affair *'84*
Ratings Game *'84*
Thief of Hearts *'84*
Fletch *'85*
Gung Ho *'86*
House *'86*
Guilty by Suspicion *'91*
Forever Young *'92*
Bye Bye Birdie *'95*
Man of the House *'95*
Alien Avengers *'96*
The Lovemaster *'97*
Space Truckers *'97*
Spice World: The Movie *'97*
Alice in Wonderland *'99*
Outside Providence *'99*
Lakeboat *'00*
The Prime Gig *'00*
Strange Relations *'02*
King of the Ants *'03*
Edmond *'05*
Kids in America *'05*
Santa Baby *'06*
Santa Buddies *'09*
Merry In-Laws *'12*
The Seven Year Hitch *'12*

John Wengraf (1897-1974)
Sahara *'43*
The Razor's Edge *'46*
Five Fingers *'52*
The Gambler from Natchez *'54*
GOG *'54*
The Pride and the Passion *'57*
Valerie *'57*
Return of Dracula *'58*
12 to the Moon *'60*

David Wenham (1965-)
Cosi *'95*
A Little Bit of Soul *'97*
Molokai: The Story of Father Damien *'99*
Better Than Sex *'00*
The Bank *'01*
Dust *'01*
Moulin Rouge *'01*
The Crocodile Hunter: Collision Course *'02*
Lord of the Rings: The Two Towers *'02*
Pure *'02*
After the Deluge *'03*
Lord of the Rings: The Return of the King *'03*
Van Helsing *'04*
The Proposition *'05*
Married Life *'07*
300 *'07*
Australia *'08*
The Children of Huang Shi *'08*
Public Enemies *'09*

Legend of the Guardians: The Owls of Ga'Hoole *'10 (V)*
Oranges and Sunshine *'10*
300: Rise of an Empire *'13*
Top of the Lake *'13*
Lion *'16*
Goldstone *'18*

Jann Wenner
Perfect *'85*
Almost Famous *'00 (C)*

Alexandra Wentworth (1965-)
Trial and Error *'96*
American Virgin *'98*
Meeting Daddy *'98*
Office Space *'98*
It's Complicated *'09*
Breathe In *'13*

Martha Wentworth (1889-1974)
Clancy Street Boys *'43*
The Stranger *'46*
Jupiter's Darling *'55*
The Sword in the Stone *'63 (V)*

Fritz Wepper (1941-)
The Bridge *'59*
Cabaret *'72*
Le Dernier Combat *'84*
Murder on the Orient Express *'01*

Devon Werkheiser (1991-)
Recipe for Disaster *'03*
Christmas in Paradise *'07*
The Prankster *'10*
Beneath the Darkness *'12*
Sundown *'16*

Barbara Werle (1928-2013)
Battle of the Bulge *'65*
Charro! *'69*
Krakatoa East of Java *'69*

Oskar Werner (1922-84)
Angel with the Trumpet *'50*
Decision Before Dawn *'51*
Lola Montes *'55*
The Life and Loves of Mozart *'59*
Jules and Jim *'62*
Ship of Fools *'65*
The Spy Who Came in from the Cold *'65*
Fahrenheit 451 *'66*
Interlude *'68*
The Shoes of the Fisherman *'68*
Voyage of the Damned *'76*

Roy Werner (1957-)
Loco Love *'03*
In Enemy Hands *'04*

Otto Wernicke (1893-1965)
M *'31*
Crimes of Dr. Mabuse *'32*

Gary Werntz
The Art of Dying *'90*
The Peacemaker *'97*
Deep Impact *'98*
Pay It Forward *'00*

Doug Wert (1961-)
Dracula Rising *'93*
Roswell: The U.F.O. Cover-Up *'94*
The Wasp Woman *'96*

Charles Wesley
Murdercycle *'99*
3 Days Gone *'08*

Paul Wesley (1982-)
Full Count *'06*
Peaceful Warrior *'06*
Killer Movie *'08*
That Russell Girl *'08*
Elsewhere *'09*
Beneath the Blue *'10*
The Baytown Outlaws *'12*
Amira & Sam *'15*

Rutina Wesley (1979-)
How She Move *'08*
13 Sins *'13*
Last Weekend *'14*

Dick Wessel (1913-65)
They Died with Their Boots On *'41*
Corky of Gasoline Alley *'51*
Flying Leathernecks *'51*
Gasoline Alley *'51*
Starlift *'51*

Dick Wesson (1919-79)
Destination Moon *'50*
Force of Arms *'51*
Jim Thorpe: All American *'51*
Calamity Jane *'53*
The Desert Song *'53*
The Errand Boy *'61*

Adam West (1928-2017)
Robinson Crusoe on Mars *'64*
The Outlaws Is Coming! *'65*
Batman *'66*
The Girl Who Knew Too Much *'69*
The Eyes of Charles Sand *'74*
The Specialist *'75*
Hooper *'78*
For the Love of It *'80*
The Happy Hooker Goes Hollywood *'80*
Time Warp *'81*
Warp Speed *'81*
One Dark Night *'82*
Young Lady Chatterly 2 *'85*
Zombie Nightmare *'86*
Omega Cop *'90*
The New Age *'94*
American Vampire *'97*
Joyride *'97*
Drop Dead Gorgeous *'99 (C)*
Baadasssss! *'03*
Chicken Little *'05 (V)*
Meet the Robinsons *'07 (V)*
National Lampoon's Ratko: The Dictator's Son *'09*
Super Capers *'09*

Billy West (1952-)
Joe's Apartment *'96 (V)*
Looney Tunes: Back in Action *'03 (V)*
Comic Book: The Movie *'04*
Queer Duck: The Movie *'06 (V)*

Chandra West (1970-)
Puppet Master 4 *'93*
Puppet Master 5: The Final Chapter *'94*
The Waiting Game *'98*
Something More *'99*
The Perfect Son *'00*
The '70s *'00*
The Salton Sea *'02*
Water's Edge *'03*
Category 6: Day of Destruction *'04*
FBI: Negotiator *'05*
The Long Weekend *'05*
White Noise *'05*
The Last Trimester *'06*
The Tooth Fairy *'06*
Badland *'07*
I Now Pronounce You Chuck and Larry *'07*
For the Love of Grace *'08*
My Neighbor's Secret *'09*

Dominic West (1969-)
The Gambler *'97*
A Christmas Carol *'99*
William Shakespeare's A Midsummer Night's Dream *'99*
28 Days *'00*
Rock Star *'01*
Chicago *'02*
Mona Lisa Smile *'03*
The Forgotten *'04*
Hannibal Rising *'07*
300 *'07*
Punisher: War Zone *'08*
Centurion *'10*
Appropriate Adult *'11*
The Awakening *'11*
Johnny English Reborn *'11*
John Carter *'12*
Burton and Taylor *'13*
Pride *'14*
Testament of Youth *'15*

Money Monster *'16*
The Square *'17*
Tomb Raider *'18*

Gregory West
Class of 1999 2: The Substitute *'93*
The Surgeon *'94*

Joel West (1975-)
Blood Surf *'00*
The Smokers *'00*

Kevin West (1965-)
Killer Tomatoes Strike Back *'90*
Killer Tomatoes Eat France *'91*
Bio-Dome *'96*

Lockwood West (1905-89)
The Leather Boys *'63*
Bedazzled *'68*

Mae West (1893-1980)
Night After Night *'32*
I'm No Angel *'33*
She Done Him Wrong *'33*
Belle of the Nineties *'34*
Goin' to Town *'35*
Go West, Young Man *'36*
Klondike Annie *'36*
Every Day's a Holiday *'38*
My Little Chickadee *'40*
The Love Goddesses *'65*
Myra Breckinridge *'70*
Sextette *'78*

Martin West (1937-2019)
Lord Love a Duck *'66*
Sweet November *'68*
Assault on Precinct 13 *'76*

Nathan West (1978-)
Home Room *'02*
The Skulls 2 *'02*
Miracle *'04*
Forever Strong *'08*
Alleged *'10*

Norma West (1943-)
And the Ship Sails On *'83*
Cause Celebre *'87*

Red West (1936-)
Hard Knox *'83*
Proud Men *'87*
John Grisham's The Rainmaker *'97*
Forty Shades of Blue *'05*
Goodbye Solo *'08*

Samuel West (1966-)
Howard's End *'92*
Carrington *'95*
Persuasion *'95*
Stiff Upper Lips *'96*
Retribution *'98*
Horatio Hornblower *'99*
Longitude *'00*
Pandaemonium *'00*
Iris *'01*
Cambridge Spies *'03*
Dark Kingdom: The Dragon King *'04*
Van Helsing *'04*
Murder on the Orient Express *'10*
Any Human Heart *'11*
Hyde Park on Hudson *'12*
On Chesil Beach *'17*

Shane West (1978-)
Get a Clue! *'98*
A Time for Dancing *'00*
Whatever It Takes *'00*
Get Over It! *'01*
A Walk to Remember *'02*
The League of Extraordinary Gentlemen *'03*
The Elder Son *'06*
What We Do Is Secret *'07*
Echelon Conspiracy *'09*
The Lodger *'09*
Red Sands *'09*
Red Sky *'14*
Awakening the Zodiac *'17*

Tegan West
Hamburger Hill *'87*
Sleep with Me *'94*
Hi-Life *'98*

Timothy West (1934-)
Edward the King *'75*
Agatha *'79*
Oliver Twist *'82*
Cry Freedom *'87*
Consuming Passions *'88*
Framed *'93*
Hiroshima *'95*
Ever After: A Cinderella Story *'98*
King Lear *'98*
102 Dalmatians *'00*
The Fourth Angel *'01*
Iris *'01*
Station Jim *'01*
Beyond Borders *'03*
Sinbad: Legend of the Seven Seas *'03 (V)*
Bleak House *'05*
A Room With a View *'08*
Endgame *'09*
Going Postal *'10*

Simon Westaway (1958-)
Sahara *'95*
The Thorn Birds: The Missing Years *'96*
When Love Comes *'98*

John Westbrook (1922-89)
Room at the Top *'59*
Tomb of Ligeia *'64*
Masque of the Red Death *'65*

Gordon Westcott (1903-35)
The Working Man *'33*
The Case of the Howling Dog *'34*
I've Got Your Number *'34*
Front Page Woman *'35*

Helen Westcott (1927-98)
Homicide *'49*
The Gunfighter *'50*
Abbott and Costello Meet Dr. Jekyll and Mr. Hyde *'52*
Battles of Chief Pontiac *'52*
With a Song in My Heart *'52*
Hot Blood *'56*

Travis Wester (1977-)
Eurotrip *'04*
All Souls Day *'05*

James Westerfield (1913-71)
The Gunfight at Dodge City *'59*
Wild River *'60*
Homicidal *'61*
That Funny Feeling *'65*
True Grit *'69*

Carlie Westerman
King of the Ants *'03*
Me and You and Everyone We Know *'05*

Floyd 'Red Crow' Westerman (1936-2007)
Dances with Wolves *'90*
Walker: Texas Ranger: One Riot, One Ranger *'93*
Buffalo Girls *'95*
The Last Assassins *'96*
Hidalgo *'04*
Comanche Moon *'08*
Swing Vote *'08*

Jennifer Westfeldt (1970-)
Kissing Jessica Stein *'02*
How to Lose Your Lover *'04*
Ira & Abby *'06*
Before You Say 'I Do' *'09*
Friends with Kids *'12*

David Westhead
Mrs. Brown *'97*
Murderland *'09*

Helen Westley (1875-1942)
The Age of Innocence *'34*
Anne of Green Gables *'34*
Death Takes a Holiday *'34*
Dimples *'36*
Stowaway *'36*
Cafe Metropole *'37*
Heidi *'37*
Alexander's Ragtime Band *'38*
Rebecca of Sunnybrook Farm *'38*
All This and Heaven Too *'40*
Lillian Russell *'40*
The Smiling Ghost *'41*
Sunny *'41*
Lady from Louisiana *'42*

Nydia Westman (1902-70)
Manhattan Love Song *'34*
Hullabaloo *'40*
The Bad Man *'41*
The Chocolate Soldier *'41*

Matt Westmore (1971-)
Hard As Nails *'01*
Charlotte Sometimes *'02*
Shakedown *'02*

James Westmoreland (1935-)
Journey Beneath the Desert *'61*
The Undertaker and His Pals *'67*
Don't Answer the Phone *'80*

Cecil Weston
Money Madness *'47*
Belles on Their Toes *'52*

Celia Weston (1951-)
Honky Tonk Freeway *'81*
Lost Angels *'89*
Little Man Tate *'91*
Dead Man Walking *'95*
Flirting with Disaster *'95*
Snow Falling on Cedars *'99*
Joe Gould's Secret *'00*
Hearts in Atlantis *'01*
In the Bedroom *'01*
K-PAX *'01*
Far from Heaven *'02*
Hulk *'03*
Undermind *'03*
The Village *'04*
Junebug *'05*
The Invasion *'07*
Joshua *'07*
No Reservations *'07*
After.life *'10*
The Extra Man *'10*
Knight and Day *'10*
Goodbye to All That *'14*
Poms *'19*

David Weston (1938-)
The Heroes of Telemark *'65*
Masque of the Red Death *'65*

Jack Weston (1924-96)
Please Don't Eat the Daisies *'60*
The Honeymoon Machine *'61*
It's Only Money *'62*
Palm Springs Weekend *'63*
The Incredible Mr. Limpet *'64*
The Cincinnati Kid *'65*
Mirage *'66*
Wait until Dark *'67*
The Thomas Crown Affair *'68*
Cactus Flower *'69*
A New Leaf *'71*
Fuzz *'72*
Deliver Us From Evil *'73*
Marco *'73*
Gator *'76*
The Ritz *'76*
Cuba *'79*
The Four Seasons *'81*
High Road to China *'83*
If Tomorrow Comes *'86*
The Longshot *'86*
Dirty Dancing *'87*
Ishtar *'87*
Short Circuit 2 *'88*

Jeff Weston (1960-)
Demonic Toys *'90*
Puppet Master 2 *'90*

Jonny Weston
Chasing Mavericks *'12*
Project Almanac *'15*
We Are Your Friends *'15*

Michael Weston (1973-)
Coyote Ugly *'00*
Lucky Numbers *'00*
Hart's War *'02*
Garden State *'04*
The Dukes of Hazzard *'05*
The Last Kiss *'06*
Pathology *'08*
Love, Wedding, Marriage *'11*
Coma *'12*
Speed Kills *'18*

Ed Westwick (1987-)
Son of Rambow *'07*
100 Feet *'08*
S. Darko: A Donnie Darko Tale *'09*
Chalet Girls *'11*
J. Edgar *'11*
Romeo & Juliet *'13*
Freaks of Nature *'15*
Billionaire Ransom *'16*

Jack Wetherall
The Victory *'81*
Third Man Out: A Donald Strachey Mystery *'05*

Virginia Wetherell (1943-)
The Crimson Cult *'68*
Demons of the Mind *'72*
Disciple of Death *'72*
Dracula *'73*

Patricia Wettig (1951-)
City Slickers *'91*
Guilty by Suspicion *'91*
City Slickers 2: The Legend of Curly's Gold *'94*
Stephen King's The Langoliers *'95*
Bongwater *'98*
Dancer, Texas-Pop. 81 *'98*
The 19th Wife *'10*

Merritt Wever (1980-)
All I Wanna Do *'98*
Series 7: The Contenders *'01*
Tiny Furniture *'10*
Remember Sunday *'13*
Welcome to Marwen *'18*

Paul Wexler
Four Skulls of Jonathan Drake *'59*
Doc Savage *'75*

Ron Weyand (1929-2003)
Child's Play *'72*
Man on a Swing *'74*

Marius Weyers (1945-)
African Rage *'78*
The Gods Must Be Crazy *'84*
Deepstar Six *'89*
Farewell to the King *'89*
Happy Together *'89*
The Power of One *'92*
Bophal *'93*
Stander *'03*
Charlie *'04*

Ruth Weyher
Warning Shadows *'23*
Secrets of a Soul *'25*

Michael Whalen (1902-74)
Professional Soldier *'35*
Career Woman *'36*
Sing, Baby, Sing *'36*
White Fang *'36*
Wee Willie Winkie *'37*
Kentucky Jubilee *'51*
The Phantom from 10,000 Leagues *'56*
Missile to the Moon *'59*

Sean M. Whalen (1964-)
The People under the Stairs *'91*
Waterworld *'95*
The Cable Guy *'96*
That Thing You Do! *'96*
Twister *'96*
Suicide Kings *'97*
Idle Hands *'99*
Never Been Kissed *'99*
Charlie's Angels *'00*
Perfect Murder, Perfect Town *'00*
The Last Shot *'04*
Chasing Ghosts *'05*
Employee of the Month *'06*
Laid to Rest *'09*

Frank Whaley (1963-)
Ironweed *'87*
Born on the Fourth of July *'89*
Cold Dog Soup *'89*
Field of Dreams *'89*
Little Monsters *'89*
The Freshman *'90*
Career Opportunities *'91*
The Doors *'91*
JFK *'91 (C)*
Hoffa *'92*
A Midnight Clear *'92*
Fatal Deception: Mrs. Lee Harvey Oswald *'93*
Swing Kids *'93*
To Dance with the White Dog *'93*
The Desperate Trail *'94*
I.Q. *'94*
Pulp Fiction *'94*
Swimming with Sharks *'94*
Broken Arrow *'95*
Homage *'95*
The Winner *'96*
Bombshell *'97*
Cafe Society *'97*
Curtain Call *'97*
Glam *'97*
Retroactive *'97*
Went to Coney Island on a Mission from God. . . Be Back by Five *'98*
When Trumpets Fade *'98*
The Wall *'99*
Chelsea Walls *'01*
The Jimmy Show *'01*
Pursuit of Happiness *'01*
Mrs. Harris *'05*
Crazy Eights *'06*
Cherry Crush *'07*
Vacancy *'07*
The Cell 2 *'09*
As Good As Dead *'10*
Janie Jones *'10*
Rob the Mob *'14*
The Shed *'19*

Justin Whalin (1974-)
The Dead Pool *'88*
Child's Play 3 *'91*
Perfect Harmony *'91*
The Fire Next Time *'93*
Serial Mom *'94*
White Wolves 2: Legend of the Wild *'94*
Miracle at Midnight *'98*
Dungeons and Dragons *'00*
Final Encounter *'00*
Super Capers *'09*

Joanne Whalley (1964-)
Pink Floyd: The Wall *'82*
Dance with a Stranger *'85*
Edge of Darkness *'86*
No Surrender *'86*
The Singing Detective *'86*
The Good Father *'87*
Willow *'88*
Kill Me Again *'89*
Scandal *'89*
To Kill a Priest *'89*
Navy SEALS *'90*
The Big Man: Crossing the Line *'91*
Shattered *'91*
Storyville *'92*
A Good Man in Africa *'94*
Mother's Boys *'94*
Scarlett *'94*
The Secret Rapture *'94*
Trial by Jury *'94*
The Man Who Knew Too Little *'97*
The Guilty *'99*
A Texas Funeral *'99*
Jackie Bouvier Kennedy Onassis *'00*
Ride the Wild Fields *'00*
Played *'06*
Flood *'07*
44 Inch Chest *'09*
Golf in the Kingdom *'10*
Twixt *'12*
Paul, Apostle of Christ *'18*

Leigh Whannell (1977-)
One Perfect Day *'04*
Saw *'04*
Insidious *'10*
Insidious: Chapter 2 *'13*
Cooties *'14*
Insidious: Chapter 3 *'15*
Insidious: The Last Key *'18*

Kevin Whately (1951-)
The English Patient *'96*
What Katy Did *'99*
Plain Jane *'02*
Joe Maddison's War *'10*

Liem Whatley
The Iron Triangle *'89*
Heaven and Earth *'93*

Alan Wheatley (1907-91)
Appointment with Crime *'45*
Brighton Rock *'47*
Counterblast *'48*
The Limping Man *'53*

Blane Wheatley
The Unnamable *'88*
Monarch of the Moon *'05*

Thomas Wheatley (1951-)
Where Angels Fear to Tread *'91*
Piglet's Big Movie *'03 (V)*

Wil Wheaton (1972-)
The Secret of NIMH *'82 (V)*
The Last Starfighter *'84*
Stand by Me *'86*
The Curse *'87*
December *'91*
Toy Soldiers *'91*
Pie in the Sky *'95*
Flubber *'97*
Deep Core *'00*
Python *'00*
Star Trek: Nemesis *'02*

Bert Wheeler (1895-1968)
Rio Rita *'29*
Dixiana *'30*
Half-Shot at Sunrise *'30*
Hook, Line and Sinker *'30*
Caught Plastered *'31*
Cracked Nuts *'31*
Girl Crazy *'32*
Hold 'Em Jail *'32*
Kentucky Kernels *'34*
The Nitwits *'35*
The Rainmakers *'35*
Mummy's Boys *'36*
High Flyers *'37*
On Again-Off Again *'37*
Las Vegas Nights *'41*

David Wheeler
Pros and Ex-cons *'05*
Newtown *'16*

Jane Wheeler
The Neighbor *'93*
The Kid *'97*
Obsessed *'02*
Blue Seduction *'09*

Dana Wheeler-Nicholson (1960-)
Mrs. Soffel *'84*
Fletch *'85*
Circuitry Man *'90*
The Night We Never Met *'93*
Tombstone *'93*
Bye Bye, Love *'94*
My Life's in Turnaround *'94*
The Pompatus of Love *'95*
Living in Peril *'97*
5 Time Champion *'11*
Angels Sing *'13*

Laura Wheelwright
Animal Kingdom *'09*
Underground: The Julian Assange Story *'12*

Arleen Whelan (1916-93)
Gateway *'38*
Kidnapped *'38*
Young Mr. Lincoln *'39*
Young People *'40*
Charley's Aunt *'41*
Ramrod *'47*
Never Wave at a WAC *'52*
The Sun Shines Bright *'53*

Julia Whelan (1984-)
The Secret of Zoey *'02*
Fading of the Cries *'10*
Beverly Lewis' The Confession *'13*

Nicky Whelan (1981-)
Paranormal Movie *'13*
The Power of Few *'13*
Left Behind *'14*
Inconceivable *'17*

Lisa Whelchel (1963-)
The Double McGuffin *'79*
Where the Red Fern Grows: Part 2 *'92*

Shea Whigham (1969-)
Tigerland *'00*
All the Real Girls *'03*
Man of the House *'05*
Wristcutters: A Love Story *'06*
First Snow *'07*
Pride and Glory *'08*
Spooner *'08*
Bad Lieutenant: Port of Call New Orleans *'09*
The Killing Room *'09*
Barry Munday *'10*
Machete *'10*
Catch.44 *'11*
The Lincoln Lawyer *'11*
Take Shelter *'11*
Silver Linings Playbook *'12*
The Wolf of Wall Street *'13*
Cop Car *'15*
Beirut *'18*
Low Tide *'19*
To the Stars *'20*

Barbara Whinnery
Crawlspace *'86*
Hot to Trot! *'88*

Joseph Whipp (1941-)
Amazons *'86*
Red Shoe Diaries: Luscious Lola *'00*

Sam Whipple (1961-2002)
Jekyll & Hyde. . . Together Again *'82*
Airheads *'94*
The Rock *'96*

Shannon Whirry (1964-)
Animal Instincts *'92*
Body of Influence *'93*
Animal Instincts 2 *'94*
Private Obsession *'94*
Omega Doom *'96*
Retroactive *'97*
The Prophet's Game *'99*
Mach 2 *'00*
Me, Myself, and Irene *'00*

Ben Whishaw (1980-)
Layer Cake *'05*
Stoned *'05*
Perfume: The Story of a Murderer *'06*
I'm Not There *'07*
Brideshead Revisited *'08*
Bright Star *'09*
The Tempest *'10*
Skyfall *'12*
Days and Nights *'14*
Lilting *'14*
Paddington *'14 (V)*
The Danish Girl *'15*
In the Heart of the Sea *'15*
Paddington 2 *'17 (V)*
Mary Poppins Returns *'18*
Little Joe *'19*

Christina Whitaker
Assault of the Killer Bimbos *'88*
Vampire at Midnight *'88*

Damon Whitaker (1970-)
Bird *'88*
Saints and Sinners *'95*

Denzel Whitaker (1990-)
The Great Debaters *'07*
Bad Lieutenant: Port of Call New Orleans *'09*
My Soul to Take *'10*

Duane Whitaker (1959-)
Eddie Presley *'92*
Tales from the Hood *'95*
From Dusk Till Dawn 2: Texas Blood Money *'98*
Spoiler *'98*
The Devil's Rejects *'05*
Feast *'06*
Albino Farm *'09*

Children of the Corn: Genesis '11

Forest Whitaker (1961-)
Fast Times at Ridgemont High '82
Vision Quest '85
The Color of Money '86
Platoon '86
Good Morning, Vietnam '87
Stakeout '87
Bird '88
Bloodsport '88
Downtown '89
Johnny Handsome '89
Diary of a Hitman '91
A Rage in Harlem '91
Article 99 '92
Consenting Adults '92
The Crying Game '92
Body Snatchers '93
Last Light '93
Blown Away '94
The Enemy Within '94
Jason's Lyric '94
Ready to Wear '94
Smoke '95
Species '95
Phenomenon '96
Rebound: The Legend of Earl 'The Goat' Manigault '96
Body Count '97
Ghost Dog: The Way of the Samurai '99
Light It Up '99
Witness Protection '99
Battlefield Earth '00
Four Dogs Playing Poker '00
Anne Rice's The Feast of All Saints '01
The Fourth Angel '01
Green Dragon '01
Panic Room '02
Phone Booth '02
First Daughter '04 (N)
American Gun '05
Jiminy Glick in LaLa Wood '05 (C)
A Little Trip to Heaven '05
Even Money '06
Everyone's Hero '06 (V)
The Last King of Scotland '06
The Air I Breathe '07
The Great Debaters '07
Ripple Effect '07
Fragments '08
Street Kings '08
Vantage Point '08
Hurricane Season '09
Powder Blue '09
Where the Wild Things Are '09 (V)
The Experiment '10
My Own Love Song '10
Our Family Wedding '10
Repo Men '10
Catch.44 '11
A Dark Truth '12
Freelancers '12
Black Nativity '13
Ernest & Celestine '13 (V)
The Last Stand '13
Lee Daniels' The Butler '13
Out of the Furnace '13
Pawn '13
Repentance '14
Southpaw '15
Taken 3 '15
Arrival '16
The Forgiven '18
Finding Steve McQueen '19

Jodie Whitaker (1982-)
Venus '06
Good '08
Tess of the D'Urbervilles '08
Perrier's Bounty '09
White Wedding '10
Attack the Block '11
One Day '11

Johnny Whitaker (1959-)
The Littlest Angel '69
Napoleon and Samantha '72
Tom Sawyer '73

Andrea Whitburn
Tell Me No Lies '07
Lonesome Dove Church '14
Wrecker '15

Alice White (1904-83)
Show Girl in Hollywood '30
Murder at Midnight '31
Employees' Entrance '33
Picture Snatcher '33
Jimmy the Gent '34
King of the Newsboys '38
Flamingo Road '49

Bernie (Bernard) White (1959-)
Body Count '87
Ain't No Way Back '89
No Way Back '90
Killing Obsession '94
Land of Plenty '04
American Dreamz '06

Betty White (1922-)
Advise and Consent '62
Hard Rain '97
Dennis the Menace Strikes Again '98
Lake Placid '99
The Story of Us '99
Whispers: An Elephant's Tale '00 (V)
Bringing Down the House '03
Annie's Point '05
Ponyo '08 (V)
Love N' Dancing '09
The Proposal '09
You Again '10
The Lost Valentine '11
Dr. Seuss' The Lorax '12 (V)

Brian White (1975-)
Mr. 3000 '04
The Family Stone '05
Brick '06
DOA: Dead or Alive '06
The Game Plan '07
Motives 2-Retribution '07
Stomp the Yard '07
In the Name of the King: A Dungeon Siege Tale '08
Fighting '09
I Can Do Bad All By Myself '09
12 Rounds '09
The Cabin in the Woods '12
Tyler Perry's Good Deeds '12
And Then There Was You '13
Where Children Play '15

Bridget Ann White
The Apostate '98
A Boyfriend for Christmas '04
Depth Charge '08
Bound by a Secret '09

Carol White (1942-91)
Never Let Go '60
A Matter of WHO '62
I'll Never Forget What's 'Isname '67
Prehistoric Women '67
Daddy's Gone A-Hunting '69
The Squeeze '77

Dan(iel) White (1908-80)
The Last Hunt '56
Creature of Darkness '09

David A.R. White (1970-)
Mercy Streets '00
Six: The Mark Unleashed '04
Revelation Road: The Beginning of the End '13
God's Not Dead '14

Deborah White
The Girl in the Empty Grave '77
The Van '77

De'voreaux White
The Children of Times Square '86
Die Hard '88

Farah White
Hate Crime '05
My Dog the Champion '14

Harriet White (1914-2005)
Paisan '46
The Ghost '63

Harrison White
Doom Asylum '88
I Got the Hook-Up '98

Jack White (1975-)
Coffee and Cigarettes '03
Cold Mountain '03
Walk Hard: The Dewey Cox Story '07
It Might Get Loud '09

Jacqueline White (1922-)
Air Raid Wardens '43
Thirty Seconds Over Tokyo '44
Night Song '47
Return of the Bad Men '48
The Capture '50
The Narrow Margin '52

Jaleel White (1976-)
Silence of the Heart '84
Quest for Camelot '98 (V)
Who Made the Potatoe Salad? '05
Miracle Dogs Too '06
Beach Kings '08
Call of the Wild 3D '09
Mega Shark *vs.* Crocosaurus '10
Judy Moody and the Not Bummer Summer '11

Jeremy White
Afterschool '08
Twelve '10

Jesse White (1919-97)
Harvey '50
Bedtime for Bonzo '51
Francis Goes to the Races '51
The Girl in White '52
Million Dollar Mermaid '52
Forever Female '53
Hell's Half Acre '54
Witness to Murder '54
The Bad Seed '56
Designing Woman '57
The Rise and Fall of Legs Diamond '60
On the Double '61
Sail a Crooked Ship '61
Three Blondes in His Life '61
It's Only Money '62
Looking for Love '64
Pajama Party '64
Ghost in the Invisible Bikini '66
The Reluctant Astronaut '67
Bless the Beasts and Children '71
Monster in the Closet '86
Matinee '92

John White (1981-)
The Legend of Gator Face '96
American Pie Presents: The Naked Mile '06
American Pie Presents: Beta House '07
Wild Cherry '09

Julie White (1961-)
The Heidi Chronicles '95
Slap Her, She's French '02
Transformers '07
Breaking Upwards '09
Monsters *vs.* Aliens '09 (V)
Transformers: Revenge of the Fallen '09
Morning '10
Inside Out '11
Transformers: Dark of the Moon '11
Hello I Must Be Going '12
Lincoln '12

Lillias White
Pieces of April '03
Game 6 '05

Liz White
A Short Stay in Switzerland '09
The Woman in Black '12

Michael Jai White (1967-)
City of Industry '96
Spawn '97
Ringmaster '98
Thick as Thieves '99
Universal Soldier: The Return '99
Freedom Song '00
Exit Wounds '01
Silver Hawk '04
Undisputed 2: Last Man Standing '06
Tyler Perry's Why Did I Get Married? '07
The Dark Knight '08
Black Dynamite '09
Blood and Bone '09
One Angry Juror '10
Tyler Perry's Why Did I Get Married Too '10
Never Back Down 2: The Beatdown '11
Tactical Force '11
Freaky Deaky '12
The Philly Kid '12
Android Cop '14
Chain of Command '15
Asian Connection '16
Never Back Down: No Surrender '16
Vigilante Diaries '16
Dragged Across Concrete '18

Mike White (1970-)
Chuck & Buck '00
The Good Girl '02
School of Rock '03
Smother '08
Gentlemen Broncos '09

Patricia White (1921-)
See Patricia Barry

Peter White (1937-)
Mother '96
Thirteen Days '00

Ron White
Cowboys Don't Cry '88
Blood Brothers '93
Guilty as Sin '93
Race to Freedom: The Story of the Underground Railroad '94
Treacherous Beauties '94
Screamers '96
ShadowZone: The Undead Express '96
The Wall '99
Jasper, Texas '03

Ruth White
Edge of the City '57
Up the Down Staircase '67

Sammy White
711 Ocean Drive '50
Pat and Mike '52

Sheila White (1950-)
Confessions of a Window Cleaner '74
Confessions of a Driving Instructor '76

Slappy (Melvin) White (1920-95)
Amazing Grace '74
Mr. Saturday Night '92

Steve White (1961-)
Just for the Hell of It '68
She-Devils on Wheels '68
Get On the Bus '96

Charles White Eagle
Three Warriors '77
Altered States '80

Fionn Whitehead
Dunkirk '17
The Children Act '18

O.Z. Whitehead (1911-98)
The Grapes of Wrath '40
My Brother Talks to Horses '47
Road House '48
Rally 'Round the Flag, Boys! '58
The Horse Soldiers '59

Paxton Whitehead (1937-)
Back to School '86
Jumpin' Jack Flash '86 (C)
Baby Boom '87
The Adventures of Huck Finn '93
My Boyfriend's Back '93
Kate & Leopold '01

Josh Whitehouse
The Knight Before Christmas '19
Valley Girl '20

Billie Whitelaw (1932-2014)
Bobbikins '59
The Flesh and the Fiends '60
Make Mine Mink '60
Strange Case of Dr. Jekyll & Mr. Hyde '68
Start the Revolution without Me '70
Frenzy '72
Gumshoe '72
Night Watch '72
The Omen '76
Leopard in the Snow '78
Water Babies '79
A Tale of Two Cities '80
Camille '84
Slayground '84
Maurice '87
The Secret Garden '87
Catherine Cookson's The Fifteen Streets '90
Lorna Doone '90
A Murder of Quality '90
Duel of Hearts '92
Jane Eyre '96
The Lost Son '98
Merlin '98
The Last of the Blonde Bombshells '00
Hot Fuzz '07

Arkie Whiteley (1965-2001)
Razorback '84
Princess Caraboo '94
The Last Musketeer '00

Jon Whiteley (1945-2020)
Hunted '52
Moonfleet '55
The Weapon '56
The Spanish Gardener '57

Paul Whiteman (1890-1967)
Strike Up the Band '40
The Fabulous Dorseys '47
Lady Frankenstein '72

Charles Malik Whitfield (1972-)
The Temptations '98
Behind Enemy Lines '01
Bound by Lies '05
The Playaz Court '07
Gun '10
Krews '10

Dondre T. Whitfield (1969-)
Two Can Play That Game '01
Mr. 3000 '04
The Salon '05
Middle of Nowhere '12

June Whitfield (1925-)
Carry On Abroad '72
Carry On Columbus '92
Catherine Cookson's The Secret '00
The Last of the Blonde Bombshells '00
Absolutely Fabulous: The Movie '16

Lynn Whitfield (1953-)
Doctor Detroit '83
The Slugger's Wife '85
Hard Lessons '86
Jaws: The Revenge '87
Johnnie Gibson F.B.I. '87
The Josephine Baker Story '90
State of Emergency '94
A Thin Line Between Love and Hate '96
Eve's Bayou '97
Gone Fishin' '97
Junior's Groove '97
Stepmom '98
Dangerous Evidence: The Lori Jackson Story '99
Love Songs '99
A Time for Dancing '00
A Girl Thing '01
The Cheetah Girls '03
Head of State '03
The Cheetah Girls 2 '06
Madea's Family Reunion '06
Kings of the Evening '08
The Women '08
The Rebound '09
Battlefield America '12
And Then There Was You '13
The Last Letter '13

Mitchell Whitfield (1964-)
Dogfight '91
My Cousin Vinny '92
I Love You, Don't Touch Me! '97
Best Men '98
Lost and Found '99
Amy's O '02
TMNT: Teenage Mutant Ninja Turtles '07 (V)

Smoki Whitfield (1918-67)
Bomba on Panther Island '49
Bomba, the Jungle Boy '49
Bomba and the Hidden City '50
The Lion Hunters '51

Bradley Whitford (1959-)
The Betty Ford Story '87
Awakenings '90
Presumed Innocent '90
Vital Signs '90
Young Guns 2 '90
Scent of a Woman '92
My Life '93
A Perfect World '93
Billy Madison '94
The Client '94
My Fellow Americans '96
Red Corner '97
Behind the Mask '99
Bicentennial Man '99
The Muse '99
Kate & Leopold '01
Little Manhattan '05
The Sisterhood of the Traveling Pants '05
An American Crime '07
Mitch Albom's Have a Little Faith '11
The Cabin in the Woods '12
Saving Mr. Banks '13
Savannah '14
Other People '16
Get Out '17
Megan Leavey '17
The Darkest Minds '18
The Call of the Wild '20

Peter Whitford (1939-)
My Brilliant Career '79
Dead End Drive-In '86
Strictly Ballroom '92

Jack Whiting (1901-61)
Give Me a Sailor '38
Sailing Along '38

Leonard Whiting (1950-)
Romeo and Juliet '68
Say Hello to Yesterday '71
Rachel's Man '75

Margaret Whiting (1924-2011)
Sinbad and the Eye of the Tiger '77
Disraeli '79

Kym E. Whitley (1961-)
Next Friday '00
What About Your Friends: Weekend Getaway '02
Deliver Us from Eva '03
Along Came Polly '04
Up Against the Eight Ball '04
L.A. Dicks '05
The Perfect Man '05
The Salon '05
College Road Trip '08
The Hustle '08
Black Dynamite '09

Group Sex '10
Heaven Ain't Hard to Find '10

Isiah Whitlock, Jr. (1954-)
25th Hour '02
Pieces of April '03
She Hate Me '04
Kettle of Fish '06
Main Street '10
Cedar Rapids '11
Gun Hill Road '11
Why Stop Now '12
Europa Report '13
Corporate Animals '19
Da 5 Bloods '20

Jill Whitlow (1963-)
Night of the Creeps '86
Ghost Chase '88
Twice Dead '88

Kari Whitman (1964-)
Phantom of the Mall: Eric's Revenge '89
Chained Heat 2 '92
Forced to Kill '93

Mae Whitman (1988-)
Bye Bye, Love '94
When a Man Loves a Woman '94
Independence Day '96
One Fine Day '96
The Gingerbread Man '97
Hope Floats '98
Invisible Child '99
A Season for Miracles '99
An American Rhapsody '01
The Jungle Book 2 '03 (V)
Disney's Teacher's Pet '04 (V)
Going Shopping '05
Jesse Stone: Death in Paradise '06
Love's Abiding Joy '06
Lost in the Dark '07
Nights in Rodanthe '08
Spring Breakdown '08
Acceptance '09
The Factory '10
Scott Pilgrim *vs.* the World '10
The Perks of Being a Wallflower '12
The DUFF '15

Stuart Whitman (1928-2020)
Silver Lode '54
Crime of Passion '57
Hell Bound '57
Darby's Rangers '58
The Decks Ran Red '58
Murder, Inc. '60
The Story of Ruth '60
The Comancheros '61
The Mark '61
The Longest Day '62
Rio Conchos '64
Sands of the Kalahari '65
Those Magnificent Men in Their Flying Machines '65
An American Dream '66
Captain Apache '71
City Beneath the Sea '71
Night of the Lepus '72
The Woman Hunter '72
Call Him Mr. Shatter '74
Crazy Mama '75
Mean Johnny Barrows '75
Eaten Alive '76
Las Vegas Lady '76
Maniac '77
Ruby '77
The White Buffalo '77
Fury '78
Oil '78
Kill Castro '80
The Mercenaries '80
Demonoid, Messenger of Death '81
Butterfly '82
First Strike '85
The Monster Club '85
The Treasure of the Amazon '85
Moving Target '89
Heaven & Earth '90 (N)
Omega Cop '90
Private Wars '93
Trial by Jury '94
Second Chances '98

Elizabeth Whitmere
The Last Hit Man '08
The Watch '08

Nigel Whitmey (1963-)
The Twilight of the Ice Nymphs '97
Helen of Troy '03
Pulse '03

Steve Whitmire (1959-)
Labyrinth '86
The Muppet Christmas Carol '92 (V)
Muppet Treasure Island '96 (V)
Muppets from Space '99 (V)
The Muppets' Wizard of Oz '05 (V)
The Muppets '11 (V)
Muppets Most Wanted '14 (V)

James Whitmore (1921-2009)
Battleground '49
The Undercover Man '49
The Asphalt Jungle '50
The Next Voice You Hear '50
The Outriders '50
It's a Big Country '51
Because You're Mine '52
Above and Beyond '53
All the Brothers Were Valiant '53
The Girl Who Had Everything '53
The Great Diamond Robbery '53
Kiss Me Kate '53
The Command '54
Them! '54
Battle Cry '55
The McConnell Story '55
Oklahoma! '55
Savage Wilderness '55
Crime in the Streets '56
The Eddy Duchin Story '56
Deep Six '58
The Restless Years '58
Face of Fire '59
Who Was That Lady? '60
Black Like Me '64
Chuka '67
Waterhole Number 3 '67
Madigan '68
Planet of the Apes '68
The Split '68
Guns of the Magnificent Seven '69
Tora! Tora! Tora! '70
Chato's Land '71
Harrad Experiment '73
Where the Red Fern Grows '74
Give 'Em Hell, Harry! '75
I Will Fight No More Forever '75
The Serpent's Egg '78
The First Deadly Sin '80
The Adventures of Mark Twain '85 (V)
Nuts '87
The Shawshank Redemption '94
The Relic '96
Swing Vote '99
The Majestic '01

James Whitmore, Jr. (1948-)
The Boys in Company C '77
The Bastard '78
The Gypsy Warriors '78
The Long Riders '80
Tricks of the Trade '88

Daniel Lawrence Whitney (1963-)
See Larry the Cable Guy

Grace Lee Whitney (1930-2015)
Star Trek: The Motion Picture '79
Star Trek 3: The Search for Spock '84
Star Trek 6: The Undiscovered Country '91

Peter Whitney (1916-72)
Blues in the Night '41
Underground '41
Rio Rita '42
Whistling in Dixie '42
Action in the North Atlantic '43
Destination Tokyo '43
Murder, He Says '45
Three Strangers '46
All the Brothers Were Valiant '53
Savage Wilderness '55
Man from Del Rio '56
Buchanan Rides Alone '58

Benjamin Whitrow (1937-)
Pride and Prejudice '95
Tom Jones '98
Chicken Run '00 (V)
Scenes of a Sexual Nature '06
Bomber '09

Garland Whitt
Blind Faith '98
Save the Last Dance '01

Jodie Whittaker (1982-)
Wired '08
The Legend of Fritton's Gold '09
A Thousand Kisses Deep '11

Ted Whittall
Between Truth and Lies '06
Mail Order Bride '08
The Other Woman '08
Daydream Nation '10
Against the Wild '14

Margaret Whitton (1950-)
The Best of Times '86
9 1/2 Weeks '86
Ironweed '87
The Secret of My Success '87
Little Monsters '89
Major League '89
Big Girls Don't Cry. . . They Get Even '92
The Man Without a Face '93
Major League 2 '94
Trial by Jury '94

May Whitty (1865-1948)
Conquest '37
Night Must Fall '37
The Lady Vanishes '38
Raffles '39
If Winter Comes '41
Suspicion '41
Mrs. Miniver '42
Thunder Birds '42
The Constant Nymph '43
Crash Dive '43
Lassie, Come Home '43
Madame Curie '43
Gaslight '44
The White Cliffs of Dover '44

Dame May Whitty (1865-1948)
Slightly Dangerous '43
Devotion '46
This Time for Keeps '47

James Whitworth
The Hills Have Eyes '77
Planet of the Dinosaurs '80

Johnny Whitworth (1975-)
Bye Bye, Love '94
Empire Records '95
Hell's Kitchen NYC '97
John Grisham's The Rainmaker '97
Valentine '01
MTV's Wuthering Heights '03
3:10 to Yuma '07
Pathology '08
Reach for Me '08
Limitless '11
Valley of the Sun '11
Ghost Rider: Spirit of Vengeance '12

Richard Whorf (1906-66)
Midnight '34
Blues in the Night '41
Juke Girl '42
Keeper of the Flame '42
Yankee Doodle Dandy '42
The Cross of Lorraine '43
Chain Lightning '50

Patrick Whyte (1907-84)
Hideous Sun Demon '59
Kitten with a Whip '64

Scott Whyte (1978-)
The Fallen Ones '05
All In '06
Ghosts of Goldfield '07
Dark House '09
Wyatt Earp's Revenge '12

Anna Wiazemsky (1947-)
Au Hasard Balthazar '66
La Chinoise '67
Teorema '68
Porcile '69

Emily Wickersham (1984-)
For One More Day '07
How I Got Lost '09
Gone '12

Mary Wickes (1916-95)
The Man Who Came to Dinner '41
Private Buckaroo '42
Who Done It? '42
I'll See You in My Dreams '51
On Moonlight Bay '51
The Story of Will Rogers '52
Young Man With Ideas '52
The Actress '53
By the Light of the Silvery Moon '53
Half a Hero '53
Ma and Pa Kettle at Home '54
Good Morning, Miss Dove '55
Dance with Me, Henry '56
It Happened to Jane '59
The Sins of Rachel Cade '61
Fate Is the Hunter '64
How to Murder Your Wife '64
Where Angels Go, Trouble Follows '68
Postcards from the Edge '90
Sister Act '92
Sister Act 2: Back in the Habit '93
Little Women '94
The Hunchback of Notre Dame '96 (V)

Jeffrey Wickham (1933-)
Another Country '84
Clarissa '91

Saskia Wickham (1967-)
Clarissa '91
Royal Deceit '94
Angels and Insects '95
Anna Karenina '96

Bernhard Wicki (1919-2000)
La Notte '60
Crime & Passion '75

Kathleen Widdoes (1939-)
The Group '66
Petulia '68
The Sea Gull '68
The Mephisto Waltz '71
Savages '72
Courage Under Fire '96

Connor Widdows (1992-)
Agent Cody Banks 2: Destination London '04
X-Men: The Last Stand '06

Johan Widerberg (1974-)
All Things Fair '95
Under the Sun '98

Richard Widmark (1914-2008)
Kiss of Death '47
Road House '48
The Street with No Name '48
Yellow Sky '48
Slattery's Hurricane '49
The Halls of Montezuma '50
Night and the City '50
No Way Out '50
Panic in the Streets '50
Don't Bother to Knock '52
Red Skies of Montana '52
Destination Gobi '53
Pickup on South Street '53
Broken Lance '54
Garden of Evil '54
The Cobweb '55
Backlash '56
Run for the Sun '56
Saint Joan '57
Time Limit '57
The Law and Jake Wade '58
The Tunnel of Love '58
The Trap '59
Warlock '59
The Alamo '60
Judgment at Nuremberg '61
Two Rode Together '61
How the West Was Won '63
Cheyenne Autumn '64
Flight From Ashiya '64
The Long Ships '64
Bedford Incident '65
Alvarez Kelly '66
The Way West '67
Madigan '68
Death of a Gunfighter '69
The Moonshine War '70
Murder on the Orient Express '74
Sell Out '76
The Sellout '76
To the Devil, a Daughter '76
The Domino Principle '77
Rollercoaster '77
Coma '78
The Swarm '78
National Lampoon Goes to the Movies '81
Hanky Panky '82
Against All Odds '84
Texas Guns '90
Murder on the Bayou '91
True Colors '91

Jane Wiedlin
Clue '85
I Want to Get Married '11

Christopher Wiehl
Cold Hearts '99
Moonlight & Mistletoe '08

Matthias Wieman (?-1969)
The Blue Light '32
The Mistress of Atlantis '32

Danielle Wiener
Traveller '96
Beethoven's 3rd '00

Kai Wiesinger (1966-)
Backbeat '94
Terror in the Mall '98
The Harmonists '99
Murder on the Orient Express '01
Dresden '06

Dianne Wiest (1948-)
Zalmen or the Madness of God '75
It's My Turn '80
Falling in Love '84
Footloose '84
The Purple Rose of Cairo '85
Hannah and Her Sisters '86
The Lost Boys '87
Radio Days '87
Bright Lights, Big City '88
September '88
Cookie '89
Parenthood '89
Edward Scissorhands '90
Little Man Tate '91
Bullets over Broadway '94
Cops and Robbersons '94
The Scout '94
The Birdcage '95
The Associate '96
Drunks '96
The Horse Whisperer '97
Practical Magic '98
The Simple Life of Noah Dearborn '99
The 10th Kingdom '00
I Am Sam '01
Category 6: Day of Destruction '04
Merci Docteur Rey '04
Robots '05 (V)
A Guide to Recognizing Your Saints '06
Dan in Real Life '07
Dedication '07
Passengers '08
Synecdoche, New York '08
Rabbit Hole '10
The Big Year '11
Darling Companion '12
The Odd Life of Timothy Green '12
Five Nights in Maine '16

Naima Wifstrand (1890-1969)
Night Is My Future '47
The Magician '58
Hour of the Wolf '68

Geoff Wigdor (1982-)
Sleepers '96
Levity '03
White Irish Drinkers '10

Chris Wiggins (1931-)
King of the Grizzlies '69
Why Shoot the Teacher '79
Kavik the Wolf Dog '80
Rock & Rule '83 (V)
Ford: The Man & the Machine '87
Babar: The Movie '88 (V)
Black Fox: The Price of Peace '94

Jennifer Lee Wiggins
King of the Lost World '06
I Am Omega '07

Josh Wiggins
Hellion '13
Max '15
Mean Dreams '17
Walking Out '17
Giant Little Ones '19
Light from Light '19

Laura Wiggins
Along Came the Devil 2 '19
Nancy Drew and the Hidden Staircase '19

Wiley Wiggins (1976-)
Dazed and Confused '93
Waking Life '01
Computer Chess '13

Shea Wigham
This Must Be the Place '12
American Hustle '13
Lila & Eve '15

Paul Wight
Knucklehead '10
Vendetta '15

Peter Wight (1950-)
Naked '93
Shiner '00
Lucky Break '01
The Statement '03
Pride and Prejudice '05
Another Year '10

Natasha Wightman
Murder on the Orient Express '01
V for Vendetta '06

Robert Wightman (1952-)
A Day for Thanks on Walton's Mountain '82
Opposing Force '87
Stepfather 3: Father's Day '92
Living in Oblivion '94

Kristen Wiig (1973-)
The Brothers Solomon '07
Knocked Up '07
Meet Bill '07
Walk Hard: The Dewey Cox Story '07
Ghost Town '08
Adventureland '09
Extract '09
Whip It '09
All Good Things '10
Date Night '10
Despicable Me '10 (V)

How to Train Your Dragon '10 (V)
MacGruber '10
Bridesmaids '11
Paul '11
Friends with Kids '12
Girl Most Likely '12
Revenge for Jolly! '12
Despicable Me 2 '13 (V)
Hateship Loveship '13
The Secret Life of Walter Mitty '13
How to Train Your Dragon 2 '14 (V)
The Skeleton Twins '14
The Diary of a Teenage Girl '15
The Martian '15
Nasty Baby '15
Welcome to Me '15
Ghostbusters '16
Masterminds '16
Sausage Party '16
Zoolander 2 '16
Despicable Me 3 '17 (V)
Downsizing '17
Where'd You Go, Bernadette '19

Crane Wilbur (1886-1973)
Captain Calamity '36
Crime School '38

George P. Wilbur
Halloween 4: The Return of Michael Myers '88
Halloween 6: The Curse of Michael Myers '95

James Wilby (1958-)
Dreamchild '85
Maurice '87
A Handful of Dust '88
A Summer Story '88
A Tale of Two Cities '89
Howard's End '92
Lady Chatterley '92
Behind the Lines '97
The Woman in White '97
Cotton Mary '99
Gosford Park '01
De-Lovely '04
Gradiva '06
Clapham Junction '07
Little Devil '07

Robin Wilcock
The Hound of the Baskervilles '00
Blind Trust '06

Frank Wilcox (1907-74)
They Died with Their Boots On '41
The Wagons Roll at Night '41
Across the Pacific '42
The Hidden Hand '42
Night Editor '46
Abbott and Costello Meet the Keystone Kops '54
A Majority of One '56
Seventh Cavalry '56
Beginning of the End '57
Man From God's Country '58

Larry Wilcox (1947-)
The Girl Most Likely to. . . '73
The Last Hard Men '76
The Last Ride of the Dalton Gang '79
The Dirty Dozen: The Next Mission '85
Mission Manila '87
National Lampoon's Loaded Weapon 1 '93

Lisa Wilcox (1964-)
A Nightmare on Elm Street 4: Dream Master '88
A Nightmare on Elm Street 5: Dream Child '89
Watchers Reborn '98

Mary Wilcox (1944-)
Beast of the Yellow Night '70
Love Me Deadly '73

Robert Wilcox (1910-55)
Dead End Kids: Little Tough Guy '38
Rascals '38
Blondie Takes a Vacation '39
Buried Alive '39
The Man They Could Not Hang '39
Dreaming Out Loud '40

Collin Wilcox-Paxton (1937-2009)
To Kill a Mockingbird '62
The Baby Maker '70
Catch-22 '70
Jaws 2 '78
Wildflower '91
Fluke '95

Henry Wilcoxon (1905-84)
Cleopatra '34
The Crusades '35
The Last of the Mohicans '36
The President's Mystery '36
Souls at Sea '37
Jericho '38
Tarzan Finds a Son '39
That Hamilton Woman '41
The Corsican Brothers '42
Mrs. Miniver '42
Unconquered '47
A Connecticut Yankee in King Arthur's Court '49
Samson and Delilah '49
Scaramouche '52
The Ten Commandments '56
The War Lord '65
Escape from Planet Earth '67
Man in the Wilderness '71
Against a Crooked Sky '75
Pony Express Rider '76
When Every Day Was the Fourth of July '78
The Two Worlds of Jenny Logan '79
Caddyshack '80

Jack Wild (1952-2006)
Oliver! '68
Pufnstuf '70
Flight of the Doves '71
Melody '71
Pied Piper '72
Robin Hood: Prince of Thieves '91

Cornel Wilde (1915-89)
High Sierra '41
Life Begins at Eight-Thirty '42
Wintertime '43
Leave Her to Heaven '45
A Song to Remember '45
The Bandit of Sherwood Forest '46
Forever Amber '47
Road House '48
Shockproof '49
At Sword's Point '51
The Greatest Show on Earth '52
Operation Secret '52
Saadia '53
Passion '54
Big Combo '55
The Scarlet Coat '55
Hot Blood '56
Omar Khayyam '57
Edge of Eternity '59
Sword of Lancelot '63
The Naked Prey '66
Beach Red '67
The Comic '69
The Fifth Musketeer '79

Gabriella Wilde (1989-)
Carrie '13
Endless Love '14

Lois Wilde (1907-95)
Caryl of the Mountains '36
Undersea Kingdom '36

Olivia Wilde (1984-)
Conversations with Other Women '05
Alpha Dog '06
Bickford Shmeckler's Cool Ideas '06
Turistas '06
Bobby Z '07
Fix '08
Year One '09
The Next Three Days '10
Tron: Legacy '10
The Change-Up '11
Cowboys & Aliens '11
In Time '11
On the Inside '11
Butter '12
Deadfall '12
People Like Us '12
The Words '12
Drinking Buddies '13
The Incredible Burt Wonderstone '13
Rush '13
Third Person '13
Better Living Through Chemistry '14
The Longest Week '14
The Lazarus Effect '15
Love the Coopers '15
Meadowland '15
Life Itself '18
Richard Jewell '19
A Vigilante '19

Gene Wilder (1933-2016)
Bonnie & Clyde '67
The Producers '68
Quackser Fortune Has a Cousin in the Bronx '70
Start the Revolution without Me '70
Willy Wonka & the Chocolate Factory '71
Everything You Always Wanted to Know about Sex (But Were Afraid to Ask) '72
Blazing Saddles '74
The Little Prince '74
Young Frankenstein '74
Silver Streak '76
World's Greatest Lover '77
The Adventures of Sherlock Holmes' Smarter Brother '78
The Frisco Kid '79
Stir Crazy '80
Hanky Panky '82
The Woman in Red '84
Haunted Honeymoon '86
See No Evil, Hear No Evil '89
Funny About Love '90
Another You '91
Alice in Wonderland '99
Murder in a Small Town '99

Glenn Wilder (1933-)
The Sand Pebbles '66
Zebra Force '76

James Wilder (1968-)
Zombie High '87
Murder One '88
Prey of the Chameleon '91
Scorchers '92
Allie & Me '97
Flypaper '97
Ivory Tower '97
Kisses in the Dark '97
First Degree '98
The Last Don 2 '98
Burning Down the House '01
Heart of Stone '01

Webb Wilder
The Thing Called Love '93
Heroes of the Heart '94

Yvonne Wilder (1937-)
West Side Story '61
The Return of Count Yorga '71
Bloodbrothers '78

Michael Wilding (1912-79)
Convoy '40
Cottage to Let '41
In Which We Serve '43
An Ideal Husband '47
Spring in Park Lane '48
Under Capricorn '49
Stage Fright '50
The Lady With the Lamp '51
The Law and the Lady '51
Derby Day '52
Torch Song '53
The Egyptian '54
The Glass Slipper '55
The Scarlet Coat '55
Zarak '56
The World of Suzie Wong '60
The Sweet Ride '68

Michael Wilding, Jr. (1953-)
A.D. '85
Sweet Bird of Youth '89

John Wildman (1961-)
My American Cousin '85
Sorority Babes in the Slimeball Bowl-A-Rama '87

Valerie Wildman (1953-)
Salvador '86
Inner Sanctum '91

Tristan Wilds (1989-)
The Secret Life of Bees '08
Red Tails '12

Dawn Wildsmith
Cyclone '87
Evil Spawn '87
Phantom Empire '87
Surf Nazis Must Die '87
Hollywood Chainsaw Hookers '88
Terminal Force '88
Warlords '88
Alienator '89
Wizards of the Demon Sword '94
Jack-O '95

Jason Wiles (1970-)
Higher Learning '94
Roadracers '94
Windrunner '94
Kicking and Screaming '95
Organizm '08

Michael Shamus Wiles (1955-)
Rock Star '01
Neo Ned '05
The Gene Generation '07
Hydra '09

Mike Wiles
Terror at Tenkiller '86
Held Up '00

Ed Wiley
Lace 2 '85
The Canterville Ghost '96

Jan Wiley (1916-93)
Rhythm Parade '43
So Proudly We Hail '43
The Underdog '43
A Fig Leaf for Eve '44
Master Key '44

Dianne Wilhite
Gruesome Twosome '67
Flesh Feast '69

Kathleen Wilhoite (1964-)
Private School '83
The Morning After '86
Murphy's Law '86
Angel Heart '87
Campus Man '87
Witchboard '87
Bad Influence '90
Everybody Wins '90
Lorenzo's Oil '92
Color of Night '94
Getting Even with Dad '94
Breast Men '97
Drowning Mona '00
Nurse Betty '00
Quicksand '01
My Sister's Keeper '02
Audrey's Rain '03
National Lampoon Presents: Endless Bummer '09
California Solo '12

Robert J. Wilke (1915-89)
Kill the Umpire '50
Cattle Town '52
High Noon '52
From Here to Eternity '53
War Paint '53
20,000 Leagues under the Sea '54
Canyon River '56
Gun the Man Down '56
Night Passage '57
Tarnished Angels '57
The Cheyenne Social Club '70

Jose Wilker (1944-2014)
Dona Flor and Her Two Husbands '78
Bye Bye Brazil '79
Medicine Man '92

Guy Wilkerson (1899-1971)
Sergeant York '41
Comin' Round the Mountain '51
The Last Posse '53
Man of the West '58

Donna Wilkes (1959-)
Baby Broker '81
Blood Song '82
Angel '84
Grotesque '87

Elaine Wilkes (1965-)
Roommate '84
Killer Party '86

Barbara Wilkin
The Flesh Eaters '64
Six in Paris '68

Adrienne Wilkinson
Death on the Set '35
Interceptor Force 2 '02

Elizabeth Wilkinson
Suburban Roulette '67
A Taste of Blood '67

Linden Wilkinson
The Wedding Party '97
The Monkey's Mask '00

Scott Wilkinson
Wish upon a Star '96
Benji: Off the Leash! '04

Tom Wilkinson (1948-)
Paper Mask '91
Prime Suspect '92
In the Name of the Father '93
Martin Chuzzlewit '94
Priest '94
Royal Deceit '94
The Full Monty '96
The Ghost and the Darkness '96
Smilla's Sense of Snow '96
Oscar and Lucinda '97
Wilde '97
The Governess '98
Rush Hour '98
Shakespeare in Love '98
David Copperfield '99 (N)
Essex Boys '99
Molokai: The Story of Father Damien '99
Ride with the Devil '99
Chain of Fools '00
The Patriot '00
Another Life '01
Black Knight '01
In the Bedroom '01
The Gathering Storm '02
The Importance of Being Earnest '02
Girl with a Pearl Earring '03
Normal '03
Eternal Sunshine of the Spotless Mind '04
A Good Woman '04
If Only '04
Stage Beauty '04
Batman Begins '05
The Exorcism of Emily Rose '05
Separate Lies '05
The Last Kiss '06
The Night of the White Pants '06
Dedication '07
Michael Clayton '07
John Adams '08
Recount '08
RocknRolla '08
Duplicity '09
44 Inch Chest '09
Burke & Hare '10
The Conspirator '10
The Debt '10
The Ghost Writer '10
The Green Hornet '11
The Kennedys '11
Mission: Impossible-Ghost Protocol '11
The Best Exotic Marigold Hotel '12
The Good Samaritan '12
Belle '13
Felony '13
The Lone Ranger '13
Good People '14
The Grand Budapest Hotel '14
Selma '14
Unfinished Business '15
The Choice '16
Denial '16
Snowden '16
This Beautiful Fantastic '17

Lee Wilkof (1951-)
Chattahoochee '89
Afterschool '08

Fred Willard (1933-2020)
Chesty Anderson USN '76
Americathon '79
Salem's Lot '79
How to Beat the High Cost of Living '80
This Is Spinal Tap '84
Moving Violations '85
Roxanne '87
The Return of Spinal Tap '92 (C)
Waiting for Guffman '96
Permanent Midnight '98
Austin Powers 2: The Spy Who Shagged Me '99
Idle Hands '99
Best in Show '00
How High '01
The Wedding Planner '01
American Wedding '03
A Mighty Wind '03
National Lampoon's Christmas Vacation 2: Cousin Eddie's Big Island Adventure '03
Anchorman: The Legend of Ron Burgundy '04
Harold and Kumar Go to White Castle '04
How to Lose Your Lover '04
Killer Diller '04
Chicken Little '05 (V)
Date Movie '06
For Your Consideration '06
I Could Never Be Your Woman '06
Ira & Abby '06
Monster House '06 (V)
Epic Movie '07
I'll Believe You '07
Harold '08
WALL-E '08 (V)
Scout's Honor: Badge to the Bone '09
A Very Mary Christmas '10
Youth in Revolt '10
My Future Boyfriend '11
12 Christmas Wishes For My Dog '11
Your Love Never Fails '11
The Magic of Belle Isle '12
The Bird Men '13
Fifty Shades of Black '16
Mascots '16

Toyah Willcox (1958-)
Quadrophenia '79
Ebony Tower '86

Jean Willes (1923-89)
So Proudly We Hail '43
Abbott and Costello Go to Mars '53
Invasion of the Body Snatchers '56
The FBI Story '59

Peter Willes
Call It a Day '37
Dawn Patrol '38

Chad Willet (1971-)
Outlaw Justice '98
The Locket '02
Carolina Moon '07

Chad Willett (1971-)
Nothing Too Good for a Cowboy '98
The Twelve Days of Christmas Eve '04

Blind Trust '06
Phantom Racer '09

will.i.am
Madagascar: Escape 2 Africa '08 (V)
X-Men Origins: Wolverine '09

Warren William (1895-1948)
The Woman From Monte Carlo '31
Skyscraper Souls '32
Under Eighteen '32
Beauty and the Boss '33
Employees' Entrance '33
Gold Diggers of 1933 '33
Lady for a Day '33
The Mind Reader '33
The Case of the Howling Dog '34
Cleopatra '34
Imitation of Life '34
Upperworld '34
The Case of the Curious Bride '35
The Case of the Lucky Legs '35
Living on Velvet '35
The Secret Bride '35
Go West, Young Man '36
Satan Met a Lady '36
The Firefly '37
Madame X '37
Arsene Lupin Returns '38
Wives under Suspicion '38
Day-Time Wife '39
The Gracie Allen Murder Case '39
The Man in the Iron Mask '39
Arizona '40
Lillian Russell '40
The Lone Wolf Meets a Lady '40
The Wolf Man '41
Counter-Espionage '42
Passport to Suez '43
Strange Illusion '45
The Private Affairs of Bel Ami '47

Adam Williams (1922-2006)
Flying Leathernecks '51
Queen for a Day '51
Vice Squad '53
Fear Strikes Out '57
The Space Children '58
North by Northwest '59
Gunfight at Comanche Creek '64

Alex Williams
Underground: The Julian Assange Story '12
The Reckoning '14

Allen Williams
The Two Worlds of Jenny Logan '79
Scorpion '86

Allison Williams (1988-)
Peter Pan Live! '14
Get Out '17
The Perfection '19

Anson Williams (1949-)
Lisa, Bright and Dark '73
I Married a Centerfold '84

Ashley Williams (1978-)
Snow '04
Montana Sky '07
Snow 2: Brain Freeze '08
The Human Centipede: First Sequence '10
Patricia Cornwell's At Risk '10
Patricia Cornwell's The Front '10
Margin Call '11
Something Borrowed '11
Lovesick '14

Barbara Williams (1953-)
Thief of Hearts '84
Jo Jo Dancer, Your Life Is Calling '86
Tiger Warsaw '87
Watchers '88
Peter Gunn '89
City of Hope '91
Spenser: Ceremony '93
Spenser: Pale Kings & Princes '94
Family of Cops '95
Bone Daddy '97
Family of Cops 2: Breach of Faith '97
Inventing the Abbotts '97
Family of Cops 3 '98
Krippendorf's Tribe '98
Love Come Down '00
Every Second Counts '08
Angels Crest '11

Barry Williams (1954-)
Wild in the Streets '68
The Brady Bunch Movie '95 (C)
Mega Piranha '10

Bill Williams (1915-92)
Deadline at Dawn '46
Till the End of Time '46
A Dangerous Profession '49
The Stratton Story '49
Operation Haylift '50
Cavalry Charge '51
Son of Paleface '52
Wiretapper '55
The Broken Star '56
The Halliday Brand '57
Storm Rider '57
Space Master X-7 '58
Buckskin '68
The Giant Spider Invasion '75

Flight of the Grey Wolf '76

Billy Dee Williams (1937-)
Black Brigade '69
The Out-of-Towners '70
Brian's Song '71
Final Comedown '72
The Glass House '72
Lady Sings the Blues '72
Hit! '73
The Take '74
Mahogany '75
Bingo Long Traveling All-Stars & Motor Kings '76
Scott Joplin '77
The Empire Strikes Back '80
Nighthawks '81
Return of the Jedi '83
Fear City '85
Courage '86
Oceans of Fire '86
The Right of the People '86
Number One with a Bullet '87
Batman '89
The Jacksons: An American Dream '92
Alien Intruder '93
Dangerous Passion '95
Triplecross '95
Moving Target '96
Mask of Death '97
Steel Sharks '97
The Contract '98
Fear Runs Silent '99
The Ladies Man '00
The Visit '00
Undercover Brother '02
Epoch: Evolution '03
iMurders '08
Barry Munday '10
The Perfect Age of Rock 'n' Roll '10

Billy 'Sly' Williams (1968-)
Voodoo Dawn '89
Lost Treasure '03

Brook Williams (1938-2005)
Plague of the Zombies '66
Where Eagles Dare '68
Absolution '81

Cara Williams (1925-)
Boomerang '47
The Girl Next Door '53
The Helen Morgan Story '57
The Defiant Ones '58
The White Buffalo '77

Caroline Williams (1957-)
The Texas Chainsaw Massacre 2 '86
Stepfather 2: Make Room for Daddy '89
Leprechaun 3 '95
Abolition '11
Contracted '13

Chris(topher) Williams (1967-)
The Courage to Love '00
Dodgeball: A True Underdog Story '04
The World's Fastest Indian '05
Swedish Auto '06
The Joneses '09

Cindy Williams (1947-)
Gas-s-s-s! '70
Beware! The Blob '72
Travels with My Aunt '72
American Graffiti '73
The Killing Kind '73
The Conversation '74
The First Nudie Musical '75
Mr. Ricco '75
More American Graffiti '79
Spaceship '81
Tricks of the Trade '88
Bingo '91
Meet Wally Sparks '97
The Biggest Fan '02
Strawberry Summer '12

Clara Williams (1888-1928)
The Italian '15
Hell's Hinges '16

Clarence Williams, III (1939-)
Purple Rain '84
52 Pick-Up '86
Tough Guys Don't Dance '87
The House of Dies Drear '88
I'm Gonna Git You Sucka '88
Maniac Cop 2 '90
Deep Cover '92
Dangerous Relations '93
Against the Wall '94
Sugar Hill '94
The Immortals '95
Tales from the Hood '95
Hoodlum '96
Rebound: The Legend of Earl 'The Goat' Manigault '96
The Silencers '96
Sprung '96
George Wallace '97
Half-Baked '97
Frogs for Snakes '98
The Legend of 1900 '98
The General's Daughter '99
Life '99
Malicious Intent '99
Reindeer Games '00
Blue Hill Avenue '01
Mindstorm '01
Mystery Woman: Mystery Weekend '05
American Gangster '07
Lee Daniels' The Butler '13

Cole Williams (1981-)
Harry and Max '04
North Country '05
Mammoth '06

Cynda Williams (1966-)
Mo' Better Blues '90
One False Move '91
Armistead Maupin's Tales of the City '93
The Ghost Brigade '93
Tales of Erotica '93
Condition Red '95
The Sweeper '95
The Tie That Binds '95
Gang in Blue '96
Spirit Lost '96
Caught Up '98
Relax. . . It's Just Sex! '98
Introducing Dorothy Dandridge '99
The Courage to Love '00
MacArthur Park '01
When Do We Eat? '05

Darnell Williams (1955-)
How U Like Me Now? '92
Firestarter 2: Rekindled '02

David Edward Williams (1971-)
See David Walliams

Dick Anthony Williams (1938-2012)
The Anderson Tapes '71
Dog Day Afternoon '75
A Woman Called Moses '78
An Almost Perfect Affair '79
Gardens of Stone '87
Tap '89
Edward Scissorhands '90
Mo' Better Blues '90
The Players Club '98
Black Listed '03

D.J. Williams (1868-1949)
The Crimes of Stephen Hawke '36
Murder in the Old Red Barn '36

Edy Williams (1942-)
Naked Kiss '64
Good Times '67
Where It's At '69
Beyond the Valley of the Dolls '70
Bad Girls from Mars '90

Emlyn Williams (1905-87)
The Citadel '38
The Stars Look Down '39
The Girl in the News '41
Another Man's Poison '52
The Wreck of the Mary Deare '59
Eye of the Devil '67
The Walking Stick '70

Esther Williams (1921-2013)
Andy Hardy's Double Life '42
Bathing Beauty '44
Thrill of a Romance '45
Easy to Wed '46
Ziegfeld Follies '46
This Time for Keeps '47
On an Island with You '48
Neptune's Daughter '49
Take Me Out to the Ball Game '49
The Duchess of Idaho '50
Pagan Love Song '50
Texas Carnival '51
Million Dollar Mermaid '52
Skirts Ahoy! '52
Dangerous When Wet '53
Easy to Love '53
Jupiter's Darling '55
The Unguarded Moment '56
That's Entertainment '74

Evan Williams
The National Tree '09
On Strike for Christmas '10

Gareth Williams
Palookaville '95
From the Earth to the Moon '98
The Cell '00
Hard Luck '01
13 Moons '02

Gary Anthony Williams (1966-)
Undercover Brother '02
Jiminy Glick in LaLa Wood '05

Gayland Williams
Natural Selection '11
Natural Selection '12

Genelle Williams
Saving God '08
The Note 2: Taking a Chance on Love '09

Grant Williams (1930-85)
Written on the Wind '56
The Incredible Shrinking Man '57
The Monolith Monsters '57
The Leech Woman '59
Susan Slade '61
The Couch '62
Escape from Planet Earth '67
Brain of Blood '71

Gregory Alan Williams (1956-)
In the Line of Fire '93
Be Cool '05
Good Intentions '10
Preacher's Kid '10
A Question of Faith '17

Guinn 'Big Boy' Williams (1899-1962)
Burning Daylight '28
Noah's Ark '28
Lucky Star '29
Liliom '30
The Bachelor Father '31
Mystery Squadron '33
Rafter Romance '33
Dangerous Appointment '34
Career Woman '36
The Vigilantes Are Coming '36
You Only Live Once '37
The Bad Man of Brimstone '38
Castle on the Hudson '40
The Fighting 69th '40
Virginia City '40
Billy the Kid '41
Mr. Wise Guy '42
The Desperadoes '43
Hands Across the Border '43
Bad Men of Tombstone '49
Rocky Mountain '50
Springfield Rifle '52
Southwest Passage '54
Hidden Guns '56
Man from Del Rio '56
The Alamo '60

Guy Williams (1924-89)
Savage Wilderness '55
Seven Angry Men '55
The Sign of Zorro '60
Damon and Pythias '62
The Prince and the Pauper '62
Captain Sinbad '63

Hal Williams (1938-)
Guess Who '05
Snow 2: Brain Freeze '08

Harland Williams (1962-)
Dumb & Dumber '94
Down Periscope '96
Half-Baked '97
RocketMan '97
Dog Park '98
There's Something about Mary '98
Superstar '99
The Whole Nine Yards '00
Freddy Got Fingered '01
Sorority Boys '02
The Dukes of Hazzard: The Beginning '06
Employee of the Month '06
Meet the Robinsons '07 (V)
Bachelor Party 2: The Last Temptation '08
My Life in Ruins '09
Spooky Buddies '11
Back in the Day '14

Heathcote Williams (1941-)
Orlando '92
Blue Juice '95
The Odyssey '97
The Tango Lesson '97
Basic Instinct 2 '06

Hugh Williams (1904-69)
Bitter Sweet '33
Bank Holiday '38
The Human Monster '39
Inspector Hornleigh '39
Wuthering Heights '39
One of Our Aircraft Is Missing '41
An Ideal Husband '47
Khartoum '66

Ian Patrick Williams
Dolls '87
Bloodmoon '90
Bad Channels '92
Heaven's a Drag '94

Jason Williams (1952-)
Flesh Gordon '72
Cop Killers '73
Cheerleaders' Wild Weekend '85
Vampire at Midnight '88

Jermaine Williams (1982-)
Fat Albert '04
The Comebacks '07
The Great Debaters '07
World's Greatest Dad '09

Jesse Williams (1981-)
The Sisterhood of the Traveling Pants 2 '08
The Cabin in the Woods '12
Snake & Mongoose '13

Jessica Williams
People Places Things '15
Booksmart '19
Corporate Animals '19

Jim Williams
The Newlydeads '87
Living to Die '91

JoBeth Williams (1948-)
Kramer vs. Kramer '79
Stir Crazy '80
The Dogs of War '81
Endangered Species '82
Poltergeist '82
Adam '83
The Big Chill '83
The Day After '83
American Dreamer '84
Teachers '84
Desert Bloom '86
Poltergeist 2: The Other Side '86
Memories of Me '88
My Name Is Bill W. '89
Welcome Home '89
Dutch '91
Switch '91
Victim of Love '91
Stop! or My Mom Will Shoot '92
Wyatt Earp '94
Jungle 2 Jungle '96
Just Write '97
Little City '97
From the Earth to the Moon '98
It Came from the Sky '98
Backlash '99
Jackie's Back '99
Crazylove '05
Fever Pitch '05
Into the Fire '05
In the Land of Women '06
Timer '09
The Big Year '11
Love's Christmas Journey '11
In My Dreams '14
Barracuda '17

John Williams (1903-83)
Dial 'M' for Murder '54
Sabrina '54
To Catch a Thief '55
D-Day, the Sixth of June '56
Island in the Sun '57
Will Success Spoil Rock Hunter? '57
Witness for the Prosecution '57
The Young Philadelphians '59
Dear Brigitte '65
Double Trouble '67
The Secret War of Harry Frigg '68

Katt Micah Williams (1973-)
Friday After Next '02
Ganked '05
Norbit '07
The Perfect Holiday '07
First Sunday '08
Internet Dating '08
Cats & Dogs: The Revenge of Kitty Galore '10

Kelli Williams (1970-)
Zapped Again '89
There Goes My Baby '92
Till Murder Do Us Part '92
Lifepod '93
Snowbound: The Jim and Jennifer Stolpa Story '94

Flowers for Algernon '00
A Boyfriend for Christmas '04
Murder on Pleasant Drive '06
Gossip '08
Any Day Now '12

Kenneth Williams (1926-88)
Carry On Sergeant '58
Carry On Constable '60
Carry On Regardless '61
Carry On Cruising '62
Carry On Jack '63
Carry On Spying '64
Carry On Cleo '65
Carry On Cowboy '66
Carry On Screaming '66
Don't Lose Your Head '66
Follow That Camel '67
Carry On Doctor '68
Carry On Up the Khyber '68
Carry On Again Doctor '69
Carry On Loving '70
Carry On at Your Convenience '71
Carry On Camping '71
Carry On Henry VIII '71
Carry On Abroad '72
Carry On Matron '72
Carry On Behind '75
Carry On Emmanuelle '78
The Thief and the Cobbler '96 (V)

Kiely Williams (1986-)
The Cheetah Girls '03
The Cheetah Girls 2 '06
The Cheetah Girls: One World '08
The House Bunny '08
Stomp the Yard 2: Homecoming '10

Kimberly Williams (1971-)
Father of the Bride '91
Indian Summer '93
Coldblooded '94
Father of the Bride Part 2 '95
The War at Home '96
Just a Little Harmless Sex '99
Safe House '99
Simpatico '99
The 10th Kingdom '00
Follow the Stars Home '01
The Christmas Shoes '02
Lucky Seven '03
Identity Theft: The Michelle Brown Story '04
How to Eat Fried Worms '06
How to Go Out on a Date in Queens '06
We Are Marshall '06
Amish Grace '10
Alvin and the Chipmunks: Road Chip '15

Lee Williams (1974-)
The Wolves of Kromer '98
In His Life: The John Lennon Story '00
The Debt '03

Lia Williams (1964-)
Firelight '97
Shot Through the Heart '98
The King Is Alive '00

Maisie Williams
The Book of Love '16
Mary Shelley '17
Early Man '18

Malinda Williams (1975-)
High School High '96
A Thin Line Between Love and Hate '96
Uninvited Guest '99
The Wood '99
Dancing in September '00
Idlewild '06
Daddy's Little Girls '07
First Sunday '08
A Day in the Life '09
A Cross to Bear '12
Percentage '13

Mark Williams (1959-)
Kill Line '91
101 Dalmatians '96
The Borrowers '97
High Heels and Low Lifes '01
Harry Potter and the Chamber of Secrets '02
Harry Potter and the Goblet of Fire '05
Tristram Shandy: A Cock and Bull Story '05
Harry Potter and the Order of the Phoenix '07
A Room With a View '08
Harry Potter and the Half-Blood Prince '09
Albert Nobbs '11

Mary Parker Williams
Sarah's Child '96
Wish upon a Star '96

Meadow Williams (1966-)
Den of Thieves '18
10 Minutes Gone '19

Michael Williams (1935-2001)
Educating Rita '83
A Dance to the Music of Time '97
The Blair Witch Project '99

Michael C. Williams (1973-)
Altered '06
The Objective '08

Michael K(enneth) Williams (1966-)
Gone Baby Gone '07
I Think I Love My Wife '07
Brooklyn's Finest '09
A Day in the Life '09
Life During Wartime '09
The Road '09
Wonderful World '09
The Perfect Age of Rock 'n' Roll '10
LUV '13
Snitch '13
12 Years a Slave '13
The Gambler '14
Kill the Messenger '14
The Purge: Anarchy '14
RoboCop '14
Captive '15
SuperFly '18

Michelle Williams (1980-)
Lassie '94
Species '95
Timemaster '95
Killing Mr. Griffin '97
A Thousand Acres '97
Halloween: H20 '98
Dick '99
If These Walls Could Talk 2 '00
Me Without You '01
Perfume '01
Prozac Nation '01
The Station Agent '03
United States of Leland '03
A Hole in One '04
Land of Plenty '04
The Baxter '05
Brokeback Mountain '05
Imaginary Heroes '05
The Hawk Is Dying '06
The Hottest State '06
I'm Not There '07
Deception '08
Incendiary '08
Synecdoche, New York '08
Wendy and Lucy '08
Mammoth '09
Shutter Island '09
Blue Valentine '10
Meek's Cutoff '10
My Week With Marilyn '11
Take This Waltz '11
Oz the Great and Powerful '13
Certain Women '16
Manchester by the Sea '16
All the Money in the World '17
The Greatest Showman '17
Wonderstruck '17
I Feel Pretty '18
Venom '18
After the Wedding '19

Olivia Williams (1968-)
Emma '97
The Postman '97
Rushmore '98
The Sixth Sense '99
Born Romantic '00
Four Dogs Playing Poker '00
Jason and the Argonauts '00
The Body '01
Lucky Break '01
The Man from Elysian Fields '01
Below '02
The Heart of Me '02
Peter Pan '03
To Kill a King '03
Agatha Christie: A Life in Pictures '04
Tara Road '05
Valiant '05 (V)
X-Men: The Last Stand '06
Miss Austen Regrets '07
Flashbacks of a Fool '08
An Education '09
The Ghost Writer '10
Sex & Drugs & Rock & Roll '10
Anna Karenina '12
Hyde Park on Hudson '12
Now Is Good '12
The Last Days on Mars '13
Maps to the Stars '14
Sabotage '14
Seventh Son '15

Paul Williams (1940-)
The Loved One '65
Watermelon Man '70
Battle for the Planet of the Apes '73
Phantom of the Paradise '74
Smokey and the Bandit '77
The Cheap Detective '78
The Muppet Movie '79 (C)
Smokey and the Bandit 2 '80
Smokey and the Bandit, Part 3 '83
Zombie High '87
Chill Factor '90
The Doors '91
A Million to Juan '94
Headless Body in Topless Bar '96
The Princess Diaries 2: Royal Engagement '04

Peter Williams (1957-)
The Bridge on the River Kwai '57
Destroy All Planets '68
Robin Hood. . . The Legend: Robin Hood and the Sorcerer '83
Jungleground '95
Soul Survivor '95
Love Come Down '00

Rebecca Williams
The Night Before the Night Before Christmas '10
Reviving Ophelia '10

Rex Williams
Tarzan Triumphs '43
The Marrying Kind '52

Rhys Williams (1897-1969)
How Green Was My Valley '41
Mrs. Miniver '42
The Corn Is Green '45
So Goes My Love '46
Kiss Tomorrow Goodbye '50
Man in the Attic '53
The Black Shield of Falworth '54
Battle Cry '55
The Boss '56
Fastest Gun Alive '56

Robin Williams (1952-2014)
Can I Do It. . . Till I Need Glasses? '77
Popeye '80
The World According to Garp '82
Survivors '83
Moscow on the Hudson '84
The Best of Times '86
Club Paradise '86
Seize the Day '86
Good Morning, Vietnam '87
The Adventures of Baron Munchausen '89 (C)
Dead Poets Society '89
Awakenings '90
Cadillac Man '90
Dead Again '91 (C)
The Fisher King '91
Hook '91
Aladdin '92 (V)
Ferngully: The Last Rain Forest '92 (V)
Shakes the Clown '92 (C)
Toys '92
Mrs. Doubtfire '93
Being Human '94
The Birdcage '95
Jumanji '95
Nine Months '95
To Wong Foo, Thanks for Everything, Julie Newmar '95 (C)
Aladdin and the King of Thieves '96 (V)
Father's Day '96
Hamlet '96
Jack '96
The Secret Agent '96
Deconstructing Harry '97
Flubber '97
Good Will Hunting '97
Patch Adams '98
What Dreams May Come '98
Bicentennial Man '99
Jakob the Liar '99
A. I.: Artificial Intelligence '01 (V)
Death to Smoochy '02
Insomnia '02
One Hour Photo '02
The Final Cut '04
House of D '04
Noel '04
The Big White '05
Robots '05 (V)
Everyone's Hero '06 (V)
Happy Feet '06 (V)
Man of the Year '06
Night at the Museum '06
The Night Listener '06
RV '06
August Rush '07
License to Wed '07
Night at the Museum: Battle of the Smithsonian '09
Old Dogs '09
Shrink '09
World's Greatest Dad '09
Happy Feet Two '11 (V)
The Big Wedding '13
The Face of Love '13
Lee Daniels' The Butler '13
The Angriest Man in Brooklyn '14
Night at the Museum: Secret of the Tomb '14
Boulevard '15
Absolutely Anything '17 (V)

Samm-Art Williams (1946-)
The Adventures of Huckleberry Finn '85
Blood Simple '85
A Rage in Harlem '91

Saul Williams (1972-)
Slam '98
K-PAX '01

Scot Williams (1972-)
Backbeat '94
In His Life: The John Lennon Story '00
The Crew '08
Perfect Victims '08

Steven Williams (1949-)
Dummy '79
The Blues Brothers '80
Twilight Zone: The Movie '83
Better Off Dead '85
Missing in Action 2: The Beginning '85
Silent Witness '85
Jason Goes to Hell: The Final Friday '93
Bloodfist 7: Manhunt '95
The Sender '98
Crash & Byrnes '99
Firetrap '01
Route 666 '01
Darkwolf '03
Kings of the Evening '08
F6 Twister '12

Timothy Williams (1967-)
Club Med '86
Tiger Heart '96

Tonya Lee Williams
Poor Man's Game '06
Cybergeddon '12

Treat Williams (1951-)
Deadly Hero '75
The Ritz '76
The Eagle Has Landed '77
Hair '79
1941 '79
Prince of the City '81
Dempsey '83
Flashpoint '84
Once Upon a Time in America '84
Smooth Talk '85
The Men's Club '86
Night of the Sharks '87
Dead Heat '88
Sweet Lies '88
The Heart of Dixie '89
Drug Wars: The Camarena Story '90
Final Verdict '91
Hand Gun '93
Where the Rivers Flow North '94
Mulholland Falls '95
Things to Do in Denver When You're Dead '95
The Devil's Own '96
The Late Shift '96
The Phantom '96
The Substitute 2: School's Out '97
The Deep End of the Ocean '98
Deep Rising '98
Escape: Human Cargo '98
Journey to the Center of the Earth '99
The Substitute 3: Winner Takes All '99
Critical Mass '00
Skeletons in the Closet '00
The Substitute 4: Failure is Not an Option '00
Extreme Limits '01
The Fraternity '01
Gale Force '01
Venomous '01
Hollywood Ending '02
Miss Congeniality 2: Armed and Fabulous '05
Moola '07
What Happens in Vegas '08
Miles from Nowhere '09
Safe Harbor '09
The Storm '09
Howl '10
Mask Maker '10
127 Hours '10
Beyond the Blackboard '11
A Little Bit of Heaven '11
Attack of the 50 Foot Cheerleader '12
Age of Dinosaurs '13
Eve of Destruction '13
In the Blood '13
Reaching for the Moon '13
Barefoot '14
The Congressman '16
Second Act '18
Drunk Parents '19

Tyler James Williams (1992-)
Unaccompanied Minors '06
Let It Shine '12
Dear White People '14
The Wedding Year '19

Vanessa Williams (1963-)
New Jack City '91
DROP Squad '94
Mother '96
Incognito '99
Like Mike '02
Our America '02
Black Listed '03
My Brother '06
Ice Spiders '07
Flirting with Forty '09
Imagine That '09
Delhi Safari '12 (V)
Tyler Perry's Temptation: Confessions of a Marriage Counselor '13
The Trip to Bountiful '14

Vanessa L(ynne) Williams (1963-)
The Pick-Up Artist '87
Full Exposure: The Sex Tape Scandals '89
Another You '91
Harley Davidson and the Marlboro Man '91
Candyman '92
The Jacksons: An American Dream '92
Bye Bye Birdie '95
Eraser '96
Hoodlum '96
The Odyssey '97
Soul Food '97
Dance with Me '98
Futuresport '98
Light It Up '99
The Courage to Love '00
Shaft '00
Winds of Terror '01
Keep the Faith, Baby '02
Johnson Family Vacation '04
My Brother '06
And Then Came Love '07

Virginia Williams (1978-)
Honeymoon with Mom '06
Revenge of the Bridesmaids '10
10 Rules for Sleeping Around '13

Wade Andrew Williams (1961-)
Route 9 '98
K-911 '99
Terror Tract '00
Bark! '02
I Witness '03
Gangster Squad '13

Zelda Williams
House of D '04
Were the World Mine '08

Kimberly Williams-Paisley (1971-)
See Kimberly Williams

Alister Williamson (1918-99)
The Oblong Box '69
Murder on the Midnight Express '74

Chase Williamson (1988-)
John Dies at the End '12
Sparks '13
Beyond the Gates '16

Felix Williamson
Strange Planet '99
Dirty Deeds '02
Haunted Echoes '08

Fred Williamson (1938-)
M*A*S*H '70
Black Caesar '73
Hell Up in Harlem '73
That Man Bolt '73
Black Eye '74
Boss '74
No Way Back '74
Three the Hard Way '74
Adios Amigo '75
Bucktown '75
Mean Johnny Barrows '75
Take a Hard Ride '75
Death Journey '76
Joshua '76
Deadly Mission '78
The Inglorious Bastards '78
Fist of Fear, Touch of Death '80
One Down, Two to Go! '82
Big Score '83
The New Gladiators '83

1990: The Bronx Warriors '83
Vigilante '83
Warriors of the Wasteland '83
Deadly Impact '84
White Fire '84
The Black Cobra '87
Delta Force Commando '87
Deadly Intent '88
Black Cobra 2 '89
Black Cobra 3: The Manila Connection '90
Steele's Law '91
South Beach '92
Silent Hunter '94
From Dusk Till Dawn '95
Original Gangstas '96
Blackjack '97
Night Vision '97
Children of the Corn 5: Fields of Terror '98
Active Stealth '99
The Independent '00 (C)
Submerged '00
Rhapsody '01
On the Edge '02
Starsky & Hutch '04
Crooked '05
Transformed '05
Last Ounce of Courage '12

Mykelti Williamson (1960-)
Streets of Fire '84
Number One with a Bullet '87
The First Power '89
Miracle Mile '89
Forrest Gump '94
Heat '95
How to Make an American Quilt '95
Waiting to Exhale '95
Soul of the Game '96
Buffalo Soldiers '97
Con Air '97
Truth or Consequences, N.M. '97
Primary Colors '98
Species 2 '98
Having Our Say: The Delany Sisters' First 100 Years '99
Three Kings '99
Holiday Heart '00
Ali '01
Our America '02
After the Sunset '04
The Assassination of Richard Nixon '05
ATL '06
Fatwa '06
Lucky Number Slevin '06
Vice '08
Black Dynamite '09
The Final Destination '09
Mitch Albom's Have a Little Faith '11
The Purge: Election Year '16
Don't Let Go '19

Nicol Williamson (1938-2011)
The Reckoning '69
The Wilby Conspiracy '75
Robin and Marian '76
The Seven-Per-Cent Solution '76
The Cheap Detective '78
The Human Factor '79
Excalibur '81
I'm Dancing as Fast as I Can '82
Venom '82
Return to Oz '85
Mountbatten: The Last Viceroy '86
Black Widow '87
Exorcist 3: Legion '90
The Advocate '93
Mr. Toad's Wild Ride '96
Spawn '97

Amanda Williford (1981-)
See Willa Ford

Noble Willingham (1930-2004)
Aloha, Bobby and Rose '74
Big Bad Mama '74
The Boys in Company C '77
Backstairs at the White House '79
Kenny Rogers as the Gambler '80
The Children Nobody Wanted '81
Coward of the County '81
First Monday in October '81
Good Morning, Vietnam '87
The Heist '89
Blind Fury '90
Career Opportunities '91
City Slickers '91
The Last Boy Scout '91
Pastime '91
Article 99 '92
Ace Ventura: Pet Detective '93
City Slickers 2: The Legend of Curly's Gold '94
Up Close and Personal '96

Bruce Willis (1955-)
Moonlighting '85
Blind Date '87
Die Hard '88
Sunset '88
In Country '89
Look Who's Talking '89 (V)
The Bonfire of the Vanities '90
Die Hard 2: Die Harder '90
Look Who's Talking, Too '90 (V)
Billy Bathgate '91
Hudson Hawk '91
The Last Boy Scout '91
Mortal Thoughts '91
Death Becomes Her '92
The Player '92
National Lampoon's Loaded Weapon 1 '93
Striking Distance '93
Color of Night '94
Nobody's Fool '94
Pulp Fiction '94
Die Hard: With a Vengeance '95
Four Rooms '95
12 Monkeys '95
Beavis and Butt-Head Do America '96 (V)
Last Man Standing '96
The Fifth Element '97
The Jackal '97
Armageddon '98
Breakfast of Champions '98
Mercury Rising '98
The Siege '98
The Sixth Sense '99
The Story of Us '99
Disney's The Kid '00
Unbreakable '00
The Whole Nine Yards '00
Bandits '01
Hart's War '02
Rugrats Go Wild! '03 (V)
Tears of the Sun '03
The Whole Ten Yards '04
Hostage '05
Sin City '05
Alpha Dog '06
Fast Food Nation '06
Lucky Number Slevin '06
Over the Hedge '06 (V)
16 Blocks '06
The Astronaut Farmer '07 (C)
Live Free or Die Hard '07
Perfect Stranger '07
Planet Terror '07
Assassination of a High School President '08
What Just Happened '08
Surrogates '09
Cop Out '10
The Expendables '10
RED '10
Catch.44 '11
Setup '11
The Cold Light of Day '12
The Expendables 2 '12
Fire With Fire '12
Lay the Favorite '12
Looper '12
Moonrise Kingdom '12
G.I. Joe: Retaliation '13
A Good Day to Die Hard '13
RED 2 '13
The Prince '14
Sin City: A Dame to Kill For '14
Extraction '15
Rock the Kasbah '15
Vice '15
Marauders '16
Precious Cargo '16
First Kill '17
Acts of Violence '18
Death Wish '18
Reprisal '18
Glass '19
Motherless Brooklyn '19
10 Minutes Gone '19

Dave Willis
Aqua Teen Hunger Force Colon Movie Film for Theaters '07 (V)
There Will Be Blood '07

Matt Willis (1913-89)
Return of the Vampire '43
A Walk in the Sun '46
The Noose Hangs High '48

Rumer Willis (1988-)
Striptease '96
Hostage '05
The House Bunny '08
Sorority Row '09
Wild Cherry '09
The Odd Way Home '13

Susan Willis (1925-2009)
What about Bob? '91
The Majestic '01

Noel Willman (1917-88)
Beau Brummell '54
The Warriors '55
Across the Bridge '57
Trouble in the Sky '60
Kiss of the Vampire '62
Doctor Zhivago '65
The Reptile '66
The Odessa File '74
21 Hours at Munich '76

Chill Wills (1903-78)
Allegheny Uprising '39
Boom Town '40
The Westerner '40
The Bad Man '41
Billy the Kid '41
Honky Tonk '41
Western Union '41
Her Cardboard Lover '42
Stand by for Action '42
Tarzan's New York Adventure '42
I'll Be Seeing You '44
Sunday Dinner for a Soldier '44
The Harvey Girls '46
The Yearling '46
That Wonderful Urge '48
Francis the Talking Mule '49 (V)
Tulsa '49
High Lonesome '50
Rio Grande '50
Francis Goes to the Races '51 (V)
Francis Goes to West Point '52 (V)
Francis Covers the Big Town '53 (V)
Man from the Alamo '53
Small Town Girl '53
Francis Joins the WACs '54 (V)
Kentucky Rifle '55
Giant '56
Santiago '56
Gun for a Coward '57
Gun Glory '57
The Alamo '60
Where the Boys Are '60
Deadly Companions '61
Gold of the Seven Saints '61
Young Guns of Texas '62
McLintock! '63
The Wheeler Dealers '63
The Rounders '65
Fireball 500 '66
The Over-the-Hill Gang '69
The Over-the-Hill Gang Rides Again '70
Pat Garrett & Billy the Kid '73
Mr. Billion '77

Maury Wills (1932-)
The Black Six '74
The Sandlot '93

Paul Willson (1945-)
Devonsville Terror '83
My Best Friend Is a Vampire '88
Office Space '98

Douglas Wilmer (1920-)
Jason and the Argonauts '63
Brides of Fu Manchu '66
The Vengeance of Fu Manchu '67
The Reckoning '69
The Vampire Lovers '70
Golden Voyage of Sinbad '73
The Adventures of Sherlock Holmes' Smarter Brother '78

Gary Wilmes
A Mighty Heart '07
Birds of America '08
I Hate Valentine's Day '09

David Wilmot
Intermission '03
Middletown '06
The Guard '11
Shadow Dancer '12
Ordinary Love '20

Andre Wilms (1947-)
Monsieur Hire '89
L'Enfer '93
Ricky '09

Channing Wilroy (1940-)
Pink Flamingos '72
Female Trouble '74
Desperate Living '77

Ajita Wilson (1950-87)
Escape from Hell '79
Contraband '80
Savage Island '85

Andreas Wilson
Evil '03
Kill Your Darlings '06

Andrew Wilson (1964-)
Bottle Rocket '95
The Big Bounce '04
Time Trap '17

Barbara Wilson (1936-)
Teenage Doll '57
Lost, Lonely, and Vicious '59
Invasion of the Animal People '62
Lies My Mother Told Me '05
Boot Camp '07
Hush Little Baby '07

Brad Wilson
Grotesque '87
Pterodactyl Woman from Beverly Hills '97

Brian Wilson (1942-)
Beach Party '63
Beach Blanket Bingo '65

Brian Anthony Wilson (1960-)
The Fields '11
6 Degrees of Hell '12

Brittney Wilson (1991-)
Best Friends '05
Chasing Christmas '05
Home By Christmas '06
12 Hours to Live '06
Ice Blues: A Donald Strachey Mystery '08
Mom, Dad and Her '08
Step Dogs '13

Charles C. Wilson (1894-1948)
Pennies from Heaven '36
The Spider's Web '38
Larceny in her Heart '46

Cherilyn Wilson
Extreme Movie '08
Parasomnia '08

David Wilson (1949-)
Hometown U.S.A. '79
Eddie and the Cruisers '83
The Inside Man '84

Don Wilson (1900-82)
The Chase '46
Niagara '52
Sailor Beware '52
The Last Sentinel '07

Don 'The Dragon' Wilson (1954-)
Bloodfist '89
Born on the Fourth of July '89
Say Anything '89
Bloodfist 2 '90
Futurekick '91
Ring of Fire '91
Black Belt '92
Bloodfist 3: Forced to Fight '92
Bloodfist 4: Die Trying '92
Magic Kid '92
Ring of Fire 2: Blood and Steel '92
Bloodfist 5: Human Target '93
Cyber-Tracker '93
Out for Blood '93
Bloodfist 6: Ground Zero '94
Ring of Fire 3: Lion Strike '94
Batman Forever '95
Bloodfist 7: Manhunt '95
Cyber-Tracker 2 '95
Night Hunter '95
Virtual Combat '95
Bloodfist 8: Hard Way Out '96
Hollywood Safari '96
Terminal Rush '96
The Capitol Conspiracy '99
Moving Target '00
Sci-Fighter '04
Crooked '05
18 Fingers of Death '05

Dooley Wilson (1894-1953)
Casablanca '42
Stormy Weather '43

Dorothy Wilson (1909-98)
Dangerous Appointment '34
His Greatest Gamble '34
In Old Kentucky '35
Last Days of Pompeii '35

Earl Wilson (1907-87)
Copacabana '47 (C)
Night of Evil '62 (N)
Beach Blanket Bingo '65

Elizabeth Wilson (1921-2015)
Patterns '56
The Goddess '58
The Tunnel of Love '58
The Graduate '67
Catch-22 '70
Little Murders '71
Prisoner of Second Avenue '74
Where Are the Children? '85
The Believers '87
Nutcracker: Money, Madness & Murder '87
The Addams Family '91
Regarding Henry '91
Queen '93
Sarah, Plain and Tall: Skylark '93
Quiz Show '94
Scarlett '94
The Boys Next Door '96

Flip Wilson (1933-98)
Cancel My Reservation '72
Uptown Saturday Night '74
The Fish that Saved Pittsburgh '79
Zora Is My Name! '90

Frank Wilson (1885-1956)
Girl from Chicago '32
Emperor Jones '33
The Green Pastures '36
Paradise in Harlem '40

George Wilson (1921-2010)
Attack of the Killer Tomatoes '77
Mesrine: Part 2-Public Enemy Number 1 '08

Georges Wilson (1921-2010)
More Than a Miracle '67
Beatrice Cenci '69

Kristen Wilson (1969-)
The Pompatus of Love '95
Bulletproof '96
Girl 6 '96
Harlem Aria '99
Dungeons and Dragons '00
Dr. Dolittle 2 '01
Confessions of a Dangerous Mind '02
Tales from the Crypt Presents Ritual '02
Walking Tall '04
Twitches '05
Crossover '06
Dr. Dolittle 3 '06
Twitches Too '07
Soccer Mom '08

Lambert Wilson (1958-)
Julia '77
Five Days One Summer '82
Rendez-vous '85
The Belly of an Architect '91
Frankenstein '93
The Leading Man '96
The Last September '99
The Matrix Reloaded '03
The Matrix Revolutions '03
Timeline '03
Catwoman '04
People '04
Sahara '05
Private Fears in Public Places '06
Flawless '07
Babylon A.D. '08
Dante 01 '08
The Lazarus Project '08
Of Gods and Men '10
The Princess of Montpensier '10
You Ain't Seen Nothin' Yet '12
Bicycling With Moliere '13

Lois Wilson (1896-1983)
Monsieur Beaucaire '24
The Vanishing American '25
The Show Off '26
The Rider of Death Valley '32
Laughing at Life '33
Bright Eyes '34

Luke Wilson (1971-)
Bottle Rocket '95
Telling Lies in America '96
Best Men '98
Bongwater '98
Dog Park '98
Home Fries '98
Blue Streak '99
Committed '99
My Dog Skip '99
Bad Seed '00
Charlie's Angels '00
Legally Blonde '01
The Royal Tenenbaums '01
Soul Survivors '01
The Third Wheel '02
Alex & Emma '03
Charlie's Angels: Full Throttle '03
Legally Blonde 2: Red White & Blonde '03
Masked and Anonymous '03
Old School '03
Anchorman: The Legend of Ron Burgundy '04
Around the World in 80 Days '04
The Family Stone '05
The Wendell Baker Story '05
Hoot '06
Idiocracy '06
My Super Ex-Girlfriend '06
Blonde Ambition '07
Vacancy '07
You Kill Me '07
Henry Poole Is Here '08
Battle for Terra '09 (V)
Tenure '09
Death at a Funeral '10

Middle Men '10
Meeting Evil '12
Straight A's '13
Playing It Cool '14
The Skeleton Twins '14
Meadowland '15
All We Had '16
Approaching the Unknown '16
Dear Eleanor '16
Outlaws and Angels '16
Brad's Status '17
Rock Dog '17
Arizona '18
The Goldfinch '19

Lulu Wilson
Ouija: Origin of Evil '16
Annabelle: Creation '17

Lydia Wilson (1984-)
South Riding '11
The Making of a Lady '12
All Is True '18

Mara Wilson (1987-)
Mrs. Doubtfire '93
Miracle on 34th Street '94
Matilda '96
Balloon Farm '97
A Simple Wish '97
Thomas and the Magic Railroad '00

Marie Wilson (1916-72)
March of the Wooden Soldiers '34
China Clipper '36
Satan Met a Lady '36
The Great Garrick '37
Boy Meets Girl '38
Flying Blind '41
Music For Millions '44
The Private Affairs of Bel Ami '47
My Friend Irma '49
My Friend Irma Goes West '50
Never Wave at a WAC '52
Mr. Hobbs Takes a Vacation '62

Mark Wilson
Personal Vendetta '96
Hangman '00
Crazy for Christmas '05

Mary Louise Wilson (1931-)
Green Card '90
The Adventures of Huck Finn '93
Stepmom '98
A Season for Miracles '99
24 Nights '99
Searching for Paradise '02

Michelle Wilson
The Trial of Billy Jack '74
Premature '20

Niamh Wilson (1997-)
Haunting Sarah '05
The House Next Door '06
They Come Back '07
The Young and Prodigious T.S. Spivet '15

Owen Wilson (1968-)
Bottle Rocket '95
Anaconda '96
The Cable Guy '96
Armageddon '98
Breakfast of Champions '98
Permanent Midnight '98
The Haunting '99
The Minus Man '99
Meet the Parents '00
Shanghai Noon '00
Behind Enemy Lines '01
The Royal Tenenbaums '01
Zoolander '01
I Spy '02
Shanghai Knights '03
Around the World in 80 Days '04
The Big Bounce '04
The Life Aquatic with Steve Zissou '04
Meet the Fockers '04
Starsky & Hutch '04
Wedding Crashers '05
The Wendell Baker Story '05
Cars '06 *(V)*
Night at the Museum '06
You, Me and Dupree '06
The Darjeeling Limited '07
Drillbit Taylor '08
Marley & Me '08
Fantastic Mr. Fox '09 *(V)*
Night at the Museum: Battle of the Smithsonian '09
How Do You Know '10
Little Fockers '10
Marmaduke '10 *(V)*
The Big Year '11
Cars 2 '11 *(V)*
Hall Pass '11
Midnight in Paris '11
Are You Here '13
Free Birds '13 *(V)*
The Internship '13
The Grand Budapest Hotel '14 *(C)*
Inherent Vice '14
Night at the Museum: Secret of the Tomb '14
No Escape '15
She's Funny That Way '15
Masterminds '16
Zoolander 2 '16
Cars 3 '17 *(V)*
Wonder '17

Patrick Wilson (1973-)
Angels in America '03
The Alamo '04
The Phantom of the Opera '04
Hard Candy '06
Little Children '06
Running with Scissors '06
Brothers Three '07
Evening '07
Purple Violets '07
Lakeview Terrace '08
Passengers '08
Watchmen '09
The A-Team '10
Barry Munday '10
Insidious '10
Morning Glory '10
The Switch '10
The Ledge '11
Young Adult '11
The Conjuring '13
Insidious: Chapter 2 '13
Let's Kill Ward's Wife '14
Space Station 76 '14
Big Stone Gap '15
The Conjuring 2 '16
The Hollow Point '16
A Kind of Murder '16
Aquaman '18
The Commuter '18
Annabelle Comes Home '19
In the Tall Grass '19
Midway '19

Perry Wilson (1916-2009)
Fear Strikes Out '57
The Matchmaker '58

Peta Wilson (1970-)
Loser '97
Mercy '00
Joe and Max '02
The League of Extraordinary Gentlemen '03
False Pretenses '04
Beautiful '09
Malibu Shark Attack '09

Rachel Wilson
Mystery, Alaska '99
Winter Break '02
Hellions '15
Backstabbing for Beginners '18

Rainn Wilson (1966-)
Permanent '17
The Meg '18

Rainn Wilson (1968-)
Baadasssss! '03
Sahara '05
My Super Ex-Girlfriend '06
The Last Mimzy '07
The Rocker '08
Monsters vs. Aliens '09 *(V)*
Transformers: Revenge of the Fallen '09
Hesher '10
Peep World '10
Super '10
Few Options '11
Cooties '14
Uncanny '15
Smurfs: The Lost Village '17 *(V)*

Rainn Dietrich Wilson (1966-)
See Rainn Wilson

Rebel Wilson (1980-)
Bachelorette '12
Pitch Perfect '12
Struck by Lightning '12
Pain & Gain '13
Night at the Museum: Secret of the Tomb '14
Pitch Perfect 2 '15
The Brothers Grimsby '16
How to Be Single '16
Pitch Perfect 3 '17
Cats '19
The Hustle '19
Isn't It Romantic '19

Reno Wilson (1970-)
City of Industry '96
She Creature '01
R.S.V.P. '02
Crank '06
Transformers '07 *(V)*

Richard Wilson (1936-)
How to Get Ahead in Advertising '89
Selling Hitler '91
The Man Who Knew Too Little '97

Rita Wilson (1956-)
The Day It Came to Earth '77
Volunteers '85
Sleepless in Seattle '93
Mixed Nuts '94
Now and Then '95
If These Walls Could Talk '96
Jingle All the Way '96
That Thing You Do! '96
From the Earth to the Moon '98
Psycho '98
Invisible Child '99
Runaway Bride '99
The Story of Us '99
The Glass House '01
Perfume '01
Auto Focus '02
Raise Your Voice '04
The Chumscrubber '05
Beautiful Ohio '06
It's Complicated '09
Old Dogs '09
The Art of Getting By '11
Larry Crowne '11
Jewtopia '12
My Big Fat Greek Wedding 2 '16
Gloria Bell '18

Rod Wilson
Darkman 2: The Return of Durant '94
Widows '02

Roger Wilson (1958-)
Porky's '82
Porky's 2: The Next Day '83
Second Time Lucky '84
The Ghost Brigade '93
Power of Attorney '94

Ruth Wilson (1982-)
Jane Eyre '06
The Prisoner '09
Small Island '09
Locke '13
The Lone Ranger '13
Saving Mr. Banks '13
How To Talk To Girls At Parties '17
Dark River '18
The Little Stranger '18

Ryan Wilson, MS III
Just Ask My Children '01
Cold Creek Manor '03

Scott Wilson (1942-)
In Cold Blood '67
Castle Keep '69
The Gypsy Moths '69
The Grissom Gang '71
The New Centurions '72
Lolly-Madonna XXX '73
The Ninth Configuration '79
The Right Stuff '83
On the Line '84
Year of the Quiet Sun '84
The Aviator '85
Blue City '86
Malone '87
The Tracker '88
Johnny Handsome '89
Exorcist 3: Legion '90
Young Guns 2 '90
Pure Luck '91
Flesh and Bone '93
Dead Man Walking '95
G.I. Jane '97
Shiloh '97
Clay Pigeons '98
The Jack Bull '99
Shiloh 2: Shiloh Season '99
Way of the Gun '00
Pearl Harbor '01
Bark! '02
Coastlines '02
The Last Samurai '03
Monster '03
Junebug '05
Behind the Mask: The Rise of Leslie Vernon '06
Come Early Morning '06
Open Window '06
Saving Shiloh '06
The Sensation of Sight '06
Big Stan '07
The Heartbreak Kid '07
Saving Grace B. Jones '09

Sheree J. Wilson (1958-)
Fraternity Vacation '85
News at Eleven '86
Walker: Texas Ranger: One Riot, One Ranger '93
Hellbound '94
Killing Down '06
Anna's Storm '07

Stuart Wilson (1946-)
The Strauss Family '73
Wallenberg: A Hero's Story '85
Lethal Weapon 3 '92
The Age of Innocence '93
Teenage Mutant Ninja Turtles 3 '93
Death and the Maiden '94
Exit to Eden '94
No Escape '94
Edie & Pen '95
Crossworlds '96
The Rock '96
Enemy of the State '98
The Mask of Zorro '98
Second Sight '99
Here on Earth '00
The Luzhin Defence '00
Slow Burn '00
Vertical Limit '00
Princess of Thieves '01
Dinotopia '02
The Rundown '03
Fascination '04
Hot Fuzz '07

Teddy Wilson (1943-91)
Cotton Comes to Harlem '70
The Ambush Murders '82
Kiss Shot '89
Life Stinks '91

Thomas F. Wilson (1959-)
Back to the Future '85
April Fool's Day '86
Let's Get Harry '87
Action Jackson '88
Back to the Future, Part 2 '89
Back to the Future, Part 3 '90
Mr. Write '92
Blood In . . . Blood Out: Bound by Honor '93
Camp Nowhere '94
Andersonville '95
Born to Be Wild '95
That Darn Cat '96
Larry the Cable Guy: Health Inspector '06
Zoom '06
Housebroken '09
The Heat '13

Tom Wilson (1880-1965)
California Straight Ahead '25
Battling Butler '26

Trey Wilson (1948-89)
Three Warriors '77
The Vampire Hookers '78
Kennedy '83
Raising Arizona '87
Bull Durham '88
End of the Line '88
Married to the Mob '88
Twins '88
Great Balls of Fire '89
Miss Firecracker '89
Welcome Home '89

Bridgette Wilson-Sampras (1973-)
Last Action Hero '93
Billy Madison '94
Mortal Kombat 1: The Movie '95
Sweet Evil '95
I Know What You Did Last Summer '97
The Real Blonde '97
Virtual Obsession '98
House on Haunted Hill '99
Love Stinks '99
The Suburbans '99
Beautiful '00
Just Visiting '01
The Wedding Planner '01
Buying the Cow '02
Extreme Ops '02
Shopgirl '05

Penelope Wilton (1946-)
The Norman Conquests, Part 1: Table Manners '78
The Norman Conquests, Part 2: Living Together '78
The Norman Conquests, Part 3: Round and Round the Garden '78
Singleton's Pluck '84
Clockwise '86
Cry Freedom '87
Blame It on the Bellboy '92
The Secret Rapture '94
Carrington '95
Iris '01
Victoria & Albert '01
Wives and Daughters '01
Calendar Girls '03
Shaun of the Dead '04
Match Point '05
Pride and Prejudice '05
The History Boys '06
Five Days '07
Half Broken Things '07
Margot '09
South Riding '11
The Best Exotic Marigold Hotel '12
The Girl '12
Belle '13
The BFG '16

Juliana Wimbles
Restless Spirits '99
Snakehead Terror '04

Mary Wimbush
Oh! What a Lovely War '69
Poldark '75

Brian Wimmer (1959-)
Dangerous Pursuit '89
Late for Dinner '91
Blue Flame '93
Lipstick Camera '93
Tank Girl '94
Bitter Sweet '98
Final Justice '98
Beneath Loch Ness '01
Heart of the Storm '04
Attack of the Sabretooth '05
The Yankles '09
6 Guns '10

Troy Winbush (1970-)
The Principal '87
The Replacements '00
Carmen: A Hip Hopera '01
Gabriela '01
A Light in the Darkness '02
What About Your Friends: Weekend Getaway '02
United States of Leland '03
The Last Shot '04
Six: The Mark Unleashed '04
Sniper 3 '04
Backwoods '08

Paul Winchell (1922-2005)
The Aristocats '70 *(V)*
The Many Adventures of Winnie the Pooh '77 *(V)*
The Fox and the Hound '81 *(V)*

Walter Winchell (1897-1972)
Wake Up and Live '37
The Bellboy '60 *(C)*
Dondi '61

Philip Winchester (1981-)
Lethal Dose '03
Thunderbirds '04
Flyboys '06
Alice '09
Maneater '09
A Walk in My Shoes '10

Jeff Wincott (1956-)
Deadly Bet '91
Martial Outlaw '93
The Killing Man '94
Last Man Standing '95
Street Law '95
Future Fear '97
The Undertaker's Wedding '97
Battle Queen 2020 '99
Paper Bullets '99
The Invasion '07

Michael Wincott (1958-)
Wild Horse Hank '79
Curtains '83
Talk Radio '88
The Doors '91
Robin Hood: Prince of Thieves '91
1492: Conquest of Paradise '92
The Crow '93
Romeo Is Bleeding '93
The Three Musketeers '93
Dead Man '95
Strange Days '95
Basquiat '96
Metro '96
Alien: Resurrection '97
Gunshy '98
Hidden Agenda '99
Before Night Falls '00
Along Came a Spider '01
Anti-Terrorist Cell: Manhunt '01
The Count of Monte Cristo '02
Treasure Planet '02 *(V)*
The Assassination of Richard Nixon '05
Seraphim Falls '06
What Just Happened '08
Hitchcock '12
Forsaken '15
Foresaken '16

Rebecca Windheim
Black Swarm '07
The Year Dolly Parton Was My Mom '11

William Windom (1923-2012)
To Kill a Mockingbird '62
Cattle King '63
For Love or Money '63
One Man's Way '63
The Americanization of Emily '64
Columbo: Prescription Murder '67
The Detective '68
The Gypsy Moths '69
Operation Heartbeat '69
Brewster McCloud '70
Escape from the Planet of the Apes '71
The Mephisto Waltz '71

Pursuit '72
Leave 'Em Laughing '81
Desperate Lives '82
Grandview U.S.A. '84
Planes, Trains & Automobiles '87
She's Having a Baby '88
Funland '89
Back to Hannibal: The Return of Tom Sawyer and Huckleberry Finn '90
Committed '91
Attack of the 50 Ft. Woman '93
Sommersby '93
Miracle on 34th Street '94
Children of the Corn 4: The Gathering '96

Barbara Windsor (1937-)
Carry On Spying '64
Carry On Doctor '68
Carry On Again Doctor '69
Carry On Camping '71
Carry On Henry VIII '71
Carry On Abroad '72
Carry On Matron '72
Not Now Darling '73

Marie Windsor (1922-2000)
Smart Alecks '42
The Fighting Kentuckian '49
Force of Evil '49
Outpost in Morocco '49
Little Big Horn '51
Japanese War Bride '52
Jungle '52
The Narrow Margin '52
Outlaw Women '52
The Sniper '52
Cat Women of the Moon '53
The Eddie Cantor Story '53
Tall Texan '53
Trouble along the Way '53
Hell's Half Acre '54
Abbott and Costello Meet the Mummy '55
Silver Star '55
Swamp Women '55
The Killing '56
Girl in Black Stockings '57
Bedtime Story '63
Critic's Choice '63
Mail Order Bride '63
Cahill: United States Marshal '73
The Outfit '73
Salem's Lot '79

Romy Windsor
Howling 4: The Original Nightmare '88
Big Bad John '90

Paul Winfield (1940-2004)
Brother John '70
R.P.M.* (*Revolutions Per Minute) '70
Sounder '72
Trouble Man '72
Gordon's War '73
The Horror at 37,000 Feet '73
Huckleberry Finn '74
It's Good to Be Alive '74
Damnation Alley '77
The Greatest '77
A Hero Ain't Nothin' but a Sandwich '78
King '78
Backstairs at the White House '79
Roots: The Next Generation '79
Carbon Copy '81
Star Trek 2: The Wrath of Khan '82
White Dog '82
Go Tell It on the Mountain '84
Mike's Murder '84
The Terminator '84
Blue City '86
Big Shots '87
Death Before Dishonor '87
The Serpent and the Rainbow '87
The Women of Brewster Place '89
Back to Hannibal: The Return of Tom Sawyer and Huckleberry Finn '90
Presumed Innocent '90
Cliffhanger '93
Dennis the Menace '93
Queen '93
Scarlett '94
The Legend of Gator Face '96
Mars Attacks! '96
Original Gangstas '96
Relax. . . It's Just Sex! '98
Catfish in Black Bean Sauce '00

Oprah Winfrey (1954-)
The Color Purple '85
The Women of Brewster Place '89
Beloved '98
Charlotte's Web '06 (V)
Bee Movie '07 (V)
The Princess and the Frog '09 (V)
Lee Daniels' The Butler '13
Selma '14
A Wrinkle in Time '18
Toni Morrison: The Pieces I Am '19

Leslie Wing
Dungeonmaster '83
Retribution '88

Toby Wing (1915-2001)
Murder at the Vanities '34
Search for Beauty '34

Adam Wingard (1982-)
V/H/S '12
24 Exposures '13
V/H/S/2 '13

Debra Winger (1955-)
Slumber Party '57 '76
Thank God It's Friday '78
French Postcards '79
Urban Cowboy '80
Cannery Row '82
E.T.: The Extra-Terrestrial '82 (V)
An Officer and a Gentleman '82
Terms of Endearment '83
Mike's Murder '84
Legal Eagles '86
Black Widow '87
Made in Heaven '87 (C)
Betrayed '88
Everybody Wins '90
The Sheltering Sky '90
Leap of Faith '92
Shadowlands '93
Wilder Napalm '93
Forget Paris '95
Big Bad Love '02
Radio '03
Eulogy '04
Sometimes in April '05
Rachel Getting Married '08
Lola Versus '12
The Red Tent '14
The Lovers '17

Peter Wingfield (1962-)
Uncovered '94
Highlander: Endgame '00
Edge of Madness '02
X2: X-Men United '03
Catwoman '04
Superbabies: Baby Geniuses 2 '04
Highlander: The Source '07
Riverworld '10
Stonehenge Apocalypse '10

Angela Winkler (1944-)
The Lost Honor of Katharina Blum '75
The Tin Drum '79
Danton '82
Sheer Madness '84
Benny's Video '92

Henry Winkler (1945-)
The Lords of Flatbush '74
Katherine '75
Heroes '77
The One and Only '78
An American Christmas Carol '79
Night Shift '82
One Christmas '95
Scream '96
Hostage High '97
National Lampoon's Dad's Week Off '97
Ground Control '98
P.U.N.K.S. '98
The Waterboy '98
Down to You '00
Holes '03
Berkeley '05
The Kid and I '05
Click '06
I Could Never Be Your Woman '06
Unbeatable Harold '06
The Most Wonderful Time of the Year '08
A Plumm Summer '08
Group Sex '10
Here Comes the Boom '12

Mel Winkler (1941-2020)
City Hall '95
Devil in a Blue Dress '95

Kitty Winn (1944-)
Panic in Needle Park '71
They Might Be Giants '71
The Exorcist '73
The Exorcist 2: The Heretic '77

Vic Winner
Horror Rises from the Tomb '72
The Rue Morgue Massacres '73

Olof Winnerstrand (1875-1956)
Torment '44
Night Is My Future '47

Katheryn Winnick (1977-)
Fabled '02
Satan's Little Helper '04
Hellraiser: Hellworld '05
Failure to Launch '06
Kiss Me Again '06
The Tipping Point '07
Amusement '08
Cold Souls '09
Killers '10
Love and Other Drugs '10
A Glimpse Inside the Mind of Charles Swan III '12
Stand Up Guys '12
The Art of the Steal '13
Speed Kills '18
Polar '19

Lucyna Winnicka (1928-2013)
First Spaceship on Venus '60
Mother Joan of the Angels '60
25 Fireman's Street '73

Charles Winninger (1884-1969)
The Canadian '26
Flying High '31
God's Gift to Women '31
Night Nurse '31
The Sin of Madelon Claudet '31
Show Boat '36
Three Smart Girls '36
Cafe Metropole '37
Nothing Sacred '37
You Can't Have Everything '37
Every Day's a Holiday '38
Hard to Get '38
Babes in Arms '39
Destry Rides Again '39
Three Smart Girls Grow Up '39
Beyond Tomorrow '40
If I Had My Way '40
Little Nellie Kelly '40
My Love Came Back '40
Pot o' Gold '41
Ziegfeld Girl '41
Coney Island '43
Lady Takes a Chance '43
Broadway Rhythm '44
Sunday Dinner for a Soldier '44
She Wouldn't Say Yes '45
State Fair '45
Living In a Big Way '47
Something in the Wind '47
Father Is a Bachelor '50
The Sun Shines Bright '53

Mare Winningham (1959-)
One Trick Pony '80
The Thorn Birds '83
St. Elmo's Fire '85
Nobody's Fool '86
Who Is Julia? '86
Made in Heaven '87
God Bless the Child '88
Miracle Mile '89
Turner and Hooch '89
Hard Promises '92
The War '94
Wyatt Earp '94
Georgia '95
The Boys Next Door '96
George Wallace '97
Under Pressure '98
Sally Hemings: An American Scandal '00
Snap Decision '01
The Maldonado Miracle '03
War Eagle, Arkansas '07
Swing Vote '08
Brothers '09
Mildred Pierce '11
Hatfields & McCoys '12
Mirror Mirror '12
Philomena '13
The Seagull '18

Marissa Jaret Winokur (1973-)
On Edge '03
Fever Pitch '05
It Was One of Us '00

Beth Winslet
Bodywork '99
The Shadow Within '07

Kate Winslet (1975-)
Heavenly Creatures '94
A Kid in King Arthur's Court '95
Sense and Sensibility '95
Hamlet '96
Jude '96
Titanic '97
Hideous Kinky '99
Holy Smoke '99
Quills '00
Enigma '01
Iris '01
The Life of David Gale '03
Eternal Sunshine of the Spotless Mind '04
Finding Neverland '04
Romance & Cigarettes '05
All the King's Men '06
Flushed Away '06 (V)
The Holiday '06
Little Children '06
The Reader '08
Revolutionary Road '08
Carnage '11
Contagion '11
Mildred Pierce '11
Labor Day '13
Movie 43 '13
Divergent '14
A Little Chaos '14
Insurgent '15
Steve Jobs '15
Triple 9 '15
Collateral Beauty '16
The Dressmaker '16
The Mountain Between Us '17
Wonder Wheel '17

George Winslow (1946-2015)
Monkey Business '52
Gentlemen Prefer Blondes '53
Mr. Scoutmaster '53
The Rocket Man '54
Artists and Models '55

Michael Winslow (1958-)
Cheech and Chong's Nice Dreams '81
Alphabet City '84
Lovelines '84
Police Academy '84
Police Academy 2: Their First Assignment '85
Police Academy 3: Back in Training '86
Police Academy 4: Citizens on Patrol '87
Spaceballs '87
Police Academy 5: Assignment Miami Beach '88
Far Out Man '89
Police Academy 6: City under Siege '89
Going Under '91
Police Academy 7: Mission to Moscow '94
National Lampoon Presents RoboDoc '08

Mary Elizabeth Winstead (1984-)
Sky High '05
Black Christmas '06
Bobby '06
Final Destination 3 '06
Death Proof '07
Live Free or Die Hard '07
Make It Happen '08
Scott Pilgrim vs. the World '10
The Thing '11
Abraham Lincoln: Vampire Hunter '12
A Glimpse Inside the Mind of Charles Swan III '12
Smashed '12
A.C.O.D. '13
A Good Day to Die Hard '13
The Spectacular Now '13
Faults '15
Swiss Army Man '16
10 Cloverfield Lane '16
All About Nina '18
Gemini Man '19
The Parts You Lose '19
Birds of Prey: And the Fantabulous Emancipation of One Harley Quinn '20

Hattie Winston (1945-)
Clara's Heart '88
Jackie Brown '97
True Crime '99

Helen Winston (1925-72)
Battle Circus '53
I Love Melvin '53
Tobor the Great '54

Helene Winston (1922-2004)
Double Trouble '67
The Shakiest Gun in the West '68
The Trouble with Girls (and How to Get into It) '69
The Witchmaker '69
The Brotherhood of Satan '71
Our Time '74
A Boy and His Dog '75
The Shaggy D.A. '76
Return from Witch Mountain '78
The Devil & Max Devlin '81
Killjoy '81

Jahi Di'Allo Winston
The Upside '17
Proud Mary '18

Matt Winston
The Boy Who Cried Werewolf '10
StarStruck '10

Jaime Winstone (1985-)
Cravings '06
Donkey Punch '08
Boogie Woogie '09

Ray Winstone (1957-)
Quadrophenia '79
Scum '79
Ladies and Gentlemen, the Fabulous Stains '82
Ladybird, Ladybird '93
Nil by Mouth '96
Face '97
Darkness Falls '98
Final Cut '98
The Sea Change '98
The Very Thought of You '98
The War Zone '98
Agnes Browne '99
Love, Honour & Obey '00
Sexy Beast '00
Last Orders '01
Ripley's Game '02
Cold Mountain '03
King Arthur '04
The Chronicles of Narnia: The Lion, the Witch and the Wardrobe '05 (V)
Doogal '05 (V)
The Proposition '05
Breaking and Entering '06
The Departed '06
Beowulf '07 (V)
Compulsion '08
Fool's Gold '08
Indiana Jones and the Kingdom of the Crystal Skull '08
The Devil's Tomb '09
44 Inch Chest '09
Ben Hur '10
Edge of Darkness '10
London Boulevard '10
Sex & Drugs & Rock & Roll '10
13 '10
Tracker '10
Great Expectations '11
Happy Feet Two '11 (V)
Hugo '11
Rango '11 (V)
Snow White and the Huntsman '12
The Sweeney '12
Noah '14
The Gunman '15
Point Break '15
Zipper '15

Maurice Dean Wint (1964-)
Rude '96
Cube '98
Hedwig and the Angry Inch '00
The Circuit '08

Alex Winter (1965-)
Death Wish 3 '85
The Lost Boys '87
Haunted Summer '88
Bill & Ted's Excellent Adventure '89
Rosalie Goes Shopping '89
Bill & Ted's Bogus Journey '91
Freaked '93
Grand Piano '13

Ariel Winter (1998-)
Opposite Day '09
The Chaperone '11
Excision '12
Mr. Peabody & Sherman '14 (V)
The Last Movie Star '17

Eric Winter (1976-)
Break-In '06
Harold & Kumar Escape from Guantanamo Bay '08
The Ugly Truth '09
Sundays at Tiffany's '10
Comet '14

Katia Winter
Night Junkies '07
Love Sick Love '12

Mark Leonard Winter
Healing '15
Escape from Pretoria '20

Vincent Winter (1947-98)
Time Lock '57
Gorgo '61
Almost Angels '62
The Horse Without a Head '63

Dean Winters (1964-)
Undercover Angel '99
Snipes '01
Hellraiser: Hellseeker '02
The Devil You Know '05
Winter of Frozen Dreams '08
Splinterheads '09
Today's Special '09
John Wick '14

Deborah Winters (1953-)
Kotch '71
Class of '44 '73
Tarantulas: The Deadly Cargo '77
Blue Sunshine '78

Jonathan Winters (1925-2013)
It's a Mad, Mad, Mad, Mad World '63
The Loved One '65
The Russians Are Coming, the Russians Are Coming '66
Eight on the Lam '67
Viva Max '69
The Fish that Saved Pittsburgh '79
More Wild, Wild West '80
Alice in Wonderland '85
The Longshot '86
Moon over Parador '88
The Flintstones '94
The Shadow '94
The Thief and the Cobbler '96 (V)
The Adventures of Rocky & Bullwinkle '00
Comic Book: The Movie '04
National Lampoon Presents Cattle Call '06
The Smurfs '11 (V)
The Smurfs 2 '13 (V)

Kristoffer Ryan Winters (1973-)
Hot Blooded '98
Fair Game '10
Judy Moody and the Not Bummer Summer '11

Roland Winters (1904-89)
The Chinese Ring '47
Docks of New Orleans '48
The Golden Eye '48
Kidnapped '48
Shanghai Chest '48
Abbott and Costello Meet the Killer, Boris Karloff '49
A Dangerous Profession '49
Malaya '49
Guilty of Treason '50
To Please a Lady '50
The Underworld Story '50
The West Point Story '50
She's Working Her Way Through College '52
Jet Pilot '57
Top Secret Affair '57
Cash McCall '60
The Iceman Cometh '60
Everything's Ducky '61
Blue Hawaii '62
Loving '70

Shelley Winters (1922-2006)
A Double Life '47
The Gangster '47
Cry of the City '48
Winchester '73 '50
A Place in the Sun '51
Behave Yourself! '52
My Man and I '52
Phone Call from a Stranger '52
Executive Suite '54
Saskatchewan '54
The Big Knife '55
I Died a Thousand Times '55
Mambo '55
The Night of the Hunter '55
The Diary of Anne Frank '59
Odds Against Tomorrow '59
The Young Savages '61
The Chapman Report '62
Lolita '62
The Balcony '63
The Greatest Story Ever Told '65
A Patch of Blue '65
Alfie '66
Harper '66
The Scalphunters '68
Wild in the Streets '68
The Mad Room '69
Bloody Mama '70
Flap '70
What's the Matter with Helen? '71
Who Slew Auntie Roo? '71
Diamonds '72
The Poseidon Adventure '72
Blume in Love '73
Cleopatra Jones '73
Poor Pretty Eddie '73
Next Stop, Greenwich Village '76
The Tenant '76
Pete's Dragon '77
Tentacles '77
Initiation of Sarah '78
King of the Gypsies '78
Elvis: The Movie '79
The French Atlantic Affair '79
The Visitor '80
S.O.B. '81
Fanny Hill '83
Deja Vu '84
Ellie '84
Alice in Wonderland '85
Delta Force '86
An Unremarkable Life '89
Superstar: The Life and Times of Andy Warhol '90
The Pickle '93
Heavy '94
Jury Duty '95
Portrait of a Lady '96

Jane Winton (1905-59)
The Patsy '28
Hell's Angels '30

Anna Wintour (1949-)
The September Issue '09
Mademoiselle C '13

Estelle Winwood (1883-1984)
Quality Street '37
The Glass Slipper '55
The Swan '56
23 Paces to Baker Street '56
Darby O'Gill & the Little People '59
The Misfits '61
The Magic Sword '62
The Notorious Landlady '62
Dead Ringer '64
Games '67
The Producers '68
Murder by Death '76

Scott Wiper (1970-)
A Better Way to Die '00
Landspeed '01
Dark Descent '02

Billy Wirth (1962-)
The Lost Boys '87
Red Shoe Diaries '92
Body Snatchers '93
Final Mission '93
The Fence '94
A Good Day to Die '95
Venus Rising '95
Last Lives '98
Relax. . . It's Just Sex! '98
Me & Will '99
The Drone Virus '04
The Talent Given Us '04
7 Mummies '06
Echoes '15

Robert Wisden
Impolite '92
The Disappearance of Vonnie '94
Captains Courageous '95
Excess Baggage '96
Outrage '98
The Snow Queen '02
A Date With Darkness '03
Above and Beyond '06
Lost Behind Bars '06
Ruslan '09

Norman Wisdom (1915-2010)
Trouble in Store '53
The Square Peg '58
The Night They Raided Minsky's '69
What's Good for the Goose '69

Robert Wisdom (1953-)
Sahara '95
Dancing at the Blue Iguana '00
Storytelling '01
Coastlines '02
Duplex '03
Live from Baghdad '03
Barbershop 2: Back in Business '04
Crazy Like a Fox '04
The Forgotten '04
Haven '04
Killer Diller '04
Ray '04
Mozart and the Whale '05
The Hawk Is Dying '06
Sex and Death 101 '07
The Loft '14

Tom Wisdom (1973-)
300 '07
Fire & Ice: The Dragon Chronicles '08
The Sisterhood of the Traveling Pants 2 '08
The Lightkeepers '09
Pirate Radio '09
Romeo & Juliet '13

DeWanda Wise
Firelight '12
Someone Great '19

Greg Wise (1966-)
The Buccaneers '95
Feast of July '95
Sense and Sensibility '95
The Moonstone '97
Sirens '02
Johnny English '03
Cranford '08
The Disappeared '08
Place of Execution '09
Return to Cranford '09
A Private War '18

Ray Wise (1947-)
Swamp Thing '82
The Journey of Natty Gann '85
RoboCop '87
Bob Roberts '92
Twin Peaks: Fire Walk with Me '92
Body Shot '93
The Chase '93
The Ghost Brigade '93
Rising Sun '93
Powder '95
Landspeed '01
Two Can Play That Game '01
The Battle of Shaker Heights '03
Jeepers Creepers 2 '03
Good Night, and Good Luck '05
Cyxork 7 '06
Peaceful Warrior '06
American East '07
The Flock '07
Strike '07
One Missed Call '08
Infestation '09
Pandemic '09
Stuntmen '09
The Aggression Scale '12
Crazy Eyes '12
Excision '12
No God, No Master '12
Tim and Eric's Billion Dollar Movie '12
Night of the Living Deb '14

William Wise (1970-)
Farewell to the King '89
In the Bedroom '01
Thirteen Conversations About One Thing '01

Joseph Wiseman (1918-2009)
Detective Story '51
Viva Zapata! '52
The Silver Chalice '54
The Prodigal '55
The Garment Jungle '57
The Unforgiven '60
The Happy Thieves '61
Dr. No '62
Bye Bye Braverman '67
Lawman '71
Pursuit '72
The Valachi Papers '72
Zalmen or the Madness of God '75
Jaguar Lives '79
Seize the Day '86

Andreas Wisniewski (1959-)
The Living Daylights '87
Urban Ghost Story '98

Googie Withers (1917-2011)
Accused '36
The Lady Vanishes '38
One of Our Aircraft Is Missing '41
The Silver Fleet '43
On Approval '44
Dead of Night '45
It Always Rains on Sunday '47
Miranda '48
Night and the City '50
Derby Day '52
Northanger Abbey '87
Country Life '95
Shine '95

Grant Withers (1904-59)
Other Men's Women '31
The Red-Haired Alibi '32
Tailspin Tommy '34
Fighting Marines '36
Let's Sing Again '36
Radio Patrol '37
Mr. Wong, Detective '38
Mr. Wong in Chinatown '39
Mystery of Mr. Wong '39
Doomed to Die '40
The Fatal Hour '40
Tomboy '40
Billy the Kid '41
Fighting Seabees '44
My Darling Clementine '46
Gunfighters '47
Tycoon '47
The Fighting Kentuckian '49
Bells of Coronado '50
Trigger, Jr. '50
Oklahoma Annie '51
Hoodlum Empire '52
Run for Cover '55

Jane Withers (1926-)
Bright Eyes '34
The Farmer Takes a Wife '35
Paddy O'Day '35
Little Miss Nobody '36
Rascals '38
High School '40
Giant '56
The Right Approach '61
Captain Newman, M.D. '63

Cora Witherspoon (1890-1957)
Libeled Lady '36
On the Avenue '37
Personal Property '37
Quality Street '37
Just Around the Corner '38
Marie Antoinette '38
Three Loves Has Nancy '38
The Bank Dick '40
Charlie Chan's Murder Cruise '40
Colonel Effingham's Raid '45
Just for You '52

Jimmy Witherspoon (1921-97)
Black Godfather '74
Georgia '95

John Witherspoon (1942-2019)
Killer Tomatoes Strike Back '90
Boomerang '92
Friday '95
Vampire in Brooklyn '95
Sprung '96
I Got the Hook-Up '98
Ride '98
The Ladies Man '00
Next Friday '00
Friday After Next '02
Little Man '06
The Hustle '08

Reese Witherspoon (1976-)
The Man in the Moon '91
Wildflower '91
A Far Off Place '93
Jack the Bear '93
Return to Lonesome Dove '93
S.F.W. '94
Freeway '95
Fear '96
Overnight Delivery '96
Cruel Intentions '98
Pleasantville '98
Twilight '98
American Psycho '99
Best Laid Plans '99
Election '99
Little Nicky '00
Legally Blonde '01
The Trumpet of the Swan '01 (V)
The Importance of Being Earnest '02
Sweet Home Alabama '02
Legally Blonde 2: Red White & Blonde '03
Vanity Fair '04
Just like Heaven '05
Walk the Line '05
Penelope '06
Rendition '07
Four Christmases '08
Monsters vs. Aliens '09 (V)
How Do You Know '10
Water for Elephants '11
Mud '12
This Means War '12
Devil's Knot '14
The Good Lie '14
Inherent Vice '14
Wild '14
Hot Pursuit '15
Sing '16
Home Again '17
A Wrinkle in Time '18

Glenn Withrow (1953-)
Lady in Red '79
The Hollywood Knights '80
Naked Lie '89

Michael Witney (1931-83)
The Way West '67
Darling Lili '70

Alicia Witt (1975-)
Bodies, Rest & Motion '93
The Disappearance of Vonnie '94
Fun '94
Four Rooms '95
Mr. Holland's Opus '95
Citizen Ruth '96
Bongwater '98
Urban Legend '98
Cecil B. Demented '00
Playing Mona Lisa '00
Vanilla Sky '01
Two Weeks Notice '02
Dark Kingdom: The Dragon King '04
The Upside of Anger '05
Last Holiday '06
Blue Smoke '07
88 Minutes '08
Peep World '10
Joint Body '11
Bending the Rules '12
Cowgirls 'n Angels '12
Cold Turkey '13
I Do '13
A Snow Globe Christmas '13
A Very Merry Mix-Up '13

Kathryn Witt (1950-)
Demon of Paradise '87
The Silence of the Lambs '91
Trapped in Paradise '94
Buffalo Girls '95

Michael Wittenborn
Yella '07
Toni Erdmann '16

Karen Witter (1961-)
Buried Alive '89
Popcorn '89
The Vineyard '89

Meg Wittner
Higher Ground '88
Born Yesterday '93

Finn Wittrock
Halloweentown High '04
Unbroken '14
My All American '15
Judy '19
Semper Fi '19

Sam Witwer (1977-)
The Return of Joe Rich '11
No God, No Master '12

Tom Wlaschiha
No One Sleeps '01
Christopher and His Kind '11

James Wlcek
Don't Tell '05
Hydra '09

David Wohl (1953-)
Armed and Dangerous '86
Chillers '88
Saving Private Ryan '98
Joe Gould's Secret '00
The Wackness '08

Johanna Wokalek (1975-)
Aimee & Jaguar '98
The Baader Meinhof Complex '08
North Face '08

Fred Wolf (1964-)
Black Sheep '96
Dirty Work '97

Hillary Wolf (1977-)
Big Girls Don't Cry. . . They Get Even '92
Home Alone 2: Lost in New York '92

Kelly Wolf
Triumph of the Spirit '89
Graveyard Shift '90
A Day in October '92

Scott Wolf (1968-)
Double Dragon '94
The Evening Star '96
White Squall '96
Go '99
Killing Emmett Young '02

Sheldon Peters Wolfchild
Miracle in the Wilderness '91
The Scarlet Letter '95

Ashley Wolfe
Tricks of a Woman '08
Immigration Tango '11

Collette Wolfe (1980-)
Young Adult '11
The Babymakers '12

David Wolfe (1915-94)
The Undercover Man '49
Kansas Raiders '50
Five Fingers '52
Salt of the Earth '54

Ian Wolfe (1896-1992)
The Barretts of Wimpole Street '34
Mutiny on the Bounty '35
Mrs. Miniver '42
The White Cliffs of Dover '44
Zombies on Broadway '44
Bedlam '45
The Judge Steps Out '49
The Magnificent Yankee '50
The Great Caruso '51
The Actress '53
Houdini '53
Moonfleet '55
Witness for the Prosecution '57
Diary of a Madman '63
One Man's Way '63
Games '67

Jim Wolfe
Chillers '88
Invasion of the Space Preachers '90

Traci Wolfe (1961-)
Lethal Weapon '87
Lethal Weapon 2 '89
Lethal Weapon 3 '92
Lethal Weapon 4 '98

Alex Wolff (1997-)
A Birder's Guide to Everything *'14*
My Friend Dahmer *'17*
Hereditary *'18*
The House of Tomorrow *'18*
Austin Wolff
A Death in the Family *'02*
Master of Disguise *'02*
13 Moons *'02*
Frank Wolff (1928-71)
The Wasp Woman *'59*
Atlas *'60*
The Awful Dr. Orloff *'62*
America America *'63*
Ringo's Mark of Vengeance *'67*
Villa Rides *'68*
The Lickerish Quartet *'70*
When Women Had Tails *'70*
Caliber 9 *'72*
Nat Wolff (1994-)
Peace, Love & Misunderstanding *'11*
Stuck in Love *'12*
Admission *'13*
The Fault In Our Stars *'14*
Palo Alto *'14*
Paper Towns *'15*
Leap! *'16*
Home Again *'17*
In Dubious Battle *'17*
Semper Fi *'19*
Finn Wolfhard
It *'17*
Dog Days *'18*
Donald Wolfit (1902-68)
The Silent Passenger *'35*
Svengali *'55*
Satellite in the Sky *'56*
The Accursed *'57*
Blood of the Vampire *'58*
The House of the Seven Hawks *'59*
Room at the Top *'59*
The Rough and the Smooth *'59*
The Hands of Orlac *'60*
The Mark *'61*
Lawrence of Arabia *'62*
Becket *'64*
The Charge of the Light Brigade *'68*
Decline and Fall...of a Birdwatcher *'68*
Wolfman Jack (1938-95)
A Session with The Committee *'68*
American Graffiti *'73*
Motel Hell *'80*
Mortuary Academy *'91*
Louis Wolheim (1880-1931)
Dr. Jekyll and Mr. Hyde *'20*
Sherlock Holmes *'22*
Little Old New York *'23*
America *'24*
Across to Singapore *'28*
Tempest *'28*
All Quiet on the Western Front *'30*
Danger Lights *'30*
The Silver Horde *'30*
James Wolk (1985-)
You Again *'10*
For a Good Time, Call... *'12*
Always Woodstock *'15*
Deborah Ann Woll (1985-)
Mother's Day *'10*
Catch.44 *'11*
Seven Days in Utopia *'11*
Someday This Pain Will Be Useful to You *'11*
Escape Room *'19*
Kirk B.R. Woller (1962-)
Killer Me *'01*
Hometown Legend *'02*
Boa *vs.* Python *'04*
Locusts: The 8th Plague *'05*
Midnight Clear *'06*
Urban Justice *'07*
The Least of These *'08*
Like Dandelion Dust *'09*
Love's Everlasting Courage *'11*
Sven Wollter (1934-)
The Sacrifice *'86*
The 13th Warrior *'99*
Kira's Reason-A Love Story *'01*
A Song for Martin *'01*
Stevie Wonder (1950-)
Bikini Beach *'64*
Muscle Beach Party *'64*
Pavarotti *'19*
Stevie (Steveland Morris) Wonder (1950-)
See Stevie Wonder
Anna May Wong (1905-61)
Peter Pan *'24*
The Thief of Baghdad *'24*
Mr. Wu *'27*
Old San Francisco *'27*
Across to Singapore *'28*
Piccadilly *'29*
Shanghai Express *'32*
A Study in Scarlet *'33*
Tiger Bay *'33*
Impact *'49*
Portrait in Black *'60*
Anthony Wong (1961-)
Full Contact *'92*
Hard-Boiled *'92*
The Heroic Trio *'93*
Organized Crime & Triad Bureau *'93*
Beast Cops *'98*
The Mission *'99*
Time and Tide *'00*
Infernal Affairs *'02*
The Matrix Revolutions *'03*
The Medallion *'03*
Vampire Effect *'03*
The Painted Veil *'06*
The Mummy: Tomb of the Dragon Emperor *'08*
The Four *'12*
Barbara Jean Wong (1924-99)
The Chinese Ring *'47*
Man from Button Willow *'65 (V)*
B.D. Wong (1960-)
The Freshman *'90*
Father of the Bride *'91*
Mystery Date *'91*
And the Band Played On *'93 (C)*
Jurassic Park *'93*
Men of War *'94*
Father of the Bride Part 2 *'95*
Executive Decision *'96*
Seven Years in Tibet *'97*
Slappy and the Stinkers *'97*
The Substitute 2: School's Out *'97*
Mulan *'98 (V)*
The Salton Sea *'02*
Mulan 2 *'04 (V)*
Stay *'05*
Marco Polo *'07*
White Frog *'12*
The Normal Heart *'14*
Focus *'15*
The Space Between Us *'17*
Benedict Wong (1970-)
Dirty Pretty Things *'03*
State of Play *'03*
On a Clear Day *'05*
Sunshine *'07*
Moon *'09*
Redemption *'13*
Doctor Strange *'16*
Annihilation *'18*
Gemini Man *'19*
Ellen Wong
Scott Pilgrim *vs.* the World *'10*
Silent Night *'12*
The Void *'17*
Faye Wong (1969-)
Chungking Express *'95*
Chinese Odyssey 2002 *'02*
2046 *'04*
Michael Wong (1965-)
Legacy of Rage *'86*
Royal Warriors *'86*
The Vineyard *'89*
Once a Thief *'96*
Beast Cops *'98*
Knock Off *'98*
House of Fury *'05*
Seven Swords *'07*
Nelson Wong
My Silent Partner *'06*
Shock to the System *'06*
Ice Blues: A Donald Strachey Mystery *'08*
On the Other Hand, Death *'08*
Russell Wong (1963-)
Tai-Pan *'86*
Eat a Bowl of Tea *'89*
China Cry *'91*
New Jack City *'91*
The Joy Luck Club *'93*
The Prophecy 2: Ashtown *'97*
Romeo Must Die *'00*
The Lost Empire *'01*
Twisted *'04*
Inside Out *'05*
Honor *'06*
Dim Sum Funeral *'08*
The Mummy: Tomb of the Dragon Emperor *'08*
The Sanctuary *'09*
Contract to Kill *'16*
Victor Wong (1927-2001)
Dim Sum: A Little Bit of Heart *'85*
Big Trouble in Little China *'86*
The Golden Child *'86*
The Last Emperor *'87*
Prince of Darkness *'87*
Eat a Bowl of Tea *'89*
Tremors *'89*
3 Ninjas *'92*
The Ice Runner *'93*
The Joy Luck Club *'93*
3 Ninjas Kick Back *'94*
3 Ninjas Knuckle Up *'95*
Seven Years in Tibet *'97*
3 Ninjas: High Noon at Mega Mountain *'97*
Petchthai Wongkamlao (1965-)
Ong-Bak *'03*
The Bodyguard *'04*
The Bodyguard 2 *'07*
Arthur Wontner (1875-1960)
The Triumph of Sherlock Holmes *'35*
Murder at the Baskervilles *'37*
Genevieve *'53*
John Woo (1946-)
A Better Tomorrow, Part 1 *'86*
A Bullet in the Head *'90*
Hard-Boiled *'92*
Twin Dragons *'92*
Andy Wood
Ghostwarrior *'86*
Brain Dead *'89*
Eye of the Eagle 2 *'89*
Clive Wood (1954-)
Treasure Island *'89*
The Crucifer of Blood *'91*
The Lion in Winter *'03*
P.D. James: Death in Holy Orders *'03*
Cynthia Wood (1950-)
Apocalypse Now *'79*
Van Nuys Blvd. *'79*
David Wood (1944-)
If. . . *'69*
Tales That Witness Madness *'73*
Edward D. Wood, Jr. (1924-78)
Glen or Glenda? *'53*
Plan 9 from Outer Space *'56*
Elijah Wood (1981-)
Back to the Future, Part 2 *'89*
Avalon *'90*
Internal Affairs *'90*
Paradise *'91*
Forever Young *'92*
Radio Flyer *'92*
The Adventures of Huck Finn *'93*
The Good Son *'93*
The War *'94*
Flipper *'96*
The Ice Storm *'97*
Oliver Twist *'97*
The Bumblebee Flies Anyway *'98*
Deep Impact *'98*
The Faculty *'98*
Black and White *'99*
Chain of Fools *'00*
Lord of the Rings: The Fellowship of the Ring *'01*
All I Want *'02*
Ash Wednesday *'02*
Lord of the Rings: The Two Towers *'02*
Lord of the Rings: The Return of the King *'03*
Spy Kids 3-D: Game Over *'03*
Eternal Sunshine of the Spotless Mind *'04*
Everything is Illuminated *'05*
Green Street Hooligans *'05*
Sin City *'05*
Bobby *'06*
Happy Feet *'06 (V)*
Paris, je t'aime *'06*
Day Zero *'07*
The Oxford Murders *'08*
9 *'09 (V)*
The Romantics *'10*
Happy Feet Two *'11 (V)*
Celeste & Jesse Forever *'12*
The Hobbit: An Unexpected Journey *'12*
Maniac *'12*
Revenge for Jolly! *'12*
Treasure Island *'12*
Grand Piano *'13*
Cooties *'14*
Open Windows *'14*
The Last Witch Hunter *'15*
The Trust *'16*
I Don't Feel at Home in This World Anymore *'17*
Come to Daddy *'20*
Evan Rachel Wood (1987-)
Digging to China *'98*
Little Secrets *'02*
Simone *'02*
The Missing *'03*
Thirteen *'03*
Down in the Valley *'05*
Pretty Persuasion *'05*
The Upside of Anger *'05*
Running with Scissors *'06*
Across the Universe *'07*
King of California *'07*
The Life Before Her Eyes *'07*
The Wrestler *'08*
Battle for Terra *'09 (V)*
Whatever Works *'09*
The Conspirator *'10*
The Ides of March *'11*
Mildred Pierce *'11*
A Case of You *'13*
Charlie Countryman *'13*
Barefoot *'14*
Strange Magic *'15 (V)*
Into the Forest *'16*
Frank Wood (1960-)
Thirteen Days *'00*
King of the Corner *'04*
Flakes *'07*
The Missing Person *'09*
Greetings from Tim Buckley *'12*
Gary Wood
Hardbodies *'84*
Martial Outlaw *'93*
G(eorge) Wood (1920-2000)
M*A*S*H *'70*
Harold and Maude *'71*
Bank Shot *'74*
Helen Wood
Charlie Chan at the Race Track *'36*
Give a Girl a Break *'53*
Janet Wood
Angels Hard As They Come *'71*
G.I. Executioner *'71*
Terror at Red Wolf Inn *'72*
Slumber Party '57 *'76*
Girl Meets Boy *'13*
John Wood (1930-2011)
Stolen Face *'52*
Postman's Knock *'62*
Just for Fun *'63*
One More Time *'70*
WarGames *'83*
Ladyhawke *'85*
The Purple Rose of Cairo *'85*
Jumpin' Jack Flash *'86*
Orlando *'92*
Shadowlands *'93*
The Young Americans *'93*
The Madness of King George *'94*
Uncovered *'94*
Citizen X *'95*
Richard III *'95*
Sabrina *'95*
Jane Eyre *'96*
The Gambler *'97*
The Avengers *'98*
Sweet Revenge *'98*
An Ideal Husband *'99*
Chocolat *'00*
The Little Vampire *'00*
Longitude *'00*
The Body *'01*
Goodbye, Mr. Chips *'02*
Napoleon *'03*
Imagining Argentina *'04*
The White Countess *'05*
John Lisbon Wood
KISS Meets the Phantom of the Park *'78*
Alligator *'80*
Karen Wood
Scalps *'83*
Loose Screws *'85*
Lana Wood (1946-)
The Searchers *'56*
Five Finger Exercise *'62*
Black Water Gold *'69*
The Over-the-Hill Gang Rides Again *'70*
Diamonds Are Forever *'71*
Grayeagle *'77*
Captain America 2: Death Too Soon *'79*
Justin Morgan Had a Horse *'81*
Demon Rage *'82*
Lawrence Wood
Scum of the Earth *'63*
Something Weird *'68*
Natalie Wood (1938-81)
The Bride Wore Boots *'46*
Tomorrow Is Forever *'46*
The Ghost and Mrs. Muir *'47*
Miracle on 34th Street *'47*
Chicken Every Sunday *'48*
The Green Promise *'49*
The Jackpot *'50*
No Sad Songs For Me *'50*
Just for You *'52*
The Star *'52*
The Silver Chalice *'54*
One Desire *'55*
Rebel without a Cause *'55*
The Burning Hills *'56*
The Girl He Left Behind *'56*
The Searchers *'56*
Bombers B-52 *'57*
Kings Go Forth *'58*
Marjorie Morningstar *'58*
Cash McCall *'60*
Splendor in the Grass *'61*
West Side Story *'61*
Gypsy *'62*
Sex and the Single Girl *'64*
The Great Race *'65*
Inside Daisy Clover *'65*
This Property Is Condemned *'66*
Bob & Carol & Ted & Alice *'69*
The Affair *'73*
Meteor *'79*
The Last Married Couple in America *'80*
Brainstorm *'83*
Peggy Wood (1892-1978)
The Right to Live *'35*
Call It a Day *'37*
The Bride Wore Boots *'46*
Magnificent Doll *'46*
The Story of Ruth *'60*
The Sound of Music *'65*
Flickers *'80*
Thomas Wood (1927-89)
See William Kerwin
Tom Wood (1963-)
Bushwhacked *'95*
Ulee's Gold *'97*
U.S. Marshals *'98*
Ty Wood
Maneater *'07*
The Haunting in Connecticut *'09*
Victoria Wood
Mr. Toad's Wild Ride *'96*
Ballet Shoes *'07*
Alfre Woodard (1952-)
Freedom Road *'79*
The Ambush Murders *'82*
Cross Creek *'83*
Code of Honor *'84*
Go Tell It on the Mountain *'84*
Words by Heart *'84*
Extremities *'86*
Unnatural Causes *'86*
Mandela *'87*
Scrooged *'88*
Miss Firecracker *'89*
Grand Canyon *'91*
The Gun in Betty Lou's Handbag *'92*
Passion Fish *'92*
Bopha! *'93*
Heart and Souls *'93*
Rich in Love *'93*
Blue Chips *'94*
Crooklyn *'94*
The Piano Lesson *'94*
Race to Freedom: The Story of the Underground Railroad *'94*
Gulliver's Travels *'95*
How to Make an American Quilt *'95*
Primal Fear *'96*
Star Trek: First Contact *'96*
Miss Evers' Boys *'97*
Down in the Delta *'98*
Mumford *'99*
Dinosaur *'00 (V)*
Holiday Heart *'00*
Love and Basketball *'00*
What's Cooking? *'00*
K-PAX *'01*
The Wild Thornberrys Movie *'02 (V)*
The Core *'03*
Radio *'03*
The Singing Detective *'03*
The Forgotten *'04*
Beauty Shop *'05*
Something New *'06*
Take the Lead *'06*
Pictures of Hollis Woods *'07*
The Family That Preys *'08*
Reach for Me *'08*
American Violet *'09*
Steel Magnolias *'12*
12 Years a Slave *'13*
Annabelle *'14*
Knucklehead *'15*
Mississippi Grind *'15*
Burning Sands *'17*
So B. It *'17*
Clemency *'19*
Juanita *'19*

The Lion King '19
Saint Judy '19

Charlaine Woodard (1953-)
Crackers '84
God Bless the Child '88
He Said, She Said '91
One Good Cop '91
Buffalo Girls '95
The Crucible '96
Around the Fire '98
The Million Dollar Hotel '99
Unbreakable '00
Sunshine State '02

Bokeem Woodbine (1973-)
Strapped '93
Jason's Lyric '94
Dead Presidents '95
Freeway '95
Panther '95
The Rock '96
Almost Heroes '97
The Big Hit '98
Caught Up '98
Wishmaster 2: Evil Never Dies '98
Blackmale '99
It's the Rage '99
Life '99
The Runner '99
Sacrifice '00
The Breed '01
Hard Cash '01
3000 Miles to Graceland '01
Sniper 2 '02
Jasper, Texas '03
Ray '04
Edmond '05
18 Fingers of Death '05
The Butcher '07
The Last Sentinel '07
The Fifth Commandment '08
Black Dynamite '09
A Day in the Life '09
The Poker House '09
Across the Line: The Exodus of Charlie Wright '10
Devil '10
Flesh Wounds '10
Total Recall '12
Riddick '13
Jarhead 2: Field of Fire '14
In the Shadow of the Moon '19
Queen & Slim '19

George Woodbridge (1907-73)
The Fallen Idol '49
The Reptile '66

Danny Woodburn (1964-)
Things You Can Tell Just by Looking at Her '00
Death to Smoochy '02
Employee of the Month '06
Santa Buddies '09
The Search for Santa Paws '10
Santa Paws 2: The Santa Pups '12
30 Nights of Paranormal Activity with the Devil Inside the Girl with the Dragon Tattoo '12
Teenage Mutant Ninja Turtles '14

Eric Woodburn
The Innocents '61
Trial & Error '62

Joan Woodbury (1915-89)
Rogue's Tavern '36
Charlie Chan on Broadway '37
Forty Naughty Girls '37
Gangs, Inc. '41
King of the Zombies '41
Paper Bullets '41
I Killed That Man '42
Yank in Libya '42
The Chinese Cat '44
Flame of the West '45
Northwest Trail '46

Jo Woodcock (1988-)
Tess of the D'Urbervilles '08
Collision '09
Land Girls '09

Margo Woode (1942-)
It Shouldn't Happen to a Dog '46
Somewhere in the Night '46
Hell Bound '57
Iron Angel '64

Pat(ricia) Woodell (1944-)
The Big Doll House '71
Twilight People '72

Nicholas Woodeson (1949-)
The Blackheath Poisonings '92
The Man Who Knew Too Little '97
Dreaming of Joseph Lees '99
Great Expectations '99
Conspiracy '01
Hannah Arendt '12
The Hustle '19

Albie Woodington
The 13th Warrior '99
The Count of Monte Cristo '02
The Hitchhiker's Guide to the Galaxy '05

Lauren Woodland (1977-)
Alien Nation: Dark Horizon '94
Alien Nation: Body and Soul '95
Alien Nation: Millennium '96
Alien Nation: The Enemy Within '96
The Doorway '00

Holly Woodlawn (1946-)
Trash '70
Is There Sex After Death? '71
Superstar: The Life and Times of Andy Warhol '90
Twin Falls Idaho '99
Milwaukee, Minnesota '03

Shailene Woodley (1991-)
A Place Called Home '04
The Descendants '11
The Spectacular Now '13
Divergent '14
The Fault In Our Stars '14
White Bird in a Blizzard '14
Insurgent '15
Allegiant '16
Snowden '16
Adrift '18
Endings, Beginnings '20

Bert Woodruff (1856-1934)
Paths to Paradise '25
Spring Fever '27
Speedy '28

Blake Woodruff (1995-)
Cheaper by the Dozen '03
Back to You and Me '05
Whisper '07

Largo Woodruff
Bill '81
Coward of the County '81
The Funhouse '81
Bill: On His Own '83

Barbara Alyn Woods (1962-)
Circuitry Man '90
Eden '93
Ghoulies 4 '93
The Wild Card '03
I Downloaded a Ghost '04

Christine Woods
The One I Wrote For You '14
I Don't Feel at Home in This World Anymore '17
Paddleton '19
Stray '19

Craig Woods
Career Girl '44
Fort Defiance '51

Donald Woods (1909-98)
Fog Over Frisco '34
The Case of the Curious Bride '35
Frisco Kid '35
Stranded '35
A Tale of Two Cities '36
The Case of the Stuttering Bishop '37
The Black Doll '38
Danger on the Air '38
The Girl From Mexico '39
If I Had My Way '40
Mexican Spitfire '40
The Mexican Spitfire Out West '40
Corregidor '43
Watch on the Rhine '43
The Bridge of San Luis Rey '44
Enemy of Women '44
Roughly Speaking '45
Never Say Goodbye '46
Bells of San Fernando '47
The Lost Volcano '50
The Beast from 20,000 Fathoms '53
13 Ghosts '60
Door to Door Maniac '61
Kissin' Cousins '64
True Grit '69

Edward (Eddie) Woods (1903-89)
Mothers Cry '30
Public Enemy '31
Hot Saturday '32
Tarzan the Fearless '33
Navy Blues '37

Harry Woods (1889-1968)
The Viking '28
Monkey Business '31
Belle of the Nineties '34
Rustlers of Red Dog '35
Savage Fury '35
Last Outlaw '36
Beau Geste '39
Winners of the West '40
Flame of the West '45
West of the Pecos '45
Colorado Territory '49
She Wore a Yellow Ribbon '49

James Woods (1947-)
Hickey & Boggs '72
The Way We Were '73
The Gambler '74
Night Moves '75
The Choirboys '77
Holocaust '78
The Black Marble '79
The Incredible Journey of Dr. Meg Laurel '79
The Onion Field '79
Eyewitness '81
Fast Walking '82
Videodrome '83
Against All Odds '84
Once Upon a Time in America '84
Cat's Eye '85
Promise '86
Salvador '86
Best Seller '87
The Boost '88
Cop '88
Immediate Family '89
My Name Is Bill W. '89
True Believer '89
The Gift of Love '90
Women & Men: Stories of Seduction '90
The Hard Way '91
In Love and War '91
Chaplin '92
Citizen Cohn '92
Diggstown '92
Straight Talk '92
The Getaway '93
Curse of the Starving Class '94
The Specialist '94
Casino '95
For Better or Worse '95
Indictment: The McMartin Trial '95
Killer: A Journal of Murder '95
Nixon '95
Ghosts of Mississippi '96
Contact '97
Hercules '97 (V)
John Carpenter's Vampires '97
Kicked in the Head '97
Another Day in Paradise '98
Any Given Sunday '99
The General's Daughter '99
True Crime '99
The Virgin Suicides '99
Dirty Pictures '00
Final Fantasy: The Spirits Within '01 (V)
Race to Space '01
Riding in Cars with Boys '01
Scary Movie 2 '01
John Q '02
Stuart Little 2 '02 (V)
Northfork '03
Rudy: The Rudy Giulani Story '03
This Girl's Life '03
Be Cool '05
Pretty Persuasion '05
End Game '06
Surf's Up '07 (V)
Hellhounds '09
Straw Dogs '11
Too Big to Fail '11
Coma '12
Jobs '13
Mary and Martha '13
White House Down '13
Jamesy Boy '14

Michael Woods (1957-2006)
Agatha Christie's Sparkling Cyanide '83
War & Remembrance '88
War & Remembrance: The Final Chapter '89
Omen 4: The Awakening '91
Red Shoe Diaries: Swimming Naked '00
Rudy: The Rudy Giulani Story '03
Not My Life '06
Shock to the System '06
Demons from Her Past '07
Secrets of an Undercover Wife '07

Ren Woods (1958-)
The Brother from Another Planet '84
Hostage High '97

Robert Woods (1936-)
Four Dollars of Revenge '66
The Perverse Countess '73
White Fang and the Hunter '85

Simon Woods (1980-)
Pride and Prejudice '05
The Queen's Sister '05
Penelope '06
Cranford '08

DB Woodside (1969-)
The Temptations '98
More Dogs Than Bones '00
Romeo Must Die '00
The Inheritance '10
Paul Blart: Mall Cop 2 '15
The Man in 3B '16

Peter Woodthorpe (1931-2004)
The Evil of Frankenstein '64
The Skull '65
The Blue Max '66
The Charge of the Light Brigade '68

Kate Woodville (1938-2013)
Sex Through a Window '72
Posse '75
Computer Wizard '77
Where's Willie? '77

John Woodvine (1929-)
An American Werewolf in London '81
The Life and Adventures of Nicholas Nickleby '81
Agatha Christie's Murder with Mirrors '85
Edge of Darkness '86
Persuasion '95
The Other Boleyn Girl '03
Joe Maddison's War '10

Edward Woodward (1930-2009)
The File of the Golden Goose '69
The Bloodsuckers '70
Sitting Target '72
Young Winston '72
The Wicker Man '75
Breaker Morant '80
Champions '84
A Christmas Carol '84
King David '85
Hands of a Murderer '90
Mister Johnson '91
Gulliver's Travels '95
Five Days '07
Hot Fuzz '07
A Congregation of Ghosts '09

Joanne Woodward (1930-)
No Down Payment '57
The Three Faces of Eve '57
The Long, Hot Summer '58
Rally 'Round the Flag, Boys! '58
From the Terrace '60
The Fugitive Kind '60
Paris Blues '61
A New Kind of Love '63
A Big Hand for the Little Lady '66
A Fine Madness '66
Rachel, Rachel '68
Winning '69
WUSA '70
They Might Be Giants '71
Summer Wishes, Winter Dreams '73
The Drowning Pool '75
Sybil '76
The End '78
Harry & Son '84
The Glass Menagerie '87
Mr. & Mrs. Bridge '90
The Age of Innocence '93 (N)
Philadelphia '93
Empire Falls '05

Jonathan M. Woodward (1973-)
Wit '01
The Notorious Bettie Page '06

Morgan Woodward (1925-)
The Gun Hawk '63
Cool Hand Luke '67
Death of a Gunfighter '69
Running Wild '73
The Killing of a Chinese Bookie '76
The Longest Drive '76
Deadly Game '77
Walking Tall: The Final Chapter '77
Which Way Is Up? '77
Battle Beyond the Stars '80
Girls Just Want to Have Fun '85

Peter Woodward (1956-)
Testament of Youth '79
Hard Cash '01
Postman Pat: The Movie '14 (V)

Shannon Marie Woodward
The Haunting of Molly Hartley '08
The Shortcut '09
Ode to Joy '19

Tim Woodward (1953-)
The Europeans '79
Personal Services '87
Piece of Cake '88
The Scarlet Letter '95
Some Mother's Son '96
B. Monkey '97
Heat of the Sun '99
RKO 281 '99
K-19: The Widowmaker '02
Barstool Cowboy '08

Marjorie Woodworth (1919-2000)
Broadway Limited '41
Road Show '41

Emily Woof (1967-)
The Full Monty '96
Photographing Fairies '97
Velvet Goldmine '98
Passion '99
Oliver Twist '00
Pandaemonium '00
Wondrous Oblivion '06

Norman Wooland (1910-89)
Angel with the Trumpet '50
Madeleine '50
The Rough and the Smooth '59
Teenage Bad Girl '59
Saul and David '64

Susan Wooldridge (1952-)
The Jewel in the Crown '84
The Last Place on Earth '85
Hope and Glory '87
How to Get Ahead in Advertising '89

Sheb Wooley (1921-2003)
High Noon '52
Hoosiers '86

Charles Woolf (1927-94)
Private Parts '72
No Way Back '74

Eric Woolfe
The Strauss Family '73
Survival of the Dead '09

Fenella Woolgar (1969-)
Bright Young Things '03
Wah-Wah '05
Scoop '06
Jekyll '07
St. Trinian's '07

Monty Woolley (1888-1963)
Live, Love and Learn '37
Arsene Lupin Returns '38
Artists and Models Abroad '38
Everybody Sing '38
Three Comrades '38
Dancing Co-Ed '39
Never Say Die '39
The Man Who Came to Dinner '41
Life Begins at Eight-Thirty '42
Holy Matrimony '43
Irish Eyes Are Smiling '44
Since You Went Away '44
Night and Day '46
The Bishop's Wife '47
Miss Tatlock's Millions '48
As Young As You Feel '51

Susan Woolridge
Pinochet's Last Stand '06
Tamara Drewe '10

Robert Woolsey (1889-1938)
Rio Rita '29
Dixiana '30
Half-Shot at Sunrise '30
Hook, Line and Sinker '30
Caught Plastered '31
Cracked Nuts '31
Girl Crazy '32
Hold 'Em Jail '32
Kentucky Kernels '34
The Nitwits '35
The Rainmakers '35
Mummy's Boys '36
High Flyers '37
On Again-Off Again '37

Gordon Michael Woolvett (1970-)
The Legend of Gator Face '96
Bride of Chucky '98
The Highway Man '99
Everything's Gone Green '06
Secrets of an Undercover Wife '07

Jaimz Woolvett (1967-)
Unforgiven '92
The Pathfinder '96
Rosewood '96
Boogie Boy '98
Sanctuary '98
The Guilty '99
Rites of Passage '99

Tail Lights Fade '99
The Stepdaughter '00
Red Water '01
Under Heavy Fire '01
Power Play '02
Rock My World '02

Tom Wopat (1951-)
Burning Rage '84
Christmas Comes to Willow Creek '87
Bonneville '06
The Hive '08
Taking Chance '09
Main Street '10
Django Unchained '12

Hank Worden (1901-92)
Red River '48
The Searchers '56
The Horse Soldiers '59
The Alamo '60
True Grit '69
Zachariah '70
Smokey and the Bandit '77
Scream '83
Almost an Angel '90

Richard Wordsworth (1915-93)
The Quatermass Experiment '56
Time Without Pity '57

Jimmy Workman (1980-)
The Addams Family '91
Addams Family Values '93
As Good As It Gets '97

Jo Anne Worley (1937-)
Beauty and the Beast '91 (V)
A Goofy Movie '94 (V)

Frederick Worlock (1886-1973)
Miracles for Sale '39
Strange Cargo '40
The Woman in Green '49
101 Dalmatians '61 (V)

Kenny Wormald (1984-)
Center Stage: Turn It Up '08
Footloose '11
Kid Cannabis '14
Centerstage: On Pointe '16
Honey 3: Dare to Dance '16

Mary Woronov (1943-)
Silent Night, Bloody Night '73
Seizure '74
Cover Girl Models '75
Death Race 2000 '75
Cannonball '76
Hollywood Boulevard '76
Hollywood Man '76
Jackson County Jail '76
Sugar Cookies '77
The Movie House Massacre '78
Lady in Red '79
Rock 'n' Roll High School '79
Heartbeeps '81
Angel of H.E.A.T. '82
Eating Raoul '82
Get Crazy '83
Night of the Comet '84
Chopping Mall '86
Nomads '86
Terrorvision '86
Black Widow '87
Let It Ride '89
Club Fed '90
Mortuary Academy '91
Motorama '91
Rock 'n' Roll High School Forever '91
Warlock '91
Grief '94
Shake, Rattle & Rock! '94
Glory Daze '96
Invisible Mom '96
Sweet Jane '98
Invisible Mom 2 '99
The Devil's Rejects '05
The House of the Devil '09

Brian Worth (1914-78)
Murder on Approval '56
The Square Peg '58
The Terror of the Tongs '61

Constance Worth (1912-63)
Windjammer '37
Criminals Within '41
G-Men *vs.* the Black Dragon '43

Harry Worth (1903-75)
Lightnin' Bill Carson '36
Adventures of Red Ryder '40

Irene Worth (1916-2002)
The Scapegoat '59
Seven Seas to Calais '62
Eyewitness '81
Deathtrap '82
The Shell Seekers '89
Lost in Yonkers '93
Just the Ticket '98
Onegin '99

Lilian Worth
The Adventures of Tarzan '21
Tarzan the Tiger '29

Mike Worth (1965-)
Final Impact '91
Street Crimes '92
To Be the Best '93
U.S. Seals 2 '01

Nicholas Worth (1937-2007)
Doin' Time '85
Darkman '90
Blood & Concrete: A Love Story '91
Fist of Honor '92
Dark Angel: The Ascent '94
Plughead Rewired: Circuitry Man 2 '94
Dangerous Cargo '96
Something About Sex '98
Slaves of Hollywood '99

Sam Worthington (1976-)
Bootmen '00
Dirty Deeds '02
Hart's War '02
Somersault '04
Pros and Ex-cons '05
Macbeth '06
Rogue '07
Avatar '09
Terminator Salvation '09
Clash of the Titans '10
The Debt '10
Last Night '10
Texas Killing Fields '11
Man on a Ledge '12
Wrath of the Titans '12
Cake '14
Sabotage '14
The Keeping Room '15
Hacksaw Ridge '16
The Shack '17
Fractured '19

Eleanor Worthington-Cox (2001-)
Action Point '18
Gwen '19

Calum Worthy (1991-)
Bond of Silence '10
Daydream Nation '10
Bodied '17

Rick Worthy
The Magnificent Seven '98
Duplicity '09

Greg Wrangler
Barbarian Queen 2: The Empress Strikes Back '89

Fay Wray (1907-2004)
Blind Husbands '19
Doctor X '32
The Most Dangerous Game '32
The Vampire Bat '32
King Kong '33
Mystery of the Wax Museum '33
One Sunday Afternoon '33
The Evil Mind '34
Woman in the Shadows '34
It Happened in Hollywood '37
Adam Had Four Sons '41
Melody for Three '41
Small Town Girl '53
The Cobweb '55
Queen Bee '55
Rock, Pretty Baby '56
Crime of Passion '57
Tammy and the Bachelor '57
Gideon's Trumpet '80

John Wray (1887-1940)
All Quiet on the Western Front '30
Safe in Hell '31
The Woman From Monte Carlo '31
Miss Pinkerton '32
The Rich Are Always With Us '32
Green Eyes '34
You Only Live Once '37
A Man to Remember '38

Aloma Wright (1950-)
Trippin' '99
Johnson Family Vacation '04
The Gospel '05
Love and Other Four Letter Words '07

Amy Wright (1950-)
The Deer Hunter '78
Girlfriends '78
The Amityville Horror '79
Breaking Away '79
Wise Blood '79
Inside Moves '80
Stardust Memories '80
Trapped in Silence '86
The Accidental Tourist '88
Crossing Delancey '88
Miss Firecracker '89
Daddy's Dyin'. . . Who's Got the Will? '90
Deceived '91
Final Verdict '91
Love Hurts '91
Hard Promises '92
To Dance with the White Dog '93
Where the Rivers Flow North '94
The Scarlet Letter '95
Tom and Huck '95

Ben Wright
The Pharaoh's Curse '57
101 Dalmatians '61 (V)

Bonnie Wright (1991-)
Harry Potter and the Chamber of Secrets '02
Harry Potter and the Goblet of Fire '05
Harry Potter and the Order of the Phoenix '07
Harry Potter and the Half-Blood Prince '09
Harry Potter and the Deathly Hallows, Part 1 '10
Harry Potter and the Deathly Hallows, Part 2 '11

Carl Wright (1932-2007)
Soul Food '97
Big Momma's House '00
Barbershop 2: Back in Business '04

Edwin Wright
Slow West '15
Turbo Kid '15

Gabriella Wright
The Transporter Refueled '15
Septembers of Shiraz '16

Gunner Wright (1973-)
J. Edgar '11
Love '11

Janet Wright (1945-)
Beyond the Call '96
The Perfect Storm '00
Blackwoods '02
Emile '03
Wisegal '08
Ramona and Beezus '10

Jeffrey Wright (1965-)
Presumed Innocent '90
Basquiat '96
Critical Care '97
Celebrity '98
Cement '99
Ride with the Devil '99
Crime and Punishment in Suburbia '00
Hamlet '00
Shaft '00
Ali '01
Eye See You '01
Boycott '02
Angels in America '03
The Manchurian Candidate '04
Broken Flowers '05
Syriana '05
Casino Royale '06
Lady in the Water '06
Chicago 10 '07 (V)
The Invasion '07
Live Free or Die Hard '07
Cadillac Records '08
Quantum of Solace '08
W. '08
Extremely Loud and Incredibly Close '11
Source Code '11
Broken City '13
Ernest & Celestine '13 (V)
The Hunger Games: Catching Fire '13
The Inevitable Defeat of Mister & Pete '13
Only Lovers Left Alive '13
A Single Shot '13
The Hunger Games: Mockingjay--Part 1 '14
The Good Dinosaur '15
Hold the Dark '18
Age Out '19
The Goldfinch '19

Jenny Wright (1962-)
The Executioner's Song '82
Pink Floyd: The Wall '82
St. Elmo's Fire '85
Near Dark '87
The Chocolate War '88
I, Madman '89
Twister '89
A Shock to the System '90
Young Guns 2 '90
The Lawnmower Man '92

Katie Wright (1981-)
Hostage High '97
Too Smooth '98
Idle Hands '99

Ken Wright
Opposing Force '87
Prince of Darkness '87
Eye of the Eagle 3 '91

Maggie Wright
One More Time '70
Twins of Evil '71

Max Wright (1943-2019)
All That Jazz '79
Fraternity Vacation '85
Konrad '85
Touch and Go '86
The Shadow '94
White Mile '94
From the Earth to the Moon '98
Snow Falling on Cedars '99
William Shakespeare's A Midsummer Night's Dream '99

Michael Wright (1956-)
Streamers '83
The Principal '87
The Five Heartbeats '91
Sugar Hill '94
Money Talks '97
Point Blank '98
Pinero '01
The Interpreter '05
Jesse '11

N'Bushe Wright (1970-)
Zebrahead '92
Fresh '94
Dead Presidents '95
Blade '98
Three Strikes '00
Civil Brand '02
Widows '02

Nicholas Wright (1982-)
Prom Wars '08
Swamp Devil '08
Afghan Luke '11

Nicolas Wright
The Tipping Point '07
Girl's Best Friend '08

Patrick Wright (1939-)
The Abductors '72
If You Don't Stop It. . . You'll Go Blind '77

Peter Wright
Vera Drake '04
Womb '10

Robin Wright (1966-)
Hollywood Vice Sqaud '86
The Princess Bride '87
State of Grace '90
The Playboys '92
Toys '92
The Crossing Guard '94
Forrest Gump '94
Moll Flanders '96
She's So Lovely '97
Hurlyburly '98
Message in a Bottle '98
The Pledge '00
Unbreakable '00
How to Kill Your Neighbor's Dog '01
The Last Castle '01
White Oleander '02
The Singing Detective '03
Virgin '03
A Home at the End of the World '04
Empire Falls '05
Nine Lives '05
Sorry, Haters '05
Breaking and Entering '06
Beowulf '07 (V)
Hounddog '08
What Just Happened '08
A Christmas Carol '09 (V)
New York, I Love You '09
The Private Lives of Pippa Lee '09
State of Play '09
The Conspirator '10
The Girl With the Dragon Tattoo '11
Moneyball '11
Rampart '11
Adore '13
The Congress '13
A Most Wanted Man '14
Everest '15
Blade Runner 2049 '17
Wonder Woman '17

Samuel E. Wright (1946-)
Bird '88
The Little Mermaid '89 (V)
Dinosaur '00 (V)

Sarah Wright (1983-)
Touchback '11
21 & Over '13
Walk of Shame '14
American Made '17

Steven Wright (1955-)
Sledgehammer '83
Desperately Seeking Susan '85
Men of Respect '91
Reservoir Dogs '92 (V)
So I Married an Axe Murderer '93 (C)
Canadian Bacon '94
Natural Born Killers '94
The Swan Princess '94 (V)
Half-Baked '97
Babe: Pig in the City '98 (V)
1999 '98
The Muse '99
Loser '00
Coffee and Cigarettes '03
Son of the Mask '05
The Emoji Movie '17 (V)

Teresa Wright (1918-2005)
The Little Foxes '41
Mrs. Miniver '42
The Pride of the Yankees '42
Shadow of a Doubt '43
Casanova Brown '44
The Best Years of Our Lives '46
Pursued '47
Enchantment '48
The Capture '50
The Men '50
Something to Live For '52
The Steel Trap '52
The Actress '53
Track of the Cat '54
The Search for Bridey Murphy '56
The Restless Years '58
The Happy Ending '69
Flood! '76
Roseland '77
Somewhere in Time '80
Bill: On His Own '83
The Good Mother '88
John Grisham's The Rainmaker '97

Tom Wright (1952-)
Creepshow 2 '87
Tales from the Hood '95
Palmetto '98
The Pentagon Wars '98
Barbershop '02
P.S. Your Cat is Dead! '02
Sunshine State '02
The Gunman '03

Tony Wright (1925-86)
Bad Blonde '53
The Beasts of Marseilles '57
The Spaniard's Curse '58
The Rough and the Smooth '59

Tracy Wright (1959-2010)
When Night Is Falling '95
Last Night '98
Trigger '10

Trevor Wright (1982-)
MXP: Most Xtreme Primate '03
Air Bud 6: Air Buddies '06
Shelter '07
Vacancy 2: The First Cut '08

Whittni Wright (1987-)
I'll Do Anything '93
Sudden Death '95

Will Wright (1891-1962)
Whispering Smith '48
Miss Grant Takes Richmond '49
They Live by Night '49
The Wayward Bus '57
Alias Jesse James '59

William Wright (1911-49)
A Night to Remember '42
The Mask of Diijon '46

Robin Wright Penn (1966-)
See Robin Wright

Maris Wrixon (1917-99)
Footsteps in the Dark '41
Waterfront '44
White Pongo '45

Chien-Lien Wu (1968-)
Eat Drink Man Woman '94
The Phantom Lover '95

Chun Wu
The Assassin's Blade '08
14 Blades '14

Constance Wu (1982-)
Crazy Rich Asians '18
Hustlers '19

Daniel Wu (1974-)
Naked Weapon '03
Around the World in 80 Days '04
New Police Story '04
House of Fury '05
Blood Brothers '07
The Man with the Iron Fists '12
Europa Report '13
Warcraft '16
Geostorm '17
Tomb Raider '18

Jing Wu
Call of Heroes '16
The Climbers '19

Kevin Wu
Rock Jocks '12
Revenge of the Green Dragons '14

Kristy Wu (1982-)
What's Cooking? '00
Cry Wolf '05
Return to Halloweentown '06

Leonard Wu
While She Was Out '08
Lost Dream '09

Ma Wu
House of Fury '05
The Guardsman '15

Sophie Wu
Wild Child '08
Kick-Ass '10

Tom Wu
Belly of the Beast '03
Out For a Kill '03

Vanessa Wu
The Kumite '03
Three Kingdoms: Resurrection of the Dragon '08

Vivian Wu (1966-)
The Guyver '91
Iron & Silk '91
The Joy Luck Club '93
Teenage Mutant Ninja Turtles 3 '93
The Pillow Book '95
A Bright Shining Lie '98
8 1/2 Women '99
Dinner Rush '00
Encrypt '03

Susanne Wuest
Goodnight Mommy '15
Sunset '18
Iceman '19

Robert Wuhl (1951-)
The Hollywood Knights '80
Flashdance '83
Good Morning, Vietnam '87
Bull Durham '88
Batman '89
Blaze '89
Mistress '91
The Bodyguard '92
Cobb '94
Open Season '95
The Last Don '97
The Last Don 2 '98

Kari Wuhrer (1967-)
The Adventures of Ford Fairlane '90
Beyond Desire '94
The Crossing Guard '94
Sensation '94
Sex and the Other Man '95
Terminal Justice: Cybertech P.D. '95
Anaconda '96
An Occasional Hell '96
Stephen King's Thinner '96
Ivory Tower '97
Luscious '97
The Undertaker's Wedding '97
Hot Blooded '98
Kissing a Fool '98
Phoenix '98
Kate's Addiction '99
Kiss Tomorrow Goodbye '00
Lip Service '00
Sand '00
The Medicine Show '01
Poison '01
Spider's Web '01
Eight Legged Freaks '02
The Hitcher 2: I've Been Waiting '03
King of the Ants '03
Hellraiser: Deader '05
Alien Storm '12
Sharknado 2: The Second One '14

Kai Wulff
Firefox '82
Jungle Warriors '84
Top Dog '95

Martin Wuttke (1962-)
The Legend of Rita '99
Rosenstrasse '03
Inglourious Basterds '09

Jane Wyatt (1911-2006)
Great Expectations '34
Lost Horizon '37
Buckskin Frontier '43
The Kansan '43
None But the Lonely Heart '44
Boomerang '47
Gentleman's Agreement '47
Task Force '49
The Man Who Cheated Himself '50
My Blue Heaven '50
Criminal Lawyer '51
Two Little Bears '61
Never Too Late '65
Katherine '75
Star Trek 4: The Voyage Home '86
Amityville 4: The Evil Escapes '89

Don Wycherley (1967-)
When Brendan Met Trudy '00
Veronica Guerin '03
Speed Dating '07
My Brothers '10

Margaret Wycherly (1881-1956)
Midnight '34
Sergeant York '41
Crossroads '42
Hangmen Also Die '42
Keeper of the Flame '42
Random Harvest '42
The Moon is Down '43
The Yearling '46
Forever Amber '47
Something in the Wind '47
White Heat '49
The Man With a Cloak '51

Karolina Wydra
Europa Report '13
A Score to Settle '19

Katya Wyeth (1949-)
Twins of Evil '71
Dressed for Death '74

Noah Wyle (1971-)
Crooked Hearts '91
A Few Good Men '92
There Goes My Baby '92
Swing Kids '93
Guinevere '94
The Myth of Fingerprints '97
The Pirates of Silicon Valley '99
Fail Safe '00
Donnie Darko '01
Scenes of the Crime '01
Enough '02
White Oleander '02
The Librarian: Quest for the Spear '04
The Librarian: Return to King Solomon's Mines '06
The Librarian: Curse of the Judas Chalice '08
Nothing But the Truth '08
W. '08
An American Affair '09
Snake & Mongoose '13
The World Made Straight '15

Gretchen Wyler (1932-2007)
The Devil's Brigade '68
The Marrying Man '91

Richard Wyler
Charge of the Lancers '54
Jungle Man-Eaters '54

Adam Wylie (1984-)
All Dogs Go to Heaven 2 '95 (V)
Balloon Farm '97
Children of the Corn 5: Fields of Terror '98
The King and I '99 (V)
Daybreak '01
Return to Sleepaway Camp '08

Daniel Wyllie (1970-)
Romper Stomper '92
Holy Smoke '99
Chopper '00
Unconditional Love '03
Animal Kingdom '09
Sanctum '11

Bill Wyman (1936-)
Gimme Shelter '70
Eat the Rich '87

Jane Wyman (1917-2007)
My Man Godfrey '36
Smart Blonde '37
Brother Rat '38
The Crowd Roars '38
Wide Open Faces '38
Tail Spin '39
Brother Rat and a Baby '40
Flight Angels '40
My Love Came Back '40
Larceny, Inc. '42
Princess O'Rourke '43
The Lost Weekend '45
Night and Day '46
The Yearling '46
Cheyenne '47
Magic Town '47
Johnny Belinda '48
It's a Great Feeling '49
A Kiss in the Dark '49
Stage Fright '50
Here Comes the Groom '51
Three Guys Named Mike '51
Just for You '52
The Story of Will Rogers '52
Let's Do It Again '53
Magnificent Obsession '54
All That Heaven Allows '55
Holiday for Lovers '59
Pollyanna '60
Bon Voyage! '62
How to Commit Marriage '69
The Incredible Journey of Dr. Meg Laurel '79

Patrick Wymark (1926-70)
Repulsion '65
The Skull '65
The Psychopath '66
Woman Times Seven '67
The Conqueror Worm '68
Where Eagles Dare '68
Battle of Britain '69
Journey to the Far Side of the Sun '69

Patrice Wymore (1926-2014)
Rocky Mountain '50
Tea for Two '50
I'll See You in My Dreams '51
Big Trees '52
She's Working Her Way Through College '52
She's Back on Broadway '53

Geraint Wyn Davies (1957-)
Hush Little Baby '93
Conspiracy of Fear '96
Trilogy of Terror 2 '96
American Psycho 2: All American Girl '02
Cube 2: Hypercube '02

H.M. Wynant (1927-)
Run Silent, Run Deep '58
Conquest of the Planet of the Apes '72
The Big Empty '98

Dennis Wyndham (1887-1973)
Men of the Sea '35
Windbag the Sailor '36
Old Mother Riley, MP '39

George Wyner (1945-)
Missiles of October '74
The Bad News Bears Go to Japan '78
Fletch '85
Spaceballs '87
Fletch Lives '89
For Richer, for Poorer '92
How to be a Serial Killer '08

Peter Wyngarde (1927-2018)
The Siege of Sidney Street '60
The Innocents '61
Burn, Witch, Burn! '62

Ed Wynn (1886-1966)
Alice in Wonderland '51 (V)
Requiem for a Heavyweight '56
Marjorie Morningstar '58
The Diary of Anne Frank '59
Cinderfella '60
The Absent-Minded Professor '61
Babes in Toyland '61
Mary Poppins '64
Dear Brigitte '65
The Greatest Story Ever Told '65
Those Calloways '65
The Gnome-Mobile '67

Keenan Wynn (1916-86)
For Me and My Gal '42
Somewhere I'll Find You '42
Lost Angel '43
See Here, Private Hargrove '44
Since You Went Away '44
Between Two Women '45
The Clock '45
Weekend at the Waldorf '45
Without Love '45
Easy to Wed '46
The Hucksters '47
Song of the Thin Man '47
B.F.'s Daughter '48
The Three Musketeers '48
My Dear Secretary '49
Neptune's Daughter '49
That Midnight Kiss '49
Annie Get Your Gun '50
Love That Brute '50
Three Little Words '50
Angels in the Outfield '51
It's a Big Country '51
Royal Wedding '51
Texas Carnival '51
The Belle of New York '52
Desperate Search '52
Fearless Fagan '52
Phone Call from a Stranger '52
Sky Full of Moon '52
All the Brothers Were Valiant '53
Battle Circus '53
Code Two '53
Kiss Me Kate '53
The Long, Long Trailer '54
Men of the Fighting Lady '54
The Glass Slipper '55
Shack Out on 101 '55
The Man in the Gray Flannel Suit '56
Naked Hills '56
Requiem for a Heavyweight '56
Don't Go Near the Water '57
Deep Six '58
A Hole in the Head '59
The Perfect Furlough '59
The Crowded Sky '60
The Absent-Minded Professor '61
The King of the Roaring '20s: The Story of Arnold Rothstein '61
Pattern for Plunder '62
Son of Flubber '63
The Americanization of Emily '64
Bikini Beach '64
Dr. Strangelove, or: How I Learned to Stop Worrying and Love the Bomb '64
The Patsy '64
Around the World Under the Sea '65
The Great Race '65
Stagecoach '66
Point Blank '67
The War Wagon '67
Warning Shot '67
Welcome to Hard Times '67
Finian's Rainbow '68
Once Upon a Time in the West '68
MacKenna's Gold '69
Smith! '69
Viva Max '69
The Desperados '70
Loving '70
Manipulator '71
Pretty Maids All In a Row '71
Cancel My Reservation '72
The Mechanic '72
Snowball Express '72
Internecine Project '73
Herbie Rides Again '74
Hit Lady '74
Devil's Rain '75
He Is My Brother '75
Nashville '75
The Killer Inside Me '76
The Longest Drive '76
The Shaggy D.A. '76
Orca '77
The Bastard '78
Coach '78
Laserblast '78
The Lucifer Complex '78
Monster '78
Piranha '78
The Clonus Horror '79
The Dark '79
Just Tell Me What You Want '80
Mission to Glory '80
Best Friends '82
The Last Unicorn '82 (V)

May Wynn (1930-)
The Caine Mutiny '54
The Violent Men '55
The White Squaw '56

Dana Wynter (1931-2011)
D-Day, the Sixth of June '56
Invasion of the Body Snatchers '56
Something of Value '57
Fraulein '58
In Love and War '58
Sink the Bismarck '60
On the Double '61
The List of Adrian Messenger '63
Airport '70
Santee '73
The Questor Tapes '74
Lovers Like Us '75
The Savage '75
Backstairs at the White House '79

Sarah Wynter (1973-)
Lost Souls '00
Race Against Time '00
The 6th Day '00
Bride of the Wind '01
Coastlines '02
Circadian Rhythm '05
L.A. Dicks '05
Shooting Livien '05

Charlotte Wynters (1899-1991)
Struggle '31
The Ivory Handled Gun '35
Smart Blonde '37
Nancy Drew-Trouble Shooter '39
Tomboy '40

Diana Wynyard (1906-64)
Cavalcade '33
Rasputin and the Empress '33
Gaslight '40
An Ideal Husband '47

Jacob Wysocki
Terri '11
Fat Kid Rules the World '12

Charles Henry Wyson
Soldier Love Story '10
Spooky Buddies '11 (V)
Treasure Buddies '12 (V)
Home Run '13

Amanda Wyss (1960-)
Fast Times at Ridgemont High '82
A Nightmare on Elm Street '84
Better Off Dead '85
Powwow Highway '89
Shakma '89
To Die For '89
Bloodfist 4: Die Trying '92
Deadly Impact '09
The Graves '10

Yu Xing
Dragon Tiger Gate '07
Flash Point '07

Lynn Xiong
Ip Man '08
Ip Man 2 '10
S.M.A.R.T. Chase '18

Xin-Xin Xiong (1965-)
Once Upon a Time in China II '92
Once Upon a Time in China III '93

Salvator Xuereb (1965-)
Blood Ties '92
Lewis and Clark and George '97
My Brother's War '97

Xzibit (1974-)
Derailed '05
Hoodwinked '05 (V)
XXX: State of the Union '05
Full Clip '06
Gridiron Gang '06
The X Files: I Want to Believe '08
American Violet '09
Bad Lieutenant: Port of Call New Orleans '09
Seal Team Six: The Raid on Osama Bin Laden '12

Kaoru Yachigusa (1931-2019)
Samurai 1: Musashi Miyamoto '55
Samurai 2: Duel at Ichijoji Temple '55
Samurai 3: Duel at Ganryu Island '56

Raghuvir Yadav (1957-)
Salaam Bombay! '88
Bandit Queen '94
Lagaan: Once upon a Time in India '01
Water '05

Missy Yager
A Fish in the Bathtub '99
Evil Alien Conquerors '02

Jeff Yagher (1961-)
Big Bad Mama 2 '87
Shag: The Movie '89
Lower Level '91
My Fellow Americans '96

James Yagi
The Gallant Hours '60
Bridge to the Sun '61

Kenichi Yajima (1956-)
Sonatine '96
Inugami '01
Onmyoji '01

Koji Yakusho (1956-)
Tampopo '86
The Eel '96
Shall We Dance? '96
Cure '97
Pulse '01
Memoirs of a Geisha '05
Babel '06
Silk '07
Tokyo Sonata '09
13 Assassins '10
Hara-Kiri: Death of a Samurai '11
The World of Kanako '15
Oh Lucy! '17

Simon Yam (1955-)
A Bullet in the Head '90
Full Contact '92
Contract Killer '98
The Mission '99
Full Time Killer '01
Breaking News '04
Exiled '06
Ip Man '08
Man of Tai Chi '13
S.M.A.R.T. Chase '18

Isuzu Yamada (1917-2012)
Osaka Elegy '36
Sisters of the Gion '36
The Lower Depths '57
Throne of Blood '57
Yojimbo '61

Mame Yamada (1965-)
Blue Spring '01
9 Souls '03
The Great Yokai War '05

Takayuki Yamada
Crows Zero '07
13 Assassins '10

Tatsuo Yamada
Another Lonely Hitman '95
Sabu '04

Isao Yamagata (1915-96)
Gate of Hell '54
Shogun Assassin 2: Lightning Swords of Death '73

Sayaka Yamaguchi
Rebirth of Mothra '96
Rebirth of Mothra 2 '97

Yoshiko (Shirley) Yamaguchi (1920-)
Scandal '50
Japanese War Bride '52
House of Bamboo '55

So Yamamura (1910-2000)
Tokyo Story '53
Barbarian and the Geisha '58
The Human Condition: No Greater Love '58
Tora! Tora! Tora! '70
Gung Ho '86

Tsutomu Yamazaki (1936-)
Kagemusha '80
The Funeral '84
Tampopo '86
A Taxing Woman '87
Rikyu '90
Doing Time '02
Departures '08

Yurei Yanagi
Ringu 2 '99
Ju-On 2 '00

Emily Yancy (1939-)
Cotton Comes to Harlem '70
Blacula '72
Jasper, Texas '03

Eduardo Yanez (1960-)
Held Up '00
Ladrones '15

Jimmy O. Yang
Juliet, Naked '18
Fantasy Island '20

Kuei-Mei Yang
Eat Drink Man Woman '94
The Hole '98

Tony Yang
Formula 17 '04
Blood Brothers '07

Edward Yankie
Deadline '00
Dead Awake '01
The Sign of Four '01

Weird Al Yankovic (1959-)
The Naked Gun: From the Files of Police Squad '88 (C)
Tapeheads '89
UHF '89
Naked Gun 2 1/2: The Smell of Fear '91 (C)
Naked Gun 33 1/3: The Final Insult '94 (C)

Jean Yanne (1933-2003)
Weekend '67
Le Boucher '69
This Man Must Die '70
Madame Bovary '91
Indochine '92
The Horseman on the Roof '95
Victory '95
Beaumarchais the Scoundrel '96
Brotherhood of the Wolf '01

Rossana Yanni (1938-)
Fangs of the Living Dead '68
White Comanche '68
Dracula's Great Love '72
The Rue Morgue Massacres '73

Atta Yaqub
A Fond Kiss '04
Nina's Heavenly Delights '06

Cedric Yarbrough (1973-)
Mulligan '00
Entry Level '07
Reno 911! Miami '07
Black Dynamite '09

Margaret Yarde (1878-1944)
The Man From Toronto '32
Tiger Bay '33
Crimes at the Dark House '39
Thursday's Child '43

Michael Yarmush (1982-)
First Do No Harm '97
Little Men '98
Crown Heights '02

Celeste Yarnall (1944-)
Beast of Blood '71
The Velvet Vampire '71
Scorpio '73
Born Yesterday '93
Midnight Kiss '93

Danika Yarosh (1998-)
Jack Reacher: Never Go Back '16
The Miracle Season '18

Amy Yasbeck (1962-)
House 2: The Second Story '87
Problem Child '90
Problem Child 2 '91
Robin Hood: Men in Tights '93
The Mask '94
Dracula: Dead and Loving It '95
The Nutt House '95
Something About Sex '98

Rikiya Yasuoka (1947-)
Tampopo '86
The Toxic Avenger, Part 2 '89

Cassie Yates (1951-)
Convoy '78
The Evil '78
F.I.S.T. '78
FM '78
Of Mice and Men '81
St. Helen's, Killer Volcano '82
Agatha Christie's A Caribbean Mystery '83
Unfaithfully Yours '84
Perry Mason Returns '85

Marjorie Yates (1941-)
The Optimists '73
The Long Day Closes '92

Yvette Yates
El Gringo '12
Bloodsucking Bastards '15

Chingmy Yau
Legend of the Liquid Sword '93
Meltdown '95

Jose Maria Yazpik (1970-)
Nicotina '03
Cronicas '04
Innocent Voices '04
Sueno '05
Beverly Hills Chihuahua '08
The Burning Plain '08
I'm So Excited '13
Everybody Loves Somebody '17

Liu Ye (1978-)
Lan Yu '01
Balzac and the Little Chinese Seamstress '02
Curse of the Golden Flower '06

Biff Yeager
Black Samurai '77
Repo Man '83
Girls Just Want to Have Fun '85
Sid & Nancy '86
Straight to Hell '87
Headless Body in Topless Bar '96

Steve Yeager (1948-)
Pink Flamingos '72
Polyester '81
Major League 3: Back to the Minors '98

Richard Yearwood (1970-)
Blood Brothers '93
Dangerous Evidence: The Lori Jackson Story '99
Breakaway '02
Webs '03

Kelvin Han Yee
A Great Wall '86
Life Tastes Good '99
Lucky You '07

Anton Yelchin (1989-2016)
A Time for Dancing '00
Along Came a Spider '01
Hearts in Atlantis '01
House of D '04
Fierce People '05
Alpha Dog '06
Charlie Bartlett '07
New York, I Love You '09
Star Trek '09
Terminator Salvation '09
The Beaver '11
Fright Night '11
Like Crazy '11
The Smurfs '11 (V)
You and I '11
The Pirates! Band of Misfits '12 (V)
Odd Thomas '13
Only Lovers Left Alive '13
The Smurfs 2 '13 (V)
Star Trek: Into Darkness '13
Dying of the Light '14
Rudderless '14
Burying the Ex '15
Cymbeline '15
Experimenter '15
5 to 7 '15
Green Room '15
The Driftless Area '16
Star Trek: Beyond '16
Porto '17
Thoroughbreds '17
We Don't Belong Here '17
Love, Antosha '19

Hannah Yelland (1976-)
Catherine Cookson's The Secret '00
Dinotopia '02

Peter Yellen
Driller Killer '79
Ms. 45 '81

Daniel Yelsky (1997-)
Meet Monica Velour '10
Another Happy Day '11
A Little Help '11

Donnie Yen (1963-)
Butterfly Sword '93
Iron Monkey '93
Wing Chun '94
Highlander: Endgame '00
Blade 2 '02
Hero '02
Shanghai Knights '03
Dragon Tiger Gate '07
Flash Point '07
Seven Swords '07
An Empress and the Warriors '08
Ip Man 2 '10
14 Blades '14
Crouching Tiger, Hidden Dragon: Sword of Destiny '16
Ip Man 3 '16
The Lost Bladesman '16
Rogue One: A Star Wars Story '16
xXx: Return of Xander Cage '17
Ip Man 4: The Finale '19

Tran Nu Yen-Khe (1968-)
The Scent of Green Papaya '93
Cyclo '95
The Vertical Ray of the Sun '00

Gwendoline Yeo (1977-)
Broken Trail '06
Dead Tone '07
The Invincible Iron Man '07 (V)
Night Skies '07

Michelle Yeoh (1962-)
Royal Warriors '86
Supercop '92
Butterfly Sword '93
The Executioners '93
The Heroic Trio '93
Supercop 2 '93
Twin Warriors '93
Wing Chun '94
Tomorrow Never Dies '97
Crouching Tiger, Hidden Dragon '00
Silver Hawk '04
Memoirs of a Geisha '05
Far North '07
Sunshine '07
Babylon A.D. '08
The Children of Huang Shi '08
The Mummy: Tomb of the Dragon Emperor '08
Reign of Assassins '10
Kung Fu Panda 2 '11 (V)
The Lady '11
Crouching Tiger, Hidden Dragon: Sword of Destiny '16
Mechanic: Resurrection '16
Crazy Rich Asians '18
Last Christmas '19

Owain Yeoman (1978-)
ChromeSkull: Laid to Rest 2 '11
Brahms: The Boy II '19

Don Yesso (1954-)
Hero '92
Out of Sync '95

Steven Yeun (1983-)
Mayhem '17
Okja '17
The Star '17
Burning '18
Sorry to Bother You '18

Bolo Yeung (1946-)
King Boxer '72
Legacy of Rage '86
Bloodsport '88
Breathing Fire '91
Tiger Claws '91
Fearless Tiger '94

Charlie Yeung (1974-)
New Police Story '04
Seven Swords '07
Bangkok Dangerous '08

Ching-Ching Yeung
Sword Masters: Two Champions of Shaolin '80
8 Diagram Pole Fighter '84

Charlyne Yi (1986-)
Paper Heart '09
Jexi '19

Murat Yilmaz
Lola and Billy the Kid '98
Out of Reach '04

Serra Yilmaz (1954-)
His Secret Life '01
Facing Windows '03
Saturn in Opposition '07

Terence Yin
Black Mask 2: City of Masks '02
Dead or Alive: Final '02

Da(nniel) Ying (1960-)
Farewell My Concubine '93
Big Shot's Funeral '01
The White Countess '05

Cecilia Yip (1963-)
Hong Kong 1941 '84
Organized Crime & Triad Bureau '93
What Time Is It There? '01 (C)

Francoise Yip (1972-)
Black Mask '96
Rumble in the Bronx '96
Futuresport '98
Romeo Must Die '00
Flatland '02
Blade: Trinity '04
The Deal '05
Dim Sum Funeral '08

Richard Yniguez (1946-)
Sniper '75
Boulevard Nights '79
World War III '86
Stalking Laura '93

Kimiko Yo
Gonin 2 '96
The Ramen Girl '08

Dwight Yoakam (1956-)
Red Rock West '93
Roswell: The U.F.O. Cover-Up '94
Painted Hero '95
Don't Look Back '96
Sling Blade '96
The Newton Boys '97
When Trumpets Fade '98
The Minus Man '99
South of Heaven, West of Hell '00
Panic Room '02
Hollywood Homicide '03
3-Way '04
The Three Burials of Melquiades Estrada '05
Wedding Crashers '05
Bandidas '06
Crank '06
Four Christmases '08
Crank: High Voltage '09
The Last Rites of Ransom Pride '09
2:13 '09
Bloodworth '10
Dirty Girl '10
90 Minutes in Heaven '15

Malik Yoba (1967-)
Cool Runnings '93
Blue in the Face '95
Smoke '95
Cop Land '97
Ride '98
Harlem Aria '99
Personals '00
Kids in America '05
Tyler Perry's Why Did I Get Married? '07
My Girlfriend's Back '10
Tyler Perry's Why Did I Get Married Too '10
Allegiance '12
Betty & Coretta '13
Awake '19

Pumwaree Yodkamol
Ong-Bak '03
The Bodyguard '04

Erica Yohn
An American Tail: Fievel Goes West '91 (V)
Corrina, Corrina '94

You Yong
Breaking News '04
Red Cliff '08

Aaron Yoo (1979-)
Disturbia '07
Nick & Norah's Infinite Playlist '08
21 '08
Friday the 13th '09
The Good Guy '10
Kid Cannabis '14

Wladimir Yordanoff (1954-)
Vincent & Theo '90
Un Air de Famille '96
The Taste of Others '00
I Do '06
The Hedgehog '09

Dick York (1929-92)
My Sister Eileen '55
Three Stripes in the Sun '55
Operation Mad Ball '57
Cowboy '58
They Came to Cordura '59
Inherit the Wind '60

Francine York (1938-2017)
Secret File of Hollywood '62
Wild Ones on Wheels '62
Curse of the Swamp Creature '66
The Doll Squad '73
The Centerfold Girls '74
Flood! '76
Astro-Zombies M3: Cloned '10

Jeff York (1912-95)
They Were Expendable '45
Up Goes Maisie '46
The Yearling '46
Kill the Umpire '50
The Lady Says No '51
Davy Crockett and the River Pirates '56
Westward Ho, the Wagons! '56
Old Yeller '57
Savage Sam '63

Kathleen York
Winners Take All '87
Checking Out '89
Cold Feet '89
Thompson's Last Run '90
Wild Hearts Can't Be Broken '91
Dream Lover '93
Nightjohn '96
Dead Men Can't Dance '97
The Big Day '99
Shelter Island '03
Fatal Desire '05
Sublime '07

Michael York (1942-)
Accident '67
Smashing Time '67
The Taming of the Shrew '67
Romeo and Juliet '68
Justine '69
Zeppelin '71
Cabaret '72
Lost Horizon '73
Murder on the Orient Express '74
The Three Musketeers '74
Conduct Unbecoming '75
The Four Musketeers '75
Logan's Run '76
The Island of Dr. Moreau '77
The Last Remake of Beau Geste '77
The Riddle of the Sands '79
Final Assignment '80
Success Is the Best Revenge '84
Weather in the Streets '84
Nevil Shute's The Far Country '85
Sword of Gideon '86
Lethal Obsession '87
The Four Minute Mile '88
Midnight Cop '88
The Lady and the Highwayman '89
Night of the Fox '90
The Heat of the Day '91
Duel of Hearts '92
Wide Sargasso Sea '93
Discretion Assured '93
Gospa '94
Not of This Earth '96
September '96
Austin Powers: International Man of Mystery '97
Dark Planet '97
True Women '97
Criminal Desire '98
54 '98 (C)
A Knight in Camelot '98
The Treat '98
Wrongfully Accused '98
Austin Powers 2: The Spy Who Shagged Me '99
The Haunting of Hell House '99
The Omega Code '99

Borstal Boy '00
Austin Powers In Goldmember '02
La Femme Musketeer '03
Moscow Heat '04
Frederick Forsyth's Icon '05
Chris & Don: A Love Story '07
Transformers: Revenge of the Fallen '09 (V)
The Mill and the Cross '11

Morgan York (1993-)
Cheaper by the Dozen '03
Cheaper by the Dozen 2 '05
The Pacifier '05

Rachel York (1971-)
One Fine Day '96
Terror Tract '00
Au Pair 2: The Fairy Tale Continues '01

Susannah York (1939-2011)
Tunes of Glory '60
Tom Jones '63
The Seventh Dawn '64
Sands of the Kalahari '65
Kaleidoscope '66
A Man for All Seasons '66
Duffy '68
Battle of Britain '69
The Killing of Sister George '69
Oh! What a Lovely War '69
They Shoot Horses, Don't They? '69
Images '72
X, Y & Zee '72
Conduct Unbecoming '75
Sky Riders '76
The Silent Partner '78
Superman: The Movie '78
The Awakening '80
Falling in Love Again '80
Superman 2 '80
We'll Meet Again '82
Loophole '83
Yellowbeard '83
A Christmas Carol '84
Alice '86
The Land of Faraway '87
Superman 4: The Quest for Peace '87 (V)
Diamond's Edge '88
A Summer Story '88
Devices and Desires '91
Romance and Rejection '96
St. Patrick: The Irish Legend '00
Visitors '03
Franklyn '08

Jade Yorker
Bomb the System '05
America '09

Bud Yorkin (1926-)
Inspector Clouseau '68
For the Boys '91

Jitsuko Yoshimura (1943-)
The Insect Woman '63
Onibaba '64

Hidetaka Yoshioka
The Sea is Watching '02
The Hidden Blade '04

Kazuko Yoshiyuki
Lady Snowblood: Love Song of Vengeance '74
The Empire of Passion '76

Ge You (1957-)
Farewell My Concubine '93
To Live '94
The Emperor's Shadow '96
Big Shot's Funeral '01

Aden Young (1972-)
Black Robe '91
Sniper '92
Metal Skin '94
Cosi '95
River Street '95
Hotel de Love '96
Cousin Bette '97
In the Shadows '98
The War Bride '01
The Crocodile Hunter: Collision Course '02
After the Deluge '03
The Starter Wife '07
Mao's Last Dancer '09
The Tree '10

Alan Young (1919-2016)
Chicken Every Sunday '48
Androcles and the Lion '52
The Time Machine '60
Baker's Hawk '76
The Great Mouse Detective '86 (V)
DuckTales the Movie: Treasure of the Lost Lamp '90 (V)
Beverly Hills Cop 3 '94
The Time Machine '02 (C)

Arthur Young (1898-1959)
Victoria the Great '37
The Lady With the Lamp '51
When a Stranger Calls '06

Bellamy Young (1970-)
Mission '00
The Freebie '10
Joint Body '11

Bill Young (1950-)
Chopper '00
Japanese Story '03

Bruce A. Young (1956-)
Basic Instinct '92
Blink '93
What Ever Happened To. . . '93
The War '94
Normal Life '96
Jurassic Park 3 '01
Addicted to Her Love '06
Into Temptation '09

Burt Young (1940-)
Carnival of Blood '71
Cinderella Liberty '73
Chinatown '74
The Gambler '74
The Killer Elite '75
Harry & Walter Go to New York '76
Rocky '76
The Choirboys '77
Convoy '78
Uncle Joe Shannon '78
Rocky 2 '79
. . .All the Marbles '81
Amityville 2: The Possession '82
Lookin' to Get Out '82
Rocky 3 '82
Once Upon a Time in America '84
The Pope of Greenwich Village '84
A Summer to Remember '84
Rocky 4 '85
Back to School '86
Blood Red '88
Beverly Hills Brats '89
Going Overboard '89
Backstreet Dreams '90
Betsy's Wedding '90
Club Fed '90
Last Exit to Brooklyn '90
Rocky 5 '90
Bright Angel '91
Excessive Force '93
Heaven Before I Die '96 (C)
North Star '96
Kicked in the Head '97
She's So Lovely '97
The Undertaker's Wedding '97
Hot Blooded '98
Mickey Blue Eyes '99
Blue Moon '00
Table One '00
The Adventures of Pluto Nash '02
Land of Plenty '04
Carlito's Way: Rise to Power '05
Shut Up and Kiss Me '05
Transamerica '05
Rocky Balboa '06
Hack! '07
Carnera: The Walking Mountain '08
Win Win '11
Rob the Mob '14

Carleton Young (1907-71)
Reefer Madness '38
Zorro's Fighting Legion '39
Adventures of Red Ryder '40
Flying Leathernecks '51
Hard, Fast and Beautiful '51
People Will Talk '51
Kansas City Confidential '52
From Here to Eternity '53
20,000 Leagues under the Sea '54
Battle Cry '55
Cry Terror! '58
The Horse Soldiers '59
The Gallant Hours '60
Sergeant Rutledge '60

Chris Young (1971-)
The Great Outdoors '88
Book of Love '91
December '91
Warlock: The Armageddon '93
P.C.U. '94
Runaway Daughters '94
Killing Mr. Griffin '97

Clara Kimball Young (1890-1960)
The Eyes of Youth '19
Kept Husbands '31
Chandu on the Magic Island '34
Return of Chandu '34
Rogue's Tavern '36
The Frontiersmen '38

Damian Young (1970-)
Amateur '94
Kill the Poor '03
Art Machine '12
Catfight '17

David Young
Banjo Hackett '76
Mary, Mary, Bloody Mary '76
Double Exposure '82

Dey Young (1955-)
Rock 'n' Roll High School '79
Strange Behavior '81
Strange Invaders '83
Doin' Time '85
Spontaneous Combustion '89
Frankie and Johnny '91
Murder 101 '91
Conflict of Interest '92
Pie in the Sky '95
The Shadow Conspiracy '96
True Heart '97
The Mod Squad '99
Protecting the King '07

Faron Young (1932-96)
Daniel Boone: Trail Blazer '56
Hidden Guns '56

Gig Young (1913-78)
Sergeant York '41
They Died with Their Boots On '41
Air Force '43
Old Acquaintance '43
Escape Me Never '47
The Three Musketeers '48
Lust for Gold '49
Tell It to the Judge '49
Wake of the Red Witch '49
Hunt the Man Down '50
Only the Valiant '50
Too Young to Kiss '51
The Girl Who Had Everything '53
Torch Song '53
Young at Heart '54
Desperate Hours '55
Desk Set '57
Teacher's Pet '58
The Tunnel of Love '58
Kid Galahad '62
That Touch of Mink '62
For Love or Money '63
Strange Bedfellows '65
Blood Island '68
They Shoot Horses, Don't They? '69
Lovers and Other Strangers '70
Bring Me the Head of Alfredo Garcia '74
The Hindenburg '75
The Killer Elite '75

Harrison Young (1930-2005)
Saving Private Ryan '98
Reptilian '99
The Adventures of Rocky & Bullwinkle '00
House of 1000 Corpses '03
The Pleasure Drivers '05

John Lloyd Young
Oy Vey! My Son is Gay! '09
Jersey Boys '14

Karen Young (1958-)
Deep in the Heart '83
Birdy '84
Maria's Lovers '84
Almost You '85
9 1/2 Weeks '86
Heat '87
Jaws: The Revenge '87
Torch Song Trilogy '88
Criminal Law '89
Little Sweetheart '90
Hoffa '92
The Wife '95
Daylight '96
Joe the King '99
Mercy '00
Heading South '05
Factotum '06
Handsome Harry '09
Conviction '10
The Green '11

Keone Young (1947-)
Uncorked '98
Return to Halloweentown '06

Lee Thompson Young (1984-2013)
Friday Night Lights '04
Akeelah and the Bee '06
The Hills Have Eyes 2 '07

Loretta Young (1913-2000)
Laugh, Clown, Laugh '28
The Squall '29
Loose Ankles '30
Road to Paradise '30
The Truth About Youth '30
Beau Ideal '31
Platinum Blonde '31
The Right of Way '31
The Hatchet Man '32
Taxi! '32
They Call It Sin '32
Employees' Entrance '33
Heroes for Sale '33
Midnight Mary '33
The Call of the Wild '35
Clive of India '35
The Crusades '35
Private Number '36
Ramona '36
The Unguarded Hour '36
Cafe Metropole '37
Love Is News '37
Second Honeymoon '37
Four Men and a Prayer '38
Kentucky '38
Suez '38
Three Blind Mice '38
Eternally Yours '39
The Story of Alexander Graham Bell '39
Wife, Husband and Friend '39
Doctor Takes a Wife '40
A Night to Remember '42
China '43
Along Came Jones '45
The Stranger '46
The Bishop's Wife '47
Come to the Stable '49
Mother Is a Freshman '49
Key to the City '50
Cause for Alarm '51
Paula '52

Mark L. Young
The Lucky Ones '08
Happiness Runs '10
The Curse of Downers Grove '15
Dirty Lies '16

Marlon Young
Blue Hill Avenue '01
SWAT: Unit 887 '15

Mary (Marsden) Young (1880-1971)
Watch on the Rhine '43
The Lost Weekend '45
Alias Jesse James '59

Nedrick Young (1913-68)
Dead Men Walk '43
Gun Crazy '49
Captain Scarlett '53
Crime Wave '54
Terror in a Texas Town '58

Neil Young (1945-)
Made in Heaven '87 (C)
Love at Large '89

Otis Young (1932-2001)
The Last Detail '73
The Capture of Bigfoot '79

Polly Ann Young (1908-97)
The Story of Alexander Graham Bell '39
The Invisible Ghost '41
Road Show '41

Ray Young (1940-99)
Blood of Dracula's Castle '69
Blue Sunshine '78
The Return of the Beverly Hillbillies '81

Ric Young
The Last Emperor '87
Dragon: The Bruce Lee Story '93
The Corruptor '99
Chain of Command '00
The Lost Empire '01
Long Life, Happiness and Prosperity '02
The Transporter '02

Richard Young
Night Call Nurses '72
Banjo Hackett '76
Cocaine Cowboys '79
Friday the 13th, Part 5: A New Beginning '85
Assassin '86
An Innocent Man '89

Robert Young (1907-98)
The Black Camel '31
The Guilty Generation '31
The Sin of Madelon Claudet '31
Kid from Spain '32
New Morals for Old '32
Strange Interlude '32
The Wet Parade '32
Today We Live '33
Tugboat Annie '33
Hollywood Party '34
Spitfire '34
The Bride Comes Home '35
Vagabond Lady '35
The Bride Walks Out '36
It's Love Again '36
The Secret Agent '36
Stowaway '36
The Bride Wore Red '37
The Emperor's Candlesticks '37
I Met Him in Paris '37
Navy Blue and Gold '37
Josette '38
Paradise for Three '38
The Shining Hour '38
Three Comrades '38
The Toy Wife '38
Honolulu '39
Maisie '39
Miracles for Sale '39
Dr. Kildare's Crisis '40
The Mortal Storm '40
Northwest Passage '40
H.M. Pulham Esquire '41
Lady Be Good '41
Western Union '41
Cairo '42
Journey for Margaret '42
Claudia '43
Slightly Dangerous '43
The Canterville Ghost '44
The Enchanted Cottage '45
Claudia and David '46
Crossfire '47
They Won't Believe Me '47
Sitting Pretty '48
Adventure in Baltimore '49
That Forsyte Woman '50
Goodbye My Fancy '51
The Half-Breed '51
The Second Woman '51
Little Women '78

Roland Young (1887-1953)
Sherlock Holmes '22
The Bishop Murder Case '30
Madam Satan '30
The Squaw Man '31
One Hour with You '32
Street of Women '32
This Is the Night '32
His Double Life '33
Here is My Heart '34
David Copperfield '35
Ruggles of Red Gap '35
Give Me Your Heart '36
One Rainy Afternoon '36
The Unguarded Hour '36
Call It a Day '37
King Solomon's Mines '37
The Man Who Could Work Miracles '37
Topper '37
Sailing Along '38
The Young in Heart '38
Irene '40
No, No Nanette '40
The Philadelphia Story '40
Star Dust '40
The Flame of New Orleans '41
Topper Returns '41
Forever and a Day '43
And Then There Were None '45
You Gotta Stay Happy '48
The Great Lover '49
Let's Dance '50
St. Benny the Dip '51

Sean Young (1959-)
Jane Austen in Manhattan '80
Stripes '81
Blade Runner '82
Young Doctors in Love '82
Dune '84
Baby. . . Secret of the Lost Legend '85
Under the Biltmore Clock '85
Blood and Orchids '86
No Way Out '87
Wall Street '87
The Boost '88
Cousins '89
Fire Birds '90
A Kiss Before Dying '91
Blue Ice '92
Once Upon a Crime '92
Sketch Artist '92
Ace Ventura: Pet Detective '93
Fatal Instinct '93
Even Cowgirls Get the Blues '94 (C)
Rebel Run '94
Dr. Jekyll and Ms. Hyde '95
The Invader '96
Men '97
Motel Blue '98
Poor White Trash '00
The House Next Door '01
Mockingbird Don't Sing '01
Sugar & Spice '01
Headspace '02
Threat of Exposure '02
Before I Say Goodbye '03
Ghosts Never Sleep '05
Third Man Out: A Donald Strachey Mystery '05
The Drop '06
A Job to Kill For '06
Jesse Stone: Sea Change '07
Haunted Echoes '08
The Man Who Came Back '08
Attack of the 50 Foot Cheerleader '12
Jug Face '13

Stephen Young (1931-)
Patton *'70*
Rage *'72*
Soylent Green *'73*
Lifeguard *'76*
Who's Harry Crumb? *'89*
The Last Debate *'00*

Tammany Young (1886-1936)
Tugboat Annie *'33*
It's a Gift *'34*
The Old-Fashioned Way *'34*
The Man On the Flying Trapeze *'35*

Tony Young (1932-2002)
Chrome and Hot Leather *'71*
Policewomen *'73*

Victor Young (1901-66)
Charlie Chan in Honolulu *'38*
Charlie Chan at Treasure Island *'39*

William Allen Young (1954-)
Johnnie Gibson F.B.I. *'87*
Stalking Laura *'93*
Serving in Silence: The Margarethe Cammermeyer Story *'95*
Fear X *'03*

Rudy Youngblood
Apocalypto *'06*
Beatdown *'10*

Barrie Youngfellow (1950-)
Nightmare in Blood *'75*
It Came Upon a Midnight Clear *'84*

Henny Youngman (1906-98)
The Unkissed Bride *'66*
The Gore-Gore Girls *'72*
History of the World: Part 1 *'81*
National Lampoon Goes to the Movies *'81*
Amazon Women on the Moon *'87*
Goodfellas *'90*

Gail Youngs (1954-)
Hockey Night *'84*
Belizaire the Cajun *'86*
Last Days of Frank & Jesse James *'86*
Timestalkers *'87*

Jim Youngs (1956-)
Wanderers *'79*
Hot Shot *'86*
Nobody's Fool *'86*
You Talkin' to Me? *'87*
Skeeter *'93*

Jade Yourell (1978-)
Waiting for Dublin *'07*
Happy Ever Afters *'09*

Chief Yowlachie (1891-1966)
Red River *'48*
Rose Marie *'54*

Ji-tae Yu
Attack the Gas Station *'99*
Natural City *'03*

Kelvin Yu
The Utopian Society *'03*
Milk *'08*

Rongguang Yu (1958-)
Iron Monkey *'93*
Supercop 2 *'93*
Jet Li's The Enforcer *'95*
Jackie Chan's The Myth *'05*
Three Kingdoms: Resurrection of the Dragon *'08*
The Karate Kid *'10*

Eugenia Yuan
Charlotte Sometimes *'02*
The Eye 2 *'04*
Mail Order Wife *'04*

Quan Yuan
Rhapsody of Spring *'98*
The White Storm *'13*

Roger Yuan (1961-)
Shanghai Noon *'00*
Bulletproof Monk *'03*
The Fifth Commandment *'08*

Shawn Yue
Infernal Affairs 2 *'03*
Dragon Tiger Gate *'07*
Reign of Assassins *'10*

Hua Yueh (1942-)
Come Drink with Me *'65*
Sword Masters: Brothers Five *'70*
Intimate Confessions of a Chinese Courtesan *'72*
Sword Masters: Web of Death *'76*
The Duel of the Century *'81*
Black Magic *'06*
Three Kingdoms: Resurrection of the Dragon *'08*

Fennie Yuen (1970-)
A Bullet in the Head *'90*
Legend of the Liquid Sword *'93*

Russell Yuen (1965-)
Long Life, Happiness and Prosperity *'02*
The Cutting Edge: Fire and Ice *'10*

Wah Yuen
Bat Without Wings *'80*
Dragon Tiger Gate *'07*

Masayuki Yui (1947-)
Ran *'85*
To End All Wars *'01*

Jimmy Yuill (1959-)
Paper Mask *'91*
Much Ado about Nothing *'93*
Love's Labour's Lost *'00*
Strictly Sinatra *'01*
Princess Kaiulani *'09*

Joe Yule (1894-1950)
New Moon *'40*
Billy the Kid *'41*

Harris Yulin (1937-)
End of the Road *'70*
Melvin Purvis: G-Man *'74*
Missiles of October *'74*
Night Moves *'75*
Dynasty *'76*
St. Ives *'76*
Victory at Entebbe *'76*
Prime Time *'77*
When Every Day Was the Fourth of July *'78*
Scarface *'83*
The Believers *'87*
Fatal Beauty *'87*
Another Woman *'88*
Bad Dreams *'88*
Judgment in Berlin *'88*
Ghostbusters 2 *'89*
Final Analysis *'92*
There Goes the Neighborhood *'92*
Clear and Present Danger *'94*
Stuart Saves His Family *'94*
Cutthroat Island *'95*
Loch Ness *'95*
Truman *'95*
If These Walls Could Talk *'96*
Looking for Richard *'96*
Multiplicity *'96*
Bean *'97*
Hostile Waters *'97*
Murder at 1600 *'97*
The Cradle Will Rock *'99*
The Hurricane *'99*
The Million Dollar Hotel *'99*
The Virginian *'99*
75 Degrees *'00*
American Outlaws *'01*
Perfume *'01*
Rush Hour 2 *'01*
Training Day *'01*
The Emperor's Club *'02*
King of the Corner *'04*
Game 6 *'05*
Fur: An Imaginary Portrait of Diane Arbus *'06*
The Treatment *'06*
Loving Leah *'09*

Muhammad Ali's Greatest Fight *'13*
The Place Beyond the Pines *'13*
A Short History of Decay *'13*

Chow Yun-Fat (1955-)
Hong Kong 1941 *'84*
A Better Tomorrow, Part 1 *'86*
Dream Lovers *'86*
City on Fire *'87*
Prison on Fire *'87*
A Better Tomorrow, Part 2 *'88*
A Better Tomorrow, Part 3 *'89*
The Killer *'90*
Once a Thief *'90*
Prison on Fire 2 *'91*
Full Contact *'92*
Hard-Boiled *'92*
The Replacement Killers *'98*
Anna and the King *'99*
The Corruptor *'99*
Crouching Tiger, Hidden Dragon *'00*
Bulletproof Monk *'03*
Curse of the Golden Flower *'06*
Pirates of the Caribbean: At World's End *'07*
The Children of Huang Shi *'08*
Dragonball: Evolution *'09*
Shanghai *'09*
The Assassins *'12*

Rick Yune (1971-)
Snow Falling on Cedars *'99*
The Fast and the Furious *'01*
Die Another Day *'02*
Alone in the Dark 2 *'08*
The Fifth Commandment *'08*
Ninja Assassin *'09*
The Man with the Iron Fists *'12*
Olympus Has Fallen *'13*

Elodie Yung (1981-)
District 13: Ultimatum *'09*
G.I. Joe: Retaliation *'13*
The Hitman's Bodyguard *'17*

Victor Sen Yung (1915-80)
Charlie Chan in Panama *'40*
Charlie Chan's Murder Cruise *'40*
The Letter *'40*
Murder over New York *'40*
Across the Pacific *'42*
Moontide *'42*
Secret Agent of Japan *'42*
China *'43*
Dangerous Money *'46*
Shadows Over Chinatown *'46*
The Trap *'46*
The Chinese Ring *'47*
Docks of New Orleans *'48*
The Golden Eye *'48*
Shanghai Chest *'48*
The Breaking Point *'50*
The Groom Wore Spurs *'51*
Men in War *'57*
The Hunters *'58*
She Demons *'58*

Blanche Yurka (1887-1974)
A Tale of Two Cities *'36*
City for Conquest *'40*
Lady for a Night *'42*
A Night to Remember *'42*
Tonight We Raid Calais *'43*
The Bridge of San Luis Rey *'44*
One Body Too Many *'44*
The Southerner *'45*
13 Rue Madeleine *'46*
At Sword's Point *'51*

Odette Yustman (1985-)
See Odette Annable

William Zabka (1965-)
The Karate Kid *'84*
Just One of the Guys *'85*
National Lampoon's European Vacation *'85*
Back to School *'86*
The Karate Kid: Part 2 *'86*

The Power Within *'95*
High Voltage *'98*
Landspeed *'01*
Antibody *'02*
Python 2 *'02*
Cake: A Wedding Story *'07*
Hot Tub Time Machine *'10*
Cross *'11*
Where Hope Grows *'15*

Grace Zabriskie (1941-)
Concrete Cowboys *'79*
East of Eden *'80*
Galaxy of Terror *'81*
Body Rock *'84*
The Big Easy *'87*
The Boost *'88*
Drugstore Cowboy *'89*
Child's Play 2 *'90*
Wild at Heart *'90*
Fried Green Tomatoes *'91*
My Own Private Idaho *'91*
Servants of Twilight *'91*
The Waterdance *'91*
Blood Ties *'92*
Ferngully: The Last Rain Forest *'92 (V)*
Twin Peaks: Fire Walk with Me *'92*
Black Widow Murders: The Blanche Taylor Moore Story *'93*
Drop Zone *'94*
The Crew *'95*
Desert Winds *'95*
The Passion of Darkly Noon *'95*
Bastard out of Carolina *'96*
A Family Thing *'96*
Dead Men Can't Dance *'97*
Houdini *'98*
Me & Will *'99*
Sparkler *'99*
A Texas Funeral *'99*
Gone in 60 Seconds *'00*
They Crawl *'01*
No Good Deed *'02*
R.S.V.P. *'02*
The Grudge *'04*
The Last Letter *'04*
Inland Empire *'06*
Bob Funk *'09*
My Son, My Son, What Have Ye Done *'09*
Wrong Cops *'13*
The Judge *'14*

Daniel Zacapa
Coronado *'03*
San Saba *'08*

Giovanna Zacarias (1976-)
Puerto Vallarta Squeeze *'04*
Border Run *'12*

Jonathan Zaccai (1970-)
My Life on Ice *'02*
They Came Back *'04*
The Beat My Heart Skipped *'05*
You and Me *'06*

Robert Zachar
Married People, Single Sex *'93*
Landspeed *'01*
Dark Waters *'03*

Steffen Zacharias
They Call Me Trinity *'72*
Revolver *'75*

John Zacherle (1918-)
Geek Maggot Bingo *'83*
Brain Damage *'88 (V)*
Frankenhooker *'90*

Krystyna Zachwatowicz (1930-)
Man of Marble *'76*
Maids of Wilko *'79*

Ramy Zada (1958-)
After Midnight *'89*
Two Evil Eyes *'90*
Dark Justice *'91*
The Judas Project: The Ultimate Encounter *'94*
Out of Sync *'95*

Bridger Zadina (1994-)
Terri *'11*
Kill or Be Killed *'15*
Sins of Our Youth *'16*

Pia Zadora (1953-)
Santa Claus Conquers the Martians *'64*
Butterfly *'82*
Fake Out *'82*
Voyage of the Rock Aliens *'87*
Hairspray *'88*
Naked Gun 33 1/3: The Final Insult *'94 (C)*

Eleni Zafirou (1916-2004)
Girl in Black *'56*
A Matter of Dignity *'57*

Frank Zagarino (1959-)
Barbarian Queen *'85*
The Revenger *'90*
Project: Eliminator *'91*
Never Say Die *'94*
Night Siege Project: Shadowchaser 2 *'94*
Project Shadowchaser 3000 *'95*
Terminal Impact *'95*
Alien Chaser *'96*
The Apocalypse *'96*
Warhead *'96*
Airboss *'97*
Convict 762 *'98*
The Stray *'00*
Lethal *'04*

Kyra Zagorsky
The ABCs of Death *'12*
Home Invasion *'16*

Alex Zahara
Ice Twisters *'09*
Lonesome Dove Church *'14*

Steve Zahn (1967-)
Reality Bites *'94*
Crimson Tide *'95*
Picture Windows *'95*
Race the Sun *'96*
That Thing You Do! *'96*
Subway Stories *'97*
From the Earth to the Moon *'98*
The Object of My Affection *'98*
Out of Sight *'98*
Safe Men *'98*
You've Got Mail *'98*
Blowin' Smoke *'99*
Forces of Nature *'99*
Happy, Texas *'99*
Stuart Little *'99 (V)*
Chain of Fools *'00*
Hamlet *'00*
Chelsea Walls *'01*
Dr. Dolittle 2 *'01 (V)*
Joy Ride *'01*
Riding in Cars with Boys *'01*
Saving Silverman *'01*
Stuart Little 2 *'02 (V)*
Daddy Day Care *'03*
National Security *'03*
Shattered Glass *'03*
Speak *'04*
Chicken Little *'05 (V)*
Sahara *'05*
Bandidas *'06*
Rescue Dawn *'06*
Comanche Moon *'08*
Strange Wilderness *'08*
Calvin Marshall *'09*
The Great Buck Howard *'09*
Management *'09*
Night Train *'09*
A Perfect Getaway *'09*
Sunshine Cleaning *'09*
Diary of a Wimpy Kid *'10*
Diary of a Wimpy Kid: Dog Days *'12*
Dallas Buyers Club *'13*
Knights of Badassdom *'13*
Captain Fantastic *'16*
War for the Planet of the Apes *'17*

Roxana Zal (1969-)
Table for Five *'83*
Testament *'83*
Shattered Spirits *'86*
River's Edge *'87*

Under the Boardwalk *'89*
Daddy's Girl *'96*
God's Lonely Man *'96*
Red Line *'96*
Broken Vessels *'98*
Big City Blues *'99*

Zbigniew Zamachowski (1961-)
The Decalogue *'88*
Trois Couleurs: Blanc *'94*
Trois Couleurs: Rouge *'94 (C)*

Del Zamora
RoboCop *'87*
Blackwater Valley Exorcism *'06*

Dominic Zamprogna (1979-)
The Boys Club *'96*
It Waits *'05*
A Valentine Carol *'07*

Gema Zamprogna (1976-)
By Way of the Stars *'92*
The Pirates of Silicon Valley *'99*

Philip Zanden (1954-)
Like It Never Was Before *'95*
Faithless *'00*

Billy Zane (1966-)
Back to the Future *'85*
Brotherhood of Justice *'86*
Critters *'86*
Back to the Future, Part 2 *'89*
Dead Calm *'89*
Going Overboard *'89*
Memphis Belle *'90*
Millions *'90*
Blood & Concrete: A Love Story *'91*
Lake Consequence *'92*
Orlando *'92*
Sniper *'92*
Posse *'93*
Tombstone *'93*
Flashfire *'94*
Only You *'94*
Tales from the Crypt Presents Demon Knight *'94*
Danger Zone *'95*
The Set Up *'95*
Head Above Water *'96*
The Phantom *'96*
Titanic *'97*
Dying to Get Rich *'98*
Cleopatra *'99*
Morgan's Ferry *'99*
Hendrix *'00*
The Believer *'01*
CQ *'01*
The Diamond of Jeru *'01*
Landspeed *'01*
Vlad *'03*
Bet Your Life *'04*
Dead Fish *'04*
Silver City *'04*
The Last Drop *'05*
The Pleasure Drivers *'05*
BloodRayne *'06*
Memory *'06*
Alien Agent *'07*
Fishtales *'07*
The Man Who Came Back *'08*
Perfect Hideout *'08*
Attack on Darfur *'09*
Blue Seduction *'09*
The Hessen Conspiracy *'09*
Love N' Dancing *'09*
The Confidant *'10*
Enemies Among Us *'10*
The Gold Retrievers *'10*
Journey to Promethea *'10*
Magic Man *'10*
Mercenaries *'11*
Mysteria *'11*
The Roommate *'11*
The Scorpion King 3: Battle for Redemption *'11*
Sniper Reloaded *'11*
Border Run *'12*
Hannah's Law *'12*
The Kill Hole *'12*
Red Clover *'12*
2 Jacks *'12*

Sniper: Ghost Shooter '16
Samson '18

Lisa Zane (1961-)
Bad Influence '90
Freddy's Dead: The Final Nightmare '91
Floundering '94
Terrified '94
The Nurse '97
The Pact '99
Wicked Ways '99
Monkeybone '01

Nick Zano (1978-)
Everything You Want '05
Beverly Hills Chihuahua '08
College '08
Joy Ride 2: Dead Ahead '08
The Final Destination '09

Angelo Zanolli
Maciste in Hell '60
Son of Samson '62

Carmen Zapata (1927-2014)
The Last Porno Flick '74
A Home of Our Own '75
Boulevard Nights '79
Gang Boys '97
The Sleepy Time Gal '01

Maya Zapata
Bordertown '06
Under the Same Moon '07

Dweezil Zappa (1969-)
Pretty in Pink '86
The Running Man '87
Jack Frost '98

Moon Zappa (1967-)
Nightmares '83
The Boys Next Door '85
Spirit of '76 '91
Heartstopper '92
Pterodactyl Woman from Beverly Hills '97
The Brutal Truth '99

William Zappa (1948-)
The Road Warrior '82
Crush '93
Zone 39 '96
Bootmen '00

Victor Zaragoza
The Damned '06
Illegal Business '06
San Franpsycho '06

Dominique Zardi (1930-2009)
Le Trou '59
La Femme Infidele '69

John Zaremba (1908-86)
20 Million Miles to Earth '57
The Gallant Hours '60

Tony Zarindast
Hardcase and Fist '89
Werewolf '95

Janet Zarish (1954-)
Danny '79
The Next Big Thing '02

Joe Zaso (1970-)
Addicted to Murder 3: Bloodlust '99
Virus X '10

David Zayas (1962-)
Washington Heights '02
Angel Rodriguez '05
The Interpreter '05
16 Blocks '06
Wake '09
Coach '10
The Expendables '10
Skyline '10
13 '10
Annie '14

Robert Z'Dar (1950-2015)
Code Name: Zebra '84
Grotesque '87
Night Stalker '87
Maniac Cop '88
Samurai Cop '89
Tango and Cash '89
The Killer's Edge '90
Maniac Cop 2 '90
Soultaker '90
Quiet Fire '91
The Legend of Wolf Mountain '92
Return to Frogtown '92
Maniac Cop 3: Badge of Silence '93
Lone Tiger '94
American Chinatown '96
Dangerous Cargo '96
Red Line '96

Rosel Zech (1942-2011)
Lola '81
Veronika Voss '82
Salmonberries '91

Antonia Zegers
No '12
The Club '16

Kevin Zegers (1984-)
Air Bud '97
Air Bud 2: Golden Receiver '98
Bram Stoker's Shadowbuilder '98
It Came from the Sky '98
Nico the Unicorn '98
Komodo '99
Treasure Island '99
Air Bud 3: World Pup '00
MVP: Most Valuable Primate '00
Air Bud 4: Seventh Inning Fetch '02
Fear of the Dark '02
The Incredible Mrs. Ritchie '03
Wrong Turn '03
Dawn of the Dead '04
The Hollow '04
Transamerica '05
It's a Boy Girl Thing '06
Zoom '06
The Jane Austen Book Club '07
Normal '07
The Stone Angel '07
Fifty Dead Men Walking '08
Gardens of the Night '08
The Narrows '08
Frozen '10
The Perfect Age of Rock 'n' Roll '10
The Entitled '11
The Mortal Instruments: City of Bones '13

Oz Zehavi
Yossi '12
The Wedding Plan '17

Nora Zehetner (1981-)
Conversations with Other Women '05
Brick '06
Beneath '07
Princess: A Modern Fairytale '08
Remarkable Power '08
Spooner '08

David Zellner (1974-)
Beeswax '09
Kumiko the Treasure Hunter '14
Damsel '18

Renée Zellweger (1969-)
Love and a .45 '94
Shake, Rattle & Rock! '94
Empire Records '95
The Low Life '95
The Texas Chainsaw Massacre 4: The Next Generation '95
Jerry Maguire '96
The Whole Wide World '96
Deceiver '97
A Price Above Rubies '97
One True Thing '98
The Bachelor '99
Me, Myself, and Irene '00
Nurse Betty '00
Bridget Jones's Diary '01
Chicago '02
White Oleander '02
Cold Mountain '03
Down With Love '03
Bridget Jones: The Edge of Reason '04
Shark Tale '04 (V)
Cinderella Man '05
Miss Potter '06
Bee Movie '07 (V)
Appaloosa '08
Leatherheads '08
Monsters vs. Aliens '09 (V)
My One and Only '09
New in Town '09
Case 39 '10
My Own Love Song '10
Bridget Jones's Baby '16
The Whole Truth '16
Same Kind of Different as Me '17
Judy '19

Michael Zelniker
Pick-Up Summer '79
Bird '88
Naked Lunch '91
Stuart Bliss '98

Roschdy Zem (1965-)
I Don't Kiss '91
Change My Life '01
Monsieur N. '03
The 36th Precinct '04
Le Petit Lieutenant '05
Days of Glory '06
The Girl From Monaco '08
London River '09
Four Lovers '10
Outside the Law '10
Point Blank '10
The Cold Light of Day '12
Collision '13
Just Like a Woman '13
Bird People '14

Tom Zembrod
Living & Dying '07
Fright Flick '10

Zendaya
The Greatest Showman '17
Smallfoot '18

Suzanne Zenor (1947-)
The Baby '72
Get to Know Your Rabbit '72
The Girl Most Likely to. . . '73

Anthony Zerbe (1936-)
Cool Hand Luke '67
Will Penny '67
The Liberation of L.B. Jones '70
They Call Me Mr. Tibbs! '70
Omega Man '71
Papillon '73
The Parallax View '74
Farewell, My Lovely '75
Rooster Cogburn '75
Centennial '78
Child of Glass '78
KISS Meets the Phantom of the Park '78
Who'll Stop the Rain? '78
Dead Zone '83
Soggy Bottom U.S.A. '84
A.D. '85
Dream West '86
Opposing Force '87
Steel Dawn '87
Onassis '88
License to Kill '89
See No Evil, Hear No Evil '89
Touch '96
Asteroid '97
Star Trek: Insurrection '98
True Crime '99
The Matrix Reloaded '03
The Matrix Revolutions '03

Catherine Zeta-Jones (1969-)
Splitting Heirs '93
Catherine Cookson's The Cinder Path '94
The Return of the Native '94
Blue Juice '95
Catherine the Great '95
The Phantom '96
Titanic '96
The Mask of Zorro '98
Entrapment '99
The Haunting '99
High Fidelity '00
Traffic '00
America's Sweethearts '01
Chicago '02
Intolerable Cruelty '03
Sinbad: Legend of the Seven Seas '03 (V)
Ocean's Twelve '04
The Terminal '04
The Legend of Zorro '05
Death Defying Acts '07
No Reservations '07
The Rebound '09
Lay the Favorite '12
Playing for Keeps '12
Rock of Ages '12
Broken City '13
RED 2 '13
Side Effects '13
Dad's Army '16

Mai Zetterling (1925-94)
Torment '44
Night Is My Future '47
Hell Is Sold Out '51
Knock on Wood '54
Pattern for Plunder '62
Hidden Agenda '90
The Witches '90

Fengyi Zhang (1956-)
Farewell My Concubine '93
Temptation of a Monk '94
The Emperor and the Assassin '99
Red Cliff '08

Jin Zhang
The Grandmaster '13
Ip Man 3 '16

Jingchu Zhang (1980-)
Jade Warrior '06
Seven Swords '07
John Rabe '09

Yi Zhang
Mountains May Depart '16
The Climbers '19

Ziyi Zhang (1979-)
Crouching Tiger, Hidden Dragon '00
Musa: The Warrior '01
The Road Home '01
Rush Hour 2 '01
Zu Warriors '01
Hero '02
Purple Butterfly '03
House of Flying Daggers '04
2046 '04
Memoirs of a Geisha '05
Princess Raccoon '05
Horsemen '09
Dangerous Liaisons '12
The Climbers '19
Godzilla: King of the Monsters '19

Tao Zhao
A Touch of Sin '13
Mountains May Depart '16
Ash Is Purest White '18

Vicki Zhao (1976-)
Shaolin Soccer '01
Chinese Odyssey 2002 '02
Red Cliff '08

Wei Zhao
So Close '02
Painted Skin: The Resurrection '12
14 Blades '14

Xun Zhou (1974-)
Perhaps Love '05
The Great Magician '11
Painted Skin: The Resurrection '12

Alexis Zibolis (1979-)
The Da Vinci Treasure '06
Consinsual '10

Malik Zidi (1975-)
Water Drops on Burning Rocks '99
Almost Peaceful '02
Changing Times '04

Alicia Ziegler
Lake Placid 2 '07
Beautiful Wave '11

Joseph Ziegler
Focus '01
Amreeka '09

Sonja Ziemann (1926-2020)
Made in Heaven '52
A Matter of WHO '62

Chip Zien (1947-)
Howard the Duck '86 (V)
Breakfast of Champions '98
The Siege '98
Rosencrantz & Guildenstern Are Undead '10

Ian Ziering (1964-)
No Way Back '96
Domino '05
The Christmas Hope '09
National Lampoon's The Legend of Awesomest Maximus '11
Sharknado '13
Snake & Mongoose '13
Sharknado 2: The Second One '14
Sharknado 3: Oh Hell No! '15
Sharknado: The 4th Awakens '16

Madeline Zima (1985-)
The Hand that Rocks the Cradle '92
Mr. Nanny '93
Second Chances '98
The Sandy Bottom Orchestra '00
A Cinderella Story '04
Legacy '08
The Collector '09
My Own Love Song '10
Crazy Eyes '12
Crazy Kind of Love '12
Lake Effects '12

Vanessa Zima (1986-)
Ulee's Gold '97
Wicked '98
Zoe '01
The Absent '11

Yvonne Zima (1989-)
The Long Kiss Goodnight '96
Storm Catcher '99
A Father's Choice '00
The Absent '11
Meeting Spencer '11

Efrem Zimbalist, Jr. (1918-2014)
House of Strangers '49
Band of Angels '57
Bombers B-52 '57
Deep Six '58
Home Before Dark '58
Too Much, Too Soon '58
Violent Road '58
The Crowded Sky '60
By Love Possessed '61
A Fever In the Blood '61
The Chapman Report '62
Wait until Dark '67
Airport '75 '75
Terror Out of the Sky '78
The Gathering: Part 2 '79
Scruples '80
Hot Shots! '91
Batman: Mask of the Phantasm '93 (V)

Stephanie Zimbalist (1956-)
The Gathering '77
Centennial '78
The Triangle Factory Fire Scandal '79
The Awakening '80
The Killing Mind '90
The Story Lady '93
Prison of Secrets '97
The Prophet's Game '99

Constance Zimmer (1970-)
Warm Blooded Killers '01
Home Room '02
Chaos Theory '08

Kim Zimmer (1955-)
Body Heat '81
The Disappearance of Vonnie '94

Joey Zimmerman (1986-)
Mother's Boys '94
Halloweentown '98
Very Bad Things '98
Treehouse Hostage '99
Halloweentown 2: Kalabar's Revenge '01
Halloweentown High '04
Return to Halloweentown '06

Bettina Zimmermann (1975-)
Post Impact '04
Lost City Raiders '08

Luca Zingaretti (1961-)
Artemisia '97
Jesus '00
Our Life '10

Victoria Zinny (1943-)
Viridiana '61
Shoot the Living, Pray for the Dead '70
Beyond the Door 3 '91

August Zirner (1956-)
Mostly Martha '01
Taking Sides '01
A Sound of Thunder '05
The Counterfeiters '07

Hanns Zischler (1947-)
Les Rendez-vous D'Anna '78
Doktor Faustus '82
The Cement Garden '93
Francesco '93
Taking Sides '01
Munich '05

Dan Ziskie
Zebrahead '92
Dangerous Passion '95
Satan's Little Helper '04

Steve Zissis (1975-)
Baghead '08
The Overbrook Brothers '09
The Do-Deca-Pentathlon '12
Jeff, Who Lives at Home '12

Adrian Zmed (1954-)
For the Love of It '80
Grease 2 '82
The Final Terror '83
Bachelor Party '84
Storm Chasers: Revenge of the Twister '98

Jean-Pierre Zola (1916-79)
Mon Oncle '58
The Train '65

Daniel Zolghadri
Eighth Grade '18
Low Tide '19

Sheri Moon Zombie (1970-)
House of 1000 Corpses '03
The Devil's Rejects '05
Halloween '07
Halloween II '09
The Haunted World of El Superbeasto '09 (V)
The Lords of Salem '13
31 '16
3 from Hell '19

Michael Zorek (1960-)
Private School '83
Hot Moves '84

Louis Zorich (1924-2018)
Vengeance Is Mine '74
The Seagull '75
Death of a Salesman '86
City of Hope '91
Commandments '96

Vera Zorina (1917-2003)
The Goldwyn Follies '38
Louisiana Purchase '41

Zouzou (1943-)
Chloe in the Afternoon '72
S*P*Y*S '74

Rod Zuanic (1968-)
Mad Max: Beyond Thunderdome '85
Danny Deckchair '03

George Zucco (1886-1960)
The Bride Wore Red '37
The Firefly '37
Saratoga '37
Souls at Sea '37
Charlie Chan in Honolulu '38
Fast Company '38
Marie Antoinette '38

Director Index

The Director Index provides a complete videography for any director with three or more video credits. The listings for the director names follow an alphabetical sort by last name (although the names appear in a first name-last name format). The videographies are listed chronologically, from directorial debut to most recent film. If a director helmed more than one film in the same year, these movies are listed alphabetically within the year. Use this index in conjunction with the **Cast** (immediately preceding this index), **Writer**, and **Cinematographer** indexes (immediately following) to see where some of today's hottest directors got their starts.

Jason Alexander (1959-)
For Better or Worse '95
Just Looking '99

John Alexander
Sense & Sensibility '07
The Shadow in the North '07
Small Island '09

Lexi Alexander
Green Street Hooligans '05
Punisher: War Zone '08
Lifted '10

Grigori Alexandrov (1903-83)
The Battleship Potemkin '25
Ten Days That Shook the World '27

Daniel Alfredson (1959-)
The Girl Who Kicked the Hornet's Nest '10
The Girl Who Played With Fire '10
Blackway '16

Tomas Alfredson (1965-)
Let the Right One In '08
Tinker Tailor Soldier Spy '11
The Snowman '17

James Nelson Algar (1913-98)
Fantasia '40
The Adventures of Ichabod and Mr. Toad '49
Fantasia/2000 '00

Daniel Algrant (1959-)
Naked in New York '93
People I Know '02
Greetings from Tim Buckley '12

Dean Alioto
L.A. Dicks '05
Shadowheart '09

Marc Allegret (1900-73)
Fanny '32
Zou Zou '34
Blanche Fury '48
Loves of Three Queens '54
Lady Chatterley's Lover '55
Plucking the Daisy '56

Billy Allen (1922-2006)
See William Allen Castleman

Corey Allen (1934-2010)
Cry Rape! '73
Thunder and Lightning '77
Avalanche '78
Brass '85
The Ann Jillian Story '88

Dave Allen (1944-99)
Dungeonmaster '83
Puppet Master 2 '90

Debbie Allen (1950-)
Out of Sync '95
The Old Settler '01

Elizabeth Allen
Aquamarine '06
Ramona and Beezus '10

Irwin Allen (1916-91)
Story of Mankind '57
The Lost World '60
Voyage to the Bottom of the Sea '61
Five Weeks in a Balloon '62
City Beneath the Sea '71
The Towering Inferno '74
The Swarm '78
Beyond the Poseidon Adventure '79

Kevin Allen (1962-)
The Big Tease '99
Agent Cody Banks 2: Destination London '04

Lewis Allen (1905-2000)
The Uninvited '44
Appointment With Danger '51
At Sword's Point '51
Suddenly '54
A Bullet for Joey '55
Illegal '55
Another Time, Another Place '58

Woody Allen (1935-)
What's Up, Tiger Lily? '66
Take the Money and Run '69
Bananas '71
Everything You Always Wanted to Know about Sex (But Were Afraid to Ask) '72
Sleeper '73
Love and Death '75
Annie Hall '77
Interiors '78
Manhattan '79
Stardust Memories '80
A Midsummer Night's Sex Comedy '82
Zelig '83
Broadway Danny Rose '84
The Purple Rose of Cairo '85
Hannah and Her Sisters '86
Radio Days '87
Another Woman '88
September '88
Crimes & Misdemeanors '89
New York Stories '89
Alice '90
Husbands and Wives '92
Shadows and Fog '92
Manhattan Murder Mystery '93
Bullets over Broadway '94
Mighty Aphrodite '95
Everyone Says I Love You '96
Deconstructing Harry '97
Celebrity '98
Sweet and Lowdown '99
Small Time Crooks '00
The Curse of the Jade Scorpion '01
Hollywood Ending '02
Anything Else '03
Match Point '05
Melinda and Melinda '05
Scoop '06
Vicky Cristina Barcelona '08
Whatever Works '09
You Will Meet a Tall Dark Stranger '10
Midnight in Paris '11
To Rome with Love '12
Blue Jasmine '13
Magic in the Moonlight '14
Café Society '16
Wonder Wheel '17

Roger Allers
The Lion King '94
Open Season '06
Kahlil Gibran's The Prophet '15

Michael Almereyda (1960-)
Twister '89
Nadja '95
The Eternal '99
The External '99
Hamlet '00
Cymbeline '15
Experimenter '15
Marjorie Prime '17

Pedro Almodóvar (1951-)
Dark Habits '84
What Have I Done to Deserve This? '85
Law of Desire '86
Matador '86
Women on the Verge of a Nervous Breakdown '88
Tie Me Up! Tie Me Down! '90
High Heels '91
Kika '94
The Flower of My Secret '95
Live Flesh '97
All About My Mother '99
Talk to Her '02
Bad Education '04
Volver '06
Broken Embraces '09
The Skin I Live In '11
I'm So Excited '13
Julieta '16
Pain and Glory '19

Paul Almond (1931-)
Final Assignment '80
Captive Hearts '87

John A. Alonzo (1934-2001)
Champions: A Love Story '78
FM '78

Mitchell Altieri
April Fool's Day '08
The Thompsons '12

Robert Altman (1925-2006)
Countdown '68
That Cold Day in the Park '69
Brewster McCloud '70
M*A*S*H '70
McCabe & Mrs. Miller '71
Images '72
The Long Goodbye '73
Thieves Like Us '74
Nashville '75
Buffalo Bill & the Indians '76
3 Women '77
A Wedding '78
Quintet '79
Popeye '80
Streamers '83
Secret Honor '85
Beyond Therapy '86
Fool for Love '86
O.C. and Stiggs '87
Aria '88
The Caine Mutiny Court Martial '88
Tanner '88 '88
Vincent & Theo '90
The Player '92
Short Cuts '93
Ready to Wear '94
Kansas City '95
The Gingerbread Man '97
Cookie's Fortune '99
Dr. T & the Women '00
Gosford Park '01
The Company '03
Tanner on Tanner '04
A Prairie Home Companion '06

Robert Alton (1906-57)
Merton of the Movies '47
Pagan Love Song '50

Fede Alvarez (1978-)
Evil Dead '13
Don't Breathe '16
The Girl in the Spider's Web '18

Kyle Patrick Alvarez (1983-)
Easier With Practice '10
C.O.G. '13
The Stanford Prison Experiment '15

Christian Alvart
Antibodies '05
Pandorum '09
Case 39 '10

Rick Alverson
Entertainment '15
The Mountain '19

Keito Amamiya (1959-)
Zeram 2 '94
Moon over Tao '97

Rod Amateau (1923-2003)
The Bushwackers '52
Pussycat, Pussycat, I Love You '70
Drive-In '76
The Seniors '78
High School USA '84
Lovelines '84
The Garbage Pail Kids Movie '87

Jorge Ameer
D'Agostino '12
The Dark Side of Love '12

Gianni Amelio (1945-)
The Stolen Children '92
Lamerica '95

Alejandro Amenabar (1972-)
Open Your Eyes '97
The Others '01
The Sea Inside '04
Agora '09
Regression '16

Jon Amiel (1948-)
The Singing Detective '86
Queen of Hearts '89
Tune in Tomorrow '90
Sommersby '93
Copycat '95
The Man Who Knew Too Little '97
Entrapment '99
The Core '03
Creation '09

Ana Lily Amirpour
A Girl Walks Home Alone at Night '14
The Bad Batch '17

Vicente Amorim
Good '08
Rio, I Love You '14

Franco Amurri (1958-)
Flashback '89
Monkey Trouble '94

Julian Amyes (1917-92)
Great Expectations '81
Jane Eyre '83
The Lady's Not for Burning '87

Jay Anania
Long Time Since '97
Shadows and Lies '10
The Letter '12

Dominic Anciano (1959-)
Final Cut '98
Love, Honour & Obey '00

Allison Anders (1954-)
Border Radio '88
Gas Food Lodging '92
Mi Vida Loca '94
Four Rooms '95
Grace of My Heart '96
Sugar Town '99
Things Behind the Sun '01
Ring of Fire '13

Sean Anders
Sex Drive '08
That's My Boy '12
Horrible Bosses 2 '14
Daddy's Home '15
Daddy's Home 2 '17
Instant Family '18

Bill Anderson
Melissa '97
Sword of Honour '01
Warrior Queen '03

Brad Anderson (1964-)
Next Stop, Wonderland '98
Happy Accidents '00
Session 9 '01
The Machinist '04
Transsiberian '08
Vanishing on 7th Street '10
The Call '13
Stonehearst Asylum '13
Beirut '18
Fractured '19

Jane Anderson (1954-)
The Baby Dance '98
If These Walls Could Talk 2 '00
Normal '03
The Prize Winner of Defiance, Ohio '05

Kurt Anderson
Martial Outlaw '93
The Killing Grounds '97

Lindsay Anderson (1923-94)
This Sporting Life '63
If... '69
O Lucky Man! '73
In Celebration '75
Britannia Hospital '82
The Whales of August '87

Michael Anderson, Sr. (1920-)
Hell Is Sold Out '51
The House of the Arrow '53
Dam Busters '55
Around the World in 80 Days '56
1984 '56
Chase a Crooked Shadow '58
The Wreck of the Mary Deare '59
Flight From Ashiya '64
Operation Crossbow '65
The Quiller Memorandum '66
The Shoes of the Fisherman '68
Conduct Unbecoming '75
Doc Savage '75
Logan's Run '76
Orca '77
Dominique '79
The Martian Chronicles: Part 1 '79
The Martian Chronicles: Part 2 '79
The Martian Chronicles: Part 3 '79
Second Time Lucky '84
Sword of Gideon '86
Millennium '89
The Jeweller's Shop '90
Young Catherine '91
Captains Courageous '95
20,000 Leagues Under the Sea '97
Summer of the Monkeys '98

Paul Thomas Anderson (1970-)
Hard Eight '96
Boogie Nights '97
Magnolia '99
Punch-Drunk Love '02
There Will Be Blood '07
The Master '12
Inherent Vice '14
Phantom Thread '17

Paul W.S. Anderson (1965-)
Shopping '93
Mortal Kombat 1: The Movie '95
Event Horizon '97
Soldier '98
Resident Evil '02
Alien vs. Predator '04
Death Race '08
Resident Evil: Afterlife '10
The Three Musketeers '11
Resident Evil: Retribution '12
Pompeii '14
Resident Evil: The Final Chapter '16

Stephen John Anderson
Meet the Robinsons '07
Winnie the Pooh '11

Steve (Stephen M.) Anderson
South Central '92
Dead Men Can't Dance '97

Wes Anderson (1969-)
Bottle Rocket '95
Rushmore '98
The Royal Tenenbaums '01
The Life Aquatic with Steve Zissou '04
The Darjeeling Limited '07
Fantastic Mr. Fox '09
Moonrise Kingdom '12
The Grand Budapest Hotel '14
Isle of Dogs '18

Mario Andreacchio (1955-)
Fair Game '86
The Dreaming '88
Napoleon '96

Casper Andreas
A Four Letter Word '07
Between Love & Goodbye '08
Violet Tendencies '10

Benedict Andrews
Una '17
Seberg '19

Jay Andrews (1950-)
See Jim Wynorski

Kaare Andrews
Altitude '10
The ABCs of Death '12

Mark C. Andrews
Seal Team '08
Brave '12

Peter Andrews (1963-)
See Steven Soderbergh

Peter Andrikidis
The Incredible Journey of Mary Bryant '05
The Diplomat '08

Chris Angel (1972-)
Beyond Redemption '99
The Fear: Halloween Night '99
Wishmaster 3: Beyond the Gates of Hell '01
Wishmaster 4: The Prophecy Fulfilled '02

Robert Angelo
Forbidden Sins '99
Dead Sexy '01

Theo Angelopoulos (1935-2012)
Landscape in the Mist '88
Ulysses' Gaze '95
Eternity and a Day '97

Ken Annakin (1914-2009)
Miranda '48
The Story of Robin Hood & His Merrie Men '52
The Sword & the Rose '53
Land of Fury '55
Value for Money '55
Three Men in a Boat '56
Across the Bridge '57
Third Man on the Mountain '59
You Know What Sailors Are '59
The Swiss Family Robinson '60
The Longest Day '62
Battle of the Bulge '65
Those Magnificent Men in Their Flying Machines '65
The Biggest Bundle of Them All '68
Those Daring Young Men in Their Jaunty Jalopies '69
Call of the Wild '72
The Fifth Musketeer '79
Pirate Movie '82
The New Adventures of Pippi Longstocking '88

Jean-Jacques Annaud (1943-)
Black and White in Color '76
Quest for Fire '82
The Name of the Rose '86
The Bear '89
The Lover '92
Seven Years in Tibet '97
Enemy at the Gates '00
Two Brothers '04
Day of the Falcon '11
Wolf Totem '15

Paul Annett
The Beast Must Die *'75*
Poldark *'75*
Tales of the Unexpected *'91*

Reverge Anselmo (1962-)
Lover's Prayer *'99*
Stateside *'04*

David Anspaugh (1946-)
Hoosiers *'86*
Fresh Horses *'88*
Rudy *'93*
Moonlight and Valentino *'95*
Swing Vote *'99*
Wisegirls *'02*
The Game of Their Lives *'05*

Nimrod Antal (1973-)
Kontroll *'03*
Vacancy *'07*
Armored *'09*
Predators *'10*
Metallica Through the Never *'13*

Joseph Anthony (1912-93)
The Rainmaker *'56*
The Matchmaker *'58*
Career *'59*
All in a Night's Work *'61*
Tomorrow *'72*

Steve Antin (1958-)
Glass House: The Good Mother *'06*
Burlesque *'10*
Proud Mary *'18*

Pedrag (Peter) Antonijevic (1959-)
Savior *'98*
Hard Cash *'01*

Lou Antonio (1934-)
Someone I Touched *'75*
The Girl in the Empty Grave *'77*
The Gypsy Warriors *'78*
A Real American Hero *'78*
Breaking Up Is Hard to Do *'79*
Agatha Christie's Thirteen at Dinner *'85*
Mayflower Madam *'87*
Pals *'87*
This Gun for Hire *'90*
Lies Before Kisses *'92*
A Taste for Killing *'92*

Michelangelo Antonioni (1912-2007)
Story of a Love Affair *'50*
The Vanquished *'52*
Il Grido *'57*
La Notte *'60*
L'Avventura *'60*
The Eclipse *'62*
The Red Desert *'64*
Blow-Up *'66*
Zabriskie Point *'70*
The Passenger *'75*
Identification of a Woman *'82*
Beyond the Clouds *'95*
Eros *'04*

Judd Apatow (1967-)
The 40 Year Old Virgin *'05*
Knocked Up *'07*
Funny People *'09*
This Is 40 *'12*
Trainwreck *'15*
The King of Staten Island *'20*

Michael Apted (1941-)
The Squeeze *'77*
Agatha *'79*
Coal Miner's Daughter *'80*
Continental Divide *'81*
Gorky Park *'83*
Critical Condition *'86*
Gorillas in the Mist *'88*
Class Action *'91*
Incident at Oglala: The Leonard Peltier Story *'92*
Thunderheart *'92*
Blink *'93*
Nell *'94*
Extreme Measures *'96*
Always Outnumbered Always Outgunned *'98*
The World Is Not Enough *'99*
Enigma *'01*
Enough *'02*
Amazing Grace *'06*
The Chronicles of Narnia: The Voyage of the Dawn Treader *'10*
Chasing Mavericks *'12*
Unlocked *'17*

Gregg Araki (1959-)
The Living End *'92*
Totally F***ed Up *'94*
The Doom Generation *'95*
Splendor *'99*
Mysterious Skin *'04*
Smiley Face *'07*
Kaboom *'11*
White Bird in a Blizzard *'14*

Vicente Aranda (1926-)
The Blood Spattered Bride *'72*
If They Tell You I Fell *'89*
Intruso *'93*
Jealousy *'99*
Mad Love *'01*
Carmen *'03*

Alfonso Arau (1932-)
Like Water for Chocolate *'93*
A Walk in the Clouds *'95*
Picking Up the Pieces *'99*
The Magnificent Ambersons *'02*
A Painted House *'03*

Denys Arcand (1941-)
The Decline of the American Empire *'86*
Jesus of Montreal *'89*
Love and Human Remains *'93*
Stardom *'00*
The Barbarian Invasions *'03*
The Fall of the American Empire *'19*

Nikolaj Arcel
A Royal Affair *'12*
The Dark Tower *'17*

George Archainbaud (1890-1959)
Alias French Gertie *'30*
Framed *'30*
The Silver Horde *'30*
The Lady Refuses *'31*
State's Attorney *'31*
Penguin Pool Murder *'32*
Murder On the Blackboard *'34*
Her Jungle Love *'38*
Thanks for the Memory *'38*
Hoppy Serves a Writ *'43*
The Kansan *'43*
The Woman of the Town *'44*
Hopalong Cassidy: The Devil's Playground *'46*
The Millerson Case *'47*
Hunt the Man Down *'50*

Louise Archambault
Familia *'05*
Gabrielle *'13*

Emile Ardolino (1943-93)
Dirty Dancing *'87*
Chances Are *'89*
Three Men and a Little Lady *'90*
Sister Act *'92*
George Balanchine's The Nutcracker *'93*
Gypsy *'93*

Asia Argento (1975-)
Scarlet Diva *'00*
The Heart Is Deceitful Above All Things *'04*

Dario Argento (1940-)
The Bird with the Crystal Plumage *'70*
The Cat o' Nine Tails *'71*
Four Flies on Grey Velvet *'72*
Deep Red: Hatchet Murders *'75*
Suspiria *'77*
Inferno *'80*
Unsane *'82*
Creepers *'85*
Opera *'88*
Two Evil Eyes *'90*
Dario Argento's Trauma *'93*
The Stendahl Syndrome *'95*
The Phantom of the Opera *'98*
Sleepless *'01*
Mother of Tears *'08*
Giallo *'09*
Argento's Dracula 3D *'13*

Adolfo Aristarain (1943-)
The Stranger *'87*
A Place in the World *'92*
Martin (Hache) *'97*

Allan Arkush (1948-)
Hollywood Boulevard *'76*
Death Sport *'78*
Rock 'n' Roll High School *'79*
Heartbeeps *'81*
Get Crazy *'83*
Caddyshack 2 *'88*
Shake, Rattle & Rock! *'94*
The Temptations *'98*
Christmas with Holly *'12*

Leslie Arliss (1901-87)
The Night Has Eyes *'42*
The Man in Grey *'43*
Love Story *'44*
The Wicked Lady *'45*
A Man About the House *'47*

George Armitage (1942-)
Private Duty Nurses *'71*
Hit Man *'72*
Vigilante Force *'76*
Miami Blues *'90*
Grosse Pointe Blank *'97*
The Big Bounce *'04*

Gillian Armstrong (1950-)
My Brilliant Career *'79*
Starstruck *'82*
Mrs. Soffel *'84*
High Tide *'87*
Fires Within *'91*
Little Women *'94*
Oscar and Lucinda *'97*
Charlotte Gray *'01*
Death Defying Acts *'07*

Moira Armstrong (1930-)
Testament of Youth *'79*
How Many Miles to Babylon? *'82*
Body & Soul *'93*
A Village Affair *'95*

Vic Armstrong
Army of One *'94*
Left Behind *'14*

Andrea Arnold
Red Road *'06*
Fish Tank *'09*
Wuthering Heights *'12*
American Honey *'16*

Frank Arnold (1938-)
A Waltz Through the Hills *'88*
Josh Kirby. . . Time Warrior: Chapter 2, The Human Pets *'95*
Josh Kirby. . . Time Warrior: Chapter 3, Trapped on Toyworld *'95*
Josh Kirby. . . Time Warrior: Chapter 6, Last Battle for the Universe *'96*

Jack Arnold (1916-92)
It Came from Outer Space *'53*
Creature from the Black Lagoon *'54*
Revenge of the Creature *'55*
Tarantula *'55*
The Incredible Shrinking Man *'57*
Man in the Shadow *'57*
High School Confidential *'58*
The Space Children *'58*
Monster on the Campus *'59*
The Mouse That Roared *'59*
No Name on the Bullet *'59*
Bachelor in Paradise *'61*
The Lively Set *'64*
Hello Down There *'69*
Black Eye *'74*
Boss *'74*
Games Girls Play *'75*
Swiss Conspiracy *'77*

Newton Arnold (1928-2000)
Hands of a Stranger *'62*
Blood Thirst *'65*
Bloodsport *'88*

Darren Aronofsky (1969-)
Pi *'98*
Requiem for a Dream *'00*
The Fountain *'06*
The Wrestler *'08*
Black Swan *'10*
Noah *'14*
mother! *'17*

Greg Aronowitz
Labou *'07*
Battle Planet *'08*

Guillermo Arriaga (1958-)
The Burning Plain *'08*
Rio, I Love You *'14*

Miguel Arteta (1965-)
Star Maps *'97*
Chuck & Buck *'00*
The Good Girl *'02*
Youth in Revolt *'10*
Cedar Rapids *'11*
Alexander and the Terrible, Horrible, No Good, Very Bad Day *'14*
Beatriz at Dinner *'17*
Like a Boss *'20*

Karen Arthur (1941-)
My Sister, My Love *'78*
Broken Badge *'85*
Bridge to Silence *'89*
The Jacksons: An American Dream *'92*
The Secret *'93*
Dead by Sunset *'95*
True Women *'97*
The Lost Child *'00*
The Song of the Lark *'01*
The Locket *'02*
The Christmas Blessing *'05*
Moonlight & Mistletoe *'08*

Dorothy Arzner (1897-1979)
Merrily We Go to Hell *'32*
Christopher Strong *'33*
The Bride Wore Red *'37*
Dance, Girl, Dance *'40*

Amma Asante
A Way of Life *'04*
Belle *'13*
A United Kingdom *'17*

Kelly Asbury (1960-2020)
Spirit: Stallion of the Cimarron *'02*
Shrek 2 *'04*
Gnomeo & Juliet *'11*
Smurfs: The Lost Village *'17*
UglyDolls *'19*

Anthony Ascot (1932-)
See Giuliano Carnimeo

Katie (Kathryn) Aselton (1978-)
The Freebie *'10*
Black Rock *'12*

Ash (1964-)
Bang *'95*
Pups *'99*
This Girl's Life *'03*

Hal Ashby (1930-88)
The Landlord *'70*
Harold and Maude *'71*
The Last Detail *'73*
Shampoo *'75*
Bound for Glory *'76*
Coming Home *'78*
Being There *'79*
Second-Hand Hearts *'81*
Lookin' to Get Out *'82*
The Slugger's Wife *'85*

John Mallory Asher (1971-)
Kounterfeit *'96*
Diamonds *'99*
Dirty Love *'05*

William Asher (1921-2012)
Shadow on the Window *'57*
The 27th Day *'57*
Beach Party *'63*
Johnny Cool *'63*
Bikini Beach *'64*
Muscle Beach Party *'64*
Beach Blanket Bingo *'65*
How to Stuff a Wild Bikini *'65*
Fireball 500 *'66*
Movers and Shakers *'85*

Peter Askin
Company Man *'00*
Trumbo *'07*
A Good Marriage *'14*

Anthony Asquith (1902-68)
I Stand Condemned *'36*
Pygmalion *'38*
Cottage to Let *'41*
We Dive at Dawn *'43*
The Way to the Stars *'45*
Man of Evil *'48*
The Winslow Boy *'48*
The Browning Version *'51*
The Importance of Being Earnest *'52*
The Doctor's Dilemma *'58*
Libel *'59*
The Millionairess *'60*
Guns of Darkness *'62*
The V.I.P.'s *'63*
The Yellow Rolls Royce *'64*

Olivier Assayas (1955-)
Irma Vep *'96*
Late August, Early September *'98*
Les Destinees *'00*
Demonlover *'02*
Clean *'04*
Paris, je t'aime *'06*
Boarding Gate *'07*
Summer Hours *'08*
Carlos *'10*
Something in the Air *'13*
Clouds of Sils Maria *'15*
Personal Shopper *'17*
Non-Fiction *'18*

Ovidio G. Assonitis (1943-)
Beyond the Door *'75*
Forever Emmanuelle *'75*
Tentacles *'77*

Ari Aster
Hereditary *'18*
Midsommar *'19*

Doug Atchison
The Pornographer *'00*
Akeelah and the Bee *'06*

Peter Atencio (1983-)
The Rig *'10*
Keanu *'16*

Rowan Athale
Wasteland *'13*
Strange But True *'19*

Mark Atkins
Night Orchid *'97*
Evil Eyes *'04*
Allan Quartermain and the Temple of Skulls *'08*
Merlin and the War of the Dragons *'08*
Dragonquest *'09*
The Haunting of Winchester House *'09*
Princess of Mars *'09*
Jack the Giant Killer *'13*
Android Cop *'14*
Awaken *'15*

Thomas Atkins
The Silver Streak *'34*
Mutiny Ahead *'35*

Yvan Attal (1965-)
My Wife is an Actress *'01*
Happily Ever After *'04*
New York, I Love You *'09*

Richard Attenborough (1923-2014)
Oh! What a Lovely War *'69*
Young Winston *'72*
A Bridge Too Far *'77*
Magic *'78*
Gandhi *'82*
A Chorus Line *'85*
Cry Freedom *'87*
Chaplin *'92*
Shadowlands *'93*
In Love and War *'96*
Grey Owl *'99*
Closing the Ring *'07*

David Attwood (1952-)
Moll Flanders *'96*
Shot Through the Heart *'98*
Fidel *'02*
The Hound of the Baskervilles *'02*
On Thin Ice *'03*

Jacques Audiard (1952-)
Read My Lips *'01*
The Beat My Heart Skipped *'05*
A Prophet *'09*
Rust and Bone *'12*
Dheepan *'16*
The Sisters Brothers *'18*

John H. Auer (1906-75)
Outside of Paradise *'38*
Hell's Half Acre *'54*

Bille August (1948-)
Twist & Shout *'84*
Pelle the Conqueror *'88*
The Best Intentions *'92*
The House of the Spirits *'93*
Smilla's Sense of Snow *'96*
Les Miserables *'97*
A Song for Martin *'01*
Convicted *'04*
The Color of Freedom *'07*
Night Train to Lisbon *'13*

Carlos Aured (1937-)
Horror Rises from the Tomb *'72*
Curse of the Devil *'73*

Jean Aurel (1925-96)
Manon *'68*
The Women *'68*

Paul Auster (1947-)
Blue in the Face *'95*
Lulu on the Bridge *'98*

Ray Austin (1932-)
The Virgin Witch *'70*
House of the Living Dead *'73*
Return of the Man from U.N.C.L.E. *'83*
Highlander: The Gathering *'92*

Steven Austin
Expert Weapon *'93*
American Streetfighter *'96*

Claude Autant-Lara (1901-2000)
Devil in the Flesh *'46*
The Red Inn *'51*
Four Bags Full *'56*

Igor Auzins (1949-)
High Rolling in a Hot Corvette *'77*
Night Nurse *'77*
We of the Never Never *'82*

Aram Avakian (1926-87)
End of the Road '70
Cops and Robbers '73
11 Harrowhouse '74

Roger Avary (1965-)
Killing Zoe '94
The Rules of Attraction '02

Pupi Avati (1938-)
Zeder '83
Revenge of the Dead '84
The Best Man '97
Incantato '03

Howard (Hikmet) Avedis
The Stepmother '71
The Teacher '74
The Specialist '75
Mortuary '81
Separate Ways '82
They're Playing with Fire '84

Brian Avenet-Bradley
Ghost of the Needle '03
Dark Remains '05

Hy Averback (1925-97)
I Love You, Alice B. Toklas! '68
Suppose They Gave a War and Nobody Came? '70
A Guide for the Married Woman '78
Pearl '78
Where the Boys Are '84 '84

Julius Avery
Son of a Gun '14
Overlord '18

John G. Avildsen (1935-2017)
Guess What We Learned in School Today? '70
Joe '70
Cry Uncle '71
Save the Tiger '73
Foreplay '75
W.W. and the Dixie Dancekings '75
Rocky '76
The Formula '80
Neighbors '81
A Night in Heaven '83
The Karate Kid '84
The Karate Kid: Part 2 '86
Happy New Year '87
For Keeps '88
The Karate Kid: Part 3 '89
Lean on Me '89
Rocky 5 '90
The Power of One '92
8 Seconds '94

Meiert Avis
Far from Home '89
Undiscovered '05

Jon Avnet (1949-)
Fried Green Tomatoes '91
The War '94
Up Close and Personal '96
Red Corner '97
Uprising '01
The Starter Wife '07
88 Minutes '08
Righteous Kill '08
Mitch Albom's Have a Little Faith '11

Gabriel Axel (1918-2014)
Babette's Feast '87
Royal Deceit '94

David Ayer (1972-)
Harsh Times '05
Street Kings '08
End of Watch '12
Fury '14
Sabotage '14
Suicide Squad '16
Bright '17

Richard Ayoade
Submarine '10
The Double '13

Steven Ayromlooi
Leprechaun 6: Back 2 Tha Hood '03
Love and Other Four Letter Words '07
My Girlfriend's Back '10

Mario Azzopardi (1950-)
Nowhere to Hide '83
Bone Daddy '97
Thrill Seekers '99
Total Recall 2070: Machine Dreams '99
Stiletto Dance '01
Savage Messiah '02
The Wives He Forgot '06
Lies and Crimes '07
Still Small Voices '07
Witchslayer Gretl '12

Jamie Babbit (1970-)
But I'm a Cheerleader '99
The Quiet '05
Itty Bitty Titty Committee '07
Addicted to Fresno '15

Hector Babenco (1946-)
Pixote '81
Kiss of the Spider Woman '85
Ironweed '87
Carandiru '03

Kevin Bacon (1958-)
Losing Chase '96
Loverboy '05

Lloyd Bacon (1890-1955)
The Singing Fool '28
Say It With Songs '29
Kept Husbands '31
Sit Tight '31
Miss Pinkerton '32
You Said a Mouthful '32
Footlight Parade '33
42nd Street '33
Picture Snatcher '33
Here Comes the Navy '34
Wonder Bar '34
Frisco Kid '35
In Caliente '35
The Irish in Us '35
Cain and Mabel '36
Gold Diggers of 1937 '36
Marked Woman '37
San Quentin '37
Boy Meets Girl '38
Cowboy from Brooklyn '38
A Slight Case of Murder '38
Invisible Stripes '39
Oklahoma Kid '39
Wings of the Navy '39
Brother Orchid '40
Knute Rockne: All American '40
Footsteps in the Dark '41
The Fighting Sullivans '42
Larceny, Inc. '42
Silver Queen '42
Action in the North Atlantic '43
Sunday Dinner for a Soldier '44
Wake Up and Dream '46
Miss Grant Takes Richmond '49
Mother Is a Freshman '49
The Fuller Brush Girl '50
Kill the Umpire '50
Call Me Mister '51
Golden Girl '51
The I Don't Care Girl '53

Malik Bader
Crush '13
Killerman '19

Clarence Badger (1880-1964)
Paths to Paradise '25
It '27
Party Husband '31

John Badham (1939-)
Bingo Long Traveling All-Stars & Motor Kings '76
Saturday Night Fever '77
Dracula '79
Whose Life Is It Anyway? '81
Blue Thunder '83
WarGames '83
American Flyers '85
Short Circuit '86
Stakeout '87
Bird on a Wire '90
The Hard Way '91
Another Stakeout '93
Point of No Return '93
Drop Zone '94
Nick of Time '95
Incognito '97
The Jack Bull '99
The Last Debate '00
Brother's Keeper '02
Obsessed '02
Footsteps '03

Reza Badiyi (1930-2011)
Death Merchants '73
The Eyes of Charles Sand '74
Of Mice and Men '81

Jeff Baena (1977-)
Life After Beth '14
Joshy '16
The Little Hours '17
Horse Girl '20

Max Baer, Jr. (1937-)
The McCullochs '75
Ode to Billy Joe '76
Hometown U.S.A. '79

Jesse Baget
Breathless '12
Cellmates '12
All Hallow's Eve 2 '15
Zombieworld '15

King Baggot (1879-1948)
Tumbleweeds '25
The Notorious Lady '27

Ramin Bahrani
Goodbye Solo '08
99 Homes '14

Charles Bail (1936-)
Black Samson '74
Cleopatra Jones & the Casino of Gold '75
Gumball Rally '76
Street Corner Justice '96

Fenton Bailey
The Eyes of Tammy Faye '00
Party Monster '03
Inside Deep Throat '05

John Bailey (1942-)
China Moon '91
Search for Signs of Intelligent Life in the Universe '91
Brief Interviews With Hideous Men '09

Norma Bailey (1949-)
Eight Days to Live '06
The Capture of the Green River Killer '08
The Christmas Hope '09
The Devil's Teardrop '10
The Pastor's Wife '11

Barnet Bain
The Lost & Found Family '09
Milton's Secret '16

Jon S. Baird
Filth '13
Stan & Ollie '18

Stuart Baird (1947-)
Executive Decision '96
U.S. Marshals '98
Star Trek: Nemesis '02
Vantage Point '08

Graham Baker
The Final Conflict '81
Impulse '84
Alien Nation '88
Born to Ride '91
Beowulf '98

Jonathan Baker
Inconceivable '17
Kin '18

Robert S. Baker (1916-2009)
Blackout '50
Jack the Ripper '60
The Siege of Sidney Street '60
The Secret of Monte Cristo '61

Roy Ward Baker (1916-2010)
Highly Dangerous '50
Morning Departure '50
I'll Never Forget You '51
Don't Bother to Knock '52
One That Got Away '57
A Night to Remember '58
Flame in the Streets '61
The Anniversary '68
Moon Zero Two '70
The Scars of Dracula '70
The Vampire Lovers '70
Dr. Jekyll and Sister Hyde '71
Asylum '72
And Now the Screaming Starts '73
The Legend of the 7 Golden Vampires '73
Vault of Horror '73
Danger UXB '81
The Flame Trees of Thika '81
The Monster Club '85

Sean Baker
Starlet '12
Tangerine '15
The Florida Project '17

Ralph Bakshi (1938-)
Fritz the Cat '72
Heavy Traffic '73
Streetfight '75
Wizards '77
The Lord of the Rings '78
American Pop '81
Hey Good Lookin' '82
Fire and Ice '83
Cool World '92
Cool and the Crazy '94

Bob Balaban (1945-)
Parents '89
My Boyfriend's Back '93
Subway Stories '97
Bernard and Doris '08
Georgia O'Keefe '09

Burt Balaban
Stranger from Venus '54
Murder, Inc. '60
Mad Dog Coll '61

Jaume Balaguero
The Nameless '99
Darkness '02
Fragile '05
[Rec] '07
[Rec] 2 '09
Sleep Tight '11
[REC] 4: Apocalyse '14

Josiane Balasko (1950-)
Hotel America '81
French Twist '95
A French Gigolo '08

Marius Balchunas
No Vacancy '99
The Elder Son '06

Kyle Balda
Dr. Seuss' The Lorax '12
Minions '15
Despicable Me 3 '17

Gianfranco Baldanello (1928-)
Great Adventure '75
The Uranium Conspiracy '78

Ferdinando Baldi (1917-2007)
David and Goliath '61
Duel of Champions '61
Texas, Adios '66

Wes Ball
The Maze Runner '14
Maze Runner: The Scorch Trials '15
Maze Runner: The Death Cure '18

Carroll Ballard (1937-)
The Black Stallion '79
Never Cry Wolf '83
Wind '92
Fly Away Home '96
Duma '05

Tony Bancroft
Mulan '98
Animal Crackers '17

Albert Band (1924-2002)
I Bury the Living '58
Face of Fire '59
She Came to the Valley '77
Zoltan. . . Hound of Dracula '78
Ghoulies 2 '87
Doctor Mordrid: Master of the Unknown '90
Robot Wars '93

Charles Band (1952-)
The Alchemist '81
Parasite '82
Dungeonmaster '83
Metalstorm: The Destruction of Jared Syn '83
Trancers '84
Crash and Burn '90
Doctor Mordrid: Master of the Unknown '90
Trancers 2: The Return of Jack Deth '90
Dollman vs Demonic Toys '93
The Creeps '97
Goobers! '97
Hideous '97

Elizabeth Banks (1974-)
Movie 43 '13
Pitch Perfect 2 '15
Charlie's Angels '19

Montague (Monty) Banks (1897-1950)
The Church Mouse '34
Great Guns '41

Norberto Barba (1963-)
Blue Tiger '94
Solo '96
Terror in the Mall '98

Ernie Barbarash
Cube: Zero '04
Stir of Echoes 2: The Homecoming '07
Hardwired '09
Meteor '09
Ticking Clock '10
6 Bullets '12
Holiday in the Wild '19

Randy Barbato
The Eyes of Tammy Faye '00
Party Monster '03
Inside Deep Throat '05

Daniel Barber
Harry Brown '09
The Keeping Room '15

Joseph Barbera (1911-)
Hey There, It's Yogi Bear '64
Jetsons: The Movie '90

Paris Barclay (1956-)
America's Dream '95
Don't Be a Menace to South Central While Drinking Your Juice in the Hood '95
The Cherokee Kid '96

Richard Bare
The Joe McDoakes Collection '42
This Side of the Law '50

Richard L. Bare (1913-)
Shoot-out at Medicine Bend '57
Wicked, Wicked '73

Clive Barker (1952-)
Hellraiser '87
Nightbreed '90
Lord of Illusions '95

Mike Barker (1966-)
The Tenant of Wildfell Hall '96
Best Laid Plans '99
Lorna Doone '01
To Kill a King '03
A Good Woman '04
Shattered '07
Moby Dick '11

Reginald Barker (1886-1945)
The Wrath of the Gods '14
The Italian '15
Civilization '16
The Great Divide '29
Seven Keys to Baldpate '29
Healer '36

Steve Barker (1971-)
Outpost '07
Outpost: Black Sun '12

Steve Barnett (1955-)
Emmanuelle 5 '87
Mindwarp '91
Scanners: The Showdown '94

Neema Barnette (1949-)
Zora Is My Name! '90
Spirit Lost '96
Civil Brand '02
Heaven Ain't Hard to Find '10

Daniel Barnz
Phoebe in Wonderland '08
Beastly '11
Won't Back Down '12
Cake '14

Allen Baron (1935-)
Blast of Silence '61
Foxfire Light '82

Douglas Barr (1949-)
Ed McBain's 87th Precinct: Heatwave '97
Confessions of an American Bride '05
The Note '07
To Be Fat Like Me '07
The Note 2: Taking a Chance on Love '09
The Jensen Project '10
Secrets of the Mountain '10
Game Time: Tackling the Past '11
The Note 3: Notes from the Heart Healer '12
Northpole '14

Christophe Barratier
The Chorus '04
Paris 36 '08
War of the Buttons '12

Bruno Barreto (1955-)
Dona Flor and Her Two Husbands '78
Gabriela '84
A Show of Force '90
Carried Away '95
Four Days in September '97
One Tough Cop '98
Bossa Nova '99
View from the Top '03
Reaching for the Moon '13

Simon Barrett
V/H/S '12
V/H/S/2 '13

Steven Barron (1956-)
Teenage Mutant Ninja Turtles: The Movie *'90*
Coneheads *'93*
The Adventures of Pinocchio *'96*
Merlin *'98*
Arabian Nights *'00*
Treasure Island *'12*

Zelda Barron (1929-2006)
Bulldance *'88*
Forbidden Sun *'89*
Shag: The Movie *'89*

Mariano Barroso
Extasis *'96*
In the Time of the Butterflies *'01*

Ian Barry
Chain Reaction *'80*
Wrangler *'88*
Crimebroker *'93*
The Seventh Floor *'93*
Crime Broker *'94*
Joey *'98*
The Diamond of Jeru *'01*

Lionel Barrymore (1878-1954)
Madame X *'29*
Ten Cents a Dance *'31*

Paul Bartel (1938-2000)
Private Parts *'72*
Death Race 2000 *'75*
Cannonball *'76*
Eating Raoul *'82*
Not for Publication *'84*
Lust in the Dust *'85*
The Longshot *'86*

Sophie Barthes
Cold Souls *'09*
Madame Bovary *'15*

Andrzej Bartkowiak (1950-)
Romeo Must Die *'00*
Exit Wounds *'01*
Cradle 2 the Grave *'03*
Doom *'05*
Street Fighter: The Legend of Chun-Li *'09*
Maximum Impact *'18*

Hall Bartlett (1922-93)
Zero Hour! *'57*
The Caretakers *'63*
Jonathan Livingston Seagull *'73*
Children of Sanchez *'79*

Richard Bartlett (1922-94)
Lonesome Trail *'55*
Silver Star *'55*
Rock, Pretty Baby *'56*

Charles T. Barton (1902-81)
The Last Outpost *'35*
Murder With Pictures *'36*
The Big Boss *'41*
The Time of Their Lives *'46*
Buck Privates Come Home *'47*
The Wistful Widow of Wagon Gap *'47*
Abbott and Costello Meet Frankenstein *'48*
Mexican Hayride *'48*
The Noose Hangs High *'48*
Abbott and Costello Meet the Killer, Boris Karloff *'49*
Africa Screams *'49*
Double Crossbones *'51*
Ma and Pa Kettle at the Fair *'52*
Dance with Me, Henry *'56*
The Shaggy Dog *'59*
Toby Tyler *'59*

Paolo Barzman
Autumn Hearts: A New Beginning *'07*
Dr. Jekyll and Mr. Hyde *'08*
The Phantom *'09*
Who Is Simon Miller? *'11*

K.C. Bascombe
The Contract *'98*
Fear of the Dark *'02*
Swindle *'02*
Hide *'08*

Giulio Base
Doc West *'09*
Triggerman *'09*

Harry Basil
The 4th Tenor *'02*
Soul's Midnight *'06*

Qasim Basir
Mooz-Lum *'10*
A Boy. A Girl. A Dream. *'18*

Jules Bass (1935-)
Mad Monster Party *'68*
The Hobbit *'78*
The Return of the King *'80*
Flight of Dragons *'82*
The Last Unicorn *'82*

Michael J. Bassett
Deathwatch *'02*
Silent Hill: Revelation 3D *'12*

Lawrence Bassoff
Weekend Pass *'84*
Hunk *'87*

Jason Bateman (1969-)
Bad Words *'13*
The Family Fang *'16*

Richard Bates, Jr.
Trash Fire *'16*
Tone-Deaf *'19*

Otto Bathurst
Five Days *'07*
Margot *'09*
Robin Hood *'18*

Zal Batmanglij
Sound of My Voice *'11*
The East *'13*

Ritesh Batra
The Lunchbox *'13*
The Sense of an Ending *'17*
Photograph *'19*

Bradley Battersby (1953-)
Blue Desert *'91*
Red Letters *'00*

Roy Battersby
Catherine Cookson's The Black Candle *'92*
Cracker: Brotherly Love *'95*
Catherine Cookson's The Moth *'96*
Red Mercury *'05*

Brian Baugh
To Save a Life *'10*
I'm Not Ashamed *'16*

Chris Baugh
Ping! *'99*
Bad Day for the Cut *'17*

Noah Baumbach (1969-)
Kicking and Screaming *'95*
Highball *'97*
Mr. Jealousy *'98*
The Squid and the Whale *'05*
Margot at the Wedding *'07*
Greenberg *'10*
Frances Ha *'13*
While We're Young *'14*
Mistress America *'15*
De Palma *'16*
The Meyerowitz Stories (New and Selected) *'17*
Marriage Story *'19*

Lamberto Bava (1944-)
Macabre *'80*
A Blade in the Dark *'83*
Demons *'86*
Demons 2 *'87*
Ghost Son *'06*

Mario Bava (1914-80)
Black Sunday *'60*
The Girl Who Knew Too Much *'63*
The Invaders *'63*
The Whip and the Body *'63*
Black Sabbath *'64*
Blood and Black Lace *'64*
Hercules in the Haunted World *'64*
Knives of the Avenger *'65*
Planet of the Vampires *'65*
Kill, Baby, Kill *'66*
Danger: Diabolik *'68*
Four Times That Night *'69*
Five Dolls for an August Moon *'70*
Hatchet for the Honeymoon *'70*
Roy Colt and Winchester Jack *'70*
Twitch of the Death Nerve *'71*
Torture Chamber of Baron Blood *'72*
Kidnapped *'74*
Lisa and the Devil *'75*
Shock *'79*

Craig R. Baxley (1949-)
Action Jackson *'88*
I Come in Peace *'90*
Stone Cold *'91*
Deep Red *'94*
The Avenging Angel *'95*
Under Pressure *'98*
Stephen King's The Storm of the Century *'99*
Sniper 2 *'02*
Stephen King's Rose Red *'02*
The Diary of Ellen Rimbauer *'03*
The Triangle *'05*
Aces 'n Eights *'08*

John Baxter (1896-1975)
Love on the Dole *'41*
Old Mother Riley's Ghosts *'41*

Michael Bay (1965-)
Bad Boys *'95*
The Rock *'96*
Armageddon *'98*
Pearl Harbor *'01*
Bad Boys 2 *'03*
The Island *'05*
Transformers *'07*
Transformers: Revenge of the Fallen *'09*
Transformers: Dark of the Moon *'11*
Pain & Gain *'13*
Transformers: Age of Extinction *'14*
13 Hours: The Secret Soldiers of Benghazi *'16*
Transformers: The Last Knight *'17*
6 Underground *'19*

Juan Antonio Bayona (1975-)
The Orphanage *'07*
The Impossible *'12*
A Monster Calls *'17*
Jurassic World: Fallen Kingdom *'18*

Camillo Bazzoni (1934-)
A Long Ride From Hell *'68*
Black Lemons *'70*

Luigi Bazzoni (1929-2012)
Man, Pride and Vengeance *'67*
Primal Impulse *'74*

David Beaird (1952-)
Octavia *'82*
Party Animal *'83*
My Chauffeur *'86*
Scorchers *'92*

Charlie Bean
The LEGO Ninjago Movie *'17*
Lady and the Tramp *'19*

Henry Bean (1945-)
The Believer *'01*
Noise *'07*

Warren Beatty (1937-)
Heaven Can Wait *'78*
Reds *'81*
Dick Tracy *'90*
Bulworth *'98*
Rules Don't Apply *'16*

William Beaudine (1892-1970)
The Canadian *'26*
Sparrows *'26*
Road to Paradise *'30*
Penrod and Sam *'31*
Make Me a Star *'32*
Three Wise Girls *'32*
The Old-Fashioned Way *'34*
Boys Will Be Boys *'35*
Windbag the Sailor *'36*
Blonde Comet *'41*
Desperate Cargo *'41*
Robot Pilot *'41*
The Panther's Claw *'42*
Clancy Street Boys *'43*
Spotlight Scandals *'43*
Black Market Babies *'45*
Don't Gamble with Strangers *'46*
The Chinese Ring *'47*
Mom & Dad *'47*
The Golden Eye *'48*
Kidnapped *'48*
Shanghai Chest *'48*
Bela Lugosi Meets a Brooklyn Gorilla *'52*
Westward Ho, the Wagons! *'56*
Ten Who Dared *'60*
Lassie's Great Adventure *'62*
Jesse James Meets Frankenstein's Daughter *'65*
Billy the Kid Versus Dracula *'66*

Gabrielle Beaumont (1942-)
Death of a Centerfold *'81*
Gone Are the Days *'84*
He's My Girl *'87*
Riders *'88*

Harry Beaumont (1888-1966)
Beau Brummel *'24*
Our Dancing Daughters *'28*
Broadway Melody *'29*
Speedway *'29*
Lord Byron of Broadway *'30*
Our Blushing Brides *'30*
Dance Fools Dance *'31*
Laughing Sinners *'31*
West of Broadway *'31*
Are You Listening? *'32*
Faithless *'32*
Made On Broadway *'33*
When's Your Birthday? *'37*
Maisie Goes to Reno *'44*
Up Goes Maisie *'46*
Undercover Maisie *'47*

Xavier Beauvois (1967-)
Le Petit Lieutenant *'05*
Of Gods and Men *'10*

Gorman Bechard (1959-)
Galactic Gigolo *'87*
Psychos in Love *'87*
Cemetery High *'89*

Steve Beck
13 Ghosts *'01*
Ghost Ship *'02*

Harold Becker (1950-)
The Black Marble *'79*
The Onion Field *'79*
Taps *'81*
Vision Quest *'85*
Big Town *'87*
The Boost *'88*
Sea of Love *'89*
Malice *'93*
City Hall *'95*
Mercury Rising *'98*
Domestic Disturbance *'01*

Jacques Becker (1906-60)
Casque d'Or *'52*
Grisbi *'53*
Le Trou *'59*

Jean Becker (1933-)
A Man Named Rocca *'61*
One Deadly Summer *'83*
My Afternoons with Margueritte *'10*

Josh Becker (1958-)
Thou Shalt Not Kill. . .Except *'87*
Alien Apocalypse *'05*

Walt Becker (1968-)
Buying the Cow *'02*
National Lampoon's Van Wilder *'02*
Wild Hogs *'07*
Old Dogs *'09*
Alvin and the Chipmunks: Road Chip *'15*

James Becket (1936-)
Plato's Run *'96*
Final Approach *'04*

James Gavin Bedford
Red Shoe Diaries 8: Night of Abandon *'97*
The Street King *'02*

Ford Beebe (1888-1978)
The Last of the Mohicans *'32*
Pride of the Legion *'32*
Shadow of the Eagle *'32*
Laughing at Life *'33*
Ace Drummond *'36*
Radio Patrol *'37*
Tim Tyler's Luck *'37*
Buck Rogers Conquers the Universe *'39*
Destination Saturn *'39*
Flash Gordon: Mars Attacks the World *'39*
The Green Hornet *'39*
The Phantom Creeps *'39*
Fantasia *'40*
Flash Gordon Conquers the Universe *'40*
Junior G-Men *'40*
Winners of the West *'40*
Riders of Death Valley *'41*
Night Monster *'42*
Overland Mail *'42*
Don Winslow of the Coast Guard *'43*
Don Winslow of the Navy *'43*
The Invisible Man's Revenge *'44*
My Dog Shep *'46*
Bomba on Panther Island *'49*
Bomba, the Jungle Boy *'49*
Bomba and the Hidden City *'50*
The Lost Volcano *'50*
Elephant Stampede *'51*
The Lion Hunters *'51*
African Treasure *'52*
Bomba and the Jungle Girl *'52*
Wagons West *'52*
Safari Drums *'53*
The Golden Idol *'54*
Killer Leopard *'54*
Lord of the Jungle *'55*
King of the Wild Stallions *'59*

Greg Beeman (1962-)
License to Drive *'88*
Mom and Dad Save the World *'92*
Bushwhacked *'95*
Miracle in Lane Two *'00*

Charles Beeson
Agatha Christie's The Pale Horse *'96*
Cider with Rosie *'99*
Second Sight *'99*

Jean-Jacques Beineix (1946-)
Diva *'82*
Moon in the Gutter *'83*
Betty Blue *'86*
Mortal Transfer *'01*

Timur Bekmambetov
Night Watch *'04*
Day Watch *'06*
Wanted *'08*
Abraham Lincoln: Vampire Hunter *'12*
Ben-Hur *'16*

Chris Bell
Bigger Stronger Faster *'08*
Prescription Thugs *'16*

Diane Bell
Obselidia *'10*
Bleeding Heart *'15*

Martin Bell
American Heart *'92*
Hidden in America *'96*
Brotherhood of Murder *'99*

Monta Bell (1891-1958)
Lady of the Night *'25*
Torrent *'26*
Downstairs *'32*

William Brent Bell
Stay Alive *'06*
The Devil Inside *'12*
The Boy *'16*
Brahms: The Boy II *'19*

Earl Bellamy (1917-2003)
Seminole Uprising *'55*
Munster, Go Home! *'66*
The Desperate Mission *'69*
Against a Crooked Sky *'75*
Seven Alone *'75*
Walking Tall: Part 2 *'75*
Flood! *'76*
Fire *'77*
Sidewinder One *'77*

Donald P. Bellisario (1935-)
Last Rites *'88*
JAG *'95*

Marco Bellocchio (1939-)
Henry IV *'85*
Devil in the Flesh *'87*
My Mother's Smile *'02*
The Wedding Director *'06*
Vincere *'09*

Andrew Bellware
Pandora Machine *'04*
Clone Hunter *'09*

Maria-Luisa Bemberg (1922-95)
Camila *'84*
I, the Worst of All *'90*
I Don't Want to Talk About It *'94*

Jack Bender
Letting Go *'85*
The Midnight Hour *'86*
Tricks of the Trade *'88*
My Brother's Wife *'89*
Child's Play 3 *'91*
Lone Justice 2 *'93*
Lone Justice 3: Showdown at Plum Creek *'96*
Killing Mr. Griffin *'97*
It Came from the Sky *'98*
My Little Assassin *'99*

Joel Bender
Gas Pump Girls *'79*
The Immortalizer *'89*
Midnight Kiss *'93*
Karla *'06*

Laszlo Benedek (1907-92)
The Kissing Bandit *'48*
Port of New York *'49*
Death of a Salesman *'51*
The Wild One *'54*
Namu, the Killer Whale *'66*
The Night Visitor *'70*

Richard Benedict (1916-84)
Winter a Go-Go *'65*
Impasse *'69*

Roberto Benigni (1952-)
The Monster '96
Life Is Beautiful '98
Pinocchio '02
The Tiger and the Snow '05

Richard Benjamin (1938-)
My Favorite Year '82
City Heat '84
Racing with the Moon '84
The Money Pit '86
Little Nikita '88
My Stepmother Is an Alien '88
Downtown '89
Mermaids '90
Made in America '93
Milk Money '94
Mrs. Winterbourne '96
The Pentagon Wars '98
Marci X '03
A Little Thing Called Murder '06

Roxanne Benjamin
Southbound '16
XX '17
Body at Brighton Rock '19

Spencer Gordon Bennet (1893-1987)
Last Frontier '32
Zorro's Black Whip '44
The Purple Monster Strikes '45
Atom Man *vs.* Superman '50
Atomic Submarine '59

Bill Bennett (1953-)
Two If by Sea '95
Tempted '01
The Nugget '02
Bollywood Hero '09

Compton Bennett (1900-74)
King Solomon's Mines '50
That Forsyte Woman '50

Rodney Bennett
The Lost Boys '78
Edwin '84
Sense & Sensibility '85

Sacha Bennett (1971-)
Bonded by Blood '09
Outside Bet '12
Get Lucky '13

Spencer Gordon Bennett
Night Alarm '34
The Oil Raider '34

Justin Benson
Spring '15
The Endless '17

Steve Benson (1936-99)
See Joe D'Amato

Thomas Bentley (1880-1950)
The Living Dead '33
Murder at the Baskervilles '37

Robert Benton (1932-)
Bad Company '72
The Late Show '77
Kramer *vs.* Kramer '79
Still of the Night '82
Places in the Heart '84
Nadine '87
Billy Bathgate '91
Nobody's Fool '94
Twilight '98
The Human Stain '03
Feast of Love '07

Luca Bercovici (1957-)
Ghoulies '84
Rockula '90
Bitter Sweet '98
Convict 762 '98
Luck of the Draw '00

Bruce Beresford (1940-)
Barry McKenzie Holds His Own '74
Don's Party '76
The Getting of Wisdom '77
Breaker Morant '80
The Club '81
Tender Mercies '83
King David '85
Crimes of the Heart '86
Aria '88
Her Alibi '88
Driving Miss Daisy '89
Black Robe '91
Mister Johnson '91
Rich in Love '93
A Good Man in Africa '94
Silent Fall '94
Last Dance '96
Paradise Road '97
Double Jeopardy '99
Bride of the Wind '01
Evelyn '02
And Starring Pancho Villa as Himself '03
The Contract '07
Mao's Last Dancer '09
Peace, Love & Misunderstanding '11
Bonnie & Clyde '13
Mr. Church '16

Amy Berg
West of Memphis '12
Every Secret Thing '15

Peter Berg (1964-)
Very Bad Things '98
The Rundown '03
Friday Night Lights '04
The Kingdom '07
Hancock '08
Virtuality '09
Battleship '12
Lone Survivor '13
Deepwater Horizon '16
Patriots Day '17
Mile 22 '18
Spenser Confidential '20

Pamela Berger
The Imported Bridegroom '89
The Magic Stone '95

Todd Berger (1979-)
The Scenesters '09
It's a Disaster '12

Bibo Bergeron
Shark Tale '04
A Monster in Paris '11

Andrew Bergman (1945-)
So Fine '81
The Freshman '90
Honeymoon in Vegas '92
It Could Happen to You '94
Striptease '96
Isn't She Great '00

Ingmar Bergman (1918-2007)
Night Is My Future '47
Port of Call '48
Devil's Wanton '49
Three Strange Loves '49
Summer Interlude '50
To Joy '50
Monika '52
Secrets of Women '52
Sawdust & Tinsel '53
Summer With Monica '53
Smiles of a Summer Night '55
The Seventh Seal '56
Brink of Life '57
Wild Strawberries '57
The Magician '58
The Virgin Spring '59
Through a Glass Darkly '61
The Winter Light '62
The Silence '63
Persona '66
Hour of the Wolf '68
The Shame '68
The Rite '69
The Passion of Anna '70
Cries and Whispers '72
The Magic Flute '73
Scenes from a Marriage '73
Face to Face '76
Autumn Sonata '78
The Serpent's Egg '78
From the Life of the Marionettes '80
Fanny and Alexander '83
Saraband '03

Dan Berk
Body '15
Villains '19

William Berke (1903-58)
Tornado '43
The Falcon in Mexico '44
Navy Way '44
That's My Baby! '44
Renegade Girl '46
Rolling Home '48
Deputy Marshal '50
Operation Haylift '50
Pygmy Island '50
Treasure of Monte Cristo '50
Fury of the Congo '51
Savage Drums '51
FBI Girl '52
Jungle '52
The Marshal's Daughter '53
Four Boys and a Gun '57
Cop Hater '58
The Lost Missile '58
Mark of the Gorilla '58
The Mugger '58

Busby Berkeley (1895-1976)
Gold Diggers of 1935 '35
Hollywood Hotel '37
Garden of the Moon '38
Babes in Arms '39
Fast and Furious '39
They Made Me a Criminal '39
Strike Up the Band '40
Babes on Broadway '41
For Me and My Gal '42
The Gang's All Here '43
Take Me Out to the Ball Game '49

Greg Berlanti
The Broken Hearts Club '00
Life As We Know It '10
Love, Simon '18

Alain Berliner (1963-)
Ma Vie en Rose '97
Passion of Mind '00

Joe Berlinger (1961-)
Brother's Keeper '92
Paradise Lost: The Child Murders at Robin Hood Hills '95
Paradise Lost 2: Revelations '99
Book of Shadows: Blair Witch 2 '00
Metallica: Some Kind of Monster '04
Crude: The Real Price of Oil '09
Paradise Lost 3: Purgatory '11
Whitey: United States of America v. James J. Bulger '14
Extremely Wicked, Shockingly Evil and Vile '19

Monty Berman (1912-2006)
Jack the Ripper '60
The Siege of Sidney Street '60
The Secret of Monte Cristo '61

Shari Springer Berman (1963-)
American Splendor '03
The Nanny Diaries '07
The Extra Man '10
Cinema Verite '11
Girl Most Likely '12
Ten Thousand Saints '15

Ted Berman (1920-2001)
The Fox and the Hound '81
The Black Cauldron '85

Zev Berman
Plain Dirty '04
Borderland '07

Edward L. Bernds (1905-2000)
Corky of Gasoline Alley '51
Gasoline Alley '51
Harem Girl '52
World Without End '56
Storm Rider '57
Queen of Outer Space '58
Space Master X-7 '58
Return of the Fly '59
The Three Stooges Meet Hercules '61
Valley of the Dragons '61
Three Stooges in Orbit '62
Gunfight at Comanche Creek '64

Jack Bernhard (1914-97)
Decoy '46
Violence '47
Blonde Ice '48
The Hunted '48
Unknown Island '48

Curtis Bernhardt (1899-1981)
My Love Came Back '40
Juke Girl '42
Conflict '45
Devotion '46
My Reputation '46
A Stolen Life '46
High Wall '47
The Possessed '47
The Doctor and the Girl '49
Payment on Demand '51
Sirocco '51
Miss Sadie Thompson '53
Beau Brummell '54
Interrupted Melody '55
Damon and Pythias '62
Kisses for My President '64

Corbin Bernsen (1954-)
Carpool Guy '05
Dead Air '08
Donna on Demand '09
Rust '09

Adam Bernstein (1960-)
It's Pat: The Movie '94
Six Ways to Sunday '99

Assaf Bernstein (1970-)
The Debt '07
Look Away '18

Molly Bernstein
Deceptive Practice: The Mysteries and Mentors of Ricky Jay '12
Deceptive Practice: The Mysteries and Mentors of Ricky Jay '13

Walter Bernstein (1919-)
Little Miss Marker '80
Women & Men: In Love There Are No Rules '91

Claude Berri (1934-2009)
The Two of Us '68
Jean de Florette '87
Manon of the Spring '87
The Housekeeper '02

John Berry (1917-99)
Tension '50
The Bad News Bears Go to Japan '78
Boesman & Lena '00

Tom Berry
Blind Fear '89
Twin Sisters '91

Bryan Bertino
The Strangers '08
The Monster '16

Bernardo Bertolucci (1940-2018)
The Grim Reaper '62
Partner '68
The Conformist '71
Last Tango in Paris '73
1900 '76
The Last Emperor '87
The Sheltering Sky '90
Little Buddha '93
Stealing Beauty '96
Besieged '98
The Dreamers '03
Me and You '12

Julie Bertuccelli (1968-)
Since Otar Left. . . '03
The Tree '10

Irvin Berwick (1914-)
The 7th Commandment '61
Malibu High '79

Carl Bessai
Emile '03
Normal '07

Luc Besson (1959-)
Le Dernier Combat '84
Subway '85
The Big Blue '88
La Femme Nikita '91
The Professional '94
The Fifth Element '97
The Messenger: The Story of Joan of Arc '99
Angel-A '05
Arthur and the Invisibles '06
The Lady '11
The Family '13
Lucy '14
Valerian and the City of a Thousand Planets '17
Anna '19

Nicole Bettauer
Zack & Reba '98
Duck '05

Matt Bettinelli-Olpin
Devil's Due '14
Ready or Not '19

Angela Bettis (1973-)
Roman '06
The ABCs of Death '12

Gil Bettman
Crystal Heart '87
Night Vision '97

Jonathan Betuel (1949-)
My Science Project '85
Theodore Rex '95

Frank Beyer (1932-2006)
Carbide and Sorrel '63
Jacob the Liar '74

Thomas Bezucha
Big Eden '00
The Family Stone '05
Monte Carlo '11

Sanjay Leela Bhansali
Devdas '02
Padmaavat '18

Andrea Bianchi (1925-)
Cry of a Prostitute: Love Kills '72
What the Peeper Saw '72
Burial Ground '85

Edward Bianchi (1942-)
The Fan '81
The Two Mr. Kissels '08

Abner Biberman (1909-77)
The Price of Fear '56
Gun for a Coward '57

Herbert Biberman (1900-71)
Meet Nero Wolfe '36
The Master Race '44
Salt of the Earth '54

Rick Bieber
Crazy '08
The 5th Quarter '10

Fabian Bielinsky (1959-2006)
Nine Queens '00
The Aura '05

Suzanne (Susanne) Bier (1960-)
Like It Never Was Before '95
Brothers '04
After the Wedding '06
Things We Lost in the Fire '07
In a Better World '10
Serena '14

Robert Bierman
Vampire's Kiss '88
Clarissa '91
A Merry War '97
The Moonstone '97

Kathryn Bigelow (1952-)
Loveless '83
Near Dark '87
Blue Steel '90
Point Break '91
Wild Palms '93
Strange Days '95
The Weight of Water '00
K-19: The Widowmaker '02
The Hurt Locker '08
Zero Dark Thirty '12
Detroit '17

Tony Bill (1940-)
My Bodyguard '80
Six Weeks '82
Five Corners '88
Crazy People '90
A Home of Our Own '93
Untamed Heart '93
One Christmas '95
Beyond the Call '96
Oliver Twist '97
Harlan County War '00
Flyboys '06
Pictures of Hollis Woods '07

Peter Billingsley (1971-)
Couples Retreat '09
Term Life '16

Kevin Billington (1934-)
Interlude '68
The Rise and Rise of Michael Rimmer '70
Light at the Edge of the World '71

Danny Bilson (1956-)
Zone Troopers '84
The Wrong Guys '88

Charles Biname
The Trojan Horse '08
Cyberbully '11

Mike Binder (1958-)
Crossing the Bridge '92
Indian Summer '93
Blankman '94
The Sex Monster '99
The Search for John Gissing '01
The Upside of Anger '05
Reign Over Me '07
Black or White '14

Steve Binder
The T.A.M.I. Show '64
Give 'Em Hell, Harry! '75

William Bindley
The Eighteenth Angel '97
Madison '01

Josh Binney (1889-1956)
Boardinghouse Blues '48
Killer Diller '48

Claude Binyon (1905-78)
Family Honeymoon '49
Mother Didn't Tell Me '50
Here Come the Girls '53

Mike Birbiglia (1978-)
Sleepwalk with Me '12
Don't Think Twice '16

Antonia Bird (1951-2013)
Priest '94
Mad Love '95
Face '97
Ravenous '99
The Hamburg Cell '04

Brad Bird (1957-)
The Iron Giant '99
The Incredibles '04
Ratatouille '07

Mission: Impossible-Ghost Protocol '11
Tomorrowland '15
Incredibles 2 '18

Andrew Birkin (1945-)
The Cement Garden '93
Desire '93

Daniel Birt (1907-55)
The Three Weird Sisters '48
Interrupted Journey '49

Larry Bishop (1948-)
Trigger Happy '96
Hell Ride '08

Matthew Bissonnette
Who Loves the Sun '06
Passenger Side '09

Bill Bixby (1934-93)
The Trial of the Incredible Hulk '89
Death of the Incredible Hulk '90
Another Pair of Aces: Three of a Kind '91
Baby of the Bride '91
The Woman Who Loved Elvis '93

Anne K. Black
Mythica 2: The Darkspore '15
Mythica: A Quest for Heroes '15

Dustin Lance Black (1974-)
The Journey of Jared Price '00
Virginia '10

Noel Black (1937-)
Pretty Poison '68
Jennifer On My Mind '71
A Man, a Woman, and a Bank '79
Prime Suspect '82
Private School '83
Promises to Keep '85

Shane Black (1961-)
Kiss Kiss Bang Bang '05
Iron Man 3 '13
The Nice Guys '16
The Predator '18

David Blair
Split Second '99
Anna Karenina '00
Tess of the D'Urbervilles '08
Going for Gold: The '48 Games '12
Mission of Honor '19

Alfonso Corona Blake (1919-99)
Samson *vs.* the Vampire Women '61
Samson in the Wax Museum '63

Michael Blakemore (1928-)
Privates on Parade '84
Country Life '95

J. Blakeson
The Disappearance of Alice Creed '09
The 5th Wave '16

Larry Blamire
The Lost Skeleton of Cadavra '01
Dark and Stormy Night '09

Jamie Blanks
Urban Legend '98
Valentine '01
Nature's Grave '08

Alessandro Blasetti (1900-87)
Fabiola '48
Too Bad She's Bad '54

Edward Blatt (1903-91)
Between Two Worlds '44
Smart Woman '48

William Peter Blatty (1928-2017)
The Ninth Configuration '79
Exorcist 3: Legion '90

Barry W. Blaustein (1955-)
The Ringer '05
Peep World '10

Jeff Bleckner (1943-)
Brotherly Love '85
White Water Summer '87
Serving in Silence: The Margarethe Cammermeyer Story '95
The Beast '96
Flowers for Algernon '00
Dean Koontz's Black River '01
Have No Fear: The Life of Pope John Paul II '05
That Russell Girl '08
Loving Leah '09
Beyond the Blackboard '11
Remember Sunday '13

Bernard Blier (1916-89)
Notre Histoire '84
How Much Do You Love Me? '05

Bertrand Blier (1939-)
Going Places '74
Get Out Your Handkerchiefs '78
Buffet Froid '79
Beau Pere '81
Menage '86
Too Beautiful for You '88

Jeffrey Blitz (1969-)
Spellbound '02
Rocket Science '07
Table 19 '17

Neill Blomkamp (1979-)
District 9 '09
Elysium '13
Chappie '15

Jason Bloom
Bio-Dome '96
Overnight Delivery '96
Dead Simple '01

Jeffrey Bloom
Dog Pound Shuffle '75
The Right of the People '86
Flowers in the Attic '87

George Bloomfield (1930-)
The Awakening '95
Jacob Two Two Meets the Hooded Fang '99

Don Bluth (1938-)
The Secret of NIMH '82
An American Tail '86
The Land Before Time '88
All Dogs Go to Heaven '89
Rock-a-Doodle '92
The Pebble and the Penguin '94
Thumbelina '94
A Troll in Central Park '94
Anastasia '97
Titan A.E. '00

John Blystone (1892-1938)
Our Hospitality '23
Too Busy to Work '32
Little Miss Nobody '36
23 1/2 Hours Leave '37
Block-heads '38
Swiss Miss '38

David Blyth (1956-)
Death Warmed Up '85
Red Blooded American Girl '90
Hot Blooded '98

Baran bo Odar
The Silence '10
Sleepless '17

James Bobin
The Muppets '11
Muppets Most Wanted '14

Alice Through the Looking Glass '16
Dora and the Lost City of Gold '19

Hart Bochner (1956-)
P.C.U. '94
High School High '96
Just Add Water '07

Richard Boddington
The Dogfather '10
Against the Wild '14
Against the Wild II: Survive the Seregenti '16

Anna Boden
Sugar '09
It's Kind of a Funny Story '10
Mississippi Grind '15
Captain Marvel '19

Sergei Bodrov (1948-)
Prisoner of the Mountains '96
Running Free '00
The Quickie '01
Mongol '07
Seventh Son '15

Budd Boetticher (1916-2001)
Bullfighter & the Lady '50
Horizons West '52
Man from the Alamo '53
Seminole '53
The Killer Is Loose '56
7 Men From Now '56
Decision at Sundown '57
The Tall T '57
Buchanan Rides Alone '58
Westbound '58
Ride Lonesome '59
Comanche Station '60
The Rise and Fall of Legs Diamond '60

Paul Bogart (1919-2012)
Marlowe '69
Halls of Anger '70
Skin Game '71
Cancel My Reservation '72
A House Without a Christmas Tree '72
Class of '44 '73
Mr. Ricco '75
You Can't Take It With You '79
Power, Passion & Murder '83
Oh, God! You Devil '84
The Canterville Ghost '86
Nutcracker: Money, Madness & Murder '87
Torch Song Trilogy '88
The Heidi Chronicles '95

Yurek Bogayevicz (1948-)
Anna '87
Three of Hearts '93
Edges of the Lord '01

Peter Bogdanovich (1939-)
Targets '68
Voyage to the Planet of Prehistoric Women '68
The Last Picture Show '71
What's Up, Doc? '72
Paper Moon '73
Daisy Miller '74
Nickelodeon '76
Saint Jack '79
They All Laughed '81
Mask '85
Illegally Yours '87
Texasville '90
Noises Off '92
The Thing Called Love '93
To Sir, With Love 2 '96
A Saintly Switch '99
The Cat's Meow '01
Hustle '04
She's Funny That Way '15

Michel Boisrond (1921-2002)
That Naughty Girl '58
Voulez-Vous Danser avec Moi? '59

Richard Boleslawski (1889-1937)
Rasputin and the Empress '33
Hollywood Party '34
Men in White '34
Operator 13 '34
The Painted Veil '34
Clive of India '35
Les Miserables '35
The Garden of Allah '36
Theodora Goes Wild '36
Three Godfathers '36
The Last of Mrs. Cheyney '37

Uwe Boll (1965-)
Sanctimony '01
Blackwoods '02
Heart of America '03
House of the Dead '03
Alone in the Dark '05
BloodRayne '06
BloodRayne 2: Deliverance '07
Postal '07
Far Cry '08
In the Name of the King: A Dungeon Siege Tale '08
Seed '08
Tunnel Rats '08
Attack on Darfur '09
The Final Storm '09
Rampage '09
Bloodrayne: The Third Reich '11
Blubberella '11
In the Name of the King 2: Two Worlds '11
In the Name of the King 3: The Last Mission '14
Rampage: Capital Punishment '14
Rampage: President Down '16

Iciar Bollain
Take My Eyes '03
Even the Rain '10

Gabriel Bologna
The Theory of the Leisure Class '01
30,000 Leagues Under the Sea '07
The Black Waters of Echo's Pond '10

Mauro Bolognini (1922-2001)
Bambole '65
The Queens '66
The Inheritance '76

Craig Bolotin (1954-)
That Night '93
Light It Up '99

Ben Bolt (1952-)
Big Town '87
Wilderness '96
The Turn of the Screw '99

James Bolton
Eban and Charley '01
The Graffiti Artist '04
Dream Boy '08

Timothy Bond (1942-)
Deadly Harvest '72
The Lost World '92
Return to the Lost World '93
Night of the Twisters '95
Diamond Girl '98
Loving Evangeline '98
Running Wild '99
Family in Hiding '06
Gospel of Deceit '06
Lesser Evil '06
The Secrets of Comfort House '06
Blue Seduction '09
The Case for Christmas '11

Bertrand Bonello
Nocturama '17
Zombi Child '20

Peter Bonerz (1938-)
Nobody's Perfekt '79
Police Academy 6: City under Siege '89

Joon-ho Bong (1969-)
Barking Dogs Never Bite '00
The Host '06
Madeo '09
Tokyo! '09
Snowpiercer '14
Okja '17
Parasite '19

John Bonito
The Marine '06
Carjacked '11

Mario Bonnard (1889-1965)
The Last Days of Pompeii '60
The Mercenaries '62

J.R. Bookwalter (1966-)
The Dead Next Door '89
Witchouse 2: Blood Coven '00
Witchouse 3: Demon Fire '01

Benny Boom
Next Day Air '09
S.W.A.T.: Firefight '11
All Eyez on Me '17

Josh Boone (1979-)
Stuck in Love '12
The Fault In Our Stars '14

John Boorman (1933-)
Having a Wild Weekend '65
Point Blank '67
Hell in the Pacific '69
Deliverance '72
Zardoz '73
The Exorcist 2: The Heretic '77
Excalibur '81
The Emerald Forest '85
Hope and Glory '87
Where the Heart Is '90
Beyond Rangoon '95
Picture Windows '95
The General '98
The Tailor of Panama '00
In My Country '04
The Tiger's Tale '06
Queen and Country '14

H. Gordon Boos (1958-2004)
Red Surf '90
Forgotten City '98

Lizzie Borden (1958-)
Working Girls '87
Erotique '94

Michael Borden
Ain't No Way Back '89
No Way Back '90

Bernard Borderie (1924-78)
Ladies' Man '62
Your Turn Darling '63
Angelique '64
Angelique: The Road to Versailles '65
Angelique and the King '66
Untamable Angelique '67
Angelique and the Sultan '68

Paul Borghese
Searching for Bobby D '05
Once Upon a Time in Brooklyn '13

Robert Boris (1945-)
Oxford Blues '84
Steele Justice '87
Frank and Jesse '94

Ole Bornedal
Nightwatch '96
Just Another Love Story '08
The Possession '12

Walerian Borowczyk (1923-2006)
The Beast '75
Emmanuelle 5 '87

Clay Borris (1950-)
Quiet Cool '86
The Gunfighters '87
Prom Night 4: Deliver Us from Evil '91
Killer Deal '99

Phillip Borsos (1954-95)
Mean Season '85
One Magic Christmas '85
Far from Home: The Adventures of Yellow Dog '94

Frank Borzage (1893-1962)
Lazybones '25
7th Heaven '27
Street Angel '28
Lucky Star '29
They Had to See Paris '29
Liliom '30
Song o' My Heart '30
Bad Girl '31
After Tomorrow '32
A Farewell to Arms '32
Young America '32
Flirtation Walk '34
No Greater Glory '34
Living on Velvet '35
Shipmates Forever '35
Stranded '35
Big City '37
The Green Light '37
History Is Made at Night '37
Mannequin '37
The Shining Hour '38
Three Comrades '38
Flight Command '40
The Mortal Storm '40
Strange Cargo '40
Smilin' Through '41
The Vanishing Virginian '41
Seven Sweethearts '42
Stage Door Canteen '43
His Butler's Sister '44
The Spanish Main '45
I've Always Loved You '46
Magnificent Doll '46
That's My Man '47
The Smallest Show on Earth '48
Journey Beneath the Desert '61

Rick Bota
Hellraiser: Hellseeker '02
Hellraiser: Deader '05
Hellraiser: Hellworld '05
Love Me '12

Huck Botko
Mail Order Wife '04
The Virginity Hit '10

Rachid Bouchareb (1959-)
Dust of Life '95
Days of Glory '06
London River '09
Outside the Law '10
Just Like a Woman '13

John Boulting (1913-85)
Brighton Rock '47
Crest of the Wave '54
Lucky Jim '58
I'm All Right Jack '59
Heavens Above '63

Roy Boulting (1913-2001)
Sailor of the King '53
Crest of the Wave '54
Run for the Sun '56
Lucky Jim '58
Carlton Browne of the F.O. '59
Heavens Above '63
There's a Girl in My Soup '70

Gilles Bourdos (1963-)
Afterwards '08
Renoir '12

Serge Bourguignon (1928-)
A Coeur Joie *'67*
Head Over Heels *'67*
The Picasso Summer *'69*

Jason Bourque
Wildfire 7: The Inferno *'02*
Termination Point *'07*
Doomsday Prophecy *'11*
Seattle Superstorm *'12*
Stonados *'13*
Drone *'17*

Darren Lynn Bousman (1979-)
Saw 2 *'05*
Saw 3 *'06*
Saw 4 *'07*
Repo! The Genetic Opera *'08*
Mother's Day *'10*
11-11-11 *'11*
The Barrens *'12*
Tales of Halloween *'15*
Abattoir *'17*

John Bowen (1948-)
Knock Outs *'92*
Dark Secrets *'95*

David Bowers (1970-)
Flushed Away *'06*
Astro Boy *'09*
Diary of a Wimpy Kid 2: Rodrick Rules *'11*
Diary of a Wimpy Kid: Dog Days *'12*
Diary of a Wimpy Kid: The Long Haul *'17*

George Bowers (1944-)
The Hearse *'80*
Body & Soul *'81*
My Tutor *'82*
Private Resort *'84*

Chuck Bowman
Threshold *'03*
The Tooth Fairy *'06*

Rob Bowman (1960-)
Airborne *'93*
The X-Files *'98*
Reign of Fire *'02*
Elektra *'05*

Muriel Box (1905-91)
Simon and Laura *'55*
Eyewitness *'56*

Tim Boxell
Aberration *'97*
Chasing Destiny *'00*
Valley of the Heart's Delight *'07*

Ross Boyask
I Am Vengeance *'18*
I Am Vengeance: Retaliation *'20*

Daniel Boyd (1956-)
Chillers *'88*
Invasion of the Space Preachers *'90*
Heroes of the Heart *'94*

Danny Boyle (1956-)
Shallow Grave *'94*
Trainspotting *'95*
A Life Less Ordinary *'97*
The Beach *'00*
Vacuuming Completely Nude in Paradise *'01*
28 Days Later *'02*
Millions *'05*
Sunshine *'07*
Slumdog Millionaire *'08*
127 Hours *'10*
Trance *'13*
Steve Jobs *'15*
T2 Trainspotting *'17*
Yesterday *'19*

Steve Boyum (1952-)
Meet the Deedles *'98*
Slap Shot 2: Breaking the Ice *'02*
La Femme Musketeer *'03*
Timecop 2: The Berlin Decision *'03*
Supercross: The Movie *'05*

Bruno Bozzetto (1933-)
Allegro Non Troppo *'76*
VIP, My Brother Superman *'90*

Charles Brabin (1883-1957)
The Raven *'15*
Twinkletoes *'26*
Sporting Blood *'31*
The Beast of the City *'32*
The Mask of Fu Manchu *'32*
New Morals for Old *'32*
Day of Reckoning *'33*

Al (Alfonso Brescia) Bradley (1930-2001)
Captive Planet *'78*
Cosmos: War of the Planets *'80*
White Fang and the Hunter *'85*
Cross Mission *'89*

David Bradley (1920-97)
12 to the Moon *'60*
They Saved Hitler's Brain *'64*

John Bradshaw (1952-)
The Big Slice *'90*
The Reaper *'97*
Specimen *'97*
The Undertaker's Wedding *'97*
Breakout *'98*
Full Disclosure *'00*
Killing Moon *'00*
Triggermen *'02*
Between Truth and Lies *'06*
Obituary *'06*
They Come Back *'07*
Every Second Counts *'08*
Darwin's Darkest Hour *'09*
You Lucky Dog *'10*
Cancel Christmas *'11*
Christmas Magic *'11*
Mistletoe Over Manhattan *'11*
The Christmas Consultant *'12*
Come Dance With Me *'12*

Eugene Brady
The Nephew *'97*
Missing Brendan *'03*

Jordan Brady (1964-)
The Third Wheel *'02*
Waking Up in Reno *'02*

Tom Brady
The Hot Chick *'02*
The Comebacks *'07*
Bucky Larson: Born to Be a Star *'11*

Zach Braff (1975-)
Garden State *'04*
Wish I Was Here *'14*
Going in Style *'17*

John Brahm (1893-1982)
Let Us Live *'39*
Tonight We Raid Calais *'43*
Wintertime *'43*
Guest in the House *'44*
Hangover Square *'45*
The Locket *'46*
Miracle of Our Lady of Fatima *'52*
The Mad Magician *'54*
Hot Rods to Hell *'67*

Marco Brambilla (1960-)
Demolition Man *'93*
Excess Baggage *'96*
Dinotopia *'02*

Risa Bramon Garcia (1956-)
200 Cigarettes *'98*
The Con Artist *'10*

Kenneth Branagh (1960-)
Henry V *'89*
Dead Again *'91*
Peter's Friends *'92*
Much Ado about Nothing *'93*
Mary Shelley's Frankenstein *'94*
A Midwinter's Tale *'95*
Hamlet *'96*
Love's Labour's Lost *'00*
As You Like It *'06*
Sleuth *'07*
Thor *'11*
Jack Ryan: Shadow Recruit *'14*
Cinderella *'15*
Murder on the Orient Express *'17*
All Is True *'18*

Rustam Branaman
Project Solitude: Buried Alive *'09*
Any Day *'15*

Larry Brand
The Drifter *'88*
Paranoia *'98*
Christina *'10*
The Girl On the Train *'13*

Charlotte Brandstrom (1959-)
Sweet Revenge *'90*
A Business Affair *'93*

Ash Brannon
Surf's Up *'07*
Rock Dog *'17*

Fred Brannon (1901-53)
The Purple Monster Strikes *'45*
Jesse James Rides Again *'47*
King of the Rocketmen *'49*
The Invisible Monster *'50*
Government Agents *vs.* Phantom Legion *'51*
Radar Men from the Moon *'52*
Zombies of the Stratosphere *'52*
Jungle Drums of Africa *'53*

Richard Brauer
The Lost Treasure of Sawtooth Island *'99*
Mr. Art Critic *'07*

Charles Braverman (1944-)
Brotherhood of Justice *'86*
Prince of Bel Air *'87*
Final Shot: The Hank Gathers Story *'92*

Kevin Bray
All About the Benjamins *'02*
Walking Tall *'04*
Linewatch *'08*

George Breakston (1920-73)
Geisha Girl *'52*
White Huntress *'57*
The Manster *'59*

Paddy Breathnach (1964-)
Blow Dry *'00*
Shrooms *'07*

Michael Scott Bregman
Table One *'00*
Carlito's Way: Rise to Power *'05*

Catherine Breillat (1948-)
A Real Young Girl *'75*
36 Fillete *'88*
Perfect Love *'96*
Romance *'99*
Sex is Comedy *'02*
Anatomy of Hell *'04*
Bluebeard *'09*
The Sleeping Beauty *'10*

Valerie Breiman
Going Overboard *'89*
Love & Sex *'00*

Herbert Brenon (1880-1958)
Peter Pan *'24*
Dancing Mothers *'26*
Laugh, Clown, Laugh *'28*
Beau Ideal *'31*

Alfonso Brescia (1930-2001)
Special Forces *'68*
War in Space *'77*
Reactor *'78*
The Beast in Space *'80*

Robert Bresson (1907-99)
The Ladies of the Bois de Bologne *'44*
Diary of a Country Priest *'50*
A Man Escaped *'57*
Pickpocket *'59*
Au Hasard Balthazar *'66*
Mouchette *'67*
Lancelot of the Lake *'74*
The Devil, Probably *'77*
L'Argent *'83*

Martin Brest (1951-)
Going in Style *'79*
Beverly Hills Cop *'84*
Midnight Run *'88*
Scent of a Woman *'92*
Meet Joe Black *'98*
Gigli *'03*

Howard Bretherton (1896-1969)
The Showdown *'40*
Rhythm Parade *'43*
The Trap *'46*
The Prince of Thieves *'48*

Eric Brevig (1957-)
Journey to the Center of the Earth *'08*
Yogi Bear *'10*

Craig Brewer (1971-)
Hustle & Flow *'05*
Black Snake Moan *'07*
Footloose *'11*
Dolemite Is My Name *'19*

Salome Breziner
An Occasional Hell *'96*
Fast Sofa *'01*

Patrick Brice
Creep *'15*
The Overnight *'15*
Corporate Animals *'19*

Marshall Brickman (1941-)
Simon *'80*
Lovesick *'83*
The Manhattan Project *'86*

Paul Brickman (1949-)
Risky Business *'83*
Men Don't Leave *'89*

Alan Bridges (1927-2013)
The Hireling *'73*
Out of Season *'75*
Return of the Soldier *'82*
The Shooting Party *'85*

James Bridges (1936-93)
The Baby Maker *'70*
The Paper Chase *'73*
September 30, 1955 *'77*
The China Syndrome *'79*
Urban Cowboy *'80*
Mike's Murder *'84*
Perfect *'85*
Bright Lights, Big City *'88*

Stephen Bridgewater
Out of the Woods *'05*
The Christmas Card *'06*
Prairie Fever *'08*

Matthew Bright (1952-)
Freeway *'95*
Freeway 2: Confessions of a Trickbaby *'99*

Steven Brill (1962-)
Heavyweights *'94*
Late Last Night *'99*
Little Nicky *'00*
Mr. Deeds *'02*
Without a Paddle *'04*
Drillbit Taylor *'08*
Movie 43 *'13*
Walk of Shame *'14*

Burt Brinckerhoff (1936-)
The Invasion of Carol Enders *'74*
Come Die With Me *'75*
Acapulco Gold *'78*
Baby Broker *'81*
A Girl of the Limberlost *'90*

Tony Britten
Draw on Sweet Night *'15*
Chicklit *'16*

Deborah Brock
Slumber Party Massacre 2 *'87*
Andy and the Airwave Rangers *'89*
Rock 'n' Roll High School Forever *'91*

Q. Allan Brocka
Boy Culture *'06*
Eating Out 4: Drama Camp *'11*
Eating Out: The Open Weekend *'11*

Henry Bromell (1947-)
Panic *'00*
Last Call: The Final Chapter of F. Scott Fitzgerald *'02*

Harry Bromley-Davenport (1950-)
Xtro *'83*
Xtro 2: The Second Encounter *'91*
Xtro 3: Watch the Skies *'95*
Mockingbird Don't Sing *'01*
Haunted Echoes *'08*

Adam Brooks (1956-)
Almost You *'85*
Red Riding Hood *'88*
Invisible Circus *'00*
Definitely, Maybe *'08*
Father's Day *'12*

Albert Brooks (1947-)
Real Life *'79*
Modern Romance *'81*
Lost in America *'85*
Defending Your Life *'91*
Mother *'96*
The Muse *'99*
Looking for Comedy in the Muslim World *'06*

James L. Brooks (1940-)
Terms of Endearment *'83*
Broadcast News *'87*
I'll Do Anything *'93*
As Good As It Gets *'97*
Spanglish *'04*
How Do You Know *'10*

Katherine Brooks
Loving Annabelle *'06*
Waking Madison *'10*

Mel Brooks (1926-)
The Producers *'68*
The Twelve Chairs *'70*
Blazing Saddles *'74*
Young Frankenstein *'74*
Silent Movie *'76*
High Anxiety *'77*
History of the World: Part 1 *'81*
Spaceballs *'87*
Life Stinks *'91*
Robin Hood: Men in Tights *'93*
Dracula: Dead and Loving It *'95*

Richard Brooks (1912-92)
Crisis *'50*
Battle Circus *'53*
The Last Time I Saw Paris *'54*
Blackboard Jungle *'55*
The Catered Affair *'56*
The Last Hunt *'56*
Something of Value *'57*
The Brothers Karamazov *'58*
Cat on a Hot Tin Roof *'58*
Elmer Gantry *'60*
Sweet Bird of Youth *'62*
Lord Jim *'65*
The Professionals *'66*
In Cold Blood *'67*
The Happy Ending *'69*
Dollars *'71*
Bite the Bullet *'75*
Wrong Is Right *'82*

Nick Broomfield (1948-)
Dark Obsession *'90*
Monster in a Box *'92*
Biggie & Tupac: The Story Behind the Murder of Rap's Biggest Superstars *'02*
Aileen: Life and Death of a Serial Killer *'03*
Marianne & Leonard: Words of Love *'19*

Eric Bross (1964-)
Restaurant *'98*
Ten Benny *'98*
Stranger than Fiction *'99*
On the Line *'01*
Vampire Bats *'05*
Vacancy 2: The First Cut *'08*
The Boy Who Cried Werewolf *'10*
We Have Your Husband *'11*

Hilary Brougher
The Sticky Fingers of Time *'97*
Stephanie Daley *'06*

Otto Brower (1895-1946)
The Light of Western Stars *'30*
Fighting Caravans *'31*
Devil Horse *'32*
Mystery Mountain *'34*
The Phantom Empire *'35*

Alan Brown
Book of Love *'04*
Superheroes *'07*
Private Romeo *'11*

Arvin Brown (1940-)
A Change of Heart *'98*
Just Ask My Children *'01*

Bruce Brown (1937-)
The Endless Summer *'66*
The Endless Summer 2 *'94*

Clarence Brown (1890-1987)
The Last of the Mohicans *'20*
The Eagle *'25*
Smouldering Fires *'25*
Kiki *'26*
The Flesh and the Devil *'27*
The Trail of '98 *'28*
Navy Blues *'29*
Anna Christie *'30*
Romance *'30*
A Free Soul *'31*
Possessed *'31*
Emma *'32*
Night Flight *'33*
Chained *'34*
Sadie McKee *'34*
Ah, Wilderness! *'35*
Anna Karenina *'35*
The Gorgeous Hussy *'36*
Wife Versus Secretary *'36*
Conquest *'37*
Of Human Hearts *'38*
Idiot's Delight *'39*
The Rains Came *'39*
Come Live With Me *'40*
Edison the Man *'40*
They Met in Bombay *'41*
The Human Comedy *'43*
National Velvet *'44*
The White Cliffs of Dover *'44*
The Yearling *'46*
Song of Love *'47*
Intruder in the Dust *'49*
To Please a Lady *'50*
Angels in the Outfield *'51*
It's a Big Country *'51*

Dana Brown
Step Into Liquid *'03*
Dust to Glory *'05*
On Any Sunday: The Next Chapter *'14*

Georg Stanford Brown (1943-)
Grambling's White Tiger '81
Miracle of the Heart: A Boys Town Story '86
Alone in the Neon Jungle '87
Dangerous Relations '93
The Long Shot '04
The Reading Room '05

Gregory Brown (1957-)
Stranger by Night '94
See No Evil '06
Frenemy '09

Karl Brown (1896-1990)
The White Legion '36
Barefoot Boy '38

Mark Brown
Two Can Play That Game '01
The Salon '05

Melville Brown (1887-1938)
Check & Double Check '30
Behind Office Doors '31
Mad About Money '37

Christopher Browne
Third World Cop '99
League of Ordinary Gentlemen '04

Tod Browning (1882-1962)
Outside the Law '21
White Tiger '23
The Unholy Three '25
The Black Bird '26
The Show '27
Dracula '31
Freaks '32
Fast Workers '33
Devil Doll '36
Miracles for Sale '39

S.F. Brownrigg (1937-96)
Don't Look in the Basement '73
Don't Open the Door! '74
Keep My Grave Open '80

James Bruce
Headless Body in Topless Bar '96
Love to Kill '97
Whacked! '02

Clyde Bruckman (1894-1955)
The General '26
Feet First '30
Movie Crazy '32
The Man On the Flying Trapeze '35

David Bruckner
V/H/S '12
Southbound '16

Mads Brügger
The Ambassador '11
Cold Case Hammarskjöld '19

Alejandro Brugues
The ABCs of Death 2 '14
Nightmare Cinema '19

Callan Brunker
Escape From Planet Earth '13
The Nut Job 2: Nutty by Nature '17

Tommy Brunswick (1970-)
Mr. Jingles '06
Born of Earth '08

James Bryan
Boogie Vision '77
Don't Go in the Woods '81
Lady Street Fighter '86

Larry Buchanan (1923-2004)
Free, White, and 21 '62
The Eye Creatures '65
Curse of the Swamp Creature '66
Mars Needs Women '66
Zontar, the Thing from Venus '66
Creature of Destruction '67
It's Alive! '68
Goodbye, Norma Jean '75

Chris Buck
Tarzan '99
Surf's Up '07
Frozen '13
Frozen II '19

Bethel Buckalew
Dirty Mind of Young Sally '72
Summer School '77
My Boys Are Good Boys '78

Bryan Buckley
The Bronze '15
The Pirates of Somalia '17

Colin Bucksey (1946-)
Dealers '89
Midnight's Child '93
September '96

Harold Bucquet (1891-1946)
Young Dr. Kildare '38
Calling Dr. Kildare '39
On Borrowed Time '39
The Secret of Dr. Kildare '39
Dr. Kildare Goes Home '40
Dr. Kildare's Crisis '40
Dr. Kildare's Strange Case '40
Dr. Kildare's Wedding Day '41
Kathleen '41
The People *vs.* Dr. Kildare '41
Calling Dr. Gillespie '42
The Adventures of Tartu '43
Without Love '45

Colin Budds
Hurricane Smith '92
Dr. Jekyll & Mr. Hyde '99
Maiden Voyage: Ocean Hijack '04

Robert Budreau
That Beautiful Somewhere '06
Born to Be Blue '15

John Carl Buechler
Dungeonmaster '83
Troll '86
Friday the 13th, Part 7: The New Blood '88
Ghoulies 3: Ghoulies Go to College '91
Watchers Reborn '98
The Eden Formula '06
The Strange Case of Dr. Jekyll and Mr. Hyde '06

Timothy Linh Bui (1969-)
Green Dragon '01
Powder Blue '09

Penelope Buitenhuis
Killer Bees '02
Mary Higgins Clark: Lucky Day '02
Past Tense '06
The Secret of Hidden Lake '06
Time and Again '07
Wide Awake '07
Whispers and Lies '08

Andrew Bujalski
Beeswax '09
Computer Chess '13
Results '15
Support the Girls '18

Luis Bunuel (1900-83)
Los Olvidados '50
Mexican Bus Ride '51
Susana '51
A Woman Without Love '51
El Bruto '52
Robinson Crusoe '54
The Criminal Life of Archibaldo de la Cruz '55
Death in the Garden '56
Fever Mounts at El Pao '59
Viridiana '61
The Young One '61
The Exterminating Angel '62
Diary of a Chambermaid '64
Belle de Jour '67
The Milky Way '68
The Discreet Charm of the Bourgeoisie '72
Phantom of Liberty '74
That Obscure Object of Desire '77

Aleksandr (Sasha) Buravsky
Out of the Cold '99
Attack on Leningrad '09

Ray Burdis (1958-)
Final Cut '98
Love, Honour & Obey '00

Stuart Burge (1918-2002)
Othello '65
Julius Caesar '70

Neil Burger
Interview with the Assassin '02
The Illusionist '06
The Lucky Ones '08
Limitless '11
Divergent '14
The Upside '17

David J. Burke (1948-)
Animal '05
Edison Force '05

Martyn Burke (1952-)
Power Play '78
Last Chase '81
Clown Murders '83
The Pirates of Silicon Valley '99
Avenging Angelo '02

Charles Burmeister
Columbus Day '08
Mercury Plains '16

Charles Burnett (1944-)
Killer of Sheep '77
To Sleep with Anger '90
The Glass Shield '95
Nightjohn '96
Selma, Lord, Selma '99
Finding Buck McHenry '00
Relative Stranger '09

Edward Burns (1968-)
The Brothers McMullen '94
She's the One '96
No Looking Back '98
Sidewalks of New York '01
Ash Wednesday '02
Looking for Kitty '04
The Groomsmen '06
Purple Violets '07
Nice Guy Johnny '10
Newlyweds '11
The Fitzgerald Family Christmas '12

Ken Burns (1953-)
The Central Park Five '12
The Vietnam War '17

Jeff Burr (1963-)
The Offspring '87
Leatherface: The Texas Chainsaw Massacre 3 '89
Stepfather 2: Make Room for Daddy '89
Eddie Presley '92
Puppet Master 4 '93
Pumpkinhead 2: Blood Wings '94
Puppet Master 5: The Final Chapter '94
Night of the Scarecrow '95
Straight into Darkness '04
Devil's Den '06
Alien Storm '12

James Burrows (1940-)
More Than Friends '78
Partners '82

Rama Burshtein
Fill the Void '12
The Wedding Plan '17

Colette Burson
Coming Soon '99
Permanent '17

Tim Burstall (1929-2004)
Attack Force Z '84
Nightmare at Bittercreek '91

Nanette Burstein
The Kid Stays in the Picture '02
American Teen '08
Going the Distance '10

David Burton (1877-1963)
Fighting Caravans '31
Brief Moment '33
Lady by Choice '34

Jeff Burton
Night Divides the Day '01
Acts of Death '07

LeVar Burton (1957-)
The Tiger Woods Story '98
Smart House '00
Reach for Me '08

Tim Burton (1960-)
Pee-wee's Big Adventure '85
Beetlejuice '88
Batman '89
Edward Scissorhands '90
Batman Returns '92
Ed Wood '94
Mars Attacks! '96
Sleepy Hollow '99
Planet of the Apes '01
Big Fish '03
Charlie and the Chocolate Factory '05
Tim Burton's Corpse Bride '05
Sweeney Todd: The Demon Barber of Fleet Street '07
Alice in Wonderland '10
Dark Shadows '12
Frankenweenie '12
Big Eyes '14
Miss Peregrine's Home for Peculiar Children '16
Dumbo '19

Steve Buscemi (1957-)
Tree's Lounge '96
Animal Factory '00
Lonesome Jim '06
Interview '07

Noah Buschel
The Missing Person '09
Glass Chin '14
The Phenom '16

Anthony Bushell (1904-97)
Angel with the Trumpet '50
The Long Dark Hall '51
The Terror of the Tongs '61

Chris Butler
ParaNorman '12
Missing Link '19

David Butler (1894-1979)
White Fang '36
Kentucky '38
Kentucky Moonshine '38
My Wild Irish Rose '47
Jump Into Hell '55
The Girl He Left Behind '56
The Right Approach '61

David Butler (1927-2006)
Bright Eyes '34
Doubting Thomas '35
The Little Colonel '35
The Littlest Rebel '35
Captain January '36
Pigskin Parade '36
East Side of Heaven '39
If I Had My Way '40
You'll Find Out '40
Caught in the Draft '41
Playmates '41
The Road to Morocco '42
Thank Your Lucky Stars '43
They Got Me Covered '43
The Princess and the Pirate '44
San Antonio '45
John Loves Mary '48
It's a Great Feeling '49
Look for the Silver Lining '49
The Story of Seabiscuit '49
The Daughter of Rosie O'Grady '50
Tea for Two '50
Lullaby of Broadway '51
Painting the Clouds With Sunshine '51
April in Paris '52
By the Light of the Silvery Moon '53
Calamity Jane '53
The Command '54
King Richard and the Crusaders '54

Joshua Butler
Prancer Returns '01
Deathlands: Homeward Bound '03

Robert Butler (1927-)
The Computer Wore Tennis Shoes '69
The Barefoot Executive '71
Scandalous John '71
Now You See Him, Now You Don't '72
Strange New World '75
James Dean '76
Mayday at 40,000 Feet '76
Hot Lead & Cold Feet '78
Up the Creek '84
Moonlighting '85
White Mile '94
Turbulence '96

Hendel Butoy
The Rescuers Down Under '90
Fantasia/2000 '00

Jorg Buttgereit (1963-)
Nekromantik '87
Nekromantik 2 '91

Edward Buzzell (1900-85)
Virtue '32
Fast Company '38
Paradise for Three '38
At the Circus '39
Honolulu '39
Go West '40
Ship Ahoy '42
Best Foot Forward '43
The Youngest Profession '43
Keep Your Powder Dry '45
Easy to Wed '46
Song of the Thin Man '47
Neptune's Daughter '49
Confidentially Connie '53

Eric Byler
Charlotte Sometimes '02
Tre '06

Jeff Byrd
Seventeen Again '00
Jasper, Texas '03
King's Ransom '05

John Byrum (1947-)
Inserts '76
Heart Beat '80
The Razor's Edge '84
The Whoopee Boys '86

Reggie Rock Bythewood (1965-)
Dancing in September '00
Biker Boyz '03

Scott Caan (1976-)
Dallas 362 '03
The Dog Problem '06

Christy Cabanne (1888-1950)
The Red-Haired Alibi '32
The World Gone Mad '33
Jane Eyre '34
Behind the Green Lights '35
The Keeper of the Bees '35
One Frightened Night '35
Last Outlaw '36
The Mummy's Hand '40
Dixie Jamboree '44

Paco Cabezas
Rage '14
Mr. Right '16

Michael Cacoyannis (1927-2011)
Stella '55
Girl in Black '56
A Matter of Dignity '57
Zorba the Greek '64
Trojan Women '71
The Story of Jacob & Joseph '74
Iphigenia '77
The Cherry Orchard '99

Andy Cadiff
Leave It to Beaver '97
Chasing Liberty '04

David Caesar
Idiot Box '97
Dirty Deeds '02

David Caffrey (1969-)
Aristocrats '99
The Aristocrats '99
Grand Theft Parsons '03

Mike Cahill (1979-)
King of California '07
Another Earth '11
I Origins '14

Edward L. Cahn (1899-1963)
Destination Murder '50
Dragstrip Girl '57
Flesh and the Spur '57
Shake, Rattle and Rock '57
Zombies of Moratau '57
Curse of the Faceless Man '58
It! The Terror from Beyond Space '58
Four Skulls of Jonathan Drake '59
Invisible Invaders '59
Cage of Evil '60
Five Guns to Tombstone '60
Noose for a Gunman '60
Twelve Hours to Kill '60
Vice Raid '60
Boy Who Caught a Crook '61
Frontier Uprising '61
Three Came to Kill '61
Incident in an Alley '62

Mario Caiano (1933-)
Ulysses Against the Son of Hercules '61
Two Gladiators '64
Erik, the Viking '65
Fighting Fists of Shanghai Joe '65
Ringo's Mark of Vengeance '67

Christopher Cain (1943-)
Sixth and Main '77
The Stone Boy '84
That Was Then. . . This Is Now '85
Where the River Runs Black '86
The Principal '87
Young Guns '88
Pure Country '92
The Next Karate Kid '94
The Amazing Panda Adventure '95
Gone Fishin' '97
Rose Hill '97
A Father's Choice '00
September Dawn '07
Pure Country 2: The Gift '10

Tom Cairns
Amongst Women '98
Marie and Bruce '04

Philippe Caland
Ripple Effect '07
Repentance '14

Mars Callahan (1971-)
Double Down '01
Poolhall Junkies '02
What Love Is '07

Art Camacho
The Power Within '95
Little Bigfoot '96
Little Bigfoot 2: The Journey Home '97
Recoil '97
Final Payback '99
Deadly Reckoning '01
Sci-Fighter '04
Confessions of a Pit Fighter '05
Crooked '05
Assassin X '16

Cody Cameron (1970-)
Open Season 3 '10
Cloudy with a Chance of Meatballs 2 '13

James Cameron (1954-)
Piranha 2: The Spawning '82
The Terminator '84
Aliens '86
The Abyss '89
Terminator 2: Judgment Day '91
True Lies '94
Titanic '97
Avatar '09

Ken Cameron (1946-)
The Good Wife '86
Brides of Christ '91
Dalva '95
Oldest Confederate Widow Tells All '95
Miracle at Midnight '98

Douglas Camfield
Danger UXB '81
Ivanhoe '82

Donald Cammell (1939-96)
Performance '70
Demon Seed '77

Joe Camp (1939-)
Benji '74
Hawmps! '76
For the Love of Benji '77
The Double McGuffin '79
Oh, Heavenly Dog! '80
Benji the Hunted '87
Benji: Off the Leash! '04

Juan J. Campanella (1959-)
Love Walked In '97
The Son of the Bride '01
The Secret in Their Eyes '09

Pasquale Festa Campanile (1927-86)
The Libertine '69
When Women Had Tails '70
When Women Lost Their Tails '75

Doug Campbell
Zapped Again '89
Perfect Tenant '99
The Tomorrow Man '01
Trapped: Buried Alive '02
Accused at 17 '09
Betrayed at 17 '11
Stalked at 17 '12
Walking the Halls '12
The Surrogate '13

Graeme Campbell (1954-)
Blood Relations '87
Into the Fire '88
Murder One '88
The Disappearance of Vonnie '94
Nico the Unicorn '98
Lip Service '00
Dangerous Child '01
Everest '07
An Old-Fashioned Thanksgiving '08
The National Tree '09
Be My Valentine '13

Martin Campbell (1940-)
The Sex Thief '74
Edge of Darkness '86
Criminal Law '89
Defenseless '91
No Escape '94
Goldeneye '95
The Mask of Zorro '98
Vertical Limit '00
Beyond Borders '03
The Legend of Zorro '05
Casino Royale '06
Edge of Darkness '10
Green Lantern '11
The Foreigner '17

Robin Campillo
They Came Back '04
BPM (Beats Per Minute) '17

Jane Campion (1954-)
Two Friends '86
An Angel at My Table '89
Sweetie '89
The Piano '93
Portrait of a Lady '96
Holy Smoke '99
In the Cut '03
Bright Star '09
Top of the Lake '13

Carlo Campogalliani (1885-1974)
Goliath and the Barbarians '60
The Mighty Ursus '61
Son of Samson '62
Ursus in the Valley of the Lions '62

Antonio Campos
Afterschool '08
Christine '16

Michael Campus
Zero Population Growth '72
The Mack '73
The Education of Sonny Carson '74
The Christmas Cottage '08

Guillaume Canet (1973-)
Whatever You Say '02
Tell No One '06
Little White Lies '10
Blood Ties '13

Danny Cannon (1968-)
The Young Americans '93
Judge Dredd '95
I Still Know What You Did Last Summer '98
Phoenix '98
Goal! The Dream Begins '06

Laurent Cantet (1961-)
Time Out '01
Heading South '05
The Class '08

Erik Canuel
Bon Cop Bad Cop '06
Barrymore '11

Michael Canzoniero
The Wedding Bros. '08
Don Peyote '14

Giorgio Capitani (1927-)
Samson and His Mighty Challenge '64
Lady of the Evening '75

Steven Caple, Jr.
The Land '16
Creed II '18

Giuseppe Capotondi
The Double Hour '09
The Burnt Orange Heresy '20

Frank Cappello
American Yakuza '94
No Way Back '96

Frank Capra (1897-1991)
Strong Man '26
That Certain Thing '28
Ladies of Leisure '30
Rain or Shine '30
The Miracle Woman '31
Platinum Blonde '31
American Madness '32
Forbidden '32
The Bitter Tea of General Yen '33
Lady for a Day '33
Broadway Bill '34
It Happened One Night '34
Mr. Deeds Goes to Town '36
Lost Horizon '37
You Can't Take It with You '38
Mr. Smith Goes to Washington '39
Meet John Doe '41
Arsenic and Old Lace '44
It's a Wonderful Life '46
State of the Union '48
Riding High '50
Here Comes the Groom '51
A Hole in the Head '59
Pocketful of Miracles '61

Luigi Capuano
Hercules and the Black Pirate '60
Tiger of the Seven Seas '62

Leos Carax (1960-)
Boy Meets Girl '84
Mauvais Sang '86
The Lovers on the Bridge '91
Pola X '99
Tokyo! '09
Holy Motors '12

Jack Cardiff (1914-2009)
Intent to Kill '58
Sons and Lovers '60
My Geisha '62
The Long Ships '64
The Liquidator '65
Young Cassidy '65
Dark of the Sun '68
The Girl on a Motorcycle '68
The Freakmaker '73

Roger Cardinal
Snowballin' '71
Malarek '89
Captive '98
Dead Silent '99

Rene Cardona, Jr. (1939-2003)
Night of the Bloody Apes '68
Night of a Thousand Cats '72
Robinson Crusoe & the Tiger '72
The Treasure of the Amazon '85
Beaks: The Movie '87

J.S. Cardone (1946-)
The Slayer '82
Shadowzone '89
Shadowhunter '93
Black Day Blue Night '95
The Forsaken '01
True Blue '01
8mm 2 '05
Wicked Little Things '07

John Cardos (1928-)
Kingdom of the Spiders '77
The Dark '79
Day Time Ended '80
Mutant '83
Skeleton Coast '89

Patricia Cardoso
Real Women Have Curves '02
Meddling Mom '13

Christian Carion (1963-)
The Girl from Paris '02
Joyeux Noel '05
Farewell '09

Carlo Carlei (1960-)
Flight of the Innocent '93
Fluke '95
Romeo & Juliet '13

Lewis John Carlino (1932-2020)
The Sailor Who Fell from Grace with the Sea '76
The Great Santini '80
Class '83

Joe Carnahan (1969-)
Blood, Guts, Bullets and Octane '99
Narc '02
Smokin' Aces '07
The A-Team '10
The Grey '12

Marcel Carne (1906-96)
Bizarre Bizarre '39
Le Jour Se Leve '39
Children of Paradise '44

Charles Robert Carner (1957-)
A Killer Among Friends '92
The Fixer '97
Echo of Murder '00
Red Water '01
Breakaway '02
Witless Protection '08

John Carney
On the Edge '00
Once '06
Begin Again '13
Sing Street '16

Giuliano Carnimeo (1932-)
Fistful of Lead '70
Gunslinger '70
Sartana's Here. . . Trade Your Pistol for a Coffin '70
The Case of the Bloody Iris '72

Marc Caro (1956-)
Delicatessen '92
The City of Lost Children '95
Dante 01 '08

Niki Caro (1967-)
Whale Rider '02
North Country '05
A Heavenly Vintage '09
McFarland USA '15
The Zookeeper's Wife '17

Adam Carolla (1964-)
Road Hard '15
Winning: The Racing Life of Paul Newman '15
The 24 Hour War '16

Glenn Gordon Caron (1954-)
Clean and Sober '88
Wilder Napalm '93
Love Affair '94
Picture Perfect '96

Heiner Carow (1929-97)
The Legend of Paul and Paula '73
Coming Out '89
The Mistake '91

John Carpenter (1948-)
Dark Star '74
Assault on Precinct 13 '76
The Fog '78
Halloween '78
Elvis: The Movie '79
Escape from New York '81
The Thing '82
Christine '84
Starman '84
Big Trouble in Little China '86
Prince of Darkness '87
They Live '88
Memoirs of an Invisible Man '92
Body Bags '93
In the Mouth of Madness '95
Village of the Damned '95
Escape from L.A. '96
John Carpenter's Vampires '97
John Carpenter's Ghosts of Mars '01
The Ward '10

Stephen Carpenter
Dorm That Dripped Blood '82
Soul Survivors '01

Jonas Carpignano
Mediterranea '15
A Ciambra '17

Steve Carr
Next Friday '00
Dr. Dolittle 2 '01
Daddy Day Care '03
Rebound '05
Are We Done Yet? '07
Paul Blart: Mall Cop '09
Movie 43 '13
Middle School: The Worst Years of My Life '16

Thomas Carr (1907-97)
Jesse James Rides Again '47
Captain Scarlett '53
The Fighting Lawman '53
Dino '57
Cast a Long Shadow '59

Kevin Carraway
7 Below '11
Way of the Wicked '14
Chain of Command '15

Michael Carreras (1927-94)
Maniac '63
Prehistoric Women '67
Call Him Mr. Shatter '74

Willard Carroll (1955-)
Playing by Heart '98
Marigold '07

Shane Carruth (1972-)
Primer '04
Upstream Color '13

David Carson
Star Trek: Generations '94
From the Earth to the Moon '98
Letters from a Killer '98
In His Life: The John Lennon Story '00
The 10th Kingdom '00
Carrie '02
Blue Smoke '07

Jack Paddy Carstairs (1910-70)
The Saint in London '39
He Found a Star '41
Tony Draws a Horse '51
Made in Heaven '52
Trouble in Store '53
The Square Peg '58

John Carter
Fatwa '06
The Way of War '08

Peter Carter (1933-82)
Klondike Fever '79
Rituals '79
Kavik the Wolf Dog '80

Thomas Carter (1953-)
Miami Vice '84
Swing Kids '93
Metro '96
Save the Last Dance '01
Coach Carter '05
Gifted Hands: The Ben Carson Story '09
When the Game Stands Tall '14

D.J. Caruso (1965-)
Black Cat Run '98
The Salton Sea '02
Taking Lives '04
Two for the Money '05
Disturbia '07
Eagle Eye '08
I Am Number Four '11
Standing Up '13
The Disappointments Room '16
xXx: Return of Xander Cage '17

Steve Carver (1945-)
The Arena '73
Big Bad Mama '74
Drum '76
An Eye for an Eye '81
Lone Wolf McQuade '83
Oceans of Fire '86
Jocks '87
Bulletproof '88
River of Death '90

Robert Cary
Anything But Love '02
Ira & Abby '06
Save Me '07

David S. Cass, Sr.
Johnson County War '02
Straight from the Heart '03
The Trail to Hope Rose '04
Back to You and Me '05
The Family Plan '05
Avenging Angel '07
Lone Rider '08
Prairie Fever '08
Bound by a Secret '09
Love Finds a Home '09
The Christmas Pageant '11
Love Begins '11
Love's Christmas Journey '11
Shadow on the Mesa '13

Henry Cass (1902-89)
The Glass Mountain '49
Last Holiday '50
No Smoking '55
Bond of Fear '56
Blood of the Vampire '58

Jon Cassar (1958-)
The Final Goal '94
Shadow Warriors 2: Hunt for the Death Merchant '97
Shadow Warriors '97
The Ultimate Weapon '97
Danger Beneath the Sea '02
24: Redemption '08
The Kennedys '11
Forsaken '15
Foresaken '16
When the Bough Breaks '16

John Cassavetes (1929-89)
Saddle the Wind '58
Shadows '60
Too Late Blues '61
Faces '68
Husbands '70
Minnie and Moskowitz '71
A Woman under the Influence '74
The Killing of a Chinese Bookie '76
Opening Night '77
Gloria '80
Big Trouble '86

Nick Cassavetes (1959-)
Unhook the Stars '96
She's So Lovely '97
John Q '02
The Notebook '04
Alpha Dog '06
My Sister's Keeper '09
The Other Woman '14

Lucien Castaing-Taylor
Sweetgrass '09
Leviathan '13

Renato Castellani (1913-85)
Romeo and Juliet '54
And the Wild, Wild Women '59

Enzo G. Castellari (1938-)
Any Gun Can Play '67
Go Kill and Come Back '68
Eagles Over London '69
Cold Eyes of Fear '70
Street Law '74
Loves & Times of Scaramouche '76
Deadly Mission '78
The Inglorious Bastards '78
Shark Hunter '79
1990: The Bronx Warriors '83

Warriors of the Wasteland '83
Day of the Cobra '84
Sinbad of the Seven Seas '89

Nick Castle (1947-)
The Last Starfighter '84
The Boy Who Could Fly '86
Tap '89
Dennis the Menace '93
Major Payne '95
Mr. Wrong '95
Connor's War '06

William Castle (1914-77)
Betrayed '44
Undertow '49
It's a Small World '50
Hollywood Story '51
Conquest of Cochise '53
Battle of Rogue River '54
Charge of the Lancers '54
Americano '55
The Gun That Won the West '55
New Orleans Uncensored '55
House on Haunted Hill '58
Macabre '58
The Tingler '59
13 Ghosts '60
Homicidal '61
Mr. Sardonicus '61
Zotz! '62
13 Frightened Girls '63
Strait-Jacket '64
The Busy Body '67
Project X '68
Shanks '74

William Allen Castleman (1922-2006)
Bummer '73
Johnny Firecloud '75

Gil Cates, Jr. (1969-)
Spent '00
Deal '08
Lucky '11

Gilbert Cates (1934-2011)
I Never Sang for My Father '70
To All My Friends on Shore '71
The Affair '73
Summer Wishes, Winter Dreams '73
The Promise '79
The Last Married Couple in America '80
Oh, God! Book 2 '80
Hobson's Choice '83
Burning Rage '84
Backfire '88
A Death in the Family '02

Joseph Cates (1924-98)
Girl of the Night '60
The Fat Spy '66

Michael Caton-Jones (1958-)
Scandal '89
Memphis Belle '90
Doc Hollywood '91
This Boy's Life '93
Rob Roy '95
The Jackal '97
City by the Sea '02
Shooting Dogs '05
Basic Instinct 2 '06

Peter Cattaneo (1964-)
The Full Monty '96
Lucky Break '01
The Rocker '08

Alberto Cavalcanti (1897-1982)
Dead of Night '45
Nicholas Nickleby '46
They Made Me a Fugitive '47

Liliana Cavani (1937-)
The Night Porter '74
The Skin '81
Beyond Obsession '82

Francesco '93
Ripley's Game '02

Joseph Cedar
Time of Favor '00
Beaufort '07
Footnote '11
Norman '17

Jeff Celentano
Gunshy '98
Moscow Heat '04
Breaking Point '09

Nuri Bilge Ceylan
Climates '06
Once Upon a Time in Anatolia '12
Winter Sleep '14
The Wild Pear Tree '18

Claude Chabrol (1930-2010)
Le Beau Serge '58
The Cousins '59
Les Cousins '59
Les Bonnes Femmes '60
Who's Got the Black Box? '67
Les Biches '68
Six in Paris '68
La Femme Infidele '69
Le Boucher '69
La Rupture '70
This Man Must Die '70
Just Before Nightfall '71
Ten Days Wonder '72
A Piece of Pleasure '74
Wedding in Blood '74
Innocents with Dirty Hands '76
The Twist '76
Violette '78
Cop Au Vin '85
The Cry of the Owl '87
The Story of Women '88
Quiet Days in Clichy '90
Madame Bovary '91
Betty '92
L'Enfer '93
La Ceremonie '95
The Swindle '97
The Color of Lies '99
Merci pour le Chocolat '00
The Bridesmaid '04
Comedy of Power '06
A Girl Cut in Two '07
Inspector Bellamy '09

Gurinder Chadha (1960-)
What's Cooking? '00
Bend It Like Beckham '02
Bride & Prejudice '04
Paris, je t'aime '06
Angus, Thongs and Perfect Snogging '08
Viceroy's House '17
Blinded by the Light '19

Justin Chadwick
Bleak House '05
The Other Boleyn Girl '08
Mandela: Long Walk to Freedom '13
Tulip Fever '17

Don Chaffey (1917-90)
Dentist In the Chair '60
Greyfriars Bobby '61
A Matter of WHO '62
The Prince and the Pauper '62
The Horse Without a Head '63
Jason and the Argonauts '63
The Three Lives of Thomasina '63
The Crooked Road '65
One Million Years B.C. '66
The Viking Queen '67
Creatures the World Forgot '70
Ride a Wild Pony '75
Pete's Dragon '77
C.H.O.M.P.S. '79
The Gift of Love '90

Youssef Chahine (1926-)
Alexandria. . . Why? '78
An Egyptian Story '82

Alexandria Again and Forever '90
Destiny '97

Gregg Champion (1956-)
The Cowboy Way '94
The Simple Life of Noah Dearborn '99
Dodson's Journey '01
The Last Brickmaker in America '01
Miracle Run '04
Amish Grace '10
Field of Vision '11
The Gabby Douglas Story '14

Benny Chan
Jackie Chan's Who Am I '98
Gen-X Cops '99
New Police Story '04
Robin-B-Hood '06
The White Storm '13
Call of Heroes '16

Fruit Chan (1959-)
Three . . . Extremes '04
Don't Look Up '08

Gordon Chan (1960-)
Fist of Legend '94
Beast Cops '98
The Medallion '03
The Four '12
Kingdom of Blood: The Final Battle '16

Jackie Chan (1954-)
Young Master '80
Project A '83
Police Story '85
Operation Condor 2: The Armour of the Gods '86
Project A: Part 2 '87
Miracles '89
Operation Condor '91
Jackie Chan's Who Am I '98

Peter Chan (1962-)
The Love Letter '99
Perhaps Love '05
Warlords '08

J.C. Chandor
Margin Call '11
All is Lost '13
A Most Violent Year '14
Triple Frontier '19

Jay Chandrasekhar (1968-)
Super Troopers '01
Club Dread '04
The Dukes of Hazzard '05
Beerfest '06
The Babymakers '12
Super Troopers 2 '18

Cheh Chang (1923-2002)
The Magnificent Trio '66
The One-Armed Swordsman '67
Golden Swallow '68
Have Sword, Will Travel '69
The Heroic Ones '70
Duel of Fists '71
The Delightful Forest '72
Heroes Two '73
The Brave Archer '77
Five Deadly Venoms '78
Heaven & Hell '78
Sword Masters: Two Champions of Shaolin '80
House of Traps '81
The Brave Archer and His Mate '82
Five Element Ninjas '82

James Chankin
The Mark '12
The Mark 2: Redemption '13

Damian Chapa (1963-)
El Padrino '04
Mexican Gangster '08

Todor Chapkanov
Monsterwolf '10
Miami Magma '11
Weather Wars '11

Charlie Chaplin (1889-1977)
The Gold Rush '25
The Circus '28
City Lights '31
Modern Times '36
The Great Dictator '40
Monsieur Verdoux '47
Limelight '52
A King in New York '57
The Chaplin Revue '58
A Countess from Hong Kong '67

Brenda Chapman
Prince of Egypt '98
Brave '12

Matthew Chapman (1950-)
Hussy '80
The Ledge '11

Michael Chapman (1935-)
All the Right Moves '83
The Clan of the Cave Bear '86
The Viking Sagas '95

Joe Chappelle
Halloween 6: The Curse of Michael Myers '95
Phantoms '97
Dracula: The Dark Prince '01
The Skulls 2 '02

Christian Charles
Full of It '07
Love Sick Love '12

Larry Charles (1956-)
Masked and Anonymous '03
Borat: Cultural Learnings of America for Make Benefit Glorious Nation of Kazakhstan '06
Religulous '08
Bruno '09
The Dictator '12
Army of One '16

Henri Charr
Caged Hearts '95
Cellblock Sisters: Banished Behind Bars '95
Hollywood Safari '96
My Uncle: The Alien '96

Amin Qamar Chaudhri (1942-)
Tiger Warsaw '87
An Unremarkable Life '89

Pascal Chaumeil
Heartbreaker '10
A Long Way Down '14

Charles Chauvel
Forty Thousand Horsemen '41
The Fighting Rats of Tobruk '44

Damien Chazelle (1985-)
Guy and Madeline on a Park Bench '09
Whiplash '14
La La Land '16
First Man '18

Stephen Chbosky (1972-)
The Perks of Being a Wallflower '12
Wonder '17

Jeremiah S. Chechik (1955-)
National Lampoon's Christmas Vacation '89
Benny & Joon '93
Tall Tale: The Unbelievable Adventures of Pecos Bill '95
Diabolique '96
The Avengers '98
American Meltdown '04
The Bronx Is Burning '07
The Right Kind Of Wrong '13

Peter Chelsom (1956-)
Funny Bones '94
The Mighty '98
Serendipity '01
Town and Country '01
Shall We Dance? '04
Hannah Montana: The Movie '09
Hector and the Search for Happiness '14
The Space Between Us '17

Joan Chen (1961-)
Xiu Xiu: The Sent Down Girl '97
Autumn in New York '00

Kuo-fu Chen (1958-)
The Personals '98
Double Vision '02

Yarrow Cheney
The Secret Life of Pets '16
The Grinch '18

Andy Cheng
End Game '06
Redline '07

Patrice Chereau (1944-2013)
L'Homme Blesse '83
Queen Margot '94
Those Who Love Me Can Take the Train '98
Intimacy '00
Gabrielle '05

Christopher Scott Cherot (1967-)
Hav Plenty '97
G '02

John R. Cherry, III
Dr. Otto & the Riddle of the Gloom Beam '86
Ernest Goes to Camp '87
Ernest Saves Christmas '88
Ernest Goes to Jail '90
Ernest Scared Stupid '91
Slam Dunk Ernest '95
Ernest Goes to Africa '97
Ernest in the Army '97
All New Adventures of Laurel and Hardy: For Love or Mummy '98

Lionel Chetwynd (1940-)
Hanoi Hilton '87
Varian's War '01

Pierre Chevalier (1915-)
Orloff and the Invisible Man '70
Dr. Orloff and the Invisible Man '72

Stephen Chiau (1962-)
See Stephen (Chiau) Chow

Austin Chick
XX/XY '02
August '08
Girls Against Boys '12

Siu-Tung Ching (1953-)
Duel to the Death '82
Belly of the Beast '03
Naked Weapon '03
An Empress and the Warriors '08
The Sorcerer and the White Snake '13

Tina Gordon Chism
Peeples '13
Little '19

Lisa Cholodenko (1964-)
High Art '98
Laurel Canyon '02
The Kids Are All Right '10
Olive Kitteridge '14

Sylvain Chomet (1963-)
The Triplets of Belleville '02
Paris, je t'aime '06
The Illusionist '10

Alejandro Chomski
Feel the Noise '07
A Beautiful Life '08

Marvin J. Chomsky (1929-)
Mongo's Back In Town '71
Evel Knievel '72
Murph the Surf '75
Victory at Entebbe '76
Little Ladies of the Night '77
Roots '77
Holocaust '78
Tank '83
Anastasia: The Mystery of Anna '86
The Deliberate Stranger '86
Billionaire Boys Club '87
The Brotherhood of the Rose '89
Robert Kennedy and His Times '90
Catherine the Great '95

Thomas Chong (1938-)
Cheech and Chong's Next Movie '80
Cheech and Chong's Nice Dreams '81
Cheech and Chong: Still Smokin' '83
Cheech and Chong's The Corsican Brothers '84
Far Out Man '89

Joyce Chopra (1938-)
Smooth Talk '85
The Lemon Sisters '90
Murder in New Hampshire: The Pamela Smart Story '91
High Stakes '93
Murder in a Small Town '99
Blonde '01
Hollywood Wives: The New Generation '03
The Last Cowboy '03

Yuen Chor (1934-)
Intimate Confessions of a Chinese Courtesan '72
Sword Masters: Web of Death '76
Bat Without Wings '80
The Duel of the Century '81
The Magic Blade '08

Elie Chouraqui (1953-)
Love Songs '84
Harrison's Flowers '02
O Jerusalem '07

Deborah Chow
The High Cost of Living '10
Flowers in the Attic '14

Stephen (Chiau) Chow (1962-)
Shaolin Soccer '01
Kung Fu Hustle '04
Journey to the West '14
The Mermaid '16

Roger Christian (1944-)
The Sender '82
Underworld '96
Battlefield Earth '00
Stranded '13

Christian-Jaque (1904-94)
La Chartreuse de Parme '48
Fanfan la Tulipe '51
Nana '55
Madame Sans-Gene '62
The Black Tulip '64

Benjamin Christiansen (1879-1959)
Haxan: Witchcraft through the Ages '22
Mockery '27

Mark Christopher
54 '98
Pizza '05

Jon M. Chu
Step Up 2 the Streets '08
Step Up 3D '10
Justin Bieber: Never Say Never '11

G.I. Joe: Retaliation '13
Jem and the Holograms '15
Now You See Me 2 '16
Crazy Rich Asians '18

Yen Ping Chu
Fantasy Mission Force '84
The Prisoner '90

Lyndon Chubbuck
Naked Souls '95
Kiss Toledo Goodbye '00
The Right Temptation '00
The War Bride '01

Byron Ross Chudnow (1926-)
The Doberman Gang '72
Daring Dobermans '73

Oxide Pang Chun
Rica 3: Juvenile's Lullaby '73
Bangkok Dangerous '00
The Tesseract '03
The Eye 2 '04
The Eye 3 '05
Re-Cycle '06

Tze Chun
Children of Invention '09
Cold Comes the Night '14

Derek Cianfrance
Blue Valentine '10
The Place Beyond the Pines '13
The Light Between Oceans '16

Gerard Ciccoritti (1956-)
Graveyard Shift '87
Paris, France '94
The Life Before This '99

Jerry Ciccoritti
Murder in the Hamptons '05
The Terrorist Next Door '08
Wisegal '08
Hostile Makeover '09
Killer Hair '09

Matt Cimber (1936-)
Single Room Furnished '68
The Black Six '74
Candy Tangerine Man '75
Lady Cocoa '75
Witch Who Came from the Sea '76
Butterfly '82
Fake Out '82
Time to Die '83

Michael Cimino (1943-2016)
Thunderbolt & Lightfoot '74
The Deer Hunter '78
Heaven's Gate '81
Year of the Dragon '85
The Sicilian '87
Desperate Hours '90
Sunchaser '96

Francesco Cinquemani
Andron: The Black Labyrinth '16
The Poison Rose '19

Osvaldo Civirani (1917-)
Hercules *vs.* the Sons of the Sun '64
Dead for a Dollar '70

Richard Clabaugh (1960-)
Python '00
Eyeborgs '09

Rene Clair (1898-1981)
Italian Straw Hat '27
Under the Roofs of Paris '29
A Nous la Liberte '31
Le Million '31
The Ghost Goes West '36
The Flame of New Orleans '41
Forever and a Day '43
It Happened Tomorrow '44
And Then There Were None '45
Beauties of the Night '52

Bob (Benjamin) Clark (1941-2007)
Children Shouldn't Play with Dead Things '72
Deathdream '72
Black Christmas '75
Murder by Decree '79
Porky's '82
A Christmas Story '83
Porky's 2: The Next Day '83
Rhinestone '84
Turk 182! '85
From the Hip '86
Loose Cannons '90
My Summer Story '94
Baby Geniuses '98
I'll Remember April '99
Now & Forever '02
Karate Dog '04
Superbabies: Baby Geniuses 2 '04

Bruce (B.D.) Clark (1945-)
The Naked Angels '69
Galaxy of Terror '81

Colbert Clark (1898-1960)
Fighting with Kit Carson '33
Mystery Squadron '33
The Three Musketeers '33
Whispering Shadow '33

Duane Clark
Shaking the Tree '92
Protector '97
XIII '08

Greydon Clark (1943-)
Bad Bunch '76
Black Shampoo '76
Hi-Riders '77
Satan's Cheerleaders '77
Without Warning '80
Joy Sticks '83
Final Justice '84
The Uninvited '88
The Forbidden Dance '90
Russian Roulette '93

James B. Clark (1908-2000)
23 Paces to Baker Street '56
A Dog of Flanders '59
One Foot in Hell '60
Misty '61
Drums of Africa '63
Flipper '63
My Side of the Mountain '69

Jim Clark (1931-)
Rentadick '72
Madhouse '74

Larry Clark (1943-)
Kids '95
Another Day in Paradise '98
Bully '01
Teenage Caveman '01
Wassup Rockers '06

Lawrence Gordon Clark
Just Another Secret '89
Death Has a Bad Reputation '90

Steve Clark
The Last International Playboy '08
Night Has Settled '14

Alan Clarke (1935-90)
Scum '79
Rita, Sue & Bob Too '87

Malcolm Clarke
Chasing Holden '01
Prisoner of Paradise '02

Noel Clarke (1975-)
4.3.2.1 '10
The Anomaly '15

Zoe Clarke-Williams (1974-)
Men '97
New Best Friend '02

James Clavell (1925-94)
To Sir, with Love '67
The Last Valley '71

William Claxton (1914-96)
Fangs of the Wild '54
Night of the Lepus '72

Jack Clayton (1921-95)
Room at the Top '59
The Innocents '61
The Pumpkin Eater '64
Our Mother's House '67
The Great Gatsby '74
Something Wicked This Way Comes '83
The Lonely Passion of Judith Hearne '87

Marc Clebanoff
The Pink Conspiracy '07
Break '09

Tom Clegg (1927-)
Destination Moonbase Alpha '75
The Inside Man '84
Mountbatten: The Last Viceroy '86
Any Man's Death '90
The Price of the Bride '90
Sharpe's Eagle '93
Sharpe's Rifles '93
Sharpe's Battle '94
Sharpe's Company '94
Sharpe's Enemy '94
Sharpe's Gold '94
Sharpe's Honour '94
Sharpe's Sword '94
Sharpe's Mission '96
Sharpe's Regiment '96
Sharpe's Siege '96
Sharpe's Justice '97
Sharpe's Revenge '97
Sharpe's Waterloo '97
Sharpe's Challenge '06
Sharpe's Peril '08

William Clemens (1905-80)
The Case of the Stuttering Bishop '37
Nancy Drew-Detective '38
Nancy Drew, Reporter '39
Nancy Drew-Trouble Shooter '39
The Falcon and the Co-Eds '43
The Falcon in Danger '43

Dick Clement (1937-)
Otley '68
A Severed Head '70
Catch Me a Spy '71
Bullshot '83
Water '85
Porridge '91

Rene Clement (1913-96)
Battle of the Rails '46
Forbidden Games '52
Gervaise '56
Purple Noon '60
Joy House '64
Is Paris Burning? '66
Rider on the Rain '70
Wanted: Babysitter '75

Ron Clements (1953-)
The Great Mouse Detective '86
The Little Mermaid '89
Aladdin '92
Hercules '97
Treasure Planet '02
The Princess and the Frog '09
Moana '16

Graeme Clifford (1942-)
Frances '82
Gleaming the Cube '89
Deception '92
The Last Don '97
The Last Don 2 '98
Caracara '00
Redeemer '02

Elmer Clifton (1892-1949)
Down to the Sea in Ships '22
Assassin of Youth '35
Custer's Last Stand '36
Ten Laps to Go '36
Mile a Minute Love '37
Pilot X '37
Seven Doors to Death '44
The Judge '49
Streets of Sin '49

Edward F. (Eddie) Cline (1892-1961)
Hook, Line and Sinker '30
Cracked Nuts '31
Peck's Bad Boy '34
Cowboy Millionaire '35
Forty Naughty Girls '37
High Flyers '37
On Again-Off Again '37
Hawaii Calls '38
Peck's Bad Boy with the Circus '38
The Bank Dick '40
My Little Chickadee '40
Never Give a Sucker an Even Break '41
The Villain Still Pursued Her '41
Private Buckaroo '42
Snuffy Smith, Yard Bird '42

Hayley Cloake
The House of Usher '06
Impact Point '08

George Clooney (1961-)
Confessions of a Dangerous Mind '02
Good Night, and Good Luck '05
The Ides of March '11
The Monuments Men '13
Suburbicon '17

Robert Clouse (1929-97)
Enter the Dragon '73
Black Belt Jones '74
Golden Needles '74
The Ultimate Warrior '75
The Pack '77
Game of Death '79
Battle Creek Brawl '80
The Big Brawl '80
Force: Five '81
Gymkata '85
China O'Brien '88

Henri-Georges Clouzot (1907-77)
The Murderer Lives at Number 21 '42
Le Corbeau '43
Jenny Lamour '47
Diabolique '55
Wages of Fear '55
Mystery of Picasso '56

E.B. (Enzo Barboni) Clucher (1922-2002)
They Call Me Trinity '72
Trinity Is Still My Name '75
Crime Busters '78
Sons of Trinity '95

Travis Cluff
The Gallows '15
The Gallows Act II '19

Craig Clyde
Little Heroes '91
The Legend of Wolf Mountain '92
Walking Thunder '94
Miracle Dogs '03
The Derby Stallion '05
The Wild Stallion '09
A Christmas Wish '11
Heaven's Door '12
Storm Rider '13

Lewis Coates (1947-)
See Luigi Cozzi

Stacy Cochran
My New Gun '92
Boys '95

Jean Cocteau (1889-1963)
Beauty and the Beast '46
Orpheus '49
The Testament of Orpheus '59

Matt Codd
Lost Colony: The Legend of Roanoke '07
Super Eruption '11

Ethan Coen (1957-)
The Ladykillers '04
Paris, je t'aime '06
No Country for Old Men '07
Burn After Reading '08
A Serious Man '09
True Grit '10
Inside Llewyn Davis '13
Hail, Caesar! '16
The Ballad of Buster Scruggs '18

Joel Coen (1954-)
Blood Simple '85
Raising Arizona '87
Miller's Crossing '90
Barton Fink '91
The Hudsucker Proxy '93
Fargo '96
The Big Lebowski '97
O Brother Where Art Thou? '00
The Man Who Wasn't There '01
Intolerable Cruelty '03
The Ladykillers '04
Paris, je t'aime '06
No Country for Old Men '07
Burn After Reading '08
A Serious Man '09
True Grit '10
Inside Llewyn Davis '13
Hail, Caesar! '16
The Ballad of Buster Scruggs '18

Scott Coffey (1967-)
Ellie Parker '05
Adult World '13

Pierre Coffin
Despicable Me '10
Despicable Me 2 '13
Minions '15
Despicable Me 3 '17

Dan Cohen
Madman '79
Corporate Affairs '07

Eli Cohen (1940-)
The Summer of Aviya '88
The Quarrel '93
The Soft Kill '94
Under the Domim Tree '95

Etan Cohen
Get Hard '15
Holmes & Watson '18

Gary P. Cohen
Video Violence '87
Video Violence Part 2. . . The Exploitation! '87

Howard R. Cohen (1942-99)
Saturday the 14th '81
Saturday the 14th Strikes Back '88
Deathstalker 4: Match of Titans '92

Larry Cohen (1947-)
Housewife '72
Black Caesar '73
Hell Up in Harlem '73
It's Alive '74
God Told Me To '76
The Private Files of J. Edgar Hoover '77
It's Alive 2: It Lives Again '78
Q (The Winged Serpent) '82
Perfect Strangers '84
Special Effects '85
The Stuff '85
It's Alive 3: Island of the Alive '87
Return to Salem's Lot '87
Wicked Stepmother '89
The Ambulance '90
Original Gangstas '96

Norman Cohen (1936-83)
Adolf Hitler: My Part in His Downfall '74
Confessions of a Driving Instructor '76

Rob Cohen (1949-)
A Small Circle of Friends '80
Dragon: The Bruce Lee Story '93
Daylight '96
Dragonheart '96
The Rat Pack '98
The Skulls '00
The Fast and the Furious '01
XXX '02
Stealth '05
The Mummy: Tomb of the Dragon Emperor '08
Alex Cross '12
The Boy Next Door '15
The Hurricane Heist '18

Steve Cohen
Devil in the Flesh '98
Bar Hopping '00

Jared Cohn
Born Bad '11
Hold Your Breath '12
12/12/12 '12

Michael Cohn
Interceptor '92
When the Bough Breaks '93
Snow White: A Tale of Terror '97

Kat Coiro
Life Happens '11
And While We Were Here '13
A Case of You '13

Isabel Coixet (1960-)
Things I Never Told You '96
My Life Without Me '03
Paris, je t'aime '06
Elegy '08
Learning to Drive '15
The Bookshop '18

Cyril Coke (1914-93)
The Duchess of Duke Street '78
Flickers '80
Pride and Prejudice '85

Harley Cokliss (1945-)
Warlords of the 21st Century '82
Black Moon Rising '86
Malone '87
Hercules the Legendary Journeys, Vol. 2: The Lost Kingdom '94
Inferno '99

Marcus Cole
The Christmas Box '95
From the Mixed-Up Files of Mrs. Basil E. Frankweiler '95
A Song From the Heart '99

Nigel Cole (1959-)
Saving Grace '00
Calendar Girls '03
A Lot Like Love '05
$5 a Day '08
Made in Dagenham '10

Randel Cole
2B Perfectly Honest '04
Real Time '08

John David Coles
Signs of Life '89
The Good Fight '92

Giuseppe Colizzi (1925-78)
Ace High '68
Boot Hill '69
All the Way, Boys '73

Richard A. Colla (1936-)
ZigZag '70
Fuzz '72
The Questor Tapes '74

Manny Coto
Cover-Up *'91*
Dr. Giggles *'92*
Star Kid *'97*

Vittorio Cottafavi (1914-98)
Goliath and the Dragon *'61*
Hercules and the Captive Women *'63*

Jack Couffer (1924-)
Nikki, the Wild Dog of the North *'61*
Ring of Bright Water *'69*
Living Free *'72*

Allen Coulter
Stephen King's Golden Years *'91*
Hollywoodland *'06*
Remember Me *'10*

Rich Cowan
The Basket *'99*
The River Murders *'11*

William J. Cowen (1886-1964)
Kongo *'32*
Oliver Twist *'33*

Gabriela Cowperthwaite
Blackfish *'13*
Megan Leavey *'17*

Alex Cox (1954-)
Repo Man *'83*
Sid & Nancy *'86*
Straight to Hell *'87*
Walker *'87*
Highway Patrolman *'91*
The Winner *'96*
Repo Chick *'09*

Brian Cox (1946-)
Scorpion Spring *'96*
Keepin' It Real *'01*
The Dead One *'07*

C. Jay Cox (1962-)
Latter Days *'04*
Kiss the Bride *'07*

Courteney Cox (1964-)
Talhotblond *'12*
Just Before I Go *'15*

James Cox (1975-)
Highway *'01*
Wonderland *'03*
Straight A's *'13*
Billionaire Boys Club *'18*

Nell Cox
Roommate *'84*
Konrad *'85*

Paul Cox (1940-)
Lonely Hearts *'82*
Man of Flowers *'84*
Cactus *'86*
Vincent: The Life and Death of Vincent van Gogh *'87*
Molokai: The Story of Father Damien *'99*
Innocence *'00*

Tim Cox
Alien Lockdown *'04*
Mammoth *'06*
Miss Nobody *'10*

Luigi Cozzi (1947-)
The Killer Must Kill Again *'75*
Star Crash *'78*
Alien Contamination *'81*
Hercules *'83*
Hercules 2 *'85*

Arthur Crabtree (1900-75)
Madonna of the Seven Moons *'45*
Caravan *'46*
Lilli Marlene *'50*
Fiend without a Face *'58*
Horrors of the Black Museum *'59*

William Crain (1949-)
Blacula *'72*
Dr. Black, Mr. Hyde *'76*

Kenneth Crane
Monster from Green Hell *'58*
When Hell Broke Loose *'58*
The Manster *'59*

Brian Crano
A Bag of Hammers *'11*
Permission *'18*

Jay Craven
Where the Rivers Flow North *'94*
A Stranger in the Kingdom *'98*
Disappearances *'06*

Wes Craven (1939-2015)
Last House on the Left *'72*
The Hills Have Eyes *'77*
Summer of Fear *'78*
Deadly Blessing *'81*
Swamp Thing *'82*
The Hills Have Eyes, Part 2 *'84*
Invitation to Hell *'84*
A Nightmare on Elm Street *'84*
Deadly Friend *'86*
The Serpent and the Rainbow *'87*
Shocker *'89*
The People under the Stairs *'91*
Wes Craven's New Nightmare *'94*
Vampire in Brooklyn *'95*
Scream *'96*
Scream 2 *'97*
Music of the Heart *'99*
Scream 3 *'00*
Cursed *'04*
Red Eye *'05*
Paris, je t'aime *'06*
My Soul to Take *'10*
Scream 4 *'11*

Guy Crawford
Starved *'97*
The Catcher *'98*
Autopsy: A Love Story *'02*

Eran Creevy (1976-)
Shifty *'08*
Welcome to the Punch *'13*
Collide *'17*

Destin Daniel Cretton
Short Term 12 *'13*
The Glass Castle *'17*
Just Mercy *'19*

Charles Crichton (1910-99)
Dead of Night *'45*
Hue and Cry *'47*
Against the Wind *'48*
The Lavender Hill Mob *'51*
Hunted *'52*
A Fish Called Wanda *'88*

Michael Crichton (1942-2008)
Pursuit *'72*
Westworld *'73*
Coma *'78*
The Great Train Robbery *'79*
Looker *'81*
Runaway *'84*
Physical Evidence *'89*
The 13th Warrior *'99*

Donald Crisp (1880-1974)
Don Q., Son of Zorro *'25*
Dress Parade *'27*
The Fighting Eagle *'27*
Dr. Ehrlich's Magic Bullet *'40*
Saddle the Wind *'58*

Armando Crispino (1925-)
Dead Are Alive *'72*
Commandos *'73*
Autopsy *'75*

Michael Cristofer (1945-)
Gia *'98*
Body Shots *'99*
Original Sin *'01*

John Cromwell (1888-1979)
Double Harness *'33*
Sweepings *'33*
Of Human Bondage *'34*
Spitfire *'34*
Little Lord Fauntleroy *'36*
Prisoner of Zenda *'37*
Algiers *'38*
In Name Only *'39*
Made for Each Other *'39*
Abe Lincoln in Illinois *'40*
So Ends Our Night *'41*
Son of Fury *'42*
Since You Went Away *'44*
The Enchanted Cottage *'45*
Anna and the King of Siam *'46*
Dead Reckoning *'47*
Night Song *'47*
Caged *'50*
The Racket *'51*
The Goddess *'58*

David Cronenberg (1943-)
They Came from Within *'75*
Rabid *'77*
Fast Company *'78*
The Brood *'79*
Scanners *'81*
Dead Zone *'83*
Videodrome *'83*
The Fly *'86*
Dead Ringers *'88*
Naked Lunch *'91*
M. Butterfly *'93*
Crash *'95*
eXistenZ *'99*
Spider *'02*
A History of Violence *'05*
Eastern Promises *'07*
A Dangerous Method *'11*
Cosmopolis *'12*
Maps to the Stars *'14*

Harold Cronk
God's Not Dead *'14*
God's Not Dead 2 *'16*
God Bless the Broken Road *'18*
Unbroken: Path to Redemption *'18*

Jeff Crook
Ghetto Dawg 2: Out of the Pits *'05*
Salvage *'06*

Josh Crook
Ghetto Dawg 2: Out of the Pits *'05*
Salvage *'06*

Alan Crosland (1894-1936)
Don Juan *'26*
The Jazz Singer *'27*
Old San Francisco *'27*
When a Man Loves *'27*
On with the Show *'29*
Big Boy *'30*
The Case of the Howling Dog *'34*
Massacre *'34*
The White Cockatoo *'35*

Cameron Crowe (1957-)
Say Anything *'89*
Singles *'92*
Jerry Maguire *'96*
Almost Famous *'00*
Vanilla Sky *'01*
Elizabethtown *'05*
Pearl Jam Twenty *'11*
We Bought a Zoo *'11*
Aloha *'15*

Christopher Crowe (1948-)
Off Limits *'87*
Whispers in the Dark *'92*

John Crowley
Intermission *'03*
Boy A *'07*
Is Anybody There? *'08*
Closed Circuit *'13*
Brooklyn *'15*
The Goldfinch *'19*

James Cruze (1884-1942)
The Great Gabbo *'29*
If I Had a Million *'32*
I Cover the Waterfront *'33*
Mr. Skitch *'33*
David Harum *'34*

Billy Crystal (1947-)
Mr. Saturday Night *'92*
Forget Paris *'95*
61* *'01*

Gabor Csupo (1952-)
Bridge to Terabithia *'07*
The Secret of Moonacre *'08*

Alfonso Cuarón (1961-)
A Little Princess *'95*
Great Expectations *'97*
Y Tu Mama Tambien *'01*
Harry Potter and the Prisoner of Azkaban *'04*
Children of Men *'06*
Paris, je t'aime *'06*
Gravity *'13*
Roma *'18*

Carlos Cuaron (1966-)
Rudo y Cursi *'09*
Sugar Kisses *'13*

Michael Cuesta (1963-)
L.I.E. *'01*
12 and Holding *'05*
Roadie *'11*
Kill the Messenger *'14*
American Assassin *'17*

George Cukor (1899-1983)
One Hour with You *'32*
What Price Hollywood? *'32*
Dinner at Eight *'33*
Little Women *'33*
David Copperfield *'35*
Sylvia Scarlett *'35*
Camille *'36*
Romeo and Juliet *'36*
Holiday *'38*
The Women *'39*
The Philadelphia Story *'40*
Susan and God *'40*
A Woman's Face *'41*
Her Cardboard Lover *'42*
Keeper of the Flame *'42*
Gaslight *'44*
A Double Life *'47*
Edward, My Son *'49*
Adam's Rib *'50*
Born Yesterday *'50*
A Life of Her Own *'50*
The Model and the Marriage Broker *'51*
The Marrying Kind *'52*
Pat and Mike *'52*
The Actress *'53*
It Should Happen to You *'54*
A Star Is Born *'54*
Bhowani Junction *'56*
Les Girls *'57*
Wild Is the Wind *'57*
Heller in Pink Tights *'60*
Let's Make Love *'60*
Song Without End *'60*
The Chapman Report *'62*
My Fair Lady *'64*
Justine *'69*
Travels with My Aunt *'72*
The Corn Is Green *'79*
Rich and Famous *'81*

Jeremiah Cullinane
Spacejacked *'98*
Dangerous Curves *'99*

Jill Culton
Open Season *'06*
Abominable *'19*

Adamo P. Cultraro (1973-)
Bad Ass *'09*
Tactical Force *'11*

Alan Cumming (1965-)
The Anniversary Party *'01*
Ghost Writer *'07*

Irving Cummings (1888-1959)
Flesh and Blood *'22*
Broken Hearts of Broadway *'23*
Behind That Curtain *'29*
Curly Top *'35*
Girl's Dormitory *'36*
Just Around the Corner *'38*
Little Miss Broadway *'38*
Hollywood Cavalcade *'39*
The Story of Alexander Graham Bell *'39*
Down Argentine Way *'40*
Louisiana Purchase *'41*
That Night in Rio *'41*
My Gal Sal *'42*
Springtime in the Rockies *'42*
The Impatient Years *'44*
The Dolly Sisters *'46*
Double Dynamite *'51*

Rusty Cundieff (1965-)
Fear of a Black Hat *'94*
Tales from the Hood *'95*
Sprung *'96*
Movie 43 *'13*

Richard Cunha (1922-2005)
Frankenstein's Daughter *'58*
Giant from the Unknown *'58*
She Demons *'58*
Missile to the Moon *'59*

David L. Cunningham
The Seeker: The Dark Is Rising *'07*
Running for Grace *'18*

Sean S. Cunningham (1941-)
Friday the 13th *'80*
A Stranger Is Watching *'82*
Spring Break *'83*
The New Kids *'85*
Deepstar Six *'89*
Terminal Invasion *'02*

Terry Cunningham
Chaos Factor *'00*
Code Hunter *'02*
Descent *'05*
Earthstorm *'06*

John Curran
Praise *'98*
We Don't Live Here Anymore *'04*
The Painted Veil *'06*
Stone *'10*
Tracks *'14*
Chappaquiddick *'17*

Andrew Currie
Fido *'06*
Barricade *'12*

Dan Curtis (1928-2006)
House of Dark Shadows *'70*
Night of Dark Shadows *'71*
The Night Strangler *'72*
Dracula *'73*
The Norliss Tapes *'73*
Melvin Purvis: G-Man *'74*
Nightmare at 43 Hillcrest *'74*
Scream of the Wolf *'74*
The Turn of the Screw *'74*
Trilogy of Terror *'75*
Burnt Offerings *'76*
Dead of Night *'77*
When Every Day Was the Fourth of July *'78*
The Last Ride of the Dalton Gang *'79*
The Long Days of Summer *'80*
The Winds of War *'83*
War & Remembrance *'88*
War & Remembrance: The Final Chapter *'89*
Me and the Kid *'93*
Trilogy of Terror 2 *'96*
The Love Letter *'98*

Richard Curtis (1956-)
Love Actually *'03*
Pirate Radio *'09*
About Time *'13*

Simon Curtis (1960-)
David Copperfield *'99*
Five Days *'07*
Cranford *'08*
Return to Cranford *'09*
A Short Stay in Switzerland *'09*
My Week With Marilyn *'11*
Woman in Gold *'15*
Goodbye Christopher Robin *'17*
The Art of Racing in the Rain *'19*

Stacey Stewart Curtis
Recipe for Revenge *'98*
What Katy Did *'99*
Gossip *'08*

Vondie Curtis-Hall (1956-)
Gridlock'd *'96*
Glitter *'01*
Waist Deep *'06*
Abducted: The Carlina White Story *'12*

Michael Curtiz (1888-1962)
Noah's Ark *'28*
Bright Lights *'30*
The Matrimonial Bed *'30*
God's Gift to Women *'31*
The Woman From Monte Carlo *'31*
Alias the Doctor *'32*
Doctor X *'32*
The Strange Love of Molly Louvain *'32*
The Kennel Murder Case *'33*
Mystery of the Wax Museum *'33*
20,000 Years in Sing Sing *'33*
British Agent *'34*
Jimmy the Gent *'34*
Black Fury *'35*
Captain Blood *'35*
The Case of the Curious Bride *'35*
Front Page Woman *'35*
The Charge of the Light Brigade *'36*
Kid Galahad *'37*
Stolen Holiday *'37*
The Adventures of Robin Hood *'38*
Angels with Dirty Faces *'38*
Four Daughters *'38*
Four's a Crowd *'38*
Gold Is Where You Find It *'38*
Daughters Courageous *'39*
Dodge City *'39*
Four Wives *'39*
The Private Lives of Elizabeth & Essex *'39*
Santa Fe Trail *'40*
The Sea Hawk *'40*
Virginia City *'40*
Dive Bomber *'41*
Captains of the Clouds *'42*
Casablanca *'42*
Yankee Doodle Dandy *'42*
Mission to Moscow *'43*
This Is the Army *'43*
Passage to Marseilles *'44*
Mildred Pierce *'45*
Roughly Speaking *'45*
Night and Day *'46*
Life with Father *'47*
The Unsuspected *'47*
Romance on the High Seas *'48*
Flamingo Road *'49*
My Dream Is Yours *'49*
The Breaking Point *'50*
Bright Leaf *'50*
Young Man with a Horn *'50*
Force of Arms *'51*
I'll See You in My Dreams *'51*
Jim Thorpe: All American *'51*
The Jazz Singer *'52*
The Story of Will Rogers *'52*
Trouble along the Way *'53*
The Boy From Oklahoma *'54*
The Egyptian *'54*
White Christmas *'54*

We're No Angels *'55*
The Helen Morgan Story *'57*
King Creole *'58*
Proud Rebel *'58*
The Hangman *'59*
The Man in the Net *'59*
The Adventures of Huckleberry Finn *'60*
Breath of Scandal *'60*
The Comancheros *'61*

R.J. Cutler
The September Issue *'09*
If I Stay *'14*

Catherine Cyran
True Heart *'97*
Christmas Do-Over *'06*
The Prince & Me 2: Royal Wedding *'06*
The Prince & Me 3: A Royal Honeymoon *'08*
The Prince & Me 4: The Elephant Adventure *'10*

Czar (1973-)
See S. Craig Zahler

Paul Czinner (1890-1972)
Catherine the Great *'34*
As You Like It *'36*

Renee Daalder (1944-)
Massacre at Central High *'76*
Habitat *'97*

Cherien Dabis
Amreeka *'09*
May in Summer *'13*
May in the Summer *'13*

Morton DaCosta (1914-89)
Auntie Mame *'58*
The Music Man *'62*
Island of Love *'63*

Olivier Dahan (1967-)
La Vie Promise *'02*
Crimson Rivers 2: Angels of the Apocalypse *'05*
La Vie en Rose *'07*
My Own Love Song *'10*
Grace of Monaco *'14*

John Dahl (1956-)
Kill Me Again *'89*
Red Rock West *'93*
The Last Seduction *'94*
Unforgettable *'96*
Rounders *'98*
Joy Ride *'01*
The Great Raid *'05*

Stephen Daldry (1960-)
Billy Elliot *'00*
The Hours *'02*
The Reader *'08*
Extremely Loud and Incredibly Close *'11*
Trash *'14*

Holly Dale (1953-)
Blood & Donuts *'95*
Absolution *'05*
Hush Little Baby *'07*

Zale Dalen (1947-)
Expect No Mercy *'95*
Call of the Wild *'04*

John Francis Daley (1985-)
Vacation *'15*
Game Night *'18*

Massimo Dallamano (1917-76)
Dorian Gray *'70*
Super Bitch *'73*

Ian Dalrymple (1903-89)
Storm in a Teacup *'37*
Esther Waters *'48*

Lance Daly
Kisses *'08*
The Good Doctor *'11*
Life's a Breeze *'14*
Black '47 *'18*

Joe D'Amato (1936-99)
Anthropophagus: The Grim Reaper *'80*
Buried Alive *'81*
Grim Reaper *'81*
Ator the Fighting Eagle *'83*
Black Cobra *'83*

Michael Damian (1962-)
Hot Tamale *'06*
Moondance Alexander *'07*
Marley & Me: The Puppy Years *'11*
A Princess for Christmas *'11*
Flicka: Country Pride *'12*
The Sweeter Side of Life *'13*
High Strung *'16*

Damiano Damiani (1922-2013)
A Bullet for the General *'68*
Confessions of a Police Captain *'72*
How to Kill a Judge *'75*
Amityville 2: The Possession *'82*

Mel Damski (1946-)
The Child Stealer *'79*
Yellowbeard *'83*
Mischief *'85*
Happy Together *'89*
Legendary *'10*

Rod Daniel (1942-2016)
Teen Wolf *'85*
Like Father, Like Son *'87*
K-9 *'89*
The Super *'91*
Beethoven's 2nd *'93*

Harold Daniels (1903-71)
Roadblock *'51*
Sword of Venus *'53*
Terror in the Haunted House *'58*
House of the Black Death *'65*

Jeff Daniels (1955-)
Escanaba in da Moonlight *'01*
Super Sucker *'03*

Lee Daniels (1959-)
Shadowboxer *'06*
Precious: Based on the Novel 'Push' by Sapphire *'09*
The Paperboy *'12*
Lee Daniels' The Butler *'13*

Brian Dannelly
Saved! *'04*
Struck by Lightning *'12*

Joe Dante (1946-)
Hollywood Boulevard *'76*
Piranha *'78*
The Howling *'81*
Twilight Zone: The Movie *'83*
Gremlins *'84*
Explorers *'85*
Amazon Women on the Moon *'87*
Innerspace *'87*
The 'Burbs *'89*
Gremlins 2: The New Batch *'90*
Matinee *'92*
Runaway Daughters *'94*
Picture Windows *'95*
The Second Civil War *'97*
Small Soldiers *'98*
Looney Tunes: Back in Action *'03*
Burying the Ex *'15*
Nightmare Cinema *'19*

Ray Danton (1931-92)
Crypt of the Living Dead *'73*
Psychic Killer *'75*
Tales of the Unexpected *'91*

Frank Darabont (1959-)
Buried Alive *'90*
The Shawshank Redemption *'94*
The Green Mile *'99*
The Majestic *'01*
The Mist *'07*

Jonathan Darby
The Enemy Within *'94*
Hush *'98*

Kieran Darcy-Smith (1965-)
Wish You Were Here *'12*
The Duel *'16*

Jean-Pierre Dardenne (1951-)
La Promesse *'96*
Rosetta *'99*
The Child *'05*
Lorna's Silence *'08*
The Kid with a Bike *'11*
Two Days, One Night *'14*
The Unknown Girl *'17*

Luc Dardenne (1954-)
La Promesse *'96*
Rosetta *'99*
The Child *'05*
Lorna's Silence *'08*
The Kid with a Bike *'11*
Two Days, One Night *'14*
The Unknown Girl *'17*

Gregory Dark (1957-)
See Gregory Brown

Eric Darnell
Antz *'98*
Madagascar *'05*
Madagascar: Escape 2 Africa *'08*
Madagascar 3: Europe's Most Wanted *'12*
Penguins of Madagascar *'14*

Damon Dash (1971-)
Paper Soldiers *'02*
State Property 2 *'05*

Julie Dash (1952-)
Daughters of the Dust *'91*
Subway Stories *'97*
Incognito *'99*
The Rosa Parks Story *'02*

Jules Dassin (1911-2008)
Reunion in France *'42*
Young Ideas *'43*
The Canterville Ghost *'44*
Two Smart People *'46*
Brute Force *'47*
The Naked City *'48*
Night and the City *'50*
Rififi *'54*
Where the Hot Wind Blows *'59*
Never on Sunday *'60*
Phaedra *'61*
Topkapi *'64*
Uptight *'68*
Circle of Two *'80*

Delmer Daves (1904-77)
Destination Tokyo *'43*
Hollywood Canteen *'44*
Pride of the Marines *'45*
Dark Passage *'47*
The Red House *'47*
A Kiss in the Dark *'49*
Task Force *'49*
Broken Arrow *'50*
Bird of Paradise *'51*
Never Let Me Go *'53*
Demetrius and the Gladiators *'54*
Drum Beat *'54*
Jubal *'56*
3:10 to Yuma *'57*
The Badlanders *'58*
Cowboy *'58*
Kings Go Forth *'58*
The Hanging Tree *'59*
A Summer Place *'59*
Parrish *'61*
Susan Slade *'61*
Rome Adventure *'62*
Spencer's Mountain *'63*
Youngblood Hawke *'64*

Lorena David
Eastside *'99*
Outta Time *'01*
Extreme Dating *'04*

Mark David (1974-)
Sweet Thing *'00*
American Cowslip *'09*

Boaz Davidson (1943-)
Last American Virgin *'82*
Salsa *'88*
American Cyborg: Steel Warrior *'94*
Solar Force *'94*
Outside the Law *'95*

Martin Davidson (1939-)
The Lords of Flatbush *'74*
Hero at Large *'80*
Eddie and the Cruisers *'83*
The Heart of Dixie *'89*
Hard Promises *'92*
Follow the River *'95*
Looking for an Echo *'99*

Gareth Davies
Oliver Twist *'85*
Unexplained Laughter *'89*
A Mind to Murder *'96*

John Davies (1953-)
Kim *'84*
A Married Man *'84*
Devices and Desires *'91*

Terence Davies (1945-)
Distant Voices, Still Lives *'88*
The Long Day Closes *'92*
The Neon Bible *'95*
House of Mirth *'00*
Of Time and the City *'08*
The Deep Blue Sea *'12*
Sunset Song *'16*
A Quiet Passion *'17*

Andrew Davis (1946-)
Stony Island *'77*
The Final Terror *'83*
Code of Silence *'85*
Above the Law *'88*
The Package *'89*
Under Siege *'92*
The Fugitive *'93*
Steal Big, Steal Little *'95*
Chain Reaction *'96*
A Perfect Murder *'98*
Collateral Damage *'02*
Holes *'03*
The Guardian *'06*

Desmond Davis (1928-)
Girl with Green Eyes *'64*
I Was Happy Here *'66*
Smashing Time *'67*
Clash of the Titans *'81*
The Sign of Four *'83*
Camille *'84*
The Man Who Lived at the Ritz *'91*

Garth Davis
Top of the Lake *'13*
Lion *'16*
Mary Magdalene *'19*

John A. Davis
Jimmy Neutron: Boy Genius *'01*
The Ant Bully *'06*

Julie Davis (1969-)
Witchcraft 6: The Devil's Mistress *'94*
I Love You, Don't Touch Me! *'97*
All Over the Guy *'01*
Amy's O *'02*
Finding Bliss *'09*

Lee Davis
3 A.M. *'01*
Christmas at Water's Edge *'04*

Michael Davis (1961-)
Eight Days a Week *'97*
100 Girls *'00*
Monster Man *'03*
Shoot 'Em Up *'07*

Mitch Davis
The Other Side of Heaven *'02*
Language of the Enemy *'07*
Christmas Eve *'15*
The Stray *'17*
The Other Side of Heaven 2: Fire of Faith *'19*

Ossie Davis (1917-2005)
Cotton Comes to Harlem *'70*
Gordon's War *'73*

Tamra Davis (1962-)
Guncrazy *'92*
CB4: The Movie *'93*
Billy Madison *'94*
Half-Baked *'97*
Best Men *'98*
Skipped Parts *'00*
Crossroads *'02*
Jean-Michel Basquiat: The Radiant Child *'10*

Anthony M. Dawson (1930-2002)
Assignment Outer Space *'61*
Battle of the Worlds *'61*
Giants of Rome *'63*
Castle of Blood *'64*
Hercules, Prisoner of Evil *'64*
Planet on the Prowl *'65*
The Virgin of Nuremberg *'65*
The War of the Planets *'65*
Wild, Wild Planet *'65*
Lightning Bolt *'67*
The Snow Devils *'67*
And God Said to Cain *'69*
Web of the Spider *'70*
Seven Deaths in the Cat's Eye *'72*
Mr. Superinvisible *'73*
Andy Warhol's Dracula *'74*
Take a Hard Ride *'75*
Death Rage *'77*
The Rip Off *'78*
Cannibal Apocalypse *'80*
The Last Hunter *'80*
The Squeeze *'80*
Ark of the Sun God *'82*
Yor, the Hunter from the Future *'83*
Code Name: Wild Geese *'84*
Codename: Wildgeese *'84*

Ernest Day (1927-2006)
Green Ice *'81*
Waltz across Texas *'83*

Robert Day (1922-)
Corridors of Blood *'58*
The Haunted Strangler *'58*
Bobbikins *'59*
First Man into Space *'59*
Tarzan the Magnificent *'60*
Two-Way Stretch *'60*
Tarzan's Three Challenges *'63*
She *'65*
Tarzan and the Valley of Gold *'65*
Tarzan and the Great River *'67*
The Big Game *'72*
A Home of Our Own *'75*
Initiation of Sarah *'78*
The Man with Bogart's Face *'80*
Peter and Paul *'81*
The Quick and the Dead *'87*
Higher Ground *'88*

Josee Dayan (1943-)
Balzac: A Life of Passion *'99*
The Count of Monte Cristo *'99*
Dangerous Liaisons *'03*

Jonathan Dayton (1957-)
Little Miss Sunshine *'06*
Ruby Sparks *'12*
Battle of the Sexes *'17*

Lyman Dayton
Baker's Hawk *'76*
The Red Fury *'84*

Fabrizio de Angelis (1940-)
Deadly Impact *'84*
The Manhunt *'86*

Jan De Bont (1943-)
Speed *'94*
Twister *'96*
Speed 2: Cruise Control *'97*
The Haunting *'99*
Lara Croft Tomb Raider: The Cradle of Life *'03*

Philippe de Broca (1933-2004)
Cartouche *'62*
The King of Hearts *'66*
Le Magnifique *'76*
On Guard! *'03*

Fred de Cordova (1910-2001)
For the Love of Mary *'48*
Buccaneer's Girl *'50*
Bedtime for Bonzo *'51*
Yankee Buccaneer *'52*
Frankie and Johnny *'65*
I'll Take Sweden *'65*

Albert de Courville (1887-1960)
There Goes the Bride *'32*
Crackerjack *'38*

Andy de Emmony
Filth *'08*
God on Trial *'08*
Framed *'10*
The Bletchley Circle *'13*

Frank De Felitta (1921-)
The Two Worlds of Jenny Logan *'79*
Dark Night of the Scarecrow *'81*
Scissors *'91*

Raymond De Felitta (1964-)
Cafe Society *'97*
Two Family House *'99*
The Thing About My Folks *'05*
City Island *'09*
Rob the Mob *'14*

Rolf de Heer (1951-)
Encounter at Raven's Gate *'88*
Dingo *'90*
Bad Boy Bubby *'93*
Alien Visitor *'95*
The Quiet Room *'96*
Ten Canoes *'06*

Alex de la Iglesia (1965-)
Dance with the Devil *'97*
800 Bullets *'02*
El Crimen Perfecto *'04*
The Oxford Murders *'08*
The Last Circus *'10*

Gerardo (Gerry) De Leon (1913-81)
Terror Is a Man *'59*
The Walls of Hell *'64*
Brides of the Beast *'68*
Mad Doctor of Blood Island *'68*

Alberto De Martino (1929-)
The Invincible Gladiator *'62*
Medusa Against the Son of Hercules *'62*
The Blancheville Monster *'63*
The Triumph of Hercules *'66*
Crime Boss *'72*
New Mafia Boss *'72*
Django Shoots First *'74*
The Chosen *'77*

Kirk De Micco
Space Chimps *'08*
The Croods *'13*

Robert De Niro (1943-)
A Bronx Tale *'93*
The Good Shepherd *'06*

Manoel de Oliveira (1908-)
Abraham's Valley *'93*
The Convent *'95*
Party *'96*

Voyage to the Beginning of the World *'96*
I'm Going Home *'00*
Belle Toujours *'06*
Eccentricities of a Blonde-Haired Girl *'10*
The Strange Case of Angelica *'10*

Armando de Ossorio (1926-2001)
Fangs of the Living Dead *'68*
Night of the Sorcerers *'70*
When the Screaming Stops *'73*
Night of the Death Cult *'75*
Return of the Evil Dead *'75*

Brian De Palma (1941-)
Greetings *'68*
The Wedding Party *'69*
Hi, Mom! *'70*
Get to Know Your Rabbit *'72*
Sisters *'73*
Phantom of the Paradise *'74*
Carrie *'76*
Obsession *'76*
The Fury *'78*
Home Movies *'79*
Dressed to Kill *'80*
Blow Out *'81*
Scarface *'83*
Body Double *'84*
Wise Guys *'86*
The Untouchables *'87*
Casualties of War *'89*
The Bonfire of the Vanities *'90*
Raising Cain *'92*
Carlito's Way *'93*
Mission: Impossible *'96*
Snake Eyes *'98*
Mission to Mars *'00*
Femme Fatale *'02*
The Black Dahlia *'06*
Redacted *'07*
Passion *'13*
Domino *'19*

Jean De Segonzac
Homicide: The Movie *'00*
Mimic 2 *'01*
Lost City Raiders *'08*

Vittorio De Sica (1902-74)
The Children Are Watching Us *'44*
Shoeshine *'47*
The Bicycle Thief *'48*
Miracle in Milan *'51*
The Gold of Naples *'54*
Umberto D *'55*
Two Women *'61*
Boccaccio '70 *'62*
Marriage Italian Style *'64*
Yesterday, Today and Tomorrow *'64*
After the Fox *'66*
Woman Times Seven *'67*
The Garden of the Finzi-Continis *'71*

Tom De Simone (1939-)
Terror in the Jungle *'68*
Chatterbox *'76*
Hell Night *'81*
Reform School Girls *'86*
Angel 3: The Final Chapter *'88*

Steven E. de Souza (1947-)
Street Fighter *'94*
Possessed *'00*

Andre de Toth (1912-2002)
Passport to Suez *'43*
Dark Waters *'44*
The Other Love *'47*
Ramrod *'47*
Slattery's Hurricane *'49*
Man in the Saddle *'51*
Carson City *'52*
Springfield Rifle *'52*
House of Wax *'53*
The Stranger Wore a Gun *'53*
Crime Wave *'54*
The Indian Fighter *'55*
The Day of the Outlaw *'59*
Man On a String *'60*
The Mongols *'60*
Gold for the Caesars *'63*

Alfredo de Villa
Washington Heights *'02*
Yellow *'06*
Adrift in Manhattan *'07*
Nothing Like the Holidays *'08*
Fugly! *'14*

Basil Dean (1888-1978)
Lorna Doone *'34*
21 Days *'40*

William Dear (1944-)
Northville Cemetery Massacre *'76*
Timerider *'83*
Harry and the Hendersons *'87*
If Looks Could Kill *'91*
Journey to the Center of the Earth *'93*
Angels in the Outfield *'94*
Balloon Farm *'97*
Wild America *'97*
The Foursome *'06*
School of Life *'06*
The Sandlot 3: Heading Home *'07*
Simon Says *'07*
Free Style *'09*
Mr. Troop Mom *'09*
The Perfect Game *'09*

Basil Dearden (1911-71)
Dead of Night *'45*
Captive Heart *'47*
The Blue Lamp *'49*
Who Done It? *'56*
The Smallest Show on Earth *'57*
Sapphire *'59*
The League of Gentlemen *'60*
Victim *'61*
All Night Long *'62*
The Mind Benders *'63*
Khartoum *'66*
The Assassination Bureau *'69*
The Man Who Haunted Himself *'70*

James Dearden (1949-)
Cold Room *'84*
A Kiss Before Dying *'91*
Rogue Trader *'98*

John DeBello (1952-)
Attack of the Killer Tomatoes *'77*
Happy Hour *'87*
Return of the Killer Tomatoes! *'88*
Killer Tomatoes Strike Back *'90*
Killer Tomatoes Eat France *'91*

Dean DeBlois (1970-)
Lilo & Stitch *'02*
How to Train Your Dragon *'10*
How to Train Your Dragon 2 *'14*
How to Train Your Dragon: The Hidden World *'19*

James D. Deck (1964-)
Two Shades of Blue *'98*
Silent Partner *'05*

David DeCoteau (1962-)
Creepozoids *'87*
Nightmare Sisters *'87*
Sorority Babes in the Slimeball Bowl-A-Rama *'87*
Dr. Alien *'88*
Puppet Master 3: Toulon's Revenge *'90*
Test Tube Teens from the Year 2000 *'93*
Beach Babes 2: Cave Girl Island *'95*
Femalien *'96*
Petticoat Planet *'96*
Prey of the Jaguar *'96*
Absolution *'97*
Curse of the Puppet Master: The Human Experiment *'98*
Femalien 2 *'98*
Frankenstein Reborn *'98*
Leather Jacket Love Story *'98*
Talisman *'98*
Ancient Evil: Scream of the Mummy *'00*
Voodoo Academy *'00*
Brotherhood 2: The Young Warlocks *'01*
The Brotherhood 3: The Young Demons *'02*
Ring of Darkness *'04*
Witches of the Caribbean *'05*
Beastly Boyz *'06*
Grizzly Rage *'07*
The Raven *'07*
The Pit and the Pendulum *'09*
Snow White: A Deadly Summer *'12*
2: Voodoo Academy *'12*

Miles Deem (1914-94)
See Demofilo Fidani

David DeFalco
Chaos *'05*
Wrong Side of Town *'10*

Edward Dein (1907-84)
Shack Out on 101 *'55*
The Leech Woman *'59*

Donna Deitch (1945-)
Desert Hearts *'86*
The Women of Brewster Place *'89*
A Change of Place *'94*
The Devil's Arithmetic *'99*

Steve DeJarnatt
Cherry 2000 *'88*
Miracle Mile *'89*

Fred Dekker (1959-)
Night of the Creeps *'86*
The Monster Squad *'87*
RoboCop 3 *'91*

Deborah Del Prete
Simple Justice *'89*
Ricochet River *'98*

Roy Del Ruth (1893-1961)
The First Auto *'27*
Three Faces East *'30*
Blonde Crazy *'31*
The Maltese Falcon *'31*
Blessed Event *'32*
Taxi! *'32*
Winner Take All *'32*
Beauty and the Boss *'33*
Bureau of Missing Persons *'33*
Employees' Entrance *'33*
Lady Killer *'33*
The Little Giant *'33*
The Mind Reader *'33*
Kid Millions *'34*
Upperworld *'34*
Broadway Melody of 1936 *'35*
Folies Bergere de Paris *'35*
Thanks a Million *'35*
Born to Dance *'36*
Private Number *'36*
Broadway Melody of 1938 *'37*
On the Avenue *'37*
Happy Landing *'38*
My Lucky Star *'38*
Tail Spin *'39*
The Chocolate Soldier *'41*
Topper Returns *'41*
Maisie Gets Her Man *'42*
Du Barry Was a Lady *'43*
Broadway Rhythm *'44*
It Happened on 5th Avenue *'47*
Babe Ruth Story *'48*
Red Light *'49*
The West Point Story *'50*
On Moonlight Bay *'51*
Starlift *'51*
Three Sailors and a Girl *'53*
Why Must I Die? *'60*

Guillermo del Toro (1964-)
Cronos *'94*
Mimic *'97*
The Devil's Backbone *'01*
Blade 2 *'02*
Hellboy *'04*
Pan's Labyrinth *'06*
Hellboy II: The Golden Army *'08*
Pacific Rim *'13*
Crimson Peak *'15*
The Shape of Water *'17*

Camille Delamarre
Brick Mansions *'14*
The Transporter Refueled *'15*

Jean Delannoy (1908-)
The Hunchback of Notre Dame *'57*
Love and the Frenchwoman *'60*
Imperial Venus *'63*
Action Man *'67*
Bernadette *'90*

Youssef Delara
ESL: English as a Second Language *'05*
Filly Brown *'12*
The Bounce Back *'16*

Jeffrey Dell (1899-1985)
The Flemish Farm *'43*
Carlton Browne of the F.O. *'59*

Gaby Dellal (1961-)
On a Clear Day *'05*
Angels Crest *'11*
3 Generations *'17*

Julie Delpy (1969-)
2 Days in Paris *'07*
The Countess *'09*
Lolo *'15*

Dom DeLuise (1933-2009)
Hot Stuff *'80*
Boys Will Be Boys *'97*

Peter DeLuise (1966-)
Beyond Sherwood Forest *'09*
16 Wishes *'10*
Garage Sale Mystery *'13*

Yann Demange
'71 *'14*
White Boy Rick *'18*

Lee Demarbre (1972-)
Jesus Christ Vampire Hunter *'01*
Summer's Moon *'09*

Johanna Demetrakas
Out of Line *'00*
Crazy Wisdom: The Life & Times of Chogyam Trungpa Rinpoche *'11*

Tulio Demicheli (1915-92)
Dracula *vs.* Frankenstein *'69*
Mean Machine *'73*

Cecil B. DeMille (1881-1959)
The Squaw Man *'14*
The Little American *'17*
Male and Female *'19*
Why Change Your Wife? *'20*
Affairs of Anatol *'21*
The Ten Commandments *'23*
The Road to Yesterday *'25*
King of Kings *'27*
Madam Satan *'30*
The Squaw Man *'31*
The Sign of the Cross *'33*
This Day and Age *'33*
Cleopatra *'34*
Four Frightened People *'34*
The Crusades *'35*
The Plainsman *'37*
Union Pacific *'39*
Reap the Wild Wind *'42*
Unconquered *'47*
Samson and Delilah *'49*
The Greatest Show on Earth *'52*
The Ten Commandments *'56*

Jonathan Demme (1944-2017)
Caged Heat *'74*
Crazy Mama *'75*
Fighting Mad *'76*
Citizens Band *'77*
Last Embrace *'79*
Melvin and Howard *'80*
Stop Making Sense *'84*
Swing Shift *'84*
Something Wild *'86*
Swimming to Cambodia *'87*
Married to the Mob *'88*
The Silence of the Lambs *'91*
Philadelphia *'93*
Subway Stories *'97*
Beloved *'98*
The Truth About Charlie *'02*
The Manchurian Candidate *'04*
Neil Young: Heart of Gold *'06*
Rachel Getting Married *'08*
Ricki and the Flash *'15*

Ted (Edward) Demme (1964-2002)
The Ref *'93*
Who's the Man? *'93*
Beautiful Girls *'96*
Subway Stories *'97*
Monument Ave. *'98*
Life *'99*
Blow *'01*
A Decade Under the Influence *'02*

James DeMonaco (1968-)
Staten Island *'09*
The Purge *'13*
The Purge: Anarchy *'14*
The Purge: Election Year *'16*

Jacques Demy (1931-90)
Lola *'61*
Umbrellas of Cherbourg *'64*
The Young Girls of Rochefort *'68*
Model Shop *'69*
Donkey Skin *'70*
Peau D'Ane *'71*
Pied Piper *'72*
A Slightly Pregnant Man *'79*

Christopher Denham (1985-)
Home Movie *'08*
Preservation *'14*

Claire Denis (1948-)
Chocolat *'88*
I Can't Sleep *'93*
Nenette and Boni *'96*
Beau Travail *'98*
Friday Night *'02*
The Intruder *'04*
35 Shots of Rum *'08*
White Material *'10*
Let the Sunshine In *'17*
High Life *'18*

Pen Densham (1947-)
The Kiss *'88*
Moll Flanders *'96*
Houdini *'98*

Tom DeNucci
Arlo the Burping Pig *'16*
Vault *'19*

Ruggero Deodato (1939-)
Live Like a Cop, Die Like a Man *'76*
Cannibal Holocaust *'80*
Cut and Run *'85*
The Lone Runner *'88*

Gerard Depardieu (1948-)
The Bridge *'00*
Paris, je t'aime *'06*

Jacques Deray (1929-2003)
La Piscine *'69*
Borsalino *'70*
Swimming Pool *'70*

John Derek (1926-98)
Once Before I Die *'65*
Fantasies *'73*
Tarzan, the Ape Man *'81*
Bolero *'84*

Scott Derrickson
Hellraiser 5: Inferno *'00*
The Exorcism of Emily Rose *'05*
The Day the Earth Stood Still *'08*
Sinister *'12*
Deliver Us From Evil *'14*
Doctor Strange *'16*

Dominique Deruddere (1957-)
Suite 16 *'94*
Everybody's Famous! *'00*

Caleb Deschanel (1941-)
The Escape Artist *'82*
Crusoe *'89*

Arnaud Desplechin (1960-)
La Sentinelle *'92*
My Sex Life. . . Or How I Got into an Argument *'96*
Esther Kahn *'00*
Kings and Queen *'04*
A Christmas Tale *'08*
Jimmy P. *'13*
My Golden Days *'15*

Howard Deutch (1950-)
Pretty in Pink *'86*
Some Kind of Wonderful *'87*
The Great Outdoors *'88*
Article 99 *'92*
Getting Even with Dad *'94*
Grumpier Old Men *'95*
The Odd Couple 2 *'98*
The Replacements *'00*
The Whole Ten Yards *'04*
My Best Friend's Girl *'08*

Jason DeVan
Along Came the Devil *'18*
Along Came the Devil 2 *'19*

Joanna DeVarona (1953-)
See Joanna Kerns

Ross Devenish (1939-)
Bleak House *'85*
A Certain Justice *'99*

Dennis Devine
Things *'93*
Vampires of Sorority Row: Kickboxers From Hell *'99*

Danny DeVito (1944-)
Ratings Game *'84*
Throw Momma from the Train *'87*
The War of the Roses *'89*
Hoffa *'92*
Matilda *'96*
Death to Smoochy *'02*
Duplex *'03*
The Oh in Ohio *'06*

Dean Devlin (1962-)
Geostorm *'17*
Bad Samaritan *'18*

John Dexter (1925-90)
The Virgin Soldiers *'69*
I Want What I Want *'72*

Maury Dexter (1928-)
Young Guns of Texas *'62*
Raiders from Beneath the Sea *'64*
Wild On the Beach *'65*
Hell's Belles *'69*

Tom Dey (1965-)
Shanghai Noon *'00*
Showtime *'02*
Failure to Launch *'06*
Marmaduke *'10*

Fernando Di Leo (1932-2003)
Slaughter Hotel '71
Caliber 9 '72
The Boss '73
Hired to Kill '73
The Italian Connection '73
Manhunt '73
Shoot First, Die Later '74
Loaded Guns '75
Kidnap Syndicate '76
Rulers of the City '76
Rulers of the City '77

Matthew Diamond
These Old Broads '01
Camp Rock '08
The Oogieloves in the Big Balloon Adventure '12
Undercover Bridesmaid '12

Saul Dibb (1968-)
The Line of Beauty '06
The Duchess '08
Journey's End '18

Tom DiCillo (1954-)
Johnny Suede '92
Living in Oblivion '94
Box of Moonlight '96
The Real Blonde '97
Double Whammy '01
Delirious '06

Kirby Dick
Derrida '02
This Film Is Not Yet Rated '06
Outrage '09
The Hunting Ground '15

Nigel Dick (1953-)
Deadly Intent '88
Final Combination '93

Ernest R. Dickerson (1952-)
Juice '92
Surviving the Game '94
Tales from the Crypt Presents Demon Knight '94
Bulletproof '96
Blind Faith '98
Futuresport '98
Bones '01
Big Shot: Confessions of a Campus Bookie '02
Monday Night Mayhem '02
Our America '02
Good Fences '03
Never Die Alone '04
For One Night '06
Last Man Standing '11

Thorold Dickinson (1903-84)
High Command '37
The Arsenal Stadium Mystery '39
Gaslight '40
The Next of Kin '42
The Queen of Spades '49

Katherine Dieckmann
A Good Baby '99
Diggers '06
Motherhood '09

Carlos Diegues (1940-)
Bye Bye Brazil '79
Quilombo '84
Tieta of Agreste '96
Orfeu '99

William Dieterle (1893-1972)
The Last Flight '31
Jewel Robbery '32
Lawyer Man '32
Fashions of 1934 '34
Fog Over Frisco '34
A Midsummer Night's Dream '35
The Secret Bride '35
The Great O'Malley '36
Satan Met a Lady '36
Another Dawn '37
The Life of Emile Zola '37
The Hunchback of Notre Dame '39
Juarez '39
Dr. Ehrlich's Magic Bullet '40
The Devil & Daniel Webster '41
Syncopation '42
I'll Be Seeing You '44
Kismet '44
Love Letters '45
Portrait of Jennie '48
Rope of Sand '49
Dark City '50
September Affair '50
Salome '53
Elephant Walk '54
Omar Khayyam '57
Quick, Let's Get Married '71

John Francis Dillon (1887-1934)
Suds '20
Sally '29
One Night at Susie's '30
Millie '31
The Reckless Hour '31
Call Her Savage '32

Steve DiMarco
Back in Action '94
Prisoner of Love '99
Cheaters' Club '06

Ross Dimsey (1943-)
Blue Fire Lady '78
Death Games '80

Dennis Dimster-Denk (1965-)
Mikey '92
Double Identity '10

Mark Dindal
Cats Don't Dance '97
The Emperor's New Groove '00
Chicken Little '05

Paul Dinello (1962-)
Strangers with Candy '06
Gym Teacher: The Movie '08

Michael Dinner
Heaven Help Us '85
Hot to Trot! '88
The Crew '00

Mark Dippe (1958-)
Spawn '97
Frankenfish '04
Halloweentown High '04
Reef 2: High Tide '12

Director X.
Centerstage: On Pointe '16
SuperFly '18

Mike Disa
Hoodwinked Too! Hood vs. Evil '11
Postman Pat: The Movie '14

Mark DiSalle
Kickboxer '89
The Perfect Weapon '91

Warren F. Disbrow
Invasion for Flesh and Blood '94
Flesh Eaters from Outer Space '05

Ivan Dixon (1931-2008)
Trouble Man '72
The Spook Who Sat by the Door '73

Jamie Dixon
Bram Stoker's Shadowbuilder '98
Bats: Human Harvest '07

Jasmin Dizdar (1961-)
Beautiful People '99
Chosen '16

Leila Djansi
And Then There Was You '13
Where Children Play '15

Edward Dmytryk (1908-99)
Golden Gloves '40
Counter-Espionage '42
The Falcon Strikes Back '43
Murder, My Sweet '44
Back to Bataan '45
Cornered '45
Till the End of Time '46
Crossfire '47
So Well Remembered '47
The Hidden Room '49
Obsession '49
Eight Iron Men '52
Mutiny '52
The Sniper '52
The Juggler '53
Broken Lance '54
The Caine Mutiny '54
End of the Affair '55
The Left Hand of God '55
Soldier of Fortune '55
The Mountain '56
Raintree County '57
The Young Lions '58
Warlock '59
Walk on the Wild Side '62
The Carpetbaggers '64
Where Love Has Gone '64
Alvarez Kelly '66
Mirage '66
Anzio '68
Shalako '68
Bluebeard '72
He Is My Brother '75
The Human Factor '75

Darren Doane (1972-)
Godmoney '97
Saving Christmas '14

David Dobkin (1969-)
Clay Pigeons '98
Shanghai Knights '03
Wedding Crashers '05
Fred Claus '07
The Change-Up '11
The Judge '14

Kevin James Dobson (1952-)
Miracle in the Wilderness '91
Gold Diggers: The Secret of Bear Mountain '95
The Thorn Birds: The Missing Years '96

Pete Docter (1968-)
Monsters, Inc. '01
Up '09
Inside Out '15

James Dodson
Behind Enemy Lines 2: Axis of Evil '06
The Other End of the Line '08

Donald M. Dohler (1946-2006)
The Alien Factor '78
Fiend '83
Night Beast '83
Galaxy Invader '85
Deadly Neighbor '91

Jacques Doillon (1944-)
Ponette '95
Petits Freres '00

Xavier Dolan (1989-)
I Killed My Mother '09
Heartbeats '11
Laurence Anyways '12
Mommy '14
The Death and Life of John F. Donovan '19

Bob Dolman
The Banger Sisters '02
How to Eat Fried Worms '06

Andrew Dominik (1967-)
Chopper '00
The Assassination of Jesse James by the Coward Robert Ford '07
Killing Them Softly '12

Roger Donaldson (1945-)
Sleeping Dogs '77
Smash Palace '82
The Bounty '84
Marie '85
No Way Out '87
Cocktail '88
Cadillac Man '90
White Sands '92
The Getaway '93
Species '95
Dante's Peak '97
Thirteen Days '00
The Recruit '03
The World's Fastest Indian '05
The Bank Job '08
Seeking Justice '12
The November Man '14

Harris Done (1963-)
Storm Tracker '99
Firetrap '01

Vincent J. Donehue (1915-66)
Peter Pan '60
Sunrise at Campobello '60

Stanley Donen (1924-)
On the Town '49
Royal Wedding '51
Fearless Fagan '52
Love Is Better Than Ever '52
Singin' in the Rain '52
Give a Girl a Break '53
Deep in My Heart '54
Seven Brides for Seven Brothers '54
It's Always Fair Weather '55
Funny Face '57
Kiss Them for Me '57
The Pajama Game '57
Damn Yankees '58
Indiscreet '58
Once More, With Feeling '60
The Grass Is Greener '61
Charade '63
Arabesque '66
Two for the Road '67
Bedazzled '68
The Little Prince '74
Movie, Movie '78
Saturn 3 '80
Blame It on Rio '84
Love Letters '99

Walter Doniger (1917-2011)
Duffy of San Quentin '54
Unwed Mother '58
House of Women '62
Mad Bull '77

Clive Donner (1926-)
What's New Pussycat? '65
Luv '67
Rogue Male '76
She Fell Among Thieves '78
The Thief of Baghdad '78
The Nude Bomb '80
Charlie Chan and the Curse of the Dragon Queen '81
Oliver Twist '82
The Scarlet Pimpernel '82
A Christmas Carol '84
To Catch a King '84

Richard Donner (1939-)
Salt & Pepper '68
Lola '69
The Omen '76
Superman: The Movie '78
Inside Moves '80
The Toy '82
The Goonies '85
Ladyhawke '85
Lethal Weapon '87
Scrooged '88
Lethal Weapon 2 '89
Lethal Weapon 3 '92
Radio Flyer '92
Maverick '94
Assassins '95
Conspiracy Theory '97
Lethal Weapon 4 '98
Timeline '03
16 Blocks '06

Vincent D'Onofrio (1959-)
Don't Go in the Woods '10
The Kid '19

Jack Donohue (1908-84)
Close-Up '48
Watch the Birdie '50
Lucky Me '54
Babes in Toyland '61
Marriage on the Rocks '65
Assault on a Queen '66

Jim Donovan
Provocateur '96
The Watch '08
The Perfect Teacher '10
Fugitive at 17 '12

Martin Donovan (1950-)
Apartment Zero '88
The Substitute '93

Paul Donovan (1954-)
Def-Con 4 '85
Northern Extremes '93

Daniel D'or
Falling Fire '97
Battle Queen 2020 '99

Drake Doremus
Spooner '08
Douchebag '10
Like Crazy '11
Breathe In '13
Equals '16
Endings, Beginnings '20

Robert Dornhelm (1947-)
The Children of Theatre Street '77
Echo Park '86
Cold Feet '89
Fatal Deception: Mrs. Lee Harvey Oswald '93
Sins of the Father '01
RFK '02
Rudy: The Rudy Giulani Story '03
Identity Theft: The Michelle Brown Story '04
The Crown Prince '06
Amanda Knox: Murder on Trail in Italy '11

Andrew Dosunmu
Mother of George '13
Where Is Kyra? '17

Shimon Dotan (1949-)
The Finest Hour '91
Sworn Enemies '96
Diamond Dogs '07

Ziad Doueiri
West Beirut '98
Lila Says '04
The Attack '13
The Insult '17

Michael Dougherty (1974-)
Trick 'r Treat '08
Krampus '15
Godzilla: King of the Monsters '19

David Douglas
Final Encounter '00
Pandas '18

Gordon Douglas (1907-93)
Broadway Limited '41
Gildersleeve on Broadway '43
Zombies on Broadway '44
Black Arrow '48
If You Knew Susie '48
Walk a Crooked Mile '48
Mr. Soft Touch '49
Between Midnight and Dawn '50
Kiss Tomorrow Goodbye '50
The Nevadan '50
Only the Valiant '50
Rogues of Sherwood Forest '50
I Was a Communist for the FBI '51
The Iron Mistress '52
Mara Maru '52
She's Back on Broadway '53
So This Is Love '53
Them! '54
Young at Heart '54
The McConnell Story '55
Sincerely Yours '55
Santiago '56
Bombers B-52 '57
The Fiend Who Walked the West '58
Fort Dobbs '58
Up Periscope '59
Claudelle Inglish '61
Follow That Dream '61
Gold of the Seven Saints '61
The Sins of Rachel Cade '61
Call Me Bwana '63
Rio Conchos '64
Robin and the 7 Hoods '64
Harlow '65
Stagecoach '66
Chuka '67
In Like Flint '67
Tony Rome '67
The Detective '68
Lady in Cement '68
They Call Me Mr. Tibbs! '70
Slaughter's Big Ripoff '73
Viva Knievel '77

Lorenzo Doumani (1962-)
Storybook '95
Bug Buster '99

Alexander Dovzhenko (1849-1956)
Zvenigora '28
Arsenal '29
Earth '30

John Erick Dowdle
Quarantine '08
Devil '10
As Above, So Below '14
No Escape '15

Chris Dowling
Rock Slyde: Private Eye '09
Where Hope Grows '15
Run the Race '19

Kevin Dowling
The Sum of Us '94
Mojave Moon '96

Robert Downey (1936-)
Putney Swope '69
Greaser's Palace '72
Up the Academy '80
Too Much Sun '90
Hugo Pool '97

Michael Dowse (1973-)
It's All Gone, Pete Tong '04
Take Me Home Tonight '11
Goon '12
What If '13
Stuber '19

Stan Dragoti (1932-2018)
Dirty Little Billy '72
Love at First Bite '79
Mr. Mom '83
The Man with One Red Shoe '85
She's Out of Control '89
Necessary Roughness '91

Tony Drazan (1955-)
Zebrahead '92
Imaginary Crimes '94
Hurlyburly '98

Lance Dreesen
Terror Tract '00
Big Bad Wolf '06

Arthur Dreifuss (1908-93)
Boss of Big Town '43
Campus Rhythm '43
The Payoff '43
The Quare Fellow '62
The Love-Ins '67
Riot on Sunset Strip '67

Di Drew (1948-)
1915 '82
The Right Hand Man '87
Trouble in Paradise '88

Carl Theodor Dreyer (1889-1968)
Leaves from Satan's Book '21
Master of the House '25
Passion of Joan of Arc '28
Vampyr '31
Day of Wrath '43
Ordet '55
Gertrud '64

Karim Dridi (1961-)
Pigalle '95
Bye-Bye '96

Dr. David Drury
Defense of the Realm '85
Forever Young '85
Split Decisions '88
Hostile Waters '97
The Unknown Soldier '98
The Take '09

Dinesh D'Souza (1961-)
2016: Obama's America '12
America: Imagine the World Without Her '14
Hillary's America: The Secret History of the Democratic Party '16
Death of a Nation '18

Frederick Du Chau (1965-)
Quest for Camelot '98
Racing Stripes '05
Underdog '07

Charles S. Dubin (1919-2011)
Cinderella '64
Murder Once Removed '71
Moving Violation '76
The Gathering: Part 2 '79
The Manions of America '81

Olivier Ducastel (1962-)
Jeanne and the Perfect Guy '98
My Life on Ice '02
Cote d'Azur '05
Born in 68 '08

Jonathan Dueck
Final Draft '07
Just Business '08

Peter Duffell (1937-)
The House that Dripped Blood '71
Inside Out '75
Flambards '78
The Far Pavilions '84

Troy Duffy (1971-)
Boondock Saints '99
The Boondock Saints II: All Saints Day '09

Dennis Dugan (1946-)
Problem Child '90
Brain Donors '92
Beverly Hills Ninja '96
Happy Gilmore '96
Big Daddy '99
Saving Silverman '01
National Security '03
The Benchwarmers '06
I Now Pronounce You Chuck and Larry '07
You Don't Mess with the Zohan '08
Grown Ups '10
Jack and Jill '11
Just Go With It '11
Grown Ups 2 '13

Michael Dugan
Mausoleum '83
Raging Hormones '99

George Dugdale
Slaughter High '86
Living Doll '90

Christian Duguay (1957-)
Live Wire '92
Snowbound: The Jim and Jennifer Stolpa Story '94
Screamers '96
The Assignment '97
Joan of Arc '99
The Art of War '00
Extreme Ops '02
Hitler: The Rise of Evil '03
Human Trafficking '05
Lies My Mother Told Me '05
Boot Camp '07
Coco Chanel '08

John Duigan (1949-)
The Winter of Our Dreams '82
The Year My Voice Broke '87
Flirting '89
Romero '89
Wide Sargasso Sea '92
Sirens '94
The Journey of August King '95
Lawn Dogs '96
The Leading Man '96
Molly '99
Head in the Clouds '04

Bill Duke (1943-)
Johnnie Gibson F.B.I. '87
Maximum Security '87
A Raisin in the Sun '89
A Rage in Harlem '91
Deep Cover '92
The Cemetery Club '93
Sister Act 2: Back in the Habit '93
America's Dream '95
Hoodlum '96
The Golden Spiders: A Nero Wolfe Mystery '00
Cover '08
Not Easily Broken '09

Daryl Duke (1929-2006)
Payday '73
Griffin and Phoenix: A Love Story '76
The Silent Partner '78
The Thorn Birds '83
Florence Nightingale '85
Tai-Pan '86

Bruno Dumont (1958-)
The Life of Jesus '96
Humanity '99
Twentynine Palms '03
Flanders '06
Hors Satan '11

Peter Duncan (1954-)
Children of the Revolution '95
A Little Bit of Soul '97
Passion '99

Duwayne Dunham
Homeward Bound: The Incredible Journey '93
Little Giants '94
Halloweentown '98
Santa and Pete '99

Griffin Dunne (1955-)
Addicted to Love '96
Practical Magic '98
Lisa Picard Is Famous '01
Fierce People '05
The Accidental Husband '08
Movie 43 '13

Philip Dunne (1908-92)
Three Brave Men '57
In Love and War '58
Wild in the Country '61
Lisa '62

Marcus Dunstan
The Collector '09
The Collection '12

Cheryl Dunye (1966-)
The Watermelon Woman '97
My Baby's Daddy '04
The Owls '09

Quentin Dupieux
Rubber '10
Wrong Cops '13

Jay Duplass (1973-)
Baghead '08
Cyrus '10
The Do-Deca-Pentathlon '12
Jeff, Who Lives at Home '12

Mark Duplass (1976-)
Baghead '08
Cyrus '10
The Do-Deca-Pentathlon '12
Jeff, Who Lives at Home '12

Ewald Andre Dupont (1891-1956)
Variety '25
Piccadilly '29
Hell's Kitchen '39
The Steel Lady '53
Return to Treasure Island '54

Fred Durst (1970-)
The Longshots '08
The Fanatic '19

David E. Durston (1921-)
I Drink Your Blood '71
Stigma '73

Charles S. Dutton (1951-)
First Time Felon '97
The Corner '00
Against the Ropes '04

Robert Duvall (1931-)
The Apostle '97
Assassination Tango '03
Wild Horses '15

Ava DuVernay
Middle of Nowhere '12
Selma '14
A Wrinkle in Time '18

Julien Duvivier (1896-1967)
Poil de Carotte '31
Pepe Le Moko '37
The Great Waltz '38
Tales of Manhattan '42
Heart of a Nation '43
Anna Karenina '48
The Burning Court '62
Diabolically Yours '67

Allan Dwan (1885-1981)
Robin Hood '22
The Iron Mask '29
Tide of Empire '29
Hollywood Party '34
Heidi '37
Josette '38
Rebecca of Sunnybrook Farm '38
Suez '38
Frontier Marshal '39
The Gorilla '39
The Three Musketeers '39
Young People '40
Look Who's Laughing '41
Here We Go Again! '42
Brewster's Millions '45
Getting Gertie's Garter '45
Sands of Iwo Jima '49
I Dream of Jeannie '52
Woman They Almost Lynched '53
Cattle Queen of Montana '54
Passion '54
Silver Lode '54
Escape to Burma '55
Pearl of the South Pacific '55
Tennessee's Partner '55
Slightly Scarlet '56
Enchanted Island '58
Most Dangerous Man Alive '61

Jesse Dylan (1966-)
How High '01
American Wedding '03
Kicking & Screaming '05

Bill Eagles
Beautiful Creatures '00
The Riverman '04
Dracula '06

B. Reeves Eason (1886-1956)
The Galloping Ghost '31
Vanishing Legion '31
The Last of the Mohicans '32
Alimony Madness '33
Law of the Wild '34
Mystery Mountain '34
The Miracle Rider '35
The Phantom Empire '35
Fighting Marines '36
Undersea Kingdom '36
Call of the Yukon '38
Rimfire '49

Eric Eason
Manito '03
Journey to the End of the Night '06

Allan Eastman (1950-)
Snapshot '77
Ford: The Man & the Machine '87
Danger Zone '95

Clint Eastwood (1930-)
Play Misty for Me '71
High Plains Drifter '73
The Eiger Sanction '75
The Outlaw Josey Wales '76
The Gauntlet '77
Bronco Billy '80
Firefox '82
Honkytonk Man '82
Sudden Impact '83
Pale Rider '85
Heartbreak Ridge '86
Bird '88
The Rookie '90
White Hunter, Black Heart '90
Unforgiven '92
A Perfect World '93
The Bridges of Madison County '95
Absolute Power '97
Midnight in the Garden of Good and Evil '97
True Crime '99
Space Cowboys '00
Blood Work '02
Mystic River '03
Million Dollar Baby '04
Flags of Our Fathers '06
Letters from Iwo Jima '06
Changeling '08
Gran Torino '08
Invictus '09
Hereafter '10
J. Edgar '11
American Sniper '14
Jersey Boys '14
Sully '16
The 15:17 to Paris '18
The Mule '18
Richard Jewell '19

James Eaves
Hellbreeder '04
The Witches Hammer '06

Thom Eberhardt (1947-)
Night of the Comet '84
Sole Survivor '84
The Night Before '88
Without a Clue '88
Gross Anatomy '89
Captain Ron '92
Ratz '99

John L'Ecuyer (1966-)
Prom Queen '04
In God's Country '07

Uli Edel (1947-)
Christiane F. '82
Last Exit to Brooklyn '90
Body of Evidence '92
Confessions of Sorority Girls '94
Purgatory '99
The Little Vampire '00
Mists of Avalon '01
King of Texas '02
Dark Kingdom: The Dragon King '04
The Baader Meinhof Complex '08
Houdini '14
Pay the Ghost '15

Joel Edgerton (1974-)
The Gift '15
Boy Erased '18

Nash Edgerton (1973-)
The Square '08
Gringo '18

Don Edmonds (1937-)
Tender Loving Care '73
Ilsa, Harem Keeper of the Oil Sheiks '76
Bare Knuckles '77

A.J. Edwards
The Better Angels '14
Age Out '19

Blake Edwards (1922-2010)
Operation Petticoat '59
The Perfect Furlough '59
High Time '60
Breakfast at Tiffany's '61
Days of Wine and Roses '62
Experiment in Terror '62
The Pink Panther '64
A Shot in the Dark '64
The Great Race '65
What Did You Do in the War, Daddy? '66
The Party '68
Darling Lili '70
Wild Rovers '71
The Carey Treatment '72
Return of the Pink Panther '74
The Tamarind Seed '74
The Pink Panther Strikes Again '76
Revenge of the Pink Panther '78
10 '79
S.O.B. '81
Trail of the Pink Panther '82
Victor/Victoria '82
Curse of the Pink Panther '83
The Man Who Loved Women '83
Micki & Maude '84
A Fine Mess '86
That's Life! '86
Blind Date '87
Sunset '88
Peter Gunn '89
Skin Deep '89
Switch '91
Son of the Pink Panther '93

Gareth Edwards
Monsters '10
Godzilla '14
Rogue One: A Star Wars Story '16

Robert Edwards
Land of the Blind '06
One More Time '15

Robert Eggers
The Witch '16
The Lighthouse '19

Jan Egleson (1946-)
A Shock to the System '90
Acts of Contrition '95
Coyote Waits '03

Atom Egoyan (1960-)
Next of Kin '84
Family Viewing '87
Speaking Parts '89
The Adjuster '91
Calendar '93
Exotica '94
The Sweet Hereafter '96
Felicia's Journey '99
Ararat '02
Where the Truth Lies '05
Adoration '08
Chloe '09
The Captive '14
Devil's Knot '14
Remember '15

Jason Eisener
Hobo With a Shotgun '11
The ABCs of Death '12
V/H/S/2 '13

Rafael Eisenman
Lake Consequence '92
Red Shoe Diaries 3: Another Woman's Lipstick '93
Red Shoe Diaries 7: Burning Up '96
Red Shoe Diaries: Four on the Floor '96
Red Shoe Diaries: Strip Poker '96
Red Shoe Diaries 8: Night of Abandon '97
Red Shoe Diaries: Swimming Naked '00

Sergei Eisenstein (1898-1948)
Strike '24
The Battleship Potemkin '25
Ten Days That Shook the World '27
Que Viva Mexico '32
Alexander Nevsky '38
Ivan the Terrible, Part 1 '44
Ivan the Terrible, Part 2 '46

Breck Eisner (1970-)
Taken '02
Sahara '05
The Crazies '09
The Last Witch Hunter '15

Richard Elfman (1942-)
Forbidden Zone '80
Modern Vampires '98

Harry Elfont (1968-)
Can't Hardly Wait '98
Josie and the Pussycats '01

Larry Elikann (1923-2004)
God Bless the Child '88
I Know My First Name Is Steven '89
Fever '91
The Great Los Angeles Earthquake '91
The Story Lady '93
Blue River '95
Robin Cook's Terminal '96

Ellory Elkayem (1972-)
Eight Legged Freaks '02
Return of the Living Dead: Rave to the Grave '05
Without a Paddle: Nature's Calling '09

Doug Ellin (1968-)
Phat Beach '96
Kissing a Fool '98
Entourage '15

Stephan Elliot
Easy Virtue '08
A Few Best Men '11

Mike Elliott
Beethoven's Big Break '08
Blue Crush 2 '11
The Scorpion King 4: Quest for Power '15

Stephan Elliott (1963-)
The Adventures of Priscilla, Queen of the Desert '94
Welcome to Woop Woop '97
Eye of the Beholder '99
Rio, I Love You '14
Swinging Safari '19

David R. Ellis (1952-2013)
Homeward Bound 2: Lost in San Francisco '96
Final Destination 2 '03
Cellular '04
Snakes on a Plane '06
The Final Destination '09
Shark Night 3D '11

Sean Ellis (1970-)
Cashback '06
The Broken '08
Metro Manila '13
Anthropoid '16

Joseph Ellison (1948-)
Don't Go in the House '80
Joey '85

Maurice Elvey (1887-1967)
Hindle Wakes '27
The Evil Mind '34
Phantom Fiend '35
Transatlantic Tunnel '35
The Gay Dog '54

Roland Emmerich (1955-)
Making Contact '86
Ghost Chase '88
Moon 44 '90
Universal Soldier '92
Stargate '94
Independence Day '96
Godzilla '98
The Patriot '00
The Day After Tomorrow '04
10,000 B.C. '08
2012 '09
Anonymous '11
White House Down '13
Stonewall '15
Independence Day: Resurgence '16
Midway '19

Cy Endfield (1914-95)
The Underworld Story '50
The Master Plan '55
Child in the House '56
Mysterious Island '61
Zulu '64
Sands of the Kalahari '65

Eric England
Contracted '13
Roadside '15

John English (1903-69)
Dick Tracy '37
Zorro Rides Again '37
The Lone Ranger '38
Zorro's Fighting Legion '39
Adventures of Red Ryder '40
Drums of Fu Manchu '40
Captain America '44
Don't Fence Me In '45
Loaded Pistols '48
Cow Town '50

Jonathan English
Ironclad '11
Ironclad: Battle for Blood '14

George Englund (1926-)
The Ugly American '63
Zachariah '70
The Vegas Strip Wars '84
Dixie: Changing Habits '85

Robert Englund (1947-)
976-EVIL '88
Killer Pad '06

Robert Enrico (1931-2001)
The Last Adventure '67
Zita '68

Ray Enright (1896-1965)
Golden Dawn '30
The Tenderfoot '32
Blondie Johnson '33
Dames '34
I've Got Your Number '34
Alibi Ike '35
China Clipper '36
Slim '37
Gold Diggers in Paris '38
Hard to Get '38
Swing Your Lady '38
Angels Wash Their Faces '39
Brother Rat and a Baby '40
The Wagons Roll at Night '41
The Spoilers '42
Gung Ho! '43
Trail Street '47
Return of the Bad Men '48
South of St. Louis '48
Kansas Raiders '50
Montana '50
Man from Cairo '54

Nora Ephron (1941-2012)
This Is My Life '92
Sleepless in Seattle '93
Mixed Nuts '94
Michael '96
You've Got Mail '98
Lucky Numbers '00
Bewitched '05
Julie & Julia '09

Robert Epstein (1955-)
Times of Harvey Milk '83
Common Threads: Stories from the Quilt '89
The Celluloid Closet '95
Howl '10
Lovelace '13

Rene Eram
Sweet Evil '95
Voodoo '95

Andrew C. Erin (1973-)
Tornado Valley '09
Confined '10

John Erman (1935-)
Alexander: The Other Side of Dawn '77
Roots '77
Child of Glass '78
My Old Man '79
Roots: The Next Generation '79
Eleanor: First Lady of the World '82
An Early Frost '85
The Attic: The Hiding of Anne Frank '88
Stella '89
The Last Best Year '90
Our Sons '91
Carolina Skeletons '92
Queen '93
Scarlett '94
The Sunshine Boys '95
The Boys Next Door '96
Ellen Foster '97
Only Love '98
Victoria & Albert '01

George Erschbamer (1954-)
Bounty Hunters '96
Bounty Hunters 2: Hardball '97
Criminal Intent '05
Stranger in My Bed '05
Double Cross '06
The Christmas Clause '08
Christmas Town '08
Courage '09

Joakim (Jack) Ersgard
Invisible: The Chronicles of Benjamin Knight '93
Mandroid '93
Living in Peril '97
Backlash '99
Rancid '04

Chester Erskine (1905-86)
Midnight '34
Egg and I '47
Androcles and the Lion '52

Andrew Erwin
October Baby '12
Moms' Night Out '14
I Can Only Imagine '18

Jon Erwin
October Baby '12
Moms' Night Out '14

Daniel Espinosa (1977-)
Easy Money '10
Safe House '12
Child 44 '15
Life '17

Harry Essex (1910-97)
Octaman '71
The Cremators '72

Jacob Aaron Estes (1972-)
Mean Creek '04
The Details '11
Don't Let Go '19

Emilio Estevez (1962-)
Wisdom '87
Men at Work '90
The War at Home '96
Rated X '00
Bobby '06
The Way '10
The Public '18

Paul Etheredge-Ouzts (1968-)
Hellbent '04
Angel of Death '09

William Eubank
Love '11
The Signal '14
Underwater '20

Corey Michael Eubanks
Bigfoot: The Unforgettable Encounter '94
Two Bits & Pepper '95

Bruce A. Evans
Kuffs '92
Mr. Brooks '07

David Evans (1893-1966)
Fever Pitch '96
The Grace Card '11

David Mickey Evans (1962-)
The Sandlot '93
First Kid '96
Beethoven's 3rd '00
Beethoven's 4th '01
The Sandlot 2 '05
The Final Season '07
Ace Ventura Jr.: Pet Detective '08

Gareth Evans
The Raid: Redemption '11
V/H/S/2 '13
Apostle '18

Marc Evans (1963-)
Thicker Than Water '93
Trauma '04
Snow Cake '06
Collision '09

Charles Evered
Adopt a Sailor '08
A Thousand Cuts '12

Nick Everhart
666: The Beast '07
2012: Doomsday '08

Heidi Ewing
Jesus Camp '06
Freakonomics '10

Chris Eyre (1969-)
Smoke Signals '98
Skins '02
Skinwalker '02
A Thief of Time '04
Hide Away '11

Richard Eyre (1943-)
The Ploughman's Lunch '83
Singleton's Pluck '84
The Insurance Man '86
King Lear '98
Iris '01
Stage Beauty '04
Notes on a Scandal '06
The Other Man '08
The Dresser '15
The Children Act '18

John Eyres
Night Siege Project: Shadowchaser 2 '94
Project Shadowchaser 3000 '95
Conspiracy of Fear '96
Judge & Jury '96
Octopus '00
Ripper: Letter from Hell '01
Irish Jam '05

Roberto Faenza (1943-)
Corrupt '84
Someday This Pain Will Be Useful to You '11

Claudio Fah
Coronado '03
Hollow Man 2 '06
Sniper Reloaded '11
Northman: A Viking Saga '15
Beyond Valkyrie: Dawn of the Fourth Reich '16

Peter Faiman
Crocodile Dundee '86
Dutch '91

Kevin Fair
Possessing Piper Rose '11
CAT. 8 '13
Lucky in Love '14
Signed, Sealed, Delivered for Christmas '14

Ferdinand Fairfax (1944-)
Danger UXB '81
Nate and Hayes '83
The Last Place on Earth '85
The Rescue '88
Frenchman's Creek '98

Philippe Falardeau
Monsieur Lazhar '11
The Good Lie '14
Chuck '17

Ben Falcone
Tammy '14
The Boss '16
Life of the Party '18

Harry Falk (1933-)
Centennial '78
Beulah Land '80

Jim Fall (1962-)
Trick '99
The Lizzie McGuire Movie '03
Wedding Wars '06
Holiday Engagement '11
Holly's Holiday '12

Rick Famuyiwa (1973-)
The Wood '99
Brown Sugar '02
Our Family Wedding '10
Dope '15

Jamaa Fanaka (1942-)
Soul Vengeance '75
Black Sister's Revenge '76
Penitentiary '79
Penitentiary 2 '82
Street Wars '91

Anthony Fankhauser
Supernova '09
8213: Gacy House '10
Rise of the Dinosaurs '13

James Fargo (1938-)
The Enforcer '76
Every Which Way But Loose '78
Forced Vengeance '82
Voyage of the Rock Aliens '87
Second Chances '98
Born to Ride '11

Asghar Farhadi (1972-)
A Separation '11
The Past '13
The Salesman '16
Everybody Knows '18

Corrado Farina (1939-)
Baba Yaga '73
Kiss Me, Kill Me '73

Ernest Farino
Josh Kirby. . .Time Warrior: Chapter 1, Planet of the Dino-Knights '95
Josh Kirby. . . Time Warrior: Chapter 5, Journey to the Magic Cavern '96

Julian Farino
Our Mutual Friend '98
Byron '03
The Oranges '12

Valerie Faris (1958-)
Little Miss Sunshine '06
Ruby Sparks '12
Battle of the Sexes '17

Leonard Farlinger
The Perfect Son '00
All Hat '07

Ned Farr
The Gymnast '06
A Marine Story '10

Bobby Farrelly (1958-)
Kingpin '96
There's Something about Mary '98
Me, Myself, and Irene '00
Osmosis Jones '01
Shallow Hal '01
Stuck On You '03
Fever Pitch '05
The Heartbreak Kid '07
Hall Pass '11
The Three Stooges '12
Dumb and Dumber To '14

Peter Farrelly (1957-)
Dumb & Dumber '94
Kingpin '96
There's Something about Mary '98
Me, Myself, and Irene '00
Osmosis Jones '01
Shallow Hal '01
Stuck On You '03
Fever Pitch '05
The Heartbreak Kid '07
Hall Pass '11
The Three Stooges '12
Movie 43 '13
Dumb and Dumber To '14
Green Book '18

John Farrow (1904-63)
Reno '39
The Saint Strikes Back '39
Wake Island '42
China '43
Commandos Strike at Dawn '43
Calcutta '47
The Big Clock '48
Copper Canyon '50
Where Danger Lives '50
His Kind of Woman '51
Hondo '53
Ride, Vaquero! '53
A Bullet Is Waiting '54
Sea Chase '55

John Fasano (1961-2014)
Rock 'n' Roll Nightmare '85
Black Roses '88

Rainer Werner Fassbinder (1946-82)
Gods of the Plague '69
Love Is Colder Than Death '69
Why Does Herr R. Run Amok? '69
The American Soldier '70
Beware of a Holy Whore '70
Whity '70
The Merchant of Four Seasons '71
The Bitter Tears of Petra von Kant '72
World on a Wire '73
Ali: Fear Eats the Soul '74
Effi Briest '74
Fear of Fear '75
Fox and His Friends '75
I Only Want You to Love Me '76
Mother Kusters Goes to Heaven '76
Satan's Brew '76
The Stationmaster's Wife '77
Despair '78
Germany in Autumn '78
In a Year of 13 Moons '78
The Marriage of Maria Braun '79
Lola '81
Veronika Voss '82
Querelle '83
Chinese Roulette '86

Don E. Fauntleroy (1953-)
The Perfect Wife '00
Today You Die '05
Seven Days of Grace '06
Urban Justice '07
Anaconda 3: The Offspring '08
Anacondas: Trail of Blood '09

Jon Favreau (1966-)
Made '01
Elf '03
Zathura '05
Iron Man '08
Iron Man 2 '10
Cowboys & Aliens '11
Chef '14
The Jungle Book '16
The Lion King '19

John Fawcett (1968-)
The Boys Club '96
Ginger Snaps '01
Taken '02

Nat Faxon (1975-)
The Way Way Back '13
Downhill '20

Feras Fayyad
Last Men In Aleppo '17
The Cave '19

Neill Fearnley
Johnny 2.0 '99
Christmas in Boston '05
A Decent Proposal '06
I Dream of Murder '06
The Bad Son '07
My Baby Is Missing '07
Daniel's Daughter '08
Christmas in Canaan '09
A Family Thanksgiving '10
Christmas Comes Home to Canaan '11

Michael Feifer
A Dead Calling '06
The Boston Strangler: The Untold Story '08
Bundy: A Legacy of Evil '08
A Christmas Proposal '08
Dear Me: A Blogger's Tale '08
The Dog Who Saved Christmas '09
Drifter '09
Abandoned '10
The Dog Who Saved Christmas Vacation '10
A Nanny for Christmas '10
A Christmas Wedding Tail '11
The Perfect Student '11
Soda Springs '11
Your Love Never Fails '11
The Dog Who Saved the Holidays '12
A Star for Christmas '12
Wyatt Earp's Revenge '12

Paul Feig (1962-)
I Am David '04
Unaccompanied Minors '06
Bridesmaids '11
The Heat '13
Spy '15
Ghostbusters '16
A Simple Favor '18
Last Christmas '19

Beda Docampo Feijoo (1948-)
The Perfect Husband '92
What Your Eyes Don't See '99

Felix Feist (1910-65)
Golden Gloves '40
George White's Scandals '45
Guilty of Treason '50
The Man Who Cheated Himself '50
Tomorrow Is Another Day '51
Battles of Chief Pontiac '52
Big Trees '52
This Woman Is Dangerous '52
Donovan's Brain '53

Jean-Loup Felicioli
A Cat in Paris '11
Phantom Boy '16

Sam Fell
Flushed Away '06
The Tale of Despereaux '08
ParaNorman '12

Federico Fellini (1920-93)
Variety Lights '51
The White Sheik '52
I Vitelloni '53
La Strada '54
Il Bidone '55
Nights of Cabiria '57
La Dolce Vita '60
Boccaccio '70 '62
8 1/2 '63
Juliet of the Spirits '65
Spirits of the Dead '68
Fellini Satyricon '69
The Clowns '71
Fellini's Roma '72
Amarcord '74
Orchestra Rehearsal '78
City of Women '81
And the Ship Sails On '83
Ginger & Fred '86
Intervista '87

Simon Fellowes
Second in Command '05
Malice in Wonderland '09

Georg Fenady (1930-)
Cave-In! '79
Hanging By a Thread '79
The Night the Bridge Fell Down '83

Leslie Fenton (1902-78)
Stronger Than Desire '39
Tomorrow the World '44
Saigon '47
Lulu Belle '48
On Our Merry Way '48
Whispering Smith '48

Charles Ferguson
No End in Sight '07
Inside Job '10
Time to Choose '16

Larry Ferguson (1940-)
Beyond the Law '92
Gunfighter's Moon '96

Guy Ferland (1966-)
The Babysitter '95
Telling Lies in America '96
Delivered '98
After the Storm '01
Dirty Dancing: Havana Nights '04

Anthony C. Ferrante
Boo! '05
Headless Horseman '07
Hansel & Gretel '13
Sharknado '13
Sharknado 2: The Second One '14
Sharknado 3: Oh Hell No! '15
Sharknado: The 4th Awakens '16

Abel Ferrara (1952-)
Driller Killer '79
Ms. 45 '81
Fear City '85
The Gladiator '86
Cat Chaser '90
King of New York '90
Bad Lieutenant '92
Body Snatchers '93
Dangerous Game '93
The Funeral '96
The Blackout '97
Subway Stories '97
New Rose Hotel '98
'R Xmas '01
4:44 Last Day on Earth '11
Welcome to New York '15

Jose Ferrer (1909-92)
Return to Peyton Place '61
State Fair '62

Marco Ferreri (1928-97)
El Cochecito '60
Dillinger Is Dead '69
La Grande Bouffe '73
Tales of Ordinary Madness '83

Darin Ferriola (1970-)
Ivory Tower '97
Mr. Fix It '06

Giorgio Ferroni (1908-81)
Mill of the Stone Women '60
The Trojan Horse '62
Conquest of Mycene '63
Hero of Rome '63
The Lion of Thebes '64
Fort Yuma Gold '66
Secret Agent Super Dragon '66
The Battle of El Alamein '68
The Night of the Devils '72

Larry Fessenden (1963-)
Habit '97
Wendigo '01
The Last Winter '06
The ABCs of Death 2 '14

Shana Feste (1976-)
The Greatest '09
Country Strong '10
Endless Love '14
Boundaries '18

Jeff Feuerzeig
The Devil and Daniel Johnston '05
Author: The JT LeRoy Story '16

Louis Feuillade (1873-1925)
Les Vampires '15
Judex '16

Jacques Feyder (1885-1948)
The Kiss '29
Knight Without Armour '37

Severin Fiala
Goodnight Mommy '15
The Lodge '19

Glenn Ficarra
I Love You Phillip Morris '10
Crazy, Stupid, Love. '11
Focus '15
Whiskey Tango Foxtrot '16

Andy Fickman
She's the Man '06
The Game Plan '07
Race to Witch Mountain '09
You Again '10
Paul Blart: Mall Cop 2 '15
Playing with Fire '19

Demofilo Fidani (1914-94)
Django and Sartana; It's the End '70
One Fine Day, When Django Met Sartana '70

Sally Field (1946-)
From the Earth to the Moon '98
Beautiful '00

Todd Field (1964-)
In the Bedroom '01
Little Children '06

Ralph Fiennes (1962-)
Coriolanus '11
The Invisible Woman '13
The White Crow '18

Mike Figgis (1948-)
Stormy Monday '88
Internal Affairs '90
Liebestraum '91
Women & Men: In Love There Are No Rules '91
Mr. Jones '93
The Browning Version '94
Leaving Las Vegas '95
One Night Stand '97

The Loss of Sexual Innocence '98
Miss Julie '99
Time Code '00
Hotel '01
Cold Creek Manor '03

Ivan Fila (1956-)
Lea '96
King of Thieves '04

Kleber Mendonca Filho
Neighboring Sounds '12
Aquarius '16
Bacurau '20

Charles Finch (1962-)
Where Sleeping Dogs Lie '91
Circle of Passion '97

Nigel Finch (1950-95)
The Lost Language of Cranes '92
Stonewall '95

David Fincher (1963-)
Alien 3 '92
Seven '95
The Game '97
Fight Club '99
Panic Room '02
Zodiac '07
The Curious Case of Benjamin Button '08
The Social Network '10
The Girl With the Dragon Tattoo '11
Gone Girl '14

Roberta Findlay
The Oracle '85
Blood Sisters '86
Lurkers '88
Prime Evil '88

Travis Fine (1968-)
The Space Between '10
Any Day Now '12

Ken Finkleman (1946-)
Airplane 2: The Sequel '82
Head Office '86

Will Finn
Home on the Range '04
Legends of Oz: Dorothy's Return '14

Laurent Firode (1963-)
Happenstance '00
My First Wedding '04

Sam Firstenberg (1950-)
Revenge of the Ninja '83
Breakin' 2: Electric Boogaloo '84
American Ninja '85
American Ninja 2: The Confrontation '87
Delta Force 3: The Killing Game '91
American Samurai '92
Cyborg Soldier '94
Motel Blue '98
Agent of Death '99
Quicksand '01
Spiders 2: Breeding Ground '01

Michael Firth
The Lazarus Syndrome '79
Heart of the Stag '84

Michael Fischa (1952-)
Crack House '89
My Mom's a Werewolf '89
Delta Heat '92

Max Fischer (1929-)
Psychopath '97
Taken '99

Chris Fisher (1973-)
Nightstalker '02
Rampage: The Hillside Strangler Murders '04
Dirty '05
S. Darko: A Donnie Darko Tale '09

Street Kings 2: Motor City '11
Meeting Evil '12

David Fisher (1948-)
Liar's Moon '82
Toy Soldiers '84

Terence Fisher (1904-80)
Man Bait '52
A Stolen Face '52
Stolen Face '52
Four Sided Triangle '53
Spaceways '53
Black Glove '54
Blackout '54
Unholy Four '54
Race for Life '55
The Curse of Frankenstein '57
Kill Me Tomorrow '57
The Horror of Dracula '58
The Revenge of Frankenstein '58
The Hound of the Baskervilles '59
The Man Who Could Cheat Death '59
The Mummy '59
The Brides of Dracula '60
The Stranglers of Bombay '60
Sword of Sherwood Forest '60
The Two Faces of Dr. Jekyll '60
The Curse of the Werewolf '61
The Phantom of the Opera '62
Sherlock Holmes and the Deadly Necklace '62
The Gorgon '64
Dracula, Prince of Darkness '66
Frankenstein Created Woman '66
Island of the Burning Doomed '67
The Devil Rides Out '68
Frankenstein Must Be Destroyed '69
Frankenstein and the Monster from Hell '74

Bill Fishman
Tapeheads '89
Car 54, Where Are You? '94

Jack Fisk (1945-)
Raggedy Man '81
Violets Are Blue '86
Daddy's Dyin'. . . Who's Got the Will? '90
Final Verdict '91

Thom Fitzgerald (1968-)
The Hanging Garden '97
Beefcake '99
The Event '03
Cloudburst '11

George Fitzmaurice (1885-1940)
Raffles '30
Strangers May Kiss '31
Mata Hari '32
Suzy '36
The Emperor's Candlesticks '37
The Last of Mrs. Cheyney '37
Live, Love and Learn '37
Arsene Lupin Returns '38

Cash Flagg (1938-2009)
See Ray Dennis Steckler

Paul Flaherty (1945-)
18 Again! '88
Who's Harry Crumb? '89
Clifford '92

Robert Flaherty (1884-1951)
Nanook of the North '22
Tabu: A Story of the South Seas '31
Man of Aran '34

Elephant Boy '37
Louisiana Story '48

Mike Flanagan (1978-)
Absentia '11
Oculus '14
Before I Wake '15
Ouija: Origin of Evil '16
Doctor Sleep '19

Ryan Fleck (1976-)
Half Nelson '06
Sugar '09
It's Kind of a Funny Story '10
Mississippi Grind '15
Captain Marvel '19

Gary Fleder (1963-)
Things to Do in Denver When You're Dead '95
Kiss the Girls '97
From the Earth to the Moon '98
Don't Say a Word '01
Impostor '02
Runaway Jury '03
The Express '08
Homefront '13

Dave Fleischer (1894-1979)
Gulliver's Travels '39
Hoppity Goes to Town '41

Richard Fleischer (1916-2006)
So This Is New York '48
Trapped '49
Armored Car Robbery '50
The Narrow Margin '52
20,000 Leagues under the Sea '54
The Girl in the Red Velvet Swing '55
Violent Saturday '55
Between Heaven and Hell '56
The Vikings '58
Compulsion '59
Barabbas '62
Fantastic Voyage '66
Doctor Dolittle '67
The Boston Strangler '68
Tora! Tora! Tora! '70
The Last Run '71
See No Evil '71
10 Rillington Place '71
The New Centurions '72
The Don Is Dead '73
Soylent Green '73
Mr. Majestyk '74
The Spikes Gang '74
Mandingo '75
The Prince and the Pauper '78
Ashanti, Land of No Mercy '79
The Jazz Singer '80
Amityville 3: The Demon '83
Tough Enough '83
Conan the Destroyer '84
Red Sonja '85
Million Dollar Mystery '87

Ruben Fleischer
Zombieland '09
30 Minutes or Less '11
Gangster Squad '13
Venom '18
Zombieland: Double Tap '19

Andrew Fleming (1964-)
Bad Dreams '88
Threesome '94
The Craft '96
Dick '99
The In-Laws '03
Nancy Drew '07
Hamlet 2 '08
Barefoot '14

Victor Fleming (1883-1949)
When the Clouds Roll By '19
Red Dust '32
The Wet Parade '32
Bombshell '33
The White Sister '33
Treasure Island '34

The Farmer Takes a Wife '35
Reckless '35
Captains Courageous '37
Test Pilot '38
Gone with the Wind '39
The Wizard of Oz '39
Dr. Jekyll and Mr. Hyde '41
Tortilla Flat '42
Joan of Arc '48

Gordon Flemyng (1934-95)
Just for Fun '63
Daleks-Invasion Earth 2150 A.D. '66
The Split '68
The Last Grenade '70
Philby, Burgess and MacLean: Spy Scandal of the Century '84

Rodman Flender (1964-)
The Unborn '91
Leprechaun 2 '94
Idle Hands '99
Nature of the Beast '07
Conan O'Brien Can't Stop '11

Anne Fletcher (1966-)
Step Up '06
27 Dresses '08
The Proposal '09
The Guilt Trip '12
Hot Pursuit '15

Dexter Fletcher (1966-)
Eddie the Eagle '16
Rocketman '19

Mandie Fletcher
Deadly Advice '93
Absolutely Fabulous: The Movie '16

Clive Fleury
Tunnel Vision '95
Big City Blues '99

Theodore J. Flicker (1930-)
The President's Analyst '67
Soggy Bottom U.S.A. '84

John Florea (1916-2000)
Island of the Lost '68
The Invisible Strangler '76
Computer Wizard '77
Where's Willie? '77

Isaac Florentine
Cold Harvest '98
High Voltage '98
Bridge of Dragons '99
U.S. Seals 2 '01
Special Forces '03
Undisputed 2: Last Man Standing '06
Assassin's Bullet '12
Close Range '15
Acts of Vengeance '17

David Flores
Boa *vs.* Python '04
Crimson Force '05
Lake Placid 2 '07

Phil Flores
April Fool's Day '08
The Thompsons '12

Robert Florey (1900-79)
The Cocoanuts '29
Those We Love '32
Girl Missing '33
The House on 56th Street '33
The Woman in Red '35
Dangerously We Live '41
The Desert Song '43
God is My Co-Pilot '45
The Beast with Five Fingers '46
Tarzan and the Mermaids '48
Outpost in Morocco '49

Per Fly (1960-)
The Inheritance '76
Backstabbing for Beginners '18

John Flynn (1932-2007)
The Sergeant '68
The Outfit '73
Rolling Thunder '77
Defiance '79
Best Seller '87
Lock Up '89
Out for Justice '91
Brainscan '94
Absence of the Good '99
Protection '01

Bryan Fogel
Jewtopia '12
Icarus '17

Susanna Fogel
Life Partners '14
The Spy Who Dumped Me '18

Dan Fogelman
Danny Collins '15
Life Itself '18

Lawrence Foldes (1959-)
Nightstalker '81
Finding Home '03

Brendan Foley
The Riddle '07
Legend of the Bog '08

James Foley (1953-)
Reckless '84
At Close Range '86
Who's That Girl? '87
After Dark, My Sweet '90
Glengarry Glen Ross '92
The Chamber '96
Fear '96
Two Bits '96
The Corruptor '99
Confidence '03
Perfect Stranger '07
Fifty Shades Darker '17
Fifty Shades Freed '18

Christopher Folino
Gamers '06
Sparks '13

Sheree Folkson
Casanova '05
The Decoy Bride '11

Ari Folman
Waltz with Bashir '08
The Congress '13

Timothy Wayne Folsome (1966-)
Uninvited Guest '99
Jacked Up '01

Peter Fonda (1940-2019)
Hired Hand '71
Idaho Transfer '73
Wanda Nevada '79

Jorge Fons (1939-)
Jory '72
Midaq Alley '95

Anne Fontaine (1959-)
Dry Cleaning '97
How I Killed My Father '03
Nathalie '03
The Girl From Monaco '08
Coco Before Chanel '09
My Worst Nightmare '11
Adore '13
Gemma Bovery '15
The Innocents '16

Frederic Fonteyne (1968-)
An Affair of Love '99
Gilles' Wife '04

Bryan Forbes (1926-2013)
Seance on a Wet Afternoon '64
King Rat '65
The Whisperers '66
The Wrong Box '66
The Madwoman of Chaillot '69
The Stepford Wives '75
The Slipper and the Rose '76
International Velvet '78
The Naked Face '84

Christopher Forbes
Basketweave '06
All Hell Broke Loose '09
A Cold Day in Hell '11

Maya Forbes
Infinitely Polar Bear '14
The Polka King '18

Howard Ford (1973-)
Mainline Run '98
The Dead 2 '13

John Ford (1895-1973)
The Iron Horse '24
Four Sons '28
Hangman's House '28
Up the River '30
Arrowsmith '31
Seas Beneath '31
Flesh '32
Doctor Bull '33
Pilgrimage '33
Judge Priest '34
The Lost Patrol '34
The World Moves On '34
The Informer '35
Steamboat Round the Bend '35
The Whole Town's Talking '35
Mary of Scotland '36
The Prisoner of Shark Island '36
The Hurricane '37
Wee Willie Winkie '37
Four Men and a Prayer '38
Drums Along the Mohawk '39
Stagecoach '39
Young Mr. Lincoln '39
The Grapes of Wrath '40
The Long Voyage Home '40
How Green Was My Valley '41
Tobacco Road '41
They Were Expendable '45
My Darling Clementine '46
Fort Apache '48
The Fugitive '48
Three Godfathers '48
She Wore a Yellow Ribbon '49
Rio Grande '50
Wagon Master '50
When Willie Comes Marching Home '50
The Quiet Man '52
What Price Glory? '52
Mogambo '53
The Sun Shines Bright '53
The Long Gray Line '55
Mister Roberts '55
The Searchers '56
The Rising of the Moon '57
Wings of Eagles '57
Gideon's Day '58
The Last Hurrah '58
The Horse Soldiers '59
Sergeant Rutledge '60
Two Rode Together '61
The Man Who Shot Liberty Valance '62
Donovan's Reef '63
How the West Was Won '63
Cheyenne Autumn '64
December 7th: The Movie '91

Tom Ford
A Single Man '09
Nocturnal Animals '16

Eugene Forde (1898-1986)
Charlie Chan in London '34
Charlie Chan at Monte Carlo '37
Charlie Chan on Broadway '37
International Settlement '38
Inspector Hornleigh '39
Charlie Chan's Murder Cruise '40
Michael Shayne: Private Detective '40
Sleepers West '41
Berlin Correspondent '42

Walter Forde (1896-1984)
Rome Express '32
The Secret Four '39
The Ghost Train '41

Milos Forman (1932-2018)
Black Peter '63
Loves of a Blonde '65
The Firemen's Ball '68
One Flew Over the Cuckoo's Nest '75
Hair '79
Ragtime '81
Amadeus '84
Valmont '89
The People vs. Larry Flynt '96
Man on the Moon '99
Goya's Ghosts '06

Jose Maria Forque (1923-95)
Autopsy '73
Beyond Erotica '74

Marc Forster (1969-)
Everything Put Together '00
Monster's Ball '01
Finding Neverland '04
Stay '05
Stranger Than Fiction '06
The Kite Runner '07
Machine Gun Preacher '11
World War Z '13
All I See Is You '17

Bill Forsyth (1948-)
That Sinking Feeling '79
Gregory's Girl '80
Local Hero '83
Housekeeping '87
Breaking In '89
Being Human '94

Ed Forsyth (1920-2004)
Superchick '71
Chesty Anderson USN '76

John Fortenberry
Jury Duty '95
A Night at the Roxbury '98

Bob Fosse (1927-87)
Sweet Charity '69
Cabaret '72
Lenny '74
All That Jazz '79
Star 80 '83

Giles Foster
Silas Marner '85
Dutch Girls '87
Northanger Abbey '87
Consuming Passions '88
The Rector's Wife '94
Coming Home '98
Relative Strangers '99
The Prince and the Pauper '01

Jodie Foster (1963-)
Little Man Tate '91
Home for the Holidays '95
The Beaver '11
Money Monster '16

Lewis R. Foster (1898-1974)
El Paso '49
Cavalry Charge '51
Dakota Incident '56
Tonka '58
The Sign of Zorro '60

Marc Foster
Quantum of Solace '08
Christopher Robin '18

Norman Foster (1900-76)
Thank you, Mr. Moto '37
Think Fast, Mr. Moto '37
Charlie Chan at Treasure Island '39
Mr. Moto's Last Warning '39
Charlie Chan in Panama '40
Tell It to the Judge '49
Father Is a Bachelor '50
Woman On the Run '50
Sky Full of Moon '52
Davy Crockett, King of the Wild Frontier '55
Davy Crockett and the River Pirates '56
The Sign of Zorro '60
Indian Paint '64
Brighty of the Grand Canyon '67
Crazy Horse and Custer: 'The Untold Story' '90

Alastair Fothergill (1960-)
Deep Blue '03
Earth '07
Chimpanzee '12
Bears '14
Monkey Kingdom '15
Penguins '19

James Fotopoulos
Zero '97
Back Against the Wall '00
Migrating Forms '00

Gene Fowler, Jr. (1917-98)
I Married a Monster from Outer Space '58
Showdown at Boot Hill '58
The Rebel Set '59

Eytan Fox (1964-)
Yossi & Jagger '02
The Bubble '06
Yossi '12

Paul Fox
Everything's Gone Green '06
Making Mr. Right '08
Before You Say 'I Do' '09

Wallace Fox (1895-1958)
Smart Alecks '42
Kid Dynamite '43
Career Girl '44
Dead Man's Eyes '44
The Great Mike '44
Men On Her Mind '44

Ciaran Foy
Citadel '12
Sinister 2 '15
Eli '19

William A. Fraker (1923-2010)
Monte Walsh '70
A Reflection of Fear '73
Legend of the Lone Ranger '81

Jonathan Frakes (1952-)
Star Trek: First Contact '96
Star Trek: Insurrection '98
Clockstoppers '02
Thunderbirds '04
The Librarian: Return to King Solomon's Mines '06
The Librarian: Curse of the Judas Chalice '08
Truth Be Told '11

Pascal Franchot (1962-)
Milo '98
Triple Dog '09

Freddie Francis (1917-2007)
Paranoiac '62
Day of the Triffids '63
Nightmare '63
The Evil of Frankenstein '64
Hysteria '64
The Skull '65
The Psychopath '66
They Came from Beyond Space '67
Torture Garden '67
Dracula Has Risen from the Grave '68
Girly '70
Trog '70
The Vampire Happening '71
The Creeping Flesh '72
Tales from the Crypt '72
Tales That Witness Madness '73
Craze '74
The Ghoul '75
The Doctor and the Devils '85

Pietro Francisci (1906-77)
Attila '54
Hercules '58
Hercules Unchained '59
Hercules, Samson and Ulysses '64

James Franco (1978-)
The Ape '05
The Broken Tower '11
Sal '11
Child of God '14
The Disaster Artist '17
In Dubious Battle '17
Future World '18
Pretenders '19
Zeroville '19

Jess (Jesus) Franco (1930-2013)
The Awful Dr. Orloff '62
Dr. Orloff's Monster '64
The Diabolical Dr. Z '65
Attack of the Robots '66
The Castle of Fu Manchu '68
Deadly Sanctuary '68
Kiss and Kill '68
99 Women '69
Venus in Furs '70
Count Dracula '71
Virgin among the Living Dead '71
Rites of Frankenstein '72
The Screaming Dead '72
Female Vampire '73
The Perverse Countess '73
Jack the Ripper '76
Ilsa, the Wicked Warden '78
Sex Is Crazy '79
Oasis of the Zombies '82
Revenge in the House of Usher '82
Bloody Moon '83
Angel of Death '86
Faceless '88
Tender Flesh '97
Devil Hunter '08

Michel Franco
Daniel & Ana '09
Chronic '16

Georges Franju (1912-87)
The Shadow Man '53
The Horror Chamber of Dr. Faustus '59
Judex '64

Melvin Frank (1913-88)
The Reformer and the Redhead '50
Above and Beyond '53
Knock on Wood '54
The Court Jester '56
The Jayhawkers '59
Li'l Abner '59
The Facts of Life '60
Strange Bedfellows '65
A Touch of Class '73
Prisoner of Second Avenue '74
The Duchess and the Dirtwater Fox '76
Lost and Found '79
Walk Like a Man '87

Scott Frank (1960-)
The Lookout '07
A Walk Among the Tombstones '14

Cyril Frankel (1921-)
Never Take Candy From a Stranger '60
The Witches '66

David Frankel (1959-)
Miami Rhapsody '95
From the Earth to the Moon '98
Band of Brothers '01
The Devil Wears Prada '06
Marley & Me '08
The Big Year '11
Hope Springs '12
One Chance '13
Collateral Beauty '16

John Frankenheimer (1930-2002)
The Young Stranger '57
Days of Wine and Roses '58
The Young Savages '61
All Fall Down '62
Birdman of Alcatraz '62
The Manchurian Candidate '62
Seven Days in May '64
The Train '65
Grand Prix '66
Seconds '66
The Gypsy Moths '69
The Horsemen '70
I Walk the Line '70
The Iceman Cometh '73
99 & 44/100 Dead '74
French Connection 2 '75
Black Sunday '77
Prophecy '79
The Holcroft Covenant '85
52 Pick-Up '86
Dead Bang '89
The Fourth War '90
Year of the Gun '91
Against the Wall '94
Andersonville '95
The Island of Dr. Moreau '96
George Wallace '97
Ronin '98
Reindeer Games '00
Path to War '02

Carl Franklin (1949-)
Eye of the Eagle 2 '89
One False Move '91
Devil in a Blue Dress '95
One True Thing '98
High Crimes '02
Out of Time '03
The Pacific '10
Bless Me, Ultima '13

Chester M. Franklin
Where the North Begins '23
A Parisian Romance '32
Vanity Fair '32

Howard Franklin
Quick Change '90
The Public Eye '92
Larger Than Life '96

Jeff Franklin (1955-)
Double Double Toil and Trouble '94
To Grandmother's House We Go '94
Love Stinks '99

Richard Franklin (1948-)
Patrick '78
Road Games '81
Psycho 2 '83
Cloak & Dagger '84
Link '86
F/X 2: The Deadly Art of Illusion '91
Flatland '02
Visitors '03

Sidney Franklin (1893-1972)
The Forbidden City '18
Heart o' the Hills '19
The Hoodlum '19
The Primitive Lover '22
Her Night of Romance '24
Her Sister from Paris '25
The Duchess of Buffalo '26
Wild Orchids '28
The Last of Mrs. Cheyney '29
Private Lives '31
Smilin' Through '32
The Barretts of Wimpole Street '34
The Good Earth '37

Veronika Franz
Goodnight Mommy '15
The Lodge '19

Harry Fraser (1889-1974)
Ghost City '32
Cavalcade of the West '36

Heroes of the Alamo '37
The Spirit of Youth '37
Chained for Life '51

James Frawley (1937-)
The Big Bus '76
The Muppet Movie '79
Fraternity Vacation '85
Spies, Lies and Naked Thighs '91

R. Ellis Frazier
Across the Line: The Exodus of Charlie Wright '10
Dead Drop '13
Misfire '14

Stephen Frears (1941-)
Gumshoe '72
The Hit '85
My Beautiful Laundrette '85
Prick Up Your Ears '87
Saigon: Year of the Cat '87
Dangerous Liaisons '88
The Grifters '90
Hero '92
The Snapper '93
Mary Reilly '95
The Van '95
The Hi-Lo Country '98
Fail Safe '00
High Fidelity '00
Liam '00
Dirty Pretty Things '03
Mrs. Henderson Presents '05
The Queen '06
Cheri '09
Tamara Drewe '10
Lay the Favorite '12
Muhammad Ali's Greatest Fight '13
Philomena '13
The Program '15
Florence Foster Jenkins '16
Victoria & Abdul '17

Riccardo Freda (1909-99)
Les Miserables '52
Sins of Rome '54
I, Vampiri '56
The Giants of Thessaly '60
Maciste in Hell '60
The Mongols '60
Devil of the Desert Against the Son of Hercules '62
The Horrible Dr. Hichcock '62
Samson and the 7 Miracles of the World '62
The Ghost '63
Double Face '70

Herb Freed
Haunts '77
Beyond Evil '80
Graduation Day '81
Tomboy '85
Subterfuge '98

Mark Freed
Shock 'Em Dead '90
Criminal Desire '98

Jerrold Freedman (1927-)
Kansas City Bomber '72
Borderline '80
Seduced '85
Thompson's Last Run '90

Thornton Freeland (1898-1987)
Be Yourself '30
Whoopee! '30
Love Affair '32
They Call It Sin '32
Flying Down to Rio '33
Accused '36
Jericho '38
Dear Mr. Prohack '49

Joan Freeman (1942-)
Streetwalkin' '85
Satisfaction '88

Morgan Freeman (1937-)
Bopha! '93
Just Like the Son '06

Morgan J. Freeman (1969-)
Hurricane Streets '96
Desert Blue '98
American Psycho 2: All American Girl '02
Born Killers '05
Homecoming '09

Hugo Fregonese (1908-87)
Saddle Tramp '47
Decameron Nights '53
Man in the Attic '53
The Beasts of Marseilles '57
Apache's Last Battle '64
Dracula *vs.* Frankenstein '69

Harold French (1900-97)
Unpublished Story '42
Encore '52
The Hour of 13 '52
Rob Roy-The Highland Rogue '53

Charles Frend (1909-77)
Scott of the Antarctic '48
The Cruel Sea '53
All at Sea '57
Trouble in the Sky '60

Juan Carlos Fresnadillo (1967-)
Intacto '01
28 Weeks Later '07
Intruders '11

Thor Freudenthal
Hotel for Dogs '09
Diary of a Wimpy Kid '10
Percy Jackson: Sea of Monsters '13

Karl Freund (1890-1969)
The Mummy '32
Mad Love '35

Bart Freundlich (1970-)
The Myth of Fingerprints '97
World Traveler '01
Catch That Kid '04
Trust the Man '06
The Rebound '09
After the Wedding '19

Ron Fricke
Baraka '93
Samsara '12

Jason Friedberg
Epic Movie '07
Disaster Movie '08
Meet the Spartans '08
Vampires Suck '10
The Starving Games '13
Best Night Ever '14

Rick Friedberg
Pray TV '80
Spy Hard '96

Richard Friedenberg
Mr. & Mrs. Loving '96
The Education of Little Tree '97
Snow in August '01

William Friedkin (1939-)
Good Times '67
The Night They Raided Minsky's '69
The Boys in the Band '70
The French Connection '71
The Exorcist '73
Sorcerer '77
Brink's Job '78
Cruising '80
Deal of the Century '83
To Live & Die in L.A. '85
Stalking Danger '86
Rampage '87
The Guardian '90
Blue Chips '94
Jailbreakers '94
Jade '95
Rules of Engagement '00
The Hunted '03
Bug '06
Killer Joe '11

Lee Friedlander
Girl Play '04
Out at the Wedding '07

Louis Friedlander (1901-62)
See Lew Landers

Jeffrey Friedman
Common Threads: Stories from the Quilt '89
The Celluloid Closet '95
Howl '10
Lovelace '13
Linda Ronstadt: The Sound of My Voice '19

Richard Friedman
Doom Asylum '88
Phantom of the Mall: Eric's Revenge '89
Forever Together '00
Darkwolf '03

Seymour Friedman (1917-2003)
Counterspy Meets Scotland Yard '50
Criminal Lawyer '51
Loan Shark '52
I'll Get You '53

Martyn Friend (1942-)
All Passion Spent '86
Love or Money '01

Harvey Frost
Midnight Heat '95
National Lampoon's Golf Punks '99
Recipe for Disaster '03
All I Want for Christmas '07
A Grandpa for Christmas '07
Battle of the Bulbs '10
Soldier Love Story '10

Lee Frost (1935-2007)
Rebel Vixens '69
Chrome and Hot Leather '71
Chain Gang Women '72
The Thing with Two Heads '72
Policewomen '73
Black Gestapo '75
Dixie Dynamite '76
Private Obsession '94

William Fruet (1933-)
Wedding in White '72
Search and Destroy '81
Funeral Home '82
Bedroom Eyes '86
Killer Party '86
Imaginary Playmate '06

Robert Fuest (1927-)
And Soon the Darkness '70
Wuthering Heights '70
The Abominable Dr. Phibes '71
Doctor Phibes Rises Again '72
The Final Programme '73
Devil's Rain '75

Toshiya Fujita
Lady Snowblood '73
Lady Snowblood: Love Song of Vengeance '74

Kinji Fukasaku (1930-2003)
The Green Slime '68
Tora! Tora! Tora! '70
Under the Flag of the Rising Sun '72
Cops *vs.* Thugs '75
Message from Space '78
Samurai Reincarnation '81
Fall Guy '82
Virus '82
Battle Royale '00

Jun Fukuda (1924-2000)
Godzilla *vs.* the Sea Monster '66
Son of Godzilla '66
Godzilla on Monster Island '72
Godzilla *vs.* the Cosmic Monster '74
Godzilla *vs.* Megalon '76

Cary Fukunaga (1977-)
Sin Nombre '09
Jane Eyre '11
Beasts of No Nation '15

Lucio Fulci (1927-96)
Beatrice Cenci '69
A Lizard in a Woman's Skin '71
Don't Torture a Duckling '72
Contraband '80
Gates of Hell '80
Zombie '80
The Black Cat '81
The Beyond '82
Manhattan Baby '82
New York Ripper '82
Conquest '83
The House by the Cemetery '83
The New Gladiators '83
Challenge to White Fang '86
Demonia '90
Voices from Beyond '90

Samuel Fuller (1911-97)
I Shot Jesse James '49
Baron of Arizona '51
Fixed Bayonets! '51
The Steel Helmet '51
Park Row '52
Pickup on South Street '53
House of Bamboo '55
China Gate '57
Forty Guns '57
The Crimson Kimono '59
Verboten! '59
Underworld U.S.A. '61
Merrill's Marauders '62
Shock Corridor '63
Naked Kiss '64
The Meanest Men in the West '67
Shark! '68
Dead Pigeon on Beethoven Street '72
The Big Red One '80
White Dog '82

Keith Fulton (1965-)
Lost in La Mancha '03
Brothers of the Head '06

Antoine Fuqua (1966-)
The Replacement Killers '98
Bait '00
Training Day '01
Tears of the Sun '03
King Arthur '04
Lighting in a Bottle '04
Shooter '07
Brooklyn's Finest '09
Olympus Has Fallen '13
The Equalizer '14
Southpaw '15
The Magnificent Seven '16
The Equalizer 2 '18

Sidney J. Furie (1933-)
A Dangerous Age '57
The Snake Woman '61
Doctor Blood's Coffin '62
The Leather Boys '63
The Ipcress File '65
The Appaloosa '66
Lady Sings the Blues '72
Hit! '73
The Boys in Company C '77
The Entity '83
Purple Hearts '84
Iron Eagle '86
Superman 4: The Quest for Peace '87
Iron Eagle 2 '88
Ladybugs '92
Hollow Point '95
Iron Eagle 4 '95
The Rage '96
Top of the World '97
The Collectors '99
Hide and Seek '00
My 5 Wives '00
The Fraternity '01
Road Rage '01
Under Heavy Fire '01
Rock My World '02
American Soldiers '05
The Veteran '06

Brad Furman
The Lincoln Lawyer '11
Runner Runner '13
The Infiltrator '16

Griff Furst (1981-)
I Am Omega '07
Universal Soldiers '07
100 Million BC '08
House of Bones '09
Wolvesbayne '09
Lake Placid 3 '10
Mask Maker '10
Swamp Shark '11

Stephen Furst (1955-)
Magic Kid 2 '94
Dragon Storm '04

Tim Fywell (1951-)
Cracker: To Be a Somebody '94
Norma Jean and Marilyn '95
The Ice House '97
The Woman in White '97
I Capture the Castle '02
Cambridge Spies '03
Ice Princess '05
Half Broken Things '07
Affinity '08

Richard Gabai (1964-)
Assault of the Party Nerds '89
Virgin High '90
Assault of the Party Nerds 2: Heavy Petting Detective '95
Vice Girls '96
Virtual Girl '00
Miracle Dogs Too '06
Call of the Wild 3D '09
InSight '11

Mike Gabriel
The Rescuers Down Under '90
Pocahontas '95

Stephen Gaghan (1965-)
Abandon '02
Syriana '05
Gold '16
Dolittle '20

Alain Gagnol (1967-)
A Cat in Paris '11
Phantom Boy '16

Philippe Gagnon
Fatal Trust '06
No Brother of Mine '07

Richard Gale
The Proposal '00
Pressure '02

Timothy Galfas
Homeboy '75
Fist '76

John A. Gallagher
The Deli '97
Blue Moon '00

Fred Gallo (1965-)
Dead Space '90
Dracula Rising '93
Termination Man '97

George Gallo (1956-)
29th Street '91
Trapped in Paradise '94
Double Take '01
Local Color '06
My Mom's New Boyfriend '08
Columbus Circle '10
Middle Men '10
The Poison Rose '19

Vincent Gallo (1961-)
Buffalo 66 '97
The Brown Bunny '03

Samuel Gallu (1918-91)
Theatre of Death '67
The Man Outside '68

Nisha Ganatra (1974-)
Chutney Popcorn '99
Cake '05
Will You Merry Me? '08
The Hunters '13
Late Night '19

Abel Gance (1889-1981)
J'accuse! '19
La Roue '23
Beethoven '36

Albert C. Gannaway (1920-)
Daniel Boone: Trail Blazer '56
Hidden Guns '56
Man or Gun '58

Christophe Gans (1960-)
Brotherhood of the Wolf '01
Silent Hill '06
Beauty and the Beast '14

Dennis Gansel (1973-)
Before the Fall '04
The Wave '08
Mechanic: Resurrection '16

Robert Ben Garant (1970-)
Balls of Fury '07
Reno 911! Miami '07

Dan Garcia
Enemies Among Us '10
Flesh Wounds '10
Journey to Promethea '10
Terror Trap '10
Mysterious Ways '15

Jon Garcia
The Falls: Testament of Love '13
The Falls: Covenant of Grace '16

Marcio Garcia (1970-)
Bed & Breakfast '10
Open Road '13

Rodrigo Garcia (1959-)
Things You Can Tell Just by Looking at Her '00
Passengers '08
Mother and Child '09
Albert Nobbs '11
Last Days in the Desert '16

Victor Garcia
Return to House on Haunted Hill '07
Mirrors 2 '10
Hellraiser: Revelations '11

Richard Harding Gardner (1949-)
Deadly Daphne's Revenge '93
Sherlock: Undercover Dog '94

Eva Gardos (1950-)
An American Rhapsody '01
Too Young to Be a Dad '02

Jack Garfein (1930-2019)
The Strange One '57
Something Wild '61

Mario Gariazzo (1930-2002)
Eyes Behind the Stars '72
White Slave '86

Alex Garland (1970-)
Ex Machina '15
Annihilation '18

Lee Garmes (1898-1978)
Angels Over Broadway '40
Actors and Sin '52

Tay Garnett (1898-1977)
The Flying Fool '29
One Way Passage '32
S.O.S. Iceberg '33
China Seas '35
Professional Soldier '35

Love Is News '37
Slave Ship '37
Stand-In '37
Joy of Living '38
Eternally Yours '39
Seven Sinners '40
Slightly Honorable '40
Cheers for Miss Bishop '41
Bataan '43
The Cross of Lorraine '43
Mrs. Parkington '44
The Valley of Decision '45
The Postman Always Rings Twice '46
A Connecticut Yankee in King Arthur's Court '49
The Fireball '50
Cause for Alarm '51
One Minute to Zero '52
Cattle King '63
The Big Push '75
Challenge To Be Free '76

Philippe Garrel (1948-)
Frontier of Dawn '08
A Burning Hot Summer '11
Jealousy '13

Otis Garrett (1893-1941)
The Black Doll '38
Danger on the Air '38
Exile Express '39
The Witness Vanishes '39

Roy Garrett (1930-2002)
See Mario Gariazzo

Mick Garris (1951-)
Critters 2: The Main Course '88
Psycho 4: The Beginning '90
Sleepwalkers '92
Stephen King's The Stand '94
Quicksilver Highway '98
Virtual Obsession '98
Steve Martini's The Judge '01
Riding the Bullet '04
Bag of Bones '11
Nightmare Cinema '19

Matteo Garrone (1968-)
The Embalmer '03
Gomorrah '08
Tale of Tales '15

Louis Gasnier (1875-1963)
Kismet '20
The Last Outpost '35
The Gold Racket '37
Reefer Madness '38

Ed Gass-Donnelly (1977-)
Small Town Murder Songs '10
The Last Exorcism Part II '13

Robert Gaston
Open Cam '05
2 Minutes Later '07

Nils Gaup (1955-)
Shipwrecked '90
North Star '96

Roberto Gavaldon (1909-86)
The Littlest Outlaw '54
Beyond All Limits '59

Julie Gavras
Blame It on Fidel '06
Late Bloomers '11

Glenn Gaylord
Eating Out 3: All You Can Eat '09
I Do '13

Joe Gayton
Warm Summer Rain '89
Wes Craven Presents Mind Ripper '95
Sweet Jane '98

Peter Geiger
The Cold Equations '96
The Colony '98
40 Days and Nights '12

Will Geiger
Elvis and Annabelle '07
Free Willy: Escape from Pirate's Cove '10

David Gelb
Jiro Dreams of Sushi '12
The Lazarus Effect '15

Augusto Genina (1892-1957)
Cyrano de Bergerac '25
Prix de Beaute '30

Xavier Gens
Hitman '07
The ABCs of Death '12
Cold Skin '18

Giacomo Gentilomo (1909-2001)
Young Caruso '51
Hercules against the Moon Men '64

Terry George (1952-)
Some Mother's Son '96
A Bright Shining Lie '98
Hotel Rwanda '04
Reservation Road '07
Stand Off '11
The Promise '17

Fred Gerber
Closer and Closer '96
Prison of Secrets '97

Marion Gering
The Devil and the Deep '32
Thirty Day Princess '34
Thunder in the City '37

Pietro Germi (1904-74)
Divorce-Italian Style '62
Seduced and Abandoned '64
Alfredo, Alfredo '72

Chris Gerolmo
Citizen X '95
Certain Prey '11

Clyde Geronimi (1901-89)
Melody Time '48
The Adventures of Ichabod and Mr. Toad '49
Alice in Wonderland '51
Lady and the Tramp '55
Sleeping Beauty '59
101 Dalmatians '61

Ricky Gervais (1961-)
The Invention of Lying '09
Cemetery Junction '10

Sacha Gervasi (1966-)
Anvil! The Story of Anvil '09
Hitchcock '12
November Criminals '17

Greta Gerwig (1983-)
Nights and Weekends '08
Lady Bird '17
Little Women '19

Nicolas Gessner (1931-)
The Peking Blond '68
Someone Behind the Door '71
The Little Girl Who Lives down the Lane '76

Bahman Ghobadi (1968-)
Marooned in Iraq '02
Turtles Can Fly '04

Francis Giacobetti
Emmanuelle, the Joys of a Woman '76
Emmanuelle 4 '84

David Giancola (1969-)
Time Chasers '95
Diamond Run '96
Lightning: Fire from the Sky '00
Peril '00

Duncan Gibbins (1952-93)
Fire with Fire '86
Eve of Destruction '90

Rodney Gibbons
The Neighbor '93
Owd Bob '97
Captive '98
Little Men '98
The Pact '99
The Hound of the Baskervilles '00
Wilder '00
The Sign of Four '01
Silent Night '02
Deadly Isolation '05

Gwyneth Gibby
Marquis de Sade '96
Isaac Asimov's Nightfall '00

Alex Gibney (1953-)
Enron: The Smartest Guys in the Room '05
Gonzo: The Life and Work of Dr. Hunter S. Thompson '08
Casino Jack and the United States of Money '10
Client 9: The Rise and Fall of Eliot Spitzer '10
Freakonomics '10
Magic Trip: Ken Kesey's Search for a Kool Place '11
Mea Maxima Culpa: Silence in the House of God '12
The Armstrong Lie '13
We Steal Secrets: The Story of WikiLeaks '13
Going Clear: Scientology and the Prison of Belief '15
Steve Jobs: The Man in the Machine '15
Zero Days '16
No Stone Unturned '17
Citizen K '19
The Inventor: Out For Blood In Silicon Valley '19

Alan Gibson (1938-87)
Crescendo '69
Dracula A.D. 1972 '72
The Satanic Rites of Dracula '73
A Woman Called Golda '82
The Charmer '87

Brian Gibson (1944-2004)
Breaking Glass '80
Poltergeist 2: The Other Side '86
Drug Wars: The Camarena Story '90
The Josephine Baker Story '90
What's Love Got to Do with It? '93
The Juror '96
Still Crazy '98

Mel Gibson (1956-)
The Man Without a Face '93
Braveheart '95
The Passion of the Christ '04
Apocalypto '06
Hacksaw Ridge '16

Coky Giedroyc (1962-)
Stella Does Tricks '96
Carrie's War '04
Oliver Twist '07
Wuthering Heights '09
Spies of Warsaw '13
How to Build a Girl '20

Gregory Gieras
The Prince and the Surfer '99
Dark Asylum '01
Centipede '05

Adam Gierasch
Autopsy '08
Night of the Demons '09
Fertile Ground '10
Tales of Halloween '15

Tony Giglio (1971-)
Soccer Dog: The Movie '98
In Enemy Hands '04

Brian Gilbert (1960-)
Vice Versa '88
Not Without My Daughter '90
Tom & Viv '94
Wilde '97
The Gathering '02

Lewis Gilbert (1920-2018)
Cosh Boy '52
Tough Guy '53
Cast a Dark Shadow '55
Reach for the Sky '56
The Admirable Crichton '57
A Cry from the Streets '57
Carve Her Name with Pride '58
Ferry to Hong Kong '59
Sink the Bismarck '60
Damn the Defiant '62
The Seventh Dawn '64
Alfie '66
You Only Live Twice '67
The Adventurers '70
Friends '71
Operation Daybreak '75
The Spy Who Loved Me '77
Moonraker '79
Educating Rita '83
Not Quite Paradise '86
Shirley Valentine '89
Haunted '95

Peter Gilbert (1957-)
A Time for Dancing '00
At the Death House Door '08

Julian Gilbey
Rise of the Footsoldier '07
A Lonely Place to Die '11
The ABCs of Death 2 '14
Plastic '14

David Giles
The Strauss Family '73
Mansfield Park '85

Stuart Gillard (1950-)
Paradise '82
A Man Called Sarge '90
Teenage Mutant Ninja Turtles 3 '93
Poltergeist: The Legacy '96
RocketMan '97
Crimes of Fashion '04
Twitches '05
The Initiation of Sarah '06
Twitches Too '07
The Cutting Edge 3: Chasing the Dream '08
WarGames: The Dead Code '08
Riverworld '10
Girl *vs.* Monster '12

Craig Gillespie
Mr. Woodcock '07
Fright Night '11
Million Dollar Arm '14
The Finest Hours '16
I, Tonya '17

Jeremy Gillespie
Father's Day '12
The Void '17

Jim Gillespie
I Know What You Did Last Summer '97
Eye See You '01
Venom '05
Billionaire Ransom '16

Tyler Gillett
V/H/S '12
Devil's Due '14
Ready or Not '19

Terry Gilliam (1940-)
And Now for Something Completely Different '72
Monty Python and the Holy Grail '75
Jabberwocky '77
Time Bandits '81
Monty Python's The Meaning of Life '83
Brazil '85

The Adventures of Baron Munchausen '89
The Fisher King '91
12 Monkeys '95
Fear and Loathing in Las Vegas '98
The Brothers Grimm '05
Tideland '05
The Imaginarium of Doctor Parnassus '09
The Zero Theorem '13
The Man Who Killed Don Quixote '18

Sidney Gilliat (1908-94)
Waterloo Road '45
Green for Danger '47
She Played With Fire '57
The Great St. Trinian's Train Robbery '66
Endless Night '71

John Gilling (1912-85)
No Trace '50
The Frightened Man '52
My Son, the Vampire '52
The Voice of Merrill '52
Recoil '53
White Fire '53
Bond of Fear '56
Odongo '56
Pickup Alley '57
Idol on Parade '59
The Flesh and the Fiends '60
It Takes a Thief '60
Night Caller from Outer Space '66
Plague of the Zombies '66
The Reptile '66
The Mummy's Shroud '67

Stuart Gilmore (1909-71)
The Virginian '46
The Half-Breed '51
1,000 Years From Now '52

Dan Gilroy (1959-)
Nightcrawler '14
Roman J. Israel, Esq. '17
Velvet Buzzsaw '19

Frank D. Gilroy (1925-)
Desperate Characters '71
From Noon Till Three '76

Tom Gilroy
Spring Forward '99
The Cold Lands '13

Tony Gilroy (1956-)
Michael Clayton '07
The Bourne Legacy '12

Milton Moses Ginsberg (1943-)
Coming Apart '69
Werewolf of Washington '73

Robert Ginty (1948-2009)
Vietnam, Texas '90
Woman of Desire '93

Jose Giovanni (1923-2004)
Gypsy '75
Le Gitan '75

Buddy Giovinazzo (1957-)
Combat Shock '84
No Way Home '96
Life is Hot in Cracktown '08

Bob Giraldi (1939-)
Club Med '86
Hiding Out '87
Dinner Rush '00

Bernard Girard (1918-97)
Dead Heat on a Merry-Go-Round '66
The Mad Room '69
A Name for Evil '70
Mind Snatchers '72
Little Moon & Jud McGraw '78

Francois Girard (1963-)
32 Short Films about Glenn Gould '93
The Red Violin '98

Silk '07
The Song of Names '19

Michael Paul Girard (1954-)
Body Parts '94
Witchcraft 7: Judgement Hour '95
Bikini House Calls '96
Illegal Affairs '96
Witchcraft 9: Bitter Flesh '96
Bikini Med School '98
Sweet Evil '98

William Girdler (1947-78)
Asylum of Satan '72
Three on a Meathook '72
Sheba, Baby '75
Grizzly '76
Day of the Animals '77
Project: Kill! '77
The Manitou '78

Amos Gitai (1950-)
Golem: The Petrified Garden '93
Kadosh '99
Kippur '00
Free Zone '05
Disengagement '07
One Day You'll Understand '08

Wyndham Gittens (1885-1967)
Tim Tyler's Luck '37
Forbidden Valley '38

Paul Michael Glaser (1943-)
Band of the Hand '86
The Running Man '87
The Cutting Edge '92
The Air Up There '94
Kazaam '96

Leslie Linka Glatter
State of Emergency '94
Now and Then '95
The Proposition '97

Richard Glatzer (1952-2015)
Grief '94
The Fluffer '01
Quinceanera '06
The Last of Robin Hood '13
Still Alice '14

Harvey Glazer
Kickin' It Old Skool '07
Van Wilder: Freshman Year '08

Jonathan Glazer (1965-)
Sexy Beast '00
Birth '04
Under the Skin '13

Francis Glebas
Fantasia/2000 '00
Piglet's Big Movie '03

David Gleeson (1966-)
Cowboys & Angels '04
The Front Line '06

John Glen (1932-)
For Your Eyes Only '81
Octopussy '83
A View to a Kill '85
The Living Daylights '87
License to Kill '89
Aces: Iron Eagle 3 '92

John Glenister (1932-)
Six Wives of Henry VIII '71
Emma '72
Love for Lydia '79

Peter Glenville (1913-96)
The Prisoner '55
Summer and Smoke '61
Term of Trial '63
Becket '64
The Comedians '67

James Glickenhaus (1950-)
Exterminator '80
Protector '85
Shakedown '88

Slaughter of the Innocents '93
Timemaster '95

Arne Glimcher (1938-)
The Mambo Kings '92
Just Cause '94
White River '99

Ben Gluck (1976-)
Brother Bear 2 '06
Alpha and Omega '10

Will Gluck
Fired Up! '09
Easy A '10
Friends With Benefits '11
Annie '14
Peter Rabbit '18

Jean-Luc Godard (1930-)
Breathless '59
Le Petit Soldat '60
A Woman Is a Woman '60
My Life to Live '62
Les Carabiniers '63
Band of Outsiders '64
Contempt '64
Une Femme Mariee '64
Alphaville '65
The Joy of Knowledge '65
A Married Woman '65
Pierrot le Fou '65
Masculine Feminine '66
Two or Three Things I Know about Her '66
La Chinoise '67
Weekend '67
Six in Paris '68
Sympathy for the Devil '70
Numero Deux '75
Every Man for Himself '79
Passion '82
First Name: Carmen '83
Detective '85
Hail Mary '85
Aria '88
Helas pour Moi '94
For Ever Mozart '96
In Praise of Love '01
Our Music '04
Film Socialisme '10
Goodbye to Language '14

Drew Goddard
The Cabin in the Woods '12
Bad Times at the El Royale '18

Jim (James) Goddard (1937-2013)
A Tale of Two Cities '80
The Life and Adventures of Nicholas Nickleby '81
Kennedy '83
Shanghai Surprise '86
The Impossible Spy '87
Reilly: Ace of Spies '87
The Four Minute Mile '88

Peter Godfrey (1899-1970)
Christmas in Connecticut '45
Cry Wolf '47
Escape Me Never '47
That Hagen Girl '47
The Two Mrs. Carrolls '47
Barricade '49
The Girl from Jones Beach '49

Bryan Goeres (1969-)
Face of Terror '04
Reflections '08

Kevin Goetz
Scenic Route '13
Martyrs '16

Michael Goetz
Scenic Route '13
Martyrs '16

Michael Goi (1959-)
Megan Is Missing '11
Mary '19

Menahem Golan (1929-)
What's Good for the Goose '69
Eagles Attack at Dawn '70
Diamonds '72
Lepke '75
Operation Thunderbolt '77
The Uranium Conspiracy '78
The Apple '80
Enter the Ninja '81
Delta Force '86
Over the Top '86
Hit the Dutchman '92
Silent Victim '92

Jack Gold (1930-)
The Reckoning '69
Catholics '73
The National Health '73
Man Friday '75
The Naked Civil Servant '75
The Medusa Touch '78
Escape from Sobibor '87
The Tenth Man '88
The Rose and the Jackal '90
The Return of the Native '94
Into the Blue '97
Goodnight, Mr. Tom '99

Sandra Goldbacher (1960-)
The Governess '98
Me Without You '01
Ballet Shoes '07

Willis Goldbeck (1898-1979)
Dr. Gillespie's New Assistant '42
Dr. Gillespie's Criminal Case '43
Three Men in White '44
Between Two Women '45
Love Laughs at Andy Hardy '46
Dark Delusion '47

Eric Goldberg (1955-)
Pocahontas '95
Fantasia/2000 '00

Evan Goldberg (1982-)
This Is the End '13
The Interview '14

Gary David Goldberg (1944-2013)
Dad '89
Must Love Dogs '05

Jake Goldberger (1977-)
Don McKay '09
Life of a King '13
Almost Friends '17

Mark Goldblatt
Dead Heat '88
The Punisher '90

Dan Golden
Saturday Night Special '92
Burial of the Rats '95
Stripteaser '95
The Haunted Sea '97

Rachel Goldenberg
Sunday School Musical '08
Sherlock Holmes '10
Grimm's Snow White '12
Love at the Christmas Table '12

Gary Goldman (1944-)
Thumbelina '94
A Troll in Central Park '94
Anastasia '97
Titan A.E. '00

Allan Goldstein (1949-)
The House of Dies Drear '88
Death Wish 5: The Face of Death '94
Synapse '95
Jungle Boy '96
Virus '96
Home Team '98
When Justice Fails '98
2001: A Space Travesty '00
One Way Out '02
Snakeman '05

Jonathan Goldstein (1969-)
Vacation '15
Game Night '18

Scott Goldstein
Walls of Glass '85
Levitation '97

James Goldstone (1931-91)
Winning '69
Brother John '70
They Only Kill Their Masters '72
Cry Panic '74
Swashbuckler '76
Rollercoaster '77
When Time Ran Out '80

Bobcat Goldthwait (1962-)
Shakes the Clown '92
Sleeping Dogs Lie '06
World's Greatest Dad '09
God Bless America '11
Willow Creek '13
Call Me Lucky '15

Tony Goldwyn (1960-)
A Walk on the Moon '99
Someone Like You '01
The Last Kiss '06
Conviction '10

Steve Gomer
Sweet Lorraine '87
Fly by Night '93
Sunset Park '96
Barney's Great Adventure '98
Expecting a Miracle '09
All Saints '17

Nick Gomez (1963-)
Laws of Gravity '92
New Jersey Drive '95
Drowning Mona '00
Lizzie Borden Took an Ax '14

Manuel Gomez Pereira (1958-)
Why Do They Call It Love When They Mean Sex? '92
Mouth to Mouth '95
Love Can Seriously Damage Your Health '96
Between Your Legs '99

Alfonso Gomez-Rejon
The Town That Dreaded Sundown '14
Me and Earl and the Dying Girl '15
The Current War: Director's Cut '19

Michel Gondry (1963-)
Human Nature '02
Eternal Sunshine of the Spotless Mind '04
Dave Chappelle's Block Party '06
The Science of Sleep '06
Be Kind Rewind '08
Tokyo! '09
The Green Hornet '11
Mood Indigo '13

Noam Gonick (1973-)
Hey, Happy! '01
Stryker '04

Saul Goodkind (1896-1962)
Buck Rogers Conquers the Universe '39
The Phantom Creeps '39

Brian Goodman (1963-)
What Doesn't Kill You '08
Black Butterfly '17

Leslie Goodwins (1899-1969)
The Girl From Mexico '39
Men Against the Sky '40
Mexican Spitfire '40
The Mexican Spitfire Out West '40
The Mexican Spitfire's Baby '41
Mexican Spitfire at Sea '42
The Mexican Spitfire Sees a Ghost '42
Silver Skates '43
Radio Stars on Parade '45

Nicholaus Goossen
Grandma's Boy '06
The Shortcut '09

Chris Gorak
Right at Your Door '06
The Darkest Hour '11

Bert I. Gordon (1922-)
Cyclops '56
Beginning of the End '57
Attack of the Puppet People '58
Earth *vs.* the Spider '58
War of the Colossal Beast '58
Tormented '60
The Magic Sword '62
Village of the Giants '65
Picture Mommy Dead '66
The Mad Bomber '72
The Witching '72
Food of the Gods '76
Empire of the Ants '77
The Big Bet '85

Bette Gordon (1950-)
Variety '83
Luminous Motion '00
Handsome Harry '09

Bryan Gordon
Career Opportunities '91
Pie in the Sky '95

Dennie Gordon
Joe Dirt '01
What a Girl Wants '03
New York Minute '04

Fiona Gordon
L'Iceberg '05
Lost in Paris '17

Josh Gordon
Blades of Glory '07
The Switch '10
Office Christmas Party '16

Keith Gordon (1961-)
The Chocolate War '88
A Midnight Clear '92
Wild Palms '93
Mother Night '96
Waking the Dead '00
The Singing Detective '03

Michael Gordon (1911-93)
The Lady Gambles '49
Woman in Hiding '49
Cyrano de Bergerac '50
I Can Get It For You Wholesale '51
Pillow Talk '59
Portrait in Black '60
Boys' Night Out '62
For Love or Money '63
Move Over, Darling '63
A Very Special Favor '65
Texas Across the River '66
The Impossible Years '68

Robert Gordon (1895-1971)
The Joe Louis Story '53
It Came from Beneath the Sea '55
Black Zoo '63
Tarzan and the Jungle Boy '68
The Gatling Gun '72

Seth Gordon
The King of Kong: A Fistful of Quarters '07
Four Christmases '08
Freakonomics '10
Horrible Bosses '11
Identity Thief '13
Baywatch '17

Stuart Gordon (1947-2020)
Re-Animator '84
From Beyond '86
Dolls '87
Robot Jox '90
The Pit & the Pendulum '91
Fortress '93
Castle Freak '95
Space Truckers '97
The Wonderful Ice Cream Suit '98
King of the Ants '03
Edmond '05
Stuck '07

Lawrence Gordon-Clark
Flambards '78
Jamaica Inn '82

Jonathan Gorman
Bikini Bloodbath '06
Bikini Bloodbath Carwash '08
Bikini Bloodbath Christmas '09

Lisa Gornick (1970-)
Do I Love You? '02
Tick Tock Lullaby '07

John Gorrie (1932-)
Macbeth '70
Edward the King '75
Cause Celebre '87
Like A Bride '94

Marleen Gorris (1948-)
Antonia's Line '95
Mrs. Dalloway '97
The Luzhin Defence '00
Carolina '03

Hideo Gosha (1929-92)
Sword of the Beast '65
Goyokin '69
Hunter in the Dark '80
The Wolves '82

Raja Gosnell (1968-)
Home Alone 3 '97
Never Been Kissed '99
Big Momma's House '00
Scooby-Doo '02
Scooby-Doo 2: Monsters Unleashed '04
Yours, Mine & Ours '05
Beverly Hills Chihuahua '08
The Smurfs '11
The Smurfs 2 '13
Show Dogs '18

Andrew Goth
B.U.S.T.E.D. '99
Cold and Dark '05

Carl Gottlieb (1938-)
Caveman '81
Amazon Women on the Moon '87

Lisa Gottlieb
Just One of the Guys '85
Across the Moon '94
Cadillac Ranch '96

Michael Gottlieb (1945-2014)
Mannequin '87
Mr. Nanny '93
A Kid in King Arthur's Court '95

Heywood Gould
One Good Cop '91
Trial by Jury '94
Mistrial '96
Double Bang '01

Edmund Goulding (1891-1959)
Grand Hotel '32
Riptide '34
That Certain Woman '37
Dawn Patrol '38
Dark Victory '39
The Old Maid '39
The Great Lie '41
Claudia '43
The Constant Nymph '43
Forever and a Day '43
The Razor's Edge '46
Nightmare Alley '47
Mister 880 '50
We're Not Married '52
Teenage Rebel '56

Anne Goursaud
Embrace of the Vampire '95
Poison Ivy 2: Lily '95
Red Shoe Diaries 6: How I Met My Husband '95
Another 9 1/2 Weeks '96

David S. Goyer (1965-)
ZigZag '02
Blade: Trinity '04
The Invisible '07
The Unborn '09

Rachel Grady
Jesus Camp '06
Freakonomics '10

Gustavo Graef-Marino
Johnny 100 Pesos '93
Diplomatic Siege '99
Instinct to Kill '01

Todd Graff (1959-)
Camp '03
Bandslam '09
Joyful Noise '12

William A. Graham (1930-2013)
Waterhole Number 3 '67
Then Came Bronson '68
Change of Habit '69
Birds of Prey '72
Deadly Encounter '72
Get Christie Love! '74
Beyond the Bermuda Triangle '75
21 Hours at Munich '76
The Amazing Howard Hughes '77
Contract on Cherry Street '77
The Guyana Tragedy: The Story of Jim Jones '80
Harry Tracy '83
Calendar Girl Murders '84
Secrets of a Married Man '84
Last Days of Frank & Jesse James '86
Proud Men '87
Return to the Blue Lagoon '91
Betrayed: A Story of Three Women '95
The Man Who Captured Eichmann '96
Acceptable Risk '01
Blood Crime '02

Gilles Grangier (1911-96)
Hijack Highway '55
Duke of the Derby '62

Pierre Granier-Deferre (1927-2007)
The Last Train '74
Widow Couderc '74

Debra Granik
Down to the Bone '04
Winter's Bone '10
Leave No Trace '18

Barra Grant (1948-)
Life of the Party '05
Love Hurts '09

Brian Grant
Sensation '94
The Immortals '95
The Cyberstalking '99

Darren Grant
Diary of a Mad Black Woman '05
Make It Happen '08

Lee Grant (1927-)
Tell Me a Riddle '80
Staying Together '89
Following Her Heart '94

Alex Grasshof (1930-)
Pepper and His Wacky Taxi '72
A Billion for Boris '90

Jorge Grau (1930-)
Let Sleeping Corpses Lie '74
We Are What We Are '11
The ABCs of Death '12

Walter Grauman (1922-)
Lady in a Cage '64
633 Squadron '64
A Rage to Live '65
Paper Man '71
They Call It Murder '71
The Streets of San Francisco '72
Scene of the Crime '85
Who Is Julia? '86
Shakedown on the Sunset Strip '88

Gary Graver (1938-2006)
Texas Lightning '81
Crossing the Line '90
Evil Spirits '91
Sexual Roulette '96

Duane Graves (1975-)
The Wild Man of the Navidad '08
Kill or Be Killed '15

Bradley Rust Gray
The Exploding Girl '09
Jack and Diane '12

F. Gary Gray (1969-)
Friday '95
Set It Off '96
The Negotiator '98
The Italian Job '03
A Man Apart '03
Be Cool '05
Law Abiding Citizen '09
Straight Outta Compton '15
The Fate of the Furious '17
Men in Black: International '19

James Gray (1969-)
Little Odessa '94
The Yards '00
We Own the Night '07
Two Lovers '09
The Immigrant '13
The Lost City of Z '17
Ad Astra '19

John Gray
Billy Galvin '86
When He's Not a Stranger '89
The Lost Capone '90
Born to Be Wild '95
The Glimmer Man '96
The Hunley '99
Brian's Song '01
The Seventh Stream '01
White Irish Drinkers '10
The Makeover '13

Gavin Grazer (1961-)
Chow Bella '98
Scorched '02

Adam Green (1975-)
Hatchet '07
Spiral '07
Frozen '10
Hatchet 2 '10

Alfred E. Green (1889-1960)
The Man Who Had Everything '20
Through the Back Door '21
Old English '30
Smart Money '31
It's Tough to Be Famous '32
Parachute Jumper '32
The Rich Are Always With Us '32
Union Depot '32
Baby Face '33
Dark Hazard '34
Housewife '34
The Merry Frinks '34
Dangerous '35
The Girl from 10th Ave. '35
The Goose and the Gander '35
Colleen '36
The Golden Arrow '36
More Than A Secretary '36
Thoroughbreds Don't Cry '37
The Gracie Allen Murder Case '39
East of the River '40
Flowing Gold '40
Adventure in Washington '41
The Mayor of 44th Street '42
Meet the Stewarts '42
There's Something About a Soldier '43
Mr. Winkle Goes to War '44
Strange Affair '44
The Jolson Story '46
Copacabana '47
The Fabulous Dorseys '47
Four Faces West '48
Cover Up '49
The Jackie Robinson Story '50
Sierra '50
Invasion U.S.A. '52
The Eddie Cantor Story '53
Top Banana '54

Dave Green
Earth to Echo '14
Teenage Mutant Ninja Turtles: Out of the Shadows '16

David Green (1948-)
Code of Honor '84
Car Trouble '86
Buster '88
Fire Birds '90

David Gordon Green (1975-)
All the Real Girls '03
Undertow '04
Snow Angels '07
Pineapple Express '08
The Sitter '11
Your Highness '11
Joe '13
Prince Avalanche '13
Manglehorn '15
Our Brand is Crisis '15
Stronger '17
Halloween '18

Guy Green (1913-2005)
Postmark for Danger '56
Sea of Sand '58
The Snorkel '58
S.O.S. Pacific '60
Light in the Piazza '61
The Mark '61
Diamond Head '62
A Patch of Blue '65
Walk in the Spring Rain '70
Luther '74
Once Is Not Enough '75
The Incredible Journey of Dr. Meg Laurel '79

Jack N. Green (1946-)
Traveller '96
Seduced: Pretty When You Cry '01

Rashaad Ernesto Green (1978-)
Gun Hill Road '11
Premature '20

Terry Green
Heavens Fall '06
No God, No Master '12

Peter Greenaway (1942-)
The Draughtsman's Contract '82
Drowning by Numbers '87
A Zed & Two Noughts '88
The Cook, the Thief, His Wife & Her Lover '90
The Belly of an Architect '91
Prospero's Books '91
The Pillow Book '95
8 1/2 Women '99
Nightwatching '07
Eisenstein in Guanajuato '15

David Greene (1921-2003)
Blood Island '68
Madame Sin '71
Godspell '73
Gray Lady Down '77
Roots '77
Friendly Fire '79
Hard Country '81
Rehearsal for Murder '82
Prototype '83
Guilty Conscience '85
Miles to Go '86
World War III '86
The Betty Ford Story '87
The Penthouse '89
In a Stranger's Hand '92
What Ever Happened To. . . '93
A Good Day to Die '95
Family of Cops 2: Breach of Faith '97

Robert Greene (1976-)
Kate Plays Christine '16
Bisbee '17 '18

Lauren Greenfield
The Queen of Versailles '12
The Kingmaker '19

Luke Greenfield (1972-)
The Animal '01
The Girl Next Door '04
Something Borrowed '11
Let's Be Cops '14

Paul Greengrass (1955-)
The One That Got Away '96
Bloody Sunday '01
The Bourne Supremacy '04
United 93 '06
The Bourne Ultimatum '07
Green Zone '10
Captain Phillips '13
Jason Bourne '16
22 July '18

Michael Greenspan
Wrecked '10
Kill for Me '12

Maggie Greenwald (1955-)
The Kill-Off '89
The Ballad of Little Jo '93
Songcatcher '99
Get a Clue '02
Comfort and Joy '03
Tempted '03

Robert Greenwald (1948-)
Xanadu '80
In the Custody of Strangers '82
The Burning Bed '85
Shattered Spirits '86
Sweet Hearts Dance '88
Hear No Evil '93
A Woman of Independent Means '94
Breaking Up '97
Steal This Movie! '00
Outfoxed: Rupert Murdoch's War on Journalism '04
Uncovered: The War on Iraq '04
Wal-Mart: The High Cost of Low Price '05

William Grefe (1930-)
The Checkered Flag '63
The Death Curse of Tartu '66
The Hooked Generation '69
Wild Rebels '71
Alligator Alley '72
Stanley '72
Impulse '74
Jaws of Death '76

Clark Gregg (1962-)
Choke '08
Trust Me '13

Colin Gregg (1947-)
To the Lighthouse '83
Lamb '85
The Guilty '92

Francesca Gregorini (1968-)
Tanner Hall '09
The Truth About Emanuel '13

Leslie Greif
Keys to Tulsa '96
10 Rules for Sleeping Around '13

Marc S. Grenier
Stalker '98
Fallen Angel '99
Cause of Death '00
Dead Awake '01
Hidden Agenda '01

Kevin Greutert
Saw 6 '09
Saw 3D: The Final Chapter '10
Visions '16

Edmond T. Greville (1906-66)
Princess Tam Tam '35
Beat Girl '60
The Hands of Orlac '60

John Greyson (1960-)
Zero Patience '94
Lilies '96

Sergio Grieco (1917-82)
Man of Legend '71
Sergeant Klems '71
Mad Dog Killer '77
Mad Dog '84

Tom Gries (1922-77)
Will Penny '67
100 Rifles '69
Fools '70
Earth II '71
The Glass House '72
Lady Ice '73
QB VII '74
Breakout '75
Breakheart Pass '76
Helter Skelter '76
The Greatest '77

Andrew Grieve (1939-)
Lorna Doone '90
All or Nothing at All '93
Horatio Hornblower '99
Horatio Hornblower: The Adventure Continues '01

Richard Griffin
Pretty Dead Things '06
Beyond the Dunwich Horror '08
Nun of That '09

Charles B. Griffith (1930-2007)
Eat My Dust '76
Up from the Depths '79
Smokey Bites the Dust '81

D.W. Griffith (1875-1948)
Avenging Conscience '14
Judith of Bethulia '14
The Birth of a Nation '15
Intolerance '16
Broken Blossoms '19
The Greatest Question '19
True Heart Susie '19
The Idol Dancer '20
The Love Flower '20
Way Down East '20
Dream Street '21
Orphans of the Storm '21
America '24
Sally of the Sawdust '25
Battle of the Sexes '28
Abraham Lincoln '30
Struggle '31

Edward H. Griffith (1894-1975)
The Animal Kingdom '32
No More Ladies '35
Next Time We Love '36
Cafe Metropole '37
My Love For Yours '39
The Sky's the Limit '43

Mark Griffiths
Running Hot '83
Hardbodies '84
Hardbodies 2 '86
A Cry in the Wild '90
Cheyenne Warrior '94
Behind Enemy Lines '96
Au Pair '99
Tactical Assault '99
Au Pair 2: The Fairy Tale Continues '01
Beethoven's 5th '03
Mystery Woman: Mystery Weekend '05
Safe Harbor '06
Love's Unending Legacy '07
Au Pair 3: Adventure in Paradise '09
Growing the Big One '09
How to Fall in Love '12
Nearlyweds '13

Megan Griffiths (1975-)
The Off Hours '11
Lucky Them '13

Nick Grinde (1893-1979)
The Bishop Murder Case '30
This Modern Age '31
Shopworn '32
Ladies Crave Excitement '35
Exiled to Shanghai '37
The Man They Could Not Hang '39

Alan Grint
Catherine Cookson's Colour Blind '98
Catherine Cookson's Tilly Trotter '99
Catherine Cookson's The Secret '00

Ferde Grofe, Jr.
The Day of the Wolves '71
The Proud and the Damned '72

Ulu Grosbard (1929-)
The Subject Was Roses '68
Straight Time '78
True Confessions '81
Falling in Love '84
Georgia '95
The Deep End of the Ocean '98

Jerry Gross (1940-2002)
Girl on a Chain Gang '65
Teenage Mother '67

Paul Gross (1959-)
Men with Brooms '02
Passchendaele '10
Hyena Road '16

Adam Grossman
Sometimes They Come Back. . . Again '96
Carnival of Souls '98

Seth Grossman
The Elephant King '06
The Butterfly Effect 3: Revelation '09

Charles Grosvenor
Once Upon a Forest '93
The Land Before Time 5: The Mysterious Island '97
The Land Before Time 6: The Secret of Saurus Rock '98
Land Before Time 7: The Stone of Cold Fire '00

Adrian Grunberg
Get the Gringo '12
Rambo: Last Blood '19

Luca Guadagnino (1971-)
I Am Love '09
A Bigger Splash '15
Call Me by Your Name '17
Suspiria '18

Robert Guediguian (1953-)
Marius and Jeannette '97
The Town Is Quiet '00
The Army of Crime '10

Ciro Guerra
Embrace of the Serpent '15
Birds of Passage '18

Romolo Guerrieri (1931-)
Johnny Yuma '66
Ring of Death '69

Christopher Guest (1948-)
The Big Picture '89
Attack of the 50 Ft. Woman '93
Waiting for Guffman '96
Almost Heroes '97
Best in Show '00
A Mighty Wind '03
For Your Consideration '06
Mascots '16

Val Guest (1911-2006)
Miss London Ltd. '43
Bees in Paradise '44
Give Us the Moon '44
Penny Princess '52
The Runaway Bus '54
The Quatermass Experiment '56
The Weapon '56
The Abominable Snowman '57
Carry On Admiral '57
Quatermass 2 '57
Further Up the Creek '58
Expresso Bongo '59
Yesterday's Enemy '59
Stop Me Before I Kill! '60
The Day the Earth Caught Fire '61
Where the Spies Are '65
Casino Royale '67
Assignment K '68
Au Pair Girls '72
Confessions of a Window Cleaner '74

Davis Guggenheim (1964-)
Gossip '99
An Inconvenient Truth '06
Gracie '07
It Might Get Loud '09
Waiting for Superman '10
He Named Me Malala '15

Martin Guigui
National Lampoon Presents Cattle Call '06
Benny Bliss & the Disciples of Greatness '07
Beneath the Darkness '12
9/11 '17

John Guillermin (1925-)
Tarzan's Greatest Adventure '59
The Day They Robbed the Bank of England '60
Never Let Go '60
Tarzan Goes to India '62
Waltz of the Toreadors '62
Guns at Batasi '64
Rapture '65
The Blue Max '66
The Bridge at Remagen '69
El Condor '70
Skyjacked '72
Shaft in Africa '73
The Towering Inferno '74
King Kong '76
Death on the Nile '78
Sheena '84
King Kong Lives '86
The Tracker '88

Fred Guiol (1898-1964)
The Rainmakers '35
Mummy's Boys '36

Alain Guiraudie
Stranger by the Lake '13
Staying Vertical '16

Sacha Guitry (1885-1957)
The Story of a Cheat '36
Napoleon '55

John Gulager (1957-)
Feast '06
Feast 2: Sloppy Seconds '08
Piranha 3DD '11

James Gunn (1970-)
Slither '06
Super '10
Guardians of the Galaxy '14

Guardians of the Galaxy Vol. 2 '17

Jon Gunn (1973-)
Mercy Streets '00
My Date With Drew '05
Like Dandelion Dust '09
Do You Believe? '15

Sturla Gunnarsson (1952-)
Such a Long Journey '98
Dangerous Evidence: The Lori Jackson Story '99
Ricky Nelson: Original Teen Idol '99
Rare Birds '01
Above and Beyond '06
Beowulf & Grendel '06
Ice Soldiers '13

Mike Gunther
Beatdown '10
Setup '11

Andrew Gurland (1971-)
Mail Order Wife '04
The Virginity Hit '10

Lawrence (Larry) Guterman
Cats & Dogs '01
Son of the Mask '05

Sebastian Gutierrez (1974-)
She Creature '01
Rise: Blood Hunter '07
Women in Trouble '09
Elektra Luxx '10

Tomas Gutierrez Alea (1926-96)
The Last Supper '76
Strawberry and Chocolate '93
Guantanamera '95

Bill Guttentag
Live! '07
Knife Fight '13

Phillip Guzman
The Lawless '07
2:22 '08

Stephen Gyllenhaal (1949-)
A Family of Spies '90
A Killing in a Small Town '90
Waterland '92
Losing Isaiah '94
Homegrown '97
Talking to Heaven '02
Girl Fight '11
So B. It '17

Charles F. Haas (1913-2011)
Screaming Eagles '56
Tarzan and the Trappers '58

Hugo Haas (1902-68)
One Girl's Confession '53
Bait '54

Philip Haas
The Music of Chance '93
Angels and Insects '95
The Blood Oranges '97
Up at the Villa '00
The Lathe of Heaven '02
The Situation '06

Taylor Hackford (1944-)
Idolmaker '80
An Officer and a Gentleman '82
Against All Odds '84
White Nights '85
Chuck Berry: Hail! Hail! Rock 'n' Roll '87
Everybody's All American '88
Blood In . . . Blood Out: Bound by Honor '93
Dolores Claiborne '94
The Devil's Advocate '97
Proof of Life '00
Ray '04
Love Ranch '10
Parker '13
The Comedian '16

Mikael Hafstrom (1960-)
Evil '03
Derailed '05
1408 '07
Shanghai '09
The Rite '11
Escape Plan '13

Jeremy Haft (1972-)
Grizzly Mountain '97
The Crimson Code '99
Tamara '05

Piers Haggard (1939-)
Quatermass Conclusion '79
The Fiendish Plot of Dr. Fu Manchu '80
Venom '82
A Summer Story '88
Back Home '90
The Shell Seekers '06

Paul Haggis (1953-)
Crash '05
In the Valley of Elah '07
The Next Three Days '10
Third Person '13

Stuart Hagmann (1942-)
The Strawberry Statement '70
Tarantulas: The Deadly Cargo '77

Charles Haid (1943-)
Iron Will '93
The Nightman '93
Riders of the Purple Sage '96
Buffalo Soldiers '97
Sally Hemings: An American Scandal '00

Andrew Haigh
Weekend '11
45 Years '15
Lean on Pete '17

Michael Haigney
Pokemon: The First Movie '99
Pokemon the Movie 2000: The Power of One '00
Pokemon 3: The Movie '01

Randa Haines (1945-)
Children of a Lesser God '86
The Doctor '91
Wrestling Ernest Hemingway '93
Dance with Me '98
The Outsider '02

Richard W. Haines (1957-)
Splatter University '84
Class of Nuke 'Em High '86

Hadi Hajaig
Cleanskin '12
Blue Iguana '18

Don Haldane (1914-)
Nikki, the Wild Dog of the North '61
The Reincarnate '71

Sonnie Hale (1902-59)
Gangway '37
Head Over Heels '37
Sailing Along '38

William (Billy) Hale (1934-)
Gunfight in Abilene '67
S.O.S. Titanic '79
One Shoe Makes It Murder '82
Lace '84
Lace 2 '85
The Murder of Mary Phagan '87

Brett Haley
I'll See You in My Dreams '15
The Hero '17
Hearts Beat Loud '18

Jack Haley, Jr. (1933-2001)
The Love Machine '71
That's Entertainment '74
That's Dancing! '85

H.B. Halicki (1941-89)
Gone in 60 Seconds '74
The Junkman '82

Alexander Hall (1894-1968)
Torch Singer '33
Little Miss Marker '34
Goin' to Town '35
Doctor Takes a Wife '40
Here Comes Mr. Jordan '41
My Sister Eileen '42
The Heavenly Body '44
She Wouldn't Say Yes '45
Down to Earth '47
The Great Lover '49
Love That Brute '50
Because You're Mine '52
Let's Do It Again '53
Forever Darling '56

Don Hall
Winnie the Pooh '11
Big Hero 6 '14

Ivan Hall
Kill or Be Killed '66
Funeral for an Assassin '77
Kill and Kill Again '81

Peter Hall (1930-)
A Midsummer Night's Dream '68
The Homecoming '73
The Camomile Lawn '92
Jacob '94
Never Talk to Strangers '95

Robert Hall (1973-)
Lightning Bug '04
Laid to Rest '09
ChromeSkull: Laid to Rest 2 '11

Daniel Haller (1926-)
Die, Monster, Die! '65
Devil's Angels '67
The Dunwich Horror '70
Pieces of Dreams '70
Buck Rogers in the 25th Century '79
Follow That Car '80

Lasse Hallstrom (1946-)
My Life As a Dog '85
Once Around '91
What's Eating Gilbert Grape '93
Something to Talk About '95
The Cider House Rules '99
Chocolat '00
The Shipping News '01
Casanova '05
An Unfinished Life '05
The Hoax '06
Hachiko: A Dog's Tale '09
Dear John '10
Salmon Fishing in the Yemen '11
Safe Haven '13
The Hundred-Foot Journey '14
A Dog's Purpose '17
The Nutcracker and the Four Realms '18

Victor Halperin (1895-1983)
Party Girl '30
The White Zombie '32
Supernatural '33
Revolt of the Zombies '36
Buried Alive '39

John Hamburg (1970-)
Safe Men '98
Along Came Polly '04
I Love You, Man '09
Why Him? '16

Bent Hamer (1956-)
Kitchen Stories '03
Factotum '06
O'Horten '09

Robert Hamer (1911-63)
Dead of Night '45
It Always Rains on Sunday '47
Kind Hearts and Coronets '49
The Long Memory '53
To Paris with Love '55
The Scapegoat '59
School for Scoundrels '60

Dean Hamilton (1961-)
Strike a Pose '93
Savage Land '94
D.R.E.A.M. Team '99
Blonde and Blonder '07

Guy Hamilton (1922-)
The Colditz Story '55
Goldfinger '64
Funeral in Berlin '66
Battle of Britain '69
Diamonds Are Forever '71
Live and Let Die '73
The Man with the Golden Gun '74
Force 10 from Navarone '78
The Mirror Crack'd '80
Evil under the Sun '82
Remo Williams: The Adventure Begins '85

John Hamilton
The Kid '97
Codename: Jaguar '98
Perpetrators of the Crime '98

Strathford Hamilton (1952-)
Blueberry Hill '88
The Set Up '95
The Proposition '96

William Hamilton (1893-1942)
Seven Keys to Baldpate '35
Murder On a Bridle Path '36

Nick Hamm (1957-)
Talk of Angels '96
The Very Thought of You '98
The Hole '01
Godsend '04
Killing Bono '11

Christopher Hampton (1946-)
Carrington '95
The Secret Agent '96
Imagining Argentina '04

Robert Hampton (1909-99)
See Riccardo Freda

Sanaa Hamri
Something New '06
The Sisterhood of the Traveling Pants 2 '08
Acceptance '09
Just Wright '10

John Hancock (1941-92)
Let's Scare Jessica to Death '71
Bang the Drum Slowly '73
California Dreaming '79
Steal the Sky '88
Prancer '89
Suspended Animation '02

John Lee Hancock (1956-)
The Rookie '02
The Alamo '04
The Blind Side '09
Saving Mr. Banks '13
The Founder '17
The Highwaymen '19

David Hand (1900-86)
Snow White and the Seven Dwarfs '37
Bambi '42

Michael Haneke (1942-)
Benny's Video '92
Funny Games '97
Code Unknown '00
The Piano Teacher '01
Time of the Wolf '03
Hidden '05
Funny Games '07
The White Ribbon '09
Amour '12
Happy End '17

Sean Hanish
Return to Zero '14
Saint Judy '19

Tom Hanks (1956-)
That Thing You Do! '96
From the Earth to the Moon '98
Band of Brothers '01
Larry Crowne '11

William Hanna (1910-2001)
Hey There, It's Yogi Bear '64
Jetsons: The Movie '90

Paul D. Hannah
Consinsual '10
The Perfect Man '11
The Last Letter '13
The Sin Seer '15

Mia Hansen-Love (1981-)
Father of My Children '09
Eden '14
Things to Come '16

Curtis Hanson (1945-)
The Arousers '70
Little Dragons '80
Losin' It '82
The Children of Times Square '86
The Bedroom Window '87
Bad Influence '90
The Hand that Rocks the Cradle '92
The River Wild '94
L.A. Confidential '97
Wonder Boys '00
8 Mile '02
In Her Shoes '05
Lucky You '07
Too Big to Fail '11
Chasing Mavericks '12

Keiichi Hara (1959-)
Colorful: The Motion Picture '10
Miss Hokusai '16

Masato Harada (1949-)
Rowing Through '96
Inugami '01

Tomoo Haraguchi
Kibakichi 2 '04
Kibakichi '04
Death Kappa '10

C.B. Harding
Delta Farce '07
Bait Shop '08

Sarah Harding
Reckless '97
Dead Gorgeous '02
Compulsion '08

Gary Hardwick
The Brothers '01
Deliver Us from Eva '03

Catherine Hardwicke (1955-)
Thirteen '03
Lords of Dogtown '05
The Nativity Story '06
Twilight '08
Red Riding Hood '11
Plush '13
Miss You Already '15
Miss Bala '19

Rob Hardy
The Gospel '05
Stomp the Yard 2: Homecoming '10

Robin Hardy (1929-2016)
The Wicker Man '75
The Wicker Tree '10

Rod Hardy (1949-)
Thirst '79
The Yearling '94

Buffalo Girls '95
Two for Texas '97
High Noon '00
December Boys '07

David Hare (1947-)
Wetherby '85
Strapless '90
The Designated Mourner '97
Page Eight '11

Sterlin Harjo
Four Sheets to the Wind '07
This May Be the Last Time '14

Tsui Hark (1951-)
Zu: Warriors from the Magic Mountain '83
Mad Mission 3 '84
A Better Tomorrow, Part 3 '89
Once Upon a Time in China '91
Once Upon a Time in China II '92
Twin Dragons '92
Green Snake '93
Once Upon a Time in China III '93
Double Team '97
Knock Off '98
Time and Tide '00
Zu Warriors '01
Black Mask 2: City of Masks '02

Veit Harlan (1899-1964)
Jud Suess '40
Kolberg '45

Renny Harlin (1959-)
Born American '86
A Nightmare on Elm Street 4: Dream Master '88
The Adventures of Ford Fairlane '90
Die Hard 2: Die Harder '90
Cliffhanger '93
Cutthroat Island '95
The Long Kiss Goodnight '96
Deep Blue Sea '99
Driven '01
Exorcist: The Beginning '04
Mindhunters '05
The Covenant '06
Cleaner '07
12 Rounds '09
5 Days of War '11
Devil's Pass '13
The Legend of Hercules '14

John Harlow (1896-1977)
Spellbound '41
Candles at Nine '44
Appointment with Crime '45
Echo Murders '45
Old Mother Riley's New Venture '49
Old Mother Riley, Headmistress '50
Those People Next Door '52

Allan Harmon
Afghan Knights '07
Second Sight '07
Uncaged Heart '07

Robert Harmon
The Hitcher '86
Eyes of an Angel '91
Nowhere to Run '93
Gotti '96
The Crossing '00
Wes Craven Presents: They '02
Highwaymen '03
Ike: Countdown to D-Day '04
Jesse Stone: Stone Cold '05
Jesse Stone: Death in Paradise '06
Jesse Stone: Night Passage '06
Jesse Stone: Sea Change '07
Jesse Stone: Thin Ice '09
Jesse Stone: No Remorse '10

Jim Henson (1936-90)
The Great Muppet Caper *'81*
The Dark Crystal *'82*
Labyrinth *'86*

Robby Henson
Pharoah's Army *'95*
The Badge *'02*
Thr3e *'07*

Marcel L'Herbier (1888-1979)
Feu Mathias Pascal *'26*
The Fantastic Night *'42*

Stephen Herek (1958-)
Critters *'86*
Bill & Ted's Excellent Adventure *'89*
Don't Tell Mom the Babysitter's Dead *'91*
The Mighty Ducks *'92*
The Three Musketeers *'93*
Mr. Holland's Opus *'95*
101 Dalmatians *'96*
Holy Man *'98*
Rock Star *'01*
Life or Something Like It *'02*
Man of the House *'05*
Picture This! *'08*
Into the Blue 2: The Reef *'09*
The Cutting Edge: Fire and Ice *'10*
The Chaperone *'11*
Dolly Parton's Coat of Many Colors *'15*
The Great Gilly Hopkins *'16*

Al(bert) Herman (1887-1967)
Whispering Shadow *'33*
The Clutching Hand *'36*
Yank in Libya *'42*
Delinquent Daughters *'44*

Jean Herman (1933-)
Honor Among Thieves *'68*
Butterfly Affair *'71*

Mark Herman (1954-)
Blame It on the Bellboy *'92*
Brassed Off *'96*
Little Voice *'98*
The Boy in the Striped Pajamas *'08*

Charles Herman-Wurmfeld (1966-)
Kissing Jessica Stein *'02*
Legally Blonde 2: Red White & Blonde *'03*
The Hammer *'07*

Jaime Humberto Hermosillo (1942-2020)
Dona Herlinda & Her Son *'86*
Homework *'90*
Esmeralda Comes by Night *'98*

Rowdy Herrington (1951-)
Road House *'89*
Gladiator *'92*
Striking Distance *'93*
A Murder of Crows *'99*
The Stickup *'01*
I Witness *'03*
Bobby Jones: Stroke of Genius *'04*

Marshall Herskovitz (1952-)
Jack the Bear *'93*
Dangerous Beauty *'98*

Michael Herz (1949-)
Sugar Cookies *'77*
First Turn On *'83*
Stuck on You *'84*
The Toxic Avenger *'86*
Troma's War *'88*
The Toxic Avenger, Part 2 *'89*
The Toxic Avenger, Part 3: The Last Temptation of Toxie *'89*
Sgt. Kabukiman N.Y.P.D. *'94*

John Herzfeld
Two of a Kind *'83*
A Father's Revenge *'88*
Two Days in the Valley *'96*
Don King: Only in America *'97*
15 Minutes *'01*
Bobby Z *'07*
S.I.S. *'08*
Reach Me *'14*

Brian Herzlinger (1976-)
My Date With Drew *'05*
Baby on Board *'08*
Finding Normal *'13*
Bus Driver *'16*

Werner Herzog (1942-)
Signs of Life *'68*
Aguirre, the Wrath of God *'72*
Heart of Glass *'74*
Every Man for Himself & God Against All *'75*
Stroszek *'77*
Woyzeck *'78*
Nosferatu the Vampyre *'79*
Fitzcarraldo *'82*
Where the Green Ants Dream *'84*
Cobra Verde *'88*
Invincible *'01*
The White Diamond *'04*
Grizzly Man *'05*
Rescue Dawn *'06*
Encounters at the End of the World *'07*
Bad Lieutenant: Port of Call New Orleans *'09*
My Son, My Son, What Have Ye Done *'09*
Cave of Forgotten Dreams *'11*
Into the Abyss *'11*
Happy People: A Year in the Taiga *'13*
Into the Inferno *'16*
Lo and Behold: Reveries of the Connected World *'16*

Jared Hess (1979-)
Napoleon Dynamite *'04*
Nacho Libre *'06*
Gentlemen Broncos *'09*
Don Verdean *'15*
Masterminds *'16*

Jon Hess
Watchers *'88*
Alligator 2: The Mutation *'90*
Excessive Force *'93*
Mars *'96*
Legion *'98*
Crash & Byrnes *'99*

Gordon Hessler (1930-)
Catacombs *'64*
The Oblong Box *'69*
Cry of the Banshee *'70*
Scream and Scream Again *'70*
Murders in the Rue Morgue *'71*
Embassy *'72*
Golden Voyage of Sinbad *'73*
Betrayal *'74*
Medusa *'74*
KISS Meets the Phantom of the Park *'78*
Pray for Death *'85*
Rage of Honor *'87*
The Girl in a Swing *'89*
Tales of the Unexpected *'91*

Charlton Heston (1924-2008)
Antony and Cleopatra *'73*
Mother Lode *'82*
A Man for All Seasons *'88*

Fraser Heston (1955-)
Treasure Island *'89*
The Crucifer of Blood *'91*
Needful Things *'93*
Alaska *'96*

David L. Hewitt (1939-)
Horrors of the Red Planet *'64*
Alien Massacre *'67*
Gallery of Horrors *'67*
Journey to the Center of Time *'67*
The Lucifer Complex *'78*

Peter Hewitt (1962-)
Bill & Ted's Bogus Journey *'91*
Wild Palms *'93*
Tom and Huck *'95*
The Borrowers *'97*
Princess of Thieves *'01*
Garfield: The Movie *'04*
Zoom *'06*
The Maiden Heist *'08*
Home Alone: The Holiday Heist *'12*
Radio Rebel *'12*

Rod Hewitt
Strip Search *'97*
The Debt *'98*

Douglas Heyes (1919-93)
Kitten with a Whip *'64*
The French Atlantic Affair *'79*

Jesse Hibbs (1906-85)
Ride Clear of Diablo *'54*
To Hell and Back *'55*
Ride a Crooked Trail *'58*

George Hickenlooper (1963-2010)
Hearts of Darkness: A Filmmaker's Apocalypse *'91*
The Ghost Brigade *'93*
The Low Life *'95*
Persons Unknown *'96*
Dogtown *'97*
The Big Brass Ring *'99*
The Man from Elysian Fields *'01*
Mayor of the Sunset Strip *'03*
Factory Girl *'06*
Casino Jack *'10*

Ben Hickernell
Lebanon, PA *'10*
Backwards *'12*

Steve Hickner
Prince of Egypt *'98*
Bee Movie *'07*

Anthony Hickox (1959-)
Waxwork *'88*
Sundown *'91*
Waxwork 2: Lost in Time *'91*
Hellraiser 3: Hell on Earth *'92*
Full Eclipse *'93*
Warlock: The Armageddon *'93*
Storm Catcher *'99*
Contaminated Man *'00*
Jill the Ripper *'00*
Last Run *'01*
Federal Protection *'02*
Blast *'04*
Submerged *'05*
Sundown: The Vampire in Retreat *'08*

Douglas Hickox (1929-88)
The Giant Behemoth *'59*
Sitting Target *'72*
Theatre of Blood *'73*
Brannigan *'75*
Sky Riders *'76*
Zulu Dawn *'79*
The Hound of the Baskervilles *'83*
Mistral's Daughter *'84*
Sins *'85*

James D.R. Hickox
Children of the Corn 3: Urban Harvest *'95*
Blood Surf *'00*
Sabretooth *'01*
The Gold Retrievers *'10*

Scott Hicks (1953-)
Shine *'95*
Snow Falling on Cedars *'99*
Hearts in Atlantis *'01*
No Reservations *'07*
The Boys Are Back *'09*
The Lucky One *'12*
Fallen *'17*

Howard Higgin (1891-1938)
The Racketeer *'29*
The Painted Desert *'31*
Hell's House *'32*

Colin Higgins (1941-88)
Foul Play *'78*
9 to 5 *'80*
The Best Little Whorehouse in Texas *'82*

Mikey Hilb
Dishdogz *'05*
Deep Winter *'08*

Zak Hilditch
Plum Role *'07*
1922 *'17*
Rattlesnake *'19*

George Roy Hill (1922-2002)
Period of Adjustment *'62*
Toys in the Attic *'63*
The World of Henry Orient *'64*
Hawaii *'66*
Thoroughly Modern Millie *'67*
Butch Cassidy and the Sundance Kid *'69*
Slaughterhouse Five *'72*
The Sting *'73*
The Great Waldo Pepper *'75*
Slap Shot *'77*
A Little Romance *'79*
The World According to Garp *'82*
The Little Drummer Girl *'84*
Funny Farm *'88*

George W. Hill (1895-1934)
Tell It to the Marines *'26*
The Flying Fleet *'29*
The Big House *'30*
Min & Bill *'30*
Hell Divers *'31*
The Secret Six *'31*
Clear All Wires! *'33*

Jack Hill (1933-)
The Terror *'63*
Spider Baby *'64*
Portrait in Terror *'66*
Track of the Vampire *'66*
Pit Stop *'67*
The Fear Chamber *'68*
The Big Doll House *'71*
The Big Bird Cage *'72*
Coffy *'73*
Foxy Brown *'74*
The Swinging Cheerleaders *'74*

James Hill (1919-94)
Trial & Error *'62*
Seaside Swingers *'65*
Born Free *'66*
A Study in Terror *'66*
Captain Nemo and the Underwater City *'69*
An Elephant Called Slowly *'69*
Black Beauty *'71*

Jody Hill
The Foot Fist Way *'08*
Observe and Report *'09*

Robert F. 'Bob' Hill (1886-1966)
The Adventures of Tarzan *'21*
Tarzan the Fearless *'33*
The Cyclone Ranger *'35*
Queen of the Jungle *'35*
Blake of Scotland Yard *'36*
A Face in the Fog *'36*
Prison Shadows *'36*
Rogue's Tavern *'36*
Shadow of Chinatown *'36*
Two Minutes to Play *'37*
Flash Gordon: Mars Attacks the World *'39*

Terence Hill (1939-)
Lucky Luke *'94*
Troublemakers *'94*
Doc West *'09*

Tim Hill
Muppets from Space *'99*
Max Keeble's Big Move *'01*
Garfield: A Tail of Two Kitties *'06*
Alvin and the Chipmunks *'07*
Hop *'11*

Walter Hill (1942-)
Hard Times *'75*
The Driver *'78*
The Warriors *'79*
The Long Riders *'80*
Southern Comfort *'81*
48 Hrs. *'82*
Streets of Fire *'84*
Brewster's Millions *'85*
Crossroads *'86*
Extreme Prejudice *'87*
Red Heat *'88*
Johnny Handsome *'89*
Another 48 Hrs. *'90*
Trespass *'92*
Geronimo: An American Legend *'93*
Wild Bill *'95*
Last Man Standing *'96*
Supernova *'99*
Undisputed *'02*
Broken Trail *'06*
Bullet to the Head *'12*
The Assignment *'17*

John Hillcoat (1961-)
The Proposition *'05*
The Road *'09*
Lawless *'12*
Triple 9 *'15*

David Hillenbrand
King Cobra *'98*
Survival Island *'02*
Gamebox 1.0 *'04*
Transylmania *'09*

Scott Hillenbrand
King Cobra *'98*
Survival Island *'02*
Gamebox 1.0 *'04*
Transylmania *'09*

Arthur Hiller (1923-)
The Careless Years *'57*
The Miracle of the White Stallions *'63*
The Wheeler Dealers *'63*
The Americanization of Emily *'64*
Tobruk *'66*
Popi *'69*
Love Story *'70*
The Out-of-Towners *'70*
The Hospital *'71*
Plaza Suite *'71*
Man of La Mancha *'72*
The Man in the Glass Booth *'75*
Silver Streak *'76*
The In-Laws *'79*
Nightwing *'79*
Author! Author! *'82*
Making Love *'82*
Romantic Comedy *'83*
The Lonely Guy *'84*
Teachers *'84*
Outrageous Fortune *'87*
See No Evil, Hear No Evil *'89*
Taking Care of Business *'90*
The Babe *'92*
Married to It *'93*
Carpool *'96*
An Alan Smithee Film: Burn, Hollywood, Burn *'97*

Richard Hilliard
The Lonely Sex *'59*
Psychomania *'63*

William B. Hillman
Double Exposure *'82*
Ragin' Cajun *'90*
Quigley *'03*

Lambert Hillyer (1889-1969)
The Cradle of Courage *'20*
The Toll Gate *'20*
Three Word Brand *'21*
The Shock *'23*
Barbara Frietchie *'24*
Forbidden Trail *'32*
The California Trail *'33*
The Defense Rests *'34*
Dracula's Daughter *'36*
The Invisible Ray *'36*
Flame of the West *'45*

Arthur Hilton (1897-1979)
Return of Jesse James *'50*
Cat Women of the Moon *'53*

Robert Hiltzik
Sleepaway Camp *'83*
Return to Sleepaway Camp *'08*

Gregory Hines (1946-2003)
Bleeding Hearts *'94*
The Red Sneakers *'01*

Bill (William Heinzman) Hinzman (1936-2012)
The Majorettes *'87*
Revenge of the Living Zombies *'88*

Alexander Gregory (Gregory Dark) Hippolyte (1954-)
Carnal Crimes *'91*
Mirror Images *'91*
Animal Instincts *'92*
Secret Games *'92*
Animal Instincts 2 *'94*
Secret Games 3 *'94*
Undercover *'94*
Animal Instincts 3: The Seductress *'95*
Object of Obsession *'95*

Oliver Hirschbiegel (1957-)
The Experiment *'01*
Downfall *'04*
The Invasion *'07*
Five Minutes of Heaven *'09*
Diana *'13*
13 Minutes *'17*

Leslie Hiscott (1894-1968)
Death on the Set *'35*
The Triumph of Sherlock Holmes *'35*
The Lady From Lisbon *'42*
The Time of His Life *'55*

Alfred Hitchcock (1899-1980)
The Pleasure Garden *'25*
The Lodger *'26*
Easy Virtue *'27*
The Ring *'27*
Champagne *'28*
The Farmer's Wife *'28*
Blackmail *'29*
The Manxman *'29*
Juno and the Paycock *'30*
Murder *'30*
Skin Game *'31*
Rich and Strange *'32*
The Man Who Knew Too Much *'34*
The 39 Steps *'35*
Sabotage *'36*
The Secret Agent *'36*
Young and Innocent *'37*
The Lady Vanishes *'38*
Jamaica Inn *'39*
Foreign Correspondent *'40*
Rebecca *'40*
Mr. & Mrs. Smith *'41*
Suspicion *'41*
Saboteur *'42*
Shadow of a Doubt *'43*
Lifeboat *'44*
Spellbound *'45*
Notorious *'46*
The Paradine Case *'47*
Rope *'48*

Reginald (Reggie) Hudlin (1961-)
House Party '90
Boomerang '92
The Great White Hype '96
The Ladies Man '00
Serving Sara '02
Marshall '17

Hugh Hudson (1936-)
Chariots of Fire '81
Greystoke: The Legend of Tarzan, Lord of the Apes '84
Revolution '85
Lost Angels '89
My Life So Far '98
I Dreamed of Africa '00
Finding Altamira '16

Brent Huff (1961-)
Final Justice '94
The Bad Pack '98
100 Mile Rule '02
Treasure Raiders '07
Welcome to Paradise '07
Cat City '08

R. John Hugh (1924-85)
Yellowneck '55
You've Ruined Me, Eddie '58

Albert Hughes (1972-)
Menace II Society '93
Dead Presidents '95
From Hell '01
The Book of Eli '10
Alpha '18

Allen Hughes (1972-)
Menace II Society '93
Dead Presidents '95
From Hell '01
Knights of the South Bronx '05
New York, I Love You '09
The Book of Eli '10
Broken City '13

Bronwen Hughes
Harriet the Spy '96
Forces of Nature '99
Stander '03

Howard Hughes (1905-76)
Hell's Angels '30
The Outlaw '43

John Hughes (1950-2009)
Sixteen Candles '84
The Breakfast Club '85
Weird Science '85
Ferris Bueller's Day Off '86
Planes, Trains & Automobiles '87
She's Having a Baby '88
Uncle Buck '89
Curly Sue '91

Ken Hughes (1922-2001)
The Atomic Man '56
The Long Haul '57
The Trials of Oscar Wilde '60
Of Human Bondage '64
Casino Royale '67
Chitty Chitty Bang Bang '68
Cromwell '70
Internecine Project '73
Oh, Alfie '75
Sextette '78
Night School '81

Patrick Hughes
Red Hill '10
The Expendables 3 '14
The Hitman's Bodyguard '17

Robert C. Hughes
Memorial Valley Massacre '88
Down the Drain '89
St. Patrick: The Irish Legend '00

Terry Hughes
Sunset Limousine '83
The Butcher's Wife '91
Mrs. Santa Claus '96

H. Bruce Humberstone (1903-84)
The Crooked Circle '32
If I Had a Million '32
Strangers of the Evening '32
Charlie Chan at the Opera '36
Charlie Chan at the Race Track '36
Charlie Chan in Honolulu '38
Rascals '38
I Wake Up Screaming '41
Tall, Dark and Handsome '41
Iceland '42
To the Shores of Tripoli '42
Hello, Frisco, Hello '43
Pin-Up Girl '44
Wonder Man '45
Three Little Girls In Blue '46
Happy Go Lovely '51
She's Working Her Way Through College '52
The Desert Song '53
Ten Wanted Men '54
Tarzan's Hidden Jungle '55
Tarzan and the Lost Safari '57
Tarzan and the Trappers '58
Tarzan's Fight for Life '58

Sammo Hung (1952-)
Spooky Encounters '80
The Prodigal Son '82
Heart of Dragon '85
The Millionaire's Express '86
Eastern Condors '87
Dragons Forever '88
Mr. Nice Guy '98
Three Kingdoms: Resurrection of the Dragon '08

Tran Anh Hung (1963-)
The Scent of Green Papaya '93
Cyclo '95
The Vertical Ray of the Sun '00

Tom Hunsinger (1952-)
Lawless Heart '01
Sparkle '07

Bonnie Hunt (1961-)
Return to Me '00
Call Me Crazy '13

Courtney Hunt
Frozen River '08
The Whole Truth '16

Jeffrey G. Hunt
Satanic '15
Saving Zoe '19

Peter H. Hunt (1938-)
1776 '72
It Came Upon a Midnight Clear '84
The Adventures of Huckleberry Finn '85

Peter R. Hunt (1925-2002)
On Her Majesty's Secret Service '69
Gulliver's Travels '77
The Beasts Are On the Streets '78
Death Hunt '81
The Last Days of Pompeii '84
Assassination '87

Neil Hunter
Lawless Heart '01
Sparkle '07

Simon Hunter (1969-)
Dead of Night '99
Mutant Chronicles '08
Edie '19

Tim Hunter (1947-)
Tex '82
Sylvester '85
River's Edge '87
The Saint of Fort Washington '93
The Maker '98
Video Voyeur: The Susan Wilson Story '02
The Far Side of Jericho '06
Kings of South Beach '07

Lawrence Huntington (1900-68)
The Upturned Glass '47
Eight Witnesses '54

Nick Hurran (1959-)
Virtual Sexuality '99
Undertaking Betty '02
Little Black Book '04
It's a Boy Girl Thing '06
The Prisoner '09

Andy Hurst
Are You Scared? '06
Wild Things: Foursome '10

Brian Desmond Hurst (1900-86)
A Christmas Carol '51
Malta Story '53
Simba '55

Michael Hurst (1973-)
New Blood '99
House of the Dead 2: Dead Aim '05
Pumpkinhead 4: Blood Feud '07

Harry Hurwitz (1938-95)
The Projectionist '71
Rosebud Beach Hotel '85

Jon Hurwitz (1977-)
Harold & Kumar Escape from Guantanamo Bay '08
American Reunion '12

Waris Hussein (1938-)
Quackser Fortune Has a Cousin in the Bronx '70
Melody '71
Divorce His, Divorce Hers '72
The Possession of Joel Delaney '72
And Baby Makes Six '79
Edward and Mrs. Simpson '80
The Henderson Monster '80
Callie and Son '81
Princess Daisy '83
Arch of Triumph '85
When the Bough Breaks '86
Onassis '88
The Shell Seekers '89

Anjelica Huston (1951-)
Bastard out of Carolina '96
Agnes Browne '99

Jimmy Huston
Final Exam '81
My Best Friend Is a Vampire '88

John Huston (1906-87)
Dr. Ehrlich's Magic Bullet '40
The Maltese Falcon '41
Across the Pacific '42
In This Our Life '42
Key Largo '48
Treasure of the Sierra Madre '48
The Asphalt Jungle '50
The African Queen '51
The Red Badge of Courage '51
Moulin Rouge '52
Beat the Devil '53
Moby Dick '56
Heaven Knows, Mr. Allison '57
Barbarian and the Geisha '58
The Unforgiven '60
The Misfits '61
The List of Adrian Messenger '63
The Night of the Iguana '64
The Bible '66
Casino Royale '67
Reflections in a Golden Eye '67
Sinful Davey '69
The Kremlin Letter '70
Fat City '72
Life & Times of Judge Roy Bean '72
Mackintosh Man '73
The Man Who Would Be King '75
Wise Blood '79
Phobia '80
Victory '81
Annie '82
Under the Volcano '84
Prizzi's Honor '85
The Dead '87

Charles (Hutchison) Hutchinson (1879-1949)
Lightning Hutch '26
Desert Guns '36
Night Cargo '36
Children of the Wild '37

Clint Hutchison
Terror Tract '00
Conjurer '08

Brian G. Hutton (1935-)
Where Eagles Dare '68
Kelly's Heroes '70
Night Watch '72
X, Y & Zee '72
The First Deadly Sin '80
High Road to China '83

Willard Huyck (1945-)
Messiah of Evil '74
French Postcards '79
Best Defense '84
Howard the Duck '86

John Hyams
Dragon Eyes '12
Universal Soldier: Day of Reckoning '12

Peter Hyams (1943-)
Busting '74
Our Time '74
Capricorn One '78
Hanover Street '79
Outland '81
The Star Chamber '83
2010: The Year We Make Contact '84
Running Scared '86
The Presidio '88
Narrow Margin '90
Stay Tuned '92
Timecop '94
Sudden Death '95
The Relic '96
End of Days '99
The Musketeer '01
A Sound of Thunder '05
Beyond a Reasonable Doubt '09
Enemies Closer '14

Andrew Hyatt
The Frozen '12
Paul, Apostle of Christ '18

Nicholas Hytner (1957-)
The Madness of King George '94
The Crucible '96
The Object of My Affection '98
Center Stage '00
The History Boys '06
The Lady in the Van '15

Armando Iannucci
In the Loop '09
The Death of Stalin '17

Juan Ibanez (1938-2000)
Dance of Death '68
The Fear Chamber '68

Leon Ichaso (1948-)
Power, Passion & Murder '83
Crossover Dreams '85
Sugar Hill '94
Bitter Sugar '96
Free of Eden '98
Hendrix '00
Pinero '01
El Cantante '06
Left to Die: The Sandra and Tammi Chase Story '12

Kon Ichikawa (1915-2008)
The Burmese Harp '56
Fires on the Plain '59
An Actor's Revenge '63
Tokyo Olympiad '66
Phoenix '78
The Makioka Sisters '83

Miguel Iglesias
Green Inferno '72
Kilma, Queen of the Amazons '75

Noboru Iguchi
RoboGeisha '06
The Machine Girl '07
The ABCs of Death '12

Toshiharu Ikeda
Evil Dead Trap '88
Beautiful Beast '95

Kazuo Ikehiro (1928-)
Zatoichi: Master Ichi and a Chest of Gold '64
Zatoichi: Zatoichi's Flashing Sword '64

Mark Illsley (1958-)
Happy, Texas '99
Bookies '03

Kwon Taek Im (1936-)
Chunhyang '00
Chihwaseon: Painted Fire '02

Sang-soo Im (1962-)
The Housemaid '10
The Taste of Money '12
Rio, I Love You '14

Tadashi Imai
Bushido: The Cruel Code of the Samurai '63
Revenge '64

Shohei Imamura (1926-2006)
The Insect Woman '63
The Pornographers '66
Vengeance Is Mine '79
The Ballad of Narayama '83
Black Rain '88
The Eel '96
Dr. Akagi '98

Hiroshi Inagaki (1905-80)
Samurai 1: Musashi Miyamoto '55
Samurai 2: Duel at Ichijoji Temple '55
Samurai 3: Duel at Ganryu Island '56
Rikisha-Man '58

Alejandro Gonzalez Inarritu (1963-)
Amores Perros '00
21 Grams '03
Babel '06
Biutiful '10
Birdman, or (The Unexpected Virtue of Ignorance) '14
The Revenant '15

Raul Inglis
Vice '08
Takedown '10

Rex Ingram (1892-1950)
The Four Horsemen of the Apocalypse '21
The Prisoner of Zenda '22
Scaramouche '23
The Magician '26

Terry Ingram
The Stranger Game '06
Ties That Bind '06
To Have and to Hold '06
A Trick of the Mind '06
All the Good Ones Are Married '07
Nightmare '07
Angel and the Badman '09
Phantom Racer '09
Christmas Lodge '11
Chupacabra vs. the Alamo '13

Boris Ingster (1904-78)
The Judge Steps Out '49
Southside 1-1000 '50

J. Christian Ingvordsen (1957-)
Firehouse '87
Hangmen '87
Mob War '88
Search and Destroy '88
Airboss '97
Blood Relic '05

Dan Ireland (1958-2016)
The Whole Wide World '96
The Velocity of Gary '98
Passionada '02
Mrs. Palfrey at the Claremont '05
Jolene '08
Living Proof '08

O'Dale Ireland (1928-81)
Date Bait '60
High School Caesar '60

Matthew Irmas
When the Party's Over '91
Edie & Pen '95
Sleep Easy, Hutch Rimes '00

John Irvin (1940-)
Tinker, Tailor, Soldier, Spy '80
The Dogs of War '81
Ghost Story '81
Champions '84
Raw Deal '86
Hamburger Hill '87
Next of Kin '89
Robin Hood '91
Firefall '94
Widow's Peak '94
A Month by the Lake '95
City of Industry '96
When Trumpets Fade '98
Noah's Ark '99
Shiner '00
The Fourth Angel '01
The Boys and Girl From County Clare '03
Dot.Kill '05
The Moon & the Stars '07
Hemingway's Garden of Eden '08

Sam Irvin (1956-)
Guilty as Charged '92
Oblivion '94
Backlash: Oblivion 2 '95
Elvira's Haunted Hills '02
Too Cool for Christmas '04

Oliver Irving
How to Be '08
Ghost Team '16

Richard Irving (1917-90)
Columbo: Prescription Murder '67
The Jesse Owens Story '84

James Isaac (1960-)
The Horror Show '89
Jason X '01
Skinwalkers '07

Antonio (Isasi-Isasmendi) Isasi (1927-)
They Came to Rob Las Vegas '68
Ricco '74

Robert Iscove (1947-)
Shattered Dreams '90
Mission of the Shark '91
Cinderella '97
She's All That '99
Boys and Girls '00
Firestarter 2: Rekindled '02
From Justin to Kelly '03
Love N' Dancing '09
Spectacular '09
On Strike for Christmas '10
Smart Cookies '13

Sleeper Cell *'05*
The Sentinel *'06*
Juanita *'19*

Craig Johnson
The Skeleton Twins *'14*
Wilson *'17*

Emory Johnson (1894-1960)
West-Bound Limited *'23*
The Non-Stop Flight *'26*

Jesse Johnson (1971-)
Pit Fighter *'05*
Alien Agent *'07*
The Butcher *'07*
The Last Sentinel *'07*
The Fifth Commandment *'08*
Green Street Hooligans 2 *'09*
The Hitman Diaries *'09*
The Package *'12*

Jesse V. Johnson
Avengement *'19*
Triple Threat *'19*

John Johnson
Alucard *'08*
Skeleton Key 2: 667, the Neighbor of the Beast *'08*

Kenneth Johnson (1942-)
The Incredible Hulk *'77*
Senior Trip *'81*
V *'83*
Hot Pursuit *'84*
Short Circuit 2 *'88*
Alien Nation: Dark Horizon *'94*
Alien Nation: Body and Soul *'95*
Alien Nation: Millennium *'96*
Alien Nation: The Enemy Within *'96*
Steel *'97*

Lamont Johnson (1922-2010)
A Covenant With Death *'67*
Kona Coast *'68*
McKenzie Break *'70*
A Gunfight *'71*
The Groundstar Conspiracy *'72*
The Last American Hero *'73*
Lipstick *'76*
One on One *'77*
Spacehunter: Adventures in the Forbidden Zone *'83*
Wallenberg: A Hero's Story *'85*
Unnatural Causes *'86*
Gore Vidal's Lincoln *'88*
Escape *'90*

Liza Johnson
Return *'11*
Hateship Loveship *'13*
Elvis & Nixon *'16*

Mark Steven Johnson (1964-)
Simon Birch *'98*
Daredevil *'03*
Ghost Rider *'07*
When in Rome *'09*
Killing Season *'13*
Finding Steve McQueen *'19*

Niall Johnson
The Ghost of Greville Lodge *'00*
Keeping Mum *'05*

Nunnally Johnson (1897-1977)
Black Widow *'54*
Night People *'54*
The Man in the Gray Flannel Suit *'56*
Oh, Men! Oh, Women! *'57*
The Three Faces of Eve *'57*

Patrick Read Johnson (1964-)
Spaced Invaders *'90*
Baby's Day Out *'94*
Angus *'95*
When Good Ghouls Go Bad *'01*

Raymond K. Johnson (1895-1964)
See Bernard B. Ray

Rian Johnson (1973-)
Brick *'06*
The Brothers Bloom *'09*
Looper *'12*
Star Wars: The Last Jedi *'17*
Knives Out *'19*

Susan Johnson
Carrie Pilby *'17*
To All the Boys I've Loved Before *'18*

Tim Johnson
Antz *'98*
Sinbad: Legend of the Seven Seas *'03*
Over the Hedge *'06*
Home *'15*

Joe Johnston (1950-)
Honey, I Shrunk the Kids *'89*
The Rocketeer *'91*
The Pagemaster *'94*
Jumanji *'95*
October Sky *'99*
Jurassic Park 3 *'01*
Hidalgo *'04*
The Wolfman *'09*
Captain America: The First Avenger *'11*
The Nutcracker and the Four Realms *'18*

Thomas Johnston
Jerome *'98*
About Fifty *'11*

Angelina Jolie (1975-)
In the Land of Blood and Honey *'11*
Unbroken *'14*
By the Sea *'15*
First They Killed My Father *'17*

Amy Holden Jones (1953-)
Slumber Party Massacre *'82*
Love Letters *'83*
Maid to Order *'87*
The Rich Man's Wife *'96*

Chuck Jones (1912-2002)
Phantom Tollbooth *'69*
Looney Looney Looney Bugs Bunny Movie *'81*

David Hugh Jones (1934-)
84 Charing Cross Road *'86*
The Christmas Wife *'88*
Jacknife *'89*
Look Back in Anger *'89*
The Trial *'93*
Is There Life Out There? *'94*
The Confession *'98*
A Christmas Carol *'99*

Duncan Jones
Moon *'09*
Source Code *'11*
Warcraft *'16*

F. Richard Jones (1894-1930)
Extra Girl *'23*
The Gaucho *'27*

Gary Jones
Mosquito *'95*
Spiders *'00*
Crocodile 2: Death Swamp *'01*
Ghouls *'07*
Boogeyman 3 *'08*
Ballistica *'10*

Harmon Jones (1911-72)
As Young As You Feel *'51*
Bloodhounds of Broadway *'52*
Pride of St. Louis *'52*
City of Bad Men *'53*
The Silver Whip *'53*
Princess of the Nile *'54*
Target Zero *'55*
Canyon River *'56*
Don't Worry, We'll Think of a Title *'66*

James Cellan Jones (1931-)
Portrait of a Lady *'67*
The Golden Bowl *'72*
Fortunes of War *'87*
A Little Piece of Sunshine *'90*

Jon Jones
The Debt *'03*
Archangel *'05*
The Secret Life of Mrs. Beeton *'06*
Northanger Abbey *'07*
The Diary of Anne Frank *'08*
Going Postal *'10*
Titanic *'12*

Justin Jones
The Apocalypse *'07*
Invasion of the Pod People *'07*

Kent Jones (1960-)
Hitchcock/Truffaut *'15*
Diane *'18*

Kirk Jones (1963-)
Waking Ned Devine *'98*
Nanny McPhee *'06*
Everybody's Fine *'09*
What to Expect When You're Expecting *'12*
My Big Fat Greek Wedding 2 *'16*

Mark Jones (1953-)
Leprechaun *'93*
Rumpelstiltskin *'96*

Pete Jones
Stolen Summer *'02*
Outing Riley *'04*

Philip Jones (1963-2003)
Cause of Death *'90*
Backflash *'01*
Asylum of the Damned *'03*

Simon Cellan Jones
The Queen's Sister *'05*
Generation Kill *'08*

Terry Jones (1942-2020)
Monty Python and the Holy Grail *'75*
Monty Python's Life of Brian *'79*
Monty Python's The Meaning of Life *'83*
Personal Services *'87*
Erik the Viking *'89*
Mr. Toad's Wild Ride *'96*
Absolutely Anything *'17*

Tommy Lee Jones (1946-)
The Good Old Boys *'95*
The Three Burials of Melquiades Estrada *'05*
The Sunset Limited *'11*
The Homesman *'14*

Spike Jonze (1969-)
Being John Malkovich *'99*
Adaptation *'02*
Where the Wild Things Are *'09*
Her *'13*

Henry Joost
Catfish *'10*
Paranormal Activity 4 *'12*
Nerve *'16*
Viral *'16*

Glenn Jordan (1936-)
Frankenstein *'73*
Picture of Dorian Gray *'74*
One of My Wives Is Missing *'76*
Les Miserables *'78*
Only When I Laugh *'81*
Lois Gibbs and the Love Canal *'82*
Mass Appeal *'84*
Dress Gray *'86*
Promise *'86*
O Pioneers! *'91*
Sarah, Plain and Tall *'91*
Barbarians at the Gate *'93*
To Dance with the White Dog *'93*
My Brother's Keeper *'95*
A Streetcar Named Desire *'95*
Legalese *'98*
The Long Way Home *'98*
Sarah, Plain and Tall: Winter's End *'99*

Gregor Jordan (1967-)
Twisted *'96*
Two Hands *'98*
Buffalo Soldiers *'01*
Ned Kelly *'03*
The Informers *'09*

Kevin Jordan (1974-)
Smiling Fish & Goat on Fire *'99*
Brooklyn Lobster *'05*

Neil Jordan (1950-)
Danny Boy *'82*
The Company of Wolves *'85*
Mona Lisa *'86*
High Spirits *'88*
We're No Angels *'89*
The Crying Game *'92*
Interview with the Vampire *'94*
Michael Collins *'96*
The Butcher Boy *'97*
In Dreams *'98*
The End of the Affair *'99*
The Good Thief *'03*
Breakfast on Pluto *'05*
The Brave One *'07*
Ondine *'09*
Byzantium *'12*
Greta *'18*

Jon Jost (1943-)
Sure Fire *'90*
All the Vermeers in New York *'91*
The Bed You Sleep In *'93*

C. Courtney Joyner
Trancers 3: Deth Lives *'92*
Lurking Fear *'94*

Mike Judge (1962-)
Beavis and Butt-Head Do America *'96*
Office Space *'98*
Idiocracy *'06*
Extract *'09*

Rupert Julian (1889-1943)
Merry-Go-Round *'23*
The Phantom of the Opera *'25*
Yankee Clipper *'27*

Miranda July (1974-)
Me and You and Everyone We Know *'05*
The Future *'11*

Brian Jun (1979-)
Steel City *'06*
Joint Body *'11*

Gil Junger (1954-)
Ten Things I Hate about You *'99*
Black Knight *'01*
If Only *'04*
My Fake Fiance *'09*
Beauty & the Briefcase *'10*
Christmas Cupid *'10*
Teen Spirit *'11*
Think Like a Dog *'20*

Nathan 'Jerry' Juran (1907-2002)
The Black Castle *'52*
Law and Order *'53*
Drums Across the River *'54*
The Crooked Web *'55*
The Brain from Planet Arous *'57*
The Deadly Mantis *'57*
Hellcats of the Navy *'57*
20 Million Miles to Earth *'57*
Attack of the 50 Foot Woman *'58*
Good Day for a Hanging *'58*
The Seventh Voyage of Sinbad *'58*
Jack the Giant Killer *'62*
East of Sudan *'64*
First Men in the Moon *'64*
Land Raiders *'69*

George Kaczender (1933-)
The Girl in Blue *'74*
In Praise of Older Women *'78*
The Agency *'81*
Where Are My Children? *'94*
Vanished *'95*

Jan Kadar (1918-79)
The Shop on Main Street *'65*
The Angel Levine *'70*
Freedom Road *'79*

Jeremy Paul Kagan (1945-)
Katherine *'75*
Heroes *'77*
Scott Joplin *'77*
The Chosen *'81*
The Sting 2 *'83*
The Journey of Natty Gann *'85*
Courage *'86*
Conspiracy: The Trial of the Chicago Eight *'87*
Descending Angel *'90*
Roswell: The U.F.O. Cover-Up *'94*
Bobbie's Girl *'02*
Crown Heights *'02*
Taken *'02*

Cedric Kahn (1966-)
L'Ennui *'98*
Red Lights *'04*

Harvey Kahn
Water's Edge *'03*
The Deal *'05*
Trophy Wife *'06*

Joseph Kahn (1972-)
Torque *'04*
Detention *'11*
Bodied *'17*

Richard C. Kahn (1897-1960)
Son of Ingagi *'40*
Guns Don't Argue *'57*

Chen Kaige (1952-)
Life on a String *'90*
Farewell My Concubine *'93*
Temptress Moon *'96*
The Emperor and the Assassin *'99*
Killing Me Softly *'01*
Together *'02*
The Promise *'05*

Mikhail Kalatozov (1903-73)
The Cranes Are Flying *'57*
I Am Cuba *'64*
Red Tent *'69*

Tom Kalin
Swoon *'91*
Savage Grace *'07*

Scott Kalvert (1964-2014)
The Basketball Diaries *'95*
Deuces Wild *'02*

Deborah Kampmeier (1964-)
Virgin *'03*
Hounddog *'08*

Joseph Kane (1897-1975)
Fighting Marines *'36*
Born to Be Wild *'38*
Hands Across the Border *'43*
Idaho *'43*
Texas Legionnaires *'43*
Dakota *'45*
Flame of the Barbary Coast *'45*
Hoodlum Empire *'52*

Rolfe Kanefsky (1969-)
There's Nothing out There *'90*
The Hazing *'04*

Shusuke (Shu) Kaneko (1955-)
Godzilla, Mothra, and King Ghidorah: Giant Monsters All-Out Attack *'01*
Azumi 2 *'05*
Death Note 2: The Last Name *'07*

Jeff Kanew (1944-)
Eddie Macon's Run *'83*
Revenge of the Nerds *'84*
Gotcha! *'85*
Tough Guys *'86*
Troop Beverly Hills *'89*
V.I. Warshawski *'91*
National Lampoon's Adam & Eve *'05*
National Lampoon's The Legend of Awesomest Maximus *'11*

Woo-suk Kang
Public Enemy *'02*
Another Public Enemy *'05*

Young Man Kang
Cupid's Mistake *'01*
The Last Eve *'05*

Charles Kanganis
Chance *'89*
Deadly Breed *'89*
Sinners *'89*
A Time to Die *'91*
No Escape, No Return *'93*
3 Ninjas Kick Back *'94*
Race the Sun *'96*
Dennis the Menace Strikes Again *'98*
K-911 *'99*
Impulse *'08*

Marek Kanievska (1952-)
Another Country *'84*
Less Than Zero *'87*
Where the Money Is *'00*
A Different Loyalty *'04*

Garson Kanin (1912-99)
A Man to Remember *'38*
Next Time I Marry *'38*
Bachelor Mother *'39*
My Favorite Wife *'40*
Tom, Dick, and Harry *'41*
Where It's At *'69*

Ellie Kanner
Crazylove *'05*
Wake *'09*
Authors Anonymous *'14*

Hal Kanter (1918-2011)
Loving You *'57*
For the Love of It *'80*

Kaos
Ballistic: Ecks *vs.* Sever *'02*
Zero Tolerance *'15*

Wych Kaosayananda
See Kaos

Asif Kapadia (1972-)
The Warrior *'01*
The Return *'06*
Far North *'07*
Senna *'11*
Amy *'15*
Diego Maradona *'19*

Deborah Kaplan
Can't Hardly Wait *'98*
Josie and the Pussycats *'01*

Jonathan Kaplan (1947-)
Night Call Nurses *'72*
The Slams *'73*
The Student Teachers *'73*
Truck Turner *'74*
White Line Fever *'75*
Mr. Billion *'77*
Over the Edge *'79*
Heart Like a Wheel *'83*
Girls of the White Orchid *'85*

Michael Keusch (1955-)
Lena's Holiday *'90*
Anything for Love *'93*
Huck and the King of Hearts *'93*
Just One of the Girls *'93*
Attack Force *'06*
Shadow Man *'06*

Franck Khalfoun
P2 *'07*
Wrong Turn at Tahoe *'09*
Maniac *'12*
Amityville: The Awakening *'17*
Prey *'19*

Callie Khouri (1957-)
Divine Secrets of the Ya-Ya Sisterhood *'02*
Mad Money *'08*

Abbas Kiarostami (1940-)
Where Is My Friend's House? *'87*
Life and Nothing More . . . *'92*
The Taste of Cherry *'96*
Shirin *'09*
Certified Copy *'10*
Like Someone in Love *'13*

Dylan Kidd (1969-)
Roger Dodger *'02*
P.S. *'04*
Get a Job *'16*

Beeban Kidron (1961-)
Oranges Are Not the Only Fruit *'89*
Used People *'92*
Shades of Fear *'93*
To Wong Foo, Thanks for Everything, Julie Newmar *'95*
Swept from the Sea *'97*
Bridget Jones: The Edge of Reason *'04*

Fritz Kiersch (1951-)
Children of the Corn *'84*
Tuff Turf *'85*
Winners Take All *'87*
Gor *'88*
Under the Boardwalk *'89*
Into the Sun *'92*
Shattered Image *'93*

Krzysztof Kieslowski (1941-96)
Camera Buff *'79*
No End *'84*
The Decalogue *'88*
The Double Life of Veronique *'91*
Trois Couleurs: Bleu *'93*
Trois Couleurs: Blanc *'94*
Trois Couleurs: Rouge *'94*

Gerard Kikoine (1946-)
Dragonard *'88*
Buried Alive *'89*
Edge of Sanity *'89*

Edward Killy (1903-81)
Seven Keys to Baldpate *'35*
Murder On a Bridle Path *'36*
Along the Rio Grande *'41*
West of the Pecos *'45*

Clare Kilner
Janice Beard *'99*
How to Deal *'03*
The Wedding Date *'05*
American Virgin *'09*

Jee-woon Kim (1964-)
The Good, the Bad, the Weird *'08*
I Saw the Devil *'10*
The Last Stand *'13*
The Age of Shadows *'16*

Ji-woon Kim
The Quiet Family *'98*
The Foul King *'00*

Ki-Duk Kim
The Isle *'01*
Samaritan Girl *'04*
Time *'06*
Moebius *'13*
Pieta *'13*

So Yong Kim
Treeless Mountain *'08*
Lovesong *'17*

Bruce Kimmel (1947-)
The First Nudie Musical *'75*
Spaceship *'81*

Anthony Kimmins (1910-62)
Mine Own Executioner *'47*
Captain's Paradise *'53*

Tim Kincaid (1952-)
Bad Girls Dormitory *'84*
Breeders *'86*
Mutant Hunt *'87*
Necropolis *'87*
Riot on 42nd Street *'87*
Maximum Thrust *'88*
The Occultist *'89*

Burton King (1877-1944)
The Houdini Serial *'20*
The Adorable Cheat *'28*

George King (1899-1966)
Matinee Idol *'33*
The Crimes of Stephen Hawke *'36*
Demon Barber of Fleet Street *'36*
Ticket of Leave Man *'37*
The Hooded Terror *'38*
Sexton Blake and the Hooded Terror *'38*
The Case of the Frightened Lady *'39*
Crimes at the Dark House *'39*
The Face at the Window *'39*
Candlelight in Algeria *'44*

Henry King (1888-1982)
Tol'able David *'21*
The White Sister *'23*
Romola *'25*
The Winning of Barbara Worth *'26*
Hell Harbor *'30*
Marie Galante *'34*
Lloyds of London *'36*
Ramona *'36*
In Old Chicago *'37*
Alexander's Ragtime Band *'38*
Jesse James *'39*
Chad Hanna *'40*
Remember the Day *'41*
A Yank in the R.A.F. *'41*
The Black Swan *'42*
The Song of Bernadette *'43*
Wilson *'44*
Captain from Castile *'47*
Deep Waters *'48*
Prince of Foxes *'49*
Twelve o'Clock High *'49*
The Gunfighter *'50*
David and Bathsheba *'51*
I'd Climb the Highest Mountain *'51*
The Snows of Kilimanjaro *'52*
King of the Khyber Rifles *'53*
Love Is a Many-Splendored Thing *'55*
Untamed *'55*
Carousel *'56*
The Sun Also Rises *'57*
The Bravados *'58*
Beloved Infidel *'59*
Tender Is the Night *'62*

Jeff King
Kill Switch *'08*
Ruslan *'09*

Louis King (1898-1962)
Charlie Chan in Egypt *'35*
Bulldog Drummond Comes Back *'37*
Thunder In the Valley *'47*
Powder River *'53*
Massacre *'56*

Michael Patrick King
Sex and the City: The Movie *'08*
Sex and the City 2 *'10*

Paul King
Bunny and the Bull *'09*
Paddington *'14*
Paddington 2 *'17*

Rick King
Hard Choices *'84*
Hot Shot *'86*
The Killing Time *'87*
Prayer of the Rollerboys *'91*
Kickboxer 3: The Art of War *'92*
Quick *'93*
Terminal Justice: Cybertech P.D. *'95*
Road Ends *'98*

Robert Lee King
Boys Life *'94*
Psycho Beach Party *'00*
Bad Actress *'11*

Zalman King (1942-2012)
Two Moon Junction *'88*
Wildfire *'88*
Wild Orchid *'90*
Red Shoe Diaries *'92*
Red Shoe Diaries 2: Double Dare *'92*
Wild Orchid 2: Two Shades of Blue *'92*
Red Shoe Diaries 3: Another Woman's Lipstick *'93*
Red Shoe Diaries 4: Auto Erotica *'93*
Delta of Venus *'95*
Red Shoe Diaries: Four on the Floor *'96*
Red Shoe Diaries: Strip Poker *'96*
In God's Hands *'98*
Red Shoe Diaries: Luscious Lola *'00*
Red Shoe Diaries: Swimming Naked *'00*

Jack Kinney (1909-92)
Fun & Fancy Free *'47*
Melody Time *'48*
1001 Arabian Nights *'59*

Keisuke Kinoshita (1912-98)
Twenty-Four Eyes *'54*
The Ballad of Narayama *'58*

Robert Kirbyson
Snowmen *'10*
Red Line *'13*

Kazuaki Kiriya
Casshern *'04*
Black House *'07*
Last Knights *'15*

Brian Kirk (1968-)
Middletown *'06*
My Boy Jack *'07*
Great Expectations *'11*
21 Bridges *'19*

Tim Kirkman (1966-)
Loggerheads *'05*
Lazy Eye *'16*

Karey Kirkpatrick
Over the Hedge *'06*
Imagine That *'09*
Smallfoot *'18*

Ryuhei Kitamura
Versus *'00*
Alive *'02*
Azumi *'03*
Godzilla: Final Wars *'04*
The Midnight Meat Train *'08*
Nightmare Cinema *'19*

Takeshi 'Beat' Kitano (1947-)
Violent Cop *'89*
Boiling Point *'90*
A Scene at Sea *'92*
Sonatine *'96*
Fireworks *'97*
Kikujiro *'99*
Brother *'00*
Dolls *'02*
Zatoichi *'03*
Outrage *'10*

Martin Kitrosser
Silent Night, Deadly Night 5: The Toymaker *'91*
Daddy's Girl *'96*
The Fiance *'96*

Robert J. Kizer (1952-)
Hell Comes to Frogtown *'88*
Death Ring *'93*

Robert Klane (1941-)
Thank God It's Friday *'78*
Weekend at Bernie's 2 *'93*

Cedric Klapisch (1961-)
Un Air de Famille *'96*
L'Auberge Espagnole *'02*
Russian Dolls *'05*
Paris *'08*
My Piece of the Pie *'11*
Chinese Puzzle *'13*

Josh Klausner
The 4th Floor *'99*
Date Night *'10*

Randal Kleiser (1946-)
The Boy in the Plastic Bubble *'76*
The Gathering *'77*
Grease *'78*
The Blue Lagoon *'80*
Summer Lovers *'82*
Grandview U.S.A. *'84*
Flight of the Navigator *'86*
Big Top Pee-wee *'88*
Getting It Right *'89*
White Fang *'91*
Honey, I Blew Up the Kid *'92*
It's My Party *'95*
Shadow of Doubt *'98*

Walter Klenhard
Disappearance *'02*
My Neighbor's Keeper *'07*

Max Kleven (1933-)
Ruckus *'81*
Deadly Stranger *'88*
Bail Out *'90*
Fugitive Champion *'99*

Elem Klimov (1933-2003)
Come and See *'85*
Rasputin *'85*

Leon Klimovsky (1907-96)
Commando Attack *'67*
The Werewolf *vs.* the Vampire Woman *'70*
Dr. Jekyll and the Wolfman *'71*
Vengeance of the Zombies *'72*
Orgy of the Vampires *'73*
The Devil's Possessed *'74*

Herbert Kline (1909-99)
The Kid From Cleveland *'49*
The Fighter *'52*

Werner Klingler (1903-72)
Secret of the Black Trunk *'62*
Testament of Dr. Mabuse *'62*

Glenn Klinker
Dark Justice *'00*
The Nickel Children *'05*

Dan Klores
The Boys of 2nd Street Park *'03*
Crazy Love *'07*

Nicolas Klotz
The Bengali Night *'88*
Heartbeat Detector *'07*

Steve Kloves (1960-)
The Fabulous Baker Boys *'89*
Flesh and Bone *'93*

Brian Knappenberger
We Are Legion: The Story of the Hacktivists *'12*
The Internet's Own Boy: The Story of Aaron Swartz *'14*

Joe Knee
Cult *'07*
Dragon Wasps *'12*

Steven Knight (1959-)
Locke *'13*
Redemption *'13*
Serenity *'19*

Travis Knight
Kubo and the Two Strings *'16*
Bumblebee *'18*

Robert Knights (1942-)
Ebony Tower *'86*
The Dawning *'88*

Edwin H. Knopf (1899-1982)
The Light of Western Stars *'30*
The Law and the Lady *'51*

Bernard Knowles (1900-75)
The Magic Bow *'47*
Norman Conquest *'53*
Murder on Approval *'56*
Frozen Alive *'64*

Michael Knowles
Room 314 *'07*
The Trouble With Bliss *'11*

Roy Knyrim
Night Skies *'07*
Death Racers *'08*

Masaki Kobayashi (1916-96)
The Human Condition: No Greater Love *'58*
The Human Condition: Road to Eternity *'59*
The Human Condition: A Soldier's Prayer *'61*
Harakiri *'62*
Kwaidan *'64*
Samurai Rebellion *'67*

Chris Koch
Snow Day *'00*
A Guy Thing *'03*

Howard W. Koch (1916-2001)
Big House, U.S.A. *'55*
Girl in Black Stockings *'57*
Untamed Youth *'57*
Andy Hardy Comes Home *'58*
Frankenstein 1970 *'58*
Violent Road *'58*
Born Reckless *'59*
The Last Mile *'59*
Badge 373 *'73*

David Koepp (1964-)
The Trigger Effect *'96*
Stir of Echoes *'99*
Secret Window *'04*
Ghost Town *'08*
Premium Rush *'12*
Mortdecai *'15*
You Should Have Left *'20*

Amos Kollek (1947-)
Forever, Lulu *'87*
Fiona *'98*

Xavier Koller (1944-)
Journey of Hope *'90*
Squanto: A Warrior's Tale *'94*
Cowboy Up *'00*

Kevin Kölsch
Holidays *'16*
Pet Sematary *'19*

Lajos Koltai (1946-)
Fateless *'05*
Evening *'07*

Andrei Konchalovsky (1937-)
Siberiade *'79*
Maria's Lovers *'84*
Runaway Train *'85*
Homer and Eddie *'89*
Tango and Cash *'89*
The Inner Circle *'91*
The Odyssey *'97*
House of Fools *'02*
The Lion in Winter *'03*

James Kondelik
Airplane *vs.* Volcano *'14*
All Hallow's Eve 2 *'15*

Jon Kondelik
Airplane *vs.* Volcano *'14*
All Hallow's Eve 2 *'15*

Jackie Kong (1954-)
The Being *'83*
Night Patrol *'85*
Blood Diner *'87*

Kern Konwiser
Stranded *'06*
Shanghai Kiss *'07*

Chuck Konzelman
The Insatiable *'06*
Unplanned *'19*

Martin Koolhoven
Winter in Wartime *'10*
Brimstone *'17*

Brian Koppelman
Knockaround Guys *'01*
Solitary Man *'10*

Barbara Kopple (1946-)
Harlan County, U.S.A. *'76*
American Dream *'90*
Havoc *'05*
Running From Crazy *'13*
Hot Type: 150 Years of The Nation *'15*

Alexander Korda (1893-1956)
The Squall *'29*
Marius *'31*
The Private Life of Henry VIII *'33*
Private Life of Don Juan *'34*
Rembrandt *'36*
The Thief of Bagdad *'40*
That Hamilton Woman *'41*
Vacation from Marriage *'45*
An Ideal Husband *'47*

Zoltan Korda (1895-1961)
Sanders of the River *'35*
Elephant Boy *'37*
Drums *'38*
The Four Feathers *'39*
The Thief of Bagdad *'40*
The Jungle Book *'42*
Sahara *'43*
Counter-Attack *'45*
Storm Over the Nile *'55*

Hirokazu Koreeda (1962-)
Maborosi *'95*
After Life *'98*
Nobody Knows *'04*
Hana: The Tale of a Reluctant Samurai *'07*
I Wish *'11*
Like Father, Like Son *'13*
Our Little Sister *'16*
After the Storm *'17*
Shoplifters *'18*

Harmony Korine (1974-)
Gummo *'97*
Julien Donkey-boy *'99*
Mister Lonely *'07*
Spring Breakers *'13*
The Beach Bum *'19*

Baltasar Kormakur (1966-)
101 Reykjavik *'00*
The Sea *'02*
A Little Trip to Heaven *'05*
White Night Wedding *'08*
Inhale *'10*
Contraband *'12*
2 Guns *'13*

Everest '15
Adrift '18

Jacob Kornbluth (1972-)
Haiku Tunnel '00
Inequality For All '13

John Korty (1936-)
The People '71
Silence '73
The Autobiography of Miss Jane Pittman '74
Oliver's Story '78
A Christmas Without Snow '80
The Haunting Passion '83
The Ewok Adventure '84
Resting Place '86
Baby Girl Scott '87
Getting Out '94

Dover Kosashvili (1966-)
Late Marriage '01
Anton Chekhov's The Duel '09

Joseph Kosinski (1974-)
Tron: Legacy '10
Oblivion '13
Only the Brave '17

Peter Kosminsky (1956-)
Emily Bronte's Wuthering Heights '92
White Oleander '02

Steven Kostanski
Manborg '11
Father's Day '12
The ABCs of Death 2 '14
The Void '17

Henry Koster (1905-88)
Three Smart Girls '36
100 Men and a Girl '37
The Rage of Paris '38
First Love '39
Three Smart Girls Grow Up '39
Spring Parade '40
It Started with Eve '41
Music For Millions '44
Two Sisters From Boston '46
The Bishop's Wife '47
The Unfinished Dance '47
The Luck of the Irish '48
Come to the Stable '49
The Inspector General '49
Harvey '50
My Blue Heaven '50
Wabash Avenue '50
Elopement '51
Mr. Belvedere Rings the Bell '51
No Highway in the Sky '51
My Cousin Rachel '52
Stars and Stripes Forever '52
The Robe '53
Desiree '54
Good Morning, Miss Dove '55
A Man Called Peter '55
The Virgin Queen '55
D-Day, the Sixth of June '56
The Power and the Prize '56
My Man Godfrey '57
Fraulein '58
The Story of Ruth '60
Flower Drum Song '61
Mr. Hobbs Takes a Vacation '62
Take Her, She's Mine '63
Dear Brigitte '65
The Singing Nun '66

Tom Kotani
The Bermuda Depths '78
The Bushido Blade '80

Ted Kotcheff (1931-)
Tiara Tahiti '62
Outback '71
The Apprenticeship of Duddy Kravitz '74
Billy Two Hats '74
Fun with Dick and Jane '77
Who Is Killing the Great Chefs of Europe? '78
North Dallas Forty '79
First Blood '82
Uncommon Valor '83
Switching Channels '88
Weekend at Bernie's '89
Winter People '89
Folks! '92
Red Shoe Diaries 3: Another Woman's Lipstick '93
Hidden Assassin '94
Family of Cops '95
Red Shoe Diaries 5: Weekend Pass '95

Jim Kouf (1951-)
Disorganized Crime '89
Gang Related '96

Bernard L. Kowalski (1929-2007)
Krakatoa East of Java '69
The Woman Hunter '72
Sssssss '73

Karl Kozak (1964-)
Out of the Black '01
Clawed: The Legend of Sasquatch '05

Lloyd Kramer (1947-)
For One More Day '07
Liz & Dick '12

Stanley Kramer (1913-2001)
Not as a Stranger '55
The Pride and the Passion '57
The Defiant Ones '58
On the Beach '59
Inherit the Wind '60
Judgment at Nuremberg '61
It's a Mad, Mad, Mad, Mad World '63
Ship of Fools '65
Guess Who's Coming to Dinner '67
The Secret of Santa Vittoria '69
R.P.M.* (*Revolutions Per Minute) '70
Bless the Beasts and Children '71
Oklahoma Crude '73
The Domino Principle '77

Wayne Kramer (1965-)
The Cooler '03
Running Scared '06
Crossing Over '09

Tony Krantz
Sublime '07
Otis '08
The Big Bang '11

John Krasinski (1979-)
The Hollars '16
A Quiet Place '18

Norman Krasna (1909-84)
Princess O'Rourke '43
The Big Hangover '50
The Ambassador's Daughter '56

Paul Krasny (1935-2001)
Joe Panther '76
Centennial '78
Terror Among Us '81
Back to Hannibal: The Return of Tom Sawyer and Huckleberry Finn '90
Two Fathers: Justice for the Innocent '94

Ron Krauss (1970-)
Alien Hunter '03
Gimme Shelter '14

Lee Toland Krieger
The Vicious Kind '09
Celeste & Jesse Forever '12
The Age of Adaline '15

John Krish (1923-)
A Wild Affair '63
Decline and Fall...of a Birdwatcher '68

Suri Krishnamma (1961-)
A Respectable Trade '98
MTV's Wuthering Heights '03

Allen Kroeker
Age Old Friends '89
Showdown at Williams Creek '91

Steve Kroschel
Running Free '94
Avalanche '99

Lisa Krueger (1961-)
Manny & Lo '96
Committed '99

Shawn Ku
The American Mall '08
Beautiful Boy '10
A Score to Settle '19

Stanley Kubrick (1928-99)
Killer's Kiss '55
The Killing '56
Paths of Glory '57
Spartacus '60
Lolita '62
Dr. Strangelove, or: How I Learned to Stop Worrying and Love the Bomb '64
2001: A Space Odyssey '68
A Clockwork Orange '71
Barry Lyndon '75
The Shining '80
Full Metal Jacket '87
Eyes Wide Shut '99

Buzz Kulik (1923-99)
The Explosive Generation '61
Warning Shot '67
Villa Rides '68
Riot '69
Brian's Song '71
Pioneer Woman '73
Shamus '73
Bad Ronald '74
Babe! '75
The Lindbergh Kidnapping Case '76
The Hunter '80
Women of Valor '86
Code Name: Dancer '87
Around the World in 80 Days '89

Edward Kull (1886-1946)
The New Adventures of Tarzan '35
Tarzan and the Green Goddess '38

Roger Kumble (1966-)
Cruel Intentions '98
Cruel Intentions 2 '99
The Sweetest Thing '02
Just Friends '05
College Road Trip '08
Furry Vengeance '10

Akira Kurosawa (1910-98)
Sanshiro Sugata '43
No Regrets for Our Youth '46
One Wonderful Sunday '47
Drunken Angel '48
A Quiet Duel '49
Stray Dog '49
Scandal '50
The Idiot '51
Rashomon '51
Ikiru '52
Seven Samurai '54
I Live in Fear '55
The Lower Depths '57
Throne of Blood '57
The Hidden Fortress '58
The Bad Sleep Well '60
Yojimbo '61
High & Low '62
Sanjuro '62
Red Beard '65
Dodes 'ka-den '70
Dersu Uzala '75
Kagemusha '80
Ran '85
Akira Kurosawa's Dreams '90
Rhapsody in August '91

Kiyoshi Kurosawa (1955-)
Cure '97
Pulse '01
Bright Future '03
Tokyo Sonata '09
Creepy '16

Alex Kurtzman (1973-)
People Like Us '12
The Mummy '17

Robert Kurtzman (1964-)
The Demolitionist '95
Wishmaster '97
Deadly Impact '09

Diane Kurys (1948-)
Entre-Nous '83
A Man in Love '87
Love After Love '94
Six Days, Six Nights '94
Children of the Century '99

Justin Kurzel
The Snowtown Murders '12
Macbeth '15
Assassin's Creed '16
True History of the Kelly Gang '20

Karyn Kusama (1968-)
Girlfight '99
Aeon Flux '05
Jennifer's Body '09
The Invitation '16
XX '17
Destroyer '18

Emir Kusturica (1954-)
When Father Was Away on Business '85
Time of the Gypsies '90
Arizona Dream '94
Underground '95

Ken Kwapis (1957-)
The Beniker Gang '83
Sesame Street Presents: Follow That Bird '85
Vibes '88
He Said, She Said '91
Dunston Checks In '95
The Beautician and the Beast '97
The Sisterhood of the Traveling Pants '05
License to Wed '07
He's Just Not That Into You '09
Big Miracle '12
A Walk in the Woods '15

Richard Kwietniowski (1957-)
Love and Death on Long Island '97
Owning Mahowny '03

Paul Kyriazi
Death Machines '76
Omega Cop '90

Gregory La Cava (1892-1952)
Feel My Pulse '28
Big News '29
Symphony of Six Million '32
Gabriel Over the White House '33
Gallant Lady '33
My Man Godfrey '36
Stage Door '37
Fifth Avenue Girl '39
Primrose Path '40
Lady in a Jam '42
Living In a Big Way '47

Steven La Rocque
Samantha '92
Above Suspicion '00

Eriq La Salle (1962-)
Rebound: The Legend of Earl 'The Goat' Manigault '96
Crazy as Hell '02

Nadine Labaki
Caramel '07
Rio, I Love You '14
Capernaum '18

Neil LaBute (1963-)
In the Company of Men '96
Your Friends & Neighbors '98
Nurse Betty '00
Possession '02
The Shape of Things '03
The Wicker Man '06
Lakeview Terrace '08
Death at a Funeral '10
Some Velvet Morning '13

Gregory LaCava (1892-1952)
See Gregory La Cava

Harry Lachman (1886-1975)
Baby, Take a Bow '34
Dante's Inferno '35
Charlie Chan at the Circus '36
Our Relations '36
It Happened in Hollywood '37
Murder over New York '40

Aldo Lado (1934-)
Short Night of Glass Dolls '71
Who Saw Her Die? '72
Night Train Murders '75

John Lafia (1957-2020)
Blue Iguana '88
Child's Play 2 '90
Man's Best Friend '93
The Rats '01

Joachim Lafosse
Private Property '06
Our Children '12

Ron Lagomarsino
Dinner at Eight '89
Running Mates '00
My Sister's Keeper '02
Snowglobe '07

Richard LaGravenese (1959-)
Living Out Loud '98
A Decade Under the Influence '02
Paris, je t'aime '06
Freedom Writers '07
P.S. I Love You '07
Beautiful Creatures '13
The Last Five Years '14

Frank Laloggia (1954-)
Fear No Evil '80
The Lady in White '88
Mother '94

Ringo Lam (1954-)
City on Fire '87
Prison on Fire '87
Prison on Fire 2 '91
Undeclared War '91
Full Contact '92
Twin Dragons '92
Maximum Risk '96
Replicant '01
In Hell '03

Mary Lambert (1951-)
Pet Sematary '89
Pet Sematary 2 '92
Dragstrip Girl '94
The In Crowd '00
Halloweentown 2: Kalabar's Revenge '01
Urban Legends: Bloody Mary '05
The Attic '06
Mega Python Vs. Gatoroid '11

Charles Lamont (1895-1993)
Circumstantial Evidence '35
A Shot in the Dark '35
The Dark Hour '36
Hit the Ice '43
Ma and Pa Kettle '49
Abbott and Costello in the Foreign Legion '50
Ma and Pa Kettle Go to Town '50
Abbott and Costello Meet the Invisible Man '51
Comin' Round the Mountain '51
Abbott and Costello Meet Captain Kidd '52
Abbott and Costello Meet Dr. Jekyll and Mr. Hyde '52
Abbott and Costello Go to Mars '53
Ma and Pa Kettle on Vacation '53
Abbott and Costello Meet the Keystone Kops '54
Ma and Pa Kettle at Home '54
Abbott and Costello Meet the Mummy '55
Francis in the Haunted House '56
The Kettles in the Ozarks '56

Lew Landers (1901-62)
Tailspin Tommy '34
Rustlers of Red Dog '35
Savage Fury '35
Flight from Glory '37
Smashing the Rackets '38
Wagons Westward '40
Ridin' on a Rainbow '41
The Boogie Man Will Get You '42
Canal Zone '42
Return of the Vampire '43
I'm from Arkansas '44
The Enchanted Forest '45
The Mask of Dijjon '46
The Adventures of Gallant Bess '48
Chain Gang '50
Davy Crockett, Indian Scout '50
Jungle Manhunt '51
The Magic Carpet '51
Captain Kidd and the Slave Girl '54

Peter Landesman (1965-)
Parkland '13
Concussion '15
Mark Felt: The Man Who Brought Down the White House '17

James Landis (1926-91)
Stakeout '62
The Sadist '63
Nasty Rabbit '64
Deadwood '65

John Landis (1950-)
Schlock '73
Kentucky Fried Movie '77
National Lampoon's Animal House '78
The Blues Brothers '80
An American Werewolf in London '81
Trading Places '83
Twilight Zone: The Movie '83
Into the Night '85
Spies Like Us '85
Three Amigos '86
Amazon Women on the Moon '87
Coming to America '88
Oscar '91
Innocent Blood '92
Beverly Hills Cop 3 '94
The Stupids '95
Blues Brothers 2000 '98
Dying to Get Rich '98
Burke & Hare '10

Jeffrey Scott Lando (1969-)
Savage Island '03
Insecticidal '05
Decoys: The Second Seduction '07
House of Bones '09
Goblin '10

Christopher Landon (1975-)
Paranormal Activity: The Marked Ones *'14*
Scout's Guide to the Zombie Apocalypse *'15*
Happy Death Day *'17*
Happy Death Day 2U *'19*

Michael Landon (1936-91)
It's Good to Be Alive *'74*
Little House on the Prairie *'74*

Michael Landon, Jr. (1964-)
Love Comes Softly *'03*
Love's Enduring Promise *'04*
Love's Long Journey *'05*
Love's Abiding Joy *'06*
Saving Sarah Cain *'07*
Beverly Lewis' The Shunning *'11*
Beverly Lewis' The Confession *'13*
The Ultimate Life *'13*
When Calls the Heart *'13*

Paul Landres (1912-2001)
Square Dance Jubilee *'51*
Man From God's Country *'58*
Return of Dracula *'58*
Go, Johnny Go! *'59*
Son of a Gunfighter *'65*

Penny Lane
Nuts! *'16*
Hail Satan? *'19*

Eric Laneuville (1952-)
Hard Lessons *'86*
Secret Witness *'88*
Pandora's Clock *'96*
The Client List *'10*

Sidney Lanfield (1898-1972)
One in a Million *'36*
Sing, Baby, Sing *'36*
Thin Ice *'37*
Wake Up and Live *'37*
Always Goodbye *'38*
The Hound of the Baskervilles *'39*
Swanee River *'39*
You'll Never Get Rich *'41*
My Favorite Blonde *'42*
Where There's Life *'47*
Sorrowful Jones *'49*
The Lemon Drop Kid *'51*
Skirts Ahoy! *'52*

Fritz Lang (1890-1976)
Spiders *'18*
Destiny *'21*
Dr. Mabuse, The Gambler *'22*
Kriemhilde's Revenge *'24*
Siegfried *'24*
Metropolis *'26*
Spies *'28*
Woman in the Moon *'29*
M *'31*
Crimes of Dr. Mabuse *'32*
Liliom *'35*
Fury *'36*
You Only Live Once *'37*
You and Me *'38*
Return of Frank James *'40*
Man Hunt *'41*
Western Union *'41*
Hangmen Also Die *'42*
Ministry of Fear *'44*
Woman in the Window *'44*
Scarlet Street *'45*
Cloak and Dagger *'46*
Secret Beyond the Door *'48*
American Guerrilla in the Philippines *'50*
Clash by Night *'52*
Rancho Notorious *'52*
The Big Heat *'53*
The Blue Gardenia *'53*
Human Desire *'54*
Moonfleet *'55*
Beyond a Reasonable Doubt *'56*
While the City Sleeps *'56*
Journey to the Lost City *'58*
The Thousand Eyes of Dr. Mabuse *'60*

Richard Lang
Fantasy Island *'76*
Vegas *'78*
A Change of Seasons *'80*
The Mountain Men *'80*
Kung Fu: The Movie *'86*
Christmas Comes to Willow Creek *'87*
Texas *'94*

Samantha Lang (1967-)
Twisted *'96*
The Well *'97*
The Monkey's Mask *'00*

Walter Lang (1898-1972)
Red Kimono *'25*
No More Orchids *'32*
Hooray for Love *'35*
Love Before Breakfast *'36*
Second Honeymoon *'37*
The Baroness and the Butler *'38*
The Little Princess *'39*
The Blue Bird *'40*
Star Dust *'40*
Moon over Miami *'41*
Week-End in Havana *'41*
Coney Island *'43*
Greenwich Village *'44*
State Fair *'45*
Claudia and David *'46*
Mother Wore Tights *'47*
Sitting Pretty *'48*
Cheaper by the Dozen *'50*
The Jackpot *'50*
With a Song in My Heart *'52*
There's No Business Like Show Business *'54*
The King and I *'56*
Desk Set *'57*
Can-Can *'60*
The Marriage-Go-Round *'61*
Snow White and the Three Stooges *'61*

Michael Lange
Intern *'00*
My Future Boyfriend *'11*

Noel Langley (1911-80)
The Pickwick Papers *'54*
The Adventures of Sadie *'55*
Svengali *'55*
The Search for Bridey Murphy *'56*

Simon Langton (1941-)
The Duchess of Duke Street *'78*
Love for Lydia *'79*
Therese Raquin *'80*
Danger UXB *'81*
I Remember Nelson *'82*
Smiley's People *'82*
The Whistle Blower *'87*
Catherine Cookson's The Cinder Path *'94*
Pride and Prejudice *'95*

Douglas Langway
Raising Heroes *'97*
BearCity *'10*

Lawrence Lanoff
Miami Hustle *'95*
The Chosen One: Legend of the Raven *'98*

Yelena Lanskaya
Hidden Places *'06*
Hybrid *'07*
The Santa Incident *'10*

Yorgos Lanthimos
Dogtooth *'09*
The Lobster *'16*
The Killing of a Sacred Deer *'17*
The Favourite *'18*

Anthony M. Lanza
The Glory Stompers *'67*
The Incredible Two-Headed Transplant *'71*

Claude Lanzmann (1925-2018)
Shoah *'85*
The Last of the Unjust *'13*

James Lapine (1949-)
Sunday in the Park with George *'86*
Impromptu *'90*
Life with Mikey *'93*
Earthly Possessions *'99*

Pablo Larrain
No *'12*
The Club *'16*
Jackie *'16*
Neruda *'16*

Sheldon Larry (1949-)
Behind Enemy Lines *'85*
Family of Strangers *'93*
Family of Cops 3 *'98*
Trial by Media *'00*
Recipe for a Perfect Christmas *'05*
Christmas in Paradise *'07*

Eric Lartigau
I Do *'06*
The Big Picture *'10*

John Lasseter (1957-)
Toy Story *'95*
A Bug's Life *'98*
Toy Story 2 *'99*
Cars *'06*
Cars 2 *'11*

Stan Lathan (1945-)
Amazing Grace *'74*
Beat Street *'84*
Go Tell It on the Mountain *'84*

Steve Latshaw (1959-)
Dark Universe *'93*
Biohazard: The Alien Force *'95*
Jack-O *'95*
Death Mask *'98*

David Michael Latt (1966-)
H.G. Wells' War of the Worlds *'05*
Megafault *'09*

Alberto Lattuada (1913-2005)
Variety Lights *'51*
Mafioso *'62*
La Cicada *'83*

Andrew Lau (1960-)
See Wai Keung (Andrew) Lau

Patrick Lau
Invasion: Earth *'98*
The Scarlet Pimpernel *'99*
The Scarlet Pimpernel 2: Mademoiselle Guillotine *'99*

Wai Keung (Andrew) Lau (1960-)
Infernal Affairs *'02*
Infernal Affairs 2 *'03*
Infernal Affairs 3 *'03*
The Flock *'07*
Revenge of the Green Dragons *'14*

Nicholas Laughland
Sirens *'02*
Like Father Like Son *'05*
Under the Greenwood Tree *'05*

Michael Laughlin
Strange Behavior *'81*
Strange Invaders *'83*
Mesmerized *'84*

Tom Laughlin (1931-2013)
Born Losers *'67*
Billy Jack *'71*
The Trial of Billy Jack *'74*
Billy Jack Goes to Washington *'77*

Frank Launder (1907-97)
Two Thousand Women *'44*
I See a Dark Stranger *'46*
Captain Boycott *'47*
The Belles of St. Trinian's *'53*
Geordie *'55*
Blue Murder at St. Trinian's *'56*
The Pure Hell of St. Trinian's *'61*
The Great St. Trinian's Train Robbery *'66*

Georges Lautner (1926-2013)
Monsieur Gangster *'63*
The Great Spy Chase *'64*
The Monocle *'64*
Icy Breasts *'75*
Le Professionnel *'81*
La Cage aux Folles 3: The Wedding *'86*

Arnold Laven (1922-2009)
Vice Squad *'53*
Down Three Dark Streets *'54*
The Rack *'56*
The Monster That Challenged the World *'57*
Rough Night in Jericho *'67*
Sam Whiskey *'69*

Clara Law (1957-)
Autumn Moon *'92*
Erotique *'94*
Temptation of a Monk *'94*
The Goddess of 1967 *'00*

Diarmuid Lawrence (1947-)
Anglo-Saxon Attitudes *'92*
Emma *'97*
Heat of the Sun *'99*
P.D. James: The Murder Room *'04*
Little Dorrit *'08*
South Riding *'11*
The Mystery of Edwin Drood *'12*
The Lady Vanishes *'13*

Francis Lawrence (1971-)
Constantine *'05*
I Am Legend *'07*
Water for Elephants *'11*
The Hunger Games: Catching Fire *'13*
The Hunger Games: Mockingjay--Part 1 *'14*
The Hunger Games: Mockingjay-Part 2 *'15*
Red Sparrow *'18*

John Lawrence (1931-92)
Cycle Psycho *'72*
Savage Abduction *'73*

Marc Lawrence (1959-)
Two Weeks Notice *'02*
Music & Lyrics *'07*
Did You Hear About the Morgans? *'09*
The Rewrite *'15*
Noelle *'19*

Quentin Lawrence
The Crawling Eye *'58*
Cash on Demand *'61*

Ray Lawrence (1948-)
Lantana *'01*
Jindabyne *'06*

Joseph J. Lawson
Age of the Hobbits *'12*
Age of Dinosaurs *'13*

J.F. Lawton (1960-)
Cannibal Women in the Avocado Jungle of Death *'89*
Pizza Man *'91*
The Hunted *'94*

Richard Laxton
Band of Gold *'95*
Poldark *'96*
Invasion: Earth *'98*
An Englishman in New York *'09*
Burton and Taylor *'13*
Effie Gray *'15*

Bart Layton
The Imposter *'12*
American Animals *'18*

Philippe Le Guay
The Women on the Sixth Floor *'10*
Bicycling With Moliere *'13*

Wilford Leach (1929-88)
The Wedding Party *'69*
The Pirates of Penzance *'83*

Philip Leacock (1917-90)
Appointment in London *'53*
The Spanish Gardener *'57*
Take a Giant Step *'59*
13 West Street *'62*
War Lover *'62*
Adam's Woman *'70*
Colditz: Escape of the Birdmen *'71*
Shattered Silence *'71*
Baffled *'72*
Dying Room Only *'73*
Three Sovereigns for Sarah *'85*

David Lean (1908-91)
In Which We Serve *'43*
Blithe Spirit *'45*
Brief Encounter *'46*
Great Expectations *'46*
This Happy Breed *'47*
Oliver Twist *'48*
Madeleine *'50*
The Sound Barrier *'52*
Hobson's Choice *'53*
Summertime *'55*
The Bridge on the River Kwai *'57*
Lawrence of Arabia *'62*
Doctor Zhivago *'65*
Ryan's Daughter *'70*
A Passage to India *'84*

Reginald LeBorg (1902-89)
Dead Man's Eyes *'44*
Great Jesse James Raid *'49*
Bad Blonde *'53*
Sins of Jezebel *'54*
The White Orchid *'54*
The Black Sleep *'56*
The Dalton Girls *'57*
War Drums *'57*
Diary of a Madman *'63*
House of the Black Death *'65*
The Sibling *'72*

Patrice Leconte (1947-)
French Fried Vacation *'79*
Monsieur Hire *'89*
The Hairdresser's Husband *'92*
The Perfume of Yvonne *'94*
Ridicule *'96*
The Girl on the Bridge *'98*
The Widow of Saint-Pierre *'00*
The Man on the Train *'02*
Intimate Strangers *'04*
My Best Friend *'06*
A Promise *'13*

Jacques LeCotier (1921-88)
See Jerry Warren

Mimi Leder (1952-)
The Peacemaker *'97*
Deep Impact *'98*
Pay It Forward *'00*
The Code *'09*
On the Basis of Sex *'18*

Paul Leder (1926-96)
I Dismember Mama *'74*
A*P*E* *'76*
Body Count *'87*
Killing Obsession *'94*

David Ross Lederman (1894-1972)
Phantom of the West *'31*
Tarzan's Revenge *'38*

Key Witness *'47*
The Tanks Are Coming *'51*

Richard Ledes
A Hole in One *'04*
The Caller *'08*

Ang Lee (1954-)
Pushing Hands *'92*
The Wedding Banquet *'93*
Eat Drink Man Woman *'94*
Sense and Sensibility *'95*
The Ice Storm *'97*
Ride with the Devil *'99*
Crouching Tiger, Hidden Dragon *'00*
Hulk *'03*
Brokeback Mountain *'05*
Lust, Caution *'07*
Taking Woodstock *'09*
Life of Pi *'12*
Billy Lynn's Long Halftime Walk *'16*
Gemini Man *'19*

Benson Lee
Miss Monday *'98*
Battle of the Year *'13*

Chang-dong Lee (1954-)
Poetry *'10*
Burning *'18*

Damian Lee (1950-)
Food of the Gods: Part 2 *'88*
Abraxas: Guardian of the Universe *'90*
Ski School *'91*
Street Law *'95*
Moving Target *'96*
Terminal Rush *'96*
Trail of a Serial Killer *'98*
Agent Red *'00*
Hearts of War *'07*
Sacrifice *'11*
A Dark Truth *'12*
A Fighting Man *'14*

Daniel Lee
Black Mask *'96*
The Kumite *'03*
Three Kingdoms: Resurrection of the Dragon *'08*
14 Blades *'14*
Dragon Blade *'15*
The Climbers *'19*

Dennis Lee
Fireflies in the Garden *'08*
Jesus Henry Christ *'12*

Jack Lee (1913-2002)
A Town Like Alice *'56*
Robbery under Arms *'57*
The Captain's Table *'60*

Malcolm Lee (1970-)
The Best Man *'99*
Undercover Brother *'02*
Roll Bounce *'05*
Soul Men *'08*
Welcome Home Roscoe Jenkins *'08*
The Best Man Holiday *'13*
Scary Movie 5 *'13*
Barbershop: The Next Cut *'16*
Girls Trip *'17*
Night School *'18*

Quentin Lee
Drift *'00*
The People I've Slept With *'09*
White Frog *'12*

Robert Lee
Virtual Assassin *'95*
Act of War *'96*
Dead Fire *'98*
The Silencer *'99*
Absolute Zero *'05*
Disaster Zone: Volcano in New York *'06*

Rowland V. Lee (1891-1975)
The Guilty Generation *'31*
The Count of Monte Cristo *'34*

Cardinal Richelieu '35
One Rainy Afternoon '36
Love from a Stranger '37
Toast of New York '37
Son of Frankenstein '39
The Tower of London '39
The Son of Monte Cristo '40
The Bridge of San Luis Rey '44
Captain Kidd '45

Spike Lee (1957-)
She's Gotta Have It '86
School Daze '88
Do the Right Thing '89
Mo' Better Blues '90
Jungle Fever '91
Malcolm X '92
Crooklyn '94
Clockers '95
Get On the Bus '96
Girl 6 '96
He Got Game '98
Summer of Sam '99
Bamboozled '00
25th Hour '02
She Hate Me '04
Sucker Free City '05
Inside Man '06
Miracle at St. Anna '08
Bad 25 '12
Red Hook Summer '12
Oldboy '13
Da Sweet Blood of Jesus '14
Chi-raq '15
BlacKkKlansman '18
Da 5 Bloods '20

Herbert I. Leeds (1900-54)
Charlie Chan in City of Darkness '39
The Cisco Kid and the Lady '39
The Return of the Cisco Kid '39
Blue, White and Perfect '42
Just Off Broadway '42
It Shouldn't Happen to a Dog '46
Bunco Squad '50

Doug Lefler
Hercules the Legendary Journeys, Vol. 3: The Circle of Fire '94
Dragonheart: A New Beginning '00
The Last Legion '07

Alexandre Lehmann
Blue Jay '16
Paddleton '19

Michael Lehmann (1957-)
Heathers '89
Hudson Hawk '91
Airheads '94
The Truth about Cats and Dogs '96
My Giant '98
40 Days and 40 Nights '02
Because I Said So '07
Flakes '07

Mike Leigh (1943-)
Bleak Moments '71
Hard Labour '73
Nuts in May '76
Abigail's Party '77
Kiss of Death '77
Who's Who '78
Grown Ups '80
Meantime '81
Home Sweet Home '82
Four Days in July '85
High Hopes '88
Life Is Sweet '90
Naked '93
Secrets and Lies '95
Career Girls '97
Topsy Turvy '99
All or Nothing '02
Vera Drake '04
Happy-Go-Lucky '08
Another Year '10
Mr. Turner '14
Peterloo '18

Danny Leiner
Dude, Where's My Car? '00
Harold and Kumar Go to White Castle '04
The Great New Wonderful '06
Balls Out: Gary the Tennis Coach '09

Mitchell Leisen (1898-1972)
Death Takes a Holiday '34
Murder at the Vanities '34
Hands Across the Table '35
Easy Living '37
Swing High, Swing Low '37
Artists and Models Abroad '38
The Big Broadcast of 1938 '38
Midnight '39
Remember the Night '40
Hold Back the Dawn '41
No Time For Love '43
Frenchman's Creek '44
Golden Earrings '47
Captain Carey, U.S.A. '50
Young Man With Ideas '52
Bedevilled '55

Christopher Leitch
Teen Wolf Too '87
Courage Mountain '89
A Nightmare Come True '97
I've Been Waiting for You '98
Secrets in the Walls '10

David Leitch
Atomic Blonde '17
Deadpool 2 '18
Fast & Furious Presents: Hobbs & Shaw '19

David Leland (1947-)
Wish You Were Here '87
Checking Out '89
The Big Man: Crossing the Line '91
Band of Brothers '01
Virgin Territory '07

Sebastián Lelio
Gloria '13
Disobedience '17
A Fantastic Woman '18
Gloria Bell '18

Claude Lelouch (1937-)
A Man and a Woman '66
Happy New Year '73
And Now My Love '74
Another Man, Another Chance '77
Bolero '82
A Man and a Woman: 20 Years Later '86
And Now Ladies and Gentlemen '02
Roman de Gare '07

Michael Lembeck (1948-)
The Santa Clause 2 '02
Connie and Carla '04
The Santa Clause 3: The Escape Clause '06
The Clique '08
Tooth Fairy '10
The Bling Ring '11
Sharpay's Fabulous Adventure '11

James (Momel) Lemmo (1949-)
Heart '87
Relentless 3 '93
Dream a Little Dream 2 '94

Kasi Lemmons (1961-)
Eve's Bayou '97
The Caveman's Valentine '01
Talk to Me '07
Black Nativity '13
Harriet '19

Rusty Lemorande
Journey to the Center of the Earth '88
The Turn of the Screw '92

Paul Leni (1885-1929)
The Cat and the Canary '27
The Man Who Laughs '27

Umberto Lenzi (1931-)
Pirates of the Seven Seas '62
Sandokan the Great '63
Sandok '65
Desert Commandos '67
Gun for 100 Graves '68
Paranoia '69
Seven Blood-Stained Orchids '72
Bruce Lee Fights Back from the Grave '76
Battleforce '78
From Hell to Victory '79
City of the Walking Dead '80
Emerald Jungle '80
Bridge to Hell '87
Welcome to Spring Break '88
Black Demons '91

Kenny Leon
A Raisin in the Sun '08
Steel Magnolias '12
The Watsons Go to Birmingham '13
In My Dreams '14
American Son '19

Brett Leonard
Dead Pit '89
The Lawnmower Man '92
Hideaway '94
Virtuosity '95
Feed '05
Highlander: The Source '07

Robert Z. Leonard (1889-1968)
A Mormon Maid '17
A Lady of Chance '28
The Divorcee '30
Let Us Be Gay '30
The Bachelor Father '31
Five and Ten '31
Susan Lenox: Her Fall and Rise '31
Lovers Courageous '32
Strange Interlude '32
Dancing Lady '33
After Office Hours '35
The Great Ziegfeld '36
The Firefly '37
Maytime '37
Girl of the Golden West '38
Broadway Serenade '39
New Moon '40
Pride and Prejudice '40
Third Finger, Left Hand '40
When Ladies Meet '41
Ziegfeld Girl '41
Stand by for Action '42
We Were Dancing '42
Weekend at the Waldorf '45
The Secret Heart '46
Cynthia '47
B.F.'s Daughter '48
The Bribe '48
In the Good Old Summertime '49
The Duchess of Idaho '50
Nancy Goes to Rio '50
Too Young to Kiss '51
Everything I Have is Yours '52
The Clown '53
The Great Diamond Robbery '53
The King's Thief '55

Anthony Leondis (1972-)
Lilo & Stitch 2: Stitch Has a Glitch '05
Igor '08

Sergio Leone (1929-89)
The Colossus of Rhodes '61
A Fistful of Dollars '64
For a Few Dollars More '65
The Good, the Bad and the Ugly '67
Once Upon a Time in the West '68
A Fistful of Dynamite '72

Once Upon a Time in America '84

John R. Leonetti (1956-)
Mortal Kombat 2: Annihilation '97
The Butterfly Effect 2 '06
Annabelle '14
Wish Upon '17

Brad Leong (1986-)
Palo Alto '07
Dorfman in Love '11

Po Chih Leong (1939-)
See Po-Chih Leung

Dan Lerner
Lone Justice 3: Showdown at Plum Creek '96
Target of Opportunity '04
Finding Rin Tin Tin '07
Direct Contact '09

Irving Lerner (1909-76)
Murder by Contract '58
City of Fear '59
Studs Lonigan '60
Cry of Battle '63

Mervyn LeRoy (1900-87)
Little Caesar '30
Show Girl in Hollywood '30
Five Star Final '31
Tonight or Never '31
I Am a Fugitive from a Chain Gang '32
Two Seconds '32
Elmer the Great '33
Gold Diggers of 1933 '33
Hard to Handle '33
Tugboat Annie '33
Happiness Ahead '34
Hi, Nellie! '34
Oil for the Lamps of China '35
Anthony Adverse '36
They Won't Forget '37
Escape '40
Waterloo Bridge '40
Blossoms in the Dust '41
Johnny Eager '42
Random Harvest '42
Madame Curie '43
Thirty Seconds Over Tokyo '44
Without Reservations '46
Homecoming '48
Any Number Can Play '49
East Side, West Side '49
Little Women '49
Quo Vadis '51
Lovely to Look At '52
Million Dollar Mermaid '52
Rose Marie '54
Mister Roberts '55
Strange Lady in Town '55
The Bad Seed '56
A Majority of One '56
Toward the Unknown '56
Home Before Dark '58
No Time for Sergeants '58
The FBI Story '59
Wake Me When It's Over '60
The Devil at 4 O'Clock '61
Gypsy '62
Mary, Mary '63

Elliott Lester
Addicted to Her Love '06
Blitz '11
Aftermath '17

Mark L. Lester (1949-)
Truck Stop Women '74
Bobbie Jo and the Outlaw '76
Stunts '77
Gold of the Amazon Women '79
Roller Boogie '79
Class of 1984 '82
Firestarter '84
Commando '85
Armed and Dangerous '86
Class of 1999 '90
Showdown in Little Tokyo '91
Extreme Justice '93

Night of the Running Man '94
Misbegotten '98
The Base '99
Blowback '99
Hitman's Run '99
The Base 2: Guilty as Charged '00
Sacrifice '00
Lady Jayne Killer '03
Stealing Candy '04
Pterodactyl '05

Richard Lester (1932-)
The Mouse on the Moon '62
Ring-a-Ding Rhythm '62
A Hard Day's Night '64
Help! '65
The Knack '65
A Funny Thing Happened on the Way to the Forum '66
How I Won the War '67
Petulia '68
The Bed Sitting Room '69
Juggernaut '74
The Three Musketeers '74
The Four Musketeers '75
Royal Flash '75
The Ritz '76
Robin and Marian '76
Butch and Sundance: The Early Days '79
Cuba '79
Superman 2 '80
Superman 3 '83

Louis Leterrier (1973-)
Transporter 2 '05
Unleashed '05
The Incredible Hulk '08
Clash of the Titans '10
Now You See Me '13
The Brothers Grimsby '16

Rob Letterman
Shark Tale '04
Monsters *vs.* Aliens '09
Gulliver's Travels '10
Goosebumps '15
Pokémon Detective Pikachu '19

Sheldon Lettich (1962-)
Lionheart '90
Double Impact '91
Only the Strong '93
Perfect Target '98
The Last Warrior '99

Po-Chih Leung (1939-)
Hong Kong 1941 '84
Immortality '98
Cabin by the Lake '00
Return to Cabin by the Lake '01
Out of Reach '04
The Detonator '06

Matthew Leutwyler
Unearthed '07
The River Why '10
Answers to Nothing '11
Uncanny '15

Brian Levant (1952-)
Problem Child 2 '91
Beethoven '92
The Flintstones '94
Jingle All the Way '96
The Flintstones in Viva Rock Vegas '00
Snow Dogs '02
Are We There Yet? '05
The Spy Next Door '10
A Christmas Story 2 '12

Michel Levesque
Werewolves on Wheels '71
Sweet Sugar '72

William A. Levey (1943-)
Blackenstein '73
Wham-Bam, Thank You Spaceman '75
Slumber Party '57 '76
The Happy Hooker Goes to Washington '77
Lightning: The White Stallion '86

Hellgate '89
Committed '91

Alan J. Levi
Last Song '80
Blood Song '82
Dead Man's Revenge '93

Henry Levin (1901-80)
The Bandit of Sherwood Forest '46
Night Editor '46
Jolson Sings Again '49
Man from Colorado '49
Mr. Soft Touch '49
Convicted '50
The Family Secret '51
Two of a Kind '51
Belles on Their Toes '52
Mr. Scoutmaster '53
The Gambler from Natchez '54
The Warriors '55
April Love '57
The Lonely Man '57
Holiday for Lovers '59
Journey to the Center of the Earth '59
The Remarkable Mr. Pennypacker '59
Where the Boys Are '60
If a Man Answers '62
Genghis Khan '65
Murderers' Row '66
The Ambushers '67
That Man Bolt '73

Marc Levin
Slam '98
White Boyz '99
Little Manhattan '05
Nim's Island '08

Peter Levin
Zalmen or the Madness of God '75
Between the Darkness and the Dawn '85
Take Down '92
A Stranger in Town '95
And Never Let Her Go '01
Homeless to Harvard: The Liz Murray Story '03
A Perfect Day '06
Queen Sized '08

Thunder Levin
Evil Lives '92
American Warships '01
American Warship '12
AE: Apocalypse Earth '13

Victor Levin
5 to 7 '15
Destination Wedding '18

Jonathan Levine
All the Boys Love Mandy Lane '06
The Wackness '08
50/50 '11
Warm Bodies '13
The Night Before '15
Snatched '17
Long Shot '19

Paul Levine
Deal of a Lifetime '99
Spider's Web '01

Barry Levinson (1942-)
Diner '82
The Natural '84
Young Sherlock Holmes '85
Good Morning, Vietnam '87
Tin Men '87
Rain Man '88
Avalon '90
Bugsy '91
Toys '92
Disclosure '94
Jimmy Hollywood '94
Sleepers '96
Sphere '97
Wag the Dog '97
Liberty Heights '99
An Everlasting Piece '00
Bandits '01
Envy '04
Man of the Year '06

What Just Happened '08
You Don't Know Jack '10
The Bay '12
Rock the Kasbah '15

Kristian Levring (1957-)
The King Is Alive '00
The Intended '02
The Salvation '14

I. Robert Levy
Can I Do It. . . Till I Need Glasses? '77
If You Don't Stop It. . . You'll Go Blind '77

Jefery Levy (1958-)
Inside Monkey Zetterland '93
S.F.W. '94

Ralph Levy (1919-2001)
Bedtime Story '63
Do Not Disturb '65

Raoul Levy (1922-66)
Hail Mafia '65
The Defector '66

Scott Levy
Midnight Tease '94
Piranha '95
Unknown Origin '95
Spectre '96

Shawn Levy (1968-)
Address Unknown '96
Big Fat Liar '02
Cheaper by the Dozen '03
Just Married '03
Night at the Museum '06
The Pink Panther '06
Night at the Museum: Battle of the Smithsonian '09
Date Night '10
Real Steel '11
The Internship '13
Night at the Museum: Secret of the Tomb '14
This Is Where I Leave You '14

Shuki Levy
Turbo: A Power Rangers Movie '96
Aussie and Ted's Great Adventure '09

Albert Lewin (1916-96)
The Moon and Sixpence '43
Picture of Dorian Gray '45
The Private Affairs of Bel Ami '47
Pandora and the Flying Dutchman '51
Saadia '53

Ben Lewin (1946-)
The Favor, the Watch, & the Very Big Fish '92
Paperback Romance '96
The Sessions '12
Please Stand By '17
The Catcher Was a Spy '18

Christopher Lewis (1944-)
Blood Cult '85
Revenge '86
The Ripper '86

Herschell Gordon Lewis (1926-)
The Prime Time '60
Blood Feast '63
Scum of the Earth '63
Color Me Blood Red '64
Moonshine Mountain '64
2000 Maniacs '64
Monster a Go-Go! '65
Jimmy, the Boy Wonder '66
Blast-Off Girls '67
Gruesome Twosome '67
Suburban Roulette '67
A Taste of Blood '67
Just for the Hell of It '68
The Psychic '68
She-Devils on Wheels '68
Something Weird '68
The Wizard of Gore '70
This Stuff'll Kill Ya! '71
The Gore-Gore Girls '72

Jerry Lewis (1926-2017)
The Bellboy '60
The Errand Boy '61
The Ladies' Man '61
The Nutty Professor '63
The Patsy '64
The Family Jewels '65
One More Time '70
Which Way to the Front? '70
Cracking Up '83

Joseph H. Lewis (1907-2000)
Criminals Within '41
The Invisible Ghost '41
So Dark the Night '46
The Swordsman '47
Gun Crazy '49
The Undercover Man '49
A Lady Without Passport '50
Desperate Search '52
Big Combo '55
A Lawless Street '55
Seventh Cavalry '56
Terror in a Texas Town '58

Kevin Lewis
Dark Heart '06
The Drop '06

Mark Lewis
Gordy '95
The Thaw '09

Richard J. Lewis
K-9 3: P.I. '01
Barney's Version '10

Robert Lewis (1909-97)
Anything Goes '56
Child Bride of Short Creek '81
Desperate Lives '82
Agatha Christie's A Caribbean Mystery '83
Agatha Christie's Sparkling Cyanide '83
A Summer to Remember '84

Marshall Lewy (1977-)
Blue State '07
California Solo '12

Peter Paul Liapis
Alone with a Stranger '99
Captured '99
The Stepdaughter '00

Leslie Libman
Path to Paradise '97
Brave New World '98

Demian Lichtenstein
3000 Miles to Graceland '01
Venus and Vegas '10

Jeff Lieberman (1947-)
Squirm '76
Blue Sunshine '78
Just Before Dawn '80
Satan's Little Helper '04

Robert Lieberman (1941-)
Table for Five '83
Fire in the Sky '93
D3: The Mighty Ducks '96
Titanic '96
Tom Clancy's Netforce '98
The Dead Zone '02
Final Days of Planet Earth '06
The Stranger '10
Eve of Destruction '13

Jonathan Liebesman (1976-)
Darkness Falls '03
The Texas Chainsaw Massacre: The Beginning '06
The Killing Room '09
Battle: Los Angeles '11
Wrath of the Titans '12
Teenage Mutant Ninja Turtles '14

Kevin Lima (1962-)
A Goofy Movie '94
Tarzan '99
102 Dalmatians '00
Eloise at the Plaza '03
Enchanted '07

Doug Liman (1965-)
Swingers '96
Go '99
The Bourne Identity '02
Mr. & Mrs. Smith '05
Jumper '08
Fair Game '10
Edge of Tomorrow '14
American Made '17
The Wall '17

Justin Lin (1973-)
Better Luck Tomorrow '02
Annapolis '06
The Fast and the Furious: Tokyo Drift '06
Fast & Furious '09
Fast Five '11
Fast & Furious 6 '13

Kevin J. Lindenmuth (1965-)
Addicted to Murder '95
Addicted to Murder 2: Tainted Blood '97
Addicted to Murder 3: Bloodlust '99

Tobias Lindholm
A Hijacking '13
A War '15

Eleanor Lindo
Crazy for Christmas '05
A Dad for Christmas '06
She Drives Me Crazy '07

Michael Lindsay-Hogg (1940-)
Let It Be '70
Nasty Habits '77
Brideshead Revisited '81
The Object of Beauty '91
Running Mates '92
Horton Foote's Alone '97
Two of Us '00

Leopold Lindtberg (1902-84)
The Last Chance '45
Four in a Jeep '51

Mark Linfield
Earth '07
Chimpanzee '12
Monkey Kingdom '15

Caroline Link (1964-)
Beyond Silence '96
Nowhere in Africa '02

Richard Linklater (1960-)
Slacker '91
Dazed and Confused '93
Before Sunrise '94
The Newton Boys '97
Tape '01
Waking Life '01
School of Rock '03
Before Sunset '04
The Bad News Bears '05
Fast Food Nation '06
A Scanner Darkly '06
Me and Orson Welles '09
Bernie '12
Before Midnight '13
Boyhood '14
Everybody Wants Some!! '16
Last Flag Flying '17
Where'd You Go, Bernadette '19

Jeff Lipsky
Flannel Pajamas '06
Once More With Feeling '08

Aaron Lipstadt (1952-)
Android '82
City Limits '85
Blood Money '99

Steven Lisberger (1951-)
Tron '82
Hot Pursuit '87
Slipstream '89

David Lister
The Story of an African Farm '04
Malibu Shark Attack '09
Beauty and the Beast: A Dark Tale '10

Peter MacKenzie Litten
Living Doll '90
Heaven's a Drag '94

Dwight Little (1947-)
Bloodstone '88
Halloween 4: The Return of Michael Myers '88
The Phantom of the Opera '89
Marked for Death '90
Rapid Fire '92
Free Willy 2: The Adventure Home '95
Murder at 1600 '97
Boss of Bosses '99
Anacondas: The Hunt for the Blood Orchid '04

Ryan Little
Saints and Soldiers '03
Everything You Want '05
Forever Strong '08
Age of the Dragons '11
Saints and Soldiers: Airborne Creed '12

Lynne Littman (1941-)
Testament '83
Having Our Say: The Delany Sisters' First 100 Years '99

Anatole Litvak (1902-74)
Mayerling '36
Amazing Dr. Clitterhouse '38
The Sisters '38
Confessions of a Nazi Spy '39
All This and Heaven Too '40
Castle on the Hudson '40
City for Conquest '40
Blues in the Night '41
Out of the Fog '41
This Above All '42
The Long Night '47
The Snake Pit '48
Sorry, Wrong Number '48
Decision Before Dawn '51
Anastasia '56
The Journey '59
Night of the Generals '67

Chia-Liang Liu
The 36th Chamber of Shaolin '78
Legendary Weapons of China '82
Heroes of the East '08

Gerry Lively
Darkness Falls '98
Body Armour '07
The Art of War 3: Retribution '08
Finish Line '08

Carlo Lizzani (1922-2013)
The Hills Run Red '67
Last Four Days '77

Luis Llosa (1951-)
Sniper '92
800 Leagues Down the Amazon '93
Fire on the Amazon '93
The Specialist '94
Anaconda '96

Frank Lloyd (1886-1960)
Oliver Twist '22
Within the Law '23
The Sea Hawk '24
The Divine Lady '29
Weary River '29
Son of the Gods '30
The Right of Way '31
Cavalcade '33
Mutiny on the Bounty '35
Maid of Salem '37
The Howards of Virginia '40
Forever and a Day '43
Blood on the Sun '45

Phyllida Lloyd (1957-)
Mamma Mia! '08
The Iron Lady '11

Ken Loach (1936-)
Kes '69
Black Jack '79
Hidden Agenda '90
Riff Raff '92
Ladybird, Ladybird '93
Raining Stones '93
Carla's Song '97
My Name Is Joe '98
Bread and Roses '00
The Navigators '01
Sweet Sixteen '02
A Fond Kiss '04
The Wind That Shakes the Barley '06
Looking for Eric '09
I, Daniel Blake '16
Sorry We Missed You '20

Sondra Locke (1944-)
Ratboy '86
Impulse '90

Chris Lofing
The Gallows '15
The Gallows Act II '19

Bob Logan
Repossessed '90
Meatballs 4 '92
The LEGO Ninjago Movie '17

Joshua Logan (1908-88)
Picnic '55
Bus Stop '56
Sayonara '57
South Pacific '58
Tall Story '60
Fanny '61
Ensign Pulver '64
Camelot '67
Paint Your Wagon '69

Dimitri Logothetis
Body Shot '93
The Lost Angel '04

Julia Loktev
Day Night Day Night '06
The Loneliest Planet '12

Ulli Lommel (1944-)
Tenderness of the Wolves '73
Cocaine Cowboys '79
The Boogey Man '80
Brainwaves '82
Devonsville Terror '83
Olivia '83
BTK Killer '06
Baseline Killer '08
Son of Sam '08
Night Stalker '09

Richard Loncraine (1946-)
Brimstone & Treacle '82
The Missionary '82
Bellman and True '88
Deep Cover '88
The Wedding Gift '93
Richard III '95
Band of Brothers '01
The Gathering Storm '02
My House in Umbria '03
Wimbledon '04
Firewall '06
My One and Only '09
The Special Relationship '10
5 Flights Up '15
Finding Your Feet '18

Jeff London
Arizona Sky '08
A Warm Wind '11

Jerry London (1937-)
Shogun '80
The Scarlet & the Black '83
If Tomorrow Comes '86
Rent-A-Cop '88
Kiss Shot '89
Victim of Love '91
A Mother's Gift '95
Stolen Women, Captured Hearts '97
Take Me Home: The John Denver Story '00
Counterstrike '03

Kenneth Lonergan (1963-)
You Can Count On Me '99
Margaret '11
Manchester by the Sea '16

Gonzalo Lopez-Gallego
Apollo 18 '11
The Hollow Point '16

Jean-Claude Lord (1943-)
Visiting Hours '82
Toby McTeague '87
Eddie and the Cruisers 2: Eddie Lives! '89
The Secrets of the Summer House '08

Peter Lord (1953-)
Chicken Run '00
The Pirates! Band of Misfits '12

Phil Lord (1975-)
Cloudy with a Chance of Meatballs '09
21 Jump Street '12
The Lego Movie '14
22 Jump Street '14

Joseph Losey (1909-84)
The Boy with the Green Hair '48
The Lawless '50
The Big Night '51
The Prowler '51
Stranger on the Prowl '52
The Sleeping Tiger '54
Time Without Pity '57
Eva '62
The Servant '63
These Are the Damned '63
King and Country '64
Modesty Blaise '66
Accident '67
The Go-Between '71
Assassination of Trotsky '72
A Doll's House '73
Romantic Englishwoman '75
Mr. Klein '76
Don Giovanni '79
La Truite '83

Ye Lou
Purple Butterfly '03
Summer Palace '06

Todd Louiso (1970-)
Love Liza '02
The Marc Pease Experience '09
Hello I Must Be Going '12

John Lounsbery
The Many Adventures of Winnie the Pooh '77
The Rescuers '77

Eugene Lourie (1903-91)
The Beast from 20,000 Fathoms '53
Colossus of New York '58
The Giant Behemoth '59
Gorgo '61

Eric Louzil (1951-)
Lust for Freedom '87
Fortress of Amerikka '89
Class of Nuke 'Em High 2: Subhumanoid Meltdown '91
Class of Nuke 'Em High 3: The Good, the Bad and the Subhumanoid '94
Dangerous Cargo '96

Nick Love (1969-)
The Business '05
Outlaw '07
The Sweeney '12

Charles Loventhal
My Demon Lover '87
Mr. Write '92
Meet Market '08

Brand Upon the Brain! '06
Keyhole '11

Madonna (1959-)
Filth and Wisdom '08
W.E. '11

Kurt Maetzig
First Spaceship on Venus '60
The Rabbit Is Me '65

Guy Magar (1948-)
Retribution '88
Stepfather 3: Father's Day '92
Showdown '94
Children of the Corn: Revelation '01

Maria Maggenti (1962-)
The Incredibly True Adventure of Two Girls in Love '95
Puccini for Beginners '06

Joe Maggio
Virgil Bliss '01
Milk and Honey '03
Bitter Feast '10
The Last Rites of Joe May '11

Albert Magnoli
Purple Rain '84
American Anthem '86
Dark Planet '97

Sharon Maguire (1960-)
Bridget Jones's Diary '01
Incendiary '08
Call Me Crazy '13
Bridget Jones's Baby '16

Brendan Maher
Flatland '02
The Road from Coorain '02
After the Deluge '03
Kidnapped '05
Wide Sargasso Sea '06
Sisters of War '10
Return to Nim's Island '13

Barry Mahon (1921-99)
Rocket Attack U.S.A. '58
Assault of the Rebel Girls '59
Pagan Island '60

Majid Majidi (1959-)
Children of Heaven '98
The Color of Paradise '99
The Song of Sparrows '08

Siu Fai Mak
Infernal Affairs 2 '03
Infernal Affairs 3 '03

Dusan Makavejev (1932-)
Man Is Not a Bird '65
The Love Affair, or The Case of the Missing Switchboard Operator '67
Innocence Unprotected '68
WR: Mysteries of the Organism '71
Sweet Movie '75
Montenegro '81
The Coca-Cola Kid '84

Mohsen Makhmalbaf (1957-)
Gabbeh '96
Kandahar '01

Kelly Makin
National Lampoon's Senior Trip '95
Kids in the Hall: Brain Candy '96
Mickey Blue Eyes '99
I Do (But I Don't) '04
Playing House '06

Karoly Makk (1925-)
Love '71
Cat's Play '74
Another Way '82
Lily in Love '85
The Gambler '97

Guido Malatesta (1919-70)
Fire Monsters Against the Son of Hercules '62
Goliath Against the Giants '63

Rob Malenfant
The Night Caller '97
The Nurse '97
The Landlady '98
Facing the Enemy '00
The Perfect Nanny '00
Lost in the Dark '07

Terrence Malick (1943-)
Badlands '74
Days of Heaven '78
The Thin Red Line '98
The New World '05
The Tree of Life '11
To the Wonder '12
Knight of Cups '15
Song to Song '17
A Hidden Life '19

Thanapon Maliwan
Brave '07
The Sanctuary '09

Laurence Malkin
Soul Assassin '01
Five Fingers '06

Louis Malle (1932-95)
Frantic '58
The Lovers '59
The Fire Within '64
Viva Maria! '65
The Thief of Paris '67
Spirits of the Dead '68
Murmur of the Heart '71
Black Moon '75
Pretty Baby '78
Atlantic City '81
My Dinner with Andre '81
Crackers '84
Alamo Bay '85
Au Revoir les Enfants '87
Damage '92
Vanya on 42nd Street '94

Jim Mallon
Blood Hook '86
Mystery Science Theater 3000: The Movie '96

Bruce Malmuth (1937-)
Foreplay '75
Nighthawks '81
The Man Who Wasn't There '83
Where Are the Children? '85
Hard to Kill '89
Pentathlon '94

Mark Malone
Bulletproof Heart '95
Hoods '98
The Last Stop '99
Dead Heat '01

William Malone (1953-)
Scared to Death '80
Creature '85
House on Haunted Hill '99
Feardotcom '02
Parasomnia '08

David Mamet (1947-)
House of Games '87
Things Change '88
Homicide '91
Oleanna '94
The Spanish Prisoner '97
The Winslow Boy '98
State and Main '00
Heist '01
Spartan '04
Redbelt '08
Phil Spector '13

Rouben Mamoulian (1897-1987)
Applause '29
Dr. Jekyll and Mr. Hyde '32
Love Me Tonight '32
Queen Christina '33
The Song of Songs '33
We Live Again '34
Becky Sharp '35
The Gay Desperado '36
High, Wide and Handsome '37
Golden Boy '39
The Mark of Zorro '40
Blood and Sand '41
Rings on Her Fingers '42
Summer Holiday '48
Silk Stockings '57

Milcho Manchevski (1959-)
Before the Rain '94
Dust '01

Don Mancini (1963-)
Seed of Chucky '04
Curse of Chucky '13

Robert Mandel
F/X '86
Touch and Go '86
Big Shots '87
Perfect Witness '89
School Ties '92
The Substitute '96
Thin Air '00
Winds of Terror '01
A Season on the Brink '02
The Secret of Zoey '02

Artie Mandelberg
Taming Andrew '00
Inside Out '11
Bending the Rules '12

Luis Mandoki (1954-)
White Palace '90
Born Yesterday '93
When a Man Loves a Woman '94
Message in a Bottle '98
Angel Eyes '01
Trapped '02
Innocent Voices '04

Neil Mandt (1969-)
Hijacking Hollywood '97
Arthur's Quest '99
The Million Dollar Kid '99
Last Stop for Paul '08

Joseph Manduke
Cornbread, Earl & Me '75
Kid Vengeance '75

James Mangold (1964-)
Heavy '94
Cop Land '97
Girl, Interrupted '99
Kate & Leopold '01
Identity '03
Walk the Line '05
3:10 to Yuma '07
Knight and Day '10
The Wolverine '13
Logan '17
Ford v Ferrari '19

Joseph L. Mankiewicz (1909-93)
Dragonwyck '46
Somewhere in the Night '46
The Ghost and Mrs. Muir '47
House of Strangers '49
A Letter to Three Wives '49
All About Eve '50
No Way Out '50
People Will Talk '51
Five Fingers '52
Julius Caesar '53
The Barefoot Contessa '54
Guys and Dolls '55
Suddenly, Last Summer '59
Cleopatra '63
The Honey Pot '67
There Was a Crooked Man '70
Sleuth '72

Tom Mankiewicz (1942-2010)
Dragnet '87
Delirious '91

Anthony Mann (1906-67)
Great Flamarion '45
The Bamboo Blonde '46
Strange Impersonation '46
Desperate '47
Railroaded '47
T-Men '47
He Walked by Night '48
Raw Deal '48
Border Incident '49
Reign of Terror '49
The Devil's Doorway '50
The Furies '50
Side Street '50
Winchester '73 '50
The Tall Target '51
Bend of the River '52
The Naked Spur '53
Thunder Bay '53
The Glenn Miller Story '54
Far Country '55
The Man from Laramie '55
Savage Wilderness '55
Strategic Air Command '55
Serenade '56
Men in War '57
The Tin Star '57
God's Little Acre '58
Man of the West '58
Cimarron '60
El Cid '61
The Fall of the Roman Empire '64
The Heroes of Telemark '65
Dandy in Aspic '68

Daniel Mann (1912-91)
Come Back, Little Sheba '52
I'll Cry Tomorrow '55
The Rose Tattoo '55
The Teahouse of the August Moon '56
Butterfield 8 '60
Ada '61
Five Finger Exercise '62
Who's Got the Action? '63
Our Man Flint '66
For Love of Ivy '68
A Dream of Kings '69
The Revengers '72
Playing for Time '80

Delbert Mann (1920-2007)
Marty '55
Desire Under the Elms '58
Separate Tables '58
Middle of the Night '59
Lover Come Back '61
That Touch of Mink '62
Dear Heart '64
Mister Buddwing '66
Fitzwilly '67
Heidi '67
David Copperfield '70
All Quiet on the Western Front '79
Torn Between Two Lovers '79
Night Crossing '81
A Death in California '85
The Last Days of Patton '86
April Morning '88

Farhad Mann
Nick Knight '89
Lawnmower Man 2: Beyond Cyberspace '95
His and Her Christmas '05
In Her Mother's Footsteps '06
The Lost Treasure of the Grand Canyon '08

Michael Mann (1943-)
Thief '81
Manhunter '86
The Last of the Mohicans '92
Heat '95
The Insider '99
Ali '01
Collateral '04
Miami Vice '06
Public Enemies '09
Blackhat '15

Scott Mann
The Tournament '09
Final Score '18

Peter Manoogian
Dungeonmaster '83
Demonic Toys '90
Seedpeople '92
Soldiers of Change '06

Mark Manos
Liquid Dreams '92
Josh Kirby. . . Time Warrior: Chapter 4, Eggs from 70 Million B.C. '95

Samuel Maoz
Lebanon '09
Foxtrot '18

Robert Marcarelli
Original Intent '91
I Don't Buy Kisses Anymore '92
The Omega Code '99
The Long Ride Home '01

Terry Marcel (1942-)
Hawk the Slayer '81
Prisoners of the Lost Universe '84
Jane & the Lost City '87
The Last Seduction 2 '98

Siro Marcellini
The Beast of Babylon Against the Son of Hercules '63
Lola Colt '67

Alex March (1921-89)
Paper Lion '68
The Big Bounce '69
Firehouse '72
The Amazing Captain Nemo '78

Gilles Marchand (1963-)
Who Killed Bambi? '03
Black Heaven '10

Greg Marcks (1976-)
11:14 '03
Echelon Conspiracy '09

David Marconi
The Harvest '92
Collision '13

Adam Marcus (1968-)
Jason Goes to Hell: The Final Friday '93
Let It Snow '99

Mitch Marcus
Boltneck '98
The Haunting of Hell House '99
Knocking on Death's Door '99

Paul Marcus (1955-)
The Break Up '98
Eye of the Killer '99

Andreas Marfori
Evil Clutch '89
Desperate Crimes '93

Antonio Margheriti (1930-2002)
See Anthony M. Dawson

Stuart Margolin (1940-)
The Long Summer of George Adams '82
How the West Was Fun '95

A. L. Mariaux (1930-2013)
See Jess (Jesus) Franco

Edwin L. Marin (1899-1951)
The Death Kiss '33
A Study in Scarlet '33
Bombay Mail '34
The Casino Murder Case '35
I'd Give My Life '36
Speed '36
A Christmas Carol '38
Everybody Sing '38
Listen, Darling '38
Fast and Loose '39
Maisie '39
Society Lawyer '39
Gold Rush Maisie '40
Hullabaloo '40
Maisie Was a Lady '41
Ringside Maisie '41
Invisible Agent '42
Show Business '44
Tall in the Saddle '44
Abilene Town '46
Mr. Ace '46
Nocturne '46
Race Street '48
Raton Pass '51

Ken Marino (1968-)
How to Be a Latin Lover '17
Dog Days '18

Peter Maris
Land of Doom '84
Viper '88
Ministry of Vengeance '89
True Blood '89
Hangfire '91

Fletcher Markle (1921-91)
Jigsaw '49
The Man With a Cloak '51
The Incredible Journey '63

Peter Markle (1946-)
Hot Dog. . . The Movie! '83
The Personals '83
Youngblood '86
Bat 21 '88
El Diablo '90
Wagons East '94
The Last Days of Frankie the Fly '96
The Tenth Circle '08
High Noon '09
Carnal Innocence '11

Robert Markowitz (1935-)
Children of the Night '85
Decoration Day '90
Too Young to Die '90
Afterburn '92
The Tuskegee Airmen '95
David '97
Into Thin Air: Death on Everest '97
The Great Gatsby '01
The Pilot's Wife '01

Arthur Marks (1927-2019)
Bonnie's Kids '73
Detroit 9000 '73
Bucktown '75
Friday Foster '75
J.D.'s Revenge '76
Monkey Hustle '77

Ross Kagen Marks
Homage '95
The Twilight of the Golds '97

Mans Marlind (1969-)
Storm '05
Underworld: Awakening '12
6 Souls '13

Christian Marquand (1927-2000)
Attila '54
Candy '68

Richard Marquand (1938-87)
The Legacy '79
Eye of the Needle '81
Return of the Jedi '83
Until September '84
The Jagged Edge '85

James Marsh (1963-)
The King '05
Man on Wire '08
Red Riding, Part 2: 1980 '09
Project Nim '11
Shadow Dancer '12
The Theory of Everything '14
The Mercy '19

Frank Marshall (1954-)
Arachnophobia '90
Alive '93
Congo '95
From the Earth to the Moon '98
Eight Below '06

Garry Marshall (1934-2016)
Young Doctors in Love '82
The Flamingo Kid '84
Nothing in Common '86

Tim McCanlies (1953-)
Dancer, Texas-Pop. 81 *'98*
Secondhand Lions *'03*
Angels Sing *'13*

Tim McCann (1968-)
Desolation Angels *'95*
Revolution #9 *'01*
Runaway *'05*
The Poker Club *'08*

Leo McCarey (1898-1969)
Indiscreet *'31*
Kid from Spain *'32*
Duck Soup *'33*
Belle of the Nineties *'34*
Ruggles of Red Gap *'35*
Milky Way *'36*
The Awful Truth *'37*
Love Affair *'39*
Once Upon a Honeymoon *'42*
Going My Way *'44*
The Bells of St. Mary's *'45*
Good Sam *'48*
My Son John *'52*
An Affair to Remember *'57*
Rally 'Round the Flag, Boys! *'58*

Ray McCarey (1898-1948)
Devil's Party *'38*
So This Is Washington *'43*
Atlantic City *'44*

Claire McCarthy
The Waiting City *'09*
Ophelia *'19*

Michael McCarthy (1917-59)
The Accursed *'57*
Operation Amsterdam *'60*

Nicholas McCarthy
The Pact *'12*
Holidays *'16*
The Prodigy *'19*

Thomas (Tom) McCarthy (1966-)
The Station Agent *'03*
The Visitor *'07*
Win Win *'11*
The Cobbler *'14*
Spotlight *'15*
Timmy Failure: Mistakes Were Made *'20*

Gregory McClatchy
Vampire at Midnight *'88*
Soccer Mom *'08*

Nelson McCormick
Where the Truth Lies *'99*
Prom Night *'08*
The Stepfather *'09*
Killing Kennedy *'13*

George McCowan (1927-95)
The Ballad of Andy Crocker *'69*
Black Brigade *'69*
The Over-the-Hill Gang Rides Again *'70*
Savage Run *'70*
Frogs *'72*
Murder on Flight 502 *'75*
Shadow of the Hawk *'76*
Return to Fantasy Island *'77*

Ian McCrudden (1971-)
The Big Day *'99*
Trailer, the Movie *'99*
Islander *'06*

Bruce McCulloch (1961-)
Dog Park *'98*
Superstar *'99*
Stealing Harvard *'02*

Jim McCullough, Sr.
Charge of the Model T's *'76*
The Aurora Encounter *'85*
Mountaintop Motel Massacre *'86*
Where the Red Fern Grows: Part 2 *'92*
The St. Tammany Miracle *'94*

John Michael McDonagh
The Guard *'11*
Calvary *'14*
War on Everyone *'17*

Martin McDonagh
In Bruges *'08*
Seven Psychopaths *'12*

Bruce McDonald (1959-)
Roadkill *'89*
Highway 61 *'91*
Dance Me Outside *'95*
Hard Core Logo *'96*
Picture Claire *'01*
Killer Wave *'07*
The Tracey Fragments *'07*
Pontypool *'09*
Hard Core Logo 2 *'10*
Trigger *'10*
Hellions *'15*

Frank McDonald (1899-1980)
Smart Blonde *'37*
Flying Blind *'41*
No Hands on the Clock *'41*
Wildcat *'42*
Wrecking Crew *'42*
Gambler's Choice *'44*
One Body Too Many *'44*
Treasure of Fear *'45*
My Pal Trigger *'46*
Sioux City Sue *'46*
Under Nevada Skies *'46*
Lights of Old Santa Fe *'47*
The Big Sombrero *'49*
The Purple Gang *'59*
Gunfight at Comanche Creek *'64*

Rodney McDonald
Scorned 2 *'96*
Steel Sharks *'97*
Nautilus *'99*
Sonic Impact *'99*
Deep Core *'00*

Edward T. McDougal
One for the Road *'82*
The Prodigy *'98*

Charles McDougall
Heart *'99*
Call Me: The Rise and Fall of Heidi Fleiss *'04*

Francine McDougall
Sugar & Spice *'01*
Cow Belles *'06*

Charlie McDowell (1983-)
The One I Love *'14*
The Discovery *'17*

Ross McElwee (1947-)
Sherman's March *'86*
Time Indefinite *'93*

Bernard McEveety (1924-2004)
The Brotherhood of Satan *'71*
A Step Out of Line *'71*
Killer by Night *'72*
Napoleon and Samantha *'72*
One Little Indian *'73*
The Bears & I *'74*
Centennial *'78*

Vincent McEveety
Firecreek *'68*
Menace on the Mountain *'70*
Million Dollar Duck *'71*
Charley and the Angel *'73*
Superdad *'73*
The Castaway Cowboy *'74*
Wonder Woman *'74*
Gus *'76*
The Treasure of Matecumbe *'76*
Herbie Goes to Monte Carlo *'77*
The Apple Dumpling Gang Rides Again *'79*
Herbie Goes Bananas *'80*
Amy *'81*
Gunsmoke: Return to Dodge *'87*

McG (1968-)
Charlie's Angels *'00*
Charlie's Angels: Full Throttle *'03*
We Are Marshall *'06*
Terminator Salvation *'09*
This Means War *'12*
3 Days to Kill *'14*
The Babysitter *'17*

William McGann (1893-1977)
The Case of the Black Cat *'36*
Blackwell's Island *'39*
American Empire *'42*
In Old California *'42*

Scott McGehee
Suture *'93*
The Deep End *'01*
Bee Season *'05*
Uncertainty *'08*
What Maisie Knew *'12*

Sean McGinly
Two Days *'03*
The Great Buck Howard *'09*

J(ohn) P(aterson) McGowan (1880-1952)
Headin' for Trouble *'31*
Hurricane Express *'32*

Michael McGowan (1966-)
One Week *'08*
Still Mine *'13*

Robert McGowan (1882-1955)
Old Swimmin' Hole *'40*
Tomboy *'40*

Tom McGowan (1959-)
Cataclysm *'81*
Savage Journey *'83*

Douglas McGrath (1958-)
Emma *'96*
Company Man *'00*
Nicholas Nickleby *'02*
Infamous *'06*
I Don't Know How She Does It *'11*
Becoming Mike Nichols *'16*

Joseph McGrath (1930-)
Casino Royale *'67*
The Bliss of Mrs. Blossom *'68*
The Magic Christian *'69*

Tom McGrath
Madagascar *'05*
Madagascar: Escape 2 Africa *'08*
Megamind *'10*
Madagascar 3: Europe's Most Wanted *'12*
The Boss Baby *'17*

Mary McGuckian (1963-)
The Bridge of San Luis Rey *'05*
The Man on the Train *'11*

Paul McGuigan (1963-)
The Acid House *'98*
Gangster No. 1 *'00*
The Reckoning *'03*
Wicker Park *'04*
Lucky Number Slevin *'06*
Push *'09*
Victor Frankenstein *'15*
Film Stars Don't Die in Liverpool *'17*

Doug McHenry
House Party 2: The Pajama Jam *'91*
Jason's Lyric *'94*
Kingdom Come *'01*
Keep the Faith, Baby *'02*

Christian McIntire (1964-)
Landspeed *'01*
Lost Voyage *'01*
Antibody *'02*

Adam McKay (1968-)
Anchorman: The Legend of Ron Burgundy *'04*
Talladega Nights: The Ballad of Ricky Bobby *'06*
Step Brothers *'08*
The Other Guys *'10*
Anchorman 2: The Legend Continues *'13*
The Big Short *'15*
Vice *'18*

Cole McKay
Star Hunter *'95*
The Underground *'97*

Jim McKay
Girls Town *'95*
Our Song *'01*
Angel Rodriguez *'05*

John McKay
Crush *'02*
A Waste of Shame *'05*

Lucky McKee (1975-)
May *'02*
The Woods *'03*
Red *'08*
The Woman *'11*
Tales of Halloween *'15*
Blood Money *'17*

Don McKellar (1963-)
Last Night *'98*
The Grand Seduction *'13*

Andrew V. McLaglen (1920-2014)
Gun the Man Down *'56*
Man in the Vault *'56*
McLintock! *'63*
Shenandoah *'65*
Monkeys, Go Home! *'66*
The Rare Breed *'66*
The Ballad of Josie *'67*
The Way West *'67*
Bandolero! *'68*
The Devil's Brigade *'68*
Hellfighters *'68*
The Undefeated *'69*
Chisum *'70*
Cahill: United States Marshal *'73*
Mitchell *'75*
Banjo Hackett *'76*
The Last Hard Men *'76*
Wild Geese *'78*
ffolkes *'80*
Sea Wolves *'81*
The Blue and the Gray *'82*
The Shadow Riders *'82*
The Dirty Dozen: The Next Mission *'85*

Greg McLean
Wolf Creek *'05*
Rogue *'07*
Wolf Creek 2 *'13*
The Darkness *'16*
The Belko Experiment *'17*
Jungle *'17*

Norman Z. McLeod (1898-1964)
Monkey Business *'31*
Horse Feathers *'32*
If I Had a Million *'32*
Alice in Wonderland *'33*
It's a Gift *'34*
Here Comes Cookie *'35*
Pennies from Heaven *'36*
Topper *'37*
Merrily We Live *'38*
Little Men *'40*
Lady Be Good *'41*
Panama Hattie *'42*
Swing Shift Maisie *'43*
The Kid from Brooklyn *'46*
The Road to Rio *'47*
The Secret Life of Walter Mitty *'47*
The Paleface *'48*
Let's Dance *'50*
My Favorite Spy *'51*
Never Wave at a WAC *'52*
Casanova's Big Night *'54*
Alias Jesse James *'59*

Tom McLoughlin (1950-)
One Dark Night *'82*
Friday the 13th, Part 6: Jason Lives *'86*
Date with an Angel *'87*
Sometimes They Come Back *'91*
The Fire Next Time *'93*
The Yarn Princess *'94*
Behind the Mask *'99*
The Unsaid *'01*
Murder in Greenwich *'02*
She's Too Young *'04*
Cyber Seduction: His Secret Life *'05*
Not Like Everyone Else *'06*
Patricia Cornwell's At Risk *'10*
Patricia Cornwell's The Front *'10*
The Wronged Man *'10*

Gerard McMurray
Burning Sands *'17*
The First Purge *'18*

David McNally
Coyote Ugly *'00*
Kangaroo Jack *'02*

Sean McNamara (1963-)
3 Ninjas: High Noon at Mega Mountain *'97*
P.U.N.K.S. *'98*
Treehouse Hostage *'99*
Wild Grizzly *'99*
The Trial of Old Drum *'00*
Race to Space *'01*
Raise Your Voice *'04*
The Cutting Edge: Going for the Gold *'05*
Bratz *'07*
Soul Surfer *'11*
Space Warriors *'13*
Field of Lost Shoes *'14*
Spare Parts *'15*
The Miracle Season *'18*

Bob McNaught
Grand National Night *'53*
Sea Wife *'57*

John McNaughton (1950-)
Henry: Portrait of a Serial Killer *'90*
Mad Dog and Glory *'93*
Girls in Prison *'94*
Normal Life *'96*
Wild Things *'98*
Lansky *'99*

Glenn McQuaid
I Sell the Dead *'09*
V/H/S *'12*

Christopher McQuarrie (1968-)
Way of the Gun *'00*
Jack Reacher *'12*
Mission: Impossible Rogue Nation *'15*
Mission: Impossible-Fallout *'18*

Steve McQueen (1969-)
Hunger *'08*
Shame *'11*
12 Years a Slave *'13*
Widows *'18*

James McTeigue
V for Vendetta *'06*
Ninja Assassin *'09*
The Raven *'12*
Breaking In *'18*

John McTiernan (1951-)
Nomads *'86*
Predator *'87*
Die Hard *'88*
The Hunt for Red October *'90*
Medicine Man *'92*
Last Action Hero *'93*
Die Hard: With a Vengeance *'95*
The 13th Warrior *'99*
The Thomas Crown Affair *'99*
Rollerball *'02*
Basic *'03*

Shane Meadows (1972-)
Once Upon a Time in the Midlands *'02*
Dead Man's Shoes *'04*
This Is England *'06*
Le Donk & Scor-Zay-Zee *'09*

Nancy Meckler
Sister My Sister *'94*
Alive and Kicking *'96*

Peter Medak (1940-)
A Day in the Death of Joe Egg *'71*
The Ruling Class *'72*
The Third Girl from the Left *'73*
The Changeling *'80*
Zorro, the Gay Blade *'81*
The Men's Club *'86*
Let Him Have It *'91*
Romeo Is Bleeding *'93*
Pontiac Moon *'94*
The Hunchback *'97*
Species 2 *'98*
Anne Rice's The Feast of All Saints *'01*
Sex & Lies in Sin City: The Ted Binion Scandal *'08*

Julio Medem (1958-)
Vacas *'91*
Tierra *'95*
Lovers of the Arctic Circle *'98*
Sex and Lucia *'01*

Justin Meeks
The Wild Man of the Navidad *'08*
Kill or Be Killed *'15*

Olivier Megaton
Red Siren *'02*
Transporter 3 *'08*
Colombiana *'11*
Taken 2 *'12*
Taken 3 *'15*

Stella Meghie
Everything, Everything *'17*
The Photograph *'20*

Deepa Mehta (1950-)
Camilla *'94*
Fire *'96*
Earth *'98*
The Republic of Love *'03*
Water *'05*

Ursula Meier
Home *'09*
Sister *'12*

Gus Meins (1893-1940)
March of the Wooden Soldiers *'34*
Hit Parade of 1937 *'37*
Nobody's Baby *'37*

Fernando Meirelles (1955-)
City of God *'02*
The Constant Gardener *'05*
Blindness *'08*
360 *'12*
Rio, I Love You *'14*
The Two Popes *'19*

Theodore Melfi
St. Vincent *'14*
Hidden Figures *'17*

George Melford (1877-1961)
The Sheik *'21*
Moran of the Lady Letty *'22*
Dracula Spanish Version *'31*
East of Borneo *'31*
Boiling Point *'32*
The Dude Bandit *'33*

James Melkonian
The Stoned Age *'94*
The Jerky Boys *'95*

Jean-Pierre Melville (1917-73)
Les Enfants Terrible '50
Bob le Flambeur '55
Le Doulos '61
Leon Morin, Priest '61
Le Deuxieme Souffle '66
Le Samourai '67
Army of Shadows '69
Le Cercle Rouge '70

Stevan Mena
Malevolence '04
Brutal Massacre: A Comedy '07
Bereavement '10

Christopher Menaul
A Dangerous Man: Lawrence after Arabia '91
Prime Suspect '92
Feast of July '95
The Passion of Ayn Rand '99
Secret Smile '05
See No Evil: The Moors Murders '06
Summer in February '13

Eric Mendelsohn (1964-)
Judy Berlin '99
3 Backyards '10

George Mendeluk (1948-)
The Kidnapping of the President '80
Doin' Time '85
Her Fatal Flaw '06
Presumed Dead '06
12 Hours to Live '06
Under the Mistletoe '06
Destination: Infestation '07
Judicial Indiscretion '07
Secrets of an Undercover Wife '07
Nightmare at the End of the Hall '08
Secret Lives of Second Wives '08
Storm Seekers '08
Bitter Harvest '17

Lothar Mendes (1894-1974)
Power '34
The Man Who Could Work Miracles '37
Moonlight Sonata '38
Tampico '44

Sam Mendes (1965-)
American Beauty '99
Road to Perdition '02
Jarhead '05
Revolutionary Road '08
Away We Go '09
Skyfall '12
Spectre '15
1917 '19

Mike Mendez
The Convent '00
The Gravedancers '06
Tales of Halloween '15
The Last Heist '16
Don't Kill It '17

Joe Menendez (1969-)
Lords of the Barrio '02
A Golden Christmas 2: The Second Tail '11
The Brittany Murphy Story '14
Ladrones '15

Ramon Menendez
Stand and Deliver '88
Money for Nothing '93

Chris Menges (1940-)
A World Apart '88
Crisscross '92
Second Best '94
The Lost Son '98

Jiri Menzel (1938-)
Closely Watched Trains '66
I Served the King of England '07

William Cameron Menzies (1896-1957)
Chandu the Magician '32
Things to Come '36
The Green Cockatoo '37
The Thief of Bagdad '40
Address Unknown '44
Drums in the Deep South '51
Invaders from Mars '53

Ismail Merchant (1936-2005)
The Courtesans of Bombay '85
In Custody '94
Cotton Mary '99
The Mystic Masseur '01

Stephen Merchant (1974-)
Cemetery Junction '10
Fighting with My Family '19

Michael Meredith (1967-)
Three Days of Rain '02
The Open Road '09

James Merendino (1967-)
Witchcraft 4: Virgin Heart '92
Hard Drive '94
Terrified '94
A River Made to Drown In '97
SLC Punk! '99
Evil Remains '04

Joseph Merhi (1953-)
The Killing Game '87
The Newlydeads '87
L.A. Heat '88
Emperor of the Bronx '89
L.A. Vice '89
Midnight Warrior '89
The Last Riders '90
Night of the Wilding '90
Repo Jake '90
Final Impact '91
C.I.A.: Code Name Alexa '92
Magic Kid '92
Maximum Force '92
Direct Hit '93
To Be the Best '93
Zero Tolerance '93
Last Man Standing '95
Rage '95
The Sweeper '95
Riot '96
Executive Target '97

Edmund Elias Merhige (1964-)
Shadow of the Vampire '00
Suspect Zero '04

Jose Luis Merino (1927-)
Hell Commandos '69
Scream of the Demon Lover '71
The Hanging Woman '72

Alex Merkin
Across the Hall '09
House of Bodies '13
Percentage '13
Altitude '17

Dagen Merrill
Beneath '07
Broken Hill '09

Keith Merrill (1940-)
Three Warriors '77
Windwalker '81
Harry's War '84
The Twelve Dogs of Christmas '05
12 Dogs of Christmas: Great Puppy Rescue '12

William Mesa
The Black Gate '95
DNA '97

Alan Metter
Girls Just Want to Have Fun '85
Back to School '86
Moving '88
Cold Dog Soup '89
Police Academy 7: Mission to Moscow '94
Billboard Dad '98
The Growing Pains Movie '00

Alan Metzger
Murder C.O.D. '90
Black Widow Murders: The Blanche Taylor Moore Story '93
Take My Advice: The Ann & Abby Story '99
My Husband's Double Life '01
Snap Decision '01

Radley Metzger (1929-)
Dark Odyssey '57
The Dirty Girls '64
Carmen, Baby '66
Therese & Isabelle '67
Camille 2000 '69
The Lickerish Quartet '70
Little Mother '71
Score '72
The Cat and the Canary '79
The Princess & the Call Girl '84

Nicholas Meyer (1945-)
Time After Time '79
Star Trek 2: The Wrath of Khan '82
The Day After '83
Volunteers '85
The Deceivers '88
Company Business '91
Star Trek 6: The Undiscovered Country '91
Vendetta '99

Russ Meyer (1922-2004)
Faster, Pussycat! Kill! Kill! '65
Motor Psycho '65
Beyond the Valley of the Dolls '70
Supervixens '75
Beneath the Valley of the Ultra-Vixens '79

Turi Meyer (1964-)
Sleepstalker: The Sandman's Last Rites '94
Candyman 3: Day of the Dead '98

Marc Meyers
Harvest '10
My Friend Dahmer '17

Nancy Meyers (1949-)
The Parent Trap '98
What Women Want '00
Something's Gotta Give '03
The Holiday '06
It's Complicated '09
The Intern '15

Menno Meyjes (1954-)
Max '02
Martian Child '07
A Matador's Mistress '08

Eric Meza
House Party 3 '94
The Breaks '99

Richard Michaels (1936-)
Once an Eagle '76
Berlin Tunnel 21 '81
The Children Nobody Wanted '81
Silence of the Heart '84
The Queen of Mean '90
Backfield in Motion '91
Father and Scout '94

Oscar Micheaux (1884-1951)
Within Our Gates '20
Body and Soul '24
Girl from Chicago '32

Roger Michell (1957-)
The Buddha of Suburbia '92
Notting Hill '99
Changing Lanes '02
The Mother '03
Enduring Love '04
Venus '06
Morning Glory '10
Hyde Park on Hudson '12
Le Week-End '14
My Cousin Rachel '17
Tea with the Dames '18

David Michod
Animal Kingdom '09
The Rover '14
War Machine '17
The King '19

Jim Mickle
Mulberry Street '06
Stake Land '10
We Are What We Are '13
Cold in July '14
In the Shadow of the Moon '19

George Mihalka (1952-)
Pick-Up Summer '79
My Bloody Valentine '81
Eternal Evil '87
Psychic '91
Relative Fear '95
Cruel and Unusual '01
Sticks and Stones '08
Hoax for the Holidays '10

Christopher R. Mihm
The Monster of Phantom Lake '06
It Came From Another World '07
Cave Women on Mars '08
Destination: Outer Space '10
Attack of the Moon Zombies '11

Takashi Miike (1960-)
Fudoh: The New Generation '96
The Way To Fight '96
Audition '99
Andromedia '00
Dead or Alive 2 '00
Dead or Alive '00
The Happiness of the Katakuris '01
Ichi the Killer '01
Red Shadow '01
Visitor Q '01
Dead or Alive: Final '02
Graveyard of Honor '02
Gozu '03
One Missed Call '03
Sabu '04
Three . . . Extremes '04
Zebraman '04
The Great Yokai War '05
Crows Zero '07
Sukiyaki Western Django '08
13 Assassins '10
Hara-Kiri: Death of a Samurai '11
Yakuza Apocalypse '15
Blade of the Immortal '17

Fouad Mikati
Operation: Endgame '10
Return to Sender '15

Ted V. Mikels (1929-)
The Black Klansman '66
The Astro-Zombies '67
Girl in Gold Boots '69
The Corpse Grinders '71
The Doll Squad '73
Blood Orgy of the She-Devils '74
Hustler Squad '76
10 Violent Women '79
Aftermath '85
Mark of the Astro-Zombies '02
Astro-Zombies M3: Cloned '10
Astro-Zombies M4: Invaders from Cyberspace '12

Nikita Mikhalkov (1945-)
An Unfinished Piece for a Player Piano '77
A Slave of Love '78
Oblomov '81
Burnt by the Sun '94
12 '07

Christopher Miles (1939-)
The Virgin and the Gypsy '70
Priest of Love '81

Terry Miles
A Night for Dying Tigers '10
Recoil '11
Dawn Rider '12
Lonesome Dove Church '14
Stagecoach: The Texas Jack Story '16

Lewis Milestone (1895-1980)
The Garden of Eden '28
All Quiet on the Western Front '30
The Front Page '31
Rain '32
Hallelujah, I'm a Bum '33
The Captain Hates the Sea '34
The General Died at Dawn '36
Of Mice and Men '39
Lucky Partners '40
Edge of Darkness '43
The North Star '43
The Purple Heart '44
The Strange Love of Martha Ivers '46
A Walk in the Sun '46
Arch of Triumph '48
The Red Pony '49
The Halls of Montezuma '50
The Australian Story '52
Pork Chop Hill '59
Ocean's 11 '60
Mutiny on the Bounty '62

John Milius (1944-)
Dillinger '73
The Wind and the Lion '75
Big Wednesday '78
Conan the Barbarian '82
Red Dawn '84
Farewell to the King '89
Flight of the Intruder '90
Rough Riders '97

Ray Milland (1905-86)
Rhubarb '51
Panic in Year Zero! '62
Hostile Witness '68

Catherine Millar
Twisted '96
13 Gantry Row '98

Gavin Millar (1938-)
Secrets '82
Dreamchild '85
A Murder of Quality '90
Catherine Cookson's The Dwelling Place '94
The Crow Road '96
Retribution '98

Bennett Miller (1966-)
Capote '05
Moneyball '11
Foxcatcher '14

Brian A. Miller
Caught in the Crossfire '10
House of the Rising Sun '11
Officer Down '13
The Outsider '14
The Prince '14
Vice '15
Reprisal '18
10 Minutes Gone '19

Christopher Miller (1975-)
Cloudy with a Chance of Meatballs '09
Puss in Boots '11
21 Jump Street '12
The Lego Movie '14
22 Jump Street '14

Claude Miller (1942-2012)
The Best Way '76
Alias Betty '01
La Petite Lili '03
A Secret '07
I'm Glad My Mother Is Alive '09
Therese '12

David Miller (1909-92)
Billy the Kid '41
Flying Tigers '42
Love Happy '50
Sudden Fear '52
Diane '55
The Opposite Sex '56
Back Street '61
Lonely Are the Brave '62
Captain Newman, M.D. '63
Hammerhead '68
Executive Action '73

Frank Miller (1957-)
Sin City '05
The Spirit '08
Sin City: A Dame to Kill For '14

George Miller (1943-)
The Man from Snowy River '82
The Aviator '85
Nevil Shute's The Far Country '85
NeverEnding Story 2: The Next Chapter '91
Over the Hill '93
Andre '94
Zeus and Roxanne '96
Journey to the Center of the Earth '99
Attack of the Sabretooth '05
Happy Feet '06

George Miller (1945-)
Mad Max '80
The Road Warrior '82
Twilight Zone: The Movie '83
Mad Max: Beyond Thunderdome '85
The Witches of Eastwick '87
Lorenzo's Oil '92
Robinson Crusoe '96
Babe: Pig in the City '98
Cybermutt '02
Happy Feet Two '11
Mad Max: Fury Road '15

Harvey Miller (1936-99)
Bad Medicine '85
Getting Away With Murder '96

Jonathan Miller (1934-)
Alice in Wonderland '66
Take a Girl Like You '70
Long Day's Journey into Night '88

Logan Miller
Touching Home '08
Sweetwater '13

Michael Miller
Street Girls '75
Jackson County Jail '76
National Lampoon's Class Reunion '82
Silent Rage '82
Silent Witness '85
Roses Are for the Rich '87
Necessity '88
Danielle Steel's Daddy '91
Danielle Steel's Palomino '91
Danielle Steel's Heartbeat '93
Danielle Steel's Star '93
Dangerous Passion '95

Neal Miller
Under the Biltmore Clock '85
Raising Flagg '06

Percy Miller (1967-)
See Master P

Randall Miller
Class Act '91
Houseguest '94
The Sixth Man '97
Marilyn Hotchkiss' Ballroom Dancing & Charm School '06
Nobel Son '08
CBGB '13

Rebecca Miller (1962-)
Angela *'94*
Personal Velocity: Three Portraits *'02*
The Ballad of Jack and Rose *'05*
The Private Lives of Pippa Lee *'09*
Maggie's Plan *'16*

Robert Ellis Miller (1932-)
Any Wednesday *'66*
The Heart Is a Lonely Hunter *'68*
Sweet November *'68*
The Buttercup Chain *'70*
The Girl from Petrovka *'74*
Brenda Starr *'86*
Hawks *'89*

Sam Miller (1962-)
Among Giants *'98*
No Good Deed *'14*

Sidney Miller (1916-2004)
The 30-Foot Bride of Candy Rock *'59*
Get Yourself a College Girl *'64*

Steven C. Miller (1981-)
Automaton Transfusion *'06*
Scream of the Banshee *'11*
The Aggression Scale *'12*
Silent Night *'12*
Extraction *'15*
Marauders *'16*
Arsenal *'17*
First Kill *'17*
Escape Plan 2: Hades *'18*

Tim Miller
Deadpool *'16*
Terminator: Dark Fate *'19*

Troy Miller
Jack Frost *'98*
Dumb and Dumberer: When Harry Met Lloyd *'03*

Andy Milligan (1929-91)
The Ghastly Ones *'68*
The Body Beneath *'70*
Torture Dungeon *'70*
Legacy of Horror *'78*
Carnage *'84*

Bill Milling
Lauderdale *'89*
Caged Fury *'90*
Body Trouble *'92*

Travis Milloy (1969-)
Street Gun *'96*
Thugs *'96*

Alec Mills (1932-)
Bloodmoon *'90*
Dead Sleep *'91*

Mike Mills (1966-)
Thumbsucker *'05*
Beginners *'10*
20th Century Women *'17*

Dan Milner
The Phantom from 10,000 Leagues *'56*
The Oh in Ohio *'06*

Sergio Mimica-Gezzan (1957-)
Taken *'02*
The Legend of Butch & Sundance *'04*
Pillars of the Earth *'10*

Matej Minac (1961-)
All My Loved Ones *'00*
Nicky's Family *'13*

Allen Miner
Ghost Town *'56*
Black Patch *'57*
The Ride Back *'57*
Chubasco *'67*

Steve Miner (1951-)
Friday the 13th, Part 2 *'81*
Friday the 13th, Part 3 *'82*
House *'86*
Soul Man *'86*
Warlock *'91*
Wild Hearts Can't Be Broken *'91*
Forever Young *'92*
My Father the Hero *'93*
Big Bully *'95*
Halloween: H20 *'98*
Lake Placid *'99*
Texas Rangers *'01*
Private Valentine: Blonde & Dangerous *'08*

Wu Ming (1966-)
See Xiaoshuai Wang

Anthony Minghella (1954-2008)
Truly, Madly, Deeply *'91*
Mr. Wonderful *'93*
The English Patient *'96*
The Talented Mr. Ripley *'99*
Cold Mountain *'03*
Breaking and Entering *'06*

Rob Minkoff
Honey, I Shrunk the Kids *'89*
The Lion King *'94*
Stuart Little *'99*
Stuart Little 2 *'02*
The Haunted Mansion *'03*
The Forbidden Kingdom *'08*
Flypaper *'11*
Mr. Peabody & Sherman *'14*

Vincente Minnelli (1903-86)
Cabin in the Sky *'43*
I Dood It *'43*
Meet Me in St. Louis *'44*
The Clock *'45*
Yolanda and the Thief *'45*
Undercurrent *'46*
Ziegfeld Follies *'46*
The Pirate *'48*
Madame Bovary *'49*
Father of the Bride *'50*
An American in Paris *'51*
Father's Little Dividend *'51*
The Bad and the Beautiful *'52*
The Band Wagon *'53*
The Story of Three Loves *'53*
Brigadoon *'54*
The Long, Long Trailer *'54*
The Cobweb *'55*
Kismet *'55*
Lust for Life *'56*
Tea and Sympathy *'56*
Designing Woman *'57*
Gigi *'58*
The Reluctant Debutante *'58*
Some Came Running *'58*
Bells Are Ringing *'60*
Home from the Hill *'60*
The Courtship of Eddie's Father *'62*
The Four Horsemen of the Apocalypse *'62*
Two Weeks in Another Town *'62*
The Sandpiper *'65*
On a Clear Day You Can See Forever *'70*
A Matter of Time *'76*

David Mirkin (1955-)
Romy and Michele's High School Reunion *'97*
Heartbreakers *'01*

Bob Misiorowski
Point of Impact *'93*
On the Border *'98*
Shark Attack *'99*
Derailed *'02*

Kenji Misumi (1921-75)
Zatoichi: The Life and Opinion of Masseur Ichi *'62*
Zatoichi: The Blind Swordsman and the Chess Expert *'65*
Lone Wolf and Cub *'72*
Lone Wolf and Cub: Baby Cart at the River Styx *'72*
Lone Wolf and Cub: Baby Cart to Hades *'72*
Shogun Assassin 2: Lightning Swords of Death *'73*

David Mitchell
The Killing Man *'94*
Ski School 2 *'94*
Downhill Willie *'96*
Mask of Death *'97*
UKM: The Ultimate Killing Machine *'06*

David Robert Mitchell
The Myth of the American Sleepover *'10*
It Follows *'15*
Under the Silver Lake *'18*

John Cameron Mitchell (1963-)
Hedwig and the Angry Inch *'00*
Rabbit Hole *'10*
How To Talk To Girls At Parties *'17*

Mike Mitchell
Deuce Bigalow: Male Gigolo *'99*
Surviving Christmas *'04*
Sky High *'05*
Shrek Forever After *'10*
Alvin and the Chipmunks: Chipwrecked *'11*
Trolls *'16*
The LEGO Movie 2: The Second Part *'19*

Monika Mitchell
Break a Leg *'03*
What Comes Around *'06*
The Knight Before Christmas *'19*

Oswald Mitchell (1890-1949)
Old Mother Riley in Paris *'38*
Old Mother Riley, MP *'39*
Mysterious Mr. Nicholson *'47*
The Greed of William Hart *'48*
House of Darkness *'48*

Akira Mitsuwa
Atomic Rulers of the World *'65*
Evil Brain from Outer Space *'65*

Hayao Miyazaki (1941-)
The Castle of Cagliostro *'80*
My Neighbor Totoro *'88*
Kiki's Delivery Service *'98*
Princess Mononoke *'98*
Spirited Away *'01*
Howl's Moving Castle *'04*
Ponyo *'08*
The Wind Rises *'13*

Kenji Mizoguchi (1898-1956)
Osaka Elegy *'36*
Sisters of the Gion *'36*
47 Ronin, Part 1 *'42*
47 Ronin, Part 2 *'42*
Utamaro and His Five Women *'46*
Ugetsu *'53*
Sansho the Bailiff *'54*
Shin Heike Monogatari *'55*
Street of Shame *'56*

Moshe Mizrahi (1931-)
I Love You Rosa *'72*
Rachel's Man *'75*
Every Time We Say Goodbye *'86*

Juan Lopez Moctezuma (1932-95)
Dr. Tarr's Torture Dungeon *'75*
Mary, Mary, Bloody Mary *'76*
To Kill a Stranger *'84*

Philip Moeller (1880-1958)
The Age of Innocence *'34*
Break of Hearts *'35*

Leonide Moguy (1899-1976)
Paris After Dark *'43*
Action in Arabia *'44*
Whistle Stop *'46*

Jose Mojica Marins (1929-)
At Midnight, I'll Take Your Soul *'63*
Awakenings of the Beast *'68*

Hans Petter Moland (1955-)
The Last Lieutenant *'94*
Zero Degrees Kelvin *'95*
Aberdeen *'00*
The Beautiful Country *'04*
A Somewhat Gentle Man *'10*
In Order of Disappearance *'14*
Cold Pursuit *'19*

Gustaf Molander (1888-1973)
Intermezzo *'36*
A Woman's Face *'38*

Ron Moler
The Runner *'99*
Local Boys *'02*

Jacinto (Jack) Molina (1934-2009)
See Paul Naschy

William H. Molina
The Last Assassins *'96*
Where Truth Lies *'96*

Edouard Molinaro (1928-2013)
Ravishing Idiot *'64*
To Commit a Murder *'67*
La Cage aux Folles *'78*
La Cage aux Folles 2 *'81*
Just the Way You Are *'84*
Beaumarchais the Scoundrel *'96*

Dominik Moll (1962-)
With a Friend Like Harry *'00*
Lemming *'05*

Craig Monahan
The Interview *'98*
Healing *'15*

William Monahan (1960-)
London Boulevard *'10*
Mojave *'15*

Karen Moncrieff (1963-)
Blue Car *'03*
The Dead Girl *'06*
The Trials of Cate McCall *'13*
Petals on the Wind *'14*

Andrew Mondshein (1962-)
Evidence of Blood *'97*
An Unfinished Life *'05*

Christopher Monger (1950-)
Waiting for the Light *'90*
The Englishman Who Went up a Hill But Came down a Mountain *'95*

Mario Monicelli (1915-2010)
Big Deal on Madonna Street *'58*
The Organizer *'64*
Casanova '70 *'65*
The Queens *'66*
Lovers and Liars *'81*

Steven R. Monroe (1964-)
House of 9 *'05*
It Waits *'05*
Storm Cell *'08*
Ice Twisters *'09*
Wyvern *'09*
I Spit on Your Grave *'10*
Mongolian Death Worm *'10*
12 Disasters *'12*
End of the World *'13*
I Spit on Your Grave 2 *'13*

Carl Monson (1932-88)
Please Don't Eat My Mother *'72*
Blood Legacy *'73*
Death Feud *'89*

Edward Montagne (1912-2003)
McHale's Navy *'64*
The Reluctant Astronaut *'67*
They Went That-a-Way & That-a-Way *'78*

Guiliano Montaldo (1930-)
Grand Slam *'67*
Machine Gun McCain *'69*
Sacco & Vanzetti *'71*
Fifth Day of Peace *'72*
Time to Kill *'89*

Jorge Montesi
Omen 4: The Awakening *'91*
Hush Little Baby *'93*
Mother, May I Sleep With Danger? *'96*
Turbulence 3: Heavy Metal *'00*
Call of the Wild *'04*
Last Chance Cafe *'06*
Cleaverville *'07*

George Montgomery (1916-2000)
The Steel Claw *'61*
Samar *'62*
Guerillas in Pink Lace *'64*

Robert Montgomery (1904-81)
Lady in the Lake *'46*
Ride the Pink Horse *'47*
Eye Witness *'49*
The Gallant Hours *'60*

Dito Montiel (1965-)
A Guide to Recognizing Your Saints *'06*
Fighting *'09*
The Son of No One *'11*
Boulevard *'15*
Man Down *'16*
The Clapper *'18*

Daniel Monzon
The Kovak Box *'06*
Cell 211 *'09*

Lukas Moodysson (1969-)
Show Me Love *'99*
Mammoth *'09*
We Are the Best! *'13*

Charles Philip Moore
Dance with Death *'91*
Black Belt *'92*
Angel of Destruction *'94*

Jason Moore
Pitch Perfect *'12*
Sisters *'15*

John Moore (1970-)
Behind Enemy Lines *'01*
Flight of the Phoenix *'04*
The Omen *'06*
Max Payne *'08*
A Good Day to Die Hard *'13*
I.T. *'16*

Michael Moore (1954-)
Roger & Me *'89*
Canadian Bacon *'94*
The Big One *'98*
Bowling for Columbine *'02*
Fahrenheit 9/11 *'04*
Sicko *'07*
Capitalism: A Love Story *'09*
Where to Invade Next *'15*
Fahrenheit 11/9 *'18*

Michael D. Moore (1914-)
Paradise, Hawaiian Style *'66*
Kill a Dragon *'67*
Buckskin *'68*
Fastest Guitar Alive *'68*

Rich Moore
Wreck-It Ralph *'12*
Zootopia *'16*

Robert Moore (1927-84)
Murder by Death *'76*
The Cheap Detective *'78*
Chapter Two *'79*

Scott Moore
21 & Over *'13*
Bad Moms *'16*
A Bad Moms Christmas *'17*
Jexi *'19*

Tom (Thomas R.) Moore
Return to Boggy Creek *'77*
'night, Mother *'86*
Danielle Steel's Fine Things *'90*
Gepetto *'00*

Vin Moore
Flirting With Danger *'35*
The Drag-Net *'36*
Children of the Wild *'37*

Jocelyn Moorhouse (1960-)
Proof *'91*
How to Make an American Quilt *'95*
A Thousand Acres *'97*
The Dressmaker *'16*

Philippe Mora (1949-)
Mad Dog Morgan *'76*
The Beast Within *'82*
Return of Captain Invincible *'83*
Howling 2: Your Sister Is a Werewolf *'85*
Howling 3: The Marsupials *'87*
Communion *'89*
Back in Business *'96*
Pterodactyl Woman from Beverly Hills *'97*
Burning Down the House *'01*

Christopher Morahan (1929-)
All Neat in Black Stockings *'69*
The Jewel in the Crown *'84*
Clockwise *'86*
Troubles *'88*
Paper Mask *'91*
Element of Doubt *'96*

Reed Morano (1977-)
Meadowland *'15*
I Think We're Alone Now *'18*
The Rhythm Section *'19*

Gael Morel (1972-)
Full Speed *'96*
Apres Lui *'07*
Our Paradise *'11*

Pierre Morel (1964-)
District B13 *'04*
Taken *'08*
From Paris With Love *'10*
The Gunman *'15*
Peppermint *'18*

Juan Martinez Moreno
Two Tough Guys *'03*
The ABCs of Death 2 *'14*

David Moreton
Edge of Seventeen *'99*
Testosterone *'03*

Nanni Moretti (1953-)
Caro Diario *'93*
The Son's Room *'00*
Mia Madre *'16*

Glen Morgan
Willard *'03*
Black Christmas *'06*

William M. Morgan (1899-1964)
Mr. District Attorney *'41*
Heart of the Rio Grande *'42*
Fun & Fancy Free *'47*

Brett Morgen
The Kid Stays in the Picture *'02*
Chicago 10 *'07*
Cobain: Montage of Heck *'15*
Jane *'17*

First Monday in October '81
Foreign Body '86

Hal Needham (1931-2013)
Smokey and the Bandit '77
Hooper '78
The Villain '79
Smokey and the Bandit 2 '80
Cannonball Run '81
Stroker Ace '83
Cannonball Run 2 '84
Body Slam '87
Hostage Hotel '00

Antonio Negret
Transit '12
Overdrive '17

Jose Antonio Negret
Towards Darkness '07
Seconds Apart '11

Alberto Negrin (1940-)
Mussolini & I '85
Tower of the Firstborn '98

Jean Negulesco (1900-93)
The Conspirators '44
The Mask of Dimitrios '44
Humoresque '46
Nobody Lives Forever '46
Three Strangers '46
Deep Valley '47
Johnny Belinda '48
Road House '48
The Forbidden Street '49
The Mudlark '50
Three Came Home '50
Lure of the Wilderness '52
Phone Call from a Stranger '52
How to Marry a Millionaire '53
Scandal at Scourie '53
Titanic '53
Three Coins in the Fountain '54
Daddy Long Legs '55
The Rains of Ranchipur '55
The Best of Everything '59

Marshall Neilan (1891-1958)
Rebecca of Sunnybrook Farm '17
Amarilly of Clothesline Alley '18
Stella Maris '18
Daddy Long Legs '19
Vagabond Lover '29

Roy William Neill (1886-1946)
The Viking '28
Whirlpool '34
The Black Room '35
Dr. Syn '37
Frankenstein Meets the Wolfman '42
Sherlock Holmes and the Secret Weapon '42
Sherlock Holmes Faces Death '43
Sherlock Holmes in Washington '43
The Pearl of Death '44
Scarlet Claw '44
House of Fear '45
Pursuit to Algiers '45
Black Angel '46
Dressed to Kill '46
The Woman in Green '49

James Neilson (1910-79)
Night Passage '57
Bon Voyage! '62
Moon Pilot '62
Johnny Shiloh '63
Summer Magic '63
Dr. Syn, Alias the Scarecrow '64
The Moon-Spinners '64
The Adventures of Bullwhip Griffin '66
Gentle Giant '67
Return of the Gunfighter '67
Where Angels Go, Trouble Follows '68
The First Time '69

Chris Nelson
Ass Backwards '13
Date and Switch '13
The Perfect Date '19

Dusty Nelson
Necromancer: Satan's Servant '88
Inferno '01

Gary Nelson
Molly & Lawless John '72
Santee '73
Freaky Friday '76
Washington: Behind Closed Doors '77
The Black Hole '79
Pride of Jesse Hallum '81
Murder in Coweta County '83
The Baron and the Kid '84
Allan Quatermain and the Lost City of Gold '86
Noble House '88
Get Smart, Again! '89

Gene Nelson (1920-96)
Kissin' Cousins '64
Your Cheatin' Heart '64
Harum Scarum '65
The Cool Ones '67

Jessie Nelson
Corrina, Corrina '94
I Am Sam '01
Love the Coopers '15

Ralph Nelson (1916-87)
Requiem for a Heavyweight '56
Requiem for a Heavyweight '62
Lilies of the Field '63
Soldier in the Rain '63
Fate Is the Hunter '64
Father Goose '64
Duel at Diablo '66
Counterpoint '67
Charly '68
Soldier Blue '70
Tick... Tick... Tick '70
Flight of the Doves '71
The Wrath of God '72
The Wilby Conspiracy '75
Embryo '76
A Hero Ain't Nothin' but a Sandwich '78

Stanley Nelson
Freedom Summer '14
The Black Panthers: Vanguard of the Revolution '15

Tim Blake Nelson (1964-)
Eye of God '97
The Grey Zone '01
O '01
Leaves of Grass '09

László Nemes
Son of Saul '15
Sunset '18

Avi Nesher (1953-)
She '83
Doppelganger: The Evil Within '90
Timebomb '91
Mercenary '96
The Taxman '98
Raw Nerve '99
Tales from the Crypt Presents Ritual '02
The Secrets '07
The Other Story '19

Sandra Nettelbeck (1966-)
Mostly Martha '01
Helen '09
Last Love '13

Kurt Neumann (1906-58)
It Happened in New Orleans '36
Let's Sing Again '36
Make a Wish '37
Wide Open Faces '38
Tarzan and the Amazons '45
Tarzan and the Leopard Woman '46
Tarzan and the Huntress '47
The Dude Goes West '48
Bad Men of Tombstone '49
Rocketship X-M '50
Hiawatha '52
The Ring '52
Tarzan and the She-Devil '53
Carnival Story '54
Party Girls for Sale '54
They Were So Young '55
Mohawk '56
Kronos '57
She Devil '57
The Fly '58
Counterplot '59

Mark Neveldine (1973-)
Crank '06
Crank: High Voltage '09
Gamer '09
Ghost Rider: Spirit of Vengeance '12

Morgan Neville
20 Feet from Stardom '13
Best of Enemies '15
Won't You Be My Neighbor? '18

Mike Newell (1942-)
The Man in the Iron Mask '77
The Awakening '80
Bad Blood '81
Dance with a Stranger '85
Amazing Grace & Chuck '87
The Good Father '87
Enchanted April '92
Into the West '92
An Awfully Big Adventure '94
Four Weddings and a Funeral '94
Donnie Brasco '96
Pushing Tin '99
Mona Lisa Smile '03
Harry Potter and the Goblet of Fire '05
Prince of Persia: The Sands of Time '10
Great Expectations '12
The Guernsey Literary & Potato Peel Pie Society '18

Sam Newfield (1899-1964)
Reform Girl '33
Lightnin' Bill Carson '36
Windjammer '37
Hitler: Beast of Berlin '39
The Mad Monster '42
Dead Men Walk '43
The Monster Maker '44
Nabonga '44
Swing Hostess '44
Thundering Gunslingers '44
I Accuse My Parents '45
The Lady Confesses '45
White Pongo '45
Blonde for a Day '46
Gas House Kids '46
Ghost of Hidden Valley '46
Larceny in her Heart '46
Money Madness '47
Miraculous Journey '48
She Shoulda Said No '49
State Department File 649 '49
Hi-Jacked '50
Three Desperate Men '50
The Lost Continent '51
The Gambler & the Lady '52
Outlaw Women '52
Scotland Yard Inspector '52

Anthony Newley (1931-99)
Those People Next Door '52
Summertree '71

Jonathan Newman
Angel in the House '11
Swinging With the Finkels '11
The Adventurer: The Curse of the Midas Box '13

Joseph M. Newman (1909-2006)
Abandoned '47
Jungle Patrol '48
Great Dan Patch '49
711 Ocean Drive '50
Love Nest '51
Red Skies of Montana '52
Dangerous Crossing '53
This Island Earth '55
Death in Small Doses '57
Fort Massacre '58
The Big Circus '59
The Gunfight at Dodge City '59
The George Raft Story '61
The King of the Roaring '20s: The Story of Arnold Rothstein '61
A Thunder of Drums '61
Twenty Plus Two '61

Kyle Newman
The Hollow '04
Fanboys '09
Barely Lethal '15

Paul Newman (1925-2008)
Rachel, Rachel '68
Sometimes a Great Notion '71
Harry & Son '84
The Glass Menagerie '87

Fred Newmeyer (1888-1967)
Safety Last '23
Girl Shy '24
The Freshman '25
Rodeo Rhythm '42

Kim Nguyen
War Witch '12
The Hummingbird Project '18

Phil Nibbelink
An American Tail: Fievel Goes West '91
We're Back! A Dinosaur's Story '93

Fred Niblo (1874-1948)
Mark of Zorro '20
Sex '20
The Three Musketeers '21
Blood and Sand '22
Ben-Hur '26
The Temptress '26

Andrew Niccol (1964-)
Gattaca '97
Simone '02
Lord of War '05
In Time '11
The Host '13
Good Kill '15

Paul Nicholas (1945-)
Daughter of Death '82
Chained Heat '83
Luckytown '00

George Nicholls, Jr. (1897-1939)
Finishing School '33
Anne of Green Gables '34
High School '40

Jeff Nichols (1978-)
Shotgun Stories '07
Take Shelter '11
Mud '12
Loving '16
Midnight Special '16

Mike Nichols (1931-2014)
Who's Afraid of Virginia Woolf? '66
The Graduate '67
Catch-22 '70
Carnal Knowledge '71
The Day of the Dolphin '73
Silkwood '83
Gin Game '84
Heartburn '86
Biloxi Blues '88
Working Girl '88
Postcards from the Edge '90
Regarding Henry '91
Wolf '94
The Birdcage '95
Primary Colors '98
What Planet Are You From? '00
Wit '01
Angels in America '03
Closer '04
Charlie Wilson's War '07

Jack Nicholson (1937-)
The Terror '63
Goin' South '78
The Two Jakes '90

William Nicholson (1948-)
Firelight '97
Hope Gap '20

Michael A. (M.A.) Nickles (1968-)
Desert Winds '95
Just Peck '09
Playback '12

Ted Nicolaou
Dungeonmaster '83
Terrorvision '86
Subspecies '90
Bad Channels '92
Bloodstone: Subspecies 2 '92
Bloodlust: Subspecies 3 '93
Vampire Journals '96
Bloodstorm: Subspecies 4 '98
LIP Service '99

John Nicolella (1946-98)
Runaway Father '91
Kull the Conqueror '97

Sebastian Niemann (1968-)
7 Days to Live '00
Ancient Relic '02

William Nigh (1881-1955)
Mr. Wu '27
Across to Singapore '28
Lord Byron of Broadway '30
The Sea Ghost '31
Headline Woman '35
The Old Homestead '35
Sweepstake Annie '35
Gangster's Boy '38
Mr. Wong, Detective '38
Romance of the Limberlost '38
Mr. Wong in Chinatown '39
Mutiny in the Big House '39
Mystery of Mr. Wong '39
Doomed to Die '40
The Fatal Hour '40
Mr. Wise Guy '42
The Strange Case of Dr. Rx '42
Corregidor '43
The Underdog '43
Where Are Your Children? '44
I Wouldn't Be in Your Shoes '48
Stage Struck '48

Rob Nilsson (1940-)
Signal 7 '83
On the Edge '86
Heat and Sunlight '87

Leonard Nimoy (1931-2015)
Star Trek 3: The Search for Spock '84
Star Trek 4: The Voyage Home '86
Three Men and a Baby '87
The Good Mother '88
Funny About Love '90
Holy Matrimony '94

Marcus Nispel (1964-)
The Texas Chainsaw Massacre '03
Pathfinder '07
Friday the 13th '09
Conan the Barbarian '11

Adrian Noble (1950-)
A Midsummer Night's Dream '96
Mrs. Lowry & Son '19

Gaspar Noé (1963-)
I Stand Alone '98
Irreversible '02
Enter the Void '09
Love '15
Climax '18

Christopher Nolan (1970-)
Following '99
Memento '00
Insomnia '02
Batman Begins '05
The Prestige '06
The Dark Knight '08
Inception '10
The Dark Knight Rises '12
Interstellar '14
Dunkirk '17

George Nolfi
The Adjustment Bureau '11
The Banker '20

Chris Noonan (1952-)
Babe '95
Miss Potter '06

Tom Noonan (1951-)
What Happened Was. . . '94
The Wife '95

Stephen Norrington (1965-)
Death Machine '95
Blade '98
The Last Minute '01
The League of Extraordinary Gentlemen '03

Aaron Norris (1951-)
Braddock: Missing in Action 3 '88
Delta Force 2: Operation Stranglehold '90
The Hitman '91
Hellbound '94
Forest Warrior '95
Top Dog '95

Eric Norris (1965-)
The President's Man '00
The President's Man 2: A Line in the Sand '02

Bill W.L. Norton (1943-)
More American Graffiti '79
Baby. . . Secret of the Lost Legend '85
Tour of Duty '87
False Arrest '92
Hercules the Legendary Journeys, Vol. 1: And the Amazon Women '94
Hercules the Legendary Journeys, Vol. 4: In the Underworld '94

Edward Norton (1969-)
Keeping the Faith '00
Motherless Brooklyn '19

Max Nosseck (1902-72)
Gambling Daughters '41
Dillinger '45

Noel Nosseck (1943-)
Best Friends '75
Las Vegas Lady '76
Return of the Rebels '81
Full Exposure: The Sex Tape Scandals '89
French Silk '94
Tornado! '96
NightScreams '97
Silent Predators '99
Another Woman's Husband '00

Jonathan Nossiter (1961-)
Sunday '96
Signs & Wonders '00
Mondovino '04
Rio Sex Comedy '10

Thierry Notz
The Terror Within '88
Watchers 2 '90
Fortunes of War '94

Jehane Noujaim (1974-)
Control Room '04
The Square '13
The Great Hack '19

Nima Nourizadeh
Project X '11
American Ultra '15

Cherie Nowlan
The Wedding Party '97
Marking Time '03
Introducing the Dwights '07

Cyrus Nowrasteh (1956-)
The Day Reagan Was Shot '01
The Stoning of Soraya M. '08
The Young Messiah '16

Phillip Noyce (1950-)
Newsfront '78
Dead Calm '89
Blind Fury '90
Patriot Games '92
Sliver '93
Clear and Present Danger '94
The Saint '97
The Bone Collector '99
The Quiet American '02
Rabbit-Proof Fence '02
Catch a Fire '06
Salt '10
Mary and Martha '13
The Giver '14

Elliott Nugent (1900-80)
If I Were Free '33
Three-Cornered Moon '33
Strictly Dynamite '34
Love in Bloom '35
And So They Were Married '36
Give Me a Sailor '38
The Cat and the Canary '39
Never Say Die '39
Nothing But the Truth '41
The Male Animal '42
Up in Arms '44
My Favorite Brunette '47
Welcome Stranger '47
My Outlaw Brother '51
Just for You '52

Victor Nunez (1945-)
A Flash of Green '85
Ulee's Gold '97
Coastlines '02

Trevor Nunn (1940-)
Lady Jane '85
Twelfth Night '96
Oklahoma! '99
Red Joan '19

Joe Nussbaum (1973-)
Sleepover '04
American Pie Presents: The Naked Mile '06
Sydney White '07
Prom '11

Raphael Nussbaum (1932-93)
Death Blow '87
Lethal Victims '87

Colin Nutley (1944-)
Under the Sun '98
Gossip '00

David Nutter (1960-)
Trancers 5: Sudden Deth '94
Disturbing Behavior '98
Band of Brothers '01
The Pacific '10

Christian Nyby (1913-93)
The Thing '51
Operation C.I.A. '65
First to Fight '67

Sven Nykvist (1922-2006)
Gorilla '56
The Ox '91

Ron Nyswaner (1956-)
Prince of Pennsylvania '88
Why Stop Now '12

Dan O'Bannon (1946-2009)
Return of the Living Dead '85
The Resurrected '91

Michael Oblowitz
The Breed '01
On the Borderline '01
The Foreigner '03
Out For a Kill '03
The Traveler '10

Arch Oboler
Five '51
One Plus One '61

Adam O'Brien
The Invoking 2 '15
Zombieworld '15

Declan O'Brien
Cyclops '08
Wrong Turn 3: Left for Dead '09
Sharktopus '10
Wrong Turn 4: Bloody Beginnings '11
Joy Ride 3: Road Kill '14

Jim O'Brien (1947-2012)
The Jewel in the Crown '84
Rebecca '97

Jeffrey Obrow
Dorm That Dripped Blood '82
Servants of Twilight '91
Bram Stoker's The Mummy '97
They Are Among Us '04

Matthew O'Callaghan
Curious George '06
Open Season 2 '08

Masayuki Ochiai
Parasite Eve '97
Shutter '08

James O'Connolly (1924-87)
Berserk! '67
The Valley of Gwangi '69
Tower of Evil '72

Gavin O'Connor
Tumbleweeds '98
Miracle '04
Pride and Glory '08
Warrior '11
The Accountant '16
Jane Got a Gun '16
The Way Back '20

Pat O'Connor (1943-)
A Month in the Country '87
The January Man '89
Circle of Friends '94
Inventing the Abbotts '97
Dancing at Lughnasa '98
Sweet November '01
Private Peaceful '12

William A. O'Connor (1900-)
Pace That Kills '28
Cocaine Fiends '36

Bob Odenkirk (1962-)
Melvin Goes to Dinner '03
Let's Go to Prison '06
The Brothers Solomon '07
Movie 43 '13

Damien O'Donnell (1967-)
East Is East '99
Rory O'Shea Was Here '04

Steve Oedekerk (1961-)
Ace Ventura: When Nature Calls '95
Nothing to Lose '96
Kung Pow! Enter the Fist '02
Barnyard '06

Peter O'Fallon
Suicide Kings '97
A Rumor of Angels '00

Jorgo Ognenovski
Warrior of Justice '96
Stalked '99

Jim O'Hanlon (1970-)
House of Saddam '08
Emma '09
Of Two Minds '12
100 Streets '17

Gerry O'Hara (1924-)
Maroc 7 '67
The Bitch '78
Leopard in the Snow '78
Fanny Hill '83
The Mummy Lives '93

Terrence O'Hara
Darkroom '90
Depth Charge '08

Tommy O'Haver (1968-2005)
Billy's Hollywood Screen Kiss '98
Get Over It! '01
Ella Enchanted '04
An American Crime '07

Michael O'Herlihy (1919-97)
The Fighting Prince of Donegal '66
The One and Only, Genuine, Original Family Band '68
Smith! '69
Kiss Me...Kill Me '76
Peter Lundy and the Medicine Hat Stallion '77
Backstairs at the White House '79
Cry of the Innocent '80
Detour to Terror '80
A Time for Miracles '80

Ataru Oikawa
Tomie '99
The Black House '00

Kihachi Okamoto (1923-2005)
Sword of Doom '67
Kill! '68
Red Lion '69
Zatoichi *vs.* Yojimbo '70

Takao Okawara (1949-)
Godzilla *vs.* Mothra '92
Godzilla *vs.* Mechagodzilla II '93
Godzilla *vs.* Destroyah '95
Godzilla 2000 '99

Sidney Olcott (1873-1949)
From the Manger to the Cross '12
Little Old New York '23
Monsieur Beaucaire '24
Ranson's Folly '26

Ken Olin (1954-)
Doing Time on Maple Drive '92
White Fang 2: The Myth of the White Wolf '94
In Pursuit of Honor '95

Ron Oliver
Prom Night 3: The Last Kiss '89
Blood Angels '05
Chasing Christmas '05
Third Man Out: A Donald Strachey Mystery '05
My Silent Partner '06
Shock to the System '06
A Dennis the Menace Christmas '07
Bridal Fever '08
Kiss Me Deadly '08
On the Other Hand, Death '08
Harriet the Spy: Blog Wars '10
Smooch '11
Cupid '12
Love at the Thanksgiving Day Parade '12

Hector Olivera (1931-)
Funny, Dirty Little War '83
Barbarian Queen '85
A Shadow You Soon Will Be '94

Laurence Olivier (1907-89)
Henry V '44
Hamlet '48
Richard III '55
The Prince and the Showgirl '57

Ermanno Olmi (1931-)
Fiances '63
The Tree of Wooden Clogs '78
Keep Walking '82

Edward James Olmos (1947-)
American Me '92
Battlestar Galactica: The Plan '09

Michael D. Olmos
Splinter '06
Filly Brown '12

Robert Olsen
Body '15
Villains '19

William Olsen (1950-)
Getting It On '83
Rockin' Road Trip '85

Sean Robert Olson (1976-)
The Dog Who Saved Easter '15
The Dog Who Saved Summer '15

David O'Malley (1944-)
Kid Colter '85
Easy Wheels '89
Dark Honeymoon '08

Robert Vincent O'Neil
Blood Mania '70
Paco '75
Angel '84
Avenging Angel '85

Kevin O'Neill
Dinocroc '04
Dinoshark '10
Attack of the 50 Foot Cheerleader '12

Morgan O'Neill
Solo '06
The Factory '10

Marcel Ophuls (1927-)
Make Your Bets Ladies '65
The Sorrow and the Pity '71
The Troubles We've Seen '94

Max Ophuls (1902-57)
Letter from an Unknown Woman '48
Caught '49
Reckless Moment '49
La Ronde '51
Le Plaisir '52
The Earrings of Madame De. . . '54
Lola Montes '55

Niels Arden Oplev (1961-)
The Girl With the Dragon Tattoo '09
Dead Man Down '13
Flatliners '17

Evan Oppenheimer
Alchemy '05
The Speed of Thought '11

Timothy O'Rawe (1962-)
The Basement '89
Ghoul School '90

Wyott Ordung (1922-2005)
Monster from the Ocean Floor '54
Walk the Dark Street '56

Paul Oremland
Like It Is '98
Surveillance 24/7 '07

Stuart Orme
The Heist '89
Hands of a Murderer '90
The Blackheath Poisonings '92
The Puppet Masters '94
Ivanhoe '97
The Sculptress '97
The Waiting Time '99
Goodbye, Mr. Chips '02
The Lost World '02
Ghostboat '06

Ron Ormond (1911-81)
Kentucky Jubilee '51
Mesa of Lost Women '52

Alan Ormsby (1944-)
Deranged '74
Popcorn '89

Gary Orona (1964-)
The Bikini Car Wash Company 2 '92
Stripshow '95

James Orr (1953-)
Mr. Destiny '90
Man of the House '95
Christmas in Wonderland '07
The Night Before the Night Before Christmas '10

Melanie Orr
The Devil's Mercy '07
Grindstone Road '07
Harm's Way '07

John Orrichio
Abduction '07
Dead Collections '12

Kenny Ortega (1950-)
Newsies '92
Hocus Pocus '93
The Cheetah Girls 2 '06
High School Musical '06
High School Musical 2 '07
High School Musical 3: Senior Year '08
Michael Jackson's This Is It '09

Aaron Osborne
Zarkorr! The Invader '96
Kraa! the Sea Monster '98

Ken Osborne
Wild Wheels '69
Jailbreakin' '72

Mark Osborne
Kung Fu Panda '08
The Little Prince '16

Mamoru Oshii (1951-)
Stray Dog '91
Ghost in the Shell '95
The Sky Crawlers '08
Garm Wars: The Last Druid '15

Nagisa Oshima (1932-2013)
Violence at Noon '66
The Empire of Passion '76
In the Realm of the Senses '76
Merry Christmas, Mr. Lawrence '83
Max, Mon Amour '86
Taboo '99

Louise Osmond
Deep Water '06
Dark Horse '16

Sam O'Steen (1923-2000)
Brand New Life '72
Sparkle '76

Ruben Ostlund
Force Majeure '14
The Square '17

Thaddeus O'Sullivan (1948-)
December Bride '91
Witness to the Mob '98
Ordinary Decent Criminal '99
The Heart of Me '02
Into the Storm '09
Stella Days '12

Olatunde Osunsanmi (1977-)
The Cavern '05
The Fourth Kind '09

Gerd Oswald (1919-89)
The Brass Legend '56
Crime of Passion '57
Paris Holiday '57
Valerie '57
Screaming Mimi '58

Dominique Othenin-Girard (1958-)
Halloween 5: The Revenge of Michael Myers '89
Omen 4: The Awakening '91
Beyond Desire '94

Jean-Paul Ouellette
The Unnamable '88
The Unnamable 2: The Statement of Randolph Carter '92

Gerard Oury (1919-2006)
La Grande Vadrouille '66
The Brain '69
Delusions of Grandeur '76

André Ovredal
The Troll Hunter '11
The Autopsy of Jane Doe '16
Scary Stories to Tell in the Dark '19

Cliff Owen (1919-93)
The Wrong Arm of the Law '63
The Magnificent Two '67
The Vengeance of She '68
No Sex Please-We're British '73

Frank Oz (1944-)
The Dark Crystal '82
The Muppets Take Manhattan '84
Little Shop of Horrors '86
Dirty Rotten Scoundrels '88
What about Bob? '91
Housesitter '92
The Indian in the Cupboard '95
In and Out '97
Bowfinger '99
The Score '01
The Stepford Wives '04
Death at a Funeral '07

Shigehiro (Sakae) Ozawa
Return of the Street Fighter '74
The Street Fighter '74

Francois Ozon (1967-)
Sitcom '97
Criminal Lovers '99
Water Drops on Burning Rocks '99
Under the Sand '00
8 Women '02
Swimming Pool '03
5x2 '04
Time to Leave '05
Angel '07
Hideaway '09
Ricky '09
Potiche '10
Young & Beautiful '13
The New Girlfriend '14
Frantz '17

Ferzan Ozpetek (1959-)
Steam: A Turkish Bath *'96*
Harem *'99*
His Secret Life *'01*
Facing Windows *'03*
Saturn in Opposition *'07*
Loose Cannons *'10*

Yasujiro Ozu (1903-63)
I Was Born But. . . *'32*
Late Spring *'49*
Early Summer *'51*
Tokyo Story *'53*
Equinox Flower *'58*
Drifting Weeds *'59*
Good Morning *'59*
An Autumn Afternoon *'62*

G.W. Pabst (1885-1967)
Joyless Street *'25*
Secrets of a Soul *'25*
The Love of Jeanne Ney *'27*
Pandora's Box *'28*
Diary of a Lost Girl *'29*
The Threepenny Opera *'31*
The Mistress of Atlantis *'32*
Don Quixote *'35*

Jose Padilha (1967-)
Rio, I Love You *'14*
RoboCop *'14*
7 Days in Entebbe *'18*

Anthony Page (1935-)
Missiles of October *'74*
I Never Promised You a Rose Garden *'77*
The Lady Vanishes *'79*
Absolution *'81*
Bill *'81*
Bill: On His Own *'83*
Grace Kelly *'83*
Monte Carlo *'86*
Pack of Lies *'87*
Middlemarch *'93*
My Zinc Bed *'08*

Marcel Pagnol (1895-1974)
Cesar *'36*
Well-Digger's Daughter *'46*

Peter Paige (1969-)
Say Uncle *'05*
Leaving Barstow *'08*

John Paizs
Invasion! *'99*
Marker *'05*

Alan J. Pakula (1928-98)
The Sterile Cuckoo *'69*
Klute *'71*
Love and Pain and the Whole Damn Thing *'73*
The Parallax View *'74*
All the President's Men *'76*
Comes a Horseman *'78*
Starting Over *'79*
Rollover *'81*
Sophie's Choice *'82*
Dream Lover *'85*
Orphans *'87*
See You in the Morning *'89*
Presumed Innocent *'90*
Consenting Adults *'92*
The Pelican Brief *'93*
The Devil's Own *'96*

George Pal (1908-80)
Tom Thumb *'58*
The Time Machine *'60*
Atlantis, the Lost Continent *'61*
7 Faces of Dr. Lao *'63*

Mark Palansky
Penelope *'06*
Rememory *'17*

Euzhan Palcy (1957-)
Sugar Cane Alley *'83*
A Dry White Season *'89*
Ruby Bridges *'98*

David Palmer
Brother's Justice *'11*
Hit and Run *'12*

Chazz Palminteri (1952-)
Women *vs.* Men *'02*
Noel *'04*

Bruce Paltrow (1943-2002)
A Little Sex *'82*
Ed McBain's 87th Precinct: Lightning *'95*
Duets *'00*

Jake Paltrow
The Good Night *'07*
Young Ones *'14*
De Palma *'16*

Jafar Panahi (1960-)
The White Balloon *'95*
The Circle *'00*
Crimson Gold *'03*
This is Not a Film *'10*
Closed Curtain *'13*
Jafar Panahi's Taxi *'15*

Norman Panama (1914-2003)
The Reformer and the Redhead *'50*
Above and Beyond *'53*
Knock on Wood *'54*
The Court Jester *'56*
The Trap *'59*
The Road to Hong Kong *'62*
How to Commit Marriage *'69*
I Will, I Will...for Now *'76*

Danny Pang (1965-)
Bangkok Dangerous *'00*
The Eye *'02*
The Eye 2 *'04*
The Eye 3 *'05*
Re-Cycle *'06*
The Messengers *'07*
Bangkok Dangerous *'08*
Out of the Inferno *'13*

Oxide Pang (1965-)
The Eye *'02*
The Messengers *'07*
Bangkok Dangerous *'08*
Out of the Inferno *'13*

Rithy Panh (1964-)
S21: The Khmer Rouge Killing Machine *'03*
The Missing Picture *'13*

Alan Pao
Toxic *'07*
Loaded *'08*

Hsueh Li Pao
The Delightful Forest *'72*
Sword Masters: The Battle Wizard *'77*

Domenico Paolella (1918-2002)
Pirates of the Coast *'61*
Hercules Against the Mongols *'63*
Hercules and the Tyrants of Babylon *'64*
Challenge of the Gladiator *'65*
Hate for Hate *'67*
Execution *'68*

Sven Pape
L.A. Twister *'04*
Hollywood Kills *'06*

Gilles Paquet-Brenner
Sarah's Key *'10*
Dark Places *'15*

Roger Paradiso
Kisses in the Dark *'97*
Tony n' Tina's Wedding *'07*

Sergei Paradjanov (1924-90)
Shadows of Forgotten Ancestors *'64*
The Color of Pomegranates *'69*
Ashik Kerib *'88*

John Paragon (1954-)
Double Trouble *'91*
Ring of the Musketeers *'93*
Twinsitters *'95*

Chuck Parello
Henry: Portrait of a Serial Killer 2: Mask of Sanity *'96*
Ed Gein *'01*
The Hillside Stranglings *'04*

Domonic Paris
Dracula's Last Rites *'79*
Splitz *'84*

Jerry Paris (1925-86)
Don't Raise the Bridge, Lower the River *'68*
How Sweet It Is! *'68*
Never a Dull Moment *'68*
The Grasshopper *'69*
Viva Max *'69*
The Passing of Evil *'70*
Evil Roy Slade *'71*
Star Spangled Girl *'71*
Only with Married Men *'74*
Police Academy 2: Their First Assignment *'85*
Police Academy 3: Back in Training *'86*

Vanessa Parise
Jack and Jill *vs.* the World *'08*
The Wedding Chapel *'13*

Dean Parisot
Framed *'90*
Home Fries *'98*
Galaxy Quest *'99*
Fun With Dick and Jane *'05*
RED 2 *'13*

Chan-wook Park (1963-)
JSA: Joint Security Area *'00*
Sympathy for Mr. Vengeance *'02*
Oldboy *'03*
Three . . . Extremes *'04*
Thirst *'09*
Stoker *'13*
The Handmaiden *'16*

Nick Park (1958-)
Chicken Run *'00*
Wallace & Gromit in The Curse of the Were-Rabbit *'05*
Early Man *'18*

Richard W. Park (2006-)
Gang Justice *'94*
American Chinatown *'96*

Alan Parker (1944-)
Bugsy Malone *'76*
Midnight Express *'78*
Fame *'80*
Pink Floyd: The Wall *'82*
Shoot the Moon *'82*
Birdy *'84*
Angel Heart *'87*
Mississippi Burning *'88*
Come See the Paradise *'90*
The Commitments *'91*
The Road to Wellville *'94*
Evita *'96*
Angela's Ashes *'99*
The Life of David Gale *'03*

Albert Parker (1887-1974)
The Eyes of Youth *'19*
Sherlock Holmes *'22*
The Black Pirate *'26*
The Third Clue *'34*

Dave Parker
The Dead Hate the Living *'99*
Tales of Halloween *'15*

Jonathan Parker
Bartleby *'01*
(Untitled) *'09*

Ol Parker (1969-)
Imagine Me & You *'06*
Now Is Good *'12*
Mamma Mia! Here We Go Again *'18*

Oliver Parker (1960-)
Othello *'95*
An Ideal Husband *'99*
The Importance of Being Earnest *'02*
I Really Hate My Job *'07*
St. Trinian's *'07*
Dorian Gray *'09*
The Legend of Fritton's Gold *'09*
Johnny English Reborn *'11*
Dad's Army *'16*

Trey Parker (1969-)
Cannibal! The Musical *'96*
Orgazmo *'98*
South Park: Bigger, Longer and Uncut *'99*
Team America: World Police *'04*

Matthew Parkhill
Dot the I *'03*
The Caller *'11*

Gordon Parks (1912-2006)
The Learning Tree *'69*
Shaft *'71*
Shaft's Big Score *'72*
The Super Cops *'74*
Three the Hard Way *'74*
Half Slave, Half Free *'85*

Gordon Parks, Jr. (1934-79)
Superfly *'72*
Aaron Loves Angela *'75*

Hugh Parks
Shakma *'89*
Fatal Passion *'94*

Gianfranco Parolini (1930-)
The Fury of Hercules *'61*
Samson *'61*
The Old Testament *'62*
Three Avengers *'64*
Kiss Kiss Kill Kill *'66*
Death is Nimble, Death is Quick *'67*
Five for Hell *'67*
Sabata *'69*
Adios, Sabata *'71*
Return of Sabata *'71*
God's Gun *'75*

Vincent Paronnauel (1970-)
Persepolis *'07*
Chicken With Plums *'11*

Robert Parrish (1916-95)
Cry Danger *'51*
The Mob *'51*
Assignment: Paris *'52*
The San Francisco Story *'52*
The Purple Plain *'54*
Fire Down Below *'57*
Saddle the Wind *'58*
The Wonderful Country *'59*
In the French Style *'63*
The Bobo *'67*
Casino Royale *'67*
Duffy *'68*
Journey to the Far Side of the Sun *'69*
A Town Called Hell *'72*
The Destructors *'74*

Gordon Parry (1908-81)
Tom Brown's School Days *'51*
Twilight Women *'52*
Tread Softly Stranger *'58*

Gabriel Pascal (1894-1954)
Major Barbara *'41*
Caesar and Cleopatra *'46*

Goran Paskalyevic (1947-)
Cabaret Balkan *'98*
How Harry Became a Tree *'01*

Pier Paolo Pasolini (1922-75)
Accatone! *'61*
Mamma Roma *'62*
The Gospel According to St. Matthew *'64*
Love Meetings *'64*
The Hawks & the Sparrows *'67*
Oedipus Rex *'67*
Teorema *'68*
Porcile *'69*
The Decameron *'70*
Medea *'70*
The Canterbury Tales *'71*
Arabian Nights *'74*
Salo, or the 120 Days of Sodom *'75*

John Pasquin
Nightmare *'91*
The Santa Clause *'94*
Jungle 2 Jungle *'96*
Joe Somebody *'01*
Miss Congeniality 2: Armed and Fabulous *'05*

Ivan Passer (1933-2020)
Born to Win *'71*
Law and Disorder *'74*
Crime & Passion *'75*
Cutter's Way *'81*
Creator *'85*
Haunted Summer *'88*
Kidnapped *'95*

Jonas Pate (1970-)
Deceiver *'97*
Shrink *'09*

Giuseppe Patroni-Griffi (1921-2005)
Driver's Seat *'73*
'Tis a Pity She's a Whore *'73*
Collector's Item *'89*

Michael Pattinson (1957-)
Moving Out *'83*
. . .Almost *'90*

Robert Patton-Spruill
Body Count *'97*
Squeeze *'97*

Peter Patzak (1945-)
Lethal Obsession *'87*
Midnight Cop *'88*

Don Michael Paul
Half Past Dead *'02*
Who's Your Caddy? *'07*
Lake Placid: The Final Chapter *'12*
Company of Heroes *'13*
Jarhead 2: Field of Fire *'14*
Sniper: Legacy *'14*
Tremors 5: Bloodlines *'15*
Kindergarten Cop 2 *'16*
Sniper: Ghost Shooter *'16*

Mark Pavia
Stephen King's The Night Flier *'96*
Fender Bender *'16*

Michael Pavone
The Reunion *'11*
That's What I Am *'11*

Pawel Pawlikowski (1957-)
My Summer of Love *'05*
The Woman in the Fifth *'11*
Ida *'13*
Cold War *'18*

Bill Paxton (1955-2017)
Frailty *'02*
The Greatest Game Ever Played *'05*

Alexander Payne (1961-)
Citizen Ruth *'96*
Election *'99*
About Schmidt *'02*
Sideways *'04*
Paris, je t'aime *'06*
The Descendants *'11*
Nebraska *'13*
Downsizing *'17*

Dave Payne
Concealed Weapon *'94*
Alien Terminator *'95*
Under Oath *'97*

Michael Pearce
Initiation *'87*
Beast *'17*

Richard Pearce (1943-)
Heartland *'81*
Country *'84*
No Mercy *'86*
The Long Walk Home *'89*
Leap of Faith *'92*
A Family Thing *'96*
Witness Protection *'99*
Rodgers & Hammerstein's South Pacific *'01*
Fatal Contact: Bird Flu in America *'06*

Kris Pearn
Cloudy with a Chance of Meatballs 2 *'13*
The Willoughbys *'20*

Max Pecas (1925-2003)
Daniella by Night *'61*
Sweet Ecstasy *'62*

Raoul Peck (1953-)
Lumumba *'01*
Sometimes in April *'05*
I Am Not Your Negro *'17*

Sam Peckinpah (1925-84)
Deadly Companions *'61*
Ride the High Country *'62*
Major Dundee *'65*
The Wild Bunch *'69*
Ballad of Cable Hogue *'70*
The Getaway *'72*
Junior Bonner *'72*
Straw Dogs *'72*
Pat Garrett & Billy the Kid *'73*
Bring Me the Head of Alfredo Garcia *'74*
The Killer Elite *'75*
Cross of Iron *'76*
Convoy *'78*
The Osterman Weekend *'83*

Jordan Peele (1979-)
Get Out *'17*
Us *'19*

Larry Peerce (1935-)
Goodbye, Columbus *'69*
Ash Wednesday *'73*
The Other Side of the Mountain *'75*
Two Minute Warning *'76*
The Other Side of the Mountain, Part 2 *'78*
The Bell Jar *'79*
Love Child *'82*
Hard to Hold *'84*
Queenie *'87*
The Abduction *'96*

Barbara Peeters
Bury Me an Angel *'71*
Summer School Teachers *'75*
Humanoids from the Deep *'80*

Kimberly Peirce (1967-)
Boys Don't Cry *'99*
Stop-Loss *'08*
Carrie *'13*

Oren Peli
Paranormal Activity *'09*
Paranormal Activity 3 *'11*
Area 51 *'15*

Anthony Pelissier (1912-88)
The Rocking Horse Winner *'49*
Encore *'52*

Jean Pellerin
For Hire *'98*
Laserhawk *'99*
Escape under Pressure *'00*
Daybreak *'01*

Mark Pellington (1962-)
Going All the Way *'97*
Arlington Road *'99*

The Fearless Vampire Killers '67
Rosemary's Baby '68
Macbeth '71
Chinatown '74
The Tenant '76
Tess '79
Frantic '88
Bitter Moon '92
Death and the Maiden '94
The Ninth Gate '99
The Pianist '02
Oliver Twist '05
The Ghost Writer '10
Carnage '11
Venus in Fur '13

Stephen Poliakoff (1952-)
Hidden City '87
Close My Eyes '91
Shooting the Past '99
Almost Strangers '01
Friends & Crocodiles '05
Gideon's Daughter '05
Glorious 39 '09

Michael Polish (1970-)
Twin Falls Idaho '99
Jackpot '01
Northfork '03
The Astronaut Farmer '07
The Smell of Success '09
Stay Cool '09
Big Sur '13
Amnesiac '15
90 Minutes in Heaven '15

Patrik-Ian Polk
Noah's Arc: Jumping the Broom '08
Blackbird '14

Jeff Pollack (1959-)
Above the Rim '94
Booty Call '96
Lost and Found '99

Sydney Pollack (1934-2008)
The Slender Thread '65
This Property Is Condemned '66
The Scalphunters '68
Castle Keep '69
They Shoot Horses, Don't They? '69
Jeremiah Johnson '72
The Way We Were '73
Three Days of the Condor '75
The Yakuza '75
Bobby Deerfield '77
The Electric Horseman '79
Absence of Malice '81
Tootsie '82
Out of Africa '85
Havana '90
The Firm '93
Sabrina '95
Random Hearts '99
The Interpreter '05
Amazing Grace '19

Harry A. Pollard (1883-1934)
California Straight Ahead '25
Uncle Tom's Cabin '27
Shipmates '31
Fast Life '32

Sarah Polley (1979-)
Away From Her '06
Take This Waltz '11

George Pollock (1907-79)
Murder She Said '61
Kill or Cure '62
Murder at the Gallop '63
Murder Ahoy '64
Murder Most Foul '65

John Polonia (1968-2008)
Feeders '96
Terror House '97
Razorteeth '05

Mark Alan Polonia (1968-)
Feeders '96
Terror House '97

Abraham Polonsky (1910-99)
Force of Evil '49
Tell Them Willie Boy Is Here '69
Romance of a Horsethief '71

Gabe Polsky
The Motel Life '12
In Search of Greatness '18

John Polson (1965-)
Siam Sunset '99
Swimfan '02
Hide and Seek '05
Tenderness '08

Barry Poltermann (1964-)
The Unearthing '93
Aswang '03

Ventura Pons (1945-)
What It's All About '95
Caresses '97
Beloved/Friend '99
To Die, Or Not '99
Food of Love '02

James Ponsoldt (1978-)
Smashed '12
The Spectacular Now '13
The End of the Tour '15
The Circle '17

Gillo Pontecorvo (1919-2006)
The Wide Blue Road '57
Kapo '59
The Battle of Algiers '66
Burn! '70

DJ Pooh
Three Strikes '00
The Wash '01

Lea Pool (1950-)
Lost and Delirious '01
The Blue Butterfly '04

Ralph Portillo (1916-95)
Hollywood Dreams '94
Stolen Hearts '95
Naked Lies '98
Bloody Murder '99
Big Brother Trouble '00
One of Them '03

Natalie Portman (1981-)
New York, I Love You '09
A Tale of Love and Darkness '16

Todd Portugal
Flooding '97
The Legend of Bloody Jack '07

Arie Posin
The Chumscrubber '05
The Face of Love '13

P.J. Posner
Last Breath '96
The Next Big Thing '02

Ted Post (1918-2013)
Hang 'Em High '67
Beneath the Planet of the Apes '70
Yuma '70
The Baby '72
The Bravos '72
Harrad Experiment '73
Magnum Force '73
Whiffs '75
Go Tell the Spartans '78
Good Guys Wear Black '78
Stagecoach '86

H.C. Potter (1904-77)
The Cowboy and the Lady '38
Shopworn Angel '38
The Story of Vernon and Irene Castle '39
Congo Maisie '40
Second Chorus '40
Mr. Lucky '43
Mr. Blandings Builds His Dream House '48
The Time of Your Life '48
You Gotta Stay Happy '48
The Miniver Story '50
Three for the Show '55
Top Secret Affair '57

Sally Potter (1947-)
Orlando '92
The Tango Lesson '97
The Man Who Cried '00
Yes '04
Ginger & Rosa '13
The Party '17

Richard Pottier (1906-94)
David and Goliath '61
The Rape of the Sabines '61

Michel Poulette
Bonanno: A Godfather's Story '99
The Tipping Point '07
Too Young to Marry '07

Dick Powell (1904-63)
Split Second '53
The Conqueror '56
Enemy Below '57
The Hunters '58

Michael Powell (1905-90)
Red Ensign '34
The Phantom Light '35
Edge of the World '37
Spy in Black '39
Contraband '40
The Thief of Bagdad '40
The Forty-Ninth Parallel '41
One of Our Aircraft Is Missing '41
The Life and Death of Colonel Blimp '43
A Canterbury Tale '44
I Know Where I'm Going '45
Stairway to Heaven '46
Black Narcissus '47
The Red Shoes '48
The Small Back Room '49
The Tales of Hoffmann '51
Ill Met By Moonlight '57
Night Ambush '57
Pursuit of the Graf Spee '57
Peeping Tom '60
Age of Consent '69

John Power (1930-)
Charles & Diana: A Palace Divided '93
Stephen King's The Tommyknockers '93
Goldrush: A Real Life Alaskan Adventure '98

Wayne Powers
Skeletons in the Closet '00
Out of Order '03

Bryan Poyser
Lovers of Hate '10
Love & Air Sex '14

Manuel Pradal (1968-)
Ginostra '02
A Crime '06

Stanley Prager (1917-72)
Bang Bang Kid '67
Madigan's Millions '67

Udayan Prasad (1953-)
My Son the Fanatic '97
Gabriel & Me '01
Opa! '05
The Yellow Handkerchief '08

Michael Preece
Prize Fighter '79
Logan's War: Bound by Honor '98

Otto Preminger (1906-86)
Danger: Love at Work '37
Margin for Error '43
In the Meantime, Darling '44
Laura '44
Fallen Angel '45
A Royal Scandal '45
Daisy Kenyon '47
Forever Amber '47
The Fan '49
Whirlpool '49
Where the Sidewalk Ends '50
Angel Face '52
The Moon Is Blue '53
Carmen Jones '54
River of No Return '54
The Court Martial of Billy Mitchell '55
The Man with the Golden Arm '55
Bonjour Tristesse '57
Saint Joan '57
Anatomy of a Murder '59
Exodus '60
Advise and Consent '62
The Cardinal '63
Bunny Lake Is Missing '65
In Harm's Way '65
Hurry Sundown '67
Skidoo '68
Such Good Friends '71
The Human Factor '79

Andrew Prendergast
Parasite '03
Hydra '09

Emeric Pressburger (1902-88)
One of Our Aircraft Is Missing '41
The Life and Death of Colonel Blimp '43
A Canterbury Tale '44
I Know Where I'm Going '45
Stairway to Heaven '46
Black Narcissus '47
The Red Shoes '48
The Small Back Room '49
The Tales of Hoffmann '51
Ill Met By Moonlight '57
Night Ambush '57

Michael Pressman (1950-)
The Great Texas Dynamite Chase '76
The Bad News Bears in Breaking Training '77
Boulevard Nights '79
Those Lips, Those Eyes '80
Some Kind of Hero '82
Doctor Detroit '83
Secret Passions '87
Capone '89
The Chinatown Murders: Man against the Mob '89
Quicksand: No Escape '91
Teenage Mutant Ninja Turtles 2: The Secret of the Ooze '91
To Gillian on Her 37th Birthday '96
A Season for Miracles '99

Carrie Preston (1967-)
29th & Gay '05
That's What She Said '12

Ruben Preuss
Almost Dead '94
The Art of Murder '99

Steve Previn (1925-93)
Almost Angels '62
Waltz King '63

David F. Price (1961-)
Children of the Corn 2: The Final Sacrifice '92
Dr. Jekyll and Ms. Hyde '95

Jason Priestley (1969-)
Kiss Tomorrow Goodbye '00
Don't Cry Now '07
The Other Woman '08
Dear Santa '11
Goodnight for Justice '11
Cas & Dylan '15

Joseph Prieto
Shanty Tramp '67
Savages from Hell '68

Prince (1958-2016)
Under the Cherry Moon '86
Graffiti Bridge '90

Harold Prince (1928-)
A Little Night Music '77
Sweeney Todd: The Demon Barber of Fleet Street '84

Gina Prince-Bythewood (1969-)
Disappearing Acts '00
Love and Basketball '00
The Secret Life of Bees '08
Beyond the Lights '14

David A. Prior
Sledgehammer '83
Future Force '89
Rapid Fire '89
Future Zone '90
Center of the Web '92
Mardi Gras for the Devil '93
Raw Justice '93
Felony '95

Franco Prosperi (1928-)
Mondo Cane 2 '64
Counter Punch '71
Meet Him and Die '76

Martin Provost
Seraphine '08
The Midwife '17

Andrew Prowse
Demonstone '89
Attack of the Gryphon '07

Alex Proyas (1965-)
The Crow '93
Dark City '97
Garage Days '03
I, Robot '04
Knowing '09
Gods of Egypt '16

Craig Pryce
I Me Wed '07
For the Love of Grace '08
The Good Witch '08
The Good Witch's Garden '09
Double Wedding '10
The Good Witch's Gift '10
The Good Witch's Family '11
The Good Witch's Charm '12
Oh Christmas Tree! '13

Vsevolod Pudovkin (1893-1953)
Mother '26
The End of St. Petersburg '27
Storm over Asia '28

Luis Puenzo (1946-)
The Official Story '85
Old Gringo '89

Cristi Puiu (1967-)
The Death of Mr. Lazarescu '05
Aurora '10

Robert Pulcini (1964-)
American Splendor '03
The Extra Man '10
Cinema Verite '11
Girl Most Likely '12
Ten Thousand Saints '15

Evelyn Purcell
Nobody's Fool '86
Borderline '02

Steve Purcell
Queens of Comedy '01
Brave '12

Jon Purdy
Dillinger and Capone '95
Joshua '02

John Putch (1961-)
Alone in the Woods '95
My Magic Dog '97
Tycus '98
Pursuit of Happiness '01
BachelorMan '03
A Time to Remember '03
The Poseidon Adventure '05
Route 30 '08
American Pie Presents: Book of Love '09
Beethoven's Christmas Adventure '11
Atlas Shrugged 2: The Strike '12

Tom Putnam
The Hottie and the Nottie '08
Burn '12

Joe Pytka (1938-)
Let It Ride '89
Space Jam '96

Albert Pyun (1954-)
Sword & the Sorcerer '82
Alien from L.A. '87
Captain America '89
Cyborg '89
Dollman '90
Kickboxer 2: The Road Back '90
Arcade '93
Nemesis '93
Kickboxer 4: The Aggressor '94
Heatseeker '95
Adrenalin: Fear the Rush '96
Omega Doom '96
Mean Guns '97
Nemesis 4: Cry of Angels '97
Crazy Six '98
Postmortem '98
Corrupt '99
Urban Menace '99
The Wrecking Crew '99
Ticker '01
Invasion '07
Tales of an Ancient Empire '11

Steven Quale
SuperFire '02
Final Destination 5 '11
Into the Storm '14
Renegades '17

Jonas Quastel
Sasquatch '02
Forced to Fight '11

James Quattrochi (1961-)
True Friends '98
The Prince and the Pauper '07

Stephen Quay (1947-)
Institue Benjamenta or This Dream People Call Human Life '95
Piano Tuner of Earthquakes '05

Timothy Quay (1947-)
Institue Benjamenta or This Dream People Call Human Life '95
Piano Tuner of Earthquakes '05

Richard Quine (1920-89)
All Ashore '53
Drive a Crooked Road '54
Pushover '54
My Sister Eileen '55
Full of Life '56
Solid Gold Cadillac '56
Operation Mad Ball '57
Bell, Book and Candle '58
It Happened to Jane '59
Strangers When We Meet '60
The World of Suzie Wong '60
The Notorious Landlady '62
How to Murder Your Wife '64
Paris When It Sizzles '64
Sex and the Single Girl '64
Synanon '65
Hotel '67
The Moonshine War '70
W '74
Prisoner of Zenda '79

Gene Quintano (1946-)
National Lampoon's Loaded Weapon 1 *'93*
Dollar for the Dead *'98*

Eduardo Quiroz
I Got Five on It *'05*
The Damned *'06*
Illegal Business *'06*
San Franpsycho *'06*

Jose Quiroz (1972-)
I Got Five on It *'05*
The Damned *'06*
Illegal Business *'06*
San Franpsycho *'06*

Mark Quod
#1 Cheerleader Camp *'10*
Mother *'13*

Marcus Raboy (1965-)
Friday After Next *'02*
The Janky Promoters *'09*

Peter Rader
Grandma's House *'88*
Hired to Kill *'91*

Michael Radford (1946-)
1984 *'84*
White Mischief *'88*
The Postman *'94*
B. Monkey *'97*
Dancing at the Blue Iguana *'00*
The Merchant of Venice *'04*
Flawless *'07*
Elsa & Fred *'14*

Robert Radler
Best of the Best *'89*
Best of the Best 2 *'93*
T.N.T. *'98*
The Substitute 3: Winner Takes All *'99*
The Substitute 4: Failure is Not an Option *'00*

Josh Radnor (1974-)
Happythankyoumoreplease *'10*
Liberal Arts *'12*

Eric Radomski
Batman: Mask of the Phantasm *'93*
Todd McFarlane's Spawn *'97*

Michael Raeburn (1943-)
Laserblast *'78*
Killing Heat *'84*

Bob Rafelson (1933-)
Head *'68*
Five Easy Pieces *'70*
The King of Marvin Gardens *'72*
Stay Hungry *'76*
The Postman Always Rings Twice *'81*
Black Widow *'87*
Mountains of the Moon *'90*
Man Trouble *'92*
Tales of Erotica *'93*
Picture Windows *'95*
Blood & Wine *'96*
Poodle Springs *'98*
No Good Deed *'02*

Gideon Raff
The Killing Floor *'06*
Train *'08*

Stewart Raffill (1945-)
Across the Great Divide *'76*
The Adventures of the Wilderness Family *'76*
Sea Gypsies *'78*
High Risk *'81*
Ice Pirates *'84*
The Philadelphia Experiment *'84*
Mac and Me *'88*
Mannequin 2: On the Move *'91*
Grizzly Falls *'99*
Croc *'07*

Alan Rafkin (1928-2001)
Ski Party *'65*
The Ghost and Mr. Chicken *'66*
The Shakiest Gun in the West *'68*
How to Frame a Figg *'71*

Sam Raimi (1959-)
Evil Dead *'83*
Evil Dead 2: Dead by Dawn *'87*
Darkman *'90*
Army of Darkness *'92*
The Quick and the Dead *'95*
A Simple Plan *'98*
For Love of the Game *'99*
The Gift *'00*
Spider-Man *'02*
Spider-Man 2 *'04*
Spider-Man 3 *'07*
Drag Me to Hell *'09*
Oz the Great and Powerful *'13*

Frank Rainone
Me and the Mob *'94*
A Brooklyn State of Mind *'97*

Alvin Rakoff (1927-)
Hoffman *'70*
Say Hello to Yesterday *'71*
King Solomon's Treasure *'76*
The First Olympics: Athens 1896 *'84*
A Voyage 'Round My Father *'89*
A Dance to the Music of Time *'97*

Harold Ramis (1944-2014)
Caddyshack *'80*
National Lampoon's Vacation *'83*
Club Paradise *'86*
Groundhog Day *'93*
Stuart Saves His Family *'94*
Multiplicity *'96*
Analyze This *'98*
Bedazzled *'00*
Analyze That *'02*
The Ice Harvest *'05*
Year One *'09*

Lynne Ramsay (1969-)
Ratcatcher *'99*
Morvern Callar *'02*
You Were Never Really Here *'17*

Peter Ramsey
Rise of the Guardians *'12*
Spider-Man: Into the Spider-Verse *'18*

Alex Ranarivelo
Born 2 Race *'11*
Born to Race: Fast Track *'14*
The Dog Lover *'16*
Bennett's War *'19*

Addison Randall (1949-)
Chance *'89*
East L.A. Warriors *'89*
The Killing Zone *'90*

Tony Randel (1956-)
Hellbound: Hellraiser 2 *'88*
Amityville 1992: It's About Time *'92*
Children of the Night *'92*
Ticks *'93*
Fist of the North Star *'95*
One Good Turn *'95*
The Hybrids Family *'16*

Arthur Rankin, Jr. (1924-)
The Hobbit *'78*
The Return of the King *'80*
Flight of Dragons *'82*

Kyle Rankin
The Battle of Shaker Heights *'03*
Infestation *'09*
Night of the Living Deb *'14*

Whitney Ransick
Hand Gun *'93*
Green Sails *'00*

Jean-Paul Rappeneau (1932-)
Lovers Like Us *'75*
The Savage *'75*
Cyrano de Bergerac *'90*
The Horseman on the Roof *'95*
Bon Voyage *'03*

Irving Rapper (1898-1999)
One Foot in Heaven *'41*
Now, Voyager *'42*
The Adventures of Mark Twain *'44*
The Corn Is Green *'45*
Rhapsody in Blue *'45*
Deception *'46*
The Voice of the Turtle *'47*
Another Man's Poison *'52*
Bad for Each Other *'53*
Forever Female *'53*
The Brave One *'56*
Marjorie Morningstar *'58*
The Christine Jorgensen Story *'70*
Born Again *'78*

Jim Rash
The Way Way Back *'13*
Downhill *'20*

Steve Rash
The Buddy Holly Story *'78*
Under the Rainbow *'81*
Can't Buy Me Love *'87*
Queens Logic *'91*
Son-in-Law *'93*
Eddie *'96*
Held Up *'00*
Good Advice *'01*
American Pie Presents Band Camp *'05*
Bring It On: All or Nothing *'06*
Bring It On: In It to Win It *'07*
Road Trip: Beer Pong *'09*
Crooked Arrows *'12*

Ian Iqbal Rashid
Touch of Pink *'04*
How She Move *'08*

George Ratliff
Joshua *'07*
Salvation Boulevard *'11*
Welcome Home *'18*

Brett Ratner (1969-)
Money Talks *'97*
Rush Hour *'98*
Family Man *'00*
Rush Hour 2 *'01*
Red Dragon *'02*
After the Sunset *'04*
X-Men: The Last Stand *'06*
Rush Hour 3 *'07*
New York, I Love You *'09*
Tower Heist *'11*
Movie 43 *'13*
Hercules *'14*

Gregory Ratoff (1897-1960)
Day-Time Wife *'39*
Intermezzo *'39*
Rose of Washington Square *'39*
Wife, Husband and Friend *'39*
Adam Had Four Sons *'41*
The Corsican Brothers *'42*
Irish Eyes Are Smiling *'44*
Do You Love Me? *'46*
Carnival in Costa Rica *'47*
Black Magic *'49*
Abdulla the Great *'56*

John Rawlins (1902-97)
Junior G-Men *'40*
Arabian Nights *'42*
Overland Mail *'42*
Sherlock Holmes and the Voice of Terror *'42*
Dick Tracy Meets Gruesome *'47*
Massacre River *'49*
Fort Defiance *'51*
Lost Lagoon *'58*

Albert Ray (1897-1944)
13th Guest *'32*
St. Louis Woman *'34*

Bernard B. Ray (1895-1964)
Caryl of the Mountains *'36*
I'll Name the Murderer *'36*
The Reckless Way *'36*
Buffalo Bill Rides Again *'47*

Billy Ray
Shattered Glass *'03*
Breach *'07*
Secret in Their Eyes *'15*

Christopher Ray (1977-)
Mega Shark *vs.* Crocosaurus *'10*
Almighty Thor *'11*
Shark Island *'12*
2-Headed Shark Attack *'12*
Asteroid *vs.* Earth *'14*

Fred Olen Ray (1954-)
Alien Dead *'79*
Bio Hazard *'85*
Armed Response *'86*
Cyclone *'87*
Phantom Empire *'87*
Star Slammer *'87*
Beverly Hills Vamp *'88*
Hollywood Chainsaw Hookers *'88*
Terminal Force *'88*
Warlords *'88*
Alienator *'89*
Bad Girls from Mars *'90*
Evil Toons *'90*
Haunting Fear *'91*
Inner Sanctum *'91*
Bikini Drive-In *'94*
Wizards of the Demon Sword *'94*
Attack of the 60-Foot Centerfold *'95*
Over the Wire *'95*
Friend of the Family 2 *'96*
Fugitive Rage *'96*
Invisible Mom *'96*
Death and Desire *'97*
Hybrid *'97*
Invisible Dad *'97*
The Shooter *'97*
Mom, Can I Keep Her? *'98*
Active Stealth *'99*
The Capitol Conspiracy *'99*
Fugitive Mind *'99*
Invisible Mom 2 *'99*
The Kid with the X-Ray Eyes *'99*
Rapid Assault *'99*
Critical Mass *'00*
Mach 2 *'00*
Submerged *'00*
Air Rage *'01*
Black Horizon *'01*
Kept *'01*
Mom's Outta Sight *'01*
Venomous *'01*
The Glass Trap *'04*
Nuclear Hurricane *'07*
Deadly Shift *'08*
Silent Venom *'08*
Tarzeena: Queen of Kong Island *'08*
American Bandits: Frank and Jesse James *'10*
Turbulent Skies *'10*
Collision Course *'12*
Abner the Invisible Dog *'13*
Sniper: Special Ops *'16*

Nicholas Ray (1911-79)
Knock on Any Door *'49*
They Live by Night *'49*
In a Lonely Place *'50*
Flying Leathernecks *'51*
On Dangerous Ground *'51*
The Lusty Men *'52*
Johnny Guitar *'53*
Rebel without a Cause *'55*
Run for Cover *'55*
Hot Blood *'56*
The True Story of Jesse James *'57*
Bitter Victory *'58*
Party Girl *'58*
The King of Kings *'61*

55 Days at Peking *'63*
We Can't Go Home Again *'73*

Satyajit Ray (1921-92)
Pather Panchali *'54*
Aparajito *'58*
Jalsaghar *'58*
The World of Apu *'59*
Devi *'60*
Charulata *'64*

Ed Raymond (1954-)
See Fred Olen Ray

David Raynr
Trippin' *'99*
Whatever It Takes *'00*
Christmas in Compton *'12*

Patrick Rea
The Empty Acre *'07*
The Invoking 2 *'15*

Bill Rebane (1937-)
Monster a Go-Go! *'65*
The Giant Spider Invasion *'75*
Rana: The Legend of Shadow Lake *'75*
The Alpha Incident *'76*
The Capture of Bigfoot *'79*

Eric Red (1961-)
Cohen and Tate *'88*
Body Parts *'91*
Bad Moon *'96*
100 Feet *'08*

Robert Redford (1936-)
Ordinary People *'80*
The Milagro Beanfield War *'88*
A River Runs Through It *'92*
Quiz Show *'94*
The Horse Whisperer *'97*
The Legend of Bagger Vance *'00*
Lions for Lambs *'07*
The Conspirator *'10*
The Company You Keep *'12*

Carol Reed (1906-76)
Men of the Sea *'35*
Bank Holiday *'38*
Climbing High *'38*
The Stars Look Down *'39*
Night Train to Munich *'40*
The Girl in the News *'41*
Immortal Battalion *'44*
The Way Ahead *'44*
Odd Man Out *'47*
The Fallen Idol *'49*
The Third Man *'49*
A Kid for Two Farthings *'55*
Trapeze *'56*
The Key *'58*
Our Man in Havana *'59*
The Agony and the Ecstasy *'65*
Oliver! *'68*
Flap *'70*

Joel M. Reed (1933-2020)
G.I. Executioner *'71*
Bloodsucking Freaks *'75*
Night of the Zombies *'81*

Luther Reed (1888-1961)
Rio Rita *'29*
Dixiana *'30*
Convention Girl *'35*

Peyton Reed (1964-)
Bring It On *'00*
Down With Love *'03*
The Break-Up *'06*
Yes Man *'08*
Ant-Man *'15*
Ant-Man and the Wasp *'18*

Theodore Reed (1887-1959)
Double or Nothing *'37*
What a Life *'39*

Tripp Reed
Manticore *'05*
Walking Tall: Lone Justice *'07*

Walking Tall: The Payback *'07*
Mandrake *'10*

Dee Rees
Pariah *'11*
Mudbound *'17*

Geoffrey Reeve (1932-)
Puppet on a Chain *'72*
Souvenir *'88*

Tom Reeve
George and the Dragon *'04*
Hard Times *'09*

Matt Reeves (1966-)
Future Shock *'93*
The Pallbearer *'95*
Cloverfield *'08*
Let Me In *'10*
Dawn of the Planet of the Apes *'14*
War for the Planet of the Apes *'17*

Michael Reeves (1944-69)
The She-Beast *'65*
The Sorcerers *'67*
The Conqueror Worm *'68*

Nicolas Winding Refn (1970-)
Pusher *'96*
Fear X *'03*
Bronson *'09*
Valhalla Rising *'09*
Drive *'11*
Only God Forgives *'13*
The Neon Demon *'16*

Godfrey Reggio (1940-)
Koyaanisqatsi *'83*
Powaqqatsi: Life in Transformation *'88*
Visitors *'13*

Kelly Reichardt
River of Grass *'94*
Old Joy *'06*
Wendy and Lucy *'08*
Meek's Cutoff *'10*
Night Moves *'13*
Certain Women *'16*
First Cow *'20*

Alastair Reid (1939-)
The Night Digger *'71*
Traffik *'90*
Selling Hitler *'91*
Teamster Boss: The Jackie Presser Story *'92*
Armistead Maupin's Tales of the City *'93*

Tim Reid (1944-)
The Little Mermaid *'75*
Once Upon a Time . . . When We Were Colored *'95*
Asunder *'99*
For Real *'02*

Roel Reine (1969-)
The Delivery *'99*
Black Ops *'07*
Pistol Whipped *'08*
The Marine 2 *'09*
Death Race 2 *'10*
The Scorpion King 3: Battle for Redemption *'11*
Death Race 3: Inferno *'12*
Seal Team 8: Behind Enemy Lines *'14*
The Condemned 2 *'16*
Hard Target 2 *'16*

Carl Reiner (1922-2020)
The Comic *'69*
Where's Poppa? *'70*
Oh, God! *'77*
The One and Only *'78*
The Jerk *'79*
Dead Men Don't Wear Plaid *'82*
The Man with Two Brains *'83*
All of Me *'84*
Summer Rental *'85*
Summer School *'87*

Bert Rigby, You're a Fool *'89*
Sibling Rivalry *'90*
Fatal Instinct *'93*
That Old Feeling *'96*

Jeff Reiner
Blood & Concrete: A Love Story *'91*
Trouble Bound *'92*
Smalltime *'96*
Deadly Game *'98*
Wilderness Love *'02*
Caught in the Act *'04*
Caprica *'09*

Rob Reiner (1947-)
This Is Spinal Tap *'84*
The Sure Thing *'85*
Stand by Me *'86*
The Princess Bride *'87*
When Harry Met Sally. . . *'89*
Misery *'90*
A Few Good Men *'92*
The American President *'95*
Ghosts of Mississippi *'96*
The Story of Us *'99*
Alex & Emma *'03*
Rumor Has It. . . *'05*
The Bucket List *'07*
Flipped *'10*
The Magic of Belle Isle *'12*
And So It Goes *'14*
Being Charlie *'16*
LBJ *'17*
Shock and Awe *'18*

Robert Reiner (1947-)
See Rob Reiner

Gottfried Reinhardt (1911-94)
Invitation *'51*
The Story of Three Loves *'53*
Betrayed *'54*
Town without Pity *'61*

John Reinhardt
Captain Calamity *'36*
For You I Die *'47*
Open Secret *'48*
Chicago Calling *'52*

Harald Reinl (1908-86)
The Return of Dr. Mabuse *'61*
The Invisible Dr. Mabuse *'62*
Strangler of Blackmoor Castle *'63*
The Torture Chamber of Dr. Sadism *'69*

Irving Reis (1906-53)
The Gay Falcon *'41*
Big Street *'42*
A Date With the Falcon *'42*
The Falcon Takes Over *'42*
Crack-Up *'46*
The Bachelor and the Bobby-Soxer *'47*
Enchantment *'48*
Three Husbands *'50*

Joel Paul Reisig
Horse Camp *'14*
Small Town Santa *'14*

Charles Reisner (1887-1962)
The Better 'Ole *'26*
Steamboat Bill, Jr. *'28*
Hollywood Revue of 1929 *'29*
Chasing Rainbows *'30*
Politics *'31*
Reducing *'31*
Stepping Out *'31*
Manhattan Merry-Go-Round *'37*
Big Store *'41*
Lost in a Harem *'44*

Karel Reisz (1926-2002)
Saturday Night and Sunday Morning *'60*
Night Must Fall *'64*
Morgan: A Suitable Case for Treatment *'66*
The Gambler *'74*
Who'll Stop the Rain? *'78*
The French Lieutenant's Woman *'81*
Sweet Dreams *'85*
Everybody Wins *'90*

Wolfgang Reitherman (1909-85)
Sleeping Beauty *'59*
101 Dalmatians *'61*
The Sword in the Stone *'63*
The Jungle Book *'67*
The Aristocats *'70*
Robin Hood *'73*
The Many Adventures of Winnie the Pooh *'77*
The Rescuers *'77*

Ivan Reitman (1946-)
Meatballs *'79*
Stripes *'81*
Ghostbusters *'84*
Legal Eagles *'86*
Twins *'88*
Ghostbusters 2 *'89*
Kindergarten Cop *'90*
Dave *'93*
Junior *'94*
Father's Day *'96*
Six Days, Seven Nights *'98*
Evolution *'01*
My Super Ex-Girlfriend *'06*
No Strings Attached *'11*
Draft Day *'14*

Jason Reitman (1977-)
Thank You for Smoking *'06*
Juno *'07*
Up in the Air *'09*
Young Adult *'11*
Labor Day *'13*
Men, Women & Children *'14*
The Front Runner *'18*
Tully *'18*

Edgar Reitz (1932-)
Germany in Autumn *'78*
Heimat 1 *'84*
Heimat 2 *'92*

Chris Renaud
Despicable Me *'10*
Dr. Seuss' The Lorax *'12*
Despicable Me 2 *'13*
The Secret Life of Pets *'16*
The Secret Life of Pets 2 *'19*

Norman Rene (1951-96)
Longtime Companion *'90*
Prelude to a Kiss *'92*

Jeff Renfroe
Paranoia 1.0 *'04*
Civic Duty *'06*
Sand Serpents *'09*
Seven Deadly Sins *'10*
He Loves Me *'11*

Jean Renoir (1894-1979)
Boudu Saved from Drowning *'32*
The Crime of Monsieur Lange *'36*
The Lower Depths *'36*
Grand Illusion *'37*
La Marseillaise *'37*
La Bete Humaine *'38*
The Rules of the Game *'39*
This Land Is Mine *'43*
The Southerner *'45*
Diary of a Chambermaid *'46*
The Woman on the Beach *'47*
The River *'51*
The Golden Coach *'52*
French Can-Can *'55*
Elena and Her Men *'56*
The Testament of Dr. Cordelier *'59*
The Elusive Corporal *'62*

Nicholas Renton (1946-)
The Ebb-Tide *'97*
Far from the Madding Crowd *'97*
Wives and Daughters *'01*
Bait *'02*
A Room With a View *'08*

John Requa
I Love You Phillip Morris *'10*
Crazy, Stupid, Love. *'11*
Focus *'15*
Whiskey Tango Foxtrot *'16*

Alain Resnais (1922-2014)
Hiroshima, Mon Amour *'59*
Last Year at Marienbad *'61*
Muriel *'63*
La Guerre Est Finie *'66*
Stavisky *'74*
Mon Oncle d'Amerique *'80*
Life Is a Bed of Roses *'83*
Melo *'86*
I Want to Go Home *'89*
Private Fears in Public Places *'06*
Wild Grass *'09*
You Ain't Seen Nothin' Yet *'12*

Dale Resteghini (1968-)
Colorz of Rage *'97*
Da Hip Hop Witch *'00*

Franc Reyes
Empire *'02*
Illegal Tender *'07*
The Ministers *'09*

Burt Reynolds (1936-2018)
Gator *'76*
The End *'78*
Sharky's Machine *'81*
Stick *'85*
The Man from Left Field *'93*
The Final Hit *'02*

Kevin Reynolds (1950-)
Fandango *'85*
The Beast *'88*
Robin Hood: Prince of Thieves *'91*
Rapa Nui *'93*
Waterworld *'95*
187 *'97*
The Count of Monte Cristo *'02*
Tristan & Isolde *'06*
Hatfields & McCoys *'12*
Risen *'16*

Scott Reynolds (1968-)
The Ugly *'96*
Heaven *'99*

Sheldon Reynolds (1924-2003)
A Place Called Glory *'66*
Assignment to Kill *'69*

Stephen Reynolds
12 Rounds 3: Lockdown *'15*
Interrogation *'16*

Phillip Rhee (1960-)
Best of the Best 3: No Turning Back *'95*
Best of the Best: Without Warning *'98*
Underdog Kids *'15*

Michael Rhodes (1935-)
The Killing Mind *'90*
Heidi *'93*
Christy *'94*

Michael Ray Rhodes (1945-)
Fourth Wise Man *'85*
Visions of Murder *'93*
Entertaining Angels: The Dorothy Day Story *'96*

Tonino Ricci (1927-)
Liberators *'69*
Thor the Conqueror *'83*

David Lowell Rich (1923-)
No Time to Be Young *'57*
Have Rocket Will Travel *'59*
Madame X *'66*
A Lovely Way to Die *'68*
The Horror at 37,000 Feet *'73*
Satan's School for Girls *'73*
That Man Bolt *'73*
Little Women *'78*
The Concorde: Airport '79 *'79*
Nurse *'80*
The Sky's No Limit *'84*
Choices *'86*

John Rich (1925-2012)
Roustabout *'64*
Boeing Boeing *'65*
Easy Come, Easy Go *'67*

Matty Rich (1971-)
Straight out of Brooklyn *'91*
The Inkwell *'94*

Richard Rich
The Fox and the Hound *'81*
The Black Cauldron *'85*
The Swan Princess *'94*
The Swan Princess 2: Escape from Castle Mountain *'97*
The King and I *'99*
The Trumpet of the Swan *'01*

Cybil (Sybil) Richards
Femalien *'96*
Virtual Encounters *'96*
Exotic House of Wax *'97*
Lolida 2000 *'97*
Femalien 2 *'98*

David Richards
Kiss and Tell *'96*
Reckless *'97*
Reckless: The Sequel *'98*
Little Devil *'07*
Albert's Memorial *'09*

Dick Richards (1934-)
Culpepper Cattle Co. *'72*
Farewell, My Lovely *'75*
March or Die *'77*
Death Valley *'81*
Man, Woman & Child *'83*

Lloyd Richards (1919-2006)
Paul Robeson *'77*
The Piano Lesson *'94*

Tony Richardson (1928-91)
Look Back in Anger *'58*
The Entertainer *'60*
The Loneliness of the Long Distance Runner *'62*
Tom Jones *'63*
The Loved One *'65*
Mademoiselle *'66*
The Charge of the Light Brigade *'68*
Ned Kelly *'70*
Joseph Andrews *'77*
The Border *'82*
The Hotel New Hampshire *'84*
The Phantom of the Opera *'90*
Women & Men: Stories of Seduction *'90*
Blue Sky *'91*

William Richert (1942-)
Winter Kills *'79*
A Night in the Life of Jimmy Reardon *'88*
The Man in the Iron Mask *'97*

Jean-Francois Richet (1966-)
Assault on Precinct 13 *'05*
Mesrine: Part 1-Killer Instinct *'08*
Mesrine: Part 2-Public Enemy Number 1 *'08*
Blood Father *'16*

Anthony Richmond (1942-)
Deja Vu *'84*
Night of the Sharks *'87*

Roland Suso Richter (1961-)
The Tunnel *'01*
The I Inside *'04*
Dresden *'06*

W.D. Richter (1945-)
The Adventures of Buckaroo Banzai Across the Eighth Dimension *'84*
Late for Dinner *'91*

Alan Rickman (1946-2016)
The Winter Guest *'97*
A Little Chaos *'14*

John Ridley (1965-)
Cold Around the Heart *'97*
Jimi: All Is by My Side *'14*

Philip Ridley
The Reflecting Skin *'91*
The Passion of Darkly Noon *'95*
Heartless *'10*

Leni Riefenstahl (1902-2003)
The Blue Light *'32*
Triumph of the Will *'34*
Tiefland *'44*

Charles Riesner
Love in the Rough *'30*
Flying High *'31*
Meet the People *'44*

Adam Rifkin (1966-)
Never on Tuesday *'88*
Tale of Two Sisters *'89*
The Dark Backward *'91*
The Chase *'93*
Psycho Cop 2 *'94*
The Nutt House *'95*
Something About Sex *'98*
Detroit Rock City *'99*
Welcome to Hollywood *'00*
Night at the Golden Eagle *'02*
National Lampoon's The Stoned Aged *'07*
The Last Movie Star *'17*

Ned Rifle (1959-)
See Hal Hartley

Patricia Riggen (1970-)
Under the Same Moon *'07*
Lemonade Mouth *'11*
Girl in Progress *'12*
The 33 *'15*
Miracles From Heaven *'16*

Dustin Rikert (1974-)
Lethal *'04*
Alien Invasion Arizona *'07*

Eran Riklis (1954-)
Cup Final *'92*
Lemon Tree *'08*

Wolf Rilla (1920-2005)
The Scamp *'57*
Village of the Damned *'60*

Arthur Ripley (1895-1961)
The Chase *'46*
Thunder Road *'58*

Maria Ripoli
Twice upon a Yesterday *'98*
Tortilla Soup *'01*

Dino Risi (1916-2008)
Il Sorpasso *'63*
Bambole *'65*
Tiger and the Pussycat *'67*
The Priest's Wife *'71*
The Scent of a Woman *'75*

Guy Ritchie (1968-)
Lock, Stock and 2 Smoking Barrels *'98*
Snatch *'00*
Swept Away *'02*
Revolver *'05*
RocknRolla *'08*
Sherlock Holmes *'09*
Sherlock Holmes: A Game of Shadows *'11*
The Man from U.N.C.L.E. *'15*
King Arthur: Legend of the Sword *'17*
Aladdin *'19*
The Gentlemen *'20*

Michael Ritchie (1938-2001)
Downhill Racer *'69*
The Candidate *'72*
Prime Cut *'72*
Smile *'75*
The Bad News Bears *'76*
Semi-Tough *'77*
An Almost Perfect Affair *'79*
The Island *'80*
Survivors *'83*
Fletch *'85*
The Golden Child *'86*
Wildcats *'86*
The Couch Trip *'87*
Fletch Lives *'89*
Diggstown *'92*
The Positively True Adventures of the Alleged Texas Cheerleader-Murdering Mom *'93*
Cops and Robbersons *'94*
The Scout *'94*
The Fantasticks *'95*
A Simple Wish *'97*

Martin Ritt (1914-90)
Edge of the City *'57*
No Down Payment *'57*
The Long, Hot Summer *'58*
Black Orchid *'59*
Paris Blues *'61*
Hud *'63*
The Outrage *'64*
The Spy Who Came in from the Cold *'65*
Hombre *'67*
The Brotherhood *'68*
The Great White Hope *'70*
The Molly Maguires *'70*
Pete 'n' Tillie *'72*
Sounder *'72*
The Front *'76*
Casey's Shadow *'78*
Norma Rae *'79*
Back Roads *'81*
Cross Creek *'83*
Murphy's Romance *'85*
Nuts *'87*
Stanley and Iris *'90*

Panna Rittikrai (1961-)
Born to Fight *'07*
Ong Bak 2 *'08*

Lance Rivera
The Cookout *'04*
The Perfect Holiday *'07*

Jacques Rivette (1928-)
La Belle Noiseuse *'90*
Jeanne la Pucelle *'94*
Va Savoir *'01*
The Story of Marie and Julien *'03*
The Duchess of Langeais *'07*
Around a Small Mountain *'09*

Hal Roach (1892-1992)
The Devil's Brother *'33*
One Million B.C. *'40*
Road Show *'41*

Jay Roach (1957-)
Austin Powers: International Man of Mystery *'97*
Austin Powers 2: The Spy Who Shagged Me *'99*
Mystery, Alaska *'99*
Meet the Parents *'00*
Austin Powers In Goldmember *'02*
Meet the Fockers *'04*
Recount *'08*
Dinner for Schmucks *'10*
The Campaign *'12*
Game Change *'12*
Trumbo *'15*
Bombshell *'19*

Alain Robbe-Grillet (1922-2008)
L'Immortelle *'63*
The Man Who Lies *'68*
Gradiva *'06*

The Perfect Man '05
Princess: A Modern Fairytale '08
Snow 2: Brain Freeze '08
William & Kate '11

Milton Rosmer (1881-1971)
Murder in the Old Red Barn '36
The Challenge '38

Craig Ross, Jr.
Blue Hill Avenue '01
Motives '03

Gary Ross (1956-)
Pleasantville '98
Seabiscuit '03
The Hunger Games '12
Free State of Jones '16
Ocean's 8 '18

Herbert Ross (1927-2001)
Goodbye Love '34
Goodbye, Mr. Chips '69
The Owl and the Pussycat '70
Play It Again, Sam '72
The Last of Sheila '73
Funny Lady '75
The Sunshine Boys '75
The Seven-Per-Cent Solution '76
The Goodbye Girl '77
The Turning Point '77
California Suite '78
Nijinsky '80
Pennies from Heaven '81
Max Dugan Returns '83
Footloose '84
Protocol '84
Dancers '87
The Secret of My Success '87
Steel Magnolias '89
My Blue Heaven '90
True Colors '91
Undercover Blues '93
Boys on the Side '94

Matt Ross (1970-)
28 Hotel Rooms '12
Captain Fantastic '16

Matthew Ross
Frank & Lola '16
Siberia '18

Roberto Rossellini (1906-77)
Open City '45
Paisan '46
Deutschland im Jahre Null '47
Germany Year Zero '48
The Flowers of St. Francis '50
Voyage in Italy '53
Era Notte a Roma '60
Vanina Vanini '61
The Rise of Louis XIV '66
Blaise Pascal '71
Generale Della Rovere '09

Robert Rossen (1908-66)
Body and Soul '47
Johnny O'Clock '47
All the King's Men '49
Alexander the Great '55
Mambo '55
Island in the Sun '57
They Came to Cordura '59
The Hustler '61
Lilith '64

Bobby Roth (1950-)
The Inheritance '97
A Secret Affair '99
A Date With Darkness '03
Brave New Girl '04
Berkeley '05
Reviving Ophelia '10
Iris Johansen's The Killing Game '11

Eli Roth (1972-)
Cabin Fever '03
Hostel '06
Hostel: Part 2 '07
The Green Inferno '14

Knock Knock '15
Death Wish '18
The House with a Clock in Its Walls '18

Joe Roth (1948-)
Revenge of the Nerds 2: Nerds in Paradise '87
Coupe de Ville '90
America's Sweethearts '01
Christmas With the Kranks '04
Freedomland '06

Phillip J. Roth (1959-)
Red Snow '91
Digital Man '94
Total Reality '97
Darkdrive '98
Interceptor Force '99
Velocity Trap '99
Boa '02
Hypersonic '02
Interceptor Force 2 '02
Dark Waters '03
Deep Shock '03

Stephanie Rothman (1936-)
Track of the Vampire '66
The Student Nurses '70
The Velvet Vampire '71
Terminal Island '73
Working Girls '75

William Rotsler (1926-97)
Agony of Love '66
Mantis in Lace '68

Nick Rotundo
Gladiator Cop: The Swordsman 2 '95
G2: Mortal Conquest '99

Russell Rouse (1913-87)
The Well '51
The Thief '52
Fastest Gun Alive '56

Roy Rowland (1902-95)
Lost Angel '43
Our Vines Have Tender Grapes '45
Killer McCoy '47
The Romance of Rosy Ridge '47
Tenth Avenue Angel '47
Scene of the Crime '49
The Outriders '50
Two Weeks with Love '50
Excuse My Dust '51
The 5000 Fingers of Dr. T '53
The Moonlighter '53
Witness to Murder '54
Hit the Deck '55
Many Rivers to Cross '55
These Wilder Years '56
Gun Glory '57
Slander '57
The Seven Hills of Rome '58
The Girl Hunters '63

William Rowland (1898-)
Follies Girl '43
Flight to Nowhere '46

Christopher Rowley
Soul Patrol '80
Bonneville '06

Richard Roy
A Deadly Encounter '04
Thrill of the Kill '06
The Double Life of Eleanor Kendall '08

Patricia Rozema (1958-)
I've Heard the Mermaids Singing '87
When Night Is Falling '95
Mansfield Park '99
Kit Kittredge: An American Girl '08
Into the Forest '16

Andy Ruben
Streets '90
Club Vampire '98

J. Walter Ruben (1899-1942)
The Public Defender '31
The Phantom of Crestwood '32
Ace of Aces '33
Riff Raff '35
The Bad Man of Brimstone '38

Joseph Ruben (1951-)
Pom Pom Girls '76
Joyride '77
Dreamscape '84
The Stepfather '87
True Believer '89
Sleeping with the Enemy '91
The Good Son '93
Money Train '95
Return to Paradise '98
The Forgotten '04

Henry Alex Rubin
Murderball '05
Semper Fi '19

Oren Rudavsky
The Treatment '06
Joseph Pulitzer: Voice of the People '18

Alan Rudolph (1943-)
Barn of the Naked Dead '73
Roadie '80
Endangered Species '82
Choose Me '84
Songwriter '84
Trouble in Mind '86
Made in Heaven '87
The Moderns '88
Love at Large '89
Mortal Thoughts '91
Mrs. Parker and the Vicious Circle '94
Afterglow '97
Breakfast of Champions '98
Trixie '00
Intimate Affairs '01
The Secret Lives of Dentists '02

Wesley Ruggles (1889-1972)
The Plastic Age '25
Cimarron '31
No Man of Her Own '32
College Humor '33
I'm No Angel '33
The Bride Comes Home '35
The Gilded Lily '35
I Met Him in Paris '37
True Confession '37
Sing You Sinners '38
Arizona '40
Too Many Husbands '40
Somewhere I'll Find You '42
Slightly Dangerous '43
See Here, Private Hargrove '44
London Town '46

Raul Ruiz (1941-2011)
Genealogies of a Crime '97
Shattered Image '98
Time Regained '99
Comedy of Innocence '00
Klimt '06
Blind Revenge '10
Mysteries of Lisbon '10
Night Across the Street '12

Richard Rush (1929-)
Too Soon to Love '60
Hell's Angels on Wheels '67
Thunder Alley '67
Psych-Out '68
Getting Straight '70
Freebie & the Bean '74
The Stunt Man '80
Color of Night '94

Josef Rusnak
Quiet Days in Hollywood '97
No Strings Attached '98
The Thirteenth Floor '99
The Contractor '07
Art of War 2: The Betrayal '08

Perfect Victims '08
Beyond '11

Chuck Russell (1958-)
A Nightmare on Elm Street 3: Dream Warriors '87
The Blob '88
The Mask '94
Eraser '96
Bless the Child '00
The Scorpion King '02
I Am Wrath '16
Junglee '19

David O. Russell (1958-)
Spanking the Monkey '94
Flirting with Disaster '95
Three Kings '99
I Heart Huckabees '04
The Fighter '10
Silver Linings Playbook '12
American Hustle '13
Accidental Love '15
Joy '15

Jay Russell (1960-)
End of the Line '88
My Dog Skip '99
Tuck Everlasting '02
Ladder 49 '04
The Water Horse: Legend of the Deep '07

Ken Russell (1927-2011)
Billion Dollar Brain '67
Women in Love '70
The Boy Friend '71
The Devils '71
Savage Messiah '72
Mahler '74
Lisztomania '75
Tommy '75
Valentino '77
Altered States '80
Crimes of Passion '84
Gothic '87
Aria '88
The Lair of the White Worm '88
Salome's Last Dance '88
The Rainbow '89
Women & Men: Stories of Seduction '90
Prisoner of Honor '91
Lady Chatterley '92
Tales of Erotica '93
Tracked '98

William D. Russell (1908-68)
The Green Promise '49
Best of the Badmen '50

Anthony Russo
Welcome to Collinwood '02
You, Me and Dupree '06
Captain America: The Winter Soldier '14
Captain America: Civil War '16
Avengers: Infinity War '18
Avengers: Endgame '19

Joe Russo
Welcome to Collinwood '02
You, Me and Dupree '06
Captain America: The Winter Soldier '14
Captain America: Civil War '16
Avengers: Infinity War '18
Avengers: Endgame '19

John A. Russo (1939-)
Midnight '81
Heartstopper '92
Midnight 2: Sex, Death, and Videotape '93

Ry Russo-Young (1981-)
You Wont Miss Me '09
Nobody Walks '12
Before I Fall '17
The Sun Is Also a Star '19

Marti Rustam
Evils of the Night '85
James Dean: Live Fast, Die Young '97

Stefan Ruzowitsky
Anatomy 2 '03
Deadfall '12

Stefan Ruzowitzky (1961-)
The Inheritors '98
Anatomy '00
All the Queen's Men '02
The Counterfeiters '07
Patient Zero '18

Frank Ryan (1947-)
Can't Help Singing '45
So Goes My Love '46

James Ryan (1958-)
The Young Girl and the Monsoon '99
Bachelor Party 2: The Last Temptation '08

Mark Rydell (1929-)
The Reivers '69
The Cowboys '72
Cinderella Liberty '73
Harry & Walter Go to New York '76
The Rose '79
On Golden Pond '81
The River '84
For the Boys '91
Intersection '93
James Dean '01
Even Money '06

Gary Rydstrom
The Secret World of Arrietty '10
Strange Magic '15

Michael Rymer (1963-)
Allie & Me '97
In Too Deep '99
Perfume '01
Queen of the Damned '02

Seung-wan Ryoo
No Blood No Tears '02
The City of Violence '06

Frank Sabatella
Blood Night: The Legend of Mary Hatchet '09
The Shed '19

Jerome Sable
The ABCs of Death 2 '14
Stage Fright '14

Gabriel Sabloff
Revelation Road: The Beginning of the End '13
Samson '18

Ira Sachs (1965-)
The Delta '97
Forty Shades of Blue '05
Married Life '07
Keep the Lights On '12
Love Is Strange '14
Little Men '16
Frankie '19

William Sachs
Incredible Melting Man '77
Van Nuys Blvd. '79
Galaxina '80

James Sadwith (1952-)
Sinatra '92
A Smile as Big as the Moon '12

Benny Safdie
Heaven Knows What '15
Good Time '17
Uncut Gems '19

Josh Safdie
Heaven Knows What '15
Good Time '17
Uncut Gems '19

Boris Sagal (1917-81)
Twilight of Honor '63
Guns of Diablo '64
Girl Happy '65
Made in Paris '65
Night Gallery '69
1,000 Plane Raid '69
Operation Heartbeat '69

Mosquito Squadron '70
Omega Man '71
Deliver Us From Evil '73
Arthur Hailey's The Moneychangers '76
The Awakening Land '78
Masada '81

Yoichi Sai
Doing Time '02
Blood and Bones '04

Henry Saine
The Last Lovecraft: Relic of Cthulhu '09
Bounty Killer '13

Malcolm St. Clair (1897-1952)
The Show Off '26
The Bashful Bachelor '42

Daniel St. Pierre
Everyone's Hero '06
Legends of Oz: Dorothy's Return '14

Michael O. Sajbel
One Night with the King '06
The Ultimate Gift '07

Gene Saks (1921-2015)
Barefoot in the Park '67
The Odd Couple '68
Cactus Flower '69
Last of the Red Hot Lovers '72
Mame '74
Brighton Beach Memoirs '86
Bye Bye Birdie '95

Carlos Saldanha (1968-)
Ice Age: The Meltdown '06
Ice Age: Dawn of the Dinosaurs '09
Rio '11
Rio 2 '14
Rio, I Love You '14
Ferdinand '17

Richard Sale (1911-93)
Spoilers of the North '47
Let's Make It Legal '51
Meet Me After the Show '51
My Wife's Best Friend '52
The Girl Next Door '53

Sidney Salkow (1909-2000)
The Lone Wolf Meets a Lady '40
Time Out for Rhythm '41
City Without Men '43
The Golden Hawk '52
Raiders of the Seven Seas '53
Sitting Bull '54
Robbers' Roost '55
Gun Brothers '56
Chicago Confidential '57
Gun Duel In Durango '57
The Iron Sheriff '57
Twice-Told Tales '63
The Last Man on Earth '64
The Quick Gun '64

Adam Salky
Dare '09
I Smile Back '15

Walter Salles (1956-)
Foreign Land '95
Central Station '98
Behind the Sun '01
Dark Water '02
The Motorcycle Diaries '04
Paris, je t'aime '06
On the Road '12

Mikael Salomon (1945-)
A Far Off Place '93
Hard Rain '97
Aftershock: Earthquake in New York '99
Band of Brothers '01
A Glimpse of Hell '01
Benedict Arnold: A Question of Honor '03
Salem's Lot '04
The Company '07
The Andromeda Strain '08

Beer for My Horses '08
Flirting with Forty '09
The Natalee Holloway Story '09
The Lost Future '10
Who Is Clark Rockefeller? '10
Blue Lagoon: The Awakening '12
Coma '12
Drew Peterson: Untouchable '12
Freezer '14

Victor Salva (1958-)
Clownhouse '88
Nature of the Beast '94
Powder '95
Rites of Passage '99
Jeepers Creepers '01
Jeepers Creepers 2 '03
Peaceful Warrior '06
Dark House '14
Jeepers Creepers 3 '17

Pierre Salvadori (1964-)
Apres-Vous '03
Priceless '06

Gabriele Salvatores (1950-)
Nirvana '97
I'm Not Scared '03

Keith Samples
A Smile Like Yours '96
Single White Female 2: The Psycho '05
Love Lies Bleeding '07

Barry Samson
The Ice Runner '93
Bloodfist 8: Hard Way Out '96

Yann Samuell (1965-)
Love Me if You Dare '03
My Sassy Girl '08

Rachel Samuels
Running Woman '98
Robert Louis Stevenson's The Game of Death '99
Dark Streets '08

Eduardo Sanchez (1968-)
The Blair Witch Project '99
Altered '06
Seventh Moon '08
V/H/S/2 '13

David F. Sandberg
Lights Out '16
Annabelle: Creation '17
Shazam! '19

Espen Sandberg (1971-)
Bandidas '06
Max Manus: Man of War '08
Kon-Tiki '12
Pirates of the Caribbean: Dead Men Tell No Tales '17

Ari Sandel
Vince Vaughn's Wild West Comedy Show '06
The DUFF '15
Goosebumps 2: Haunted Halloween '18

Chris (Christopher) Sanders (1962-)
Lilo & Stitch '02
How to Train Your Dragon '10
The Croods '13
The Call of the Wild '20

Denis Sanders (1929-87)
Crime and Punishment, USA '59
War Hunt '62
One Man's Way '63
Invasion of the Bee Girls '73

Rupert Sanders
Snow White and the Huntsman '12
Ghost in the Shell '17

Scott Sanders
Thick as Thieves '99
Black Dynamite '09

Helma Sanders-Brahms
Earthquake in Chile '74
Under the Pavement Lies the Strand '75

Helmer Sanders-Brahms (1940-)
Germany, Pale Mother '80
The Future of Emily '85

Allan Sandler
Time Warp '81
Warp Speed '81

Jay Sandrich (1932-)
Seems Like Old Times '80
For Richer, for Poorer '92

Mark Sandrich (1900-45)
The Gay Divorcee '34
Top Hat '35
Follow the Fleet '36
A Woman Rebels '36
Shall We Dance '37
Carefree '38
Buck Benny Rides Again '40
Holiday Inn '42
So Proudly We Hail '43
Here Come the Waves '45

Arlene Sanford
A Very Brady Sequel '96
I'll Be Home for Christmas '98
Frank McKlusky, C.I. '02
12 Men of Christmas '09

Jimmy Sangster (1924-2011)
The Horror of Frankenstein '70
Lust for a Vampire '71
Dynasty of Fear '72

Alfred Santell (1895-1981)
Polly of the Circus '32
Winterset '36
Breakfast for Two '37
Internes Can't Take Money '37
Having a Wonderful Time '38
Beyond the Blue Horizon '42
The Hairy Ape '44
Jack London '44
That Brennan Girl '46

Cirio H. Santiago (1936-)
Cover Girl Models '75
TNT Jackson '75
The Muthers '76
She Devils in Chains '76
Fighting Mad '77
Death Force '78
The Vampire Hookers '78
Caged Fury '80
Firecracker '81
Demon of Paradise '87
Eye of the Eagle '87
Nam Angels '88
Eye of the Eagle 3 '91
Beyond the Call of Duty '92
Raiders of the Sun '92
One Man Army '93
Stranglehold '94

Joseph Santley (1889-1971)
The Cocoanuts '29
Harmony Lane '35
She's Got Everything '37
Melody Ranch '40
Music in My Heart '40
Down Mexico Way '41
Call of the Canyon '42

Jeff Santo (1963-)
Liar's Poker '99
Jake's Corner '08

Damon Santostefano
Three to Tango '99
Bring It On Again '03
Another Cinderella Story '08
A Cinderella Story: Once Upon a Song '11

Ken Sanzel
Scarred City '98
Lone Hero '02

David Saperstein (1937-)
A Killing Affair '85
Beyond the Stars '89

Deran Sarafian (1968-)
To Die For '89
Death Warrant '90
Gunmen '93
Terminal Velocity '94
The Road Killers '95

Richard Sarafian (1930-2013)
Fragment of Fear '70
Man in the Wilderness '71
Vanishing Point '71
Lolly-Madonna XXX '73
Man Who Loved Cat Dancing '73
The Arab Conspiracy '76
Eye of the Tiger '86
Solar Crisis '92

Joseph Sargent (1925-)
Colossus: The Forbin Project '70
Maybe I'll Come Home in the Spring '71
White Lightning '73
The Taking of Pelham One Two Three '74
Hustling '75
MacArthur '77
The Manions of America '81
Nightmares '83
Jaws: The Revenge '87
Day One '89
The Incident '89
Never Forget '91
Sarah, Plain and Tall: Skylark '93
Abraham '94
World War II: When Lions Roared '94
Larry McMurtry's Streets of Laredo '95
Mandela and de Klerk '97
Miss Evers' Boys '97
A Lesson Before Dying '99
The Wall '99
For Love or Country: The Arturo Sandoval Story '00
Bojangles '01
The Salem Witch Trials '02
Out of the Ashes '03
Something the Lord Made '04
Sweet Nothing in My Ear '08

Vic Sarin (1945-)
Spenser: Pale Kings & Princes '94
The Legend of Gator Face '96
In His Father's Shoes '97
Hard to Forget '98
The Waiting Game '98
Sea People '00
Flatland '02
Love on the Side '04
Partition '07
A Shine of Rainbows '09

Marcel Sarmiento
Heavy Petting '07
Deadgirl '08

Michael J. Sarna (1965-)
Doomsdayer '00
LA Apocalypse '14

Peter Sasdy (1935-)
Taste the Blood of Dracula '70
Hands of the Ripper '71
Doomwatch '72
Nothing But the Night '72
I Don't Want to Be Born '75
King Arthur, the Young Warlord '75
Young Warlord '75

Oley Sassone
Bloodfist 3: Forced to Fight '92
Future Shock '93

Relentless 4 '94
Cradle of Lies '06

Ron Satlof
Perry Mason Returns '85
Misconceptions '08

Marjane Satrapi (1969-)
Persepolis '07
Chicken With Plums '11
The Voices '15

Ernest G. Sauer
Bikini Bistro '94
Broadcast Bombshells '95

Jeremy Saulnier
Blue Ruin '13
Green Room '15
Hold the Dark '18

Charles Saunders (1904-97)
Love in Pawn '53
Meet Mr. Callaghan '54
The Womaneater '59

Hubert Sauper (1966-)
Darwin's Nightmare '04
We Come As Friends '14

Carlos Saura (1932-)
The Hunt '65
Cria Cuervos '76
Blood Wedding '81
Carmen '83
El Amor Brujo '86
Outrage '93
Tango '98
Goya in Bordeaux '99

Claude Sautet (1924-2000)
Classe Tous Risque '60
Cesar & Rosalie '72
Mado '76
Un Coeur en Hiver '93
Nelly et Monsieur Arnaud '95

Matthew Saville
Cloudstreet '11
Felony '13

Philip Saville (1930-)
The Best House in London '69
Secrets '71
Count Dracula '77
Those Glory, Glory Days '83
Mandela '87
Family Pictures '93
The Buccaneers '95
Metroland '97
Deacon Brodie '98
My Uncle Silas '01
The Gospel of John '03

Victor Saville (1897-1979)
Friday the Thirteenth '33
The Good Companions '33
First a Girl '35
It's Love Again '36
Dark Journey '37
Storm in a Teacup '37
If Winter Comes '41
Forever and a Day '43
Tonight and Every Night '45
The Green Years '46
Green Dolphin Street '47
Conspirator '49
Kim '50
The Silver Chalice '54

Nancy Savoca (1960-)
True Love '89
Dogfight '91
If These Walls Could Talk '96
The 24 Hour Woman '99

Leopoldo Savona
The Mongols '60
Byleth: The Demon of Incest '72

Geoffrey Sax
Framed '93
Broken Trust '95
Doctor Who '96
Othello '01
Tipping the Velvet '02

Widows '02
White Noise '05
Alex Rider: Operation Stormbreaker '06
Frankie and Alice '10
Christopher and His Kind '11
Murder On the Home Front '13

John Sayles (1950-)
Return of the Secaucus 7 '80
Baby It's You '82
Lianna '83
The Brother from Another Planet '84
Matewan '87
Eight Men Out '88
City of Hope '91
Passion Fish '92
The Secret of Roan Inish '94
Lone Star '95
Hombres Armados '97
Limbo '99
Sunshine State '02
Casa de los Babys '03
Silver City '04
Honeydripper '07
Go for Sisters '13

Lorene Scafaria
Seeking a Friend for the End of the World '12
The Meddler '15
Hustlers '19

Stefan Scaini
Under the Piano '95
Double Play '96
Anne of Green Gables: The Continuing Story '99
Spirit Bear: The Simon Jackson Story '05

Joseph L. Scanlan
Spenser: A Savage Place '94
Spenser: The Judas Goat '94
Flatland '02

Dan Scanlon
Monsters University '13
Onward '20

Steven Schachter
Above Suspicion '95
A Slight Case of Murder '99
The Mermaid Chair '06
The Deal '08
Unanswered Prayers '10

Armand Schaefer (1898-1967)
Lightning Warrior '31
Hurricane Express '32
Sinister Hands '32
Fighting with Kit Carson '33
The Three Musketeers '33
Law of the Wild '34
The Lost Jungle '34
The Miracle Rider '35

George Schaefer (1920-97)
Doctors' Wives '70
Once Upon a Scoundrel '73
In This House of Brede '75
The Last of Mrs. Lincoln '76
An Enemy of the People '77
The People vs. Jean Harris '81
Children in the Crossfire '84

Eric Schaeffer (1962-)
My Life's in Turnaround '94
If Lucy Fell '95
Fall '97
Wirey Spindell '99
Never Again '01
Mind the Gap '04
After Fall, Winter '11

Akiva Schaffer (1977-)
The Watch '12
Popstar: Never Stop Never Stopping '16

Franklin J. Schaffner (1920-89)
The Best Man '64
The War Lord '65
The Double Man '67
Planet of the Apes '68
Patton '70
Nicholas and Alexandra '71
Papillon '73
Islands in the Stream '77
Our Town '77
The Boys from Brazil '78
Sphinx '81
Yes, Giorgio '82
Lionheart '87
Welcome Home '89

Don Schain
The Abductors '72
Ginger '72
Girls Are for Loving '73

Jerry Schatzberg (1927-)
Panic in Needle Park '71
Scarecrow '73
Sweet Revenge '76
The Seduction of Joe Tynan '79
Honeysuckle Rose '80
No Small Affair '84
Street Smart '87
Blood Money: The Story of Clinton and Nadine '88

Daniel Schechter
Goodbye Baby '07
Life of Crime '13
Supporting Characters '13

Peter Scheerer
Alone in the Dark 2 '08
Brotherhood of Blood '08

Robert Scheerer (1929-)
Hans Brinker '69
Adam at 6 a.m. '70
The World's Greatest Athlete '73
Ants '77
How to Beat the High Cost of Living '80

Daniel Scheinert
Swiss Army Man '16
The Death of Dick Long '19

Carl Schenkel (1948-2003)
Eye of the Demon '87
The Mighty Quinn '89
Knight Moves '93
Beyond Betrayal '94
The Surgeon '94
In the Lake of the Woods '96
Tarzan and the Lost City '98
Murder on the Orient Express '01

Richard Schenkman (1958-)
The Pompatus of Love '95
Went to Coney Island on a Mission from God. . . Be Back by Five '98
And Then Came Love '07
The Man from Earth '07
Abraham Lincoln vs. Zombies '12
Mischief Night '13

Fred Schepisi (1939-)
The Devil's Playground '76
The Chant of Jimmie Blacksmith '78
Barbarosa '82
Iceman '84
Plenty '85
Roxanne '87
A Cry in the Dark '88
The Russia House '90
Mr. Baseball '92
Six Degrees of Separation '93
I.Q. '94
Fierce Creatures '96
Last Orders '01
It Runs in the Family '03
Empire Falls '05
Words and Pictures '13

Lone Scherfig (1959-)
Italian for Beginners *'01*
Wilbur Wants to Kill Himself *'02*
An Education *'09*
One Day *'11*
The Riot Club *'15*
Their Finest *'17*

Victor Schertzinger (1890-1941)
The Woman Between *'31*
Uptown New York *'32*
Something to Sing About *'36*
Rhythm on the River *'40*
The Road to Singapore *'40*
Birth of the Blues *'41*
The Road to Zanzibar *'41*

Ryan Schifrin
Abominable *'06*
Tales of Halloween *'15*

Lawrence Schiller (1936-)
The Executioner's Song *'82*
The Plot to Kill Hitler *'90*
American Tragedy *'00*
Perfect Murder, Perfect Town *'00*
Master Spy: The Robert Hanssen Story *'02*

Thomas Schlamme (1950-)
Miss Firecracker *'89*
Crazy from the Heart *'91*
So I Married an Axe Murderer *'93*
You So Crazy *'94*

John Schlesinger (1926-2003)
Billy Liar *'63*
Darling *'65*
Far from the Madding Crowd *'67*
Midnight Cowboy *'69*
Sunday, Bloody Sunday *'71*
The Day of the Locust *'75*
Marathon Man *'76*
Yanks *'79*
Honky Tonk Freeway *'81*
The Falcon and the Snowman *'85*
The Believers *'87*
Madame Sousatzka *'88*
Pacific Heights *'90*
A Question of Attribution *'91*
The Innocent *'93*
Cold Comfort Farm *'94*
An Eye for an Eye *'95*
The Next Best Thing *'00*

Volker Schlondorff (1939-)
The Lost Honor of Katharina Blum *'75*
Coup de Grace *'78*
Germany in Autumn *'78*
The Tin Drum *'79*
Swann in Love *'84*
Death of a Salesman *'86*
The Handmaid's Tale *'90*
Murder on the Bayou *'91*
The Ogre *'96*
Palmetto *'98*
The Legend of Rita *'99*
The Ninth Day *'04*

Hayden Schlossberg (1978-)
Harold & Kumar Escape from Guantanamo Bay *'08*
American Reunion *'12*

Rob Schmidt (1965-)
Speed of Life *'99*
Crime and Punishment in Suburbia *'00*
Wrong Turn *'03*
The Alphabet Killer *'08*

Wolfgang Schmidt (1938-2009)
See Ray Dennis Steckler

Oliver Schmitz (1960-)
Paris, je t'aime *'06*
Life, Above All *'10*

David Schmoeller (1947-)
Tourist Trap *'79*
The Seduction *'82*
Crawlspace *'86*
Puppet Master *'89*
Netherworld *'90*
Mysterious Museum *'99*
2 Little Monsters *'15*

Julian Schnabel (1951-)
Basquiat *'96*
Before Night Falls *'00*
The Diving Bell and the Butterfly *'07*
Miral *'10*
At Eternity's Gate *'18*

Paul Schneider
Babycakes *'89*
Cries in the Dark *'06*
Seventeen and Missing *'06*
Behind the Wall *'08*
Pretty Bird *'08*

Ernest B. Schoedsack (1893-1979)
Chang: A Drama of the Wilderness *'27*
The Most Dangerous Game *'32*
King Kong *'33*
Son of Kong *'33*
Last Days of Pompeii *'35*
Dr. Cyclops *'40*
Mighty Joe Young *'49*

Bruce Schooley
Hillary's America: The Secret History of the Democratic Party *'16*
Death of a Nation *'18*

Paul Schrader (1946-)
Blue Collar *'78*
American Gigolo *'79*
Hardcore *'79*
Cat People *'82*
Mishima: A Life in Four Chapters *'85*
Patty Hearst *'88*
The Comfort of Strangers *'91*
Light Sleeper *'92*
Touch *'96*
Affliction *'97*
Forever Mine *'99*
Auto Focus *'02*
Dominion: Prequel to the Exorcist *'05*
The Walker *'07*
Adam Resurrected *'08*
The Canyons *'13*
Dying of the Light *'14*
Dog Eat Dog *'16*
First Reformed *'17*

Jake Schreier
Robot & Frank *'12*
Paper Towns *'15*

Rick Schroder (1970-)
Black Cloud *'04*
Hellhounds *'09*
Our Wild Hearts *'13*

Barbet Schroeder (1941-)
More *'69*
The Valley Obscured by the Clouds *'70*
Maitresse *'76*
Tricheurs *'84*
Barfly *'87*
Reversal of Fortune *'90*
Single White Female *'92*
Kiss of Death *'94*
Before and After *'95*
Desperate Measures *'98*
Our Lady of the Assassins *'01*
Murder by Numbers *'02*

Michael Schroeder (1952-)
Out of the Dark *'88*
Damned River *'89*
Mortuary Academy *'91*
Relentless 2: Dead On *'91*
Cyborg 2 *'93*
Cyborg 3: The Recycler *'95*

Ariel Schulman
Catfish *'10*
Paranormal Activity 4 *'12*
Nerve *'16*

Carl Schultz (1939-)
Blue Fin *'78*
Careful, He Might Hear You *'84*
The Seventh Sign *'88*
To Walk with Lions *'99*

John Schultz
Bandwagon *'95*
Drive Me Crazy *'99*
Like Mike *'02*
The Honeymooners *'05*
Aliens in the Attic *'09*
Judy Moody and the Not Bummer Summer *'11*

Michael A. Schultz (1938-)
Honeybaby *'74*
Cooley High *'75*
Car Wash *'76*
Greased Lightning *'77*
Which Way Is Up? *'77*
Sgt. Pepper's Lonely Hearts Club Band *'78*
Carbon Copy *'81*
Krush Groove *'85*
The Last Dragon *'85*
Disorderlies *'87*
The Spirit *'87*
Timestalkers *'87*
Livin' Large *'91*
The Great American Sex Scandal *'94*
Woman, Thou Art Loosed *'04*

Douglas Schulze
Hellmaster *'92*
Dark Fields *'09*
Mimesis *'11*

Joel Schumacher (1939-2020)
The Virginia Hill Story *'76*
The Incredible Shrinking Woman *'81*
D.C. Cab *'84*
St. Elmo's Fire *'85*
The Lost Boys *'87*
Cousins *'89*
Flatliners *'90*
Dying Young *'91*
Falling Down *'93*
The Client *'94*
Batman Forever *'95*
A Time to Kill *'96*
Batman and Robin *'97*
8mm *'98*
Flawless *'99*
Tigerland *'00*
Bad Company *'02*
Phone Booth *'02*
Veronica Guerin *'03*
The Phantom of the Opera *'04*
The Number 23 *'07*
Blood Creek *'09*
Twelve *'10*
Trespass *'11*

Reinhold Schunzel (1886-1954)
Balalaika *'39*
Ice Follies of 1939 *'39*

Harold Schuster (1902-86)
Dinner at the Ritz *'37*
Wings of the Morning *'37*
My Friend Flicka *'43*
Breakfast in Hollywood *'46*
So Dear to My Heart *'49*
Kid Monk Baroni *'52*
Loophole *'54*
Portland Expose *'57*

Eric Schwab
The Learning Curve *'01*
My Lucky Elephant *'13*

Douglas Schwartz
Peacekillers *'71*
Thunder in Paradise *'93*
Thunder in Paradise 2 *'94*
Thunder in Paradise 3 *'94*

Hanns Schwarz (1888-1945)
Hungarian Rhapsody *'28*
The Return of the Scarlet Pimpernel *'37*

Robert Schwentke (1968-)
Flightplan *'05*
The Time Traveler's Wife *'09*
RED *'10*
R.I.P.D. *'13*
Insurgent *'15*
Allegiant *'16*

David Schwimmer (1966-)
Since You've Been Gone *'97*
Run, Fatboy, Run *'07*
Trust *'10*

Alberto Sciamma (1961-)
Killer Tongue *'96*
Jericho Mansions *'03*

Céline Sciamma
Girlhood *'14*
Portrait of a Lady on Fire *'19*

Ettore Scola (1931-)
A Special Day *'77*
We All Loved Each Other So Much *'77*
Macaroni *'85*

Martin Scorsese (1942-)
Who's That Knocking at My Door? *'68*
Boxcar Bertha *'72*
Mean Streets *'73*
Alice Doesn't Live Here Anymore *'74*
Taxi Driver *'76*
New York, New York *'77*
The Last Waltz *'78*
Raging Bull *'80*
King of Comedy *'82*
After Hours *'85*
The Color of Money *'86*
The Last Temptation of Christ *'88*
New York Stories *'89*
Goodfellas *'90*
Cape Fear *'91*
The Age of Innocence *'93*
Casino *'95*
Kundun *'97*
Bringing Out the Dead *'99*
Gangs of New York *'02*
The Aviator *'04*
The Departed *'06*
Shine a Light *'08*
Shutter Island *'09*
George Harrison: Living in the Material World *'11*
Hugo *'11*
The Wolf of Wall Street *'13*
Silence *'16*
The Irishman *'19*
Rolling Thunder Revue: A Bob Dylan Story by Martin Scorsese *'19*

Campbell Scott (1961-)
Big Night *'95*
Final *'01*
Hamlet *'01*
Off the Map *'03*

Darin Scott
Caught Up *'98*
Dark House *'09*

George C. Scott (1927-99)
The Andersonville Trial *'70*
Rage *'72*
Savage Is Loose *'74*
Descending Angel *'90*

Jake Scott (1965-)
Plunkett & Macleane *'98*
Welcome to the Rileys *'10*
American Woman *'19*

Ken Scott
Delivery Man *'13*
Unfinished Business *'15*

Leigh Scott
King of the Lost World *'06*
Pirates of Treasure Island *'06*

Transmorphers *'07*
Flu Birds *'08*
Cyborg Conquest *'09*
The Witches of Oz *'11*

Michael Scott
Lost in the Barrens *'91*
Spirit Rider *'93*
Heck's Way Home *'95*

Michael M. Scott
Ladykiller *'92*
Best Friends *'05*
Personal Effects *'05*
Possessed *'05*
Gradiva *'06*
Her Sister's Keeper *'06*
Murder on Pleasant Drive *'06*
Tell Me No Lies *'07*
Special Delivery *'08*
Mrs. Miracle *'09*
Call Me Mrs. Miracle *'10*
Debbie Macomber's Trading Christmas *'11*
Hitched for the Holidays *'12*

Oz Scott (1950-)
Bustin' Loose *'81*
Spanish Judges *'99*
The Cheetah Girls *'03*
Home Run Showdown *'10*

Ridley Scott (1939-)
The Duellists *'77*
Alien *'79*
Blade Runner *'82*
Legend *'86*
Someone to Watch Over Me *'87*
Black Rain *'89*
Thelma & Louise *'91*
1492: Conquest of Paradise *'92*
White Squall *'96*
G.I. Jane *'97*
RKO 281 *'99*
Gladiator *'00*
Black Hawk Down *'01*
Hannibal *'01*
Matchstick Men *'03*
Kingdom of Heaven *'05*
A Good Year *'06*
American Gangster *'07*
Body of Lies *'08*
Robin Hood *'10*
Prometheus *'12*
The Counselor *'13*
Exodus: Gods and Kings *'14*
The Martian *'15*
Alien: Covenant *'17*
All the Money in the World *'17*

Sherman Scott (1954-)
See Fred Olen Ray

Tony Scott (1944-2012)
The Hunger *'83*
Top Gun *'86*
Beverly Hills Cop 2 *'87*
Days of Thunder *'90*
Revenge *'90*
The Last Boy Scout *'91*
True Romance *'93*
Crimson Tide *'95*
The Fan *'96*
Enemy of the State *'98*
Spy Game *'01*
Man on Fire *'04*
Domino *'05*
Deja Vu *'06*
The Taking of Pelham 123 *'09*
Unstoppable *'10*

James Seale
Scorcher *'02*
Momentum *'03*
Juncture *'07*

Francis Searle (1909-2002)
Things Happen at Night *'48*
Cloudburst *'51*
The Marked One *'63*

Fred F. Sears (1913-57)
Ambush at Tomahawk Gap *'53*
The Miami Story *'54*

Cell 2455, Death Row *'55*
Wyoming Renegades *'55*
Earth *vs.* the Flying Saucers *'56*
Rumble on the Docks *'56*
The Werewolf *'56*
The Giant Claw *'57*
Crash Landing *'58*
The World Was His Jury *'58*

George Seaton (1911-79)
Junior Miss *'45*
Miracle on 34th Street *'47*
The Shocking Miss Pilgrim *'47*
Apartment for Peggy *'48*
Chicken Every Sunday *'48*
The Big Lift *'50*
For Heaven's Sake *'50*
Country Girl *'54*
The Proud and Profane *'56*
Teacher's Pet *'58*
The Counterfeit Traitor *'62*
The Hook *'63*
36 Hours *'64*
Airport *'70*
Showdown *'73*

Mike Sedan
Married People, Single Sex *'93*
Night Fire *'94*
Lap Dancing *'95*

Edward Sedgwick (1892-1953)
The Phantom of the Opera *'25*
Spring Fever *'27*
The Cameraman *'28*
Spite Marriage *'29*
Doughboys *'30*
Free and Easy *'30*
Parlor, Bedroom and Bath *'31*
The Passionate Plumber *'32*
Speak Easily *'32*
Mister Cinderella *'36*
Fit for a King *'37*
Pick a Star *'37*
Air Raid Wardens *'43*
A Southern Yankee *'48*
Ma and Pa Kettle Back On the Farm *'51*

Paul Seed (1947-)
House of Cards *'90*
To Play the King *'93*
The Affair *'95*
A Rather English Marriage *'98*
Every Woman Knows a Secret *'99*
Heat of the Sun *'99*
Dirty Tricks *'00*
Dr. Bell and Mr. Doyle: The Dark Beginnings of Sherlock Holmes *'00*
Strange Relations *'02*

Shawn Seet
Storm Boy
The Mystery of a Hansom Cab *'12*

Paul V. Seetachitt
Rock Jocks *'12*
Precious Cargo *'16*

Alex Segal (1915-77)
Ransom! *'56*
The Story of David *'76*

Peter Segal (1962-)
Naked Gun 33 1/3: The Final Insult *'94*
Tommy Boy *'95*
My Fellow Americans *'96*
Nutty Professor 2: The Klumps *'00*
Anger Management *'03*
50 First Dates *'04*
The Longest Yard *'05*
Get Smart *'08*
Grudge Match *'13*
Second Act *'18*
My Spy *'19*

Peter Sehr (1951-)
Kaspar Hauser '93
Obsession '97
Love the Hard Way '01

Arthur Allan Seidelman
Hercules in New York '70
Echoes '83
Kate's Secret '86
The Caller '87
Glory Years '87
Poker Alice '87
Harvest of Fire '95
By Dawn's Early Light '00
The Runaway '00
Sex & Mrs. X '00
Puerto Vallarta Squeeze '04
The Sisters '05

Susan Seidelman (1952-)
Smithereens '82
Desperately Seeking Susan '85
Making Mr. Right '86
Cookie '89
She-Devil '89
Tales of Erotica '93
Gaudi Afternoon '01
Power and Beauty '02
The Boynton Beach Club '05
The Hot Flashes '13

Ulrich Seidl (1952-)
Paradise: Faith '12
Paradise: Hope '13

Lewis Seiler (1890-1964)
Charlie Chan in Paris '35
Paddy O'Day '35
Career Woman '36
Crime School '38
Dust Be My Destiny '39
Hell's Kitchen '39
King of the Underworld '39
You Can't Get Away With Murder '39
Flight Angels '40
It All Came True '40
The Smiling Ghost '41
The Big Shot '42
Pittsburgh '42
Guadalcanal Diary '43
Something for the Boys '44
Doll Face '46
If I'm Lucky '46
Whiplash '48
Breakthrough '50
The Tanks Are Coming '51
Operation Secret '52
The Winning Team '52
The System '53
Women's Prison '55
Over-Exposed '56

William A. Seiter (1890-1964)
Little Church Around the Corner '23
The Family Secret '24
The White Sin '24
Skinner's Dress Suit '26
Why Be Good? '29
Going Wild '30
Sunny '30
The Truth About Youth '30
Caught Plastered '31
Girl Crazy '32
Hot Saturday '32
If I Had a Million '32
Chance at Heaven '33
Rafter Romance '33
Sons of the Desert '33
The Daring Young Man '35
Orchids to You '35
Roberta '35
Dimples '36
If You Could Only Cook '36
The Moon's Our Home '36
Stowaway '36
Room Service '38
Sally, Irene and Mary '38
Three Blind Mice '38
Allegheny Uprising '39
Susannah of the Mounties '39
Broadway '42
You Were Never Lovelier '42
Destroyer '43
Lady Takes a Chance '43
Four Jills in a Jeep '44
It's a Pleasure '45
Little Giant '46
One Touch of Venus '48
Up in Central Park '48
Borderline '50

George B. Seitz (1888-1944)
The Vanishing American '25
Danger Lights '30
Arizona '31
Drums of Jeopardy '31
Shadow of Doubt '35
Exclusive Story '36
The Last of the Mohicans '36
A Family Affair '37
You're Only Young Once '37
Judge Hardy's Children '38
Love Finds Andy Hardy '38
Out West With the Hardys '38
The Hardys Ride High '39
Judge Hardy and Son '39
Andy Hardy Meets Debutante '40
Gallant Sons '40
Kit Carson '40
Sky Murder '40
Andy Hardy's Private Secretary '41
Life Begins for Andy Hardy '41
Andy Hardy's Double Life '42
The Courtship of Andy Hardy '42
Andy Hardy's Blonde Trouble '44

Steve Sekely (1899-1979)
Women in Bondage '43
Waterfront '44
The Scar '48
Day of the Triffids '63
Kenner '73

Andrzej Sekula (1954-)
Voodoo Dawn '99
Cube 2: Hypercube '02
The Pleasure Drivers '05

Lesley Selander (1900-79)
Empty Saddles '36
The Frontiersmen '38
Buckskin Frontier '43
Colt Comrades '43
Hopalong Cassidy: Riders of the Deadline '43
Robin Hood of Texas '47
Panhandle '48
Stampede '49
Short Grass '50
Cavalry Scout '51
Fort Osage '51
Battle Zone '52
Flat Top '52
Flight to Mars '52
Fort Vengeance '53
War Paint '53
Dragonfly Squadron '54
Fort Yuma '55
Shotgun '55
The Broken Star '56
Quincannon, Frontier Scout '56
Outlaw's Son '57
The Texican '66
Arizona Bushwackers '67

Henry Selick (1952-)
The Nightmare Before Christmas '93
James and the Giant Peach '96
Monkeybone '01
Coraline '09

Michael D. Sellers
Vlad '03
Eye of the Dolphin '06
Beneath the Blue '10

Charles E. Sellier
Silent Night, Deadly Night '84
Snowballing '85

Aaron Seltzer
Date Movie '06
Disaster Movie '08
Meet the Spartans '08
Vampires Suck '10
The Starving Games '13
Best Night Ever '14

David Seltzer (1940-)
Lucas '86
Punchline '88
Shining Through '92
Nobody's Baby '01

Edgar Selwyn (1875-1944)
The Sin of Madelon Claudet '31
Skyscraper Souls '32
Turn Back the Clock '33

Ousmane Sembene (1923-2007)
Black Girl '66
Mandabi '68
Xala '75
Moolaade '04

David Semel
Campfire Tales '98
Lone Star State of Mind '02

Dean Semler (1943-)
Firestorm '97
The Patriot '99

Dominic Sena (1949-)
Kalifornia '93
Gone in 60 Seconds '00
Swordfish '01
Whiteout '09

Lorraine Senna
A Long Way Home '01
Paradise, Texas '05

Mack Sennett (1880-1960)
Tillie's Punctured Romance '14
Mickey '17

Giorgio Serafini
Game of Death '10
Ambushed '13

Julien Seri (1971-)
The Great Challenge '04
Darkness Falls '20

Yahoo Serious (1953-)
Young Einstein '89
Reckless Kelly '93
Mr. Accident '99

Andy Serkis (1964-)
Breathe '17
Mowgli: Legend of the Jungle '18

Koldo Serra
The Backwoods '06
Guernica '16

Coline Serreau (1947-)
Three Men and a Cradle '85
Chaos '01

Ishai Setton
The Big Bad Swim '06
The Kitchen '12

Vernon Sewell (1903-2001)
The Silver Fleet '43
Frenzy '46
Ghosts of Berkeley Square '47
The Jack of Diamonds '49
Ghost Ship '53
Radio Cab Murder '54
Terror Ship '54
Where There's a Will '55
Spin a Dark Web '56
Missiles from Hell '58
Blood Beast Terror '67
The Crimson Cult '68
Horrors of Burke & Hare '71

Thomas Edward Seymour
Bikini Bloodbath '06
Bikini Bloodbath Carwash '08
Bikini Bloodbath Christmas '09

Joann Sfar (1971-)
Gainsbourg: A Heroic Life '10
The Rabbi's Cat '11
The Lady in the Car with Glasses and a Gun '16

Tom Shadyac (1960-)
Ace Ventura: Pet Detective '93
The Nutty Professor '96
Liar Liar '97
Patch Adams '98
Dragonfly '02
Bruce Almighty '03
Evan Almighty '07
I Am '11
Brian Banks '18

Krishna Shah (1938-)
Rivals '72
The River Niger '76
Deadly Thief '78
Hard Rock Zombies '85

Steven Shainberg (1963-)
Hit Me '96
Secretary '02
Fur: An Imaginary Portrait of Diane Arbus '06

Karen Shakhnazarov (1952-)
The Vanished Empire '08
Ward No. 6 '09

Maxwell Shane (1905-83)
Fear in the Night '47
The Glass Wall '53

Tom Shankland
The Killing Gene '07
The Children '08

Adam Shankman (1964-)
The Wedding Planner '01
A Walk to Remember '02
Bringing Down the House '03
Cheaper by the Dozen 2 '05
The Pacifier '05
Hairspray '07
Bedtime Stories '08
Rock of Ages '12
What Men Want '19

John Patrick Shanley (1950-)
Joe Versus the Volcano '90
Doubt '08

Alan Shapiro (1957-)
Tiger Town '83
The Crush '93
Flipper '96

Dana Adam Shapiro
Murderball '05
Monogamy '10

Ken Shapiro (1943-)
The Groove Tube '72
Modern Problems '81

Paul Shapiro (1955-)
Hockey Night '84
Choices of the Heart: The Margaret Sanger Story '95
Murder at Devil's Glen '99
Ann Rule Presents: The Stranger Beside Me '03
Plain Truth '04
Deadly Honeymoon '10

Jim Sharman (1945-)
The Rocky Horror Picture Show '75
Shock Treatment '81

Don Sharp (1922-2011)
Kiss of the Vampire '62
The Devil-Ship Pirates '64
The Face of Fu Manchu '65
Bang! Bang! You're Dead! '66
Brides of Fu Manchu '66
Rasputin the Mad Monk '66
Those Fantastic Flying Fools '67
Psychomania '73
Hennessy '75
The Four Feathers '78
The Thirty-Nine Steps '79
A Woman of Substance '84
Hold the Dream '86
Tears in the Rain '88

Ian Sharp (1946-)
Robin Hood. . . The Legend: Robin Hood and the Sorcerer '83
Pride and Extreme Prejudice '90
R.P.M. '97
Tess of the D'Urbervilles '98
Tracker '10

Ben Sharpsteen (1895-1980)
Fantasia '40
Pinocchio '40

William Shatner (1931-)
Star Trek 5: The Final Frontier '89
TekWar '94
Groom Lake '02

Melville Shavelson (1917-2007)
The Seven Little Foys '55
Houseboat '58
The Five Pennies '59
It Started in Naples '60
On the Double '61
A New Kind of Love '63
Cast a Giant Shadow '66
Yours, Mine & Ours '68
Legend of Valentino '75

Helen Shaver (1951-)
Summer's End '99
Due East '02

Larry Shaw
Don't Look Down '98
Jackie, Ethel, Joan: The Kennedy Women '01

Robert Shaye (1939-)
Book of Love '91
The Last Mimzy '07

Andrew Shea
Santa Fe '97
Forfeit '07

Katt Shea (1957-)
Stripped to Kill '87
Stripped to Kill 2: Live Girls '89
Streets '90
Poison Ivy '92
The Rage: Carrie 2 '99
Nancy Drew and the Hidden Staircase '19

Barry Shear (1923-79)
Wild in the Streets '68
The Todd Killings '71
Across 110th Street '72
The Deadly Trackers '73
Strike Force '75
Undercover With the KKK '78

Donald Shebib (1938-)
Fish Hawk '79
The Little Kidnappers '90
The Pathfinder '96

Todd Sheets
Goblin '93
Prehistoric Bimbos in Armageddon City '93

Adrienne Shelly (1966-2006)
Sudden Manhattan '96
I'll Take You There '99
Waitress '07

Lynn Shelton (1946-2020)
My Effortless Brilliance '08
Humpday '09
Your Sister's Sister '11
Laggies '13
Outside In '17
Sword of Trust '19

Ron Shelton (1945-)
Bull Durham '88
Blaze '89
White Men Can't Jump '92
Cobb '94
Tin Cup '96
Play It to the Bone '99
Dark Blue '03
Hollywood Homicide '03
Just Getting Started '17

Dax Shepard (1975-)
Brother's Justice '11
Hit and Run '12
CHIPS '17

Richard Shepard
Cool Blue '88
The Linguini Incident '92
Mercy '96
Oxygen '99
Mexico City '00
The Matador '06
The Hunting Party '07
Dom Hemingway '13
The Perfection '19

Sam Shepard (1943-2017)
Far North '88
Silent Tongue '92

John Shepphird
Snowboard Academy '96
The Santa Trap '02
Chupacabra Terror '05
Jersey Shore Shark Attack '12

Jack Sher (1913-88)
The Three Worlds of Gulliver '59
The 3 Worlds of Gulliver '60

Adrian Shergold
Christabel '89
Stalag Luft '93
Heat of the Sun '99
Clapham Junction '07
Persuasion '07

Jim Sheridan (1949-)
My Left Foot '89
The Field '90
In the Name of the Father '93
The Boxer '97
In America '02
Get Rich or Die Tryin' '05
Brothers '09
Dream House '11

Kristen Sheridan (1976-)
Disco Pigs '01
August Rush '07

Edwin Sherin (1930-)
Valdez Is Coming '71
The Father Clements Story '87

Adam Sherman
Happiness Runs '10
Crazy Eyes '12

Gary Sherman (1945-)
Raw Meat '72
Dead and Buried '81
Mysterious Two '82
Vice Squad '82
Wanted Dead or Alive '86
Poltergeist 3 '88

George Sherman (1908-91)
South of the Border '39
The Bandit of Sherwood Forest '46
Border River '47
Feudin', Fussin', and A-Fightin' '48
Tomahawk '51
Against All Flags '52
War Arrow '53
Dawn at Socorro '54
Panic Button '62
Revenge of Sartana '65
Big Jake '71

Lowell Sherman (1885-1934)
The Royal Bed '31
False Faces '32
Three Broadway Girls '32
Morning Glory '33
She Done Him Wrong '33

Vincent Sherman (1906-2006)
Crime School '38
Saturday's Children '40
Underground '41
All Through the Night '42
The Hard Way '43
Old Acquaintance '43
Mr. Skeffington '44
Nora Prentiss '47
Adventures of Don Juan '49
Backfire '50
The Damned Don't Cry '50
Goodbye My Fancy '51
Affair in Trinidad '52
Lone Star '52
The Garment Jungle '57
The Young Philadelphians '59
Ice Palace '60
A Fever In the Blood '61
The Second Time Around '61

Amir Shervan
Hollywood Cop '87
Samurai Cop '89

John Sherwood (1959-)
The Creature Walks among Us '56
The Monolith Monsters '57

Dominic Shiach
Blackheart '98
Dark Side '02

Brent Shields (1963-)
Cupid & Cate '00
Brush with Fate '03

Steve Shill
Obsessed '09
Ben Hur '10

Barry Shils
Motorama '91
Wigstock: The Movie '95

Hyung Rae Shim (1958-)
Reptilian '99
Dragon Wars '07
The Last Godfather '10

Takashi Shimizu (1972-)
Ju-On 2 '00
Ju-On: The Grudge '03
The Grudge '04
The Grudge 2 '06
7500 '12
Flight 7500 '16

Ten Shimoyama
Shinobi '05
Blood '09

Kaneto Shindo (1912-2012)
Onibaba '64
Kuroneko '68

Masahiro Shinoda (1931-)
Pale Flower '64
Double Suicide '69

Akihiko Shiota
Moonlight Whispers '99
Dororo '07

Jack Sholder (1945-)
Alone in the Dark '82
A Nightmare on Elm Street 2: Freddy's Revenge '85
The Hidden '87
By Dawn's Early Light '89
Renegades '89
12:01 '93
Wishmaster 2: Evil Never Dies '98
Arachnid '01

Lee Sholem (1913-2000)
Tarzan's Magic Fountain '48
Tarzan and the Slave Girl '50
The Redhead from Wyoming '53
Jungle Man-Eaters '54
Tobor the Great '54
Ma and Pa Kettle at Waikiki '55
Hell Ship Mutiny '57
The Pharaoh's Curse '57
Escape from Planet Earth '67

Gary Shore
Dracula Untold '14
Holidays '16

Cate Shortland (1968-)
Somersault '04
The Silence '06
Lore '13
Berlin Syndrome '17

Michael Showalter (1970-)
The Baxter '05
The Big Sick '17
The Lovebirds '20

Trey Edward Shults
Krisha '15
It Comes at Night '17
Waves '19

Mina Shum
Double Happiness '94
Long Life, Happiness and Prosperity '02

Herman Shumlin
Watch on the Rhine '43
Confidential Agent '45

M. Night Shyamalan (1970-)
Wide Awake '97
The Sixth Sense '99
Unbreakable '00
Signs '02
The Village '04
Lady in the Water '06
The Happening '08
The Last Airbender '10
After Earth '13
The Visit '15
Split '16
Glass '19

Charles Shyer (1941-)
Irreconcilable Differences '84
Baby Boom '87
Father of the Bride '91
I Love Trouble '94
Father of the Bride Part 2 '95
The Affair of the Necklace '01
Alfie '04

Nicholas Siapkaris
Warm Blooded Killers '01
From Mexico With Love '09

Alex Sichel (1963-)
All Over Me '96
If These Walls Could Talk 2 '00

Andy Sidaris (1933-)
Malibu Express '85
Hard Ticket to Hawaii '87
Picasso Trigger '89
Savage Beach '89
Guns '90
Do or Die '91
Hard Hunted '92
Fit to Kill '93
The Dallas Connection '94
Day of the Warrior '96
Return to Savage Beach '97

George Sidney (1916-2002)
Pilot No. 5 '43
Thousands Cheer '43
Bathing Beauty '44
Anchors Aweigh '45
The Harvey Girls '46
Holiday in Mexico '46
Cass Timberlane '47
The Three Musketeers '48
Annie Get Your Gun '50
Key to the City '50
The Red Danube '50
Show Boat '51
Scaramouche '52
Kiss Me Kate '53
Young Bess '53
Jupiter's Darling '55
The Eddy Duchin Story '56
Jeanne Eagels '57
Pal Joey '57
Who Was That Lady? '60
Bye, Bye, Birdie '63
Viva Las Vegas '63
Half a Sixpence '67

Trish Sie
Step Up: All In '14
Pitch Perfect 3 '17

Marcos Siega (1969-)
Pretty Persuasion '05
Underclassman '05
Chaos Theory '08

Bill Siegel
The Weather Underground '02
The Trials of Muhammad Ali '13

David Siegel
Suture '93
The Deep End '01
Bee Season '05
Uncertainty '08
What Maisie Knew '12

Donald Siegel (1912-91)
Big Steal '49
Night Unto Night '49
Duel at Silver Creek '52
Private Hell 36 '54
Riot in Cell Block 11 '54
Crime in the Streets '56
Invasion of the Body Snatchers '56
The Gun Runners '58
The Lineup '58
Edge of Eternity '59
Flaming Star '60
Hell Is for Heroes '62
The Killers '64
Coogan's Bluff '68
Madigan '68
Death of a Gunfighter '69
The Beguiled '70
Two Mules for Sister Sara '70
Dirty Harry '71
Charley Varrick '73
The Shootist '76
Telefon '77
Escape from Alcatraz '79
Jinxed '82
The Most Wonderful Time of the Year '08

Robert Siegel
Swimming '00
Big Fan '09
Cruise '18

James Signorelli
Easy Money '83
Elvira, Mistress of the Dark '88

Joel Silberg (1927-)
Breakin' '84
Rappin' '85
Catch the Heat '87
Lambada '89

Brad Silberling (1962-)
Casper '95
City of Angels '98
Moonlight Mile '02
Lemony Snicket's A Series of Unfortunate Events '04
10 Items or Less '06
Land of the Lost '09
An Ordinary Man '18

Jerome Silberman (1933-2016)
See Gene Wilder

Radio Silence
V/H/S '12
Southbound '16

Sebastian Silva (1979-)
The Maid '09
Crystal Fairy & the Magical Cactus '13
Magic Magic '13
Nasty Baby '15

Adam Silver
Countdown: Jerusalem '09
The 7 Adventures of Sinbad '10

Joan Micklin Silver (1935-)
Hester Street '75
Between the Lines '77
Crossing Delancey '88
Loverboy '89
Big Girls Don't Cry. . . They Get Even '92
A Private Matter '92
In the Presence of Mine Enemies '97
A Fish in the Bathtub '99
Invisible Child '99
Charms for the Easy Life '02
Hunger Point '03

Marisa Silver (1960-)
Old Enough '84
Permanent Record '88
Vital Signs '90
He Said, She Said '91

Scott Silver
johns '96
The Mod Squad '99

Lori Silverbush
On the Outs '05
A Place at the Table '13

Elliot Silverstein (1937-)
Cat Ballou '65
A Man Called Horse '70
Nightmare Honeymoon '73
The Car '77
Jailbait: Betrayed By Innocence '86
Flashfire '94

Lloyd A. Simandl (1948-)
Chained Heat 2 '92
Escape Velocity '99
Lethal Target '99
Crackerjack 3 '00
Last Stand '00

Francois Simard
Turbo Kid '15
Summer of 84 '18

Anthony Simmons (1922-)
Four in the Morning '65
The Optimists '73
Little Sweetheart '90

Adam Simon (1962-)
Brain Dead '89
Body Chemistry 2: Voice of a Stranger '91
Carnosaur '93

J(uan) Piquer Simon (1934-)
Where Time Began '77
Supersonic Man '78
Pieces '83
Slugs '87

S. Sylvan Simon (1910-51)
Dancing Co-Ed '39
Those Glamour Girls '39
Two Girls on Broadway '40
Whistling in the Dark '41
Grand Central Murder '42
Rio Rita '42
Tish '42
Whistling in Dixie '42
Salute to the Marines '43
Whistling in Brooklyn '43
Abbott and Costello in Hollywood '45
Son of Lassie '45
Her Husband's Affairs '47
Lust for Gold '49

Yves Simoneau (1955-)
Amelia Earhart: The Final Flight '94
Mother's Boys '94
Larry McMurtry's Dead Man's Walk '96
Dean Koontz's Intensity '97
Free Money '99
Nuremberg '00
Ignition '01
44 Minutes: The North Hollywood Shootout '03
Napoleon '03
Bury My Heart at Wounded Knee '07
America '09
Betty & Coretta '13

Jane Simpson
Number One Fan '94
Little Witches '96

John Simpson
Freeze Frame '04
Amusement '08

Michael A. Simpson
Sleepaway Camp 2: Unhappy Campers '88
Fast Food '89
Funland '89
Sleepaway Camp 3: Teenage Wasteland '89

Jeremy Sims
Beneath Hill 60 '10
Last Cab to Darwin '16

Robert B. Sinclair
I'll Wait for You '41
That Wonderful Urge '48

Gerald Seth Sindell (1944-)
Teenager '74
H.O.T.S. '79

Alexander Singer (1932-)
Psyche 59 '64
Love Has Many Faces '65
Captain Apache '71
The Million Dollar Rip-Off '76
Pearl '78

Bryan Singer (1966-)
Public Access '93
The Usual Suspects '95
Apt Pupil '97
X-Men '00
X2: X-Men United '03
Superman Returns '06
Valkyrie '08
Jack the Giant Slayer '13
X-Men: Days of Future Past '14
X-Men: Apocalypse '16
Bohemian Rhapsody '18

Tarsem Singh (1961-)
The Cell '00
The Fall '06
Immortals '11
Mirror Mirror '12
Self/Less '15

John Singleton (1968-)
Boyz N the Hood '91
Poetic Justice '93
Higher Learning '94
Rosewood '96
Shaft '00
Baby Boy '01
2 Fast 2 Furious '03
Four Brothers '05
Abduction '11

David Sington
In the Shadow of the Moon '07
The Fear of 13 '15

Bruce Sinofsky (1956-2015)
Brother's Keeper '92
Paradise Lost: The Child Murders at Robin Hood Hills '95
Paradise Lost 2: Revelations '99
Metallica: Some Kind of Monster '04
Paradise Lost 3: Purgatory '11

Gary Sinyor (1962-)
Leon the Pig Farmer '93
Stiff Upper Lips '96
The Bachelor '99
Bob the Butler '05
In Your Dreams '07

Curt Siodmak (1902-2000)
Bride of the Gorilla '51
The Magnetic Monster '53

Robert Siodmak (1900-73)
Son of Dracula '43
Cobra Woman '44
Phantom Lady '44
The Strange Affair of Uncle Harry '45
Dark Mirror '46
The Killers '46
The Spiral Staircase '46
Criss Cross '48
Cry of the City '48
The Great Sinner '49
The File on Thelma Jordon '50
Crimson Pirate '52
The Rough and the Smooth '59

Florent Emilio Siri (1965-)
The Nest '02
Hostage '05

Douglas Sirk (1900-87)
A Scandal in Paris '46
Lured '47
Sleep, My Love '48
Shockproof '49
Slightly French '49
Thunder on the Hill '51
Has Anybody Seen My Gal? '52
No Room for the Groom '52
All I Desire '53
Magnificent Obsession '54
Taza, Son of Cochise '54
All That Heaven Allows '55
Captain Lightfoot '55
There's Always Tomorrow '56
Written on the Wind '56
Battle Hymn '57
Tarnished Angels '57
Imitation of Life '59

Rob Sitch (1962-)
The Castle '97
The Dish '00

Santosh Sivan
The Terrorist '98
Before the Rains '07

Tom Six
The Human Centipede: First Sequence '10
The Human Centipede 2: Full Sequence '11
The Human Centipede 3: The Final Sequence '15

Alf Sjoberg (1903-80)
Torment '44
Miss Julie '50

John Sjogren (1966-)
Red Line '96
Choke '00

Victor Sjostrom (1879-1960)
The Outlaw and His Wife '17
The Phantom Chariot '20
The Phantom Carriage '21
He Who Gets Slapped '24
Under the Red Robe '36

Erik Skjoldbjaerg
Insomnia '97
Prozac Nation '01

Keri Skogland
White Lies '98
Children of the Corn 666: Isaac's Return '99
The Courage to Love '00
Zebra Lounge '01

Liberty Stands Still '02
Banshee '06
The Stone Angel '07
Fifty Dead Men Walking '08

Jerzy Skolimowski (1938-)
Moonlighting '82
Success Is the Best Revenge '84
The Lightship '86
Torrents of Spring '90

Tim Skousen
The Sasquatch Gang '06
Raiders!: The Story of the Greatest Fan Film Ever Made '16

David Slade
Hard Candy '06
30 Days of Night '07
The Twilight Saga: Eclipse '10
Nightmare Cinema '19

Bohdan Slama (1967-)
Something Like Happiness '05
The Country Teacher '08

Bob Slatzer (1927-2005)
Hellcats '68
Bigfoot '70

Brian Sloan
Boys Life '94
I Think I Do '97

Holly Goldberg Sloan (1958-)
The Big Green '95
The Secret Life of Girls '99

Paul Sloane (1893-1963)
Half-Shot at Sunrise '30
The Sun Sets at Dawn '50

Rick Sloane (1961-)
The Movie House Massacre '78
Hobgoblins '87
Vice Academy '88
Vice Academy 2 '90
Vice Academy 3 '91
Mind, Body & Soul '92

Edward Sloman (1886-1972)
Up the Ladder '25
The Lost Zeppelin '29

Karl Slovin
Sex and the Other Man '95
On Edge '03

George Sluizer (1932-)
The Vanishing '88
The Vanishing '93
Crimetime '96

Leslie Small
Hair Show '04
Kevin Hart: Let Me Explain '13
Kevin Hart: What Now? '16
Holiday Rush '19

Jack Smight (1926-2003)
The Third Day '65
Harper '66
Kaleidoscope '66
No Way to Treat a Lady '68
The Secret War of Harry Frigg '68
The Illustrated Man '69
Rabbit, Run '70
The Traveling Executioner '70
Airport '75 '75
Midway '76
Airport '77 '77
Damnation Alley '77
Fast Break '79
Loving Couples '80
Holocaust Survivors. . . Remembrance of Love '83
Number One with a Bullet '87
Intimate Power '89

Adam Smith
Little Dorrit '08
Trespass Against Us '16

Alex Smith
The Slaughter Rule '01
Walking Out '17

Andrew J. Smith
The Slaughter Rule '01
Walking Out '17

Brian J. Smith
Body of Influence 2 '96
Tarzan 2 '05

Bruce Smith
Bebe's Kids '92
The Proud Family Movie '05

Carter Smith (1971-)
The Ruins '08
Jamie Marks is Dead '13

Charles Martin Smith (1953-)
Trick or Treat '86
Air Bud '97
The Snow Walker '03
Frederick Forsyth's Icon '05
Dolphin Tale '11
Dolphin Tale 2 '14
A Dog's Way Home '19

Chris Smith (1970-)
American Movie '99
The Yes Men '03
Severance '06
Collapse '09
Triangle '09
Black Death '10

Christopher Smith (1970-)
Labyrinth '12
Detour '17

Cliff(ord) Smith (1894-1937)
The Back Trail '24
Radio Patrol '37

Jim Field Smith (1979-)
She's Out of My League '10
Butter '12

John N. Smith (1943-)
The Boys of St. Vincent '93
Dangerous Minds '95
Sugartime '95
A Cool, Dry Place '98

Kevin Smith (1970-)
Clerks '94
Mallrats '95
Chasing Amy '97
Dogma '99
Jay and Silent Bob Strike Back '01
Jersey Girl '04
Clerks 2 '06
Zack and Miri Make a Porno '08
Cop Out '10
Red State '11
Tusk '14
Holidays '16
Yoga Hosers '16
Jay and Silent Bob Reboot '19

Mark Smith
Overnight '03
Seance '06

Mel Smith (1952-2013)
The Tall Guy '89
Radioland Murders '94
Bean '97
High Heels and Low Lifes '01

Peter Smith
No Surrender '86
The Alchemists '99

Richard Curson Smith
Agatha Christie: A Life in Pictures '04
Pinochet's Last Stand '06
The Making of a Lady '12

Roy Allen Smith (1954-)
The Land Before Time 2: The Great Valley Adventure '94
The Land Before Time 3: The Time of the Great Giving '95
The Land Before Time 4: Journey Through the Mists '96

Sarah Adina Smith
Holidays '16
Buster's Mal Heart '17

Simon J. Smith
Bee Movie '07
Penguins of Madagascar '14

Alan Smithee
Iron Cowboy '68
Ghost Fever '87
I Love N.Y. '87
Let's Get Harry '87
Morgan Stewart's Coming Home '87
Bloodsucking Pharoahs of Pittsburgh '90
The Shrimp on the Barbie '90
Fatal Charm '92
Solar Crisis '92
Call of the Wild '93
Hellraiser 4: Bloodline '95
Sub Down '97

Stephen Smoke
Final Impact '91
Street Crimes '92

Phil Smoot
Alien Outlaw '85
The Dark Power '85

Jack Snyder (1960-)
Ghost Image '07
Fatal Call '12

Zack Snyder (1966-)
Dawn of the Dead '04
300 '07
Watchmen '09
Legend of the Guardians: The Owls of Ga'Hoole '10
Sucker Punch '11
Man of Steel '13
Batman v Superman: Dawn of Justice '16
Justice League '17

Michele (Michael) Soavi (1957-)
Stagefright '87
The Devil's Daughter '91
Cemetery Man '95
The Church '98

Mark Sobel (1956-)
Sweet Revenge '87
Ordeal in the Arctic '93
Storm Chasers: Revenge of the Twister '98

Jonathan Sobol
A Beginner's Guide to Endings '10
The Art of the Steal '13
The Padre '18

Steven Soderbergh (1963-)
sex, lies and videotape '89
The Underneath '95
Gray's Anatomy '96
Schizopolis '97
Out of Sight '98
The Limey '99
Erin Brockovich '00
Traffic '00
Ocean's Eleven '01
Full Frontal '02
Solaris '02
Eros '04
Ocean's Twelve '04
Bubble '06
The Good German '06
Ocean's Thirteen '07
Che '08
The Girlfriend Experience '09
The Informant! '09
And Everything Is Going Fine '10
Contagion '11
Haywire '12
Magic Mike '12
Behind the Candelabra '13
Side Effects '13
Logan Lucky '17
Unsane '18
High Flying Bird '19
The Laundromat '19

Iain Softley (1958-)
Backbeat '94
Hackers '95
The Wings of the Dove '97
K-PAX '01
The Skeleton Key '05
Inkheart '09
Trap for Cinderella '13
Curve '16

Joel Soisson
Maniac Cop 3: Badge of Silence '93
Pulse 2: Afterlife '08
Children of the Corn: Genesis '11

Alexandr Sokurov (1951-)
Mother and Son '97
Father and Son '03
The Sun '05
Alexandra '07

Russell Solberg
Forced to Kill '93
Raven '97

Silvio Soldini (1958-)
Bread and Tulips '01
Days and Clouds '07

Alfred Sole (1943-)
Alice Sweet Alice '76
Tanya's Island '81

Paul Solet
Tales of Halloween '15
Bullet Head '17

Peter Sollett
Raising Victor Vargas '03
Nick & Norah's Infinite Playlist '08
Freeheld '15

Sergio Sollima (1921-)
The Big Gundown '66
The Family '70
Revolver '75

Cary Solomon
The Insatiable '06
Unplanned '19

Courtney Solomon (1971-)
Dungeons and Dragons '00
An American Haunting '05
Getaway '13

Todd Solondz (1960-)
Welcome to the Dollhouse '95
Happiness '98
Storytelling '01
Palindromes '04
Life During Wartime '09
Dark Horse '11
Wiener-Dog '16

Ben Sombogaart
Crusade: A March through Time '06
Bride Flight '08

Stephen Sommers (1962-)
The Adventures of Huck Finn '93
Rudyard Kipling's The Jungle Book '94
Deep Rising '98
The Mummy '99
The Mummy Returns '01
Van Helsing '04
G.I. Joe: The Rise of Cobra '09
Odd Thomas '13

Barry Sonnenfeld (1953-)
The Addams Family '91
Addams Family Values '93
For Love or Money '93
Get Shorty '95
Men in Black '97
Wild Wild West '99
Big Trouble '02
Men in Black 2 '02
RV '06
Men in Black 3 '12
Nine Lives '16

Warren Sonoda
Merlin and the Book of Beasts '09
Sexting '11
The Masked Saint '16

Dror Soref
The Seventh Coin '92
Not Forgotten '09

David Soren
Turbo '13
Captain Underpants: The First Epic Movie '17

Fumihiko Sori
Ping Pong '02
Ichi '08

Paolo Sorrentino (1970-)
This Must Be the Place '12
The Great Beauty '13
Rio, I Love You '14
Youth '15
Loro '19

Lodovico Sorret (1951-)
See Tom Noonan

Jen Soska
The ABCs of Death 2 '14
Vendetta '15

Sylvia Soska
The ABCs of Death 2 '14
Vendetta '15

John V. Soto
Crush '09
Needle '10
The Reckoning '14

Kevin Spacey (1959-)
Albino Alligator '96
Beyond the Sea '04

Robert Sparr (1915-69)
More Dead Than Alive '68
Once You Kiss a Stranger '69

Will Speck
Blades of Glory '07
The Switch '10
Office Christmas Party '16

Greg Spence
Children of the Corn 4: The Gathering '96
The Prophecy 2: Ashtown '97

Richard Spence (1957-)
Blind Justice '94
Different for Girls '96
New World Disorder '99

Brenton Spencer
Blown Away '93
Call of the Wild '04
Never Cry Werewolf '08

Robert Spera
Witchcraft '88
Leprechaun 5: In the Hood '99
Bloody Murder 2 '03

Penelope Spheeris (1945-)
Suburbia '83
The Boys Next Door '85
Hollywood Vice Sqaud '86
Wayne's World '92
The Beverly Hillbillies '93
The Little Rascals '94
Black Sheep '96
Senseless '98

The Kid and I '05
Five '11

Bryan Spicer
Mighty Morphin Power Rangers: The Movie '95
For Richer or Poorer '97
McHale's Navy '97
Taken '02

Marcus Spiegel
Eye of the Storm '98
Devil in the Flesh 2 '00

Scott Spiegel (1957-)
Intruder '88
From Dusk Till Dawn 2: Texas Blood Money '98
My Name is Modesty: A Modesty Blaise Adventure '04
Hostel: Part 3 '11

Steven Spielberg (1947-)
Night Gallery '69
Columbo: Murder by the Book '71
Duel '71
The Sugarland Express '74
Jaws '75
Close Encounters of the Third Kind '77
1941 '79
Raiders of the Lost Ark '81
E.T.: The Extra-Terrestrial '82
Twilight Zone: The Movie '83
Indiana Jones and the Temple of Doom '84
The Color Purple '85
Empire of the Sun '87
Always '89
Indiana Jones and the Last Crusade '89
Hook '91
Jurassic Park '93
Schindler's List '93
Amistad '97
The Lost World: Jurassic Park 2 '97
Saving Private Ryan '98
A. I.: Artificial Intelligence '01
Catch Me If You Can '02
Minority Report '02
The Terminal '04
Munich '05
War of the Worlds '05
Indiana Jones and the Kingdom of the Crystal Skull '08
The Adventures of Tintin '11
War Horse '11
Lincoln '12
Bridge of Spies '15
The BFG '16
The Post '17
Ready Player One '18

Michael Spierig
Undead '05
Daybreakers '09
Predestination '15
Jigsaw '17
Winchester '18

Peter Spierig
Undead '05
Daybreakers '09
Predestination '15
Jigsaw '17
Winchester '18

Bob Spiers
That Darn Cat '96
Spice World: The Movie '97
Chilly Dogs '01

Philip Spink
Ronnie and Julie '97
Big and Hairy '98
The Duke '99
Voyage of the Unicorn '00
Kung Fu Killer '08
Knights of Bloodsteel '09

Lev L. Spiro
Alien Avengers '96
Minutemen '08
The Wizards of Waverly Place: The Movie '09

Beverly Hills Chihuahua 3: Viva La Fiesta! '12

Roger Spottiswoode (1945-)
Terror Train '80
Under Fire '83
The Best of Times '86
Shoot to Kill '88
Turner and Hooch '89
Air America '90
Stop! or My Mom Will Shoot '92
And the Band Played On '93
Mesmer '94
Hiroshima '95
Tomorrow Never Dies '97
The 6th Day '00
Shake Hands With the Devil '07
The Children of Huang Shi '08
The Journey Home '14
A Street Cat Named Bob '16

Jill Sprecher
Clockwatchers '97
Thirteen Conversations About One Thing '01
Thin Ice '12

R.G. Springsteen (1904-89)
The Red Menace '49
Oklahoma Annie '51
Track the Man Down '55
Cole Younger, Gunfighter '58
Revolt in the Big House '58
King of the Wild Stallions '59
Operation Eichmann '61
Johnny Reno '66
Hostile Guns '67

Morgan Spurlock (1970-)
Super Size Me '04
Where in the World Is Osama Bin Laden? '06
Freakonomics '10
Comic-Con Episode IV: A Fan's Hope '11
POM Wonderful Presents: The Greatest Movie Ever Sold '11
One Direction: This Is Us '13
Super Size Me 2: Holy Chicken! '19

Salvatore Stabile
Gravesend '97
Where God Left His Shoes '07

Nick Stagliano
The Florentine '98
Good Day for It '11

Chad Stahelski
John Wick '14
John Wick: Chapter 2 '17
John Wick: Chapter 3-Parabellum '19

Eric Steven Stahl (1959-)
Safe House '99
I-See-You.Com '06

John M. Stahl (1886-1950)
Imitation of Life '34
Magnificent Obsession '35
Parnell '37
Letter of Introduction '38
Holy Matrimony '43
Immortal Sergeant '43
The Keys of the Kingdom '44
Leave Her to Heaven '45
The Foxes of Harrow '47

John Stalberg, Jr.
High School '10
Crypto '19

Sylvester Stallone (1946-)
Paradise Alley '78
Rocky 2 '79
Rocky 3 '82
Staying Alive '83
Rocky 4 '85
Rocky Balboa '06
Rambo '08
The Expendables '10

Kimo Stamboel
Killers '14
Headshot '17

Daniel Stamm (1976-)
The Last Exorcism '10
13 Sins '13

Richard Standeven
Band of Gold '95
Falling for a Dancer '98

Sean Stanek
A Crack in the Floor '00
Played '06

Jeremy Stanford
Stepmonster '92
Watchers 3 '94

Richard Stanley (1966-)
Hardware '90
Dust Devil '93
Color Out of Space '19

Stanislav Stanojevic
Diary of a Suicide '73
Subversion '79

Andrew Stanton (1965-)
A Bug's Life '98
Finding Nemo '03
WALL-E '08
John Carter '12
Finding Dory '16

Jeff Stanzler
Jumpin' at the Boneyard '92
Sorry, Haters '05

Jack Starrett (1936-89)
Run, Angel, Run! '69
Cry Blood, Apache '70
The Losers '70
Slaughter '72
Cleopatra Jones '73
Race with the Devil '75
Hollywood Man '76
A Small Town in Texas '76
Walking Tall: The Final Chapter '77

Ben Stassen
Fly Me to the Moon '08
The Wild Life '16

Ralph Staub (1899-1969)
Sitting On the Moon '36
Join the Marines '37
The Mandarin Mystery '37
Navy Blues '37

Riley Stearns
Faults '15
The Art of Self-Defense '19

Ray Dennis Steckler (1938-2009)
Wild Guitar '62
Incredibly Strange Creatures Who Stopped Living and Became Mixed-Up Zombies '63
The Thrill Killers '65
Rat Pfink a Boo-Boo '66
Sinthia: The Devil's Doll '70
The Hollywood Strangler Meets the Skid Row Slasher '79
Las Vegas Serial Killer '86

Justin Steele
Death and Cremation '10
Gutshot Straight '14

Burr Steers (1966-)
Igby Goes Down '02
17 Again '09
Charlie St. Cloud '10
Pride and Prejudice and Zombies '16

Giorgio Stegani (1928-)
Beyond the Law '68
The Gentleman Killer '69

Mark Steilen
The Settlement '99
Wieners '08

Bjorn Stein (1970-)
Storm '05
Underworld: Awakening '12
6 Souls '13

Darren Stein (1973-)
Jawbreaker '98
Sparkler '99
G.B.F. '13

Paul Stein (1892-1951)
Lottery Bride '30
One Romantic Night '30
Sin Takes a Holiday '30
The Saint Meets the Tiger '43
Counterblast '48
The Twenty Questions Murder Mystery '50

David Steinberg (1942-)
Going Berserk '83
The Wrong Guy '96

Michael Steinberg (1959-)
The Waterdance '91
Bodies, Rest & Motion '93
Wicked '98

Danny Steinmann
Savage Streets '83
Friday the 13th, Part 5: A New Beginning '85

Gerard Stembridge (1958-)
About Adam '00
Alarm '08

Kriv Stenders
Red Dog '11
Danger Close '19

Barbara Stepansky
Hurt '09
Taken for Ransom '13

Frederick Stephani
Rocketship '36
Flash Gordon: Rocketship '40

A.C. (Stephen Apostoloff) Stephen (?-2005)
Orgy of the Dead '65
Lady Godiva Rides '68

Martha Stephens (1984-)
Land Ho! '14
To the Stars '20

Mora Stephens
Conventioneers '05
Zipper '15

James D. Stern
It's the Rage '99
Every Little Step '08

Joshua Michael Stern
Swing Vote '08
Jobs '13

Ricki Stern
The Devil Came on Horseback '07
Joan Rivers: A Piece of Work '10
In My Father's House '15

Sandor Stern (1936-)
Assassin '86
Shattered Innocence '87
Pin. . . '88
Amityville 4: The Evil Escapes '89
Dangerous Pursuit '89

Steven Hilliard Stern (1937-)
Harrad Summer '74
I Wonder Who's Killing Her Now? '76
Anatomy of a Seduction '79
Portrait of an Escort '80
The Devil & Max Devlin '81
Miracle on Ice '81
The Ambush Murders '82
Forbidden Love '82
Mazes and Monsters '82
Portrait of a Showgirl '82
Hostage Flight '85

The Park Is Mine '85
Morning Glory '93
Black Fox: Good Men and Bad '94
Black Fox: The Price of Peace '94
Breaking the Surface: The Greg Louganis Story '96

Josh Sternfeld
Winter Solstice '04
Meskada '10

Patrick Stettner
The Business of Strangers '01
The Night Listener '06

Andrew Stevens (1955-)
The Skateboard Kid 2 '94
Virtual Combat '95
Crash Dive '96
The White Raven '98
Fire From Below '09
Tommy and the Cool Mule '09

Fisher Stevens (1963-)
Just a Kiss '02
Stand Up Guys '12
Before the Flood '16

George Stevens (1904-75)
Kentucky Kernels '34
Alice Adams '35
Annie Oakley '35
The Nitwits '35
Swing Time '36
A Damsel in Distress '37
Quality Street '37
Vivacious Lady '38
Gunga Din '39
Vigil in the Night '40
Penny Serenade '41
Talk of the Town '42
Woman of the Year '42
The More the Merrier '43
I Remember Mama '48
A Place in the Sun '51
Something to Live For '52
Shane '53
Giant '56
The Diary of Anne Frank '59
The Greatest Story Ever Told '65

Leslie Stevens (1924-98)
Hero's Island '62
Incubus '65

Michael Stevens (1966-)
Sin '02
Thurgood '11
Herblock: The Black & the White '13

Robert Stevens (1920-89)
The Big Caper '57
In the Cool of the Day '63

Dr. John Stevenson
Kung Fu Panda '08
Sherlock Gnomes '18

Robert Stevenson (1905-86)
Nine Days a Queen '36
King Solomon's Mines '37
Non-Stop New York '37
Tom Brown's School Days '40
Back Street '41
Joan of Paris '42
Forever and a Day '43
Jane Eyre '44
Dishonored Lady '47
The Woman on Pier 13 '50
My Forbidden Past '51
Old Yeller '57
Johnny Tremain & the Sons of Liberty '58
Darby O'Gill & the Little People '59
Kidnapped '60
The Absent-Minded Professor '61
I Thank a Fool '62
In Search of the Castaways '62

The Misadventures of Merlin Jones '63
Son of Flubber '63
Mary Poppins '64
Monkey's Uncle '65
That Darn Cat '65
Blackbeard's Ghost '67
The Gnome-Mobile '67
The Love Bug '68
My Dog, the Thief '69
Bedknobs and Broomsticks '71
Herbie Rides Again '74
The Island at the Top of the World '74
One of Our Dinosaurs Is Missing '75
The Shaggy D.A. '76

Jean Stewart
Cracker: Men Should Weep '94
Butterfly Collectors '99

Jon Stewart (1962-)
Rosewater '14
Irresistible '20

Scott Stewart
Legion '10
Priest '11
Holidays '16

Alex Steyermark
Prey for Rock and Roll '03
One Last Thing '05

Ben Stiller (1965-)
Reality Bites '94
The Cable Guy '96
Zoolander '01
Tropic Thunder '08
The Secret Life of Walter Mitty '13
Zoolander 2 '16

Mauritz Stiller (1883-1928)
Treasure of Arne '19
The Atonement of Gosta Berling '24
Hotel Imperial '27

John Whitney Stillman (1952-)
See Whit Stillman

Whit Stillman (1952-)
Metropolitan '90
Barcelona '94
The Last Days of Disco '98
Damsels in Distress '11
Love & Friendship '16

John Stimpson
The Legend of Lucy Keyes '06
The March Sisters at Christmas '12
Sexting in Suburbia '12

John Stockwell (1961-)
Cheaters '00
crazy/beautiful '01
Blue Crush '02
Into the Blue '05
Turistas '06
Cat Run '11
Dark Tide '12
Seal Team Six: The Raid on Osama Bin Laden '12
In the Blood '13
Kid Cannabis '14
Countdown '16
Kickboxer: Vengeance '16

Josh Stolberg (1971-)
Kids in America '05
The Hungover Games '14

Bryan Michael Stoller (1960-)
Turn of the Blade '97
Undercover Angel '99
Miss Cast Away '04
First Dog '10

Nicholas Stoller
Forgetting Sarah Marshall '08
Get Him to the Greek '10

The Five-Year Engagement '12
Neighbors '14
Neighbors 2: Sorority Rising '16
Storks '16

Ben Stoloff (1895-1960)
Palooka '34
To Beat the Band '35
The Hidden Hand '42

Philipp Stolzl (1967-)
North Face '08
Young Goethe in Love '11
Erased '12

Andrew L. Stone (1902-99)
Hi Diddle Diddle '43
Stormy Weather '43
Sensations of 1945 '44
Highway 301 '50
The Steel Trap '52
A Blueprint for Murder '53
The Night Holds Terror '55
Julie '56
Cry Terror! '58
The Decks Ran Red '58
The Last Voyage '60
The Password Is Courage '62

Charles Stone, III (1966-)
Drumline '02
Paid in Full '02
Mr. 3000 '04
Lila & Eve '15
Uncle Drew '18

Jason Stone
The Calling '14
At First Light '18

Norman Stone
Catherine Cookson's The Black Velvet Gown '92
Catherine Cookson's The Gambling Man '98

Oliver Stone (1946-)
Seizure '74
The Hand '81
Platoon '86
Salvador '86
Wall Street '87
Talk Radio '88
Born on the Fourth of July '89
The Doors '91
JFK '91
Heaven and Earth '93
Natural Born Killers '94
Nixon '95
U-Turn '97
Any Given Sunday '99
Alexander '04
World Trade Center '06
W. '08
South of the Border '09
Wall Street 2: Money Never Sleeps '10
Savages '12
Snowden '16

Virginia Lively Stone (1921-97)
The Treasure of Jamaica Reef '74
Run If You Can '87

Lynne Stopkewich (1964-)
Kissed '96
Suspicious River '00

Michael Storey
We'll Meet Again '02
Before I Say Goodbye '03

Tim Story (1970-)
Barbershop '02
Taxi '04
Fantastic Four '05
Fantastic Four: Rise of the Silver Surfer '07
Hurricane Season '09
Think Like a Man '12
Kevin Hart: Let Me Explain '13
Ride Along '14
Think Like a Man Too '14

Ride Along 2 '16
Shaft '19

Mark Stouffer
Man Outside '88
Dog Gone '08
Creature of Darkness '09

Colin Strause
Aliens *vs.* Predator: Requiem '07
Skyline '10

Greg Strause
Aliens *vs.* Predator: Requiem '07
Skyline '10

Todd Strauss-Schulson (1980-)
A Very Harold & Kumar Christmas '11
The Final Girls '15
Isn't It Romantic '19

Frank Strayer (1891-1964)
Murder at Midnight '31
The Crusader '32
The Vampire Bat '32
Dangerous Appointment '34
Fugitive Road '34
The Ghost Walks '34
Condemned to Live '35
Death from a Distance '36
Blondie '38
Blondie Brings Up Baby '39
Blondie Meets the Boss '39
Blondie Takes a Vacation '39
Blondie Has Trouble '40
Blondie On a Budget '40
Blondie Plays Cupid '40
Blondie in Society '41
Blondie Goes Latin '42
Blondie Goes to College '42

Barbra Streisand (1942-)
Yentl '83
The Prince of Tides '91
The Mirror Has Two Faces '96

Susan Streitfeld
Female Perversions '96
Golf in the Kingdom '10

Joseph Strick (1923-)
The Balcony '63
Ulysses '67
Tropic of Cancer '70
Road Movie '72
James Joyce: A Portrait of the Artist as a Young Man '77

Wesley Strick (1954-)
The Tie That Binds '95
Hitched '01

Peter Strickland
Berberian Sound Studio '12
The Duke of Burgundy '14
In Fabric '18

Herbert L. Strock (1918-2005)
The Magnetic Monster '53
GOG '54
Blood of Dracula '57
How to Make a Monster '58
Rider on a Dead Horse '62
The Crawling Hand '63
Monster '78

James C. Strouse
Grace Is Gone '07
The Winning Season '09
People Places Things '15

Jeb Stuart (1961-)
Switchback '97
Blood Done Sign My Name '10

Mel Stuart (1928-2012)
If It's Tuesday, This Must Be Belgium '69
Willy Wonka & the Chocolate Factory '71
The Triangle Factory Fire Scandal '79

John Sturges (1910-92)
The Capture '50
The Magnificent Yankee '50
Mystery Street '50
Right Cross '50
It's a Big Country '51
The People Against O'Hara '51
The Girl in White '52
Escape from Fort Bravo '53
Jeopardy '53
Bad Day at Black Rock '54
The Scarlet Coat '55
Backlash '56
Gunfight at the O.K. Corral '57
The Law and Jake Wade '58
The Old Man and the Sea '58
Last Train from Gun Hill '59
Never So Few '59
The Magnificent Seven '60
By Love Possessed '61
Sergeants 3 '62
The Great Escape '63
The Hallelujah Trail '65
The Satan Bug '65
Hour of the Gun '67
Ice Station Zebra '68
Marooned '69
Joe Kidd '72
McQ '74
Chino '75
The Eagle Has Landed '77

Preston Sturges (1898-1959)
Christmas in July '40
The Great McGinty '40
The Lady Eve '41
Sullivan's Travels '41
The Palm Beach Story '42
The Great Moment '44
Hail the Conquering Hero '44
Miracle of Morgan's Creek '44
The Sin of Harold Diddlebock '47
Unfaithfully Yours '48
The Beautiful Blonde from Bashful Bend '49

Charles Sturridge (1951-)
Brideshead Revisited '81
Aria '88
A Handful of Dust '88
Where Angels Fear to Tread '91
A Foreign Field '93
Gulliver's Travels '95
FairyTale: A True Story '97
Longitude '00
Shackleton '02
Lassie '05
The Road to Coronation Street '10
The Scapegoat '12

Antoni Stutz
The Killing Club '01
Rushlights '13

Eric Styles (1967-)
Dreaming of Joseph Lees '99
Relative Values '99
Tempo '03
Miss Conception '08

Michael Sucsy
Grey Gardens '09
The Vow '12
Every Day '18

Sara Sugarman (1962-)
Very Annie Mary '00
Confessions of a Teenage Drama Queen '04
House of Versace '13

John Suits
The Scribbler '14
3022 '19

Brett Sullivan
Ginger Snaps: Unleashed '04
A Christmas Horror Story '15

John Sullivan
2016: Obama's America '12
America: Imagine the World Without Her '14

Kevin Sullivan (1955-)
Wild Pony '83
Anne of Green Gables '85
Anne of Avonlea '87

Kevin Rodney Sullivan (1958-)
America's Dream '95
Soul of the Game '96
How Stella Got Her Groove Back '98
Conviction '02
Barbershop 2: Back in Business '04
Guess Who '05

Peter Sullivan (1976-)
The Dog Who Saved Halloween '11
12 Christmas Wishes For My Dog '11
F6 Twister '12
Hidden Away '13

Tim Sullivan
Jack and Sarah '95
2001 Maniacs '05
2001 Maniacs: Field of Screams '10

Jeremy Summers (1931-)
Five Golden Dragons '67
The House of 1000 Dolls '67
The Vengeance of Fu Manchu '67
Danger UXB '81

Annie Sundberg
The Devil Came on Horseback '07
Joan Rivers: A Piece of Work '10

Cedric Sundstrom
American Ninja 3: Blood Hunt '89
The Revenger '90
American Ninja 4: The Annihilation '91

Stephen Surjik
Wayne's World 2 '93
Weapons of Mass Distraction '97
I Want Candy '07

David Sutherland
Guns '08
Home Again '13

Edward Sutherland (1895-1974)
It's the Old Army Game '26
Mr. Robinson Crusoe '32
International House '33
Mississippi '35
Every Day's a Holiday '38
The Flying Deuces '39
Beyond Tomorrow '40
The Invisible Woman '40
One Night in the Tropics '40

Kiefer Sutherland (1966-)
Last Light '93
Truth or Consequences, N.M. '97
Woman Wanted '98

Tim Sutton
Dark Night '17
Donnybrook '18

Seijun Suzuki (1923-)
Detective Bureau 2-3: Go to Hell Bastards! '63
Gate of Flesh '64
Fighting Elegy '66
Branded to Kill '67
Princess Raccoon '05

Peter Svatek
Witchboard 3: The Possession '95
Sci-Fighters '96
Bleeders '97

Jack London's The Call of the Wild '97
Silver Wolf '98
The Rendering '02
Student Seduction '03
Widow on the Hill '05
Proof of Lies '06
The Christmas Choir '08
Girl's Best Friend '08

Jan Sverak (1965-)
Kolya '96
Dark Blue World '01

E.W. Swackhamer (1927-94)
Man & Boy '71
Gidget Gets Married '72
Death Sentence '74
Death at Love House '75
Once an Eagle '76
The Dain Curse '78
The Winds of Kitty Hawk '78
The Oklahoma City Dolls '81
Cocaine and Blue Eyes '83
The Rousters '90

Bob Swaim (1943-)
Half Moon Street '86
Masquerade '88
The Climb '97

Joe Swanberg (1981-)
Hannah Takes the Stairs '07
Nights and Weekends '08
Alexander the Last '09
V/H/S '12
All the Light in the Sky '13
Drinking Buddies '13
24 Exposures '13
Happy Christmas '14
Digging for Fire '15

Bruce Sweeney
Last Wedding '01
American Venus '07

Robin Swicord (1952-)
The Jane Austen Book Club '07
Wakefield '17

David Swift (1919-2001)
Pollyanna '60
The Parent Trap '61
The Interns '62
Love Is a Ball '63
Under the Yum-Yum Tree '63
Good Neighbor Sam '64
How to Succeed in Business without Really Trying '67

Saul Swimmer (1936-2007)
Force of Impulse '60
Mrs. Brown, You've Got a Lovely Daughter '68

Michael Switzer
Nitti: The Enforcer '88
Stalking Laura '93
Unlikely Angel '97
Forever Love '98
Fallen Angel '03
Annie's Point '05
Vanished '06

Peter Sykes (1939-)
Demons of the Mind '72
To the Devil, a Daughter '76

Joe Syracuse (1967-)
Amateur Night '16
Dear Dictator '18

Istvan Szabo (1938-)
Father '67
Love Film '70
25 Fireman's Street '73
Mephisto '81
Meeting Venus '91
Sunshine '99
Taking Sides '01
Being Julia '04

Janos Szasz
Woyzeck '94
Opium: Diary of a Madwoman '07
The Notebook '13

Jeannot Szwarc (1937-)
Sex Through a Window '72
Lisa, Bright and Dark '73
Bug '75
Jaws 2 '78
Somewhere in Time '80
Enigma '82
Supergirl '84
Santa Claus: The Movie '85
The Murders in the Rue Morgue '86
Grand Larceny '92

Juan Carlos Tabio
Strawberry and Chocolate '93
Guantanamera '95

Johnny Tabor
Day of the Mummy '14
Eaters '15

Kristoffer Tabori (1952-)
Anna's Storm '07
Fireball '09
High Plains Invaders '09
Goodnight for Justice: The Measure of a Man '12
My Gal Sunday '14

Jorma Taccone (1977-)
MacGruber '10
Popstar: Never Stop Never Stopping '16

Gabriela Tagliavini (1968-)
Without Men '11
Border Run '12

Tibor Takacs (1954-)
The Gate '87
I, Madman '89
Gate 2 '92
Red Shoe Diaries 2: Double Dare '92
Sabotage '96
Sabrina the Teenage Witch '96
Redline '97
Sanctuary '98
Kraken: Tentacles of the Deep '06
Ice Spiders '07
Megasnake '07
NYC: Tornado Terror '08
Lies and Illusions '09
Meteor Storm '10
Spiders '13

Isao Takahata (1935-2018)
Grave of the Fireflies '88
Pom Poko '94
The Tale of the Princess Kaguya '13
Only Yesterday '16

Sophia Takal
Always Shine '16
Black Christmas '19

Beat Takeshi (1947-)
See Takeshi 'Beat' Kitano

Yojiro Takita
Onmyoji '01
When the Last Sword is Drawn '02
Onmyoji 2 '03
Ashura '05
Departures '08

Rachel Talalay
Freddy's Dead: The Final Nightmare '91
Ghost in the Machine '93
Tank Girl '94
Hannah's Law '12

David E. Talbert (1966-)
First Sunday '08
Baggage Claim '13
Almost Christmas '16

Paul Talbot
Freakshow '95
Hellblock 13 '97

Gregg Tallas (1915-)
Summer Storm '44
Prehistoric Women '50

Espionage in Tangiers '65
Cataclysm '81

Lee Tamahori (1950-)
Once Were Warriors '94
Mulholland Falls '95
The Edge '97
Along Came a Spider '01
Die Another Day '02
XXX: State of the Union '05
Next '07
The Devil's Double '11

Kevin Tancharoen
Fame '09
Glee: The 3D Concert Movie '11

William (Bill) Tannen
Flashpoint '84
Hero and the Terror '88
The Cutter '05

Danis Tanovic
No Man's Land '01
Triage '09

Daniel Taplitz
Commandments '96
Breakin' All The Rules '04

Michael Tarantini
Crimebusters '79
Massacre in Dinosaur Valley '85

Quentin Tarantino (1963-)
Reservoir Dogs '92
Pulp Fiction '94
Four Rooms '95
Jackie Brown '97
Kill Bill Vol. 1 '03
Kill Bill Vol. 2 '04
Death Proof '07
Inglourious Basterds '09
Django Unchained '12
The Hateful Eight '15
Once Upon A Time... In Hollywood '19

Andrei Tarkovsky (1932-86)
My Name Is Ivan '62
Andrei Rublev '66
Solaris '72
The Mirror '75
Stalker '79
Nostalghia '83
The Sacrifice '86

Genndy Tartakovsky
Hotel Transylvania '12
Hotel Transylvania 2 '15
Hotel Transylvania 3: Summer Vacation '18

Frank Tashlin (1913-72)
The Fuller Brush Man '48
The First Time '52
Son of Paleface '52
Susan Slept Here '54
Artists and Models '55
The Girl Can't Help It '56
Hollywood or Bust '56
Rock-A-Bye Baby '57
Will Success Spoil Rock Hunter? '57
The Geisha Boy '58
Say One for Me '59
Cinderfella '60
Bachelor Flat '62
It's Only Money '62
Who's Minding the Store? '63
Disorderly Orderly '64
The Alphabet Murders '65
The Glass Bottom Boat '66
Caprice '67
Private Navy of Sgt. O'Farrell '68

Nadia Tass (1956-)
Malcolm '86
Rikky and Pete '88
Pure Luck '91
The Miracle Worker '00
Child Star: The Shirley Temple Story '01
Fatal Honeymoon '12

Jacques Tati (1908-82)
Mr. Hulot's Holiday *'53*
Mon Oncle *'58*
Playtime *'67*
Traffic *'71*

John Tatoulis
The Silver Stallion: King of the Wild Brumbies *'93*
Zone 39 *'96*

Norman Taurog (1899-1981)
Sunny Skies *'30*
Hold 'Em Jail *'32*
If I Had a Million *'32*
Mrs. Wiggs of the Cabbage Patch *'34*
We're Not Dressing *'34*
Rhythm on the Range *'36*
You Can't Have Everything *'37*
The Adventures of Tom Sawyer *'38*
Boys Town *'38*
Mad About Music *'38*
Broadway Melody of 1940 *'40*
Little Nellie Kelly *'40*
Young Tom Edison *'40*
Design for Scandal *'41*
Men of Boys Town *'41*
A Yank at Eton *'42*
Girl Crazy *'43*
Presenting Lily Mars *'43*
The Bride Goes Wild *'48*
Words and Music *'48*
That Midnight Kiss *'49*
The Toast of New Orleans *'50*
Rich, Young and Pretty *'51*
Room for One More *'51*
The Stooge *'51*
Jumping Jacks *'52*
The Caddy *'53*
Living It Up *'54*
You're Never Too Young *'55*
Birds & the Bees *'56*
Bundle of Joy *'56*
Pardners *'56*
Onionhead *'58*
G.I. Blues *'60*
All Hands on Deck *'61*
Blue Hawaii *'62*
Girls! Girls! Girls! *'62*
It Happened at the World's Fair *'63*
Palm Springs Weekend *'63*
Sergeant Deadhead *'65*
Tickle Me *'65*
Dr. Goldfoot and the Bikini Machine *'66*
Spinout *'66*
Double Trouble *'67*
Live a Little, Love a Little *'68*
Speedway *'68*

Bertrand Tavernier (1941-)
The Clockmaker *'73*
Death Watch *'80*
Coup de Torchon *'81*
A Sunday in the Country *'84*
Round Midnight *'86*
Life and Nothing But *'89*
Daddy Nostalgia *'90*
L'Appat *'94*
Revenge of the Musketeers *'94*
Capitaine Conan *'96*
It All Starts Today *'99*
Safe Conduct *'01*
In the Electric Mist *'08*
The Princess of Montpensier *'10*
The French Minister *'13*

Paolo Taviani (1931-)
St. Michael Had a Rooster *'72*
Padre Padrone *'77*
The Night of the Shooting Stars *'82*
Kaos *'85*
Night Sun *'90*
Fiorile *'93*
The Lark Farm *'07*

Vittorio Taviani (1929-2018)
St. Michael Had a Rooster *'72*
Padre Padrone *'77*
The Night of the Shooting Stars *'82*
Kaos *'85*
Night Sun *'90*
Fiorile *'93*
The Lark Farm *'07*

Alan Taylor (1965-)
Palookaville *'95*
The Emperor's New Clothes *'01*
Kill the Poor *'03*
Thor: The Dark World *'13*
Terminator Genisys *'15*

Brian Taylor
Crank *'06*
Crank: High Voltage *'09*
Gamer *'09*
Ghost Rider: Spirit of Vengeance *'12*

Deon Taylor
Dead Tone *'07*
The Hustle *'08*
Chain Letter *'10*
Meet the Blacks *'16*
Traffik *'18*
Black and Blue *'19*
The Intruder *'19*

Don Taylor (1920-98)
Everything's Ducky *'61*
Ride the Wild Surf *'64*
The Five Man Army *'69*
Escape from the Planet of the Apes *'71*
Tom Sawyer *'73*
Great Scout & Cathouse Thursday *'76*
The Island of Dr. Moreau *'77*
Damien: Omen 2 *'78*
The Final Countdown *'80*
Secret Weapons *'85*

Finn Taylor (1958-)
Dream with the Fishes *'97*
Cherish *'02*
The Darwin Awards *'06*

Jud Taylor (1940-)
Winter Kill *'74*
Search for the Gods *'75*
Mary White *'77*
License to Kill *'84*
Broken Vows *'87*
Foxfire *'87*
Danielle Steel's Kaleidoscope *'90*
The Old Man and the Sea *'90*
Guinevere *'94*

Ray Taylor (1888-1952)
Battling with Buffalo Bill *'31*
Chandu on the Magic Island *'34*
The Perils of Pauline *'34*
Return of Chandu *'34*
The Ivory Handled Gun *'35*
The Vigilantes Are Coming *'36*
Dick Tracy *'37*
Flaming Frontiers *'38*
The Spider's Web *'38*
The Green Hornet *'39*
Flash Gordon Conquers the Universe *'40*
Winners of the West *'40*
Riders of Death Valley *'41*
Gang Busters *'42*
Junior G-Men of the Air *'42*
Adventures of Smilin' Jack *'43*
Don Winslow of the Coast Guard *'43*
Don Winslow of the Navy *'43*
Master Key *'44*
Raiders of Ghost City *'44*
Lost City of the Jungle *'45*
Son of Billy the Kid *'49*

S. Lee Taylor (1957-)
See Steve Taylor

Sam Taylor (1895-1958)
Safety Last *'23*
The Freshman *'25*
Exit Smiling *'26*
My Best Girl *'27*
Tempest *'28*
The Taming of the Shrew *'29*
Ambassador Bill *'31*
Vagabond Lady *'35*
Nothing But Trouble *'44*

Steve Taylor (1957-)
Social Intercourse *'01*
The Second Chance *'06*
Blue Like Jazz *'12*

Tate Taylor
Pretty Ugly People *'08*
The Help *'11*
Get On Up *'14*
The Girl on the Train *'16*
Ma *'19*

Sam Taylor-Johnson (1967-)
Nowhere Boy *'09*
Fifty Shades of Grey *'15*

Sam Taylor-Wood (1967-)
See Sam Taylor-Johnson

Julie Taymor (1952-)
Titus *'99*
Frida *'02*
Across the Universe *'07*
The Tempest *'10*

Colin Teague (1970-)
Shooters *'00*
The Last Drop *'05*
Dragonheart 3: The Sorcerer's Curse *'15*

Lewis Teague (1941-)
Lady in Red *'79*
Alligator *'80*
Fighting Back *'82*
Cujo *'83*
Cat's Eye *'85*
The Jewel of the Nile *'85*
Collision Course *'89*
Navy SEALS *'90*
Deadlock *'91*
The Triangle *'01*

Andre Techine (1943-)
Barocco *'76*
The Bronte Sisters *'79*
Hotel America *'81*
Rendez-vous *'85*
Scene of the Crime *'87*
I Don't Kiss *'91*
Ma Saison Preferee *'93*
Wild Reeds *'94*
Les Voleurs *'96*
Strayed *'03*
Changing Times *'04*
The Witnesses *'07*
The Girl on the Train *'09*
Unforgivable *'11*

Julien Temple (1953-)
The Secret Policeman's Other Ball *'82*
Absolute Beginners *'86*
Aria *'88*
Earth Girls Are Easy *'89*
Bullet *'94*
The Filth and the Fury *'99*
Pandaemonium *'00*

Andy Tennant (1955-)
The Amy Fisher Story *'93*
It Takes Two *'95*
Fools Rush In *'97*
Ever After: A Cinderella Story *'98*
Anna and the King *'99*
Sweet Home Alabama *'02*
Hitch *'05*
Fool's Gold *'08*
The Bounty Hunter *'10*
Wild Oats *'16*

Del Tenney (1930-)
Curse of the Living Corpse *'64*
Horror of Party Beach *'64*
I Eat Your Skin *'64*

Kevin S. Tenney (1955-)
Witchboard *'87*
Night of the Demons *'88*
Peacemaker *'90*
Pinocchio's Revenge *'96*
The Arrival 2 *'98*
Tick Tock *'00*
Endangered Species *'02*

Pearry Reginald Teo
The Gene Generation *'07*
Necromentia *'09*
Witchville *'10*

Jonathan Teplitzky
Better Than Sex *'00*
Burning Man *'11*
The Railway Man *'13*
Churchill *'17*

John Terlesky (1961-)
Judgment Day *'99*
Supreme Sanction *'99*
Chain of Command *'00*
The Guardian *'01*
Cerberus *'05*
Not My Life *'06*
Fire Serpent *'07*
Smoke Jumpers *'08*

Jessy Terrero
Soul Plane *'04*
Gun *'10*
NYC Underground *'13*

Don Terry
Legacy of Fear *'06*
A Near-Death Experience *'08*

Hiroshi Teshigahara (1927-2001)
Woman in the Dunes *'64*
Face of Another *'66*
Rikyu *'90*

Duccio Tessari (1926-94)
The Cats *'68*
Sundance and the Kid *'69*
Zorro *'74*
Beyond Justice *'92*

Ted Tetzlaff (1903-95)
A Dangerous Profession *'49*
Johnny Allegro *'49*
The Window *'49*
The White Tower *'50*
Terror on a Train *'53*
The Young Land *'59*

Joan Tewkesbury (1936-)
Old Boyfriends *'79*
Sudie & Simpson *'90*

Peter Tewkesbury (1923-2003)
Sunday in New York *'63*
Emil and the Detectives *'64*
Stay Away, Joe *'68*
The Trouble with Girls (and How to Get into It) *'69*

Masaaki Tezuka
Godzilla *vs.* Megaguirus *'00*
Godzilla Against Mechagodzilla *'02*
Godzilla-Tokyo S.O.S. *'03*

Graham Theakston
The Mill on the Floss *'97*
Money Kings *'98*
Sherlock: Case of Evil *'02*

Wilhelm Thiele (1890-1975)
Tarzan Triumphs *'43*
Tarzan's Desert Mystery *'43*

Betty Thomas (1948-)
Only You *'92*
The Brady Bunch Movie *'95*
The Late Shift *'96*
Private Parts *'96*
Dr. Dolittle *'98*
28 Days *'00*
I Spy *'02*
John Tucker Must Die *'06*
Alvin and the Chipmunks: The Squeakuel *'09*

Gerald Thomas (1920-93)
Time Lock *'57*
Carry On Sergeant *'58*
Carry On Nurse *'59*
Carry On Constable *'60*
No Kidding *'60*
Carry On Regardless *'61*
Carry On Cruising *'62*
Carry On Cabby *'63*
Carry On Jack *'63*
Carry On Spying *'64*
Carry On Cleo *'65*
Carry On Cowboy *'66*
Carry On Screaming *'66*
Don't Lose Your Head *'66*
Follow That Camel *'67*
Carry On Doctor *'68*
Carry On Up the Khyber *'68*
Carry On Again Doctor *'69*
Carry On Loving *'70*
Carry On Up the Jungle *'70*
Carry On at Your Convenience *'71*
Carry On Camping *'71*
Carry On Henry VIII *'71*
Carry On Abroad *'72*
Carry On Matron *'72*
Carry On Behind *'75*
Carry On Dick *'75*
Carry On England *'76*
Carry On Emmanuelle *'78*
Carry On Columbus *'92*

John G. Thomas (1948-)
Tin Man *'83*
Banzai Runner *'86*

Ralph Thomas (1915-2001)
Appointment With Venus *'51*
Doctor in the House *'53*
Mad About Men *'54*
Above Us the Waves *'55*
Doctor at Sea *'56*
The Iron Petticoat *'56*
Campbell's Kingdom *'57*
Doctor at Large *'57*
A Tale of Two Cities *'58*
The Wind Cannot Read *'58*
Upstairs and Downstairs *'59*
Conspiracy of Hearts *'60*
Doctor in Love *'60*
Doctor in Distress *'63*
Hot Enough for June *'64*
The High Bright Sun *'65*
Doctor in Clover *'66*
Deadlier Than the Male *'67*
Quest for Love *'71*
The Big Scam *'79*

Ralph L. (R.L.) Thomas (1939-)
Carry On Regardless *'61*
Ticket to Heaven *'81*
Young Ivanhoe *'95*

Scott Thomas
Deranged *'01*
Latin Dragon *'03*
Flight of the Living Dead: Outbreak on a Plane *'07*

Harry Z. Thomason (1940-)
Encounter with the Unknown *'75*
Hootch Country Boys *'75*
Visions of Evil *'75*
The Day It Came to Earth *'77*
The Hunting of the President *'04*
The Last Ride *'12*

Barnaby Thompson
St. Trinian's *'07*
The Legend of Fritton's Gold *'09*

Caroline Thompson (1956-)
Black Beauty *'94*
Buddy *'97*
Snow White: The Fairest of Them All *'02*

Daniele Thompson (1942-)
La Buche *'00*
Jet Lag *'02*
Avenue Montaigne *'06*
Change of Plans *'09*

Ernest Thompson (1949-)
1969 *'89*
Out of Time *'00*

J. Lee Thompson (1914-2002)
An Alligator Named Daisy *'55*
Flame Over India *'59*
North West Frontier *'59*
Tiger Bay *'59*
Cape Fear *'61*
The Guns of Navarone *'61*
Taras Bulba *'62*
Kings of the Sun *'63*
Eye of the Devil *'67*
Before Winter Comes *'69*
The Chairman *'69*
MacKenna's Gold *'69*
Conquest of the Planet of the Apes *'72*
Battle for the Planet of the Apes *'73*
Huckleberry Finn *'74*
St. Ives *'76*
The White Buffalo *'77*
The Greek Tycoon *'78*
The Passage *'79*
Cabo Blanco *'81*
Happy Birthday to Me *'81*
Ten to Midnight *'83*
The Ambassador *'84*
The Evil That Men Do *'84*
King Solomon's Mines *'85*
Firewalker *'86*
Murphy's Law *'86*
Death Wish 4: The Crackdown *'87*
Messenger of Death *'88*
Kinjite: Forbidden Subjects *'89*

Chris Thomson (1945-)
1915 *'82*
Swimsuit *'89*
The Morrison Murders *'96*
Trucks *'97*

Youngyooth Thongkonthun
The Iron Ladies *'00*
The Iron Ladies 2 *'03*

Billy Bob Thornton (1955-)
Sling Blade *'96*
Daddy & Them *'99*
All the Pretty Horses *'00*
Jayne Mansfield's Car *'13*

Jerry Thorpe (1930-)
The Venetian Affair *'67*
Day of the Evil Gun *'68*
Kung Fu *'72*
Smile Jenny, You're Dead *'74*
The Possessed *'77*
Blood and Orchids *'86*

Richard Thorpe (1896-1986)
The Lone Defender *'32*
The Midnight Lady *'32*
Notorious But Nice *'33*
City Park *'34*
Green Eyes *'34*
The Quitter *'34*
Tarzan Escapes *'36*
Double Wedding *'37*
Night Must Fall *'37*
The Crowd Roars *'38*
Three Loves Has Nancy *'38*
The Toy Wife *'38*
The Adventures of Huckleberry Finn *'39*
Tarzan Finds a Son *'39*
The Earl of Chicago *'40*
The Bad Man *'41*
Tarzan's Secret Treasure *'41*
Tarzan's New York Adventure *'42*
Above Suspicion *'43*
Cry Havoc *'43*
The Thin Man Goes Home *'44*
Two Girls and a Sailor *'44*
Her Highness and the Bellboy *'45*
Thrill of a Romance *'45*
This Time for Keeps *'47*

A Date with Judy '48
On an Island with You '48
Malaya '49
The Sun Comes Up '49
Three Little Words '50
The Great Caruso '51
It's a Big Country '51
Vengeance Valley '51
Carbine Williams '52
Ivanhoe '52
Prisoner of Zenda '52
All the Brothers Were Valiant '53
The Girl Who Had Everything '53
Knights of the Round Table '53
Athena '54
The Student Prince '54
The Prodigal '55
Quentin Durward '55
Jailhouse Rock '57
Ten Thousand Bedrooms '57
Tip On a Dead Jockey '57
The House of the Seven Hawks '59
The Honeymoon Machine '61
The Tartars '61
The Horizontal Lieutenant '62
Follow the Boys '63
Fun in Acapulco '63
That Funny Feeling '65
The Last Challenge '67

Rawson Marshall Thurber (1975-)
Dodgeball: A True Underdog Story '04
The Mysteries of Pittsburgh '08
We're the Millers '13
Central Intelligence '16
Skyscraper '18

Michael Thurmeier
Ice Age: Continental Drift '12
Ice Age: Collision Course '16

Antonio Tibaldi
Little Boy Blue '97
Kiss of Fire '98

Michael Tiddes
A Haunted House '13
A Haunted House 2 '14
Fifty Shades of Black '16

Greg Tiernan
Sausage Party '16
The Addams Family '19

Jacob Tierney (1979-)
Twist '03
The Trotsky '09
Good Neighbors '10

Eric Till (1929-)
Hot Millions '68
The Walking Stick '70
An American Christmas Carol '79
Wild Horse Hank '79
Buffalo Jump '90
To Catch a Killer '92
The Girl Next Door '98
Luther '03

George Tillman, Jr. (1969-)
Soul Food '97
Men of Honor '00
Notorious '09
Faster '10
The Inevitable Defeat of Mister & Pete '13
The Longest Ride '15
The Hate U Give '18

James Tinling (1889-1967)
Charlie Chan in Shanghai '35
Mr. Moto's Gamble '38

Robert Tinnell (1961-)
Kids of the Round Table '96
Believe '99

Stacy Title
The Last Supper '96
Let the Devil Wear Black '99
The Bye Bye Man '17

Timo Tjahjanto
The ABCs of Death '12
V/H/S/2 '13
Killers '14
Headshot '17

Johnny To (1955-)
The Heroic Trio '93
The Mission '99
Running out of Time '99
Full Time Killer '01
Running on Karma '03
Breaking News '04
Exiled '06
Running Out of Time 2 '06

Tony To
Band of Brothers '01
The Pacific '10

James Toback (1944-)
Fingers '78
Love and Money '80
The Pick-Up Artist '87
Two Girls and a Guy '98
Black and White '99
Harvard Man '01
When Will I Be Loved '04
Tyson '08

Janet Tobias
No Place on Earth '12
Unseen Enemy '17

Ricky Tognazzi (1955-)
La Scorta '94
Excellent Cadavers '99

Norman Tokar (1920-79)
Big Red '62
Savage Sam '63
A Tiger Walks '64
Those Calloways '65
The Ugly Dachshund '65
Follow Me, Boys! '66
The Happiest Millionaire '67
The Horse in the Gray Flannel Suit '68
The Boatniks '70
Snowball Express '72
Where the Red Fern Grows '74
The Apple Dumpling Gang '75
No Deposit, No Return '76
Candleshoe '78
The Cat from Outer Space '78

Eric Toledano
The Intouchables '12
Samba '14

Michael Tolkin (1950-)
The Rapture '91
The New Age '94

Stephen Tolkin
Stephen King's Golden Years '91
Daybreak '93
Carolina Moon '07
What If God Were the Sun? '07
A Day Late and a Dollar Short '14

Mike Tollin (1956-)
Summer Catch '01
Radio '03

Stanley Tong (1960-)
Supercop '92
Supercop 2 '93
Jackie Chan's First Strike '96
Rumble in the Bronx '96
Mr. Magoo '97
Jackie Chan's The Myth '05

Burt Topper (1928-2007)
The Strangler '64
The Hard Ride '71
Soul Hustler '76

Giuseppe Tornatore (1956-)
Cinema Paradiso '88
A Pure Formality '94
The Star Maker '95
The Legend of 1900 '98
Malena '00
The Unknown Woman '06
Baaria '09
The Best Offer '13

Joe Tornatore
Zebra Force '76
Code Name: Zebra '84
Grotesque '87

Fina Torres (1951-)
Oriana '85
Celestial Clockwork '94
Woman on Top '00

Gabe Torres
December '91
Brake '12

Robert Totten (1938-95)
Death of a Gunfighter '69
The Wild Country '71
Pony Express Rider '76
The Sacketts '79

Jacques Tourneur (1904-77)
Nick Carter, Master Detective '39
Phantom Raiders '40
Cat People '42
Days of Glory '43
I Walked with a Zombie '43
The Leopard Man '43
Experiment Perilous '45
Canyon Passage '46
Out of the Past '47
Berlin Express '48
Easy Living '49
The Flame & the Arrow '50
Stars in My Crown '50
Way of a Gaucho '52
Appointment in Honduras '53
Stranger on Horseback '55
Nightfall '56
Curse of the Demon '57
The Fearmakers '58
Timbuktu '59
The Giant of Marathon '60
The Comedy of Terrors '64

Maurice Tourneur (1876-1961)
Pride of the Clan '18
The Last of the Mohicans '20
Lorna Doone '22

Robert Towne (1936-)
Personal Best '82
Tequila Sunrise '88
Without Limits '97
Ask the Dust '06

Bud Townsend (1921-97)
Nightmare in Wax '69
Terror at Red Wolf Inn '72
Coach '78

Robert Townsend (1957-)
Hollywood Shuffle '87
The Five Heartbeats '91
The Meteor Man '93
B.A.P.'s '97
Jackie's Back '99
Love Songs '99
Holiday Heart '00
Little Richard '00
Carmen: A Hip Hopera '01
10,000 Black Men Named George '02
Black Listed '03
Phantom Punch '09
Playin' For Love '15

Ian Toynton
Piece of Cake '88
Annie: A Royal Adventure '95

Phil Traill
All About Steve '09
Chalet Girls '11

Josh Trank (1985-)
Chronicle '12
Fantastic Four '15
Capone '20

Pablo Trapero
Rolling Family '04
Lion's Den '08
Carancho '10

Andrew Traucki
Black Water '07
The Reef '10
The ABCs of Death '12

Pete Travis
Vantage Point '08
Dredd '12

Joey Travolta (1950-)
Hard Vice '94
Vegas Vice '94
Navajo Blues '97
Matter of Trust '98
Partners '99
Enemies of Laughter '00
The House Next Door '01
Arizona Summer '03
Final Move '06

Peter S. Traynor
Death Game '77
Seducers '77

Jeff Tremaine
Jackass: The Movie '02
Jackass Number Two '06
Jackass 3D '10
Jackass Presents: Bad Grandpa '13

Brian Trenchard-Smith (1946-)
Escape 2000 '81
BMX Bandits '83
Dead End Drive-In '86
Day of the Panther '88
The Siege of Firebase Gloria '89
Night of the Demons 2 '94
Leprechaun 3 '95
Sahara '95
Escape Clause '96
Leprechaun 4: In Space '96
Britannic '00
The Paradise Virus '03
DC 9/11: Time of Crisis '04
In Her Line of Fire '06
Long Lost Son '06
Absolute Deception '13
Drive Hard '14

John Trent (?-1983)
Vengeance Is Mine '74
It Seemed Like a Good Idea at the Time '75
Crossbar '79

Blair Treu
Wish upon a Star '96
Little Secrets '02
The Last Days of Summer '07

Monika Treut (1954-)
Virgin Machine '88
Seduction: The Cruel Woman '89
Erotique '94
Ghosted '09

Dale Trevillion
One Man Force '89
Play Time '94
Heart of Stone '01

Colin Trevorrow
Safety Not Guaranteed '12
Jurassic World '15
The Book of Henry '17

Joachim Trier
Reprise '06
Oslo, August 31st '11
Louder Than Bombs '16
Thelma '17

Gus Trikonis (1938-)
The Evil '78
She's Dressed to Kill '79

Take This Job & Shove It '81
Miss All-American Beauty '82
Dempsey '83
The Rumor Mill '86

Lawrence Trilling
Dinner and Driving '97
Group Sex '10

Rose Troche
Go Fish '94
Bedrooms and Hallways '98
The Safety of Objects '01

Jan Troell (1931-)
The New Land '72
Zandy's Bride '74
Hurricane '79
Hamsun '96
Everlasting Moments '08
The Last Sentence '12

Jason Trost
All Superheroes Must Die '11
The FP '12

Gary Trousdale (1960-)
Beauty and the Beast '91
The Hunchback of Notre Dame '96
Atlantis: The Lost Empire '01

Fernando Trueba (1955-)
Twisted Obsession '90
Belle Epoque '92
Two Much '96
The Girl of Your Dreams '99
Chico & Rita '10

Francois Truffaut (1932-84)
The 400 Blows '59
Jules and Jim '62
Shoot the Piano Player '62
The Soft Skin '64
Fahrenheit 451 '66
The Bride Wore Black '68
Stolen Kisses '68
Mississippi Mermaid '69
Bed and Board '70
The Wild Child '70
Two English Girls '72
Day for Night '73
The Story of Adele H. '75
Small Change '76
The Man Who Loved Women '77
The Green Room '78
Love on the Run '78
The Last Metro '80
The Woman Next Door '81
Confidentially Yours '83

Douglas Trumbull (1942-)
Silent Running '71
Brainstorm '83

Ming-liang Tsai
The Hole '98
What Time Is It There? '01
Goodbye, Dragon Inn '03
Stray Dogs '13

Shinya Tsukamoto (1960-)
Tetsuo: The Iron Man '92
Tetsuo 2: Body Hammer '97
Nightmare Detective '06

Slava Tsukerman
Liquid Sky '83
Perestroika '09

Stanley Tucci (1960-)
Big Night '95
The Imposters '98
The Impostors '98
Joe Gould's Secret '00
Blind Date '08
Final Portrait '17

Michael Tuchner (1934-)
Villain '71
Haywire '80
The Hunchback of Notre Dame '82
Adam '83
Trenchcoat '83
Trapped in Silence '86

Back to the Secret Garden '01
A Place Called Home '04

Anand Tucker (1963-)
Hilary and Jackie '98
Shopgirl '05
When Did You Last See Your Father? '07
Red Riding, Part 3: 1983 '09
Leap Year '10

David Tucker
Behaving Badly '89
A Year in Provence '89

James Tucker
Skinned Alive '08
Superman: Unbound '13

Roger Tucker
Deadly Recruits '86
Waiting for Dublin '07

Michael Tully
Cocaine Angel '06
Ping Pong Summer '14
Don't Leave Home '18

Montgomery Tully (1904-88)
Boys in Brown '49
Paid to Kill '54
Terror Street '54
The Way Out '56
The Counterfeit Plan '57
The Electronic Monster '57
Strange Awakening '58
Battle Beneath the Earth '68

Ching Siu Tung (1953-)
The Executioners '93
The Heroic Trio '93

Sandy Tung (1950-)
Across the Tracks '89
Shiloh 2: Shiloh Season '99
Saving Shiloh '06

Gary J. Tunnicliffe (1968-)
Within the Rock '96
Jack and the Beanstalk '09

Rosemarie Turko (1951-)
Dungeonmaster '83
Scarred '84

Alex Turner
Dead Birds '04
Red Sands '09

Ann Turner (1960-)
Hammers over the Anvil '91
Irresistible '06

Brad Turner
The Inspectors '98
This Matter of Marriage '98
Roswell: The Aliens Attack '99
The Inspectors 2: A Shred of Evidence '00
Prison Break: The Final Break '09

Jon Turteltaub (1963-)
3 Ninjas '92
Cool Runnings '93
While You Were Sleeping '95
Phenomenon '96
From the Earth to the Moon '98
Instinct '99
Disney's The Kid '00
National Treasure '04
National Treasure: Book of Secrets '07
The Sorcerer's Apprentice '10
Last Vegas '13
The Meg '18

John Turturro (1957-)
Mac '93
Illuminata '98
Romance & Cigarettes '05
Fading Gigolo '13
Rio, I Love You '14

Frank Tuttle (1892-1963)
This Is the Night *'32*
Here is My Heart *'34*
Waikiki Wedding *'37*
This Gun for Hire *'42*
Don Juan Quilligan *'45*
Suspense *'46*
Island of Lost Women *'59*

David N. Twohy (1955-)
Grand Tour: Disaster in Time *'92*
The Arrival *'96*
Pitch Black *'00*
Below *'02*
The Chronicles of Riddick *'04*
A Perfect Getaway *'09*
Riddick *'13*

Tom Tykwer (1965-)
Winter Sleepers *'97*
Run Lola Run *'98*
The Princess and the Warrior *'00*
Heaven *'01*
Paris, je t'aime *'06*
Perfume: The Story of a Murderer *'06*
The International *'09*
3 *'10*
Cloud Atlas *'12*
A Hologram for the King *'16*

Morten Tyldum
Headhunters *'11*
The Imitation Game *'14*
Passengers *'16*

Liv Ullmann (1939-)
Sofie *'92*
Faithless *'00*
Miss Julie *'14*

Edgar G. Ulmer (1904-72)
The Black Cat *'34*
The Singing Blacksmith *'38*
The Light Ahead *'39*
Moon over Harlem *'39*
American Matchmaker *'40*
Tomorrow We Live *'42*
Girls in Chains *'43*
Isle of Forgotten Sins *'43*
Bluebeard *'44*
Strange Illusion *'45*
Detour *'46*
Her Sister's Secret *'46*
The Strange Woman *'46*
Carnegie Hall *'47*
Ruthless *'48*
The Pirates of Capri *'49*
The Man from Planet X *'51*
St. Benny the Dip *'51*
Loves of Three Queens *'54*
Murder Is My Beat *'55*
The Daughter of Dr. Jekyll *'57*
Naked Venus *'58*
Beyond the Time Barrier *'60*
Journey Beneath the Desert *'61*

Ron Underwood (1953-)
Tremors *'89*
City Slickers *'91*
Heart and Souls *'93*
Speechless *'94*
Mighty Joe Young *'98*
The Adventures of Pluto Nash *'02*
Stealing Sinatra *'04*
In the Mix *'05*
Santa Baby *'06*
Holiday in Handcuffs *'07*
Santa Baby 2: Santa Maybe *'09*

Lee Unkrich
Toy Story 2 *'99*
Toy Story 3 *'10*
Coco *'17*

Peter Ustinov (1921-2004)
Billy Budd *'62*
Lady L *'65*

Roar Uthaug
Escape *'12*
The Wave *'15*
Tomb Raider *'18*

Jamie Uys (1921-96)
The Gods Must Be Crazy *'84*
The Gods Must Be Crazy 2 *'89*

Roger Vadim (1928-2000)
And God Created Woman *'57*
The Night Heaven Fell *'57*
Dangerous Liaisons *'60*
Blood and Roses *'61*
Please Not Now! *'61*
Le Repos du Guerrier *'62*
Love on a Pillow *'62*
Circle of Love *'64*
The Game Is Over *'66*
Barbarella *'68*
Spirits of the Dead *'68*
Pretty Maids All In a Row *'71*
Don Juan (Or If Don Juan Were a Woman) *'73*
Game of Seduction *'76*
And God Created Woman *'88*

Kerry Valderrama
Garrison *'07*
Sanitarium *'13*

Luis Valdez (1940-)
Zoot Suit *'81*
La Bamba *'87*
The Cisco Kid *'94*

Tonino Valerii (1934-)
A Reason to Live, a Reason to Die *'73*
My Name Is Nobody *'74*

Eric Valette
One Missed Call *'08*
Super Hybrid *'10*
The Prey *'11*

Amir Valinia
Lords of the Street *'08*
Mutants *'08*

Jean-Marc Vallee
The Young Victoria *'09*
Dallas Buyers Club *'13*
Wild *'14*
Demolition *'15*

Nick Vallelonga (1959-)
All In *'06*
Stiletto *'08*

Jaco Van Dormael (1957-)
Toto le Heros *'91*
Mr. Nobody *'13*
The Brand New Testament *'15*

Shane Van Dyke (1979-)
6 Guns *'10*
Titanic 2 *'10*

W.S. Van Dyke (1889-1943)
The Pagan *'29*
White Shadows in the South Seas *'29*
Tarzan, the Ape Man *'32*
Penthouse *'33*
The Prizefighter and the Lady *'33*
Manhattan Melodrama *'34*
The Thin Man *'34*
Forsaking All Others *'35*
I Live My Life *'35*
Naughty Marietta *'35*
After the Thin Man *'36*
The Devil Is a Sissy *'36*
Love on the Run *'36*
Rose Marie *'36*
San Francisco *'36*
Personal Property *'37*
They Gave Him a Gun *'37*
Marie Antoinette *'38*
Rosalie *'38*
Sweethearts *'38*
Andy Hardy Gets Spring Fever *'39*
Another Thin Man *'39*
It's a Wonderful World *'39*
Stand Up and Fight *'39*
Bitter Sweet *'40*
I Love You Again *'40*
I Take This Woman *'40*
Rage in Heaven *'41*
Shadow of the Thin Man *'41*
Cairo *'42*
Dr. Kildare's Victory *'42*
I Married an Angel *'42*
Journey for Margaret *'42*

Felix van Groeningen
The Broken Circle Breakdown *'12*
Beautiful Boy *'18*

Andre Van Heerden (1971-)
Revelation *'00*
Tribulation *'00*

Buddy Van Horn (1929-)
Any Which Way You Can *'80*
The Dead Pool *'88*
Pink Cadillac *'89*

Erik van Looy
The Memory of a Killer *'03*
The Loft *'14*

Mario Van Peebles (1957-)
New Jack City *'91*
Posse *'93*
Panther *'95*
Gang in Blue *'96*
Love Kills *'98*
Baadasssss! *'03*
Redemption Road *'10*
Red Sky *'14*
USS Indianapolis: Men of Courage *'16*

Melvin Van Peebles (1932-)
The Story of a Three Day Pass *'68*
Watermelon Man *'70*
Sweet Sweetback's Baadasssss Song *'71*
Identity Crisis *'90*
Tales of Erotica *'93*
Gang in Blue *'96*

Gus Van Sant (1952-)
Drugstore Cowboy *'89*
My Own Private Idaho *'91*
Even Cowgirls Get the Blues *'94*
To Die For *'95*
Good Will Hunting *'97*
Psycho *'98*
Finding Forrester *'00*
Gerry *'02*
Elephant *'03*
Last Days *'05*
Paris, je t'aime *'06*
Paranoid Park *'07*
Milk *'08*
Restless *'11*
Promised Land *'12*
The Sea of Trees *'16*
Don't Worry, He Won't Get Far on Foot *'18*

Andrew Van Slee (1965-)
Totally Blonde *'01*
Net Games *'03*

Alex Van Warmerdam
The Dress *'96*
Borgman *'13*

Norman Thaddeus Vane
Frightmare *'81*
The Black Room *'82*

Kevin VanHook
The Fallen Ones *'05*
Voodoo Moon *'05*

Carlo Vanzina (1952-)
The Gamble *'88*
Millions *'90*

Agnes Varda (1928-)
Cleo from 5 to 7 *'61*
Le Bonheur *'65*
Daguerreotypes *'75*
Vagabond *'85*
One Hundred and One Nights *'95*
The Beaches of Agnes *'08*
Faces Places *'17*

Giuseppe Vari (1916-93)
Revenge of the Barbarians *'60*
Conquest of the Normans *'62*
Django: Last Killer *'67*
Shoot the Living, Pray for the Dead *'70*
The Legend of Sea Wolf *'75*

Marcel Varnel (1894-1947)
Chandu the Magician *'32*
Good Morning, Boys *'37*
Ask a Policeman *'38*
Hey! Hey! USA! *'38*

Joseph B. Vasquez (1962-95)
The Bronx War *'90*
Hangin' with the Homeboys *'91*
Manhattan Merenque! *'95*

Tom Vaughan (1969-)
He Knew He Was Right *'04*
Starter for 10 *'06*
What Happens in Vegas *'08*
Extraordinary Measures *'10*
Playing House *'10*
So Undercover *'13*
Some Kind of Beautiful *'15*

Matthew Vaughn (1971-)
Layer Cake *'05*
Stardust *'07*
Kick-Ass *'10*
X-Men: First Class *'11*
Kingsman: The Secret Service *'15*
Kingsman: The Golden Circle *'17*

Francis Veber (1937-)
La Chevre *'81*
Les Comperes *'83*
Three Fugitives *'89*
The Dinner Game *'98*
The Closet *'00*
The Valet *'06*

Malcolm Venville
44 Inch Chest *'09*
Henry's Crime *'10*

Gore Verbinski (1964-)
Mouse Hunt *'97*
The Mexican *'01*
The Ring *'02*
Pirates of the Caribbean: The Curse of the Black Pearl *'03*
The Weather Man *'05*
Pirates of the Caribbean: Dead Man's Chest *'06*
Pirates of the Caribbean: At World's End *'07*
Rango *'11*
The Lone Ranger *'13*
A Cure for Wellness *'17*

Michael Verhoeven (1929-)
Blitz *'85*
The Nasty Girl *'90*
My Mother's Courage *'95*

Paul Verhoeven (1938-)
Business is Business *'71*
Turkish Delight *'73*
Katie Tippel *'75*
Soldier of Orange *'78*
The 4th Man *'79*
Spetters *'80*
Flesh and Blood *'85*
RoboCop *'87*
Total Recall *'90*
Basic Instinct *'92*
Showgirls *'95*
Starship Troopers *'97*
Hollow Man *'00*
Black Book *'06*
Elle *'16*

Henri Verneuil (1920-2002)
The Sheep Has Five Legs *'54*
Any Number Can Win *'63*
Greed In the Sun *'64*
The 25th Hour *'67*
Night Flight from Moscow *'73*

Conrad Vernon (1968-)
Monsters *vs.* Aliens *'09*
Madagascar 3: Europe's Most Wanted *'12*
Sausage Party *'16*
The Addams Family *'19*

Marion Vernoux (1966-)
Love, etc. *'96*
Bright Days Ahead *'14*

Stephen Verona (1940-)
The Lords of Flatbush *'74*
Boardwalk *'79*

Todd Verow (1966-)
Frisk *'95*
Little Shots of Happiness *'97*
Between Something & Nothing *'08*
The Boy With the Sun in His Eyes *'09*

Charles Vidor (1900-59)
The Lady in Question *'40*
Ladies in Retirement *'41*
The Desperadoes *'43*
Cover Girl *'44*
Over 21 *'45*
A Song to Remember *'45*
Gilda *'46*
The Loves of Carmen *'48*
It's a Big Country *'51*
Hans Christian Andersen *'52*
Rhapsody *'54*
Love Me or Leave Me *'55*
The Swan *'56*
A Farewell to Arms *'57*
Song Without End *'60*

King Vidor (1894-1982)
Wild Oranges *'24*
The Big Parade *'25*
Bardelys the Magnificent *'26*
La Boheme *'26*
The Patsy *'28*
Show People *'28*
Hallelujah! *'29*
Billy the Kid *'30*
Street Scene *'31*
Bird of Paradise *'32*
The Champ *'32*
Our Daily Bread *'34*
The Wedding Night *'35*
The Texas Rangers *'36*
Stella Dallas *'37*
The Citadel *'38*
Comrade X *'40*
Northwest Passage *'40*
H.M. Pulham Esquire *'41*
Together Again *'43*
An American Romance *'44*
Duel in the Sun *'46*
On Our Merry Way *'48*
The Fountainhead *'49*
Lightning Strikes Twice *'51*
Japanese War Bride *'52*
Ruby Gentry *'52*
Man Without a Star *'55*
War and Peace *'56*
Solomon and Sheba *'59*

Berthold Viertel (1885-1954)
The Man From Yesterday *'32*
The Passing of the Third Floor Back *'35*

Joel Viertel
Devil's Pond *'03*
Strictly Sexual *'08*

Nacho Vigalondo
The ABCs of Death *'12*
Open Windows *'14*
Colossal *'17*

Reynaldo Villalobos (1940-)
Conagher *'91*
Hollywood Confidential *'97*

Denis Villeneuve (1967-)
Maelstrom *'00*
Incendies *'10*
Enemy *'13*
Prisoners *'13*
Sicario *'15*
Arrival *'16*
Blade Runner 2049 *'17*

Joseph Vilsmaier (1939-2020)
Stalingrad *'94*
Brother of Sleep *'95*
The Harmonists *'99*

Robert Vince
MVP: Most Valuable Primate *'00*
MVP2: Most Vertical Primate *'01*
Air Bud 4: Seventh Inning Fetch *'02*
MXP: Most Xtreme Primate *'03*
Air Bud 6: Air Buddies *'06*
Snow Buddies *'08*
Space Buddies *'08*
Santa Buddies *'09*
The Search for Santa Paws *'10*
Spooky Buddies *'11*
Santa Paws 2: The Santa Pups *'12*
Treasure Buddies *'12*
Super Buddies *'13*

Christian Vincent (1955-)
The Separation *'94*
La Separation *'98*

Chuck Vincent (1940-91)
Preppies *'82*
Deranged *'87*
Slammer Girls *'87*
Thrilled to Death *'88*

Thomas Vinterberg (1969-)
The Celebration *'98*
It's All About Love *'03*
Dear Wendy *'05*
Submarino *'10*
The Hunt *'13*
Far from the Madding Crowd *'15*

Albert T. Viola
Cry of the Penguins *'71*
Preacherman *'83*

Joe Viola
Angels Hard As They Come *'71*
Hot Box *'72*

Norton Virgien
The Rugrats Movie *'98*
Rugrats Go Wild! *'03*

Clement Virgo (1966-)
Rude *'96*
Junior's Groove *'97*
Love Come Down *'00*
Poor Man's Game *'06*

Paolo Virzi
Caterina in the Big City *'03*
The Leisure Seeker *'17*

Luchino Visconti (1906-76)
Ossessione *'42*
La Terra Trema *'48*
Bellissima *'51*
Senso *'54*
White Nights *'57*
Rocco and His Brothers *'60*
Boccaccio '70 *'62*
The Leopard *'63*
The Damned *'69*
Death in Venice *'71*
Ludwig *'72*
Conversation Piece *'75*
The Innocent *'76*

Tony Vitale
Kiss Me, Guido *'97*
One Last Ride *'03*

Virgil W. Vogel (1920-96)
The Mole People *'56*
The Kettles on Old MacDonald's Farm *'57*
The Land Unknown *'57*
Invasion of the Animal People *'62*
Centennial *'78*
Beulah Land *'80*

Spider-Man: Far from Home '19

Ric Roman Waugh (1968-)
In the Shadows '01
Felon '08
Snitch '13
Angel Has Fallen '19

Scott Waugh
Act of Valor '12
Need for Speed '14
6 Below: Miracle on the Mountain '17

Keoni Waxman (1968-)
Almost Blue '93
Serial Bomber '96
The Highway Man '99
The Suspect '05
Unthinkable '07
The Keeper '09
Hunt to Kill '10
Maximum Conviction '12
Force of Execution '13
A Good Man '14
Mercenary: Absolution '15
Contract to Kill '16
End of a Gun '16

Keenen Ivory Wayans (1958-)
I'm Gonna Git You Sucka '88
A Low Down Dirty Shame '94
Scary Movie '00
Scary Movie 2 '01
White Chicks '04
Little Man '06

John Wayne (1907-79)
The Alamo '60
The Green Berets '68

David Weaver
Siblings '04
Holiday Wishes '06
Love Notes '07
Charlie & Me '08
Fairfield Road '10
The Good Samaritan '12

Jack Webb (1920-82)
Dragnet '54
Pete Kelly's Blues '55
D.I. '57
30 '59

Lewin Webb
Gone Dark '03
The Confessor '04

Marc Webb
(500) Days of Summer '09
The Amazing Spider-Man '12
The Amazing Spider-Man 2 '14
Gifted '17
The Only Living Boy in New York '17

Robert D. Webb (1903-90)
Beneath the 12-Mile Reef '53
The Glory Brigade '53
Seven Cities of Gold '55
Love Me Tender '56
Pirates of Tortuga '61
The Jackals '67

Peter Webber (1968-)
Girl with a Pearl Earring '03
Hannibal Rising '07
Emperor '12
Earth: One Amazing Day '17

Nicholas Webster (1912-2006)
Gone Are the Days '63
Purlie Victorious '63
Santa Claus Conquers the Martians '64

Chris Wedge (1957-)
Ice Age '02
Robots '05
Epic '13
Monster Trucks '16

Stephen Weeks (1948-)
I, Monster '71
Sword of the Valiant '83

Apichatpong Weerasethakul
Tropical Malady '04
Uncle Boonmee Who Can Recall His Past Lives '10
Cemetery of Splendor '15

Lo Wei (1918-96)
Chinese Connection '73
Fists of Fury '73
New Fist of Fury '76

Samuel Weil (1945-)
See Lloyd Kaufman

Paul Weiland (1953-)
Leonard Part 6 '87
Bernard and the Genie '91
City Slickers 2: The Legend of Curly's Gold '94
For Roseanna '96
Made of Honor '08

Claudia Weill (1947-)
Girlfriends '78
It's My Turn '80

Daryl Wein
Breaking Upwards '09
Sex Positive '09
Lola Versus '12

Yossi Wein
Lethal Ninja '93
Never Say Die '94
Terminal Impact '95
Mission of Death '97
Operation Delta Force 2: Mayday '97
U.S. Seals '98
Operation Delta Force 5: Random Fire '00
Shark Attack 2 '00
Octopus 2: River of Fear '02

Jed Weintrob
On_Line '01
Scar '07

Peter Weir (1944-)
The Cars That Ate Paris '74
Picnic at Hanging Rock '75
The Last Wave '77
Plumber '79
Gallipoli '81
The Year of Living Dangerously '82
Witness '85
The Mosquito Coast '86
Dead Poets Society '89
Green Card '90
Fearless '93
The Truman Show '98
Master and Commander: The Far Side of the World '03
The Way Back '10

Don Weis (1922-2000)
It's a Big Country '51
The Affairs of Dobie Gillis '53
Half a Hero '53
I Love Melvin '53
A Slight Case of Larceny '53
The Gene Krupa Story '59
Critic's Choice '63
Looking for Love '64
Pajama Party '64
Billie '65
Ghost in the Invisible Bikini '66
The Munsters' Revenge '81

Gary Weis
All You Need Is Cash '78
Wholly Moses! '80

Jack Weis
Crypt of Dark Secrets '76
Mardi Gras Massacre '78

Sam Weisman
Bye Bye, Love '94
D2: The Mighty Ducks '94
George of the Jungle '97

The Out-of-Towners '99
What's the Worst That Could Happen? '01
Dickie Roberts: Former Child Star '03

Michael Cole Weiss (1979-)
Standing Still '05
Deceit '06

Adam Weissman
The Modern Adventures of Tom Sawyer '99
Infected '08

Martin Weisz
Grimm Love '06
The Hills Have Eyes 2 '07

Chris Weitz (1969-)
American Pie '99
Down to Earth '01
About a Boy '02
The Golden Compass '07
The Twilight Saga: New Moon '09
A Better Life '11
Operation Finale '18

Paul Weitz (1965-)
American Pie '99
Down to Earth '01
About a Boy '02
In Good Company '04
American Dreamz '06
Cirque du Freak: The Vampire's Assistant '09
Little Fockers '10
Being Flynn '12
Admission '13
Grandma '15
Bel Canto '18

Orson Welles (1915-85)
Citizen Kane '41
The Magnificent Ambersons '42
The Stranger '46
The Lady from Shanghai '48
Macbeth '48
Othello '52
Mr. Arkadin '55
Touch of Evil '58
David and Goliath '61
The Trial '63
Chimes at Midnight '67
Don Quixote '92
It's All True '93
The Other Side of the Wind '18

David Wellington (1963-)
The Carpenter '89
A Man in Uniform '93
Restless Spirits '99
Would Be Kings '08

William A. Wellman (1896-1975)
Wings '27
Beggars of Life '28
Eleven Men and a Girl '30
Night Nurse '31
Other Men's Women '31
Public Enemy '31
Safe in Hell '31
The Conquerors '32
Frisco Jenny '32
The Hatchet Man '32
The Purchase Price '32
Central Airport '33
Heroes for Sale '33
Midnight Mary '33
Wild Boys of the Road '33
Stingaree '34
The Call of the Wild '35
Nothing Sacred '37
A Star Is Born '37
Men with Wings '38
Beau Geste '39
The Great Man's Lady '42
Roxie Hart '42
Thunder Birds '42
Lady of Burlesque '43
The Ox-Bow Incident '43
Buffalo Bill '44
The Story of G.I. Joe '45
Magic Town '47
Yellow Sky '48
Battleground '49

The Happy Years '50
The Next Voice You Hear '50
Across the Wide Missouri '51
It's a Big Country '51
Westward the Women '51
My Man and I '52
Island in the Sky '53
The High and the Mighty '54
Track of the Cat '54
Blood Alley '55
Goodbye, My Lady '56
Darby's Rangers '58
Lafayette Escadrille '58

Audrey Wells (1960-)
Guinevere '99
Under the Tuscan Sun '03

John Wells (1956-)
The Company Men '10
August: Osage County '13
Burnt '15

Simon Wells (1961-)
An American Tail: Fievel Goes West '91
We're Back! A Dinosaur's Story '93
Balto '95
Prince of Egypt '98
The Time Machine '02
Mars Needs Moms '11

Laurie Weltz
Wrestling with Alligators '98
About Scout '15

Wim Wenders (1945-)
The Scarlet Letter '73
The American Friend '77
The Wrong Move '78
Hammett '82
Paris, Texas '83
Tokyo-Ga '85
Wings of Desire '88
Until the End of the World '91
Faraway, So Close! '93
Lisbon Story '94
Beyond the Clouds '95
The End of Violence '97
Buena Vista Social Club '99
The Million Dollar Hotel '99
Land of Plenty '04
Don't Come Knocking '05
Pina '11
The Salt of the Earth '14
Every Thing Will Be Fine '15
Submergence '18

Paul Wendkos (1922-)
The Burglar '57
The Case Against Brooklyn '58
Tarawa Beachhead '58
Battle of the Coral Sea '59
Gidget '59
Because They're Young '60
Angel Baby '61
Gidget Goes Hawaiian '61
Gidget Goes to Rome '63
Guns of the Magnificent Seven '69
Cannon for Cordoba '70
Hell Boats '70
The Mephisto Waltz '71
The Tattered Web '71
The Delphi Bureau: The Merchant of Death Assignment '72
Honor Thy Father '73
Death Among Friends '75
The Legend of Lizzie Borden '75
The Death of Richie '76
Betrayal '78
A Woman Called Moses '78
The Ordeal of Dr. Mudd '80
Cocaine: One Man's Seduction '83
The Bad Seed '85
The Execution '85
Blood Vows: The Story of a Mafia Wife '87
From the Dead of Night '89
The Chase '91

White Hot: The Mysterious Murder of Thelma Todd '91

Richard Wenk (1956-)
Vamp '86
Just the Ticket '98

Alfred Werker (1896-1975)
Gateway '38
Kidnapped '38
The Adventures of Sherlock Holmes '39
Whispering Ghosts '42
Shock! '46
He Walked by Night '48
Lost Boundaries '49
Walk East on Beacon '52
The Last Posse '53
Three Hours to Kill '54
Rebel in Town '56

Byron Werner
Death Valley: The Revenge of Bloody Bill '04
Starkweather '04

Constantin Werner
Dead Leaves '98
The Pagan Queen '09

Jeff Werner
Die Laughing '80
Cheerleaders' Wild Weekend '85

Peter Werner (1947-)
Hard Knox '83
I Married a Centerfold '84
The Alamo: Thirteen Days to Glory '87
No Man's Land '87
The Image '89
The Substitute Wife '94
Mama Flora's Family '98
The '70s '00
Call Me Claus '01
Ruby's Bucket of Blood '01
Killer Instinct: From the Files of Agent Candice DeLong '03
Gracie's Choice '04
Mom at Sixteen '05
Why I Wore Lipstick to My Mastectomy '06
Girl, Positive '07
The Circuit '08
A Dog Named Christmas '09
Bond of Silence '10
Prosecuting Casey Anthony '13

Lina Wertmuller (1928-)
Seduction of Mimi '72
Love and Anarchy '73
All Screwed Up '74
Swept Away. . . '75
Seven Beauties '76
A Night Full of Rain '78
Belle Starr '79
Blood Feud '79
Summer Night with Greek Profile, Almond Eyes & Scent of Basil '87
Ciao, Professore! '94

Jake West
Razor Blade Smile '98
Pumpkinhead 3: Ashes to Ashes '06
The ABCs of Death '12

Roland West (1885-1952)
The Monster '25
The Bat '26
Alibi '29
The Bat Whispers '30
Corsair '31

Simon West (1961-)
Con Air '97
The General's Daughter '99
Lara Croft: Tomb Raider '01
When a Stranger Calls '06
The Mechanic '11
The Expendables 2 '12
Stolen '12
Wild Card '15
Gun Shy '17

Ti West (1980-)
Cabin Fever 2: Spring Fever '08
The House of the Devil '09
The Innkeepers '11
The ABCs of Death '12
V/H/S '12
The Sacrament '13
In a Valley of Violence '16

Wash Westmoreland
Quinceanera '06
The Last of Robin Hood '13
Still Alice '14
Earthquake Bird '19

Eric Weston
Evilspeak '82
The Iron Triangle '89
To Protect and Serve '92
Hyenas '10

Haskell Wexler (1926-)
Medium Cool '69
Latino '85

Tanya Wexler
Finding North '97
Hysteria '11
Buffaloed '20

James Whale (1896-1957)
Frankenstein '31
The Old Dark House '32
The Invisible Man '33
The Bride of Frankenstein '35
Show Boat '36
The Great Garrick '37
Wives under Suspicion '38
The Man in the Iron Mask '39

Frank Whaley (1963-)
Joe the King '99
The Jimmy Show '01

Leigh Whannell (1977-)
Insidious: Chapter 3 '15
Upgrade '18
The Invisible Man '20

Tony Wharmby
Love for Lydia '79
Covert Assassin '94
Like A Bride '94

Claude Whatham (1927-2008)
Elizabeth R '72
That'll Be the Day '73
All Creatures Great and Small '74
Disraeli '79
Sweet William '79
Agatha Christie's Murder is Easy '82

Jim Wheat (1952-)
The Ewoks: Battle for Endor '85
After Midnight '89
Pitch Black '00

Ken Wheat (1950-)
The Ewoks: Battle for Endor '85
After Midnight '89
Pitch Black '00

Ben Wheatley
Down Terrace '10
The ABCs of Death '12
Kill List '12
Sightseers '12
A Field in England '14
High-Rise '16
Free Fire '17

David Wheatley (1950-)
Catherine Cookson's The Fifteen Streets '90
Catherine Cookson's The Girl '96
Catherine Cookson's The Rag Nymph '96
Catherine Cookson's The Tide of Life '96
Catherine Cookson's The Wingless Bird '97

Joss Whedon (1964-)
Serenity *'05*
The Avengers *'12*
Much Ado About Nothing *'13*
Avengers: Age of Ultron *'15*

Anne Wheeler (1946-)
Cowboys Don't Cry *'88*
Better Than Chocolate *'99*
Edge of Madness *'02*
Mail Order Bride *'08*
Mom, Dad and Her *'08*
The Gambler, the Girl and the Gunslinger *'09*
Knockout *'11*
The Horses of McBride *'12*
The Bouquet *'13*

Gary Wheeler
The List *'07*
The Trial *'10*

Tim Whelan (1893-1957)
The Murder Man *'35*
The Divorce of Lady X *'38*
Sidewalks of London *'38*
The Mill on the Floss *'39*
The Thief of Bagdad *'40*
Seven Days' Leave *'42*
Swing Fever *'43*
Higher and Higher *'44*
Step Lively *'44*
Badman's Territory *'46*
Rage at Dawn *'55*
Texas Lady *'56*

Anouk Whissell
Turbo Kid *'15*
Summer of 84 *'18*

Yoann-Karl Whissell
Turbo Kid *'15*
Summer of 84 *'18*

Forest Whitaker (1961-)
Strapped *'93*
Waiting to Exhale *'95*
Hope Floats *'98*
First Daughter *'04*

Alan White
Risk *'00*
Reclaim *'14*

Andrew White (1925-)
See Andrea Bianchi

Jules White (1900-85)
Dogville Shorts *'30*
Sidewalks of New York *'31*
The Robert Benchley Miniatures Collection *'35*

Michael Jai White (1967-)
Never Back Down 2: The Beatdown *'11*
Never Back Down: No Surrender *'16*

Mike White (1970-)
Year of the Dog *'07*
Brad's Status *'17*

Susanna White
Bleak House *'05*
Jane Eyre *'06*
Generation Kill *'08*
Nanny McPhee Returns *'10*
Our Kind of Traitor *'16*
Woman Walks Ahead *'17*

Sylvain White
Stomp the Yard *'07*
The Losers *'10*
Slender Man *'18*

Trevor White
Jamesy Boy *'14*
A Crooked Somebody *'18*

Mat Whitecross
The Road to Guantanamo *'06*
Sex & Drugs & Rock & Roll *'10*
Oasis: Supersonic *'16*

Greg Whiteley
New York Doll *'05*
Mitt *'14*

John Whitesell
See Spot Run *'01*
Malibu's Most Wanted *'03*
Big Momma's House 2 *'06*
Deck the Halls *'06*
Big Mommas: Like Father, Like Son *'11*
Thunderstruck *'12*

Philip H. (Phil, P.H.) Whitman (1893-1935)
Air Eagles *'31*
Girl from Calgary *'32*
His Private Secretary *'33*

Preston A. Whitmore, II (1962-)
Crossover *'06*
This Christmas *'07*

Tom Whitus
Threat of Exposure *'02*
The Wild Card *'03*
Jr. Detective Agency *'09*

Richard Whorf (1906-66)
Blues in the Night *'41*
Till the Clouds Roll By *'46*
It Happened in Brooklyn *'47*
Luxury Liner *'48*
Champagne for Caesar *'50*
The Groom Wore Spurs *'51*

William Wiard (1928-87)
Snowblind *'78*
Tom Horn *'80*

David Wickes
Silver Dream Racer *'83*
Jack the Ripper *'88*
Jekyll and Hyde *'90*
Frankenstein *'93*

Bernhard Wicki (1919-2000)
The Bridge *'59*
The Longest Day *'62*
The Visit *'64*
Morituri *'65*

Bo Widerberg (1930-97)
Elvira Madigan *'67*
All Things Fair *'95*

Dennis Widmyer
Holidays *'16*
Pet Sematary *'19*

Ken Wiederhorn
Shock Waves *'77*
Eyes of a Stranger *'81*
Meatballs 2 *'84*
Return of the Living Dead 2 *'88*

Robert Wiemer (1938-)
Anna to the Infinite Power *'84*
Somewhere Tomorrow *'85*

Robert Wiene (1881-1938)
The Cabinet of Dr. Caligari *'19*
The Hands of Orlac *'25*

Gavin Wiesen
The Art of Getting By *'11*
All Nighter *'17*

Crane Wilbur (1886-1973)
The Devil on Horseback *'36*
Yellow Cargo *'36*
Crime School *'38*
The Devil on Wheels *'47*
Inside the Walls of Folsom Prison *'51*
The Bat *'59*

Fred M. Wilcox (1905-64)
Lassie, Come Home *'43*
Courage of Lassie *'46*
The Hills of Home *'48*
Three Daring Daughters *'48*
The Secret Garden *'49*
Code Two *'53*
Forbidden Planet *'56*

Herbert Wilcox (1892-1977)
Bitter Sweet *'33*
Victoria the Great *'37*
Sixty Glorious Years *'38*
Nurse Edith Cavell *'39*
Irene *'40*
No, No Nanette *'40*
Sunny *'41*
Forever and a Day *'43*
I Live in Grosvenor Square *'46*
Spring in Park Lane *'48*
The Lady With the Lamp *'51*
Derby Day *'52*
Trouble in the Glen *'54*
Let's Make Up *'55*
The Lady Is a Square *'58*
Teenage Bad Girl *'59*

Cornel Wilde (1915-89)
Sword of Lancelot *'63*
The Naked Prey *'66*
Beach Red *'67*
No Blade of Grass *'70*

Ted Wilde (1893-1929)
The Kid Brother *'27*
Speedy *'28*
Clancy in Wall Street *'30*
Loose Ankles *'30*

Billy Wilder (1906-2002)
Mauvaise Graine *'33*
The Major and the Minor *'42*
Five Graves to Cairo *'43*
Double Indemnity *'44*
The Lost Weekend *'45*
Emperor Waltz *'48*
Sunset Boulevard *'50*
Ace in the Hole *'51*
Stalag 17 *'53*
Sabrina *'54*
The Seven Year Itch *'55*
Love in the Afternoon *'57*
Spirit of St. Louis *'57*
Witness for the Prosecution *'57*
Some Like It Hot *'59*
The Apartment *'60*
One, Two, Three *'61*
Irma La Douce *'63*
Kiss Me, Stupid! *'64*
The Fortune Cookie *'66*
The Private Life of Sherlock Holmes *'70*
Avanti! *'72*
The Front Page *'74*
Fedora *'78*

Gene Wilder (1933-2016)
World's Greatest Lover *'77*
The Adventures of Sherlock Holmes' Smarter Brother *'78*
The Woman in Red *'84*
Haunted Honeymoon *'86*

W. Lee Wilder (1904-82)
The Pretender *'47*
Woman in Brown *'48*
Three Steps North *'51*
Phantom from Space *'53*
Killers from Space *'54*
The Snow Creature *'54*
Big Bluff *'55*
Fright *'56*
Manfish *'56*
Spy in the Sky *'58*

Gavin Wilding
Stag *'97*
Premonition *'98*
Christina's House *'99*
Spliced *'03*

Gordon Wiles (1902-50)
Charlie Chan's Secret *'35*
Prison Train *'38*
The Gangster *'47*

Jason Wiles (1970-)
Full Count *'06*
Play Dead *'09*

Ethan Wiley
House 2: The Second Story *'87*
Children of the Corn 5: Fields of Terror *'98*
Blackwater Valley Exorcism *'06*

Chris Williams
Bolt *'08*
Big Hero 6 *'14*

Elmo Williams (1913-)
Tall Texan *'53*
Hell Ship Mutiny *'57*

Larry Williams (1951-99)
Path to Paradise *'97*
Brave New World *'98*

Lester Williams (1903-58)
See William Berke

Matt Williams
Where the Heart Is *'00*
Walker Payne *'06*

Oscar Williams (1944-)
Final Comedown *'72*
Hot Potato *'76*

Pat Williams
Deep Evil *'04*
Dead Rising: End Game *'16*

Paul Williams (1940-)
Dealing: Or the Berkeley-to-Boston Forty-Brick Lost-Bag Blues *'72*
Miss Right *'81*

Rob Williams
Long-Term Relationship *'06*
Make the Yuletide Gay *'09*
Role/Play *'10*
The Men Next Door *'12*

Stephen Williams
Soul Survivor *'95*
ShadowZone: The Undead Express *'96*
My Teacher Ate My Homework *'98*
A Killing Spring *'02*
Verdict in Blood *'02*

Tod Harrison Williams (1968-)
The Adventures of Sebastian Cole *'99*
The Door in the Floor *'04*
American Loser *'07*
Paranormal Activity 2 *'10*
Cell *'16*

Fred Williamson (1938-)
No Way Back *'74*
Adios Amigo *'75*
Mean Johnny Barrows *'75*
Death Journey *'76*
One Down, Two to Go! *'82*
Big Score *'83*
Steele's Law *'91*
South Beach *'92*
Silent Hunter *'94*
On the Edge *'02*

Nick Willing (1961-)
Photographing Fairies *'97*
Alice in Wonderland *'99*
Jason and the Argonauts *'00*
Close Your Eyes *'02*
The River King *'05*
Alice *'09*
Neverland *'11*

J. Elder Wills (1900-70)
Tiger Bay *'33*
Song of Freedom *'36*
Big Fella *'37*

Hugh Wilson (1943-2018)
Police Academy *'84*
Rustler's Rhapsody *'85*
Burglar *'87*
Guarding Tess *'94*
The First Wives Club *'96*
Blast from the Past *'98*
Dudley Do-Right *'99*

Jim Wilson
Stacy's Knights *'83*
Head Above Water *'96*
Whirlygirl *'04*
50 to 1 *'14*

Lana Wilson
After Tiller *'13*
The Departure *'17*

Richard Wilson (1915-91)
The Big Boodle *'57*
Al Capone *'59*
Wall of Noise *'63*
Invitation to a Gunfighter *'64*
It's All True *'93*

Sheldon Wilson
Shallow Ground *'04*
Carny *'09*
Screamers: The Hunting *'09*
Mothman *'10*
Red: Werewolf Hunter *'10*
Super Storm *'12*

S.S. Wilson
Tremors 2: Aftershocks *'96*
Tremors 4: The Legend Begins *'04*

Kurt Wimmer (1964-)
One Man's Justice *'95*
Equilibrium *'02*
Ultraviolet *'06*

James R. Winburn
The Death Merchant *'91*
Miami Beach Cops *'93*

Simon Wincer (1943-)
The Night After Halloween *'79*
Dark Forces *'83*
D.A.R.Y.L. *'85*
Lonesome Dove *'89*
Quigley Down Under *'90*
Harley Davidson and the Marlboro Man *'91*
Free Willy *'93*
Lightning Jack *'94*
Operation Dumbo Drop *'95*
The Phantom *'96*
Escape: Human Cargo *'98*
Flash *'98*
P.T. Barnum *'99*
Crocodile Dundee in Los Angeles *'01*
Crossfire Trail *'01*
Monte Walsh *'03*
Comanche Moon *'08*
The Cup *'11*

Bretaigne Windust (1906-60)
Winter Meeting *'48*
Perfect Strangers *'50*
Pretty Baby *'50*
The Enforcer *'51*
The Pied Piper of Hamelin *'57*

Harry Winer (1947-)
SpaceCamp *'86*
JFK: Reckless Youth *'93*
House Arrest *'96*
Jeremiah *'98*
A Memory In My Heart *'99*
Lucky Seven *'03*
The Dive from Clausen's Pier *'05*

Jason Winer
Arthur *'11*
Ode to Joy *'19*

Jonathan Winfrey
Black Scorpion *'95*
Bloodfist 7: Manhunt *'95*
Excessive Force 2: Force on Force *'95*
Black Scorpion 2: Ground Zero *'96*
Carnosaur 3: Primal Species *'96*
Legend of the Lost Tomb *'97*

Adam Wingard (1982-)
Home Sick *'08*
A Horrible Way to Die *'10*
The ABCs of Death *'12*
V/H/S *'12*
V/H/S/2 *'13*
You're Next *'13*
The Guest *'14*
Blair Witch *'16*

Gary Winick (1961-2011)
Curfew *'88*
The Tic Code *'99*
Tadpole *'02*
13 Going on 30 *'04*
Charlotte's Web *'06*
Bride Wars *'09*
Letters to Juliet *'10*

Charles Winkler
You Talkin' to Me? *'87*
Rocky Marciano *'99*
The Net 2.0 *'06*
Streets of Blood *'09*

David Winkler
Finding Graceland *'98*
Devour *'05*
A Daughter's Conviction *'06*
The Obsession *'06*
Christmas Caper *'07*
How I Married My High School Crush *'07*

Henry Winkler (1945-)
Memories of Me *'88*
Cop and a Half *'93*
The Most Wonderful Time of the Year *'08*

Irwin Winkler (1934-)
Guilty by Suspicion *'91*
Night and the City *'92*
The Net *'95*
At First Sight *'98*
Life as a House *'01*
De-Lovely *'04*
Home of the Brave *'06*

Max Winkler
Ceremony *'10*
Flower *'18*

Terence H. Winkless
The Nest *'88*
Bloodfist *'89*
Corporate Affairs *'90*
Rage and Honor *'92*
White Wolves 2: Legend of the Wild *'94*
Not of This Earth *'96*
Lady Killer *'97*
Get a Clue! *'98*

Michael Winner (1935-2013)
The System *'64*
You Must Be Joking! *'65*
The Girl Getters *'66*
I'll Never Forget What's 'Isname *'67*
Hannibal Brooks *'69*
Chato's Land *'71*
Lawman *'71*
The Mechanic *'72*
The Nightcomers *'72*
Scorpio *'73*
The Stone Killer *'73*
Death Wish *'74*
The Sentinel *'76*
The Big Sleep *'78*
Firepower *'79*
Death Wish 2 *'82*
Death Wish 3 *'85*
A Chorus of Disapproval *'89*
Bullseye! *'90*
Parting Shots *'98*

Michael Winnick
Shadow Puppets *'07*
Guns, Girls and Gambling *'11*
Code of Honor *'16*

David Winning (1961-)
Killer Image *'92*
Turbo: A Power Rangers Movie *'96*
He Sees You When You're Sleeping *'02*
Call of the Wild *'04*
Past Sins *'06*
Black Swarm *'07*
Something Beneath *'07*
Swamp Devil *'08*

Alice Winocour
Augustine *'12*
Disorder *'16*

Terry Winsor
Fool's Gold: The Story of the Brink's-Mat Robbery *'92*
The Magician *'93*

Essex Boys '99
In the Spider's Web '07

Alex Winter (1965-)
Freaked '93
Fever '99

Michael Winterbottom (1961-)
Butterfly Kiss '94
Jude '96
Welcome to Sarajevo '97
Wonderland '99
The Claim '00
24 Hour Party People '01
Code 46 '03
In This World '03
Tristram Shandy: A Cock and Bull Story '05
The Road to Guantanamo '06
A Mighty Heart '07
A Summer in Genoa '08
The Killer Inside Me '10
The Trip '10
Trishna '11
Everyday '12
The Look of Love '13
The Face of an Angel '14
The Trip to Italy '14
The Trip to Spain '17
The Wedding Guest '18

David Winters (1939-)
Dr. Jekyll and Mr. Hyde '73
Fanatic '82
Mission. . . Kill '85
Thrashin' '86
Space Mutiny '88

Peter Winther
The Librarian: Quest for the Spear '04
Touch the Top of the World '06
Painkillers '15

Scott Wiper (1970-)
A Better Way to Die '00
The Condemned '07
The Marine 3: Homefront '11

Tommy Wirkola (1979-)
Dead Snow '09
Hansel & Gretel: Witch Hunters '12
Dead Snow: Red vs. Dead '14

Herbert Wise (1924-)
Castle of the Living Dead '64
Elizabeth R '72
The Norman Conquests, Part 1: Table Manners '78
The Norman Conquests, Part 2: Living Together '78
The Norman Conquests, Part 3: Round and Round the Garden '78
Reunion at Fairborough '85
Woman in Black '89
The 10th Kingdom '00

Kirk Wise (1963-)
Beauty and the Beast '91
The Hunchback of Notre Dame '96
Atlantis: The Lost Empire '01

Robert Wise (1914-2005)
The Magnificent Ambersons '42
Curse of the Cat People '44
The Body Snatcher '45
Born to Kill '47
The Set-Up '49
Three Secrets '50
The Day the Earth Stood Still '51
The Captive City '52
Something for the Birds '52
The Desert Rats '53
Destination Gobi '53
Executive Suite '54
Helen of Troy '56
Somebody Up There Likes Me '56
Tribute to a Bad Man '56
Until They Sail '57
I Want to Live! '58
Run Silent, Run Deep '58
Odds Against Tomorrow '59
West Side Story '61
Two for the Seesaw '62
The Haunting '63
The Sound of Music '65
The Sand Pebbles '66
Star! '68
The Andromeda Strain '71
The Hindenburg '75
Audrey Rose '77
Star Trek: The Motion Picture '79
Rooftops '89

Len Wiseman (1973-)
Underworld '03
Underworld: Evolution '05
Live Free or Die Hard '07
Total Recall '12

Doris Wishman (1920-2002)
Nude on the Moon '61
Bad Girls Go to Hell '65
The Amazing Transplant '70
Deadly Weapons '70
Double Agent 73 '80

William Witney (1915-2002)
Zorro Rides Again '37
Dick Tracy Returns '38
The Lone Ranger '38
Zorro's Fighting Legion '39
Adventures of Red Ryder '40
Drums of Fu Manchu '40
Dick Tracy vs. Crime Inc. '41
G-Men vs. the Black Dragon '43
Apache Rose '47
Home in Oklahoma '47
Grand Canyon Trail '48
Under California Stars '48
The Golden Stallion '49
Susanna Pass '49
Bells of Coronado '50
Trail of Robin Hood '50
Trigger, Jr. '50
Colorado Sundown '52
The WAC From Walla Walla '52
The Secret of the Purple Reef '60
Master of the World '61
Apache Rifles '64
Arizona Raiders '65
40 Guns to Apache Pass '67

Peter Wittman
Play Dead '81
Ellie '84

Bryan Wizemann (1973-)
Think of Me '11
About Sunny '12

Jay Woelfel (1962-)
Beyond Dream's Door '88
Things '93
Unseen Evil '99
Trancers 6: Life After Deth '02

Bethany Ashton Wolf
Little Chenier: A Cajun Story '06
Forever My Girl '18

Fred Wolf (1964-)
The House Bunny '08
Strange Wilderness '08
Drunk Parents '19

Andy Wolk
Traces of Red '92
Mr. Rock 'n' Roll: The Alan Freed Story '99
Deliberate Intent '01
The Christmas Shoes '02
Fighting the Odds: The Marilyn Gambrell Story '05
A Stranger's Heart '07

M. Wallace Wolodarsky
Coldblooded '94
Sorority Boys '02
Seeing Other People '04

Chun-Chun Wong
The Cave of the Silken Web '67
Six Strong Guys '04

James Wong (1940-2004)
Final Destination '00
The One '01
Final Destination 3 '06
Dragonball: Evolution '09

Kar-Wai Wong
As Tears Go By '88
Days of Being Wild '91

Kirk Wong (1949-)
Crime Story '93
Organized Crime & Triad Bureau '93
The Big Hit '98

Petchthai Wongkamlao (1965-)
The Bodyguard '04
The Bodyguard 2 '07

John Woo (1946-)
Last Hurrah for Chivalry '78
A Better Tomorrow, Part 1 '86
Heroes Shed No Tears '86
A Better Tomorrow, Part 2 '88
A Bullet in the Head '90
The Killer '90
Once a Thief '90
Hard-Boiled '92
Hard Target '93
Broken Arrow '95
Once a Thief '96
Blackjack '97
Face/Off '97
Mission: Impossible 2 '00
Windtalkers '02
Paycheck '03
Red Cliff '08

Edward D. Wood, Jr. (1924-78)
Glen or Glenda? '53
Jail Bait '54
Bride of the Monster '55
Plan 9 from Outer Space '56
Night of the Ghouls '59
The Sinister Urge '60

Martin Wood
Teenage Space Vampires '99
The Impossible Elephant '02
Stargate: Continuum '08
Goodnight for Justice: Queen of Hearts '13

Sam Wood (1883-1949)
Beyond the Rocks '22
It's a Great Life '29
So This Is College '29
The Girl Said No '30
Paid '30
The Man in Possession '31
Huddle '32
The Barbarian '33
Hold Your Man '33
Let 'Em Have It '35
A Night at the Opera '35
Whipsaw '35
The Unguarded Hour '36
A Day at the Races '37
Madame X '37
Navy Blue and Gold '37
Goodbye, Mr. Chips '39
Raffles '39
Kitty Foyle '40
Our Town '40
The Devil & Miss Jones '41
Kings Row '41
The Pride of the Yankees '42
For Whom the Bell Tolls '43
Casanova Brown '44
Guest Wife '45
Saratoga Trunk '45
Heartbeat '46
Command Decision '48
The Stratton Story '49
Ambush '50

Aaron Woodley (1971-)
Tennessee '08
The Entitled '11
Spark: A Space Tail '17
Arctic Dogs '19

Bille Woodruff
Honey '03
Beauty Shop '05
Bring It On: Fight to the Finish '09
Rags '12
Addicted '14
Honey 2 '14
Honey 3: Dare to Dance '16

John Woods
Kings in Grass Castles '97
Plain Jane '02

Rowan Woods (1959-)
Do or Die '01
Little Fish '05
Fragments '08

Timothy Woodward, Jr.
SWAT: Unit 887 '15
Decommissioned '16
Traded '16
Weaponized '16
American Violence '17
The Outsider '19

Jeff Woolnough
First Degree '95
Lost Souls '98
Strange Frequency 2 '01
Taken '02
The House Next Door '06
Celine '08

Chuck Workman
The Money '75
Kill Castro '80
The Mercenaries '80
Superstar: The Life and Times of Andy Warhol '90

Wallace Worsley, II (1878-1944)
The Penalty '20
The Ace of Hearts '21
The Hunchback of Notre Dame '23

David Worth
Soldier's Revenge '84
Warrior of the Lost World '84
Lady Dragon '92
Chain of Command '95
The Prophet's Game '99
Shark Attack 2 '00
Time Lapse '01
Shark Attack 3: Megalodon '02
Honor '06

John Griffith Wray (1896-1929)
Anna Christie '23
Soul of the Beast '23

Alexander Wright
The First 9 1/2 Weeks '98
Styx '00

Edgar Wright (1974-)
Shaun of the Dead '04
Hot Fuzz '07
Scott Pilgrim vs. the World '10
The World's End '13
Baby Driver '17

Geoffrey Wright (1959-)
Romper Stomper '92
Metal Skin '94
Cherry Falls '00
Terror Tract '00
Macbeth '06

Joe Wright (1972-)
Pride and Prejudice '05
Atonement '07
The Soloist '09
Hanna '11
Anna Karenina '12
Pan '15
Darkest Hour '17

Jonathan Wright
Psychotica '10
A Very Merry Mix-Up '13
Awakening the Zodiac '17

Mack V. Wright (1895-1965)
Robinson Crusoe of Clipper Island '36
The Vigilantes Are Coming '36

Thomas J. Wright
Torchlight '85
No Holds Barred '89
The Fatal Image '90
Highlander: The Gathering '92
Taken '02
Unspeakable '02

Donald Wrye
Born Innocent '74
Ice Castles '79
Divorce Wars: A Love Story '82
Lucky Day '91
Range of Motion '00

David Wu
The Bride with White Hair 2 '93
Formula 51 '01
The Snow Queen '02
Webs '03
Merlin's Apprentice '06
The Party Never Stops '07
Iron Road '08

Rupert Wyatt (1972-)
The Escapist '08
Rise of the Planet of the Apes '11
The Gambler '14
Captive State '19

William Wyler (1902-81)
The Love Trap '29
Hell's Heroes '30
Counsellor-at-Law '33
The Gay Deception '35
The Good Fairy '35
Come and Get It '36
Dodsworth '36
Dead End '37
Jezebel '38
Wuthering Heights '39
The Letter '40
The Westerner '40
The Little Foxes '41
Mrs. Miniver '42
The Best Years of Our Lives '46
The Heiress '49
Detective Story '51
Carrie '52
Roman Holiday '53
Desperate Hours '55
Friendly Persuasion '56
The Big Country '58
Ben-Hur '59
The Children's Hour '61
The Collector '65
How to Steal a Million '66
Funny Girl '68
The Liberation of L.B. Jones '70

Paul Wynne
Destination Vegas '95
Bombshell '97
Barrio Wars '02
Makin' Baby '02
Alien 51 '04

Jim Wynorski (1950-)
Chopping Mall '86
Big Bad Mama 2 '87
Deathstalker 2: Duel of the Titans '87
Not of This Earth '88
The Return of Swamp Thing '89
The Return of the Swamp Thing '89
Transylvania Twist '89
The Haunting of Morella '91
976-EVIL 2: The Astral Factor '91
Munchie '92
Sorority House Massacre 2: Nighty Nightmare '92
Body Chemistry 3: Point of Seduction '93
Ghoulies 4 '93
Home for Christmas '93
Hard Bounty '94
Sorceress '94
Body Chemistry 4: Full Exposure '95
Demolition High '95
Vampirella '96
The Wasp Woman '96
Against the Law '98
Storm Trooper '98
Desert Thunder '99
Final Voyage '99
Militia '99
Stealth Fighter '99
Ablaze '00
Rangers '00
Extreme Limits '01
Gale Force '01
Poison '01
Project Viper '02
Lost Treasure '03
Komodo vs. Cobra '05
Shockwave '06
Bone Eater '07
Fire From Below '09
Dinocroc Vs. Supergator '10
Camel Spiders '11

Greg Yaitanes (1970-)
Hard Justice '95
Children of Dune '03

Boaz Yakin (1944-)
Fresh '94
A Price Above Rubies '97
Remember the Titans '00
Uptown Girls '03
Death in Love '08
Max '15

Yoji Yamada (1931-)
The Twilight Samurai '02
The Hidden Blade '04
Kabei: Our Mother '08

Kazuhiko Yamaguchi
Sister Street Fighter 2: Hanging by a Thread '74
Sister Street Fighter '76

Satsuo Yamamoto (1910-83)
Shinobi no Mono '62
Shinobi no Mono 2: Vengeance '63

Jean Yarbrough (1900-75)
Under Western Stars '38
The Devil Bat '41
King of the Zombies '41
South of Panama '41
In Society '44
Here Come the Co-Eds '45
The Naughty Nineties '45
House of Horrors '46
Shed No Tears '48
Jack & the Beanstalk '52
Lost in Alaska '52
Saintly Sinners '62
Hillbillies in a Haunted House '67
The Over-the-Hill Gang '69

Kimiyoshi Yasuda
100 Monsters '68
Zatoichi: The Blind Swordsman and the Fugitives '68
Along with Ghosts '69

David Yates (1963-)
The Way We Live Now '02
State of Play '03
The Girl in the Cafe '05
Harry Potter and the Order of the Phoenix '07
Harry Potter and the Half-Blood Prince '09
Harry Potter and the Deathly Hallows, Part 1 '10
Harry Potter and the Deathly Hallows, Part 2 '11
Fantastic Beasts and Where to Find Them '16
The Legend of Tarzan '16

Blood Diamond *'06*
Defiance *'08*
Love and Other Drugs *'10*
Pawn Sacrifice *'15*
Jack Reacher: Never Go Back *'16*
Trial by Fire *'18*

Joel Zwick (1942-)
Second Sight *'89*
My Big Fat Greek Wedding *'02*
Elvis Has Left the Building *'04*
Fat Albert *'04*

Terry Zwigoff (1948-)
Crumb *'94*
Ghost World *'01*
Bad Santa *'03*
Art School Confidential *'06*

Writer Index

The Writer Index provides a videography for any writer with three or more video credits. The listings for the writer names follow an alphabetical sort by last name (although the names appear in a first name-last name format). The videographies are listed chronologically, from earliest film credit to most recent. If a writer wrote more than one film in the same year, these movies are listed alphabetically within the year. Used in conjunction with the **Cast** index, this index will let you find actors and actresses who wrote themselves juicy parts (with varying degrees of success). Directors also tend to show up here, either before their directorial ambitions surfaced, or after they'd gained enough clout to get one of their scripts to the screen.

Kim Fupz Aakeson
A Somewhat Gentle Man *'10*
Perfect Sense *'11*

Douglas Aarniokoski
Puppet Master 4 *'93*
Puppet Master 5: The Final Chapter *'94*
Nurse 3D *'13*

Paul Aaron
Octagon *'80*
In Too Deep *'99*

George Abbott (1887-1995)
All Quiet on the Western Front *'30*
The Pajama Game *'57*

Paul Abbott (1960-)
Reckless *'97*
Touching Evil *'97*
Reckless: The Sequel *'98*
Butterfly Collectors *'99*
State of Play *'03*
Twenty8k *'12*

Scott Abbott
Winchell *'98*
Introducing Dorothy Dandridge *'99*
The Wall *'99*
Queen of the Damned *'02*
Rosemary's Baby *'14*

Kobe Abe (1924-93)
Woman in the Dunes *'64*
Face of Another *'66*

Dominique Abel
L'Iceberg *'05*
Lost in Paris *'17*

Lewis Abernathy
Deepstar Six *'89*
Terminal Invasion *'02*

Dustin Lee Abraham
The Runner *'99*
How High *'01*

Jim Abrahams (1944-)
Kentucky Fried Movie *'77*
Airplane! *'80*
Top Secret! *'84*
The Naked Gun: From the Files of Police Squad *'88*
Hot Shots! *'91*
Hot Shots! Part Deux *'93*
Mafia! *'98*
Scary Movie 4 *'06*

Terry Abrahamson
Wilder *'00*
Dead Awake *'01*

J.J. (Jeffrey) Abrams (1966-)
Taking Care of Business *'90*
Regarding Henry *'91*
Forever Young *'92*
Gone Fishin' *'97*
Armageddon *'98*
Joy Ride *'01*
Mission: Impossible 3 *'06*
Super 8 *'11*
Star Wars: The Force Awakens *'15*
Star Wars: The Rise of Skywalker *'19*

Hany Abu-Assad
Paradise Now *'05*
Omar *'13*
The Idol *'15*

Peter Ackerman
Ice Age *'02*
Ice Age: Dawn of the Dinosaurs *'09*
The Angry Birds Movie 2 *'19*

Rodney Ackland (1908-91)
Bank Holiday *'38*
The Forty-Ninth Parallel *'41*
Thursday's Child *'43*

Allen Actor
Terror at Red Wolf Inn *'72*
Dungeonmaster *'83*

Gilbert Adair (1944-2011)
The Dreamers *'03*
Blind Revenge *'10*

Daniel Adams
A Fool and His Money *'88*
The Golden Boys *'08*
The Lightkeepers *'09*
An L.A. Minute *'18*

Douglas Adams (1952-2001)
The Hitchhiker's Guide to the Galaxy *'81*
The Hitchhiker's Guide to the Galaxy *'05*

Gerald Drayson Adams (1900-88)
Big Steal *'49*
Armored Car Robbery *'50*
Duel at Silver Creek *'52*
The Gambler from Natchez *'54*
Princess of the Nile *'54*
Taza, Son of Cochise *'54*
Gun Brothers *'56*
Three Bad Sisters *'56*
War Drums *'57*
Harum Scarum *'65*

Max Adams
Extraction *'15*
Precious Cargo *'16*

Richard DeLong Adams
The Slams *'73*
A Family of Spies *'90*

Steve Adams (1960-2012)
Envy *'04*
Waiting for Forever *'11*

Andrew Adamson (1966-)
Shrek 2 *'04*
The Chronicles of Narnia: The Lion, the Witch and the Wardrobe *'05*
The Chronicles of Narnia: Prince Caspian *'08*
Cirque du Soleil: Worlds Away *'12*

Ewart Adamson (1882-1945)
Inside the Lines *'30*
Circumstantial Evidence *'35*

Lisa Addario (1968-)
Surf's Up *'07*
Parental Guidance *'12*
Amateur Night *'16*
Dear Dictator *'18*

Milo Addica (1963-)
Monster's Ball *'01*
Birth *'04*
The King *'05*

Alice Addison
The Silence *'06*
The Hunter *'12*

Maren Ade
Everyone Else *'09*
Toni Erdmann *'16*

Bear Aderhold
Delta Farce *'07*
Bait Shop *'08*
Knucklehead *'10*

Robert Adetuyi
Turn It Up *'00*
Code Name: The Cleaner *'07*
Stomp the Yard *'07*

Alan J. Adler
The Giant Behemoth *'59*
The Alchemist *'81*
Parasite *'82*
Metalstorm: The Destruction of Jared Syn *'83*

Duane Adler
Save the Last Dance *'01*
Step Up *'06*
Make It Happen *'08*
Step Up Revolution *'12*
Make Your Move *'13*

Gilbert Adler
Children of the Corn 2: The Final Sacrifice *'92*
Tales from the Crypt Presents Bordello of Blood *'96*

Eleonore Adlon
Bagdad Cafe *'88*
Rosalie Goes Shopping *'89*

Felix Adlon
Salmonberries *'91*
Eat Your Heart Out *'96*

Percy Adlon (1935-)
Bagdad Cafe *'88*
Rosalie Goes Shopping *'89*
Salmonberries *'91*

Ed Adlum (1944-)
Invasion of the Blood Farmers *'72*
Shriek of the Mutilated *'74*

Frank (Franklyn) Adreon (1902-79)
S.O.S. Coast Guard *'37*
Zorro's Fighting Legion *'39*
Adventures of Red Ryder *'40*
Drums of Fu Manchu *'40*

Gilles Adrien
Delicatessen *'92*
The City of Lost Children *'95*

Ben Affleck (1972-)
Good Will Hunting *'97*
Gone Baby Gone *'07*
The Town *'10*
Live by Night *'16*

James Agee (1909-55)
The African Queen *'51*
The Night of the Hunter *'55*

John Aglialoro
Atlas Shrugged: Part 1 *'11*
Atlas Shrugged 3: Who Is John Galt? *'14*

Jim Agnew
Giallo *'09*
Game of Death *'10*
Rage *'14*
Broken Vows *'16*

Roberto Aguirre-Sacasa
Carrie *'13*
The Town That Dreaded Sundown *'14*

Joe Ahearne (1963-)
Ultraviolet *'98*
Perfect Parents *'06*
Trance *'13*

Kamal Ahmed
The Jerky Boys *'95*
Rapturious *'07*

Jonathan Aibel
Kung Fu Panda *'08*
Alvin and the Chipmunks: The Squeakuel *'09*
Monsters *vs.* Aliens *'09*
Alvin and the Chipmunks: Chipwrecked *'11*
Kung Fu Panda 2 *'11*
The SpongeBob Movie: Sponge Out of Water *'15*
Kung Fu Panda 3 *'16*
Monster Trucks *'16*
Trolls *'16*
Trolls World Tour *'20*

Karim Ainouz (1966-)
Behind the Sun *'01*
Madame Sata *'02*

Alexandre Aja (1978-)
High Tension *'03*
P2 *'07*
Mirrors *'08*
Piranha 3D *'10*
Maniac *'12*

Chantal Akerman (1950-2015)
News from Home *'76*
Les Rendez-vous D'Anna *'78*
A Couch in New York *'95*
Almayer's Folly *'12*
No Home Movie *'15*

Michael D. Akers
Gone, But Not Forgotten *'03*
Matrimonium *'05*
Phoenix *'06*
Morgan *'12*

Desiree Akhavan
Appropriate Behavior *'14*
The Miseducation of Cameron Post *'18*

Yasushi Akimoto
One Missed Call *'03*
One Missed Call 2 *'05*

Fatih Akin (1973-)
Head On *'04*
The Edge of Heaven *'07*
New York, I Love You *'09*
In the Fade *'17*

Zoë Akins (1886-1958)
Camille *'36*
The Toy Wife *'38*
Desire Me *'47*

Haifaa Al-Mansour
Wadjda *'13*
Mary Shelley *'17*

Mikko Alanne (1972-)
5 Days of War *'11*
The 33 *'15*

Jeff Albert
Never Say Die *'94*
Danger Zone *'95*
Live Wire: Human Timebomb *'95*
Terminal Impact *'95*
Warhead *'96*
The Base *'99*
The Base 2: Guilty as Charged *'00*

Barbara Alberti (1943-)
I'm for the Hippopotamus *'79*
I Am Love *'09*

Mitch Albom
For One More Day *'07*
Mitch Albom's Have a Little Faith *'11*

Karin Albou
La Petite Jerusalem *'05*
The Wedding Song *'09*

Luis Alcoriza (1918-92)
Death in the Garden *'56*
The Exterminating Angel *'62*

Todd Alcott (1961-)
Curtain Call *'97*
Antz *'98*

Alan Alda (1936-)
The Seduction of Joe Tynan *'79*
The Four Seasons *'81*
M*A*S*H: Goodbye, Farewell & Amen *'83*
Sweet Liberty *'86*
Betsy's Wedding *'90*

Will Aldis
Back to School *'86*
The Couch Trip *'87*
Stealing Home *'88*
Clifford *'92*
Avenging Angelo *'02*
Black Cadillac *'03*
Stealing Cars *'16*

Matthew Aldrich
Cleaner *'07*
Coco *'17*
Spinning Man *'18*

Robert Aldrich (1918-83)
Four for Texas *'63*
Too Late the Hero *'70*

David Alexander
The Long Shot *'04*
A Grandpa for Christmas *'07*
Cancel Christmas *'11*

J. Grubb Alexander (1887-1932)
Svengali *'31*
The Hatchet Man *'32*

Lexi Alexander
Green Street Hooligans *'05*
Lifted *'10*

Scott M. Alexander (1963-)
Problem Child *'90*
Problem Child 2 *'91*
Ed Wood *'94*
The People *vs.* Larry Flynt *'96*
That Darn Cat *'96*
Man on the Moon *'99*
Screwed *'00*
Agent Cody Banks *'03*
1408 *'07*
Big Eyes *'14*
Goosebumps *'15*
Dolemite Is My Name *'19*

Grigori Alexandrov (1903-83)
Ten Days That Shook the World *'27*
Que Viva Mexico *'32*

Sherman Alexie (1966-)
Smoke Signals *'98*
The Business of Fancydancing *'02*

Richard Alfieri (1952-)
Echoes *'83*
Harvest of Fire *'95*
Puerto Vallarta Squeeze *'04*
The Sisters *'05*

Daniel Algrant (1959-)
Naked in New York *'93*
Greetings from Tim Buckley *'12*

Dean Alioto
L.A. Dicks *'05*
Shadowheart *'09*

Keith Allan
Rise of the Zombies *'12*
Mother *'13*

James Allardice
Sailor Beware *'52*
Money from Home *'53*

Adam Alleca (1983-)
The Last House on the Left *'09*
Cell *'16*
Standoff *'16*

Marc Allegret (1900-73)
Loves of Three Queens *'54*
Plucking the Daisy *'56*

Curt Allen
Walking the Edge *'83*
Bloodstone *'88*
Alligator 2: The Mutation *'90*

Irwin Allen (1916-91)
Story of Mankind *'57*
The Big Circus *'59*
The Lost World *'60*
Voyage to the Bottom of the Sea *'61*
Five Weeks in a Balloon *'62*

Jay Presson Allen (1922-2006)
Marnie *'64*
The Prime of Miss Jean Brodie *'69*
Cabaret *'72*
Travels with My Aunt *'72*
Forty Carats *'73*
Funny Lady *'75*
Just Tell Me What You Want *'80*
Prince of the City *'81*
Deathtrap *'82*
Year of the Gun *'91*

Jim Allen (1926-99)
Hidden Agenda *'90*
Raining Stones *'93*

J.T. Allen
Geronimo *'93*
The Good Old Boys *'95*
Jesse Stone: Death in Paradise *'06*

Woody Allen (1935-)
What's New Pussycat? *'65*
What's Up, Tiger Lily? *'66*
Take the Money and Run *'69*
Bananas *'71*
Everything You Always Wanted to Know about Sex (But Were Afraid to Ask) *'72*
Play It Again, Sam *'72*
Sleeper *'73*
Love and Death *'75*
Annie Hall *'77*
Interiors *'78*
Manhattan *'79*
Stardust Memories *'80*
A Midsummer Night's Sex Comedy *'82*
Zelig *'83*
Broadway Danny Rose *'84*
The Purple Rose of Cairo *'85*
Hannah and Her Sisters *'86*
Radio Days *'87*
Another Woman *'88*
September *'88*
Crimes & Misdemeanors *'89*
New York Stories *'89*
Alice *'90*
Husbands and Wives *'92*
Shadows and Fog *'92*
Manhattan Murder Mystery *'93*
Bullets over Broadway *'94*
Mighty Aphrodite *'95*
Everyone Says I Love You *'96*
Deconstructing Harry *'97*
Celebrity *'98*
Sweet and Lowdown *'99*
Small Time Crooks *'00*
The Curse of the Jade Scorpion *'01*
Hollywood Ending *'02*
Anything Else *'03*
Match Point *'05*
Melinda and Melinda *'05*
Scoop *'06*
Vicky Cristina Barcelona *'08*
Whatever Works *'09*
You Will Meet a Tall Dark Stranger *'10*
Midnight in Paris *'11*
To Rome with Love *'12*
Blue Jasmine *'13*
Magic in the Moonlight *'14*
Café Society *'16*
Wonder Wheel *'17*

Bradley Allenstein
Juwanna Mann *'02*
Who's Your Caddy? *'07*

Gila Almagor (1939-)
The Summer of Aviya *'88*
Under the Domim Tree *'95*

Michael Almereyda (1960-)
Cherry 2000 *'88*
Twister *'89*
Search and Destroy *'94*
Nadja *'95*
The Eternal *'99*
Hamlet *'00*
Cymbeline *'15*
Experimenter *'15*
Marjorie Prime *'17*

Pedro Almodóvar (1951-)
Dark Habits *'84*
What Have I Done to Deserve This? *'85*
Law of Desire *'86*
Matador *'86*
Women on the Verge of a Nervous Breakdown *'88*
Tie Me Up! Tie Me Down! *'90*
High Heels *'91*
Kika *'94*
The Flower of My Secret *'95*
Live Flesh *'97*
All About My Mother *'99*
Talk to Her *'02*
Bad Education *'04*
Volver *'06*
Broken Embraces *'09*
The Skin I Live In *'11*
I'm So Excited *'13*
Julieta *'16*
Pain and Glory *'19*

Kayla Alpert
Confessions of a Shopaholic *'09*
Flowers in the Attic *'14*
Petals on the Wind *'14*

Arthur Alsberg (1917-2004)
Gus *'76*
No Deposit, No Return *'76*
Herbie Goes to Monte Carlo *'77*
Hot Lead & Cold Feet *'78*

Eric Alter
Hardbodies *'84*
Hardbodies 2 *'86*

Daniel Altiere
Gym Teacher: The Movie *'08*
Dr. Dolittle: Million Dollar Mutts *'09*
Beethoven's Christmas Adventure *'11*
Norm of the North *'16*

Steven Altiere
Gym Teacher: The Movie *'08*
Dr. Dolittle: Million Dollar Mutts *'09*
Beethoven's Christmas Adventure *'11*
Norm of the North *'16*

Mitchell Altieri
April Fool's Day *'08*
The Thompsons *'12*

Sergio D. Altieri (1952-)
Blind Fear *'89*
Silent Trigger *'97*

Mark Altman
Free Enterprise *'98*
House of the Dead *'03*
All Souls Day *'05*

Robert Altman (1925-2006)
McCabe & Mrs. Miller *'71*
Images *'72*
Thieves Like Us *'74*
Buffalo Bill & the Indians *'76*
3 Women *'77*
A Wedding *'78*
Quintet *'79*
Beyond Therapy *'86*
Aria *'88*
Short Cuts *'93*
Ready to Wear *'94*
Kansas City *'95*

John Altschuler
Blades of Glory *'07*
Action Point *'18*

Fede Alvarez (1978-)
Evil Dead *'13*
Don't Breathe *'16*
The Girl in the Spider's Web *'18*

Kyle Patrick Alvarez (1983-)
Easier With Practice *'10*
C.O.G. *'13*

Rick Alvarez
A Haunted House *'13*
A Haunted House 2 *'14*
Fifty Shades of Black *'16*

Sofia Alvarez
To All the Boys I've Loved Before *'18*
To All the Boys: P.S. I Still Love You *'20*

Christian Alvart
Antibodies *'05*
Pandorum *'09*
Case 39 *'10*

D. Alvelo (1965-2004)
Spider's Web *'01*
Bound by Lies *'05*

Rick Alverson
Entertainment *'15*
The Mountain *'19*

Silvio Amadio (1926-95)
The Inveterate Bachelor *'58*
Assassination in Rome *'65*

Rod Amateau (1923-2003)
Hook, Line and Sinker *'30*
Pussycat, Pussycat, I Love You *'70*
The Wilby Conspiracy *'75*
The Garbage Pail Kids Movie *'87*
Sunset *'88*

Eric Ambler (1909-98)
Immortal Battalion *'44*
The Way Ahead *'44*
Highly Dangerous *'50*
Encore *'52*
The Promoter *'52*
The Cruel Sea *'53*
The Purple Plain *'54*
A Night to Remember *'58*
The Wreck of the Mary Deare *'59*

David Ambrose (1943-)
The Fifth Musketeer *'79*
The Final Countdown *'80*
Survivor *'80*
Dangerous Summer *'82*
Amityville 3: The Demon *'83*
D.A.R.Y.L. *'85*
Taffin *'88*
Year of the Gun *'91*

Jorge Ameer
D'Agostino *'12*
The Dark Side of Love *'12*

Arash (A.E.) Amel
Erased *'12*
Grace of Monaco *'14*
A Private War *'18*

Gianni Amelio (1945-)
The Stolen Children *'92*
Lamerica *'95*

Deborah Amelon (1955-)
Exit to Eden *'94*
Hunger Point *'03*

Alejandro Amenabar (1972-)
Open Your Eyes *'97*
The Others *'01*
The Sea Inside *'04*
Agora *'09*
Regression *'16*

Sergio Amidei (1904-81)
Open City *'45*
Shoeshine *'47*
Tales of Ordinary Madness *'83*
Generale Della Rovere *'09*

Jack Amiel
The Prince & Me *'04*
Raising Helen *'04*
The Shaggy Dog *'06*
Big Miracle *'12*

Cesar Amigo
The Walls of Hell *'64*
The Ravagers *'65*

Santiago Amigorena
After Sex *'97*
A Few Days in September *'06*

Mark Amin
Diplomatic Siege *'99*
The Prince & Me *'04*

Hossein Amini (1966-)
Jude *'96*
The Wings of the Dove *'97*
The Four Feathers *'02*
Killshot *'09*
Shanghai *'09*
Drive *'11*
Snow White and the Huntsman *'12*
47 Ronin *'13*
The Two Faces of January *'14*
Our Kind of Traitor *'16*
The Snowman *'17*

Ana Lily Amirpour
A Girl Walks Home Alone at Night *'14*
The Bad Batch *'17*

Martin Amis
Saturn 3 *'80*
London Fields *'18*

Niccolo Ammaniti
I'm Not Scared *'03*
Me and You *'12*

Guillermo Amoedo
Aftershock *'12*
The Green Inferno *'14*
Knock Knock *'15*
The Stranger *'15*

Michelle Amor (1971-)
Of Boys and Men *'08*
Playin' For Love *'15*

Jay Anania
Long Time Since *'97*
Shadows and Lies *'10*
The Letter *'12*

Dominic Anciano (1959-)
Final Cut *'98*
Love, Honour & Obey *'00*

Allison Anders (1954-)
Border Radio *'88*
Gas Food Lodging *'92*
Mi Vida Loca *'94*
Four Rooms *'95*
Grace of My Heart *'96*
Sugar Town *'99*
Things Behind the Sun *'01*

Sean Anders
Never Been Thawed *'05*
Sex Drive *'08*
She's Out of My League *'10*
Mr. Popper's Penguins *'11*
We're the Millers *'13*
Dumb and Dumber To *'14*
Horrible Bosses 2 *'14*
Daddy's Home *'15*
Daddy's Home 2 *'17*
Instant Family *'18*

Brad Anderson (1964-)
Next Stop, Wonderland *'98*
Happy Accidents *'00*
Session 9 *'01*

Clyde Anderson (1951-)
See Claudio Fragasso

Doris Anderson (1897-1971)
And So They Were Married *'36*
Give Me a Sailor *'38*

Edward A. Anderson
Flawless *'07*
Shuttle *'09*

Elizabeth Anderson
Lassie *'94*
Three Wishes *'95*

Gerry Anderson
Journey to the Far Side of the Sun *'69*
Blonde and Blonder *'07*

Jace Anderson
Crocodile *'00*
Crocodile 2: Death Swamp *'01*
Derailed *'02*
Mortuary *'05*
Autopsy *'08*
Mother of Tears *'08*
Night of the Demons *'09*
Fertile Ground *'10*

Jane Anderson (1954-)
The Positively True Adventures of the Alleged Texas Cheerleader-Murdering Mom *'93*
It Could Happen to You *'94*
How to Make an American Quilt *'95*
The Baby Dance *'98*
If These Walls Could Talk 2 *'00*
Normal *'03*
The Prize Winner of Defiance, Ohio *'05*
Olive Kitteridge *'14*
The Wife *'17*

Josef Anderson
Stephen King's Golden Years *'91*
Safe Harbor *'09*

Maxwell Anderson (1888-1959)
All Quiet on the Western Front *'30*
Rain *'32*
Death Takes a Holiday *'34*

Paul Thomas Anderson (1970-)
Hard Eight *'96*
Boogie Nights *'97*
Magnolia *'99*
Punch-Drunk Love *'02*
There Will Be Blood *'07*
The Master *'12*
Inherent Vice *'14*
Phantom Thread *'17*

Paul W.S. Anderson (1965-)
Shopping *'93*
Resident Evil *'02*
Alien *vs.* Predator *'04*

Resident Evil: Apocalypse '04
Resident Evil: Extinction '07
Death Race '08
Resident Evil: Afterlife '10
Resident Evil: Retribution '12
Resident Evil: The Final Chapter '16

Robert Anderson (1923-)
Tea and Sympathy '56
Until They Sail '57
The Nun's Story '59
The Sand Pebbles '66
I Never Sang for My Father '70

Steve Anderson
The Big Empty '04
The River Murders '11

Wes Anderson (1969-)
Bottle Rocket '95
Rushmore '98
The Royal Tenenbaums '01
The Life Aquatic with Steve Zissou '04
The Darjeeling Limited '07
Fantastic Mr. Fox '09
Moonrise Kingdom '12
The Grand Budapest Hotel '14
Isle of Dogs '18

Mario Andreacchio (1955-)
The Dreaming '88
Napoleon '96

Casper Andreas
A Four Letter Word '07
Between Love & Goodbye '08

Guy Andrews
All or Nothing at All '93
The Infiltrator '95
Lost in Austen '08
Appointment With Death '10

Jack Andrews (1900-65)
Berlin Correspondent '42
Dark Delusion '47

Jay Andrews (1950-)
See Jim Wynorski

Jesse Andrews (1982-)
Me and Earl and the Dying Girl '15
Every Day '18

Mark C. Andrews
Seal Team '08
Brave '12
John Carter '12

Peter Andrews (1963-)
See Steven Soderbergh

Robert D. (Robert Hardy) Andrews (1903-76)
Gangster's Boy '38
Sherlock Holmes and the Voice of Terror '42
Bataan '43
The Woman on Pier 13 '50
The Tanks Are Coming '51
Tarzan Goes to India '62

Tina Andrews (1951-)
Why Do Fools Fall in Love? '98
Jackie Bouvier Kennedy Onassis '00
Sally Hemings: An American Scandal '00

Mark Andrus
Late for Dinner '91
As Good As It Gets '97
Life as a House '01
Divine Secrets of the Ya-Ya Sisterhood '02
Georgia Rule '07
And So It Goes '14
Otherhood '19

Dan Angel
Body Bags '93
R.L. Stine's The Haunting Hour: Don't Even Think About It '07

Mikel Angel (1917-2005)
Psychic Killer '75
Grotesque '87
Evil Spirits '91

Michael Angeli
Conflict of Interest '92
Sketch Artist '92
Killing Mr. Griffin '97

Kate Angelo (1958-)
The Back-Up Plan '10
Sex Tape '14

Theo Angelopoulos (1935-2012)
Landscape in the Mist '88
Ulysses' Gaze '95
Eternity and a Day '97

Edna Anhalt (1914-)
Return of the Frontiersman '50
Sierra '50

Edward Anhalt (1914-2000)
Panic in the Streets '50
The Member of the Wedding '52
Not as a Stranger '55
The Pride and the Passion '57
In Love and War '58
The Restless Years '58
The Young Lions '58
The Sins of Rachel Cade '61
The Young Savages '61
Girls! Girls! Girls! '62
Becket '64
Boeing Boeing '65
The Satan Bug '65
Hour of the Gun '67
The Boston Strangler '68
The Madwoman of Chaillot '69
Jeremiah Johnson '72
Luther '74
QB VII '74
The Man in the Glass Booth '75
Contract on Cherry Street '77
Escape to Athena '79
Green Ice '81
The Holcroft Covenant '85

Erik Anjou (1961-)
976-EVIL 2: The Astral Factor '91
The Cool Surface '92

Ken Annakin (1914-2009)
Very Important Person '61
Those Magnificent Men in Their Flying Machines '65
Those Daring Young Men in Their Jaunty Jalopies '69
The New Adventures of Pippi Longstocking '88

Jean-Jacques Annaud (1943-)
Black and White in Color '76
The Lover '92
Enemy at the Gates '00
Two Brothers '04
Day of the Falcon '11
Wolf Totem '15

Jean Anouilh (1910-87)
Monsieur Vincent '47
Circle of Love '64

Reverge Anselmo (1962-)
Lover's Prayer '99
Stateside '04

Nimrod Antal (1973-)
Kontroll '03
Metallica Through the Never '13

Joseph Anthony (1912-93)
Meet Nero Wolfe '36
Wedding Present '36

Stuart Anthony (1891-1942)
Mutiny Ahead '35
The Shepherd of the Hills '41

Walter Anthony
Golden Dawn '30
Old English '30
Tarzan the Fearless '33

Steve Antin (1958-)
Inside Monkey Zetterland '93
Gloria '98
Chasing Papi '03
Burlesque '10

Michelangelo Antonioni (1912-2007)
Story of a Love Affair '50
The Vanquished '52
Il Grido '57
La Notte '60
L'Avventura '60
The Eclipse '62
The Red Desert '64
Blow-Up '66
Zabriskie Point '70
The Passenger '75
Identification of a Woman '82
Beyond the Clouds '95
Eros '04

John Antrobus (1933-)
Idol on Parade '59
The Bed Sitting Room '69

Judd Apatow (1967-)
Heavyweights '94
The Cable Guy '96
Celtic Pride '96
The 40 Year Old Virgin '05
Fun With Dick and Jane '05
Knocked Up '07
Walk Hard: The Dewey Cox Story '07
You Don't Mess with the Zohan '08
Funny People '09
This Is 40 '12
The King of Staten Island '20

Josh Appelbaum
Teenage Mutant Ninja Turtles: Out of the Shadows '16
Wonder Park '19

Max Apple
Smokey Bites the Dust '81
The Air Up There '94
Roommates '95

Josh Applebaum
Mission: Impossible-Ghost Protocol '11
Teenage Mutant Ninja Turtles '14

William Applegate, Jr. (1972-)
Skyscraper '95
The Sweeper '95
The Big Fall '96
Pure Danger '96
Riot '96
The Silencers '96
Tiger Heart '96

Theodore Apstein (1918-98)
Whatever Happened to Aunt Alice? '69
Baffled '72

Yuri Arabov
Mother and Son '97
The Sun '05

Gregg Araki (1959-)
The Living End '92
Totally F***ed Up '94
The Doom Generation '95
Splendor '99
Mysterious Skin '04
Kaboom '11
White Bird in a Blizzard '14

Shimon Arama (1941-)
Black Eagle '88
Triumph of the Spirit '89

Vicente Aranda (1926-)
The Blood Spattered Bride '72
If They Tell You I Fell '89
Intruso '93
Jealousy '99

Mad Love '01
Carmen '03

David Arata
Brokedown Palace '99
Spy Game '01

Denys Arcand (1941-)
The Decline of the American Empire '86
Jesus of Montreal '89
Stardom '00
The Barbarian Invasions '03
The Fall of the American Empire '19

Nikolaj Arcel (1972-)
The Girl With the Dragon Tattoo '09
A Royal Affair '12
The Dark Tower '17

Jeffrey Arch
Iron Will '93
Sleepless in Seattle '93

Louise Archambault
Familia '05
Gabrielle '13

Jesse Archer
A Four Letter Word '07
Violet Tendencies '10

William Archibald (1917-70)
I Confess '53
The Innocents '61

Robert Ardrey (1908-80)
The Green Years '46
Song of Love '47
The Secret Garden '49
Quentin Durward '55
The Power and the Prize '56
The Wonderful Country '59
Khartoum '66

Asia Argento (1975-)
Scarlet Diva '00
The Heart Is Deceitful Above All Things '04

Dario Argento (1940-)
Once Upon a Time in the West '68
The Five Man Army '69
The Bird with the Crystal Plumage '70
The Cat o' Nine Tails '71
Four Flies on Grey Velvet '72
Commandos '73
Deep Red: Hatchet Murders '75
Suspiria '77
Inferno '80
Unsane '82
Creepers '85
Demons '86
Demons 2 '87
Opera '88
Two Evil Eyes '90
The Devil's Daughter '91
Dario Argento's Trauma '93
The Stendahl Syndrome '95
The Church '98
The Phantom of the Opera '98
Sleepless '01
Mother of Tears '08
Giallo '09
Argento's Dracula 3D '13

Anne Argula (1938-)
See Darryl Ponicsan

Adolfo Aristarain (1943-)
A Place in the World '92
Martin (Hache) '97

Alice Arlen
Silkwood '83
Alamo Bay '85
Cookie '89
The Weight of Water '00
Then She Found Me '07

Leslie Arliss (1901-87)
Good Morning, Boys '37
The Man in Grey '43
The Saint Meets the Tiger '43
Love Story '44
The Wicked Lady '45

Giorgio Arlorio (1929-2019)
Burn! '70
Zorro '74

Michael Armbruster
Beautiful Boy '10
Feel the Beat '20

George Armitage (1942-)
Gas-s-s-s! '70
Private Duty Nurses '71
Hit Man '72
Night Call Nurses '72
Vigilante Force '76
The Last of the Finest '90
Miami Blues '90
The Late Shift '96

Steve Armogida
Attack of the 60-Foot Centerfold '95
Masseuse '95
Death and Desire '97

Jesse Armstrong
In the Loop '09
Four Lions '10
The Day Shall Come '19
Downhill '20

Mike Armstrong
Two If by Sea '95
Monument Ave. '98

Scot Armstrong (1970-)
Road Trip '00
Old School '03
Starsky & Hutch '04
School for Scoundrels '06
The Heartbreak Kid '07
Semi-Pro '08
The Hangover, Part 2 '11

Shayne Armstrong
Acolytes '08
The Darkness '16

Adam Armus
Frederick Forsyth's Icon '05
Final Approach '08

Michael Arndt
Little Miss Sunshine '06
Toy Story 3 '10
The Hunger Games: Catching Fire '13
Oblivion '13
A Walk in the Woods '15

Andrea Arnold
Red Road '06
Fish Tank '09
Wuthering Heights '12
American Honey '16

Danny Arnold (1925-95)
The Caddy '53
Fort Yuma '55
Rebel in Town '56

Elliott Arnold
Kings of the Sun '63
Flight From Ashiya '64
Alvarez Kelly '66

Jack Arnold (1916-92)
Tarantula '55
The Monolith Monsters '57

David Arnott (1976-)
The Adventures of Ford Fairlane '90
Last Action Hero '93

Darren Aronofsky (1969-)
Pi '98
Requiem for a Dream '00
Below '02
The Fountain '06
Noah '14
mother! '17

Greg Aronowitz
Labou '07
Battle Planet '08

Eric Aronson
On the Line '01
Mortdecai '15

Guillermo Arriaga (1958-)
Amores Perros '00
21 Grams '03
The Three Burials of Melquiades Estrada '05
Babel '06

The Burning Plain '08
Rio, I Love You '14

Emmanuelle Arsan (1932-)
Forever Emmanuelle '75
Good-bye, Emmanuelle '77

Art Arthur
Day-Time Wife '39
Birds Do It '66

Brooks Arthur
Adam Sandler's 8 Crazy Nights '02
I Now Pronounce You Chuck and Larry '07

Ash (1964-)
Bang '95
Pups '99
This Girl's Life '03

William Asher (1921-2012)
Bikini Beach '64
Muscle Beach Party '64
Beach Blanket Bingo '65
How to Stuff a Wild Bikini '65
Fireball 500 '66

Piers Ashworth
Sherlock: Case of Evil '02
St. Trinian's '07
The Legend of Fritton's Gold '09
Burke & Hare '10
Fisherman's Friends '19

Peter Askin
Smithereens '82
Company Man '00

Olivier Assayas (1955-)
Rendez-vous '85
Scene of the Crime '87
Irma Vep '96
Late August, Early September '98
Les Destinees '00
Demonlover '02
Clean '04
Paris, je t'aime '06
Boarding Gate '07
Summer Hours '08
Carlos '10
Something in the Air '13
Clouds of Sils Maria '15
Personal Shopper '17
Non-Fiction '18

Ovidio G. Assonitis (1943-)
Beyond the Door '75
Red Riding Hood '03

Ari Aster
Hereditary '18
Midsommar '19

Tom J. Astle
Failure to Launch '06
Get Smart '08
Home '15

Doug Atchison
The Pornographer '00
Akeelah and the Bee '06
The Longshots '08
Brian Banks '18

Rowan Athale
Wasteland '13
Revolt '17

David Atkins
Arizona Dream '94
Novocaine '01

Eileen Atkins (1934-)
Mrs. Dalloway '97
Vita & Virginia '19

Mark Atkins
The Haunting of Winchester House '09
Princess of Mars '09
Dragon Wasps '12
Jack the Giant Killer '13
Android Cop '14
Awaken '15

Peter Atkins (1955-)
Hellbound: Hellraiser 2 '88
Hellraiser 3: Hell on Earth '92
Hellraiser 4: Bloodline '95
Wishmaster '97

Leopold Atlas (1907-54)
Tomorrow the World '44
The Story of G.I. Joe '45
Raw Deal '48

Yvan Attal (1965-)
My Wife is an Actress '01
Happily Ever After '04
New York, I Love You '09

Paul Attanasio
Rapid Fire '92
Disclosure '94
Quiz Show '94
Donnie Brasco '96
Sphere '97
The Sum of All Fears '02
The Good German '06

Kin-Yee Au
Running on Karma '03
Running Out of Time 2 '06

David Auburn (1970-)
Proof '05
The Lake House '06

Jacques Audiard (1952-)
Baxter '89
Read My Lips '01
The Beat My Heart Skipped '05
A Prophet '09
Rust and Bone '12
Dheepan '16
The Sisters Brothers '18

Michel Audiard (1920-85)
Hijack Highway '55
Les Miserables '57
Taxi for Tobruk '60
Any Number Can Win '63
Monsieur Gangster '63
The Great Spy Chase '64
Greed In the Sun '64
Le Professionnel '81

Bille August (1948-)
Twist & Shout '84
Pelle the Conqueror '88
The House of the Spirits '93
A Song for Martin '01

John August (1970-)
Go '99
Charlie's Angels '00
Titan A.E. '00
Big Fish '03
Charlie's Angels: Full Throttle '03
Charlie and the Chocolate Factory '05
Tim Burton's Corpse Bride '05
The Nines '07
Dark Shadows '12
Frankenweenie '12
Aladdin '19

Joe Augustyn
Night of the Demons '88
Night of the Demons 2 '94

Jean Aurel (1925-96)
Le Trou '59
Manon '68
The Women '68
Confidentially Yours '83

Jean Aurenche (1904-92)
Devil in the Flesh '46
The Red Inn '51
Forbidden Games '52
The Hunchback of Notre Dame '57
The Clockmaker '73

Robert Alan Aurthur (1922-78)
Edge of the City '57
Warlock '59
All That Jazz '79

Paul Auster (1947-)
Blue in the Face '95
Smoke '95
Lulu on the Bridge '98

Carl Austin (1968-)
Sexual Malice '93
Telling Lies '06

Michael Austin
Five Days One Summer '82
Greystoke: The Legend of Tarzan, Lord of the Apes '84
Princess Caraboo '94

Ronald Austin (1934-)
Paper Man '71
Harry in Your Pocket '73
The Horror at 37,000 Feet '73

Roger Avary (1965-)
Killing Zoe '94
Pulp Fiction '94
The Rules of Attraction '02
Silent Hill '06
Beowulf '07

Antonio Avati
Macabre '80
Zeder '83

Pupi Avati (1938-)
Zeder '83
The Best Man '97
Incantato '03

Howard (Hikmet) Avedis
The Specialist '75
Mortuary '81
They're Playing with Fire '84

Brian Avenet-Bradley
Ghost of the Needle '03
Dark Remains '05

Stephen Morehiouse Avery (1893-1948)
The Gay Deception '35
Four Mothers '41

Robert J. Avrech (1950-)
Body Double '84
A Stranger Among Us '92
Into Thin Air: Death on Everest '97
Brotherhood of Murder '99
The Devil's Arithmetic '99

Nicole Avril
Hollywood Wives: The New Generation '03
Make It Happen '08

George Axelrod (1922-2003)
Phffft! '54
The Seven Year Itch '55
Bus Stop '56
Rally 'Round the Flag, Boys! '58
Breakfast at Tiffany's '61
The Manchurian Candidate '62
How to Murder Your Wife '64
Paris When It Sizzles '64
Lord Love a Duck '66
The Lady Vanishes '79
The Holcroft Covenant '85
The Fourth Protocol '87

Alan Ayckbourn (1939-)
The Norman Conquests, Part 1: Table Manners '78
The Norman Conquests, Part 2: Living Together '78
The Norman Conquests, Part 3: Round and Round the Garden '78
A Chorus of Disapproval '89
Private Fears in Public Places '06

David Ayer (1972-)
U-571 '00
The Fast and the Furious '01
Training Day '01
Dark Blue '03
S.W.A.T. '03
Harsh Times '05
End of Watch '12
Fury '14
Sabotage '14
Suicide Squad '16

Frederick Ayeroff
Ace of Hearts '08
Soccer Mom '08

Clay Ayers
Sword of Honor '94
The Watcher '00

Dan Aykroyd (1952-)
The Blues Brothers '80
Ghostbusters '84
Spies Like Us '85
Dragnet '87
Ghostbusters 2 '89
Nothing But Trouble '91
Coneheads '93
Blues Brothers 2000 '98

Richard Ayoade
Submarine '10
The Double '13

Gerald Ayres
Foxes '80
Rich and Famous '81
Crazy in Love '92

Rafael Azcona (1926-)
El Cochecito '60
Mafioso '62
Autopsy '73
La Grande Bouffe '73
Blood and Sand '89
Belle Epoque '92
Butterfly '98
The Girl of Your Dreams '99

Bahareh Azimi
Goodbye Solo '08
99 Homes '14

Masuru Baba
Pale Flower '64
Vengeance Is Mine '79

Dwight V. Babcock (1909-79)
Dead Man's Eyes '44
Loophole '54

Hector Babenco (1946-)
Pixote '81
Carandiru '03

Michael Bacall (1973-)
Manic '01
Bookies '03
Scott Pilgrim *vs.* the World '10
Project X '11
21 Jump Street '12
22 Jump Street '14

Danilo Bach
Beverly Hills Cop '84
April Fool's Day '86
Escape Clause '96

Lawrence Bachmann (1911-2004)
Dr. Gillespie's New Assistant '42
Dr. Gillespie's Criminal Case '43

Jean-Pierre Bacri (1951-)
Un Air de Famille '96
The Taste of Others '00
Look at Me '04
Let It Rain '08

Nicola Badalucco
Death in Venice '71
Escape from Death Row '73

Randall Badat
Hear No Evil '93
The Cutting Edge 3: Chasing the Dream '08
WarGames: The Dead Code '08
Riverworld '10

Kenneth M. Badish
Alien Lockdown '04
Attack of the Gryphon '07

Jeff Baena (1977-)
I Heart Huckabees '04
Life After Beth '14
Joshy '16
The Little Hours '17
Horse Girl '20

Emily Baer
Four and a Half Women '05
A Family Thanksgiving '10

Geoffrey Baere
School Spirit '85
Campus Man '87
Corporate Affairs '90

Michael Bafaro
Act of War '96
Behind the Wall '08
Wrecker '15

Steven Bagatourian
American Gun '05
All Eyez on Me '17

Jesse Baget
Breathless '12
Cellmates '12
All Hallow's Eve 2 '15

Alison Bagnall
Buffalo 66 '97
The Dish & the Spoon '11

Fax Bahr
Hearts of Darkness: A Filmmaker's Apocalypse '91
Son-in-Law '93
In the Army Now '94
Jury Duty '95
Malibu's Most Wanted '03

Ramin Bahrani
Goodbye Solo '08
99 Homes '14

Steven Baigelman
Feeling Minnesota '96
Brother's Keeper '02
Miles Ahead '16

Fenton Bailey
Party Monster '03
Inside Deep Throat '05

Frederick Bailey
Demon of Paradise '87
Raiders of the Sun '92
Quick '93
Terminal Justice: Cybertech P.D. '95
Threat of Exposure '02

Barnet Bain
The Celestine Prophecy '06
Milton's Secret '16

Sam Bain
Four Lions '10
Corporate Animals '19

John Baines (1909-)
Dead of Night '45
Derby Day '52
I'll Get You '53
The Beasts of Marseilles '57
The Hands of Orlac '60

Robert L. Baird
Monsters University '13
Big Hero 6 '14
Ferdinand '17

Jon Robin Baitz (1961-)
The Substance of Fire '96
People I Know '02
Stonewall '15

Nick Bakay
Paul Blart: Mall Cop '09
Zookeeper '11
Paul Blart: Mall Cop 2 '15

Bart Baker
Baby of the Bride '91
Live Wire '92
Supercross: The Movie '05

C. Graham Baker
The Singing Fool '28
You Only Live Once '37

Chris Baker
Mean Machine '01
The Reeds '09

Elliott Baker (1922-2007)
A Fine Madness '66
Breakout '75
Lace '84
Lace 2 '85

Herbert Baker (1920-83)
So This Is New York '48
Big Leaguer '53
Dream Wife '53
Scared Stiff '53
Artists and Models '55
The Girl Can't Help It '56
King Creole '58
Murderers' Row '66
The Ambushers '67
Sextette '78
The Jazz Singer '80

Melville Baker
One Romantic Night '30
Downstairs '32
Next Time We Love '36

Sean Baker
Starlet '12
Tangerine '15
The Florida Project '17

Ralph Bakshi (1938-)
Fritz the Cat '72
Heavy Traffic '73
Streetfight '75
Wizards '77
Hey Good Lookin' '82
Fire and Ice '83
Cool and the Crazy '94

Jaume Balaguero
The Nameless '99
Darkness '02
Fragile '05
[Rec] '07
[Rec] 2 '09
[REC] 4: Apocalyse '14

Josiane Balasko (1950-)
Hotel America '81
French Twist '95
A French Gigolo '08

Bela Balazs (1884-1949)
The Threepenny Opera '31
The Blue Light '32

Jaime Jesus Balcazar
Four Dollars of Revenge '66
The Gentleman Killer '69
Twice a Judas '69

Nigel Balchin
23 Paces to Baker Street '56
Barabbas '62

Marius Balchunas
No Vacancy '99
The Elder Son '06

John Lloyd Balderston (1889-1954)
Frankenstein '31
The Mummy '32
The Bride of Frankenstein '35
The Lives of a Bengal Lancer '35
Mad Love '35
The Mystery of Edwin Drood '35
Prisoner of Zenda '37
Stand by for Action '42
Gaslight '44
Red Planet Mars '52

Ferdinando Baldi (1917-2007)
The Tartars '61
Texas, Adios '66

Earl Baldwin (1901-70)
Doctor X '32
The Tenderfoot '32
Blondie Johnson '33
Wild Boys of the Road '33
Here Comes the Navy '34
Wonder Bar '34
Go Into Your Dance '35
The Irish in Us '35
Cowboy from Brooklyn '38
Gold Diggers in Paris '38
A Slight Case of Murder '38
My Love Came Back '40
Greenwich Village '44
Irish Eyes Are Smiling '44
Africa Screams '49
South Sea Woman '53

Micheal Baldwin
Landspeed '01
Antibody '02

Paul Bales
The Da Vinci Treasure '06
Megafault '09
Sherlock Holmes '10
2010: Moby Dick '10

Alan Ball (1957-)
American Beauty '99
Towelhead '07

Peter Baloff
Quicksand: No Escape '91
A Job to Kill For '06

D. R. Banat (1920-2012)
See Ray Bradbury

Albert Band (1924-2002)
The Red Badge of Courage '51
Face of Fire '59
Gunfight at Red Sands '63
She Came to the Valley '77

John Banville
The Last September '99
Albert Nobbs '11

Jack Baran
Band of the Hand '86
Great Balls of Fire '89
Uncovered '94

Steve Barancik (1961-)
The Last Seduction '94
No Good Deed '02
Domino '05

Ernie Barbarash
Cube: Zero '04
Stir of Echoes 2: The Homecoming '07

Bob Barbash (1919-95)
The Plunderers '60
Tarzan and the Great River '67
The Gambler, the Girl and the Gunslinger '09

Randy Barbato
Party Monster '03
Inside Deep Throat '05

David Barenbaum
Elf '03
The Haunted Mansion '03

Frank Barhydt
Quintet '79
Short Cuts '93
Kansas City '95

Ike Barinholtz (1977-)
Central Intelligence '16
The Oath '18

Leora Barish
Desperately Seeking Susan '85
Venus Rising '95
Basic Instinct 2 '06

Clive Barker (1952-)
Hellraiser '87
Rawhead Rex '87
Nightbreed '90
Lord of Illusions '95

Kim Barker
License to Wed '07
All About Steve '09

Steve Barker (1971-)
Outpost '07
Outpost: Black Sun '12

Bob Barlen
Escape From Planet Earth '13
The Nut Job 2: Nutty by Nature '17
Arctic Dogs '19

Jeff Barmash (1957-)
Power of Attorney '94
Bounty Hunters 2: Hardball '97
Stranger in My Bed '05
Double Cross '06
A Trick of the Mind '06
Hidden Away '13

Joseph John Barmettler, Jr.
Time Barbarians '90
Rage '95
Pure Danger '96
Riot '96
The Silencers '96
Timelock '99

Peter Barnes (1931-2004)
The Ruling Class *'72*
Enchanted April *'92*
Alice in Wonderland *'99*
A Christmas Carol *'99*
The Magical Legend of the Leprechauns *'99*
Noah's Ark *'99*
Arabian Nights *'00*
The Moon & the Stars *'07*

Kevin Barnett
The Heartbreak Kid *'07*
Hall Pass *'11*

Daniel Barnz
Phoebe in Wonderland *'08*
Beastly *'11*
Won't Back Down *'12*

Alexander Baron (1917-99)
Poldark 2 *'75*
Oliver Twist *'85*

David Baron (1930-2008)
See Harold Pinter

Sacha Baron Cohen (1971-)
Borat: Cultural Learnings of America for Make Benefit Glorious Nation of Kazakhstan *'06*
Bruno *'09*
The Dictator *'12*
The Brothers Grimsby *'16*

Jessica Barondes
Wish upon a Star *'96*
Little Secrets *'02*
Lucky Seven *'03*

Douglas Barr (1949-)
The Note 2: Taking a Chance on Love *'09*
Secrets of the Mountain *'10*
The Note 3: Notes from the Heart Healer *'12*

Jackson Barr
Body Chemistry *'90*
Body Chemistry 2: Voice of a Stranger *'91*
Bad Channels *'92*
Seedpeople *'92*
Body Chemistry 3: Point of Seduction *'93*
800 Leagues Down the Amazon *'93*
Mandroid *'93*

Christophe Barratier
The Chorus *'04*
Paris 36 *'08*
War of the Buttons *'12*

Bruno Barreto (1955-)
Dona Flor and Her Two Husbands *'78*
Gabriela *'84*

James Lee Barrett (1929-89)
The Greatest Story Ever Told *'65*
Shenandoah *'65*
The Green Berets *'68*
Tick... Tick... Tick *'70*
The Awakening Land *'78*
Poker Alice *'87*
April Morning *'88*

Simon Barrett
Dead Birds *'04*
Frankenfish *'04*
Red Sands *'09*
A Horrible Way to Die *'10*
The ABCs of Death *'12*
V/H/S *'12*
V/H/S/2 *'13*
You're Next *'13*
The Guest *'14*
Blair Witch *'16*

H.E. Barrie
She Demons *'58*
Missile to the Moon *'59*

J.M. Barrie (1860-1937)
As You Like It *'36*
Quality Street *'37*

Michael Barrie
Ratings Game *'84*
Amazon Women on the Moon *'87*

Oscar *'91*
Bad Boys *'95*

Michael Barringer
Death on the Set *'35*
The Lady From Lisbon *'42*

Kenya Barris
Barbershop: The Next Cut *'16*
Girls Trip *'17*
Shaft *'19*

Fred Barron
Between the Lines *'77*
Something Short of Paradise *'79*

Janet Barron
Clarissa *'91*
The Tenant of Wildfell Hall *'96*

Julian Barry (1931-)
Lenny *'74*
The River *'84*

Odile Barski
Violette *'78*
The Cry of the Owl *'87*
The Color of Lies *'99*
Comedy of Power *'06*
The Girl on the Train *'09*
Inspector Bellamy *'09*

Peter Barsocchini
Drop Zone *'94*
High School Musical 2 *'07*
High School Musical 3: Senior Year *'08*

Paul Bartel (1938-2000)
Cannonball *'76*
Eating Raoul *'82*
Not for Publication *'84*

Phillip J. Bartell
Eating Out 2: Sloppy Seconds *'06*
Eating Out 3: All You Can Eat *'09*
Eating Out 4: Drama Camp *'11*
Eating Out: The Open Weekend *'11*

Sophie Barthes
Cold Souls *'09*
Madame Bovary *'15*

Hall Bartlett (1922-93)
Zero Hour! *'57*
Jonathan Livingston Seagull *'73*
Children of Sanchez *'79*

Richard Bartlett (1922-94)
Lonesome Trail *'55*
Silver Star *'55*

Sy Bartlett (1900-78)
13 Rue Madeleine *'46*
Twelve o'Clock High *'49*
The Big Country *'58*
Beloved Infidel *'59*

Jay Baruchel (1982-)
Goon *'12*
Goon: Last of the Enforcers *'17*

Hal Barwood
The Sugarland Express *'74*
Bingo Long Traveling All-Stars & Motor Kings *'76*
MacArthur *'77*
Corvette Summer *'78*
Dragonslayer *'81*
Warning Sign *'85*

Ben Barzman (1911-89)
The Lady in Question *'40*
Stranger on the Prowl *'52*
Time Without Pity *'57*
The Ceremony *'63*
The Visit *'64*
The Heroes of Telemark *'65*
The Blue Max *'66*

Marc Basch
I'll See You in My Dreams *'15*
The Hero *'17*
Hearts Beat Loud *'18*

K.C. Bascombe
Fear of the Dark *'02*
Swindle *'02*

Ron Base
First Degree *'95*
Deadline *'00*

Harry Basil
Meet Wally Sparks *'97*
My 5 Wives *'00*
The 4th Tenor *'02*

Qasim Basir
Mooz-Lum *'10*
A Boy. A Girl. A Dream. *'18*

Ronald Bass (1942-)
Code Name: Emerald *'85*
Black Widow *'87*
Gardens of Stone *'87*
Rain Man *'88*
Sleeping with the Enemy *'91*
The Joy Luck Club *'93*
The Enemy Within *'94*
When a Man Loves a Woman *'94*
Dangerous Minds *'95*
Waiting to Exhale *'95*
My Best Friend's Wedding *'97*
How Stella Got Her Groove Back *'98*
Stepmom *'98*
What Dreams May Come *'98*
Entrapment *'99*
Snow Falling on Cedars *'99*
Swing Vote *'99*
Passion of Mind *'00*
Mozart and the Whale *'05*
Amelia *'09*
Before We Go *'14*

Seth Bass
The Twilight of the Golds *'97*
Martian Child *'07*

Michael J. Bassett
Deathwatch *'02*
Silent Hill: Revelation 3D *'12*

Lawrence Bassoff
Weekend Pass *'84*
Hunk *'87*

William Bast (1931-)
Hammerhead *'68*
The Valley of Gwangi *'69*
The Legend of Lizzie Borden *'75*
James Dean *'76*
The Betsy *'78*
Power and Beauty *'02*

Janet Scott Batchler
Batman Forever *'95*
My Name is Modesty: A Modesty Blaise Adventure *'04*
Pompeii *'14*

Lee Batchler
Batman Forever *'95*
My Name is Modesty: A Modesty Blaise Adventure *'04*
Pompeii *'14*

Richard Bates, Jr.
Excision *'12*
Trash Fire *'16*
Tone-Deaf *'19*

Zal Batmanglij
Sound of My Voice *'11*
The East *'13*

Ritesh Batra
The Lunchbox *'13*
Photograph *'19*

Joe Batteer
Blown Away *'94*
Chasers *'94*
Windtalkers *'02*
Anna Nicole *'13*
Bonnie & Clyde *'13*

Bradley Battersby (1953-)
Blue Desert *'91*
Red Letters *'00*

Lucio Battistrada
Crime Boss *'72*
Dead Are Alive *'72*

Commandos *'73*
Autopsy *'75*

John Tucker Battle (1902-62)
Irish Eyes Are Smiling *'44*
Invaders from Mars *'53*
Shoot-out at Medicine Bend *'57*

Hans Bauer
Anaconda *'96*
Komodo *'99*
Highwaymen *'03*
The Flock *'07*

Thomas Baum
Carny *'80*
Simon *'80*
The Sender *'82*
The Manhattan Project *'86*
Journey to the Center of the Earth *'99*
Dracula: The Dark Prince *'01*
Journey to the Center of the Earth *'08*

Noah Baumbach (1969-)
Kicking and Screaming *'95*
Highball *'97*
Mr. Jealousy *'98*
The Life Aquatic with Steve Zissou *'04*
The Squid and the Whale *'05*
Margot at the Wedding *'07*
Fantastic Mr. Fox *'09*
Greenberg *'10*
Madagascar 3: Europe's Most Wanted *'12*
Frances Ha *'13*
While We're Young *'14*
Mistress America *'15*
The Meyerowitz Stories (New and Selected) *'17*
Marriage Story *'19*

Jason Baumgardner
Samson *'18*
Run the Race *'19*

Lamberto Bava (1944-)
Shock *'79*
Macabre *'80*
Demons *'86*
Demons 2 *'87*
Ghost Son *'06*

Mario Bava (1914-80)
Black Sunday *'60*
The Girl Who Knew Too Much *'63*
Black Sabbath *'64*
Blood and Black Lace *'64*
Knives of the Avenger *'65*
Planet of the Vampires *'65*
Kill, Baby, Kill *'66*
Danger: Diabolik *'68*
Hatchet for the Honeymoon *'70*
Twitch of the Death Nerve *'71*
Lisa and the Devil *'75*

George L. Baxt (1923-2003)
Circus of Horrors *'60*
Horror Hotel *'60*
Burn, Witch, Burn! *'62*
Thunder in Dixie *'65*

Peter Baynham
Borat: Cultural Learnings of America for Make Benefit Glorious Nation of Kazakhstan *'06*
Arthur *'11*
Arthur Christmas *'11*
The Brothers Grimsby *'16*

Sergio Bazzini
Dillinger Is Dead *'69*
The Inheritance *'76*

Wayne Beach
The Shadow Conspiracy *'96*
Murder at 1600 *'97*
The Art of War *'00*
Slow Burn *'05*

Travis Beacham
Clash of the Titans *'10*
Pacific Rim *'13*

Peter S. Beagle (1939-)
The Dove *'74*
The Lord of the Rings *'78*
The Last Unicorn *'82*

David Beaird (1952-)
Octavia *'82*
Party Animal *'83*
My Chauffeur *'86*
Scorchers *'92*

John Beaird (1953-93)
Happy Birthday to Me *'81*
My Bloody Valentine *'81*

Will Beall
Gangster Squad *'13*
Aquaman *'18*

Henry Bean (1945-)
Running Brave *'83*
Internal Affairs *'90*
Deep Cover *'92*
Desperate Measures *'98*
The Believer *'01*
Basic Instinct 2 *'06*
Noise *'07*

Richard Beattie
Prom Night 4: Deliver Us from Evil *'91*
Cold Sweat *'93*
Face the Evil *'97*
Grizzly Falls *'99*
The Highway Man *'99*
Almost Heaven *'06*
The Baby Formula *'08*
High Plains Invaders *'09*
Maximum Conviction *'12*
Eve of Destruction *'13*
Force of Execution *'13*
Mercenary: Absolution *'15*

Stuart Beattie
Joey *'98*
Collateral *'04*
Derailed *'05*
30 Days of Night *'07*
Australia *'08*
G.I. Joe: The Rise of Cobra *'09*
I, Frankenstein *'13*
Danger Close *'19*

Warren Beatty (1937-)
Shampoo *'75*
Heaven Can Wait *'78*
Reds *'81*
Love Affair *'94*
Bulworth *'98*
Rules Don't Apply *'16*

D.D. Beauchamp (1908-69)
Feudin', Fussin', and A-Fightin' *'48*
The San Francisco Story *'52*
Abbott and Costello Go to Mars *'53*
Law and Order *'53*
Jesse James' Women *'54*
Ride Clear of Diablo *'54*
Tennessee's Partner *'55*
Massacre *'56*
Shoot-out at Medicine Bend *'57*
Alias Jesse James *'59*

Simon Beaufoy (1967-)
The Full Monty *'96*
Among Giants *'98*
Blow Dry *'00*
This Is Not a Love Song *'02*
Miss Pettigrew Lives for a Day *'08*
Slumdog Millionaire *'08*
127 Hours *'10*
Salmon Fishing in the Yemen *'11*
The Hunger Games: Catching Fire *'13*
Everest *'15*
Battle of the Sexes *'17*

Jerome Beaujour
A Single Girl *'96*
Seventh Heaven *'98*
Change My Life *'01*
La Moustache *'05*

Phil Beauman
Don't Be a Menace to South Central While Drinking Your Juice in the Hood *'95*
Not Another Teen Movie *'01*

Charles Beaumont (1929-67)
Queen of Outer Space *'58*
Shame *'61*
Burn, Witch, Burn! *'62*
Premature Burial *'62*
The Haunted Palace *'63*
7 Faces of Dr. Lao *'63*
Masque of the Red Death *'65*
Brain Dead *'89*

Xavier Beauvois (1967-)
Le Petit Lieutenant *'05*
Of Gods and Men *'10*

Scott Beck
A Quiet Place *'18*
Haunt *'19*

Jacques Becker (1906-60)
Casque d'Or *'52*
Grisbi *'53*
Le Trou *'59*

Jean Becker (1933-)
A Man Named Rocca *'61*
My Afternoons with Marguerite *'10*

Josh Becker (1958-)
Thou Shalt Not Kill. . .Except *'87*
Alien Apocalypse *'05*

Barry Beckerman (1943-96)
Shamus *'73*
St. Ives *'76*

James Becket (1936-)
Plato's Run *'96*
Latin Dragon *'03*
Final Approach *'04*

Ann Beckett
Portrait of an Escort *'80*
The Oklahoma City Dolls *'81*
First Do No Harm *'97*

Michael Frost Beckner (1963-)
Sniper *'92*
Spy Game *'01*

Dick Beebe
Into the Badlands *'92*
House on Haunted Hill *'99*
Book of Shadows: Blair Witch 2 *'00*

Ford Beebe (1888-1978)
Pride of the Legion *'32*
My Dog Shep *'46*
Bomba on Panther Island *'49*
Elephant Stampede *'51*
The Lion Hunters *'51*
African Treasure *'52*
Bomba and the Jungle Girl *'52*
Safari Drums *'53*
The Golden Idol *'54*
Killer Leopard *'54*
Lord of the Jungle *'55*
King of the Wild Stallions *'59*

Erica Beeney
The Battle of Shaker Heights *'03*
Captive State *'19*

Jim Beggarly
Free Samples *'12*
The Kitchen *'12*

Michael Begler
The Prince & Me *'04*
Raising Helen *'04*
The Shaggy Dog *'06*
Big Miracle *'12*

Marc Behm (1925-2007)
Help! *'65*
The Peking Blond *'68*
Someone Behind the Door *'71*

Harry Behn (1898-1973)
The Big Parade *'25*
Hell's Angels *'30*

S.N. Behrman (1893-1973)
Liliom *'30*
Hallelujah, I'm a Bum *'33*
Anna Karenina *'35*
A Tale of Two Cities *'36*

Jon Bernstein
Ringmaster '98
Beautiful '00
Max Keeble's Big Move '01
Larry the Cable Guy: Health Inspector '06
Meet the Robinsons '07

Jonathan Bernstein
The Spy Next Door '10
Unsane '18

Marcos Bernstein (1970-)
Foreign Land '95
Central Station '98

Richard Bernstein (1922-83)
Force of Impulse '60
Why Must I Die? '60
The Oh in Ohio '06

Sarah Bernstein
Trial and Error '96
Call Me Claus '01

Walter Bernstein (1919-)
Heller in Pink Tights '60
Paris Blues '61
Fail-Safe '64
The Money Trap '65
The Train '65
The Molly Maguires '70
The Front '76
Semi-Tough '77
The Betsy '78
An Almost Perfect Affair '79
Yanks '79
Little Miss Marker '80
The House on Carroll Street '88
Doomsday Gun '94
Miss Evers' Boys '97
Fail Safe '00
Hidden '11

Eric Bernt
Surviving the Game '94
Virtuosity '95
Romeo Must Die '00
Bachelor Party Vegas '05
The Hitcher '07

Claude Berri (1934-2009)
The Two of Us '68
Jean de Florette '87
Manon of the Spring '87
The Housekeeper '02

Peter Berry
The Luzhin Defence '00
The Incredible Journey of Mary Bryant '05
The Last Enemy '08

Bryan Bertino
The Strangers '08
The Monster '16
The Strangers: Prey at Night '18

Christopher Bertolini
The General's Daughter '99
Battle: Los Angeles '11

Bernardo Bertolucci (1940-2018)
Once Upon a Time in the West '68
Partner '68
The Conformist '71
Last Tango in Paris '73
1900 '76
The Last Emperor '87
The Sheltering Sky '90
Stealing Beauty '96
Besieged '98
The Triumph of Love '01
Me and You '12

Giuseppe Bertolucci (1947-)
1900 '76
Berlinguer I Love You '77

Julie Bertuccelli (1968-)
Since Otar Left... '03
The Tree '10

Andrew Rai Berzins
Blood & Donuts '95
Beowulf & Grendel '06

Eric Besnard
Babylon A.D. '08
Cash '08

Luc Besson (1959-)
Le Dernier Combat '84
Subway '85
The Big Blue '88
La Femme Nikita '91
The Professional '94
The Fifth Element '97
The Messenger: The Story of Joan of Arc '99
Kiss of the Dragon '01
Wasabi '01
The Transporter '02
District B13 '04
Angel-A '05
Crimson Rivers 2: Angels of the Apocalypse '05
Transporter 2 '05
Unleashed '05
Arthur and the Invisibles '06
Bandidas '06
Taken '08
Transporter 3 '08
District 13: Ultimatum '09
Colombiana '11
Lockout '12
Taken 2 '12
The Family '13
Brick Mansions '14
Lucy '14
3 Days to Kill '14
Taken 3 '15
The Transporter Refueled '15
Enter the Warriors Gate '17
Renegades '17
Valerian and the City of a Thousand Planets '17
Anna '19

Ben Best
The Foot Fist Way '08
Your Highness '11

Christian Piers Betley
Dark Hearts '12
Stranded '13

Jonathan Betuel (1949-)
The Last Starfighter '84
My Science Project '85
Theodore Rex '95

Alberto Bevilacqua (1934-2013)
Atom Age Vampire '61
Black Sabbath '64
Planet of the Vampires '65

Troy Beyer (1964-)
B.A.P.'s '97
Love Don't Cost a Thing '03

Thomas Bezucha
Big Eden '00
The Family Stone '05
Monte Carlo '11
The Guernsey Literary & Potato Peel Pie Society '18

A(lbert) I(saac) Bezzerides (1908-2007)
Juke Girl '42
Action in the North Atlantic '43
Beneath the 12-Mile Reef '53
Track of the Cat '54
A Bullet for Joey '55
Kiss Me Deadly '55

Sanjay Leela Bhansali
Devdas '02
Padmaavat '18

Jenny Bicks
What a Girl Wants '03
Rio 2 '14
The Greatest Showman '17

Thomas Bidegain
The Chateau '01
A Prophet '09
Our Children '12
Rust and Bone '12
Dheepan '16
The Sisters Brothers '18

Ann Biderman
Copycat '95
Primal Fear '96
Smilla's Sense of Snow '96
Public Enemies '09

Rick Bieber
Crazy '08
The 5th Quarter '10

Fabian Bielinsky (1959-2006)
Nine Queens '00
The Aura '05

Kathryn Bigelow (1952-)
Loveless '83
Near Dark '87
Blue Steel '90

Luca Biglione
Doc West '09
Triggerman '09

Danny Bilson (1956-)
Trancers '84
Zone Troopers '84
The Wrong Guys '88
The Rocketeer '91
Trancers 6: Life After Deth '02
Company of Heroes '13
Da 5 Bloods '20

Carl Binder
Pocahontas '95
He Sees You When You're Sleeping '02

John Binder (1940-)
Honeysuckle Rose '80
Endangered Species '82

Mike Binder (1958-)
Coupe de Ville '90
Crossing the Bridge '92
Indian Summer '93
The Sex Monster '99
The Search for John Gissing '01
The Upside of Anger '05
Reign Over Me '07
Black or White '14

Scott Bindley
Madison '01
The Nut Job 2: Nutty by Nature '17

Steve Bing (1965-2020)
Missing in Action 2: The Beginning '85
Kangaroo Jack '02

Joe Bini
Roman Polanski: Wanted and Desired '08
The Tillman Story '10

Claude Binyon (1905-78)
College Humor '33
Search for Beauty '34
The Bride Comes Home '35
The Gilded Lily '35
Mississippi '35
I Met Him in Paris '37
True Confession '37
Sing You Sinners '38
Arizona '40
Too Many Husbands '40
No Time For Love '43
Mother Didn't Tell Me '50
My Blue Heaven '50
Rally 'Round the Flag, Boys! '58

Mike Birbiglia (1978-)
Sleepwalk with Me '12
Don't Think Twice '16

Brad Bird (1957-)
*batteries not included '87
The Incredibles '04
Ratatouille '07
Tomorrowland '15
Incredibles 2 '18

Brian Bird
Bopha! '93
Saving Sarah Cain '07
Not Easily Broken '09
Game Time: Tackling the Past '11
Beverly Lewis' The Confession '13
The Ultimate Life '13
Captive '15
The Case for Christ '17

Sarah Bird
Don't Tell Her It's Me '90
The Oh in Ohio '06

David Birke
13 Sins '13
Elle '16
Slender Man '18

Paul A. Birkett
Not My Life '06
Hellhounds '09
The Keeper '09
Altitude '10
Weather Wars '11
Alien Storm '12
Drone '17

Andrew Birkin (1945-)
Pied Piper '72
The Lost Boys '78
The Final Conflict '81
King David '85
The Name of the Rose '86
The Cement Garden '93
The Messenger: The Story of Joan of Arc '99
Perfume: The Story of a Murderer '06

Lajos Biro (1880-1948)
The Private Life of Henry VIII '33
The Scarlet Pimpernel '34
Dark Journey '37
The Return of the Scarlet Pimpernel '37
The Four Feathers '39
The Thief of Bagdad '40
An Ideal Husband '47

John Bishop (1929-2006)
The Package '89
Drop Zone '94

Larry Bishop (1948-)
Trigger Happy '96
Underworld '96
Hell Ride '08

Wes Bishop (1933-93)
Black Gestapo '75
Race with the Devil '75

Wesley Bishop
Dream Chasers '82
Dead by Sunset '95
The Christmas Shoes '02
On Thin Ice '03
The Christmas Blessing '05
Cyber Seduction: His Secret Life '05
The Christmas Hope '09
A Walk in My Shoes '10
Field of Vision '11
Truth Be Told '11

Matthew Bissonnette
Who Loves the Sun '06
Passenger Side '09

Shem Bitterman
Halloween 5: The Revenge of Michael Myers '89
Off the Lip '04
Full Count '06
The Job '09
Play Dead '09
Betty & Coretta '13
Whitney '15

Rick Bitzelberger
Embrace of the Vampire '95
Crazy for Christmas '05

Jerome Bixby (1923-98)
Curse of the Faceless Man '58
It! The Terror from Beyond Space '58
The Man from Earth '07

Anne K. Black
Mythica 2: The Darkspore '15
Mythica: A Quest for Heroes '15

Dustin Lance Black (1974-)
The Journey of Jared Price '00
Milk '08
Virginia '10
J. Edgar '11

Ian Stuart Black (1915-97)
Spin a Dark Web '56
The High Bright Sun '65

Jennifer Black
Recipe for Revenge '98
The Waiting Game '98

John D.F. Black
Gunfight in Abilene '67
Shaft '71
The Carey Treatment '72
Trouble Man '72
Wonder Woman '74

Michael Ian Black (1971-)
Wedding Daze '06
Run, Fatboy, Run '07

Shane Black (1961-)
Lethal Weapon '87
The Monster Squad '87
The Last Boy Scout '91
Last Action Hero '93
The Long Kiss Goodnight '96
Kiss Kiss Bang Bang '05
Iron Man 3 '13
The Nice Guys '16
The Predator '18

Stephen Black
Love Among Thieves '86
Eden '93

Richard Blackburn
Lemora, Lady Dracula '73
Eating Raoul '82

Thomas W. Blackburn (1913-92)
Short Grass '50
Raton Pass '51

Tom Blackburn
Cattle Town '52
Orwell Rolls in His Grave '03

Dirk Blackman
Outlander '08
Underworld: Rise of the Lycans '09

Peter Blackmore (1909-84)
Miranda '48
Mad About Men '54
Simon and Laura '55
The Magnificent Two '67

April Blair
Christmas Caper '07
Private Valentine: Blonde & Dangerous '08
Lemonade Mouth '11
Monte Carlo '11

Macon Blair
I Don't Feel at Home in This World Anymore '17
Hold the Dark '18

Rikki Beadle Blair
Stonewall '95
Blackbird '14

Michael Blake (1945-)
Stacy's Knights '83
Dances with Wolves '90

Richard Blake (1906-54)
Invaders from Mars '53
Counterplot '59

J. Blakeson
The Descent 2 '09
The Disappearance of Alice Creed '09

Larry Blamire
The Lost Skeleton of Cadavra '01
Dark and Stormy Night '09

Alain-Michel Blanc
The Concert '09
Free Men '12

Michael Blankfort (1907-82)
The Halls of Montezuma '50
The Juggler '53
The Caine Mutiny '54
Untamed '55
Tribute to a Bad Man '56

Philippe Blasband (1964-)
An Affair of Love '99
Gilles' Wife '04
Irina Palm '07
Romantics Anonymous '10

Joel Blasberg
Family of Cops '95
Family of Cops 2: Breach of Faith '97

Vera Blasi
Woman on Top '00
Tortilla Soup '01
Emperor '12

William Peter Blatty (1928-2017)
A Shot in the Dark '64
What Did You Do in the War, Daddy? '66
Darling Lili '70
The Exorcist '73
The Ninth Configuration '79
Exorcist 3: Legion '90

Raphael David Blau (1913-96)
Fear Strikes Out '57
Girl of the Night '60

Barry W. Blaustein (1955-)
Police Academy 2: Their First Assignment '85
Coming to America '88
Boomerang '92
The Nutty Professor '96
Nutty Professor 2: The Klumps '00
The Honeymooners '05

Alan Bleasdale (1946-)
No Surrender '86
G.B.H. '91
Melissa '97
Oliver Twist '00
The Sinking of the Laconia '10

Corey Blechman
Dominick & Eugene '88
Free Willy '93
Free Willy 2: The Adventure Home '95

Robert Blees (1925-)
All I Desire '53
Cattle Queen of Montana '54
Magnificent Obsession '54
One Desire '55
Slightly Scarlet '56
The Black Scorpion '57
High School Confidential '58
Screaming Mimi '58
Who Slew Auntie Roo? '71
Doctor Phibes Rises Again '72
Frogs '72

Bernard Blier (1916-89)
Notre Histoire '84
How Much Do You Love Me? '05

Bertrand Blier (1939-)
Going Places '74
Get Out Your Handkerchiefs '78
Buffet Froid '79
Beau Pere '81
Menage '86
Too Beautiful for You '88

William Blinn (1938-)
Brian's Song '71
Roots '77
The Lazarus Syndrome '79
Purple Rain '84
The Boys Next Door '96
Brian's Song '01

Ricky Blitt
The Ringer '05
Hit By Lightning '14

Robert Bloch (1917-94)
The Couch '62
Strait-Jacket '64
The Psychopath '66
Torture Garden '67
The House that Dripped Blood '71
Asylum '72
The Amazing Captain Nemo '78

Larry Block (1943-2012)
The Funhouse '81
My Blueberry Nights '07

Ralph Block (1889-1974)
Dark Hazard *'34*
Massacre *'34*
The Right to Live *'35*

Michael Blodgett (1940-2007)
Hero and the Terror *'88*
Rent-A-Cop *'88*
Turner and Hooch *'89*
The White Raven *'98*

Marnie Blok
Jackie *'12*
Simon and the Oaks *'12*

Neill Blomkamp (1979-)
District 9 *'09*
Elysium *'13*
Chappie *'15*

George Arthur Bloom
The Last Flight of Noah's Ark *'80*
Any Day Now *'12*

Harold Jack Bloom (1925-99)
The Naked Spur *'53*
Land of the Pharaohs *'55*
A Gunfight *'71*

Jeffrey Bloom
11 Harrowhouse *'74*
Dog Pound Shuffle *'75*
Swashbuckler *'76*
Nightmares *'83*
Flowers in the Attic *'87*

Steven L. Bloom
The Sure Thing *'85*
Like Father, Like Son *'87*
Tall Tale: The Unbelievable Adventures of Pecos Bill *'95*
Overnight Delivery *'96*
Jack Frost *'98*

Jill Blotevogel
Wilderness Love *'02*
That Russell Girl *'08*
Iris Johansen's The Killing Game *'11*

Edwin Blum (1906-95)
Kidnapped *'38*
The Adventures of Sherlock Holmes *'39*
Young People *'40*
The Boogie Man Will Get You *'42*
The Canterville Ghost *'44*
Down to Earth *'47*
South Sea Woman *'53*
Stalag 17 *'53*
Pearl of the South Pacific *'55*

Len Blum
Meatballs *'79*
Heavy Metal *'81*
Stripes *'81*
Spacehunter: Adventures in the Forbidden Zone *'83*
Feds *'88*
Beethoven's 2nd *'93*
Private Parts *'96*
Over the Hedge *'06*
The Pink Panther *'06*

Stuart Blumberg (1969-)
Keeping the Faith *'00*
The Girl Next Door *'04*
The Kids Are All Right *'10*
Thanks for Sharing *'13*

Don Bluth (1938-)
The Secret of NIMH *'82*
All Dogs Go to Heaven *'89*
Thumbelina *'94*

Henry Blyth
The Square Peg *'58*
Very Important Person *'61*

Mark Boal (1973-)
The Hurt Locker *'08*
Zero Dark Thirty *'12*
Detroit *'17*
Triple Frontier *'19*

Jeffrey Boam (1949-2000)
Straight Time *'78*
Dead Zone *'83*
Innerspace *'87*
The Lost Boys *'87*
Funny Farm *'88*
Indiana Jones and the Last Crusade *'89*
Lethal Weapon 2 *'89*
Lethal Weapon 3 *'92*
The Phantom *'96*

Paul Harris Boardman
Hellraiser 5: Inferno *'00*
Urban Legends 2: Final Cut *'00*
The Exorcism of Emily Rose *'05*
Deliver Us From Evil *'14*
Devil's Knot *'14*

Al Boasberg (1892-1937)
Battling Butler *'26*
The General *'26*
Hollywood Revue of 1929 *'29*
It's a Great Life *'29*
So This Is College *'29*
Cracked Nuts *'31*
Freaks *'32*
A Night at the Opera *'35*
The Nitwits *'35*

Steven Bochco (1943-2018)
Columbo: Murder by the Book *'71*
Silent Running *'71*

Richard Boddington
Against the Wild *'14*
Against the Wild II: Survive the Seregenti *'16*

DeWitt Bodeen (1908-88)
Cat People *'42*
Night Song *'47*
I Remember Mama *'48*
12 to the Moon *'60*

Anna Boden
Half Nelson *'06*
Sugar *'09*
It's Kind of a Funny Story *'10*
Mississippi Grind *'15*
Captain Marvel *'19*

Sergei Bodrov (1948-)
Somebody to Love *'94*
Prisoner of the Mountains *'96*
East-West *'99*
The Quickie *'01*
Schizo *'04*
Mongol *'07*

Sydney (Sidney) Boehm (1908-90)
High Wall *'47*
The Undercover Man *'49*
Mystery Street *'50*
Side Street *'50*
Union Station *'50*
When Worlds Collide *'51*
The Big Heat *'53*
Siege at Red River *'54*
The Tall Men *'55*
Violent Saturday *'55*
Woman Obsessed *'59*
One Foot in Hell *'60*
Seven Thieves *'60*
Rough Night in Jericho *'67*

Timothy Scott Bogart
The I Inside *'04*
Touched *'05*

Yurek Bogayevicz (1948-)
Anna *'87*
Edges of the Lord *'01*

Peter Bogdanovich (1939-)
The Wild Angels *'66*
Targets *'68*
The Last Picture Show *'71*
Nickelodeon *'76*
Saint Jack *'79*
They All Laughed *'81*
Texasville *'90*
She's Funny That Way *'15*

Roger Bohbot
The Dreamlife of Angels *'98*
Since Otar Left. . . *'03*
Kings and Queen *'04*
Lady Chatterley *'10*

Endre Bohem (1900-90)
Monster from Green Hell *'58*
Twenty Bucks *'93*

Leslie Bohem (1952-)
The Horror Show *'89*
A Nightmare on Elm Street 5: Dream Child *'89*
Nowhere to Run *'93*
Twenty Bucks *'93*
Daylight *'96*
Dante's Peak *'97*
Taken *'02*
The Alamo *'04*
Safe Haven *'13*

Charles F. Bohl
He's My Girl *'87*
Swimfan *'02*

Don Bohlinger
The Killing Time *'87*
Women *'97*
The Experiment *'01*

Tewd A. Bohus
Vampire Vixens from Venus *'94*
This Thing of Ours *'03*

Jon Bokenkamp
Bad Seed *'00*
Taking Lives *'04*

Bridget Boland (1913-88)
Gaslight *'40*
He Found a Star *'41*
War and Peace *'56*
Anne of the Thousand Days *'69*

Uwe Boll (1965-)
Sanctimony *'01*
Blackwoods *'02*
Heart of America *'03*
Postal *'07*
Seed *'08*
Tunnel Rats *'08*
Attack on Darfur *'09*
Rampage *'09*
Blubberella *'11*
Rampage: Capital Punishment *'14*
Rampage: President Down *'16*

Gabriel Bologna
The Theory of the Leisure Class *'01*
The Black Waters of Echo's Pond *'10*

Joseph Bologna (1934-)
Lovers and Other Strangers *'70*
Love Is All There Is *'96*

Charles Bolon
Monsterwolf *'10*
Swamp Shark *'11*

Craig Bolotin (1954-)
Black Rain *'89*
Straight Talk *'92*
That Night *'93*
Light It Up *'99*
Jodi Picoult's Salem Falls *'11*
The Longest Ride *'15*

Robert Bolt (1924-95)
Lawrence of Arabia *'62*
Doctor Zhivago *'65*
A Man for All Seasons *'66*
Ryan's Daughter *'70*
The Bounty *'84*
The Mission *'86*

Guy Bolton (1884-1979)
The Love Parade *'29*
Angel *'37*
Weekend at the Waldorf *'45*

James Bolton
Eban and Charley *'01*
The Graffiti Artist *'04*
Dream Boy *'08*

Adriano Bolzoni (1919-2005)
The Slave *'62*
Diary of a Rebel *'68*
Night of the Assassin *'70*
Your Vice is a Closed Room and Only I Have the Key *'72*

Mark Bomback (1971-)
Godsend *'04*
Live Free or Die Hard *'07*
Deception *'08*
Race to Witch Mountain *'09*
Unstoppable *'10*
Total Recall *'12*
The Wolverine *'13*
Dawn of the Planet of the Apes *'14*
Insurgent *'15*
War for the Planet of the Apes *'17*
The Art of Racing in the Rain *'19*

Julian Bond (1930-)
Choice of Weapons *'76*
The Duchess of Duke Street *'78*
Love for Lydia *'79*
The Shooting Party *'85*
The Whistle Blower *'87*

Bertrand Bonello
Nocturama *'17*
Zombi Child *'20*

Joon-ho Bong (1969-)
Barking Dogs Never Bite *'00*
The Host *'06*
Madeo *'09*
Tokyo! *'09*
Snowpiercer *'14*
Okja *'17*
Parasite *'19*

Vittorio Bonicelli (1919-94)
The Bible *'66*
Barbarella *'68*
Moses *'76*

Pascal Bonitzer (1946-)
The Bronte Sisters *'79*
La Belle Noiseuse *'90*
Jeanne la Pucelle *'94*
Genealogies of a Crime *'97*
Lumumba *'01*
Va Savoir *'01*
The Story of Marie and Julien *'03*
Changing Times *'04*
The Duchess of Langeais *'07*
Gemma Bovery *'15*
The Innocents *'16*

Taro Bonten
Rica *'72*
Rica 2: Lonely Wanderer *'73*
Rica 3: Juvenile's Lullaby *'73*

Josh Boone (1979-)
Stuck in Love *'12*
All We Had *'16*
Pretenders *'19*

John Boorman (1933-)
Zardoz *'73*
Excalibur *'81*
Hope and Glory *'87*
Where the Heart Is *'90*
The General *'98*
The Tailor of Panama *'00*
The Tiger's Tale *'06*
Queen and Country *'14*
The Professor and the Madman *'19*

Telsche Boorman (1957-97)
Where the Heart Is *'90*
French Twist *'95*

James Booth (1927-2005)
Pray for Death *'85*
American Ninja 2: The Confrontation *'87*

Teena Booth
A Little Thing Called Murder *'06*
Sex & Lies in Sin City: The Ted Binion Scandal *'08*
The Natalee Holloway Story *'09*
Amish Grace *'10*
Bond of Silence *'10*
The Pregnancy Pact *'10*
Reviving Ophelia *'10*
The Wronged Man *'10*
Cyberbully *'11*
The Hunt for the I-5 Killer *'11*
Jodi Picoult's Salem Falls *'11*
Justice for Natalee *'11*
Drew Peterson: Untouchable *'12*
Fatal Honeymoon *'12*
The Pregnancy Project *'12*
In My Dreams *'14*

William G. Borchert
My Name Is Bill W. *'89*
When Love Is Not Enough: The Lois Wilson Story *'10*

Lizzie Borden (1958-)
Working Girls *'87*
Erotique *'94*

Bernard Borderie (1924-78)
Ladies' Man *'62*
Your Turn Darling *'63*
Angelique and the King *'66*
Angelique and the Sultan *'68*

Max Borenstein
Godzilla *'14*
Kong: Skull Island *'17*

Allen Boretz (1900-86)
It Ain't Hay *'43*
Up in Arms *'44*
Copacabana *'47*
Where There's Life *'47*

Alvin Boretz
Brass Target *'78*
The Night the Bridge Fell Down *'83*

Paul Borghese
Searching for Bobby D *'05*
Once Upon a Time in Brooklyn *'13*

Robert Boris (1945-)
Electra Glide in Blue *'73*
Some Kind of Hero *'82*
Doctor Detroit *'83*
Oxford Blues *'84*
Steele Justice *'87*
Extreme Justice *'93*
Frank and Jesse *'94*
Diplomatic Siege *'99*

Ole Bornedal
Nightwatch *'96*
Just Another Love Story *'08*

Christopher Borrelli
Whisper *'07*
The Marine 2 *'09*

Craig Borten
Dallas Buyers Club *'13*
The 33 *'15*

Michael Bortman
The Good Mother *'88*
Crooked Hearts *'91*
Chain Reaction *'96*
Resurrecting the Champ *'07*
Taken From Me: The Tiffany Rubin Story *'10*

Aida Bortnik (1938-)
The Official Story *'85*
Old Gringo *'89*

Ray Boseley
Criminal Ways *'03*
Return to Nim's Island *'13*

Luc Bossi
The Prey *'11*
Mood Indigo *'13*

Pierre Bost (1901-75)
Devil in the Flesh *'46*
The Red Inn *'51*
Forbidden Games *'52*
The Clockmaker *'73*

Max Botkin (1979-)
Opposite Day *'09*
Show Dogs *'18*

Huck Botko
Mail Order Wife *'04*
The Last Exorcism *'10*
The Virginity Hit *'10*
Lucky Them *'13*

Rachid Bouchareb (1959-)
Dust of Life *'95*
Days of Glory *'06*
London River *'09*
Outside the Law *'10*

Daniel Boulanger (1922-2014)
The King of Hearts *'66*
Who's Got the Black Box? *'67*
Spirits of the Dead *'68*
Game of Seduction *'76*

Roy Boulting (1913-2001)
Crest of the Wave *'54*
Run for the Sun *'56*
Carlton Browne of the F.O. *'59*

Emmanuel Bourdieu
My Sex Life. . . Or How I Got into an Argument *'96*
Esther Kahn *'00*
A Christmas Tale *'08*

Gilles Bourdos (1963-)
Afterwards *'08*
Renoir *'12*

David Bourla
When Time Expires *'97*
Push *'09*

Jason Bourque
Art of War 2: The Betrayal *'08*
Hellhounds *'09*
Phantom Racer *'09*
Polar Storm *'09*
Wyvern *'09*
Doomsday Prophecy *'11*
Metal Tornado *'11*
Collision Course *'12*
End of the World *'13*
Drone *'17*

Darren Lynn Bousman (1979-)
Saw 2 *'05*
11-11-11 *'11*
The Barrens *'12*

Kate Boutilier
Rugrats in Paris: The Movie *'00*
The Wild Thornberrys Movie *'02*
Rugrats Go Wild! *'03*

Andrew Bovell (1962-)
Head On *'98*
Lantana *'01*
Edge of Darkness *'10*
A Most Wanted Man *'14*

Susan Bowen
The Power Within *'95*
Storybook *'95*

T.R. Bowen (1942-)
The Body in the Library *'84*
Catherine Cookson's The Rag Nymph *'96*
Catherine Cookson's The Gambling Man *'98*
Catherine Cookson's The Secret *'00*

William Bowers (1916-87)
Seven Days' Leave *'42*
Abandoned *'47*
Something in the Wind *'47*
Convicted *'50*
Cry Danger *'51*
The Mob *'51*
Assignment: Paris *'52*
Split Second *'53*
5 Against the House *'55*
My Man Godfrey *'57*
Imitation General *'58*
The Sheepman *'58*
Alias Jesse James *'59*
30 *'59*
Advance to the Rear *'64*
Support Your Local Sheriff *'69*
Sidekicks *'74*

Chris Bowman
Masterminds *'16*
Middle School: The Worst Years of My Life *'16*

Ross Boyask
I Am Vengeance *'18*
I Am Vengeance: Retaliation *'20*

Brandon Boyce
Apt Pupil '97
Wicker Park '04
Venom '05
Bad Samaritan '18

Frank Cottrell Boyce (1959-)
Millions '05
God on Trial '08
Framed '10
The Railway Man '13
Earth: One Amazing Day '17
Goodbye Christopher Robin '17
Sometimes Always Never '19

Brent Boyd
Aurora Borealis '06
Crazy '08

Daniel Boyd (1956-)
Chillers '88
Invasion of the Space Preachers '90
Heroes of the Heart '94

William Boyd (1952-)
Tune in Tomorrow '90
Mister Johnson '91
Chaplin '92
A Good Man in Africa '94
The Trench '99
Sword of Honour '01
A Waste of Shame '05
Any Human Heart '11

Philippa Boyens
Lord of the Rings: The Fellowship of the Ring '01
Lord of the Rings: The Two Towers '02
Lord of the Rings: The Return of the King '03
King Kong '05
The Lovely Bones '09
The Hobbit: An Unexpected Journey '12
The Hobbit: The Desolation of Smaug '13
The Hobbit: The Battle of the Five Armies '14
Mortal Engines '18

Francois Boyer
Forbidden Games '52
The 25th Hour '67

Malcolm Stuart Boylan (1897-1967)
Hangman's House '28
Hell Divers '31
Mr. District Attorney '41
One Too Many '51

Bruno Bozzetto (1933-)
Allegro Non Troppo '76
VIP, My Brother Superman '90

Gerard Brach (1927-2006)
Repulsion '65
Cul de Sac '66
The Fearless Vampire Killers '67
The Tenant '76
Tess '79
Identification of a Woman '82
Quest for Fire '82
Maria's Lovers '84
The Name of the Rose '86
Jean de Florette '87
Manon of the Spring '87
Frantic '88
The Bear '89
Bitter Moon '92
The Lover '92
The Phantom of the Opera '98

Charles Brackett (1892-1969)
The Last Outpost '35
Live, Love and Learn '37
Bluebeard's Eighth Wife '38
Midnight '39
What a Life '39
Ball of Fire '41
Hold Back the Dawn '41
The Major and the Minor '42
Five Graves to Cairo '43
The Lost Weekend '45
Emperor Waltz '48
Miss Tatlock's Millions '48
Sunset Boulevard '50
The Model and the Marriage Broker '51
Niagara '52
Titanic '53
The Girl in the Red Velvet Swing '55
Teenage Rebel '56
Journey to the Center of the Earth '59

Leigh Brackett (1915-78)
The Big Sleep '46
Rio Bravo '59
Gold of the Seven Saints '61
Hatari! '62
The Long Goodbye '73
The Empire Strikes Back '80

Jacob Brackman (1943-)
The King of Marvin Gardens '72
Times Square '80

Ray Bradbury (1920-2012)
It Came from Outer Space '53
Moby Dick '56
The Picasso Summer '69
Something Wicked This Way Comes '83
The Wonderful Ice Cream Suit '98

Sue Bradford
The Indestructible Man '56
The Atomic Brain '64

Clive Bradley
A Harlot's Progress '06
The Killing Gene '07

John Bradshaw (1952-)
The Big Slice '90
The Undertaker's Wedding '97

Pam Brady
South Park: Bigger, Longer and Uncut '99
Team America: World Police '04
Hot Rod '07
Hamlet 2 '08

Tom Brady
The Animal '01
The Hot Chick '02

Zach Braff (1975-)
Garden State '04
Wish I Was Here '14

Brannon Braga (1965-)
Star Trek: Generations '94
Star Trek: First Contact '96

Kenneth Branagh (1960-)
Henry V '89
Much Ado about Nothing '93
A Midwinter's Tale '95
Hamlet '96
Love's Labour's Lost '00
As You Like It '06

Rustam Branaman
Love to Kill '97
Project Solitude: Buried Alive '09
Any Day '15

Chris Brancato
Hoodlum '96
Species 2 '98

John Brancato
Flight of Black Angel '91
Mindwarp '91
The Unborn '91
Interceptor '92
Into the Sun '92
The Net '95
The Game '97
Terminator 3: Rise of the Machines '03
Catwoman '04
Primeval '07
Surrogates '09
Terminator Salvation '09

Houston Branch (1899-1968)
Alias the Doctor '32
Mr. Wong, Detective '38
Women in Bondage '43

Benjamin Brand
November '05
Bollywood Hero '09

Larry Brand
Backfire '88
The Drifter '88
Paranoia '98
Halloween: Resurrection '02
Christina '10
The Girl On the Train '13
A Perfect Man '13

David Brandes
Dirt Bike Kid '86
The Quarrel '93

Richard Brandes
Party Line '88
The Nurse '97
Devil in the Flesh 2 '00

Michael Brandman
Monte Walsh '03
Jesse Stone: Stone Cold '05
Jesse Stone: Death in Paradise '06
Jesse Stone: No Remorse '10
Jesse Stone: Innocents Lost '11
Jesse Stone: Benefit of the Doubt '12

Gary Brandner (1933-)
Howling 2: Your Sister Is a Werewolf '85
Cameron's Closet '89

Clark Brandon (1958-)
Fast Food '89
Skeeter '93

Michael Brandt (1968-)
2 Fast 2 Furious '03
Catch That Kid '04
3:10 to Yuma '07
Wanted '08
The A-Team '10
The Double '11
Overdrive '17

Caliope Brattlestreet
Showdown in Little Tokyo '91
The Watsons Go to Birmingham '13

Maurizio Braucci
Gomorrah '08
Piranhas '19

Guillaume Breaud
Le Petit Lieutenant '05
Bird People '14

Irving Brecher (1914-2008)
New Faces of 1937 '37
At the Circus '39
Go West '40
Ship Ahoy '42
Best Foot Forward '43
Du Barry Was a Lady '43
Bye, Bye, Birdie '63

Andy Breckman (1955-)
Arthur 2: On the Rocks '88
Moving '88
I.Q. '94
Sgt. Bilko '95
Rat Race '01

Don Bredes
Where the Rivers Flow North '94
A Stranger in the Kingdom '98

Richard L. Breen (1918-67)
Miss Tatlock's Millions '48
Appointment With Danger '51
The Model and the Marriage Broker '51
Titanic '53
Stopover Tokyo '57
The FBI Story '59
Wake Me When It's Over '60
Mary, Mary '63
Do Not Disturb '65
Tony Rome '67

Michael Scott Bregman
Table One '00
Carlito's Way: Rise to Power '05

Catherine Breillat (1948-)
A Real Young Girl '75
Police '85
36 Fillete '88
Perfect Love '96
Romance '99
Sex is Comedy '02
Anatomy of Hell '04
Bluebeard '09
The Sleeping Beauty '10

Fred Breinersdorfer
Sophie Scholl: The Final Days '05
13 Minutes '17

Frederick Hazlitt Brennan (1901-62)
Killer McCoy '47
Fearless Fagan '52

Neal Brennan
Half-Baked '97
The Female Brain '18

Yoni Brenner
Ice Age: Dawn of the Dinosaurs '09
Rio 2 '14
Ice Age: Collision Course '16

Alfonso Brescia (1930-2001)
Two Gladiators '64
War in Space '77
Reactor '78
The Beast in Space '80

Lou Breslow (1900-87)
Paddy O'Day '35
Little Miss Nobody '36
City Streets '38
International Settlement '38
Sleepers West '41
Blondie Goes to College '42
Whispering Ghosts '42
Murder, He Says '45
Merton of the Movies '47
On Our Merry Way '48
Bedtime for Bonzo '51
You Never Can Tell '51
The Crooked Web '55

Eric Bress
Final Destination 2 '03
The Butterfly Effect '04
The Final Destination '09

Robert Bresson (1907-99)
The Ladies of the Bois de Bologne '44
Diary of a Country Priest '50
A Man Escaped '57
Pickpocket '59
Au Hasard Balthazar '66
Lancelot of the Lake '74
The Devil, Probably '77
L'Argent '83

Martin Brest (1951-)
Going in Style '79
Gigli '03

Jonathan Brett
Tales of Erotica '93
Turbulence '96

Craig Brewer (1971-)
Pressure '02
Water's Edge '03
Hustle & Flow '05
Black Snake Moan '07
Footloose '11
The Legend of Tarzan '16

Jameson Brewer (1916-2003)
Ghost Town '56
The Incredible Mr. Limpet '64
The Over-the-Hill Gang '69

Monte Brice (1891-1962)
The Mexican Spitfire Sees a Ghost '42
Radio Stars on Parade '45

Patrick Brice
Creep '15
The Overnight '15

George Bricker (1898-1955)
King of the Underworld '39
Murder by Invitation '41
Dead Man's Eyes '44
Gas House Kids '46
House of Horrors '46
If I'm Lucky '46
Roadblock '51
Loophole '54

Marshall Brickman (1941-)
Sleeper '73
Annie Hall '77
Manhattan '79
Simon '80
Lovesick '83
The Manhattan Project '86
For the Boys '91
Intersection '93
Manhattan Murder Mystery '93
Jersey Boys '14

Paul Brickman (1949-)
The Bad News Bears in Breaking Training '77
Citizens Band '77
Deal of the Century '83
Risky Business '83
Men Don't Leave '89
True Crime '99
Uprising '01

Leslie Bricusse (1931-)
Doctor Dolittle '67
Scrooge '70
Bullseye! '90

James Bridges (1936-93)
The Appaloosa '66
The Baby Maker '70
Colossus: The Forbin Project '70
The Paper Chase '73
September 30, 1955 '77
The China Syndrome '79
Urban Cowboy '80
Mike's Murder '84
Perfect '85
White Hunter, Black Heart '90

Elisa Briganti
Zombie '80
Manhattan Baby '82
The New Gladiators '83

John Bright (1908-89)
Blonde Crazy '31
Public Enemy '31
Smart Money '31
The Crowd Roars '32
Taxi! '32
Union Depot '32
She Done Him Wrong '33
San Quentin '37
Broadway '42
Sherlock Holmes and the Voice of Terror '42
Close-Up '48
I Walk Alone '48
The Kid From Cleveland '49

Matthew Bright (1952-)
Forbidden Zone '80
Wildfire '88
Guncrazy '92
Dark Angel: The Ascent '94
Freeway '95
Modern Vampires '98
Freeway 2: Confessions of a Trickbaby '99

Irena Brignull
Skellig: The Owl Man '09
The Boxtrolls '14
The Little Prince '16

John Briley (1925-)
Invasion Quartet '61
Postman's Knock '62
Children of the Damned '63
The Medusa Touch '78
Eagle's Wing '79
Enigma '82
Gandhi '82
Marie '85
Tai-Pan '86
Cry Freedom '87
Molokai: The Story of Father Damien '99

Steven Brill (1962-)
The Mighty Ducks '92
D2: The Mighty Ducks '94
Heavyweights '94
D3: The Mighty Ducks '96
Little Nicky '00
Ready to Rumble '00
Walk of Shame '14

Ron L. Brinkerhoff
Eye See You '01
The Guardian '06

Brian Brinkman
Dragonquest '09
Meteor Apocalypse '10

Mort Briskin (1919-2000)
The Second Woman '51
Walking Tall '73
Framed '75

Tony Britten
Draw on Sweet Night '15
Chicklit '16

Holly Brix
The Butterfly Effect 3: Revelation '09
The Cutting Edge: Fire and Ice '10

Eduardo Brochero (1919-)
Ringo's Big Night '66
Ringo's Mark of Vengeance '67
Gun for 100 Graves '68
The Case of the Scorpion's Tail '71
The Night of the Devils '72

Deborah Brock
Slumber Party Massacre 2 '87
Rock 'n' Roll High School Forever '91

Jeremy Brock (1959-)
Mrs. Brown '97
Charlotte Gray '01
Driving Lessons '06
The Last King of Scotland '06
Brideshead Revisited '08
The Eagle '11
How I Live Now '13
A Little Chaos '14
Dark Crimes '16

Tricia Brock
Due East '02
Killer Diller '04

Q. Allan Brocka
Boy Culture '06
Eating Out 2: Sloppy Seconds '06
Eating Out 4: Drama Camp '11
Eating Out: The Open Weekend '11

Kevin Brodbin (1964-)
The Glimmer Man '96
Constantine '05
Mindhunters '05

Brendan Broderick
Bloodfist 6: Ground Zero '94
Bloodfist 7: Manhunt '95
Spectre '96
Route 9 '98
Spacejacked '98
Turbulence 2: Fear of Flying '99

Oscar Brodney (1907-2008)
For the Love of Mary '48
Mexican Hayride '48
Harvey '50
Double Crossbones '51
Francis Goes to the Races '51
Francis Goes to West Point '52
Francis Covers the Big Town '53
The Black Shield of Falworth '54
The Glenn Miller Story '54

Captain Lightfoot '55
Lady Godiva '55
Tammy and the Bachelor '57
When Hell Broke Loose '58
Bobbikins '59
Tammy Tell Me True '61
The Brass Bottle '63
Tammy and the Doctor '63
Ghost Fever '87

Henry Bromell (1947-)
Panic '00
Last Call: The Final Chapter of F. Scott Fitzgerald '02

Ronald Bronstein
Heaven Knows What '15
Uncut Gems '19

Peter Brook (1925-)
Lord of the Flies '63
Swann in Love '84

Kate Brooke
Secret Smile '05
Wired '08
The Making of a Lady '12

Ralph Brooke (1920-63)
Giant from the Unknown '58
Bloodlust '59

Nathan Brookes
12 Rounds 3: Lockdown '15
Eliminators '16

William Brookfield
Rough Magic '95
Close Your Eyes '02

Adam Brooks (1956-)
French Kiss '95
Subway Stories '97
Beloved '98
Practical Magic '98
Invisible Circus '00
Bridget Jones: The Edge of Reason '04
Wimbledon '04
Definitely, Maybe '08
Father's Day '12

Albert Brooks (1947-)
Real Life '79
Modern Romance '81
Lost in America '85
Defending Your Life '91
The Scout '94
Mother '96
The Muse '99
Looking for Comedy in the Muslim World '06

James L. Brooks (1940-)
Starting Over '79
Terms of Endearment '83
Broadcast News '87
I'll Do Anything '93
As Good As It Gets '97
Spanglish '04
The Simpsons Movie '07
How Do You Know '10

Katherine Brooks
Loving Annabelle '06
Waking Madison '10
Guns for Hire '15

Mel Brooks (1926-)
The Producers '68
The Twelve Chairs '70
Blazing Saddles '74
Young Frankenstein '74
Silent Movie '76
High Anxiety '77
History of the World: Part 1 '81
Spaceballs '87
Life Stinks '91
Robin Hood: Men in Tights '93
Dracula: Dead and Loving It '95
The Producers '05

Richard Brooks (1912-92)
Cobra Woman '44
Brute Force '47
Key Largo '48
Any Number Can Play '49
Crisis '50
Mystery Street '50
Storm Warning '51
Battle Circus '53
The Last Time I Saw Paris '54
Blackboard Jungle '55
The Last Hunt '56
Something of Value '57
The Brothers Karamazov '58
Cat on a Hot Tin Roof '58
Elmer Gantry '60
Sweet Bird of Youth '62
Lord Jim '65
The Professionals '66
In Cold Blood '67
The Happy Ending '69
Dollars '71
Bite the Bullet '75
Wrong Is Right '82

Stephen Brooks
The Mangler '94
Spiders 2: Breeding Ground '01

Larry Brothers
An Innocent Man '89
Fever '91
Two for Texas '97

Joyce Heft Brotman
Forever Love '98
Circle of Friends '06
He Loves Me '11

Hilary Brougher
The Sticky Fingers of Time '97
Stephanie Daley '06

Alan Brown
Book of Love '04
Superheroes '07
Private Romeo '11

Andrew Brown
High Tide '80
Bad Blood '81

Bruce Brown (1937-)
The Endless Summer '66
The Endless Summer 2 '94

Dana Brown
The Endless Summer 2 '94
Step Into Liquid '03
Dust to Glory '05
On Any Sunday: The Next Chapter '14

George Carleton Brown
Atlantic City '44
McHale's Navy '64

Harry Brown (1917-86)
A Walk in the Sun '46
The Other Love '47
Arch of Triumph '48
Sands of Iwo Jima '49
Wake of the Red Witch '49
Only the Valiant '50
A Place in the Sun '51
Eight Iron Men '52
The Sniper '52
All the Brothers Were Valiant '53
Many Rivers to Cross '55
Between Heaven and Hell '56
Ocean's 11 '60

Jamie Brown (1945-98)
Toby McTeague '87
The Brylcreem Boys '96

Jon Brown
Cuban Fury '14
A Shaun the Sheep Movie: Farmageddon '19

Karl Brown (1896-1990)
City Park '34
Dangerous Appointment '34
Mr. District Attorney '41

Leigh Brown (1939-98)
A Christmas Story '83
My Summer Story '94

Mark Brown
Def Jam's How to Be a Player '97
Jackie's Back '99
Two Can Play That Game '01
Barbershop '02
The Salon '05
Three Can Play That Game '07

Michael Henry Brown
Dead Presidents '95
In Too Deep '99

Randy Brown
Trouble with the Curve '12
Miracles From Heaven '16

Riwia Brown
Once Were Warriors '94
The Legend of Johnny Lingo '03

Rowland Brown (1897-1963)
State's Attorney '31
What Price Hollywood? '32
Angels with Dirty Faces '38
Johnny Apollo '40
Nocturne '46
The Nevadan '50
Kansas City Confidential '52

Christopher Browne
Third World Cop '99
The Walk '15

Janet Brownell
Sweet Revenge '90
Christmas in Connecticut '92
The Amy Fisher Story '93
Eloise at the Plaza '03
Angels Fall '07
Northern Lights '09

Michael Browning
Six Days, Seven Nights '98
More Dogs Than Bones '00
Bad Company '02

Rod Browning (1942-)
Oh, Heavenly Dog! '80
Agatha Christie's Thirteen at Dinner '85
Cruel and Unusual '01

Tod Browning (1882-1962)
Intolerance '16
The Black Bird '26

John Brownjohn
Bitter Moon '92
The Ninth Gate '99

William Broyles, Jr. (1944-)
JFK: Reckless Youth '93
Apollo 13 '95
Entrapment '99
Cast Away '00
Planet of the Apes '01
Unfaithful '02
Jarhead '05
Flags of Our Fathers '06

George Bruce (1898-1974)
Navy Blue and Gold '37
The Crowd Roars '38
The Man in the Iron Mask '39
Kit Carson '40
The Son of Monte Cristo '40
The Corsican Brothers '42
Stand by for Action '42
Salute to the Marines '43
Keep Your Powder Dry '45
Walk a Crooked Mile '48
Rogues of Sherwood Forest '50
Kansas City Confidential '52

Clyde Bruckman (1894-1955)
Our Hospitality '23
The General '26

David Bruckner
V/H/S '12
Southbound '16

Mads Brügger
The Ambassador '11
Cold Case Hammarskjöld '19

Alejandro Brugues
The ABCs of Death 2 '14
Nightmare Cinema '19

Claude Brule
Blood and Roses '61
Please Not Now! '61
Angelique '64
Angelique: The Road to Versailles '65
Who's Got the Black Box? '67
Barbarella '68

Andre G. Brunelin
The Desert of the Tartars '76
Madame Claude '77

James Bruner
An Eye for an Eye '81
Missing in Action '84
Invasion U.S.A. '85
Delta Force '86
Braddock: Missing in Action 3 '88

Callan Brunker
Escape From Planet Earth '13
The Nut Job 2: Nutty by Nature '17
Arctic Dogs '19

Bob Brunner
Exit to Eden '94
The Other Sister '98

Rae Brunton
Outpost '07
Outpost: Black Sun '12
Outpost: Rise of the Spetsnaz '13

Franco Brusati (1922-93)
Romeo and Juliet '68
Bread and Chocolate '73

Peter Bryan
The Hound of the Baskervilles '59
The Brides of Dracula '60
Plague of the Zombies '66
Blood Beast Terror '67

Chris Bryant (1936-)
Don't Look Now '73
The Girl from Petrovka '74
Spiral Staircase '75
Joseph Andrews '77
The Awakening '80
Sword of Gideon '86
Young Catherine '91
Miracle at Midnight '98

Bill Bryden (1942-)
The Long Riders '80
Aria '88

Larry Buchanan (1923-2004)
Mars Needs Women '66
Zontar, the Thing from Venus '66
It's Alive! '68

Harold Buchman (1912-90)
Paris After Dark '43
Cynthia '47
The Sleeping Tiger '54

Peter Buchman (1967-)
Jurassic Park 3 '01
Eragon '06
Che '08

Sidney Buchman (1902-75)
The Sign of the Cross '33
His Greatest Gamble '34
Adventure in Manhattan '36
Theodora Goes Wild '36
Holiday '38
Mr. Smith Goes to Washington '39
Here Comes Mr. Jordan '41
Over 21 '45
The Mark '61
Billy Jack Goes to Washington '77

Sharon Buckingham
Owd Bob '97
Sticks and Stones '08

Kristen Buckley
102 Dalmatians '00
How to Lose a Guy in 10 Days '03

Robert Buckner (1906-89)
Gold Is Where You Find It '38
Jezebel '38
Angels Wash Their Faces '39
You Can't Get Away With Murder '39
My Love Came Back '40
Santa Fe Trail '40
Dive Bomber '41
Yankee Doodle Dandy '42
The Desert Song '43
Confidential Agent '45
Love Me Tender '56

Benjamin Budd (1976-)
Dead Drop '13
Misfire '14

Robert Budreau
That Beautiful Somewhere '06
Born to Be Blue '15

John Carl Buechler
The Eden Formula '06
The Strange Case of Dr. Jekyll and Mr. Hyde '06

Adele Buffington (1900-73)
The Keeper of the Bees '35
Flame of the West '45

Moira Buffini
Tamara Drewe '10
Jane Eyre '11
Byzantium '12
Viceroy's House '17

Takashi Bufford (1952-)
House Party 3 '94
Booty Call '96
Set It Off '96
The Tiger Woods Story '98

Ray Buffum (1904-80)
The Black Dakotas '54
The Brain from Planet Arous '57
Island of Lost Women '59

Jeff Buhai
Revenge of the Nerds '84
Last Resort '86
The Whoopee Boys '86
Jocks '87
Johnny Be Good '88
Revenge of the Nerds 3: The Next Generation '92
Eddie '96

Jeff Buhler
Insanitarium '08
The Midnight Meat Train '08
Pet Sematary '19
The Prodigy '19

Timothy Linh Bui (1969-)
Green Dragon '01
Powder Blue '09

Andrew Bujalski
Beeswax '09
Computer Chess '13
Results '15
Support the Girls '18
Lady and the Tramp '19

Donald Bull (1913-93)
Storm in a Teacup '37
Dear Mr. Prohack '49

Walter Bullock (1907-53)
Springtime in the Rockies '42
Greenwich Village '44
Out of the Blue '47
Golden Girl '51
The I Don't Care Girl '53

Keith Bunin
Horns '13
Onward '20

Edward (Eddie) Bunker (1933-2005)
Straight Time '78
Runaway Train '85
Animal Factory '00

Luis Bunuel (1900-83)
Robinson Crusoe '54
The Criminal Life of Archibaldo de la Cruz '55
Death in the Garden '56
Fever Mounts at El Pao '59
Viridiana '61
The Young One '61
The Exterminating Angel '62
Diary of a Chambermaid '64
Belle de Jour '67
The Discreet Charm of the Bourgeoisie '72
Phantom of Liberty '74
That Obscure Object of Desire '77

Aleksandr (Sasha) Buravsky
Out of the Cold '99
Attack on Leningrad '09

Betty Burbridge (1895-1987)
South of the Border '39
Texas Legionnaires '43

Ron Burch
Head Over Heels '01
Yours, Mine & Ours '05

Ray Burdis (1958-)
Final Cut '98
Love, Honour & Obey '00

Andy Burg
Alaska '96
Trojan War '97

Neil Burger
Interview with the Assassin '02
The Illusionist '06
The Lucky Ones '08

Anthony Burgess (1917-93)
Moses '76
Jesus of Nazareth '77
A.D. '85

Tony Burgess
Pontypool '09
Septic Man '14

David J. Burke (1948-)
Women vs. Men '02
Dark Town '04
Edison Force '05

Edwin J. Burke (1889-1944)
Bad Girl '31
Call Her Savage '32
Bright Eyes '34
The Farmer Takes a Wife '35

Gregory Burke
'71 '14
7 Days in Entebbe '18

Martyn Burke (1952-)
Power Play '78
Last Chase '81
Top Secret! '84
Sugartime '95
The Second Civil War '97
The Pentagon Wars '98
Animal Farm '99
The Pirates of Silicon Valley '99

Simon Burke (1961-)
The Guilty '92
Faith '94
Tom Jones '98
Persuasion '07
The Exception '17

Susan Burke
Smashed '12
Southbound '16

Howard Burkons
Take My Advice: The Ann & Abby Story '99
Smooch '11
My Gal Sunday '14

Charles Burmeister
Columbus Day '08
Mercury Plains '16

Alan Burnett (1949-)
DuckTales the Movie: Treasure of the Lost Lamp '90
Batman: Mask of the Phantasm '93

Allison Burnett
Bloodfist 3: Forced to Fight '92
Red Meat '98
Autumn in New York '00
Feast of Love '07
Resurrecting the Champ '07
Untraceable '08
Fame '09

Gone '12
Underworld: Awakening '12

Charles Burnett (1944-)
Killer of Sheep '77
To Sleep with Anger '90
The Glass Shield '95

W.R. Burnett (1899-1982)
The Westerner '40
High Sierra '41
This Gun for Hire '42
Wake Island '42
Action in the North Atlantic '43
Background to Danger '43
Crash Dive '43
San Antonio '45
The Man I Love '46
Nobody Lives Forever '46
Yellow Sky '48
The Asphalt Jungle '50
Captain Lightfoot '55
I Died a Thousand Times '55
Illegal '55
Sergeants 3 '62
Four for Texas '63
The Great Escape '63
The Jackals '67
Ice Station Zebra '68

Allan Burns (1935-)
Butch and Sundance: The Early Days '79
A Little Romance '79
Just the Way You Are '84
Just Between Friends '86

Brian Burns
You Stupid Man '02
Daddy's Home '15

Dominic Burns (1983-)
Alien Uprising '12
Madness in the Method '19

Edward Burns (1968-)
The Brothers McMullen '94
She's the One '96
No Looking Back '98
Sidewalks of New York '01
Ash Wednesday '02
Flight of the Phoenix '04
Looking for Kitty '04
The Groomsmen '06
Purple Violets '07
Generation Kill '08
Nice Guy Johnny '10
Newlyweds '11
The Fitzgerald Family Christmas '12

Mark Burns (1936-2007)
Married to the Mob '88
She-Devil '89

Rich Burns
Snow '04
Brother Bear 2 '06
The Fox and the Hound 2 '06
Snow 2: Brain Freeze '08

Scott Z. Burns
PU-239 '06
The Bourne Ultimatum '07
The Informant! '09
Contagion '11
Side Effects '13
The Laundromat '19
The Mercy '19
The Report '19

Tim Burns (1953-)
Freaked '93
An American Werewolf in Paris '97
Jacob Two Two Meets the Hooded Fang '99

Jim Burnstein
Renaissance Man '94
D3: The Mighty Ducks '96

Jeff Burr (1963-)
The Offspring '87
Straight into Darkness '04

Richard Burridge (1951-)
Absolute Beginners '86
The Fourth Protocol '87

Abe Burrows (1910-85)
Solid Gold Cadillac '56
How to Succeed in Business without Really Trying '67

Rama Burshtein
Fill the Void '12
The Wedding Plan '17

Colette Burson
Coming Soon '99
Permanent '17

Guy Burt (1972-)
Ghostboat '06
The Bletchley Circle '13

Jeff Burton
Night Divides the Day '01
Acts of Death '07

Mark Burton
Madagascar '05
Wallace & Gromit in The Curse of the Were-Rabbit '05
Aliens in the Attic '09
Gnomeo & Juliet '11
Shaun the Sheep Movie '15
Early Man '18

Michael Burton
Flight of the Navigator '86
Shoot to Kill '88

Tim Burton (1960-)
Edward Scissorhands '90
The Nightmare Before Christmas '93

Steve Buscemi (1957-)
Tree's Lounge '96
Interview '07

Charles Busch (1954-)
Psycho Beach Party '00
Die Mommie Die! '03
A Very Serious Person '06

Niven Busch (1903-91)
The Crowd Roars '32
Miss Pinkerton '32
The Man with Two Faces '34
Angels Wash Their Faces '39
The Westerner '40
The Postman Always Rings Twice '46
The Moonlighter '53

Noah Buschel
The Missing Person '09
Glass Chin '14
The Phenom '16

Jared Bush
Moana '16
Zootopia '16

John Bushelman
The Iron Triangle '89
Violent Zone '89

Adrian Butchart
I Love Your Work '03
Goal! The Dream Begins '06

Oliver Butcher
Dr. Jekyll and Ms. Hyde '95
Unknown '11

Chris Butler
ParaNorman '12
Kubo and the Two Strings '16
Missing Link '19

David Butler
The Strauss Family '73
Voyage of the Damned '76
Disraeli '79
Mountbatten: The Last Viceroy '86
Like A Bride '94

Frank Butler (1890-1967)
Untamed '29
Montana Moon '30
This Modern Age '31
College Humor '33
March of the Wooden Soldiers '34
Search for Beauty '34
Vagabond Lady '35
The Princess Comes Across '36
Waikiki Wedding '37
Give Me a Sailor '38
Never Say Die '39
The Road to Singapore '40
The Road to Zanzibar '41
Beyond the Blue Horizon '42
My Favorite Blonde '42
The Road to Morocco '42
Wake Island '42
China '43
Going My Way '44
Golden Earrings '47
Whispering Smith '48
The Road to Bali '53
Strange Lady in Town '55

Hugo Butler (1914-68)
Big City '37
Young Tom Edison '40
The Southerner '45
The Prowler '51
The First Time '52
Robinson Crusoe '54
The Young One '61
Eva '62
Sodom and Gomorrah '62
The Legend of Lylah Clare '68

Michael Butler
The Don Is Dead '73
Brannigan '75
The Car '77
The Gauntlet '77
Flashpoint '84
Code of Silence '85
Pale Rider '85
White Mile '94

William Butler (1968-)
Madhouse '04
Return of the Living Dead: Rave to the Grave '05

Jez Butterworth (1969-)
Birthday Girl '02
The Last Legion '07
Fair Game '10
Edge of Tomorrow '14
Get On Up '14
Black Mass '15
Spectre '15
Ford v Ferrari '19

John-Henry Butterworth (1976-)
Edge of Tomorrow '14
Get On Up '14
Ford v Ferrari '19

Tom Butterworth (1967-)
Birthday Girl '02
The Last Legion '07
Molly Moon and The Incredible Book of Hypnotism '15

Jorg Buttgereit (1963-)
Nekromantik '87
Nekromantik 2 '91

Floyd Byars
Making Mr. Right '86
Compulsion '13

Eric Byler
Charlotte Sometimes '02
Tre '06

Johnny Byrne (1935-2008)
Adolf Hitler: My Part in His Downfall '74
Heaven's a Drag '94

Jim Byrnes (1948-)
The Shadow Riders '82
Miracle in the Wilderness '91
Dead Man's Revenge '93
The Pledge '08

John Byrum (1947-)
Mahogany '75
Harry & Walter Go to New York '76
Inserts '76
Valentino '77
Heart Beat '80
Sphinx '81
The Razor's Edge '84
Duets '00

Reggie Rock Bythewood (1965-)
Get On the Bus '96
Dancing in September '00
Biker Boyz '03
Notorious '09

Scott Caan (1976-)
Dallas 362 '03
The Dog Problem '06
Mercy '09

Stephane Cabel
Brotherhood of the Wolf '01
The Clearstream Affair '15

Michael Cacoyannis (1927-2011)
Stella '55
Girl in Black '56
A Matter of Dignity '57
Iphigenia '77
The Cherry Orchard '99

Jerome Cady (1903-48)
Charlie Chan at Monte Carlo '37
Mr. Moto's Gamble '38
The Mexican Spitfire's Baby '41
Play Girl '41
The Saint in Palm Springs '41
Guadalcanal Diary '43
Silver Skates '43
A Wing and a Prayer '44
Thunder In the Valley '47
Call Northside 777 '48

Arthur Caesar (1892-1953)
Three Faces East '30
The Tenderfoot '32
Adventure in Washington '41

David Caesar
Idiot Box '97
Dirty Deeds '02

Josh A. Cagan
Bandslam '09
The DUFF '15
Kim Possible '19

Mike Cahill (1979-)
King of California '07
Another Earth '11
I Origins '14

Mario Caiano (1933-)
Ulysses Against the Son of Hercules '61
Medusa Against the Son of Hercules '62
Two Gladiators '64
Erik, the Viking '65
Ringo's Mark of Vengeance '67
Ringo, the Lone Rider '68

Alan Caillou (1914-2006)
Clarence, the Cross-eyed Lion '65
Village of the Giants '65
The Losers '70
Kingdom of the Spiders '77

Christopher Cain (1943-)
Sixth and Main '77
September Dawn '07
Pure Country 2: The Gift '10

Jeffrey Caine
Goldeneye '95
Rory O'Shea Was Here '04
The Constant Gardener '05
Exodus: Gods and Kings '14
The Song of Names '19

Yule Caise (1964-)
Free of Eden '98
Way Past Cool '00

Joseph M. Cala (1932-)
Angel '84
Avenging Angel '85

Guillermo Calderon
The Club '16
Neruda '16

Michael Caleo
The Last Time '06
The Family '13

David Callaham
Doom '05
Horsemen '09
The Expendables '10

Dan Callahan
College '08
Demoted '11

George Callahan (1902-89)
Red Light '49
Bunco Squad '50

Mars Callahan (1971-)
Double Down '01
Poolhall Junkies '02
What Love Is '07

Dayton Callie (1946-)
The Last Days of Frankie the Fly '96
Executive Target '97

Paul Callisi
Josh Kirby. . .Time Warrior: Chapter 1, Planet of the Dino-Knights '95
Josh Kirby. . . Time Warrior: Chapter 2, The Human Pets '95

Art Camacho
Little Bigfoot 2: The Journey Home '97
Confessions of a Pit Fighter '05

James Cameron (1954-)
The Terminator '84
Rambo: First Blood, Part 2 '85
Aliens '86
The Abyss '89
Terminator 2: Judgment Day '91
True Lies '94
Strange Days '95
Titanic '97
Avatar '09
Alita: Battle Angel '19

Lorne Cameron
Like Father, Like Son '87
Deadly Game '98
The Extreme Adventures of Super Dave '98
Brother Bear '03
Over the Hedge '06
The Nut Job '14

Tassie Cameron
Cake '05
Would Be Kings '08

W. Bruce Cameron (1960-)
A Dog's Purpose '17
A Dog's Journey '19
A Dog's Way Home '19

Augusto Caminito
Django: Last Killer '67
Hallelujah for Django '67
Long Days of Revenge '67

Donald Cammell (1939-96)
Duffy '68
Performance '70
Wild Side '95

Alessandro Camon
The Messenger '09
Bullet to the Head '12

Brandon Camp
Dragonfly '02
Love Happens '09

Joe Camp (1939-)
Benji '74
For the Love of Benji '77
Oh, Heavenly Dog! '80
Benji the Hunted '87
Benji: Off the Leash! '04

Juan J. Campanella (1959-)
Love Walked In '97
The Son of the Bride '01
The Secret in Their Eyes '09

Alan Campbell (1904-63)
The Moon's Our Home '36
Tales of Manhattan '42
Woman On the Run '50

Darren O. Campbell
The Foreigner '03
Black Dawn '05

Doug Campbell
Walking the Halls '12
The Surrogate '13

Kevin Campbell
The Return of Jafar '94
Backslash '05

Robert W(right) Campbell (1927-2000)
Gun for a Coward '57
Quantez '57
Teenage Caveman '58
Masque of the Red Death '65
Hell's Angels on Wheels '67
Captain Nemo and the Underwater City '69

Robin Campillo
Time Out '01
They Came Back '04
Heading South '05
The Class '08
BPM (Beats Per Minute) '17

Anna Campion (1952-)
Loaded '94
Holy Smoke '99

Jane Campion (1954-)
Sweetie '89
The Piano '93
Holy Smoke '99
In the Cut '03
Bright Star '09
Top of the Lake '13

Cam'ron (1976-)
Killa Season '06
Percentage '13

Christopher Canaan
Drug Wars: The Camarena Story '90
Robinson Crusoe '96
The Apocalypse Watch '97
No Good Deed '02
A Date With Darkness '03
Little Girl Lost: The Delimar Vera Story '08

Guillaume Canet (1973-)
Whatever You Say '02
Tell No One '06
Little White Lies '10
Blood Ties '13

Stephen J. Cannell (1942-2010)
The Rousters '90
It Waits '05
The Tooth Fairy '06

Doran William Cannon
Skidoo '68
Brewster McCloud '70
Charms '73

Kay Cannon
Pitch Perfect '12
Pitch Perfect 2 '15
Pitch Perfect 3 '17
Let It Snow '19

Laurent Cantet (1961-)
Time Out '01
Heading South '05
The Class '08

Michael Canzoniero
The Wedding Bros. '08
Don Peyote '14

Leon Capetanos
Gumball Rally '76
Greased Lightning '77
The Tempest '82
Moscow on the Hudson '84
Down and Out in Beverly Hills '86
Moon over Parador '88
Fletch Lives '89

Truman Capote (1924-84)
Beat the Devil '53
The Innocents '61

Frank Cappello
Suburban Commando '91
No Way Back '96
Constantine '05

James (Jim) Carabatsos
Heroes '77
Heartbreak Ridge '86
No Mercy '86
Hamburger Hill '87
Lost Battalion '01

Steven W. Carabatsos
El Condor '70
Tentacles '77
The Last Flight of Noah's Ark '80
Hot Pursuit '87

Leos Carax (1960-)
Boy Meets Girl '84
Mauvais Sang '86
The Lovers on the Bridge '91
Pola X '99
Tokyo! '09
Holy Motors '12

Julien Carbon
Black Mask 2: City of Masks '02
Running Out of Time 2 '06

Rene Cardona, Jr. (1939-2003)
Night of the Bloody Apes '68
The Treasure of the Amazon '85

J.S. Cardone (1946-)
The Slayer '82
Shadowzone '89
Crash and Burn '90
Shadowhunter '93
Black Day Blue Night '95
The Forsaken '01
True Blue '01
Alien Hunter '03
Sniper 3 '04
The Covenant '06
Prom Night '08
The Stepfather '09

Mark Patrick Carducci (1955-97)
Pumpkinhead '88
Buried Alive '90

Topper Carew (1943-)
D.C. Cab '84
Talkin' Dirty after Dark '91

C. Robert Cargill (1975-)
Sinister '12
Sinister 2 '15
Doctor Strange '16

Christian Carion (1963-)
The Girl from Paris '02
Plain Dirty '04
Joyeux Noel '05
Farewell '09

Carlo Carlei (1960-)
Flight of the Innocent '93
Fluke '95

John Carlen
Blind Side '93
Sonny '02

Lewis John Carlino (1932-2020)
Seconds '66
The Brotherhood '68
The Mechanic '72
A Reflection of Fear '73
The Sailor Who Fell from Grace with the Sea '76
I Never Promised You a Rose Garden '77
The Great Santini '80
Resurrection '80
Haunted Summer '88
The Mechanic '11

Joe Carnahan (1969-)
Blood, Guts, Bullets and Octane '99
Narc '02
Smokin' Aces '07
Pride and Glory '08
The Grey '12
Death Wish '18
Bad Boys for Life '20

Matthew Carnahan
Black Circle Boys '97
The Kingdom '07
Lions for Lambs '07
State of Play '09

Matthew Michael Carnahan
World War Z '13
Deepwater Horizon '16
Dark Waters '19

Charles Robert Carner (1957-)
Gymkata '85
Let's Get Harry '87
Blind Fury '90
A Killer Among Friends '92
The Fixer '97
Echo of Murder '00
Crossfire Trail '01
Breakaway '02
Witless Protection '08

Michael Carnes
Mr. Woodcock '07
Furry Vengeance '10

John Carney
On the Edge '00
Once '06
Begin Again '13
Sing Street '16

Marc Caro (1956-)
Delicatessen '92
The City of Lost Children '95

Niki Caro (1967-)
Whale Rider '02
A Heavenly Vintage '09

Reid Carolin (1982-)
Magic Mike '12
Magic Mike XXL '15

Adam Carolla (1964-)
Road Hard '15
Winning: The Racing Life of Paul Newman '15

Glenn Gordon Caron (1954-)
Condorman '81
Moonlighting '85
Picture Perfect '96

A.J. Carothers (1931-2007)
The Miracle of the White Stallions '63
Emil and the Detectives '64
The Happiest Millionaire '67
Never a Dull Moment '68
Hero at Large '80
Making of a Male Model '83
The Secret of My Success '87

John Carpenter (1948-)
Dark Star '74
Assault on Precinct 13 '76
Eyes of Laura Mars '78
The Fog '78
Halloween '78
Zuma Beach '78
Escape from New York '81
Halloween 2: The Nightmare Isn't Over! '81
Black Moon Rising '86
Prince of Darkness '87
They Live '88
El Diablo '90
Village of the Damned '95
Escape from L.A. '96
John Carpenter's Vampires '97
Silent Predators '99
John Carpenter's Ghosts of Mars '01

Richard Carpenter (1933-)
The Scarlet Pimpernel '99
The Scarlet Pimpernel 2: Mademoiselle Guillotine '99
The Scarlet Pimpernel 3: The Kidnapped King '99

Stephen Carpenter
Dorm That Dripped Blood '82
Servants of Twilight '91
Blue Streak '99
Soul Survivors '01
The Man '05

Tito Carpi
Revenge of the Musketeers '63
Eagles Over London '69
Cold Eyes of Fear '70
Fistful of Lead '70
Sartana's Here. . . Trade Your Pistol for a Coffin '70
Tentacles '77

Shark Hunter '79
Thor the Conqueror '83

Jonas Carpignano
Mediterranea '15
A Ciambra '17

Allan Carr (1937-99)
Grease '78
Can't Stop the Music '80

Benjamin Carr
Head of the Family '96
Zarkorr! The Invader '96
The Creeps '97
Goobers! '97
Hideous '97
Shrieker '97
Curse of the Puppet Master: The Human Experiment '98
Kraa! the Sea Monster '98
Talisman '98
Timekeeper '98
Murdercycle '99
Retro Puppet Master '99
Super Hybrid '10

Caleb Carr (1955-)
Exorcist: The Beginning '04
Dominion: Prequel to the Exorcist '05

Richard Carr (1929-88)
Man from Del Rio '56
Too Late Blues '61
Hell Is for Heroes '62
Heaven With a Gun '69
The Over-the-Hill Gang Rides Again '70
Americana '81

Rodney Carr-Smith
Bartleby '70
Lolly-Madonna XXX '73

Joan Carr-Wiggin
My First Wedding '04
If I Were You '12

Kevin Carraway
Caged Animal '10
7 Below '11
Chain of Command '15

Michael Carreras (1927-94)
Unholy Four '54
Prehistoric Women '67
Creatures the World Forgot '70
Moon Zero Two '70

Jean-Claude Carriere (1931-)
Diary of a Chambermaid '64
The Diabolical Dr. Z '65
Viva Maria! '65
Attack of the Robots '66
Belle de Jour '67
The Thief of Paris '67
The Milky Way '68
La Piscine '69
Borsalino '70
The Discreet Charm of the Bourgeoisie '72
Phantom of Liberty '74
That Obscure Object of Desire '77
The Associate '79
Every Man for Himself '79
The Tin Drum '79
Danton '82
The Return of Martin Guerre '83
Swann in Love '84
Max, Mon Amour '86
The Unbearable Lightness of Being '88
Valmont '89
Cyrano de Bergerac '90
Circle of Deceit '94
The Night and the Moment '94
The Horseman on the Roof '95
The Ogre '96
Chinese Box '97
Birth '04
Goya's Ghosts '06
The Patience Stone '13
At Eternity's Gate '18

James Carrington
Fluke '95
Joseph '95
Caravaggio '07

Robert B. Carrington
Kaleidoscope '66
Wait until Dark '67
Venom '82

Sidney Carroll (1913-88)
A Big Hand for the Little Lady '66
Dynasty '76

Willard Carroll (1955-)
Playing by Heart '98
Marigold '07

Shane Carruth (1972-)
Primer '04
Upstream Color '13

L.M. Kit Carson (1941-2014)
David Holzman's Diary '67
Breathless '83
Paris, Texas '83
The Texas Chainsaw Massacre 2 '86
Perfume '01
Tempo '03

Robert Carson (1913-83)
Men with Wings '38
Beau Geste '39
Western Union '41
The Desperadoes '43
Just for You '52

William Carson
Judgment Day '99
Militia '99

Bill Carter (1918-95)
The Late Shift '96
Monday Night Mayhem '02

Chris Carter (1956-)
The X-Files '98
The X Files: I Want to Believe '08

Natalie Carter
A Secret '07
Love Crime '10
Therese '12

Tim Carter
The Chateau Meroux '11
Dead Rising: End Game '16

Carroll Cartwright
Dungeons and Dragons '00
Where the Money Is '00
What Maisie Knew '12

Dee Caruso
Which Way to the Front? '70
The World's Greatest Athlete '73
Doin' Time '85

D.J. Caruso (1965-)
Standing Up '13
The Disappointments Room '16

Sergio Casci
American Cousins '02
The Caller '11
The Lodge '19

Patrick Casey
Gamebox 1.0 '04
Transylmania '09
Sonic the Hedgehog '20

Jim Cash (1940-2000)
Legal Eagles '86
Top Gun '86
The Secret of My Success '87
Turner and Hooch '89
Dick Tracy '90
Anaconda '96
The Flintstones in Viva Rock Vegas '00

Vera Caspary (1904-87)
Lady from Louisiana '42
Claudia and David '46
Out of the Blue '47
I Can Get It For You Wholesale '51

John Cassavetes (1929-89)
Saddle the Wind '58
Too Late Blues '61
Faces '68
Husbands '70
Minnie and Moskowitz '71
A Woman under the Influence '74
The Killing of a Chinese Bookie '76
Opening Night '77
She's So Lovely '97

Nick Cassavetes (1959-)
Unhook the Stars '96
Blow '01
Alpha Dog '06
My Sister's Keeper '09

Rickie Castaneda
Christmas Magic '11
Mistletoe Over Manhattan '11

Enzo G. Castellari (1938-)
Eagles Over London '69
Cold Eyes of Fear '70

Sergio Castellitto (1953-)
Around a Small Mountain '09
Twice Born '12

Nick Castle (1947-)
Pray TV '80
Escape from New York '81
The Boy Who Could Fly '86
Tap '89
Hook '91
August Rush '07

William Castle (1914-77)
It's a Small World '50
Bug '75

Robert Caswell (1946-2006)
A Cry in the Dark '88
The Doctor '91
A Far Off Place '93
Over the Hill '93
Something the Lord Made '04

Victor Andres Catena
Sandokan the Great '63
A Fistful of Dollars '64

Gil Cates, Jr. (1969-)
Spent '00
Deal '08

Jean Cau (1925-93)
Borsalino '70
Don Juan (Or If Don Juan Were a Woman) '73

Liliana Cavani (1937-)
The Night Porter '74
The Skin '81
Beyond Obsession '82
Francesco '93
Ripley's Game '02

Fred Cavaye
The Next Three Days '10
Point Blank '10

Nick Cave (1957-)
The Proposition '05
Lawless '12
20,000 Days on Earth '14

Frank Cavett (1905-73)
Syncopation '42
Going My Way '44

Joseph Cedar
Time of Favor '00
Beaufort '07
Footnote '11
Norman '17

Vincenzo Cerami (1940-2013)
The Monster '96
Life Is Beautiful '98
Pinocchio '02
The Tiger and the Snow '05

Mike Cerrone (1957-)
Me, Myself, and Irene '00
The Three Stooges '12
Dumb and Dumber To '14

Ebru Ceylan
Once Upon a Time in Anatolia '12
Winter Sleep '14
The Wild Pear Tree '18

Nuri Bilge Ceylan
Climates '06
Once Upon a Time in Anatolia '12
Winter Sleep '14
The Wild Pear Tree '18

Michael Chabon
Spider-Man 2 '04
John Carter '12

Claude Chabrol (1930-2010)
Le Beau Serge '58
The Cousins '59
Les Cousins '59
Les Biches '68
Six in Paris '68
La Femme Infidele '69
Le Boucher '69
La Rupture '70
Just Before Nightfall '71
Wedding in Blood '74
Cop Au Vin '85
The Cry of the Owl '87
The Story of Women '88
Quiet Days in Clichy '90
Madame Bovary '91
Betty '92
L'Enfer '93
La Ceremonie '95
The Swindle '97
The Color of Lies '99
Merci pour le Chocolat '00
The Bridesmaid '04
Comedy of Power '06
A Girl Cut in Two '07
Inspector Bellamy '09

Gurinder Chadha (1960-)
What's Cooking? '00
Bend It Like Beckham '02
Bride & Prejudice '04
The Mistress of Spices '05
Paris, je t'aime '06
Angus, Thongs and Perfect Snogging '08
Viceroy's House '17
Blinded by the Light '19

Youssef Chahine (1926-)
Alexandria. . . Why? '78
An Egyptian Story '82
Alexandria Again and Forever '90
Destiny '97

Ilene Chaiken
Barb Wire '96
Dirty Pictures '00

Kitty Chalmers
Journey to the Center of the Earth '88
Cyborg '89

John C. Champion (1923-94)
Panhandle '48
Stampede '49
Hellgate '52
Dragonfly Squadron '54
Zero Hour! '57
The Texican '66

Eric Champnella
Eddie '96
Mail to the Chief '00
Mr. 3000 '04
Thunderstruck '12

Benny Chan
Gen-X Cops '99
Robin-B-Hood '06
The White Storm '13

Gordon Chan (1960-)
Dragons Forever '88
The Bodyguard from Beijing '94
Beast Cops '98
The Medallion '03
The Four '12

Hing-Ka Chan
Contract Killer '98
The Mermaid '16

Christian Clavier (1952-)
The Visitors '95
Just Visiting '01

Thomas McKelvey Cleaver
The Terror Within '88
Raiders of the Sun '92

Marc Clebanoff
The Pink Conspiracy '07
Break '09

John Cleese (1939-)
The Magic Christian '69
The Rise and Rise of Michael Rimmer '70
And Now for Something Completely Different '72
Rentadick '72
Monty Python and the Holy Grail '75
Monty Python's Life of Brian '79
Monty Python's The Meaning of Life '83
A Fish Called Wanda '88
Fierce Creatures '96

Brian Clemens (1931-2015)
The Tell-Tale Heart '60
And Soon the Darkness '70
Dr. Jekyll and Sister Hyde '71
See No Evil '71
Golden Voyage of Sinbad '73
Captain Kronos: Vampire Hunter '74
Murder on the Midnight Express '74
The Watcher in the Woods '81

Dick Clement (1937-)
Otley '68
Hannibal Brooks '69
Catch Me a Spy '71
Villain '71
Prisoner of Zenda '79
Water '85
Vice Versa '88
The Commitments '91
Excess Baggage '96
Still Crazy '98
Archangel '05
Flushed Away '06
Goal! The Dream Begins '06
Across the Universe '07
The Bank Job '08
Killing Bono '11
Spies of Warsaw '13

Rene Clement (1913-96)
Battle of the Rails '46
Forbidden Games '52
Purple Noon '60
Joy House '64

Ron Clements (1953-)
The Great Mouse Detective '86
The Little Mermaid '89
Aladdin '92
Hercules '97
Treasure Planet '02
The Princess and the Frog '09

Gianfranco Clerici
Cannibal Holocaust '80
New York Ripper '82

Rick Cleveland
Jerry and Tom '98
Runaway Jury '03

Howard Clewes (1912-88)
One That Got Away '57
The Day They Robbed the Bank of England '60

Ernest Cline (1972-)
Fanboys '09
Ready Player One '18

George Clooney (1961-)
Good Night, and Good Luck '05
The Ides of March '11
The Monuments Men '13
Suburbicon '17

Harry Clork (1888-1978)
Las Vegas Nights '41
Whistling in the Dark '41
Ship Ahoy '42
Broadway Rhythm '44
Painting the Clouds With Sunshine '51
Ma and Pa Kettle at Waikiki '55

Robert Clouse (1929-97)
The Ultimate Warrior '75
The Pack '77
Battle Creek Brawl '80
The Big Brawl '80
Force: Five '81
China O'Brien '88

Henri-Georges Clouzot (1907-77)
The Murderer Lives at Number 21 '42
Diabolique '55
Wages of Fear '55
L'Enfer '93

Daniel Clowes (1961-)
Ghost World '01
Art School Confidential '06
Wilson '17

Travis Cluff
The Gallows '15
The Gallows Act II '19

Craig Clyde
Little Heroes '91
The Legend of Wolf Mountain '92
Walking Thunder '94
Miracle Dogs '03
The Wild Stallion '09
A Christmas Wish '11
Heaven's Door '12
Storm Rider '13

Lewis Coates (1947-)
See Luigi Cozzi

Sharon Y. Cobb
Lighthouse Hill '04
June '15

Stacy Cochran
My New Gun '92
Boys '95

Francis Cockrell (1906-87)
The Family Secret '51
Rhubarb '51

Jay Cocks (1944-)
The Age of Innocence '93
Strange Days '95
Gangs of New York '02
De-Lovely '04
Silence '16

Jean Cocteau (1889-1963)
The Ladies of the Bois de Bologne '44
Beauty and the Beast '46
Orpheus '49
Les Enfants Terrible '50
The Testament of Orpheus '59

Diablo Cody (1978-)
Juno '07
Jennifer's Body '09
Young Adult '11
Ricki and the Flash '15
Tully '18

Amanda Coe
Filth '08
Margot '09

Ethan Coen (1957-)
Blood Simple '85
Raising Arizona '87
Miller's Crossing '90
Barton Fink '91
The Hudsucker Proxy '93
Fargo '96
The Big Lebowski '97
O Brother Where Art Thou? '00
The Man Who Wasn't There '01
Intolerable Cruelty '03
The Ladykillers '04
Paris, je t'aime '06
No Country for Old Men '07
Burn After Reading '08
A Serious Man '09
True Grit '10
Gambit '12
Inside Llewyn Davis '13
Unbroken '14
Bridge of Spies '15
Hail, Caesar! '16
Suburbicon '17
The Ballad of Buster Scruggs '18

Franklin Coen (1912-90)
The Glory Brigade '53
The Train '65
Alvarez Kelly '66
Black Gunn '72
The Take '74

Joel Coen (1954-)
Blood Simple '85
Raising Arizona '87
Miller's Crossing '90
Barton Fink '91
The Hudsucker Proxy '93
Fargo '96
The Big Lebowski '97
O Brother Where Art Thou? '00
The Man Who Wasn't There '01
Intolerable Cruelty '03
The Ladykillers '04
Paris, je t'aime '06
No Country for Old Men '07
Burn After Reading '08
A Serious Man '09
True Grit '10
Gambit '12
Inside Llewyn Davis '13
Unbroken '14
Bridge of Spies '15
Hail, Caesar! '16
Suburbicon '17
The Ballad of Buster Scruggs '18

Lenore Coffee (1896-1984)
Chicago '27
The Bishop Murder Case '30
Mothers Cry '30
The Squaw Man '31
Downstairs '32
Torch Singer '33
Evelyn Prentice '34
Four Frightened People '34
Four Daughters '38
Old Acquaintance '43
Lightning Strikes Twice '51
Sudden Fear '52
End of the Affair '55
Footsteps in the Fog '55
Cash McCall '60

David Coggeshall
The Haunting in Connecticut 2: Ghosts of Georgia '13
Prey '19

Andrew Jay Cohen
Neighbors '14
Mike and Dave Need Wedding Dates '16
Neighbors 2: Sorority Rising '16
The House '17

Barney Cohen
Friday the 13th, Part 4: The Final Chapter '84
Killer Party '86
Sabrina the Teenage Witch '96
Guernica '16

Bennett Cohen (1890-1964)
Midnight Faces '26
The Three Musketeers '33

David Aaron Cohen
V.I. Warshawski '91
The Devil's Own '96
Friday Night Lights '04
The Miracle Season '18
Speed Kills '18

David Steven Cohen
Balto '95
Mean Girls 2 '11

Etan Cohen
Idiocracy '06
Tropic Thunder '08
Men in Black 3 '12
Get Hard '15
Holmes & Watson '18

Howard R. Cohen (1942-99)
The Young Nurses '73
Saturday the 14th '81
Deathstalker '83
Barbarian Queen '85
Saturday the 14th Strikes Back '88
Barbarian Queen 2: The Empress Strikes Back '89

Joel Cohen
Sister, Sister '87
Toy Story '95
Money Talks '97
Goodbye, Lover '99
Cheaper by the Dozen '03
Garfield: The Movie '04
Garfield: A Tail of Two Kitties '06

Larry Cohen (1947-)
Return of the Magnificent Seven '66
Daddy's Gone A-Hunting '69
El Condor '70
Housewife '72
Black Caesar '73
Hell Up in Harlem '73
It's Alive '74
God Told Me To '76
The Private Files of J. Edgar Hoover '77
It's Alive 2: It Lives Again '78
I, the Jury '82
Q (The Winged Serpent) '82
Perfect Strangers '84
Into Thin Air '85
Special Effects '85
The Stuff '85
Best Seller '87
It's Alive 3: Island of the Alive '87
Return to Salem's Lot '87
Maniac Cop '88
Wicked Stepmother '89
The Ambulance '90
Maniac Cop 2 '90
Guilty as Sin '93
Maniac Cop 3: Badge of Silence '93
Uncle Sam '96
Ed McBain's 87th Precinct: Heatwave '97
Misbegotten '98
Phone Booth '02
Cellular '04
Captivity '07
The Gambler, the Girl and the Gunslinger '09

Lawrence D. Cohen
Carrie '76
Ghost Story '81
Stephen King's The Tommyknockers '93
Rodgers & Hammerstein's South Pacific '01

Lawrence J. Cohen (1938-)
Start the Revolution without Me '70
S*P*Y*S '74
The Big Bus '76
Delirious '91

Lester Cohen (1901-63)
One Man's Journey '33
Sweepings '33
Of Human Bondage '34

Martin B. Cohen
Rebel Rousers '69
Humanoids from the Deep '80

Rob Cohen (1949-)
Dragon: The Bruce Lee Story '93
The Last Ride '04

Ronald M. Cohen (1939-98)
Blue '68
The Good Guys and the Bad Guys '69
Last Stand at Saber River '96
Aces 'n Eights '08

Art Cohn (1909-58)
The Set-Up '49
The Tall Target '51
Tomorrow Is Another Day '51
Carbine Williams '52
Men of the Fighting Lady '54
Ten Thousand Bedrooms '57
The Seven Hills of Rome '58

Jared Cohn
Born Bad '11
12/12/12 '12

Kat Coiro
Life Happens '11
And While We Were Here '13

Isabel Coixet (1960-)
Things I Never Told You '96
My Life Without Me '03
Paris, je t'aime '06
The Bookshop '18

Cheo Hodari Coker
Notorious '09
Lowriders '17
Creed II '18

Anthony Coldeway (1887-1963)
Old San Francisco '27
Noah's Ark '28
The Hidden Hand '42

Brandon Cole
Mac '93
Illuminata '98
Pete Smalls Is Dead '10

Lester Cole (1904-85)
Follow Your Heart '36
The Invisible Man Returns '40
Footsteps in the Dark '41
Blood on the Sun '45
Objective, Burma! '45
High Wall '47
The Romance of Rosy Ridge '47
Operation Eichmann '61
Born Free '66

Randel Cole
2B Perfectly Honest '04
Real Time '08

Tom Cole (1933-2009)
Smooth Talk '85
High Stakes '93

Warren Coleman
Happy Feet '06
Happy Feet Two '11

Lewis Colick
Dirt Bike Kid '86
Unlawful Entry '92
Judgment Night '93
Bulletproof '96
Ghosts of Mississippi '96
October Sky '99
Domestic Disturbance '01
Beyond the Sea '04
Ladder 49 '04
Charlie St. Cloud '10

Bill Collage
New York Minute '04
Accepted '06
Exodus: Gods and Kings '14
The Transporter Refueled '15
Allegiant '16
Assassin's Creed '16

Dave Collard
Out of Time '03
Annapolis '06

Michael Colleary
Darkman 3: Die Darkman Die '95
Face/Off '97
Firehouse Dog '07

Robert Collector
Memoirs of an Invisible Man '92
Believe in Me '06

John Collee (1955-)
Paper Mask '91
Master and Commander: The Far Side of the World '03
Happy Feet '06
Creation '09
Walking with Dinosaurs 3D '13
Wolf Totem '15
Hotel Mumbai '18

John Collier (1901-80)
Sylvia Scarlett '35
Her Cardboard Lover '42
The War Lord '65

Max Allan Collins (1948-)
Mommy '95
Mommy 2: Mommy's Day '96
Real Time: Siege at Lucas Street Market '00
The Last Lullaby '08

Monte (Monty) Collins, Jr. (1898-1951)
The Green Promise '49
Utopia '51

Richard Collins (1914-2013)
Riot in Cell Block 11 '54
My Gun Is Quick '57
The Badlanders '58
Edge of Eternity '59

Laurie Collyer
Sherrybaby '06
Sunlight Jr. '13

Harry Colomby
Johnny Dangerously '84
Touch and Go '86

Carl Colpaert (1963-)
The Crew '95
Black Limousine '10

John Colton (1891-1946)
Werewolf of London '35
The Invisible Ray '36

Chris Columbus (1958-)
Gremlins '84
Reckless '84
The Goonies '85
Young Sherlock Holmes '85
Heartbreak Hotel '88
Only the Lonely '91
Little Nemo: Adventures in Slumberland '92
Nine Months '95
Christmas With the Kranks '04

Adele Comandini (1898-1987)
Jane Eyre '34
Three Smart Girls '36
Beyond Tomorrow '40
Strange Illusion '45

Ryan Combs (1974-)
Straight out of Compton '99
I Accidentally Domed Your Son '04
The Hit '06
Phantom Punch '09
Caged Animal '10
Mafia '11

Betty Comden (1915-2006)
Good News '47
The Barkleys of Broadway '49
On the Town '49
Singin' in the Rain '52
The Band Wagon '53
It's Always Fair Weather '55
Auntie Mame '58
Bells Are Ringing '60

Bob Comfort
Dogfight '91
Good Luck '96

Kevin Commins
Cybermutt '02
Cheaters' Club '06
Every Second Counts '08
The Santa Suit '10
You Lucky Dog '10
Come Dance With Me '12

Richard Compton (1938-2007)
Angels Die Hard '70
The California Kid '74

Chuck Conaway
Dilemma '97
Waiting for Dublin '07

Paul Cox (1940-)
Lonely Hearts '82
Man of Flowers '84
Cactus '86
Vincent: The Life and Death of Vincent van Gogh '87
Innocence '00
Tim Cox
Mammoth '06
Attack of the Gryphon '07
Lucinda Coxon (1962-)
The Heart of Me '02
Wild Target '10
The Crimson Petal and the White '12
The Danish Girl '15
The Little Stranger '18
Adam Cozad
Jack Ryan: Shadow Recruit '14
The Legend of Tarzan '16
Underwater '20
Luigi Cozzi (1947-)
The Killer Must Kill Again '75
Star Crash '78
Alien Contamination '81
Hercules '83
Hercules 2 '85
Kerry Crabbe
The Playboys '92
Innocent Lies '95
Peter Crabbe
Car 54, Where Are You? '94
McHale's Navy '97
Dean Craig (1974-)
Caffeine '06
Death at a Funeral '07
Death at a Funeral '10
A Few Best Men '11
Moonwalkers '16
H.A.L. Craig (1921-78)
Anzio '68
The Message '77
Lion of the Desert '81
Laurie Craig
Modern Girls '86
Paulie '98
Ella Enchanted '04
Ramona and Beezus '10
Peter Craig (1969-)
The Town '10
The Hunger Games: Mockingjay--Part 1 '14
The Hunger Games: Mockingjay-Part 2 '15
Blood Father '16
12 Strong '18
Bad Boys for Life '20
Brian Crano
A Bag of Hammers '11
Permission '18
Frank Craven (1875-1945)
Sons of the Desert '33
Our Town '40
Jay Craven
Where the Rivers Flow North '94
A Stranger in the Kingdom '98
Disappearances '06
Jonathan Craven (1965-)
Wes Craven Presents Mind Ripper '95
The Hills Have Eyes 2 '07
Wes Craven (1939-2015)
Last House on the Left '72
The Hills Have Eyes '77
Deadly Blessing '81
Swamp Thing '82
The Hills Have Eyes, Part 2 '84
A Nightmare on Elm Street '84
A Nightmare on Elm Street 3: Dream Warriors '87
Shocker '89
The People under the Stairs '91
Wes Craven's New Nightmare '94
Paris, je t'aime '06
Pulse '06
The Hills Have Eyes 2 '07
My Soul to Take '10
Darlene Craviotto
Angel Dusted '81
Squanto: A Warrior's Tale '94
Wayne Crawford
Valley Girl '83
Jake Speed '86
Chad Gomez Creasy
Sydney White '07
Legally Blondes '09
James A. Creelman (1901-41)
Vagabond Lover '29
The Most Dangerous Game '32
King Kong '33
Eran Creevy (1976-)
Shifty '08
Welcome to the Punch '13
Collide '17
James Cresson (1934-2004)
The Morning After '86
Chattahoochee '89
Defenseless '91
Destin Daniel Cretton
Short Term 12 '13
The Glass Castle '17
The Shack '17
Just Mercy '19
Michael Crichton (1942-2008)
Sex Through a Window '72
Westworld '73
Coma '78
The Great Train Robbery '79
Looker '81
Runaway '84
Jurassic Park '93
Rising Sun '93
Twister '96
The 13th Warrior '99
Armando Crispino (1925-)
Dead Are Alive '72
Commandos '73
Autopsy '75
Michael Cristofer (1945-)
Falling in Love '84
The Witches of Eastwick '87
The Bonfire of the Vanities '90
Mr. Jones '93
Breaking Up '97
Gia '98
Original Sin '01
Georgia O'Keefe '09
Chuck '17
David Cronenberg (1943-)
They Came from Within '75
Rabid '77
Fast Company '78
The Brood '79
Scanners '81
Videodrome '83
The Fly '86
Dead Ringers '88
Naked Lunch '91
Crash '95
eXistenZ '99
Cosmopolis '12
Karen Croner
One True Thing '98
Admission '13
Allison Cross
Serving in Silence: The Margarethe Cammermeyer Story '95
Blood & Wine '96
Beverley Cross (1932-98)
Jason and the Argonauts '63
The Long Ships '64
Genghis Khan '65
Half a Sixpence '67
Sinbad and the Eye of the Tiger '77
Clash of the Titans '81
Shauna Cross (1976-)
Whip It '09
What to Expect When You're Expecting '12
If I Stay '14
Bad Santa 2 '16
Bill Crounse
9 1/2 Ninjas '90
American Cyborg: Steel Warrior '94
Lance Crouther (1962-)
Down to Earth '01
Good Hair '09
Cameron Crowe (1957-)
Fast Times at Ridgemont High '82
Say Anything '89
Singles '92
Jerry Maguire '96
Almost Famous '00
Vanilla Sky '01
Elizabethtown '05
Pearl Jam Twenty '11
Aloha '15
Christopher Crowe (1948-)
Last Chase '81
Nightmares '83
Mean Season '85
Off Limits '87
The Last of the Mohicans '92
Whispers in the Dark '92
Fear '96
John Crowther
Kill and Kill Again '81
The Evil That Men Do '84
Damned River '89
Jim Cruickshank
Tough Guys '86
Three Men and a Baby '87
Mr. Destiny '90
Sister Act 2: Back in the Habit '93
Man of the House '95
Christmas in Wonderland '07
The Night Before the Night Before Christmas '10
My Future Boyfriend '11
Jon Cryer (1965-)
The Pompatus of Love '95
Went to Coney Island on a Mission from God. . . Be Back by Five '98
Billy Crystal (1947-)
Memories of Me '88
Mr. Saturday Night '92
City Slickers 2: The Legend of Curly's Gold '94
Forget Paris '95
America's Sweethearts '01
Alfonso Cuarón (1961-)
Y Tu Mama Tambien '01
Children of Men '06
Paris, je t'aime '06
Gravity '13
Roma '18
Carlos Cuaron (1966-)
Who the Hell is Juliette? '98
Y Tu Mama Tambien '01
Rudo y Cursi '09
Sugar Kisses '13
Jonas Cuaron
Gravity '13
Desierto '16
Allan Cubitt
St. Ives '98
Anna Karenina '00
The Hound of the Baskervilles '02
The Boys Are Back '09
Milo G. Cuccia
Venus in Furs '70
Count Dracula '71
Tom Cudworth
Restaurant '98
Ten Benny '98
Gerald Cuesta
L.I.E. '01
Roadie '11
Michael Cuesta (1963-)
L.I.E. '01
Roadie '11
Alma Cullen
A Village Affair '95
All the King's Men '99
Mike Cullen
Horatio Hornblower '99
Bloodlines '05
Robert Cullen
As You Like It '36
Cop Out '10
Adamo P. Cultraro (1973-)
Bad Ass '09
Tactical Force '11
Carmen Culver
Agatha Christie's Murder is Easy '82
The Last Days of Pompeii '84
If Tomorrow Comes '86
David Cummings
The Last Seduction 2 '98
Kevin & Perry Go Large '00
Rusty Cundieff (1965-)
House Party 2: The Pajama Jam '91
Fear of a Black Hat '94
Tales from the Hood '95
Sprung '96
Jack Cunningham (1882-1941)
Beyond the Rocks '22
Don Q., Son of Zorro '25
The Black Pirate '26
Captain Salvation '27
The Viking '28
The Guilty Generation '31
The Rider of Death Valley '32
It's a Gift '34
The Old-Fashioned Way '34
Mississippi '35
Jere P. Cunningham
The Last of the Finest '90
Boss of Bosses '99
Michael Cunningham (1952-)
Splatter University '84
A Home at the End of the World '04
Evening '07
Terry Cunningham
Land of the Free '98
The Stray '00
Code Hunter '02
Pat Cupo
Smalltime '96
One Last Ride '03
Tim Curnen
Forbidden World '82
Ghostwarrior '86
Brian Currie
Two Tickets to Paradise '06
Green Book '18
Valerie Curtin (1945-)
And Justice for All '79
Inside Moves '80
Best Friends '82
Unfaithfully Yours '84
Toys '92
Dan Curtis (1928-2006)
Burnt Offerings '76
Trilogy of Terror 2 '96
Nathaniel Curtis (1909-83)
Blood on the Sun '45
Jack & the Beanstalk '52
Richard Curtis (1956-)
The Tall Guy '89
Four Weddings and a Funeral '94
Bean '97
Notting Hill '99
Bridget Jones's Diary '01
Love Actually '03
Bridget Jones: The Edge of Reason '04
The Girl in the Cafe '05
Pirate Radio '09
War Horse '11
About Time '13
Mary and Martha '13
Trash '14
Mamma Mia! Here We Go Again '18
Yesterday '19
Vondie Curtis-Hall (1956-)
Gridlock'd '96
Waist Deep '06
Stephen J. Curwick (1960-)
Police Academy 5: Assignment Miami Beach '88
Police Academy 6: City under Siege '89
John Cusack (1966-)
Grosse Pointe Blank '97
High Fidelity '00
War, Inc. '08
Carlton Cuse
San Andreas '15
Rampage '18
Neil Cuthbert
The Return of the Swamp Thing '89
Hocus Pocus '93
Mystery Men '99
The Adventures of Pluto Nash '02
Ron Cutler
Blood Red '88
Article 99 '92
Catherine Cyran
Bloodfist 2 '90
A Cry in the Wild '90
Slumber Party Massacre 3 '90
Futurekick '91
Fire on the Amazon '93
True Heart '97
Werewolf: The Beast Among Us '12
Honey 3: Dare to Dance '16
Czar (1973-)
See S. Craig Zahler
Renee Daalder (1944-)
Massacre at Central High '76
Habitat '97
Jean-Loup Dabadie (1938-)
Cesar & Rosalie '72
The Savage '75
Ingram D'Abbes
Song of Freedom '36
Big Fella '37
Cherien Dabis
Amreeka '09
May in Summer '13
May in the Summer '13
Abdel Raouf Dafri
Mesrine: Part 1-Killer Instinct '08
Mesrine: Part 2-Public Enemy Number 1 '08
Don DaGradi
Lady and the Tramp '55
Blackbeard's Ghost '67
Bedknobs and Broomsticks '71
Olivier Dahan (1967-)
La Vie en Rose '07
My Own Love Song '10
John Dahl (1956-)
Kill Me Again '89
Red Rock West '93
Julia Dahl
Uptown Girls '03
Flirting with Forty '09
Roald Dahl (1916-90)
36 Hours '64
You Only Live Twice '67
Chitty Chitty Bang Bang '68
The Night Digger '71
Willy Wonka & the Chocolate Factory '71
Minako Daira
One Missed Call '03
One Missed Call 2 '05
Art D'Alessandro
The Final Season '07
She Drives Me Crazy '07
Mayor Cupcake '11
John Francis Daley (1985-)
Horrible Bosses '11
Cloudy with a Chance of Meatballs 2 '13
The Incredible Burt Wonderstone '13
Vacation '15
Spider-Man: Homecoming '17
Herbert Dalmas (1902-89)
Address Unknown '44
An American Romance '44
Ian Dalrymple (1903-89)
The Good Companions '33
Storm in a Teacup '37
Dear Mr. Prohack '49
Darren Dalton (1965-)
Hourglass '95
The Day the Earth Stopped '08
The Land That Time Forgot '09
Lance Daly
Kisses '08
The Pagan Queen '09
Life's a Breeze '14
Black '47 '18
Janeen Damian (1961-)
Hot Tamale '06
Moondance Alexander '07
Marley & Me: The Puppy Years '11
A Princess for Christmas '11
The Sweeter Side of Life '13
A Royal Christmas '14
High Strung '16
Michael Damian (1962-)
Hot Tamale '06
Moondance Alexander '07
Marley & Me: The Puppy Years '11
A Princess for Christmas '11
The Sweeter Side of Life '13
A Royal Christmas '14
High Strung '16
Damiano Damiani (1922-2013)
Confessions of a Police Captain '72
How to Kill a Judge '75
Nick Damici
Mulberry Street '06
Stake Land '10
We Are What We Are '13
Cold in July '14
Bushwick '17
Suso Cecchi D'Amico (1914-2010)
Bellissima '51
Too Bad She's Bad '54
White Nights '57
Big Deal on Madonna Street '58
Rocco and His Brothers '60
The Leopard '63
The Queens '66
Man, Pride and Vengeance '67
Conversation Piece '75
The Innocent '76
Jesus of Nazareth '77
The Sky Is Falling '00
Matt Damon (1970-)
Good Will Hunting '97
Gerry '02
Promised Land '12
Oniroku Dan
Flower & Snake '74 '74
Flower & Snake '04
Flower & Snake 2 '05
Clemence Dane (1888-1965)
Anna Karenina '35
Fire Over England '37
Sidewalks of London '38
Vacation from Marriage '45

Massimo De Rita
Companeros *'70*
Street Law *'74*
War Goddess *'74*
Chino *'75*
Revolver *'75*
The Switch *'76*

Everett De Roche (1946-)
The Night After Halloween *'79*
Road Games *'81*
Razorback *'84*
Link *'86*
Visitors *'03*
Nature's Grave *'08*

Gino De Santis
Atom Age Vampire *'61*
Fury of Achilles *'62*

Guiseppe de Santis (1917-97)
Ossessione *'42*
Bitter Rice *'49*

Vittorio De Sica (1902-74)
The Children Are Watching Us *'44*
The Bicycle Thief *'48*
Umberto D *'55*
Two Women *'61*

Steven E. de Souza (1947-)
48 Hrs. *'82*
Return of Captain Invincible *'83*
Commando *'85*
The Running Man *'87*
The Spirit *'87*
Bad Dreams *'88*
Die Hard *'88*
Seven Hours to Judgment *'88*
Die Hard 2: Die Harder *'90*
Hudson Hawk *'91*
Ricochet *'91*
Beverly Hills Cop 3 *'94*
The Flintstones *'94*
Street Fighter *'94*
Judge Dredd *'95*
Knock Off *'98*
Possessed *'00*
Blast *'04*

Pedro De Urdimalas
Over the Waves *'49*
Pepe El Toro *'53*

Marina de Van (1971-)
Under the Sand *'00*
8 Women *'02*

Alfredo de Villa
Washington Heights *'02*
Adrift in Manhattan *'07*

Gary De Vore (1941-97)
Back Roads *'81*
The Dogs of War *'81*
Raw Deal *'86*
Running Scared *'86*
Timecop *'94*

Karen De Wolf (1909-89)
Blondie Plays Cupid *'40*
Blondie in Society *'41*
Blondie Goes Latin *'42*

Annie de Young
The Day the World Ended *'01*
Earth *vs.* the Spider *'01*
MTV's Wuthering Heights *'03*

Zach Dean
Deadfall *'12*
24 Hours to Live *'17*

Geoff Deane
It's a Boy Girl Thing *'06*
Kinky Boots *'06*

Nick Dear (1955-)
Persuasion *'95*
The Gambler *'97*
The Turn of the Screw *'99*
Byron *'03*

William Dear (1944-)
Timerider *'83*
Harry and the Hendersons *'87*
Simon Says *'07*

James Dearden (1949-)
Fatal Attraction *'87*
A Kiss Before Dying *'91*
Rogue Trader *'98*

Frank Deasy (1959-2009)
Captives *'94*
Prozac Nation *'01*
The Rats *'01*

John DeBello (1952-)
Attack of the Killer Tomatoes *'77*
Happy Hour *'87*
Return of the Killer Tomatoes! *'88*
Killer Tomatoes Strike Back *'90*
Killer Tomatoes Eat France *'91*

Dean DeBlois (1970-)
Lilo & Stitch *'02*
How to Train Your Dragon *'10*
How to Train Your Dragon 2 *'14*
How to Train Your Dragon: The Hidden World *'19*

Denise DeClue
About Last Night. . . *'86*
For Keeps *'88*
The Cherokee Kid *'96*

Didier Decoin (1945-)
Balzac: A Life of Passion *'99*
The Count of Monte Cristo *'99*
Jakob the Liar *'99*
Napoleon *'03*
The Crown Prince *'06*

David DeCoteau (1962-)
Femalien *'96*
Femalien 2 *'98*
Beastly Boyz *'06*

Edward Decter (1959-)
There's Something about Mary *'98*
The Santa Clause 2 *'02*
The Lizzie McGuire Movie *'03*
The Santa Clause 3: The Escape Clause *'06*
The Wild *'06*

Miles Deem (1914-94)
See Demofilo Fidani

Frank Deese
The Principal *'87*
Josh and S.A.M. *'93*

David DeFalco
Gangland *'00*
Chaos *'05*
Wrong Side of Town *'10*

Christopher DeFaria (1959-)
Amityville 1992: It's About Time *'92*
Amityville: A New Generation *'93*

James DeFelice
Why Shoot the Teacher *'79*
Out of the Dark *'88*

Michael DeForrest
Camille 2000 *'69*
The Lickerish Quartet *'70*

Brian Degas (1935-)
Barbarella *'68*
Danger: Diabolik *'68*

Michael deGuzman
Jaws: The Revenge *'87*
Hidden in America *'96*

Paul Dehn (1912-76)
Goldfinger *'64*
The Spy Who Came in from the Cold *'65*
Beneath the Planet of the Apes *'70*
Fragment of Fear *'70*
Escape from the Planet of the Apes *'71*
Conquest of the Planet of the Apes *'72*
Murder on the Orient Express *'74*

Len Deighton (1929-)
Billion Dollar Brain *'67*
Oh! What a Lovely War *'69*

Edward Dein (1907-84)
The Falcon Strikes Back *'43*
Shack Out on 101 *'55*

Steve DeJarnatt
Strange Brew *'83*
Miracle Mile *'89*

Fred Dekker (1959-)
Night of the Creeps *'86*
The Monster Squad *'87*
If Looks Could Kill *'91*
RoboCop 3 *'91*
The Predator *'18*

Alvaro del Amo
Intruso *'93*
Jealousy *'99*

Remigio del Grosso (1912-)
Neapolitan Carousel *'54*
Mill of the Stone Women *'60*
Conquest of Mycene *'63*

Hampton Del Ruth (1879-1958)
Tillie's Punctured Romance *'14*
Air Eagles *'31*

Guillermo del Toro (1964-)
Cronos *'94*
The Devil's Backbone *'01*
Hellboy *'04*
Pan's Labyrinth *'06*
Hellboy II: The Golden Army *'08*
Don't Be Afraid of the Dark *'11*
The Hobbit: An Unexpected Journey *'12*
The Hobbit: The Desolation of Smaug *'13*
Pacific Rim *'13*
The Hobbit: The Battle of the Five Armies *'14*
Crimson Peak *'15*
The Shape of Water *'17*
Scary Stories to Tell in the Dark *'19*

Jean Delannoy (1908-)
Imperial Venus *'63*
Action Man *'67*

Matthieu Delaporte
Renaissance *'06*
22 Bullets *'10*

Youssef Delara
ESL: English as a Second Language *'05*
Filly Brown *'12*
The Bounce Back *'16*

R.F. Delderfield
Value for Money *'55*
Where There's a Will *'55*

Walter DeLeon (1884-1947)
Lonely Wives *'31*
Girl Crazy *'32*
Make Me a Star *'32*
Union Depot *'32*
Ruggles of Red Gap *'35*
The Princess Comes Across *'36*
Rhythm on the Range *'36*
Artists and Models *'37*
Waikiki Wedding *'37*
The Big Broadcast of 1938 *'38*
College Swing *'38*
The Cat and the Canary *'39*
Union Pacific *'39*
The Ghost Breakers *'40*
Birth of the Blues *'41*
Pot o' Gold *'41*
Little Giant *'46*
Scared Stiff *'53*

Francis Delia
Freeway *'88*
Trouble Bound *'92*

Jeffrey Dell (1899-1985)
The Flemish Farm *'43*
Lucky Jim *'58*

Vina Delmar (1903-90)
The Awful Truth *'37*
Make Way for Tomorrow *'37*

Julie Delpy (1969-)
Before Sunset *'04*
2 Days in Paris *'07*
The Countess *'09*
Before Midnight *'13*
Lolo *'15*

Rudy DeLuca
Silent Movie *'76*
High Anxiety *'77*
Caveman *'81*
Transylvania 6-5000 *'85*
Million Dollar Mystery *'87*
Life Stinks *'91*
Dracula: Dead and Loving It *'95*
Screw Loose *'99*

Paul DeMeo
Zone Troopers *'84*
The Wrong Guys *'88*
The Rocketeer *'91*

William DeMeo (1971-)
Wannabes *'01*
Searching for Bobby D *'05*

Jonathan Demme (1944-2017)
Angels Hard As They Come *'71*
Hot Box *'72*
Caged Heat *'74*
Fighting Mad *'76*
The Truth About Charlie *'02*

James DeMonaco (1968-)
Jack *'96*
The Negotiator *'98*
Assault on Precinct 13 *'05*
Skinwalkers *'07*
Staten Island *'09*
The Purge *'13*
The Purge: Anarchy *'14*
The Purge: Election Year *'16*
The First Purge *'18*

Albert DeMond (1901-73)
The Love Trap *'29*
Skyway *'33*
Flirting With Danger *'35*
The Purple Monster Strikes *'45*
The Red Menace *'49*

Jacques Demy (1931-90)
Umbrellas of Cherbourg *'64*
The Young Girls of Rochefort *'68*
Model Shop *'69*
Donkey Skin *'70*
Pied Piper *'72*
A Slightly Pregnant Man *'79*

Christopher Denham (1985-)
Home Movie *'08*
Preservation *'14*
Area 51 *'15*

Claire Denis (1948-)
Chocolat *'88*
I Can't Sleep *'93*
Nenette and Boni *'96*
Beau Travail *'98*
Friday Night *'02*
The Intruder *'04*
35 Shots of Rum *'08*
White Material *'10*
Let the Sunshine In *'17*
High Life *'18*

Chris Denk
Bats: Human Harvest *'07*
Alpha and Omega *'10*
Reef 2: High Tide *'12*

Henry Denker (1912-2012)
Time Limit *'57*
The Hook *'63*
Twilight of Honor *'63*

Wilton Denmark
Cain's Cutthroats *'71*
Johnny Firecloud *'75*

Gill Dennis
Return to Oz *'85*
Riders of the Purple Sage *'96*

Without Evidence *'96*
Walk the Line *'05*

Robert C. Dennis (1915-83)
Terror in the Haunted House *'58*
The Amazing Captain Nemo *'78*

Pen Densham (1947-)
Robin Hood: Prince of Thieves *'91*
Lifepod *'93*
Moll Flanders *'96*
Houdini *'98*

Alan Dent (1905-78)
Henry V *'44*
Hamlet *'48*

Greg DePaul
Killer Bud *'00*
Saving Silverman *'01*

Jacques Deray (1929-2003)
La Piscine *'69*
Borsalino *'70*

Arpad DeRiso
Hercules and the Black Pirate *'60*
Caesar the Conqueror *'63*

Everett DeRoche (1946-)
See Everett De Roche

Bob DeRosa
The Air I Breathe *'07*
Killers *'10*

Scott Derrickson
Hellraiser 5: Inferno *'00*
Urban Legends 2: Final Cut *'00*
The Exorcism of Emily Rose *'05*
Sinister *'12*
Deliver Us From Evil *'14*
Devil's Knot *'14*
Sinister 2 *'15*
Doctor Strange *'16*

Georges des Esseintes
Animal Instincts *'92*
Secret Games *'92*

Gino DeSanctis
See Gino De Santis

Arnaud Desplechin (1960-)
La Sentinelle *'92*
My Sex Life. . . Or How I Got into an Argument *'96*
Esther Kahn *'00*
Kings and Queen *'04*
A Christmas Tale *'08*
Jimmy P. *'13*
My Golden Days *'15*

Helen Deutsch (1906-92)
National Velvet *'44*
Golden Earrings *'47*
The Loves of Carmen *'48*
Shockproof *'49*
King Solomon's Mines *'50*
It's a Big Country *'51*
Valley of the Dolls *'67*

Andrew Deutschman
Paranormal Activity 5: The Ghost Dimension *'15*
Project Almanac *'15*

Jacques Deval (1895-1972)
Cafe Metropole *'37*
Balalaika *'39*
Her Cardboard Lover *'42*

Jason DeVan
Along Came the Devil *'18*
Along Came the Devil 2 *'19*

D.V. DeVincentis
Grosse Pointe Blank *'97*
High Fidelity *'00*
Lay the Favorite *'12*

Dennis Devine
Things *'93*
Vampires of Sorority Row: Kickboxers From Hell *'99*
Chain of Souls *'00*

Scott Devine (1969-)
Shark Attack *'99*
Shark Attack 2 *'00*
Shark Attack 3: Megalodon *'02*

Dean Devlin (1962-)
Universal Soldier *'92*
Stargate *'94*
Independence Day *'96*
Godzilla *'98*
The Triangle *'05*
Independence Day: Resurgence *'16*
Geostorm *'17*

Christopher DeVore
The Elephant Man *'80*
Frances *'82*
Hamlet *'90*

Jack DeWitt (1900-81)
Bells of San Fernando *'47*
Bomba, the Jungle Boy *'49*
The Lost Volcano *'50*
Battles of Chief Pontiac *'52*
Sitting Bull *'54*
Cell 2455, Death Row *'55*
Women's Prison *'55*
Rumble on the Docks *'56*
Portland Expose *'57*
The Purple Gang *'59*
Five Guns to Tombstone *'60*
A Man Called Horse *'70*
Man in the Wilderness *'71*
Neptune Factor *'73*
The Return of a Man Called Horse *'76*
Sky Riders *'76*

Karen DeWolf (1909-89)
Meet the Stewarts *'42*
Getting Gertie's Garter *'45*
Johnny Allegro *'49*
Slightly French *'49*

Pete Dexter (1943-)
Rush *'91*
Mulholland Falls *'95*
Michael *'96*

Annie DeYoung
Return to Halloweentown *'06*
Princess Protection Program *'09*
16 Wishes *'10*
StarStruck *'10*
Girl *vs.* Monster *'12*

Elize D'Haene
Red Shoe Diaries: Strip Poker *'96*
Red Shoe Diaries: Luscious Lola *'00*

Fernando Di Leo (1932-2003)
Johnny Yuma *'66*
Hate for Hate *'67*
Long Days of Revenge *'67*
Caliber 9 *'72*
The Boss *'73*
Hired to Kill *'73*
The Italian Connection *'73*
Shoot First, Die Later *'74*
Kidnap Syndicate *'76*
Live Like a Cop, Die Like a Man *'76*
Rulers of the City *'76*

Edward Di Lorenzo
A Place Called Glory *'66*
Lady Frankenstein *'72*

Vince Di Meglio
Smother *'08*
Marmaduke *'10*

Catherine Di Napoli
Bartleby *'01*
(Untitled) *'09*

Mario di Nardo
The Cats *'68*
Five Dolls for an August Moon *'70*
Roy Colt and Winchester Jack *'70*
Mean Machine *'73*

Gerald Di Pego (1941-)
Sharky's Machine *'81*
Phenomenon *'96*
Message in a Bottle *'98*
Instinct *'99*
Angel Eyes *'01*
The Forgotten *'04*

David Diamond
Body Count *'97*
Family Man *'00*

Appointment With Danger '51

Brian Duffield
Insurgent '15
Jane Got a Gun '16
The Babysitter '17
Underwater '20

Jo Duffy
Puppet Master 4 '93
Puppet Master 5: The Final Chapter '94

Troy Duffy (1971-)
Boondock Saints '99
The Boondock Saints II: All Saints Day '09

John Duigan (1949-)
The Year My Voice Broke '87
Flirting '89
Wide Sargasso Sea '92
Sirens '94
The Leading Man '96
Head in the Clouds '04

Bruno Dumont (1958-)
The Life of Jesus '96
Humanity '99
Twentynine Palms '03
Flanders '06
Hors Satan '11

Don Carlos Dunaway
Cujo '83
Impulse '84

David Duncan (1913-99)
The Leech Woman '59
Monster on the Campus '59
The Time Machine '60

Patrick Duncan (1963-)
A Home of Our Own '93
Nick of Time '95

Patrick Sheane Duncan (1947-)
Mr. Holland's Opus '95
Courage Under Fire '96
The Wall '99
A Painted House '03

Peter Duncan (1954-)
Children of the Revolution '95
A Little Bit of Soul '97

Lena Dunham (1986-)
Tiny Furniture '10
Nobody Walks '12

Winifred Dunn
Sparrows '26
Twinkletoes '26

John Gregory Dunne (1932-2003)
Panic in Needle Park '71
A Star Is Born '76
True Confessions '81
Broken Trust '95
Up Close and Personal '96

Philip Dunne (1908-92)
The Count of Monte Cristo '34
Suez '38
The Rains Came '39
Swanee River '39
Johnny Apollo '40
How Green Was My Valley '41
Son of Fury '42
Forever Amber '47
The Ghost and Mrs. Muir '47
The Luck of the Irish '48
Pinky '49
David and Bathsheba '51
Way of a Gaucho '52
The Robe '53
Demetrius and the Gladiators '54
The Egyptian '54
Three Brave Men '57
The Agony and the Ecstasy '65

Marcus Dunstan
Feast '06
Saw 4 '07
Feast 2: Sloppy Seconds '08
Saw 5 '08
The Collector '09
Saw 6 '09
Saw 3D: The Final Chapter '10
Piranha 3DD '11
The Collection '12

Cheryl Dunye (1966-)
The Watermelon Woman '97
The Owls '09

Quentin Dupieux
Rubber '10
Wrong Cops '13

Jay Duplass (1973-)
Baghead '08
Cyrus '10
The Do-Deca-Pentathlon '12
Jeff, Who Lives at Home '12
Outside In '17
Table 19 '17

Mark Duplass (1976-)
Baghead '08
Cyrus '10
Black Rock '12
The Do-Deca-Pentathlon '12
Jeff, Who Lives at Home '12
Creep '15
Blue Jay '16
Table 19 '17
Paddleton '19

Carl DuPre
Detroit Rock City '99
The Prophecy 3: The Ascent '99
Hellraiser: Hellseeker '02
Hellraiser: Hellworld '05

Marguerite Duras (1914-96)
Hiroshima, Mon Amour '59
Nathalie Granger '72

Brook Durham
Mammoth '06
Showdown at Area 51 '07
Merlin and the Book of Beasts '09
Red: Werewolf Hunter '10
Witchslayer Gretl '12

Arnaud d'Usseau (1916-90)
Just Off Broadway '42
Horror Express '72
Psychomania '73

Robert Duvall (1931-)
The Apostle '97
Assassination Tango '03
Wild Horses '15

Julien Duvivier (1896-1967)
Pepe Le Moko '37
Anna Karenina '48

Allie Dvorin
The Sandlot 3: Heading Home '07
A Novel Romance '11

Jim Dwyer (1970-)
Frisk '95
Little Shots of Happiness '97
The Boy With the Sun in His Eyes '09

H. Kaye Dyal
Lone Wolf McQuade '83
Project: Eliminator '91

Eric Eason
Manito '03
Journey to the End of the Night '06
A Better Life '11

Robert Easter (1945-2002)
The Toolbox Murders '78
Sworn to Justice '97
Kiss Toledo Goodbye '00

Charles Eastman (1929-2009)
The All-American Boy '73
Second-Hand Hearts '81

George Eastman (1854-1932)
Anthropophagus: The Grim Reaper '80
Tower of the Firstborn '98

James Eastwood
Devil Girl from Mars '54
The Counterfeit Plan '57

James Eaves
Hellbreeder '04
The Witches Hammer '06

Thom Eberhardt (1947-)
Night of the Comet '84
The Night Before '88
All I Want for Christmas '91
Captain Ron '92
Honey, I Blew Up the Kid '92
Ratz '99

Roger Ebert (1942-2013)
Beyond the Valley of the Dolls '70
Beneath the Valley of the Ultra-Vixens '79

Uli Edel (1947-)
Dark Kingdom: The Dragon King '04
The Baader Meinhof Complex '08

David Edgar (1948-)
The Life and Adventures of Nicholas Nickleby '81
Lady Jane '85

Marriott Edgar
Windbag the Sailor '36
Good Morning, Boys '37
Ask a Policeman '38
Hey! Hey! USA! '38
The Ghost Train '41
Miss London Ltd. '43
Bees in Paradise '44

Joel Edgerton (1974-)
The Square '08
Felony '13
The Gift '15
Jane Got a Gun '16
Boy Erased '18
The King '19

Patrick Edgeworth (1942-)
BMX Bandits '83
Raw Deal '86

Eric Edson
The Rose and the Jackal '90
Uncaged Heart '07

A.J. Edwards
The Better Angels '14
Age Out '19

Blake Edwards (1922-2010)
Panhandle '48
Stampede '49
All Ashore '53
The Atomic Kid '54
Drive a Crooked Road '54
My Sister Eileen '55
Operation Mad Ball '57
The Notorious Landlady '62
Soldier in the Rain '63
The Pink Panther '64
A Shot in the Dark '64
What Did You Do in the War, Daddy? '66
The Party '68
Darling Lili '70
Wild Rovers '71
Return of the Pink Panther '74
The Tamarind Seed '74
Revenge of the Pink Panther '78
10 '79
S.O.B. '81
Trail of the Pink Panther '82
Victor/Victoria '82
Curse of the Pink Panther '83
The Man Who Loved Women '83
City Heat '84
A Fine Mess '86
That's Life! '86
Sunset '88
Skin Deep '89
Switch '91
Son of the Pink Panther '93

Cheryl Edwards
Save the Last Dance '01
Against the Ropes '04
Frankie and Alice '10

Cory Edwards
Hoodwinked '05
Hoodwinked Too! Hood *vs.* Evil '11

Paul F. Edwards
Fire Birds '90
Ordeal in the Arctic '93

Robert Edwards
Land of the Blind '06
One More Time '15

Todd Edwards (1971-)
Hoodwinked '05
Hoodwinked Too! Hood *vs.* Evil '11

Sam Egan
Elvira, Mistress of the Dark '88
Knights of Bloodsteel '09

Dave Eggers (1970-)
Away We Go '09
Where the Wild Things Are '09
Promised Land '12
The Circle '17

Robert Eggers
The Witch '16
The Lighthouse '19

Atom Egoyan (1960-)
Next of Kin '84
Family Viewing '87
Speaking Parts '89
The Adjuster '91
Calendar '93
Exotica '94
The Sweet Hereafter '96
Felicia's Journey '99
Ararat '02
Where the Truth Lies '05
Adoration '08
The Captive '14

Kerry Ehrin
Mr. Wrong '95
Inspector Gadget '99

Bernd Eichinger (1949-2011)
Downfall '04
Perfume: The Story of a Murderer '06
The Baader Meinhof Complex '08

Robert Eisele (1948-)
The Great Debaters '07
Hurricane Season '09

Lee Eisenberg
Year One '09
Bad Teacher '11
Good Boys '19

Sergei Eisenstein (1898-1948)
Strike '24
The Battleship Potemkin '25
Ten Days That Shook the World '27
Que Viva Mexico '32
Alexander Nevsky '38
Ivan the Terrible, Part 1 '44
Ivan the Terrible, Part 2 '46

Jo Eisinger (1909-91)
Gilda '46
Night and the City '50
The System '53
Bedevilled '55
The Big Boodle '57
Crime of Passion '57
The House of the Seven Hawks '59
They Came to Rob Las Vegas '68

Philip Eisner
Event Horizon '97
Firestarter 2: Rekindled '02
Mutant Chronicles '08

John (Anthony Hinds) Elder (1922-)
The Curse of the Werewolf '61
Kiss of the Vampire '62
The Phantom of the Opera '62
The Evil of Frankenstein '64
Dracula, Prince of Darkness '66
Frankenstein Created Woman '66
Plague of the Zombies '66
Rasputin the Mad Monk '66
The Reptile '66
Dracula Has Risen from the Grave '68
The Scars of Dracula '70
Taste the Blood of Dracula '70
Frankenstein and the Monster from Hell '74

Lonnie Elder, III (1926-96)
Sounder '72
A Woman Called Moses '78
Bustin' Loose '81

Kevin Elders
Iron Eagle '86
Iron Eagle 2 '88
Echelon Conspiracy '09

John Eldridge (1917-60)
The Smallest Show on Earth '57
Operation Amsterdam '60

Laurice Elehwany
My Girl '91
The Amazing Panda Adventure '95
The Brady Bunch Movie '95

Harry Elfont (1968-)
A Very Brady Sequel '96
Can't Hardly Wait '98
The Flintstones in Viva Rock Vegas '00
Josie and the Pussycats '01
Surviving Christmas '04
Made of Honor '08
Leap Year '10

Caroline Eliacheff
La Ceremonie '95
Merci pour le Chocolat '00

Michael Elias (1940-)
The Frisco Kid '79
The Jerk '79
Serial '80
Young Doctors in Love '82

Joyce Eliason (1934-)
Tell Me a Riddle '80
Babycakes '89
A Good Day to Die '95
Oldest Confederate Widow Tells All '95
Titanic '96
The Last Don '97
The Last Don 2 '98
Blonde '01
Gracie's Choice '04
A Perfect Day '06
America '09

Edward Eliscu (1902-98)
Paddy O'Day '35
Little Miss Nobody '36

Thomas Ellice (1939-)
Devices and Desires '91
Albert's Memorial '09

Doug Ellin (1968-)
Phat Beach '96
Kissing a Fool '98
Entourage '15

David Elliot
Four Brothers '05
Catacombs '07
G.I. Joe: The Rise of Cobra '09

Michael Elliot
Carmen: A Hip Hopera '01
Brown Sugar '02
Like Mike '02
Just Wright '10
Aaliyah: The Princess of R&B '14

Pearse Elliott
The Mighty Celt '05
Shrooms '07

Stephan Elliott (1963-)
The Adventures of Priscilla, Queen of the Desert '94
Eye of the Beholder '99
Rio, I Love You '14
Swinging Safari '19

Ted Elliott (1961-)
Little Monsters '89
Aladdin '92
The Puppet Masters '94
The Mask of Zorro '98
Small Soldiers '98
The Road to El Dorado '00
Shrek '01
Pirates of the Caribbean: The Curse of the Black Pearl '03
Pirates of the Caribbean: Dead Man's Chest '06
Pirates of the Caribbean: At World's End '07
Pirates of the Caribbean: On Stranger Tides '11
The Lone Ranger '13

William Elliott (1920-2012)
See Ray Bradbury

Bob Ellis (1942-)
Man of Flowers '84
Cactus '86
The Nostradamus Kid '92

Bret Easton Ellis (1964-)
The Informers '09
The Canyons '13
The Curse of Downers Grove '15

Kirk Ellis
Anne Frank: The Whole Story '01
John Adams '08

Michael Ellis
Bounty Hunters 2: Hardball '97
The Wedding Planner '01
An Invisible Sign '11

Robert Ellis (1892-1974)
Dangerous Appointment '34
The Quitter '34
Charlie Chan in Egypt '35
Charlie Chan at the Circus '36
Charlie Chan at the Race Track '36
Charlie Chan at the Olympics '37
Rascals '38
Charlie Chan in City of Darkness '39
Star Dust '40
Iceland '42
Hello, Frisco, Hello '43
Four Jills in a Jeep '44
Something for the Boys '44
Do You Love Me? '46
If I'm Lucky '46

Sean Ellis (1970-)
Cashback '06
The Broken '08
Metro Manila '13
Anthropoid '16

Trey Ellis (1962-)
The Inkwell '94
The Tuskegee Airmen '95
Good Fences '03

Joseph Ellison (1948-)
Don't Go in the House '80
Joey '85

James Ellroy
Street Kings '08
Rampart '11

Carl Ellsworth
Red Eye '05
Disturbia '07
The Last House on the Left '09

Neil Elman
Mongolian Death Worm '10
I Spit on Your Grave 2 '13
LA Apocalypse '14

Guy Elmes (1920-98)
Bad Blonde '53
Across the Bridge '57
Serious Charge '59
The Big Scam '79

Kirsten Elms
Banshee *'06*
Texas Chainsaw 3D *'13*
Ben Elton (1959-)
Maybe Baby *'99*
All Is True *'18*
Sheri Elwood
Deeply *'99*
The Christmas Clause *'08*
Kevin Elyot (1951-2014)
Clapham Junction *'07*
Christopher and His Kind *'11*
Matt Ember (1961-)
Failure to Launch *'06*
Get Smart *'08*
Home *'15*
John Emerson (1874-1956)
His Picture in the Papers *'16*
Struggle *'31*
The Girl from Missouri *'34*
Roland Emmerich (1955-)
Ghost Chase *'88*
Stargate *'94*
Independence Day *'96*
Godzilla *'98*
The Day After Tomorrow *'04*
10,000 B.C. *'08*
2012 *'09*
Independence Day: Resurgence *'16*
Toby Emmerich (1963-)
Frequency *'00*
The Last Mimzy *'07*
E.V.H. Emmett (1902-71)
Sabotage *'36*
Non-Stop New York *'37*
John Enbom (1968-)
The Low Life *'95*
The Good Doctor *'11*
Cy Endfield (1914-95)
The Master Plan *'55*
Child in the House *'56*
Zulu *'64*
Sands of the Kalahari *'65*
Guy Endore (1900-70)
Mad Love *'35*
Devil Doll *'36*
Lady from Louisiana *'42*
The Story of G.I. Joe *'45*
Johnny Allegro *'49*
Tomorrow Is Another Day *'51*
Captain Sinbad *'63*
Samuel G. Engel (1904-84)
Johnny Apollo *'40*
Blue, White and Perfect *'42*
My Darling Clementine *'46*
Eric England
Contracted *'13*
Roadside *'15*
Otto Englander (1906-69)
Snow White and the Seven Dwarfs *'37*
Fantasia *'40*
Pinocchio *'40*
Ryan Engle
Non-Stop *'14*
Breaking In *'18*
The Commuter *'18*
Rampage *'18*
Diane English (1948-)
The Lathe of Heaven *'80*
The Women *'08*
Jonathan English
Ironclad *'11*
Ironclad: Battle for Blood *'14*
Richard English (1910-57)
Sweet and Low-Down *'44*
711 Ocean Drive *'50*
Ken Englund (1914-93)
Artists and Models Abroad *'38*
Nothing But the Truth *'41*
Rings on Her Fingers *'42*
Springtime in the Rockies *'42*
The Secret Life of Walter Mitty *'47*
Good Sam *'48*
Nick Enright (1950-2003)
Lorenzo's Oil *'92*
Blackrock *'97*
Max Enscoe
The Day the World Ended *'01*
Earth *vs.* the Spider *'01*
MTV's Wuthering Heights *'03*
Return to Halloweentown *'06*
Delia Ephron (1944-)
This Is My Life *'92*
Mixed Nuts *'94*
Michael *'96*
Hanging Up *'99*
Bewitched *'05*
The Sisterhood of the Traveling Pants *'05*
Henry Ephron (1911-92)
Bride by Mistake *'44*
John Loves Mary *'48*
Look for the Silver Lining *'49*
The Jackpot *'50*
Belles on Their Toes *'52*
There's No Business Like Show Business *'54*
Daddy Long Legs *'55*
Carousel *'56*
Desk Set *'57*
Nora Ephron (1941-2012)
Silkwood *'83*
Heartburn *'86*
Cookie *'89*
When Harry Met Sally. . . *'89*
My Blue Heaven *'90*
This Is My Life *'92*
Sleepless in Seattle *'93*
Mixed Nuts *'94*
Michael *'96*
You've Got Mail *'98*
Hanging Up *'99*
Bewitched *'05*
Julie & Julia *'09*
Phoebe Ephron (1914-71)
Bride by Mistake *'44*
John Loves Mary *'48*
Look for the Silver Lining *'49*
The Jackpot *'50*
Belles on Their Toes *'52*
There's No Business Like Show Business *'54*
Daddy Long Legs *'55*
Carousel *'56*
Desk Set *'57*
Tom Epperson
One False Move *'91*
Don't Look Back *'96*
A Family Thing *'96*
A Gun, a Car, a Blonde *'97*
Camouflage *'00*
The Gift *'00*
Jesse Stone: Night Passage *'06*
Jayne Mansfield's Car *'13*
Jack Epps, Jr. (1949-)
Legal Eagles *'86*
Top Gun *'86*
The Secret of My Success *'87*
Turner and Hooch *'89*
Dick Tracy *'90*
Anaconda *'96*
The Flintstones in Viva Rock Vegas *'00*
Adam Jay Epstein
Not Another Teen Movie *'01*
Extreme Movie *'08*
Julius J. Epstein (1909-2000)
In Caliente *'35*
Living on Velvet *'35*
Four Daughters *'38*
Daughters Courageous *'39*
Four Wives *'39*
No Time For Comedy *'40*
Saturday's Children *'40*
The Bride Came C.O.D. *'41*
The Man Who Came to Dinner *'41*
Strawberry Blonde *'41*
Casablanca *'42*
The Male Animal *'42*
Arsenic and Old Lace *'44*
Romance on the High Seas *'48*
Forever Female *'53*
The Last Time I Saw Paris *'54*
Young at Heart *'54*
The Tender Trap *'55*
Kiss Them for Me *'57*
Take a Giant Step *'59*
Tall Story *'60*
Fanny *'61*
Light in the Piazza *'61*
Send Me No Flowers *'64*
Any Wednesday *'66*
Pete 'n' Tillie *'72*
Once Is Not Enough *'75*
Cross of Iron *'76*
Philip G. Epstein (1909-52)
Mummy's Boys *'36*
New Faces of 1937 *'37*
Daughters Courageous *'39*
Four Wives *'39*
No Time For Comedy *'40*
Saturday's Children *'40*
The Bride Came C.O.D. *'41*
The Man Who Came to Dinner *'41*
Strawberry Blonde *'41*
Casablanca *'42*
The Male Animal *'42*
Arsenic and Old Lace *'44*
Forever Female *'53*
The Last Time I Saw Paris *'54*
Greg Erb
RocketMan *'97*
Senseless *'98*
Playmobil: The Movie *'19*
Carl Erickson (1908-35)
Girl Missing *'33*
Mystery of the Wax Museum *'33*
Dave Erickson
Murder in Greenwich *'02*
Power and Beauty *'02*
Paul Erickson (1920-91)
Track the Man Down *'55*
The Marked One *'63*
Andrew C. Erin (1973-)
Ice Twisters *'09*
Tornado Valley *'09*
George Erschbamer (1954-)
Power of Attorney *'94*
Bounty Hunters *'96*
Bounty Hunters 2: Hardball *'97*
Criminal Intent *'05*
Stranger in My Bed *'05*
Double Cross *'06*
Joakim (Jack) Ersgard
Living in Peril *'97*
Rancid *'04*
Patrick Ersgard (1964-)
Living in Peril *'97*
Backlash *'99*
Rancid *'04*
Chester Erskine (1905-86)
Midnight *'34*
Witness to Murder *'54*
Jon Erwin
October Baby *'12*
Moms' Night Out *'14*
I Can Only Imagine *'18*
John Eskow
Pink Cadillac *'89*
The Mask of Zorro *'98*
John Esposito
Graveyard Shift *'90*
Russell Mulcahy's Tale of the Mummy *'99*
Harry Essex (1910-97)
The Killer That Stalked New York *'47*
Kansas City Confidential *'52*
It Came from Outer Space *'53*
Creature from the Black Lagoon *'54*
Southwest Passage *'54*
The Lonely Man *'57*
Sons of Katie Elder *'65*
Octaman *'71*
Howard Estabrook (1884-1978)
Hell's Angels *'30*
The Woman Between *'31*
David Copperfield *'35*
Orchids to You *'35*
The Bridge of San Luis Rey *'44*
Heavenly Days *'44*
Lone Star *'52*
Julian Esteban (1953-)
Zombie Lake *'80*
Devil Hunter *'08*
Erik Estenberg
Monster *'08*
Almighty Thor *'11*
LA Apocalypse *'14*
Jacob Aaron Estes (1972-)
Mean Creek *'04*
Nearing Grace *'05*
The Details *'11*
Rings *'17*
Don't Let Go *'19*
Emilio Estevez (1962-)
That Was Then. . . This Is Now *'85*
Men at Work *'90*
Bobby *'06*
The Way *'10*
The Public *'18*
Robin Estridge
Campbell's Kingdom *'57*
North West Frontier *'59*
No Kidding *'60*
Escape From Zahrain *'62*
Drums of Africa *'63*
Eye of the Devil *'67*
Jonathan Estrin
Jewels *'92*
Jasper, Texas *'03*
Joe Eszterhas (1944-)
Flashdance *'83*
The Jagged Edge *'85*
Big Shots *'87*
Betrayed *'88*
Checking Out *'89*
Music Box *'89*
Basic Instinct *'92*
Nowhere to Run *'93*
Sliver *'93*
Jade *'95*
Showgirls *'95*
Telling Lies in America *'96*
An Alan Smithee Film: Burn, Hollywood, Burn *'97*
Peter Ettedgui
Onegin *'99*
McQueen *'18*
Carlyle Eubank
The Signal *'14*
Crypto *'19*
William Eubank
Love *'11*
The Signal *'14*
Corey Michael Eubanks
Forced to Kill *'93*
Bigfoot: The Unforgettable Encounter *'94*
Two Bits & Pepper *'95*
Rich Eustis
Serial *'80*
Young Doctors in Love *'82*
Bruce A. Evans
A Man, a Woman, and a Bank *'79*
Starman *'84*
Made in Heaven *'87*
Kuffs *'92*
Jungle 2 Jungle *'96*
Mr. Brooks *'07*
David Mickey Evans (1962-)
Journey to the Center of the Earth *'93*
The Sandlot *'93*
Ed *'96*
Mickey, Donald, Goofy: The Three Musketeers *'04*
The Sandlot 2 *'05*
Ace Ventura Jr.: Pet Detective *'08*
Gareth Evans
The Raid: Redemption *'11*
V/H/S/2 *'13*
Apostle *'18*
Shelley Evans
Ladykiller *'92*
Beyond Betrayal *'94*
Footsteps *'03*
A Girl Like Me: The Gwen Araujo Story *'06*
An Old-Fashioned Thanksgiving *'08*
Wisegal *'08*
The Bling Ring *'11*
Vincent B. Evans
Chain Lightning *'50*
Battle Hymn *'57*
Charles Evered
Adopt a Sailor *'08*
A Thousand Cuts *'12*
Nick Everhart
666: The Beast *'07*
2012: Doomsday *'08*
Clive Exton (1930-2007)
Night Must Fall *'64*
10 Rillington Place *'71*
Doomwatch *'72*
The Awakening *'80*
The Infinite Worlds of H.G. Wells *'01*
David Eyre
Wolfen *'81*
Pastime *'91*
Richard Eyre (1943-)
King Lear *'98*
Iris *'01*
The Other Man *'08*
The Dresser *'15*
John Eyres
Judge & Jury *'96*
Irish Jam *'05*
Diego Fabbri (1911-80)
Barabbas *'62*
Generale Della Rovere *'09*
Steve Faber
Wedding Crashers *'05*
We're the Millers *'13*
Andre Fabrizio
The Prince *'14*
Vice *'15*
Nicholas Factor
Sabrina the Teenage Witch *'96*
Hostage Hotel *'00*
Alejandro Fadel
Lion's Den *'08*
Carancho *'10*
Roberto Faenza (1943-)
Corrupt *'84*
Someday This Pain Will Be Useful to You *'11*
Anthony Faia
Death Toll *'07*
Father of Lies *'07*
Julia Fair
Alien Raiders *'08*
Higher Power *'18*
Douglas Fairbanks, Sr. (1883-1939)
Mark of Zorro *'20*
The Three Musketeers *'21*
Robin Hood *'22*
The Black Pirate *'26*
The Iron Mask *'29*
Mr. Robinson Crusoe *'32*
William Fairchild (1919-2000)
Morning Departure *'50*
Value for Money *'55*
Star! *'68*
Marion Fairfax (1875-1970)
Through the Back Door *'21*
The Lost World *'25*
Gerald Fairlie (1899-1983)
Charlie Chan in Shanghai *'35*
Conspirator *'49*
Aleksey Fajko (1893-1978)
Aelita: Queen of Mars *'24*
The Cigarette Girl of Mosselprom *'24*
Ben Falcone
Tammy *'14*
The Boss *'16*
Life of the Party *'18*
Pamela Falk
The Wedding Planner *'01*
An Invisible Sign *'11*
Jason Faller
Mythica 2: The Darkspore *'15*
Mythica: A Quest for Heroes *'15*
Mythica: The Necroromancer *'15*
Mythica: The Iron Crown *'16*
David Fallon
Split Decisions *'88*
White Fang *'91*
White Fang 2: The Myth of the White Wolf *'94*
Call of the Wild *'04*
Kevin Falls
The Temp *'93*
Summer Catch *'01*
Rick Famuyiwa (1973-)
The Wood *'99*
Brown Sugar *'02*
Talk to Me *'07*
Our Family Wedding *'10*
Dope *'15*
Jamaa Fanaka (1942-)
Soul Vengeance *'75*
Black Sister's Revenge *'76*
Penitentiary *'79*
Penitentiary 2 *'82*
Street Wars *'91*
Barry Fanaro
The Crew *'00*
Men in Black 2 *'02*
I Now Pronounce You Chuck and Larry *'07*
Hampton Fancher (1938-)
Blade Runner *'82*
The Mighty Quinn *'89*
The Minus Man *'99*
Blade Runner 2049 *'17*
Anthony Fankhauser
Supernova *'09*
8213: Gacy House *'10*
Cowboys vs Dinosaurs *'15*
John Fante (1909-83)
My Man and I *'52*
Full of Life *'56*
Jeanne Eagels *'57*
Walk on the Wild Side *'62*
Francis Edwards Faragoh (1895-1966)
Little Caesar *'30*
Frankenstein *'31*
The Right of Way *'31*
Jean-Pol Fargeau
Chocolat *'88*
I Can't Sleep *'93*
Nenette and Boni *'96*
Beau Travail *'98*
Pola X *'99*
The Intruder *'04*
35 Shots of Rum *'08*
High Life *'18*
Asghar Farhadi (1972-)
Low Heights *'02*
A Separation *'11*
The Past *'13*
The Salesman *'16*
Everybody Knows *'18*
Corrado Farina (1939-)
Baba Yaga *'73*
Kiss Me, Kill Me *'73*
Ernest Farino
Beverly Hills Vamp *'88*
Wizards of the Demon Sword *'94*

Jeff Farley
Thunderstruck *'12*
More Money More Family *'15*

Todd Farmer (1968-)
Jason X *'01*
Messengers 2: The Scarecrow *'09*
My Bloody Valentine 3D *'09*
Drive Angry *'11*

Joe Farnham (1884-1931)
West Point *'27*
Across to Singapore *'28*
Laugh, Clown, Laugh *'28*
So This Is College *'29*
Speedway *'29*
Tide of Empire *'29*
Love in the Rough *'30*
Montana Moon *'30*

Dorothy Farnum
Bardelys the Magnificent *'26*
The Temptress *'26*
Torrent *'26*
The Pagan *'29*

David Farr
Hanna *'11*
The Ones Below *'16*

Ned Farr
The Gymnast *'06*
A Marine Story *'10*

Daniel Farrands (1969-)
Halloween 6: The Curse of Michael Myers *'95*
The Haunting of Sharon Tate *'19*

Henry Farrell (1920-2006)
Hush, Hush, Sweet Charlotte *'65*
The Eyes of Charles Sand *'74*

Bobby Farrelly (1958-)
Dumb & Dumber *'94*
Kingpin *'96*
There's Something about Mary *'98*
Outside Providence *'99*
Me, Myself, and Irene *'00*
Shallow Hal *'01*
Stuck On You *'03*
The Heartbreak Kid *'07*
Hall Pass *'11*
The Three Stooges *'12*
Dumb and Dumber To *'14*

Peter Farrelly (1957-)
Dumb & Dumber *'94*
There's Something about Mary *'98*
Outside Providence *'99*
Me, Myself, and Irene *'00*
Shallow Hal *'01*
Stuck On You *'03*
The Heartbreak Kid *'07*
Hall Pass *'11*
The Three Stooges *'12*
Dumb and Dumber To *'14*
Green Book *'18*

John Fasano (1961-2014)
The Hunchback *'97*
Universal Soldier: The Return *'99*
Darkness Falls *'03*
The Legend of Butch & Sundance *'04*
Jesse Stone: Stone Cold *'05*
Woke Up Dead *'09*
Sniper Reloaded *'11*
The Eleventh Victim *'12*
Hannah's Law *'12*
Sniper: Legacy *'14*

Walter Fasano
Mother of Tears *'08*
I Am Love *'09*

Rainer Werner Fassbinder (1946-82)
Love Is Colder Than Death *'69*
Why Does Herr R. Run Amok? *'69*
The American Soldier *'70*
Beware of a Holy Whore *'70*
Whity *'70*
The Merchant of Four Seasons *'71*
The Bitter Tears of Petra von Kant *'72*
World on a Wire *'73*
Ali: Fear Eats the Soul *'74*
Effi Briest *'74*
Fear of Fear *'75*
I Only Want You to Love Me *'76*
Mother Kusters Goes to Heaven *'76*
Satan's Brew *'76*
The Stationmaster's Wife *'77*
In a Year of 13 Moons *'78*
The Marriage of Maria Braun *'79*
Lola *'81*
Querelle *'83*
Chinese Roulette *'86*

Alvin L. Fast
Bummer *'73*
Eaten Alive *'76*
Satan's Cheerleaders *'77*

Matthew Faulk
Jason and the Argonauts *'00*
The Infinite Worlds of H.G. Wells *'01*
Vanity Fair *'04*

William Faulkner (1897-1962)
Today We Live *'33*
The Road to Glory *'36*
Gunga Din *'39*
Air Force *'43*
To Have & Have Not *'44*
The Southerner *'45*
The Big Sleep *'46*

Jon Favreau (1966-)
Swingers *'96*
Made *'01*
The First $20 Million is Always the Hardest *'02*
Couples Retreat *'09*
Chef *'14*

Nat Faxon (1975-)
The Descendants *'11*
The Way Way Back *'13*
Downhill *'20*

Feras Fayyad
Last Men In Aleppo *'17*
The Cave *'19*

Jacqueline Feather
The Rumor Mill *'86*
Goldrush: A Real Life Alaskan Adventure *'98*
The King and I *'99*
By Dawn's Early Light *'00*
Kung Fu Killer *'08*

Terence Feely (1928-2000)
Destination Moonbase Alpha *'75*
The Lady and the Highwayman *'89*
Duel of Hearts *'92*

F.X. Feeney (1953-2020)
Frankenstein Unbound *'90*
The Big Brass Ring *'99*

Michael Feifer
A Dead Calling *'06*
The Boston Strangler: The Untold Story *'08*
Drifter *'09*
Soda Springs *'11*
Your Love Never Fails *'11*

Jules Feiffer (1929-)
Carnal Knowledge *'71*
Little Murders *'71*
Oh! Calcutta! *'72*
Popeye *'80*
I Want to Go Home *'89*

Paul Feig (1962-)
Spy *'15*
Ghostbusters *'16*

Beda Docampo Feijoo (1948-)
The Perfect Husband *'92*
What Your Eyes Don't See *'99*

Steve Feinberg
Prime Time *'77*
Fortress *'93*
Fortress 2: Re-Entry *'99*

Bruce Feirstein (1956-)
Tomorrow Never Dies *'97*
The World Is Not Enough *'99*

Steve Feke
When a Stranger Calls *'79*
Flatland *'02*

Mark Feldberg
Disorderlies *'87*
Beverly Hills Ninja *'96*

Dennis Feldman
The Golden Child *'86*
Species *'95*
Virus *'98*

Jonathan Marc Feldman
Swing Kids *'93*
From the Earth to the Moon *'98*

Rachel Feldman
Recipe for a Perfect Christmas *'05*
Love Notes *'07*

Randy Feldman
Hell Night *'81*
Tango and Cash *'89*
Nowhere to Run *'93*
Metro *'96*
The Reading Room *'05*

Federico Fellini (1920-93)
Open City *'45*
Paisan *'46*
The Flowers of St. Francis *'50*
Variety Lights *'51*
The White Sheik *'52*
I Vitelloni *'53*
La Strada *'54*
Il Bidone *'55*
Nights of Cabiria *'57*
La Dolce Vita *'60*
Boccaccio '70 *'62*
8 1/2 *'63*
Juliet of the Spirits *'65*
Spirits of the Dead *'68*
Fellini Satyricon *'69*
The Clowns *'71*
Fellini's Roma *'72*
Amarcord *'74*
Orchestra Rehearsal *'78*
City of Women *'81*
And the Ship Sails On *'83*
Ginger & Fred *'86*
Intervista *'87*

Julian Fellowes (1949-)
Gosford Park *'01*
Vanity Fair *'04*
Separate Lies *'05*
The Young Victoria *'09*
The Tourist *'10*
Titanic *'12*
Romeo & Juliet *'13*
Downton Abbey *'19*

Earl Felton (1909-72)
Armored Car Robbery *'50*
20,000 Leagues under the Sea *'54*

Andrew J. Fenady (1928-2020)
Chisum *'70*
Mayday at 40,000 Feet *'76*
The Man with Bogart's Face *'80*

Pablo F. Fenjves (1956-)
The Affair *'95*
Trophy Wife *'06*
Man on a Ledge *'12*

Suzanne Fenn
Dancehall Queen *'97*
Third World Cop *'99*

Frank Fenton (1903-71)
The Gay Falcon *'41*
A Date With the Falcon *'42*
Nocturne *'46*
Night Song *'47*
Malaya *'49*
His Kind of Woman *'51*
The Man With a Cloak *'51*
The Wild North *'52*
Escape from Fort Bravo *'53*
Ride, Vaquero! *'53*
Garden of Evil *'54*
River of No Return *'54*
Untamed *'55*
These Wilder Years *'56*

Mark Fergus
First Snow *'07*
Iron Man *'08*
Cowboys & Aliens *'11*

Charles Ferguson
No End in Sight *'07*
Inside Job *'10*
Time to Choose *'16*

Craig Ferguson (1962-)
The Big Tease *'99*
Saving Grace *'00*
I'll Be There *'03*

Larry Ferguson (1940-)
Highlander *'86*
Beverly Hills Cop 2 *'87*
The Presidio *'88*
The Hunt for Red October *'90*
Talent for the Game *'91*
Beyond the Law *'92*
Gunfighter's Moon *'96*
Maximum Risk *'96*
Rollerball *'02*

Harvey Fergusson (1890-1971)
It Happened in Hollywood *'37*
Stand Up and Fight *'39*

Pascale Ferran (1960-)
Lady Chatterley *'10*
Bird People *'14*
The Red Turtle *'17*

Anthony C. Ferrante
Boo! *'05*
Headless Horseman *'07*
House of Bones *'09*
Scream of the Banshee *'11*
Red Clover *'12*

Abel Ferrara (1952-)
Bad Lieutenant *'92*
The Blackout *'97*
New Rose Hotel *'98*
'R Xmas *'01*
4:44 Last Day on Earth *'11*
Welcome to New York *'15*

Will Ferrell (1968-)
A Night at the Roxbury *'98*
Anchorman: The Legend of Ron Burgundy *'04*
Talladega Nights: The Ballad of Ricky Bobby *'06*
Step Brothers *'08*
Anchorman 2: The Legend Continues *'13*

Heidi Ferrer
The Hottie and the Nottie *'08*
Princess: A Modern Fairytale *'08*

Marco Ferreri (1928-97)
El Cochecito *'60*
Mafioso *'62*
Dillinger Is Dead *'69*
La Grande Bouffe *'73*
Tales of Ordinary Madness *'83*

Linda Ferri
The Son's Room *'00*
Light of My Eyes *'01*

Franco Ferrini (1944-)
Once Upon a Time in America *'84*
Creepers *'85*
Demons *'86*
Opera *'88*
Two Evil Eyes *'90*
The Church *'98*
Sleepless *'01*
Carnera: The Walking Mountain *'08*

Darin Ferriola (1970-)
Ivory Tower *'97*
Mr. Fix It *'06*

Michael Ferris (1961-)
Mindwarp *'91*
Interceptor *'92*
Into the Sun *'92*
The Net *'95*
The Game *'97*
Terminator 3: Rise of the Machines *'03*
Catwoman *'04*
Primeval *'07*
Surrogates *'09*
Terminator Salvation *'09*
Dead Rising: End Game *'16*

Walter Ferris (1882-1965)
Death Takes a Holiday *'34*
Lloyds of London *'36*
Heidi *'37*
Four Men and a Prayer *'38*
The Little Princess *'39*
At Sword's Point *'51*

Giorgio Ferroni (1908-81)
Mill of the Stone Women *'60*
Conquest of Mycene *'63*
The Lion of Thebes *'64*

Jean Ferry (1906-75)
Nana *'55*
Daughters of Darkness *'71*

Larry Fessenden (1963-)
Habit *'97*
Wendigo *'01*
The Last Winter *'06*

Michael Fessier (1905-88)
Exclusive Story *'36*
Speed *'36*
Angels Wash Their Faces *'39*
Wings of the Navy *'39*
It All Came True *'40*
You'll Never Get Rich *'41*
Greenwich Village *'44*
Red Garters *'54*

Shana Feste (1976-)
The Greatest *'09*
Country Strong *'10*
Endless Love *'14*
Boundaries *'18*

Rob Festinger
In the Bedroom *'01*
Trust *'10*

Will Fetters
Remember Me *'10*
The Lucky One *'12*
The Best of Me *'14*
A Star Is Born *'18*

Darrell Fetty
Freeway *'88*
Trouble Bound *'92*

Jeff Feuerzeig
The Devil and Daniel Johnston *'05*
Author: The JT LeRoy Story *'16*
Chuck *'17*

Tina Fey (1970-)
Mean Girls *'04*
Date Night *'10*

Severin Fiala
Goodnight Mommy *'15*
The Lodge *'19*

Glenn Ficarra
Cats & Dogs *'01*
Bad Santa *'03*
The Bad News Bears *'05*
I Love You Phillip Morris *'10*
Focus *'15*

Demofilo Fidani (1914-94)
Django and Sartana; It's the End *'70*
One Fine Day, When Django Met Sartana *'70*

David Field
Invisible Child *'99*
Passion of Mind *'00*

Todd Field (1964-)
In the Bedroom *'01*
Little Children *'06*

Pat Fielder
The Monster That Challenged the World *'57*
Return of Dracula *'58*

Richard Fielder
A Distant Trumpet *'64*
Adam's Woman *'70*
Stolen Women, Captured Hearts *'97*

Helen Fielding (1958-)
Bridget Jones's Diary *'01*
Bridget Jones: The Edge of Reason *'04*
Bridget Jones's Baby *'16*

Herbert Fields (1897-1958)
Hands Across the Table *'35*
Mississippi *'35*
Love Before Breakfast *'36*
Honolulu *'39*
Up in Central Park *'48*

Joseph Fields (1895-1966)
The Girl From Mexico *'39*
Mexican Spitfire *'40*
Two Girls on Broadway *'40*
Louisiana Purchase *'41*
My Sister Eileen *'42*
A Night in Casablanca *'46*

W.C. Fields (1879-1946)
The Bank Dick *'40*
My Little Chickadee *'40*
Never Give a Sucker an Even Break *'41*

Jacques Fieschi
Un Coeur en Hiver *'93*
Nelly et Monsieur Arnaud *'95*
Place Vendome *'98*
Les Destinees *'00*
Sade *'00*
How I Killed My Father *'03*
Nathalie *'03*
The Girl From Monaco *'08*

Mike Figgis (1948-)
Stormy Monday *'88*
Liebestraum *'91*
Leaving Las Vegas *'95*
One Night Stand *'97*
The Loss of Sexual Innocence *'98*
Time Code *'00*
Hotel *'01*

Ivan Fila (1956-)
Lea *'96*
King of Thieves *'04*

Jason Filardi
Bringing Down the House *'03*
17 Again *'09*

Peter Filardi (1962-)
Flatliners *'90*
The Craft *'96*
Salem's Lot *'04*

Jackie Filgo
Diary of a Wimpy Kid *'10*
Take Me Home Tonight *'11*

Jeff Filgo
Diary of a Wimpy Kid *'10*
Take Me Home Tonight *'11*

Kleber Mendonca Filho
Neighboring Sounds *'12*
Aquarius *'16*
Bacurau *'20*

Efthymis Filippou
Dogtooth *'09*
Chevalier *'16*
The Lobster *'16*
The Killing of a Sacred Deer *'17*

Hal Fimberg (1907-74)
Big Store *'41*
In Society *'44*
Our Man Flint *'66*
In Like Flint *'67*

Brian Finch (1936-2007)
Goodnight, Mr. Tom *'99*
Goodbye, Mr. Chips *'02*
The Shell Seekers *'06*

Michael Finch
Predators *'10*
The November Man *'14*
Hitman: Agent 47 *'15*
Countdown *'16*
Interrogation *'16*

American Assassin '17
Blood Brother '18

Scot (Scott) Finch
Shalako '68
Catlow '71

Diane Fine
Firetrap '01
Lost Treasure '03
Art Heist '05

Travis Fine (1968-)
The Space Between '10
Any Day Now '12

Anthony Fingleton
Drop Dead Fred '91
Swimming Upstream '03

Harry Julian Fink
Major Dundee '65
Dirty Harry '71

Abem Finkel (1889-1948)
Hi, Nellie! '34
The Black Legion '37
Jezebel '38
Sergeant York '41
The Big Shot '42
God is My Co-Pilot '45

Fred Finklehoffe (1910-77)
Mr. Ace '46
At War with the Army '50
The Stooge '51

Melanie Finn
Lake Consequence '92
Red Shoe Diaries: Swimming Naked '00

Augusto Finocchi
Hallelujah for Django '67
Count Dracula '71
The Italian Connection '73

Tim Firth (1964-)
Calendar Girls '03
Kinky Boots '06
Confessions of a Shopaholic '09
G-Force '09

Antwone Fisher (1959-)
Antwone Fisher '02
ATL '06

Bob Fisher
I'll Take Sweden '65
Eight on the Lam '67
Wedding Crashers '05
We're the Millers '13
Overboard '18

Carrie Fisher (1956-2016)
Postcards from the Edge '90
These Old Broads '01

Chris Fisher (1973-)
Nightstalker '02
Taboo '02
Rampage: The Hillside Strangler Murders '04
Dirty '05
Meeting Evil '12

Steve Fisher (1912-80)
I Wake Up Screaming '41
Berlin Correspondent '42
Lady in the Lake '46
Dead Reckoning '47
That's My Man '47
The Hunted '48
I Wouldn't Be in Your Shoes '48
Roadblock '51
Battle Zone '52
Flat Top '52
Woman They Almost Lynched '53
Hell's Half Acre '54
Terror Street '54
Top Gun '55
Johnny Reno '66
Hostile Guns '67

Steve(n) Fisher
The Woman Inside '83
Alien Trespass '09

Jeffrey Alladin Fiskin
Angel Unchained '70
Cutter's Way '81
From the Earth to the Moon '98
The '60s '99

Micah Fitzerman-Blue
The Motel Life '12
A Beautiful Day in the Neighborhood '19
Maleficent: Mistress of Evil '19

Benedict Fitzgerald (1949-)
In Cold Blood '96
The Passion of the Christ '04

Edith Fitzgerald (1889-1968)
Five and Ten '31
Brief Moment '33
Today We Live '33
The Painted Veil '34
The Wedding Night '35

F. Scott Fitzgerald (1896-1940)
Marie Antoinette '38
Three Comrades '38

Kieran Fitzgerald
The Homesman '14
Snowden '16

Thom Fitzgerald (1968-)
The Hanging Garden '97
Beefcake '99
The Event '03
Cloudburst '11

Jennifer Flackett
Madeline '98
Wimbledon '04
Little Manhattan '05
Journey to the Center of the Earth '08
Nim's Island '08

Cash Flagg (1938-2009)
See Ray Dennis Steckler

Ennio Flaiano (1910-72)
Variety Lights '51
The White Sheik '52
I Vitelloni '53
La Strada '54
Too Bad She's Bad '54
Il Bidone '55
Nights of Cabiria '57
La Dolce Vita '60
La Notte '60
Boccaccio '70 '62
8 1/2 '63
Juliet of the Spirits '65
10th Victim '65
Sundance and the Kid '69

Mike Flanagan (1978-)
Absentia '11
Oculus '14
Before I Wake '15
Ouija: Origin of Evil '16
Doctor Sleep '19

Sara Flanigan (1931-2006)
Wildflower '91
Other Voices, Other Rooms '95

Harvey Flaxman (1939-)
Grizzly '76
Preacherman '83

Ryan Fleck (1976-)
Half Nelson '06
Sugar '09
It's Kind of a Funny Story '10
Mississippi Grind '15
Captain Marvel '19

Andrew Fleming (1964-)
Bad Dreams '88
Threesome '94
The Craft '96
Dick '99
Nancy Drew '07
Hamlet 2 '08

R. Lee Fleming, Jr. (1970-)
She's All That '99
Get Over It! '01

Charlie Fletcher
Fair Game '95
Mean Machine '01

Lucille Fletcher (1912-2000)
Sorry, Wrong Number '48
The Hitch-Hiker '53

Clive Fleury
Tunnel Vision '95
Big City Blues '99

Pat C. Flick
The Singing Kid '36
Nobody's Baby '37

Ruth Brooks Flippen (1921-81)
Love Is Better Than Ever '52
Sail a Crooked Ship '61
Looking for Love '64

Phil Flores
April Fool's Day '08
The Thompsons '12

Richard Flournoy (1901-67)
Mister Cinderella '36
Blondie '38
Blondie Brings Up Baby '39
Blondie Meets the Boss '39
Blondie Takes a Vacation '39
Blondie Has Trouble '40
Blondie On a Budget '40
Blondie Plays Cupid '40
Blondie Goes Latin '42
A Night to Remember '42

Frank E. Flowers
Haven '04
Metro Manila '13

Per Fly (1960-)
The Inheritance '76
Backstabbing for Beginners '18

Gillian Flynn (1971-)
Gone Girl '14
Widows '18

Tom Flynn (1980-)
Gifted '17
Togo '19

Ladislas Fodor (1989-78)
The Other Love '47
The Great Sinner '49
Tom Thumb '58
Testament of Dr. Mabuse '62
Strangler of Blackmoor Castle '63
Apache's Last Battle '64

Bryan Fogel
Jewtopia '12
Icarus '17

Susanna Fogel
Life Partners '14
The Spy Who Dumped Me '18
Booksmart '19

Dan Fogelman
Cars '06
Fred Claus '07
Bolt '08
Tangled '10
Crazy, Stupid, Love. '11
The Guilt Trip '12
Last Vegas '13
Danny Collins '15
Zootopia '16
Life Itself '18

Lawrence Foldes (1959-)
Nightstalker '81
Finding Home '03

Brendan Foley
Johnny Was '05
The Riddle '07
Legend of the Bog '08

Dave Foley (1963-)
The Wrong Guy '96
Suck '09

James Foley (1953-)
After Dark, My Sweet '90
S.F.W. '94

Christopher Folino
Gamers '06
Sparks '13

Ari Folman
Waltz with Bashir '08
The Congress '13

Timothy Wayne Folsome (1966-)
Uninvited Guest '99
Jacked Up '01

Marcello Fondato (1924-)
Black Sabbath '64
Blood and Black Lace '64

Naomi Foner (1946-)
Violets Are Blue '86
Running on Empty '88
Losing Isaiah '94
Bee Season '05
Very Good Girls '13

Eddie Ling-Ching Fong (1954-)
Erotique '94
Temptation of a Monk '94
The Goddess of 1967 '00

Anne Fontaine (1959-)
Dry Cleaning '97
How I Killed My Father '03
Nathalie '03
The Girl From Monaco '08
Coco Before Chanel '09
My Worst Nightmare '11
Gemma Bovery '15
The Innocents '16

Tom Fontana
Fourth Wise Man '85
Homicide: The Movie '00

Dennis Foon
White Lies '98
Long Life, Happiness and Prosperity '02
Torso '02
A Shine of Rainbows '09
Life, Above All '10

Bradbury Foote (1894-1995)
Of Human Hearts '38
Young Tom Edison '40

Horton Foote (1916-2009)
To Kill a Mockingbird '62
Baby, the Rain Must Fall '64
The Chase '66
Hurry Sundown '67
Tomorrow '72
Tender Mercies '83
1918 '85
The Trip to Bountiful '85
On Valentine's Day '86
Of Mice and Men '92
Lily Dale '96
Horton Foote's Alone '97
Main Street '10
The Trip to Bountiful '14

John Taintor Foote (1881-1950)
Kentucky '38
Swanee River '39
The Mark of Zorro '40
Great Dan Patch '49

Bryan Forbes (1926-2013)
Of Human Bondage '64
King Rat '65
The Whisperers '66
Eye Witness '70
The Man Who Haunted Himself '70
The Slipper and the Rose '76
The Naked Face '84
Chaplin '92

Christopher Forbes
Basketweave '06
All Hell Broke Loose '09
A Cold Day in Hell '11

Maya Forbes
Seeing Other People '04
The Rocker '08
Monsters *vs.* Aliens '09
Infinitely Polar Bear '14
A Dog's Purpose '17
The Polka King '18
A Dog's Journey '19
Trolls World Tour '20

Christian Ford
Kazaam '96
Slow Burn '00
Category 7: The End of the World '05
Final Days of Planet Earth '06
Merlin's Apprentice '06

Christopher Ford
Robot & Frank '12
Cop Car '15
Clown '16
Spider-Man: Homecoming '17

Derek Ford (1932-95)
Black Torment '64
Estate of Insanity '64
Hell Boats '70

Donald Ford
Black Torment '64
Estate of Insanity '64
Hell Boats '70

Katie Ford
Double Platinum '99
Prayers for Bobby '09

Ron Ford (1958-)
The Fear '94
Witchcraft 11: Sisters in Blood '00

Tom Ford
A Single Man '09
Nocturnal Animals '16

Carl Foreman (1914-84)
So This Is New York '48
Champion '49
Cyrano de Bergerac '50
The Men '50
High Noon '52
The Sleeping Tiger '54
The Bridge on the River Kwai '57
The Key '58
A Hatful of Rain '59
The Guns of Navarone '61
MacKenna's Gold '69
High Noon '00

Adam Forgash
Everything Put Together '00
The Last New Yorker '07

Milos Forman (1932-2018)
Black Peter '63
Loves of a Blonde '65
The Firemen's Ball '68
Goya's Ghosts '06

Eric Forsberg
30,000 Leagues Under the Sea '07
War of the Worlds 2: The Next Wave '08
Mega Piranha '10
Age of the Hobbits '12

Bill Forsyth (1948-)
That Sinking Feeling '79
Gregory's Girl '80
Local Hero '83
Housekeeping '87
Being Human '94

Garrett Fort (1900-45)
The Letter '29
Dracula '31
Dracula Spanish Version '31
Frankenstein '31
The Lost Patrol '34
Devil Doll '36
Dracula's Daughter '36
Ladies in Retirement '41

Will Forte (1970-)
The Brothers Solomon '07
MacGruber '10

Jan Fortune (1892-1979)
The Vanishing Virginian '41
Mokey '42

Bob Fosse (1927-87)
All That Jazz '79
Star 80 '83

Lewis R. Foster (1898-1974)
Golden Gloves '40
Adventure in Washington '41
The Mayor of 44th Street '42
Can't Help Singing '45
Never Say Goodbye '46
El Paso '49
Billy Jack Goes to Washington '77

Nora Kay Foster
Frederick Forsyth's Icon '05
Mysterious Island '05

Norman Foster (1900-76)
Thank you, Mr. Moto '37
Think Fast, Mr. Moto '37
Woman On the Run '50
Sky Full of Moon '52

Robert Foster
Dead Bang '89
The Contractor '07

Alastair Fothergill (1960-)
Deep Blue '03
Earth '07
Chimpanzee '12

James Fotopoulos
Back Against the Wall '00
Migrating Forms '00

Vincent Fotre
Missile to the Moon '59
Torture Chamber of Baron Blood '72

Alyson Fouse
Scary Movie 2 '01
Bring It On: All or Nothing '06
Bring It On: In It to Win It '07
Bring It On: Fight to the Finish '09
Honey 2 '14

David Fowler
Born in China '17
Penguins '19

Gene Fowler, Sr. (1890-1960)
State's Attorney '31
What Price Hollywood? '32
The Call of the Wild '35
Professional Soldier '35
White Fang '36
Nancy Steele Is Missing '37
Billy the Kid '41

Amy Fox
Heights '04
Equity '16

Dana Fox
The Wedding Date '05
What Happens in Vegas '08
Couples Retreat '09
How to Be Single '16
Isn't It Romantic '19

Robbie Fox
So I Married an Axe Murderer '93
Playing for Keeps '12

Victoria Foyt (1958-)
Babyfever '94
Last Summer In the Hamptons '96
Deja Vu '98
Going Shopping '05

Claudio Fragasso (1951-)
Meet Him and Die '76
Hell of the Living Dead '83
Troll 2 '92

Randall Frakes
Hell Comes to Frogtown '88
Blowback '99
Instinct to Kill '01

Michael France (1962-)
Cliffhanger '93
Goldeneye '95
Hulk '03
The Punisher '04
Fantastic Four '05

Dan Franck
The Separation '94
La Separation '98
One Day You'll Understand '08
Carlos '10

James Franco (1978-)
The Ape '05
The Broken Tower '11
Child of God '14

Jess (Jesus) Franco (1930-2013)
The Awful Dr. Orloff '62
The Diabolical Dr. Z '65
Venus in Furs '70
Count Dracula '71
Rites of Frankenstein '72

Jack the Ripper '76
Ilsa, the Wicked Warden '78
Zombie Lake '80
Oasis of the Zombies '82
Bloody Moon '83
Tender Flesh '97
Devil Hunter '08

Michel Franco
Daniel & Ana '09
Chronic '16

Bruno Frank (1887-1945)
The Hunchback of Notre Dame '39
A Royal Scandal '45

Debra Frank
Mr. St. Nick '02
The Muppets' Wizard of Oz '05

Frederic M. Frank (1911-77)
Unconquered '47
The Ten Commandments '56

Harriet Frank, Jr. (1917-)
Whiplash '48
Ten Wanted Men '54
The Long, Hot Summer '58
Home from the Hill '60
Hud '63
Hombre '67
The Reivers '69
The Carey Treatment '72
The Cowboys '72
The Spikes Gang '74
Norma Rae '79
Murphy's Romance '85
Stanley and Iris '90

Jonathan Frank
The Tournament '09
Final Score '18

Melvin Frank (1913-88)
Star Spangled Rhythm '42
Monsieur Beaucaire '46
The Road to Utopia '46
Mr. Blandings Builds His Dream House '48
The Reformer and the Redhead '50
Above and Beyond '53
Knock on Wood '54
The Facts of Life '60
Strange Bedfellows '65
A Funny Thing Happened on the Way to the Forum '66

Scott Frank (1960-)
Dead Again '91
Little Man Tate '91
Malice '93
Get Shorty '95
Heaven's Prisoners '95
Out of Sight '98
Minority Report '02
Flight of the Phoenix '04
The Interpreter '05
The Lookout '07
Marley & Me '08
Night at the Museum: Battle of the Smithsonian '09
The Wolverine '13
A Walk Among the Tombstones '14
Logan '17

David Frankel (1959-)
Funny About Love '90
Nervous Ticks '93
Miami Rhapsody '95

Al Franken (1951-)
Stuart Saves His Family '94
When a Man Loves a Woman '94

Carl Franklin (1949-)
Eye of the Eagle 3 '91
Devil in a Blue Dress '95
Bless Me, Ultima '13

Howard Franklin
The Name of the Rose '86
Someone to Watch Over Me '87
Quick Change '90
The Public Eye '92
The Man Who Knew Too Little '97

Antitrust '00
The Big Year '11

Jeff Franklin (1955-)
Summer School '87
Double Double Toil and Trouble '94
To Grandmother's House We Go '94
Love Stinks '99

Veronika Franz
Paradise: Faith '12
Paradise: Hope '13
Goodnight Mommy '15
The Lodge '19

David Franzoni
Jumpin' Jack Flash '86
Citizen Cohn '92
Amistad '97
Gladiator '00
King Arthur '04

Brad Fraser (1959-)
Love and Human Remains '93
Leaving Metropolis '02

George MacDonald Fraser (1925-2008)
The Three Musketeers '74
The Four Musketeers '75
Royal Flash '75
The Prince and the Pauper '78

Garrett Frawley
Santa Baby '06
Snowglobe '07
Santa Baby 2: Santa Maybe '09

F. Scott Frazier
The Numbers Station '13
Collide '17
xXx: Return of Xander Cage '17

R. Ellis Frazier
Confessions of a Pit Fighter '05
The Line '08
Across the Line: The Exodus of Charlie Wright '10

Riccardo Freda (1909-99)
I, Vampiri '56
The Ghost '63
Double Face '70

Donald Freed
Secret Honor '85
Of Love and Shadows '94

Mark Freed
Shock 'Em Dead '90
Criminal Desire '98

Robert Freedman
Cinderella '97
Life with Judy Garland-Me and My Shadows '01
Murder in the Hamptons '05

David Freeman
Street Smart '87
Carry On Columbus '92

Devery Freeman (1913-2005)
The Guilt of Janet Ames '47
Three Sailors and a Girl '53

Everett Freeman (1911-91)
George Washington Slept Here '42
Larceny, Inc. '42
The Princess and the Pirate '44
It Happened on 5th Avenue '47
The Secret Life of Walter Mitty '47
Lulu Belle '48
Pretty Baby '50
Destination Gobi '53
My Man Godfrey '57
The Glass Bottom Boat '66

Fred Freeman
Start the Revolution without Me '70
The Big Bus '76

Gillian Freeman (1929-)
The Leather Boys '63
The Girl on a Motorcycle '68
That Cold Day in the Park '69

Leonard Freeman
Claudelle Inglish '61
Gold of the Seven Saints '61
Hang 'Em High '67

Morgan J. Freeman (1969-)
Hurricane Streets '96
Desert Blue '98

Fred Freiberger (1915-2003)
The Beast from 20,000 Fathoms '53
The Weapon '56
Beginning of the End '57
Crash Landing '58

Kelly Fremon Craig
Post Grad '09
The Edge of Seventeen '16

Robert M. Fresco (1928-)
Tarantula '55
The Monolith Monsters '57

Juan Carlos Fresnadillo (1967-)
Intacto '01
28 Weeks Later '07

Bart Freundlich (1970-)
The Myth of Fingerprints '97
World Traveler '01
Trust the Man '06
The Rebound '09
After the Wedding '19

Anthony Frewin
Color Me Kubrick '05
Anthropoid '16

Ron Fricke
Koyaanisqatsi '83
Baraka '93
Samsara '12

Jason Friedberg
Spy Hard '96
Date Movie '06
Epic Movie '07
Disaster Movie '08
Meet the Spartans '08
Vampires Suck '10
The Starving Games '13
Best Night Ever '14

Richard Friedenberg
Promise '86
Dying Young '91
A River Runs Through It '92
Mr. & Mrs. Loving '96
The Education of Little Tree '97
Snow in August '01
The 19th Wife '10
Of Two Minds '12
Ring of Fire '13
Unbroken: Path to Redemption '18

William Friedkin (1939-)
Cruising '80
To Live & Die in L.A. '85
Rampage '87
The Guardian '90

Brent Friedman (1962-)
Ticks '93
Mortal Kombat 2: Annihilation '97

Josh Friedman
War of the Worlds '05
The Black Dahlia '06

Ken Friedman
White Line Fever '75
Mr. Billion '77
Heart Like a Wheel '83
Johnny Handsome '89
Cadillac Man '90
Bad Girls '94

Lewis Friedman
BASEketball '98
The Comedian '16

Ron J. Friedman
Brother Bear '03
Chicken Little '05

Cats & Dogs: The Revenge of Kitty Galore '10

Collin Friesen (1964-)
The Big White '05
The Con Artist '10

Ketti Frings (1909-81)
Guest in the House '44
The File on Thelma Jordon '50

James Fritzell (1920-79)
Good Neighbor Sam '64
The Ghost and Mr. Chicken '66
The Reluctant Astronaut '67
The Shakiest Gun in the West '68

George Froeschel (1891-1979)
The Mortal Storm '40
Waterloo Bridge '40
Mrs. Miniver '42
Random Harvest '42
We Were Dancing '42
The White Cliffs of Dover '44
Command Decision '48
The Miniver Story '50
Never Let Me Go '53
The Story of Three Loves '53
Quentin Durward '55

Clayton Frohman
Under Fire '83
Defiance '08

Pea Frolich
The Marriage of Maria Braun '79
Veronika Voss '82

Lee Frost (1935-2007)
Black Gestapo '75
Race with the Devil '75
Dixie Dynamite '76
Private Obsession '94

Mark Frost (1953-)
The Believers '87
Storyville '92
Fantastic Four '05
The Greatest Game Ever Played '05
Fantastic Four: Rise of the Silver Surfer '07

Cesare Frugoni
The Big Alligator River '79
Cut and Run '85

Roy Frumkes
Street Trash '87
The Substitute '96
The Substitute 2: School's Out '97
The Substitute 3: Winner Takes All '99
The Sweet Life '03

Christopher Fry (1907-2005)
Beggar's Opera '54
Barabbas '62
The Bible '66
The Brontes of Haworth '73
The Lady's Not for Burning '87

E. Max Frye
Something Wild '86
Amos and Andrew '93
Palmetto '98
Where the Money Is '00
Band of Brothers '01
Foxcatcher '14

Carol Fuchs
Alaska '96
No Reservations '07

Daniel Fuchs (1909-93)
The Hard Way '43
Between Two Worlds '44
Criss Cross '48
Storm Warning '51
Jeanne Eagels '57
The Underneath '95

Jason Fuchs (1986-)
Ice Age: Continental Drift '12
Rags '12
Pan '15

Robert Fuest (1927-)
Doctor Phibes Rises Again '72
The Final Programme '73

Katherine Fugate (1965-)
Carolina '03
The Prince & Me '04
Valentine's Day '10
New Year's Eve '11

Kinji Fukasaku (1930-2003)
Under the Flag of the Rising Sun '72
Message from Space '78
Samurai Reincarnation '81

Cary Fukunaga (1977-)
Sin Nombre '09
Beasts of No Nation '15
It '17

Lucio Fulci (1927-96)
Beatrice Cenci '69
A Lizard in a Woman's Skin '71
Don't Torture a Duckling '72
Contraband '80
Gates of Hell '80
The Black Cat '81
The Beyond '82
New York Ripper '82
The House by the Cemetery '83
Demonia '90
Wax Mask '97

Charles Fuller (1939-)
A Soldier's Story '84
Love Songs '99
The Wall '99

David Fuller
Necessary Roughness '91
Gang in Blue '96

Kim Fuller
Spice World: The Movie '97
High Heels and Low Lifes '01
From Justin to Kelly '03

Samuel Fuller (1911-97)
It Happened in Hollywood '37
I Shot Jesse James '49
Shockproof '49
Baron of Arizona '51
Fixed Bayonets! '51
The Steel Helmet '51
Park Row '52
Pickup on South Street '53
China Gate '57
Forty Guns '57
The Crimson Kimono '59
Verboten! '59
Underworld U.S.A. '61
Merrill's Marauders '62
Shock Corridor '63
Naked Kiss '64
Shark! '68
Dead Pigeon on Beethoven Street '72
The Klansman '74
The Big Red One '80
White Dog '82
Let's Get Harry '87
Girls in Prison '94

Maude Fulton
Other Men's Women '31
Safe in Hell '31

Sidney J. Furie (1933-)
A Dangerous Age '57
The Boys in Company C '77
Purple Hearts '84
Iron Eagle '86
Iron Eagle 2 '88

Jules Furthman (1888-1966)
Shanghai Express '32
China Seas '35
Mutiny on the Bounty '35
Come and Get It '36
Spawn of the North '38
Only Angels Have Wings '39
The Shanghai Gesture '42
The Outlaw '43
To Have & Have Not '44
The Big Sleep '46
Nightmare Alley '47
Rio Bravo '59

John Fusco
Crossroads '86
Young Guns '88
Young Guns 2 '90
The Babe '92
Thunderheart '92
Loch Ness '95
Spirit: Stallion of the Cimarron '02
Hidalgo '04
The Forbidden Kingdom '08
Crouching Tiger, Hidden Dragon: Sword of Destiny '16
The Shack '17
The Highwaymen '19

Dan Futterman (1967-)
Capote '05
Foxcatcher '14

Richard Gabai (1964-)
Virgin High '90
Assault of the Party Nerds 2: Heavy Petting Detective '95

Frank Gabrielson (1910-80)
Something for the Boys '44
Don Juan Quilligan '45
Flight of the Doves '71

Antonio Gades (1936-2004)
Blood Wedding '81
Carmen '83

Reg Gadney
Kennedy '83
The Sculptress '97

Marjorie Gaffney (1897-1963)
First a Girl '35
Head Over Heels '37

Christos N. Gage
The Breed '01
Teenage Caveman '01

Stephen Gaghan (1965-)
Rules of Engagement '00
Traffic '00
Abandon '02
The Alamo '04
Havoc '05
Syriana '05
Dolittle '20

Alain Gagnol (1967-)
A Cat in Paris '11
Phantom Boy '16

Neil Gaiman (1960-)
Neil Gaiman's NeverWhere '96
Princess Mononoke '98
MirrorMask '05
Beowulf '07

Karl Gajdusek (1968-)
Trespass '11
Oblivion '13
The November Man '14
Blood Brother '18

Bob Gale (1951-)
1941 '79
Used Cars '80
Back to the Future '85
Back to the Future, Part 2 '89
Back to the Future, Part 3 '90
Trespass '92
Interstate 60 '02

John A. Gallagher
The Deli '97
Blue Moon '00

Michelle Gallagher
Road to Riches '01
The Marine '06

Thomas Gallagher
Ghost Writer '07
Stand Off '11

George Gallo (1956-)
Midnight Run '88
29th Street '91
Trapped in Paradise '94
Double Take '01
See Spot Run '01
The Whole Ten Yards '04

Code Name: The Cleaner '07
My Mom's New Boyfriend '08
Columbus Circle '10
Middle Men '10

Vincent Gallo (1961-)
Buffalo 66 '97
The Brown Bunny '03

Steve Galluccio
Mambo Italiano '03
Funkytown '11

Michael M.B. Galvin (1970-)
Blowin' Smoke '99
Fat Kid Rules the World '12

Kenneth Gamet (1903-71)
The Case of the Stuttering Bishop '37
Smart Blonde '37
Nancy Drew-Detective '38
Nancy Drew-Trouble Shooter '39
You Can't Get Away With Murder '39
Flowing Gold '40
The Smiling Ghost '41
Pittsburgh '42
Tampico '44
Blonde Ice '48
Wake of the Red Witch '49
Flying Leathernecks '51
Man in the Saddle '51
Santa Fe '51
The Last Posse '53
A Lawless Street '55

Nisha Ganatra (1974-)
Chutney Popcorn '99
The Cheetah Girls: One World '08
Centerstage: On Pointe '16

Abel Gance (1889-1981)
J'accuse! '19
La Roue '23
Beethoven '36

Joesph Gangemi
Wind Chill '07
Stonehearst Asylum '13
Blackway '16

Brad Gann
Invincible '06
Black Irish '07

Ernest K. Gann (1910-91)
Island in the Sky '53
The High and the Mighty '54
Soldier of Fortune '55

Roberts Gannaway
Cats Don't Dance '97
Leroy and Stitch '06

Joe Gannon
Solar Crisis '92
The Cyberstalking '99

Lucy Gannon (1948-)
Plain Jane '02
The Best of Men '12

Russell Gannon
The Last Letter '04
Purple Heart '05

Christophe Gans (1960-)
Brotherhood of the Wolf '01
Beauty and the Beast '14

Dennis Gansel (1973-)
Before the Fall '04
The Wave '08

Lowell Ganz (1948-)
Night Shift '82
Splash '84
Spies Like Us '85
Gung Ho '86
Vibes '88
Parenthood '89
City Slickers '91
A League of Their Own '92
Mr. Saturday Night '92
City Slickers 2: The Legend of Curly's Gold '94
Greedy '94
Forget Paris '95
Father's Day '96
Multiplicity '96
EDtv '99
Where the Heart Is '00
Fever Pitch '05
Robots '05
Tooth Fairy '10

Robert Ben Garant (1970-)
Taxi '04
Herbie: Fully Loaded '05
The Pacifier '05
Let's Go to Prison '06
Night at the Museum '06
Balls of Fury '07
Reno 911! Miami '07
Night at the Museum: Battle of the Smithsonian '09

Dan Garcia
Death Toll '07
Lords of the Street '08
Enemies Among Us '10
Journey to Promethea '10
Kiss the Bride '10
Terror Trap '10

Eric Garcia
Repo Men '10
Strange But True '19

Jon Garcia
The Falls: Testament of Love '13
The Falls: Covenant of Grace '16

Rodrigo Garcia (1959-)
Things You Can Tell Just by Looking at Her '00
Nine Lives '05
Mother and Child '09
Last Days in the Desert '16

Yolanda Garcia Serrano (1958-)
Between Your Legs '99
Km. 0 '00

Louis Gardel
Fort Saganne '84
Indochine '92
East-West '99

Herb Gardner (1934-2003)
A Thousand Clowns '65
I'm Not Rappaport '96

Pierce Gardner (1951-)
Lost Souls '00
Dan in Real Life '07

Richard Harding Gardner (1949-)
Deadly Daphne's Revenge '93
Sherlock: Undercover Dog '94

Jeremy Garelick (1975-)
The Break-Up '06
The Wedding Ringer '15

Leo Garen
Charms '73
Band of the Hand '86

Brian Garfield (1939-)
Fleshburn '84
Necessity '88

Louis Garfinkle (1928-2005)
I Bury the Living '58
Face of Fire '59
Little Cigars '73
The Deer Hunter '78

Alex Garland (1970-)
28 Days Later '02
The Tesseract '03
Sunshine '07
Never Let Me Go '10
Dredd '12
Ex Machina '15
Annihilation '18

Robert Garland
The Electric Horseman '79
No Way Out '87

Tony Garnett (1936-)
Kes '69
Deep in the Heart '83
Fat Man and Little Boy '89

Philippe Garrel (1948-)
Frontier of Dawn '08
A Burning Hot Summer '11
Jealousy '13

David Garrett
Corky Romano '01
Deuce Bigalow: European Gigolo '05

Oliver H.P. Garrett (1894-1952)
Three Faces East '30
A Farewell to Arms '32
The Man From Yesterday '32
Night Flight '33
Manhattan Melodrama '34
The Hurricane '37
One Third of a Nation '39
The Man I Married '40
Duel in the Sun '46
Dead Reckoning '47

Mick Garris (1951-)
Critters 2: The Main Course '88
The Fly 2 '89
Hocus Pocus '93
Quicksilver Highway '98
Virtual Obsession '98
Riding the Bullet '04
Nightmare Cinema '19

Matteo Garrone (1968-)
The Embalmer '03
Gomorrah '08
Tale of Tales '15

Ed Gass-Donnelly (1977-)
Small Town Murder Songs '10
The Last Exorcism Part II '13

Harold Gast (1918-2003)
A Woman Called Golda '82
The Jesse Owens Story '84
Shakedown on the Sunset Strip '88

Ernesto Gastaldi (1934-)
Giants of Rome '63
The Whip and the Body '63
The Case of the Scorpion's Tail '71
The Scorpion's Tail '71
The Case of the Bloody Iris '72
Your Vice is a Closed Room and Only I Have the Key '72
The Grand Duel '73
Torso '73
Lady of the Evening '75
The Big Alligator River '79
The Great Alligator '81
Scorpion with Two Tails '82

Robert Gaston
Open Cam '05
2 Minutes Later '07

Harvey Gates (1894-1948)
Paint and Powder '25
Hell Divers '31
Clancy Street Boys '43
Don't Gamble with Strangers '46

Tudor Gates (1930-2007)
Barbarella '68
Danger: Diabolik '68
The Vampire Lovers '70
Fright '71
Lust for a Vampire '71
Twins of Evil '71
The Optimists '73

John Gatins
Hardball '01
Summer Catch '01
Coach Carter '05
Dreamer: Inspired by a True Story '05
Real Steel '11
Flight '12
Need for Speed '14
Power Rangers '17

Massimo Gaudioso (1958-)
The Embalmer '03
Gomorrah '08
Tale of Tales '15

Stephane Gauger
The Owl and the Sparrow '07
Powder Blue '09

Peter Gaulke
Black Knight '01
Say It Isn't So '01
Ice Age: The Meltdown '06
Strange Wilderness '08
The Babymakers '12
Drunk Parents '19

Bart Gavigan
Luther '03
End of the Spear '06
The Journey Home '14

Julie Gavras
Blame It on Fidel '06
Late Bloomers '11

John Gay (1924-)
Run Silent, Run Deep '58
Separate Tables '58
The Happy Thieves '61
The Courtship of Eddie's Father '62
The Four Horsemen of the Apocalypse '62
The Hallelujah Trail '65
No Way to Treat a Lady '68
The Power '68
Soldier Blue '70
Sometimes a Great Notion '71
Hennessy '75
A Tale of Two Cities '80
The Long Summer of George Adams '82

Henry Gayden
Earth to Echo '14
Shazam! '19

Joe Gayton
Bulletproof '96
Sweet Jane '98
The Shepherd: Border Patrol '08
Faster '10

Tony Gayton (1959-)
Murder by Numbers '02
The Salton Sea '02
Faster '10

Michael V. Gazzo (1923-95)
King Creole '58
A Hatful of Rain '59

Fred Gebhardt (1925-72)
12 to the Moon '60
The Phantom Planet '61

Paul Gegauff (1922-83)
Les Cousins '59
Purple Noon '60
This Man Must Die '70
A Piece of Pleasure '74

Peter Geiger
The Cold Equations '96
The Colony '98

Will Geiger
Elvis and Annabelle '07
Free Willy: Escape from Pirate's Cove '10

Larry Gelbart (1928-2009)
The Notorious Landlady '62
The Wrong Box '66
Oh, God! '77
Movie, Movie '78
Neighbors '81
Tootsie '82
Blame It on Rio '84
Barbarians at the Gate '93
Weapons of Mass Distraction '97
Bedazzled '00
And Starring Pancho Villa as Himself '03

Stephen Geller
Slaughterhouse Five '72
The Valachi Papers '72

Milton S. Gelman (1919-90)
Cabo Blanco '81
One Man's Hero '98

Erwin Gelsey (1900-88)
Jewel Robbery '32
The Strange Love of Molly Louvain '32
Double or Nothing '37

Jonathan Gems
Mars Attacks! '96
The Treat '98

Kevin Gendreau
Deep Evil '04
Warbirds '08

Pierre Gendron (1896-1956)
Bluebeard '44
The Monster Maker '44
Fog Island '45

Michael Genet (1958-)
She Hate Me '04
Talk to Me '07

Robert Geoffrion
Eternal Evil '87
The Peacekeeper '98
Cruel and Unusual '01

Dean Georgaris
Lara Croft Tomb Raider: The Cradle of Life '03
Paycheck '03
The Manchurian Candidate '04
Tristan & Isolde '06
The Meg '18

George W. George (1920-2007)
The Nevadan '50
City of Bad Men '53
The Rocket Man '54
The Halliday Brand '57
Apache Territory '58
Fort Dobbs '58
Two Little Bears '61

Nelson George
CB4: The Movie '93
Life Support '07

Rob George (1950-)
Fair Game '86
The Dreaming '88

Terry George (1952-)
In the Name of the Father '93
Some Mother's Son '96
The Boxer '97
A Bright Shining Lie '98
Hart's War '02
Stand Off '11
The Promise '17

Gerald Geraghty (1906-54)
South of the Border '39
The Falcon and the Co-Eds '43
The Falcon Strikes Back '43
The Falcon in Mexico '44
The Red Menace '49
Trigger, Jr. '50

Maurice Geraghty (1908-87)
Whiplash '48
Tomahawk '51
Robbers' Roost '55
Mohawk '56

Tom Geraghty (1883-1945)
Elmer the Great '33
The Church Mouse '34
Wings of the Morning '37

Gary Gerani
Pumpkinhead '88
Vampirella '96
Trading Paint '19

Glenn German
Racing for Time '08
At Middleton '13

Pietro Germi (1904-74)
Divorce-Italian Style '62
Seduced and Abandoned '64
Alfredo, Alfredo '72

Chris Gerolmo
Mississippi Burning '88
Citizen X '95
Certain Prey '11

Glen Gers
Off Season '01
Brother's Keeper '02
Fracture '07
Mad Money '08

Daniel Gerson (1966-2016)
Monsters, Inc. '01
Monsters University '13
Big Hero 6 '14

Paul Gerstenberger
Fakers '04
Bad Meat '11

Ricky Gervais (1961-)
The Invention of Lying '09
Cemetery Junction '10

Sacha Gervasi (1966-)
The Big Tease '99
The Terminal '04
Henry's Crime '10
November Criminals '17

Greta Gerwig (1983-)
Hannah Takes the Stairs '07
Nights and Weekends '08
Frances Ha '13
Mistress America '15
Lady Bird '17
Little Women '19

Nicolas Gessner (1931-)
The Peking Blond '68
Someone Behind the Door '71

Robert Getchell
Alice Doesn't Live Here Anymore '74
Bound for Glory '76
Mommie Dearest '81
Sweet Dreams '85
Stella '89
Point of No Return '93
This Boy's Life '93
The Client '94

Russell Gewirtz
Inside Man '06
Righteous Kill '08

Bahman Ghobadi (1968-)
Marooned in Iraq '02
Turtles Can Fly '04

Alfredo Giannetti (1924-95)
Divorce-Italian Style '62
L'Automobile '71

Robert Gianviti
Revenge of the Musketeers '63
The Triumph of Hercules '66
Gunslinger '70
A Lizard in a Woman's Skin '71
Don't Torture a Duckling '72

Roberto Gianviti
Revenge of the Musketeers '63
The Triumph of Hercules '66
Beatrice Cenci '69
Gunslinger '70
A Lizard in a Woman's Skin '71
Don't Torture a Duckling '72
Seven Blood-Stained Orchids '72

Daniel Giat (1955-)
Path to War '02
Bury My Heart at Wounded Knee '07
The Legend of Hercules '14

Andrea Gibb
Dear Frankie '04
Nina's Heavenly Delights '06

Alex Gibney (1953-)
Enron: The Smartest Guys in the Room '05
Casino Jack and the United States of Money '10
Client 9: The Rise and Fall of Eliot Spitzer '10
Freakonomics '10
Magic Trip: Ken Kesey's Search for a Kool Place '11
Mea Maxima Culpa: Silence in the House of God '12
The Armstrong Lie '13

We Steal Secrets: The Story of WikiLeaks *'13*
Going Clear: Scientology and the Prison of Belief *'15*
Zero Days *'16*
No Stone Unturned *'17*
Citizen K *'19*
The Inventor: Out For Blood In Silicon Valley *'19*

Sheridan Gibney (1904-88)
The House on 56th Street *'33*
Massacre *'34*
Anthony Adverse *'36*
The Locket *'46*

Channing Gibson
Lethal Weapon 4 *'98*
Walking Tall *'04*

Mark Gibson
The In Crowd *'00*
Lush *'01*
Snow Dogs *'02*
The Wild *'06*

Mel Gibson (1956-)
The Passion of the Christ *'04*
Apocalypto *'06*
Get the Gringo *'12*

Nelson Gidding (1919-2004)
The Helen Morgan Story *'57*
I Want to Live! *'58*
Onionhead *'58*
Odds Against Tomorrow *'59*
Lisa *'62*
The Haunting *'63*
The Andromeda Strain *'71*
The Hindenburg *'75*
The Mummy Lives *'93*

Raynold Gideon
A Man, a Woman, and a Bank *'79*
Starman *'84*
Stand by Me *'86*
Made in Heaven *'87*
Kuffs *'92*
The River Wild *'94*
Jungle 2 Jungle *'96*
Mr. Brooks *'07*

Gregory Gieras
Dark Asylum *'01*
Centipede *'05*
Beyond *'11*

Adam Gierasch
Crocodile *'00*
Crocodile 2: Death Swamp *'01*
Derailed *'02*
Mortuary *'05*
Autopsy *'08*
Mother of Tears *'08*
Night of the Demons *'09*
Fertile Ground *'10*

Barry Gifford (1946-)
Lost Highway *'96*
Dance with the Devil *'97*
City of Ghosts *'03*

Tony Giglio (1971-)
In Enemy Hands *'04*
Death Race 2 *'10*
Death Race 3: Inferno *'12*

Mateo Gil (1972-)
Open Your Eyes *'97*
The Sea Inside *'04*
Agora *'09*

Josh Gilbert
Mr. Woodcock *'07*
Furry Vengeance *'10*

Lewis Gilbert (1920-2018)
Cosh Boy *'52*
Carve Her Name with Pride *'58*
Haunted *'95*

Julian Gilbey
Rise of the Footsoldier *'07*
A Lonely Place to Die *'11*
The ABCs of Death 2 *'14*
Plastic *'14*

Will Gilbey
Rise of the Footsoldier *'07*
A Lonely Place to Die *'11*
Plastic *'14*

Gail Gilchriest
My Dog Skip *'99*
The Greening of Whitney Brown *'11*

Berne Giler (1908-67)
Westbound *'58*
Tarzan's Greatest Adventure *'59*
Tarzan the Magnificent *'60*
Tarzan's Three Challenges *'63*
Gunfight in Abilene *'67*

David Giler
Myra Breckinridge *'70*
The Parallax View *'74*
Fun with Dick and Jane *'77*
Southern Comfort *'81*
The Money Pit *'86*
Undisputed *'02*

Cameron Giles (1976-)
See Cam'ron

David Giles
Paradise Road *'97*
Under the Lighthouse Dancing *'97*

Frank Gill, Jr. (1907-70)
Atlantic City *'44*
McHale's Navy *'64*

Stuart Gillard (1950-)
Paradise *'82*
Teenage Mutant Ninja Turtles 3 *'93*

Jeremy Gillespie
Father's Day *'12*
The Void *'17*

Terry Gilliam (1940-)
And Now for Something Completely Different *'72*
Monty Python and the Holy Grail *'75*
Jabberwocky *'77*
Monty Python's Life of Brian *'79*
Time Bandits *'81*
Monty Python's The Meaning of Life *'83*
Brazil *'85*
The Adventures of Baron Munchausen *'89*
Fear and Loathing in Las Vegas *'98*
Tideland *'05*
The Imaginarium of Doctor Parnassus *'09*
The Man Who Killed Don Quixote *'18*

Sidney Gilliat (1908-94)
Rome Express *'32*
The Lady Vanishes *'38*
Jamaica Inn *'39*
Night Train to Munich *'40*
The Girl in the News *'41*
Two Thousand Women *'44*
Waterloo Road *'45*
The Belles of St. Trinian's *'53*
Geordie *'55*
She Played With Fire *'57*
Endless Night *'71*

Vince Gilligan (1967-)
Wilder Napalm *'93*
Home Fries *'98*
Hancock *'08*

John Gilling (1912-85)
House of Darkness *'48*
The Frightened Man *'52*
The Voice of Merrill *'52*
Recoil *'53*
Bond of Fear *'56*
Odongo *'56*
The Flesh and the Fiends *'60*
It Takes a Thief *'60*
The Gorgon *'64*
The Mummy's Shroud *'67*

Rob Gilmer
Out of Time *'00*
Second Sight *'07*

Bettina Gilois
Glory Road *'06*
McFarland USA *'15*

Dan Gilroy (1959-)
Freejack *'92*
Chasers *'94*
Two for the Money *'05*
The Fall *'06*
The Bourne Legacy *'12*
Nightcrawler *'14*
Kong: Skull Island *'17*
Roman J. Israel, Esq. *'17*
Velvet Buzzsaw *'19*

Frank D. Gilroy (1925-)
Fastest Gun Alive *'56*
The Gallant Hours *'60*
The Subject Was Roses *'68*
Desperate Characters *'71*
From Noon Till Three *'76*
Jinxed *'82*

Henry Gilroy
Bionicle 3: Web of Shadows *'05*
Star Wars: The Clone Wars *'08*
Mass Effect: Paragon Lost *'12*

Tom Gilroy
Spring Forward *'99*
Bait *'00*
The Cold Lands *'13*

Tony Gilroy (1956-)
The Cutting Edge *'92*
Dolores Claiborne *'94*
Extreme Measures *'96*
The Devil's Advocate *'97*
Proof of Life *'00*
The Bourne Identity *'02*
The Bourne Supremacy *'04*
The Cutting Edge: Going for the Gold *'05*
The Bourne Ultimatum *'07*
Michael Clayton *'07*
State of Play *'09*
The Bourne Legacy *'12*
Rogue One: A Star Wars Story *'16*
The Great Wall *'17*
Beirut *'18*

Michael Gilvary
According to Greta *'08*
Transit *'12*

Milton Moses Ginsberg (1943-)
Coming Apart *'69*
Werewolf of Washington *'73*

Aaron Ginsburg
InSight *'11*
Home Alone: The Holiday Heist *'12*

Jose Giovanni (1923-2004)
Le Trou *'59*
Classe Tous Risque *'60*
Le Deuxieme Souffle *'66*
Le Gitan *'75*

Buddy Giovinazzo (1957-)
Combat Shock *'84*
No Way Home *'96*
Life is Hot in Cracktown *'08*

Bernard Girard (1918-97)
Breakthrough *'50*
The Rebel Set *'59*
Dead Heat on a Merry-Go-Round *'66*
The Mad Room *'69*

Francois Girard (1963-)
32 Short Films about Glenn Gould *'93*
The Red Violin *'98*
Silk *'07*

Michael Paul Girard (1954-)
Body Parts *'94*
Bikini House Calls *'96*
Illegal Affairs *'96*
Bikini Med School *'98*
Sweet Evil *'98*

William Girdler (1947-78)
Asylum of Satan *'72*
Three on a Meathook *'72*
Sheba, Baby *'75*
The Manitou *'78*

Karin Gist
Jump In! *'07*
Camp Rock *'08*
Camp Rock 2: The Final Jam *'10*

Amos Gitai (1950-)
Golem: The Petrified Garden *'93*
Kadosh *'99*
Kippur *'00*
Free Zone *'05*
Disengagement *'07*

Kubec Glasmon (1889-1938)
Blonde Crazy *'31*
Public Enemy *'31*
Smart Money *'31*
Taxi! *'32*
Union Depot *'32*

Sydney Glass
Roots: The Next Generation *'79*
Detour to Terror *'80*

Leonard Glasser
Out Cold *'89*
Mojave Moon *'96*

Richard Glatzer (1952-2015)
Grief *'94*
Quinceanera *'06*
The Last of Robin Hood *'13*
Still Alice *'14*

Benjamin Glazer (1887-1956)
The Merry Widow *'25*
7th Heaven *'27*
Beggars of Life *'28*
The Trail of '98 *'28*
A Farewell to Arms *'32*
No Man of Her Own *'32*

Jonathan Glazer (1965-)
Birth *'04*
Under the Skin *'13*

Mitch Glazer (1953-)
Moon over Miami *'41*
Mr. Mike's Mondo Video *'79*
Scrooged *'88*
Great Expectations *'97*
The Recruit *'03*
Passion Play *'10*
Rock the Kasbah *'15*

James Gleason (1886-1959)
The Flying Fool *'29*
Beyond Victory *'31*

David Gleeson (1966-)
Cowboys & Angels *'04*
The Front Line *'06*
Tolkien *'19*

Tom Gleisner
The Castle *'97*
The Dish *'00*

John Glenn
Eagle Eye *'08*
The Lazarus Project *'08*

James Glickenhaus (1950-)
Exterminator *'80*
Shakedown *'88*
Slaughter of the Innocents *'93*
Timemaster *'95*

Greg Glienna (1963-)
A Guy Thing *'03*
Relative Strangers *'06*

Will Gluck
Friends With Benefits *'11*
Annie *'14*
Peter Rabbit *'18*

Richard Gnolfo
The Dog Who Saved Christmas *'09*
The Dog Who Saved Christmas Vacation *'10*
A Nanny for Christmas *'10*
12 Christmas Wishes For My Dog *'11*
The Dog Who Saved the Holidays *'12*
Jersey Shore Shark Attack *'12*
The Dog Who Saved Summer *'15*

Alain Godard
Enemy at the Gates *'00*
Day of the Falcon *'11*
Wolf Totem *'15*

Jean-Luc Godard (1930-)
Breathless *'59*
Le Petit Soldat *'60*
A Woman Is a Woman *'60*
My Life to Live *'62*
Les Carabiniers *'63*
Band of Outsiders *'64*
Contempt *'64*
Une Femme Mariee *'64*
Alphaville *'65*
The Joy of Knowledge *'65*
A Married Woman *'65*
Pierrot le Fou *'65*
Two or Three Things I Know about Her *'66*
La Chinoise *'67*
Weekend *'67*
Six in Paris *'68*
Numero Deux *'75*
Every Man for Himself *'79*
Passion *'82*
Hail Mary *'85*
Aria *'88*
Helas pour Moi *'94*
For Ever Mozart *'96*
In Praise of Love *'01*
Our Music *'04*
Film Socialisme *'10*
Goodbye to Language *'14*

Stephen Godchaux
Five *'11*
Call Me Crazy *'13*

Drew Goddard
Cloverfield *'08*
The Cabin in the Woods *'12*
World War Z *'13*
The Martian *'15*
Bad Times at the El Royale *'18*

Ivan Goff (1910-99)
My Love Came Back *'40*
White Heat *'49*
Backfire *'50*
Captain Horatio Hornblower *'51*
Goodbye My Fancy *'51*
King of the Khyber Rifles *'53*
White Witch Doctor *'53*
Green Fire *'55*
Serenade *'56*
Band of Angels *'57*
Man of a Thousand Faces *'57*
Portrait in Black *'60*
Legend of the Lone Ranger *'81*

Michael Golamco
Please Stand By *'17*
Always Be My Maybe *'19*

Menahem Golan (1929-)
What's Good for the Goose *'69*
Eagles Attack at Dawn *'70*
Operation Thunderbolt *'77*
The Apple *'80*

Michael Goldbach
Daydream Nation *'10*
Down a Dark Hall *'18*

Sandra Goldbacher (1960-)
The Governess *'98*
Me Without You *'01*

Willis Goldbeck (1898-1979)
Scaramouche *'23*
Peter Pan *'24*
Freaks *'32*
Penguin Pool Murder *'32*
Murder On the Blackboard *'34*
Young Dr. Kildare *'38*
Calling Dr. Kildare *'39*
The Secret of Dr. Kildare *'39*
Dr. Kildare Goes Home *'40*
Dr. Kildare's Crisis *'40*
Dr. Kildare's Strange Case *'40*
Dr. Kildare's Wedding Day *'41*
The People *vs.* Dr. Kildare *'41*
Calling Dr. Gillespie *'42*
Dr. Gillespie's New Assistant *'42*
Dr. Kildare's Victory *'42*
Sergeant Rutledge *'60*
The Man Who Shot Liberty Valance *'62*

Adam F. Goldberg (1976-)
The Muppets' Wizard of Oz *'05*
Aliens in the Attic *'09*
Fanboys *'09*

Brent Goldberg
National Lampoon's Van Wilder *'02*
The Girl Next Door *'04*
My Baby's Daddy *'04*
Underclassman *'05*

Dan Goldberg
Heavy Metal *'81*
Feds *'88*

Evan Goldberg (1982-)
Superbad *'07*
Pineapple Express *'08*
The Green Hornet *'11*
Goon *'12*
The Watch *'12*
This Is the End *'13*
The Night Before *'15*
Neighbors 2: Sorority Rising *'16*
Sausage Party *'16*

Gary David Goldberg (1944-2013)
Dad *'89*
Bye Bye, Love *'94*
Must Love Dogs *'05*

Harris Goldberg (1972-)
I'll Be Home for Christmas *'98*
Deuce Bigalow: Male Gigolo *'99*
Master of Disguise *'02*
Without a Paddle *'04*
Numb *'07*

Howard Goldberg
Spontaneous Combustion *'89*
Eden *'98*

Ian Goldberg
The Autopsy of Jane Doe *'16*
Eli *'19*

Marshall Goldberg
The Abduction *'96*
Where the Truth Lies *'99*

Mel Goldberg
The Lively Set *'64*
Hang 'Em High *'67*

Michael Goldberg
Cool Runnings *'93*
Little Giants *'94*
Bushwhacked *'95*
The Lovemaster *'97*
Snow Dogs *'02*
Harry Potter and the Order of the Phoenix *'07*

Paula Goldberg
In Her Line of Fire *'06*
Out at the Wedding *'07*
The Perfect Family *'11*

Jake Goldberger (1977-)
Don McKay *'09*
Homecoming *'09*
Life of a King *'13*
Almost Friends *'17*

Kenny Golde
The Smokers *'00*
The Job *'03*
Walking with the Enemy *'13*

Dan Golden
Wizards of the Demon Sword *'94*
Venomous *'01*

David Golden
Personal Effects *'05*
Safe Harbor *'06*
The Secret of Hidden Lake *'06*
Nightmare *'07*
Time and Again *'07*
Mrs. Miracle *'09*

Jeffrey Goldenberg
Blowback *'99*
Looking for an Echo *'99*

Michael Goldenberg (1965-)
Bed of Roses *'95*
Contact *'97*
Peter Pan *'03*
Green Lantern *'11*

Peter Goldfinger
Sorority Row *'09*
Jigsaw *'17*

Joshua Goldin
Darkman *'90*
Wonderful World *'09*

Marilyn Goldin
Barocco *'76*
Sweet Revenge *'76*
Camille Claudel *'89*
The Triumph of Love *'01*

Bo Goldman (1932-)
One Flew Over the Cuckoo's Nest *'75*
Melvin and Howard *'80*
Shoot the Moon *'82*
Swing Shift *'84*
Little Nikita *'88*
Scent of a Woman *'92*
City Hall *'95*
Meet Joe Black *'98*

Gary Goldman (1944-)
Big Trouble in Little China *'86*
Navy SEALS *'90*
Total Recall *'90*
Next *'07*

James Goldman (1927-98)
The Lion in Winter *'68*
Nicholas and Alexandra *'71*
They Might Be Giants *'71*
Oliver Twist *'82*
Anastasia: The Mystery of Anna *'86*
The Lion in Winter *'03*

Jane Goldman (1970-)
Stardust *'07*
The Debt *'10*
Kick-Ass *'10*
X-Men: First Class *'11*
The Woman in Black *'12*
Kingsman: The Secret Service *'15*
Miss Peregrine's Home for Peculiar Children *'16*
Kingsman: The Golden Circle *'17*

Lawrence Louis Goldman
Kronos *'57*
The Viking Women and the Sea Serpent *'57*
War of the Satellites *'58*

William Goldman (1931-)
Harper *'66*
Butch Cassidy and the Sundance Kid *'69*
The Great Waldo Pepper *'75*
The Stepford Wives *'75*
All the President's Men *'76*
Marathon Man *'76*
A Bridge Too Far *'77*
Magic *'78*
Heat *'87*
The Princess Bride *'87*
Casual Sex? *'88*
Misery *'90*
Chaplin *'92*
Year of the Comet *'92*
Maverick *'94*
The Chamber *'96*
The Ghost and the Darkness *'96*
Absolute Power *'97*
The General's Daughter *'99*
Hearts in Atlantis *'01*
Dreamcatcher *'03*
Wild Card *'15*

Akiva Goldsman (1962-)
The Client *'94*
Silent Fall *'94*
Batman Forever *'95*
A Time to Kill *'96*
Batman and Robin *'97*
Lost in Space *'98*
Practical Magic *'98*
A Beautiful Mind *'01*
I, Robot *'04*
Cinderella Man *'05*
The Da Vinci Code *'06*
I Am Legend *'07*
Angels & Demons *'09*
Winter's Tale *'14*
Insurgent *'15*
The 5th Wave *'16*
The Dark Tower *'17*
Rings *'17*

John Goldsmith
The Old Curiosity Shop *'94*
Catherine the Great *'95*
Kidnapped *'95*
The Apocalypse Watch *'97*
The Island on Bird Street *'97*
Coming Home *'98*
Agnes Browne *'99*
Victoria & Albert *'01*
The Gospel of John *'03*
Darwin's Darkest Hour *'09*

Josh Goldsmith (1970-)
What Women Want *'00*
13 Going on 30 *'04*

Martin Goldsmith (1913-94)
Detour *'46*
Fort Massacre *'58*
Cast a Long Shadow *'59*
The Gunfight at Dodge City *'59*

Allan Goldstein (1949-)
Rooftops *'89*
Death Wish 5: The Face of Death *'94*
Jungle Boy *'96*
Snakeman *'05*

Gary Goldstein
Hitched for the Holidays *'12*
Strawberry Summer *'12*

Jonathan M. Goldstein (1969-)
Horrible Bosses *'11*
Cloudy with a Chance of Meatballs 2 *'13*
The Incredible Burt Wonderstone *'13*
Vacation *'15*
Spider-Man: Homecoming *'17*

P'nenah Goldstein
Loving Leah *'09*
November Christmas *'10*
Christmas with Holly *'12*

Deena Goldstone
Safe Passage *'94*
Identity Theft: The Michelle Brown Story *'04*

Bobcat Goldthwait (1962-)
Shakes the Clown *'92*
Sleeping Dogs Lie *'06*
World's Greatest Dad *'09*
God Bless America *'11*
Willow Creek *'13*

Larry Golin
Final Combination *'93*
Rebound: The Legend of Earl 'The Goat' Manigault *'96*
Hostage High *'97*
Love Walked In *'97*
Rocky Marciano *'99*

Bryan Goluboff
The Affair *'95*
The Basketball Diaries *'95*

Sy Gomberg (1918-2001)
Summer Stock *'50*
Bloodhounds of Broadway *'52*
Three Warriors *'77*

Nick Gomez (1963-)
Laws of Gravity *'92*
New Jersey Drive *'95*

Manuel Gomez Pereira (1958-)
Why Do They Call It Love When They Mean Sex? *'92*
Mouth to Mouth *'95*
Love Can Seriously Damage Your Health *'96*
Between Your Legs *'99*

Michel Gondry (1963-)
Eternal Sunshine of the Spotless Mind *'04*
The Science of Sleep *'06*
Be Kind Rewind *'08*
Tokyo! *'09*
Mood Indigo *'13*

Noam Gonick (1973-)
Hey, Happy! *'01*
Stryker *'04*

Reuben Gonzalez
Mambo Cafe *'00*
Once Upon a Wedding *'05*

Gregory Goodell
Shattered Spirits *'86*
My Brother's Keeper *'95*
Don't Look Down *'98*
Behind the Mask *'99*
Lost Holiday: The Jim & Suzanne Shemwell Story *'07*

J. Mills Goodloe (1971-)
A Gentleman's Game *'01*
Pride *'07*
The Best of Me *'14*
The Age of Adaline *'15*
Everything, Everything *'17*
The Mountain Between Us *'17*
To All the Boys: P.S. I Still Love You *'20*

Cory Goodman
Priest *'11*
The Last Witch Hunter *'15*
Underworld: Blood Wars *'16*

David Zelag Goodman (1930-2011)
The Stranglers of Bombay *'60*
Lovers and Other Strangers *'70*
Monte Walsh *'70*
Straw Dogs *'72*
Man on a Swing *'74*
Farewell, My Lovely *'75*
Logan's Run *'76*
March or Die *'77*
Eyes of Laura Mars *'78*
Fighting Back *'82*
Monte Walsh *'03*

Frances Goodrich (1890-1984)
The Thin Man *'34*
Society Lawyer *'39*
It's a Wonderful Life *'46*
The Virginian *'46*
Easter Parade *'48*
Father of the Bride *'50*
Father's Little Dividend *'51*
Too Young to Kiss *'51*
The Long, Long Trailer *'54*
Seven Brides for Seven Brothers *'54*
Five Finger Exercise *'62*

Alex Gordon (1922-2003)
Jail Bait *'54*
Bride of the Monster *'55*

Bernard Gordon (1918-2007)
The Lawless Breed *'52*
Crime Wave *'54*
Earth *vs.* the Flying Saucers *'56*
Chicago Confidential *'57*
Hellcats of the Navy *'57*
The Man Who Turned to Stone *'57*
The Case Against Brooklyn *'58*
Day of the Triffids *'63*
The Thin Red Line *'64*
Krakatoa East of Java *'69*

Bert I. Gordon (1922-)
War of the Colossal Beast *'58*
Tormented *'60*
The Witching *'72*
Empire of the Ants *'77*

Dan Gordon
Gulliver's Travels *'39*
Tank *'83*
Gotcha! *'85*
Highlander: The Gathering *'92*
Passenger 57 *'92*
Surf Ninjas *'93*
Wyatt Earp *'94*
Murder in the First *'95*
Terror in the Mall *'98*
The Hurricane *'99*
The Celestine Prophecy *'06*
A Very Mary Christmas *'10*
Let There Be Light *'17*

Fiona Gordon
L'Iceberg *'05*
Lost in Paris *'17*

Gordon Gordon (1906-2002)
Down Three Dark Streets *'54*
Experiment in Terror *'62*

Jill Gordon
Angus *'95*
Five *'11*

Keith Gordon (1961-)
Static *'87*
The Chocolate War *'88*
A Midnight Clear *'92*

Leo Gordon (1922-2000)
Black Patch *'57*
The Wasp Woman *'59*
Tower of London *'62*
The Terror *'63*
Tobruk *'66*

Leon Gordon (1894-1960)
Freaks *'32*
Kongo *'32*
Tarzan and His Mate *'34*
The Unguarded Hour *'36*
Balalaika *'39*
They Met in Bombay *'41*
The Hour of 13 *'52*

Mildred Gordon (1905-79)
Down Three Dark Streets *'54*
Experiment in Terror *'62*

Robert Gordon
Addicted to Love *'96*
Galaxy Quest *'99*
Men in Black 2 *'02*
Lemony Snicket's A Series of Unfortunate Events *'04*

Ruth Gordon (1896-1985)
Dr. Ehrlich's Magic Bullet *'40*
A Double Life *'47*
Adam's Rib *'50*
The Marrying Kind *'52*
Pat and Mike *'52*
The Actress *'53*
It Should Happen to You *'54*

Stuart Gordon (1947-2020)
Re-Animator *'84*
Honey, I Shrunk the Kids *'89*
Body Snatchers *'93*
The Dentist *'96*

Graham Gordy
War Eagle, Arkansas *'07*
The Love Guru *'08*

Kristin Gore (1977-)
Arctic Tale *'07*
War Story *'14*
Accidental Love *'15*

Jonathan Gorman
Bikini Bloodbath *'06*
Bikini Bloodbath Carwash *'08*
Bikini Bloodbath Christmas *'09*

Lisa Gornick (1970-)
Do I Love You? *'02*
Tick Tock Lullaby *'07*

Laszlo Gorog (1903-97)
The Mole People *'56*
The Land Unknown *'57*
Earth *vs.* the Spider *'58*
Too Soon to Love *'60*

Rene Goscinny (1926-77)
The Holes *'72*
Lucky Luke *'94*

Hideo Gosha (1929-92)
Sword of the Beast *'65*
Goyokin *'69*
The Wolves *'82*

Philippa Goslett
Little Ashes *'09*
How To Talk To Girls At Parties *'17*
Mary Magdalene *'19*

Carl Gottlieb (1938-)
Jaws *'75*
Which Way Is Up? *'77*
Jaws 2 *'78*
The Jerk *'79*
Caveman *'81*
Doctor Detroit *'83*
Jaws 3 *'83*

Alfred Gough (1967-)
Shanghai Noon *'00*
Showtime *'02*
Shanghai Knights *'03*
Spider-Man 2 *'04*
Herbie: Fully Loaded *'05*
The Mummy: Tomb of the Dragon Emperor *'08*
I Am Number Four *'11*

Heywood Gould
Rolling Thunder *'77*
The Boys from Brazil *'78*
Fort Apache, the Bronx *'81*
Cocktail *'88*
One Good Cop *'91*
Trial by Jury *'94*
Mistrial *'96*
Double Bang *'01*

Peter Gould
Double Dragon *'94*
Meeting Daddy *'98*
Too Big to Fail *'11*

Edmund Goulding (1891-1959)
Tol'able David *'21*
A Lady of Chance *'28*
No Man of Her Own *'32*
Riptide *'34*
That Certain Woman *'37*

David S. Goyer (1965-)
Death Warrant *'90*
Arcade *'93*
The Puppet Masters *'94*
The Crow 2: City of Angels *'96*
Dark City *'97*
Blade *'98*
Blade 2 *'02*
ZigZag *'02*
Blade: Trinity *'04*
Batman Begins *'05*
Jumper *'08*
The Unborn *'09*
Man of Steel *'13*
Batman v Superman: Dawn of Justice *'16*
Terminator: Dark Fate *'19*

Jean-Francois Goyet
Western *'96*
Lulu *'02*

Todd Graff (1959-)
Used People *'92*
Fly by Night *'93*
The Vanishing *'93*
Angie *'94*
The Beautician and the Beast *'97*
Coyote Ugly *'00*
Camp *'03*
Bandslam *'09*
Joyful Noise *'12*

Benoit Graffin (1966-)
The New Yorker *'98*
Apres-Vous *'03*
Priceless *'06*
The Girl From Monaco *'08*

Sue Grafton (1940-)
Lolly-Madonna XXX *'73*
Agatha Christie's A Caribbean Mystery *'83*
Agatha Christie's Sparkling Cyanide *'83*

Bruce Graham
Dunston Checks In *'95*
Anastasia *'97*
Steal This Movie! *'00*
Gradiva *'06*
Debbie Macomber's Trading Christmas *'11*

Ronny Graham (1919-99)
To Be or Not to Be *'83*
Spaceballs *'87*

Seth Grahame-Smith (1976-)
Abraham Lincoln: Vampire Hunter *'12*
Dark Shadows *'12*
The LEGO Batman Movie *'17*

Michael Grais
Death Hunt *'81*
Poltergeist *'82*
Poltergeist 2: The Other Side *'86*
Marked for Death *'90*
Cool World *'92*

Charles de Grandcourt
Victoria the Great *'37*
Sixty Glorious Years *'38*

Jean-Christophe Grange (1961-)
The Crimson Rivers *'01*
Crimson Rivers 2: Angels of the Apocalypse *'05*
Empire of the Wolves *'05*

Derek Granger
A Handful of Dust *'88*
Where Angels Fear to Tread *'91*

Debra Granik
Down to the Bone *'04*
Winter's Bone *'10*
Leave No Trace *'18*

Barra Grant (1948-)
Life of the Party *'05*
Love Hurts *'09*

James Edward Grant (1905-66)
Danger: Love at Work *'37*
Josette *'38*
Miracles for Sale *'39*
Johnny Eager *'42*
Gambler's Choice *'44*
Angel and the Badman *'47*
Sands of Iwo Jima *'49*
Flying Leathernecks *'51*
Two of a Kind *'51*
Hondo *'53*
Three Violent People *'57*
The Sheepman *'58*
The Alamo *'60*
Donovan's Reef *'63*
McLintock! *'63*
Circus World *'64*
Support Your Local Gunfighter *'71*

John Grant (1891-1955)
Buck Privates *'41*
Hold That Ghost *'41*
In the Navy *'41*
It Ain't Hay *'43*
In Society *'44*
Here Come the Co-Eds *'45*
Buck Privates Come Home *'47*
Abbott and Costello Meet Frankenstein *'48*
Abbott and Costello Meet the Killer, Boris Karloff *'49*
Abbott and Costello in the Foreign Legion *'50*
Abbott and Costello Meet the Invisible Man *'51*
Comin' Round the Mountain *'51*
Abbott and Costello Meet Dr. Jekyll and Mr. Hyde *'52*

Ma and Pa Kettle at the Fair '52
Abbott and Costello Go to Mars '53
Abbott and Costello Meet the Keystone Kops '54
Abbott and Costello Meet the Mummy '55

Shaun Grant
The Snowtown Murders '12
Berlin Syndrome '17
True History of the Kelly Gang '20

Susannah Grant (1963-)
Pocahontas '95
Ever After: A Cinderella Story '98
Erin Brockovich '00
28 Days '00
In Her Shoes '05
Charlotte's Web '06
Catch and Release '07
The Soloist '09
The 5th Wave '16

Robert Grasmere
A Million to Juan '94
Baby Geniuses '98

Duane Graves (1975-)
The Wild Man of the Navidad '08
Kill or Be Killed '15

Bradley Rust Gray
The Exploding Girl '09
Jack and Diane '12
Lovesong '17

James Gray (1969-)
Little Odessa '94
The Yards '00
We Own the Night '07
Two Lovers '09
Blood Ties '13
The Immigrant '13
The Lost City of Z '17
Ad Astra '19

John Gray
Billy Galvin '86
The Lost Capone '90
Showdown at Williams Creek '91
The Hunley '99
Brian's Song '01
The Seventh Stream '01
White Irish Drinkers '10

Mike Gray (1935-2013)
The China Syndrome '79
Code of Silence '85

Pamela Gray
Music of the Heart '99
A Walk on the Moon '99
Conviction '10
Megan Leavey '17

William Gray
The Changeling '80
Prom Night '80
Humongous '82
Killer Deal '99
Killer Wave '07

Charles Grayson (1903-73)
The Boys From Syracuse '40
One Night in the Tropics '40
Underground '41
Outpost in Morocco '49
The Woman on Pier 13 '50
Battle Hymn '57

Brian Grazer (1951-)
Armed and Dangerous '86
Housesitter '92

Claudio Grazioso
Bring It On Again '03
Are We There Yet? '05

Adam Green (1975-)
Hatchet '07
Frozen '10
Hatchet 2 '10

Adolph Green (1915-2002)
The Barkleys of Broadway '49
On the Town '49
Singin' in the Rain '52
It's Always Fair Weather '55
Auntie Mame '58
Bells Are Ringing '60

Clifford Green
Picnic at Hanging Rock '75
Bless the Child '00

David Gordon Green (1975-)
All the Real Girls '03
Undertow '04
Snow Angels '07
Prince Avalanche '13
Goat '16
Halloween '18

Howard J. Green (1893-1965)
Blessed Event '32
I Am a Fugitive from a Chain Gang '32
They Call It Sin '32
If You Could Only Cook '36
Meet Nero Wolfe '36
The Big Boss '41
George White's Scandals '45
Chain Gang '50

Janet Green (1914-93)
Eyewitness '56
Victim '61

Lewis Green
The Spy Within '94
Never Talk to Strangers '95

Michael Green
Green Lantern '11
Blade Runner 2049 '17
Logan '17
Murder on the Orient Express '17
The Call of the Wild '20

Rashaad Ernesto Green (1978-)
Gun Hill Road '11
Premature '20

Terry Green
Heavens Fall '06
No God, No Master '12

Walon Green (1936-)
The Wild Bunch '69
Sorcerer '77
Brink's Job '78
The Border '82
Solarbabies '86
Crusoe '89
RoboCop 2 '90
Eraser '96
The Hi-Lo Country '98

Peter Greenaway (1942-)
The Draughtsman's Contract '82
Drowning by Numbers '87
A Zed & Two Noughts '88
The Cook, the Thief, His Wife & Her Lover '90
The Belly of an Architect '91
Prospero's Books '91
The Pillow Book '95
8 1/2 Women '99
Nightwatching '07
Eisenstein in Guanajuato '15

Everett Greenbaum (1920-99)
Good Neighbor Sam '64
The Reluctant Astronaut '67
The Shakiest Gun in the West '68

Dan Greenberg
Oh! Calcutta! '72
The Guardian '90

Matt Greenberg
The Ghost Brigade '93
The Prophecy 2: Ashtown '97
Halloween: H20 '98
Reign of Fire '02
1408 '07

Rob Greenberg
Meet Dave '08
Overboard '18

Seth Jared Greenberg (1976-)
See Seth Grahame-Smith

Stanley R. Greenberg (1928-2002)
Skyjacked '72
Soylent Green '73

Anthony Laurence Greene
Number One Fan '94
Dead Sexy '01

Clarence Greene (1913-95)
D.O.A. '49
The Thief '52

Eve Greene
Day of Reckoning '33
Tugboat Annie '33
Operator 13 '34
Strange Affair '44

Graham Greene (1904-91)
21 Days '40
Brighton Rock '47
The Fallen Idol '49
The Third Man '49
Saint Joan '57
Our Man in Havana '59
The Comedians '67

Harold Greene (1915-2000)
The House of the Seven Gables '40
Counterspy Meets Scotland Yard '50
Criminal Lawyer '51
Kansas City Confidential '52
Texas Across the River '66

Paul Greengrass (1955-)
The One That Got Away '96
Bloody Sunday '01
United 93 '06
Jason Bourne '16
22 July '18

Matt Greenhalgh
Control '07
Nowhere Boy '09
The Look of Love '13
Film Stars Don't Die in Liverpool '17

Seth Greenland
Who's the Man? '93
My Teacher's Wife '95

Adam Greenman
Three of Hearts '93
And Never Let Her Go '01

Maggie Greenwald (1955-)
The Kill-Off '89
The Ballad of Little Jo '93
Songcatcher '99

Edwin Greenwood (1895-1939)
The Man Who Knew Too Much '34
Young and Innocent '37

James Greer
Max Keeble's Big Move '01
Larry the Cable Guy: Health Inspector '06
The Spy Next Door '10
Unsane '18

William Grefe (1930-)
The Checkered Flag '63
The Death Curse of Tartu '66
The Hooked Generation '69

Clark Gregg (1962-)
What Lies Beneath '00
Choke '08
Trust Me '13

Francesca Gregorini (1968-)
Tanner Hall '09
The Truth About Emanuel '13

Alex Gregory
A Good Old Fashioned Orgy '11
What Men Want '19

Andre Gregory (1934-)
My Dinner with Andre '81
Vanya on 42nd Street '94

Frederic Grendel (1924-2001)
Diabolique '55
Violette '78

Sergio Grieco (1917-82)
Sergeant Klems '71
Mad Dog Killer '77
Deadly Mission '78
The Inglorious Bastards '78

Tom Gries (1922-77)
Will Penny '67
100 Rifles '69

Eleanore Griffin (1904-95)
War of the Wildcats '43
Tenth Avenue Angel '47
Good Morning, Miss Dove '55
Back Street '61
One Man's Way '63

Kynan Griffin
Mythica 2: The Darkspore '15
Mythica: A Quest for Heroes '15

Richard Griffin
Pretty Dead Things '06
Beyond the Dunwich Horror '08
Nun of That '09

Ted Griffin (1970-)
Best Laid Plans '99
Ravenous '99
Ocean's Eleven '01
Matchstick Men '03
Killers '10
Tower Heist '11
Solace '16

Charles B. Griffith (1930-2007)
The Gunslinger '56
Not of This Earth '57
Teenage Doll '57
The Undead '57
A Bucket of Blood '59
Atlas '60
Creature from the Haunted Sea '60
Little Shop of Horrors '60
The Wild Angels '66
Devil's Angels '67
Death Race 2000 '75
Eat My Dust '76
Not of This Earth '88

D.W. Griffith (1875-1948)
Judith of Bethulia '14
The Birth of a Nation '15
Intolerance '16
Broken Blossoms '19
The Love Flower '20
Way Down East '20
Orphans of the Storm '21
Struggle '31

Thomas Ian Griffith (1962-)
Night of the Warrior '91
Excessive Force '93
Black Point '01
Mr. Troop Mom '09

David Griffiths (1952-)
Collateral Damage '02
The Hunted '03

Leon Griffiths (1928-92)
The Flesh and the Fiends '60
The Secret of Monte Cristo '61
The Grissom Gang '71
Piece of Cake '88

Peter Griffiths (1950-)
Collateral Damage '02
The Hunted '03

Jean (Giovanni Grimaldi) Grimaud (1917-2001)
The Slave '62
The Blancheville Monster '63
Castle of Blood '64
Four Dollars of Revenge '66

Tony Grisoni (1952-)
The Island on Bird Street '97
Fear and Loathing in Las Vegas '98
In This World '03
Tideland '05
Brothers of the Head '06
Death Defying Acts '07
Red Riding, Part 1: 1974 '09
Red Riding, Part 2: 1980 '09
Red Riding, Part 3: 1983 '09
The Unloved '09
How I Live Now '13
The Man Who Killed Don Quixote '18

Ferde Grofe, Jr.
Guerillas in Pink Lace '64
The Walls of Hell '64
The Day of the Wolves '71

Adam Gross
Devour '05
DOA: Dead or Alive '06

Ethan Gross
Klepto '03
Ad Astra '19

Jerry Gross (1940-2002)
Girl on a Chain Gang '65
Teenage Mother '67

Larry Gross (1953-)
48 Hrs. '82
Streets of Fire '84
Geronimo: An American Legend '93
Chinese Box '97
David '97
Gunshy '98
True Crime '99
The Virginian '99
Crime and Punishment in Suburbia '00
The Beautiful Country '04
We Don't Live Here Anymore '04
Veronika Decides to Die '15
Porto '17

Paul Gross (1959-)
Men with Brooms '02
Passchendaele '10
Hyena Road '16

Seth Gross
Devour '05
DOA: Dead or Alive '06

Norman Grossfeld (1963-)
Pokemon 3: The Movie '01
Yu-Gi-Oh! The Movie: Pyramid of Light '04

Adam Grossman
Sometimes They Come Back. . . Again '96
Carnival of Souls '98

Jean Gruault (1924-)
Jules and Jim '62
The Wild Child '70
The Story of Adele H. '75
The Green Room '78
Mon Oncle d'Amerique '80
Life Is a Bed of Roses '83
Love Unto Death '84

Frank Gruber (1904-69)
The Mask of Dimitrios '44
Dressed to Kill '46
Denver and the Rio Grande '52
White Comanche '68

J. Mackye Gruber
Final Destination 2 '03
The Butterfly Effect '04

Jean-Claude Grumberg (1939-)
The Last Metro '80
Amen '02
Capital '12

John Guare (1938-)
Atlantic City '81
Six Degrees of Separation '93
Subway Stories '97

Paul Guay
The Little Rascals '94
Liar Liar '97
Heartbreakers '01

Richard Guay
True Love '89
The 24 Hour Woman '99

Bill Gucwa
No Code of Conduct '98
Storm Catcher '99

Christian Gudegast
A Man Apart '03
London Has Fallen '16
Den of Thieves '18

Mac Gudgeon
Wind '92
Last Ride '09
Fatal Honeymoon '12

Robert Guediguian (1953-)
Marius and Jeannette '97
The Town Is Quiet '00
The Army of Crime '10

Robert Guenette (1935-2003)
The Defector '66
Children of the Night '85

Tonino Guerra (1920-2012)
La Notte '60
L'Avventura '60
The Eclipse '62
The Red Desert '64
Saul and David '64
Casanova '70 '65
10th Victim '65
Blow-Up '66
More Than a Miracle '67
Zabriskie Point '70
Amarcord '74
The Night of the Shooting Stars '82
And the Ship Sails On '83
Nostalghia '83
Henry IV '85
Ginger & Fred '86
Landscape in the Mist '88
Night Sun '90
Golem: The Petrified Garden '93
Beyond the Clouds '95
Ulysses' Gaze '95
The Truce '96

Jorge Guerricaechevarria
Dance with the Devil '97
Live Flesh '97
El Crimen Perfecto '04
The Oxford Murders '08
Cell 211 '09

Christopher Guest (1948-)
This Is Spinal Tap '84
The Big Picture '89
The Return of Spinal Tap '92
Waiting for Guffman '96
Best in Show '00
A Mighty Wind '03
For Your Consideration '06
Mascots '16

Val Guest (1911-2006)
Good Morning, Boys '37
Ask a Policeman '38
Hey! Hey! USA! '38
The Ghost Train '41
Miss London Ltd. '43
Bees in Paradise '44
Give Us the Moon '44
Happy Go Lovely '51
Another Man's Poison '52
Penny Princess '52
The Runaway Bus '54
Carry On Admiral '57
Quatermass 2 '57
Further Up the Creek '58
Dentist In the Chair '60
Stop Me Before I Kill! '60
The Day the Earth Caught Fire '61
Where the Spies Are '65
Assignment K '68
Au Pair Girls '72
Confessions of a Window Cleaner '74

Davis Guggenheim (1964-)
Waiting for Superman '10
Safe House '12
He Named Me Malala '15

Marc Guggenheim (1970-)
Green Lantern '11
Percy Jackson: Sea of Monsters '13

Martin Guigui
National Lampoon Presents Cattle Call '06

Stewart Harcourt
Dracula *'06*
Murder on the Orient Express *'10*
Treasure Island *'12*

Gary Hardwick
Todd McFarlane's Spawn *'97*
Trippin' *'99*
The Brothers *'01*
Deliver Us from Eva *'03*

Catherine Hardwicke (1955-)
Thirteen *'03*
Plush *'13*

Martin Hardy (1959-)
See Frank Cottrell Boyce

Rene Hardy
Bitter Victory *'58*
Triple Cross *'67*

David Hare (1947-)
Plenty *'85*
Wetherby *'85*
Saigon: Year of the Cat *'87*
Strapless *'90*
Damage *'92*
The Secret Rapture *'94*
The Hours *'02*
My Zinc Bed *'08*
The Reader *'08*
Page Eight *'11*
Denial *'16*
The White Crow *'18*

Lance Z. Hargreaves
First Man into Space *'59*
Devil Doll *'64*

Marion Hargrove (1919-2003)
Cash McCall *'60*
40 Pounds of Trouble *'62*
The Music Man *'62*

Sterlin Harjo
Four Sheets to the Wind *'07*
This May Be the Last Time *'14*

Tsui Hark (1951-)
Once Upon a Time in China *'91*
Once Upon a Time in China II *'92*
Twin Dragons *'92*
Wicked City *'92*
Iron Monkey *'93*
Once Upon a Time in China III *'93*
Black Mask *'96*
Time and Tide *'00*
Zu Warriors *'01*
Black Mask 2: City of Masks *'02*

Robert Harling (1951-)
Steel Magnolias *'89*
Soapdish *'91*
The Evening Star *'96*
The First Wives Club *'96*
Laws of Attraction *'04*

John Harlow (1896-1977)
Appointment with Crime *'45*
Echo Murders *'45*
Those People Next Door *'52*

David Harmon
Shadow on the Window *'57*
Killer by Night *'72*
Rescue from Gilligan's Island *'78*

Phil Harnage
Banzai Runner *'86*
Inspector Gadget's Biggest Caper Ever *'05*

Joby Harold
Awake *'07*
King Arthur: Legend of the Sword *'17*

Sam Harper
Rookie of the Year *'93*
Cheaper by the Dozen *'03*
Just Married *'03*
Cheaper by the Dozen 2 *'05*
Housebroken *'09*

Noah Harpster
The Motel Life *'12*
A Beautiful Day in the Neighborhood *'19*
Maleficent: Mistress of Evil *'19*

Chris Harrald
Photographing Fairies *'97*
The Infinite Worlds of H.G. Wells *'01*

Stephen Harrigan
Lone Justice 3: Showdown at Plum Creek *'96*
Cleopatra *'99*
Take Me Home: The John Denver Story *'00*
Murder on the Orient Express *'01*
King of Texas *'02*
Widow on the Hill *'05*

Curtis Harrington (1928-2007)
Night Tide *'61*
Planet of Blood *'66*
Queen of Blood *'66*

Damian Harris (1958-)
The Rachel Papers *'89*
Mercy *'00*
Gardens of the Night *'08*
The Wilde Wedding *'17*

Daniel P. 'Dan' Harris (1979-)
X2: X-Men United *'03*
Imaginary Heroes *'05*
Superman Returns *'06*

Elmer Harris (1878-1966)
Tess of the Storm Country *'22*
Stepping Out *'31*
The Barbarian *'33*

Eoghan Harris
Sharpe's Eagle *'93*
Sharpe's Rifles *'93*
Sharpe's Enemy *'94*
Sharpe's Sword *'94*
Sharpe's Mission *'96*
Sharpe's Regiment *'96*
Sharpe's Siege *'96*
Sharpe's Revenge *'97*

James B. Harris (1928-)
Cop *'88*
Boiling Point *'93*

Joe Harris
Darkness Falls *'03*
The Tripper *'06*

Kirk Harris
Loser *'97*
Hard Luck *'01*

Mark Harris
Black Coffee *'14*
Five Came Back *'17*

Mark Jonathan Harris
Into the Arms of Strangers: Stories of the Kindertransport *'00*
Foster *'18*

Ray Harris (1885-1971)
Three-Cornered Moon *'33*
Hooray for Love *'35*
The Man On the Flying Trapeze *'35*

Robert Harris (1957-)
Selling Hitler *'91*
The Ghost Writer *'10*

Timothy Harris (1946-)
Trading Places *'83*
Brewster's Millions *'85*
My Stepmother Is an Alien *'88*
Twins *'88*
Kindergarten Cop *'90*
Pure Luck *'91*
Astro Boy *'09*

Vernon Harris (1905-99)
Three Men in a Boat *'56*
The Admirable Crichton *'57*
Carve Her Name with Pride *'58*
Oliver! *'68*

Jim Harrison (1937-)
Cold Feet *'89*
Revenge *'90*
Wolf *'94*
Dalva *'95*

Joan Harrison (1911-94)
Jamaica Inn *'39*
Foreign Correspondent *'40*
Rebecca *'40*
Dark Waters *'44*

John Harrison
Dinosaur *'00*
Dune *'00*
Children of Dune *'03*
Experiment *'05*
Clive Barker's Book of Blood *'08*

John Kent Harrison
Shock Waves *'77*
Beautiful Dreamers *'92*
City Boy *'93*
You Know My Name *'99*
Game of Your Life *'11*

Lindsay Harrison
Fraternity Vacation *'85*
A Memory In My Heart *'99*

Matthew Harrison (1960-)
Rhythm Thief *'94*
Kicked in the Head *'97*

Mary Harron (1953-)
I Shot Andy Warhol *'96*
American Psycho *'99*
The Notorious Bettie Page *'06*
The Moth Diaries *'11*

Jacobsen Hart
Cyber-Tracker *'93*
Direct Hit *'93*
Zero Tolerance *'93*
Steel Frontier *'94*
The Power Within *'95*
Rage *'95*
Raven *'97*

James V. Hart (1960-)
Bram Stoker's Dracula *'92*
Muppet Treasure Island *'96*
Jack and the Beanstalk: The Real Story *'01*
Tuck Everlasting *'02*
Sahara *'05*
August Rush *'07*
Epic *'13*

Julia Hart
The Keeping Room *'15*
Miss Stevens *'16*
Fast Color *'18*

Kevin Hart (1979-)
Kevin Hart: What Now? *'16*
Night School *'18*

Kyle Hart (1981-)
Storm Seekers *'08*
Toxic Skies *'08*

Moss Hart (1904-61)
Flesh *'32*
Gentleman's Agreement *'47*
Hans Christian Andersen *'52*
A Star Is Born *'54*

Chad Hartigan
This is Martin Bonner *'13*
Morris from America *'16*

Hal Hartley (1959-)
Trust *'90*
The Unbelievable Truth *'90*
Simple Men *'92*
Amateur *'94*
Henry Fool *'98*
No Such Thing *'01*
Fay Grim *'06*

Don Hartman (1900-58)
The Gay Deception *'35*
Here Comes Cookie *'35*
The Princess Comes Across *'36*
Waikiki Wedding *'37*
Never Say Die *'39*
The Road to Singapore *'40*
Nothing But the Truth *'41*
The Road to Zanzibar *'41*
My Favorite Blonde *'42*
The Road to Morocco *'42*
The Princess and the Pirate *'44*
Up in Arms *'44*
Wonder Man *'45*
The Kid from Brooklyn *'46*
Mr. Imperium *'51*

Edmund L. Hartmann (1911-2003)
Time Out for Rhythm *'41*
Ali Baba and the Forty Thieves *'43*
In Society *'44*
The Lemon Drop Kid *'51*
My Favorite Spy *'51*
Casanova's Big Night *'54*

Steven Hartov
Mars *'96*
Mercenary *'96*

Joey Hartstone
LBJ *'17*
Shock and Awe *'18*

Frank Harvey
The Long Memory *'53*
Crest of the Wave *'54*
Upstairs and Downstairs *'59*

Johanna Harwood
Dr. No *'62*
Call Me Bwana *'63*
From Russia with Love *'63*

Ronald Harwood (1934-)
Operation Daybreak *'75*
The Dresser *'83*
The Doctor and the Devils *'85*
A Fine Romance *'92*
The Browning Version *'94*
Taking Sides *'01*
The Pianist *'02*
The Statement *'03*
Being Julia *'04*
Oliver Twist *'05*
The Diving Bell and the Butterfly *'07*
Australia *'08*
Quartet *'12*

Adi Hasak
From Paris With Love *'10*
3 Days to Kill *'14*

Shinobu Hashimoto (1918-)
Rashomon *'51*
Ikiru *'52*
Seven Samurai *'54*
I Live in Fear *'55*
Throne of Blood *'57*
The Hidden Fortress *'58*
The Bad Sleep Well *'60*
Harakiri *'62*
Revenge *'64*
Samurai Rebellion *'67*
Dodes 'ka-den *'70*

Michael Hastings (1938-)
The Nightcomers *'72*
Tom & Viv *'94*
The American *'01*

Gregory Hatanaka
Mad Cowgirl *'06*
Violent Blue *'10*

Jeffrey Hatcher
Stage Beauty *'04*
Casanova *'05*
The Duchess *'08*
Mr. Holmes *'15*
The Good Liar *'19*

Richard Hatem (1966-)
Under Siege 2: Dark Territory *'95*
The Mothman Prophecies *'02*

Fanny Hatton (?-1939)
Painted Faces *'29*
Tonight or Never *'31*

Frederic Hatton (1879-1946)
Painted Faces *'29*
Tonight or Never *'31*

Jeffrey Hause
Once Bitten *'85*
BachelorMan *'03*

Wings Hauser (1947-)
No Safe Haven *'87*
Gang Boys *'97*

Chris Hauty
Homeward Bound 2: Lost in San Francisco *'96*
Never Back Down *'08*
Never Back Down 2: The Beatdown *'11*
Sniper: Ghost Shooter *'16*

Anthony Havelock-Allan (1904-2003)
Blithe Spirit *'45*
Brief Encounter *'46*

Jean C. Havez (1870-1925)
Our Hospitality *'23*
Safety Last *'23*

Ethan Hawke (1971-)
Before Sunset *'04*
The Hottest State *'06*
Before Midnight *'13*
Blaze *'18*

John Hawkesworth (1920-2003)
Tiger Bay *'59*
The Duchess of Duke Street *'78*
The Flame Trees of Thika *'81*

Lowell S. Hawley (1908-2003)
The Swiss Family Robinson *'60*
The One and Only, Genuine, Original Family Band *'68*

Noah Hawley
Lies & Alibis *'06*
Lucy in the Sky *'19*

Ian Hay (1876-1952)
The 39 Steps *'35*
Sabotage *'36*

Phil Hay
crazy/beautiful *'01*
Aeon Flux *'05*
Clash of the Titans *'10*
R.I.P.D. *'13*
Ride Along *'14*
The Invitation *'16*
Ride Along 2 *'16*
Destroyer *'18*

Will Hay (1888-1949)
Boys Will Be Boys *'35*
Windbag the Sailor *'36*

Al Hayes (1911-85)
The Double Man *'67*
The Gingerbread Man *'97*

Alfred Hayes (1911-85)
Clash by Night *'52*
A Hatful of Rain *'59*

Carey Hayes (1961-)
House of Wax *'05*
The Reaping *'07*
Whiteout *'09*
The Conjuring *'13*
The Conjuring 2 *'16*

Chad Hayes (1961-)
House of Wax *'05*
The Reaping *'07*
Whiteout *'09*
The Conjuring *'13*
The Conjuring 2 *'16*

John Michael Hayes (1919-)
Thunder Bay *'53*
War Arrow *'53*
Rear Window *'54*
It's a Dog's Life *'55*
To Catch a Thief *'55*
The Trouble with Harry *'55*
The Man Who Knew Too Much *'56*
Peyton Place *'57*
The Matchmaker *'58*
Butterfield 8 *'60*
The Children's Hour *'61*
The Carpetbaggers *'64*
The Chalk Garden *'64*
Where Love Has Gone *'64*
Harlow *'65*
Nevada Smith *'66*
Winter Kill *'74*
Iron Will *'93*

Joseph Hayes (1918-2006)
Stolen Hours *'63*
Desperate Hours *'90*

Steve Hayes
Fantastic Planet *'73*
Mr. St. Nick *'02*
The Muppets' Wizard of Oz *'05*

Terry Hayes (1951-)
The Road Warrior *'82*
Mad Max: Beyond Thunderdome *'85*
Dead Calm *'89*
Payback *'98*
Vertical Limit *'00*
From Hell *'01*

Todd Haynes (1961-)
Poison *'91*
Safe *'95*
Office Killer *'97*
Velvet Goldmine *'98*
Far from Heaven *'02*
I'm Not There *'07*
Mildred Pierce *'11*

David Hayter (1969-)
X-Men *'00*
The Scorpion King *'02*
Watchmen *'09*

Justin Haythe (1973-)
The Clearing *'04*
Revolutionary Road *'08*
The Lone Ranger *'13*
Snitch *'13*
A Cure for Wellness *'17*
Red Sparrow *'18*

Lillie Hayward (1891-1977)
Miss Pinkerton *'32*
They Call It Sin *'32*
Lady Killer *'33*
Housewife *'34*
Front Page Woman *'35*
The White Cockatoo *'35*
Her Jungle Love *'38*
Margin for Error *'43*
Tarzan's Hidden Jungle *'55*
Tarzan and the Lost Safari *'57*
Proud Rebel *'58*

Eric Haywood (1970-)
Relative Stranger *'09*
Four of Hearts *'13*

Lawrence Hazard (1897-1959)
Hooray for Love *'35*
Mannequin *'37*

Ping He (1957-)
Swordsmen in Double Flag Town *'91*
Rhapsody of Spring *'98*

Gary Heacock
Alien Massacre *'67*
Gallery of Horrors *'67*

Jim Head
On Strike for Christmas *'10*
Strawberry Summer *'12*

Leslye Headland
Bachelorette *'12*
About Last Night *'14*
Sleeping with Other People *'15*

Josh Heald (1977-)
Hot Tub Time Machine *'10*
Mardi Gras: Spring Break *'11*
Hot Tub Time Machine 2 *'15*

Jennifer Heath (1955-)
Ella Enchanted *'04*
Sundays at Tiffany's *'10*

Laurence Heath (1928-2007)
Valerie *'57*
The Beasts Are On the Streets *'78*
Triumph of the Spirit *'89*

David Heavener (1958-)
Twisted Justice *'89*
Prime Target *'91*

Eye of the Stranger '93
Outlaw Prophet '01

Julie Hebert
Female Perversions '96
Ruby's Bucket of Blood '01

Ben Hecht (1894-1964)
The Great Gabbo '29
Design for Living '33
Hallelujah, I'm a Bum '33
Turn Back the Clock '33
Twentieth Century '34
Nothing Sacred '37
Gunga Din '39
It's a Wonderful World '39
Let Freedom Ring '39
Wuthering Heights '39
Angels Over Broadway '40
Comrade X '40
The Black Swan '42
China Girl '42
Tales of Manhattan '42
Spellbound '45
Notorious '46
Ride the Pink Horse '47
Cry of the City '48
The Miracle of the Bells '48
Whirlpool '49
Where the Sidewalk Ends '50
The Thing '51
Actors and Sin '52
Monkey Business '52
The Indian Fighter '55
The Iron Petticoat '56
A Farewell to Arms '57
Circus World '64

Amy Heckerling (1954-)
Look Who's Talking '89
Look Who's Talking, Too '90
976-EVIL '88
Clueless '95
Loser '00
I Could Never Be Your Woman '06
Vamps '12

Rob Hedden (1954-)
Friday the 13th, Part 8: Jason Takes Manhattan '89
The Colony '95
Clockstoppers '02
Boxboarders! '07
The Condemned '07
You May Not Kiss the Bride '12

Roger Hedden
Bodies, Rest & Motion '93
Sleep with Me '94
Hi-Life '98

Peter Hedges (1962-)
What's Eating Gilbert Grape '93
A Map of the World '99
About a Boy '02
Pieces of April '03
Dan in Real Life '07
The Odd Life of Timothy Green '12
Ben Is Back '18

Victor Heerman (1893-1977)
Little Women '33
The Age of Innocence '34
Little Minister '34
Break of Hearts '35
Magnificent Obsession '35
Stella Dallas '37
Golden Boy '39

Kevin Heffernan (1968-)
Super Troopers '01
Club Dread '04
Preaching to the Choir '05
Beerfest '06
The Slammin' Salmon '09
Super Troopers 2 '18

Tim Heidecker
Tim and Eric's Billion Dollar Movie '12
Entertainment '15
Mister America '19

Carol Heikkinen (1966-)
The Thing Called Love '93
Empire Records '95
Center Stage '00

Jo Heims (1930-78)
The Gun Hawk '63
Double Trouble '67
Play Misty for Me '71

Eric Heisserer
A Nightmare on Elm Street '10
Final Destination 5 '11
The Thing '11
Hours '13
Arrival '16
Lights Out '16
Bloodshot '20

Rasmus Heisterberg
The Girl With the Dragon Tattoo '09
A Royal Affair '12

Jalmari Helander
Rare Exports: A Christmas Tale '10
Big Game '15

Ian Helfer
The Oranges '12
Why Him? '16

Ross Helford
Alien Lockdown '04
Sniper 3 '04
Wild Things 2 '04
Single White Female 2: The Psycho '05
Wild Things 3: Diamonds in the Rough '05

Brian Helgeland (1961-)
A Nightmare on Elm Street 4: Dream Master '88
976-EVIL '88
Assassins '95
Conspiracy Theory '97
L.A. Confidential '97
The Postman '97
Payback '98
A Knight's Tale '01
Blood Work '02
Mystic River '03
The Order '03
Man on Fire '04
Cirque du Freak: The Vampire's Assistant '09
The Taking of Pelham 123 '09
Green Zone '10
Robin Hood '10
Salt '10
42 '13
Legend '15
Spenser Confidential '20

Jake Helgren
Finding Mr. Wright '11
Bloody Homecoming '12
A Belle for Christmas '14
Varsity Blood '14

Lukas Heller (1930-88)
What Ever Happened to Baby Jane? '62
Hot Enough for June '64
Hush, Hush, Sweet Charlotte '65
The Dirty Dozen '67
The Killing of Sister George '69
Damnation Alley '77
Blue City '86
Monte Walsh '03

Lillian Hellman (1905-84)
Dead End '37
The Little Foxes '41
The North Star '43
Watch on the Rhine '43
The Chase '66

Oliver Hellman (1943-)
See Ovidio G. Assonitis

Sam Hellman (1885-1950)
Little Miss Marker '34
Murder at the Vanities '34
Thirty Day Princess '34
The Daring Young Man '35
In Old Kentucky '35
A Message to Garcia '36
Slave Ship '37
The Baroness and the Butler '38
Frontier Marshal '39
The Three Musketeers '39

The Horn Blows at Midnight '45
My Darling Clementine '46

Axel Hellstenius
The Last Lieutenant '94
Elling '01

Zach Helm (1975-)
Stranger Than Fiction '06
Mr. Magorium's Wonder Emporium '07

Jim Hemphill
Bad Reputation '05
The Trouble with the Truth '11

Kevin Hench
The Hammer '07
Road Hard '15

Chris Henchy
Land of the Lost '09
The Other Guys '10
The Campaign '12

Eric Hendershot
The Robin Hood Gang '98
Down and Derby '05

Frank Henenlotter (1950-)
Basket Case '82
Brain Damage '88
Basket Case 2 '90
Frankenhooker '90
Basket Case 3: The Progeny '92

James Henerson
The Fire Next Time '93
Getting Gotti '94
The Love Letter '98

Liu Heng
Ju Dou '90
The Story of Qiu Ju '91

Paul Hengge
Double Face '70
The Rose Garden '89

Kim Henkel
The Texas Chainsaw Massacre '74
Eaten Alive '76
The Texas Chainsaw Massacre 4: The Next Generation '95

Hilary Henkin (1962-)
Fatal Beauty '87
Romeo Is Bleeding '93
Wag the Dog '97

Beth Henley (1952-)
Crimes of the Heart '86
Nobody's Fool '86
True Stories '86
Miss Firecracker '89

Jack Henley (1896-1958)
Ma and Pa Kettle Back On the Farm '51
Ma and Pa Kettle on Vacation '53
The Rocket Man '54
Ma and Pa Kettle at Waikiki '55

Paul Henning (1911-2005)
The Return of the Beverly Hillbillies '81
Dirty Rotten Scoundrels '88
The Hustle '19

Robert Henny
Who's Your Caddy? '07
Beyond Valkyrie: Dawn of the Fourth Reich '16

Buck Henry (1930-2020)
The Graduate '67
Candy '68
Catch-22 '70
The Owl and the Pussycat '70
What's Up, Doc? '72
The Day of the Dolphin '73
First Family '80
Protocol '84
To Die For '95
Town and Country '01

Todd Henschell
Puppet Master 4 '93
Puppet Master 5: The Final Chapter '94

Jim Henshaw (1949-)
Another Woman '94
Broken Lullaby '94
A Change of Place '94
Treacherous Beauties '94

Jonathan Hensleigh
A Far Off Place '93
Die Hard: With a Vengeance '95
Jumanji '95
The Rock '96
The Saint '97
Armageddon '98
The Punisher '04
Next '07
Kill the Irishman '11

Jim Henson (1936-90)
Labyrinth '86
Witchcraft 2: The Temptress '90

Robby Henson
Pharoah's Army '95
The Badge '02

F. Hugh Herbert (1897-1958)
The Great Gabbo '29
Road to Paradise '30
A Parisian Romance '32
Those We Love '32
The Secret Bride '35
The Case of the Black Cat '36
Colleen '36
Together Again '43
Sitting Pretty '48
Let's Make It Legal '51

Marcel L'Herbier (1888-1979)
Feu Mathias Pascal '26
The Fantastic Night '42

Laurent Herbiert (1961-)
Wild Grass '09
You Ain't Seen Nothin' Yet '12

Tim Herlihy (1966-)
Happy Gilmore '96
The Wedding Singer '97
The Waterboy '98
Big Daddy '99
Little Nicky '00
Mr. Deeds '02
Bedtime Stories '08
Grown Ups 2 '13
Pixels '15

Mark Herman (1954-)
Blame It on the Bellboy '92
Brassed Off '96
Little Voice '98
The Boy in the Striped Pajamas '08

Pee-wee Herman (1952-)
See Paul (Pee-wee Herman) Reubens

Jaime Humberto Hermosillo (1942-2020)
Dona Herlinda & Her Son '86
Homework '90
Esmeralda Comes by Night '98

Gyula Hernadi (1926-2005)
The Red and the White '68
Electra, My Love '74
Adoption '75

Michael Herr (1940-)
Apocalypse Now '79
Full Metal Jacket '87
John Grisham's The Rainmaker '97

Rowdy Herrington (1951-)
Striking Distance '93
A Murder of Crows '99
The Stickup '01
Bobby Jones: Stroke of Genius '04

W(illiam) Blake Herron
A Texas Funeral '99
The Bourne Identity '02

Marshall Herskovitz (1952-)
Special Bulletin '83
Glory '89
The Last Samurai '03
Love and Other Drugs '10
Jack Reacher: Never Go Back '16
American Assassin '17

David Hertz
Three Loves Has Nancy '38
Stronger Than Desire '39
Pilot No. 5 '43
Daisy Kenyon '47

Harry Hervey (1900-51)
The Cheat '31
His Greatest Gamble '34

Adam Herz (1973-)
American Pie '99
American Pie 2 '01
American Wedding '03

Michael Herz (1949-)
First Turn On '83
Stuck on You '84

Jim Herzfeld
Meet the Deedles '98
Meet the Parents '00
Meet the Fockers '04

John Herzfeld
Two Days in the Valley '96
15 Minutes '01
S.I.S. '08
Reach Me '14

Sid Herzig (1897-1985)
Old Man Rhythm '35
Colleen '36
Varsity Show '37
Four's a Crowd '38
They Made Me a Criminal '39
Meet the People '44
London Town '46

Werner Herzog (1942-)
Signs of Life '68
Aguirre, the Wrath of God '72
Heart of Glass '74
Every Man for Himself & God Against All '75
Stroszek '77
Woyzeck '78
Nosferatu the Vampyre '79
Fitzcarraldo '82
Cobra Verde '88
Invincible '01
Rescue Dawn '06
Encounters at the End of the World '07
My Son, My Son, What Have Ye Done '09
Cave of Forgotten Dreams '11
Happy People: A Year in the Taiga '13
Into the Inferno '16
Lo and Behold: Reveries of the Connected World '16

Martyn Hesford
The Old Curiosity Shop '07
Mrs. Lowry & Son '19

Grant Heslov (1963-)
Good Night, and Good Luck '05
The Ides of March '11
The Monuments Men '13
Suburbicon '17

Eugene Hess
Don't Do It '94
Cruel World '05
Streets of Blood '09

Jared Hess (1979-)
Napoleon Dynamite '04
Nacho Libre '06
Gentlemen Broncos '09
Don Verdean '15

Jerusha Hess (1980-)
Napoleon Dynamite '04
Nacho Libre '06

Gentlemen Broncos '09
Austenland '13
Don Verdean '15

Fraser Heston (1955-)
The Mountain Men '80
Treasure Island '89

Olivia Hetreed
What Katy Did '99
Girl with a Pearl Earring '03
Wuthering Heights '12
Finding Altamira '16

Jason Hewitt (1973-)
Death Toll '07
Blood Out '10

Peter Hewitt (1962-)
Thunderbirds '04
I Want Candy '07

Rod Hewitt
Sworn Enemies '96
The Debt '98

Douglas Heyes (1919-93)
Battle of Rogue River '54
Kitten with a Whip '64
Ice Station Zebra '68
The French Atlantic Affair '79

Louis M. Heyward (1920-2002)
Pajama Party '64
Planet of the Vampires '65
Sergeant Deadhead '65
Ghost in the Invisible Bikini '66
The Conqueror Worm '68

Guy Hibbert
Shot Through the Heart '98
Five Minutes of Heaven '09
Eye in the Sky '15
A United Kingdom '17

Winston Hibler (1910-76)
The Adventures of Ichabod and Mr. Toad '49
Peter Pan '53
Nikki, the Wild Dog of the North '61
Charlie the Lonesome Cougar '67

George Hickenlooper (1963-2010)
Hearts of Darkness: A Filmmaker's Apocalypse '91
The Low Life '95
Dogtown '97
The Big Brass Ring '99
Mayor of the Sunset Strip '03

Anthony Hickox (1959-)
Waxwork '88
Waxwork 2: Lost in Time '91
Last Run '01
Submerged '05
Sundown: The Vampire in Retreat '08

Regina Hicks
Jump In! '07
Camp Rock '08
Camp Rock 2: The Final Jam '10

Scott Hicks (1953-)
Snow Falling on Cedars '99
The Boys Are Back '09

Julie Hickson
Homeward Bound 2: Lost in San Francisco '96
Snow White: The Fairest of Them All '02

Howard Higgin (1891-1938)
The Painted Desert '31
Revolt of the Zombies '36

Colin Higgins (1941-88)
Harold and Maude '71
Silver Streak '76
Foul Play '78
The Best Little Whorehouse in Texas '82

John C. Higgins (1908-95)
The Murder Man '35
Railroaded '47
T-Men '47
He Walked by Night '48
Raw Deal '48

Border Incident '49
Big House, U.S.A. '55
The Black Sleep '56
The Broken Star '56
Quincannon, Frontier Scout '56
Untamed Youth '57
Robinson Crusoe on Mars '64
The File of the Golden Goose '69
Impasse '69

Charles Higson (1958-)
Suite 16 '94
King of the Ants '03

Zak Hilditch
Plum Role '07
1922 '17
Rattlesnake '19

David Hill
Shattered Dreams '90
Too Young to Die '90

Debra Hill (1950-2005)
The Fog '78
Halloween '78
Halloween 2: The Nightmare Isn't Over! '81
Jailbreakers '94
Escape from L.A. '96

Elizabeth Hill (1901-78)
Our Daily Bread '34
H.M. Pulham Esquire '41

Ethel Hill (1898-1954)
Whirlpool '34
Public Menace '35
It Happened in Hollywood '37
The Little Princess '39
War of the Wildcats '43
Two Smart People '46

Gladys Hill (1981-)
The Kremlin Letter '70
The Man Who Would Be King '75

Jack Hill (1933-)
The Terror '63
Spider Baby '64
Pit Stop '67
The Fear Chamber '68
The Big Bird Cage '72
Coffy '73
Foxy Brown '74

Jody Hill
The Foot Fist Way '08
Observe and Report '09

John Hill
Heartbeeps '81
Little Nikita '88
Quigley Down Under '90
Griffin & Phoenix '06

Robert Hill
Female On the Beach '55
Sex Kittens Go to College '60
Confessions of an Opium Eater '62

Robert F. 'Bob' Hill (1886-1966)
The Adventures of Tarzan '21
The Cat and the Canary '27

Walter Hill (1942-)
The Getaway '72
Hickey & Boggs '72
Mackintosh Man '73
The Drowning Pool '75
Hard Times '75
The Driver '78
The Warriors '79
Southern Comfort '81
48 Hrs. '82
Streets of Fire '84
Aliens '86
Blue City '86
Red Heat '88
The Getaway '93
Wild Bill '95
Last Man Standing '96
Undisputed '02
The Assignment '17

David Hillenbrand
King Cobra '98
Survival Island '02

Scott Hillenbrand
King Cobra '98
Survival Island '02

Richard Hilliard
The Lonely Sex '59
Horror of Party Beach '64

Lambert Hillyer (1889-1969)
The Cradle of Courage '20
The Toll Gate '20
Barbara Frietchie '24
The California Trail '33

David Hilton
The Young Americans '93
The Delivery '99

James Hilton (1900-54)
Camille '36
Foreign Correspondent '40
Mrs. Miniver '42

Jim Hilton
All Hell Broke Loose '09
A Cold Day in Hell '11

Robert Hiltzik
Sleepaway Camp '83
Return to Sleepaway Camp '08

David Himmelstein
Power '86
Talent for the Game '91
Village of the Damned '95
Soul of the Game '96

Alan Hines
Square Dance '87
Breaking the Surface: The Greg Louganis Story '96
My Husband's Double Life '01
The Interrogation of Michael Crowe '02
A Dad for Christmas '06
Save Me '07

David Hines
Once Bitten '85
BachelorMan '03

Jonathan Hirschbein
Bad Country '14
Road to Paloma '14
A Prayer Before Dawn '18

Roger O. Hirson (1926-)
Pieces of Dreams '70
Demon Seed '77
Pippin '81
A Christmas Carol '84
The Old Man and the Sea '90

Michael Hirst (1952-)
The Ballad of the Sad Cafe '91
Meeting Venus '91
Uncovered '94
Elizabeth '98
Have No Fear: The Life of Pope John Paul II '05
Elizabeth: The Golden Age '07

Alfred Hitchcock (1899-1980)
The Lodger '26
The Ring '27
Champagne '28
The Farmer's Wife '28
Blackmail '29
Juno and the Paycock '30
Murder '30
Skin Game '31
Rich and Strange '32
Saboteur '42

Michael Hitchcock (1958-)
Where the Day Takes You '92
House Arrest '96

Carl K. Hittleman (1907-99)
36 Hours '64
Jesse James Meets Frankenstein's Daughter '65
Billy the Kid Versus Dracula '66

Eliza Hittman
It Felt Like Love '14
Beach Rats '17
Never Rarely Sometimes Always '20

Ken Hixon
Inventing the Abbotts '97
City by the Sea '02
Welcome to the Rileys '10
Unbroken: Path to Redemption '18
Finding Steve McQueen '19

Patrick Hobby
Hollywood Boulevard '76
Love at the Christmas Table '12

Danny Hoch (1970-)
Subway Stories '97
White Boyz '99

John Hodge (1964-)
Shallow Grave '94
Trainspotting '95
A Life Less Ordinary '97
The Beach '00
The Seeker: The Dark Is Rising '07
The Sweeney '12
Trance '13
The Program '15
T2 Trainspotting '17

Adrian Hodges
Tom & Viv '94
Metroland '97
Amongst Women '98
David Copperfield '99
Lorna Doone '01
The Lost World '02
Ruby in the Smoke '06
The History of Mr. Polly '07
The Shadow in the North '07
My Week With Marilyn '11
Labyrinth '12

Mike Hodges (1932-)
Get Carter '71
Pulp '72
The Terminal Man '74
Damien: Omen 2 '78
Black Rainbow '91

Christina Hodson
Shut In '16
Unforgettable '17
Bumblebee '18
Birds of Prey: And the Fantabulous Emancipation of One Harley Quinn '20

Erich Hoeber
Whiteout '09
RED '10
Battleship '12
RED 2 '13
The Meg '18
My Spy '19

Jon Hoeber
Whiteout '09
RED '10
Battleship '12
RED 2 '13
The Meg '18
My Spy '19

Arthur Hoerl (1891-1968)
The Shadow Laughs '33
The Spirit of Youth '37
Reefer Madness '38

Monckton Hoffe
The Emperor's Candlesticks '37
Derby Day '52

Samuel Hoffenstein (1890-1947)
An American Tragedy '31
Dr. Jekyll and Mr. Hyde '32
Love Me Tonight '32
The Song of Songs '33
White Woman '33
Tales of Manhattan '42
The Phantom of the Opera '43
His Butler's Sister '44
Laura '44
Carnival in Costa Rica '47

Charles Hoffman (1911-72)
That Hagen Girl '47
The West Point Story '50
The Blue Gardenia '53

Joseph Hoffman (1909-97)
The Man with Two Lives '42
Carolina Blues '44
Buccaneer's Girl '50
At Sword's Point '51
Has Anybody Seen My Gal? '52
No Room for the Groom '52

Michael Hoffman (1956-)
Promised Land '88
William Shakespeare's A Midsummer Night's Dream '99
The Last Station '09

Tamar Simon Hoffs (1934-)
Stony Island '77
The Allnighter '87
Red Roses and Petrol '03
Pound of Flesh '10

Michael Hogan (1893-1977)
The Passing of the Third Floor Back '35
King Solomon's Mines '37
Arabian Nights '42
Lady from Louisiana '42
Forever and a Day '43

Paul Hogan (1939-)
Crocodile Dundee '86
Crocodile Dundee 2 '88
Almost an Angel '90
Lightning Jack '94

P.J. Hogan (1962-)
Muriel's Wedding '94
Peter Pan '03
Unconditional Love '03

Brian Hohlfeld
He Said, She Said '91
The Mighty Ducks '92
Piglet's Big Movie '03

Jihad Hojeily
Caramel '07
Capernaum '18

Jay Holben
All Hallow's Eve 2 '15
The Invoking 2 '15

Kara Holden
Middle School: The Worst Years of My Life '16
Carrie Pilby '17

Carlton Holder (1962-)
Bridge of Dragons '99
El Padrino '04

Bill Holderman
A Walk in the Woods '15
Book Club '18

Jeremy Hole
A Killing Spring '02
Verdict in Blood '02

Agnieszka Holland (1948-)
Danton '82
Angry Harvest '85
Anna '87
To Kill a Priest '89
Europa, Europa '91
Trois Couleurs: Bleu '93
The Healer '02

Mandel Holland
The Other Brother '02
Love and Other Four Letter Words '07
My Girlfriend's Back '10

Savage Steve Holland (1960-)
Better Off Dead '85
One Crazy Summer '86

Tom Holland (1943-)
The Beast Within '82
Class of 1984 '82
Psycho 2 '83
Cloak & Dagger '84
Fright Night '85
Child's Play '88
Stephen King's The Langoliers '95
Stephen King's Thinner '96

David Hollander (1969-)
Rated X '00
Personal Effects '09

Jean Holloway (1917-89)
Till the Clouds Roll By '46
Madame X '66

Matt Holloway
Iron Man '08
Punisher: War Zone '08
Transformers: The Last Knight '17
Men in Black: International '19

Brown Holmes (1907-74)
The Strange Love of Molly Louvain '32
Street of Women '32
20,000 Years in Sing Sing '33
Dark Hazard '34
The Case of the Lucky Legs '35
Three Blind Mice '38
Castle on the Hudson '40
Three Little Girls In Blue '46
Shed No Tears '48

Geoffrey Holmes (1902-77)
See Daniel Mainwaring

Milton Holmes (1907-87)
Salty O'Rourke '45
Johnny O'Clock '47

Nicole Holofcener (1960-)
Walking and Talking '96
Lovely & Amazing '02
Friends with Money '06
Please Give '10
Enough Said '13
Every Secret Thing '15
Can You Ever Forgive Me? '18
The Land of Steady Habits '18

Robert I. Holt
Rampage '63
White Comanche '68

Edward Holzman
Forbidden Games '95
Friend of the Family '95

Geoffrey Homes (1902-77)
See Daniel Mainwaring

Ishiro Honda (1911-93)
Godzilla '54
Godzilla, King of the Monsters '56
Destroy All Monsters '68
War of the Gargantuas '70

Christophe Honore (1970-)
Girls Can't Swim '99
Close to Leo '02
Inside Paris '06
Apres Lui '07
Love Songs '07
The Beautiful Person '08
Making Plans for Lena '09
Beloved '11
Let My People Go! '11

Brendan William Hood
Wes Craven Presents: They '02
The Deaths of Ian Stone '07

Gavin Hood (1963-)
In Desert and Wilderness '01
Tsotsi '05
Ender's Game '13
Official Secrets '19

Kevin Hood
Becoming Jane '07
A Royal Night Out '15
The Guernsey Literary & Potato Peel Pie Society '18

Sean Hood (1966-)
Cube 2: Hypercube '02
Halloween: Resurrection '02
The Crow: Wicked Prayer '05
Conan the Barbarian '11
The Legend of Hercules '14

William Hooke
Shark Attack '99
Shark Attack 2 '00
Shark Attack 3: Megalodon '02

Tobe Hooper (1946-)
The Texas Chainsaw Massacre '74
Spontaneous Combustion '89
The Mangler '94

Arthur Hopcraft (1932-2004)
Tinker, Tailor, Soldier, Spy '80
A Perfect Spy '88
A Tale of Two Cities '89
Rebecca '97

Edward Hope (1986-58)
The Long Gray Line '55
Three for the Show '55

Joel Hopkins
Last Chance Harvey '08
The Love Punch '13

John Hopkins
Thunderball '65
The Virgin Soldiers '69
The Offence '73
Murder by Decree '79
Smiley's People '82
The Holcroft Covenant '85
Dunston Checks In '95
Hiroshima '95

Karen Leigh Hopkins
Stepmom '98
A Woman's a Helluva Thing '01
Because I Said So '07
Miss Meadows '14

Robert Hopkins (1886-1966)
Hollywood Revue of 1929 '29
Love in the Rough '30
Flying High '31
Stepping Out '31
Saratoga '37

Brian Horiuchi
America So Beautiful '01
Parts Per Billion '14

Arthur T. Horman (1905-64)
Buck Privates '41
In the Navy '41
Captains of the Clouds '42
Here Come the Co-Eds '45
Undertow '49
The WAC From Walla Walla '52

Douglas Horn
Entry Level '07
Babysitters Beware '08

Robert Horn
Good Advice '01
Sharpay's Fabulous Adventure '11
Teen Beach Movie '13

Nick Hornby (1957-)
Fever Pitch '96
An Education '09
Wild '14
Brooklyn '15

Israel Horovitz (1939-)
The Strawberry Statement '70
Author! Author! '82
A Man in Love '87
Sunshine '99
James Dean '01

Adam Horowitz
Confessions of an American Bride '05
Tron: Legacy '10

Anthony Horowitz (1955-)
Diamond's Edge '88
The Gathering '02
Alex Rider: Operation Stormbreaker '06
Collision '09

Ed Horowitz
- On Deadly Ground '94
- Exit Wounds '01
- K-9 3: P.I. '01

Jordan Horowitz
- Miss Stevens '16
- Fast Color '18

H. Perry Horton (1977-)
- 40 Days and Nights '12
- Shark Island '12
- 2-Headed Shark Attack '12

Jason Horwitch
- Finding Graceland '98
- Joe and Max '02

David Hoselton
- Deadly Game '98
- Brother Bear '03
- Over the Hedge '06

Jim Hosking
- The ABCs of Death 2 '14
- The Greasy Strangler '16

Mamoru Hosoda
- Summer Wars '09
- Mirai '18

Hou Hsiao-hsien (1947-)
- Flight of the Red Balloon '08
- The Assassin '15

Coleman Hough
- Full Frontal '02
- Bubble '06

Don Houghton (1930-91)
- Dracula A.D. 1972 '72
- The Legend of the 7 Golden Vampires '73
- The Satanic Rites of Dracula '73

Lionel Houser (1908-49)
- Public Menace '35
- Smashing the Rackets '38
- First Love '39
- The Girl From Mexico '39
- Third Finger, Left Hand '40
- Design for Scandal '41
- A Yank at Eton '42
- Courage of Lassie '46
- Adventure in Baltimore '49

Dianne Houston (1954-)
- Knights of the South Bronx '05
- Take the Lead '06

Cy Howard (1915-93)
- My Friend Irma '49
- My Friend Irma Goes West '50
- That's My Boy '51
- Marriage on the Rocks '65

David Howard (1896-1941)
- Galaxy Quest '99
- Flick '07

Gregory Allen Howard (1962-)
- Remember the Titans '00
- Harriet '19

Jeff Howard
- Oculus '14
- Before I Wake '15
- Ouija: Origin of Evil '16

Jeffrey M. Howard
- Planes '13
- Planes: Fire & Rescue '14

Karin Howard
- NeverEnding Story 2: The Next Chapter '91
- The Tigress '93

Ron Howard (1954-)
- Grand Theft Auto '77
- Parenthood '89

Sidney Howard (1891-1939)
- Raffles '30
- Arrowsmith '31
- Dodsworth '36
- Gone with the Wind '39
- Raffles '39

C. Thomas Howell (1966-)
- Hourglass '95
- Hope Ranch '02

Dorothy Howell (1899-1971)
- Rain or Shine '30
- The Miracle Woman '31
- Platinum Blonde '31
- Love Affair '32
- Whirlpool '34

Maude Howell (1887-1964)
- Old English '30
- The Man Who Played God '32
- A Successful Calamity '32
- The Working Man '33
- Cardinal Richelieu '35
- East Meets West '36

Perry Howze
- Maid to Order '87
- Mystic Pizza '88
- Chances Are '89

Rita Hsiao
- Mulan '98
- Toy Story 2 '99
- My Little Pony: The Movie '17

Hou Hsiao-Hsien (1947-)
- *See Hou Hsiao-hsien*

King Hu (1931-97)
- Come Drink with Me '65
- Painted Skin '93

George Huang
- Swimming with Sharks '94
- How to Make a Monster '01
- Hard Target 2 '16

Lucien Hubbard (1888-1971)
- Outside the Law '21
- The Vanishing American '25
- Paid '30
- Smart Money '31
- The Squaw Man '31

Norman Hudis
- Bond of Fear '56
- Carry On Constable '60
- No Kidding '60
- Midsummer Madness '07

Reginald (Reggie) Hudlin (1961-)
- House Party '90
- Bebe's Kids '92

Brent Huff (1961-)
- Final Justice '94
- Power Play '02
- Face of Terror '04
- Welcome to Paradise '07
- Cat City '08
- Magic Man '10

John Huff
- Hunter's Moon '97
- Cyxork 7 '06

Clair Huffaker (1926-90)
- Flaming Star '60
- The Second Time Around '61
- Tarzan and the Valley of Gold '65
- The War Wagon '67
- Hellfighters '68
- 100 Rifles '69
- Flap '70
- Chino '75

Matthew Huffman
- The Adventurer: The Curse of the Midas Box '13
- The Hunters '13

Roy Huggins (1914-2002)
- The Lady Gambles '49
- Too Late for Tears '49
- Woman in Hiding '49
- Pushover '54
- Three Hours to Kill '54
- A Fever In the Blood '61

Gwyneth Hughes
- Five Days '07
- Miss Austen Regrets '07
- The Girl '12
- The Mystery of Edwin Drood '12

John Hughes (1950-2009)
- National Lampoon's Class Reunion '82
- Mr. Mom '83
- National Lampoon's Vacation '83
- Sixteen Candles '84
- The Breakfast Club '85
- National Lampoon's European Vacation '85
- Weird Science '85
- Ferris Bueller's Day Off '86
- Pretty in Pink '86
- Planes, Trains & Automobiles '87
- Some Kind of Wonderful '87
- The Great Outdoors '88
- She's Having a Baby '88
- National Lampoon's Christmas Vacation '89
- Uncle Buck '89
- Home Alone '90
- Career Opportunities '91
- Curly Sue '91
- Dutch '91
- Beethoven '92
- Home Alone 2: Lost in New York '92
- Dennis the Menace '93
- Baby's Day Out '94
- Miracle on 34th Street '94
- 101 Dalmatians '96
- Flubber '97
- Home Alone 3 '97
- Just Visiting '01

Ken Hughes (1922-2001)
- The Trials of Oscar Wilde '60
- Chitty Chitty Bang Bang '68
- Cromwell '70
- Oh, Alfie '75

Russell S. Hughes (1910-58)
- This Side of the Law '50
- The Command '54
- Savage Wilderness '55
- Jubal '56

Jojo Hui
- The Eye '02
- The Eye 2 '04
- Warlords '08

Cyril Hume (1900-66)
- Live, Love and Learn '37
- They Gave Him a Gun '37
- The Bad Man of Brimstone '38
- High Barbaree '47
- A Lady Without Passport '50
- Tarzan's Savage Fury '52
- Forbidden Planet '56
- Ransom! '56

Edward Hume
- A Reflection of Fear '73
- Two Minute Warning '76

Steve Humphrey
- Agatha Christie's A Caribbean Mystery '83
- Agatha Christie's Sparkling Cyanide '83

Ted Humphrey
- The Triangle '01
- The Code '09

Sammo Hung (1952-)
- Spooky Encounters '80
- The Millionaire's Express '86

Tran Anh Hung (1963-)
- The Scent of Green Papaya '93
- Cyclo '95
- The Vertical Ray of the Sun '00

Tom Hunsinger (1952-)
- Lawless Heart '01
- Sparkle '07

Elizabeth Hunter
- The Fighting Temptations '03
- Jumping the Broom '11
- Abducted: The Carlina White Story '12

Evan Hunter (1926-2005)
- High & Low '62
- The Birds '63
- Dream West '86

Ian McLellan Hunter (1915-91)
- Young Ideas '43
- The Amazing Mr. X '48
- Captain Sinbad '63

John Hunter (1911-)
- Never Take Candy From a Stranger '60
- Pirates of Blood River '62
- Hollywood North '03

Kyle Hunter
- The Night Before '15
- Sausage Party '16

Neil Hunter
- Lawless Heart '01
- Sparkle '07

Tim Hunter (1947-)
- Over the Edge '79
- Tex '82

William Hurlbut (1878-1957)
- Imitation of Life '34
- The Bride of Frankenstein '35
- The Daring Young Man '35
- Orchids to You '35
- It Happened in New Orleans '36

Andy Hurst
- Wild Things 2 '04
- Single White Female 2: The Psycho '05
- Wild Things 3: Diamonds in the Rough '05
- Are You Scared? '06

Michael Hurst (1973-)
- New Blood '99
- Mosquito Man '05
- Pumpkinhead 4: Blood Feud '07
- Hardwired '09

Harry Hurwitz (1938-95)
- The Projectionist '71
- Under the Rainbow '81

Jon Hurwitz (1977-)
- Harold and Kumar Go to White Castle '04
- Harold & Kumar Escape from Guantanamo Bay '08
- A Very Harold & Kumar Christmas '11
- American Reunion '12

Chuck Hustmyre
- House of the Rising Sun '11
- End of a Gun '16

John Huston (1906-87)
- Amazing Dr. Clitterhouse '38
- Jezebel '38
- Juarez '39
- Dr. Ehrlich's Magic Bullet '40
- High Sierra '41
- The Maltese Falcon '41
- Sergeant York '41
- The Killers '46
- Three Strangers '46
- Key Largo '48
- Treasure of the Sierra Madre '48
- The African Queen '51
- Moulin Rouge '52
- Beat the Devil '53
- Moby Dick '56
- Heaven Knows, Mr. Allison '57
- The Night of the Iguana '64
- The Kremlin Letter '70
- The Man Who Would Be King '75
- Mr. North '88

Paul Huston
- Junior G-Men of the Air '42
- Overland Mail '42

Tony (Walter Anthony) Huston (1950-)
- The Sidehackers '69
- The Dead '87

Ron Hutchinson
- Blue Ice '92
- Against the Wall '94
- The Tuskegee Airmen '95
- The Island of Dr. Moreau '96
- Marco Polo '07
- The Devil's Teardrop '10
- Betty & Coretta '13

Clint Hutchison
- Terror Tract '00
- Conjurer '08

Willard Huyck (1945-)
- American Graffiti '73
- Messiah of Evil '74
- French Postcards '79
- More American Graffiti '79
- Best Defense '84
- Indiana Jones and the Temple of Doom '84
- Howard the Duck '86
- Radioland Murders '94

David Henry Hwang (1957-)
- Golden Gate '93
- M. Butterfly '93
- The Lost Empire '01
- Possession '02

Peter Hyams (1943-)
- Busting '74
- Our Time '74
- Telefon '77
- Capricorn One '78
- Hanover Street '79
- The Hunter '80
- Outland '81
- The Star Chamber '83
- 2010: The Year We Make Contact '84
- Narrow Margin '90
- Beyond a Reasonable Doubt '09

Andrew Hyatt
- The Frozen '12
- Paul, Apostle of Christ '18

Daniel Hyatt (1911-88)
- *See Daniel James*

Chris Hyde
- Chained Heat 2 '92
- Chained Heat 3: Hell Mountain '98
- Lethal Target '99
- Last Stand '00

Dick Irving Hyland (1906-76)
- Kilroy Was Here '47
- New Orleans '47
- Night Song '47

Frances Hyland (1927-2004)
- The Lost Zeppelin '29
- The Cisco Kid and the Lady '39

Marc Hyman
- Osmosis Jones '01
- The Perfect Score '04
- Show Dogs '18

Jeremy Iacone
- Blood In . . . Blood Out: Bound by Honor '93
- One Tough Cop '98
- The Bone Collector '99

Tobias Iaconis
- Behind Enemy Lines 3: Colombia '08
- The Curse of La Llorona '19
- Five Feet Apart '19

Armando Iannucci
- In the Loop '09
- Alan Partridge '13
- The Death of Stalin '17

Juan Luis Iborra (1959-)
- Mouth to Mouth '95
- Between Your Legs '99
- Km. 0 '00

Rustam Ibragimbekov (1939-)
- Burnt by the Sun '94
- East-West '99

Ice Cube (1969-)
- Friday '95
- The Players Club '98
- Next Friday '00
- All About the Benjamins '02
- Friday After Next '02
- The Janky Promoters '09

Leon Ichaso (1948-)
- Crossover Dreams '85
- Bitter Sugar '96
- Pinero '01
- El Cantante '06

Kon Ichikawa (1915-2008)
- Tokyo Olympiad '66
- The Makioka Sisters '83

Masato Ide (1922-)
- Kagemusha '80
- Ran '85

Eric Idle (1943-)
- And Now for Something Completely Different '72
- Monty Python and the Holy Grail '75
- All You Need Is Cash '78
- Monty Python's Life of Brian '79
- Monty Python's The Meaning of Life '83
- National Lampoon's European Vacation '85
- Splitting Heirs '93

Alexander Ignon
- Ransom '96
- Billionaire Ransom '16

Noboru Iguchi
- RoboGeisha '06
- The Machine Girl '07
- The ABCs of Death '12

W. Peter Iliff (1957-)
- Point Break '91
- Prayer of the Rollerboys '91
- Patriot Games '92
- Varsity Blues '98
- Under Suspicion '00
- Rites of Passage '12

Sang-soo Im (1962-)
- The Housemaid '10
- The Taste of Money '12
- Rio, I Love You '14

Shohei Imamura (1926-2006)
- The Ballad of Narayama '83
- Black Rain '88
- The Eel '96
- Dr. Akagi '98

Hiroshi Inagaki (1905-80)
- Samurai 1: Musashi Miyamoto '55
- Samurai 2: Duel at Ichijoji Temple '55
- Samurai 3: Duel at Ganryu Island '56

Alejandro Gonzalez Inarritu (1963-)
- Biutiful '10
- Birdman, or (The Unexpected Virtue of Ignorance) '14
- The Revenant '15

Thomas Ince (1882-1924)
- The Wrath of the Gods '14
- The Italian '15

Agenore Incrocci (1919-2005)
- Mafioso '62
- The Good, the Bad and the Ugly '67

William Inge (1913-73)
- Splendor in the Grass '61
- All Fall Down '62

Brad Ingelsby
- The Dynamiter '11
- Out of the Furnace '13
- Run All Night '15
- American Woman '19
- The Way Back '20

Raul Inglis
- Premonition '98
- Greenmail '01
- Cerberus '05
- Vice '08
- The Killing Machine '09
- Sand Serpents '09
- Goblin '10
- Takedown '10
- American Heist '15

Boris Ingster (1904-78)
Thin Ice *'37*
Happy Landing *'38*
Southside 1-1000 *'50*
Something for the Birds *'52*

J. Christian Ingvordsen (1957-)
Firehouse *'87*
Hangmen *'87*
Mob War *'88*
Search and Destroy *'88*
Blood Relic *'05*

Sheldon Inkol
Carver's Gate *'96*
Specimen *'97*
Dark Side *'02*

Caroline Ip
The Hole *'01*
Cracks *'09*

Oliver Irving
How to Be *'08*
Ghost Team *'16*

Stanley Isaacs
Megalodon *'03*
Raptor Island *'04*

Christopher Isherwood (1904-86)
Rage in Heaven *'41*
Forever and a Day *'43*
The Great Sinner *'49*
Diane *'55*
The Loved One *'65*

Toshiro Ishido (1932-)
Black Rain *'88*
Hiroshima *'95*

Kazuo Ishiguro (1954-)
The Saddest Music in the World *'03*
The White Countess *'05*

Takashi Ishii (1946-)
Evil Dead Trap *'88*
Gonin 2 *'96*
Flower & Snake *'04*
Flower & Snake 2 *'05*

Ira Israel (1966-)
Dilemma *'97*
American Virgin *'98*

Neal Israel (1945-)
Americathon *'79*
Police Academy *'84*
Real Genius *'85*
Look Who's Talking, Too *'90*
All I Want for Christmas *'91*
National Lampoon's Dad's Week Off *'97*

Juzo Itami (1933-97)
The Funeral *'84*
Tampopo *'86*
A Taxing Woman *'87*

Daisuke Ito (1898-1981)
An Actor's Revenge *'63*
Zatoichi: The Blind Swordsman and the Chess Expert *'65*

Junji Ito
Tomie *'99*
Uzumaki *'00*

James Ivory (1928-)
Shakespeare Wallah *'65*
Maurice *'87*
A Soldier's Daughter Never Cries *'98*
Call Me by Your Name *'17*

William Ivory (1964-)
American Women *'00*
Women in Love *'11*
Going for Gold: The '48 Games *'12*
Burton and Taylor *'13*

Shunji Iwai (1963-)
All About Lily Chou-Chou *'01*
Hana & Alice *'04*
New York, I Love You *'09*

Renato Izzo (1929-2009)
Sabata *'69*
Adios, Sabata *'71*
Return of Sabata *'71*
Night Train Murders *'75*

David S. Jackson
Mystery Mansion *'83*
Detonator *'93*
Detonator 2: Night Watch *'95*
Do or Die *'03*

Felix Jackson (1902-92)
Mad About Music *'38*
Destry Rides Again *'39*
Three Smart Girls Grow Up *'39*
Spring Parade *'40*
Back Street *'41*
Broadway *'42*

Horace Jackson (1898-1952)
Beyond Victory *'31*
The Animal Kingdom *'32*
We're Not Dressing *'34*
No More Ladies *'35*

Joseph Jackson (1894-1932)
The Singing Fool *'28*
Say It With Songs *'29*
Eleven Men and a Girl *'30*
God's Gift to Women *'31*
Safe in Hell *'31*
Smart Money *'31*
Beauty and the Boss *'33*

Peter Jackson (1961-)
Bad Taste *'88*
Meet the Feebles *'89*
Dead Alive *'93*
Heavenly Creatures *'94*
Jack Brown, Genius *'94*
Forgotten Silver *'96*
The Frighteners *'96*
Lord of the Rings: The Fellowship of the Ring *'01*
Lord of the Rings: The Two Towers *'02*
Lord of the Rings: The Return of the King *'03*
King Kong *'05*
The Lovely Bones *'09*
The Hobbit: An Unexpected Journey *'12*
The Hobbit: The Desolation of Smaug *'13*
The Hobbit: The Battle of the Five Armies *'14*

Tracey Jackson
The Guru *'02*
The Other End of the Line *'08*
Confessions of a Shopaholic *'09*

Alan Jacobs
Nina Takes a Lover *'94*
Just One Night *'00*
American Gun *'02*

Alexander Jacobs (1927-79)
Hell in the Pacific *'69*
Sitting Target *'72*
An Enemy of the People *'77*

Evan Jacobs
Doughboys *'08*
Knockout *'11*

Gregory Jacobs
Criminal *'04*
Blackway *'16*

Harrison Jacobs (1892-1968)
Borderland *'37*
Wagons Westward *'40*

Jillian Jacobs
Truth or Dare *'18*
Fantasy Island *'20*

Jon Jacobs (1966-)
The Girl with the Hungry Eyes *'94*
Welcome Says the Angel *'01*

Matthew Jacobs (1956-)
Smart Money *'88*
Lorna Doone *'90*
Lassie *'94*
Doctor Who *'96*

Robert Nelson Jacobs
Out to Sea *'97*
Chocolat *'00*

Dinosaur *'00*
The Shipping News *'01*
The Water Horse: Legend of the Deep *'07*
Extraordinary Measures *'10*

Andrew Jacobson
Not Another Teen Movie *'01*
Extreme Movie *'08*

Danny Jacobson
Out to Sea *'97*
The Honeymooners *'05*

David Jacobson
Dahmer *'02*
Down in the Valley *'05*

Hans Jacoby (1904-63)
Tarzan and the Amazons *'45*
Tarzan and the Slave Girl *'50*
Tarzan's Savage Fury *'52*
Carnival Story *'54*
Stranger from Venus *'54*

John Jacoby
The Amazing Mrs. Holiday *'43*
She Wouldn't Say Yes *'45*

Michael Jacoby
The Charge of the Light Brigade *'36*
The Mystery of Marie Roget *'42*

Benoit Jacquot (1947-)
The Disenchanted *'90*
A Single Girl *'96*
Seventh Heaven *'98*
Farewell, My Queen *'12*
Diary of a Chambermaid *'16*

Rick Jaffa
An Eye for an Eye *'95*
The Relic *'96*
Rise of the Planet of the Apes *'11*
Dawn of the Planet of the Apes *'14*
Jurassic World *'15*

Robert Jaffe
Demon Seed *'77*
Motel Hell *'80*

Henry Jaglom (1938-)
A Safe Place *'71*
Tracks *'76*
Sitting Ducks *'80*
Can She Bake a Cherry Pie? *'83*
Always *'85*
Someone to Love *'87*
New Year's Day *'89*
Eating *'90*
Venice, Venice *'92*
Babyfever *'94*
Last Summer In the Hamptons *'96*
Deja Vu *'98*
Festival at Cannes *'02*
Going Shopping *'05*
Irene in Time *'09*
The M Word *'14*

Randall Jahnson
See Randall Johnson

Don Jakoby
Blue Thunder *'83*
The Philadelphia Experiment *'84*
Lifeforce *'85*
Invaders from Mars *'86*
Arachnophobia *'90*
Double Team *'97*
Evolution *'01*

Jonathan Jakubowicz
Hands of Stone *'16*
Resistance *'20*

Daniel James
The Giant Behemoth *'59*
Gorgo *'61*
On the Edge *'00*

Kevin James (1965-)
Paul Blart: Mall Cop *'09*
Here Comes the Boom *'12*

Mark James
Ruslan *'09*
Reaper *'15*

Polly James
Mrs. Parkington *'44*
The Redhead from Wyoming *'53*

Rian James (1899-1953)
Lawyer Man *'32*
Central Airport *'33*
42nd Street *'33*
To Beat the Band *'35*
Internes Can't Take Money *'37*
Down Argentine Way *'40*

Steve Jankowski
Demolition High *'95*
Chupacabra Terror *'05*

Orin Jannings (1912-66)
Mr. Soft Touch *'49*
Force of Arms *'51*
She's Back on Broadway *'53*

Susan Estelle Jansen
The Lizzie McGuire Movie *'03*
Bratz *'07*

Karen Janszen
The Matchmaker *'97*
Digging to China *'98*
From the Earth to the Moon *'98*
A Walk to Remember *'02*
Duma *'05*
Gracie *'07*
Dolphin Tale *'11*

Michael January
Firepower *'93*
To Be the Best *'93*
C.I.A. 2: Target Alexa *'94*
Deadly Target *'94*
The Heist *'96*

Naomi Janzen
Treacherous Beauties *'94*
Breakout *'98*

Agnes Jaoui (1964-)
Un Air de Famille *'96*
The Taste of Others *'00*
Look at Me *'04*
Let It Rain *'08*

Sebastien Japrisot (1931-2003)
Honor Among Thieves *'68*
The Story of O *'75*

Petr Jarchovsky (1966-)
Divided We Fall *'00*
Zelary *'03*

Pascal Jardin (1934-80)
Classe Tous Risque *'60*
A Coeur Joie *'67*

Eugene Jarecki
The Opponent *'01*
Freakonomics *'10*
The House I Live In *'12*

Nicholas Jarecki
The Informers *'09*
Arbitrage *'12*

Derek Jarman (1942-94)
Sebastiane *'79*
Caravaggio *'86*
The Last of England *'87*
Aria *'88*
Edward II *'92*
Blue *'93*
Wittgenstein *'93*

Jim Jarmusch (1953-)
Stranger than Paradise *'84*
Down by Law *'86*
Mystery Train *'89*
Night on Earth *'91*
Dead Man *'95*
Ghost Dog: The Way of the Samurai *'99*
Coffee and Cigarettes *'03*
Broken Flowers *'05*
The Limits of Control *'09*
Only Lovers Left Alive *'13*
Paterson *'16*
The Dead Don't Die *'19*

Kevin Jarre (1954-2011)
Glory *'89*
Tombstone *'93*
The Devil's Own *'96*

John Jarrell
Restraining Order *'99*
Romeo Must Die *'00*
Terminal Invasion *'02*

Paul Jarrico (1915-97)
Tom, Dick, and Harry *'41*
Thousands Cheer *'43*
The Search *'48*
The White Tower *'50*
All Night Long *'62*
Messenger of Death *'88*

Anthony Jaswinski
Backwoods *'08*
Vanishing on 7th Street *'10*
Satanic *'15*
The Shallows *'16*
Mary *'19*

Griffin Jay (1905-54)
Air Hawks *'35*
The Mummy's Hand *'40*
Junior G-Men of the Air *'42*
The Mummy's Tomb *'42*
Return of the Vampire *'43*
The Devil Bat's Daughter *'46*
The Mask of Diijon *'46*

Mark Jean
Homecoming *'96*
Finn on the Fly *'09*

Vadim Jean (1963-)
Nightscare *'93*
Hogfather *'06*
The Color of Magic *'08*

Henri Jeanson (1900-70)
Pepe Le Moko *'37*
Nana *'55*

Richard Jefferies
Cold Creek Manor *'03*
Organizm *'08*
Tron: Legacy *'10*

Ian Mackenzie Jeffers
Death Sentence *'07*
The Grey *'12*

Stephen Jeffreys (1950-)
The Libertine *'05*
Diana *'13*

Erik Jendresen
Deadlocked *'00*
Band of Brothers *'01*
Crazy as Hell *'02*
Sublime *'07*
Otis *'08*
The Big Bang *'11*
Killing Lincoln *'13*
Ithaca *'16*

Guy Jenkin (1955-)
The Sleeping Dictionary *'02*
What We Did on Our Holiday *'15*

Barry Jenkins
Medicine for Melancholy *'08*
Moonlight *'16*
If Beale Street Could Talk *'18*

Tamara Jenkins (1962-)
Slums of Beverly Hills *'98*
The Savages *'07*
Juliet, Naked *'18*

Jim Jennewein
The Flintstones *'94*
Getting Even with Dad *'94*
Richie Rich *'94*

Garth Jennings (1972-)
Son of Rambow *'07*
Sing *'16*

Talbot Jennings (1894-1985)
Mutiny on the Bounty *'35*
Spawn of the North *'38*
Frenchman's Creek *'44*
Anna and the King of Siam *'46*
The Black Rose *'50*
Untamed *'55*

Anders Thomas Jensen (1972-)
Mifune *'99*
The King Is Alive *'00*
Flickering Lights *'01*
Wilbur Wants to Kill Himself *'02*

The Green Butchers *'03*
Brothers *'04*
Adam's Apples *'05*
After the Wedding *'06*
The Duchess *'08*
In a Better World *'10*
The Salvation *'14*
Men & Chicken *'15*
The Dark Tower *'17*

Caytha Jentis
And Then Came Love *'07*
The One *'11*
Bad Parents *'12*

Jean-Pierre Jeunet (1955-)
Delicatessen *'92*
The City of Lost Children *'95*
Amelie *'01*
Micmacs *'09*
The Young and Prodigious T.S. Spivet *'15*

Jack Jevne (1892-1972)
Our Relations *'36*
Merrily We Live *'38*
Wintertime *'43*
Wonder Man *'45*

Ruth Prawer Jhabvala (1927-2013)
The Householder *'63*
Shakespeare Wallah *'65*
Bombay Talkie *'70*
Roseland *'77*
Hullabaloo over Georgie & Bonnie's Pictures *'78*
The Europeans *'79*
Jane Austen in Manhattan *'80*
Quartet *'81*
Heat and Dust *'82*
The Bostonians *'84*
A Room with a View *'86*
Madame Sousatzka *'88*
Mr. & Mrs. Bridge *'90*
Howard's End *'92*
The Remains of the Day *'93*
Jefferson in Paris *'94*
Surviving Picasso *'96*
A Soldier's Daughter Never Cries *'98*
The Golden Bowl *'00*
Le Divorce *'03*
The City of Your Final Destination *'09*

Zhangke Jia
Mountains May Depart *'16*
Ash Is Purest White *'18*

Neal Jimenez (1960-)
River's Edge *'87*
For the Boys *'91*
The Waterdance *'91*
Hideaway *'94*
Sleep with Me *'94*
Desperate Measures *'98*

Zou Jingzhi
Riding Alone for Thousands of Miles *'05*
The Grandmaster *'13*

Peter Jobin (1944-)
Happy Birthday to Me *'81*
Queen's Messenger II *'01*

Richard Jobson (1960-)
16 Years of Alcohol *'03*
The Purifiers *'04*

Alejandro Jodorowsky (1929-)
El Topo *'71*
The Holy Mountain *'73*
Santa Sangre *'90*
The Dance of Reality *'14*

Roland Joffé (1945-)
Fat Man and Little Boy *'89*
Brighton Rock *'10*
There Be Dragons *'11*
The Forgiven *'18*

Rowan Joffe (1972-)
28 Weeks Later *'07*
The American *'10*
Before I Go to Sleep *'14*

Tim John
Dr. Jekyll and Ms. Hyde *'95*
Call of the Wild *'04*
A Street Cat Named Bob *'16*

Bayard Johnson
Rudyard Kipling's the Second Jungle Book: Mowgli and Baloo *'97*
Tarzan and the Lost City *'98*

Catherine Johnson (1957-)
Mamma Mia! *'08*
Mamma Mia! Here We Go Again *'18*

Charles Johnson
Beyond Atlantis *'73*
Slaughter's Big Ripoff *'73*

Charles Eric Johnson
Hard Lessons *'86*
Steele's Law *'91*

David C(lark) Johnson (1962-)
DROP Squad *'94*
Woo *'97*
Animal *'05*

David Leslie Johnson
Orphan *'09*
Red Riding Hood *'11*
Wrath of the Titans *'12*
The Conjuring 2 *'16*
Unforgettable *'17*

Denis Johnson (1949-)
Hit Me *'96*
Dog Gone *'08*

Eric Johnson
The Fighter *'10*
The Finest Hours *'16*

J. Randall Johnson
See Randall Johnson

Jesse Johnson (1971-)
Pit Fighter *'05*
The Butcher *'07*
The Last Sentinel *'07*
The Hitman Diaries *'09*

Kenneth Johnson (1942-)
V *'83*
Hot Pursuit *'84*
Alien Nation: Millennium *'96*
Steel *'97*

Kristine Johnson
Imaginary Crimes *'94*
I Am Sam *'01*

Laurence E. Johnson (1869-1933)
The Bachelor Father *'31*
The Passionate Plumber *'32*
Polly of the Circus *'32*

Mark Steven Johnson (1964-)
Grumpy Old Men *'93*
Big Bully *'95*
Grumpier Old Men *'95*
Jack Frost *'98*
Simon Birch *'98*
Daredevil *'03*
Ghost Rider *'07*

Matt Johnson
Torque *'04*
Into the Blue *'05*
Tracers *'15*
Operation Avalanche *'16*

Monica Johnson (1956-)
Americathon *'79*
Real Life *'79*
Modern Romance *'81*
Jekyll & Hyde. . . Together Again *'82*
Lost in America *'85*
The Scout *'94*
Mother *'96*
The Muse *'99*

Niall Johnson
The Ghost of Greville Lodge *'00*
Keeping Mum *'05*
White Noise *'05*

Nunnally Johnson (1897-1977)
Kid Millions *'34*
Thanks a Million *'35*
The Prisoner of Shark Island *'36*
Jesse James *'39*
Rose of Washington Square *'39*
Wife, Husband and Friend *'39*
Chad Hanna *'40*
The Grapes of Wrath *'40*
Tobacco Road *'41*
Life Begins at Eight-Thirty *'42*
Roxie Hart *'42*
Holy Matrimony *'43*
The Moon is Down *'43*
Casanova Brown *'44*
The Keys of the Kingdom *'44*
Woman in the Window *'44*
Along Came Jones *'45*
The Mudlark *'50*
Three Came Home *'50*
My Cousin Rachel *'52*
Phone Call from a Stranger *'52*
We're Not Married *'52*
How to Marry a Millionaire *'53*
Black Widow *'54*
Night People *'54*
Oh, Men! Oh, Women! *'57*
The Three Faces of Eve *'57*
Flaming Star *'60*
Mr. Hobbs Takes a Vacation *'62*
Take Her, She's Mine *'63*
The World of Henry Orient *'64*
The Dirty Dozen *'67*

Randall Johnson
The Doors *'91*
Sunset Strip *'99*

Rian Johnson (1973-)
Brick *'06*
The Brothers Bloom *'09*
Looper *'12*
Star Wars: The Last Jedi *'17*
Knives Out *'19*

Robert Lee Johnson (1908-80)
Huddle *'32*
Canal Zone *'42*

Robert P. Johnson
The Temptations *'98*
Bojangles *'01*

Toni Johnson
Ruby Bridges *'98*
The Courage to Love *'00*
Crown Heights *'02*
Step Up 2 the Streets *'08*

Kurt Johnstad
300 *'07*
Act of Valor *'12*
300: Rise of an Empire *'13*
Atomic Blonde *'17*

Aaron Kim Johnston
For the Moment *'94*
Tornado Valley *'09*

Agnes Christine Johnston (1896-1978)
Daddy Long Legs *'19*
Three Wise Girls *'32*
Out West With the Hardys *'38*
The Hardys Ride High *'39*
Andy Hardy's Double Life *'42*
The Courtship of Andy Hardy *'42*
Andy Hardy's Blonde Trouble *'44*
Stage Struck *'48*

Becky Johnston
The Prince of Tides *'91*
Seven Years in Tibet *'97*

Phil Johnston
Wreck-It Ralph *'12*
The Brothers Grimsby *'16*
Zootopia *'16*
Ralph Breaks the Internet *'18*

Rory Johnston
Prey of the Jaguar *'96*
The Secret Agent Club *'96*

Stephen Johnston
Ed Gein *'01*
Starkweather *'04*

Thomas Johnston
Jerome *'98*
About Fifty *'11*

Tony Johnston (1960-)
Replikator: Cloned to Kill *'94*
Full Disclosure *'00*
Killing Moon *'00*
Triggermen *'02*
Hollywood North *'03*

Angelina Jolie (1975-)
In the Land of Blood and Honey *'11*
By the Sea *'15*
First They Killed My Father *'17*

Amy Holden Jones (1953-)
Love Letters *'83*
Mystic Pizza *'88*
Beethoven *'92*
The Getaway *'93*
Indecent Proposal *'93*
The Relic *'96*
The Rich Man's Wife *'96*

Arthur V. Jones (1904-76)
Mister Cinderella *'36*
Along the Rio Grande *'41*

Brennon Jones
Makin' Baby *'02*
Alien 51 *'04*

Ed Jones
Ninja in the U.S.A. *'88*
Carried Away *'95*

Evan Jones (1976-)
Eva *'62*
These Are the Damned *'63*
King and Country *'64*
Funeral in Berlin *'66*
Modesty Blaise *'66*
Outback *'71*
Champions *'84*
A Show of Force *'90*

Grover Jones (1893-1940)
Trouble in Paradise *'32*
One Sunday Afternoon *'33*
The Lives of a Bengal Lancer *'35*
The Trail of the Lonesome Pine *'36*
Souls at Sea *'37*
The Shepherd of the Hills *'41*

Jerry Jones
Dolemite *'75*
Dolemite 2: Human Tornado *'76*

Kent Jones (1960-)
Jimmy P. *'13*
Hitchcock/Truffaut *'15*
Diane *'18*

Kirk Jones (1963-)
Waking Ned Devine *'98*
Everybody's Fine *'09*

Laura Jones (1951-)
High Tide *'87*
An Angel at My Table *'89*
Portrait of a Lady *'96*
Oscar and Lucinda *'97*
A Thousand Acres *'97*
The Well *'97*
Angela's Ashes *'99*
Possession *'02*

Mark Jones (1953-)
Leprechaun *'93*
Rumpelstiltskin *'96*

Matthew F. Jones
Tomorrow You're Gone *'12*
A Single Shot *'13*

Pete Jones
Stolen Summer *'02*
Outing Riley *'04*
Hall Pass *'11*

Robert Jones
Lennon Naked *'10*
Secret State *'12*

Robert C. Jones
Coming Home *'78*
P.D. James: Death in Holy Orders *'03*
P.D. James: The Murder Room *'04*

Terry Jones (1942-2020)
And Now for Something Completely Different *'72*
Monty Python and the Holy Grail *'75*
Monty Python's Life of Brian *'79*
Monty Python's The Meaning of Life *'83*
Labyrinth *'86*
Erik the Viking *'89*
Mr. Toad's Wild Ride *'96*
Absolutely Anything *'17*

Todd R. Jones
Johnson Family Vacation *'04*
Rio *'11*

Tommy Lee Jones (1946-)
The Good Old Boys *'95*
The Homesman *'14*

Spike Jonze (1969-)
Where the Wild Things Are *'09*
Her *'13*

Gregor Jordan (1967-)
Two Hands *'98*
Buffalo Soldiers *'01*

Kevin Jordan (1974-)
Smiling Fish & Goat on Fire *'99*
Brooklyn Lobster *'05*

Neil Jordan (1950-)
Danny Boy *'82*
The Company of Wolves *'85*
Mona Lisa *'86*
High Spirits *'88*
The Crying Game *'92*
Michael Collins *'96*
The Butcher Boy *'97*
In Dreams *'98*
The End of the Affair *'99*
The Good Thief *'03*
Breakfast on Pluto *'05*
Ondine *'09*
Greta *'18*

Rafael Jordan
Lost Colony: The Legend of Roanoke *'07*
Yeti *'08*
Super Eruption *'11*
Dragon Wasps *'12*
Rise of the Dinosaurs *'13*
Stonados *'13*
Cowboys vs Dinosaurs *'15*

Curtis Joseph
They Crawl *'01*
Project Viper *'02*

Rajiv Joseph
Draft Day *'14*
Army of One *'16*

Robert L. Joseph (1923-2002)
The Hitch-Hiker *'53*
World War III *'86*

Julien Josephson (1881-1959)
The Man Who Played God *'32*
A Successful Calamity *'32*
Chance at Heaven *'33*
Suez *'38*
The Rains Came *'39*

Jon Jost (1943-)
Sure Fire *'90*
All the Vermeers in New York *'91*
The Bed You Sleep In *'93*

Leland Jourdan (1986-)
The Mark *'12*
The Mark 2: Redemption *'13*

Adrien (Carole Eastman) Joyce (1934-2004)
The Shooting *'66*
Model Shop *'69*
Five Easy Pieces *'70*
Man Trouble *'92*

C. Courtney Joyner
The Offspring *'87*
Class of 1999 *'90*
Puppet Master 3: Toulon's Revenge *'90*
Vietnam, Texas *'90*
Trancers 3: Deth Lives *'92*
Lurking Fear *'94*
Nautilus *'99*
The Base 2: Guilty as Charged *'00*
Trancers 6: Life After Deth *'02*
Lady Jayne Killer *'03*
Stealing Candy *'04*

Jeff Judah
Diary of a Wimpy Kid *'10*
Diary of a Wimpy Kid 2: Rodrick Rules *'11*

Mike Judge (1962-)
Beavis and Butt-Head Do America *'96*
Office Space *'98*
Idiocracy *'06*
Extract *'09*

Jerry Juhl (1938-2005)
The Muppet Movie *'79*
Muppet Treasure Island *'96*
Muppets from Space *'99*

Lenny Juliano
Desert Thunder *'99*
Stealth Fighter *'99*

Miranda July (1974-)
Me and You and Everyone We Know *'05*
The Future *'11*

Amy Jump
Kill List *'12*
A Field in England *'14*
High-Rise *'16*
Free Fire *'17*

Brian Jun (1979-)
Steel City *'06*
Joint Body *'11*

Doug Jung
Confidence *'03*
Star Trek: Beyond *'16*

Nathan 'Jerry' Juran (1907-2002)
Boy Who Caught a Crook *'61*
Jack the Giant Killer *'62*

Jason Kabolati (1967-)
Mad Bad *'07*
The Final *'10*

Cedric Kahn (1966-)
L'Ennui *'98*
Red Lights *'04*

Gordon Kahn (1902-62)
Navy Blues *'37*
Lights of Old Santa Fe *'47*
Ruthless *'48*
Whiplash *'48*

Chen Kaige (1952-)
Life on a String *'90*
The Emperor and the Assassin *'99*
Together *'02*
The Promise *'05*

David Kajganich (1969-)
The Invasion *'07*
Blood Creek *'09*
A Bigger Splash *'15*
Suspiria *'18*

Michael Kalesniko (1961-)
Private Parts *'96*
Spoiler *'98*
How to Kill Your Neighbor's Dog *'01*

Tom Kalin
Swoon *'91*
Office Killer *'97*

Bert Kalmar (1884-1947)
Horse Feathers *'32*
Kid from Spain *'32*
Duck Soup *'33*
A Night at the Opera *'35*

Laeta Kalogridis (1965-)
Alexander *'04*
Pathfinder *'07*
Shutter Island *'09*
Terminator Genisys *'15*
Alita: Battle Angel *'19*

Steven Kaman
Firehouse *'87*
Hangmen *'87*

Karl Kamb (1903-88)
Carnegie Hall *'47*
Lulu Belle *'48*
Luxury Liner *'48*
Whispering Smith *'48*
The Captive City *'52*
Tarzan and the She-Devil *'53*

Robert Mark Kamen
Taps *'81*
The Karate Kid *'84*
The Karate Kid: Part 2 *'86*
The Karate Kid: Part 3 *'89*
Gladiator *'92*
Lethal Weapon 3 *'92*
The Power of One *'92*
A Walk in the Clouds *'95*
Kiss of the Dragon *'01*
The Transporter *'02*
Transporter 2 *'05*
Bandidas *'06*
Taken *'08*
Transporter 3 *'08*
The Karate Kid *'10*
Colombiana *'11*
Taken 2 *'12*
Taken 3 *'15*
Enter the Warriors Gate *'17*
Angel Has Fallen *'19*

Kazuo Kamimura
Lady Snowblood *'73*
Lady Snowblood: Love Song of Vengeance *'74*
The Princess Blade *'02*

Steven Kampmann (1947-)
Back to School *'86*
The Couch Trip *'87*
Stealing Home *'88*
Clifford *'92*

Deborah Kampmeier (1964-)
Virgin *'03*
Hounddog *'08*

John Kamps
Mighty Morphin Power Rangers: The Movie *'95*
The Borrowers *'97*
Zathura *'05*
Ghost Town *'08*
Premium Rush *'12*

Aben Kandel (1897-1993)
They Won't Forget *'37*
The Fighter *'52*
Blood of Dracula *'57*
Horrors of the Black Museum *'59*
Black Zoo *'63*
Trog *'70*

Stephen Kandel
Battle of the Coral Sea *'59*
Cannon for Cordoba *'70*

David Kane (1961-)
Born Romantic *'00*
The River King *'05*
Murder On the Home Front *'13*

Henry Kane
Cop Hater *'58*
The Mugger *'58*

Joany Kane
The Christmas Card *'06*
Moonlight & Mistletoe *'08*
Christmas Magic *'11*

Michael Kane
Hot Stuff *'80*
Smokey and the Bandit 2 *'80*
Hard Country *'81*
Legend of the Lone Ranger *'81*
Southern Comfort *'81*
All the Right Moves *'83*
The Bear *'89*
The Cisco Kid *'94*

Rolfe Kanefsky (1969-)
There's Nothing out There *'90*
Red Line *'96*

The Hazing '04
Blonde and Blonder '07

Young Man Kang
Cupid's Mistake '01
The Last Eve '05

Charles Kanganis
A Time to Die '91
Fist of Honor '92
No Escape, No Return '93
Impulse '08

Fay Kanin (1917-2013)
Rhapsody '54
The Opposite Sex '56
Teacher's Pet '58
The Right Approach '61
Friendly Fire '79

Garson Kanin (1912-99)
A Double Life '47
Adam's Rib '50
The Marrying Kind '52
Pat and Mike '52
It Should Happen to You '54
Where It's At '69

Michael Kanin (1910-93)
Woman of the Year '42
The Cross of Lorraine '43
Honeymoon '47
Rhapsody '54
The Opposite Sex '56
Teacher's Pet '58
The Right Approach '61
Swordsman of Siena '62
The Outrage '64
How to Commit Marriage '69

Hal Kanter (1918-2011)
Here Come the Girls '53
Money from Home '53
The Road to Bali '53
Casanova's Big Night '54
Artists and Models '55
The Rose Tattoo '55
Loving You '57
Bachelor in Paradise '61
Pocketful of Miracles '61
Blue Hawaii '62
Move Over, Darling '63
Dear Brigitte '65

Asif Kapadia (1972-)
The Warrior '01
Far North '07

Prakash Kapadia
Devdas '02
Padmaavat '18

Deborah Kaplan
A Very Brady Sequel '96
Can't Hardly Wait '98
The Flintstones in Viva Rock Vegas '00
Josie and the Pussycats '01
Surviving Christmas '04
Made of Honor '08
Leap Year '10

Jonathan Kaplan (1947-)
White Line Fever '75
Mr. Billion '77

Marty Kaplan
The Distinguished Gentleman '92
Noises Off '92
Striking Distance '93

Mitchell Kapner
The Whole Nine Yards '00
The Whole Ten Yards '04
Into the Blue 2: The Reef '09
Oz the Great and Powerful '13

Wong Kar-Wai (1958-)
Ashes of Time '94
Chungking Express '95
Fallen Angels '95
Happy Together '96
In the Mood for Love '00
Eros '04
2046 '04
My Blueberry Nights '07
Ashes of Time Redux '08
The Grandmaster '13

Larry Karaszewski (1961-)
Problem Child '90
Problem Child 2 '91

Ed Wood '94
The People vs. Larry Flynt '96
That Darn Cat '96
Man on the Moon '99
Screwed '00
Agent Cody Banks '03
1408 '07
Big Eyes '14
Goosebumps '15
Dolemite Is My Name '19

Maria Karlsson
Easy Money '10
Easy Money: Hard to Kill '12

Kazuo Kasahara (?-2002)
Cops vs. Thugs '75
Ronin Gai '90

Jake Kasdan (1975-)
Zero Effect '97
The TV Set '06
Walk Hard: The Dewey Cox Story '07
Jumanji: The Next Level '19

Jonathan Kasdan
In the Land of Women '06
The First Time '12
Solo: A Star Wars Story '18

Lawrence Kasdan (1949-)
The Empire Strikes Back '80
Body Heat '81
Continental Divide '81
The Big Chill '83
Return of the Jedi '83
Silverado '85
The Accidental Tourist '88
Grand Canyon '91
The Bodyguard '92
Wyatt Earp '94
Mumford '99
Dreamcatcher '03
Darling Companion '12
Star Wars: The Force Awakens '15
Solo: A Star Wars Story '18

Meg Kasdan
Grand Canyon '91
Darling Companion '12

Hiroshi Kashiwabara
Godzilla vs. SpaceGodzilla '94
Godzilla 2000 '99
Godzilla vs. Megaguirus '00

Bryce Kass
Outlaw Prophet: Warren Jeffs '14
Lizzie '18

Sam Henry Kass
The Search for One-Eye Jimmy '94
Body and Soul '98

Mathieu Kassovitz (1967-)
Cafe au Lait '94
Hate '95
The Crimson Rivers '01
Babylon A.D. '08

Brian Katkin
If I Die Before I Wake '98
Hard As Nails '01
Shakedown '02
Vipers '08

Norman Katkov
It Happened to Jane '59
Once You Kiss a Stranger '69
The Amazing Captain Nemo '78
Cave-In! '79
Blood and Orchids '86

Monte Katterjohn (1891-1949)
The Sheik '21
Moran of the Lady Letty '22

Aaron Katz (1981-)
Land Ho! '14
Gemini '17

A.L. Katz
Children of the Corn 2: The Final Sacrifice '92
Tales from the Crypt Presents Bordello of Blood '96

E.L. Katz
Autopsy '08
Home Sick '08

Gloria Katz
American Graffiti '73
Messiah of Evil '74
French Postcards '79
More American Graffiti '79
Best Defense '84
Indiana Jones and the Temple of Doom '84
Howard the Duck '86
Radioland Murders '94

Jordan Katz (1960-)
Trial by Jury '94
Incognito '97
Valiant '05

Pamela Katz
Rosenstrasse '03
Hannah Arendt '12

Stephen Katz (1946-2005)
Charms '73
From the Earth to the Moon '98
The Contract '07

Steven Katz
Shadow of the Vampire '00
Wind Chill '07

Charles Kaufman (1958-)
Breakfast for Two '37
Cynthia '47
Squeeze Play '79
Mother's Day '80
Waitress '81
Ferocious Female Freedom Fighters '88

Charles A. Kaufman (1904-91)
Return to Paradise '53
Bridge to the Sun '61

Charlie Kaufman (1958-)
Being John Malkovich '99
Adaptation '02
Confessions of a Dangerous Mind '02
Human Nature '02
Eternal Sunshine of the Spotless Mind '04
Synecdoche, New York '08
Anomalisa '16

George S. Kaufman (1889-1961)
The Cocoanuts '29
A Night at the Opera '35
Star Spangled Rhythm '42

Ken Kaufman (1963-)
In the Army Now '94
Space Cowboys '00
The Missing '03
Curious George '06

Lloyd Kaufman (1945-)
First Turn On '83
Stuck on You '84
Class of Nuke 'Em High '86
Troma's War '88
The Toxic Avenger, Part 2 '89
The Toxic Avenger, Part 3: The Last Temptation of Toxie '89
Class of Nuke 'Em High 2: Subhumanoid Meltdown '91
Class of Nuke 'Em High 3: The Good, the Bad and the Subhumanoid '94
Sgt. Kabukiman N.Y.P.D. '94
Citizen Toxie: The Toxic Avenger 4 '01

Millard Kaufman (1917-)
The War Lord '65
Living Free '72

Philip Kaufman (1936-)
Goldstein '64
The Great Northfield Minnesota Raid '72
The Outlaw Josey Wales '76
Wanderers '79
Raiders of the Lost Ark '81
The Right Stuff '83
The Unbearable Lightness of Being '88

Henry & June '90
Rising Sun '93

Robert Kaufman (1931-91)
Ski Party '65
The Cool Ones '67
Love at First Bite '79

Aki Kaurismaki (1957-)
Ariel '89
The Match Factory Girl '90
The Man Without a Past '02
Lights in the Dusk '06
The Other Side of Hope '17

Gina Kaus (1894-1985)
The Red Danube '50
Three Secrets '50
All I Desire '53

Ivan Kavanagh
The Canal '14
Never Grow Old '19

Kikuo Kawasaki
Private Passions '85
Lured Innocence '97

Minoru Kawasaki
The Calamari Wrestler '04
Executive Koala '06

Dan Kay
Pay the Ghost '15
I.T. '16

Stephen Kay (1963-)
The Last Time I Committed Suicide '96
The Mod Squad '99
Lizzie Borden Took an Ax '14

Tony Kayden
Slipstream '89
When Justice Fails '98

John Kaye
Where the Buffalo Roam '80
Along for the Ride '00

Elia Kazan (1909-2003)
Blues in the Night '41
America America '63
The Arrangement '69

Nicholas Kazan (1950-)
Frances '82
Impulse '84
At Close Range '86
Patty Hearst '88
Reversal of Fortune '90
Mobsters '91
Dream Lover '93
Matilda '96
Fallen '97
Homegrown '97
Bicentennial Man '99
Enough '02

Zoe Kazan (1983-)
Ruby Sparks '12
Wildlife '18

Tim Kazurinsky (1950-)
About Last Night. . . '86
For Keeps '88
The Cherokee Kid '96
Strange Relations '02

James Keach (1947-)
Slashed Dreams '74
The Long Riders '80
Armed and Dangerous '86

Gene R. Kearney (1930-79)
Games '67
Night of the Lepus '72
The Invasion of Carol Enders '74

James Kearns
John Q '02
Held Hostage '09

David Keating
The Last of the High Kings '96
Wake Wood '10

Buster Keaton (1895-1966)
Go West '25
The General '26

Abdellatif Kechiche (1960-)
Games of Love and Chance '03

Blue is the Warmest Color '13

Joe Keenan (1958-)
Sleep with Me '94
Flushed Away '06

Brad Keene
The Gravedancers '06
The Grudge 3 '09

Jon Keeyes (1969-)
American Nightmare '00
Living & Dying '07

Harvey Keith
Jezebel's Kiss '90
Stand-Ins '97

Woody Keith
Bride of Re-Animator '89
Dementia '98

Ed Kelleher (1944-2005)
Invasion of the Blood Farmers '72
Shriek of the Mutilated '74
Lurkers '88
Stand-Ins '97

Tim Kelleher
First Kid '96
Grudge Match '13

Jason Keller (1971-)
Big Shot: Confessions of a Campus Bookie '02
Machine Gun Preacher '11
Mirror Mirror '12
Escape Plan '13
Ford v Ferrari '19

Sean Keller
Kraken: Tentacles of the Deep '06
Mammoth '06
Attack of the Gryphon '07
Giallo '09
Rage '14
Broken Vows '16

Cindy Kelley
Love Comes Softly '03
Love's Enduring Promise '04
Love's Unfolding Dream '07
Saving Sarah Cain '07

David E. Kelley (1956-)
To Gillian on Her 37th Birthday '96
Lake Placid '99
Mystery, Alaska '99

John T. Kelley (1921-72)
A Rage to Live '65
ZigZag '70

Bob Kelljan (1930-82)
Count Yorga, Vampire '70
The Return of Count Yorga '71

Bill Kelly
Blast from the Past '98
Enchanted '07
Premonition '07

Justin Kelly
King Cobra '16
I Am Michael '17

Karen Kelly
Hard Bounty '94
Body Chemistry 4: Full Exposure '95
Poison Ivy 3: The New Seduction '97
The Last Best Sunday '98

Patrick Smith Kelly
A Perfect Murder '98
Don't Say a Word '01

Richard Kelly (1975-)
Donnie Darko '01
Domino '05
Southland Tales '06
The Box '09

Tim Kelly (1931-98)
Cry of the Banshee '70
Sugar Hill '74
Homeboy '75
Fist '76

David Kendall
The Growing Pains Movie '00

The New Guy '02
Nature of the Beast '07
Revenge of the Bridesmaids '10
Teen Spirit '11

Alex Kendrick
Fireproof '08
Courageous '11
War Room '15
Overcomer '19

Stephen Kendrick
Fireproof '08
Courageous '11
War Room '15
Overcomer '19

James Kennaway
The Mind Benders '63
Battle of Britain '69

Anne Kennedy (1959-)
Crush '93
The Monkey's Mask '00

Burt Kennedy (1922-2001)
Gun the Man Down '56
Man in the Vault '56
7 Men From Now '56
The Tall T '57
Fort Dobbs '58
Ride Lonesome '59
Comanche Station '60
Mail Order Bride '63
The Rounders '65
Welcome to Hard Times '67
Hannie Caulder '72
Train Robbers '73
Texas Guns '90
White Hunter, Black Heart '90

Jane Kennedy (1964-)
The Castle '97
The Dish '00

William Kennedy (1928-)
The Cotton Club '84
Ironweed '87

Troy Kennedy-Martin (1932-)
Kelly's Heroes '70
Hostile Waters '97

Doug Kenney
National Lampoon's Animal House '78
Caddyshack '80

Jennifer Kent
The Babadook '14
The Nightingale '18

Robert E. Kent (1911-84)
The Spider's Web '38
Gildersleeve on Broadway '43
Zombies on Broadway '44
Radio Stars on Parade '45
The Golden Hawk '52
Charge of the Lancers '54
The Miami Story '54
The Gun That Won the West '55
Seminole Uprising '55
The Werewolf '56
Noose for a Gunman '60
Three Came to Kill '61
Diary of a Madman '63
Twice-Told Tales '63
Get Yourself a College Girl '64
The Quick Gun '64
When the Boys Meet the Girls '65
Hot Rods to Hell '67
The Christine Jorgensen Story '70

Chris Kentis (1962-)
Grind '96
Open Water '03

Earl Kenton
Invisible: The Chronicles of Benjamin Knight '93
Mandroid '93
LIP Service '99

Charles Kenyon (1880-1961)
The Penalty '20
The Iron Horse '24

Michael Knowles
Room 314 '07
The Trouble With Bliss '11

Hirohoshi Kobayashi
Death Note 3: L Change the World '08
Negative Happy Chainsaw Edge '08

Masaki Kobayashi (1916-96)
The Human Condition: No Greater Love '58
The Human Condition: Road to Eternity '59

Arthur Kober (1900-75)
Make Me a Star '32
Me and My Gal '32
Hollywood Party '34
Having a Wonderful Time '38
In the Meantime, Darling '44
Don Juan Quilligan '45

Chris Kobin
2001 Maniacs '05
2001 Maniacs: Field of Screams '10

Flip Kobler
The Lion King: Simba's Pride '98
Jack and the Beanstalk '09

Howard Koch (1901-95)
The Letter '40
The Sea Hawk '40
Sergeant York '41
Casablanca '42
Mission to Moscow '43
Rhapsody in Blue '45
Three Strangers '46
Letter from an Unknown Woman '48
No Sad Songs For Me '50
War Lover '62

Anya Kochoff (1969-)
Monster-in-Law '05
Mother's Day '16

David Koepp (1964-)
Apartment Zero '88
Death Becomes Her '92
Carlito's Way '93
Jurassic Park '93
The Paper '94
The Shadow '94
Mission: Impossible '96
The Trigger Effect '96
The Lost World: Jurassic Park 2 '97
Snake Eyes '98
Stir of Echoes '99
Panic Room '02
Spider-Man '02
Secret Window '04
War of the Worlds '05
Zathura '05
Ghost Town '08
Indiana Jones and the Kingdom of the Crystal Skull '08
Angels & Demons '09
Men in Black 3 '12
Premium Rush '12
Jack Ryan: Shadow Recruit '14
Inferno '16
The Mummy '17
You Should Have Left '20

Wolfgang Kohlhaase (1931-)
The Gleiwitz Case '61
The Legend of Rita '99

Abby Kohn
Never Been Kissed '99
He's Just Not That Into You '09
Valentine's Day '10
The Vow '12
How to Be Single '16
I Feel Pretty '18

Frederick Kohner (1905-86)
Three Daring Daughters '48
Hollywood Story '51

Kazuo Koike (1936-)
Lady Snowblood '73
Shogun Assassin 2: Lightning Swords of Death '73
Lady Snowblood: Love Song of Vengeance '74
Shogun Assassin '80
The Princess Blade '02

Vincent Kok (1965-)
Contract Killer '98
Gorgeous '99

Stefan Kolditz
Burning Life '94
Dresden '06
Generation War '13

Amy Kolquist
Border Run '12
Amnesiac '15

Derek Kolstad
One In the Chamber '12
The Package '12
John Wick '14
John Wick: Chapter 2 '17
John Wick: Chapter 3-Parabellum '19

Todd Komarnicki (1965-)
Resistance '03
Perfect Stranger '07
Sully '16
The Professor and the Madman '19

Andrei Konchalovsky (1937-)
Andrei Rublev '66
Siberiade '79
Maria's Lovers '84
Runaway Train '85
The Inner Circle '91
The Odyssey '97
House of Fools '02

James Kondelik
Airplane vs. Volcano '14
All Hallow's Eve 2 '15

Jon Kondelik
Airplane vs. Volcano '14
All Hallow's Eve 2 '15

Kate Kondell (1973-)
Legally Blonde 2: Red White & Blonde '03
First Daughter '04

Larry Konner
The Jewel of the Nile '85
Desperate Hours '90
Sometimes They Come Back '91
The Beverly Hillbillies '93
For Love or Money '93
Mercury Rising '98
Mighty Joe Young '98
Planet of the Apes '01
Mona Lisa Smile '03
Flicka '06

Michael Konyves
Descent '05
Solar Attack '06
Fire & Ice: The Dragon Chronicles '08
Storm Cell '08
Barney's Version '10
Last Knights '15

Chuck Konzelman
Earth vs. the Spider '01
The Insatiable '06
Finding Normal '13
Do You Believe? '15
God's Not Dead 2 '16
Unplanned '19

Martin Koolhoven
Winter in Wartime '10
Brimstone '17

Peter Koper
Headless Body in Topless Bar '96
Island of the Dead '00

Arthur Kopit (1937-)
The Phantom of the Opera '90
Roswell: The U.F.O. Cover-Up '94

Brian Koppelman
Rounders '98
Knockaround Guys '01
Runaway Jury '03
Walking Tall '04
Ocean's Thirteen '07
The Girlfriend Experience '09
Solitary Man '10
Runner Runner '13

Howard Korder (1957-)
My Little Assassin '99
The Passion of Ayn Rand '99
Stealing Sinatra '04
Lakeview Terrace '08

Hirokazu Kore-eda (1962-)
After Life '98
Nobody Knows '04
I Wish '11
Like Father, Like Son '13
Our Little Sister '16
After the Storm '17
Shoplifters '18

Steve Koren
A Night at the Roxbury '98
Superstar '99
Bruce Almighty '03
Click '06
Jack and Jill '11
A Thousand Words '12

Avi Korine
Mister Lonely '07
The Double '13

Harmony Korine (1974-)
Kids '95
Gummo '97
Julien Donkey-boy '99
Mister Lonely '07
Spring Breakers '13
The Beach Bum '19

Baltasar Kormakur (1966-)
101 Reykjavik '00
The Sea '02
A Little Trip to Heaven '05
White Night Wedding '08

Jacob Kornbluth (1972-)
Haiku Tunnel '00
Inequality For All '13

Mari Kornhauser
Zandalee '91
The Last Ride '94
Kitchen Privileges '00

Scott Kosar
The Texas Chainsaw Massacre '03
The Machinist '04
The Crazies '09

Jacob Koskoff
The Marc Pease Experience '09
Macbeth '15
Marshall '17

Ron Koslow
Lifeguard '76
Into the Night '85
Last Dance '96

Steven Kostanski
Manborg '11
Father's Day '12
The Void '17

Carlos Kotkin
Rio 2 '14
The Star '17

Jim Kouf (1951-)
Class '83
The Hidden '87
Stakeout '87
Disorganized Crime '89
Another Stakeout '93
Operation Dumbo Drop '95
Gang Related '96
Rush Hour '98
Snow Dogs '02
National Treasure '04
Taxi '04
Money Monster '16

Paul Koval
Psychic '91
Dead Silent '99

Janet Kovalcik
Married to It '93
My Girl 2 '94

Yu Koyama
Azumi '03
Azumi 2 '05

Karl Kozak (1964-)
Out of the Black '01
Clawed: The Legend of Sasquatch '05

Andrzej Krakowski (1946-)
Triumph of the Spirit '89
Looking for Palladin '08

Hans Kraly (1884-1950)
Her Night of Romance '24
Her Sister from Paris '25
The Duchess of Buffalo '26
Kiki '26
The Garden of Eden '28
The Last of Mrs. Cheyney '29
Private Lives '31

Larry Kramer (1935-)
Women in Love '70
Lost Horizon '73
The Normal Heart '14

Richard Kramer
All I Want for Christmas '91
Armistead Maupin's Tales of the City '93

Wayne Kramer (1965-)
The Cooler '03
Mindhunters '05
Running Scared '06
Crossing Over '09

John Krasinski (1979-)
Promised Land '12
A Quiet Place '18

Norman Krasna (1909-84)
Hands Across the Table '35
Wife Versus Secretary '36
The Devil & Miss Jones '41
The Flame of New Orleans '41
It Started with Eve '41
Mr. & Mrs. Smith '41
Princess O'Rourke '43
The Big Hangover '50
The Ambassador's Daughter '56
Indiscreet '58
Let's Make Love '60
Who Was That Lady? '60
My Geisha '62
Sunday in New York '63

Shane Krause
Acolytes '08
The Darkness '16

Howard B. Kreitsek
The Illustrated Man '69
Rabbit, Run '70
Breakout '75

Stu Krieger (1952-)
The Parent Trap II '86
The Land Before Time '88
In the Army Now '94
Monkey Trouble '94
A Troll in Central Park '94
Cow Belles '06

Peter Krikes
Star Trek 4: The Voyage Home '86
Anna and the King '99

Milton Krims (1904-88)
Forbidden Trail '32
The Great O'Malley '36
The Green Light '37
Confessions of a Nazi Spy '39
Prince of Foxes '49
Tennessee's Partner '55
Mohawk '56

Dave Krinsky
Blades of Glory '07
Action Point '18

John Krizanc
Men with Brooms '02
The Summit '08

Jerzy Kromolowski (1953-)
The Pledge '00
In the Electric Mist '08

Lisa Krueger (1961-)
Manny & Lo '96
Committed '99

Ehren Kruger (1972-)
Arlington Road '99
New World Disorder '99
Reindeer Games '00
Scream 3 '00
Impostor '02
The Ring '02
The Brothers Grimm '05
The Ring 2 '05
The Skeleton Key '05
Blood & Chocolate '07
Transformers: Revenge of the Fallen '09
Transformers: Dark of the Moon '11
Transformers: Age of Extinction '14
Ghost in the Shell '17
Dumbo '19

Joseph Krumgold (1908-80)
Jim Hanvey, Detective '37
Join the Marines '37

Shawn Ku
Beautiful Boy '10
Feel the Beat '20

Stanley Kubrick (1928-99)
Killer's Kiss '55
The Killing '56
Paths of Glory '57
Dr. Strangelove, or: How I Learned to Stop Worrying and Love the Bomb '64
2001: A Space Odyssey '68
A Clockwork Orange '71
Barry Lyndon '75
The Shining '80
Full Metal Jacket '87
Eyes Wide Shut '99

Kankuro Kudo
Ping Pong '02
Zebraman '04

Kurt Kuenne
Dear Zachary: A Letter to a Son About His Father '08
Batkid Begins '15

Robert Kuhn
The Cure '95
Mickey Blue Eyes '99

Shane Kuhn
The Scorpion King 3: Battle for Redemption '11
Seal Team 8: Behind Enemy Lines '14

Roger Kumble (1966-)
National Lampoon's Senior Trip '95
Cruel Intentions '98
Cruel Intentions 2 '99

Hanif Kureishi (1954-)
My Beautiful Laundrette '85
The Buddha of Suburbia '92
My Son the Fanatic '97
The Mother '03
Venus '06
Le Week-End '14

Harry Kurnitz (1908-68)
Fast Company '38
Fast and Furious '39
Fast and Loose '39
Ship Ahoy '42
They Got Me Covered '43
The Heavenly Body '44
See Here, Private Hargrove '44
Something in the Wind '47
One Touch of Venus '48
The Inspector General '49
A Kiss in the Dark '49
Pretty Baby '50
The Happy Road '57
Witness for the Prosecution '57
Once More, With Feeling '60
How to Steal a Million '66

Akira Kurosawa (1910-98)
No Regrets for Our Youth '46
One Wonderful Sunday '47
A Quiet Duel '49
Scandal '50
Rashomon '51
Ikiru '52
Seven Samurai '54
I Live in Fear '55
The Lower Depths '57
Throne of Blood '57
The Hidden Fortress '58
The Bad Sleep Well '60
Yojimbo '61
High & Low '62
Sanjuro '62
Dodes 'ka-den '70
Dersu Uzala '75
Kagemusha '80
Ran '85
Akira Kurosawa's Dreams '90
Rhapsody in August '91
The Sea is Watching '02

Kiyoshi Kurosawa (1955-)
Cure '97
Pulse '01
Bright Future '03
Tokyo Sonata '09
Creepy '16

Richard Kurti
Kidnapped '05
Going Postal '10
Treasure Guards '11

Alex Kurtzman (1973-)
The Island '05
The Legend of Zorro '05
Mission: Impossible 3 '06
Transformers '07
Star Trek '09
Transformers: Revenge of the Fallen '09
Cowboys & Aliens '11
People Like Us '12
Star Trek: Into Darkness '13
The Amazing Spider-Man 2 '14

Andrew Kurtzman
Number One with a Bullet '87
See No Evil, Hear No Evil '89
Camp Nowhere '94
Down Periscope '96

Diane Kurys (1948-)
Entre-Nous '83
A Man in Love '87
Love After Love '94
Six Days, Six Nights '94
Children of the Century '99

Karyn Kusama (1968-)
Girlfight '99
XX '17

Tony Kushner (1956-)
Angels in America '03
Munich '05
Lincoln '12

Alex Kustanovich
Out of the Cold '99
Red Serpent '02
Mirror Wars: Reflection One '05
A Thousand Kisses Deep '11

Emir Kusturica (1954-)
Arizona Dream '94
Underground '95

Richard Kwietniowski (1957-)
Love and Death on Long Island '97
Owning Mahowny '03

Christopher Kyle
The Weight of Water '00
K-19: The Widowmaker '02
Alexander '04
Serena '14

Craig Kyle
The Invincible Iron Man '07
Thor: Ragnarok '17

Smash-Up: The Story of a Woman '47
The Careless Years '57

J.F. Lawton (1960-)
Cannibal Women in the Avocado Jungle of Death '89
Pretty Woman '90
Mistress '91
Pizza Man '91
Under Siege '92
Blankman '94
The Hunted '94
Chain Reaction '96
DOA: Dead or Alive '06

Beirne Lay, Jr. (1909-82)
Twelve o'Clock High '49
Above and Beyond '53
Toward the Unknown '56
The Gallant Hours '60

Cooper Layne
The Core '03
The Fog '05

Peter Layton
The Paradise Virus '03
Criminal Intent '05

Charles Lazar
Diamond Girl '98
Loving Evangeline '98

Michael Lazarou (1964-)
Heat Wave '90
Possessed '00

Martin Lazarus
Interceptor Force '99
Deep Core '00

Philip LaZebnik
Pocahontas '95
Mulan '98

Mike Le
Amnesiac '15
Patient Zero '18

Philippe Le Guay
The Women on the Sixth Floor '10
Bicycling With Moliere '13

Alain Le Henry
Entre-Nous '83
Subway '85

Didier Le Pecheur (1959-)
Don't Let Me Die on a Sunday '98
Harrison's Flowers '02

David Lean (1908-91)
Brief Encounter '46
Great Expectations '46
This Happy Breed '47
Oliver Twist '48
Summertime '55
A Passage to India '84

Norman Lear (1922-)
Come Blow Your Horn '63
Divorce American Style '67
The Night They Raided Minsky's '69
Cold Turkey '71

Charles Leavitt
Sunchaser '96
The Mighty '98
K-PAX '01
Blood Diamond '06
The Express '08
In the Heart of the Sea '15
Seventh Son '15
Warcraft '16

Keith Ross Leckie
Lost in the Barrens '91
The Morrison Murders '96
To Walk with Lions '99
Shattered City: The Halifax Explosion '03
Everest '07

Patrice Leconte (1947-)
Monsieur Hire '89
The Hairdresser's Husband '92
The Perfume of Yvonne '94
Intimate Strangers '04
My Best Friend '06
A Promise '13

Herbert J. Leder (1922-83)
Fiend without a Face '58
The Frozen Dead '66

Paul Leder (1926-96)
A*P*E* '76
Killing Obsession '94

Richard Leder
A Father's Choice '00
The Last Brickmaker in America '01
Scared Silent '02
The Suspect '05
The Bad Son '07
Unthinkable '07
Primal '19

Charles Lederer (1911-76)
Double or Nothing '37
Broadway Serenade '39
Comrade X '40
His Girl Friday '40
Slightly Dangerous '43
The Youngest Profession '43
Ride the Pink Horse '47
I Was a Male War Bride '49
Wabash Avenue '50
The Thing '51
Fearless Fagan '52
Monkey Business '52
Gentlemen Prefer Blondes '53
Kismet '55
Tip On a Dead Jockey '57
Ocean's 11 '60
Follow That Dream '61
Mutiny on the Bounty '62

Richard Ledes
A Hole in One '04
The Caller '08

Ang Lee (1954-)
Pushing Hands '92
The Wedding Banquet '93
Eat Drink Man Woman '94

Bruce Lee (1940-73)
Fists of Fury '73
Return of the Dragon '73
Circle of Iron '78

Chang-dong Lee (1954-)
Poetry '10
Burning '18

Damian Lee (1950-)
Abraxas: Guardian of the Universe '90
The Killing Man '94
Street Law '95
Jungle Boy '96
Specimen '97
Agent Red '00
Sacrifice '11
A Dark Truth '12
A Fighting Man '14

Daniel Lee
The Kumite '03
Three Kingdoms: Resurrection of the Dragon '08
14 Blades '14
Dragon Blade '15
The Climbers '19

Dennis Lee
Fireflies in the Garden '08
Jesus Henry Christ '12

Gerard Lee
Sweetie '89
Top of the Lake '13

James H. Lee (1923-2002)
Counterpoint '67
Roots '77
Napoleon and Josephine: A Love Story '87

Jennifer Lee (1968-)
Wreck-It Ralph '12
Frozen '13
Zootopia '16
A Wrinkle in Time '18
Frozen II '19

Lilian Lee
Farewell My Concubine '93
Three . . . Extremes '04

Malcolm Lee (1970-)
The Best Man '99
Welcome Home Roscoe Jenkins '08
The Best Man Holiday '13

Mark Lee (1958-)
Fortunes of War '94
The Next Karate Kid '94

Mu-yeong Lee
JSA: Joint Security Area '00
Sympathy for Mr. Vengeance '02

Robert N. Lee (1890-1964)
The Kennel Murder Case '33
Fog Over Frisco '34
The Tower of London '39

Spike Lee (1957-)
She's Gotta Have It '86
School Daze '88
Do the Right Thing '89
Mo' Better Blues '90
Jungle Fever '91
Malcolm X '92
Clockers '95
He Got Game '98
Summer of Sam '99
Bamboozled '00
She Hate Me '04
Red Hook Summer '12
Da Sweet Blood of Jesus '14
Chi-raq '15
BlacKkKlansman '18
Da 5 Bloods '20

Timothy Lee
Street Gun '96
2103: Deadly Wake '97

William Lee
Psychopath '97
The Pact '99

Tony Leech
Hoodwinked '05
Hoodwinked Too! Hood *vs.* Evil '11

Robert Lees (1912-2004)
The Invisible Woman '40
The Black Cat '41
Hold That Ghost '41
Buck Privates Come Home '47
Abbott and Costello Meet Frankenstein '48
Abbott and Costello Meet the Invisible Man '51
Comin' Round the Mountain '51

Michael Leeson
Jekyll & Hyde. . . Together Again '82
Survivors '83
The War of the Roses '89
I.Q. '94
What Planet Are You From? '00
The Tuxedo '02

Philippe Lefebvre
Whatever You Say '02
Tell No One '06

Ernest Lehman (1915-2005)
Executive Suite '54
Sabrina '54
The King and I '56
Somebody Up There Likes Me '56
Sweet Smell of Success '57
North by Northwest '59
From the Terrace '60
West Side Story '61
The Prize '63
The Sound of Music '65
Who's Afraid of Virginia Woolf? '66
Hello, Dolly! '69
Family Plot '76
Black Sunday '77

Gladys Lehman (1892-1993)
White Woman '33
Death Takes a Holiday '34
Little Miss Marker '34

A Message to Garcia '36
Slave Ship '37
Blondie Brings Up Baby '39
Her Highness and the Bellboy '45
This Time for Keeps '47
Luxury Liner '48
Golden Girl '51

Joshua Leibner
Free Style '09
Krews '10

Jerry Leichtling (1948-)
Peggy Sue Got Married '86
Blue Sky '91

Mike Leigh (1943-)
Bleak Moments '71
Nuts in May '76
Kiss of Death '77
Who's Who '78
Grown Ups '80
Home Sweet Home '82
High Hopes '88
Life Is Sweet '90
Naked '93
Secrets and Lies '95
Career Girls '97
Topsy Turvy '99
All or Nothing '02
Vera Drake '04
Happy-Go-Lucky '08
Another Year '10
Mr. Turner '14
Peterloo '18

Rowland Leigh (1903-63)
The Charge of the Light Brigade '36
Vigil in the Night '40
The Master Race '44
Summer Storm '44
Tarzan and the Huntress '47

Warren Leight
Mother's Day '80
The Night We Never Met '93
Dear God '96

David Leland (1947-)
Mona Lisa '86
Personal Services '87
Wish You Were Here '87
White River '99
Virgin Territory '07

Sebastián Lelio
Gloria '13
Disobedience '17
A Fantastic Woman '18
Gloria Bell '18

Claude Lelouch (1937-)
A Man and a Woman '66
Happy New Year '73
And Now My Love '74
Another Man, Another Chance '77
Bolero '82
A Man and a Woman: 20 Years Later '86
And Now Ladies and Gentlemen '02
Roman de Gare '07

Guillaume Lemans
The Next Three Days '10
Point Blank '10

Alan LeMay (1899-1964)
Reap the Wild Wind '42
The Adventures of Mark Twain '44
Cheyenne '47
Gunfighters '47
High Lonesome '50
Rocky Mountain '50

Darren Lemke
Lost '05
Jack the Giant Slayer '13
Turbo '13
Goosebumps '15
Gemini Man '19
The Parts You Lose '19

Jonathan Lemkin
The Devil's Advocate '97
Red Planet '00
Shooter '07

Steve Lemme (1968-)
Super Troopers '01
Club Dread '04

Beerfest '06
The Slammin' Salmon '09
Super Troopers 2 '18

James (Momel) Lemmo (1949-)
Relentless 3 '93
Nowhere in Sight '01

Kasi Lemmons (1961-)
Eve's Bayou '97
Black Nativity '13
Harriet '19

Kay Lenard (1911-97)
Ma and Pa Kettle at Home '54
The Kettles in the Ozarks '56

Vicente Lenero (1933-)
Midaq Alley '95
The Crime of Father Amaro '02

Rebecca Lenkiewicz
Ida '13
Disobedience '17

Peter M. Lenkov
Demolition Man '93
Dr. Jekyll & Mr. Hyde '99

Isobel Lennart (1915-71)
Lost Angel '43
Holiday in Mexico '46
The Kissing Bandit '48
A Life of Her Own '50
It's a Big Country '51
My Wife's Best Friend '52
The Girl Next Door '53
Merry Andrew '58
Please Don't Eat the Daisies '60
Period of Adjustment '62
Two for the Seesaw '62
Fitzwilly '67
Funny Girl '68

Gary Lennon
Drunks '96
.45 '06

Thomas Lennon (1896-1963)
Murder On a Bridle Path '36
The Crowd Roars '38

Thomas Lennon (1970-)
Taxi '04
Herbie: Fully Loaded '05
Let's Go to Prison '06
Night at the Museum '06
Balls of Fury '07
Reno 911! Miami '07
Night at the Museum: Battle of the Smithsonian '09

Robert W. Lenski (1927-2002)
Decoration Day '90
The Return of the Native '94
Hole in the Sky '95
What the Deaf Man Heard '98
A Death in the Family '02

Umberto Lenzi (1931-)
Sandokan the Great '63
Desert Commandos '67
Seven Blood-Stained Orchids '72
Emerald Jungle '80
Welcome to Spring Break '88
Black Demons '91

Maurice Leo
Hard to Get '38
Swing Your Lady '38
Flight Angels '40

Albert Leon
Feel the Noise '07
Stomp the Yard 2: Homecoming '10
Holiday Spin '12

Elmore Leonard (1925-2013)
The Moonshine War '70
Joe Kidd '72
Mr. Majestyk '74
Stick '85
52 Pick-Up '86
Cat Chaser '90

Hugh Leonard (1926-2009)
Interlude '68
The Moonstone '72
Widow's Peak '94

Jack Leonard (1913-54)
His Kind of Woman '51
My Man and I '52

Megan Leonard
Finding Your Feet '18
Fisherman's Friends '19

Niall Leonard
Fifty Shades Darker '17
Fifty Shades Freed '18

Doriana Leondeff (1962-)
Bread and Tulips '01
Days and Clouds '07

Sergio Leone (1929-89)
The Last Days of Pompeii '60
The Colossus of Rhodes '61
A Fistful of Dollars '64
For a Few Dollars More '65
The Good, the Bad and the Ugly '67
Once Upon a Time in the West '68
Once Upon a Time in America '84

Alan Jay Lerner (1918-86)
An American in Paris '51
Royal Wedding '51
Brigadoon '54
Gigi '58
My Fair Lady '64
Camelot '67
On a Clear Day You Can See Forever '70
The Little Prince '74

Danny Lerner
Operation Delta Force 5: Random Fire '00
Out For a Kill '03

Ali LeRoi
Down to Earth '01
Head of State '03

Michael LeSieur
You, Me and Dupree '06
The Maiden Heist '08
Keeping Up with the Joneses '16
The Grinch '18

Mimi Lesseos (1964-)
Pushed to the Limit '92
Beyond Fear '93
Personal Vendetta '96

Elana Lesser
Balto '95
Cats Don't Dance '97
Beethoven's 5th '03
Mean Girls 2 '11

Michael Lesslie
Macbeth '15
Assassin's Creed '16

Rob Letterman
Shark Tale '04
Monsters *vs.* Aliens '09
Pokémon Detective Pikachu '19

Sheldon Lettich (1962-)
Lionheart '90
Double Impact '91
Only the Strong '93
Legionnaire '98
Max '15

Tracy Letts (1965-)
Bug '06
Killer Joe '11
August: Osage County '13

Lai-Yin Leung
Ip Man 3 '16
Ip Man 4: The Finale '19

Matthew Leutwyler
Unearthed '07
Answers to Nothing '11

Gregory Levasseur
High Tension '03
The Hills Have Eyes '06
P2 '07

Issa Lopez
Pulling Strings *'13*
600 Miles *'16*
Tigers Are Not Afraid *'19*

Matt Lopez
Bedtime Stories *'08*
Race to Witch Mountain *'09*
The Sorcerer's Apprentice *'10*

Nicolas Lopez (1983-)
Aftershock *'12*
Knock Knock *'15*

Phil Lord (1975-)
Cloudy with a Chance of Meatballs *'09*
The Lego Movie *'14*
Spider-Man: Into the Spider-Verse *'18*
The LEGO Movie 2: The Second Part *'19*

Phillips Lord (1902-75)
Gang Busters *'42*
Guns Don't Argue *'57*

Robert Lord (1900-76)
On with the Show *'29*
Five Star Final *'31*
The Conquerors *'32*
Frisco Jenny *'32*
It's Tough to Be Famous *'32*
One Way Passage *'32*
The Purchase Price *'32*
Winner Take All *'32*
You Said a Mouthful *'32*
Hard to Handle *'33*
Heroes for Sale *'33*
The Little Giant *'33*
The Mind Reader *'33*
20,000 Years in Sing Sing *'33*

Olivier Lorelle
Days of Glory *'06*
London River *'09*
Outside the Law *'10*

Anna Lorenzo
In Her Line of Fire *'06*
Nuclear Hurricane *'07*

Dean Lorey (1967-)
Jason Goes to Hell: The Final Friday *'93*
My Boyfriend's Back *'93*
Major Payne *'95*
Animal Crackers *'17*

Hope Loring (1894-1959)
Shadows *'22*
It *'27*
My Best Girl *'27*
Wings *'27*

Joseph Losey (1909-84)
The Big Night *'51*
Don Giovanni *'79*

Ye Lou
Purple Butterfly *'03*
Summer Palace *'06*

David Loucka
The Dream Team *'89*
Eddie *'96*
Borderline *'02*
Dream House *'11*
House at the End of the Street *'12*
Rings *'17*

David Loughery
Star Trek 5: The Final Frontier *'89*
Passenger 57 *'92*
The Three Musketeers *'93*
Money Train *'95*
Tom and Huck *'95*
Lakeview Terrace *'08*
Obsessed *'09*
Nurse 3D *'13*
The Intruder *'19*

Todd Louiso (1970-)
The Marc Pease Experience *'09*
Macbeth *'15*

Eugene Lourie (1903-91)
The Beast from 20,000 Fathoms *'53*
Revolt in the Big House *'58*
The Giant Behemoth *'59*

Eric Louzil (1951-)
Fortress of Amerikka *'89*
Class of Nuke 'Em High 2: Subhumanoid Meltdown *'91*

Nick Love (1969-)
The Business *'05*
Outlaw *'07*
The Sweeney *'12*

Paul Lovett
Four Brothers *'05*
G.I. Joe: The Rise of Cobra *'09*

Michelle A. Lovretta
Playing House *'06*
To Be Fat Like Me *'07*
Sorority Wars *'09*

Robert Lovy
Circuitry Man *'90*
Plughead Rewired: Circuitry Man 2 *'94*

Steven Lovy
Circuitry Man *'90*
Plughead Rewired: Circuitry Man 2 *'94*

Edward T. Lowe (1890-1973)
The Hunchback of Notre Dame *'23*
The Crusader *'32*
The Midnight Lady *'32*
The Red-Haired Alibi *'32*
The Vampire Bat *'32*
Curtain at Eight *'33*
The World Gone Mad *'33*
Charlie Chan in Shanghai *'35*
Charlie Chan at the Race Track *'36*
Bulldog Drummond Escapes *'37*
Tarzan's Desert Mystery *'43*
House of Frankenstein *'44*
House of Dracula *'45*

Sherman Lowe (1894-1968)
Night Cargo *'36*
Frolics on Ice *'39*
Yank in Libya *'42*
Parole, Inc. *'49*

Jeff Lowell (1973-)
John Tucker Must Die *'06*
Over Her Dead Body *'08*
Hotel for Dogs *'09*

Richard Lowenstein (1959-)
Dogs in Space *'87*
He Died With a Falafel in His Hand *'01*

Andrew Lowery (1970-)
Simon Sez *'99*
Boys and Girls *'00*

David Lowery
Ain't Them Bodies Saints *'13*
Pete's Dragon *'16*
A Ghost Story *'17*
The Yellow Birds *'17*
The Old Man & the Gun *'18*

Sam Lowry (1963-)
See Steven Soderbergh

John Loy
The Land Before Time 3: The Time of the Great Giving *'95*
The Land Before Time 5: The Mysterious Island *'97*
The Land Before Time 6: The Secret of Saurus Rock *'98*
Beethoven's 4th *'01*

Chuan Lu
The Missing Gun *'02*
City of Life and Death *'09*
Born in China *'17*

Ernst Lubitsch (1892-1947)
One Arabian Night *'20*
The Smiling Lieutenant *'31*
To Be or Not to Be *'42*

Craig Lucas (1950-)
Longtime Companion *'90*
Prelude to a Kiss *'92*
The Secret Lives of Dentists *'02*
The Dying Gaul *'05*

George Lucas (1944-)
THX 1138 *'71*
American Graffiti *'73*
Star Wars *'77*
Raiders of the Lost Ark *'81*
Return of the Jedi *'83*
Star Wars: Episode 1-The Phantom Menace *'99*
Star Wars: Episode 2-Attack of the Clones *'02*
Star Wars: Episode 3-Revenge of the Sith *'05*

Jon Lucas
Rustin *'01*
Rebound *'05*
Full of It *'07*
Four Christmases *'08*
Ghosts of Girlfriends Past *'09*
The Hangover *'09*
The Change-Up *'11*
Flypaper *'11*
21 & Over *'13*
Bad Moms *'16*
A Bad Moms Christmas *'17*
Jexi *'19*

Ralph Lucas
The Child *'76*
Planet of the Dinosaurs *'80*

Daniele Luchetti (1960-)
Ginger and Cinnamon *'03*
My Brother Is an Only Child *'07*
Our Life *'10*

Michael Lucker
Vampire in Brooklyn *'95*
Mulan 2 *'04*

John Ludin
The Land Before Time 2: The Great Valley Adventure *'94*
The Land Before Time 3: The Time of the Great Giving *'95*

Graham Ludlow
Jack London's The Call of the Wild *'97*
Storm Cell *'08*

William Ludwig (1912-99)
Love Finds Andy Hardy *'38*
Out West With the Hardys *'38*
The Hardys Ride High *'39*
Stronger Than Desire *'39*
An American Romance *'44*
Andy Hardy's Blonde Trouble *'44*
Love Laughs at Andy Hardy *'46*
The Hills of Home *'48*
The Sun Comes Up *'49*
It's a Big Country *'51*
Athena *'54*
Interrupted Melody *'55*
Oklahoma! *'55*
Gun Glory *'57*
Ten Thousand Bedrooms *'57*
Back Street *'61*

Kurt Luedtke (1939-)
Absence of Malice *'81*
Out of Africa *'85*
Random Hearts *'99*

John Luessenhop
Takers *'10*
Speed Kills *'18*

Baz Luhrmann (1962-)
Strictly Ballroom *'92*
William Shakespeare's Romeo and Juliet *'96*
Moulin Rouge *'01*
Australia *'08*
The Great Gatsby *'13*

Eric Luke
Explorers *'85*
Gargoyles, The Movie: The Heroes Awaken *'94*

Sergey Lukyanenko (1968-)
Night Watch *'04*
Day Watch *'06*

Jenny Lumet (1967-)
Rachel Getting Married *'08*
Remember Me *'10*

Sidney Lumet (1924-2011)
Prince of the City *'81*
Q & A *'90*
Night Falls on Manhattan *'96*
Find Me Guilty *'06*

Bigas Luna (1946-2013)
Reborn *'81*
Anguish *'88*
The Chambermaid on the Titanic *'97*

Israel Luna (1972-)
The Deadbeat Club *'04*
Fright Flick *'10*

Dolph Lundgren (1957-)
Missionary Man *'07*
Command Performance *'09*

Ida Lupino (1914-95)
Streets of Sin *'49*
The Hitch-Hiker *'53*
Private Hell 36 *'54*

Gwyn Lurie
The Music Never Stopped *'11*
Nine Lives *'16*

Rod Lurie (1962-)
The Contender *'00*
Deterrence *'00*
Nothing But the Truth *'08*
Straw Dogs *'11*

Patrick Lussier
Dracula 2: Ascension *'03*
Dracula 3: Legacy *'05*
Terminator Genisys *'15*

Jan Lustig (1902-79)
The White Cliffs of Dover *'44*
Homecoming *'48*
The Story of Three Loves *'53*
Young Bess *'53*

Karen McCullah Lutz
Ten Things I Hate about You *'99*
Legally Blonde *'01*
Ella Enchanted *'04*
She's the Man *'06*
The House Bunny *'08*

Brian Lynch
Love and Rage *'99*
Hop *'11*
Minions *'15*
The Secret Life of Pets *'16*
The Secret Life of Pets 2 *'19*

David Lynch (1946-)
Eraserhead *'78*
The Elephant Man *'80*
Dune *'84*
Blue Velvet *'86*
Wild at Heart *'90*
Twin Peaks: Fire Walk with Me *'92*
Lost Highway *'96*
Mulholland Drive *'01*
Inland Empire *'06*

Barre Lyndon (1896-1972)
Hangover Square *'45*
House on 92nd Street *'45*
To Please a Lady *'50*
Man in the Attic *'53*
The War of the Worlds *'53*

Jonathan Lynn (1943-)
Clue *'85*
Nuns on the Run *'90*

Fibe Ma
Supercop *'92*
Rumble in the Bronx *'96*
Mr. Nice Guy *'98*

Jingle Ma
Silver Hawk *'04*
Seoul Raiders *'05*
The Assassin's Blade *'08*

Jon Maas
The Last Debate *'00*
12 Men of Christmas *'09*

Lindsay MacAdam
Under the Mistletoe *'06*
My Neighbor's Keeper *'07*

Charles MacArthur (1895-1956)
Billy the Kid *'30*
The Girl Said No *'30*
Paid *'30*
Rasputin and the Empress *'33*
Twentieth Century *'34*
Wuthering Heights *'39*

Richard Macaulay (1909-69)
Hollywood Hotel *'37*
Varsity Show *'37*
Brother Rat *'38*
Garden of the Moon *'38*
Hard to Get *'38*
The Roaring Twenties *'39*
Torrid Zone *'40*
Manpower *'41*
Out of the Fog *'41*
Across the Pacific *'42*
Captains of the Clouds *'42*

Ruggero Maccari (1919-89)
Adua and Her Friends *'60*
Il Sorpasso *'63*
The Queens *'66*
The Priest's Wife *'71*
The Scent of a Woman *'75*
A Special Day *'77*

Nora MacCoby
Bongwater *'98*
Buffalo Soldiers *'01*

Ian MacDonald (1914-78)
Montana *'50*
Silver Star *'55*

Philip MacDonald (1901-80)
Charlie Chan in London *'34*
The Last Outpost *'35*
Whispering Ghosts *'42*
The Body Snatcher *'45*
The Man Who Cheated Himself *'50*

Sharman MacDonald (1951-)
The Winter Guest *'97*
The Edge of Love *'08*

Ranald MacDougall (1915-73)
Mildred Pierce *'45*
Objective, Burma! *'45*
The Unsuspected *'47*
The Breaking Point *'50*
Bright Leaf *'50*
I'll Never Forget You *'51*
Mr. Belvedere Rings the Bell *'51*
Queen Bee *'55*
We're No Angels *'55*

Seth MacFarlane (1973-)
A Million Ways to Die In the West *'14*
Ted 2 *'15*

Daniel MacIvor (1962-)
Marion Bridge *'02*
Whole New Thing *'05*
Trigger *'10*

Willard Mack (1873-1934)
The Monster *'25*
It's a Great Life *'29*
Madame X *'29*
Untamed *'29*
The Voice of the City *'29*
Lord Byron of Broadway *'30*
Sporting Blood *'31*

Steve Mackall
Avenging Angelo *'02*
Stealing Cars *'16*

Aeneas MacKenzie (1889-1962)
Juarez *'39*
They Died with Their Boots On *'41*
Fighting Seabees *'44*
The Ten Commandments *'56*

David Mackenzie (1966-)
Young Adam *'03*
Mister Foe *'07*
Outlaw King *'18*

Angus MacLachlan
Junebug *'05*
Stone *'10*
Goodbye to All That *'14*

Patricia MacLachlan (1938-)
Sarah, Plain and Tall: Skylark *'93*
Baby *'00*

Bernard MacLaverty (1942-)
Lamb *'85*
The Real Charlotte *'91*

Alistair MacLean (1922-87)
Where Eagles Dare *'68*
When Eight Bells Toll *'71*
Breakheart Pass *'76*

Mike MacLean
Dinocroc Vs. Supergator *'10*
Sharktopus *'10*
Attack of the 50 Foot Cheerleader *'12*

Angus MacPhail (1903-62)
The Good Companions *'33*
The Secret Four *'39*
The Next of Kin *'42*
Dead of Night *'45*

Don MacPherson
Absolute Beginners *'86*
The Big Man: Crossing the Line *'91*
The Avengers *'98*
The Gunman *'15*

Jeanie Macpherson (1887-1946)
The Little American *'17*
Male and Female *'19*

Malcolm MacRury
The Man Without a Face *'93*
Mr. Hockey: The Gordie Howe Story *'13*

Jon Macy
Merlin and the War of the Dragons *'08*
Supernova *'09*

William H. Macy (1950-)
A Slight Case of Murder *'99*
Rudderless *'14*

Guy Maddin (1956-)
Tales from the Gimli Hospital *'88*
Careful *'92*
The Saddest Music in the World *'03*
Brand Upon the Brain! *'06*
Keyhole *'11*

Brent Maddock
Short Circuit *'86*
*batteries not included *'87*
Short Circuit 2 *'88*
Tremors *'89*
Ghost Dad *'90*
Heart and Souls *'93*
Tremors 2: Aftershocks *'96*
Wild Wild West *'99*

Ben Maddow (1909-92)
Framed *'47*
The Asphalt Jungle *'50*
Men in War *'57*
No Down Payment *'57*
The Balcony *'63*
The Chairman *'69*
The Secret of Santa Vittoria *'69*

Robert Madero
Mausoleum *'83*
All Tied Up *'92*

Madonna (1959-)
Filth and Wisdom *'08*
W.E. *'11*

David Magee (1962-)
Finding Neverland *'04*
Miss Pettigrew Lives for a Day *'08*
Life of Pi *'12*
Mary Poppins Returns *'18*

Doug Magee
Somebody Has to Shoot the Picture '90
Beyond the Call '96

Maria Maggenti (1962-)
The Incredibly True Adventure of Two Girls in Love '95
The Love Letter '99
Puccini for Beginners '06
Monte Carlo '11
Before I Fall '17

Joe Maggio
Virgil Bliss '01
Milk and Honey '03
Bitter Feast '10
The Last Rites of Joe May '11

Mark Magidson
Baraka '93
Samsara '12

Jeff Maguire
Victory '81
In the Line of Fire '93
Timeline '03
Gridiron Gang '06

John Lee Mahin (1902-84)
The Beast of the City '32
Red Dust '32
The Wet Parade '32
The Devil Is a Sissy '36
Love on the Run '36
Wife Versus Secretary '36
The Last Gangster '37
Boom Town '40
Dr. Jekyll and Mr. Hyde '41
Johnny Eager '42
My Son John '52
Mogambo '53
Elephant Walk '54
The Bad Seed '56
Heaven Knows, Mr. Allison '57
No Time for Sergeants '58
The Horse Soldiers '59

Derek Mahon (1941-)
How Many Miles to Babylon? '82
The Death of the Heart '87

Wilkie Mahoney (1897-1976)
Whistling in Dixie '42
Whistling in Brooklyn '43
Brewster's Millions '45

Richard Maibaum (1909-91)
Live, Love and Learn '37
The Bad Man of Brimstone '38
Ransom! '56
Zarak '56
The Day They Robbed the Bank of England '60
Battle at Bloody Beach '61
Dr. No '62
From Russia with Love '63
Goldfinger '64
Thunderball '65
On Her Majesty's Secret Service '69
The Spy Who Loved Me '77
The Living Daylights '87
License to Kill '89

Norman Mailer (1923-2007)
Tough Guys Don't Dance '87
American Tragedy '00
Master Spy: The Robert Hanssen Story '02

David Main
Vengeance Is Mine '74
It Seemed Like a Good Idea at the Time '75

Daniel Mainwaring (1902-77)
Treasure of Fear '45
Swamp Fire '46
Out of the Past '47
Big Steal '49
The Lawless '50
Cavalry Charge '51
This Woman Is Dangerous '52
The Hitch-Hiker '53
Powder River '53
Southwest Passage '54
A Bullet for Joey '55
The Phenix City Story '55
The Phenix City Story '55
Invasion of the Body Snatchers '56
Cole Younger, Gunfighter '58
The Gun Runners '58
Space Master X-7 '58
Atlantis, the Lost Continent '61
The George Raft Story '61
Catacombs '64

Jennifer Maisel
Double Wedding '10
The March Sisters at Christmas '12

Arduino (Dino) Maiuri (1916-84)
Danger: Diabolik '68
Companeros '70
Street Law '74
War Goddess '74
Chino '75
Revolver '75

Majid Majidi (1959-)
Children of Heaven '98
The Color of Paradise '99
The Song of Sparrows '08

Siu Fai Mak
Infernal Affairs 2 '03
Infernal Affairs 3 '03

Dusan Makavejev (1932-)
Man Is Not a Bird '65
The Love Affair, or The Case of the Missing Switchboard Operator '67
Innocence Unprotected '68
WR: Mysteries of the Organism '71
Sweet Movie '75
Montenegro '81

Mohsen Makhmalbaf (1957-)
Gabbeh '96
Kandahar '01

James Makichuk
Greenmail '01
Maiden Voyage: Ocean Hijack '04

Guido Malatesta (1919-70)
Barrier of the Law '54
Fire Monsters Against the Son of Hercules '62

Justin Malen
Office Christmas Party '16
Father Figures '17

Terrence Malick (1943-)
Pocket Money '72
Badlands '74
Days of Heaven '78
The Thin Red Line '98
The New World '05
The Tree of Life '11
To the Wonder '12
Knight of Cups '15
Song to Song '17
A Hidden Life '19

Robert Malkani
Dot.Kill '05
The Chaos Experiment '09

Laurence Malkin
Soul Assassin '01
Five Fingers '06

Louis Malle (1932-95)
The Lovers '59
Zazie dans le Metro '61
The Fire Within '64
Viva Maria! '65
The Thief of Paris '67
Spirits of the Dead '68
Murmur of the Heart '71
Black Moon '75
Au Revoir les Enfants '87

Miles Malleson (1888-1969)
Night Birds '31
Perfect Understanding '33
Lorna Doone '34
Nine Days a Queen '36
Victoria the Great '37
Sixty Glorious Years '38
The Thief of Bagdad '40

Tom Malloy (1974-)
The Attic '06
The Alphabet Killer '08
Love N' Dancing '09

Mark Malone
Dead of Winter '87
Signs of Life '89
Bulletproof Heart '95
Hoods '98
Dead Heat '01

William Malone (1953-)
Universal Soldier: The Return '99
Parasomnia '08

H.F. Maltby (1880-1963)
Ticket of Leave Man '37
Crimes at the Dark House '39

Albert (John B. Sherry) Maltz (1908-85)
This Gun for Hire '42
Pride of the Marines '45
Cloak and Dagger '46
The Naked City '48
Broken Arrow '50
The Robe '53
The Last Challenge '67
The Beguiled '70
Two Mules for Sister Sara '70

David Mamet (1947-)
The Postman Always Rings Twice '81
The Verdict '82
House of Games '87
The Untouchables '87
Things Change '88
We're No Angels '89
Homicide '91
Glengarry Glen Ross '92
Hoffa '92
A Life in the Theater '93
Oleanna '94
Vanya on 42nd Street '94
American Buffalo '95
The Edge '97
The Spanish Prisoner '97
Wag the Dog '97
Ronin '98
The Winslow Boy '98
Lansky '99
Lakeboat '00
State and Main '00
Hannibal '01
Heist '01
Spartan '04
Edmond '05
Redbelt '08
Phil Spector '13

Milcho Manchevski (1959-)
Before the Rain '94
Dust '01

Don Mancini (1963-)
Child's Play '88
Child's Play 2 '90
Child's Play 3 '91
Bride of Chucky '98
Seed of Chucky '04
Curse of Chucky '13

Babaloo Mandel (1949-)
Night Shift '82
Splash '84
Spies Like Us '85
Gung Ho '86
Vibes '88
Parenthood '89
City Slickers '91
A League of Their Own '92
Mr. Saturday Night '92
City Slickers 2: The Legend of Curly's Gold '94
Greedy '94
Forget Paris '95
Father's Day '96
Multiplicity '96
EDtv '99
Where the Heart Is '00
Fever Pitch '05
Robots '05

David Mandel (1971-)
Dr. Seuss' The Cat in the Hat '03
EuroTrip '04
The Dictator '12

John Mandel
Terror in the Mall '98
Kung Fu Killer '08

Neil Mandt (1969-)
Hijacking Hollywood '97
Last Stop for Paul '08

Matt Manfredi (1971-)
crazy/beautiful '01
Aeon Flux '05
Clash of the Titans '10
R.I.P.D. '13
Ride Along '14
The Invitation '16
Ride Along 2 '16
Destroyer '18

Gino Mangini (1921-91)
David and Goliath '61
Hyena of London '62

Giuseppe Mangione
The Mighty Ursus '61
Mole Men Against the Son of Hercules '61

James Mangold (1964-)
Oliver & Company '88
Heavy '94
Cop Land '97
Girl, Interrupted '99
Kate & Leopold '01
Walk the Line '05
Logan '17
Ford v Ferrari '19

Don Mankiewicz (1922-)
Trial '55
I Want to Live! '58
The Chapman Report '62

Herman J. Mankiewicz (1897-1953)
Man of the World '31
Girl Crazy '32
Dinner at Eight '33
After Office Hours '35
Citizen Kane '41
The Pride of the Yankees '42
Stand by for Action '42
Pride of St. Louis '52

Joseph L. Mankiewicz (1909-93)
Alice in Wonderland '33
Manhattan Melodrama '34
Forsaking All Others '35
I Live My Life '35
The Keys of the Kingdom '44
Dragonwyck '46
Somewhere in the Night '46
A Letter to Three Wives '49
All About Eve '50
No Way Out '50
People Will Talk '51
Julius Caesar '53
The Barefoot Contessa '54
Guys and Dolls '55
Cleopatra '63
The Honey Pot '67

Tom Mankiewicz (1942-2010)
The Sweet Ride '68
Diamonds Are Forever '71
Live and Let Die '73
The Man with the Golden Gun '74
The Cassandra Crossing '76
Mother, Jugs and Speed '76
The Eagle Has Landed '77
Ladyhawke '85
Dragnet '87

Wolf Mankowitz (1925-98)
A Kid for Two Farthings '55
Expresso Bongo '59
The Two Faces of Dr. Jekyll '60
The Day the Earth Caught Fire '61
Waltz of the Toreadors '62
Where the Spies Are '65
Casino Royale '67
The 25th Hour '67
The Hireling '73

Abby Mann (1927-2008)
Judgment at Nuremberg '61
Ship of Fools '65
The Detective '68
Report to the Commissioner '75
King '78
Indictment: The McMartin Trial '95

Edward Andrew (Santos Alcocer) Mann (1923-95)
The Freakmaker '73
Seizure '74

Michael Mann (1943-)
Vegas '78
Thief '81
Manhunter '86
The Last of the Mohicans '92
Heat '95
The Insider '99
Ali '01
Miami Vice '06

Stanley Mann (1928-)
The Mouse That Roared '59
The Collector '65
Rapture '65
Meteor '79
Eye of the Needle '81
Conan the Destroyer '84
Firestarter '84

Ted Mann
Space Truckers '97
Hatfields & McCoys '12

Albert Mannheimer (1913-72)
Dancing Co-Ed '39
Whistling in the Dark '41
Three Daring Daughters '48
Born Yesterday '50

Bruce Manning (1902-65)
Meet Nero Wolfe '36
100 Men and a Girl '37
Mad About Music '38
That Certain Age '38
First Love '39
Three Smart Girls Grow Up '39
Spring Parade '40
Back Street '41
Guest Wife '45
So Goes My Love '46
Hoodlum Empire '52

Vincenzo Mannino
I'm for the Hippopotamus '79
New York Ripper '82

Max Mannix
Rain Fall '09
Tokyo Sonata '09

John Mantley (1920-2003)
The 27th Day '57
My Blood Runs Cold '65

Braulio Mantovani
City of God '02
The Year My Parents Went on Vacation '07

Russell V. Manzatt
Rush Week '88
Trapper County War '89

Samuel Maoz
Lebanon '09
Foxtrot '18

Patrick Marber (1964-)
Closer '04
Asylum '05
Notes on a Scandal '06

Scott Marcano
Bio-Dome '96
Sanitarium '13

Kelly Marcel (1974-)
Saving Mr. Banks '13
Fifty Shades of Grey '15
Venom '18

Siro Marcellini
The Beast of Babylon Against the Son of Hercules '63
Lola Colt '67

Joseph Moncure March (1899-1977)
Hell's Angels '30
Her Jungle Love '38
Wagons Westward '40

Gilles Marchand (1963-)
With a Friend Like Harry '00
Bon Voyage '03
Lemming '05
Black Heaven '10
The Lady in the Car with Glasses and a Gun '16

Tony Marchant (1959-)
Different for Girls '96
Great Expectations '99

Francesca Marciano (1955-)
Iris Blond '98
I'm Not Scared '03
Don't Tell '05
Escobar: Paradise Lost '15
Me, Myself and Her '16

David Marconi
The Harvest '92
Enemy of the State '98
Collision '13
The Foreigner '17

Art Marcum
Iron Man '08
Punisher: War Zone '08
Transformers: The Last Knight '17
Men in Black: International '19

Adam Marcus (1968-)
Texas Chainsaw 3D '13
Momentum '15

Cindy Marcus
The Lion King: Simba's Pride '98
Jack and the Beanstalk '09

Larry Marcus
Dark City '50
The Unguarded Moment '56

Lawrence B. Marcus (1917-2001)
Backfire '50
A Covenant With Death '67
Petulia '68
Justine '69
Going Home '71
The Stunt Man '80

Andreas Marfori
Evil Clutch '89
Desperate Crimes '93

Antonio Margheriti (1930-2002)
See Anthony M. Dawson

Herbert Margolis
Smart Woman '48
Ma and Pa Kettle '49
Francis in the Haunted House '56
The Kettles on Old MacDonald's Farm '57

Paul B. Margolis
Ticker '01
Between Truth and Lies '06
Dr. Jekyll and Mr. Hyde '08

Donald Margulies
Dinner with Friends '01
The End of the Tour '15

A. L. Mariaux (1930-2013)
See Jess (Jesus) Franco

Richard 'Cheech' Marin (1946-)
Cheech and Chong's Up in Smoke '79
Cheech and Chong's Next Movie '80
Cheech and Chong's Nice Dreams '81
Cheech and Chong: Things Are Tough All Over '82

Cheech and Chong: Still Smokin' '83
Cheech and Chong's The Corsican Brothers '84
Born in East L.A. '87
Cheech & Chong's Animated Movie! '13

Alberto Marini
Sleep Tight '11
Summer Camp '16
Feedback '20

Ken Marino (1968-)
The Ten '07
Role Models '08
Wanderlust '12

Charles Marion
Campus Rhythm '43
Apache Territory '58

Frances Marion (1888-1973)
Rebecca of Sunnybrook Farm '17
Amarilly of Clothesline Alley '18
Stella Maris '18
The Love Light '21
The Primitive Lover '22
Within the Law '23
Lazybones '25
The Winning of Barbara Worth '26
The Red Mill '27
Their Own Desire '29
The Big House '30
Let Us Be Gay '30
The Secret Six '31
The Champ '32
Dinner at Eight '33
Camille '36

George Marion, Jr.
Love Me Tonight '32
This Is the Night '32
Kiss and Make Up '34

Giorgio Mariuzzo
Contraband '80
The Beyond '82

Gene Markey (1895-1980)
Baby Face '33
Midnight Mary '33
The Merry Frinks '34
Girl's Dormitory '36
Private Number '36
On the Avenue '37

Mitch Markowitz
Good Morning, Vietnam '87
Crazy People '90

Jack Marks (1895-1987)
Old Mother Riley's New Venture '49
Old Mother Riley, Headmistress '50

Justin Marks
Street Fighter: The Legend of Chun-Li '09
The Jungle Book '16

William Marks
Don't Worry, We'll Think of a Title '66
Kill a Dragon '67

Ben Markson (1892-1971)
What Price Hollywood? '32
Girl Missing '33
Lady Killer '33
The Case of the Howling Dog '34
Here Comes the Navy '34
Upperworld '34
The Case of the Lucky Legs '35
The White Cockatoo '35
Danger: Love at Work '37

Christopher Markus
The Chronicles of Narnia: The Lion, the Witch and the Wardrobe '05
You Kill Me '07
The Chronicles of Narnia: Prince Caspian '08
The Chronicles of Narnia: The Voyage of the Dawn Treader '10
Captain America: The First Avenger '11
Pain & Gain '13
Thor: The Dark World '13
Captain America: The Winter Soldier '14
Captain America: Civil War '16
Avengers: Infinity War '18
Avengers: Endgame '19

Russell P. Marleau (1965-)
3-Way '04
The Curiosity of Chance '06

Brit Marling (1983-)
Another Earth '11
Sound of My Voice '11
The East '13

Brian Marlow (1893-1949)
Brief Moment '33
Supernatural '33

Andrew Marlowe
Air Force One '97
End of Days '99
Hollow Man '00

Malcolm Marmorstein
S*P*Y*S '74
Whiffs '75
Mary, Mary, Bloody Mary '76
Pete's Dragon '77
Return from Witch Mountain '78
Konrad '85
Dead Men Don't Die '91

Barbara Marshall
Triple Dog '09
Wish Upon '17

Garry Marshall (1934-2016)
The Grasshopper '69
Evil Roy Slade '71
The Flamingo Kid '84
The Other Sister '98

Neil Marshall (1970-)
The Flamingo Kid '84
Dog Soldiers '01
The Descent '05
Doomsday '08
Centurion '10
Tales of Halloween '15

Roger Marshall (1934-)
Theatre of Death '67
And Now the Screaming Starts '73

Joshua Marston (1968-)
Maria Full of Grace '04
New York, I Love You '09
Complete Unknown '16

Lucrecia Martel (1966-)
Holy Girl '04
The Headless Woman '08
Zama '17

William C. Martell
Virtual Combat '95
Crash Dive '96
Invisible Mom '96
Steel Sharks '97
Black Thunder '98
The Base '99
Crooked '05

Peter Marthesheimer (1937-2004)
The Marriage of Maria Braun '79
Lola '81
Veronika Voss '82

Al Martin (1897-1971)
Prison Shadows '36
The Invisible Ghost '41
Money Madness '47

Charles Martin (1910-83)
My Dear Secretary '49
Death of a Scoundrel '56

Darnell Martin (1964-)
I Like It Like That '94
Cadillac Records '08

Don Martin (1911-85)
The Pretender '47
Destination Murder '50
Stranger on Horseback '55
The Brass Legend '56
Hot Cars '56
Quincannon, Frontier Scout '56

Donald Martin
Spenser: A Savage Place '94
The Secrets of Comfort House '06
Celine '08
The Christmas Choir '08
Dim Sum Funeral '08
Carnal Innocence '11
The Craigslist Killer '11
CAT. 8 '13
Milton's Secret '16

Francis Martin (1900-79)
We're Not Dressing '34
Mississippi '35
The Princess Comes Across '36
Rhythm on the Range '36
Artists and Models '37
Waikiki Wedding '37
The Big Broadcast of 1938 '38
College Swing '38
One Night in the Tropics '40

Gregory Mars Martin (1971-)
See Mars Callahan

Helen Martin (1909-2000)
The Invisible Ghost '41
The Lady Confesses '45

John Benjamin Martin
The House Next Door '01
We'll Meet Again '02
Wishmaster 4: The Prophecy Fulfilled '02
Before I Say Goodbye '03
Gospel of Deceit '06
Legacy of Fear '06
The Secrets of Comfort House '06
Thrill of the Kill '06
The Secrets of the Summer House '08

J.P. Martin
The Last Cowboy '03
A Place Called Home '04

Mardik Martin (1937-)
Revenge Is My Destiny '71
Mean Streets '73
New York, New York '77
Valentino '77
Raging Bull '80

Megan Martin
Ginger Snaps: Unleashed '04
The Right Kind Of Wrong '13

Robert Martin (1948-)
Frankenhooker '90
Basket Case 3: The Progeny '92

Steve Martin (1945-)
The Jerk '79
Dead Men Don't Wear Plaid '82
The Man with Two Brains '83
Three Amigos '86
Roxanne '87
L.A. Story '91
A Simple Twist of Fate '94
Bowfinger '99
Shopgirl '05
The Pink Panther '06
The Pink Panther 2 '09

Suzanne Martin
Maneater '09
The Client List '10

Wyre Martin
The Unearthing '93
Aswang '03

Jacques Martineau (1963-)
Jeanne and the Perfect Guy '98
My Life on Ice '02
Cote d'Azur '05
Born in 68 '08

Renzo Martinelli
The Stone Merchant '06
Carnera: The Walking Mountain '08
Sword of War '09

Derick Martini (1975-)
Smiling Fish & Goat on Fire '99
Lymelife '08
The Curse of Downers Grove '15

Steven Martini (1978-)
Smiling Fish & Goat on Fire '99
Lymelife '08

Luciano Martino (1933-)
The Old Testament '62
Giants of Rome '63
The Whip and the Body '63
Hercules and the Tyrants of Babylon '64
Your Vice is a Closed Room and Only I Have the Key '72

Raymond Martino
American Born '89
Angels of the City '89
DaVinci's War '92
To the Limit '95

Sergio Martino (1938-)
Torso '73
Mannaja: A Man Called Blade '77
The Big Alligator River '79
The Great Alligator '81
The Opponent '89

Miho Maruo
Colorful: The Motion Picture '10
Miss Hokusai '16

Arthur Marx (1921-2011)
I'll Take Sweden '65
Eight on the Lam '67
Cancel My Reservation '72

R.J. Marx (1955-)
Dragonard '88
Gor '88
Master of Dragonard Hill '89

Francesco Maselli (1930-)
Story of a Love Affair '50
Kill Me Quick, I'm Cold '67

David Mason
They Crawl '01
Project Viper '02

Richard Mason (1919-97)
A Town Like Alice '56
The Wind Cannot Read '58

Sarah Y. Mason (1896-1980)
The Girl Said No '30
The Man in Possession '31
Chance at Heaven '33
Little Women '33
The Age of Innocence '34
Magnificent Obsession '35
Stella Dallas '37
Golden Boy '39

Patrick Massett
Lara Croft: Tomb Raider '01
Gold '16

Elan Mastai
MVP2: Most Vertical Primate '01
Alone in the Dark '05
The Good Samaritan '12
What If '13

Master P (1967-)
Foolish '99
Internet Dating '08

Ed Masterson
No Code of Conduct '98
Storm Catcher '99

Kelly Masterson
Before the Devil Knows You're Dead '07
Killing Kennedy '13
Good People '14
Snowpiercer '14

Nico Mastorakis (1941-)
Blood Tide '82
Blind Date '84
Zero Boys '86
The Wind '87
Bloodstone '88
Glitch! '88
In the Cold of the Night '89
Hired to Kill '91

William Mastrosimone
Extremities '86
The Beast '88
Sinatra '92
With Honors '94
Benedict Arnold: A Question of Honor '03

Berkely Mather (1909-96)
Dr. No '62
The Long Ships '64

John C. Mather
Devil Girl from Mars '54
Satellite in the Sky '56

Ali Matheson
Halloweentown '98
Halloweentown 2: Kalabar's Revenge '01
Before I Say Goodbye '03

Chris Matheson
Bill & Ted's Excellent Adventure '89
Bill & Ted's Bogus Journey '91
A Goofy Movie '94
Mr. Wrong '95
Evil Alien Conquerors '02

Richard Matheson (1926-2013)
The Incredible Shrinking Man '57
The Fall of the House of Usher '60
Master of the World '61
The Pit and the Pendulum '61
Burn, Witch, Burn! '62
Tales of Terror '62
The Raven '63
The Comedy of Terrors '64
The Last Man on Earth '64
Die! Die! My Darling! '65
The Devil Rides Out '68
Duel '71
The Night Stalker '71
The Night Strangler '72
Dracula '73
Dying Room Only '73
The Legend of Hell House '73
Scream of the Wolf '74
Trilogy of Terror '75
Somewhere in Time '80
Jaws 3 '83
Twilight Zone: The Movie '83
Trilogy of Terror 2 '96

Richard Christian Matheson (1953-)
Three O'Clock High '87
Loose Cannons '90
Full Eclipse '93
It Waits '05
Nightmare Cinema '19

Temple Mathews
Return to Never Land '02
Picture This! '08
Holiday Breakup '16

June Mathis (1892-1927)
The Four Horsemen of the Apocalypse '21
The Saphead '21
Blood and Sand '22

Melissa Mathison (1950-)
The Black Stallion '79
The Escape Artist '82
E.T.: The Extra-Terrestrial '82
The Indian in the Cupboard '95
Kundun '97
The BFG '16

Francisca Matos
A Million to Juan '94
Baby Geniuses '98

Elissa Matsueda
Spare Parts '15
Dog Days '18
The Miracle Season '18

Hitoshi Matsumoto
Big Man Japan '07
R100 '15

Taiyo Matsumoto
Blue Spring '01
Ping Pong '02

Zenzo Matsuyama (1925-)
The Human Condition: No Greater Love '58
The Human Condition: Road to Eternity '59

Paul Matthews
Grim '95
The Proposition '96
Breeders '97
Hooded Angels '00

John Mattson
Milk Money '94
Free Willy 2: The Adventure Home '95
Free Willy 3: The Rescue '97

Nat Mauldin
The Preacher's Wife '96
Dr. Dolittle '98
The In-Laws '03
Open Season '06
The Perfect Holiday '07
A Christmas Story 2 '12

J. Stephen Maunder
Tiger Claws '91
Talons of the Eagle '92
Expect No Mercy '95
The Veteran '06

Armistead Maupin (1944-)
The Celluloid Closet '95
The Night Listener '06

Joseph Maurer
The Sandy Bottom Orchestra '00
The Song of the Lark '01

Captain Mauzner
Wonderland '03
Factory Girl '06
Billionaire Boys Club '18

Garth Maxwell (1963-)
Jack Be Nimble '94
When Love Comes '98

Ronald F. Maxwell (1947-)
Gettysburg '93
Gods and Generals '03

Elaine May (1932-)
A New Leaf '71
Such Good Friends '71
Mikey & Nicky '76
Heaven Can Wait '78
Ishtar '87
The Birdcage '95
Primary Colors '98

Carl Mayer (1894-1944)
The Cabinet of Dr. Caligari '19
The Last Laugh '24
Tartuffe '25

Edwin Justus Mayer (1896-1960)
Our Blushing Brides '30
Merrily We Go to Hell '32
Thirty Day Princess '34
Exile Express '39
They Met in Bombay '41
To Be or Not to Be '42

Paul Mayersberg (1941-)
The Man Who Fell to Earth '76
Merry Christmas, Mr. Lawrence '83
Croupier '97

Wendell Mayes (1918-92)
Spirit of St. Louis '57
The Hunters '58
Anatomy of a Murder '59
The Hanging Tree '59
Advise and Consent '62
In Harm's Way '65
Von Ryan's Express '65

Hotel *'67*
The Poseidon Adventure *'72*
The Revengers *'72*
Bank Shot *'74*
Death Wish *'74*
Go Tell the Spartans *'78*
Love and Bullets *'79*
Monsignor *'82*

Gonzalo Maza
Gloria *'13*
A Fantastic Woman *'18*

Adam Mazer
Breach *'07*
You Don't Know Jack *'10*

Dan Mazer (1971-)
Borat: Cultural Learnings of America for Make Benefit Glorious Nation of Kazakhstan *'06*
I Give It a Year *'13*
Bridget Jones's Baby *'16*
Office Christmas Party *'16*

Craig Mazin (1971-)
RocketMan *'97*
Senseless *'98*
Scary Movie 3 *'03*
Scary Movie 4 *'06*
The Hangover, Part 2 *'11*
The Hangover, Part III *'13*
Identity Thief *'13*
The Huntsman: Winter's War *'16*

Dan Mazur
Night of the Scarecrow *'95*
Brave New World *'98*

Stephen Mazur
The Little Rascals *'94*
Liar Liar *'97*
Heartbreakers *'01*
Wedding Wars *'06*
Without a Paddle: Nature's Calling *'09*
Jingle All the Way 2 *'14*

Paul Mazursky (1930-2014)
I Love You, Alice B. Toklas! *'68*
Bob & Carol & Ted & Alice *'69*
Alex in Wonderland *'70*
Blume in Love *'73*
Harry and Tonto *'74*
Next Stop, Greenwich Village *'76*
An Unmarried Woman *'78*
The Tempest *'82*
Moscow on the Hudson *'84*
Down and Out in Beverly Hills *'86*
Moon over Parador *'88*
Enemies, a Love Story *'89*
Scenes from a Mall *'91*
The Pickle *'93*

Danny McBride (1976-)
Underworld *'03*
Underworld: Evolution *'05*
The Foot Fist Way *'08*
Underworld: Rise of the Lycans *'09*
Your Highness *'11*
Halloween *'18*

James McBride (1957-)
Miracle at St. Anna *'08*
Red Hook Summer *'12*

Jim McBride (1941-)
David Holzman's Diary *'67*
Glen and Randa *'71*
Breathless *'83*
Great Balls of Fire *'89*
Uncovered *'94*

Patrick McCabe
The Butcher Boy *'97*
Breakfast on Pluto *'05*

Howard McCain
Outlander *'08*
Underworld: Rise of the Lycans *'09*

Mary C. McCall (1904-86)
Street of Women *'32*
A Midsummer Night's Dream *'35*
The Secret Bride *'35*
The Woman in Red *'35*
Maisie *'39*
Congo Maisie *'40*
Gold Rush Maisie *'40*
Kathleen *'41*
Maisie Was a Lady *'41*
Ringside Maisie *'41*
The Fighting Sullivans *'42*
Maisie Gets Her Man *'42*
Swing Shift Maisie *'43*
Maisie Goes to Reno *'44*
Keep Your Powder Dry *'45*

Tim McCanlies (1953-)
Dancer, Texas-Pop. 81 *'98*
Dennis the Menace Strikes Again *'98*
The Iron Giant *'99*
Secondhand Lions *'03*

Tim McCann (1968-)
Desolation Angels *'95*
Revolution #9 *'01*

Leo McCarey (1898-1969)
Love Affair *'39*
My Favorite Wife *'40*
Going My Way *'44*
My Son John *'52*
An Affair to Remember *'57*
Rally 'Round the Flag, Boys! *'58*
Move Over, Darling *'63*

Anthony McCarten (1961-)
The Theory of Everything *'14*
Darkest Hour *'17*
Bohemian Rhapsody *'18*
The Two Popes *'19*

Brendan McCarthy
Wake Wood *'10*
Mad Max: Fury Road *'15*

Charles McCarthy, Jr. (1933-)
See Cormac McCarthy

Cormac McCarthy (1933-)
The Sunset Limited *'11*
The Counselor *'13*

Melissa McCarthy (1970-)
Tammy *'14*
The Boss *'16*
Life of the Party *'18*

Michael McCarthy (1917-59)
The Accursed *'57*
Operation Amsterdam *'60*

Peter McCarthy (1951-2004)
Tapeheads *'89*
Car 54, Where Are You? *'94*
Floundering *'94*

Thomas (Tom) McCarthy (1966-)
The Station Agent *'03*
The Visitor *'07*
Win Win *'11*
The Cobbler *'14*
Million Dollar Arm *'14*
Spotlight *'15*
Christopher Robin *'18*
Timmy Failure: Mistakes Were Made *'20*

Henry McCarty (1882-1954)
Bright Lights *'30*
Going Wild *'30*
Sunny *'30*

Jim McClain
Sniper 2 *'02*
24 Hours to Live *'17*

Karen McClellan
Bridal Fever *'08*
Will You Merry Me? *'08*

Hamish McColl
Mr. Bean's Holiday *'07*
Johnny English Reborn *'11*
Dad's Army *'16*

Bernard McConville (1887-1961)
Heart o' the Hills *'19*
Monte Cristo *'22*

Brent McCorkle
Unconditional *'12*
I Can Only Imagine *'18*

Mark McCorkle
Aladdin and the King of Thieves *'96*
Sky High *'05*
Hotel for Dogs *'09*
Kim Possible *'19*

Pete McCormack
The Blue Butterfly *'04*
Whirlygirl *'04*

John McCormick
Victim *'61*
Living on Tokyo Time *'87*

Randall McCormick
Speed 2: Cruise Control *'97*
The Scorpion King 2: Rise of a Warrior *'08*
Blue Crush 2 *'11*

Horace McCoy (1897-1955)
The Trail of the Lonesome Pine *'36*
There's Something About a Soldier *'43*
The Fireball *'50*
The Lusty Men *'52*
Bad for Each Other *'53*
Rage at Dawn *'55*

Karen McCullah
The Ugly Truth *'09*
Crazy Kind of Love *'12*

Michael McCullers
Austin Powers 2: The Spy Who Shagged Me *'99*
Austin Powers In Goldmember *'02*
Undercover Brother *'02*
Thunderbirds *'04*
Baby Mama *'08*
The Boss Baby *'17*
Hotel Transylvania 3: Summer Vacation *'18*

Bruce McCulloch (1961-)
Kids in the Hall: Brain Candy *'96*
Dog Park *'98*

Jim McCullough, Jr.
Creature from Black Lake *'76*
The Aurora Encounter *'85*
Mountaintop Motel Massacre *'86*
The St. Tammany Miracle *'94*

John Michael McDonagh
Ned Kelly *'03*
The Guard *'11*
Calvary *'14*
War on Everyone *'17*

Martin McDonagh (1970-)
In Bruges *'08*
Seven Psychopaths *'12*
Three Billboards Outside Ebbing, Missouri *'17*

Bruce McDonald (1959-)
Dance Me Outside *'95*
Hard Core Logo 2 *'10*

Michael James McDonald (1964-)
Revenge of the Red Baron *'93*
The Crazysitter *'94*
Alien Avengers *'96*

Michael McDowell (1950-99)
Beetlejuice *'88*
Tales from the Darkside: The Movie *'90*
The Nightmare Before Christmas *'93*
Stephen King's Thinner *'96*

Matthew McDuffie
A Cool, Dry Place *'98*
Ann Rule Presents: The Stranger Beside Me *'03*
The Face of Love *'13*

Alan B. McElroy
Halloween 4: The Return of Michael Myers *'88*
Rapid Fire *'92*
Spawn *'97*
Todd McFarlane's Spawn *'97*
Left Behind: The Movie *'00*
Ballistic: Ecks *vs.* Sever *'02*
Wrong Turn *'03*
The Marine *'06*
Thr3e *'07*
The Condemned 2 *'16*
Fractured *'19*

Ross McElwee (1947-)
Sherman's March *'86*
Time Indefinite *'93*

Donald McEnery
Hercules *'97*
A Bug's Life *'98*

Ian McEwan (1948-)
The Good Son *'93*
The Innocent *'93*
On Chesil Beach *'17*
The Children Act *'18*

Stephen McFeely
The Chronicles of Narnia: The Lion, the Witch and the Wardrobe *'05*
You Kill Me *'07*
The Chronicles of Narnia: Prince Caspian *'08*
Captain America: The First Avenger *'11*
Pain & Gain *'13*
Thor: The Dark World *'13*
Captain America: The Winter Soldier *'14*
Captain America: Civil War *'16*
Avengers: Infinity War *'18*
Avengers: Endgame *'19*

Mark Thomas McGee
Bad Girls from Mars *'90*
Sorceress *'94*

Ron McGee
The Last Ride *'04*
Maiden Voyage: Ocean Hijack *'04*
Fatal Contact: Bird Flu in America *'06*
Shock to the System *'06*
Christmas Town *'08*
Finish Line *'08*
On the Other Hand, Death *'08*
Deadly Honeymoon *'10*
Girl *vs.* Monster *'12*

Scott McGehee
Suture *'93*
The Deep End *'01*
Uncertainty *'08*

Kathleen McGhee-Anderson
Sunset Park *'96*
Dear Viola *'14*

Josann McGibbon
Worth Winning *'89*
Three Men and a Little Lady *'90*
The Favor *'92*
Runaway Bride *'99*
The Starter Wife *'07*

David McGillivray (1947-)
Frightmare *'74*
House of Whipcord *'75*
The Terror *'79*

Sean McGinly
Scorned 2 *'96*
Sexual Roulette *'96*
Fugitive Mind *'99*
Venomous *'01*
Two Days *'03*
The Great Buck Howard *'09*

Kele McGlohon
The Bouquet *'13*
The Wedding Chapel *'13*

Jimmy McGovern (1949-)
Cracker: Men Should Weep *'94*
Cracker: The Big Crunch *'94*
Cracker: To Be a Somebody *'94*
Priest *'94*
Cracker: Brotherly Love *'95*
Heart *'99*
Liam *'00*

Michael McGowan (1966-)
One Week *'08*
Still Mine *'13*
The Etruscan Smile *'19*

Douglas McGrath (1958-)
Born Yesterday *'93*
Bullets over Broadway *'94*
Emma *'96*
Company Man *'00*
Nicholas Nickleby *'02*
Infamous *'06*

John McGrath
Billion Dollar Brain *'67*
The Reckoning *'69*

Tom McGrath
Madagascar *'05*
Madagascar: Escape 2 Africa *'08*

John McGreevey
Hot Rod Girl *'56*
Death in Small Doses *'57*
Cast a Long Shadow *'59*
Hello Down There *'69*
Gidget Gets Married *'72*
Night Crossing *'81*
Captains Courageous *'95*

Tim McGregor
UKM: The Ultimate Killing Machine *'06*
The Final Storm *'09*

Thomas McGuane (1939-)
Rancho Deluxe *'75*
Missouri Breaks *'76*
92 in the Shade *'76*
Tom Horn *'80*
Cold Feet *'89*

Frank McGuinness (1953-)
Talk of Angels *'96*
Dancing at Lughnasa *'98*
A Short Stay in Switzerland *'09*

James Kevin McGuinness (1893-1950)
Tarzan and His Mate *'34*
China Seas *'35*
Arsene Lupin Returns *'38*
I Take This Woman *'40*
Rio Grande *'50*

Don McGuire (1919-99)
The Delicate Delinquent *'56*
Suppose They Gave a War and Nobody Came? *'70*
Tootsie *'82*

William Anthony McGuire (1881-1640)
Kid from Spain *'32*
The Great Ziegfeld *'36*
Lillian Russell *'40*

Douglas Lloyd McIntosh
Love's Long Journey *'05*
Love's Abiding Joy *'06*

Wade McIntyre
InSight *'11*
Home Alone: The Holiday Heist *'12*

Adam McKay (1968-)
Anchorman: The Legend of Ron Burgundy *'04*
Talladega Nights: The Ballad of Ricky Bobby *'06*
Step Brothers *'08*
The Other Guys *'10*
Anchorman 2: The Legend Continues *'13*
Ant-Man *'15*
The Big Short *'15*
Vice *'18*

Jim McKay
Girls Town *'95*
Our Song *'01*
Angel Rodriguez *'05*
Life Support *'07*

Neil McKay
See No Evil: The Moors Murders *'06*
Appropriate Adult *'11*

Steven McKay
Hard to Kill *'89*
Diggstown *'92*
Darkman 2: The Return of Durant *'94*

Michael McKean (1947-)
This Is Spinal Tap *'84*
The Big Picture *'89*
The Return of Spinal Tap *'92*

Lucky McKee (1975-)
May *'02*
Roman *'06*
The Woman *'11*
Tales of Halloween *'15*

Don McKellar (1963-)
Roadkill *'89*
Highway 61 *'91*
32 Short Films about Glenn Gould *'93*
Dance Me Outside *'95*
Last Night *'98*
The Red Violin *'98*
Blindness *'08*

Aline Brosh McKenna (1967-)
Three to Tango *'99*
Laws of Attraction *'04*
The Devil Wears Prada *'06*
27 Dresses *'08*
Morning Glory *'10*
I Don't Know How She Does It *'11*
We Bought a Zoo *'11*
Annie *'14*

Bruce McKenna
Band of Brothers *'01*
The Pacific *'10*

Chris McKenna (1977-)
Igor *'08*
Jumanji: Welcome to the Jungle *'17*
The LEGO Batman Movie *'17*
Spider-Man: Homecoming *'17*
Ant-Man and the Wasp *'18*
Spider-Man: Far from Home *'19*

David McKenna (1968-)
American History X *'98*
Body Shots *'99*
Get Carter *'00*
Blow *'01*
S.W.A.T. *'03*

Charles McKeown
Brazil *'85*
The Adventures of Baron Munchausen *'89*
Plunkett & Macleane *'98*
Ripley's Game *'02*
The Imaginarium of Doctor Parnassus *'09*

Vince McKewin
Fly Away Home *'96*
The Climb *'97*
The Replacements *'00*

Rob McKittrick (1973-)
Waiting *'05*
Still Waiting *'08*
Tag *'18*

Sean McLain
Safe House *'99*
I-See-You.Com *'06*

John McLaughlin
The Great Gatsby *'01*
Man of the House *'05*

John J. McLaughlin
Coma *'12*
Hitchcock *'12*
Parker *'13*

Greg McLean
Wolf Creek *'05*
Rogue *'07*
Wolf Creek 2 *'13*
The Darkness *'16*

Tom McLoughlin (1950-)
Friday the 13th, Part 6: Jason Lives *'86*
Date with an Angel *'87*

John McMahon
Broken Vessels *'98*
Rip It Off *'02*

James McManus
The Big Empty '98
ABCD '99
La Cucaracha '99

Susan McMartin
Mr. Church '16
After '19

Larry McMurtry (1936-)
The Last Picture Show '71
Falling from Grace '92
Larry McMurtry's Streets of Laredo '95
Larry McMurtry's Dead Man's Walk '96
Johnson County War '02
Brokeback Mountain '05
Comanche Moon '08

Terrence McNally (1938-2020)
The Ritz '76
Frankie and Johnny '91
Love! Valour! Compassion! '96

Sean McNamara (1963-)
3 Ninjas: High Noon at Mega Mountain '97
Soul Surfer '11
Space Warriors '13

Tony McNamara
The Rage In Placid Lake '03
The Favourite '18

Dennis McNicholas
The Ladies Man '00
Land of the Lost '09

Patterson McNutt (1896-1948)
George White's Scandals of 1935 '35
Come Live With Me '40

William Slavens McNutt (1885-1938)
One Sunday Afternoon '33
Mrs. Wiggs of the Cabbage Patch '34
The Lives of a Bengal Lancer '35

Glenn McQuaid
I Sell the Dead '09
V/H/S '12

Christopher McQuarrie (1968-)
Public Access '93
The Usual Suspects '95
Way of the Gun '00
Valkyrie '08
The Tourist '10
Jack Reacher '12
Jack the Giant Slayer '13
Edge of Tomorrow '14
Mission: Impossible Rogue Nation '15
The Mummy '17
Mission: Impossible-Fallout '18

Steve McQueen (1969-)
Hunger '08
Shame '11
Widows '18

Will McRobb
Snow Day '00
Alvin and the Chipmunks '07
Angus, Thongs and Perfect Snogging '08

Anna McRoberts
MXP: Most Xtreme Primate '03
Air Bud 6: Air Buddies '06
Snow Buddies '08
Space Buddies '08
Santa Buddies '09
The Search for Santa Paws '10
Spooky Buddies '11
Treasure Buddies '12

Geoff Mead
I Am Omega '07
Bermuda Tentacles '14

Herb Meadow (1912-95)
The Strange Woman '46
The Redhead from Wyoming '53
Stranger on Horseback '55
Lone Ranger '56
The Unguarded Moment '56

Shane Meadows (1972-)
Once Upon a Time in the Midlands '02
Dead Man's Shoes '04
This Is England '06
Le Donk & Scor-Zay-Zee '09

Irene Mecchi
The Lion King '94
The Hunchback of Notre Dame '96
Hercules '97
Annie '99
Brave '12
Peter Pan Live! '14
Strange Magic '15

Julio Medem (1958-)
Vacas '91
Tierra '95
Lovers of the Arctic Circle '98
Sex and Lucia '01

Harold Medford (1911-77)
The Damned Don't Cry '50
Operation Secret '52
The Killer Is Loose '56
Incident in an Alley '62
Fate Is the Hunter '64

Enrico Medioli (1925-)
Rocco and His Brothers '60
The Leopard '63
Conversation Piece '75
The Innocent '76
Once Upon a Time in America '84
Coco Chanel '08

Mark Medoff (1940-)
Good Guys Wear Black '78
Children of a Lesser God '86
Clara's Heart '88
City of Joy '92
Homage '95
Santa Fe '97

Geoff Meed (1965-)
Universal Soldiers '07
6 Guns '10
Hold Your Breath '12

Elizabeth Meehan (1894-1967)
Laugh, Clown, Laugh '28
Beau Ideal '31

John Meehan (1890-1954)
Strangers May Kiss '31
The Painted Veil '34
Madame X '37
Seven Sinners '40
Kismet '44
The Valley of Decision '45
Three Daring Daughters '48

Thomas Meehan
Annie '82
One Magic Christmas '85
Spaceballs '87
The Producers '05
Hairspray '07

Justin Meeks
The Wild Man of the Navidad '08
Kill or Be Killed '15

Steve Meerson
Star Trek 4: The Voyage Home '86
Anna and the King '99

Leslie Megahey
The Advocate '93
Earth '07

Robert T. Megginson
F/X '86
Wolverine '96

Deepa Mehta (1950-)
Fire '96
Earth '98
The Republic of Love '03

Ursula Meier
Home '09
Sister '12

Gordon Melbourne
Bulletproof Heart '95
White Tiger '95

Ib Melchior (1917-)
The Angry Red Planet '59
Journey to the Seventh Planet '62
Reptilicus '62
Robinson Crusoe on Mars '64
Planet of the Vampires '65

Theodore Melfi
St. Vincent '14
Going in Style '17
Hidden Figures '17

Austin Melford (1884-1971)
It's Love Again '36
He Found a Star '41

Louis Mellis
Sexy Beast '00
44 Inch Chest '09

Kay Mellor (1950-)
Band of Gold '95
Jane Eyre '97

Greg Mellott
Jackie Chan's First Strike '96
The Rage '96
Black Point '01
Road Rage '01
Under Heavy Fire '01
American Soldiers '05

George Melly (1926-2007)
Smashing Time '67
Take a Girl Like You '70

Patrick Melton (1975-)
Feast '06
Saw 4 '07
Feast 2: Sloppy Seconds '08
Saw 5 '08
The Collector '09
Saw 6 '09
Saw 3D: The Final Chapter '10
Piranha 3DD '11
The Collection '12

Lewis Meltzer (1911-95)
The Jazz Singer '52
The Man with the Golden Arm '55
New Orleans Uncensored '55
The Brothers Rico '57
High School Confidential '58

Jean-Pierre Melville (1917-73)
Les Enfants Terrible '50
Bob le Flambeur '55
Le Samourai '67
Army of Shadows '69
Le Cercle Rouge '70

Stevan Mena
Malevolence '04
Brutal Massacre: A Comedy '07
Bereavement '10

Ivan Menchell
The Cemetery Club '93
Blended '14

Aaron Mendelsohn (1966-)
Air Bud '97
Air Bud 2: Golden Receiver '98
A Change of Heart '98

Eric Mendelsohn (1964-)
Judy Berlin '99
3 Backyards '10

George Mendeluk (1948-)
Doin' Time '85
Secrets of an Undercover Wife '07
Bitter Harvest '17

Stacey Menear
The Boy '16
Brahms: The Boy II '19

Richard Menello
Two Lovers '09
The Immigrant '13

Ramon Menendez
Stand and Deliver '88
Money for Nothing '93
Tortilla Soup '01

Joe Menosky
Hiding Out '87
Anonymous Rex '04

Jiri Menzel (1938-)
Closely Watched Trains '66
I Served the King of England '07

Stephen Merchant (1974-)
Cemetery Junction '10
Fighting with My Family '19

Nicolas Mercier
Times Have Been Better '06
My Worst Nightmare '11

Anne Meredith
Bastard out of Carolina '96
Losing Chase '96
Rated X '00
Out of the Ashes '03
Secrets of Eden '12
The Red Tent '14

Michael Meredith (1967-)
Land of Plenty '04
The Open Road '09

Bess Meredyth (1890-1969)
The Red Lily '24
Don Juan '26
When a Man Loves '27
Chasing Rainbows '30
Our Blushing Brides '30
West of Broadway '31
Folies Bergere de Paris '35
That Night in Rio '41

James Merendino (1967-)
Hard Drive '94
Terrified '94
SLC Punk! '99
Evil Remains '04

Joseph Merhi (1953-)
The Newlydeads '87
Angels of the City '89
Emperor of the Bronx '89
Last Man Standing '95

Monte Merrick
Staying Together '89
Memphis Belle '90
Mr. Baseball '92
8 Seconds '94
Oliver Twist '97
Miracle at Midnight '98
The Miracle Worker '00

Dagen Merrill
Beneath '07
Broken Hill '09

Keith Merrill (1940-)
The Twelve Dogs of Christmas '05
12 Dogs of Christmas: Great Puppy Rescue '12

Brett Merryman
Glass House: The Good Mother '06
Impact Point '08

Keith Merryman
Friends With Benefits '11
Think Like a Man '12
Think Like a Man Too '14

Adam Mervis (1960-)
The Philly Kid '12
21 Bridges '19

Alex Metcalf
The Crimson Code '99
An American Affair '09
God's Pocket '14

Stephen Metcalfe
Cousins '89
Jacknife '89
Roommates '95
Beautiful Joe '00

Tim Metcalfe (1956-)
Revenge of the Nerds '84
Million Dollar Mystery '87
Fright Night 2 '88
Iron Maze '91
Kalifornia '93
Killer: A Journal of Murder '95
44 Minutes: The North Hollywood Shootout '03
Higher Ground '11

Radley Metzger (1929-)
Dark Odyssey '57
The Cat and the Canary '79

Nicholas Meyer (1945-)
Invasion of the Bee Girls '73
The Seven-Per-Cent Solution '76
Time After Time '79
Star Trek 4: The Voyage Home '86
Company Business '91
Star Trek 6: The Undiscovered Country '91
Sommersby '93
The Human Stain '03
Elegy '08
The Hessen Conspiracy '09
Houdini '14

Russ Meyer (1922-2004)
Faster, Pussycat! Kill! Kill! '65
Motor Psycho '65
Supervixens '75
Beneath the Valley of the Ultra-Vixens '79

Turi Meyer (1964-)
Leprechaun 2 '94
Chairman of the Board '97
Candyman 3: Day of the Dead '98
Wrong Turn 2: Dead End '07

Ashley Scott Meyers
Dish Dogs '98
Rushlights '13

Marc Meyers
Harvest '10
My Friend Dahmer '17

Nancy Meyers (1949-)
Private Benjamin '80
Irreconcilable Differences '84
Protocol '84
Baby Boom '87
Father of the Bride '91
I Love Trouble '94
Father of the Bride Part 2 '95
The Parent Trap '98
Something's Gotta Give '03
The Holiday '06
It's Complicated '09
The Intern '15

Menno Meyjes (1954-)
The Color Purple '85
Empire of the Sun '87
Foreign Student '94
The Siege '98
Max '02
A Matador's Mistress '08
Day of the Falcon '11

Roger Michell (1957-)
The Buddha of Suburbia '92
My Cousin Rachel '17

Dave Michener
The Fox and the Hound '81
The Great Mouse Detective '86

David Michod
Animal Kingdom '09
Hesher '10
The Rover '14
War Machine '17
The King '19

Cathryn Michon
A Dog's Purpose '17
A Dog's Journey '19
A Dog's Way Home '19

William Mickelberry
Black Dog '98
Escape: Human Cargo '98

Elizabeth (Lizzie) Mickery
The Ice House '97
Love or Money '01
The State Within '06
The 39 Steps '09

Jim Mickle
Mulberry Street '06
Stake Land '10
We Are What We Are '13
Cold in July '14

Anne-Marie Mieville (1945-)
Numero Deux '75
Every Man for Himself '79
First Name: Carmen '83

Masakazu Migita
The Calamari Wrestler '04
Executive Koala '06
Death Kappa '10

Romano Migliorini
The Bloody Pit of Horror '65
The Night of the Devils '72
Deadly Mission '78

Christopher R. Mihm
The Monster of Phantom Lake '06
It Came From Another World '07
Cave Women on Mars '08
Destination: Outer Space '10
Attack of the Moon Zombies '11

Takashi Miike (1960-)
The Great Yokai War '05
Sukiyaki Western Django '08

Ted V. Mikels (1929-)
The Astro-Zombies '67
The Corpse Grinders '71
The Doll Squad '73
Blood Orgy of the She-Devils '74
10 Violent Women '79
Mark of the Astro-Zombies '02
Astro-Zombies M3: Cloned '10
Astro-Zombies M4: Invaders from Cyberspace '12

Nikita Mikhalkov (1945-)
Burnt by the Sun '94
12 '07

Jean-Louis Milesi (1956-)
Marius and Jeannette '97
The Town Is Quiet '00

Lewis Milestone (1895-1980)
Lucky Partners '40
Arch of Triumph '48

Djordje Milicevic (1942-)
Victory '81
Runaway Train '85
Toby McTeague '87
Iron Will '93

Frank Military
Buffalo Soldiers '97
Blind Faith '98

John Milius (1944-)
Evel Knievel '72
Jeremiah Johnson '72
Life & Times of Judge Roy Bean '72
Dillinger '73
Magnum Force '73
The Wind and the Lion '75
Big Wednesday '78
Apocalypse Now '79
1941 '79
Conan the Barbarian '82
Red Dawn '84
Farewell to the King '89
Geronimo: An American Legend '93
Clear and Present Danger '94
Rough Riders '97

Miles Millar (1970-)
Shanghai Noon '00
Showtime '02
Shanghai Knights '03
Spider-Man 2 '04
Herbie: Fully Loaded '05
The Mummy: Tomb of the Dragon Emperor '08
I Am Number Four '11

Ronald Millar (1919-98)
The Miniver Story '50
Never Let Me Go '53

Sound City '13
The Summit '13
Fed Up '14
Before the Flood '16
Icarus '17
The Biggest Little Farm '18
Pavarotti '19

Eric Monte (1944-)
Nine Lives of Fritz the Cat '74
Cooley High '75

Luigi Montefiore (1942-)
The Great Alligator '81
Stagefright '87
Beyond Justice '92

Art Monterastelli (1957-)
The Hunted '03
Rambo '08

Doreen Montgomery (1916-92)
The Man in Grey '43
Love Story '44

Michael Thomas Montgomery
Eye of the Tiger '86
Night Vision '97

Dito Montiel (1965-)
A Guide to Recognizing Your Saints '06
Fighting '09
The Son of No One '11
Man Down '16
The Clapper '18

Daniel Monzon
The Kovak Box '06
Cell 211 '09

Lukas Moodysson (1969-)
Show Me Love '99
Mammoth '09
We Are the Best! '13

Martin Mooney (1896-1967)
Gangs, Inc. '41
Paper Bullets '41
The Panther's Claw '42
I Escaped from the Gestapo '43
The Monster Maker '44

Nick Moorcroft
St. Trinian's '07
The Legend of Fritton's Gold '09
Burke & Hare '10
Finding Your Feet '18
Fisherman's Friends '19

Brian Moore (1921-99)
Torn Curtain '66
Black Robe '91

Charles Philip Moore
Black Belt '92
The Last Assassins '96
Not of This Earth '96
Termination Man '97
Heaven's Fire '99

Dudley Moore (1935-2002)
Bedazzled '68
The Hound of the Baskervilles '77

Kevin Moore
Today You Die '05
Showdown at Area 51 '07

Michael Moore (1954-)
Roger & Me '89
Canadian Bacon '94
Bowling for Columbine '02
Fahrenheit 9/11 '04
Sicko '07
Capitalism: A Love Story '09
Fahrenheit 11/9 '18

Rich Moore
Zootopia '16
Ralph Breaks the Internet '18

Ronald D. Moore (1964-)
Star Trek: Generations '94
Star Trek: First Contact '96
Caprica '09
Virtuality '09

Scott Moore
Rebound '05
Full of It '07
Four Christmases '08
Ghosts of Girlfriends Past '09
The Hangover '09
The Change-Up '11
Flypaper '11
21 & Over '13
Bad Moms '16
A Bad Moms Christmas '17
Jexi '19

Simon Moore (1958-)
Traffik '90
Under Suspicion '92
Gulliver's Travels '95
The Quick and the Dead '95
Dinotopia '02
The Snow Queen '02

Jocelyn Moorhouse (1960-)
Proof '91
Unconditional Love '03
The Dressmaker '16

Philippe Mora (1949-)
Howling 3: The Marsupials '87
Pterodactyl Woman from Beverly Hills '97

Eddie Moran
Merrily We Live '38
Wonder Man '45

Patrick Moran (1960-)
Dark Universe '93
Jack-O '95

Julian More (1928-)
The Valley of Gwangi '69
The Bloodsuckers '70

Gael Morel (1972-)
Full Speed '96
Apres Lui '07
Our Paradise '11

Rob Moreland
Happily N'Ever After '07
Space Chimps '08

Juan Martinez Moreno
Two Tough Guys '03
The ABCs of Death 2 '14

Robert Moresco
Crash '05
10th & Wolf '06

Nanni Moretti (1953-)
Caro Diario '93
The Son's Room '00
Quiet Chaos '08
Mia Madre '16

Renato Moretti
The War of the Planets '65
The Snow Devils '67

Rafael Moreu
Hackers '95
The Rage: Carrie 2 '99

Abi Morgan (1968-)
The Iron Lady '11
Shame '11
Birdsong '12
The Invisible Woman '13
Suffragette '15

Byron Morgan (1889-1963)
The Smart Set '28
Five Star Final '31
Fast Life '32
High Flyers '37

Chris Morgan (1968-)
Cellular '04
The Fast and the Furious: Tokyo Drift '06
Wanted '08
Fast & Furious '09
Fast Five '11
Fast & Furious 6 '13
47 Ronin '13
Furious 7 '15
The Fate of the Furious '17
Fast & Furious Presents: Hobbs & Shaw '19

George Morgan (1854-1936)
Headin' for Trouble '31
Her Forgotten Past '33
The Oil Raider '34

Glen Morgan
The Boys Next Door '85
Final Destination '00
The One '01
Willard '03
Black Christmas '06
Final Destination 3 '06

Guy Morgan
Hell Is Sold Out '51
Love in Pawn '53

Peter Morgan (1963-)
The Very Thought of You '98
The Last King of Scotland '06
Longford '06
The Queen '06
Frost/Nixon '08
The Other Boleyn Girl '08
The Damned United '09
Hereafter '10
The Special Relationship '10
360 '12
Rush '13
Bohemian Rhapsody '18

Brett Morgen
The Kid Stays in the Picture '02
Chicago 10 '07
Cobain: Montage of Heck '15
Jane '17

Louis Morheim
Smart Woman '48
Ma and Pa Kettle '49
The Beast from 20,000 Fathoms '53
Tall Lie '53
Rumble on the Docks '56

Louis Morneau
Bet Your Life '04
Werewolf: The Beast Among Us '12

Tony Morphett (1938-)
The Last Wave '77
Sweet Talker '91
Crimebroker '93
Crime Broker '94
Kings in Grass Castles '97
13 Gantry Row '98

Christopher Morris (1965-)
Four Lions '10
The Day Shall Come '19

Edmund Morris (1912-98)
Walk on the Wild Side '62
Project X '68

Errol Morris (1948-)
The Thin Blue Line '88
Standard Operating Procedure '08
The Unknown Known '14

Grant Morris
The Return of the Swamp Thing '89
Dead Dog '00

Howard J. Morris
Mr. Write '92
Five '11
Call Me Crazy '13

John Morris
Never Been Thawed '05
Sex Drive '08
She's Out of My League '10
Mr. Popper's Penguins '11
We're the Millers '13
Dumb and Dumber To '14
Horrible Bosses 2 '14
Daddy's Home '15
Daddy's Home 2 '17
Instant Family '18

Judy Morris (1947-)
Babe: Pig in the City '98
Happy Feet '06

Linda Morris
Shannon's Rainbow '09
Multiple Sarcasms '10

Richard Morris (1924-96)
Ma and Pa Kettle at the Fair '52
If a Man Answers '62
Thoroughly Modern Millie '67

Wendell Morris
The Medicine Show '01
Eye of the Dolphin '06
Beneath the Blue '10

Paul Morrison (1944-)
Solomon and Gaenor '98
Wondrous Oblivion '06

Rebecca Morrison
Legionnaire '98
Scorcher '02

Paul Morrissey (1939-)
Flesh '68
Trash '70
Heat '72
Andy Warhol's Dracula '74
Andy Warhol's Frankenstein '74
The Hound of the Baskervilles '77
Mixed Blood '84

William Morrissey
Shattered '07
The Entitled '11

Barry Morrow (1948-)
Rain Man '88
Race the Sun '96
Remember Sunday '13

Douglas S. Morrow (1913-94)
The Stratton Story '49
Jim Thorpe: All American '51
Beyond a Reasonable Doubt '56

William Morrow (1907-71)
Buck Benny Rides Again '40
The Road to Bali '53

Cynthia Mort
The Brave One '07
Nina '16

John Mortimer (1923-2009)
The Innocents '61
Guns of Darkness '62
Bunny Lake Is Missing '65
No Sex Please-We're British '73
Edwin '84
Cider with Rosie '99
Tea with Mussolini '99
In Love and War '01

Penelope Mortimer (1918-99)
Bunny Lake Is Missing '65
A Summer Story '88

Lisa Morton
The Glass Trap '04
Blood Angels '05

Stefania Moscato
Breathless '12
Cellmates '12
Zombieworld '15

Guy Moshe
Holly '07
Bunraku '10

Jared Moshe
Dead Man's Burden '12
The Ballad of Lefty Brown '17

April Moskowitz
Body Strokes '95
Friend of the Family '95

Craig Moss
Breaking Wind '12
30 Nights of Paranormal Activity with the Devil Inside the Girl with the Dragon Tattoo '12

Jamie Moss
Ghost in the Shell '17
Hunter Killer '18

Marc Moss
Along Came a Spider '01
Alex Cross '12

Nat Moss
Washington Heights '02
Adrift in Manhattan '07

Jonathan Mostow (1961-)
Breakdown '96
U-571 '00

Greg Mottola (1964-)
The Daytrippers '96
Superbad '07
Adventureland '09

Marcel Moussey (1924-95)
The 400 Blows '59
Shoot the Piano Player '62

Oren Moverman
Jesus' Son '99
I'm Not There '07
Married Life '07
The Messenger '09
Rampart '11
The Quiet Ones '14
Time Out of Mind '14
Love & Mercy '15
The Dinner '17
Puzzle '18

Allan Moyle (1947-)
Pump Up the Volume '90
The Thing Called Love '93

Niels Mueller (1961-)
Tadpole '02
The Assassination of Richard Nixon '05

Domonic Muir
Critters '86
Contract Killer '98

Robin Mukherjee
Poldark '96
Lore '13

Jim Mulholland
Ratings Game '84
Amazon Women on the Moon '87
Oscar '91
Bad Boys '95

Don Mullaly (?-1933)
Girl Missing '33
Mystery of the Wax Museum '33

Peter Mullan (1959-)
Orphans '97
The Magdalene Sisters '02

Paul Alfred Muller (1901-70)
Kiss Kiss Kill Kill '66
Death is Nimble, Death is Quick '67

Mark Mullin
The Killing Jar '96
Eye of the Beast '07
Something Beneath '07

Sean Mullin
Amira & Sam '15
Semper Fi '19

Kieran Mulroney (1965-)
Paper Man '09
Sherlock Holmes: A Game of Shadows '11

Michele Mulroney
Paper Man '09
Sherlock Holmes: A Game of Shadows '11

Annie Mumolo
Bridesmaids '11
Megan Leavey '17

Christopher Munch (1962-)
Color of a Brisk and Leaping Day '95
The Sleepy Time Gal '01
Harry and Max '04

Lance Mungia (1972-)
Six-String Samurai '98
The Crow: Wicked Prayer '05

Cristian Mungiu (1968-)
4 Months, 3 Weeks and 2 Days '07
Beyond the Hills '13
Graduation '17

Robert Munic (1968-)
In a Class of His Own '99
They Call Me Sirr '00
Fighting '09

Rona Munro (1959-)
Ladybird, Ladybird '93
Aimee & Jaguar '98
Oranges and Sunshine '10

Kevin Munroe
TMNT: Teenage Mutant Ninja Turtles '07
Ratchet & Clank '16

Takeo Murata (1910-)
Godzilla '54
Godzilla, King of the Monsters '56

Jane Murfin (1892-1955)
Seven Keys to Baldpate '29
What Price Hollywood? '32
Spitfire '34
Come and Get It '36
The Shining Hour '38
Stand Up and Fight '39
Andy Hardy's Private Secretary '41

John Murlowski
Black Cadillac '03
Possessed '05
Whispers and Lies '08

Charles Murphy
Vampire in Brooklyn '95
Norbit '07

David Murphy
Border Lost '08
Lost Treasure of the Maya '08

Dennis Murphy
Eye of the Devil '67
The Sergeant '68

Nick Murphy
The Casino Job '08
The Awakening '11

Richard Murphy (1912-93)
Flying Blind '41
Wrecking Crew '42
Boomerang '47
Cry of the City '48
Deep Waters '48
Slattery's Hurricane '49
You're In the Navy Now '51
Three Stripes in the Sun '55
Compulsion '59

Richard D. (R.D.) Murphy (1966-)
Betty '97
Milwaukee, Minnesota '03

Ryan Murphy (1966-)
Running with Scissors '06
Eat, Pray, Love '10
Ready or Not '19

Tab Murphy
My Best Friend Is a Vampire '88
The Last of the Dogmen '95
The Hunchback of Notre Dame '96
Tarzan '99
Atlantis: The Lost Empire '01
Brother Bear '03
Dark Country '09

Warren B. Murphy (1933-)
The Eiger Sanction '75
Remo Williams: The Adventure Begins '85

John Fenton Murray (1917-96)
Everything's Ducky '61
It's Only Money '62
Robin and the 7 Hoods '64
Pufnstuf '70

Kiel Murray
Cars '06
Cars 3 '17

Michael J. Murray
Acceptable Risk '01
My Neighbor's Secret '09
Blue-Eyed Butcher '12
Duke '12

Paul T. Murray
Cruel World *'05*
What Doesn't Kill You *'08*

Tom Musca
Stand and Deliver *'88*
Money for Nothing *'93*
Race *'99*
Tortilla Soup *'01*

John Musker (1953-)
The Little Mermaid *'89*
Aladdin *'92*
Hercules *'97*
Treasure Planet *'02*
The Princess and the Frog *'09*

Floyd Mutrux (1941-)
Dusty and Sweets Mcgee *'71*
Aloha, Bobby and Rose *'74*
The Hollywood Knights *'80*
American Me *'92*
There Goes My Baby *'92*
Blood In . . . Blood Out: Bound by Honor *'93*

Anna Muylaert
The Year My Parents Went on Vacation *'07*
The Second Mother *'15*

Cindy Myers
Gossip *'08*
All Roads Lead to Rome *'15*

Claudia Myers
Kettle of Fish *'06*
Wild Oats *'16*

Henry Myers (1893-1975)
The Black Room *'35*
Destry Rides Again *'39*

Mike Myers (1963-)
Wayne's World *'92*
So I Married an Axe Murderer *'93*
Wayne's World 2 *'93*
Austin Powers: International Man of Mystery *'97*
Austin Powers 2: The Spy Who Shagged Me *'99*
Austin Powers In Goldmember *'02*
The Love Guru *'08*

Scott Myers
K-9 *'89*
Trojan War *'97*

John Myhers (1921-92)
The Private Eyes *'80*
The Longshot *'86*

Daniel Myrick
The Blair Witch Project *'99*
Believers *'07*
The Objective *'08*

Fred Myton (1885-1955)
The Great Divide *'29*
Hitler: Beast of Berlin *'39*
Dead Men Walk *'43*
Thundering Gunslingers *'44*
Blonde for a Day *'46*
Miraculous Journey *'48*
Hi-Jacked *'50*

Jeffrey Nachmanoff
The Day After Tomorrow *'04*
Traitor *'08*

Michael Nachoff
Bloodrayne: The Third Reich *'11*
In the Name of the King 2: Two Worlds *'11*

Phyllis Nagy (1962-)
Mrs. Harris *'05*
Carol *'15*

Ed Naha (1950-)
Troll *'86*
Dolls *'87*
Honey, I Shrunk the Kids *'89*
Omega Doom *'96*

Richard Naing
The Autopsy of Jane Doe *'16*
Eli *'19*

Olivier Nakache
The Intouchables *'12*
Samba *'14*

Takehiro Nakajima (1935-)
Okoge *'93*
Village of Dreams *'97*
When the Last Sword is Drawn *'02*
Genghis Khan: To the Ends of the Earth and Sea *'07*

Masa Nakamura
The Way To Fight *'96*
Andromedia *'00*
Dead or Alive 2 *'00*
Dororo *'07*
Sukiyaki Western Django *'08*

Yoshihiro Nakamura
Doing Time *'02*
The Booth *'06*

Desmond Nakano (1953-)
American Me *'92*
White Man's Burden *'95*

Hiroyuki Nakano
Samurai Fiction *'99*
Red Shadow *'01*

Kazuki Nakashima
Ashura *'05*
Promare *'19*

Tetsuya Nakashima
Kamikaze Girls *'04*
The World of Kanako *'15*

Hideo Nakata (1961-)
Ringu 2 *'99*
Dark Water *'02*
The Ring 2 *'05*
Death Note 3: L Change the World *'08*

Yin Nam
Prison on Fire *'87*
Full Contact *'92*

Michael Nankin (1955-)
The Gate *'87*
Gate 2 *'92*

Susan Nanus
If These Walls Could Talk *'96*
Recipe for a Perfect Christmas *'05*

Paul Naschy (1934-2009)
Dracula *vs.* Frankenstein *'69*
The Fury of the Wolfman *'70*
The Werewolf *vs.* the Vampire Woman *'70*
Dr. Jekyll and the Wolfman *'71*
Dracula's Great Love *'72*
Horror Rises from the Tomb *'72*
Curse of the Devil *'73*
Exorcism *'74*
Inquisition *'76*
Human Beasts *'80*

Gustin Nash
Charlie Bartlett *'07*
Youth in Revolt *'10*

Jamie Nash (1971-)
Altered *'06*
Adventures of a Teenage Dragonslayer *'10*
V/H/S/2 *'13*

N. Richard Nash (1913-2000)
Nora Prentiss *'47*
Mara Maru *'52*
Helen of Troy *'56*
The Rainmaker *'56*
Between the Darkness and the Dawn *'85*

Jack Nasser
Angel and the Badman *'09*
Courage *'09*

Joseph Nasser
FBI: Negotiator *'05*
WWJD: What Would Jesus Do? *'10*
Dawn Rider *'12*

Roberto Natale (1921-)
The Bloody Pit of Horror *'65*
A Long Ride From Hell *'68*

Vincenzo Natali (1969-)
Cube *'98*
Paris, je t'aime *'06*
Splice *'10*
In the Tall Grass *'19*

Mort Nathan
Kingpin *'96*
Boat Trip *'03*

Robert Nathan (1894-1985)
Pagan Love Song *'50*
In the Deep Woods *'91*

Jeff Nathanson
For Better or Worse *'95*
Speed 2: Cruise Control *'97*
Bait *'00*
Rush Hour 2 *'01*
Catch Me If You Can *'02*
The Last Shot *'04*
The Terminal *'04*
Rush Hour 3 *'07*
New York, I Love You *'09*
Tower Heist *'11*
Pirates of the Caribbean: Dead Men Tell No Tales *'17*
The Lion King *'19*

Maria Nation
The Awakening *'95*
Blue River *'95*
Ellen Foster *'97*
The Inheritance *'97*
A Season for Miracles *'99*
The Salem Witch Trials *'02*
Little Girl Lost: The Delimar Vera Story *'08*
The Tenth Circle *'08*
The Two Mr. Kissels *'08*
Held Hostage *'09*
The Gabby Douglas Story *'14*
A Street Cat Named Bob *'16*

Rick Natkin
The Boys in Company C *'77*
Necessary Roughness *'91*
Gang in Blue *'96*

Jack Natteford (1894-1970)
Lightning Hutch *'26*
The Dude Bandit *'33*
St. Louis Woman *'34*

Gregory Nava (1949-)
El Norte *'83*
My Family *'94*
Selena *'96*
Frida *'02*
Bordertown *'06*

Lex Neal (1896-1940)
Go West *'25*
Battling Butler *'26*

Christopher Neame (1947-)
Zeta One *'69*
Feast of July *'95*

Ronald Neame (1911-)
Brief Encounter *'46*
Great Expectations *'46*
This Happy Breed *'47*

Hal Needham (1931-2013)
Smokey and the Bandit *'77*
Stroker Ace *'83*

Oleg Negin
Elena *'11*
Leviathan *'14*
Loveless *'18*

Troy Neighbors
Fortress *'93*
Fortress 2: Re-Entry *'99*

Paul Jan Nelissen
Nothing to Lose *'08*
Winter in Wartime *'10*

Hank Nelken
Killer Bud *'00*
Saving Silverman *'01*
Are We Done Yet? *'07*
Mama's Boy *'07*

Arty Nelson
Beautiful Losers *'08*
Plush *'13*

Bob Nelson (1956-)
Ryder P.I. *'86*
Nebraska *'13*
The Confirmation *'16*

Brian Nelson
Hard Candy *'06*
30 Days of Night *'07*
Devil *'10*

Don Nelson
Past Sins *'06*
My Baby Is Missing *'07*

Jessie Nelson
Corrina, Corrina *'94*
Stepmom *'98*
The Story of Us *'99*
I Am Sam *'01*
Because I Said So *'07*

John Allen Nelson (1959-)
Best of the Best 2 *'93*
American Yakuza *'94*

Peter W. Nelson
Untamed Love *'94*
Buying the Cow *'02*

Richard Nelson (1950-)
Ethan Frome *'92*
Hyde Park on Hudson *'12*

Sean Nelson (1980-)
Godmoney *'97*
My Effortless Brilliance *'08*

Stanley Nelson
Freedom Summer *'14*
The Black Panthers: Vanguard of the Revolution *'15*

Tim Blake Nelson (1964-)
Eye of God *'97*
The Grey Zone *'01*
Leaves of Grass *'09*

André Nemec
Mission: Impossible-Ghost Protocol *'11*
Teenage Mutant Ninja Turtles *'14*
Teenage Mutant Ninja Turtles: Out of the Shadows *'16*
Wonder Park *'19*

Dennis Nemec
Murder in Coweta County *'83*
God Bless the Child *'88*
Deadly Relations *'93*
The Avenging Angel *'95*

László Nemes
Son of Saul *'15*
Sunset *'18*

Avi Nesher (1953-)
Doppelganger: The Evil Within *'90*
Timebomb *'91*
Mercenary *'96*
The Taxman *'98*
Tales from the Crypt Presents Ritual *'02*
The Secrets *'07*
The Other Story *'19*

Sandra Nettelbeck (1966-)
Mostly Martha *'01*
Helen *'09*
Last Love *'13*

E. Jack Neuman (1921-98)
The Venetian Affair *'67*
A Death in California *'85*

Sam Neuman
Career Girl *'44*
Hitler *'62*

Kurt Neumann (1906-58)
Rocketship X-M *'50*
Carnival Story *'54*
Party Girls for Sale *'54*
She Devil *'57*

Edward Neumeier
RoboCop *'87*
Starship Troopers *'97*
Anacondas: The Hunt for the Blood Orchid *'04*
Starship Troopers 2: Hero of the Federation *'04*
Starship Troopers 3: Marauder *'08*

Scott Neustadter (1977-)
(500) Days of Summer *'09*
The Pink Panther 2 *'09*

The Spectacular Now *'13*
The Fault In Our Stars *'14*
Paper Towns *'15*
The Disaster Artist *'17*

Mark Neveldine (1973-)
Crank *'06*
Gamer *'09*
Jonah Hex *'10*

John Thomas 'Jack' Neville (1886-1970)
Malay Nights *'32*
Alimony Madness *'33*
Barefoot Boy *'38*
The Devil Bat *'41*
Never Give a Sucker an Even Break *'41*

Craig J. Nevius
Black Scorpion *'95*
Black Scorpion 2: Ground Zero *'96*
Marquis de Sade *'96*
Lady Killer *'97*

David Newman (1937-2003)
Oh! Calcutta! *'72*
Think Like a Man *'12*

David Newman (1954-)
Bonnie & Clyde *'67*
There Was a Crooked Man *'70*
Bad Company *'72*
What's Up, Doc? *'72*
Superman: The Movie *'78*
Superman 2 *'80*
Jinxed *'82*
Still of the Night *'82*
Superman 3 *'83*
Sheena *'84*
Santa Claus: The Movie *'85*

David A. Newman
Friends With Benefits *'11*
Think Like a Man Too *'14*

Eric Newman
Christmas Child *'03*
Home Run *'13*

John Stuart Newman
Proud Mary *'18*
A Score to Settle *'19*

Jonathan Newman
Angel in the House *'11*
Swinging With the Finkels *'11*

Samuel Newman
Shanghai Chest *'48*
Jungle Manhunt *'51*
Tarzan's Peril *'51*
Jungle Man-Eaters *'54*
Invisible Invaders *'59*

Walter Newman (1916-93)
Ace in the Hole *'51*
The Man with the Golden Arm *'55*
The True Story of Jesse James *'57*
Crime and Punishment, USA *'59*
The Interns *'62*

Kim Nguyen
War Witch *'12*
The Hummingbird Project *'18*

Kuang Ni
The One-Armed Swordsman *'67*
Have Sword, Will Travel *'69*
Sword Masters: Brothers Five *'70*
Duel of Fists *'71*
The Delightful Forest *'72*
Heroes Two *'73*
Infra-Man *'76*
Sword Masters: Web of Death *'76*
The Brave Archer *'77*
Sword Masters: The Battle Wizard *'77*
Five Deadly Venoms *'78*
Heaven & Hell *'78*
The 36th Chamber of Shaolin *'78*
The Master *'80*
Sword Masters: Two Champions of Shaolin *'80*

House of Traps *'81*
The Brave Archer and His Mate *'82*
Five Element Ninjas *'82*
8 Diagram Pole Fighter *'84*
Black Magic *'06*
Heroes of the East *'08*
The Magic Blade *'08*

Sloan Nibley (1908-90)
Carson City *'52*
Hostile Guns *'67*

Fred Niblo, Jr. (1903-73)
The Criminal Code *'31*
City Streets *'38*
Hell's Kitchen *'39*
East of the River *'40*
The Wagons Roll at Night *'41*
You Can't Escape Forever *'42*
The Falcon in Danger *'43*
Tampico *'44*
Convicted *'50*

Andrew Niccol (1964-)
Gattaca *'97*
The Truman Show *'98*
Simone *'02*
The Terminal *'04*
Lord of War *'05*
In Time *'11*
The Host *'13*
Good Kill *'15*

David Nicholls (1966-)
Simpatico *'99*
Much Ado About Nothing *'05*
Starter for 10 *'06*
When Did You Last See Your Father? *'07*
Tess of the D'Urbervilles *'08*
One Day *'11*
Great Expectations *'12*
Far from the Madding Crowd *'15*

Dudley Nichols (1895-1960)
Seas Beneath *'31*
Pilgrimage *'33*
The Lost Patrol *'34*
The Crusades *'35*
The Informer *'35*
She *'35*
The Hurricane *'37*
Bringing Up Baby *'38*
Stagecoach *'39*
Man Hunt *'41*
Air Force *'43*
For Whom the Bell Tolls *'43*
Government Girl *'43*
This Land Is Mine *'43*
It Happened Tomorrow *'44*
And Then There Were None *'45*
The Bells of St. Mary's *'45*
The Fugitive *'48*
Pinky *'49*
Prince Valiant *'54*
Run for the Sun *'56*
The Tin Star *'57*
The Hangman *'59*

Jeff Nichols (1978-)
Shotgun Stories *'07*
Take Shelter *'11*
Mud *'12*
Loving *'16*
Midnight Special *'16*

Peter Nichols (1927-)
Having a Wild Weekend *'65*
Georgy Girl *'66*
The National Health *'73*

Jack Nicholson (1937-)
Ride in the Whirlwind *'66*
The Trip *'67*
Head *'68*

William Nicholson (1948-)
A Private Matter *'92*
Sarafina! *'92*
Shadowlands *'93*
Nell *'94*
First Knight *'95*
Firelight *'97*
Grey Owl *'99*
Gladiator *'00*
Les Miserables *'12*

Mandela: Long Walk to Freedom '13
Unbroken '14
Everest '15
Breathe '17
Hope Gap '20

Nicholas Niciphor
Death Sport '78
Fatal Charm '92

Michael A. (M.A.) Nickles (1968-)
Desert Winds '95
Playback '12

Ted Nicolaou
Terrorvision '86
Assault of the Killer Bimbos '88
Bloodstone: Subspecies 2 '92
Bloodlust: Subspecies 3 '93
Vampire Journals '96
Bloodstorm: Subspecies 4 '98

Grant Nieporte
Seven Pounds '08
Breakthrough '19

Steve Niles
30 Days of Night '07
30 Days of Night: Dark Days '10

Rob Nilsson (1940-)
Signal 7 '83
On the Edge '86
Heat and Sunlight '87

Brian Nissen
The Swan Princess '94
The Swan Princess 2: Escape from Castle Mountain '97

John Niven
Cat Run '11
Kill Your Friends '16

Gaspar Noé (1963-)
I Stand Alone '98
Irreversible '02
Enter the Void '09
Love '15
Climax '18

Marie Noelle
Obsession '97
Love the Hard Way '01

David Nokes
Clarissa '91
The Tenant of Wildfell Hall '96

Christopher Nolan (1970-)
Following '99
Memento '00
Batman Begins '05
The Prestige '06
The Dark Knight '08
Inception '10
The Dark Knight Rises '12
Interstellar '14
Dunkirk '17

Jonathan Nolan (1976-)
The Prestige '06
The Dark Knight '08
The Dark Knight Rises '12
Interstellar '14

Ken Nolan
Black Hawk Down '01
The Company '07
Only the Brave '17
Transformers: The Last Knight '17

William F. Nolan (1928-)
The Norliss Tapes '73
Trilogy of Terror 2 '96

George Nolfi
Timeline '03
Ocean's Twelve '04
The Sentinel '06
The Bourne Ultimatum '07
The Adjustment Bureau '11
The Banker '20

Tom Noonan (1951-)
What Happened Was. . . '94
The Wife '95

Tommy Noonan (1921-68)
The Rookie '59
Promises! Promises! '63

Denis Norden (1922-)
Love in Pawn '53
The Best House in London '69

Eric Norden
Please Don't Eat My Mother '72
Blood Legacy '73

Marc Norman (1941-)
Oklahoma Crude '73
Zandy's Bride '74
Breakout '75
The Killer Elite '75
The Aviator '85
Bat 21 '88
Cutthroat Island '95
Waterworld '95
Shakespeare in Love '98

Marsha Norman (1947-)
'night, Mother '86
The Audrey Hepburn Story '00

Brock Norman Brock
Bronson '09
The Mustang '19

Stephen Norrington (1965-)
Death Machine '95
The Last Minute '01

Chuck Norris (1940-)
Braddock: Missing in Action 3 '88
Logan's War: Bound by Honor '98

Edmund H. North (1911-90)
Murder On a Bridle Path '36
Colorado Territory '49
Flamingo Road '49
Only the Valiant '50
The Day the Earth Stood Still '51
The Far Horizons '55
Cowboy '58
Sink the Bismarck '60
Damn the Defiant '62
Patton '70

Bill W.L. Norton (1943-)
Losin' It '82
Back to the Beach '87

William W. Norton, Sr. (1925-)
The Scalphunters '68
Sam Whiskey '69
McKenzie Break '70
White Lightning '73
Big Bad Mama '74
I Dismember Mama '74
Brannigan '75
Gator '76
Moving Violation '76
A Small Town in Texas '76
Day of the Animals '77

Todd Norwood
Tricks of a Woman '08
Immigration Tango '11

Jonathan Nossiter (1961-)
Sunday '96
Signs & Wonders '00
Rio Sex Comedy '10

Jennifer Notas
Gift of the Magi '10
A Taste of Romance '12

T.S. Nowlin
The Maze Runner '14
Maze Runner: The Scorch Trials '15
Phoenix Forgotten '17
Maze Runner: The Death Cure '18
Pacific Rim: Uprising '18

Louis Nowra (1950-)
Map of the Human Heart '93
Cosi '95
Heaven's Burning '97
The Matchmaker '97

Betsy Giffen Nowrasteh
Under Pressure '98
The Stoning of Soraya M. '08
The Young Messiah '16

Cyrus Nowrasteh (1956-)
The Day Reagan Was Shot '01
10,000 Black Men Named George '02
The Stoning of Soraya M. '08
The Young Messiah '16

Marti Noxon (1964-)
Just a Little Harmless Sex '99
Fright Night '11
I Am Number Four '11

Frank Nugent (1908-66)
Fort Apache '48
She Wore a Yellow Ribbon '49
Angel Face '52
The Quiet Man '52
Mister Roberts '55
The Tall Men '55
The Searchers '56
The Rising of the Moon '57
The Last Hurrah '58
Two Rode Together '61
Donovan's Reef '63

Victor Nunez (1945-)
A Flash of Green '85
Ulee's Gold '97
Coastlines '02

Tom Nursall
I'll Be Home for Christmas '98
Without a Paddle '04

Colin Nutley (1944-)
Under the Sun '98
Gossip '00

Ron Nyswaner (1956-)
Smithereens '82
Mrs. Soffel '84
Purple Hearts '84
Swing Shift '84
Prince of Pennsylvania '88
Gross Anatomy '89
Love Hurts '91
Philadelphia '93
Soldier's Girl '03
The Painted Veil '06
Why Stop Now '12
Freeheld '15

Tsugumi Oba
Death Note '06
Death Note 2: The Last Name '07
Death Note 3: L Change the World '08

Dan O'Bannon (1946-2009)
Dark Star '74
Alien '79
Dead and Buried '81
Blue Thunder '83
Lifeforce '85
Return of the Living Dead '85
Invaders from Mars '86
Total Recall '90
Screamers '96
Bleeders '97
Alien *vs.* Predator '04

Rockne S. O'Bannon (1955-)
Alien Nation '88
Robin Cook's Invasion '97
Fatal Error '99
The Triangle '05

Sean O'Bannon
Invisible Mom '96
Hybrid '97
Mom, Can I Keep Her? '98
Invisible Mom 2 '99
The Kid with the X-Ray Eyes '99
Air Rage '01
Mom's Outta Sight '01
Poison '01

Takeshi Obata
Death Note '06
Death Note 2: The Last Name '07
Death Note 3: L Change the World '08

Margaret Grieco Oberman
Troop Beverly Hills '89
The Man '05
The American Mall '08

Arch Oboler
Escape '40
Five '51
One Plus One '61

Brendan O'Brien
Neighbors '14
Mike and Dave Need Wedding Dates '16
Neighbors 2: Sorority Rising '16
The House '17

Declan O'Brien
Snakeman '05
The Marine 3: Homefront '11
Miami Magma '11
Wrong Turn 4: Bloody Beginnings '11
Joy Ride 3: Road Kill '14

Edna O'Brien (1930-)
Girl with Green Eyes '64
I Was Happy Here '66
X, Y & Zee '72

Jeff O'Brien (1965-)
Blind Heat '00
Insecticidal '05

John O'Brien (1962-)
The Big Dis '89
Cradle 2 the Grave '03
Starsky & Hutch '04

Liam O'Brien (1913-96)
Chain Lightning '50
Young at Heart '54
The Awakening Land '78

Richard O'Brien (1942-)
The Rocky Horror Picture Show '75
Shock Treatment '81

Robert O'Brien (1918-2005)
Lady on a Train '45
The Lemon Drop Kid '51
By the Light of the Silvery Moon '53
Say One for Me '59

Jeffrey Obrow
Bram Stoker's The Mummy '97
They Are Among Us '04

Joey O'Bryan
Full Time Killer '01
Triple Threat '19

Harriet O'Carroll
Aristocrats '99
The Aristocrats '99

Michael O'Connell
Sleep Easy, Hutch Rimes '00
The Living Wake '07

James O'Connolly (1924-87)
Night Caller from Outer Space '66
Tower of Evil '72

Deirdre O'Connor
Five '11
Call Me Crazy '13

Gavin O'Connor
Tumbleweeds '98
Pride and Glory '08
Warrior '11

Tom O'Connor
Fire With Fire '12
The Hitman's Bodyguard '17

John O'Dea (1908-72)
Raiders of the Seven Seas '53
Robbers' Roost '55
Wiretapper '55

David Odell
Cry Uncle '71
Dealing: Or the Berkeley-to-Boston Forty-Brick Lost-Bag Blues '72
The Dark Crystal '82
Supergirl '84
Masters of the Universe '87

Clifford Odets (1906-63)
The General Died at Dawn '36
None But the Lonely Heart '44
Deadline at Dawn '46
Humoresque '46
Sweet Smell of Success '57
Wild in the Country '61

Jerome Odlum (1905-54)
Strange Affair '44
Cover Up '49
The Fast and the Furious '54

Jack O'Donnell
The Gentleman from Arizona '39
Stephen King's The Night Flier '96

Steve Oedekerk (1961-)
Ace Ventura: When Nature Calls '95
Nothing to Lose '96
The Nutty Professor '96
Patch Adams '98
Nutty Professor 2: The Klumps '00
Jimmy Neutron: Boy Genius '01
Kung Pow! Enter the Fist '02
Bruce Almighty '03
Barnyard '06
Evan Almighty '07

Mo Ogrodnik (1966-)
Ripe '97
Uptown Girls '03

Hideo Oguni (1904-96)
Ikiru '52
Seven Samurai '54
I Live in Fear '55
The Lower Depths '57
Throne of Blood '57
The Hidden Fortress '58
The Bad Sleep Well '60
Yojimbo '61
High & Low '62
Sanjuro '62
Dodes 'ka-den '70
Tora! Tora! Tora! '70
Ran '85

Colo Tavernier O'Hagan
A Sunday in the Country '84
The Story of Women '88
Daddy Nostalgia '90
L'Appat '94

James O'Hanlon (1910-69)
Sahara '43
Destination Moon '50
Calamity Jane '53
Revenge of Sartana '65

Tommy O'Haver (1968-2005)
Billy's Hollywood Screen Kiss '98
An American Crime '07

Paul Ohl
Highlander: The Final Dimension '94
North Star '96

Kazuki Ohmori
Godzilla *vs.* Mothra '92
Godzilla *vs.* Destroyah '95

Ataru Oikawa
Tomie '99
The Black House '00

Tetsuya Oishi
Death Note '06
Death Note 2: The Last Name '07
Blade of the Immortal '17

Mark O'Keefe
Bruce Almighty '03
Click '06

Joel Oliansky (1935-2002)
Counterpoint '67
The Todd Killings '71
Bird '88

Deanna Oliver
Casper '95
My Favorite Martian '98

Ron Oliver
Hello Mary Lou: Prom Night 2 '87
Prom Night 3: The Last Kiss '89
Ice Blues: A Donald Strachey Mystery '08

Tracy Oliver
Barbershop: The Next Cut '16
Girls Trip '17
Little '19
The Sun Is Also a Star '19

Hector Olivera (1931-)
Funny, Dirty Little War '83
A Shadow You Soon Will Be '94
The Road '00

Marcello Olivieri
Doc West '09
Triggerman '09

Ermanno Olmi (1931-)
Fiances '63
The Tree of Wooden Clogs '78
Keep Walking '82

Jesus Olmo
28 Weeks Later '07
Cold Skin '18

Arne Olsen
Red Scorpion '89
Cop and a Half '93
All Dogs Go to Heaven 2 '95
Mighty Morphin Power Rangers: The Movie '95
Grizzly Rage '07
Hybrid '07
Distorted '18

Dana Olsen
The 'Burbs '89
George of the Jungle '97

Robert Olsen
Body '15
Don't Kill It '17
Villains '19

David C. Olson
Anaconda 3: The Offspring '08
Anacondas: Trail of Blood '09

Josh Olson
On the Border '98
Infested: Invasion of the Killer Bugs '02
A History of Violence '05

David O'Malley (1944-)
House of the Dead '78
Hangar 18 '80
Kid Colter '85
Easy Wheels '89
Edge of Honor '91
Fatal Instinct '93
Dark Honeymoon '08

Charles 'Blackie' O'Neal (1904-96)
The Seventh Victim '43
Return of the Bad Men '48
Montana '50
Golden Girl '51
Lassie's Great Adventure '62

George O'Neil (1898-1940)
Magnificent Obsession '35
High, Wide and Handsome '37

Robert Vincent O'Neil
Paco '75
Vice Squad '82

Morgan O'Neill
Solo '06
The Factory '10

Suzan-Lori Parks (1963-)
Girl 6 *'96*
Native Son *'19*

Gianfranco Parolini (1930-)
The Old Testament *'62*
Three Avengers *'64*
Kiss Kiss Kill Kill *'66*
Sabata *'69*
Adios, Sabata *'71*
Return of Sabata *'71*

Vincent Paronnaud (1970-)
Persepolis *'07*
Chicken With Plums *'11*

Sara Parriott
Worth Winning *'89*
Three Men and a Little Lady *'90*
The Favor *'92*
Runaway Bride *'99*
The Starter Wife *'07*

Marion Parsonnet (1905-60)
Miracles for Sale *'39*
Those Glamour Girls *'39*
Gallant Sons *'40*
Dangerously We Live *'41*
I'll Be Seeing You *'44*
Gilda *'46*
My Forbidden Past *'51*

Michael Part (1949-)
A Kid in King Arthur's Court *'95*
A Kid in Aladdin's Palace *'97*

Frank Partos (1901-56)
Thirty Day Princess *'34*
The Last Outpost *'35*
Wings in the Dark *'35*
Honolulu *'39*
The Uninvited *'44*
The Snake Pit *'48*

Justin Partridge
Mythica 2: The Darkspore *'15*
Mythica: The Necroromancer *'15*

Ernest Pascal (1896-1966)
Lloyds of London *'36*
Kidnapped *'38*
Hollywood Cavalcade *'39*
Canyon Passage *'46*

Goran Paskalyevic (1947-)
Cabaret Balkan *'98*
How Harry Became a Tree *'01*

Pier Paolo Pasolini (1922-75)
Accatone! *'61*
The Grim Reaper *'62*
Mamma Roma *'62*
The Gospel According to St. Matthew *'64*
Love Meetings *'64*
The Hawks & the Sparrows *'67*
Porcile *'69*
The Decameron *'70*
The Canterbury Tales *'71*
Arabian Nights *'74*
Salo, or the 120 Days of Sodom *'75*

Ivan Passer (1933-2020)
Loves of a Blonde *'65*
The Firemen's Ball *'68*
Born to Win *'71*
Law and Disorder *'74*

Jeremy Passmore
Special *'06*
The Prince *'14*
Vice *'15*

Alex Pastor
Carriers *'09*
Self/Less *'15*

David Pastor
Carriers *'09*
Self/Less *'15*

Michael Pate (1920-2008)
Most Dangerous Man Alive *'61*
Tim *'79*

David Paterson (1966-)
Love, Ludlow *'05*
Bridge to Terabithia *'07*
The Great Gilly Hopkins *'16*

John Patrick (1905-95)
International Settlement *'38*
Enchantment *'48*
Love Is a Many-Splendored Thing *'55*
Daniel Boone: Trail Blazer *'56*
The World of Suzie Wong *'60*

Vincent Patrick
The Pope of Greenwich Village *'84*
Family Business *'89*
The Devil's Own *'96*

Giuseppe Patroni-Griffi (1921-2005)
More Than a Miracle *'67*
Driver's Seat *'73*

Erik Patterson
A Cinderella Story: Once Upon a Song *'11*
Radio Rebel *'12*

John Patus
The Mark 2: Redemption *'13*
Left Behind *'14*

Cinco Paul
Bubble Boy *'01*
The Santa Clause 2 *'02*
Dr. Seuss' Horton Hears a Who! *'08*
Despicable Me *'10*
Hop *'11*
Dr. Seuss' The Lorax *'12*
Despicable Me 2 *'13*
The Secret Life of Pets *'16*
Despicable Me 3 *'17*

Don Michael Paul
Harley Davidson and the Marlboro Man *'91*
Half Past Dead *'02*
Who's Your Caddy? *'07*
Sniper: Legacy *'14*
Beyond Valkyrie: Dawn of the Fourth Reich *'16*

Elliot Paul (1891-1958)
A Woman's Face *'41*
It's a Pleasure *'45*
London Town *'46*
New Orleans *'47*

Jarrad Paul (1976-)
Yes Man *'08*
The D Train *'15*

Steven Paul (1954-)
Baby Geniuses *'98*
Karate Dog *'04*

David Paulsen
The Uranium Conspiracy *'78*
Savage Weekend *'80*

Mark Pavia
Stephen King's The Night Flier *'96*
Fender Bender *'16*

Anna Pavignano
The Postman *'94*
Elsa & Fred *'14*

Michael Pavone
The Reunion *'11*
That's What I Am *'11*

Pawel Pawlikowski (1957-)
My Summer of Love *'05*
The Woman in the Fifth *'11*
Ida *'13*
Cold War *'18*

John Paxton (1911-85)
Murder, My Sweet *'44*
Crossfire *'47*
So Well Remembered *'47*
Rope of Sand *'49*
The Wild One *'54*
Pickup Alley *'57*
On the Beach *'59*

Alexander Payne (1961-)
Citizen Ruth *'96*
Election *'99*
Jurassic Park 3 *'01*
About Schmidt *'02*
Sideways *'04*
Paris, je t'aime *'06*
I Now Pronounce You Chuck and Larry *'07*
The Descendants *'11*
Downsizing *'17*

Don Payne
My Super Ex-Girlfriend *'06*
Fantastic Four: Rise of the Silver Surfer *'07*
Thor *'11*

Keith Payson
Puppet Master 4 *'93*
Puppet Master 5: The Final Chapter *'94*

Steve Peace (1953-)
Return of the Killer Tomatoes! *'88*
Killer Tomatoes Eat France *'91*

Ann Peacock
A Lesson Before Dying *'99*
Cora Unashamed *'00*
In My Country *'04*
The Chronicles of Narnia: The Lion, the Witch and the Wardrobe *'05*
Pictures of Hollis Woods *'07*
Kit Kittredge: An American Girl *'08*
Nights in Rodanthe *'08*
The Killing Room *'09*

Craig Pearce
Strictly Ballroom *'92*
William Shakespeare's Romeo and Juliet *'96*
Moulin Rouge *'01*
Charlie St. Cloud *'10*
The Great Gatsby *'13*

Drew Pearce
Iron Man 3 *'13*
Hotel Artemis *'18*
Fast & Furious Presents: Hobbs & Shaw *'19*

Barry Pearson
Bloody Birthday *'80*
Iron Road *'08*

Ben Pearson
The Second Chance *'06*
Blue Like Jazz *'12*

Humphrey Pearson (1894-1937)
Bright Lights *'30*
Going Wild *'30*
Sunny *'30*

Raoul Peck (1953-)
Lumumba *'01*
Sometimes in April *'05*

Anthony Peckham
Don't Say a Word *'01*
Invictus *'09*
Sherlock Holmes *'09*
The Book of Eli *'10*

Sam Peckinpah (1925-84)
Invasion of the Body Snatchers *'56*
Major Dundee *'65*
Villa Rides *'68*
The Wild Bunch *'69*
Straw Dogs *'72*
Bring Me the Head of Alfredo Garcia *'74*

Jordan Peele (1979-)
Keanu *'16*
Get Out *'17*
Us *'19*

Quinton Peeples
Joyride *'97*
The Circuit *'08*

Bill Peet (1915-2002)
Call of the Yukon *'38*
Fantasia *'40*
Peter Pan *'53*
101 Dalmatians *'61*
The Sword in the Stone *'63*

Simon Pegg (1970-)
Shaun of the Dead *'04*
Hot Fuzz *'07*
Paul *'11*
The World's End *'13*
Star Trek: Beyond *'16*

Pedro Peirano
The Maid *'09*
No *'12*

Kimberly Peirce (1967-)
Boys Don't Cry *'99*
Stop-Loss *'08*

Oren Peli
Paranormal Activity *'09*
Paranormal Activity 3 *'11*
Chernobyl Diaries *'12*
Area 51 *'15*

Louis Pelletier (1907-2000)
Big Red *'62*
Those Calloways *'65*
Follow Me, Boys! *'66*
The Horse in the Gray Flannel Suit *'68*
Smith! *'69*

Joe Penhall
Enduring Love *'04*
The Road *'09*
Hanna *'11*

Sean Penn (1960-)
The Indian Runner *'91*
The Crossing Guard *'94*
Into the Wild *'07*
The Gunman *'15*

Zak Penn (1968-)
P.C.U. *'94*
Inspector Gadget *'99*
Behind Enemy Lines *'01*
Suspect Zero *'04*
Elektra *'05*
X-Men: The Last Stand *'06*
The Incredible Hulk *'08*
The Avengers *'12*
Ready Player One *'18*

Erdman Penner (1905-56)
Pinocchio *'40*
The Adventures of Ichabod and Mr. Toad *'49*
Peter Pan *'53*
Lady and the Tramp *'55*

Jonathan Penner (1962-)
Let the Devil Wear Black *'99*
The Bye Bye Man *'17*

John Penney
Return of the Living Dead 3 *'93*
Matter of Trust *'98*
Contaminated Man *'00*
In Pursuit *'00*
The Enemy *'01*

Phil Penningroth
Silence of the Heart *'84*
Promises to Keep *'85*
In the Line of Duty: Ambush in Waco *'93*

David Peoples (1940-)
Blade Runner *'82*
The Blood of Heroes *'89*
Leviathan *'89*
Hero *'92*
Unforgiven *'92*
Deadfall *'93*
12 Monkeys *'95*
Soldier *'98*

Clare Peploe (1942-)
Zabriskie Point *'70*
High Season *'88*
Rough Magic *'95*
Besieged *'98*
The Triumph of Love *'01*

Mark Peploe (1943-)
Pied Piper *'72*
The Passenger *'75*
The Last Emperor *'87*
High Season *'88*
The Sheltering Sky *'90*
Afraid of the Dark *'92*
Little Buddha *'93*
Victory *'95*

Stacy Peralta (1957-)
Riding Giants *'04*
Lords of Dogtown *'05*

S.J. Perelman (1904-79)
Monkey Business *'31*
Horse Feathers *'32*
Around the World in 80 Days *'56*

Evgenia Peretz
Our Idiot Brother *'11*
Juliet, Naked *'18*

Mark Perez
The Country Bears *'02*
Frank McKlusky, C.I. *'02*
Accepted *'06*
Game Night *'18*

Frank Ray Perilli
The Doberman Gang *'72*
Little Cigars *'73*
Mansion of the Doomed *'76*
Laserblast *'78*
Zoltan. . . Hound of Dracula *'78*
Alligator *'80*

Ivo Perilli (1902-94)
War and Peace *'56*
Barabbas *'62*

Oz (Osgood) Perkins, II (1974-)
Cold Comes the Night *'14*
The Blackcoat's Daughter *'17*

Ted Perkins
Where Truth Lies *'96*
Compadres *'16*

Arnold Perl
Gold for the Caesars *'63*
Malcolm X *'92*

Steven Peros (1966-)
The Cat's Meow *'01*
The Undying *'09*

Jacques Perrin (1941-)
Winged Migration *'01*
Oceans *'09*

Nat Perrin (1905-98)
Duck Soup *'33*
Kid Millions *'34*
Dimples *'36*
New Faces of 1937 *'37*
On Again-Off Again *'37*
The Gracie Allen Murder Case *'39*
Hullabaloo *'40*
Whistling in Dixie *'42*
Swing Fever *'43*
Whistling in Brooklyn *'43*
I'll Take Sweden *'65*

Alex Ross Perry
The Color Wheel *'11*
Listen Up Philip *'14*
Queen of Earth *'15*
Golden Exits *'17*
Christopher Robin *'18*
Nostalgia *'18*
Her Smell *'19*

Eleanor Perry (1914-81)
David and Lisa *'62*
Man Who Loved Cat Dancing *'73*

Fred C. Perry
Zero Boys *'86*
The Wind *'87*

Michael R. Perry
Paranormal Activity 2 *'10*
The Voices *'15*

Nickolas Perry (1967-)
Speedway Junky *'99*
The Hunting of the President *'04*

Tyler Perry (1969-)
Diary of a Mad Black Woman *'05*
Madea's Family Reunion *'06*
Daddy's Little Girls *'07*
Tyler Perry's Why Did I Get Married? *'07*
Tyler Perry's Meet the Browns *'08*
I Can Do Bad All By Myself *'09*
Madea Goes to Jail *'09*
For Colored Girls *'10*
Tyler Perry's Why Did I Get Married Too *'10*
Madea's Big Happy Family *'11*
Madea's Witness Protection *'12*
Tyler Perry's Good Deeds *'12*
Tyler Perry's A Madea Christmas *'13*
Tyler Perry's Temptation: Confessions of a Marriage Counselor *'13*
Tyler Perry's Hell Hath No Fury Like a Woman Scorned: The Play *'14*
Tyler Perry's The Single Moms' Club *'14*
Boo! A Madea Halloween *'16*
Boo 2! A Madea Halloween *'17*
Acrimony *'18*
Nobody's Fool *'18*
A Madea Family Funeral *'19*

Michael Pertwee (1916-91)
Crackerjack *'38*
The Mouse on the Moon *'62*
Ladies Who Do *'63*
Strange Bedfellows *'65*
A Funny Thing Happened on the Way to the Forum *'66*
Salt & Pepper *'68*
One More Time *'70*

Roland Pertwee (1885-1963)
The Ghoul *'34*
King Solomon's Mines *'37*
Non-Stop New York *'37*
The Secret Four *'39*
Madonna of the Seven Moons *'45*
Caravan *'46*
The Magic Bow *'47*

Nicolas Pesce (1990-)
The Eyes of My Mother *'16*
Piercing *'18*

P.J. Pesce (1961-)
The Desperate Trail *'94*
Smokin' Aces 2: Assassins' Ball *'10*

Matthew Peterman (1975-)
Stay Alive *'06*
The Devil Inside *'12*

Charlie Peters
Kiss Me Goodbye *'82*
Blame It on Rio *'84*
Her Alibi *'88*
Hot to Trot! *'88*
Three Men and a Little Lady *'90*
Passed Away *'92*
My Father the Hero *'93*
Music from Another Room *'97*
Krippendorf's Tribe *'98*
My One and Only *'09*
5 Flights Up *'15*

Stephen Peters (1947-)
The Park Is Mine *'85*
Wild Things *'98*

Wolfgang Petersen (1941-)
Das Boot *'81*
The NeverEnding Story *'84*
Shattered *'91*

Bob Peterson (1961-)
Finding Nemo *'03*
Up *'09*
Cars 3 *'17*

Cassandra Peterson (1951-)
Elvira, Mistress of the Dark *'88*
Elvira's Haunted Hills *'02*

Lou Peterson
Take a Giant Step *'59*
In the Blood *'06*

Steven Palmer Peterson
Cop Dog *'08*
Christmas Mail *'10*

Denne Bart Petitclerc (1929-2006)
Islands in the Stream *'77*
Forgotten City *'98*
Papa: Hemingway in Cuba *'16*

Sandro Petraglia (1947-)
The Stolen Children '92
Fiorile '93
The Truce '96
Best of Youth '03
The Girl by the Lake '07
My Brother Is an Only Child '07
Our Life '10

Elio Petri (1929-82)
10th Victim '65
A Quiet Place in the Country '69

Daniel Petrie, Jr. (1952-)
Beverly Hills Cop '84
The Big Easy '87
Shoot to Kill '88
Toy Soldiers '91
In the Army Now '94
Pictures of Hollis Woods '07

Michael Petroni
The Dangerous Lives of Altar Boys '02
Till Human Voices Wake Us '02
Possession '08
The Rite '11
The Book Thief '13
Backtrack '16

Wilfred Pettitt (1910-48)
The Bandit of Sherwood Forest '46
The Swordsman '47

Pamela Pettler
Tim Burton's Corpse Bride '05
Monster House '06
9 '09
The Addams Family '19

J.T. Petty
Soft for Digging '01
Mimic 3: Sentinel '03

Christian Petzold
Yella '07
Phoenix '14
Jerichow '15
Transit '18

Julie Peyr
Four Lovers '10
Jimmy P. '13
My Golden Days '15

Harley Peyton
Less Than Zero '87
Heaven's Prisoners '95
Keys to Tulsa '96
Elmore Leonard's Gold Coast '97
Bandits '01

Chuck Pfarrer
Darkman '90
Hard Target '93
Darkman 2: The Return of Durant '94
Barb Wire '96
The Jackal '97
Virus '98
Red Planet '00

Anna Hamilton Phelan
Mask '85
Gorillas in the Mist '88
In Love and War '96
Girl, Interrupted '99
Amelia '09

Sarah Phelps
Oliver Twist '07
Great Expectations '11

Bill (William) Phillips (1908-57)
Christine '84
Fire with Fire '86
Physical Evidence '89
El Diablo '90

Glasgow Phillips
Undead or Alive '07
Smiley '12

Jeff Phillips
3 Ninjas: High Noon at Mega Mountain '97
Treehouse Hostage '99
I Downloaded a Ghost '04
Space Warriors '13

Patrick Phillips
Interceptor Force 2 '02
Dragon Storm '04
Good People, Bad Things '08

Todd Phillips (1970-)
Road Trip '00
Old School '03
Starsky & Hutch '04
School for Scoundrels '06
Due Date '10
The Hangover, Part 2 '11
The Hangover, Part III '13
War Dogs '16
Joker '19

Robert Phippeny
The Night of the Following Day '69
Simon, King of the Witches '71

Nicholas Phipps (1913-80)
Spring in Park Lane '48
Madeleine '50
Appointment With Venus '51
Captain's Paradise '53
I'll Get You '53
The Lady Is a Square '58
Doctor in Love '60

Maurice Pialat (1925-2003)
Loulou '80
A Nos Amours '84
Van Gogh '92

Fabio Piccioni
Thor and the Amazon Women '60
Cjamango '67

Giuseppe Piccioni (1953-)
Not of This World '99
Light of My Eyes '01
Giulia Doesn't Date at Night '09

Francesco Piccolo (1964-)
Days and Clouds '07
Quiet Chaos '08
Mia Madre '16
The Leisure Seeker '17

Robbie Pickering
Natural Selection '11
Natural Selection '12
The Book of Love '16

Darci Picoult
Mother of George '13
Where Is Kyra? '17

Jim Piddock (1956-)
Traces of Red '92
One Good Turn '95
The Man '05
Mascots '16

John Pielmeier
Agnes of God '85
The Shell Seekers '89
Acts of Contrition '95
Flowers for Algernon '00
Dodson's Journey '01
Sins of the Father '01
Talking to Heaven '02
Hitler: The Rise of Evil '03
The Capture of the Green River Killer '08
The Memory Keeper's Daughter '08
Gifted Hands: The Ben Carson Story '09
Patricia Cornwell's At Risk '10
Patricia Cornwell's The Front '10
Pillars of the Earth '10

Arthur C. Pierce (1923-87)
The Cosmic Man '59
Invasion of the Animal People '62
Destination Inner Space '66
The Invisible Strangler '76

Charles B. Pierce (1938-)
Grayeagle '77
Boggy Creek II '83
Sacred Ground '83

Shirley Pierce
Incognito '99
For Real '02

Frank Pierson (1925-2012)
Cat Ballou '65
Cool Hand Luke '67
The Looking Glass War '69
The Anderson Tapes '71
Dog Day Afternoon '75
A Star Is Born '76
King of the Gypsies '78
In Country '89
Presumed Innocent '90

Krzysztof Piesiewicz (1945-)
No End '84
The Decalogue '88
The Double Life of Veronique '91
Trois Couleurs: Bleu '93
Trois Couleurs: Blanc '94
Trois Couleurs: Rouge '94
Heaven '01

Tseng Pik-Yin
The Bride with White Hair '93
Iron Monkey '93

Jeremy Pikser
The Lemon Sisters '90
Bulworth '98
War, Inc. '08

Vlady Pildysh
Alien Agent '07
The Frankenstein Theory '13

Nicholas Pileggi (1933-)
Goodfellas '90
Casino '95
City Hall '95
Kings of South Beach '07

Michael Piller (1948-2005)
Star Trek: Insurrection '98
The Dead Zone '02

Drew Pillsbury
100 Mile Rule '02
About Fifty '11

Tullio Pinelli (1908-)
Variety Lights '51
The White Sheik '52
La Strada '54
Il Bidone '55
Nights of Cabiria '57
La Dolce Vita '60
Boccaccio '70 '62
8 1/2 '63
Juliet of the Spirits '65
Ginger & Fred '86

Sidney W. Pink (1916-2002)
The Angry Red Planet '59
Journey to the Seventh Planet '62
Reptilicus '62
The Castilian '63

Steve Pink (1966-)
Grosse Pointe Blank '97
High Fidelity '00

Jeff Pinkner
The Amazing Spider-Man 2 '14
The 5th Wave '16
The Dark Tower '17
Jumanji: Welcome to the Jungle '17
Venom '18
Jumanji: The Next Level '19

Harold Pinter (1930-2008)
The Servant '63
The Pumpkin Eater '64
The Quiller Memorandum '66
Accident '67
The Go-Between '71
The Homecoming '73
The Last Tycoon '76
The French Lieutenant's Woman '81
The Handmaid's Tale '90
The Comfort of Strangers '91
The Heat of the Day '91
The Trial '93
Sleuth '07

Bret Piper
A Nymphoid Barbarian in Dinosaur Hell '94

Arachnia '03
Screaming Dead '03

David Pirie (1953-)
The Woman in White '97
Dr. Bell and Mr. Doyle: The Dark Beginnings of Sherlock Holmes '00
The Wyvern Mystery '00
Murderland '09

Robert Pirosh (1910-89)
A Day at the Races '37
Up in Arms '44
Battleground '49
Go for Broke! '51
Hell Is for Heroes '62

Mark Pirro (1956-)
Curse of the Queerwolf '87
Deathrow Gameshow '88
My Mom's a Werewolf '89

Glen Pitre
Belizaire the Cajun '86
The Home Front '02
The Man Who Came Back '08

Montgomery Pittman
Tarzan's Hidden Jungle '55
Tarzan and the Lost Safari '57

Angelo Pizzo
Hoosiers '86
Rudy '93
The Game of Their Lives '05
My All American '15

Alan Plater (1935-)
The Virgin and the Gypsy '70
Priest of Love '81
The Inside Man '84
Coming Through '85
Fortunes of War '87
A Very British Coup '88
A Merry War '97
The Last of the Blonde Bombshells '00
Joe Maddison's War '10

Polly Platt (1939-2011)
Pretty Baby '78
A Map of the World '99

Paco Plaza
[Rec] '07
[Rec] 2 '09
[REC] 3: Genesis '12

George Plympton (1889-1972)
Battling with Buffalo Bill '31
The Spider's Web '38
The Green Hornet '39
Flash Gordon Conquers the Universe '40
Junior G-Men '40
Gang Busters '42
Junior G-Men of the Air '42

Amos Poe
The Foreigner '78
Alphabet City '84
Rocket Gibraltar '88
Frogs for Snakes '98
The Guitar '08

James Poe (1921-80)
Paula '52
Scandal Sheet '52
Around the World in 80 Days '56
Attack! '56
Cat on a Hot Tin Roof '58
Lilies of the Field '63
Toys in the Attic '63
Riot '69
They Shoot Horses, Don't They? '69
The Nightman '93

S. Lee Pogostin (1926-)
Synanon '65
Hard Contract '69
Nightmare Honeymoon '73
Golden Needles '74

Charles Edward Pogue
The Hound of the Baskervilles '83
The Sign of Four '83
The Fly '86

Psycho 3 '86
D.O.A. '88
Hands of a Murderer '90
Dragonheart '96
Kull the Conqueror '97

John Pogue
U.S. Marshals '98
The Skulls '00
Ghost Ship '02
Rollerball '02
The Quiet Ones '14

Jean-Marie Poire (1945-)
The Visitors '95
Just Visiting '01

Gregory Poirier (1961-)
Rosewood '96
Gossip '99
Tomcats '01
A Sound of Thunder '05

Mark Jude Poirier
Smart People '08
Goats '12
Hateship Loveship '13

Roman Polanski (1933-)
Knife in the Water '62
Repulsion '65
Cul de Sac '66
The Fearless Vampire Killers '67
Rosemary's Baby '68
Macbeth '71
The Tenant '76
Tess '79
Frantic '88
Bitter Moon '92
The Ninth Gate '99
The Ghost Writer '10
Carnage '11
Venus in Fur '13

Stephen Poliakoff (1952-)
Close My Eyes '91
Shooting the Past '99
Almost Strangers '01
Friends & Crocodiles '05
Gideon's Daughter '05
Glorious 39 '09

Mark Polish (1970-)
Twin Falls Idaho '99
Jackpot '01
Northfork '03
The Astronaut Farmer '07
The Smell of Success '09
Stay Cool '09

Michael Polish (1970-)
Twin Falls Idaho '99
Jackpot '01
Northfork '03
The Astronaut Farmer '07
The Smell of Success '09
Big Sur '13
90 Minutes in Heaven '15

Patrik-Ian Polk
Noah's Arc: Jumping the Broom '08
Blackbird '14

Jack Pollexfen (1908-2003)
The Man from Planet X '51
1,000 Years From Now '52
Captain Kidd and the Slave Girl '54
Return to Treasure Island '54
The Daughter of Dr. Jekyll '57
The Atomic Brain '64

Sarah Polley (1979-)
Away From Her '06
Take This Waltz '11

Gene Pollock
Incredibly Strange Creatures Who Stopped Living and Became Mixed-Up Zombies '63
The Thrill Killers '65

Vicki Polon
Girlfriends '78
Mr. Wonderful '93

Mark Alan Polonia (1968-)
Feeders '96
Terror House '97

Abraham Polonsky (1910-99)
Body and Soul '47
Golden Earrings '47
Force of Evil '49
I Can Get It For You Wholesale '51
Odds Against Tomorrow '59
Madigan '68
Tell Them Willie Boy Is Here '69
Avalanche Express '79
Monsignor '82

Abe Polsky
Rebel Rousers '69
The Baby '72

Barry Poltermann (1964-)
The Unearthing '93
Aswang '03

Darryl Ponicsan
Cinderella Liberty '73
Taps '81
Vision Quest '85
Nuts '87
The Boost '88
School Ties '92
The Enemy Within '94

Ventura Pons (1945-)
What It's All About '95
Caresses '97
To Die, Or Not '99
Food of Love '02

James Ponsoldt (1978-)
Smashed '12
The Circle '17

Gillo Pontecorvo (1919-2006)
The Wide Blue Road '57
Kapo '59
The Battle of Algiers '66

Federica Pontremoli
Days and Clouds '07
Giulia Doesn't Date at Night '09

DJ Pooh
Friday '95
Three Strikes '00
The Wash '01

Robert Roy Pool
Big Town '87
Outbreak '94

Duane Poole
One Christmas '95
I've Been Waiting for You '98
Shattered Image '98
A Deadly Encounter '04
Honeymoon with Mom '06
Moonlight & Mistletoe '08
7 Things to Do Before I'm 30 '08

Marty Poole
Diamond Run '96
Reptilian '99

Aaron Pope
Vampire Clan '02
Rampage: The Hillside Strangler Murders '04
Pandemic '09
The Gold Retrievers '10

Elaine Pope
These Old Broads '01
Alfie '04

Jeff Pope
Fool's Gold: The Story of the Brink's-Mat Robbery '92
The Magician '93
Essex Boys '99
Philomena '13
Stan & Ollie '18

Tom Pope
Don't Look in the Basement '73
The Manitou '78
Cold Dog Soup '89

Eric Poppen
Virtual Assassin '95
Borderland '07

Gregory Poppen (1963-)
Boys Will Be Boys '97
Superbabies: Baby Geniuses 2 '04

Natalie Portman (1981-)
New York, I Love You '09
A Tale of Love and Darkness '16

Todd Portugal
Flooding '97
The Legend of Bloody Jack '07

Joel Posner
Last Breath '96
The Next Big Thing '02

P.J. Posner
Last Breath '96
The Next Big Thing '02

Dennis Potter (1935-94)
Pennies from Heaven '81
Brimstone & Treacle '82
Gorky Park '83
Dreamchild '85
Track 29 '88
Christabel '89
Mesmer '94
The Singing Detective '03

Sally Potter (1947-)
Orlando '92
The Tango Lesson '97
The Man Who Cried '00
Ginger & Rosa '13
The Party '17

Michael Powell (1905-90)
Perfect Understanding '33
Red Ensign '34
Edge of the World '37
Contraband '40
One of Our Aircraft Is Missing '41
A Canterbury Tale '44
I Know Where I'm Going '45
Stairway to Heaven '46
Black Narcissus '47
The Red Shoes '48
Ill Met By Moonlight '57

Donna Powers
Deep Blue Sea '99
Skeletons in the Closet '00
Valentine '01
The Italian Job '03
Out of Order '03

Wayne Powers
Deep Blue Sea '99
Skeletons in the Closet '00
Valentine '01
The Italian Job '03
Out of Order '03

Bryan Poyser
Lovers of Hate '10
Love & Air Sex '14

Manuel Pradal (1968-)
Ginostra '02
A Crime '06

Tim Prager
Haunted '95
Heat of the Sun '99
Vendetta '99
Quicksand '01

Leonard Praskins (1896-1968)
Emma '32
Flesh '32
The Call of the Wild '35
One in a Million '36
Ice Follies of 1939 '39
So This Is Washington '43
Mr. Scoutmaster '53

Dennis A. Pratt
Leprechaun 4: In Space '96
Britannic '00
Depth Charge '08
The Storm '09

John Prebble (1915-2001)
Mysterious Island '61
Zulu '64
Elizabeth R '72

Jose Prendes
Countdown: Jerusalem '09
The Terminators '09
Hansel & Gretel '13

David Prentiss
Alien Massacre '67
Gallery of Horrors '67

Robert Presnell, Jr. (1914-86)
Man in the Attic '53
Screaming Eagles '56
Conspiracy of Hearts '60
13 West Street '62
The Third Day '65

Robert Presnell, Sr. (1894-1969)
What Price Hollywood? '32
Bureau of Missing Persons '33
Employees' Entrance '33
The Kennel Murder Case '33
The Real Glory '39
They Shall Have Music '39
Meet John Doe '41
For You I Die '47

Emeric Pressburger (1902-88)
The Forty-Ninth Parallel '41
One of Our Aircraft Is Missing '41
A Canterbury Tale '44
I Know Where I'm Going '45
Stairway to Heaven '46
Black Narcissus '47
The Red Shoes '48
Ill Met By Moonlight '57
Operation Crossbow '65

Steven Pressfield (1943-)
King Kong Lives '86
Above the Law '88
Freejack '92
Army of One '94
Separate Lives '94

Jason Preston
The Utopian Society '03
Trapped '06

Richard Preston, Jr.
Cyber-Tracker 2 '95
Little Bigfoot '96
The Silencers '96
Recoil '97
The Sender '98
Firetrap '01
Final Move '06

Trevor Preston
Thicker Than Water '93
I'll Sleep When I'm Dead '03

Jacques Prevert (1900-77)
The Crime of Monsieur Lange '36
Bizarre Bizarre '39
Children of Paradise '44
The Hunchback of Notre Dame '57

Eugene Price
Corky '72
Concrete Cowboys '79

Jeffrey Price (1949-)
Trenchcoat '83
Who Framed Roger Rabbit '88
Doc Hollywood '91
Wild Wild West '99
Dr. Seuss' How the Grinch Stole Christmas '00
Last Holiday '06
Shrek the Third '07

Kathryn Price
The Game Plan '07
Fallen '17

Richard Price (1949-)
The Color of Money '86
New York Stories '89
Sea of Love '89
Night and the City '92
Mad Dog and Glory '93
Kiss of Death '94
Clockers '95
Ransom '96
Shaft '00
Freedomland '06
Child 44 '15

Tim Rose Price
Dark Obsession '90
A Dangerous Man: Lawrence after Arabia '91
Rapa Nui '93
The Serpent's Kiss '97

Adam Prince
Red Sky '14
Junglee '19

Peter Prince
The Hit '85
Waterland '92

Gina Prince-Bythewood (1969-)
Love and Basketball '00
The Secret Life of Bees '08
Beyond the Lights '14

David A. Prior
Sledgehammer '83
Future Force '89
Raw Nerve '91
Mardi Gras for the Devil '93
Raw Justice '93
Felony '95

David Pritchard
Slashed Dreams '74
Violent Zone '89

Pat Proft (1947-)
Bachelor Party '84
Police Academy '84
Moving Violations '85
Real Genius '85
Lucky Stiff '88
The Naked Gun: From the Files of Police Squad '88
Hot Shots! '91
Naked Gun 2 1/2: The Smell of Fear '91
Brain Donors '92
Hot Shots! Part Deux '93
Naked Gun 33 1/3: The Final Insult '94
High School High '96
Mr. Magoo '97
Wrongfully Accused '98
Scary Movie 3 '03
Scary Movie 5 '13

Biagio Proietti (1940-)
Taste of Death '68
The Black Cat '81

Chip Proser
Iceman '84
Innerspace '87

Giorgio Prosperi
The Seven Hills of Rome '58
The Old Testament '62

Mark Protosevich (1961-)
The Cell '00
Poseidon '06
I Am Legend '07
Oldboy '13

Martin Provost
Seraphine '08
The Midwife '17

Alex Proyas (1965-)
Dark City '97
Garage Days '03

Kelli Pryor
More of Me '07
A Stranger's Heart '07
Secret Lives of Second Wives '08
Hostile Makeover '09
Smart Cookies '13

Richard Pryor (1940-2005)
Blazing Saddles '74
Bustin' Loose '81
Jo Jo Dancer, Your Life Is Calling '86

Luis Puenzo (1946-)
The Official Story '85
Old Gringo '89

Frank Pugliese
Shot in the Heart '01
Undefeated '03

Cristi Puiu (1967-)
The Death of Mr. Lazarescu '05
Aurora '10

Robert Pulcini (1964-)
American Splendor '03
The Extra Man '10
Ten Thousand Saints '15

Jack Pulman (1925-79)
Portrait of a Lady '67
The Golden Bowl '72
War and Peace '73
Poldark '75

Daniella Purcell
Midnight Tease '94
The Wasp Woman '96
Spacejacked '98

Gertrude Purcell (1895-1963)
No More Orchids '32
If You Could Only Cook '36
Destry Rides Again '39
The Invisible Woman '40
One Night in the Tropics '40

Charles Purpura (1945-2005)
Heaven Help Us '85
Satisfaction '88

David Pursall (1917-86)
Murder She Said '61
Kill or Cure '62
The Longest Day '62
The Alphabet Murders '65
The Blue Max '66
The Southern Star '69

Neal Purvis (1961-)
Let Him Have It '91
Plunkett & Macleane '98
The World Is Not Enough '99
Die Another Day '02
Johnny English '03
Convicted '04
Stoned '05
Casino Royale '06
Quantum of Solace '08
Skyfall '12
Spectre '15

Nick Pustav
Camille '07
Ramona and Beezus '10

Mario Puzo (1920-99)
The Godfather '72
Earthquake '74
The Godfather, Part 2 '74
Superman: The Movie '78
Superman 2 '80
The Cotton Club '84
The Godfather, Part 3 '90

Daniel Pyne (1955-)
Pacific Heights '90
Doc Hollywood '91
The Hard Way '91
White Sands '92
Where's Marlowe? '98
The Sum of All Fears '02
The Manchurian Candidate '04
Fracture '07
Backstabbing for Beginners '18

Albert Pyun (1954-)
Sword & the Sorcerer '82
Alien from L.A. '87
Adrenalin: Fear the Rush '96
Nemesis 4: Cry of Angels '97

John Quaintance
Aquamarine '06
Material Girls '06
Hot Pursuit '15

Paris Qualles
Blood Brothers '93
The Inkwell '94
The Tuskegee Airmen '95
The Rosa Parks Story '02
A Raisin in the Sun '08

Darryl Quarles (1954-)
Big Momma's House '00
Black Knight '01

Jonas Quastel
Sasquatch '02
Forced to Fight '11

Stephen Quay (1947-)
Institue Benjamenta or This Dream People Call Human Life '95
Piano Tuner of Earthquakes '05

Timothy Quay (1947-)
Institue Benjamenta or This Dream People Call Human Life '95
Piano Tuner of Earthquakes '05

Ben Queen
Proximity '00
Cars 2 '11

Pascal Quignard
Tous les Matins du Monde '92
A Pure Formality '94

Richard Quine (1920-89)
All Ashore '53
Drive a Crooked Road '54
My Sister Eileen '55

Paul Quinn
This Is My Father '99
Growing Up Smith '17

Gene Quintano (1946-)
Making the Grade '84
King Solomon's Mines '85
Allan Quatermain and the Lost City of Gold '86
Police Academy 3: Back in Training '86
Police Academy 4: Citizens on Patrol '87
National Lampoon's Loaded Weapon 1 '93
Operation Dumbo Drop '95
Sudden Death '95
Dollar for the Dead '98
Outlaw Justice '98
The Musketeer '01

Eduardo Quiroz
I Got Five on It '05
The Damned '06
Illegal Business '06
San Franpsycho '06

Jose Quiroz (1972-)
I Got Five on It '05
The Damned '06
Illegal Business '06
San Franpsycho '06

David Rabe (1940-)
I'm Dancing as Fast as I Can '82
Streamers '83
Casualties of War '89
Hurlyburly '98

Martin Rackin (1918-76)
Fighter Squadron '48
Race Street '48
A Dangerous Profession '49
Three Secrets '50
The Enforcer '51
The Stooge '51
Loan Shark '52
Sailor Beware '52
The Clown '53
The Great Diamond Robbery '53
Long John Silver '54
Santiago '56
The Horse Soldiers '59
Revak the Rebel '60

Michael Radford (1946-)
White Mischief '88
The Postman '94
Dancing at the Blue Iguana '00
The Merchant of Venice '04
Elsa & Fred '14

Vivienne Radkoff
Tempted '03
Living Proof '08

Josh Radnor (1974-)
Happythankyoumoreplease '10
Liberal Arts '12

Edward A. Radtke (1962-)
The Dream Catcher '99
A Loving Father '02

Bob Rafelson (1933-)
Head '68
Five Easy Pieces '70
Stay Hungry '76
Mountains of the Moon '90
Tales of Erotica '93

Gideon Raff
The Killing Floor '06
Train '08

Stewart Raffill (1945-)
Napoleon and Samantha '72
Across the Great Divide '76
The Adventures of the Wilderness Family '76
Sea Gypsies '78
High Risk '81
Ice Pirates '84
Mac and Me '88

John Raffo
Dragon: The Bruce Lee Story '93
The Relic '96
Johnny Skidmarks '97

Martin Ragaway (1923-89)
Abbott and Costello in the Foreign Legion '50
Ma and Pa Kettle Go to Town '50
Lost in Alaska '52

Philip Railsback
The Stars Fell on Henrietta '94
Flash of Genius '08

Ivan Raimi (1956-)
Easy Wheels '89
Darkman '90
Army of Darkness '92
Spider-Man 3 '07
Drag Me to Hell '09

Sam Raimi (1959-)
Evil Dead '83
Evil Dead 2: Dead by Dawn '87
Darkman '90
Army of Darkness '92
The Hudsucker Proxy '93
The Nutt House '95
Spider-Man 3 '07
Drag Me to Hell '09

Norman Reilly Raine (1894-1971)
The Life of Emile Zola '37
The Adventures of Robin Hood '38
Each Dawn I Die '39
The Fighting 69th '40
Captains of the Clouds '42
Captain Kidd '45
Nob Hill '45

Frank Rainone
Me and the Mob '94
A Brooklyn State of Mind '97

Ron Raley
Edge of Sanity '89
Cupid & Cate '00
The Runaway '00
The Locket '02

Rick Ramage
The Proposition '97
Stigmata '99

Hans Rameau (1901-80)
Waterloo Bridge '40
We Were Dancing '42

Harold Ramis (1944-2014)
National Lampoon's Animal House '78
Meatballs '79
Caddyshack '80
Stripes '81
National Lampoon's Vacation '83
Ghostbusters '84
Armed and Dangerous '86
Back to School '86
Club Paradise '86
Caddyshack 2 '88
Ghostbusters 2 '89
Rover Dangerfield '91

Groundhog Day *'93*
Multiplicity *'96*
Analyze This *'98*
Bedazzled *'00*
Analyze That *'02*
Year One *'09*

Lynne Ramsay (1969-)
Ratcatcher *'99*
Morvern Callar *'02*
You Were Never Really Here *'17*

Robert Ramsey (1962-)
Life *'99*
Big Trouble *'02*
Intolerable Cruelty *'03*
Man of the House *'05*
Soul Men *'08*

Alex Ranarivelo
Born 2 Race *'11*
Bennett's War *'19*

Cathy Randall
Hey Hey It's Esther Blueberger *'08*
Return to Nim's Island *'13*

Charles Randolph
The Life of David Gale *'03*
The Interpreter *'05*
Love and Other Drugs *'10*
The Big Short *'15*
Bombshell *'19*

Joe Ranft (1960-2005)
The Rescuers Down Under *'90*
A Bug's Life *'98*
Cars *'06*

Caleb Ranson
Take Me *'01*
Me & Mrs. Jones *'02*
First Light *'10*

Frederic Raphael (1931-)
Darling *'65*
Far from the Madding Crowd *'67*
Two for the Road *'67*
A Severed Head *'70*
Daisy Miller *'74*
Rogue Male *'76*
The King's Whore *'90*
Coast to Coast *'04*

June Diane Raphael (1980-)
Bride Wars *'09*
Ass Backwards *'13*

Samson Raphaelson (1894-1983)
The Smiling Lieutenant *'31*
One Hour with You *'32*
Trouble in Paradise *'32*
Angel *'37*
The Shop Around the Corner *'40*

Anne Rapp
Cookie's Fortune *'99*
Dr. T & the Women *'00*

Philip Rapp (1907-96)
Wonder Man *'45*
The Secret Life of Walter Mitty *'47*
The Inspector General *'49*

Ezra D. Rappaport
Deja Vu *'84*
Harry and the Hendersons *'87*

Mark Rappaport
From the Journals of Jean Seberg *'95*
Uncaged *'16*

Jean-Paul Rappeneau (1932-)
Lovers Like Us *'75*
The Savage *'75*
Cyrano de Bergerac *'90*
The Horseman on the Roof *'95*
Bon Voyage *'03*

Judith Rascoe (1941-)
Road Movie *'72*
Who'll Stop the Rain? *'78*
Endless Love *'81*
Eat a Bowl of Tea *'89*
Havana *'90*

Jim Rash
The Descendants *'11*
The Way Way Back *'13*
Downhill *'20*

Michael Rasmussen (1974-)
The Ward *'10*
Crawl *'19*

Shawn Rasmussen
The Ward *'10*
Crawl *'19*

Tim Rasmussen
License to Wed *'07*
Marmaduke *'10*

Harry Ratchford
Kevin Hart: What Now? *'16*
Night School *'18*

George Ratliff
Joshua *'07*
Salvation Boulevard *'11*

Terence Rattigan (1911-77)
The Way to the Stars *'45*
The Winslow Boy *'48*
The Sound Barrier *'52*
The Prince and the Showgirl *'57*
The V.I.P.'s *'63*
The Yellow Rolls Royce *'64*

Michael Rauch
Stalker *'98*
In the Weeds *'00*

Herman Raucher (1928-)
Sweet November *'68*
Watermelon Man *'70*
Summer of '42 *'71*

Stanley Rauh
Michael Shayne: Private Detective *'40*
Sleepers West *'41*

Irving Ravetch (1920-)
Living In a Big Way *'47*
The Outriders *'50*
Vengeance Valley *'51*
Ten Wanted Men *'54*
The Long, Hot Summer *'58*
Home from the Hill *'60*
Hud *'63*
Hombre *'67*
The Reivers *'69*
The Carey Treatment *'72*
The Cowboys *'72*
The Spikes Gang *'74*
Norma Rae *'79*
Murphy's Romance *'85*
Stanley and Iris *'90*

Rand Ravich
Candyman 2: Farewell to the Flesh *'94*
The Maker *'98*
The Astronaut's Wife *'99*

A.R. Rawlinson (1894-1984)
The Man Who Knew Too Much *'34*
Ticket of Leave Man *'37*
Crackerjack *'38*
The Hooded Terror *'38*
Gaslight *'40*

Billy Ray
Color of Night *'94*
Hidden Assassin *'94*
Volcano *'97*
Legalese *'98*
Hart's War *'02*
Shattered Glass *'03*
Suspect Zero *'04*
Flightplan *'05*
Breach *'07*
State of Play *'09*
The Hunger Games *'12*
Captain Phillips *'13*
Secret in Their Eyes *'15*
Overlord *'18*
Gemini Man *'19*
Richard Jewell *'19*
Terminator: Dark Fate *'19*

David Ray (1968-)
Ice Quake *'10*
Mandrake *'10*
Seattle Superstorm *'12*
Super Storm *'12*
End of the World *'13*

Fred Olen Ray (1954-)
Alien Dead *'79*
Phantom Empire *'87*
Hollywood Chainsaw Hookers *'88*
Bad Girls from Mars *'90*
Haunting Fear *'91*
American Bandits: Frank and Jesse James *'10*
Turbulent Skies *'10*
Collision Course *'12*
Sniper: Special Ops *'16*

Nicholas Ray (1911-79)
They Live by Night *'49*
Bitter Victory *'58*
We Can't Go Home Again *'73*

Satyajit Ray (1921-92)
Pather Panchali *'54*
Aparajito *'58*
Jalsaghar *'58*
The World of Apu *'59*
Devi *'60*
Charulata *'64*

David Rayfiel (1923-2011)
Castle Keep *'69*
Valdez Is Coming *'71*
Three Days of the Condor *'75*
Lipstick *'76*
Death Watch *'80*
Round Midnight *'86*
Havana *'90*
The Firm *'93*
Intersection *'93*
Sabrina *'95*

Ed Raymond (1954-)
See Fred Olen Ray

Jonathan Raymond
Old Joy *'06*
Wendy and Lucy *'08*
Meek's Cutoff *'10*
Night Moves *'13*
First Cow *'20*

William Raynor (1920-94)
Francis in the Haunted House *'56*
The Kettles on Old MacDonald's Farm *'57*

Patrick Rea
The Empty Acre *'07*
The Invoking 2 *'15*

Jan Read (1917-)
The Haunted Strangler *'58*
Jason and the Argonauts *'63*
First Men in the Moon *'64*

Simon Reade
Private Peaceful *'12*
Journey's End *'18*

Jim Reardon
WALL-E *'08*
Zootopia *'16*
Ralph Breaks the Internet *'18*

Michael Reaves (1950-)
Batman: Mask of the Phantasm *'93*
Gargoyles, The Movie: The Heroes Awaken *'94*

Theresa Rebeck
Harriet the Spy *'96*
Gossip *'99*

Paulo Rebelo
O Fantasma *'00*
Two Drifters *'05*

Eric Red (1961-)
The Hitcher *'86*
Near Dark *'87*
Cohen and Tate *'88*
Blue Steel *'90*
Body Parts *'91*
The Last Outlaw *'93*
Bad Moon *'96*
100 Feet *'08*

Jeffrey Reddick
Final Destination *'00*
Return to Cabin by the Lake *'01*
Tamara *'05*

James Redford (1962-)
Cowboy Up *'00*
Skinwalker *'02*
Spin *'04*

Robert Redlin
After Dark, My Sweet *'90*
Bare Knuckles *'10*

David Reed
Lake Placid 3 *'10*
Lake Placid: The Final Chapter *'12*
Company of Heroes *'13*

Joel M. Reed (1933-2020)
Bloodsucking Freaks *'75*
Night of the Zombies *'81*

Luther Reed (1888-1961)
Little Old New York *'23*
Rio Rita *'29*

Tom Reed (1901-61)
Hell's Heroes *'30*
S.O.S. Iceberg *'33*
Bombay Mail *'34*
The Man with Two Faces *'34*
The Case of the Curious Bride *'35*
The Great O'Malley *'36*
Pittsburgh *'42*
David Harding, Counterspy *'50*
Back to God's Country *'53*

Calvin Reeder
My Effortless Brilliance *'08*
The Rambler *'13*

Dee Rees
Pariah *'11*
Mudbound *'17*

Rhett Reese
Clifford's Really Big Movie *'04*
Cruel Intentions 3 *'04*
Zombieland *'09*
G.I. Joe: Retaliation *'13*
Deadpool *'16*
Life *'17*
Deadpool 2 *'18*
6 Underground *'19*
Zombieland: Double Tap *'19*

Tom Reeve
Retrograde *'03*
George and the Dragon *'04*

Matt Reeves (1966-)
The Pallbearer *'95*
The Yards *'00*
Let Me In *'10*
War for the Planet of the Apes *'17*

Michael Reeves (1944-69)
The She-Beast *'65*
The Sorcerers *'67*
The Conqueror Worm *'68*

Theodore Reeves (1910-73)
Internes Can't Take Money *'37*
National Velvet *'44*
The Doctor and the Girl *'49*

Garfield Reeves-Stevens
My Teacher Ate My Homework *'98*
Fire Serpent *'07*

Judith Reeves-Stevens
My Teacher Ate My Homework *'98*
Fire Serpent *'07*

Nicolas Winding Refn (1970-)
Pusher *'96*
Fear X *'03*
Bronson *'09*
Valhalla Rising *'09*
Only God Forgives *'13*
The Neon Demon *'16*

Brian Regan
102 Dalmatians *'00*
How to Lose a Guy in 10 Days *'03*

Godfrey Reggio (1940-)
Koyaanisqatsi *'83*
Visitors *'13*

Piero Regnoli (1921-2001)
I, Vampiri *'56*
The Hills Run Red *'67*
City of the Walking Dead *'80*
Demonia *'90*
Voices from Beyond *'90*

Frank Rehwaldt
The Fiance *'96*
The Night Caller *'97*
The Landlady *'98*
The Perfect Wife *'00*

Kelly Reichardt
River of Grass *'94*
Old Joy *'06*
Wendy and Lucy *'08*
Night Moves *'13*
Certain Women *'16*
First Cow *'20*

Dorothy Davenport Reid (1895-1977)
Prison Break *'38*
Tomboy *'40*
Impact *'49*
Rhubarb *'51*
Footsteps in the Fog *'55*

J. Reifel
The House on Tombstone Hill *'92*
Convict 762 *'98*

Ethan Reiff (1965-)
Men of War *'94*
Tales from the Crypt Presents Demon Knight *'94*
Josh Kirby. . .Time Warrior: Chapter 1, Planet of the Dino-Knights *'95*
Josh Kirby. . . Time Warrior: Chapter 2, The Human Pets *'95*
Josh Kirby. . . Time Warrior: Chapter 5, Journey to the Magic Cavern *'96*
Josh Kirby. . . Time Warrior: Chapter 6, Last Battle for the Universe *'96*
Bulletproof Monk *'03*
Sleeper Cell *'05*

William Reilly
Men of Respect *'91*
Mortal Thoughts *'91*

Carl Reiner (1922-2020)
The Thrill of It All! *'63*
The Comic *'69*
Dead Men Don't Wear Plaid *'82*
The Man with Two Brains *'83*
Bert Rigby, You're a Fool *'89*

Ivan Reiner (1911-97)
The War of the Planets *'65*
The Snow Devils *'67*
The Green Slime *'68*

Jeff Reiner
Blood & Concrete: A Love Story *'91*
Smalltime *'96*

Rob Reiner (1947-)
More Than Friends *'78*
This Is Spinal Tap *'84*
Flipped *'10*

Al Reinert
Apollo 13 *'95*
From the Earth to the Moon *'98*
Final Fantasy: The Spirits Within *'01*

Elizabeth Reinhardt (1909-54)
Gold Rush Maisie *'40*
Maisie Was a Lady *'41*
Maisie Gets Her Man *'42*
Laura *'44*
Carnival in Costa Rica *'47*

Walter Reisch (1903-83)
That Uncertain Feeling *'41*
Seven Sweethearts *'42*
Somewhere I'll Find You *'42*
Gaslight *'44*
The Heavenly Body *'44*
The Fan *'49*
The Model and the Marriage Broker *'51*
Niagara *'52*
Titanic *'53*
The Girl in the Red Velvet Swing *'55*
Teenage Rebel *'56*
Stopover Tokyo *'57*
Journey to the Center of the Earth *'59*
The Remarkable Mr. Pennypacker *'59*

Mike Reiss (1960-)
Queer Duck: The Movie *'06*
The Simpsons Movie *'07*
Ice Age: Dawn of the Dinosaurs *'09*
My Life in Ruins *'09*

Jason Reitman (1977-)
Thank You for Smoking *'06*
Up in the Air *'09*
Labor Day *'13*
Men, Women & Children *'14*
The Front Runner *'18*

Edgar Reitz (1932-)
Heimat 1 *'84*
Heimat 2 *'92*

Robert Reneau
Action Jackson *'88*
Demolition Man *'93*

Jeff Renfroe
Paranoia 1.0 *'04*
Seattle Superstorm *'12*

Jeff Reno
Radioland Murders *'94*
Meet Joe Black *'98*

Jean Renoir (1894-1979)
Boudu Saved from Drowning *'32*
The Crime of Monsieur Lange *'36*
The Lower Depths *'36*
Grand Illusion *'37*
La Marseillaise *'37*
La Bete Humaine *'38*
The Rules of the Game *'39*
The Southerner *'45*
The Woman on the Beach *'47*
The River *'51*
The Golden Coach *'52*
The Testament of Dr. Cordelier *'59*

John Requa
Cats & Dogs *'01*
Bad Santa *'03*
The Bad News Bears *'05*
I Love You Phillip Morris *'10*
Focus *'15*

Alain Resnais (1922-2014)
Last Year at Marienbad *'61*
Melo *'86*
Private Fears in Public Places *'06*

Adam Resnick
Cabin Boy *'94*
Lucky Numbers *'00*
Death to Smoochy *'02*

Patricia Resnick
3 Women *'77*
A Wedding *'78*
Quintet *'79*
9 to 5 *'80*
Maxie *'85*
Second Sight *'89*
Straight Talk *'92*

Dale Resteghini (1968-)
Colorz of Rage *'97*
Da Hip Hop Witch *'00*

Paul (Pee-wee Herman) Reubens (1952-)
Pee-wee's Big Adventure *'85*
Big Top Pee-wee *'88*

Alex Reval
Wild Grass *'09*
You Ain't Seen Nothin' Yet *'12*

Alma Reville (1899-1982)
Rich and Strange *'32*
The Passing of the Third Floor Back *'35*
The 39 Steps *'35*
Sabotage *'36*
Young and Innocent *'37*
Shadow of a Doubt *'43*
It's in the Bag! *'45*

Franc Reyes
Empire *'02*
Illegal Tender *'07*
The Ministers *'09*

Clarke Reynolds (1917-94)
Genghis Khan *'65*
Son of a Gunfighter *'65*
The Viking Queen *'67*
Shalako *'68*

Dave Reynolds
The Emperor's New Groove *'00*
Finding Nemo *'03*

Jonathan Reynolds
Micki & Maude *'84*
Leonard Part 6 *'87*
My Stepmother Is an Alien *'88*
Switching Channels *'88*

Kevin Reynolds (1950-)
Red Dawn *'84*
Fandango *'85*
Rapa Nui *'93*
Risen *'16*

Lee Reynolds
Allan Quatermain and the Lost City of Gold *'86*
Delta Force 2: Operation Stranglehold *'90*
Storyville *'92*
Jackie Chan's Who Am I *'98*

Scott Reynolds (1968-)
The Ugly *'96*
Heaven *'99*

Shonda Rhimes (1970-)
Introducing Dorothy Dandridge *'99*
Crossroads *'02*
The Princess Diaries 2: Royal Engagement *'04*

Don Rhymer
Carpool *'96*
Big Momma's House *'00*
The Santa Clause 2 *'02*
Agent Cody Banks 2: Destination London *'04*
The Honeymooners *'05*
Big Momma's House 2 *'06*
Deck the Halls *'06*
Surf's Up *'07*
Rio *'11*

Pamela Ribon (1975-)
Smurfs: The Lost Village *'17*
Ralph Breaks the Internet *'18*

Luke Ricci
Fast Girl *'07*
How to be a Serial Killer *'08*

Elmer Rice (1892-1967)
Street Scene *'31*
Counsellor-at-Law *'33*

John Rice
Blown Away *'94*
Chasers *'94*
Windtalkers *'02*
Anna Nicole *'13*
Bonnie & Clyde *'13*

Jolene Rice
Still Small Voices *'07*
Last Man Standing *'11*

Susan Rice
Taming Andrew *'00*
Mrs. Washington Goes to Smith *'09*

Wayne Allan Rice
Only You *'92*
Suicide Kings *'97*

Mike Rich (1959-)
Finding Forrester *'00*
The Rookie *'02*
Radio *'03*
The Nativity Story *'06*
Secretariat *'10*
Cars 3 *'17*

Richard Rich
The Black Cauldron *'85*
The Swan Princess *'94*

Jean-Louis Richard (1927-2012)
The Soft Skin *'64*
Fahrenheit 451 *'66*
The Bride Wore Black *'68*
Day for Night *'73*
Emmanuelle *'74*
Le Choc *'82*
After Sex *'97*

Cybil (Sybil) Richards
Femalien *'96*
Femalien 2 *'98*

George Richards
Redemption Road *'10*
Seconds Apart *'11*

John C. Richards (1957-)
Nurse Betty *'00*
Sahara *'05*

Robert L. Richards
Act of Violence *'48*
One Sunday Afternoon *'48*
Kansas Raiders *'50*
The Indian Fighter *'55*
Gorgo *'61*

Doug Richardson
Die Hard 2: Die Harder *'90*
Money Train *'95*
Welcome to Mooseport *'04*
Hostage *'05*

Tony Richardson (1928-91)
Ned Kelly *'70*
The Hotel New Hampshire *'84*

William Richert (1942-)
Law and Disorder *'74*
Winter Kills *'79*
A Night in the Life of Jimmy Reardon *'88*
The Man in the Iron Mask *'97*

Jean-Francois Richet (1966-)
Mesrine: Part 1-Killer Instinct *'08*
Mesrine: Part 2-Public Enemy Number 1 *'08*

Mordecai Richler (1931-2001)
The Apprenticeship of Duddy Kravitz *'74*
Fun with Dick and Jane *'77*

Maurice Richlin (1930-90)
Operation Petticoat *'59*
Pillow Talk *'59*
Come September *'61*
Don't Make Waves *'67*
For Pete's Sake *'74*

Jason Richman
Bad Company *'02*
Bangkok Dangerous *'08*
Swing Vote *'08*

Bill Richmond
The Nutty Professor *'63*
The Family Jewels *'65*

W.D. Richter (1945-)
Slither *'73*
Nickelodeon *'76*
Invasion of the Body Snatchers *'78*
Dracula *'79*
Brubaker *'80*
All Night Long *'81*
Big Trouble in Little China *'86*
Needful Things *'93*
Home for the Holidays *'95*
Stealth *'05*

Alan Rickman (1946-2016)
The Winter Guest *'97*
A Little Chaos *'14*

Tom Rickman
Kansas City Bomber *'72*
The White Dawn *'75*
W.W. and the Dixie Dancekings *'75*
Hooper *'78*
Truman *'95*
Tuesdays with Morrie *'99*
Bless the Child *'00*
The Reagans *'04*
A Smile as Big as the Moon *'12*

Tom Ricostronza (1962-)
See Trey Ellis

Brad Riddell
American Pie Presents Band Camp *'05*
Road Trip: Beer Pong *'09*
Crooked Arrows *'12*

John Ridley (1965-)
Cold Around the Heart *'97*
U-Turn *'97*
Undercover Brother *'02*
Red Tails *'12*
12 Years a Slave *'13*
Jimi: All Is by My Side *'14*
Ben-Hur *'16*

Philip Ridley
The Reflecting Skin *'91*
The Passion of Darkly Noon *'95*
Heartless *'10*

Georgina Garcia Riedel
How the Garcia Girls Spent Their Summer *'05*
Pulling Strings *'13*

Leni Riefenstahl (1902-2003)
The Blue Light *'32*
Triumph of the Will *'34*

August Rieger (1914-84)
The Vampire Happening *'71*
The Uranium Conspiracy *'78*

Ernest Riera (1977-)
The Other Side of the Door *'16*
47 Meters Down *'17*
47 Meters Down: Uncaged *'19*

Dean Riesner (1918-2002)
Operation Haylift *'50*
The Helen Morgan Story *'57*
Coogan's Bluff *'68*
Dirty Harry *'71*
Play Misty for Me *'71*
Charley Varrick *'73*
High Plains Drifter *'73*
Arthur Hailey's The Moneychangers *'76*
Fatal Beauty *'87*

Adam Rifkin (1966-)
Never on Tuesday *'88*
The Dark Backward *'91*
The Chase *'93*
Mouse Hunt *'97*
Small Soldiers *'98*
Something About Sex *'98*
Night at the Golden Eagle *'02*
Zoom *'06*
National Lampoon's The Stoned Aged *'07*
Underdog *'07*
Knucklehead *'10*
The Last Movie Star *'17*

Ned Rifle (1959-)
See Hal Hartley

Ray Rigby
The Hill *'65*
Operation Crossbow *'65*

Lynn Riggs (1899-1954)
The Garden of Allah *'36*
Sherlock Holmes and the Voice of Terror *'42*
Oklahoma! *'99*

Wolf Rilla (1920-2005)
The Scamp *'57*
Village of the Damned *'60*

Joe Rinaldi (1914-74)
The Adventures of Ichabod and Mr. Toad *'49*
Peter Pan *'53*

Frederic Rinaldo (1913-92)
The Invisible Woman *'40*
The Black Cat *'41*
Hold That Ghost *'41*
Buck Privates Come Home *'47*
Abbott and Costello Meet Frankenstein *'48*
Abbott and Costello Meet the Invisible Man *'51*
Comin' Round the Mountain *'51*

David W. Rintels (1938-)
Scorpio *'73*
Washington: Behind Closed Doors *'77*
Day One *'89*
The Last Best Year *'90*
Not Without My Daughter *'90*
World War II: When Lions Roared *'94*
Andersonville *'95*
Nuremberg *'00*
A Season on the Brink *'02*

Ben Ripley
Species 4: The Awakening *'07*
The Watch *'08*
Source Code *'11*
Flatliners *'17*

Gabriel Ripstein
Pulling Strings *'13*
Compadres *'16*
600 Miles *'16*

Dino Risi (1916-2008)
Il Sorpasso *'63*
The Scent of a Woman *'75*

Robert Riskin (1897-1955)
Arizona *'31*
American Madness *'32*
Shopworn *'32*
Three Wise Girls *'32*
Virtue *'32*
Lady for a Day *'33*
Broadway Bill *'34*
It Happened One Night *'34*
The Whole Town's Talking *'35*
Mr. Deeds Goes to Town *'36*
Lost Horizon *'37*
You Can't Take It with You *'38*
Meet John Doe *'41*
Magic Town *'47*
Mister 880 *'50*
Riding High *'50*

Steven Ritch (1921-95)
Plunder Road *'57*
City of Fear *'59*

Guy Ritchie (1968-)
Lock, Stock and 2 Smoking Barrels *'98*
Snatch *'00*
Swept Away *'02*
Revolver *'05*
RocknRolla *'08*
Sherlock Holmes *'09*
The Man from U.N.C.L.E. *'15*
King Arthur: Legend of the Sword *'17*
Aladdin *'19*
The Gentlemen *'20*

Panna Rittikrai (1961-)
Born to Fight *'07*
Ong Bak 2 *'08*

Thomas Ritz
Martial Outlaw *'93*
The Killing Grounds *'97*

Stephen J. Rivele (1949-)
Nixon *'95*
Ali *'01*
Like Dandelion Dust *'09*

Jose Rivera (1955-)
The Motorcycle Diaries *'04*
Trade *'07*

Letters to Juliet *'10*
On the Road *'12*

Jacques Rivette (1928-)
La Belle Noiseuse *'90*
Va Savoir *'01*
The Story of Marie and Julien *'03*
The Duchess of Langeais *'07*
Around a Small Mountain *'09*

Allen Rivkin (1903-90)
What Price Hollywood? *'32*
Dancing Lady *'33*
Picture Snatcher *'33*
Let Us Live *'39*
Till the End of Time *'46*
Dead Reckoning *'47*
The Guilt of Janet Ames *'47*
Tension *'50*
It's a Big Country *'51*

Christopher Roach
Non-Stop *'14*
Truth or Dare *'18*
Fantasy Island *'20*

David Roach
Young Einstein *'89*
Beneath Hill 60 *'10*

Janet Roach
Prizzi's Honor *'85*
Mr. North *'88*

Alain Robbe-Grillet (1922-2008)
Last Year at Marienbad *'61*
L'Immortelle *'63*
The Man Who Lies *'68*
Gradiva *'06*

Matthew Robbins (1945-)
The Sugarland Express *'74*
Bingo Long Traveling All-Stars & Motor Kings *'76*
MacArthur *'77*
Corvette Summer *'78*
Dragonslayer *'81*
Warning Sign *'85*
*batteries not included *'87*
Mimic *'97*
The Concert *'09*
Don't Be Afraid of the Dark *'11*
Crimson Peak *'15*

Tim Robbins (1958-)
Bob Roberts *'92*
Dead Man Walking *'95*
The Cradle Will Rock *'99*

Jacques Robert
The Monocle *'64*
Make Your Bets Ladies *'65*

Ben Roberts (1916-84)
South of Panama *'41*
White Heat *'49*
Backfire *'50*
Goodbye My Fancy *'51*
King of the Khyber Rifles *'53*
White Witch Doctor *'53*
Green Fire *'55*
Serenade *'56*
Portrait in Black *'60*

Charles E. Roberts (1894-1951)
Corruption *'33*
Mummy's Boys *'36*
Mexican Spitfire *'40*
The Mexican Spitfire Out West *'40*
The Mexican Spitfire's Baby *'41*
The Mexican Spitfire Sees a Ghost *'42*

Johannes Roberts (1976-)
Hellbreeder *'04*
When Evil Calls *'06*
The Other Side of the Door *'16*
47 Meters Down *'17*
47 Meters Down: Uncaged *'19*

Jonathan Roberts
Once Bitten *'85*
The Sure Thing *'85*
The Lion King *'94*

The Hunchback of Notre Dame *'96*
Jack Frost *'98*

Jordan Roberts
Around the Bend *'04*
March of the Penguins *'05*
3, 2, 1...Frankie Go Boom *'12*
Big Hero 6 *'14*

Marguerite Roberts (1905-89)
Escape *'40*
If Winter Comes *'41*
Somewhere I'll Find You *'42*
Undercurrent *'46*
Desire Me *'47*
The Sea of Grass *'47*
The Bribe *'48*
Ambush *'50*
Ivanhoe *'52*
Rampage *'63*
Five Card Stud *'68*
True Grit *'69*
Shoot Out *'71*

Scott Roberts
Riders of the Storm *'88*
K2: The Ultimate High *'92*
The Hard Word *'02*

Stanley Roberts (1916-82)
Death of a Salesman *'51*
The Story of Will Rogers *'52*
The Caine Mutiny *'54*
Made in Paris *'65*

William Roberts (1913-97)
Easy to Love *'53*
The Mating Game *'59*
The Magnificent Seven *'60*
The Devil's Brigade *'68*
The Bridge at Remagen *'69*
Red Sun *'71*
The Last American Hero *'73*
Posse *'75*
Legend of the Lone Ranger *'81*
Ten to Midnight *'83*

R.J. Robertson
Forbidden World *'82*
Big Bad Mama 2 *'87*
Not of This Earth *'88*
Transylvania Twist *'89*
The Haunting of Morella *'91*
Home for Christmas *'93*

Geneva Robertson-Dworet
Tomb Raider *'18*
Captain Marvel *'19*

Gillian Robespierre
Obvious Child *'14*
Landline *'17*

Angela Robinson (1971-)
D.E.B.S. *'04*
Professor Marston and the Wonder Women *'17*

Bruce Robinson (1946-)
The Killing Fields *'84*
Withnail and I *'87*
Fat Man and Little Boy *'89*
How to Get Ahead in Advertising *'89*
Jennifer 8 *'92*
In Dreams *'98*
Return to Paradise *'98*
The Rum Diary *'11*

Butch Robinson
DROP Squad *'94*
Crazy as Hell *'02*

Casey Robinson (1903-79)
Captain Blood *'35*
Give Me Your Heart *'36*
Call It a Day *'37*
It's Love I'm After *'37*
Stolen Holiday *'37*
Four's a Crowd *'38*
Dark Victory *'39*
Kings Row *'41*
One Foot in Heaven *'41*
Now, Voyager *'42*
Passage to Marseilles *'44*
Saratoga Trunk *'45*
The Snows of Kilimanjaro *'52*
The Egyptian *'54*

Mark Rosman (1959-)
The House on Sorority Row '83
Evolver '94
The Invader '96
Life-Size '00
Dead in a Heartbeat '02
Sorority Row '09

Arthur Ross
Star Spangled Rhythm '42
Creature from the Black Lagoon '54
The Creature Walks among Us '56
The Three Worlds of Gulliver '59
The 3 Worlds of Gulliver '60
Satan's School for Girls '73
Brubaker '80

David Ross
The Woods '03
The Babysitters '07

Dev Ross
The Land Before Time 2: The Great Valley Adventure '94
The Land Before Time 3: The Time of the Great Giving '95
The Land Before Time 4: Journey Through the Mists '96

Gary Ross (1956-)
Big '88
Mr. Baseball '92
Dave '93
Lassie '94
Pleasantville '98
Seabiscuit '03
The Tale of Despereaux '08
The Hunger Games '12
Free State of Jones '16
Ocean's 8 '18

Kenneth Ross (1941-)
The Day of the Jackal '73
The Odessa File '74

Kevin Ross
Mulligan '00
Vernie '04

Matt Ross (1970-)
28 Hotel Rooms '12
Captain Fantastic '16

Michael Arlen Ross
Turistas '06
Fallen '17

Stanley Ralph Ross (1936-2000)
Death Among Friends '75
Gold of the Amazon Women '79

Roberto Rossellini (1906-77)
Paisan '46
Germany Year Zero '48
The Flowers of St. Francis '50
Voyage in Italy '53
Era Notte a Roma '60
Blaise Pascal '71
Generale Della Rovere '09

Gregg Rossen
The Christmas Consultant '12
The Seven Year Hitch '12
Undercover Bridesmaid '12
Northpole '14

Robert Rossen (1908-66)
They Won't Forget '37
Dust Be My Destiny '39
The Roaring Twenties '39
Blues in the Night '41
Out of the Fog '41
Edge of Darkness '43
The Strange Love of Martha Ivers '46
A Walk in the Sun '46
Johnny O'Clock '47
All the King's Men '49
The Hustler '61
Billy Budd '62
Lilith '64

Mick Rossi
Played '06
2:22 '08

Terry Rossio (1960-)
Little Monsters '89
Aladdin '92
The Puppet Masters '94
The Mask of Zorro '98
Small Soldiers '98
The Road to El Dorado '00
Shrek '01
Pirates of the Caribbean: The Curse of the Black Pearl '03
Deja Vu '06
Pirates of the Caribbean: Dead Man's Chest '06
Pirates of the Caribbean: At World's End '07
Pirates of the Caribbean: On Stranger Tides '11
The Lone Ranger '13

Leo Rosten (1908-97)
The Conspirators '44
Dark Corner '46
Lured '47
Sleep, My Love '48
Walk East on Beacon '52

Eli Roth (1972-)
Cabin Fever '03
Hostel '06
Hostel: Part 2 '07
Aftershock '12
The Man with the Iron Fists '12
The Green Inferno '14
Knock Knock '15

Eric Roth (1945-)
The Nickel Ride '74
The Concorde: Airport '79 '79
The Onion Field '79
Suspect '87
Memories of Me '88
Mr. Jones '93
Forrest Gump '94
The Horse Whisperer '97
The Postman '97
The Insider '99
Ali '01
Munich '05
The Good Shepherd '06
Lucky You '07
The Curious Case of Benjamin Button '08
Extremely Loud and Incredibly Close '11
A Star Is Born '18

Phillip J. Roth (1959-)
Digital Man '94
Total Reality '97
Interceptor Force '99
Velocity Trap '99
Boa '02
Dark Descent '02
Hypersonic '02
Dark Waters '03
Deep Shock '03

Jeff Rothberg (1957-2009)
Hiding Out '87
The Amazing Panda Adventure '95
A Simple Wish '97
The Whole Shebang '01

Creighton Rothenberger
Olympus Has Fallen '13
The Expendables 3 '14
London Has Fallen '16

Rodney Rothman (1974-)
Grudge Match '13
22 Jump Street '14
Spider-Man: Into the Spider-Verse '18

Scott Rothman
Draft Day '14
Army of One '16

Jayson Rothwell
Second in Command '05
Malice in Wonderland '09
Silent Night '12
Polar '19

Talbot Rothwell (1916-81)
Carry On Cabby '63
Carry On Jack '63
Carry On Spying '64
Carry On Cowboy '66
Don't Lose Your Head '66
Carry On Up the Khyber '68
Carry On Again Doctor '69
Carry On Loving '70
Carry On Up the Jungle '70
Carry On Camping '71
Carry On Henry VIII '71
Carry On Abroad '72
Carry On Matron '72

Nick Rotundo
Gladiator Cop: The Swordsman 2 '95
G2: Mortal Conquest '99

Russell Rouse (1913-87)
D.O.A. '49
The Thief '52
Fastest Gun Alive '56

Francois Olivier Rousseau
Children of the Century '99
Change My Life '01
The Princess of Montpensier '10

Kathleen Rowell
The Outsiders '83
Hear No Evil '93
Vanished '95
Killing Mr. Griffin '97
Video Voyeur: The Susan Wilson Story '02

J. K. Rowling (1965-)
Fantastic Beasts and Where to Find Them '16
Fantastic Beasts: The Crimes of Grindelwald '18

Patricia Rozema (1958-)
When Night Is Falling '95
Mansfield Park '99
Grey Gardens '09
Into the Forest '16

Andy Ruben
The Patriot '86
Stripped to Kill '87
Streets '90
Poison Ivy '92
Club Vampire '98

J. Walter Ruben (1899-1942)
The Royal Bed '31
Symphony of Six Million '32

Benny Rubin (1899-1986)
High Flyers '37
On Again-Off Again '37

Bruce Joel Rubin (1943-)
Brainstorm '83
Deadly Friend '86
Ghost '90
Jacob's Ladder '90
My Life '93
Deep Impact '98
Stuart Little 2 '02
The Last Mimzy '07
The Time Traveler's Wife '09

Mann Rubin (1927-)
The Best of Everything '59
An American Dream '66
Warning Shot '67
The First Deadly Sin '80

Cliff Ruby
Balto '95
Cats Don't Dance '97
Beethoven's 5th '03

Harry Ruby (1895-1974)
Horse Feathers '32
Kid from Spain '32
Duck Soup '33
A Night at the Opera '35

Oren Rudavsky
The Treatment '06
Joseph Pulitzer: Voice of the People '18

Paul Rudd (1969-)
Role Models '08
Ant-Man '15
Ant-Man and the Wasp '18

David Rudkin (1936-)
Fahrenheit 451 '66
December Bride '91

Paul Rudnick (1957-)
Addams Family Values '93
Jeffrey '95
In and Out '97
Isn't She Great '00
Marci X '03
The Stepford Wives '04

Steve Rudnick
The Santa Clause '94
Kicking & Screaming '05

Alan Rudolph (1943-)
Barn of the Naked Dead '73
Buffalo Bill & the Indians '76
Roadie '80
Endangered Species '82
Choose Me '84
Trouble in Mind '86
The Moderns '88
Love at Large '89
Afterglow '97
Breakfast of Champions '98
Trixie '00
Intimate Affairs '01

Ed Rugoff
Mannequin '87
Mannequin 2: On the Move '91
Mr. Nanny '93

Raoul Ruiz (1941-2011)
Genealogies of a Crime '97
Time Regained '99
Comedy of Innocence '00
Night Across the Street '12

Mogens Rukov (1943-)
The Celebration '98
Reconstruction '03

Stefano Rulli (1949-)
The Stolen Children '92
The Truce '96
Best of Youth '03
My Brother Is an Only Child '07
Our Life '10

Simon Rumley
Red White & Blue '10
The ABCs of Death '12

Terry Runte (1960-94)
Mystery Date '91
Super Mario Bros. '93

Peter Ruric (1902-66)
The Black Cat '34
Grand Central Murder '42

Jane Rusconi
Hush '98
Swing Vote '99

Richard Rush (1929-)
Too Soon to Love '60
Psych-Out '68
The Stunt Man '80
Air America '90
Color of Night '94

Harry Ruskin (1894-1969)
Paradise for Three '38
Young Dr. Kildare '38
Calling Dr. Kildare '39
Miracles for Sale '39
The Secret of Dr. Kildare '39
Dr. Kildare Goes Home '40
Dr. Kildare's Crisis '40
Dr. Kildare's Strange Case '40
Andy Hardy's Private Secretary '41
Dr. Kildare's Wedding Day '41
The People *vs.* Dr. Kildare '41
Calling Dr. Gillespie '42
Dr. Gillespie's New Assistant '42
Dr. Kildare's Victory '42
Tish '42
Dr. Gillespie's Criminal Case '43
Andy Hardy's Blonde Trouble '44
Three Men in White '44
Between Two Women '45
Love Laughs at Andy Hardy '46
The Postman Always Rings Twice '46
Dark Delusion '47
Tenth Avenue Angel '47
The Happy Years '50
Lady Godiva '55

Josef Rusnak
Quiet Days in Hollywood '97
The Thirteenth Floor '99

Lou Rusoff (1911-63)
Day the World Ended '55
The Phantom from 10,000 Leagues '56
The She-Creature '56
Shake, Rattle and Rock '57
The Ghost of Dragstrip Hollow '59
Beach Party '63

Chuck Russell (1958-)
Dreamscape '84
A Nightmare on Elm Street 3: Dream Warriors '87
The Blob '88
Junglee '19

David O. Russell (1959-)
Spanking the Monkey '94
Flirting with Disaster '95
Three Kings '99
I Heart Huckabees '04
The Fighter '10
Silver Linings Playbook '12
American Hustle '13
Joy '15

Ken Russell (1927-2011)
The Boy Friend '71
The Devils '71
Mahler '74
Lisztomania '75
Tommy '75
Valentino '77
Aria '88
The Lair of the White Worm '88
Salome's Last Dance '88
The Rainbow '89
Lady Chatterley '92

Ray Russell (1924-99)
Mr. Sardonicus '61
Premature Burial '62
Zotz! '62
X: The Man with X-Ray Eyes '63

Vivian Russell
The Atomic Brain '64
The Rainbow '89

Willy Russell (1947-)
Educating Rita '83
Shirley Valentine '89

Joe Russo
Welcome to Collinwood '02
Extraction '20

John A. Russo (1939-)
Night of the Living Dead '68
Return of the Living Dead '85
The Majorettes '87
Voodoo Dawn '89
Night of the Living Dead '90
Heartstopper '92

Richard Russo (1949-)
Twilight '98
Brush with Fate '03
Empire Falls '05
The Ice Harvest '05
Keeping Mum '05

Ry Russo-Young (1981-)
You Wont Miss Me '09
Nobody Walks '12

Marti Rustam
Eaten Alive '76
Evils of the Night '85

Micho Rutare
Dragonquest '09
Mega Shark *vs.* Crocosaurus '10
Meteor Apocalypse '10

Morrie Ruvinsky (1943-)
A Woman Hunted '03
Lies and Crimes '07

Stefan Ruzowitzky (1961-)
The Inheritors '98
Anatomy '00
Anatomy 2 '03
The Counterfeiters '07

Don Ryan (1889-1978)
Smart Blonde '37
You Can't Get Away With Murder '39

Frank Ryan (1947-)
The Amazing Mrs. Holiday '43
Can't Help Singing '45

Sean Ryan
Decommissioned '16
Weaponized '16
The Outsider '19

Florence Ryerson (1892-1965)
The Reckless Hour '31
The Casino Murder Case '35
Everybody Sing '38
Ice Follies of 1939 '39

Michael Rymer (1963-)
Allie & Me '97
Perfume '01

Seung-wan Ryoo
No Blood No Tears '02
The City of Violence '06

Morrie Ryskind (1895-1985)
The Cocoanuts '29
Animal Crackers '30
A Night at the Opera '35
My Man Godfrey '36
Room Service '38
Penny Serenade '41
Claudia '43

Ichiro Ryu
Dead or Alive '00
Dead or Alive: Final '02

Joseph Sabo
Fantasia '40
Pinocchio '40

Dardano Sacchetti (1944-)
Shock '79
Cannibal Apocalypse '80
Gates of Hell '80
Zombie '80
The Beyond '82
Manhattan Baby '82
New York Ripper '82
A Blade in the Dark '83
The House by the Cemetery '83
The New Gladiators '83
Demons '86

Gabe Sachs
Diary of a Wimpy Kid '10
Diary of a Wimpy Kid 2: Rodrick Rules '11
Diary of a Wimpy Kid: Dog Days '12

Ira Sachs (1965-)
The Delta '97
Forty Shades of Blue '05
Married Life '07
Keep the Lights On '12
Love Is Strange '14
Little Men '16
Frankie '19

William Sackheim (1920-2004)
Border River '47
Barricade '49
Homicide '49
Paula '52

Benny Safdie
Good Time '17
Uncut Gems '19

Josh Safdie
Heaven Knows What '15
Good Time '17
Uncut Gems '19

Farhad Safinia
Apocalypto '06
The Professor and the Madman '19

Yoichi Sai
Doing Time '02
Blood and Bones '04

Arthur St. Claire (1899-1950)
Yank in Libya '42
Submarine Base '43
The Mask of Diijon '46
Rimfire '49

Adela Rogers St. John
The Great Man's Lady '42
Smart Woman '48

Chad St. John
London Has Fallen '16
Peppermint '18
Replicas '18

Nicholas St. John
Driller Killer '79
Ms. 45 '81
Fear City '85
King of New York '90
Body Snatchers '93
Dangerous Game '93
The Funeral '96

Stewart St. John
Seventeen Again '00
Dark Metropolis '10

Cecil Saint-Laurent (1919-2000)
Manon '68
The Women '68

Hiroshi Saito
Rubber's Lover '97
Samurai Fiction '99

Koji Steven Sakai
The People I've Slept With '09
Santa & Me '13

Richard Sale (1911-93)
The Dude Goes West '48
Mother Is a Freshman '49
When Willie Comes Marching Home '50
Meet Me After the Show '51
Let's Do It Again '53
Suddenly '54
Torpedo Run '58
Assassination '87

Kario Salem (1955-)
Don King: Only in America '97
The Rat Pack '98
The Score '01
Chasing Mavericks '12

Shane Salerno
Aliens vs. Predator: Requiem '07
Savages '12

Sidney Salkow (1909-2000)
Murder With Pictures '36
Rhythm on the Range '36
Raiders of the Seven Seas '53
Sitting Bull '54
Robbers' Roost '55

Sy Salkowitz (1926-91)
Thunder Alley '67
The Biggest Bundle of Them All '68

Walter Salles (1956-)
Foreign Land '95
Behind the Sun '01
Paris, je t'aime '06

Roy Sallows
Conspiracy of Fear '96
Fall Down Dead '07

Jennifer Salt (1944-)
Tempo '03
Eat, Pray, Love '10

Waldo Salt (1914-87)
Shopworn Angel '38
Tonight We Raid Calais '43
Mr. Winkle Goes to War '44
Flight From Ashiya '64
Midnight Cowboy '69
Serpico '73

Claudia Salter
Running Mates '00
Man in the Mirror: The Michael Jackson Story '04

Mark Saltzman
The Adventures of Milo & Otis '89
Milo & Otis '89
Iron & Silk '91
3 Ninjas Kick Back '94
Mrs. Santa Claus '96
Napoleon '96
The Red Sneakers '01
Third Man Out: A Donald Strachey Mystery '05

Victor Salva (1958-)
Nature of the Beast '94
Powder '95
Rites of Passage '99
Jeepers Creepers '01
Jeepers Creepers 2 '03
Peaceful Warrior '06
Dark House '14
Jeepers Creepers 3 '17

Pierre Salvadori (1964-)
Apres-Vous '03
Priceless '06

Todd Samovitz
Wonderland '03
Black Swarm '07

Jon Robert Samsel
Carnal Crimes '91
Animal Instincts '92

Lesser Samuels (1894-1980)
It's Love Again '36
Gangway '37
Climbing High '38
Sailing Along '38
Bitter Sweet '40
The Earl of Chicago '40
Strange Cargo '40
No Way Out '50
Ace in the Hole '51
The Silver Chalice '54

Eduardo Sanchez (1968-)
The Blair Witch Project '99
Altered '06
Seventh Moon '08

Sergio G. Sanchez (1973-)
The Orphanage '07
The Impossible '12

Matthew Sand
Ninja Assassin '09
Deepwater Horizon '16

Duke Sandefur
The Phantom of the Opera '89
Atlas Shrugged 2: The Strike '12

Chris (Christopher) Sanders (1962-)
Mulan '98
Lilo & Stitch '02
How to Train Your Dragon '10
The Croods '13

Scott Sanders
Thick as Thieves '99
Black Dynamite '09

Helma Sanders-Brahms
Earthquake in Chile '74
Under the Pavement Lies the Strand '75

Helmer Sanders-Brahms (1940-)
Germany, Pale Mother '80
The Future of Emily '85

Mark Sanderson
I'll Remember April '99
Silent Venom '08

Adam Sandler (1966-)
Billy Madison '94
Happy Gilmore '96
The Waterboy '98
Big Daddy '99
Little Nicky '00
Adam Sandler's 8 Crazy Nights '02
You Don't Mess with the Zohan '08
Grown Ups '10
Bucky Larson: Born to Be a Star '11
Just Go With It '11
Grown Ups 2 '13
Hotel Transylvania 2 '15

Barry Sandler
The Duchess and the Dirtwater Fox '76
The Mirror Crack'd '80
Making Love '82
Crimes of Passion '84
All-American Murder '91

Anna Sandor
Family of Strangers '93
Amelia Earhart: The Final Flight '94
My Louisiana Sky '02
Mom, Dad and Her '08
Growing the Big One '09

Donald S. Sanford
1,000 Plane Raid '69
Mosquito Squadron '70
Midway '76

Jimmy Sangster (1924-2011)
X The Unknown '56
The Curse of Frankenstein '57
Blood of the Vampire '58
The Crawling Eye '58
The Horror of Dracula '58
Intent to Kill '58
The Revenge of Frankenstein '58
The Snorkel '58
The Man Who Could Cheat Death '59
The Mummy '59
The Brides of Dracula '60
The Siege of Sidney Street '60
Scream of Fear '61
The Terror of the Tongs '61
Paranoiac '62
Maniac '63
Nightmare '63
The Devil-Ship Pirates '64
Hysteria '64
The Nanny '65
Deadlier Than the Male '67
The Anniversary '68
Crescendo '69
The Horror of Frankenstein '70
Dynasty of Fear '72
Concrete Cowboys '79
Once Upon a Spy '80
Phobia '80
The Devil & Max Devlin '81

Marie-Jose Sanselme
Kippur '00
Free Zone '05
Disengagement '07

Danny Santiago (1911-88)
See Daniel James

Jeff Santo (1963-)
Liar's Poker '99
Jake's Corner '08

Nick Santora
The Longshots '08
Punisher: War Zone '08
Prison Break: The Final Break '09

Ken Sanzel
The Replacement Killers '98
Scarred City '98
Lone Hero '02

Alvin Sapinsley (1922-2002)
Moon of the Wolf '72
The Scarlet Letter '79

Lawrence Sara
Caged Animal '10
7 Below '11
Chain of Command '15

Tedi Sarafian (1966-)
Solar Crisis '92
Tank Girl '94
The Road Killers '95
The Possession of Michael King '14

Jan Sardi
Shine '95
The Notebook '04
Mao's Last Dancer '09

Barney A. Sarecky (1895-1968)
Fighting Marines '36
Zorro's Fighting Legion '39
Adventures of Red Ryder '40
Drums of Fu Manchu '40
The Purple Monster Strikes '45
Buffalo Bill Rides Again '47

Alvin Sargent (1931-)
Gambit '66
The Stalking Moon '69
The Sterile Cuckoo '69
I Walk the Line '70
Love and Pain and the Whole Damn Thing '73
Paper Moon '73
Bobby Deerfield '77
Julia '77
Straight Time '78
Ordinary People '80
Nuts '87
Dominick & Eugene '88
White Palace '90
Other People's Money '91
What about Bob? '91
Bogus '96
Anywhere But Here '99
Unfaithful '02
Spider-Man 2 '04
Spider-Man 3 '07
The Amazing Spider-Man '12

Vic Sarin (1945-)
Partition '07
A Shine of Rainbows '09

Arlene Sarner
Peggy Sue Got Married '86
Blue Sky '91
Ricky Nelson: Original Teen Idol '99
The Healer '02

Vaclav Sasek
Loves of a Blonde '65
The Firemen's Ball '68

Oley Sassone
Wild Hearts Can't Be Broken '91
Cradle of Lies '06

Marjane Satrapi (1969-)
Persepolis '07
Chicken With Plums '11

Harry Sauber (1885-1967)
Happiness Ahead '34
Adventure in Manhattan '36
Outside of Paradise '38

Oscar Saul (1912-94)
Strange Affair '44
Road House '48
Woman in Hiding '49
Thunder on the Hill '51
The Helen Morgan Story '57
The Second Time Around '61
Major Dundee '65
The Silencers '66

Jeremy Saulnier
Blue Ruin '13
Green Room '15

George Saunders (1959-)
Bloodsport 4: The Dark Kumite '98
The Landlady '98
The Perfect Wife '00
Magic Man '10

John Monk Saunders (1895-1940)
Wings '27
The Last Flight '31
Ace of Aces '33

Hubert Sauper (1966-)
Darwin's Nightmare '04
We Come As Friends '14

Carlos Saura (1932-)
Cria Cuervos '76
Blood Wedding '81
Carmen '83
Outrage '93
Tango '98
Goya in Bordeaux '99

Claude Sautet (1924-2000)
Classe Tous Risque '60
Borsalino '70
Cesar & Rosalie '72
Nelly et Monsieur Arnaud '95

Jody Savin
Witchcraft '88
Marilyn Hotchkiss' Ballroom Dancing & Charm School '06
CBGB '13

Nancy Savoca (1960-)
True Love '89
If These Walls Could Talk '96
The 24 Hour Woman '99

Gerald Savory (1909-96)
Young and Innocent '37
Count Dracula '77

Brian Sawyer
The Christmas Consultant '12
The Seven Year Hitch '12
Undercover Bridesmaid '12
Northpole '14

Rodo Sayagues
Evil Dead '13
Don't Breathe '16

John Sayles (1950-)
Piranha '78
Lady in Red '79
Alligator '80
Battle Beyond the Stars '80
Return of the Secaucus 7 '80
The Howling '81
Baby It's You '82
Lianna '83
The Brother from Another Planet '84
The Clan of the Cave Bear '86
Unnatural Causes '86
Matewan '87
Eight Men Out '88
Breaking In '89
City of Hope '91
Passion Fish '92
Men of War '94
The Secret of Roan Inish '94
Lone Star '95
Hombres Armados '97
Mimic '97
Limbo '99
Sunshine State '02
Casa de los Babys '03
Silver City '04
Honeydripper '07
The Spiderwick Chronicles '08
Go for Sisters '13

George Wallace Sayre (1898-1962)
Reform Girl '33
Where Are Your Children? '44
Black Market Babies '45
Stage Struck '48
Untamed Women '52

Joel Sayre (1901-79)
The Road to Glory '36
Gunga Din '39

Matt Sazama
Dracula Untold '14
The Last Witch Hunter '15
Gods of Egypt '16

Lorene Scafaria
Nick & Norah's Infinite Playlist '08
Seeking a Friend for the End of the World '12
The Meddler '15
Hustlers '19

Newt Scamander (1965-)
See J. K. Rowling

Dan Scanlon
Monsters University '13
Onward '20

David Scarpa
The Last Castle '01
The Day the Earth Stood Still '08
All the Money in the World '17

Furio Scarpelli (1919-2010)
Big Deal on Madonna Street '58
Mafioso '62
The Good, the Bad and the Ugly '67
Time to Kill '89
The Postman '94

Sauro Scavolini (1934-)
The Case of the Scorpion's Tail '71
The Scorpion's Tail '71
Your Vice is a Closed Room and Only I Have the Key '72

Steven Schachter
A Slight Case of Murder '99
The Deal '08

Johnathon Schaech (1969-)
Road House 2: Last Call '06
The Poker Club '08

Eric Schaeffer (1962-)
My Life's in Turnaround '94
If Lucy Fell '95
Fall '97
Wirey Spindell '99
Never Again '01
Mind the Gap '04
After Fall, Winter '11

Jac Schaeffer
Timer '09
The Hustle '19

Scott Schafer (1958-)
Fatwa '06
The Way of War '08

Dylan Schaffer (1964-)
Inside Out '11
Bending the Rules '12

Jeff Schaffer
Dr. Seuss' The Cat in the Hat '03
Eurotrip '04
The Dictator '12

Don Schain
The Abductors '72
Ginger '72
Girls Are for Loving '73

James Schamus (1959-)
The Wedding Banquet '93
Eat Drink Man Woman '94
The Ice Storm '97
Ride with the Devil '99
Crouching Tiger, Hidden Dragon '00
Hulk '03
Lust, Caution '07
Taking Woodstock '09
Indignation '16

Dore Schary (1905-80)
Big City '37
Young Tom Edison '40
It's a Big Country '51
Sunrise at Campobello '60

Richard Schayer (1880-1956)
Tell It to the Marines '26
The Flying Fleet '29
Parlor, Bedroom and Bath '31
Private Lives '31
The Devil Is a Sissy '36
Davy Crockett, Indian Scout '50
The Bandits of Corsica '53
The Steel Lady '53
Top Gun '55
Gun Brothers '56
Five Guns to Tombstone '60

Daniel Schechter
The Big Bad Swim *'06*
Goodbye Baby *'07*
Life of Crime *'13*
Supporting Characters *'13*

David Schechter
Interview *'07*
Blind Date *'08*

Jeff Schechter
Beethoven's 3rd *'00*
Out of the Woods *'05*
Exploding Sun *'13*
The Hunters *'13*

Peter Scheerer
Alone in the Dark *'05*
Alone in the Dark 2 *'08*
Brotherhood of Blood *'08*
Far Cry *'08*

Adam Scheinman
Little Big League *'94*
Mickey Blue Eyes *'99*
Bait *'00*

Andrew Scheinman
Bait *'00*
Flipped *'10*

George Schenck
Don't Worry, We'll Think of a Title *'66*
Kill a Dragon *'67*
More Dead Than Alive *'68*
The Phantom of Hollywood *'74*
Futureworld *'76*
Escape 2000 *'81*
Kiss Me Deadly *'08*

Nick Schenk
Gran Torino *'08*
The Judge *'14*
The Mule *'18*

Robert Schenkkan (1953-)
The Quiet American *'02*
The Andromeda Strain *'08*
The Pacific *'10*
Hacksaw Ridge *'16*

Richard Schenkman (1958-)
The Pompatus of Love *'95*
Went to Coney Island on a Mission from God. . . Be Back by Five *'98*
Abraham Lincoln *vs.* Zombies *'12*
Mischief Night *'13*

Fred Schepisi (1939-)
The Devil's Playground *'76*
The Chant of Jimmie Blacksmith *'78*
A Cry in the Dark *'88*
Last Orders *'01*

Shawn Schepps
Encino Man *'92*
Son-in-Law *'93*
Lip Service *'00*
Drumline *'02*
You and I *'11*

Lone Scherfig (1959-)
Italian for Beginners *'01*
Wilbur Wants to Kill Himself *'02*

Jay Scherick
I Spy *'02*
Serving Sara *'02*
National Security *'03*
Guess Who *'05*
Norbit *'07*
The Smurfs *'11*

Paul Scheuring
A Man Apart *'03*
The Experiment *'10*

Stephen Schiff
Lolita *'97*
The Deep End of the Ocean *'98*
True Crime *'99*
Wall Street 2: Money Never Sleeps *'10*
American Assassin *'17*

Michael Schiffer
Colors *'88*
Lean on Me *'89*
Crimson Tide *'95*
The Peacemaker *'97*
The Four Feathers *'02*

Karl Schiffman
Back in Action *'94*
Bullet Down Under *'94*
Dead End *'98*
Riddler's Moon *'98*

Suzanne Schiffman (1930-2001)
Day for Night *'73*
The Story of Adele H. *'75*
Small Change *'76*
The Man Who Loved Women *'77*
The Last Metro *'80*
The Woman Next Door *'81*
Confidentially Yours *'83*
Sorceress *'88*

Ryan Schifrin
Abominable *'06*
Tales of Halloween *'15*

Vivian Schilling (1968-)
Soultaker *'90*
Future Shock *'93*

Murray Schisgal (1926-)
Luv *'67*
Tootsie *'82*

George Schlatter (1932-)
Norman, Is That You? *'76*
Fire and Ice *'87*

Volker Schlondorff (1939-)
The Tin Drum *'79*
The Ogre *'96*
The Legend of Rita *'99*

Hayden Schlossberg (1978-)
Harold and Kumar Go to White Castle *'04*
Harold & Kumar Escape from Guantanamo Bay *'08*
A Very Harold & Kumar Christmas *'11*
American Reunion *'12*

Wolfgang Schmidt (1938-2009)
See Ray Dennis Steckler

David Schmoeller (1947-)
Tourist Trap *'79*
Day Time Ended *'80*
The Seduction *'82*
Crawlspace *'86*
2 Little Monsters *'15*

Julian Schnabel (1951-)
Basquiat *'96*
Before Night Falls *'00*
At Eternity's Gate *'18*

Marco Schnabel
The Librarian: Return to King Solomon's Mines *'06*
The Librarian: Curse of the Judas Chalice *'08*

Charles Schnee (1916-63)
I Walk Alone *'48*
The Prince of Thieves *'48*
Red River *'48*
Scene of the Crime *'49*
They Live by Night *'49*
The Furies *'50*
Right Cross *'50*
Westward the Women *'51*
The Bad and the Beautiful *'52*
Butterfield 8 *'60*
The Crowded Sky *'60*

Barry Schneider
Ruby *'77*
Harper Valley P.T.A. *'78*
Roller Boogie *'79*
Take This Job & Shove It *'81*
Mother's Boys *'94*

Dan Schneider (1966-)
Good Burger *'97*
Big Fat Liar *'02*

David Schneider (1963-)
All the Queen's Men *'02*
Stark Raving Mad *'02*
The Death of Stalin *'17*

Paul Schneider (1976-)
All the Real Girls *'03*
Pretty Bird *'08*

Rob Schneider (1963-)
Deuce Bigalow: Male Gigolo *'99*
The Animal *'01*
Deuce Bigalow: European Gigolo *'05*

Bernard C. Schoenfeld (1907-90)
Phantom Lady *'44*
Dark Corner *'46*
Caged *'50*
Down Three Dark Streets *'54*
There's Always Tomorrow *'56*
The Space Children *'58*
13 West Street *'62*

Bruce Schooley
America: Imagine the World Without Her *'14*
Hillary's America: The Secret History of the Democratic Party *'16*
Death of a Nation *'18*

Robert Schooley
Aladdin and the King of Thieves *'96*
Sky High *'05*
Hotel for Dogs *'09*
Kim Possible *'19*

David J. Schow (1955-)
Leatherface: The Texas Chainsaw Massacre 3 *'89*
Critters 3 *'91*
Critters 4 *'91*
The Crow *'93*

Leonard Schrader (1943-2006)
The Yakuza *'75*
Blue Collar *'78*
Old Boyfriends *'79*
Kiss of the Spider Woman *'85*
Mishima: A Life in Four Chapters *'85*

Paul Schrader (1946-)
The Yakuza *'75*
Obsession *'76*
Taxi Driver *'76*
Rolling Thunder *'77*
Blue Collar *'78*
American Gigolo *'79*
Hardcore *'79*
Old Boyfriends *'79*
Raging Bull *'80*
Mishima: A Life in Four Chapters *'85*
The Mosquito Coast *'86*
The Last Temptation of Christ *'88*
Light Sleeper *'92*
City Hall *'95*
Touch *'96*
Affliction *'97*
Bringing Out the Dead *'99*
Forever Mine *'99*
The Walker *'07*
Dying of the Light *'14*
First Reformed *'17*

Joseph Schrank (1900-84)
A Slight Case of Murder *'38*
Swing Your Lady *'38*
Cinderella *'64*

Carol Schreder
In Love and War *'91*
Mama Flora's Family *'98*

Liev Schreiber (1967-)
Everything is Illuminated *'05*
Chuck *'17*

Raymond L. Schrock (1892-1950)
Where the North Begins *'23*
The Phantom of the Opera *'25*
Sitting On the Moon *'36*
The Hidden Hand *'42*
Men On Her Mind *'44*
White Pongo *'45*
Danny Boy *'46*
Gas House Kids *'46*
Larceny in her Heart *'46*
Shadows Over Chinatown *'46*
Key Witness *'47*
Hi-Jacked *'50*

Rick Schroder (1970-)
Black Cloud *'04*
Our Wild Hearts *'13*

Allison Schroeder
Mean Girls 2 *'11*
Hidden Figures *'17*
Christopher Robin *'18*

Bernard Schubert (1895-1988)
The Public Defender *'31*
Symphony of Six Million *'32*

Budd Schulberg (1914-2009)
Government Girl *'43*
On the Waterfront *'54*
A Face in the Crowd *'57*

Arnold Schulman (1925-)
Wild Is the Wind *'57*
A Hole in the Head *'59*
Cimarron *'60*
Goodbye, Columbus *'69*
The Night They Raided Minsky's *'69*
Funny Lady *'75*
A Chorus Line *'85*
Tucker: The Man and His Dream *'88*
And the Band Played On *'93*

Roger S.H. Schulman
Balto *'95*
Shrek *'01*
Mulan 2 *'04*
The Fox and the Hound 2 *'06*

Tom Schulman (1951-)
Dead Poets Society *'89*
Honey, I Shrunk the Kids *'89*
Second Sight *'89*
What about Bob? *'91*
Medicine Man *'92*
8 Heads in a Duffel Bag *'96*
Holy Man *'98*
Welcome to Mooseport *'04*

Dave Schultz
Don't Cry Now *'07*
The Other Woman *'08*
Scout's Honor: Badge to the Bone *'09*

Douglas Schulze
Hellmaster *'92*
Dark Fields *'09*
Mimesis *'11*

Joel Schumacher (1939-2020)
Car Wash *'76*
Sparkle *'76*
The Wiz *'78*
D.C. Cab *'84*
St. Elmo's Fire *'85*
Batman and Robin *'97*
Flawless *'99*
The Phantom of the Opera *'04*

Eric Schwab
The Learning Curve *'01*
My Lucky Elephant *'13*

Mark Schwahn (1966-)
Whatever It Takes *'00*
The Perfect Score *'04*
Coach Carter *'05*

David R. Schwartz (1911-2003)
Island of Love *'63*
Robin and the 7 Hoods *'64*
Sex and the Single Girl *'64*
That Funny Feeling *'65*
The Bobo *'67*

Deborah Schwartz
Thunder in Paradise 3 *'94*
Soul Surfer *'11*

Elroy Schwartz
Wackiest Wagon Train in the West *'77*
Rescue from Gilligan's Island *'78*

Mark Evan Schwartz
Little Men *'98*
Wanted *'98*

Sherwood Schwartz (1916-2011)
Wackiest Wagon Train in the West *'77*
Rescue from Gilligan's Island *'78*

S.S. Schweitzer
Hornets' Nest *'70*
A Step Out of Line *'71*

Alberto Sciamma (1961-)
Killer Tongue *'96*
Jericho Mansions *'03*

Céline Sciamma
Girlhood *'14*
My Life as a Zucchini *'16*
Portrait of a Lady on Fire *'19*

Aleksander Scibor-Rylski (1928-83)
Man of Marble *'76*
Man of Iron *'81*

David Scinto
Sexy Beast *'00*
44 Inch Chest *'09*

Ettore Scola (1931-)
Two Nights with Cleopatra *'54*
Adua and Her Friends *'60*
Il Sorpasso *'63*
A Special Day *'77*
Macaroni *'85*

Kathryn Scola (1891-1982)
One Night at Susie's *'30*
Night After Night *'32*
Baby Face *'33*
Midnight Mary *'33*
The Merry Frinks *'34*
Second Honeymoon *'37*
Alexander's Ragtime Band *'38*
Always Goodbye *'38*
The Baroness and the Butler *'38*
One Night in the Tropics *'40*
The Constant Nymph *'43*
Colonel Effingham's Raid *'45*
Night Unto Night *'49*

Nino Scolaro (1921-)
Caesar the Conqueror *'63*
Hercules against the Moon Men *'64*

Martin Scorsese (1942-)
Mean Streets *'73*
Goodfellas *'90*
The Age of Innocence *'93*
Casino *'95*
Silence *'16*

Allan Scott (1907-95)
Top Hat *'35*
Joy of Living *'38*
Lucky Partners *'40*
Remember the Day *'41*
So Proudly We Hail *'43*
The 5000 Fingers of Dr. T *'53*
Top Secret Affair *'57*
Don't Look Now *'73*
The Girl from Petrovka *'74*
Spiral Staircase *'75*
Joseph Andrews *'77*
The Awakening *'80*
D.A.R.Y.L. *'85*
Castaway *'87*
The Witches *'90*
Cold Heaven *'92*
Two Deaths *'94*
In Love and War *'96*
The Preacher's Wife *'96*
Samson and Delilah *'96*
Behind the Lines *'97*

Darin Scott
Tales from the Hood *'95*
Sprung *'96*
Caught Up *'98*
Waist Deep *'06*
Dark House *'09*

Don D. Scott
Barbershop *'02*
Barbershop 2: Back in Business *'04*

Evan Scott
Death Toll *'07*
Father of Lies *'07*

Gavin Scott (1950-)
The Borrowers *'97*
Small Soldiers *'98*
Mists of Avalon *'01*
Beauty and the Beast: A Dark Tale *'10*
Absolutely Anything *'17*

Jessica Scott
Another Cinderella Story *'08*
A Cinderella Story: Once Upon a Song *'11*
Radio Rebel *'12*

Kelsey Scott
Motives *'03*
Motives 2-Retribution *'07*

Ken Scott
Delivery Man *'13*
The Grand Seduction *'13*

Leigh Scott
King of the Lost World *'06*
Pirates of Treasure Island *'06*
Invasion of the Pod People *'07*
Transmorphers *'07*
Cyborg Conquest *'09*
Wolvesbayne *'09*
The Witches of Oz *'11*

Michael Scott
Slappy and the Stinkers *'97*
The Mark 2: Redemption *'13*

Sherman Scott (1954-)
See Fred Olen Ray

Steven Seagal (1952-)
Belly of the Beast *'03*
Attack Force *'06*
Kill Switch *'08*
Born to Raise Hell *'10*

Peter S. Seaman (1951-)
Trenchcoat *'83*
Who Framed Roger Rabbit *'88*
Doc Hollywood *'91*
Wild Wild West *'99*
Dr. Seuss' How the Grinch Stole Christmas *'00*
Last Holiday *'06*
Shrek the Third *'07*

Ted Sears (1900-58)
Snow White and the Seven Dwarfs *'37*
Pinocchio *'40*
The Adventures of Ichabod and Mr. Toad *'49*
Peter Pan *'53*

Zelda Sears (1873-1935)
Emma *'32*
New Morals for Old *'32*
Dancing Lady *'33*
Day of Reckoning *'33*
Tugboat Annie *'33*
Operator 13 *'34*

George Seaton (1911-79)
A Day at the Races *'37*
Doctor Takes a Wife *'40*
Charley's Aunt *'41*
That Night in Rio *'41*
Coney Island *'43*
Junior Miss *'45*
Miracle on 34th Street *'47*
The Shocking Miss Pilgrim *'47*
Apartment for Peggy *'48*
Chicken Every Sunday *'48*
For Heaven's Sake *'50*
Country Girl *'54*
The Proud and Profane *'56*
The Counterfeit Traitor *'62*
36 Hours *'64*
Airport *'70*
Miracle on 34th Street *'94*

Cheryl Seban
Au Pair *'99*
Au Pair 2: The Fairy Tale Continues *'01*

Jack Seddon (1924-2001)
Murder She Said *'61*
Kill or Cure *'62*

John Scott Shepherd (1964-)
Joe Somebody '01
Life or Something Like It '02

John Shepphird
The Santa Trap '02
Chupacabra Terror '05

Eyal Sher
Under the Domim Tree '95
Axe '06

Jack Sher (1913-88)
My Favorite Spy '51
Shane '53
The Three Worlds of Gulliver '59
The 3 Worlds of Gulliver '60
Paris Blues '61
Critic's Choice '63
Move Over, Darling '63
Goodbye, Raggedy Ann '71

Ted Sherdeman (1909-87)
Breakthrough '50
Scandal Sheet '52
The Eddie Cantor Story '53
Them! '54
Away All Boats '56
Misty '61
Latitude Zero '69

Bob Sheridan
Sorority House Massacre 2: Nighty Nightmare '92
Against the Law '98

Jim Sheridan (1949-)
My Left Foot '89
The Field '90
Into the West '92
In the Name of the Father '93
Some Mother's Son '96
The Boxer '97
In America '02

Michael J. Sheridan
That's Entertainment, Part 3 '93
When the Sky Falls '99

Taylor Sheridan
Sicario '15
Hell or High Water '16
Wind River '17
Sicario: Day of the Soldado '18

Fenn Sherie (1896-1953)
Song of Freedom '36
Big Fella '37

Adam Sherman
Happiness Runs '10
Crazy Eyes '12

Eric P. Sherman
Carnival of Wolves '96
Eastside '99

Gary Sherman (1945-)
Phobia '80
Poltergeist 3 '88

Jeffrey C. Sherman
Au Pair '99
Au Pair 2: The Fairy Tale Continues '01
Au Pair 3: Adventure in Paradise '09

Martin Sherman (1938-)
Alive and Kicking '96
Bent '97
Callas Forever '02
The Roman Spring of Mrs. Stone '03
Mrs. Henderson Presents '05

Teddi Sherman (1924-)
Tennessee's Partner '55
Four for Texas '63

R.C. Sherriff (1896-1975)
The Old Dark House '32
The Invisible Man '33
The Four Feathers '39
Goodbye, Mr. Chips '39
This Above All '42
Odd Man Out '47
No Highway in the Sky '51
Storm Over the Nile '55

David Sherwin (1942-)
If. . . '69
Britannia Hospital '82

Robert Sherwood (1896-1955)
The Scarlet Pimpernel '34
The Ghost Goes West '36
The Adventures of Marco Polo '38
Abe Lincoln in Illinois '40
Rebecca '40
The Best Years of Our Lives '46
The Bishop's Wife '47
Man on a Tightrope '53

Zach Shields
Krampus '15
Godzilla: King of the Monsters '19

Susan Shilliday
Legends of the Fall '94
I Dreamed of Africa '00

Hyung Rae Shim (1958-)
Dragon Wars '07
The Last Godfather '10

Takashi Shimizu (1972-)
Ju-On 2 '00
Ju-On: The Grudge '03
The Grudge '04

Shintaro Shimosawa
The Echo '08
Repentance '14

Kaneto Shindo (1912-2012)
Kuroneko '68
Rica '72
Under the Flag of the Rising Sun '72
Rica 2: Lonely Wanderer '73
Rica 3: Juvenile's Lullaby '73

Masahiro Shinoda (1931-)
Pale Flower '64
Double Suicide '69

Barry Shipman (1912-94)
S.O.S. Coast Guard '37
Flash Gordon Conquers the Universe '40

Ryan Shiraki
Poster Boy '04
Spring Breakdown '08

John Shirley (1953-)
The Crow '93
The Tomb '09

Jack Sholder (1945-)
Alone in the Dark '82
Wishmaster 2: Evil Never Dies '98

Del Shores (1957-)
Daddy's Dyin'. . . Who's Got the Will? '90
Sordid Lives '00

Cate Shortland (1968-)
Somersault '04
Lore '13

Michael Showalter (1970-)
Wet Hot American Summer '01
The Baxter '05
They Came Together '14

Joe Shrapnel (1976-)
Race '16
The Aftermath '19
Seberg '19

Dennis Shryack (1936-)
The Car '77
Pale Rider '85
Aces 'n Eights '08

Takeshi Shudo
Pokemon: The First Movie '99
Pokemon the Movie 2000: The Power of One '00
Pokemon 3: The Movie '01

Irving Shulman (1913-95)
The Ring '52
Rebel without a Cause '55

Max Shulman (1919-88)
The Affairs of Dobie Gillis '53
Confidentially Connie '53
Half a Hero '53

Trey Edward Shults
Krisha '15
It Comes at Night '17
Waves '19

Mina Shum
Double Happiness '94
Long Life, Happiness and Prosperity '02

Harold Shumate (1893-1983)
The Kansan '43
Abilene Town '46
Saddle Tramp '47
Buccaneer's Girl '50

Ronald Shusett
Phobia '80
Dead and Buried '81
King Kong Lives '86
Freejack '92
Bleeders '97

M. Night Shyamalan (1970-)
Wide Awake '97
The Sixth Sense '99
Stuart Little '99
Unbreakable '00
Signs '02
The Village '04
Lady in the Water '06
The Happening '08
The Last Airbender '10
After Earth '13
The Visit '15
Split '16
Glass '19

Charles Shyer (1941-)
Smokey and the Bandit '77
Goin' South '78
House Calls '78
Private Benjamin '80
Irreconcilable Differences '84
Protocol '84
Baby Boom '87
Father of the Bride '91
I Love Trouble '94
Father of the Bride Part 2 '95
The Parent Trap '98
Alfie '04

Sylvia Sichel
All Over Me '96
If These Walls Could Talk 2 '00

Andy Sidaris (1933-)
Hard Ticket to Hawaii '87
Picasso Trigger '89
Guns '90
Do or Die '91
Hard Hunted '92
Fit to Kill '93
Day of the Warrior '96
Return to Savage Beach '97

Alastair Siddons
Trespass Against Us '16
Tomb Raider '18

Lynn Siefert
Cool Runnings '93
Cousin Bette '97

David Siegel
Suture '93
The Deep End '01
Uncertainty '08

Robert Siegel
Swimming '00
The Wrestler '08
Big Fan '09
Turbo '13
The Founder '17
Cruise '18

Brian Sieve
Boogeyman 2 '07
Boogeyman 3 '08

Cas Sigers
A Cross to Bear '12
Hamlet & Hutch '14

Christoph Silber (1971-)
North Face '08
The Von Trapp Family: A Life of Music '15

Brad Silberling (1962-)
Moonlight Mile '02
10 Items or Less '06
An Ordinary Man '18

Jerome Silberman (1933-2016)
See Gene Wilder

Katie Silberman
Booksmart '19
Isn't It Romantic '19

Robert Silliphant (1937-99)
Incredibly Strange Creatures Who Stopped Living and Became Mixed-Up Zombies '63
Creeping Terror '64

Stirling Silliphant (1918-96)
5 Against the House '55
Nightfall '56
The Lineup '58
Village of the Damned '60
The Slender Thread '65
In the Heat of the Night '67
Charly '68
Marlowe '69
The Liberation of L.B. Jones '70
Walk in the Spring Rain '70
Murphy's War '71
The New Centurions '72
The Poseidon Adventure '72
Shaft in Africa '73
The Towering Inferno '74
The Killer Elite '75
The Enforcer '76
Telefon '77
Circle of Iron '78
Pearl '78
The Swarm '78
When Time Ran Out '80
Over the Top '86
Catch the Heat '87
The Grass Harp '95

Sebastian Silva (1979-)
The Maid '09
Crystal Fairy & the Magical Cactus '13
Magic Magic '13
Nasty Baby '15

Amanda Silver
The Hand that Rocks the Cradle '92
An Eye for an Eye '95
The Relic '96
Rise of the Planet of the Apes '11
Dawn of the Planet of the Apes '14
Jurassic World '15

Scott Silver
johns '96
The Mod Squad '99
8 Mile '02
The Fighter '10
The Finest Hours '16
Joker '19

Peter Silverman
American Heart '92
Hidden in America '96
Harlan County War '00
Something the Lord Made '04
Touch the Top of the World '06

Nancey Silvers
Battling for Baby '92
One Special Night '99
Mom at Sixteen '05
Home By Christmas '06
Why I Wore Lipstick to My Mastectomy '06
Girl, Positive '07
How I Married My High School Crush '07
Call Me Mrs. Miracle '10
Sundays at Tiffany's '10
William & Kate '11
Love at the Thanksgiving Day Parade '12

Marc Silverstein
Never Been Kissed '99
He's Just Not That Into You '09
Valentine's Day '10
The Vow '12
How to Be Single '16
I Feel Pretty '18

David Simkins
Adventures in Babysitting '87
Alien Raiders '08

Anthony Simmons (1922-)
Four in the Morning '65
The Optimists '73

Richard Alan Simmons
War Paint '53
Three Hours to Kill '54
Female On the Beach '55
Outlaw's Son '57
Tarawa Beachhead '58

Jay Simms
The Giant Gila Monster '59
The Killer Shrews '59
Creation of the Humanoids '62
Panic in Year Zero! '62

Adam Simon (1962-)
Brain Dead '89
Carnosaur '93
Bones '01

Alex Simon (1967-)
Piranha '95
Unknown Origin '95
Bloodfist 8: Hard Way Out '96
My Brother's War '97

Ellen Simon
Moonlight and Valentino '95
One Fine Day '96

Neil Simon (1927-)
After the Fox '66
Barefoot in the Park '67
The Odd Couple '68
The Out-of-Towners '70
Plaza Suite '71
Star Spangled Girl '71
The Heartbreak Kid '72
Last of the Red Hot Lovers '72
Prisoner of Second Avenue '74
The Sunshine Boys '75
Murder by Death '76
The Goodbye Girl '77
California Suite '78
The Cheap Detective '78
Chapter Two '79
Seems Like Old Times '80
Only When I Laugh '81
Max Dugan Returns '83
The Slugger's Wife '85
Brighton Beach Memoirs '86
Biloxi Blues '88
The Marrying Man '91
Lost in Yonkers '93
The Sunshine Boys '95
The Odd Couple 2 '98

Nick Simon (1973-)
Cold Comes the Night '14
The Pyramid '14

Giovanni Simonelli
The Old Testament '62
Assassination in Rome '65
Kiss Kiss Kill Kill '66
One After Another '68
Gunslinger '70

Rocco Simonelli
The Substitute '96
The Substitute 2: School's Out '97
The Substitute 3: Winner Takes All '99
The Sweet Life '03

Albert Simonin (1905-80)
Any Number Can Win '63
Cold Sweat '71

Theodore Simonson
The Blob '58
The 4D Man '59

Charles Sinclair
Chase a Crooked Shadow '58
The Green Slime '68

Joshua Sinclair (1953-)
Judgment in Berlin '88
Shaka Zulu: The Last Great Warrior '01

Stephen Sinclair
Meet the Feebles '89
Dead Alive '93
Lord of the Rings: The Two Towers '02

Bryan Singer (1966-)
Public Access '93
The Triangle '05
Superman Returns '06

Eric Warren Singer
The International '09
American Hustle '13
Only the Brave '17

Josh Singer
The Fifth Estate '13
Spotlight '15
The Post '17
First Man '18

Randi Mayem Singer
Mrs. Doubtfire '93
Tooth Fairy '10
Alvin and the Chipmunks: Road Chip '15

Raymond Singer
NightScreams '97
Mulan '98

John Singleton (1968-)
Boyz N the Hood '91
Poetic Justice '93
Higher Learning '94
Baby Boy '01

Gary Sinyor (1962-)
Leon the Pig Farmer '93
Stiff Upper Lips '96
Bob the Butler '05
In Your Dreams '07

Curt Siodmak (1902-2000)
Non-Stop New York '37
Black Friday '40
The Invisible Man Returns '40
The Wolf Man '41
Frankenstein Meets the Wolfman '42
Invisible Agent '42
I Walked with a Zombie '43
The Climax '44
The Beast with Five Fingers '46
Tarzan's Magic Fountain '48
Bride of the Gorilla '51
The Magnetic Monster '53

Bryan Sipe
Demolition '15
The Choice '16

Rosemary Anne Sisson (1923-2017)
Elizabeth R '72
The Littlest Horse Thieves '76
Candleshoe '78
The Duchess of Duke Street '78
The Bretts '88
A Change of Place '94

Rob Sitch (1962-)
The Castle '97
The Dish '00

Chris Sivertson
Wicked Lake '08
Marauders '16

Tom Six
The Human Centipede: First Sequence '10
The Human Centipede 2: Full Sequence '11
The Human Centipede 3: The Final Sequence '15

Victor Sjostrom (1879-1960)
The Outlaw and His Wife '17
The Phantom Chariot '20

David Spade (1964-)
Lost and Found *'99*
Joe Dirt *'01*
Dickie Roberts: Former Child Star *'03*

Jon Spaihts
The Darkest Hour *'11*
Prometheus *'12*
Doctor Strange *'16*
Passengers *'16*

Esta Spalding (1966-)
Falling Angels *'03*
The Republic of Love *'03*
In God's Country *'07*
Would Be Kings *'08*

Harry Spalding (1913-2008)
Young Guns of Texas *'62*
Raiders from Beneath the Sea *'64*
Wild On the Beach *'65*

Chris Sparling
Buried *'10*
ATM *'12*
The Sea of Trees *'16*
Down a Dark Hall *'18*

David Sparling
Mission of Death *'97*
Operation Delta Force 2: Mayday *'97*
Operation Delta Force 3: Clear Target *'98*

Douglas Spaulding (1920-2012)
See Ray Bradbury

Leonard Spaulding (1920-2012)
See Ray Bradbury

Peter Speakman
Blowin' Smoke *'99*
Fat Kid Rules the World *'12*

Aaron Spelling
One Foot in Hell *'60*
Black Brigade *'69*

Greg Spence
Children of the Corn 4: The Gathering *'96*
The Prophecy 2: Ashtown *'97*

Ralph Spence (1890-1949)
A Lady of Chance *'28*
The Patsy *'28*
Caught Plastered *'31*
Cracked Nuts *'31*
Fast Life *'32*
The Passionate Plumber *'32*
Stand Up and Cheer *'34*
Strictly Dynamite *'34*
The Flying Deuces *'39*
Down Argentine Way *'40*

Rod C. Spence
The Good Witch *'08*
The Good Witch's Gift *'10*

Don Spencer
The Student Nurses *'70*
The Big Doll House *'71*

Milton Sperling (1912-88)
Sing, Baby, Sing *'36*
Thin Ice *'37*
Happy Landing *'38*
The Return of the Cisco Kid *'39*
Merrill's Marauders *'62*

Bella Spewack (1899-1990)
Clear All Wires! *'33*
The Nuisance *'33*
The Cat and the Fiddle *'34*
Rendezvous *'35*
Boy Meets Girl *'38*
Three Loves Has Nancy *'38*
My Favorite Wife *'40*
Weekend at the Waldorf *'45*

Samuel Spewack (1899-1971)
Clear All Wires! *'33*
The Nuisance *'33*
The Cat and the Fiddle *'34*
Rendezvous *'35*
Boy Meets Girl *'38*
Three Loves Has Nancy *'38*
My Favorite Wife *'40*
Weekend at the Waldorf *'45*

Penelope Spheeris (1945-)
Suburbia *'83*
The Little Rascals *'94*

Matt Spicer
Ingrid Goes West *'17*
Flower *'18*

Scott Spiegel (1957-)
Evil Dead 2: Dead by Dawn *'87*
Thou Shalt Not Kill. . .Except *'87*
The Nutt House *'95*
From Dusk Till Dawn 2: Texas Blood Money *'98*

Steven Spielberg (1947-)
The Sugarland Express *'74*
Close Encounters of the Third Kind *'77*
Poltergeist *'82*
The Goonies *'85*
A. I.: Artificial Intelligence *'01*

Michael Spierig
Undead *'05*
Daybreakers *'09*
Predestination *'15*
Winchester *'18*

Peter Spierig
Undead *'05*
Daybreakers *'09*
Predestination *'15*
Winchester *'18*

Adrian Spies (1920-98)
Dark of the Sun *'68*
Hanging By a Thread *'79*

Leonard Spigelgass (1908-85)
The Boys From Syracuse *'40*
Big Street *'42*
I Was a Male War Bride *'49*
The Law and the Lady *'51*
Scandal at Scourie *'53*
Athena *'54*
A Majority of One *'56*
Ten Thousand Bedrooms *'57*
Gypsy *'62*

Evan Spiliotopoulos
Art Heist *'05*
Battle for Terra *'09*
Hercules *'14*
The Huntsman: Winter's War *'16*
Beauty and the Beast *'17*

Gary Spinelli
Stash House *'12*
American Made *'17*

Tony Spiridakis (1959-)
Queens Logic *'91*
If Lucy Fell *'95*
The Last Word *'95*

Marian Spitzer (1899-1983)
The Dolly Sisters *'46*
Look for the Silver Lining *'49*

Frank Spotnitz
The X-Files *'98*
The X Files: I Want to Believe *'08*

Simon Sprackling
Funnyman *'94*
The Reeds *'09*

Jill Sprecher
Clockwatchers *'97*
Thirteen Conversations About One Thing *'01*
Thin Ice *'12*

Karen Sprecher
Clockwatchers *'97*
Thirteen Conversations About One Thing *'01*
Thin Ice *'12*

Morgan Spurlock (1970-)
Super Size Me *'04*
Where in the World Is Osama Bin Laden? *'06*
Freakonomics *'10*
Comic-Con Episode IV: A Fan's Hope *'11*
POM Wonderful Presents: The Greatest Movie Ever Sold *'11*
Super Size Me 2: Holy Chicken! *'19*

Salvatore Stabile
Gravesend *'97*
Where God Left His Shoes *'07*

Bima Stagg
Inside *'96*
Stander *'03*

Rama Laurie Stagner
Blue Sky *'91*
House of Versace *'13*

Eric Steven Stahl (1959-)
Safe House *'99*
I-See-You.Com *'06*

Jerry Stahl (1953-)
Bad Boys 2 *'03*
Hemingway & Gelhorn *'12*
Urge *'16*
Chuck *'17*

Kent Staines
Prom Queen *'04*
Spirit Bear: The Simon Jackson Story *'05*

Laurence Stallings (1894-1968)
Fast Workers *'33*
The Jungle Book *'42*
On Our Merry Way *'48*
She Wore a Yellow Ribbon *'49*
The Sun Shines Bright *'53*

Sylvester Stallone (1946-)
The Lords of Flatbush *'74*
Rocky *'76*
F.I.S.T. *'78*
Paradise Alley *'78*
Rocky 2 *'79*
First Blood *'82*
Rocky 3 *'82*
Staying Alive *'83*
Rhinestone *'84*
Rambo: First Blood, Part 2 *'85*
Rocky 4 *'85*
Cobra *'86*
Over the Top *'86*
Rambo 3 *'88*
Rocky 5 *'90*
Cliffhanger *'93*
Driven *'01*
Rocky Balboa *'06*
Rambo *'08*
The Expendables *'10*
The Expendables 2 *'12*
Homefront *'13*
The Expendables 3 *'14*
Creed II *'18*
Rambo: Last Blood *'19*

Sean Stanek
A Crack in the Floor *'00*
Played *'06*

Zac Stanford
The Chumscrubber *'05*
Sleepwalking *'08*

Justin Stanley (1973-)
The Last Assassins *'96*
Beneath Loch Ness *'01*
Black Butterfly *'17*

Richard Stanley (1966-)
Dust Devil *'93*
The Island of Dr. Moreau *'96*
Color Out of Space *'19*

Eliot Stannard (1888-1944)
The Pleasure Garden *'25*
The Lodger *'26*
The Manxman *'29*

Stanislav Stanojevic
Diary of a Suicide *'73*
Subversion *'79*

Andrew Stanton (1965-)
A Bug's Life *'98*
Toy Story 2 *'99*
Monsters, Inc. *'01*
Finding Nemo *'03*
WALL-E *'08*
John Carter *'12*
Finding Dory *'16*
Toy Story 4 *'19*

Jeff Stanzler
Jumpin' at the Boneyard *'92*
Sorry, Haters *'05*

Lynn Starling (1888-1955)
Torch Singer *'33*
More Than A Secretary *'36*
Thanks for the Memory *'38*
Three Blind Mice *'38*
The Cat and the Canary *'39*
Wintertime *'43*
The Climax *'44*
It's a Pleasure *'45*

Ben Starr
Our Man Flint *'66*
Texas Across the River *'66*
The Busy Body *'67*
How to Commit Marriage *'69*

Jean Stawarz
Powwow Highway *'89*
Spirit Rider *'93*

Riley Stearns
Faults *'15*
The Art of Self-Defense *'19*

Ray Dennis Steckler (1938-2009)
The Thrill Killers *'65*
Las Vegas Serial Killer *'86*

Andrew Steele
The Ladies Man *'00*
Casa de mi Padre *'12*

Burr Steers (1966-)
Igby Goes Down *'02*
How to Lose a Guy in 10 Days *'03*
Pride and Prejudice and Zombies *'16*

Joseph Stefano (1922-2006)
Black Orchid *'59*
Psycho *'60*
Blackout *'78*
Psycho 4: The Beginning *'90*
Two Bits *'96*
Psycho *'98*

Darren Stein (1973-)
Jawbreaker *'98*
Sparkler *'99*

Jeff Stein
The Kids Are Alright *'79*
The Perfect Holiday *'07*

David H. Steinberg
Slackers *'02*
American Pie Presents: Book of Love *'09*
Kindergarten Cop 2 *'16*

Hank Steinberg (1969-)
61* *'01*
RFK *'02*

Michael Steinberg (1959-)
Sleep with Me *'94*
The Cave *'05*

Norman Steinberg (1939-)
Blazing Saddles *'74*
My Favorite Year *'82*
Yes, Giorgio *'82*
Johnny Dangerously *'84*
Funny About Love *'90*

Reed Steiner
Night of the Scarecrow *'95*
S.W.A.T.: Firefight *'11*

Peter Steinfeld
Drowning Mona *'00*
Analyze That *'02*
Be Cool *'05*
21 *'08*

J. David Stem
The Rugrats Movie *'98*
Jimmy Neutron: Boy Genius *'01*
Clockstoppers *'02*
Shrek 2 *'04*
Are We There Yet? *'05*

Gerard Stembridge (1958-)
Ordinary Decent Criminal *'99*
About Adam *'00*
Nora *'00*
Alarm *'08*

Robert A. Stemmle (1903-73)
Testament of Dr. Mabuse *'62*
Apache's Last Battle *'64*

Rick Stempson
Balls Out: Gary the Tennis Coach *'09*
The Goods: Live Hard, Sell Hard *'09*

Zack Stentz
Agent Cody Banks *'03*
Thor *'11*
X-Men: First Class *'11*

Mora Stephens
Devil's Pond *'03*
Conventioneers *'05*
Zipper *'15*

Todd Stephens
Edge of Seventeen *'99*
Gypsy 83 *'01*

Jeff Stephenson
Smoke Jumpers *'08*
Not Since You *'09*

John Steppling
52 Pick-Up *'86*
Animal Factory *'00*

Brett Sterling (1920-2012)
See Ray Bradbury

Dan Sterling
The Interview *'14*
Long Shot *'19*

Daniel I. Stern
Open Season 2 *'08*
Open Season 3 *'10*

David Stern (1909-2003)
Swamp Women *'55*
Gepetto *'00*

Emil Stern
The Life Before Her Eyes *'07*
Tenderness *'08*
Legend of the Guardians: The Owls of Ga'Hoole *'10*

Henry Stern
Love Among Thieves *'86*
Eden *'93*

J. David Stern
Daddy Day Camp *'07*
The Smurfs *'11*

Jared Stern
Mr. Popper's Penguins *'11*
The Watch *'12*
The Internship *'13*
The LEGO Batman Movie *'17*
The LEGO Ninjago Movie *'17*

Joshua Michael Stern
Amityville Dollhouse *'96*
The Contractor *'07*
Swing Vote *'08*

Leonard Stern (1923-)
Abbott and Costello in the Foreign Legion *'50*
Ma and Pa Kettle Go to Town *'50*
The Jazz Singer *'52*
Lost in Alaska *'52*
Three for the Show *'55*

Noah Stern
The Opposite Sex and How to Live With Them *'93*
The Invisibles *'99*

Ricki Stern
The Devil Came on Horseback *'07*
In My Father's House *'15*

Sandor Stern (1936-)
The Amityville Horror *'79*
Assassin *'86*
Shattered Innocence *'87*
Pin. . . *'88*
Amityville 4: The Evil Escapes *'89*

Stewart Stern (1922-2015)
Rebel without a Cause *'55*
The Rack *'56*
The Ugly American *'63*
Rachel, Rachel *'68*
Summer Wishes, Winter Dreams *'73*

Tom Stern (1940-)
Hell's Angels '69 *'69*
Freaked *'93*
An American Werewolf in Paris *'97*

Josh Sternfeld
Winter Solstice *'04*
Meskada *'10*

Joshua Sternin
Surviving Christmas *'04*
Tooth Fairy *'10*
Yogi Bear *'10*

Patrick Stettner
The Business of Strangers *'01*
The Night Listener *'06*

Andrew Stevens (1955-)
Fire From Below *'09*
Tommy and the Cool Mule *'09*

Dana Stevens
Blink *'93*
City of Angels *'98*
For Love of the Game *'99*
Life or Something Like It *'02*
Safe Haven *'13*

David Stevens
Breaker Morant *'80*
Queen *'93*
The Sum of Us *'94*
The Thorn Birds: The Missing Years *'96*
Mama Flora's Family *'98*
Merlin *'98*
Aftershock: Earthquake in New York *'99*
Jackie, Ethel, Joan: The Kennedy Women *'01*

George Stevens, Jr. (1932-)
Separate but Equal *'91*
Thurgood *'11*

Leslie Stevens (1924-98)
The Marriage-Go-Round *'61*
Hero's Island *'62*
Incubus *'65*
Probe *'72*
Gordy *'95*

Louis Stevens (1899-1963)
The Texas Rangers *'36*
Border River *'47*
Massacre River *'49*
Horizons West *'52*
Gun Duel In Durango *'57*

Neal Marshall Stevens
13 Ghosts *'01*
Hellraiser: Deader *'05*

Philip Stevenson (1896-1965)
The Story of G.I. Joe *'45*
The Girl in White *'52*

Robert Stevenson (1905-86)
Nine Days a Queen *'36*
Jane Eyre *'44*

Donald Stewart (1930-99)
The White Sister *'33*
Cannonball *'76*
Jackson County Jail *'76*
Death Sport *'78*
Missing *'82*
The Hunt for Red October *'90*
Patriot Games *'92*
Clear and Present Danger *'94*
Dead Silence *'96*

Donald Ogden Stewart (1894-1980)
Dinner at Eight *'33*
Going Hollywood *'33*
No More Ladies *'35*
Prisoner of Zenda *'37*
Holiday *'38*

Bruce Sweeney
Last Wedding '01
American Venus '07

Julia Sweeney (1959-)
It's Pat: The Movie '94
God Said 'Ha!' '99

Edithe Swensen
Too Young to Be a Dad '02
Student Seduction '03
Bond of Silence '10
Who Is Clark Rockefeller? '10

Michael Swerdlick
Can't Buy Me Love '87
Love Don't Cost a Thing '03

Tommy Swerdlow (1962-)
Cool Runnings '93
Little Giants '94
Bushwhacked '95
Snow Dogs '02

Jo Swerling (1893-1964)
Ladies of Leisure '30
Rain or Shine '30
The Miracle Woman '31
Platinum Blonde '31
Ten Cents a Dance '31
Forbidden '32
Love Affair '32
Shopworn '32
East of Fifth Avenue '33
The Defense Rests '34
Lady by Choice '34
No Greater Glory '34
The Whole Town's Talking '35
Pennies from Heaven '36
Double Wedding '37
Made for Each Other '39
The Real Glory '39
The Westerner '40
Blood and Sand '41
Confirm or Deny '41
The Pride of the Yankees '42
Crash Dive '43
Lifeboat '44
Leave Her to Heaven '45
It's a Wonderful Life '46

John Swetnam
Into the Storm '14
Step Up: All In '14

Robin Swicord (1952-)
Shag: The Movie '89
Little Women '94
The Perez Family '94
Matilda '96
Practical Magic '98
Memoirs of a Geisha '05
The Jane Austen Book Club '07
The Promise '17
Wakefield '17

David Swift (1919-2001)
Pollyanna '60
The Parent Trap '61
The Interns '62
Love Is a Ball '63
Under the Yum-Yum Tree '63
Good Neighbor Sam '64
How to Succeed in Business without Really Trying '67
Candleshoe '78
The Parent Trap '98

Mark Swift
Freddy vs. Jason '03
Friday the 13th '09
Baywatch '17

Musa Syeed
Valley of Saints '12
Menashe '17

Joe Syracuse (1967-)
Surf's Up '07
Parental Guidance '12
Amateur Night '16
Dear Dictator '18

Istvan Szabo (1938-)
Father '67
Love Film '70
25 Fireman's Street '73
Mephisto '81
Meeting Venus '91
Sunshine '99

Janos Szasz
Woyzeck '94
The Notebook '13

Andras Szeker
Opium: Diary of a Madwoman '07
The Notebook '13

Kam-yuen Szeto
Dog Bite Dog '06
Exiled '06
Flash Point '07
Out of the Inferno '13

On Szeto
Corpse Mania '81
The Magic Blade '08

Roy Szeto
Mr. Vampire '86
Dragons Forever '88
Wicked City '92
The Phantom Lover '95

Damian Szifron
The Bottom of the Sea '03
Wild Tales '14

Thomas Szollosi
Three O'Clock High '87
Bone Daddy '97
Snow White: A Tale of Terror '97
It Waits '05

Adam Sztykiel
Made of Honor '08
Due Date '10
Alvin and the Chipmunks: Road Chip '15
Rampage '18
Scoob! '20

Matthew Tabak
Beyond Suspicion '00
Obsessed '02
Point of Origin '02
Ann Rule Presents: The Stranger Beside Me '03
Plain Truth '04

George Tabori (1914-)
I Confess '53
The Journey '59

Paul Tabori (1908-74)
Four Sided Triangle '53
Spaceways '53
Paid to Kill '54

Jorma Taccone (1977-)
MacGruber '10
Popstar: Never Stop Never Stopping '16

Massy Tadjedin
Leo '02
The Jacket '05
Last Night '10

Brian Taggert
Visiting Hours '82
Of Unknown Origin '83
The New Kids '85
Wanted Dead or Alive '86
Poltergeist 3 '88
What Ever Happened To. . . '93
Dangerous Passion '95
Trucks '97

Hajime Taikawa
Shinobi no Mono '62
Shinobi no Mono 2: Vengeance '63
Shinobi No Mono 3: Resurrection '09

Don Tait
Hell's Angels '69 '69
The North Avenue Irregulars '79
Unidentified Flying Oddball '79

Tibor Takacs (1954-)
Redline '97
Spiders '13

Koji Takada (1934-)
Legends of the Poisonous Seductress 1: Female Demon Ohyaku '68
Legends of the Poisonous Seductress 2: Quick Draw Okatsu '69
Legends of the Poisonous Seductress 3: Okatsu the Fugitive '69
Return of the Street Fighter '74
The Street Fighter '74

Hiroshi Takahashi
Ringu '98
Ringu 2 '99
Ringu 0 '01
Crows Zero '07

Isao Takahata (1935-2018)
Grave of the Fireflies '88
Pom Poko '94
The Tale of the Princess Kaguya '13
Only Yesterday '16

Shigenori Takechi
Graveyard of Honor '02
Blood '09

Beat Takeshi (1947-)
See Takeshi 'Beat' Kitano

David E. Talbert (1966-)
First Sunday '08
Baggage Claim '13
Almost Christmas '16

Tim Talbott
The Lather Effect '06
The Stanford Prison Experiment '15

Amy Talkington
Brave New Girl '04
The Night of the White Pants '06
Valley Girl '20

Ted Tally (1952-)
White Palace '90
The Silence of the Lambs '91
Before and After '95
The Juror '96
All the Pretty Horses '00
Red Dragon '02
12 Strong '18

Frankie Tam
The Four '12
Kingdom of Blood: The Final Battle '16

Paul Tamasy
Air Bud '97
Air Bud 2: Golden Receiver '98
The Fighter '10
The Finest Hours '16

Anthony Tambakis
Warrior '11
Jane Got a Gun '16
Gringo '18

Edward Tang (1946-)
Project A '83
Operation Condor 2: The Armour of the Gods '86
Project A: Part 2 '87
Operation Condor '91
Supercop '92
The Legend of Drunken Master '94
Rumble in the Bronx '96
Mr. Nice Guy '98

Robert Tannen
Even Money '06
Seeking Justice '12

Danis Tanovic
No Man's Land '01
Triage '09

Daniel Taplitz
Commandments '96
Little Richard '00
Dean Koontz's Black River '01
Winds of Terror '01
Breakin' All The Rules '04
Chaos Theory '08
Red Dog '11
The Angriest Man in Brooklyn '14

Daniel Taradash (1913-2003)
Golden Boy '39
Knock on Any Door '49
Don't Bother to Knock '52
Rancho Notorious '52
From Here to Eternity '53
Desiree '54
Picnic '55
Storm Center '56
Bell, Book and Candle '58
Morituri '65
Hawaii '66
Castle Keep '69
Doctors' Wives '70
The Other Side of Midnight '77

Paul Tarantino
Newsbreak '00
Headhunter '05

Quentin Tarantino (1963-)
Reservoir Dogs '92
True Romance '93
Pulp Fiction '94
Four Rooms '95
From Dusk Till Dawn '95
Jackie Brown '97
Kill Bill Vol. 1 '03
Kill Bill Vol. 2 '04
Death Proof '07
Inglourious Basterds '09
Django Unchained '12
The Hateful Eight '15
Once Upon A Time... In Hollywood '19

Sooni Taraporevala
Salaam Bombay! '88
Mississippi Masala '92
My Own Country '98
Such a Long Journey '98
The Namesake '06
Girl Rising '13

Andrei Tarkovsky (1932-86)
Andrei Rublev '66
Solaris '72
The Mirror '75
Nostalghia '83
The Sacrifice '86

Frank Tarloff (1916-99)
Father Goose '64
The Double Man '67
A Guide for the Married Man '67
Once You Kiss a Stranger '69

Susan Tarr
Cousin Bette '97
My Sister's Keeper '02

Frank Tashlin (1913-72)
A Night in Casablanca '46
One Touch of Venus '48
The Fuller Brush Girl '50
Kill the Umpire '50
Love Happy '50
The Lemon Drop Kid '51
Son of Paleface '52
Artists and Models '55
The Girl Can't Help It '56
Rock-A-Bye Baby '57
Will Success Spoil Rock Hunter? '57
Cinderfella '60
Bachelor Flat '62
Who's Minding the Store? '63
Caprice '67
Private Navy of Sgt. O'Farrell '68

Robert Tasker (1898-1944)
Doctor X '32
San Quentin '37

Terri Tatchell
District 9 '09
Chappie '15

Jacques Tati (1908-82)
Mr. Hulot's Holiday '53
Mon Oncle '58
Traffic '71

Gilles Taurand (1943-)
Hotel America '81
Wild Reeds '94
Les Voleurs '96
Dry Cleaning '97
Time Regained '99
Strayed '03
The Beautiful Person '08
The Army of Crime '10
Farewell, My Queen '12

Catherine Tavel (1959-)
Married People, Single Sex '93
Night Fire '94

Bertrand Tavernier (1941-)
The Clockmaker '73
Death Watch '80
Coup de Torchon '81
A Sunday in the Country '84
Round Midnight '86
Life and Nothing But '89
L'Appat '94
Capitaine Conan '96
It All Starts Today '99
Safe Conduct '01
The Princess of Montpensier '10
The French Minister '13

Paolo Taviani (1931-)
St. Michael Had a Rooster '72
Padre Padrone '77
The Night of the Shooting Stars '82
Kaos '85
Night Sun '90
Fiorile '93
The Lark Farm '07

Vittorio Taviani (1929-2018)
St. Michael Had a Rooster '72
Padre Padrone '77
The Night of the Shooting Stars '82
Kaos '85
Night Sun '90
Fiorile '93
The Lark Farm '07

Alison Taylor
The Cheetah Girls '03
The Cheetah Girls 2 '06

Brian Taylor
Crank '06
Crank: High Voltage '09
Gamer '09
Jonah Hex '10

Bruce Taylor
Hell Swarm '00
The Brave One '07
Open Graves '09

David Taylor
Get Crazy '83
DROP Squad '94
Tracked '98

Delores Taylor (1932-2018)
Billy Jack '71
The Trial of Billy Jack '74
Billy Jack Goes to Washington '77

Deon Taylor
Dead Tone '07
The Hustle '08
Chain Letter '10
Meet the Blacks '16
Traffik '18

Doug Taylor
The Carpenter '89
In the Name of the King: A Dungeon Siege Tale '08
Splice '10
A Christmas Horror Story '15

Dwight Taylor (1902-86)
Are You Listening? '32
If I Were Free '33
Today We Live '33
Top Hat '35
Head Over Heels '37
Rhythm on the River '40
I Wake Up Screaming '41
Something to Live For '52
We're Not Married '52

Eric Taylor (1897-1952)
Navy Blues '37
Black Friday '40
The Black Cat '41
The Phantom of the Opera '43
Son of Dracula '43
Dick Tracy Meets Gruesome '47

Finn Taylor (1958-)
Pontiac Moon '94
Dream with the Fishes '97
Cherish '02
The Darwin Awards '06

Greg Taylor
Prancer '89
The Christmas Box '95
Summer of the Monkeys '98
Santa and Pete '99
Prancer Returns '01

Jim Taylor (1962-)
Citizen Ruth '96
Election '99
Jurassic Park 3 '01
About Schmidt '02
I Now Pronounce You Chuck and Larry '07
Downsizing '17
Juliet, Naked '18

Kenneth Taylor (1922-)
Cause Celebre '87
The Camomile Lawn '92

Lawrence Taylor
The Spider Returns '41
The Jackie Robinson Story '50

Renee Taylor (1933-)
Lovers and Other Strangers '70
Love Is All There Is '96

Rex Taylor (1889-1968)
My Friend from India '27
Sit Tight '31
The Oil Raider '34
Junior G-Men '40

Roderick Taylor
The Star Chamber '83
Hell Swarm '00
American Outlaws '01
The Brave One '07
Open Graves '09

S. Lee Taylor (1957-)
See Steve Taylor

Sam Taylor (1895-1958)
Safety Last '23
Girl Shy '24
The Freshman '25
Exit Smiling '26

Samuel A. Taylor (1912-2000)
The Eddy Duchin Story '56
Vertigo '58
Topaz '69
The Love Machine '71

Steve Taylor (1957-)
Social Intercourse '01
The Second Chance '06
Blue Like Jazz '12

Tate Taylor
Pretty Ugly People '08
The Help '11

Vanessa Taylor
Hope Springs '12
Divergent '14
The Shape of Water '17

Julie Taymor (1952-)
Titus '99
The Tempest '10

Andre Techine (1943-)
Barocco '76
The Bronte Sisters '79
Hotel America '81
Ma Saison Preferee '93
Wild Reeds '94
Les Voleurs '96
Strayed '03
Changing Times '04
The Witnesses '07
The Girl on the Train '09
Unforgivable '11

Dave Tedder
Shock 'Em Dead '90
Criminal Desire '98

Miguel Tejada-Flores
Fright Night 2 '88
Almost Dead '94
Screamers '96
The Unsaid '01
Solar Attack '06
Decoys: The Second Seduction '07
Screamers: The Hunting '09
Sundown '16

Frank Telford
The Bamboo Saucer '68
Hello Down There '69

William Templeton
The Fallen Idol '49
Midnight Episode '50
1984 '56

Daisuke Tengan (1959-)
The Eel '96
Dr. Akagi '98
Audition '99
13 Assassins '10

Andy Tennant (1955-)
Ever After: A Cinderella Story '98
Fool's Gold '08

Kevin S. Tenney (1955-)
Witchboard '87
Peacemaker '90
Witchboard 3: The Possession '95
Pinocchio's Revenge '96
Tick Tock '00
Endangered Species '02

Jonathan Teplitzky
Better Than Sex '00
Burning Man '11

John Terlesky (1961-)
Supreme Sanction '99
The Guardian '01

Courtney Terrett (1903-50)
Made On Broadway '33
20,000 Years in Sing Sing '33
Castle on the Hudson '40

Chris Terrio
Argo '12
Batman v Superman: Dawn of Justice '16
Justice League '17
Star Wars: The Rise of Skywalker '19

Bridget Terry
Shadrach '98
Love's Abiding Joy '06

Gay Partington Terry
The Toxic Avenger, Part 2 '89
The Toxic Avenger, Part 3: The Last Temptation of Toxie '89

Steve Tesich (1942-96)
Breaking Away '79
Eyewitness '81
Four Friends '81
The World According to Garp '82
American Flyers '85

Duccio Tessari (1926-94)
A Fistful of Dollars '64
The Cats '68

Joan Tewkesbury (1936-)
Thieves Like Us '74
Nashville '75
A Night in Heaven '83

Sylvia Thalberg (1907-88)
Untamed '29
Montana Moon '30
This Modern Age '31
Now and Forever '34

Rudy Thauberger
12 Disasters '12
Independence Daysaster '13

Justin Theroux (1971-)
Tropic Thunder '08
Iron Man 2 '10
Rock of Ages '12
Zoolander 2 '16

Daniel Therriault (1953-)
First Time Felon '97
Witness Protection '99

Alex Theurer
Sleight '17
Stray '19

Harvey Thew (1883-1946)
Uncle Tom's Cabin '27
The Matrimonial Bed '30
Show Girl in Hollywood '30
Illicit '31
Public Enemy '31
The Woman From Monte Carlo '31
Two Seconds '32
She Done Him Wrong '33
Supernatural '33
Operator 13 '34
The Trail of the Lonesome Pine '36

Nick Thiel
Fire Birds '90
Shipwrecked '90
V.I. Warshawski '91
White Fang '91
The Associate '96

Robert Thoeren (1903-57)
Rage in Heaven '41
Mrs. Parkington '44
Summer Storm '44
Captain Carey, U.S.A. '50

Robert Thom (1929-79)
Wild in the Streets '68
Bloody Mama '70
Crazy Mama '75
Death Race 2000 '75

Michael Thoma
The Set Up '95
We'll Meet Again '02

Anna Thomas (1948-)
El Norte '83
My Family '94
Frida '02

Daniela Thomas
Foreign Land '95
Paris, je t'aime '06

Heidi Thomas
Kiss and Tell '96
I Capture the Castle '02
Ballet Shoes '07
Cranford '08
Return to Cranford '09
Upstairs Downstairs '11

Jim Thomas
Predator '87
The Rescue '88
Predator 2 '90
Executive Decision '96
Mission to Mars '00

John Thomas
Predator '87
The Rescue '88
Predator 2 '90
Executive Decision '96
Mission to Mars '00

Lucy Thomas (1970-)
See Dave Eggers

Michael Thomas (1962-)
The Hunger '83
Ladyhawke '85
Scandal '89
Deception '92
Backbeat '94
B. Monkey '97
Welcome to Woop Woop '97
The Night We Called It a Day '03
The Devil's Double '11
The 33 '15

Rob Thomas (1965-)
Drive Me Crazy '99
Veronica Mars '14

Scott Thomas
Deranged '01
Flight of the Living Dead: Outbreak on a Plane '07

Camille Thomasson
Luther '03
When Love Is Not Enough: The Lois Wilson Story '10
Beyond the Blackboard '11

Brett Thompson
Britannic '00
The Glass Trap '04
Blood Angels '05

Caroline Thompson (1956-)
Edward Scissorhands '90
The Addams Family '91
Homeward Bound: The Incredible Journey '93
The Nightmare Before Christmas '93
The Secret Garden '93
Black Beauty '94
Buddy '97
Snow White: The Fairest of Them All '02
Tim Burton's Corpse Bride '05
City of Ember '08
Welcome to Marwen '18

Christopher Thompson (1966-)
La Buche '00
Jet Lag '02
Change of Plans '09

Daniele Thompson (1942-)
The Brain '69
Queen Margot '94
Those Who Love Me Can Take the Train '98
La Buche '00
Belphegor: Phantom of the Louvre '01
Jet Lag '02
Avenue Montaigne '06
Change of Plans '09

Donald G. Thompson (1938-)
Project: Kill! '77
The Evil '78

Emma Thompson (1959-)
Sense and Sensibility '95
Wit '01
Nanny McPhee '06
Nanny McPhee Returns '10
Effie Gray '15
Bridget Jones's Baby '16
Last Christmas '19

Ernest Thompson (1949-)
On Golden Pond '81
Sweet Hearts Dance '88
1969 '89
Out of Time '00

Galen Thompson (1938-)
See Donald G. Thompson

Gary Scott Thompson (1959-)
Split Second '92
K-911 '99
The Fast and the Furious '01
K-9 3: P.I. '01
Timecop 2: The Berlin Decision '03
88 Minutes '08

Jim Thompson (1906-77)
The Killing '56
Paths of Glory '57

Keene Thompson (1886-1937)
Paths to Paradise '25
No More Orchids '32
Love in Bloom '35

Mike Thompson
Dragonfly '02
Love Happens '09

Peggy Thompson
Men of the Sea '35
King of the Newsboys '38
Better Than Chocolate '99

Rob Thompson
Hearts of the West '75
Ratboy '86
The Cowboy Way '94

Robert E. Thompson (1924-2004)
They Shoot Horses, Don't They? '69
Kiss Me...Kill Me '76
The Trial of Lee Harvey Oswald '77
White Hot: The Mysterious Murder of Thelma Todd '91

Youngyooth Thongkonthun
The Iron Ladies '00
The Iron Ladies 2 '03

Chaz Thorne
Poor Man's Game '06
Just Buried '07

Jack Thorne
A Long Way Down '14
Wonder '17
The Aeronauts '19

Billy Bob Thornton (1955-)
One False Move '91
Don't Look Back '96
A Family Thing '96
Sling Blade '96
Daddy & Them '99
Camouflage '00
The Gift '00
Jayne Mansfield's Car '13

Ralph Thornton (1897-1993)
See Aben Kandel

Sarah Thorp
Twisted '04
The Bounty Hunter '10

Rawson Marshall Thurber (1975-)
Dodgeball: A True Underdog Story '04
The Mysteries of Pittsburgh '08
Central Intelligence '16
Skyscraper '18

George Tibbles (1913-87)
Munster, Go Home! '66
How to Frame a Figg '71

Ernest Tidyman (1928-84)
The French Connection '71
Shaft '71
Shaft's Big Score '72
High Plains Drifter '73
Dummy '79
Brotherly Love '85

Gary Tieche
The First $20 Million is Always the Hardest '02
Tribute '09
Seven Deadly Sins '10

Chu Tien-Wen (1956-)
See Tien-wen Chu

Jacob Tierney (1979-)
Twist '03
The Trotsky '09
Good Neighbors '10

Robert Tiffe
Sword of Honor '94
Face of Terror '04

Patrick Tilley
Wuthering Heights '70
The People That Time Forgot '77

David Titcher
Around the World in 80 Days '04
The Librarian: Quest for the Spear '04
The Curse of King Tut's Tomb '06
Be My Valentine '13

Craig Titley
Scooby-Doo '02
Percy Jackson & The Olympians: The Lightning Thief '10

Timo Tjahjanto
V/H/S/2 '13
Killers '14
Headshot '17

Raymond To
7 Grand Masters '04
Perhaps Love '05

James Toback (1944-)
The Gambler '74
Fingers '78
Love and Money '80
The Pick-Up Artist '87
Bugsy '91
Two Girls and a Guy '98
Black and White '99
Harvard Man '01
When Will I Be Loved '04

Janet Tobias
No Place on Earth '12
Unseen Enemy '17

Peter Tolan
My Fellow Americans '96
Analyze This '98
Bedazzled '00
What Planet Are You From? '00
America's Sweethearts '01
Analyze That '02
Stealing Harvard '02
Guess Who '05
Just like Heaven '05
Finding Amanda '08

Eric Toledano
The Intouchables '12
Samba '14

George Toles (1948-)
Careful '92
The Twilight of the Ice Nymphs '97
The Saddest Music in the World '03
Brand Upon the Brain! '06
Keyhole '11

Jonathan Tolins
The Twilight of the Golds '97
Martian Child '07

Michael Tolkin (1950-)
Gleaming the Cube '89
The Rapture '91
Deep Cover '92
The Player '92
The New Age '94
Deep Impact '98
Changing Lanes '02
Nine '09

Stephen Tolkin
Captain America '89
Daybreak '93
Dean Koontz's Intensity '97
Dean Koontz's Mr. Murder '98
Fidel '02
Carolina Moon '07
Midnight Bayou '09
The Craigslist Killer '11

Maurice Tombragel (1913-2000)
The Prince of Thieves '48
Kentucky Jubilee '51
The Dalton Girls '57
Fort Bowie '58

Stanley Tong (1960-)
Supercop 2 '93
Jackie Chan's First Strike '96
Jackie Chan's The Myth '05

Jerome Tonnerre
Un Coeur en Hiver '93
Belphegor: Phantom of the Louvre '01
On Guard! '03
Intimate Strangers '04
My Best Friend '06
The Women on the Sixth Floor '10
Renoir '12
A Promise '13
On My Way '14

Rhet Topham
Trick or Treat '86
976-EVIL '88

Tom Topor
Nuts '87
The Accused '88
Judgment '90

Perfect Murder, Perfect Town '00

Tim Tori
Prowl '10
Dragon Eyes '12

Tracy Torme (1959-)
Spellbinder '88
Fire in the Sky '93

Giuseppe Tornatore (1956-)
Cinema Paradiso '88
A Pure Formality '94
The Star Maker '95
The Legend of 1900 '98
Malena '00
The Unknown Woman '06
Baaria '09
The Best Offer '13

Antonio Toro
Amityville 1992: It's About Time '92
Amityville: A New Generation '93

Peter Torokvei
Real Genius '85
Armed and Dangerous '86
Back to School '86
Caddyshack 2 '88
Guarding Tess '94

Fina Torres (1951-)
Oriana '85
Celestial Clockwork '94
From Prada to Nada '11

Ivan Tors (1916-83)
Song of Love '47
The Glass Wall '53
The Magnetic Monster '53
GOG '54
Island of the Lost '68

Laura Toscano (1944-2009)
Deadly Mission '78
The Inglorious Bastards '78

Dan Totheroh (1894-1976)
The Dawn Patrol '30
Dawn Patrol '38

Jacques Toulemonde Vidal
Embrace of the Serpent '15
Birds of Passage '18

Joelle Touma
Lila Says '04
The Attack '13
Just Like a Woman '13
The Insult '17

Harry Alan Towers (1920-2009)
The Face of Fu Manchu '65
Brides of Fu Manchu '66
The Vengeance of Fu Manchu '67
The Castle of Fu Manchu '68
Count Dracula '71
Call of the Wild '72
Black Venus '83
The Mangler '94
Queen's Messenger II '01
Sea Wolf: The Pirate's Curse '05

Juliette Towhidi
Calendar Girls '03
Death Comes to Pemberley '13
Testament of Youth '15

Gene Towne (1904-79)
Loose Ankles '30
You Only Live Once '37
Joy of Living '38
Top Banana '54

Robert Towne (1936-)
The Last Woman on Earth '61
Tomb of Ligeia '64
Villa Rides '68
The Last Detail '73
Chinatown '74
Shampoo '75
The Yakuza '75
Personal Best '82
Tequila Sunrise '88
Days of Thunder '90
The Two Jakes '90

The Firm '93
Love Affair '94
Mission: Impossible '96
Without Limits '97
Mission: Impossible 2 '00
Ask the Dust '06

Roger Towne
The Natural '84
The Recruit '03

Jack Townley (1896-1960)
Mummy's Boys '36
The Plot Thickens '36

James Townsend
Belly of the Beast '03
Out of Reach '04
Undisputed 2: Last Man Standing '06

Leo Townsend (1908-87)
It Started with Eve '41
Seven Sweethearts '42
Southside 1-1000 '50
Dangerous Crossing '53
Four Boys and a Gun '57
Shadow on the Window '57
Fraulein '58
Bikini Beach '64
Beach Blanket Bingo '65
How to Stuff a Wild Bikini '65
Fireball 500 '66

Robert Townsend (1957-)
Hollywood Shuffle '87
The Five Heartbeats '91
The Meteor Man '93
Black Listed '03
Playin' For Love '15

Michael Traeger
Dead Man on Campus '97
The Moguls '05

Josh Trank (1985-)
Fantastic Four '15
Capone '20

Pablo Trapero
Rolling Family '04
Lion's Den '08
Carancho '10

Andrew Traucki
Black Water '07
The Reef '10

Bill Travers (1922-94)
An Elephant Called Slowly '69
Ring of Bright Water '69

John Travis
The Haunting of Molly Hartley '08
The New Daughter '10

Joey Travolta (1950-)
Hard Vice '94
Vegas Vice '94
To the Limit '95

Caspian Tredwell-Owen
Beyond Borders '03
The Island '05

Brian Trenchard-Smith (1946-)
Britannic '00
Drive Hard '14

Monika Treut (1954-)
Virgin Machine '88
Seduction: The Cruel Woman '89
Erotique '94
Ghosted '09

Ken Trevey (1929-92)
The Hanged Man '74
Banjo Hackett '76

Dale Trevillion
One Man Force '89
Beyond Desire '94

Colin Trevorrow
Jurassic World '15
Jurassic World: Fallen Kingdom '18

Joachim Trier
Reprise '06
Oslo, August 31st '11
Louder Than Bombs '16
Thelma '17

Lawrence Trilling
Dinner and Driving '97
Delivered '98
Group Sex '10

Josie Trinidad
Zootopia '16
Ralph Breaks the Internet '18

Dorothy Tristan (1942-)
Suspended Animation '02
The Looking Glass '16

Victor Trivas (1896-1970)
The Stranger '46
The Head '59

Barry Trivers (1907-81)
The Wagons Roll at Night '41
There's Something About a Soldier '43

Anne-Louise Trividic
Intimacy '00
Gabrielle '05

Pierre Trividic
Those Who Love Me Can Take the Train '98
Lady Chatterley '10

Rose Troche
Go Fish '94
The Safety of Objects '01

Jan Troell (1931-)
The New Land '72
Everlasting Moments '08
The Last Sentence '12

Guy Trosper (1911-63)
I'll Wait for You '41
Crossroads '42
Eyes in the Night '42
The Stratton Story '49
The Devil's Doorway '50
Many Rivers to Cross '55
The Girl He Left Behind '56
Jailhouse Rock '57
Darby's Rangers '58
Birdman of Alcatraz '62
The Spy Who Came in from the Cold '65

Jason Trost
All Superheroes Must Die '11
The FP '12

Lamar Trotti (1900-52)
Life Begins at Forty '35
Steamboat Round the Bend '35
Career Woman '36
Ramona '36
In Old Chicago '37
Slave Ship '37
Alexander's Ragtime Band '38
The Baroness and the Butler '38
Gateway '38
Kentucky '38
The Story of Alexander Graham Bell '39
Young Mr. Lincoln '39
Brigham Young: Frontiersman '40
Hudson's Bay '40
Thunder Birds '42
Guadalcanal Diary '43
Immortal Sergeant '43
The Ox-Bow Incident '43
Wilson '44
The Razor's Edge '46
Captain from Castile '47
Mother Wore Tights '47
Yellow Sky '48
American Guerrilla in the Philippines '50
Cheaper by the Dozen '50
My Blue Heaven '50
I'd Climb the Highest Mountain '51
With a Song in My Heart '52

Pascal Trottier
A Christmas Horror Story '15
Hellions '15

David Trueba
Two Much '96
Dance with the Devil '97
The Girl of Your Dreams '99

Fernando Trueba (1955-)
Two Much '96
Chico & Rita '10

Guerdon (Gordon) Trueblood
Welcome Home, Soldier Boys '72
The Last Hard Men '76
Ants '77
Tarantulas: The Deadly Cargo '77
The Bastard '78
Terror Out of the Sky '78
The Chase '91

Francois Truffaut (1932-84)
The 400 Blows '59
Jules and Jim '62
Shoot the Piano Player '62
The Soft Skin '64
Fahrenheit 451 '66
The Bride Wore Black '68
Stolen Kisses '68
Mississippi Mermaid '69
Bed and Board '70
The Wild Child '70
Two English Girls '72
Day for Night '73
Small Change '76
The Man Who Loved Women '77
The Last Metro '80
Confidentially Yours '83

Dalton Trumbo (1905-76)
A Man to Remember '38
Thirty Seconds Over Tokyo '44
Our Vines Have Tender Grapes '45
Gun Crazy '49
Rocketship X-M '50
The Prowler '51
Roman Holiday '53
The Boss '56
The Brave One '56
Terror in a Texas Town '58
Exodus '60
Spartacus '60
The Last Sunset '61
Lonely Are the Brave '62
Hawaii '66
The Horsemen '70
Johnny Got His Gun '71
Papillon '73

Alan R. Trustman (1930-)
Bullitt '68
The Thomas Crown Affair '68
They Call Me Mr. Tibbs! '70
Hit! '73
Lady Ice '73
The Arab Conspiracy '76

Glenn Tryon (1894-1970)
The Daring Young Man '35
Orchids to You '35

Ming-liang Tsai
The Hole '98
What Time Is It There? '01
Goodbye, Dragon Inn '03
Stray Dogs '13

Kan-Cheung (Sammy) Tsang
Shaolin Soccer '01
Kung Fu Hustle '04
The Mermaid '16

Alex Tse
Sucker Free City '05
Watchmen '09
SuperFly '18

Shinya Tsukamoto (1960-)
Tetsuo: The Iron Man '92
Tetsuo 2: Body Hammer '97
Nightmare Detective '06

Slava Tsukerman
Liquid Sky '83
Perestroika '09

Stanley Tucci (1960-)
Big Night '95
The Imposters '98
The Impostors '98
Joe Gould's Secret '00
Blind Date '08
Final Portrait '17

Wanda Tuchock (1898-1985)
Billy the Kid '30
Sporting Blood '31
New Morals for Old '32
Sunday Dinner for a Soldier '44
Nob Hill '45
The Foxes of Harrow '47

Larry Tucker (1933-2001)
I Love You, Alice B. Toklas! '68
Bob & Carol & Ted & Alice '69
Alex in Wonderland '70

Harry Tugend (1897-1989)
Pigskin Parade '36
Sing, Baby, Sing '36
Love Is News '37
Wake Up and Live '37
You Can't Have Everything '37
My Lucky Star '38
Sally, Irene and Mary '38
Seven Sinners '40
Birth of the Blues '41
Caught in the Draft '41
Star Spangled Rhythm '42
Take Me Out to the Ball Game '49
Wabash Avenue '50
Pocketful of Miracles '61
Who's Minding the Store? '63

Michael Tully
Ping Pong Summer '14
Don't Leave Home '18

Karl Tunberg (1909-92)
You Can't Have Everything '37
Down Argentine Way '40
Tall, Dark and Handsome '41
Week-End in Havana '41
My Gal Sal '42
Orchestra Wives '42
Up in Central Park '48
You Gotta Stay Happy '48
Love That Brute '50
The Law and the Lady '51
Scandal at Scourie '53
Beau Brummell '54
The Scarlet Coat '55
Ben-Hur '59
Libel '59
I Thank a Fool '62
The Seventh Dawn '64

William Tunberg
That's My Baby! '44
Old Yeller '57

Gary J. Tunnicliffe (1968-)
Within the Rock '96
The Guardian '01
Megalodon '03
Hellraiser: Revelations '11

Gregg Turkington
Entertainment '15
Mister America '19

John Turman
Hulk '03
Ticking Clock '10

Ann Turner (1960-)
Hammers over the Anvil '91
Irresistible '06

Barbara Turner
Georgia '95
Pollock '00
The Company '03
Hemingway & Gelhorn '12

Bonnie Turner
Wayne's World '92
Coneheads '93
Wayne's World 2 '93
The Brady Bunch Movie '95
Tommy Boy '95

Brian Turner
Santa Baby '06
Snowglobe '07
Santa Baby 2: Santa Maybe '09

Dennis Turner
Between the Darkness and the Dawn '85
Poor Little Rich Girl: The Barbara Hutton Story '87

Guinevere Turner (1968-)
Go Fish '94
American Psycho '99
BloodRayne '06
The Notorious Bettie Page '06

Laurent Turner
Ultimate Heist '09
The Prey '11

Sheldon Turner
The Longest Yard '05
The Texas Chainsaw Massacre: The Beginning '06
Up in the Air '09

Terry Turner
Wayne's World '92
Coneheads '93
Wayne's World 2 '93
The Brady Bunch Movie '95
Tommy Boy '95

Thadd Turner
Miracle at Sage Creek '05
7 Mummies '06

Catherine Turney (1906-98)
The Man I Love '46
My Reputation '46
Cry Wolf '47
Winter Meeting '48
Japanese War Bride '52

John Turturro (1957-)
Mac '93
Illuminata '98
Romance & Cigarettes '05
Fading Gigolo '13
Rio, I Love You '14

Casey Twenter
Rudderless '14
The Scent of Rain & Lightening '17

Derek Twist (1905-79)
Non-Stop New York '37
Angels One Five '54

John Twist (1898-1976)
Reno '39
Pittsburgh '42
Sinbad, the Sailor '47
Tycoon '47
Colorado Territory '49
King Richard and the Crusaders '54
Helen of Troy '56
Santiago '56
Serenade '56
Band of Angels '57
The FBI Story '59
Marines, Let's Go '61
A Distant Trumpet '64

David N. Twohy (1955-)
Critters 2: The Main Course '88
Warlock '91
Grand Tour: Disaster in Time '92
The Fugitive '93
Terminal Velocity '94
Waterworld '95
The Arrival '96
G.I. Jane '97
Pitch Black '00
Below '02
Impostor '02
The Chronicles of Riddick '04
A Perfect Getaway '09
Riddick '13

Jonathan Tydor
The King's Guard '01
Ice Soldiers '13

Tom Tykwer (1965-)
Winter Sleepers '97
Run Lola Run '98
The Princess and the Warrior '00
Paris, je t'aime '06
Perfume: The Story of a Murderer '06
3 '10
Cloud Atlas '12
A Hologram for the King '16

Evan Tylor
Stag '97
Wrecker '15

Steve Tymon (1956-)
Dark Secrets '95
Mirror, Mirror 3: The Voyeur '96

Bob Tzudiker
Newsies '92
The Hunchback of Notre Dame '96
Anastasia '97
Tarzan '99
102 Dalmatians '00
Tarzan 2 '05

Cory Udler
Astro-Zombies M3: Cloned '10
Astro-Zombies M4: Invaders from Cyberspace '12

Yale Udoff
Bad Timing: A Sensual Obsession '80
Eve of Destruction '90

Keinosuke Uegusa
One Wonderful Sunday '47
Drunken Angel '48

Jim Uhls
Fight Club '99
Jumper '08

Alfred Uhry (1936-)
Mystic Pizza '88
Driving Miss Daisy '89
Rich in Love '93

Daniel Ullman (1918-79)
Cavalry Scout '51
Fort Osage '51
Square Dance Jubilee '51
Hiawatha '52
Wagons West '52
Wild Stallion '52
The Fighting Lawman '53
Fort Vengeance '53
Seven Angry Men '55
The Warriors '55
Canyon River '56
The First Texan '56
Good Day for a Hanging '58
Battle of the Coral Sea '59
The Gunfight at Dodge City '59
Mysterious Island '61

Elwood Ullman (1903-85)
The Stooge '51
Harem Girl '52
Ma and Pa Kettle at Waikiki '55
Snow White and the Three Stooges '61
The Three Stooges Meet Hercules '61
The Outlaws Is Coming! '65

Liv Ullmann (1939-)
Sofie '92
Miss Julie '14

Loung Ung (1970-)
Girl Rising '13
First They Killed My Father '17

Gladys Unger (1885-1940)
Great Expectations '34
The Mystery of Edwin Drood '35
Sylvia Scarlett '35

Eve Unsell (1887-1937)
Shadows '22
The Plastic Age '25

Leon Uris (1924-2003)
Battle Cry '55
Gunfight at the O.K. Corral '57

Peter Ustinov (1921-2004)
Immortal Battalion '44
The Way Ahead '44
Billy Budd '62

Cyrus Voris
Men of War '94
Tales from the Crypt Presents Demon Knight '94
Josh Kirby. . .Time Warrior: Chapter 1, Planet of the Dino-Knights '95
Josh Kirby. . . Time Warrior: Chapter 2, The Human Pets '95
Josh Kirby. . . Time Warrior: Chapter 5, Journey to the Magic Cavern '96
Josh Kirby. . . Time Warrior: Chapter 6, Last Battle for the Universe '96
Bulletproof Monk '03
Sleeper Cell '05

Niels Vorsel (1953-)
The Element of Crime '84
Zentropa '92
The Kingdom '95
The Kingdom 2 '97

Kurt Voss (1963-)
Border Radio '88
Where the Day Takes You '92
Baja '95
Highway Hitcher '98
Sugar Town '99
Things Behind the Sun '01

William W. Vought
Stricken '98
When Trumpets Fade '98

Ariel Vromen (1973-)
Rx '06
The Iceman '12

Andy Wachowski (1967-)
See Lilly Wachowski

Lana Wachowski (1965-)
Assassins '95
Bound '96
The Matrix '99
The Matrix Reloaded '03
The Matrix Revolutions '03
V for Vendetta '06
Speed Racer '08
Cloud Atlas '12
Jupiter Ascending '15

Larry Wachowski (1965-)
See Lana Wachowski

Lilly Wachowski (1967-)
Assassins '95
Bound '96
The Matrix '99
The Matrix Reloaded '03
The Matrix Revolutions '03
V for Vendetta '06
Speed Racer '08
Cloud Atlas '12
Jupiter Ascending '15

Natto Wada (1920-83)
The Burmese Harp '56
Fires on the Plain '59
An Actor's Revenge '63

Kevin Wade (1954-)
Working Girl '88
Mr. Baseball '92
Junior '94
Meet Joe Black '98
Maid in Manhattan '02

Robert Wade (1962-)
Let Him Have It '91
Plunkett & Macleane '98
The World Is Not Enough '99
Die Another Day '02
Johnny English '03
Convicted '04
Stoned '05
Casino Royale '06
Quantum of Solace '08
Skyfall '12
Spectre '15

Annette Wademant (1928-)
The Earrings of Madame De. . . '54
Voulez-Vous Danser avec Moi? '59

Maggie Wadey
The Duchess of Duke Street '78
Northanger Abbey '87
The Buccaneers '95
Mansfield Park '07

Jeff Wadlow (1976-)
Cry Wolf '05
Kick-Ass 2 '13
Truth or Dare '18
Bloodshot '20
Fantasy Island '20

George Waggner (1894-1984)
The Keeper of the Bees '35
The Fatal Hour '40
Man From God's Country '58

Andrew Wagner
The Talent Given Us '04
Starting Out in the Evening '07

Bruce Wagner (1954-)
A Nightmare on Elm Street 3: Dream Warriors '87
Wild Palms '93
I'm Losing You '98
Maps to the Stars '14

David T. Wagner
National Lampoon's Van Wilder '02
The Girl Next Door '04
My Baby's Daddy '04
Underclassman '05
Restraint '08

Jane Wagner (1935-)
The Incredible Shrinking Woman '81
Search for Signs of Intelligent Life in the Universe '91

Ka-Fai Wai
Fulltime Killer '01
Running on Karma '03
Drug War '13

David Wain
Wet Hot American Summer '01
The Ten '07
Role Models '08
Wanderlust '12
They Came Together '14

Taika Waititi (1975-)
Eagle *vs.* Shark '07
What We Do in the Shadows '14
Hunt for the Wilderpeople '16
Jojo Rabbit '19

Andrzej Wajda (1927-)
Ashes and Diamonds '58
Innocent Sorcerers '60
Lotna '64
Everything for Sale '68
Landscape After Battle '70
Land of Promise '74
Danton '82
Zemsta '02
Katyn '07

Tokuhei Wakao (1918-)
Samurai 1: Musashi Miyamoto '55
Samurai 3: Duel at Ganryu Island '56

Eliot Wald (1946-2003)
See No Evil, Hear No Evil '89
Camp Nowhere '94
Down Periscope '96

Jerry Wald (1911-62)
In Caliente '35
Living on Velvet '35
Hollywood Hotel '37
Varsity Show '37
Brother Rat '38
Garden of the Moon '38
Hard to Get '38
Brother Rat and a Baby '40
Torrid Zone '40
Manpower '41
Out of the Fog '41

Frank Waldman (1919-90)
High Time '60
Love Is a Ball '63
Inspector Clouseau '68
Return of the Pink Panther '74
The Pink Panther Strikes Again '76
Revenge of the Pink Panther '78
Trail of the Pink Panther '82

Tom Waldman (1922-85)
High Time '60
Love Is a Ball '63
Inspector Clouseau '68

Andrew Kevin Walker (1964-)
Brainscan '94
Hideaway '94
Seven '95
8mm '98
Sleepy Hollow '99
The Wolfman '09

Chuck Walker
Ryder P.I. '86
Retribution Road '07
The Man Who Came Back '08

H.M. Walker (1878-1937)
Pardon Us '31
Pack Up Your Troubles '32

Michael Walker
Relative Values '99
Chasing Sleep '00

Gary Walkow
Notes from Underground '95
Beat '00
Crashing '07

Jake Wade Wall
When a Stranger Calls '06
The Hitcher '07

Irving Wallace (1916-90)
The West Point Story '50
Bad for Each Other '53
Split Second '53
The Gambler from Natchez '54
Jump Into Hell '55
Sincerely Yours '55
The Burning Hills '56
Bombers B-52 '57
The Big Circus '59

Pamela Wallace
Straight from the Heart '03
Last Chance Cafe '06
Though None Go With Me '06
Love's Unending Legacy '07
Finding a Family '10
Soldier Love Story '10

Randall Wallace (1949-)
Braveheart '95
The Man in the Iron Mask '98
Pearl Harbor '01
We Were Soldiers '02
Heaven Is for Real '14

Tommy Lee Wallace (1949-)
Amityville 2: The Possession '82
Halloween 3: Season of the Witch '82
Fright Night 2 '88
John Carpenter Presents Vampires: Los Muertos '02

Earl W. Wallace
Witness '85
Rose Hill '97

Ira Wallach (1913-95)
Boys' Night Out '62
Don't Make Waves '67
Hot Millions '68

Melisa Wallack
Meet Bill '07
Mirror Mirror '12
Dallas Buyers Club '13

Anthony Waller (1959-)
Mute Witness '95
An American Werewolf in Paris '97

Hugh Walpole (1884-1941)
David Copperfield '35
Little Lord Fauntleroy '36

Bill Walsh (1913-75)
The Absent-Minded Professor '61
Mary Poppins '64
Blackbeard's Ghost '67
Bedknobs and Broomsticks '71
One of Our Dinosaurs Is Missing '75

Enda Walsh
Disco Pigs '01
Hunger '08
Chatroom '10

Fran Walsh (1959-)
Meet the Feebles '89
Dead Alive '93
Heavenly Creatures '94
Jack Brown, Genius '94
The Frighteners '96
Lord of the Rings: The Fellowship of the Ring '01
Lord of the Rings: The Two Towers '02
Lord of the Rings: The Return of the King '03
King Kong '05
The Lovely Bones '09
The Hobbit: An Unexpected Journey '12
The Hobbit: The Desolation of Smaug '13
The Hobbit: The Battle of the Five Armies '14
Mortal Engines '18

Mary Walsh (1952-)
Bailey's Billion$ '05
The Silence '06

Matthew Jason Walsh (1970-)
Petticoat Planet '96
Witchouse '99
Ring of Darkness '04
The Raven '07

Raoul Walsh (1887-1980)
Regeneration '15
Sadie Thompson '28
Big Brown Eyes '36
Esther and the King '60

Douglas Walton
Face of Terror '04
Cat City '08

Fred Walton
When a Stranger Calls '79
When a Stranger Calls Back '93

James Wan (1977-)
Insidious: Chapter 2 '13
The Conjuring 2 '16
Aquaman '18

Bin Wang
Hero '02
House of Flying Daggers '04
The Assassins '12

Hui-Ling Wang
Eat Drink Man Woman '94
Jackie Chan's The Myth '05

Patrick Wang
In the Family '11
A Bread Factory, Part One '18
A Bread Factory, Part Two '18

Wayne Wang (1949-)
Chan Is Missing '82
Blue in the Face '95
Chinese Box '97
The Center of the World '01

Xiaoshuai Wang (1966-)
Beijing Bicycle '01
In Love We Trust '07

David S. Ward (1947-)
Steelyard Blues '73
The Sting '73
Cannery Row '82
The Sting 2 '83
The Milagro Beanfield War '88
Major League '89
King Ralph '91
The Program '93
Sleepless in Seattle '93
Flyboys '06

Donal Lardner Ward (1964-)
My Life's in Turnaround '94
The Suburbans '99

Jason Ward
Corky Romano '01
Deuce Bigalow: European Gigolo '05

Kelly Ward (1956-)
Once Upon a Forest '93
All Dogs Go to Heaven 2 '95

Kyle Ward (1969-)
Machete Kills '13
Underworld: Blood Wars '16

Lucille Ward (1907-69)
A Woman of the World '25
Texas Legionnaires '43

Morgan Ward
A Pyromaniac's Love Story '95
Riding in Cars with Boys '01

Vincent Ward (1956-)
The Navigator '88
Map of the Human Heart '93
River Queen '05

Darrell Ware
Second Honeymoon '37
Tall, Dark and Handsome '41
My Gal Sal '42
Orchestra Wives '42
Love That Brute '50

David Warfield
Kill Me Again '89
Linewatch '08

Regis Wargnier (1948-)
Indochine '92
East-West '99

Dave Warner (1953-)
Cut '00
Garage Days '03

Charles Marquis Warren (1912-90)
Hellgate '52
Day of the Evil Gun '68
Charro! '69

John Warren (1953-)
Naked in New York '93
Flashfire '94
Major League 3: Back to the Minors '98

Deric Washburn
Silent Running '71
The Deer Hunter '78
The Border '82
Extreme Prejudice '87

Art Washington
Hendrix '00
Keep the Faith, Baby '02

Wendy Wasserstein (1950-2006)
The Heidi Chronicles '95
The Object of My Affection '98
Trial by Media '00

Anna Waterhouse
The Lost & Found Family '09
Frankie and Alice '10
Race '16
The Aftermath '19
Seberg '19

Daniel Waters (1962-)
Heathers '89
The Adventures of Ford Fairlane '90
Hudson Hawk '91
Batman Returns '92
Demolition Man '93
Happy Campers '01
Sex and Death 101 '07
Vampire Academy '14

John Waters (1946-)
Pink Flamingos '72
Female Trouble '74
Desperate Living '77
Polyester '81
Hairspray '88
Cry-Baby '90
Serial Mom '94
Pecker '98
Cecil B. Demented '00
A Dirty Shame '04

Lawrence Edward Watkin (1901-81)
The Great Locomotive Chase '56
Darby O'Gill & the Little People '59

Maurine Watkins (1896-1969)
Up the River '30
No Man of Her Own '32
Strictly Dynamite '34
Libeled Lady '36

Peter Watkins (1935-)
Privilege '67
Edvard Munch '74

Carol Watson
Friday the 13th, Part 3 '82
Crazylove '05

Don Watson (1949-)
Passion '99
The Man Who Sued God '01

Kim Watson
What About Your Friends: Weekend Getaway '02
Honey '03

Sarah Watson
Absolute Zero '05
Disaster Zone: Volcano in New York '06

Sarah Watt (1958-2011)
Look Both Ways '05
My Year Without Sex '09

Jon Watts
Cop Car '15
Clown '16
Spider-Man: Homecoming '17

Ric Roman Waugh (1968-)
In the Shadows '01
Felon '08
Snitch '13
Angel Has Fallen '19

Keoni Waxman (1968-)
Lost Treasure '03
A Good Man '14
Mercenary: Absolution '15
Contract to Kill '16
End of a Gun '16

Craig Wayans
Scary Movie 2 '01
Dance Flick '09

Damon Wayans (1960-)
Mo' Money '92
Blankman '94
Major Payne '95

Keenen Ivory Wayans (1958-)
Hollywood Shuffle '87
I'm Gonna Git You Sucka '88
The Five Heartbeats '91
A Low Down Dirty Shame '94
Most Wanted '97
White Chicks '04
Little Man '06
Dance Flick '09

Marlon Wayans (1972-)
Don't Be a Menace to South Central While Drinking Your Juice in the Hood '95
Scary Movie '00
Scary Movie 2 '01
White Chicks '04
Little Man '06
Dance Flick '09
A Haunted House '13
A Haunted House 2 '14
Fifty Shades of Black '16

Anne Wheeler (1946-)
Edge of Madness '02
The Horses of McBride '12

Gary Wheeler
The List '07
The Trial '10

Martin Wheeler
Black Dawn '05
The Detonator '06

Rene Wheeler (1912-2000)
Fanfan la Tulipe '51
Utopia '51

Tom Wheeler
Puss in Boots '11
The LEGO Ninjago Movie '17

William Wheeler
The Prime Gig '00
The Hoax '06
Queen of Katwe '16
Ghost in the Shell '17
The LEGO Ninjago Movie '17

Tim Whelan (1893-1957)
Safety Last '23
Exit Smiling '26
My Best Girl '27
Girl Crazy '32
The Murder Man '35
Sidewalks of London '38
The Mill on the Floss '39

John Whelpley
Tremors 3: Back to Perfection '01
Tremors 5: Bloodlines '15

Kennilworthy Kathleen Whisp (1965-)
See J. K. Rowling

Duane Whitaker (1959-)
Eddie Presley '92
From Dusk Till Dawn 2: Texas Blood Money '98

Cynthia Whitcomb (1951-)
Grace Kelly '83
I Know My First Name Is Steven '89
Buffalo Girls '95
Degree of Guilt '95
Emma's Wish '98
Selma, Lord, Selma '99
Caught in the Act '04
I Dream of Murder '06

David A.R. White (1970-)
Six: The Mark Unleashed '04
The Mark 2: Redemption '13

Garry Michael White
Scarecrow '73
Sky Riders '76
The Promise '79

James Gordon White
Hell's Belles '69
Bigfoot '70
The Incredible Two-Headed Transplant '71
The Tormentors '71
The Thing with Two Heads '72

J.B. White
The Beast '96
The Spring '00
Counterstrike '03
The Twelve Days of Christmas Eve '04
Come Dance at My Wedding '09
The National Tree '09
We Have Your Husband '11
The Christmas Ornament '13

Michael Jai White (1967-)
Black Dynamite '09
Never Back Down: No Surrender '16

Mike White (1970-)
Dead Man on Campus '97
Chuck & Buck '00
The Good Girl '02
Orange County '02
School of Rock '03
Nacho Libre '06
Year of the Dog '07
Gentlemen Broncos '09
Beatriz at Dinner '17
Brad's Status '17
The Emoji Movie '17
Pitch Perfect 3 '17

Noni White
The Hunchback of Notre Dame '96
Anastasia '97
Tarzan '99
102 Dalmatians '00
Tarzan 2 '05

Robb White (1909-)
House on Haunted Hill '58
Macabre '58
The Tingler '59
13 Ghosts '60
Homicidal '61

Robertson White
The Witness Vanishes '39
Charlie Chan's Murder Cruise '40
Dick Tracy Meets Gruesome '47

Stiles White
Knowing '09
The Possession '12
Ouija '14

Ted Whitehead
Cracker: The Big Crunch '94
Tess of the D'Urbervilles '98
The Mayor of Casterbridge '03

Hugh Whitemore (1936-)
Elizabeth R '72
All Creatures Great and Small '74
I Remember Nelson '82
Pack of Lies '87
The Rector's Wife '94
Jane Eyre '96
A Dance to the Music of Time '97
The Gathering Storm '02
My House in Umbria '03
Into the Storm '09

Preston A. Whitmore, II (1962-)
Fled '96
Lockdown '00
Blood Crime '02
Civil Brand '02
Crossover '06
This Christmas '07

Stanford Whitmore (1925-2014)
War Hunt '62
Your Cheatin' Heart '64
The Eyes of Charles Sand '74
Arthur Hailey's The Moneychangers '76
The Dark '79

Steven Whitney
Anti-Terrorist Cell: Manhunt '01
Flatland '02

Gary Whitta
The Book of Eli '10
After Earth '13

Jack Whittingham (1910-72)
Hunted '52
The Prince and the Pauper '62

John Whittington
The LEGO Batman Movie '17
The LEGO Ninjago Movie '17

Tom Whitus
The Wild Card '03
Jr. Detective Agency '09

Cormac Wibberley (1959-)
Motel Blue '98
The 6th Day '00
I Spy '02
Charlie's Angels: Full Throttle '03
National Treasure '04
The Shaggy Dog '06
National Treasure: Book of Secrets '07
G-Force '09

Marianne S. Wibberley (1965-)
Motel Blue '98
The 6th Day '00
I Spy '02
Charlie's Angels: Full Throttle '03
National Treasure '04
The Shaggy Dog '06
National Treasure: Book of Secrets '07
G-Force '09

David Wickes
Jack the Ripper '88
Jekyll and Hyde '90
Frankenstein '93

Christopher Wicking (1943-)
Cry of the Banshee '70
Scream and Scream Again '70
Blood from the Mummy's Tomb '71
Demons of the Mind '72
To the Devil, a Daughter '76

Gregory Widen
Highlander '86
Backdraft '91
The Prophecy '95
Green Sails '00

Bo Widerberg (1930-97)
Elvira Madigan '67
All Things Fair '95

Ken Wiederhorn
Shock Waves '77
Return of the Living Dead 2 '88

John Wierick
Bopha! '93
The Dive from Clausen's Pier '05
A Life Interrupted '07

Joe Wiesenfeld
Anne of Green Gables '85
The Yearling '94
At the Midnight Hour '95
20,000 Leagues Under the Sea '97
A Knight in Camelot '98
The Hound of the Baskervilles '00
Back to the Secret Garden '01
Child Star: The Shirley Temple Story '01
The Sign of Four '01
A Killing Spring '02
St. Urbain's Horseman '07

Lionel Wigram
The Man from U.N.C.L.E. '15
King Arthur: Legend of the Sword '17

Crane Wilbur (1886-1973)
Lord Byron of Broadway '30
The Devil on Horseback '36
Yellow Cargo '36
Crime School '38
Blackwell's Island '39
Hell's Kitchen '39
The Devil on Wheels '47
I Was a Communist for the FBI '51
Inside the Walls of Folsom Prison '51
House of Wax '53
Crime Wave '54
The Mad Magician '54
The Phenix City Story '55
The Phenix City Story '55
Women's Prison '55
The Bat '59
The George Raft Story '61
Mysterious Island '61
House of Women '62

Wellesley Wild
Ted '12
A Million Ways to Die In the West '14
Ted 2 '15

Cornel Wilde (1915-89)
Beach Red '67
No Blade of Grass '70

Billy Wilder (1906-2002)
Mauvaise Graine '33
Bluebeard's Eighth Wife '38
Midnight '39
Ninotchka '39
Ball of Fire '41
Hold Back the Dawn '41
The Major and the Minor '42
Five Graves to Cairo '43
Double Indemnity '44
The Lost Weekend '45
Emperor Waltz '48
A Song Is Born '48
Sunset Boulevard '50
Ace in the Hole '51
Stalag 17 '53
Sabrina '54
The Seven Year Itch '55
Love in the Afternoon '57
Spirit of St. Louis '57
Witness for the Prosecution '57
Some Like It Hot '59
The Apartment '60
One, Two, Three '61
Irma La Douce '63
Kiss Me, Stupid! '64
The Fortune Cookie '66
The Private Life of Sherlock Holmes '70
Avanti! '72
The Front Page '74
Fedora '78

Gene Wilder (1933-2016)
Young Frankenstein '74
World's Greatest Lover '77
The Adventures of Sherlock Holmes' Smarter Brother '78
The Woman in Red '84
Haunted Honeymoon '86
See No Evil, Hear No Evil '89
Murder in a Small Town '99

John Wilder (1936-)
Centennial '78
Return to Lonesome Dove '93
Anne Rice's The Feast of All Saints '01

Robert Wilder (1901-74)
Flamingo Road '49
The Big Country '58

Thornton Wilder (1897-1975)
Shadow of a Doubt '43
Our Town '03

Jason Wiles (1970-)
Full Count '06
Play Dead '09

Ethan Wiley
House '86
House 2: The Second Story '87
Children of the Corn 5: Fields of Terror '98
Black Ops '07

Wolfgang Wilhelm
The Saint Meets the Tiger '43
Captain Boycott '47

Rich Wilkes (1966-)
Airheads '94
The Jerky Boys '95
Glory Daze '96
XXX '02

Christopher Wilkinson (1950-)
Nixon '95
Ali '01

Brock Williams
Candlelight in Algeria '44
Meet Mr. Callaghan '54

Delondra Williams
Rise of the Zombies '12
Mother '13
Blood Lake '14

Emlyn Williams (1905-87)
Friday the Thirteenth '33
The Man Who Knew Too Much '34

Nigel Williams
Dirty Tricks '00
Elizabeth I '05
Moby Dick '11

Rob Williams
Long-Term Relationship '06
Make the Yuletide Gay '09
Role/Play '10
The Men Next Door '12

Sarah Williams
The Secret Life of Mrs. Beeton '06
Becoming Jane '07
Small Island '09

Tennessee Williams (1911-83)
A Streetcar Named Desire '51
The Rose Tattoo '55
Baby Doll '56
Cat on a Hot Tin Roof '84
The Glass Menagerie '87
The Roman Spring of Mrs. Stone '03
The Loss of a Teardrop Diamond '08

Tod Harrison Williams (1968-)
The Adventures of Sebastian Cole '99
The Door in the Floor '04
American Loser '07

Tyger Williams
Menace II Society '93
The Perfect Guy '15

David Williamson (1942-)
Don's Party '76
The Club '81
Gallipoli '81
The Year of Living Dangerously '82
The Four Minute Mile '88
On the Beach '00

Fred Williamson (1938-)
Boss '74
Adios Amigo '75

Kevin Williamson (1965-)
Scream '96
I Know What You Did Last Summer '97
Scream 2 '97
The Faculty '98
Teaching Mrs. Tingle '99
Cursed '04
Scream 4 '11

Nick Willing (1961-)
Photographing Fairies '97
Close Your Eyes '02
Alice '09
Neverland '11

Calder Willingham (1922-95)
Paths of Glory '57
The Strange One '57
The Vikings '58
One-Eyed Jacks '61
The Graduate '67
Little Big Man '70
Thieves Like Us '74
Rambling Rose '91

Willard Willingham (1909-97)
Battle at Bloody Beach '61
40 Guns to Apache Pass '67

Kevin Willmott
The '70s '00
Chi-raq '15
BlacKkKlansman '18
Da 5 Bloods '20

Tim Willocks
Swept from the Sea '97
Sin '02

August Wilson
The Piano Lesson '94
Fences '16

Caleb Wilson
Four Christmases '08
Nine Lives '16

Carey Wilson (1889-1962)
He Who Gets Slapped '24
Why Be Good? '29
Behind Office Doors '31
Faithless '32
Polly of the Circus '32
Gabriel Over the White House '33
Mutiny on the Bounty '35
Judge Hardy and Son '39

Casey Wilson
Bride Wars '09
Ass Backwards '13

David Wilson (1949-)
The Perfect Weapon '91
Strangers in Good Company '91

Erin Cressida Wilson (1964-)
Secretary '02
Fur: An Imaginary Portrait of Diane Arbus '06
Chloe '09
Call Me Crazy '13
Men, Women & Children '14
The Girl on the Train '16

Gerald Wilson
Chato's Land '71
Lawman '71
Scorpio '73

Henry Wilson (1921-91)
See Gino Mangini

Hugh Wilson (1943-2018)
Stroker Ace '83
Police Academy '84
Rustler's Rhapsody '85
Burglar '87
Guarding Tess '94
Down Periscope '96
Rough Riders '97
Blast from the Past '98
Dudley Do-Right '99

Lana Wilson
After Tiller '13
The Departure '17

Michael Wilson (1914-78)
A Place in the Sun '51
Five Fingers '52
Salt of the Earth '54
Friendly Persuasion '56
The Bridge on the River Kwai '57
Lawrence of Arabia '62
Planet of the Apes '68

Michael G. Wilson (1943-)
For Your Eyes Only '81
Octopussy '83
A View to a Kill '85
The Living Daylights '87
License to Kill '89

Michael J. Wilson
Ice Age '02
The Tuxedo '02
Shark Tale '04

Owen Wilson (1968-)
Bottle Rocket '95
Rushmore '98
The Royal Tenenbaums '01

S.S. Wilson
Short Circuit '86
*batteries not included '87
Short Circuit 2 '88
Tremors '89
Ghost Dad '90
Heart and Souls '93
Tremors 2: Aftershocks '96
Wild Wild West '99

Kurt Wimmer (1964-)
The Neighbor '93
Relative Fear '95
The Thomas Crown Affair '99
Equilibrium '02
The Recruit '03
Ultraviolet '06

Street Kings '08
Law Abiding Citizen '09
Salt '10
Total Recall '12
Point Break '15

Arthur Wimperis (1874-1953)
The Private Life of Henry VIII '33
The Scarlet Pimpernel '34
The Green Cockatoo '37
The Return of the Scarlet Pimpernel '37
The Four Feathers '39
If Winter Comes '41
Mrs. Miniver '42
Random Harvest '42
Young Bess '53

Jenny Wingfield
The Outsider '02
A Dog Named Christmas '09

Charles Winkler
You Talkin' to Me? '87
Rocky Marciano '99

Max Winkler
Ceremony '10
Flower '18

Terence H. Winkless
The Howling '81
He's My Girl '87
Corporate Affairs '90
Rage and Honor '92

Michael Winner (1935-2013)
The Sentinel '76
The Big Sleep '78
Firepower '79
A Chorus of Disapproval '89
Bullseye! '90
Parting Shots '98

Michael Winnick
Shadow Puppets '07
Guns, Girls and Gambling '11
Code of Honor '16

Alice Winocour
Augustine '12
Mustang '15
Disorder '16

Don Winslow
Full Ride '02
Savages '12

Terry Winsor
Fool's Gold: The Story of the Brink's-Mat Robbery '92
Essex Boys '99

Alex Winter (1965-)
Freaked '93
Fever '99

Terence Winter
Get Rich or Die Tryin' '05
Brooklyn Rules '07
The Wolf of Wall Street '13

Michael Winterbottom (1961-)
A Mighty Heart '07
A Summer in Genoa '08
Trishna '11
Everyday '12
The Trip to Italy '14
The Wedding Guest '18

Scott Wiper (1970-)
A Better Way to Die '00
The Condemned '07
The Marine 3: Homefront '11
The Cold Light of Day '12

Tommy Wirkola (1979-)
Dead Snow '09
Hansel & Gretel: Witch Hunters '12
Dead Snow: Red vs. Dead '14

Mildred Wirt Benson
Nancy Drew-Detective '38
Nancy Drew-Trouble Shooter '39

Aubrey Wisberg (1909-90)
Counter-Espionage '42
They Came to Blow Up America '43
So Dark the Night '46
The Man from Planet X '51
1,000 Years From Now '52
Captain Kidd and the Slave Girl '54
Return to Treasure Island '54
Murder Is My Beat '55
Hercules in New York '70

Len Wiseman (1973-)
Underworld: Evolution '05
Underworld: Awakening '12

Jerome Wish
The Gay Deceivers '69
Run, Angel, Run! '69

William Wisher
Judge Dredd '95
Exorcist: The Beginning '04
Dominion: Prequel to the Exorcist '05
I.T. '16

Doris Wishman (1920-2002)
Nude on the Moon '61
Bad Girls Go to Hell '65
The Amazing Transplant '70
Double Agent 73 '80

Theodore Witcher
Love Jones '96
Body Count '97

Wolfram Witt
Coming Out '89
The Mistake '91

Dirk Wittenborn
Fierce People '05
The Lucky Ones '08

William D. Wittliff (1940-)
The Black Stallion '79
Honeysuckle Rose '80
Raggedy Man '81
Barbarosa '82
Country '84
Lonesome Dove '89
Lone Justice 2 '93
The Cowboy Way '94
Legends of the Fall '94
The Perfect Storm '00

Bryan Wizemann (1973-)
Think of Me '11
About Sunny '12

Bethany Ashton Wolf
Little Chenier: A Cajun Story '06
Forever My Girl '18

Dick Wolf (1946-)
Skateboard '77
No Man's Land '87
Masquerade '88
School Ties '92

Fred Wolf (1964-)
Black Sheep '96
Dirty Work '97
Joe Dirt '01
Dickie Roberts: Former Child Star '03
Without a Paddle '04
Strange Wilderness '08
Grown Ups '10
Grown Ups 2 '13
Drunk Parents '19

Robert Hewitt Wolfe
Futuresport '98
Riverworld '10

P.J. Wolfson (1903-79)
Dancing Lady '33
Picture Snatcher '33
Mad Love '35
Rendezvous '35
Love on a Bet '36
Vigil in the Night '40

Dave Wollert
Quicksand: No Escape '91
A Job to Kill For '06

M. Wallace Wolodarsky
Coldblooded '94
Seeing Other People '04
The Rocker '08
The Polka King '18
A Dog's Journey '19
Trolls World Tour '20

Wally Wolodarsky
Monsters vs. Aliens '09
A Dog's Purpose '17

Barry Wong (1946-92)
Heart of Dragon '85
Hard-Boiled '92
Twin Dragons '92

Chun-Chun Wong
The Cave of the Silken Web '67
Six Strong Guys '04

Edmond Wong
Dragon Tiger Gate '07
Ip Man '08
Ip Man 2 '10
Ip Man 3 '16
Ip Man 4: The Finale '19

James Wong
The Boys Next Door '85
Final Destination '00
The One '01
Final Destination 3 '06
Rosemary's Baby '14

Jing Wong
The Prodigal Son '82
Legend of the Liquid Sword '93
Naked Weapon '03

Kar-Wai Wong
As Tears Go By '88
Days of Being Wild '91

Manfred Wong
Dream Lovers '86
The White Storm '13

Maria Wong
The Four '12
Kingdom of Blood: The Final Battle '16

Raymond Wong (1948-)
Mad Mission 3 '84
The Phantom Lover '95

Petchthai Wongkamlao (1965-)
The Bodyguard '04
The Bodyguard 2 '07

John Woo (1946-)
Last Hurrah for Chivalry '78
A Better Tomorrow, Part 1 '86
Heroes Shed No Tears '86
A Better Tomorrow, Part 2 '88
A Bullet in the Head '90
The Killer '90
Once a Thief '90
Hard-Boiled '92
Red Cliff '08

Charles Wood (1932-)
Help! '65
The Knack '65
How I Won the War '67
The Charge of the Light Brigade '68
Cuba '79
An Awfully Big Adventure '94
Sharpe's Company '94
Iris '01
The Other Man '08

Christopher Wood (1935-)
Confessions of a Window Cleaner '74
Confessions of a Driving Instructor '76
The Spy Who Loved Me '77
Moonraker '79
Remo Williams: The Adventure Begins '85
Dangerous Curves '99

Edward D. Wood, Jr. (1924-78)
Glen or Glenda? '53
Jail Bait '54
Bride of the Monster '55
Plan 9 from Outer Space '56
The Bride & the Beast '58
Night of the Ghouls '59
The Sinister Urge '60
Orgy of the Dead '65

Christopher Wooden
Body Chemistry 2: Voice of a Stranger '91
The Showgirl Murders '95

William Read Woodfield
The Hypnotic Eye '60
Earth II '71

Aaron Woodley (1971-)
Spark: A Space Tail '17
Arctic Dogs '19

Bryan Woods
A Quiet Place '18
Haunt '19

Jack Woods
Equinox '71
Beware! The Blob '72

Lotta Woods (1869-1957)
The Three Musketeers '21
The Gaucho '27

Skip Woods
Swordfish '01
X-Men Origins: Wolverine '09
The A-Team '10
A Good Day to Die Hard '13
Sabotage '14
Hitman: Agent 47 '15

Abbe Wool
Sid & Nancy '86
Roadside Prophets '92

Edgar Allan Woolf (1881-1943)
Flesh '32
Freaks '32
The Casino Murder Case '35
Everybody Sing '38
Ice Follies of 1939 '39

Linda Woolverton (1959-)
Beauty and the Beast '91
Homeward Bound: The Incredible Journey '93
Alice in Wonderland '10
Maleficent '14
Alice Through the Looking Glass '16
Maleficent: Mistress of Evil '19

Hank Woon, Jr.
Age of Dinosaurs '13
500 MPH Storm '13

Tom Woosley
Attack of the Sabretooth '05
Army of the Dead '08

Peter Martin Wortmann
The Breed '06
Who Do You Love '08

John Wrathall
Good '08
The Liability '12

Ardel Wray (1907-83)
The Falcon and the Co-Eds '43
I Walked with a Zombie '43
The Leopard Man '43
Isle of the Dead '45

Alexander Wright
The First 9 1/2 Weeks '98
Wishmaster 3: Beyond the Gates of Hell '01

Brad Wright
Poltergeist: The Legacy '96
Stargate: Continuum '08

Edgar Wright (1974-)
Shaun of the Dead '04
Hot Fuzz '07
Scott Pilgrim vs. the World '10
The Adventures of Tintin '11
The World's End '13
Ant-Man '15
Baby Driver '17

Geoffrey Wright (1959-)
Romper Stomper '92
Metal Skin '94
Macbeth '06

Jonathan Wright
Psychotica '10
Awakening the Zodiac '17

Ralph Wright (1908-88)
Peter Pan '53
Lady and the Tramp '55
Nikki, the Wild Dog of the North '61

Ray Wright
Fatal Desire '05
Pulse '06
The Crazies '09
Case 39 '10
Greta '18

Donald Wrye
Ice Castles '79
Divorce Wars: A Love Story '82

David Wu
The Bride with White Hair '93
The Bride with White Hair 2 '93

Rudy Wurlitzer (1938-)
Glen and Randa '71
Two Lane Blacktop '71
Pat Garrett & Billy the Kid '73
Walker '87
Wind '92
Little Buddha '93

Rupert Wyatt (1972-)
The Escapist '08
Captive State '19

Robert Wyler (1900-71)
Detective Story '51
The Big Country '58

J.H. (Joel Howard) Wyman (1967-)
Mr. Rice's Secret '00
The Mexican '01
Dead Man Down '13

Tracy Keenan Wynn (1945-)
The Autobiography of Miss Jane Pittman '74
The Longest Yard '74
The Drowning Pool '75
The Deep '77
In the Line of Duty: The FBI Murders '88
Capone '89
Carolina Skeletons '92
Robinson Crusoe '96

Paul Wynne
Destination Vegas '95
Bombshell '97
Barrio Wars '02

Jim Wynorski (1950-)
Forbidden World '82
Screwballs '83
Chopping Mall '86
Big Bad Mama 2 '87
Deathstalker 2: Duel of the Titans '87
Not of This Earth '88
The Haunting of Morella '91
Home for Christmas '93
Final Voyage '99
Komodo vs. Cobra '05
Shockwave '06
Bone Eater '07
Fire From Below '09
Dinocroc Vs. Supergator '10
Camel Spiders '11

Frank Yablans (1935-)
North Dallas Forty '79
Mommie Dearest '81

Boaz Yakin (1966-)
The Punisher '90
Fresh '94
A Price Above Rubies '97
Dirty Dancing: Havana Nights '04
Death in Love '08
Now You See Me '13
Max '15
Boarding School '18

Kazuo Yamada
Godzilla vs. the Sea Monster '66
What's Up, Tiger Lily? '66

Yoji Yamada (1931-)
The Twilight Samurai '02
The Hidden Blade '04
Kabei: Our Mother '08

Kikumi Yamagishi
The Happiness of the Katakuris '01
Hara-Kiri: Death of a Samurai '11

Yudai Yamaguchi
Versus '00
Alive '02
The ABCs of Death '12

Shugoro Yamamoto
Kill! '68
The Sea is Watching '02
Sabu '04

Geling Yan
Dangerous Liaisons '12
Earth: One Amazing Day '17

Pi-ying Yang
The Hole '98
What Time Is It There? '01

Brock Yates
Smokey and the Bandit 2 '80
Cannonball Run '81

George Worthing Yates (1901-75)
The Falcon in Mexico '44
Cavalry Charge '51
The Tall Target '51
This Woman Is Dangerous '52
Earth vs. the Flying Saucers '56
Attack of the Puppet People '58
Earth vs. the Spider '58
Frankenstein 1970 '58
Space Master X-7 '58
War of the Colossal Beast '58
Tormented '60

Nai-Hoi Yau
The Mission '99
Running on Karma '03
Running Out of Time 2 '06
Drug War '13

Peter Yeldham (1927-)
The Liquidator '65
24 Hours to Kill '65
Bang! Bang! You're Dead! '66
Age of Consent '69
1915 '82

Jack Yellen (1892-1991)
George White's Scandals of 1935 '35
Pigskin Parade '36
Sing, Baby, Sing '36
Love Is News '37
Wake Up and Live '37
You Can't Have Everything '37
My Lucky Star '38
Sally, Irene and Mary '38

Bennett Yellin
Dumb & Dumber '94
Joy Ride 2: Dead Ahead '08
In the Blood '13
Dumb and Dumber To '14

Valentin Yezhov (1921-2004)
Ballad of a Soldier '60
Siberiade '79

Rafael Yglesias
Fearless '93
Death and the Maiden '94
Les Miserables '97
From Hell '01
Dark Water '02

Tin-Shing Yip
Running on Karma '03
Exiled '06

Yoshikata Yoda (1909-91)
Osaka Elegy '36
Sisters of the Gion '36
47 Ronin, Part 1 '42
47 Ronin, Part 2 '42

Utamaro and His Five Women '46
Ugetsu '53
Sansho the Bailiff '54
Bushido: The Cruel Code of the Samurai '63

Masahiro Yokotani
Godzilla, Mothra, and King Ghidorah: Giant Monsters All-Out Attack '01
Godzilla-Tokyo S.O.S. '03

Jeff Yonis
Bloodfist 5: Human Target '93
Humanoids from the Deep '96

Philip Yordan (1914-2003)
Syncopation '42
Betrayed '44
Johnny Doesn't Live Here Any More '44
Dillinger '45
The Chase '46
Whistle Stop '46
Bad Men of Tombstone '49
House of Strangers '49
Reign of Terror '49
Detective Story '51
Drums in the Deep South '51
Mutiny '52
Houdini '53
Johnny Guitar '53
Broken Lance '54
Naked Jungle '54
Big Combo '55
The Man from Laramie '55
Savage Wilderness '55
The Harder They Fall '56
Four Boys and a Gun '57
Men in War '57
The Bravados '58
The Fiend Who Walked the West '58
God's Little Acre '58
The Day of the Outlaw '59
Studs Lonigan '60
El Cid '61
The King of Kings '61
Day of the Triffids '63
55 Days at Peking '63
The Fall of the Roman Empire '64
Battle of the Bulge '65
Captain Apache '71
Bad Man's River '72
Night Train to Terror '84
Bloody Wednesday '87
The Unholy '88

Tetsuro Yoshida
100 Monsters '68
Along with Ghosts '69
Zatoichi *vs.* Yojimbo '70

Christopher Yost (1973-)
Max Steel '16
Thor: Ragnarok '17

Graham Yost
Speed '94
Broken Arrow '95
Hard Rain '97
From the Earth to the Moon '98
Mission to Mars '00
Band of Brothers '01
The Last Castle '01
The Pacific '10

Bob Young (1923-)
Nature of the Beast '07
Revenge of the Bridesmaids '10

Brian D. Young
Ghouls '07
Bond of Silence '10

Carroll Young (1908-92)
Tarzan Triumphs '43
Tarzan and the Leopard Woman '46
Tarzan and the Mermaids '48
Bomba and the Hidden City '50
Pygmy Island '50
Fury of the Congo '51
Tarzan and the She-Devil '53
She Devil '57
Mark of the Gorilla '58

Clarence Upson Young (1895-1969)
The Plot Thickens '36
Night Monster '42
The Strange Case of Dr. Rx '42

Dalene Young (1939-)
Panic in Echo Park '77
Cross Creek '83
Is There Life Out There? '94
The Yarn Princess '94
The Baby-Sitters' Club '95
Evidence of Blood '97

Gary Young
The Last Drop '05
Harry Brown '09

John G. Young
Parallel Sons '95
The Reception '05

John Sacret Young
Chandler '71
Champions: A Love Story '78
Testament '83
Romero '89
Deceit '04

Mark Young
Once Upon a Forest '93
All Dogs Go to Heaven 2 '95
The Least Among You '09
Wicked Blood '13

Mark H. Young
Tooth and Nail '07
The Killing Jar '10

Mike Young
My Man Is a Loser '14
A Stand Up Guy '16

Nedrick Young (1913-68)
Decoy '46
The Defiant Ones '58
Inherit the Wind '60
Inherit the Wind '99

Robert M. Young (1924-)
Nothing but a Man '64
Alambrista! '77
Agatha Christie's Sparkling Cyanide '83
Triumph of the Spirit '89

Robinson Young
Bugs '03
Encrypt '03
Webs '03

Terence Young (1915-94)
On Approval '44
Mayerling '68
War Goddess '74

Waldemar Young (1878-1938)
The Show '27
Sally '29
Tide of Empire '29
Penrod and Sam '31
Island of Lost Souls '32
Love Me Tonight '32
The Sign of the Cross '33
Men in White '34
The Crusades '35
The Lives of a Bengal Lancer '35
Peter Ibbetson '35
Test Pilot '38

A.P. Younger (1890-1931)
A Lady of Chance '28
Five and Ten '31
Flying High '31

Ben Younger (1972-)
Boiler Room '00
Prime '05
Bleed for This '16

Henry Younger (1927-94)
See Michael Carreras

Vlad Yudin
Last Day of Summer '10
Generation Iron '13

Baku Yumemakura
Onmyoji '01
Onmyoji 2 '03

Cathy Yuspa (1971-)
What Women Want '00
13 Going on 30 '04

Larry Yust (1930-)
Trick Baby '72
Testimony of Two Men '77

Brian Yuzna (1951-)
From Beyond '86
Bride of Re-Animator '89
Silent Night, Deadly Night 5: The Toymaker '91
The Dentist 2: Brace Yourself '98

Bruce Zabel
Mortal Kombat 2: Annihilation '97
Pandemic '07

Bryce Zabel
The Poseidon Adventure '05
Blackbeard '06
Miles from Nowhere '09

Jackie Zabel
Pandemic '07
Miles from Nowhere '09

Mauricio Zacharias
Keep the Lights On '12
Love Is Strange '14
Rio, I Love You '14
Little Men '16
Frankie '19

Steve Zacharias
Revenge of the Nerds 3: The Next Generation '92
Revenge of the Nerds 4: Nerds in Love '94
Eddie '96

Jon Zack
Out Cold '01
The Perfect Score '04
Shrek the Third '07
How to Be a Latin Lover '17

Justin Zackham
Going Greek '01
The Bucket List '07
The Big Wedding '13
Second Act '18

S. Craig Zahler (1973-)
Bone Tomahawk '15
Brawl in Cell Block 99 '17
Dragged Across Concrete '18
Puppet Master: The Littlest Reich '18

Steven Zaillian (1953-)
The Falcon and the Snowman '85
Awakenings '90
Jack the Bear '93
Schindler's List '93
Searching for Bobby Fischer '93
Clear and Present Danger '94
A Civil Action '98
Hannibal '01
Gangs of New York '02
The Interpreter '05
All the King's Men '06
American Gangster '07
The Girl With the Dragon Tattoo '11
Moneyball '11
Exodus: Gods and Kings '14
The Irishman '19

Alex Zamm
Chairman of the Board '97
Inspector Gadget 2 '02
Dr. Dolittle: Million Dollar Mutts '09
Beverly Hills Chihuahua 2 '10
The Little Rascals Save the Day '14

Darryl F. Zanuck (1902-79)
The Better 'Ole '26
The First Auto '27
Noah's Ark '28

Bernardino Zapponi (1927-2000)
Spirits of the Dead '68
Fellini Satyricon '69
The Clowns '71
The Priest's Wife '71
Deep Red: Hatchet Murders '75

Tony Zarindast
Hardcase and Fist '89
Werewolf '95

Cesare Zavattini (1902-89)
The Children Are Watching Us '44
Shoeshine '47
The Bicycle Thief '48
Bellissima '51
Miracle in Milan '51
Umberto D '55
Two Women '61
Boccaccio '70 '62
After the Fox '66
The Garden of the Finzi-Continis '71

Ben Zazove
Tooth Fairy 2 '12
Sherlock Gnomes '18

Franco Zeffirelli (1923-2019)
The Taming of the Shrew '67
Romeo and Juliet '68
Brother Sun, Sister Moon '73
Jesus of Nazareth '77
Hamlet '90
Jane Eyre '96
Tea with Mussolini '99
Callas Forever '02

Rudolf Zehetgruber (1926-)
Death is Nimble, Death is Quick '67
Superbug Super Agent '76

J.D. Zeik
Ronin '98
Pistol Whipped '08

Laurent Zeitoun
I Do '06
Heartbreaker '10
Leap! '16

Nathan Zellner (1975-)
Kumiko the Treasure Hunter '14
Damsel '18

Daniel Zelman (1967-)
Anacondas: The Hunt for the Blood Orchid '04
Fool's Gold '08

Yuri Zeltser (1962-)
Black & White '99
High Crimes '02
Seeking Justice '12

Robert Zemeckis (1952-)
I Wanna Hold Your Hand '78
1941 '79
Used Cars '80
Back to the Future '85
Back to the Future, Part 2 '89
Back to the Future, Part 3 '90
Trespass '92
A Christmas Carol '09
The Walk '15
Welcome to Marwen '18

Bo Zenga
Soul Plane '04
Stan Helsing '09

Enid Zentelis
Evergreen '04
Bottled Up '13

Joshua Zetumer
RoboCop '14
Patriots Day '17

Yimou Zhang (1951-)
Hero '02
House of Flying Daggers '04
Curse of the Golden Flower '06
Shadow '18

Chloé Zhao
Songs My Brother Taught Me '15
The Rider '17

Stuart Zicherman
Elektra '05
A.C.O.D. '13

Scott Ziehl
Red Line '96
Broken Vessels '98
Exit Speed '08

Lester Ziffren
Charlie Chan in Panama '40
Charlie Chan's Murder Cruise '40

Paul Ziller
Moving Target '00
Firefight '03
Ba'al: The Storm God '08
Sea Beast '08
Polar Storm '09
Ice Quake '10
Stonehenge Apocalypse '10
Metal Shifters '11
Seeds of Destruction '11

Julian Zimet
Saigon '47
Circus World '64
Psyche 59 '64
Crack in the World '65
Horror Express '72
Pancho Villa '72

Bruce Zimmerman
The Inspectors '98
The Inspectors 2: A Shred of Evidence '00

Paul Zimmerman
Lovers and Liars '81
King of Comedy '82
Consuming Passions '88
A Modern Affair '94

Vernon Zimmerman
Charms '73
Fade to Black '80

Paul Zindel (1936-2003)
Up the Sandbox '72
Mame '74
Maria's Lovers '84
Alice in Wonderland '85
Runaway Train '85

John Zinman
Lara Croft: Tomb Raider '01
Gold '16

Stephen Zito
Hostage Flight '85
Full Exposure: The Sex Tape Scandals '89
Diana: Her True Story '93
Two Fathers: Justice for the Innocent '94

Craig Zobel
Great World of Sound '07
Compliance '12

Chris Zois
The Blackout '97
New Rose Hotel '98

Rob Zombie (1965-)
House of 1000 Corpses '03
The Devil's Rejects '05
Halloween '07
Halloween II '09
The Haunted World of El Superbeasto '09
The Lords of Salem '13
31 '16
3 from Hell '19

Erick Zonca
The Dreamlife of Angels '98
Julia '08

Tom Zuber
Lansdown '01
Little Athens '05

David Zucker (1947-)
Kentucky Fried Movie '77
Airplane! '80
Top Secret! '84
The Naked Gun: From the Files of Police Squad '88
Naked Gun 2 1/2: The Smell of Fear '91
Naked Gun 33 1/3: The Final Insult '94
High School High '96
BASEketball '98
Scary Movie 4 '06
An American Carol '08
Scary Movie 5 '13

Jerry Zucker (1950-)
Kentucky Fried Movie '77
Airplane! '80
Top Secret! '84
The Naked Gun: From the Files of Police Squad '88

George Zuckerman (1916-96)
Border Incident '49
Dawn at Socorro '54
Ride Clear of Diablo '54
Taza, Son of Cochise '54
Written on the Wind '56
Tarnished Angels '57

Andrzej Zulawski
Possession '81
Cosmos '16

Andrey Zvyagintsev
Elena '11
Leviathan '14
Loveless '18

Ron Zwang
Doin' Time '85
The Nutt House '95

Alan Zweibel (1950-)
Dragnet '87
The Story of Us '99

Edward Zwick (1952-)
Special Bulletin '83
The Siege '98
The Last Samurai '03
Defiance '08
Love and Other Drugs '10
Jack Reacher: Never Go Back '16
American Assassin '17

Video Sources

The **Video Sources** section provides full contact information, including address, phone, fax and toll-free numbers, as well as web site address and e-mail when available, for mail order and retail resources for videos reviewed in this book. They are listed alphabetically. Some of the videos have no currently known distributor, but copies may still be available. Others are **On Moratorium**, meaning their distributor, or more likely, their producer, has pulled them out of circulation for a certain amount of time. These videos may still be available from local or mail sources because they were distributed at one time. Many video stores provide an ordering service. If your local video store doesn't have a title you want, you can ask them to order it for you, or you can find someone here who will. To find additional web-based and specialty distributors, please check our **Web Site Guide**.

A24 FILMS LLC
31 W 27th St., 11th Fl.
New York, NY 10001
(646)568-6015
HomePage: http://www.a24films.com

A&E TELEVISION NETWORKS, LLC
235 E 45th St.
New York, NY 10017
Email: feedback@aenetworks.com
HomePage: http://www.aetv.com

ACORN MEDIA GROUP INC.
8515 Georgia Ave., Ste. 650
Silver Spring, MD 20910
(301)608-2115
800-999-0212
Fax: (301)608-9312
HomePage: http://www.acorn-tv.com

AFA ENTERTAINMENT
HomePage: http://afaentertainment.com/index.html

AFRICAN-AMERICAN IMAGES
PO Box 1799
Chicago Heights, IL 60412
(708)672-4909
800-552-1991
Fax: (708)672-0466
Email: customersvc@africanamericanimages.com
HomePage: http://www.africanamericanimages.com

ALCHEMY WORLDWIDE L.L.C.
15250 Ventura Blvd., 3 Fl.
Sherman Oaks, CA 91403
877-776-8432
Email: customercare@provida.com
HomePage: http://providalifesciences.com

ALCON ENTERTAINMENT L.L.C.
10390 Santa Monica Blvd., Ste. 250
Los Angeles, CA 90025
(310)789-3040
Fax: (310)789-3060
HomePage: http://www.alconent.com

ALL DAY ENTERTAINMENT
IL
HomePage: http://www.alldayentertainment.com

ALLIED ARTISTS INTERNATIONAL
655 North Central Ave., 17th Fl
Glendale, CA 91203
(626)330-0600
Fax: (626)961-0411
HomePage: http://alliedartists.com

ALLIED VAUGHN
7600 Parklawn, Ste. 300
Minneapolis, MN 55435
(952)832-3100
800-323-0281
Fax: (952)832-3179
Email: mlxolhelp@alliedvaughn.com
HomePage: http://www.alliedvaughn.com

ALLUMINATION FILMWORKS
21250 Califa St., Ste. 102
Woodland Hills, CA 91367
(818)712-9000
Fax: (818)712-9074
Email: info@alluminationfilmworks.com
HomePage: http://www.alluminationfilmworks.com

ALPHA OMEGA PUBLICATIONS INC. (AOP)
804 N 2nd Ave. E
Rock Rapids, IA 51246
800-622-3070
HomePage: http://www.aop.com

ALPHA VIDEO
PO Box 101
Narberth, PA 19072-0101
(610)649-7565
800-336-4627
Fax: (610)649-0315
HomePage: http://www.oldies.com

ALPHA VIDEO DISTRIBUTORS
255 Old New Brunswick Rd.
Piscataway, NJ 08854
(732)981-0110

ALTERNATIVE CINEMA INC.
PO Box 132
Butler, NJ 07405
Email: store@alternativecinema.com
HomePage: http://www.alternativecinema.com

ALTERNATIVE DISTRIBUTION ALLIANCE
72 Spring St., 12th Fl.
New York, NY 10012
Email: sales@ada-music.com
HomePage: http://ada-music.com

AMAZON STUDIOS
410 Terry Ave. N
Seattle, WA 98109-5210
(206)266-7010
Email: copyright@amazon.com
HomePage: http://studios.amazon.com

AMAZON.COM, INC.
410 Terry Ave. N
Seattle, WA 98109-5210
(206)266-1000
HomePage: http://www.amazon.com

AMSELL ENTERTAINMENT INC.
12001 Ventura Pl., Ste. 404
Studio City, CA 91604

ANCHOR BAY ENTERTAINMENT
1699 Stutz Dr.
Troy, MI 48084

ANCHOR BAY ENTERTAINMENT INC.
9242 Beverly Blvd., Ste. 201
Beverly Hills, CA 90210
877-230-2756
HomePage: http://www.anchorbayentertainment.com

ANDERSON DIGITAL L.L.C.
530 S Hewitt St., Ste. 535
Los Angeles, CA 90013
(949)258-2000
800-218-7888
HomePage: http://www.anderson-digital.com

ANIMEIGO INC.
6810 Finian Dr.
Wilmington, NC 28409
(910)251-1850
Email: questions@animeigo.com
HomePage: http://www.animeigo.com

ANTHEM PICTURES
5137 Clareton Dr., Ste. 120
Agoura Hills, CA 91301

ANTON PICTURES
4249 Vineland Ave.
North Hollywood, CA 91601
HomePage: http://www.antonpictures.com

ARAB FILM DISTRIBUTION
Seattle, WA 98121
(206)322-0882
Fax: (206)322-4586
Email: info@arabfilm.com
HomePage: http://www.arabfilm.com

ARC ENTERTAINMENT L.L.C.
3212 Nebraska Ave.
Santa Monica, CA 90404

ARIZTICAL ENTERTAINMENT, INC.
12400 Ventura Blvd., Ste. 686
Studio City, CA 91604-2406
(818)760-3740
Email: info@ariztical.com
HomePage: http://www.ariztical.com

ARTE FRANCE S.A.
8 rue Marceau
92785 Issy-les-Moulineaux, France
Email: infosales@artefrance.fr
HomePage: http://sales.arte.tv

ARTIST VIEW ENTERTAINMENT INC.
5775 E Los Angeles Ave., Ste. 218
Simi Valley, CA 93063
(818)752-2480
Fax: (818)301-3272
Email: info@artistviewent.com
HomePage: http://www.artistviewent.com

THE ASYLUM
440 W Los Feliz Rd.
Burbank, CA 91501
(323)850-1214
Fax: (323)260-9811
HomePage: http://www.theasylum.cc

ASYMMETRICAL ENTERTAINMENT, INC.
110 Remsen St., Ste 1A
Brooklyn, NY 11201
(718)237-6031
Fax: (718)237-6031
Email: info@asymmetricalvideo.com

ATLANTIC VIDEO
c/o Atlantic Records
1290 Avenue of the Americas
New York, NY 10019
(212)707-2000
HomePage: http://www.atlanticrecords.com

BAKER & TAYLOR INC.
2550 W Tyvola Rd., Ste. 300
Charlotte, NC 28217
(704)998-3100
800-775-1800
Email: btinfo@baker-taylor.com
HomePage: http://www.baker-taylor.com

BANDAI ENTERTAINMENT INC. (BEI)
5551 Katella Ave.
Cypress, CA 90630
(714)816-9500
Fax: (714)816-6708
Email: support@bandai-ent.com
HomePage: http://www.bandai.com

BASEBALL DIRECT
PO Box 7563
Charlottesville, VA 22906
888-244-8837
Fax: (434)974-4986
Email: info@baseballdirect.com
HomePage: http://baseballdirect.com

BAYVIEW ENTERTAINMENT, LLC.
210 W Pky., Ste. 7
Pompton Plains, NJ 07444
(201)488-6110
Fax: (973)835-2672
Email: sales@bayviewent.com

HomePage: http://www .bayviewentertainment .com

BBC AMERICA INC.
747 3rd Ave., 7th Fl.
New York, NY 10017-2803
(212)705-9300
Email: info-amc@amc.com
HomePage: http://www .bbcamerica.com

BBC MAGAZINES
201 Wood Ln.
London W6 7BT, United Kingdom
44 20 84332000
Email: online@bbc.co.uk
HomePage: http://www .bbcmagazines.com

BBC STUDIOS AMERICAS INC
1120 Ave. of the Americas, 5th Fl.
New York, NY 10036-6700
(212)705-9300
HomePage: http://www .bbcstudios.com

BBC WORLDWIDE AMERICA INC.
1120 Avenue of the Americas, 5th Fl.
New York, NY 10036-6700
(212)705-9300
HomePage: http://www .bbcworldwide.com

BBC WORLDWIDE LTD.
101 Wood Ln.
London W12 7FA, United Kingdom
44 20 843-320-00
Fax: 44 20 874-905-38
HomePage: http://www .bbcworldwide.com

BBC WORLDWIDE PUBLISHING LTD.
Media Ctr.
201 Wood Ln.
London W12 7TQ, United Kingdom
HomePage: http://www .bbcworldwide.com

BEDFORD ENTERTAINMENT INC.
14216 SW 136th St.
Miami, FL 33186
(305)255-8684
Fax: (305)233-6943
HomePage: http://www .mtivideo.com

BENNETT MARINE VIDEO
210 W Parkway, Ste. 7
Pompton Plains, NJ 07444
800-433-6769
Email: customerservice@bennettmarine.com
HomePage: http://www .bennettmarine.com

BFS VIDEO
360 Newkirk Rd.
Richmond Hill, ON, Canada L4C 3G7
HomePage: http://www .bfsent.com

BIFROST DISTRIBUTION L.L.C.
6529 Lakeside Cir.
Littleton, CO 80125
HomePage: http:// bifrostdistribution.com

BLAIR & ASSOCIATES LTD.
11333 E 60th Pl.
Tulsa, OK 74146-6828
800-331-4077
Fax: (918)254-6117
HomePage: http://www .vcientertainment.com

BLEECKER STREET MEDIA
381 Park Ave. S, Ste. 1401
New York, NY 10016
(212)951-5700
HomePage: http://www .bleeckerstreetmedia.com

BLUE UNDERGROUND INC.
1049 Havenhurst Dr., Ste. 187
West Hollywood, CA 90046-6002
Email: info@blue-underground.com
HomePage: http://www.blue-underground.com

BMG ENTERTAINMENT
1540 Broadway
New York, NY 10036
(212)930-4000
Fax: (212)930-4862
HomePage: http://www.bmg .com

BRAIN DAMAGE FILMS
6929 N Hayden Rd., Ste. C4-246
Scottsdale, AZ 85250
HomePage: http://www .braindamagefilms.com

BRAINSTORM MEDIA
280 S Beverly Dr., Ste. 208
Beverly Hills, CA 90212
(310)285-0812
Email: info@brainmedia.com
HomePage: http:// brainmedia.net

BREAKING GLASS PICTURES
133 N Fourth St.
Philadelphia, PA 19106
(267)324-3934
Fax: (267)687-7533
Email: customerservice@bgpics.com
HomePage: http://www .bgpics.com

BRENTWOOD COMMUNICATIONS INC.
2508 S Barrington Ave.
Los Angeles, CA 90064-2806
(310)476-6363
Fax: (310)207-5566
Email: info@brentwoodcomm.com
HomePage: http://www .brentwoodcomm.com

BRIDGESTONE MULTIMEDIA GROUP INC. (BMG)
Phoenix, AZ
866-774-3774
Fax: (888)890-4884
HomePage: http://www .gobmg.com

BRIMSTONE MEDIA PRODUCTIONS, LLC
3 W 102nd, Ste. 4B
New York, NY 10025
HomePage: http://www .lindenmuth.com

BROAD GREEN PICTURES
HomePage: http:// broadgreen.com

BUENA VISTA HOME ENTERTAINMENT, INC.
500 S Buena Vista St.
Burbank, CA 91521
HomePage: http://www.bvhe .com

CABLE FILMS/I2BS ONLINE WORLD
Country Club Sta. 7171
2026 E 63rd St.
Mission Hills, KS 66208
(913)362-2804
800-514-2804
Fax: (913)341-7365

CALIFORNIA NEWSREEL
44 Gough St., Ste. 303
San Francisco, CA 94103-5424
(415)284-7800
Fax: (415)284-7801
Email: contact@newsreel.org
HomePage: http://www .newsreel.org

CAPITOL RECORDS INC.
1750 N Vine St.
Hollywood, CA 90028-5209
HomePage: http://www .capitolrecords.com

CAV DISTRIBUTING CORP.
389 Oyster Point Blvd., Ste. 6
South San Francisco, CA 94080
(650)588-2228
Email: sales@cavd.com
HomePage: http://www.cavd .com

CBS FILMS INC.
11800 Wilshire Blvd.
Los Angeles, CA 90025-6602
HomePage: http://www .cbsfilms.com

CELEBRITY VIDEO DISTRIBUTION, INC.
6380 Wilshire Blvd., Ste. 115
Los Angeles, CA 90048
(323)655-0303
323-655-0548
Email: info@cvdistributes.com
HomePage: http://www .cvdistributes.com

CENTER FOR HUMANITIES INC.
31 Pine View Rd.
Mount Kisco, NY 10549
(914)420-2363
800-431-1242
Fax: (914)666-5319
Email: willg1961@gmail.com
HomePage: http://www .guidanceassociates.com

CHEEZY FLICKS ENTERTAINMENT INC.
6700 N New York Ave.
Portland, OR 97086
Email: sales@cheezyflicks.com
HomePage: http:// cheezyflicks.com

CINEDIGM CORPORATION
45 W 36th St., 7th Fl.
New York, NY 10018
(212)206-8600
Email: infobox@cinedigm.com
HomePage: http://www .cinedigm.com

CINEDIGM ENTERTAINMENT GROUP
902 Broadway, 9th Fl.
New York, NY 10010-6036
(212)206-8600
800-314-8822
Fax: (212)206-9001
Email: info@newvideo.com
HomePage: http://www .newvideo.com

CINEMA CLASSICS
(212)243-4905
Email: cinemaclassicsny@gmail.com
HomePage: http://www .cinemaclassics.com

CINEMA EPOCH
2600 W Olive Ave., 5th Fl.
Burbank, CA 91505
(818)753-2345
Email: info@cinemaepoch.com
HomePage: http://www .cinemaepoch.com

THE CINEMA GUILD
115 W 30th St., Ste. 800
New York, NY 10001
(212)685-6242
800-723-5522
Fax: (212)685-4717
Email: info@cinemaguild.com
HomePage: http://www .cinemaguild.com

CINEMA INTERNATIONAL CANADA
8275 Mayrand
Montreal, QC, Canada H4P 2C8
(514)336-9696
Fax: (514)336-9696

CINEMA LIBRE STUDIO
8328 De Soto Ave.
Canoga Park, CA 91304
(818)349-8822
Fax: (818)349-9922
Email: info@cinemalibrestudio.com
HomePage: http://www .cinemalibrestudio.com

CINEMANOW INC.
4553 Glencoe Ave., Ste. 200
Marina del Rey, CA 90292-7909
(310)314-3000
HomePage: http://www .cinemanow.com

CINEQUEST
PO Box 720040
San Jose, CA 95172-0040
(408)295-3378
Fax: (408)995-5713
HomePage: http://www .cinequestonline.org

CISNEROS MEDIA DISTRIBUTION L.L.C.
121 Alhambra Plz., Ste. 1400
Coral Gables, FL 33134

CITY LIGHTS MEDIA GROUP
Six E 39th St.
New York, NY 10016
(646)519-5200
Fax: (212)679-4482
HomePage: http://www .citylightsmedia.com

CJ ENTERTAINMENT
Seoul, South Korea
HomePage: http://cj-entertainment.com

CLASSIC MEDIA L.L.C.
85 Fifth Ave., 6th Fl.
New York, NY 10003
HomePage: http://www .myolivia.com

CLEAR VUE INC.
905 Delaware St.
Safety Harbor, FL 34695-3840
(727)726-5386
HomePage: http://www .clearvuewindows.net

CLOUD TEN PICTURES
PO Box 1466
Niagara Falls, NY 14302
(905)684-5561
Email: info@cloudtenpictures.com
HomePage: http:// cloud10pictures.com

COBRA ENTERTAINMENT
HomePage: http://www .cobra-entertainment.com/

CODEBLACK ENTERTAINMENT
1626 Ocean Park Blvd.
Santa Monica, CA 90405

THE COLUMBIA HOUSE!
1400 N Fruitridge Ave.
Terre Haute, IN 47804-1776
HomePage: http://www .columbiahouse.com

COLUMBIA PICTURES INDUSTRIES INC.
10202 W Washington Blvd.
Culver City, CA 90232
(310)244-4000
HomePage: http://www .sonypictures.com

COMET VIDEO
PO Box 750
Franklin, NC 28744-0750
(828)524-5251
Email: cowboys@cometwesterns.com
HomePage: http:// cometwesterns.com

CONTENT MEDIA CORPORATION LTD.
225 Arizona Ave., Ste. 250
Santa Monica, CA 90401
(310)576-1059
Fax: (310)576-1859
Email: admin@contentmediacorp.com
HomePage: http://www .contentmediacorp.com

CORINTH FILMS INC.
3117 Bursonville Rd.
Riegelsville, PA 18077
(610)509-8350
Fax: (610)346-6345
HomePage: http://www .corinthfilms.com

CRITERION COLLECTION INC.
215 Park Ave. S, 5th Fl.
New York, NY 10003
Email: orders@criterion.com
HomePage: http://criterion .com

CRITICAL MASS RELEASING
312 Adelaide St. W, 6th Fl.
Toronto, ON, Canada M5V 1R2
(416)673-5275
HomePage: http://www .criticalmass.com

CRITICS' CHOICE VIDEO
PO Box 642
Itasca, IL 60143
(630)919-2285
800-367-7765
HomePage: http://www .ccvideo.com

CROWN ENTERTAINMENT
15397 117th Ave.
Edmonton, AB, Canada T5M 3X4

CRYSTAL PRODUCTIONS
5320 Carpinteria Ave, Ste. K
Carpinteria, CA 93013-2107
(847)657-8144
800-255-8629
Email: custserv@crystalproductions.com
HomePage: http://www .crystalproductions.com

CULT EPICS
3129 Griffith Path Blvd.
Los Angeles, CA 90027
Email: info@cultepics.com
HomePage: http://www .cultepics.com

DEFA FILM LIBRARY
502 Herter Hall, Univ. of Massachusetts, 161 Presidents Dr.
Amherst, MA 01003-9312
(413)545-6681
Fax: (413)577-3808
Email: defa@german.umass.edu
HomePage: http:// ecommerce.umass.edu/ defa

DESERT ISLAND FILMS INC.
30 Portico Way
Plymouth, MA 02360
(774)773-9223
Fax: (774)404-7947

DIRECT HOLDINGS AMERICAS INC.
8280 Willow Oaks, Corporate Dr.
Fairfax, VA 22031-4511
(703)663-4500
Fax: (703)663-4620
Email: elienne.anoriscat@timelife.com
HomePage: http://www .timelife.com

DIRECT SOURCE SPECIAL PRODUCTS INC.
392 Dorval Ave., Ste. 137
Montreal, QC, Canada H9S 3H7

DISNEY EDUCATIONAL PRODUCTIONS
3900 W Alameda Ave.
Burbank, CA 91505
HomePage: http://dep .disney.go.com

DISTRIMAX
2401 Worthington Drive, Suite 103
Denton, TX 76207
HomePage: http://www .distrimaxinc.com

DOCURAMA
902 Broadway, 9th Fl.
New York, NY 10010
(212)206-8600
Fax: (212)598-4898
HomePage: http://www .docurama.com

DREAMWORKS ANIMATION LLC
1000 Flower St.
Glendale, CA 91201
(818)695-5000
Email: befeldman@dreamworksanimation.com
HomePage: http://www .dreamworksanimation .com

DREAMWORKS ANIMATION LLC.
400 R St., Ste. 1080
Sacramento, CA 95814
(916)445-1254
HomePage: http://www .dreamworks.com

DRIVEN BY DESIGN
8440 Carmel Valley Rd.
Carmel, CA 93923-9538
(831)625-1393

EAGLE ENTERTAINMENT
3800 S. Ocean Dr., Ste. 206
Hollywood, FL 33019
(954)455-8445
800-923-2453
Fax: (954)455-8515
Email: info@regalgames.com
HomePage: http://www .regalgames.com

EAST WEST
144 W 37th St., 4th Fl.
New York, NY 10018
HomePage: http://www .eastwestentgrp.com

ECHO BRIDGE HOME ENTERTAINMENT
PO Box 2798
La Crosse, WI 54602
(608)784-6620
HomePage: http://www .echobridgeentertainment .com

ECHOLIGHT STUDIOS
HomePage: http://www .echolight.com/

ECUFILM
810 12th Ave. S
Nashville, TN 37203
(615)242-6277
800-251-4091

EDUCATION 2000 INC.
2705 E Commercial Blvd.
Fort Lauderdale, FL 33308
(954)565-8888
HomePage: http://www .education2000i.com

EDUCATION INC.
407 Fair Hill Ct.
Annapolis, MD 21403

ELITE ENTERTAINMENT INC.
2 Hartford Dr., Ste. 106
Tinton Falls, NJ 07701
(732)935-7500
888-354-8380
Email: info@EliteEntertainment.com
HomePage: http:// eliteentertainment.com

EMERGING PICTURES CORP.
49 W 27th St. 8th F.
New York, NY 10001

EMILY RIDDELL PHOTOGRAPHY
HomePage: http://www .emilyriddell.com

EMPIRE PICTURES
595 Madison Ave., 39th Fl.
New York, NY 10022
Fax: (212)629-3629
Email: info@empirepicturesusa.com
HomePage: http://www .empirepicturesusa.com

ENTERTAINMENT ONE
45 Warren St.
London W1T 6AG, United Kingdom

Email: info@ipc.on.ca
HomePage: http://entertainmentone.com

ENTERTAINMENT ONE LTD.
134 Peter St., Ste. 700
Toronto, ON, Canada M5V 2H2
(416)646-2400
Fax: (416)979-9255
Email: eone@redleafpr.com
HomePage: http://www.entertainmentone.com

ENTERTAINMENT ONE US L.P.
10 Harbor Park Dr.
Port Washington, NY 11050
Email: info@ipc.on.ca
HomePage: http://WWW.ENTERTAINMENTONE.COM/DISTRIBUTION

EPIC RECORDS
25 Madison Ave., 22nd Fl.
New York, NY 10010
HomePage: http://www.epicrecords.com

ERGO MEDIA INC.
PO Box 2132
Teaneck, NJ 07666
(201)692-0404
HomePage: http://www.ergomedia.com

EROS INTERNATIONAL
550 County Ave.
Secaucus, NJ 07094
800-962-4284
Email: customerservice1@erosintl.com
HomePage: http://www.erosplc.com

ESPN INC.
ESPN Plz.
Bristol, CT 06010
888-549-3776
HomePage: http://www.espn.com

EUROPACORP S.A.
137 rue du Faubourg St.-Honore
75008 Paris, France
HomePage: http://www.europacorp.com

FACETS INC.
401 First St., Ste. 205
Richmond, CA 94801

FACETS MULTIMEDIA INC.
1517 W Fullerton Ave.
Chicago, IL 60614-2096
(773)281-9075
800-331-6197
HomePage: http://www.facets.org

FACTORY 25
274 Willoughby Ave., Ste. 4R
Brooklyn, NY 11205
HomePage: http://www.factorytwentyfive.com

FAST FORWARD
1901 Carnegie Ave.
Santa Ana, CA 92701
Email: support@ffv.com
HomePage: http://www.ffv.com

FEATURE FILMS FOR FAMILY
PO Box 572410
Murray, UT 84157
(801)263-0053
800-326-4598
Fax: (801)284-7313
HomePage: http://www.familytv.com

FESTIVAL FILMS
6115 Chestnut Ter.
Shorewood, MN 55331
(952)470-2172
Fax: (952)470-2172
Email: fesfilms@aol.com
HomePage: http://www.fesfilms.com

FILM CHEST MEDIA GROUP
100 Congress St.
Bridgeport, CT 06604-4046
(203)212-3333
HomePage: http://www.filmchestmediagroup.com

FILM MOVEMENT
109 W 27th St., Ste. 9B
New York, NY 10001
866-937-3456
Email: info@filmmovement.com
HomePage: http://www.filmmovement.com

FILM THREAT VIDEO
5042 Wilshire Blvd.
Los Angeles, CA 90036
HomePage: http://www.filmthreat.com

FILM4 LIBRARY
HomePage: http://www.film4library.com

FILMS FOR THE HUMANITIES AND SCIENCES
132 W 31st St., 16th Fl.
New York, NY 10001
(609)671-1000
800-257-5126
Fax: (609)671-0266
Email: custserv@films.com
HomePage: http://films.com

FILMS MEDIA GROUP OF COS.
132 W 31st St., 16th Fl.
New York, NY 10001
800-322-8755
Fax: (800)678-3633
Email: custserv@films.com
HomePage: http://www.films.com

FIRST INDEPENDENT PICTURES L.L.C.
528 Palisades Dr., Ste. 141
Pacific Palisades, CA 90272
HomePage: http://www.firstindependentpictures.com

FIRST LOOK STUDIOS INC.
2000 Ave. of the Stars, Ste. 410
Century City, CA 90067-4704
(424)202-5000
Email: info@firstlookmedia.com
HomePage: http://www.firstlookmedia.com

FIRST RUN FEATURES (FRF)
The Film Center Bldg., 630 Ninth Ave., Ste. 1213
New York, NY 10036
(212)243-0600
800-229-8575
Fax: (212)989-7649
Email: info@firstrunfeatures.com
HomePage: http://www.firstrunfeatures.com

FIRST RUN/ICARUS FILMS
32 Court St., 21st Fl.
Brooklyn, NY 11201
(718)488-8900
Fax: (718)488-8642
Email: mail@icarusfilms.com
HomePage: http://www.icarusfilms.com

FLICKER ALLEY
PO Box 931762
Los Angeles, CA 90093
(323)851-1905
Email: info@flickeralley.com
HomePage: http://www.flickeralley.com

FOCUS FEATURES L.L.C.
c/o Nbcuniversal 30 Rockefeller Plz., Bldg. 5ts - 10th Fl.
New York, NY 10112
HomePage: http://focusfeatures.com

FOX ENTERTAINMENT GROUP INC.
10201 W Pico Blvd.
Los Angeles, CA 90035
HomePage: http://www.fox.com

FOX SEARCHLIGHT PICTURES
10201 W Pico Blvd., Bldg. 38, 1st Fl.
Los Angeles, CA 90035
(310)369-1530
Fax: (310)369-0563
HomePage: http://www.searchlight.comi

FREESTYLE RELEASING
1925 Century Pk. E, 10th Fl.
Los Angeles, CA 90067
(310)277-3500
Email: info@freestyledigitalmedia.tv
HomePage: http://www.freestyledigitalmedia.tv

FRONT ROW ENTERTAINMENT
135 Fieldcrest Ave.
Edison, NJ 08837
(732)225-8896
HomePage: http://frontrowent.com/en

FULL MOON FEATURES
1626 Wilcox Ave., Ste. 474
Hollywood, CA 90028
(323)822-2100
800-315-6666
Fax: (323)627-4615
HomePage: http://www.fullmoonfeatures.com

FULL MOON PICTURES
1626 N Wilcox Ave., Ste. 474
Hollywood, CA 90028
(323)822-2100
Email: orderdesk@fullmoonfeatures.com
HomePage: http://www.fullmoondirect.com

FUNIMATION ENTERTAINMENT
1200 Lakeside Pky., Bldg. 1
Flower Mound, TX 75028
(972)355-7300
Email: feedback@funimation.com
HomePage: http://www.funimation.com

FUSION VIDEO
100 Fusion Way
Country Club Hills, IL 60478

GAIA, INC.
833 W S Boulder Rd.
Louisville, CO 80027
(303)222-3809
877-989-6321
Fax: (303)222-3445
Email: customerservice@gaiam.com
HomePage: http://www.gaiam.com

GAIAM INTERNATIONAL INC.
9107 Meridian Way
West Chester, OH 45069
877-989-6321
Email: customerservice@gaiam.com
HomePage: http://www.gaiam.com

GENIUS ENTERTAINMENT
3301 Exposition, Ste. 100
Santa Monica, CA 90404
(310)453-1222

GERMAN LANGUAGE VIDEO CENTER
7625 Pendleton Pke.
Indianapolis, IN 46226-5298
(317)547-1257
Fax: (317)547-1263
HomePage: http://www.germanvideo.com

GIANT NETWORK GROUP CO., LTD.
China
86 21 3397-9999
Fax: 86 21 3397-9990
Email: baihailei@ztgame.com
HomePage: http://www.ga-me.com

GLENN VIDEO VISTAS LTD.
6924 Canby Ave., Ste. 103
Reseda, CA 91335

GOTHAM DISTRIBUTING CORP.
60 Portland Rd.
West Conshohocken, PA 19428

GRAPEVINE VIDEO
4021 W San Juan Ave.
Phoenix, AZ 85019
(602)973-3661
Fax: (602)973-2973
HomePage: http://www.grapevinevideo.com

GRAVITAS VENTURES L.L.C.
300 Continental Blvd., Ste. 160
El Segundo, CA 90245
(310)648-8430
HomePage: http://www.gravitasventures.com

GREEN APPLE ENTERTAINMENT, INC.
5111 Sabal Gardens Ln., Ste 1
Boca Raton, FL 33487

GRINDHOUSE RELEASING
Email: grndhouse@aol.com
HomePage: http://www.grindhousereleasing.com

HAAS ANIMATION STUDIOS
3355 Havencroft Ct.
Reynoldsburg, OH 43068
(614)751-9906

HALESTONE DISTRIBUTION
5132 North 300 West
Provo, UT 84604
(801)655-5180
Fax: (801)655-5181
HomePage: http://www.halestormentertainment.com

HALLMARK HALL OF FAME
4346 Belgium Rd.
Riverside, MO 64150
877-323-1199

HANNOVER HOUSE
1428 Chester St.
Springdale, AR 72764
(479)751-4500
Fax: (479)751-4999
Email: info@hannoverhouse.com
HomePage: http://www.hannoverhouse.com

HENS TOOTH VIDEO
800-668-4344
Email: info@henstoothvideo.com
HomePage: http://www.henstoothvideo.com

HERE! FILMS
10990 Wilshire Blvd., Penthouse
Los Angeles, CA 90024
HomePage: http://www.heretv.com

HERETIC FILMS
2043 Green St
San Francisco, CA 94123

HOME BOX OFFICE INC. (HBO)
1100 Avenue of the Americas
New York, NY 10036
Email: general@hbo.com
HomePage: http://www.hbo.com

HUAYI BROTHERS MEDIA CO., LTD.
No. 2, Xinyuan South Rd., Chaoyand District
Beijing 100027, Beijing, China
86 10 658-058-88
HomePage: http://www.huayimedia.com

HULU L.L.C.
12312 W Olympic Blvd.
Los Angeles, CA 90064
(310)571-4700
Fax: (310)571-4883
HomePage: http://www.hulu.com

IFC FILMS
11 Penn Plz., 18th Fl.
New York, NY 10001
Email: ifcfilmsinfo@ifcfilms.com
HomePage: http://www.ifcfilms.com

IGNATIUS PRESS
PO Box 1339
Fort Collins, CO 80522
800-651-1531
Fax: (415)387-0896
Email: info@ignatius.com
HomePage: http://www.ignatius.com

IMAGE ENTERTAINMENT CORPORATION INC.
790 Principale Ouest
Magog, QC, Canada
(514)994-1204
Email: cv@image-cie.com
HomePage: http://www.image-cie.com

IMAGE ENTERTAINMENT INC.
20525 Nordhoff St., Ste. 200
Chatsworth, CA 91311
(818)407-9100
Email: inquiries@rljentertainment.com
HomePage: http://www.image-entertainment.com

IMPERIAL ENTERTAINMENT CORP.
11846 Ventura Blvd., Ste. 300
Studio City, CA 91604
(818)762-0005
Fax: (818)762-0006

INCEPTION MEDIA GROUP
13412 Ventura Blvd., Ste. 200
Sherman Oaks, CA 91423
(310)582-5948
HomePage: http://www.inceptionmediagroup.com

INDICAN PICTURES
1041 North Formosa Ave., Formosa Bldg., Ste. 221A
West Hollywood, CA 90046
(323)850-2667
Fax: (800)862-6234
Email: contact@indicanpictures.com
HomePage: http://www.indicanpictures.com

INDIEFLIX
4111 E Madison St.
Seattle, WA 98112
(206)940-3549
HomePage: http://indieflix.com

INDIEPIX FILMS
31 E 32nd St., 12th Fl.
New York, NY 10016
HomePage: http://www.indiepixfilms.com

INFINITY ENTERTAINMENT GROUP
2300 E Katella
Anaheim, CA 92806

INGRAM ENTERTAINMENT INC. (IEI)
Two Ingram Blvd.
La Vergne, TN 37089
(615)287-4000
800-621-1333
HomePage: http://www.ingramentertainment.com

INTERAMA INC.
301 W 53rd St., Ste. 19E
New York, NY 10019
Fax: (212)581-6582

INTERNATIONAL FILM CIRCUIT INC.
383 Lafayette st.
New York, NY 10003

INTERNATIONAL HISTORIC FILMS INC.
PO Box 5796
Chicago, IL 60680
(773)927-2900
Fax: (773)927-9211
Email: info@ihffilm.com
HomePage: http://ihffilm.com

INTERNET ARCHIVE
300 Funston Ave.
San Francisco, CA 94118
(415)561-6767
Fax: (415)840-0391
Email: info@archive.org
HomePage: http://www.archive.org

INTERVISION
PO Box 268
Eugene, OR 97440
(541)343-7993
Email: info@intervisionmedia.com
HomePage: http://www.intervisionmedia.com

IRS MEDIA INC.
3520 Hayden Ave.
Culver City, CA 90232-2413
(310)838-7800

ITV GLOBAL ENTERTAINMENT LTD.
15303 Ventura Bvld., Bdlg. C, Ste. 800
15303 Ventura Blvd., Bldg. C, Ste. 800
Sherman Oaks, CA 91403
(818)455-4600
HomePage: http://www.itvstudios.com

IVY CLASSICS VIDEO
Nine SW Pack Sq., Ste. 202
Asheville, NC 28801
(828)285-9995
800-669-4057
Fax: (828)285-9997

J2 GLOBAL, INC.
6922 Hollywood Blvd.
Los Angeles, CA 90028
800-878-7151
HomePage: http://www.j2global.com

J4HI
PO Box 123
Bloomfield, NJ 07003
Email: info@j4hi.com
HomePage: http://www.j4hi.com

JAMES AGEE FILM PROJECT
PO Box 73
Riverdale, MD 20738
(301)277-3880
Email: jagee@cstone.net
HomePage: http://www.ageefilms.org

JANSON MEDIA
The Cunningham House, 118 Main St.
Tappan, NY 10983
(845)359-8488
Email: info@janson.com
HomePage: http://www.janson.com

JEF FILMS, INC.
143 Hickory Hill Cir.
Osterville, MA 02655-1322
(508)428-7198
Email: finchleyrd@aol.com

JEZEBEL INC.
2860 State Hwy. 14 N
Madrid, NM 87010
(505)471-3795
866-539-3235
Email: sales@jezebelgallery.com
HomePage: http://www.jezebelgallery.com

KAROL FULFILLMENT
Hanover Industrial Estates
375 Stewart Rd.
Wilkes Barre, PA 18773-7600
(570)822-8899
800-526-4773
Email: sales@karolmedia.com
HomePage: http://karolmedia.com

KARTEMQUIN FILMS LTD. (KTQ)
1901 W Wellington St.
Chicago, IL 60657-4029

(773)472-4366
Fax: (773)472-3348
Email: info@kartemquin.com
HomePage: http://www.kartemquin.com

KIM'S VIDEO AND MUSIC (KIM)
124 First Ave.
New York, NY 10009
HomePage: http://www.mondokims.com

KINO INTERNATIONAL CORP.
333 W 39th St., Ste. 503
New York, NY 10018-1380
(212)629-6880
800-562-3330
Fax: (212)714-0871
Email: contact@kinolorber.com
HomePage: http://www.kino.com

KINO ON VIDEO
333 W 39th St., Ste. 503
New York, NY 10018
(212)629-6880
800-562-3330
Fax: (212)714-0871
Email: contact@kino.com
HomePage: http://www.kinolorber.com

KIT PARKER FILMS
c/o Central Park Media
331 W, 57th St., Ste. 554
New York, NY 10019
Email: kit@kitparker.com
HomePage: http://www.kitparker.com

KNOWLEDGE UNLIMITED, INC.
PO Box 52
Madison, WI 53701
(608)836-6660
800-356-2303
Fax: (608)836-6684
Email: help@knowledgeunlimited.com
HomePage: http://www.knowledgeunlimited.com

KULTUR INTERNATIONAL FILMS LTD.
PO Box 755
Forked River, NJ 08731
888-329-2580
Email: support@kultur.com
HomePage: http://www.kulturvideo.com

LAGUNA PRODUCTIONS
20640 Plummer St.
Chatsworth, CA 91311
800-852-9840
Email: info@lagunaproductios.com
HomePage: http://www.lagunaproductions.com

LEGACY ENTERTAINMENT
5348 Cleon Ave.
North Hollywood, CA 91601
(818)505-0025
Fax: (818)505-0545
HomePage: http://www.legacyus.com

LEGEND FILMS
8328 Clairemont Mesa Blvd., Ste. 201
San Diego, CA 92111
Email: marketing@legendfilms.com
HomePage: http://www.legendfilms.com

LEO FILMS
6548 Country Squire Ln.
Omaha, NE 68152
(323)459-5574

LES BLANK FILMS
10341 San Pablo Ave.
El Cerrito, CA 94530
(510)525-0942
HomePage: http://lesblank.com

LEVAIRE
233 N Walnut St.
Lansing, MI 48933
(517)394-3000
HomePage: http://levaire.com

LIBERATION ENTERTAINMENT INC.
1990 Westwood Blvd., Penthouse
Los Angeles, CA 90025-4650
(310)474-4456
Fax: (310)474-7455
Email: info@libertyinteractive.com
HomePage: http://www.libertyinteractive.com

LIBERTY INTERNATIONAL ENTERTAINMENT
1990 Westwood Blvd.
Los Angeles, CA 90025

LIFESIZE ENTERTAINMENT
194 Elmwood Dr., Ste. 2
Parsippany, NJ 07054
(973)884-4884
Fax: (973)428-9550
Email: info@lifesizeentertainment.com
HomePage: http://lifesizeentertainment.com

LIGHTYEAR ENTERTAINMENT
4011 Alcove Ave.
Studio City, CA 91604
(818)855-1318
HomePage: http://www.lightyear.com

LION ENTERTAINMENT INC.
2700 Colorado Ave.
Santa Monica, CA 90404
(310)449-9200
800-650-7099
Fax: (310)255-3870
Email: homevideocustomerservice@lionsgate.com
HomePage: http://www.lionsgate.com

LIONS GATE ENTERTAINMENT CORP.
2700 Colorado Ave.
Santa Monica, CA 90404
(310)449-9200
HomePage: http://lionsgatefilms.com

LIONS GATE HOME ENTERTAINMENT
2700 Colorado Ave.
Santa Monica, CA 90404
(310)449-9200
HomePage: http://www.lionsgatefilms.com

LIONS GATE TELEVISION INC.
2700 Colorado Ave., 2nd Fl.
Santa Monica, CA 90404
HomePage: http://www.lionsgate.com

LIONSGATE
2700 Colorado Ave., Ste. 200
Santa Monica, CA 90404
(310)255-3726
Email: lionshares@lionsgate.com
HomePage: http://www.lionsgate.com

LUCASFILM LTD.
PO Box 29901
San Francisco, CA 94129-0901
(415)623-1000
Email: publicity@lucasfilm.com
HomePage: http://www.lucasfilm.com

LUMINOUS FILM & VIDEO WURKS (LFV)
PO Box 289
Hampton Bays, NY 11946
(785)538-9383
Fax: (631)728-3111
Email: info@lfvw.com
HomePage: http://www.lfvw.com

LUNACY UNLIMITED PRODUCTIONS INC.
1158 26th St., Ste. 429
Santa Monica, CA 90403
HomePage: http://lunacyunlimited.com

MACKINAC MEDIA INC.
337 Upper Ranch View Dr.
Granby, CO 80446

MADACY ENTERTAINMENT
3333 Graham Blvd., Ste. 102
Montreal, QC, Canada H3R 3L5

MAGNOLIA HOME ENTERTAINMENT
60 W 23rd St.
New York, NY 10001
(212)366-1373
877-643-9682
Email: online@magnoliaav.com
HomePage: http://www.magnoliaav.com

MANAGEMENT COMPANY ENTERTAINMENT GROUP (MCEG) INC.
1888 Century Pk. E, Ste. 1777
Los Angeles, CA 90067-1721

MANGA ENTERTAINMENT L.L.C..
727 Hudson St., Ste. 100
Chicago, IL 60610
Email: info@manga.com
HomePage: http://www.manga.com

MARENGO FILMS
27206 Waterfall Hill Pky.
Spicewood, TX 78669
(972)365-0406
Email: cosgray@outlook.com
HomePage: http://www.marengofilms.com

MAVERICK ENTERTAINMENT GROUP (MEG)
1166 W Newport Center Dr., Ste. 214
Deerfield Beach, FL 33442
Email: acquisitions@maverickentertainment.cc
HomePage: http://www.maverickentertainment.cc

MAYA ENTERTAINMENT
1201 W 5th St., Ste. T-210
Los Angeles, CA 90017
(213)542-4420
HomePage: http://www.maya-entertainment.com

MEDIA BLASTERS INC.
PO Box 20743
New York, NY 10023
HomePage: http://www.media-blasters.com

MEDIA EDUCATION FOUNDATION (MEF)
60 Masonic St.
Northampton, MA 01060
(413)584-8500
800-897-0089
Fax: (800)659-6882
Email: info@mediaed.org
HomePage: http://www.mediaed.org

MEGAFORCE RECORDS INC.
130 W 57th St.
New York, NY 10019
(212)741-8861
HomePage: http://megaforcerecords.com

MENTOROM MULTIMEDIA
Richmond Hill, ON, Canada L4C 3G7
HomePage: http://www.bfsent.com

MERCURY INTERNATIONAL PRODUCTIONS INC.
5353 Westpath way
Bethesda, MD 20816

METRO-GOLDWYN-MAYER INC. (MGM)
245 N Beverly Dr.
Beverly Hills, CA 90210
(310)449-3000
Fax: (310)449-3100
HomePage: http://www.mgm.com

METRO-GOLDWYN-MAYER STUDIOS INC.
245 N Beverly Dr.
Beverly Hills, CA 90210
(310)449-3000
HomePage: http://www.mgm.com

MGM HOME ENTERTAINMENT
245 N Beverly Dr.
Beverly Hills, CA 90210-5317

MIDNIGHT LEGACY L.L.C.
5010 Church Dr.
Coplay, PA 18037

MILESTONE FILM & VIDEO
PO Box 128
Harrington Park, NJ 07640-0128
(201)767-3117
Email: milefilms@gmail.com
HomePage: http://milestonefilms.com

MILITARY/COMBAT STOCK FOOTAGE LIBRARY
The National Combat History Archive
5801 NW Cornelius Pass Rd.
Hillsboro, OR 97124

MILL CREEK ENTERTAINMENT L.L.C.
2445 Nevada Ave. N
Golden Valley, MN 55427-3611
866-410-9000
Email: support@millcreekent.com
HomePage: http://www.millcreekent.com

MILLENNIUM ENTERTAINMENT L.L.C.
5900 Wilshire Blvd., 18th Fl.
Los Angeles, CA 90036-5013
HomePage: http://www.ouralchemy.com

MILLENNIUM MEDIA INC.
300 W Aztec Ave.
Gallup, NM 87301
HomePage: http://www.gallupradio.com

A MILLION AND ONE WORLD-WIDE VIDEOS (MWW)
1239 Pine Creek Dr.
Woodstock, GA 30188

MIRAMAX L.L.C.
1901 Avenue of the Stars, Ste. 2000
Los Angeles, CA 90067
(310)409-4321
Email: publicity@miramax.com
HomePage: http://www.miramax.com

MLB PRODUCTIONS
HomePage: http://www.mlb.com

MNTEX ENTERTAINMENT INC.
500 Kirts Blvd.
Troy, MI 48084-5225
800-786-8777

MONARCH HOME ENTERTAINMENT
Two Ingram Blvd.
La Vergne, TN 37089-2000

MONDO MACABRO
Boum Productions Ltd.
Bridport DT6 6DU, United Kingdom
HomePage: http://www.mondomacabrodvd.com

MONTEREY HOME VIDEO
566 St. Charles Dr.
Thousand Oaks, CA 91360-3953
(805)494-7199
800-424-2593
Fax: (805)496-6061
Email: customerservice@montereymedia.com
HomePage: http://www.montereymedia.com

MOVIECRAFT HOME VIDEO
PO Box 438
Orland Park, IL 60462
(708)460-9082
Fax: (708)460-9099
HomePage: http://www.moviecraft.com

MOVIES UNLIMITED
3015 Darnell Rd.
Philadelphia, PA 19154
800-668-4344
HomePage: http://www.moviesunlimited.com

MPI MEDIA GROUP, L.L.C.
16101 S 108th Ave.
Orland Park, IL 60467
(708)460-0555
HomePage: http://www.mpihomevideo.com

MUSE ENTERTAINMENT
3451 Rue St-Jacques
Montreal, QC, Canada H4C 1H1
(514)866-6873
Fax: (514)876-3911
HomePage: http://www.muse.ca

MUSIC BOX FILMS
173 N Morgan St.
Chicago, IL 60607
(312)241-1320
Email: info@musicboxfilms.com
HomePage: http://www.musicboxfilms.com

MUSIC FOR LITTLE PEOPLE (MFLP)
1881 Barnett Ct., Ste. 7
Redway, CA 95560

MUSIC VIDEO DISTRIBUTORS INC.
203 Windsor Rd.
Pottstown, PA 19464
(610)650-8200
HomePage: http://musicvideodistributors.com

MYSTIC FIRE VIDEO
687 Marshall Ave.
Williston, VT 05495

NATIONAL CENTER FOR JEWISH FILM (NCJF)
Brandeis University
Lown 102 MS053
Waltham, MA 02454
(781)736-8600
Fax: (781)736-2070
Email: jewishfilm@brandeis.edu
HomePage: http://www.jewishfilm.org

NATIONAL GEOGRAPHIC
1145 17th St. NW
Washington, DC 20036
(202)835-0021
888-966-8687
Email: natgeocreative@natgeo.com
HomePage: http://www.nationalgeographic.com

NEOCLASSICS FILMS LTD.
1153 56th St.
Box 11553
Vancouver, BC, Canada V4L 2P8
(604)240-7676
Email: info@neoclassicsfilms.com
HomePage: http://www.neoclassicsfilms.com

NETFLIX, INC.
100 Winchester Cir.
Los Gatos, CA 95032
(408)540-3700
866-579-7172
Email: info@netflix.com
HomePage: http://help.netflix.com

NEW HORIZONS PICTURE CORP.
11600 San Vincente Blvd.
Los Angeles, CA 90049
HomePage: http://www.newhorizonspictures.com

NEW LINE CINEMA L.L.C.
4000 Warner Blvd.
Burbank, CA 91522
HomePage: http://www.newline.com

NEW LINE HOME ENTERTAINMENT
116 N Robertson Blvd.
Los Angeles, CA 90048-3103
(310)854-5811
Fax: (310)854-0602
Email: dvdteam@newline.com
HomePage: http://www.newline.com

NEW LINE PRODUCTIONS INC.
116 N Robertson Blvd., Ste. 200
Los Angeles, CA 90048-3103
HomePage: http://www.warnerbros.com

NEW YORKER FILMS
New York, NY
Email: info@newyorkerfilms.com
HomePage: http://www.newyorkerfilms.com

NOBILITY STUDIOS
Email: contact@nobilitystudios.com
HomePage: http://www.nobilitystudios.com

NORTH AMERICAN MOTION PICTURES, LLC
Email: Email is a form at the site.
HomePage: http://www.northamericanmotionpictures.com

NOSTALGIA COLLECTIBLES
(609)513-6895
HomePage: http://www.nostalgiacollectibles.net

NOSTALGIA FAMILY VIDEO, INC.
1833 Main St.
Baker City, OR 97814

OLIVE FILMS
312 N May St., Ste. 102
Chicago, IL 60607
(630)444-1757
HomePage: http://www.olivefilms.com

THE ORCHARD
23 E 4th St., 3rd Fl.
Washington, DC 20003
Email: communications@theorchard.com
HomePage: http://www.theorchard.com

OSIRIS ENTERTAINMENT
9428Eton Ave.
Chatsworth, CA 91311
Email: info@osirisent.com
HomePage: http://www.osirisent.com

PALISADES TARTAN VIDEO
(212)265-2323
Email: support@palisadestartan.com
HomePage: http://www.palisadestartan.com

PALM PICTURES
76 Ninth Ave., Ste. 1110
New York, NY 10011
(646)790-1211
Email: kevin.yatarola@palmpictures.com
HomePage: http://www.palmpictures.com

PARABOX MEDIA GROUP
11 Stewart Pl.
Fairfield, NJ 07004

PARAGON HOME VIDEO
55 S. Atlantic
Seattle, WA 98134

(206)808-7600
800-874-9044
Fax: (206)808-7601
Email: stevec@paragongroup.com
HomePage: http://www.paragongroup.com

PARAMOUNT PICTURES CORP.
5555 Melrose Ave.
Hollywood, CA 90038
HomePage: http://www.paramount.com

PARLOUR PICTURES
Email: info@parlourpictures.com
HomePage: http://www.parlourpictures.com

PASSION RIVER
154 Mount Bethel Rd.
Warren, NJ 07059
(732)321-0711
Email: info@passionriver.com
HomePage: http://www.passionriver.com

PASSPORT INTERNATIONAL ENTERTAINMENT L.L.C.
10520 Magnolia Blvd.
North Hollywood, CA 91601

PATHFINDER PICTURES
801 Ocean Front Walk, Ste. 7
Venice, CA 90291
800-953-9666
Fax: (310)664-0400
Email: info@pathfinderpictures.com
HomePage: http://www.pathfinderpictures.com

PBS HOME VIDEO
2100 Crystal Dr.
Arlington, VA 22202
(703)739-5051
Fax: (703)299-2985
HomePage: http://www.pbs.org

PEACE ARCH ENTERTAINMENT GROUP
1867 Yonge St., Ste. 650
Toronto, ON, Canada M4S 1Y5

PEARTREE ENTERTAINMENT
2938 30th Ave.
Astoria, NY 11102
HomePage: http://www.peartree-entertainment.com

PHASE 4/KABOOM ENTERTAINMENT
20 Eglinton Ave. W, Ste. 603
Toronto, ON, Canada M4R 1K8
(416)783-8383
866-495-3650
HomePage: http://www.phase4films.com

PHOENIX LEARNING GROUP INC.
141 Millwell Dr., Ste. A
Saint Louis, MO 63101
Email: customerservice@phoenixlearninggroup.com
HomePage: http://www.phoenixlearninggroup.com

PICTURE THIS! HOME VIDEO
PO Box 292668
Los Angeles, CA 90029
HomePage: http://www.picturethisent.com

POMERANIAN PICTURES
20236 Leadwell St.
Winnetka, CA 91306
(818)998-1983
Email: pompix@aol.com
HomePage: http://www.pompixweb.com

PORCHLIGHT ENTERTAINMENT
14724 Ventura Blvd., Ste. 1105
Sherman Oaks, CA 91403-3510
(310)477-8400
Fax: (310)477-5555
HomePage: http://www.porchlight.com

PRINCETON BOOK COMPANY PUBLISHERS
15 W Front St., 3rd Fl.
Trenton, NJ 08608
(609)426-0602
800-220-7149
Fax: (609)426-1344
Email: pbc@dancehorizons.com
HomePage: http://www.dancehorizons.com

PROMARK ENTERTAINMENT GROUP
3599 Cahuenga Blvd., W 3rd Fl.
Los Angeles, CA 90068

PURE FLIX ENTERTAINMENT L.L.C.
18940 N Pima Rd., Ste. 110
Scottsdale, AZ 85255
(480)991-2258
855-517-6566
Email: support@support.pureflix.com
HomePage: http://www.pureflix.com

QUALITY INFORMATION PUBLISHERS, INC.
441 N Louisiana Ave., Ste. P
Asheville, NC 28806
(828)423-0504
Email: qualityinformationpublishers@gmail.com
HomePage: http://www.qualityinformationpublishers.com

QUESTAR INC.
307 N Michigan Ave.
Chicago, IL 60601
(312)266-9400
HomePage: http://www.questarentertainment.com

R SQUARED INC.
11211 E Arapahoe Rd.
Englewood, CO 80112
(303)784-7030
Fax: (303)799-9297
HomePage: http://www.Vangard.com

RARO VIDEO
Email: www.rarovideousa.com
HomePage: http://www.rarovideousa.com

RAZOR & TIE DIRECT L.L.C.
214 Sullivan St., Ste. 4a
New York, NY 10012
HomePage: http://www.razorandtie.com

RAZOR DIGITAL
947 Hamilton Ave.
Menlo Park, CA 94025
(631)404-6561
HomePage: http://www.razordigital.net

REEL MEDIA INTERNATIONAL
7801 Alma Dr. Ste. 105-335
Plano, TX 75025
(214)521-3301
Fax: (214)522-3448
HomePage: http://www.reelmediainternational.com

REGENT RELEASING
10990 Wilshire Blvd., Penthouse
Los Angeles, CA 90024
HomePage: http://www.regentreleasing.com

RELATIVITY MEDIA, LLC
9242 Beverly Blvd., Ste. 300
Beverly Hills, CA 90210
(310)724-7700
HomePage: http://www.relativitymediallc.com

RELIANCE ENTERTAINMENT PRIVATE LTD.
Grandeur, 8th Fl., Veera Desai Extension Rd., Andheri W
Mumbai 400053, Maharashtra, India
91 22 49666000
HomePage: http://www.relianceentertainment.net

REMSTAR CORP.
Montreal, QC, Canada
HomePage: http://www.remstarcorp.com

RETROMEDIA ENTERTAINMENT INC.
6553 Louise Ave.
Lake Balboa, CA 91406

REVOLVER ENTERTAINMENT
7083 Hollywood Blvd., 1st Fl.
Los Angeles, CA 90028
HomePage: http://revolverentertainment.com

RHI ENTERTAINMENT
HomePage: http://www.rhitv.com

THE RIGHT COOPERATIVE ASSOCIATION
10881 Main St.
Wright, KS 67882
HomePage: http://www.rightcoop.com

RIVERCOAST MEDIA
Email: Email is a form at the site.
HomePage: http://www.rivercoastmedia.com

RLJ ENTERTAINMENT, INC.
8515 Georgia Ave., Ste. 650
Silver Spring, MD 20910
(301)608-2115
Email: inquiries@rljentertainment.com
HomePage: http://www.rljentertainment.com

RM FILMS INTERNATIONAL INC.
PO Box 3748
Hollywood, CA 90078
(323)466-7791
Email: rmf@rmfilms.com
HomePage: http://www.rmfilms.com

ROAN GROUP
361 River Sound Village
Hayesville, NC 28904

RUBICON PRODUCTIONS
(541)686-1238
Fax: (541)686-1239
Email: nealmiller@rubicon-films.com
HomePage: http://www.rubicon-films.com

RUSS DOUGHTEN FILMS INC.
5907 Meredith Dr.
Des Moines, IA 50322-1204
(515)278-4737
800-247-3456
Fax: (515)278-4738
HomePage: http://www.rdfilms.com

SALIENT MEDIA
Email: info@salientmedia.com
HomePage: http://www.salientmedia.com

SAMUEL GOLDWYN FILMS
8675 Washington Blvd., Ste. 203, Los Angeles
Culver City, CA 90232
(310)860-3100
Fax: (310)872-5077
Email: info@samuelgoldwyn.com
HomePage: http://www.samuelgoldwynfilms.com

SANKOFA
2714 Georgia Ave. NW
Washington, DC 20001
(202)234-4755
Email: store@sankofa.com
HomePage: http://www.sankofa.com

SCORPION RELEASING
Email: info@scorpionreleasing.com
HomePage: http://www.scorpionreleasing.com

SCREEN ARCHIVES ENTERTAINMENT
PO Box 550
Linden, VA 22642-0550
(540)635-2575
888-345-6335
Email: info@screenarchives.com
HomePage: http://www.screenarchives.com

SCREEN MEDIA VENTURES L.L.C.
800 Third Ave., 3rd Fl.
New York, NY 10022
(212)308-1790
Fax: (212)308-1791
Email: info@screenmedia.net
HomePage: http://screenmedia.net

SEVERIN FILMS
Email: Email is a form at the site.
HomePage: http://www.severin-films.com

SHANACHIE ENTERTAINMENT CORP.
37 E Clinton St.
Newton, NJ 07860-1870
(973)579-7763
HomePage: http://www.shanachie.com

SHOUT! FACTORY
Los Angeles, CA
Email: info@shoutfactory.com
HomePage: http://www.shoutfactory.com

SHOWCASE ENTERTAINMENT INC.
4500 Park Granada Ste. 202
Calabasas, CA 91302
(818)918-4905
HomePage: http://thescmediagroup.com

SHOWTIME NETWORKS INC. (SNI)
1633 Broadway
New York, NY 10019
877-474-6984
HomePage: http://www.sho.com

SIGNALS VIDEO
1000 Westgate Dr.
Saint Paul, MN 55114
800-669-5225
Fax: (800)454-3718

SILVER MINE VIDEO INC.
31316 Via Colinas, Ste. 104
Westlake Village, CA 91362-6715
(818)707-0300

SIMON WIESENTHAL CENTER (SWC)
1399 S Roxbury Dr.
Los Angeles, CA 90035
(310)553-9036
800-900-9036
Fax: (310)553-4521
Email: information@wiesenthal.com
HomePage: http://www.wiesenthal.com/site/pp.asp

SINISTER CINEMA
PO Box 4369
Medford, OR 97501-0168
(541)773-6860
Fax: (541)779-8650
HomePage: http://www.sinistercinema.com

SISU HOME ENTERTAINMENT INC.
340 W 39th St., 6th Fl.
New York, NY 10018
(212)947-7888
800-223-7478
Fax: (212)947-8388
Email: sisu@sisuent.com
HomePage: http://www.sisuent.com

S'MORE ENTERTAINMENT
4335 Van Nuys Blvd., Ste. 313
Sherman Oaks, CA 91403
(818)905-7267
Email: info@smoreent.com
HomePage: http://www.smoreent.com

SOMERVILLE HOUSE
131 Bloor St. W, Ste. 808
Toronto, ON, Canada M5S 1S3
(416)921-3088
877-499-3700
Email: info@somervillehouse.org
HomePage: http://www.somervillehouse.org

SOMETHING WEIRD VIDEO (SWV)
PO Box 33664
Seattle, WA 98133
(425)290-5830
Email: somethingweirdauctions@gmail.com
HomePage: http://www.somethingweird.com

SONAR ENTERTAINMENT
423 W 55th St., 12th Fl.
New York, NY 10019
HomePage: http://www.sonarent.com

SONY CORPORATION OF AMERICA
25 Madison Ave.
New York, NY 10010
(212)833-6800
HomePage: http://www.sony.com

SONY MUSIC ENTERTAINMENT GERMANY GMBH
Balanstrasse 73, Haus 31
81541 Muenchen, Germany
Email: mail@centurymedia.de
HomePage: http://www.sonymusic.de

SONY PICTURES ENTERTAINMENT INC.
10202 W Washington Blvd.
Culver City, CA 90232-3195
888-476-6972
HomePage: http://www.sonypictures.com

SONY PICTURES HOME ENTERTAINMENT INC.
10202 W Washington Blvd.
Culver City, CA 90232
(310)244-4000
HomePage: http://www.sonypictures.com

SP DISTRIBUTION P.L.C.
1 Atlantic Quay
Glasgow G2 8SP, United Kingdom
Email: crfeedback@scottishpower.com
HomePage: http://www.scottishpower.com

SPEED COMMERCE INC.
7400 49th Ave. N
Minneapolis, MN 55428-4258
(763)535-8333
800-728-4000
Fax: (763)533-2156
Email: info@navarre.com
HomePage: http://www.navarre.com

STAGESTEP
4701 Bath St., Ste. 46B
Philadelphia, PA 19137
(215)636-9000
800-523-0960
Fax: (267)672-2912
Email: stagestep@stagestep.com
HomePage: http://www.stagestep.com

STARDANCE ENTERTAINMENT
1951 W Carson St.
Torrance, CA 90501
(310)326-2348
HomePage: http://www.stardancestudio.com

STARZ ACQUISITION LLC
8900 Liberty Cir.
Englewood, CO 80112
(720)852-7700
855-247-9175
Email: help@starz.com
HomePage: http://www.starz.com

STERLING ENTERTAINMENT
PO Box 336
Bogota, NJ 07603
HomePage: http://sterlingwwe.wix.com

STRAND RELEASING
6140 W Washington Blvd.
Culver City, CA 90232
(310)836-7500
Fax: (310)836-7510
Email: strand@strandreleasing.com
HomePage: http://strandreleasing.com

STREAMLINE PICTURES LLC
6220 Enterprise Dr.
Knoxville, TN 37909
(865)384-1204
HomePage: http://streamline-productions.com

STX ENTERTAINMENT
3900 W. Alameda Ave.
Burbank, CA 91505

SUBVERSIVE CINEMA
1037 NE 65th St., Ste. 200
Seattle, WA 98155

SUMMIT ENTERTAINMENT
1630 Stewart St., Ste. 120
Santa Monica, CA 90404
(310)309-8400
HomePage: http://www.summit-ent.com

SUNDANCE INSTITUTE (SI)
1825 Three Kings Dr.
Park City, UT 84060
(435)658-3456
Fax: (435)658-3457
Email: institute@sundance.org
HomePage: http://www.sundance.org

SUNDANCETV L.L.C.
11 Penn Plz., 21st Fl.
New York, NY 10001
Email: feedback@sundance.tv
HomePage: http://www.sundancetv.com

SUNWORLD PICTURES
Email: info@sunworldpictures.com
HomePage: http://www.sunworldpictures.com

SYNAPSE
15400 Oakwood Dr.
Romulus, MI 48174
(734)494-3502
Fax: (734)494-3504
HomePage: http://www.synapse-films.com

SYNERGY ENTERPRISES INC.
220 2nd Ave. S
Franklin, TN 37064

SYNERGY ENTERTAINMENT INC.
1747 1st Ave., 3rd Fl.
New York, NY 10128
HomePage: http://www.synergyent.com

SYNKRONIZED USA
19370 Collins Ave., Ste. B-3
Miami, FL 33160

HomePage: http://www.skddvd.com

TAI SENG VIDEO MARKETING
170 S Spruce Ave., Ste. 200
South San Francisco, CA 94080
(415)871-8118
800-888-3836
Fax: (415)871-2392

TANGO ENTERTAINMENT
746 E 4th Ave.
Escondido, CA 92025
(858)774-1638

TAPEWORM VIDEO DISTRIBUTORS INC.
25876 The Old Rd., Ste. 141
Stevenson Ranch, CA 91381

TELEVISTA INTERNATIONAL INC.
3151 E Harding St.
Lakewood, CA 90805-3726

TERRA ENTERTAINMENT INC.
1345 Avenue of The Americas
New York, NY 10105

THINKFILM COMPANY INC.
10960 Wilshire Blvd., Ste. 700
Los Angeles, CA 90024
(310)286-7200
Fax: (212)444-7901
Email: info@thinkfilmcompany.com
HomePage: http://www.thinkfilmcompany.com

TIMELESS MEDIA GROUP
2480 W 7th Pl.
Eugene, OR 97402
800-547-6014
HomePage: http://www.shoutfactory.com

TLA RELEASING
234 Market St., 5th Fl.
Philadelphia, PA 19106
(215)733-0608
800-333-8521
HomePage: http://www.tlareleasing.com

TOUCHSTONE PICTURES
500 S Buena Vista St.
Burbank, CA 91521
HomePage: http://www.touchstonepictures.go.com

TRINITY FILMS
c/o Elliott Films
4018 31st Ave., S
Minneapolis, MN 55406-3308

TRISTAR PICTURES INC.
10202 W Washington Blvd.
Culver City, CA 90232
(310)244-4000
Email: groupsales@sonypictures.com
HomePage: http://www.sonypictures.com

TROMA ENTERTAINMENT INC.
36-40 11th St.
Queens, NY 11106
(718)391-0110
Fax: (718)391-0255
HomePage: http://www.troma.com

TURNER BROADCASTING SYSTEM INC.
One CNN Ctr.
Atlanta, GA 30303
Email: turnersportspr@turner.com

TURNER CLASSIC MOVIES, INC. (TCM)
1050 Techwood Dr., NW
Atlanta, GA 30318
Fax: (404)885-0600
HomePage: http://www.tcm.com

TVA FILMS
1 600 Blvd., de Maisonneuve E
Montreal, QC, Canada H2L 4P2
(514)284-2525
Fax: (514)985-4461

TWENTIETH CENTURY FOX FILM CORP.
10201 W Pico Blvd.
Los Angeles, CA 90035
HomePage: http://www.foxmovies.com

20TH CENTURY FOX HOME ENTERTAINMENT (TCFHE)
2121 Avenue of the Stars, 7th Fl.
Los Angeles, CA 90067
888-223-4369
Email: support@sharp.ru
HomePage: http://www.foxconnect.com

TWENTIETH CENTURY FOX HOME ENTERTAINMENT LTD.
31-32 Soho Sq.
London W1D 3AP, United Kingdom
HomePage: http://www.fox.co.uk

TWENTIETH CENTURY FOX HOME ENTERTAINMENT L.L.C.
PO Box 900
Beverly Hills, CA 90213
877-369-7867
HomePage: http://www.foxconnect.com

TWENTIETH CENTURY FOX LICENSING AND MERCHANDISING CORP.
2121 Avenue of the Stars, Ste. 400
Los Angeles, CA 90067-5010
(310)369-1000
Fax: (310)369-2939
Email: feedback@fox.com
HomePage: http://www.fox.com

UFO CENTRAL
2321 Abbot Kinney Blvd.
Venice, CA 90291
(310)578-5300
800-350-4639
Fax: (310)578-5308

UNEARTHED
7185 Farmington Terr.
Citrus Springs, FL 34434
Email: heneverdies@aol.com
HomePage: http://www.unearthedfilms.com

UNITED ARTISTS CORP.
245 N Beverly Dr.
Beverly Hills, CA 90210-5317

UNIVERSAL MUSIC AND VIDEO DISTRIBUTION
111 Universal Hollywood Dr., Ste. 400
Universal City, CA 91608
(818)286-4400
HomePage: http://www.universalmusic.com

UNIVERSAL PICTURES HOME ENTERTAINMENT
100 Universal City
Universal City, CA 91608
HomePage: http://www.uphe.com

UNIVERSAL PICTURES INC.
100 Universal City Plaza Dr.
Universal City, CA 91608
HomePage: http://WWW.UNIVERSALPICTURES.COM

UNIVERSAL PICTURES INTERNATIONAL FRANCE S.A.S.
21 Rue Francois 1er
75008 Paris, France
HomePage: http://www.universalpictures-film.fr

UNIVERSAL STUDIOS INC.
10 Universal City Plz.
Universal City, CA 91608
(818)777-1000
HomePage: http://www.universalstudios.com

UNKNOWN PRODUCTIONS INC.
1891 Goodyear Ave., Ste. 616
Ventura, CA 93003
877-666-8646

URBAN VISION ENTERTAINMENT INC. (UV)
5120 W Goldleaf Cir., Ste. 280
Los Angeles, CA 90025
800-338-6827

VANGUARD FILMS INC.
8703 W Olympic
Los Angeles, CA 90035-1907
HomePage: http://vanguardanimation.com

VCX LTD.
3430 Precision Dr.
North Las Vegas, NV 89032-7979
HomePage: http://www.vcx.com

VELOCITY HOME ENTERTAINMENT
906-2300 Yonge St.
Toronto, ON, Canada M4P 1E4

VENTURA DISTRIBUTION INC.
2961 Morvale Dr.
Thousand Oaks, CA 91361

VERTICAL ENTERTAINMENT
HomePage: http://www.vert-ent.com

VIACOM INTERNATIONAL INC.
1515 Broadway - 52nd Fl.
New York, NY 10036
(212)846-6700
800-516-4399
Email: corpcomm@viacom.com
HomePage: http://www.viacom.com

VICTORY MULTIMEDIA
222 N Sepulveda Blvd., Ste. 1306
El Segundo, CA 90245
(310)416-9140

VIDCREST
PO Box 69642
Los Angeles, CA 90069
(323)822-1740
HomePage: http://www.vidcrest.net

VIDEO ACTION
800 W 1st St., Ste. 1606
Los Angeles, CA 90012
(213)687-8262
800-422-2241
Fax: (213)687-8425
Email: info@videoaction.net
HomePage: http://www.videoaction.net

VIDEO ARTISTS INTERNATIONAL INC. (VAI)
109 Wheeler Ave.
Pleasantville, NY 10570
800-477-7146
Fax: (914)769-5407
Email: inquiries@vaimusic.com
HomePage: http://www.vaimusic.com

THE VIDEO BEAT
Email: Email is a form at the site.
HomePage: http://www.thevideobeat.com

VIDEO COLLECTIBLES
PO Box 385
Lewiston, NY 14092-0385
800-268-3891
Fax: (800)269-8877
HomePage: http://sites01.lsu.edu

VIDEO SEARCH OF MIAMI
PO Box 492768
Lawrenceville, GA 30049
(678)836-5838

VIDEO SERVICES CORP.
240 Pegasus Ave.
Northvale, NJ 07647-1904
(201)784-2856
Fax: (201)784-2878
Email: jpolne@vscx.com
HomePage: http://www.vscx.com

VIDEO VAULT (VVA)
113 S Columbus St.
Old Town
Alexandria, VA 22314
HomePage: http://videovault.com

VIRGIL FILMS & ENTERTAINMENT (VFE)
22 Terry Dr., No. 649
Newtown, PA 18940-9998
Email: info@virgilfilmsent.com
HomePage: http://www.virgilfilmsent.com

VISION VIDEO
2030 Wentz Church Rd.
Worcester, PA 19490
(610)584-3500
800-523-0226
Fax: (610)584-6643
Email: info@visionvideo.com
HomePage: http://www.visionvideo.com

VISION VIDEO/GATEWAY FILMS
PO Box 540
Worcester, PA 19490-0540
(610)584-3500
800-523-0226
Fax: (610)584-4610
Email: info@visionvideo.com
HomePage: http://www.visionvideo.com

VISTA STREET ENTERTAINMENT
10536 Culver Blvd., Ste. P
Culver City, CA 90232
HomePage: http://www.vistastreet.com

VISUAL ENTERTAINMENT INC.
73 Galaxy Blvd., Ste. 2
Toronto, ON, Canada M9W 5T4
(416)259-9100
Email: returns@visualentertainment.tv
HomePage: http://www.visualentertainment.tv

VIVENDI VISUAL ENTERTAINMENT
111 Universal Hollywood Dr., Ste. 400
Universal City, CA 91608
877-252-4144
HomePage: http://www.vivendient.com/home.htm

VIZ MEDIA L.L.C.
295 Bay St.
San Francisco, CA 94133
(415)546-7073
Fax: (415)546-7086
HomePage: http://www.viz.com

THE WALT DISNEY COMPANY
500 S Buena Vista St.
Burbank, CA 91521-0931
(818)560-1000
Fax: (818)560-4299
Email: presidential.service@disneystore.com
HomePage: http://thewaltdisneycompany.com

WALT DISNEY PICTURES
500 S Buena Vista St.
Burbank, CA 91521
(818)560-1000
Fax: (818)560-4299
HomePage: http://www.disneytermsofuse.com

THE WALT DISNEY STUDIOS
PO Box 7667
Burbank, CA
HomePage: http://waltdisneystudios.com

WARNER BROS. ENTERTAINMENT INC. (WB)
4000 Warner Blvd., Bldg.
Burbank, CA 91522
(818)954-2451
Fax: (818)954-6710
HomePage: http://www.warnerbros.com

WARNER HOME VIDEO INC.
4000 Warner Blvd.
Burbank, CA 91522
(818)954-3000
HomePage: http://www.warnerbros.com

WARNERARCHIVE.COM
Email: Email is a form at the site.
HomePage: http://www.wbshop.com

WARNERVISION
4000 Warner Blvd.
Burbank, CA 91522

WATER BEARER FILMS INC.
3239 Gateway Cir.
Charlottesville, VA 22911-7476
800-551-8304
HomePage: http://waterbearerfilms.com

WAXWORKS INC.
325 E 3Rd. St.
Owensboro, KY 42303
(270)926-0008
800-825-8558
Fax: (270)663-0737
HomePage: http://www.waxworksonline.com

THE WEINSTEIN COMPANY (TWC)
345 Hudson St., 13th Fl.
New York, NY 10014
(508)655-3838
HomePage: http://www.weinsteinco.com

WELL GO USA INC.
1601 E Plano Pky., Ste. 110
Plano, TX 75074
HomePage: http://wellgousa.com

WELLSPRING MEDIA
A Division of Genius Products, Inc.
25000 Ave. Stanford, Ste. 96
Valencia, CA 91355
800-514-1314
Fax: (800)861-3759
Email: info@wellspring.com
HomePage: http://www.wellspring.com

WGBH/BOSTON
PO Box 55875
Boston, MA 02205-5875
(617)300-5400
Email: stock_sales@wgbh.org
HomePage: http://www.wgbh.org

WHITE STAR
121 State Route 36
West Long Branch, NJ 07764-1304
(732)229-2343
800-458-5887

WILD EAST PRODUCTIONS
PO Box 286863
New York, NY 10128
HomePage: http://wildeast.net

WNET/THIRTEEN NON-BROADCAST
825 Eighth Ave.
New York, NY 10019
(212)560-1313
Fax: (212)560-1314
Email: communications@thirteen.org
HomePage: http://www.thirteen.org

WOLFE VIDEO
PO Box 64
New Almaden, CA 95042
(408)268-6782
800-438-9653
Fax: (408)268-9449
Email: media@wolfevideo.com
HomePage: http://www.wolfevideo.com

WOMEN MAKE MOVIES (WMM)
115 W 29th St., Ste. 1200
New York, NY 10001
(212)925-0606
Fax: (212)925-2052
Email: info@wmm.com
HomePage: http://www.wmm.com

WOODHAVEN ENTERTAINMENT
Intermedia Video Products
9144 Deering Ave.
Chatsworth, CA 91311
Fax: (800)228-2209

WORD ENTERTAINMENT L.L.C.
25 Music Sq. W
Nashville, TN 37203
HomePage: http://www.wordentertainment.com

WORLD VIDEO & SUPPLY INC.
247 Utah Ave.
South San Francisco, CA 94080

WORLD WRESTLING ENTERTAINMENT, INC. (WWE)
1241 E Main St.
Stamford, CT 06902-3520
(203)352-8600
Email: talent.marketing@wwe.com
HomePage: http://www.wwe.com

XENON PICTURES
1440 Ninth St.
Santa Monica, CA 90401
(310)451-5510
800-829-1913
Fax: (310)395-4058
Email: info@xenonpictures.com
HomePage: http://www.xenonpictures.com

XENON PICTURES INC.
3521 Jack Northrop Ave.
Hawthorne, CA 90250
(310)451-5510
Fax: (310)395-4058
Email: info@xenonpictures.com
HomePage: http://www.xenonpictures.com

YASH RAJ FILMS PVT. LTD.
2417 Jericho Tpke., Ste. 284
Garden City Park, NY 11040
(516)280-5662
Email: usoffice@yashrajfilms.com
HomePage: http://www.yashrajfilms.com

YORK ENTERTAINMENT
4565 Sherman Oaks Ave.
Sherman Oaks, CA 91403
800-846-6843
Fax: (818)647-6677

YORK PICTURES INC.
1925 Century Park East, Ste. 850
Los Angeles, CA 90067
(310)684-3628
Fax: (818)647-6677

THE ZALMAN KING COMPANY
HomePage: http://www.zalmanking.com

ZEITGEIST FILMS LTD.
247 Centre St.
New York, NY 10013
Fax: (212)274-1644

Email: orders@
zeitgeistfilms.com

HomePage: http://www
.zeitgeistfilms.com

ZENGER MEDIA
10200 Jefferson Blvd.
Culver City, CA 90232
(310)839-2436
800-421-4246
Fax: (800)944-5432

HomePage: http://
zengermedia.com

Web Site Guide

The Internet is an important resource for movie information, appreciation, and (especially) obsession. For your web surfing enjoyment, we have compiled a comprehensive list of many of the top entertainment websites that will expand your movie knowledge. If you're looking for information on how to make your own film, there are sites for that, too. The guide is divided into seven categories: cult movie resources, film magazines, film studios, filmmaker resources, film reviews, general entertainment, and video outlets. The sites are listed alphabetically within each category, and each site includes name and URL address information. The general information websites briefly describe what you can expect to find. Just as you can spend hours flipping through *VideoHound,* you can spend hours cruising the web with the sites listed below since a majority of these homepages can link you to other interesting sites.

CULT MOVIE RESOURCES

Alamo Drafthouse
https://drafthouse.com/
Web site devoted to a chain of Austin, Texas movie theatres that *Entertainment Weekly* calls 0dquo;the best theatre in America.0dquo; Check out their unbelievably cool theme screenings and Quentin Tarantino-sponsored film festival.

Animated Views
https://animatedviews.com/
Animation and CGI news (all animation not just Japanese anime).

Animation Insider
http://www.animationinsider.com/
More Animation and anime news.

Anime News Network
http://www.animenewsnetwork.com/
Yet more Anime news and a handy encyclopedia of anime related terms.

AsianCineFest
http://asiancinefest.blogspot.com/
News and reviews of Asian films and other media.

Asian Movie Pulse
http://www.asianmoviepulse.com/
News of upcoming Asian film releases, along with reviews, a discussion forum, and profiles of major stars and directors.

ASIFA Hollywood Animation Archive
http://www.asifa-hollywood.org/about-us/animation-archive/
Blog dedicated to archiving animation for the benefit of the public and the industry.

A Slash Above
https://aslashabove.com/
Slasher movies, and nothing but slasher movies.

Bad Movies
www.badmovies.org
Reviews bad movies in a good way (clever, funny, witty). Includes reviews by visitors to the site. Rating system is from five teardrops (0dquo;pinnacle of bad movies0dquo;) to a skull (0dquo;this is gonna hurt, lots.0dquo;)

Bloody-Disgusting.com
www.bloody-disgusting.com
Interviews, reviews, features--anything your sick little mind might want to know about the Horror film genre.

Bollywood.com
http://www.bollywood.com/
Bollywood music and movie reviews and information.

Bollywood Hungama
http://www.bollywoodhungama.com/
News on all things Bollywood.

Bob Burns
http://bobburns.mycottage.com/
Bob's web site has a lot of neat stuff, but none quite as neat as his amazing links section.

Brian's Drive-In Movie Theater
http://www.briansdriveintheater.com/index.html
Has Photos and information on B movie actors/actresses from the 30's to the 80's. Also has a very extensive links section.

British Horror Films
http://www.britishhorrorfilms.co.uk/
Site dedicated to British horror movies. There really aren't enough of them, you know.

Bruce Campbell Online
www.bruce-campbell.com/
Home page of the Tom Cruise of cult movie actors, Bruce Campbell, the star of director Sam Raimi's *Evil Dead* series. Site features frequently updated Bruce-News, a filmography, and a schedule of public appearances.

Buried
http://www.buried.com/
Horror film and fiction news, reviews, and interviews.

Cartoon Brew
http://www.cartoonbrew.com/
Cartoons and animation resource site.

City on Fire
http://www.cityonfire.com/
Reviews of Hong Kong and martial arts cinema.

Classic Horror Film Board
https://www.tapatalk.com/groups/monsterkidclassichorrorforum/index.php?sid=e26afd9f587912f9e9ccdafa6e9b6dfa
Bela Lugosi demands you visit the forum. You will look into his spoookity hypnotic eyes. . .

ComicBookMovie.com
http://www.comicbookmovie.com/
Page devoted to comic book films.

Cult Movies Info
www.cultmovies.info/
Offers searchable reviews and summaries of cult movies, categorized into such sub-groups as European Horror Cinema and U.S. Horror Directors.

Dark Angel's Horror Realm
http://www.realmofhorror.co.uk/
British site for news and reviews of horror films, including a history of the genre's battles with censorship.

Den of Geek
http://www.denofgeek.com/
News and reviews of films, television, comics, and games from a geek perspective.

Dread Central
http://www.dreadcentral.com/index.php
Horror film, DVD, and book reviews with a forum and several podcasts.

Dreams: The Terry Gilliam Fanzine
www.smart.co.uk/dreams/
Managed by Phil Stubbs, this is the ultimate online resource for anything having to do with ex-Python and notorious film director Terry Gilliam.

Eat My Brains
http://www.eatmybrains.com/index.php
Originally a zombie-only horror film site, it is slowly including the horror genre as a whole.

Fantastic Movie Musings and Ramblings
https://fantasticmoviemusings.com/
Sci-fi, fantasy, and horror movies. Has reviews, and upcoming movie and DVD news.

Fiction into Film Database
http://fifdb.com/
Database of fantasy, horror, and sci-fi films based on works of fiction.

Film Bizarre
http://www.filmbizarro.com/
Reviews of underground horror and arthouse films.

FrankensteinFilms
http://www.frankensteinfilms.com/
Dedicated to all things Frankenstein, especially movies.

Girls with Guns
http://www.girlswithguns.org/
For the action heroine fan in everyone.

Godzilla Temple
www.godzillatemple.com/
A home page devoted to the glory of the world's finest man-in-suit, Godzilla. Showcases reviews, audio and video clips, and an exhaustive Godzilla FAQ.

Gojipedia
https://godzilla.fandom.com/wiki/Main_Page
Massive wiki for all things Kaiju, with links to other wikis on Asian fantasy film and television.

Gorgon Video
http://gorgon-video.com/
Formerly exclusive to the Faces of Death series, it now contains other horror related stuff as well.

Han Cinema
http://www.hancinema.net/index.php
Online database and news site for Korean films.

Harvey Deneroff
http://deneroff.com/blog/
Blog on animated films from around the world.

Hong Kong Movie Database
http://www.hkmdb.com/
Database of Hong Kong cinema in Chinese and English.

Horror Asylum
http://www.horror-asylum.com/
Reviews of horror films and DVD releases.

Horror DVDs
http://www.horrordvds.com/

Upcoming horror film releases, links, and a neat forum.

Horror Movie a Day
http://horror-movie-a-day.blogspot.com/
Blogger reviews a horror film every day of the week.

Horrorhound
http://www.horrorhound.com/
Horror movie news and reviews.

House of Horrors
http://www.houseofhorrors.com/
Horror film news, reviews, and interviews.

Japanese Horror Movie Database
http://jhmd.jp/
In English and Japanese.

Joe Bob Report
www.joebobbriggs.com/
Home page of the most prolific bad movie critic of our time, King of the Drive-In, Joe Bob Briggs. Site features archives of Briggs' reviews of schlock classics and his hilarious Ultimate B-Movie Guide.

Kaijuphile
http://www.kaijuphile.com/
Portal to five other websites on giant monsters.

Keyframe
http://www.keyframeonline.com/
Information resource for animation in all its forms.

Korean Film
http://www.koreanfilm.org/
Online database and news site for Korean cinema that includes a history of Korean film, several essays, and a discussion board.

Love and Bullets
http://www.loveandbullets.com/
Reviews of Hong Kong films on DVD, and comparisons of quality between different releases.

Love HK Film
www.lovehkfilm.com/
Fans of Jackie Chan and John Woo will love this comprehensive site, which offers copious information on the Hong Kong film industry. Includes an update of new Hong Kong films, filmographies, interviews, reviews, and a searchable database of Hong Kong actors and actresses.

Micro Brew Reviews
http://microbrewreviews.blogspot.com/
Reviews of little known, low budget, and sometimes just plain godawful B films.

M.J. Simpson
http://mjsimpson-films.blogspot.com/
News and reviews of horror and sci-fi films by former staff writer for SFX magazine.

Mondo Digital
http://www.mondo-digital.com/
DVD, video, and theatrical reviews of horror movies and unusual films (especially foreign ones).

Monster Island News
http://robojapan.blogspot.com/
Blog for the comic book, sci-fi, and Godzilla fan in you.

Muppet Central
www.muppetcentral.com
The coolest and most comprehensive fan-made resource to Jim Henson's ageless creations, *The Muppets*.

Origins of American Animation
http://www.loc.gov/collection/origins-of-american-animation/about-this-collection/
Library of Congress site chronicling the history of Animation in the states.

Planet of Dinosaurs
http://www.wsu.edu/~delahoyd/dinosource.html
Your resource for dinosaurs in movies.

Polish Movie Posters
www.polishposter.com/
Check out this archive of original movie poster artwork from Poland and marvel at how scary Polish advertising can be. Their *Weekend at Bernie's* poster looks like something out of *Eraserhead*.

Quiet Earth
http://www.quietearth.us/
Film reviews with an emphasis on post-apocalyptic movies.

Sci-fi Japan
http://www.scifijapan.com/
News and reviews of oriental sci-fi, horror, and fantasy films and DVD releases.

Sci-Fi Movie Page
http://www.scifimoviepage.com/
Sci-fi movie reviews, articles, scripts, and trailers.

Scifi-Movies
http://www.scifi-movies.com/
Huge database of science fiction films and television series.

Shivers of Horror
http://www.shiversofhorror.com/
Forum for horror movies, and a second site devoted to the Friday the 13th movies.

Shock Cinema
http://www.shockcinemamagazine.com/
Online version of magazine catering to fans of bizarre and unconventional cinema.

Slice of SciFi
http://www.sliceofscifi.com/
News and review site for science fiction films that also includes tech news.

The Spaghetti Western Database
http://www.spaghetti-western.net/index.php/Main_Page
Fairly exhaustive database of Spaghetti Western films and info.

The Spinning Image
http://www.thespinningimage.co.uk/index.asp
News, articles, and reviews of cult films from the world over.

Superhero Hype
http://www.superherohype.com/
Comics and some horror movies on the screen and DVD.

Tabula Rasa
http://www.tabula-rasa.info/
A history of horror in Australia, including horror movies.

Toho Kingdom
http://www.tohokingdom.com/
Oriental film news and reviews.

Upcoming Horror Movies
http://www.upcominghorrormovies.com/
Trailers, image gallery, reviews, etc.

The Video Graveyard
http://www.thevideograveyard.com/
Horror movie reviews and trailers.

FILM FESTIVALS

ACB Sacramento Film and Music Festival
http://www.sacfilm.com/
A centerpiece for the arts community of Sacramento and a celebration of both visual and musical works from around the world.

AFI Los Angeles International Film Festival (USA)
http://www.afi.com/afifest/
Features attractions from this huge film festival held every October. Also lists synopses of the films appearing each year.

African Diaspora Film Festival
http://nyadiff.org/
Highlights the works of African-American filmmakers.

Ann Arbor Film Festival
https://www.aafilmfest.org/
Not-for-profit festival showcases independent and experimental films.

Ashland Independent Film Festival
http://www.ashlandfilm.org/
Supports independent film and film education.

Aspen Filmfest
http://www.aspenfilm.org/
Indie and short film festivals.

Atlanta Film Festival
http://www.atlantafilmfestival.com/
Features animation, shorts, docs, narrative, and full length films.

Atlantic Film Festival
http://www.finfestival.ca/
Festival for International and Canadian film.

Austin Film Festival
http://www.austinfilmfestival.com/

Bicycle Film Festival
http://www.bicyclefilmfestival.com/
Festival celebrating the bicycle in film, music, and art.

Big List of Horror Film Festivals
http://www.biglistofhorrorfilmfestivals.com/
Attempt at cataloguing links to horror film festivals.

Big Muddy Film Festival
http://bigmuddyfilm.com/
Independent film festival held in Illinois.

The Big Queer Film Festival List
http://www.queerfilmfestivals.org/
List of LGBT oriented film festivals.

Boston Irish Film Festival
http://www.irishfilmfestival.com/

Calgary International Film Festival
http://www.calgaryfilm.com

California Independent Film Festival
http://www.caiff.org/

Cannes Film Festival
http://www.festival-cannes.fr/
Searchable site with each year's film schedule, a FAQ, and jury and press information.

Chicago Asian American Showcase
http://www.faaim.org/
Promoting Asian American films.

Chicago International Film Festival
http://www.chicagofilmfestival.com/
Answers questions in the area of awards, entries, juries, and transportation.

Chicago Lesbian and Gay International Film Festival
http://www.reelingfilmfestival.org/
Offers a rundown of films featured in this alternative film festival.

Chicago Underground Film Festival
http://www.cuff.org/

Cine Las Americas
http://www.cinelasamericas.org/
Latino film festival in Texas.

Cine Tropical
http://www.cinematropical.com/
Open air celebration of Latin American films, food, culture, and music.

Cinecon
http://www.cinecon.org/
Hollywood event screening silent and early talking films.

Cinefest Sudbury
http://www.cinefest.com/
Annual Canadian film festival.

Cinevent Classic Film Convention
http://www.cinevent.com/
Annual event in Columbus, Ohio.

Cinema St. Louis
http://cinemastlouis.org
Ten-day festival showing foreign film, shorts, documentaries, and American Indie movies.

Cleveland International Film Festival
http://clevelandfilm.org

DC Shorts
http://www.dcshorts.com/
Short film festival in Washington, DC.

DC Independent Film Festival
http://dciff-indie.org/

Denver International Film Festival
http://www.denverfilm.org
Besides information on the entries, this site offers insight into the Denver Film Society.

East Lansing Film Festival
http://www.elff.com/

Edmonton International Film Festival
http://www.edmontonfilmfest.com/
Annual independent film festival in Canada.

Eerie Horrorfest
https://eerie-horror-film-festival.site123.me/
Held in (are you ready for it?) Erie, Pennsylvania.

Fairy Tales International Queer Film Festival
https://www.calgaryqueerartssociety.com/fairy-tales-calgarys-queer-film-festival
Canadian event presenting films by and/or about the gay, lesbian, bi, transgender, and twin spirited community.

Film Festival Server
http://www.filmfestivals.com
Searchable database of international film and video festivals.

Film Festival Today
http://www.filmfestivaltoday.com/
Magazine covering the film festival circuit.

Filmfest DC
http://www.filmfestdc.org/
Premieres international cinema in Washington DC.

48 Hour Film Project
http://www.48hourfilm.com/
Film competition for films done entirely within 48 hours.

Freeze Frame
http://www.freezeframeonline.org/
International festival of children's films held in Canada.

Full Frame Documentary Film Festival
http://www.fullframefest.org/
Large Documentary fest in the states.

Hartford Jewish Film Festival
http://www.hjff.org/
Showcases films highlighting the Jewish international experience.

Hawaii International Film Festival
http://www.hiff.org/

Heartland Film Festival
http://heartlandfilm.org/festival/

H.P. Lovecraft Film Festival
http://www.hplfilmfestival.com/
Promotes cinematic adaptations of weird tales from professional and amateur filmmakers.

Human Rights Watch International Film Festival
http://www.hrw.org/iff/
Highlights films dealing with the worldwide struggle for Human Rights.

Image Out Rochester Lesbian & Gay Film & Video Festival
http://www.imageout.org
Highlights films dealing with gay and lesbian issues.

Imagenation
http://imagenation.us/
Year-round film festival promoting independent art-house films about the African Diaspora.

Images Festival
https://www.facebook.com/imagesfestival/
Experimental film festival held every spring in Toronto.

Independent Film Festival of Boston
http://www.iffboston.org/
Indie filmfest held in, of course, Boston.

Independent Lens Online https://www.pbs.org/filmfestival/2019-festival/Shorts Festival
http://www.pbs.org/filmfestival/2018-festival/
Annual online festival of short films from the PBS series.

Indianapolis International Film Festival
http://indyfilmfest.org/
Midwest film fest screening feature and short films.

The Indie Gathering
http://theindiegathering.com/
Independent film festival in Cleveland, Ohio.

Indian Film Festival of Los Angeles
http://www.indianfilmfestival.org/
Los Angeles event showcasing films about India.

Inside Film Online
http://www.insidefilm.com/
Festival news, listings, and articles.

Inside Out
https://www.insideout.ca/
GLBT festival in Toronto.

International Buddhist Film Festival
http://www.ibff.org/
Films about Buddhist culture, history, etc.

International Wildlife Film Festival
http://www.wildlifefilms.org/
Film festival dedicated to wildlife and it's conservation.

Israel Film Festival
http://www.israelfilmfestival.com/
Showing subtitled films in LA, New York, and Miami.

Italian Film Festival
http://www.italianfilm.com/
Held every year in Marin County, California.

Jackson Hole Wildlife Film Festival
http://www.jhfestival.org/
Nature festival in Grand Teton National Park.

James River Film Festival
http://jamesriverfilm.com/
Indie film and video festival in Virginia.

Kansas International Film Festival
http://www.kansasfilm.com/
Shows independent and classic cinema.

Kansas Silent Film Festival
http://www.kssilentfilmfest.org/
Annual silent film festival in Wichita, Kansas.

LA Femme Film Festival
http://www.lafemme.org/
Focuses on works by female filmmakers.

Last Remaining Seats
https://www.laconservancy.org/node/961
Classic films shown in downtown LA.

London Lesbian Film Festival
http://www.llff.ca/
Celebrating lesbian film making in Canada.

Lone Pine Film Festival
http://www.lonepinefilmfestival.org/
Festival featuring movies filmed in or around Lone Pine California.

Los Angeles Film Festival
https://www.filmindependent.org/la-film-festival/

Maine International Film Festival
http://www.miff.org
Includes 100 screenings of new, old, and student films in a non-competitive, free-spirited atmosphere.

Maine Jewish Film Festival
http://www.mjff.org/
Features and documentaries on Jewish themes.

Malibu International Film Festival
http://www.malibufilmfestival.org/
Held every year during the American Film Market.

Manhattan Short Film Festival
http://www.msfilmfest.com/
New York based festival.

Margaret Mead Film and Video Festival
http://www.amnh.org/explore/margaret-mead-film-festival
Largest ethnographic/documentary film festival in US.

Maryland Film Festival
https://mdfilmfest.com/
Features restored classics, indies, docs, shorts, and full length films.

Maui Film Festival
http://www.mauifilmfestival.com/
Annual film festival in Hawaii.

Miami Latin Film Festival
http://www.miamifilmfestival.com/

Mill Valley Film Festival
http://www.mvff.com/
Sponsored by California Film Institute.

Monster Bash
http://www.monsterbashnews.com/bash.html
Pennsylvania based monster movie festival.

Moondance International Film Festival
http://www.moondancefilmfestival.com/
Promotes and encourages the best work in screenwriting, filmmaking, stage plays, radio plays, TV scripts, musical scores, lyrics, librettos, musical videos, puppetry theatre, and short stories.

Mountainfilm Festival
http://www.mountainfilm.org/
Celebrates cultures of the mountain communities.

Nantucket Film Festival
http://www.nantucketfilmfestival.org/
Shows films of various length and genre, studio or indie.

Nashville Independent Film Festival
http://www.nashvillefilmfestival.org/
Tennessee festival showing films of all genres.

New Jersey Film Festival
http://www.njfilmfest.com/
Indie, classic, international, and experimental films.

New Jersey Jewish Film Festival
https://jccmetrowest.org/programs/njjff/#overview
Jewish themed festival in the Garden State.

New Orleans Film Festival
http://www.nuff.no/
Features, shorts, documentaries, and music videos.

Newport Beach Film Festival
http://www.newportbeachfilmfest.com/
Features, shorts, documentaries, and animation from around the world.

New York City Independent Horror Film Festival
http://www.nychorrorfest.com/
Indie horror movies.

New York Film Festival
https://www.filmlinc.org/
International features and shorts.

New York International Children's Film Festival
http://nyicff.org/
Showcase of children's films.

Noir City
http://www.filmnoirfoundation.org/
Classic film noir movies in San Francisco.

NSI FilmExchange
http://www.nsi-canada.ca/
Short and feature films from Canada.

NYC Midnight Movie Making Madness
http://www.nycmidnight.com/
Competition for digital films.

Ohio Independent Film Festival
http://www.ohiofilms.com/

Ottawa International Animation Festival
http://www.animationfestival.ca/
Largest animated film festival in North America.

Out on Film
http://www.outonfilm.org
LGBT film festival in Georgia.

Pan African Film Festival
http://www.paff.org/
LA festival showing African American themed films.

Philadelphia Film Festival
http://www.filmadelphia.org/
Annual event put on by Philadelphia Film Society.

Phoenix Film Festival
http://www.phoenixfilmfestival.com/
Annual film event in Arizona.

Picture This Film Festival
http://www.ptff.org/
Highlights films for, by, and about people with disabilities.

Pioneer Valley Jewish Film Festival
http://www.pvjff.org/
3-week event in Massachusetts.

Planet in Focus
http://www.planetinfocus.org/
Environmental film and video festival based in Toronto.

Polish Film Festival in LA
http://www.polishfilmla.org/
Also has info on other Polish events and films.

Portland International Film Festival
http://www.nwfilm.org/
Annual Film Festival held at the Portland Art Museum.

Port Townsend Film Festival
http://www.ptfilmfest.com/
Independent film festival in Washington.

Providence Latin American Film Festival
http://www.plaff.org/
Competition held in Rhode Island.

Q Cinema
http://www.qcinema.org/
Fort Worth's Gay and Lesbian film festival.

Real to Reel Film Festival
http://www.ccartscouncil.org/realtoreel/
Independent film festival in North Carolina.

Red Rock Film Festival
http://www.redrockfilmfestival.com/
Utah film festival showing movies of all genres.

Reel Affirmations
http://thedccenter.org/reelaffirmations/
International gay and lesbian film festival in Washington DC.

ReelWorld Film Festival
http://www.reelworld.ca/
Toronto festival showcasing diverse types of film and video.

Rehoboth Beach Independent Film Festival
https://www.rehobothfilm.com/
Sponsored by the Rehoboth Beach Film Society.

Rhode Island International Film Festival
http://www.film-festival.org/
International film festival in Providence. They also hold a horror festival.

RiverRun International Film Festival
http://www.riverrunfilm.com/
International festival for indie films in North Carolina.

Rochester International Film Festival
http://www.rochesterfilmfest.org/
Independent film festival in New York.

Roger Ebert's Film Festival
http://www.ebertfest.com/
Annual spring festival of movies to honor the late Roger Ebert.

Sacramento French Film Festival
http://www.sacramentofrenchfilmfestival.org/
Canadian festival celebrating historic and modern French cinema.

Sacramento Horror Film Festival
http://www.sachorrorfilmfest.com/
Californian horror and sci-fi film festival.

San Diego Asian Film Festival
http://pacarts.org/sdaff/

San Diego International Film Festival
http://sdfilmfest.com
Competition for documentaries, short films, and music video. Also presents films by Native American and Women filmmakers.

San Diego Latino Film Festival
http://www.sdlatinofilm.com/
Celebration of Latin film, art, and music.

San Francisco Asian American Film Festival
http://caamfest.com
Films about the Asian American experience.

San Francisco Black Film Festival
http://www.sfbff.org/
Festival celebrating African-American cinema and the African cultural Diaspora.

San Francisco Silent Film Festival
http://www.silentfilm.org/
Annual celebration of silent films in California.

San Francisco Transgender Film Festival
http://www.sftff.org/
Transgender film and video festival.

San Luis Obispo International Film Festival
http://slofilmfest.org/
Competitive event in California.

Santa Barbara International Film Festival
http://sbiff.org/
Shows features, shorts, animation, documentaries, and indie films.

Santa Cruz Film Festival
http://www.santacruzfilmfestival.org/
Indie film festival in California.

Santa Fe Film Festival
http://www.santafefilmfestival.com/
Premieres new local and foreign films and has several mini-festivals.

Sarasota Film Festival
http://www.sarasotafilmfestival.com/
Also shows movies and holds year-round events.

Savanna Film and Video Festival
http://filmfest.scad.edu/
Independent festival in Georgia.

Scottsdale International Film Festival
http://www.scottsdalefilmfestival.com/
Arizona festival that features newer films.

Screamfest LA
http://www.screamfestla.com/
SciFi/Horror film and screenplay festival/competition in LA.

Sedona International Film Festival and Workshop
http://www.sedonafilmfestival.com/
Independent film showcase and workshop.

SF Shorts
http://www.sfshorts.org/
Short films from around the world.

Shriek Fest
http://www.shriekfest.com/
Scifi/horror film festival in LA.

Sidewalk Moving Picture Festival
http://sidewalkfest.com/
Shows narrative features, documentaries, shorts, and a competition for teens.

Silent Clowns Film Series
http://www.silentclowns.com/
Show of silent comedies presented by the New York Historical Society.

Silverdocs
http://afi.com/afidocs/
Documentary festival sponsored by the American Film Institute and the Discovery Channel.

Slamdance Film Festival
http://www.slamdance.com/

Sound Unseen
http://www.soundunseen.com/
Underground films and documentaries about music.

South Asian Film Festival
http://www.thirdi.org/festival/
Indian arthouse classics, documentaries, and independent films from South Asia.

Sprout Film Festival
http://www.gosprout.org/film/
Film and video devoted to developmental disabilities.

Studentfilms
http://www.studentfilms.com/
Online showcase of student short films.

Sundance-A Festival Virgin's Guide
http://www.sundanceguide.net/
Online companion to a guide about the festival.

Sundance Film Festival
http://www.sundance.org/festival/
Official site may not be as exciting as actually rubbing elbows among the hot talent, but it does come close. Sections include a daily report, listings of films competing, and a guide for getting around. Also has an archive for past festivals.

SXSW
http://sxsw.com/
South by Southwest is an annual film, music, and multimedia festival held in Austin, Texas.

Tampa International Gay and Lesbian Film Festival
http://www.tiglff.com/
GLBT film festival from Florida.

Telluride Film Festival
http://www.telluridefilmfestival.org/
Clint Eastwood calls this film festival the 0dquo;best,0dquo; and who are you to argue with the Outlaw Josey Wales?

Tiburon International Film Festival
http://www.tiburonfilmfestival.com/
California event promoting heightened cultural awareness.

Toronto Jewish Film Festival
http://www.tjff.com/
Films, documentaries, and shorts about Jewish culture and identity.

Toronto International Film Festival
http://www.torontointernationalfilmfestival.ca/
Take off to the Great White North and enjoy one of the largest film festivals in North America.

Trash Film Orgy
https://www.facebook.com/Trash-Film-Orgy-118004334907627/
Bizarre film festival of some of the weirdest, goriest, and most disturbing films ever.

Trenton Film Festival
http://trentonfilmsociety.org/trenton-film-festival/
Narrative films, documentaries, shorts, foreign movies, animation, and experiments.

Tribeca Film Festival
http://tribecafilm.com/festival/
Co-founded by Robert De Niro in 2002, this uber-trendy lower Manhattan film fete has evolved into one of the most respected festivals in the country.

TromaDance Film Festival
http://www.tromadance.com

Twin Rivers Multimedia Festival
http://www.twinriversmediafestival.com/
Festival encompassing film, video, and internet media formats.

United Nations Association Film Festival
http://www.unaff.org/
Documentaries about human rights, the environment, racism, homelessness, war, and women's issues.

USA Film Festival
http://www.usafilmfestival.com/
Nonprofit dedicated to recognizing excellence in film.

US International Film and Video Festival
http://www.filmfestawards.com/
Competition for documentary, educational, corporate, student, and entertainment films.

Vail Film Festival
http://www.vailfilmfestival.com/
Dedicated to American indie films, showing features, shorts, documentaries, tv pilots, commercials, and sports.

Valley Film Festival
http://www.valleyfilmfest.com/
Indie film fest in San Fernando Valley.

Vancouver Asian Film Festival
http://www.vaff.org/
Forum for North American Asian filmmakers.

Vancouver Jewish Film Festival
http://vjff.org/
Canada's longest running Jewish film festival.

Vancouver Latin American Film Festival
http://www.vlaff.org/
Canadian festival for Latin American cinema.

VCU French Film Festival
http://frenchfilmfestival.us/
French films premiered in Virginia.

Victoria Independent Film and Video Festival
http://victoriafilmfestival.com/
Competition in British Columbia.

Virginia Film Festival
http://www.virginiafilmfestival.org/
Weekend long annual event in Charlottesville.

Washington DC Independent Film Festival
http://dciff-indie.org/
Annual competition for indie films.

Washington Jewish Film Festival
http://washingtondcjcc.org/center-for-arts/film/WJFF/
Celebration of Jewish culture, films, and filmmakers.

Westchester Film Festival
http://www.westchesterfilmfestival.com/
Annual showcase of films of 60 minutes or less.

Wild and Scenic Environmental Film Festival
http://www.wildandscenicfilmfestival.org/
Nevada celebration of environmental and adventure films.

Williamsburg Brooklyn Film Festival
http://www.wbff.org/
Festival for new independent filmmakers.

Woods Hole Film Festival
http://www.woodsholefilmfestival.com/
Cape Cod event for New England based independent film makers.

Woodstock Film Festival
http://www.woodstockfilmfestival.com/
Concerts and independent films.

Women's Film Festival
http://www.womensfilmfestival.org/
Benefit for the Women's Crisis Center in Windham County, Vermont.

WorldFest
http://www.worldfest.org/
International independent and short film festival in Houston, Texas.

FILM MAGAZINES

Animation Magazine
http://www.animationmagazine.net/
Magazine on animation.

Box Office
http://pro.boxoffice.com/
One of the first trade publications to go online, reporting the latest on current films and films in production.

Cinefex
http://www.cinefex.com/
Online version of the renowned special-effects magazine. Offers synopses of articles, back issues, and a cover archive. Issues are indexed by artist, company, and film name.

Empire Online
http://www.empireonline.co.uk
The web companion to the U.K.'s coolest film magazine

Entertainment Weekly
http://www.ew.com/
Vast amount of content from the best-selling movie, TV, and pop culture weekly.

Fangoria
http://www.fangoria.com
Scream in terror thanks to original content and reviews from the world's leading horror film magazine.

G-Fan
http://www.g-fan.com/
Magazine and site devoted to Japanese giant monster films and their loving fans.

The Hollywood Reporter
http://www.hollywoodreporter.com/
Provides the latest scoop on all major studio happenings.

Images
http://www.imagesjournal.com/index.html
Online film journal published quarterly, though the site itself updates with movie reviews weekly.

Millennium Film Journal
http://mfj-online.org/
Presents articles about independent, experimental, and avant-garde cinema, video, and, more recently, works that use newer technologies. Also has an archive for past issues.

Rue Morgue
http://www.rue-morgue.com/
Magazine devoted to horror in culture and entertainment.

Screem
http://screemag.com/
Magazine devoted to bizarre cinema, mostly in the horror genre.

Variety
http://www.variety.com
The classic trade magazine brings industry news, reviews, and box office info to the web.

FILM STUDIOS

Dreamworks SKG
http://www.dreamworksanimation.com/
Browse info on upcoming movie, TV, and music projects from one of the best-known studios in Hollywood.

Electric Entertainment
http://www.electricentertainment.com/
Production studio for films and for TNT.

Focus Features
http://www.focusfeatures.com
Check out the home page of one of the major players in modern independent cinema. Includes a link to their more commercial arm, Rogue Pictures.

Lionsgate Films
http://www.lionsgatefilms.com/
Takes you behind the scenes of their latest releases and gives you a glimpse of future films.

MGM Lion's Den
http://www.mgm.com/
Home of the revamped *ShowGirls* site, also has coverage on the huge distributor's large slate of theatrical releases. Divided into MGM's niches, such as MGM television and home video.

Miramax
http://www.miramax.com/
Walk into a smorgasbord of Miramax's post-Weinstein delectables. Click on their week's specials and get a glimpse into their upcoming and current releases.

MPI Home Video
http://www.mpimedia.com/
Answers questions on availability for MPI video releases.

Paramount Pictures
http://www.paramount.com/
Click on any of the film icons to receive information on production and cast.

Pixar Animation Studios
http://www.pixar.com/
There's a reason why Disney bought Pixar--they've consistently put out the best animated movies of the past twenty years. Click around their web site and learn volumes about how they develop their award-winning CGI animated features.

Sony Classics
http://www.sonyclassics.com/
Focuses on Sony's independent releases and offers links to other sites.

Sony Pictures Entertainment
http://www.sonypictures.com/
Sony (which includes Columbia and TriStar) gives you the latest on their crop of films. Along with film and studio information, you can enter their contests to win movie t-shirts or trips to a Hollywood premiere.

Troma
http://www.troma.com/
With its Number 1 citizen, Toxie, welcoming you, indulge in the finest in camp cinema. Features information on such classics as *Toxic Avenger, Class of Nuke'em High* and *Sgt. Kabukiman NYPD.*

Twentieth Century Fox Home Entertainment
http://www.foxmovies.com/
Promotes the studio's library of films, listing films currently in theaters or that are coming soon...

United International Pictures
http://www.uip.com/
Comes in a variety of languages and has materials on their films which can be downloaded.

Universal Studios
http://www.universalstudios.com
Learn all about the upcoming films and awesome theme park rides of Universal Studios.

Walt Disney Studios
http://disney.com/
Divided into nine categories where you can find the latest on Disney books, home video, movies, music, shopping, software, television, theater and theme parks.

Warner Brothers
http://www.warnerbros.com/
Get the latest on WB's films, TV programs, music, merchandise, DC comics and kid's programming.

FILMMAKER RESOURCES

Adrienne Shelly Foundation
https://www.facebook.com/pg/TheAdrienneShellyFoundation/posts/?ref=page_internal
Founded in memory of actress/director/writer/indie icon Adrienne Shelly by her husband Andy Ostroy. Goal is to fund and mentor female filmmakers.

American Film Institute
http://www.afi.com/
The American Film Institute created this site to further its cause of finding talent that will prolong the life of art and film. The site lists the various courses, study facilities, and grants that this non-profit organization offers.

American Zoetrope
http://www.zoetrope.com/
A virtual tour of Francis Ford Coppola's Zoetrope Studios, which offers screenwriting contests and seminars as well as post-production information.

The Clay and Stop Motion Animation How-To Page
http://www.animateclay.com/
Tutorials and community based around stop motion animation.

Daily Script
http://www.dailyscript.com/
Don't know how to write a blockbuster screenplay? Check out this online archive of hundreds of TV and movie scripts and see how it's done.

Film-Makers.com
http://www.filmmakers.com/
Offers hundreds of links to film resource sites.

Filmmaking.net
http://www.filmmaking.net/
Features a comprehensive film school database and an internet filmmaker's FAQ.

Film Underground
http://www.cyberfilmschool.com/
Want to become the next Quentin or Spike, but can't afford film school? Try this informative and entertaining venue that teaches the tricks of the trade in areas such as screenwriting, cinematography, and producing.

Independent Film & Television Alliance (IFTA)
http://www.ifta-online.org/
Formerly known as the American Film Marketing Association, this group speaks to those who exclusively license, distribute, and produce independent films.

Industry Central
http://www.industrycentral.net/
Links to film industry related sites.

Mandy's Film and Television Production Directory
http://www.mandy.com/
An international geographical listing of film technicians, facilities, and producers. Helpful site for anyone looking for a film crew.

Screenwriter's Utopia
http://www.screenwritersutopia.com/
A screenwriter's one-stop resource site. Learn about the format and structure of scripts, how to market your script, network among your peers, receive tips from the pros, and become informed of the latest events and seminars.

Stop Motion Animation
http://www.stopmotionanimation.com/
Tutorials on stop motion animation and puppet making.

FILM REVIEWS

AV Maniacs
https://www.facebook.com/AV-Maniacs-61835441295/
Cult films on DVD, formerly known as DVD Maniacs.

Bigfanboy
http://bigfanboy.com/wp/
News, reviews, and interviews of current film (and some not so current film).

CinemaReview
http://www.cinemareview.com/
Includes detailed synopses and content ratings, and sometimes images from the film.

Classic B-Movies on Video
http://www3.sympatico.ca/bmovieguy/
Reviews of classic B films, and where you can find them on tape or DVD.

Cranky Critic
http://www.crankycritic.com/
Rates movies in a way that will speak to people: i.e. was the film worth the price of the ticket it cost to see it.

Deep Focus
http://www.deep-focus.com
Offers up five years' worth of reviews by New York cinephile Bryant Frazer, listed alphabetically or by grade.

DVD Drive-In
http://www.dvddrive-in.com/
Reviews and announces upcoming sci-fi, horror, and cult films being released on DVD.

DVD Movie Guide
http://www.dvdmg.com/index.shtml
Reviews upcoming films on DVD.

DVD Review
http://www.dvdreview.com/
DVD (and high definition DVD) news, reviews, and easter eggs.

Four Word Film Reviews
http://www.fwfr.com
Movies summed up in four words.

Fuds on Film
https://www.fudsonfilm.com/

Sardonic movie reviews done as only the British can do them.

Kids in Mind
http://www.kidsinmind.com
Reviews movies with an eye toward whether or not they're suitable for the kiddies. Offers a sex, violence, and language rating system for parents.

The Man Who Viewed Too Much
http://www.panix.com/~dangelo/
A New York screenwriting student with a soft touch for the art house fluff and mediocre gems, like *Joe Versus the Volcano*.

Metacritic
http://www.metacritic.com
Compiles and provides links to new and recent release movie reviews from various magazines and newspapers, creating an overall rating (on a 1-100 scale) based on the consensus of the reviews. Also reviews DVD/video releases, music, books, and video games in the same way.

The Movie Mom's Guide to Movies and Videos for Families
http://moviemom.com/
Created by movie critic and mother, Nell Minow, who gives critiques and advice on how to get children to watch movies that aren't doused in violence.

Movie Review Query Engine
http://www.mrqe.com
Allows you to search on any movie and find all available reviews appearing in the Usernet group *rec.arts.movies.reviews*.

The Movies Made Me Do It
http://www.moviesmademe.com/home
Film reviews, usually genre or not so mainstream films.

1000 Misspent Hours and Counting
http://www.1000misspenthours.com/
El Santo reviews films so you don't have to.

Onion A.V. Club
http://www.avclub.com/
Spin-off of the popular satirical newspaper that features movie and DVD reviews, filmmaker interviews, and more.

Out Magazine Movie Reviews
http://www.out.com/
Online version of the magazine that includes movie reviews and commentary on gay and lesbian cinema.

Roger Ebert
http://rogerebert.suntimes.com/
Newspapers, books, television, now Ebert storms the web. Offers his newspaper film reviews, with a searchable archive that goes back to 1985.

Rotten Tomatoes
http://www.rottentomatoes.com/
Collects reviews of newly released movies from various newspapers and ranks the overall critical reaction to the film.

Teen Movie Critic
http://www.dreamagic.com/roger/teencritic.html
Teenaged movie buff from Minnesota offers his thoughts on current theatrical releases. Also has a link to a listing of many video rental stores around America.

Women Studies Film Reviews
http://mith.umd.edu/womensstudies/FilmReviews/
Movie reviews with a feminist angle written by Florida radio personality Linda Lopez McAlister and film scholar Cynthia Fuchs.

GENERAL ENTERTAINMENT

Academy of Motion Picture Arts and Sciences
http://www.oscars.org/
Site proves that the AMPAS does more than just hand out gold statuettes every year. This homepage reveals this organization's dedication to spreading the love of film around the world. Includes information on AMPAS's various fellowships, educational, and historical activities.

A Futurist at the Movies
http://www.futuristmovies.com/
A site dedicated to films depicting the future.

Ain't It Cool News
http://www.aintitcool.com
Get the latest on upcoming releases before they even hit theaters with website originator Harry Knowles's inside scoop on their test screenings. He's the geekiest of web master film fanatics, but his information is usually reliable.

American Memory
http://memory.loc.gov/ammem/index.html
Collection of historical film stock that can be downloaded from the Library of Congress. Time frame is from 1897 to 1916 and includes such archival footage as President William McKinley's funeral and 0dquo;actuality films0dquo; showing panoramic views of old San Francisco policemen and firemen in action.

Angry Alien Productions
http://www.angryalien.com/
Movies re-enacted within 30 seconds. . . With bunnies. We'd like to say more, but we're speechless.

Animation Resources
http://animationresources.org/
Blog dedicated to supporting the education of aspiring animators.

The Big Cartoon Database
http://www.bcdb.com/
Like IMDB, but for cartoons.

The Black Film Center/Archive
https://bfca.sitehost.iu.edu/home/
An academic reference devoted to sharing resources on black cinema.

Blackfilm
http://www.blackfilm.com
Provides a forum for filmmakers, scholars, and organizations to discuss and express their artistic views. Includes info on upcoming releases, films in production, casting calls, jobs, and film festivals. There's also a gallery of film clips.

Black Flix
http://www.blackflix.com
Highlights the contributions of black movie stars, filmmakers, writers, and directors who mainstream reviews and web sites often overlook.

Box Office Guru
http://www.boxofficeguru.com
Classic site devoted to box office results. See what came in first this week or check out their database of film grosses for over 2,700 movies.

Box Office Mojo
http://www.boxofficemojo.com/
Similar to the above (e.g. Box Office Guru).

Box Office Prophets
http://www.boxofficeprophets.com/
Blogs, reviews, and research tools for movie buffs.

Bright Lights Film Journal
https://brightlightsfilm.com/
Film blog and articles.

British Council
http://film.britishcouncil.org/
The official online database of British films.

Celluloid Dreams
http://www.celluloiddreams.net/
web site for the Celluloid Dreams radio show. Features interviews, reviews, and interesting movie topics.

Cinema Blend
http://www.cinemablend.com
One of the Hound's favorite places for movie news on the net. Features thousands of mildly interesting, occasionally exciting editorials, reviews, reports, previews, and half-crazed rants, perfect for the film literate or merely film curious.

CinemaNerdz
http://cinemanerdz.com
Fun and informative site contains reviews of recent releases, feature articles, and interviews, as well as reviews of trailers. Brought to you by a close friend of VideoHound himself (it's the Editor folks).

Cinemaniac
http://web.archive.org/web/20120118181447/http://frank.mtsu.edu/~jpurcell/Cinema/maincinema2.htm
Collection of links to cinema related sites online.

Cinemorgue
http://www.cinemorgue.com/
List of actors/actresses who have died onscreen with descriptions of the events. Kinda creepy.

Classic Hollywood Biographies
http://www.classichollywoodbios.com/
Also has many magazine covers featuring stars of the times.

Classic Movie Favorites
http://www.classicmoviefavorites.com/
Impressive effort by one tireless fan.

Classic Movie Guide
http://www.classicmovieguide.com/content/category/3/7/56/
Classic film and TV reviews, as well as other information.

Classic Movies Online
http://www.classiccinemaonline.com/
Blog that streams classic and silent films online.

Classic Noir Online
http://www.classicnoir.com/
For fans of classic films and film noir.

Cliffhanger Corner
http://members.tripod.com/~fedora_2/
Fan page devoted to the old cliffhanger serials.

ComingSoon.net
http://www.comingsoon.net
Presents news, features, interviews, and images of upcoming movies, updated daily.

The Complete Index to World Film
http://www.citwf.com/index.htm
Searchable database of films, actors, and professionals in the film industry compiled by Alan Goble.

Creepy Classics
http://www.creepyclassics.com/
Lists upcoming classic sci-fi and horror films on DVD. Also sells them.

Dark City
http://www.eskimo.com/~noir/
Dedicated to all things noir.

Dark Horizons
http://www.darkhorizons.com
Movie rumors are aplenty here and it's updated regularly. The site is regulated by Garth (yes, Garth) Franklin, an Australian entertainment journalist.

The Deadbolt
http://www.thedeadbolt.com
This ultimate hub site collects daily links related to the coolest in movies, music, entertainment, and more--plus they offer their own original reviews, features, and interviews. One-stop shopping for internet media addicts.

Digitally Obsessed
http://www.digitallyobsessed.com
Provides information, reviews, contests, and inside information on new DVD releases.

Don Markstein's Toonopedia
http://www.toonopedia.com/
Cartoon Reference site run by the former editor of Comics Revue.

Drive-Ins
http://www.drive-ins.com/
Drive-In movie theater database.

DriveIn Movie
http://www.driveinmovie.com/
List of Drive-Ins and some of their history.

E! Online
http://www.eonline.com
Filled with tons of entertainment news, this is a fun site to visit come Oscar time, thanks to their habit of creating online games at the expense of the stars not nominated.

The 80's Movies Rewind
http://www.fast-rewind.com/
Reviews, trivia, plot synopses, and more in this homage to eighties cinema.

The Electronic Urban Report
http://www.EURweb.com/
Supports the positive images of African Americans in film and offers the latest celebrity news on the top black stars.

Every Frame a Painting
https://www.youtube.com/user/everyframeapainting/featured
A video analysis of how to edit films. Also has chanels on Vimeo, Facebook, and Tumblr.

Fiction into Film Database
http://www.fifdb.com/
Database of films and television based on fictional works.

Film and Video Resources
http://guides.lib.umich.edu/film
Created by the folks at the University of Michigan School of Information and Library Studies, this site leads you to many of the textual resources available that deal with film and video. Organized according to reviews, filmographies, discussions, and other databases.

Film Jerk
http://www.filmjerk.com/
Despite the name, they seem like nice people.

Film Monthly
http://www.filmmonthly.com/
News, reviews, and articles. Has an emphasis on genre films.

Film Noir
https://www.crimeculture.com/?page_id=1515
The Crime Culture websites historical guide to film noir.

Film Noir, Suspense, and Classic Action Movies
http://www.suspense-movies.com/
Huzzah for Carol Landis!

Film Resources on the Web
http://people.duke.edu/~kenneth/filmsite.html
Links to movie resources on sites on the web.

Film Sound Cliches
http://www.filmsound.org/cliche/
Popular movie sound clichés and logic flaws, and some articles on sound in films.

FilmJabber
http://www.filmjabber.com/
A blog with movie and film reviews, trailers from upcoming films, and photos and posters.

Films 101
http://www.films101.com/
Database of films chosen by critics and filmmakers to be the best in their genre.

FilmSpot
http://www.cinemaspot.com/
Site listing film related resources and sites.

Find Your Video Store
http://myvideostore.com/
Enter your zip code into their search engine to find movie stores in your area.

The Flying Inkpot's Incredible Movie Links Page
https://web.archive.org/web/20150405064744/http://inkpot.com/movielinks/other.html
Gotta love the name.

The Force
http://www.theforce.net
Articles, gossip, news, fan submissions on all things Star Wars.

ForMovies
http://formovies.com/
Movie news and trivia, and a directory of local video stores allowing users to search them for a specific title.

German-Hollywood Connection
http://www.german-way.com/history-and-culture/germany/cinema-in-germany/germans-in-hollywood/
Site about the impact the Germans, Austrians, and Swiss have had on Hollywood and it's films with essays on everything from Noir to Tarzan.

Glamour Girls of the Silver Screen
http://www.glamourgirlsofthesilverscreen.com/
Images and profiles of famous actresses from the 40's to the 60's.

Golden Age Cartoons
https://www.facebook.com/GoldenAgeCartoons/
Central site for 7 dedicated carton historians who have banded together.

Golden Silents
http://www.goldensilents.com/
Bios and film clips from Hollywood's Silent Age.

Home Theater Forums
http://www.hometheaterforum.com/
Hardware and film reviews, and an excellent forum that contains a variety or resources.

The Hot Blog
https://moviecitynews.com/the-podcast-section/

Critic Dave Poland discusses Hollywood gossip, future films, and weekly box office reports.

Hollywood Elsewhere
http://www.hollywood-elsewhere.com
Movie journalist Jeffrey Wells posts articles on upcoming films, the movie industry, and the vagaries of Hollywood.

Hollywood Online
http://www.hollywood.com
Feast your eyes at movie trailers, movie trivia, movie chat, vote on the latest contest, or check out some real estate in California.

Hollywood Sign
http://www.hollywoodsign.org/
Offers snapshots and a historical overview of the world famous Hollywood sign.

IGN
http://www.ign.com
Testosterone fueled site focuses on sci-fi, wrestling, and video games. Movie fans will find interviews, features, opinions, and trivia in three film areas.

IndieWire
http://www.indiewire.com
Up-to-date info on the latest in independent film festivals and wide releases.

Insultingly Stupid Movie Physics
http://www.intuitor.com/moviephysics/
Rails on scenes from movies that disregard the laws of physics and explains why they're impossible. Lists generic 0dquo;bad movie physics,0dquo; examples of cliches that show up in movie after movie, as well as serious scientific gaffes.

International Film and Video Center
http://ifvc.com/
Film database, links to film festivals, and they produce their own films and documentaries.

The Internet Entertainment Network
http://www.hollywoodnetwork.com/dealmaking/index.html
Enables you to become a member of the Screenwriters, Producers, or Writers Network. Divided into various sites like deal-making, box office, in-production, and script sales.

The Internet Movie Database
http://www.imdb.com
The mother of all entertainment databases. Users can frequently update the information and submit their own film reviews. With thousands of movies stored in its database, you can search by title, actor, director, country, and even by character name.

Jerry Beck's Cartoon Research
http://www.cartoonresearch.com/
Comprehensive resource for animation.

Lumiere
http://lumiere.obs.coe.int/web/search/
Record of annual film ticket sales of films released in Europe since 1996. Entries include a breakdown by individual country.

Martin's Film Noir Page
http://www.martinsfilmnoir.com/
Extensive site on the popular genre of film noir.

Media Resource Center
http://www.lib.berkeley.edu/MRC/
List of resources for movie fans and makers.

Meredith
https://www.meredith.com/national-media/brands
Created by Time Warner, this site links to their variety of magazines that check the pulse of popular culture such as *People, Vibe, Groove* and *Entertainment Weekly.*

Moderntimes
https://web.archive.org/web/20170810084727/http://www.moderntimes.com/
Has, among other things, a history of how B films began to exist.

Motion Pictures Association of America (MPAA)
http://www.filmratings.com
Tells what a film is rated and why it received that rating.

Movie-A-Minute
http://www.rinkworks.com/movieaminute/
Humorous synopses of films.

The Movie Cliches List
http://www.moviecliches.com/
A vast list of common film stereotypes and instances that stifle logic. Divided into over fifty topics including bodily functions, minorities, teenagers, and wood. A growing site since people can submit their own materials.

Movie Mistakes
http://www.moviemistakes.com/
Identifies mistakes of continuity, fact, and omission in movies.

Movie Poster Web Page
http://www.musicman.com/mp/mp.html
No, you're not seeing double. This one is a catalog of movie posters available for sale. Includes foreign films.

The Movie Posters Archive
http://www.filmsondisc.com/movieposterarchives.htm
An online vault of old movie posters, categorized by lead actor.

Movie Theology
http://www.cmu.ca/library/faithfilm.html
Directory of websites offering film information from a Christian perspective.

Moviepooper
http://www.moviepooper.com/
Collection of spoilers revealing the ends of movies.

Movies.com
http://www.movies.com/
Trailers, clips, and reviews of upcoming films. Also reviews films coming out on DVD.

MovieWEB
http://movieweb.com/
Groups together info from every film studio and offers production data and still photos of their new releases. Also offers the latest box office statistics.

Musicals 101
http://www.musicals101.com/
A history of musical theatre and film.

Netflix
http://www.netflix.com/
The coolest mail-order DVD rental service around. Browse through their 75,000-title movie catalog and enjoy DVDs delivered right to your mailbox.

Not Starring
http://www.notstarring.com/
A database of your favorite stars and the movie roles they didn't get.

The Old Corral
http://www.b-westerns.com/
B movie westerns. Strange cowboy get-ups included.

Prelinger Archives
http://www.archive.org/details/prelinger
Archive dedicated to the collection of historic films that haven't been collected elsewhere.

Ravin' Maven
http://www.themave.com/
Collection of mini-sites devoted to classic actors and actresses.

Razzies
http://www.razzies.com/
Visitors can vote for the 0dquo;Golden Raspberry Awards0dquo; for the year's worst films and performances.

Reel Classics
http://www.reelclassics.com/
Classic films, actors, filmmakers, and more.

Reel Faces
http://www.chasingthefrog.com/reelfaces/reel_faces.php
Looks at films based on real life events and people and compares them to actual events.

Rifftrax
http://www.rifftrax.com/
Mystery Science Theater 3000 fans unite! Mike and the boys are once again skewering bad film.

The Serial Squadron
http://www.serialsquadron.com/
The cliffhanger serial appreciation society.

Shobary's Spaghetti Westerns
http://spaghettiwesterns.1g.fi/
Even has a bloopers section!

Silent and Sound Cliffhanger Serials
http://www.themaverick.us/home/serial.html
Lists serials by year, A-Z, and by studio.

Silent Era
http://www.silentera.com/
Scads of info on Silent Films, including what is available on DVD.

Silents Are Golden
http://www.silentsaregolden.com/
Devoted to silent movies, and the idea that they are. . .well, you know.

Slipups
http://www.slipups.com/
Highlights amusing oopsies in film.

Surf Classics
http://www.surfclassics.com/
Site devoted to lobby cards and posters for surf movies from the 60's.

Temporal Anomalies in Time Travel Movies
http://www.mjyoung.net/time/
Now this site is fun.

Those Golden Movie Musicals
https://web.archive.org/web/20161028180639/http://www.classicmoviemusicals.com/
Dedicated to classic musicals.

TV Tropes
https://tvtropes.org/
Site collecting tropes used in the media, a trope being a literary device or motif used in writing.

VideoHelp
http://www.videohelp.com/
Ostensibly a site on how to make your own DVD's, it also has reviews of DVD players, specifically how to access the hidden menu's that will allow you to play DVD's of any region code.

Welcome to Silent Movies
http://www.welcometosilentmovies.com/
News on silent films available on VFS and DVD, and articles of various sorts.

The Western Posters Page
http://www.westernposterpage.com/
Seller of reproductions of posters from the classic western films.

Westerns
http://www.lewestern.com/
The Western movie internet database.

Where Did They Film That
http://www.wheredidtheyfilmthat.co.uk/
Location listings for films shot in the UK or Ireland.

Women in Animation
http://womeninanimation.org/
Professional non-profit group established to help the advancement of women in the animation industry.

The Worldwide Guide to Movie Locations
http://www.movie-locations.com/
Photographic history of the locales of movie shoots. Can be searched by place, film, or cast member.

VIDEO OUTLETS

Amazon.com
http://www.amazon.com
The largest online store on the internet, with a huge DVD catalog and options to pre-order releases or buy used copies of out-of-print movies.

AnimEigo
http://www.animeigo.com
Japanese animation and classic samurai films, including extensive translation notes on cultural quirks in the film that would otherwise be lost on western viewers.

BBC America Shop
https://shop.bbc.com/
For your British tv and film needs.

Best Video
http://www.bestvideo.com
With over 24,000 titles, you can search their inventory via various topics and subject categories. Also includes brief monthly reviews of current releases.

Captain Bijou
http://www.captainbijou.com/
Video and DVD sales, and all sorts of posters and memorabilia.

Carpel Video
http://www.carpelvideo.com/
If you're only interested in purchasing blank and recycled video tapes, then you've hit the jackpot with this site.

CD Universe
http://www.cduniverse.com/
Primarily a music seller, but it also carries DVDs.

Christmas Movies
http://www.christmasmovies.us/
Xmas films only, other holidays need not apply.

The Criterion Collection
http://www.criterion.com/
Collection of classic and contemporary films considered to be important.

Critics' Choice Video & DVD
http://www.ccvideo.com
Online ordering service. Includes new release, upcoming releases, classics, kid's video, and bargain sections.

DDD House
http://www.dddhouse.com/v3/index.php
English language version of the Asian site. Carries DVD, VCD, games, and other stuff. Please make sure to pay attention to the Region Code and Format of your order to ensure it plays on your DVD player.

Deep Discount DVD
http://www.deepdiscountdvd.com
Online ordering service, with a lowest price guarantee, for DVD releases.

Draculina
http://www.draculina.com/
Magazine publisher that also carries some niche horror and exploitation films.

DVD Empire
http://www.dvdempire.com/

Facets
http://www.facets.org/
Distributor of hard to find art, cult, and foreign videos. Please make sure to pay attention to the Region Code and Format of your order to ensure it plays on your DVD player.

Family Home Video
http://www.familyvideo.com/catalog/
Online ordering service for over 25,000 titles that are also linked to the Internet Movie Database.

GKids
http://www.gkids.com/
Distributor of animated films from around the world.

HBO Home Video Online
http://www.hbo.com
Along with information of their productions released on video, this site includes program summaries, sound and video clips, and celebrity photos.

iNetVideo
https://www.inetvideo.com/
Sells movies, music, and games.

J Store
http://japanimation.com
Anime and Japanese products.

Kino on Video
http://www.kinolorber.com/
Kino International showcases a breadth of films from world cinema.

Manga Video
http://www.manga.com/
Spin-off retailer site offering comic books, soundtracks, and fan club information.

Mondo Macabro DVD
http://www.mondomacabrodvd.com/
Foreign horror and exploitation film.

Rare Hollywood
http://www.rarehollywood.com/
Specialists in finding rare and out of print films. They also sell Hollywood memorabilia and posters.

RightStuf
https://www.rightstufanime.com/
Importer of Japanese merchandise, films, and anime.

RLJ Entertainment
http://us.rljentertainment.com/
Films of all kinds, many of which are hard to find.

Robert's Hard to Find Videos
http://robertsvideos.com/
Video catalog searchable by genre as well as format.

Russ Meyer Films International
http://www.rmfilms.com/
The man who gave many large busted women their first acting roles.

Scarecrow Video
http://blog.scarecrow.com/
Rare and hard to find films for sale or rent.

Sci-Fi Station
http://www.scifistation.com/
Classic and modern science fiction films and collectibles.

Science Fiction Continuum
http://www.sfcontinuum.com/
Guide to a diverse collection of sci-fi and horror films as well as animation, television and UFO documentaries on video and DVD. Please make sure to check the Region/Format to make sure it plays on your DVD player.

Synapse Films
http://synapse-films.com/
Horror, scifi, indie, and cult films.

Tempe Entertainment
http://www.tempevideo.com/catalog/
Direct to video horror and scifi movies.

Turner Classic Movies
http://www.tcm.com/index.jsp
Aside from its catalog the site also has trailers and clips from classic films.

Wolfe Video
http://www.wolfevideo.com
Online video outlet specializing in gay and lesbian themed films.